Geschenk an die
Universität Witten-Herdecke

H.R. (5.8.89)

DICTIONARY OF INTERNATIONAL BIOGRAPHY

2013

36th Edition

All communications to: International Biographical Centre
St. Thomas' Place, ELY, CB7 4GG, GREAT BRITAIN

© COPYRIGHT 2013 by Melrose Press Ltd., Cambridge, England
ALL RIGHTS RESERVED. No part of this publication may be reproduced, stored in a retrieval system, or transmitted in any form or by any means, electronic, mechanical, photocopying or otherwise, without the prior written permission of the publisher.

PUBLISHER
Nicholas S. Law

EDITOR IN CHIEF
Sara Rains

PRODUCTION/DESIGN
Scott Gwinnett

ISBN: 978 1 903986 39 4

Printed and bound in United Kingdom by:
CPI Group (UK) Ltd, Croydon, CR0 4YY

Contents

Foreword by the Director General	IV - V
Range of IBC Titles	VI
Deputy Directors General of the IBC	VII - XV
Advisers to the Director General	XVI - XVII
Lifetime Achievement Award	XVIII - XX
Vice Consuls of the IBC	XXI
The Worldwide Honours List	XXII - XLIII
Director General's Roll of Honour	XLIV - XLVI
Dedications	XLVII - LXVII
Biographies	1 - 1114
21st Century Honours List	1115 - 1134

FOREWORD BY THE PUBLISHER

I am delighted to offer the Thirty Sixth Edition of the Dictionary of International Biography, the flagship publication of the International Biographical Centre of Cambridge, England, to its many readers or 'users' throughout the world.

The Dictionary of International Biography attempts to reflect contemporary achievement in every profession and field of interest within as many countries as possible. It is an ever growing reference source since very few biographical entries are repeated from one edition to the next and only then when they have been updated with relevant new material. In this way each new Edition adds thousands of new biographies to those already published in the series; to date more than 225,000 biographies have been presented from information supplied and checked by those individuals who are featured.

As with previous Editions of the Dictionary, the Thirty Sixth has been dedicated to a number of individuals who have been chosen by our Editorial Board to represent the thousands whose lives and work have received notice in this title over the years. They are, in alphabetical order:

- **Marjorie Ruth Burns**
- **Professor Dr Haruo Hyodo**
- **Professor Gabriel Ampah Johnson**
- **Professor Dr Seon Bong Kim**
- **MUDr Pavel Novosad**
- **Paul Bartlett Ré**
- **Professor Tso-Min Shih**
- **Dr Troy Alvin Smith**
- **Madhavji (Mark) A. Unde**

To those in the Dedication Section and to all who are mentioned in this Thirty Sixth Edition I offer my congratulations and admiration.

I am often asked how we select individuals for inclusion in the Dictionary of International Biography and for that matter other titles published by the IBC. Readers and researchers should know that we publish only information which has been provided by those listed and in every case we have had their permission to publish it. Selection is made on the grounds of achievement and contribution on a professional, occupational, national or international level, as well as interest to the reader. An additional intention is to provide librarians of major libraries with a cumulative reference work consisting of Volumes published annually.

It cannot be emphasised too strongly that there is no charge or fee of any kind for inclusion in the Dictionary. Every entrant was sent at least one typescript for approval before publication in order to eliminate errors and to ensure accuracy and relevance. While great care has been taken by our Editors it is always possible that in a work of this size a few errors may have been made. If this is the case, my apologies in advance.

I would be grateful to hear from readers and researchers who feel that particular individuals should appear in future Volumes of the Dictionary of International Biography or any other relevant IBC works of reference. Such recommendations may be sent to the IBC's Research Department. Since our researchers have great difficulty in contacting some important figures it is always helpful to us to have addresses.

Nicholas S. Law
Director General
International Biographical Centre
Cambridge

April 2013

INTERNATIONAL BIOGRAPHICAL CENTRE
RANGE OF REFERENCE TITLES

From one of the widest ranges of contemporary biographical reference works published under any one imprint, some IBC titles date back to the 1930's. Each edition is compiled from information supplied by those listed, who include leading personalities of particular countries or professions. Information offered usually includes date and place of birth; family details; qualifications; career histories; awards and honours received; books published or other creative work; other relevant information including postal address. Naturally there is no charge or fee for inclusion. New editions are freshly compiled and contain on average 80-90% new information. New titles are regularly added to the IBC reference library.

Titles include:

2000 Eminent Scientists of Today
Dictionary of International Biography
Who's Who in Asia and the Pacific Nations
2000 Outstanding People
Who's Who in the 21st Century
2000 Outstanding Scientists - 2010
2000 Outstanding Scholars of the 21st Century
2000 Outstanding Intellectuals of the 21st Century
Living Science
The Cambridge Blue Book

Enquires to:
Editorial Offices
International Biographical Centre
St. Thomas' Place
ELY
CB7 4GG
GREAT BRITAIN

DEPUTY DIRECTORS GENERAL OF THE IBC

Prof Frank A Abban LPIBA DDG, Ghana
Prof Hamed S-Hillmi Abbas DDG, Saudi Arabia
Mr Aliyy M Abdalrahaman-Barri DDG, Sudan
Prof Dr Aly Ismail Nageeb Abdel-Aal DDG, Egypt
Mr Azmi Abdulazid DDG, Malaysia
Mr Alhaji Umar Faruk Abdullahi DDG, Nigeria
Dr Sarsengali A Abdymanapov DDG, Kazakhstan
Dr Hiroyuki Abe DDG, Japan
Prof Olayiwola O Abegunrin DDG, USA
Prof Antonio A Acosta IOM DDG, USA
Prof Peter O Adeniyi DDG, Nigeria
Dr Moses Adibo DDG, Ghana
Prof Emmanuel Chia Agishi DDG, Nigeria
Ms Nefertari Abena Ahmose DDG IOM DO MOIF, USA
Dr Kyung Chun Ahn DDG, Korea
Mr Chong Tek Aik DDG, Indonesia
Sir Chief (Dr) Ezekiel A Ainabe DDG, Nigeria
Mr Thomas Ernest Ainlay FWLA DDG, Japan
Dr Adeniyi Gabriel Ajewole DDG, Nigeria
Dr Manuwa Idowu Akenroye DDG, Nigeria
Prof Muhammed Salim Akhter DDG, Pakistan
Mr Edet Effiong Akpan DDG, Nigeria
Mrs Ayla Akyol DDG LFIBA AdVAh, Turkey
Dr Zohair A Al Aseri DDG, Saudi Arabia
Mr Mohamed Y A Al Beshir DDG LFIBA AdVAh, United Arab Emirates
Prof Abubakar Abdou Al Tobaiqi DDG, Saudi Arabia
Prof E M Alahuhta DDG LPIBA HonDG AIOM MOIF CH AdVAh DO, Finland
Dr Ayse A Alaylioglu DDG, South Africa
Mr Abdullah Khaled Al-Ayoub DDG, Kuwait
Mr T Hamid Al-Bayati DDG, USA
Prof Hassan Al-Chalabi DDG, Lebanon
Engineer Mr Yasser Ali Alhabibi DDG, Egypt
Prof Jalal Alirza Aliyev DDG HonDG, Azerbaijan
Dr Hanadi Mubarak Al-Mubaraki LFIBA DDG, Kuwait
Prof Fatima Al-Omran DDG, Kuwait
Dr Khalil Al-Shamma' LFIBA DDG MOIF, Jordan
Dr Ramadan Alsharrah DDG, Kuwait
Dr Rowland Iwu Amadi DDG LFIBA, Nigeria
Mr Jacob Oladele Amao DDG LFIBA, Nigeria
Dr Kazuo Amaya DDG, Japan
Dr Khaled B Amer DDG, Egypt
Rev Dr D L Amerasinghe LFIBA DDG, Sri Lanka
Prof Zhixin An DDG MOIF, China
Dr Masanori Ando DDG, Japan
Prof Raoelina Andriambololona DDG, Madagascar
Mr Vikuotuolie Angami FABI(USA) DDG, India
Prof B Angelopoulos LPIBA DDG HonDG, Greece
Dr Jaume Anguera LFIBA MOIF DDG, Spain
Rt Rev John K A Aniagwu DDG, Nigeria
Prof Anatoly V Anisimov DDG, Ukraine
Prof John Joseph Ansbro IOM DDG AdVAh, USA
Ms Bella Aouad DDG LPIBA, Lebanon
Maj Gen Dr Faisal Sadiq Arab DDG, Saudi Arabia
Mr M A Aranda-Gomez DDG, Mexico
Prof Soli Jal Arceivala DDG, India
Prof Aurel Ardelean DDG, Romania
Dr Alvina K Ardounis DDG, Greece
Dr Eitoku Arima DDG, Japan
Mario Vernon Arroyo-Gomez LPIBA DDG LFWLA IOM MOIF AdVAh, Gibraltar
Hon Justice Abdulkareem A Aruwa DDG, Nigeria
Prof Luisa Maria Arvide Cambra DDG, Spain
Prof Andrei Vasil'evich Arzhannikov DDG, Russia
Dr Muhammad Asif DDG, Pakistan
Prof Katsutoshi Ayano DDG LPIBA IOM MOIF, Japan
Prof Dr Ismail Hakki Aydin DDG, Turkey

Dr Maryam Babangida DDG, Nigeria
Prof Solomon Olufunmilayo Badejo DDG, Nigeria
Dr Charles E Bagg LPIBA DDG, England
Prof Bai Geng Yan MOIF DDG, China
Ms Rhea Bailey DDG, Cyprus
Rev Prof Juvenalis Rwelamira Baitu DDG, Kenya
Vjekoslav Bakasun MD PhD MOIF DDG LPIBA, Croatia
Dr K Bala IOM DDG, Malaysia
Prof Kamaldeen A-A Balogun DDG, Nigeria
Mr Sergio Estrada Cajigal Barrera DDG, Mexico
Dr Leonard Octavius Barrett DDG MD MOIF, USA
Ms Everlyn Bass DDG, USA
Mr Elijah Sarwat Bassily MOIF DDG LFIBA, Egypt
Dr Sarwat S Bassily DDG, Egypt
Mr Abdul R Batal LPIBA LFWLA DDG AdVBus, Syria
Prof Valentin D Batukhtin DDG, Russia
Prof Yuriy Bazhora DDG, Ukraine
Prof Charles P Beardsley DDG IOM, USA
Ms Georgia M Zeigler Beasley DDG HonDG, USA
Prof Pier Franco Beatrice LPIBA AdVAh DDG, Italy
Prof Sergei Belotserkovsky DDG IOM, Russia
Mr Roger Benebig DDG, New Caledonia
Dr (Sir) Moses Gordon Bestman DDG LFIBA CH, Nigeria
Mr Ismail Bhamjee DDG, Botswana
Dr I B Bhatti LPIBA IOM MOIF DDG, Pakistan
Dr Jay Narayan Bhore MD DDG DO, USA
Dr Chongthu Biakmawia DDG, India
Mr Nguyen Ngoc Bich DDG, USA
Dr Vitomir Bilic IOM DDG, Croatia
Dr Shazia Billal DDG, USA
Ms Irene M Bisiachi MOIF LPIBA DDG AdVAh, Italy
Dr Leikny Annadotter Bjørkli LPIBA MOIF DDG AdVAh HonDG AIOM, Sweden
Prof Hans Peter Blankholm DDG, Norway
Ms Claude Alexia Blondel DDG, France
Dr Emmanuel Oti Boateng DDG HonDG, Ghana
Ms Grethe Boe LPIBA MOIF AIOM DO DDG HonDG AdVSci, Norway
Mr Karic J Bogoljub DDG, Serbia
Prof Alexander Bogoljubov DDG, Russia
Dr Guy Boillat DDG LFIBA MOIF, France
Prof Nikolay Lilov Bojkov DDG, Bulgaria
Mr Vassil Kroumov Bojkov DDG HonDG AdVFin, Bulgaria
Prof Vladimir I Bolshakov LPIBA IOM DDG, Ukraine
Prof V Bondarenko DDG, Russia
Ms Opal J Bontrager LFIBA DDG, USA
Prof Nikolai Borisevich DDG, Belarus
Ms Shauna D Boulton LFIBA DDG, USA
Dr Manolis Bountioukos DDG, Greece
Mme Chantal-Marie Bourdet DDG, France
Prof Romano Bozac DDG, Croatia
Mr Nikolai T Bozhilov MOIF DDG, Bulgaria
Lady of Soul Eleonora Bregu MOIF DDG, Albania
Dr Sandra Breitenbach LFIBA IOM DDG DO, Norway
Dr C Da Rocha Brito LFIBA DDG, Brazil
Dr Y S K Brobbey DDG, Ghana
Mr Sabit Brokaj DDG, Albania
Dr Daniel D Brunda DDG LPIBA MOIF AIOM AdVSci DO HonDG, USA
Dr Josef Buchberger DDG, Switzerland
Prof Anatoly Alekseevich Buganov DDG, Russia
Prof Giuseppe R Burgio DDG, Italy
Dr D Busumtwi-Sam LFIBA DDG IOM, Ghana
Mr Valery S Buyanov DDG, Russia
Mr Dimiter M Buyukliiski DDG, Bulgaria
Mrs Merlene Hutto Byars DDG LFIBA, USA
Mr Shaun Byrne DDG, USA
Dr Eun Sun Byun DDG, Korea

Ms Margot Cairnes LFIBA DDG, Australia
Dr Maria Caloianu-Iordachel DDG, Romania
Dr Angelo Cammarata DDG, USA
Ms Sondra L Campian DDG, USA
Dr Guoping Cao LFIBA DDG, China
Dr Birger Carlqvist LPIBA DDG, Sweden
Mrs Gertrude E Carper DDG IOM, USA
Prof Alberto Carpinteri LFIBA DDG MOIF, Italy
Dr Jorge M-G Carpizo DDG, Mexico
Dr Xavier Castellon DDG, France
Dr Dorel A Cernomazu DDG, Romania
Prof Han-Jung Chae DDG, Korea
Dr Balaram Chakravarti DDG, India
Prof Chan Han Shui DDG IOM, Hong Kong
Mr Peter Kam Fan Chan DDG, Hong Kong
Mr Yee Kwong Chan DDG, Hong Kong
Prof Mutale William Chanda DDG, Zambia
Ms Colleen Chanel DDG, USA
Mr Scott Clay Chaney DDG, USA
Dr Wen-Ying Chang LPIBA MOIF DDG IOM HonDG AWCASC, Taiwan ROC
Dr Chang Wan-Hsi (Mo Jen) DDG, Taiwan ROC
Mr Xuping Chang DDG, China
Dr Kuk Won Chang LFIBA IOM AdVAh DDG, USA
Dr Patrick Peat Cheon Chang DDG, Hong Kong
Mr David Dah-Chung Chang LFIBA DDG, USA
Dr Sung-Goo Chang DDG, Korea
Dr Shan-Tsan Chao DDG, Taiwan ROC
Dr Ronal Charles DDG, USA
Dr Tapan Kumar Chatterjee LFIBA DDG, Mexico
Mr Mousallam Maher Chatty DDG, United Arab Emirates
Dr Chakwing Chau DDG, China
Mr John M Cheesman LFIBA IOM DDG, USA
Dr Ricardo Chequer Chemas LFIBA DDG MOIF, Brazil
Prof Chen Weixian DDG, China
Prof Yi-Feng Chen DDG, China
Dr Pang-Chi Chen DDG MOIF IOM LPIBA, Taiwan ROC
Prof Chen Qi Qi DDG, China
Mr Chen Feng DDG, China
Mr Tsung-Hsin Chen DDG, Taiwan ROC
Mr Fai Chut Cheng LFIBA DDG MOIF, Hong Kong
Prof Juei-Tang Cheng DDG LFIBA, Taiwan ROC
Mr Charles Yang Chee Chew DDG, Australia
Ms Elsie Childers IOM DDG, USA
Dr Victoria H P Chi-Lough DDG, USA
Dr Robert S K Chiluwe DDG, Zambia
Mr Chen-Ting Ch'in DDG, China
Dr C Juliana Ching LPIBA AIOM MOIF DDG HonDG AdVBus DO, Hong Kong
Dr Vera M Chirwa LFIBA DDG, Malawi
Dr Seong Yun Cho DDG, Korea
Dr Jae Lim Cho DDG LFIBA, Korea
Dr Byoung-Soo Cho DDG, Korea
Prof Young-Kil Choi DDG, Korea
Dr Hyo Choi DDG, Korea
Prof Jeong Ryeol Choi LFIBA DDG IOM MOIF, Korea
Dr Sang Yoon Choi DDG, Korea
Mr Shyam Kishore Chowdhary DDG, India
Dr Christodoulos Christodoulou HonDG DDG, Cyprus
Mr Lowell Koon Wa Chun DDG, USA
Prof Young Nam Chun DDG, Korea
Prof Kyu-bok Chung DDG AdVAh HonDG, Korea
Prof Kwansoo Chung DDG, Korea
Prof Keun Hee Chung DDG, Korea
Prof Wha Soon Chung DDG, Korea
Dr Ihn Hwa Chung DDG MOIF, Korea
Prof Dr Esther Una Cidon DDG LFIBA, Spain
Dr Lorenzo F A Cimino DDG, Italy

Dr J Civasaqui LPIBA LFWLA DDG, Japan
Prof Paula K Clarke DDG LFIBA, USA
Mr Irwin Cohen LFIBA LFWLA DDG, USA
Prof Vasko Solomon Colanceski DDG, Macedonia
Dr Solon R Cole DDG, USA
Ms Paula Anita Compo-Pratt DDG, USA
Dr Paolo C Conti DDG, Italy
Ms Jenik S Cook DDG, USA
Lt Col Fred Charles Cooke DDG LFIBA, USA
Dr Gonzalo Cordoba Candanedo DDG, Panama
Dr Oana Costan DDG, Romania
Prof Colin Crampton DDG, Canada
Dr Deborah Craven IOM DDG, USA
Dr Eva A Czajkowski DDG FIBA, USA
Prof Dai Duy Ban DDG, Vietnam
Ms Sonia Margarita Centeno Dainty LFIBA DDG, USA
Dr Mamudu Dako DDG, Nigeria
Mr Luciano Damarati DDG AWCASC, Italy
Mr Alhaji M Danmadami LFIBA DDG, Nigeria
Mrs Joan Kikel Danylak DDG, USA
Prof Marie Hoang-Nga Dao DDG HonDG IOM DG OIA WL AGE FABI, Australia
Dr Ram Das DDG, India
Mr Jaideep Das LFIBA DDG MOIF, India
Dr Bimal Krishna Das DDG, India
Ms Sandra Lynn Daves LFIBA DDG MOIF, USA
Dr Hugh Nicholas Dawes DDG HonDG, USA
Hon Mr E M G De Zylva DDG LFIBA, Sri Lanka
Dr Ann Maree Delahunty DDG LFIBA, Australia
Edmund N Delle MD DDG, Ghana
Prof Ziji Deng LFIBA DDG IOM, China
Prof Andrzej Denys DDG, Poland
Ms Beemakolam Devikarani DDG, India
Dr Dharam Pal Dhall MOIF LFIBA DDG, Australia
Mr Vishnu Prasad Dhital DDG, Nepal
Prof Maghawry Shehata Diab DDG, Egypt
Prof Donaldo De Souza Dias DDG, Brazil
Maestro Florentino Dias DDG IOM MOIF, Brazil
Dr C C Dickinson III LFIBA DDG, USA
Mrs Doris Dillon DDG, USA
Prof Dr Mile Dimitrovski DDG, Macedonia
Mr Maxim Jekov Dimov DDG, Bulgaria
Dr Robert Ding Pooi Huat DDG IOM MOIF CH HonDG, Malaysia
Prof Dr Deog-Hee Doh LFIBA DDG, Korea
Mr Dong Lisheng DDG, China
Prof Dolphi Drimer DDG, Romania
Miss Du Ying IOM DDG, China
Prof Klavdiya V Dubych DDG, Ukraine
Prof Ha Minh Duc DDG, Vietnam
Mr Hasan Duman DDG, Turkey
Dr Doina Dumitrescu-Ionescu DDG, Romania
Dr Willie J Duncan DDG, USA
Linda K Duntley MA LFIBA MOIF DDG, USA
Dr Pushparanee Durai DDG, Malaysia
Ms P Dureska MOIF LPIBA IOM DDG, USA
Dr Webster Sterling Edwards DDG, Jamaica
Mr Finn Egil Eide DDG, Norway
Mrs Zena El Khoury DDG, Lebanon
Mr Elhamy Mostafa El Zayat DDG, Egypt
Prof Mohammad H S El-Ahl DDG MOIF IOM, Egypt
Dr M F Elkady DDG IOM LFIBA, Saudi Arabia
Mr Farid M Elsayed DDG AWCASC HonDG, Kuwait
Prof Mohamed K El-Sorougi DDG, Egypt
Ms Jacquelyn Rose Ely DDG, USA
Dr Huseyin Engin IOM DDG, Turkey
Mr Andrew J Entwistle IOM MOIF DDG LFIBA, USA
Prof Charles Osayande Eregie DDG, Nigeria

Dr Periklis Ergatis DDG LFIBA MOIF AdVSci, Greece
Dr Alexei M Ermolaev DDG, England
Mr Ole Kristian Ersgaard CBEcon DDG, Denmark
Dr Hernani Esteban DDG AdVAh, Philippines
Dr Duk-Soo Eun LFIBA DDG, Korea
Dr Jong-Pil Eun PhD DDG, Korea
Mrs Elisabeth Anne Rooney-Ewing DDG MOIF, USA
Dr James E Ewing DDG MOIF, USA
Dr Festus A Fadeyi DDG, USA
Prof Samir Qasim Fakhro DDG, Bahrain
Dr Victor Olusegun Falaiye DDG, USA
Prof Gong-Xiu Fan DDG, China
Prof Christine Faulk-Miles DDG, USA
Dr Oladiran Fawibe DDG, Nigeria
Dr Reza Fekrazad DDG, Iran
Mr Jacob Feldman LFIBA DDG IOM, Australia
Mr Shun-Hua Feng DDG LFIBA, China
Mr James Ferguson LFIBA DDG MOIF AWCASC, Australia
Prof Dr Antony Fernando ThD PhD DDG, Sri Lanka
Prof Antonio G Ferreira DDG, Portugal
Mr Pietro Camillo Ferrigno AIOM DDG AdVMed HonDG MOIF DO AWCASC WCOIM, Italy
Mrs Ruth Kinniebrew Fields LFIBA AdVAh DDG, USA
Dr David E Flinchbaugh LFIBA DDG, USA
Ms LuAnn F Florio LFIBA DDG, USA
Ms Maryanne Tam-Po Fong DDG IOM AdVBus HonDG MOIF, Canada
Prof Foo Check-Teck DDG, Singapore
Dr Francis Frandeau de Marly MOIF DDG HonDG, France
Prof Irmtraut Freiberg LFIBA DDG, Austria
Dr Errol Friedberg DDG, USA
Mr Jeffrey S Fu DDG, Singapore
Dr Takemi Fujikawa DDG LFIBA, Malaysia
Prof Tanefusa Fukatsu LPIBA IOM DDG MOIF, Japan
Dr Hajime Fukazawa LFIBA MOIF DDG IOM CH, Japan
Prof Dr Tetsuo Fukuda LFIBA DDG, Japan
Ms Barbara Lynn Funk DDG, USA
Dr Erzsebet Galantai DDG, Hungary
Mr Xiechu Gao DDG, China
Dr Ashok Garg DDG, India
Mr Allenby T Gargour DDG, Lebanon
Mr Barry Pere Gbe DDG, Nigeria
Prof Jinsheng Geng DDG, China
Prof Dr Nikolai Genov DDG, Bulgaria
Dr Borislav Georgiev DDG, Bulgaria
Dr Isam Ghanem DDG, Yemen
Dr Curtis A Gibson LFIBA DDG, USA
Dr Devinder Singh Gill DDG AdVSci MOIF HonDG IOM, India
Mr Allen Fletcher Gilliard DDG AdVAh IOM, USA
Prof Trajan Gocevski DDG, Macedonia
Prof Dr Vasyl Goch DDG LFIBA AdVSci HonDG, Ukraine
Ms Gisela Erika W Goettling DDG, USA
Prof T Goino DDG IOM MOIF LFWLA LPIBA, Japan
Dr Tangis V Golashvili DDG, Russia
Dr M Goldston-Morris OAM DDG LPIBA MOIF DDG, Australia
Dr Dora Maria Gomez DDG, Venezuela
Prof Petr L Goncharov DDG AdVSci CH, Russia
Mr Naichang Gong DDG, China
Prof Zhong Lin Gong DDG, China
Mr Alhaji M Goni DDG HonDG, Nigeria
Mr Isaac T Goodine DDG IOM MOIF AdVAh HonDG, Canada
Mr Timothy A Goodwin LPIBA DO IOM CH DDG MOIF HonDG, USA
Mr Mookeshwarsing Gopal DDG, Mauritius
Ms Melba J Goree DDG, USA
Dr Masae Goseki-Sone DDG IOM, Japan
Prof Hiroki Gotoh DDG IOM, Japan
Dr Carlos A M Gottschall IOM DDG, Brazil
Prof Saneshan Govender DDG, South Africa
Dr Michael E Grant DDG, USA
Ms Joanne Greene DDG, USA
Prof Dr Ovidiu N Grivu LPIBA DDG, Romania
Dietrich H W Gronemeyer MD DDG, Germany
Mr Borys Gryadushchyy DDG, Ukraine
Mr Vladimir Gryaznov DDG, Russia
Dr Gu Juan LFIBA MOIF DDG, China
Dr Meen-Wah Gui DDG, Taiwan ROC
Mr Sardar Narinder Singh Gujral DDG, India
Mrs Padmin Gunaratnam DDG, Singapore
Prof Dr Benny Gunawan DDG, Indonesia
Mr Gaston Gunewardena DDG, Sri Lanka
Dr Guo Minyuan DDG, China
Prof Guillermo T Gutierrez DDG IOM, Philippines
Ms M D C Gwinn DDG IOM LFIBA, USA
Mr Chang-Sik Ha DDG, Korea
Prof Jeong Hyo Ha DDG IOM AdVAh MOIF, Korea
Mr H M Habib DDG, United Arab Emirates
Prof Ghassan Haddad LPIBA DDG, France
Prof Datuk Dr A Hamid A Hadi DDG, Malaysia
Prof Naoyuki Hagiwara LPIBA MOIF DDG, Japan
Mr Joji Hagiwara LFIBA DDG MOIF, Japan
Dr Thomas J Hammons LPIBA DDG, Scotland
Dr Ahmed M Hamza Sayed El-Ahl LFIBA DDG MOIF, Egypt
Prof Youngmo Han DDG HonDG, Korea
Ms Nancy Sue Hardwig LFIBA DDG, USA
Dr David E Harmon LFIBA MOIF DDG IOM, USA
Mr Kiyoshi Hasegawa IOM DDG MOIF, Japan
Dr Kohji Hasunuma LFIBA DDG, Japan
Prof Dr Kazuyuki Hatada LFIBA DDG IOM, Japan
Ms Susanne S Hathaway LPIBA DDG, USA
Dr Constantine N Hatjiyiannakis DDG LFIBA DO, Greece
Prof Hisashi Hayashi DDG, Japan
Prof Dr Ali A Hebeish DDG, Egypt
Mrs Roberta M Helming HonDG MOIF AdVAh DDG, USA
Prof Yasar Metin Hepguler DDG, Switzerland
Ms Kathy A Hesterwerth LFIBA DDG MOIF, USA
The Most Rev Dr Daddy Hezekiah IOM DDG DO LFIBA, Nigeria
Dr Paul Stephen Higgs DDG, USA
Mr Tatsuya Hirata MOIF DDG, Japan
Dr Takeshi Thomas Hirayama DDG HonDG, Japan
Dr Morooka Hiroshi DDG, Japan
Prof Hoang Vu Tuyen MOIF DDG, Vietnam
Mme Dr Hoang Thi Bach Bich AdVMed DDG IOM, France
Dr Hoang Trung Du DDG, Romania
Mr Antonio Holley DDG HonDG, USA
Dr Branton K Holmberg DDG, USA
Dr Jiann-Ruey Hong DDG, Taiwan ROC
Dr Tohru Horiuchi LPIBA IOM DDG MOIF AdVMed, Japan
Ms June M Horne IOM DDG, USA
Mr S Nevin House DDG, USA
Prof Zuey-Shin Hsu LFIBA DDG IOM MOIF, Taiwan ROC
Prof John Wen-Chain Hsu DDG, Taiwan ROC
Dr Tien-Pen Hsu LFIBA DDG, Taiwan ROC
Dr Tien-tung Hsueh LFIBA DDG, Hong Kong
Mr Kwong Yuen Hu DDG, Hong Kong
Prof Hua Lesun DDG, China
Dr Pai-Tsang Huang AdVMed IOM DDG HonDG, Taiwan ROC
Ms Beryl Hughes DDG, USA
Dr Max Lin Hui-Bon-Hoa DDG, Hong Kong
Mr Charles Orvis Hunter DDG, USA
Mr Barney Hurwitz MOIF DDG, South Africa

Dr Ali Abbass Hussain Saleh DDG, Bahrain
Prof Gamil M Hussein DDG HonDG, Egypt
Prof Hassan Mohamed Ali Hussein DDG AdVSci, Sudan
Dr Kuei-Hsiang Hwang LPIBA MOIF DDG IOM LFWLA, Taiwan ROC
Rev Dr Prof Tzu-Yang Hwang LPIBA AdVAh AIOM MOIF CH DO DDG HonDG AWCASC WCOIM, USA
Dr Wen-Jyi Hwang DDG LFIBA, Taiwan ROC
Prof Haruo Hyodo AdVMed AWCASC DDG HonDG, Japan
Dr M H C J Ian DDG, Sri Lanka
Sir Anthony O Ibe DDG, Nigeria
Sir Peter Chukwunwike Ibekwe DDG, Nigeria
Alhaji Idris Ibrahim DDG LFIBA, Nigeria
Mr John Igo DDG, USA
Prof Ljiljana Igric DDG, Croatia
Mr Yukisato Iida LFIBA IOM DDG, Japan
Dr Dozie Ikedife LPIBA DDG, Nigeria
Mr Patrick Allen Ikekhua DDG HonDG, Nigeria
Prof Moon Whan Im LFIBA MOIF AWCASC DDG HonDG, Korea
Dr Chai-sit Intuwongse DDG, Thailand
Prof Ouranios Ioannides DDG LFIBA IOM, Cyprus
Dr Lorenzo Iorio DDG, Italy
Prof Alexander Iosebashvili PhD MD DDG IOM, USA
Dr David Ip LPIBA MOIF DDG AdVMed DO IOM, Hong Kong
Bishop Dr K Isaac DDG, India
Dr Hamlet Abdulla Isaxanli DDG IOM, Azerbaijan
Mr Masamichi Ishihara LFIBA DDG, Japan
Prof Peter Uche Isichei DDG MOIF, New Zealand
Prof Dr Tagir A Ismailov DDG, Daghestan
Dr Seishi Isobe DDG, Japan
Dr Tetsuya Isobe DDG, Japan
Chief Ebenezer Isokariari DDG HonDG AdVBus, Nigeria
Prof S Issaragrisil IOM LPIBA DDG, Thailand
Mr Hideki Iwamoto IOM DDG, Japan
Dr Tomio Iwasaki DDG HonDG, Japan
Prof Algirdas Jackevicius DDG, Lithuania
Dr S M Jacobsen BCA LFIBA FABI DDG DG LDAF IOM MOIF CH AGE, USA
Mr Neil H Jacoby Jr LPIBA IOM AdVSci CH DO DDG, USA
Prof Dr George V Jandieri DDG, Georgia
Prof Yong-Woong Jang DDG, Korea
Dr Abdullah Jafar Ali Jassbi DDG CH, Iran
Mr Amin Hassanali Javer LFIBA DDG, Kenya
Mrs Marie Jocelyne Jean-Baptiste DDG, USA
Dr Jong Gi Jee DDG, Korea
Dr Magali R Jerez DDG, USA
Prof Dinesh Chhaganlal Jinabhai DDG, South Africa
Dr Yasushi Joh MOIF DDG, Japan
Dr Bengt W Johansson IOM LFIBA DDG, Sweden
Dr Jane P Johnson IOM MOIF DDG, USA
Ms Margaret H Johnson LFIBA DDG, USA
Prof Gabriel Ampah Johnson DDG AdVSci IOM HonDG, Togo
Prof John B Jordanoglou DDG, Greece
Dr Prem Chandra Joshi DDG, India
Dr Nicolina L Joubert DDG, South Africa
Prof Dehua Ju DDG IOM AdVSci LFIBA, China
Dr Gonzalez M Juana MOIF DDG IOM, Sierra Leone
Prof Tae-Youn Jun DDG, Korea
Prof Natalia Juristo DDG, Spain
Dr Kamaruzaman Jusoff DDG, Malaysia
Dr Sci Habil Nella Kacergiene MOIF DDG LFIBA DO, Lithuania
Prof Joseph M N Kakooza DDG, Uganda
Dr Mirja Kalliopuska DDG IOM MOIF, Finland
Prof Yuliya Emilova Kamenova DDG LFIBA DDG, Bulgaria

Mr Tetsuo Kaneko LPIBA DDG AdVSci IOM, Japan
Prof Sam Suk Kang IOM MOIF DDG, Korea
Mr Hyungwoo Kang DDG, Korea
Dr Richard Willy Kanzler DDG IOM MOIF, South Africa
Dr Paul E Kaplan DDG, USA
Dr Isak Karabegovic DDG, Bosnia and Herzegovina
Associate Prof Strashimir Karanov DDG, Bulgaria
Dr Milan Karvas DDG, Slovakia
Prof Serafim Kastanakis DDG, Greece
Mr Neimat Abbasuli Oglu Kasumov DDG, Azerbaijan
Dr Satoshi Katai DDG MOIF, Japan
Ms M M Katchur LPIBA DDG MOIF AdVMed, USA
Dr Satish K Kaushik DDG, Australia
Prof Shunji Kawamoto DDG LFIBA, Japan
Dr Ahmed Kazim DDG, United Arab Emirates
Mrs Terri Lilya Keanely LFIBA DDG AWCASC, USA
Mr Richard Kemoli DDG, Kenya
Prof Dr Hans J Kempe DDG AWCASC, Germany
Dr Christine M Kennefick LFIBA IOM DDG MOIF, USA
Prof Jovanka Kepeska PhD LFIBA DDG, Macedonia
Mr Askhad S Khabibullaev LFIBA DDG, Uzbekistan
Prof Alexander A Khadartsev DDG HonDG, Russia
Ms Lurey Khan DDG DO, USA
Mr Qadir Bakhsh Khan DDG, USA
Dr Kazim Ali Khan DDG, India
Commodore Anand Khandekar (Retd) DDG, India
Dr Rustom A Khatib DDG, Lebanon
Prof Vladimir Kh Khavinson DDG, Russia
Prof Ramaz Khetsuriani MD PhD DDG IOM, Georgia
Mr George Khizanishvili DDG, Georgia
Dr Khoo Boo-Chai AdVMed DDG IOM MOIF HonDG, Singapore
Dr Noriyasu Kihara DDG IOM LFIBA DO, Japan
Dr Adem Kilicman DDG LFIBA, Malaysia
Prof Rev Dr Kim Kwang Tae LFIBA DDG, Korea
Prof Pill Soo Kim LPIBA DDG IOM AdVSci CH, Korea
Dr Seok Kwun Kim DDG, Korea
Dr Kyoung Soo Kim LPIBA IOM MOIF HonDG DDG AdVSci, Korea
Prof Yoon Soo Kim DDG, Korea
Dr Chan-Ki Kim DDG, Korea
Dr Jae Hyo Kim DDG, Korea
Mr Yong Kuk Kim DDG, Korea
Prof Seock-Sam Kim DDG, Korea
Prof Jin Kyu Kim DDG, Korea
Dr Jeongsu Kim DDG, Korea
Prof Jinsul Kim DDG, Korea
Prof Dong Ha Kim DDG, Korea
Prof Dr Dong Ho Kim DDG LFIBA, Korea
Prof Changsu Kim DDG, Korea
Dr Hyeun Sung Kim LFIBA DDG, Korea
Dr Yong Ho Kim DDG, Korea
Prof Dae-Soung Kim DDG, Korea
Dr Hyung Hun Kim DDG, Korea
Mr Young Jae Kim DDG, Korea
Prof Katsumi Kimura DDG, Japan
Mr Masashi Kimura MOIF DDG IOM DO HonDG AdVSci, Japan
Rev Dr Harold Ivor Edwin Kingdon DDG, USA
Dr Vihar Nikolov Kiskinov DDG, Bulgaria
Prof Hirohisa Kitano DDG, Japan
Dr Aggrey Kiyingi DDG, Australia
Mr Tor G Kjoelberg DDG, Norway
Prof Eliezer I Klainman LPIBA IOM AdVMed DDG, Israel
Prof Ir Pierre Klees DDG HonDG IOM, Belgium
Prof Wlodzimierz Klonowski DDG, Poland
Prof Vladimir V Klyuev DDG, Russia
Mr Dagfinn Andreas Knudsen DDG MOIF HonDG, Norway

Prof Il Seok (Franz) Ko DDG, Korea
Dr Edvard Kobal DDG, Slovenia
Mr Nikolai Mykola I Kobasko DDG, USA
Prof Toshiro Kobayashi MOIF DDG HonDG, Japan
Prof Yukio Kobayashi DDG LFIBA MOIF, Japan
Dr Venkata Surya Ramam Koduri DDG, Chile
Dr Spincer Sih-Ping Koh DDG, Taiwan ROC
Ms Ladi Comfort Tanko Kokwain DDG, Nigeria
Prof Oleg A Kolobov DDG, Russia
Prof Victor G Komar DDG IOM, Russia
Prof Changduk Kong DDG, Korea
Prof Dr Toshihiko Kono DDG, USA
Prof Chong Min Koo DDG, Korea
Dr Yoon-Ah Kook DDG, Korea
Ms CheriLyn Korth DDG, USA
Prof Dr Annikki M Koskensalo DDG, Finland
Prince Molum Owolabi Kosoko DDG, Nigeria
Prof Gennady P Kotelnikov DDG, Russia
Dr Allabhax D Kotnal DDG, India
Dr Vitaly Kovalchuk DDG, Russia
Prof Ryszard Kozlowski DDG, Poland
Prof Dr Nadezhda Krasnoyarova DDG HonDG AWCASC MOIF, Kazakhstan
Mr Nicholaos Kretsis DDG LFIBA, Greece
Dr Walter Kreyszig DDG, Canada
Dr Alexei Krivolutsky DDG, Russia
Bishop Navasard Ktshoyan CH DDG, Armenia
Prof Ryszard Kucha LFIBA IOM DDG, Poland
Dr Dietmar Alfred Kumm LFIBA DDG, Germany
Dr Joy T Kunjappu DDG, USA
Prof Dr Heinrich W Kunstmann DDG AWCASC, Germany
Dr Soji Kurimoto IOM AdVMed DDG, Japan
Marvin Z Kurlan MD FACS LFIBA DDG IOM, USA
Prof Vladimir G Kuz DDG, Ukraine
Dr Oleg Kuzichkin DDG, Russia
Dr Vladimir Kuznetsov DDG, Singapore
Prof Hyuk-Joon Kwon DDG, Korea
Prof Bernhard Kytzler DDG, South Africa
Prof Aris Lacis DDG, Latvia
Prof Romans Lacis LFIBA DDG, Latvia
Mrs Elly A Ladas DDG, Greece
Dr Armando Vicente Lago IOM DDG CH, Argentina
Dr Eric P S Lai DDG, Hong Kong
Mr Chin-Hung Lai LFIBA DDG AdVSci IOM, Taiwan ROC
Mr Paul F Lalande MOIF DDG, France
Mr Billy Lam LFIBA DDG, Hong Kong
Dr Luc Johan Lambrecht LPIBA DDG MOIF IOM HonDG, Belgium
Ms Lilly Katherine Lane DDG, USA
Dr Martti Johannes Larikka DDG, Finland
Dr Benedicte Laursen DDG MOIF LFIBA AdVMed HonDG AWCASC, Denmark
Dr John L Lawson Jr DDG MOIF DO, USA
Dr Dale P Layman PhD MOIF DDG LPIBA AdVMed AIOM HonDG, USA
Dr Harry C Layton DDG IOM LHD, USA
Dr Elhang Howard Lee DDG, Korea
Dr Irene Lee DDG, USA
Mr Andrew Siu-Woo Lee MOIF DDG LPIBA, Hong Kong
Dr Don Yoon Lee PhD LFIBA DDG, USA
Ms Angela W Y Lee DDG, Hong Kong
Prof Jeong Y Lee DDG LFIBA, Korea
Dr Shyh-Dye Lee DDG, Taiwan ROC
Ms Emily H M Kuo Lee DDG, USA
Mr Doyung Lee IOM DDG HonDG, USA
Prof Sang Hee Lee IOM DDG, Korea
Dr Chi Shing Lee DDG HonDG, Hong Kong
Prof Dr Keun-Young Lee DDG, Korea

Dr Dongwoon Lee DDG, Korea
Prof Jehee Lee DDG, Korea
Prof Chang-Myung Lee DDG, Korea
Dr Seung Hwan Lee DDG, Korea
Dr Sang-Cheol Lee DDG, Korea
Prof Dr Geuk Lee DDG, Korea
Dr Jeong-Phil Lee DDG, Korea
Dr Hyun Chong Lee DDG, Korea
Prof Seung Hwan Lee DDG, USA
Dr Laurence A Lees LFIBA DDG, Australia
Miss Joy LeRoy LPIBA MOIF DDG HonDG AIOM OIA AGE CG OAA AWASC, USA
Prof Gorazd Lesnicar DDG, Slovenia
Prof Jerzy Leszczynski DDG, USA
Dr Winston G Lewis LPIBA MOIF DDG IOM AWCASC, Trinidad & Tobago
Prof Li Zhongying DDG, USA
Prof Liang Dan-Fong LPIBA DDG, Taiwan ROC
Dr Lila Lila DDG, Australia
Ms Joan Pek Bee Lim LFIBA IOM DDG, Malaysia
Dr Phillip K Lim LPIBA DDG, USA
Prof Chung-sheng Lin DDG, Taiwan ROC
Prof Lin Tiezheng DDG, China
Prof Zone-Ching Lin DDG MOIF LFIBA, Taiwan ROC
Prof Yuh-Ling Lin DDG, Taiwan ROC
Mr Chia-Hsiang Lin DDG AdVSci, Taiwan ROC
Ms J C McKee Lindsay LPIBA IOM DDG MOIF, USA
Ms Joanne M Lindsey IOM DDG MOIF, USA
Dr Savvas John Lionis DDG LFIBA, Greece
Mr Yeh Chyn Kuo Liou DDG, USA
Mr Liu Guohui DDG, China
Prof Yanpei Liu DDG, China
Mr Zhaorong Liu DDG, China
Prof HsinChih F Liu DDG MOIF IOM, Taiwan ROC
Dr Chun Ming Liu DDG HonDG, Taiwan ROC
Mr Chiu-Yuen Benson Lo LFIBA DDG, Hong Kong
Dr Otto-Robert Loesener DDG, USA
Prof Harti Hanns Löffler di Casagiove DDG, Italy
Sir George Lofgren DDG, USA
Dr Kheng Min Loi DDG, Malaysia
Mr Ho-Quang Long DDG, Vietnam
Hon Gov Prof Dr Elizeu Pereira Lopes LFIBA MOIF AdVSci DDG AIOM HonDG DG HE, Brazil
Hon Gov Prof Dr Eliezer Pereira Lopes LFIBA MOIF AIOM DDG AdVSci HonDG DG HE, Brazil
Mrs Julia M LoTempio DDG, USA
Dr Alan Louis LPIBA MOIF IOM DDG HonDG, England
Dr Timothy Low LFIBA DDG, Singapore
Prof Dr Ramon Lucas Lucas LFIBA DDG, Italy
Prof Vladimir Luchkevich DDG, Russia
Dr ing Drita Lulo LPIBA IOM DDG AdVSci MOIF, Albania
Prof Luo Yuanzheng DDG, China
Dr Edward Ching-Ruey Luo DDG, Taiwan ROC
Prof T Maghiar DDG AdVSci IOM LFIBA MOIF, Romania
Mr Ki Choong Mah DDG, Korea
Mr Russell J Maharaj IOM DDG, Trinidad & Tobago
Prof Abel Maharramov DDG, Azerbaijan
Dr Florence Omolara Mahoney DDG AdVAh, The Gambia
Dr Moses Makayoto DDG, Kenya
Mr Vladimir G Makhankov DDG, USA
Prof Mohammad S Makki DDG HonDG LFIBA, Saudi Arabia
Mr Faramaz Maksudov DDG, Azerbaijan
Prof Lyubov T Malaya DDG, Ukraine
Mr Hamid A Malik DDG, Saudi Arabia
Dr H Malin LPIBA LFWLA DDG IOM MOIF AdVMed CH, USA
Prof Efim M Malitikov DDG, Russia
Dr John J Manolakakis MD LPIBA DDG IOM, Zimbabwe

Ms Patricia J S Mapel DDG, USA
Prof Giorgio Marcou DDG, Greece
Mr Israel Arieh Mark DDG, Israel
Dr Koshi Maruyama DDG, Japan
Mr Jean-Francois Mascari DDG, Italy
Sir Paulias Matane DDG, Papua New Guinea
Mr Om Prakash Mathur DDG, India
Dr Nobuhito Matsushiro DDG AdVSci IOM HonDG, Japan
Dr Clarice Chris Matteson PhD DDG, USA
Prof Vladimir Matvienko IOM DDG, Ukraine
Dr Dmitry Mavlo MOIF DDG, Russia
Dr Patricia J Maybin IOM DDG, USA
Prof Wolfgang Mayer-Koenig DDG, Austria
Dr Ivan I Mazur DDG IOM, England
Ms Mabel Mazzini IOM DDG, Argentina
Dr Colette Grace Mazzucelli DDG HonDG, USA
Dr Lucie Mba DDG, Gabon
Mr Tito Titus Mboweni DDG, South Africa
Dr James Ndungu Mburu DDG, Kenya
Dr Leland McClanahan DDG MOIF LFIBA, USA
Mr Gary Albert McConnell MOIF DDG, Norway
Prof Marianne McDonald LFIBA IOM CH AdVAh DDG, USA
Mr Paul McDonald Smith DDG MOIF, Australia
Prof Nasip Mecaj DDG, Albania
Mr David G Mehr DDG, USA
Mr Ioannis Melissanidis DDG, Greece
Prof Dr Parakkat Ramakrishnan Menon DDG, India
Mr Paul J Meyer IOM LFIBA DDG, USA
Dr Isaac L Mgemane LPIBA IOM DDG CH DO HonDG, South Africa
Prof Dr Alexandru Mica DDG, Romania
Prof Dr H A Michalek MOIF DDG, Austria
Dr P Mierzejewski Count of Calmont DDG, Poland
Dr Magdy Mikhail DDG, USA
Prof Peter Mikhailenko DDG MOIF IOM, Ukraine
Dr Victor N Mikhailov LFIBA IOM DDG, Russia
Prof Aleksandr T Mikhailov DDG, Spain
Dr Yoshitsugu Miki LFIBA DDG IOM, Japan
Dr Errol C Miller DDG LFIBA, Jamaica
Ms Carol Ann Mills DDG, USA
Prof Nairmen Mina DDG, Puerto Rico
Prof Tetsuya Mine DDG, Japan
Mr Mohamed A Mitkees DDG, United Arab Emirates
Dr Elpis Mitropoulou DDG, Greece
Mr Akihiko Miura DDG, Japan
Prof Iwao Miyachi LPIBA IOM MOIF DDG AdVSci HonDG DO, Japan
Mr Gu-Zi Mo DDG, China
Mrs Veena Modi DDG, India
Mr Henry Stanley Rawle Moe DDG, Antigua
Dr Amir-Naser Moezi DDG, Iran
Prof Sureswar Mohanty DDG, India
Dr Victoria I Mojekwu LFIBA DDG, Nigeria
Mr Ho Ming Joseph Mok LFIBA MOIF DDG, Hong Kong
Dr Ntsu Mokhehle MOIF DDG, South Africa
Mr Eric Bhamuza Molefe IOM DDG AdVFin CH HonDG, South Africa
Mr Eric Mathew Moles DDG AdVFin, Canada
Dr Alexander Kaoranu Molokwu DDG, Nigeria
Ms Elizabeth Monteree-Zaleski DDG, Australia
Mr Ralph E Montijo LPIBA DDG IOM, USA
Dr Felicia Nwanne Monye DDG, Nigeria
Prof Sinyong Moon DDG, Korea
Mr Michael Moraitis LFIBA DDG, Greece
Prof Masahiko Mori DDS DDG, Japan
Prof Hirotoshi Morii DDG, Japan
Dr Naofumi Morita DDG HonDG, Japan

Prof Mineo Moritani DDG, Japan
Mr Benjamin Moshwana DDG, South Africa
Mr Vladimir Dmitrievich Moukha DDG, Russia
Dr Chi Cheung Moy DDG, Hong Kong
Prof N Mulabegovic LFIBA DDG IOM, Bosnia and Herzegovina
Mrs Sharon R Mulkey DDG, USA
Dr Margit Gabriele Muller DDG, United Arab Emirates
Dr Edwin Muniz Jr DDG, USA
Dr Tadeusz K Murawski DDG MOIF LFIBA IOM, Poland
Prof Dr Omar M S Mustafa DDG, Cyprus
Mr George K Mwai LPIBA DDG IOM, Kenya
Prof John Gowland Mwangi DDG, Kenya
Dr Sang Ho Na LFIBA DDG, Korea
Mr Mohinder Singh Nadala DDG HonDG, India
Dr Yukio Nagamachi DDG IOM, Japan
Dr Kazunori Nagashima DDG IOM, Japan
Prof Akira Nagatomi LPIBA MOIF AdVSci DO DDG, Japan
Mrs Yong-Gyun Nah LFIBA DDG, Korea
Dr Shrinivas H Naidu LFIBA DDG, USA
Princess Kaoru Nakamaru DDG MOIF, Japan
Dr Shigehisa Nakamura LFIBA DDG IOM, Japan
Dr Ho-Yun Nam DDG LFIBA WCOIM, Korea
Prof Jatinder Nath Nanda DDG, India
Mr Shiv Sahai Naraine DDG, Guyana
Dr Eva Mae Nash-Isaac DDG IOM, USA
Dr M Natarajan MOIF DDG, India
Prof Ahmed Nawar IOM DDG, Egypt
Mr Philemon Ndesamburo DDG, Tanzania
Mr Frederick L Neff DDG, USA
Mr Syoum Michael Negassi DDG, France
Prof Johan Theron Nel LFIBA DDG MOIF IOM AdVMed DO, South Africa
Prof Eviatar Nevo DDG LFIBA MOIF, Israel
Prof Heung-Tat Ng DDG, Taiwan ROC
Dr Frankie M C Ng IOM MOIF DDG, Hong Kong
Prof Dr Ngo Dat Tam DDG, Vietnam
Prof Thu The Nguyen DDG, USA
Prof Nguyen Canh Toan MOIF DDG HonDG, Vietnam
Mr Huu Thai Hoa (Henry) Nguyen DDG, Vietnam
Dr Hiroshi Niimura LFIBA DDG IOM, Japan
Mr Alexander G M Nijbakker LFIBA DDG, Netherlands
Dr Victor Alekseevich Nikerov DDG, Russia
Dr Ekaterini Nikolarea DDG, Greece
Dr Blazho Nikolov DDG, Bulgaria
Dr Massimiliano Nisati DDG AdVAh, Italy
Prof Tasuku Noguchi DDG LFIBA, Japan
Dr Takuma Nomiya LFIBA MOIF DDG IOM AdVMed, Japan
Dr Khalida I Noor LPIBA DDG, Saudi Arabia
Grand Dr Jury Noskov DDG LFIBA, Russia
Dr Pavel Novosad DDG LFIBA MOIF IOM HonDG, Czech Republic
Prof Jozef Novotny LFIBA DDG IOM, Slovakia
Mr Benson Iroabuchi Nwoji DDG, Nigeria
Dr Soe Nyunt DDG, Singapore
Prof Nzele David Nzomo DDG, Kenya
Ms Rosaline Odeh DDG, Nigeria
Dr Henrietta Ingo Ogan DDG, Nigeria
Rev Anthony E Ogba DDG, Nigeria
Prof Dr Takashi Oguchi DDG AIOM DO HonDG AdVSci MOIF LPIBA, Japan
Dr Joo Han Oh DDG, Korea
Dr Masaki Ohkawa DDG MOIF, Japan
Dr Akihide Ohkuchi LPIBA DDG MOIF AdVMed IOM DO, Japan
Emeritus Prof Katsuichiro Ohsaki DDG MOIF HonDG, Japan
Mr Shozo Ohtsuka LPIBA DDG, Japan

Mr Masa Aki Oka DDG, Japan
Prof Masahiro Oka DDG, Japan
Prof Anthony Olisaemeka Okafor DDG, Nigeria
Prof Christopher Uchefuna Okeke DDG, Nigeria
Prof Emmanuel Chukwuemeka Okereke DDG, Nigeria
Sir Josiah Onyebuchi Johnson Okezie DDG, Nigeria
Dr Bartholomew E Okoduwa DDG, Nigeria
Mr Akira Okuyama LFIBA DDG, Japan
Dr Ing Paul-Christian Olaru DDG, Romania
Mr David V F Olateru-Olagbegi DDG, Nigeria
Dr (Mrs) Ayoka Mopelola Olusakin DDG, Nigeria
Mr Patrick Chizoba Omabu DDG, Nigeria
Prof Iwao Omae DDG, Japan
Dr Bernard O'Meara LFIBA DDG, Australia
Dr Tadanori Ondoh DDG LFIBA, Japan
Prof Saime Ulker Ones DDG, Turkey
Dr Vladimir I Onopriev IOM DDG, Russia
Dr Sazrar Opata DDG, Ghana
Dr Siddalingeswara Orekondy MOIF DDG, Australia
Dr C G Orvell IOM DDG MOIF AdVMed DO, Sweden
Mr Alfred Abiodun Oshowole DDG, Nigeria
Dr Gladys S Ostrom MOIF DDG, USA
A A Oteng-Amoako PhD MOIF DDG, Ghana
Dr Akeeb O Bola Oyefolu DDG, Nigeria
Mr Nick Pahys Jr DDG CH AdVAh, USA
Dr Bojan Pajic WCOIM LFIBA AdVMed DDG, Switzerland
Dr Pritam S Panesar LFIBA DDG, Kenya
Mr Henry K Pangelinan DDG, Saipan
Prof Paolo Pantani DDG IOM, Italy
Ms Eva Papai DDG, Hungary
Dr Choon-Keun Park DDG, Korea
Dr Il-Kwon Park LFIBA DDG, Korea
Mr Yongwan Park DDG, Korea
Prof Dr Kwang Joo Park DDG, Korea
Prof Hong-Seok Park DDG AdVSci IOM DO HonDG, Korea
Prof Wansu Park DDG, Korea
Mr Manoel Carlos F F Parolari DDG, Brazil
Dr Eugenia Pasternak CM PhD DDG LPIBA IOM, Canada
Dr D V R Pasupuleti DDG LFIBA MOIF DO AdVMed IOM, USA
Mr Abdullah Suleman Patel DDG, Zambia
Dr Howard John Peak DDG, Australia
Dr Mette K Pedersen DDG MOIF HonDG, Denmark
Dr Bozena Pejkovic DDG, Slovenia
Dr Sergey Nikolayevich Pelykh DDG, Ukraine
Ms Nancy Pencherek-Jackson DDG, USA
Dr Liviu Pendefunda DDG IOM, Romania
Mr I R Perumal DDG, India
Dr Sergio G Petersen DDG, Brazil
Dr Barbara B Peterson DDG, USA
Prof Petko Stoyanov Petkov DDG, Bulgaria
Prof L A Petrov MOIF DDG, Bulgaria
Mr Horst Willy Petzold IOM DDG MOIF, USA
Mr Karel Pexidr DDG, Czech Republic
Dr Sulejman Peza DDG, Albania
Prof Phan Huu Dat DDG, Vietnam
Ms Thresia Pierce LFIBA DDG AdVAh, USA
Dr Vimolvan Pimpan LFIBA DDG, Thailand
Prof Dr E N Pinguli CH LPIBA AdVSci IOM MOIF DDG DO, Albania
Mr Jozsef Pinter DDG, Hungary
Prof Dr Drozda Pisseva-Stoyanova DDG, Bulgaria
Ms Bernarda Polanc DDG, Slovenia
Mr Ion Popescu DDG, Romania
Prof Katarina Popov-Pergal DDG, Serbia
Dr M L Porter LPIBA DDG HonDG, USA
Mr Malcolm Frederick Potter DDG, Australia
Dr Odon Prado Loredo DDG, Mexico

Ms Letricia E C Preston DDG, USA
Dr Zbigniew Jerzy Przerembski DDG, Poland
Dr Raisa I Pshenichnikova DDG AWCASC, Russia
Dr Alexandru Puiu DDG, Romania
Prof Qu Lian Bi DDG, China
Prof Roger Rafanomezantsoa DDG, Madagascar
Dr Mariam Rajab DDG, Lebanon
Dr Srinivasa S Rajan LFIBA DDG, India
Mr Anumolu Ramakrishna DDG, India
Dr Sundaram Ramaswamy DDG, India
Mr Harold Radj Ramdhani DDG, Suriname
Dr Aspy Phiroze Rana DDG, India
Dr Usha Rao DDG, India
Dr A Satyanarayana Rao DDG, India
Dr Harun Ar Rashid DDG, Bangladesh
Dr Gerald Lee Ratliff DDG, USA
Dr Paul Ratnayake DDG, Switzerland
Dr Md Abdur Razzaque DDG, Bangladesh
Reverend Heinrich Reinhardt PhD DDG, Switzerland
Dr Milan Remko LPIBA MOIF DDG, Slovakia
Dr Jaidev Singh Retola DDG IOM, India
Dr Lonnie Royce Rex DDG, USA
Mr Eugene E Rhemann LPIBA DDG DO AdVAh, USA
Mr Richard David Rhimes DDG IOM AdVSci MOIF DO, Australia
Ms Sharron Maye Riddle DDG, USA
Prof Oueslati Ridha DDG, Tunisia
Mrs Dorothy Ringlesbach LFIBA DDG, USA
Dr Roberto Miguel Rodriguez DDG LFIBA, USA
Dr Grayce M Roessler DDG, USA
Dr Belle Sara Rosenbaum IOM DDG, USA
Dr Yuriy A Rossikhin DDG, Russia
Ms C I Rouchdy LFIBA MOIF DDG, Saudi Arabia
Mr Zoliana Royte DDG, India
Dr Seth Isaiah Rubin IOM DDG, USA
Mr Shimon Rubinstein AdVAh DDG IOM MOIF, Israel
Dr P A Rubio MD PhD LPIBA DDG, USA
Prof Vladimir A Rusol LPIBA DDG MOIF, Russia
Ms Phyllis Ann Ruth MOIF DDG HonDG, USA
Dr Tongmin Sa DDG, Korea
Amb Josefa Leonel Correia Sacko DDG, Ghana
Prof Victoria Safonova DDG, Russia
Mr Irek Safargaleev LFIBA DDG AdVAh, Russia
Dr Pascal Marie Saffache DDG, Martinique
Dr Bindeshwar Prasad Sah DDG, India
Mrs Shikiko Saitoh LPIBA IOM DDG, Japan
Prof Ahmad Salahuddin DDG LFIBA MOIF, Zimbabwe
Mr Mohammad Abdul Saleem LFIBA DDG, United Arab Emirates
Dr Holem M Saliba DDG IOM AdVSci CH LFIBA, Lebanon
Dr Uday Salunkhe DDG, India
Mr Anatoly Samokhin DDG, Russia
Dr Gilbert Carlos San Diego LFIBA MOIF IOM DDG HonDG, Philippines
Dr Luis Enrique Sanchez Crespo DDG, Spain
Mr E F Sanguinetti DDG, Argentina
Dr Antonio Santangelo DDG, Italy
Dr Emmanuel T Santos DDG, Philippines
Mr Masakazu Sarai DDG, Japan
Mrs Arlene Sarkoyan DDG, USA
Dr Mitsuo Sato DDG, Japan
Dr Kazuo Sato DDG, Japan
Mr Sagandyk Satubaldin DDG DO, Kazakhstan
Prof Dr Bhavanari Satyanarayana DDG, India
Prof Vladimir V Saveliev DDG, Korea
Ms Mariann D Savilla DDG, USA
Mr Anton I Savvov DDG, Ukraine
Prof Alfred Schauer DDG, Germany

Prof Dr Adolf E Schindler DDG LFIBA, Germany
Prof Judith T Scholl LFIBA DDG, USA
Mr Jorg U Schroeder LFIBA MOIF DDG, Germany
HE A A Sedacca SFO DDG LFIBA MOIF OIA LDAF, USA
Prof Baik Lin Seong DDG, Korea
Jukka Tapani Seppinen DDG, Finland
Dr Elsa C Servy DDG, Argentina
Mrs Afsaneh Shaaban Nejad CH DDG, Iran
Dr Shirish Shah LFIBA DDG MOIF HonDG AdVSci, USA
Prof Mrad Shahia DDG, South Africa
Prof Dr Alexei N Shamin DDG, Russia
Dr Isadore Shapiro DDG IOM, USA
Dr Hari Shanker Sharma DDG, Sweden
Mr Hamzeh Mohammed Shaweesh DDG, Jordan
Prof George V Shchokin DDG LFIBA MOIF, Ukraine
Dr Muhammad M Mukram Sheikh DDG HLFIBA IOM, Botswana
Dr Nimish Shelat LPIBA DDG, India
Master Ronger Shen DDG, USA
Dr Chai Cheng Sheng DDG, Singapore
Ms Shi Bingxia DDG, China
Prof Tso-Min Shih DDG, Taiwan ROC
Prof Chun-Jen Shih LFIBA DDG, Taiwan ROC
Dr Sang-Tai Shim DDG, Korea
Dr Yasuyuki Shimada LFIBA MOIF DDG, Japan
Prof Koki Shimoji DDG LFIBA, Japan
Mr Min-Ku Shin DDG LFIBA MOIF HonDG, Korea
Ms Marina V Shitikova DDG, Russia
Dr Leonid Vassilievich Shmakov DDG, Russia
Mrs Galia Shulga DDG, Latvia
Prof Andrei Vasilii Shulga DDG HonDG, Russia
Prof Dr Jau-Ying Shyr (Stone) DDG, Taiwan ROC
Ms Monique S Sidaross DDG AdVSci, USA
Mr Robert D Siedle LPIBA DDG AdVBus IOM, USA
Prof G S Siklosi DDG LPIBA MOIF IOM CH, Hungary
Dr Velimir N Simicevic MD IOM DDG LFIBA, Croatia
Dr Teja Singh LFIBA IOM DDG, Canada
Dr Navin Kumar Sinha DDG, India
Dr Jimmy Ong Sio MOIF LFIBA IOM DDG DO, USA
Mr Fred Dean Sisk LFIBA DDG, USA
Mr Aleksandre Sitnikov DDG, Russia
Prof Krzysztof Sliwa DDG LFIBA CH, USA
Ms Ina Smiley Clayton PhD DDG AdVAh, USA
Dr Valery K Smirnov LFIBA MOIF DDG, Russia
Mr Christopher L Snyder DDG WCIOM, USA
Ms Beatriz Lizama Soberanis DDG, Mexico
Prof Dr A M M Solaiman DDG, Saudi Arabia
Prof Vladimir Solenov DDG, Russia
Mr Alexander Igorevich Solovey DDG, Russia
Dr Olateju Abiola Somorin DDG, Nigeria
Ms Anne-Marie A Sondakh DDG, Indonesia
Prof Song Zhongyue DDG, China
Dr Yo Han Song AdVMed DDG, Korea
Dr Igor Sourovtzev DDG, Russia
Miss Callie J Spady FIBA DDG, USA
Mr Ion G Spanulescu DDG HonDG, Romania
Dr Vera Spatenkova DDG, Czech Republic
Mr Ramesh Kumar Srivastava DDG, India
Mr Peter Stadler DDG LFIBA, Denmark
Mr Charles D Stallworth DDG, USA
Ms Ursula Helena Stanescu DDG, Romania
Ms Barbara Anne (Bond) Steiner DDG, USA
Ms Izabela Steinka DDG, Poland
Ms Annette Michelle Stokes IOM DDG, USA
Prof Dr Boyko S Stoyanov LPIBA DDG IOM MOIF, Japan
Prof Roman G Strongin LFIBA DDG, Russia
Prof Hyontai Sug LFIBA MOIF AdVSci DDG AIOM DO, Korea

Prof Chizuko Sugita DDG, Japan
Prof Qian Zhang Sun DDG MOIF, China
Prof Dr A Sun IOM MOIF LPIBA DDG CH AdVMed HonDG, Taiwan ROC
Mr Ulf L Sundblad DDG, Sweden
Dr E Sundermoorthy HPSM DHMS DDG, India
Prof Dr Shin'ichi Suzuki DDG, Japan
Dr Srikanta M N Swamy LFIBA DDG IOM, Canada
Dr Andrzej Szczerbakow DDG, Poland
Mr Norio Takeoka DDG, Japan
Prof Yukio Takizawa IOM DDG, Japan
Dr Masaki Tan DDG, Japan
Prof Yoshihiro Tanaka DDG LFIBA, Japan
Prof Hiroshige Tanaka DDG LFIBA AdVFin, Japan
Dr Zhichun Tang DDG, China
Prof Giulio F Tarro DDG IOM, Italy
Dr Aslan Kitovich Thakushinov DDG, Russia
Ms Marie Alice Theard DDG, Haiti
Mr V T Thiayagarajan DDG AWCASC, Singapore
Dr M Thiel IOM LPIBA DDG MOIF AAAS CH DO, Germany
Prof Dr Georges Emile Andre Thill DDG HonDG AdVAh, Belgium
Mr Daniel Edward Thomas DDG, USA
HRH Admiral Steven Roy Thomashow LFIBA DDG IOM DG HE(IOA) FABI, USA
Mrs Theresa M Thombs DDG, USA
Captain Dr Ivica Tijardovic DDG LPIBA MOIF AIOM HonDG AdVSci DO, Croatia
Mr Gary L Tipton LFIBA DDG, USA
Dr Ljerka Tiska-Rudman DDG, Croatia
Dr Brigitte Simone Tison DDG, France
Mr Criton P Tomazos DDG, England
Dr Pui To Tong DDG, Hong Kong
Prof Florin Nicolai Topoliceanu DDG, Romania
Dr Felix Toran DDG IOM, France
Ms Lillian Del Toro DDG, USA
Dr Dimitrios T Trafalis DDG, Greece
Dr Tran Quang Hai LFIBA DDG, France
Prof Tran Van Truong DDG, Vietnam
Prof Tsai Chiu-Lai LFIBA DDG MOIF, Taiwan ROC
Ir Philip Kui Tse DDG AdVSci, Canada
Prof Cheng Kui Tseng DDG, China
Mr Tang-Kuang Tseng DDG, Taiwan ROC
Dr Ming-Shium Tu DDG WCOIM, Taiwan ROC
Prof P Tuglaci IOM LFWLA DDG MOIF LPIBA HonDG, Turkey
Prof Oleksiy Tymofyeyev DDG, Ukraine
Dr Kenneth O Udeh DDG, Poland
Prof Edward Ueno LPIBA MOIF DDG IOM AdVSci, Japan
Dr David O Ukaegbu DDG, Nigeria
Reverend Dr James Udogu Ukaegbu DDG, Nigeria
Mr Isyaku Tofa Umar IOM DDG AdVBus LFIBA MOIF, Nigeria
Dr Diclehan Unsal DDG, Turkey
Prof Vitaly Nicolaevich Uvarov DDG, Kazakhstan
Prof Dr Lehel Vadon DDG, Hungary
Dr Alexander Valendo DDG, Belarus
Dr Reinier Jan Van Meerten IOM HonDG DDG, Netherlands
Dr Carrie Temple Vance IOM DDG, USA
Ms J Egenes Vander Naald LFIBA DDG IOM, USA
Dr Marilene Batista Vargas DDG, Brazil
Prof Baidya Varma DDG, USA
Mrs Peggy T Vaughan DDG HonDG MOIF DO, USA
Mr Juan Garbin Vereda DDG, Spain
Constantin K Vereketis LPIBA DDG, Greece
Dr Rajesh Kumar Verma DDG HonDG AdVAh LFIBA, India
Dr Ruslana Vernickaite MOIF DDG LFIBA IOM, Lithuania

Dr Steven A Vladem LFIBA DDG IOM, USA
Mr James Yaovi Vodzi DDG, Ghana
Mt Rev Dr Robert A Voice DDG, Canada
Prof Vyacheslav T Volov DDG, Russia
Ms Annita C Walker DDG LFIBA IOM, USA
Ms Annette Walker DDG, USA
Mr Albert Fred Walker Jr DDG, USA
W W Walley MD DDG AdVMed, USA
Prof Wang Tao LFIBA DDG, China
Prof Zhong Gao Wang DDG, China
Dr Jong Wang DDG, China
Mr Rollin M Warner Jr LFIBA DDG, USA
Prof Atsushi Watanabe DDG, Japan
Mr Menizibeya Osain Welcome LFIBA DDG, Belarus
Dr Don B Wethasinghe LPIBA DDG, Sri Lanka
Mr Roger James Whitbeck IOM DDG, USA
Ms Clara Jo White MGA LFIBA DDG, USA
Mr Brooks Morris Whitehurst DDG HonDG, USA
Mr Bruce Lincoln Whyte IOM DDG, USA
Dr M R Wiemann Jr LPIBA LFWLA DDG IOM MOIF, USA
Dr Joseph R Williams DDG, USA
Ms Cynthia Ann Williams LFIBA DDG FABI, USA
Mr James L Williams DDG, USA
Dr Samuel Jeyakumar Williams BSc DDG, India
Dr Babatunde Adebayd Akintola Williams DDG, Nigeria
Mr Emmanuel A Winful LPIBA DDG, Ghana
Dr Azi Wolfenson LPIBA DDG, USA
Mr Vincent W S Wong LPIBA IOM DDG, Malaysia
Dr Baron C K W Wong MD LFIBA MOIF DO DDG, USA
Prof Dr Albert Wing Kuen Wong MOIF HonDG DDG LFIBA, Hong Kong
Prof Sung-Il Woo DDG, Korea
Ms Dixie Lee Wood DDG IOM, USA
Prof Eugen-Georg Woschni DDG, Germany
Prof Ching-Yi Wu DDG, Taiwan ROC
Dr Christina Xinyan Xie LFIBA MOIF AdVAh DDG HonDG, Hong Kong
Prof Xu Benli DDG, China
Mr Yadugiri Kiran Kumar DDG, India
Prof Kohei Yamada MOIF LFIBA DDG, Japan
Prof Toshiro Yamada DDG, Japan
Prof Masayoshi Yamaguchi IOM DDG, Japan
Dr Etsuo Yamamura MOIF DDG IOM HonDG, Japan
Prof Masami Yamanaka DDG LPIBA AdVSci IOM MOIF, Japan
Prof Ichiro Yamashita IOM DDG LFIBA MOIF, Japan
Prof Chen-Chung Yang DDG LFIBA, Taiwan ROC
Mr Yang Shi Liang DDG, China
Dr Czau-Siung Yang DDG, Taiwan ROC
Dr Anne Yarrow DDG, USA
Prof Nikolai Yatsenko DDG, USA
Ms Meira Yedidsion DDG, USA
Dr Gili Yen IOM DDG, Taiwan ROC
Prof Jung-Sou Yeo DDG, Korea
Dr Momoh Lawani Yesufu DDG, Nigeria
Mrs Olufemi Adedotun Yesufu DDG, Nigeria
Mr Miu Leong Yew LPIBA DDG, Hong Kong
Dr Cheong-Ho Yi DDG, Korea
Dr Ahmet Yildizhan LPIBA MOIF DDG AdVMed AIOM HonDG, Turkey
Prof Yulong Yin DDG, China
Mr Antti Juhani Ylikoski DDG LFIBA WCOIM, Finland
Dr Vak Y Yoo MOIF DDG LPIBA AdVMed IOM DO HonDG, Korea
Prof Dr Jung Han Yoo DDG, Korea
Prof Keum-Rok Yoo DDG LFIBA, Korea
Dr Won Ku Yoon DDG, Korea
Prof Dr K Yoshihara LPIBA DDG IOM MOIF AdVAh, Japan

Dr Yong-Ouk You LFIBA DDG, Korea
Ms Hala Fousad Youssef DDG, Egypt
Dr Yu Xiaohui LFIBA DDG, China
Prof Yu Bao Ming MOIF DDG, China
Prof Yu Shen DDG, China
Mr Chang Hee Yun DDG, Korea
Dr Constantinos Zachariou DDG, Greece
Dr Vladimir S Zagriadsky DDG, Russia
Dr Branimir Zamola DDG, Croatia
Dr Wendell E Zehel DDG MOIF IOM HonDG, USA
Prof Wanxin Zhang DDG, China
Prof Zhang Zhixiang DDG IOM, China
Dr Zhang Fushan LFIBA MOIF DDG, USA
Mr Shengcai Zhao DDG, China
Mr Jixue Zhong DDG, China
Prof Guoxing Zhou DDG, China
Prof Zhou Fangcheng LFIBA DDG, China
Prof Boris N Zhukov DDG, Russia
Dr Dhyana Ziegler IOM DDG, USA
Dr Jamil Gad Zilkha DDG, Israel
Prof Dr Jasenka Zivko-Babic DDG, Croatia
Mr Vladimir Zolotarev DDG, Russia
Prof Stanislav F Zubovich IOM DDG, Belarus
Mrs Alevtina N Zvonova DDG, Russia

ADVISERS TO THE DIRECTOR GENERAL

Dr Byung Moon Ahn AdVMed HonDG, Korea
Mrs Ayla Akyol DDG LFIBA AdVAh, Turkey
Mr Osman Refik Akyuz AdVAh, Turkey
Mr Mohamed Y A Al Beshir DDG LFIBA AdVAh, United Arab Emirates
Prof E M Alahuhta DDG LPIBA HonDG AIOM MOIF CH AdVAh DO, Finland
Prof Salah El-Din Allam AdVAh, Egypt
Prof John Joseph Ansbro IOM DDG AdVAh, USA
Mario Vernon Arroyo-Gomez LPIBA DDG LFWLA IOM MOIF AdVAh, Gibraltar
Prof Dalia Atlas AdVAh, Israel
Mr Abdul R Batal LPIBA LFWLA DDG AdVBus, Syria
Ms Soussan Bathaee DO AdVSci, USA
Prof Pier Franco Beatrice LPIBA AdVAh DDG, Italy
Dr Khalid A Bin Abdulrahman AdVMed, Saudi Arabia
Ms Irene M Bisiachi MOIF LPIBA DDG AdVAh, Italy
Dr Leikny Annadotter Bjørkli LPIBA MOIF DDG AdVAh HonDG AIOM, Sweden
Dr Ingrid Blakstad IOM AdVAh, Norway
Ms Grethe Boe LPIBA MOIF AIOM DO DDG HonDG AdVSci, Norway
Mr Vassil Kroumov Bojkov DDG HonDG AdVFin, Bulgaria
Dr Daniel D Brunda DDG LPIBA MOIF AIOM AdVSci DO HonDG, USA
Mr Imad J Bukhamseen AdVBus WCOIM, Kuwait
Mr Craig Edward Burgess LFIBA MOIF IOM AdVAh, USA
Dr Kuk Won Chang LFIBA IOM AdVAh DDG, USA
Dr C Juliana Ching LPIBA AIOM MOIF DDG HonDG AdVBus DO, Hong Kong
Dr Bazlul Mobin Chowdhury AdVSoc, Bangladesh
Prof Kyu-bok Chung DDG AdVAh HonDG, Korea
Prof Chomchark Chuntrasakul AWCASC HonDG MOIF AdVMed, Thailand
Mrs Ranjini S Deraniyagala LFIBA AdVAh HonDG AWCASC, USA
Dr Periklis Ergatis DDG LPIBA MOIF AdVSci, Greece
Dr Hernani Esteban DDG AdVAh, Philippines
Ms Ann C Falkner AdVAh, USA
Chief (Dr) Ephraim F Faloughi LFIBA AdVBus, Nigeria
Mr Edward Farell AdVBus, Canada
Mr Pietro Camillo Ferrigno AIOM DDG AdVNed HonDG MOIF DO AWCASC WCOIM, Italy
Mrs Ruth Kinniebrew Fields LFIBA AdVAh DDG, USA
Ms Maryanne Tam-Po Fong DDG IOM AdVBus MOIF, Canada
Prof Dr James M Fragomeni LPIBA MOIF AdVSci HonDG IOM, USA
Dr Devinder Singh Gill DDG AdVSci MOIF HonDG IOM, India
Mr Allen Fletcher Gilliard DDG AdVAh IOM, USA
Prof Dr Vasyl Goch DDG LFIBA AdVSci HonDG, Ukraine
Prof Petr L Goncharov DDG AdVSci CH, Russia
Mr Isaac T Goodine DDG IOM MOIF AdVAh HonDG, Canada
Mr Fabio Paolo Guffanti LFIBA IOM AdVBus, Italy
Prof Krassimir Borissov Guigov AdVMed, Bulgaria
Dr Elisabeth van der Gulik LPIBA AdVMed, Netherlands
Prof Jeong Hyo Ha DDG IOM AdVAh MOIF, Korea
Dr Tommy Hansson IOM AdVAh, Sweden
Mr Sadamoto Harito AdVFin, Japan
Prof Syed Tajuddin Syed Hassan AdVSci, Malaysia
Mrs Roberta M Helming HonDG MOIF AdVAh DDG, USA
Dr Mahmoud H Hijazy AdVMed, Saudi Arabia
Mme Dr Hoang Thi Bach Bich AdVMed DDG IOM, France
Dr Tohru Horiuchi DDG LPIBA IOM MOIF AdVMed, Japan
Mr Hui-Wen Hsia AdVAh, Taiwan ROC
Dr Jinlian Hu AdV, Hong Kong
Dr Pai-Tsang Huang AdVMed IOM DDG HonDG, Taiwan ROC
Prof Hassan Mohamed Ali Hussein DDG AdVSci, Sudan
Rev Dr Prof Tzu-Yang Hwang LPIBA AdVAh AIOM MOIF CH DO DDG HonDG AWCASC WCOIM, USA
Prof Haruo Hyodo AdVMed AWCASC DDG HonDG, Japan
Dr David Ip LPIBA MOIF DDG AdVMed DO IOM, Hong Kong
Chief Ebenezer Isokariari DDG HonDG AdVBus, Nigeria
Ms Olga O Ivanjicki AdVAh, Serbia
Prof Peter Jacobs AdVSci, South Africa
Mr Neil H Jacoby Jr LPIBA IOM AdVSci CH DO DDG, USA
Prof Gabriel Ampah Johnson DDG AdVSci IOM HonDG, Togo
Dr Hajime Jozuka AdVMed, Japan
Prof Dehua Ju DDG IOM AdVSci LFIBA, China
Mr Tetsuo Kaneko LPIBA DDG AdVSci IOM, Japan
Ms M M Katchur LPIBA DDG MOIF AdVMed, USA
Dr Khoo Boo-Chai AdVMed DDG IOM MOIF HonDG, Singapore
Prof Pill Soo Kim LPIBA DDG IOM AdVSci CH, Korea
Dr Kyoung Soo Kim LPIBA IOM MOIF HonDG DDG AdVSci, Korea
Mr Masashi Kimura MOIF DDG IOM DO HonDG AdVSci, Japan
Mrs Nagiko Sato Kiser LFIBA AdVAh, USA
Prof Eliezer I Klainman LPIBA IOM AdVMed DDG, Israel
Prof Kowan Young Ko AdVSci, Korea
Dr Patricia J Kole-Harf IOM MOIF AdVMed, USA
Dr Soji Kurimoto IOM AdVMed DDG, Japan
Mr Chin-Hung Lai LFIBA DDG AdVSci IOM, Taiwan ROC
Dr Benedicte Laursen DDG MOIF LFIBA AdVMed HonDG AWCASC, Denmark
Dr Dale P Layman PhD MOIF DDG LPIBS AdVMed AIOM HonDG, USA
Prof Carla Ann Bouska Lee IOM AdVMed, USA
Dr Hee Jun Lee AdVSci, Korea
Mr Chia-Hsiang Lin DDG AdVSci, Taiwan ROC
Hon Gov Prof Dr Elizeu Pereira Lopes LFIBA MOIF AdVSci DDG AIOM HonDG DG HE, Brazil
Hon Gov Prof Dr Eliezer Pereira Lopes LFIBA MOIF AIOM DDG AdVSci HonDG DG HE, Brazil
Dr ing Drita Lulo LPIBA IOM DDG AdVSci MOIF, Albania
Prof William Lyakurwa AdVBus, Kenya
Mr Nobuaki Maeda AdVSci, Japan
Prof T Maghiar DDG AdVSci IOM LFIBA MOIF, Romania
Dr Florence Omolara Mahoney DDG AdVAh, The Gambia
Dr H Malin LPIBA LFWLA DDG IOM AdVMed CH, USA
Dr Michael Malkiel AdVMed, Latvia
Mr David Markish AdVAh, Israel
Ms Veronica Martin AdVMed, USA
Dr Nobuhito Matsushiro DDG AdVSci IOM HonDG, Japan
Prof Marianne McDonald LFIBA IOM CH AdVAh DDG, USA
Prof Iwao Miyachi LPIBA IOM MOIF DDG AdVSci HonDG DO, Japan
Mr Eric Bhamuza Molefe IOM DDG AdVFin CH HonDG, South Africa
Mr Eric Mathew Moles DDG AdVFin, Canada
Prof Akira Nagatomi LPIBA MOIF AdVSci DO DDG, Japan
Prof Dr Stefan Neagu HonDG AdVMed, Romania
Prof Johan Theron Nel LPIBA DDG MOIF IOM AdVMed DO, South Africa
Dr Massimiliano Nisati DDG AdVAh, Italy
Dr Takuma Nomiya LFIBA MOIF DDG IOM AdVMed, Japan
Prof Dr Takashi Oguchi DDG AIOM DO HonDG AdVSci MOIF LPIBA, Japan

Dr Akihide Ohkuchi LPIBA DDG MOIF AdVMed IOM DO, Japan
Mr Oladayo Akinwumi Oladeji AdVFin, Nigeria
Mrs Florence N Onochie AdVFin HonDG AWCASC, USA
Dr Chester D Opalsky AdVMed, USA
Dr C G Orvell IOM DDG MOIF AdVMed DO, Sweden
Dr Bella Eugenia Oster AdVAh, USA
Dr Brankica Pacic AdVAh, Serbia
Mr Nick Pahys Jr DDG CH AdVAh, USA
Dr Bojan Pajic WCOIM LFIBA AdVMed, Switzerland
Prof Hong-Seok Park DDG AdVSci IOM DO HonDG, Korea
Dr D V R Pasupuleti DDG LFIBA MOIF DO AdVMed IOM, USA
Ms Thresia Pierce LFIBA DDG AdVAh, USA
Prof Dr E N Pinguli CH LPIBA AdVSci IOM MOIF DDG DO, Albania
Ms Claire Power Murphy FIBA HonDG AdVAh, USA
Mr Eugene E Rhemann LPIBA DDG DO AdVAh, USA
Mr Richard David Rhimes DDG IOM AdVSci MOIF DO, Australia
Mr Shimon Rubinstein AdVAh DDG IOM MOIF, Israel
Mr Irek Safargaleev LFIBA DDG AdVAh, Russia
Prof Makoto Saito LFIBA MOIF AdVFin AIOM AWCASC, Japan
Dr Holem M Saliba DDG IOM AdVSci CH LFIBA, Lebanon
Dr Mitsuo Samata LFIBA MOIF AdVSci, Japan
Prof Dr Sunil Kumar Sarkar HonDG MBBS MD PhD DSc AdVMed AWCASC IOM WCOIM, USA
Mr Maksim Sedej AdVAh, Slovenia
Count H C von Seherr-Thoss LFIBA AdVSci DO, Germany
Dr Shirish Shah LFIBA DDG MOIF HonDG AdVSci, USA
Mr Shrideo Sharma AdVSci, India
Prof Dr Sadao Shirayama AdVAh, Japan
Ms Monique S Sidaross DDG AdVSci, USA
Mr Robert D Siedle LPIBA DDG AdVBus IOM, USA
Prof Radomir Ivanovitch Silin AdVAh, Ukraine
Ms Ina Smiley Clayton PhD DDG AdVAh, USA
Prof Elise S Sobol AdVAh LFIBA HonDG, USA
Dr Yo Han Song AdVMed DDG, Korea
Ms Agnes F Stradley MOIF IOM HonDG AdVBus, USA
Prof Hyontai Sug LFIBA MOIF AdVSci DDG AIOM DO, Korea
Prof Dr A Sun IOM MOIF LPIBA DDG CH AdVMed HonDG, Taiwan ROC
Mr Christian Tamas AdVAh, Romania
Prof Hiroshige Tanaka DDG LFIBA AdVFin, Japan
Prof Dr Georges Emile Andre Thill DDG HonDG AdVAh, Belgium
Captain Dr Ivica Tijardovic DDG LPIBA MOIF AIOM HonDG AdVSci DO, Croatia
Ir Philip Kui Tse DDG AdVSci, Canada
Prof Hsien Ho Tsien AdVSci, Taiwan ROC
Dr Yutaka Tsutsumi AdVMed, Japan
Prof Edward Ueno LPIBA MOIF DDG IOM AdVSci, Japan
Mr Isyaku Tofa Umar IOM DDG AdVBus LFIBA MOIF, Nigeria
Prof Birasak Varasundharosoth PhD AdVSci, Thailand
Dr Rajesh Kumar Verma DDG HonDG AdVAh LFIBA, India
Dr Panayiotis M Vlamos AdVAh, Greece
W W Walley MD DDG AdVMed, USA
Prof Sonia Viktoria Wanner AdVAh, Sweden
Rev Father Cletus M Watson TOR LPIBA AdVAh, USA
Prof Shinq-Jen Wu LFIBA AdVSci, Taiwan ROC
Dr Christina Xinyan Xie LFIBA MOIF AdVAh DDG HonDG, Hong Kong
Prof Masami Yamanaka DDG LPIBA AdVSci IOM MOIF, Japan
Prof Dr Yassin Mohamed Yassin LPIBA AdVMed MOIF IOM DO, Egypt
Prof Michiru Yasuhara LFIBA IOM AdVSci, Japan
Dr Ahmet Yildizhan LPIBA MOIF DDG AdVMed AIOM HonDG, Turkey
Dr Vak Y Yoo MOIF DDG LPIBA AdVMed IOM DO HonDG, Korea
Prof Dr K Yoshihara LPIBA DDG IOM MOIF AdVAh, Japan

LIFETIME ACHIEVEMENT AWARD

Mrs Benigna G Able-Thomas IOM, The Gambia
Prof Antonio A Acosta IOM DDG, USA
Dr Marion Darlyne Adinolfi IOM HonDG, USA
Mr Peter A Aduja MOIF IOM, USA
Most Hon Maitre Artiste Afewerk Tekle IOM CH, Ethiopia
Dr Pius Anozie C Agwaramgbo, Nigeria
Ms Geraldine Ahearn AIOM HonDG, USA
Ms Nefertari Abena Ahmose DDG IOM DO MOIF, USA
Ryoko Akamatsu, Japan
Dr Mohammed Akmal, USA
Prof E M Alahuhta DDG LPIBA HonDG AIOM MOIF CH AdVAh DO, Finland
Dr Monica Albu, Romania
Prof Jalal Alirza Aliyev DDG HonDG, Azerbaijan
Prof Nihal Amerasinghe, Philippines
Mr Hans H Amtmann, USA
Prof B Angelopoulos LPIBA DDG HonDG, Greece
Prof John Joseph Ansbro IOM DDG AdVAh, USA
Prof Kurt April, South Africa
Prof Ioannis Konstantinos Argyros, USA
Dr S Michael Awad, Canada
Dr Detlev Baller, Germany
Dr Leonard Octavius Barrett DDG MD MOIF, USA
Dr Christine Baxter, Australia
Mr Peter James Bazeley, India
Prof Pier Franco Beatrice LPIBA AdVAh DDG, Italy
Dr (Sir) Moses Gordon Bestman DDG LFIBA CH, Nigeria
Prof Rodger Bick LFIBA, USA
Dr Nicola Bietolini HonDG, Italy
Ms Irene M Bisiachi MOIF LPIBA DDG AdVAh, Italy
Dr Leikny Annadotter Bjørkli LPIBA MOIF DDG AdVAh HonDG AIOM, Sweden
Ms Grethe Boe LPIBA MOIF AIOM DO DDG HonDG AdVSci, Norway
Dr Athar Ali Bokhari, Saudi Arabia
Ms Barbara Sue Bolin, USA
Dr Lutgart Elizabeth Bonte IOM, Belgium
Prof Carlos Soares Borrego, Portugal
Dr Bruno Bosbach, Germany
Dr Sandra Breitenbach LFIBA IOM DDG DO, Norway
Dr Charles Edward Brodine LFIBA WCOIM DO AWCASC, USA
Dr Daniel D Brunda DDG LPIBA MOIF AIOM AdVSci DO HonDG, USA
Miss Marjorie R Burns MOIF IOM, Australia
Dr Hinko Cackovic AIOM MOIF, Germany
Prof Kan Ip Philip Chan HonDG, Hong Kong
Dr Chang Wan-Hsi (Mo Jen) DDG, Taiwan ROC
Dr Barry Lloyd Chapman LFIBA, Australia
Mr Valentinos Christou Charalambous, Cyprus
Prof Yam-Cheng Chee, Singapore
Dr Pang-Chi Chen DDG MOIF IOM LPIBA, Taiwan ROC
Prof Cecil Chin Hin Chew, Singapore
Dr C Juliana Ching LPIBA AIOM MOIF DDG HonDG AdVBus DO, Hong Kong
Dr Cho Kwungsoo LFIBA, Korea
Prof Jeong Ryeol Choi LFIBA DDG IOM MOIF, Korea
Dr Sunchai Churesigaew, Thailand
Dr Karen A Clarke LPIBA IOM, USA
Dr Kenneth Louis Coenegrachts LFIBA MOIF HonDG IOM, Belgium
Prof Freddie C Colston MOIF HonDG AWCASC, USA
Ms Paula Anita Compo-Pratt DDG, USA
Ms Jacqueline Turner Copeland, USA
Mr Donald Mercer Cormie IOM, USA
Prof Ignacio Cornejo Aguirre IOM, Spain
Mr Ronald Lloyd Cox IOM LFIBA MOIF, USA
Mr Dominick Vincent Crea, USA

Ms Arlene Dahl, USA
Dr Osei Kofi Darkwa, Ghana
Mr Sadhu Narayan Prasad Das, India
Prof Predrag Dasic HonDG, Serbia
Ms Sandra Lynn Daves LFIBA DDG MOIF, USA
Rev Dr Gommar A De Pauw, USA
Ms Handunnetti S V De Silva IOM DO, USA
Dr Richard E Devey LFIBA, USA
Dr Michael William Doll, USA
Mr Charles Douglas, USA
Mr Terry Dowel MOIF LFIBA AIOM, Australia
Prof Dr Joze Duhovnik, Slovenia
Mr Emmanuel C Duncan, West Indies
Mrs Kathleen M Duyck AWCASC DO, USA
Dr Allen Broderick Edmundson, USA
Prof Mohammad H S El-Ahl DDG MOIF IOM, Egypt
Dr M F Elkady DDG IOM LFIBA, Saudi Arabia
Mr Andrew J Entwistle IOM MOIF DDG LFIBA, USA
Ms Eden P Espina, USA
Prof Margaret E Fahey, USA
Mr James Ferguson LFIBA DDG MOIF AWCASC, Australia
Prof Antonio G Ferreira DDG, Portugal
Mr Pietro Camillo Ferrigno AIOM DDG AdVMed HonDG MOIF DO AWCASC WCOIM, Italy
Dr Brady J Fletcher LPIBA, USA
Dr Hajime Fukazawa LFIBA MOIF DDG IOM CH, Japan
Ms Vivian T Gamble, USA
Prof Dr Pedro Garaguso, Argentina
Prof Maurice P Gautier MOIF, France
Prof Xindu Geng, China
Ms Susan Gibson, USA
Dr Devinder Singh Gill DDG AdVSci MOIF HonDG IOM, India
Prof Dr Vasyl Goch DDG LFIBA AdVSci HonDG, Ukraine
Dr M Goldston-Morris OAM DDG LPIBA MOIF HonDG, Australia
Mr Timothy A Goodwin LPIBA DO IOM CH DDG MOIF HonDG, USA
Dr Masae Goseki-Sone DDG IOM, Japan
Ms Lynn C Green, USA
Mr Bruce A Grindley LFIBA, Spain
Mr Can Cheng Guo, China
Mr Rajesh Gupta, Canada
Dr Yeugeniy M Gusev, Russia
Prof Lars Haarr, Norway
Prof Doug-Woong Hahn LFIBA, Korea
Prof Dr Palma Hamm HonDG, Switzerland
Dr Raymond Kenneth Hart IOM, USA
Dr Daryl E Hartter, USA
Prof Dr Kazuyuki Hatada LFIBA DDG IOM, Japan
Dr Nobuhiko Hayashi LPIBA HonDG IOM AWCASC, Japan
Prof Albert A Hayden LFIBA IOM, USA
Pastor J B Hays Jr, USA
Ms Kathy A Hesterwerth LFIBA DDG MOIF, USA
Dr Mahmoud H Hijazy AdVMed, Saudi Arabia
Dr Yoshitaka Hirooka LFIBA, Japan
Dr Sun Ig Hong, Korea
Dr In Pyo Hong LPIBA IOM MOIF HonDG, Korea
Dr Jiann-Ruey Hong DDG, Taiwan ROC
Dr Tohru Horiuchi LPIBA DDG IOM MOIF AdVMed, Japan
Prof John Wen-Chain Hsu DDG, Taiwan ROC
Dr Bingkun Hu, USA
Dr Pai-Tsang Huang AdVMed IOM DDG HonDG, Taiwan ROC
Dr Xianya Huang, Singapore
Mrs Stacy Huey, USA
Dr Max Lin Hui-Bon-Hoa DDG, Hong Kong

Rev Dr Prof Tzu-Yang Hwang LPIBA AdVAh AIOM MOIF CH DO DDG HonDG AWCASC WCOIM, USA
Dr Der-Yan Hwang, Taiwan ROC
Dr Samuel Wilson Hynd CBE, Swaziland
Prof Moon Whan Im LFIBA MOIF AWCASC DDG HonDG, Korea
Prof Ouranios Ioannides DDG LFIBA IOM, Cyprus
Dr David Ip LPIBA MOIF DDG AdVMed DO IOM, Hong Kong
Prof Akira Ishibashi, Japan
Dr Tetsuya Isobe DDG, Japan
Dr Tomio Iwasaki DDG HonDG, Japan
Mr Neil H Jacoby Jr LPIBA IOM AdVSci CH DO DDG, USA
Mrs Renu Jain IOM MOIF, India
Mr John Eric Janke CH, USA
Mrs Marie Jocelyne Jean-Baptiste DDG, USA
Dr Rudra Narayan Jha HonDG, Nepal
Dr Satish D Joglekar, India
Prof Stein Erik Johansen LFIBA IOM, Norway
Dr Jane P Johnson IOM MOIF DDG, USA
Prof Gabriel Ampah Johnson DDG AdVSci IOM HonDG, Togo
Dr Roger Anthony Charles Jones IOM, Australia
Prof Gudrun Kalmbach HE, Germany
Mr Yuji Kanaori, Japan
Prof Dr Rustem Sultan-Hamit Kashaev, Russia
Dr Stefan Kassay, Slovakia
Dr Satoshi Katai DDG MOIF, Japan
Dr Satish K Kaushik DDG, Australia
Mrs Terri Lilya Keanely LFIBA DDG AWCASC, USA
Prof Jovanka Kepeska PhD LFIBA DDG, Macedonia
Dr (Ms) Pushpa Khanna HonDG, India
Dr Tawfik Khoja, Saudi Arabia
Ms Won Andrea Kim, Korea
Prof Pill Soo Kim LPIBA DDG IOM AdVSci CH, Korea
Prof Jong Gurl Kim, Korea
Dr Su-Gwan Kim LFIBA, Korea
Dr Kyoung Soo Kim LPIBA IOM MOIF HonDG DDG AdVSci, Korea
Dr Sang-Ha Kim, Korea
Prof Sungwon Kim LFIBA MOIF IOM, Korea
Dr Jung Whee Kim, Korea
Dr Bong-Hyun Kim LFIBA AWCASC, Korea
Mr Hyungil Kim, Korea
Mr Masashi Kimura MOIF DDG IOM DO HonDG AdVSci, Japan
Mrs Nagiko Sato Kiser LFIBA AdVAh, USA
Dr Vladimir Kislik, Israel
Mr Shizuo Kitahara, Japan
Dr Jindrich Ludvik Klapka HonDG IOM, Czech Republic
Prof Kowan Young Ko AdVSci, Korea
Prof Toshiro Kobayashi MOIF DDG HonDG, Japan
Prof Hamilah Koesoemahardja, Indonesia
Mr Heinz-Peter Kohler LFIBA, Switzerland
Dr Kok Wai Peng, Malaysia
Prof Changduk Kong DDG, Korea
Dr Cuneyt Konuralp LFIBA, Turkey
Ms CheriLyn Korth DDG, USA
Dr Vitaly Kovalchuk DDG, Russia
Dr Hiroshi Kubota, Japan
Mr Nikolay I Kuchersky IOM MOIF HonDG, Uzbekistan
Dr Takashi Kumagai LFIBA, Japan
Dr Soji Kurimoto IOM AdVMed DDG, Japan
Dr Jack Kushner HonDG, USA
Mr Bernard Kuttner, USA
Dr Grigorios Kyriakopoulos, Greece
Dr Luc Johan Lambrecht LPIBA DDG MOIF IOM HonDG, Belgium
Mrs Clara Maria Laura Marrama Lanaro LFIBA, USA
Mr Andy Lee Lang CH DO, Austria
Ms Lila M Larson, Canada
Prof Dr Cecilia Popescu Latis, Romania
Ms Margaret E Lawrence, Australia
Dr Dale P Layman PhD MOIF DDG LPIBA AdVMed AIOM HonDG, USA
Prof Carla Ann Bouska Lee IOM AdVMed, USA
Dr Kenneth Bok Lee, USA
Prof Sang Hee Lee IOM DDG, Korea
Prof Sang-Go Lee, Korea
Dr Jeong-Phil Lee DDG, Korea
Prof Dr Christian Lehmann IOM HonDG DO, Switzerland
Prof Dr Hans Albert Paul Lenk, Germany
Miss Joy LeRoy LPIBA MOIF DDG HonDG AIOM OIA AGE CG OAA AWCASC, USA
Prof Valery I Levitas, USA
Dr Yu-Chu Maxwell Li, Taiwan ROC
Dr Tae-Gyoon Lim, Korea
Dr Han-Shou Liu IOM HonDG, USA
Mr Zhaorong Liu DDG, China
Prof HsinChih F Liu DDG MOIF IOM, Taiwan ROC
Dr Liu Xiangming, China
Dr Jasna Loboda-Cackovic AIOM MOIF, Germany
Hon Gov Prof Dr Elizeu Pereira Lopes LFIBA MOIF AdVSci DDG AIOM HonDG DG HE, Brazil
Hon Gov Prof Dr Eliezer Pereira Lopes LFIBA MOIF AIOM DDG AdVSci HonDG DG HE, Brazil
Dr Alan Louis LPIBA MOIF IOM DDG HonDG, UK
Ms Chen Lu, Hong Kong
Dr ing Drita Lulo LPIBA IOM DDG AdVSci MOIF, Albania
Prof T Maghiar DDG AdVSci IOM LFIBA MOIF, Romania
Dr Madhuri Majumder, Malaysia
Dr H Malin LPIBA LFWLA DDG IOM MOIF AdVMed CH, USA
Mr Constantin Mandruleanu, Romania
Dr John J Manolakakis MD LPIBA DDG IOM, Zimbabwe
Mrs Cora DeMunck Manthe, USA
Prof James W Marchand, USA
Dean Towle Mason MD IOM MOIF HonDG, USA
Dr Nobuhito Matsushiro DDG AdVSci IOM HonDG, Japan
Ms Royetta A McBain, USA
Prof Marianne McDonald LFIBA IOM CH AdVAh DDG, USA
Dr George C Messenger, USA
Dr Isaac L Mgemane LPIBA IOM DDG CH DO HonDG, South Africa
Dr Jun-Hong Min, Korea
Dr Pitabasa Misra, Saudi Arabia
Prof Dr Aruna Kumari Misra, India
Prof Eva Misurova, Slovakia
Ms Elizabeth Mittelstaedt, Germany
Mr Ho Ming Joseph Mok LFIBA MOIF DDG, Hong Kong
Dr Sandra Morgan, USA
Dr Naofumi Morita DDG HonDG, Japan
Dr Chi Cheung Moy DDG, Hong Kong
Mr J M Mwanakatwe LFIBA, Zambia
Dr Yukio Nagamachi DDG IOM, Japan
Mr Miklos Nagy, USA
Dr Endre László Nagy HonDG IOM, Japan
Dr Eva Mae Nash-Isaac DDG IOM, USA
Mr Gary Mei-Cheong Ngai, Macao
Mrs Angela C Nicols, USA
Dr Takuma Nomiya LFIBA MOIF DDG IOM AdVMed, Japan
Dr Abraham Noordergraaf IOM, USA
Prof Stig H M Nystrom IOM, Finland
Dr Soe Nyunt DDG, Singapore
Mr Nils Kornelius Oeijord, Norway

Prof Dr Takashi Oguchi DDG AIOM DO HonDG AdVSci MOIF LPIBA, Japan
Dr Akihide Ohkuchi LPIBA DDG MOIF AdVMed IOM DO, Japan
Dr C G Orvell IOM DDG MOIF AdVMed DO, Sweden
A A Oteng-Amoako PhD MOIF DDG, Ghana
Mr Ericson Omotayo Oyetibo, Nigeria
Mr Nick Pahys Jr DDG CH AdVAh, USA
Dr Bojan Pajic WCOIM LFIBA AdVMed, Switzerland
Prof Jiun Pang, Taiwan ROC
Prof Dr Ivan Panin, Russia
Dr Soo-Jin Park CH, Korea
Dr Won Kuk Park MOIF, Korea
Prof Dong Gon Park, Korea
Dr Il-Kwon Park LFIBA DDG, Korea
Prof Dr Jung Yul Park LFIBA, Korea
Prof Hong-Seok Park DDG AdVSci IOM DO HonDG, Korea
Mr Heung Sik Park, Korea
Dr D V R Pasupuleti DDG LFIBA MOIF DO AdVMed IOM, USA
Dr Bindeshwar Pathak LFIBA AWCASC, India
Dr Norman Pearson LFIBA IOM MOIF, Canada
Mr Tuyen Pham, Vietnam
Prof Dr E N Pinguli CH LPIBA AdVSci IOM MOIF DDG DO, Albania
Mr Jozsef Pinter DDG, Hungary
Ms Marina Pirtskhalava, Georgia
Dr Sitaram Poddar IOM LFIBA, Jamaica
Dr Alexander M Ponizovsky, Israel
Dr Witold Poplawski, Canada
Ms Claire Power Murphy FIBA HonDG AdVAh, USA
Ms Harriett Kinloch H Price, USA
Mr Eddie B Pue, USA
Mr Henry James Rainford LFIBA, Jamaica
Prof Dr Melkote Ramdas Ramsay IOM, Australia
Dr Hugo Francis Murchison Reid, Trinidad & Tobago
Dr Stuart Glen Rice, USA
Dr Pierre Rioux LFIBA IOM, USA
Dr Gary S Roubin, USA
Dr Seth Isaiah Rubin IOM DDG, USA
Mr Shimon Rubinstein AdVAh DDG IOM MOIF, Israel
Ms Phyllis Ann Ruth MOIF DDG HonDG, USA
Prof Dr Abdel Fattah A K Saad, Egypt
Prof Makoto Saito LFIBA MOIF AdVFin AIOM AWCASC, Japan
Dr Masakiyo Sakaguchi, Japan
Prof Dr Sunil Kumar Sarkar HonDG MBBS MD PhD DSc AdVMed AWCASC IOM WCOIM, USA
Dr Kazuo Sato DDG, Japan
Mr Arthur V Savage, USA
Prof Vladimir V Saveliev DDG, Korea
Prof Yoshinari Sawada, Japan
Mr Gilbert L Scott, USA
Dr Masafumi Seki, Japan
Dr Isadore Shapiro DDG IOM, USA
Ms Lois E Landis Shenk LFIBA MOIF IOM HonDG DO, USA
Dr Atsuyoshi Shimada, Japan
Mr Alhaji Umaru Ali Shinkafi CH, Nigeria
Mr Taku Shirai, Japan
Mr Robert D Siedle LPIBA DDG AdVBus IOM, USA
Mrs Lois Oliver Sigler, USA
Prof G S Siklosi DDG LPIBA MOIF IOM CH, Hungary
Dr Sergey Victorovich Simonenko HonDG, Russia
Dr Navin Kumar Sinha DDG, India
Dr Jimmy Ong Sio MOIF LFIBA IOM DDG DO, USA
Dr Gregorio Skromne-Kadlubik IOM, Mexico
Dr Troy Alvin Smith, USA
Ms Ruth O'Dell Gillespie Snowden IOM, USA
Prof Uy Dong Sohn IOM, Korea
Dr Yo Han Song AdVMed DDG, Korea
Mrs Mary Spencer, Spain
Dr Chandrika Prasad Srivastava, India
Mr Robert Steiner DO CH LFIBA, Australia
Ms Margaret C Sticht, Nigeria
Mr Sava Stojkov, Serbia
Dr Sharron Stroud, USA
Prof Hyontai Sug LFIBA MOIF AdVSci DDG AIOM DO, Korea
Ms Wilma Warren Sukapdjo LFIBA MOIF, USA
Prof Dr A Sun IOM MOIF LPIBA DDG CH AdVMed HonDG, Taiwan ROC
Mr Noriyasu Suzuki, Japan
Dr Srikanta M N Swamy LFIBA DDG IOM, Canada
Dr Yasuo Tahama LPIBA IOM, Japan
Mr Yen-Po Tang IOM, Taiwan ROC
Dr Gerhard M Tarmann, Austria
Mr Sylvester Taylor, USA
Prof Paul B Tchounwou ScD IOM, USA
Prof Albert Tezla CH, USA
Dr M Thiel IOM LPIBA DDG MOIF AAAS CH DO, Germany
Captain Dr Ivica Tijardovic DDG LPIBA MOIF AIOM HonDG AdVSci DO, Croatia
Mrs Anne Tooby CH, USA
Dr Zdzislawa Traczyk, Poland
Dr Jerry R Trevino, USA
Dr Ming-Shium Tu DDG WCOIM, Taiwan ROC
Prof P Tuglaci IOM LFWLA DDG MOIF LPIBA HonDG, Turkey
Dr Kazuo Uejima, Japan
Prof Dr Lehel Vadon DDG, Hungary
Mrs Peggy T Vaughan DDG HonDG MOIF DO, USA
David Lynn Vesely MD PhD, USA
Mr Carlos Jose Gomes Vieira IOM, Portugal
Dr Lazar J Vukadinovich IOM, Australia
Prof Takao Wada, Japan
Ms Reba Faye Wade, USA
Dr Florence Muringi Wambugu, Kenya
Dr Jong Wang DDG, China
Ms Veronica Welgemoed, South Africa
Mr Brooks Morris Whitehurst DDG HonDG, USA
Dr Mitchell Albert Wick, USA
Dr-Ing Hans Wittfoht LFIBA HonDG IOM MOIF, Germany
Dr Baron C K W Wong MD LFIBA MOIF DO DDG, USA
Prof Dr Albert Wing Kuen Wong MOIF HonDG DDG LFIBA, Hong Kong
Prof Thomas S Woods, USA
Prof Yun Xia, China
Prof Masayoshi Yamaguchi IOM DDG, Japan
Dr Etsuo Yamamura MOIF DDG IOM HonDG, Japan
Prof Dr Yassin Mohamed Yassin LPIBA AdVMed MOIF IOM DO, Egypt
Mr Sachio Yasufuku, Japan
Prof Michiru Yasuhara LFIBA IOM AdVSci, Japan
Mr Anson A Yeager Sr LFIBA, USA
Dr Gili Yen IOM DDG, Taiwan ROC
Dr Ahmet Yildizhan LPIBA MOIF DDG AdVMed AIOM HonDG, Turkey
Mr Antti Juhani Ylikoski DDG LFIBA WCOIM, Finland
Dr Sang Jin Yoon, Korea
Prof Dr K Yoshihara LPIBA DDG IOM MOIF AdVAh, Japan
Prof Yu Bao Ming MOIF DDG, China
Dr Oleg Zayratiyants, Russia
Prof Yonggao Zhao, China
Prof Fulian Zhuang, China
Dr Dhyana Ziegler IOM DDG, USA

VICE CONSULS OF THE IBC

Prof E M Alahuhta DDG LPIBA HonDG AIOM MOIF CH
  AdVAh, Finland
Mario Vernon Arroyo-Gomez LPIBA DDG LFWLA IOM
  MOIF AdVAh, Gibraltar
Ms Marilyn A Bennett, USA
Dr Sandra Breitenbach LFIBA IOM DDG DO, Norway
Mr Craig Edward Burgess LFIBA MOIF IOM AdVAh, USA
Juseon Byun PhD, Korea
Ms Margot Cairnes LFIBA DDG, Australia
Dr Wen-Ying Chang LPIBA MOIF DDG IOM HonDG
  AWCASC, Taiwan ROC
Mr John Davies, Australia
Dr M F Elkady DDG IOM LFIBA, Saudi Arabia
Dr James E Ewing DDG MOIF, USA
Mrs Elisabeth Anne Rooney-Ewing DDG MOIF, USA
Mr Joji Hagiwara LFIBA DDG MOIF, Japan
Dr Tohru Horiuchi LPIBA DDG IOM MOIF AdVMed, Japan
Dr Seishi Isobe DDG, Japan
Dr Rustom A Khatib DDG, Lebanon
Prof Pill Soo Kim LPIBA DDG IOM AdVSci CH, Korea
Mr Kong Hyung-Yun, Korea
Mr Nikolay I Kuchersky IOM MOIF HonDG, Uzbekistan
Mr Temirgali A Kuketaev, Kazakhstan
Mrs Elly A Ladas DDG, Greece
K Jameson Lawrence Esq, USA
Professor Jeong Y Lee DDG LFIBA, Korea
Miss Joy LeRoy LPIBA MOIF DDG HonDG AIOM OIA AGE
  CG OAA AWCASC, USA
Ms Joanne M Lindsey IOM DDG MOIF, USA
Mr Liu Dao-shun, Taiwan ROC
Dr H Malin LPIBA LFWLA DDG IOM MOIF AdVMed CH,
  USA
Dr Clarice Chris Matteson PhD DDG, USA
Professor Vladimir Matvienko IOM DDG, Ukraine
Professor Albert Nikolaevich Nikitin, Russia
Mr Shozo Ohtsuka LPIBA DDG, Japan
Professor Vladimir Okrepilov, Russia
Dr Gladys S Ostrom MOIF DDG, USA
Mr Nick Pahys Jr DDG CH AdVAh, USA
Professor Jeom K Paik PhD, Korea
Dr A Robertson-Pearce DDG IOM, Sweden
Professor Valery Sagaidatchny, Greece
Dr Isadore Shapiro DDG IOM, USA
Professor Tamaz Shilakadze IOM DDG HonDG, Georgia
Prof Dr A Sun IOM MOIF LPIBA DDG CH AdVMed
  HonDG, Taiwan ROC
Mr Alexander Yakovitski IOM, Belarus
Dr Vak Y Yoo MOIF DDG LPIBA AdVMed IOM DO
  HonDG, Korea
Professor Taek Rim Yoon MD PhD, Korea

THE WORLDWIDE HONOURS LIST

PETER A ADUJA

FOR AN OUTSTANDING CONTRIBUTION TO

COMMUNITY, STATE AND NATION

INAUGURATED IN THE YEAR 2003

★ ★ ★ ★ ★

EDWARD DUA AGYEMAN

FOR AN OUTSTANDING CONTRIBUTION TO

GOOD GOVERNANCE AND FIGHTING CORRUPTION IN GHANA

INAUGURATED IN THE YEAR 2006

★ ★ ★ ★ ★

PROFESSOR AMOS ENIOLA AKINGBOHUNGBE

FOR AN OUTSTANDING CONTRIBUTION TO

ENTOMOLOGY

INAUGURATED IN THE YEAR 2003

★ ★ ★ ★ ★

DR YALLAPRAGADA RAMESH BABU

FOR AN OUTSTANDING CONTRIBUTION TO

INDUSTRIAL ENGINEERING

INAUGURATED IN THE YEAR 2003

★ ★ ★ ★ ★

PROF DR CLAUS BALDUS

FOR AN OUTSTANDING CONTRIBUTION TO

PHILOSOPHY AND THEORY OF ARCHITECTURE

INAUGURATED IN THE YEAR 2005

★ ★ ★ ★ ★

SANDRA E BEGUHN

FOR AN OUTSTANDING CONTRIBUTION TO

POETRY

INAUGURATED IN THE YEAR 2003

★ ★ ★ ★ ★

DR ALI BEHFAR

INAUGURATED IN THE YEAR 2004

★ ★ ★ ★ ★

PROFESSOR DR GUIDO BIMBERG

FOR AN OUTSTANDING CONTRIBUTION TO

MUSICOLOGY AND MEDIA ENTERTAINMENT BUSINESS

INAUGURATED IN THE YEAR 2003

★ ★ ★ ★ ★

IURII BOTNARI

FOR AN OUTSTANDING CONTRIBUTION TO

SYMPHONY CONDUCTING

INAUGURATED IN THE YEAR 2005

★ ★ ★ ★ ★

DANIEL DONALD BRUNDA

FOR AN OUTSTANDING CONTRIBUTION TO

AEROSPACE AND ELECTROMAGNETIC POWERLINE RADIATION ENGINEERING

INAUGURATED IN THE YEAR 2003

FLORIANA BULIC-JAKUS

FOR AN OUTSTANDING CONTRIBUTION TO

DIFFERENTAL EXPRESSION OF BB PROTEIN

INAUGURATED IN THE YEAR 2003

PROFESSOR YUNG FRANK CHIANG

FOR AN OUTSTANDING CONTRIBUTION TO

LAW AND LEGAL EDUCATION

INAUGURATED IN THE YEAR 2003

DR C JULIANA CHING

FOR AN OUTSTANDING CONTRIBUTION TO

BUSINESS AND MEDICINE

INAUGURATED IN THE YEAR 2003

DR SARA CIAMPI

FOR AN OUTSTANDING CONTRIBUTION TO

LITERATURE AND PHILOSOPHY

INAUGURATED IN THE YEAR 2003

★ ★ ★ ★ ★

DONALD MERCER CORMIE

FOR AN OUTSTANDING CONTRIBUTION TO

ARTS AND LAW

INAUGURATED IN THE YEAR 2003

★ ★ ★ ★ ★

JASPER L. CUMMINGS

FOR AN OUTSTANDING CONTRIBUTION TO

EDUCATION

INAUGURATED IN THE YEAR 2003

★ ★ ★ ★ ★

PROFESSOR PAUL DIESING

FOR AN OUTSTANDING CONTRIBUTION TO

PHILOSOPHY OF SOCIAL SCIENCE

INAUGURATED IN THE YEAR 2004

★ ★ ★ ★ ★

PROFESSOR DR DONCHO DONEV

FOR AN OUTSTANDING CONTRIBUTION TO

SOCIAL MEDICINE & PUBLIC HEALTH

INAUGURATED IN THE YEAR 2002

★ ★ ★ ★ ★

DR MARY JOSEPHINE DRAYTON

FOR AN OUTSTANDING CONTRIBUTION TO

EDUCATION AND LOCAL AND REGIONAL GOVERNMENT

INAUGURATED IN THE YEAR 2003

★ ★ ★ ★ ★

PROFESSOR (HR) HARRY EDWARDS

FOR AN OUTSTANDING CONTRIBUTION TO

ECONOMICS, POLITICS AND THIRD-WORLD DEVELOPMENT

INAUGURATED IN THE YEAR 2003

★ ★ ★ ★ ★

FINN EGIL EIDE

FOR AN OUTSTANDING CONTRIBUTION TO

PHILOSOPHY AND ART

INAUGURATED IN THE YEAR 2004

★ ★ ★ ★ ★

DR M F ELKADY

FOR AN OUTSTANDING CONTRIBUTION TO

ECONOMIC, FINANCE AND BUSINESS ADMINISTRATION AND STRENGTHENING THE RELATION AMONG ENTERPRISES

INAUGURATED IN THE YEAR 2003

★ ★ ★ ★ ★

DR WILLIAM O FOYE

FOR AN OUTSTANDING CONTRIBUTION TO

RESEARCH AND SCHOLARSHIP

INAUGURATED IN THE YEAR 2003

★ ★ ★ ★ ★

DR HAJIME FUKIZAWA

FOR AN OUTSTANDING CONTRIBUTION TO

HEAD AND NECK CANCER THERAPY

AND ORAL SURGERY

INAUGURATED IN THE YEAR 2004

★ ★ ★ ★ ★

ALLEN FLETCHER GILLIARD, JR.

FOR AN OUTSTANDING CONTRIBUTION TO

LAW

INAUGURATED IN THE YEAR 2004

★ ★ ★ ★ ★

DR JUVENAL GUTIERREZ-MOCTEZUMA

FOR AN OUTSTANDING CONTRIBUTION TO

PAEDIATRIC NEUROLOGY IN MEXICO

INAUGURATED IN THE YEAR 2003

★ ★ ★ ★ ★

PROFESSOR RAMI W HAMDALLAH

FOR AN OUTSTANDING CONTRIBUTION TO

EDUCATION

INAUGURATED IN THE YEAR 2004

★ ★ ★ ★ ★

E R HANKS

FOR AN OUTSTANDING CONTRIBUTION TO

REAL ESTATE DEVELOPMENT IN THE 20TH CENTURY

INAUGURATED IN THE YEAR 2003

★ ★ ★ ★ ★

PROFESSOR DR KAZUYUKI HATADA

FOR AN OUTSTANDING CONTRIBUTION TO

NUMBER THEORY OF SIEGEL CUSP FORMS

INAUGURATED IN THE YEAR 2003

★ ★ ★ ★ ★

PROFESSOR ALBERT A HAYDEN

FOR AN OUTSTANDING CONTRIBUTION TO

HISTORY

INAUGURATED IN THE YEAR 2003

★ ★ ★ ★ ★

DR RODOLFO HERRERA-LLERANDI

FOR AN OUTSTANDING CONTRIBUTION TO

SURGERY AND MEDICAL EDUCATION

INAUGURATED IN THE YEAR 2003

★ ★ ★ ★ ★

PROFESSOR CHIAKI ITOH

FOR AN OUTSTANDING CONTRIBUTION TO

UNIFIED GAUGE THEORY OF WEAK, ELECTROMAGNETIC AND STRONG INTERACTIONS

INAUGURATED IN THE YEAR 2003

★ ★ ★ ★ ★

NEIL H JACOBY JR

FOR AN OUTSTANDING CONTRIBUTION TO

ASTRODYNAMICS AND ASTRONAUTICS

INAUGURATED IN THE YEAR 2003

★ ★ ★ ★ ★

DR SATISH D JOGLEKAR

FOR AN OUTSTANDING CONTRIBUTION TO

THEORETICAL HIGH ENERGY PHYSICS

INAUGURATED IN THE YEAR 2003

★ ★ ★ ★ ★

JOSEPH SEYMOUR JONES

FOR AN OUTSTANDING CONTRIBUTION TO

POETRY

INAUGURATED IN THE YEAR 2004

★ ★ ★ ★ ★

ROGER ANTHONY CHARLES JONES

FOR AN OUTSTANDING CONTRIBUTION TO

AGRICULTURAL SCIENCE - PLANT VIROLOGY

INAUGURATED IN THE YEAR 2004

★ ★ ★ ★ ★

SALLY D P JONES

FOR AN OUTSTANDING CONTRIBUTION TO

UNITED NATIONS ORGANISATIONS

INAUGURATED IN THE YEAR 2003

★ ★ ★ ★ ★

DR INDIRA YASHWANT JUNGHARE

FOR AN OUTSTANDING CONTRIBUTION TO

SOUTH ASIAN LANGUAGES AND CULTURES

INAUGURATED IN THE YEAR 2004

★ ★ ★ ★ ★

PROFESSOR DR GUDRUN KALMBACH HE

FOR AN OUTSTANDING CONTRIBUTION TO

SCIENCE AND SOCIETY

INAUGURATED IN THE YEAR 2003

★ ★ ★ ★ ★

COMMODORE ANAND KHANDEKAR (RETD)

FOR AN OUTSTANDING CONTRIBUTION TO

INFORMATION TECHNOLOGY

INAUGURATED IN THE YEAR 2003

★ ★ ★ ★ ★

DR NORIYASU KIHARA

FOR AN OUTSTANDING CONTRIBUTION TO

HIBAKUSHA AS A MEMBER OF NGO TO THE U.N.

INAUGURATED IN THE YEAR 2003

★ ★ ★ ★ ★

DR SU GWAN KIM

FOR AN OUTSTANDING CONTRIBUTION TO

ORAL AND MAXILLOFACIAL SURGERY

INAUGURATED IN THE YEAR 2004

★ ★ ★ ★ ★

DR VLADIMIR KISLIK

FOR AN OUTSTANDING CONTRIBUTION TO

CHEMISTRY, SEPARATION SCIENCE

INAUGURATED IN THE YEAR 2003

★ ★ ★ ★ ★

CHARLES JOSEPH KOCIAN

FOR AN OUTSTANDING CONTRIBUTION TO

BIOSTATISTICS

INAUGURATED IN THE YEAR 2005

★ ★ ★ ★ ★

JULIE ANN LAHOOD

FOR AN OUTSTANDING CONTRIBUTION TO

HISTORIC BUILDINGS AND POETRY

INAUGURATED IN THE YEAR 2004

★ ★ ★ ★ ★

BEULAH ENFIELD "BOO" LAW

FOR AN OUTSTANDING CONTRIBUTION TO

EDUCATION AND HELPING THE COMMUNITY

INAUGURATED IN THE YEAR 2004

★ ★ ★ ★ ★

MISS JOY LEROY

FOR AN OUTSTANDING CONTRIBUTION TO

LEADERSHIP AND THE ARTS

INAUGURATED IN THE YEAR 2003

★ ★ ★ ★ ★

CHEE-PENG LIM PHD

FOR AN OUTSTANDING CONTRIBUTION TO

ARTIFICIAL INTELLIGENCE

INAUGURATED IN THE YEAR 2004

★ ★ ★ ★ ★

DR ING DRITA LULO

FOR AN OUTSTANDING CONTRIBUTION TO

THE FIELD OF CONSTRUCTION ENGINEERING

INAUGURATED IN THE YEAR 2003

★ ★ ★ ★ ★

DR JOHN J MANOLAKAKIS MD

FOR AN OUTSTANDING CONTRIBUTION TO

MEDICINE, HEALTHCARE AND LANGUAGES

INAUGURATED IN THE YEAR 2003

★ ★ ★ ★ ★

DR AJAX MENEKRATIS

FOR AN OUTSTANDING CONTRIBUTION TO

ORAL RECONSTRUCTION

INAUGURATED IN THE YEAR 2002

★ ★ ★ ★ ★

PROFESSOR EMERITUS ALBERT J MILLER

FOR AN OUTSTANDING CONTRIBUTION TO

LIBRARYAND INFORMATION SCIENCES

INAUGURATED IN THE YEAR 2005

★ ★ ★ ★ ★

PROFESSOR J W F MULDER

FOR AN OUTSTANDING CONTRIBUTION TO

LINGUISTICS

INAUGURATED IN THE YEAR 2002

★ ★ ★ ★ ★

DR IVKA MARIA MUNDA

FOR AN OUTSTANDING CONTRIBUTION TO

MARINE BIOLOGY - PHYCOLOGY

INAUGURATED IN THE YEAR 2003

★ ★ ★ ★ ★

PROFESSOR AKIRA NAGATOMI

FOR AN OUTSTANDING CONTRIBUTION TO

ENTOMOLOGY

INAUGURATED IN THE YEAR 2003

★ ★ ★ ★ ★

DR SHIGEHISA NAKAMURA

FOR AN OUTSTANDING CONTRIBUTION TO

GEOPHYSICAL SCIENCES

INAUGURATED IN THE YEAR 2002

★ ★ ★ ★ ★

DR W R OGG

FOR AN OUTSTANDING CONTRIBUTION TO

THE ARTS, LAW AND PHILOSOPHY

INAUGURATED IN THE YEAR 2003

★ ★ ★ ★ ★

EUGENE THOMAS OUZTS

FOR AN OUTSTANDING CONTRIBUTION TO

EDUCATION AND RELIGION

INAUGURATED IN THE YEAR 2003

DR ARIE PEDDEMORS

FOR AN OUTSTANDING CONTRIBUTION TO

MUSIC AND ARCHAEOLOGY

INAUGURATED IN THE YEAR 2004

PROFESSOR DR RUDIGER PFEIFFER

FOR AN OUTSTANDING CONTRIBUTION TO

MUSICOLOGY AND MEDIA ENTERTAINMENT BUSINESS

INAUGURATED IN THE YEAR 2003

PROFESSOR DR E N K PINGULI

FOR AN OUTSTANDING CONTRIBUTION TO

THE FIELD OF CONSTRUCTION ENGINEERING

INAUGURATED IN THE YEAR 2003

★ ★ ★ ★ ★

PROFESSOR DR ZDZŁSLAW W PUŚLECKI

FOR AN OUTSTANDING CONTRIBUTION TO

ECONOMIC SCIENCE

INAUGURATED IN THE YEAR 2003

★ ★ ★ ★ ★

DR MARIA REVERTE BERNAL

FOR AN OUTSTANDING CONTRIBUTION TO

PHARMACOLOGY

INAUGURATED IN THE YEAR 2003

★ ★ ★ ★ ★

DR BHAGWAN SAHAY

FOR AN OUTSTANDING CONTRIBUTION TO

PETROLEUM GEOLOGICAL ENGINEERING

INAUGURATED IN THE YEAR 2002

★ ★ ★ ★ ★

DR SWAMI PRANAVANANDA SARASWATI

FOR AN OUTSTANDING CONTRIBUTION TO

WORKING FOR WORLD PEACE AND WELFARE OF HUMANITY FOR MORE THAN HALF A CENTURY

INAUGURATED IN THE YEAR 2003

★ ★ ★ ★ ★

HONORABLE KAZUO SATO

FOR AN OUTSTANDING CONTRIBUTION TO

MECHANICAL ENGINEERING AND INVENTING THE TWO CYCLE ENGINE

INAUGURATED IN THE YEAR 2003

★ ★ ★ ★ ★

PROFESSOR DR ROBERT M SCHMIDT

FOR AN OUTSTANDING CONTRIBUTION TO

MEDICAL RESEARCH, EDUCATION AND ADMINISTRATION

INAUGURATED IN THE YEAR 2003

★ ★ ★ ★ ★

LUIS M SESÉ

FOR AN OUTSTANDING CONTRIBUTION TO

QUANTUM STATISTICAL MECHANICS

INAUGURATED IN THE YEAR 2005

★ ★ ★ ★ ★

TROY ALVIN SMITH

FOR AN OUTSTANDING CONTRIBUTION TO

NUMERICAL ANALYSIS OF SHELLS

INAUGURATED IN THE YEAR 2003

★ ★ ★ ★ ★

SVEN STROMQVIST

FOR AN OUTSTANDING CONTRIBUTION TO

LINGUISTIC AND COGNITIVE SCIENCES

INAUGURATED IN THE YEAR 2003

★ ★ ★ ★ ★

PROFESSOR DR A SUN

FOR AN OUTSTANDING CONTRIBUTION TO

IMMUNOLOGY AND MEDICINE

INAUGURATED IN THE YEAR 2003

★ ★ ★ ★ ★

DR KATHLEEN DAS SUNEJA

FOR AN OUTSTANDING CONTRIBUTION TO

THE FIELD OF INTERNATIONAL RELATIONS

INAUGURATED IN THE YEAR 2003

★ ★ ★ ★ ★

DR WILLIAM H THUEME

FOR AN OUTSTANDING CONTRIBUTION TO

PEACE THROUGH UNDERSTANDING

INAUGURATED IN THE YEAR 2003

★ ★ ★ ★ ★

DR GARNIK TONOYAN

FOR AN OUTSTANDING CONTRIBUTION TO

MATHEMATICS

INAUGURATED IN THE YEAR 2004

★ ★ ★ ★ ★

GLORIA VADUS

FOR AN OUTSTANDING CONTRIBUTION TO

SCIENTIFIC DOCUMENT EXAMINATION

INAUGURATED IN THE YEAR 2004

★ ★ ★ ★ ★

DR JONG WANG

FOR AN OUTSTANDING CONTRIBUTION TO

EDUCATION & LITERATURE

INAUGURATED IN THE YEAR 2003

★ ★ ★ ★ ★

BABATUNDE O WILLIAMS

FOR AN OUTSTANDING CONTRIBUTION TO

REFINERIES PROCESS DESIGN AND CONSTRUCTION

INAUGURATED IN THE YEAR 2003

★ ★ ★ ★ ★

DR ALAN WONG YUN SANG

FOR AN OUTSTANDING CONTRIBUTION TO

ART AND LITERATURE

INAUGURATED IN THE YEAR 2004

★ ★ ★ ★ ★

DR ETSUO YAMAMURA

FOR AN OUTSTANDING CONTRIBUTION TO

MODEL REFERENCE ADAPTIVE ECONOMICS

INAUGURATED IN THE YEAR 2004

★ ★ ★ ★ ★

VLADIMIR ZAKHAROV

FOR AN OUTSTANDING CONTRIBUTION TO

FLOURINE CHEMISTRY

INAUGURATED IN THE YEAR 2003

★ ★ ★ ★ ★

PROFESSOR STEFAN ZAREA

INAUGURATED IN THE YEAR 2004

★ ★ ★ ★

PROFESSOR URI ZEHAVI

FOR AN OUTSTANDING CONTRIBUTION TO

BIOCHEMISTRY

INAUGURATED IN THE YEAR 2003

★ ★ ★ ★ ★

DR WENDELL E ZEHEL

FOR AN OUTSTANDING CONTRIBUTION TO

BIOTECHNOLOGY

INAUGURATED IN THE YEAR 2003

★ ★ ★ ★ ★

DR YUMING ZHOU

FOR AN OUTSTANDING CONTRIBUTION TO

POETIC LITERATURE

INAUGURATED IN THE YEAR 2003

★ ★ ★ ★ ★

DIRECTOR GENERAL'S ROLL OF HONOUR

EDGARDO GALPO ADVINCULA
Medical Doctor
FOR CONTRIBUTIONS TO
Medicine and Surgery

❀❀❀❀❀❀❀❀

URSULA MARY ANDERSON
Paediatrician
FOR CONTRIBUTIONS TO
Services to Humanity

❀❀❀❀❀❀❀❀

CHARLES E. BRODINE
Physician
FOR CONTRIBUTIONS TO
Medicine and Healthcare

❀❀❀❀❀❀❀❀

DR. DANIEL D. BRUNDA
Mechanical Engineer
FOR CONTRIBUTIONS TO
Scientific Excellence

❀❀❀❀❀❀❀❀

PAULO DE CARVALHO
Sociologist
FOR CONTRIBUTIONS TO
Sociology and Journalism

❀❀❀❀❀❀❀❀

PROF. FRANCISCO FERREIRA DE CASTRO
Lawyer, Educator
FOR CONTRIBUTIONS TO
Law

❀❀❀❀❀❀❀❀

PROFESSOR CHOMCHARK CHUNTRASAKUL
Medical Doctor
FOR CONTRIBUTIONS TO
Medicine in the Field of Surgery

❀❀❀❀❀❀❀❀

DR. FREDDIE C. COLSTON
Professor of Political Science
FOR CONTRIBUTIONS TO
Political Science

❀❀❀❀❀❀❀❀

BARONESS DR JOY BEAUDETTE CRIPPS
Poet; Writer
FOR CONTRIBUTIONS TO
Humanity, Peace, Culture, Education, Literature

❀❀❀❀❀❀❀❀

IGA B. DELAPALME
Engineer
FOR CONTRIBUTIONS TO
Research and Innovation

❀❀❀❀❀❀❀❀

ALLEN FLETCHER GILLIARD, JR
Attorney
FOR CONTRIBUTIONS TO
Law

❀❀❀❀❀❀❀❀

NICOLAAS JOHANNES GROBBELAAR
General Surgeon
FOR CONTRIBUTIONS TO
Medicine: General Surgery

❀❀❀❀❀❀❀❀

DIRECTOR GENERAL'S ROLL OF HONOUR

JOSIPA SANJA GRUDEN POKUPEC

Specialist in Oral Medicine
FOR CONTRIBUTIONS TO
Medicine

❁❁❁❁❁❁❁❁❁

BENEDICTE LAURSEN

Doctor of Medical Science
FOR CONTRIBUTIONS TO
The Clinical Practice of Medicine and Haematology

❁❁❁❁❁❁❁❁❁

THE HON. DR. DALE LAYMAN

Professor; Author
FOR CONTRIBUTIONS TO
The Future Survival of Mankind

❁❁❁❁❁❁❁❁❁

MUDR PAVEL NOVOSAD

Doctor of Medicine
FOR CONTRIBUTIONS TO
Medicine for Patients, Metabolic Medicine

❁❁❁❁❁❁❁❁❁

PROF. NICK PAHYS, JR

Author; Museum Curator
FOR CONTRIBUTIONS TO
the US Presidency

❁❁❁❁❁❁❁❁❁

PROF. DR. BOJAN PAJIC

Ophthalmologist; Ophthalmic Surgeon; Researcher & Scientist.
FOR CONTRIBUTIONS TO
Ophthalmology Research Science

❁❁❁❁❁❁❁❁❁

IR. KIRTI PENIWATI

Decision Making Facilitator
FOR CONTRIBUTIONS TO
The Analytic Hierarchy / Network Process

❁❁❁❁❁❁❁❁❁

KAREL PEXIDR

Lawyer; Philosopher; Composer; Writer
FOR CONTRIBUTIONS TO
Philosophy, Music, Literature

❁❁❁❁❁❁❁❁❁

PROF. ELENA RADULESCU

Professor; Senior Specialist in Haematology; Immunocytochemist; Researcher
FOR CONTRIBUTIONS TO
Haematology

❁❁❁❁❁❁❁❁❁

DR. HORST R. RÖHLING

Retired Librarian
FOR CONTRIBUTIONS TO
Slavistics Librarianship Eastern Churches

❁❁❁❁❁❁❁❁❁

DR. GILBERT C. SAN DIEGO

Businessman
FOR CONTRIBUTIONS TO
Education

❁❁❁❁❁❁❁❁❁

DIRECTOR GENERAL'S ROLL OF HONOUR

THE HON. DR. SERGEY V. SIMONENKO

Engineer; Physicist

FOR CONTRIBUTIONS TO

The Cosmic Physics and Earthquakes Prediction

✤✤✤✤✤✤✤✤

DR. MING-SHIUM TU

Physician

FOR CONTRIBUTIONS TO

Human Spirituality and Medicine

✤✤✤✤✤✤✤✤

PROF. DR. PARS TUGLACI

Linguist; Historian; Lexicographer

FOR CONTRIBUTIONS TO

Linguistics and History

✤✤✤✤✤✤✤✤

DR. CHRISTINA XINYAN XIE

Language Educator

FOR CONTRIBUTIONS TO

Language Education

✤✤✤✤✤✤✤✤

DEDICATIONS

DEDICATIONS

MARJORIE RUTH BURNS, B.A., MOIF, IOM

For an Outstanding Contribution to Research and Music

MARJORIE RUTH BURNS, B.A., MOIF, IOM

Born on the 16th August 1929 in Adelaide, South Australia, Marjorie Ruth Burns held the appointments of Clerk to Elders Trustee Company in 1951, Library Assistant at Barr Smith Library between 1952-62, Librarian for the Commonwealth of Australia Public Services from 1962-67 and Librarian, and Parliamentary Librarian for South Australia Parliament Library between 1967-88. Miss Burns is the author of numerous professional publications, including: "Australia: Some Facts", "Human Rights in Australia", "Songs of the Hebrides: Commentary on Marjory Kennedy Fraser's Edition V.1", "Centenary of Robert Burns Statue" and "Scottish in South Australia". She is the recipient of a Gold Medal of Honour, an International Cultural Diploma of Honour in 1987, the World Decoration in 1989, Musician of the Year of 1989, Woman of the Year of 1990 and 1993-95, Grand Ambassador of Achievement in 1991, Silver Shield of Valour in 1992, congress Medallion of the 22nd Congress, Sydney in 1995 and Most Admired Woman of the Decade in 1996. Miss Burns is a member of several societies and associations. In her leisure time, she enjoys playing the piano and going to concerts and the theatre.

The biography of Marjorie Ruth Burns, B.A.,MOIF, IOM appears in the main section of this edition.

DEDICATIONS

**PROFESSOR DR HARUO HYODO,
AdVMed, AWCASC, DDG,
HonDG, HonDL**

*For an Outstanding Contribution to
Radiology*

PROFESSOR DR HARUO HYODO, AdVMed, AWCASC, DDG, HonDG, HonDL

Dr Haruo Hyodo was born on 3 March 1928 in Ehime. He graduated in 1959 from the Tokushima University School of Medicine, and received a Medical Doctor degree from Tokushima University seven years later.

Dr Hyodo has held a variety of positions during his career. He served as Chief of the Division of Radiology at Ehime Prefecture Central Hospital from 1970 to 1977. During this time he also held several other positions. Then joined Dokkyo University School of Medicine as a Professor, and held this post until 1990. After three years, he joined Fukuda Memorial Hospital as a Voice Director and Chief of Health Medical Center at Mooka Tochigi.

Interestingly, in 1982, Dr Hyodo dedicated a panel of early gastric cancer to the German Roentgen Museum at Remschid-Lennep in Germany. The panel is displayed in an exhibiting hall; it contains double contrast X-ray imaging, freshly respected specimens, cross sections of the specimen, and histological pictures. Also of note, he obtained two Japanese patents for a table of X-ray CT in 1994, and a method of observation concerning three-dimensional imaging in 2003.

As befits a professional of his stature, Dr Hyodo is a member of the Japan Radiological Society. Moreover, an honorary member of the Japan Biliary Association, the Japanese Society of Interventional Radiology and special member of the Japanese Society of Medical Images Technology. To acknowledge his outstanding contributions, Dr Hyodo was given the Award of MIKI-Kourakukai from Tokushima University in 1958, and the International Hippocrates Award for medical achievement from IBC in Cambridge, England in 2009.

Dr Hyodo is married to Keiko Tomita and the couple have a son and two daughters. In his leisure time, Dr Hyodo enjoys photography and motoring.

A biography of Professor Dr Haruo Hyodo, AdVMed, AWCASC, DDG, HonDG, HonDL appears in the main section of this edition.

DEDICATIONS

PROFESSOR GABRIEL AMPAH JOHNSON, DDG, AdVSci, IOM, HonDG

For an Outstanding Contribution to Biology and University Administration

PROFESSOR GABRIEL AMPAH JOHNSON, DDG, AdVSci, IOM, HonDG

Professor of Biology, Gabriel Ampah Johnson, was educated at the Universite de Poitiers, France. He received his Licence-es-Sciences in 1954 and his Doctorat-es- Sciences d'État in 1959. Between 1958-60 Professor Johnson was a research fellow at CNRS, France and was later appointed as a Professor and Chair of Biology. As Founding Rector of the Universite du Benin in Lome, Togo, he held the post of rector from 1970 until 1986. Professor Johnson has been Chancellor of Togolese Universities since 1998. He is the author of numerous articles and papers that have been published in professional scientific journals worldwide.

In the course of his career, Professor Johnson has received many honours and awards in recognition of his achievements. In 1966 he was awarded the Chevalier de l'Ordre National de la Côte-d'Ivoire. During the 1970s he was appointed Officier de la Légion d'Honneur of France, Commandeur de l'Ordre National du Gabon, and Grand Officier de la Croix du Sud of the Ordre du Cruzeiro do Sul of Brazil. He received the Commandeur de l'Ordre du Mérite of France and a Certificate of Merit from the IBC in 1983, and three years later was presented with the titles Commandeur de l'Ordre des Palmes Académiques, France, and Commandeur de l'Ordre National de Mérite de la Tunisie. More recently, the professor has gained the following honours: Commandeur de l'Ordre du Mono, Togo (2000), Commandeur de l'Ordre des Palmes Académiques, Togo (2006), the Universal Award of Accomplishment, ABI (2006), the International Medal of Honor, IBC (2006), and the American Medal of Honor, ABI (2006). He currently holds membership of The Africa Club, the World Association of Social Prospective and UNESCO.

Professor Johnson was born on 13 October 1930 in Aneho, Togo. He and his wife, Louise Chipan, have three sons and three daughters.

A biography of Professor Gabriel Ampah Johnson, DDG, AdVSci, IOM, HonDG appears in the main section of this edition.

PROFESSOR DR SEON BONG KIM

For an Outstanding Contribution to Food Science and Technology

PROFESSOR DR SEON BONG KIM

Professor Kim was born on 28 November 1955 in Namhae, Gyeongsangnamdo, Republic of Korea. He is married to Jin Sook Cho and they have two children, Yeong Min and Yeong Gyeong.

Professor Kim achieved his PhD at the University of Tokyo in 1985, before joining Pukyong National University as a Professor in the Department of Flood Science & Technology in 1986. He has subsequently been appointed Director of the Flood Analysis & Inspection Center, and is currently Director of the Institute of Flood Science. In the course of is career, Professor Kim has been an invited researcher at the National Cancer Research Institute in Japan, and an invited Professor at Kyoto University. He has also worked as a Research Fellow at the Institute of Pathology at Case Western Research University, USA for one year. Among his many publications are the following titles: "Seafood Processing & Utilization" (1994), "Introduction to Fisheries Processing" (1997), and "Fisheries Processing" (2003).

In 1988 Professor Kim received the Korean Fisheries Society Award. He is also the recipient of the 1990 Foundation for Promotion of Cancer Research Fellowship, the 1993 Rotary Yoneyama Memorial Fellowship, and the 1995 Ochi Young Scholarship Award. Professor Kim is a Fellow of the Korean Academy of Science and Technology and Editor-in-chief of the Korean Journal of Fisheries & Aquatic Science.

A biography of Professor Dr Seon Bong Kim appears in the main section of this edition.

DEDICATIONS

MUDr PAVEL NOVOSAD, DDG, LFIBA, MOIF, IOM, HonDG

For an Outstanding Contribution to Metabolic Medicine for Patients

MUDR PAVEL NOVOSAD, DDG, LFIBA, MOIF, IOM, HonDG

MUDr Pavel Novosad is a doctor of medicine. He was born on 13 June 1945 in Zlin, Czech Republic. He is married to Paula, and they have two sons.

MUDr Novosad attended the Medical Faculty, UJEP BRNO in 1969. He achieved two postgraduate diplomas, the first in Internal Medicine in 1974, and a second in Clinical Chemistry in 1979. Between 1979 and 1992, MUDr Novosad was chief of the Special Science Laboratory specializing in Metabolic Diseases at the Internal Teaching Clinic in Zlin. Since 1992 he has been chief of Mediekos Labor Ltd, and since 2007 he has been chief of the Osteology Academy. Further study led to a postgraduate diploma in Clinical Osteology in 2010. In the course of his career he has published numerous articles in professional journals. MUDr Novosad has also been chief of a Workgroup for Problematic Metabolic Diseases of Bones with the Czech Medicine Society. He is a member of the International Osteoporosis Foundation, the Society of J E Purkyne and the Osteology and Clinical Chemistry.

A biography of MUDr Pavel Novosad, DDG, LFIBA, MOIF, IOM, HonDG appears in the main section of this edition.

DEDICATIONS

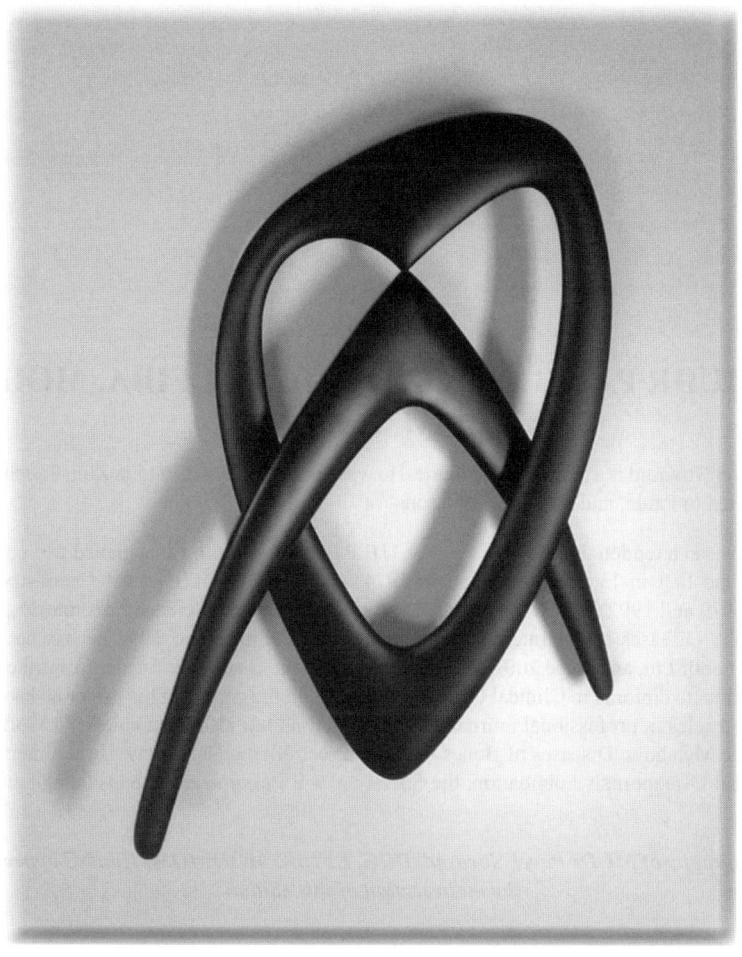

PAUL BARTLETT RÉ

*For an Outstanding Contribution to
Elevating, Universal Art that
Harmonizes the World*

PAUL BARTLETT RÉ

Paul Ré (pronounced Ray) was born on 18 April 1950 in Albuquerque, New Mexico where he still resides. He is an artist, writer, poet and peace worker. Ré explains the process of his art unfolding inside its viewers: "If we have in our consciousness clear and harmonious images, these can act as powerful statements of hope and faith. They are a kind of meditation and visual mantra." He continues, "The derivation of my art from closed curves is significant. It represents the interconnectedness of everything in existence, from the scale of the universe down to the subatomic and is philosophically related to String Theory of modern physics which holds promise of being a 'Theory of Everything.' In sociology, my curves constitute a prayer and visual model for the peaceful, constructive interaction of human beings. In ecology, these closed curves symbolize the dynamic interdependence of all species and encourage humankind to conserve and use thoughtfully the physical and spiritual bounty of nature. When reverence for our natural, cultural and scientific heritage guides our practical actions, then our diverse world civilization can evolve to that higher fulfillment which I believe is the intent of life."

Mr. Ré earned a Bachelor's Degree in physics with high honours from Caltech in 1972 and this has served him well as an artist expressing the beauty of science. He has been acclaimed by art critics as "a virtuoso of the pencil" for his art of "quiet greatness and noble simplicity." In 13 states, he has had 22 solo exhibits including those at the University of New Mexico Jonson Gallery, Albuquerque Museum, Triangle Gallery, Wichita Museum, Sumter Gallery, J B Speed Museum, the Colorado Springs Museum and the Karpeles Museum. His traveling exhibition of Touchable Art For The Blind And Sighted has been shown 18 times in North America. A documentary film on his Touchable Art was produced by SCETV in 1990 and a companion book was created. He is now making a second tactile exhibit, Inspired By Nature, which is dedicated to environmental conservation.

In 1993, his monograph The Dance Of The Pencil: Serene Art by Paul Ré was published. The Journal of the Print World reviewed it as "one of the outstanding art books of the year." Included are 71 full page plates and discussions of these examples from every stage of the first two decades of Mr. Ré's career: the Growth Series ('ancient' symbolic drawings and motifs); the Mandala Series (beautifully balanced designs); the Animal Series (real and mythical beasts); as well as three series of abstract works. Other writings by Ré appear in Leonardo 13, 14 and 15, Spirit of Enterprise: The 1990 Rolex Awards, The Journal of Visual Impairment, New America, La Mamelle and Design Journal. Mr. Ré is prominently included in Contemporary Graphic Artists, Great Minds of the 21st Century and Greatest Geniuses plus many other reference volumes worldwide. Also an accomplished guitarist, poet and humorist he is editing his collected poems The Iris Ballet and compiling his 48 volumes of aphorisms and micro-essays into The Récycled Dictionary. In addition, a book and traveling exhibit of his Réograms (hybrid hand-digital artworks) are being developed. Further information and examples of his work may be found at www.paulre.org

Mr. Ré has received twenty major awards including the Legion of Honor and the International Peace Prize from the United Cultural Convention, the Order of American Ambassadors, the World Lifetime Achievement Award, Genius Laureate and Albert Einstein Award from the American Biographical Institute, plus the Da Vinci Laureate, Director General's Roll of Honour, and the Hall of Fame from the International Biographical Centre in Cambridge, England. He has been named to The Global 100. Extending his decades of work promoting harmony in the world, the Paul Bartlett Ré Peace Prize has been established at the University of New Mexico. Emphasis is on promoting both internal and external peace and fostering discussion of what really constitutes peace. Included is conflict resolution, but conflict prevention is particularly strongly emphasized.

Beyond the joy of doing the art itself, Mr. Ré's greatest reward is when people are moved by his work toward peace and fulfillment. He greatly enjoys walking and meditating in nature. From the hundreds of articles and letters about Ré's work, we offer these insights:

DEDICATIONS

"The Dance of the Pencil should firmly establish Paul Ré as a national and world treasure." Fred Shair, Professor Emeritus, California Institute of Technology, past President of Sigma Xi

"The singular purity of his basic shapes gives them a unique place in modern art." Dennis Wepman, Contemporary Graphic Artists

"I spent several hours viewing your drawings; they are sensitive and exhilarating… I expect many more hours of enjoyment." Subrahmanyan Chandrasekhar, Astrophysicist, Nobel Laureate, Enrico Fermi Institute

"Since his earliest work, Ré has sought to integrate the aesthetic and the intellectual and to use art as a spiritual exercise." Dennis Wepman, The Journal of the Print World

"Looking at its beautiful images has been providing me with a deep feeling of serenity and inner peace." Moustafa Chahine, Chief Scientist, Jet Propulsion Laboratory (JPL)

"I really like this work. I find it very peaceful and relaxing." Richard Feynman, Physicist, Nobel Laureate, California Institute of Technology

"I shall treasure this book. It shows tremendous artistic creativity of a form I have not enjoyed before. I find I enjoy (your pictures) immensely and can study them for a long time, learning as each moment passes…I intend to keep the book on a table in my office so that people who believe Caltech turns out narrow and creative scientists only can see first hand what a least one of our students has done…The Institute is truly proud of you." Thomas E. Everhart, President Emeritus, California Institute of Technology

"I received the notice of your show, and thought the drawing on the front to be very nice. If you are passing through this area and have any of your other work with you I would be interested in seeing it. Luck to you." Georgia O'keeffe

In closing, the following poem written by Ré in 2004 is a good summary of his work:

Bridging to Peace

My life has been a journey

of bridging –

art and science,

East and West,

the worlds of the blind and sighted,

humankind with nature,

and most basically,

a bridging to the serenity

deep within me.

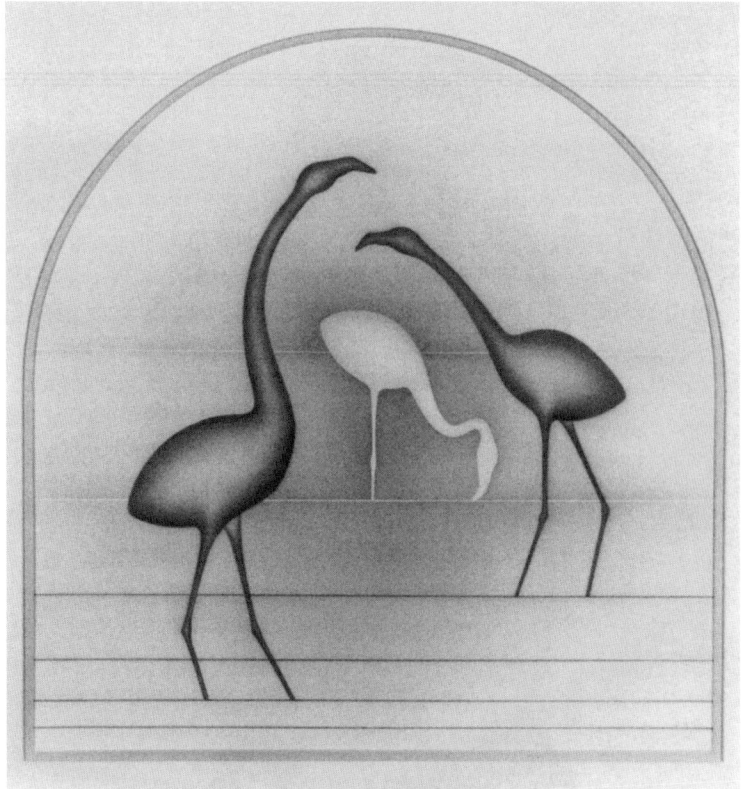

"Flamingos", Paul Ré, pencil on rag paper, 27" x 26", 1973

Continuing this journey,

may my art

help others to nurture

their tranquil center.

And may they then build bridges

spreading outward

from their inner harmony

to a Global Peace.

A biography of Paul Bartlett Ré appears in the main section of this edition.

PROFESSOR TSO-MIN SHIH, DDG

For an Outstanding Contribution to Engineering Education

DICTIONARY OF INTERNATIONAL BIOGRAPHY 35th EDITION

PROFESSOR TSO-MIN SHIH, DDG

The son of Ren-Yeng and Sun-Sum Shih, Tso-Min Shih was born on 4 April 1935 in Ying-Chen, in the Province of Shantung, China. His father, a Lieutenant-Colonel in the Chinese Army, died for his country during World War II, while his mother also lost her life in the war. He is married to Ching-Chi Hsia, who teaches at Taiwan Provincial Tainan Deaf and Blind School; the wedding took place on 1 June 1961. The couple have three children, Rosa Hung-Chen, Kim Hung-Wei and Sophia Hung-Jui, all now adult.

In 1958 Professor Shih graduated from the Taiwan Provincial Cheng-Kung University in Tainan, where he earned a BSc degree. He then embarked on further education in Canada, obtaining his MSc degree from McGill University in Montreal in 1965 and completing his postgraduate study at the University of British Columbia in 1968.

While in Canada, Professor Shih worked as a Research Assistant at the Nova Scotia Technical College in Halifax. Since returning to Taiwan in 1968 he has been on the academic staff at the National Cheng-Kung University, where he held positions as Lecturer, Associate Professor and Department Chairman, and in 1980 was appointed to his present post of Full Professor of Rock Mechanics and then he retired from NCKU on 1 August 2000. He has been employed as a full professor in Diwan University, Tainan county since 2003. In addition, from 1976-78 he served as Director of the Chinese Institute of Mining and Metallurgical Engineering.

Professor Shih has published more than fifty articles in professional journals, as well as authoring two books in Chinese, namely, 'Diamond', which appeared in 1996, and 'The Exploitation and Utilization of Graphite Materials', as recently as 1999. In recognition of his research activities, he was the recipient of awards from Pi Epsilon Tau, the National Petroleum Engineering Honor Society, in 1989. Further recognition came his way in 1993 through the awards of the Taiwan Provincial Government's Department of Reconstruction.

Just as Professor Shih achieved an advanced education, his children have also furthered their academic backgrounds. His son, Kim, graduated from Feng-Chia University, Taichung, in 1989, receiving a BSc degree and then went on to the University of Massachusetts, USA, to obtain a PhD degree, which was followed by a Fellowship at Harvard University. At that time his daughter Rosa had already earned a BSc degree at Tam-Kang University, Taipei, in 1984; her MSc degree followed in 1987 from the University of Missouri-Rolla, USA. His younger daughter, Sophia, obtained her BSc degree from Taipei Medical College in 1998. She then spent one year on research at the Academica Sinica, after which she, too, travelled to the USA, to pursue graduate studies at the Northeastern University in Boston, Massachusetts. Sophia obtained her first MS degree in June 2002 and her second MS degree from UC Davis California in June 2004.

As a young man, Professor Shih served as a Second Lieutenant in the ROTC from 1958-60. He holds permanent membership of the Chinese Institute of Mining and Metallurgical Engineering, from which he received awards in 1972 and 1992. He is also a permanent member of the Chinese Institute of Engineers, as well as the Mining Association of China, serving as a director of the latter from 1988-94 and again from 1996 up to the present and from which he received an award in 1996.

On a more personal note, Professor Shih is a member of the Association of Chinese Kung-Fu. For relaxation he enjoys the various forms of Chinese Kung-Fu, such as Tai-Chi Chu'uan, Tai-Chi Sword and Tai-Chi Fan.

A biography of Professor Tso-Min Shih, DDG appears in the main section of this edition.

DR TROY ALVIN SMITH

*For an Outstanding Contribution to
Civil Engineering and Engineering Mechanics*

DR TROY ALVIN SMITH

Troy Alvin Smith is an Aerospace Research Engineer. He was born the son of Wade Hampton and Augusta Mabel (Lindsey) Smith on 4 July 1922 in Sylvatus, Virginia, USA. He graduated from Sylvatus High School on 24 May 1940 as class valedictorian. On 24 November 1990 he married Grace Marie (Peacock) Dees.

Dr Smith served in the US Navy Reserve in the Pacific Theatre of Operations between 1942-46. The naval unit with which he was serving was awarded the Presidential Unit Citation for naval action during the Battle of Leyte Gulf on 23-26 October 1944. At the end of World War II, he returned to his studies in engineering at the University of Virginia and was awarded the earned BCE degree by the University of Virginia in June 1948.

Dr Smith was employed as a civilian Structural Engineer with the Corps of Engineers of the US Army during the period from 1948-59. During the period from June 1951 to June 1952 he pursued graduate study at the University of Michigan from which he was awarded the MSE degree in June 1952. He was employed as Chief Structural Engineer of Brown Engineering Company Inc, Huntsville, Alabama for one year during 1959-60. He was employed as a Structural Research Engineer with the US Army Missile Command, Redstone Arsenal, Alabama from 1960-63, as an Aerospace Engineer from 1963-80, and as an Aerospace Research Engineer from 1980-96. Throughout his career, Dr Smith has continued his studies, earning his PhD degree in Engineering Mechanics at the University of Michigan, which was awarded in May 1970.

During the period 1996-2003, Dr Smith served as an Aerospace Engineer Emeritus with the US Army Aviation and Missile Command, Redstone Arsenal, Alabama. Since 2003, he has served as an Aerospace Engineer Emeritus with the US Army Research, Development, and Engineering Command, Aviation and Missile Research, Development, and Engineering Center, Redstone Arsenal, Alabama. He has been a Registered Professional Engineer in Virginia since 1948 and in Alabama since 1959. Dr Smith has published 18 major US Army technical reports on analysis of shells and other structures as well as articles in the AIAA Journal and the Journal of Sound and Vibration on analysis of shells. His doctoral dissertation was entitled "Numerical Solution for the Dynamic Response of Rotationally Symmetric Shells of Revolution under Transient Loadings". Dr Smith is a member of Sigma Xi, the New York Academy of Sciences, and the Association of the US Army. He has received honours for his achievements, and in 1969 was awarded a Secretary of the Army Research and Study Fellowship for Graduate Study at the University of Michigan. He received the awards of IBC Leading Engineers of the World, 2006; IBC Director General's Roll of Honour, 2007; Top Two Hundred of the IBC, 2008; IBC Distinguished Service to Engineering Award, 2008; IBC Hall of Fame, 2008; IBC Lifetime Achievement Award, 2008; IBC Top 100 Engineers, 2009; ABI World Laureate, 2009; and ABI Magna Cum Laude, 2009.

A biography of Dr Troy Alvin Smith appears in the main section of this edition.

DEDICATIONS

MADHAVJI (MARK) A. UNDE

For an Outstanding Contribution to Science and Engineering

MADHAVJI (MARK) A. UNDE

Mr Madhav Unde is a welding scientist and an engineer. He was born in Pune, India on 28 June 1934 and is father to one son and two adopted daughters.

Mr Unde's first position was as a Senior Scientific Officer in Defence R&D with the Government of India between 1965-74. He travelled to the USA where he earned his MS in Welding Engineering in 1978 at the Ohio State University, Columbus. Mr Unde joined the Fruehauf Corporation as a Division Welding Engineer and then became a Tool Design Engineer with Danly Machines/Ingersol Milling Machines Inc. Following this, he took up the post of Mechanical Engineer for the Sacramento Army Depot in Sacramento, California, USA. Mr Unde is currently President of California Consulting Engineers.

As an author, Mr Unde has published the following titles: "Effect of back-up on Welding of Thin Sections of Aluminium Alloy", "Mathematical Theory of Heat Diffusion" (1994), "A Brief on IPSR technology for weld-joints" (2nd revision, 2003), and several other professional articles. He has patented processes in casting, non-destructive testing, mechanisms and welding including: IPSR, the in process stress relief of welds (US patent 1983); EHS the equivalent heat sink process for in-process production of welds without defects and reduced residual stress (US patent 1991); and Mind Engineering. Mr Unde's US patents include: "Covered Trailing Edge of Weld" (2000); "Trailing Edge Stress Relief" (2001); a total of four processes in IPSR technology to produce a metal joint without defect and known value residual stress during welding; and "IPSR technology eliminates 70% of the welding labour".

Mr Unde is a UK Chartered Engineer, a MIProdE, London and a MIE, India. He also belongs to the AWS and ASM International. In acknowledgement of his development of the IPSR process, Mr Unde was awarded the ARPA Presidential Award.

A biography of Madhavji (Mark) A. Unde appears in the main section of this edition.

BIOGRAPHIES

A

AAKER Everett, b. 20 April 1954, Wigan, Lancashire, England. Author. Education: HNC, Business Studies, Wirral College of Technology. 1982-86. Appointments: Professional career in business in England; Feature Writer, TV Scene Magazine, 1987-90. Publication: Television Western Players of the Fifties: A Biographical Encyclopaedia of All Regular Cast Members in Western Series, 1949-59, 1997; Encyclopaedia of Early Television Crime Fighters All Regular Cast Members in American Crime and Mystery Series 1948-1959, 2006; The Films of George Raft, 2012. Honour: Associate, London Academy of Music and Dramatic Art, 1977. Membership: Institute of Purchasing and Supply, 1987. Address: c/o McFarland & Co, PO Box 611, Jefferson, North Carolina 28640, USA.

AARÅS Arne, b. 7 March 1937, Holla, Norway. Physician. m. Astrid, 1 son, 2 daughters. Education: Graduate, Medical School, 1964, PhD, 1987, University of Oslo; Hospital training in Ear, Nose and Throat, Gynaecology, Geriatric Medicine, Surgery, Internal Medicine; Occupational Medicine Courses: Arbetsmedisinske Institutet, Karolinska Institutet, Stockholm, Sweden, 1971, Norwegian Employer Federation and Johns Hopkins Hospital, Baltimore, USA, 1987-88. Appointments: District Doctor in Sweden, 3 years; Concurrently, Occupational Physician with a large packaging company; Occupational Doctor, Centre for Occupational Medicine, Sweden, 5 years; Co-ordinator for Occupational Medicine, Standard Telefon og Kabelfabrikk A/S (ITT Norway, later, Alcatel STK A/S), 1974-; Co-operator with Work Physiology Institute in Oslo, 1977-; Associate Chairman, Work Inspectorate, Oslo, 10 years; Co-ordinator for an international study of musculoskeletal, visual and psychosocial stress for VDU workers with 5 participating countries, 1990-; Professor, Department of Optometry and Visual Sciences, Buskerud University College. Publications: Approximately 90 papers. Honours: Award, Nordic Ergonomic Society, 1995; Distinguished International Colleague Award, Human Factors and Ergonomics Society, 1999. Memberships: International Committee of Occupational Medicine; Norwegian Research Council (5 years); Ergonomic Society, UK. Address: Finstadkroken 12, 1475 Finstadjordet, Norway. E-mail: arne.aaras@alcatel.no

AARONSON Edward John (Jack), b. 16 August 1918. Company Director. m. Marian Davies, 2 sons. Education: CFS, London. Appointments: RA, Palestine to Tunisia, 1940-44, India, 1945-46, W/S Captain; Articled, Jackson Pixley & Co, 1946-49; Founder, General Secretary, The Anglo Israel Chamber of Commerce, 1950-53; Economic Advisor (Export), GEC, 1954-61, later General Manager Overseas Operations, 1961-63; Economic Advisor, Celmac Ltd, 1964-65; Deputy Chairman and part-time Chief Executive, The Steel Barrel Scammells & Associated Engineers Ltd, later Anthony Carrimore Ltd, 1965-68; Industrial Advisor, later Director, Armitage Industrial Holdings Ltd, 1965-68, Director, later Chairman, George Turton Platt, 1966-68; Director, E R & F Turner Ltd, 1967-68; Chairman Br Northrop Ltd, 1968-73; Chairman and Chief Executive, Scheme Manager and Creditors Committee Chairman, The G R A Property Trust Ltd, 1975-83; Non-Executive Chairman, Wand FC Bonham & Sons Ltd, 1981-89; Non-Executive Director, Camlab Ltd, 1982-89; Non-Executive Chairman, The Reject Shop plc, 1985-90. Memberships: FBI Standing Committees on overseas credit and overseas investment from inception, 1958-63; Council, The Export Group for the Construction Industries, 1960-63; Member, British Greyhound Racing Board, 1975-83; Chairman, NGRC Race Course Promoters Association, 1978-83; FCA, 1960; FInstD, 1980; Member General Committee, 1976-79, 1980-83, Chairman Pension Fund Trustees, 1985-2005, Reform Club. Address: 2 The Paddock, The Street, Bishops Cannings, Devizes SN10 2LD, England.

AARSETH Sverre Johannes, b. 20 July 1934, Steinkjer, Norway. Astronomer. Education: BSc, Oslo, 1959; PhD, Cantab, 1963. Appointments: Research Scientist, Institute of Astronomy, University of Cambridge, 1967-2001; Retired, 2001. Publications: Over 100 research papers in dynamical astronomy; Gravitational N-Body Simulations, 2003. Honours: Dirk Brouwer Award, American Astronomical Society; Asteroid #9836 named Aarseth. Memberships: Royal Astronomical Society; Royal Geographical Society; Alpine Club. Address: Institute of Astronomy, Madingley Road, Cambridge CB3 0HA, England. Website: www.ast.cam.ac.uk/~sverre

ABADIR Karim Maher, b. 6 January 1964, Egypt. Professor of Financial Econometrics. Education: Bachelor of Arts, Economics, Master of Arts, Economics, The American University in Cairo; DPhil, Economics, Oxford University, England. Appointments: Board of Directors, NACITA Corp, Cairo, 1985-; Lecturer, Economics, Lincoln College, Oxford, England, 1988-92; Board of Directors, FOREX Corp, Cairo, 1991-; Research Fellow, Economics, American University in Cairo, 1992-93; Senior Lecturer, Statistics and Econometrics, 1993-94, Reader, Econometrics, 1994-96, University of Exeter, England; Professor, Econometrics and Statistics, Departments of Mathematics and Economics, University of York, England, 1996-2005; Professor of Financial Econometrics, Imperial College London, 2005-; Co-Director, Londar Investments Ltd, London, 2010-; Co-Director, Greycourt Ltd, London, 2011-; Founding Member and member of political office, 2011-, Chair of Data Analysis and Information Committee, Initiator and Co-leader of Operations Room for parliamentary elections, 2011-12, Al Masreyeen El Ahrrar liberal party. Publications: Numerous publications in professional journals and books; Numerous papers presented at national and international conferences. Honours: Invited lecturer at many conferences; ESRC Grants, 1996-98, 2001-04, 2003-06, 2008-10; Multa Scripsit Award, 1997; University of York Grant, 1998; Plura Scripsit Award, 2001. Memberships: Econometric Society; Institute of Mathematical Statistics; Fellow, Royal Statistical Society; European Science Foundation's Network on Econometric Methods for the Modelling of Nonstationary Data, Policy Analysis and Forecasting; Professional Association of Diving Instructors; Founder and Director, various undergraduate and graduate degrees; Editor of various journals. Address: Business School, Imperial College London, South Kensington Campus, London SW7 2AZ, England. E-mail: k.m.abadir@imperial.ac.uk

ABBASOV Ali M, b. 1 January 1953, Nakhichevan, Azerbaijan. Minister. m. Shafag, 1 son, 1 daughter. Education: Azerbaijan Oil and Chemistry Institute, 1969-72; Moscow Power Engineering Institute, 1971-76; Moscow Power Engineering Institute, 1971-76; PhD, Ukraine Academy of Sciences, 1977-80; Full Member, International Academy of Informatization, Moscow, 1998; Full Member, Azerbaijan National Academy of Sciences, 2001. Appointments: Laboratory Engineer, 1976-77, Junior Research Worker, 1981-82, Laboratory Manager, 1982-88, Chief Engineer, 1988-92, Automated Management Systems Department, Director, Information-Telecommunications Centre, 1992-2000, Institute of Cybernetics of Azerbaijan National Academy of Science; President, Azerbaijan Research and Educational Network Association, 1995-; Professor, Azerbaijan Technical University, 1995-2000; Member, Azerbaijan Parliament and Parliamentary Assembly of Council of Europe, 2000-04; Rector, Azerbaijan State University of Economics, 2000-04; Minister, Ministry of Communications and Information Technologies, 2004-. Publications: Numerous articles in professional journals. Honours: Professor in the field of Informatics, 1996; Listed in biographical dictionaries. Memberships: IEEE; Broadband Commission; New York Academy of Sciences; International Academy of Informatization; UNESCO; Representative of Azerbaijan Republic in European Association of International Computer Network INTERNET. Address: Zarifa Aliyeva street 33, AZ1000 Baku, Azerbaijan. E-mail: us@mincom.gov.az

ABBOTT Gerry, b. 13 February 1935, Bow, London, England. University Teacher. m. Khin-Thant Han, 1 son, 2 daughters. Education: BA Honours, English, University College, London, 1958; PGCE with TEFL, Institute of Education, London, 1959; PhD, Education, University of Manchester, 1998. Appointments: National Service, 1953-55; Commissioned, 1955; Lecturer, College of Education, Bangkok, 1959-63; British Council Education Officer, Jordan, 1963-65; Lecturer, Teaching of English Overseas, Manchester University including numerous postings in Asia and Africa, 1965-92; Honorary Fellow, Manchester University, 1992-. Publications: Relative Clauses, 1969; Conditionals, 1970; Question-Word Questions, 1970; The Teaching of English as an International Language (with Peter Wingard), 1981; Back to Mandalay, 1990; Inroads in Burma, 1997; Traveller's History of Burma, 1998; Conformity and variety in the global diffusion of English, 1998; The folk-tales of Burma (with Khin Thant Han), 2000; English all over the place (with Bob Jordan), 2001; Numerous articles. Honours: 1st Prize, English Speaking Union Essay Competition, 1978; Appointed Honorary Fellow, Manchester University, 1992. Memberships: IATEFL; Amnesty International; Friends of the Earth; World Development Movement; Britain-Burma Society. Address: 16 Manor Drive, Manchester M21 7GQ, England.

ABBS Peter Francis, b. 22 February 1942, Cromer, Norfolk, England. Author; Lecturer. m. Barbara Beazeley, 10 June 1963, 1 son, 2 daughters. Education: BA, University of Bristol, England; DPhil, University of Sussex, England. Appointments: Lecturer, Senior Lecturer, Reader, Professor of Creative Writing, 1999-, University of Sussex, England. Publications: Poetry: For Man and Islands; Songs of a New Taliesin; Icons of Time; Personae; Love After Sappho, 2000; Viva la Vida, 2005; Voyaging Out, 2009; Non-Fiction: English for Diversity; Root and Blossom - The Philosophy, Practice and Politics of English Teaching; English Within the Arts; The Forms of Poetry; The Forms of Narrative; Autobiography in Education; Proposal for a New College (with Graham Carey); Reclamations - Essays on Culture, Mass-Culture and the Curriculum; A is for Aesthetic - Essays on Creative and Aesthetic Education; The Educational Imperative; The Polemics of Education; Editor, The Black Rainbow - Essays on the Present Breakdown of Culture; Living Powers - The Arts in Education; The Symbolic Order - A Contemporary Reader on the Arts Debate; The Polemics of Imagination: Essays on Art, Culture and Society; Against the Flow: Education, the Arts and Postmodern Culture, 2004; The Flowering of Flint: New edition selected poems, 2007. Contributions to: Times Higher Education Supplement; Agenda; Independent; Acumen; Stand; Daily Telegraph. Membership: Founding Member, New Metaphysical Art; Fellow, English Association. Address: Graduate Research Centre in the Humanities, University of Sussex, Falmer, Brighton BN1 9RG, England. E-mail: p.f.abbs@sussex.ac.uk

ABDANK KOZUBSKI Rafal, b. 22 February 1955, Cieszyn, Poland. Physicist. m. Bogna Partyka, 1 daughter. Education: MSc, Physics, 1977, PhD, 1984, DSc (habilitation), 1997, Jagellonian University. Appointments: Assistant and Senior Assistant, 1978-87, Adjunct Professor (Lecturer), 1987-97, Associate Professor, 1997-2005, Professor, 2006-, Jagellonian University. Publications: Over 100 publications in scientific journals; 2 books edited. Honours: Lise Meitner Fellowship, University of Vienna, Austria, 1993-95; Professor of Physics, title awarded by President of the Republic of Poland, 2005. Memberships: Materials Research Society, USA; Polish Physical Society; Committee for Crystallography, Polish Academy of Sciences. E-mail: rafal.kozubski@uj.edu.pl

ABDEL MEGUID Eiman, b. 2 September 1962, Alexandria, Egypt. Professor. m. Ashraf Amr, 2 sons. Education: Bachelor of Medicine and Surgery, 1985; Master, 1990, Doctor, 1996, Anatomy and Embryology. Appointments: Demonstrator, Anatomy, Alexandria University, 1987; Scholarship to finish PhD, Tubingen, Germany, 1992-94; Assistant Professor, Damam University, Saudi Arabia, 1999; Professor, Faculty of Medicine, Alexandria University. Publications: Mode of insertion of abductor allicus, 2009; An Anatomical study of Frahyoid, 2009; An Anatomical study of modiolus, 2009; The lip: A histological and Analytical Approach of relevance to surgery, 2009. Honours: DAAD German Scholarship for PhD; Scientific research grants from Saudi universities. Memberships: American Association of Clinical Anatomists; Alumni of Deutsch Akademis de Austaush Drenst. Address: 12 Ismail Helmy Street, Sporting Club Building, Apartment 14, Smouha, Alexandria, Egypt. E-mail: eimanmeguid@yahoo.com

ABDEL REHIM Mona H, b. 23 June 1968, El-Fayohm, Egypt. Researcher. m. Gamal Turky, 2 sons, 1 daughter. Education: BSc, Chemistry Department, Faculty of Science, Cairo University, 1989; MSc, Organic Chemistry, Faculty of Science, Halwan University, 2001; PhD, Faculty of Mathematics and Natural Science, TUD, Dresden, Germany, 2004. Appointments: Assistant Researcher, Institute of Polymer Research, IPF, Dresden, Germany, 2001-04; Research, National Research Center, Packing and Packaging Materials, 2006-. Publications: 2 articles in professional journals. Honours: NRC Award for Distinguished Scientific Work, 2009; Misr El-Khir Foundation Award for Best Scientific Article, 2010. Memberships: Egyptian Society for Polymer Science. E-mail: monaabdelrehim@yahoo.com

ABDEL-RAHIM Muddathir, b. 19 July 1932, Ad-Damar, Sudan. University Professor; Former Ambassador. m. Zainab Muhammad Badri, 5 sons, 3 daughters. Education: BA, Economics, History and Arabic, University of London, England, 1955; BA (First Class Hons), Politics, University of Nottingham, England, 1958; PhD, Economic and Social Studies (Government), University of Manchester, England, 1964. Appointments: Lecturer in Government, Manchester University, 1960-65; Senior Lecturer then Professor, University of Khartoum, Sudan, 1965-70, 1980-88; Visiting Professor, Temple University, Philadelphia, USA, 1984-85; Vice Chancellor, Omdurman Islamic University, Sudan, 1988-91; Professor, International Institute of Islamic Thought and Civilization, Kuala Lumpur, Malaysia, 1997-. Publications include: Imperialism and Nationalism in the Sudan, 1969; The Problem of the Southern Sudan (in Arabic), 1970; The Human

Rights Tradition in Islam, 2004; Editor: Human Rights in Theory and Practice (in Arabic), 1968; Islam in The Sudan, 1988; Islam in Africa, 2007; Al-Ghazali's Political Thought and Other Essays on Hajjatul-Islam, 2011. Honours: Listed in international biographical dictionaries. Memberships include: International Institute for Strategic Studies, London; British Association of Middle Eastern Studies; Arab Thought Forum, Amman, Jordan. Address: International Institute of Islamic Thought and Civilization, No 24, Persiaran Duta, Taman Duta, 50480 Kuala Lumpur, Malaysia.

ABDUL Ahmad Bustamam, b. 13 August 1960, Muar, Johore, Malaysia. Lecturer. Scientist. m. Munirah Khudri, 1 son. Education: BSc (Hons), Biochemistry, University of Malaya, Kuala Lumpur, 1984; PhD, Clinical Biochemistry, University of Newcastle Upon Tyne, England, 1998. Appointments: Researcher, Malaysian Institute of Nuclear Technology, 1985-2001; Lecturer, Scientist, University Putra of Malaysia, Serdang, 2001-. Publication: Numerous articles in professional journals. Honours: Best Researcher Award, University Putra of Malaysia, 2006; Silver Medal, IENA International, Nurnberg, Malaysia, 2006; Gold Medal, ITEX International, Kuala Lumpur, 2006; Gold Medal, MTE National, Koala Lumpur, 2008. Memberships: European Society of Gynocological Society; NIH AIDS Research and Reference Reagent Program. Address: No 65, Jalan Chenderai, Taman Lucky, Kuala Lumpur 59100, Malaysia. E-mail: ahmadbstmm@yahoo.com

ABDUL Paula, b. 19 June 1962, Los Angeles, California, USA. Singer; Dancer; Choreographer. Education: Television and Radio Studies, Cal State, Northridge College. Musical Education: Studied jazz and tap dance. Career: Choreographer, LA Laker basketball cheerleaders; Scenes in films: Bull Durham; Coming To America; The Waiting Game; Appeared in a Saturday Night Live sketch with David Duchovny. Choreographer, pop videos including: The Jacksons and Mick Jagger: Torture; George Michael: Monkey; with Janet Jackson: Nasty; When I Think Of You; What Have You Done For Me Lately; Fitness video, Cardio Dance. Worldwide performances as singer include: Tours throughout US, UK, Japan and Far East; Prince's Trust Rock Gala, London Palladium, 1989; America Has Heart (earthquake and hurricane benefit concert), 1989; LIFEbeat's Counteraid (AIDS benefit concert), 1993; Own dance company, Co Dance; Judge, American Idol, 2002-09; Judge, Live to Dance, American version of The X Factor, 2011: Recordings: Solo albums: Forever Your Girl (Number 1, US), 1989; Shut Up And Dance (The Dance Mixes), 1990; Spellbound (Number 1, US), 1991; Head Over Heels, 1995; Contributor, Disney charity album For Our Children, 1991; Greatest Hits, 2000; US Number 1 singles include: Straight Up; Forever Your Girl; Cold Hearted; Opposites Attract; Rush Rush; The Promise Of A New Day. Honours: MTV Video Award, Best Choreography, Janet Jackson's Nasty, 1987; Emmy, Best Choreography, for Tracey Ullman Show, 1989; Rolling Stone Awards, including Best Female Singer, 1989; American Music Awards include: Favourite Pop/Rock Female Vocalist, 1989, 1992; Billboard Magazine, Top Female Pop Album, 1990; Grammy, Best Music Video, Opposites Attract, 1991; Star on Hollywood Walk Of Fame, 1993; Humanitarian of the Year, Starlight Foundation, Los Angeles, 1992; Numerous Gold and Platinum discs. Address: Third Rail Entertainment, Tri-Star Bldg, 10202 W Washington Avenue, Suite 26, Culver City, CA 90232, USA.

ABDUL GHANI Ahmad Khairiri, b. 15 August 1965, Ipoh, Perak, Malaysia. m. Nor Aziah Ahmad, 1 son, 5 daughters. Education: BSc, Mechanical Engineering; Master, Business Administration. Appointments: Petronas Carigali Sdn, BHD; OGP Technical Services Sdn, BHD; Petronas Gas, BHD. Publications: Conference papers and proceedings. Memberships: Project Management Institute; Institute of Engineers, Malaysia; Malaysian Society of Engineers & Technologists. Address: 4 Jln Suasana 5/1, BDR Tun Hussein ONN, 43200 Cheras, Selangor, Malaysia.

ABDULGANI Hafil Budianto, b. 9 May 1948, Yogyakarta, Indonesia. Cardiothoracic Surgeon. m. Nana Riwayatie, 2 daughters. Education: BA, Biology, State University of New York at Buffalo, 1971; D Med, University of Hawaii, 1976; D Phil, Padjadjaran University. Appointments: Consultant Surgeon, National Cardiac Centre, Indonesia, 1984-94; Head, Cardiothoracic Surgery, Hasan Sadikin General Hospital, Indonesia, 1994-2002; Associate Professor, Padjadjaran University, Indonesia, 2002-07; Professor, Universiti Teknologi Mara, Malaysia, 2007-. Honours: Fellow, American College of Surgeons; Fellow, American College of Cardiology. Memberships: Asian Society for Cardiovascular and Thoracic Surgery; American College of Surgeons; American College of Cardiology. Address: 17-19-1 Majestic Tower, Mont Kiara Palma, Jalan Kiara, 50480 Kuala Lumpur, Malaysia.

ABDULJALIL Mustafa, b. 1952, Al-Baidha, Libya. Chairman. m. Hawwa Boufares, 3 sons, 5 daughters. Education: BA, Law and Legislation, 1975. Appointments: Prosecuting Attorney, 1975-78; Judge, 1978-96; Consultant, 1996-99; Attorney, Court of Appeal, -2002; Court of Appeal, -2005; Minister of Justice, 2007-11; Chairman, National Transitional Council, 2011-. Memberships: Alakhdar Club, Al-Baidha; League of Old Athletes, Green Mountain.

ABDULLAH Mohd Azmuddin, b. 16 February 1970, Malaysia. Academician. Education: MEng, Chemical Engineering and Biotechnology, University of Manchester Institute of Science and Technology, England, 1994; PhD, Bioprocess Engineering, Universiti Putra, Malaysia, 1999. Appointments: Research Assistant, 1994, Tutor, 1994-99, Universiti Putra, Malaysia; Visiting Scientist, Plant Tissue Culture and Plant Physiology Laboratory, Kinki University, Japan, 1997; Visiting Scientist, Biomaterials Science and Engineering Laboratory, Massachusetts Institute of Technology, USA, 2000-01; Associate Researcher, Mathematical Sciences and Application Laboratory, Institute for Mathematical Research, 2003-, Associate Researcher, Natural Product Laboratory, Institute of Bioscience, 2003-, Lecturer, Department of Biotechnology, 1999-2004, Universiti Putra, Malaysia; Senior Lecturer, 2004-08, Associate Professor, 2008-, Department of Chemical Engineering, Universiti Teknologi Petronas. Publications: Numerous articles in professional journals. Honours: Best Undergraduate project, 7th MSMBB Conference, 1996; Research Award, Japanese Society for the Promotion of Science, 1997; Research Award, Malaysia-MIT Biotechnology Partnership Programme, 2000-01; Gold Medal, Research & Design Exhibition, 2003; Silver Medal, Research & Design Exhibition, 2004; Silver Medal, Exhibition of Invention & Research, 2005; Bronze Medal, 16th International Exhibition on Invention, Innovation, Industrial Design & Technology, 2005; Overall Champion, EDX 15, 2005; Overall Champion, Engineering & Innovation Design Competition, 2006; Bronze Medal, 17th International Exhibition on Invention, Innovation, Industrial Design & Technology, 2006; Listed in international biographical dictionaries. Memberships:

Subcommittee, Malaysian Society of Molecular Biology and Biotechnology; Academic Staff Association of UPM; Subcommittee, Society of Malaysian Chemical Engineers; Member, Institute of Chemical Engineers, UK; Secretary, Petronas Anugerah Merdeka Health, Science and Technology, 2008; Institute of Chemical Engineers. Address: Department of Chemical Engineering, Universiti Teknologi Petronas, Bandar Sri Iskandar, 31750, Perak, Malaysia. E-mail: azmuddin@petronas.com.my

ABE Hiroyuki, b. 20 September 1938, Hokkaido, Japan. Physician. m. Midori Abe, 1 daughter. Education: Graduate, Sapporo Medical University, 1964; Doctor of Medicine, 1965, Doctor of Philosophy, 1974, Sapporo. Appointments: Clinical Fellow, Cleveland Clinic, Ohio, USA, 1972-74; Instructor, Juntendo University, Tokyo, Japan, 1975-81; Associate Professor, Nihon University, Tokyo, 1981-88; President, Kudan Clinic, Tokyo, 1988-. Publications: Numerous articles in professional journals. Honours: Fellow, American College of Cardiology; Fellow, American College of Chest Physicians; Contribution for Cancer Immunology, Cancer Control Society, USA, 2005; Contribution for Cancer Treatment, LifeScience Institute, USA, 2005. Memberships: International Society of Integrative Medicine; Dendritic Cell and Vaccine Science; Japan Society of Oncology; Japan Society of Cardiology. Address: 3-11 Hayabusacho, Chiyoda-ku, Tokyo 102-0092, Japan. E-mail: drabeqqq@yahoo.co.jp

ABEDI Saied, b. 12 July 1966, Salmas, Iran. Principal Research Engineer. m. Sanaz Noubakhti Afshar. Education: BSc, Telecommunications, Sharif University of Technology, Tehran, Iran, 1989; MSc, Artificial Intelligence and Signal Processing, 1996, PhD, Mobile Communications, 2000, University of Surrey, England. Appointments: Research and Development Engineer, Fajre Research Company, Tehran, Iran, 1990-95; Research Fellow, Centre for Communications Systems Research, University of Surrey, England, 1998-2001; Principal Research Engineer, Fujitsu Laboratories of Europe Ltd, Hayes, Middlesex, England, 2001-. Publications: Articles in scientific journals include most recently as first author: A Genetic Multiuser Receiver for Code Division Multiple Access Communications, 2000; A New CDMA Multiuser Detection Technique Using an Evolutionary Algorithm, 2001; Genetically Modified Multiuser Detection for Code Division Multiple Access Systems, 2002; A Genetic Approach for Downlink Packet Scheduling in HSDPA System, Accepted paper; 9 papers presented at conferences; 9 UK Patents. Honours: NTL Prize for Research Excellence, 1999; Vodaphone Airtouch Prize for Research Excellence, 2000; Both these prizes were jointly awarded by a board of scientists and experts from a group of companies including: Nokia, Vodaphone, NTL, Marconi, INMARSAT and CCSR, University of Surrey. Membership: Member, IEEE. Address: Mobile Radio Technology, Fujitsu Laboratories of Europe Ltd, Hayes Park Central, Hayes End Road, Hayes, Middlesex UB4 8FE, England. E-mail: saeid_abedi@hotmail.com

ABETZ Peter, b. 17 December 1952, Stuttgart, Germany. Member of Parliament. m. Jenny, 3 sons, 2 daughters. Education: Agricultural Science (Honours), University of Tasmania, 1973; Divinity, Reformed Theological College, Geelong, Victoria, Australia. Appointments: Pastor, Willetton Christian Reformed Church, 1991-2004; Pastor, Grace Christian Reformed Church, 2004-08; Member of Parliament (West Australia), 2008-. Address: Unit 4, 2 Furley Road, Southern River, WA 6110, Australia.

ABLE Graham George, b. 28 July 1947, Norwich, England. School Principal. m. Mary Susan Munro, 1 son, 1 daughter. Education: BA (later MA), Natural Sciences, 1968, PGCE, 1969, Trinity College, Cambridge; MA (by research and thesis), Social Sciences, Durham University, 1983. Appointments: Teacher of Chemistry, 1969-83, Housemaster (Boarding), 1976-83, Sutton Valence School; Second Master, Barnard Castle School, 1983-88; Headmaster, Hampton School, 1988-96; Master (Principal), Dulwich College, London, 1997-2009; Chairman, Dulwich College Enterprises Ltd, 1997-2009; Senior Vice President (Academic), Dulwich College Management International, 2009-; Chief Executive Officer, Alpha Plus Group Ltd, 2009-. Publications: MA Thesis on boarding education, 1983; Head to Head (co-author), 1992; Various newspaper and magazine articles. Memberships: Chairman, Academic Policy, 1998-2001, Chairman, 2003, Headmasters and Headmistresses Conference; President, 2006-09, International Boy's School Coalition; Member of Council, Imperial College, 1999-2006; Member of Council, Roedean School, 2000-09. Address: The Old Smithy, High Street, Wighton, Norfolk NR23 1AL, England. E-mail: ablegm@btinternet.com

ABOROWA Gabriel Duro, b. 8 August 1969, Ifon, Ondo State, Nigeria. Sport Administrator. Appointments: Chairman, Technical Committee, Ondo State Football Association; Team Manager, Sunshine Stars FC (Premiership Team), Ondo State, Nigeria. Memberships: Ondo State Coaches Association. Address: Ondo State Football Association, Ondo State Sports Council, Akure, Ondo State, Nigeria. Website: www.gabrielaborowa.com

ABOU-HELAL Mohummad Osamah, b. 5 January 1965, Canada. Academic Doctor. m. Hanan Tharwat Abdel Zaher, 2 sons. Education: Researcher, Atomic Energy Authority, Egypt, 1987-90; Administrative Part-time Job, Scientific Service Company, 1987-90. Appointments: Assistant, Canada, 1992-93; Postgraduate courses in Solid State Physics, Quantum Mechanics and Electronics, DAAD, Germany; Assistantship to PhD, 1995; Associate Professor, 2004-; Staff member, Information Technology Faculty, Isra University, Amman, Jordan, 2008-11. Publications: Numerous articles in professional journals. Memberships: DAAD, Germany; Egyptian Materials Research Society, Egypt. Address: National Research Center NRC, Solid State Physics Department, 12622 Doki, Cairo, Egypt. E-mail: mabouhelal@mailer.scu.eun.eg

ABRAHAMS Sidney Cyril, b. 28 May 1924, London, England (US citizen, 1963). Physicist. m. Rhoda Banks, 2 sons, 1 daughter. Education: BSc, 1946, PhD, 1949, DSc, 1957, University of Glasgow, Scotland; Doctor (honoris causa), University of Uppsala, Sweden, 1981; Docteur (honoris causa), University of Bordeaux, France, 1997. Appointments: Research Fellow, University of Minnesota, 1949-50; Member of Staff, Massachusetts Institute of Technology, 1950-54; Research Fellow, University of Glasgow, 1954-57; Guest Scientist, Brookhaven National Laboratory, 1957-90; Member of Technical Staff, Bell Laboratories, 1957-82; Visiting Professor, University of Bordeaux, France, 1979; Distinguished Member of Technical Staff, 1982-88, Retired, 1988, AT&T Bell Laboratories; Alexander von Humboldt Foundation Senior US Scientist, University of Tübingen, 1989-90; Visiting Professor, University of Bordeaux, 1990, 1993; Adjunct Professor of Physics, Southern Oregon University, 1990-; Visiting Professor, University of Tübingen, 1995. Honours: Humboldt-Prize Winner, Alexander von Humboldt-Foundation, 1989 and 1995. Memberships:

American Crystallographic Association; USA National Committee for Crystallography of National Academy of Sciences; American Institute of Physics; Fellow, American Association for the Advancement of Science; Fellow, American Physical Society; Sigma Xi; Royal Society of Chemistry, London; Book Review Editor, Taylor & Francis Ferroelectrics. Address: Physics Department, Southern Oregon University, Ashland, OR 97520, USA.

ABRAMSKY Dame Jennifer, b. 7 October 1946. Chairman, National Heritage Memorial Fund. m. Alasdair Liddell, 1976, 1 son, 1 daughter. Education: BA, University of East Anglia. Appointments: Programme Operations Assistant, 1969, Producer, The World at One, 1973, Editor, PM, 1978, Producer, Radio Four Budget Programmes, 1979-86, Editor, Today Programme, 1986-87, Editor, News and Current Affairs Radio, 1987-93, established Radio Four News FM, 1991, Controller, Radio Five Live, 1993-96, Director, Continuous News, including Radio Five Live, BBC News 24, BBC World, BBC News Online, Ceefax, and Director, 1998-2000, BBC Radio and Music, 2000-08, BBC Radio; News International Visiting Professor of Broadcast Media, 2002; Chairman, National Heritage Memorial Fund, 2008-. Honours: Woman of Distinction, Jewish Care, 1990; Honorary Professor, Thames Valley University, 1994; Sony Radio Academy Award, 1995; Honorary MA, Salford University, 1997; Royal Academy Fellowship, 1998; Honorary RAM, 2002; Dame Commander of the Order of the British Empire, 2009. Memberships: Editorial Board, British Journalism Review, 1993-; Member, Board of Governors, BFI, 2000-; Vice-Chair, Digital Radio Development Bureau, 2002-; News International Visiting Professor of Broadcast Media, Exeter College, Oxford, 2002; Director, Hampstead Theatre, 2003-; The Radio Academy.

ABRAMYAN Evgeny, b. 3 August 1930, Tbilisi, USSR. Scientist. Education: Moscow Engineering Physics Institute, 1953; Professor, 1968; Doctor of Engineering Sciences, 1968. Appointments: Department Head, Badker Institute of Nuclear Physics, 1958-72; Institute of High Temperatures of USSR Academy of Sciences, 1973-93. Publications: More than 90 scientific articles in professional journals; 100 inventions. Honours: USSR State Prize, 1969. Address: Apt 32, 8 Ostryakov St, Moscow 125057, Russia. E-mail: let@savefuture.net Website: www.savefuture.net

ABSATOVA Marfuga, b. 25 May 1974, Kzilorda oblast, Kazakhstan. Doctor of Pedagogical Science; Assistant Professor. m. Arnur, 2 sons. Education: Candidate thesis, 2002, Doctoral thesis, 2007, Almaty State Pedagogical University. Appointments: Teacher of Pedagogies, Kzilorda Pedagogical Institute, 1995-97; Researcher, 1997-98, Post Graduator, 1998-2001, Almaty State Pedagogical University; Assistant Professor, Daryn Social-Humanitarian Institute, 2001-04; Doctor of Pedagogical Science, Assistant Professor, Abay Kazakh State Pedagogical University, 2007-11. Publications: 90 articles in professional journals. Honours: Certificates of Merit. Memberships: Head of Master' Program, Pedagogical conditions of upbringing Kazakh youth to a national idea in a condition of a multinational state; Scientific secretary, Scientific council of PhD, Almaty State Pedagogical University. Address: Flat No 22, Kluchkova street 20, Almaty, Kazakhstan. E-mail: absatovamar@mail.ru

ABSE Dannie, b. 22 September 1923, Cardiff, Glamorgan, Wales. Physician; Poet; Writer; Dramatist. m. Joan Mercer, 1951 (deceased 2005), 1 son, 2 daughters. Education: St Illtyd's College, Cardiff; University of South Wales and Monmouthshire, Cardiff; King's College, London; MD, Westminster Hospital, London, 1950. Appointments: Manager, Chest Clinic, Central Medical Establishment, London, 1954-82; Senior Fellow in Humanities, Princeton University, New Jersey, 1973-74. Publications: Poetry: Funland and Other Poems, 1973; Lunchtime, 1974; Way Out in the Centre, 1981; White Coat, Purple Coat: Collected Poems, 1948-88, 1989; Remembrance of Crimes Past, 1990; On the Evening Road, 1994; Intermittent Journals, 1994; Twentieth-Century Anglo-Welsh Poetry, 1997; A Welsh Retrospective, 1997; Arcadia, One Mile, 1998; Goodbye Twentieth Century, 2001; New and Collected Poems, 2003; The Two Roads Taken, 2003, Yellow Bird, 2004; Running Late, 2006; 100 Great Poems of Love and Lust: Homage to Eros, 2007; The Presence, 2007; Volume of Collected Poems, 2009. Editor: The Music Lover's Literary Companion, 1988; The Hutchinson Book of Post-War British Poets, 1989; Fiction: Ash on a Young Man's Sleeve, 1954; Some Corner of an English Field, 1956; O Jones, O Jones, 1970; Voices in the Gallery, 1986; Ask the Bloody Horse, 1986; There was a Young Man from Cardiff, 2001; The Strange Case of Dr Simmonds and Dr Glas, 2002. Contributions to: BBC and various publications in UK and USA. Honours: Foyle Award, 1960; Welsh Arts Council Literature Prizes, 1971, 1987; Cholmondeley Award, 1985; Wales Book of the Year (The Presence), 2008; Commander of the Order of the British Empire, 2012. Memberships: Poetry Society, President, 1979-92; Royal Society of Literature, Fellow, 1983; Welsh Academy, Fellow, 1990, President, 1995. Address: c/o PFD, Drury House, 34-43 Russell Street, London, WC2B 5HA, England.

ACHARYA Manjulaben, b. 7 February 1959, Sukhpur, Roha, India. Primary Teacher. m. Ramesh Bhatt, 1 daughter. Education: New SSC, 1979; HSC, 1985; BA, 1994; MA, 1997; PhD, 2004; ND, 1993; PTC, 1981. Appointments: Joint in Service, 1983-. Publications: Numerous articles in profound journals; 20 radio talks on education of women, social awareness, saving, literacy and art. Honours: Different Cast Felicitations for Creation and Education, 1983-2007; Special Honour, Rotary Club of Nakhatrana for Patriotic Competitions for students; Different Institutional Felicitations for Creation, Study and Teaching Skills; State Award, Government of Gujarat; Best Teacher, Zydus Cadilla AMA, Ahmedabad; Best Teacher, IIM, Ahmedabad; BMC Bank Higher Education Award, 2004; Gyati Gauraw Award for PhD, 2004; Jiyapar Vishu Samaj Journalist Award, 2004; Indian Institute of Management, Ahmedabad Best Innovative Teacher Award, 2004; Ahmedabad Management Association Best Teacher Award, 2006; J R Upadhyay Memorial Best Teacher Award, 2005; Runner Up, Air India Bolt Award (District Level); Alexander Prize Award, CASTME, Winchester University, 2009. Memberships: Ex-Cluster Resource Centre; Rotary Club of Nakhatrana; Shri Aurobindo Society; Shri Raman Kendram; Gujarat State Awardee, Teacher's Federation; Samasta Brahima Samaj; Kachchhi Sahitay Kala-Sangh; Junior Chambers, Nakhatrana; President, Innerwheel Club, Nakhatrana. Address: 20 Kekarav Umiyadham, Navovas, Nakha Trana 370615, Dist Kachchhi Gujarat, India.

ACHARYULU K V L N, Lecturer. Education: MSc, AO Mathematics (1st class), Bapatla Engineering College, 1999; M Phil, Mathematics, R K M Vivekananda College, Madras University, 2001; PhD, Mathematics, Acharya Nagarjuna University, 2011. Appointments: Lecturer, Mathematics, National Institute of Mathematics, 1 year; Lecturer, Mathematics, Bapatla Engineering College, 2001-. Publications: 44 international publications; Member of 13 editorial boards; Member of 15 reviewer boards; Participated in seminars and presented papers on various topics. Honours:

Bhavapuri Rachayitala Sangam, 2011; Grama Siri, 2011. Memberships include: Indian Mathematical Society; Ramanujan Mathematical Society; International Association of Engineers; Institute of Advanced Scientific Research; International Association of Computer Science & Information Technology. Address: Faculty of Science, Department of Mathematics, Bapatla Engineering College, Bapatla 522101, Andhra Pradesh, India. E-mail: kvlna@yahoo.com

ADACHI Kozaburo, b. 3 January 1933, Osaka, Japan. Physician. m. Yasuko, 3 sons. Education: MD, Osaka University Medical School, 1958; PhD, Medical Science, Osaka University, 1963. Appointments: Assistant, 1963-65, Lecturer, 1968-75, Biochemistry, Osaka University Dental School, Osaka, Japan; Postdoctoral Fellow, Biochemistry, Brandeis University, Massachusetts, USA, 1965-67; Postdoctoral Fellow, Physiological Chemistry, University of Wisconsin, USA, 1967-68; Professor, Biochemistry, Kanazawa Medical University, Uchinada, Ishikawa, Japan, 1974-83; Professor, Nutritional Physiology, Kobe College, Department of Food and Nutrition Studies, Nishinomiya, Hyogo, 1983-99; Chairman, Kobe College Department of Food and Nutrition Studies, 1989-93; Chief, Health Service Centre, Kobe College, 1983-99; Physician, Board of Directors, Agape Kabutoyama Hospital, Nishinomiya, Hyogo, 1999-. Publications: Several books on enzymology and nutrition; Numerous articles in professional journals. Honours: Encouragement Award, Japanese Association of Nutrition and Foods, 1990. Memberships: Overseas Fellow, Royal Society of Medicine, UK; Japanese Society of Internal Medicine; Japan Geriatrics Society. Address: 10-20 Mondoso, Nishinomiya, Hyogo, 662-0825, Japan.

ADAIR Hilary, b. 29 May 1943, Sussex, England. Painter; Printmaker. m. Julian Marshall, 2 sons. Education: Chichester High School for Girls; Brighton College of Art; St Martin's School of Art. Appointments: Freelance Painter and Printmaker; Work exhibited widely and held in many private and public collections. Publications: Arts Review; The Observer Colour Magazine; The Athenian; The English Garden; The Exmoor Magazine; Somerset Life; Printmakers' Secrets. Memberships: Royal Society of Painter-Printmakers. E-mail: info@hilaryadair.co.uk Website: www.hilaryadair.co.uk

ADAM Gottfried W J, b. 1 December 1939, Treysa, Germany. Professor. 3 sons. Education: Dr Theol, University of Bonn, 1968; Dr Theol, Habil, University of Marburg, 1975. Appointments: Assistant, Theology Faculty, University of Bonn, 1966-67; Assistant, 1968-75, Lecturer, Professor, Practical Theology, 1976-78, 1980, University of Marburg; Professor, University of Goettingen, 1978-79; Professor, Protestant Theology, Chair, Philosophy Faculty, University of Wuerzburg, 1981-92; Professor, Religious Education, Chair, Faculty of Protestant Theology, Vienna, 1992-2008; Dean, Faculty of Protestant Theology, University of Vienna, 1999-2006. Publications: Author: 6 books; Editor, Co-editor: 24 books; 3 periodicals; 3 book series; 430 articles on theological and religious educational questions. Honours: Diploma of Theology, honoris causa, Sibiu, Romania, 1996; Károli Gáspár Református University, Budapest, Hungary, 2000. Memberships: Wissenschaftliche Gesellschaft für Theologie; Rudolf-Bultmann-Gesellschaft für Hermeneutische Theologie; Arbeitskreis für Religionspaedagogik; Religious Education Association, USA. Address: Sedanstr 42, 30161 Hannover, Germany. E-mail: gottfried.adam@univie.ac.at

ADAM Robert, b. 10 April 1948, Bournemouth, England. Architect. m. Sarah, 1 son, 1 daughter. Education: Rome Scholarship, University of Westminster, 1973. Appointments: Director, Adam Architecture (formerly Robert Adam Architects), 1977-; Chair, College of Chapters, INTBAU, 2000-. Publications: Classical Architecture: A Complete Handbook, 1990; Buildings by Design, 1994; Editor, Tradition Today, 2008; Robert Adam, The Search for a Modern Classicism, 2010; Contributor & Editor, Tradition Today; Author of numerous articles and papers for publications including national and international newspapers, magazines and journals; Contributions to many TV and radio programmes. Honours: Commendation London Borough of Richmond-Upon-Thames Conservation and Design Awards Scheme, 1991; Winner, Copper Roofing Competition Copper Development Association, 1995; Elmbridge BC Design/Conservation Award, 1998; RIBA Southern Region National Housebuilder Design Award; Best Partnership Development Commendation for Roman Court, Rocester, 2000; Marsh Country Life Awards, 2001; Best Private Housing Development, Brick Awards, 2004; Award for a New Building in the Classical Tradition, The Georgian Group Awards, 2007; Award of Excellence for Masterplan for Western Harbour, Edinburgh, Congress for the New Urbanism Charter Awards, 2008. Memberships: RIBA; Brother, The Artworkers Guild; Fellow, Royal Society of Arts; Architecture Club Committee; Academy of Urbanism; Athenaeum and Home House. Address: Adam Architecture, 9 Upper High Street, Winchester, Hampshire SO23 8UT, England. E-mail: robert.adam@adamarchitecture.com

ADAMS Anna Theresa, (Theresa Butt, Anna Butt as painter), b. 9 March 1926, London, England. Writer; Artist. m. Norman Adams, deceased 2005, 2 sons. Education: NDD Painting, Harrow School of Art, 1945; NDD, Sculpture, Hornsey College of Art, 1950. Appointments: Teaching at various schools; Designer, Chelsea Pottery, 1953-55; Part-time Art Teacher, Manchester, 1966-86; Exhibited terracotta sculptures widely, various galleries in the North of England, 1969-86; Works in several public collections, including Rochdale Museum, Bradford University and Blackwell at Bowness; Art Teacher, Settle High School, 1971-74; Exhibited watercolours in RA Summer Show, 1986-2005; Poetry Editor, Green Book, 1989-92; Small retrospective, Peter Scott Gallery, Lancaster University, 2007. Publications: Journey Through Winter, 1969; Rainbow Plantation, 1971; Memorial Tree, 1972; A Reply to Intercepted Mail, 1979; Brother Fox, 1983; Trees in Sheep Country, 1986; Dear Vincent, 1986; Six Legs Good, 1987; Angels of Soho, 1988; Nobodies, 1990; Island Chapters, 1991; Life on Limestone, 1994; Green Resistance: Selected and New Poems, 1996; A Paper Ark, 1996; The Thames: Anthology of River Poems, 1999; London in Verse & Prose, 2002; Flying Underwater, 2004. Contributions to: Poetry Review; P N Review; The Countryman; 10th Muse; Country Life; Yorkshire Life; Dalesman; Pennine Platform; Western Mail; Stand; Sunday Telegraph; Poetry Durham; Poetry Canada; Poetry Nottingham; Poetry Matters; Encounter; Spokes: Meridian; Acumen; Aquarius; Orbis; Spectator; The North; Yorkshire Journal; Rialto; Scintilla; The Interpreter's House; The London Magazine; Magma; Temenos; Included in many anthologies, most recently: The Virago Anthology of the Joys of Shopping; Writers on Islands; Writing Yourself. Honours: 1st Prize, Yorkshire Poets, 1974, 1976, 1977; 1st Prize, Arnold Vincent Bowen, 1976; Several Prizes, Lancaster Festival Poetry Competition; 1st Prize, Lincoln Open, 1984; 1st Prize, Rhyme International, 1986; 2nd Prize, Cardiff Festival Poetry Competition, 1987. Memberships: Poetry Society, London.

DICTIONARY OF INTERNATIONAL BIOGRAPHY 36th EDITION

ADAMS Bryan, b. 5 November 1959, Kingston, Ontario, Canada. Singer; Songwriter; Musician. 1 daughter with girlfriend Alicia Grimaldi, 2011. Career: International Recording Artist; Signed contract with A&M Records, 1979; 45 million albums sold world-wide, 1995; Numerous worldwide tours. Creative Works: Albums: Bryan Adams; Cuts Like A Knife, 1983; You Want It You Got It; Reckless, 1984; Into The Fire, 1987; Waking Up The Neighbours, 1991; Live! Live! Live!; 18 'Til I Die, 1996; The Best of Me, 2000; Room Service, 2004; Live in Lisbon, 2005; 11, 2008; Singles: Kids Wanna Rock; Summer of 69; Heaven; Run To You; Can't Stop This Thing We've Started; It's Only Love; Everything I Do, I Do It For You; Have You Ever Really Loved A Woman; I Finally Found Someone; Back to You; When You're Gone; Cloud Number Nine; Don't Give Up; Here I Am; Open Road; Soundtrack: Spirit: Stallion of the Cimarron, 2002; Room Service, 2004. Photography exhibitions: Toronto; Montreal; Saatchi Gallery, London; Royal Jubilee Exhibition, Windsor Castle, 2002. Publications: Bryan Adams: The Official Biography, 1995; Made in Canada; Photographs by Bryan Adams. Honours: Longest Standing No 1 in UK Singles Charts, 16 weeks, 1994; Diamond Sales Award; 12 Juno Awards; Recording Artist of the Decade; Order of Canada; Order of British Columbia. Address: c/o Press Department, A&M Records, 136-144 New King's Road, London, SW6 4LZ, England.

ADAMS Jad, b. 27 November 1954, London, England. Writer; TV Producer. Education: BA, University of Sussex, 1976; MA, University of London Birkbeck College, 1982; Fellow of the Royal Historical Society, 1997. Appointments: Television Professional, 1982-; Currently series producer; Councillor, London Borough of Lewisham, 1978-86; Chair, Nightwatch (homeless charity), 1992-; Research Fellow, Institute of English, School of Advanced Study, University of London, 2006. Publications: Tony Benn: A Biography, 1992; The Dynasty: The Nehru-Gandhi Story, 1997; Madder Music, Stranger Wine: The Life of Ernest Dowson, 2000; Pankhurst, 2003; Hideous Absinthe, 2004; Kipling, 2006; Gandhi: Naked Ambition, 2010. Honours: Young Journalist of the Year, British Press Awards, 1977; Best International Current Affairs Documentary, Royal Television Society, 1987. Membership: Institute of Historical Research. Address: 2 Kings Garth, 29 London Road, London SE23 3TT, England. E-mail: jadadams@btinternet.com Website: www.jadadams.co.uk

ADAMS Nicola Virginia, b. 26 October 1982, Leeds, England. Boxer. Career: English Amateur Champion, 2003-06; Silver medal (bantamweight), European Championships, Denmark, 2007; Silver medal, World Championships, China, 2008; Silver (flyweight), World Championships, Barbados, 2010; Winner, GB Amateur Boxing Championships, Liverpool, 2010; Gold medal, European Union Amateur Boxing Championships, Katowice, 2011; Gold medal, London Olympics, 2012.

ADAMS Richard, b. 9 May 1920. Author. m. Barbara Elizabeth Acland, 1949, 2 daughters. Education: Bradfield College, Berkshire, 1938; Worcester College, Oxford, 1938; MA, Modern History, Oxford University, 1948. Appointments: Army service, 1940-46; Civil Servant, 1948-74; Assistant Secretary, Department of the Environment, 1974; Writer-in-Residence, University of Florida, 1975; Writer-in-Residence, Hollins College, VA, 1976. Publications: Watership Down, 1972, 2nd edition, 1982; Shardik, 1974; Nature Through the Seasons, co-author Max Hooper, 1975; The Tyger Voyage (narrative poem), 1976; The Ship's Cat (narrative poem), 1977; The Plague Dogs, 1977; Nature Day and Night, (co-author Max Hooper), 1978; The Girl in a Swing, 1980; The Iron Wolf (short stories), 1980; Voyage Through the Antarctic (co-author Ronald Lockley), 1982; Maia, 1984; The Bureaucats, 1985; A Nature Diary, 1985; Occasional Poets, anthology, 1986; The Legend of Te Tuna, narrative poem, 1986; Traveller, 1988; The Day Gone By, autobiography, 1990; Tales from Watership Down, 1996; The Outlandish Knight, 2000; Daniel, 2006; Gentle Footprints, 2010. Honours: Carnegie Medal for Watership Down, 1972; Guardian Award for Children's Fiction for Watership Down, 1972. Memberships: President, RSPCA, 1980-82. Address: 26 Church Street, Whitchurch, Hampshire RG28 7AR, England.

ADAMSON Donald, b. 30 March 1939, Culcheth, Cheshire, England. Critic; Biographer; Historian; Diarist. m. Helen Freda Griffiths, 24 September 1966, 2 sons. Education: Magdalen College, Oxford, England, 1956-59; University of Paris, France, 1960-61; MA, MLitt, DPhil (Oxon). Appointment: Visiting Fellow, Wolfson College, Cambridge. Publications: T S Eliot: A Memoir, 1971; The House of Nell Gwyn, jointly, 1974; Les Romantiques Français Devant La Peinture Espagnole, 1989; Blaise Pascal: Mathematician, Physicist, And Thinker About God, 1995; Rides Round Britain, The Travel Journals of John Byng, 5th Viscount Torrington, 1996; The Curriers' Company: A Modern History, 2000; Oskar Kokoschka at Polperro, 2009; Researching Kokoschka, 2010; various translations of Balzac and Maupassant. Honours: JP, Cornwall, England, 1993; KStJ, 1998. Membership: FSA, 1979; FRSL, 1983; FCIL, 1989; FRHistS, 2007. Address: Dodmore House, Meopham, Kent, DA13 0AJ, England. E-mail: aimsworthy@tesco.net

ADCOCK Fleur, b. 10 February 1934, Papakura, New Zealand. Poet. m. (1) Alistair Teariki Campbell, 1952, divorced, 1958, 1 son, (2) Barry Crump, 1962, divorced 1966. Education: MA Victoria University of Wellington, 1955. Appointments: Assistant Lecturer, 1958, Assistant Librarian, 1959-61, University of Otago; with Alexander Turnbull Library, 1962; with FCO, 1963-79; Freelance writer, 1979-; Northern Arts Fellowship in Literature, Universities of Newcastle-upon-Tyne and Durham, 1979-81; Eastern Arts Fellowship, University of East Anglia, 1986; Writer-in-Residence, University of Adelaide, 1986. Publications: The Eye of the Hurricane, 1964; Tigers, 1967; High Tide in the Garden, 1971; The Scenic Route, 1974; The Inner Harbour, 1979; Below Loughrigg, 1979; Selected Poems, 1983; The Virgin and the Nightingale, 1983; The Incident Book, 1986; Time Zones, 1991; Looking Back, 1997; Poems 1960-2000, 2000; Dragon Talk, 2010: Contributor, The 2nd Wellington International Poetry Festival Anthology, 2004; Editor: The Oxford Book of Contemporary New Zealand Poetry, 1982; The Faber Book of 20th Century Women's Poetry, 1987; Translator and Editor, Hugh Primas and the Archpoet, 1994; Editor (with Jacqueline Simms), The Oxford Book of Creatures, 1995; Looking Back, 1997. Honours: Buckland Award, 1967, 1979; Jessie MacKay Award, 1968, 1972; Cholmondeley Award, 1976; New Zealand Book Award, 1984; Order of the British Empire, 1996; recipient of the prestigious Queen's Gold Medal for Poetry, 2006; Companion of the New Zealand Order of Merit, 2008. Membership: Poetry Society. Address: 14 Lincoln Road, London N2 9DL, England.

ADEJUYIGBE Olusanya, b. 4 August 1952, Akure, Nigeria. Paediatric Surgery. m. Ebunduluwa, 2 sons, 3 daughters. Education: MBBS, University of Ibadan, 1975; Fellow, Medical College of Surgeons, Nigeria, 1984; Fellow, West African College of Surgeons, 1994. Appointments: Chief Medical Director, Obafemi Awolowo University Teaching

Hospitals Complex, Ile-Ife, 2005-. Publications: Over 75 publications and articles. Honours: Over 15 honours and awards. Memberships: Nigerian Medical Association; West African Society of Gastroenterology; Medical and Dental Consultants Association of Nigeria. Address: Obafemi Awolowo University Teaching Hospitals Complex, PMB 5538, Ile-Ife, Osun State, Nigeria.

ADELE (Adele Laurie Blue Adkins), b. 5 May 1988, London, England. Singer; Songwriter. 1 son. Education: Graduate, BRIT School for Performing Arts & Technology, 2006. Career: Singer and Songwriter, XL Recordings, 2006-. Publications: Singles include: Hometown Glory, 2007; Chasing Pavements, Cold Shoulder, Make You Feel My Love, 2008; Rolling in the Deep, 2010; Someone Like You, Set Fire to the Rain, 2011; Rumour Has It, 2012; Skyfall, 2012; Albums: 19, 2008; 21, 2011. Honours: Critics' Choice Award, 2007; BBC Sound of 2008; 8 Grammy Awards; 3 BRIT Awards; Golden Globe Award for Best Original Song, 2013; Academy Award for Best Original Song, 2013.

ADELMAN Saul Joseph, b. 18 November 1944, Atlantic City, New York, USA. Astronomer; College Professor. m. Carol, 3 sons. Education: BS, Physics, University of Maryland, 1966; PhD, Astronomy, California Institute of Technology, 1972. Appointments: Postdoctorate, NASA Space Flight Center, 1972-74, 1984-86; Assistant Astronomer, Boston University, 1974-78; Assistant Professor, Associate Professor, Professor, The Citadel, 1978-. Publications: 340 papers; 7 articles; 1 book; 9 proceedings (co-editor). Honours: Phi Beta Kappa; Phi Kappa Phi; Sigma Pi Sigma; Sigma Xi; South Carolina Governor's Award for Excellence in Research at a Predominantly Undergraduate Institution, 2011. Memberships: International Astronomical Union; American Astronomical Society; Astronomical Society of the Pacific. Address: The Citadel Department of Physics, 171 Moultrie St, Charleston, SC 29409, USA.

ADEMOLA Michale Oluwole, b. 29 September 1975, Edunabon, Nigeria. Lecturer. m. Christianah Adedoyin Odewole, 1 son, 1 daughter. Education: NCE, French/Yoruba, Osun State College of Education, 1997; BA, French, University of Ilorin, 2002. Appointments: French Lecturer, Shehu Shagari College of Education, Sokoto, 2002-05; French Lecturer, Federal College of Education, Kontagora, 2005-. Memberships: Teachers Registration Council of Nigeria; Inter-Colleges Association of French Teachers. Address: French Department, School of Languages, Federal College of Education, PMB 39, Kontagora, Niger State, Nigeria. E-mail: michadem2009@yahoo.co.uk

ADEMUJIMI Kolawole Jones, b. 30 June 1953, Idanre, Ondo State, Nigeria. Medicine. m. Iyabode, 2 sons, 1 daughter. Education: MBBS, Premier University, Ibadan, 1980. Appointments: Schoolteacher, Methodist Modern School, Idanre; Housemanship, State Specialist Hospital, Akure; National Youth Service, Primary Health Centre, Ikeji-Ile, Osun State; Medical Practice, Dairo and Dairo Hospital, Akure, 1984; State Specialist Hospital, Ado-Ekiti, 1986; Medical Director, Hope Hospital and Maternity, Odode, Idanre, 1988; Managing Director, Hope Health Care Services Ltd, Odode, Idanre; Supervisor for Health and Finance, Idanre/Ifedore Local Government Area, 1990; Member, Health Council, Ondo State, 1990; Director, Owena Motels Ltd, 1994-96; Executive Chairman, Ondo State Housing Corporation, Akure, 1999-2003; Chairman, State Congress of Alliance for Democracy, 2000. Honours: National Merit University Award, 1975-76; Otunba-Ajiroba of Idanre Land, 1991; Akaiyejo of Iropora-Ekiti, 1992; Jerusalem Pilgrim, 1992; Justice of Peace, 1993; Ondo State Achievers' Award, 1994. Memberships: Youth Wing, Unity Party of Nigeria; Social Democratic Party; Alliance for Democracy; Nigerian Medical Association Ondo State; Association of General and Private Medical Practitioners of Nigeria; Klub 20; Owena Lions Club International; Akure Recreation Club; Love Brothers' Club. Address: Governor's Office, Ondo State Government, Alagbaka, Akure, Ondo State, Nigeria.

ADE-OJO Gordon O, Educational Researcher. Education: Doctorate in Education; MA PCET; MA ESL; BA, English. Appointments: Lecturer, English University of Ife, 1981-95; Trainer and Assessor in Basic Skills, Connex South East Train Company, 1995-99; ESOI and Basic Skills Lecturer, IELTS Co-ordinator, College of North West London, 1999-2000; Entry level ESOL and Literacy Course Team Leader, 2000-01, Faculty Senior Tutor, 2000-02, Lead IV/ESOL, Basic Skills and Teacher Training, 2002-05, Co-ordinator and Skills for Life Teacher Training, 2001-05, Programme Manager/Head of School for ESOL/Basic Skills, 2002-05, Southwark College, London; Principal Lecturer, Department of Professional Learning Development, 2005-, LLUK Sector Network Director, 2007-, University of Greenwich; External Examiner, Anglia Ruskin University, University of Bolton and Leeds Metropolitan University, 2005-. Publications: Numerous articles in professional journals; Book in progress. Memberships: Fellow, Institute for Learning, UK; Professional Member, Institute of Linguists, UK; Fellow, Higher Education Academy, UK; Qualified Teacher Status. Address: Department of Professional Learning Development, University of Greenwich, Southwood Site, Avery Hill Campus, Avery Hill Road, London SE9 2UG, England. E-mail: ag22@gre.ac.uk

ADER Robert, b. 20 February 1932, New York, USA. Psychologist. m. Gayle Simon, 4 daughters. Education: BS, Tulane University, New Orleans, USA, 1953; PhD, Cornell University, Ithaca, New York, USA, 1957. Appointments: Teaching and Research Assistantships, Department of Psychology, Cornell University, 1953-57; Research Instructor, Psychiatry, University of Rochester School of Medicine and Dentistry, 1957-59; Research Senior Instructor, 1959-61; Research Assistant Professor, 1961-64; Associate Professor, 1964-68; Professor, Department of Psychiatry, University of Rochester, 1968-; Visiting Professor, Rudolf Magnus Institute for Pharmacology, University of Utrecht, The Netherlands, 1970-71; Dean's Professor, University of Rochester School of Medicine and Dentistry, 1982-83; Professor of Medicine, 1983-; George L Engel Professor, Psychosocial Medicine, 1983-2002; Distinguished University Professor, 2002-; Fellow, Centre for Advanced Study in the Behavioural Sciences, 1992-93. Publications: Behaviourally conditioned immunosuppression; Behaviour and the Immune System; Psychoneuroimmunology; The role of conditioning in pharmacotherapy; Many other publications. Honours: Research Scientist Award; Institutional Training Grant; Editor-in-Chief, Brain Behaviour and Immunity; Honorary MD; Honorary ScD; Many other honours. Memberships: Academy of Behavioural Medicine Research, President, 1984-85; American Psychosomatic Society, President, 1979-80; International Society for Developmental Psychobiology, President, 1981-82; Psychoneuroimmunology Research Society, Founding President, 1993-94; Many other memberships. Address: 7 Moss Creek Ct, Pittsford, NY 14534-1071, USA.

DICTIONARY OF INTERNATIONAL BIOGRAPHY 36th EDITION

ADIE Kathryn (Kate), b. 19 September 1945, England. Television News Correspondent. Education: Newcastle University. Appointments: Technician and Producer, BBC Radio, 1969-76; Reporter, BBC TVS, 1977-79; BBC TV News, 1979-81; Correspondent, 1982-; Chief Correspondent, 1989-2003; Freelance Journalist, Broadcaster and TV Presenter, 2003-. Publications: The Kindness of Strangers, autobiography, 2002; Corsets to Camouflage: Women and War, 2003; Nobody's Child; Into Danger. Honours: RTS News Award, 1981, 1987; Monte Carlo International News Award, 1981, 1990; Honorary MA, Bath University, 1987; BAFTA Richard Dimbleby Award, 1989; Honorary DLitt, City University, 1989; Honorary MA, Newcastle University, 1990; Freeman of Sunderland, 1990; Honorary DLitt, Sunderland University, 1991; Loughborough University, 1991; Order of the British Empire, 1993; Honorary Professor, Sunderland University, 1995. Address: c/o BBC Television, Wood Lane, London W12 7RJ, England.

ADJANI Isabelle, b. 27 June 1955, France. Actress. 1 son with Bruno Nuytten, 1 son with Daniel Day-Lewis. Education: Lycée de Courbevoie. Appointment: President, Commission d'avances sur recettes, 1986-88. Career: Films include: Faustine et le bel été, 1972, Barocco, 1977; Nosferatu, 1978; Possession, 1980; Quartet, 1981; l'Eté Meurtrier, 1983; Camille Claudel, 1988; La Reine Margot, 1994; Diabolique, 1996; Paparazzi, 1998; La Repentie, 2002; Adolphe, 2002; Bon Voyage, 2003; Monsieur Ibrahim et les Fleurs du Coran, 2003; La Journée de la Jupe, 2008; Mammuth, 2010; De Force, 2011: Theatre includes: La Maison de Bernada Alba, 1970; l'Avare, 1972-73 Port-Royal, 1973; Ondine, 1974; TV includes: Le Petit Bougnat, 1969; l'Ecole des Femmes, 1973; Top á Sacha Distel, 1974; Princesse aux Petit Pois, 1986. Honours: Best Actress, Cannes, Possession, 1981; Best Actress, Cannes, Quartet, 1982; Best Actress César, Best Actress Award, Berlin Film Festival, Camille Claudel, 1989; Best Actress César, La Reine Margot, 1995. Address: c/o Phonogram, 89 Boulevard Auguste Blanqui, 75013 Paris, France.

ADLER Samuel, b. 4 March 1928, Mannheim, Germany. Professor. m. Emily Freeman Brown, 2 daughters. Education: BM, Boston University, 1948; MA, Harvard University, 1950; Honorary Doctorates: Southern Methodist University; Wake Forest University; St Mary's of Notre Dame College; The St Louis Conservatory. Appointments: Music Director, Temple Emanuel, Dallas, Texas, 1953-66; Music Director, Dallas Lyric Theater, 1955-60; Professor of Composition, University of North Texas, 1956-66; Professor of Composition, Eastman School of Music, 1966-95; Chair, Composition Department, 1971-94, Professor of Composition, 1997-, The Juilliard School. Publications: Over 400 compositions including: 5 operas; 6 symphonies; 9 string quartets; 14 concerti; 4 oratorios; and many other pieces; 3 books: Choral Conducting, 1971, 1985; Sight Singing, 1979, 1997; The Study of Orchestration, 1982, 1989, 2001, 2011. Honours: Special US Army Citation for Outstanding Service, 1952; American Academy of Arts and Letters, 2001; Chilean Academy of the Arts, 1993; German Akademie der Kunste, 1999; Classical Music Hall of Fame, 2008. Memberships: ASCAP; American Music Center; Sinfonia. Address: 9412 Sheffield Road, Perrysburg, OH 43551, USA.

ADLERSHTEYN Leon, b. 28 October 1925, St Petersburg, Russia. Naval Architect; Researcher; Educator. m. Irina Bereznaya. Education: MS, Shipbuilding Institute, St Petersburg, Russia 1945-51; DSc, Central Research Institute for Shipbuilding Technology, St Petersburg, Russia, 1970. Appointments: Private, Soviet Army, 1943-45; Foreman, Deputy Chief, Hull Shop, Baltic Shipyard, St Petersburg, Russia, 1951-63; Chief Technologist, Team Leader, 1963-74, Chief Researcher, 1993-94, Central Research Institute for Shipbuilding Technology; Head of the Chair, Professor, Shipbuilding Academy, 1974-94; Retired 1994. Publications: Author or co-author of 11 books which include: Accuracy in Ship Hull Manufacturing; Mechanisation and Automation of Ship Manufacturing; Modular Shipbuilding; Ship Examiner (2 editions); Handbook of Ship Marking and Examining Works and over 160 brochures and scientific articles; 9 Russian Patents. Honours: Order of the Patriotic War, 1st Class; 13 Russian Military Medals; 3 Medals of American Legion; 5 Medals of Russian Industrial Exhibition; Listed in numerous Who's Who and biographical publications. Memberships: Fellow, Institute of Marine Engineering, Science and Technology, UK; Society of Naval Architects and Marine Engineers, USA; American Association of Invalids and Veterans of WWII from the former Soviet Union. Address: 72 Montgomery Street, Apt 1510, Jersey City, NJ 07302-3827, USA. E-mail: bereznaya@gmail.com

ADLINGTON Rebecca, b. 17 February 1989, Mansfield, England. Freestyle Swimmer. Education: The Brunts School, Mansfield. Career: 2 Gold Medals (400m and 800m), Olympic Games, Beijing, 2008. Honours: Sportswoman of the Year, Sport Journalists' Association, 2008; OBE, 2009.

ADOMAYTIS Valentyn V, b. 23 February 1953, Ukraine. Ambassador of Ukraine to Australia and New Zealand. m. 1 daughter. Education: Graduate, Kyiv State Taras Shevchenko University, 1978. Appointments: English Language Travel Guide, Kyiv Branch of State Committee for Foreign Tourism of USSR, 1974-77; Senior Staff Member, Department of International Relations, Committee of Physical Culture and Sports under the Council of Ministers of Ukrainian Soviet Socialist Repblic, 1979-82; Member, Organising Committee, 1980 Olympic Games in Ukraine, 1980; Interpreter, Engineer, Commercial and Legal Directorate of the Soviet Erection Organisation, V/O Tiajpromexsport, Nigeria, 1982-85; Deputy Director, Ukrainian Society for Friendship and Cultural Relations with Foreign Countries, 1985-92; Director, Asia-Pacific Department, Ministry of Foreign Affairs of Ukraine, 1992-93; Counselor, Embassy of Ukraine to India, 1993-94; Deputy Director General, Asia-Pacific, Middle East and Africa Directorate General, MFA of Ukraine, 1994-98; Member, Ukrainian Delegation, 52nd UN General Assembly Session, New York, USA, 1997; Numerous official missions to India, Philippines, Republic of Korea, People's Democratic Republic of Korea, Sri Lanka, Nepal, Bangladesh, Indonesia, Japan, Pakistan, Vietnam, Thailand, China, Colombia, Cuba, Germany, Great Britain, USA, Russia and Georgia, 1992-2000; Ambassador Extraordinary and Plenipotentiary of Ukraine to the Republic of India, 1998; Non-Resident Ambassador Extraordinary and Plenipotentiary of Ukraine to the Kingdom of Nepal and the People's Republic of Bangladesh, 1998; Non-Resident Ambassador Extraordinary and Plenipotentiary of Ukraine to the Democratic Socialist Republic of Sri Lanka, 1999; Director, Foreign Economic Relations, Joint Stock Bank Etalon, President, Etalon Corporation, Kyiv, 2000-04; Consultant to Director of State Foreign Trade Fir Ukrinmash, Director, Burc Contracting Inc, Kyiv, 2004-05; Ambassador at Large, Ministry of Foreign Affairs of Ukraine, 2005-07; Ambassador Extraordinary and Plenipotentiary of Ukraine to Commonwealth of Australia, 2007-; Ambassador Extraordinary and Plenipotentiary of Ukraine to New Zealand, 2007-. Address: Embassy of Ukraine in Australia, GPO Box 1567, Canberra, ACT 2601, Australia. Website: www.mfa.gov.ua/australia

DICTIONARY OF INTERNATIONAL BIOGRAPHY 36ᵗʰ EDITION

ADOOR Gopalakrishnan, b. 3 July 1941, Adoor, Kerala, India. m. Sunanda, 1972, 1 daughter. Education: Postgraduate diplomas in Screenplay Writing & Elements of Direction and Advanced Film Direction, Film Institute of India. Appointments: Film maker, 1969-; Director, National Film Development Corporation, 1980-83; Chairman, Film and TV Inst India, 1987-89 and 1993-96; Chairman, 7th International Children's Film Festival of India, 1991; Chairman, Public Service Broadcasting Trust of India, 2000-; Jury Chairman, Singapore International Film Festival; Jury Chairman, international film festivals of Fribourg, Dubai, and Cairo, 2009, and Valladolid, 2010. Publications: 2 plays; 11 screenplays; 3 books on cinema. Honours: British Film Institute Award (Elippathayam); 6 times winner, International Film Critics' Prize; Commander of the Order of Arts & Letters, France; Dada Saheb Award for Lifetime Achievement in Cinema; Lifetime Achievement Awards, International Film Festivals of Denver, Cairo, and New Jersey; India's top civilian honour, title of Padma Vibhushan, 2006; Honorary Degree, D Litt, Mahatma Gandhi University and the Kerala University; many others. Memberships: Indian International Centre. Address: Darsanam, Trivandrum, 695 017, Kerala, India.

ADVINCULA Edgardo Galpo, b. 20 March 1940, Manila, Philippines. Medical Doctor. m. Erlinda, 3 sons. Education: Doctor of Medicine & Surgery, 1963; Echocardiography & Vascular Doppler Studies Course; American Board Int Medicine, 2007-17. Appointments: Chief Medical Staff; Director, MMH Family Health Clinic; Worshipful Master, The Ancient St John's Lodge #3, Kingston, Ontario, Canada, 1993; Assistant, Department of Medicine, Queens University; Medical Acupuncture Lecture, Queens University Nurses' Conference. Publications: Orthostatic Hypotension, 1967; Myelocyte Transit, Time in Acute Leukemia, presented to New York Academy of Science, 1972. Honours: Top Physician, American, 2005, 2006, 2008; Fellowship, American, Canadian, Royal Society of Medicine College of Physician (by Examination); International Hippocrates Award for Medical Achievement; Lifetime Achievement Award in Medicine & Humanity, 2010; Man of the Year, 2010. Memberships: FACP; FRCP(C); FRSM; FACIP; CAFCI; ACP Executive; Fellow, Disability Medicine; Master, American Academy Cardiology; New York Academy of Sciences. Address: PO Box #687, 1071 N Maple, Muenster, TX 76252, USA.

AFFLECK Ben, b. 15 August 1972, Berkeley, California, USA. Actor, Director, Screenwriter and Producer. m. Jennifer Garner, 2005, 2 daughters. Career: Appeared in films including School Ties, 1992, Buffy the Vampire Slayer, Dazed and Confused, Mallrats, 1995, Glory Daze, Office Killer, Chasing Amy, Going All the Way, Good Will Hunting, film and screenplay, 1997, Phantoms, Armageddon, Shakespeare in Love, 1998; Reindeer Games, Forces of Nature, Dogma, Daddy and Them, The Boiler Room, 200 Cigarettes, 1999; Bounce, The Third Wheel (also producer), 2000; Pearl Harbor, 2001; The Sum of All Fear, Changing Lanes, 2002; Daredevil, Gigli, Paycheck, 2003; Jersey Girl, Surviving Christmas, 2004; Man About Town, 2005; Hollywoodland, 2006; Gone Baby Gone, 2007; Smoking Aces, 2007; He's Just Not That Into You, State of Play, Extract, 2009; The Company Men, The Town, 2010; Argo, 2012. Television appearances include: Voyage of the Mimi, Against the Grain, Lifestories: Family in Crisis, Hands of a Stranger, Daddy. Honours: Academy Award for Good Will Hunting, 1997; Golden Globe for Best Original Screenplay, 1997. Address: c/o Creative Artists Agency, 9830 Wilshire Boulevard, Beverly Hills, CA 90212, USA.

AGARWAL Manojkumar, b. 19 October 1963, India. Eye Surgeon. m. Suman, 1 son. Education: MBBS, 1985; MS, 1990; DOMS, 1989; FCPS, 1990; DNB, 1991; MFCO, 1991; FRF, 1991; DIT, 1999; DHM, 2004. Appointments: Lecturer, 1991-95, Associate Professor, 1995-2001, Ophthalmology, Sir J J Hospital; Professor & Head, Ophthalmology, Dr V M Medical College, 2002; Consultant, Godrej Hospital, Pramukhswami Hospital, Shitij Eyecare Centre; Consultant, Karuna Hospital; Consultant, Gokuldham Medical Centre, Rotary Eye Hospital. Publications: Numerous articles in professional journals. Honours: Dr L H Hiranandani Prize for First in Mumbai University; Dr Menino Desouza Prize for Best Student; Farish & Merit Scholarships; Many other awards in sports, education and cultural events; Listed in international biographical dictionaries. Memberships: All India Ophthalmology Society; Bombay Ophthalmologists Association; Maharashtra Ophthalmic Society; Vitreo Retinal Society of India; Intra Ocular Implant & Refractive Society of India; Association of Medical Consultants. Address: Shitij Eye Care Centre, Kaveri-D-002, Vasant Sagar, Thakur Village, Kandivali-E, Mumbai 400101, India.

AGASSI Andre, b. 29 April 1970, Las Vegas, USA. Tennis Player. m. (1) Brooke Shields, 1997, divorced 1999; (2) Steffi Graf, 2001, 1 son, 1 daughter. Education: Coached from age of 13 by Nick Bolletieri; Strength coach Gil Reyes. Appointments: Semi Finalist, French Open, 1988; US Open, 1988, 1989; Member, US Team which defeated Australia in Davis Cup Final, 1990; Defeated Stefan Edberg to win inaugural ATP World Championships, Frankfurt, 1991; Finalist, French Open, 1990, 1991; US Open, 1990, 1995, 2002; Australian Open, 1994; Wimbledon, 1999; Men's Singles Wimbledon Champion, 1992; Won, US Open, 1994; Canadian Open, 1995; Australian Open, 1995, 2000, 2001, 2003; Winner, Olympic Games Tennis Tournament, 1996; Association of Tennis Professionals World Champion, 1990. Cincinnati Masters, 2004. Retired from professional tennis 3 September 2006. Address: International Management Group, 1 Brieview Plaza, Suite 1300, Cleveland, OH 44114, USA.

AGATA Koichiro, b. 30 January 1956, Kobe, Japan. Professor. m. Masako Onisawa, 1 son, 1 daughter. Education: BA, 1979, MA, 1982, Political Science, Waseda University; Dr rer publ, Hochschule fur Verwaltungswissenschaften Speyer, Germany, 1992. Appointments: Assistant Professor, 1990-92, Associate Professor, 1992-97, Professor, Public Administration, 1997-, Dean, Okuma School of Public Management, Waseda University; Ambassador Scientist of Alexander von Humboldt Foundation, 2008-. Publications: Staatliche Forderprogramme fur Gemeinden, 1992; Convergence of Telecommunications and Broadcasting, 2001; Kolleg Policy Research, 2007. Honours: Scholarship, German Academic Exchange Service, 1984-88; Scholarship, Alexander von Humboldt Foundation, 1994-95; Vordienstkreuz am Barde des Verdeinstordans der Bundesrepublik, 2006. Memberships: Japanese Society for Public Administration, Science Council of Japan.

AGIUS Marcus Ambrose Paul, b. 22 July 1946, Walton-on-Thames, England. Group Chairman of Barclays plc. m. Katherine Juliette de Rothschild, 2 daughters. Education: MA, Mechanical Sciences and Economics, Cambridge University, 1971; MBA, Harvard Business School, 1972; Vickers Scholarship, 1970. Appointments: Director, Exbury Gardens Limited, 1977-; Director. Exbury Gardens Retail Limited, 1998-; Deputy Chairman, Lazard LLC, 2002-; Chairman, The Foundation and Friends of the Royal Botanic Gardens, Kew, 2004-; Trustee to the Board of the Royal Botanic Gardens, Kew, 2006-; Chairman,

BAA plc, 2002-2006; Chairman, Lazard London, 2001-06; Senior Independent Director, BBC Executive Board, 2006-; Non-Executive Director, Barclays plc, 2006; Group Chairman, Barclays plc, 2007-; Chairman, British Bankers' Association, 2010; Business Ambassador, UK Trade and Investment; Member, Advisory Council, TheCityUK; Member, Executive Committee, IIEB, Member, The Takeover Panel. Memberships: Whites; Swinley Forest; The Garden Society; Beaulieu River Sailing Club; Brokenhurst Manor Golf Club.

AGNEW Jonathan Geoffrey William, b. 30 July 1941, Windsor, England. Investment Banker. m. (1) Honourable Joanna Campbell, 1966, divorced 1985, 1 son, 2 daughters, (2) Marie-Claire Dreesmann, 1990, 1 son, 1 daughter. Education: MA Cantab, Trinity College, Cambridge. Appointments: with The Economist, 1964-65, IBRD, 1965-67; Various positions, 1967-73, Director, 1971, Hill Samuel & Co; Non-Executive Director, Thos Agnew & Sons Ltd, 1969-2007, Thos Agnew & Sons (Holdings) Limited, 2007-; Positions, 1973-82, Managing Director, 1977, Morgan Stanley & Co; with J G W Agnew & Co, 1983-86; Chief Executive, ISRO, 1986; Positions, 1987-93, Chief Executive, 1989-93, Kleinwort Benson Group plc; Chairman, Limit plc, 1993-2000; Member, Council, Lloyd's, 1995-98; Chairman, Henderson Geared Income and Growth Trust plc, 1995-2003; Non-Executive Director, 1997, Deputy Chairman, 1999-2002, Chair, 2002-07, Nationwide Building Society; Chairman, Gerrard Group plc, 1998-2000; Non Executive Director, 2002-, Chair, Beazley Group plc, 2003-09, Beazley plc, 2009-; Chairman, LMS Capital plc, 2006-10; Chairman, The Cayenne Trust plc, 2006-; Senior Independent Director, Rightmove plc, 2006-; Chairman, Ashmore Global Opportunities Ltd, 2007-. Address: Flat E, 51 Eaton Square, London SW1W 9BE, England. E-mail: jgwagnew@yahoo.co.uk

AGOPIAN Antoine Antranig Hagop, b. 22 December 1957, Addis-Adeba, Ethiopia. Dental Surgeon. m. Yesenya Gasparyan, 1 daughter. Education: Studies in odontology, Universities of Marseilles and Nice, France; Postdoctoral diplomas in different specialities. Appointments: Research, Hensson International Society, Vienna, Austria; Bertin and Company, Aix-en-Provence, France; Founder President, Azadakroutioun Association, 1983; Founder Member, International Academy of Computerized Dentistry, 1988; Founder President, International Association for Odontological Aid to Armenia, 1989; Editorial Staff Member, Armenia monthly magazine, 1987-89; Editor, France-Arménie monthly magazine, Marseilles, 1989-95. Publications: More than 1,000 articles in French and Armenian newspapers and magazines; 500 hours of radio broadcasts; 11 books published in French. Memberships: International Academy of Computerized Dentistry; Azadakroutioun Association. Address: Residence le Parc de Camille Bat B, 152 Bd de la Comtesse, 13012 Marseille, France.

AGRAWAL Ajay, b. 15 February 1965, Agra, India. Consultant. m. Alpna Agrawal, 2 sons. Education: BSc, Combined Sciences, 1981-83, MSc, Chemistry, 1983-85, Agra University, India; PhD, Central Drug Research Institute, Lucknow, India, 1985-90. Appointments: Postdoctoral Fellow, Faculty of Medicine, University of Alberta, Canada, 1991-93; Senior Postdoctoral Fellow, Molecular Cell Pathology, Royal Free Hospital Medical School, London, 1993-95; Principal Scientist, polyMASC Pharmaceuticals plc, London, 1995-2001; Senior Consultant, numerous biotech and pharma companies worldwide (Board member of Immupharma plc, London and Clinova UK and member of Advisory Board of Commonwealth British Council, London), 2001-. Publications: Numerous research articles and reviews, including some pioneer work on infectious diseases documented in peer-reviewed journals and books; Several international presentations and invited lectures. Honours: Co-founder, polyMASC Pharmaceuticals, London, 1995; Member, Editorial Advisory Board of four international journals; Honorary Research Fellow, Royal Free and University College Medical School, London; National Merit Award and Research Fellowships, WHO and CSIR; Gold Medal, 1st place, Master's Exam. Memberships: London Technology Network; London Biotechnology Network; Camden Badminton Club. Address: 12 Grange Avenue, Cambridgeshire PE1 4HH, England. E-mail: ajaymedpharm@aol.com

AGUILERA Christina, b. 18 December 1980, Staten Island, New York, USA. Singer; Songwriter; Actress. m. Jordan Bratman, 2005, 1 son. Career: Singer: Albums: Christina Aguilera, 1999; Mi Reflejo, 2000; My Kind of Christmas, 2000; Stripped, 2002; Back to Basics, 2006; Keeps Gettin' Better: A Decade of Hits, 2008; Light & Darkness, 2010; DVDs: Genie Gets Her Wish, 1999; My Reflection, 2001; Stripped Live in the UK, 2004; Back to Basics: Live and Down Under, 2008; Tours: Christina Aguilera: In Concert Tour, 2000-01; Justified/Stripped Tour/Stripped World Tour, 2003; Back to Basics Tour, 2006-07. Honours: 4 Grammy Awards, 2000, 2002, 2004, 2007; Latin Grammy Award, 2001.

AGUTTER Jenny, b. 20 December 1952, Taunton, Somerset, England. Actress; Dancer. m. Johan Tham, 1990, 1 son. Education: Elmhurst Ballet School. Career: Film debut East of Sudan, 1964; Appeared in numerous films for both cinema and TV, dramas, plays and series on stage; Plays include: Spring Awakening; Tempest; Betrayal; Breaking the Code; Love's Labour's Lost; Peter Pan, 1997-98; Films include: Ballerina, 1964; The Railway Children, 1969; Logan's Run, 1975; Equus, 1975; The Eagle has Landed, Sweet William, 1980; An American Werewolf in London, 1981; Secret Places, 1983; Dark Tower, 1987; King of the Wind, 1989; Child's Play 2, 1991; Freddie as Fro 7, 1993; Blue Juice, 1995; English Places, English Faces, 1996; The Parole Officer, 2001; At Dawning, 2001; Number 1, Longing, Number 2, Regret, 2004; TV includes: Amy, 1980; Not a Penny More, Not a Penny Less, 1990; The Good Guys, 1991; Love Hurts, Heartbreak, 1994; The Buccaneers, 1995; And the Beat Goes On, 1996; A Respectable Trade, 1997; Bramwell, 1998; The Railway Children, 2000; Spooks, 2002; The Alan Clarke Diaries, 2004; New Tricks, 2005; Diamond Geezer, 2005; Irina Palm, 2007; The Invisibles, 2008; Monday Monday, 2009. Publication: Snap, 1983. Honour: Emmy Award for The Snow Goose, 1972; BAFTA Award for Equus, 1978. Address: c/o Marmont Management, Langham House, 308 Regent Street, London W1B 3AT, England.

AHARONI Herzl, b. 18 December 1937, Haifa, Israel. Professor Emeritus. m. Miriam, 2 sons, 2 daughters. Education: BSc, 1964, MSc, 1967, Dip Ing, 1970, DSc, 1972, Electrical Engineering Faculty, Technion, Israel Institute of Technology, Haifa, Israel; Research on Semiconductor devices breakdown mechanisms and CVD of Si-Ge hetroepitaxial layers. Appointments: Professor, 1973-2007, Professor Emeritus, 2007-, Department of Electrical and Computer Engineering, specialising in new processing development in microelectrics, Ben Gurion University; Sabbatical activities include: Visiting Associate Professor, University of California at San Diego, lectures on semiconductor technology and circuit analysis, 1978-79; Advanced Photovoltaic Development Group Jet

Propulsion Laboratory, Pasadena, California, USA, 1979-80; ITO/InP photovoltaic devices, Solar Energy Research Institute, Golden, Colorado, USA, 1984-86; Invention of Integrated single crystal Silicon Light Emiting Devices, University of Pretoria, Pretoria, South Africa, 1993-94; Research on low temperature Si devices processing using plasma techniques, Tohoku University, Sendai, Japan, 1994-96, 1999-2001 and 2006-07. Publications: 10 patents; Over 200 scientific publications including 4 conference invited papers and 2 plenary papers; Poetry books: Poems in the Rain, 1989; Poems From Heaven and Earth, 1993. Honours: Research Associateship Award by NASA, National Research Council, for research at the Jet Propulsion Laboratory, Pasadena, California, USA, 1979-80; Faculty of Engineering Best Teacher Awards, Ben Gurion University, 1987, 1988; Esteemed Teacher Citation, Student Association, Ben Gurion University, 1988-89; Distinguished Research Professor, Rand Afrikaans University, Johannesburg, South Africa, 1990; Ben-Gurion University Annual Prize in Applied Electronics, donated by the Polish Jewish Ex-Servicemen's Association of London, 1998; Supervised and co-authored a student conference paper which received the Young Researcher Award, SSDM, 2000; Fellow, Institute of Engineering and Technology, 2003; Distinguished Lecturer, IEEE, 2003; BGU Dean of Engineering Faculty, Excellence in Teaching Awards, 2004, 2005, 2006; Fellow, Institute of Physics, 2005; Ben-Gurion University President and Rector Outstanding Teaching Award, 2005, 2006; Fellow, American Physical Society, 2007; Certificate of Recognition and Appreciation awarded by the President of the IEEE Electron Device Society, 2009; The 2010 International Network for Engineering Education & Research (iNEER) Achievement Award; Fellow, International Society for Optical Engineering, 2011. Memberships: Senior Member, IEEE; Optical Society of America; American Vacuum Society; Israel Association of Crystal Growth; The Israel Vacuum Society; The Israel Physical Society. Address: Department of Electrical & Computer Engineering, Ben Gurion University of the Negev, PO Box 653, Beer Sheva 84105, Israel.

AHERN Bertie, b. 12 September 1951, Dublin, Ireland. Former Irish Politician. m. Miriam Patricia Kelly, 1975, separated, 2 daughters. Education: Rathmines College of Commerce, Dublin; University College, Dublin. Appointments: Elected to Dáil, constituency of Dublin-Finglas, 1977-2011, represented Dublin Central, 1981-; Member, Dublin City Council, 1978-88, Lord Mayor, 1986-87; Assistant Government Whip, 1980-81; Fianna Fáil Front Bench spokesman on Youth, 1981-82; Minister of State, Department of the Taoiseach and at Department of Defence, and Government Chief Whip, 1982; Opposition Chief Whip, 1982-84; Fianna Fáil Front Bench spokesman on Labour, 1984-87; Minister for Labour, 1987-91; Chairman Dublin Millennium Committee, 1988; Chairman, European Investment Bank, 1991-92; Member, Board of Governors, World Bank, 1991-94; Member, Board of Governors, IMF, 1991-94; Minister for Finance, 1991-94; Minister for Industry and Commerce, 1993; Leader, Fianna Fáil Party, 1994-; Tánaiste (Deputy Prime Minister), 1994; Minister for Arts, Culture and the Gaeltacht, 1994; Taoiseach, 1997-2002, 2002-08. Honours: Grand Cross, Order of Merit with Star and Sash, Germany, 1991; Thomas J Dodd Prize in International Justice and Human Rights (jointly awarded to Taoiseach and British Prime Minister Mr Tony Blair MP), 2003; European Voice Statesman of the Year, 2004; The Stara Planina, Bulgaria, 2005; American Lung Association Chairman's Award, 2005; Golden Statuette, Business Centre Club, Poland, 2005; Polio Eradication Champion Award, Rotary International, 2006; 7 honorary degrees.

AHLSEN Leopold, b. 12 January 1927, Munich, Germany. Author. m. Ruth Gehwald, 1964, 1 son, 1 daughter. Publications: 13 plays, 23 radio plays, 68 television plays, 7 novels. Honours: Gerhart Hauptmann Prize; Schiller-Förderungspreis; Goldener Bildschirm; Hörspielpreis der Kriegsblinden; Silver Nymph of Monte Carlo; Bundesverdienstkreuz. Address: Waldschulstrasse 58, 81827 Munich, Germany.

AHLSKOG J Eric, b. 14 September 1945, Chicago, Illinois, USA. Neurologist. m. Faye Wayland, 3 sons. Education: BA, Michigan State University, 1967; PhD, Princeton University, 1973; MD, Dartmouth Medical School, 1976. Appointments: Instructor of Neurology, 1981-86, Assistant Professor of Neurology, 1986-93, Associate Professor of Neurology, 1993-98, Professor of Neurology, 1998-, Mayo Medical School, Rochester; Chair, Division of Movement Disorders, Department of Neurology, Rochester, 1992-2001; Consultant and Chair, Section of Movement Disorders, Mayo Clinic, Rochester, 2002-. Publications: Over 190 peer reviewed publications; Co-editor, Parkinson's Disease and Movement Disorders, 2000; Author: The Parkinson's Disease Treatment Book, 2005; Parkinson's Treatment Guide for Physicians, 2009. Honours: Honors College, Michigan State University, 1967; Alpha Omega Alpha, Dartmouth Medical School, 1975; Distinguished Mayo Clinician, 2005; Fred Springer Award, American Parkinson's Disease Association, 2007. Memberships: American Academy of Neurology; Movement Disorder Society. Address: Department of Neurology, Mayo Clinic, 200 First St SW, Rochester, MN 55905, USA.

AHMAD Mukhtar, b. 22 March 1948, Hamirpur, India. Teacher. m. Maimoona, 2 sons, 3 daughters. Education: BS, Electrical Engineering, 1969; MSc, Engineering, 1972; PhD, Engineering, 1991. Appointments: Reader, 1986-98, Professor, Electrical Engineering, 1998-, AMU, Aligarh; Associate Professor, University Puta, Malaysia, 1997-99; Associate Professor, Multimedia University, Malaysia, 2001-02. Publications: Books: High Performance AC Drives, 2010; Power System State Estimation, 2013; 14 technical papers in international journals; 8 international conferences; 6 national conferences; 18 popular science articles in science magazines and newspapers. Memberships: Senior Member, IEEE. Address: 4/1307 New Sir Syed, Nagar, Aligarh, India. E-mail: mukhtar@ieee.org

AHMED E M E, b. 27 December 1954, Mansoura, Egypt. Professor. m. L Abd-Al-Wahab, 1 daughter. Education: BSc, 1977, MSc, 1980, Mathematics, Mansoura University, Egypt; PhD, Applied Mathematics, London University, England, 1986. Appointments: Lecturer, 1986-91, Associate Professor, 1991-97, Professor, 1997-, Mathematics Department, Mansoura University. Publications: More than 100 papers in international journals. Honours: ORS, ORS UK, 1984, 1985; Amin Lotfy, Egyptian Academy of Science, 1988, 1994; Best Lecturer, Mansoura University, 2006. Memberships: European Society of Complex Systems; Multi Criteria Decision Making Society; Egyptian Society of Mathematics; Reviewer, Zentrlablatt Mathematics; Reviewer, American Mathematical Society. Address: Mathematics Department, Faculty of Science, Mansoura 35516, Egypt. E-mail: magd45@yahoo.com

AHMED Khurshid, b. 13 July 1936, Lahore, Pakistan. Trade Unionist. m. Sahra, 2 sons, 4 daughters. Education: Law Graduate, University of Punjab, 1960; Diploma, Industrial Relations, Turkey and UK, 1967. Appointments: Pakistan Workers Confederation; Editor, monthly Pak Workers;

Member, ILO Governing Body, 1972-2011. Publications: Many books including: Labour Movement of Pakistan, Past & Present; ILO for Decent Work & Social Justice; Numerous articles in professional journals. Honours: Sitara Imtiaz National Award. Memberships: ILO Governing Body, Workers Group; Tripartite Standing Labour Commission of Pakistan; National Industrial Relations Commission. Address: Bukhtiar Labour Hall, 28 Nibat Road, Lahore, Pakistan.

AHN Byung Moon, b. 11 June 1951, Goheung, Jeollanamdo, Korea. Superintendent. m. Mee Sook Lee, 1982, 2 daughters. Education: MD, Seoul National University, 1976; PhD, Chung-Ang University, 1982; CEO Course, Graduate School of Public Health,Yonsei University, 1999. Appointments: Staff Surgeon, Department of Orthopaedic Surgery, Hangang Sacred Heart Hospital, Hallym University, 1981-83; Member, Medical Advisory Committee, Incheon District Prosecutor's Office, 1990-94; Superintendent, Sungmin General Hospital, 1993-; Director of the Board, Chairman of Committee for International Affairs, Korean Hospital Association, 1996-; Member, Special Task Team for Healthcare, Presidential Council for Future and Vision, 2010-; Chairman, National Forum for Digital Hospital Export, 2011-. Publications: Over 60 articles including: Fibromastosis: Report of Two Cases, 1981; Lunate Dislocation, 1983; Clinical Failures of Internal Fixation, 1985; Co-author, The Textbook of Anti-Ageing Medicines, 2006. Honours: Choongwae Humanitarian Award, 2008; Government Citation for Specialty Hospital of Excellence, Ministry of Health and Welfare, 2010; Minister's Award for Healthcare Contribution, Ministry of Health and Welfare, 2010. Memberships: Korean Hospital Association; National Forum for Digital Hospital Export; HIMSS. Address: Seognamdong 522-1, Seo-gu, Incheon, 404-220, Korea. E-mail: bm-ahn@hanmail.net

AHN Gan Hun, b. 19 October 1945, Hyeungseong-gun, Gangwon-do, Korea. Professor. m. Young Sook Lee, 1 son, 1 daughter. Education: BA, 1974, MA, 1979, PhD, 1987, Philosophy, Korea University; MA, Education, 1976, Seoul National University; MA, Philosophy, Michigan State University, USA, 1983; PhD, Interdisciplinary, University of Missouri, USA, 1999. Appointments: Research Fellow, Korean Educational Development Institute, 1977-79; Professor, Kangwon National University, 1987-2010; President, Korean Society for the Study of Environmental Philosophy, 1994-2000; Associate Dean, College of Humanities, Kangwon National University, 1995-96; President, Korean Society for the Study of Philosophy of History, 2003-10; Chair of Section of Environmental Philosophy, XXII World Congress of Philosophy, 2008; Vice President, Korean Philosophical Association, 2009-10. Publications: Author: Symbolic Logic I; Science, Technology and Philosophy; Logic and Inquiry; An Analysis of Causation; Symbolic Logic and Its Applications; Freewill and Determinism; Contemporary British and American Philosophy; History and Historical View; The Quest for Certainty; The Problems of Philosophy; Environmental Culture and Ecodemocracy; Translator: Philosophical Analysis; Ten Moral Paradoxes. Honours: Recipient, Outstanding Faculty in Teaching, Kangwon National University. Address: 211-105 Hyunjin Evervill 2, Seoksa dong, Chuncheon Si, Gangwondo, 200-972, Republic of Korea. E-mail: ghahn@kangwon.ac.kr

AHN Namsu, b. 5 May 1977, Seoul, Korea. Researcher. m. YoonGyeong Gwack. Education: MS, Pennsylvania State University, USA; PhD, KAIST. Appointments: Researcher, Defense Agency for Technology and Quality; Researcher, LG Electronics.

AHN Yangkeun, b. 19 April 1973, Miryang, South Korea. Computer Engineer. m. Yejung. Education: B Eng, 1995, M Eng, 1997, Control and Instrumentation Engineering, Korea Maritime University. Appointments: Electric Power Network Simulaton System Design, Korea Electric Power Research Institute, 1997; ADSL and VDSL Communication System Development, HaeDong Telecom, 2000-04; Research, Embedded Systems and Digital Communications, Korea Electronics Technology Institute, 2005-; Research, HCI/UI/UX/3D Systems. Address: 8 Floor, #1599, Sangam-dong, Mapo-gu, Seoul, South Korea. E-mail: ykahn@keti.re.kr

AHN Yeh-Jin, b. 10 July 1972, Seoul, Korea. Assistant Professor. m. Lin-Woo Kang, 2 daughters. Education: BA, Horticulture, Korea University, 1997; MS, Environmental Engineering, Pohang University of Science & Technology, 2000; PhD, Plant Physiology, University of Maryland, USA, 2004. Appointments: Researcher, US Department of Agriculture, ARS, Albany, USA, 2004-06; Assistant Professor, Sangmyung University, Seoul, 2006-. Publications: Numerous articles in professional journals. Honours: Outstanding Performance Award, US Department of Agriculture, 2006; Teaching Award, Sangmyung University, 2007, 2008; Research Award, Sangmyung University, 2011. Memberships: American Society of Plant Biologists; Korean Society for Horticultural Science. Address: Department of Green Life Science, College of Convergence, Sangmyung University, 20 Hongjimun 2-gil, Jongno-gu, Seoul 110-743, Korea. E-mail: yjahn@smu.ac.kr

AHN Young Chull, b. 27 July 1973, Suwon, Korea. Professor. m. Bogum Kang, 1 son, 1 daughter. Education: Bachelor of Engineering, Mechanical Engineering, 1996; Master of Engineering, Mechanical Engineering, 1998; PhD, Thermal and Fluid Engineering, 2004. Appointments: Researcher, Janwoo Machinery Co Ltd, 2000-02; Associate Professor, Research Institute of Mechanical Technology, Pusan National University, 2004-06; Professor, Department of Architectural Engineering, Pusan National University, 2006-. Publications: Numerous articles in professional journals. Honours: Best Paper Award, 5th International Conference on Cooling and Heating Technologies, 2010; Best Paper Award, 7th International Conference on Fluid and Thermal Energy Conversion, 2011; Best Paper Award, Winter Meeting of the Society of Air-Conditioning and Refrigerating Engineers of Korea, 2011. Memberships: Society of Air-conditioning and Refrigerating Engineers of Korea; Architectural Institute of Korea. Address: Department of Architectural Engineering, Pusan National University, San 30, Jangjeondong, Keumjunggu, Busan 609-735, Korea. E-mail: ycahn@pusan.ac.kr Website: www.archieng.pusan.ac.kr

AHNIYAZ Anwar, b. 18 February 1969, Aksu, Xinjiang, China. Material Scientist. m. Dilnur Halik, 2 sons. Education: BSc, Chemistry, Xinjiang University, China, 1991; Dr Sci, Material Science and Engineering, Tokyo Institute of Technology, Japan, 2005. Appointments: Postdoctorate, Tokyo Institute of Technology, 2002-05; Postdoctorate, Stockholm University, 2005-07; Project Manager, Powder Technology, 2007-11, Area Manager, Nanotechnology, 2011-, Ytkemiska Institut AB, Sweden. Publications: More than 20 articles; Proceedings, National Academy of Sciences of the USA, 2007. Honours: Monbusho Scholarship, Japan, 1991-2002; Distinguished Young Asian Scholar Millennium Awards, Japanese Ceramic Society, 2001. Memberships: Materials Research Society. Address: Morbydalen 8, Stockholm 18252, Sweden. E-mail: anwar218@yahoo.com

AHRENDS Peter, b. 30 April 1933, Berlin, Germany. Architect. m. Elizabeth Robertson, 1954, 2 daughters. Education: AA (Hons) School of Architecture; ARIBA. Appointments: Denys Lasdun and Partners, 1959-60; Teacher, Architectural Association School of Architecture, 1960-61; Partner, Director, Consultant, Ahrends, Burton and Koralek architectural practice, London, 1961-; Professor, Bartlett School of Architecture and Planning, University College, London, 1987-90; Chair, Architects Support Group South Africa; Chair, Camden Design Advisory Group; Member, RIBA Annual Awards Group; Chair, Newham Design Review Panel; Principal projects include British Embassy, Moscow, 2000 Dublin Corporation Convent Lands Master Plan, 2000; Dublin Corporation/NEIC Civic Centre, 2001; Great Egyptian Museum Competition Entry, 2002; Whitworth Art Gallery Development Plan Review, 2002; Designs on Democracy Stockport winning competition entry, 2002; Riverside Building, London Docklands, 2003; Institute of Technology, Blanchardstown, Dublin, Masterplan & Phase I buildings, 2003; Bexhill Town Centre Masterplan, 2004; John Wheatley College, Glasgow, 2007; Civic Offices, Cork, 2007; St Thomas More Catholic School, London, in progress. Publications: Ahrends, Burton and Koralek (monograph), 1991; Collaborations: The Architecture of ABK, August/Birkhäuser; Numerous articles in professional journals. Honours: Good Design in Housing Award, 1977, Architecture Awards, 1978, 1993, 1996, 1999, Structural Steel Design Award, 1980, Structural Steel Commendation, 1993; Gulbenkian Museum of the Year Award, 1999. Memberships: Royal Institute of British Architects; Design Council; Chairman, UK Architects Against Apartheid, 1988-93; Chair, Newham Design Review Panel. Address: 16 Rochester Road, London NW1 9JH, England. E-mail: abk@abklondon.com Website: www.abk.co.uk

AHRENS Renate Katharina Elisabeth, b. 6 June 1955, Herford, Germany. Author. m. Alan Kramer. Education: English and French Literature, universities of Marburg, Lille and Hamburg; Teachers' training, Hamburg. Appointments: Teacher; Freelance writer (TV, radio, stage and novels), 1986-. Publications: Back to Berlin (radio play), 1991; When the Wall Came Down (stage play), 1998; Der Wintergarten (novel), 2001; Der Nachlass (stage play), 2002; Zeit der Wahrheit (novel), 2003; SOS in Dublin! (children's novel), 2009; Over the Wall (children's novel), 2010; Give Us The Money, Or Else! (children's novel), 2010; Fremde Schwestern (novel), 2011; many others. Honours: Kulturpreis des Kreises Herford, 1989; Christophorus-Autoren-Preis, 1994; Goldener Telix, 1999; Förderpreis des Club Bertelsmann, 2000; 1st Prize, Children's Jury Limburg, 2001. Memberships: Irish Writers' Centre; PEN Centre for German-Speaking Writers Abroad. Address: Rockingham, Nerano Road, Dalkey, Co Dublin, Republic of Ireland. E-mail: info@renate-ahrens.de Website: www.renate-ahrens.de

AHTIALA Pekka, b. 12 June 1935, Helsinki, Finland. Professor of Economics. m. Anna-Maija, 1 son, 2 daughters. Education: BBA, 1956, MBA, 1958, Helsinki School of Economics and Administration; PhD, Harvard University, USA, 1964. Appointments: Teaching Fellow, Instructor, Harvard, early 1960s; Professor of Economics, 1965-99, Dean, Faculty of Economics and Administration, 1969-71, University of Tampere; Minister of the Chancery responsible for Economic Policy, Finnish Government; Visiting Professor of Economics, Northwestern University and Princeton University. Publications: 4 books; Articles in several professional journals. Honours: Blue Cross of Finland; Earhart Prize, Harvard University; Knight Commander of the Order of the Lion of Finland; World Culture Prize: Statue of Victory, Centro Studi e Ricerche Delle Nazioni, Italy, 1985; Best Paper Award, Multinational Finance Journal, 1999; Honorary Member, Junior Chamber International; Honorary Member, Omicron Delta Epsilon. Memberships: Nomination College of the Nobel Prize Committee on Economics; Finnish Economic Association; American Economic Association; European Economic Association. Address: Liutunkuja 3, 36240 Kangasala, Finland.

AICHINGER Ilse, b. 1 November 1921, Vienna, Austria. Novelist; Playwright. Education: University of Vienna, 1945-48. Appointment: Member of Grupe 47, 1951-. Publications: Die Grössere Hoffnung, 1948; Rede Unter dem Galgen, 1953; Eliza, Eliza, 1965; Selected Short Stories and Dialogue, 1966; Nachricht und Tag: Erzählungen, 1970; Schlechte Worter, 1976; Meine Sprache und Ich Erzählungen, 1978; Spiegelesichte: Erzählungen und Dialoge, 1979; Kleist, Moos, Fasane, 1987; Film und Verhängnis, 2001; Plays, Zu Keiner Stunde, 1957, 1980; Besuch im Pfarrhaus, 1961; Auckland: 4 Horspiele, 1969; Knopfe, 1978; Weisse Chrysanthemum, 1979; Radio Plays, Selected Poetry and Prose of Ilse Aichinger, 1983; Collected Works, 8 volumes, 1991. Honours: Belgian Europe Festival Prize, 1987; Town of Solothurn Prize, 1991. Address: c/o Fischer Verlag, Postfach 700480, 6000 Frankfurt, Germany.

AIELLO Danny, b. 20 May 1933, New York City, New York, USA. Actor. m. Sandy Cohen, 1955, 3 sons, 1 daughter. Career: Numerous film appearances including Bang the Drum Slowly, 1973; The Godfather II, 1976; Once Upon a Time in America, 1984; The Purple Rose of Cairo, 1985; Moonstruck, 1987; Do the Right Thing, Harlem Nights, 1989; Jacob's Ladder, 1990; Once Around, Hudson Hawk, The Closer, 29th Street, 1991; Mistress, Ruby, The Pickle, The Cemetery Club, 1992; The Professional, Prêt-à-Porter, Léon, 1994; City Hall, Power of Attorney, 1995; Two Days in the Valley, Mojave Moon, Two Much, 1996; A Brooklyn State of Mind, 1997; Bring Me the Head of Mavis Davis, 1998; Dust, 1999; Prince of Central Park, Dinner Rush, 2000; Off Key, 2001; The Russian Job, Marcus Timberwolf, The Last Request, 2002; Mail Order Bride, 2003; Zeyda and the Hit Man, 2004; Brooklyn Lobster, 2005; Stiffs, Lucky Number Slevin, The Last Request, The Shoemaker, 2006; Theatre appearances including Lamppost Reunion, 1975, Gemini, 1977, Hurlyburly, 1985; The House of Blue Leaves; Appeared in TV films including The Preppie Murder, 1989; A Family of Strangers, 1993; The Last Don, mini-series, Dellaventura, series, 1997; The Last Don II, mini-series, 1998. Honours: Theatre World Award for Lamppost Reunion, 1975; Obie Award for Gemini, 1977; Boston Critics Award, Chicago Critics Award, Los Angeles Critics Award, all for Best Supporting Actor in Do the Right Thing, 1989; Emmy Award for A Family of Strangers, 1993. Address: William Morris Agency, 151 South El Camino Drive, Beverly Hills, CA 90212, USA.

AINSLIE Sir Ben (Charles Benedict), b. 5 February 1977, Macclesfield, England. Competitive Sailor. Education: Truro School; Peter Symonds College, Winchester. Career: Gold (Laser radial), World Championships, Takapuna, 1993; Bronze (Laser), World Championships, Simon's Town, 1996; Silver (Laser), Atlanta Olympics, 1996; Bronze (Laser), World Championships, Algarrobo, 1997; Gold (Laser), World Championships, Melbourne, 1999; Bronze (Laser), World Championships, Cancun, 2000; Gold (Laser), Sydney Olympics, 2000; Gold (Finn), World Championships, Athens, 2002; Gold (Finn), World Championships, Cadiz, 2003; Gold (Finn), World Championships, Rio de Janeiro,

2004; Gold (Finn), Athens Olympics, 2004; Gold (Finn), World Championships, Moscow, 2005; Gold (Finn), World Championships, Melbourne, 2008; Gold (Finn), Beijing Olympics, 2008; Bronze (Etchells), World Championships, Brighton, 2009; Gold (Finn), World Championships, Falmouth, 2012; Gold (Finn), London Olympics, 2012. Honours: British Yachtsman of the Year, 1995, 1999, 2000 and 2002; ISAF World Sailor of the Year, 1998, 2002 and 2008; MBE, 2001; OBE, 2005; CBE, 2009; 5 Olympic Gold Medals, 2012; Knighted, 2013.

AITKIN Don, b. 4 August 1937, Australia. m. (3) Beverley, 9 children. Writer; Strategist; Consultant; Director. Education: MA (1st class honours), History, University of New England, 1961; PhD, Political Science, 1964, later Research Fellow, Australia National University; Travelling Postdoctoral Fellowship, Oxford, England; Institute of Social Research, University of Michigan in Ann Arbor. Appointments: Foundation Professor, Politics, Macquarie University, 1971; Professor, Political Science, Australia National University, 1980; Chairman of the Board, Institute of Advanced Studies, Australian National University, mid 1980s; Member, Australian Science and Technology Council, mid 1980s; Vice Chancellor and President, 1991-2002, Professor Emeritus, 2002, University of Canberra; Vice President, Australian Vice Chancellors Committee, 1994-95; Chairman, Cultural Facilities Corporation of the ACT. Publications: Author/Editor, 13 books, including a novel and a family memoir; Numerous articles in professional and popular journals. Honours: Elected Fellow, Academy of Social Sciences in Australia, 1975; Chairman, Australian Research Grants Committee, mid 1980s; First Chairman, Australian Research Council, 1988; Elected Fellow, Australian College of Educators, 1995; Officer of the Order of Australia, 1998; Honorary Fellow, Royal Australian Planning Institute, 2001; Doctor honoris causa, University of Canberra, 2002; Doctor of Letters honoris causa, University of New England, 2004; Chairman, Australia's National Capital Authority. Memberships: Life Member, Australasian Political Studies Association. Address: 80 Banks Street, Yarralumla, ACT 2600, Australia. E-mail: donaitkin@grapevine.com.au

AKAY Mehmet Fatih, b. 8 May 1977, Adana, Turkey. Academician. m. Emel, 1 daughter. Education: BSc, 1999, MSc, 2001, Electrical and Electronics Engineering, Cukurova University; PhD, Electrical Engineering, Drexel University, 2005. Appointments: Research and Teaching Assistant, 1999-2007, Assistant Professor, 2007-, Cukurova University. Publications: 14 articles; 12 international conference papers; 8 national conference papers. Honours: Design of PC Based Data Collecting and Processing Unit; Third highest degree, Rotary Club Creative Thought Project Competition; Second highest degree, Siemens Creative Thought Project Competition;President's Award, Cukurova University, 1999; Full Scholarship, Turkey Council of Higher Education, 2001-05; Certificate of Appreciation, 2004, Leadership Award, 2005, International House of Philadelphia. Address: Cukurova University, Department of Computer Engineering, Adana, Turkey. E-mail: mfakay@cu.edu.tr Website: http://bmb.cu.edu.tr/fakay

AKSEL Mehmet Haluk, b. 26 December 1953, Ankara, Turkey. Mechanical Engineer. m. Emine Asli Aksel. Education: BS. Mechanical Engineering, 1976, MS, Mechanical Engineering, 1978, Middle East Technical University; PhD, Mechanical Engineering, Lehigh University, Bethlehem, Pennsylvania, USA, 1981. Appointments: Visiting Professor, Department of Mechanical Engineering and Mechanics, Lehigh University, Bethlehem, Pennsylvania, USA, 1981-82; Assistant Professor, Mechanical Engineering, 1982-84, Associate Professor, Mechanical Engineering, 1984-90, Assistant Chairman, Aero Engineering, 1985-87, Professor of Mechanical Engineering, 1990-, Middle East Technical University, Ankara, Turkey; Consultant, Scientific and Technical Research Council of Turkey, 1991-94; Consultant, Turkish Aerospace Industries, 2002-05. Publications: Author or co-author: A Study of Frontogenesis Using the Finite Element and Finite Difference Methods, 1980; A Finite Element Study of Frontogenesis, 1984; A Numerical Simulation of Axisymmetric Vortex Breakdown in a Tube, 1992; Gas Dynamics, 1994. Honour: Research Promotion Grantee, Parlar Foundation, 1992. Memberships: Chamber of Mechanical Engineers, Turkey; Turkish Scientific and Technical Heat Transfer Association; Mechanical Design and Construction Associates. Address: Room G-208, Department of Mechanical Engineering, Middle East Technical University, 06531 Ankara, Turkey. E-mail: aksel@metu.edu.tr Website: http://www.me.metu.edu.tr/people/aksel

AKŞIN I Sina, b. 1937. Professor. m. Tülin, 2 daughters. Education: Graduate, Robert College, 1955; Graduate, Law School, Istanbul University, 1959; MA, 1960, MALD, 1961, International Relations, Fletcher School of Law and Diplomacy, Boston, USA; PhD, Contemporary History, School of Literature, Istanbul University, 1968. Appointments: Instructor, History of Civilization, Robert College, School of Higher Education, 1961-67; Military Service, 1967-69; Teaching Assistant, Turkish Politics, School of Political Science, 1969, Associate Professor, 1975, Elected Chair, Turkish Politics, 1980, Assistant Director, Institute of Social Sciences, 1988, Full Professor, 1989, Chair, Department of Public Administration, 1991, Ankara University; Researcher, British State Archives, United Nations Fellowship, 1971-72; Researcher, 1978-79, 1989-90, French Foreign Ministry Archives; Retired, 2004. Publications: Numerous articles in professional journals; 5 books. Honours: Fulbright Award, 1960-61; Grand Prize, Türkiye İş Bankasi, 1994. Address: Siyasal Bilgiler Fakültesi, Cebeci, 06590 Ankara, Turkey.

AKSIROV Mukhamkhan, b. 10 September 1936, Psygansu, USSR. Senior Research Officer. 2 sons, 2 daughters. Education: PhD, Kalardino Balcorian State University. Appointments: Senior Research Officer, Institute for Informatics and Problems of Regional Management of RAS. Publications: Numerous articles in professional journals; 5 monographs. Honours: RF Medal for Valorous Work. Address: Shortanova 17 FL65K, Kalardino Balcarian Republic, Nalchik 360017, Russia.

AKTAR Md Wasim, b. 4 October 1981, West Bengal, India. Researcher. Education: Diploma, HRD, MSPI, New Delhi; BSc (Hons), Agriculture, 2004, MSc, 2006, PhD, 2010, Agricultural Chemicals, Bidhan Ch Krishi Viswavidyalaya, Mohanpur. Appointments: Research Fellow, BCKV, 2006-07; Analyst, 2007-08, Lab-in-Charge, 2008-09, Export Testing Lab, Nadia; Research Scientist, Krish Biotech Research Pvt Ltd, Nadia, 2009-10; Section-In-Charge, Residue Section, Multilaboratories, SGS India Pvt Ltd, Kolkata, 2010-. Publications: 35 international and 2 national research papers; 1 international review article; 9 international book chapters; many others. Honours: Gold Medal, BCKV; Medal of Achievement, Management Studies Promotion Institute (MSPI), New Delhi. Memberships: Fellow Member, MSPI, New Delhi; Life Member of 8 prestigious societies. Address: S/o Sk Ansar Ali, Namaz Gram (West), Pandua, Hooghly, 712149, West Bengal, India. E-mail: wasim04101981@yahoo.co.in

DICTIONARY OF INTERNATIONAL BIOGRAPHY 36th EDITION

AKULOV Nikolay Ivanovich, b. 1 January 1956, Chita, Transbaikal Edge, Russia. Geologist. m. Barbara Victorovna Koroleva, 1 son, 1 daughter. Education: Diploma in Higher Education, Geological Faculty, Irkutsk Polytechnic Institute, 1978; DSc, Institute of the Earth's Crust, SB RAS, 1985; Professorial diploma, 2005. Appointments: Junior Scientific Worker, 1985-90; Docent, Scientific Worker, 1990-93; Senior Scientific Worker, 1994-2010. Publications: Over 120 scientific articles in professional journals. Honours: Silver Sigma, Academy of Sciences. Memberships: Scientific Council for Awarding Scientific Degrees. Address: 297 "B", 135 Lermontov St, Irkutsk 664033, Russia. E-mail: akulov@crust.irk.ru

AKYOL Ayla, b. 19 April 1940, Istanbul, Turkey. Artist; Art Gallery Owner. m. Selahattin Akyol, 2 sons, 1 daughter. Education: English Literature, Istanbul University; Illumination and Miniature Course with Professor Dr Süheyl Ünver; Studied with artists including Deniz Orkuş, Dara Abadi, Hasan Taşdemir, Ümmet Karaca and Ildar Ahmet Veli. Appointments: Paintings Organiser, Love and Tolerance Train of Mevlana from Konya to Madrid, Turkish Ministry of Culture and Ministry of Foreign Affairs; Exhibitions of work at Akyol Art House, 2003-, and at Büyükada Anadolu Club for Prince Islands Resident Painters; Organiser, Jury Member, Children and Youth Paintings Competition, Anadolu Club. Publications: Subject of numerous articles in newspapers, magazines and books; Listed in international biographical dictionaries. Honours: One painting, The House of Atatürk in Trabzon, continuously exhibited in Beşiktaş Marine Museum; Antalya Golden Orange Film Festival Award, 2002; Listed in international biographical dictionaries; Decree of Excellence in Art, IBC; Deputy Director General for Europe, IBC; 2000 Outstanding Intellectuals of the 21st Century, 2007; Woman of the Year, 2008; Commemorative Golden Medal, Gold Medal for Turkey, ABI, 2009; Director General's Roll of Honour, IBC; The International Medal of Honour, IBC; Award 2009, given by artists of Akyol Art House; Da Vinci Diamond, 2009; Lifetime of Greatness Award, IBC, 2010; Award, Yacht and Sports Club of Princess Islands for Art, 2010; Top Two Hundred of IBC, 2010; Recreation Association Award, 2010; The Final Honours List, IBC, 2011. Memberships: Fine Arts Union; Artists Community; International Plastic Arts Association, UNESCO; Life Fellow, IBC; Anatolian Club of Ankara; Sedef Island's Association; Recreation Association, Turkey. Address: Nisantasi Ihlamur yolu, Demir Palas Apt No 36 D4, Topağaci, Istanbul, Turkey. E-mail: akyolsanat@akyolsanat.com Website: www.akyolsanat.com

AL KHATEEB Mutaz I K M Fakhry, b. 1 January 1962, Baghdad, Iraq. Consultant Cardiothoracic and Vascular Surgeon. m. Nagham Abdul Sattar. Education: Bachelor in Surgery and Medicine, MBchB, Baghdad University, College of Medicine, 1986; Cardiothoracic and Vascular Surgery Board, FIBMS, MD, Fellow, Iraqi Commission for Medical Specialities, MD, 1996; ABSA, USA, 2008; Fundamentals of Clinical Research 101, 2009, Clinical Research 201, 2010, Albert Einstein College of Medicine, USA. Appointments: MD, Internship and Residency program, Baghdad Teaching Hospital, Ibn Alnafis Hospital, Ibn Albitar Hospital, etc; Fellow, Iraqi Board, Cardiovascular and Thoracic Surgery, 1992-96; Specialist Cardiothoracic and Vascular Surgeon, 1996-97; Specialist Cardiothoracic and Vascular Surgeon, Basrah Teaching Hospital, 1997-99; Specialist Cardiothoracic and Vascular Surgery, 1999-2001, Vice Chief, Surgery Department, 2001-03, Head of Surgery Department, 2003-05, Ibn Albitar Centre for Cardiac Surgery, Baghdad; Cardiothoracic and Vascular Surgeon, FIBMS, MD, Head of Thoracic and Vascular Surgery Department, Prince Hamza Hospital, Amman, Jordan, 2005-08; Faculty Member, 2009, Director of Education, 2010-, Drake College of Business, USA. Publications: Numerous articles in professional journals; Surgery in patient ductus arteriosus/Ligation versus excision; Ventricular septal defect, surgery in severe pulmonary hypertension; Cardiac myxoma, the outcome; Cardiac nydatiol cyst, the outcome; Myocardial Revascularization, in severe Lv Function; Adequate versus complete revacularization in CABG; Traumtic vascular injuries of the neck. Honours: Leading World Health Professionals, 2009-11; Man of the Year, 2010; American Order of Merit in Cardiothoracic and Vascular Surgery, 2010; Great Minds of the 21st Century, 2010; Pinnacle of Achievement, 2011; Many recognitions and letters of appreciation from Ministry of Health, Baghdad and Ministry of Health, Jordan; Participation in over 60 national and international congresses; Various recognition and awards by many societies and assemblies; Listed in international biographical dictionaries. Memberships: New Jersey Business/Technology Education Association; Afro-Middle East Hernia Society; STS; ISS; EACTS; Iraqi Medical Association; Jordanian Medical Association; Jordanian Cardiothoracic and Vascular Surgeons; Jordanian Cardiology Society; Albasil Heart Institute; Scientific Assembly of Iraqi Cardiothoracic and Vascular Surgeons; Canadian Thoracic Surgery Society; Fellow, ABI. Address: Drake College of Business, 800 Broad Street, Newark, NJ 07102, USA. E-mail: mutaz_alkhateeb@yahoo.com

AL-ABDULLAH Her Majesty Queen Rania, b. 31 August 1970, Kuwait. Queen of Jordan. m. His Majesty King Abdullah bin Al-Hussein, 2 sons, 2 daughters. Education: Bachelor's degree, Business Administration, American University, Cairo, 1991. Appointments: Career in banking; Worked in field of information technology. Publications: The King's Gift, children's book. Honours: North-South Prize, Council of Europe, 2008. Memberships: Founder, Chairperson, Jordan River Foundation; Foundation Board Member, World Economic Forum; Board Member, GAVI Fund (Global Alliance for Vaccines and Immunization); Board Member, International Youth Foundation; Member, UNICEF Global Leadership Initiative for Children; Regional Ambassador of INJAZ (Junior Achievements World Wide). Address: Royal Hashemite Court, Amman, Jordan.

AL-AMIEDY Munir, b. 1 July 1946, Babylon, Iraq. Specialist Rheumatologist. m. Rugzanattia, 1 son, 3 daughters. Education: MBChB, University of Mosul, Iraq, 1969; Diploma, Rheumatology Rehabilitation, Royal College of Physicians, London University, UK, 1981; Diploma TCM, Chinese Medicine, Shenzhou University, Amsterdam, Netherlands, 2002. Appointments: Lecturer, Rheumatology & Rehabilitation, Al-Mustansiriya University, Kufa Medical College, Iraq, 1983-96. Publications: Rehabilitation Programs in Iraq; International Seminar, Disability & Developing Countries, 1988. Honours: ACR Fellowship; Leading Health Professional, 2011. Memberships: Iraqi Medical Association; Iraqi Rehabilitation & Rheumatology Association; Federation Internationale de Medicine Sportie; UAE Medical Association; Zhong Netherlands Society for Chinese Medicine; PEFOTS; FACRI. Address: Al Biraa Arthritis Clinic, Al Wasl Road, PO Box 191422, Dubai, United Arab Emirates. E-mail: munirdy@yahoo.com

AL-ARRAYED Jalil Ebrahim, b. 26 January 1933. Emeritus Professor; University Administrator. Education: BA, Chemistry, American University, Beirut, Lebanon, 1954; MEd, Science Education, Leicester University, England,

DICTIONARY OF INTERNATIONAL BIOGRAPHY 36th EDITION

1964; PhD, Comparative Science Education and Management of Curriculum Development, Bath University, England, 1974. Appointments: Teacher, Sciences, Maths, 1954-59, Science Inspector, 1959-66, Bahrain Government Department of Education; Principal, Bahrain Men's Teachers Training College, 1966-72; Under-Secretary, Bahrain Ministry of Education, 1974-82; Executive Council Member (Bahrain Rep), 1975-82, Deputy Chairman, 1978-79; Chairman, 1979-80, Arab Bureau of Education for the Gulf States; Member, Bahrain Representative, Council for Higher Education in the Gulf States, 1976-92; Member, Board of Trustees, Bahrain University College of Arts, Science and Education, 1979-86; Member Founding Committee, Arabian Gulf University, 1980-85; Member, IIEP Council of Consultant Fellows, Paris, 1984-92; Rector, Bahrain University College of Arts, Science and Education, 1982-87; Professor of Education, Vice President, Academic Affairs, University of Bahrain, 1987-91, Acting President, 1991; Participant, various regional and international conferences on education reform, and Chair, several committees. Publications: Author of books: A Critical Analysis of Arab School Science Teaching, 1980, Development and Evaluation of University Faculty in Arab Gulf States, 1994, Some Aspects of Contemporary Management Thought, 1996; More than 50 articles on educational issues in general and science education in particular, 1956-78. Honours: Gold Medal for Academic Achievement, Bahrain Government Department of Education, 1969; Prize for Academic Achievement, Bahrain Ministry of Education, 1975; American Biographical Institute Commemorative Medal of Honour, 1988; State Award for Outstanding Citizens, Government of Bahrain, 1992; International Association of University Presidents Certificate for Outstanding Contributions, 1996; Baharat Excellence Award and Gold Medal, Friendship Forum of India, 2009; International Gold Star Award and Gold Medal, 2009. Memberships: Life Fellow, International Biographical Association; Life Member, Indian Institute of Public Administration; Various organizations including: Chartered Management Institute; Institute of Administrative Management, UK; International Association of University Presidents; Royal Society of Chemistry (UK); Listed in numerous biographical dictionaries. Address: PO Box 26165, Adlia, Manama, Bahrain.

AL-ASSAD Asma, b. 11 August 1975, London, England. First Lady of Syria. m. Bashar al-Assad, 2 sons, 1 daughter. Education: BSc (Honours), Computer Science & French, King's College London, 1996; Honorary Doctorate, Archaeology, La Sapienza University, Rome, Italy, 2004. Appointments: Analyst, Hedge Fund Management section of Sales and Trading, Deutsche Morgan Grenfell, London (now Deutsche Bank), 1997; Mergers and Acquisitions for Biotechnology and Pharmaceutical companies, investment banking division of JP Morgan, London (also Paris and New York offices), 1998 –2000; First Lady of Syria, 2000. Address: Presidential Palace, Rawda Square, Damascus, Syrian Arab Republic. E-mail: ofl@mopa.gov.sy

AL-BAYATI T Hamid, b. 1 July 1952, Iraq. Ambassador. Education: BA, 1974; MA, 1980; PhD, 1990. Appointments: Deputy Minister, Foreign Affairs, 2004-06; Ambassador of Iraq to the United Nations, 2006-. Publications: The coup of February 8, 1963 in Iraq: In the British Secret Documents, 1995; The Shia of Iraq: Between Sectarianism and Suspicions, 1996; The Bloody History of Saddam Al Takriti, 1997; The Defeat: The Secret of the Israeli-Arab War of 1967 in the British Secret Reports about Israel and Arab states, 1998; Saddam Hussein and the Great Conspiracy: The Secrets of 17 July 1968 Coup in the US Secret Documents, 2000; The Terrorism Game: 11 September Attacks and New Alliances, 2001; Fall of the Evil, the US and the Iraqi Opposition Plans to Overthrow Saddam Hussein and Iraq's Future, 2003; Quarter of a Century with Mohamad Baqir Al Hakim, 2004; The Iraqi Constitutions, 2005; Terrorism in Iraq: And the Danger of Its Expansion to the Region and the World, 2005; Federalism, 2006; From Dictatorship to Democracy: An Insider's Account of the Iraqi Opposition to Saddam, 2011. Honours: Bronze Medal from Pope Benedict XVI, 2005; Medal of Marine Corps Installation West, 2006; Honoured by Imam Al-Khoei Islamic Center, 2006; Inaugural Lecture, Global Law Society, Fordham University Law School, 2007; Award of People to People, Students Leader Programs, 2007; Medal of Marine Corps University, 2008; Honoured by Iraqi Community, 2008; Doctor of Laws degree, Ignatius University, 2008; Ambassador for Peace, Universal Peace Federation, 2008; Award of Lotus Club, New York, 2009; Spirit of the United Nations Award, NGOs Committee, New York, 2010; Medal of Excellence, Commander of US Central Command General David H Petraeus, 2010; Honoured for Great Services at the United Nations, 2011; Honoured as Guest Professor, Utah Valley University, 2011; Silver Medal, Outstanding People of the 21st Century, 2012; Listed in biographical dictionaries. Address: 14 East 79th Street, New York, NY 10075, USA. E-mail: hamid.al-bayati@un.int

AL-DABBAGH Riadh H, b. 10 September 1946, Mosul, Iraq. Professor. m. 3 children. Education: BSc, Geology, Mosul University, Iraq, 1968; Diploma, Hydrogeology, University College, UK, 1972; MSc, 1972, PhD, 1975, Hydrogeology, London University, England. Appointments: Lecturer, 1968-75, Head, 1975-78, Geology Department, Acting Dean, College of Science, 1976-77, Vice President, Academic Affairs, 1977-82, President, 2001-02, Mosul University, Iraq; Acting President, Diala University, Iraq, 1999-2001; President, Mustansiria University, Iraq, 1982-2001; Professor/Advisor to the President, Ajman University, UAE, 2003-. Publications: Science in Response to Basic Human Needs with Special Reference to Water, 1999. Memberships: Iraqi Academy of Science; Iraq Scientific Research Organization; Iraqi National Committee for Geodesy; Iraqi National Committee for Hydrological Program; IAHS, UNESCO; Arab Universities Union; International Universities Union; Iraq-German Friendship Society; Arab Council for Training University Students in Arab countries. E-mail: riadhdabbagh@yahoo.com

AL-DUWAISAN Khaled Abdelaziz, b. 15 August 1947, Kuwait. Ambassador. m. Dalal Yacoub Al-Homaizi, 1 son, 1 daughter. Education: BA Commerce, Cairo University, Egypt; Postgraduate Diploma, Public Administration, University of Kuwait. Appointments: Diplomatic Attaché, Ministry of Foreign Affairs, 1970-74; Appointed Second Secretary, 1974; Joined Kuwait Embassy in Washington DC, USA, 1975; Appointed Ambassador to the Netherlands, 1984-90; Accredited Ambassador to Romania, 1988; Chairman, Kuwait Delegation for supervision of de-militarised zone between Iraq and Kuwait and Chief Co-ordinator for the return of stolen property, 1991; Ambassador to the United Kingdom, 1993 and accredited to Denmark, Norway and Sweden 1994-95, accredited to The Republic of Ireland, 1995; Joined Advisory Board, Centre of Near and Middle East Studies, School of Oriental and African Studies, 1998. Honours: GCVO (UK), 1995; Freedom of the City of London, 2001; Doyen of the Diplomatic Corps at the Court of St James, 2003; Honorary Certificate, Management of Public Sector Projects and Facilities (Executive Program for Kuwait), Harvard University,

2005; Participant in Workshop of International Diplomacy in the New Century, Kuwait Foundation for the Advancement of Sciences and John F Kennedy School of Government, Harvard University, Cambridge, Massachusetts, 2007; Award of Excellence, British Business Forum and British Ambassador in Kuwait, 2009; Lifetime Contribution to Diplomacy in London, Diplomat Magazine, 2009; Three Faiths Forum Gold Medallion, 2010. Address: Kuwait Embassy, 2 Albert Gate, Knightsbridge, London SW1X 7JU, England.

AL-HAGGAR Mohammad Moh Saleh, b. 15 March 1962, Mansoura, Egypt. Professor. m. Nermin Ahmad, 2 sons, 1 daughter. Education: M B Bch, 1986; MSc, Pediatrics, 1991; MD, Pediatrics, 1995; Practical Training Courses, Biostatics, Dysmorphology, Clinical Genetics, Medical Genetic Counseling, Molecular Genetics. Appointments: Lecturer, Pediatrics, 1998; Assistant Professor, Pediatrics, 2001; Director of Medical Training, Mansoura University Children's Hospital, 2007-; Professor, Pediatrics, 2008-. Publications: Numerous articles in professional journals. Honours: Top 3 Scientific Speakers in Kingdom of Saudi Arabia, 2005; Best Scientific Research Award in Genetics, 2009. Memberships: European Society of Pediatric Research; Egyptian Genetic Society. Address: 2 Aki Street, Gehan Street, Mansoura 35516, Egypt. E-mail: m.alhaggar@yahoo.co.uk

AL-ISSA Mohammed Abdul Kareel, b. 10 June 1965, Saqraa, Kingdom of Saudi Arabia. Minister of Justice. m. Munera N Al-Jofan, 3 sons, 1 daughter. Education: BA, Islamic Law, MA, Comparative Juris Prudence, PhD, Comparative Juris Prudence, Higher Institute of Judiciary Islamic University of Imam Mohammed B Saud. Appointments: Judge, Ministry of Justice; Scientific Researcher, Senior Scholars Commission; Vice-President, Board of Grievances; Lecturer, Faculty of Law; Minister of Justice, 2009-. Publications: Author of various books on judicial topics and all aspects of general administrative law. Honours: Many medals and appreciation certificates from various legal international and local organizations. Memberships: Various legal societies; Supreme Council of Islamic Affairs; SSC; Arab Arbitration Board. Address: BOB 7775, Riyadh 11472, Kingdom of Saudi Arabia. E-mail: muhamd999@gmail.com

AL-MUBARAKI Hanadi Mubarak, b. 1 December 1968, Kuwait City, Kuwait. Assistant Professor; Civil Engineer; Educator. Education: BS (Hons), Civil Engineering, 1992, MSc, Project Management, 1996, Kuwait University; PhD, Business Administration, Washington International University, 2007. Appointments: Intensive Training Programme, Gleeds International UK, 1992; Project Engineer, Amiri Diwan Projects MPW-Turner International, 1993-99; Financial Analyst, Kuwaiti Co, Kuwait City, 1999-2001; Teaching Assistant, Kuwait University, Kuwait City, 2002-; Volunteer, International Community for Helping Human, Kuwait City, 1993-2000; Assistant Professor, Civil Engineering, Kuwait University. Publications: scientific articles in different academic journals; 1 book; Research papers presented in many countries. Honours: Master Degree Medal, Kuwait University, 1996; International Who's Who of Professional Educators, 2003-04; Life Fellow, IBA, 2004; International Peace Prize, United Cultural Convention, 2004; International Educator of the Year, IBC, 2004; IBC Medal, 2005; DDG Medal, 2005; International Computer Driving License Course ICDL, 2005; Who's Who in Science and Engineering, 2005-06; Madison Who's Who of Professionals, 2005-06; International Who's Who of Professionals, 2005-06; Key of Success, Teaching Excellence, USA, 2006; International Who's Who of Professional Educators, 2006-07; Who's Who in the World, 2009-12; Deputy Director General of Asia, IBC; 21st Century Award for Achievement, IBC; Shike Jabar Alahmed, Kuwait University; Presidential Seal of Honor, Professional Education, USA; Deputy Director General of Asia, IBC; International Peace Prize, United Cultural Convention. Memberships: Institution of Civil Engineering, UK; Kuwait Society of Engineers; Harvard Business School; Forbers Global; IAPA; IBC; ABI; IWW; NBIA; IBA; ECONOMIS; MTI. Address: PO Box 39964, Nuzha 39964, Kuwait. E-mail: pro5383526@yahoo.com Website: www.hm-almubaraki.org

AL-MURRANI Waleed, b. June 1938, Iraq. University Professor. Selma Al-Sam, 1 son, 3 daughters. Education: BVM and S, Veterinary Sciences, Iraq, 1961; Training diploma, Bradford University, England, 1968; PhD, Edinburgh University, Scotland, 1973. Appointments: Lecturer, 1961-66, Assistant Professor, 1974-82, Head, Department of Veterinary Public Health, 1974-82, 1990-99, 2003-04, Professor, Genetics and Biostatistics, 1990-99, 1999-2003, 2003-04, College of Veterinary Medicine, Director of Higher Studies & Scientific Affairs, Professor of Genetics, Breeding and Biostatistics, 1986-90, Professor, Genetics, Biostatics and Transgenesis, Institute of Genetic Engineering and Biotechnology for Higher Studies, 2004-06, Baghdad University, Iraq; Technical Adviser to the Director General, Arab Organization for Agricultural Development, Khartoum, Sudan, 1982-86; Professor, School of Biological Sciences, Plymouth University, England, 2006-. Publications: Around 100 international, regional and local journals. Honours: Holder, First Class National Iraqi Award for Scientific Achievements, 1999-2002;Listed in international biographical dictionaries. Memberships: Iraqi Society of Veterinary Sciences; Iraqi Association of Translators.

AL-NAJJAR Mohammad A A, b. 26 February 1972, Kuwait. Scientist. m. Siham al-Amoush, 2 sons, 1 daughter. Education: BSc, Biology, Yarmouk University, Jordan, 1994; Masters, 2007, PhD, 2010, Marine Microbiology, Max-Planck Institute, Bremen, Germany. Appointments: Microbiology Laboratory Supervisor, Jordan, 1994-99; Microbiology Laboratory Specialist, United Arab Emirates University, UAE, 1999-2005; Postdoctorate, Max-Planck Institute, Bremen, Germany, 2011-. Publications: Microbiological and Chemical Quality of Drinking water in Mafraq Area, 2001; Effect of temperature on photosynthesis, oxygen consumption and sulfide production in an extremely hypersaline cynobacterial mat, 2006; Modular Spectral Imaging System for Discrimination of Pigments in Cells and Microbial Communities, 2009; Hyper-spectral imaging of biofilm growth dynamics, 2009; Conversion and conservation of light energy in a photosynthetic microbial mat ecosystem, 2010; Comparison of light utilization efficiency in photosynthetic microbial mats. Honours: MPI Scholarship for Masters Studies. Memberships: Dutch Society for Microbiology; International Society for Microbial Ecology. Address: Max-Planck Institute, Celsius str 1, 28359 Bremen, Germany. E-mail: malnajja@mpi-bremen.de

AL-RUBAYE Kadhim Qasim Ali, b. 1 July 1947, Maysanm, Iraq. Consultant Dermatologist. m. Ashwaq Isaac, 2 sons, 3 daughters. Education: Bachelor's degree, Medicine & Surgery, Basra, 1973; Diploma, Dermatology, 1982, Diploma, History of Medicine, 1982, London, UK; Tropical Medicine and Hygiene, Liverpool, UK, 1982; Diploma, Veneriology, Liverpool, 1983; PhD, Dermatoepidemiology, Basra, 2001. Appointments: Assistant Professor, Dermatology, Basra College of Medicine; Examiner, Iraqi Board of Dermatology,

DICTIONARY OF INTERNATIONAL BIOGRAPHY 36th EDITION

1987-, Chief Executive, 1992-93, Clinical Director, 1993-, Examiner, Arab Board of Dermatology, 1993-, Head, Out-patient Department, 1998-, Head, Department of Dermatology, 1998-, Head, Dermatology Research and Development Office, 1998-, Basra General Hospital; Lead Consultant, Medical Library of Basra College of Medicine, 2000-; Editor, Al-Tahreer Medical Journal, 2002-; Chief Editor, AlFida's Journal of the Iraqi Red Cross, 2003. Publications: Numerous articles in professional journals. Honours: Patent, Lecitithin is an inhibitor of the exfoliative exotoxin of staphylococcus aureus, 1997; Head, Anthrax Research Center, Basra Medical Directorate; Member, Scientific Research Center, Basra College of Veterinary Medicine; Research Distinction Certificate, Minister of Health for reporting 2 cases of Miaysis for the first time in Basra, 1992; Clinical Director, Basra Research Center, Basra General Hospital. Memberships: International Dermatoepidemiology Association; Dermatology Association; American Medical Association; Iraqi Dermatology Association; Arabic Dermatology Association; Iraqi Diabetes Association. Address: College of Medicine, University of Basra, Basra, Iraq. E-mail: k.alrubaye@gmail.com

AL-THANI Hamad bin Jassim bin Jabor (Sheikh), b. 1959, Doha, Qatar. Prime Minister; Minister of Foreign Affairs. Appointments: Director, Office of the Minister of Municipality Affairs and Agriculture, 1982-89; Minister of Municipality Affairs and Agriculture, 1989; Minister of Urban Affairs and Agriculture, and responsibilities of Ministry of Electricity and Water, 1990; Minster of Foreign Affairs, 1995-; First Deputy Prime Minister, 2003; Prime Minister, 2007-. Honours: Grand officier de la légion d'honneur, France, 1958; Grand-croix de l'ordre national du Mérite, France, 2007; Grand Cordon of the National Order of the Cedar, Lebanon, 2007; Diploma Magistralle dei Onorificenza, Italy, 2007; Honorary Special Medal, Ministry of the Interior of the Russian Federation, 2010; Honorary Doctorate, State Institute of International Relations, Moscow, 2010; Honorary Doctorae, Lebanese American University, Beirut, 2010. Memberships: Arab Thought Forum, Amman; Club de Monaco, France; Advisory Council of the Brookings Institution, USA; International Advisory Council, Brookings Doha Centre. Address: Ministry of Foreign Affairs, POB 250, Doha, Qatar.

AL-TURKI Abdullah Bin Abdul Mohsen, b. 1940. Secretary General of the Muslim World League. Education: BA, Islamic Law, Shari'ah College, Riyadh, 1963; MA, Higher Institute of Justice, Riyadh, 1969; PhD, Fundamentals of Islamic Jurisprudence, Al-Azhar University, Cairo, 1973. Appointments: Ministry of Islamic Affairs, Endowments, Call and Guidance, Riyadh, Saudi Arabia, 1995-99; Secretary General, Muslim World League, Makkah, Al-Mukarramah, Saudi Arabia, 2000-; General Supervisor, King Fahad Complex for printing the Holy Quran. Address: Muslim World League, PO Box 537, Makkah, Saudi Arabia.

ALAGIAH George, b. 21 November 1955, Sri Lanka. Journalist; Television News Presenter. m. 2 sons. Education: Graduate, Durham University. Appointments: Journalist, South Magazine, 7 years; Contributed to The Guardian, the Daily Telegraph, The Independent, the Daily Express; Joined BBC, 1989; Foreign Correspondent and specialist on Africa and the developing world; Currently Co-Presenter BBC's Six O'Clock News, 2003-; Launched BBC4's international news programme, 2004; Presenter of a new programme on BBC World, World News Today, 2006; Has reported on: Trade in human organs in India; Murder of street children in Brazil; Civil war and famine in Somalia; Genocide in Rwanda and its aftermath; Plight of marsh Arabs in southern Iraq; Civil wars in Afghanistan, Liberia and Sierra Leone; Truth and Reconciliation Commission in South Africa; Fall of Mobuto Sese Seko in Zaire; Effects of Hurricane Mitch on Honduras; Kosovan refugee crisis; NATO liberation of Pristina; International intervention in East Timor; Farm invasions in Zimbabwe, Intifada in the West Bank; Aftermath of the terror attacks on New York; Documentaries and features include: Saddam Hussein's genocidal campaign against the Kurds of northern Iraq; The last reunion of the veterans of Dunkirk and a BBC 1 Special on the trial and conviction of Jill Dando's murderer. Publications: Book, A Passage to Africa, 2001; Essay, Shaking the Foundations, in the BBC's book on the aftermath of September 11. Honours include: Critics Award and Golden Nymph Award, Monte Carlo Television Festival, 1992; Award for Best International Report, Royal Television Society, 1993; Commendation, BAFTA, 1993; Amnesty International's Best TV Journalist Award, 1994; One World Broadcasting Trust Award, 1994; James Cameron Memorial Trust Award, 1995; Bayeux Award for War Reporting, 1996; Media Personality of the Year, Ethnic Minority Media Award, 1998; BAFTA Award for coverage of the Kosovo conflict (BBC Team), 2000; Madoc Award, Hay Literary Festival, 2002; OBE, 2008. Memberships: Patron: The Presswise Trust; NAZ Project; Parenting, Education and Support Forum; Fairtrade Foundation. Address: British Broadcasting Corporation, BBC News Publicity, Television Centre, Wood Lane, London W12 7RJ, England.

ALAGNA Roberto, b. 7 June 1963, Clichy-sur-Bois, France. Singer (Tenor). m. (1) Florence Lancien, deceased 1994, 1 daughter, (2) Angela Gheorghiu, 1996. Education: Studied in France and Italy. Debut: Plymouth, 1988, as Alfredo in La Traviata for Glyndebourne Touring Opera. Career: Sang Rodolfo at Covent Garden (1990) and has returned for Gounod's Roméo and Don Carlos, 1994-96; sang Donizetti's Roberto Devereux at Monte Carlo (1992) and the Duke of Mantua at the Vienna Staatsoper (1995); Sang Don Carlos at the Théâtre du Châtelet, Paris, 1996; American appearances at Chicago and New York (debut at Met 1996, as Rodolfo); Alfredo at La Scala, Milan; Opened the 2006-07 season in Aida at La Scala, Milan. Recordings include: video of Gounod's Roméo et Juliette (Pioneer); La Traviata, from La Scala (Sony) and Don Carlos, Paris; Duets and Arias (with Angela Gheorghiu), La Boheme 1996, Don Carlos 1996, La Rondine 1997. Honours include: Winner, Pavarotti Competition, 1988; Chevalier des Arts et des Lettres; Personalite Musicale de l'Annee, 1994; Laurence Olivier Award for Outstanding Achievement in Opera, 1995; Victor Award for Best Singer, 1997. Address: c/o Lévon Sayan, 9 chemin de Plonjon, Geneva, Switzerland.

ALAGOA Ebiegberi Joe, b. 14 April 1933, Nembe, Nigeria. Historian. m. Mercy, 1 son, 1 daughter. Education: St Luke's School, 1943-48; Government College, Umuahia, 1948-54; University College, Ibadan, (London University) 1954-59; University of Wisconsin, Madison, Wisconsin, USA, 1962-65. Appointments: Deputy Vice-Chancellor, University of Port Harcourt, 1980-81; Pro-Chancellor, Niger Delta University, 2001-03; Chairman, Governing Board, Rev D O Ockiya College of Theology and Management Sciences, Emeyal, Bayelsa State, 2004-. Publications: 29 books; 3 archival monographs; 49 contributions to books; 47 journal articles. Honours: Fellow, Historical Society of Nigeria, 1981; Officer of the Order of the Niger, 2000; Fellow, Nigerian Academy of Letters, 2001; Award of Excellence, Bayelsa State Government, 2004; Emeritus Professor of History, University of Port Harcourt, 2005; various research fellowships. Memberships: Historical Society of Nigeria; Diabetes Association of Nigeria; Diabetes UK. Address: 11 Orogbum Crescent, GRA Phase II, Port Harcourt, Rivers State, Nigeria. E-mail: kala_joe@yahoo.com

ALBA Jessica, b. 28 April 1981, Pomona, California, USA. Actress. m. Cash Warren, 2008, 1 daughter. Career: Films: Camp Nowhere, 1994; Venus Rising, 1995; PUNKS, Never Been Kissed, Idle Hands, 1999; Paranoid, 2000; The Sleeping Dictionary, Honey, 2003; Sin City, Fantastic Four, Into the Blue, 2005; Knocked Up, Fantastic Four: Rise of the Silver Surfer, The Ten, Good Luck Chuck, Awake, 2007; The Eye, Meet Bill, The Love Guru, 2008; An Invisible Sign of My Own, 2009; The Killer Inside Me, Sin City 2, Machete, Valentine's Day, 2010; TV: Flipper, 1995-97; Dark Angel, 2000-02; many guest appearances on other TV programmes. Honours: ALMA Award, 2001; Young Hollywood Awards, 2005; Spike TV Guy's Choice Awards, 2007.

ALBARELLA Joan, b. 22 September 1944, New York, New York, USA. Teacher of English; Poet. Education: BSc, 1962, MSEd, 1966, State University of New York at Buffalo. Appointments: Publisher, Alpha Press, 1971-2003; Journalist, Western New York Catholic, 1975-88; Professor of English, State University of Buffalo, 1996-2005. Publications: Nikki Barnes Mysteries: Agenda for Murder, 1999; Called to Kill, 2000; Close to You, 2003; Sister Amnesia, 2009; Four books of poetry: Mirror Me; Poems for the Asking; Women, Flowers, Fantasy; Spirit of Joy; Two plays: Katherine Hepburn's Brownies; Mother Cabrini's Mission to America. Honours: EOC Eighteen, 1988; Oxner-Lytle Distinguished Service Award, 1999; Sisters of Social Service Appreciation Award, 2003; Professor Emeritus. Memberships: Mystery Writers of America; Sisters in Crime; Italian-American Writers; Poets & Writers. Address: 337 Summit Ave, Buffalo, NY 14224, USA.

ALBARN Damon, b. 23 March 1968, Whitechapel, London, England. Singer; Songwriter. 1 daughter with partner Suzi Winstanley. Education: Drama School, Stratford East, 1 year. Musical Education: Part-time Music course, Goldsmith's College. Career: First solo concerts, Colchester Arts Centre; Member, Blur; Numerous television and radio appearances, include: Later With Jools Holland; Top Of The Pops; Loose Ends, Radio 4; Later With... Britpop Now; Extensive tours, concerts include: Alexandra Palace, Reading Festival, 1993; Glastonbury, 1994; Mile End, 1995; V97, UK Arena Tour, 1997; Glastonbury, 1998; T in the Park, Reading and Leeds Festival, 1999; Actor, film, Face, 1997; Score for Ravenous, 1998; Score for Ordinary Decent Criminal, 1999; score for 101 Reykjavik (with Einar Benediktsson), 2000; Score for Monkey: Journey to the West, 2008. Recordings: Albums: with Blur: Leisure, 1991; Modern Life Is Rubbish, 1993; Parklife, 1994; The Great Escape, 1995; Blur, 1997; 13, 1999; Best of Blur 2000; Think Tank, 2003; (with Gorillaz) Gorillaz, 2001; G-Slides, 2002; Phase One: Celebrity Take Down, 2002; We Are Happy Landfill, 2005; Demon Days, 2005; The Good, the Bad & the Queen, 2007; D-Sides, 2007; Midlife: a Beginner's Guide to Blur, 2009; Singles: She's So High, 1990; There's No Other Way, Bang, 1991; Popscene, 1992; For Tomorrow, Chemical World, Sunday Sunday, 1993; Girls And Boys, To The End, Parklife, End Of A Century, 1994; Country House, The Universal, 1995; Stereotypes, 1996; Beetlebum, Song 2, On Your Own, MOR, 1997; Tender, Coffee and TV, No Distance Left To Run, 1999; Music is My Radar, (with Gorillaz) Clint Eastwood, 2000; 19-2000, Rock the House, 2001; Tomorrow Comes Today, 2002; Solo: Original score for film Ravenous, directed by Antonia Bird, with Michael Nyman, 1998; Score for film Ordinary Decent Criminal, directed by Thasseus O'Sullivan, 1999; Mali Music, various contributors, 2002; Democrazy, 2003. Honours: Mercury Prize Nomination; Platinum album, Parklife; BRIT Awards: Best Single, Video, Album and Band, 1995; Q Awards, Best Album, 1994, 1995; Mercury Music Prize nomination, 1999; Platinum albums. Honorary MA, University of East London, 2006. Current Management: CMO Management, Unit 32, Ransome Dock, 35-37 Parkgate Road, London SW11 4NP, England.

ALBEE Edward (Franklin III), b. 12 March 1928, Virginia, USA. Playwright. Education: Trinity College, Hartford, Connecticut, 1946-47. Appointments: Lecturer at various US colleges and universities. Publications: Plays: The Zoo Story, 1958; The Death of Bessie Smith, The Sandbox, 1959; The American Dream, 1960; Who's Afraid of Virginia Woolf?, 1962; Tiny Alice, 1963; A Delicate Balance, 1966; Box, Quotations from Chairman Mao, 1970; All Over, 1971; Seascape, 1975; Counting the Ways, 1976; Listening, 1977; The Lady from Dubuque, 1979; Finding the Sun, 1982; The Man Who Had Three Arms, 1983; Marriage Play, 1987; Three Tall Women, 1991; Fragments, 1993; The Play about the Baby, 1996; The Goat, or, Who is Sylvia? 2000; Occupant, 2001; Peter and Jerry (Act 1: Home Life, Act 2: The Zoo Story), 2004; Me, Myself and I, 2007; At Home At The Zoo, 2009. Adaptions of: Carson McCuller's The Ballad of the Sad Café, 1963; James Purdy's Malcolm, 1965; Giles Cooper's Everything in the Garden, 1967; Vladimir Nabokov's Lolita, 1980. Honours: Tony Awards, 1963, 1965, 2002, 2005; Pulitzer Prizes in Drama, 1967, 1975, 1994; American Academy and Institute of Arts and Letters Gold Medal, 1980; Theater Hall of Fame, 1985; Tony Award for Lifetime Achievement, 2005. Memberships: Dramatists Guild Council; Edward F Albee Foundation, president. Address: 14 Harrison Street, New York, NY 10013, USA.

ALBERT II, b. 6 June 1934, Belgium. King of Belgium. m. Donna Paola Ruffo Di Calabria, 1959, 2 sons, 1 daughter. Appointments: Formerly Prince of Liege; Former Vice Admiral of Navy; President, Caisse d'Epargne et de Retraite, 1954-92; President, Belgian Red Cross, 1958-93; President, Belgian Office of Foreign Trade, 1962; Appointed by Council of Europe as President of Conference of European Ministers responsible for protection of Cultural and Architectural Heritage, 1969; Participant in Numerous Conferences on environment including UN Conference, Stockholm, 1972; Chair, Belgian Olympic and Interfed Committee; Succeeded to the throne 9 August 1993 following death of his brother King Baudouin I. Address: Cabinet of the King, The Royal Place, rue Bréderode, 1000 Brussels, Belgium.

ALBERT II, His Serene Highness Prince Albert Alexandre Louis Pierre, b. 14 March 1958. Sovereign Prince of Monaco and Marquis of Baux. Education: Albert I High School; Amherst College, Massachusetts, USA. Appointments: 1st Class Ensign (Sub-Captain); President, Monegasque Delegate to General Assembly, UN, 1993-; Chair, several sports federations and committees; Chair, Organising Committee, Monte Carlo International Television Festival, 1988-; Deputy Chair, Princess Grace Foundation of Monaco; named Sovereign Prince of Monaco, 2005; Honorary President, International Athletic Foundation, International Modern Pentathlon Union, World Beach Volleyball; Honorary Citizen of Fort Worth, 2000; Honorary Chair, Jeune Chambre Economique, Monaco Aide et Presence; Honorary Member, St Petersburg Naval Association; International Institute for Human Rights; Honorary Professor of International Studies, Tarrant County College, Fort Worth, 2000. Honours: Grand Cross, Order of Grimaldi, 1958; Grand Officier, National

Order of the Lion of Senegal, 1977; Grand Cross, Order of Saint-Charles, 1979; Knight Grand Cross, Equestrian Order of the Holy Sepulchre of Jerusalem, 1983; Grand Officer, Legion of Honour, 1984; Colonel of the Carabineers, 1986; Chevalier, Order of Malta, 1989; Grand Officer, Merite International du Sang, 1994; Grand Cross, National Order of Merit, 1997; Grand Cross, National Order of Niger, 1998; Grand Cross of the Jordanian Renaissance (Nahdah Medal), 2000; Grand Cross, Order of the Sun of Peru, 2003; Grand Cross, Order Juan Mora Fernandez, Costa Rica, 2003; Order of Stara Planina, Bulgaria, 2004; Dr hc, Pontifical University, Maynooth, 1996. Address: Palais Princier, BP 518, MC 98015, Monaco. Website: www.palais.mc

ALBERTI Luiz Ronaldo, b. 11 November 1976, Varginha, Brazil. Physician. m. Roberta Gazzi Salum. Education: Graduate, Medicine, 2001; General Surgeon, 2003; Master of Science, 2003; PhD, 2005; Paediatric Surgeon, 2006; Gastroenterologist, 2007. Appointments: General Surgeon; Paediatric Surgeon; Gastroenterologist; Professor of Surgery, Surgery Department of the Federal University of Minas Gerais. Publications: 100 articles published in international journals; Many book chapters; Over 400 presentations in congress. Honours: 38 national and international honours and awards. Memberships: Brazilian College of Surgeons; Brazilian Federation of Gastroenterology; Brazilian Society of Digestive Endoscopy. Address: Rua Professor Baroni 151/ Apt 0401, Bairro Gutierrez, Belo Horizonte, 30440-140, Brazil. E-mail: luizronaldo@zipmail.com.br

ALBRIGHT Carol Rausch, b. 20 March 1936, Evergreen Park, Illinois, USA. Writer; Editor; Retired Foundation Administrator. m. (1) Saul Gorski, deceased, 2 sons, (2) John Albright, 1991. Education: BA, Augustana College, Rock Island, Illinois, 1956; Graduate Study, Lutheran Schools of Theology, Chicago, Berkeley, Washington University, St Louis. Appointments: Director, Lutheran Campus Ministry, Oregon State University, 1958-61; Publishing Consultant, 1966-70; Assistant Editor, World Book Encyclopaedia, 1970-75; Publishing Consultant, 1975-98; Contributing Editor, Doctor I've Read...., 1983-93; Executive Editor, Zygon: Journal of Religion and Science, 1989-98; Managing Editor, Science and Religion South, 1995-99; Publisher, Bridge Building, 1999; Co-Director, John Templeton Foundation Science and Religion Course Programme, Southern US, 1995-99; Co-Director, CTNS Science and Religion course programme, Midwestern US,1999-2001; Visiting Professor of Religion and Science, Lutheran School of Theology at Chicago, 2006-. Publications: Beginning with the end: God, Science, and Wolfhart Pannenberg; The Humanizing Brain; Where God Lives in the Human Brain; Growing in the Image of God; NeuroTheology. Honours: Academic Achievement Award, Institute for Religion in an Age of Science; Phi Beta Kappa; Chicago Women in Publishing: Award for Excellence in Periodical Writing. Memberships: Treasurer, Centre for Advanced Study in Religion and Science; Board Member, Copenhagen University Science and Religion Network; Executive Council, American Theological Society, Midwest Division; Institute for Religion in an Age of Science; Augustana Lutheran Church of Hyde Park; European Society for the study of Science and Theology; Society of Midland Authors. Address: 5436 S Hyde Park Blvd, Chicago, IL 60615, USA.

ALBRIGHT Madeleine Korbel, b. 15 May 1937, Prague, Czechoslovakia (US citizen). Former Government Official; Diplomatist; International Affairs Adviser. m. Joseph Albright, 1959, divorced 1983, 3 daughters. Education: Wellesley College; Columbia University. Appointments: Professor, International Affairs, Georgetown University, 1982-83; Head, Centre for National Policy, 1985-93; Chief Legislative Assistant to Democratic Senator Edmund Muskie, 1976-78; Member, National Security Council Staff in Carter Administration, 1978-81; Advisor, Democratic candidates, Geraldine Ferraro, 1984, and Michael Dukakis, 1988; Permanent Representative to United Nations, 1993-97; Secretary of State, 1997-2001; Co-founder, Principal, The Albright Group LLC, 2001-; Chair, National Democratic Institute for International Affairs, Washington DC, 2001-; Chair, The PEW Global Attitudes Project; President, Truman Scholarship Foundation. Publications: Poland: the Role of the Press in Political Change, 1983; Madam Secretary: A Memoir, 2003; The Mighty and the Almighty: Reflections on America, God, and World Affairs, 2006; Memo to the President Elect: How We Can Restore America's Reputation and Leadership, 2008; Read My Pins, 2009; numerous articles. Honours: Menschen In Europa Award, 2006. Memberships: Board, New York Stock Exchange; Council on Foreign Relations; American Political Science Association; American Association for Advancement of Slavic Studies. Address: 901 15th Street, NW, Suite 1000, Washington, DC 20005, USA.

ALBU Dragos Nicolae, b. 18 September 1974, Pitesti, Romania. Medical Educator. m. Alice Ioana Alimanescu, 2000, 1 daughter. Education: MD, 1999, Assistant Professor, 2005, Master, Management, 2007, PhD, Ecocardiography, 2009, UMF Carol Davila. Appointments: Resident, Ob-Gyn, 2001-05, Assistant Professor, 2005-, UMF Carol Davila. Publications: Numerous articles in professional journals. Honours: Listed in international biographical dictionaries. Memberships: RSUOG; FIGO. Address: Panait Cerna, Sector 3, Bl. M52, Sc3, Ap67, Bucharest 030991, Romania. E-mail: dragosnicolaealbu@yahoo.com

ALCAINO Gonzalo, b. 28 May 1936, Santiago, Chile. Architect; Astronomer. 1 son, 1 daughter. Education: Architect, Catholic University of Chile, 1960; Graduate Studies, Astronomy, Indiana University, USA, 1961-64. Appointments: Founder and President, Isaac Newton Institute of Astronomy, 1978-. Publications: Numerous articles in professional journals. Memberships: International Astronomical Union; American Astronomical Society. Address: Fernandez Concha 472, Las Condes, Santiago, Chile.

ALCARAZ Jose Luis, b. 3 July 1963, Hellin, Albacete, Spain. Engineering University Professor. Education: Bachelor, Murcia, Spain, 1981; Graduated in Industrial Engineering, Valencia, Spain, 1988; Doctor in Industrial Engineering, San Sebastian, Spain, 1993. Assistant Lecturer, Valencia, Spain, 1988-89; San Sebastian, Spain, 1989-93, Bilbao, Spain, 1993-94; Full Professor, Bilbao, Spain, 1994-. Publications: Books: Theory of Plasticity and Applications, 1993; Elasticity and Strength of Materials, 1995; Elastic, Plastic and Viscous Behaviour of Materials, 2002; Contributed papers to international journals. Honour: Graduation Special Award, 1988. Memberships: European Mechanics Society; New York Academy of Sciences; Spanish Association for Mechanical Engineering. Address: Dep Ingenieria Mecánica, Escuela Superior de Ingenieros, Alameda Urquijo, s/n, 48013 Bilbao, Spain.

ALDA Alan, b. 28 January 1936, New York, USA. Actor. m. Arlene Weiss, 3 daughters. Education: Fordham University. Appointments: Performed with Second City, 1963; Broadway roles in The Owl and the Pussycat, Purlie Victorious, Fair Game of Lovers, The Apple Tree, Our Town, London, 1991, Jake's Women, 1992. Creative Works: Films include: Gone are the Days, 1963; Paper Lion, The Extraordinary Seaman,

1968; The Moonshine War, Jenny, 1970; The Mephisto Waltz, 1971; To Kill a Clown, 1972; California Suite, Same Time Next Year, 1978; The Seduction of Joe Tynan, also wrote screenplay, 1979; Four Seasons, 1981; Sweet Liberty, 1986; A New Life, 1987; Crimes and Misdemeanours, 1989; Betsy's Wedding, 1990; Whispers in the Dark, 1992; And the Band Played On, Manhattan Murder Mystery, 1993; White Mile, 1994; Canadian Bacon, 1995; Everybody Says I Love You, 1996; Murder at 1600, Mad City, 1997; The Object of My Affection, 1998; What Women Want, 2000; The Aviator, 2004; The West Wing, 2004-06; Resurrecting the Champ, 2007; Diminished Capacity, Flash of Genius, Nothing But the Truth, 2008; Numerous TV includes: The Glass House, 1972; MASH, 1972-83; The West Wing, 1999; Club Land, The Killing Yard, 2001; 30 Rock, 2009. Honours: Theatre World Award; 5 Emmy Awards; 2 Directors Guild Awards; Writers Guild Award; 7 Peoples Choice Awards; Humanities Award for Writing; 5 Golden Globe Awards. Memberships: Trustee, Museum of TV and Radio; Rockefeller Foundation; President, National Commission for Observance of International Women's Year, 1976; Co-chair, National ERA Countdown Campaign, 1982. Address: c/o Martin Bregman Productions, 641 Lexington Avenue, NY 10022, USA.

ALDERMAN Minnis Amelia, b. 14 October 1928, Douglas, Georgia, USA. Counsellor; Psychologist; Business Woman, Executive. Education: AB, Music and Speech Dramatics, Georgia State College at Milledgeville, 1949; MA, Guidance, Counselling, Psychology, Supervision, Murray State University, Kentucky, 1960; PhD, Psychology and Performing Arts, ongoing. Appointments: Private music instructor, piano, violin, voice, organ 1981-; Band Director for Sacred Heart School 1982-98; Associate Dean, Professor and Head of Fine Arts Department, Wassuk College 1986-87; Academic Dean, Wassuk College 1987-90; Choir Director and Organist, Sacred Heart Church; Director, Ely Shoshone Tribal Child and Family Center and the Family and Community Center (ICWA and Social Services) 1988-93; Professor, Music Appreciation, General Psychology, Educational Psychology, Human Resource Management, Human Relations, Humanities, Great Basin College. Publications: Numerous articles, pamphlets, handbooks, journals and newsletters on guidance-counselling, functions and organisation in education, pupil personnel programs, music instruction and practice, social services programs, youth problems, mental health, problems of ageing and geriatrics, tribal law; news articles and feature stories for newspapers and state organisations' publications. Honours include: Fellowship recipient to University of Utah in geriatric psychology 1974; Fellowship, University of Utah, 1975; American Biographical Institute, nominee for Most Admired Woman of the Decade, 1994; Delta Kappa Gamma Rose of Recognition Award, 1994. Memberships include: Delta Kappa Gamma; International Platform Association; American Association of University Women; National Federation of Business and Professional Women; Eastern Nevada Child and Family Services Advisory Committee; Society of Descendants of Knights of the Most Noble Order of the Garter; National Association of Parliamentarians. Address: P O Box 150457, East Ely, NV 89315, USA.

ALDINGTON Peter John, b. 14 April 1933, Preston, Lancashire, England. Architect. m. Margaret, 2 daughters. Education: University of Manchester, School of Architecture. Appointments: Architect, London County Council Architects Housing Division, 1956-62; Timber Research and Development Association, 1962-63; Own Practice, Peter Aldington, 1963-70; Aldington & Craig, 1970-80; Aldington, Craig & Collinge, 1980-86; Visiting Critic, Sheffield University, 1975-95; Visiting lecturer at many Schools of Architecture; External Examiner, Birmingham, 1978-81, Newcastle, 1980-82, Leicester, 1982-85, London South Bank, 1983-87, Leeds, 1985-89; Lecturer, Vienna School of Architecture, 1979, and Cincinnati Centre for Urban Design, 1991; RIBA Council Member, 1976-79; Sat on seven RIBA committees (represented RIBA on others); Royal Gold Medal jury member, 1978, 1979; Assessor for many design awards and competitions; Retired, 1986; Garden Designer, 1986-; Practice archive (1963-86) donated to British Architectural Library; Formed Turn End Charitable Trust to ensure the future of Turn End and associated buildings 'to foster the integration of architecture and landscape thinking', 1998-; Member, English Heritage Post War Steering Group, 2000-03. Publications: Work published in 40 books in UK and Europe; 1 monograph, 2009; Work published over 300 times in 11 countries worldwide, 1963-88. Honours: Order of the British Empire, 1987; 14 Design Awards; 1 award for landscape; Two buildings listed as of Special Architectural or Historic Interest at Grade 2*, and five at Grade 2. Memberships: Associate, Royal Institute of British Architects; Member, Chartered Society of Designers. Address: Turn End, Townside, Haddenham, Aylesbury, Buckinghamshire HP17 8BG, England. E-mail: turnend@gotadsl.co.uk

ALDISS Brian Wilson, b. 18 August 1925, East Dereham, England. Literary Editor; Writer; Critic. m. (2) Margaret Manson, 11 December 1965, 2 sons, 2 daughters. Appointments: President, British Science Fiction Association, 1960-64; Guest of Honour at World Science Fiction Convention, London, 1965, World Science Fiction Convention Brighton, 1979; Chairman, Committee of Management, Society of Authors, 1977-78; Arts Council Literature Panel, 1978-80; Booker McConnell Prize Judge, 1981; Fellow, Royal Society of Literature, 1990; Prix Utopia, 1999; Grand Master of Science Fiction, 2000. Publications: Novels include: Hothouse, 1962; Frankenstein Unbound, 1973; The Malacia Tapestry, 1976; Life in the West, 1980; The Helliconia Trilogy, 1982, 1983, 1985, 1996; Forgotten Life, 1988; Dracula Unbound, 1991; Remembrance Day, 1993; Somewhere East of Life, 1994; Story collections include: Seasons in Flight, 1984; Best SF Stories of Brian W Aldiss, 1988; A Romance of the Equator, Best Fantasy Stories, 1989; A Tupolev Too Far, 1993; The Secret of This book, 1995; Non-Fiction includes: Cities and Stones: A Traveller's Jugoslavia, 1966; Bury My Heart at W H Smith's: A Writing Life, 1990; The Detached Retina (essays), 1995; At the Caligula Hotel (collected poems), 1995; Songs From the Steppes of Central Asia, 1996; The Twinkling of an Eye, My Life as a Englishman, 1998; When the Feast is Finished, 1998; White Mars (with Roger Penrose), 1999; Supertoys Last All Summer Long (made into Kubrick-Spielberg film, AI), 2001; The Cretan Teat, 2001; Super-State, Researches and Churches in Serbia, The Dark Sun Rises, poems, 2002; Affairs in Hampden Ferrers, 2004; Jocasta, Sanity and the Lady, 2005; Harm, 2007; Opera: Oedipus on Mars; Plays: SF Blues; Kindred Blood in Kensington Gore; Monsters of Every Day, Oxford Literary Festival, 2000; Drinks with the Spider King, Florida, 2000; Acted in own productions, 1985-2002; Contributions to: Times Literary Supplement; Nature. Honours: Hugo Awards, 1962, 1987; Nebula Award, 1965; various British Science Fiction Association awards; Ferara Cometa d'Argento, 1977; Prix Jules Verne, Sweden, 1977; Science Fiction Research Association Pilgrim Awards, 1978; First International Association of the Fantastic in the Arts Distinguished Scholarship Award, 1986; J Lloyd Eaton Award, 1988; World Science Fiction President's Award, 1988; Hugo Nomination, 1991; Order of the British Empire, 2005.

ALDRICH Christiaan, b. 7 July 1960, Bloemfontein, South Africa. Chemical Engineer. m. Annemarie Aldrich, 1 son, 1 daughter. Education: BEng (Chem), 1982; MEng (Metall) 1985; PhD (Engineering) 1993. Appointments: Process Engineer, Sasol, 1985-87; Senior Researcher, 1992-93, Senior Lecturer, 1994-95, Associate Professor, 1996-98, Professor, Process Engineering, 1999-, Head, Department of Chemical Engineering, 2010-, University of Stellenbosch; Director of Institute for Mineral Processing and Intelligent Process Systems, 1999-2005; Founding Director, Anglo Platinum Centre of Excellence in Process Monitoring. Publications: Over 100 peer reviewed papers in international journals since 1994; Numerous contributions to the proceedings of international conferences, symposia and workshops. Honours: British Association Silver (S_2A_3) Medal, 2000; FRD President's Award, 1996. Memberships: FSAAE; MSAIMM, MAAS, MIEE. Address: Department of Process Engineering, University of Stellenbosch, Private Bag X1, Matieland, 7602, Stellenbosch, South Africa. E-mail: ca1@sun.ac.za

ALDRIDGE (Harold Edward) James, b. 10 July 1918, England. Author; Journalist. m. Dina Mitchnik, 1942, 2 sons. Appointments: with Herald and Sun, Melbourne, Australia, 1937-38; Daily Sketch and Sunday Dispatch, London, 1939; Australian Newspaper Service, North American Newspaper Alliance (as war correspondent), Finland, Norway, Middle East, Greece, USSR, 1939-45; Correspondent, Time and Life, Tehran, 1944. Plays: 49th State, 1947; One Last Glimpse, 1981. Publications: Signed with Their Honour, 1942; The Sea Eagle, 1944; Of Many Men, 1946; The Diplomat. 1950; The Hunter, 1951; Heroes of the Empty View, 1954; Underwater Hunting for Inexperienced Englishmen, 1955; I Wish He Would Not Die, 1958; Gold and Sand, short stories, 1960; The Last Exile, 1961; A Captive in the Land, 1962; The Statesman's Game, 1966; My Brother Tom, 1966; The Flying 19, 1966; Living Egypt, with Paul Strand, 1969; Cairo: Biography of a City, 1970; A Sporting Proposition, 1973; The Marvellous Mongolian, 1974; Mockery in Arms, 1974; The Untouchable Juli, 1975; One Last Glimpse, 1977; Goodbye Un-America, 1979; The Broken Saddle, 1982; The True Story of Lilli Stubek, 1984; The True Story of Spit Mac Phee, 1985; The True Story of Lola MacKellar, 1993; The Girl from the Sea, 2003; The Wings of Kitty St Clair, 2006. Honours: Rhys Memorial Award, 1945; Lenin Peace Prize, 1972; Australian Childrens Book of the Year, 1985; Guardian Children's Fiction Prize. Address: c/o Curtis Brown, 28/29 Haymarket, London, SW1Y 4SP, England.

ALDRIN Buzz, b. 20 January 1930, Montclair, New Jersey. American Astronaut. m. (1) Joan Archer, divorced 1978, 2 sons, 1 daughter, (2) Beverley Zile, (3) Lois Driggs-Cannon, 1988. Education: US Military Academy; MA Institute of Technology. Appointments: Former Member, US Air Force; Completed Pilot Training, 1952; Flew Combat Mission during Korean War; Aerial Gunnery Instructor, Nellis Air Force Base, Nevada; Attended Squadron Officers School, Air University, Maswell Air Force Base, Alabama; Flight Commander, 36th Tactical Fighter Wing, Bitburg, Germany; Completed Astronautics Studies, MIT, 1963; Selected by NASA as Astronaut, 1963; Later assigned to Manned Spacecraft Centre, Houston, Texas; Pilot of Backup Crew for Gemini IX Mission, 1966; Pilot, Gemini XII, 1966; Backup Command module pilot for Apollo VIII; Lunar Module Pilot for Apollo XI; Landed on the moon, 20 July 1969; Commandant Aerospace Research Pilot School, 1971-72; Scientific Consultant, Beverly Hills Oil Co, Los Angeles; Chair, Starcraft Enterprises; Fellow, American Institute of Aeronautics and Astronautics; Retired from USAF, 1972; President, Research and Engineering Consultants Inc, 1972-; Consultant, JRW Jet Propulsion Laboratory. Publications: First on the Moon: A Voyage with Neil Armstrong, 1970; Return to Earth, 1973; Men from Earth, 1989; Encounter with the Tiber, 1996; Encounter with the Tiber – the Return, 2000. Honours: Honorary Member, Royal Astronautical Society; Several honorary degrees; Numerous decorations and awards. Address: 233 Emerald Bay, Laguna Beach, CA 92651, USA.

ALEKPEROV Chingiz, b. 16 July 1954, Baku, Azerbaijan, USSR. m. Larisa Jeny, 2 sons. Education: MSc, Land Survey Engineering, Moscow Institute of Engineers, Moscow, 1976; PhD, Agronomist-Soil Scientist, Soil Erosion Research Department, Institute of Soil Science and Agrochemistry, Baku, Azerbaijan, 1985. Appointments: Agronomist-Soil Scientist, Reseracher, George S Wise Faculty of Life Sciences, Tel Aviv University, Israel, 2004-. Publications: More than 28 papers. Honours: Member of KAMEA, Israel. Memberships: Soil Science Society of America; American Society of Agronomy; European Water Resources Association; International Union of Soil Science; USSR Soil Science Society. Address: Levi Eshkol, 82, apt 8, Tel Aviv, Israel.

ALEKSANDROV Aleksandr Pavlovich, b. 20 February 1943, Moscow, Russia. Cosmonaut; Flight Engineer. m. Natalia Valentinovna Aleksandrova, 1 son, 1 daughter. Education: Baumann Technical Institute, Moscow; PhD. Appointments: Served in Soviet Army; Space Programme, 1964-; Participant, elaboration of control system of spacecraft, Cosmonaut, from 1978; Participant, Soyuz-T and Salyut programmes; Successful completion of 149-day flight to Salyut-T orbital station, 1983; Spacewalk, July 1987; Return to Earth, 1987; Completed 160-day flight on Mir Space Station; Chief, Department of Crew Training and Extra Vehicular Activity, Energya design and production firm; resigned from Cosmonaut team in 1993, became chief of NPOE Cosmonaut group; Chief flight test directorate of RKKE, 1996-. Member, Extra Vehicular Activity Committee, IAF, 1994-. Honours: Hero of Soviet Union, 1983, 1987; Hero of Syria. Memberships: Academician, International Informatization Academy, 1997. Address: Khovanskaya Str 3-27, 129515 Moscow, Russia.

ALEKSIN Anatoliy Georgievich, b. 3 August 1924, Moscow, Russia. Writer. m. Tatyana Alexina, 1 son, 1 daughter. Education: Moscow Institute of Oriental Studies, 1950. Career: Writer, 1951-; Playwright; Scriptwriter; Member, Russian Academy of Education, 1982-; Secretary, Union of the Writers of Russia, 1970-89; President of the Association, Peace to the Children of the World, 1986-90; Chairman, Council of Children's and Youth Literature of Russia, 1970-90; Host of monthly TV show, Friend's Faces, 1971-86; Writer of film, television scripts and numerous plays, staged in Russia and abroad. Publications: More than 220 books translated into 48 languages (over 120 million printed copies); More than 60 Russian books published between 1993-2009; Translated into English, French, Dutch, Greek, Spanish, Japanese, Chinese, Korean, Finnish, Hebrew, Arabic, Hindi, Czech and others; Collected works published in 3 volumes, 1979-81, 5 volumes, 1998-99, 9 volumes, 2000-2001; More than 1,000 magazine articles; Editorial Board, Yunost Magazine, 1973-93. Honours: Mildred Batchelder Award Nomination for "A Late Born Child", Association of American Libraries, USA, 1973; Russian

Government Award, 1974; USSR Government Award, 1978; Two Orders of the Labour Banner; Included in Hans Christian Andersen Awards; IBBY Honor List; The International Board on Books for Young People for 'Deistvujuschtye Litsa I Ispolnitely'; Chosen as an Outstanding Example of Literature with International Importance, 1976; International European Maxim Gorky Award for "Bezumnaya Evdokia" (Crazy Evdokia), 1980; Award of Federation of Unions of Writers of Israel, 1999; Jubilee Medal, 200th Anniversary of A S Pushkin, 1999; Compassion Award for Assistance to People Suffering from Cancer, 1998, 2000; Title, Man of Legend, 2004; Gold Medal of Janush Korchik, 2005; Great Golden Medal, International Association Knowledge for outstanding contribution in Enlightenment, Russian and World Literature, 2010. Memberships: Writers Union of Moscow; International PEN Club; Russian Writers Union of Israel; Russian Academy of Education; The International Academy of Science, Education, Industry and Art, USA, 2007. Address: Rubinstein Street 39/17, Jaffo-Dalet 68212, Tel-Aviv, Israel.

ALENCAR Eunice M L Soriano de, b. 15 January 1945, Teófilo Otôni, MG, Brazil. University Professor. m. Geraldo de Alencar, 4 sons. Education: BA, Psychology, 1966, Teacher's Certificate in Psychology, 1966, Certificate of Post-Graduate Studies, 1967, Federal University of Minas Gerais; MS, 1970, PhD, 1974, Purdue University, USA. Appointments: Assistant Professor, Federal University of Minas Gerais, Brazil, 1967-71; Associate Professor, 1972-87, Professor of Psychology, 1987-97, University of Brasilia; Professor, Psychology and Education, Catholic University of Brasilia, 1997-. Publications: Over 150 articles in professional journals; Books include most recently: The Creativity Process, 1999; Creativity and Gifted Education, 2001; Giftedness: Determinants, Education and Adjustment, 2001; Creativity: Multiple Perspectives, 2003; Talents and High Ability Development. Guidance to Parents and Teachers, 2007; Creativity Measurements. Theory and Practice, 2010. Honours: Educator of the Year, Federal District, Brazil, 1998; Honorary Citizen of Brasilia, 2002; Member, Permanent Honorary Council, Brazilian Council for Giftedness; Professor Emeritus, University of Brasilia, 2005. Memberships: Fellow, Psychology Academy of São Paulo, Brazil; World Council for Gifted and Talented Children; Brazilian Society of Psychology; School and Educational Psychology Association. Address: Programa de Pós-Gradua çao em Educaçao, Universidade Católica de Brasilia, SGAN 916 Módulo B Asa Norte, 70790-160 Brasilia, DF, Brazil. E-mail: ealencar@pos.ucb.br

ALESSENDRE Angelina, b. 3 November 1946, Beaconsfield, Buckinghamshire, England. Ballet Dancer; Dance Teacher. 1 son, 1 daughter. Education: Lycèe Français, London; French Institute, Budapest, 1959; Trained as a dancer under Miss Ballantyne, Betty Haines, Dr Ronald Heavey MBE. Career: Professional Ballet Dancer; Performances in England and Italy including The Scala and the Cambridge Theatres, London; Became interested in teaching dance to children with learning difficulties in 1990; Founded the Alessendre Special Needs Dance School, 1992; Won international recognition for uncovering latent talents in people with special needs and helping them to develop into well adjusted and confident individuals more able to lead active, happy and fulfilled lives; Developed an innovative curriculum able to suit all sorts of learning difficulties including children with Down's Syndrome; The Larondina Dance Company (established in 1992) acts as a showcase for the School's work; Pupils have performed with great success in London's West End, also in Moscow, France, Germany and Guernsey; Performances in Ecuador and Nigeria are planned. Publications: Articles in Moscow Times, local papers and educational magazines. Honours: MBE, 2010. Membership: British Theatre Dance Association. Address: 17 Whistlers Avenue, Battersea, London SW11 3TS, England. E-mail: info@asneeds.org.uk Website: www.asneeds.org.uk

ALEXANDER Bill, b. 23 February 1948, Hunstanton, Norfolk, England. Theatre Director. m. Juliet Harmer, 1977, 2 daughters. Education: Keele University. Appointments: Directed Shakespeare and classical and contemporary drama, Bristol Old Vic; Joined, 1977, Associate Director, 1984-91, Artistic Director, 1991-, Royal Shakespeare Company, productions including Tartuffe, Richard III, 1984, Volpone, The Accrington Pals, Clay, Captain Swing, School of Night, A Midsummer Night's Dream, The Merry Wives of Windsor; Other theatre work, Nottingham Playhouse, Royal Court Theatre, Victory Theatre, New York and Shakespeare Theatre, Washington DC; Artistic Director, Birmingham Repertory Company, 1993-2000, productions including Othello, The Snowman, Macbeth, Dr Jekyll and Mr Hyde, The Alchemist, Awake and Sing, The Way of the World, Divine Right, The Merchant of Venice, Old Times, Frozen, Hamlet, The Tempest, The Four Alice Bakers, Jumpers, Nativity, 1999; Quarantine, Twelfth Night, 2000; An Enemy of the People, Frozen, Mappa Mundi, The Importance of Being Ernest, 2002; Titus Andronicus, RSC, 2003; King Lear, RSC, 2004. Publications: Film, The Snowman, 1998. Honours: Olivier Award for Director of the Year, 1986. Address: Rose Cottage, Tunley, Gloucestershire GL7 6LP, England.

ALEXANDER Michael Joseph, b. 21 May 1941, Wigan, Lancashire, England. Writer. m. (1) Eileen McCall, deceased, (2) Mary Sheahan, 1 son, 2 daughters. Education: Downside School; BA, 1962, MA, 1967, University of Oxford; University of Perugia; Princeton University. Appointments: Lecturer d'anglais, Cahors; Editor, Wm Collins, 1963; English-Speaking Union Fellow, Princeton University, USA, 1965; Lecturer, University of California SB, 1966; Editor, André Deutsch, 1967; Lecturer, University of East Anglia, 1968; Lecturer, University of Stirling, 1969; Senior Lecturer, Reader; Berry Professor of English Literature, University of St Andrews, 1985-2003. Publications: The First Poems in English; Beowulf; The Poetic Achievement of Ezra Pound; A History of English Literature; Medievalism; and others. Honours: Ford Foundation Award to translate Beowulf; Arts Council Awards for translation of Old English Riddles and for critical book on the poetry of Ezra Pound; Represents Scotland on Round Britain Quiz, BBC Radio Four. Memberships: The Athenaeum; Fellow, English Association. Address: 21 Stapleton Road, Headington, Oxford, OX3 7LX, England. E-mail: michael.j.alex@googlemail.com

ALEXANDER (Robert) McNeill, b. 7 July 1934, Lisburn, Northern Ireland. Emeritus Professor of Zoology. m. Ann Elizabeth Coulton, 1 son, 1 daughter. Education: BA, 1955, PhD, 1958, MA, 1959, Cambridge University; DSc, University of Wales, 1969. Appointments: Assistant Lecturer, 1958-61, Lecturer, 1961-68, Senior Lecturer, 1968-69, University College of North Wales; Professor of Zoology, 1969-99, Research Professor, 1999-2008, Emeritus Professor, 1999-, University of Leeds; Editor: Proceedings of the Royal Society B, 1998-2004. Publications: Books: Functional Design in Fishes, 1967; Animal Mechanics, 1968, 1983; Size and Shape, 1971; The Chordates, 1975, 1981; Biomechanics, 1975; The Invertebrates, 1979; Locomotion of Animals, 1982; Optima for Animals, 1982, 1996; Elastic Mechanisms for Animal Movement, 1988; Dynamics of

Dinosaurs and other Extinct Giants, 1989; Animals, 1990; The Human Machine, 1992; Exploring Biomechanics: Animals in Motion, 1992; Bones, 1994; How Animals Move (a multimedia CD-ROM), 1995; Energy for Animal Life, 1999; Principles of Animal Locomotion, 2003; Human Bones, 2004; About 270 scientific papers most of them on human and animal biomechanics. Honours include: Scientific Medal, Zoological Society of London, 1969; Linnean Medal for Zoology, Linnean Society of London, 1979; Fellow of the Royal Society, 1987; Muybridge Medal, International Society for Biomechanics, 1991; Member, Academia Europaea, 1996; CBE, 2000; Honorary DSc, University of Aberdeen, 2002; Honorary Doctor, University of Wageningen, 2003; Honorary Fellow, Zoological Society of London, 2003; Borelli Award, American Society of Biomechanics, 2004; Member, European Academy of Sciences, 2004. Memberships: Royal Society; Zoological Society of London, Secretary, 1992-99; Society for Experimental Biology, President, 1995-97; Honorary Member, Society for Integrative and Comparative Biology; International Society for Vertebrate Morphology, President, 1997-2001; Foreign Honorary Member, American Academy of Arts and Sciences; International Society for Biomechanics. Address: Institute for Integrative and Comparative Biology, University of Leeds, Leeds LS2 9JT, England. E-mail: r.m.alexander@leeds.ac.uk

ALEXANDER-SKIPNES Ingrid, b. 19 July 1949, New York, USA. Art Historian; Educator. m. Kolbjørn Skipnes. Education: BA, Emmanuel College, Boston, Massachusetts, 1971; MFA, Villa Schifanoia Graduate School of Fine Arts, Florence, Italy, 1975; PhD, Université Catholique de Louvain, Belgium, 1990. Appointments: Art Conservation Consultant, Sotherby's, Belgium, 1981-88; Consultant, US Department of State, Art Embassies' Program, American Embassy, Brussels, 1986; Research Art Historian, Smithsonian Institution, Washington DC, 1988-96; Associate Professor, Art History, University of Stavanger, 1997-2011; Lecturer, University of Freiburg, 2012. Publications: Cultural Exchange Between the Low Countries and Italy 1400-1600, 2007; Bound with wond'rous beauty: Eastern Codices in the Library of Federico da Montefeltro, in Mediterranean Studies vol 19, 2010; Greek Mathematics in Rome and the Aesthetics of Geometry in Piero della Francesca, in Early Modern Rome 1341-1667, 2011. Honours: Myron Taylor Scholarship, 1973; Pre-doctoral Fellowship, Université Catholique de Louvain, 1979-81; Smithsonian Institution Awards for Outstanding Achievement 1989-95. Memberships: Board of Directors, International Council of Museums, Committee for Conservation.

ALEXANDRA Liana, b. 27 May 1947, Bucharest, Romania. Computer; University Professor. m. Serban Nichifor. Education: George Enescu Scholarship, Ciprian Porumbescu University of Music, Bucharest, 1965-71; International courses of compositions, Darmstadt, West Germany, 1974, 1978, 1980, 1984; USIA stipendium, USA, 1983; PhD, Musicology. Appointments: Master in Music, Professor, National University of Music of Bucharest; Member, Duo Intermedia; Co-director, Nuova Musica Consonante-Living Music Foundation Inc, USA; National Expert for Music, National Register of Experts, 2005. Publications: Numerous symphonic, concerto, chamber music and computer works. Honours include: Prize of the Union of Romanian Composers, 1975, 1979, 1980, 1982, 1984, 1987, 1988; Gaudeamus Prize, 1979, 1980; First Prize, Carl Maria von Weber, Dresden, 1979; Prize of Romanian Academy, 1980; Prize of Beer-Sheva, Israel, 1986; 2nd Prize, Mannheim-Gedock, Germany, 1989; 3rd Prize, Fanny Mendelssohn, Dortmund-Unna, Germany, 1991; Prize Gaudeamus, Magadino, Switzerland, 1992; ISCM Prize, Mexico, 1993; many others; Listed in international biographical dictionaries. Memberships: Union of Romanian Composers; International Society Frau and Musik; GEMA, Germany; many others. Address: Str Rosia Montana nr 4, Bloc 05, scara 4, apt 165, 77584 Bucharest, Sector 6, Romania. E-mail: lianaalexandra@yahoo.com

ALEXEEV Boris, b. 2 May 1938, Orechovo-Zuevo, Moscow Region. Physicist; Educator. Divorcee, 1 daughter. Education: Degree in Physics, Engineering, 1961, PhD, 1964, Moscow Institute of Physics and Technology; DSc, Computer Centre of USSR Academy of Sciences, 1973; Professor of Physics, Higher Attestation Commission of USSR, 1974. Appointments: Senior Research Scientist, Computer Centre, USSR Academy of Sciences, 1964-73; Head of Physics Department, Moscow Aviation Institute, 1973-83; Head of Physics Department, Moscow Fine Chemical Technology Institute, 1983-; Visiting Professor, University of Provence (Marseilles), 1992-95; University of Alabama (Huntsville, USA), 1995, 1997; Head, Centre of the Theoretical Foundations in Nanotechnology, 2007-. Publications: Over 280 scientific works including 22 books including: Mathematical Kinetics of Reacting Gases (author), 1982; Transport Processes in Reacting Gases and Plasma (co-author), 1994, Generalized Boltzmann Physical Kinetics (author), Esevier, 2004. Honours: Meritorious Science and Technics Worker of Russia, USSR, 1989-; Presidents Stipend for Outstanding Russian Scientists, 1994-; Meritorious Worker, Higher Professional Education of Russia, 1998-; Man of the Year, Medal of Honor, ABI, 1999; Meritorious Science & Technics Worker of Russia, Russian Federation, 2008-; Meritorious DSc, Moscow Academy of Fine Chemical Technology, 2010. Memberships: Russian National Committee on Theoretical and Applied Mechanics, 1987-; Organising Committee, Russian Academy of Sciences and Head of the Moscow Regional Committee, Moscow, 1991; Academician of the International Higher Education Academy of Sciences (General Physics and Astronomy) 1993-; New York Academy of Sciences, 1995-. Address: 3rd Frunzenskaya h 9, ap 130 Moscow 119270, Russia.

ALEXIU Lucian, b. 2 February 1950, Timisoara. Romania. Poet; Literary Critic; Essayist; Translator; Editor. m. Adara-Monica Blaga. Education: Scholarship from Avignon-Marseille, Faculty of Letters, Romanian-French Section, West University of Timisoara, 1974. Appointments: Publisher, academic journals, Cercetari Experimentale si Medico-Chirurgicale, British and American Studies, Revue d'Etude Interculturelle; Editor of literary magazines; General Manager of cultural magazines; Member, Steering Committee, National Council, and Management Committee of Timisoara Branch,, Writers' Union of Romania. Publications: 14 books on poetry and literary criticism in Romania and abroad; 27 books translated from world literature in Romania and abroad; Contribution of articles to over 30 literary magazines and General Dictionary of Literature, and others. Honours: Decorated by French, Romanian and Serbian high cultural orders; Order of Cultural Merit in the Rank of Officer; Order Les Palmes Academiques in the Rank of Knight; Distinguished with many literary prizes. Memberships: Writers' Union of Romania; Romanian Pen Club; Copy Ro.

ALFKIN William P, b. 30 November 1941, Hoopa, California, USA. Social Services. Education: Certified in Computer Design Drafting, Completed 60 semester units, Community College Level, 1978-80; Completed 40 semester units, California State University System, 1990-91. Appointments: Summer Internship, State Water Resources Control Board, (State Board) Nonpoint Source Unit, 1990; Survey Technologist and

Design Drafter, engineering and architectural offices, 25 years; Vocational Assistant, County of Humboldt Social Services Branch, 1997-. Honours: Motivational Coaching, 2009; Youth Services, 2009; Professional of the Year, 2010; Listed in international biographical dictionaries. Memberships: Hoopa Valley Tribe. Address: 2546 Hubbard Ln, Apt A, Eureka, CA 95501-3484, USA.

ALI Mahbub, Scientist Emeritus. Appointments: Agricultural/Research Assistant, 1942-55, Assistant Botanist, Cotton, 1955-58, Department of Agriculture, Government of the Punjab; Cotton Botanist, Cotton Research Station, 1958-70, Director, Central Cotton Research Institute, 1970-79, Pakistan Central Cotton Committee, Government of Pakistan; Managing Director, Punjab Seed Corporation, Government of the Punjab, 1979-85; Scientist Emeritus, Government of the Punjab, 1985-; Scientist Emeritus, Government of Pakistan, 2000-. Publications: Over 80 articles in professional journals; Book, Cotton Plant in Pakistan. Honours: President's Medal for Pride of Performance, 1971; Appreciation of PhD Examination Committee in the USA; Scientist Emeritus, Government of the Punjab; Gold Medal, Pakistan Academy of Sciences, 1980; Shield of Distinction, University of Agriculture, Faisalabad, 1981; Award of Fellowship, Pakistan Academy of Sciences, 1985; President of Pakistan's Shield, 1995; Award of Status of Scientist Emeritus, Government of Pakistan, 1999; Many other honours and awards. Memberships: Fellow, Pakistan Academy of Sciences; Pakistan Association for Advancement of Science; Honor Scientific Societies of Sigma Xi and Phi Kappa Phi, USA; Academic Council, Bahaudin Zakariya University, Multan; Academic Council, University of Agriculture, Faisalabad; Pakistan Central Cotton Committee, Ministry of Food & Agriculture, Government of Pakistan; Agriculture Sub-Committee, Pakistan Central Cotton Committee, Ministry of Agriculture, Pakistan. Address: 77 Industrial Estate, Multan, Pakistan.

ALI Md Hossain, b. 31 December 1966, Jamalpur, Bangladesh. Service. m. Anjuman Ara Begum, 1 son, 1 daughter. Education: BSc, 1991, MSc, 1997, Agricultural Engineering, Bangladesh Agricultural University; M Engg Sci, University of Melbourne, Australia, 2000; PhD, 2008, Bangladesh Agricultural University; Postdoctoral, School of Civil Engineering, University Sains Malaysia, 2011. Appointments: Assistant General Manager, Bangladesh Rural Electrification Board, 1993-94; Scientific Officer, 1994-2001, Senior Scientific Officer, 2001-11, Bangladesh Institute of Nuclear Agriculture; Visiting Senior Lecturer, University Malaysia Pahang, 2011-. Publications: 4 books; 5 book chapters; Numerous articles in professional journals. Memberships: Association of Agrometeorologists; Bangladesh Association for the Advancement of Science; Progressive Agriculturalists; International Society of Agricultural Meteorologists; Asia Pacific Water Forum; Water Environment Forum; Institution of Engineers, Bangladesh; Bangladesh Society of Agricultural Engineers; Bangladesh Association of Environmental Development; Krishibid Institution. Address: Agricultural Engineering Division, Bangladesh Institute of Nuclear Agriculture, BAU Campus, Mymensingh-2202, Bangladesh. E-mail: hossain.ali.bina@gmail.com

ALI Muhammad, b. 17 January 1942, Louisville, Kentucky, USA. Boxer. m. (1) Sonji Roi, divorced, (2) Belinda Boyd, divorced, (3) Veronica Porsche, 1977, divorced, (4) Yolanda Williams; 2 sons, 7 daughters. Education: Louisville. Appointments: Amateur Boxer, 1954-60; Olympic Games Light-Heavyweight Champion, 1960; Professional Boxer, 1960-; Won World heavyweight title, 1964; Stripped of title after refusing to be drafted into US Army, 1967; Returned to Professional Boxing, 1970; Regained World Heavyweight, 1974; Lost Title to Leon Spinks, 1978; Regained Title, Spinks, 1978; 56 victories in 61 fights, 1981; Lost to Larry Holmes, 1980; Acted in films, The Greatest; Freedom Road. Publications: The Greatest: My Own Story, 1975; Healing, 1996; More Than a Hero (with Hana Ali), 2000. Honours: Named Messenger of Peace, UN; Athlete of the Century, GQ Magazine; Lifetime Achievement Award, Amnesty International; Honorary Consul General for Bangladesh in Chicago; Named Messenger of Peace, UN, 1999; Presidential Medal of Freedom, 2005; Otto Hahn Peace Medal in Gold, 2005; Honorary doctorate, Princeton University, 2007. Memberships: Black Muslim Movement; Peace Corps Advisory Council. Address: P O Box 160, Berrien Springs, MI 49103, USA.

ALKER (John) Stephen, b. 1 July 1953, Wigan, England. Priest. Education: St Joseph's College, Upholland, 1966-75; St Cuthbert's College, Durham, 1975-78. Appointments: Ordained Priest, 1978; RC Chaplain, British Army (Great Britain, Northern Ireland, Germany, Australia, Cyprus & Germany), 1983-2009; Principal RC Chaplain (Army) and Vicar General, 2006-09; Pastor, St Leonhard's, Frankfurt am Main, Germany; Pastor, St Mary's, Liederbach, Germany. Publications: Various articles in professional journals. Honours: MBE,1997; Knight of the Holy Sepulchre, 2002; Honorary Chaplain to the Queen, 2007-09; Prelate of Honour to the Pope (Monsignor), 2006; Operational medals: GSM (NI); UN Cyprus; UNPROFOR (Balkans); NATO (Former Yugoslavia); Queen's Jubilee Medal, 2002; Knight Commander of the Holy Sepulchre, 2010. Memberships: Equestrian Order of the Holy Sepulchre of Jerusalem; Royal British Legion; RSPB; Society for the Protection of Unborn Children. Address: St Leonhard's International English Speaking Roman Catholic Parish, Vilbeler Strasse 36, 60313 Frankfurt am Main, Germany. Website: www.stleonards.org

ALKOOT Fuad, b. 1 November 1963, Kuwait. Lecturer; Trainer. m. Maryam Ahmad, 2 daughters. Education: BSc, Fairleigh Dickinson University, Teaneck, New Jersey, USA, 1986; MSc, Rochester Institute of Technology, Rochester, New York, USA, 1989; PhD, University of Surrey, Guildford, United Kingdom, 2001. Appointments: Trainer/Lecturer A, 1991-98, Specialized Trainer/Lecturer C, 1998-2004, Head of Switching Department, 2003-08, Specialized Trainer/Lecturer B, 2004-, Telecommunication & Navigation Institute, PAAET. Publications: Sum vs Vote Fusion in multiple classifier Systems, 2003; Moderating K-NN Classifiers, 2002; Modified Product Fusion, 2002; Experimental evaluation of expert fusion Strategies, 1999; An Artificual neural network for decoding linear Hamming Codes, 1999; A survey of GSM radiation the State of Kuwait, 2010. Honours: IDB Merit, PhD Scholarship, 1998-2001. Memberships: IAPR-TC1, 2001; Arbitration Committee, HHSSAA Informatics Award, 2008, 2009, 2010; Scientific committee member of many conferences. Address: PO Box 4575, Alsalmia 22046, Kuwait.

ALLAM Salah El-Din, b. 30 December 1940, Cairo, Egypt. Professor. m. Kamilia Abdelmageed, 1 son, 1 daughter. Education: BSc, Mathematics and Education, 1960, Higher Diploma in Education, 1964, MEd, Educational Psychology, 1971, Ain Shams University, Egypt; PhD, Educational and Psychological Measurement, Evaluation and Statistics, University of Michigan, USA, 1980. Appointments: Assistant Researcher (part time), University of Michigan, 1977-79;

Lecturer, University of Kuwait, 1983-87; Consultant Eduational Bureau for the Gulf Arab States, Kuwait, 1984-87; Visiting Professor, Um Al-Kora University, Saudi Arabia, 1989; Professor, College of Education, Al-Azhar University, Cairo, 1991-; Consultant for UNESCO, Kuwait, Jordan, 1985-93; Visiting Professor, College of Education, Emirates University, United Arab Emirates, 1996; Head of Evaluation Department, National Center for Examinations and Educational Evaluation, Cairo, Egypt, 1996-97; Consultant, Ministry of Education, United Arab Emirates, 1999-2001; Visiting Professor, College of Education, Bahrain University, Bahrain, 2003; Consultant, National Accreditation and Quality Assurance in Education, Egypt. Publications: Numerous books and articles and research papers in national, regional and international journals. Honours: Award for PhD dissertation, University of Michigan, 1981; Kuwait University Award, 1986; Ministry of Education Award, Quatar, 1995; NWL-Alhussein Association, Jordan, 1996; Dar Al-Fekr Alarabi Award, 2004; Advisor to the Director General, IBC, England, 2007; World Lifetime Achievement Award, ABI, USA, 2008; Named 500 Greatest Geniuses of the 21st Century, ABI, USA, 2008; Vice President of the Recognition Board, World Congress of Arts, Science and Communications, England, 2007; Master, The World Academy of Letters, ABI, 2008; International Peace Prize, The United Cultural Convention, ABI, 2008; Inducted, Hall of Fame, ABI, 2008; Leading Scientists of the World, IBC, England, 2008; Lifetime Secretary-General Award, United Cultural Convention, ABI, 2011; Listed in international biographical dictionaries. Memberships: American Educational Research Association; Egyptian Psychological Association; Arab Council for Gifted and Talented, Amman, Jordan; People to People Ambassador Programs, USA; Science Age Society, Egypt. Address: 52 Al-Nozha Street, Rabaa Bldgs, Madinet Nasr, Cairo, Egypt. E-mail: salaheldinallam@hotmail.com

ALLAN Terrence William, b. 8 October 1947, Forres, United Kingdom. Retired, Emeritus Head of Computer Education. m. Linda Myra Janet Low, 1 son, 1 daughter. Education: BSc (Eng) Hons, 1970, M Ed, 1981, University of Aberdeen; PGCE (Further Education), Jordanhill College, 1973; PGCE (Secondary Education), Dundee College of Education, 1982. Appointments: Lecturer, Computing, Aberdeen College of Commerce, 1970-81; Lecturer, Northern College, 1981-88; Senior Lecturer, Deputy Head, 1988-94, Head, 1994-2001, Computer Education, Northern College of Education; Head of Computer Education, University of Aberdeen, 2001-10. Honours: Listed in international biographical dictionaries. Memberships: General Teaching Council, Scotland; Scottish National Party. Address: 32 Middleton Circle, Bridge of Don, Aberdeen, AB22 8NZ, Scotland. E-mail: terry@allans.org

ALLEN Blair H, b. 2 July 1933, Los Angeles, California, USA. Writer; Poet; Editor; Artist; Photographer. m. Juanita Aguilar Raya, 27 January 1968, 1 son, 1 daughter. Education: AA, San Diego City College, 1964; University of Washington, 1965-66; BA, San Diego State University, 1970. Appointments: Sargeant, Honorable Discharge, US Marine Corps, 1953-59; Assistant Display Organiser for Art Building in LA County Fair, 1975-77; Book Reviewer, Los Angeles Times, 1977-78; Special Feature Editor, Cerulean Press and Kent Publications, 1982-. Publications: Televisual Poems for Bloodshot Eyeballs, 1973; Malice in Blunderland, 1974; N/Z, 1979; The Atlantis Trilogy, 1982; Dreamwish of the Magician, 1983; Right Through the Silver Lined 1984 Looking Glass, The Magical World of David Cole (editor), 1984; Snow Summits in the Sun (anthology, editor), 1988; Trapped in a Cold War Travelogue, 1991; May Burning into August, 1992; The Subway Poems, Bonfire on the Beach, by John Brander (editor), 1993; The Cerulean Anthology of Sci-Fi/Outer Space/Fantasy/Poetry and Prose Poems (anthology, editor), 1995; When the Ghost of Cassandra Whispers in My Ears, 1996; Ashes Ashes All Fall Down, 1997; Around the World in 56 Days, 1998; Thunderclouds from the Door, Jabberbunglemerkeltoy, 1999; The Athens Café, 2000; The Day of the Jamberee Call, 2001; Assembled I Stand, Wine of Starlight, 2002; Snow Birds in Cloud Hands (anthology, editor), Trek into Yellowstone's Cascade Corner Wilderness, Hour of Iced Wheels, 2003; Light in the Crossroads, 2004; Shot Doves, 2005; What Time Does: One Man Show (artbook retrospective), 2006; Moon Hiding in the Orange Tree, In the Face of Gateless High Walls, the Sound of Purple Horns, 2007; Opossum in the Fig Tree, When Morning is Still Night, 2008; Rain Hiking in Nikko, Flight to the Green Dream (photobook with poems), 2009; Glimpsing Margins (poetry), 2010; Nikko Reborn (photos), 2010; The Restless Years (photobook with prose), 2011; Contributions to: Numerous periodicals and 21 anthologies. Honours: Nominated for "Pushcart Prize", for Poetry, 1982; 1st Prize for Poetry, Pacificus Foundation Competition, 1992; Pacificus Foundation Literary Prize for Lifetime Achievement in Poetry and Story Writing, 2003; IBC International Writer of the Year Award, 2008; Special Guest Editorial in Small Press Review: on National Affairs, 2008 (and how it influenced my writing prose and poetry); Listed in international biographical dictionaries; Various other honours and awards. Memberships: The Academy of American Poets; Poets and Writers; Association for Applied Poetry; Beyond Baroque Foundation; California State Poetry Society; Medina Foundation; Democratic Party National Committee. Address: PO Box 162, Colton, CA 92324, USA. Website: http://www.pw.org/directory/writer-detail.php?writer_id=14154B

ALLEN Geoffrey (Sir), b. 29 October 1928, Clay Cross, Derbyshire, England. Polymer Scientist; Administrator. m. Valerie Frances Duckworth, 1972, 1 daughter. Education: PhD, University of Leeds. Appointments: Postdoctoral Fellow, National Research Council, Canada, 1952-54; Lecturer, 1955-65, Professor of Chemical Physics, 1965-75, University of Manchester; Professor of Polymer Science, 1975-76, Professor of Chemical Technology, 1976-81, Imperial College of Science and Technology, University of London; Chair, Science Research Council, 1977-81; Visiting Fellow, Robinson College, Cambridge, 1980-; Head of Research, 1981-90, Director for Research and Engineering, 1982-90; Unilever PLC, 1981-90; Visiting Fellow: St Catherine's College, Oxford, 1982; St Cross College, Oxford, 1983; Non-Executive Director, Courtaulds, 1987-93; President, Society of Chemical Industry, Plastics and Rubber Institute, 1990-92, Institute of Materials, 1994-95; Executive Adviser, Kobe Steel Ltd, 1990-2000; Member, National Consumer Council, 1993-96; Chancellor, University of East Anglia, 1994-2003. Honours: Honorary MSc, Manchester; Dr Univ, Open University; Honorary DSc, Durham, East Anglia, 1984, Bath, Bradford, Keele, Loughborough, 1985, Essex, Leeds, 1986, Cranfield, 1988, Surrey, 1989, North London, 1999; Monbu Daijin Sho, Monbusho, Japan, 2000. Memberships: Fellow, Royal Society, Vice-President, 1991-93; Fellow, Institute of Physics; Fellow, Plastics and Rubber Institute; Honorary Fellow, Institute of Materials & Mining; Fellow, Royal Society of Chemistry; Honorary Fellow, Institute of Chemical Engineering; Fellow, Royal Academy of Engineering. Address: 18 Oxford House, 52 Parkside, London SW19 5NE, England.

ALLEN John Anthony, b. 27 May 1926, West Bridgford, England. Marine Biologist. m. Margaret Porteous Aitken, 1 son, 1 stepson, 1 daughter. Education: University College, Nottingham, 1946-48; Chelsea Polytechnic & University College, Southampton, 1946-48 (part time while in HM Forces); BSc, University College, Southampton, 1950; PhD, London, 1955; DSc, London, 1963. Appointments: HM Foresters, 1945-46; RAMC, 1946-48; Development Commission Award, Scottish Marine Biological Association, Millport, 1950-51; Assistant Lecturer, Department of Zoology, University of Glasgow, 1951-54; Lecturer, 1954-64, Senior Lecturer, 1964-68, Department of Zoology, Member, Academic Board and various committees of Court & Senate, 1954-75, Reader in Marine Biology, 1968-76, Scientist in Charge, Dove Marine Lab, 1967-76, Chairman, Board of Studies in Zoology, 1972-75, University of Newcastle-upon-Tyne; Professor Emeritus, University of London, 1991-; Honorary Fellow, University Marine Biological Station, Millport. Publications: Author and co-author of more than 100 research papers in professional scientific journals. Honours: John Murray Student of the Royal Society, 1952-54; NSF Research Fellow, Scripps Oceanographic Institute, 1968; Scientist, Scripps Oceanographic Institute, 1975; Guest Investigator, Woods Hole Oceanographic Institution, 1967-2006; British Council Lecturer, University of Bergen, Norway, 1972; Visiting Professor, University of Washington, Seattle, 1968, 1970, 1971; Royal Society Visiting Professor, University of the West Indies, 1976. Memberships: Fellow, Royal Society of Edinburgh; Fellow, Society of Biology. Address: 21 Clyde Street, Millport, Isle of Cumbrae, KA28 0EP, Scotland. E-mail: jallen@udef.gla.ac.uk

ALLEN Lily Rose Beatrice, b. 2 May 1985, Hammersmith, London, England. Recording Artist; Talk Show Host; Actress. m. Sam Cooper, 2 daughters. Career: TV/film appearances: The Comic Strip Presents..., 1988; Elizabeth, 1998; Music: First demo tracks appeared on community website MySpace.com, 2005; Albums: Alright, Still, 2006; It's Not Me, It's You, 2009. Honours: Best Pop Artist, Digital Music Awards, 2006; Editors Special Award, Glamour Women of the Year Awards, 2008; BMI Award, 2008; Woman of the Year, GQ, 2009.

ALLEN Thomas (Sir), b. 10 September 1944, Seaham, County Durham, England. Opera Singer. m. (1) Margaret Holley, 1968, divorced 1986, 1 son, (2) Jeannie Gordon Lascelles, 1988, 1 stepson, 1 stepdaughter. Education: Royal College of Music. Appointments: Principal Baritone: Welsh National Opera, 1968-72; Royal Opera House, Covent Garden, 1972-78; Glyndebourne Opera, 1973; ENO, London Coliseum, 1986; La Scala, 1987; Chicago Lyric Opera, 1990; Royal Albert Hall, 2000; London Proms, 2002; Royal Opera House, Covent Garden, 2003. Performances include: Die Zauberflote, 1973; Le Nozze di Figaro, 1974; Cosi fan Tutte, 1975; Don Giovanni, 1977; The Cunning Little Vixen, 1977; Simon Boccanegra, Billy Budd, La Boheme, L'Elisir d'Amore, Faust, Albert Herring, Die Fledermaus, La Traviata, A Midsummer Night's Dream, Die Meistersinger von Nurnberg; as producer Albert Herring, 2002; Film: Mrs Henderson Presents, 2005. Publications: Foreign Parts: A Singer's Journal, 1993. Art Exhibitions: Chelsea Festival, 2001; Salisbury Playhouse, 2001. Honours: Honorary Fellow, University of Sunderland; Queen's Prize, 1967; Gulbenkian Fellow, 1968; MA Hon, Newcastle, 1984; RAM Hon, 1988; DMus Hon, Durham, 1988; Commander of the British Empire, 1989; Knight Bachelor, 1999; BBC Radio 3 Listeners' Award, 2004; Hon DMus, Birmingham, 2004. Address: c/o Askonas Holt Ltd, Lonsdale Chambers, 27 Chancery Lane, London WC2A 1PF, England.

ALLEN Tim, b. 13 June 1953, Denver, USA. Actor. m. (1) Laura Diebel, 1984, divorced 2003, 1 daughter, (2) Jane Hajduk, 2006, 1 daughter. Education: West Michigan University; University of Detroit. Career: Creative Director, advertising agency; Comedian, Showtime Comedy Club All Stars, 1988; TV series include: Tim Allen: Men are Pigs, 1990; Home Improvement, 1991-; Tim Allen Rewrites America; Showtime Comedy Club All-Stars II, 1988; Jimmy Neutron: Win, Lose and Kaboom (voice), 2004; Films include: Comedy's Dirtiest Dozen; The Santa Clause, 1994; Toy Story, 1995; Meet Wally Sparks, Jungle 2 Jungle, For Richer for Poorer, 1997; Galaxy Quest, 1999; Toy Story 2, Buzz Lightyear of Star Command: the Adventure Begins, 2000; Who is Cletis Tout?, Joe Somebody, 2001; Big Trouble, The Santa Clause 2, 2002; Christmas with the Kranks, 2004; The Shaggy Dog, Cars (voice), Zoom, The Santa Clause 3: The Escape Clause, Fired (documentary), Wild Hogs, 2007; Redbelt, 2008; The Six Wives of Henry Lefay, 2009; Toy Story 3, Crazy on the Outside, 2010. Publications: Don't Stand Too Close to a Naked Man, 1994; I'm Not Really Here, 1996. Honours: Favourite Comedy Actor, People's Choice Award, 1995, 1997-99. Address: c/o Commercial Unlimited, 8883 Wilshire Boulevard, Suite 850, Beverly Hills, CA 90211, USA.

ALLEN Woody (Allen Stewart Konigsberg), b. 1 December 1935, Brooklyn, New York, USA. Actor; Writer. m. (1) Harlene Rosen, divorced, (2) Louise Lasser, divorced, 1 son with Mia Farrow, (3) Soon-Yi Previn, 2 adopted daughters. Education: City College, New York; New York University. Career: Wrote for TV Performers: Herb Shriner, 1953; Sid Caesar, 1957; Art Carney, 1958-59; Jack Parr and Carol Channing; Also wrote for Tonight Show and the Gary Moore Show; Debut performance, Duplex, Greenwich Village, 1961; Performed in a variety of nightclubs across the US; Plays: Play It Again Sam; Don't Drink the Water, 1966; The Floating Light Bulb, 1981; Death Defying Acts, 1995; Films Include: What's New Pussycat?, 1965; Casino Royale, What's Up, Tiger Lily?, 1967; Take the Money and Run, 1969; Bananas, 1971; Everything You Always Wanted to Know About Sex, Play it Again Sam, 1972; Sleeper, 1973; Love and Death, 1976; The Front, 1976; Annie Hall, 1977; Interiors, 1978; Manhattan, 1979; Stardust Memories, 1980; A Midsummer Night's Sex Comedy, 1982; Zelig, 1983; Broadway Danny Rose, 1984; The Purple Rose of Cairo, Hannah and her Sister, 1985; Radio Days, September, 1987; Another Woman, 1988; Oedipus Wrecks, Crimes and Misdemeanors, 1989; Alice, 1990; Scenes from a Mall, Shadows and Fog, 1991; Husbands and Wives, 1992; Manhattan Murder Mystery, 1993; Bullets Over Broadway, Mighty Aphrodite, 1995; Everybody Says I Love You, Deconstructing Harry, 1997; Celebrity, Wild Man Blues, Stuck on You, 1998; Company Men, Sweet and Lowdown, 1999; Small Town Crooks, 2000; The Curse of the Jade Scorpion, Hail Sid Caesar! 2001; Hollywood Ending, 2002; Anything Else, 2003; Melinda and Melinda, 2004; Match Point, 2005; Scoop, 2006; Cassandra's Dream, 2007; Vicky Cristina Barcelona, 2008; Whatever Works, 2008; Midnight in Paris, 2011. Publications: Getting Even, 1971; Without Feathers, 1975; Side Effects, 1980; The Complete Prose, 1994; Telling Tales (contribution to charity anthology), 2004; Contributions to Playboy and New Yorker. Honours: Academy Award for Best Director; Best Writer; D W Griffith Award, 1996. Address: 930 Fifth Avenue, New York, NY 10021, USA.

ALLENDE Isabel, b. 2 August 1942, Lima, Peru. Writer. m. (1) Miguel Frias, 1962, 1 son, 1 daughter (deceased), (2) William C Gordon, 1988. Appointments: Journalist, Paula Magazine, 1967-74, Mampato Magazine, 1969-74; Channel 13 World Hunger Campaign, 1964; Channel 7, various humourous programmes, 1970-74; Maga-Cine-Ellas, 1973; Administrator, Marroco School, Caracas, 1978-82; Freelance journalist, El Nacional newspaper, Caracas, 1976-83; Visiting teacher, Montclair State College, New Jersey, 1985, University of Virginia, Charlottesville, 1988, University of California, Berkeley, 1989; Writer, 1981-; President, Chamber of Deputies, Chile, 2003-; Goodwill Ambassador for Hans Christian Andersen bicentennial, 2005. Publications: The House of the Spirits, 1982; Of Love and Shadows, La Gorda de Porcelana, 1984; Eva Luna, 1989; Tales of Eva Luna, 1990; The Infinite Plan, 1992; Paula, 1995; Aphrodite, a memoir of the senses, 1998; Daughter of Fortune, 1999; Portrait in Sepia, 2000; The Kingdom of the Golden Dragon, My Invented Country: A Nostalgic Journey Through Chile, 2003; Zorro, 2005; The Sum of Our Days: A Memoir, 2008; Plays: Paula; Stories of Eva Luna, 1989; The House of the Spirits ; Eva Luna, 1987; My Invented Country, 2003; Forest of the Pygmies, 2005; Ines of my Soul, 2006. Honours: Novel of the Year, Panorama Literario, Chile, 1983; Point de Mire, Belgium, 1985; Author of the Year and Book of the Year, Germany, 1984; Grand Priz d'Evasion, France, 1984; Colima for Best Novel, Mexico, 1985; Author of the Year, Germany, 1986; Mulheres Best Novel, Portugal, 1987; Dorothy and Jillian Gish Prize, 1998; Sara Lee Frontrunner Award, 1998; GEMS Women of the Year Award, 1999; Donna Dell'Anno Award, Italy, 1999; WILLA Literary Award, USA, 2000; Honorary Doctor of Humane Letters degree, San Francisco State University, 2008. Address: 116 Caledonia Street, Sausalito, CA 94965, USA.

ALLEY Kirstie, b. 12 January 1951, Wichita, Kansas, USA. Actress. m. Parker Stevenson, 1983-1997, 1 son, 1 daughter. Education: University of Kansas. Appointments: Stage appearances include: Cat on a Hot Tin Roof; Answers; Regular TV Show Cheers, 1987-93; Other appearances in TV films and series: Star Trek II, The Wrath of Khan, 1982; One More Chance, Blind Date, Champions, 1983; Runaway, 1984; Summer School, 1987; Look Who's Talking Too, Madhouse, 1990; Look Who's Talking Now, 1993; David's Mother (TV Film), 1994; Village of the Damned, It Takes Two, 1995; Sticks and Stones, Nevada, 1996; For Richer or Poorer, Victoria's Closet, Deconstructing Harry, Toothless, 1997; Drop Dead Gorgeous, The Mao Game, 1999; Blonde, 2001; Salem Witch Trials, Back By Midnight, 2002; Profoundly Normal, Family Sins, 2003; While I Was Gone, 2004; Fat Actress (series), 2005; Nailed, 2009. Publications: How To Lose Your Ass and Regain Your Life, 2005. Honours: 2 Emmy Awards; Golden Globe for Best Actress. Address: Jason Weinberg and Associates, 122 East 25th Street, 2nd Floor, New York, NY 10010, USA.

ALLI Waheed, Baron of Norbury in the London Borough of Croydon, b. 16 November 1964. Business Executive. Appointments: Co-Founder, Joint Managing Director, Planet 24 Productions Ltd, formerly 24 Hour Productions, 1992-99; Managing Director, Production, Carlton Productions, 1988-2000; Director, Carlton TV, 1998-2000; Director, 2002, Non-Executive Chair, 2003-, Chorion; Vice President, UNICEF UK, 2003-; Chairman, Asos; Director, Olga Television. Memberships: Member, Teacher Training Agency, 1997-98; Panel 2000, Creative Industry Taskforce; Board member, English National Ballet, 2001-; Director, Shine Entertainment Ltd; Shine M; Castaway TV; Digital Radio Group Ltd. Address: House of Lords, London SW1A 0PW, England.

ALLIANCE David (Baron Alliance), b. 15 June 1932, Kashan, Iran. Business Executive. Appointments: 1st acquisition, Thomas Hoghton, Oswaldtwistle, 1956; Chair, N Brown Group, 1968-; Acquired Spirella, 1968, Vantona Ltd to form Vantona Group, 1975; Group Chief Executive, 1975-90, Chair, 1989-99, Coats Viyella; Acquired Carrington Viyella to form Vantona Viyella, 1983, Nottingham Manufacturing, 1985, Coats Patons to form Coats Viyella, 1986; Chair, Tootal Group PLC, 1991-99. Honours: Commander, Order of the British Empire, 1984; Honorary Fellow, University of Manchester Institute of Science and Technology; Honorary LLD, Manchester, 1989; GBE, 1989; Honorary FCGI, 1991; Honorary DSc, Heriot-Watt, 1991; Honorary LLD, Liverpool, 1996; Life Peer, 2004. Memberships: Fellow, Royal Society of Arts; Companion, British Institute of Management. Address: N Brown Group, 53 Dale Street, Manchester M60 6ES, England.

ALLISON John William Francis, b. 31 March 1962, Durban, South Africa. Lecturer in Law. Education: BA, 1982, LLB, 1984, University of Stellenbosch; LLM, 1986, M Phil, 1987, PhD, 1992, Cambridge University. Appointments: Junior Lecturer, University of Stellenbosch, 1985; Bigelow Fellow and Lecturer in Law, University of Chicago Law School, USA, 1987-88; Lecturer, Queen Mary College, University of London, 1989-91; Research Fellow, Queens' College, University of Cambridge, 1991-94; Senior Lecturer, Department of Roman and Comparative Law, University of Cape Town, South Africa, 1994-95; University Lecturer, 1995-2001, University Senior Lecturer, 2001-, University of Cambridge. Publications include: The Procedural Reason for Judicial Restraint (journal article), 1994; A Continental Distinction in the Common Law: A Historical and Comparative Perspective on English Public Law (book), 1996; Parliamentary Sovereignty, Europe and the Economy of Common Law in M Andenas (editor), Liber Amicorum in Honour of Lord Slynn of Hadley: Judicial Review in International perspective, 2000; The English Historical Constitution: Continuity, Change and European Effects (book), 2007; History in the Law of Consitution, (journal article), 2007. Honours: Jubilee Scholarship, Rondebosch Boys' High School, 1985-87; Elsie Ballot Scholarship, 1985-87; W M Tapp Studentship, Gonville and Caius College, Cambridge, 1988-89, 1990-91; Yorke Prize, Cambridge Law Faculty, 1993. Memberships: Fellow of Queens' College; European Group of Public Law. Address: Queens' College, Cambridge CB3 9ET, England.

ALMEIDA Rui Manuel de Sousa Sequeira Antones de, b. 2 July 1955, Inhahbane, Brazil. Medical Doctor. m. Andrea, 2 sons. Education: Graduate, Medicine, 1980, MSc, 1993, PhD, Surgery, 2000, Federal University of Parana. Appointments: Resident, Cardiovascular Surgery, Evangelical Hospital, Curitiba, 1981-84; Senior House Officer, Pediatric Cardiothroacic Surgery, 1985-86, Honorary Resarch Fellow, 1986, Hospital for Sick Children, London; Registrar, National Heart Hospital, 1986, 1987; Registrar, Harley Street Clinic, London, 1987; Chief Surgeon, Western Parana Institute of Cardiovascular Surgery, 1992-; Head, Department of Cardiology and Cardiovascular Surgery, 2001-, Head, Residency Program in Cardiology, 2010-, University Hospital of the Parana Western State University; Chief Surgeon, Cardiovascular Surgery, University Hospital of the Western Parana State University, 2007-; Dean, Medical School of Assis Gurgacz University, 2008-. Publications: Over 200 papers presented at medical meetings; Invited speaker at 100 lectures; Numerous articles in professional journals. Honours: Motion of Recognition, Parana State Legislative Assembly, 1996; Recognition, Medical School, Parana Western State University, 2004, 2006; Motion of Recognition, Cascavel's Municipality, 2008; Motion of Recognition, Parana State Medical Association, 2008; Student Medical Organization,

Assis Gurgacz University, 2008; Latin American Integration Award, 2009; Oral and poster presentation prizess, Brazilian Congress of Cardiovascular Surgery, 2009. Memberships: Brazilian Societies of Cardiovascualr Surgery, Cardiology, Arrhythmias and Pace Makers and Endovascular Surgery; European Association of Cardiothoracic Surgery; Latin American Society of Cardiovascular and Thoracic Surgery. Address: Rua Terra Roxa, 1425, Regiao do Lago 2, Cascavel – Parana, CEP 85816-360, Brazil. E-mail: ruimsalmeida@iccop.com.br Website: www.iccop.com.br

ALON Azaria, b. 15 November 1918, Wollodarsk, Ukraine. In Israel since 1925. Biologist. m. Ruth Diamant, 2 sons, 1 daughter. Appointments: Member of Kibbutz Beit-Hashitta, 1938-; Agricultural Worker; Youth Movement Leader; Educator; Teacher of Biology; One of Founders of Society for the Protection of Nature in Israel, 1951, General Secretary, 1969-77, Publication Editor; Played major part in campaign to save the wild flowers of Israel, 1964-; Created Governmental Nature Reserves Authority, Board Member, 1964-76; Mapping nature reserves and national parks of Israel, 1951-65; Numerous campaigns to save wildlife and environment; Created Field Study Centres; Took part in Stockholm Convention, 1972, IUCN and UNESCO Conference, Tbilisi, 1977, and IUCN conferences, 1963-90; Writer, Lecturer, Broadcaster on conservation of nature and the environment, 1951-; Senior Lecturer on Landscape, Technion, Haifa, Israel, 1992-. Publications: Hundreds of articles in daily papers, periodicals on nature, environment and conservation; 33 books: 8 books on flowers and trees; 3 books on Sinai and Israel's deserts; 5 books on landscape and animals; 3 books on environmental education; 7 books on plants and animals for children; 2 guidebooks to nature trails in Israel; 1 book on flower trails; 1 book on seven species in the Bible; Books in English, Russian and Arabic; Numerous booklets and brochures; Editor, Encyclopaedia of Plant and Animal Life of Israel, 12 volumes; Nature and landscape photographs: More than 1000 published in books and papers; Weekly radio programme, The Landscape of Our Country, over 2,600 programmes broadcast, 1959-. Honours: Kol Israel (Israel Radio) Prize, 1962; Zimmerman Prize for Environmental Activity, 1977; Israel Prize, co-winner, 1980; Knesset (Israel Parliament) Prize for Environmental Activity, 1984; 500 Global Role of Honor, UNEP, 1987; Dr Honoris Causa, Weizman Institute, 1991; Yigal Alon Prize for Life Activity, 1994; Lions Israel Honour Roll for Life Activity, 2004; Prize for Life Activity, Israeli Minister of Environment, 2008; Golden Microphone – Pioneer of Media on Nature and Environment, Israel Broadcasting Authority, 2009; Herzl Prize, 2010; Dr Honoris Causa, 2011. Memberships: Society for the Protection of Nature in Israel; Life & Environment. Address: Beit Hashitta, Israel 10801. E-mail: azaralon@bethashita.org.il

ALPERT Herb, b. 31 March 1935, Los Angeles, California, USA. Musician (trumpet); Songwriter; Arranger; Record Company Executive. m. Lani Hall, 1 son, 2 daughters. Education: University of Southern California. Career: 3 television specials; Leader, own group Tijuana Brass; Multiple world tours; Owner, Dore Records; Manager, Jan And Dean; Co-founder with Jerry Moss, A&M Records (formerly Carnival), 1962-89; Artists have included: The Carpenters; Captain And Tennille; Carole King; Cat Stevens; The Police; Squeeze; Joe Jackson; Bryan Adams. Compositions include: Wonderful World, Sam Cooke (co-writer with Lou Adler). Recordings: The Lonely Bull; A Taste Of Honey; Spanish Flea; Tijuana Taxi; Casino Royale; This Guy's In Love With You (Number 1, UK and US), 1968; Rise (Number 1, US), 1979; Albums include: The Lonely Bull, Tijuana Brass, 1963; Tijuana Brass Vol 2, 1964; South Of The Border, Whipped Cream And Other Delights, 1965; Going Places, 1966; SRO, Sounds Like Us, 1967; Herb Alpert's 9th, The Best Of The Brass, 1968; Warm, 1969; Rise, Keep Your Eyes On Me, 1979; Magic Man, 1981; My Abstract Heart, 1989; Midnight Sun, 1992; Second Wind, 1996; Passion Dance, 1997; Colors, 1999; Definitive Hits, 2001; Lost Treasures, 2005; Whipped Cream & Other Delights Rewhipped, 2006; Rise (reissue), 2007; Anything Goes, 2009. Honours: Numerous Grammy Awards. Address: c/o Kip Cohen, La Brea Tours, Inc., 1414 Sixth Street, Santa Monica, CA 90401, USA.

ALSADOON Imad Ouda, b. 1951, Iraq. Professor; Medical Director. Education: MB CH B, Medical College, University of Basrah, Iraq, 1976; GMC Registration, 1982; MRCP, Edinburgh, 1983; FRCP, Edinburgh, 1995. Appointments: House Officer, 1976-77, Senior House Officer and Registrar, General Paediatrics, 1978-81, Basrah Teaching Hospital; General Practitioner in rural areas, 1977-78; Doctor, Hospital for Sick Children, Edinburgh, 1981-83; Consultant, Paediatric Department, Basrah Maternity & Child Hospital; Lecturer, 1984, Head of Paediatrics Department, 1986-2001, Assistant Professor, 1987, Professor of Paediatrics, 1996, Dean of Medical College, 2001-04, Basra Medical College; Senior Consultant and Head of Paediatric Department, 2004-, Medical Director, 2004-, Kalba Hospital, Sharjah, United Arab Emirates. Publications: Numerous articles in professional journals. Address: Kalba Hospital, PO Box 145093, Kalba Sharjah, United Arab Emirates. E-mail: alsadoon9@yahoo.co.uk

ALSOP William Allen, b. 12 December 1947, Northampton, England. Architect. m. Sheila Bean, 1972, 2 sons, 1 daughter. Education: Architectural Association. Career: Teacher of Sculpture, St Martin's College; Worked with Cedric Price; In practice with John Lyall; Designed ferry terminal, Hamburg; Design work on Cardiff barrage; Feasibility studies to recycle former De Lorean factory, Belfast; Designed government building, Marseilles; Established own practice, collaborates with Bruce Maclelan in producing architectural drawings; Principal, Alsop and Störmer Architects, 1979-2000; Principal, Director and Chair, Alsop Architects, 2001; Chair, Architecture Foundation, 2001-; Projects include: North Greenwich Station, 2000; Peckham Library and Media Centre, 2000; Commissioned to design Fourth Grace, Liverpool, 2002; Fawood Children's Centre, 2005; Alsop Toronto Sales Centre, 2006. Publications: City of Objects, 1992; William Alsop Buildings and Projects, 1992; William Alsop Architect: Four Projects, 1993; Will Alsop and Jan Störmer, Architects, 1993; Le Grand Bleu-Marseille, 1994; SuperCity, 2004; Alsop and Störmer: Selected and Current Works. Honours: Officer, Order of the British Empire; Honorary LLD, Leicester; Stirling Prize, 2000; Honorary DCL, University of East Anglia, 2001. Memberships: Fellow, Royal Society of Arts. ddress: 72 Pembroke Road, London W8 6NX, England. E-mail: walsop@alsopandstormer.co.uk Website: www.alsopandstormer.com

ALSTON Richard, b. 19 December 1941, Perth, Western Australia. Company Director. m. Megs, 1973, 1 son, 1 daughter. Education: Bachelor degrees in Law, Arts and Commerce, Melbourne University; Masters degrees in Law and Business Administration, Monash University. Appointments: Barrister in common law, commercial and administrative law; Senator for Victoria, 1986-2005; Deputy Leader of the Senate, over 10 years; Minister for Communications, Information Technology and the Arts, Australian Federal Parliament,

1996-2003; Company director, having served on the boards of listed Australian companies; Chairman, Broadcasting Services Australia; Member, International Advisory Board of London-based hedge fund CQS; Non-Executive Director, Chime plc, UK; Adjunct Professor, Information Technology, Bond University, Queensland, 2004-; Australian High Commissioner (Ambassador) to the United Kingdom, 2005-08; Prime Minister's Special Envoy and Leader of the Australian delegation to the Commonwealth Heads of Government Meeting, Uganda, 2007. Honours: Outstanding Contribution to IT industry, Asia-Oceania Computing Industry Organization, 1999; Best Asian Communications Minister, 2002; Outstanding Service Award, Australian Venture Capital Association, 2003; Charles Todd Medal for Outstanding Services to the Australian telecommunications industry, 2004. Address: 362 Albert Road, South Melbourne, 3205, Australia.

ALTARAC Silvio, b. 30 December 1958, Zagreb, Croatia. Urological Surgeon. m. Lidija Lopičić, 1 son, 1 daughter. Education: MD, 1983, PhD, 1989, School of Medicine, Zagreb. Appointments: Teaching Assistant, 1985-89, Scientific Associate, 1993, Scientific Adviser, 2007, Department of Physiology and Immunology, Zagreb; Clinical Research Fellow: University Hospital Pittsburgh, 1990, Royal Hallamshire Hospital, Sheffield, 1993-94, University Hospital Innsbruck, 1995, Brigham and Women's Hospital, Harvard University, Boston, 1995-96; Scientific Associate, 1993; Scientific Adviser, 2007; Chief of Staff, Primarius. Publications: Numerous articles in professional journals; Expert columnist, Salud (i) Ciencia, Buenos Aires, Argentina; Citations, Campbell's Urology, Smith's General Urology; European Association of Urology: Guidelines on Urological Trauma; Reviewer, Liječnički Vjesnik, Croatian Medical Journal. Honours: Academician Drago Perović's Medal; Rector's Award for academic excellence; Listing in numerous biographical publications. Memberships: European Association of Urology; American Urological Association; The Academy of Medical Sciences of Croatia. Address: Bukovačka cesta 229C, 10 000 Zagreb, Croatia.

ALTENBURGER Otto Andreas, b. 29 October 1951, Vienna, Austria. Professor. m. Veronika Maria Weber, 1981, 5 daughters. Education: Mag rer soc oec, 1975, Dr rer soc oec, 1979, habil 1990, Vienna University of Economics and Business Administration (WU), CPA. Appointments: Research & Teaching Assistant, WU, Vienna, 1974-79, 1981-88; Lecturer: Vienna Board of Trade, 1975-78, WU, 1975-92, Austrian Chamber of Accountants, 1976-91, University of St Gallen for Business Administration, Economics, Law and Social Sciences, Switzerland, 1982-2001, University of Linz, Austria, 1989; Auditor, Alpen Treuhand Group, Vienna, 1979-81; Clerk, KPMG, Austria, 1988-90; Professor, Business Administration, University of Regensburg, Germany, 1990-2002, University of Vienna, 2002-, Head, Department of Business Administration, 2008-; External Examiner, University of Limerick, Ireland, 1999-2003; Deputy Member, Austrian Financial Reporting & Auditing Committee, 2005-. Publications: Elements of a Theory of Production of Services, 1980; Commentary on the Austrian Financial Reporting Act, 1993; Financial Accounting and Uncertainty, 1995; Editor, Achievements in Accounting, 1999, 2nd edition 2000; Contributor to journals and books. Honours: Cardinal Innitzer Encouragement Award, 1981; W Wilfling Research Encouragement Award, 1990. Memberships: Austrian Society of Ins Science; German Association of Ins Science; Association of University Teachers of Business Administration. Address: University of Vienna, Department of Business Administration, Bruenner Strasse 72, Vienna 1210, Austria. E-mail: otto.altenburger@univie.ac.at

ALTER Robert B(ernard), b. 2 April 1935, New York, USA. Professor; Literary Critic. m. Carol Cosman, 1974, 3 sons, 1 daughter. Education: BA, Columbia College, 1957; MA, 1958, PhD, 1962, Harvard University. Appointments: Instructor, Assistant Professor of English, Columbia University, 1962-66; Associate Professor of Hebrew and Comparative Literature, 1967-69, Professor of Hebrew and Comparative Literature, 1969-89, Class of 1937 Professor, 1989-, University of California, Berkeley. Publications: Partial Magic, 1975; Defenses of the Imagination, 1978; Stendhal: A Biography, 1979; The Art of Biblical Narrative, 1981; Motives for Fiction, 1984; The Art of Biblical Poetry, 1985; The Pleasures of Reading in an Ideological Age, 1989; Necessary Angels, 1991; The World of Biblical Literature, 1992; Hebrew and Modernity, 1994; Genesis: Translation and Commentary, 1996; The David Study: Translation and Commentary, 1999; Canon and Creativity, 2000; The Five Books of Moses: A Translation with Commentary, 2004; Imagined Cities, 2005; The Book of Psalms, 2007; Pen of Iron, 2010; The Wisdom Books: Translation and Commentary, 2010. Contributions to: Commentary; New Republic; New York Times Book Review; London Review of Books; Times Literary Supplement. Honours: English Institute Essay Prize, 1965; National Jewish Book Award for Jewish Thought, 1982; Present Tense Award for Religious Thought, 1986; Award for Scholarship, National Foundation for Jewish Culture, 1995; Pen USA Award for Literary Translation, 2007; Robert Kirsch Award for Contribution to American Letters, 2009. Memberships: Association for Jewish Studies; Association of Literary Scholars and Critics; Council of Scholars of the Library of Congress; American Academy of Arts and Sciences; American Philosophical Society. Address: 1475 Le Roy Avenue, Berkeley, CA 94708, USA.

ALTEZ Rogelio, b. 15 June 1964, Montevideo, Uruguay. Anthropologist; Historian. m. Inés Quintero, 2 sons. Education: Anthropology; Master, American History. Appointments: Anthropologist, 1991-; Researcher, Earth Sciences Department, Venezuelan Foundation of Seismological Research, 1996-97; Teacher, Metropolitan University; Teacher, Andrés Bello Catholic University; Professor, Anthropology School, Century University of Venezuela, 1998-; Researcher, National Academy of Natural, Physical and Mathematical Sciences, 1998-2000. Publications: Numerous articles in professional journals. Honours: Biennial Award, 2008; Invited Professor and Researcher, Institut des Hautes Études de l'Amerique Latine, Paris; Centro de Investigaciones y Estudios Superiores en Antropologia Social, Mexico; Esuela de Estudios Hispanoamericanos, Seville; Istituto Nazionale de Geofisica e Vulcanologia, Milan; Instituto de Geofisica, Universidad Autonoma de Mexico; Universidad del Quindio, Colombia; Universidad Jaume I, Castellon, Spain; Universidad Industrial de Santander, Colombia. Memberships: International Commission on the History of Geological Sciences; Sociedad Venezolana de Historia de las Geociencias; Editorial Board, Revista geografica Venezolana. Address: 3a avenida de Santa Eduvigis, Edificio El Pionio, piso 4, apto 4-B, Caracas, Venezuela. E-mail: ryaltez@yahoo.com

ALTON Roger Martin, b. 20 December 1947, Oxford, England. Journalist. Divorced, 1 daughter. Education: Exeter College, Oxford. Appointments: Graduate Trainee, then General Reporter and Deputy Features Editor, Liverpool

Post, 1969-73; Sub-Editor, News, 1973-76, Chief Sub-Editor, News, 1976-81, Deputy Sports Editor, 1981-85, Arts Editor, 1985-90, Weekend Magazine Editor, 1990-93, Features Editor, 1993-96, Assistant Editor, 1996-98, The Guardian; Editor, The Observer, 1998-2007; Editor, The Independent, 2008-. Honours: Editor of the Year, What the Papers Say Awards, 2000; Editor of the Year, GQ Men of the Year Awards, 2005. Address: Office of the Editor, The Independent, 2 Derry Street, London W8 5HF, England.

ALVAREZ-CASTRO José María, b. 23 October 1970, Noia, Galiza, Spain. Researcher. 1 son. Education: Degrees in Mathematics and Biology, 1995 and 1998; Advanced Studies Diploma, Genetics, 2000; PhD, Theoretical Population Genetics, 2003. Appointments: Postdoctoral Researcher, Biologie II Department, Ludwig Maximillian University, Munich, Germany, 2003-05; Postdoctoral Researcher, Linnaeus Centre for Bioinformatics, Uppsala University, Sweden, 2006-07; Researcher, Associate Professor, Animal Breeding and Genetics Department, Swedish University of Agricultural Sciences, Uppsala, 2008-; Researcher, Genetics Department, University of Santiago de Compostela, Galiza, Spain, 2008-. Publications: Numerous articles in professional journals. Address: Genetics Department, Veterinary Faculty – PAV IV, Av de Carvalho Calero s/n, ES-27002 Lugo, Galiza, Spain. E-mail: jose.alvarez.castro@usc.es

ALZAMIL Waleed, Doctoral Student. Education: BSc (Hons), MSc, Urban Planning, King Saud University, Saudi Arabia; Master of Community Planning, University of Cincinnati, USA, 2010; Doctoral Student, Urban Planning & Environmental Policy, Texas Southern University, USA, in progress. Appointments: Adjunct Teacher, King Saud University, 2001-08; Affordable Housing, Community Design Center, Cincinnati Uptown, 2010. Publications: Author, The Experiences of Governments in Dealing with Squatter Settlements, 2011. Memberships: American Planning Association; Urban Affairs Association; Urban Land Institute; International Society of City and Regional Planners. Address: 3806 Childress St, Houston, Texas 77005-1114, USA. Website: www.al-zamil.org

AMANO Toshihiko, b. 7 May 1955, Shizuoka, Japan. Professor. m. Tomoko, 1 son, 1 daughter. Education: Bachelor, 1978, Master, 1984, Literature, Tsukuba University. Appointments: Lecturer, 1988, Associate Professor, 1992, Shizuoka Gakuen College; Associate Professor, 1998, Professor, 2002, Shizuoka Sangyo University. Publications: La transitivité, l'hétérogénéité et l'implexe, in Semiotics by the Japanese Association of Semiotic Studies, 1988; A Case Study of the Effectiveness of Distance Learning Materials in Higher Education and Suggestions for Improvement, at IEEE International Conference on Systems, Man and Cybernetics, 1999. E-mail: amano@ssu.ac.jp

AMANPOUR Christiane, b. 12 January 1958, London, England. Broadcasting Correspondent. m. James Rubin, 1998, 1 son. Education: New Hall, Cambridge; University of Rhode Island, USA. Appointments: Radio Producer and Research Assistant, BBC Radio, London, 1980-82; Radio Reporter, WBRU, Brown University, USA, 1981-83; Electronic Graphics Designer, WJAR, Providence, Rhode Island, 1983; Assistant, CNN International Assignment Desk, Atlanta, Georgia, 1983; News Writer, CNN, Atlanta, 1984-86; Reporter, Producer, CNN, New York, 1987-90; International Correspondent, 1990, Senior International Correspondent, 1994, Chief International Correspondent, 1996, CNN; Assignments include Gulf War coverage, 1990-91, USSR break-up and subsequent war in Tbilisi, 1991, extensive reports on conflict in former Yugoslavia and civil unrest and crises coverage, Haiti, Algeria, Somalia and Rwanda; Contracted to CBS, 1996-2005; Anchor, Amanpour, 2009-. Honours: Dr hc, Rhode Island; 3 Dupont-Columbia Awards, 1986-96; 2 News and Documentary Emmy Awards, 1999; George Foster Peabody Award, 1999; George Polk Award, 1999; University of Missouri Award for Distinguished Service to Journalism, 1999; Edward R Murrow Award, 2002; Goldsmith Career Award for Excellence, 2002; International Emmy, 2006; Honorary Citizen, Sarajevo, 2006; Honorary doctorate degree, University of Michigan, 2006; CBE, 2007; Persian Woman of the Year, 2007; Fourth Estate Award, 2008. Memberships: Fellow, Society of Professional Journalists; Honorary Member, Daniel Pearl Foundation; Committee to Protect Journalists. Address: c/o CNN International, CNN House, 19-22 Rathbone Place, London W1P 1DF, England.

AMATO Giuliano, b. 13 May 1938, Turin, Italy. Politician; Professor. m. Diana, 1 son, 1 daughter. Appointments: Joined Italian Socialist Party, 1958; Member, Central Committee, 1978-; Assistant Secretary; elected Deputy for Turin-Novara-Vercelli, 1983, 1987; Former Under-Secretary of State; President and Vice-President, Council of Ministers; Minister of the Treasury, 1987-89; Professor, Italian and Comparative Constitutional Law, University of Rome; National Deputy Secretary, Italian Socialist Party, 1988-92; Foreign debt negotiator for Albanian government, 1991-92, Prime Minister of Italy, 1992-93, 2000-01; Minister for Treasury, 1999-2001; Vice President, EU Special Convention on a Pan-European Constitution, 2001; Minister of the Interior in Romano Prodi's government, 2006-08. Publications: Antitrust and the Bounds of Power, 1997; Tornare al Futuro, 2001. Honours: Foreign Honorary Member, American Academy of Arts and Sciences, 2001. Address: Special Convention on a European Constitution, European Union, 200 rue de la Loi, 1049 Brussels, Belgium.

AMBACHE Stella Maude Ellen, b. 12 July 1917, Lastingham, Yorkshire, England. Medicine; Psychoanalysis. m. Nachman Ambache (deceased), 2 sons (1 deceased), 1 daughter. Education: St Margarets School, Bushey, Hertfordshire, 1926-34; BA, Newnham College, Cambridge, 1936-39; MRCS LRCP, Royal Free Hospital, London, 1939-42; MB BCh (Camb), 1943. Appointments: Principal in General Practice, 1946-68; Foundation Member, RCGPS, 1952; Clinic Staff Member, The London Clinic of PsychoAnalysis, 1966-73; Private practice, Psycho Analysis and Psychotherapy, 1968-2004; Committee work, British PsychoAnalytical Society, 1968-80; Honorary Secretary, The British PsychoAnalytical Society, 1977-80; Retired. Memberships: Fellow, British PsychoAnalytical Society; Affiliate, The Royal College of Psychiatrists; Member and Honorary Secretary, The Winnicott Clinic of Psychotherapy; Foundation and Registration of Charitable Status, The Bromley Clinic for Psychotherapy, now The South East Psychotherapy Group. Address: 23 Parkfields, London SW15 6NH, England. E-mail: stella@ambache.wanadoo.co.uk

AMETEMBUN Nikolaus Aloysius, b. 19 November 1933, Tanimbar, Indonesia. Educator. m. Pia Kelyombar, 1 son, 4 daughters. Education: Master, Educational Administration; PhD, Institute of Teacher Training & Education, Bandung, West Java, Indonesia. Appointments: Lecturer, 1967-98, Professor of Educational Administration, 1993-98, Professor Emeritus, 1999-, Institute of Teacher Training and Education, Bandung. Publications: The Role of Principal in Educational Reformation in Indonesia, 2004; Educational Supervision:

A handbook, 8th edition, 2006; Management of Human Resources in Education: A Handbook for the Educational Managers in Indonesia, 2011; Management of Human Behavior at Work: A Handbook for the Managers of Business and Government in Indonesia, 2013. Honours: Medal of Honor, President of Republic of Indonesia, 1990; Listed in international biographical dictionaries. Memberships: Association for Supervision & Curriculum Development, USA; National Association of Indonesia Educators; Association of Indonesia Catholic Intelligentsia; Listed in international biographical dictionaries. Address: Jalan Melati Raya E22 No 9, Desa Melatiwangi-Ujung Berung, Bandung 40618, Indonesia.

AMIRALI Evangelia-Lila, b. 28 November 1962. Medical Doctor; Psychiatrist. m. J Hadjinicolaou, 4 sons. Education: MD, University of Athens, Greece, 1986; Candidate, Canadian Institute of Psychoanalysis. Appointments: Research Fellow, McGill University, 1988-90, Clinical Fellow, 1990-92; Psychiatrist, Child Psychiatrist, Universite de Montreal, 2001; Assistant Professor, Universite de Montreal; Assistant Professor, McGill University; Medical Director, Pediatric Psychiatric Care Program, Montreal Children's Hospital, McGill University, Health Centre. Honours: A S Onassis Scholarship, 1990-92; Berta Mizne Award, 1988-90; Best Promising Clinician Prize, Department of Psychiatry, McGill University, 1999-2000; American Psychiatric Association Women Fellowship, 2001. Memberships: APA; CPA; QMA; AMPQ. Address: 2875 Douglas Avenue, Montreal, QC H3R 2C7, Canada.

AMIS Martin Louis, b. 25 August 1949, Oxford, England. Author. m. (1) Antonia Phillips, 2 sons, (2) Isabel Fonseca, 3 daughters. Education: BA, Exeter College, Oxford. Appointments: Fiction and Poetry Editor, Times Literary Supplement, 1974; Literary Editor, New Statesman, 1977-79; Special Writer, Observer Newspaper, 1980-; Professor of Creative Writing, University of Manchester, 2007-. Publications: The Rachel Papers, 1973; Dead Babies, 1975; Success, 1978; Other People: A Mystery Story, 1981; Invasion of the Space Invaders, 1982; Money: A Suicide Note, 1984; The Moronic Inferno and Other Visits to America, 1986; Einstein's Monsters: Five Stories, 1987; London Fields, 1989; Time's Arrow, 1991; Visiting Mrs Nabokov and Other Excursions,1993; The Information, 1995; Night Train, 1997; Heavy Water and Other Stories, 1999; Experience, 2000; The War Against Cliché, 2001; Koba the Dread: Laughter and the Twenty Million, 2002; Yellow Dog, 2003; House of Meetings, 2006; The Second Plane: September 11, 2008; The Pregnant Widow, 2010. Honours: Somerset Maugham Award, 1974; James Tait Black Memorial Prize, 2000. Address: c/o Wylie Agency (UK), 17 Bedford Square, London WC1B 3JA, England. E-mail: mail: wylieagency.co.uk

AMLIE Jan Peder, b. 23 September 1940, Bøverbru, V Toten, Norway. Physician. m. May Lisbet, 1 son, 2 daughters. Education: C and Med, 1965, Dr Med, 1981, Oslo University; Speciality Internal Medicine and Cardiology, Sweden and Norway, 1973; Professor in Cardiology, 1991-. Appointments: Assistant Doctor, Sweden, 1966-73; University Lecturer, 1973-75, Research Fellow, 1975-80, Cardiologist, 1981-89, Professor, 1990-, Rikshospitalet, Oslo, Norway. Publications: 150 papers in medical journals and conference proceedings include: Prolonged Ventricular Repolarization, 1983; Books include: Dispersion of Repolarization, 2000. Honour: President, UEMS, Cardiology Section, 2002-06. Memberships: Norwegian Society of Cardiology. Address: Risbakken 10, Oslo 0374, Norway.

AMMAR Mohammed Shokry Ahmed, b. 22 August 1962, Guiza, Egypt. Professor. m. Nadra, 3 sons. Education: BSc, Zoology, 1984, MSc, 1994, PhD, 1997, Coral Reefs, Cairo University; Fellowship, Johannes Güttenberg University, Germany, 2002; 3 Star Diver, 1998; Rescue Diver, 2000; Underwater Photography, 2000. Appointments: Researcher Assistant, 1989-93, Assistant Lecturer, Coral Reefs, 1994-96, Lecturer, Coral Reefs, 1997-2002, Associate Professor, Coral Reefes, 2002-08, Professor, Coral Reefs, 2008; Head of Hurghada Marine Station, 2004-05; Professor, Marine Invertebrates/Coral Reefs. Publications: 40 publications in national and international scientific journals. Honours: Vice Director, National Institute of Oceanography, 2004; Head of Hurghada Marine Station, 2004-05; Listed in international biographical dictionaries. Memberships: Sinai Environmental Center; National Institute of Oceanography; Syndicate of Scientific Professions. Address: PO Box 182, Suez, Egypt.

AMOROSO Santi, b. 17 June 1925, Italy. Physician. m. Gabriella Malanga, 3 sons, 1 daughter. Education: Graduate, 1949, Specialist in Pulmonary Diseases, 1951, Medical School, University "La Sapienza", Rome Italy; Licensed to practice medicine in Italy, Maryland, USA, Virginia, USA, 1959; Certified by ABFP, USA, 1978. Appointments: Internship and Residency, St Mary's Memorial Hospital, Knoxville, Tennessee, 1953-59; General Practitioner, Overlea Medical Group, Baltimore, Maryland, 1959-62; General Practitioner, Perry Hall Medical Group, Baltimore, Maryland, 1962-64; Private Practice, Rome, Italy, 1964-2005; Retired, 2005. Publications: 2 medical articles in an Italian medical journal; 2 books of poetry: Gocciole di rugiada (Dewdrops) and Versi affidati al vento (Lines relying on the wind). Honours: 2nd Place, Poetry Competition sponsored by Association of Italian Physicians Writers, 1996; Translator of English medical books and of "Treatment Guidelines" for CIS Publisher, Italy. Memberships: Former Member, AMA and AAFP; Member, Italian Medical Association. Address: Via Villa Belardi 24, 00154 Rome, Italy. E-mail: santi.amoroso@libero.it

AMOS Tim (Timothy Robert), b. 13 January 1964, Bedford, England. Barrister; Collaborative Lawyer; Resolution Mediator. m. Elke Mund-Amos. Education: King's College Choir School, Cambridge; The King's School, Canterbury; MA, History, Oriel College, Oxford; Diploma in Law, University of Westminster (Polytechnic of Central London). Appointments: Standing Counsel to the Queen's Proctor, 2001-08; Queen's Counsel, 2008; Recorder, 2009. Publications: Essential Family Practice; W(h)ither Forensic Accountancy in English Matrimonial Finance? Honours: Queen's Counsel. Memberships: Fellow, International Academy of Matrimonial Lawyers; Family Law Bar Association; Affiliate Member, Resolution. Address: Queen Elizabeth Building, Temple, London EC4Y 9BS, England. E-mail: t.amos@qeb.co.uk

AMOS William Henry, b. 14 March 1927, Durham, USA. Chief Apostle. m. Myrtle G, 1 son, 2 daughters. Education: DD, 1973; B Th, 1974; BA, 1977; M Div, 1981; PhD, Ministry, 1998. Appointments: Chief Apostle, Church of God in Christ Jesus New Deal Inc. Honours: The Presidential Leadership Circle, Bill Clinton, 1999; Man of the Year, ABI, 2008; Listed in international biographical dictionaries. Memberships: 32nd Degree Mason and Shriner. Address: 4007 Booker Street, Durham, NC 27713, USA.

AN Beongku, b. 18 September 1960, Republic of Korea. Professor. m. Jeongran Baeck, 1 son. Education: BS, Kyungpook National Universitym, Korea, 1988; MS,

Polytechnic University, USA, 1996; PhD, New Jersey Institute of Technology, USA, 2002. Appointments: Senior Researcher, RIST, Republic of Korea, 1989-94; Lecturer & RA, New Jersey Institute of Technology, USA, 1997-2002; Professor, Hongik University, Republic of Korea, 2003-. Publications: 15 articles in professional international journals. Honours: Best Award Paper, KSEA, USA, 2001; Listed in international biographical dictionaries. Memberships: Institute of Electronics Engineering of Korea; Korea Information and Communications Society; Institute of Webcasting and Internet Television; Korea Multimedia Society; Korea Society of Transportation. Address: Department of Computer & Information Communications Engineering, Hongik University, Shinan-Ri, Jochiwon, Yeong-Gun, Chungnam, 339-701, Republic of Korea. E-mail: beongku@wow.hongik.ac.kr

ANAND Amaladass, b. 24 October 1943, Irumathi, Tamil Nadu, India. Professor. Education: BA, English Literature, 1968; Licentiate in Philosophy, 1971; MA, Sanskrit, 1973; PhD, University of Madras, 1981. Appointments: Dean, Faculty, Satya Nilayam, Chennai, 1996-2000; Director, Satya Nilayam Research Institute, Chennai, 1992-2007; Co-editor, Journal of Hindu Christian Studies, 1998-2008; Founder & Editor, Satya Nilayam Chennai Journal of Intercultural Philosophy, 2002-07. Publications: 20 books; 30 articles in English. Honours: Intercultural Philosophy, 2002-07. Address: Satya Nilayam, Institute of Philosophy & Culture, 201, Kalki Krishnamurthi Road, Thiruvanmiyur, Chennai 600041, India. E-mail: amaladass24@gmail.com

ANASRAJ Robert J, b. 29 May 1968, Kerala, India. m. Achamma E Alex, 1 son, 1 daughter. Education: PhD. Appointments: Teaching. Publications: Numerous articles in professional journals. Memberships: ISTE; IE (India). Address: Department of Electrical and Electronics Engineering, Government Engineering College, Thrissur, Kerala, India.

ANDERSON Elizabeth Lang, b. 3 March 1960, Orange, New Jersey, USA. Composer; m. David S Baltuch. Education: BA, Music, Gettysburg College, Gettysburg, Pennsylvania, 1982; Master of Music in Composition, Peabody Institute, Baltimore, Maryland, 1987; Certificate, Composition, Royal Conservatory of Brussels, 1990; Diploma, Electronic Music Composition, Royal Conservatory, Antwerp, 1993; Premier Prix in Electroacoustic Music Composition, Royal Conservatory of Mons, 1997; Superior Diploma In Electroacoustic Music Composition, Royal Conservatory of Mons, 1998; PhD, Electroacoustic Music Composition, in progress, City University, London, 2010. Appointments: Instructor of Musicianship (Creative Music Theory), Peabody Preparatory, Baltimore, Maryland, 1985-87; Professor, Electroacoustic Music Composition, Academy of Soignies, Belgium, 1994-2002; Lecturer in the Electroacoustic Music Department, Royal Conservatory of Mons, 2003-04. Publications: The following works are available on compact disc Mimoyecques, 1995, L'éveil,1997-98, Chat Noir, 2000, Neon, 2005, Les Forges de l'Invisible, 2004; Protopia/Tesseract, 2007. Honours: Music honoured in several competitions specialising in electroacoustic music including: Ascap/Seamus, Bourges, Città di Udine, Cimesp, Métamorphoses, Noroit, Stockholm; Commissions from Musiques & Recherches, Belgium and La Chambre d'Ecoute, Belgium; Numerous performances and conferences at international venues; Overseas Research Students Award Scheme Grant funded by the Committee of Vice-Chancellors and Principals of the Universities of the United Kingdom; Grant, British Federation of Women Graduates Charitable Foundation; Grant, Foundation SPES, Belgium. Memberships: Federation Belge de Musique Electroacoustique, International Computer Music Association, SACEM, Sonic Arts Network, Society for Electro-Acoustic Music in the United States. Address: Avenue de Monte Carlo, 11, 1190 Brussels, Belgium. E-mail: e.anderson@skynet.be

ANDERSON Gillian, b. 9 August 1968, Chicago, USA. Actress. m. (1) Errol Clyde Klotz, divorced, 1 daughter; (2) Julian Ozanne, 2004-06; 2 sons with Mark Griffiths, 2006. Education: DePaul University, Chicago; Goodman Theatre School, Chicago. Appointments: Worked at National Theatre, London; Appeared in two off-broadway productions; Best Known Role as Special Agent Dana Scully in TV Series, The X Files (Feature Film 1998); Films include: Chicago Cab, 1995; The Turning, 1997; The X-Files, The Mighty, Playing By Heart, 1998; Princess Mononoke, 1999; House of Mirth, 2000; The Mighty Celt, Tristam Shandy: A Cock and Bull Story, 2005; The Last King of Scotland, 2006; Straightheads, 2007; The X-Files: I Want to Believe, How to Lose Friends & Alienate People, 2008; Plays include: Absent Friends, Manhattan Theater Club, 1991; The Philanthropist, Along Wharf Theater, 1992; What the Night is For, Comedy Theatre, London, 2002; The Sweetest Swing in Baseball, Royal Court Theatre, London, 2004; A Doll's House, Donmar Warehouse, London, 2009; TV films include: Home Fire Burning, 1992; When Planes Go Down, 1996; Presenter, Future Fantastic, BBC TV; Bleak House, BBC TV, 2005. Honours: Theater World Award, 1991; Golden Globe Awards, 1995, 1997; Screen Actors' Guild Awards, 1996, 1997; Emmy Award, 1997. Address: William Morris Agency, 151 El Camino Drive, Beverly Hills, CA 90212, USA. Website: www.gilliananderson.ws

ANDERSON John Anthony (Sir), b. 2 August 1945, Wellington, New Zealand. Banker. m. Carol M Tuck, 1970, 2 sons, 1 daughter. Education: Christ's College; Victoria University of Wellington; FCA. Appointments: Deloitte Haskins and Sells chartered accountants, Wellington, 1962-69; Guest and Bell sharebrokers, Melbourne, Victoria, Australia, 1969-72; Joined, 1972, Chief Executive, Director, 1979, South Pacific Merchant Finance Ltd, Wellington; Deputy Chief Executive, 1988, Chief Executive, Director, 1990-2003, National Bank of New Zealand; Chair, Petroleum Corporation of New Zealand Ltd, 1986-88; Director, New Zealand Steel Ltd, 1986-87, Lloyds Merchant Bank, London, 1986-92, Lloyds Bank NZA, Australia, 1989-97; New Zealand Bankers' Association, 1991-92, 1999-2000; President, New Zealand Bankers Institute, 1990-2001; Chair, New Zealand Cricket Board, 1995-, New Zealand Sports Foundation Inc, 1999-2002; Managing Director, ANZ National Bank Ltd, 2003-05; Chair, Television New Zealand, 2006-; Chairman, Capital and Coast District Health Board, 2007; Commissioner, Hawkes Bay District Health Board, 2008; Other professional and public appointments. Honours: NZ Commemoration Medal, 1990; Knight Commander, Order of the British Empire, 1994; Blake Medal, 2005. Memberships: Chair, New Zealand Merchant Banks Association, 1982-89; Chair, New Zealand Bankers Association, 1992-. Address: 5 Fancourt Street, Karori, Wellington 5, New Zealand.

ANDERSON Katrina Marysia Tomaszewska, b. 7 December 1947, Springfield by Cupar, Fife, Scotland. Community Educator. m. William Anderson, 1 son, 2 daughters. Education: General Scottish Vocational Qualification, National Certificate Level III, Care with Merit, 1994; Master of Arts, English Literature (Honours), University of Dundee, 1999; Open University Postgraduate

Diploma in Community Education, Northern College, Dundee, 2001. Appointments: Personal Assistant to husband in the family business, 1986-; Community Educator; Member, Volunteer, Tracing and Message Co-ordinator. Publications: Numerous poems published by International Society of Poets, 1998, 2000; Triumph House, 1997-2001; Brownstone Books, 1997; Poets 2008; Poetry, Forward Press, 2010. Honours: National Award, Higher National Certificate, Social Services, 1995; Cultural Relations Attache to Scotland, HRP (Title: The Hon); Medal, HRP, 1998; Honoured Poet, 1998; One of the Best Poets of the 20th Century; Woman of the Year, ABI, 2006; Member, ABI's Professional Women's Advisory Board; International Peace Prize; Nominated for Gold Medal, 2008; Listed in Who's Who publications and biographical dictionaries. Memberships: Environmental Officer, Students Union, Glenrothes College; International Society of Poets; University of Dundee Alumni; British Red Cross; Lifetime Partronage, Hutt River Province, Australia. Address: 31 Clyde Court, Rimbleton, Glenrothes, Fife KY6 2BN, Scotland.

ANDERSON Kevin, b. 15 June 1994, Skelleftea, Sweden. Student; Philanthropist. Education: Undergoing gymnasium education. Appointments: Founder/President of the local UN association; Board of Directors, Social Democratic Youth; Founder, local Red Cross office. Publications: Book, The Global Hunger. Honours: Numerous leadership award on a global scale; President's Education Program Award; Branting Medal; Certificate of Academic Excellence; President's Volunteer Award Service; Nominee, Children's International Peace Prize. Memberships: UN; SSU; Red Cross; Young Leaders. E-mail: kevin_harno@hotmail.com

ANDERSON Michael, b. 30 January 1920, London, England. Film Director. m. (1) Betty Jordan, 1939, 5 children; (2) Vera Carlisle, 1969, 1 child; (3) Adrianne Ellis, 1977, 2 stepchildren. Education: France. Appointments: Co-Director with Peter Ustinov, film, Private Angelo, 1949; Director, films: Waterfront, 1950; Hell Is Sold Out, 1952; Night Was Our Friend; Dial 17; Will Any Gentleman?; The House of the Arrow, 1952; The Dam Busters, 1954; Around the World in Eighty Days, 1956; Yangtse Incident, 1957; Chase a Crooked Shadow, 1957; Shake Hands with the Devil, 1958; Wreck of the Mary Deare, 1959-60; All the Fine Young Cannibals, 1960; The Naked Edge, 1961; Flight from Ashyia, 1962; Operation Crossbow, 1964; The Quiller Memorandum, 1966; Shoes of The Fisherman, 1969; Pope Joan, 1970-71; Doc Savage, 1973; Conduct Unbecoming, 1974; Logan's Run, 1975; Orca - Killer Whale, 1976; Dominique, 1977; The Martian Chronicles, 1978; Bells, 1979-80; Millennium; Murder by Phone; Second Time Lucky; Separate Vacations; Sword of Gideon; Jeweller's Shop; Young Catherine; Millennium; Summer of the Monkeys; The New Adventures of Pinocchio, 1999. Address: c/o Film Rights Ltd, 113-117 Wardour Street, London W1, England.

ANDERSON Ursula Mary, b. Cheshire, England. Medicine; Research; Writing. Education: MB, ChB, DPH, Liverpool University, England; MD; MRCS; DCH; FAAP; DSc (Hon). Appointments: Distinguished Professor and Research Professor, Forest institute of Professional Psychology; Chief, Division of Community Pediatrics and Associate Professor of Pediatrics, University of Toronto, Canada; Consultant, Division of Research, World Health Organisation, Geneva, Switzerland; Clinical Professor of Pediatrics, Emory University, Georgia, USA; Medical Director, Interagency Programs for Children and Regional Medical Consultant, US Department of Health Education and Welfare; Consultant, USA National Perinatal Association; Consultant, USA National & Regional Head Start Programs; Director, Maternal and Child Health, Buffalo and Erie County, New York, USA; Associate Professor of Pediatrics, New York State University, Buffalo; Chair, New York State Task Force on Health Manpower, Governor's Office, Albany, New York. Publications: Over 60 articles in professional journals; 9 books. Honours: Listed in international biographical dictionaries; Several major grants; United Nations Open University Merit of Excellence Award. Memberships: American Academy of Pediatrics; Center for Mind/Being Research; Institute of Noetic Sciences; Yale University Alumni, USA. Website: www.drursulaanderson.com www.andersonbeyondgenome.com

ANDERSON (William) Eric (Kinloch), b. 27 May 1936, Edinburgh, Scotland. Education. m. Elizabeth (Poppy) Mason, 1 son, 1 daughter. Education: George Watson's College, Edinburgh; St Andrew's University; Balliol College, Oxford. Appointments: Assistant Master, Fettes College; Assistant Master, Gordonstoun; Headmaster, Abingdon School; Headmaster, Shrewsbury School; Headmaster, Eton; Chairman, Heritage Lottery Fund; Rector, Lincoln College, Oxford; Provost of Eton. Publications: Journal of Sir Walter Scott, 1972; Percy Letters Vol IX, 1988; Sayings of Sir Walter Scott, 1992; (with Adam Nicolson) About Eton, 2010. Honours: KT; Hon D Litt: St Andrews University; Hull University; Siena University; Birmingham University; Visitor of Harris-Manchester College, Oxford. Memberships: FRSE. Address: The Homestead, Kingham, Oxfordshire, OX7 6YA, England.

ANDO Nisuke, b. 6 August 1935, Kyoto, Japan. Professor Emeritus of International Law. m. Noriko Fujimoto, 1 son, 2 daughters. Education: LLB, 1959, LLM, 1961, Kyoto University; PhD, Fletcher School of Law and Diplomacy, 1971. Appointments: Lecturer and Associate Professor, 1965-68, 1968-81, Kyoto University; Professor, 1981-90, Kobe University; Professor, Kyoto University, 1990-98; Professor, Doshisha University, 1998-2006; Director, Kyoto Human Rights Research Institute, 2001-. Publications: Surrender, Occupation and Private Property in International Law, 1991; Japan and International Law - Past, Present and Future, editor, 1999; Liber Amicorum Judge Shigeru Oda, co-editor, 2002; Towards Implementing Universal Human Rights, editor, 2004. Honours: Fulbright Graduate Student, 1962-64; Fulbright Research Fellow, 1969-70; British Council Fellow, 1976-78; Fulbright 50th Anniversary Distinguished Fellow, 1996; Japanese Government's Order of Sacred Treasure, Double Light Degree, 2008. Memberships: Human Rights Committee under the International Covenant on Civil and Political Rights, 1987-2006; Judge, Administrative Tribunal of the International Monetary Fund, 1994-; Member, Permanent Court of Arbitration, 2001-. Address: 922-66 Kokubu 2-chome, Otsu-shi, Shiga-ken 520-0844, Japan.

ANDO Tsugio, b. 15 November 1935, Morioka City, Japan. Law Professor. m. Nagako Musha, 2 sons. Education: LLB, 1959, Doctor of Laws, 1980, Tohoku University, Japan; LLM, Yale University Law School, 1964. Appointments: Lecturer, Associate, Main Professor, Professor Emeritus, Tohoku University, 1965-90; Professor, Tsukuba University Graduate Course, 1990-96; Professor, Tohoku Gakuin University, Sendai, Japan, 1996-. Publications: Book, Law and Legal Process, 1986; Articles: Finance lease and tax law, 1980; Comparative studies of risk of loss in sales, 1983-84. Memberships: Japanese American Society for Legal Studies; Association of Japanese Private Law. Address: 1-3-7 Sogodai, Natori-City, Miyagi-ken, 981-1246, Japan. E-mail: tsugio-ando5@lagoon.ocn.ne.jp/

DICTIONARY OF INTERNATIONAL BIOGRAPHY 36th EDITION

ANDRAE Anders Sven Gunnar, b. 11 July 1973, Västervik, Sweden. Researcher. Education: MSc, Chemical Engineering, Royal Institute of Technology, Stockholm, Sweden, 1997; PhD, Electronics Production, Chalmers University of Technology, Gothenburg, Sweden, 2005. Appointments: Environmental Engineer, Ericsson, Stockholm, Sweden, 1997-2001; PhD student, Chalmers University of Technology, Gothenburg, Sweden, 2001-05; Postdoctoral Research Scientist, National Institute of Advanced Industrial Science and Technology, Tsukuba, Japan, 2006-07; Postdoctoral JSPS Fellow, AIST, Tsukuba, Japan, 2007-08; Senior Expert, Huawei Technologies, Stockholm, 2008-. Publications: Numerous articles in professional journals; 2 books, 2009. Honours: IEEE Young Award, 2006; JSPS Postdoctoral Fellowship, 2007; Expert Evaluator for European Commission, 2010; Listed in international biographical dictionaries. Memberships: Djurgardens IF Fotbollsförening. Address: Wiboms väg 8, 17160 Solna, Sweden. E-mail: andersandrae@gmail.com

ANDREANI Pascale, b. 6 April 1955, Paris, France. Diplomat. m. Gilles Andreani, 3 sons. Education: Masters degree, Public Law, 1976; Graduate (magna cum laude), Insitut d'Etudes Politiques de Paris, 1978; ENA (Promotion Henri François d'Aguesseau), 1980-82; DEA of Community Law, 1988. Appointments: First Secretary, Foreign Affairs, French Mission to the United Nations, New York, 1982; Economic Affairs, Ministry of Foreign Affairs, 1984; Head of the Community Internal Market Bureau, Ministry of Foreign Affairs, 1989; General Secretary, Interministerial Mission for Central and Eastern Europe, 1990; Deputy Head of the European Secretariat (SGCI), 1990; Head of the Private Office of the Minister for European Affairs, 1993; Head of the CFSP Bureau, 1995; Head of the Private Office of the Minister for Budget, Government Spokesperson, 1995; Deputy Head, United Nations and International Organisations Directorate, 1997; Adviser on European Affairs to the President of the Republic, 1997; Deputy Chief of Mission, French Embassy to the UK, London, 1998; Head of the European Co-operation Directorate, Ministry of Foreign Affairs, 2000; Adviser on European Affairs to the Prime Minister, 2002; General Secretary of European Secretariat (SGCI), 2002; General Secretary for European Affairs (SGAE), 2005; Spokesperson for the Ministry of Foreign and European Affairs, 2007; Ambassador, Permanent Representative to NATO, 2008. Publications: Numerous articles in professional journals, including: The Constitutional Enlargement of Europe, 2004. Address: Permanent Representation of France to NATO, Boulevard Leopold III, 1110 Brussels, Belgium.

ANDREEV Rumen Dimov, b. 20 March 1955, Sofia, Bulgaria. Engineer. Education: Master of Science, 1980, PhD, 1987, Sofia Technical University, Sofia, Bulgaria. Appointments: Constructor, Institute of Computer Technique, 1980-82; Research Fellow, Central Institute of Computer Technique and Technology, 1982-88; Research Associate, Central Laboratory of Automation and Scientific Instrumentation, 1988-93; Associate Professor, Institute of Computer and Communication Systems, Bulgarian Academy of Sciences, 1994-2010; Associate Professor, Institute of Information and Communication Technologies, 2010-. Publications: Monograph: Graphics Systems: Architecture and Realization, 1993; Articles in scientific journals including: Computer Graphics Forum; Computers and Graphics; Interacting with Computers; Communication and Cognition; Lecture notes on Artificial Intelligence. Honours: Medal, Ministry of Defence, Republic of Bulgaria, 1974; Nominated for International Scientist of the Year 2003, Diploma of Achievement in Science, IBC; Listed in Who's Who publications and biographical dictionaries. Memberships: Bulgarian Union of Automation and Informatics, British Computer Society; New York Academy of Sciences. Address: Institute of Information and Communication Technologies, Bulgarian Academy of Sciences, str Acad. G Bonchev Bl 2, 1113 Sofia, Bulgaria. E-mail: rumen@isdip.bas.bg

ANDRETTI Mario Gabriele, b. 28 February 1940, Montona, Italy. Racing Driver. m. Dee Ann Hoch, 1961, 2 sons, 1 daughter. Appointments: Began midget car racing in US, graduating to US Auto Club National Formula; Indy Car National Champion, 1965, 1966, 1969, 1984; USAC Champion, 1965, 1966, 1969, 1974; Winner, Indianapolis 500 Miles, 1969; Winner, Daytona 500 Miles NASCAR Stock Car Race, 1967; Began Formula 1 Racing in 1968; World Champion, 1978; Third, 1977; Winner, International Race of Champions, 1979; President, MA 500 Inc, 1968-; Newman/Haas Racing, 1983; Honours: Driver of the Year, 1967, 1978, 1984; Driver of the Quarter Century, 1992; Driver of the Century, 1999-2000; All Time Indy Car Lap Leader (7587); Grand Prix Wins: South African (Ferrari); Japanese (Lotus Ford), 1976; US (Lotus Ford), 1977; Spanish (Lotus Ford), 1977; French (Lotus Ford), 1977; Italian (Lotus Ford), 1977; Argentine (Lotus Ford), 1978; Belgian (Lotus Ford), 1978; Spanish (Lotus Ford), 1978; French (Lotus Ford), 1978; German (Lotus Ford), 1978; Dutch (Lotus Ford), 1978; Commendatore dell'Ordine al Merito della Repubblica Italiana (known as the Commendatore), 2006. Address: 475 Rose Inn Avenue, Nazareth, PA 18064, USA.

ANDREW Jon, b. 29 March 1932, New Zealand. Vocal Coach; Retired Opera Singer. m. Victoria Julia Maud, 4 sons. Education: Fielding Agricultural College, New Zealand. Appointments: International Opera Singer, 1958-82; Sang for New Zealand Opera Co, 1958-62, Sadler's Wells Opera, 1962-69; Appeared with Royal Opera, Glyndebourne Festival Opera, Scottish Opera, Welsh National Opera; In Germany contracted to: Badische Staatsoper, Mannheim National Oper, Deutsche Oper am Rhein, Düsseldorf; Also appeared with La Scala, Milan, La Fenice, Venice, Paris Opera, Rome Opera, San Diego, Chicago, Pittsburgh, Baltimore; Sang under conductors: Wolfgang Sawallisch, Taijiro Iimori, Sir Georg Solti, Sir Colin Davis, Sir Charles Mackerras, James Levine, Karl Bohm, Erich, Leinsdorf, Sir John Prichard, etc; Repertoire includes: Il Trovatore, La Traviata, Un Ballo in Maschera, Aida, Otello, Attilla, Rigoletto (Verdi); Tannhäuser, Lohengrin, Die Meistersinger, Das Rheingold, Die Valküre, Siegfried, Parsifal, Der Fliegende Holländer (Wagner); Il Barbiere di Siviglia (Rossini); Jenufa, From the House of the Dead, (Janacek); La Bohème, Tosca, Madama Butterfly, La Fancuilla del West, Il Tabarro, La Rondine, Turandot, (Puccini); Salome, Der Rosenkavalier, Ariadne auf Naxos, Electra (Richard Strauss); Cavalleria Rusitcana (Mascagni); Der Freischütz (Weber); The Knife (Daniel Jones); Die Fledermaus (Johann Strauss); Peter Grimes (Britten); Faust (Gounod); Boris Godunov (Mussorgsky); Pique Dame, Eugene Onegin (Tchaikovsky); Fidelio (Beethoven); Anna Bolena (Donizetti); Pagliacci, Oedipus Rex (Leoncavallo); Le Nozze di Figaro (Mozart); Requiem (Verdi); Vocal Coach, pupils include: Kate Royal (soprano), David Habbin (tenor), Jonathan Prentice (baritone), Hannah Pedley (mezzo), 1991-; Founder/Director, Silhouette Opera, 1998-. Honours: Kammersanger, Deutsche Staatsoper, 1973. Memberships: Charitable Fundraiser, Associated Children's Hospices, Julia's House, Anthony Nolan Trust, NSPCC, Lord's Taverners,

Tenovus, Bournemouth Hospital Jigsaw Appeal, Help and Care. Address: 37 St Alban's Crescent, Bournemouth, Dorset BH8 9EW, England. E-mail: royaltoria@ntlworld

ANDREWS Anthony, b. 12 January 1948, Hampstead, London, England. Actor. m. Georgina Simpson, 1 son, 2 daughters. Career: Started acting, 1967; TV appearances include: Doomwatch, Woodstock, 1972, A Day Out, Follyfoot, Fortunes of Nigel, 1973, The Pallisers, David Copperfield, 1974, Upstairs Downstairs, 1975, French Without Tears, The Country Wife, Much Ado About Nothing, 1977, Danger UXB, 1978, Romeo and Juliet, 1979, Brideshead Revisited, 1980, Ivanhoe, 1982, The Scarlet Pimpernel, 1983, Colombo, 1988, The Strange Case of Dr Jekyll and Mr Hyde, 1989, Hands of a Murderer, 1990, Lost in Siberia, 1990, The Law Lord, 1991, Jewels, 1992, Ruth Rendell's Heartstones, Mothertime; David Copperfield, 2000; Love in a Cold Climate, 2001; Cambridge Spies, 2003; Marple: By the Pricking of my Thumbs, 2006. Films include: The Scarlet Pimpernel, Under the Volcano, A War of the Children, Take Me High, 1973, Operation Daybreak, 1975, Les Adolescents, 1976, The Holcroft Covenant, 1986, Second Victory, 1987, Woman He Loved, 1988, The Lighthorsemen, 1988, Hannah's War, 1988, Lost in Siberia, as actor and producer, 1990, Haunted, as actor and producer, 1995; Appeared in plays: 40 Years On, A Midsummer Night's Dream, Romeo and Juliet, One of Us, 1986, Coming into Land, 1986, Dragon Variation, Tima and the Conways; My Fair Lady, 2003; The Woman in White, 2005. Address: c/o Peters Fraser and Dunlop Ltd, 503 The Chambers, Chelsea Harbour, London SW10 0XF, England.

ANDREWS Julie (Dame), b. 1 October 1935, Walton-on-Thames, Surrey, England. Singer; Actress. m. (1) Tony Walton, May 1959, divorced, 1 daughter; (2) Blake Edwards, 1969. Musical Education: Voice lessons with Lillian Stiles-Allen. Career: As actress: Debut, Starlight Roof, London Hippodrome, 1947; Appeared: Royal Command Performance, 1948; Broadway production, The Boy Friend, NYC, 1954; My Fair Lady, 1956-60; Camelot, 1960-62; Putting It Together, 1993; Film appearances include: Mary Poppins, The Americanization Of Emily, 1964; Torn Curtain, The Sound Of Music, Hawaii, 1966; Thoroughly Modern Millie, 1967; Stark, 1968; Darling Lili, 1970; The Tamarind Seed, 1973; 10, 1979; Little Miss Marker, 1980; S.O.B., 1981; Victor/Victoria, 1982; The Man Who Loved Women, 1983; That's Life!, Duet For One, 1986; The Sound of Christmas, TV, 1987; Relative Values, 1999; The Princess Diaries, 2001; Shrek 2 (voice), The Princess Diaries 2: Royal Engagement, 2004; Shrek the Third (voice), 2007; Enchanted (voice), 2007; Television debut, 1956; Host, The Julie Andrews Hour, 1972-73; Julie (comedy series), ABC-TV, 1992; Eloise at the Plaza, 2003; Eloise at Christmastime, 2003; Television films include Our Sons, 1991. Recordings: Albums: A Christmas Treasure, 1968; The Secret Of Christmas, 1977; Love Me Tender, 1983; Broadway's Fair, 1984; Love Julie, 1989; Broadway: The Music Of Richard Rogers, 1994; Here I'll Stay, Nobody Sings It Better, 1996; with Carol Burnett: Julie And Carol At Carnegie Hall, 1962; At The Lincoln Center, 1989; Cast and film soundtacks: My Fair Lady (Broadway cast), 1956; Camelot (Broadway cast), 1961; Mary Poppins (film soundtrack), 1964; The Sound Of Music (film soundtrack), 1965; The King And I (studio cast), 1992. Publications: Mandy (as Julie Edwards), 1971; The Last Of The Really Great Whangdoodles, 1974; Home: A Memoir of My Early Years (autobiography), 2008. Honours: Oscar, Mary Poppins, 1964; Golden Globe Awards, Hollywood Foreign Press Association, 1964, 1965; BAFTA Silver Mask, 1989; Dame Commander of the Order of the British Empire, 2000; Kennedy Center Honor, 2001; SAG Life Achievement Award, 2007; Lifetime Musical Achievement, UCLA George and Ira Gershwin Award, 2009. Address: c/o Triad Artists, 10100 Santa Monica Boulevard, 16th Floor, Los Angeles, CA 90067, USA.

ANDREWS Kevin, b. 9 November 1955, Sale, Victoria, Australia. Member of Australian Parliament. m. Margaret Mary Ryan, 3 sons, 2 daughters. Education: BA, LLB, University of Melbourne; LLM, Monash University. Appointments: Research Solicitor, Law Institute of Victoria, 1980-81; Co-ordinator of Continuing Legal Education, Law Institute of Victoria, 1981-83; Associate to the Hon Justice James Gobbo, Supreme Court of Victoria, 1983-85; Barrister-at-Law, 1985-91; Member for Menzies, Australian House of Representatives, 1991-; Parliamentary Secretary to the Leader of the Opposition, 1992-93; Shadow Minister for Schools, Vocational Education and Training, 1993-94; Parliamentary Secretary to the Deputy Leader of the Opposition, 1994-96; Chairman, House of Representatives Legal and Constitutional Affairs Committee, 1996-2001; Minister for Ageing, 2001-03; Minister Assisting the Prime Minister for the Public Service, 2003-07; Minister for Employment and Workplace Relations, 2003-07; Minsiter for Immigration and Citizenship, 2007; Deputy Chairman, House of Representatives Economics Committee, 2009; Chair, Coalition Policy Review, 2008-09; Deputy Chairman, House of Representatives Economics Committee, 2008-09; Shadow Minister for Families, Housing and Human Services, 2009-. Publications: Elderly and the Law, 1982; Issues in Biomedical Ethics (contributor), 1990; Trends in Biomedical Regulation (contributor), 1990; Rights and Freedoms in Australia (contributor), 1990; The Heart of Liberalism, 1994; Changing Australia, 1998; The Australian Polity, 2008-; Numerous journal articles. Honours: Australian Young Lawyer of the Year, 1987, 1988; Centenary Medal, 2003. Address: PO Box 124, Doncaster 3108, Victoria, Australia. E-mail: kevin.andrews.mp@aph.gov.au Website: www.kevinandrews.au.com

ANDRONIKOU Andonakis Yiannagou, b. 29 November 1931, Kythrea-Nicosia, Cyprus. Retired. m. Klelia Avraamides, 1 son, 1 daughter. Education: LLB, London University, 1961; Postgraduate diploma, Development Administration, London School of Economics and Political Science, 1967; Diploma, Management, University of Michigan, 1981; PhD, Management, Pacific Western University, 1989. Appointments: Director-General, Economic Planning Commission, 1967-71; Cabinet Secretary, 1971-73, Government of Cyprus; Director-General, Cyprus Tourism Organisation, 1973-91; Executive Director, Cyprus Anti-Cancer Organisation, 1997-2009. Publications: Book, Cyprus Tourism-Harmonization of Tourism with the Environment; Book chapter, Tourism Passport to Development; Many articles on Cyprus Tourism and the Role of Non-Governmental Philanthropic Institutions. Honours: Eisenhower Exchange Fellow, 1981. Memberships: Cyprus Bar Association; International Association of Scientific Experts in Tourism; Fellow, British Institute of Management. Address: 38 Archimedes Str, Strovolos, 2018, Nicosia, Cyprus. E-mail: supire@cytanet.com.cy

ANDSNES Leif Ove, b. 7 April 1970, Karmoy, Norway. Pianist. Education: Studied at the Music Conservatory of Bergen with Jiri Hlinka. Debut: Oslo, 1987; British debut, Edinburgh Festival with the Oslo Philharmonic, Mariss Jansons, 1989; US Debut, Cleveland Symphony, Neeme Järvi. Career: Appearances include: Schleswig-Holstein Festival and with orchestras such as Los Angeles Philharmonic, Japan Philharmonic, Berlin Philharmonic, London Philharmonic, Philharmonia, City of Birmingham Symphony Orchestra,

Royal Scottish National Orchestra, BBC Philharmonic Orchestra for his debut at the Proms, 1992 and Chicago Symphony Orchestra; Soloist, Last Night of the Proms, 2002; Artistic Director, Risor Festival; Recitals at Teatro Communale, Bologna, Wigmore Hall, Barbican Hall, London, Herkulesaal, Munich, Concertgebouw, Amsterdam, Konzerthaus Vienna and Glasgow Royal Concert Hall. Recordings include: Grieg: A Minor and Liszt A Major concerti; Grieg: Lyric Pieces; Janacek, Solo Piano Music; Chopin, Sonatas and Grieg, Solo Piano Music; Brahms and Schumann works for piano and viola with Lars Anders Tomter. Honours include: First Prize, Hindemith Competition, Frankfurt am Main; Levin Prize, Bergen, 1999; Norwegian Music Critics' Prize, 1988; Grieg Prize, Bergen, 1990; Dorothy B Chandler Performing Art Award, Los Angeles, 1992; Gilmore Prize, 1997; Instrumentalist Award, Royal Philharmonic Society, 2000; Gramophone Award, Best Concerto Recording, 2000; Best Instrumental Recording, 2002; Commander, Royal Norwegian Order of St Olav, 2002; Sibelius Prize, 2005; Spellemannpris, 2006; Classical Brit Award, Best Instrumentalist, 2007. Address: c/o Kathryn Enticott, IMG Artists (Europe), Lovell House, 616 Chiswick High Road, London W4 5RX, England.

ANG Peng Hwa, b. 20 November 1957, Singapore. Company Director. m. Caroline Sai Lin Loy, 1 daughter. Education: Bachelor of Law, National University of Singapore, 1982; Postgraduate Practice Law Course, Board of Legal Education, Singapore, 1982; MA, Communication Management, University of Southern California, USA, 1988; PhD, Mass Media, Michigan State University, 1993. Appointments: Chair, Wee Kim Wee School of Communication and Information, 2003-08; Professor; Dean, Mudra Institute of Communications Research, 2008-09; Chairman, Asian Media Information and Communication Centre, 2004-13; Director, Singapore Internet Research Centre. Publications: 4 books; 20 book chapters; 13 peer reviewed publications; 11 invited publications; many others. Honours: Top Paper, 1993; Fellow, Harvard Information Infrastructure Project, 2000; Fulbright Award, 2000; Visiting Fellow, University of Oxford, 2001; Honorary Fellow, International University of Japan, 2001-07; Governor, Intellectual Property Academy, Singapore, 2005-; Member, United Nation's Working Group on Internet Governance, 2004-05; Chairman, Inaugural Steering Committee, Global Internet Governance Academic Network, 2006; Public Service Medal, 2007; Listed in international biographical dictionaries. Memberships: International Communication Association, USA. Address: Wee Kim Wee School of Communication and Information, Nanyang Technological University, 31 Nanyang Link, Singapore 637718. E-mail: tphang@ntu.edu.sg

ANGELINI Cristiana, b. 6 June 1937, Tuscany, Italy. Art Lecturer. m. Alfred, 3 daughters. Education: Scuola di Belle Arti, Carrara, 1952; Diploma, Fine Art & Art History, 1955. Appointments: Artist; 8 solo exhibitions in England; Over 40 mixed shows in England and abroad, including Royal Academy Summer Shows and Whitechapel Gallery Open Exhibition; Visiting Lecturer, Adult Education College, Bexley. Publications: Artists in Britain Since 1945; The Drawing and Painting Course; Several articles and reproductions in professional and popular journals in England and abroad; Listed in international biographical dictionaries. Honours: Long Service Award for over 20 years of Service in Education, Bexley Council, 2007; 1st Prize, Laing Collection Exhibition, London and South East of England, 1990. Website: www.blueforce.demon.co.uk/cristiana.angelini

ANGELOU Maya, b. 4 April 1928, St Louis, Missouri, USA. Author. Appointments: Associate Editor, Arab Observer, 1961-62; Assistant Administrator, Teacher, School of Music and Drama, University of Ghana, 1963-66; Feature Editor, African Review, Accra, 1964-66; Reynolds Professor of American Studies, Wake Forest University, 1981-; Teacher of modern dance, Rome Opera House, Hambina Theatre, Tel Aviv; Member, Board of Governors, Maya Angelou Institute for the Improvement of Child and Family Education, Winston-Salem State University, North Carolina, 1998-; Theatre appearances include: Porgy and Bess, 1954-55; Calypso, 1957; The Blacks, 1960; Mother Courage, 1964; Look Away, 1973; Roots, 1977; How to Make an American Quilt, 1995; Plays: Cabaret for Freedom, 1960; The Least of These, 1966; Getting' Up Stayed On My Mind, 1967; Ajax, 1974; And Still I Rise, 1976; Moon On a Rainbow Shawl (producer), 1988. Film: Down in the Delta (director), 1998. Publications include: I Know Why the Caged Bird Sings, 1970; Just Give Me A Cool Drink of Water 'Fore I Die, 1971; Georgia, Georgia (screenplay), 1972; Oh Pray My Wings Are Gonna Fit Me Well, 1975; Singin' and Swingin' and Gettin' Merry Like Christmas, 1976; And Still I Rise, 1976; The Heart of a Woman, 1981; Shaker, Why Don't You Sing, 1983; All God's Children Need Travelling Shoes, 1986; Now Sheba Sings the Song, 1987; I Shall Not Be Moved, 1990; Gathered Together in My Name, 1991; Wouldn't Take Nothing for my Journey Now, 1993; Life Doesn't Frighten Me, 1993; Collected Poems, 1994; My Painted House, My Friendly Chicken and Me, 1994; Phenomenal Woman, 1995; Kofi and His Magic, 1996; Even the Stars Look Lonesome, 1997; Making Magic in the World, 1998; A Song Flung up to Heaven, 2002. Honours: Horatios Alger Award, 1992; Grammy Award Best Spoken Word or Non-Traditional Album, 1994; Honorary Ambassador to UNICEF, 1996-; Lifetime Achievement Award for Literature, 1999; National Medal of Arts; Distinguished visiting professor at several universities; Chubb Fellowship Award, Yale University; Nominated, National Book Award, I Know Why the Caged Bird Sings; Tony Award Nomination, Performances in Look Away; Over 30 honorary degrees; Golden Eagle Award; First Reynolds Professor; The Matrix Award; American Academy of Achievements Golden Plate Award; Distinguished Woman of North Carolina; Essence Woman of the Year; Many others. Memberships: The Directors Guild of America; Equity; AFTRA; Woman's Prison Association; Harlem Writers Guild; Horatio Alger Association of Distinguished Americans; National Society for the Prevention of Cruelty to Children. Address: Care Dave La Camera, Lordly and Dame Inc, 51 Church Street, Boston, MA 02116-5417, USA.

ANGUS Beverley Margaret, b. 18 November 1934, Lautoka, Fiji. Parasitologist. m. James Robert Angus, 1 son, 1 daughter. Education: BSc, 1979, PhD, 1994, University of Queensland, Australia; Graduate Diploma, Education, Queensland University of Technology, Australia. Appointments: Scientific Researcher, 1980-; Research Associate and Honorary Consultant, Queensland Museum, Australia, 1997-. Publications: Books: Tick Fever and Cattle Tick in Australia 1829-1996, 1998, 2nd edition 2003; Parasitology and the Queensland Museum; A History of Parasitology in Queensland, 2007; My Colonial Fiji, 2013; Publications in refereed jounals, 1975-2000; Contributor, From Many Nations, 1995. Memberships: Australian & New Zealand Society for Parasitology; Australian Society for History of Medicine; Australian Federation of University Women. Address: 20/3 Bronberg Court, Southport, Queensland 4215, Australia. E-mail: bmangus@live.co.uk

DICTIONARY OF INTERNATIONAL BIOGRAPHY 36th EDITION

ANGUS Kenneth William, (Ken Angus), b. 13 August 1930, Rhu, Dunbartonshire, Scotland. Veterinary Pathologist. m. Marna Renwick Redpath, 1977, 1 son. Education: BVMS, Glasgow, 1955; FRCVS, 1976; DVM, Glasgow, 1985. Publications: Scotchpotch, 1995; Eechtie-Peechtie-Pandy, 1996; Wrack and Pinion, 1997; Breakfast with Kilroy, 2000; Only the Sound of Sparrows, 2001; Conversations with Hamsters, 2002; A Little Overnight Rain, 2004; Combating After-Dribble, 2008; Spirit of the Highlands, 2009. Contributions to: New Writing Scotland; First Time; Cencrastus; Orbis; Poetry Scotland; Poetry Monthly; Poetry Life; Scarp (University of Wollongong, Berrima, Australia); Staple. Honours: Scottish International Poetry Competition, 1998. Memberships: Scottish Poetry Library; Poetry Association of Scotland. Address: 12 Temple Village, Gorebridge, Midlothian EH23 4SQ, Scotland.

ANIKA ZAFIAH Mohd Rus, b. 3 October 1973, Perak, Malaysia. Associate Professor. m. Mohammad Faiz Liew Abdullah, 3 sons, 2 daughters. Education: Degree (Hons), Mechanical Engineering, Master, Technical and Vocational, UTM, Malaysia; PhD, Engineering Chemistry, Warwick University, England. Appointments: Head of Metallurgy Laboratory. Publications: Degradation of Polyurethane Based on Vegetable Oils, 2008; Degradation of Polyurethane Based on Vegetable Oils, 2009; Polymer from Renewable Materials, 2010. Honours: Gold Medal, ITEX, 2010; Gold Medal, RnI Fest, 2010; Foreign Special Award, MTE, Kuala Lumpur, 2011; Double Gold, BIS, London, 2011; Women Inventor of the Year, MTE, 2012. Memberships: Board of Engineer, Malaysia. Address: 17 Jalan Manis 5, Taman Manis 2, 86400 Johor, Malaysia. E-mail: zafiah@uthm.edu.my

ANISTON Jennifer, b. 11 February 1969, Sherman Oaks, California, USA. Actress. m. Brad Pitt, 2000, divorced 2005. Education: New York High School of the Performing Arts. Appointments: Theatre includes: For Dear Life; Dancing on Checker's Grave; Films include: Leprechaun, 1993; She's The One, Dream for an Insomniac, 'Til There Was You, 1996; Picture Perfect, 1997; The Object of My Affection, 1998; Office Space, The Iron Giant, 1999; Rock Star, 2001; The Good Girl, 2002; Bruce Almighty, 2003; Along Came Polly, 2004; Derailed, Rumor Has It, 2005; Friends with Money, The Break-Up, 2006; The Senator's Wife, Diary, 2007; Marley & Me, 2008; He's Just Not That Into You, Management, Love Happens, 2009; The Bounty Hunter, The Switch, 2010. TV includes: Molloy (series), 1989; The Edge; Ferris Bueller; Herman's Head; Friends, 1994-2004; Dirt, 2007; 30 Rock, 2008. Honours: Screen Actors Guild Award, 1996; 5 People's Choice Awards, 2001, 2002, 2003, 2004, 2007; 54th Primetime Emmy Award, 2002; 5 Teen Choice Awards, 2002, 2003 (2), 2004, 2006; Golden Globe Award, 2003; 3 Logie Awards, 2003, 2004 (2); Vanguard Award, GLAAD Media Awards, 2007. Address: c/o CAA, 9830 Wilshire Boulevard, Beverly Hills, CA 90212, USA.

ANNIS Francesca, b. 14 May 1944, London, England. Actress. 1 son, 2 daughters. Appointments: with Royal Shakespeare Company, 1975-78; Plays include: The Tempest; The Passion Flower Hotel; Hamlet; Troilus and Cressida; Comedy of Errors; The Heretic; Mrs Klein; Rosmersholm; Lady Windermere's Fan; Hamlet; Films include: Cleopatra; Saturday Night Out; Murder Most Foul; The Pleasure Girls; Run With the Wind; The Sky Pirates; The Walking Stick; Penny Gold; Macbeth; Krull; Dune; Under the Cherry Moon; Golden River; El Rio de Oro; The Debt Collector, 1999; Milk, 1999; The End of the Affair; The Libertine, Revolver, 2005; Shifty, 2008; TV includes: Great Expectations; Children in Uniform; Love Story; Danger Man; The Human Jungle; Lily Langtry (role of Lily); Madam Bovary; Partners in Crime; Coming Out of Ice; Why Didn't They Ask Evans?; Magnum PI; Inside Story; Onassis - The Richest Man in the World, 1990; Parnell and the Englishwoman, Absolute Hell, The Gravy Train, Weep No More My Lady, 1991; Between the Lines, 1993; Reckless, Deadly Summer, 1997; Wives and Daughters, 1999; Deceit, 2000; Copenhagen, 2002; Jericho, 2005; Jane Eyre, 2006; Marple: At Bertram's Hotel, Cranford, 2007. Address: c/o ICM, 76 Oxford Street, London, W1N 0AX, England.

ANN-MARGRET, b. 28 April 1941, Stockholm, Sweden. Actress; Singer; Dancer. m. Roger Smith, 1967. Appointments: Film Debut, Pocketful of Miracles, 1961; Films include: State Fair; Bye Bye Birdie; Once a Thief; The Cincinnati Kid; Stagecoach; Murderer's Row; C C & Co; Carnal Knowledge; RPM; Train Robbers; Tommy; The Twist; Joseph Andrews; Last Remark of Beau Geste; Magic; Middle Age Crazy; Return of the Soldier; I Ought to be in Pictures; Looking to Get Out; Twice in a Lifetime; 52 Pick-Up, 1987; New Life, 1988; Something More; Newsies, 1992; Grumpy Old Men, 1993; Grumpier Old Men, 1995; Any Given Sunday, 1999; The Last Producer, 2000; A Woman's a Helluva Thing, 2000; Interstate 60, 2002; Taxi, 2004; Mem-o-re, 2005; Tales of the Rat Fink (voice), The Break Up, The Santa Clause 3: The Escape Clause, 2006; The Loss of a Teardrop Diamond, 2008; All's Faire in Love, 2009; TV includes: Who Will Love My Children?, 1983; A Streetcar Named Desire, 1984; The Two Mrs Grenvilles, 1987; Our Sons, 1991; Nobody's Children, 1994; Following her Heart; Seduced by Madness; The Diana Borchardt Story, 1996; Blue Rodeo, 1996; Pamela Hanniman, 1999; Happy Face Murders, 1999; Perfect Murder, Perfect Town, 2000; The Tenth Kingdom, 2000; Third Watch, 2003; A Place Called Home, 2004; Also appears in cabaret. Publications: (with Todd Gold) Ann-Margaret: My Story, 1994. Honours: Five Golden Globe Awards; Three Female Star of the Year Awards. Address: William Morris Agency, 151 S, El Camino Drive, Beverly Hills, CA 90212, USA.

ANNWEILER Cedric, b. 13 August 1981, Schiltigheim, France. Medical Doctor. m. Marie-Elodie. Education: MSc, University Jean Monnet, St Etienne, France, 2007; MD, University Medical School Jacques Lisfranc, St Etienne, France, 2007; Diplomate, Gerontology and Geriatric Medicine, 2009; PhD, 2011, Angers University; Diplomate, Biostatistics, University of Lyon, France, 2009. Appointments: Postgraduate Junior Attending, 2008-09, Alzheimer's Researcher, 2009-, Angers University Hospital. Publications: Research into implication of vitamin D in central nervous system and cognitive functions; Typology of gait and gait disorders in demented older adults. Honours: Listed in international biographical dictionaries. Memberships: Association des Jeunes Gériatres Hospitaliers; Ageing Balance and Cognition research group; International Society for Posture and Gait; Société Française de Gériatrie et Gérontologie; Alzheimer's Association International Society to Advance Alzheimer Research and Treatment. Address: Angers University Hospital, 4 rue Larrey, F-49933 Angers, France. E-mail: ceannweiler@chu-angers.fr

ANSELME Jean-Pierre Louis Marie, b. 22 September 1936, Port-au-Prince, Haiti. Professor. m. Marie-Céline Carrié, 3 daughters. Education: BA, Letters and Philosophy, St Martial College, Port-au-Prince, Haiti, 1955; BSc, Chemistry, Fordham University, Bronx, New York, 1959; PhD, Organic Chemistry, Polytechnic Institute of Brooklyn, New York, 1963. Appointments: Postdoctoral Fellow, 1963, 1965, Instructor, 1965, Polytechnic Institute of Brooklyn, New York; Assistant

Professor, 1965-68, Associate Professor, 1968-70, Professor, 1970-, University of Massachusetts at Boston, Massachusetts; Visiting Professor, Kyushu University, Fukuoka, Japan, 1972; Visiting Professor, University of Miami, Florida, 1979. Publications: 117 publications as author and co-author in professional national and international journals; Co-author and editor of 2 books; Founder and Executive Editor, Organic Preparations and Procedures International, the New Journal for Organic Synthesis; Numerous invited lectures; Papers at international, national, regional and local meetings. Honours: 15 sponsored projects; Seymour Shapiro Award as Outstanding Graduate Student, Polytechnic Institute of Brooklyn, 1963; NSF Postdoctoral Fellow, Institut für Organische Chemie, Munich, Germany, 1964; Fellow, A P Sloan Foundation, 1969-71; Invited Lecturer, Fourth Cork Conference, Ireland, 1971; Invited Lecturer, Chemical Society of Japan, 1972; Fellow, Japan Society for the Promotion of Science, 1972; Honoree, Citizens' Committee for Immigration Reform, New York, 1982; Listed in numerous national and international biographical dictionaries and Who's Who publications. Memberships: Sigma Xi; Phi Lambda Upsilon; American Chemical Society; Royal Chemical Society, London. Address: Department of Chemistry, University of Massachusetts, Harbor Campus, Boston, MA 02125-3393, USA.

ANSTEE John Howard, b. 25 April 1943, Neyland, Milford Haven, England. Scientific Director. m. Angela J Young. Education: Milford Haven Grammar School; BSc, PhD, Nottingham University. Appointments: Senior Demonstrator, Zoology, 1968, Lecturer, Senior Lecturer, Professor, 1996-, Biological Sciences, Deputy Dean, Faculty of Science, 1991-94, Dean of Science, 1994-97, Pro Vice Chancellor, 1997-2000, Pro Vice Chancellor and Subwarden, 2000-04, Emeritus Professor of Biological Sciences, 2004-, Chairman, Business School, 2007-08, University of Durham; Netpark Scientific Director, 2004-09, County Durham Development Company; Directorships held in a number of companies involved in knowledge and technology transfer. Publications: Contributed chapters to books; Numerous articles to peer-reviewed scientific journals. Honours: Deputy Lieutenant for County Durham. Memberships: Fellow, Royal Entomological Society; Fellow, Zoological Society; Member, Society for Experimental Biology; Member, Company of Biologists. Address: 35 Albert Street, Western Hill, Durham DH1 4RJ, England. E-mail: johnanstee@btinternet.com

ANSTEE Margaret Joan (Dame), b. 25 June 1926, Writtle, Essex, England. United Nations Official; Lecturer; Consultant; Author. Education: Modern and Medieval Languages, Newnham College, Cambridge, 1944-47; MA, Newnham College, 1955; BSc, Economics, London University, 1964. Appointments: Lecturer in Spanish, Queen's University, Belfast, 1947-48; Third Secretary, Foreign Office, 1948-52; Administrative Officer, UN Technical Assistance Board, Manila, 1952-54; Spanish Supervisor, University of Cambridge, 1955-56; Officer-in-Charge, UN Technical Assistance Board, Bogota, 1956-57; Resident Representative, Uruguay, 1957-59, Bolivia, 1960-65; Resident Representative, UNDP Ethiopia and UNDP Liaison Officer, ECA, 1965-67; Senior Economic Adviser, Office of Prime Minister, London, 1967-68; Senior Assistant to Commissioner in charge of study of Capacity of UN Development System, 1968-69; Resident Representative, UNDP, Morocco, 1969-72, Chile (also UNDP Liaison Officer with ECLA) 1972-74; Deputy to UN Under Secretary General in charge of UN Relief Operation to Bangladesh and Deputy Co-ordinator of UN Emergency Assistance to Zambia, 1973; Deputy Regional Director for Latin America, UNDP, New York, 1974-78; Deputy Assistant Administrator and Head, UNDP Administrator's Special Unit, 1975-77; Assistant Secretary-General of UN, Department of Technical Co-operation for Development), 1978-87; Special Representative of Secretary-General to Bolivia, 1982-92, for co-ordination of earthquake relief assistance to Mexico, 1985-87; Under Secretary-General, UN, 1987-93, Director-General of UN office at Vienna, Head of Centre for Social Development and Humanitarian Affairs, 1987-92, Special Representative of Secretary-General for Angola and Head of Angolan Verification Mission, 1992-93; Adviser to UN Secretary-General on peacekeeping, post-conflict peacebuilding and training troops for UN peacekeeping missions, 1994-2004; Chair, Advisory Group of Lessons Learned Unit, Department of Peacekeeping Operations, UN, 1996-2002; Co-ordinator of UN Drug Control Related Activities, 1987-90, of International Co-operation for Chernobyl, 1991-92; Secretary-General, 8th UN Congress on Prevention of Crime and Treatment of Offenders, August 1990; Writer, lecturer, consultant and adviser (ad honorem) to Bolivian Government, 1993-97, 2002-05. Publications: The Administration of International Development Aid, 1969; Gate of the Sun: A Prospect of Bolivia, 1970; Africa and the World, 1970; Orphan of the Cold War: The Inside Story of the Collapse of the Angolan Peace Process, 1992-93, 1996; Never Learn to Type: A woman at the United Nations, 2003, 2nd edition, 2004; The House on the Sacred Lake (And Other Bolivian Dreams – and Nightmares), 2009; What Price Security?, 2011. Honours: Honorary Fellow, Newnham College, Cambridge, 1991; Hon DU (Essex), 1994; Honorary LLD (Westminster), 1996; Honorary DSc (Economics) (London), 1998; Hon LLD, (Cambridge) 2004; Reves Peace Prize, William & Mary College, USA, 1993; Commander, Ouissam Alaouite, Morocco, 1972; Dama Gran Cruz Condor of the Andes, Bolivia, 1986; Grosse Goldene Ehrenzeichen am Bande, Austria, 1993; Dame Commander of the Most Distinguished Order of St Michael and St George, 1994; Gran Caballero, Orden de Bernardo O'Higgins, Chile, 2007. Memberships: Member, Advisory Board, UN Studies at Yale University, 1996-; Member, Advisory Council, Oxford Research Group, 1997-; Member, Advisory Board, UN Intellectual History Project, 1999-; Trustee, Helpage International, 1994-97; Patron and Board Member, British Angola Forum, 1998-2010; Member, President Carter's International Council for Conflict Resolution, 2001-; Vice President, UK UN Association, 2002-; Member, Editorial Board, Global Governance, 2004-; Elected Honorary Life Vice President of British Association of Former UN Civil Servants, 2010; Member, Strategic Development Board, Durham Global Security Institute, Durham University, 2011-. Address: c/o PNUD, Casilla 9072, La Paz, Bolivia; c/o The Walled Garden, Knill, Nr Presteigne, Powys LD8 2PR, United Kingdom.

ANTONOVA Natalia Vladimirovna, b. 14 January 1954, Krasnoyarsk city, Russia. Teacher. 1 daughter. Education: Diploma (distinction), Krasnoyarsk State Teacher Training University, 1976; Certificate, Deakin University, Australia, 1994; Certificate, Central School of English, London, England, 1997; 2 certificates, British Council, International Education Centre, DFID York Associates, 1999, 2000; KELTA certificate, 2008; Modern Quality Management certificate, 2008; Internal Audit certificate, Krasnoyarsk, 2009. Appointments: Teacher, boarding school, Bograd village, 1976-79; Senior Teacher, Omsk Militia Higher School, Krasnoyarsk, 1980-84; Senior Instructor, Deputy Chairman, 1984-87, Head of Department for Work Organisation, Deputy Chairman, 1987-89, All-Russia Voluntary Fire Protecting Association, Krasnoyarsk; Senior Teacher, Krasnoyarsk Institute of Aerospace Engineering, 1989-93; Docent, Head of Foreign Languages Chair, Dean of International Faculty, Director, Institute of International Management and Business, Krasnoyarsk State Agrarian University, 1993-. Publications: More than 200 articles in professional journals. Honours: Letter of Gratitude, Krasnoyarsk Regional Administration, 2003; Letter of Gratitude for Elaboration of New Curricula, 2007; Labor of Honor Medal of the 1st degree, 2009; Diploma for many years of diligent work in the system of agro industrial complex, 2009; Yaroslav Mudriy Diploma in nomination for Elite of Science and Education, 2009. Memberships: University and Institute Scientific and Methodical Board, Krasnoyarsk State Agrarian University, Russia. Address: 75A Lado Ketskhovely St, apt 116, Krasnoyarsk, Russia. E-mail: natan@kgau.ru

ANTONSSON Haukur, b. 6 April 1947, Dalvik, Iceland. Education: Menntaskolinn A Akureyri, 1967. Appointments: Astrophysics; Cosmology; Mathematics. Publications: The Big Bang Paradox: Mathematics Changing with Time. Memberships: New York Academy of Sciences. Address: Lokastig 4 NH-TH, PO Box 33, IS-620 Dalvik, Iceland.

ANTZELEVITCH Charles, b. 25 March 1951, Israel. Executive Director. m. Brenda, 1973, 1 son, 1 daughter. Education: BA, Queens College, City University of New York, Flushing, 1973; PhD, University of New York at Syracuse, 1978. Appointments: Postdoctoral Fellow, Experimental Cardiology Department, Masonic Medical Research Laboratory, Utica, New York, 1977-80; Assistant Professor, Pharmacology Department, SUNY Health Science Centre, Syracuse, 1980-83; Research Scientist, Experimental Cardiology, Masonic Medical Research Laboratory, 1980-83; Associate Professor, Pharmacology Department, SUNY Health Science Centre, 1983-86; Senior Research Scientist, Experimental Cardiology, Masonic Medical Research Laboratory, 1984; Executive Director, Director of Research, 1984-, Gordon K Moe Scholar, 1987-, Masonic Medical Research Laboratory; Professor of Pharmacology, SUNY Health Science Centre, 1995-. Publications: Over 400 original papers and reviews. Honours include: Distinguished Service Award, RAM Medical Research Foundation, 1994; Charles Henry Johnson Medal, Grand Lodge F and AM, NYS, 1996; Distinguished Scientist Award, NASPE, 2002; Excellence in Cardiovascular Science Award, NE Affiliate AHA, 2003; Carl J Wiggers Lecturer, American Journal of Physiology, 2007; Gordon K Moe Lecturer, Cardiac Electrophysiology Society, 2006; Distinguished Scientist Award, American College of Cardiology, 2011. Memberships: AHA; Association for the Advancement of Science; FASEB; APS; Cardiac Electrophysiology Society; Upstate New York Cardiac Electrophysiology Society; New York Academy of Sciences; Heart Rhythm Society; ISHR; ISCE. Address: Masonic Medical Research Laboratory, 2150 Bleecker Street, Utica, NY 13501, USA.

ANUBHAV Naresh, b. 1 November 1982, Chandigarh, India. Doctor. Education: BDS; PGDHHM; PGDMLS. Appointments: Director, Break Loose; Director, Provider; Consultant, Tooth Healers; Organizing Secretary, Virasat; General Secretary, Urdu Parishad. Publications: More than 500 articles in different newspapers and magazines; Delivered numerous talks on radio. Memberships: IDA. Address: #169, Sector-17, Panchkula 134109, Haryana, India. Website: www.providergraphics.com

ANWAR Ul-Haque, b. 27 March 1977, Lahore, Pakistan. Engineer. m. Sara, 1 daughter. Education: BE, Aerospace, College of Aeronautical Engineering, National University of Science and Technology, Risalpur Campus, 1998; MSc, Advanced Mechanical Engineering for Aerospace, University of Sheffield, England, 2004. Appointments: Aircraft Maintenance Engineer, 1998-99; Research Associate, 1999-2005, Manager, 2005-. Publications: Validation of 2D Multiblock; Effect of various Reduced Frequencies; Power Law Fluid Modeling; Influence of turbulence Modeling; many others. Honours: Fully funded scholarship for Postgraduate Studies; UNESCO Sponsorship for Summer School; Travel grant, Pakistan Science Foundation; Merit Scholarship by Government for HSSC. Memberships: Pakistan Engineering Council; Pakistan Engineering Congress; World Congress on Engineering; American Society of Mechanical Engineers. Address: House No 305, Street No 80, G11/2, Islamabad, 44000, Pakistan. E-mail: ulhaque.anwar@gmail.com

ANWYL Shirley Anne, b. 10 December 1940, Johannesburg, South Africa. Circuit Judge. m. Robin H C Anwyl, 2 sons. Education: BA, 1960, LLB, 1963, Rhodes University South Africa. Appointments: Called to South African Bar, 1963; Called to Bar of England and Wales by Inner Temple, 1966; Master of the Bench of Inner Temple, 1985; Recorder, 1981-95; Member of Criminal Injuries Compensation Board, 1980-95; President, Mental Health Review Tribunals, 1983-95; Deputy High Court Judge (Family Division), 1981-2008; Circuit Judge, 1995-2008; Resident Judge of Woolwich Crown Court, 1999-2007; Retired, 2008. Honours: Queen's Counsel, 1979; Freeman of the City of London, 1994. Memberships: Senate of Inns of Court and Bar, 1978-81; General Council of the Bar, 1987-88; Chairman, Barristers Benevolent Association, 1989-95; Royal Society of Arts, 1989-; Worshipful Company of Fruiterers, 1996-. Address: 27 Prusom's Island, 135 Wapping High Street, London E1W 3NH, England.

AOYAGI Keishiro, b. 29 December 1958, Fukuoka, Japan. Gastroenterological Surgery. m. Naoko, 2 daughters. Education: MD, Resident, Department of Surgery, 1984, PhD, 2nd Department of Pathology, 1988, Kurume University School of Medicine. Appointments: Clinical and Research Associate, 2nd Department of Pathology, 1988-89, Clinical and Research Associate, 1st Department of Surgery, 1989-96, Clinical and Research Associate, Department of Surgery, 1998-2003, Kurume University School of Medicine; Visiting Scientist, Department of Pathology, and Laboratory of Medicine, Allegheny University of Health Sciences, Philadelphia, USA, 1996-98; Assistant Professor, Department of Surgery, Kurume University, 2003-. Publications: Numerous articles in professional journals. Honours: PhD, 1988; Board Certified Surgeon, 1992; Board Certified Gastroenterological Surgeon, 1994; Board Certified Gastroenterological Endoscopist, 2000; Board Certified Gastroenterologist, 2001; Clinical Instructor, Japanese Society of Gastroenterological Surgery, 2001; Board Certified Cancer Therapist, 2008. Memberships: International College of Surgeons; International Society of Surgery; American Association for Cancer Research. Address: 8-10-703 Jounan-machi, Kurume city, Fukuoka 830-0022, Japan. E-mail: keishiro@med.kurume-u.ac.jp

APPIAH James Peter King, b. 16 February 1951, Baman, Kumasi, Ghana. Writer; Poet; Apostle. m. Angela Mabel Asare, 1 daughter. Education: Unesco Certificate in Writing and Publishing, 1972; Certificate of Completion, Morris Cerullo School of Ministry, San Diego, 1981; BA, Literary Studies, Pacific Western University, 1990; Diploma in Journalism, Story Writing, ICS Scranton, 1993; PhD, English Grade A, Washington International University, USA, 2001; Masters Degree in Biblical Studies, 2004, Grade A, Florida Christian University, Orlando, Florida. USA. Appointments: Library Assistant, Ghana Library, 1973-76; Founder,

President, Followers of Christ International Church, FOCIC, 1974; Director, Adonten Literary Works, Kumasi, 1976-95; Ordained Bishop, Universal Ministries, 1980 President, Founder, Director, Editor in Chief, Appiah Esthermat Ltd, 1995; Feed the Poor and Preach the Gospel Ministries, 2002. Publications: The Lord of Praise, 1988; Prayer, The Key to a Triumphant Christian Living, 1992; Overcomers in the Blood, 1995; The Meaning of Pentecost, 1995; Ode to the Dead, Dedicated to the Princess of the People, 1998; Inventor, Father and Founder, Colours of Formation, acrostic novel, 2008; Acrostic Kingdom Book, The Earth, Heavens and Crown Lands, 2008; Many other publications. Honours: Mondello Poetry International Award, First Prize, 1987; Honoured, City of Palermo (Unione Quartieri), 1988; Deputy Governor, ABI, 1999; Appointed to Research Board of Advisors, ABI, 2002; Selected among 500 Leading Intellectuals of the World and Great Minds of the Century, ABI, 2002; American Medal of Honor, ABI, 2003; Ambassador of Grand Eminence, ABI, 2004. Memberships: Morris Cerullo World Evangelism, Italy 1995-; United Christians Association in Italy, 1996; United Christians Association, 1998-; Ghana Young Pioneers; Ghana Youth Club; Ghana Association of Writers; United Christian Association; Christian Writers Forum; Member of the Adonten Royal Family of Asante, Mansa Nana. Address: Via Tignale del Garde 60, 41125 Modena, Italy. Website: www.drjamespeterkingappiah.blog.spot.com

APPLEBY Malcolm Arthur, b. 6 January 1946, West Wickham, Kent, England. Artist, Designer and Engraver. m. Philippa Swann, 1 daughter. Education: Beckenham School of Art; Ravensbourne College of Art; Central School of Arts and Crafts; Sir John Cass School of Art; Royal College of Art. Career: Held one-man art exhibition, Aberdeen Art Gallery, 1998: Is now the top gun engraver in the UK, famous for his Raven Gun which is housed in the Royal Armouries: the seal for the Victoria and Albert Museum and the silver centrepiece for the New Scottish Parliament. Honours: Littledale Scholar, 1969; Liveryman, Worshipful Company of Goldsmiths, 1991; Hon D Litt, Heriot-Watt, 2000; Gold Award, Silver Award and Commended, Craftsmanship and Design Awards, 2006. Memberships: Founder member and Chairman of the British Art Postage Stamp Society; Member of the British Art Medal Society and the Society for the Protection of Ancient Buildings. Address: Aultbeag, Grandtully, by Aberfeldy, Perthshire PH15 2QU, Scotland.

APPLEMAN Philip (Dean), b. 8 February 1926, Kendallville, Indiana, USA. Professor; Writer. m. Marjorie Ann Haberkorn, 1950. Education: BS, 1950, PhD, 1955, English, Northwestern University; AM, English, University of Michigan, 1951. Appointments: Fulbright Scholar, University of Lyon, 1951-52; Instructor to Professor, 1955-67, Professor, 1967-84, Distinguished Professor of English, 1984-86, Distinguished Professor Emeritus, 1986-, Indiana University; Director and Instructor, International School of America, 1960-61, 1962-63; Visiting Professor, State University of New York College at Purchase, 1973, Columbia University, 1974; Visiting Scholar, New York University, University of Southern California at Los Angeles; John Steinbeck Visiting Writer, Long Island University of Southampton, 1992. Publications: Non-Fiction: The Silent Explosion, 1965; Novels: In the Twelfth Year of the War, 1970; Shame the Devil, 1981; Apes and Angels, 1989. Poetry: Kites on a Windy Day, 1967; Summer Love and Surf, 1968; Open Doorways, 1976; Darwin's Ark, 1984; Darwin's Bestiary, 1986; Let There Be Light, 1991; New and Selected Poems, 1956-1996, 1996; Karma, Dharma, Pudding & Pie, 2009; Perfidious Proverbs, 2011; Contributor and editor of numerous other publications. Honours: Ferguson Memorial Award, Friends of Literature Society, 1969; Christopher Morley Awards, Poetry Society of America, 1970, 1975; Castagnola Award, Poetry Society of America, 1975; National Endowment for the Arts Fellowship, 1975; Pushcart Prize, 1985; Humanist Arts Award, American Humanist Association, 1994; Long Island School of Poetry Award, Walt Whitman Birthplace, 1999; National Center for Science Education, Friend of Darwin Award, 2002. Memberships: Academy of American Poets; American Association of University Professors; Authors Guild of America; Modern Language Association; National Council of Teachers of English; PEN American Center; Poetry Society of America; Poets and Writers. Address: PO Box 5058, East Hampton, NY 11937, USA. E-mail: phil.appleman@gmail.com

APTED Michael, b. 10 February 1941, Aylesbury, England. Film Director. Education: Cambridge University. Career: Researcher, Granada TV, 1963; Investigative Reporter, World in Action; Director debut as feature film director, The Triple Echo, 1972; Other films include Stardust, 1975; The Squeeze, 1977; Agatha, 1979; Coal Miner's Daughter, 1980; Continental Divide, 1981; Gorky Park, 1983; Firstborn, 1984; Critical Condition, Gorillas in the Mist, 1988; Class Action, 1991; Incident at Oglala, Thunderheart, 1992; Moving the Mountain, 1993; Nell, Blink, 1994; Extreme Measures, 1996; Enigma, 2001; Enough, 2002; Amazing Grace, 2006; The Power of the Game, 2007; The Chronicles of Narnia: The Voyage of the Dawn Treader, 2010; Television films and direction: Coronation Street episodes; The Lovers comedy series; Folly Foot children's series; Another Sunday and Sweet F A, Kisses at Fifty, Poor Girl; Jack Point; P'tang Yang Kipperbang, 1984; New York News, 1994; Rome (mini-series), 2006; UP document series including 28 UP, 35 UP, 42 UP; Always Outnumbered. Honours: Several British Academy Awards including Best Dramatic Director. Memberships: President of the Directors Guild of America. Address: Michael Apted Film Co, 1901 Avenue of the Stars, Suite 1245, Los Angeles, CA 90067, USA.

ARADAG Selin, b. 25 May 1979, Ankara, Turkey. Academician; Mechanical and Aerospace Engineer. m. Kutay Celebioglu, 1 son. Education: BS, 2000, MS, 2002, Mechanical Engineering, Middle East Technical University; PhD, Mechanical and Aero Engineer, Rutgers University, 2006. Appointments: Teaching and Research Assistant, Middle East Technical University, 2000-02; Teaching and Research Assistant, Rutgers University, 2002-06; Research Engineer, US Air Force Academy, 2006-08; Assistant Professor, TOBB University, 2008-. Publications: Over 40 articles in professional journals; Book, CFD for High Speed Flows in Engineering, 2006. Memberships: American Institute of Aeronautics and Astronautics; American Society of Mechanical Engineers; Society of Women Engineers; American Physical Society. E-mail: selinaradag@gmail.com

ARAGALL GARRIGA Giacomo (Jaime), b. 6 June 1939, Barcelona, Spain. Tenor. Education: Studied with Francesco Puig in Barcelona and with Vladimiro Badiali in Milan. Debut: La Fenice, Venice, 1963 in the first modern performance of Verdi's Jerusalem. Career: La Scala Milan in 1963 as Mascagni's Fritz; In 1965 sang in Haydn's Le Pescatrici with Netherlands Opera and at the Edinburgh Festival; Vienna Staatsoper debut in 1966 as Rodolfo in La Bohème; Covent Garden debut in 1966 as the Duke of Mantua; Metropolitan Opera debut in 1968; Guest appearances in Berlin, Italy, San Francisco and at the Lyric Opera Chicago; Sang at San Carlo Opera Naples in 1972 in a revival of Donizetti's Caterina

Cornaro; Festival appearances at Bregenz and Orange in 1984 as Cavaradossi and Don Carlos; Sang Gabriele Adorno at Barcelona in 1990 and Don Carlos at the Orange Festival in 1990; Sang Rodolfo at Barcelona in 1991 and Don Carlos at the Deutsche Opera Berlin, 1992; Sang Cavaradossi at the Opéra Bastille, 1994. Other roles include Pinkerton, Romeo in I Capuleti e i Montecchi, Werther and Gennaro in Lucrezia Borgia. Recordings: La Traviata; Lucrezia Borgia; Faust; Rigoletto; Simon Boccanegra; Madama Butterfly. Address: c/o Stafford Law Associates, 6 Barham Close, Weybridge, Surrey KT13 9PR, England.

ARAI Asao, b. 10 January 1954, Chichibu, Saitama. Mathematician; Mathematical Physicist; University Professor. m. Sayoko Anada, 1 daughter. Education: BS, Chiba University, 1976; MS, University of Tokyo, 1979; DS, Gakushuin University, 1986. Appointments: Assistant Professor, Tokyo Institute of Technology, 1980-86; Lecturer, 1986-92, Associate Professor, 1992-95, Professor, 1995-, Hokkaido University. Publications: Mathematics of Symmetry, 1993, in Japanese; Hilbert Space and Quantum Mechanics, 1997, in Japanese; Quantum Field Theory and Statistical Mechanics, 1988, in Japanese; Mathematical Structures of Quantum Mechanics, 1999, in Japanese; Fock Spaces and Quantum Fields, 2000, in Japanese; Mathematical Principles of Physical Phenomena, 2003, in Japanese; Handbook of Modern Mathematical Physics, 2005, in Japanese; Mathematical Principles of Quantum Phenomena, 2006, in Japanese; Complex Analysis and Its Applications, in Japanese, 2006; Modern Vector Analysis: Principles and Applications, in Japanese, 2006; Symmetries in Physics, in Japanese, 2008; Mathematical Principles of Quantum Statistical Mechanics, in Japanese, 2008; Symmetries in Aesthetics, in Japanese, 2009; Functional Integral Methods in Quantum Mathematical Physics, in Japanese, 2010; Many articles in professional journals; Listed in biographical publications. Memberships: New York Academy of Sciences; International Association of Mathematical Physics; The Mathematical Society of Japan. Address: Department of Mathematics, Hokkaido University, Sapporo 060 0810, Japan.

ARAKAKI Francisco Kioshi, b. 30 October 1957, Catanduva, SP, Brazil. Research & Development Engineer. m. Ilayne Marmius Diniz, 2 daughters. Education: BE, Mechanical Engineer, UNESP, 1980; MS, Aeronautical Engineer, ITA, 1986-. Appointments: Professor, Institute of Aeronautical Technology, 1981-87; Senior Engineering Specialist, Composite Structures, Embraersa, 1987-; Professor, Vale do Paraiza University, 1992-; Engineering Credencial Representative, Agency National of the Aviation Civil, 2005-. Publications: Numerous articles in professional journals. Honours: Technical Standards Board, Outstanding Contribution Award, Engineering Society for Advancing Mobility on Land, Sea, Air and Space, 2003; Listed in international biographical dictionaries. Memberships: Commercial Aircraft Composite Repair Committee; Composite Material Handbook Seventee; Brazilian Aerospacial Association. Address: Rua Coronel Manoel martins Jr, 190, Sao Jose dos Campos, 12242-810, Sao Paulo, Brazil. E-mail: francisco.arakaki@gmail.com

ARANAS Primo Jr, b. 5 January 1971, Ajong, Philippines. Social Science Instructor. Education: Bachelor of Secondary Education, Social Science Major. Appointments: Observer, Asia-Pacific Conference for East Timor, 1994; Observer, Asia-Pacific Coalition for East Timor, 1994; Classroom Instructor, Silliman University, 1998-; Co-ordinator, Silliman University High School, 1999-2002, 2005-06; Member, Steering Committee, Global Map School, 2006-08. Honours: Award of Academic Excellence, Metro Manila College, 1994; Nominee, Field of Education, Metro Bank Foundation, 2004; Awardee, Silliman University Alumni Association, 2004. Memberships: Asia-Pacific Coalition for East Timor, 1994; Global Map School Steering Committee, 2006-08. Address: Ajong, Sibulan, 6201, Negros Oriental, Philippines. E-mail: junsuhs_1571@yahoo.com

ARBUTHNOTT Robert, b. 28 September 1936, Kuala Lumpur, Malaysia. British Council Officer. m. (Sophie) Robina Axford, 1 son, 2 daughters. Education: BA, MA, Modern Languages, Emmanuel College, Cambridge, 1957-60; Institute of Education, London and School of Oriental and African Studies, 1972-73; Royal College of Defence Studies, 1986. Appointments: Military Service, 2nd Lieutenant The Black Watch, 1955-57; British Council Service, 1960-94: Karachi, Lahore, 1960-64, London, 1964-67, Representative, Nepal, 1967-72, Representative, Malaysia, 1973-76, Director, Educational Contracts, 1977-78, Controller Personnel, 1978-81, Representative, Germany, 1981-85; RCDS, 1986; Controller, Asia, Pacific and Americas Division, 1987; Minister (Cultural Affairs), British High Commission and Director British Council in India, 1988-93. Honours: Exhibitioner, Emmanuel College, Cambridge; CBE, 1991. Memberships: Fellow, Royal Asiatic Society; Council Member (1996-2002); Royal Society for Asian Affairs, Council Member, 2006-09; Oxford-Cambridge Club. Address: Killicks, The Green, Mannings Heath, Horsham, West Sussex, RH13 6JX, England.

ARBUZ Joseph, b. 23 November 1949, New York, USA. Attorney. Divorced, 1 daughter. Education: Juris Doctor; Doctor of Divinity; Master of Public Administration; Master of Divinity; Bachelor of Arts. Appointments: Church Pastor; Assistant Attorney General; Assistant Staff Judge Advocate; American Express Financial Advisors; Joseph R Arbuz, PA. Publications: Commander's Guide; Many other airforce manuals and newspaper articles. Honours: JFK Teaching Scholarship; National Defence Service Medal; Air Force Service Medal; Listed in international biographical directories. Memberships: The Florida Bar; Federal District Court; Federal Court of Appeals; US Supreme Court; US Court of Military Appeals; DADE County Bar Association. Address: PO Box 398843, Miami Beach, FL 33239-8843, USA. E-mail: joearbuz@aol.com

ARCANGELI Massimo, b. 17 July 1960, Rome, Italy. Linguistics Professor. Education: Italian Linguistics, La Sapienza University, Rome, 1987; Italian Language & Literature, University of Milan, 1996. Appointments: Adjunct Professor, 1997-2001, Associate Professor, 2002-04, Italian Linguistics Professor, 2005-, Sociolinguistics, 2007-, Dean, Faculty of Foreign Languages and Literatures, 2008-10, University Cagliari; Adjunct Professor, University of Luiss-Guido Carli, Rome, 2010-. Publications: La Scapigliatura Poetica Milanese e la Poesia Italiana fra Otto e Novecento, 2003; Lingua e Società nell'Era Gobale, 2005; Lingua e Identità, 2007; Giovani Scrittori Scritture Giovani, 2007; Il Linguaggio Pubblicitario, 2008; Il Medioevo alle Porte, 2009; Itabolario, 2011; Cercasi Dante disperatamente, 2012. Honours: Guarantor, University Banska-Bystrica, 2008-; Director, Lexical Atlas of Ancient Italian Dialects, 2008-; Director, Plida Dante Alighieri Society, 2010-; Director, Linguistic Observatory Zanichelli, 2009-. Memberships: ASLI; SLI; ANILS. Address: via Acqua, Donzella 27, 00179 Rome, Italy. E-mail: maxarcangeli@tin.it Website: www.massimoarcangeli.com

DICTIONARY OF INTERNATIONAL BIOGRAPHY 36th EDITION

ARCHANGELSKY Sergio, b. 27 March 1931, Morocco. Palaeontologist. m. Jos Ballester, 1 son, 1 daughter. Education: PhD, Natural Sciences, Buenos Aires University, 1957. Appointments: Professor, La Plata University, 1961-78; Superior Researcher, National Research Council, Argentina, 1985-; Head, Paleobotany Division, Argentine Museum of Natural History, 1985-2006. Publications: Fundamentals of Palaeobotany, 1970; Fossil Flora of the Baqueró Group, Cretaceous, Patagonia, 2003. Honours: Visiting Professor, Ohio State University, USA, 1984; Corresponding Member, Botanical Society America, 1975; Academician, National Academy Sciences, Cordoba, 1990; Honorary Vice-President, XVI International Botanical Congress, St Louis, USA, 1999. Memberships: Argentine Geological Society; Argentine Palaeontological Society; British Palaeontological Association; Fellow, Palaeobotanical Society, India. Address: Urquiza 1132 Vicente López B1638BWJ, Buenos Aires, Argentina.

ARCHEGOVA Inna Borisovna, b. 28 August 1931, Kutaisy, Georgia, Russia. Research Scientist. m. Vladimir Afanasievich Molin, 1 daughter. Education: Diploma, Soil Science, Leningrad State University, 1954. Appointments: Employee, Stationary Academy of Sciences, USSR, Arkhangelsk, 1954-57; Institute of Biology, Komi Science Centre, 1957-68, Senior Employee, 1981-85, Leading Employee, 1985-, Ural Branch Russian Academy of Science; Doctor of Biology, Group Leader, Lecturer, Institute of Management & Business, Ukhta, Komi Republic, Russia. Publications: Ecosystems of post-technogenic areas of the Russian North, St Petersburg, Nauka, 2002; Nature exploitation specificity and nature restoration prospects in the Far North of Russia, 1998; Land restoration in the Far North, 2000; Ecological principles of nature usage and nature restoration in the North, 2009. Honours: Medal, Russian Federation, 2007; Silver Medal, Komi Science Centre Vet, 2007; Patents for biosorbent for cleaning reservoir from oil and oil products. Memberships: Russian Society of Soil Scientists. Address: Institute of Biology, Kommunisticheskaya 28, Syktyvkar, 167982, Russia. E-mail: directorat@ib.komisc.ru

ARCHER Richard Donald, b. 3 July 1947, Leicester, England. Teacher. Education: BA, University of Durham; PGCE, Christ's College of Education, University of Liverpool; MusB, Trinity College, Dublin; MMus, University of Sheffield; MPhil, University of East Anglia; FRCO; ADCM; FTCL; LRAM; ARCM. Appointments: Organist, Recitals Locally, Solo Organist at Concerts; Organist, Leicester Philharmonic Society; Radio Broadcasts, Conductor, Hinckley Choral Union and City of Leicester Singers; Guest Conductor, Accompanist, Director of Music, St John the Baptist, Leicester; Head of Languages, Stoneygate School, Leicester. Publications: Works for Local Choirs in Manuscript, including 2 Sonnets, Fire of the Spirit; Recording, Fire of the Spirit. Honours: Prizes, organ playing competitions. Memberships: RCO; ATL; ISM; MU; Hymn Society of Great Britain and Ireland; Methodist Church Music Society; Leicester and District Organists' Association. Address: 11 Frampton Avenue, Leicester LE3 0SG, England.

ARCHER OF WESTON-SUPER-MARE, Baron of Mark in the County of Somerset; Jeffrey Howard Archer, b. 15 April 1940, Mark, Somerset, England. Author; Politician. m. Mary Weeden, 2 sons. Education: Brasenose College, Oxford. Appointments: Member, GLC for Havering, 1966-70; Member of Parliament for Louth (Conservative), 1969-74; Deputy Chair, Conservative Party, 1985-86; Served two years of a four year prison sentence for perjury and perverting the course of justice, 2001-03. Publications: Not a Penny More, Not a Penny Less, 1975; Shall We Tell the President?, 1977; Kane & Abel, 1979; A Quiver Full of Arrows (short stories), 1980; The Prodigal Daughter, 1982; First Among Equals, 1984; A Matter of Honour, 1986; A Twist in the Tale (short stories), 1988; As The Crow Flies, 1991; Honour Among Thieves, 1993; Twelve Red Herrings (short stories), 1994; The Fourth Estate, 1995; Collected Short Stories, 1997; The Eleventh Commandment, 1998; To Cut a Long Story Short (short stories), 2000; A Prison Diary, Volumes I and II, 2002; Sons of Fortune, 2003; A Prison Diary, Volume III, 2004; False Impression, Cat O'Nine Tales (short stories), 2006; The Gospel According to Judas, 2007; A Prisoner of Birth, 2008; Paths of Glory, 2009; And Thereby Hangs a Tale (short stories), 2010; Plays: Beyond Reasonable Doubt, 1987; Exclusive, 1989; The Accused, 2000. Honours: Lord Archer of Western super Mare, Queen's Birthday Honours, 1992. Address: Peninsula Heights, 93 Albert Embankment, London SE1 7TY, England.

ARCHER OF WESTON-SUPER-MARE, Lady Mary Doreen Archer, b. 22 December 1944, England. Scientist. m. Jeffrey Archer (Lord Archer of Weston-Super-Mare), 2 sons. Education: Cheltenham Ladies' College; St Anne's College, Oxford, Imperial College, London. Appointments: Junior Research Fellow, St Hilda's College, Oxford, 1968-71; Chemistry Lecturer, Somerville College, Oxford, temporary 1971-72; Research Fellow, Royal Institute of Great Britain, 1972-76; Chemistry Lecturer, Trinity College, Cambridge and Chemistry Fellow & Lecturer, Newnham College, Cambridge, 1976-86; Senior Academic Fellow, DeMontfort University, 1990-; Visiting Professor: Imperial College, London, 1991-2000; Centre for Energy Policy and Technology, 2001-03; University of Hertfordshire, 1993-; Director, 1992-, Vice Chair, 2000-02, Chair, 2002-, Addenbrooke's Hospital Trust, NHS Trust. Publications: Rupert Brooke and the Old Vicarage, Grantchester, 1989; Clean Energy from Photovoltaics, 2001-; Molecular to Global Photosynthesis, 2004; Transformation and Change: the 1702 Chair of Chemistry at Cambridge, 2004; Contributes to various chemistry journals. Honours: Hon ScD (Herts), 1994; Energy Institute Melchett Medal, 2002. Memberships: Council Member, Royal Institute, 1984-85, 1999-2001; Director, Anglia TV Group, 1987-95; Director, Mid Anglia Radio, 1988-94; Director, Q103 FM (formerly Cambridge and Newmarket Radio,) 1988-97; Member, Council of Lloyd's, 1989-92; President, Guild of Church Musicians, 1989-; Chair, 1990-2000, President, 2000-, National Energy Foundation; Trustee, Science Museum, 1990-2000; Cheltenham Ladies' College, 1991-2000; President, Solar Energy Society, 2001-; Chair, East of England Stem Cell Network, 2004-. Address: The Old Vicarage, Grantchester, Cambridge, CB3 9ND, England. Website: www.addenbrookes.org.uk

ARCULUS Ronald (Sir), b. 11 February 1923, Birmingham, England. Retired Diplomat and Company Director. Education: MA, Exeter College, Oxford, 1941, 1945-47. Appointments: 4th Queen's Own Hussars, 1942-45; HM Diplomatic Service, 1947-83; Ambassador to Italy, 1979-83; Director, Trustee and Consultant, Glaxo Holdings, 1983-92. Honours: KCMG; KCVO; Knight Grand Cross, Italian Order of Merit. Memberships: Army and Navy Club; Cowdray Park Polo Club; Hurlingham Club. Address: 20 Kensington Court Gardens, London W8 5QF, England.

ARDEN John, b. 26 October 1930, Barnsley, Yorkshire, England. Playwright/Novelist. m. Margaretta Ruth D'Arcy, 4 sons, 1 deceased. Education: King's College, Cambridge; Edinburgh College of Art. Publications include: Fiction:

Silence Among the Weapons, 1982; Books of Bale, 1988; Cogs Tyrannic, 1991; Jack Juggler and the Emperor's Whore, 1995; The Stealing Steps, 2003; Gallows, 2009. Essays: To Present the Pretence, 1977; Awkward Corners (with M D'Arcy), 1988. Plays produced include: All Fall Down, 1955; The Life of Man, 1956; The Waters of Babylon, 1957; When Is A Door Not A Door?, Live Like Pigs, 1958; Serjeant Musgrave's Dance, 1959; Soldier Soldier, 1960; Wet Fish, 1961; The Workhouse Donkey, Ironhand, 1963; Armstrong's Last Goodnight, 1964; Left-Handed Liberty, 1965; Squire Jonathan, 1968; The Bagman, 1970; Pearl, 1978; Don Quixote, 1980; Garland for a Hoar Head, The Old Man Sleeps Alone, 1982; The Little Novels of Wilkie Collins, 1998; Woe alas, the Fatal Cashbox, 2000; Wild Ride to Dublin, Poor Tom, thy Horn is Dry, 2003; Scam, 2007. With M D'Arcy: The Happy Haven, The Business of Good Government, 1960; Ars Longa Vita Brevis, 1964; The Royal Pardon, Friday's Hiding, 1966; Harold Muggins is a Martyr, The Hero Rises Up, 1968; The Ballygombeen Bequest, The Island of the Mighty, 1972; The Non-Stop Connolly Show, 1975; Vandaleur's Folly, 1978; The Manchester Enthusiasts, 1984; Whose is the Kingdom?, 1988; A Suburban Suicide, 1994.

ARDEN-GRIFFITH Paul, b. 18 January 1952, Stockport, England. Opera, Oratorio and Concert Singer. Education: GRSM (Teachers), ARMCM (Teachers), pianoforte and singing, ARMCM (Performers), Singing, Royal Northern College of Music, Manchester. Career: A Midsummer Night's Dream, Sadlers Wells Theatre, 1973; The Merry Widow, English National Opera, 1975; Paul Bunyan, Aldeburgh Festival, 1976; We Come To the River, Royal Opera Covent Garden, 1976; Of Mice and Men, Wexford Festival Opera, Eire, 1980; Carmina Burana, Singapore Festival of the Arts, Singapore, 1984; Phantom of the Opera, Her Majesty's Theatre, 1986; The Duenna, Wexford Festival Opera, Eire, 1989; The Legendary Lanza, Wexford Festival Opera, Eire, 1989; The Barber of Seville, Opera East, UK Tour, 1992; Sunset Boulevard, Rhein-Main Theatre, Frankfurt, Germany, 1998; Sweeney Todd, Royal Opera Covent Garden, London, 2003; Die Fledermaus, Opera Holland Park, London, 2004; The Tales of Hoffman, White Horse Opera, UK, 2005; The Pocket Orchestra: The Unlikely Lives of the Great Composers, London, 2006; Musical Director, 42nd Street, West Side Story, Honk!, 2007, Musical Director, Guys and Dolls, The Music Man, Phantom, 2008, Stagedoor Manor Performing Arts, New York, USA; The Great American Songbook, UK Tour, 2009; A Foreign Field, Redgrave Theatre, Bristol, 2010; Aladdin, Assembly Rooms, Derby, 2010. Recordings: Paul Arden-Griffith – The Song Is You, 1986; Phantom of the Opera (Original Cast Album), 1987; An Evening with Alan Jay Lerner, 1987; Minstrel Magic (Black & White Minstrel Cast Album), 1993; A Minstrel on Broadway, 1994; Encore! – Paul Arden Griffith in Concert, 1995; The Classic Collection, 1995; Accolade!, 1996. Honours: Gwilym, Gwalchmai Jones Scholarship for Singing; Listed in several Who's Who and biographical publications. Memberships: British Actors Equity Association; Musicians' Union; PAMRA; Concert Artistes' Association. Address: c/o Ken Spencer Personal Management, 138 Sandy Hill Road, London SE 18 7BA, England. E-mail: pagtenor@tesco.net

AREM Joel Edward, b. 28 December 1943, New York, USA. Mineralogist; Gemologist. m. Deborah, 1 son, 1 daughter. Education: BS, Geology, Brooklyn College, 1964; MA, Geology, Harvard University, 1967; PhD, Mineralogy, 1970. Appointments include: Consultant, US Department of Commerce, 1975-76; Consultant, Encyclopaedia Britannica Educational Corp, 1975-76; Consultant, Jewellers Circular-Keystone, 1978-85; President, Accredited Gemologists Association, 1977-79; Co-Founder, Editorial Board, PreciouStones Newsletter, 1978-84. Publications: Crystal Chemistry and Structure of Idocrase, PhD Dissertation, 1970; Man-Made Crystals, 1973; Rocks and Minerals, 1973; Gems and Jewelry, 1975, 2nd edition, 1992; Color Encyclopedia of Gemstones, 1977, 2nd edition, 1987; Discovering Rocks and Minerals, 1991. Honours include: Harvard University Scholarships, 1964-66; National Science Foundation Scholarships, 1966-68; Sigma Xi; Phi Beta Kappa. Memberships: Fellow, Gemmological Association of Great Britain; Fellow, Canadian Gemmological Association; Mineralogical Society of America; American Association for Crystal Growth; Mineral Museums Advisory Council; Friends of Mineralogy. Address: PO 5056, Laytonsville, MD 20882, USA.

ARENDT Josephine, b. 13 February 1941, Newark, England. Scientist. m. John Harry, 1 son, 1 daughter. Education: Ladies College, Guernsey; University College, London. Appointments: Research Assistant, Senior Research Assistant, University of Geneva, 1966-77; Reader, Senior Lecturer, Experimental Officer, 1977-90, Professor of Endocrinology, 1990-2003, Professor Emeritus, 2003-, University of Surrey. Publications: Numerous articles in professional journals. Honours: President, European Pineal and Biological Rhythms Society, 1987-90; Vice President, 1996-98, President, 1998-2000, Gordon Research Conference on Pineal Cell Biology; Vice President, The Melatonin Club; Medal, St Joran's Hospital, Karolinska Institute, Sweden; Medal, Justus Liebig Institute, University of Giessen, Germany; Ernst and Berta Scharrer Medal for Neuroendocrinology; Doctor Honoris Causa, University of Lodz, Poland. Memberships: Fellow, Royal College of Pathology; Fellow, Royal Society of Medicine; Society for Endocrinology; European Pineal and Biological Rhythms Society; Society for the Study of Fertility; Society for Research into Biological Rhythms; Society for Light Treatment and Biological Rhythms; European Sleep Research Society; British Sleep Research Society; British Neuroendocrine Group. Address: Centre for Chronobiology, FHMS, University of Surrey, Guildford, Surrey, GU2 7XH, England. E-mail: arendtjo@aol.com

ARFEEN Sultan ul, b. 12 April 1941, Delhi, India. Corporate Professional. m. Nighat Bano, 1968, 3 children. Education: BS, Karachi University, Pakistan, 1960. Appointments: Professional Engineer Trainee, 1960-63, Junior Executive, Executive, 1963-66, Shamsul Arfeen & Co, Karachi; Managing Partner, Arfeen International, Karachi, 1966-69; Chairman, Pakcom Ltd, Clifton, Karachi, 1990; Chairman, Telecard Ltd; Chairman, Gates Ltd; Chairman, Grand Leisure Corp; Chairman, Arfeen International (Pvt) Ltd. Memberships: Karachi Golf Club. Address: Arfeen International (Pvt) Ltd, World Trade Center, Karachi, 75600, Pakistan. E-mail: sa@super.net.pk

ARGHIR Mariana, b. 1 April 1946, Borsa, Cluj, Romania. Mechanical Engineer. m. (1) Paraschiv Tudorancia, 1964, divorced 1971, 1 daughter, (2) Sorin Macovescu, 2009. Education: Diploma, Engineering, Machine Building Technology, Faculty of Mechanics, Cluj, 1971; Doctoral degree, Mechanics, Cluj-Napoca, 1991. Appointments: Engineer, 1971-79, Instructor, 1979-83, Department of Mechanics, Polytechnic Institute, Cluj; Assistant Professor, 1983-92, Associate Professor, 1992-98, Professor, 1998-, Faculty of Machine Building, Department of Mechanics, Technical University of Cluj-Napoca; Editor, Acta Technica Napocensis, series: Applien Mathematics and Mechanics. Publications: 240

scientific papers; 12 textbooks; 19 handbooks; 13 compilers for Romanian computers. Honours: Excellent Diploma & Gold Medal, Proinvent, 2009. Memberships: 8 scientific international societies. Address: Technical University of Cluj-Napoca, Faculty of Building Machines (Design), Department of Mechanics and Computer Programming, C Daicoviciu str, 15, Cluj-Napoca 1, RO-3400, Romania.

ARIBAS Bilgin Kadri, b. 15 July 1961, Posof, Turkey. Radiologist. m. Leyla, 1 daughter. Education: Graduate, Hacettepe University Medical School, Ankara, Turkey, 1985; Postgraduate, Radiology Fellowship, Department of Radiology, Ankara Numune Education and Research Hospital, 1990. Appointments: Assistant Professor, Radiology and Interventional Radiology, Dr A Y Ankara Oncology Education and Research Hospital, Ankara. Publications: Many articles in Radiology and Interventional Radiology; Book chapters; Many oral and written presentations in Radiology and Oncology. Honours: Man of the Year in Medicine and Healthcare, 2011. Memberships: Turkish Interventional Radiology Society; CIRSE fellow; Turkish Society of Radiology. E-mail: bilginaribas@hotmail.com

ARIKAWA Setsuo, b. 29 April 1941, Kagoshima, Japan. President of Kyushu University. Education: BS, 1964, MS, 1966, Mathematics, DSc, 1969, Kyushu University. Appointments: Assistant Professor, Faculty of Science, 1966, Associate Professor, 1973, Professor, 1985, Research Institute of Fundamental Information Science, Dean, Computer Center, 1994, Director General, University Library, 1998, Vice President, 2002, Executive Vice President, 2004, President, 2008-, National Corporation Kyushu University. Publications: Articles: Learning Elementary Formal Systems, 1992; Towards a Mathematical Theory of Machine Discover from Facts, 1995; Book: Progress in Discovery Science, 2002. Honours: 1st Best Paper Award, Japanese Society for Artificial Intelligence, 1987; Best Paper Award, Information Processing Society of Japan, 1996; PAKDD 2000 Paper With Merit Awrad, The Pacific-Asia Conference on Knowledge Discovery and Data Mining, 2000; Best Paper Award, DEWS 2002, Institute of Electronics, Information and Communication Engineers, 2002; many others. Memberships: Japanese Society for Artificial Intelligence; Information Processing Society of Japan; Japan Society for Software Science and Technology; Japan Society of Information and Knowledge. Website: www.kyushu-u.ac.jp

ARKHIPOV Andrei, b. 8 September 1946, Karaganda, Kazakhstan, USSR. Physicist. 2 sons. Education: Graduate, Leningrad State University, Russia, 1970; PhD, 1973, DSc, 1993, Institute of High Energy Physics, Russia. Appointments: Scientist of Theoretical Physics Division, 1973-1985, Senior Scientist, 1985-95, Principal Researcher, 1995-, Institute of High Energy Physics, Russia; Lecturer, Physics, Moscow State University, 1978-98. Publications: Articles in scientific journals including: Soviet Journal of Theoretical and Mathematical Physics, 1990; Nuclear Physics, 2001; Hadron Spectroscopy, 2002. Honours: Nominated for International Scientist of the Year, 2003; Nominated as inaugural member of the Leading Scientist of the World 2005; Diploma of Achievement in Science Award, IBC, 2005; Nominated for Outstanding Scientists of the 21st Century, IBC, 2007; Laureate of the Archimedes Award, 2007; American Order of Merit for Professional Achievements, 2009; Top 100 Scientists, IBC, 2010; International Einstein Award for Scientific Achievements, 2010; The Albert Einstein Award of Excellence, ABI, 2011; Gold Medal for Russia, 2011; International Cultural Diploma of Honor, ABI, 2011; Man of Achievements Award, ABI, 2011; Listed in international biographical dictionaries. Address: Theoretical Physics Division, Institute for High Energy Physics, 142280 Protvino, Moscow Region, Russia. E-mail: Andrei.Arkhipov@ihep.ru

ARKIN Alan Wolf, b. 26 March 1934, USA. Actor; Director. m. (1) Jeremy Yaffe (divorced), 2 sons, (2) Barbara Dana (divorced), 1 son, (3) Suzanne Newlander, 1996. Education: Los Angeles City College; Los Angeles State Col; Bennington College. Appointments: Made professional theatre debut with the Compass Players, St Louis, 1959; Director, The Sunshine Boys, Eh?, 1972; Molly, 1973; Joan Lorraine, 1974; Films include: The Heart is a Lonely Hunter, 1968; Catch 22, 1970; Little Murders (also director), 1971; Last of the Red Hot Lovers, 1972; Freebie and the Bean, 1974; The In-laws, 1979; Simon, 1980; Chu Chu and the Philly Flash, 1981; The Last Unicorn, 1982; Joshua Then and Now (also director), 1985; Coupe de Ville, 1989; Havana, Edward Scissorhands, 1990; The Rocketeer, 1991; Glengarry Glen Ross, 1992; Indian Summer, 1993; So I Married an Axe Murderer, 1993; Mother Night, 1995; Grosse Point Blank, 1997; Gattaca, 1998; Slums of Beverly Hills, 1998; Jakob the Liar, 1999; Arigo, 2000; America's Sweethearts, 2001; Thirteen Conversations About One Thing, 2002; Noel, Eros, The Novice, 2004; Firewall, Little Miss Sunshine, The Santa Clause 3: The Escape Clause, Raising Flagg, 2006; Rendition, 2007; Sunshine Cleaning, Get Smart, Marley & Me, 2008; City Island, The Private Lives of Pippa Lee, 2009; Various TV appearances, including Escape from Sobibor, Necessary Parties; Cooperstown; Taking the Heat; Doomsday Gun; Varian's War, 2001; The Pentagon Papers, 2003; And Starring Pancho Villa as Himself, 2003; Will & Grace, 2005; Boston Legal, 2006-07. Publications: Tony's Hard Work Day; The Lemming Condition; Halfway Through the Door; The Clearing, 1986; Some Fine Grampha, 1995. Honours: Theatre World Award; Award Best Supporting Actor. Address: c/o William Morris Agency, 151 El Camino Drive, Beverly Hills, CA 90212, USA.

ARMANI Giorgio, b. 11 July 1934, Piacenza, Italy. Fashion Designer. Education: University of Milan. Appointments: Window dresser; Assistant buyer for La Rinascente, Milan, 1957-64; Designer and Product Developer, Hitman (menswear co of Cerruti Group), 1964-70; Freelance designer for several firms, 1970; founded Giorgio Armani SpA with Sergio Galeotti, 1975; Appeared on cover of Time, 1982. Honours: Dr hc (Royal College of Art), 1991; Numerous awards including Cutty Sark, 1980, 198l, 1984, 1986, 1987; First Designer Laureate, 1985; Ambrogino D'Oro, Milan, 1982; International Designer Award, Council of Fashion Designer of America, 1983; L'Pacchio D'Oro, 1984, 1986, 1987, 1988; L'Occhiolino D'Oro, 1984, 1986, 1987, 1988; Time-Life Achievement Award, 1987; Cristobal Balenciaga Award, 1988; Woolmark Award, New York, 1989, 1992; Senken Award, Japan, 1989; Award from People for the Ethical Treatment of Animals, USA, 1990; Fiorino d'Oro, Florence, for promoting Made in Italy image, 1992; Honorary Nomination from Brera Academy, Milan, 1993; Aguja de Oro Award, Spain, for best International Designer, 1993; Grand'Uffciale dell'ordine al merito, 1986; Gran Cavaliere, 1987. Address: Via Borgonuovo 21, 20121, Milan, Italy.

ARMATRADING Joan, b. 9 December 1950, Basseterre, St Kitts, West Indies. Singer; Songwriter; Musician (guitar). Musical Education: Self-taught piano and guitar. Career: Songwriting, performing partnership, with Pam Nestor, 1969-73; Solo artiste, 1973-; Appearances include: Regular international tours; Concerts include: Prince's Trust Gala, Wembley Arena, 1986; Nelson Mandela's 70th Birthday

Tribute, Wembley Stadium, 1988; Numerous world tours, 1973-96. Compositions include: Down To Zero; Willow, 1977. Recordings: Singles: Love And Affection, 1976; Rosie, 1980; Me Myself I, 1980; All The Way From America, 1980; I'm Lucky, 1981; Drop The Pilot, 1983; Perfect Day, 1997; Albums include: Whatever's For Us, 1973; Joan Armatrading, 1976; Show Some Emotion, 1977; Stepping Out, 1979; Me Myself I, 1980; Walk Under Ladders, 1981; The Key, 1983; Track Record, 1983; The Shouting Stage, 1988; The Very Best Of..., 1991; What's Inside, 1995; Living For You; Greatest Hits, 1996; Love And Affection, 1997; Lovers Speak, 2003; Into the Blues, 2007; DVD: All the Way from America, 2004; Also appears on: Listen To The Music: 70's Females, 1996; Carols Of Christmas Vol 2, 1997; Prince's Trust 10th Anniversary Birthday, 1997; Film soundtrack, The Wild Geese, 1978. Honour: BASCA Ivor Novello Award for Outstanding Contemporary Collection, 1996; MBE, 2001. Membership: President, Women of the Year, UK. Address: c/o F Winter and Co, Ramillies House, 2 Ramillies Street, London W1F 7LN, England.

ARMFIELD Diana Maxwell, b. 11 June 1920, Ringwood, England. Artist; Educator. m. Bernard Dunstan, 3 sons, 1 deceased. Education: Bedales School; Bournemouth Art School; Slade School; Central School, London. Appointments: Arts Teacher, Byam Shaw School of Art, 1959-89; Crafts, Central School, 1950; Artist-in-residence, Perth, Australia, 1985, Jackson, Wyoming, 1989; One-woman shows include: Browse & Darby, London, 1989-2003, 2006, 2010; 90th Birthday Show, Royal Academy Friends Room Gallery, 1995, 2004-05; Royal Cambrian Academy, 2001; Albany Gallery, Cardiff, 2001; Albany Gallery, Cardiff, 2002, 2005, 2006; New Academy Gallery, 2005; Curwen & New Academy Gallery 50th Anniversary Show, 2008; Exhibition, Pure Gold, 50 Years FBA, 2011; Featured Artist, RWS Spring Exhibition, 2011; Respresented in public collections at: Yale Centre for British Art, Government of England, Faringdon, Mercury Assat Management, Lancaster City, Victoria and Albert Museum, Textiles, Commissioner, HRH Prince of Wales, Reuters, Contemporary Art Society of Wales, National Trust. Publications: Mitchell Beazley Pocket Guide to Painting in Oils; Mitchell Beazley Pocket Guide to Drawing; The Art of Diana Armfield (Julian Halsby). Memberships: Royal Academy of Art; Honorary Member, New English Art Club; Hon Rt, Royal Cambrian Academy; Honorary Member, Pastel Society; Royal Watercolour Society; Hon Rt, Royal West of England Academy. Address: 10 High Park Road, Kew, Richmond, TW9 4BH, England.

ARMOUR Sir James, b. 17 September 1929, Basra, Iraq. Academic Veterinarian. m. Christine Strickland, 2 sons, 2 daughters. Education: MRCVS, PhD, University of Glasgow, 1947-52. Appointments: Veterinary Officer, Veterinary Research Officer, Colonial Service, Nigeria, 1952-60; Research Scientist, Cooper McDougall, Robertson, 1960-63; Lecturer, Senior Lecturer, Reader, Veterinary Parasitology, 1963-75, Professor in Veterinary Parasitology, 1975-96, Dean of the Veterinary School, 1986-91, Vice Principal, 1991-96, Dean of Faculties, 1996-99, Emeritus Professor, 1999-, University of Glasgow; Chairman Veterinary Products Committee (Part of Medicines Commission), 1988-97; Chairman, Glasgow Hospitals NHS Dental Trust, 1995-99; Chairman, Moredun Foundation, 2000-2004; Chairman, St Andrew's Clinics for Children in Africa; Vice-Chairman, Hannah Research. Publications: 150 articles on veterinary parasitology: Pathogenesis, immunology and control of internal parasites of livestock; Joint author of textbook on veterinary parasitology, translated into Spanish, Portuguese, Italian, Arabic and Russian. Honours: CBE, 1989; Kt, 1995; Honorary Degrees: Dr hc, Utrecht, DVM&S, Edinburgh, DU, Glasgow; DU, Stirling; Fellow, Royal Society of Edinburgh; Fellow, Academy of Medical Sciences; Honorary Fellow, Royal College of Veterinary Surgeons; Honorary Fellow, Institute of Biology; Honorary Doctorate, University of Stirling, 2005; Honorary Fellow, European Society for Veterinary Parasitology; Listed in biographical dictionaries. Memberships: Royal College of Veterinary Surgeons; British Veterinary Association; World Association for Advancement of Veterinary Parasitology; British Association for Veterinary Parasitology; Vice-Chairman, Hannah Trust. Address: 4b Towans Court, Prestwick, KA9 2AY, Scotland.

ARMSTRONG Fiona Kathryn, b. 28 November 1956, Preston, England. Broadcaster; Writer. m. Malcolm MacGregor, 1 daughter. Education: St Thomas More School, Preston; W R Tuson College, Preston; BA (Hons), German, UCL. Appointments: Reporter, local radio; Production Journalist, BBC, 1983; Reporter, ITV Border; Presenter, News at Ten, and News at 5.40, 1987-; Reporter/Newcaster, ITN; Presenter, GMTV, 1993; Presenter/Reporter, ITV Border; Architect, Scottish Border River Trail, 2006; Producer/ Presenter, 18 films on Scottish clans and families; Presenter, Under The Hammer; Presenter, Executive Lifestyles; Presenter/Writer, ITV's River Journeys series; Contributor, Sky TV's Tight Lines Fishing Programme; Freelance Features Correspondent, ITV Tyne Tees & Border, 2009-. Publications: F is for Fly Fishing; Let's Start Fly Fishing; The Commuter's Cookbook; Big Food for Wee Macs; Monthly articles in Scotbanner Newspaper, USA, and Scottish Field. Honours: Fellow, University of Central Lancashire. Memberships: Tyburn Angling Club; Reform Club, Pall Mall, London; President, North Cumbria NSPCC; Patron, Angling for Youth Development; Director, Clan Armstrong Trust.

ARMSTRONG Joe C W, b. 30 January, 1934, Toronto, Canada. Author; Historian. 2 sons, 2 daughters. Education: BA, History and Philosophy, Bishop's University, 1958. Appointments: Investment Director, Charterhouse Canada Ltd, Investment Bankers: 29 directorships held, 18 private and 11 public corporations, Canada, UK, USA, 1963-67; Executive Vice-President and Director, Canadian Manoir Industries, Montreal, Quebec, Canada, 1968-69; Senior Industrial Development Officer, Government of Canada, 1972-96; Senior Industrial Development Officer for Canada at World's Fair, Expo '86, Vancouver, British Columbia, Canada, 1986; Director, Economic Development, Canadian Council for Native Business, 1987; Owner, Publicist, "Canadiana Collection: Art & Discovery Maps of Canada", 1978-93; National Speaker to 30 Canadian Clubs, 1997-98; Over 200 national and international radio and television broadcasts on history, heritage and politics, 1978-2003; Author, Historian, Heritage Publicist, 1978-2004; Founding Member, O'Connor Irish Heritage House. Publications: Books: From Sea unto Sea: Art & Discovery Maps of Canada, 1982; Champlain, 1987 (French, 1988); Magna for Canada Scholarship Fund, Inaugural Invitational Author, As Prime Minister I Would..., Essay "Days of Our Lives", 1995; Farewell the Peaceful Kingdom: The Seduction and Rape of Canada, 1963-1994, 1995; Oral and written public presentations on Canada's constitution, heritage, cartography and politics. Honours: Personal interview with HRH Lord Louis Mountbatten, First Sea Lord, Royal Naval College, Greenwich, 1951; Personal interview with Rt Hon Winston S Churchill, St James's Palace, Westminster, 1951; Honorary Director, Canadian Institute of Surveyors, 1983; Director, Ontario Heritage Foundation, 1986; Ontario Advisory Committee on Land Registry Records,

History Committee, Archaeology Committee, 1989; Honorary Member, Le Mouvement Francité, 1990; Cartographic Film Consultant, Black Robe, 1991. Memberships: Fellow, Royal Geographical Society, UK, 1980; Fellow, Royal Canadian Geographical Society, Canada, 1981; Freemason. Address: The Torontonian, 45 Dunfield Avenue, Suite 2821, Toronto, Ontario, M4S 2H4, Canada.

ARMYANOV Stephan, b. 4 May 1942, Sofia, Bulgaria. Professor. m. Eugenia Valova, 1 son. Education: MS, Metallurgical Engineering, Moscow Institute of Steel & Alloys, 1968; PhD, 1975, DSi, 1995, Chemistry, Institute of Physics and Chemistry, Bulgarian Academy of Science. Appointments: Research Associate, 1971, Associate Professor, 1982, Professor, 1998, Institute of Physics and Chemistry, Bulgarian Academy of Science. Publications: Numerous articles in professional journals. Memberships: Electrochemical Society; International Society of Electrochemistry. Address: Bulgarian Academy of Sciences, Bldg 11, Sofia 1113, Bulgaria. E-mail: drmyanov@ipc.bas.bg

ARNARDOTTIR Oddyny Mjoll, b. 16 January 1970, Reykjavik, Iceland. Professor. m. Gylfi Gislason, 2 sons. Education: Cand Jur, University of Iceland, 1994; PhD, University of Edinburgh, 2002. Appointments: Adjunct, Bifrost University, Iceland, 1999-2000; Director, University of Iceland, Human Rights Institute and the Reykjavik Academy, 2001; Partner, Acta Advocates, Iceland, 2002-06; Lecturer, 2005-06, Professor, 2006-, Reykjavik University, Iceland. Publications: Equality and Non-Discrimination under the European Convention on Human Rights, 2003; The UN Convention on the Rights of Persons with Disabilities – European and Scandinavian Perspectives, 2009; Numerous articles in professional journals. Honours: The University of Edinburgh Post-Graduate Studentship; The British Chevening Scholarship; The NATO Science Fellowship; The British Federation of Women Graduates Scholarship; Outstanding Student Award, Delta Theta Phi (International).

ARNAUD Gilles, b. 4 September 1964, Neuilly-sur-Seine, France. Professor. m. Annie Dutech, 2 sons. Education: Master, I/O Psychology, 1988; PhD, Management Sciences, 2001. Appointments: Research Fellow, University of Nice, 1989-91; Professor, Toulouse Business School, 1992-2011; Professor, ESCP Europe Business School, 2011-. Publications: Organization Studies; Human Relations; Journal of Organizational Change Management; Management Decision; Journal of Managerial Psychology. Memberships: CIRFIP, Board; ISPSO; EGOS; EAWOP; Academy of Management. Address: ESCP Europe Business School, 79, avenue de la République, 75543 Paris, France. E-mail: garnaud@escpeurope.eu

ARNAUTOVIC Samir, b. 12 February 1965, Ljubuski, Bosnia & Herzegovina. University Professor. 1 daughter. Education: BA, Philosophy, 1989, MA, Contemporary Philosophy, 1994, PhD, 1997, Department of Philosophy & Sociology, Faculty of Philosophy, University of Sarajevo. Appointments: Research Assistant, Department of Philosophical Investigations, Academy of Sciences and Arts, Sarajevo, 1991; Assistant Lecturer, German Classical Idealism and Contemporary Philosophy, Department of Philosophy & Sociology, UNSA, 1996; Senior Lecturer, 1998, Associate Professor, 2001, Professor, 2001, Vice Rector, 2006-, International Co-operation. Publications: The Perspectivism of Nietzsche's Thought and Critique of Modernity, 1997; Nietzsche's Nihilism and Metaphysics, 1999; Contemporary Philosophy and Philosophical Inheritance, 2001; Phenomenological Interpretation of Aristotle, 2002; Aspects of Modernity, 2003; Philosophical Origins of Modernity, 2004; Transcendental Philospy and Determinants of Modernity, 2005; Dividing Lines of Hegel's Philosophy, in progress. Memberships: International Hegel Society, Berlin; Member, Board of Philosophical Review Prolegomena in Zagreb, Croatia; World University Service BiH; Theoria Philosophical Society. E-mail: samir.arnautovic@unsa.ba

ARNOLD Thomas Richard (Sir), b. 25 January 1947, London, England. Theatre Producer; Publisher; Consultant, Middle East Affairs. m. Elizabeth Jane, dissolved 1993, 1 daughter. Education: MA, Pembroke College, Oxford. Appointments: Member of Parliament (Conservative), Hazel Grove, Manchester, 1974-97; Parliamentary Private Secretary to Secretary of State for Northern Ireland, 1979-81; Parliamentary Private Secretary to Lord Privy Seal, Foreign and Commonwealth Office, 1981-82; Vice-Chairman, Conservative Party, 1983-92; Member, 1992-94, Chairman, 1994-97, Treasury and Civil Service Select Committee. Honours: Freeman of the City of London (Baker's Company), 1969; Knighted, 1990. Address: No 1 Manchester Square, London, W1U 3AB, England.

ARORA Prince Kumar, b. 15 November 1947, Delhi, India (US Citizen, 1981). Immunologist; Neuroimmunologist. m. Kit-ying Barbara Chin, 3 children. Education: BS (Hons), 1970, MS (Hons), 1973, Panjab University; PhD, Microbiology, Michigan State University, 1978. Appointments: Graduate Research Assistant, Michigan State University, 1976-78; John E Fogarty International Visiting Fellow, Laboratory of Immunodiagnosis, 1978-79, John E Fogarty International Visiting Fellow, Immunology Branch, 1979-82, National Cancer Institute, NIH; NIH Staff Fellow, Laboratory of Molecular Genetics, National Institute of Child Health and Human Development, NIH, 1982-83; NIH Staff Fellow, Laboratory of Developmental and Molecular Immunity, National Institute of Child Health and Human Development, NIH, 1983-87; Senior Scientist, Laboratory of Neuroscience, NIDDK, NIH, 1987-92; Interim Acting Chief, Laboratory of Neuroscience, NIDDK, NIH, Bethesda, 1989-92; Consultant, 1992-95, Assistant Vice President of Research, American Institute of Neuroimmunomodulation, Carlsbad, California, 1995-. Publications: Articles in professional journals; Author of several book chapters; Book reviewer for: American Society for Microbiology News, 1990; Immunopharmacology Journal, 1991; Quarterly Review of Biology, 1993; First to demonstrate: The role of protease inhibitor, Alpha-1-Antitryspin in immune regulation; The role of non-MHC linked genetic control of cytotoxic T lymphocytes to hapten modified syngeneic cells; Modulation of immune response by benzodiazepine receptor inverse agonists; The effect of pertussis toxin on cytotoxic T lymphocytes; That morphine induces programmed cell death (PCD) in thymic cells; Editor: International Journal of Neuroscience; Reviewing Editor, various professional journals. Honours include: Gold Medal, 1971, Merit Scholar, 1967-72, Panjab University; International Travel Awards, NIH, 1983, 1988, 1989; American Medical Association Certificate of Recognition, 1990; International Science and Engineering Fair Commendation, Teacher-Sponsor of 1990 ISEF Finalist, 1990; First President, American Society for NeuroImmunoModulation, 2003-; Research Grants from NIH (intramural), Office of Naval Research, Department of Defense, Upjohn Corporation and others. Memberships: American Society for Microbiology; New York Academy of

Sciences; American Association of Immunologists; Sigma Xi. Address: 10108 Ashburton Lane, Bethesda, MD 20817-1730, USA. E-mail: prince20817@yahoo.com

ARQUETTE Patricia, b. 8 April 1968, Chicago, Illinois. Actress. m. (1) Nicholas Cage, divorced, (2) Thomas Jane, 2006, 1 daughter, 1 son from a previous relationship. Appointments: Films include: Pretty Smart, 1986; A Nightmare on Elm Street 3: Dream Warriors, 1987; Far North, 1988; The Indian Runner, Prayer of the Rollerboys, 1991; Trouble Bound, Inside Monkey Zetterland, 1992; True Romance, 1993; Ed Wood, 1994; Beyond Rangoon, 1995; Infinity, Flirting with Disaster, 1996; Lost Highway, Nightwatch, 1997; Goodbye Lover, Stigmata, Bringing Out the Dead, 1999; Little Nicky, 2000; Human Nature, 2001; Holes, Tiptoes, Deeper than Deep, 2003; Fast Food Nation, 2006; A Single Woman, 2009; TV includes: Daddy, 1987; Dillinger, 1991; Wildflower, 1991; Betrayed by Love, 1994; Toby's Story, 1998; The Hi -Lo Country, 1998; The Badge, 2002; Medium, 2005-. Address: c/o UTA, 9560 Wilshire Blvd, 5th Floor, Beverley Hills, CA 90212, USA.

ARQUETTE Rosanna, b. 10 August 1959, New York, USA. Actress, Director, Producer. m. (1) Anthony Greco (divorced), (2) James N Howard, divorced, (3) John Sidel, divorced, 1 daughter. Appointments: Actress; Founder, Flower Child Productions; Films include: Gorp, 1980; SOB, 1981; Off The Wall, 1983; The Aviator, Desperately Seeking Susan, 1985; 8 Million Ways to Die, After Hours, Nobody's Fool, 1986; The Big Blue, 1988; Life Lessons, Black Rainbow, Wendy Cracked a Walnut, 1989; Sweet Revenge, Baby, It's You, Flight of the Intruder, 1990; The Linguini Incident, Fathers and Sons, 1992; Nowhere to Run, 1993; Pulp Fiction, 1994; Search and Destroy, 1995; Crash, 1996; Liar, Gone Fishin', Buffalo '66, 1997; Palmer's Pick Up, I'm Losing You, Homeslice, Floating Away, Hope Floats, Fait Accompli, 1998; Sugar Town, Palmer's Pick Up, Pigeonholed, Interview with a Dead Man, 1999; The Whole Nine Yards, Too Much Flesh, 2000; Things Behind the Sun, Big Bad Love, Good Advice, Diary of a Sex Addict, 2001; Gilded Stones, Dead Cool, 2004; Max and Grace, 2005; What About Brian, I-See-You.Com, 2006; Terra (voice), 2007; Ball Don't Lie, Growing Op, 2008; Northern Lights, 2009; Directed and Produced: Searching for Debra Winger, 2002; All We Are Saying, 2005; TV includes: Harvest Home; The Wall; The Long Way Home; The Executioner's Song; One Cooks, the Other Doesn't; The Parade; Survival Guide; A Family Tree; Promised a Miracle; Sweet Revenge; Separation; The Wrong Man; Nowhere to Hide; I Know What You Did; Grey's Anatomy; Medium. Address: 8033 West Sunset Boulevard, #16, Los Angeles, CA 90046, USA.

ARSENJEV Serghey, b. 3 December 1937, Tiraspol Town, Moldova. Mechanical Engineer. m. Victoria Arsenjeva, deceased, 1 son, 1 daughter. Education: MEng for Lifting and Transporting Machines and Equipment, Polytechnic Institute of Odessa, USSR, 1958-63. Appointments: Principal Investigator, Leading Theorist, The Fundamentals of Liquid and Gas Motion Physics, Organiser of Physical Technical Group, Informal Scientific Association, Pavlograd, Ukraine, 1990-. Publications: 28 articles, more than 200 of R&D accounts, reports, methods, 25 author's certificates and patent. Honours: World Record Holder, 2007; Gold Medal for Ukraine, 2007; International Profiles of Accomplished Leaders & Lifetime Achievement Award, 2007; 2007 Man of Science Award; Order of International Merit, 2008. Address: Physical Technical Group, Dobroljubova Street, 2, 29; Pavlograd Town, 51400 Ukraine. E-mail: ptglecus@yahoo.com Website: www.lozik.h1.ru

ARSHAD Waheed Ud Din, b. 21 March 1926, India. Engineer. Widower, 1 son. Education: Graduate, Engineering University of Punjab, Pakistan, 1947; Practical Training, Loughborough Technical College, England, 1948-49; Postgraduate Studies, Royal Military College of Science, England, 1955-56; Defence Resource Management Course, 1976. Appointments: Highest rank of Major General, Commissioned Service, Pakistan Army's Corps of Electrical and Mechanical Engineers, 1948-80; Chairman and Chief Executive of Pakistan Ordnance Factories; Additional Secretary, Civil Service, Ministry of Defence, Government of Pakistan, 1980-86; Executive Trustee, Munir Arshad Memorial Welfare Trust, 1990-. Publications: Articles on Pakistan Defence Production Effort. Honours: Tamgha-e-Imtiaz (M), Government of Pakistan. Memberships: Fellow, Institute of Mechanical Engineers, London; Fellow, Institute of Engineers, Pakistan; Member, Pakistan Engineering Council. Address: 20-H, Tipu Sultan Road, Multan Cantt, Pakistan.

ARTHUR Rasjid Arthur James, b. 7 June 1928, Stirling, Scotland. Journalist. Education: MA, Honours, English, Edinburgh University, 1950. Appointments: National Service, RAF, 1950-52; Local Reporter, Stirling, 1952-54; Sub Editor, 1954-55, Leader Writer, 1955-64, The Scotsman; Features Editor, News Editor and Writer, Central Office of Information, London, 1965-78; Freelance Writer on environment, development and related topics, 1978-. Publications: The Edge of Time, poetry, 2010; Many articles on environmental subjects for British and international magazines of the water industry and for the London Press Service of the Press Association. Membership: Chartered Institute of Journalists. Address: 236 (Attic) High Street, Perth PH1 5QJ, Scotland.

ARUL MOZHI SELVAN V, b. 15 May 1972, Kadavoor, India. Professor. m. Meena, 1 son, 1 daughter. Education: BE, Mechanical Engineering, 1994; M Tech, Energy Engineering, 1999; PhD, Mechanical Engineering, 2010. Appointments: Lecturer, JJCET, Trichy, 1996-2006; Assistant Professor, Department of Mechanical Engineering, National Institute of Technology, Tiruchirappalli, 2006-. Publications: Numerous articles in professional journals. Honours: Listed in international biographical dictionaries. Memberships: Indian Society for Technical Education. Address: Department of Mechanical Engineering, National Institute of Technology, Tiruchirappalli 620015, India. E-mail: arulmozhi@nitt.edu Website: www.nitt.edu

ARUNKUMAR G, b. 2 July 1975, Vellore, Tamil Nadu, India. IT Consultant, Engineering Services. m. G Mahalakshmi, 1 son. Education: BE, Mechanical Engineering, University of Madras, Chennai, 1997; ME, Engineering Design, Bharathiyar University, Coimbatore, 2000; PhD, Mechanical Engineering, Anna University, Chennai, 2009. Appointments: M/S Sakthi Auto Components Pvt Ltd, Erode, 1997-98; M/S Thirumaal Auto Components Pvt Ltd, Vellore, 1998-99; Kongu Engineering College, Erode, 2000-06; RMK Engineering College, Chennai, 2007-08; ITC Infotech Ltd, 2008-. Publications: 15 articles and research papers in professional journals. Honours: Best Manager, IBS; Best Staff Gold Medal. Memberships: AMIE; LMISTE; FIV; LMIET. Address: 66A Parthasarathy Street, Vellala Teynampet, Chennai – 600086, Tamil Nadu, India. E-mail: garun77@yahoo.co.in

ARVIDE CAMBRA Luisa Maria, b. 10 August 1956, Almeria, Spain. Professor. 2 daughters. Education: Graduate, Hispanic Philology, 1978, Graduate, Semitic Philology, 1978, Doctor in Arabic Philology, 1982, University of Granada, Spain. Appointments: Research Scholar, 1979-82, Professor

Assistant, 1982-87, University of Granada; Chair Professor, University of Almeria, 1987-. Publications: Tratado de polvos medicinales en al-Zahrawi; Tratado de pastillas medicinales en Abulcasis; Tratado de oftalmologia en Abulcasis; Tratado de odontoestomatologia en Abulcasis; Tratado de estetica y cosmetica en Abulcasis; Relatos de Ibn Qutayba; Maqamas de al-Hariri; Las Cuestiones Sicilianas de Ibn Sabin; many others. Honours: Doctorate Award, University of Granada, 1982; Listed in international biographical dictionaries. Memberships: International Institute of Informatics and Systemics, USA. Address: Dpto Filologia, Facultad de Humanidades, Universidad de Almeria, La Canada de San Urbano S/N, 04120 Almeria, Spain. E-mail: lmarvide@ual.es

ASCHERI Mario, b. 7 February 1944, Ventimiglia, Italy. Professor of Legal History. m. Cecilia Papi, 2 sons. Education: Law Degree, Siena, 1967. Appointments: Professor, University of Siena, 1971; Professor, University of Sassari, 1972-76; Professor of Legal History, University of Rome 3, 2002-. Publications include: Books: Istituzioni medievali, 1999; I diritti del Medioevo italiano (secoli XI-XV), 2000; Siena nella storia, 2000; Lo spazio storico di Siena, 2001; Introduzione storica al diritto moderno e contemporaneo, 2003; Le città – Stato, Bologna, 2006; Jurists and Institutions from Middle Ages to Early Modern (c10th-18th), 2009; Giuristi e istituzioni dal medioevo all'eta moderna (sec XI-XVIII), 2010. Honours: Doctor honoris causa, Université d'Auvergne, Clermont-Ferrand, France, 2001; Beirat Max-Planck-Institut für europäische Rechtsgeschichte, Frankfurt/Main, Germany; Consiglio Direttivo Deputazione di Storia patria per la Toscana, Florence; Direttore Sezione di Storia Accademia Senese degli Intronati, Siena; Premio della Città di Siena (Mangia d'oro), 2003; Premio della Città di Ventimiglia (San Segundin), 2003. Memberships: Editorial Member of historical periodicals published in Florence, Turin, Siena, Saragoza, Madrid. Address: Via G Duprè 99, I-53100 Siena, Italy. E-mail: ascheri@uniroma3.it

ASHDOWN OF NORTON SUB-HAMDON, Baron Ashdown of Norton Sub-Hamdon in the County of Somerset; Sir Jeremy John Durham (Paddy), b. 27 February 1941, New Delhi, India. Member of Parliament. m. Jane Courtenay, 1962, 1 son, 1 daughter. Appointments: Served RM and 42 Commando, 1959-71; Commanded 2 Special Boat Section; Captain, Royal Marines; HM Diplomatic Service, 1st Secretary, UK Mission to United Nations, Geneva, 1971-76; Commercial Managers Department, Westlands Group, 1976-78; Senior Manager, Morlands Ltd, 1978-81; Liberal Candidate, 1979; Dorset County Council, 1982-83, Spokesman for Trade and Industry, 1983-86; Liberal Member of Parliament for Yeovil, 1983-88; Liberal/SDP Alliance Spokesman on Education and Science, 1987; Liberal Democrat Member of Parliament for Yeovil, 1988-2001; Liberal Democrat Spokesman on Northern Ireland, 1988-; Leader, Liberal Democrats, 1988-99; Appointed Privy Counsellor, 1989; Appointed Non-Executive Director of Time Companies Ltd and Independent Newspapers Ltd, 1999; UN International High Representative to Bosnia and Herzegovina, 2002-06. Publications: Citizen's Britain: A Radical Agenda for the 1990s, 1989; Beyond Westminster, 1994; Making Change our Ally, 1994; The Ashdown Diaries 1988-97, 2000; The Ashdown Diaries Vol II, 1997-99, 2001. Honours: Knight Grand Cross of the Most Distinguished Order of Saint Michael and Saint George (GCMG), 2006. Address: c/o House of Lords, Westminster, London SW1A 0PW, England.

ASHE Geoffrey Thomas, b. 29 March 1923, London, England. Writer; Lecturer. m. (1) Dorothy Irene Train, 3 May 1946, deceased, 4 sons, 1 daughter, (2) Maxine Lefever, 8 December 1992, divorced, (3) Patricia Chandler, 3 April 1998. Education: BA, University of British Columbia, Canada, 1943; BA, Trinity College, Cambridge University, 1948. Appointment: Associate Editor, Arthurian Encyclopaedia, 1986. Publications: King Arthur's Avalon, 1957; From Caesar to Arthur, 1960; Land to the West, 1962; The Land and the Book, 1965; Gandhi, 1968; The Quest for Arthur's Britain, 1968; Camelot and the Vision of Albion, 1971; The Art of Writing Made Simple, 1972; The Finger and the Moon, 1973; The Virgin, 1976; The Ancient Wisdom, 1977; Miracles, 1978; Guidebook to Arthurian Britain, 1980; Kings and Queens of Early Britain, 1982; Avalonian Quest, 1982; The Discovery of King Arthur, 1985, re-issue 2003; Landscape of King Arthur, 1987; Mythology of the British Isles, 1990; King Arthur: The Dream of a Golden Age, 1990; Dawn Behind the Dawn, 1992; Atlantis, 1992; The Traveller's Guide to Arthurian Britain, 1997; The Book of Prophecy, 1999; The Hell-Fire Clubs, 2005; Merlin: The Prophet and His History, 2006; The Off-Beat Radicals, 2007. Contributions to: Numerous magazines and journals. Honour: Fellow, Royal Society of Literature, 1963. Memberships: Medieval Academy of America; Camelot Research Committee, secretary; International Arthurian Society. Address: Chalice Orchard, Well House Lane, Glastonbury, Somerset BA6 8BJ, England.

ASHER Jane, b. 5 April 1946. Actress; Author; Businesswoman. m. Gerald Scarfe, 2 sons, 1 daughter. Career: As Cook: Owner Jane Asher's Party Cake Shop and Sugarcraft, 1990-; Cake Designer and Consultant for Sainsbury's, 1992-99; Spokesperson and Consultant, Heinz Frozen Desserts, 1999-2001; Cookware and Gift Food Designer, Debenhams, 1998-2005; Creator, Home Baking Mixes for Victoria Foods, 1999-; Actress: Films include: Greengage Summer; Masque of the Red Death; Alfie; Dreamchild; Tirant Lo Blanc, 2005; Death at a Funeral, 2006; TV Appearances include: Brideshead Revisited, 1981; Murder Most Horrid, 1991; The Choir, 1995; Good Living, 1997-99; Tricks Of The Trade, 1999; Crossroads, 2003; Murder at the Vicarage, 2004; New Tricks, 2005; A for Andromeda, 2006; Holby City, 2007; Maestro, 2008; Stage Appearances include: Making it Better, Hampstead and Criterion Theatres, 1992; Things We Do for Love, Yvonne Arnaud and Gielgud Theatres, 1998; Is Everybody Happy, 2000; House and Garden, Royal National Theatre, 2000; What the Butler Saw, National Tour 2001; Festen, Almeida Theatre, 2004; Festen, Lyric Theatre, London, 2004-05; The World's Biggest Diamond, Royal Court Theatre. Publications include: The Moppy Stories, 1987, 2005; Calendar of Cakes, 1989; Eats for Treats, 1990; Time to Play, 1993; Jane Asher's Book of Cake Decorating Ideas, 1993; The Longing (novel), 1996; The Question (novel), 1998; Losing It (novel), 2002; Cakes for Fun, 2005; Beautiful Baking, 2007. Honour: Honorary LLD, Bristol University, 2001. Memberships: BAFTA; FORUM UK; Associate, RADA; Fellow, Royal Society of Arts; Charity Work: President: National Autistic Society, Arthritis Care, West London Family Service Unit; Vice-President: Child Accident Prevention Trust, Mobility Trust, National Deaf Children's Society. Address: c/o Actual Management, 7 Great Russell Street, London, WC1B 3NH, England.

ASHER Lila Oliver, b. 15 November 1921, Philadelphia, Pennsylvania, USA. Artist. m. (1) Kenneth P Crawford (deceased), (2) Sydney S Asher Jr (deceased), 1 son (deceased), 1 daughter. Education: Student of: Jos Grossman, Philadelphia, Professor Gonippo Raggi, Orange, New Jersey,

DICTIONARY OF INTERNATIONAL BIOGRAPHY 36th EDITION

Frank B A Linton, Philadelphia; Fleisher Memorial Art School, Philadelphia College of Art (now University of the Arts). Appointments: Volunteer USO Artist, during WWII; Instructor, 1948, Full Professor, 1991, Howard University. Publications: Men I Have Met in Bed, 2008; Represented in museums in US and abroad. Honours: Over 50 solo exhibitions in US and abroad; Certificate for Outstanding Service to Prinkmaking, National Museum of American Art, 1981. Memberships: Cosmos Club, Washington, DC; Washington Printmakers Gallery. Address: 4100 Thornapple St, Chevy Chase, MD 20815-5130, USA. Website: www.lilaoliverasher.com

ASHER Ronald E, b. 23 July 1926, Gringley-on-the-Hill, Nottinghamshire, England. University Professor. 2 sons. Education: BA, University of London, 1950; Certificate in Phonetics of French, University College London, 1951; PhD, University of London, 1955; DLitt, University of Edinburgh, 1993. Appointments: Lecturer, Linguistics, 1953-57, Lecturer in Tamil, 1957-65, School of Oriental and African Studies, University of London; Visiting Professor of Linguistics, University of Chicago, 1961-62; Senior Lecturer, 1965-70, Reader, 1970-77, Professor of Linguistics, 1977-93, Vice-Principal, 1990-93, Honorary Fellow, Faculty of Arts/ School of Humanities and Social Sciences, 1993-99, 2001-, University of Edinburgh; Visiting Professor of Linguistics and International Communication, International Christian University, Tokyo, 1994-95; First occupant of Vaikom Muhammad Basheer Chair, Mahatma Gandhi University, Kottayam, Kerala, India, 1995-96. Publications: Books include most recently: Critical essays on the novels and stories of Vaikom Muhammad Basheer, 1999; Colloquial Tamil (joint author), 2002; What the Sufi said (Translation from the Malayalam of novel by K P Ramanunni; joint translator), 2002; Wind Flowers: Contemporary Short Fiction from Kerala (joint editor and translator), 2004; Atlas of the World's Languages (joint editor), 2007. Honours: Honorary Fellow, Sahitya Akademi (India's National Academy of Letters), 2007; Fellow, Kerala Sahitya Akademi, 1983; Basheer Purasakaram (Basheer memorial award, Kerala), 2010. Address: Linguistics and English Language, The University of Edinburgh, Dugald Stewart Building, 3 Charles Street, Edinburgh EH8 9AD, Scotland.

ASHFAQ Muhammad, b. 18 November 1952, Jhang, Pakistan. Meritorious Professor; Dean. m. Shaheen Kausar, 3 sons, 1 daughter. Education: BSc (Hons), 1972, MSc (Hons), 1975, PhD, 1985, University of Agriculture, Faisalabad; LLB, Punjab University, Lahore, 1995; H Post Doctorate, Ibraki University, Japan, 2007. Appointments: Research Officer, 1976-77, Agricultural Officer, 1978, Lecturer, 1978-83, Assistant Professor, 1983-86, Senior Research Officer, 1986-87, Associate Professor, 1987-92, Director, Student Affairs, 1991-95, Professor, 1992-2004, Head, Department of Library, 1996-2002, Hall Warden, 1999-2004, Principal Officer, Engineering Cons, 2001-04, Chairman, Department of Agricultural Entomology, 2002-04, 2007-09, Principal Officer, Student Affairs, 2003-04, Dean, Faculty of Agriculture, 2003-06, 2009-, Meritorious Professor, 2004-, University of Agriculture, Faisalabad. Publications: Numerous articles in professional journals. Honours: Many awards including: Civil Award, 2003-04; Shield of Honour, 2006; Gold Medal, 2007; Education Excellence Award, AUSPAK, 2008; 19th Bolan Excellence Award, 2008; Zoologist of the Year Award, 2009; Asian Peace Seminar Award of Honor, 2010. Memberships: Zoological Society of Pakistan; Pakistan Science Academya; many other professional organisations. Address: Faculty of Agriculture, University of Agriculture, Faisalabad, Pakistan.

ASHKENAZY Vladimir, b. 6 July 1937, Gorky, USSR. Musician. m. Thorunn Sofia Johannsdottir, 2 sons, 3 daughters. Education: Central School of Music, Moscow, 1945-55; Moscow Conservatory, 1955-62. Appointments: Conductor, Philharmonia Orchestra, Royal Philharmonic Orchestra, Cleveland Orchestra, Deutsches Symphonie-Orchester Berlin; Guest conductor, Berlin Philharmonic, Boston Symphony, Los Angeles Philharmonic, San Francisco Symphony, Philadelphia and Concertgebouw Orchestras; Chief Conductor of the Czech Philharmonic Orchestra, 1998-2003; Conductor Laureate, Philharmonia Orchestra; Music Director, NHK Symphony Orchestra, 2004-05; Music Director, European Union Youth Orchestra; Conductor Laureate, Iceland Symphony Orchestra; Chief Conductor and Artistic Director, Sydney Symphony, 2009-. Honours: 2nd prize, Chopin Competition, Warsaw, 1955; 1st prize, Queen Elisabeth Competition, Brussels, 1956; 1st prize, Tchaikovsky Competition, Moscow, 1962; Six Grammy awards, -1999; Order of the Falcon, highest civil decoration of Iceland; Hanno R Ellenbogen Citizenship Award, 2000. Memberships: Rachmaninoff Society. Address: Savinka, Kappelistrasse 15, 6045 Meggen, Switzerland.

ASHLEY Bernard, b. 2 April 1935, London, England. Writer. Education: Teachers Certificate; Advanced Diploma, Cambridge Institute of Education. Publications: The Trouble with Donovan Croft, 1974; Terry on the Fence, 1975; All My Men, 1977; A Kind of Wild Justice, 1978; Break in the Sun, 1980; Dinner Ladies Don't Count, 1981; Dodgem, 1982; High Pavement Blues, 1983; Janey, 1985; Running Scared, 1986; Bad Blood, 1988; The Country Boy, The Secret of Theodore Brown, 1989; Clipper Street, 1990; Seeing off Uncle Jack, 1992; Cleversticks, Three Seven Eleven, 1993; Johnnie's Blitz, 1995; I Forgot, Said Troy, A Present for Paul, 1996; City Limits, 1997; Tiger Without Teeth, 1998; Growing Good, Little Soldier, 1999; Revenge House, 2002; Freedom Flight, 2003; Ten Days to Zero, 2005; Smokescreen, Down to the Wire, 2006; Flashpoint, Angel Boy, 2007; Solitaire, 2008; No Way to Go, 2009; Ronnie's War, 2010; Aftershock, 2011. Contributions to: Guardian; Books for Your Children; Junior Education; Books for Keeps; Times Educational Supplement; School Librarian. Honours: The Other Award, 1976; Runner Up, Carnegie Medal, 1979, 1986, 1999; Royal TV Society Best Children's Entertainment Programme, 1993; Runner Up, Guardian Award, 2000; Honorary Doctorate in Education, Greenwich University, 2003; Honorary Doctorate in Letters, Leicester University, 2004. Memberships: Writers Guild. Address: 128 Heathwood Gardens, London SE7 8ER, England. Website: www.bashley.com

ASHLEY Leonard Raymond Nelligan, b. 5 December 1928, Miami, Florida, USA. Professor Emeritus of English; Author; Editor. Education: BA, 1949, MA, 1950, McGill University; AM, 1953, PhD, 1956, Princeton University. Appointments: Instructor, University of Utah, 1953-56; Assistant to the Air Historian, Royal Canadian Air Force, 1956-58; Instructor, University of Rochester, 1958-61; Faculty, New School for Social Research (part-time), 1962-72; Faculty, Brooklyn College of the City University, New York, 1961-95; Professor Emeritus, 1995-. Publications include: A Military History of Modern China (collaborator); Shakespeare's Jest Book (editor); What's in a Name?; Phantasms of the Living (editor); Ballad Poetry of Ireland (editor); Elizabethan Folklore; Colley Cibber; George Peele: The Man and His Work; Relics of Irish Poetry (editor); Language in Contemporary Society (co-editor); Language in Action; Language in Modern Society; Language in The Era of Globalization (co-editor); Language and Identity (co-editor); Eleven books on the occult; Geolinguistic Perspectives (co-editor); Language and Politics (co-editor); Phantasms of the Living (editor); Language in Modern Society; Animal Crackers; George Alfred Henty and the Victorian Mind, and Nordic Folklore and Tradition (with Ola J Holten), etc; Regular reviewer in Bibliotheque d'Humanisme et Renaissance, etc. Contributions to: Anthologies such as Modern American Drama: The Female Canon and Art, Glitter and Glitz, its Mainstream Playwrights… 1920s America; Reference books such as: Great Writers of the English Language; History of the Theater; Encyclopaedias (US and abroad); DLB; New DNB; Numerous works on names and naming including: Names of Places, Names in Literature, Names in Popular Culture, Art Attack: Essays on Names in Satire, Cornish Names; Last Days: Armageddon, The Messiah, The Rapture, The Last Judgement; Mexico: The Smart Traveler's Guide to All the Names; Animal Crackers: An Alphabestiary; Over 180 articles in periodicals and scholarly journals in US, UK, India, etc; Poetry in over 60 publications; Co-editor of conference proceedings; Over 5000 pages of book reviews; Many other collaborations. Honours: Shakespeare Gold Medal, 1949; LHD (honoris causa), Columbia Theological, 1998; American Name Society Best Article Award; Fellowships and grants; American Name Society, president 1979, 1987, long-time member editorial board, executive board; American Name Society; International Linguistic Association, Secretary, 1980-82; American Name Society, President, 1979, 1987; American Association of University Professors, former president, Brooklyn College Chapter; McGill Graduates Society of New York, President, 1970-75; American Society of Geolinguistics, president 1991-; Princeton Club of New York; New York Academy of Sciences; Modern Language Association. Address: Library Technical Services, Brooklyn College of the City University of New York, Brooklyn, NY 11210, USA.

ASHMORE Biba Victoria, b. 29 November 1952, Trieste, Italy. Artist. Education: St Marys, The Town and Country School, London, 1964-69; The Camden Arts Centre, London, 1969-70; Camberwell School of Art and Crafts, London, 1970-74. Appointments: Artist; Work held in private and public collections including Harrison Wier Fund, Royal Academy of Arts, 1978; Group and solo exhibitions, 1973-; RA Summer Exhibition, 1975, 1976, 1978, 1996, 1997; Exhibited with The London Group, 1975; Exhibited with Llewelyn Alexander Gallery, 2000; Exhibited, The Brix St Mathews, 2010; Solo Exhibition, Tate Library, 2010; Solo Exhibition, Carnegie Library Gallery, 2011. Publications: Listed in international biographical dictionaries; Article in popular press. Honours: Dip Ad Fine Art, 1974; David Murray Scholarship, Landscape Painting, 1972; City & Guilds Certificates in Interior Décor and Additional Decorative Techniques, 1996-98; Edexel Level 2 BTEC Certificate in Photography, 2006; Exhibited with the Hunting Art Prizes: The Royal College of Art, 2001; Edexel Level 3 BTEC Certificate in Photography, 2007. Memberships: Friend of the Royal Academy of Arts; Friend of Tate Britain/Tate Modern; Member, Alumni of University of the Arts. Address: 134 Leander Road, London SW2 2LJ, England. E-mail: ashmorebiba@tiscali.co.uk

ASIF Anila, b. 8 February 1972, Lahore, Pakistan. Associate Professor. m. Muhammad Asif. Education: FSc, Pre-Med Group, BISE, Lahore, 1989; BSc, Chemistry, Zoology, Botany, Punjab University, Lahore, 1992; PhD, Polymer Chemistry and Physics, University of Science and Technology of China, 2005. Appointments: Lecturer, Chemistry, Higher Education Department, Government of the Punjab, Pakistan, 1997-98, 2006-08; Lecturer, Chemistry, Lahore College for Women University, Lahore, 1998-2006; Assistant Professor, Interdisciplinary Research Center in Biomedical Materials, COMSATS Institute of Information Technology, Lahore, 2008-10; Associate Professor, Interdisciplinary Research Centre in Biomedical Materials, COMSATS, Institute of Information Technology, Lahore, 2010-. Publications: 18 articles in professional journals; 1 book chapter. Honours: President, Talent Scholarship in BSc; Cultural Exchange Scholarship for PhD studies in P R China; Research Productivity Allowance, 2005-06; Listed in international biographical dictionaries. Address: House No 430, Sirhindi Road, Main Samanabad, Lahore, Pakistan. E-mail: anila.asif@gmail.com

ASIF Muhammad, b. 4 September 1968, Lahore, Pakistan. Research; Teaching/Research. m. Anila. Education: MSc, Physics, 1992, M Phil, Physics, 1995, PhD, Plasma Physics, 2005, Chinese Academy of Science. Appointments: Associate Professor, Physics, COMSATS Institute of Information Technology, Lahore. Publications: 30 articles in professional journals. Honours: Listed in international biographical dictionaries. Address: 430 Sirhindi Road, Main Samanabad, Lahore, Pakistan. E-mail: dr.muh.asif@gmail.com

ASKEW Reginald James Albert, b. 16 May 1928, Aberdeen, Scotland. Clerk in Holy Orders. m. Kate Wigley, 1 son, 2 daughters. Education: BA, 1951, MA, 1956, Corpus Christi College, Cambridge; Scholae Cancelarii, Lincoln, 1955-57; King's College London, 1957-61. Appointments: Ordained Deacon, Church of England, 1957; Ordained Priest, 1958; Curate of Highgate, 1957-61; Lecturer and Vice-Principal, Wells Theological College, 1961-69; Priest Vicar, Wells Cathedral, 1961-69; Vicar, Christ Church, Lancaster Gate, 1969-73; Principal, Salisbury and Wells Theological College, 1973-87; Dean, King's College London, 1987-93; Retired, 1993. Publications: The Tree of Noah, 1971; Muskets and Altars, Jeremy Taylor and the Last of the Anglicans, 1997; Contributor: The Reality of God, 1986. Honours: Pilkington Prize, 1957, 1958; Canon, 1975-87, Canon Emeritus, 1988-, Salisbury Cathedral; Chaplain, Worshipful Company of Merchant Taylors, 1996-97. Memberships: Corrymeela Community, 1971-; President, Bath and Wells Clerical Society, 1996-. Address: Carters Cottage, North Wootton, Shepton Mallet, Somerset BA4 4AF, England. E-mail: reginald.askew@virgin.net

ASLAKSEN Erik Waldemar, b. 2 November 1938, Oslo, Norway. Engineer. m. Elfriede Seidl, 1 son, 2 daughters. Education: Dipl Ing, ETH, 1962; Graduate Study Program, Bell Telephone Laboratories, 1965; PhD, Physics, Lehigh University, 1968; Certified Professional Logistician, Society of Logistics Engineers, 1993; Certified Systems Engineering Professional, International Society of Systems Engineering, 2004. Appointments: Member of Technical Staff, Microwave Ferrite Device Development Department, Bell Telephone Laboratories Inc, Pennsylvania, USA, 1963-67; Teaching Assistant, Physics Department, Lehigh University, USA, 1967-68; Member of Technical Staff, Quantum Electronics Research Department, Bell Telephone Laboratories Inc, New Jersey, USA, 1968-70; Senior Research Scientist, Theoretical Physics Group, Corporate Research Center, Brown Boveri & Company, Switzerland, 1970-73; Technical Director, GUTOR-Group, Wettingen, Switzerland, 1974-77; Own consulting firm, Aslaksen AG, 1977-81; Senior Consultant, Ewbank Belford Pty Ltd, Australia, 1982; Visiting Professor, School of Electrical Engineering, Adjunct Professor, Faculty of Engineering, University of Technology, Sydney, 1983-2000; Deputy Manager, Electrical Division, 1982-84, Manager, Systems Division, 1984-85, Brown Boveri (Australia) Pty Ltd; Technical Manager, Racal Electronics Pty Ltd, 1985-88;

Director, Ewbank Preece Sinclair Knight, 1988-93, Principal and Senior Consultant, Sinclair Knight Merz Pty Ltd, 1988-. Publications: 4 books; Numerous articles in professional journals. Memberships: Fellow, Institute of Engineers, Australia; Fellow, INCOSE; Member, Australian Institute of Physics. Address: Sinclair Knight Merz Pty Ltd, 100 Christie Street, St Leonards, NSW 2065, Australia. E-mail: erik.aslaksen@bigpond.com

ASSAAD Fawzia, b. 17 July 1929, Cairo, Egypt. Author. m. Fakhry Assaad, 1 son, 2 daughters. Education: French Baccalaureate, Cairo, 1946; BA, 1949, PhD, 1956, Sorbonne, University of Paris; Arabic Baccalaureate, Cairo, 1957. Appointments: Lecturer in Philosophy, University of Ain Shams, Cairo, 1957-64, Universities of Taipei and Dunghai, Taiwan, 1960-64. Publications: Fiction (in French): L'Egyptienne, 1975, English translation, 2005; Des Enfants et des Chats, 1987; La Grande Maison de Louxor, 1992, Arabic translation, 2004; Ahlam et les Eboueurs du Caire, 2004, Arabic translation, 2008. Non-Fiction: Soren Kierkegaard (in Arabic), 1960, 2nd edition revised 2009; Les Préfigurations Egyptiennes de la Pensée de Nietzsche (French), 1986; Hatshepsout, Woman Pharao, (French) 2000, (Arabic translation), 2003; Les Pharaons Hérétiques: Hatshepsout, Akhenaton, Nefertiti, 2007; contributions to journals. Honours: Prix de Société Genevoise des Ecrivains, 1985, 1991; Prix Afrique Méditerrannée, 2005. Memberships: Association des Critiques Littéraires; PEN International; Association de Ecrivains de langue Française; Association Internationale de Cerisy-la-Salle; President, PEN Suisse Romande, 2002-; President, Société Genevoise des Ecrivains, 2004-06; Observer for PEN Int, Human Rights United Nations Council, 1989-; Founding Member, Lavigny's Writers Retreat, Switzerland. Address: 2 ch. de Sous-Cherre, 1245 Collonge-Bellerive, Geneva, Switzerland. E-mail: fassaad@worldcom.ch Website: www.arabworldbooks/com/authors/fawzia_assaad.html

ASSUMPCÃO Francisco B Jr, b. 7 September 1951, São Paulo, Brazil. Psychiatrist. 2 daughters. Education: MD, Medical School FUABC, S Andre, Brazil, 1974; Doctor, Psychology PUC, São Paulo, Brazil, 1988; Professor, Child Psychiatry, Medicine School, Universidade De São Paulo, Brazil, 1993-2000. Appointments: Professor of Psychopathology, Psychology Institute, São Paulo University, 2005-. Publications: Child and Adolescent Psychiatry Handbook; Psychology and Comics; Psiquiatria Infantil Brasileira; Psiquiatria da Infância e Adolescência; Autismo; Adolescência Normal e Patologica; Semiologia em Psiquiatria da Infância e da Adolescência; Handbook of Child and Adolescent Psychiatry, 2003; Sexuality and Mental Retardation, 2005; Psychopharmacotherapy in Children; Psychoscial Situations in Children and Adolescents; Sexuality, Cinema and Handicap; Evolutive Psychopathology, 2009. Honours: Colar Gran Cruz Merito Da Medicina; Medal for Science and Peace; Listed in 2000 Most Admired Physicians in Brazil, 2007-08, 2008-09; Medal of Immigration, 2008. Memberships: Brazilian Psychiatry Society; APAL; Brazilian Child Psychiatry Association; President, Child Psychiatry Department, Brazilian Psychiatric Association, 2004-; Paulista Academy of Psychology. Address: R Otonis 697-V, Clementino, Sao Paolo, SP 04325 002, Brazil. E-mail: cassiterides@bol.com.br

ASTASHKIN Sergey, b. 15 April 1956, Kuibyshev, USSR. Mathematician. m. Aset Yakubova, 2 sons. Education: MS, Mathematics, Kuibyshev University, 1978; PhD, Mathematics, Voronezh State University, 1982; DSc, Mathematics, Institute of Mathematics, Russian Academy of Sciences, 1999. Appointments: Snr Lecturer, Kuibyshev State University, 1982-87; Associate Professor, Mathematics, 1999, Chair Professor, 1999-, Professor, Mathematics, 2000-, Samara State University, Russia. Publications: Contributor of more than 90 articles to professional journals. Honours: Grantee, Research Grant, Royal Swedish Academy of Sciences, 2003-06, 2009-11; Russian Fund of Fundamental Research, 2007-08, 2010-11; Australian Research Council, 2005-08; 2010-11. Memberships: American Mathematical Society. Address: Department of Mathematics and Mechanics, Samara State University, Acad Pavlov Str 1, 443011 Samara, Russia. E-mail: astashkn@ssu.samara.ru

ASTBURY Paul (John), b. 11 December 1945, Cheshire, England. Artist. m. Lesley, 2 sons, 1 daughter. Education: College of Art, Stoke-on-Trent, 1960-68; MA (Hons), Royal College of Art, London, 1968-71. Career: Artist in oil and sculpture; Solo and group exhibitions around the UK, Europe, Japan, Australia and New Zealand, Scandinavia, Taiwan and USA, 1971-; Art held in public and private collections around the world; Exhibition, Postmodernism: Style and Subversion 1970-1990, Victoria & Albert Museum, London, 2011. Publications: Document, a Body of Raw Clay Sculpture; Work also appears in many professional journals, reviews and books. Honours: Awards and sponsorships from: Crafts Advisory Committee, 1974; British Arts Council, 1977; Crafts Council, 1984; Middlesex University Research Board, 1995, 1999; British Council, Western Japan, 1997; Kodak Professional Motion Imaging Ltd, 1999; The Widescreen Centre, 1999. E-mail: pja_62@hotmail.com Website: www.paul-astbury.co.uk

ATABEK Osman Melek, b. 28 April 1946, Istanbul, Turkey. Research Director; Physicist. m. Rosemarie. Education: Chemical Engineering Diploma, Ecole Nationale Supérieure de Chimie de Paris, 1970; PhD, Physics University Paris 6, 1973; Doctorate d'Etat, Physics University Pierre and Marie Curie, Paris, 1976. Appointments: Assistant Professor, University Pierre and Marie Curie, Paris, 1974-76; Research Assistant, Centre National de la Recherche Scientifique, CNRS, Paris, 1976-78; Research Associate, CNRS, Paris, 1978-88; Research Director, CNRS, Paris, 1988-; Mathematics Professor, Ecole Nationale Supérieure de Chimie de Paris, 1988-2003. Publications: Over 160 peer-reviewed publications; 11 chapters in books; Over 50 invited talks at international conferences; Over 15 PhD thesis supervision; Group leader, Quantum Modelisation and Laser Control, Laboratoire de Photophysique Moléculaire du CNRS. Honours: Chemical Physics Medal, Ecole Nationale Supérieure de Chimie de Paris, 1970; Nominated Outstanding Referee, American Physical Society, 2011; Listed in biographical dictionaries. Memberships: Associate Member, International Society of Theoretical Chemical Physics; Active Member, Scientific Committee, Turkish Physical Society. Address: ISMO Institut des Sciences Moleculaires d'Orsay, Universite Paris-Sud 11, Bat 350, Campus d'Orsay, 91405 Orsay Cedex, France. E-mail: osman.atabek@u-psud.fr

ATHERTON Richard, b. 15 February 1928, Liverpool, England. Catholic Priest. Education: St Francis de Sales School; St Francis Xavier Grammar School; Upholland College. Appointments: Assistant Priest, St Philip, St Cecilia's, 1954-60, Liverpool, 1960-65; RC Chaplain, HMP Walton, 1965-75; Senior RC Chaplain, HMP Appleton Thorn, 1975-77; Principal RC Chaplain, Prison Department, Home Office, 1977-89; Parish Priest, St Joseph's, Leigh, 1989-91; President, Ushaw College, Durham, 1991-96; Chaplain to

Archbishop of Liverpool, 1996-2001; Retired. Publications: Summons to Serve, 1987; New Light, 1993; Praying the Prayer of the Church, 1998; Praying the Sunday Psalms (Year A) 2001, (Year B) 2002, (Year C) 2003; Let's Meet the Prophets, 2008. Honours: BA; MA; Dip Crim; OBE. Address: 8 Lindley Road, Elland, HX5 0TE, England. E-mail: r.atherton@rcaolp.co.uk

ATHILL Diana, b. 21 December 1917, London, England. Publisher; Writer. Education: Lady Margaret Hall, Oxford. Appointments: Editorial Director, André Deutsch Ltd, 1952-92. Publications: Instead of a Letter (memoir), 1962; An Unavoidable Delay (stories), 1962; Don't Look at Me Like That (novel), 1967; After a Funeral (documentary), 1986; Make Believe (documentary), 1993; Stet: A Memoir (memoir), 2000; Yesterday Morning (memoir), 2003; Somewhere Towards the End (memoir), 2009. Honours: OBE; Winner, The Costa Prize for Biography, 2009. Memberships: Fellow, Royal Society of Literature. Address: 30 Kekewich House, 1 View Road, Highgate, London N6 4DJ, England.

ATKINS (Dame) Eileen June, b. 16 June 1934, Clapton, London, England. Actress. m. (1) Julian Glover, (2) William B Shepherd. Education: Parkside Preparatory School, Tottenham; Latymer Grammer School, Edmonton; Guildhall School of Music & Drama, London. Career: Co-creator: Upstairs, Downstairs; The House of Eliot; Screenplay: Mrs Dalloway, 1997; As an actress: Theatre: Open Air Theatre, 1953; Semi-Detached, 1962; The Killing of Sister George, 1966; Vivat! Vivat Regina!, 1972; Vita and Virginia; Cymbeline, Mountain Language, 1988; A Room of One's Own, 1991;A Night of the Iguana, 1992; Indiscretions, 1995; John Gabriel Borkman, 1996; A Delicate Balance, 1997; The Unexpected Man, 1998, 2001; Honour, 2003; The Retreat from Moscow, 2004; The Birthday Party, 2005; Doubt, 2006; The Sea, The Female of the Species, 2008; TV: Three Sisters, 1970; A Midsummer Night's Dream, 1971; The Lady from the Sea, Electra, 1974; She Fell Among Thieves, 1977; Sons and Lovers, 1981; Oliver Twist, Smiley's People, 1982; Titus Andronicus, The Burston Rebellion, A Better Class of Person, 1985; Roman Holiday, 1987; A Room of One's Own, 1990; The Lost Language of Cranes, 1991; Cold Comfort Farm, 1995; Talking Heads, 1998; Madame Bovary, David Copperfield, 2000; Wit, 2001; Bertie and Elizabeth, 2002; Cranford, 2007; Psychoville, 2009; Film: Equus, 1977; The Dresser, 1983; Wolf, 1994; Jack and Sarah, 1995; Gosford Park, 2001; The Hours, 2002; Cold Mountain, 2003; Vanity Fair, 2004; Ask the Dusk, 2006; Wild Target, 2009. Honours: CBE, 1990; DBE, 2001; Drama Desk Award for Outstanding One-Person Show; BAFTA Award, 2008; Emmy Award, 2008; Honorary degree, City of London University; 3 Evening Standard Best Actress Awards; 3 Olivier Best Actress Awards; 1 Evening Standard Best Screenplay Awards; Numerous US awards.

ATKINSON David John, b. 5 September 1943. Retired Bishop. m. Suzan, 1969, 1 son, 1 daughter. Education: BSc, 1965, AKC, 1965, PhD, 1969, University of London; Diploma in Theology, 1970, M Litt, Theology, 1973, Trinity College, Bristol; Certificate in Student Counselling, University of London, 1979; MA, University of Oxford, 1984. Appointments: Teacher, Maidstone Technical High School for Boys, 1968-69; Ordained Deacon, 1972; Curate in Charge, Smithills Hall Chapel, St Peter Halliwell, Bolton, 1972-74; Ordained Priest, 1973; Senior Curate, St John the Baptist Harborne, Birmingham, 1974-77; Librarian, Latimer House, Oxford, 1977-80; Chaplain, Corpus Christi College, Oxford, 1977-93; Lecturer, Christian Ethics, Oxford Diocese NSM course, 1978-81; Visiting Lecturer, Christian Ethics, London Bible College, 1980-83; Theological Consultant to Care and Counsel, 1980-87; Part time Staff Member, Oxford University Student Counselling Service, 1981; Fellow, Lecturer in Theology, Corpus Christi College, Oxford, 1984-93; Visiting Chaplain, Fuller Theological Seminary, Pasadena, USA, 1983; Visiting Lecturer, Christian Ethics and Pastoral Theology, Wycliffe Hall, Oxford, 1983-93; Tutor, Oxford University Faculty of Theology in Psychology of Religion, Christian Ethics and Moral Theology (Final Honours School), 1984-93; Northrup Visiting Professor, Hope College, Holland, Michigan, USA, 1986, 1991; Canon Chancellor of Southwark Cathedral and Canon Missioner, Diocese of Southwark, 1993-96; Visiting Lecturer, South Asia Institute of Advanced Christian Studies, Bangalore, India, 1999; Martin Lecturer, St John's College, University of Hong Kong, 2000; Archdeacon of Lewisham, 1996-2001; Bishop of Thetford (Norwich), 2001-09. Publications: Booklets: Prophecy, 1977; Tasks for the Church in Marriage Debate, 1979; The Values of Science, 1980; Life and Death, 1985; The Moral Teaching of the Apostle Paul, 1991; The Ethics of the Johannine Literature, 1993; Books: The Have and To Hold: The Marriage Covenant and the Discipline of Divorce, 1979; Homosexuals and the Christian Fellowship, 1979; Bible Speaks Today: Ruth, 1983, Genesis I-II, 1990, Job, 1991, Proverbs, 1996; Peace in Our Time?, 1985; Pastoral Ethics, 1989, 1994; Counselling in Context, 1994, 1998; New Dictionary of Christian Ethics and Pastoral Theology, 1995; Jesus, Lamb of God, 1996; God So Loved the World, 1999; Renewing the Face of the Earth: Theological and Pastoral Responses to Climate Change, 2008. Address: 6 Bynes Road, South Croydon, CR2 0PR, England.

ATKINSON Rowan Sebastian, b. 6 January 1955, Newcastle-upon-Tyne, England. Actor; Author. m. Sunetra Sastry, 1990, 1 daughter, 1 son. Education: Universities of Newcastle and Oxford. Appointments: Stage appearances include: Beyond a Joke, Hampstead, 1978; Oxford University, Revues at Edinburgh Fringe, One Man Show, London, 1981; The Nerd, 1985; The New Revue, 1986; The Sneeze, 1988; Oliver, 2008-09; TV appearances: Not the Nine O'Clock News, 1979-82; Blackadder, 1983; Blackadder II, 1985; Blackadder the Third, 1987; Comic Relief, 1988-; Blackadder Goes Forth, 1989; Mr Bean (13 episodes), 1990-96; Rowan Atkinson on Location in Boston, 1993; Full Throttle, 1994; The Thin Blue Line, 1995; Blackadder: Back and Forth, 1999; We are Most Amused, 2008; Blackadder Rides Again, 2008; Films include: Never Say Never Again; The Tall Guy, The Appointments of Dennis Jennings, 1989; The Witches, 1990; Four Weddings and a Funeral, Hot Shots - Part Deux, 1994; Bean: The Ultimate Disaster Movie, 1997; Blackadder – Back and Forth, Maybe Baby, 2000; Rat Race, Scooby Doo, 2002; Johnny English, Love Actually, Mickey's PhilharMagic (voice), 2003; Keeping Mum, 2005; Mr. Bean's Holiday, 2007. Honours: Variety Club Award, BBC Personality of the Year, 1980; BAFTA Best Light Entertainment Performance, 1989. Address: c/o PBJ Management Ltd, 7 Soho Street, London W1D 3DQ, England. E-mail: general@pbjmgt.co.uk

ATLASOV Kirill, b. 5 January 1980, St Petersburg, Russia. Research Associate. Education: Master, Physics, The National Research University of Information Technologies, Mechanics and Optics, Russia, 2003; PhD, Physics, Swiss Federal Institute of Technology, Switzerland, 2009. Appointments: Research Assistant, Laser Technology, IFMO, 2000-04; Research Assistant, 2004-09, Research Associate, Visiting Science, 2009-10, 2011, Laboratory of Physics of Nanostructures, EPFL. Publications: Numerous articles in professional journals. Honours: Sokrates International Program, Institute fuer Lasertechnik, Germany, 20000; Personal grant for young scientists, IFMO, Russian Federal Progam, 2002. Address: Spassky str 1/46-16, 190031 St Petersburg, Russia.

ATSUJI Shigeo, b. 24 January 1959, Kyoto, Japan. Social Scientist. Education: Doctor, Business Administration, 1996; PhD, Policy Sciences, 2003. Appointments: Associate Professor, St Andrew's University, Japan, 1989-94; Professor, Kansai University, 1994-. Publications: Author: Organization and Intelligence, 1996; The Sciences of Organizational Decisions, 1999; Management Policy Against Organizational Disasters, 2003; Co-author, The Thinking Organization, 2001. Memberships: International Society for the System Sciences; International Federation of Scholarly Associations of Management. Address: 2-1 Ryozenji Takatsuki, Osaka 569-1095, Japan. E-mail: atsuji@res.kutc.kansai-u.ac.jp

ATTENBOROUGH David Frederick (Sir), b. 8 May 1926, London, England. Naturalist; Film-Maker; Author. Education: Zoology, Clare College, Cambridge, England. Appointments: Military Service, Royal Navy, 1947-49; Editorial Assistant, educational publishing; Joined BBC Television, Trainee Producer, 1952; First expedition to West Africa, 1954; Many trips to study wildlife and human cultures, 1954-64; TV series, Zoo Quest; Controller, BBC2, 1965-68; Director of Television Programmes, BBC, 1969-72; Member, Board of Management; TV Series include: Life on Earth, 1979, The Living Planet, 1983, The Trials of Life, 1990; The Private Life of Plants, 1995; The Life of Birds, 1998; Life of Mammals, 2002; Life in the Undergrowth, The Life Collection, 2005; Planet Earth, 2007. Publications: Zoo Quest to Guiana, 1956; Zoo Quest for a Dragon, 1957; Zoo Quest in Paraguay, 1959; Quest in Paradise, 1960; Zoo Quest to Madagascar, 1961; Quest under Capricorn, 1963; The Tribal Eye, 1976; Life on Earth, 1979; The Living Planet, 1984; The First Eden, 1987; The Trials of Life, 1990; The Private Life of Plants, 1994; The Life of Birds, 1998; The Life of Mammals, 2002; Life on Air, autobiography, 2002; Life in the Undergrowth, 2005. Honours include: Silver Medal, Zoological Society of London, 1966; Gold Medal Royal Geographical Society; Kalinga Prize, UNESCO; Honorary Degrees: Leicester, London, Birmingham, Liverpool, Heriot-Watt, Sussex, Bath, Ulster, Durham, Bristol, Glasgow, Essex, Cambridge, Oxford; Knighted, 1985; Encyclopaedia Britannica Award, 1987; Edinburgh Medal, Edinburgh Science Festival, 1998; BP Natural World Book Prize, 1998; Faraday Prize, Royal Society, 2003; International Documentary Association Career Achievement Award, 2003; Raffles Medal, Zoological Society of London, 2004; Caird Medal, National Maritime Museum, 2004; British Book Awards Lifetime Achievement Award, 2004; British Naturalists' Association Peter Scott Memorial Award, 2007; BAFTA (Life in Cold Blood), 2009; Prince of Asturias Award, 2009. Memberships include: Fellow, Royal Society, Honorary Fellow, British Academy of Film and Television Arts, The Culture Show British Icon Award, 2006. Address: 5 Park Road, Richmond, Surrey, England.

ATTENBOROUGH, Baron Attenborough of Richmond-upon-Thames, Sir Richard Samuel Attenborough, b. 29 August 1923, Cambridge, England. Actor; Producer; Director. m. Sheila Beryl Grant Sim, 1945, 1 son, 2 daughters (1 deceased). Education: Royal Academy of Dramatic Art, London. Appointments: First Stage Appearance as Richard Miller in Ah! Wilderness, Palmers Green 1941; West End Debut, Awake and Sing, 1942; First Film Appearance, In Which We Serve, 1942; Joined RAF, 1943; Seconded to RAF Film Unit for Journey Together, 1944; Demobilised, 1946; Returned to Stage, 1949; Formed Beaver Films, with Bryan Forbes, 1959; Allied Film Makers, 1960; Goodwill Ambassador for UNICEF, 1987-; Director, Chelsea Football Club, 1969-82; Many stage appearances; Film appearances: School for Secrets; The Man Within; Dancing With Crime; Brighton Rock; London Belongs to Me; The Guinea Pig; The Lost People; Boys in Brown; Morning Departure; The Magic Box; The Great Escape; Dr Doolittle; David Copperfield; Jurassic Park; Miracle on 34th Street; The Lost World: Jurassic Park; Elizabeth; Snow Prince, 2006; Many others; Produced: Whistle Down the Wind, 1961; The L Shaped Room; Directed: Young Winston, 1972; A Bridge Too Far, 1976; Magic, 1978; A Chorus Line, 1985; Puckoon, 2002; Closing the Ring, 2004; Produced and Directed: Oh! What a Lovely War, 1968; Gandhi, 1981; Cry Freedom!, 1987; Chaplin, 1992; Shadowlands, 1993; In Love and War, 1997; Grey Owl, 1999; Closing the Ring, 2007. Publications: In Search of Gandhi, 1982; Richard Attenborough's Chorus Line, 1986; Cry Freedom, A Pictorial Record, 1987. Honours: 8 Oscars; 5 BAFTA Awards; 5 Hollywood Golden Globes; Directors Guild of America Award; others. Memberships: Tate Foundation; Royal Academy of Dramatic Arts; Help a London Child; President of RADA; President of BAFTA; Others. Address: Old Friars, Richmond Green, Surrey, TW9 1NQ, England.

ATTFIELD Robin, b. 20 December 1941, St Albans, England. University Professor. 1 son, 2 daughters. Education: Christ Church, Oxford, 1960-64; Regent's Park College, Oxford, 1964-66; Manchester University, 1967. Appointments: Lecturer, 1968-77, Senior Lecturer, 1977-81, Reader, 1982-91, Professor, 1991-, Philosophy, Cardiff University. Publications: God and The Secular, 1978; The Ethics of Environmental Concern, 1983; A Theory of Value and Obligation, 1987; Environmental Philosophy: Principles and Prospects, 1994; Value, Obligation and Meta-Ethics, 1995; The Ethics of the Global Environment, 1999; Environmental Ethics: An Overview for the Twenty-First Century, 2003; Creation, Evolution and Meaning, 2006; The Ethics of the Environment, 2008. Honours: Chair, Conference Session on Environmental Philosophy at World Congress of Philosophy, 1998; Visiting Research Fellow, National Research Council, Republic of South Africa, 1999; Member, UNESCO Expert Working Party on Environmental Ethics, 2004; Research Fellow, Arts and Humanities Research Council, 2005-06; D Litt, 2008. Memberships: University and College Union; Society for Applied Philosophy; International Society for Environmental Ethics; International Society for Value Inquiry; British Society for Ethical Theory; British Society of the Philosophy of Religion; British Society for the History of Philosophy; Royal Institute of Philosophy; Religious Society of Friends (Quakers).

ATWOOD Margaret (Eleanor), b. 18 November 1939, Ottawa, Ontario, Canada. Poet; Author; Critic. m. Graeme Gibson, 1 daughter. Education: BA, Victoria College, University of Toronto, 1961; AM, Radcliffe College, Cambridge, Massachusetts, 1962; Harvard University, 1962-63, 1965-67. Appointments: Teacher, University of British Columbia, 1964-65, Sir George Williams University, Montreal, 1967-68, University of Alberta, 1969-70, York University, 1971-72; Writer-in-Residence, University of Toronto, 1972-73, University of Alabama, Tuscaloosa, 1985, Macquarie University, Australia, 1987; Berg Chair, New York University, 1986. Publications: Poetry: Double Persephone, 1961; The Circle Game, 1964; Kaleidoscopes Baroque, Talismans for Children, 1965; Speeches for Doctor Frankenstein, 1966; The Animals in That Country, 1968; The Journals of Susanna Moodie, Procedures for Underground, Oratorio for Sasquatch, Man and Two Androids, 1970; Power

Politics, 1971; You Are Happy, 1974; Selected Poems, 1976; Marsh Hawk, 1977; Two-Headed Poems, 1978; True Stories, Notes Towards a Poem That Can Never Be Written, 1981; Snake Poems, 1983; Interlunar, 1984; Selected Poems II: Poems Selected and New, 1976-1986, 1986; Selected Poems 1966-1984, 1990; Margaret Atwood Poems 1965-1975, 1991; Morning in the Burned House, 1995; The Door, 2007; Fiction: The Edible Woman, 1969; Surfacing, 1972; Lady Oracle, 1976; Dancing Girls, 1977; Life Before Man, 1979; Bodily Harm, 1981; Encounters With the Element Man, 1982; Murder in the Dark, Bluebeard's Egg, Unearthing Suite, 1983; The Handmaid's Tale, 1985; Cat's Eye, 1988; Wilderness Tips, 1991; Good Bones, 1992; The Robber Bride, 1993; Alias Grace, 1996; The Blind Assassin, 2000; Oryx and Crake, 2003; Telling Tales (contribution to charity anthology), 2004; The Penelopiad, 2005; The Year of the Flood, 2009; Juvenile: Up in the Tree, 1978; Anna's Pet, 1980; For the Birds, 1990; Princess Prunella and the Purple Peanut, 1995; Rude Ramsay and the Roaring Radishes, 2003; Bashful Bob & Doleful Dorinda, 2006; Non-Fiction: Survival: A Thematic Guide to Canadian Literature, 1972; Days of The Rebels 1815-1840, 1977; Second Words: Selected Critical Prose, 1982; The Oxford Book of Canadian Verse in English (editor), 1982; The Best American Short Stories (editor with Shannon Ravenel), 1989; Strange Things: The Malevolent North in Canadian Literature, 1995; Negotiating with the Dead: A Writer on Writing, 2002; Moving Targets: Writing with Intent 1982-2004, 2004; Curious Pursuits: Occasional Writings, 2005; Contributions to: Books in Canada; Canadian Literature; Globe and Mail; Harvard Educational Review; The Nation; New York Times Book Review; Washington Post. Honours: Guggenheim Fellowship, 1981; Companion of the Order of Canada, 1981; Fellow, Royal Society of Canada; Foreign Honorary Member, American Academy of Arts and Sciences, 1988; Order of Ontario, 1990; Centennial Medal, Harvard University, 1990; Commemorative Medal, 125th Anniversary of Canadian Confederation, 1992; Giller Prize, 1996; Author of the Year, Canadian Book Industry Award, 1997; Marian McFadden Memorial Lecturer, Indianapolis-Marion County Public Library Foundation, 1998; Booker Prize, 2000; International Crime Writers' Association Dashiell Hammett Award, 2001; Radcliffe Medal, 2003; Harold Washington Literary Award, 2003; Prince of Asturias Award for Letters, 2008; Honorary degrees. Memberships: Writers Union of Canada, president, 1981-82; PEN International, president, 1985-86. Address: McClelland & Stewart, 481 University Ave, Suite 900, Toronto, Ontario, Canada M5G 2E9.

AUGSBACH Linda Jean Keller, b. 7 June 1951, Glendale, West Virginia, USA. Elementary School Teacher. m. Charles William Augsbach. Education: AA Degree, Minnesota Bible College; Postgraduate studies, Kentucky Christian College, 1973-74; BS Degree, Malone College, Canton, Ohio, 1975. Appointments: Grades 1-8 Tutor, Minerva Local School, Ohio, 1976-77; Grades 1 and 2 Teacher, Christian School of Cincinnati, Ohio, 1977-78; Substitute Teacher, Canton (Ohio) City School, 1978-82; Substitute Teacher, Pasco County School, Florida, 1982-83; Grade 6 Teacher, Dade City, Florida, 1983-87; Grade 4 Teacher, New Port Richey, Florida, 1987-88; Grade 6 Teacher, 1988-91, Grade 4 Teacher, 1991-96, alternately Grade 4 and Grade 5 Teacher, 1996-99; Alternately Grade 4 and Grade 5 Teacher, 2000-07, Grade 5 Teacher, 2008-, Mittye P Locke Elementary, Elfers, Florida. Publications: Article in Learning Magazine, 1991; Copyright secured, 1999, for large curriculum: Learning: It's Just a Game – Science, History, Word Structure, Grammar, Writing and More, All Rolled Into One Exciting Unit, currently preparing for publication. Honours: The Best Teachers in America Selected by the Best Students, 1996; Selected attendee of Governor Bush's Second Annual Educators' Leadership Summit, 2002; Listed in Who's Who publications and biographical dictionaries. Membership: Christian Educators' Association International. Address: 1441 Wegman Drive, Tarpon Springs, FL 34689, USA.

AUGUSTYN Józef, b. 21 March 1950, Olpiny, Poland. Jesuit; Theologian. Education: BA Philosophical Studies, Jesuit School of Philosophy, Krakow, Poland, 1971-73; Theological Studies, Jesuit School of Theology, Warsaw, Poland, 1973-76; Graduate Studies, ThL, Religious Education, ATK University, Warsaw; Christian Spirituality, Gregorian University Rome, 1981-82; Research, The Center of Ignatian Spirituality, Quebec, Canada, 1989; PhD, Theology, Catholic University, Warsaw, 1994; Habilitation (qualification as a University Professor), 2002. Appointments: Professor, University School of Philosophy and Education "Ignatianum", Krakow, Poland; Editor, Pastores, 1996-2001; Currently Editor, Spiritual Life; Advisor, Polish Government, Department of Education, 1996-; Reviewer of Textbooks on sexual education and family values and public health and education, 1997-2000. Publications: 45 books and over 220 articles in the fields of spiritual life, Christian education, psychology and religion include: A Practice of Spiritual Direction, 1993; Sexual Integration. A Guidebook for discovering and maturing human sexuality, 1994; Homosexuality and Love, 1996; Sexual education in schools and families, 1997; Fatherhood: Pedagogical and spiritual dimensions, 1999; Know Yourself, 1999; Celibacy: Pedagogical and spiritual dimensions, 1999; Meditations based on the Spiritual Exercises of St Ignatius Loyola, 6 volumes, 2001; Deeply Shaken: The Church's Self-Cleaning, 2002, The Lustration of Priests, 2006, The Art of Confessing (editor), 2006, The Art of Spiritual Direction (editor), 2007; Jerusalem Meditations, 2010; The Art of Being a Priest, 2010; A Quarter of Sincerity, 2011; Around 30 books translated into Slavic languages. Honour: Award from the journal Powsciagliwosc I Praca, 1991. Memberships: Fellow of the State Committee, Department of Education, responsible for creating and implementing the school subject, Human Development and Sexuality, 1998; Advisor, Committee for Christian Education, Polish Conference of Catholic Bishops. Address: ul Kopernika 26, PL-31-501 Cracow, Poland.

AULLEN Jean-Patrice, b. 26 April 1948, Annaba, Algeria. Public Health Service Officer. m. Marie-Isabelle Celeyron, 1 son, 1 daughter. Education: PhD, Medicine, University of Paris St Louis-Lariboisière, Paris, 1974; Certificate in Preventive Pediatry, University Necker-Enfants Malades, Paris V, 1975; Degree in Public Health, University Pierre et Marie Curie, Paris VI, 1981; Diploma, National School in Public Health, Rennes, 1982; Diploma, National Center of Health Economic Programs Studies – National Institute of Economic Studies, Paris, 1991; Diploma, Institute for Development of Applied Epidemiology, 1996. Appointments: Practice and Research, Health Infancy Community and Pediatric Hospital, Paris, 1973-81; Medical Inspector, Departmental Direction of Health Ministry, Nantes, Pays de la Loire, 1982-83; Chief Medical Inspector, Regional Direction of Health Ministry, Rennes, Bretagne, 1983-85; Chief Medical Inspector, Regional Direction of Health Ministry, Nantes, Pays de la Loire, 1985-95; Chairman's Adviser, Public Health and Haemovigilance Network, French Blood Agency, Paris, 1995-99; Medical Inspection Officer, 2nd Group of Public Hospitals in France, Lyon, 1999-2002; Medical Inspection Officer, Sanitary Crisis, Marseille, 2002-04; Medical Inspection Officer, Regional Co-ordinator in Charge, Regional System of Haemovigilance, 2004-10, Member,

French National Haemovigilance Commission. Publications: 30 publications including: Blood pressure in infants and adolescents – Influences of age, sex, high, height, cardiac frequency, 1980; For a French accreditation system, 1993; Serious events in transfusion chain, 2008; 40 thesis; 18 thesis tutor; 106 lectures, conferences, seminars and presentations. Honours: Diabetes-HTA, Ricaut Award of French National Academy of Medicine, 1975; Award of French National Foundation for Cardiology, 1977; Pediatrics, Renault Award of French National Academy of Medicine, 1980; Award of Quality of Life in Labor and Ergonomy, 1982; Award of High Medical Committee of French Social Insurance, 1990. Memberships: Association of Medicine Inspectors in Public Health; French Society of Vigilance and Therapeutic Blood Transfusion; College of Health Economists. Address: 13 Montée du Roucas Blanc, 13 007 Marseille, France. E-mail: jean-patrice.aullen@wanadoo.fr

AUNG Kyi, b. 1 November 1946, Yangon, Myanmar. Minister. m. Thet Thet Swe, 2 daughters. Education: BSc, 1967; HGP, 1982; IOAC, Fort Benning, US Army, 1986. Appointments: Primary Teacher, 1964-66; High School Teacher, 1967-69; Army Officer Cadet, 1969; TOC Commander, Northeast Command Headquarters, 1994; Commandant of Officer's Training School, 1995; Commandant of Myanmar Army Combat Forces School, 1998; Director of Military Training, 1999, Vice Chief of Armed Forces Training, 2001, Ministry of Defence; Deputy Minister for Immigration and Population, 2006; Deputy Minister for Labour, 2006; Minister for Labour, 2007; Union Minister for Ministry of Labour and Ministry of Social Welfare, Relief and Resettlement, 2011; Met with Daw Aung San Su Kyi four times in 2011; Led drafting party of new labour organisation in line with ILO convention 87, Freedom of Association and Protection of the Right to Organize. Publications: Articles on leadership and management. Honours: Thiri Pyanchi Title; Medal for Famed Heroes. Memberships: Overseas Employment Supervisory Committee; Supervisory Committee of Cutting, Making and Packaging Enterprises; Myanmar Women's Affairs Federation. Address: No 1072, Yarza Thingaba Housing (1), NayPyiTaw, Myanmar. E-mail: mol@mptmail.net.mm

AUSTIN SUTHANTHIRARAJ Samuel, b. 15 August 1958, Valparai, Tamil Nadu, India. Researcher. m. Ayyadurai Sheela Subashini, 1 son. Education: BSc, Scott Christian College, Nagercoil, India, 1978; MSc, The American College, Madurai, India, 1980; PhD, Indian Institute of Technology, Madras, 1984. Appointments: Junior Research Fellow, 1980-83, Senior Research Fellow, 1983-85, Research Associate, 1985-86, Indian Institute of Technology, Madras; Lecturer, 1986-91, Senior Lecturer, 1991-92, Reader, 1992-98, Professor, 1998-, Professor & Head, 2006-, University of Madras; Postdoctoral Fellow, Harwell Laboratory, Oxford, UK, 1990-91. Publications: 87 in journals; 161 in conferences. Honours: Boyscast Fellow, Ministry of Science & Technology, India, 1990-91; University Grants Commission Research Award, 1999-2002; Bharat Jyoti Award, India International Friendship Society, 2006; Indira Gandhi Shiromani Award, 2006; Glory of India Award, 2006; Mother Teresa Excellence Award, Integrated Coun Socio-Econ Progress, India, 2010. Memberships: Fellow, Indian Chemical Society; Society for the Advancement of Electrochemical Science and Technology, India; Indian Solid State Ionics Society; Tamil Nadu Academy of Sciences; American Physics Society; Electrochemical Society of India. Address: 67 Bajanai Koil Street, Pallipet, Chennai 600113, Tamil Nadu, India. E-mail: suthan98@gmail.com

AUSTIN-COOPER Richard Arthur, b. 21 February 1932. International Banking Personnel Manager (Retired). m. (1) Sylvia Anne Shirley Berringer; (2) Valerie Georgina Drage, 1 son, 1 daughter; (3) Mariola Danuta Sikorska; (4) Rosemary Swaisland (née Gillespie). Education: Wellingborough Grammar School; Tottenham Grammar School. Appointments: Served RA, 1950-52 and TAVR in the RA, Intelligence Corps, 21 SAS Regt (Artist's Rifles), Essex ACF, 1952-68 and the Hon Artillery Co, 1978-79 (Commissioned 2 Lt TAVR 1968), OC ACF Canvey Island; Honorary Colonel Polish Militia, 1981; With Barclays Bank, 1948-60; Head Cashier, Bank of Baroda, 1960-63, Lloyd's Bank, 1963-69; Deputy Head, Stocks and Shares Department, Banque de Paris et des Pays Bas, 1969-74; Assistant Manager, Banking Division, Brook Street Bureau of Mayfair Ltd, 1974-75; Chief Custodian and London Registrar, Canadian Imperial Bank of Commerce and Registrar in Britain for Angostura Bitters Ltd, 1975-78; Personnel Officer, Deutsche Bank AG London Branch, 1978-85; Senior Manager, Head of Human Resources, Deutsche Bank Capital Markets Ltd, 1985-90; Partner Charsby Associates Recruitment Consultants, London, 1989-91; Retired, 1991. Publications: Books: Butterhill and Beyond, 1991; The Beavers of Barnack, 1995; The de Gidlow Family of Ince, 1996; The Peisley Family of Clifton Hampden, Oxon, 1996. Honours: Prizes for: Athletics, Operatic Singing (Tenor), Painting; Freeman, City of London, 1964; Hon LLD, Hon MA (USA), FHG, 1965; FRSA, 1974; FRSAIre, 1980, FCIB, 1987. Memberships: Founder Fellow, Institute of Heraldic and Genealogical Studies; Treasurer, Irish Genealogical Research Society; Irish Peers Association, 1964-; Life Governor Sherriff's and Recorder's Fund at the Old Bailey, 1979-; Vice-President, Bourne Lincs Family History Society, 1993-; Chairman, Arthritis Care, Stamford, Lincolnshire, 1993-94; Chairman, Eastbourne Branch, British Cardiac Patients Association, 2003-06; Vice-Chairman, Trustee and Member Executive Committee, Friends of Eastbourne Hospitals, 2003-06; Governor, American College in Oxford; Governor, City of London School for Girls; Governor, Freeman's School; Governor, Lansbury Adult Education Institute; Representative, City of London Corporation on the Greater London Arts Council; Trustee, City of London Imperial Volunteers; Member, City of London-TAVR Association; A Manager, Barbican School of Music and Drama; Member, City of London Mayor's Court of Common Council for Cripplegate Ward, 1978-81; President, Royal Artillery Association, Eastbourne, East Sussex, 2006-; SAS Regimental Association; Intelligence Corps OCA; Artists Rifles Association; Hospital Visitor, Royal British Legion, Eastbourne, 2007-. Address: 2 Lea House, 1 Mill Road, Eastbourne, East Sussex BN21 2LY, England.

AVAGYAN Armen Borisovich, b. 1953, Yerevan, Armenia. Biotechnology; Biophysics; Economist. 1 son, 1 daughter. Education: MD, Biophysics, 1976; PhD, Biophysics, Moscow State University, 1979; MD, Economics, Armenian University. Appointments: Senior Researcher, Agriculture Institute, Ministry of Agriculture of Armenia, 1980-89; Senior Researcher, Technological Institute of Amino Acids, Ministry of Medicine and Biological Industry, USSR, 1989-93; Solo Founder, Research & Industry Center of Photosynthesizing Organisms, Feed Additives and Physiologically Active Compounds LLC, 1991-; Executive Director, Yerevan Vitamin Plant, JOC, Armenia, 1998-; Executive Director, Institute of Biotechnology, JCC, Ministry of Trade and Industry, Armenia, 1998-2000; Deputy Director, Chloroprene Rubber Nairit, JCC, Yerevan, Armenia, 2000-09. Publications: Numerous articles in professional journals. Honours: Awards from USSR and Armenia in area of Science and Technology;

Award, Journal of Clean Technology and Environment Policy, 2008; Top 100 Professionals of 2010; Laureate, The International Presidents Award for Iconic Achievement, IBC, 2010; Listed in international biographical dictionaries. Memberships: Academic Council, Institute of Agriculture and Institute of Biotechnology of RA; Expert, Council of Chemistry and Petrochemistry of the CIS countries, Program FP7 and International Co-operation of EU, INTAS; American Chemical Society; Board, Armenian Producers Union; President and Head, Economic Development and Investments Sub-Commission of Public Consil of RA. Address: Nalbandyan St, 51/5, Yerevan, 0025, Armenia. E-mail: armin.av@hotmail.com

AVERY Charles Henry Francis, b. 26 December 1940, London, England. Fine Art Consultant. m. (Kathleen) Mary, 3 daughters (triplets). Education: MA, PhD, St John's College, Cambridge; Academic Diploma, Courtauld Institute of Art, London. Appointments: Deputy Keeper of Sculpture, Victoria and Albert Museum, 1965-69; Director, Sculpture Department, Christie's, 1979-90; Currently, Independent Fine Art Consultant. Publications: Books: Florentine Renaissance Sculpture, 1970; Studies in European Sculpture, 1981, 1987; Giambologna the Complete Sculpture, 1987; Renaissance and Baroque Bronzes in the Frick Art Museum, 1993; Donatello: An Introduction, 1994; David Le Marchand (1674-1726). An Ingenious Man for Carving in Ivory, 1996; Bernini, Genius of the Baroque, 1997; Studies in Italian Sculpture, 2001; Bertos: The Triumph of Motion, 2008; A School of Dolphins, 2009. Honours: Cavaliere Dell'ordine Al Merito della Repubblica Italiana, 1979; Medal of the Ministry of Culture, Poland; FSA, 1985; Leverhulme Research Fellow, 1997-99; Honorary Life Member, Venice in Peril; Association Internationale des Critiques d'Art; Vetting Committees: Maastricht European Fine Art Fair; Biennale des Antiquaires, Paris; Gotha, Parma; Biennale Internazionale di Antiquariato; Palazzo Venezia, Rome; Biennale del Antiquariato, Florence; Masterpiece, London; Collezioni d'Arte, Milan. Memberships: British Italian Society; United Oxford and Cambridge. Address: Holly Tree House, 20 Southend Road, Beckenham, Kent BR3 1SD, England.

AVETISSIAN Vahan, b. 4 July 1947, Yerevan, Armenia. Radiophysics. m. Ida, 1 son, 1 daughter. Education: Master, Radiophysics, 1972, Doctor of Physics, 1996, Doctor of Sciences, Engineering, 2007, Physical Faculty, Yerevan State University. Appointments: Signal Officer, USSR Army, 1972-74; Group Leader, Institute of Readiophysic and Electronics, Armenian National Academy of Sciences, 1974-1981; Senior Staff Scientists, All-Union Research Institute of Radiophysical Pleasurements, Yerevan, 1981-93; Deputy Director on Science, Yerevan Research Telecommunication Institute, 2005-; Head, Subdepartment of Telecommunication, Russian-Armenian (Slavon) University, 2010-. Publications: Over 50 scientific works; 18 inventions. Honours: President of Republic of Armenia's Prize for Technical Sciences and Information Technologies, 2009. Memberships: IEEE. Address: Yerevan Telecommunication Research Institute, Deoraphy 26, Yerevan, 0015, Armenia. E-mail: avahan@mail.ru

AVRAMI Shirley, b. 31 July 1960, Israel. Director of Research Center. m. Gideon, 2 sons, 1 daughter. Education: BA, Occupational Therapy, 1985, MA, Social Work, 1999, Hebrew University, Israel; PhD, Haifa University, 2003. Appointments: Director, Knesset (Israeli Parliament) Research and Information Center. Publications: Numerous articles in professional journals. Honours: Annual Award for PhD dissertations by Israeli Parliamentary Association, 2005. Memberships: Esparot Israel. Address: Research and Information Center, The Knesset, Kiryat Ben Guryon, Jerusalem 91950, Israel. E-mail: avrami@knesset.gov.il Website: www.knesset.gov.il/mmm

AXELSSON OLSSON Diana, b. 10 November 1973, Kalmar, Sweden. Professor. m. Henrik Olssson. Education: MSc, Biomedical Chemistry, 2003; PhD, Microbiology, University of Kalmar, 2009. Appointments: Researcher, Kalmar County Hospital, 2003-04; Researcher, University of Kalmar, 2004-06, 2009; Laboratory Engineer, 2010, Postdoc, 2010-, Linneaus University. Publications: Numerous articles in professional journals. Memberships: Infecton Ecology and Epidemiology Network, Sweden; One Health Initiative; Society for Zoonotic Ecology and Epidemiology, Sweden. Address: Section for Zoonotic Ecology and Epidemiology, School of Natural Sciences, Linneaus University, SE 391 82 Kalmar, Sweden.

AXFORD Elizabeth Carole, b. 21 December 1958, Van Nuys, California, USA. Music Instructor; Publisher. Education: BA Music, University of Illinois, Urbana-Champaign, 1982; MA Musicology, San Diego State University, 1995. Appointments: Owner, Piano Press Studio; Music Instructor; Published Author, Arranger, Composer, Songwriter and Poet. Publications: Traditional World Music Influences in Contemporary Solo Piano Literature, 1997; Song Sheets to Software – A guide to print music, software, instructional media and websites for musicians, 2001, 2004, 2009. Honours: Illinois State Scholarship, 1976; Pi Kappa Lambda, National Music Honor Society, 1996; Nashville Songwriters Association International Awards of Appreciation, 1997, 2008, 2010. Memberships: ASCAP; NARAS; NSAI; MTNA; MTAC; CAPMT; TAXI; SCBWI; NGPT. Address: PO Box 85, Del Mar, CA 92014-0085, USA. E-mail: lizaxford@pianopress.com Website: www.pianopress.com

AYAZ Iftikhar Ahmad, b. 18 January 1936, Tanzania. Educator. m. Amatul Basit, 5 daughters, 1 son. Education: BEd, University of Newcastle upon Tyne; Diploma of Comparative Education, Dip TEFL, MA, University of London; PhD, International University Foundation, USA. Appointments: Teacher, District Education Officer, Regional Inspector of Schools, Chairman, Teacher Education Panel, Head, Department of Education, Tanzania, 1960-78; Senior Curriculum Advisor, Institute of Education, University of Dar es Salaam, Tanzania, 1978-81; Publications Officer, Centre on Integrated Rural Development, Arusha, Tanzania, 1981-85; Education Advisor and Consultant, Commonwealth Secretariat, 1985-92; UNESCO Co-ordinator and Manager of Education For Life Programme, 1992-95; UN Human Rights Commission Workshop on Minority Group Rights, 1997-; Honorary Consul of Tuvalu in the UK, 1995-; Attended numerous international conferences including: World Conference against Racism, Racial Discrimination, Xenophobia and related Intolerance, Durban, South Africa, 2001; World Peace Summit in South Korea, 2003; Poverty Alleviation in SE Asia Conference, New Delhi, 2004; International Leadership Summit, South Korea, 2007; Broadcaster, Education programmes for teachers, Tanzania, 1979-81, Tuvalu, 1985-88; Co-ordinator, Language Support for Immigrant Workers, 1989; Conferences attended: Climate Change Challenges for Small Island States, Scotland, 2008; World Forum, USA, 2009; Copenhagen Summit on Climate Change, Poland, 2009; Interfaith Dialogue for Peace, Iceland, 2010. Publications: Numerous publications on education theory, philosophy and sociology, linguistics, literature, curriculum development, HR development, culture in education, peace education, education in small States. Honours: OBE, 1998; Alfred Nobel Medal, 1991; Hind Ratan and Hind Ratan Gold Medal, India, 2002; Nav Ratan and Nav Ratan Gold Medal, India, 2003; Federation for World Peace, USA, Ambassador for Peace Award; D Ed, Emeritus International University Foundation, USA; International Education Fellow, Commonwealth Institute, London, 1976-77; Commonwealth Fellowship for Higher Education; Vice-President, India's International Congress of Intellectuals, 2004; Great Minds of the 21st Century Medal, American Biographical Institute; Man of the Year, ABI, 2004; Senator, World Nations Congress, 2005; Founder, IA Foundation for Poverty Alleviation, 2007; Genius Laureate in the Field of Human Development, 2007; Vice Chancellor, International Academy of Letters, 2007; Lifetime Achievement Award, 2008; Deputy Governor, ABI Research Institute, 2008; USA Presidential Inaugural Award, World Forum, Washington, 2009; Ambassador of Knowledge, Cambridge University, 2010; Man of the Year in Human Rights, 2010. Memberships: The London Diplomatic Corps; The Commonwealth Association; The Royal Commonwealth Society; Commonwealth Education Council; Commonwealth Human Ecology Council; Universal Peace Federation; Pacific Peace Forum. Address: Tuvalu House, 230 Worple Road, London SW20 8RH, England. E-mail: tuvaluconsulate@netscape.net

AYCKBOURN Alan (Sir), b. 12 Apr 1939, London, England. Theatre Director; Playwright; Artistic Director. Plays: Mr Whatnot, 1963; Relatively Speaking, 1965; How the Other Half Loves, 1969; Time and Time Again, 1971; Absurd Person Singular, 1972; The Norman Conquests, 1973; Absent Friends, 1974; Confusions, 1975; Bedroom Farce, 1975; Just Between Ourselves, 1976; Ten Times Table, 1977; Joking Apart, 1978; Sisterly Feelings, 1979; Taking Steps, 1979; Season's Greetings, 1980; Way Upstream, 1981; Intimate Exchanges, 1982; A Chorus of Disapproval, 1984; Woman in Mind, 1985; A Small Family Business, 1986; Henceforward, 1987; Man of the Moment, 1988; The Revengers' Comedies, 1989; Time of My Life, 1992; Dreams From a Summer House, 1992; Communicating Doors, 1994; Hunting Julia, 1994; The Musical Jigsaw Play, 1994; A Word From Our Sponsor, 1995; By Jeeves (with Andrew Lloyd Webber), 1996; The Champion of Paribanou, 1996; Things We Do For Love, 1997; Comic Potential, 1998; The Boy Who Fell into a Book, 1998; Gizmo, 1998; House Garden, 1999; Callisto #7, 1999; Virtual Reality, 2000; Whenever, 2000; Game Plan, 2001; Flat Spin, 2001. Honours: Hon DLitt, Hull, 1981, Keele, 1987, Leeds, 1987, York, 1992, Bradford, 1994, Cardiff University of Wales, 1996, Open University, 1998; Commander of the Order of the British Empire, 1987; Cameron Mackintosh Professor of Contemporary Theatre, 1992; Knighthood, 1997. Memberships: Garrick Club; Fellow, Royal Society of Arts. Address: c/o Casarotto Ramsay and Associates Ltd, National House, 60-66 Wardour Street, London W1V 4ND, England.

AYDAL Dogan, b. 23 September 1953, Mardin, Turkey. University Lecturer. m. Nilgün, 1 son, 1 daughter. Education: BSc, MSc, Hacettepe University, Turkey, 1976; PhD, University of Leeds, England, 1980. Appointments: Engineer, MTA (Mineral Research and Exploration Institute of Turkey), 1976; Engineer, MTA, and part time Lecturer, University of Firat, 1981-82; Director, Kastamonu Polytechnic, Ankara University, and Member, Ankara University Senate, 1982-87; Assistant Professor, 1987, Associate Professor, 1991, Professor Doctor, 2000-, Department of Geological Engineering, Faculty of Engineering, Ankara University; Election Candidacy of Member of Parliament from Istanbul to Turkish National Assembly, 1995; Advisor, Turkish National Assembly, 1996-97; Advisor, Prime Minister, 1996-97; Member, Executive Committee, Sümer Holding, 1997; Undersecretary of the Prime Minister, 1997. Publications: 28 papers; 12 books. Memberships: Turkish Geological Society. Address: Ankara Universitesi, Mühendislik Fakültesi, Jeoloji Müh Böl, 06100 Besevler Ankara, Turkey. Website: www.doganaydal.com

AYDINGÜN Sengül, b. 19 November 1959, Ankara, Turkey. Archaeologist. m. Haldun. Education: Degree, Art History & Archaeology, Master's degree, Doctorate degree, Archaeology, Hacettepe University. Appointments: Curator, Istanbul Archaeological Museums, Ministry of Culture; Curator, Hagia Sophia Museum, Ministry of Culture; Assistant Professor, Archaeology Department, Kocaeli University; Head, Ancient Bathonea Excavations. Publications: 2 books: Mysterious Women of the Bronze Age, and Antalya – Antike Stadte; 300 articles. Honours: Adviser to documentary film, Tunnel to a Lost World (National Geographic International), which won Telly Award, 2009; Social Sciences Honor Award of the Year, 2009, Social Sciences Award, 2010, Kocaeli University; International Women's Day Honor Award, Istanbul Kalamis Rotary Club, 2011. Memberships: National Geographic in Turkey; Protection of Cultural Heritage Council of Turkey. Address: Science, Arts and Archaeology Department, Kocaeli University, Turkey. Website: www.aydingun.com/sengul

AYKROYD Dan (Daniel Edward), b. 1 July 1952, Ottawa, Canada. Actor. m. (1) Maureen Lewis, 1974, divorced, 3 sons, (2) Donna Dixon, 1983, 3 daughters. Education: Carleton University, Ottawa. Appointments: Started as stand up comedian and worked on Saturday Night Live, 1975-79; Created and performed as the Blues Brothers; Albums include: Made in America; Films include: 1941, 1979; Mr Mike's Mondo Video, 1979; The Blues Brothers, 1980; Neighbors, 1981; Doctor Detroit, Trading Places, Twilight Zone, 1983; Ghostbusters, Nothing Lasts for Ever, 1984; Into the Night, Spies Like Us, 1985; Dragnet, 1987; Caddyshack II, The Great Outdoors, My Stepmother is an Alien, 1988; Ghostbusters II, 1989; Driving Miss Daisy, 1990; My Girl; Loose Cannons; Valkemania; Nothing But Trouble, 1991; Coneheads, 1993; My Girl II, 1994; North; Casper, 1995; Sergeant Bilko, 1996; Grosse Point Blank, The Arrow, 1997; Blues Brothers 2000, Susan's Plan, 1998; Antz, Diamonds, 1999; The House of Mirth, Stardom, Dying to Get Rich, 2000; The Devil and Daniel Webster, Not A Girl, Pearl Harbour, Evolution, 2001; Crossroads, Who Shot Victor Fox, The Curse of the Jade Scorpion, Unconditional Love, 2002; Bright Young Things, 2003; 50 First Dates, Intern Academy, Christmas with the Kranks, 2004; Dan Aykroyd Unplugged on UFOs, 2005; I now Pronounce You Chuck and Larry, 2007; War, Inc, 2008; Family Guy, 2009; Dorothy of Oz, 2010. Honours: Emmy Award, 1976-77; Honorary Doctor of Literature, Carleton University, 1994; Member, Order of Canada, 1998. Address: c/o CAA, 9830 Wilshire Boulevard, Beverly Hills, CA 90212, USA.

AYLETT Holly, Filmmaker; Cultural Sector Director; Lecturer; Consultant. Education: South Hampstead High School, London, 1967-73; TEFL certificate, Bell School of Languages, Cambridge, 1977; BA (Hons), 1978, MA, 1985, Cambridge University; Screenwriting certificate, Birkbeck College, London, 1997; Certificate of Education (1st class), London Metropolitan University, 2003. Appointments: Independent Producer/Director, 1980-95; Managing Director, Director and Screenwriter, Luna Films, 1989-;

Series Director, OR Media, 1995/1996; Visiting Lecturer, The London Guildhall and The London College of Printing, 1998-2000; Course Tutor, City University, 1998-2003; Founding Director & Managing Editor, Vertigo Magazine, 2000-10; Senior Lecturer, London Metropolitan University, 2002-; Founding Trustee & Director, Independent Film Parliament, 2003-07; Founding Director, UK Coalition for Cultural Diversity, 2006-; Senior Research Fellow, Global Policy Institute, 2007-. Publications: Numerous articles in professional journals. Honours: 1st Prize for Documentary, Philadelphia Peace Festival, 1985; 1st Prize for Documentary, Havana Film Festival, 1989. Memberships: Luna Films Ltd; Vertigo Productions Ltd; Indpendent Film Parliament; UK Coalition for Cultural Diversity; UK National Commission for UNESCO. Address: 59 Oakfield Road, London N4 4LD, England. E-mail: ayletth@gmail.com

AZNAVOUR Charles (Varenagh Aznavourian), b. 22 May 1924, Paris, France. Singer; Actor. m. (1) Micheline Rugel, 1946, (2) Evelyene Plessis, 1955, (3) Ulla Thorsel, 1967, 5 children (1 deceased). Education: Ecole Centrale de TSF. Career: Centre de Spectacle, Paris; Jean Dasté Company, 1941; Les Fâcheux, Arlequin, 1944; Numerous film appearances, 1964-; Compositions include: Songs: Il Pleut; Le Feutre Tropez; Jezebel (all recorded by Edith Piaf); Hier Encore (Yesterday When I Was Young); The Old Fashioned Way; She (theme for ITV series, The Seven Faces Of Woman); What Makes A Man; Happy Anniversary. Recordings: Albums include: Charles Aznavour Sings, 1963; Qui, 1964; Et Voici, 1964; Sings His Love Songs In English, 1965; Encore, 1966; De T'Avoir Aimée, 1966; Désormais, 1972; Chez Lui A Paris, 1973; A Tapestry Of Dreams, 1974; I Sing For You, 1975; In Times To Be, 1983; Aznavour, 1990; En Espanol, Vols I-III, 1991; The Old Fashioned Way, 1992; Jezabel, 1993; Toi Et Moi, 1994; Il Faut Savior, 1995; Paris Palais Des Congres, 1996; Jazznavour, 1999; Aznavour, 2000. He started his global farewell tour in late 2006. Honours: Chevalier Légion d'Honneur, Des Arts et Lettres; Grand Prix National de la Chanson, 1986; César d'honneur, 1997; Molière amical, 1999; Time Magazine Entertainer of the Century; Honorary President, Belgrade Film Festival, 2003; Commandeur, Légion d'honneur, 2004; Commandeur des Arts et des Lettres; Honorary Officer of the Order of Canada, 2008; Citizenship of the Republic of Armenia, 2008; MIDEM Lifetime Achievement Award, 2009; Grigor Lusavorich Award, 2009. Address: c/o Lévon Sayan, 76-78 Avenue des Champs Elysées, Bureau 322, 75008 Paris, France.

AZUMA Takehiro, b. 21 November 1976, Hokkaido, Japan. Physicist. Education: Graduate, Todaiji-Gakuen High School, 1995; BSc, 1999, MSc, 2001, PhD, 2004, Kyoto University. Appointments: JSPS DC2 Predoctoral Fellowship, Kyoto University, 2002-04; JSPS Postdoctoral Fellowship, High Energy Accelerator Research Organisation, 2004-06; Visiting Fellowship, Tata Institute of Fundamental Research, 2006-08; Full-time Instructor, Setsunan University, 2008-. Publications: Monte Carlo of the GWW Phase Transion in Large-N Gauge Theories, 2008; A General Approach to the Sign Problem: The Factorization Method with Multiple Observables, 2011. Honours: Listed in international biographical dictionaries. Memberships: Soryushiron Group; The Physical Society of Japan; Consortium for Computational Fundamental Science. Address: Setsunan University, 17-8 Ikeda Nakamachi, Neyagawa, Osaka 572-8508, Japan. E-mail: azuma@mpg.setsunan.ac.jp Website: www2.yukawa.kyoto-u.ac.jp/~azuma/index.html

B

BABAEV Agajan Geldievich, b. 10 May 1929, Mary city, Turkmenistan. Scientist. m. Dunyagozel, 2 sons, 6 daughters. Education: Turkmen State University. Appointments: Scientist. Publications: 380 articles in professional journals. Honours: Sovient Union State Prize, 1981; German State International Prize, 1990; USA International Prize, 1993. Memberships: Turkmen Academy of Science, 1975; Russian Academy of Science, 1976; Islamic Academy of Science, 1994. Address: Kosayev str 113, Ashgabat city, Turkmenistan.

BABAN Serwan M J, b. 23 April 1958, Kirkuk, Iraq. University Professor. m. Judith Anne, 2 daughters. Education: BSc, Geology, 1980, MSc, Geophysics, 1983, University of Baghdad, Iraq; PhD, Environmental Remote Sensing, University of East Anglia, UK, 1991. Appointments: Research Associate, Senior Research Associate, University of East Anglia, UK; Lecturer, Senior Lecturer, Coventry University, UK; Professor of Surveying and Land Information, 2000-07, Chairman, School of Graduate Studies and Research, 2004-07, The University of the West Indies, Trinidad and Tobago; Professor, Environmental Geoinformatics and Head of School, Southern Cross University, Australia, 2007-09; Professor and Vice Chancellor, University of Kurdistan-Hawler, Iraq, 2009-. Publications: Over 100 articles in international and national journals, international conference proceedings, chapters in books as well as consultancy reports including most recently: Modelling Sites for Reservoirs in Tropical Environments, 2003; Responding to the Effects of Climate Change, 2003; Flooding and Landslides in the West Indies, 2004; Information Poverty and Decision-Making, 2004; Mapping Landslide Susceptibility in the Tropics, 2004, 2005; Examining land use changes due to irrigated agriculture in Jordan using Geoinformatics, 2005; Evaluating Water Circulation and Contaminant Transport Models for the Intra-American Seas, 2005; Accomplishing Sustainable Development in Southern Kurdistan Using Geoinformatics, 2005. Memberships: Fellow, Royal Geographical Society, 1999-; Remote Sensing Society Council, 1999-2001; Fellow, Geological Society, 2000-; Fellow, Remote Sensing and Photogrammetry Society, 2001; Fellow, International Congress of Disaster Management; Visiting Fellow, School of Environmental Sciences, University of East Anglia, UK, 2002-; Member and National Representative, International Association of Hydrological Sciences. Address: University of Kurdistan-Hawler, 30 Meter Avenue, Hawler (Erbil), Federal Region of Kurdistan, Iraq. E-mail: vice.chancellor@ukh.com

BABIAK Jerzy Kazimierz, b. 27 May 1943, Kepno, Poland. Academic. m. Krystyna, 2 daughters. Education: Master of Economics, 1968, Doctor of Economics, 1974, Postdoctoral Degree, 1990, Poznan University of Economics. Appointments: Professor, Vice Dean, Institute of Political Sciences and Journalism,Adam Mickiewicz University, Poznan; Professor, Deputy Vice Chancellor, The Greater Poland University of Social Affairs and Economics, USAE, Sroda Wielkopolska. Publications: Numerous articles in professional journals. Honours: Two awards from the Minister of National Education. Memberships: Polish Economic Society; Polish Political Sciences Society. E-mail: jerzy.babiak@amu.edu.pl

BABICH Alexander, b. 12 November 1952, Donetsk, Ukraine. Metallurgist; Educator. m. Eugenia Goldstein, 1 son. Education: Metallurgy Engineering, Donetsk Polytechnic Institute, 1974; PhD (Tech), 1984; Associate Professor, 1989. Appointments: Furnace Worker, Foreman, Donetsk Steel Plant, 1974-76; Engineer, Scientific worker, Donetsk Polytechnic Institute, 1978-85; Associate Professor, Donetsk State University of Technology, 1985-96; Visiting Researcher, National Centre for Metallurgical Investigation, Madrid, 1997-98; Researcher, 1998-2009, Group Leader, 2009-, BWTH Aachen University. Publications: Over 190 publications including a monograph, 2 textbooks and 20 patents. Honours: Grant, Ministry of Education and Science, Spain; Who's Who in the World Diploma, 1999; Listed in several biographical publications. Address: Aachen, Germany. E-mail: babich@iehk.rwth-aachen.de

BABITSKY Vladimir, b. 4 April 1938, Gomel, USSR. Mechanical Engineer; Researcher; Educator; Inventor; Consultant. m. Eleonora Lublina, 1 son. Education: MSc Mechanical Engineering, Moscow State Technological University, 1960; PhD, 1964, DSc, 1973, USSR Academy of Sciences. Appointments: Engineer, 1960-61, Research Assistant, 1961-67, Senior Research Assistant and a Head of a research group, 1967-87, Founder and Head, Vibrations Systems Laboratory, 1987-91, Institute for Machine Studies, USSR Academy of Sciences; Guest Professor, Institute B for Mechanics, Munich, Germany, 1990; Consultant, HILTI AG, 1992-95; Professor of Dynamics, Loughborough University, England, 1995-; Visiting Professor: Tokyo Institute of Technology, Japan, 2006; Northeastern University, Shenyang, P R China, 2008. Publications: Books: Theory of vibro-impact systems and applications, 1998 (translation from Russian 1978); Vibration of strongly nonlinear discontinuous systems (co-author), 2001 (translation from Russian, 1985); Dynamics and Control of Machines (co-author), 2000; Resonant Robotic Systems (co-author), 2003; Ultrasonic Processes and Machines (co-author), 2007; Founder and Editor, Springer book series, Foundations of Engineering Mechanics, 1996-; Contributed articles to handbooks and professional journals; Patentee in field; Inventor, patented JCB low vibration hand-held breaker. Honours: President, International Centre of Vibro-Impact Systems, 2004-. Memberships: Euromech; FICoVIS; IFAC. Address: Wolfson School of Mechanical and Manufacturing Engineering, Loughborough University, Loughborough LE11 3TU, England. E-mail: v.i.babitsky@lboro.ac.uk

BABU Yallapragada Ramesh, b. 14 January 1952, Bhattiprolu, India. Engineer. Education: Graduate, Mechanical Department, College of Engineering, Jawaharlal Nehru Technological University, 1975; MEng, Industrial Engineering, College of Engineering, Sri Venkateswara University, 1979; PhD, Mechanical Department, College of Engineering, Andhra University, 1993. Appointments: Lecturer, Mechanical Department, Bapatla Engineering College, 1982-86; Faculty, College of Engineering, Gandhi Institute of Technology and Management, Visakhapatnam, 1986-. Publications: 24 profesional papers for National and International Conferences and Scientific Journals. Honours: World Life Time Achievement Award, 1997; 20th Century Award for Achievement, 1998, Outstanding Man of the 20th Century, 1999; International Man of the Millennium, 1999; 2000 Millenium Medal of Honour, 1998; International Scientist of the Year, 2001; 21st Century Award for Achievement, 2003; Order of International Ambassadors, 2005; Salute to Greatness Award, 2005; Global Year of Engineering, 2006; The Brunel Award, 2006; Listed in 56 biographical publications. Memberships: Indian Institution of Industrial Engineering; Institution of Engineers, India; Research Board of Advisors, American Biographical Institute, USA and Advisory Council, International Biographical Centre, England. Address: VNR College of Engineering, GBC Road, Ponnur,522124, Guntur (Dt) A.P, India.

DICTIONARY OF INTERNATIONAL BIOGRAPHY 36th EDITION

BACALL Lauren, b. 16 September 1924, New York, USA. Actress. m. (1) Humphrey Bogart, 1945, died 1957, 1 son, 1 daughter, (2) Jason Robards, 1961, divorced, 1 son. Career: Films include: Two Guys from Milwaukee, 1946; The Big Sleep; Young Man with a Horn; How to Marry a Millionaire; Blood Alley, Sex and the Single Girl; Murder on the Orient Express, 1974; Appointment with Death, 1988; Misery, 1990; All I Want for Christmas, 1991; The Field, 1993; Pret á Porter, 1995; Le Jour et la Nuit, 1996; The Mirror Has Two Faces, 1996; My Fellow Americans; Day and Night; Diamonds; The Venice Project; Presence of Mind; Dogville, 2003; The Limit, 2003; Birth, 2004; Manderlay, 2005; Those Foolish Things, 2006; The Walker, 2007; Eve, 2008. Publications: Lauren Bacall by Myself, 1978; Lauren Bacall Now, 1994; By Myself and Then Some, 2005. Honours: 2 Tony Awards, 1970, 1981; Woman of the Year Award, 1981; Golden Globe Award, 1996; Screen Actors' Guild Award, 1997; Kennedy Center Honors, 1997; Bette Davis Medal of Honor, 2008; Honorary Academy Award, 2009. Address: c/o Johnnies Planco, William Morris Agency, 1325 Avenue of the Americas, New York, NY 10019, USA.

BACANI Mirko, b. 6 August 1979, Varazdin, Croatia. Physicist. Education: Diploma, Physics, 2007, PhD, Physics, in progress, University of Zagreb. Appointments: Research Assistant, Solid State Physics and Polymer Science, University of Zagreb, 2008-. Honours: Multiple Winner, Croatian national competitions in science. Memberships: Department of Physics, Zagreb University, Bijenicka 32, 10000 Zagreb, Croatia. E-mail: mbacani@phy.hr

BACCI Stefano, b. 24 July 1963, Florence, Italy. Research Assistant. Education: BS, 1990; PhD, 1997. Appointments: Research Assistant, 2002; Aggregate Professor, Histology, 2005; Research field: Mast cells and dendritic cells: localization, differentiation, responses to different stimuli. Publications: More than 100 publications in cellular immunology, forensic medicine and neurology. Honours: Research Fellow, The Schepens Eye Research Institute, Harvard Medical School, 1994-96. Memberships: Association of Cellular Biology and Differentiation. E-mail: stefano.bacci@unifi.it

BACH Jan Morris, b. 11 December 1937, Forrest, Illinois, USA. University Music Professor; Composer. m. Dalia Zakaras, 2 daughters. Education: BM, 1959, MM, 1961, Dr MA, 1971, University of Illinois at Urbana-Champaign; Additional study, Yale Summer School, Berkshire Music Centre, University of Virginia at Arlington. Appointments: Assistant Football Band Director, University of Illinois, 1959-61; Graduate Research Assistant, IBID, 1961-62; Associate First Horn, US Army Band, Ft Myer, Virginia, 1962-65; Instructor in Music, University of Tampa, 1965-66; Professor of Music, Northern Illinois University, 1966-98; Retired, part time Professor of Music, 1998-2005. Publications: Many compositions; Works included on more than 20 CDs. Honours: First Prize, BMI Student Composers Contest, 1957; Koussevitzky Composition Award, 1961; Mannes College Opera Award, 1974; Nebraska Sinfonia Composition Contest, 1979; NYC Opera Contest, 1980; 6 Pulitzer nominations, 1974, 1979, 1980, 1981, 1983 and 1991; Excellence in Undergraduate Education Award, 1978; Distinguished Presidential Research Professor, 1982-86, Northern Illinois University; Fox Valley Arts Hall of Fame inductee, 2004; Listed in international biographical dictionaries. Memberships: Broadcast Music Inc; Phi Eta Sigma; Phi Mu Alpha; Phi Kappa Phi; Pi Kappa Lambda; Omicron Delta Kappa. Address: PO Box 403, Wasco, IL 60183, USA. E-mail: janbach@janbach.com Website: www.janbach.com

BACHMANN Fedor Wolfgang, b. 23 May 1927, Zurich, Switzerland. Hematology Educator; Scientist. m. Edith I Derendinger, 1957, 1 son. Education: MD, University of Zurich, 1954; Diplomate, Swiss Board of Internal Medicine and Hematology. Appointments: Intern, Resident, Medical School, University of Zurich, 1955-61; Trainee, USPHS, 1961-64, Assistant Professor, 1964-68, Medical School, Washington University, St Louis; Associate Professor, Medical School, Rush-Presbyterian, St Luke's Hospital, Chicago, 1968-73; Director, Medical Research, Schering Corp, USA, Lucerne, Switzerland, 1973-76; Professor, 1976-92, Professor Emeritus, 1992-, Medicine, Medical School, University of Lausanne, Switzerland; Director, Hematology Laboratories, 1976-92, Acting Chairman, Department of Medicine, 1980-81, Provost, 1987-91, University of Lausanne Medical Centre; Scientific Co-ordinator, Thrombosis Research Institute, London, 1995-98; Visiting Scholar, Pathology Department, Stanford, California University, 1986; Visiting Professor, University of Paris VI, 1991-95; International Director, Thrombosis/Vascular Training Centre Programme, 1994-2005. Publications: Editor, Progress in Fibrinolytics, 1983; Fibrinolytics and Antifybrinolytics, 2000; Associate Editor, Fibrinolysis; Over 200 articles in professional journals; Editorial board member of international journals. Honours: International Committee of Fibrinolysis, Amsterdam, 1988; Distinguished Career Award, International Society of Thrombosis and Haemostasis, 1997; Grantee of many professional associations. Memberships: Fellow, ACP; International Society of Thrombosis and Haemostasis; American Heart Association; New York Academy of Sciences; International Society of Haematology; International Society of Fibrinolysis and Thrombosis; American Federation of Clinical Research; American Society of Hematology; American Physiological Society; Central Society of Clinical Research; Swiss Medical Society; Swiss Hematological Society; Society of Medicine Vaudois; Swiss Society of Internal Medicine; German-Austrian Society of Thrombosis and Haemostasis; Argentinian Medical Society; Medical Society of Vienna; European Thrombosis Research Association; World Heart Federation; European Society of Cardiology Working Group on Thrombosis, 2006-12; Sigma Xi. Address: Chemin de Praz-Mandry 20, 1052 Le Mont, Switzerland. E-mail: fedor.bachmann@unil.ch

BACK Lloyd, b. 13 February 1933, San Francisco, USA. Mechanical Engineer. m. Carol Peterson, 1 son, 2 daughters. Education: BS, 1959, PhD, 1962, University of California at Berkeley. Appointments: Supervisor, Fluid Dynamics, Reactive Processes and Biomedical Research, Jet Propulsion Laboratory, California Institute of Technology, Pasadena, 1962-92; Clinical Assistant Professor of Medicine, University of Southern California, 1974-92; Volunteer Faculty Member, School of Medicine, University of Southern California, Los Angeles, 1992-. Publications: Over 150 experimental and analytical publications in technical journals including investigations in rocket propulsion and blood flow through diseased arteries. Honours: Exceptional Service Award, NASA, 1979; ASME Fellow, Heat Transfer Division; Distinguished Service Award, 1987; 50th Anniversary Award, 1988. Memberships: ASME; AIAA. Address: 16 Rushingwind, Irvine, CA 92614-7409, USA.

BACKLEY Steve, b. 12 February 1969, Sidcup, Kent, England. Athlete. m. Clare. Career: Specialist in Javelin; Coached by John Trower; Commonwealth record holder, 1992 (91,46m); Gold Medal European Junior Championships, 1987; Silver Medal, World Junior Championships, 1988; Gold Medal European Cup, 1989, 1997; Bronze Medal, 1995; Gold Medal World Student Games, 1989, 1991; Gold Medal World Cup, 1989, 1994, 1998; Gold Medal Commonwealth Games, 1990, 1994, 2002; Silver Medal, 1998; Gold Medal European Championships, 1990, 1994, 1998, 2002; Bronze Medal Olympic Games, 1992; Silver Medal, 1996, 2000; Silver Medal World Championships, 1995, 1997; Athlete of the Year, UK Athletics, 2000; MBE, 1995; OBE, 2003. Publication: The Winning Mind.

BACON Kevin, b. 8 July 1958, Philadelphia, USA. Actor. m. Kyra Sedgewick, 1 son, 1 daughter. Education: Manning St Actor's Theatre. Appointments: Stage appearances include: Getting On, 1978; Glad Tidings, 1979-80; Mary Barnes, Album, 1980; Forty-Deuce, 1981; Flux, Poor Little Lambs, 1982; Slab Boys, 1983; Men Without Dates, 1985; Loot, 1986; Road; Spike Heels; TV appearances include: The Gift, 1979; Enormous Changes at the Last Minute, 1982; The Demon Murder Case, 1983; Tender Age, Lemon Sky; Frasier; Happy Birthday Elizabeth: A Celebration of Life, 1997; Will & Grace, 2002; Film appearances include: National Lampoon's Animal House, 1978; Starting Over, 1979; Hero at Large, Friday the 13th, 1980; Only When I Laugh, 1981; Diner, 1982; Footloose, 1984; Quicksilver, 1985; White Water Summer, Planes, Trains and Automobiles, 1987; End of the Line, She's Having A Baby, 1988; Criminal Law, The Big Picture, 1989; Tremors, Flatliners, 1990; Queens Logic, He Said/She Said, Pyrates, 1991; JFK, A Few Good Men, 1992; The Air Up There, The River Wild, 1994; Murder in the First, Apollo 13, 1995; Sleepers, 1996; Telling Lies in America, Picture Perfect, Digging to China, 1997; Wild Things, 1998; My Dog Skip, The Hollow Man, Stir of Echoes, 1999; Novocain, We Married Margo, 2000; 24 Hours, 2001; Trapped, 2002; In the Cut, Mystic River, 2003; The Woodsman, Cavedweller, 2004; Loverboy, Beauty ShopWhere the Truth Lies, 2005; Saving Angelo, The Air I Breathe, Black Water Transit, 2006; Death Sentence, The 1 Second Film, 2007; The Air I Breathe, Frost/Nixon, 2008; Taking Chance, The Magic 7, New York, I Love You, My One and Only, 2009. Honours: BFCA Award for Best Actor, 1996; Blockbuster Entertainment Award, 2001; BSFC Award for Best Cast, 2003. Address: c/o Kevin Huvane, Creative Artists Agency, 9830 Wilshire Boulevard, Beverley Hills, CA 90212, USA.

BAČOSKA Gordana, b. 3 September 1948, Tetovo, Macedonia. Pianist. m. Mathias Vogrič, 1 son. Education: Seminars with Ms Jeanne Blancard, Mr Aldo Cicolini, Ms Monique Deschaussees, Mr Evgenij Timakin, Mr Leonid Eftimovich Brumberg, 1968-81; Diploma, Higher Conservatory of Music, Skopje, Macedonia, 1973; Certificate of study, Higher Conservatory of Music, Warsaw, Poland, 1974-75; Diploma, Postgraduate Studies, Masterium and title of Master of Piano, University of Kiril I Metodi, College of Musical Art, Skopje, 1982. Appointments: Concert Pianist, France, Italy, Macedonia, Italy, Serbia, Slovenia, Belgium and Poland, 1966-87; Professor, 1976-. Publications: Articles in newspapers, 1973-83; TV appearances, 1980, 1981; Subject of many articles and publications. Honours: Golden Medal, Association of Professional Women Artists, Italy, 1978; Golden Medal, Association of Classical Music, Italy, 1978; Golden Medal, Tourist and Cultural Association, Italy, 1978; Secretary General, Union of Music Teachers Association of Ex-Yugoslavia, 1979; Representative of Ex-Yugoslavia, European Union National Music Competition for Youth, 1979, 1980; Secretary General, Federal Competition of the Union of Music Teachers Association of Ex-Yugoslavia, 1980; Certificate of Honour: Musical Youth of Macedonia, 1978; Association of Music Teachers from Macedonia, Serbia, Croatia and Slovenia, 1978-82; Music Conservatory of Prilep, Macedonia, 1979; Leopold-Bellan competition, Paris, France, 1992. Memberships: Music Teachers Association of Macedonia; Musical Artists Association of Macedonia; Union for Professional Music Artists of Paris.

BADER Erwin, b. 10 October 1943, Schladming, Austria. Professor. m. Barbara, 2 daughters. Education: Dr phil, University of Salzburg, 1972; Theology Faculty, Vienna, 1975-79. Appointments: Lecturer, Political Science University, Salzburg, 1973-75; Scientific Secretary, Ministry of Science, Wien, Austria, 1973-75; Teacher, Roman Catholic Religion, Vienna, 1977-97; Assistant, 1987, Habil, 1993, University Professor, 1997, University of Vienna. Publications: Books: Karl Vogelang, 1990; Christliche Sozialreform, 1991; Karl Kummer, 1993; Die Macht des Geistes, 2003; Dialog der Religionen, 2005; Terrorismus, 2007; Weltcthos, 2007; Globalisierung, 2008; K Marx, 2009; 10 Gebote Reloaded, 2010. Honours: Karl Vogelsang State Award, 1992; many others. Memberships: Societas Ethica; IVR; Weltcthos Osterreich; and others. Address: Gablenzgasse 93/56, A-1150 Wien, Austria. E-mail: erwin.bader@univie.ac.at

BADRINATH Srinivas G, b. 4 July 1981, Kolan Gold Fields, India. PhD Scholar. Education: BE, Computer Science and Engineering, Visveswariah Technological University, Karnataka, 2003; ME, Information Technology, Bangalore University, 2005; PhD, Computer Science and Engineering, Indian Institute of Technology, Kanpur, in progress. Appointments: Teaching Assistant, Data Structures and Algorithms, University Visveswarya College of Engineering, Bangalore University, 2003-04; Guest Faculty, Wireless Networks, Alpha College of Engineering, Bangalore, 2004-05; Teaching Assistant, Multimodal Biometrics, 2007-, Teaching Assistant, Digital Watermarking and Stenography, 2010, Research Assistant, 2010-, Indian Institute of Technology, Kanpur. Publications: Numerous articles in professional journals. Honours: Best Paper Award, 2006; Best Paper Award nomination, 2008; Travel Grant, International Conference on Contemporary Computing, 2009; 1st Prize, SKOCH Summit, 2009; Microsoft Scholarship, 2010; Invited Speaker, International Workshop on Biometrics and its applications in Forensic Science, 2010; Listed in international biographical dictionaries. Memberships: IEEE; ACM; BMVA. Address: CS-213, Department of Computer Science & Engineering, Indian Institute of Technology, Kanpur, PIN 208016, India. E-mail: badri@cse.iitk.ac.in

BAE Chang Hoon, b. 19 February 1970, Daegu, Republic of Korea. Otorhinolaryngologist. m. Hye Gyoung Kang, 2 sons. Education: College of Medicine, 1988-94, Master of Medical Science, 1998, Doctor of Medical Science, 2002, Graduate School, Yeungnam University. Appointments: Clinical Fellow, 1999, Full-time Instructor, 2005-07, Assistant Professor, 2007-11, Associate Professor, 2011-, Department of Otorhinolaryngology, Yeungnam University Medical Centre; Practitioner, Dr Bae's Otorhinolaryngology Clinic, 2001-04. Publications: Diallyl disulphide induces MUC5B expression via ERK2 in human airway epithelial cells, 2012; Insulin-like growth factor-1 induces MUC8 and MUC5B expression via ERK1 and p38 MAPK in human airway epithelial cells, 2013; and others. Honours: Listed in international biographical dictionaries. Memberships:

Korean Society of Otorhinolaryngology – Head and Neck Surgery; The Korean Otologic Society; The Korean Balance Society. Address: #1406-1402 Castle Goldpark 4 Danji, 261, Cheongsu-ro, Suseong-gu, Daegu, 706-934, Republic of Korea. E-mail: baech@ynu.ac.kr

BAE Jinho, b. 21 July 1968, Busan, Korea. Professor. m. Jeongyeon Kim, 1 son, 1 daughter. Education: BS, Ajou University, Suwon, Korea, 1993; MS, 1996, PhD, 2001, Korea Advanced Institute of Science and Technology, Daejon. Appointments: Technical Staff, Daeyang Electric Co, Busan, 1993-2002; Visiting Professor, KAIST, 2002; Associate Professor, Jeju National University, Jeju, Korea, 2002-; Visiting Professor, Texas A & M University, USA, 2006-07. Publications: 28 papers in journals; 39 conference papers. Honours: Listed in national and international biographical directories. Memberships: Optical Society of Korea; Optical Society of America. Address: Department of Ocean System Engineering, Jeju National University, 66 Jejudaehakro, Jeju 690-756, Republic of Korea. E-mail: baejh@cheju.ac.kr

BAE Jungok, Professor. Education: PhD, Applied Linguistics, UCLA, 2000. Appointments: English Teacher, Daegu City Board of Education, 1983; Professor, English Education, Kyungpook National University, Daegu, 2008-. Honours: International Language Testing Award, 1999. Address: English Education Department, Kyungpook National University, 1370 Sanguk-dong, Daegu 702-701, Republic of Korea. E-mail: jungokbae@knu.ac.kr

BAE Kyung Dong, b. 19 May 1966, Yousu, Korea. Researcher; Company Worker. m. YooNa Song, 1 son, 1 daughter. Education: Bachelor in Chemical Engineering, Inha University, 1987; Master in Biochemical Engineering, 1992, PhD, Biochemical Engineering, 2003, Inha Graduate School, Korea. Appointments: Researcher, Hanhyo Institute of Hanil Synthetic Fiber Co, 1992-98; Researcher, BernaBiotech Korea Corp, 1998-; Part time Lecturer, Inha Graduate School, 2006-. Publications: More than 12 papers in professional scientific journals. Honours: Listed in international biographical dictionaries. Address: 504-103, Kolong APT, Kugal Dong, Yongin, 449-903, Republic of Korea. E-mail: kdbae@bernabiotech.co.kr

BAEDECKER Philip Ackerman, b. 19 December 1939, East Orange, New Jersey, USA. Research Chemist. m. Mary Jo LaFuze, 1 daughter. Education: BS, Chemistry, Ohio University, Athens, Ohio, 1957-61; MS, Chemistry, University of Kentucky, Lexington, Kentucky, 1964; PhD, Chemistry, 1967. Appointments: Research Associate, Massachusetts Institute of Technology, 1967-68; Assistant Professor, 1970-71, Assistant Research Chemist, 1968-73, University of California, Los Angeles; Research Chemist, Branch of Analytical Laboratories, 1974-81, Chief, 1981-86, Research Chemist,1986-96, Branch of Geochemistry, US Geological Survey. Publications: Published reports, abstracts. Honours: Haggin Fellow; Paul I Murrill Fellow; Tennessee Eastman Fellow; NSF Fellow; NASA Citatation; NAPAP Citation. Memberships: American Chemical Society; Meteoritical Society; American Association for the Advancement of Science; Sigma Xi; Geological Society of Washington. Address: 2221 Terra Ridge Drive, Vienna, VA 22181-3276, USA.

BAEK Sun-Hee, b. 25 January 1969, Korea. Professor. m. Yeon-Myung Kim, 2 sons. Education: BA, 1991, MA, 1993, PhD, 1999, Social Welfare, Chung-Ang University, Seoul. Appointments: Professor, Seoul Theological University, 2000-; International Research Fellow, The Martha N Ozawa Center for Social Policy Studies, Washington University, USA, 2006-07; Expert Adviser, Presidential Committee on Ageing and Future Society, 2004-05. Publications: The impact of social transfers on children in female-headed households. A comparison between Korea and the United States, 2009. Honours: Listed in international biographical dictionaries. Memberships: Women versus Men: Comparisons of three types of transfers in Korea and the US, 2010. Address: Department of Social Welfare, Seoul Theological University, 52 489th St, Hohyun-ro Sosa-gu, Bucheon-si Gyeonggi-cho, 422-742, Korea. E-mail: shbaek@stu.ac.kr

BAEK Yong Gu, b. 3 September 1965, Chuncheon, Korea. Researcher. m. Young Mi Lee, 2 sons. Education: BS, Chemistry, Hallym University, 1988; MS, 1993, PhD, 1997, Organic Synthesis, Ajou University. Appointments: Postdoctor, Chemistry, ETH, Switzerland, 1997-99; Senior Researcher, Chirotech Laboratory, C-TRI Co Ltd, 2000-02; CTO, Vice President, ELM Co Ltd, 2002-. Memberships: Korean Chemical Society. Address: 1-43, Geumjeong-dong, Gunpo-si, Gyeonggi-do, 435-824, Republic of Korea. E-mail: ygbaek@elmk.co.kr

BAEK Yong Hyeon, b. 5 April 1970, South Korea. Professor; Oriental Medical Doctor. m. Sang Hee Song, 1 son, 1 daughter. Education: Bachelor, 1999, Master, 2003, Doctor of Medicine, 2006, Kyung Hee University. Appointments: Specialist in Acupuncture and Medicine, 1999-; Professor, Oriental Medical College, Kyung Hee University, 2006-; Chief, Facial Palsy Center and Joints Center, Kyung Hee University Hospital, Gangdong, 2006-; Chief, Department of Acupuncture and Moxibustion, Kyung Hee University Medical Center, 2010-; Board of Korean Oriental Medicine Education and Evaluation Institute, 2011-. Publications: Therapeutic effect of Arailia Cordata extracts on, 2009; Bee venom inhibits tumor angiogenesis and metasis, 2010; Formononetin accelerates wound repair by the regulation, 2011; Gastroprotective and safety of WIN-34B, a novel treatment of osteoarthritis, 2011. Honours: Medical Research Award, Kyung Hee University, 2006; Medical Research Award, Kyung Hee University, 2009; Listed in biographical dictionaries. Memberships: Korean Acupuncture & Moxibustion Society; Korean Oriental Medical Society. Address: #149 Sangil-dong, Gangdong-gu, Seoul 134-727, South Korea. E-mail: byhacu@khu.ac.kr

BAEK Young Hyun, b. 10 November 1976, Jeonju, Korea. Image Processing Engineer. m. Mi Rim Lee, 2 daughters. Education: Bachelor, 2002, Master, 2004, Doctor, 2007, Engineering, Wonkwang University. Appointments: Assistant Professor, Electronics and Control Engineering, Wonkwang University, 2007-09; Image Processing Engineer, New Technology Development Team, Union Community Co Ltd, 2009-. Publications: Numerous articles in professional journals. Honours: Scientific Award of Excellence, 2011. Memberships: IEEE; KES; IEEK; KIIS.

BAI Zhan-Wu, b. 23 March 1962, Hebei Province, China. Professor. m. Xin-Li Zhang, 1 daughter. Education: BA, 1982, MA, 1986, Southwest Jiaotong University, China; PhD, Beijing Normal University, 2006. Appointments: Assistant Professor, 1986-88, Lecturer, 1988-91, Southwest Jiaotong University; Lecturer, 1991-2001, Associate Professor, 2001-10, Professor, 2011-, North China Electric Power University. Publications: Numerous articles in professional journals. Honours: International Excellent Article Prize, World Chinese Interchange Association, World Cultural and Arts Research Centre, Hong Kong, 2001, 2002; China Theory

Innovation Excellent Scholarship Result (First Class), China Management Science Academy Human Institute, 2003; many others. E-mail: baizhanwu@126.com

BAIGUNCHEKOV Zhumadil, b. 8 July 1947, Zhambyl city, Kazakhstan. Mechanical Engineer. m. Gulzada Esbergenova, 3 sons. Education: Mechanical Engineer, Kazakh Politechnical Institute, 1971; PhD, 1977; Doctor of Technical Sciences, 1985. Appointments: Post-graduate Student, Senior Teacher, Assistant Professor, Professor, Kazakh State University, 1971-91; Deputy Director, Science, Director of the Institute of Mechanics and Mechanical Engineering, Kazakhstan National Academy of Sciences, 1991-2002; Visiting Professor, Middlesex University, London, UK, 1996-98; Director, Institute of Mechanical Engineering, Technologies and Ecology, Kazakh National Technical University, 2000-02; Vice Rector for Research, Professor, Kazakh-British Technical University, 2002-. Publications: More than 300 articles; 80 patents in field of theory of machines and mechanisms, mechatronics and robotics. Honours: Kazakhstan Komsomol Laureate, 1980; V G Shukhov's Golden Medal, International and Russian Union of Engineers, 1992. Memberships: Kazakhstan National Academy of Sciences, Engineering Academy of Kazakhstan; Robotics and Mechatronics Technical Committee, International Federation on the Theory of Machines and Mechanisms. E-mail: bzh47@mail.ru Website: www.kbtu.kz

BAIKINA Nina Grigorievna, b. 18 July 1942, Russia. Pedagogy. 1 daughter. Education: MPC Doctor, Teacher of PE and Sport, Anatomy and Physiology, Uzbek State University of Physical Education, Tashkent, 1964; Doctor of Pedagogical Science, Correctional Pedagogy Institute, Moscow, 1992; Professor, Zaporizhzhya State University, 1994. Appointments: Teacher of Choreography, Republican Boarding School for Deaf Children, Tashkent, 1964-67; Teacher, PE and Sport, Tashkent State University, 1967-71; Lecturer, Chair of Sport, 1971-82, Head, Chair of Sport, 1983-87, Zaporizhzhya State University; Head, Chair of Correctional Pedagogy, 2003-06, Professor, Physical Education and Tourism Theory and Methods, 2007-11, Zaporizhzhya National University. Publications: 380 articles in professional journals. Honours: Lecturer's Certificate, Moscow, 1992; Doctor of Pedagogic Science, 1994; Professor, Ukraine; Honour of Real Member of Academy, 2001; Education High Achiever of Ukraine. Memberships: Board of Academics, INV; Technical Board of Academics, K D V Schyksky South Ukrainian National Pedagogical University. Address: Depovska Str, 83, Flat 12, Zaporizhzhya, Ukraine 69086.

BAILEY David, b. 2 January 1938, London, England. Photographer; Film Director. m. (1) Rosemary Bramble, 1960, (2) Catherine Deneuve, 1965; (3) Marie Helvin, divorced, (4) Catherine Dyer, 1986, 2 sons, 1 daughter. Appointments: Self taught photographer for Vogue, UK, USA, France, Italy; Advertising Photography, 1959-; Director, Commercials, 1966-; TV Documentaries, 1968-; Exhibition National Portrait Gallery, 1971; Photographers Gallery, 1973; Olympus Gallery, 1980, 1982, 1983; Victoria and Albert Museum, 1983; International Centre of Photography, New York, 1984; Hamilton Gallery, 1990, 1992; Director, Producer, TV Film Who Dealt?, 1993; Documentary: Models Close Up, 1998; Director, feature film, The Intruder, 1999. Publications: Box of Pinups, 1964; Goodbye Baby and Amen, 1969; Warhol, 1974; Beady Minces, 1974; Mixed Moments, 1976; Trouble and Strife, 1980; NW1, 1982; Black and White Memories, 1983; Nudes, 1981-84, 1984; Imagine, 1985; The Naked Eye: Great Photographers of the Nude (with Martin Harrison), 1988; If

We Shadows, 1992; The Lady is a Tramp, 1995; Rock and Roll Heroes, 1997; Archive, 1999; Chasing Rainbows, 2001; Bailey's Democracy, 2005; Havana, 2006; 8 Minutes: Hirst & Bailey, 2009. Honours: Dr hc, Bradford University, 2001. Address: c/o Robert Montgomery and Partners, 3 Junction Mews, Sale Place, London, W2, England.

BAILYN Bernard, b. 10 September 1922, Hartford, Connecticut, USA. Professor Emeritus of History; Writer. m. Lotte Lazarsfeld, 18 June 1952, 2 sons. Education: AB, Williams College, 1945; MA, 1947, PhD, 1953, Harvard University. Appointments: Instructor, 1953-54, Assistant Professor, 1954-58, Associate Professor, 1958-61, Professor of History, 1961-66, Winthrop Professor of History, 1966-81, Adams University Professor, 1981-93, Director, Charles Warren Center for Studies in American History, 1983-94, James Duncan Phillips Professor of Early American History, 1991-93, Professor Emeritus, 1993-, Harvard University; Trevelyan Lecturer, 1971, Pitt Professor of American History, 1986-87, Cambridge University; Fellow, British Academy, and Christ's College, Cambridge, 1991. Publications: The New England Merchants in the Seventeenth Century, 1955; Massachusetts Shipping, 1697-1714: A Statistical Study (with Lotte Bailyn), 1959; Education in the Forming of American Society: Needs and Opportunities for Study, 1960; Pamphlets of the American Revolution, 1750-1776, Vol 1 (editor), 1965; The Apologia of Robert Keayne: The Self-Portrait of a Puritan Merchant (editor), 1965; The Ideological Origins of the American Revolution, 1967, new edition, 1992; The Origins of American Politics, 1968; The Intellectual Migration: Europe and America, 1930-1960 (editor with Donald Fleming), 1969; Religion and Revolution: Three Biographical Studies, 1970; Law in American History (editor with Donald Fleming), 1972; The Ordeal of Thomas Hutchinson, 1974; The Great Republic: A History of the American People (with others), 1977, 4th edition, 1992; The Press and the American Revolution (editor with John B Hench), 1980; The Peopling of British North America: An Introduction, 1986; Voyagers to the West: A Passage in the Peopling of America on the Eve of the Revolution, 1986; Faces of Revolution: Personalities and Themes in the Struggle for American Independence, 1990; Strangers within the Realm: Cultural Margins of the First British Empire (editor with Philip B Morgan), 1991; The Debate on the Constitution: Federalist and Antifederalist Speeches, Articles and Letters during the Struggle over Ratification, 2 volumes, 1993;On the Teaching and Writing of History, 1994; To Begin the World Anew, 2003; Atlantic History: Concept and Contours, 2005. Contributions to: Scholarly journals. Honours: Bancroft Prize, 1968; Pulitzer Prizes in History, 1968, 1987; National Book Award in History, 1975; Thomas Jefferson Medal, American Philosophical Society, 1993; Honorary doctorates: Catton Prize, Society of American Historians, 2000. Memberships: American Academy of Arts and Sciences; American Historical Association, president, 1981; American Philosophical Society; National Academy of Education; Royal Historical Society. Address: 170 Clifton Street, Belmont, MA 02178, USA.

BAIN James Keith, b. 1 October 1929, Sydney, Australia. Retired Stockbroker. m. Janette Isabelle Grace King, 1958, 1 son, 1 daughter. Education: The Armidale School, 1941-43; The Scots College, 1944-47; Accountancy Degree, FCPA (night school). Appointments: Senior Partner, Bain & Company Stockbrokers, 1972-87; Senior Vice President and Executive Member, National Trust NSW Division, 1980-88; Chairman, Sydney Stock Exchange, 1983-87; Chairman, NatWest Australia Bank Ltd, 1985-91; Chairman, State Library of NSW (President of the Library Council of NSW), 1988-95; Founding Donor, Sydney Institute, 1989; Chairman,

Centenary Institute of Cancer Medicine & Cell Biology, 1990-93; Chairman, International Air Services Commission, 1993-98; Director, National Portrait Gallery, 1998-2000; Chairman, National Library of Australia, 1998-2001. Publications: Author: The Remarkable Roller Coaster, 2001; A Financial Tale of Two Cities, 2007; Uncertain Beginnings, 2011. Honours: Member, Order of Australia, 1985; Centenary Medal, 2003; Listed in international biographical dictionaries. Memberships: Fellow, Certified Public Accountants; Senior Fellow, FINSIA; Fellow, The Australian Institute of Management; Fellow, The Institute of Directors in Australia; Honorary Fellow, Australian Stock Exchange. Address: Apartment 55, The Bennelong, 3 Macquarie Street, Sydney, NSW 2000, Australia. E-mail: bainco@bigpond.net.au

BAIN Robert Gowrie, b. 1955, Brisbane, Australia. Law. m. Lana Jane Tier, 1 son, 1 daughter. Education: Brisbane Grammar School; University of Queensland. Appointments: Private practice: Bars of Federal Jurisdictions; States of Queensland, New South Wales and Victoria; Northern Territory, 1977-; QC (QLD), 1992-; QC (NSW & VIC), 1993.

BAKER Alan, b. 19 August 1939, London, England. Mathematician. Education: BSc, Mathematics, University of London, 1961; PhD, Cambridge University, 1964. Appointments: Research Fellow, 1964-68, Director of Studies, Mathematics, 1968-74, Trinity College, Cambridge; Professor of Pure Mathematics, Cambridge University, 1974; Numerous Visiting Professorships in the USA and Europe; First Turán Lecturer, János Bolyai Mathematical Society, Hungary, 1978; Research into transcendental numbers. Publications: Numerous papers; Transcendental Number Theory, 1975; A Concise Introduction to the Theory of Numbers, 1984; New Advances in Transcendence Theory, as editor, 1988. Memberships: Fellow, Royal Society, 1973; Honorary Fellow, Indian National Science Academy, 1980; European Academy, 1998; Doctor Honoris Causa, University of Louis Pasteur, Strasbourg, 1998; Honorary Member, Hungarian Academy of Sciences, 2001. Address: Department of Pure Mathematics and Mathematical Statistics, 16 Mill Lane, Cambridge, CB2 1SB, England.

BAKER Carleton Harold, b. 2 August 1930, Utica, New York, USA. Physiology Educator. m. Sara Frances Johnson, 1963, 2 daughters. Education: BA, Utica College of Syracuse University, 1952; MA, 1954, PhD, 1955, Princeton University. Appointments: Assistant Instructor, 1952-54, Assistant in Research, 1954-55, Princeton University, New Jersey; Assistant Professor, 1955-61, Associate Professor, 1961-67, Professor, 1967, Medical College, Augusta, Georgia; Professor, Physiology and Biophysics, University of Louisville Health Sciences Center, 1967-71; Professor, Chairman, Department of Physiology and Biophysics, 1971-92, Deputy Dean for Research and Graduate Studies, 1980-82, Professor of Surgery, Physiology and Biophysics, Director of Surgical Research, 1992-95, University of South Florida, College of Medicine, Tampa; Professor Emeritus, University of South Florida, 1995-; Research Professor, Physiology, University of South Carolina, College of Medicine, Columbia, 1994-2001. Publications: Contributor of numerous articles in field. Honours: Service Awards, American Heart Association, 1974, 1977; Distinguished Scientist Award, University of South Florida, College of Medicine, 1981; Outstanding Artist/Scholar Award, Phi Kappa Phi, 1991; Dean's Citation, University of South Florida, College of Medicine, 1991; Founder Award, 1991. Memberships: Fellow, American Physiology Society; Member, Shock Society; European Microcirculatory Society; Microcirculatory Society; Torch Club International; Fellow, American Heart Association. Address: 4039 Old Waynesboro Road, Augusta, GA 30906, USA. E-mail: microves@bellsouth.net

BAKER (Lawrie) Lawrence Rae, b. 25 July 1935, Geelong, Victoria, Australia. Emeritus Professor; Consultant. m. (1) Beverly Margret, 1958 (dissolved 1981), 1 son, 3 daughters, (2) Carol Elizabeth, 1985. Education: Geelong Junior Technology School; AGInstTech, BCE, Gordon Institute of Technology; M Eng Sc, University of Melbourne; PhD, Deakin University; CPEng; FIEAust. Appointments: Assistant Engineer, State Rivers and Water Supply Commission, 1957-59; Design/Senior Design Engineer, Geelong Harbor Trust, 1959-64; Lecturer/Senior Lecturer, Gordon Institute of Technology, 1964-78; Chairman, Civil Engineering Division, 1978-82; Director, Masonry Research Centre, Deakin University, 1980-93; Dean, School of Architecture, 1983-86; Head, School of Engineering and Technology, 1991-99; Professor, Engineering, 1993-99, Emeritus Professor, 1998-, Deakin University, Victoria; External Examiner, University Sains, Malaysia, 1995-98; Deputy Leader (Academic), Thailand-Australia Science and Engineering Assistance Project (TASEAP), Bangkok, 1999-2001; Consultant, 2002-. Publications: Masonry Code of Practice, 1984; Australian Masonry Manual, 1991; Masonry Structures: Behaviour and Design, 1993, revised 1999. Honours: Member, General Division, Order of Australia. Memberships: Central Region Coastal Board, 1996-98; Board Member, Water Training Centre, Werribee, 1995-99; Director, Barwon Region Water Authority, 1994-99; Foreshore Committee of Management, Lorne, 1998-99; President, Lorne Planning and Preservation League, 1999-93; Western Region Coastal Board, 2003-05; Chair, Great Ocean Road Coast Committee, 2004-07.

BAKER William, b. 6 July 1944, Shipston, Warwickshire, England. Professor. m. 1969, 2 daughters. Education: BA Hons, Sussex University, 1963-66; MPhil, London University, 1966-69; PhD, 1974; MLS, Loughborough, 1986. Appointments: Lecturer; Thurrock Technical College, 1969-71; Ben-Gurion University, 1971-77; University of Kent, 1977-78; West Midlands College, 1978-85; Professor, Pitzer College, Claremont, California, 1981-82; Housemaster, Clifton College, 1986-89; Professor, Northern Illinois University, 1989-; Presidential Research Professor (Distinguished Professor), Northern Illinois University, 2003-; University Trustee Distinguished Professor, Northern Illinois University, 2009-14; Editor, The Year's Work in English Studies, 2000-; George Eliot – G.H. Lewes Studies, 1981-. Publications: Harold Pinter, 1973; George Eliot and Judaism, 1975; The Early History of the London Library, 1992; Literary Theories: A Case Study in Critical Performance, 1996; Nineteenth Century British Book Collectors and Bibliographers, 1997; Twentieth Century British Book Collectors and Bibliographers, 1999; Pre-Nineteenth Century British Book Collectors and Bibliographers, 1999; The Letters of Wilkie Collins, 1999; Twentieth Century Bibliography and Textual Criticism, 2000; George Eliot: A Bibliographical History, 2002; Shakespeare: The Critical Tradition: The Merchant of Venice, 2005; Harold Pinter: A Bibliographical History, 2005; The Public Face of Wilkie Collins, 4 vols, 2005; The English Association One Hundred Years On, 2006; A Wilkie Collins Chronology, 2007; Harold Pinter (Continuum Writers' Lives Series), 2008; Critical Companion to Jane Austen: A Literary Reference to her Life and Work, 2008; David Daiches: A Celebration of his Life and Work, 2008; Shakespeare (Continuum Writers' Lives Series), 2009; Tom Stoppard: A Bibliographical History, 2010. Other: Editions of letters by George Henry Lewes, George

Eliot, and Wilkie Collins, 2000-. Honours: Ball Brothers Foundation Fellowship, Lilly Library, Indiana University, 1993; Bibliographical Society of America, Fellowship, 1994-95; American Philosophical Society Grant, 1997; National Endowment for the Humanities Senior Fellowship, 2002-03; Choice Outstanding Academic Book of the Year Award, 2000, 2006. Memberships: Bibliographical Society of America; ALA; MLA; SHARP. Address: Department of English, Northern Illinois University, DeKalb, Illinois, USA.

BAKEWELL Joan Dawson, b. 16 April 1933, Stockport, England. Broadcaster; Writer. m. (1) Michael Bakewell, 1955, 1 son, 1 daughter, (2) Jack Emery, 1975. Education: Newnham College, Cambridge. Appointments: TV Critic, The Times, 1978-81; Columnist, Sunday Times, 1988-90; Associate, Newnham College, Cambridge, 1980-91; Associate Fellow, 1984-87; Gov BFI, 1994-99; Chair, 1999-2003; TV Includes: Sunday Break, 1962; Home at 4.30 (writer and producer), 1964; Meeting Point, The Second Sex, 1964; Late Night Line Up, 1965-72; The Youthful Eve, 1968; Moviemakers, National Film Theatre, 1971; Film 72; Film 73; Holiday, 74, 75, 76, 77, 78 (series); Reports Action (series) 1976-78; Arts UK: OK?, 1980; Heart of the Matter, 1988-2000; My Generation, 2000; One Foot in the Past, 2000; Taboo (series), 2001; Radio includes: Artist of the Week, 1998-99; The Brains Trust, 1999-; Belief, 2000. Publications; The New Priesthood: British Television Today, 1970; A Fine and Private Place, 1977; The Complete Traveller, 1977; The Heart of the Heart of the Matter, 1996; The Centre of the Bed: An Autobiography, 2003; Contributions to journals. Honours: CBE, 1999; Chairman, British Film Institute, 2000-02; Dame Commander of the Order of the British Empire, 2008; Appointed Voice for Older People, UK Government, 2008. Address: c/o Knight Ayton Management, 10 Argyll Street, London, W1V 1AB, England.

BAKHOUM Habiboullah, b. 1 April 1952, Ziguinehor, Senegal. Professor. m. 2 sons. Education: Degree, University of Dakar, Senegal, 1979; Degree, Business English, University of Graz, Austria, 1980; Postgraduate, International Economics, Business Administration, Vienna University of Economics & Business, Vienna Diplomatic Academy, 1982; PhD, Strategic Studies, University of Sorbonne Novelle, Paris, France, 1984; Certificate in Management Training, Zürich, Switzerland, 1986; M, Linguistics, Islamic Science, Vienna University, 2001; Degree, Fiscal Academy, Vienna, 2003; Degree, Vienna Business Academy, 2010; Certified Project Manager, Didactica Academy, Vienna, 2011. Appointments: Director, Conference Services Division, Geneva, 1994-95; Translator, Interpreter (English, French, German), Interlingua Translations GmbH, Vienna, 1995-2008; Communal Support Manager, Conduit Enterprises GmbH, 1999-2001; Senior Co-ordinating Manager, Siemens Österreich, 2001-02; President, Senegal Austrian Association, Mbooloo, 2002-; Lecturer, Comparative Linguistics, Compared Religions, Translator and Interpreter, University of Vienna, 2002-; Peace Ambassador, IFWP, 2002-; Language Trainer (Arabic, business English, French, German), Wolof Verband Wiener Volksbildung, Vienna, 2003-; Senior Sales Manager, Business Forum, Vermögensbertatungs GmbH, 2004; African Business Board, Economic Federation, Vienna, 2005-; Visiting Professor, Political Science, Webster University, Vienna, 2005-; Financial Analyst, Euro-Financial Service AG, Vienna, 2005-08; Executive General Manager, Global Environmental Management Groups, 2006-; Visiting Lecturer, Austrian Defense Academy, Vienna; Executive General Manager, SENFUMSEC; Executive General Manager, Bantamba Mining (SL) Ltd, 2010. Publications: Numerous articles in professional journals. Memberships: Advisory Board, Institute of Cultural Diplomacy. Address: Meidlinger Hauptstrasse 12-14/9/3, Wien 1120, Austria. Emial habiboulah.bakhoum@univie.ac.at

BAKIEV Saydamin, b. 13 March 1942, Chirchik city, Uzbekistan. Physicist. m., 1 son, 1 daughter. Education: Tashkent State University, Uzbekistan, 1959-62; Master's degree, Physics Sciences, Moscow State University, Russia, 1962-66; Doctoral course, Physics and Mathematics, 1966-70, PhD, Physics and Mathematics, 1973, Institute of Nuclear Physics of Moscow State University, Russia; Doctor of Technical Sciences, All Russia Institute of Technical Physics and Automation, Moscow, 1993. Appointments: Junior Research Scientist, 1970-76, Senior Research Scientist, 1976-78, Head of Laboratory, Zarafshan city, 1978-88, Leading Research Scientist, 1988-93, Head of Sector, 1993-94, Deputy Director, Radiopreperat enterprise, 1994-96, Head of Laboratory, 1996-97, Scientific Secretary, Head of Laboratory, 1997-, Institute of Nuclear Physics, Uzbekistan Academy of Sciences. Publications: More than 100 professional publications; 2 books: Murphy's Law and Other Reasons Causing Things to go Wrong, 2005; Murphology, or the Laws Under which we Live. The Laws of Being. The Laws of Living. The Laws of Drinking, 2009. Honours: Breastplate for Productive Activity; Listed in international biographical dictionaries. Memberships: Scientific Council, Institute of Nuclear Physics; Problem Council, Uzbekistan Academy of Sciences. Address: Institute of Nuclear Physics, Ulugbek Twn, Tashkent, Mirzo Ulugbek 100214, Uzbekistan. E-mail: bakiev@inp.uz

BAKRADZE David, b. 1 July 1972, Tbilisi, Georgia. Politician. m. Maka Metreveli, 2 daughters. Education: Master's degree, Public Administration, US National Academy of Public Administration, 1996; PhD, Physics, Georgian Academy of Sciences, 1998. Appointments: Various senior and mid-level positions at the Foreign Affairs Ministry; Director, Political Security Department, NSC of Georgia, 2004; MP, Chairman of the Committee on European Integration, 2004-07; State Minister for Conflict Resolution Issues, 2007-08; Minister for Foreign Affairs, 2008; Special Envoy of the President of Georgia for European and Euro-Atlantic Integration Issues, 2008; Chairman, Parliament of Georgia, 2008-. Publications include: From Peacekeeping to State-Building: New Role for NATO Military Forces, 2001; Building a New Silk Road from Japan to Europe: Security of Eurasia, Global Challenges and Common Approaches, 2002. Honours: Commander's Cross of the Order of Merit of the Republic of Poland, 2010; Featured Graduate of the Month, Marshall Center, 2009; Special gratification for significant professional achievements, 2000; Decree of the President of Georgia. Memberships: International Board of the Community of Democracies Parliamentary Forum, 2008; Several State Commissions, 2005-08. Address: 8 Rustaveli Avenue, Tbilisi, 0118, Georgia. Website: www.parliament.ge

BAKUNTS Henry O, b. 18 March 1946, Yerevan, Armenia. Doctor of Medical Sciences; Professor of Neurology. m. 2 children. Education: Yerevan State Medical Institute, 1964-70; Doctoral Degree, II Medical Moscow Institute, Department of Neurology and Neurosurgery, 1985-90. Appointments: Research Assistant, Neurology Department, Yerevan State Medical Institute; Head, Cerebral Circulation Disorders, Yerevan First Aid Hospital, 1977-88; Head, Laboratory of Cerebral Pathology, Yerevan State Medical Institute and Head, Angioneurology Clinic of Yerevan First Aid Hospital, 1988-90; Director, Disaster Neurology Research Centre of Health Ministry of Armenia and Head of Angioneurology

Clinic, 1990-98; Professor, Neurology Department, Yerevan State Institute, 1993-96; Professor, Neurology and Neurosurgery Department, National Health Institute, 1996-98; Head, Angioneurology Department, National Institute of Health, 1998-; Director, Angioneurology Centre Nairi, Head of Clinic, 1998-2002; Head, Angioneurology Clinic, Nairi Medical Centre, 2002-; General Director, STROKE European Medical Centre, 2008-. Publications: Over 100 scientific publications and inventions. Memberships: International Brain Research Organization; International Academy of Ecology and Life Protection Sciences; European Federation of Neurological Societies; World Stroke Organization. Address: 0028, Kievyan 4/4, Apt 18, Yerevan, Armenia.

BALAKRISHNAN Uckath Variyath, b. 3 May 1953, Pampadi, Thrissur, India. Research. m. Sudha, 1989, 1 son. Education: BSc, 1974, MSc, 1976, Calicut University; PhD, University of Bombay, 1985. Appointments: Research Assistant, TIFR, Mumbai, 1976-95; SIM, Singapore, 1995-2000; Professor, Sona College, India, 2000-05; Professor, EIT, Eritrea, 2005-11; Professor, Sharda University, India, 2011-. Publications: On the mean value of Dirichlet Series, 1984; Extreme values of Dedekind Zeta Function, 1986; Laurent Expansion of Dirichlet Serives; A Series for SCA; On the Sum of Divisors Function, 1995; and others. Honours: National Scholarship, 1971-76; Endowment Gold Medal, 1976; Grant, Swiss National Research Fund, 1994, 1996, 1999. Membership: TATA Institute. Address: Someswarath Varriam, Pampadi West (PD), Thiruvilwamala, Thrissur (DT), Kerala 680597, India.

BALALI-MOOD Mahdi, b. 6 September 1942, Birdjand, Iran. Professor of Medicine and Clinical Toxicology. m. Maryam Khordi-Mood, 1 son, 1 daughter. Education: BSc, Chemistry, Teacher Training University, Tehran, 1964; MD, Tehran University Medical School, 1970; Medical Army Certificate, 1971; Advanced Management Certificate, 1978; PhD, Clinical Pharmacology and Toxicology, Edinburgh University Medical School, 1981; Speciality in Therapeutics, 1981; Sub-Speciality in Poisonings, 1984. Appointments: Lecturer, Forensic and Clinical Toxicology, Faculty of Medicine, Ferdowsi University, Director, Poisons Treatment Centre, 1972-77; Research Fellow, Department of Clinical Pharmacology, Edinburgh University, 1978-81; Lecturer, Clinical Pharmacology, Edinburgh University, 1981-82; Associate Professor, Clinical Toxicology, 1982-89, Professor of Medicine, Director, Medical Toxicology Centre, Imam Reza Hospital, Mashhad University of Medical Sciences (MUMS), 1989-; Regional Secretary of the World Federation of Clinical Toxicology and Poison Centre, 1994-; President, Asia Pacific Association of Medical Toxicology, 1993-2001; President, Iranian Society of Toxicology, 1990-98, 2001-03; Vice-Chairman, Scientific Advisory Board, OPCW, 2005-; Director, Medical Toxicology Research Centre, MUMS, 2007-. Publications: 21 books and monographs, 5 chapters in international textbooks, 116 original papers and articles published in national and international journals, 260 short papers and abstracts published in journals, abstract books and proceedings of international conferences. Honours: Teaching Award in Chemistry, 1964; Research Award in Clinical Toxicology, Mashad University, 1983; Medical Care Award, Minister of Higher Education, 1986; Medical Management Award of Chemical War Gas Victims, 1987; Award of Medical Council of IR Iran, 2000; Research Awards, Ministry of Sciences, Research and Technology, Iran and Best Researcher, MUMS, 2005; State Gold Medal of Medical Research, 2010; Premier Research Award of Khorassam Razavi, 2010; Best Pioneer Award in Medical Research, Khorssan Razavi Province, 2010. Memberships: Medical Council of Iran, 1970-; European Association of Poisons Control Centres and Clinical Toxicologists, 1984-; Fellow, Academy of Sciences for Developing World (new name for the third World Academy of Science), 1997-; Iranian Academy of Medical Sciences, 1990-; Member of National Board for Toxicology, 1990-. Address: Medical Toxicology Research Centre, Faculty of Medicine, Mashhad University of Medical Sciences, Mashhad 91779-48564, Iran. E-mail: mbalalimood@hotmail.com

BALÁSHÁZY Imre, b. 14 December 1956, Szekszárd, Hungary. Physicist. m. Sylvia, 2 daughters. Education: MSc, 1980; PhD (summa cum laude), 1983; CSc, 1993; DSc, 2011. Appointments: IAEA Fellowship, US EPA, North Carolina, USA, 1987-88; Lise Meitner Fellowship, 1993-96, Marie Curie Expert, EU Research Fellowship, 2001-02, University of Salzburg, Austria; Head, Low Dose Group, MTA KFKI Atomic Energy Research Institute, 2002-. Publications: 7 book chapters; 137 papers; 177 conference materials; 33 scientific reports. Honours: Medicina Thoracalis Nívó Prize. Memberships: International Society for Aerosols in Medicine; Gesellschaft fuer Aerosolforschung; Aerosol Society. Address: MTA Centre for Energy Research, Konkoly Thege Miklós út 29-33, Hungary. E-mail: imre.balashazy@energia.inta.hu Website: www.kfki.hu

BALA'ZS András, b. 15 November 1949, Budapest, Hungary. Biophysicist. m. Mária Majoros, 1 son. Education: BA, Biology, 1974, MSc, Theoretical Chemistry, 1976, Eötvös L University; PhD (Candidate) Biology, Hungarian Academy of Sciences. Appointments: Research Assistant, 1974-81, Research Worker, 1981-95, Consultant, 1995-, Eötvös L University, Theoretical Chemistry Group, Departments of Atomic/Biological Physics. Publications: In professional journals. Honours: Listed in biographical publications. Memberships: European Cell Biology Organisation; Union of Hungarian Chemists; Hungarian Biochemical Society; Hungarian Theoretical Biological Society; Molecular Electronics and Biocomputing Society; Vienna Freud Museum; World Wild Fund. Address: Department of Biological Physics, Eötvös L University, Pa'zmány Sétány 1, H-1117 Budapest, Hungary.

BALDERSTON Jean Merrill, b. 29 August 1936, Providence, Rhode Island, USA. Psychotherapist; Poet. m. David Chase Balderston, 1957. Education: BA, University of Connecticut, 1957; MA, 1965, EdD, 1968, Teachers College, Columbia University. Appointments: Adjunctive University Faculty, Douglass College for Women, Rutgers University, Mountclair State College, New Jersey, Hunter, Mt St Vincent College, Halifax, Nova Scotia and Queen's Colleges, City University of New York and Teachers College, Columbia University, 1965-70; Psychotherapist in private practice, 1968-. Publications: Contributions to anthologies and literary journals. Honours: Co-winner of The Writer Magazine / Emily Dickinson Award, Poetry Society of America, 2000. Memberships: American Psychological Association; Poetry Society of America; American Association for Marital and Family Therapy; Emily Dickinson International Society; The Academy of American Poets; The American-Scandinavian Foundation; Friends of Poets and Writers Organization; Poets House, NYC; Maine Writers and Publishers Alliance; Society of Children's Book Writers and Illustrators; The Emily Dickinson Museum. Address: 1225 Park Avenue #8C, New York, NY 10128-1758, USA.

BALDWIN Alec (Alexander Rae Baldwin III), b. 3 April 1958, Masapequa, New York, USA. Actor. m. (1) Kim Basinger, 1993, divorced, 1 daughter, (2) Hilaria Thomas, 2012. Education: George Washington University; New York University; Lee Strasberg Theatre Institute; Studied with Mira Rostova and Elaine Aiken. Appointments: Stage appearances include: Loot, 1986; Serious Money, 1988; Prelude to a Kiss, 1990; A Streetcar named Desire, 1992; TV Appearances Include: The Doctors, 1980-82; Cutter to Houston, 1982; Knot's Landing, 1984-85; Love on the Run, 1985; A Dress Gray, The Alamo: 13 Days to Glory, 1986; Sweet Revenge, 1990; Nuremberg, Path to War, 2000; Second Nature, 2002; Friends, 2002; Dreams and Giants, 2003; Thomas and Friends: The Best of Gordon, 2004; Will and Grace; 30 Rock; Film appearances include: Forever Lulu, She's Having A Baby, 1987; Beetlejuice, Married to the Mob, Talk Radio, Working Girl, 1988; Great Balls of Fire, 1989; The Hunt for Red October, Miami Blues, Alice, 1990; The Marrying Man, 1991; Prelude to a Kiss, Glengarry Glen Ross, 1992; Malice, 1993; The Getaway, The Shadow, 1994; Heaven's Prisoners, 1995; Looking for Richard, The Juror, Ghosts of Mississippi, 1996; Bookworm, The Edge, 1997; Thick as Thieves, Outside Providence, Mercury Rising (producer), 1998; The Confession, Notting Hill, 1999; Thomas and the Magic Railroad, State and Main, 2000; Pearl Harbor, Final Fantasy: The Spirit's Within, The Royal Tenenbaums, The Devil and Daniel Webster, 2001; Path to War, 2002; Dr Seuss' The Cat in the Hat, The Cooler, 2003; Along Came Polly, The Last Shot, The Aviator, 2004; Elizabethtown, Fun with Dick and Jane, 2005; The Good Shepherd, The Departed, Running with Scissors, Mini's First Time, 2006; Suburban Girl, Brooklyn Rules, Shortcut to Happiness, 2007; My Best Friend's Girl, Madagascar: Escape 2 Africa, Lymelife, 2008; My Sister's Keeper, It's Complicated, 2009. Publications: A Promise to Ourselves, 2008. Honours: 3 Screen Actors Guild Awards, 2007, 2008; 2 Golden Globe Awards, 2007, 2008; 2 Emmy Awards, 2008, 2009. Memberships: Screen Actors Guild; American Federation of TV and Radio Artists; Actors Equity Association.

BALDWIN Mark, b. 29 July 1944, Simla, India. Publisher; Author. m. Myfanwy Dundas, 1977, 3 sons. Education: BA, MA, St Catharine's College, Cambridge, 1962-65; MSc, DIC, PhD, Imperial College, 1970-86. Appointments: Engineer with Mott Hay & Anderson, 1965-70; Lecturer, Imperial College, London, England, 1971-86; Publisher & Bookseller, 1986-; Lecturer, Intelligence Studies, Buckingham University. Publications: British Freight Waterways Today and Tomorrow, 1980; Canals - A New Look, 1984; Canal Books, 1984; Simon Evans - His Life and Later Work, 1992; Cleobury 2000, 1999. Contributions to: Proc Institution Civil Engineers; Waterways World; Canal and Riverboat, Antiquarian Book Monthly Review, Book and Magazine Collector; Speaker on Second World War Codebreaking, Intelligence, U-Boats, SOE. Address: 24 High Street, Cleobury Mortimer, Kidderminster DY14 8BY, England.

BALDWIN Michael, b. 1 May 1930, Gravesend, Kent, England. Author; Poet. Education: Open Scholar, 1949, Senior Scholar, 1953, St Edmund Hall, Oxford, 1950-55. Appointments: Assistant Master, St Clement Danes Grammar School, 1955-59; Lecturer, Senior Lecturer, Principal Lecturer, Head of English and Drama Department, Whitelands College, 1959-78; Writer and Presenter, 5 series of Thames TV's Writer's Workshop, 1970-77; Many BBC radio broadcasts, 1963-70. Publications: Poetry: The Silent Mirror, 1951; Voyage From Spring, 1956; Death on a Live Wire, 1962; How Chas Egget Lost His Way in a Creation Myth, 1967; Hob, 1972; Buried God, 1973; Snook, 1980; King Horn, 1983; Fiction includes: Grandad with Snails, 1960; In Step with a Goat, 1962; Miraclejack, 1963; Sebastian, 1967; Underneath and Other Situations, 1968; There's a War On, 1970; The Great Cham, 1967; The Gamecock, 1980; The Rape of Oc, 1993. The First Mrs Wordsworth, 1996; Dark Lady, 1998. Contributions to: Listener; Encounter; New Statesman; Texas Review; BBC Wildlife Magazine; Outposts. Honours: Rediffusion Prize, 1970; Cholmondeley Award, 1984; Fellow, Royal Society of Literature, 1985. Memberships: Vice Chairman, Arvon Foundation, 1974-90; Chairman, Arvon Foundation at Lumb Bank, 1980-89; Crime Writer's Association; The Colony Room; The Athenaeum. Address: 35 Gilbert Road, Bromley, Kent BR1 3QP, England.

BALDWIN William, b. 7 August 1948, Bolton, England. Clerk in Holy Orders. m. Sheila Margaret, 1 son, 1 daughter. Education: Bolton Technical College (part-time student), 1965-68; Nursing and Midwifery Council State Registration (General and Psychiatric Nursing), Bolton School of Nursing (Royal Bolton Hospital) and Whittingham Hospital, Preston, 1968-73; Further Education Teacher's Certificate/Registered Clinical Nurse Tutor, 1974-75; Examiners Qualification, Royal College of Nursing Study Centre, Birmingham, 1996; North West Ordination Course, General Ministry Examination, 1975-78; B Th (Hons), MA, Church History, PhD, Greenwich School of Theology (distance learning student), 1991-97. Appointments include: Various NHS appointments, 1968-78; Ordained Deacon, 1978; Ordained Priest, 1979; Assistant Curate, St Anne Royton, 1978-82; Vicar, St Thomas Halliwell, 1982-87; Rector of Atherton Team Ministry, 1987-2002; Team Vicar of Atherton and Hindsford with Howe Bridge St Michael, 2002-08; Area Dean of Leigh, 2001-08; Vicar of Christ Church, Walmsley 2008-; Part-time Chaplain to: Oldham General Hospital/ Kershaw's Cottage Hospital, 1978-82; Royal Bolton Hospital, 1983-87; Royal Naval Association/White Ensign Association, 1987-2002; Advisor on healing to the Lord Bishop of Manchester, 1991-2001; Tutor for distance learning students, Greenwich School of Theology, 1996-2007; Personal Tutor, Manchester, Ordained Local Ministry Course; Member, Manchester Diocesan Synod, 1982-97, 2001-06; Member, Wigan Metropolitan Borough Council's Faith Forum, 2001; Board Member SRB5 (single regeneration budget board) Atherton Building Communities Partnership, 2001-05; Board Member, Leigh Primary Care Group, 1998-2002; Non-Executive Director, 5 Boroughs NHS Trust, 2002-08; Mental Health Act Manager, 2002-. Publications include: Booklets: Agape: A Devotion on 1 Corinthians 13, 1987; Christian Discipleship and the Created Order; Recognising Holiness in the Ordinary, 2000; Pastoral Letters of a Parish Priest, 2002; Poetry Address Book, 2003; Book: The Doctrine of Humanity Revisited, 2003; Several religious and secular poems published in anthologies. Honours: Elected Fellow of the Royal Society of Health, 1983-2008; Awarded Serving Brother of the Order of St John of Jerusalem for service to humanity by H M the Queen, 1988; Elected Fellow, Royal Society of Medicine, 2006-08. Memberships: Associate, St George's House, Windsor Castle; Friend of St George's Chapel; Institute of Advanced Motorists. Address: Walmsley Vicarage, Blackburn Road, Egerton, Bolton, BL7 9RZ, England. E-mail: frbill@fsmail.net

BALE Christian Charles Philip, b. 30 January 1974, Haverfordwest, Wales. Actor. m. Sibi Blazic, 2000, 1 daughter. Career: Empire of the Sun, 1987; Newsies, 1992; Swing Kids, 1993; Prince of Jutland, Little Women, 1994; Pocahontas (voice), 1995; The Secret Agent, The Portrait of a Lady, 1996;

Metroland, 1997; Velvet Goldmine, All the Little Animals, 1998; A Midsummer Night's Dream, 1999; American Psycho, Shaft, 2000; Captain Corelli's Mandolin, 2001; Laurel Canyon, Reign of Fire, Equilibrium, 2002; El Maquinista, 2004; Howl's Moving Castle (voice), 2004; Batman Begins, Harsh Times, The New World, 2005; The Prestige, Rescue Dawn, Harsh Times, 2006; 3:10 to Yuma, 2007; I'm Not There, 2007; Dark Knight, 2008; Terminator Salvation, Public Enemies, 2009. Honours: Best Juvenile Performance, National Board of Review, 1987; Young Artist Awards, 1989; Best Actor, Chlotrudis Award, 2001; Best Actor, CIFF, 2004; Best Hero, MTV Movie Awards, 2006; San Diego Film Critics Society Awards, 2007; Independent Spirit Award, 2008; Best Superhero, Scream Awards, 2008; Best Actor, Empire Award, 2009; 3 People's Choice Awards, 2009.

BALL Michael Ashley, b. 27 June 1962, Bromsgrove, England. Actor, Singer, Entertainer. Partner, Cathy McGowan. Education: Plymouth College. Musical Education: Guildford School of Acting, 1981-84. Career: The Pirates of Penzance, 1984; Les Miserables, West End, 1985; Phantom of the Opera, West End, 1987; Aspects of Love, West End & New York, 1989-1990; Passion, London, 1996; Alone Together, London, 2001; Chitty Chitty Bang Bang, London, 2002-04; Patience, 2005; The Woman in White, 2005; The Rocky Horror Show, 2006; Kismet, 2007; Hairspray, 2007-08; Represented UK, Eurovision Song Contest, 1992; UK tours, 1992, 1993, 1994, 1996, 1999; Television appearances: Host, own series, Michael Ball, 1993, 1994; Soapstar Superstar, 2007; Guest appearances on many TV shows; Film appearance: England My England, 1995. Recordings: Albums: Michael Ball, 1992; Always, 1993; West Side Story, 1993; One Careful Owner, 1994; The Best Of Michael Ball, 1994; First Love, 1996; Michael Ball: The Musicals, 1996; The Movies, 1998; Christmas, 1999; Live at the Royal Albert Hall, 1999; This Time It's Personal, 2000; Centre Stage, 2001; Music, 2005; One Voice, 2006; Michael Ball: The Silver Collection, 2007; Bach to Bacharach, 2007; Singles include: Love Changes Everything; The First Man You Remember; It's Still You; One Step Out of Time; Sunset Boulevard; From Here to Eternity; The Lovers We Were; Wherever You Are; Something Inside So Strong; Appears on cast albums: Les Miserables; Aspects of Love; Encore!, Andrew Lloyd Webber collection; West Side Story; Passion; Sang on Rugby World Cup album; Chitty Chitty Bang Bang, 2002. Honours: 6 Gold albums; 1 Platinum album; What's on Stage Theatre Award, 2008; Olivier Award, 2008. Address: Phil Bowdery Management, 144 Wigmore Street, London W1H 9FF, England.

BALLAL Vasudeva, b. 22 February 1977, Manipal, India. Dentist. Education: BDS, 1999; MDS, 2004; PhD, 2011. Appointments: Assistant Professor, 2004-07, Reader, 2007-10, Associate Professor, 2010-. Publications: Articles in several international journals such as British Dental Journal, International Endodontic Journal, Australian Dental Journal, Australian Endodontic Journal, American Journal of Orthodontics & Dentofacial Orthopaedics, and Esthetic & Restorative Dentistry. Honours: Reviewer of several international journals; Listed in international biographical dictionaries. Memberships: Scientific Advisory Board Member, Journal of Endodontics, American Association of Endodontics. Address: Department of Conservative Dentistry & Endodontics, Manipal College of Dental Sciences, Manipal 576104, Karnataka, India. E-mail: drballal@yahoo.com

BALLANTYNE Colin Kerr, b. 7 June 1951, Glasgow, Scotland. University Professor. m. Rebecca Trengove, 1 son, 1 daughter. Education: MA, University of Glasgow, 1973; MSc, McMaster University, Canada, 1975; PhD, University of Edinburgh; DSc, University of St Andrews, 2000. Appointments: Lecturer, Geography, 1980-89, Warden of McIntosh Hall, 1985-95, Senior Lecturer in Geography and Geology, 1989-94, Professor in Physical Geography, 1994-, University of St Andrews; Visiting Professor, UNIS, Svalbard, Norway, 1998-; Visiting Erskine Fellow, University of Christchurch, New Zealand, 2003. Publications: 145 scientific papers; Books include: The Quaternary of the Isle of Skye, 1991; The Periglaciation of Great Britain, 1994; Classic Landforms of the Isle of Skye, 2000; Paraglacial Geomorphology, 2002. Honours: Fellow, Royal Geographical Society, 1983; Warwick Award, British Geomorphological Research Group, 1987; President's Medal, Royal Scottish Geographical Society, 1991; Newbigin Prize, Royal Scottish Geographical Society, 1992; Fellow, Royal Society of Edinburgh, 1996; Scottish Science Award, Saltire Society, 1996; Fellow, Royal Society of Arts, 1996; Wiley Award, British Geomorphological Research Group, 1999; Clough Medal, Edinburgh Geological Society, 2010. Memberships: Quaternary Research Association; British Geomorphological Research Group; Royal Scottish Geographical Society; International Permafrost Association; Edinburgh Geological Society. Address: School of Geography and Geosciences, University of St Andrews, Fife KY16 9AL, Scotland. E-mail: ckb@St-and.ac.uk

BALLIN Torben Bjarke, b. 21 August 1957, Frederikshavn, Denmark. Archaeologist. m. Beverley Smith. Education: Librarian, Danmarks Biblioteksskole, Denmark, 1981; Cand Phil Prehist Archaeology, 1991, PhD Prehist Archaeology, 1999, University of Aarhus, Denmark. Appointments: Project Manager, Specialist, 1992-98; Consultant Archaeologist, Specialist at Lithic Research, 1999-. Publications: Numerous articles in professional journals. Honours: Grants from: Historic Scotland, 2000-01, 2002-03, 2004-05, 2005-06, 2006-07, 2007-08, 2008-09, 2009-10, 2010-11; National Museums Scotland, 2000-01, 2002-03, 2005-06, 2008-09, 2009-10; Society of Antiquaries Scotland, 2005-06, 2006-07, 2007-08, 2010-11; Russell Trust, 2001-02; Catherine Mackichan Bursary Trust, 2002-03, 2007-08, 2008-09; Shetland Amenity Trust, 2006-07; Robert Kiln Trust, 2007-08, 2008-09; Hunter Trust, 2009-10, 2010-11. Memberships: Member, Institute of Field Archaeologists; Fellow, Society of Antiquarians of Scotland; Member, Lithic Studies Society; Member, International Association for Obsidian Studies; Implement Petrology Group. Address: Banknock Cottage, Denny, Stirlingshire FK6 5NA, Scotland.

BALLINGER Charles Edwin, b. 3 June 1935, West Mansfield, Ohio, USA. Education. m. Venita D Riggs, 1982. Education: BA, DePauw University, 1957; MA, The Ohio State University, 1958; PhD, The Ohio State University, 1971. Appointments: Administrator, Teacher, various schools in Ohio and California, 1958-98; Curriculum Co-ordinator, San Diego County Office of Education, 1971-98; Executive Director, 1980-2000, Executive Director Emeritus, 2000-, National Association for Year-Round Education. Publication: Co-author, School Calendar Reform: Learning in All Seasons; Co-editor, Balancing the School Calendar: Perspectives from the Public and Stakeholders; Contributor of numerous professional magazine articles. Memberships: American Educational Research Association; Phi Delta Kappa; Association for Supervision and Curriculum Development. Address: 4891 Jellett St, San Diego, CA 92110, USA.

BALNAVE Derick, b. 17 June 1941, Lisburn, Northern Ireland. Academic. m. Maureen Dawson, 1 son, 1 daughter. Education: BSc, 1963, PhD, 1966, DSc, 1983, Queen's University, Belfast, Northern Ireland. Appointments: Scientific, 1966-69, Senior Scientific, 1969-73, Principal Scientific, 1973-77, Officer, Department of Agriculture, Northern Ireland; Assistant Lecturer, 1967-71, Lecturer, 1971-75, Senior Lecturer, 1975-77, Reader, 1977, Queen's University, Belfast; Senior Lecturer, 1978-81, Associate Professor, 1981-2001, University of Sydney, Australia; Research Director, Poultry Research Foundation, University of Sydney, 1978-2001; Honorary Governor, Poultry Research Foundation, University of Sydney, 2001-; Adjunct Professor, North Carolina State University, 1995-2005; Visiting Fellow, Cornell University, 1989. Publications: Approximately 150 scientific papers in professional journals; Over 200 conference and trade publications. Honours: Recipient, World's Poultry Science Association Australia Poultry Award, 1998. Memberships: Poultry Science Association Inc. Address: 26 Valley View Drive, Narellan, New South Wales, 2567 Australia. E-mail: derickbalnave@bigpond.com

BALOUET Jean-Christophe, b. France. Environmental Expert. Education: Graduate, Earth Sciences, University Paris VI, 1981; Degree of Advanced Studies, Evolutionary Biology and Genetics, University Paris VII, 1982; Doctorate, Earth Sciences, University Paris VI, Jussieu/La Sorbonne, 1984. Appointments: Research Scientist, National Museum of Natural History, Paris, and University Paris VI, 1978-86; Post Doctorate Scientist, Smithsonian Institution, Washington DC, 1984-86; Consultant, United Nations Environment Program, 1989-94; Manager, Environment International, 1993-. Publications: 43 scientific publications; 14 international newsletters; 26 books; 7 book chapters; 12 book adaptions; 3 publications pending. Honours: Fondation Singer Polignac, 1979; Compagnie Française des Pétroles, 1980; Fondation de la Vocation, 1980; Académie de Sciences, Paris, 1983; Academia dei Lincei, Rome, 1984; Government of New Caledonia, 1984; American Government, Smithsonian Institute, 1985/86; Prix Litteraire F Sommer, 1988; Fondation, Ushuaia, 1992; Society of Automotive Engineers, Standards Development Program, Aerospace Branch, Certificate of Appreciation, 2003, 2005; Listed in international biographical dictionaries. Memberships: International Society of Environmental Forensics; Pollution Investigation by Trees; Aerospace Medical Association; ASTM E60; International Society of Automotive Engineers; ASHRAE; President Planet CO2. Address: 2 ruelle du Hamet, 60129 Orrouy, France. E-mail: jcbalouet@aol.com

BALTĂ Petru, b. 22 January 1930, Republic Moldova. University Professor. m. Eugenia Cristea, 1 son. Education: Diplomat Chemist Engineer, Faculty of Industrial Chemistry, University Politehnica of Bucharest, 1952; PhD, University Politehnica, Bucharest, 1960; Honorary Member, Romanian Academy of Technical Sciences, ASTR, 2005. Appointments: Teacher, UPB, 1956-, Professor, 1971-, Consulting Professor, 2000-, Deputy Dean, Faculty of Industrial Chemistry, 1967-72, Head of Chair, Science and Engineering, of Oxidic Materials, 1980-96, Co-ordinator, European TEMPUS Program 2820, 1991-94, University Politehnica, Bucharest; Head of Research Laboratory, Structure and Properties of Silicates, Institute of Inorganic Chemistry, Romanian Academy, 1964-72; President, Department of Oxide Materials, Romanian Association of Engineers, 1981-88. Publications: Over 150 articles in professional journals,1954-; 5 books, including Introduction to the Physics and Chemistry of the Vitreous State, 1971 in Romanian, 1976 in English, 1983 in Chinese, 1992 in Korean; Glass Technology, 1966 and 1984; Energetic of Glass Elaboration, 1985. Honours: Evidenced University Professor, MEI, 1987; Gradation of Merit, University Politehnica, Bucharest, 1998; Diploma of Honor, TEMPUS activity, 2001; Diploma of Excellency, University Politehnica, Bucharest, 2002 and 2008; Diploma of Honor, Romanian Society of Chemistry, 2004; Grant of Merit, Romanian Ministry of Education, 2005. Memberships: Founding and Council Member, Balkan Society of Glass Science and Technology; Council Member, European Society of Glass Science and Technology ESG; President, Romanian Association of Glass; Member, Romanian Society of Ceramics; Romanian Society of Chemistry; Romanian Society of Chemical Engineering.

BALTAS Nicholas Constantinos, b. 20 August 1946, Kastania, Evrytania, Greece. Professor of Economics. m. Maria (Tsamboula) Balta, 1 son, 1 daughter. Education: Athens School of Economics and Business Science, Department of Economics, 1965-70; MSoc Sc, 1970-72, PhD, 1972-74, University of Birmingham. Appointments: Research Assistant, Department of Econometrics and Social Statistics, University of Birmingham, 1972; Lecturer, Economics, British Institute of Marketing, 1975-76; Lecturer, Econometrics, Department of Economics, Aristotelion University of Thessaloniki, 1976-79; Senior Economist, Research and Planning Division, Agricultural Bank of Greece, 1976-1986; Associate Professor of Economics, 1985-90, Professor of Economics, 1990-, Head of Department, 1999-2003, Athens University of Economics and Business, Department of Economics; Expert, Ministry of Agriculture, Greece, 2002-03; Expert, European Commission (DGRTD and DG TREN), 2002-03; Expert, Economic and Social Committee, Greece, 2003 and 2004; Chairman of the Board of Directors and Managing Director, Hellenic Railways, 2004-07; Vice-President, Board of Directors, Centre of Greek Public Enterprises and Organisations, 2005-08; Chairman, Board of Directors of the Community Support Framework of Management Organisation Unit, 2007-10; Board of Directors, Agricultural Bank of Greece. Publications include: Books and Research Monographs: Development Strategy and Investment in the Processing and Marketing of Agricultural Products, 2001; Co-editor, The Global Economics of a Changing Environment, 2009; Numerous journals, book chapters and conference proceedings and articles including: Investment in the Greek Processing of Agricultural Products and Food: A Panel Data Approach, 2007; An Analysis of Investment Activity in the Greek Agricultural Products and Food Manufacturing Sector, 2008; Cost Structure Efficiency and Productivity in Hellenic Railways, 2008; Rail Infrastructure Charging in Hellenic Railways, 2011; Book review: The Greek Economy: Sources of Growth in the Postwar Era, 1993. Honours: Fulbright Scholarship, 1991; British Council Scholarship, 1993; Jean Monnet Chair: EU Institutions and Economic Policy, 1999. Memberships include: Hellenic University Association for European Studies, President, 1999-2000 and 2002-03; European Community Studies Association; The Agricultural Economics Society; Greek Agricultural Economic Society; Hellenic Economic Association, Hellenic Operational Research Society; Athenian Policy Forum; European Summer Academy. Address: Athens University of Economics and Business, 76 Patission Str, 104 34 Athens, Greece. E-mail: baltas@aueb.gr

BALTAY Charles, b. 15 April 1937, Budapest, Hungary. Professor. m. Virginia Rohan, 4 sons, 1 daughter. Education: BSc, Union College, 1958; MSc, Yale University, 1959; PhD, Yale University, 1963. Appointments: Professor of Physics, Columbia University, 1964-88; Higgins Professor of Physics,

Yale University, 1988-. Publications; 3 books; 300 journal articles. Honours: Director, Nevis Laboratory, Columbia University, 1976-88; Chairman, Physics Department, Yale University, 1995-2001. Memberships: Fellow, American Physical Society Sigma Xi. Address: 86 Lower Road, Guilford, CT 06437, USA. E-mail: charles.baltay@yale.edu

BALZHINIMAEVA Darima Baldorzhievna, b. 5 September 1970, Chita, Russia. Doctor of Medicine. m. Ngawang Tenzin, 2 sons, 1 daughter. Education: Medical Doctor, Chita State Medical Academy, 1994; Doctor of Internal Medicine, Irkutsk Medical University, 2004, 2009; Naturopathic Doctor's certificate, 2005; Pharmacy, Tibetan Medical & Astro Institute, 2005; Doctor of Tibetan Medicine, India; MSc, Health Policy and Management, Brandeis University, USA, 2011. Appointments: Doctor, 1994-2004, Head, 2004-09, Centre of Oriential Medicine; Founder and Director, Dr Duparett Health Care Centre, 2011-. Publications: Numerous articles in professional journals. Honours: Local awards, Ford Foundation Fellowship; Woman 2011, American Biographical Institute. Memberships: International AIDS Society. Address: 4 Krasnoflotskaya Street, Apt 58, Ulan-Ude, Buryatia, 670033, Russia. E-mail: darima970@gmail.com

BAMBER Juliette Madeleine, b. 21 August 1930, Tidworth, England. Writer; Artist; Occupational Therapist; Counsellor. m. Donald Liddle, 1957, divorced 1972, 2 sons. Education: Art School, Foundation Course, 1947-49; Psychology, Honours, Birkbeck College, 1957-60. Publications: Breathing Space, 1991; On the Edge, 1993; Altered States, 1995; Touch Paper, 1996; The Ring of Words, 1996; The Wasting Game, 1997; The Long Pale Corridor, 1998; Flying Blind, 2000; 5 collections of poetry. Honours: 1st Prize, London Writers; 1st Prize, National Poetry Foundation; A Blue Nose Poet of the Year, 1998; Commended in Houseman Prize, 2000. Memberships: Highgate Poets; British Association of Occupational Therapists. Address: 9 Western Road, East Finchley, London N2 9JB, England.

BANA Eric, b. 9 August 1968, Melbourne, Australia. Actor. m. Rebecca Gleeson, 1997, 1 son, 1 daughter. Education: National Institute of Dramatic Art, Sydney, Australia. Career: Barman; Comedian; Actor: TV: Full Frontal, 1993; Eric, 1996, 1997; Something in the Air, 2000; Love The Beast, 2009; Films: The Castle, 1997; Chopper, 2000; Black Hawk Down, 2001; The Nugget, 2002; Finding Nemo (voice), 2003; Hulk, 2003; Troy, 2004; Munich, 2005; Romulus My Father, Lucky You, 2007; The Other Boleyn Girl, Mary and Max, Star Trek, 2008; The Time Traveller's Wife, Funny People, 2009. Honours: Logie Award, 1997; Best Actor, Australian Film Institute Award, 2001.

BANARASI Das, b. 16 October 1955, Akorhi, Mirzapur, India. Teacher; Poet. m. Vimala Devi, 10 March 1972, 1 son. Education: Sahityacharya (Equivalent to MA in Sanskrit), 1982; BTC, 1988; MA, Hindi Literature, 1993. Appointments: Headmaster, Government Basic School, Mirzapur, India. Publications: Srihanumadvandana, 1982; Srivindhyavasinicharitamrit, 1989; Sriashtabhujakathamanjari, 1991; Paryavarankaumudi in Sanskrit, Hindi, English, 1993; Utsarg, 1995; Hymn to Lord (Hanuman), 1995; Gandhari, 1996; Adyatan, 1997; Silver Poems, 1998. Contributions to: Poet International, Anthologised in Poems 96, World Poetry, 1996-2000. Honours: Sanskrit Literature Award, Uttar Pradesh Government Sanskrit Academy, 1995; Gram Ratna Award by Gram Panchayat Akorhi, Mirzapur, 1996; Winged Word Award, International Socio-Literary Foundation, 1997. Address: s/o Srimolai, Village-Post Akorhi, District, Mirzapur 231307, UP, India.

BANAT Mohamed, b. 15 July 1949, Algeria. Company Vice-President; Scientific Consultant; Professor. m. Yoko Matsuda, 2 sons. Education: Bachelor's Degree, Physics, University of Algiers, 1972; DEA's Degree, Physics, University of Toulouse, France, 1973; PhD, Physics, with special honours, University Paul Sabatier, Toulouse, France, 1975; DSc, with special honours, National Polytechnic Institute, Toulouse, France, 1985. Appointments: Researcher Scientist, IMFT/CNRS, Toulouse, France, 1980-85, Tokyo Institute of Technology, Japan, 1986-87; Consultant Scientist, Tokyo, Japan, 1987-88; Visiting Scientist, Tsukuba University, Japan, 1988-90; Senior Consultant Scientist, R&D Project Leader, Tokyo, 1990-99; R&D Project Supervisor, Riken/Science and Technology Agency, Japan, 1999-2000; Vice-President, Bell-Consulting Ltd, Tokyo, 1999-; R&D Consultant to numerous companies and institutions including: Mitsubishi-Atomic-Power-Industry, Japan Gasoline Corporation, Nuclear Fuel Industry. Publications include: Original Results related to the interfacial-turbulence physical phenomena (in the physics of fluids), 1992; Discovery of the mechanism of the void-drift phenomena in thermalhydraulics with the down stream applications for the power and process industries, 1995. Honours: Special Honours PhD and DSc; Visiting Scientist, Long Term Invited Distinguished Scientists Programme, Tsukuba University, Japan, 1988-90; Listed in Who's Who publications and biographical dictionaries. Memberships: American Society of Mechanical Engineers; Japan Society of Mechanical Engineers.

BANATVALA Jangu, b. 7 January 1934, London, England. Doctor of Medicine. m. Roshan Mugaseth, 3 sons, 1 daughter, deceased. Education: Gonville and Caius College, Cambridge; The London Hospital Medical College; Fulbright Fellow, Department of Epidemiology and Health, Yale University, USA. Appointments: Polio Fund Research Fellow, Department of Pathology, University of Cambridge, 1961-64; Research Fellow, Department of Epidemiology and Health, University of Yale, 1964-65; Senior Lecturer and Reader, 1965-75, Professor, Clinical Virology, Honorary Consultant to the Hospitals (NHS trusts), 1975-99, St Thomas' Hospital Medical School later United Medical and Dental Schools of Guy's and St Thomas' Hospitals; Registrar, 1985-87, Vice President, 1987-90, Royal College of Pathologists; Honorary Consultant Microbiologist to the Army, 1992-97; Chairman, Department of Health Advisory Group on Hepatitis, 1990-98; Emeritus Professor, Clinical Virology, Guy's King's and St Thomas' School of Medicine and Dentistry, 1999-. Publications include: About 250 peer reviewed original papers published in General Medical journals and specialist Medical Journals; 50 Editorials for Lancet and BMJ; 30 Chapters in books; Editor, 3 books including Editions 1-6 of Principles and Practice of Clinical Virology (joint editor); Various reports on blood borne virus infections for Royal Colleges of Pathologists, Senate of Surgery, Cl Br Ireland and Royal College of Surgeons and Obstetrics in Gynaecology. Honours: Lionel Whitby Medal, University of Cambridge, 1964; Founder Member, Academy of Medical Sciences, 1998; CBE, 1999; Listed in biographical dictionary. Memberships: Council of Governors, Forrest School, London, Mill Hill School, London; President, European Association Against Virus Diseases, 1981-83; Freeman, City of London, 1987; Council of the Medical Defence Union, 1987-2003; Liveryman, Society of Apothecaries, 1986; Athenaeum; MCC; Leander, Henley on Thames; Honorary member,

Hawks, Cambridge. Address: Church End, Henham, Bishops Stortford, Hertfordshire, CM22 6AN, England. E-mail: jangu@btopenworld.com

BANDARA Thennakoon Mudiyanselage Wijendra Jayalath, b. 11 July 1968, Ettempitiya, Sri Lanka. Senior Lecturer. m. Chamisha de Silva, 2 daughters. Education: BSc (special honours), 1996; Master of Philosophy, 2001; PhD, 2010. Appointments: Assistant Lecturer, University of Ruhuna, Sri Lanka; Senior Lecturer, Rajarata University, Sri Lanka. Publications: Numerous articles in professional journals. Honours: Sri Lanka President's Research Award. Address: Highland Nursery, Badulla Road, Bandarawela, Sri Lanka. E-mail: awijendr@yahoo.com

BANDERAS Antonio, b. 10 August 1960, Málaga, Spain. Film Actor. m. (1) Anna Leza, divorced, (2) Melanie Griffith, 1996, 1 child. Appointments: Began acting aged 14; Performed with National Theatre, Madrid, 6 years; Films include: Labyrinth of Passion; El Senor Galindez; El Caso Almeria; The Stilts; 27 Hours; Law of Desire; Matador; Tie Me Up! Tie Me Down!; Woman on the Verge of a Nervous Breakdown; The House of Spirits; Interviews with the Vampire; Philadelphia; The Mambo King; Love and Shadow; Miami Rhapsody; Young Mussolini; Return of Mariaolu; Assassins; Desperado; Evita; Never Talk to Strangers; Crazy in Alabama (director); The 13th Warrior; Dancing in the Dark, The Body, 2000; Spy Kids, 2001; Femme Fatale, Frida, Spy Kids 2: Island of Lost Dreams, 2002; Spy Kids 3-D: Game Over, Once Upon a Time in Mexico, Imagining Argentina, 2003; Shrek II(voice), 2004; Legend of Zorro, 2005; Take the Lead, Bordertown, 2006; Shrek the Third, 2007; My Mom's New Boyfriend, The Other Man, 2008; Thick as Thieves, 2009. Address: c/o CAA, 9830 Wilshire Boulevard, Beverley Hills, CA 90212, USA.

BANERJEE Pushan, b. 20 December 1975, Kolkata, India. Professor. Education: MSc, Physics, University of Calcutta (Kolkata), 1999; Master of Technology, Energy Science & Technology, Jadavpur University, Kolkata, 2002; PhD, Engineering, Jadavpur University, Kolkata, 2008. Appointments: UGC-Project Fellow, 2002-03; CSIR Senior Research Fellow, 2003-07; CSIR Research Associate, 2007-10; Assistant Professor, Physics, Vidyasagar Evening College, Kolkata, 2010-. Publications: 16 articles in international refereed journals. Honours: Listed in international biographical dictionaries. Memberships: Life Member, Indian Association for the Cultivation of Science. Address: 85 PWD Road, Kolkata 700108, India. E-mail: b_pushan@rediffmail.com

BANG Jae-Wook, b. 28 June 1948, Seoul, Korea. Professor. m. Hei-Kyung Yeum, 1 son, 1 daughter. Education: BS, 1975, MS, 1977, Biology, PhD, Botany, 1984, Seoul National University, Korea. Appointments: Assistant Professor, Mokp National University, Mokpo, Korea, 1981-86; Professor, Chungnam National University, Daejeon, Korea, 1986-; Visiting Scientist, Rothamsted Experimental Station, UK, 1988-89; Visiting Professor, Texas A&M University, Texas, USA, 1999-2000. Publications: 110 published articles; 180 scientific presentations; 16 books. Honours: Outstanding Teaching Award, Chungnam National University, 2004. Memberships: Korean Association of Biological Sciences; The Genetic Society of Korea; Korean Society of Medicinal Crop Science. Address: Department of Biology, Chungnam National University, 220 Kung-dong, Yuseong-Ku, Daejeon 305-764, Korea. E-mail: bangjw@cnu.ac.kr

BANG Je-Sung, b. 23 July 1973, Incheon, Korea. Researcher. Education: BS, Aerospace Engineering, Inha University, 1999; MS, Mechanical and Aerospace Engineering, Seoul National University, 2002. Appointments: Senior Engineer, Electronics PLM Business Team, Samsung SDS, 2002-04; Senior Researcher, Systems Engineering Research Division, Korea Institute of Machinery & Materials, 2005-. Publications: Integration of PDM System and Web-Based CAE Supporting System for Small and Medium Enterprise, 2007; An Automation of Fatigue Durability Analysis for Welded Bogie Frame Using Multi-Agent Based Engineering Framework, 2006; Characteristic analysis of electrodynamic suspension device with permanent magnet Halbach Array, 2009. Honours: Listed in international biographical dictionaries. Memberships: American Society for Mechanical Engineers. Address: Korea Institute of Machinery & Materials, 171 Jang-dong, Yuseong-gu, Daejeon 305-343, Korea. E-mail: jsbang@kimm.re.kr

BANGAARI Ashish, b. 11 September 1978, New Delhi, India. Consultant Anaesthesiologist. Education: MBBS, University College of Medical Sciences and Guru Teg Bahadur Hospital, Delhi, 2000; MD, Anaesthesia & Critical Care, Postgraduate Institute of Medical Education & Research, 2005. Appointments: Intern, University College of Medical Sciences and Guru Teg Bahadur Hospital, Delhi, 2001; Junior Resident (MD), 2003-05, Senior Resident, 2006, Postgraduate Institute of Medical Education & Research, Chandigarh, India; Consultant Anaesthesiologist, MIOT Hospitals, 2006-. Publications: Numerous articles in professional journals. Honours: KC Mahindra Scholarship, 1995; MN Kapur Gold Medal, 1996; First Prize, Technology in Anaesthesia & Intensive Care, 2005; Excellence Performance Award, MIOT Hospitals, 2007; Listed in biographical dictionaries. Memberships: India Society of Anaesthesiologists; Delhi Medical Council Registration. Address:

BANGERTER Michael, b. Brighton, England. Actor; Playwright; Lecturer; Freelance Tutor; Poet. m. Katya Wyeth, 8 May 1971, 1 son, 1 daughter. Education: Graduate Diploma, RADA, Teaching Certificate, Certificate in Advanced Writing; MA, Lancaster. Appointments: Actor in many television, film and theatre productions; Playwright in theatre and radio; Freelance Reviewer, Senior Tutor and Assessor, Open College of the Arts, 1999-2005; Literary Consultant, Oxford Literary Consultancy. Publications: A Far Line of Hills, 1996; Freezing the Frame, 2001; Eyelines, 2002; Post Scripts, 2005; The Fat Lady Sings, 2006. Contributions to: Envoi; Pause; Iota; Blithe Spirit; Pennine Platform; New Hope International Writing; Others; CDs: Dancing Bears, 2002 (Poetry and Music); Passions and Phantoms (Hardy Voice and Music), 2003. Honour: Award Winner, Kent and Sussex National Open Competition, 1991. Memberships: Union of University and College Teachers; British Haiku Society; Poetry Society. Address: Botriphnie Stables, Drummuir, Keith, Banffshire AB55 5JE, England.

BANKA Baldeo Prasad, b. 2 June 1948, Calcutta, India. Director. m. Manju Devi, 1973, 1 daughter. Education: Master of Commerce, 1971, Bachelor of Law, 1973, Calcutta University. Appointments: Sahu Jain Services Ltd, India, 1965-74; Jay Engineering Works, India, 1974-81; Director, PT Ispat Indo, Indonesia, 1981-; Director, Indo Investments Pte Ltd, Singapore, 2008-. Honours: Best Executive Award, Asian Programme Consultants, Jakarta, 1996. Memberships: Rotary Foundation/Club; Association of Iron and Steel Technology,

USA; Steel Association, Indonesia; Chamber of Commerce, Indonesia. Address: Ispat Indo PT, Taman Sidoarjo, P O Box 1083, Surabaya, Indonesia. E-mail: bankabp@bankanet.net

BANKS Alicia, b. 10 August 1963, Chicago, USA. Educator; Columnist; Radio Producer; Host. Education: BA, University of Illinois at Urbana-Champaign, 1984; MA, University of Arkansas at Little Rock, 2001; Arkansas Teacher's License, Arkansas Department of Education, 2006. Appointments: Educator, Columnist; Administrative Team Medical Network. Publications: Eloquent Fury & Outlook. Honours: UIUC Black Alumni Association Potential Leadership Award, 1982; UIUC 5.0 GPA Award, 1982; UIUC Black Alumni Association Earl Dickerson Achievement Award, 1983; UIUC Dean's List, 1984; UIUC Senior 100 Honorary, 1984; Outstanding Young Woman of America, 1986; Trailblazer Award, University of Illinois at Urbana-Champaign, 1996; Summa Cum Laude, University of Arkansas at Little Rock MAIOC, 2001; Listed in international biographical dictionaries. Address: POB 55596, Little Rock, Arkansas 72215, USA. E-mail: ambwww@yahoo.com Website: www.aliciabanks.xanga.com

BANKS Iain, b. 16 February 1954, Fife, Scotland. Author. m. 1992. Education: Stirling University. Appointments: Technician, British Steel, 1976; IBM, Greenock, 1978. Publications: The Wasp Factory, 1984; Walking on Glass, 1985; The Bridge, 1986; Espedair Street, 1987; Canal Dreams, 1989; The Crow Road (adapted as TV series, 1996), 1992; Complicity, 1993; Whit, 1995; Science Fiction: Consider Phlebas, 1987; The Player of Games, 1988; Use of Weapons, 1990; The State of the Art, 1991; Against a Dark Background, 1993; Feersum Endjinn, 1994; Excession, 1996; A Song of Stone, 1998; Inversions, 1998; The Business, 1999; Look to Windward, 2000; Dead Air, 2002; Raw Spirit: In Search of the Perfect Dram, 2003; The Algebraist, 2004; The Steep Approach to Goarbadale, 2007; Matter, 2008; Transition, 2009. Honours: British Science Fiction Association Best Novel, 1997; Hon DUniv, Stirling, 1997, St Andrews, 1997; Hon DLitt, Napier, 2003. Address: c/o Little, Brown, Brettenham House, Lancaster Place, London, WC2E 7EN, England.

BANKS Russell, b. 28 March 1940, Barnstead, USA. Author. m. (1) Darlene Bennett, divorced, 1962, 1 daughter, (2) Mary Gunst, divorced 1977, 3 daughters, (3) Kathy Walton, divorced 1988, (4) Chase Twichell. Education: Colgate University; University of North Carolina, Chapel Hill. Appointments: Teacher, Creative Writing, Emerson College, Boston; University of New Hampshire, Durham; University of Alabama; New England College; Teacher, Creative Writing, Princeton University, 1982-97; President, Parliament Internationale des Ecrivains, 2001-. Publications: Waiting to Freeze, 1967; 30/6, 1969; Snow; Meditation of a Cautious Man in Winter, 1974; Novels: Family Life, 1975; Hamilton Stark, 1978; The Book of Jamaica, 1980; The Relation of My Imprisonment, 1984; Continental Drift, 1985; Affliction, 1989; The Sweet Hereafter, 1991; Rule of the Bone, 1995; Cloudsplitter, 1998; The Darling, 2004; The Reserve, 2008; Non-fiction: Invisible Stranger, 1998; Dreaming Up America, 2008; Collected Short Stories; Searching for Survivors, 1975; The New World, 1978; Trailerpark, 1981; Success Stories, 1986; The Angel on the Roof, 2000; Short Stories in literary magazines. Honours: Best American Short Stories Awards, 1971, 1985; Fels Award for Fiction, 1974; O Henry Awards, 1975; St Lawrence Award for Fiction, 1976; Guggenheim Fellowship, 1976; National Endowment for the Arts Fellowship, 1977, 1983; John Dos Passos Award, 1985; American Academy of Arts and Letters Award, 1985. Address: 1000 Park Avenue, New York, NY 10028, USA.

BANKS William McKerrell, b. 28 March 1943, Dreghorn, Ayrshire, Scotland. Professor of Engineering. m. Martha Ruthven Hair, 3 sons. Education: BSc (1st class honours), 1965, MSc, 1966, PhD, 1977, Mechanical Engineering, Strathclyde University; FIMechE, 1987; FIMMM, 1993. Appointments: Indentured Senior Student Apprenticeship, Glacier Metal Co Ltd, 1961-65; Senior Research Engineer, G & J Weir Ltd, 1966; Teacher, Solid Mechanics; Teacher, specialist courses in Composite Materials and Structures for Industry in the context of Continuing Professional Development in the UK, Russia, Singapore, China, Greece and Norway; Research work on the structural exploitation of composites; Former Director, Centre for Advanced Structural Materials; Past President, Institution of Mechanical Engineers. Publications: Over 175 research papers; 80 reports for industry; Numerous book reviews, invited lectures and seminar presentations. Memberships: Fellow, Royal Academy of Engineering; Fellow, Royal Society of Edinburgh. Address: 19 Dunure Drive, Hamilton, ML3 9EY, Scotland.

BANNISTER Roger G (Sir), b. 23 March 1929, London, England. Athlete; Consultant Physician; Neurologist; University Administrator. m. Moyra Elver Jacobsson, 2 sons, 2 daughters. Education: University College School Exeter; Merton College; Oxford St Mary's Hospital, Medical School, London. Appointments: Winner, Oxford and Cambridge Mile, 1947-50; President, Oxford University, Athletic Club, 1948; British Mile Champion, 1951, 1953, 1954; World Record One Mile, 1954; First Sub Four Minute Mile, 1954; Master Pembroke College, Oxford, 1985-93; Honorary Consultant Neurologist, St Mary's Hospital, Medical School, National Hospital for Neurology and Neurosurgery, London (non-executive director); London and Oxford District and Region; Chair, St Mary's Hospital Development Trust; Chair, Government Working Group on Sport in the Universities, 1995-97; Chair, Clinical Autonomic Research Society, 1982-84. Publications: First Four Minutes, 1955 (republished as 50th Anniversary Edition, 2004); Editor, Brain and Bannister's Clinical Neurology, 1992; Autonomic Failure (co-editor), 1993; Various Medical Articles on Physiology and Neurology. Honours: Honorary Fellow, Exeter College, Oxford, 1950; Merton College, Oxford, 1986; Honorary Fellow, UMIST, 1974; Honorary LLD, Liverpool, 1972; Honorary DSc, Sheffield, 1978; Grinnell, 1984; Bath, 1984; Rochester, 1986; Williams, 1987; Dr hc, Jvvaskyla, Finland; Honorary MD, Pavia, 1986; Honorary DL, University of Victoria, Canada, 1994; University of Wales, Cardiff, 1995; Loughborough, 1996; University of East Anglia, 1997; Hans-Heinrich Siegbert Prize, 1977. Memberships: Physiological Society; Medical Research Society; Association of British Neurologists; Fellow, Imperial College; Leeds Castle Foundation, 1988-; St Mary's Hospital Medical School Trust, 1994-; First Lifetime Award, American Academy of Neurology, 2005. Address: 21 Bardwell Road, Oxford, OX2 6SU, England.

BARAŃSKI Andrzej, b. 31 October 1934, Wilno, Poland. Chemist. m. Barbara Reiss, 1961, 2 sons. Education: Master, Chemistry, 1955, Doctor, Natural Sciences, 1961, Habilitated Doctor of Physical Chemistry, 1965, Jagiellonian University, Krakow, Poland. Appointments: Assistant, 1955-62, Adjunct, 1962-63, Institute of Fertilizers, Tarnow, Poland; Adjunct, 1963-65, Assistant Professor, 1965-75, Associate Professor, 1975-87, Full Professor, 1987-, Emeritus Professor, 2005-, Director, Regional Laboratory of Physicochemical Analyses and Structural Research, 1972-95, Jagiellonian University, Krakow; Postdoctoral Fellow, National Research Council, Kinetics and Catalysis Laboratory, Ottawa, 1968-70; Visitor, Haldor Topsoe Research Laboratories, Copenhagen, 1974;

Plenipotentiary of Jagiellonian University Rector to Acid Paper Governmental Programme, 2001-08; Responsible for implementation of books deacidification technology in South Poland, 2005-06. Publications: Co-author: Physical Chemistry, 1980; Catalysis on Zeolites, 1988; Ageing and Stabilisation of Paper, 2005; Over 100 articles in professional journals. Honours: Research Awards, Polish Minister of Higher Education, 1973, 1974, 1985; J Furgal Award, Utica College of Syracuse University, New York, 1992; Rodziewicz-Bielewicz Award, Academy of Mining & Metallurgy, Krakow, 1996. Memberships: Polish Chemical Society; Polish Catalysis Club. E-mail: baranski@chemia.uj.edu.pl

BARANYI László, b. 23 November 1951, Jászapáti, Hungary. Professor. m. Robin Lee Nagano, 1 son, 2 daughters. Education: M Eng, 1975, Doctor's degree, 1980, University of Miskolc; Candidate of Technical Science, PhD, Hungarian Academy of Sciences, 1990. Appointments: Researcher, MMG, Automation Works, Budapest, 1975-77; Researcher, 1977-79, Lecturer, 1979-83, Senior Lecturer, 1983-91, Vice Dean, Faculty of Mechanical Engineering, 1991-94, Associate Professor, 1991-95, 1997-2009, Professor, 2009-, University of Miskolc; Associate Professor, Nagaoka University of Technology, Japan, 1995-97. Publications: Papers and articles in professional scientific journals. Honours: Jubilee Faculty Medal, University of Miskolc, 1999; Széchenyi Professor's Scholarship, 1998-2001; University Award for Outstanding Research, 2009. Memberships: Hungarian Committee of IUTAM; Committee of Fluid and Heat Engineering, Hungarian Academy of Sciences, 1999-. Address: Department of Fluid and Heat Engineering, University of Miskolc, Miskolc, Egyetemváros, H-3515, Hungary. E-mail: arambl@uni-miskolc.hu

BARASSI Ron (Ronald Dale), b. 27 February 1936. Public Speaker; Retired Australian Rules Football Player. m. (1) Nancy Kellet, 2 sons, 1 daughter, (2) Cherryl Copeland, 1980. Education: Guildford State School; Castlemaine and Preston Technical College; Footscray Institute of Technology; RMIT. Appointments: Australian Rules Football Player, 1953-64, Leading Goalkicker, 1958-59, Club Captain, 6 Premierships, 1960-64, Best & Fairest, 1961, 1964, Melbourne FC; Played for Victoria, 1956, 1958-63, Captain, 1961; All-Australian Team, 1956 and 1958, Captain, 1961; Captain/Coach, Carlton FC, 1965-68, Coach, 1969-71, 2 Premierships, 1968, 1970, Coach, North Melbourne FC, 1973-80, 2 Premierships, 1975, 1977; Captain/Coach, Australian Irish Football team, 1967-68; Business Proprietor, 1969-77; Coached Victoria 1969, 1971, 1977, 1978; Public Speaker, 1976-; Coach, Melbourne FC, 1981-85; Coach, Sydney Swans FC, 1993-95; Coached over 500 VFL/AFL games; Director, Sport Australia Hall of Fame, 2002-; Member, Advisory Board, AFL Foundation, 2003-. Honours: Member of Order of Australia (AM), 1978; Inducted Sport Australia Hall of Fame, 1987, elevated to Legend, 2006; Ambassador for the Republican Movement, 1994; Senior Citizen of the Year, 1994; Inducted and elevated to Legend, AFL Hall of Fame, Named in AFL Team of the Century, 1996; Centenary Medal, 2003; Subject of Bronze Statue unveiled MCG, 2003; Australian Sports Medal, ASM, 2000; Torchbearer, Olympic Games, Sydney, 2000; Legend, MFC Hall of Fame, 2003; "Walked on water" as Torchbearer, Opening Ceremony, Commonwealth Games, 2006; Healthy Ageing Citizen of the Year, 2006; Melburnian of the Year, 2006; Melbourne FC No 1 Ticketholder, 2009-; Knight of the Order of St Thomas of Acre (KStT), Victorian of the Year, 2009; AFL Coaching Legend, 2010. Memberships: Life Member: AFL; Melbourne FC; Carlton FC; North Melbourne FC; Sydney Swans FC; Melbourne Cricket Club; Carbine

(Melb); Lords Taverners; Vingt Cinq; RACV. Address: Saxton Speakers Bureau, Suite 4/Level 4, 695 Burke Road, Camberwell, VIC 3124, Australia.

BARBANTI Sergio, Ambassador. Education: Law (magna cum laude), La Sapienza University, Rome and University of Edinburgh, Scotland. Appointments: Directorate for Economic Issues, 1987-90, Deputy Director for Africa, Head of Mission for Negotiations in the Paris Club, Directorate General for Political Affairs, 1994-98, Ministry of Foreign Affairs, Italy; Deputy Chief of Mission, Harare, Zimbabwe, 1990-94; Counsellor for Press and Information, and Representative to the Organization of American States, Italian Embassy in Washington, 1994-98; Deputy Director, Directorate for NATO; Diplomatic Advisor to the Minister for Public Administration, Government of Italy, 2002-04; Consul General, Madrid; Ambassador of Italy to Montenegro, 2009-13. Honours: High State Honours of the Republic of Italy, Commendatore dell'Ordine al Merito della Repubblica Italiana.

BARBARA John Anthony James, b. 2 April 1946, Cairo, Egypt (British). Transfusion Microbiologist. m. Gillian, 1 son, 1 daughter. Education: BA (Hons) Natural Sciences, Trinity College, Cambridge, 1968; MSc, Medical School, Birmingham University, 1969; MA, Cantab, PhD, Department of Microbiology, Reading University, 1972. Appointments: Lecturer, Department of Virology, Reading University, 1972-74; Examiner, Oxford University, GCE A Level Biology, 1974-85; Head of Microbiology, North London Blood Transfusion Centre, 1974-96; Honorary Associate Research Fellow, Brunel University, Middlesex, 1984-90; Open University Research Student Supervisor, 1988-99; Lead Scientist in Microbiology, London and South East Zone, 1996-2000; Principal, Transfusion Microbiology National Laboratories and Microbiology Consultant, 2000-06, Emeritus Consultant, 2006-, National Blood Authority; External Examiner, Bristol University, 2003-05; Visiting Professor, University of West of England, 2004. Publications: Over 300 papers, chapters, abstracts and reviews. Honours: Hong Kong Red Cross Foundation Lecturer, 1996; Kenneth Goldsmith memorial prize of the BBTS, 1991; Iain Cook Memorial Award of the SNBTS, 2002; Gold Medal of the BBTS, 2003; Oliver Memorial Award, 2003; International Society of Blood Transfusion Award, 2005; Medal, Polish Association of Haematology and Transfusion Medicine, 2005. Memberships: Institute of Biology; Past President, British Blood Transfusion Society; American Association of Blood Banks, -2006; Past Vice President, International Society of Blood Transfusion; Royal College of Pathologists; Association of Clinical Microbiologists. Address: National Transfusion Microbiology Laboratories, National Blood Service, North London, Colindale Avenue, London NW9 5BG, England. E-mail: john.barbara@nhsbt.nhs.uk Website: www.blood.co.uk

BARBER Francis, b. 13 May 1957, Wolverhampton, England. Actress. Education: Bangor University; Cardiff University. Appointments: Hull Truck Theatre Company; Glasgow Citizens Theatre; Tricycle Theatre; RSC; TV appearances include: Clem Jack Story; Home Sweet Home; Flame to the Phoenix; Reilly; Ace of Spies; Those Glory Glory Days; Hard Feelings; Behaving Badly; The Nightmare Year; Real Women; Just in Time; The Ice House; Dalziel & Pascoe; Plastic Man; Love in a Cold Climate; The Legend of the Tamworth Two, Trial and Retribution VIII, 2004; Marple: A Murder Is Announced, Funland, The IT Crowd, 2005; The Royal, 2009-; Film Appearances include: The Missionary, 1982; A Zed and Two Noughts; White City Castaway; Prick Up

Your Ears; Sammy and Rosie Get Laid; We Think the World of You; The Grasscutter; Separate Bedrooms; Young Soul Rebels; Secret Friends; The Lake; Soft Top, Hard Shoulder; The Fish Tale; Three Steps to Heaven; Photographing Fairies; Shiner; Still Crazy; Esther Kahn; Mauvaise passe; 24 heures de la vie d'une femme, Flyfishing, 2002; Boudica, 2003; Evilenko, His Passionate Bride, 2004; Suzie Gold, 2004; King Lear, 2008; Stage appearances include: Night of the Iguana; Pygmalion; Closer; Uncle Vanya; Antony and Cleopatra; The Seagull; King Lear; many others. Honours: Olivier Award, Most Promising Newcomer, 1984; Honorary Fellowship, University of Wolverhampton, 2006.

BARBOSA Pedro, b. 12 May 1948, Porto, Portugal. Writer; Professor; Researcher. 1 daughter. Education: BA, Romance Philology, Universidade de Coimbra, 1974; MA, Semiotics, Université Louis Pasteur, Strasbourg, France, 1988; PhD, Communication Sciences, Universidade Nova Lisboa, 1993. Appointments: Former Full Professor, Instituto Politécnico do Porto; Visiting Scholar, UFP, Portugal and PUC of São Paulo, Brazil; Researcher, CECL, Universidade Nova de Lisboa, Portugal; Researcher, CERTEL, Université Artois, France; Lecturer, University of Siena, Italy. Publications: Essay: Teoria do Teatro Moderno, 1982; Renovação Dramatúrgica na Trilogia do Teatro-no-Teatro de Pirandello, 1993; Metamorfoses do Real: arte, imaginário e conhecimento estético, 1995; A Ciberliteratura: criação literária e cumputador, 1996; Arte, Comunição & Semiótica, 2002; Theatre: Eróstrato, 1984; Anticleia ou os Chapéus-de-Chuva do Sonho, 1992; PortoMetropolitanoLento, 1993; PortoImaginárioLento, 2001; Alletsator – XPTO.Kosmos.2001; Fiction: O Guardador de Retretes, 1976; Histórias da Menina Minhó-Minhó, 1988; Prefácio para uma Personagem Só, 1993; Cyberliterature includes: A Literatura Cibernética I, II, III, 1977-86; Teoria do Homem Sentado, 1996; O Motor Textual, 2001; Ciberliterature, Inteligencia Artificial e Teoria Quantica, 2012. Honours: Essay Prize, Association of Portuguese Writers, 1982. Memberships: Association of Portuguese Authors; Association of Portuguese Writers; Researcher, CETIC and CTEC, Universidade Fernando Pessoa, Porto. Address: Rua Aleixo, 99-Bl, Da-Hab 04, 4150-043, Porto, Portugal. E-mail: pedro_seriot_barbosa@hotmail.com Website: www.pedrobarbosa.net

BARBOT Henry Claude, b. 27 July 1950, Port-au-Prince, Haiti. Physician. m. Joseline, 1 son, 4 daughters. Education: School of Medicine and Pharmacy; Howard University Hospital. Appointments: Alexandria Community Service Board; Arlington County Mental Health; Comprehensive Psychiatric Emergency Program; Spring Road Clinic; St Elizabeth Hospital. Publications: Viewpoint of a Mental Health Professional; American Journey. Honours: 8 times winner, American Medical Association Award; 3 times nominee, America's Top Psychiatrists Award, 2009, 2010, 2011; Listed in biographical dictionaries. Memberships: American Society of Psychopharmacology; American Board of Addiction Medicine. Address: 13700 Hotomtot Dr, Upper Marlboro, MD 20774, USA. E-mail: barbotist@hotmail.com

BARBULESCU Maria, b. 2 January 1941, Blaj-Veza, Romania. Professor. m. Haralambie Barbulescu. Education: History Department, Faculty of History, Babes-Bolyai University, Cluj-Napoca, 1960-65; Study scholarships: Ravenna, Italy, 1974; University of Sofia, Bulgaria, 1973; Munich, Germany, 1981, 1990. Appointments: Lecturer, History, Pedagogical Institute of Constanta, 1965-73; Museologist, 1973-93, Scientific Researcher, 1993-2002, National Museum of Archaeology and History, Constanta; Reader Dr, Faculty of History, Constanta Ovidius University, 1993-2008. Publications: 2 monographs; Over 110 articles in specialised reviews. Honours: PhD, History, Babes-Bolyai University, 1991; The Cultural Distinction for scientific research, President's Office, 2004. Memberships: Classical Studies Society of Romania; The Archaeologists of Romania; The Consultative International Commission for Promoting IndoEuropean and Thracian Studies. Address: Str Cpt Dobrila Eugeniu, Nr 2, Bl H, Sc A, Ap 19, Constanta, Code 900512, Romania. E-mail: mariabarbulescu@yahoo.fr

BARCLAY Linwood L, b. 20 March 1955, New Haven, Connecticut, USA. Journalist; Author. m. Neetha, 1 son, 1 daughter. Education: BA (Hons), English, Trent University, Peterborough, Ontario, Canada. Appointments: Journalist, 1981, Columnist, 1993-2008, Toronto Star, Toronto, Canada; Public Speaker. Publications: Father Knows Zilch, 1996; This House is Nuts, 1997; Mike Harris Made Me Eat My Dog, 1998; Last Resort, 2000; Bad Move, 2004; Bad Guys, 2005; Lone Wolf, 2006; Stone Rain, 2007; No Time For Goodbye, 2007; Too Close to Home, 2008; Fear the Worst, 2009; Never Look Away, 2010; Clouded Vision, The Accident, 2011; Trust Your Eyes, 2012; Never Saw It Coming, 2013; A Tap on the Window, 2013. Honours: Best Columnist Award, Canadian Community Newspaper Association, 1981; Stephen Leacock Award of Merit (and Finalist for Stephen Leacock Award for Humour) for Book "Last Resort", 2001; Winner, The Richard and Judy Summer Read (for No Time For Goodbye), 2008; Arthur Ellis Award for Best Crime Novel (Too Close to Home), 2010. Memberships: Writers Union of Canada; Crime Writers of Canada; Mystery Writers of America. Address: Oakville, Ontario, Canada. E-mail: linwoodbarclay@mac.com

BAR-COHEN Yoseph, b. 3 September 1947, Baghdad, Iraq. Physicist. m. Yardena, 1 son, 1 daughter. Education: BSc, Physics, 1971, MSc, Materials Science, 1973, PhD, Physics, 1979, Hebrew University, Jerusalem, Israel. Appointments: Senior NDE Specialist, Israel Aircraft Industry, 1971-79; Postdoctorate, National Research Council, 1979-80; Senior Physicist, Systems Research Laboratory, Dayton, Ohio, 1980-83; Principal Specialist, McDonnell Douglas Corporation, Long Beach, California, 1983-91; Senior Research Scientist and Group Supervisor, Advanced Technologies, Jet Propulsion Laboratory, Pasadena, California, 1991-. Publications: Over 340 journals and proceedings papers and 6 books; 21 patents. Honours: National Research Council Fellowship Award, 1979; Nova Award, Outstanding Achievement in Technology, 1996; Nova Award, Technical Innovation and Leadership, 1998; Two SPIE Lifetime Achievement Award, 2001 and 2005; NASA Exceptional Engineering Achievement Medal, 2001; NASA Exceptional Technology Achievement Medal, 2006. Memberships: Fellow, American Society for Non-destructive Testing; Fellow, International Society for Optical Engineering. Address: Jet Propulsion Laboratory, MS-67-119, 4800 Oak Grove Drive, Pasadena, CA 91109-8099, USA.

BARDINTZEFF Jacques-Marie, b. 30 December 1953, La Tronche, France. Volcanologist. m. Isabelle Boyaud, 1 daughter. Education: Ecole Normale Supérieure de St Cloud, 1973-77; Agrégation, 1977; Doctorat (Dr Sc), 1985. Appointments: Assistant agrégé, 1977, Maître de Conférences, 1991, Université Paris-Sud, Orsay; Scientific Military, French Atomic Energy Commission, Bruyères-le-Châtel, France, 1980-81; Professor, Université Paris-Sud, Orsay and Université de Cergy-Pontoise, France, 2000-; Redactor in Chief, 1988-95, Director, 1995-, Géochronique magazine, Paris, France; Vice Président, Société Géologique de France,

1989; Member, jury agrégation, 1989-96; Member, jury CAPES, 2002-05, 2010-13; Scientific contributor, Petit Larousse, Dictionary, France, 2003-. Publications: Numerous books and articles in professional journals. Honours: Prix Furon, Société Géologique de France, 1992; Prize Earth Sciences, Bulgarian Academy of Sciences, 2000; Golden A of Adventure, 2006. Memberships: Société Géologique de France; Comité Français pour le Patrimoine Géologique; Association Française pour l'Etude du Quaternaire. Address: Laboratoire de Pétrographie-Volcanologie, bât 504, Université Paris-Sud, 91405 Orsay, France. E-mail: jacques-marie.bardintzeff@u-psud.fr Website: www.lave-volcans.com/bardintzeff.html

BARDOT Brigitte, b. 28 September 1934, Paris, France. Actress and Animal Rights Campaigner. m. (1) Roger Vadim, 1952, divorced 1957, (2) Jacques Charrier, 1959, divorced 1962, 1 son, (3) Gunter Sachs, 1966, divorced 1969, (4) Bernard d'Ormale, 1992. Education: Paris Conservatoire. Career: Films include: Manina: La fille sans voile; Futures vedettes; Le grandes manouveures; En effueillent la marguerite; Une parisienne; En case de malheur; Voulez-vous danser avec moi?; Please not now?; Viva Maria; Les femmes, 1969; Don Juan, 1973. Publications: Initiales BB, 1996; Le Carré de Pluton, 1999; Un Cri Dans Le Silence, 2003. Memberships: President Fondation Brigitte Bardot. Honours: Etoile de Cristal, Academy of Cinema, 1966; Chevalier Légion d'honneur. Address: Fondation Brigitte Bardot, 45 rue Vineuse, 75016 Paris, France. E-mail: fbb@fondationbrigittebardot.fr

BARKER Dennis Malcolm, b. 21 June 1929, Lowestoft, England. Journalist; Novelist. m. Sarah Katherine Alwyn, 1 daughter. Education: National Diploma in Journalism, 1959. Appointments: Reporter and Sub-Editor, Suffolk Chronicle & Mercury, Ipswich, 1947-48; Reporter, Feature Writer, Theatre and Film Critic, 1948-58, East Anglian Daily Times; Estates and Property Editor 1958-63, also Theatre Critic, 1960-63, Express & Star, Wolverhampton; Midlands Correspondent, 1963-67, Reporter, Feature Writer, Columnist, The Guardian, 1967-91. Publications: Novels: Candidate of Promise, 1969; The Scandalisers, 1974; Winston Three Three Three, 1987; Games with The General, 2007; The Clients of Miss May, 2008; Non-fiction: The People of the Forces Trilogy (Soldiering On, 1981, Ruling the Waves, 1986, Guarding the Skies, 1989); One Man's Estate, 1983; Parian Ware, 1985; Fresh Start, 1990; The Craft of the Media Interview, 1998; How to Deal with the Media, 2000; Seize the Day (contributor), 2001; The Guardian Book of Obituaries (contributor), 2003; Oxford Dictionary of National Biography (contributor), 2004-; Tricks Journalists Play, 2007; Contributions to: BBC; Punch; East Anglian Architecture & Building Review (editor and editorial director, 1956-58); The Guardian, 1991-. Memberships: National Union of Journalists, Secretary, Suffolk Branch, 1953-58, Chairman 1958; Chairman, Home Counties District Council, 1956-57; Life Member, 1991; Life Member, Journalists' Charity; Writers Guild of Great Britain; Broadcasting Press Guild; Society of Authors. Address: 67 Speldhurst Road, London W4 1BY, England.

BARKER Sebastian Smart, b. 16 April 1945, Moreton-in-the-Marsh, Gloucestershire, England. Poet; Editor; University Fellow. m. Hilary Susan Davies, 1 son, 3 daughters. Education: King's School, Canterbury; MA, Corpus Christi College, Oxford; MA, University of East Anglia. Appointments: Fireman, Carpenter & Furniture Restorer, 1971-76; Cataloguer of Modern First Editions, Sotheby's, 1976-77; Writer-in-Residence, South Hill Park Arts Centre, 1980-83; Writer-in-Residence, Stamford Arts Centre, 1984-85; Chairman, Poetry Society, 1988-92; Founder-Director, English College Foundation, Prague, 1991-; Self-Employed Writer, 1977-2011; Editor, London Magazine, 2002-08; Royal Literary Fund Fellow, University of Middlesex, 2009-11. Publications: Poetry: Poems, 1974; The Dragon, 1976; On the Rocks, 1977; Epistles, 1980; A Fire in the Rain, 1982; A Nuclear Epiphany, 1984; Boom, 1985; The Dream of Intelligence, 1992; Guarding the Border: Selected Poems, 1992; The Hand in the Well, 1996; Damnatio Memoriae: Erased from Memory, 2004; The Matter of Europe, 2005; The Erotics of God, 2005; Sebastian Barker Reading from His Poems, 2006; Prose: Who is Eddie Linden, 1979; Rowan Williams' Theology of Art & Other Essays, 2010; The Wheels of Ezekiel: A Theology of Poetry, 2010. Honours: Arts Council Award for Poetry, 1976; Ingram Merrill Foundation Award for Poetry, 1988; Judge, Dylan Thomas Award for Poetry, 1989; Hawthornden Fellow, 1990; Society of Authors Award, 1990; Judge, Bournemouth International Poetry Competition, 1991; Judge, London Writing Competition, 1992; Royal Literary Fund Award, 1993; Fellow, Royal Society of Literature, 1997; Judge, V S Pritchett Memorial Prize, Royal Society of Literature, 2003-07; Judge, Strokestown International Poetry Competition, 2010. Memberships: Director of Literary Festivals: Bracknell, Berkshire, 1980-83, Epsom, Surrey, 1984, First Royal Berkshire Poetry Festival, 1985; Executor of the Literature Panel, Brighton Festival, 1989-91; English PEN, 1990-92; Friedrich Nietzsche Society of Great Britain, 1991-94. Address: 70 Wargrave Avenue, London, N15 6UB, England. E-mail: sebastianbarker@gmail.com

BARKIN Ellen, b. 16 April 1955, New York, USA. Actress. m. (1) Gabriel Byrne, 1988, divorced 1999, 1 son, 1 daughter, (2) Ronald Perelman, 2000, divorced 2006. Education: City University of New York; Hunter College, Indiana. Appointments: Stage appearances include: Shout Across the River, Killings on the Last Line, 1980; Extremities, 1982; Eden Court; TV appearances include: Search for Tomorrow, Kent State, We're Fighting Back, 1981; Terrible Joe Moran, 1984; Before Women Had Wings, 1998; Films include: Diner, 1982; Daniel, Tender Mercies, Eddie and the Cruisers, 1983; The Adventures of Buckaroo Banzai, Harry and Son, 1984; Enormous Changes at the Last Minute, 1985; Down by Law, 1986; The Big Easy, Siesta, 1987; Sea of Love, 1989; Johnny Handsome; Switch; Man Trouble, 1992; Mac, This Boy's Life, Into the West, 1993; Bad Company, Wild Bill, 1995; Mad Dog Times, The Fan, 1996; Fear and Loathing in Las Vegas; Popcorn; Drop Dead Gorgeous; The White River Kid, 1999; Crime and Punishment in Suburbia, Mercy, 2000; Someone Like You, 2001; She Hate Me, 2004; Palindromes, 2005; Trust the Man, 2006; Ocean's Thirteen, 2007; Brooklyn's Finest, 2009; Rogue's Gallery, 2009. Honour: Sant Jordi Award, 1987; Emmy Award, 1997; Golden Satellite Award, 1997. Address: c/o CAA, 9830 Wilshire Boulevard, Beverly Hills, CA 90212, USA.

BARLOW Matthew B, b. 30 January 1935, Carlisle, England. Senior Project Manager. m. Mary Alice Jenkins, 1 son. Education: BA, Ealing College; BSc, University of Petroleum and Minerals, Dhahran, Saudi Arabia, 1978; BS, University of Oriental African Studies, Lagos, Nigeria, 1981; MSc, Aston University, Birmingham, England, 1986. Appointments: Departmental Managing Director, Finance and Administration, National Bank of Nigeria, Lagos, 1979-82; Project Manager, Chemsult, Sacramento, California and Johannesburg, South Africa, 1978-91; Loss Leaders Representative, Arabian Oil, Saudi Arabia, 1977-97; From

Assistant Superintendent to Superintendent, Complant International, Saudi Arabia, 1989-; Associate Assistant, Life Insurance Pension Service, Gloucester, England, 1979-; General Manager, Western Executive, Cheltenham, England, 1986-; Technical Manager, Wescott Freight, Gloucestershire, 1990-; Chartered Accountant, PES Middleborough, Lucern, Switzerland, 1977-97. Memberships: Fellow: Institute of International Accountants, Royal Institute of British Architects, British Institute of Management, Institute of Cost and Management Accountants, Institute of Accountants, American Institute of Cost and Consulting Engineers; Member, New York Academy of Sciences. Address: Edgewood Villa, 10 Vectis Close, Tudor Park Estate, Lincoln Hill Road, Ross on Wye, Herefordshire HR9 8CR, England.

BARNABY (Charles) Frank, b. 27 September 1927, Andover, Hampshire, England. Physicist; Author. m. 19 December 1972, 1 son, 1 daughter. Education: BSc, 1951, MSc, 1954, PhD, 1960, London University. Appointments: Physicist, UK Atomic Energy Authority, 1950-57; Member, Senior Scientific Staff, Medical Research Council, University College Medical School, 1957-68; Executive Secretary, Pugwash Conferences on Science and World Affairs, 1968-70; Director, Stockholm International Peace Research Institute (SIPRI), 1971-81; Professor of Peace Studies, Frei University, Amsterdam, 1981-85; Director, World Disarmament Campaign (UK), 1982-; Chair, Just Defence, 1982-; Consultant, 1998-2009, Consultant Emeritus, 2009-, Oxford Research Group; Editor, International Journal of Human Rights. Publications: Man and the Atom, 1971; Disarmament and Arms Control, 1973; Nuclear Energy, 1975; The Nuclear Age, 1976; Prospects for Peace, 1980; Future Warfare, 1983; The Automated Battlefield, 1986; Star Wars Brought Down to Earth, 1986; The Invisible Bomb, 1989; The Gaia Peace Atlas, 1989; The Role and Control of Arms in the 1990's, 1992; How Nuclear Weapons Spread, 1993; Instruments of Terror, 1997; How to Build a Nuclear Bomb ad Other Weapons of Mass Destruction, 2003; The Future of Terror, 2007. Contributions to: Ambio; New Scientist; Technology Review. Honours: Honorary Doctorates: Frei University, Amsterdam, 1982; University of Southampton, 1996; University of Bradford, 2007. Address: Brandreth, Station Road, Chilbolton, Stockbridge, Hampshire SO20 6AW, England.

BARNARD Robert, b. 23 November 1936, Burnham on Crouch, Essex, England. Crime Writer. m. Mary Louise Tabor, 1963. Education: Balliol College, Oxford, 1956-59; Dr Phil, University of Bergen, Norway, 1972. Publications: Death of an Old Goat, 1974; Sheer Torture, 1981; A Corpse in a Gilded Cage, 1984; Out of the Blackout, 1985; Skeleton in the Grass, 1987; At Death's Door, 1988; Death and the Chaste Apprentice, 1989; Masters of the House, 1994; A Cry from the Dark, 2003. As Bernard Bastable: Dead, Mr Mozart, 1995; Too Many Notes, Mr Mozart, 1995; A Brontë Encyclopaedia (with M L Barnard), 2007. Honours: Seven Times Nominated for Edgar Awards; Recipient of Diamond Dagger for Lifetime's Achievement in Crime Fiction, 2003. Memberships: Crime Writers Association; Chairman, Brontë Society, 1996-99, 2002-2005; Society of Authors. Address: Hazeldene, Houghley Lane, Leeds LS13 2DT, England.

BARNDT Helen Grace, b. 11 December 1928, Santa Rosa, California, USA. Artist. Education: Santa Rosa High School; Chicago Art Institute; San Francisco Academy of Art. Appointments: Museum of Nature and Science, Denver; Treasurers of Ancient Egypt murals; Commissions. Publications: San Francisco Chronicle; Museum of Natural History; Listed in international biographical dictionaries. Honours: Anna Lee Stacy Scholarship; Honorable Mention, State Fair. Memberships: Denver Art League; Denver Art Museum. Address: Apt 9, 940E, 8th Ave, Denver, Colorado 80218, USA.

BARNES Michael Allan, b. 19 June 1955, Sydney, Australia. Lawyer. 2 daughters. Education: BA, LLB, LLM, University of Queensland. Appointments: Aboriginal Legal Service; Chief Officer, Complaints, Criminal Justice Commission; Head, School of Justice Studies, Queensland University of Technology; State Coroner, Queensland, 2003-. Honours: Adjunct Professor of Law, Queensland University of Technology. Memberships: Police Education Advisory Council; Queensland Government Suicide Prevention Strategy Advisory Committee. Address: State Coroner Office, GPO Box 1649, Brisbane, Q 4001, Australia. E-mail: state.coroner@justice.qld.gov.au

BARNETT Correlli (Douglas), b. 28 June 1927, Norbury, Surrey, England. Author. m. Ruth Murby, 1950, 2 daughters. Education: BA, 1951, MA, 1955, Exeter College, Oxford. Appointments: Keeper of the Churchill Archives Centre, 1977-95; Fellow, Churchill College, 1977-; Development Fellow, Churchill College, 1997-99. Publications: The Hump Organisation, 1957; The Channel Tunnel (co-author), 1958; The Desert Generals, 1960, new enlarged edition 1984; The Swordbearers, 1963; Britain and Her Army, 1970; The Collapse of British Power, 1972; Marlborough, 1974; Strategy and Society, 1975; Bonaparte, 1978; The Great War, 1979; The Audit of War, 1986; Engage the Enemy More Closely: The Royal Navy in the Second World War, 1991; The Lost Victory: British Dreams, British Realities 1945-1950, 1995; The Verdict of Peace: Britain Between Her Yesterday and the Future, 2001; Television: The Great War (co-author), 1964; The Lost Peace (co-author), 1966; The Commanders, 1973. Honours: Best Television Documentary Script Award, Screenwriters Guild, 1964; Royal Society of Literature Award, 1970; Chesney Gold Medal, Royal United Services Institute for Defence Studies, 1991; Yorkshire Post Book of the Year Award, 1991; DSc Honoris Causa, Cranfield University, 1993; CBE, 1997. Address: Catbridge House, East Carleton, Norwich NR14 8JX, England.

BARNIE John Edward, b. 27 March 1941, Abergavenny, Gwent, Wales. Editor; Writer; Poet. m. Helle Michelsen, 28 October 1980, 1 son. Education: BA, Honours, 1963, MA, 1966, PhD, 1971, Birmingham University; Dip Ed, Nottingham University, 1964. Appointments: Lecturer, English Literature, University of Copenhagen, 1969-82; Assistant, then Editor, Planet: The Welsh International, 1985-2006. Publications: Borderland, 1984; Lightning Country, 1987; Clay, 1989; The Confirmation, 1992; Y Felan a Finnau, 1992; The City, 1993; Heroes, 1996; No Hiding Place, 1996; The Wine Bird, 1998; Ice, 2001; At the Salt Hotel, 2003; The Green Buoy, 2006; Sea Lilies: Selected Poems 1984-2003, 2006; Trouble in Heaven, 2007; West Jutland Suite, Vestjysk Suite, 2009; Tales of the Shopocracy, 2009; The Forest Under the Sea, 2010; Fire Drill: Notes on the Twenty-First Century, 2010; Contributions to: American Poetry Review; Critical Quarterly; Poetry Wales; New Welsh Review; Anglo-Welsh Review; Kunapipi; Juke Blues. Honour: Welsh Arts Council Prize for Literature, 1990. Memberships: Yr Academi Gymreig; Harry Martinson-Sällskapet. Address: Greenfields, Comins Coch, Aberystwyth, SY23 3BG, Ceredigion, Wales. E-mail: john.barnie@googlemail.com

BARR Geoffrey Samuel, b. 1 November 1952, Liverpool, England. Head and Neck Surgeon. m. Rowena M Bickerton, 1984, 2 sons, 1 daughter. Education: Queen's College, University of St Andrews, 1971-77. Appointments: Department of Head and Neck Surgery, University of Liverpool, 1980-84; Department of Head and Neck Surgery, University of Dundee, 1984-93; Department of Head and Neck Surgery, University of Birmingham, 1989-93; Consultant Otolaryngologist, Head and Neck Surgeon, Gwynedd Hospital, 1993-; Part time advisor to National Health Service Executive on Medical Research and Computing. Publications: Over 50 articles in peer reviewed medical and surgical journals. Honours: MBChB, University of Dundee, 1977; Fellow, Royal College of Surgeons, 1984; Master of Surgery, University of Dundee, 1989; Honorary Member, Oriole Society; Honorary Archivist, Schofield Statistical Society. Memberships: Royal Society of Medicine; Royal College of Surgeons; British Association of Otolaryngology, Head and Neck Surgery; British Association of Head and Neck Oncologists; Hospital Consultants and Specialists Association. Address: Department of Head and Neck Surgery, Gwynedd Hospital, Bangor, Gwynedd LL57 2PW, Wales, United Kingdom. E-mail: gsbarr@doctors.org.uk

BARR Patricia Miriam, b. 25 April 1934, Norwich, Norfolk, England. Writer. Education: BA, University of Birmingham; MA, University College, London. Publications: The Coming of the Barbarians, 1967; The Deer Cry Pavilion, 1968; A Curious Life for a Lady, 1970; To China with Love, 1972; The Memsahibs, 1976; Taming the Jungle, 1978; Chinese Alice, 1981; Uncut Jade, 1983; Kenjiro, 1985; Coromandel, 1988; The Dust in the Balance, 1989. Honour: Winston Churchill Fellowship for Historical Biography, 1972. Membership: Society of Authors. Address: 6 Mount Pleasant, Norwich NR2 2DG, England.

BARRA Ornella, b. Chiavari, near Genoa, Italy. Chief Executive. Education: Pharmacy degree, University of Genoa. Appointments: Pharmacist, 1979-84; Founder and Managing Director, Di Pharma, 1984-86; Managing Director, Alleanza Salute Italia, 1986; Member, Board of Directors, Alliance Santé, 1990-97; Executive Director, Alliance UniChem Board, 1997-2006; Board Member, Wholesale & Commercial Affairs Director, 2006-09, Chief Executive, Pharmaceutical Wholesale Division, Chair of Social Responsibilities Committee, 2009-, Alliance Boots. Honours: Honorary Professor, University of Nottingham School of Pharmacy; Highest Honour Prize, International Federation of Pharmaceutical Wholesalers, 2002; Listed in biographical dictionaries. Memberships: Pharmaceutical Wholesalers Association; International Federation of Pharmaceutical Wholesalers; Efficient Consumer Response Europe; Business in the Community International; European Pharmacists Forum. Address: Pharmaceutical Wholesale Division, Alliance Boots, 4th Floor, 361 Oxford Street, London, W1C 2JL, England. E-mail: pharmaceuticalwholesaledivision@alliance-healthcare.co.uk

BARRETT Philip, b. 26 May 1925, Donoughmore, Co Cork, Eire. Roman Catholic Priest. Education: Diplomas with Honours in Arts, Philosophy, Theology and Canon Law, St Kieran's College, Kilkenny, Eire, 1950; BA, 1975, BA with Honours, 1993, Open University; MPhil Thesis, Crime and Punishment in a Lancashire Industrial Town: Law and Social Change in the Borough of Wigan 1800-1950, Polytechnic University, Liverpool, 1980; Ordained Priest, Roman Catholic Church, 1950. Appointments: Assistant Priest, St Oswald's, Ashton-in-Makerfield, near Wigan, England, 1950-58; Assistant Priest, St Benet's Netherton, Bootle, 1958-59; Assistant Priest, St Ambrose's, Speke, Liverpool, England, 1959-69; Assistant Priest, St Jude's, Wigan, England, 1969-76; Parish Priest, St Winefred's, Bootle, Liverpool, England, 1977-81; Parish Priest, Holy Family, Platt Bridge, Wigan, England, 1981-2003; Liverpool Archdiocesan Religious Inspector of Schools, 1950's. Publications: Unpublished M Phil Thesis available for reference purposes in Wigan Public Reference Library (History Shop). Honours: Numerous global awards and nominations; Listed in national and international biographical dictionaries. Address: Spring View Cottage, 244 Warrington Road, Spring View, Wigan, Lancashire WN3 4NH, England.

BARROERO Liliana, b. 18 November 1947, Barbaresco, Italy. Professor. Education: Laureate, Art History, 1971. Appointments: Associate Professor, Musaeology, 1992, Full Professor, Art Criticism, 2002, Dean, Cultural Heritage Faculty, 1999-2006, Director, Art History and Archaeology Department, 2007-. Publications: About 150 articles, exhibitions and museum catalogues and books. Address: Piazza Della Republica 10, Rome, Italy. E-mail: barroero@uniroma3.it

BARRON Christine Angela, b. 9 May 1949, Birmingham, England. Composer; Musician; Author; Adjudicator; Music Teacher. Education: Moseley School of Art, Birmingham. Musical Education: School of Contemporary Pop and Jazz; University of Leeds. Career: Began as freelance percussionist, including work with Birmingham Symphony Orchestra; Theatre, cabaret musician with top entertainers including: Bruce Forsyth; Des O'Connor; Leslie Crowther; Val Doonican. Part-time lecturer, percussion and composition; North Warwickshire and Hinkley College of Technology and Art, Nuneaton, Warwickshire; Well known in the UK for innovative percussion workshops and master classes featuring percussion; Presents new professional training packages for the Boosey & Hawkes and Schott Music Composer Workshop Scheme; Adjudicator and Member, British and International Federation of Festivals for Music, Dance and Speech. Compositions include: Television signature tunes: Shut That Door (also released as single); Where Are They Now; Commissioned by Chappell Music Library for album, short pieces as jingles, theme, incidental music for television, radio, films (distributed worldwide); Collaboration with Boosey and Hawkes Music Publishers on albums, including album recorded by Royal Philharmonic Orchestra; Also wrote for their educational catalogue under pseudonyms: Chris Barron, Christine Barron. Publications: Comprehensive tutors for Learn As You Play series: Learn As You Play Drums with cassette; Learn As You Play Tuned Percussion and Timpani; New edition of Learn As You Play Drums with CD; Drum Styles Made Easy with CD, 2009. Memberships: The British Academy of Songwriters, Composers and Authors; British and International Federation of Festivals for Music, Dance and Speech. Address: 27 Madeira Croft, Coventry, Warwickshire CV5 8NX, England.

BARROSO DA SILVA Fernando Luis, b. 27 November 1972, Sao Paulo, SP, Brazil. Associate Professor. Divorced, 1 son, 1 daughter. Education: Bach, Physics, DEC, 1994; PhD, Chemistry, 2000; Habilitation/Docent, Physical Chemistry, 2008. Appointments: PhD Student, Lunds Universitet, Sweden; Associate Researcher, UNESP, Brazil; Assistant Professor, Associate Professor, Head of Laboratory of Computational Biophysical Chemistry, University of Sao Paulo, Brazil. Publications: Numerous articles in professional journals. Memberships: SBBq; SBF; and others. Address: Av Café, Sln3 – FCRP/Bloco A, Sala 64D-A, Campus DA USP, BR-14040-903 Ribeirao Preto, SP, Brazil. E-mail: fernando@fcfrp.usp.br Website: http://glu.fcfrp.usp.br

DICTIONARY OF INTERNATIONAL BIOGRAPHY 36th EDITION

BARRY Dana Malloy, b. 26 May 1949, New York, USA. Senior Technical Writer; Editor; Administrator. m. James, 4 sons. Education: BA, 1971; MS, Education, 1972; MS, Chemistry, 1974; PhD, 1985; Certified Professional Chemist; Permanent Certification by NASA to borrow lunar rocks, 1998; PhD, Engineering, Osaka University, 2011. Appointments: College Faculty Member; Chemist; Chemical Consultant; Administration; University Senior Technical Writer; Organiser, world's first MoonLink and NEARLink missions, Clarkson University, 1998; Organiser, world's first Marslink Mission, Clarkson University, 2000; External Professor, Ansted University, Malaysia, and Visiting Professor, 2001, 2004 and 2007; Presented Space/Science Education Seminars in Kuala Lumpur and Penang, Malaysia, 2001; Creative Editor and Visiting Professor collaborating in a chemistry project, Japan, 2002, 2005 and 2008; Visiting Professor in England, 2003; Professor and Scientific Board President, Ansted University; Presenter of Invited Lectures, Osaka University, 2010; Visiting Professor, Suzuka National College of Technology, Japan, 2010; Visiting Professor & Keynote Speaker, Xiamen, China, 2011; Visiting Professor, Suzuka Natl College of Technology, Japan, 2012. Publications: Over 150 professional publications including: 11 books including: Science Fair Fun in Japan, 2005, 2nd edition 2009; Science Fair Projects: Helping Your Child Create a Super Science Fair Project, 2000; Creative Science Books, 2007; Science Projects, 2008; The Power of Prayer: A Science Educator's Experience by Strategic Book Publishing, 2010; Numerous journal features including: Chem-Is-Tree, 1997; Chemical-Mechanical Polishing, 1999; Chemistry and Space Exploration, 2001; Host and Scriptwriter of the television series, Sensational Science, 1996-97; Composer and Lyricist, Chemical Sensation, science education music cassette, 1996; Engineering Education, conference paper, Korea & Japan, 2009. Honours: Apex Awards for Publication Excellence, 1996 - 2010; International Woman of the Year, 1999-2000; 20th Century Award for Achievement; Honorary Appointment, Ansted University, Malaysia, Advisory Council, 2000; Honorary Doctorate, Ansted University, Malaysia, 2001; International Medal for Scientific Excellence, ABI, 2001; International Scientist of the Year, 2001; National Award, American Chemical Society, 2004; Woman of the Year, ABI, 2005, 2006; Keynote Speaker of an Education Symposium, Suzuka City, Japan, 2008; Participant, NASA's Kepler Mission, 2009; APEX Awards for Publication Excellence, 1996-2012; Listed in Who's Who publications and biographical dictionaries. Memberships: Member, American Institute of Chemists; National Science Teachers' Association; Officer, American Chemical Society; ACS Chemistry Ambassador. Address: 46 Farmers Street, Canton, NY 13617, USA.

BARRYMORE Drew, b. 22 February 1975, Culver City, California, USA. Film Actress. m. (1) Jeremy Thomas, 1994, divorced, (2) Tom Green, 2001, divorced 2002, (3) Will Kopelman, 2012, 1 daughter. Appointments: Appeared in dog food commercial, 1976; Films include: Altered States, 1980; ET, The Extra Terrestrial, 1982; Irreconcilable Differences, Firestarter, 1984; Cat's Eye, 1985; See You in the Morning, 1988; Guncrazy, Poison Ivy, Beyond Control: The Amy Fisher Story, 1992; Wayne's World 2, 1993; Bad Girls, 1994; Boys in the Side, Batman Forever, Mad Love, 1995; Scream, Everyone Says I Love You, 1996; All She Wanted, Best Men, 1997; Never Been Kissed, Home Fries, The Wedding Singer, Ever After, 1998; Charlie's Angels (also producer), 2000; Donnie Darko (also producer), Riding in Cars With Boys, 2001; Confessions of a Dangerous Mind, 2002; Duplex (also producer); So Love Returns (also producer); Charlie's Angels: Full Throttle (also producer), Duplex, 2003; 50 First Dates, 2004; Fever Pitch, 2005; Curious George, 2006; Music and Lyrics, Lucky You, 2007; Beverley Hills Chihuahua, 2008; He's Just Not That Into You, 2009; Grey Gardens, 2009; Everybody's Fine, 2009; Whip It, 2009. Publications: Little Girl Lost, autobiography, 1990. Address: c/o EMA, 9025 Wilshire Boulevard, Suite 450, Beverly Hills, CA 90211, USA

BARTHOLD Kenneth van, b. 10 December 1927, Surabaya, Java, Indonesia. Concert Pianist; Teacher. m. (1) Prudence C M (2) Sarianne M C (3) Gillian R, 2 sons, 2 daughters. Education: Music Scholar, Bryanston School; British and French Government Scholar, Paris National Conservatoire of Music (class of Yves Nat), Laureat du Conservatoire National de Musique; LRAM. Career: Debut: Bournemouth Municipal Orchestra, 1944; Wigmore Hall, 1956; Frequent recitals in London Piano Series, Queen Elizabeth Hall and throughout the UK; Concerts in Canada, France, Israel and Eire including broadcasts; Concerto appearances with many orchestras including London Symphony Orchestra, British Concert Orchestra, English Chamber Orchestra, London Classical Players, Polyphonia under such conductors as: Sir Adrian Boult, Raymond Leppard, Sir Roger Norrington, Royalton Kisch, Bryan Fairfax; Teaching: Director of Studies, Victoria College of Music, 1953-59; Professor of Piano, Trinity College of Music, 1959-65; Head of Music, City Literary Institute, 1960-83; Edinburgh University Annual Master Classes during the International Festival, 1968-; Senior Piano Tutor, ILEA, 1983-90; Lecturer on 19th and 20th Century Opera, Wimbledon College of Art, 1983-94; Master Classes in Israel, Canada and throughout the UK; International Juror in France and Canada; Wrote and presented 21 hour-long documentaries on television including the first ever full length studio documentary, BBC, 1964; Further frequent appearances interviewing, linking, profiling and performing on BBC and ITV. Recordings: Decca/Argo-Mozart Recital; Chopin Recital; Schumann Recital; Chopin Compilation; Darmo-Chopin/Liszt; Hommage à Pierre Max Dubois; Publications: Co-author, The Story of the Piano, 1976; Reviewer BBC Music Magazine; Various articles. Honour: Critics Award (television), 1972. Address: Arvensis, Stour Lane, Stour Row, Shaftesbury, Dorset SP7 0QJ, England. E-mail: kvanbarthold@aol.com Website: www.kennethvanbarthold.com

BARTHOLOMEW Debra Lee, b. 11 September 1958, New York, USA. Writer. m. Richard Ray Bartholomew, 1 son, 2 daughters. Education: Richmondville School, 1977. Appointments: Owner, Debi Lee Publishing, 2000. Publications: Author, Hope: Discovering the Power of No; Songwriter, Believing in Myself. Honours: Merit, Writer's Digest, 2001; Listed in international biographical dictionaries. Memberships: International Society of Poets. Address: 297 Main Street, Richmondville, New York, NY 12149-0150, USA. E-mail: rbartho1@nycap.rr.com

BARTLETT Paul Thomas, b. 7 July 1955, Birmingham, England. Artist; Tutor. Education: BA (Hons), Fine Art, Falmouth College of Art, 1976; MA, Painting, Royal Academy Schools, London, 1980; David Murray Summer Scholarship for Landscape Painting, 1975, 1978, 1979, 1980; Elizabeth Greenshield Foundation Scholarship, 1980-81; City & Guilds FE & AE Adult Teaching Certificate, 1986-87; Postgraduate Diploma, History of Art & Design, University of Central England in Birmingham, 1987-90. Appointments: Artist with 28 years of tutoring other artists via workshops and teaching; Adult Education Tutor: Birmingham Council, 1985-; Midlands Arts Centre, 1992-2008, 2010-; St Anne's

Church Hall, Moseley, and Birmingham Printmakers, 2008-; Previous venues: Cadbury Sixth Form College, North Birmingham College, Wolverhampton University, Bournville College of Art (University of Central England & Birmingham City University), Sutton Coldfield School of Art & Design, Birmingham Museum & Art Gallery, Birmingham Pastel Society, East Staffordshire Arts Community Workshop Scheme, Campaign for Drawing, Walsall Community Arts Network, Winsor & Newton Leisure Painter magazine, West Dean College (Chichester), Artscape. Publications: Works appeared over 40 art books; Numerous articles in professional journals; Poems in over 20 mixed anthologies. Honours include most recently: First prizes: Daily Mail NOT the Turner Prize, 2004; RBSA Prize Show, 1996, 2004; Birmingham Pastel Society, 1994, 1995; RBSA: Members & Associates, 2003, 2004; Open Drawing & Pastel, 1995, 2002; Open Oils, 1996; Commission Prize, FBA Women on Canvas Portrait Competition, 1991; Listed in international biographical dictionaries. Memberships: Royal Society of British Artists; Royal Birmingham Society of Artists; Birmingham & Midland Pastel Society; Birmingham Print Workshop; Institute for Learning. Address: 144 Wheelers Lane, Kings Heath, Birmingham, B13 0SG, England. Website: www.rbsa.org.uk

BARYSHNIKOV Mikhail, b. 28 January 1948, Riga, Latvia. Ballet Dancer. m. Lisa Rinehart, 2 daughters, 1 son; 1 daughter with Jessica Lange. Education: Riga Ballet School; Kirov Ballet School, Leningrad. Career: Member, Kirov Ballet Company, 1969-74; Guest Artist with many leading ballet companies, including American Ballet Theatre, National Ballet of Canada; Royal Ballet; Hamburg Ballet; Federal Republic of Germany; Ballet Victoria, Australia; Stuttgart Ballet, Federal Republic of Germany; Alvin Ailey Co, USA, 1974-; Joined New York City Ballet Company, 1978, resigned 1979; Artistic Director, American Ballet Theatre, 1980-90; Co-Founder, White Oak Dance Project, 1990-2002; Stage debut in Metamorphosis, 1989; Launched perfume Misha, 1989; Founder, Baryshnikov Arts Center, New York, 2004; Ballets (world premieres) Vestris, 1969; Medea, 1975; Push Comes to Shove, Hamlet Connotations, Other Dances, Pas de Duke, 1976; La Dame de Pique, L'Apres-midi d'un Faune, Santa Fe Saga, 1978; Opus 19, 1979; Rhapsody, 1980; Films: The Turning Point, 1977; White Nights, 1985; Giselle, Dancers, 1987; Dinosaurs, 1991; Choreography: Nutcracker, 1976; Don Quixote, 1978; Cinderella, 1984; TV: Sex and the City, 2003-04. Publications: Baryshnikov at Work, 1977. Honours: Gold Medal, Varna Competition, Bulgaria, 1966; First International Ballet Competition, Moscow, USSR, 1968; Nijinsky Prize, First International Ballet Competition, Paris Academy de Danse, 1968; Kennedy Centre Honors, National Medal of Honour, Commonwealth Award. Address: c/o Vincent & Farrell Associates, 481 Eighth Avenue, Suite 740, New York, NY 10001, USA.

BASHIROV Ferid, b. 31 July 1940, Elabouga, Russia. Professor. m. Khadytcha, 1 son, 1 daughter. Education: Physicist, Kazan State University, 1963; Candidate of Sciences, Physics and Mathematics, 1972; Doctor of Sciences, Physics and Mathematics, 2006. Appointments: Professor of Physics, Kazan Federal University, Russia, 1963-; Professor of Physics (by invitation), Oran University, Algeria, 1975-78 and Professor of Physics, University of Conakry, Guinea Republic, West Africa, 1998-2010. Publications: 105 titles including: Spectroscopic techniques and hindered molecular motion, CRC Press Pub, 2011. Honours: Listed in biographical dictionaries. Address: 420015, Malaya Krasnaya St, 6-7, Kazan, Russia. fbashir@mail.ru

BASINGER Kim, b. 8 December 1953, Athens, Georgia, USA. Actress. m. (1) Ron Britton, divorced, (2) Alec Baldwin, divorced, 1 daughter. Career: Model, 1971-76; Actress: Films include: Never Say Never Again, 1982; The Man Who Loved Women, 1983; 9 1/2 Weeks, 1985; Batman, 1989; Too Hot to Handle, 1991; The Real McCoy, 1993; Wayne's World, The Getaway, Prêt-à-Porter, 1994; LA Confidential, 1997; I Dreamed of Africa, Bless the Child, 2000; 8 Mile, People I Know, 2002; Elvis Has Left The Building, Cellular, The Door in the Floor, 2004; Jump Shot, 2005; The Sentinel, 2006; Even Money, 2007; While She Was Out, 2008; The Informers, The Buring Plain, 2009. Honours: Academy Award and Golden Globe for Best Supporting Actress, 1997; Screen Actors Guild Award, 1997. Address: 3960 Laurel Canyon Boulevard, #414, Studio City, CA 91604, USA.

BASKAKOV Albert Pavlovich, b. 1 March 1928, Mojjarino, Kalinin, USSR. Professor. m. N G Martinova, 1 son, 1 daughter. Education: Engineer, Moscow Power Institute, 1950; Candidate of Sciences, 1953; DSc, Ural State Technical University, 1965. Appointments: Assistant, Ural State Technical University, Sverdlovsk, 1953-56; Assistant Professor, 1956-64, Professor, Head of Power Engineering Department, 1964-98; Head of Scientific Laboratory, Ural Branch of the Academy of Sciences of Russia, Ekaterinburg, 1961-64; Professor, Power Engineering, Ural Federal University, Ekaterinburg, 1998-. Publications: 10 scientific books; 9 text books; 500 articles. Honours: Honorary Scientist, RSFSR, 1988; Honorary Professor, Ural State Technical University, 1997. Memberships: Scientific Metals Association; International Power Academy. Address: Ural Federal University, Mira St 19, 620002, Ekaterinburg, Russia. E-mail: baskakovap@e1.ru

BASKARAN R, b. 3 May 1971, Tamil Nadu, India. Professor. m. B Antoinette, 1 son. Education: BSc, 1988-91; BE, 1991-95; MS (by research), 2001-04; PhD, 2004-08. Appointments: Industry, 1995-96; Lecturer, 1996-2004, Assistant Professor, 2004-08, Professor, 2008-, Head of Department, 2012-, St Joseph's College of Engineering; Conducted conferences and workshops; 6 PhD students under guidance. Publications: 30 papers in international journals; 27 papers at international conferences. Honours: Best Teacher Award (4 times), Jeppiaar Education Trust; Gouri Dutta Award, Chemcon, 2006; Best Citizen Award, International Publishing House, 2010. Memberships: Life Member, Indian Society of Technical Education. Address: H13, Block II, Riviera, 120 Velachery Main Road, Medavakkam, Chennai 100, Tamil Nadu, India. E-mail: rbaskaran2000@yahoo.com Website: www.professor.baskaran.webs.com

BASSEY Shirley, b. 8 January 1937, Tiger Bay, Cardiff, Wales. Singer; Entertainer. m. (1) Kenneth Hume, divorced 1965, deceased, (2) Sergio Novak, 1968, divorced 1977, 2 daughters, 1 deceased, 1 adopted son. Appointments: Variety and Revue Singer, 1950s; Concerts and TV appearances world-wide; Semi-Retired, 1981-; Artist for Peace, UNESCO, 2000; International Ambassador, Variety Club, 2001. Creative Works: I'm In the Mood For Love, 1981; Love Songs, 1982; All By Myself, 1984; I Am What I Am, 1984; Playing Solitaire, 1985; I've Got You Under My Skin, 1985; Sings The Songs From The Shows, 1986; Born To Sing the Blues, 1987; Let Me Sing And I'm Happy, 1988; Her Favourite Songs, 1988; Keep The Music Playing, 1991; Great Shirley Bassey (album), 1999; Thank You for the Years, 2003; The Columbia/EMI Singles Collection, 2006; The Performance, 2009; Various compilations. Publications: Diamond Diva, biography, 2008. Honours include most recently: Legion d'Honneur, France, 1999; DBE, 1999; Most Successful British Female Singer, Guinness Book of Records, 2000; Greatest Black Briton, BBC, 2004; Artist for Peace Award, UNESCO, 2004; Avenue of Stars, London, 2005; Inductee, Grammy Hall of Fame, 2008. Address: c/o CSS Stellar Management, Drury House, 34-43 Russell Street, London, WC2B 5HA, England.

BATABYAL Amitrajeet A, b. 6 September 1965, Chittaranjan, India. University Professor. m. Swapna B, 1 daughter. Education: BS, Cornell University, 1987; MS, University of Minnesota, 1990; PhD, University of California, Berkeley, 1994. Appointments: Visiting Assistant Professor, Economics, College of William & Mary, 1994-95; Assistant Professor, 1995-98, Associate Professor, 1998-2000, Utah State University; Arthur J Gosnell Professor of Economics, Rochester Institute of Technology, 2000-. Publications: 6 books; 170 articles in various professional journals; 16 book chapters; 302 book reviews. Honours include: Geoffrey J D Hewings Award, North American Regional Science Council, 2003; Moss Madden Memorial Medal, British and Irish Section of the Regional Science Association International, 2004; Outstanding Achievement in Research Award, Society for Range Management, 2006; Trustees Scholarship Award, Rochester Institute of Technology, 2007; Warren Samuels Prize, Runner Up, Association for Social Economics, 2010; J Wayne Reitz Seminar, University of Florida, 2010; Best Paper, Studies in Regional Science Award, Japan Section, Regional Science Association International, 2011; Listed in international biographical dictionaries. Memberships: American Economic Association; Agricultural & Applied Economics Association; Regional Science Association International; Association of Environmental & Resource Economists. Address: 35 Crandon Way, Rochester, NY 14618, USA. E-mail: aabgsh@rit.edu

BATCHELOR John Barham, b. 15 March 1942, Farnborough, England. Professor of English Literature; Writer; Editor. m. Henrietta Jane Letts, 1968, 2 sons, 1 daughter. Education: MA, 1964, PhD, 1969, Magdalene College, Cambridge; MA, University of New Brunswick, 1965. Appointments: Lecturer in English, Birmingham University, 1968-76; Fellow and Tutor, New College, Oxford, 1976-90; Joseph Cowen Professor of English Literature, 1990-2007, Emeritus Professor, 2009-, University of Newcastle upon Tyne. Publications: Mervyn Peake, 1974; Breathless Hush (novel), 1974; The Edwardian Novelists, 1982; H G Wells, 1985; Virginia Woolf, 1991; The Life of Joseph Conrad: A Critical Biography, 1994; The Art of Literary Biography (editor), 1995; Shakespearean Continuities (joint editor), 1997; John Ruskin: No Wealth But Life, 2000; Lady Trevelyan and the Pre-Raphaelite Brotherhood (biography), 2006; Editor (English and American), Modern Language Review; General Editor, Yearbook of English Studies; Contributions to: Dictionary of National Biography; Times Literary Supplement; Observer; Economist; Articles in English, Yearbook of English Studies; Review of English Studies. Honours: Visiting Professor, University of Lancaster. Membership: International Association of Professors of English; English Association; MHRA. Address: School of English, Newcastle University, Newcastle upon Tyne NE1 7RU, England.

BATCHELOR Ronald Ernest, b. 15 July 1934, Southampton, England. Retired University Teacher. m. Patricia Anne, 1 son, 1 daughter. Education: Graduated French, Spanish, Latin (Hons), 1953-56, Certificate of Education, 1956-57, MA, thesis on the novels of Julian Green, 1958-61, University of Southampton; PhD Thesis, La Francophobie de Miguel de Unamuno, University of Nottingham, 1962-67. Appointments: Lecturer, University of Besançon, France, 1957-59; Teacher of English, S Sebastián, Spain, 1959-61; Teacher of French, Spanish, Southampton, 1961-62; Lecturer in French, 1962-67, Senior Lecturer in French, 1967-97, University of Nottingham. Publications: Unamuno Novelist A European Perspective, 1972; Using French A Guide to Contemporary Usage (co-author), 1982; Using Spanish A Guide to Contemporary Usage (co-author), 1992; Using French Synonyms (co-author), 1993; Using Spanish Synonyms, 1994; French for Marketing The Language of Media and Communications (co-author), 1997; Usage pratique et courant des synonymes anglais (co-author), 1998; Using Spanish Vocabulary (co-author), 2003; A Student Grammar of Spanish, 2006; A Reference Grammar of Spanish (including Spanish America), 2010; Using Spanish Synonyms: L'Uso dei sinonimi SPAGNOLO, 2000; Usage Pratique et courant des synonymes anglais: L'Uso dei sinonimi INGLESE, 2001; A Reference Grammar of French (co-author), 2011; Adventures of a Linguist, ongoing; 2nd and 3rd editions of some of the above; Numerous articles in learned journals on literary, philosophical and historical topics. Honours: Listed in several biographical dictionaries; Member, Research Board of Advisors, ABI; Member of advisory board of Anales de la Literatura Española Contemporánea, University of Colorado; Cambridge University Press Academic Best Seller. Address: 20 Moor Lane, Bramcote, Nottingham NG9 3FH, England. E-mail: ronaldbatchelor@btinternet.com

BATE (Andrew) Jonathan, b. 26 June 1958, Sevenoaks, Kent, England. Professor of English Literature; Critic; Novelist. m. (1) Hilary Gaskin, 1984, divorced 1995, (2) Paula Byrne, 1996, 3 children. Education: MA, 1980, PhD, 1984, St Catharine's College, Cambridge. Appointments: Harkness Fellow, Harvard University, 1980-81; Research Fellow, St Catharine's College, Cambridge, 1983-85; Fellow, Trinity Hall, and Lecturer, Trinity Hall and Girton College, Cambridge, 1985-90; Visiting Associate Professor, University of California at Los Angeles, 1989; King Alfred Professor of English Literature, 1991-2003, Leverhulme Personal Research Professor, 1999-, University of Liverpool; Research Reader, British Academy, 1994-96; Professor of Shakespeare and Renaissance Literature, University of Warwick, 2003-. Publications: Shakespeare and the English Romantic Imagination, 1986; Charles Lamb: Essays of Elia (editor), 1987; Shakespearean Constitutions: Politics, Theatre, Criticism 1730-1830, 1989; Romantic Ecology: Wordsworth and the Environmental Tradition, 1991; The Romantics on Shakespeare (editor), 1992; Shakespeare and Ovid, 1993; The Arden Shakespeare: Titus Andronicus (editor), 1995, reissued 2008; Shakespeare: An Illustrated Stage History (editor), 1996; The Genius of Shakespeare, 1997; The Cure for Love, 1998; The Song of the Earth, 2000; John Clare: A Biography, 2003; Editor, I Am: The Selected Poetry of John Clare, 2004; Soul of the Age: The Life, Mind and World of William Shakespeare, 2008; Contributions to: Scholarly publications. Honours: Calvin and Rose Hoffman Prize, 1996; FBA, 1999; Honorary Fellow, St Catherine's College, Cambridge, 2000; James Tait Black Memorial Prize, 2005; Commander of the British Empire, 2006. Memberships: Fellow, British Academy; Royal Society of Literature; Honorary Fellow, St Catharine's College, Cambridge. Address: c/o Department of English, University of Liverpool, PO Box 147, Liverpool L69 3BX, England.

BATE Weston Arthur, b. 24 September 1924, Melbourne, Australia. m. Janice St John Wilson, 1955, 5 sons, 1 daughter. Author; Historian. Education: Scotch College, University of Melbourne. Appointments: RAAF Air Crew, WWII; Master, Brighton Grammar School and Melbourne Grammar School;

Professor, Australian Studies, Deakin University, Geelong, Victoria, 1978-89; Lecturer, 1952-53, Senior Lecturer, 1965-73, Reader, History, 1974-76, University of Melbourne. Publications: A History of Brighton; Lucky City (Ballarat 1851-1901); Private Lives: Public Heritage; Victorian Gold Rushes; Having a Go: Bill Boyd's Mallee; Light Blue Down Under (Geelong Grammar School History); Life After Gold: Twentieth Century Ballarat; Essential But Unplanned: The Story of Melbourne's Lanes, 1994; Here's to Grandpa! The Watercolours 1900-1940 of C A Wilson, 1995; Sustaining Their Dream: The Metropolitan Golf Club 1901-2002, 2001; Challenging Traditions: A History of Melbourne Grammar, 2002; Heads You Win! A History of the Barwon Heads Golf Club, 2007. Honours: Recipient, Ernest Scott Prize for best work in Australian History, 1978-79; OAM, 1997. Memberships: FRHistS (Vic); FFAHS; President, Royal Historical Society, Victoria, 1991-97, 2002-05; Life Member, Ballarat Historical Park, Sovereign Hill; Patron, Bendigo Historical Society, Maritime Museum, Victoria; Ballarat Reform League; Brighton History Society; Prospectors' Association, Sovereign Hill. Address: 6 Chapman Street, Brighton, East Victoria 3187, Australia.

BATEMAN Robert McLellan, b. 1930, Toronto, Canada. Artist. m. (1) Suzanne Bowerman, 1961, 2 sons, 1 daughter, (2) Birgit Freybe, 1975, 2 sons. Education: BA, University of Toronto, 1954; Ontario College of Education, 1955. Appointments: High School Art Teacher, Nelson High School, Burlington, Ontario, 1958-63, 1965-69, Government College, Umuahia, Nigeria, 1963-65, Lord Elgin High School, 1970-76; Lecturer, Resource Person in Art, Photography, Nature and Conservation. Creative Works: Major Exhibitions: Tryon Gallery, London, 1975, 1979; National Museum of Natural Sciences, Ottawa, 1981-82; Joslyn Art Museum, Omaha, Nebraska, 1987; Leigh Yawkey Woodson Art Museum, Wausau, Wisconsin, 1986-97; Smithsonian Institute, Museum of Natural History, Washington, 1987; Frye Art Museum, Seattle, Washington, 1988; Colorado Springs Fine Arts Museum, 1991; Carnegie Museum of Natural History, 1991; Canadian Embassy, Tokyo, 1992; Suntory Museum, Osaka and Tokyo, 1995-96; National Museum of Wildlife Art, 1997; Everard Read Gallery, Johannesburg, South Africa, 2000; Gerald Peters Gallery, Santa Fe, New Mexico, 2004; Masters Gallery, Calgary, Alberta, 2006; Art of Robert Bateman Retrospective Tour, 2007-09; Russia, 2009-10; Several works in permanent collections. Publications: Books: The Art of Robert Bateman, 1981; The World of Robert Bateman, 1985; Robert Bateman: Artist in Nature, 1990; Robert Bateman: Natural Worlds, 1996; Safari, 1998; Thinking Like a Mountain, 2000; Birds, 2002; Backyard Birds, 2005; Birds of Prey, 2007; Polar Worlds, 2008; Vanishing Habitats, 2009; Bateman New Works, 2010. Honours include: Queen Elizabeth Silver Jubilee Medal, 1977; Master Artist, Leigh Yawkey Woodson Art Museum, 1982; Officer of the Order of Canada, 1984; Governor General's Award for Conservation, Quebec City, 1987; Society of Animal Artists Award of Excellence, 1979, 1980, 1986, 1990; Rachel Carson Award, Society of Environmental Toxicology and Chemistry, 1996; Golden Plate Award, American Academy for Achievement, 1998; Order of British Columbia, 2001; Awards include 12 honorary doctorates; 3 Canadian schools named after him. Memberships include: Royal Canadian Academy of Arts; Sierra Club; Harmony Foundation; Jane Goodall Institute, Canada; Kenya Wildlife Fund; Audubon Society; EcoTrust Canada. Address: PO Box 115, Fulford Harbour, Salt Spring Island, BC V8K 2P2, Canada. Website: www.batemancentre.ca

BATES Kathy, b. 28 June 1948, Memphis, Tennessee, USA. Actress. m. Tony Campisi, 1991, divorced 1997. Education: Southern Methodist University. Career: Various jobs before acting; Theatre includes: Varieties, 1976; Chocolate Cake, 1980; 'night Mother, 1983; Rain of Terror, 1985; Films include: Taking Off, 1971; Arthur 2: On the Rocks, 1988; High Stakes, 1989; Dick Tracy, Misery, 1990; Prelude to a Kiss, Fried Green Tomatoes at the Whistle Stop Café, 1991; North, 1994; Diabolique, The War at Home, 1996; Primary Colors, Titanic, 1998; A Civil Action, Dash and Lilly, My Life as a Dog, 1999; Bruno, 2000; Rat Race, American Outlaws, 2001; About Schmidt, Love Liza, 2002; Evelyn, The Tulse Luper Suitcases: The Moab Story, 2003; The Ingrate, Little Black Book, Around the World in 80 Days, The Bridge of San Luis Rey, 2004; Warm Springs, Relative Strangers, Rumor Has It, 2005; Failure to Launch, Charlotte's Web (voice), Christmas Is Here Again (voice), Bonneville, 2006; Bee Movie (voice), Have Mercy, The Golden Compass (voice), 2007; The Day the Earth Stood Still, Revolutionary Road, 2008; Cheri, The Blind Side, 2009. TV films and appearances include: No Place Like Home; Murder Ordained; The Love Boat; St Elsewhere; LA Law; Cagney & Lacey; Annie, 1999; My Sister's Keeper, 2002. Honours: Pulitzer Prize, 1981; Outer Circle Critic's Award, 1983; Obie Award, 1987; Academy Award for Best Actress and Golden Globe, 1990. Address: c/o Susan Smith Associates, 121 N San Vincente Boulevard, Beverly Hills, CA 90211-2303, USA.

BATT Jürgen Otto Helmut, b. 18 August 1933, Gumbinnen, Germany. Professor of Mathematics. m. Hannelore Ulbricht, 2 daughters. Education: State Examination for Gymnasium Teachers, 1959; Dr. rer.nat. Technical College, Aachen, Germany, 1962; Habilitation, University of Munich, 1969. Appointments: Assistant, Nuclear Centre, Jülich, 1962-64; Assistant, Heidelberg University, 1964-66; Visiting Professor, 1967-68, Associate Professor, 1970-71, Kent State University, USA; Supernumerary Professor, 1974, Full Professor, Applied Mathematics, 1976-99, Dean of the Faculty of Mathematics, 1977-79, University of Munich. Publications: Many scientific articles in the area of differential equations and functional analysis in professional journals. Honours: Member of the University Senate, 1986-88; Member of the Assembly, 1988-98; Scholarly invitations to the following countries: Romania, USA, Switzerland, France, Austria, Italy, Netherlands, Australia, Brazil, India, Spain, Canada, China, Bulgaria, Greece, Colombia, Czechoslovakia, Israel and Russia. Memberships: Deutsche Mathematiker-Vereinigung; American Mathematical Society; International Federation of Nonlinear Analysts. Address: Bauschneiderstrasse 11, 81241 Munich, Germany. E-mail: batt@rz.mathematik.uni-muenchen.de

BATTERHAM Robin John, b. 3 April 1941, Brighton, Victoria, Australia. Group Chief Scientist, Rio Tinto P/L. Education: BE, University of Melbourne; LLD (Hon), PhD, DSc (Hon), University of Technology, Sydney; AMusA, Post Nominals, AO, FAA, FTSE, FREng, CE, CPE, CSci, FNAE, FAusIMM, FISS, FIChemE; FIEAust; FICD; FAIM. Appointments: Chief, CSIRO Division of Mineral Engineering, 1984-88; Vice President, Resource & Processing Development CRA Ltd, 1988-94; President, International Mineral Processing Congress, 1989-; Deputy-Chair, Co-op Research Centres, 1992-2005; G K William Co-op Research Centre, 1993-99; Chair, Australian IMM Proceedings Committee, 1995-99; Deputy Director, Music, Scot's Church, Melbourne; Chairman, International Network for Acid Prevention, 1998-2009; Chief Scientist of Australia, 1999-2006; Australia Research Council Member, 1999-2006;

Member, Major National Research Facilities Commission, 2001-06; President, Institution of Chemical Engineers, 2004-06; President, Academy of Technical Science, 2006-; Kernof Professor of Engineering, University of Melbourne; Group Chief Scientist, Rio Tinto, 2006-10. Publications: 77 refereed papers in international journals and conferences. Honours: Officer of the Order of Australia; Presidents Medal, Australian Society of Sugar Cane Technologists; Fellow, Academy of Technology and Engineering Sciences; Fellow, Australian Academy of Science; Foreign Fellow, National Academy of Engineering, USA; Foreign Fellow, Swiss Academy of Engineering Sciences; CSIRO Postdoctorate Award; Esso Award of Excellence in Chemical Engineering, 1992; Distinguished Lecturer, University of British Columbia, University of Waterloo, University of California, Berkeley, University of Utah; Kernot Medal, University of Melbourne, 1996; Chemeca Medal, 2003; Centenary Medal of Australia, 2003; Australasian Institute of Mining and Metallurgy Medal, 2004. Memberships: Fellow, Iron Steel Society, America; Fellow, Australia Institute of Mining Metallurgy; Fellow, Institution of Chemical Engineers; Fellow, Institute of Australian Engineers; Fellow, Australian Institute of Management; Fellow, Australian Academy of Sciences; Fellow, Australian Academy of Technological Sciences and Engineering; Fellow, Royal Academy of Engineering. Address: 153 Park Drive, Parkville, Vic 3052, Australia.

BATTERSBY Cameron, b. 21 January 1935, Brisbane, Australia. Surgeon. m. (1) Petah, 1961, dissolved 1975, 2 sons, (2) Jacqueline, 1996, deceased 2001. Education: CEGS, Brisbane; University of Queensland. Appointments: Visiting Surgeon, Royal Brisbane Hospital, 1977-2000; Senior Lecturer, Reader in Surgery, University of Queensland, 1967-77; Director, Australia Cricket Board, 1988-2002; Chairman, Queensland Cricket, 1993-2000; Director, 1972-2002; Manager, Australian Cricket Team (various occasions), 1990-96; Member, Australia-India Council, 1999-2002. Publications: 35 articles in medical journals. Honours: Queensland Open Scholarship, 1952; Member of the Order of Australia (AM), 2000; Award for Service to Medicine as a surgeon in the area of education and research into liver transplantation and to cricket administration. Memberships: Queensland Cricketers. Address: 30/30 O'Connell Street, Kangaroo Point, Brisbane, QLD 4169, Australia.

BATTEY Bonnie Weaver, b. 23 July 1933, Stuttgart, Arkansas, USA. Nurse Educator. m. Robert W Battey. Education: BS, Nursing, Wagner College, 1955; MSN, Vanderbilt University, 1960; PhD, University of Kansas, 1978; Advanced Quantitative Methodology Institute, 1992. Appointments: Staff Nurse, Veterans Administration Hospital, Little Rock, Arkansas, 1956; Instructor & Clinical Co-ordinator, 1957-63, Associate Director, 1964-67, St Vincent's Infirmary, Little Rock, Arkansas; Assistant Professor & Chair, Department of Nursing, University of Arkansas, Little Rock, 1967-71; Professor & Chair, Department of Nursing, University of Central Arkansas, 1977-79; Professor & Chair, Department of Nursing, Memphis State University, Tennessee, 1979-83; Professor, University of North Dakota, 1983-84; Professor & Assistant Dean, 1984-86, Tenured Professor, 1984-94, East Carolina University, North Carolina; Staff Nurse, Pitt County Memorial Hospital, Greenville, North Carolina, 1992; Adjunct Associate Professor, 1993, 1999-2003, George Mason University, Fairfax, Virginia; Professor, Shenandoah University, Virginia, 1994-97; President & Consultant, Duldt & Associates Inc, Virginia, 1985-2003; Adjunct Professor, Samuel Merritt College, Oakland, California, 2003-06; Consultant, Nursing Education, private practice, 2003-, Healing Touch Practitioner, private practice, 2005-, Antioch, California. Publications: 9 books including: Administrator's Guide to Implementing Spiritual Care into Nursing Practice, 2008; Humanism, Nursing Communication and Holistic Care, 2009; Theory of Spiritual Care for Nursing Practice, 2009; Manual for Nursing Communication Observation Tool, 2009; Spiritual Communication Satisfaction Importance (SCSI) Questionnaire Manual for Research & Education, 2010; The spiritual dimension of holistic care, 2010; Perspectives of spiritual care for nurse managers, 2012; 3 book chapters; 1 video; Numerous articles in professional journals; 4 computer assisted instruction programmes including Spirituality in Nursing Practice, 2010. Honours: Nurse Scientists Scholarship, 1970-72; Author of the Month, July 1982; Book of the Year Award, American Journal of Nursing, 1989; Listed in biographical dictionaries. Memberships: Sigma Theta Tau International; The American Holistic Nurses' Association; The Society for Spirituality, Theology and Health; Health Ministries Association. Address: 2921 Bellflower Drive, Antioch, CA 94531, USA. Website: http://www.bwbatteyconsult.com

BATVINIONAK Aliaksandr Vladzimiravich, b. 3 May 1957, Braslaw, Belarus. Sculptor. m. Irina Mikalaewna, 2 sons. Education: Theatre and Art Institute, 1977-83; Art Studios of USSR Art Academy, Minsk, 1983-86. Publications: Catalogue of Belarusian Art of the Twentieth Century, 2001; Numerous articles in professional journals. Honours: Belarusian Medal of the Union of Artists. Memberships: Belarusian Union of Artists. Address: 20-43 Golubeva str, Minsk 220116, Republic of Belarus.

BAUDOUIN Jean-Louis, b. 8 August 1938. Justice; Associate Professor; Counsel. Education: BA, Unversité de Paris, 1955; BCL (1st class honours), McGill University, 1958; Quebec Bar, 1959; DES Comparative Law, Madrid & Strasbourg, 1962; PhD, Université de Paris, 1962; Queen Counsel, 1978. Appointments: Professor, Law School, University of Montreal, 1962-89; Member, Quebec Bar, 1959-89; Vice Chairman, Law Reform Commission of Canada, 1976-80; Vice Chairman, Institut international de droit des pays d'expression française, 1973-; Chairman, Association Henri Capitant, 1977-; Justice, Quebec Court of Appeal, 1989-2008; Associate Professor, Law School, University of Montreal, 1996-; Counsel, Fasken Martineau DuMoulin LLP, 2009-. Publications: Author: Les Obligations; La Responsibilité civile; Le Code civil annoté du Québec; Civil Codes; Produire l'homme: de quel droit?; Éthique de la mort et droit à la mort. Honours: Medal of Honor of the Quebec Bar, 1988; Honorary PhD, Sherbrooke University, 1990; Honorary PhD, l'Université René Descartes, Paris V, 1994; Honorary PhD, l'Université Notre-Dame de la Paix, Namur, Belgique, 1998; Honorary PhD, University of Ottawa, 2001; Yves Pélicier Award, International Academy of Mental Health, 2001; Medal, 125th Anniversary, Faculty of Law, University of Montreal, 2004; Ramon John Hnatyshyn Award, 2004; Creation of la Chaire Jean-Louis Baudouin in Civil Law, Faculty of Law, Montreal University, 2006; Honorary PhD, McGill University, 2007; Medal, Faculty of Law, University of Montreal, 2009; Advocatus Emeritus of the Quebec Bar, 2009; Honorary PhD, l'Université Jean Moulin Lyon 3, 2009. Memberships: Royal Society of Canada; Academician, International Academy of Comparative Law; Academician of l'Académie de lettres du Québec; Academician, Academia Puertorriquena de Jurisprudencia y Legislacion de Puerto Rico. Address: 875 Antonine Maillet Avenue, Outremont (Quebec), H2V 2Y6, Canada.

DICTIONARY OF INTERNATIONAL BIOGRAPHY 36th EDITION

BAUMAN Zygmunt, b. 19 November 1925, Poznan, Poland. Sociologist. m. Janina Bauman, 18 August 1948, 3 daughters. Education: MA, 1954; PhD, 1956. Appointments: Warsaw University, 1953-68; Tel Aviv University, 1968-75; University of Leeds, 1971-91. Publications: Modernity and the Holocaust; Legislators and Interpreters; Intimations of Postinedermity; Thinking Sociologically; Modernity and Ambivalence; Freedom; Memories of Class; Culture as Praxis; Between Class and Elite; Mortality, Immortality and Other Life Strategies; Postmodernity and its Discontents, 1997; In Search of Politics, 1999; Liquid Modernity, 2000; Individualized Society, 2000; Community: Seeking Safety in an Uncertain World, 2001; Society Under Siege, 2002; Liquid Love: On the Frailty of Human Bonds, Wasted Lives: Modernity and its Outcasts, 2003; Europe: An Unfinished Adventure, Identity: Conversations with Benedetto Vecchi, 2004; Liquid Life, 2005; Liquid Fear, Liquid Times, 2006; Consuming Life, 2007. Contributions to: Times Literary Supplement; New Statesman; Professional Periodicals. Honour: Amalfi European Prize for Sociology; Theodor Adorno Prize, 1998; Dr honoris causa: Oslo, 1997, Lapland, 1999, Uppsala, 2000, West of England, 2001, London, 2002, Sofia, 2002, Charles University, Prague, 2002, Copenhagen, 2002, University of Leeds, 2004. Memberships: British Sociological Association; Polish Sociological Association. Address: 1 Lawnswood Gardens, Leeds LS16 6HF, England.

BAUMANN Herbert Karl Wilhelm, b. 31 July 1925, Berlin, Germany. Composer; Conductor. m. Marianne Brose, 2 sons. Education: Composing (with Paul Hoeffer and Boris Blacher) and Conducting (with Sergiu Celibidache), International Music Institute, Berlin. Appointments: Composer and Conductor, Deutsches Theater Berlin, 1947-53; Composer and Conductor, State Theatres Berlin, 1953-70; Musical Head Manager, Composer and Conductor, Bavarian State Theatre, 1970-79; Freelance Composer, 1979-. Publications: Music for more than 500 theatre plays and over 40 TV plays; Libretto and music for 2 ballets: Alice in Wonderland and Rumpelstilzgen; Numerous CDs; Text for: Moritat vom eigensinnigen Eheweibe; Der unzufriedene Schneemann; Das blaue Kaninchen; Vom Millerburschen, dem ein Bauer das Pferd nahm; Der wohlfeile Gaensebraten; Work collected in German National Library and Bavarian State Library; Numerous works for orchestra, for choir, and for chamber orchestra; Many chamber music works. Honours: Man of Achievement, 1973; Diploma of Honour, 1981; Bundesverdienstkreuz (Order of the Federal Republic of Germany); Member of Honour, Bund Deutscher Zupfmusiker, 1990; Diploma of Honour for 50 years' membership, GEMA, 1998. Memberships: GEMA; Bund Deutscher Zupfmusiker; Verband Muenchener Tonkuenstler. Address: Weitlstrasse 66/2049, 8035 München, Germany. E-mail: hkwbau@augustinum.net Website: www.komponisten.net

BAUROV Yuriy Alexeevich, b. 14 March 1947, Russia. Physicist. m. 2 sons. Education: Moscow Aviation Institute, 1972; PhD, 1978. Appointments: Chief of Laboratory, Central Research Institute of Machine Building; Presidency of Council of Directors, Closed Joint-Stock Company, Research Institute of Cosmic Physics. Publications: Books: On the Structure of Physical Vacuum and a New Interaction in Nature (Theory, Experiment, Applications), 2000; Global Anisotropy of Physical Space, Experimental and Theoretical Basis, Nova Science, New York, 2004; Several articles in professional journals. Honour: Diplôme 26 Salon International des Inventions, Genève, 1998; Gold Award, Seoul International Invention Fair, 2004; Gold Award, Brussels Eureka! 2004. Membership: New York Academy of Sciences, 1994-98. Address: Central Research Institute for Machine Building, 141070, Koroloyov, Moscow Region, Pionerskaya 4, Russia.

BAYARSAIKHAN Batsukh, b. 5 September 1970, Gobi-Altai province, Mongolia. Lawyer. m. A Battuya, 2 sons. Education: LLB, 1995, LLM, 1997, Dr Jur, 2004, National University of Mongolia; LLM, University of Bayreuth, Bavaria, Germany, 2000. Appointments: Lecturer, 1995-98, Head in Charge of Education, School of Law, 2001-04, Director of Research Center for Mongolian State and Legal History, 2004-, Lecturer, Department of History and Theory of Law and State, School of Law, 2004-, Member, Board of Directors, 2007-, National University of Mongolia; Member, Advocates Association and certified Lawyer, 1997-2008; Legal Advisor to Member of Parliament of Mongolia, 2004-08; Co-ordinator and Senior Researcher, "Khalkh Juram Law" Joint Project with Mongol Studies Center, Inner Mongolia University, China, 2005-09; Co-ordinator and Senior Researcher, "20 volumes of Mongolia Legislation: 1206-2009" project, 2006-09; General Consultant, Law firm "Civil Rights", 2006-08; National Legal Consultant, "Index-based livestock insurance" project, World Bank, 2006-08; Advisor to General Director, Altai Construction LLC, 2007-08; Director, Public Administration and Management Department, Ministry of Foreign Affairs and Trade, 2008-. Publications: 20 scientific works; 40 articles and reports; 6 edited books. Honours: Best Young Researcher, National University of Mongolia, 2005. Address: Management Department, Ministry of Foreign Affairs and Trade, Peace Avenue 7A, Ulaanbaatar 14210, Mongolia. E-mail: bayarsaikhan@mfat.gov.mn

BAYLISS Peter, b. 1 September 1936, Luton, England. Mineralogist. m. Daphne Phyllis Webb. Education: BE, 1959, MSc, 1962, PhD, 1967, University of New South Wales, Australia. Appointments: Professor, University of Calgary, Calgary, Alta, Canada, 1967-92; Professor Emeritus, 1992-; Research Associate, Australian Museum 1993-. Publications: 105 papers; 15 monographs; 41 book reviews; 61 X-ray powder diffraction data. Honours: University Soccer Blue, 1961; Commonwealth Scholarship, 1964; Fellow, Mineralogical Society of America, 1970; Killam Fellowship, 1981; New mineral named peterbaylissite, 1995; Fellow, International Centre Diffraction Data, 2000; Fellow, Mineralogical Society, Great Britain, 2000; Listed in national and international biographical dictionaries. Memberships: Mineralogical Association of Canada; Mineralogical Record. Address: Department of Mineralogy, Australian Museum, 6 College Street, Sydney, NSW 2010, Australia.

BEALE Hugh Gurney, b. 4 May 1948. Professor of Law. m. Jane Wilson Cox, 2 sons, 1 daughter. Education: BA (Hons), Jurisprudence, Exeter College, Oxford. Appointments: Lecturer, Law, University of Connecticut, 1969-71; Lecturer, Law, University College of Wales, Aberystwyth, 1971-73; Lecturer, Law, 1973-86, Reader, Law, 1986-87, University of Bristol; Professor of Law, University of Warwick, 1987-; Law Commissioner, 2000-07. Publications: Remedies for Breach of Contract, 1980; Principles of European Contract Law: Parts I & II, joint editor with Ole Lando, 2000; Contract cases and materials, joint editor, 5th edition, 2008; Casebooks on the Common Law of Europe: Contract Law, joint editor, 2nd edition, 2010; Chitty on Contracts, general editor, 30th edition, 2008. Honours: Honorary Bencher, Lincoln's Inn, 1999; Honorary QC, 2002; Fellow, British Academy, 2004. Address: School of Law, University of Warwick, Coventry CV4 7AL, England. E-mail: hugh.beale@warwick.ac.uk

BEALES Derek (Edward Dawson), b. 12 June 1931, Felixstowe, England. Emeritus Professor of Modern History; Writer. Education: BA, 1953, MA, PhD, 1957, Sidney Sussex College, Cambridge University. Appointments: Research Fellow, 1955-58, Fellow, 1958-, Tutor, 1961-70, Vice Master, 1973-75, Sidney Sussex College, Cambridge University; Assistant Lecturer, 1962-65, Lecturer, 1965-80, Chairman, Faculty Board of History, 1979-81, Professor of Modern History, 1980-97, Emeritus Professor, 1997-, Sidney Sussex College, Cambridge University; Editor, Historical Journal, 1971-75; Member of Council, Royal Historical Society, 1984-87; British Academy Representative, Standing Committee for Humanities, European Science Foundation, 1993-99; Recurring Visiting Professor, Central European University, Budapest, 1995-. Publications: England and Italy 1859-60, 1961; From Castlereagh to Gladstone 1815-85, 1969; The Risorgimento and the Unification of Italy, 1971, 2nd edition, with E F Biagini, 2002; History and Biography, 1981; History, Society and the Churches: Essays in Honour of Owen Chadwick (editor with G F A Best), 1985; Joseph II: In the Shadow of Maria Theresa 1741-80, 1987; Mozart and the Habsburgs, 1993; Sidney Sussex College Quatercentenary Essays, (editor with H B Nisbet), 1996; Prosperity and Plunder: European Catholic Monasteries in the Age of Revolution, 1650-1815, 2003; Enlightenment and Reform in the Eighteenth Century, 2005; Joseph II: Against the World 1780-1790, 2009. Honours: Prince Consort Prize, 1960; Doctor of Letters, 1988; Fellow, British Academy, 1989; Stenton Lecturer, University of Reading, 1992; Birkbeck Lecturer, Trinity College, Cambridge, 1993; Leverhulme 2000 Emeritus Fellowship, 2001-2003; Paolucci/Bagehot Prize, Intercollegiate Studies Institute, Wilmington, Delaware, USA, 2004. Memberships: Fellow, Royal Historical Society; Member, Athenaeum. Address: Sidney Sussex College, Cambridge CB2 3HU, England. E-mail: deb1000@cam.ac.uk

BEAN Sean, b. 17 April 1959, Sheffield, Yorkshire, England. Actor. m. (1) Debra James, 1981, divorced, (2) Melanie Hill, 1990, divorced 1997, 2 daughters, (3) Abigail Cruttenden, 1997, divorced 2000, 1 daughter, (4) Georgina Sutcliffe, 2008. Education: Royal Academy of Dramatic Art. Creative Works: Appearances include: the Last Days of Mankind and Der Rosenkavalier at Citizen's Theatre, Glasgow, Who Knew Mackenzie? and Gone, Theatre Upstairs, Roy Court, Romeo in Romeo and Juliet, RSC, Stratford-upon-Avon, 1986, Captain Spencer in The Fair Maid of the West, RSC, London; TV Appearances include: Clarissa; Fool's Gold; Role of Mellors in BBC Dramatization of Lady Chatterley's Lover; Inspector Morse; Role Sharpe in TV Series; A Woman's Guide to Adultery; Jacob; Bravo Two Zero; Extremely Dangerous; Crusoe, 2008; Red Riding, 2009; Films: Caravaggio, Stormy Monday, War Requiem, The Field, Patriot Games, Gone With the Wind, Goldeneye, When Saturday Comes, Anna Karenina, Ronin; The Lord of the Rings: The Fellowship of the Ring; Don't Say a Word; Equilibrium; Tom and Thomas; The Big Empty; Windprints; Essex Boys; Troy, Pride (voice), National Treasure, 2004; The Island, North Country, Flightplan, 2005; The Dark, Silent Hill, The Elder Scrolls IV: Oblivion (video game), 2006; Outlaw, The Hitcher (remake), Far North, 2007. Address: c/o ICM Ltd, Oxford House, London W1R 1RB, England.

BEAR Isabel Joy, b. 4 January 1927, Camperdown, Victoria, Australia. Research Scientist. Education: Associate Diploma in Applied Chemistry, MTC, 1950; Associate Diploma in Applied Science, 1950; Fellowship Diploma Applied Chemistry, RMIT 1972; D App Sc, 1978. Appointments: Experimental Scientist, AERE Harwell, 1950-51; Research Assistant, University of Birmingham, UK, 1951-53; Experimental Scientist, CSIRO Division of Industrial Chemistry/Mineral Chemistry, 1953-67; Senior Research Scientist, CSIRO Division of Mineral Chemistry/Products, 1967-72; Principal Research Scientist, 1972-79; Senior Principal Research Scientist, 1979-92; Honorary Fellow, 1992-2006. Publications: More than 70 refereed papers in scientific journals; Co-author: Alumina to Zirconia – The History of the CSIRO Division of Mineral Chemistry, 2001. Honours: Appointed, Member of the Order of Australia for Services to Science; Leighton Medallist, Royal Australian Chemical Institute; Listed on the Victorian Honour Roll of Women, 2005. Memberships: Royal Australian Chemical Institute; Australasian Institute of Mining and Metallurgy. Address: 2/750 Waverley Road, Glen Waverley, VIC 3150, Australia.

BEASLEY Arthur Wynyard, b. 25 January 1926, Auckland, New Zealand. Surgeon; Writer. m. Alice Margaret Clarke, 4 sons, 1 deceased. Education: Mount Albert Grammar School; University of Otago; Royal College of Surgeons of England; MB ChB (NZ), 1951; FRCS (Edin), 1956; FRACS, 1957; FACS, 1979; FRCS (Eng), 2001. Appointments: Orthopaedic Registrar, Palmerston North Hospital, Heatherwood Hospital, Ascot, 1955; St Margaret's Hospital, Epping, 1955-56; Visiting Orthopaedic Surgeon: Wellington Hospital, 1958-89; Wairau Hospital, Blenheim, 1959-69; Dannevirke Hospital, 1964-69; Consultant Surgeon, Wellington Artificial Limb Centre, 1962-; Clinical Reader in Surgery, University of Otago, 1981-89; Professorial Research Fellow, Central Institute of Technology, 1996-2000. Publications: The Light Accepted, 1992; Portraits at the Royal Australasian College of Surgeons, 1993; Fellowship of Three, 1993; Borne Free, 1995; The Club on The Terrace, 1996; Home Away from Home, 2000; The Mantle of Surgery, 2002; Papers include: The Disability of James VI & I, 1995; Transplanting Hunter, 2003; Churchill, Moran and the struggle for survival, 2010. Honours: OBE (Mil), 1971; Winston Churchill Memorial Fellowship, 1973; ED, 1974; Colonel Commandant, Royal New Zealand Medical Corps, 1986-90; Hunterian Professorship, 2002; CNZM, 2005; Court of Honour, Royal Australasian College of Surgeons, 1986. Memberships: Senior Fellow, British Orthopaedic Association; Senior Fellow, New Zealand Orthopaedic Association; Trustee, Past-president, Wellington Club; Fellow, Royal Society of Medicine. Address: 37 Hay Street, Oriental Bay, Wellington 6011, New Zealand. E-mail: alwynbeasley@hotmail.com

BEASLEY John David, (David Sellers), b. 26 October 1944, Hornsea, Yorkshire, England. Social Worker. m. Marian Ruth Orford, 1969, 1 son, 2 daughters. Education: London University Diploma in Sociology; Certificate of Qualification in Social Work, Polytechnic of North London, England. Appointments: United Kingdom Band of Hope Union, 1960-70; Social Worker, London Borough of Tower Hamlets, 1970-94. Publications: Who Was Who in Peckham, 1985; The Bitter Cry Heard and Heeded, 1989; 500 Quotes and Anecdotes, 1992; Origin of Names in Peckham and Nunhead, 1993; Peckham and Nunhead Churches, 1995; Peckham Rye Park Centenary, 1995; Peckham and Nunhead, 1995; Another 500 Quotes and Anecdotes, 1996; Transport in Peckham and Nunhead, 1997; East Dulwich, 1998, revised 2008; The Story of Peckham and Nunhead, 1999; Peckham and Nunhead Remembered, 2000; Southwark Remembered, 2001; East Dulwich Remembered, 2002; Southwark Revisited, 2004; Peckham and Nunhead Through Time, 2009; East Dulwich Through Time, 2009; Origin of Place Names in Peckham and Nunhead, 2010; Camberwell Through Time, 2010; Contributions to: Challenge; South London Press;

Editor, Peckham Society News, 1987-. Honour: Southwark Civic Award, 1997. Memberships: Society of Authors; Royal Historical Society. Address: South Riding, 6 Everthorpe Road, London SE15 4DA, England.

BEATRIX Wilhelmina Armgard (Queen of the Netherlands), b. 31 January 1938, Baarn, The Netherlands. m. Claus George Willem Otto Frederik Geert von Amsberg, March 1966, deceased 2002, 3 sons. Education: Leiden State University. Invested as Queen of the Netherlands, 30 April 1980-. Honour: Hon K.G. Address: c/o Government Information Service, Press & Publicity Department, Binnenhof 19, 2513 AA The Hague, The Netherlands.

BEATTIE Ann, b. 8 September 1947, Washington, District of Columbia, USA. Writer; Poet. m. Lincoln Perry. Education: BA, American University, Washington, DC, 1969; MA, University of Connecticut, 1970. Appointments: Visiting Assistant Professor, 1976-77, Visiting Writer, 1980, University of Virginia, Charlottesville; Briggs Copeland Lecturer in English, Harvard University, 1977; Guggenheim Fellow, 1977. Publications: Secrets and Surprises, 1978; Where You'll Find the Other Stories, 1986; What Was Mine and Other Stories, 1991; With This Ring, 1997; My Life, Starring Dara Falcon, 1998; Park City: New and Selected Stories, 1998; New and Selected Poems, 1999; Perfect Recall, 2001; The Doctor's House, 2002; Follies: New Stories, 2005. Contributions to: Various publications. Memberships: American Academy and Institute of Arts and Letters; PEN; Authors' Guild. Honours: Award in literature, 1980; Hon LHD, American University. Address: c/o Janklow and Nesbit, 598 Madison Avenue, New York, NY 10022, USA.

BEATTY Warren, b. 30 March 1937, Richmond, Virginia, USA. Actor. m. Annette Bening, 1992, 4 children. Education: Stella Adler Theatre School. Creative Works: Film Appearances include: Splendor in the Grass, Roman Spring of Mrs Stone, 1961; All Fall Down, 1962; Lilith, Mickey One, 1965; Promise Her Anything, Kaleidoscope, 1966; Bonnie and Clyde, 1967; The Only Game in Town, 1969; McCabe and Mrs Miller, 1971; Dollars, 1972; The Parallax View, 1974; Shampoo, 1975; The Fortune, 1976; Heaven Can Wait, 1978; Reds, 1981; Ishtar, 1987; Dick Tracy, 1989; Bugsy, 1991; Love Affair, Bulworth, 1998; Town and Country, 2001; Dean Tavoularis: The Magician of Hollywood, 2003; One Bright Shining Moment, 2005. TV Appearances include: Studio One; Playhouse 90; A Salute to Dustin Hoffman, 1999. Theatre Roles include: A Loss of Roses, 1960. Honours include: Academy Award, Best Director, 1981; Commander, Ordre des Arts et des Lettres; Irving Thalberg Special Academy Award, 2000; Fellow, BAFTA, 2002; Honorary Chair, Stella Adler School of Acting, 2004; Kennedy Center Honors, 2004. Cecil B. Demille Award, 2007. Address: CAA, 9830 Wilshire Boulevard, Beverly Hills, CA 90212, USA.

BEAUMONT Mary Rose, b. 6 June 1932, Petersfield, Hampshire, England. Art Historian. m. Lord Beaumont of Whitley, deceased, 1 son, 2 daughters. Education: Prior's Field, Godalming, Surrey; Courtauld Institute of Art, University of London, 1975-78. Appointments: Founder, Centre for the Study of Modern Art, ICA, 1972; Lecturer, Modern Art Studies, Christie's Education, 1978-2001; Lecturer in Humanities, City & Guilds School of Art, 1996-2008. Publications include: Jean Macalpine-Intervals in Light, 1998; Carole Hodgson, London, 1999; George Kyriacou, London, 1999; Contributions include: Jock McFadyen, A Book about a Painter, 2000; New European Artists; an Annual of contemporary European artists introduced by prominent art critics, Amsterdam, 2001; Albert Irvin: The Complete Prints. Memberships: AICA, Association Internationale de Critiques d'Art; Arts Club; Chelsea Arts Club; Royal Overseas League; Honorary Fellow, Royal Society of British Sculptors. Address: 40 Elms Road, London, SW4 9EX, England.

BEAVEN Freda, b. 30 July 1923, Croydon, Surrey, England. Musician; Singer; Accompanist. m. C H J Beaven, 1945, 1 son. Education: Piano tuition from childhood; Private singing tuition, 1940-, later with Henry Cummings FRAM. Career: LRAM Teacher, 1967; LRAM Performer, 1968; Choral Experience at BBC, 1963-70; Recitals in London, 1968-; Director, The Lindsey Singers, Madrigals, 1970-74; Private Teaching, Singing, Piano and Theory, 1967-; Professional Choralist, London, 1970-74; Voice Tutor and Accompanist, Westwood Centre, Oldham, 1980-88; Singing and Theory Specialist; Voice and Language Tutor, Oldham Further Education College, 1980-88; Currently gives specialist voice training and advanced coaching to singers of the English Song, French Song, Italian and German Lieder repertoires, Southport; Adjudicator, British Federation of Music Festivals, 10 years. Publications: Music Theory Makes Sense, textbook, 1985; Established Roselle Publications, 1985; Contributions to: SINGING, publication of the Association of Teachers of Singing. Memberships: Royal Society of Musicians; Member Emeritus, Association of Teachers of Singing. Address: Southport, Merseyside PR8 2AF, England.

BEBB Prudence, b. 20 March 1939, Catterick, North Yorkshire, England. Writer. Education: BA, 1960, Diploma in Education, 1961, Sheffield University. Appointments: Teacher, Snaith School, 1961-63; History Teacher, Howden School, 1963-90. Publications: The Eleventh Emerald, 1981; The Ridgeway Ruby, 1983; The White Swan, 1984; The Nabob's Nephew, 1985; Life in Regency York, 1992; Butcher, Baker, Candlestick Maker, 1994; Georgian Poppleton, 1994; Life in Regency Harrogate, 1994; Life in Regency Scarborough, 1997; Life in Regency Whitby, 2000; Life in Regency Beverley, 2004; Life in Regency Bridlington, 2006. Contributions to: Impressions, the Journal of the Northern Branch of the Jane Austen Society. Membership: English Centre of International PEN. Address: 12 Bracken Hills, Upper Poppleton, York YO26 6DH, England.

BECK JORGENSEN Torben, b. 7 March 1946, Copenhagen, Denmark. Professor. m. Jette, 2 sons. Education: MS, Economics, 1972; PhD, 1981. Appointments: Various positions at Ministry of Finance, Stanford University, University of York and University of Georgia; Professor, Chair, University of Copenhagen, 1987; Professor Emeritus, Department of Political Science, University of Copenhagen, 2011; Visiting Professor, Danish Institute of Governmental Research, 2011; Adjunct Professor, Copenhagen Business School, 2011. Publications: Value Consciousness and Public Management, 2006; Public Values – their Nature, Stability and Change. The Case of Denmark, 2007; Public Values: An Inventory, Administration and Society, 2007; Accountability as a differentiated value in supranational governance, 2010; Value Dynamics: Towards a Framework for Analyzing Public Value Changes, 2011; An aftermath of NPM: Regained Relevance of Public Values and Public Service Motivation, 2011; Weber and Kafka: The rational and enigmatic bureaucracy, 2012; Public Value Dimensions. Developing and testing a multidimensional classification, 2012; Codes of Good Governance. National and Global Public Values? 2013. Honours: The Tietgen Gold Medal for PhD dissertation, 1981; The Royal Order of Dannebrog, 1998; First Class, 2011. Memberships: Public Administration; The American

Review of Public Administration; Scandinavian Journal of Organizational Studies; The Public Value Consortium; European Group of Public Administration. Address: Fresiavej 11, DK-2970 Horsholm, Denmark. E-mail: tbj@ifs.ku.dk

BECKER Boris, b. 22 November 1967, Leimen, Germany. Tennis Player. m. (1) Barbara Feltus, divorced, 2001, 2 sons, 1 daughter by Angela Ermakova, (2) Sharlely "Lilly" Kerssenberg, 2009. Appointments: Started playing tennis at Blau-Weiss Club, Leimen; Won W German Junior Championship, 1983; Runner-up, US Junior Championship; Coached by Ion Tiriac, 1984-; Quarter Finalist, Australia Championship; Winner, Young Masters Tournament, Birmingham, England, 1985; Grand Prix Tournament, Queen's, 1985; Won Men's Singles Championship, Wimbledon, 1985, 1986, 1989, Finalist, 1988, 1990, 1991, 1995; Finalist, Benson & Hedges Championship, Wembley, London, 1985; Masters Champion, 1988, Finalist, 1989; US Open Champion, 1989; Semi Finalist, French Open, 1989; Winner, Davis Cup, 1989, Australian Open Championship, 1991, 1996, IBM/ATP Tour Championship, 1992, 1995, Grand Slam Cup, 1996; Principal Owner, tennis division, Völkl Inc, 2000-; Boris Becker TV, 2009. Publications: The Player (autobiography), 2004. Honours: Sportsman of the Year, 1985; Hon Citizen of Leimen, 1986; Named World Champion, 1991; 64 titles (49 singles). Memberships: Board member, Bayern Munich Football Club, 2001-; Chair, Laureus Sport for Good Foundation, 2002-.

BECKER Uwe Yü Eugen, b. 17 May 1947, Chemnitz, Germany. Physicist. m. Sigrid, 1 son, 1 daughter. Education: Diploma, Physics, 1971, PhD, Physics, 1977, Habilitation, Experimental Physics, 1985, Technical University of Berlin. Appointments: Postdoctoral Fellow, Free University of Berlin, 1978-79; Lawrence Berkeley Laboratory, Berkeley, California, 1980-82; Assistant Professor, Faculty of Physics, Technical University of Berlin, 1982-86; Associate Professor, Faculty of Physics and Astronomy, University of Würzburg, 1987-89; Head, VUV Radiation and X-Ray Physics Group, Fritz-Haber-Institute, Max-Planck Society, 1990-; Adjunct Professor, Faculty of Mathematics and Natural Sciences, Technical University of Berlin, 1991-; Head, Atomic Physics Division, German Physical Society, 2007-; Professor, College of Science, King Saud University, Riyadh, 2009-. Publications: The 4d-4f Giant Resonances (in Giant Resonances in Atoms, Molecules and Solids, 1987); VUV and Soft X-Ray Photoionization, 1996; Complete Photoionization Experiments, 1998; Correlation and Coherence Phenomena Studied by Photoelectron Spectroscopy, 2009. Honours: Honours Medal, Technical University of Berlin, 1971; Research Fellow, German Research Counsel, 1988; Fellow, American Physical Society, 1997; Highly Cited Researcher, Institute of Scientific Information, 2003; Fellow, World Innovation Foundation, 2004; Award, Distinguished Scientist Program of King Saud University, 2009; Fellow, American Biographical Institute and International Biographical Centre, 2010; Fellow, Institute of Physics, UK, 2011; Listed in international biographical dictionaries. Memberships: German Physical Society; European Physical Society; American Physical Society; Institute of Physics, UK. Address: Fritz-Haber-Institute, Max-Planck-Society, Faradayweg 4-6, D-14195 Berlin, Germany and Faculty of Science, King Saud University, Riyadh, Saudi Arabia. E-mail: becker_u@fhi-berlin.mpg.de

BECKETT Kenneth Albert, b. 12 January 1929, Brighton, Sussex, England. Horticulturist; Technical Advisor; Editor. m. Gillian Tuck, 1 August 1973, 1 son. Education: Diploma, The Royal Horticultural Society. Appointments: Technical Editor, Gardener's Chronicle, Reader's Digest; Retired. Publications: The Love of Trees, 1975; Illustrated Dictionary of Botany, 1977; Concise Encyclopaedia of Garden Plants, 1978; Amateur Greenhouse Gardening, 1979; Growing Under Glass, 1981; Complete Book of Evergreens, 1981; Growing Hardy Perennials, 1981; Climbing Plants, 1983; The Garden Library, 4 volumes: Flowering House Plants, Annuals and Biennials, Roses, Herbs, 1984; The RHS Encyclopaedia of House Plants, 1987; Evergreens, 1990; Alpine Garden Society Encyclopaedia of Alpines, 2 volumes, 1993-94. Contributions to: The Garden; The Plantsman. Honours: Veitch Memorial Medal, Royal Horticultural Society, 1987; Lyttel Trophy, 1995 and Clarence Elliott Memorial Award, 1995, Alpine Garden Society. Memberships: The Royal Horticultural Society; Botanical Society of the British Isles; The Plantsman; International Dendrology Society; Alpine Garden Society. Address: Bramley Cottage, Docking Road, Stanhoe, King's Lynn, Norfolk PE31 8QF, England.

BECKETT Lucy, b. 10 August 1942, Windsor, England. Writer; Teacher. m. John Warrack, 2 sons, 2 daughters. Education: Cranborne Chase School, 1955-59; MA, New Hall, Cambridge, University, 1960-63. Appointments: Teacher, Head of English, Head of VI Form, Monastic Tutor, Ampleforth Abbey and College, 1980-2001. Publications: Books: Wallace Stevens, 1974; Richard Wagner: Parsifal, 1981; York Minster, 1981; The Returning Wave, 1996; Rievaulx, Fountains, Byland and Jervaulx, 1998; The Time Before You Die, 1999; In the Light of Christ: Writings in the Western Tradition, 2006; A Postcard from the Volcano, 2009; Many articles, book reviews, etc. Address: Beck House, Rievaulx, York YO62 5LB, England. E-mail: lucy@aelred.demon.co.uk

BECKETT Margaret Mary, b. 15 January 1943, Ashton-under-Lyne, Lancashire, England. Politician. m. Leo Beckett, 2 step-sons. Education: Manchester College of Science and Technology, John Dalton Polytechnic. Appointments: Engineering Apprentice, Association of Electrical Industries, Manchester; Experimental Officer, University of Manchester; Researcher, Labour Party Headquarters; Special Adviser at ODA February-October 1974; Parliamentary Private Secretary, Minister for Overseas Development, 1974-75; Assistant Government Whip, 1975-76; Minister, Department of Education, 1976-79; Labour MP Lincoln, 1974-79; Sponsored by TGWU, 1977-; Principal Researcher, Granada TV, 1979-83; Labour Party National Executive Committee, 1980-97; MP, Derby South, 1983-; Opposition Spokesperson, Social Security, 1984-89; Shadow Chief Secretary, 1989-92; Shadow Leader of the House, Campaigns Coordinator, Deputy Leader of the Opposition, 1992-94; Appointed to Privy Council, 1993; Leader of the Opposition, 1994; Shadow Secretary of State for Health, 1994-95; Shadow President, 1995-97, President, 1997-98, Board of Trade, President of Privy Council, Leader, House of Commons, 1998-2001; Secretary of State, Department of Environment, Food and Rural Affairs, 2001-06; Secretary of State for Foreign and Commonwealth Affairs, 2006-07; Minister of State for Housing and Planning, 2008-09. Publications: The Need for Consumer Protection, 1972; The National Enterprise Board; The Nationalisation of Shipbuilding, Shiprepair and Marine Engineering; Relevant Sections of Labour's Programme, 1972, 1973; Renewing the NHS, 1995; Vision for Growth - A New Industrial Strategy for Britain, 1996. Memberships: Transport and General Workers' Union, Parliamentary Labour Party Group, National Executive Committee, 1988-98; National Union of Journalists; BECTU; Fabian Society; Tribune Group; Socialist Education Committee; Labour Women's Action Committee; Derby Co-op Party; Socialist Environment and Resources Association; Amnesty International; Council of St George's College, Windsor, 1976-1982. Address: House of Commons, London SW1A 0AA, England.

BECKHAM David Robert Joseph, b. 2 May 1975, Leytonstone, London, England. Footballer. m. Victoria Adams, 1999, 3 sons, 1 daughter. Career: Player with Manchester United, trainee, 1991, team debut, 1992, League debut, 1995, 386 appearances, 80 goals, December 2002; 7 caps for England Under 21s, represented England 1996-, Captain, 2000-2006; Player with Real Madrid, 2003-07; Player with Los Angeles Galaxy, American Soccer League, 2007-; On loan to AC Milan, 2009. Publications: Beckham: My World, 2001; David Beckham: My Side, 2002; Beckham: Both Feet on the Ground, 2003. Honours: Bobby Charlton Skills Award, 1987; Manchester United Player of the Year, 1996-97; Young Player of the Year Professional Football Association, 1996-97; Sky Football Personality of the Year, 1997; 5 Premiership Medals; 2 Football Association Medals; European Cup Medal; 2 Charity Shield Winner Medals; OBE, 2003; English Football Hall of Fame, 2008.

BECKHAM Victoria, (Posh Spice), b. 17 April 1974, Cuffley, England. Vocalist. m. David Beckham, 1999, 3 sons, 1 daughter. Career: Member, Spice Girls; Numerous TV and radio appearances, magazine interviews; Film, Spiceworld: The Movie, 1997; Victoria Beckham: Coming to America, 2007; World tour including dates in UK, Europe, India and USA; Solo artist, 2000-. Recordings: Albums: The Spice Girls: Spice, 1996; Spiceworld, 1997; Forever, 2000; Singles: Wannabe, Say You'll Be There, 2 Become 1, 1996; Mama/Who Do You Think You Are, Step To Me, Spice Up Your Life, Too Much, 1997; Stop, (How Does It Feel To Be) On Top of the World, with England United, Move Over/Generation Next, Viva Forever, Goodbye, 1998; Holler/Let Love Lead the Way, 2000. Solo: Out of Your Mind, 2000; Not Such an Innocent Girl, 2001; A Mind of Its Own, 2002; This Groove/Let Your Head Go, 2003; Solo albums: Victoria Beckham, 2001; Not Such An Innocent Girl, 2004. Honours: Best Video (Say You'll Be There), Best Single (Wannabe), Brit Awards, 1997; 2 Ivor Novello song writing awards, 1997; Best Band, Smash Hits Award, 1997; 3 American Music Awards, 1998; Special Award for International Sales, Brit Awards, 1998. Publications: Learning to Fly, autobiography, 2001; That Extra Half an Inch: Hair, Heels and Everything In Between, 2006. Address: c/o Lee & Thompson, Green Garden House, 15-22 St Christopher's Place, London, W1M 5HE, England. Website: c3.vmg.co.uk/spicegirls

BECKINSALE Kate, b. 26 July 1973, London, England. Actress. m. Len Wiseman, 2004, 1 daughter with Michael Sheen. Education: French and Russian Literature, New College, Oxford University, 1991-94. Career: TV includes: One Against the Wind, 1991; Cold Comfort Farm, 1995; Emma, 1996; Alice Through the Looking Glass, 1998; Films include: Much Ado About Nothing, 1993; Haunted, 1995; Emma, Shooting Fish, 1997; The Golden Bowl, 2000; Pearl Harbor, Serendipity, 2001; Laurel Canyon, 2002; Underworld, Tiptoes, 2003; Van Helsing, The Aviator, 2004; Underworld: Evolution, Click, 2006; Vacancy, 2007; Snow Angels, Nothing But the Truth, 2008; Whiteout, Fragments, Everybody's Fine, 2009; Play: The Seagull, 1995. Honours: Best Actress, Sitges – Catalonian International Film Festival, 1997; Best Supporting Actress, London Critics Circle Film Awards, 1999; IGN Babe Election, 2008. Address: International Creative Management, Oxford House, 76 Oxford Street, London W1N 0AX, England.

BECKWITH Merle Ray, b. 16 July 1942, East Grand Rapids, Michigan, USA. Writer: Poet. m. Barbara Cutler, 1982. Education: BA, Political Science, Western Michigan University, 1964; Graduate Student, Anthropology and Education, University of California at Los Angeles, 1966-68. Appointments: Teaching positions. Publications: Nature, 1980; Nature and Love, 1980; Meditations: A Collection of Contemplative Reflections, 1991; Contributions to many journals and periodicals. Honours: Golden Poetry Awards, World of Poetry, 1985, 1986, 1987; Listed in international biographical dictionaries. Memberships: American Society of Composers, Authors, and Publishers; California Chapparal Poets; California State Poetry Society; Christian Writers League; Academy of American Poets; National Amateur Press Association. Address: 3732 Monterey Pine, No A109, Santa Barbara, CA 93105, USA.

BECUCCI Stefano, b. 27 May 1964, Tavarnelle, Italy. Senior Lecturer. m. Monica Massari, 1 daughter. Education: Degree in Political Science, 1995; Specialization in Criminology, 1998; PhD, International Criminal Law, 2003. Appointments: Lecturer, 2001, Senior Lecturer, 2004-, Sociology, University of Florence. Publications: New Players in an Old Game: Sex Exploitation Market in Italy, 2008; Criminal Infiltration and Social Mobilisation Against Mafia. Gela: A City Between Tradition and Modernity, 2011. Memberships: Italian Sociological Association; Italian Criminological Association. Address: v le Giacomo, Matteotti, 70, Certaldo, 50052 Florence, Italy. E-mail: Stefano.becucca@unifi.it Website: www.unifi.it

BEDDINGTON John Richard, b. 15 September 1942, Haslemere, Surrey, England. Sports Manager; Sponsorship Consultant. m. Roseann Madden, 1972, 2 sons. Education: Eton College, 1956-60; Goethe Institute, 1960-61; College of Law, 1962-65. Appointments: Articled Clerk, Birkbeck, Julius, Coburn and Broad, 1962-65; Marketing Department, BP Chemicals (UK) Ltd, 1966-72; European Director, Grand Prix Tennis Circuit, 1972-77; Vice President, International Management Group, 1977-82; Chairman, Chief Executive Officer, Beddington Sports Management Inc, Toronto, Canada, 1982-; Executive Vice President, Tennis Canada, 1983-95; Tournament Director, Chairman, Canadian Open Tennis Championships, Toronto and Montreal, 1979-95; Chairman, Canadian Open Squash Championships, 1985-95; Group Managing Director, Masters International Ltd, 1995-97; Consultant, Tennis Canada, 1995-98; Chairman, Chief Executive Officer, Beddington Sports Management Ltd, 1997-; Consultant, Squash Rackets Association, 1997-99; Chairman, British Open Squash Championships, 2003-05; Founder, Tournament Director, The Masters Tennis at the Royal Albert Hall, 1997-2006; Chairman, Tennis World Cup, 2003-10; Save the Children Tennis Tournament Advisory Board, 2007-10; Chairman, Toronto Tennis Champions, 2007-10; Tennis Consultant to Barclays Bank plc, 2007-; Consultant, Dubai Duty Free, 2010-. Publications include: Play Better Squash, 1974; Several articles in a wide variety of sports publications. Honours: Several organisation awards for sports events; Inducted into Hall of Fame of Canadian Tennis, 2006; Listed in several Who's Who publications. Memberships: Director, WTA Tour, 1993-98; Duke of Edinburgh Award, Toronto, 1990-95; Professional Squash Association, 1998-2000; Cambridge Club, Toronto; All England Lawn Tennis Club, Wimbledon;

Huntercombe Golf Club. Address: The Old School House, Hook End, Checkendon, Oxon RG8 0UL, England. E-mail: jrbeddington@btinternet.com.

BEECHEY Gwilym Edward, b. 12 January 1938, London, England. Composer; Organist; Pianist. m. Joyce Downing, 1 son, 2 daughters. Education: Royal College of Music, 1948-56; MA, Mus B, PhD (Cantab), Magdalene College, Cambridge, 1956-62; FRCO; FTCL; LRAM; ARCM. Appointments: Lecturer, Music, Glasgow University, 1965-68; Lecturer, Music, Hull University, 1969-88; Organ Recitalist; Harpsichordist; Pianist; Church Musician; Recorder Player. Publications: Compositions: Organ pieces, anthems and canticle settings; Many arrangements for organ, many carols and carol arrangements; Many articles in learned journals on subjects from the 16th-20th centuries; Many editions of music from the 16th-18th centuries. Memberships: The Dolmetsch Foundation; Northamptonshire Organists Association. Address: 184 Mayor's Walk, Peterborough, PE3 6HQ, England.

BEERBAUM Frederik, b. 1942, Hilversum, The Netherlands. Artist. m. Mary Byrde, 1995, 1 daughter. Education: Graduate, Gerrit Rietveld Academy, Amsterdam, 1969. Career: Artist living and working in The Netherlands and Portugal; Exhibitions from 1971, including most recently: The Observer Observed, Portugal, 2005; Landscapes and City Scenes of Amsterdam, 2005; Landscapes and city scenes from the seventies, Helmond; Frederik Beerbaum, 65 Years Young, Amsterdam, 2007; Galerie 2 haaks bergen, 2007; Galerie Brummelkamp, AMC Amsterdam, 2007; Works in collections: Stedelijk Museum for Modern and Contemporary Art, Amsterdam; Amsterdam Council; Arts Council Drenthe; NAM (Dutch Petroleum Company); Ericsson Holland, Enschede, Amsterdam; Slotervaart Hospital, Amsterdam; Insurance Company "Het Groene Land", Lelystad; SBK: Amsterdam, Assen, Leeuwarden, Hilversum, Tilburg, Arnhem, Maastricht, Utrecht; Hogeschool Utrecht; Brummelkamp AMC collections; Photographic Atlas, Amsterdam. Publications: Works featured in newspapers and magazines; Exhibition catalogues; Book cover, Children, Problems at School and Stress, 1991; Book cover and 24 drawings, Silent Terror, 1995; Book Cover, Stress theoretical aspects of remedial education, 1999; Book cover and 12 paintings commissioned by the Hogeschool Utrecht for a book (In the Teacher's Mind, 2003); Eros and Thanatos 44 drawings, 2007; Bookcover illustration: Van der Wolf en Van Beukering Gedragsproblemen in scholen, ; Publisher Acco-Leuven Belgium; Listed in international biographical dictionaries. Membership: Arti et Amicitiae, 1978-. Address: CP 1366 Azenha, 8670-115 Aljezur, Algarve, Portugal; Kerkstraat 167, 1017 GH Amsterdam, The Netherlands. E-mail: frederikbeerbaum@yahoo.co.uk Website: www.beerbaumart.com

BEHME Thomas Joachim Walter, b. 5 April 1957, Braunschweig, Germany. Historian. Education: Teaching degree for secondary school, History & Philosophy, 1983, PhD (magna cum laude), Medieval and Modern History, 1992, University of Göttingen. Appointments: Archivist in radio archive, Südwestrundfunk Baden-Baden, 1995-96; Faculty Member, Institute for Philosophy, Freie Universität Berlin, 1997-. Publications: Samuel von Pufendorf: Naturrecht und Staat, 1995; Numerous articles in conference publications, several editions of works of Samuel Pufendorf and Erhard Weigel. Memberships: Erhard-Weigel-Gesellschaft, Wolfenbütteler Arbeitskreis für Barockforschung. E-mail: behme@zedat.tu-berlin.de

BELAFONTE Harry, b. 1 March 1927, New York, USA. Singer. m. (1) Marguerite Byrd, 1948, 2 daughters, (2) Julie Robinson, 1957, 1 son, 1 daughter. Education: Jamaica, 1935-39. Appointments: US Navy, 1943-45; American Negro Theatre; President, Belafonte Enterprises include; Goodwill Ambossador for UNICEF, 1987; Host, Nelson Mandela Birthday Concert, Wembley, 1988. Creative Works: Recordings: Mark Twain and other Folk Favorites, 1954; Belafonte, Calypso, 1956; An Evening with Belafonte, Belafonte Sings of the Caribbean, 1957; To Wish You a Merry Christmas, Belafonte Sings the Blues, 1958; Love is a Gentle Thing, Porgy and Bess, Belafonte at Carnegie Hall, My Lord What a Morning, 1959; Belafonte Returns to Carnegie Hall, Swing Dat Hammer, 1960; Jump Up Calypso, 1961; Midnight Special, The Many Moods of Belafonte, 1962; Streets I Have Walked, 1963; Belafonte at The Greek Theatre, Ballads, Blues and Boasters, 1964; An Evening with Belafonte/Makeba, 1965;En Gränslös Kväll På Operan, An Evening with Belafonte/Mouskouri, In My Quiet Room, Calypso in Brass, 1966; Belafonte on Campus, 1967; Belafonte Sings of Love, 1968; Homeward Bound, 1969; Belafonte By Request, Harry & Lena, For the Love of Life, 1970; The Warm Touch, Calypso Carnival, 1971; Belafonte... Live, 1972; Play Me, 1973; Concert in Japan, 1974; Turn the World Around, 1977; Loving You is Where I Belong, 1981; We Are the World, 1985; Paradise in Gazankulu, 1988; Belafonte '89, 1989; An Evening with Harry Belafonte and Friends, 1997; The Long Road to Freedom, An Anthology of Black Music, 2001; Belafonte Live Europe, 2003; European Tours, 1958, 1976, 1981, 1983, 1988; Broadway appearances: Three For Tonight; Almanac; Belafonte At The Palace; Films: Bright Road; Carmen Jones, 1952; Island in the Sun, 1957; The World, the Flesh and the Devil, 1958; Odds Against Tomorrow, 1959; The Angel Levine, 1969; Grambling's White Tiger, 1981; White Man's Burden; Buck and the Preacher, 1971; Uptown Saturday Night, 1974; White Man's Burden, 1995; Kansas City, 1996; Bobby, 2006; Motherland, 2009; Concerts in USA, Europe, 1989, Canada, 1990, USA and Canada, 1991, North America, Europe and Far East, 1996. Honours include: Golden Acord Award, Bronx Community College, 1989; Mandela Courage Award, 1990; National Medal of the Arts, 1994; New York Arts and Business Council Award, 1997; Distinguished American Award, John F Kennedy Library, Boston, 2002; Several honorary doctorates. Membership: Board Member, New York State Martin Luther King JR Institute for Non-violence, 1989-.

BELIAEV Yevgeny Ivanovich, b. 26 January 1939, Republic of Georgia. Educator. m. Ludmila Fedorova, 1 daughter. Education: Diploma, Teacher of Philosophy, 1961-66, Candidate of Philosophy, 1973, Moscow State University; Doctor of Philosophy, Saratov SU, 2002. Appointments: Assistant, 1966-69, Senior Teacher, 1969, Lecturer, 1973-98, Professor of Philosophy, 1999-, Saratov State University; Researcher, 1984-85, Scientific Secretary, 1975-85, Saratov State University. Publications: Numerous articles in professional journals. Honours: Long Standing Service Award, Medal of USSR, 1990; Medal of Honour, 100 Years of Saratov State University, 2009. Memberships: European Analytical Philosophy; Proceedings of Saratov University Ser Philosophy, Psychology, Pedagogy; Dissertation Committee, Saratov State University. Address: Posadsky Street, 193/199, rb 51, 410065 Saratov, Russia.

BELIKOV Sergey Borisovitch, b. 26 June 1953, Zaporizhzhye, Ukraine. Rector. Education: Engineer, Automobile Sciences, 1975; PhD, Material Sciences, 1982; Doctor of Sciences, Material Sciences, 1996. Appointments:

Scientific Worker, 1979, Assistant Professor, 1985, Machine Construction Institute, Zaporizhzhye; Rector, National Technical University, Zaporizhzhye, 1997-. Publications: Metal Science and Heat Treatment, 2001; Archives of Foundry, 2006; Archives of Metallurgy and Materials, 2007; Metal Science and Treatment, 2008; Problems of Modern Techniques in Engineering and Education, 2008. Honours: Order of Merit, III grade, 2000; Honoured Worker in Education, 2003; Honoured Diploma of Supreme Soviet of Ukraine, 2004; Order of Merit, II grade, 2009. Memberships: Academy of High School of Ukraine, 1999; Transport Academy of Ukraine, 2003. Address: Zhukovskogo str 64, Zaporizhzhye 69063, Ukraine. E-mail: rector@zntu.edu.ua

BELKIN Boris David, b. 26 January 1948, Sverdlovsk, Russia. Violinist. m. Dominique, 1 son, 1 daughter. Education: Began violin studies aged 6; Central Music School, Moscow; Moscow Conservatory with Yankelevitz and Andrievsky. Career: Public appearances from 1955; Debut in West, 1974 with Zubin Mehta and the Israel Philharmonic; Performances with Berlin Philharmonic, Concertgebouw, IPO, Los Angeles Philharmonic, Philadelphia, Cleveland, Season 1987-88, Pittsburgh, Royal Philharmonic and Tokyo Philharmonic Orchestras. Recordings: Paganini Concerto No 1 with the Israel Philharmonic; Tchaikovsky and Sibelius Concertos with the Philharmonia Orchestra; Prokofiev's Concertos with the Zurich Tonhalle Orchestra; Brahms Concerto with the London Symphony; Glazunov and Shostakovich Concerto No 1 with the Royal Philharmonic; Brahms Sonatas with Dalberto. Honour: Won Soviet National Competition for Violinists, 1972. Address: c/o Terry Harrison Artists Management, The Orchard, Market Street, Charlbury, Oxon OX7 3PJ, England.

BELL (Jared) Drake, b. 27 June 1986, Orange County, California, USA. Actor; Musician. Appointments: Actor in commercials from the age of 5 years; Several small roles in TV and film; Regular appearances on The Amanda Show, 1999-2002; Co-star, Drake & Josh, 2004-06; Films include: Jerry Maguire, 1996; The Jack Bull, 1999; High Fidelity, Perfect Game, 2000; Yours, Mine and Ours, 2005; Superhero Movie, College, Unstable Fables: Tortoise vs Hare (voice), The Nutty Professor (voice), 2008; Singer, Composer and Musician. Publications: Albums: Telegraph, 2005; It's Only Time, 2006; Singles: Found a Way, 2005; I Know, 2006; Makes Me Happy, 2007; Superhero! Song, 2008. Honours: Blimp Awards, Favorite TV Actor, 2006, 2008. Website: www.drakebell.com

BELL (John) Robin (Sinclair), b. 28 February 1933, Edinburgh, Scotland. Writer to the Signet. m. Patricia Upton, 4 sons, 1 deceased. Education: BA, Worcester College, Oxford; LLB, Edinburgh University. Appointments: National Service: Commissioned, The Royal Scots (Berlin), 1951-53; Captain, Territorial Army, 1953-63; Solicitor, Coward Chance, London, 1961-62; Solicitor, 1963-94, Partner, 1963, Senior Partner, 1987-94, Tods Murray WS, Edinburgh; Member, Company Law Committee of Council of Bars and Law Societies of European Union, 1976-94; Council Member, 1975-78, Member, Company Law Committee, 1975-91, Law Society of Scotland; Non-Executive Director: Edinburgh Financial Trust plc, 1983-87, Upton and Southern Holdings plc, 1984-93, Citizens Advice Scotland, 1997-99, East of Scotland Water Authority, 1995-2002; Scottish Charities Nominee, 1995-2001. Honour: MBE, 1999; Memberships: New Club, Edinburgh; The Royal Scots Club, Edinburgh. Address: 29 Saxe Coburg Place, Edinburgh EH3 5BP, Scotland.

BELL Martin, b. 31 August 1938. Broadcaster. m. (1) Nelly Gourdon, 1971, 2 daughters, (2) Rebecca Sobel, 1983, (3) Fiona Goddard, 1998. Education: King's College, Cambridge. Appointments: Joined BBC, 1962; News Assistant, Norwich, 1962-64; General Reporter, London and Overseas, 1964-76; Diplomatic Correspondent, 1976-77; Chief, North American Correspondent, 1977-89; Berlin Correspondent, BBC TV News, 1989-93; Vienna Correspondent, 1993-94; Foreign Affairs Correspondent, 1994-96; Special Correspondent, Nine O'Clock News, 1997; Reported in over 70 countries, covered wars in Vietnam, Middle East, 1967, 1973, Angola, Rhodesia, Biafra, El Salvador, Gulf, 1991, Nicaragua, Croatia, Bosnia; Independent Member of Parliament for Tatton, 1997-2001; Humanitarian Ambassador for UNICEF, 2001-. Publication: In Harms Way, 1995; An Accidental MP, 2000; Through Gates of Fire, 2003; The Truth That Sticks: New Labour's Breach of Trust, 2007; A Very British Revolution: The Expenses Scandal and How to Save Our Democracy, 2009. Honours include: Order of the British Empire, 1992; Royal TV Society Reporter of the Year, 1995; Institute of Public Relations President's Medal, 1996; Several honorary degrees. Address: 71 Denman Drive, London W11 6RA, England.

BELL BURNELL (Susan) Jocelyn, b. 15 July 1943, Belfast, Northern Ireland. Astrophysicist m. Martin Burnell, (dissolved), 1 son. Education: BSc, University of Glasgow, 1965; PhD, Cambridge University, 1968. Appointments: Worked with Gamma-Ray Astronomy, University of Southampton, 1968-73; X-Ray Astronomy, Mullard Space Science Laboratory, 1974-82; Senior Research Fellow, Royal Observatory, Edinburgh, Scotland, 1982-86; Head, James Clerk Maxwell Telescope Section, 1986-90; Professor of Physics, Open University, Milton Keynes, England, 1991-99; Visiting Professor for Distinguished Teaching, Princeton University, 1999-2000; Dean of Science, University of Bath, 2001-04; President, Royal Astronomical Society, 2002-04; Visiting Professor, University of Oxford, 2004-; Discovered first four pulsating radio stars (pulsars); President, Institute of Physics, 2008-10; Research contributions in astronomy; Frequent radio and TV broadcaster on science, on being a woman in science and on science and religion. Publications: 3 books; About 70 scientific papers and 35 Quaker publications. Honours: 23 honorary doctorates; Joseph Black Medal and Cowie Book Prize, Glasgow University, 1962; Michelson Medal, Franklin Institute, USA, 1973; J Robert Oppenheimer Memorial Prize, Center for Theoretical Studies, Florida, 1978; Beatrice M Tinsley Prize, American Astronomical Society, 1987; Herschel Medal, Royal Astronomical Society, 1989; Honorary Fellow, New Hall, Cambridge, 1996; CBE, 1999; Magellanic Premium, American Philosophical Society, 2000; Joseph Priestly Award, Dickinson College, Pennsylvania, 2002; Robinson Medal, Armagh Observatory, 2004. Memberships: FRAS, 1969; International Astronomical Union, 1979; FInstP, 1992; American Astronomical Society, 1992; FRSA, 1999; President, Royal Astronomical Society, 2002-04; Fellow, Royal Society, 2003; Fellow, Royal Society of Edinburgh, 2004; Foreign Associate, US National Academy of Sciences, 2005; DBE, 2007. Address: University of Oxford, Astrophysics, Denys Wilkinson Building, Keble Road, Oxford OX1 3RH, England.

BELLAMY Christopher David, b. 28 October 1955, Perivale, Middlesex, England. University Professor; Writer. m. Heather Kerr. Education: Forest School, London, 1967-73; Lincoln College, Oxford, 1973-76; Royal Military Academy, Sandhurst, 1976-77; King's College, London, 1977-78; Polytechnic of Central London, 1977-87; PhD, University of Edinburgh, 1991. Appointments: Army Officer, 1973-77;

Civil Servant, UK Ministry of Defense, 1978-87; Defence Correspondent, The Independent, 1990-97; Director, Security Studies Institute, Cranfield University, Defence Academy of the UK, 1997-2010; Professor and Director, Greenwich Martime Institute, University of Greenwich, 2010-. Publications: Knights in White Armour: The New Art of War and Peace, 1996; Absolute War: Soviet Russia in the Second World War, 2007; The Gurkhas: Special Force, 2011. Honours: RUSI, Duke of Westminster's Medal for Military Literature, 2008. Memberships: Editorial board, Civil Wars, Journal of Slavic Military Studies. Address: Greenwich Martime Institute, University of Greenwich, Park Row, Greenwich, SE10 9LS, England. E-mail: c.d.bellamy@gre.ac.uk

BELLAMY David James, b. 18 January 1933, England. Botanist; Writer. m. Rosemary Froy, 1959, 2 sons, 3 daughters. Education: Chelsea College of Science and Technology; PhD, Bedford College, London University. Appointments: Lecturer, Botany, 1960-68, Senior Lecturer, Botany, 1968-82, Honorary Professor, Adult Education, 1982-, University of Durham; Television and radio presenter, scriptwriter of series including: Bellamy's New World, 1983; Seaside Safari, 1985; The End of the Rainbow Show, 1986; Bellamy on Top of the World, 1987; Turning the Tide, 1987; Bellamy's Bulge, 1987-88; Bellamy's Birds Eye View, 1988; Moa's Ark, 1989-90; Special Professor of Botany, University of Nottingham, 1987-; Visiting Professor, Natural Heritage Studies, Massey University, New Zealand, 1989-91; Director, Botanical Enterprises, David Bellamy Associates, National Heritage Conservation Fund, New Zealand, Conservation Foundation, London. Publications: The Great Seasons, 1981; Discovering the Countryside with David Bellamy, 4 volumes, 1982-83; The Mouse Book, 1983; The Queen's Hidden Garden, 1984; Bellamy's Ireland, 1986; Bellamy's Changing World, 4 volumes, 1988; England's Last Wilderness, 1989; How Green are You?, 1991; Tomorrow's Earth, 1991; World Medicine, 1992; Poo, You and the Poteroo's Loo, 1997; Bellamy's Changing Countryside, 1998; The Glorious Trees of Great Britain, 2002; Jolly Green Giant, autobiography, 2002; A Natural Life, 2002; The Bellamy Herbal, 2003; Various books connected with television series. Honours: Officer of the Order of the British Empire; Dutch Order of the Golden Ark; UNEP Global 500 Award; Duke of Edinburgh's Award for Underwater Research; British Academy of Film and Television Arts; BSAC Diver of the Year; Richard Dimbleby Award; Chartered Institute of Water and Environmental Management, fellow. Memberships: Fellow, Linnaean Society; Founder-Director, Conservation Foundation; President, WATCH, 1982-83; President, Youth Hostels Association, 1983; President, Population Concern; President, National Association of Environmental Education. Address: Mill House, Bedburn, Bishop Auckland, County Durham DL13 3NW, England.

BELLIN Howard, b. 30 October 1933, New York City, USA. Chairman. m. Barbara Ann Box, 1962, 1 son, 1 daughter. Education: BSc, Carnegie-Mellon University, Pittsburgh, Pennsylvania, USA, 1955. Appointments: Manufacturing Management, Gillette Company; Manufacturing Management, Allied Corporation; Managing Director, Avin Plating; Founder and Chairman, IF Consulting; Editorial Board, Journal of Marketing Channels; Chairman, IE International, 1969-. Publications: Contributor, articles to professional journals. Honours: Listed in biographical dictionaries. Memberships: Member, Franchise Division, Singapore Productivity Board; St James' Club, London. Address: 17 Moule Avenue, Brighton, Vic 3186, Australia.

BELOZEROV Ilya R, b. 3 December 1985, Krasnoyarsk, Russia. Scientist; Educator. Education: BS, Mining, Siberian Federal University, Krasnoyarsk, 2009. Appointments: Postgraduate Student, 2009-, Assistant Lecturer, 2010-, Department of Mining Machines and Complexes, Institute of Mining, Geology and Geotechnologies, Siberian Federal University; Adviser, Krasnoyarsk Branch, Russian Academy of Natural History, 2011-. Publications: Over 40 published scientific works. Honours: Laureate, Competition of Gifted Persons, 2010; Diploma of III degree, 2010, and I degree, 2011, All Russian Scientific Conferences; Prize, Siberian Federal University Administration, 2010. Memberships: Institute of Electrical & Electronics Engineers, USA; Russian Academy of Natural History. Address: PO Box 16142, Krasnoyarsk 660001, Russia. E-mail: ilya.belozerov@inbox.ru

BELYAEVA Elena A, b. 31 January 1961, St Petersburg, Russia. Scientist. m. Alexander V Dubinin, 1 daughter. Education: MS, Biophysics, St Petersburg Polytechnic University, 1985; PhD, Biochemistry and Physiology of Man and Animals, Sechenov Institute of Evolutionary Physiology and Biochemistry of Russian Academy of Sciences, 1989. Appointments: Junior Scientific Researcher, Sechenov Institute of Evolutionary Physiology and Biochemistry, Russian Academy of Sciences, St Petersburg, 1990-97; Scientific Researcher, 1997-2003; Senior Scientific Researcher, 2004-08; Leading Scientific Researcher, 2009-. Publications: 33 articles published in professional scientific journals. Honours: International Scientist of the Year, 2005; The Archimedes Award, IBC, 2006; Woman of the Year, American Biographical Institute, 2006. Memberships: Federation of European Biochemical Societies; Federation of European Societies on Trace Elements and Minerals. Address: Nepokorennych pr 10/1-185, St Petersburg, 195220, Russia. E-mail: Belyaeva@iephb.ru

BENAUD Richard, b. 6 October 1930. Cricketer. m. Daphne Elizabeth Surfleet, 1967, 2 sons. Appointments: Right-Hand Middle-Order Batsman and Right-Arm Leg-Break & Googly Bowler, Played for New South Wales, 1948-49 to 1963-64 (Captain, 1958-59, 1963); Played in 63 Tests for Australia, 1951-52 to 1963-64 as Captain, 28 as Captain, scoring 2,201 runs, including 3 hundreds, taking 248 wickets; First to score 2,000 runs and take 200 wickets in tests; Scored 11,719 runs and took 945 wickets in 1st Class Cricket; Toured England, 1953, 1956, 1961; International Sports Consultant; TV Commentator, BBC, 1960-99, Channel Nine, 1977-, Channel 4, 1999-2005. Publications: Way of Cricket, 1960; Tale of Two Tests, 1962; Spin Me A Spinner, 1963; The New Champions, 1965; Willow Patterns, 1972; Benaud on Reflection, 1984; The Appeal of Cricket, 1995; Anything But...An Autobiography, 1998. Honours: OBE; Wisden Cricketer of the Year, 1962; Inducted in the Australian Cricket Hall of Fame, 2007. Address: 19/178 Beach Street, Coogee, New South Wales 2034, Australia.

BENCSIK Gabor, b. 20 November 1970, Bacstopolya, Former Yugoslavia. Medical Doctor. Education: Doctor of Medicine, 1996, Internal Medicine, 2001, Cardiology, 2004, PhD, 2011, University of Szeged, Hungary. Appointments: Assistant Professor, University of Szeged. Publications: Acute Effects of Complex Fractionated Atrial Electrogram Ablation on Dominant Frequency for Fibrillatory Process, 2009; Randomized trial of intracardiác echocardiography during corotricuspiol isthmus ablation, 2012. Honours: Fellow, European Heart Rhythm Association, 2008; European Accreditation in Invasive Electrophysiology and Cardiac Pacing and Defibrillators, 2009. Memberships: Hungarian

Society of Cardiology; European Society of Cardiology. Address: Zsitva Sor 6/A V17, 6724 Szeged, Hungary. E-mail: blackdoor@t-online.hu

BENDON Christopher Graham (Chris), b. 27 March 1950, Leeds, Yorkshire, England. Freelance Writer; Critic. m. Sue Moules, 30 August 1979, 1 daughter. Education: BA, English, St David's University College, Lampeter, 1980. Appointments: Editor, Spectrum Magazine, 1983-88. Publications: Books: In Praise of Low Music, 1981; Software, 1984; Matter, 1986; Cork Memory, 1987; Ridings Writings - Scottish Gothic, 1990; Constructions, 1991; Perspective Lessons, Virtual Lines..., 1992; Jewry, 1995; Crossover, 1996; Novella, 1997. Chapbooks: Testaments, 1983; Quanta, 1984; Aetat 23, 1985; The Posthumous Poem, 1988; A Dyfed Quartet, 1992. Contributions to: Anthologies, magazines and journals. Honours: Hugh MacDiarmid Memorial Trophy, 1st Prize, Scottish Open Poetry Competition, 1988; £1000 Prize, Guardian/WWF Poetry Competition, 1989; several awards, Royal Literary Fund. Membership: The Welsh Academy. Address: 14 Maesyderi, Lampeter, Ceredigion SA48 7EP, Wales.

BENEDICT Stewart Hurd, b. 27 December 1924, Mineola, New York, USA. Writer; Editor. Education: AB, summa cum laude, Drew University, 1944; MA, The Johns Hopkins University, 1945; Study at New York University, 1946-49, 1961-64. Appointments: Instructor in German New York University, 1946-49; Assistant Professor, Humanities, Michigan Technical University, 1951-54, 1955-61; Assistant Professor of English, New Jersey City University, 1961-64; Adjunct Professor of English: City College of New York, Rutgers University, Hudson County Community College, Essex County Community College, 1964-95; Drama Reviewer: Jersey Journal, 1964-71; Michael's Thing, 1990-2000, Stage Press Weekly, 2002-03; Book Reviewer for Publishers Weekly, 1970-98. Publications: Books include: Tales of Terror and Suspense, 1963; The Teacher's Guide to ..., several books in a series, 1966-73; The Literary Guide to the United States, 1981; Street Beat, 1982; Curtain Going Up, 2002 Numerous plays, 1967-2003, include most recently: The Robbery, Absolutely Fabulous Fairy Tales, Fancy Bread, Be Still My Liver, Yuletide Treasure, 1996; The Hero, 1999; Homicidal Murders, 2002; The Gap, 2003; Humanoids Using Goodness, 2003; Monody, 2004; Wow! 2005; Fox, Cinderella, Part II, 2007; Chapters in books; Periodical articles; Translations; Encyclopaedia articles. Honours: Various prizes, North Jersey Press Association. Memberships: Dramatists Guild; Communications Workers of America; Democratic Party. Address: Apt 4-A, 27 Washington Square N, New York, NY 10011-9165, USA.

BENEDICT XVI, His Holiness Pope, (Joseph Ratzinger), b. 16 April 1927, Bavaria, Germany. Head of the Roman Catholic Church. Education: University of Münich; Traunstein seminary; Ordained Priest, Freising, Southern Germany, 1951. Appointments: Professor of Theology, Freising, 1958, Bonn, 1959-63, Münster, 1963-66, Tübingen, 1966-69, Regensburg, 1969; Co-founder, Communio (theological journal), 1972; Archbishop, Munich-Freising, 1977-82; Created Cardinal of Munich by Pope Paul VI, 1977; Cardinal Bishop of the Episcopal See of Velletri-Segni, 1993; Former Chair, Bavarian Bishops' Conference; Prefect, Sacred Congregation for the Doctrine of the Faith, 1981-2005; Vice-Dean, 1998-2002, Dean, 2002-05, College of Cardinals; Titular Bishop of Ostia, 2002; Presided over funeral of Pope John Paul II, 2005; Elected Pope Benedict XVI, 2005, resigned 2013; President, International Theological Commission; Pontifical Biblical Commission. Honours: Dr hc (Navarra), 1998; Dr hc mult. Memberships: Congregations for the Oriental Churches, for the Divine Worship and the Discipline of the Sacrament, for the Bishops, for the Evangelization of Reapers, for Catholic Education; Member, Pontifical Council for the Promotion of Christian Unity. Address: Apostolic Palace, 00120 Vatican City, Rome, Italy.

BENEDIKTER Roland Anton Josef, b. 7 May 1965, Brunico-Bruneck, Italy. Professor. m. Judith Hilber, 1 daughter. Education: Dott Dr Dr phil; Dr rer pol. Appointments: European Foundation Professor, Sociology, UC Santa Barbara and Stamford University, USA; Former Speaker of the Cultural Minister, Autonomous Province of South Tyrol and Cultural Council of the European Regions; Fellow, Georgetown University, Washington, DC, USA; Fellow, Potomac Institute for Policy Studies, Arlington, VA, USA; Visiting Professor, School of Globalism, RMIT University Melbourne, Australia, 2008-09; Visiting Professor, School of Social Sciences, University of Northampton, England, 2007-09; External Adviser and Examiner, School of Social Sciences and School of Educational Sciences, University of Plymouth, England. Publications: Over 100 papers and articles; Co-author, Report to the Club of Rome, 2003. Honours: Research Fellowship, Damus Foundation, Mannheim, Future European Human Sciences, 2005-07; Dr Otto Siebert Prize for Scientific Publications, University of Innsbruck, 2005; European Foundation Award, 2008; Listed in international biographical dictionaries. E-mail: rbenedikter@unibz.it

BENGTSSON Erling Blöndal, b. 8 March 1932, Copenhagen, Denmark. Classical Cellist; Educator. m. Merete Bloch-Jørgensen, 2 sons. Education: Diploma, Curtis Institute of Music, Philadelphia, 1950. Career: Assistant Teacher of Cello, 1949-50, Teacher of Cello, 1950-53; Professor of Music, Royal Danish Conservatory, Copenhagen, 1953-90; Teacher of Cello, Swedish Radio's Institute of Advanced String Studies, Stockholm, 1958-78; Professor of Music, Staatliche Hochschule für Musik, Cologne, Germany, 1978-82; Professor of Cello, University of Michigan School of Music, Ann Arbor, 1990-2006; Teacher of cello masterclasses at conservatories and universities throughout Europe and the USA, 1953-; Appearances with most of the world's leading orchestras including: Royal Philharmonic, St Petersburg Philharmonic, English Chamber Orchestra, Salzburg's Mozarteum Orchestra, the Hague's Residentie Orchestra under the direction of many leading maestros including Yuri Temirkanov, Mariss Jansons, David Zinmann, Sixten Ehrling, Herbert Blomstedt, Sergiu Commissiona; Duo with the pianist Nina Kavtaradze, 1986-2007. Recordings: More than 50 albums include: Six Cello Suites of J S Bach, 1985; Zoltán Kodály Solo Sonata, 1998; The Cello and I, DVD, 2006. Publications: Erling Blöndal Bengtsson's edition of the 6 Bach Suites & the 3 Recer Suites. Honours: Grand Knight Order of Falcon, President of Iceland, 1970; Bronze statue of him erected in front of Reykjavik's University Concert Hall, 1970; Knight 1st Class, Order of Dannebrog, Queen of Denmark, 1972; Chevalier du Violoncello, Indiana University Eva Janzer Memorial Cello Centre, 1993; Award of Distinction, International Cello Festival, Manchester, England, 2001; English Hyam Morrison Gold Medal for Cello; Named Premier Master Cellist 2005, The Detroit Cello Society, USA; Honorary Award, International Federation of the Phonographic Industry, Denmark, 2006; Man of the Year, ABI, 2009. Memberships: Royal Swedish Academy of Music; Board of Directors, Symphonicum Europae, New York, 1997. Address: 1217 Westmoorland, Ypsilanti, MI 48197, USA. E-mail: cellist@erlingbb.com Website: www.erlingbb.com

DICTIONARY OF INTERNATIONAL BIOGRAPHY 36th EDITION

BENHAM Helen Wheaton, b. 4 December 1941, New York, New York, USA. Professor of Music. m. Samuel S Kim, 1 daughter. Education: Junior year abroad, Mozarteum, Salzburg, Austria, 1960-61; Mus.B, Piano, Oberlin Conservatory of Music, Oberlin, Ohio, 1962; BA, German, Oberlin College, Oberlin, Ohio, 1963; MS, Piano, The Juilliard School, New York City, 1965; Diploma in Teaching, The Diller-Quaile School of Music, New York City, 1966; PhD, Musicology and Theory, The Graduate Program in Music, Rutgers, The State University of New Jersey, 2001. Appointments: Faculty Member, The Diller-Quaile School of Music, 1964-75; Faculty Member, Preparatory School, Mannes College, 1966-82; Faculty Member, Monmouth Conservatory of Music, 1967-92; Instructor, 1973-75, Assistant Professor, 1975-81, Associate Professor, 1981-89, Professor, 1989-2010, Brookdale Community College; Performances as pianist and harpsichordist in the United States, Canada, Europe and the Far East. Publications: Piano for the Adult Beginner, Book I, 1977; Piano for the Adult Beginner, Book II, 1977; The Life and Work of Anthony Louis Scarmolin (Dissertation), 2002. Honours: Phi Kappa Lambda, Honour Society, Oberlin Conservatory of Music, 1962; Mu Phi Epsilon Professional Music Sorority, 1963; Outstanding Young Women of America Award, 1978; Included in 1989 edition of American Keyboard Artists; Outstanding Colleague Award, Brookdale Community College, 1991; Listed in Who's Who publications and biographical dictionaries. Memberships: National Guild of Piano Teachers; Music Teachers National Association; The Piano Teachers Congress; The American Musicological Society; Trustee, Secretary, A Louis Scarmolin Trust. Address: 960 Elberon Avenue, Elberon, NJ 07740, USA.

BENIGNI Roberto, b. 27 October 1952, Misericordia, Tuscany, Italy. Actor; Director; Writer. Creative Works: Films include: Beliungua ti voglio bene, 1977; Down By Law, Tutto Benigni, 1986; Johnny Stecchino, Night on Earth, 1992; Son of the Pink Panther, 1993; Mostro, Life is Beautiful, 1998; Asterisk & Obelisk, 1999; Pinocchio, 2002; Coffee and Cigarettes, 2003; The Tiger and the Snow, 2005; One man show, TuttoDante, 2006-07. Publications: E l'alluce fu monoleghi e gags, 1996. Honours include: Academy Award, Best Actor and Best Foreign Film, 1998; Dr hc (Bologna), 2002; Awarded the degree of Doctor Honoris Causa by the Katholieke Universiteit Leuven, Belgium, 2007.

BENING Annette, b. 29 May 1958, Topeka, USA. Actress. m. (1) Steven White, divorced, (2) Warren Beatty, 1992, 1 son, 3 daughters. Creative Works: Stage appearances in works by Ibsen, Chekhov and Shakespeare in San Diego and San Francisco; Other roles in Coastal Disturbances, The Great Outdoors; Films: Valmont; The Grifters; Regarding Henry; Guilty By Suspicion; Bugsy; Love Affair; The American President; Richard III; Blue Vision; Mars Attacks!; Against All Enemies; The Siege; In Dreams; American Beauty; Forever Hollywood; What Planet Are You From?; Open Range, 2003; Being Julia, 2004; Diva, Mrs Harris, 2005; Running with Scissors, 2006; 14 Women, 2007; The Women, 2008. Honours: BAFTA Award, Best Actress in a Leading Role, 1999; Two Screen Actors Guild Awards, 1999; European Achievement in World Cinema Award, 2000; Best Actress Award, National Board of Review, 2005; Best Actress in a Musical or Comedy, Golden Globe Awards, 2005. Address: c/o Kevin Huvane, CAA, 9830 Wilshire Boulevard, Beverly Hills, CA 90212, USA.

BENJAMIN Ellen, Private and Public Policy Analyst. Education: BA, Social Service Administration and Policy, Park College, Parkville, Missouri, USA, 1976; Graduate Credits, Political Science, Public Administration and Labour Market Analysis, University of New Hampshire; Urban Studies Graduate Level Public Administration and Policy, Portland State University, Portland, Oregon, 1991-93. Appointments: Director of Policy, New England Council Inc; Senior Policy Analyst for the Council of the State Government's Northeastern Committee on Human Service, New York City; Policy Advisor to the President of the New Hampshire State Senate, Director of Research for the entire Senate, Legislative Analyst for the Legislative Committee on Review of Agencies and Programs (Sunset Committee), Research Assistant in the Office of Legislative Services, Concord, New Hampshire; Research Associate for the Small Business Development Program, University of New Hampshire, Durham, New Hampshire; Committee Assistant, Maine Legislative Committee on Health and Institutional Services, Augusta, Maine; Assistant Director, Grant Writer, York County Employment and Training Agency, York County, Maine; Assistant Director of Adult Education, South Berwick, Maine; Sole Assistant to the Director of Planning and Research for all the programs administered by the Missouri Department of Social Services, Jefferson City Missouri. Publications: Human Capital: The Key to New England's Increased Productivity and Competitiveness, CSG Government News and ERC Conference Report Articles; Proceedings on productions of DC Seminar on Health Care Cost Containment in 1985, NYC, and 1986 Annual AIDS Sessions. Honours most recently include: International Professional of the Year, 2005; Lifetime of Achievement One Hundred, 2005; Legion of Honour, United Cultural Convention, 2005; The World Medal of Freedom, 2005; American Hall of Fame, 2006; Woman of the Year, 2006; Secretary-General, United Cultural Convention, 2004-07; Lifetime Ambassador-General, United Cultural Convention, 2006; Salute to Greatness Award, 2006; The Excellence Award, 2006; IBC Awards Roster, 2005; American Order of Merit, 2009; Magna Cum Laude, ABI, 2009; International Peace Prize, 2009; Gold Medal for the United States, 2009; Listed in national and international biographical directories. Website: www.beyondmeasureenterprises.com

BENJAMIN Leanne, b. 13 July 1964, Rockhampton, Australia. Principal Ballet Dancer. 1 son. Education: Trained with Valerie Hansen, Queensland; The Royal Ballet Upper School, London. Appointments: Sadler's Wells Royal Ballet, 1983-88, promoted to Soloist, 1985, Principal, 1987; Principal, London Festival Ballet, 1988-90; Principal, Deutsche Oper Ballet, 1990-92; The Royal Ballet, 1992-, First Soloist promoted to Principal, 1993; Roles include: Odette/Odile (Swan Lake); Giselle; Sugar Plum Fairy (The Nutcracker); Aurora (The Sleeping Beauty); Nikiya & Kitri (La Bayadére); Swanilda (Coppélia); Firebird; Cinderella; Lise (La Fille Mal Gardée); Titania (The Dream); Manon; Anastasia; Juliet (Romeo and Juliet); Mary Vetsera (Mayerling); The Judas Tree; Song of the Earth; Gloria; Requiem; Rhapsody; Les Biches; Apollo; Études; Mat Ek's Carmen; Electric Counterpoint; Emeralds (Jewels); Rushes - Fragments of a Lost Story; Dances at a Gathering; L'Invitation au voyage; Voluntaries; Sphinx; Symphony in C; Different Drummer; Winter Dreams; Created roles in: Metamorphosis; 'Earth' in Homage to The Queen; Mr Worldly Wise; Ashley Page's Two Part Invention; Masquerade; Qualia; Infra; Tanglewood; Children of Adam; DGV; Danse a grande vitesse; Sensorium; Invitus Invitam; Limen. Honours: Adeline Genée Gold Medal, 1980; Prix de Lausanne, 1981; OBE, 2005. Address: c/o Royal Opera House, Covent Garden, London WC2E 9DD, England.

BENJILLALI Mustapha, Professor; Engineer. Education: B Eng, Mobile Communications, INPT, Morocco, 2003; MSc, 2005, PhD, 2009, Telecommunications, INRS, Canada. Appointments: Postdoctoral Research Fellow, KAUST, KSA, 2009-11; Professor, Telecommunications, INPT, Morocco, 2011-. Honours: Best Paper Award, IEEE Communications Society, 2010. Memberships: IEEE. Address: INPT, 2 Av Allal El Fassi, Rabat 10100, Morocco.

BENNETT Alan, b. 9 May 1934, Leeds, England. Dramatist. Education: BA, Modern History, Oxford, 1957. Career: Junior Lecturer, Modern History, Magdalen College, Oxford, 1960-62; Co-author and Actor, Beyond the Fringe, Edinburgh, 1960, London, 1961, New York, 1962; Fellow, Royal Academy; Author and Actor, On the Margin, TV series, 1966. Plays: Forty Years On, 1968; Getting On, 1971; Habeas Corpus, 1973; The Old Country, 1977; Enjoy, 1980; Kafka's Dick, 1986; Single Spies, 1988; The Wind in the Willows, 1990; The Madness of King George II, 1991, film, 1995; The Lady in the Van, 1999; The History Boys, 2004; Radio: The Last of the Sun, 2004; TV scripts: A Day Out, 1972; Sunset Across the Bay, 1975; A Little Outing, A Visit from Miss Prothero, 1977; Doris and Doreen, The Old Crowd, Me! I'm Afraid of Virginia Woolf, All Day on the Sands, Afternoon Off, One Fine Day, 1978-79; Intensive Care, Our Winnie, A Woman of No Importance, Rolling Home, Marks, Say Something Happened, An Englishman Abroad, 1982; The Insurance Man, 1986; 102 Boulevard Haussmann, A Question of Attribution, 1991; Talking Heads, 1992; Talking Heads 2, 1998; Films: A Private Function, 1984; Prick Up Your Ears, 1987; The Madness of King George, 1994; TV documentaries: Dinner at Noon, 1988; Poetry in Motion, 1990; Portrait or Bust, 1994; The Abbey, 1995; Telling Tales, 1999. Publications: Beyond the Fringe, 1962; Forty Years On, 1969; Getting On, 1972; Habeas Corpus, 1973; The Old Country, 1978; Enjoy, 1980; Office Suite, 1981; Objects of Affection, 1982; The Writer in Disguise, 1985; Two Kafka Plays, 1987; Talking Heads, 1988; Single Spies, 1989; The Lady in the Van, The Wind in the Willows, 1991; The Madness of King George III, 1992, screenplay, 1995; Writing Home, 1994; The Clothes They Stood Up In, Talking Heads 2, The Complete Talking Heads, 1998; A Box of Alan Bennett, 2000; The Laying on of Hands, 2001; The Clothes They Stood Up In, 2001; Untold Stories, 2005; The Uncommon Reader, 2007; A Life Like Other People's, 2009; regular contributions to London Review of Books. Screenplays: A Private Function, 1984; Prick Up Your Ears, 1987; The Madness of King George, 1995; The History Boys, 2006. Honours: Honorary Fellow, Exeter College, Oxford; Honorary DLitt, Leeds; Evening Standard Award, 1961, 1969; Hawthornden Prize, 1988; 2 Olivier Awards, 1993; Evening Standard Award, 1996; Lifetime Achievement Award, British Book Awards, 2003; Evening Standard Award for Best Play, 2004; Critics Circle Theatre Award for Best New Play, 2005; Olivier Award for Best New Play, 2005; Olivier Award for outstanding contribution to British theatre, 2005. Address: Peter, Fraser and Dunlop, The Chambers, Chelsea Harbour, London, SW10 0XF, England.

BENNETT Roger, b. 9 April 1948, Sheffield, England. Professor of Marketing. Education: BA (1st class honours), Business Studies, Kingston University, 1972; MSc (Econ), University College, London, 1973; PhD, University of Sussex, 1978. Appointments: Lecturer in Economics, Birkbeck College, London, 1975-82; Director, RHA Management Services, 1982-91; Senior Lecturer, 1991-95, Reader, Business Studies, 1995-2001, London Guildhall University; Professor of Marketing, London Metropolitan University, 2002-. Publications: 26 books (translated into 19 foreign languages) including Organisation and Management, 1988; Choosing and Using Management Consultants, 1990; Management, 1991; Organisational Behaviour, 1991; Selling to Europe, 1993; Handbook of European Advertising, 1995; European Business, 1997; Small Business Survival, 1998; International Business, 1999; Over 150 articles published in academic journals. Honours: Several best paper awards at academic conferences and for academic journals; Founder, International Colloqium on Nonprofit, Social and Voluntary Sector Marketing, 2002. Memberships: Chartered Marketer; MCIM. Address: London Metropolitan University, 84 Moorgate, London EC2M 6SQ, England. E-mail: r.bennett@londonmet.ac.uk

BENNETT Tony (Anthony Dominick Benedetto), b. 3 August 1926, Astoria, USA. Singer; Entertainer, Artist. m. (1) Patricia Beech, 1952, 2 children, (2) Sandra Grant, 1971, 2 daughters, (3) Susan Crow, 2007. Education: American Theatre Wing, New York; University Berkeley, California. Appointment: Owner, Improv Records. Creative Works: Paintings exhibited at Butler Institute of American Art, Youngstown, Ohio, 1994; Records include: The Art of Excellence, 1986; Bennett/Berlin, 1988; Astoria: Portrait of the Artist, 1990; Perfectly Frank, 1992; Steppin Out, 1993; The Essence of Tony Bennett, 1993; MTV Unplugged, 1994; Here's to the Ladies, 1995; The Playground, 1998; Cool, 1999; The Ultimate Tony, 2000; A Wonderful World (with kd lang), 2003; The Art of Romance, 2006; Duets: An American Classic, 2007; For Once in My Life, 2007. Publication: Tony Bennett: What My Heart Has Seen, 1996; The Good Life: The Autobiography of Tony Bennett, 1998; Tony Bennett in the Studio: A Life of Art & Music, 2007. Honours include: Grammy Awards: Best Traditional Pop Vocal, 1998; Best Traditional Vocal Performance, 1992; Album of the Year, 1994; Best Traditional Pop Vocal Album, 2004; Kennedy Center Honoree, 2006; Long Island Music Hall of Fame; Humanitarian Award, UN High Commissioner for Refugees, 2006; Jazz Masters Award, National Endowment for the Arts, 2006.

BENNING Wilhelm Heinrich, b. 31 July 1954, Vardingholt, Germany. Professor. m. Evi Petropoulov, 2 sons, 1 daughter. Education: Lecturer, German Academic Exchange Service, 1980-85, Associate Professor, 1988, Full Professor, 1993, Head of Department, 1989-95, 1999-2001, University of Athens; Assistant Professor, 1987, Assistant Professor, 1988, Corfu University. Publications: Tonio Kröger – Interpretation einer Technik – Technik einer Interpretation, 1987; Editor, Festschrift für Klaus Betzen, 1995; Mentalität im Vergleich – Sentimentalität und Sensualismus, 2010; Numerous articles in professional journals. Honours: Fellowship for Studies; Fellowship for Graduation; Dissertation with Distinction; Prize of the University of Bochum for Dissertation. Memberships: Philadelphia, Athens; Greek Association of Germanists; German Association of Germanists. Address: Gr Lambraki 73, GR-15238 Athens Chanlandri, Greece. E-mail: wbenning@gs.uoa.gr

BENSE László, b. 6 July 1941, Budapest, Hungary. Medical Doctor. m. Gyöngyi Temesi, 1 son. Education: MD, Semmelweis Medical University Budapest, 1965; Specialisation of Internal Medicine, Hungary, 1971; MD, Specialisation of Internal Medicine, Sweden, 1980; Specialisation of Internal Medicine, Sweden, 1981; Specialisation of Pulmonary Medicine, Sweden, 1983; PhD, Pathogenetic Mechanism and Treatment of Spontaneous Pneumothorax, 1987. Appointments: Postgraduate, Medical School, 1970; Department of Country Institute of Medical Experts, 1970; Medical Consultant, Hungarian Airlines, 1973; General Practitioner, Budapest, 1974; Medical Clinician, Södertälje Hospital, Sweden, 1977; Psychiatric Clinic, 1979,

Department of Pulmonary Medicine, 1980, Occupational and Environmental Medicine, 1992, Huddinge University Hospital; Founder, Arno Nordic Co Ltd, 2001; Advisor, Gerson Lehrman Group, 2004-10. Publications: Numerous articles in professional medical journals; 2 patents; Listed in national and international biographical dictionaries. Honours: Listed in international biographical dictionaries. Address: Postängsv 232, 14552 Norsborg, Sweden. E-mail: la.ben@swipnet.se

BENSIMON Aaron, b. 27 January 1957, Switzerland. Professor. m. Shulamit, 1 son, 2 daughters. Education: PhD, Weizman Institute, Israel. Appointments: Professor, Pasteur Institute, Paris. Publications: More than 50 publications in review journals. Honours: Jacques Monod Prize. Address: 5 rue du clos de l'abbaye, 92160 Antony, France.

BENTLEY George, b. 19 January 1936, Sheffield, England. Professor of Orthopaedic Surgery. m. Ann Hutchings, 2 sons, 1 daughter. Education: Rotherham Grammar School, 1943-54; MBChB, 1959, ChM, 1972, DSc, 2002, Sheffield University. Appointments: House Surgeon, House Physician and Senior House Officer in Orthopaedics, Sheffield Royal Infirmary, 1959-61; Lecturer in Anatomy, University of Birmingham, 1961-62; Senior House Officer in Surgery, Manchester Royal Infirmary, 1962-63; Rotating Surgical Registrar, Sheffield Royal Infirmary and Children's Hospital, 1963-65; Registrar in Orthopaedics, Orthopaedic Hospital, Oswestry, 1965-67; Senior Registrar in Orthopaedics, Nuffield Orthopaedic Centre, Oxford and Radcliffe Infirmary, Oxford, 1967-69; Instructor in Orthopaedics, University of Pittsburgh, USA, 1969-70; Lecturer, Senior Lecturer, Clinical Reader in Orthopaedics, Nuffield Orthopaedic Centre, University of Oxford, 1971-76; Professor of Orthopaedics and Trauma, University of Liverpool, 1976-82; Professor and Director, Institute of Orthopaedics, University College, London, 1982-2002; Honorary Consultant Orthopaedic Surgeon, Royal National Orthopaedic and Middlesex Hospital, 1982-2002; Emeritus Professor, UCL and Consultant Orthopaedic Surgeon, Royal National Orthopaedic Hospital, 2002-; Robert Jones Lecturer, Royal College of Surgeons of England and Orthopaedic Association, 2007. Publications: Over 350 publications on osteoarthritis, accident surgery, joint replacement, scoliosis, cartilage cell-engineering; 5 text books. Honours: President, British Orthopaedic Research Society, 1985-87, British Orthopaedic Association, 1991-92; Honorary Fellow, Romanian Orthopaedic Association, 1997; Membre d'Honneur, French Orthopaedic Association, 1999; Fellow, Medical Academy of Science, 1999; Honorary Fellow, Royal College of Surgeons of Edinburgh, 1999; Vice President, Royal College of Surgeons of England, 2002-04; Honorary Fellow, Argentinean Orthopaedic Association, 2000; Honorary Fellow, European Federation of National Associations of Orthopaedics and Traumatology, 2002; Honorary Member, Royal Society of Medicine, 2004; Honorary Fellow, Czech Orthopaedic Association, 2004; Honorary Fellow, British Orthopaedic Association, 2004; President, EFORT (European Federation of National Associations of Orthopaedics and Traumatology), 2004-06; Honorary Fellow, Royal Society of Medicine, 2009; Visiting Professor at universities and orthopaedic associations in USA, South America, Australasia, Malaysia, Hong Kong, South Africa, India, Singapore, Japan and Scandinavia. Memberships: Royal College of Surgeons of England (Council, 1982-2004) and Edinburgh; British Orthopaedic Association; British Orthopaedic Research Society; SOFCOT – French Orthopaedic Society; SICOT, International Orthopaedic Society; Eastern Orthopaedic and Mid-Western Orthopaedic Associations, USA; Australian Orthopaedic Association; New Zealand Orthopaedic Association; South African Orthopaedic Association; Polish, Czech, Bulgarian & Argentinean Orthopaedic Associations; Orthopaedic Research Society of USA; Oxford Medical Society; European Editor-in-Chief, Journal of Arthroplasty, 2001-. Address: 16 Park Street, Woodstock, Oxfordshire OX20 1SP, England. E-mail: profgbentley@talktalk.net

BENYOUNIS Khaled Younis, b. 9 February 1968, Benghazi, Libya. Research Scientist. m. Hayat Eltawahni, 3 sons, 3 daughters. Education: BSc (honours), 1995, MSc (honours), 2001, Industrial Engineering, Garyounis University, Libya; PhD, Laser Welding Technology and Optimization, Dublin City University, 2007. Appointments: Teaching Assistant, 1998-99, Assistant Lecturer, 2001-02, Industrial Engineering, Garyounis University; Postdoctoral Researcher, Dublin City University, 2007-. Publications: Numerous articles in professional journals; Editor of peer-reviewed journals. Honours: Silver Medal, Conf AMPT, 2005; Study Grant, Libyan Government, 2002-07. Memberships: Libyan Association for Engineering; Garyounis University Association of Teachers; Society of Science and Technology, Dublin City University. Address: School of Mechanical Engineering, Dublin City University, DUC, Dublin D9, Ireland. E-mail: khaled.benyounis2@mail.dcu.ie

BENZING Rosemary Anne, b. 18 September 1945, South India. Teacher; Counsellor; Freelance Journalist; Poet. m. Richard Benzing, 1969, 1 son (deceased), 1 daughter. Education: BA, Honours, English and Philosophy, University College of North Wales, Bangor, 1968; Diploma in Education, 1969; Diploma in Counselling, 1990. Appointments: Teacher, Edward Shelley High School, Walsall, 1968-71; Supply Teacher, Shropshire LEA, 1980-; Counsellor, SRCC, 1988-98. Contributions to: Hybrid; Foolscap; Folded Sheets; Smoke; Borderlines; Envoi; First Time; Purple Patch; Shropshire Magazine; Plowman; White Rose; Poetry Nottingham; Symphony; Psyco Poetica; Third Half; Krax; Bare Wires; Housewife Writers' Forum. Honour: Anglo Welsh Poetry Competition, 1986. Membership: Poetry Society. Address: Roden House, Shawbury, Shrewsbury, Shropshire, England.

BERA Raghu Nath, b. 26 November 1970, Midnapur, India. Professor. m. Poulamy Mandal, 1 son. Education: MSc, Physics (1st class), Vidyasagar University, India; PhD, Indian Association for the Cultivation of Science. Appointments: STA Fellow, 2000-02, Postdoctoral Fellow, 2002-03, AIST, Japan; Postdoctoral Fellow, University of St Andrews, UK, 2003-05; Assistant Professor, Basirhat College, India. Publications: More than 20 publications in high impact international journals. Honours: Winner, University Gold Medla for the rank in 1st in MSc examination; STA Fellowship, Government of Japan. Memberships: Life Member, Indian Association for the Cultivation of Science. Address: Jamunotry Aptt (Flat 2C), Panchavati Complex, VIP Road, Kolkata 700 052, India.

BERCELI Tibor, b. 7 August 1929, Budapest, Hungary. Engineer. m. Maria Balla, 1 son, 1 daughter. Education: Diploma, Electrical Engineering, 1951; PhD, 1955; Doctor of Science, 1965. Appointments: Head of Research, Telecom Research Institute, 1962-87; Professor, Technical University of Budapest, 1970-. Publications: 152 papers at international conferences and in international journals. Honours: State Prize, 1980. Memberships: Life Fellow, IEEE; European Microwave Association. E-mail: berceli@mht.bme.hu

DICTIONARY OF INTERNATIONAL BIOGRAPHY 36th EDITION

BERECZ Endre, b. 10 January 1925, Csorna, Hungary. Professor Emeritus. m. Maria Illés, 1 son, 1 daughter. Education: Chemist, 1949; Candidate of Chemical Sciences, CSc, 1954; Dr rer nat, 1960; Doctor of Chemical Science, DSc, 1974; Doctor honoris causa, University of Miskolc, 1995. Appointments: Assistant, First Assistant, Assistant Professor, Eötvös L University, 1949-63; Full Professor, Head of Department of Physical Chemistry, Technical University of Heavy Industries, Miskolc, 1963-92; Dean of the Faculty of Metallurgy, University of Miskolc, 1965-68. Publications: 283 science and professional articles; Monographs: 1 Hungarian, 1 English; 8 chapters in monographs; 13 textbooks for university students; 7 patents; 101 reports on research works sponsored by grants and state foundations. Honours: Outstanding Worker of Education, 1968, Metallurgy, 1972; Silver Class Medal of the Order of Labour, 1976; Medals for the Human Environment, 1982, 1989; A Szent-Györgyi Prize, 1995. Memberships: Science and Technology Advisory Committee, 1983-95; Board of Administration, European Federation of Corrosion 1995-2001; National Representative, 1.2 Committee of IUPAC, 1985-97; President, 1992-2004, Honorary President, 2005-, Hungarian Corrosion Association. Address: H-1025 Budapest, Zöldmáli lejtő 5, Hungary.

BERENGER Tom, b. 31 May 1950, Chicago, USA. Actor. M. (1) Barbara Wilson, 1976-84, 2 children, (2) Lisa Williams, 1986-97, 3 children, (3) Patricia Alvaran, 1998, 1 child. Education: University of Missouri. Career: Stage: Regional theatre and off-Broadway including The Rose Tattoo; Electra; A Streetcar Named Desire; End as a Man; Films: Behind the Door, 1975; Sentinel; Looking for Mr Goodbar; In Praise of Older Women; Butch and Sundance: The Early Days; The Dogs of War; The Big Chill; Eddie and the Cruisers; Fear City; Firstborn; Rustler's Rhapsody; Platoon; Someone to Watch Over Me; Shoot to Kill; Betrayed; Last Rites; Major League; Love at Large; The Field; Shattered; Chasers; Sniper, Sliver, 1993; Major League 2, Last of the Dogmen, Gettysburg, 1994; The Substitute, An Occasional Hell, 1996; The Gingerbread Man, 1997; One Man's Hero (also producer), Diplomatic Siege, A Murder of Crows, 1999; Takedown, The Hollywood Sign, Fear of Flying, 2000; Training Day, Watchtower, Eye See You, 2001; Sniper 2, D-Tox, 2002; Sniper 3, 2004; Into the West, 2005; Nightmare & Dreamscapes, 2006; The Christmas Miracle of Jonathon Toomey, 2007; Stiletto, 2008; Silent Venom, 2009; Charlie Valentine, 2009; Order of Redemption, 2009; Last Will, 2009; Sinners & Saints, 2009; TV: One Life to Live (series); Johnny We Hardly Knew Ye; Flesh and Blood; If Tomorrow Comes; Johnson County War, Junction Boys, 2002; Peacemakers, 2003; Captial City, The Detective, 2004; October Road, 2007-08; Desperate Hours: An Amber Alert, 2008. Address: c/o CAA, 9830 Wilshire Boulevard, Beverly Hills, CA 90212, USA.

BERESFORD-WILLIAMS Mary Edwina, b. 30 April 1931, London, England. Artist. m. David, 1 son. Education: BA (Hons), Fine Art (Class I), 1953, Teaching Certificate, 1954, Reading University. Appointments: Teacher, Leigh-on-Sea and Rolle College; Adult Education Teacher, Exmouth and Paignton; Artist; Group and solo exhibitions around the UK; Works held in public and private collections. Address: 11 Langdon Lane, Galmpton, Brixham, Devon TQ5 0PQ, England. E-mail: beresford-williams@hotmail.co.uk

BERESTYCKI Henri, b. 25 March 1951, Paris, France. Professor. m. Marie-Anne Toledano, 2 sons, 2 daughters. Education: Ecole Normale Superieure, Paris, 1975; PhD, 1975, Habilitation, 1981, Universite Paris VI, Paris. Appointments: Professor, Ecole Polytechnique, 1987-99; Professor, University Paris VI, 1988-2001; Professor, Ecole Normale Superieure, Paris, 1994-99; Visiting Professor, University of Chicago; Director, Centre d'Analyse et Mathematiques Sociales, joint research unit of CNRS and EHESS; Professor, EHESS, Paris. Publications: Over 120 scientific publications in professional journals. Honours: Grand Prize Sophie Germain, Paris Academy of Sciences; Humboldt-Gay-Lussac Prize, 2005; Chevalier de la Legion d'Honneur, 2010; Listed in international biographical dictionaries. Memberships: American Mathematical Society. Address: Ecole des Hautes Etudes en Sciences Sociales (CAMS), 190-198 avenue de France, F-75013, Paris, France. E-mail: hb@ehess.fr

BEREZHNOY Vadim Leonidovich, b. 28 February 1938, Krasnodar Region, Russia. Scientist; Metallurgist; Physicist. m. Svetlana I Naryshkina, 1 son. Education: CMEng, Diploma, Technical University, Rostov-on-Don, Russia, 1960; Certificate, Philosophical faculty on Higher Courses, Rostov State University, 1964; MSc, Institute of Steel and Alloys, Moscow, Russia, 1968; Certificate, Pedagogical Craftsmanship Faculty of Technical University, Rostov-on-Don; DSc, Doctor of Science for Metal Working by Pressure, All-Russia Institute of Light Alloys, Moscow, 1992. Appointments: Senior Engineer, Metallurgist, Rostov Radar Navigation Plant, 1960-64; Assistant Professor (Docent) and R&D Group Leader for the Technical University, Rostov-on-Don, 1968-77; Contributing Expert for Control-Research Board in the USSR Committee of Invertions and Discoveries, 1983-91; Visiting Professional Lecturer and Expert, Russian and Foreign Countries, 1988-; Head of R&D Sector of Novel Technologies, 1978-93, Chief Scientist, Researcher and Expert, 1993-, All-Russia Institute of Light Alloys; Extrusion Consultant, LG Cable, South Korea, 1997-98; Independent Industry Consultant for Technology, Equipment, Alloys, 2001-; Academic Secretary of Institute Doctor Dissertation Council, 2002-. Publications: Author, several books including Monograph: Extrusion with Active Friction Forces, Russia, 1988; Making of Novotechnocrat: Chroniques and Essays, Russia, 2010; 240 scientific papers which include: Deformation Techniques with Peripheral-Flow Acceleration, 1973; Friction-Assisted Extrusion as an Alternative to the Indirect and Direct Extrusion of Hard Aluminium Alloys, 1997; Non-Traditional Process Techniques of Extrusion and Pressing, 2000; Technological Principles of Maximizing Strength in the Case of Production of Press-Quenched Al-Mg-Si Alloy Extrusions, 2000; Multi-functional friction-assisted and controlled extrusion production of special shapes with uniform or/and gradient mechanical properties, 2000; Innovations: 35 inventions and one Discovery of Bulk Friction and Sheer Effect as a Physical Base for a High Speed Metal Outflow, and Mechanical Properties and Structure Control, 1965; More than 30 new projects including: Friction-assisted extrusion and briquetting of heated and cold light alloys and powder materials as well as the hydraulic and mechanical presses for these methods; Developed Theory of Friction-Assisted Extrusion and the Principles of the Novel Technologies; Assisted Friction Effect as a Physical Base for a High Speed Metal Outflow and Mechanical Properties Control; Theory of Friction-Assisted Extrusion and Novel Presses and Technology; Pressing and Briquetting with Intensive Plastical Shear; New hypotheses: Matter and Anti-matter Interaction as a Limits and Base for the Finite Universe Power and Black Holes Collapse, 1998; Gulf Stream and Gulf of Mexico in System of Communicating Vessels with Tunnel Solenoids under Florida Peninsula as an Action Base for the Bermuda Triangle Phenomenon, 1997; Directed Impulse Exposure for Excitation of Local Earthquake, 1997; Novotechnology conception, political technocrats in exchange of the non-technocrats political leaders – 'liberals' as a real base for the decisions of many Global problems, 2007; 10 presentations on the 10 world conferences and congresses, 1990-2008. Honours: Several medals: 1962, 1986, 1989, 1997, 2005, 2006; Honorary Award for New Technology, Russian Government, 1995; American Medal of Honor, 2003; Man of the Year 2003, ABI; Listed in Who's Who publications, biographical dictionaries, ABI, IBC and Russia Edition. Memberships: APMI International; Research Board of Advisors and Fellows, ABI; Research Council, IBC; 3 science and 3 editorial boards of science journals in Russia. Address: Marshal Katukov Street 14-1-142, Moscow 123592, Russia.

BEREZKIN Vladimir Ivanovich, b. 27 September 1950, Petropavlovsk, Kamchatskiisity, Russia. Physiciast. m. Svetlana, 2 sons. Education: Physical Diplomate, Polytechnical University, St Petersburg, USSR, 1973; PhD, Physics and Mathematics, Ioffe Physico-Technical Institute, 1983; DSc, Physics and Mathematics, V Novgorod State University, 2010. Appointments: USSR Army Officer, 1973-75; Scientist, Ioffe Physico-Technical Institute, 1975-88; Senior Scientist, Research Centre for Ecological Safety, 1988-. Publications: Numerous articles in professional journals. Honours: Medal for Student Best Scientifical Work of the USSR in the field of Natural Sciences, 1973; Medal for Inventor of the USSR, 1983. Address: Research Centre for Ecological Safety, 18 Korpusnaya Street, St Petersburg 197110, Russia. E-mail: v.berezkin@inbox.ru

BERG Adrian, b. 12 March 1929, London, England. Artist; Painter. Education: Gonville and Caius College, Cambridge; Trinity College, Dublin; St Martin's and Chelsea Schools of Art; Royal College of Art. Career: One-man exhibitions in London, Florence, Düsseldorf, Montreal, Toronto, Chicago; Arts Council, Serpentine Gallery; Paintings 1977-86, Piccadilly Gallery; Touring Exhibition, A Sense of Place, Barbican Centre, London, Bath, Plymouth, Gwent, Sheffield, Newcastle upon Tyne, Edinburgh, 1993-94; Royal Academy, 1992-94, watercolours, 1999, 2009; Work in Collections: Arts Council; British Museum; European Parliament; Government Picture Collection; Hiroshima City Museum of Contemporary Art; Tate Gallery, Tokyo Metropolitan Art Museum. Honours: Gold Medal, Florence Biennale, 1973; Major Prize, Tolly Cobbold Eastern Arts Association Exhibition, 1981; Third Prize, John Moores Liverpool Exhibition, 1982-83; First National Trust Foundation for Art Award, 1987; First Prize, RWS Open, 2001. Memberships: RA; Honorary Fellow RCA, 1994. Address: c/o Royal Academy of Arts, Burlington House, Piccadilly, London W1J 0BD, England.

BERGADÀ GRAÑÓ Josep M, b. 5 July 1962, Vallfogona de Riucorb, Spain. Engineer; Reader. Education: Mechanical Engineer, 1990; PhD, Mechanical Engineering, 1996. Appointments: Lecturer, Fluid Mechanics, 1993; Reader, Fluid Mechanics, 2009. Publications: A direct solution for flowrate and force along a cone seated poppet valve for laminar flow, 2004; Vorticity Analysis Associated with Drafting Cylinders for Pneumatic Spinning, 2006; Flow Characterization of Cylinders for Pneumatic Spinning, 2007; Pressure, flow, force and torque between the barrel and port plate in an axial piston pump, 2008; Leakage and groove pressure of an axial piston pump slipper with multiple lands, 2008; Axial piston pump grooved slipper analysis by CFD simulation of three dimensional NVS equation in cylindrical coordinates, 2009; The hydrostatic/hydrodynamic behaviour of an axial piston pump slipper with multiple lands, 2010. Honours: Listed in international biographical dictionaries. Memberships: Col legi d'Enginyers Industrials de Catalunya; Associacio d'Amics de la UPC. Address: c/Salva 135 5e 1a, 08224 Terrassa, Spain. E-mail: bergada@mf.upc.edu

BERGANT Boris, b 19 April 1948, Maribor, Slovenia. Journalist; Television Executive. m. Verena. Education: Studied at University in Ljubljana, Slovenia. Appointments: Journalist; Experience in Broadcasting: Editor, foreign affairs, Editor-in-Chief, news and current affairs, Deputy Director General RTV, Slovenia in charge of international relations and programme co-operation, 1989-2008; President, Circom Regional, European Association of Regional Television 1990-92; Member Administrative Council, European Broadcasting Union (EBU), 1990-92, 1996-; Vice Chairman. TV Committee, EBU, EBU Radio Committee, 1993-98; Secretary-General, Circom Regional, 1995-2001; Vice President, European Broadcasting Union, 1998-2008; Representative of the Republic of Slovenia in different media committees of the Council of Europe. Publications: Several in the field of foreign politics and broadcasting. Honours: Tomšičeva nagrada for the Best Journalistic Achievement in Slovenija; Prizes at the TV Festivals at Monte Carlo, New York, Leipzig. Membership: President, Slovenian Journalist Association, 1986-90; Member, International Academy of TV Arts & Sciences, New York; Member, World Standardisation Committee for ISAS. Address: BorBER Media Activities, Boris Bergant sp, Abramova ulica 8, 1000 Ljubljana, Slovenia. E-mail: boris.bergant@borber.si

BERGEN Candice Patricia, b. 9 May 1946, Beverly Hills, USA. Actress; Photojournalist. m. (1) Louis Malle, 1980, deceased, 1995, 1 daughter, (2) Marshall Rose. Education: Westlake School for Girls; University of Pennsylvania. Career: Photojournalist work has appeared in Vogue, Cosmopolitan, Life and Esquire; Films: The Group, The Sand Pebbles, 1966; The Day the Fish Came Out, Vivre Pour Vivre, 1967; The Magus, 1968; Getting Straight, Soldier Blue, The Adventurers, 1970; Carnal Knowledge, The Hunting Party, 1971; T R Baskin, 1972; 11 Harrowhouse, 1974; Bite the Bullet, 1975; The Wind and the Lion, 1976; The Domino Principle, A Night Full of Rain, 1977; Oliver's Story, 1978; Starting Over, 1979; Rich and Famous, 1981; Gandhi, 1982; Stick, 1985; Au Revoir les Enfants (co-director), 1987; Miss Congeniality, 2000; Sweet Home Alabama, 2002; View from the Top, The In-Laws, 2003; Sex and the City, The Women, 2008; Bride Wars, 2009; TV: Murphy Brown (series), 1989; Mary and Tim, 1996; Footsteps, 2003; Will & Grace, 2004; Boston Legal (series), 2005; Law & Order: Trial by Jury, 2005. Publications: The Freezer, 1968; Knock Wood (autobiography), 1984. Honours: Best Short Plays, 1968; Emmy Award, 1989, 1990. Address: c/o William Morris Agency, 151 El Camino, Beverly Hills, CA 90212, USA.

BERGER André, b. 30 July 1942, Acoz, Belgium. Professor. m. M A Lallemand, 3 daughters. Education: MS, Meteorology, MIT, 1971; DSc, Catholic University Louvain, Belgium, 1973; Dr Honoris Causa, University Aix-Marseille, France, 1989; Docteur honoris causa de l'Université Paul Sabatier, Toulouse, 2000; Dr honoris causa, Faculté Polytechnique de Mons, 2004. Appointments: Assistant, 1965-73, Suppléant, 1973-76, Chargé de Cours, 1976-84, Head Institute of Astronomy and Geophysics, 1978-2001, Professor, 1984-89, Ordinary Professor, 1989-2007, Emeritus Professor and Senior Researcher, 2007-, University Catholic Louvain; Visiting Professor, Vrij Universiteit, Brussels, 1982-92, maitre de conference, University Liège, Belgium, 1985-93; Chaire Francqui, 1989; Chairman, Panel Special Program on Science of Global Environment Change NATO,

1992-93; Chairman, Special Program Panel in Air-Sea Interactions, 1981; Chairman International Commission Climate, 1987-93; Chairman, Paleoclimate Commission International Quaternary Association, 1987-95; President of European Geophysical Society, 2000-02; Member, Hearings Board European Parliament and Belgium Ministry of Research; Member, Science Council Gaz de France, 1994-99, Member Environment Council Electricité de France, 1998-2008; Member of the Scientific Committee of European Environment Agency, 2002-08; Member, Scientific Council of Meteo-France, 2001-11; Vice Chairman, 1998-99, Chairman, 2000-03, Expert Advisory Group on Global Change, Climate and Biodiversity of the European Commission; Member, Scientific Council of Centre National de le Recherche Scientifique, France, 2002-04; Member, Comité d'Orientation Scientifique et Stratégique du Collège de France, 2003-06. Publications: Le Climat de la Terre, un passé pour quel avenir?, 1992; Editor: Climatic Variations and Variability: Facts and Theories, 1981; Co-Editor: Milankovitch and Climate, Understanding the Response to Orbital Forcing, 1984; Understanding Climate Change, 1989; Contributor, research articles on climatic variations and climate modelling to professional journals. Honours include most recently: Associate Foreign Member, Académie des Sciences, Paris, 2000; Member of the Royal Academy of Sciences, Letters and Arts Belgium, 2002; Associate, The Royal Astronomical Society, 2003; Foreign Member, Serbian Academy of Sciences and Arts, 2006; Foreign Fellow, Royal Society of Canada, 2007. Honorary President of European Geo-Sciences Union; Officier de la Legíon d'Honneur in France, 2010; Grand Officier de l'Ordre de la Couronne. Memberships: International Union of Geodesy and Geophysics, Lecturer, 1987; World Institute Science; American Geophysical Union; American Meteorological Society; Royal Meteorological Society, Foreign Member. Address: Catholic University Louvain, Institute Astronomy and Geophysics G Lemaitre, 2 Chemin du Cyclotron, B-1348 Louvain-la-Neuve, Belgium. E-mail: berger@astr.ucl.ac.be

BERGER John, b. 5 November 1926, London, England. Author; Art Critic. Education: Central School of Art; Chelsea School of Art, London. Appointments: Painter, Teacher of Drawing; Visiting Fellow, BFI, 1990-; Numerous TV appearances and exhibitions. Publications include: Novels: A Painter of Our Time, 1958; The Foot of Clive, 1962; Corker's Freedom, 1964; A Fortunate Man, 1967; Art and Revolution; The Moment of Cubism and Other Essays; The Look of Things: Selected Essays and Articles; The Way of Seeing, 1972; G, 1972; Pig Earth, 1979; About Looking, 1980; Another Way of Telling, 1982; And Our Faces; My Heart; Brief as Photos, 1984; The White Bird, 1985; Once in Europa, 1989; Lilac and Flag, 1991; Keeping a Rendezvous (essays and poems), 1992; To The Wedding, 1995; Titian: Nymph and Shepherd, 1996; Steps Towards a Small Theory of the Visible, 1996; Photocopies, 1996; King: A Street Story, 1999; The Shape of a Pocket, 2001; John Berger Selected Essays, 2001; I Send You This Cadmium Red; Titian: Nymph and Shepherd; Here is Where We Meet; Hold Everything Dear; From A to X, 2008. Radio: Will It Be A Likeness? 1996; Poetry and translations. Honours include: Booker Prize, 1972; New York Critics Prize, Best Scenario of Year, 1976; George Orwell Memorial Prize, 1977; Prize, Best Reportage, Union of Journalists and Writers, Paris, 1977. Address: Quincy, Mieussy, 74440 Taninges, France.

BERGER Thomas (Louis), b. 20 July 1924, Cincinnati, Ohio, USA. Author. m. Jeanne Redpath, 12 June 1950. Education: BA, University of Cincinnati, 1948; Postgraduate Studies, Columbia University, 1950-51. Appointments: Librarian, Rand School of Social Science, New York City, 1948-51; Staff, New York Times Index, 1951-52; Associate Editor, Popular Science Monthly, 1952-53; Distinguished Visiting Professor, Southampton College, 1975-76; Visiting Lecturer, Yale University, 1981, 1982; Regent's Lecturer, University of California at Davis, 1982. Publications: Crazy in Berlin, 1958; Reinhart in Love, 1962; Little Big Man, 1964; Killing Time, 1967; Vital Parts, 1970; Regiment of Women, 1973; Sneaky People, 1975; Who is Teddy Villanova?, 1977; Arthur Rex, 1978; Neighbors, 1980; Reinhart's Women, 1981; The Feud, 1983; Nowhere, 1985; Being Invisible, 1987; The Houseguest, 1988; Changing the Past, 1989; Orrie's Story, 1990; Meeting Evil, 1992; Robert Crews, 1994; Suspects, 1996; The Return of Little Big Man, 1999; Best Friends, 2003; Adventures of the Artificial Woman, 2004. Other: Plays and screenplays: Other People, Stockbridge Theatre festival, 1970. Honours: Dial Fellow, 1962; Rosenthal Award, National Institute of Arts and Letters, 1965; Western Heritage Award, 1965; Ohioana Book Award, 1982; Pulitzer Prize Nomination, The Feud, 1984; LittD, Long Island University, 1986; Listed in numerous Who's Who and biographical publications. Address: PO Box 11, Palisades, NY 10964, USA. E-mail: thosberg@earthlink.net

BERISHA Sali, b. 15 October 1944, Tropoje, Albania. Professor of Medicine; Cardiologist; Prime Minister. m. Liri Rama, 1 son, 1 daughter. Education: Medical Doctor, 1967, Professor of Medicine, 1989, Tirana University Medical School; Graduate studies in Medicine, UNESCO Fellow, Paris, 1978. Appointments: Assistant Professor, Professor of Medicine, Tirana University Medical School, Cardiologist, Tirana General Hospital, 1967-90; Chairman, Democratic Party, 1991-; President, Republic of Albania, 1992-97; Leader, coalition of centre right wing parties, 2001-; Prime Minister of Albania, 2005-. Publications: Numerous works on cardiologist research studies in professional medical and scientific journals; Many articles and speeches published in Albanian and foreign magazines and journals. Memberships: European Medical Research Committee, WHO, Copenhagen, 1986. Address: Blv Dëshmorët e Kombit Nr 1, Council of Ministers, Tirana, Albania.

BERKOFF Steven, b. 3 August 1937, London, England. Writer; Director; Actor. m. (1) Alison Minto, 1970, (2) Shelley Lee, 1976, divorced. Education: Webber-Douglas Academy of Dramatic Art, London, 1958-59; École Jacques Lecoq, Paris, 1965. Appointments: Director of plays and actor in numerous plays, films and TV; Founding Director, London Theatre Group, 1973; Massage, performed at Edinburgh Festival, 1997; Shakespeare's Villains, Theatre Royal, Haymarket, UK and World Tour, 1998, 1999. Plays: In the Penal Colony, 1968; Metamorphosis, 1969; Agamemnon, 1973, 1984; The Fall of the House of Usher, 1974; The Trial, 1976; East, 1978; Hamlet, 1980, 2001; Greek, 1980; Decadence, 1981; West, 1983; Harry's Christmas, 1985; Kvetch and Acapulco, Sink the Belgrano!, 1986; With Massage, 1987; Lunch, Dog, actor, Brighton Beach Scumbags, Dahling You Were Marvellous, 1994; Coriolanus, Mermaid, 1996; Massage, 1997; Shakespeare's Villains, 1998; Messiah, 2000; Films include: Octopussy; First Blood 2; Beverley Hills Cop; Absolute Beginners; War and Remembrance; The Krays; Decadence, 1994; Rancid Aluminium, 2000; Head in the Clouds, Brides, 2004; Forest of the Gods, 2005; The Flying Scotsman, The half Life of Timofey Berezin, The 10th Man, 2006; Say It In Russian, Heavenly Sword, 2007; The Dot Man, Perfect Live, 2008; The Big I Am, 44 Inch Chest, At World's End, 2009; Publications: America, 1988; I am Hamlet, A Prisoner in Rio,

1989; The Theatre of Steven Berkoff: Photographic Record, Coriolanus in Deutschland, 1992; Overview, collected essays, 1994; Free Association, autobiography, 1996; Graft: Tales of an Actor, 1998; Shopping in the Santa Monica Mall, Ritual in Blood, Messiah, Oedipus, 2000; The Secret Love Life of Ophelia, 2001; Tough Acts, 2003. Honours: Los Angeles Drama Critics Circle Award, 1983; Comedy of the Year Award, Evening Standard, 1991. Address: c/o Joanna Marston, Rosica Colin Ltd, 1 Clareville Grove Mews, London SW7 5AH, England.

BERLIOCCHI Henri Dominique, b. 19 April 1948, Nice, France. Lecturer. m. Roseline Détappe, 1 son, 1 daughter. Education: Baccalaureat, 1965; Ecole Normale Superieure Saint-Cloud, France, 1967; PhD, Mathematics, 1970. Appointments: Lecturer, Paris 13 University, Villentaneuse, France. Publications: 5 articles in professional journals; 5 books. Address: 4 Rue du Cottage, 91120 Palaiseau, France. E-mail: henri.berliocchi@wanadoo.fr.

BERLUSCONI Silvio, b. 29 September 1936, Milan, Italy. Politician; Businessman. m. (1) Carla Dall'Oglio, 1965, (2) Veronica Lario, 1985. Education: University of Milan. Appointments: Owner, building and property development company, 1962-; Business interests include: Fininvest; Milan 2 Housing project, 1969; Canale 5 Network, 1980-; Owner, Italia 1 TV network, 1983; Owner, Rete 4 TV network, 1984; Stakeholder, La Cinq commercial TV network, 1985; Stakeholder, Chain, Cinema 5; Owner, Estudios Roma, 1986; Owner, Milan AC Football Club, 1986; Owner, La Standa department store, 1988; Chairman, Arnoldo Mondadori Editore SpA, 1990, half-share, 1991; Founder, President, Forza Italia political movement, 1993-; Full time political career, 1994-; Prime Minister of Italy, 1994-95, 2001-06, 2008-; MEP, 1999; Minister of Foreign Affairs, 2002; Stood trial on corruption charges; President, EU Council, 2003. Publications: Album, Meglio 'ne Canzone, 2003. Address: Office of the Prime Minister, Palazzo Chigi Piazza Colonna 370, 00187 Rome, Italy.

BERNE Stanley, b. Port Richmond, Staten Island, New York, USA. Research Professor; Writer. m. Arlene Zekowski, 1952. Education: BS, Rutgers University, 1947; MA, New York University, 1950; Graduate Fellow, Louisiana State University, Baton Rouge, 1954-59; PhD, Marlborough University, 1990. Appointments: Associate Professor, English, 1960-80, Research Professor, English, 1980-, Eastern New Mexico University, Portales; Host, Co-Producer, TV series, Future Writing Today, KENW-TV, PBS, 1984-85. Publications: A First Book of the Neo-Narrative, 1954; Cardinals and Saints: On the aims and purposes of the arts in our time, 1958; The Dialogues, 1962; The Multiple Modern Gods and Other Stories, 1969; The New Rubaiyat of Stanley Berne (poetry), 1973; Future Language, 1976; The Great American Empire, 1981; Every Person's Little Book of P-L-U-T-O-N-I-U-M (with Arlene Zekowski), 1992; Alphabet Soup: A Dictionary of Ideas, 1993; To Hell with Optimism, 1996; Dictionary of the Avant-Gardes, 1998; Gravity Drag, 1998; The Living Underground, 1999; Swimming to Significance, 1999; Extremely Urgent Messages, 2000; Empire Sweets - or How I Learned to Live and Love in the Greatest Empire on Earth!; Legal Tender - or It's All About Money!; You and Me - or How to Survive in the Greatest Empire on Earth!; Now Playing, 2009; Haiku America, 2009; Contributions to: Anthologies and other publications. Honours: Literary research awards, Eastern New Mexico University, 1966-76. Memberships: PEN; New England Small Press Association; Rio Grande Writers Association; Santa Fe Writers. Address: 2400 Legacy Court, Suite 313B, Santa Fe, NM 87507, USA.

BERNSTEIN Carl, b. 14 February 1944, Washington, District of Columbia, USA. Journalist; Writer. m. Nora Ephron, 14 April 1976, divorced, 2 sons. Education: University of Maryland, 1961-64. Appointments: Copyboy to Reporter, Washington Star, 1960-65; Reporter, Elizabeth Journal, New Jersey, 1965-66, Washington Post, 1966-76; Washington Bureau Chief, 1979-81, Correspondent, 1981-84, ABC-TV; Correspondent, Contributor, Time magazine, 1990-91; Visiting Professor, New York University, 1992-93; Contributing Editor to Vanity Fair, 1997-; Executive Vice President and Executive Director, Voter.com, -2001. Publications: All the President's Men (with Bob Woodward), 1973; The Final Days (with Bob Woodward), 1976; Loyalties: A Son's Memoir, 1989; His Holiness (with Marco Politi), 1996; A Woman in Charge: The Life of Hillary Rodham Clinton, 2007. Honours: Drew Pearson Prize for Investigative Reporting, 1972; Pulitzer Prize Citation, 1972; Honorary LLD, Boston University, 1975. Address: c/o Janklow and Nesbit Associates, 598 Madison Avenue, New York, NY 10022, USA.

BERRY Chuck (Charles Edward Anderson Berry), b. 18 October 1926, Overland, Missouri, USA. Singer; Composer. m. Thermetta Suggs, 1948, 4 children. Appointments: TV Appearances, 1955-. Creative Works: Albums: After School Sessions, One Dozen Berry's, 1958; New Juke Box Hits, Chuck Berry, More Chuck Berry, On Stage, 1960; You Can Never Tell, Greatest Hits, Two Great Guitars, 1964; Chuck Berry in London, Fresh Berrys, 1965; St Louis to Liverpool, 1966; Golden Hist, At the Fillmore, Medley, 1967; Concerto in B Goods, 1969; Home Again, 1971; The London Sessions, Golden Decade, St Louis to Frisco to Memphis, In Memphis, 1972; Let the Good Times Roll, Golden Decade vol II, 1973, vol V, 1974; Bio, Back in the USA, 1973; I'm a Rocker, Chuck Berry 75, 1975; Motovatin, 1976; Rockit, 1979; Chess Masters, 1983; The Chess Box, 1989; Missing Berries, Rarities, 1990; On the Blues Side, 1993; Anthology, 2000. Films: Go, Johnny Go, Rock, Rock, Rock, 1956; Jazz on a Summer's Day, 1960; Let the Good Times Roll, 1973; Hail! Hail! Rock 'n' Roll, 1987. Publication: Chuck Berry: The Autobiography, 1987. Honours include: Grammy Award for Life Achievement, 1984. Address: Berry Park, 691 Buckner Road, Wentzville, MO 63385, USA.

BERRY Halle, b. 14 August 1966, Cleveland, Ohio, USA. Actress; Model. m. (1) David Justice, 1993, divorced 1997, (2) Eric Benet, 2001, divorced 2005, partner, Gabriel Aubry, 1 daughter. Career: Numerous formal beauty contests in 1980s; TV and Film actress, 1989-; Films: Strictly Business, Jungle Fever, The Last Boy Scout, 1991; Boomerang, 1992; Father Hood, Alex Haley's Queen, The Program, 1993; The Flintstones, 1994; Losing Isaiah, 1995; The Rich Man's Wife, Executive Decision, Race the Sun, Girl 6, 1996; B.A.P.S, 1997; Why Do Fools Fall in Love, The Wedding, Bulworth, 1998; Victims of Fashion, Ringside, Introducing Dorothy Dandridge (also producer), 1999; X-Men, 2000; Swordfish, Monster's Ball, 2001; James Bond: Die Another Day, 2002; X-Men 2, Gothika, 2003; Catwoman, 2004; Robots (voice), 2005; X-Men: The Last Stand, 2006; Perfect Stranger, Things We Lost in the Fire, 2007; Frankie and Alice, 2009; TV appearances: TV debut in sitcom Living Dolls, 1989; Knots Landing, 1991-92; Their Eyes Were Watching God, 2005. Honours: Harvard Foundation for Intercultural and Race Relations Award; Golden Globe for Best Actress, Screen

Actor's Guild Award, 1999; Oscar, Actress in a Leading Role, 2001; Academy Award, 2002; NAACP Award for Best Supporting Actress, 2003. Membership: National Breast Cancer Coalition. Address: c/o William Morris Agency, 151 South El Camino Drive, Beverly Hills, LA 90212, USA.

BERRY Robert James, b. 26 October 1934, Preston, England. University Teacher. m. Caroline, 1 son, 2 daughters. Education: Gonville and Caius College Cambridge; University College London. Appointments: Professor of Genetics, University College London, 1978-2000; President: Linnean Society, 1982-85, British Ecological Society, 1987-89, European Ecological Federation, 1990-92, Mammal Society, 1995-98. Publications: Books: Teach Yourself Genetics, 1965; Adam and the Ape, 1972, 1975; Inheritance and Natural History, 1977; Natural History of Shetland, 1980; Neo-Darwinism, 1982; Free to Be Different, 1984; Natural History of Orkney, 1985; God and Evolution, 1988, 2000; God and the Biologist, 1996; Science, Life and Christian Belief, 1998; Orkney Nature, 2000; God's Stewards, 2002; God's Book of Works, 2003; Islands, 2009; Ecology and the Environment, 2011; Editor of 13 books; About 200 papers in scientific and other journals. Honours: UK Templeton Award for long and distinguished advocacy of the Christian faith among scientists, 1996; Marsh Award for Ecology, 2001. Memberships: Natural Environment Research Council, 1981-87; Human Fertilisation and Embryology Authority, 1990-96; Trustee, National Museums and Galleries on Merseyside, 1985-94; Chairman, 1968-87, President, 1993-95, Christians in Science; General Synod of the Church of England, 1970-90; Moderator, Environmental Issues Network of Churches Together in Britain and Ireland, 1989-2008. Address: Quarfseter, Sackville Close, Sevenoaks, Kent TN13 3QD, England.

BERRY Roger Julian, b. 6 April 1935, New York, USA. Physician. m. (Joseline) Valerie (Joan) Butler. Education: BA, New York University, 1954; BSc, 1957, MD, 1958, Duke University, Durham, North Carolina; DPhil, 1967, MA, Magdalen College, Oxford; MRCP, 1971; FRCP; 1978; FRCR, 1979; Honorary FACR, 1983; MFOM, 1988; FFOM, 1993. Appointments: Head, Radiobiology Laboratory, Churchill Hospital, Oxford, 1969-74; Royal Naval Reserve, 1971-92, Principal Medical Officer (Reserves), 1987-88, Captain Medical Training (Reserves) on staff of Commander-in-Chief, Naval Home Command, 1988-90; Head, Neutrons and Therapeutic Effects Group, MRC Radiobiology Unit, Harwell, 1974-76; Sir Brian Windeyer Professor of Oncology, Middlesex Hospital School of Medicine (University of London), 1976-87; Director, Health Safety and Environmental Protection, British Nuclear Fuels plc, 1987-92; Director, Westlakes Research Institute, Cumbria, 1992-95; Commissioner, International Commission on Radiological Protection, 1985-89; Chairman, British Committee on Radiation Units and Measurements, 1995-2000; Visiting Professor, Institute of Environmental and Natural Sciences, Lancaster University, 1993-2003; Trustee, Bishop Barrow's Charity and Governor King William's College, 2000-; County Commander, 2005-, Chair of Council, 2008-, St John Ambulance. Publications: Book: Manual on Radiation Dosimetry (with N W Holm), 1970; Contributions to: Oxford Textbook of Medicine; Florey's Textbook of Pathology; Hunter's Diseases of Occupation; Over 190 scientific papers in medical journals. Honours include: Academic: Roentgen Prize, 1970, Silvanus Thompson Memorial Lecturer, 1991, British Institute of Radiology; Douglas Lea Memorial Lecturer, Institute of Physical Sciences in Medicine, 1993; Civil: Freeman of the City of London, 1982; Reserve Decoration, 1986; Honorary Physician to HM The Queen, 1987-90; CStJ. Memberships: President, 1986-87, British Institute of Radiology; Yeoman, 1981, Liveryman, 1984, Worshipful Society of Apothecaries of London; Fellow, Society for Radiological Protection, 1991-; Associate Member, The Nautical Institute, 1998-2008; Royal Overseas League; Royal Naval Sailing Association. Address: 109 Fairways Drive, Mount Murray, Santon, Douglas, Isle of Man IM4 2JE, United Kingdom. E-mail: r.j.b@advsys.co.uk

BERTOLAMI Orfeu, b. 3 January 1959, São Paulo, Brazil. Physicist. m. M C Bento, October 1992, 1 daughter. Education: Graduate, Physics, São Paulo University, 1980; MSc, Inst Fís Teórica, São Paulo, 1983; Advanced Degree, Mathematics, University of Cambridge, England, 1984; PhD, Physics, University of Oxford, England, 1987. Appointments: Post-doctoral Positions; Institut für Theoretische Physik; University of Heidelberg, Germany, 1987-89; Instituto de Física and Mat, Lisbon, Portugal, 1989-91; Associate Professor, Departmento Física, Instituto Superior Técnico, Lisbon, 1991-2010; Scientific Associate, Theory Division, CERN, 1993-95; Research Associate, Istituto Nazionale Fisica Nucleare, Turim, 1994-95; Visiting Scholar, Physics Department, New York University, 1999; Full Professor, Departmento de Física e Astronomia, Universidade do Porto, 2010-. Publications: Over 210 publications, over 135 of which in specialised international Physics Journals; 2 books. Honours: Honorary Mentions in the Essay Contest, Gravity Research Foundation, USA, 1995, 1997, 2001, 2003, 2007 and 2009; Third Prize, 1999; Prémio União Latina (Latin America, Portugal), 2001; Prize, UTL/Santander Totta for scientific excellence in biophysics and physics, 2007; Listed in national and international biographical dictionaries. Memberships: Sociedade Portuguesa de Física; Sociedade Portuguesa de Astronomia. Address: Departmento de Física e Astronomia, Faculdade de Ciensias, Universidade de Porto, Rua de Campo Alegre, 687, 4169-007, Porto, Portugal. E-mail: orfeu.bertolami@fc.up.pt Website: http://web.ist.utl.pt/orfeu.bertolami/homeorfeu.html

BERTOLUCCI Bernardo, b. 16 March 1940, Parma, Italy. Film Director. m. (1) Adriana Asti, (2) Clare Peploe, 1978. Career: Director: La Commare Secca, 1962; Prima della Rivoluzione, 1964; Il Fico Infruttuoso in Vangelo 70, 1968; Partner, 1970; La Strategia del Ragno, 1970; Il Conformista, 1970; Last Tango in Paris, 1972; 1900, 1975; La Luna, 1979; Tragedy of a Ridiculous Man, 1981; The Last Emperor, 1986; The Sheltering Sky, 1989; Little Buddha, 1993; Stealing Beauty, 1995; I Dance Alone, 1996; Besieged, 1998; Ten Minutes Older: The Cello (segment), 2002; The Dreamers, 2003. Publications: In cerca del mistero (poems), 1962; Paradiso e inferno (poems), 1999. Honours: Viareggio Prize, 1962; European Film Award, 1988; Dr hc (Turin), 2000. Address: c/o Jeff Berg, ICM, 8942 Wilshire Boulevard, Beverly Hills, CA 90211, USA.

BERTONECHE Caroline Sophie Chantal, b. 29 September 1977, Pau, France. University Professor. Education: BA, English, Sorbonne, 1998; MA, 2000, PhD, 2006, English Literature, Sorbonne Nouvelle; M Phil, British Romantic Studies, Oxford, 2000. Appointments: University Lecturer, Post-doctoral Fellow, University of Reims, 2001-08; University Lecturer, Junior Research Fellow, 2002-05, 2005-06, Sorbonne Nouvelle, Paris; Senior Lecturer, Associate Professor, University Stendhal, Grenoble, 2008-. Publications: Numerous articles in professional journals; Book, John Keats: The Poet and the Myth, 2011; 2 books of poems in French. Honours: Keats-Shelley Second Essay

Prize Award, 2001; Fulbright Scholarship, 2003-04; Listed in international biographical dictionaries. Memberships: MLA; Keats-Shelley Memorial Association; Keats House, London; Harvard Club de France; Fulbright Alumni Association; Oxford Alumni Society. Address: 25bis Cours Berriat, 38000 Grenoble, France. E-mail: carolineberto@aol.com

BESSELL Eric Michael, b. 17 December 1946, Stony Stratford, Buckinghamshire, England. Medical Practitioner. m. Deborah Jane, 1 son, 1 daughter. Education: BSc, University of Bristol, 1967; PhD, Institute of Cancer Research, London, 1970; MBBS, St Mary's Hospital Medical School, London, 1978; FRCR, 1984; FRCP, 1993. Appointments: Registrar, Royal Postgraduate Medical School, Hammersmith Hospital, London, 1980-83; Senior Registrar, Royal Marsden Hospital, London, 1983-85; Consultant Oncologist, Nottingham University Hospitals NHS Trust, 1985-. Publications: Author, 80 papers on malignant lymphomas and cancer in learned journals. Honours: Clinical Director, Department of Clinical Oncology, Nottingham, 1986-96, 2003-07; Examiner, Royal College of Radiologists (London and Hong Kong), 1993-98. Memberships: British Medical Association; 1951 Radiotherapy Club/RAD Society. Address: 13 Dovedale Road, West Bridgford, Nottingham NG2 6JB, England. E-mail: eric.bessell@nuh.nhs.uk

BESSHO Takeshi, b. 10 April 1959, Moriguchi, Osaka, Japan. Professor. m. Akiko Oogai, 1 son, 1 daughter. Education: Graduate, Osaka University School of Engineering Science; Doctorate, Kanto Gakuin University of Engineering. Appointments: Project General Manager, Advanced Material Engineering Division; Project General Manager, Electronics Development Division 3, Toyota Motor Corporation; Guest Associate Professor, 2008-, Guest Professor, 2009-, Osaka University; Visiting Professor, Nagoya University, 2009-. Honours: Plenary Lecture Award, Interfinish 2008 World Congress & Exposition. Memberships: Director, Japan Institute of Electronics Packaging; Councilor, Japan Society of Heat Treatment. Address: 3-23-49 Suigen-cho, Toyota-city, Aichi-pref, 471-0822, Japan.

BESSON Luc, b. 18 March 1959, Paris, France. Film Director. m. (1) Anne Parillaud, 1 daughter, 1 daughter with Maiwenn Le Besco, (2) Milla Jovovich, 1997, divorced 1999, (3) Virginie Silla, 2004, 1 son, 2 daughters. Appointments: Assistant, Films in Hollywood and Paris; 1st Assistant for several advertising films. Creative Works: Films directed and produced: Le Dernier Combat, 1982; Subway, 1984; The Big Blue, 1988; Nikita, 1990; Atlantis, 1991; The Professional, Leon, 1994; The Fifth Element, 1996; The Messenger: the Story of Joan of Arc, 1999; The Dancer, Exit, 2000; Yamakasi, Baiser mortel du dragon, 2001; Le Transporteur, 2002; Taxi 3, Tristan, Cheeky, Vice & Versa, 2003; Crimson Rivers 2: Angels of the Apocalypse, 2004; Arthur and the Invisibles, Bandidas, Love and Other Disassters; Tell No One, 2006; The Secret, Taxi 4, Hitman, Frontier(s), 2007; Taken, Transporter 3, 2008. Address: Leeloo Productions, 53 rue Boissée, 91540 Mennecy, France.

BEST Keith Lander, b. 10 June 1949, Brighton, England. Chief Executive; Barrister. m. Elizabeth Gibson, 2 daughters. Education: BA (Hons) Jurisprudence, MA, Keble College, Oxford. Appointments: Called to the Bar, 1971; Lecturer in Law, Central London Polytechnic, 1973; General common law practice as barrister, 1973-87; Brighton Borough Councillor, 1976-80: Chairman of Lands Committee; Member of Parliament, Anglesey/Ynys Môn, 1979-87; Parliamentary Private Secretary to Secretary of State for Wales, 1981-84; Chairman (voluntary, unpaid), Executive Committee, World Federalist Movement/Institute for Global Policy, 1987-; Director, Prisoners Abroad (national charity), 1989-93; Chairman, Conservative Action for Electoral Reform, 1992-; Chief Executive Immigration Advisory Service (national charity), 1993-2009; Chief Executive Medical Foundation for the Care of Victims of Torture (Freedom from Torture) (national charity), 2010-; Chairman, Bangladesh Female Academy (charity); Chairman, Electronic Immigration Network, 1996-2006; Chairman, Electoral Reform Society, 1997-2003; Chairman, Association of Registered Immigration Advisers, 2003-09; Trustee, Cranstoun Drug Services, 2006-10; Chairman, Electoral Reform International Services; Named on Society Guardian as one of the 100 Most Influential People in Public Services in the UK, September 2003; Served in airborne and commando forces leaving with the rank of Major, Territorial Army, 1967-87. Publications: Write Your Own Will, 1978; The Right Way to Prove a Will, 1981; Various articles in magazines, Wall Street Journal, newspapers; Former Deputy Editor District Council Revue. Honours: Territorial Decoration; Freeman of the City of London. Memberships include: management Committee, Brighton Housing Trust; Chairman, Vauxhall Conservative Association, 1997-98; Amnesty; FRSA. Address: 15 St Stephen's Terrace, London SW8 1DJ, England. E-mail: kbest@torturecare.org.uk

BEST Ronald O'Neal, b. 25 May 1957, London, England. Artist. Education: Byam Shaw School of Art; Croydon College of Art; RCA, London; Assistant to Winston Branch, painter. Career: Painter and printmaker, oils, etchings, watercolours; Teacher, Essendine Centre, 1989-91, Kensington and Chelsea College, 1994; Litho Teacher, Heatherley School of Fine Art, London, 1997-2001; Co-ordinator, Visual Arts, Portobello Festival; Founder, Chelsea Painters and Printmakers, 1999; Manager, Notting Hill Fine Art Gallery; Co-ordinator, Art for the Unemployed, Portobello Academy of Drawing. Exhibitions: Royal Institute of Oil Painters; New English Art Club; Pastel Society; Society of Graphic Art; Salon des National, Paris; Lynn Stern Young Artists, London; Eva Jekel Gallery; Twentieth Century British Art Fair; Royal College of Art, London; 1492-1992 Un Nouveau Regard sur les Caraibes, Paris; Art House, Amsterdam; Pall Mall Deposit Gallery; Chelsea Printmakers; The Portobello Group; Portobello Printmakers; W11 Gallery; Gallery Café; Portobello Printmakers; Notting Hill Fine Art. Work in collections: Royal College of Art; Croydon College; Grange Museum, London. Address: 50 Berkhamsted Avenue, Wembley, Middlesex, England.

BEST Ulrich-Peter, b. 9 March 1959, Mainz, Germany. Physician. m. Doris Renate, 1 son. Education: Graduation and diploma, Technical High School, Mainz, 1978; Physician's License, 1984; Doctorate in Physiological Chemistry and Microbiology, 1989. Appointments: Surgeon Major, Medical Officer, German Armed Forces, 1987-88; Consultant, Specialist and Senior Physician, Ophthalmology, Municipal Clinical Hospitals of Frankfurt/Main-Hoechst, 1993; Project Director, Eye Care Programme Surigao, University of the Philippines, Metro, Manila, 1994-97; Freelance Specialist, Tropical Ophthalmology, Christoffel-Blindenmission, Aravind Eye Hospitals (India), Sagarmatha Chaudhary Eye Hospital, Lahan (Nepal), Kano (Nigeria), Sabatia (Kenya), and Lunsar (Sierra Leone); Medical Director, Eye Clinic and Eye Laser Clinic, Mainfranken, Schweinfurt, 2005-. Publications: Long-term Results after Selective Laser Trabeculoplasty (SLT) – a Clinical Study on 269 Eyes, 2005; Pressure Reduction after Selective Laser Trabeculoplasty (SLT) with Two Different Laster Systems and after Argon Laser Trabeculoplasty (ALT) – a Controlled Prospective Clinical

DICTIONARY OF INTERNATIONAL BIOGRAPHY 36th EDITION

Trial on 284 Eyes, 2007. Memberships: German Committee for the Prevention of Blindness. Address: Maininsel 16, D-97424 Schweinfurt, Germany. E-mail: dr.up.best@web.de Website: www.doktorbest.de

BEST William Robert, b. 14 July 1922, Chicago, Illinois, USA. Physician. m. Ruth Johanna Stuchlik, 2 daughters. Education: BS, 1945, MD, 1947, MS, Medicine, 1951, University of Illinois College of Medicine; Postdoctorate, Mathematical Biology, University of Chicago, 1964-65. Appointments: Assistant/Associate Professor of Medicine, 1953-70, Assistant Director, Research Resources Laboratory, 1964-67, Professor of Medicine, 1970-81, Associate Dean, Abraham Lincoln School of Medicine, 1972-81, University of Illinois College of Medicine, Chicago; Acting Director, VA Cooperative Studies Program, Washington, 1972; Chief, VA Midwest Research Support Center, Hines, Illinois, 1967-72; Chief of Staff, University of Illinois Hospital, Chicago, 1975-81; Chief of Staff, 1981-92, Acting Director, Rehabilitation R&D Center, 1993-94, Consultant, Senior Research Scientist, CMC[3], 1996-2008, Edward Hines Jr VA Hospital, Hines; Associate Dean for Veterans Affairs, 1981-92, Professor of Medicine, 1981-96, Clinical Professor of Medicine, 1996-2008, Stritch School of Medicine, Loyola University of Chicago. Publications: Numerous articles in professional journals. Honours: Alumnus of the Year, 1980; Listed in international biographical dictionaries. Address: 1712 Waverly Circle, St Charles, IL 60174, USA.

BETHELL John, b. 9 April 1940, Salford, England. Musician. Administrator. Career: Music Librarian, BBC, 1956-90; Isle of Man Arts Council 1966-; General Administrator Erin Arts Centre 1971-; Founder and Director of Mananan International Festival of Music and the Arts, 1974-; Director and Chairman of the Lionel Tertis International Viola Competition and Workshop, 1980-; Conductor and Musical Director of Manx Festival Chorus, 1967-; Conductor and Musical Director of Oldham Choral Society, 1971-98; Conductor Emeritus, 1998-; Musical Director, Manchester University Gilbert and Sullivan Society, 1972-86; Musical Director, Philharmonic Choir of Manchester, 1989-2000; Founder and Director Latour International Festival of Music And The Arts (France), 1993-; Part-time Lecturer, The University of Liverpool, 1997, Vice President Gale Force – Music Theatre Group; Director and Chairman, Barbirolli International Oboe Festival and Competition, 2005-; Chairman, Manx Ballet Company, 2000; Director/Founder, Uzerche International Festival of Music (France), 2007-. Publications: Recordings: With Manx Festival Chorus, Manx Folk Songs, National Songs with Douglas Town Band; Contributions to: Manx Life; Manx Radio. Honours: Catenian Association Gold Medal. Honorary Doctorate of Music, Marquis Guiseppe International University, 1988; Albert Einstein International Academy Foundation Medal; Rotary Club International Ambassador Award, 1999, MBE, 2001. Memberships: Vice President of the Rushen Band; Royal Society of Musicians; Making Music/North West Council. Address: B House, Darrag Port Erin, Isle of Man IM9 6JB, British Isles.

BETTANY Paul, b. 27 May 1971, Harlesdon, London, England. Actor. m. Jennifer Connelly, 2003, 1 son, 1 daughter, 1 stepson. Education: Drama Centre. Career: Films: Bent, 1997; The Land Girls, 1998; After the Rain, 1999; The Suicide Club, Kiss Kiss (Bang Bang), Gangster No 1, Dead Babies, 2000; A Knight's Tale, A Beautiful Mind, 2001; The Heart of Me, 2002; Dogville, The Reckoning, Master and Commander: The Far Side of the World, 2003; Euston Road, Wimbledon, 2004; Stories of Lost Souls, 2005; Firewall, The Da Vinci Code, 2006; Iron Man (voice), Broken Lines, The Secret Life of Bees, Inkheart, 2008; The Young Victoria, Creation, 2009; TV: Sharpe's Waterloo, 1997; Coming Home, Killer Net, 1998; Every Woman Knows a Secret, 1999; David Copperfield, 2000. Honours: British Supporting Actor of the Year, ALFS Award, 2002; Best Actor, Evening Standard British Film Award, 2004; British Actor of the Year, ALFS Award, 2004; Ensemble Acting of the Year, Hollywood Film Award, 2008. Memberships: Academy of Motion Picture Arts and Sciences.

BEWES Richard Thomas, b. 1 December 1934, Nairobi, Kenya. Anglican Clergyman; Writer. m. Elisabeth Ingrid Jaques, deceased 2006, 2 sons, 1 daughter. Education: Marlborough School, 1948-53; MA, Emmanuel College, Cambridge, 1954-57; Ridley Hall Theological College, Cambridge, 1957-59. Publications include: The Church Reaches Out, 1981; The Church Marches On, When God Surprises, 1986; A New Beginning, The Resurrection, 1989; Speaking in Public - Effectively, 1998; The Lamb Wins, Talking About Prayer, The Bible Truth Treasury, 2000; The Stone That Became a Mountain, Wesley Country, 2001; The Top 100 Questions, Words That Circled the World, 2002; Beginning the Christian Life, 150 Pocket Thoughts, 2004; The Goodnight Book, 2009. Contributions to: Decision Magazine. Honours: OBE, 2005. Membership: Guild of British Songwriters. Address: 50 Curzon Road, Ealing, London W5 1NF, England.

BEYER Guenter, b. 24 September 1952, Aachen, Germany. m. Else, 1 son. Education: PhD, RWTH Aachen University, 1984. Appointments: R&D, Kabelwer University, Laboratory Manager, EUPEN AG, Belgium. Publications: More than 200 publications and conference contributions. Honours: Jack Spergel Memorial Award, 2003; Fundamental Research on Nanotechnology for Cable Industry, 2004. Memberships: Gesellschaft Deutscher Chemiker. Address: Auenweg 14, B-4700 Eupen, Belgium.

BEYONCÉ (Beyoncé Knowles), b. 4 September 1981, Houston, Texas, USA. Singer; Songwriter; Producer, Actress. m. Jay-Z, 2008, 1 daughter. Career: Founding Member, GirlsTyme vocal group, 1989, renamed Something Fresh, then Dolls, and then Destiny's Child; Signed to Columbia Records, 1996; Live performances in USA and UK; Simultaneous solo career, 2001-; Established clothing label Touch of Couture. Recordings: Albums with Destiny's Child: Destiny's Child, 1998; The Writing's on the Wall, 1999; Survivor, Eight Days of Christmas, 2001; Destiny Fulfilled, 2004; Solo albums: Soul Survivors, 2002; Dangerously in Love, 2003; Live at Wembley, 2004; Singles with Destiny's Child: No No No, 1997; With Me, She's Gone, 1998; Get On The Bus, Bills Bills Bills, Bug-A-Boo, 1999; Say My Name, Jumpin' Jumpin' Independent Woman, 2000; Survivor, Bootylicious, Emotion, Eight Days of Christmas, 2001; Nasty Girl, This is the Remix, 2002; Lose My Breath, 2004; B'Day, 2006; I Am … Sasha Fierce, 2008; Solo singles: Crazy in Love, The Closer I Get to You, Baby Boy, Check on it, 2003; Déjà vu, Irreplaceable, 2006; Beautiful Liar, 2007; Film appearances: Carmen: A Hip Hopera (TV), 2001; Austin Powers in Goldmember, 2002; The Fighting Temptations, 2003; Dreamgirls, 2007; Cadillac Records, 2007; Obsessed, Wow! Wow! Wubbzy! (voice), 2009. Honours: Billboard Awards for Artist of the Year; Group of the Year; Hot 100 Singles Artist of the Year; New Female Artist of the Year; New R&B Artist; American Music Awards; Soul Train Award; Billboard R&B/Hip Hop Awards for Top Female Artist; Grammy Award, Best R&B Song; NAACP Image Award; MTV Video Award; Grammy Award, Best R&B Song; Hot 100 Group of the Year, 2000; Favourite Soul/ R&B Group, 2001; Sammy Davis Jr Award for Entertainer of the Year, 2001; American Music Award, Favorite Pop/Rock Album, 2001; Grammy Award, Best R&B Performance by a Duo or Group with Vocal, 2001; Outstanding Duo or Group, 2001; Best R&B Video, 2001; Favourite Pop/Rock Band, Duo or Group, 2002; BRIT Awards for Best International Group, 2002; Hot 200 Female Artist, 2003; Best International Female Solo Artist, 2004; Grammy Award for Best Contemporary R&B Album, 2004; New Artist, 2004; Best Rap/Sung Collaboration, 2004; Grammy Award for Best R&B performance by a Duo or Group, 2004; Grammy Award for Best Female R&B Vocal Performance, 2004.

BHAGAT Nirmal Chander, b. 5 September 1935, Lahore, Pakistan. Civil Engineer. m. Swarn Kanta, 1 son. Education: BA; Dip, Civil Engineering; BE, (AMIE Sections A&B) Civil Engineering; Dip, Project Management; Dip, Production Planning & Control. Appointments: Overseer (Junior Engineer), Civil – Capital Project, Chandigarh, India, 1955-63; Assistant Engineer, Civil, Border Roads Organisation of India, 1963-66; Senior Scientific Assistant to Scientist F, Deputy Director (retired), Central Building Research Institute, Roorkee, India, 1966-95. Publications: More than 3 dozen technical papers related to building maintenance and construction. Honours: IGS Smt Indra Joshi Annual Prize, 1991; Best Citizens of India Award, 2003; Leading Scientists of the World, 2011. Memberships: Fellow, Institution of Engineers, India; Indian Concrete Institute, Chennai; Indian Geotechnical Society, New Delhi; Indian Society of Earthquake Technology, Roorkee. Address: House No 364, Sector 15A, Chandigarh, 160015, India.

BHANGOO Nirmal Singh, b. 14 April 1950, Panjab, India. Businessman. m. Sardarth Premkaur, 1 son, 2 daughters. Education: PhD, Business Administration, Lorenz University, USA. Appointments: Chairman, Pearls Group, 1994-. Publications: Numerous articles in professional journals. Honours: Vikas Ratan Award, 1991; Vijay Shree Award, 1991; Pride of India Gold Medal, 1991; Pride of Asia International Award, 1992; Lok Shree Award, 1992; International Excellence Award, 1993; Excellence Award, 2008. Memberships: Federation of Indian Chamber of Commerce and Industry.

BHARGAVA Pushpa Mittra, b. 22 February 1928, Rajasthan, India. Scientist; Writer; Consultant. m. Edith, 1958, 1 son, 1 daughter. Education: BSc, 1944; MSc, 1946; PhD, 1949. Appointments: Lecturer, Chemistry, Lucknow University; Research Fellow, National Institute of Sciences; Project Associate, McArdle Memorial Laboratory for Cancer Research, University of Wisconsin, USA; Special Wellcome Research Fellow, National Institute of Medical Research, London, UK, 1949-58; Appointed Scientist B, Regional Research Laboratory, Hyderabad, India, 1958; Promoted to Scientist C, E and F; Scientist in Charge, Director, CCMB, Hyderabad, 1977-1990; CSIR Distinguished Fellow, 1990-93; Director, Anveshna Consultants, Hyderabad, 1993-. Publications: Over 125 major science publications; 500 articles; 5 books. Honours: Over 100 major national and international honours and awards; Padma Bhushan from the President of India; Chevalier de la Legion d'Honneur; Honorary DSc; National Citizen Award; Visiting Professorship, College de France; Life Fellow, Clare Hall, Cambridge; Wattumal Memorial Prize for Biochemistry; FICCI Award, Medical Sciences; Ranbaxy Award for Medical Sciences; SICO Award for Biotechnology; Goyal Prize; R D Birla Award for Medical Sciences; Lifetime Achievement Award for Biotechnology. Memberships: President or Past President: Society of Biological Chemicals of India; Indian Academy of Social Sciences; Association for Promotion of DNA Fingerprinting and Other DNA Technologies; Society for Scientific Values; Former Vice Chairman, National Knowledge Commission; Member, National Security Advisory Board, Government of India; 125 major national and international standing committees. Address: Anveshna, Manorama Ghar, 2nd Floor, 2-16-137/1 Road no 3, Prashanthi Nagar, Hyderabad – 500039, India. E-mail: bhargava.pm@gmail.com

BHARGAVA Samir, b. 5 April 1965, Mumbai, India. Ear, Nose and Throat Surgeon. m. Shalini, 1 son, 1 daughter. Education: DORL, College of Physicians and Surgeons, 1990; Diplomate of National Board, Delhi, 1991; MS (ENT) University of Bombay, 1991; DLO, Royal College of Surgeons, London, UK, 1993. Appointments: Associate Professor, Ear, Nose and Throat, GS Medical College and KEM Hospital, -1997; Honorary Consultant, Guru Nanak Hospital, Asian Heart Institute, R N Cooper Hospital. Publications: Co-author: A Short Textbook of ENT Diseases; More than 20 articles in national and international journals and books. Honours: Homi Gandhi Research Scholarship; Dr Manubhai Mehta Prize, CPS, 1990; Seth Gagalbhai Nathubhai Prize, MS (ENT), 1991; Best Surgeon Award, All India Medical Professional, Delhi, 2001. Memberships: Association of Otolaryngologists of India; Indian Society of Otology; Indian Medical Association; Consultants' Association. Address: Bhargava Nursing Home, Gopal Bhuvan, Tagore Road, Santacruz (W), Mumbai 400 054, India. E-mail: bhargavanursinghome@gmail.com

BHARUCHA Manchi, b. 19 April 1941, Mumbai, India. Public Healthcare; Medicine. 1 son, 1 daughter. Education: PhD. Appointments: Consultant, Reproductive Endocrinologist and Assisted Reproductive Technologies; Deputy Director, Marketing Services, Fertility Products, India. Publications: Monographs on infertility subjects; Contributed chapters in text-books on infertility; Numerous articles in professional journals. Memberships: European Society of Human Reproduction and Embryology.

BHATT Babaraju Kikubhai, b. 28 December 1961, Baroda, India. School Director. Education: BA (1st class), 1980, MA (1st class), 1982, Economics, PhD, Economics of Water Management, 1991, Sardar Patel University, Gujarat State. Appointments: Principal, MTB Arts College, Surat, 1983-2009; Director, Smt VB Nandola MBA College, 2010; Director, Naran Lala School of Industrial Management & Computer Science, Navsari, 2010-. Publications: Over 40 books; Numerous articles in professional journals. Honours include: UGC Teacher's Fellowship, 1989; Medal for India, 2008; Men of the Year, 2008; Listed in international biographical dictionaries. Memberships: Indian Economic Association; Gujarat Economic Association; Indian Econometric Society; Surat Officer's Gynkhana, Surat; Indian Society of Labour Economics.

BHAUMIK Bidhan Kumar, b. 10 June 1955, Naihati, India. Scientist. m. Arundhati. Education: MSc, Physics (Electronics), Calcutta University, India, 1979; Statistical Theories Studies, Indian Statistical Institute, 1980-82; PhD, Application of Statistical Theory in Uranium Exploration, Osmania University, India, 1989. Career: Scientific Officer, Department of Atomic Energy, 1983; Head, Physics Laboratory, 1992-. Honours: Distinguished Leadership Award, American Biographical Institute, 1998; Gold Medal for India, 2009. Memberships: Fellow, Institute of Electronics and Telecommunication Engineers, India. Address: 8C "B" Road, Anandapuri, Nonachandanpukur 700 122, India.

BHOPAL Rajinder S, b. 10 April 1953, British citizen. Professor of Public Health. m. 4 children. Education: BSc (Hons), Physiology, 1975, MBChB, 1978, MD, 1991, University of Edinburgh; MPH, Glasgow University, 1985. Appointments: Professor of Epidemiology and Public Health, Head of Department of Epidemiology and Public Health, University of Newcastle upon Tyne, 1991-99; Honorary Consultant, Public Health Medicine, 1991-99; Non-Executive Director, Newcastle and North Tyneside Health Authority, 1992-96; Visiting Professor, School of Public Health, North Carolina, USA, 1996-97; Non-Executive Director, Health Education Authority, 1996-99; Bruce and John Usher Chair of Public Health, University of Edinburgh, 1999-; Honorary Consultant in Public Health Medicine, Lothian Health Board, 1999-; Head of Department, Division of Community Health Services, University of Edinburgh, 2000-03. Publications: Around 200 articles in peer reviewed journals and chapters in books; 2 textbooks: Concepts of Epidemiology, 2002, 2nd edition, 2008; Ethnicity, Race and Health in Multicultural Societies, 2007; and 2 edited volumes, Public Health: Past, Present and Future, and The Epidemic of Coronary Heart Disease in South Asian Populations, 2002. Honours: Littlejohn Gairdner Prize, 1985; John Maddison Research Prize, 1992; J T Neech Prize, 1994; J W Starkey Silver Medal, 2000; CBE, 2001; Honorary DSc, Queen Margaret University College, 2005; Sikh Heritage in Scotland, 2007; British Association of Physicians of Indian Origin, 2008; South Asian Health Foundation, 2008. Memberships: Fellow, Royal College of Physicians (UK); Fellow, Faculty of Public Health. Address: Centre for Population Health Sciences, University of Edinburgh Medical School, Teviot Place, Edinburgh EH8 9AG, Scotland. E-mail: raj.bhopal@ed.ac.uk

BHUIYAN Lutful Bari, b. 8 July 1951, Barisal, Bangladesh. Academic. m. Leena Ferdous Khan, 2 daughters. Education: BSc (Hons), 1972, MSc, 1974, University of Dhaka; DIC, 1975, PhD, 1977, Imperial College, London. Appointments: Assistant Professor, 1983-86, Associate Professor, 1986-91, Professor, 1991-, University of Puerto Rico. Publications: Over 110 articles in professional journals. Honours: Commonwealth Scholarship, 1974; Academic Excellence and Productivity Award, 1998; Numerous grants. Memberships: Life Member, Bangladesh Physical Society; Member, American Physical Society; Member, American Chemical Society. Address: Laboratory of Theoretical Physics, Department of Physics, Faculty of Natural Sciences, Box 70377, University of Puerto Rico, San Juan, PR 00936-8377, USA. E-mail: beena@beena.cnnet.clu.edu

BHUMIBOL ADULYADEJ (King of Thailand), b. 5 December 1927, Cambridge, Massachusetts, USA. m. Queen Sirikit, 28 April 1950, 1 son, 3 daughters. Education: Bangkok; Lausanne, Switzerland. Ascended to the Throne of Thailand 9 June 1946-. Address: Chitralada Villa, Bangkok, Thailand.

BHUSHAN Braj, b. 2 October 1971, Sitamarhi, India. Academic. m. Amrita, 1 son. Education: MA, Banaras Hindu University, 1995; PhD, BRAB University, 1999. Appointments: Lecturer, Vasanta College for Women, Varanasi, 1996; Senior Lecturer, IIT Guwahati, 2003-06; Assistant Professor, 2006-10, Associate Professor, 2010-, IIT Kanpur; Visiting Professor, Kyushu University, Japan, 2007. Publications: 2 books; 6 book chapters; 1 booklet; 26 articles in professional journals; 3 conference proceedings. Honours: Best Announcer Award, National Youth Week, 1993, BHU Merit and Prize Award, 1991, Banaras Hindu University; Young Scientist Award, Indian Science Congress Association, 2002; In Search of Excellence Award, IAAP and NAOP-I, 2004; Man of the Year Award, 2005; Abstract Award, International Association for Suicide Prevention, 2009; Listed in international biographical dictionaries. Memberships: Life Member, Indian Science Congress Association; Life Member, Indian Academy of Applied Psychology; National Academy of Psychology, India; Life Member, Community Psychology Association of India; International Affiliate, American Psychological Association. Address: Department of HSS, IIT Kanpur, Kanpur 208016, India. E-mail: brajb@iitk.ac.in Website: http://home.iitk.ac.in/~brajb/

BIBICU Ion, b. 4 December 1944, Unirea, Braila County, Romania. Physicist Engineer. m. (1) Elena Melente, deceased, (2) Miruna Ganciu, 1 son. Education: Faculty, Electronics Faculty, 1963-68, Graduate, Electronics, MSc, Physical Engineering, 1968, Technical University, Bucharest; PhD, Solid State Physics, Engineering, Institute of Atomic Physics, Bucharest, 1981. Appointments: Diplomat Engineer, 1969-75, Researcher, 1975-77, Institute of Atomic Physics, Bucharest-Magurele; Researcher, 1977-90, Associate Technology Professor, 1990-91, Associate Research Professor, 1991-95, Research Professor, 1995-96, Institute of Physics and Technology of Materials, Bucharest-Magurele; Research Professor, National Institute of Materials Physics, Bucharest-Magurele, 1996-; Assistant Professor, 1999-2002, Associate Professor, 2002-09, Technical University-Electronics Faculty, Bucharest. Publications: 38 scientific papers in international journals; 1 scientific papers accepted to be published in international journals; 57 scientific papers in Romanian journals; 12 scientific papers in proceedings at international conferences; 6 scientific reports to AIEA Agency; 3 abstracts; 1 report of the KFKI Institute Budapest; 68 communications at international conferences; 63 communications at national conferences; 2 Romanian patents; Book, The corrosion of the carbon steel in ammonia media, 2006. Honours: Visiting Research Fellow, AIEA Vienna-Agency, Budapest, Hungary, 1972; Nominated for Prize of the Professional Association of Romanian Engineering, 1994; Visiting Research Fellow, Venice University, Italy, 1994-95; Stefan Procopiu Prize, Romanian Academy, 1996; Listed in international biographical dictionaries. Memberships: European Physical Society; Romanian Academy of Technical Sciences; Romanian Physical Society; Romanian Engineering Society; Romanian Catalysis Society. Address: 5 Valea Ialomitei Street, Bl D 21, Sc E, Ap 46, Bucharest 061962, Romania. E-mail: bibicu@infim.ro

BIDEN Joseph Robinette (Joe), b. 20 November 1942, Scranton, Pennsylvania, USA. 47th Vice President of the United States. m. (1) Neilia Hunter, 1966, deceased 1972, 2 sons, 1 daughter, deceased. (2) Jill Jacobs, 1977, 1 daughter. Education: Archmere Academy, Claymont; BA, University of Delaware, Newark, 1965. Appointments: Admitted to Delaware Bar, 1969; Public Defender, Wilmington, Delaware, 1969; Lawyer, Biden & Walsh; Democrat Representative, New Castle County Coucnil, 1970-72; Elected US Senator, Delaware, 1972, 1978, 1984, 1990, 1996, 2002, 2008-09; Adjunct Professor, Widener University School of Law, 1991-; 47th Vice President of the United States, 2009-. Honours: Honorary degress: University of Scranton, 1976; St Joseph's University, 1981; Widener University School of Law, 2000; Emerson College, 2003; University of Delaware, 2004; Suffolk University Law School, 2006; Syracuse University, 2009; Chancellor Medal, Syracuse University, 1980; George Arents Pioneer Medal, 2005; Best of Congress Award, 2008; Hilal-i-Pakistan Award, 2008; Gold Medal of Freedom, Kosovo, 2009; Inductee, Delaware Volunteer

DICTIONARY OF INTERNATIONAL BIOGRAPHY 36th EDITION

Firemen's Association Hall of Fame, 2009; Named in Little League Hall of Excellence, 2009. Memberships: US Senate Committee on the Judiciary; International Narcotics Control Caucus; US Senate Committee on Foreign Relations; NATO Observer Group; Subcommittee on European Affairs; Close Up Foundation; American Civil Liberties Union; National Education Association.

BIEBER Justin, b. 1 March 1994, Ontario, Canada. Singer; Songwriter. Career: Signed to Island Records, 2008; Albums: My World, 2009; My World 2.0, 2010; Under the Mistletoe, 2011; Singles: One Time, 2009; One Less Lonely Girl; Baby, 2010; Somebody to Love; U Smile; Pray; Never Say Never, 2011; Mistletoe; Many TV appearances.

BIENAYMÉ Alain, b. 22 May 1934, Toulon, France. Professor. m. Marie Helene Sifflet, 1 son, 2 daughters. Education: CPE, English British Institute, 1955; MEcon, 1956, Master Privat Law, 1957, PhD, 1957, Paris University; Agrege des Facultes de Sciences Economiques, 1964. Appointments: Assistant Professor, University of Paris, 1959-60; Junior Professor, University of Rennes, 1961-64; Tenured Professor, Dijon, 1964-68; Professor of Economics, 1969-2003, Emeritus, 2003-, Paris-Dauphine University; Head of a Master Degree Program in Applied Economics, 1980-2003; President, Committee of Economics, Paris-Dauphine University; Member of the Franco-British Council, 2001-07; Director of CEDIMES-France, 2006-. Publications: More than 100 articles in periodicals; Books include, Entreprises, Marche, Etat, 1982; Le Capitalisme Adulte, 1992; Principes de Concurrence, 1998; Les grandes questions d'économie contemporaine, 2006. Honours: Silver Medal in Economics, CNRS, 1977; Ugo Papi and Gaston Leduc Prize, 1988; Emile Girardeau Prize, Academie des Sciences Morales et Politique, 1992; Chevalier de la Légion d'honneur; Officier de l'Ordre du Merite; Commandeur de l'Ordre d'Alphonse X El Sabio; Officier des Palmes Academiques; Docteur Honoris Causa, University of Valahia, Romania. Memberships: Societe d'Economie Politique. Address: 31 Avenue Duquesne, 75007 Paris, France.

BIETOLINI Nicola, b. 8 August 1967, Rome, Italy. Researcher; Essayist; Humanities Educator. Education: BA, University La Sapienza, Rome, 1992; PhD, Comparative Literature University, Ostiense. Appointments: University of Ostiense, Rome, 1998; Postdoctorate, University of Tor Vergata, 2004; Research Assistant, German Literature Tor Vergata, Rome, 2004-09; Consultant in Field. Publications: Ludvig Holberg. A Pioneer of Modern Scandinavian Culture and Literature, Rome, 2007; Numerous articles in professional journals. Honours: Listed in international biographical dictionaries. Memberships: Italian Society of 18th Century Studies; Italian Association of Germanic Studies. Address: Via Cerveteri, 48 Int 8 II Floor, 00183 Rome, Italy. E-mail: nicola.bietolini@alice.it

BIGELOW Kathryn, b. 27 November 1951, San Carlos, California, USA. Film Director; Producer. m. James Cameron, 1989, divorced 1991. Education: San Francisco Art Institute; Whitney Museum's Independent Study Program; Columbia Film School. Career: Films: The Loveless, 1982; Near Dark, 1987; Blue Steel, 1989; Point Break, 1991; Strange Days, 1995; The Weight of Water, 2000; K-19: The Widowmaker, 2002; Mission Zero, 2007; The Hurt Locker, 2008; TV: Homicide: Life on the Street, 1998-99; Karen Sisco, 2004. Honours: First woman to win Director's Guild of America Award for Outstanding Direction of a Feature Film, 2008; Dallas Star Award, 2009; Best Director, and Best Film, BAFTA, 2010; First woman to win Oscar for Best Director, and Best Motion Picture of the Year, Academy Awards, 2010.

BIHAIN Bernard E, b. 26 March 1958, Belgium. Professor. m. Pascale, 1 son, 3 daughters. Education: MD, Free University of Brussels, Belgium, 1984. Appointments: Postdoctoral Research Fellow, Columbia University, New York, 1988-89; Instructor, 1989-91, Assistant Professor, 1991-92, Louisiana State University Medical Center, New Orleans; Director, Founder, INSERM U391, Rennes, France, 1992-; Professor and Chairman, Department of Biochemistry, Faculty of Pharmacy, University of Rennes, 1992; Vice President, Functional Genomics, Genset Corporation, San Diego, USA, 1998-2001; Director, Laboratory of Medicine and Molecular Therapeutics, Nancy, 2002-; President, Genclis SAS, 2005-. Publications: Over 45 peer reviewed articles in the field of metabolics, allergy and cancer research. Honours: Professor Victor Connard Research Prize, Free University of Brussels, 1984; Whaba Fellowship, 1985, Ajinomoto Fellowship, 1986, Travel Fellowship, 1989, European Society of Parenteral and Enteral Nutrition; M Horlait-Dapsens Foundation Fellowship, 1986; Institutional Biomedical Support Grant NIH Award, 1990; George S Bel Memorial Research Award, 1991, Irvine H Page Award Finalist, 1991, American Heart Association. Memberships: AAAS. Address: 15 rue du Bois de la Champelle, 54500 Vandoeuvre-les-Nancy, France. E-mail: bbihain@genclis.com

BILK Acker (Bernard Stanley), b. 28 January 1929, Pensford, Somerset, England. Musician (clarinet); Composer; Bandleader. m. Jean, 1 son, 1 daughter. Career: Began playing clarinet in Royal Engineers, 1948; Clarinet, Ken Colyer's Band; Formed Bristol Paramount Jazz Band; Currently freelance artiste; Guest musician on numerous records; Tours world-wide with Paramount Jazz Band; Played with Reunion Paramount Jazz Band, Isle of Bute Jazz Festival, 1995; Performed with Van Morrison, Prague, 2004, Oxford, 2005. Recordings with Van Morrison, 2001; 3B Concerts reuniting Acker and his Band with the Big Chris Barber Band and Kenny Ball and his Jazzmen, 2004; Giants of Jazz Concerts with Humphrey Lyttelton and George Melly, 2004; Owner of publishing company. Recordings: Singles include: Somerset; Aria; Stranger On The Shore (Number 1, US and UK, 1961); Albums include: The One For Me; Sheer Magic; Evergreen; Chalumeau-That's My Home; Three In The Morning (with Humphrey Lyttelton, John Barnes, Dave Green, Dave Cliff, Bobby Worth); Giants Of Jazz (with Paramount Jazz Band, Kenny Ball and his Jazzmen, Kenny Baker Don Lusher All Stars); Chris Barber and Acker Bilk, That's It Then!; Clarinet Moods, Acker Bilk, with string orchestra; Acker Bilk - The Oscars; Clarinet Moods with Acker Bilk; All the Hits and More; The Christmas Album; Acker Bilk And His Paramount Jazz Band; Acker Bilk In Holland; It Looks Like A Big Time Tonight; Hits Blues And Class; Great Moments; Best of Acker Bilk; As Time Goes By, 2004. Honour: MBE, 2001; BMI Award, London, 2004; Honorary Degree of Master of the Arts, University of Bristol, 2005. Address: c/o Acker's Agency, 53 Cambridge Mansions, Cambridge Road, London SW11 4RX, England.

BILLINGS Stephen Alec, b. 14 August 1951, Staffordshire, England. Professor of Signal Processing and Complex Systems. m. Catherine Grant Billings, 1 son, 1 daughter. Education: First Class Honours Degree, Electrical Engineering, Liverpool University, 1969-72; PhD, Control Systems, Sheffield University, 1972-75. Appointments: Lecturer, 1975-83, Senior Lecturer, 1983-85, Department of Control Engineering, Reader, 1985-90, Professor of Signal

Processing and Complex Systems, 1990-, Department of Automatic Control and Systems Engineering, University of Sheffield. Publications: Over 330 journal articles and over 110 conference papers. Honours: Honoured by the Institute of Scientific Information (ISA), USA as one of the worlds most highly cited researchers in all branches of engineering, 1980-; Awarded D. Eng., Liverpool University, 1990. Memberships: Fellow, Institute of Electrical Engineers (UK); Chartered Engineer and Chartered Scientist; Fellow, Institute of Mathematics and its Applications; Chartered Mathematician. Address: Department of Automatic Control and Systems Engineering, University of Sheffield, Mappin Street, Sheffield S1 3JD, England. E-mail: s.billings@sheffield.ac.uk

BILLINGTON Rachel (Mary), b. 11 May 1942, Oxford, England. Writer. m. 16 December 1967, 2 sons, 2 daughters. Education: BA, English, London University. Publications: Over 20 books, including: Loving Attitudes, 1988; Theo and Matilda, 1990; The First Miracles, 1990; Bodily Harm, 1992; The Family Year, 1992; The Great Umbilical, 1994; Magic and Fate, 1996; The Life of Jesus (for children), 1996; Perfect Happiness, 1996; Tiger Sky, 1998; The Life of St Francis (for children), 1999; A Woman's Life, 2002; Far Out! (for children), 2002; The Space Between, 2004; One Summer, 2006; There's More to Life (for children), 2006; Lies and Loyalties, 2008; The Missing Boy, 2010; Contributions to: Reviewer, Columnist and short story writer for various publications; co-editor of Inside Time, the national newspaper for prisoners; 2 plays for BBC TV; 4 plays for Radio. Memberships: Society of Authors; President, PEN, 1997-2000; Trustee, The Longford Trust; The Tablet Trust; The Siobhan Dowd Trust. Address: c/o David Higham Associates, 5/8 Lower John Street, London, W1F 9HA, England.

BILLINGTON Sandra, b. 10 September 1943, Eccles, England. Self-Employed Writer. Education: Guildhall School of Music and Drama, 1961-63; RADA, 1965-67; BA (Cantab), 1975, PhD (Cantab), 1980, Lucy Cavendish College, Cambridge. Appointments: Actress, BBC Radio Manchester, 1955-59; Theatre/Film, 1967-72; Lecturer, 1979-92, Reader, 1992-2003, Department of Theatre, Film and TV, University of Glasgow; Writer, 2003-. Publications: A Social History of the Fool, 1984; Mock Kings in Medieval Society and Renaissance Drama, 1991; The Concept of the Goddess (co-editor), 1996; Midsummer: A Cultural sub-text from Chrétien de Troyes to Jean Michel, 2000; Between Worlds, 2005; The midsummer solstice as it was, or was not, observed in pagan Germany, Scandinavia, and Anglo-Saxon England Folklore, 2008; Comping Up for the Third Time, 2010. Honours: Katharine Briggs Prize for Folklore, 1984; Michaelis Jena Ratcliff Prize for Folklore, 1991; FRSE, 1998. Membership: The Folklore Society. Address: 43 Franks Lane, Cambridge CB4 1RR, England.

BILSKI Benjamin, b. 1 December 1979, Amsterdam, Netherlands. Lecturer. Education: BSc, Biochemistry and Philosophy, Brandeis University, 2002; MSc, Philosophy and History, London School of Economics, 2005; PhD, Law School, Leiden University, 2012. Appointments: Biochemist, 2000-03; Researcher, MEMRI, 2003-04; Researcher, IISS, 2004-05; Lecturer, Legal Philosophy, Leiden University, 2005-11. Publications: Machiavelli, Teacher of Evil? (chapter in Dutch), 2006; Towards a Grand Strategy for an Uncertain World (book), 2008; Religion, Politics & Law (chapter), 2009; Plato's Political Ontology, 2009. Memberships: International Institute for Strategic Studies; European Convention for Liberal Democracy; Netherlands Atlantic Commission; Henry Jackson Society. Address: Torenlaan 10, 2103AC, Heemstede, Netherlands.

BILWANI Prahlad Kumar, b. 29 April 1945, Sultankot, Sindh, India. Plastic Surgeon. m. Ratna, 1 son, 1 daughter. Education: MBBS, 1967; MS, Surgery, 1971; M Ch, Plastic Surgery, 1975. Appointments: Professor, Plastic Surgery; Director, Gujarat Burns Hospital & Research Centre; Visiting Plastic Surgeon, Sterling Hospital, Ahmedabad. Publications: Burns in Elderly, 1994; Epidemiological Profile of Burn Patients in L G Hospital, Ahmedabad, 2003; Skin Donation, an overview of 26 years experience. Honours: Gillies Oration Award, Association of Plastic Surgeons of India; Phoolan Devi Award; Dr B C Roy National Award, 2008; Brig R Ganguli Oration Award, Association of Surgeons of India, 2010. Memberships: International Society for Burn Injuries; Association of Plastic Surgeons of India. Address: 24 Sarthi-3, Memnagar, Ahmedabad, 380052, India.

BINOCHE Juliette, b. 9 March 1964, Paris, France. Actress. 1 son, 1 daughter. Education: National Conservatory of Drama; Private Theatrical Studies. Creative Works: Films include: Les nanas; La vie de famille; Rouge Baiser; Rendez-Vous; Mon beau-frère a tué ma soeur; Mauvais Sang; Un tour de manège; Les amants du Pont-Neuf; The Unbearable Lightness of Being; Wuthering Heights, Damage, 1992; Trois Couleurs: Bleu, 1993; Le Hussard sur le Toit, 1995; The English Patient, 1996; Alice et Martin, Les Enfants du Siècle, 1999; La Veuve de Saint-Pierre, 2000; Chocolat, Code Unknown, 2001; Décalage horaire, 2002; Country of My Skull, 2004; Bee Season, Mary, Caché, 2005; Breaking and Entering, 2006; Le Voyage du Balloon Rouge, Dan in Real Life, Paris, Disengagement, 2007; Paris, L'Heure d'été, Shirin, 2008; Play: Naked, 1998. Honours: Academy Award, Best Supporting Actress, 1996; Berlin Film Festival Award, 1996; BAFTA Award, 1997. Address: c/o UTA, 9560 Wilshire Boulevard, Floor 5, Beverly Hills, CA 90212, USA.

BIRCH Clive Francis William, b. 22 December 1931, Edgware, Middlesex, England. Publisher; Author. Education: Uppingham School. Appointments: RAF National Service, 1950; Office Junior, Stretford Telegraph, 1952; Reporter, Stockport Express, 1954; Editor, Bucks Examiner, 1956; Public Relations Officer, Frigidaire Division, General Motors, 1958; Product Development, Metro-Cammell Weymann Ltd, 1959; Group Advertisement Manager, Modern Transport Publishing Company Ltd, 1965; Manager, Electrical Press Ltd, 1966; Director, Illustrated Newspapers Ltd, 1969 (including, Editor, Illustrated London News, 1970); Director, Northwood Publications Ltd, 1971; Managing Director designate, Textile Trade Publications Ltd, 1972; Publishing Director, Mercury House Ltd, 1973; Chairman, Barracuda Books Ltd, 1974-92; Managing Director, Quotes Ltd, 1985-97; Principal, Radmore Birch Associates (including Baron Books), 1991-; Visiting Tutor, RCA Vehicle Design Department, 2004-; Publishing Director, Boltneck Publications, 2006-10. Publications: Book of Chesham; Book of Amersham (co-author) Book of Aylesbury; Book of Beaconsfield (co-author); Yesterday's Town: Chesham; Yesterday's Town: Amersham (co-author); Maps of Bucks (editor); Chesham Century (co-author); Remember Chesham; In Camera Series - Vale of Aylesbury; Buckingham; Chesham; Chiltern Thames; Milton Keynes (2); The Missendens; Chalfont St Giles; Chorleywood & Chenies; Wish you were here series – Buckingham; Chesham; The Freedom - City of London (co-author); On the Move - Road Haulage Association (co-author); Carr and Carman - London's Transport; A Decent Man (novel), 2006;

Royal College of Art vehicle design yearbook (editor), 2006, 2007, 2008, 2009, 2010. Honours: Honorary Life Member, Chiltern Car Club, 1956; Fellow, Royal Society of Arts, 1980; Fellow, Society of Antiquaries of London, 1981; Honorary Life Member, Institution of the Royal Corps of Transport, 1985; MBE, 2000; Princess Royal Gold Medal, 2008. Memberships include: Founder Chairman, Buckingham and District Chamber of Trade, Commerce and Industry, 1983-87; Founder and Chairman, Buckingham Heritage Trust, 1985-97; Freeman City of London, 1960; Liveryman, Worshipful Company of Carmen, 1960, Court of Assistants, 1966, Master 1984-85; Founder Chairman, Carmen's Ball, 1985; Deputy Master, 1988-89; Chevalier de la Confrerie des Chevaliers du Trou Normand, 1991; Chairman, RSA Carmen Lectures, 1991-; Chairman, Carmen Marketing and Media, 1994-2007; Chairman, Carmen Awards Committee, 1999-2007; Founder, Carmen RCA Research Fellowship, 2001; RCA Readership, 2009; Honorary Editor, 2002-; Chairman, Carmen Past Masters, 2004-07; Senior Past Master, Carmen, 2005-; Chairman, Transport Committee, 2007-08; Chairman, Livery Committee, 2007-10; Trustee, Camberwell Housing Society, 2002-. Address: King's Cote, Valley Road, Finmere, Oxon MK18 4AL, England.

BIRD Harold Dennis (Dickie), b. 19 April 1933, Barnsley, Yorkshire, England. Retired County Cricket, Test & World Cup Final Umpire. Education: Burton Road Primary School; Raley Secondary Modern School, Barnsley. Appointments: Played for Yorkshire & Leicestershire County Cricket Clubs; County Cricket, Test & World Cup Umpire, retired 1998; Fully Qualified MCC Advanced Cricket Coach; Umpired following: 4 World Cups; 3 World Cup Finals; West Indies v Australia, 1975; West Indies v England, 1979; India v West Indies, 1983; Both men's and women's World Cup Finals; International matches in Sharjah (UAE); Best Batsman in the World; World Double Wicket & Best All-Rounder competitions all over the world; The Rest of the World XI against a World XI, Wembley Stadium, 1983; Bi-Centenary Test Match World XI v The Rest of the World Lords, 1987; Asia v The Rest of the World, The Oval, 2000; The Princes Trust XI v The Rest of the World, Edgbaston, 1989; Brylcream Top of the World Cricket Tournament; 68 Test Matches; 93 one-day international matches; Test matches for 25 years; First Class County Matches for 30 years; All major cup finals in England including Gillette, Nat West, Benson & Hedges and Refuge Assurance Cup Finals; Queens Silver Jubilee Test Match, Trent Bridge, England v Australia, 1977; Centenary Test Match, Lords, England v Australia, 1980; 159 international matches; Other test matches and international matches including: Shell Shield Final, Christchurch, New Zealand; Wellington v Christchurch, 1981; National Grid Award, 60th Diamond test, Pakistan v Australia, Karachi, 1994; Asia Cub, Sri Lanka, 1984; Zimbabwe v New Zealand Test Series, 1993; New Zealand v Pakistan Test Series, 1994; Pakistan v Australia Test Series, 1994; India v West Indies Test Series, 1994; Australia v Pakistan Test Series, 1996; England U19s v South Africa U19s Test Series, 1995; England U19s v Pakistan U19s Test Series, 1998. Publications: Not Out; That's Out; From the Pavilion End; Dickie Bird, My Autobiography, 1997; White Cap and Bails, 1999; Dickie Bird's Britain, 2002. Honours: Voted Yorkshire Personality of Year, 1977; MBE, Queen's Birthday Honours List, 1986; Rose Bowl, Barnsley Council for 100th International Match, 1988; Variety Club of Great Britain Yorkshire Award, 1988; National Grid Award for 49th Test Zimbabwe v New Zealand, 1992; Honorary Doctorate, Hallam University, 1996; Yorkshire Man of the Year, 1996; People of the Year Award, 1996; EADAR National People of the Year Award, 1996; Variety Club of Great Britain Award, 1997; Honorary Doctorate in Law, Leeds University, 1997; Life Long Achievement Award, 1998; Special Merit Award, The Professional Cricketers Association, 1998; Services to Cricket Award, Yorkshire CC, 1998, Warwickshire CC, 1998; Freedom of the Borough of Barnsley, 2000; Commemorative Clock, Headingley, 2002; TCCB 25 years service; Barnsley Millennium Award of Merit, 2000; 30 Years of Service Award, ECB; Anglo American Sporting Club Award; Founder, The Dickie Bird Foundation for Underprivileged Children, 2004; Numerous appearances on radio and television. Memberships: MCC; Yorkshire County Cricket Club; Leicestershire County Cricket Club; Barnsley Football Club; Cambridge University Cricket Club. Address: White Rose Cottage, 40 Paddock Road, Staincross, Barnsley, South Yorkshire S75 6LE, England.

BIRKETVEDT Grethe Stoa, b. 17 September 1942, Sarpsborg, Norway. Professor. Divorced, 1 daughter. Education: Teacher's training College, 1964; Fulbright Scholar Music, 1967-68; Master of Music, 1969; Master, University of Sports, 1972; MD, Medicine, 1983; MD, PhD, Doctorate, 1995. Appointments: Visiting Professor, University of Pennsylvania, 1995-2000; Research Professor, Mount Sinai School of Medicine, 2000-05; MD, PhD, Oslo University Hospital, 2005-. Publications: 4 poetry collections; 2 song books for children; 2 musicals for children; 2 weightloss textbooks. Honours: Honorary Professor, Albert Schweitzer International University; Poetry Awards, International Society of Poets. Memberships: Fulbright Association; International Society of Poets; Norway Association of Medicine; Association of Ingestive Behaviour. Address: 74 Oak Knoll Drive, Berwyn, PA 19312, USA.

BIRSHTEIN Tatiana, b. 20 December 1928, Leningrad, USSR. Physicist; Researcher. m. David Mirlin, 1 son, 1 daughter. Education: Graduate, Leningrad University, 1951; Postgraduate, Pedagogical Institute, Leningrad, 1954-58; PhD, 1960, Diploma, Physics, Mathematics and Science, 1974, Institute of Macromolecular Compounds, RAS, Leningrad. Appointments: Industrial Researcher, Leningrad, 1951-54; Junior Researcher, 1958-66, Senior Researcher, 1966-86, Principal Researcher, 1986-, SPb University Professor, 1965-, Institute of Macromolecular Compounds of Russian Academy of Science. Publications: Monograph, Conformations of macromolecules, 1966; More than 270 scientific papers; Editor, collections of papers. Honours: Defence of Leningrad Medal, 1944; Honored Research Scientist, Russia, 1998; L'Oreal-UNESCO award for Women in Science, 2007; Kargin Award, RAS, 2008; Order of Merit for the Fatherland Medal, 2010. Memberships: Chair, International Symposium, 1996, 2002, 2008; Member, Scientific Councils: RAS; IMC RAS; Grand Juries of Scientific Prizes. Address: 199004 SPb, 31 Bolshoi pr, IMC RAS, Russia. E-mail: birshtein@imc.maro.ru

BIRT John, Baron of Liverpool, b. 10 December 1944, Liverpool, England. Broadcasting Executive. m. (1) Jane Frances Lake, 1965, divorced, 1 son, 1 daughter, (2) Eithne Wallis, 2006. Education: St Mary's College, Liverpool; St Catherine's College, Oxford. Appointments: TV Producer, Nice Time, 1968-69; Joint Editor, World in Action, 1969-70; Producer, The Frost Programme, 1971-72; Executive Producer, Weekend World, 1972-74; Head, Current Affairs, London Weekend TV, 1974-77; Co-Producer, The Nixon Interviews, 1977; Controller, Features and Current Affairs, LWT, 1977-81; Director of Programmes, 1982-87; Deputy Director General, 1987-92, Director General, 1992-2000, BBC; Vice President, Royal TV Society, 1994-2000; Adviser to Prime Minister on criminal justice, 2000-01, Strategy Adviser, 2001-; Adviser to McKinsey and Co Inc; Chair,

Capital Ventures Fund, 2000. Publications: The Harder Path – The Autobiography. Honours: Visiting Fellow, Nuffield College, Oxford, 1991-99; Honorary Fellow: University of Wales, Cardiff, 1997; St Catherine's College, Oxford, 1992; Hon DLitt, Liverpool John Moores, 1992; City, 1998; Bradford, 1999; Emmy Award, US National Academy of Television, Arts and Sciences; Life Peerage, 2000. Memberships: Media Law Group, 1983-94; Working Party on New Technologies, 1981-83; Broadcasting Research Unit, Executive Committee, 1983-87; International Museum of TV and Radio, New York, 1994-2000; Opportunity 2000 Target Team, Business in the Community, 1991-98. Address: House of Lords, London SW1A 0PW, England.

BIRTS Peter William, b. 9 February 1946, Brighton, England. Circuit Judge. m. Angela, 1 son, 2 daughters. Education: Lancing College, Sussex; MA, St John's College, Cambridge. Appointments: Called to the Bar, 1968; Recorder, 1989; Queen's Counsel, 1990; Judicial Studies Board, 1992-96; Chairman, Mental Health Tribunals, 1994-; Queen's Counsel Northern Ireland, 1996; Deputy High Court Judge, 2000-05; Appointed Circuit Judge, 2005; Legal Member Parole Board, 2006. Publications: Trespass – Summary Procedure for Possession of Land, 1987; Remedies for Trespass, 1990; Contributor to Butterworths Costs Service, 2000-10; Articles in various journals on legal costs, countryside law and civil procedure. Honours: Choral Scholarship to St John's College, Cambridge, 1964; MA (Cantab), 1973. Memberships: Hurlingham Club; Liveryman, Carpenters Company; Bencher of Gray's Inn, 1998-. Address: Kingston Crown Court, 6-8 Penrhyn Road, Kingston-upon-Thames, Surrey KT1 2BB, England.

BIRTWISTLE Harrison (Sir), b. 15 July 1934, Accrington, Lancashire, England. Composer. m. Sheila, 1958, 3 sons. Education: Royal Manchester College of Music; Royal Academy of Music, London. Career: Director of Music, Cranborne Chase School, 1962-65; Visiting Fellow (Harkness International Fellowship), Princeton, University, 1966; Cornell Visiting Professor of Music, Swarthmore College, Pennsylvania, 1973-74; Slee Visiting Professor, New York State University, Buffalo, New York, 1975; Associate Director, National Theatre, 1975-88; Composer-in-Residence, London Philharmonic Orchestra, 1993-98; Henry Purcell Professor of Composition, King's College, London University, 1994-2001; Visiting Professor, University of Alabama at Tuscaloosa, 2001-02; Director of Contemporary Music, RAM, 1996-2001; Works widely performed at major festivals in Europe; Formed (with Sir Peter Maxwell Davies), The Pierrot Players. Honours: Grawemeyer Award, University of Louisville, Kentucky, USA, 1987; Honorary Fellow, Royal Northern College of Music, 1990; Chevalier des Arts et Lettres; Siemens Prize, 1995. Allied Artists Agency, 42 Montpelier Square, London SW7 1JZ, England.

BISDAS Sotirios, b. 25 March 1978, Athens, Greece. Neuroradiologist. Education: Bachelor, Medicine & Surgery, 2002; MD, Medicine, 2003; PhD, Radiology & Medicine, 2011. Appointments: Resident, Neuroradiology, Hannover Medical School, Germany, 2003-04; Resident, Radiology, University of Frankfurt, Germany, 2005-09; Consultant, Neuroradiology, University of Tuebingen, Germany, 2010-. Publications: 65 original articles in professional journals; 8 chapters in radiology books. Honours: Outstanding Presentation Award, American Society of Neuroradiology, 2008; Outstanding Presentation Award, European Society of Head and Neck Radiology, 2010. Memberships: American Society of Neuroradiology; European Society of Head and Neck Radiology; German Society of Neuroradiology. Address: Department of Neuroradiology, Eberhard Karls University Hospital, Hoppe-Seyler Str 3, D-72076, Tuebingen, Germany. E-mail: sbisdas@gmail.com

BISHOP James Drew, b. 18 June 1929, London, England. Journalist. m. 1959, 2 sons. Education: BA, History, Corpus Christi College, Cambridge, 1953. Appointments: Foreign Correspondent, 1957-64, Foreign News Editor, 1964-66, Features Editor, 1966-70, The Times; Editor, 1971-87, Editor-in-Chief, 1987-94, The Illustrated London News. Publications: Social History of Edwardian Britain, 1977; Social History of the First World War, 1982; The Story of The Times (with Oliver Woods), 1983; Illustrated Counties of England, editor, 1985; The Sedgwick Story, 1998. Contributions to: Books, newspapers and magazines. Membership: Association of British Editors (Chairman, 1987-96); National Heritage (Chairman, 1998-); The Annual Register Advisory Board. Address: Black Fen, Stoke By Nayland, Suffolk, CO6 4QD, England.

BISHOP Jonathan Edward, b. 8 November 1979, Llantwit Fardre, Pontypridd, Wales. Chartered IT Professional Fellow. Education: HND, Multimedia, 2002, BSc (Hons), Multimedia Studies, 2002, MSc, E-Learning, 2004, Master of Laws, European Union Law, 2007, University of Glamorgan, Higher Education Institution; Master of Economics and Social Studies, Information Systems, Aberystwyth University, Higher Education Institution, 2011; Doctor of Information Systems, Human-Computer Interaction, University of Wales Institute Cardiff, Higher Education Institution, in progress. Appointments: Company Director, Auntie Rosie's Bee Products, 1994-95; Multimedia Analyst, Broadway Studios, Treforest, 1999-2004; Community Councillor, Llantwit Fardre Community Council, 2003-04; Chair of Research, Centre for Research into Online Communities and E-Learning Systems, Swansea University, 2004-09; Research Associate, Kingston University, 2007-09; Company Secretary, Glamorgan Blended Learning Ltd, Swansea, 2006-; Town Councillor, Pontypridd Town Council, 2008-; Company Director, Jonathan Bishop Ltd, Abercynon, 2009-; Associate Tutor, University of Wales Institute Cardiff, Llandaff, 2011-. Publications: Numerous articles in professional journals. Honours: Finalist, New Statesman's Innovation Award, and Bright Sparks Award, 2004; Outstanding Newcomer, Pontypridd Labour Party, 2004. Memberships: Fellow, Royal Society of Arts; Fellow, BSC – The Chartered Institute for IT; Chartered IT Professional. Address: 8 Heol-y-Parc, Efail Isaf, Pontypridd, Wales CF38 1AN, United Kingdom. E-mail: jonathan@jonathanbishop.com

BISSET Jacqueline, b. 13 September 1944, Weybridge, Surrey, England. Education: French Lycée, London. Career: Films include: The Knack, debut, 1965; Casino Royale, 1967; Bullitt, The Detective, 1968; Airport, 1970; Believe in Me, 1971; Stand Up and Be Counted, 1972; The Thief Who Came to Dinner, 1973; Murder on the Orient Express, 1974; The Deep, 1976; Le Manifique, 1977; Secrets, 1978; When Time Ran Out, 1980; Rich and Famous, 1981; Class, 1982; Forbidden, 1986; High Season, 1988; Wild Orchid, 1989; September, 1994; La Cérémonie, End of Summer, 1995; Once You Meet a Stranger, Courtesan, 1996; Let the Devil Wear Black, Dangerous Beauty, 1998; Joan of Arc, 1999; In the Beginning, Jesus, Britannic, 2000; The Sleepy Time Gal, 2001; Sundance Holiday Gift Pack, Latter Days, 2003; Swing, Fascination, 2004; The Fine Art of Love: Mine Ha-Ha, Domino, Summer Solstice, 2005; Save the Last Dance2, Nip/Tuck, 2006; Carolina Moon, 2007; Death in Love, 2008; An

Old Fashioned Thanksgiving, 2008; The Last Film Festival, Vivaldi, 2009. Address: William Morris Agency, 151 El Camino Drive, Beverly Hills, CA 90212, USA.

BISWAS Amal Kanti, b. 8 January 1941, Kolkata, India. Consulting Engineer. m. Sarmila, 1 son, 1 daughter. Education: B Tech (Hons), Civil Engineering, Indian Institute of Technology, Kharagpur, 1963. Appointments: Assistant Engineer, CPWD; Executive Engineer, Department of Space; University Engineer, Viswa Bharati Central University; Chief Engineer, UCO Bank; Managing Director, AB Consultants Pvt Ltd, Kolkata. Publications: Numerous articles in professional journals. Honours: Chairman, Association of Multi-disciplinary Engineering Consultants, Kolkata. Memberships: Fellow, Institution of Engineers, India; Chartered Engineer; Fellow, Institution of Public Health Engineers, India; Fellow, Institution of Valuers; Fellow, Institution of Civil Engineers, India. Address: CJ 276, Sector II, Salt Lake, Kolkata 700 091, India. E-mail: biswasamal@in.com Website: www.abcpl.net

BITTERLICH Joachim, b. 10 July 1948, Saarbrücken-Dudweiler, Germany. Reserve Officer. m. Martine, 3 children. Education: Studies in law, Economics and Politics, University of Saarbrücken; French National School of Administration, Paris, France, 1974-75; Second State Examination in Law, 1976. Appointments: Joined Federal Foreign Office, 1976, posted to Algiers, 1978-81, and Permanent Representation to the European Communities, Brussels, 1981-85; Advisor, Minister of Foreign Affairs, Hans-Dietrich Genscher, 1985-87; Head, European Policy Department, Federal Chancellor's Office, 1987-93; Director General of Foreign Policy, Economic Co-operation and External Security, Federal Chancellor's Office, and Foreign and Security Policy Advisor to Federal Chancellor, Helmut Kohl, 1993-98; Ambassador, Permanent Representative of the Federal Republic of Germany, North Atlantic Council, Brussels, 1998-99; Ambassador of the Federal Republic of Germany to the Kingdom of Spain and the Principality of Andorra, 1999-2002; Executive Vice President, International Affairs, Veolia Environment, Paris, 2003-; Chairman, Veolia Environment, Germany, 2009; Professor, ESCP-Europe, Paris. Publications: Author and co-author of 20 reports and articles in professional journals including most recently: Europe's Future, 2004; Europe – mission impossible, 2005; France – Germany: mission impossible? How to relaunch the European integration, 2005; EU Treaties (juridical commentary), 5th edition, 2010. Honours: Comendador da Ordem du Mérito, 1991; Commendatore Ordine Merito de Republica Italiana, 1992; Honorary Commander of the British Empire, 1992; Gold Rays with Neck Ribbon, Order of the Rising Sun, 1993; Großes Goldenes Ehrenzeichen, 1993; Officer des Palmes Académiques; Kommandeur m Stern-Kgl Norske Fortjenstorden, 1994; Encomienda de Numero de la Orden de Isabel la Católica, 1994; Suomen Valkoisen Ruusun ritarikunnan 1 luckan, 1994; Großes Silbernes Ehrenzeichen mit Stern, 1994; Grand officier de l'Ordre de Mérite, 1995; Grand Officier de l'Ordre de la Couronne, 1995; Grande Oficial do Ordem de Rio Branco, 1995; Officier de la Legión d'Honneur, 1996; Grand Commandeur de l'Ordre de l'Honneur, 1996; Grande ufficiale n'ell Ordine al Mérito della Repubblica Italiana, 1997; Encomienda de Número de la Orden de Isabel la Católica, 1997; Placa, Orden Mexicana del Aguila Azteca, 1997; Gran Cruz de la Orden del Mérito Civil, 1998; Orden de Mayo al Mérito – Gran Cruz, 1998; Orden do Infante Don Henrique, 1998; Comendador del Orden del Liberator Simon Bolivar, 1998; Cross of Commander of the Order of Grand Duke Gediminas of Lithuania, 2002.

Memberships: Board of Directors: Veolia Environmental Services, Paris; Veolia Transport, Paris; DEKRA e V Stuttgart; Ecole Nationale d'Administration, Paris; MEDEF International, Paris; Notre Europe, Paris; Friends of Europe, Brussels; Franco-German Business Club, Paris; IISS; Rotarian (RC Paris Concorde); and others. Address: Veolia Environnement Head Office, 36-38 avenue Kleber, 75116, Paris, France. E-mail: joachim.bitterlich@veolia.com

BITTNER Wolfgang, b. 29 July 1941, Gleiwitz, Germany. Author. m. Renate Schoof, 2 sons, 1 daughter. Education: Law, Philosophy and Sociology, Universities of Goettingen and Munich, 1966-70; First Juridical Diploma, 1970, Dr Juridical, 1972, University of Goettingen; Second Juridical Diploma, Supreme Court, Braunschweig, 1973. Appointments: Government Official, Niedersachsen, 1963-1966; Lawyer, 1973; Professional author, 1974-; Member of Board of German Writers' Association, Verband deutscher Schriftsteller, 1997-2001; Member of Board, West German Radio, WDR, 1996-99. Publications: About 50 books including novels, poems, satire, children's literature, journalism, non-fiction, features, radio plays, scripts for tv, publications of literature, journalism and science in broadcasting, newspapers, journals and anthologies. Memberships: PEN; Verband deutscher Schriftsteller (German Writers' Association). Address: Merkelstrasse 63, D-37085, Göttingen, Germany. Website: http://www.wolfgangbittner.de

BJÖRK (Björk Godmunsdottir), b. 21 November 1965, Reykjavik, Iceland. Singer. 1 son, 1 daughter. Career: Solo release, aged 11; Singer, various Icelandic groups include: Exodus; Tappi Tikarras; Kukl; Singer, The Sugarcubes, 1987-92; Solo artiste, 1992-; Recent appearances include Reading Festival, 1995; Later.. with Jools Holland, Glastonbury Festival, 2007. Recordings: Albums: with the Sugarcubes: Life's Too Good, 1988; Here Today, Tomorrow, Next Week, 1989; Stick Around for Joy, 1992; It's It, 1992; Solo albums: Björk, 1977; Debut, 1993; Post, 1995; Telegram, 1996; Homogenic, 1997; Selmasongs, 2000; Vespertine, 2001; Dancer in the Dark, 2001; Greatest Hits, 2002; Family Tree, 2002; Medulla, 2004; Army of Me: Remixes and Covers (charity album), 2005; Volta, 2007; Hit singles: with The Sugarcubes: Birthday; Solo singles: Venus As A Boy; Violently Happy; Human Behaviour; Big Time Sensuality; Play Dead; Army Of Me; Isobel; It's Oh So Quiet; Possibly Maybe; I Miss You/Cover Me; Hyperballad; Hunter; Bachelorette; All Is Full Of Love; Alarm Call; Selmasongs, 2000; Triumph of a Heart, 2005; Other recordings: Gling-Go, Trio Gudmundar Ingolfssonar, 1990; Ex-El, Graham Massey, 1991; Tank Girl, 1995; Mission Impossible, 1996; Nearly God, 1996; Archive, 1997; Tibetan Freedom Concert, 1997; Not For Threes, 1998; Great Crossover Potential, 1998; Y2K Beat The Clock Version 1, 1999; Film: Dancer in the Dark, 2000. Honours: BRIT Award, Best International Female Artist, 1994,96,98; MOJO Award, 2007. Platinum and Gold records. Address: One Little Indian, 250 York Road, London SW11 3SJ, England.

BLACK Jack, b. 28 August 1969, Hermosa Beach, California, USA. Actor, Musician. m. Tanya Haden, 2006, 2 sons. Education: University of California at Los Angeles. Career: Films: Bob Roberts, 1992; Airborne, Demolition Man, 1993; Blind Justice, The NeverEnding Story III, 1994; Bye Bye, Love, Waterworld, Dead Man Walking, 1995; Crossworlds, Bio-Dome, The Cable Guy, Mars Attacks!, 1996; Bongwater, The Jackal, 1997; Johnny Skidmarks, Enemy of the State, 1998; Cradle Will Rock, Jesus' Son, 1999; High Fidelity, 2000; Saving Silverman, Frank's Book, Shallow Hal, 2001;

Run Ronnie Run, Orange County, Ice Age (voice), 2002; The School of Rock, 2003; LaserFart, Envy, Shark Tale (voice), 2004; King Kong, 2005; Tenacious D in: The Pick of Destiny, Nacho Libre, The Holiday, 2006; Be Kind Rewind, Margot at the Wedding, 2007; Kung Fu Panda (voice), Tropic Thunder, 2008; Year One, 2009; Gulliver's Travels, 2010; Kung Fu Panda 2, 2011; Bernie, The Big Year, The Muppets, 2011; Bailout, Frank or Francis, 2013. TV: Our Shining Moment, 1991; Marked for Murder, 1993; The Innocent, 1994; Heat Vision and Jack, 1999; Tenacious D, 1999; Lord of the Piercing, 2002; Jack Black: Spider-Man, 2002; Bobobo-bo Bo-bobo, 2003; Computerman, 2003; The Simpsons, 2007; The Office, Yo Gabba Gabba, 2009; Community, iCarly, 2010; Take Two with Phineas and Ferb, 2010-11; Fish Hooks, Big Time Rush, 2011; Kids' Choice Awards, American Idol, 2011; Conan, 2012.

BLACK Shirley Temple, b. 23 April 1928, Santa Monica, California, USA. Actress; Diplomat. m. (1) John Agar Jr 1945, divorced 1950, 1 daughter; m. (2) Charles A Black, 1950, deceased 2005, 1 son, 1 daughter. Education: Privately and Westlake School for Girls. Appointments: Career as film actress commenced at 3½ years; First full-length film was Stand Up and Cheer; Narrator/actress in TV series Shirley Temple Storybook, 1958; Hostess/Actress Shirley Temple Show, 1960; Delegation to UN New York, 1969-70; Ambassador to Ghana, 1974-76; White House Chief of Protocol, 1976-77; Ambassador to Czechoslovakia, 1989-92; Director, National Multiple Sclerosis Society. Publication: Child Star, 1988. Films include: Little Miss Marker; Baby Take a Bow; Bright Eyes; Our Little Girl; The Little Colonel; Curly Top; The Littlest Rebel; Captain January; Poor Little Rich Girl; Dimples; Stowaway; Wee Willie Winkie; Heidi; Rebecca of Sunnybrook Farm; Little Miss Broadway; Just Around the Corner; The Little Princess; Susannah of the Mounties; The Blue Bird; Kathleen; Miss Annie Rooney; Since You Went Away; Kiss and Tell; That Hagen Girl; War Party; The Bachelor and the Bobby-Soxer; Honeymoon. Honours: Dame Order of Knights of Malta - Paris - 1968; American Exemplar Medal, 1979; Gandhi Memorial International Foundation Award, 1988; Screen Actors guild, Lifetime Achievement Award, 2005: Numerous state decorations. Memberships: Member US Commission for UNESCO, 1973-; Member, US Delegation on African Refugee Problems Geneva, 1981. Address: c/o Academy of Motion Picture Arts and Sciences, 8949 Wilshire Blvd, Beverly Hills, CA 90211, USA.

BLACKBURN Alexander Lambert, b. 6 September 1929, Durham, North Carolina, USA. Novelist; Editor. m. Inés Dölz, 1975, 2 sons, 1 daughter. Education: BA, Yale University, 1947-51; MA, English, University of North Carolina, 1954-55; PhD, English, Cambridge University, England, 1959-60, 1961-63. Appointments: Instructor, Hampden-Sydney College, 1960-61; University of Pennsylvania, 1963-65; Lecturer, University of Maryland Euro Division, 1967-72; Professor of English, University of Colorado at Colorado Springs, 1973-95; Emeritus Professor English, 1996-. Publications: The Myth of the Picaro, 1979; The Cold War of Kitty Pentecost, novel, 1979; Editor, The Interior Country: Stories of the Modern West, 1987; A Sunrise Brighter Still: The Visionary Novels of Frank Waters, 1991; Editor, Higher Elevations: Stories from the West, 1993; Suddenly a Mortal Splendor, novel, 1995; Creative Spirit: Toward a Better World: Essays, 2001; Meeting the Professor: Growing up in the William Blackburn family, autobiography, 2004; Editor, Gifts from the Heart: Stories, Memories & Chronicles of Lucille Gonzales Oller, 2010; Unpublished books, 2013: The Door of the Sad People (novel); Intrepid Compassion (novel);

Remembering Time (short stories); Editor, Literary Titan: the Emergence of Frank Waters (critical essays). Contributions to: Founder and Editor-in-Chief; Writers Forum, 1974-95. Honours: Faculty Book Award, Colorado University, 1993; Runnerup, Colorado Book Award, 1996; International Peace-Writing Award, 2003; Frank Waters Award for Excellence in Literature, 2005; Runnerup, Colorado Book Award, 2011. Memberships: Authors Guild; Colorado Authors League. Address: 6030 Twin Rock Court, Colorado Springs, CO 80918-3239, USA.

BLACKMAN Honor, b. 12 December 1927, London, England. Actress. m. (1) Bill Sankey, 1946-56; (2) Maurice Kaufmann, 1963, divorced 1975, 2 adopted children. Creative Works: Films include: Fame is the Spur, 1947; Green Grow the Rushes, 1951; Come Die My Love, 1952; The Rainbow Jacket, 1953; The Glass Cage, 1954; Dead Man's Evidence, 1955; A Matter of Who, 1961; Goldfinger, 1964; Life at the Top, 1965; Twist of Sand, 1967; The Virgin and the Gipsy, 1970; To the Devil a Daughter, 1975; Summer Rain, 1976; The Cat and the Canary, 1977; Talos - The Mummy; To Walk with Lions; Bridget Jones's Diary, Jack Brown and the Curse of the Crown, 2001; Plays include: Madamoiselle Colombe, 2000; Cabaret, 2007: TV appearances include: Four Just Men, 1959; Man of Honour, 1960; Ghost Squad, 1961; Top Secret, 1962; The Avengers, 1962-64; The Explorer, 1968; Visit From a Stranger, 1970; Out Damned Spot, 1972; Wind of Change, 1977; Robin's Nest, Never the Twain, 1982; The Secret Adversary, 1983; Lace, 1985; The First Modern Olympics, Minder on the Orient Express, Dr Who, William Tell, 1986; The Upper Hand (TV series); Jack and the Beanstalk: The Real Story, Revolver, 2001; The Royal, 2003; Coronation Street, 2004; New Tricks, Summer Solstice, 2005; Sound, 2007; Hotel Babylon, 2009. Address: c/o Jean Diamond, London Management, 2-4 Noel Street, London W1V 3RB, England.

BLACKWELL Colin Roy, b. 4 September 1927, South Molton, Devon, England. Consulting Engineer. m. Susan Elizabeth Hunt. Education: BSc, Honours, Civil Engineering, University of Bristol, 1948-51. Appointments: Commissioned 83 LAA Regiment Royal Artillery, served Middle East, 1946-48; Joined, 1951, Site Engineer, Gold Coast (later Ghana), 1955-57, Senior Engineer, 1957-68, Principal Engineer, 1969-82, Freeman Fox & Partners, Consulting Engineers; Director, Freeman Fox Ltd, 1983-87; Consultant on telescopes and observatories to Hyder Consulting Ltd (formerly Acer Consultants Ltd, formerly Acer Freeman Fox), 1987-; Member, CIRIA Research Committee, 1976-79; Member, British Council Mission to Saudi Arabia, 1985; BSI CSB Committee, 1986-91. Publications: Das 64m Radioteleskop in Parkes (Australien), 1966; The reflector dishes of the 210 ft radio telescope at Parkes, Australia and the 150 ft diameter radio telescope at Lake Transverse, Ontario, 1966. Memberships: Fellow, Institution of Civil Engineers; Fellow, American Society of Civil Engineers; Fellow Royal Astronomical Society. Address: 14 St Mary's Court, Old Beaconsfield, Bucks HP9 2LG, England.

BLAGA Adara-Monica, b. 25 July 1978, Sibiu, Romania. Mathematician; Writer. m. Lucian G Blaga. Education: Graduate, Pure Mathematics, 2001, Master's degree, Differential Geometry and Analysis, 2003, PhD, Symplectic Geometry, 2006, West University of Timisoara. Appointments: Instructor, 2002-06, Teaching Assistant, 2006-09, Assistant Professor, 2009-, Department of Mathematics, West University of Timisoara. Publications: 50 scientific articles; 10 mathematical books; 3 poetry books; 1 translation. Honours: Romanian Union of Writers Award, 2000; Nikolaus Berwanger

Award, 2000. Memberships: American Mathematical Society; Balkan Society of Geometers; Tensor Society; Romanian Mathematical Society; Romanian Union of Writers; Copyro; and others. E-mail: adarablaga@yahoo.com

BLAINEY Geoffrey Norman, b. 11 March 1930, Melbourne, Victoria, Australia. Writer. Education: Ballarat High School; Wesley College, Melbourne; Queen's College, University of Melbourne. Publications: The Peaks of Lyell, 1954; A Centenary History of the University of Melbourne, 1957; Gold and Paper, 1958; Mines in the Spinifex, 1960; The Rush That Never Ended, 1963; A History of Camberwell, 1965; If I Remember Rightly: The Memoirs of W S Robinson, 1966; Wesley College: The First Hundred Years (co-author and editor), 1967; The Tyranny of Distance, 1966; Across a Red World, 1968; The Rise of Broken Hill, 1968; The Steel Master, 1971; The Causes of War, 1973; Triumph of the Nomads, 1975; A Land Half Won, 1980; The Blainey View, 1982; Our Side of the Country, 1984; All for Australia, 1984; The Great Seesaw, 1988; A Game of our Own: The Origins of Australian Football, 1990; Odd Fellows, 1991; Eye on Australia, 1991; Jumping Over the Wheel, 1993; The Golden Mile, 1993; A Shorter History of Australia, 1994; White Gold, 1997; A History of the AMP, 1999; In Our Time, 1999; A History of the World, 2000; This Land is All Horizons, 2002; Black Kettle and Full Moon, 2003; A Very Short History of the World, 2004-; A Short History of the 20th Century, 2005; Sea of Dangers: Captain Cook and His Rivals, 2008. Honours: Gold Medal, Australian Literature Society, 1963; Encyclopaedia Britannica Gold Award, New York, 1988; Companion of the Order of Australia, 2000. Memberships: Australia Council, chairman, 1977-81; Commonwealth Literary Fund, chairman, 1971-73; Professor of Economic History and History, University of Melbourne, 1968-88; Professor of Australian Studies, Harvard, 1982-83; Inaugural Chancellor of University of Ballarat, 1994-98; Chairman, National Council for Centenary of Federation, 2001; Chairman, Australia-China Council, 1979-84; Governor, Ian Potter Foundation, 1991-. Address: PO Box 257, East Melbourne, Victoria 8002, Australia.

BLAIR Anna Dempster, b. 12 February 1927, Glasgow, Scotland. Author. m. Matthew Blair, 13 June 1952, 1 son, 1 daughter. Education: Dunfermline College, Graduated 1947. Appointment: Teacher, Glasgow Education Authority, 1947-52, 1965-75. Publications: A Tree in the West; The Rowan on the Ridge, 1980; Historical Novels: Tales of Ayrshire (Traditional Tales Retold), 1993; Tea at Miss Cranston's Reminiscences/ Social History, 1985; Croft and Creel, Scottish Tales, 1987; The Goose-Girl of Eriska, Seed Corn, 1989; Traditional Tales: More Tea at Miss Cranston's, 1991. Contributions to: Old Giffnock (local history); Various others. Address: 20 Barrland Drive, Giffnock, Glasgow G46 7QD, Scotland.

BLAIR Anthony Charles Lynton (Tony), b. 6 May 1953, Edinburgh, Scotland. Labour Politician. m. Cherie Booth, 1980, 3 sons, 1 daughter. Education: Fettes College, Edinburgh; St Johns College, Oxford. Appointments: Barrister, Trade Union and Employment Law; MP, Sedgefield, 1983-2007; Shadow Treasury Spokesman, 1984-87, Trade and Industry Spokesman, 1987-88, Energy Spokesman, 1988-89, Employment Spokesman, 1989-92, Home Affairs Spokesman, 1992-94; Leader, Labour Party, 1994-2007; Prime Minister, First Lord of the Treasury and Minister for the Civil Service, 1997-2007; Middle East Envoy for the United Nations, United States, European Union and Russia, 2007. Publication: New Britain: My Vision of a Young Country, 1996; The Third Way, 1998. Honours: Honorary Bencher, Lincolns Inn, 1994; Honorary LLD, Northumbria; Charlemagne Prize, 1999; Honorary Law Doctorage, Queen's University Belfast, 2008; Presidential Medal of Freedom, USA, 2009; Dan David Prize, Israel, 2009.

BLAIR David Chalmers Leslie Jr, b. 8 April 1951, Long Beach, California, USA. Alternative Rock Artist; Composer; Artist; Author; Actor; Ladies' Fashion Designer. Education: BA, French, ESL certificate, California State University at Long Beach, 1979; Postgraduate Studies, Université de Provence, Aix-en-Provence, France, 1979-80. Publications: Novels: Death of an Artist, 1982; Vive la France, 1993; Death of America, 1994; Mother, 1998; Evening in Wisconsin, 2001; The Girls (and Women) I Have Known, 2001; A Small Snack Shop in Stockholm, Sweden, 2002; Composer, Writer and Recorder of 108 albums including: Her Garden of Earthly Delights; Sir Blair of Rothes; Europe; St Luke Passion. Membership: Libertarian Party, USA. Address: 19331 105th Avenue, Cadott, WI 54727, USA.

BLAIR John Samuel Greene, b. 31 December 1928, Wormit, Fife, Scotland, UK. Medical Historian; Former Surgeon. m. Ailsa Jean Bowes, MBE, 2 sons, 1 daughter. Education: High School of Dundee, Harris Gold Medal for Dux of School, Dux in English, 1946; Harkness Scholar, St Andrews University 1946-50; MB ChB, 1951; ChM, 1961; Clinical part of MD, St Andrews, 1953; D (Obst) RCOG, 1952; FRCS (Ed), 1958; FICS, 1983; BA (External), London, 1955. Appointments include: RAMC National Service 1952-55; Joined TA via St Andrews OTC (CO, 1967-71); Commanded RAMC and other Reserve Units, retired as Honorary Colonel, 225 (Highland) Field Ambulance, RAMC; Consultant Surgeon, as part of Security Forces Northern Ireland Command, Musgrave Park Military Hospital, BAOR, Berlin, Cyprus, and Nepal, 1975-76; Consultant Surgeon, Perth Royal Infirmary, 1965-90; Honorary Senior Lecturer in Surgery, Dundee University, Postgraduate Clinical Tutor, Perth, 1966-71; Honorary Senior Lecturer, 1990-97, Reader, 1997-2001, History of Medicine, University of St Andrews; Current appointment: Honorary Senior Teaching Fellow, Medical History, Faculty of Medicine, University of Dundee. Publications: 14 articles in medical and surgical journals;12 major historical articles; Books include: History of St Andrews OTC, 1982; History of Medicine in St Andrews University, 1987; Ten Tayside Doctors, 1988; History of the Bridge of Earn Hospital 1940-1990, 1990; History of the Royal Perth Golfing Society and County and City Club, 1997; In Arduis Fidelis. Definitive Centenary History of the Royal Army Medical Corps, 1989-1998, 1998, second edition, 2001; The Conscript Doctors: Memories of National Service, 2001; History of Tayforth Officers Training Corps, 2003; History of Medicine in Dundee University, 2007; Numerous invited lectures. Honours include: OBE (Military), 1974; Doctor of Letters, honoris causa, St Andrews, 1991; John Blair Fund set up by British Society for the History of Medicine, 1996; Honorary Fellow, Royal College of Physicians of Edinburgh, 2000; Fellow, Society of Antiquaries (Scotland), 1997; Captain, Royal Perth Golfing Society, 1997-99; Fellow, Royal Historical Society, 2001; Honorary Member, SSHM, 2003; President, Friends of Millbank, 2009-. Memberships: Fellow BMA, 1993; Knight of St John - Hospitaller, Priory of Scotland, 1992-2000; President, Scottish Society of the History of Medicine, 1991-94; President, British Society for the History of Medicine, 1993-95; Apothecaries Lecturer, Worshipful Society of Apothecaries, London, 1994-; Ostler Club of London, 1996; Vice-President, International Society for the History of Medicine, 2000-04; American Ostler Society, 2002. Address: "The Brae", 143 Glasgow Road, Perth PH2 0LX, Scotland. E-mail: jgb143@btinternet.com

BLAKE Martin Joseph, b. 31 October 1952, Dublin, Ireland. Retired Farmer. Education: Ambleforth College, York, 1961-71; Shuttleworth Agricultural College, Biggleswade, Bedfordshire,1971-75; Abbeyleix Further Education College, 2004; Part time study, All Hallows College, Dublin, 2000/2004. Appointments: Farmer, 1975-2003; Member, St Vincent de Paul Society, Durrow, 1986-2008; Member, Legion of Mary, Durrow, 1990-; Minister of the Word, Durrow Parish; Eucharistic Minister, Abbeyleix Parish. Publications: In Sickness and In Health, 1990; Lumen Christi, 1995. Honours: Knight of the Equestrian Order of the Holy Sepulchre of Jerusalem, 2005. Memberships: Probus (retired businessmen's association); Oblate of Clenstal Abbey, 1994; Legion of Mary, Durrow Oblate Clenstal Abbey, Probus. Address: Castlewood House, Durrow, Co Laois, Ireland.

BLAKE Quentin Saxby, b. 16 December 1932, Sidcup, Kent, England. Artist; Illustrator; Teacher. Education: Downing College, Cambridge; London Institute of Education; Chelsea School of Art. Appointments: Freelance Illustrator, 1957-; Tutor, Royal College of Art, 1965-86, Head, Illustration Department, 1978-86, Visiting Professor, 1989-, Senior Fellow, 1988; Children's Laureate, 1999-2001. Publications: Patrick, 1968; Mister Magnolia, 1980; Quentin Blake's Nursery Rhyme Book, 1983; Mrs Armitage on Wheels, 1987; Mrs Armitage Queen of the Road; Mrs Armitage and the Big Wave; The Story of the Dancing Frog; Quentin Blake's ABC, 1989; Angelo, 1990; All Join In, Cockatoos, 1992; Simpkin, 1993; La Vie de la Page, 1995; The Puffin Book of Nonsense Verse, 1996; The Green Ship, Clown, 1998; Drawing for the Artistically Undiscovered (with John Cassidy), Fantastic Daisy Artichoke, 1999; Words and Pictures, The Laureate's Party, Zagazoo, 2000; Tell Me a Picture, 2001; Loveykins, A Sailing Boat in the Sky, Laureate's Progress, 2002; Angel Pavement, 2004; You're Only Young Twice, 2008; Daddy Lost his Head, 2009; Illustrations for over 250 works for children and adults, including collaborations with Roald Dahl, Russell Hoban, Joan Aiken, Michael Rosen, John Yeoman; Exhibitions: Quentin Blake – 50 Years of Illustration, The Gilbert Collection, Somerset House, London, 2003-04; Quentin Blake at Christmas, Dulwich Picture Gallery, London, 2004-05. Honours: Honorary Fellow: Brighton University, 1996; Downing College, Cambridge, 2000; Honorary RA; Chevalier des Arts et des Lettres, 2002; Dr hc: London Institute, 2000, Northumbria, 2001, RCA, 2001; Hon D Litt, Cambridge University, 2004; Chevalier des Arts et des Lettres, 2004; CBE, 2005; Officier de l'Ordre des Arts et des Lettres, 2007. Address: Flat 8, 30 Bramham Gardens, London SW5 0HF, England.

BLAKEMORE Colin, b. 1 June 1944, Stratford-on-Avon, England. Neurophysiologist; Professor of Physiology. m. Andrée Elizabeth Washbourne, 1965, 3 daughters. Education: Natural Sciences, Corpus Christi College, Cambridge, 1965; PhD, Physiological Optics, Neurosensory Laboratory, University of California at Berkeley, 1968. Appointments: Demonstrator, Physiological Laboratory, Cambridge University, 1968-72; Lecturer in Physiology, Cambridge University, 1972-79; Fellow and Director of Medical Studies, Downing College, 1971-79; Professorial Fellow of Magdalen College, Oxford, 1979-; Wayneflete Professor of Physiology, Oxford University, 1979-2007; Chief Executive European Dana Alliance for the Brain, 1996-; President, 1997-98, Vice President, 1990-, British Association for the Advancement of Science; President, British Neuroscience Association, 1997-2000; President, Physiological Society, 2001-; Director, McDonnell-Pew Centre for Cognitive Neuroscience, Oxford, 1990-2003; Director, MRC Interdisciplinary Research Centre for Cognitive Neuroscience, Oxford, 1996-2003; Chief Executive, Medical Research Council, 2003-07; Associate Director, MRC Research Centre in Brain and Behaviour, Oxford, 1990-; Professor of Neuroscience, Oxford University and Warwick University, 2007-. Publications: Editor, Handbook of Psychobiology, 1975; Mechanics of the Mind, 1977; Editor, Mindwaves, 1987; The Mind Machine, 1988, Editor, Images and Understanding, Vision: Coding and Efficiency, 1990; Sex and Society, 1999; Oxford Companion to the Body, 2001; The Physiology of Cognitive Processes (co-editor), The Roots of Visual Awareness (co-editor), 2003; Contributions to: Constraints on Learning, Illusion in Art and Nature, 1973; The Neurosciences Third Study Program, 1974; and to professional journals. Honours: Robert Bing Prize, 1975; Man of the Year, 1978; Christmas Lectures for Young People, Royal Institute, 1982; John Locke Medal, 1983; Netter Prize, 1984; Bertram Louis Abrahams Lecture, Cairns Memorial Lecture and Medal, 1986; Norman McAllister Gregg Lecture and Medal, 1988; Royal Society Michael Faraday Medal, Robert Doyne Medal, 1989; John P McGovern Science and Society Lecture and Medal, 1990; Montgomery Medal, Sir Douglas Robb Lectures, 1991; Honorary DSc, Aston, 1992; Honorary Osler Medal, Ellison-Cliffe Medal, 1993; DSc, Salford, Charles F Prentice Award, 1994; Annual Review Prize Lecture, 1995; Century Lecture, Alcon Prize, 1996; Newton Lecture, Cockcroft Lecture, 1997; Memorial Medal, 1998; Alfred Meyer Award, British Neuroscience Association Outstanding Contribution to Neuroscience, Menzies Medal, Menzies Foundation, Melbourne, 2001; Bioindustry Association Award for Outstanding Personal Contribution to Bioscience, Lord Crook Gold Medal, Worshipful Company of Spectacle Makers, 2004; Edinburgh Medal, City of Edinburgh, Science Educator Award, 2005; Kenneth Myer Medal, 2006; Honorary Fellow: Cardiff University of Wales, 1998; Downing College, Cambridge, 1999-; Royal College of Physicians, 2004-; Institute of Biology, 2004-. Memberships: Editorial Board, Perception, 1971; Behavioural and Brain Sciences, 1977; Journal of Developmental Physiology, 1978-86; Experimental Brain Research, 1979-89; Language and Communication, 1979; Reviews in the Neurosciences, 1984-; News in Physiological Sciences, 1985; Clinical Vision Sciences, 1986; Chinese Journal of Physiological Sciences, 1988; Advances in Neuroscience, 1989-; Vision Research, 1993-; Honorary Member, Physiological Society, 1998; Associate Editor, NeuroReport, 1989-; Honorary Associate, Rationalist Press Association, 1986-; Editor-in-Chief, IBRO News, 1986-; Leverhulme Fellowship, 1974-75; BBC Reith Lecturer, 1976; Lethaby Professor, RCA, London, 1978; Storer Lecturer, University of California at Davis, 1980; Regents' Professor, 1995-96; Macallum Lecturer, University of Toronto, 1984; Fellow, World Economic Forum, 1994-98; Honorary Fellow, Corpus Christi College, Cambridge, 1994-; Founder, Fellow, Academy of Medical Sciences, 1998-; Foreign Member, Royal Netherlands Academy of Arts and Sciences, 1993; Member, Worshipful Company of Spectacle Makers and Freemen of the City of London, 1997; Member, Livery, 1998; Patron and Member, Professional Advisory Panel Headway (National Head Injuries Association), 1997-; Patron, Association for Art, Science, Engineering and Technology, 1997-. Address: Medical Research Council, 20 Park Crescent, London W1B 1AL, England. E-mail: colin.blakemore@headoffice.mrc.ac.uk

BLANC Raymond Rene Alfred, b. 19 November 1949, Besançon, France. Chef, Restaurant Owner. 2 sons. Education: Besançon Technical College. Career: Various positions, 1968-76; Military Service, 1970-71; Manager and Chef de cuisine, Bleu, Blanc, Rouge, Oxford, 1976-77; Chef Proprietor, Les Quat'Saisons, Oxford, 1977; Director and Chair, 1978-88, Maison Blanc, 1978-; Le Manoir aux Quat'Saisons, 1984; Le Petit Blanc: Oxford, 1996, Cheltenham, 1998; Birmingham, 1999; Manchester, 2000; Tunbridge Wells, 2004; Re-launched as Brasserie Blanc, 2006; Leeds and Milton Keynes, 2007; Winchester and Bristol, 2008; Weekly recipe column in the Observer, 1988-90; TV series: Blanc Mange, 1994; Passion for Perfection, 2002; The Restaurant, 2007-. Publications: Recipes from Le Manoir aux Quat'Saisons, 1989; Cooking for Friends, 1991; Blanc Mange, 1994; Best A Blanc Christmas, 1996; A Taste of My Life, 2009. Contributions to: Take Six Cooks, 1986; Taste of Health, 1987; Masterchefs of Europe, 1998; Blanc Vite, 1998; Restaurants of Great Britain, 1989; Gourmet Garden, 1990; European Chefs, 1990; Foolproof French Cooking, 2002. Honours: Representative of Great Britain at Grand Final of Wedgwood World Master of Culinary Arts, Paris, 2002; Hon DBA, Oxford Brookes University, 1999; European Chef of the Year, 1989; Personalité de l'Année, 1990; Craft Guild of Chefs Special Award, 2002; AA Restaurant Guide Chef of the Year, 2004; AA's Chefs' Chef of the Year, 2005; Honorary Member, Culinary Division, International Food, Wine and Travel Writers Association, 2005; Honorary Award, Craft Guild of Chefs, 2006; OBE, 2007; Lord Taverner of The Lady Tavener's, 2008; Catey Lifetime Achievement Award, 2009; many other awards. Memberships: Academie Culinaire de France; British Gastronomic Academy; Restaurateurs Association of Great Britain. Address: Le Manoir aux Quat'Saisons, Church Road, Great Milton, Oxford OX44 7PD, England. Website: www.manoir.com

BLANCHETT Cate, b. 14 May 1969, Melbourne, Australia. Actress. m. Andrew Upton, 1997, 3 sons. Education: Melbourne University, National Institute of Dramatic Art. Appointments: Plays include: Top Girls; Kafka Dances; Oleanna; Hamlet; Sweet Phoebe; The Tempest; The Blind Giant is Dancing; Plenty; The Vagina Monologues; Hedda Gabler; The War of the Roses Cycle; A Streetcare Named Desire; Films include: Parkland; Paradise Road, Thank God He Met Lizzie, Oscar and Lucinda, 1997; Elizabeth, 1998; Dreamtime Alice, also co-producer; The Talented Mr Ripley; An Ideal Husband; Pushing Tin, 1999; Bandit, The Man Who Cried, The Gift, Bandits, 2000; Heaven, The Lord of the Rings: The Fellowship of the Ring, Charlotte Gray, 2001; The Shipping News, The Lord of the Rings: The Two Towers, 2002; The Lord of the Rings: The Return of the King, Coffee and Cigarettes, 2003; The Life Aquatic, The Aviator, 2004; Stories of Lost Souls, Little Fish, 2005; Babel, The Good German, Notes on a Scandal, 2006; Hot Fuzz (cameo), The Golden Age, I'm Not There, 2007; Indiana Jones and the Kingdom of the Crystal Skull, The Curious Case of Benjamin Button, 2008; Ponyo (voice), 2009; Robin Hood, 2010; The Hobbit, 2013-; TV includes: Heartland, 1994; GP Police Rescue. Honours: Newcomer Award, 1993; Rosemont Best Actress Award; Golden Globe Award, 1998; BAFTA Award for Best Actress, 1999; Best Actress, National Board of Review, 2001; Golden Camera Award, 2001; Oscar, Best Actress in a Supporting Role, 2004; Best Supporting Actress, Screen Actors Guild Awards, 2005; Best Actress in a Supporting Role, BAFTA Awards, 2005; Best Supporting Actress, Academy Awards, 2005; Australian Film Institute Award for Best Actress in a Leading Role, 2007; Golden Globe Award for Best Supporting Actress, 2007; many others. Address: c/o Robyn Gardiner, PO Box 128, Surry Hill, 2010 NSW, Australia.

BLANK Eugene, b. 8 May 1924, Baltimore, USA. Paediatrician; Radiologist; Educator. m. Esther Honikberg, 1958, 3 daughters. Education: BA, 1948, MD, 1954, Johns Hopkins University. Appointments: 2nd Lieutenant, USMC, South Pacific, 1942-45; Diplomate, American Board of Paediatrics, 1960; American Board Radiology, 1965; Professor Emeritus in Paediatrics and Radiology, Oregon Health Sciences University, Portland, 1991. Publications: Paediatric Images Casebook of Differential Diagnosis, 1997; USMC457703, 2010. Address: 4940 SW Humphrey Park Road, Portland, OR 97221, USA.

BLASHFORD-SNELL John Nicholas, b. 22 Oct 1936, Hereford, England. Soldier; Colonel; Explorer; Writer. Education: Victoria College, Jersey, Channel Islands; Royal Military Academy, Sandhurst. Publications: A Taste for Adventure, 1978; Operation Drake, 1981; In the Wake of Drake (with M Cable), 1982; Mysteries: Encounters with the Unexplained, 1983; Operation Raleigh: The Start of an Adventure, 1985; Operation Raleigh: Adventure Challenge (with Ann Tweedy), 1988; Operation Raleigh: Adventure Unlimited (with Ann Tweedy), 1990; Something Lost Behind the Ranges, 1994; Mammoth Hunt (with Rula Lenska), 1996; Kota Mama: Retracing the lost trade routes of ancient South American peoples (with Richard Smailham), 2000. Contributions to: Expedition: The Field; Explorers Journal; British Army Review; Gun Digest; Spectator; Yorkshire Post; Scotsman; Traveller; Guardian; You Magazine; Daily Telegraph; Sunday Telegraph; Country Life. Address: c/o The Scientific Exploration Society, Expedition Base, Motcombe, Dorset SP7 9PB, England.

BLASIG Winfried H J, b. 6 November 1932, Breslau, Germany. Professor. Education: Ex Synodale, 1957; Promotion in Catholic Theology, 1968. Appointments: Chaplain, 1959; Docent, Homiletics, 1967; Extraordinary Professor, Homiletics, Linz, Austria, 1972; Relegation by Roman Congregation of Faith, 1985. Publications: Kirche Gottes – Kirche der Menschen, 1968; Von Jesus bis heute, 1973; Christ im Jahr 2000, 1984; Abendmahl in Jahr 2000, 2000; Für eine Erneuerung des Sonntagsgottesdienstes, 2009. Honours: Geistlicher Rat, 1972. Memberships: Lions Club; European Society for Catholic Theology. Address: Hallgrafenstrasse 28, 83512 Wasserburg, Germany.

BLATNÝ Pavel, b. 14 September 1931, Brno, Czech Republic. m. Danuse Spirková, 19 June 1982, 1 son, 1 daughter. Education: Studied Piano, Conducting and Composition; Musicology, University of Brno, 1958; Berklee School of Music, Boston, USA, 1968. Career: Composer; Conductor; Pianist; Chief, Music Department, Czech Television, to 1992; Professor, Janácek's Academy, Brno, to 1990. Compositions include: Concerto for Jazz Orchestra, 1962-64; Cantatas: Willow; Christmas Eve and Noonday Witch; Bells; Twelfth Night, based on Shakespeare's play, 1975; Full-length Musical for Children, Dilia, 1979; Two Movements for brasses, 1982; Signals for jazz orchestra, 1985; Prologue for mixed choir and jazz orchestra, 1984; Per organo e big band, 1983; Ring a Ring o' Roses, for solo piano, 1984; Symphony "Erbeniada" written for the festival "Prague Spring", world premier, 2004; An Old Song, symphonic variations on melody of Thomas Aquin, 2008; Book, Storries, 2008. Honours: Prize of Leos Jánácek, 1984; Antiteatro D'Argento for the Life's Work, Italy, 1988; Award for Life's Work, City of Brno,

2004. Honour: First place award, International Composer Composition, Prague Jazz Festival, 1966-67; Voted 5th place, 1967 and 3rd place, 1968, Composer category, Down Beat. Membership: President, Club of Moravian Composers. Address: Absolonova 35, 62400 Brno, Czech Republic.

BLAŽIĆ Helena, b. 23 March 1966, Rijeka, Croatia. University Professor. 1 son, 1 daughter. Education: BA, Faculty of Economics, University of Rijeka, 1988; MA, Faculty of Economics, University of Ljubljana, 1989-93; Alpen-Adria Scholarship, University of Klagenfurt, Austria, 1994; Croatia Mentor Program, US Government Fellowship, Carol Martin Gatton College of Business and Economics, University of Kentucky, October 1997; PhD, Economics, University of Rijeka, 1999. Appointments: Research Assistant, 1989-93, Assistant, 1993-99, Senior Assistant, 1999-2000, Assistant Professor, 2000-2003, Associate Professor, 2003-08, Full Professor, 2008-, Director of Postgraduate Academic Study in Public Administration, 2004-09, Faculty of Economics, University of Rijeka; Part-time Lecturer, University of Zagreb, 1996-97; Editorial Board Member of professional journals; President, Publishing Committee, Faculty of Economics, Member, Publishing Committee, 2000-07, Director, International Relations Office, Faculty of Economics, 2007-, University of Rijeka; Participant in numerous international conferences. Publications include most recently: Tax Compliance Costs of Companies in Croatia (journal article), 2007; Personal Income Tax Compliance Costs at an Individual Level in Croatia (journal article), 2004; The Investment Effects of PTAs in Southeast Europe (conference paper, co-author), 2004; Family Tax Treatment: A Comparative Analysis of Croatia and CEE (conference paper, co-author), 2005; Tax Compliance Costs for Companies in Slovenia and Croatia (journal article, co-author), 2005; Compliance Costs of Taxation in a Transition Country: The Example of Croatia (conference paper), 2005; The Croatian Tax System: From Consumption-based to Income-based, 2008. Memberships: National Tax Association, USA; Croatian Society of Economists; Croatian Society of Accountants and Employees in Finance; Society for Development of High Education "Universitas" Croatia. Address: Faculty of Economics, University of Rijeka, Ivana Filipovića 4, 51000 Rijeka, Croatia. E-mail: helena@efri.hr

BLEASDALE Alan, b. 23 March 1946. Playwright; Novelist. m. Julia Moses, 1970, 2 sons, 1 daughter. Education: Teachers Certificate, Padgate Teachers Training College. Publications: Scully, 1975; Who's Been Sleeping in My Bed, 1977; No More Sitting on the Old School Bench, 1979; Boys From the Blackstuff (televised), 1982; Are You Lonesome Tonight?, 1985; No Surrender, 1986; Having a Ball, 1986; It's A Madhouse, 1986; The Monocled Mutineer (televised), 1986; GBH (TV series), 1992; On the Ledge, 1993; Jake's Progress (TV), 1995; Oliver Twist, 1999. Honours: BAFTA Writer's Award, 1982; RTS Writer's Award, 1982; Broadcasting Press Guild TV Award for Best Series, 1982; Best Musical, London Stand Drama Awards, 1985; Hon DLitt, Liverpool Polytechnic, 1991; Best Writer, Monte Carlo International TV Festival, 1996; Best Drama Series, TV and Radio Industries Club, 2000. Address: c/o Harvey Unna and Stephen Durbridge Ltd, 24 Pottery Lane, Holland Park, London, W11 4LZ, England.

BLETHYN Brenda Anne, b. 20 February 1946, Ramsgate, Kent, England. Actress. m. Alan James Blethyn, 1964, divorced 1973, partner, Michael Mayhew, 1977. Education: Thanet Technical College; Guildford School of Acting. Creative Works: Theatre appearances include: Mysteries, 1979; Steaming, 1981; Double Dealer, 1982; Benefactors, 1984; Dalliance, A Doll's House, 1987; Born Yesterday, 1988; The Beaux' Stratagem, 1989; An Ideal Husband, 1992; Wildest Dreams, 1993; The Bed Before Yesterday, 1994; Habeas Corpus, Absent Friends, 1996; Mrs Warren's Profession, 2002-03. Films: The Witches, A River Runs Through It, 1992; Secrets and Lies, Remember Me, 1996; Music From Another Room, Girls' Night, 1997; Little Voice, Night Train, Daddy and Them, RKO 281, On the Nose, In the Winter Dark, 1999; The Sleeping Dictionary, Saving Grace, Yellow Bird, Pumpkin, Plots with a View, 2000; Anne Frank – The Whole Story, Lovely and Amazing, 2001; Sonny, Blizzard, 2002; Piccadilly Jim, Beyond the Sea, A Way of Life, 2004; On a Clear Day, Pooh's Heffalump Movie, Pride and Prejudice, 2005; Clubland, Atonement, War & Peace, 2007; London River, Tigger & Pooh and a Musical Too, The Calling, Dead Man Running, My Angel, 2009; TV includes: Henry VI (Part I), 1981; King Lear, 1983; Chance in a Million, 1983-85; The Labours of Erica, 1987; The Bullion Boys, 1993; The Buddah of Suburbia, 1993; Sleeping with Mickey, 1993; Outside Edge, 1994-96; First Signs of Madness, 1996; Between the Sheets, 2003; Belonging, 2004. Publications: Autobiography, Mixed Fancies, 2006. Honours include: Best Actress Award, Cannes Film Festival, 1996; Boston Film Critics Award, 1997; LA Film Critics Award, 1997; Golden Globe, 1997; London Film Critics Award, 1997; BAFTA, 1997; Honorary Dr of Letters, 1999; OBE, 2003. Membership: Poetry Society, 1976-. Address: c/o ICM, 76 Oxford Street, London W1N 0AX, England.

BLIGE Mary J, b. 11 January 1971, New York, USA. Singer, Actress. m. Martin Kendu Isaacs, 2003, 3 stepchildren. Career: Solo recording artiste; Support to Jodeci, UK tour, 1995. Recordings: Albums: What's The 411, 1992; My Life, 1994; Mary Jane, 1995; Share My World, 1997; The Tour, 1998; Mary, 1999; No More Drama, Ballads, 2001; Love & Life, 2003; The Breakthrough, 2005; Growing Pains, 2007; Stronger, 2009; Singles: What's The 411, 1992; Sweet Thing, 1993; My Love, 1994; You Bring Me Joy, All Night Long, 1995; Not Gon' Cry, 1996; Love Is All We Need, Everything, 1997; Seven Days, All That I Can Say, As, with George Michael, 1999; Also appears on: Father's Day, 1990; Changes, Close To You, 1992; Panther, Show, MTV Party To Go, Waiting To Exhale, 1995; Nutty Professor, Case, Ironman, 1996; Love And Consequences, Miseducation Of Lauryn Hill, Nu Nation Project, 1998; Dance for Me, Rainy Dayz, 2002; Love @ 1st Sight, 2003; Be Without You, 2005; Runaway Love, 2006. Address: Steve Lucas Associates, 156 W 56th Street, New York, NY 10019, USA.

BLOOM Claire, b. 15 February 1931, London, England. Actress. m. (1) Rod Steiger, 1959, 1 daughter. (2) Hillard Elkins, 1969, (3) Philip Roth, divorced 1995. Education: London, Bristol and New York. Appointments: Oxford Repertory Theatre, 1946; Stratford-on-Avon, 1948. Creative Works: Performances include: Mary, Queen of Scots in Vivat, Vivat Regina!, New York, 1972; A Streetcare Named Desire, London, 1974; The Innocents, USA, 1976; Rosmersholm, London, 1977; The Cherry Orchard, Chichester Festival, 1981; When We Dead Awaken, 1990; The Cherry Orchard, USA, 1994; Long Day's Journey into Night, USA, 1996; Electra, New York, 1998; Conversations after a Burial, London, 2000; A Little Night Music, 2003; Six Dance Lessons in Six Weeks, 2006. Films include: A Doll's House, 1973; Islands in the Stream, 1975; The Clash of the Titans, 1979; Always, 1984; Sammy and Rosie Get Laid, 1987; Brothers, 1988; Crimes and Misdemeanours, 1989; Mighty Aphrodite, 1994; Daylight, 1995; Shakespeare's Women and Claire Bloom; The Book of Eve, 2001; Imagining Argentina, 2002; Daniel and the Superdogs, 2003; Kalamazoo? 2006; TV appearances include: A Shadow in the Sun, 1988; The

Camomile Lawn, 1991; The Mirror Crack'd From Side to Side, 1992; Remember, 1993; A Village Affair, 1994; Family Money, 1996; The Lady in Question; Love and Murder; Yesterday's Children; Law and Order: Criminal Intent, 2004; Jericho, 2005; Dr Martin, 2005; Marple: By the Pricking of My Thumbs, 2006; Trial & Retribution, 2006; The Chatterley Affair, 2006; The Ten Commandments, 2006; New Tricks, 2008; Fiona's Story, 2008; One woman shows: Enter the Actress; These are the Women: A Portrait of Shakespeare's Heroines. Publications: Limelight and After, 1982; Leaving a Doll's House, 1996. Honours include: Evening Standard Drama Award for Best Actress, 1974. Address: c/o Jeremy Conway, 18-21 Jermyn Street, London SW1Y 6HB, England.

BLOOM Orlando, b. 13 January 1977, Canterbury, Kent, England. Actor. m. Miranda Kerr, 2010, 1 son. Education: National Youth Theatre, London; Scholarship, British American Drama Academy; Guildhall School of Music and Drama, 3 years. Career: Assistant, shooting club. Film appearances include: Wilde, 1997; The Lord of the Rings: The Fellowship of the Ring, 2001; The Lord of the Rings: The Two Towers, 2002; The Lord of the Rings: The Return of the King, Pirates of the Caribbean: Curse of the Black Pearl, 2003; Troy, The Calcium Kid, 2004; Kingdom of Heaven, Elizabethtown, 2005; Love and Other Disasters, Pirates of the Caribbean: Dead Man's Chest, Haven, 2006; Pirates of the Caribbean: At World's End, 2007; New York, I Love You, Sympathy for Delicious, Main Street, 2009; The Cross, 2010. TV appearances include: TV series "Casualty"; Midsomer Murders, Smack The Pony, 2000; The Saturday Show, 2001; So Graham Norton, 2002; The Tonight Show with Jay Leno, Primetime Live, V Graham Norton, 2003; The Brendan Leanard Show, Access Hollywood, 2003; GMTV, T4, 2004. Honours: Internet Movie Awards, 2002; Best Debut, Empire Award, 2002; MTV Movie Awards, 2002; Hollywood Discovery Awards; MTV Movie Awards, 2004; UNICEF Goodwill Ambassador, 2009.

BLOOMBERG Michael R, b. 14 February 1942, Medford, Massachusetts, USA. Mayor of the City of New York. Education: MBA, Harvard University. Appointments: Joined staff, 1966, Partner, 1972, Salmon Brothers, Wall Street; Established Bloomberg LP, 1982; Served on boards of 20 different civic, cultural, educational and medical institutions including: High School of Economics and Finance; Lincoln Center for the Performing Arts; Metropolitan Museum of Art; Police & Fire Widows' & Children's Benefits Fund; SLE (Lupus) Foundation and Prep for Prep. Publications: Bloomberg by Bloomberg, 1997. Honours: School of Hygiene and Public Health renamed The Bloomberg School of Public Health. Memberships: Chairman, Board of Trustees, Johns Hopkins University, -2002. Address: The Mayor's Press Office, City Hall, New York, NY 10007, USA.

BLOW DARLINGTON Joyce, b. 4 May 1929, Morecambe, England. Retired. m. J A B Darlington. Education: MA, University of Edinburgh. Appointments: Council of Industrial Design, 1953-63; Publicity and Advertising Manager, Heal & Son Ltd, 1963-65; Board of Trade, 1965-67; Monopolies Commission, 1967-70; Assistant Secretary, Department of Trade & Industry, 1970-72; Assistant Secretary, Department of Prices and Consumer Protection, 1972-74; Under-Secretary, Office of Fair Trading, 1977-80; Under Secretary, Department of Trade and Industry, 1980-84; Vice-President, Trading Standard Institute, 1985-; Chairman, Mail Order Publishers Authority, 1985-92; Chairman, Direct Marketing Association Authority, 1992-97; Board Member, 1987-97, Chairman, Consumer Policy Committee, 1987-93, British Standards Institution; Trustee, University of Edinburgh Development Trust, 1990-94; Chairman, East Sussex Family Health Services Authority, 1990-96; President, Association for Quality in Healthcare, 1991-94; Chairman, Public Relations Education Trust, 1992-97; Chairman, Child Accident Prevention Trust, 1996-2002. Publication: Consumers and International Trade: A Handbook, 1987. Honours: Freeman City of London, 1984; OBE, 1994. Memberships: Hon FCIPR; FCMI; FRSA. Address: 17 Fentiman Road, London SW8 1LD, England

BLUM Igor Robert, b. 24 October 1969, Frankfurt am Main, Germany. Dentist; Researcher, Educator. Education: DDS, Dental Surgery, Semmelweis University, Budapest, Hungary, 1990-95; MSc, Oral Surgery, 1995-97, PhD, Restorative Dentistry, 1998-2002, University of Manchester, UK; Dr Med Dent, (Magna cum laude), Dental Medicine, Goethe University of Frankfurt, Germany, 2000-2002. Appointments: Associate Clinician in Dental Implantology, 1998-2001, Associate Clinician in Oral Medicine, 1998-2001, University of Manchester, UK; Founder and Chief Executive Officer, Globaldentistry, 2002-05; Clinical Teacher in Oral Surgery, 2004-05, Clinical Teacher in Prosthodontics, 2004-05, University of Manchester, UK; Lecturer at international conferences; Lecturer in Restorative Dentistry, University of Bristol, England, 2005-. Publications: Numerous articles in scientific dental journals as author, first author and co-author include most recently: Contemporary views on dry socket (alveolar osteitis): A clinical appraisal of standardisation, aetiopathogenesis and management: a critical review, 2002; The teaching of the repair of direct composite restorations, 2002; The repair of direct composite restorations: an international survey of the teaching of operative techniques and materials, 2003; Defective direct composite restorations – replace or repair? A Comparison of teaching between Scandinavian dental schools, 2003. Honours: First Class Achievement for Oral Health Sciences Thesis, National Institute of Dentistry, 1995; Achievement in introducing a standardised definition for alveolar osteitis (dry socket) to the dental profession. Listed in Who's Who publications and biographical dictionaries. Memberships: Postgraduate Membership in Oral Surgery; Postgraduate Membership in Prosthodontics; General Dental Council, England; Hessian Dental Chamber of Germany; British Dental Association; Royal College of Surgeons of England; Royal College of Surgeons of Edinburgh; European Association of Osseointegration; Association of Dental Educators in Europe; International Association for Dental Research. Address: 109 Pinkers Mead, Emersons Green, Bristol BS16 7EJ, England.

BLUM Yehuda Zvi, b. 2 Oct 1931, Bratislava, Czechoslovakia. Professor. m. Moriah, 30 June 1966, 2 sons, 1 daughter. Education: MJur, Jerusalem, 1955; PhD, London, 1961. Appointments: Asst to Judge Advocate Gen, Israel Def Forces, 1956-59; Asst Legal Advsr, Israel Min, For Affairs, 1962-65; Lectr, Snr Lectr, Assoc Prof, Prof, Hebrew Univ, Jerusalem, 1965-; Amb, Perm Rep of Israel, UN, NY, 1978-84. Publications: Historic Titles in International Law, 1965; Secure Boundaries and Middle East Peace, 1971; For Zion's Sake, 1987; Eroding the United Nations Charter, 1993. Honours: Arlozorov Prize; Nordau Prize; Dr Jur, H C Yeshiva Univ, NY; Jabotinsky Prize. Memberships: Intl Law Assn; Amn Law Soc of Intl Law. Address: Faculty of Law, Hebrew University, Mount Scopus, Jerusalem, Israel.

BLUME Judy, b. 12 February 1938, Elizabeth, New Jersey, USA. Writer. m. (1) John M Blume, 1959, divorced 1975, 1 son, 1 daughter; (2) George Cooper, 1 stepdaughter. Education: New York University. Career: Founder and

Trustee, The Kids Fund, 1981; Author of non-fiction and juvenile and adult fiction. Publications: Juvenile: The One in the Middle is the Green Kangaroo, 1969; Iggie's House, 1970; Are You There God? It's Me, Margaret, 1970; Then Again, Maybe I Won't, 1971; Freckle Juice, 1971; It's Not the End of the World, 1972; Tales of a Fourth Grade Nothing, 1972; Otherwise Known as Sheila the Great, 1972; Deenie, 1973; Blubber, 1974; Forever, 1975; Starring Sally J Freedman as Herself, 1977; Superfudge, 1980; Tiger Eyes, 1981; The Pain and the Great One, 1984; Just As Long As We're Together, 1987; Fudge-a-mania, 1990; Here's to You, Rachel Robinson, 1993; Summer Sisters, 1998; Places I Never Meant to Be (editor), 1999; Double Fudge, 2002; Soupy Saturdays with the Pain and the Great One, 2007; Going, Going, Gone! With the Pain and the Great One, 2008; Adult: Wifey, 1978; Smart Women, 1983; Non-fiction: Letters to Judy: What Kids Wish They Could Tell You, 1986; The Judy Blue Memory Book, 1988. Honours: Honorary LHD, Kean College, 1987; Chicago Public Library Carl Sandburg Freedom to Read Award, 1984; American Civil Liberties Union Award, 1986; American Library Association Margaret A Edwards Award for Lifetime Achievement, 1996; National Book Foundation Medal for Distinguished Contribution to American Letters, 2004. Memberships: PEN Club; Authors' Guild; National Coalition Against Censorship; Society of Children's Book Writers. Address: Harold Ober Associates, 425 Madison Avenue, New York, NY 10017-1110, USA. Website: www.judyblume.com

BLUNKETT Rt Hon David, b. 6 June 1947, England. Politician. 3 sons. Education: Sheffield University. Appointments: Worker, East Midlands Gas Board; Teacher, Industrial Relations and Politics, Barnsley College of Technology; Joined Labour Party, 1963; Member, Sheffield City Council, 1970-87, Leader, 1980-87; Member, South Yorkshire County Council, 1973-77; MP for Sheffield Brightside, 1987-; National Executive Committee (NEC) of Labour Party, 1983; Chair, NEC Local Government Committee, 1984; Local Government Front Bench Spokesman in Opposition's Environment Team, 1988-92; Shadow Secretary of State for Health, 1992-94, for Education, 1994-95, for Education and Employment, 1995-97; Secretary of State for Education and Employment, 1997-2001, for the Home Department, 2001-04, for Work and Pensions, 2005 (resigned, 2005). Publications: Local Enterprise and Workers' Plans, 1981; Building From the Bottom: The Sheffield Experience, 1983; Democracy in Crisis: The Town Halls Respond, 1987; On a Clear Day (autobiography), 1995; Politics and Progress, 2001. Address: House of Commons, London SW1A 0AA, England.

BLYTHE Ronald George, b. 6 November 1922, Acton, Suffolk, England. Author. Appointments: Associate Editor, New Wessex Edition of the Works of Thomas Hardy, 1978. Publications: A Treasonable Growth, 1960; Immediate Possession, 1961; The Age of Illusion, 1963; Akenfield, 1969; William Hazlitt: Selected Writings, editor, 1970; The View in Winter, 1979; From the Headlands, 1982; The Stories of Ronald Blythe, 1985; Divine Landscapes, 1986; Each Returning Day, 1989; Private Words, 1991; Word from Wormingford, 1997; First Friends, 1998; Going to meet George, 1998; Talking About John Clare, 1999; Out of the Valley, 2000; The Circling Year, 2001; Talking to the Neighbours, 2002; The Assassin, 2004; Borderland, 2005; Field Work, 2007; Outsiders: A Book of Garden Friends, 2008; Aftermath, 2010; Critical Studies of Jane Austen, Thomas Hardy, Leo Tolstoy, Literature of the Second World War, Henry James; Contributions to: Observer; Sunday Times; New York Times; Listener; Atlantic Monthly; London Magazine; Tablet; New Statesman; Bottegue Oscure; Guardian; Church Times. Honours: Heinemann Award, 1969; Society of Authors Travel Scholarship, 1971; Angel Prize for Literature, 1986; Honorary MA, University of East Anglia, 1991; Hon DLitt, Anglia Ruskin University, 2001; MLitt, Lambeth; Hon DLitt, University of Essex, 2002; Lay Canon, St Edmundsbury Cathedral, 2003; Benson Medal for Literature, 2006. Memberships: Fellow, Royal Society of Literature; Society of Authors; President, The John Clare Society; President, The Robert Bloomfield Society; President, The Kilvert Society; Vice President, The Hazlitt Society; Lay Canon, St Edmundsbury Cathedral. Address: Bottengoms Farm, Wormingford, Colchester, Essex, England.

BNINSKI Kazimierz Andrzej, b. 28 February 1939, Gdynia, Poland. Physician in General Practice. m. Teresa Maria de Gallen Bisping, 2 July 1988, 2 sons, 1 daughter. Education: MD, University of Gdansk, Poland, 1964. Appointments: Senior House Officer, Nelson Hospital, London, England, 1967; Senior House Officer, St Mary Abbots Hospital, London, England, 1968; Registrar in Medicine, St Mary's Hospital, 1972-77; Physician, 7th US Army, Germany, 1977-81; Junior Partner, General Practice, 1981-87; Senior Doctor, Director-in-Charge Polish Clinic, London, 1988-. Memberships: Fellow, Royal Society of Medicine, London, 2008. Address: 17 Childs Place, London SW5 9RX, England.

BOATENG Paul (Yaw), b. 14 June 1951, Hackney, England. Diplomatist; Politician; Lawyer; Broadcaster. m. Janet Alleyne, 1980, 2 sons, 3 daughters. Education: Ghana International School; Accra Academy; Apsley Grammar School; University of Bristol. Appointments: Solicitor, Paddington Law Centre, 1976-79; Solicitor and Partner, B M Birnberg & Co, 1979-87; Called to the Bar, Gray's Inn, 1989; Legal Adviser, Scrap Sus Campaign, 1977-81; Member, GLC (Labour) for Walthamstow, 1981-86; Chair, Police Committee, 1981-86; Vice-Chair, Ethnic Minorities Committee, 1981-86; MP (Labour) for Brent South, 1987-2005; Home Office Member, House of Commons Environment Committee, 1987-89; Opposition Frontbench Spokesman on Treasury and Economic Affairs, 1989-92, on Legal Affairs, Lord Chancellor's Department, 1992-97; Parliamentary Under-Secretary of State, Department of Health, 1997-98; Minister of State, 1998-2001; Deputy Home Secretary, 1999-2001; Minister for Young People, 2000-01; Finanical Secretary to HM Treasury, 2001-02; Chief Secretary, 2002-05; High Commissioner to South Africa, 2005-09. Publications: Reclaiming the Ground (contributor), 1993. Memberships: Chair, Afro-Caribbean Education Resource Project, 1978-86, Westminster CRC, 1978-81; Govenor Police Staff College, Bramshill, 1981-84; Member, Home Secretary's Advisory Council on Race Relations, 1981-86; WCC Commission on Programme to Combat Racism, 1984-91; Police Training Council, 1981-85; Executive, National Council for Civil Liberties, 1980-86; Member, Court of University of Bristol, 1994-; Member, Board ENO, 1984-97. Address: High Commission of the United Kingdom, 255 Hill Street, Arcadia, Pretoria 0002, South Africa. Website: www.britain.org.za

BOBIER Claude-Abel, b. 18 March 1934, France. m. Manissier Arlette, 4 September 1959, 3 daughters. Education: BS, 1953; ENS St Cloud, 1956-60; Agreg SN, 1960; Doctor, 1971. Appointments: University of Paris VI, 1960-75; Professor, University of Tunis, 1975-86; MC University of Bordeaux I, 1986-99; Retired as Consultant, 1999. Publications include: Les éléments structuraux recents essentiels de la Tunisie nord-orientale, 1983; Morphologie de la marge Caraibe Colombienne: Relation avec la structure et la sedimentation, 1991; The Post-Triassic Sedimentary

Cover of Tunisa: Seismic Sequences and Structure, 1991; Apports de l'analyse morphostructurale dans la connaissance de la physiographie du golfe de Tehuantepec (Mexique est-pacifique), 1993; Sequence stratigraphy, Basin dynamics and Petroleum geology of the Miocene from Eastern Tunisia, 1996; Recent tectonic activity in the South Barbados Prism. Deep towed side scan sonar imagery, 1998; Distribution des sédiments sur la marge du Golfe de Tehuantepec (Pacifique oriental). Example d'interaction tectonique-eustatisme, 2000; Rôle de l'halocinese dans l'evolution du Bassin d'Essaouira/Sud Ouest Morocain), 2004; Rôle du systeme de failles E-W dans l'evolution geódynamique de l'Avant Pays de la chaîne alpine de Tunisie. Example de l'accident de Sbiba-Cherishira Tunisie Centrale, 2003; The role of shearing on the sedimentary and morphostructural evolution of the southern part of the Barbados ridge at the Latitude of Trinidad. Honour: International Ambassador's Order, 1998. Memberships: American Geophysical Union; Past Member, American Association of Petrololeum Geololgists; Past Member, New York Academy of Sciences. Address: 6 Square du Gue, F-33170 Gradignan, France.

BOBKO Nataliya Andreyevna, b. 30 November 1960, Kiev, Ukraine. Psychophysiologist. Education: Biologist-Physiologist of Humans and Animals, Teacher of Biology and Chemistry (MSc equivalent), Biological Department, Kiev State University, 1982; Candidate of Biological Science, Hygiene (PhD equivalent), Kiev Research Institute of Labour Hygiene and Occupational Diseases, 1992. Appointments: Senior High-Educated Laboratory Assistant, 1982-84, Junior Research Scientist, 1984-85, Laboratory of Mental Labour Physiology, Junior Research Scientist, 1985-91, Research Scientist, Laboratory of Labour Physiology of Process Operators, 1991-92, Senior Research Scientist, Laboratory of Chronobiology Problems in Labour, 1992-95, Senior Research Scientist, Laboratory of Mental Labour Physiology, 1995-2011, Laboratory of Shift Work Hygiene and Physiology, 2011-, Department of Labour Physiology, Institute for Occupational Health, Kiev, Ukraine (before 1992, Kiev Research Institute of Labour Hygiene and Occupational Diseases). Publications: Over 160 publications in national and international peer reviewed journals, collections and presented at conferences as author and co-author include most recently: Time-of-day and time-of-duty effects on human-operator cognitive performance under time pressure, 2009; Age changes in cognitive activity and blood circulation of human-operator of the tense shift work, 2010; Workload dynamics and its reflection in parameters of functional state in electricity distribution network controllers, 2010; Ergonomic characters of labour of unit machinists at the thermal power plants of Ukraine in the dynamics of industry restructuring in 1990-2010 years, 2011; Labour tension as the leading harmful ergonomic factor in control room shiftworkers at the modern technological processes in electric energy, 2011. Honours: 15 travel grants to attend international congresses, symposiums and conferences, 1995-2011; International Peace Prize, 2005, 2006, 2007, 2009; American Medal of Honour, 2005, 2006; Gold Medal for the Ukraine, 2006, 2008, 2009; Invitation for induction into both the American Order of Merit and Hall of Fame, 2009; Title: Senior Research Scientist (Associate Professor equivalent), Institute for Occupational Health, Kiev, Ukraine, 1994; International Scientist of the Year, 2002, 2007; Woman of the Year, 2005, 2006, 2007, 2009; Great Woman of the Year, 2008; Woman of Achievement, 2006; Listed in many international biographical directories. Memberships: International Commission on Occupational Health, 2001-; National Secretary to Ukraine; Member, Joint Board of Shiftwork and Working Time Committee and Working Time Society; Member, Scientific Committee on Neurotoxicology and Psychophysiology; Member, Sigma Xi, The Scientific Research Society, USA, 2002-; Patents: 2001, 2003, 2004, 2010, 2011. Address: Institute for Occupational Health, Saksagansky St 75, Kiev, 01033 Ukraine. E-mail: nbobko@bigmir.net

BOCELLI Andrea, b. 22 September 1958, Lajatico, Pisa, Italy. Singer (tenor). m. Enrica, 1992, divorced 2002, 2 sons. Recordings: Albums: Bocelli, Viaggio Italiano, 1995; Romanza, 1997; Aria, 1998; Sogno, Sacred Arias, 1999; Verdi, La Boheme, 2000; Cieli di Toscana, 2001; Cieli di Toscana, Verdi Requiem, 2001; Sentimento, 2002; Tosca, 2003; Il trovatore, Andrea, 2004; Werther, 2005; Amore, Leoncavallo: Pagliacci, 2006; The Best of Andrea Bocelli: Vivere, 2007; Incanto, 2008; My Christmas, 2009; numerous singles. Honours: Winner (Newcomers Section), Sanremo Music Festival, 1994; ECHO Award, 1997; 3 ECHO Klassiks, 1997, 1998, 2000; 6 World Music Awards, 1998, 2002, 2006; Classical BRIT Award, 2000; Goldene Europa, 2000; Platinum Europe Award, 2001; Special award, Federation of the Italian Music Industry, 2001; Goldene Kamera Award, 2002; 2 Telegatto Awards, 2002, 2008; Classical BRIT Award, 2002; 2 Classical BRIT Awards, 2003; Diamond CD, 2004; 4 times Diamond Disc, 2009. Address: MT Opera and Blues Production and Management, via Irnerio 16, 40162 Bologna, Italy. Website: www.andreabocelli.org

BOCHMANN Christopher Consitt, b. 8 November 1950, Chipping Norton, Oxfordshire, England. Musician; Composer; Teacher; Conductor. m. Celia Williams, 2 daughters. Education: Teacher, Escola de Musica de Brasilia, Brazil, 1978-80; Composition Teacher, 1984-2006, Head of Composition, 1990-2006, Director, 1995-2001, Escola Superior de Musica de Lisboa, Portugal; Full Professor, 2006-, Dean of the Arts, 2009-, University of Evora, Portugal. Publications: Articles in professional journals. Honours: Medal of Cultural Merit, Ministry of Culture, Portugal, 2004; OBE, 2005. Memberships: Performing Rights Society. Address: R 23, No 32, Bairro da Encarnacao, 1800-374 Lisboa, Portugal. E-mail: bochmann@uevora.pt Website: www.christopherbochmann.com

BODO Michael, b. 10 September 1947, Debrecen, Hungary. Research Scientist. m. Janice Meer, 1 son, 4 daughters. Education: MD, Semmelweis University Medical School, Budapest, 1972; Student in Psychology, University of Eotvos L, Budapest, 1971-72; PhD, Biology, Sechenov Institute of Evolutionary Physiology & Biochemistry, Academy of Sciences of the USSR, 1990. Appointments: Fellow, Electroencephalographer, National Institute of Neurosurgery, Budapest, 1972-78; Research Associate, Department of Psychophysiology, Institute of Psychology, Hungarian Academy of Sciences, 1979-83; Research Associate, Department of Neurophysiology, 1984-92, Product Manager, Department of Strategic Marketing, 1993, Chemical Works of G Richter Ltd, Budapest; Visiting Scholar and Research Associate, Department of Neurology, University of Miami School of Medicine, Miami, Florida, USA, 1993-96; Consultant, Life Resuscitation Technologies Inc, Chicago, Illinois, USA, 1996-98; Consultant, National Naval Medical Center, NMRI, Bethesda, Maryland, USA, 1996-97; Director, Medical Research and Development, AHTC, Fairfax, Virginia, USA, 1997-99; Senior Research Associate, 2000-03; Senior Staff Scientist, 2004-09, Department of Resuscitative Medicine, Walter Reed Army Institute of Research, Silver Spring, Maryland; Senior Scientist, Naval Medical Research Center, Silver Spring, Maryland, 2010-. Publications: 18

book chapters; 40 journal articles; 113 abstracts; 5 medical electronics patents; 27 chemical patents; 4 copyrights. Honours: President's Award, Hungarian Academy of Sciences, Budapest, 1980; Award, French Minister of Scientific Research, Concours Lepine, Paris, 1993; 2 Teaching Awards, Walter Reed Army Institute of Research, 2001 and 2002; Medal of US Army Medical Command, 2008. Memberships: International Society for Cerebral Blood Flow and Metabolism; World Stroke Organization; International Society for Electrical Bio-Impedance. Address: Naval Medical Research Center, Undersea Medicine Department, 503 Robert Grant Avenue, Silver Spring, MD 20910-7500, USA. E-mail: michael.bodo@med.navy.mil

BOE Grethe, b. 11 March 1958, Oslo, Norway. Systems Engineer; Editor; Webmaster. m. Oyvind K Myhre, 1 son, 1 daughter. Education: BA, English (major), Political Science, Astronomy, University of Oslo, 1982. Appointments: Systems Engineer, IBM, Norway, 1983-92; Freelance Computer Consultant, 1992-. Honours: IBM Professional Excellence Award, 1986; IBM Professional Marketing Award, 1988, 1990; Listed in various Who's Who publications and biographical dictionaries. Address: Skolebakken 5, 2750 Gran, Norway. E-mail: gboee@online.no

BOERSMA Lawrence Allan (Larry Allan), b. 24 April 1932, London, Ontario, Canada. Animal Advocate. m. June E Boersma, 3 sons, 1 daughter. Education: BA, 1953, MS, 1955, University of Nebraska, Omaha; PhD, Sussex, 1972; Postdoctoral Study, University of Oxford, 1996; ScD (hon), University of Berkeley. Appointments include: Journalism Teacher, Technical High School, Omaha, Nebraska, 1953-55; Director of Public Relations and Chair, Journalism Department, Adams State College, Alamosa, Colorado, 1955-59; Advertising Executive, Better Homes and Gardens, 1959-63; Account Executive, This Week Magazine, 1963-66; Eastern Sales Director and Marketing Director, Ladies Home Journal, 1966-75; Vice-President, Publisher, The Country Gentleman, Vice-President, Associate Publisher, Saturday Evening Post, 1975; Vice-President, Director, Marketing and Advertising Sales, Photo World Magazine, 1975-77; Advertising Manager, La Jolla Light, 1977-80; Owner, Photographer, Allan-The Animal Photographers, San Diego and Sarasota, 1980-; President, Chief Executive Officer, The Photographic Institute International, 1982-86; Director of Development and Community Relations, San Diego Humane Society/Society for the Prevention of Cruelty to Animals, 1985-94; Associate Executive Director, The Centre for Humane Education for Southern California, 1994-98; Owner, Animal Art, San Diego and Sarasota, 1999-; Chairman and Chief Executive Officer, International Dolphin Project; Chairman, Chief Executive Officer & Advocate-General, Preserve Our Wildlife Organisation; California State Humane Officer; Volunteer/Consultant, The Raptor Center, College of Veterinary Medicine, University of Minnesota, 2008-. Publications: Numerous wildlife books include: Wildcats of North America Series – Bobcat, Cougar, Feral Cat, Lynx, 1998; Wild Canines of North America Series – Coyote, Foxes and Wolf, 2000; Creative Canine Photography, 2004; ASPCA Guide to Cats; Keep Wild Animals in Our Lives, 2005; The Dove Family Tale, 2008; ASPCA Guide to Dogs; Little Lost Mountain Lion, 2009; Wildlife/Environmental Columnist Venice (FL) Gondolier Sun, 2005-09; Photographs appear in numerous magazines, calendars, greeting cards and other printed media, DVDs and motion pictures. Honours include: Fellow Royal Photographic Society of Great Britain; Award of Appreciation, Committee for a Cruelty Free California; Gold Mercury Award, International Academy of Communication Arts and Sciences; Finalist, International Wildlife Photographer of the Year, British Natural History Museum and the BBC, 2003; Ansel Adams Award, Sierra Club, 2005; Lifetime Achievement Award, University of Nebraska/Omaha, 2007; Sierran of the Month, Sierra Club, 2007; Executive Board, Southwest Florida Council, Boy Scouts of America, 2010; Master of Photography and Photographic Craftsman awards; Professional Photographers of America; Fellow, Professional Photographers of California. Memberships include: Society of Animal Welfare Administrators; National Society of Fund Raising Executives; Public Relations Society of America; Defenders of Wildlife; Sierra Club; Masons; Natural Resources Defense Council; Center for Biological Diversity; Audubon Society. Address: 4238 65th Terrace East, Sarasota, FL 34243, USA.

BOEV Zlatozar Nikolaev, b. 20 October 1955, Sofia, Bulgaria. Zoologist; Ornithologist. m. Education: Graduate, Department of Zoology of the Vertebrate Animals, Faculty of Biology, University of Sofia, 1975-80; Postgraduate, Zoology Department, National Museum of Natural History, 1984-86. Appointments: Doctor of Philosophy, 1986; Associate Professor, 1992; Doctor of Sciences, 1999; Professor of Zoology, 2001. Publications: Over 256 papers in scientific journals chiefly on fossil and sub-fossil birds; Over 289 articles in popular science journals; 5 textbooks; 13 popular books; Over 20 translated foreign popular books; 17 countries in Europe, North America and Asia. Memberships include: Society of Avian Palaeontology and Evolution; International Council for Archaeology; Society of European Avian Curators; Association for Environmental Archaeology; Ethnoornithology Research and Study Group. Address: National Museum of Natural History, Bulgarian Academy of Sciences, 1 Blvd Tsar Osvoboditel, 1000 Sofia, Bulgaria. E-mail: boev@mnmhs.com

BOGDANOFF Stewart R, b. 16 August 1940, London, England. Educator. m. Eileen Dolan, 1 son, 2 daughters. Education: BSc, Kings College, Briarcliff Manor, New York, 1963; MA and Professional Degree, New York University, 1965; Graduate Work NYU, SUNY New Platz, Harvard University, 1972-; Certificate in Administration and Supervision, 1988. Appointments: Coach, intramural director, curriculum writer, fundraiser Thomas Jefferson Elementary School, Lakeland School District, 1965-96; Physical Education Teacher, Lakeland School District, 1965-96; Head Teacher, Thomas Jefferson Elementary School, Lakeland School District, 1984-96; Acting Principal, Thomas Jefferson Elementary School, 1985-86; Educational Consultant, Speaker, Writer, 1996-. Honours include: New York State Teacher of Year, honoured at White House by President Reagan, 1983; Project Inspiration Award, National Association for Sport and Physical Education, 1992; Point of Light Award, President Bush, 1992; International Man of Year Award and Men of Achievement Award, International Biographical Centre, England, 1993; 1st teacher from NYS inducted into National Teachers Hall of Fame, Emporia, Kansas, honoured by President Clinton at Rose Garden Ceremony; Scholarship in name of Stewart Bogdanoff established by Servicemaster, 1993; Founders 2000 Award from American Alliance for Health, Physical Education Recreation and Dance with room dedicated in his honour, National Center in Reston, Virginia, 1995; J C Penny Golden Rule Award, Westchester County United Way Volunteer of Year, 1995; Inducted into Briarcliff High School Hall of Distinguished Alumni, 1995; Golden Years Award, New York State Association for Health, Physical Education, Recreation and Dance; Selected as one of the Fifty Most Influential People in Westchester and Putnam

Counties during the 20th Century, Journal News; American Medal of Honor, ABI, 2003; Inducted into King's College Hall of Distinguished Alumni, 2005; Listed in numerous Who's Who and biographical publications including: Who's Who in American Education; Contemporary Who's Who, ABI, 2003; Great Minds of the 21st Century, ABI, 2003-04; Top 100 Teachers in the World, 2006; International Peace Prize, 2010. Memberships include: Kappa Delta Pi; New York State Teachers of the Year; Harvard Principals Center, others. Address: 402 Villa Court, Carmel, NY 10512, USA.

BOGDANOV Faik Gasanovich, b. 28 November 1956, Tbilisi, Georgia. Radiophysicist; Scientist, Lecturer. m. Leila Z Gamidova, 2 sons. Education: MS, Radiophysics, Tbilisi State University, 1978; PhD, Physics and Mathematics, 1983; Doctor of Science, Physics and Mathematics, 1993. Appointments: Scientist, Senior Engineer, Senior Scientist, 1980-82, Senior Scientist, Laboratory of Applied Electrodynamics, 1996-2001, Tbilisi State University, Tbilisi; Senior Scientist, Institute of Space Construction, Tbilisi, 1983-90; Associate Professor, 1984-93, Professor, 1994-2003, Full Professor, 2003-, Georgian Technical University; Senior Scientist, TriD Team Manager, Senior Scientist, EM Software and Consulting (EMCoS), Tbilisi, 2001-. Publications: 1 monograph; 7 textbooks; 2 book chapters; 60 referred journal papers; 45 conference proceeding papers; 20 conference abstracts. Honours: State Education Ministry's prize for best student scientific work, 1978; Georgian Republic Education Ministry's Special Prize for best scientific-methodical work, 1989; International Scientific Foundation personal scientific Grant, 1994; International Scientific Foundation personal educational Grants, 1996, 1997, 1998, 1999. Memberships: IEEE; ED/MTT/AP Societies; Dissertation Councils of Georgian Technical University. E-mail: faik.bogdanov@emcos.com

BOGDANOVICH Peter, b. 30 July 1939, Kingston, New York, USA. Film Director; Writer; Producer; Actor. m. (1) Polly Platt, 1962, divorced 1970, 2 daughters, (2) L B Straten, 1988, divorced 2001. Appointments: Film Feature-Writer, Esquire, New York Times, Village Voice, Cahiers du Cinema, Los Angeles Times, New York Magazine, Vogue, Variety and others, 1961-. Publications: The Cinema of Orson Welles, 1961; The Cinema of Howard Hawks, 1962; The Cinema of Alfred Hitchcock, 1963; John Ford, 1968; Fritz Lang in America, 1969; Allan Dwan: The Last Pioneer, 1971; Pieces of Time: Peter Bogdanovich on the Movies (in UK as Picture Shows), 1961, enlarged edition, 1985; The Killing of the Unicorn: Dorothy Stratten (1960-1980), 1984; A Year and a Day Calendar (editor), 1991; This is Orson Welles, 1992; Who the Devil Made It, 1997; Who the Hell's In It? 2004. Films: The Wild Angels, 1966; Targets, 1968; The Last Picture Show, 1971; What's Up Doc? 1972; Paper Moon, 1973; Daisy Miller, 1974; At Long Last Love, 1975; Nickelodeon, 1976; Saint Jack, 1979; They All Laughed, 1981; Mask, 1985; Illegally Yours, 1988; Texasville, 1990; Noises Off, 1992; The Thing Called Love, 1993; Who The Devil Made It (director), Mr Jealousy, Highball, 1997; Coming Soon, 1999; Rated X, The Independent, 2000; The Cat's Meow (director), Scene Stealer (actor), 2003; Hustle, 2004; The Sopranos, (1999-2007); Infamous, 2006; Dedication, Runnin' Down a Dream, 2007; Humboldt County, 2008. Honours: New York Film Critics' Award for Best Screenplay, British Academy Award for Best Screenplay, 1971; Writer's Guild of America Award for Best Screenplay, 1972; Silver Shell, Mar del Plata, Spain, 1973; Best Director, Brussels Festival, 1974; Pasinetti Award, Critic Prize, Venice Festival, 1979. Memberships: Directors Guild of America; Writer's Guild of America; Academy of Motion Picture Arts and Sciences. Address: c/o William Pfeiffer, 30 Lane of Acres, Haddonfield, NJ 08033, USA.

BOGLE Joanna Margaret, (Julia Blythe), b. 7 September 1952, Carshalton, Surrey, England. Author; Journalist. m. James Stewart Lockhart Bogle, 1980. Education: St Philomena's School, Carshalton. Appointments: Local Borough Councillor, London Borough of Sutton, 1974-81; Governor, London Oratory School, 1976-86. Publications: A Book of Feasts and Seasons, 1986; When the Summer Ended (with Cecylia Wolkowinska), 1991; A Heart for Europe (with James Bogle), 1992; Caroline Chisholm, 1993; Come On In - It's Awful!, editor, 1994; We Didn't Mean to Start a School, 1998; The Pope Benedict Code, 2006; A Nun with a Difference, 2009; English Catholic Heroines (editor), 2010; Contributions to: local newspapers, 1970-74; South London News, 1984-86; Catholic Times, 1994-; Various newspapers in Britain, the USA and Australia, 1980-; Broadcaster, Eternal World Television Network, 2000-. Address: Christian Projects, PO Box 44741, London SWIP 2XA, England.

BOGOROSH Alexander Terentyvitch, b. 3 January 1946, Maykop, Russia. Physicist. m. Svetlana, 1 son, 1 daughter. Education: Kyiv National University, 1972; PhD, Moscow State University, 1977; Technology Institute, 1996; Full Doctor, Israeli Independent Academy for Development of Sciences, 2008. Publications: 12 monographs; 3 textbooks; More than 750 articles; 57 patents. Honours: Diplomas of Russian Academy of Sciences; Israeli Independent Academy for Development of Sciences. Memberships: Russian Academy of Sciences; Israeli Independent Academy for Development of Sciences. Address: 24 Lunacharskogo St, Apt 107, Kiev 02002, Ukraine. E-mail: fondfti@kpi.ua

BOICE Martha Hibbert, b. 1 October 1931, Toledo, Ohio, USA. Writer; Publisher. m. William V Boice, 1 son, 2 daughters. Education: BA, Ohio Wesleyan University, 1953; MSW, University of Michigan School of Social Work, 1955. Appointments: Caseworker, Travelers Aid, Toledo, Ohio, 1955-57; Publisher, Knot Garden Press, Dayton, Ohio, 1986-. Publications: Organiser, compiler, A Sense of Place, 1977; Author, compiler, Shaker Herbal Fare, 1985; The Wreath Maker, 1987; The Herbal Rosa, 1990; Maps of the Shaker West, 1997; Columnist, Centerville-Bellbrook Times, 1984. Honours: Distinguished Service Award, National Association of Monnett Clubs, Ohio Wesleyan University, 1974; Volunteer of the Year, Dayton-Montgomery County Park District, 1985; Centerville, Ohio' Mayor's Award for Community Service, 1988; Award of Excellence, OAHSM, 1998; Listed in biographical publications. Memberships: Phi Beta Kappa; Centerville-Washington Township Historical Society, Landmark Chair, 1972-78, 1980-84, 1997-2000; Landmarks Foundation of Centerville-Washington Township, Trustee, 1995-2008, Chair, 1997-2001; Herb Society of America, Library Committee Chair, 1988-1991; Western Shaker Study Group, Program Chair, 1988-91, 2003-04, Secretary, 1992-94, 2001, Chair, 2005-06; Dayton-Montgomery County Bicentennial Literature Committee Chair, 1994-96; Friends of White Water Shaker Village, Director, 2002-08, Secretary, 2004-06, Membership Chair, 2004-08. Address: 7712 Eagle Creek Drive, Dayton, OH 45459, USA. E-mail: marthaboice@aol.com

BOKSENBERG Alexander, b. 18 March 1936. Astronomer. m. Adella Coren, 1960, 1 son, 1 daughter. Education: BSc, Physics, University of London; PhD, 1961. Appointments: SRC Research Assistant, Department of Physics and

Astronomy, University College London, 1960-65; Lecturer in Physics, 1965-75; Head of Optical and Ultraviolet Astronomy Research Group, 1969-81; Reader in Physics, 1975-78; SRC Senior Fellow, 1976-81; Professor of Physics and Astronomy, 1978-81; Sherman Fairchild Distinguished Scholar, California Institute of Technology, 1981-82; Director, Royal Greenwich Observatory, 1981-93; Royal Observatories, 1993-96; Research Professor, University of Cambridge and PPARC Senior Research Fellow, Universities of Cambridge and London, 1996-; Extraordinary Fellow, Churchill College, Cambridge, 1996-, member of Council, 1998-2003. Honours: Chair, New Industrial Concepts Ltd, 1969-81; President, West London Astronomical Society, 1978-; Chair, SRC Astronomy Committee, 1980-81; Numerous other committees on astronomy, 1980-; Visiting Professor, Department of Physics and Astronomy, University College, London, 1981-, Astronomy Center, University of Sussex, 1981-89; Honorary Doctorate, Paris Observatory, 1982; Asteroid (3205) named Boksenberg, 1988; Honorary Professor of Experimental Astronomy, University of Cambridge, 1991-; Hon DSc (Sussex), 1991; Executive Editor, Experimental Astronomy, 1995-; Honorary President, Astronomical Society of Glasgow; Hannah Jackson Medal, 1998; Hughes Medal, Royal Society, 1999; Glazebrook Medal and Prize, 2000. Membership: Past member of over 30 other councils, boards, committees, etc, 1970-; ESA Hubble Space Telescope Instrument Definition Team, 1973-; Fellow, Royal Society, 1978; SA Astronomical Observatory Advisory Committee, 1978-85; Freeman, Clockmakers Co, 1984; British Council Science Advisory Committee, 1987-91; Liveryman, 1989; Fachbeirat of Max Planck Institut für Astronomie, 1991-95; Fellow, University College, London, 1991-; Member of Court, 1994. Address: University of Cambridge, Institute of Astronomy, The Observatories, Madingley Road, Cambridge, CB3 0HA, England.

BOLGER Dermot, b. 6 February 1959, Finglas, Ireland. Novelist; Dramatist; Poet; Editor. m. Bernadette Clifton, 1988, 2 sons. Education: Finglas and Benevin College, Finglas. Appointments: Factory hand, library assistant, professor author; Founder and Editor, Raven Arts Press, 1979-92; Founder and Executive Editor, New Island Books, Dublin, 1992-. Publications: Novels: Night Shift, 1985; The Woman's Daughter, 1987, augmented edition, 1991; The Journey Home, 1990; Emily's Shoes, 1992; A Second Life, 1994; Father's Music, Finbar's Hotel (collaborative novel), 1997; Ladies Night at Finbar's Hotel (collaborative novel), 1999; Temptation, 2000; The Valparaiso Voyage, 2001; The Family on Paradise Pier, 2005. Plays: The Lament for Arthur Cleary, 1989; Blinded by the Light, In High Germany, The Holy Ground, 1990; One Last White Horse, 1991; The Dublin Bloom, 1994; April Bright, 1995; The Passion of Jerome, 1999; Consenting Adults, 2000; From These Green Heights, 2005; The Townlands of Brazil, 2006; Walking the Road, 2007; Ranelagh Bus, 2007; The Consequences of Lightning, 2008. Poetry: The Habit of Flesh, 1979; Finglas Lilies, 1980; No Waiting America, 1981; Internal Exiles, 1986; Leinster Street Ghosts, 1989; Taking My Letters Back: New and Selected Poems, 1998; The Chosen Moment, 2004; External Affairs, 2008. Editor: The Dolmen Book of Irish Christmas Stories, The Bright Wave: Poetry in Irish Now, 1986; 16 on 16: Irish Writers on the Easter Rising, Invisible Cities: The New Dubliners: A Journey through Unofficial Dublin, 1988; Invisible Dublin: A Journey through Its Writers, 1992; The Picador Book of Contemporary Irish Fiction, 12 Bar Blues (with Aidan Murphy), 1993; The New Picador Book of Contemporary Irish Fiction, 2000; Druids, Dudes and Beauty Queens: The Changing Face of Irish Theatre, 2001. Contributions to: Anthologies. Honours: A E Memorial Prize, 1986; Macauley Fellowship, 1987; A Z Whitehead Prize, 1987; Samuel Beckett Award, 1991; Edinburgh Fringe First Award, 1991, 1995; Stewart Parker BBC Award, 1991; Playwright in Association, Abbey Theatre, Dublin, 1998; Writer Fellow, Trinity College, Dublin, 2003. Address: c/o A P Watt, 20 John Street, London WC1N 2DR, England.

BOLKIAH MU'IZUDDIN WADDAULAH, HM Sultan Sir Muda Hassanal, b. 15 July 1946, Brunei. m. (1) Rajah Isteri Anak Saleha, 1965-, 2 sons, 4 daughters, (2) Pengiran Isteri Hajjah Mariam, divorced 2003, 2 sons, 2 daughters, (3) Azrinaz Mazhar Hakim, 2005, 1 son, 1 daughter. Education: Victoria Institute, Kuala Lumpur, Malaysia; Royal Military Academy, Sandhurst, England. Appointments: Crown Prince and Heir Apparent, 1961; Ruler of State of Brunei, 1967-; Prime Minister of Brunei, 1984-; Minister of Finance and Home Affairs, 1984-86, of Defence, 1986-, also Finance and Law. Honours include: Honorary Captain, Coldstream Guards, 1968; Honorary Marshall, RAF, 1992; Sovereign and Chief of Royal Orders, Sultans of Brunei; Honoray Doctor of Law, University of Oxford; Honorary Doctor of Letters, University of Aberdeen, Scotland; Honorary Doctorate, Chulalongkorn University, Thailand; Honorary Doctorate in Humanities and Culture, Gadjah Mada University, 2003; Honorary Doctor of Laws, National University of Singapore, 2005. Address: Istana Darul Hana, Bandar Seri Begawan, BA 1000, Brunei. E-mail: pro@jpm.gov.bn

BOLSHAKOV Vladimir Ivanovich, b. 13 May 1946, Dniepropetrovsk, Ukraine. m. Iryna Rossykhyna. Professor. Education: Graduate, Technology Faculty, Dniepropetrovsk Metallurgical Institute, 1969; PhD, Moscow Institute of Civil Engineering, 1973; Dr Sc, 1985. Appointments: Forge and Shop, Dniepropetrovsk Steam Locomotive Repair Plant, 1963; Junior Research Worker, Dniepropetrovsk Institute of Civil Engineering; Professor, Doctor, Technical Sciences, 1985-, Head, Metal Technology Department, 1986-, Rector, Pridneprovskaya State Academy, 1987-. Publications: Over 1350 scientific works including 62 monographs, methodical books and brochures; 230 USSR author certificates and Ukrainian patents. Honours: Officer of French Order of Palm Branch, 1994; State Prizewinner, Ukraine, 1999; The Order for Public Service, 2000; Honoured Engineer of Russia, 2000; Listed in international biographical reference works. Memberships: Academy of Higher Education, International Engineering Academy, Moscow; Society of Ferrous Metals, USA; Royal Institute of Materials, London; European Society of Mathematicians & Mechanics, Germany.

BOLSHOV Leonid Aleksandrovich, b. 23 July 1946, Moscow, Russia. Physicist. m. Anna, 1 son, 2 daughters. Education: MV Lomonosov Moscow State University, 1964-70; PhD, Physics and Mathematics, 1973; Doctoral thesis, Physics and Mathematics, 1982; Professor, Physical Electronics specialisation, 1985; Corresponding Member, Russian Academy of Sciences, Energy Division, 1997. Appointments: Junior Researcher, I V Kurchatov Institute of Atomic Energy, 1970-73; Senior Researcher, Head of Laboratory, Branch of I V Kurchatov Institute of Atomic Energy, 1973-91; Director, Nuclear Safety Institute, Russian Academy of Sciences, 1991-. Publications: Author and co-author of more than 300 scientific works including monographs: Effect of Laser radiation on materials, 1989; Magnetic fields in laser plasma, 1991; Physical models of NPP severe accidents, 1992; Papers in leading professional journals. Honours: Laureate of USSR State Prize, Science & Engineering, 1988; Order of Courage for Participation in Elimination of Chernobyl Accident, 1997. Memberships: SAYNE, IAEA; Co-chair, JCCRER Agreement Executive Committee; EBRA Safety Review Group; Scientific Secretary of Joint US-RF Academies Committee; and others. Address: 52 Bolshaya Tulskaya Str, Moscow 115131, Russia. E-mail: bolshov@ibrae.ac.ru Website: www.brae.ac.ru

BOLT Usain St Leo, b. 21 August 1986, Jamaica. Sprinter. Career includes: Gold medals: Olympic Games: 4x100m relay, 200m, 100m, Beijing, 2008; 4x100m relay, 200m, 100m, London, 2012; World Championships: 4x100m relay, 200m, 100m, Berlin, 2009; 4x100m relay, 200m, Daegu, 2011. Honours: IAAF World Athlete of the Year, 2008, 2009; Track and Field Athlete of the Year, 2008, 2009; Laureus Sportsman of the Year, 2009, 2010; BBC Overseas Sports Personality of the Year, 2008, 2009.

BOND (Thomas) Michael, b. 13 January 1926, Newbury, Berkshire, England. Author. m. (1) Brenda May Johnson, 1950, divorced 1981, 1 son, 1 daughter; (2) Susan Rogers, 1981. Education: Presentation College, 1934-40. Publications: Children's Books: A Bear Called Paddington, 1958; More About Paddington, 1959; Paddington Helps Out, 1960; Paddington Abroad, 1961; Paddington at Large, 1962; Paddington Marches On, 1964; Paddington at Work, Here Comes Thursday, 1966; Thursday Rides Again, Paddington Goes to Town, 1968; Thursday Ahoy, Parsley's Tail, Parsley's Good Deed, 1969; Parsley's Problem Present, Parsley's Last Stand, Paddington Takes the Air, Thursday in Paris, 1970; Michael Bond's Book of Bears, Michael Bond's Book of Mice, 1971; The Day the Animals Went on Strike, Paddington Bear, Paddington's Garden, Parsley Parade, The Tales of Olga de Polga, 1972; Olga Meets Her Match, Paddington's Blue Peter Story Book, Paddington at the Circus, Paddington Goes Shopping, 1973; Paddington at the Seaside, Paddington at the Tower, Paddington on Top, 1974; Windmill, How to Make Flying Things, Eight Olga Readers, 1975; Paddington's Cartoon Book, 1979; J D Polson and the Dillogate Affair, Paddington on Screen, 1981; Olga Takes Charge, 1982; The Caravan Puppets, 1983; Paddington at the Zoo, 1984; Paddington's Painting Exhibition, Elephant, 1985; Paddington Minds the House, Paddington at the Palace, 1986; Paddington's Busy Day, Paddington and the Magical Maze, 1987; Paddington and the Christmas Surprise, 1997; Paddington at the Carnival, Paddington Bear, 1998; Olga Moves House, 2001; Olga Follows Her Nose, 2002; Paddington's Grand Tour, 2003. Adult Books: Monsieur Pamplemousse, 1983; Monsieur Pamplemousse and the Secret Mission, 1984; Monsieur Pamplemousse Takes the Cure, 1987; The Pleasures of Paris, Guide Book, 1987; Monsieur Pamplemousse Aloft, 1989; Monsieur Pamplemousse Investigates, 1990; Monsieur Pamplemousse Rests His Case, 1991; Monsieur Pamplemousse Stands Firm, Monsieur Pamplemousse on Location, 1992; Monsieur Pamplemousse Takes the Train, 1993; Bears and Forebears (autobiography), 1996; Monsieur Pamplemousse Afloat, 1998; Monsieur Pamplemousse on Probation, 2000; Monsieur Pamplemousse on Vacation, 2002; Monsieur Pamplemousse Hits the Headlines, 2003; Monsieur Pamplemousse and The Militant Midwives, 2006; Monsieur Pamplemousse and the French Solution, 2007; Paddington Here and Now, 2008; Monsieur Pamplemousse and the Carbon Footprint, 2010. Honour: Officer of the Order of the British Empire, 1997; Honorary Doctor of Letters, Reading University, 2007. Address: The Agency, 24 Pottery Lane, Holland Park, London W11 4LZ, England.

BONDARENKO Evgeny Anatol'evich, b. 4 April 1954, Kiev, Ukraine. Aerospace Engineer. m. Tat'yana Vladimirovna, 2 sons. Education: Engineer's degree, Gyroscopic Instruments and Devices, 1977, PhD, Gyroscopes and Navigation Systems, 2005, Kiev Polytechnic Institute. Appointments: Junior Research Worker, 1977-90, Research Worker, 1990-2005, Senior Teacher, Faculty of Aerospace Systems, 1994-2005, Senior Research Worker, 2005-06, Assistant Professor, 2005-, Kiev Polytechnic Institute; Leading Engineer, Arsenal Special Device Production State Enterprise, Kiev, 2006-. Publications: Geometrical optics construction of axis contour in misaligned ring laser gyroscope resonator, 2005; Analysis of slowly rotating vibrating ring laser gyroscope metrological parameters deviations caused by its resonator geometry change, 2005; Formulae for calculation of parameters of a system of differential equations describing the dynamics of laser gyroscope with nonzero $\Delta Q/Q$ resonator and slightly detuned frequency, 2007; Calculation of optical lengths of arms of misaligned resonator of laser gyro, 2008; Laser gyroscope dynamic equations. Formulae for calculation of active medium parameters and parameters of oppositely directed traveling waves linear coupling, 2009; Expressions for counterpropagating waves beat frequency of uniformly rotating laser gyro, 2010. E-mail: ea.bndrk@gmail.com

BONHAM CARTER Helena, b. 26 May 1966, Golders Green, London, England. Actress. 1 son and 1 daughter with Tim Burton. Career: Films include: Lady Jane; A Room with a View; Maurice; Francesco; The Mask; Getting it Right; Hamlet; Where Angels Fear to Tread; Howard's End, 1991; A Dark Adapted Eye (TV), Mary Shelley's Frankenstein, The Glace Bay Miners' Museum, 1994; A Little Loving, Mighty Aphrodite, 1995; Twelfth Night, Margaret's Museum, 1996; Parti Chinois, 1996; The Theory of Flight, Keep the Aspidistra Flying, 1997; The Wings of the Dove, The Revengers' Comedies, 1998; Women Talking Dirty, Fight Club, 1999; Until Human Voices Wake Us, 2000; Planet of the Apes, The Heart of Me, Novocaine, 2002; Till Human Voices Wake Us, 2003; Charlie and the Chocolate Factory, Conversations with Other Women, Wallace & Gromit in The Curse of the Were-Rabbit (voice), The Corpse Bride (voice), Magnificent 7, 2005; Sixty Six, 2006; Sweeney Todd: The Demon Barber of Fleet Street, Harry Potter and the Order of the Phoenix, 2007; Harry Potter and the Half-Blood Prince, Terminator Salvation, Enid, The Gruffalo, 2009; Alice in Wonderland, Harry Potter and the Deathly Hallows: Part I, 2010, Part II, 2011; The King's Speech, 2010; The Gruffalo's Child, 2011; Dark Shadows, 2012; A Therapy, 2012; Great Expectations, 2012; Les Miserables, 2012; The Lone Ranger, 2013; Television appearances include: A Pattern of Roses; Miami Vice; A Hazard of Hearts; The Vision; Arms and the Man; Beatrix Potter; Live from Baghdad, 2002; Henry VIII, 2003. Honours: CBE, 2012. Address: c/o Conway van Gelder Limited, 18/21 Jermyn Street, London, SW1Y 6HP, England.

BONINGTON Sir Christian (John Storey), b. 6 August 1934. Mountaineer; Writer; Photographer. m. Muriel Wendy Marchant, 1962, 2 sons. Education: University College School, London. Appointments: RMA Sandhurst, 1955-56; Commissioned, Royal Tank Regiment, 1956-61; Unilever Management Trainee, 1961-62; Writer and Photographer, 1962-; Mountaineer of: Annapurna II, 1960, Central Pillar Freney, Mont Blanc, 1961, Nuptse, 1961, North Wall of Eiger, 1962, Central Tower of Paine, Patagonia, 1963; Member of Team, 1st descent of Blue Nile, 1968; Leader, Annapurna South Face Expedition, 1970; British Everest Expedition, 1972; Brammah Himalayas, 1973; Co-Leader, Changabang, Himalayas, 1974; British Everest Expedition,

1975; Ogre, 1977; Joint Leader, Kongur, North West China, 1981; Panch Chuli II, Kumaon, Himalayas, 1992; Mejslen, Greenland, 1993; Rang Rik Rank, Kinnaur, Himalayas, 1994, Drangnag Ri, Nepal, 1995; Sepu Kangri Expedition, 1998; 1st ascent of Danga II, 2000. Publications: I Chose to Climb (autobiography), 1966; Annapurna South Face, 1971; The Next Horizon (autobiography), 1973; Everest, South West Face, 1973; Everest the Hard Way, 1976; Quest for Adventure, 1981; Kongur: China's Elusive Summit, 1982; Everest: The Unclimbed Ridge (co-author), 1983; The Everest Years, 1986; Mountaineer (autobiography), 1989; The Climbers, 1992; Sea, Ice and Rock (with Robin Knox-Johnston), 1992; Tibet's Secret Mountain, 1999; Quest for Adventure, 2000; Chris Bonington's Everest, 2002. Honours include: Founder Medal, Royal Geographical Society, 1971; Lawrence of Arabia Medal, 1986; Livingstone Medal, 1991; CBE; Honorary DSc, Sheffield; Honorary MA, Salford; Honorary DSc, Lancaster; Honorary DSc, Northumbria; Honorary Doctor of Letters, University of Bradford; Chancellor, Lancaster University, 2005-. Memberships include: Army Mountaineering Association; British Mountaineering Council; Council for National Parks; The Alpine Club. Address: Badger Hill, Nether Row, Hesket Newmarket, Wigton, Cumbria CA7 8LA, England.

BONO (Paul Hewson), 10 May 1960, Dublin, Ireland. Singer; Lyricist. m. Alison, 2 daughters, 2 sons. Career: Founder member, lead singer, rock group U2, 1978-; Regular national, international and worldwide tours; Major concerts include: US Festival, 1983; The Longest Day, Milton Keynes Bowl, Live Aid, Wembley, 1985; Self Aid, Ireland, A Conspiracy Of Hope (Amnesty International US tour), 1986; Smile Jamaica (hurricane relief concert), Very Special Arts Festival, White House, 1988; New Year's Eve Concert, Dublin (televised throughout Europe), 1989; Yankee Stadium, New York (second concert ever), 1992; Group established own record company, Mother Records. Compositions include: Co-writer, Jah Love, Neville Brothers; Lyrics, Misere, Zucchero and Pavarotti; Screenplay, Million Dollar Hotel. Recordings: Albums: with U2: Boy, 1980; October, 1981; War, Under A Blood Red Sky, 1983; The Unforgettable Fire, 1984; Wide Awake In America, 1985; The Joshua Tree, 1987; Rattle And Hum, also film, 1988; Achtung Baby, 1991; Zooropa, 1993; Passengers (film soundtrack), with Brian Eno, 1995; Pop, 1997; All Than You Can't Leave Behind, The Best of 1990-2000, 2000; How To Dismantle An Atomic Bomb, 2004; Hit singles include: Out Of Control, 1979; Another Day, 1980; New Year's Day, 1983; Two Hearts Beat As One, 1983; Pride (In The Name Of Love), 1984; The Unforgettable Fire, 1985; With Or Without You, I Still Haven't Found What I'm Looking For, Where The Streets Have No Name, 1987; Desire, Angel Of Harlem, 1988; When Love Comes To Town, with B B King, All I Want Is You, 1989; The Fly, 1991; Mysterious Ways, One, Even Better Than The Real Thing, Who's Gonna Ride Your Wild Horses, 1992; Stay, 1993; Hold Me, Thrill Me, Kiss Me (from film soundtrack Batman Forever), 1995; Discotheque, 1997; If God Will Send His Angels, Sweetest Thing, 1998; Beautiful Day, 2000; Stuck In A Moment You Can't Get Out Of, Walk On, Elevation, 2001; Electrical Storm, The Hands That Built America, 2002; Vertigo, 2004; Contributor, Do They Know It's Christmas?, Band Aid, Sun City, Little Steven, 1985; In A Lifetime, Clannad, 1986; Mystery Girl, Roy Orbison, 1988; Special Christmas, charity album, 1987; Folkways - A Vision Shared (Woody Guthrie tribute), 1988; Live For Ireland, 1989; Red Hot + Blue (Cole Porter tribute), 1990; Tower Of Song (Leonard Cohen tribute), 1995; Pavarotti And Friends, 1996; Forces Of Nature, 1999. Honours: Numerous Grammy Awards, BRIT Awards, Q Awards; Ivor Novello Award for Best Song Musically and Lyrically, 2002; Grammy, Album of the Year, 2006; Honorary Knight Commander of the Order of the British Empire, 2007; Many poll wins and awards, Billboard and Rolling Stone magazines; Gold and Platinum discs; Many awards for humanitarian work. Address: Principle Management, 30-32 Sir John Rogersons Quay, Dublin 2, Ireland.

BONTING Sjoerd Lieuwe, b. 6 October 1924, Amsterdam, The Netherlands. Biochemist; Anglican Priest-Theologian. m. (1) Susan Maarsen, deceased, 2 sons, 2 daughters, (2) Erica Schotman. Education: BSc, Chemistry, 1944, MSc, cum laude, Biochemistry, 1950, PhD, Biochemistry, 1952, University of Amsterdam; Ordained Priest, Episcopal Church, Washington, 1964. Appointments: Research Associate, University of Iowa, 1952-55; Assistant Professor, University of Minnesota, 1955-56; Assistant Professor, Biochemistry, University of Illinois, Chicago, USA, 1956-60; Section Chief, National Institutes of Health, Bethesda, Maryland, 1960-65; Professor, Head, Department of Biochemistry, University of Nymegen, Netherlands, 1965-85; Scientific Consultant, NASA-Ames Research Centre, Moffett Field, 1985-93; Assistant Priest, St Thomas Episcopal Church, Sunnyvale, USA, 1985-90; Assistant Priest, St Mark's Episcopal Church, Palo Alto, California, 1990-93; Anglican Chaplain, Church of England, Netherlands, 1965-85, 1993-. Publications: Scientific publications: 363 articles, 9 books including: Transmitters in the Visual Process, 1976; Membrane Transport, 1981; Advances in Space Biology and Medicine, vols 1-7, 1989-99; Theological publications: 102 articles, 7 books including: Evolution and Creation, 1978; Word and World, 1989; Creation and Evolution, 1996, 2nd edition, 1997; Humanity, Chaos, Reconciliation, 1998; Belief and Unbelief, 2000; Chaos Theology, a Revised Creation Theology, 2002; Creation and Double Chaos, 2005. Honours: Rudolf Lehmann Scholar, Amsterdam, 1941-46; Postdoctoral Fellowship, USPHS, Iowa City, USA, 1952-54; Fight for Sight Citation, National Council to Combat Blindness and Association for Research in Ophthalmology, 1961, 1962; Arthur S Flemming Award, Jaycees, Washington DC, USA, 1964; Prize for Enzymology on Leucocytes, Karger Foundation, Basel, Switzerland, 1964; Honorary Licentiate in Theology, St Mark's Institute of Theology, London, 1975; Citation by Archbishop of Canterbury for 20 years chaplaincy work in the Netherlands, 1985. Memberships: Sigma Xi, 1955-; American Society of Biology Chemists, 1958-; AAAS, 1960-; American Society of Cell Biology, 1960-; Netherlands Biochemical Society, 1965-; Board of Directors, Multidisciplinary Center for Church and Society, The Netherlands, 1981-85; Society of Ordained Scientists, 1989-. Address: Specreyse 12, 7471 TH Goor, The Netherlands. E-mail: s.l.bonting@wxs.nl Website: www.chaostheologie.nl

BOO Jin-Hyo, b. 11 August 1961, Jeju, Korea. Professor. m. Hye-Eun Son, 2 sons, 1 daughter. Education: BA, Chemistry, 1985, MA, Physical Chemistry, 1987, PhD, Surface & Materials Chemistry, 1992, Sungkyunkwan University. Appointments: Research Scientist, Korea Research Institute of Chemical & Technology, 1992-94; Post-doctor, Bonn University, Germany, 1994-95; Visiting Scientist, Cornell University, USA, 1996-97; Professor, Sungkyunkwan University, Korea, 1997-; Visiting Professor, Bochum University, Germany, 2004; Visiting Professor, West Bohemia University, Czech Republic, 2004-05; Visiting Professor, Fraunhofer-IST Institute, Germany, 2005; Visiting Professor, Kyushu University, Japan, 2011. Publications: Numerous articles in professional journals. Honours: Best Paper Award, Korean Federation of Science & Technology Society, 2004; Wiley International Science Award, 2005; GJ-NST Best Paper

Award, 2006; PCSI Best Paper Award, 2007. Memberships: Korean Chemical Society; Korean Vacuum Society; American Vacuum Society; Materials Research Society; American Chemical Society. Address: Department of Chemistry, Sungkyunkwan University, 300 Chunchun dong, Suwon 440-746, Korea. E-mail: jhboo@skku.edu

BOONRUANGRUTANA Samrerng, b. 23 February 1943, Ayutthaya, Thailand. m. Charweewon, 2 sons. Education: B Ed, Chemistry, 1966, M Ed, Test and Measurement, 1969, College of Education, Thailand; Certificate in Educational Innovation and Technology, INNOTECH Center, Singapore, 1972; PhD, Curriculum Research and Development, University of Illinois, USA, 1978; Certificate of National Defense, National Defense College, Thailand, 1993. Appointments: Teacher, Suravithayakarn School, 1966-67; Instructor, 1969-79, Assistant Professor, 1979-82, Associate Professor, 1982-87, Professor in Educational Measurement and Evaluation, 1987-2003, Director, Educational and Psychological Test Bureau, 1983-87, Vice President for Academic Affairs, 1987-93, Srinakharinwirot University, Thailand; National Research Co-ordinator, Second Mathematics Study of the International Association for the Evaluation of Educational Achievement, 1978-87; Professor, Educational Measurement and Evaulation, Vongchavalitkul University, 2003-. Publications: Over 50 research papers and 200 articles in various national and international journals. Honours: Knight Grand Cordon (Special Class) of the Most Exalted Order of the White Elephant; Knight Grand Cordon (Special Class) of the Most Noble Order of the Crown of Thailand; Knight Grand Cross (First Class) of the Most Exalted of the White Elephant; Knight Grand Cross (First Class) of the Most Noble Order of the Crown of Thailand; Best Research in Education Award, 1986; Best Instructor of Srinakharinwirot University Award, 1997; Princess Prem Purachatra Award, 2001; Best University Instructor of the Nation Award, 2001; One of fifteen, Thai Wisdom in the Celebration of 400 years of the Death of King Naresuan the Great, 2005; Distinguished Alumni Award, College of Education, University of Illinois, 2007. Memberships: Kappa Delta Pi; American Educational Research Association. Address: 4/357 Soi 16 Sahakorn Village, Seri Thai Road, Klongkum, Bungkum, Bangkok 10240, Thailand.

BOOTH Cherie, b. 23 September 1954, Bury, Lancashire, England. Barrister. m. A C L (Tony) Blair, 1980, 3 sons, 1 daughter. Education: London School of Economics. Appointments: Lincoln's Inn Bar, 1976; In Practice, 1976-77; New Court Chambers, 1977-91; Gray's Inn Square Chambers, 1991-2000; Queens Council, 1995; Assistant Recorder, 1996-99; Governor, London School of Economics, 1998-; Recorder, 1999-; Matrix Chambers, 2000-. Publication: Contributor, Education Law, 1997; The Goldfish Bowl, 2004. Honours: FJMU; FRSA; Fellow, John Moores University, Liverpool, Chancellor, 1998-; Patron, CLIC-Sargent Cancer Care for Children, 1998-; Patron, Breast Cancer Care, 1997-; Islington Music Centre, 1999-; Honorary Degree, Open University, 1999; Honorary LLD, Westminster University; Fellow of LSE; Fellow of International Society of Lawyers in Public Service; Hon Bencher, King's Inn, Dublin, 2002; Hon Fellow: LSE, 2003; Open University; Institute of Advanced Legal Studies; Hon President, Plater College, Hon Patron, Genesis Appeal; Hon DUniv, UMIST, 2003. Memberships: Fellow, Institute of Advisory Legal Studies. Address: Matrix Chambers, Griffin Building, Grays Inn, London WC1R 5LN, England.

BORIÇI LACUKU Justina, b. 4 August 1951, Tirana, Albania. Agronomist. m. Mikel Borici, 2 sons. Education: Agronomist, University of Tirana, High Institute for Agriculture, 1974; Master degree, 1988; PhD, 1995; Professor, 1995; Professor Doctor (Academic title), 2005. Appointments: Agronomist, Agriculture Enterprise in Kamza, Tirana, 1973-78; Scientific Expert, Water Problems in Agriculture, 1978-96, Deputy Diretor, 1996-97, Secretary, Scientific Council, 1996-2001, Director, 2005-06, Institute of Soil Sciences, Tirana; Member, Steering Board, Bulletin of the Agricultural Sciences magazine, 1989-91; Director, Agency for Return and Compensation of the Properties, 2006-07; Adviser to the Minister of Agriculture, Food and Protection of the Consumer, 2007. Publications: Numerous articles in professional journals; 2 books: Soil Drainage, 2002; The Water and Its Quality. Honours: Listed in international biographical dictionaries. Address: Rruga "Myslym Shyri", Pallati 102, Shk 2, Ap 14, Tirana, Albania. E-mail: justi_borici@hotmail.com

BORN Gustav Victor Rudolf, b. 29 July 1921. Professor Emeritus. m. (1) Wilfreda Ann Plowden-Wardlaw, 2 sons, 1 daughter, (2) Faith Elizabeth Maurice-Williams, 1 son, 1 daughter. Education: Vans Dunlop Scholar, MB, ChB, University of Edinburgh, 1943; DPhil (Oxford), 1951, MA, 1956. Appointments include: Medical Officer, RAMC, 1943-47; Member, Scientific Staff, Medical Research Council, 1952-53, Research Officer, Nuffield Institute for Medical Research, 1953-60, Departmental Demonstrator in Pharmacology, 1956-60, University of Oxford; Vandervell Professor of Pharmacology, RCS and University of London, 1960-73; Sheild Professor of Pharmacology, University of Cambridge and Fellow, Gonville and Caius College, Cambridge, 1973-78; Professor of Pharmacology, King's College, University of London, 1978-86, Professor Emeritus, 1986-; Research Director, The William Harvey Research Institute, St Bartholomew's Hospital Medical College, 1989-; Visiting Professor in Chemistry, Northwestern University, Illinois, 1970; William S Creasey Visiting Professor in Clinical Pharmacology, Brown University, 1977; Professor of Fondation de France, Paris, 1982-84; Honorary Director, Medical Research Council Thrombosis Research Group, 1964-73; Scientific Advisor, Vandervell Foundation, 1967-2001; President, International Society on Thrombosis and Haemostasis, 1977-79; Adviser, Heineman Medical Research Center, Charlotte, North Carolina, USA, 1981-; Kuratorium, Shakespeare Prize, Hamburg, 1991-98; Forensic Science Advisory Group, Home Office; Numerous invited lectures. Publications: Articles in scientific journals and books. Honours include: FRS, 1972; FRCP, 1976; Hon FRCS, 2002; FKC, 1988; Honorary Fellow, St Peter's College, Oxford, 1972; Ten Honorary Degrees; Albrecht von Haller Medal, Göttingen University, 1979; Chevalier de l'Ordre National de Mérite, France, 1980; Auenbrugger Medal, Graz University, 1984; Royal Medal, Royal Society, 1987; Robert Pfleger Prize, Bamberg, 1990; Alexander von Humboldt Award, 1995; Gold Medal for Medicine, Ernst Jung Foundation, Hamburg, 2001; Wellcome Gold Medal and Prize, British Pharmacological Society, 2009. Memberships include: Honorary Life Member, New York Academy of Sciences; Akademia Leopoldina; Honorary Member, German Physiological Society; Honorary Member, British Pharmacological Society; Corresponding Member, German Pharmacological Society; Royal Belgian Academy of Medicine. Address: 5 Walden Lodge, 48 Wood Lane, Highgate, London N6 5UU, England.

BOSKOVIC Bojan Obrad, b. 27 March 1969, Belgrade, Serbia, Yugoslavia. Engineer; Physicist. m. Olivera Spasic-Boskovic, 2 daughters. Education: Dipl Ing, Faculty of Electrical Engineering, University of Belgrade, Yugoslavia, 1989-95; PhD, University of Surrey, England, 1998-2001. Appointments: Research and Teaching Assistant, Faculty of Electrical Engineering, 1995-97, Assistant Lecturer, Faculty of Mechanical Engineering, 1997-98, University of Belgrade, Yugoslavia; Senior Specialist, Morgan Group Technology, The Morgan Crucible plc, 2001-03; Research Associate, Department of Engineering, 2003-04, Research Associate & Visiting Scientist, Departments of Materials Science & Metallurgy, 2004-06, University of Cambridge; Principal Engineer, Carbon Scientist, Meggitt Aircraft Braking Systems, Meggitt plc, 2006-08; R&D Manager, Nanocyl SA, 2009; Director, Cambridge Nanomaterials Technology Ltd, 2009-. Publications: Numerous articles in professional journals about carbon nanotechnology; 2 granted patents; Invited review articles and book chapters. Memberships: Board Member, Institute of Materials, Minerals and Mining, Composite Division, 2007-. Honours: Listed in international biographical dictionaries. Address: 14 Orchard Way, Cambourne, Cambridge, CB23 5BN, England. E-mail: boboskovic@yahoo.com

BOŠKOVIĆ Bruno, b. 27 May 1956, Jesenice, Yugoslavia. Civil Engineer. Education: Civil Engineering Diploma, University of Ljubljana, 1982. Appointments: General Construction Works, 1982, 1984, 1988-95, Ilija Bošković, Nova Gorica, Yugoslavia; General Construction Works, 1984-88, 1995-97, Bruno Bošković, Nova Gorica, Slovenia. Honours: Professional Membership, Association for Computer Machinery, 1999. Memberships: Institute of Electric and Electronic Engineers; Association for Computing Machinery. Address: Fermo Posta, Gorizia Verdi, Corso Verdi, Gorizia, 34170, Italy. E-mail: bruno.boskovic@siol.net

BOTAN Paul Antoniu Adrian, b. 30 August 1953, Bucharest, Romania. Plastic Surgeon. Divorced, 1 son, 3 daughters. Education: Graduate, Michael the Great National College, Bucharest, 1972; Graduate, Faculty of Medicine, Bucharest, 1978; PhD, University of Targu Mures Medical School, 2007. Appointments: Intern, Department of Surgery, 1978-81; Resident, Plastic Surgery, 1981-85; Attending Surgeon, 1985-, Senior Consultant, 2001-, Founder and Chief, The Burns Centre and Plastic Surgery Department, Teaching Hospital of Targu Mures Medical School. Publications: Numerous articles in professional journals. Honours: Honorary Member, Commemorative Silver Plate, International Society for Dermatologic Surgery, 2006. Memberships: International Society for hand Surgery; Euro-Mediterranean Council for Burns; International Society for Dermatologic Surgery. Address: Targu Mures, OPS COD 540 506, BD Pandurilor 21/12, Romania. E-mail: dr_botan@yahoo.com

BOTHAM (Sir) Ian Terence, b. 24 November 1955, Heswall, Cheshire, England. Cricketer. m. Kathryn Waller, 1976 1 son, 2 daughters. Career: Debut for Somerset, 1974; Awarded County Cap, 1976; Test debut, 1977; Tours of Pakistan and New Zealand, 1977-78; Australia, 1978-79; Australia and India, 1979-80; West Indies, 1981; India and Sri Lanka, 1981-892; Australia, 1982-83; New Zealand and Pakistan, 1983-84; Captain, England, 1980-81; Captain, Somerset County Cricket Club, 1983-85; Worcestershire 1987-91; Durham, 1992-93; Retired, 1993; Player for Queensland, Australia, and Worcestershire County Cricket Club, 1987; Became 1st player to score century and take 8 wickets in an innings in a Test Match v Pakistan, Lord's, 1978; Took 100th wicket in test cricket record time of 2 years 9 days, 1979 Achieved double of 1000 runs and 100 wickets in Tests to create world record of fewest Tests (21) and English records of shortest time (2 years 33 days) and at youngest age (23 years 279 days), 1979; Became 1st player to have scored 3000 runs and taken 250 wickets in Tests (55), 1982; 1st player to score century and take 10 wickets in Test Match v India; Scorer of over 1000 runs and taken more than 100 wickets in Tests gainst Australia; Won 100th Test cap for England, 1992; Has also played soccer for Scunthorpe Utd. Publications include: It Sort of Clicks, 1986; Cricket My Way, 1989; Botham: My Autobiography: Don't Tell Kath..., 1994; The Botham Report, 1997; Head On – Ian Botham: The Autobiography, 2007. Honours: Hon MSc (UMIST); Wisden Cricketer of the Year, 1978; OBE, 1992; Lifetime Achievement Award, BBC Sports Personality of the Year, 2004; Knighted by the queen in 2007. Address: Mission Sports Management, Kirmington Vale, Barnetby, North Lincolnshire, DN38 6AF, England.

BOTTOMLEY OF NETTLESTONE Rt Hon Baroness, Virginia Hilda Brunette Maxwell, b. 12 March 1948. Politician. m. Peter Bottomley, 1967, 1 son, 2 daughters. Education: London School Economics. Appointments: Various positions before election as Conservative MP for Surrey South, 1984-2005; Parliamentary Private Secretary to Chris Patten, 1985-87; Parliamentary Private Secretary for Foreign and Commonwealth Affairs Sir Geoffrey Howe QC MP, 1987-88; Parliament Under-Secretary, Department of the Environment, 1988-89; Ministry for Health, 1989-92; Secretary of State, Department of Health, 1992-95, with responsibility for family policy, 1994-95; Chairman, Millennium Commission, 1995-97; Secretary of State, Department of National Heritage, 1995-97; Vice Chairman, British Council, 1997-2000; House of Commons Select Committee on Foreign Affairs, 1997-99; Supervisory Board, Akzo Nobel, NV; Executive Director, Odger Ray and Berndtson; President, Abbeyfield Society; Council Member, Ditchley Foundation; Governor, London School of Economics, London University of the Arts; UK Advisory Council; International Chamber of Commerce; Advisory Council, Cambridge University Judge School of Management Studies. Address: House of Lords, London SW1A 0PW, England.

BOTTONI Maurizio, b. 5 December 1941, Ferrara, Italy. Researcher. Divorced, 1 daughter. Education: Degree, Humanistic High School, 1960; Absolved Biennium of Mathematical and Physical Sciences, University of Ferrara, 1962; Doctor of Nuclear Engineering, University of Bologna, 1965. Appointments: Geophysical Researcher, Schlumberger Company, Parma, Italy, 1968-70; Researcher, European Space Research Organization, Darmstadt, Germany, 1970-74; Researcher, Kernforschungszentrum Karlsruhe, Germany, 1974-90; Researcher, Argonne National Laboratory, Illinois, USA, 1990-96. Publications: 73 peer-reviewed publications; 30 non-peer-reviewed publications; 1 book. Honours: Augusto Righi Prize, Bologna University, 1966; Guest Professor, Tokodai (Tokyo), Tsinghua University (Beijing), and Ferrara University (Italy), 1996-2009; Senior Scientist, Sistema Gmbh (Wien), 2010; Consultant, Sistema, 2011-; Dr hc, International Institute for Advanced Studies, 2011. Memberships: Italian Astronomical Society; Atomic Energy Society of Japan; National Geographic Society, USA. Address: Steinackerstrasse 4, 76846 Bruchsal, Germany. E-mail: bottoni_m@hotmail.com

BOULIER Jean François, b. 14 March 1956, Caen, France. Executive. m. Marianne, 1 son, 2 daughters. Education: Ecole Polytechnique, 1977-80; ENGREF, 1980-82; Doctorate in

Fluid Mechanics, Grenoble University, 1985. Appointments: Researcher, CNRS, 1985-87; Head of Quantative Analysis, Credit Commercial de France, 1987-89; Head of Research and Innovation, 89-99, Head of Market Risk Management, 1996-99, CCF; Chief Investment Officer, President, Sinopia Asset Management, 1999-2002; Professor of Finance, University Paris Dauphine, 2000-03; Head of Euro Fixed Income and Credits, Credit Aquicole Asset Management, 2004-; Associate Professor, Paris Dauphine University, 2000-06; Deputy Chief Investment Officer, Head of Fixed Income, Credit Lyonnais Asset Management, 2002-04; Head of Euro Fixed Income and Credit, Agricole Asset Management, 2004-; Chief Investment Officer, Executive Managing Director, 2008-09, Chief Executive Officer, 2009-, Avira Investors, France; Executive Officer, Aviva Investors Europe, 2010-. Publications: Numerous articles and reports in professional journals; Editor, Creator, Quants, quarterly journal of CCF; editor, Banque et Marchés, journal of the French Finance Association. Honour: Institute of Quantative Investment Research award, 1993; Banque & Marché Award, 2005; Listed in numerous publications. Memberships: Honorary Chairman, French Finance Association; Honorary Chairman, French Asset and Liability Managers' Association; Board Member, French Pension Fund Association; Chairman of the Asset Management Technical Committee of the French Fund Manager's Association, 1999-2010; Board Member, AFG, 2010-; Steering Committee Member, Louis Bachelier Institute. Address: 5 quai de l'Orme de Sully, 78230 Le Pecq, France. E-mail: jean-francois.boulier@ca-assetmanagement.fr

BOULTON James Thompson, b. 17 February 1924, Pickering, Yorkshire, England. Emeritus Professor of English Studies. m. Margaret Helen Leary, 1949, 1 son, 1 daughter. Education: BA, University College, University of Durham, 1948; BLitt, Lincoln College, University of Oxford, 1952; PhD, University of Nottingham, 1960. Appointments: Lecturer, Senior Lecturer, Reader in English Literature, 1951-63, Professor, 1964-75, Dean of Faculty of Arts, 1970-73, University of Nottingham; Professor of English Studies and Head of Department, 1975-88, Dean of Faculty of Arts, 1981-84, Public Orator, 1984-88, Director of Institute for Advanced Research in Arts and Social Sciences, 1987-99, Deputy Director, 1999-2006, Director Emeritus, 2006-, University of Birmingham; Honorary Professor of English, Bangor University, 2007. Publications: Edmund Burke: Sublime and Beautiful (editor), 1958, 3rd edition, 1987, pb 2008; The Language of Politics in the Age of Wilkes and Burke, 1963, 2009; Samuel Johnson: The Critical Heritage, 1971; Defoe: Memoirs of a Cavalier (editor), 1972; The Letters of D H Lawrence (editor), 8 volumes, 1979-00; Selected letters of D H Lawrence (editor), 1997, 2008, 2011; Volume I, The Early Writings: The Writings and Speeches of Edmund Burke (co-editor), 1997; D H Lawrence: Late Essays and Articles (editor), 2004; James Boswell: An Account of Corsica (co-editor), 2005; Further Letters of D H Lawrence, 2006, 2007, 2008, 2009. Honours: Fellow, Royal Society of Literature, 1968; Hon DLitt, Durham University, 1991, Nottingham University, 1993; Fellow, British Academy, 1994; Listed in Who's Who publications and biographical dictionaries. Address: Tyn y Ffynnon, Nant Peris, Caernarfon, LL55 4UH, Wales.

BOUND John Pascoe, b.13 November 1920, Redhill, Surrey, England. Paediatrician, Consultant (Retired). m. Gwendoline, deceased 1998, 2 daughters. Education: MB, BS, DCH, 1943, MD, 1950, University College, London and University College Hospital Medical School; MRCP (Lond), 1950; FRCP, 1971; FRCPCH, 1997. Appointments: House Physician, University College Hospital, 1943; Assistant Medical Officer, Alder Hey Children's Hospital, Liverpool, 1943-44; RAMC, 1944-47; Member, Sprue Research Team, Poona, India for 1 year; House Physician, North Middlesex Hospital, 1947; Paediatric Registrar and Senior Registrar, Hillingdon Hospital, Middlesex, 1948-53; Paediatric Registrar, 1953-54, First Assistant, Department of Paediatrics, 1954-56, University College Hospital, London; Consultant Paediatrician, Victoria Hospital, Blackpool, Lancashire, 1956-83. Publications: Articles on neonatal conditions and perinatal mortality; Articles on congenital malformations including: Incidence of congenital heart disease in the Fylde of Lancashire 1957-71; Seasonal prevalence of major congenital malformations, 1957-81; Neural tube defects, maternal cohorts and age: a pointer to aetiology; Down's Syndrome: prevalence and ionising radiation in an area of North West England, 1957-91; Involvement of deprivation and environmental lead in neural tube defects, 1957-81; Book, Borrowdale Beauty. Honours: International Medal of Honour, International Biographical Centre, Cambridge, 2003; American Medal of Honor, American Biographical Institute, Raleigh, North Carolina, USA, 2005; Order of International Ambassadors Medal, ABI, 2006; Legion of Honor Medal, United Cultural Convention, USA, 2006; American Hall of Fame, ABI, 2007; Gold Medal for England, ABI, 2007; The John Pascoe Bound Award Foundation, ABI, 2007; Master Diploma, World Academy of Letters, ABI, 2008. Memberships: British Medical Association, 1943-; Expert Group on Special Care for Babies, Department of Health and Social Security, London, 1969-70; British Paediatric Association, 1960-97, Academic Board, 1972-75. Address: 48, St Annes Road East, Lytham St Annes, Lancashire FY8 1UR, England.

BOURAS Abdelaziz, b. 9 August 1964, Algeria. Professor. m. Zaia, 1 son, 1 daughter. Education: Engineer, Industrial Engineering, 1987; PhD, Computer Science, 1992; Habilitation degree, 2000. Appointments: Associate Professor, 1993-99, Full Professor, 2000-, University of Lyon; Guest Researcher, NIST National Institute of Standards and Technology, USA, 2005-06. Publications: Editor-in-Chief, International Journal of Product Lifecycle Management; Associate Editor, International Journal of Product Development; 100 papers in international journals and conferences; Chair, 10 international conferences. Honours: Honoris Causa PhD in Science, Chaing Mai University; NATO Award; Honorary Researcher, NIST (USA) and CAMT (Thailand). Memberships: Design Society; Micado Association; IFIP; SEE; V-Laboratory; ASME. Address: University of Lyon, Lumiere Technology Institute, 160 Bd University, 69676 - Bron - Cedex, France. E-mail: abdelaziz.bouras@univ-lyon2.fr

BOURNE Malcolm Cornelius, b. 18 May 1926, Moonta, Australia. Professor of Food Science; Active Emeritus. m. (1) Elizabeth Schumacher, deceased 2007, 3 sons, 2 daughters, (2) Janice Stone, 2008. Education: BSc, Chemistry, University of Adelaide, 1949; MS, Food Science, 1961, PhD, Agricultural Chemistry, 1962, University of California, Davis, USA. Appointments: Chief Chemist, Brookers (Australia) Ltd, 1949-58; Research Assistant, University California, Davis, 1958-62; Professor, Food Science, 1962-95, Emeritus Professor, Food Science, 1995-, Cornell University. Publications: Many publications in refereed journals; 4 patents; Author, Food Texture and Viscosity, 1982, reprinted, 1994, second edition, 2002; Editor in Chief, Journal of Texture Studies, 1980-2006. Honours: Fellow, Institute of Food Science and Technology, UK, 1966; Fellow, Institute of Food Technologists, 1985 and International Award, 1992; Inaugural Fellow, 1998, Vice President, 2001-03, President, 2003-06,

International Academy Food Science and Technology; Honorary Fellow, Australian Institute of Food Science and Technology, 1999; Fellow, Royal Australian Chemical Institute, 2003. Address: NYSAES, Cornell University, 630 West North Street, Geneva, NY 14456, USA.

BOUTROS-GHALI Boutros, b. 14 November 1922, Cairo, Egypt. Diplomat. m. Maria Leia Nadler. Education: LLB, Cairo University, 1946; PhD, Paris University, 1949. Appointments: Professor, International Law and International Relations, Head, Department of Political Sciences, Cairo University, 1949-77; Founder, Editor, Al Ahram Iktisadi, 1960-75; Ministry of State, Foreign Affairs, Egypt, 1977-91; Member, UN Commission of International Law, 1979-92; Member, Secretariat, National Democratic Party, 1980-92; MP, 1987-92; Deputy PM, Foreign Affairs, 1991-92; Secretary-General, UN, 1992-97; Secretary-General, Organisations Internationales de la Francophonie, 1997-2002; Chairman of the Board, South Centre, 2003-06; President, Curatorium Administrative Council, Hague Academy of International Law; Director, Egyptian National Council of Human Rights, 2003-. Publications: Contribution a l'étude des ententes régionales, 1949; Cours de diplomatie et de droit diplomatique et consulaire, 1951; Le problème du Canal de Suez (jtly), 1957; Egypt and the United Nations (jtly), 1957; Le principe d'égalité des états et les organisations internationales, 1961; Contribution a une théorie générale des Alliances, 1963; Foreign Policies in a World of Change, 1963; L'Organisation de l'unité africaine, 1969; Le mouvement Afro-Asiatique, 1969; Les difficultés institutionelles du panafricanisme, 1971; La ligue des états arabes, 1972; Les Conflits de frontières en Afrique, 1973; Egypt's Road to Jerusalem, 1997; Unvanquished: A US-UN Saga, 1999; Numerous books in Arabic and contributions to periodicals. Address: 2 avenue Epnipgiza, Cairo, Egypt.

BOWES Donald Ralph, b. 9 September 1926, Brighton, South Australia. Retired University Teacher. m. Annie Mary Morris, 2 sons, 1 daughter. Education: BSc, Geology and Chemistry, 1945; BSc (Hons 1st class), Mineralogy and Petrology, 1946, MSc, 1948, Adelaide University, Australia; PhD, 1950, DIC, 1950, Imperial College, London University, England; DSc, University of Glasgow, Scotland, 1968. Appointments: Lecturer, Geology, Adelaide University, Australia, 1950-52; Lecturer, Geology, University College of Swansea, Wales, 1953-56; Senior Lecturer, Geology, 1956-72, Reader, Geology, 1972-75, Professor of Geology, 1975-91, Emeritus Professor, 1991-, University of Glasgow, Scotland. Publications: 250 publications in international journals; Editor, Crustal Evolution in Northwestern Britain and Adjacent Regions, 1978; Editor, The Encyclopedia of Igneous and Metamorphic Petrology, 1989; Editor, Transactions of the Royal Society of Edinburgh: Earth Sciences, 1978-85; International Consulting Editor, American Journal of Industrial Medicine, 1980-2002. Honours: James Barrans Scholar, University of Adelaide, 1946; 1851 Exhibitioner for Australia, 1947, award held at Imperial College, London, 1948-49; Tate Medal for Geology, University of Adelaide, 1948; Fulbright Scholar, Columbia University, New York, USA 1966; Gold Medal, Charles University, Prague, Czech Republic, 1998; Emanuel Bôrický Medal, Charles University, Prague, 2003. Memberships: Fellow, Royal Society of Edinburgh, Vice-president, 1980-83; Fellow, Geological Society, London; Fellow, Geological Society of America; Fellow, Mineralogical Society. Address: School of Geographical & Earth Sciences, University of Glasgow, Glasgow G12 8QQ, Scotland. E-mail: don.bowes@glasgow.ac.uk

BOYCOTT Geoffrey, b. 21 October 1940. Cricket Commentator. m. Rachael Swinglehurst, 2003, 1 daughter. Education: Hemsworth Grammar School. Appointments: Played Cricket for Yorkshire, 1962-86; County Captain, 1963; Played for England, 1964-74, 1977-82; Captain of Yorkshire, 1970-78; Cricket Commentator, BBC TV, TWI, Channel 9, SABC, Talk Radio; Channel 4 TV; ESPN/STAR TV; BBC Radio. Publications: Geoff Boycott's Book for Young Cricketers, 1976; Put to the Test: England in Australia 1978-79, 1979; Geoff Boycott's Cricket Quiz, 1979; On Batting, 1980; Opening Up, 1980; In the Fast Lane, 1981; Master Class, 1982; Boycott, The Autobiography, 1987; Boycott on Cricket, 1990; Geoffrey Boycott on Cricket, 1999; The Best XI, 2008; Geoff Boycott on Batting; Geoff Boycott Master Class; Articles in the Daily Telegraph. Honour: OBE. Membership: Honorary Life Member, Yorkshire County Cricket Club, 1984-93; Honorary Life Member, MCC. Address: c/o Yorkshire County Cricket Club, Headingley Cricket Ground, Leeds, Yorks LS6 3BY, England.

BOYD Graham, b. 26 April 1928, Bristol, England. Artist. m. Pauline Lilian, 1 son, 1 daughter. Education: NDD, Watford School of Art, 1951; ATD, Institute of Education, London. Appointments: Army Service, 1946-48; Resident in Southern Rhodesia (Zimbabwe), 1953-55; Exchange Associate Professor, Plymouth State College, University of New Hampshire, USA, 1972-73; Visiting Artist, Reading University, 1975-83; Principal Lecturer in Fine Art, Head of Painting, Course Leader P/T BA/BA Honours Fine Art Degree Course, Herts College of Art & Design, St Albans/University of Hertfordshire, 1976-93; Participant in 2nd Triangle Workshop, New York, USA, 1983; Visiting Artist, Exeter College of Art and Design, 1983; Artists in Essex Exhibitions Selector, 1985; Guest Artist, Triangle Workshop, Barcelona, 1987; Anglo-Dutch Artists Workshop, Rounton, North Yorkshire, 1992; Guest Artist, International Multi-Media Symposium, Faial, Azores, 1995; Intuition and Reason Lecture to Tate Gallery Guides and Hertfordshire Visual Artists Forum, 2003; Exhibitions: Solo exhibitions, 1962 onwards include most recently: Colour Transactions, deli Art, Charterhouse Street, London, 1999; Graham Boyd – Disruptive Tendencies, University of Hertfordshire, 2001; The Energy of Colour, 2 person exhibition with Sheila Girling, Pilgrim Gallery, London, 2003; Striking Lights, Recent Painting, deli Art, 2004; The Long Haul, Bushey Museum and Art Gallery, 2004; The Alchemy of Colour, The Pavilion Gallery, Chenies Manor, Rickmansworth, 2004; Dancing with Colour, 2004, Recent Painting by Graham Boyd, 2006, The Salt Gallery, Hayle, Cornwall; Graham Boyd, Courtyard Gallery, Hertford, 2007; Graham Boyd, Light/Space/Colour, SE1 Gallery, London, 2007; Graham Boyd at 80, Parndon Mill, Harlow, Essex, 2008; Painting the Sublime, Campden Gallery, Gloucester, 2009; Visual Metaphors, Early Works by Graham Boyd, Bushey Museum & Art Gallery, 2010; The Primacy of Colour, Recent Paintings by Graham Boyd, Watford Museum, 2011; Group Exhibitions, 1950 onwards include most recently: Driven to Abstraction, Bell Gallery, Winchester, 2000; deli Art in Bristol, The Crypt Gallery, Summer Exhibition, Lemon Street Gallery, Truro, 2002; Confluence, The Pilgrim Gallery, London, 2004; Summer Exhibition, The Salt Gallery, Hayle, 2004 and 2006; Summer Exhibitions, The Campden Gallery, Gloucester, 2008, 2009; Works in public and private collections. Publications: Works featured in numerous newspaper and journal articles and exhibition catalogues. Address: Blackapple, 54 Scatterdells Lane, Chipperfield, Herts WD4 9EX, England. Website: www.grahamboyd.co.uk

DICTIONARY OF INTERNATIONAL BIOGRAPHY 36th EDITION

BOYD Robert David Hugh (Sir), b. 14 May 1938, Cambridge, England. Physician. m. Meriel Cornelia Boyd, 1 son, 2 daughters. Education: Cambridge University; University College Hospital Medical School. Appointments: MRC Fellow, University of Colorado, USA, 1971-72; Senior Lecturer, University College Hospital Medical School, 1973-80; Professor of Child Health, 1981-96, Dean of the Medical Faculty, 1989-93, University of Manchester; Chair Manchester Health Authority, 1994-96; Principal, St George's Hospital Medical School, 1996-2003; Pro-Vice Chancellor, Medicine, University of London, 2001-2003; Chair, Council of Heads of UK Medical Schools, 2001-2003; Chair, Lloyds TSB Foundation for England and Wales, 2003-09; Chair, Council for Assisting Refugee Academics, 2004-10. Publications: Paediatric Problems in General Practice (Joint), 3rd edition, 1996; Scientific articles on placenta, foetus, childhood illness, medical education. Honours: KB; Honorary DSc, Kingston University; Hon DSc, Keele University; Hon FRCPCH; Honorary Member, American Pediatric Society; Fellow, St George's University of London. Memberships: F Med Sci; FRCP (London); FFPH. Address: The Stone House, Adlington, Macclesfield, Cheshire, SK10 4NU, England.

BOYDE Andreas, b. 13 November 1967, Oschatz, Germany. Pianist. Education: Spezialschule and Musikhochschule, Dresden; Guildhall School of Music and Drama, London; Masterclasses, Musikfestwochen Luzern. Debut: With Berlin Symphony Orchestra, 1989. Career: Concerts with Dresden Philharmonic Orchestra, 1992, 1996; Recital, Munich Philharmonic Hall, Gasteig, 1992; Festival La Roque d'Antheron, France, 1993; Concert, Zurich Tonhalle with Zurich Chamber Orchestra, 1994; Concerts with Freiburg Philharmonic Orchestra, 1994, 1997, 1999; Dresden State Orchestra, 1994, 1995; Recitalist in Schumann Cycle Dusseldorf, 1995; South American debut, recital in Teatro Municipal Santiago, Chile, 1996; Concert, Munich Herkulessaal with Munich Symphony, Concert tour with Northwest German Philharmonic Orchestra, Recital, Munich Prinzregenten Theatre, Concert tour with Odessa Philharmonic Orchestra, including Cologne Philharmonic Hall and Stuttgart Liederhalle, 1997; Recital, Dresdner Musikfestspiele, Gave European premiere of Piano Concerto, Four Parables by Schoenfield with Dresdner Sinfoniker, 1998; Concerts with Halle Philharmonic, 1999, 2004; Schumann recital tour including own reconstruction of Schubert Variations in New York, Germany, London Wigmore Hall, World premiere of Piano Concerto by John Pickard with Dresdner Sinfoniker, Concerts, Konzertsaal KKL Lucerne with Lucerne Symphony Orchestra, 2000; Concerts with Bamberger Symphoniker, 2000, 2001; Concert tour with National Symphony Orchestra of Ukraine in the United Kingdom, Concert with Bournemouth Symphony Orchestra, Recital tour in the United Kingdom, Concerts with Israel Northern Symphony Orchestra, Beethoven Fest Bonn, Concert tour with Bolshoi Symphony Orchestra in the United Kingdom, Recital, London Wigmore Hall, 2001; Concerts with Bucharest Philharmonic Orchestra, Concerts with Slovak Philharmonic Orchestra, Concerts, London Royal Festival Hall with London Philharmonic Orchestra, 2002; Concert, Manchester Bridgewater Hall with Hallé Orchestra, 2002, 2003, 2005; Concert tour with NYOS, including Birmingham Symphony Hall and Concertgebouw Amsterdam, 2002; Concert, Prague Autumn Festival with Prague Radio Orchestra in Prague Rudolfinum, Beethoven recital, Teatro Municipal Santiago, Chile, Concerts with Malaysian Philharmonic Orchestra, 2003; Concerts with London Mozart Players, Concert, Munich Prinzregenten Theatre, 2004; Concert, Cologne Philharmonic Hall with Weimar Staatskapelle, Masterclass, Concordia College, Minnesota, 2005; Concerts with Stuttgart Philharmonic Orchestra, Recitals, Schumann Fest Düsseldorf, Concerts with El Paso Symphony Orchestra, USA, Recital, Saint Louis, USA, Concert with Munich Symphony, 2006; Brahms Cycle with Westdeutsche Rundfunk, 2007, 2008; Concert, Spartanburg Philharmonic, 2007; Concert, Graz Philharmonic, 2007; Cologne Philharmonic Hall with Virtuosi Saxoniae, 2009; Recital, Saint Louis, USA, 2009; Masterclass, Valor Summer Conservatory, 2009, 2010; Concerts with Stuttgart Philharmonic Orchestra, 2009, 2011; Concert with Munich Symphony, 2009; Concerts with Winnipeg Symphony, 2010; Recitals, Dresden, 2010; Concert with Auckland Philharmonia, 2010. Publications: Schumann, Variationen über ein Thema von Schubert, reconstructed score by Andreas Boyde, 2000. Recordings: CD releases including works by Schumann, Tchaikovsky, Mussorgsky, Ravel, Dvorak, Schoenfeld, Brahms, Skryabin and Rachmaninoff; Frequent broadcasts with most German Radio Stations and the BBC. Address: c/o Columbia Artists Management, Mark Z Alpert, 1790 Broadway, New York, NY 10019-1412, USA.

BOYLE Danny, b. 20 October 1956, Radcliffe, Lancashire, England. Film Director. Appointments: Artistic Director, Royal Court Theatre, 1982-87; Producer, Elephant, TV film, 1989; Director, The Greater Good, TV series, 1991; Mr Wroe's Virgins, TV, Not Even God is Wise Enough, TV, 1993; Executive Producer, Twin Town, 1996. Creative Works: Films: Shallow Grave, 1994; Trainspotting, A Life Less Ordinary, 1996; The Beach, 1999; Vacuuming Completely Nude in Paradise, Strumpet, 2001; Alien Love Triangle, 28 Days Later, 2002; Millions, 2004; Sunshine, 28 Days Later (Producer), 2007; Slumdog Millionaire, 2008; 127 Hours, 2010; Artistic Director, Isles of Wonder (opening ceremony of London Olympics), 2012; Trance, 2013. Honour: Alexander Korda Award, 1995; Golden Ephebe Award, 1997; British Independent Film Award, 2008; BAFTA Award, 2009; Oscar, 2009. Address: c/o ICM, 6th Floor, 76 Oxford Street, London W1N 0AX, England.

BOZZO BARRERA Italo Humberto, b. 1 August 1939, Santiago, Chile. Divorced. 3 sons, 1 daughter. Education: Medical Degree, Catholic University, 1963; Medico-cirujano, Universidad de Chile, 1964; Resident, General Surgery, 1964-67; Fellowship, Barcelona, Spain, 1974-75. Appointments: Specialist, General Surgery, Escuela Portgredo, University of Chile; Surgical Chief, Hospital Rancagua, 2001-; Chair, Professor of Surgery, University of Santiago, 2008; Magister, Salut Putlice, Catholic University, 2008. Publications: Numerous articles in professional journals. Honours: Fellow, American College of Surgeons, 1996; President, Sociedad Chilene de Coloproctologie, 1996. Memberships: American College of Surgeons; Sociedad de Cirujano de Chile; Sociedad Chilene de Coloproctologie. Address: Caceres 361, Rancagua, Chile. E-mail: ilbozzo@hotmail.com

BRABHAM John Arthur (Jack) (Sir), b. 2 April 1926, Hurstville, New South Wales, Australia. Racing Driver; Company Director. m. (1) Betty Evelyn Beresford, dissolved, 3 sons, (2) Margaret Taylor. Education: Hurstville Technical College; Kogarah Technical College. Career: Former Member, Commonwealth Government Road Safety Committee; World Champion Racing Driver, 1959, 1960, 1966; Ferodo World Trophy for Motor Sport, 1966; 3 times winner, Australian Grand Prix; Constructors Champion of the World, 1966, 1967. Publications: When The Flag Drops, 1971; The Sir Jack Brabham Story, 2004. Honours: Honorary Ambassador for Motor Sport for South Australia; Australia Day Ambassador;

OBE, 1966; Australian of the Year, 1966; Knight, 1979; Named Legend of Australian Sport, Sport Australia Hall of Fame, 2003; Centenary Medal, 2003; Participant, Queen's Baton Relay Commonwealth Games, Melbourne, 2006; AC, 2008. Memberships: RAC(Lon); BRDC(Lon); ARDC(Aust). Address: Suite 404, Locked Mail Bag 1, Robina Town Centre, QLD 4230, Australia.

BRADFORD Barbara Taylor, b. Leeds, Yorkshire, England. Journalist; Novelist. m. Robert Bradford, 1963. Appointments: Editor, Columnist, UK and US periodicals. Publications: Complete Encyclopedia of Homemaking Ideas, 1968; How to Be the Perfect Wife, 1969; Easy Steps to Successful Decorating, 1971; Making Space Grow, 1979; A Woman of Substance, 1979; Voice of the Heart, 1983; Hold the Dream, 1985; Act of Will, 1986; To Be the Best, 1988; The Women in His Life, 1990; Remember, 1991; Angel, 1993; Everything to Gain, 1994; Dangerous to Know, 1995; Love in Another Town, 1995; Her Own Rules, 1996; A Secret Affair, 1996; Power of a Woman, 1997; A Sudden Change of Heart, 1998; Where You Belong, 2000; The Triumph of Katie Byrne, 2001; Three Weeks in Paris, 2002; Emma's Secret, 2003; Unexpected Blessings, 2004-05; Just Rewards, 2006; The Deravenel Triology – The Ravenscar Dynasty, 2006, Heirs of Ravenscar, 2007. Honours: OBE, 2007. Address: c/o Bradford Enterprises, 450 Park Avenue, Suite 1903, New York, NY 10022, USA.

BRADFORD Sarah Mary Malet, b. 3 September 1938, Bournemouth, England. Author; Journalist; Critic; Broadcaster. m. (1) Anthony John Bradford, 1959, 1 son, 1 daughter (2) Viscount Bangor, 1976. Education: Lady Margaret Hall, Oxford, England, 1956-59. Appointment: Manuscript Expert, Christie's, 1975-78. Publications: The Story of Port, 1978, 1983; Portugal and Madeira, 1969; Portugal, 1973; Cesare Borgia, 1976; Disraeli, 1982; Princess Grace, 1984; King George VI, 1989; Elizabeth: A Biography of Her Majesty The Queen, 1996; America's Queen, The Life of Jacqueline Kennedy Onassis, 2000; Lucrezia Borgia, Life, Love and Death in Renaissance Italy, 2004; Diana, 2006. Contributions to: Reviews in Daily Telegraph, Sunday Telegraph, The Times, Sunday Times, Times Literary Supplement, Literary Review; Mail on Sunday; Daily Mail; Spectator; Evening Standard. Address: c/o Aitken Alexander Associates, 18-21 Cavaye Place, London SW10 9PT, England

BRADLEY Patrick James, b. 10 May 1949, Thurles, Co Tipperary, Ireland. Medical Doctor; ENT Surgeon. m. Sheena, 3 sons, 2 daughters. Education: MB, BCh, BAO, 1973, DCH, 1975, University College Medical School, Dublin; MBA, Public Health, Nottingham Business School, Nottingham University, 2002. Appointments: Registrar and Senior Registrar, Royal Liverpool Hospital, 1977-82; Consultant Head and Neck Oncologic Surgeon, Nottingham University Hospitals, Queens Medical Centre campus, 1982-2009; Special Professor of Head and Neck Oncologic Surgery, Nottingham University Medical School, 2007-; Honorary Senior Lecturer, 2003-07, Honorary Professor, Faculty of Medicine and Social Sciences, 2007-, Middlesex University London; National Clinical Lead for Head and Neck Cancer, NHS England and Wales, 2003-08; Huntarian Professor, Royal College of Surgeons, London, 2007-08. Publications: Over 28 book chapters; Over 150 peer reviewed articles in professional journals. Honours: ACCEA Platinum Award, NHS, 2008; Runner Up, BMJ Lifetime Achievement Award, 2009. Memberships: Royal College of Surgeons in Ireland; Royal College of Surgeons of Edinburgh; Royal College of Surgeons London; Honorary Fellowship, Royal College of Speech and Language Therapy, 2006; Fellowship, Hong Kong College of Otolaryngology Head and Neck Surgery, 2007; Honorary Fellowship, Royal Australasian College of Surgeons, 2007; Fellowship, American College of Surgeons, 2007; British Association of Head and Neck Oncologists; Otorhinolaryngological Research Society; British Association of Surgical Oncologists; British Association of Otolaryngologists, Head and Neck Surgeons; Royal Society of Medicine; Midlands Institute of Otology; Young Consultant Head and Neck Surgeons; European Laryngological Society; European Head and Neck Society; European Academy of Otorhinolaryngology, Head and Neck Surgery; European Salivary Gland Society; International Academy of Oral Oncology; National Association of Laryngectomy Clubs (UK); The Head and Neck Foundation; Nottingham Rhinological Research Fund. Address: 37 Lucknow Drive, Mapperley Park, Nottingham NG3 5EU, England. E-mail: pjbradley@zoo.co.uk

BRADY Patricia Veronica, b. 5 January 1929, Melbourne, Australia. Academic; Catholic Nun. Education: Loreto Convent, Toorak, Victoria; BA (Hons), University of Melbourne; MA, PhD, University of Toronto. Appointments: Senior English/History Mistress, Loreto Schools, Melbourne and Sydney; Lecturer, English & Fine Arts, Teachers' College, Melbourne; Senior Tutor, Lecturer, Senior Lecturer, Associate Professor, Honorary Senior Research Fellow, Department of English, University of Western Australia. Publications: Over 100 articles on Australian literature, culture and belief in national and international journals. Honours: Honorary Doctorate, University of Western Australia, 2009; Board Member, Australian Broadcasting Corporation; Library & Information Service of Western Australia; Member, Appeals Board, Department of Social Services; Chair, Older Australians' Advisory Council. Memberships: Australian Society of Authors; PEA International; The Australian Greens; Amnesty international. Address: 20/26 Broome Street, Nedlands, WA 6009, Australia. E-mail: vbrady@cyllose.uwa.edu.au

BRAGADÓTTIR Ragnheidur, b. 10 May 1956, Reykjavik, Iceland. Professor. m. Bjarni Kristjansson, 2 daughters. Education: Cand jur, Faculty of Law, University of Iceland, 1982; Additional Criminal Law Education, University of Copenhagen, 1983. Appointments: Assistant Judge, Criminal Court, Reykjavik, 1984; Legal Expert, Ministry of Justice, Reykjavik, 1984-85; Lecturer, 1985-89, Reader, 1989-95, Associate Professor, 1995-99, Professor, 2000-, Faculty of Law, University of Iceland; Com Pardon, Ministry of Justice, 1993-; Member, Editorship, Nordisk Tidsskrift for Kriminalvidenskab, 1999-; Board member, Scandinavian Research Council for Criminology, 1998-; Faculty of Law's Com Doctoral Studies, 2005-10; Vice Chairman, 2007-09, Chairman, 2010-, Scandinavian Research Council for Criminology. Publications: Books and articles to professional journals; Research in Icelandic criminal law, environmental criminal law and violence in the perspective of women's law. Memberships: Centre of Women's Studies, University of Iceland; Com Edn Brokers, Ministry of Economics. E-mail: rb@hi.is

BRAGG Melvyn (Baron Bragg of Wigton in the County of Cumbria), b. 6 October 1939, Wigton, Cumbria, England. Author; Broadcaster. m. Lisa Roche, 1961, deceased 1971, 1 daughter, (2) Cate Haste, 1973, 1 son, 1 daughter. Education: 2nd Class Honours, Modern History, Wadham College, Oxford, 1961. Appointments: General Trainee, BBC, 1961; Producer on Monitor, 1963; Director, films including portrait of Sir John Barbirolli, 1963; Writer, Debussy film for Ken Russell, 1963; Editor, for BBC2, New Release (Arts Magazine) which became Review, then Arena, 1964; Documentary, Writers World, 1964; Take It or Leave It (Literary Panel Game), 1964; Presenter, for Tyne Tees TV, In the Picture (local arts programme), 1971; Presenter/Producer, for BBC, Second House, 1974-8; Editor/Presenter, BBC, Read All About It, 1974-78; Interviewer for BBC, Tonight, 1974-78; Editor, Presenter, The South Bank Show, 1978; Head of Arts LWT, 1982-90; Programmes for Channel Four, 1982-90; Controller of Arts, LWT, 1990; Director, LWT Productions, 1992; Deputy Chairman, 1985-90, Chairman, 1990-95, Border TV, 1990-95; Governor LSE, 1997; Presenter, In Our Time, BBC Radio 4, 1998-. Publications: Books include: For Want of a Nail, 1965; The Second Inheritance, 1966; Without a City Wall, 1968; The Nerve, 1971; Josh Lawton, 1972; The Silken Net, 1974; Autumn Manoeuvres, 1978; The Cumbrian Trilogy, The Christmas Child, Love and Glory, 1984; A Time to Dance (BBC TV adaption 1992), 1991; Crystal Rooms, 1992; CREDO, 1996; The Sword and The Miracle (USA publication), 1997; The Soldier's Return, 1999; A Son of War, 2001; The Adventure of English (executive producer/presenter of television series), 2001; Crossing The Lines, 2003; Remember Me..., 2008; Screenplays: Isadora; The Music Lovers; Jesus Christ Superstar; A Time to Dance, 1992; Musicals: Mardi Gras, 1976; The Hired Man, 1985; Play: King Lear In New York, 1992; Journalist in various newspapers. Honours include: Numerous for the South Bank Show, including 3 Prix Italias; Ivor Novello Award for Best Musical, 1985; Richard Dimbleby Award for Outstanding Contribution to TV, 1987; 2 TRIC Awards, 1990, 1994; VLV Award, 2000; WHSmith Literary Award, 2000; Numerous honorary degrees. Memberships: President, MIND; President, The National Campaign for the Arts (NCA). Address: 12 Hampstead Hill Gardens, London, NW3 2PL, England.

BRAMALL, Field Marshal Baron, Edwin Noel Westby, b. 18 December 1923, Tunbridge Wells, Kent. Army Officer; Lord Lieutenant of Greater London. m. Avril, The Lady Bramall, 1 son, 1 daughter. Education: Eton College, 1937-42; Student, Army Staff College, Camberley, 1952; Imperial Defence College, 1970. Appointments: Joined Army 1942; Commissioned into KRRC, 1943; Served in NW Europe, 1944-45; Occupation of Japan, 1946, War Office, 1947-48; Instructor, School of Infantry, 1949-51; PSC, 1952; Middle East, 1953-58; Instructor Staff College, 1958-61; Staff of Lord Mountbatten, Ministry of Defence, 1963-64; CO 2 Green Jackets, Malaysia, 1965-66; Command, 5 Airportable Brigade, 1967-69, IDC 1970; GOC, 1 Division BAOR, 1971-73; Lieutenant General, 1973; Commander, British Forces Hong Kong, 1973-76; General, 1976; Colonel Commandant 3 Battalion Royal Green Jackets, 1973-84; Colonel, 2 Gurkhas, 1976-86; Commander-in-Chief, UK Land Forces, 1976-78; Vice-Chief of Defence Staff, Personnel and Logistics, 1978-79; Chief of General Staff, 1979-82; ADC General to H M The Queen, 1979-82; Field Marshal, 1982; Chief of the Defence Staff, 1982-85. Publication: The Chiefs: The Story of the UK Chiefs of Staff (co-author). Honours: Lord Lieutenant of Greater London, 1986-98; KG; GCB; OBE; MC; JP. Memberships include: President, Gurkha Brigade Association, 1987-; President, Greater London Playing Fields Association, 1990-; President, MCC, 1988-89; Izingari Cricket Club; Free Foresters Cricket Club; Travellers; Army and Navy; Pratts. Address: House of Lords, Westminster, London SW1A 0PW, England.

BRANAGH Kenneth, b. 10 December 1960, Belfast, Northern Ireland. Actor; Director. m. (1) Emma Thompson, divorced, (2) Lindsay Brunnock, 2003. Education: Royal Academy of Dramatic Art. Appointments: Numerous Theatre and Radio Work. Creative Works: Films: High Season; A Month in the Country; Henry V, 1989; Dead Again, 1991; Peter's Friends, Swing Kids, Swan Song, 1992; Much Ado About Nothing, 1993; Mary Shelley's Frankenstein; Othello, In the Bleak Midwinter, 1995; Hamlet, 1996; The Theory of Flight, The Proposition, The Gingerbread Man, 1997; Celebrity, Wild, Wild West, 1998; Love's Labour's Lost, 2000; How to Kill Your Neighbor's Dog, Rabbit Proof Fence, Harry Potter and the Chamber of Secrets, Alien Love Triangle, Shackleton, 2002; Five Children and It, 2004; Warm Springs, 2005; The Magic Flute (directed), As You Like It (directed), 2006; Sleuth (directed), 2007; Valkyrie, Wallander (TV), 2008; The Boat That Rocked, 2009; My Week with Marilyn, 2011. Publications: Public Enemy (play), 1988; Beginning (memoirs), 1989; The Making of Mary Shelley's Frankenstein, 1994; In the Bleak Midwinter, 1995; Screenplays for Henry V, Much Ado About Nothing, Hamlet. Honours: Evening Standard Best Film Award; New York Film Critics Circle Best Director Award; Hon DLitt, Queens University, Belfast, 1990; BAFTA Award, Best Director, 1990; Nominated, London Evening Standard Theatre Award for Best Actor, 2003; Nominated, Laurence Olivier Theatre Award for Best Actor, 2004. Memberships: RADA Council. Address: Shepperton Studios, Studio Road, Shepperton, Middlesex TW17 0QD, England.

BRAND Russell, b. 4 June 1975, Grays, Essex, England. Comedian; Actor; Columnist; Author; TV and Radio Presenter. Education: Grays School; Italia Conti Academy; Drama Centre, London. Career: Standup Comedian: Hackney Empire New Act of the Year final, 2000; Better Now, Edinburgh Festival, 2004; Eroticised Humour, Edinburgh Festival, 2005; Shame, nationwide tour, 2006; Secret Policeman's Ball, 2006; Co-host, Teenage Cancer Trust, 2007; Royal Variety Performance, 2007; Russell Brand: Only Joking, nationwide tour, 2007; Russell Brand: Scandalous, tour of UK, America and Australia, 2009; Presenter: MTV, 2000-01, 2008; Big Brother, Channel 4, 2004-07; The Russell Brand Show, Channel 4, 2007; BRIT Awards, 2007; Comic Relief, 2007; Russell Brand's Ponderland, 2007-08; MTV Video Music Awards, 2008, 2009; Actor: various TV roles; Films: Forgetting Sarah Marshall; Bedtime Stories; St Trinian's; Get Him to the Greek; Despicable Me. Publications: Autobiography, My Booky Wook, 2007.

BRANDOLINO Rosario Giovanni, b. 1 January 1955, Reggio Calabria, Italy. Architecture Educator; Architect. Education: Diploma, Art School, Mattia Preti, Reggio Calabria 1973; Degree in Architecture, University of Study of Reggio Calabria, 1984; PhD, University of Study of Palermo, 1994. Appointments: Member, Scientific Committee for the Master's in Architecture and Archaeology of the City, High School of Classical Architecture and Classical Archaeology of the City, Reggio Calabria; Member of Laboratory Models, Faculty of Architecture, University of Reggio Calabria, 2010. Publications: Numerous articles in professional journals. Honours: Luigi Vagnetti Award, 1984; Fiat Award, 1985. Memberships: Ordine degli Architetti, Pianificatori, Paesaggisti Conservatori della Provincia di Reggio Calabria, Italy.

BRANDON Peter Samuel, b. 4 June 1943, Writtle, Essex, England. Chartered Surveyor. m. Mary A E Canham, 1 son, 2 daughters. Education: MSc, Architecture, University of Bristol, 1978; DSc, Information Systems, University of Salford, 1996; DEng, Heriot-Watt University, 2006. Appointments: Surveyor, Surveying Practice, 1963-67; Surveyor, Local Government, 1968-70; Lecturer, 1969-73, Head of Surveying Department, 1981-85, Portsmouth Polytechnic; Principal

Lecturer, Bristol Polytechnic, 1973-81; Head of Surveying Department, University of Salford 1985-93, Pro Vice Chancellor, 1993-2001, Director, Strategic Programmes and Public Orator, 2001-2003, University of Salford; Director of Strategic Programmes, School of the Built Environment, 2003-10; Director, Salford University Think Lab, 2005-10; Professor Emeritus, University of Salford, 2010-; Freelance Adviser on Research and Educational Matters, 2003-. Publications: Numerous articles including: Microcomputers in Building Appraisal (with G Moore), 1983; Computer Programs for Building Cost Appraisal (with G Moore and P Main), 1985; An Integrated Database for Quantity (with J Kirkham), 1989; Editor: Building, Cost Modelling and Computers, 1987; Quantity Surveying Techniques: New Direction, 1990; Investment, Procurement & Performance in Construction, 1991; Integrated Construction Information, 1995; Evaluation of the Built Environment for Sustainability, 1997; Cities & Sustainability: Sustaining Cultural Heritage, 2000; Evaluating Sustainable Development in the Built Environment (co-author Patrizia Lombardi), 2005; Virtual Futures for Design, Construction and Procurement (co-editor with Tuba Kocaturk), 2008; Clients Driving Innovation (co-editor with Shu-Ling Lu), 2008; Over 150 publications in more than 30 countries worldwide. Honour: Honorary Member, South African Association of Quantity Surveyors for services to Quantity Surveying worldwide, 1994. Membership: Fellow, Royal Institute of Chartered Surveyors. Address: 3 Woodland Drive, Lymm, Cheshire, WA13 0BL, England. E-mail: p.s.brandon@salford.ac.uk

BRANDSTRUP Birgitte, b. 4 April 1965, Virum, Denmark. Surgeon; Clinical Associate Professor. m. Peter Starup, 1 son, 1 daughter. Education: Medical Doctor Certificate, 1992, PhD (Medicine), 2003, University of Copenhagen. Appointments: Junior Resident: Grindsted Hospital, 1992-94; Surgical Resident, Hvidovre University Hospital, 1994-95; Rigshospitalet, 1996; Glostrup University Hospital, 1996-98; Research Fellowship, Bispebjerg University Hospital, 1999-2002; Senior Resident: Glostrup University Hospital, 2002-04; Slagelse University Hospital, 2005-06; Bispebjerg University Hospital, 2006-08; Consultant Surgeon, Chief of Endoscopic Department, Glostrup University Hospital, 2008-10; Consultant Surgeon, Chief of the Endoscopic Unit and the Intensive Surveillance Unit, Surgical Department, Hvidovre University Hospital, 2010-; Clinical Associate Professor, University of Copenhagen, 2010-. Publications: Thesis, Restricted Intravenous Fluid Therapy in Colorectal Surgery, 2003; Book, Rationel Fluid and Electrolyte Therapy and Nutrition, in Danish, 2004; Book chapters in Perioperative Fluid Therapy; Articles in Perioperative Fluid Management. Honours: 1st Prize, Best Research & Presentation, Danish Gastro-Enterological Society, 2001, 2002 and Danish Surgical Society, 2003. Memberships: The Danish Surgical Society; The Danish Gastro-Enterological Society. Address: Farumgaards Alle 14, DK-3520 Farum, Denmark. E-mail: bbrandstrup@hotmail.com

BRANFIELD John Charles, b. 19 January 1931, Burrow Bridge, Somerset, England. Writer; Teacher. m. Kathleen Elizabeth Peplow, 2 sons, 2 daughters. Education: MA, Queens' College, Cambridge University; MEd, University of Exeter. Publications: Nancekuke,1972; Sugar Mouse, 1973; The Scillies Trip, 1975; Castle Minalto, 1979; The Fox in Winter, 1980; Brown Cow, 1983; Thin Ice, 1983; The Falklands Summer, 1987; The Day I Shot My Dad, 1989; Lanhydrock Days, 1991; A Breath of Fresh Air, 2001; Ella and Charles Naper: Life and Art at Lamorna, 2003; Charles Simpson: Painter of Animals and Birds, Coastline and Moorland, 2005; Tony Giles: Painter of Cornwall's Man-Made Landscape, 2005; Mingoose and Chapel Porth: The Story of a Cornish Valley, 2006; Geoffrey and Jill Garnier, a Marriage of the Arts, 2010. Address: Mingoose Villa, Mingoose, Mount Hawke, Truro, Cornwall TR4 8BX, England.

BRANSON (Sir) Richard Charles Nicholas, b. 18 July 1950, Shamley Green, Surrey, England. Founder; Chairman; President. m. (1) Kristen Tomassi, 1972, divorced 1979, (2) Joan Templeman, 1989, 1 son, 1 daughter. Education: Stowe. Appointments: Editor, Student Magazine, 1968-69; Founder, Student Advisory Centre (now Help), 1970; Founder, Virgin Mail-Order Company, 1969, First Virgin record shop, 1971; Recording Company, 1973; Nightclub (The Venue), 1976; Virgin Atlantic Airways, 1984; Founder and Chairman, Virgin Retail Group, Virgin Communications, Virgin Travel Group, Voyager Group; Group also includes publishing, broadcasting, contraction, heating systems, holidays; Chairman, 1986-88, President, 1988-, UK 2000; Director, Intourist Moscow Ltd, 1988-90; Founder, The Healthcare Foundation, 1987; Founder, Virgin Radio, 1993; Founder, Virgin Rail Group Ltd, 1996; Launched Virgin Cola drink, 1994, Babylon Restaurant, 2001; Crossed Pacific in hot air balloon with Per Lindstrand, 1991; World Record for fastest crossing of the Channel in an Amphibious Vehicle, 2004. Honours: Blue Riband Title for Fastest Atlantic Crossing, 1986; Seagrave Trophy, 1987. Publication: Losing My Virginity, autobiography, 1998. Address: c/o Virgin Group PLC, 120 Campden Hill Road, London W8 7AR, England.

BRASFIELD James, b. 19 January 1952, Savannah, Georgia, USA. University Senior Lecturer; Poet. m. Charlotte Holmes, 1983, 1 son. Education: BA, English, Armstrong State College (now Armstrong-Atlantic State University), 1975; MFA, Columbia University, 1979. Appointments: Editorial Assistant, Paris Review, 1981-82; Assistant Professor, Western Carolina University, 1984-87; Visiting Assistant Professor, University of Memphis, 2008-09; Senior Lecturer, Pennsylvania State University, University Park, 1987-. Publications: Inheritance and Other Poems, chapbook, 1983; Translation, with the author, The Selected Poems of Oleh Lysheha, 1999; Ledger of Crossroads, poems. Contributions to: Agni; Antaeus; Black Warrior Review; Chicago Review; Columbia; Iowa Review; Poetry Wales; Prairie Schooner; Quarterly West; Seattle Review; Stand; The Southern Review; Other literary magazines and professional journals. Honours: Fulbright Creative Arts Award to Ukraine, 1993-94; Fulbright Award to Ukraine, 1999; The American Association for Ukrainian Studies Prize for Translation, 1999; The 2000 PEN Award for Poetry in Translation; Creative Writing Fellowship in Poetry, National Endowment for the Arts, 2001-02; Poetry Fellowship, Pennsylvania Council on the Arts, 2004; The Pushcart Prize, XXIV: Best of the Small Presses, for translation; Notable Alumnus, Armstrong-Atlantic State University, 2011. Memberships: Academy of American Poets; PEN American Centre. Address: Department of English, 119 Burrowes Building, Pennsylvania State University, University Park, PA 16802, USA.

BRASSEAUX Carl Anthony, b. 19 August 1951, Opelousas, Louisiana, USA. Historian. m. Glenda, 21 July 1973, 2 sons, 1 daughter. Education: BA, Political Science, cum laude, University of Southwestern Louisiana, 1974; MA, History, 1975; Doctorat de 3e cycle, University of Paris, 1982. Appointments: Assistant Director, Center for Louisiana Studies, 1975-2000; Professor, History and Geography Department, University of Louisiana, Lafayette, 1998-; Director, Center for Louisiana Studies, 2003-; Director,

Center for Cultural and Eco-Tourism, University of Louisiana at Lafayette, 2001-; Director, Center for Louisiana Studies, 2004-. Publications: 102 scholarly publications in journals in North America and Europe; 33 book length works. Honours: Kemper Williams Prize, 1979; Robert L Brown Prize, 1980; President's Memorial Award, Louisiana Historical Association, 1986; Book Prize, French Colonial Historical Society, 1987; Chevalier, L'Ordre des Palmes Academiques, 1994; University Distinguished Professor, History, 1995; National Daughters of the American Revolution Award, 1995; Fellow, Louisiana Historical Association, 2000-; Louisiana Writer of the Year, 2003; Louisiana Humanist of the Year, 2005-; Archibald Hanna Jr Fellowship in American History, Yale University, 2008; Rivers Prize, 2009. Membership: Louisiana Historical Association. Address: 201 Parliament Drive, Lafayette, LA 70506, USA.

BRAVO-INCLÁN Luis Alberto, b. 21 April 1958, Mexico City, Mexico. Hydrobiologist; Researcher in Limnology. m. Cecilia Tomasini-Ortiz, 2 daughters. Education: BSc, Biology, National Autonomous University of Mexico, 1983; MSc, Biology, UNAM, 1995. Appointments: Junior Researcher, Research Center for the Control of Water Quality, Mexico City, 1986-91; Senior Researcher, Mexican Institute of Water Technology, Jiutepec, Morelos, Mexico, 1991-2010; Professor, Limnology, Engineering Faculty, UNAM, Jiutepec, 2004-10. Publications: Co-author, Valle de Bravo Reservoir, 1988; Author, Zimapan Reservice, 2008; Co-author, Pátzcuaro Lake, 2008. Honours: Fellow Founder, IMTA – 20 years Diploma, 1986-2006; Contributor, National Congress, Mexican Federation of Sanitary Engineering and Environmental Science, 2000; Medal for Best Technical Work, 2000; Listed in international biographical dictionaries. Memberships: International Water Association; North American Lake Management Society. Address: Paseo Cuauhnáhuac 8532, Col Progreso, Jiutepec, Morelos, 62550, Mexico. E-mail: lubravo@tlaloc.imta.mx Website: www.imta.gob.mx

BRAWN Ross, b. 23 November 1954, Manchester, England. Motorsport Engineer; Formula Team Owner. Education: Reading School, Berkshire. Career: Trainee Engineer, United Kingdom Atomic Energy Authority, Harwell, Oxfordshire; Milling Machine Operator (later mechanic to Formula 3 racing team), March Engineering, Bicester, 1976; Machinst (later R&D and Aerodynamicist), Williams team, 1978; Engineer, Jaguar, 1989; Technical Director, Benetton team, 1991; Technical Director, Ferrari F1, 1996-2006; Team Principal, Honda F1, 2007; Brawn GP, 2009; Mercedes GP, 2009-. Honours: Honorary Doctor of Engineering, Brunel University, 2006.

BRAZHNIKOV Andrey V, b. 28 October 1959, Kostroma, Russia. Scientist; Educator. m. Elena S Karpenko, 1 daughter. Education: BS, Electrical Engineering, major in Automatics and Telemechanics, Honours Degree, cum laude, 1982; PhD, Electromechanics 1985. Appointments: Chief of Laboratory, Research Institute, Krasnoyarsk, 1987-88; Chief of several scientific projects among them 2 international projects, 1991-2, 1993-99; Associate Professor, Department of Mining Machines and Complexes, Siberian Federal University, 1996-; Professor, Krasnoyarsk Branch of Russian Academy of Natural History, Moscow, Russia, 2007-. Publications: More than 120 scientific works. Honours: Bortnik's Fund, Moscow, 2007; Federal Educational Agency of Russia, 2006; Russian Research and Higher Educational Institutes, 1980-; Prizes for organising scientific work, Siberian Federal University, Krasnoyarsk, Russia, 1997-2005; Honoured Worker of Science and Education, Moscow, 2008; Vernadsky Medal for Valuable Contribution to Russian Science, Moscow, 2008; Listed in Who's Who publications and biographical dictionaries. Memberships: Institute of Electrical and Electronics Engineers; Research Board of Advisors, American Biographical Institute; Russian Academy of Natural History. Address: PO Box 16142, Krasnoyarsk 660001, Russia. E-mail: multypha@mail.ru

BRAZIER Marcus, b. 13 February 1971, Victoria, Australia. Biomedical Research Scientist. Education: PhD, Neuroscience, Department of Pathology, University of Melbourne. Appointments: Demonstrator, Pathology classes (3 years), 2001-10; Research Assistant, University of Bath, England, 2004-06; Research Associate, University of Melbourne, 2006-. Publications: Numerous articles in professional journals. Honours: Personal Licence (Animals) UK Home Office; Zeiss trained in use of PALM laser microdissection; Melbourne Abroad Travel Scholarship. Memberships: National Honors Society.

BREAM Julian, b. 15 July 1933, London, England. Classical Guitarist and Lutenist. m. (1) Margaret Williamson, 1 adopted son, (2) Isobel Sanchez, 1980, divorced. Education: Royal College of Music. Career: Cheltenham, 1947; London debut, Wigmore Hall, 1950; Many transcriptions for guitar of Romantic and Baroque works; Commissioned new works from Britten, Walton, Henze and Arnold; Tours throughout the world; Recitals as soloist and with the Julian Bream Consort (formed 1960); Many recitals with Sir Peter Pears and Robert Tear; Guitar duo with John Williams; 60th Birthday Concert, Wigmore Hall, London, 1993. Honours: Fellow, Royal Northern College of Music, 1983; Honorary DUniv (Surrey), 1968; Honorary DMus (Leeds), 1984; Villa-Lobos Gold Medal, 1976; Numerous recording awards. Address: Hazard Chase, Norman House, Cambridge Place, Cambridge, CB2 1NS, England. Website: www.hazardchase.co.uk

BREED William Godfrey, b. 27 June 1941, Redruth, Cornwall, England. University Professor. m. Esther Elizabeth, 1972, 3 sons. Education: BSc (Hons), Aberdeen University, 1965; DPhil, Oxford University, 1968. Appointments: Research Fellow, University of California, Los Angeles, USA, 1968-69; Research Fellow, Birmingham University, 1969-73; Lecturer, Senior Lecturer, Associate Professor, Professor, University of Adelaide, 1973-. Publications: Around 160 scientific publications; Book, Native Mice & Rats, 2007. Honours: Honorary Life Member, Australian Mammal Society. Membership: Australian Mammal Society; American Society of Mammalogists; Society of Reproductive Biology. Address: 69 Harrow Road, St Peters, SA 5069, Australia. E-mail: bill.breed@adelaide.edu.au

BREEZE David John, b. 25 July 1944, Blackpool, England. Civil Servant. m. Pamela Diane Silvester, 2 sons. Education: BA, Honours, Modern History, 1965, PhD, 1970, University College, University of Durham; Hon D Litt, Glasgow, 2008. Appointments: Inspector of Ancient Monuments, 1969-89; Chief Inspector of Ancient Monuments, Scotland, 1989-2005; Co-ordinator, Antonine Wall World Heritage Site, 2008-09. Publications: Books: The Northern Frontiers of Roman Britain, 1982; Roman Forts in Britain, 1983; A Queen's Progress, 1987; Roman Officers and Frontiers (with B Dobson), 1993; Roman Scotland: Frontier Country, 1996, 2nd edition, 2006; The Stone of Destiny (with G Munro), 1997; Historic Scotland, 1998; Hadrian's Wall, 4th edition (with B Dobson), 2000; Historic Scotland, People and Places, 2002; The Antonine Wall, 2006; Frontiers of the Roman Empire (with S Jilek and

A Thiel), 2005; Handbook to the Roman Wall, 14th edition, 2006; Roman Frontiers in Britain, 2007; Edge of Empire, The Antonine Wall, 2008; Papers in British and foreign journals. Honours: Trustee, Senhouse Roman Museum, Maryport, 1985-; President, Society of Antiquaries of Scotland, 1987-90; Chairman, Hadrian's Wall Pilgrimages, 1989, 1999, 2009; Chairman, British Archaeological Awards, 1993-2009; Visiting Professor of Archaeology, University of Durham, 1994-; Honorary Professor, University of Edinburgh, 1996-; Vice-President, Cumberland and Westmorland Antiquarian and Archaeological Society, 2002-; Honorary Professor, University of Newcastle, 2003-; President, Newcastle Society of Antiquaries, 2008-11; Archaeologist of the Year, 2009; The European Archaeological Heritage Prize, 2010; President, Royal Archaeological Institute, 2009-12. Memberships: FSA, 1975; Hon FSA Scot, 1970; FRSE, 1991; Hon MIfA, 1990; Corresponding Member, German Archaeological Institute, 1979. Address: 36 Granby Road, Edinburgh EH16 5NL, Scotland. E-mail: davidbreeze@hotmail.co.uk

BREMNER Rory Keith Ogilvy, b. 6 April 1961, Edinburgh, Scotland. Impressionist; Satirist. m. (1) Susie Davies, 1986, divorced 1994, (2)Tessa Campbell Fraser, 1999, 2 daughters. Education: BA (Hons), French and German, Kings College, London, 1984. Career: TV series, BBC, 1985-92; TV series, Channel 4, 1993-; Translation, The Silver Lake, Weill, 1998; Translation, Bizet's Carmen, Broomhill Opera, 2000. Honours: BAFTA, 1994, 1995; RTS, 1994, 1998, 1999; British Comedy Award, 1992; Channel 4 Political Humourist of the Year, 1999, 2001; Fellowship, Kings College London, 2005; James Joyce Award, Literary and Historical Society, 2008. Address: The Richard Stone Partnership, 2 Henrietta Street, London WC2E 8PS, England.

BREMZE Sarmīte, b. 19 September 1951, Latvia. Philologist; Lecturer. m. Jānis, 1 son, 1 daughter. Education: English Language and Literature, Latvia State University, 1977; Candidate of Pedagogical Sciences, Vilnius State University, 1990; Doctor of Pedagogy, Dr paed, Daugavpils Pedagogical University, 1993. Appointments: Assistant Professor, 1993, 1998, Associate Professor, 2006, Latvia University of Agriculture; Head, Department of Pedagogy and Psychology, RPIVA, 1996-98. Publications: English for Sociology Students; Changes in Lectures Lifelong Educations, 2007. Honours: Certificate awarded by Rector of LLU for Significant Contributions in the Upbringing of New Specialists at University No 48, 2011. Memberships: Academically Educated Women. E-mail: sarma325@cs.llu.lv

BRENNER Sydney, b. 13 January 1927, Germiston, South Africa (British Citizen). Molecular Biologist. m. May Woolf Balkind, 3 sons, 1 stepson, 2 daughters. Education: MSc, 1947, MB, BCh, 1951, University of Witwatersrand, Johannesburg; PhD, Oxford University, 1954. Appointments: Virus Laboratory, University of California at Berkeley, 1954; Lecturer in Physiology, University of Witwatersrand, 1955-57; Researcher, 1957-79, Director, Molecular Biology Laboratory, 1979-86, Director, Molecular Genetics Unit, 1986-92, Medical Research Council, Cambridge; Member, Scripps Institute, La Jolla, California, 1992-94; Director, Molecular Sciences Institute, Berkeley, California, 1996-2001; Distinguished Research Professor, Salk Institute, La Jolla, California, 2001-. Honours: Honorary DSc: Dublin, Witwatersrand, Chicago, London, Leicester, Oxford; Honorary LLD, Glasgow, Cambridge; Honorary DLitt, Singapore; Warren Triennial Prize, 1968; William Bate Hardy Prize, Cambridge Philosophical Society, 1969; Gregor Mendel Medal of German Academy of Science Leopoldina, 1970; Albert Lasker Medical Research Award, 1971; Gairdner Foundation Annual Award, Canada, 1978; Royal Medal of Royal Society, 1974; Prix Charles Leopold Mayer, French Academy, 1975; Krebs Medal, Federation of European Biochemical Societies, 1980; Ciba Medal, Biochemical Society, 1981; Feldberg Foundation Prize, 1983; Neil Hamilton Fairley Medal, Royal College of Physicians, 1985; Croonian Lecturer, Royal Society of London, 1986; Rosenstiel Award, Brandeis University, 1986; Prix Louis Jeantet de Médecine, Switzerland, 1987; Genetics Society of America Medal, 1987; Harvey Prize, Israel Institute of Technology, 1987; Hughlings Jackson Medal, Royal Society of Medicine, 1987; Waterford Bio-Medical Science Award, The Research Institute of Scripps Clinic, 1988; Kyoto Prize, Inamori Foundation, 1990; Gairdner Foundation Award, Canada, 1991; Copley Medal, Royal Society, 1991; King Faisal International Prize for Science (King Faisal Foundation), 1992; Bristol-Myers Squibb Award for Distinguished Achievement in Neuroscience Research, 1992; Albert Lasker Award for Special Achievement, 2000; Nobel Prize for Physiology or Medicine, 2002. Memberships: Member, Medical Research Council, 1978-82, 1986-90; Fellow, King's College, Cambridge, 1959-; Honorary Professor of Genetic Medicine, University of Cambridge, Clinical School, 1989-; Foreign Associate, NAS, 1977; Foreign Member, American Philosophical Society, 1979; Foreign Member, Real Academia de Ciencias, 1985; External Scientific Member, Max Planck Society, 1988; Member, Academy Europea, 1989; Corresponding Scientifique Emerite de l'INSERM, Associe Etranger Academie des Sciences, France; Fellow, American Academy of Microbiology; Foreign Honorary Member, American Academy of Arts and Sciences, 1965; Honorary Member, Deutsche Akademie der Natursforsche Leopoldina, 1975; Society for Biological Chemists, 1975; Honorary FRSE; Honorary Fellow, Indian Academy of Sciences, 1989; Honorary Member, Chinese Society of Genetics, 1989; Honorary Fellow, Royal College of Pathologists, 1990; Honorary Member, Associate of Physicians of GB and Ireland, 1991. Address: Kings College, Cambridge, CB2 1ST, England.

BRERETON Richard Geoffrey, b. 5 January 1955, Westminster, London, England. University Professor. Education: BA, 1976, MA, 1980, PhD, 1981, Cambridge. Appointments: Researcher, Cambridge University, 1979-83; University Lecturer, Reader, Professor, 1983-, Director, Centre for Chemometrics, 2004-, Bristol University. Publications: 7 books; 15 book chapters; 153 journal papers; 9 conference contributions; 144 short articles including: Chemometrics: Applications of Maths and Statistics to Laboratory Systems, 1990 and 1993; Chemometrics: Data Analysis for the Laboratory and Chemical Plant, 2003, 2004 and 2007; Applied Chemometrics for Scientists, 2007. Honours: Theophilus Redwood Lectureship, 2006; Royal Society of Chemistry; 159 invited and plenary conference lectures; Research Awards from 11 organisations. Memberships: Fellow, Royal Society of Chemistry; Fellow, Royal Statistical Society; Fellow, Royal Society of Medicine. Address: School of Chemistry, University of Bristol, Cantocks Close, Bristol BS8 1TS, England. E-mail: r.g.brereton@bris.ac.uk

BRESENHAM Jack E, b. USA. Chief Technical Officer; Emeritus Professor of Computer Science. Education: BSEE, University of New Mexico, 1959; MSIE, 1960, PhD, 1964, Stanford University. Appointments: Senior Technical Staff Member, Manager, Engineer, Planner, Programmer, Analyst, IBM, 1960-87; Teacher, Professor of Computer Science, Winthrop University, 1987-2003; Chief Technical Officer, Bresenham Consulting. Publications include: Algorithm for computer control of a digital plotter, 1965, reprinted, 1980, reprinted, 1998; Pixel processing fundamentals, 1996; Teaching the graphics processing pipeline: cosmetic and geometric attribute implications, 2001; The Analysis and Statistics of Line Distribution, 2002; 9 US Patents. Honours include: IBM Outstanding Contribution Award, 1967, 1984 and 1989; Distinguished Citizen Award, Wofford College National Alumni Association, 1993; Honorary Director and Invited Lecturer, University of Cantabria, Santander, Spain, July 2000; Jury Member of habilitation a diriger les recherches panel, University of Paris-8 for Jean Jaques Bourdin, 2000; Golden Quill Award in recognition of work to improve writing skills among computer science students, Winthrop University, 2001; Honorary Chair, The 11th International Conference in Central Europe on Computer Graphics, Visualization and Computer Vision, 2003; Named Distinguished Alumnus, School of Engineering, University of New Mexico, 2003. Address: 303 Palo Alto Drive, Rio Rancho, NM 87124, USA.

BREUR Hans, b. 17 May 1977, Arnhem, Netherlands. Paediatric Cardiologist. m. Gudule, 1 son, 2 daughters. Education: MD, 2003, PhD, 2003, Utrecht University, Netherlands. Appointments: Resident, Paediatrics, 2003-08, Fellow, Paediatric Cardiology, 2008-10, Paediatric Cardiologist, 2011-, Paediatrics Department, University Medical Centre, Utrecht. Publications: 20 ISI publications. Honours: Hippocrates Study Prize, 2002; Netherlands Heart Foundation Travel Grant, 2000. Memberships: Association for European Paediatric Cardiology. Address: Wilhelmina Children's Hospital University Medical Center, PO Box 85090, 3508 AB Utrecht, The Netherlands. E-mail: h.breur@umcutrecht.nl

BRIDGEMAN, Viscountess Victoria Harriet Lucy, b. 30 March 1942, Durham, England. Library Director; Writer. m. Viscount Bridgeman, 1966, 4 sons. Education: MA, Trinity College, Dublin, 1964. Appointment: Executive Editor, The Masters, 1965-69; Editor, Discovering Antiques, 1970-72; Established own company producing books and articles on fine and decorative arts; Founder and Managing Director, Bridgeman Art Library, London, New York, Paris and Berlin. Publications: An Encyclopaedia of Victoriana, 1974; An Illustrated History, The British Eccentric, 1975; Society Scandals, 1976; Beside the Seaside, 1976; A Guide to Gardens of Europe, 1979; The Last Word, 1983; 8 titles in Connoisseur's Library series. Honours: European Woman of the Year Award, Arts Section, 1997; FRSA. Address: The Bridgeman Art Library, 17-19 Garway Road, London W2 4PH, England. Website: www.bridgeman.co.uk

BRIDGES Jeff, b. 4 December 1949, Los Angeles, USA. Actor. m. Susan Geston, 3 daughters. Creative Works: Films include: Halls of Anger, 1970; The Last Picture Show, Fat City, 1971; Bad Company, 1972; The Last American Hero, The Iceman Cometh, 1973; Thunderbolt and Lightfoot, 1974; Hearts of the West, Rancho Deluxe, 1975; King Kong, Stay Hungry, 1976; Somebody Killed Her Husband, 1978; Winter Kills, 1979; The American Success Company, Heaven's Gate, 1980; Cutter's Way, 1981; Tron, Kiss Me Goodbye, The Last Unicorn, 1982; Starman, Against All Odds, 1984; Jagged Edge, 1985; 8 Million Ways to Die, The Morning After, 1986; Nadine, 1987; Tucker, the Man and His Dream, 1988; See You in the Morning, Texasville, The Fabulous Baker Boys, 1990; The Fisher King, 1991; American Heart, The Vanishing, Blown Away, Fearless, 1994; Wild Bill, White Squall, 1995; The Mirror Has Two Faces, 1996; The Big Lebowski, 1997; Arlington Road, 1998; Simpatico, The Muse, 1999; The Contender, Raising the Mammoth (TV voice), 2000; K-Pax, 2002; Masked and Anonymous, Seabiscuit, 2003; The Door in the Floor, 2004; The Moguls, Tideland, 2005; Stick It, 2006; Surf's Up (voice), 2007; A Dog Year, Iron Man, How to Lose Friends & Alienate People, The Open Road, 2008; Crazy Heart, The Men Who Stare at Goats, 2009; The Giver, Tron Legacy, 2010; Best Actor, Golden Globes, 2010. Address: c/o Creative Artists Agency, 9830 Wilshire Boulevard, Beverly Hills, CA 90212, USA.

BRIGGS Edward Samuel, b. 4 October 1926, St Paul, Minnesota, USA. Naval Officer. m. Nanette Parks, 1 son. Education: Graduate, US Naval Academy, 1949; Command and Staff School, US Naval War College, 1961; Joint Services Staff College, Latimer, England, 1965. Appointments: Midshipman to Vice Admiral, US Navy, 1945-84; Commanding Officer, USS Turner Joy (DD951), 1966-68; Commanding Officer, USS Jouett (DLG 29), 1971-72; Deputy Commander/Chief of Staff, US Seventh Fleet, 1972-73; Rear Admiral, Commander, Cruiser-Destroyer Group Three, US Pacific Fleet, 1975-76; Commander, US Navy Recruiting Command, 1976-78; Commander, Naval District Pearl Harbor, 1978-79; Commander, Naval Logistics Command, US Pacific Fleet, 1978-79; Vice Admiral, Deputy Commander/Chief of Staff, US Pacific Fleet, 1980-82; Commander, US Naval Surface Forces, US Atlantic Fleet, 1982-84; Retired, 1984; Chairman, Escondido High School District Curriculum Review Council, 1994-98; Member, San Diego Unified School District History Curriculum and Instruction Advisory Committee, 1986-98. Publications: A Biography – Charles W Briggs; A Return to Liberal Education; The War We Are In, I/II, An Appraisal of the Iraq War and the Broader War Between Civilizations; The Promised Land. Honours: Distinguished Service Medal; 5 Legion of Merits; 2 Air Medals; 3 Navy Commendation Medals; 2 Meritorious Unit Citations; 2 Bronze Stars. Memberships: US Naval Academy Alumni Association; Veterans of Foreign Wars; Navy League of the United States; San Diego Military Advisory Council.

BRIGGS Raymond Redvers, b. 18 January 1934, Wimbledon, England. Writer; Illustrator; Cartoonist. m. Jean T Clark, 1963, deceased 1973. Education: Wimbledon School of Art; Slade School of Fine Art, London. Appointments: Freelance Illustrator, 1957-; Children's Author, 1961-. Publications: The Strange House, 1961; Midnight Adventure, 1961; Sledges to the Rescue, 1963; Ring-a-Ring o' Roses, 1962; The White Land, 1963; Fee Fi Fo Fum, 1964; The Mother Goose Treasury, 1966; Jim and the Beanstalk, 1970; The Fairy Tale Treasury, 1972; Father Christmas, 1973; Father Christmas Goes on Holiday, 1975; Fungus the Bogeyman, 1977; The Snowman, 1978; Gentleman Jim, 1980; When the Wind Blows, 1982; The Tinpot Foreign General and the Old Iron Women, 1984; The Snowman Pop-Up, 1986; Unlucky Wally, 1987; Unlucky Wally Twenty Years On, 1989; The Man, 1992; The Bear, 1994; Ethel and Ernest, 1998; UG: Boy Genius of the Stone Age, The Adventures of Bert, 2001; A Bit More Bert, 2002; The Puddleman, 2004. Honours include: Kate Greenaway Medal, 1966, 1973; BAFTA Award, 1982; Francis Williams Illustration Award, Victoria & Albert Museum, 1982; Broadcasting Press Guild Radio Award, 1983; Children's Author of the Year, 1992; Kurt Maschler Award, 1992; Illustrated Book of the Year Award, 1998; Smarties Silver Award, 2001. Address: Weston, Underhill Lane, Westmeston, Nr Hassocks, Sussex, England.

BRIGHTMAN Sarah, b. 14 August 1960, Berkhamsted, England. Singer; Actress. Career: Dancer with Pan's People and Hot Gossip; Stage roles include: I and Albert, 1973; Cats, 1981; The Pirates of Penzance, 1982; Masquerade, 1982;

Nightingale, 1982; Song and Dance, 1984; Requiem, 1985; The Merry Widow, 1985; The Phantom of the Opera, 1986, 1988; Aspects of Love, 1990; Trelawney of the Wells, 1992; Relative Values, 1993; Dangerous Obsession, 1994; The Innocents, 1995; Films: Granpa, 1989; Zeit Der Erkenntnis, 2000; Repo! The Genetic Opera, 2008; Amalfi, 2009. Recordings: Albums: Dive, 1993; Fly, 1996; Time to Say Goodbye, 1997; Eden, 1998; Fly 2, 2000; La Luna, 2000; Classics, 2001; The Very Best of 1990-2000, 2001; Harem, 2003; The Harem World Tour: Live from Las Vegas, 2004; Diva: The Singles Collection, 2006; Classics: The Best of Sarah Brightman, 2006; Symphony, 2008; A Winter Symphony, 2008; Symphony: Live in Vienna, 2009. Address: c/o Sunhand Ltd, 63 Grosvenor Street, London W1X 9DA, England.

BRINSMADE Akbar Fairchild, b. 31 May 1917, Puebla, State of Puebla, Mexico. Chemical Engineer Consultant, PE. m. Juanita Phillips, 1 son, 2 daughters. Education: BS, Chemistry, University of Wisconsin, Madison, 1935-39; MS, Chemical Engineering Practice, Massachusetts Institute of Technology, Cambridge, Massachusetts, 1940-42; Postgraduate studies: University of Houston, 1943-44, Polytechnic Institute, Brooklyn, New York, 1945-46, New York University, 1947-49, Tulane University, 1967-73; Registered Professional Engineer, North Carolina, 1958, Louisiana, 1979. Appointments: General Manager, Cia Minera San Francisco y Anex, San Luis Potosi, Mexico 1939-40; Senior Research Engineer, Shell Oil Company, Houston and New York City, 1942-48; Project Manager, International Industrial Consultants, New York City and Caracas, Venezuela, 1949-50; Managing Director, Promotora Nacional de Industrias, Caracas, Venezuela, 1952-57; Research and Development Engineer, Hercules Powder Co, Rocket Center, West Virginia, 1959-64; Research Engineering Specialist, Chrysler Space Division, New Orleans, Louisiana, 1966-69; Chemical Engineer Consultant to major US and foreign corporations, 1969-. Publications: Book Chapters in Solid Rocket Technology, 1967, and Author, Travel to the Stars, 1996; Author: The Expansion of the Universe - Revisited, 2000; Author, The Origin and Cure for Cancer, A Theory, 2009; US Patent: Gravity Habitat Module for Space Vehicle, 2001. Honours: Phi Eta Sigma; Military ROTC Bombardiers, University of Oklahoma, 1935; Phi Lambda Upsilon, University of Wisconsin, 1937. Memberships (current): Fellow, American Institute of Chemists; American Institute of Chemical Engineers; American Chemical Society; National Society of Professional Engineers; Louisiana Engineering Society; Sigma Alpha Epsilon Fraternity. Address: 486 Channel Mark Drive, Biloxi, MS 39531, USA

BRISSAUD Florent, b. 16 August 1984, Vitry-le-François, France. Industrial Risk Consultant; Researcher in Safety & Reliability. Education: Engineering Degree, Dependability, Risk and Environment, 2007, Master of Science & Technology, Systems Optimization and Safety, 2007, PhD, Dependability of Safety-Related Systems, 2010, Troyes University of Technology. Appointments: Trainee, Quantitative Risk Analysis, SINTEF Technology and Society, 2006; Engineer & PhD candidate, Dependability of Safety-Related Systems, INERIS, 2007-10; Researcher, RAMS, Troyes University of Technology, 2010-11; Consultant, Reliability, Availability, Maintainability, Safety (RAMS), DNV France, 2011-12; Consultant, Industrial Risk, Safety & Reliability, 2012-. Publications: Handling Parameters and Model Uncertainties by Continuous Gates in Fault Tree Analyses, 2010; Reliability analysis for new technology-based transmitters, 2011; Dynamic Reliability of Digital-Based Transmitters, 2011; Probability of failure on demand of safety systems: impact of partial test distribution, 2012. E-mail: florent.brissaud.2007@utt.fr

BROADBENT Jim, b. 24 May 1949, Lincolnshire, England. Actor. m. Anastasia Lewis, 1987. Education: Graduate, London Academy of Music and Dramatic Arts, 1972. Career: Actor: Royal National Theatre; Royal Shakespeare Company; Co-founder, National Theatre of Brent; Films include: The Shout, 1978; The Hit, 1984; Time Bandits, 1981; Brazil, 1985; Life is Sweet, 1990; The Crying Game, Enchanted April, 1992; Bullets Over Broadway, Princess Caraboo, Widows' Peak, 1994; Little Voice, 1998; Topsy-Turvy, 1999; Bridget Jones's Diary, Moulin Rouge!, Iris, 2001; The Gangs of New York, 2002; Bright Young Things, 2003; Vanity Fair, Vera Drake, Bridget Jones: The Edge of Reason, 2004; The Magic Roundabout (voice), Robots (voice), Valiant (voice), The Chronicles of Narnia: The Lion, The Witch and The Wardrobe, 2005; Hot Fuzz, And When Did You Last See Your Father?, 2007; Indiana Jones and the Kingdom of the Crystal Skull, Inkheart, 2008; The Young Victoria, The Damned United, Harry Potter and the Half-Blood Prince, Perrier's Bounty, 2009; Harry Potter and the Deathly Hallows – Part II, 2011; TV includes: The Peter Principle, 1995; And Starring Pancho Villa as Himself, 2003; The Young Visiters, 2003; Pride (voice), 2004; Spider-Plant Man, 2005; The Street, Longford, 2006; Einstein and Eddington, 2008. Honours: Best Supporting Actor, BAFTA Award, 2001; Best Supporting Actor, Oscar, 2001; Richard Harris Award, British Independent Film Awards, 2007. Memberships: Honorary President, Lindsey Rural Players.

BROCKINGTON Ian Fraser, b. 12 December 1935, Chillington, Devon, England. Psychiatrist. m. Diana Pink, 2 sons, 2 daughters. Education: Winchester College; Gonville & Caius College, Cambridge. Appointments: Professor of Psychiatry, University of Birmingham, 1983-2001; Visiting Professorships: University of Chicago, 1980; Washington University of St Louis, 1981; University of Nagoya, 2002; University of Kumamoto, 2003; Institute of Psychiatry, 2009. Publications: Articles on: African Cardiopathies; The Classification of the Psychoses; Methods of Clinical Psychiatric Observation; Puerperal Mental Disorders; Author: Motherhood and Mental Health, 1996; Eiliethyia's Mischief: the Organic Psychoses of Pregnancy, Parturition and the Puerperium, 2006; Editor: Motherhood and Mental Illness, 1982, 1988; The Closure of Mental Hospitals, 1990; Menstrual Psychosis and the Catamenial Process, 2008. Memberships: Founder, The Marcé Society; Founder, Section on Women's Mental Health, World Psychiatric Association; Fellow, European Psychiatric Association. Address: Lower Brockington Farm, Bredenbury, Bromyard, Herefordshire HR7 4TE, England. E-mail: i.f.brockington@bham.ac.uk

BRÖDER Ernst-Günther, b. 6 January 1927, Cologne, Germany. Banker; Consultant. Education: PhD, Economics; University of Cologne; University of Mayence; University of Freiburg; University of Paris. Appointments: Corporate Staff, Bayer AG, Leverkusen, 1956-61; Projects Department, The World Bank, Washington, DC, USA, 1961-64; Banker, 1964-84, Deputy Manager, 1968-69, Manager, 1969-74, Member of Board Management, 1975-84, Spokesman, 1980-84, KfW-Bankengruppe, Frankfurt, Germany; President, 1984-93, Honorary President, 1993-, European Investment Bank, Luxembourg; Chairman, Inspection Panel, The World Bank, 1994-99. Honours: High decorations in

Germany, Belgium, Italy and Luxembourg. Memberships: Panel of Conciliators; International Center for the Settlement of Investment Disputes.

BRODERICK Laurence, b. 18 June 1935, Bristol, England. Sculptor. m. Ingrid, 3 sons. Education: Design, National Diploma; Sculpture, Regent Street Polytechnic; Sculpture, Hammersmith School of Art. Appointments: Historical and educational Illustrator and Painter; Teacher of Art, 1959, Director of Art, 1965-81, Haberdashers Askes School, Elstree; Freelance Artist and Sculptor; Full time Sculptor, 1981-; Joint President, International Otter Survival Fund. Publications: Persia The Immortal Kingdom; Everyday Life in Imperial Japan; Everyday Life in Traditional Japan; Soapstone Carving; Ports and Harbours; Henry Purcell and his Times; Uncle Matt's Mountain. Honours: Listed in international biographical dictionaries. Memberships: Associate, Royal Society of British Sculptors; Fellow, Royal Society of the Arts. Address: Thane Studios, Vicarage Road, Waresley, Cambridgeshire SG19 3DA, England. Website: www.laurencebroderick.co.uk

BRODERICK Matthew, b. 21 March 1962, New York, USA. Actor. m. Sarah Jessica Parker, 1997, 1 son, 2 daughters. Theatre includes: Valentine's Day; Torch Song Trilogy; Bright Beach Memoirs; Biloxi Blues; The Widow Claire; How to Succeed in Business Without Really Trying; The Producers; The Foreigner; the Odd Couple; The Philanthropist; The Starry Messenger; Films include: War Games; Ladyhawke; 1918; On Valentine's Day; Ferris Bueller's Day Off; Project X; Biloxi Blues; Torch Song Trilogy; Glory; Family Business; The Freshman; Lay This Laurel; Out on a Limb; The Night We Never Met; The Lion King (voice); Road to Welville; Mrs Parker and the Vicious Circle; Infinity (also director); The Cable Guy; Addicted to Love; The Lion King II: Simba's Pride (voice); Godzilla; Election; Inspector Gadget, 1999; Walking to the Waterline, 1999; You Can Count on Me, 2000; Suspicious Minds, 2001; Good Boy! (voice), 2003; Marie and Bruce, 2004; Lion King 1 ½ (voice), 2004; Stepford Wives, 2004; Last Shot, 2004; Strangers with Candy, 2005; The Producers, 2005; Deck the Halls, 2006; Margaret, 2007; The She Found Me, 2007; Bee Movie, 2007; Diminished Capacity, Finding Amanda, The Tale of Despereaux, 2008; Wonderful World, Margaret, 2009; TV includes: Master Harold... and the Boys; Cinderella; Jazz, 2001; The Music Man, 2003; 30 Rock, 2008; Cyberchase, 2009. Honours: 2 Tony Awards. Address: c/o CAA, 9830 Wilshire Boulevard, Beverly Hills, CA 90212, USA.

BRODINE Charles Edward, b. 10 May 1925, Sioux City, Iowa, USA. Physician. m. Lois Bliss, 1 son, 2 daughters. Education: BS, Iowa State University, Ames, Iowa, 1948; MD, Washington University School of Medicine, St Louis, 1953. Appointments: Gunnery Officer, aircraft carrier, World War II; Intern, 1953-54, Resident, Internal Medicine, 1954-55, St Louis County Hospital; Fellow, Hematology, Clinical Instructor in Medicine, University of Cincinnati and Cincinnati General Hospital, 1955-57; Resident, Internal Medicine, US Naval Hospital, Oakland, California, 1957-59; Head, Hematology Service, US Naval Hospital, Oakland, 1959-61; Head, Hematology Service, Naval Hospital, Bethesda, Maryland, 1961-62; Consultant in Hematology, 1962-73, Naval Hospital, Bethesda, Maryland; Head, Division of Research Hematology, 1962-66, Chairman, Department of Clinical Investigation, 1966-70, Executive Officer, 1970-73, Naval Medical Research Institute, Bethesda; Program Manager, Navy Frozen Blood and Trauma Research Program, 1962-71, Director, 1973-74, Research Division, Bureau of Medicine and Surgery, US Department, Navy, Washington; Established and co-ordinated activities of combat surgical research team for several months each year, USN Hospital, Da Nang, South Vietnam, 1965-69; Clinical Associate Professor, Department of Medicine, Georgetown University, Washington, 1971-; Board of Directors, Gorgas Memorial Institute of Tropical and Preventive Medicine, 1973-89; Special Assistant, Medical Research and Development to Surgeon General, US Navy, 1974-77; Member, Bureau of Medicine and Surgery Policy Council, 1974-77; Navy rep to the NIH Hematology Study Section and the National Research Council Committees on Blood, Plasma Expanders and Trauma; Served on Advisory Committee, National Sickle Cell Disease, NIH, 1974-77; Commanding Officer, Naval Medical Research and Development Command, National Naval Medical Centre, Bethesda, 1974-77; Career Member, Senior Foreign Service Class of Minister Consular Officer, 1977-90; Assistant Medical Director, Environmental Health and Preventive Medicine, Office of Medical Services, Department of State, Washington, 1977-90; Member, Agent Orange Working Group, 1982-90; Executive Committee, National Council for International Health, 1982-90; Member, Committee on Biomedical Research, US-Egypt Joint Working Group, 1975-77; Medical Adviser, ARC, 1975-79; Member, White House Working Group on International Health, 1977; Department of State Member, National Council for International Health, 1978-89. Publications: Numerous articles in professional journals. Honours: Navy Legion of Merit for service in Vietnam, 1968; Meritorious Service Medal, 1973; 2nd Legion of Merit for Leadership as Commanding Officer, Naval Medical Research and Development Command, 1977; Secretary of the Navy, Robert Dexter Conrad Award (Navy's highest scientific award), 1977; Biography listed in Marquis Who's Who in America, Who's Who in the World, Who's Who in Medicine, and Who's Who in Science and Engineering, 1978-2010; Man of the Year in Medicine and Healthcare, ABI, 2010; Fellow, ABI; Great Minds of the 21st Century, 5th edition; National Honor Society Who's Who, 2010-2011; IBC Inner Circle; IBC Lifetime Achievement Award; IBC Director General's Leadership Award, 2010; IBC Man of the Year in Medicine and Healthcare; IBC World Congress of Arts, Science and Communication Order of International Merit; ABI International Profiles of Accomplished Leaders; ABI Ambassador of Knowledge. Memberships: AMA; Association of Military Surgeons; Academy of Medicine of Washington; Society of Federal Medical Agencies; Western Society for Clinical Investigation; Society for Medical Consultants in the Armed Forces. Address: 211 Russell Av, Apt 57, Gaithersburg, MD 20877, USA. E-mail: cebrodinemd@gmail.com

BROGÅRDH Hans Torgny, b. 18 October 1947, Tranås, Sweden. Executive Engineer. m. Margareta Krull, 1 son, 2 daughters. Education: Master, Electrical Engineering, 1971, Doctor of Technology, 1975, Assistant Professor, 1976, University of Lund. Appointments: Lecturer, 1972-73, R&D Manager, 1978-80, Instrumentation Technology; Research Assistant, Wallenberg Laboratory, 1974-76; R&D Engineer, ASEA, 1976-78; R&D Manager, Electrical Engineering, 1980-86; R&D Engineer, ABB Robotics, 1986-91; Senior Specialist, 1991-96; Company Senior Specialist, 1996-; Corporate Executive Engineer, 2009-, ABB Corporate Research; Associate Professor, Royal Institute of Technology, Stockholm, 1982-86; Chairman of the Board, ISIS and LINK-SIC, University of Linköping. Publications: Over 175 industrial and academic reports and articles including: The Tau PKM structures in Smart Devices and Machines for Advanced Manufacturing; Present and future robot control development – an industrial perspective in Annual Reviews in Control, 2008; 69 patents. Honours: Wenstrom Award,

1990; The Gold Medal of the Swedish Royal Academy of Engineering Sciences, 1998; EURON Technology Transfer Award, 2005; Listed in international biographical dictionaries. Address: ABB Robotics, Hydrovägen 10, SE 72168, Västerås, Sweden. E-mail: torgny.brogardh@se.abb.com

BRON Eleanor, b. 14 March 1938, Stanmore, England. Actress; Author. m. Cedric Price, deceased 2003. Education: North London Collegiate School; Newnham College, Cambridge. Career: Appeared at Establishment Night Club; Toured USA, 1961; TV satire, Not So Much a Programme, More a Way of Life; Co-writer and appeared in TV series, Where was Spring?, After That This, Beyond a Joke; Director, Actors' Centre, 1982-93; Director, Soho Theatre Co, 1993-2000; Stage appearances: Private Lives; Hedda Gabler; Antony and Cleopatra; Madwoman of Chaillot; Hamlet; Uncle Vanya, Heartbreak House, Oedipus; The Prime of Miss Jean Brodie; Present Laughter; The Duchess of Malfi; The Cherry Orchard; The Real Inspector Hound; The Miser; The White Devil; Desdemona – If You Had Only Spoken! (one woman show); Dona Rosita The Spinster; A Delicate Balance; Be My Baby; Making Noise Quietly; Twopence To Cross The Mersey, 2005; TV: Rumpole; Dr Who; French and Saunders; Absolutely Fabulous; Vanity Fair; BBC TV Play for Today: Nina; A Month in the Country; The Hour of the Lynx; The Blue Boy; Ted and Alice; Fat Friends; Casualty 1909; Films: Help!; Alfie; Two for the Road; Bedazzled; Women in Love; The National Health; Turtle Diary; Little Dorrit; The Attic; Deadly Advice, 1994; Black Beauty, 1993; A Little Princess, 1994; The House of Mirth, 2000; Iris, 2001; The Heart of Me, 2002; Love's Brother, 2003; Wimbledon, 2004; Concert appearance's as narrator include: Façade; Carnival des Animaux; Peter and the Wolf; Bernstein's Symphony No 3 with BBC Symphony Orchestra. Publications include: Song Cycle (with John Dankworth), 1973; Verses for Saint-Saëns Carnival of the Animals, 1975; Is Your Marriage Really Necessary? (with John Fortune), 1972; Life and Other Punctures, 1978; The Pillow Book of Eleanor Bron, 1985; Desdemona – If You Only Had Spoken! 1992; Double Take (novel), 1996. Address: c/o Rebecca Blond, 69A King's Road, London SW3 4NX, England.

BRONKAR Eunice Dunalee (Connor), b. 8 August 1934, New Lebanon, Ohio, USA. Visual Artist; Teacher. m. Charles William Bronkar, 1 daughter. Education: BFA, Wright State University, Dayton, Ohio, 1971; M Art Ed, with WSU and teacher certification, 1983; Additional studies, Dayton Art Institute, 1972, Wright State University, 1989; Participation in 12 workshops, 1972-93. Appointments: Part-time Teacher, Springfield Museum of Art, 1967-77; Education Chairman, 1973-74; Lead Teacher, Commercial Art Program, Clark State Community College, Springfield, Ohio, 1984-94; Assistant Professor Rank, 1989; Adjunct Instructor, 1974-84; Adjunct Assistant Professor, 1998-2000; Numerous solo exhibitions; Juried exhibitions: Over 100 national, regional, state and area shows; Cleaned and restored art collections: Seven public and numerous private collections; Advisory Board, Clark County Joint Vocational Commercial Art Program. Publications: Work featured in American Artist Renown, 1981; Catalogues and magazines. Honours: Teacher Excellence Award, Clark State community College, 1992; Over 50 art awards at exhibitions including 4 Best of Shows; 2 commissioned portraits, Continental Hall, Washington DC; Commissioned by Ohio 4H Foundation to paint portrait of the founder of the 4H movement, "A B Graham and granddaughter", 1976; Medal, SFLD, Ohio Bicentennial Celebration, 1976; Outstanding Alumni, Springfield (Ohio) High School, Class of 1953, 2009. Memberships include: Pastel Society of America; Allied Artists of America; Ohio Plein Aire Society; Ohio Watercolor Society; Portrait Society of America. Commissions and Creative Works: Work in public and private collections in Massachusetts, New Mexico, New York, Ohio and others, Athens, Greece, Jerusalem and Jaffa, Israel; Commissioned portraits and landscapes.

BROOK Adrian Gibbs, b. 21 May 1924, Toronto, Canada. Professor. m. Margaret (Peg) Dunn, 2 sons, 1 daughter. Education: BA, Physics and Chemistry, 1947; PhD, Organic Chemistry, 1950, University of Toronto. Appointments: Lecturer, University of Sakatchewan, Saskatoon, 1950-51; Lecturer, 1953-56, Assistant Professor, 1956-60, Associate Professor, 1960-62, Professor of Chemistry, 1962-89, Acting Chairman and Chairman, Department of Chemistry, 1969-74, University Professor, 1987-89, Professor Emeritus, 1989-, University of Toronto. Publications: Numerous articles in professional journals. Honours: Fellow, Chemical Institute of Canada, 1967; Kipping Award, American Chemical Society, 1973; Fellow, Royal Society of Canada, 1977; CIC Medal, 1985; University Professor, 1987; Killan Memorial Prize, 1994; DSc, Honoris Causa, University of Toronto, 2006. Memberships: American Chemical Society. Address: 603-52 McMurrich St, Toronto, M5S 3T3, Canada. E-mail: abrook@chem.utoronto.ca

BROOKE Christopher Nugent Lawrence, b. 23 June 1927, United Kingdom. Historian. m. Rosalind Beckford Clark, 3 sons, 1 deceased. Education: BA, MA, DLitt, Gonville and Caius College, Cambridge. Appointments: National Service, 1948-50; Fellow, Gonville and Caius College, 1949-56 and 1977-, Assistant Lecturer in History, 1953-54, Lecturer in History, 1965-56; Dixie Professor of Ecclesiastical History, 1977-94, University of Cambridge; Professor of Medieval History, University of Liverpool, 1956-67; Professor of History, Westfield College London, 1967-77. Publications: Books include: From Alfred to Henry III, 1961; The Saxon and Norman Kings, 1963, 3rd edition, 2001; Europe in the Central Middle Ages, 1964, 3rd edition, 2000; The Monastic World 1000-1300 (with Wim Swaan), 1974, 2nd edition as The Age of the Cloister, 2003, 3rd edition as The Rise and Fall of the Medieval Monastery, 2006; A History of Gonville and Caius College, 1985; Oxford and Cambridge (with Roger Highfield and Wim Swaan), 1988; The Medieval Idea of Marriage, 1989; A History of the University of Cambridge IV, 1870-1990, 1993; Jane Austen, Illusion and Reality, 1999; A History of Emmanuel College, Cambridge (with S Bendall and P Collinson), 1999; Churches and Churchmen in Medieval Europe, 1999; The Monastic Constitutions of Lanfranc (with D Knowles), 2002. Honours include: FSA, 1964; FBA, 1970; FRHistS; Fellow, Società di Studi Francescani (Assisi); Honorary DUniv York. Memberships include: Royal Commission on Historical Monuments, 1977-84; President, Society of Antiquaries, 1981-84; Vice-President, Cumberland and Westmorland Antiquarian and Archaeological Society, 1985-89; Northamptonshire Record Society, 1987-; CBE, 1995. Address: Gonville and Caius College, Cambridge CB2 1TA, England.

BROOKE Rosalind Beckford, b. 5 November 1925, United Kingdom. Historian. m. Christopher N L Brooke, 3 sons. Education: BA, 1946, MA, PhD, 1950, LittD, 2007, Girton College, Cambridge. Appointments: Temporary Senior History Mistress, Mitcham County Grammar School for Girls, 1949-50; Regular Supervisor of Cambridge undergraduates for the History Tripos for various colleges, 1951-56; Part-time History Mistress, Birkenhead High School, 1958-59; Lecturer, Palaeography, 1963, Tutorial Teacher, part-time,

1964-66, University of Liverpool; Lecturer, part-time, Medieval History, 1968-73, Honorary Research Fellow, 1973-77, University College, London; Regular Supervisor of Cambridge Undergraduates for History Tripos and Theology Tripos for various colleges, 1977-94; Approved course of lectures for the History Faculty, Cambridge University, 1978-81. Publications: Books: Early Franciscan Government: From Elias to Bonaventure, 1959, reprinted 2004; The Writings of Leo, Rufino and Angelo, Companions of St Francis (editor and translator), 1970, reprinted 1990; The Coming of the Friars, 1975; Popular Religion in the Middle Ages (with CNL Brooke), 1985; The Image of St Francis: Responses to Sainthood in the 13th Century, 2006; Contributions to learned journals and The Oxford Dictionary of National Biography, 2004. Honours: Exhibitioner, Girton College, Cambridge, 1943; Bryce-Tebb Scholarship, 1946-48; Old Girtonian's Studentship, 1948-49; Pennsylvania State International Fellowship (Paris and Normandy), International Federation of University Women, 1950-51; FRHistS, 1959; Fellow, Società Internazionale di Studi Francescani (Assisi), 1972; FSA, 1989. Memberships: Honorary Member, Lucy Cavendish College, 1977; Senior Member, Clare Hall, 1985. Address: The Old Vicarage, Ulpha, Broughton in Furness, Cumbria LA20 6DU, England.

BROOKING Barry Alfred, b. 2 February 1944. Chief Executive. Divorced. Education: Teacher's Certificate, University of Wales, 1962-65; Chartered Teacher's Certificate, College of Preceptors, 1970; BA, History and Education, Open University, 1974-76; Advanced Television Production Certificate, University of London, 1976; MA, Manpower Studies, University of London, 1978-80; Business Management Certificate, University of Westminster, 1981. Appointments: Commissioned Officer, retiring as Lieutenant Commander, 1965-81; Business Management Administrator, Medical Protection Society, 1981-92; Regional Director, St John Ambulance, 1992-95; Chief Executive, Parkinson's Disease Society of the United Kingdom, 1995-99; Chief Executive, British Psychological Society, 2000-04. Honours: MBE. Memberships: Chartered Institute of Management; Royal Television Society; Chartered Institute of Personnel and Development. Address: 9 Hawkmoor Parke, Bovey Tracey, Devon TQ13 9NL, England.

BROOKNER Anita, b. 16 July 1928, London, England. Novelist; Art Historian. Education: BA, King's College, London; PhD, Courtauld Institute of Art, London. Appointments: Visiting Lecturer in Art History, University of Reading, 1959-64; Lecturer, 1964-77, Reader in Art History, 1977-88, Courtauld Institute of Art; Slade Professor of Art, Cambridge University, 1967-68. Publications: Fiction: A Start in Life, 1981; Providence, 1982; Look at Me, 1983; Hotel du Lac, 1984; Family and Friends, 1985; A Misalliance, 1986; A Friend from England, 1987; Latecomers, 1988; Lewis Percy, 1989; Brief Lives, 1990; A Closed Eye, 1991; Fraud, 1992; A Family Romance, 1993; A Private View, 1994; Incidents in the Rue Laugier, 1995; Visitors, 1998; Undue Influence, 1999; The Bay of Angels, 2000; The Next Big Thing, 2002; The Rules of Engagement, 2003; Leaving Home, 2005; Strangers, 2009; Non-Fiction: An Iconography of Cecil Rhodes, 1956; J A Dominique Ingres, 1965; Watteau, 1968; The Genius of the Future: Studies in French Art Criticism, 1971; Greuze: The Rise and Fall of an Eighteenth-Century Phenomenon, 1972; Jacques-Louis David, a Personal Interpretation: Lecture on Aspects of Art, 1974; Jacques-Louis David, 1980, revised edition, 1987. Editor: The Stories of Edith Wharton, 2 volumes, 1988, 1989. Contributions to: Books and periodicals. Honours: Fellow, Royal Society of Literature, 1983; Booker McConnell Prize, National Book League, 1984; Commander of the Order of the British Empire, 1990. Address: 68 Elm Park Gardens, London SW10 9PB, England.

BROOKS James, b. 11 October 1938, West Cornforth, County Durham, UK. Consultant; Academic. m. Jan, 1 son, 1 daughter. Education: BTech(Hons), Applied Chemistry, 1964; MPhil, Analysis of wool wax and related products, 1966; PhD, chemical constituents of various plant spore walls, 1970; Fellow, Geological Society (FGS), 1974; Fellow, Royal Society of Chemistry (FRSC), 1976; Chartered Chemist (CChem), 1976; DSc, research work in chemistry, geology, petroleum sciences and the origin of life, 2001; Chartered Geologist (CGeol), 2001; Chartered Scientist (CSci), 2004. Appointments: Research Geochemist, BP Research Centre, British Petroleum, 1969-75; Senior Research Fellow, University of Bradford, 1975-77; Visiting Scientist, Norwegian Continental Shelf Institute, 1975-78; Research Associate, Exploration Co-ordinator, Senior Scientist, Section Head of Production Geology, British National Oil Corporation/Britoil, 1977-86; Visiting Lecturer, University of Glasgow, 1978-99; Technical Director, Sutherland Oil and Gas Investments, 1996-98; Brooks Associates, 1986-; Chairman/Director, Petroleum Geology '86 Ltd, 1986-99; Executive Member, Scottish Baptist College, 2001-09; Myron Spurgeon Visiting Professor in Geological Sciences, Ohio University, Athens, Ohio, USA, 2003; Collaborative research, teaching, professional and conference activities at numerous universities and research institutes throughout the USA, Canada, Europe, Russia, Australia and parts of Asia. Publications include: 15 books as author or editor and over 100 scientific research papers published in peer-refereed journals including: Chemical Structure of the Exine of Pollen Walls and a new function for carotenoids in nature; Chemistry and Morphology of Precambrian Microorganisms; Origin and Development of Living Systems; A Critical Assessment of the Origin of Life; Biological Relationships of Test Structure and Models for calcification and test formation in the Globigerinacea; The Chemistry of Fossils: biochemical stratigraphy of fossil plants; Organic Matter in Meteorites and Precambrian Rocks - clues about the origin of life; Origin of Life: from the first moments of the universe to the beginning of life on earth; Tectonic Controls on Oil & Gas occurrences in the Northern North Sea; Classic Petroleum Source Rocks; Cosmochemistry and Human Significance. Honours include: UK Government Exchange Scientist to USSR, 1971; Royal Society Visiting Scientist to India, 1977 and to USSR, 1991; Vice-President, Geological Society, 1984-89; Geological Society Christmas Lecture on Origin of Life, 1983; Golden Medallion and Order of Merit for book Origin of Life, 1985; Secretary, Geological Society, 1988-92; Life Member, American Association of Petroleum Geologists, 1993-; Distinguished Achievement Award, AAPG, 1993; Distinguished Service Award, The Geological Society, 1999; President of the Baptist Union of Scotland, 2002; First holder of Myron Sturgeon Visiting Professor in Geological Sciences, Ohio University, 2003; Honorary Member (who has distinguished himself by his accomplishments to the profession of petroleum geology), AAPG, 2006. Memberships: International IPU Committee, 1972-81; NERC Higher Degrees Research Committee, 1981-84; UK Consultative Committee on Geological Sciences, 1987-92; External Examiner, University of London, 1992-97; Series Editor, Geological Special Publications, 1989-93; International Editorial Board of Marine and Petroleum Geology, 1984-96; Council of Geological Society, 1984-92; Chairman, Shawlands Academy School Board, 1991-96; Board of Ministry of the Baptist Union of Scotland, 1998-; Member, West of Scotland NHS Research

Ethics Committee, 2006-; Member, Geological Society Scrutineer Committee for award of Charter Geologist (CGeol) professional status, 2007-; Chairman, SCORE - Scotland. Address: 12 Terringzean View, Cumnock, Ayrshire, KA18 1FB, UK. E-mail: dr.jim.brooks@googlemail.com

BROOKS Mel (Melvin Kaminsky), b. 28 June 1926, New York, USA. Actor; Writer; Producer; Director. m. (1) Florence Baum, 2 sons, 1 daughter, (2) Anne Bancroft, 1964, deceased 2005, 1 son. Appointments: Script writer, TV Series, Your Show of Shows, 1951-54, Caesar's Hour, 1954-57, Get Smart, 1965; Founder, Feature Film Production Company, Brooksfilms. Creative Works: Films include: The Critic (cartoon), 1963; The Producers, 1968; The Twelve Chairs, 1970; Blazing Saddles, 1974; Young Frankenstein, 1974; Silent Movie, 1976; High Anxiety, 1977; The Elephant Man (producer), 1980; History of the World Part I, 1981; My Favorite Year (producer), 1982; To Be or Not to Be (actor, producer), 1983; Fly I, 1986; Spaceballs, 1987; 84 Charing Cross Road, 1987; Fly II, 1989; Life Stinks (actor, director, producer), 1991; Robin Hood: Men in Tights, 1993; Dracula: Dead and Loving It, 1995; Svitati, 1999; It's A Very Merry Muppet Christmas Movie (voice), 2002; Jakers! The Adventures of Piggley Winks (TV series), 2003; Robots (voice), 2005; The Producers (voice), 2005. Musical: The Producers: The New Mel Brooks Musical (producer, co-writer, composer), 2001; Young Frankenstein (composer, lyricist, co-book-writer, producer), 2007; Honours: Academy Awards, 1964, 1968; Emmy Awards for Outstanding Guest Actor in a Comedy Series, 1997, 1998, 1999; Tony Awards for Best Book, Best Score, Best Musical, 2001; Evening Standard Award for Best Musical, 2004; Critics Circle Theatre Award for Best Musical, 2005. Address: c/o The Culver Studios, 9336 West Washington Boulevard, Culver City, CA 90232, USA.

BROOKS (Troyal) Garth, b. 7 February 1962, Tulsa, Oklahoma, USA. Country Music Singer; Songwriter; Musician (guitar). m. (1) Sandra Mahl, 1986, 3 daughters, divorced 2001, (2) Trisha Yearwood, 2005. Education: BS, Journalism and Advertising, Oklahoma State University, 1985. Career: Television specials include: This Is Garth Brooks, 1992; This Is Garth Brooks Too!, 1994; Garth Brooks - The Hits, 1995; Garth Brooks Live in Central Park, 1997; Best selling country album ever, No Fences (over 13 million copies). Recordings: Albums: Garth Brooks, 1989; No Fences, 1990; Ropin' The Wind, 1991; The Chase, 1992; Beyond The Season, 1992; In Pieces, 1993; The Hits, 1994; Fresh Horses, 1995; Sevens, 1997; In The Life Of Chris Gaines, 1999; The Colors Of Christmas, 1999; Scarecrow, 2001; Singles: If Tomorrow Never Comes, 1989; Tour EP, 1994; To Make You Feel My Love, 1998; One Heart At A Time, 1998; Lost In You, 1999; Call Me Claus, 2001; The Thunder Rolls; We Shall Be Free; Somewhere Other Than The Night; Learning to Live Again; TV Specials: This is Garth Brooks, 1992; This is Garth Brooks Too, 1994; Garth Brooks: The Hits, 1995; Garth Brooks Live in Central Park, 1997. Honours: Academy of Country Music Entertainer of the Year, 1991-94; Male Vocalist of the Year Award, 1991; Horizon Award, 1991; Country Music Association Entertainer of the Year Award, 1991, 1992; Academy of Country Music Album of the Year, 1991; CMA Award for Best Album, 1991; Academy of Country Music Song of Year, 1991; CMA Award for Best Single, 1991; Academy Country Music Single Record of the Year, 1991; American Music Country Song of the Year, 1991; Grammy Award for Best Male Country Vocalist, 1992; Best Male Country Music Performer, 1992, 1993; Best Male Musical Performer, People's Choice Awards, 1992-95; Country Music Award for Artist of the Decade, 1999; American Music Award for Favorite Country Artist, 2000; Special Award of Merit, 2002. Memberships: Inducted into Grand Ole Opry; ASCAP; CMA; ACM. Address: c/o Scott Stern, GB Management Inc, 1111 17th Avenue South, Nashville, TN 37212, USA.

BROOM Donald Maurice, b. 14 July 1942, London, England. University Professor. m. Sally Elizabeth Mary, 3 sons. Education: Whitgift School; MA, PhD, ScD, St Catharine's College, Cambridge. Appointments: Lecturer, Reader, Department of Pure and Applied Zoology, University of Reading, 1967-86; Colleen Macleod Professor of Animal Welfare, Department of Veterinary Medicine, University of Cambridge, 1986-; Fellow, St Catharine's College, 1987-. Publications: 8 books and over 300 scientific papers and articles in professional journals. Honours: President, International Society for Applied Ethology, 1987-89; Chairman, E U Scientific Veterinary Committee, 1990-97; Honorary DSc, De Montfort University, 2000; BSAS/RSPCA Award, 2001; President, St Catharine's College, 2001-04; Eurogroup Medal, 2001; Vice Chairman, EFSA Scientific Panel on Animal Health and Animal Welfare, 2003-; Professor Honoris Causa, University of Salvador, Argentina, 2004; Honorary Dr, Norwegian University of Life Sciences, 2005; Honorary Socio Corrispondanti, Accademia Peloritana dei Pericolanti, Messina, 2005; President, St Catharine's Society, 2005-06. Memberships: Seven scientific societies. Address: Department of Veterinary Medicine, Madingley Road, Cambridge CB3 0ES, England. E-mail: dmb16@cam.ac.uk Website: www.vet.cam.ac.uk/research/welfare/

BROSNAN Pierce, b. 16 May 1953, Ireland. Actor. m. (1) Cassandra Harris, deceased, 1 son, 1 adopted son, 1 adopted daughter, (2) Keely Shaye Smith, 2001, 2 sons. Education: Drama Centre. Creative Works: Stage appearances include: Wait Until Dark; The Red Devil; Sign; Filumenia. TV: The Manions of America, 1981; Nancy Astor, 1982; Remington Steele, 1982-87; Noble House, 1988; Around the World in 80 Days, 1989; Murder 101, Victim of Love, 1991; Running Wilde, 1992; Death Train, The Broken Chain, 1993; Don't Talk to Strangers, 1994; Night Watch, 1995; Films: Resting Rough, 1979; The Carpathian Eagle, The Long Good Friday, 1980; Nomads, 1986; The Fourth Protocol, 1987; Taffin, The Deceivers, 1988; Mister Johnson, 1990; The Lawnmower Man, Live Wire, 1992; Mrs Doubtfire, Entangled, 1993; Goldeneye Love Affair, 1994; Mars Attacks!, The Mirror Has Two Faces, 1996; Dante's Peak, Robinson Crusoe, Tomorrow Never Dies 1997; The Nephew, 1998; The Thomas Crown Affair, The Match, Grey Owl, The World is Not Enough 1999; The Tailor of Panama, 2001; Die Another Day, Evelyn, 2002; Everything or Nothing, Laws of Attraction, After the Sunset, 2004; The Matador, 2005; Seraphim Falls, 2006; Butterfly on a Wheel, Married Life, 2007; Mamma Mia, 2008; The Greatest, 2009; The Ghost, Percy Jackson & the Olympians: The Lightning Thief, Remember Me, 2010. Honours: Honorary degrees, Dublin Institute of Technology, 2002, University College Cork, 2003; Honorary OBE, 2003. Address: c/o Guttman Associates, 118 South Beverly Drive, Suite 201, Beverly Hills, CA 90212, USA.

BROUGHTON Peter, b. 8 September 1944, Keighley, Yorkshire, England. Civil Engineer. m. Jan, 2 sons. Education: BSc, Hons, Civil Engineering, 1963-66, PhD, Structural Engineering, 1966-70, Manchester University; FREng; FICE; FIStructE; FRINA; FIMarEST. Appointments: Research Student, Research Assistant, Department of Civil Engineering, University of Manchester, 1966-71; Structural Engineering Surveyor, Lloyds Register of Shipping, London, 1971-74; Partner, Subsidiary Practice, Campbell Reith and Partner,

1974-75; Structural Engineer, Burmah Oil Trading Ltd, 1975-77; Supervising Structural Engineer, British National Oil Corporation, 1977-79; Senior Structural Engineer, 1979-82, Civil Engineering Supervisor, 1982-86, Project Manager, 1990-94, Project Manager, 1998-2003, Phillips Petroleum UK Ltd; Project Engineer, 1986-90, Project Manager, 1994-98, Phillips Petroleum Company Norway; Visiting Professor, Department of Civil Engineering, Imperial College, University of London, 1991-2005; Royal Academy of Engineering Visiting Professor, Department of Engineering Science, University of Oxford, 2004-07; Consultant, Peter Fraenkel and Partners Ltd, 2003-. Publications include: Book: The Analysis of Cable and Catenary Structures, 1994; Numerous articles in journals including: The Ekofisk Protective Barrier, 1992; Cast Steel Nodes for the Ekofisk 2/4J Jacket, 1997; The Effects of Subsidence on the Steel Jacket and Piled Foundations Design for the Ekofisk 2/4X and 2/4J Platforms, 1996; Foundation Design for the Refloat of the Maureen Steel Gravity Platform, 2002; The Refloat of the Maureen Steel Gravity Platform, 2002; Deconstruction and Partial Re-Use of the Maureen Steel Gravity Platform and Loading Column, 2004. Honours include: Stanley Grey Award, The Institute of Marine Engineers, 1992; The George Stephenson Medal, 1993; Bill Curtin Medal, 1997; Overseas Premium, 1998; David Hislop Award, 1999, Certificate for Contribution to Institution Activity, 2002, The Institution of Civil Engineers; Phillips Petroleum Presidential Shield Award, 2002. Address: Peter Frankel & Partners Ltd, 21-37 South Street, Dorking, Surrey RH4 2JZ, England.

BROWN D Norman (formerly known as Paul John Green), b. 27 July 1936, Racine, Wisconsin, USA. Scholar. Education: BA, Seattle Pacific College, 1957; MA, University of Washington, 1958; MLS, University of California at Berkeley, 1968; PhD, Washington State University, 1981; Further part-time language study, University of Oregon, 2003-05. Appointments: Teaching Assistant, English, University of Washington, 1963-66; Instructor in English, Central Washington University, 1966-67; Research Assistant in Librarianship, University of California, Berkeley, 1967-68; Assistant Serials Librarian, University of Oregon, 1968-69; Teaching Assistant in English, Washington State University, 1974-76; Bibliographic Searching Assistant, Washington State University, 1984-2001. Publications: Contributor of numerous articles, reviews, notes and translations, bibliographies, poems, letters and an abstract; Editor, Student Writing, 1966-67, 1967; Novel: The Life of Jack Gray, (privately printed), 1991, new expanded edition, 2002; Previously unpublished literary reviews, 1997-99, 2001; Previously unpublished literary essays, 1992-2000, 2001; From Russia with Love and a Literary Potpourri, 2003; Collected Writings on the Fiction of Franz Kafka, with a Germanics Supplement, 2003; Eighteenth Century Salad with French and Italian Dressing: Swift-Voltaire, Fielding-Manzoni and Reviews Franco-Italian, and Italian, 2003; On Our Mutual Friend and Other Dickensiana, 2003; The Song of Eugene, with expanded introductory materials and nine Heinrich Heine translated poems, 2004; The Song of Eugene with Translations from the Poetry of Heinrich Heine and René Char, 2006; Studies in European Fiction: Swift-Voltaire, Fielding-Manzoni, Dickens, a Dostoevsky Duo, and Kafka, 2006; In and Against in This, Our Century of the Living Dead (play), 2006; Ye Olde XerOxenford Annuaire (collection of essays), 2006, 2007; Berkeley Then and Now; Elegy for Mario; Ah, Madison! and Other Poems 2002-2007, 2008; Ye Olde XerOxenford Annuaire, 2007, 2007; Ye Olde XerOxenford Annuaire, 2008-09, 2009; Leconte de Lisle and Swinburne Early and Late, with the Rossettis and Heredia in Tow, 2010. Honours: Freshman Scholarship, Seattle Pacific College, 1954-55; Non-resident Tuition Waiver, University of California, Berkeley, 1967-68; Editorial Board Member, Works and Days, 1984-94; Editorial Board Member, Recovering Literature, 1994-2000; Phi Sigma Iota Consultant, Language Pedagogy, China, 1997; Cavalier, World Order of Science, Education and Culture; Legion of Honor, United Cultural Convention. Memberships: MLA; Order of International Ambassadors; LFIBA; DGABIRA; Life Member, London Diplomatic Academy; Industrial Workers of the World; Sierra Club; Benjamin Ide Wheeler Society, University of California, Berkeley; Fine Arts Museums, San Francisco; Life Member, University of California Alumni Association; Life Member, University of Washington Alumni Association; American Association for the Advancement of Science; Southern Poverty Law Center; Alexander C Roberts Society; San Francisco State University; Democratic Socialists of America; Union of Concerned Scientists. Address: 279 Dwight St, 2nd Floor, New Haven, CT 06511-3234, USA.

BROWN Dan, b. 22 June 1964, Exeter, New Hampshire, USA. Author. m. Blythe Newlon, 1997. Education: Phillips Exeter; Amherst College; University of Seville. Career: Songwriter and Pop Singer: Synth Animals (children's cassette); Perspective (CD), 1990; Teacher, Beverly Hills Preparatory School, 1991; Dan Brown (CD), 1993; Angels & Demons (CD), 1994; Musica Animalia (children's CD), 2003; English Teacher, Phillips Exeter, 1993; Writer: 187 Men to Avoid: A Survival Guide for the Romantically Frustrated Woman, 1995; The Bald Book, 1998; Digital Fortress, 1998; Angels and Demons, 2000; Deception Point, 2001; Da Vinci Code, 2003 (film, 2006); The Lost Symbol, 2009 (film, 2009); Memberships: National Academy of Songwriters.

BROWN Hamish Macmillan, (James Macmillan), b. 13 August 1934, Colombo, Sri Lanka. Author; Lecturer; Photographer. Education: Dollar Academy, 1944-53; Mountaineering Instructors Certificate, No 1, 1968. Appointments: National Service, RAF, Canal Zone, Kenya, etc, 1953-55; Assistant, Paisley Martyrs Memorial Church, 1957-59; Teacher, Braehead School (pioneering outdoor education), 1960-71; County Adviser on Outdoor Education, Fife, 1972-73; Freelance Writer, Photographer, Lecturer, 1973-. Publications: Time Gentlemen (poems), 1983; Climbing the Corbetts, 1988; The Bothy Brew (stories), 1993; Seton Gordon's Scotland, 2005; The Mountains Look on Marrakech, 2007; Achnashellach (poems), 2008; A Scottish Graveyard Miscellany, 2008; Seton Gordon's Cairngorms, 2009; Hamish's Mountain Walk, 2010; Hamish's Groats End Walk, 2011; Editor: Poems of the Scottish Hills, 1982; Speak to the Hills, 1985; Articles, photographs, etc in over 100 publications worldwide. Honours: Honorary DLitt, St Andrew's University, 1997; Fellow, RSGS, 1997; MBE, 2001; Honorary D University (Open), 2007. Membership: Alpine Club; Scottish Mountaineering Club; Honorary Member, Burntisland & Kingham Rotary Club. Address: 3 Links Place, Burntisland, Fife KY3 9DY, Scotland.

BROWN Malcolm Watson, b. 24 February 1946, Sheffield, England. Professor. m. Geraldine Ruth Hassall, 1 son, 1 daughter. Education: BA, 1968, MA, 1972, PhD, 1974, University of Cambridge. Appointments: Visiting Research Scientist, National Institutes of Health, USA, 1973; Research Assistant, Department of Anatomy, 1972-74; Research Fellow, Downing College, 1973-74, University of Cambridge; Research Assistant, 1974-75, Lecturer, Anatomy, 1975-91, Senior Lecturer, Anatomy, 1991-94, Reader, 1994-98, Professor, 1998-, Anatomy and Cognitive

Neuroscience, Deputy Head, 1996-98, Head, 1998-2004, Department of Anatomy, Executive Member, MRC Centre for Synaptic Plasticity, 1999-2010; Research Director, Faculty of Medical and Veterinary Sciences, 2003-2010. Publications: Numerous articles in professional journals. Honours: Open Scholarship, 1964, Wright Prize, 1966, Hockin Prize, 1968, Research Scholarship, 1968, St John's College, Cambridge; Research Fellowship, Downing College, Cambridge, 1973; Merit Awards, University of Bristol, 1989, 1990, 1997; Special Research Fellowship, Agricultural and Food Research Council, 1991-92; Fellow, Royal Society, 2004. Memberships: British Neuroscience Association; European Neuroscience Association; European Brain and Behaviour Society; Royal Society, Elder, Christ Church, Nailsworth, Gloucestershire. Address: University of Bristol, School of Physiology and Pharmacology, Medical Sciences Building, Bristol, BS8 1TD, England. E-mail: m.w.brown@bristol.ac.uk

BROWN Paul Ray Beck, b. 20 July 1944, Uxbridge, Middlesex, England. Journalist. m. Maureen McMillan, 1 daughter. Education: Churchers College, Petersfield, Hampshire. Appointments: Indentured Reporter: East Grinstead Courier, 1963-65, Lincolnshire Standard, 1965-66, Leicester Mercury, 1966-68, Birmingham Post, 1968-74; Post-Echo, Hemel Hempstead, 1974-81, News Editor, 1980-81; The Sun, 1981-82; The Guardian, 1982-2005, Environment Correspondent, 1989-2005; Teacher of Journalism, Guardian Foundation, 1998-; Freelance Journalist and Writer. Publications: The Last Wilderness, 80 Days in Antarctica, 1991; Greenpeace History, 1993; Global Warming, Can Civilisation Survive? 1996; Anita Roddick and the Body Shop, 1996; Energy and Resources, 1998; Just the Facts, Pollution, 2002; North South East West, 2005; Global Warning, Last Chance for Change, 2006, US edition 2007; Leighton Buzzard and Linslade: A History, 2008. Honours: Midlands Journalist of the Year, 1974; New York Library Prize, Best Childrens Book of the Year, 1994; Press Fellow, Wolfson College, Cambridge, 2007. Memberships: Fellow, Geologists Association; Fellow, Royal Geographical Society; Fellow, Royal Society of Arts, Manufacture and Commerce; Life Member, National Union of Journalists. E-mail: paulbrown5@mac.com

BROWN Theodis, b. 31 January 1949, Roe, Arkansas, USA. Township Committeeman; Countywide Central Committee Sergeant at Arms; Fire Chief; Publisher; Paralegal. m. Gail, 4 sons, 1 daughter. Education: Graduate, St Louis Police Academy and St Louis Fire Academy; Blackstone School of Law, Indiana University; St Louis Community College; Fire Officer I, State Fire Marshal Training School for State Investigator and State Inspector; Fire Service Instructor, State Fire and Rescue Training, University of Missouri; Certified Fire District Board Training; Kinloch Chief of Police Detective, St Louis Major Case Squad School Homocide Training Class, 1977. Appointments: St Louis Policeman, 1969; St Louis Fireman, 1978; Local Chief of Police Detectives, Assistant Chief of Police, Acting Police Chief, Colonel, 1970s, 1980s, 1990s and 2000s; Fire Chief, Fire Marshal, more than 40 years service; St Louis County Government Paralegal, Missouri, 1997; St Louis County Government Operation Safe Inspector, 1997; Trustee, Board of Directors, Office of Sergeant at Arms, Castlepoint Subdivision; Sergeant at Arms, Officer, Missouri Department of Mental Health; Elected County Public Official Committeeman, 2002-. Publications: Publisher, author and CEO, St Louis Private Eye newspaper; Author of many articles. Honours: Won the downbeat musicfest jazz band best band category, 1987, 1988, 1989; St Louis City election nomination; St Louis City Aldermanic Award, Civic Award; Police Valor Award as Hero Policeman; Listed in international biographical dictionaries. Memberships: International Association of Chiefs of Police; St Louis Police Veteran Association; Missouri State Investigators Association; Missouri Peace Officer Association; Fire Marshal Association of Missouri; National Paralegal Association. Address: PO Box 52255, St Louis, MO 63136, USA. E-mail: castlepointfiredept@yahoo.com Website: www.usafireandrescue.com

BROWNE Jackson, b. 9 October 1948, Heidelberg, Germany. Singer; Songwriter; Musician (guitar, piano). Career: Brief spell with Nitty Gritty Dirt Band, 1966; Solo singer, songwriter, musician, 1967-; Tours and concerts with Joni Mitchell; The Eagles; Bruce Springsteen; Neil Young; Major concerts include: Musicians United For Safe Energy (MUSE), Madison Square Garden (instigated by Browne and Bonnie Raitt), 1979; Glastonbury Festival, 1982; Montreux Jazz Festival, 1982; US Festival, 1982; Benefit concerts for: Amnesty International, Chile, 1990; Christie Institute, Los Angeles, 1990; Victims of Hurricane Inki, Hawaii, 1992; Various concerts for other environmental causes; Nelson Mandela Tributes, Wembley Stadium, 1988, 1990; Sang with Bonnie Raitt and Stevie Wonder, memorial service for Stevie Ray Vaughan, Dallas, Texas, 1990; Compositions: Songs recorded by Tom Rush; Nico; Linda Ronstadt; The Eagles; Co-writer with Glenn Frey, Take It Easy. Recordings: Albums: Jackson Browne, 1972; For Everyman, 1973; Late For The Sky, 1974; The Pretender, 1976; Running On Empty, 1978; Hold Out (Number 1, US), 1980; Lawyers In Love, 1983; Lives In The Balance, 1987; World In Motion, 1989; I'm Alive, 1993; Looking East, 1996; Also featured on No Nukes album, 1980; Sun City, Artists United Against Apartheid, 1985; For Our Children, Disney AIDS benefit album, 1991; The Next Voice You Hear: The Best of Jackson Browne, 1997; Singles include: Doctor My Eyes, 1972; Here Come Those Tears Again, 1977; Running On Empty, 1978; Stay, 1978; That Girl Could Sing, 1980; Somebody's Baby, used in film Fast Times At Ridgemont High, 1982; Tender Is The Night, 1983; You're A Friend Of Mine, with Clarence Clemons, 1986; For America, 1987. Current Management: Donald Miller, 12746 Kling Street, Studio City, CA 91604, USA.

BROWNJOHN J(ohn Nevil) Maxwell, b. Rickmansworth, Hertfordshire, England. Literary Translator; Screenwriter. Education: MA, Lincoln College, Oxford. Publications: Night of the Generals, 1962; Memories of Teilhard de Chardin, Klemperer Recollections, 1964; Brothers in Arms, Goya, 1965; Rodin, The Interpreter, 1967; Alexander the Great, 1968; The Poisoned Stream, 1969; The Human Animal, 1971; Hero in the Tower, 1972; Strength Through Joy, Madam Kitty, 1973; A Time for Truth, The Boat, 1974; A Direct Flight to Allah, 1975; The Manipulation Game, 1976; The Hittites, 1977; Willy Brandt Memoirs, 1978; Canaris, Life with the Enemy, 1979; A German Love Story, 1980; Richard Wagner, The Middle Kingdom, 1983; Solo Run, 1984; Momo, The Last Spring in Paris, 1985; Invisible Walls, Mirror in the Mirror, 1986; The Battle of Wagram, Assassin, 1987; Daddy, The Marquis of Bolibar, 1989; Eunuchs for Heaven, Little Apple, Jaguar, 1990; Siberian Transfer, The Swedish Cavalier, Infanta, 1992; The Survivor, Acts, Love Letters From Cell 92, 1994; Turlupin, Nostradamus, 1995; The Karnau Tapes, 1997; Heroes Like Us, 1998; The Photographer's Wife, Carl Haffner's Love of the Draw, 1999; Birds of Passage, Eduard's Homecoming, The 13 ½ Lives of Captain Bluebear, 2000; The Stone Flood, Libidissi, Where do We Go From Here?, The Alexandria Semaphore, 2001; Headhunters, 2002; Berlin Blues, 2003; The Russian Passenger, Rumo, 2004; The City of Dreaming Books, Mimus, 2005; Ice Moon, Please, Mr Einstein, 2006; The Sinner, Elizabeth I & Mary Stuart, 2007; A Perfect Waiter, Night Work, 2008; A Matter of Time, 2009; Sailing by Starlight, 2010; Splinter, 2011; Screen Credits: Tess (with Roman Polanski), 1979; The Boat, 1981; Pirates, The Name of the Rose, 1986; The Bear, 1989; Bitter Moon (with Roman Polanski), 1992; The Ninth Gate (with Roman Polanski), 2000. Honours: Schlegel Tieck Special Award, 1979; US Pen Prize, 1981; Schlegel Tieck Prize, 1993, 1999; US Christopher Award, 1995; Helen and Kurt Wolff Award, US, 1998. Memberships: Translators Association; Society of Authors. Address: Bookend House, Hound Street, Sherborne, Dorset DT9 3AA, England.

BROWNLEE Alistair Edward, b. 23 April 1988, Dewsbury, Yorkshire, England. Triathlete. Education: Bradford Grammar School, Yorkshire; Girton College, Cambridge; Sports Science and Physiology degree, University of Leeds, 2010; MSc, Finance, Leeds Metropolitan University, in progress. Career: Gold medals, ITU Triathlon World Championships: Junior Men, Lausanne, 2006; U23, Vancouver, 2008; Elite, Gold Coast, 2009; Team, Lausanne, 2011; Elite, Beijing, 2011; Elite, Kitzbuehel, 2012; Gold medals, ETU Triathlon European Championships: Junior, Copenhagen, 2007; Elite, Athlone, 2010; Elite, Pontevedra, 2011; Gold medal (triathlon), London Olympics, 2012.

BROWNLOW Bertrand (John), b. 13 January 1929, Nazeing, Essex, England. Aviation Consultant. m. Kathleen Shannon, 2 sons, 1 deceased, 1 daughter. Education: Beaufort Lodge School; Royal Air Force. Appointments: Group Captain, Defence and Air Attache, Sweden, 1969-71; Group Captain, Commanding Officer, Experimental Flying, RAF Farnborough, 1971-73; Air Commodore, Assistant Commandant, RAF College Cranwell, 1973-74; Air Commodore, Director of Flying (Research and Development), Ministry of Defence Procurement Executive, 1974-77; Air Commodore, Commandant, Aeroplane and Armament Experimental Establishment, 1977-80; Air Vice-Marshal, Commandant, RAF College Cranwell, 1980-82; Air Vice-Marshal, Director General, RAF Training, 1982-84; Director, Airport and Flight Operations, Marshall Aerospace, -1994; Non-Executive Director, Civil Aviation Authority Board, 1994-97; Aviation Consultant, 1994-. Publications: Articles in professional magazines and publications. Honours: Air Force Cross, 1961; OBE, 1966; CB, 1982; Royal Aero Club Silver Medal, 1983; Clark Trophy for Contribution to Air Safety, Popular Flying Association, 1996; Freeman of the City of London, 1997; Liveryman, The Guild of Air Pilots and Air Navigators, 1997; Sword of Honour, The Guild of Air Pilots and Air Navigators, 2000. Memberships: Fellow, Royal Aeronautical Society; Empire Test Pilots' School Association; Liveryman, The Guild of Air Pilots and Air Navigators; Light Aircraft Association; General Aviation Confidential Incident Reporting Programme Advisory Board; CAA, General Aviation Safety Review Working Group; President, The Canberra Association; Board Member, General Aviation Safety Council. Address: Woodside, Abbotsley Road, Croxton, St Neots, Cambridgeshire PE19 6SZ, England. E-mail: john.brownlow1@btinternet.com

BROWNLOW Kevin, b. 2 June 1938, Crowborough, Sussex, England. Author; Film Director; Film Historian. Publications: The Parade's Gone By, 1968; How It Happened Here, 1968, 2005; Adventures with D W Griffith, (editor), 1973; Hollywood: The Pioneers, 1979; The War, the West, and the Wilderness, 1979; Napoleon: Abel Gance's Classic Film, 1983, 2004; Behind the Mask of Innocence, 1990; David Lean - A Biography, 1996; Mary Pickford Rediscovered, 1999; The Search for Charlie Chaplin, 2005; Winstanley, Warts and All, 2009. Address: c/o Photoplay, 21 Princess Road, London NW1 8JR, England.

BROZOVSKY John A, b. 30 April 1951, Spokane, Washington, USA. Accounting Editor. m. Sue Ellen King, 1 son. Education: BBA, International Business, 1975, MPA, Accounting, 1978, University of Texas; PhD, Accounting, University of Colorado, 1990. Appointments: Computer Programmer, University of Texas, 1974-77; Teaching Assistant, University of Texas, 1977; Texas State Health Department, 1978-80; EDP Auditor, City of Austin, 1980-81; Senior Internal Auditor, Enserch Corporation, 1981-83; Lecturer, California State University-Fresno, 1983-86; Research/Teaching Assistant, University of Colorado, 1986-89; Assistant Professor, 1989-1996, Associate Professor, 1996-, Wayne Lieninger Fellow, 2009-, Virginia Tech. Publications include: Section 530 Worker Classification Relief Provisions After the Small Business Act of 1996, 1997; Some Implications of Homogenizing Restrictions on the Audit Profession: An Experimental Study, 1998; The Effect of Information Availability on the Benefits Accrued from Enhancing Audit-firm Reputation, 1998; The FASB's Codification Project: A Critical Step Forward Simplification, 2006; Ethical Judgements in Accounting: An Examination on the Ethics of Managed Earnings, 2008; Incorporating IFRS in Intermediate Accounting, 2009; Accounting for Small Business: The Role of IFRS, 2010; Residential Solar Voltaic Solutions: A Case from North Carolina, 2012. Honours include: Several grants; ANBAR Electronic Intelligence Citation of Excellence, 1997; Lybrand Certificate of Merit, Institute of Management Accountants, 1998. Memberships: American Accounting Association; American Tax Association. Address: Department of Accounting and Information Systems, Pamplin 3007 (0101), Virginia Tech, Blacksburg, VA 24061, USA.

BRUCK Yuri, b. 8 October 1931, Kharkov, Ukraine. Radio Physics. m. Tatiana, 2 daughters. Education: MS, State Polytechnical University, 1955; PhD diploma, 1967, SRW diploma, 1970, IRE Institute Radio Physics and Electronics Academy Science of Ukraine. Appointments: Electronics engineer, Radio Electronics Plant, Kharkov, 1955-57; Senior Research Worker, State Polytechnic University, Kharkov, 1957-61; Senior Research Worker, IRE Institute Radio Physics and Electronics (now Radioastronomical Institute), Academy of Science of Ukraine, 1961-95; Shapira's Allowance, Communication Department, CTECH college, Tel-Aviv, Israel, 1997-99; Researcher, IBM Haifa Israel, Laboratory of High Speed Circuits, 1999-2005. Publications: More than 100 articles and patents. Honours: Soros's Personal Grant, 1994; Grant, Ukrainian Committee on Fundamental Research, 1993-95; Grant, European South Observatory, 1993-95; Grant, European Committee INTAS, 1995-97; Listed in international biographical dictionaries, 2011. Memberships: IEEE. Address: Shaar Hagay st 115, apt 27, 21995, Karmiel, Israel. E-mail: yuri_bruck@yahoo.com

BRUCKHEIMER Jerry, b. 1945, Detroit, Michigan, USA. Film Producer. m. (1) Bonnie, 1 son, (2) Linda, 1 stepdaughter. Education: University of Arizona. Appointments: Former producer, TV commercials; Formed Don Simpson/Jerry Bruckheimer Productions, 1983; Formed Jerry Bruckheimer Films, 1997; Producer; Films include: Culpepper Cattle Company, 1972; Rafferty and the Gold Dust Twins, 1975; Farewell My Lovely, 1975; March or Die, 1977; Defiance, 1980; American Gigolo, 1980; Thief, 1981; Cat People, 1982; Young Doctors in Love, 1982; Flashdance, 1983;

Beverly Hills Cop, 1984; Thief of Hearts, 1984; Top Gun, 1986; Beverly Hills Cop II, 1987; Days of Thunder, 1990; The Ref, 1994; Dangerous Minds, 1995; Bad Boys, 1995; Crimson Tide, 1995; The Rock, 1996; Con Air, 1997; Enemy of the State, 1998; Armageddon, 1998; Gone in 60 Seconds, 2000; Coyote Ugly, 2000; Remember the Titans, 2000; Pearl Harbor, 2001; Black Hawk Down, 2002; Bad Company, 2002; Kangaroo Jack, 2003; Pirates of the Caribbean, 2003; Bad Boys, 2003; Veronica Guerin, 2003; King Arthur, 2004; National Treasure, 2004; Pirates of the Caribbean: Dead Man's Chest, 2006; Pirates of the Caribbean: At World's End, 2007; National Treasure 2: Book of Secrets, 2007; G-Force, 2009; TV: CSI: Crime Scene Investigation; The Amazing Race; CSI: Miami; Without a Trace; Cold Case; CSI: New York; Close to Home; E-Ring; Justice; Eleventh Hour; Dark Blue; The Forgotten. Honours: 5 Academy Awards; 5 Grammy Awards; 4 Golden Globes; 6 Emmy Awards; 4 People's Choice awards; Numerous MTV Awards; ShoWest Producer of the Year, 1998; David O Selznick Lifetime Achievement Award, 2000; National Board of Review Producers Award, 2004; Doctor of Fine Arts Degree, University of Arizona's College of Fine Arts, 2006. Address: Jerry Bruckheimer Films Inc, 1631 10th Street, Santa Monica, CA 90404, USA. Website: www.jbfilms.com

BRUDNER Helen G, b. New York City, USA. Professor. m. Harvey J Brudner, 2 sons, 1 daughter. Education: BS, 1959, MA, 1960, NYU; PhD, Fairleigh Dickinson University, 1973. Appointments: Teacher, NYC Board of Education, 1959-60; Instructor, Pratt Institute, Brooklyn, 1959-61; Assistant Professor, History, 1961-63, Director of Guidance, 1962-63, NY Institute of Technology, New York City; Associate Professor, Fairleigh Dickinson University, Rutherford, New Jersey, 1963-73; Vice President, HJB Enterprises, Highland Park, NJ, 1970-; Consultant, Auto Educational Systems, 1971-; Professor, History, Political Science, Teaneck, New Jersey, 1974-; Director, 1972-84, Chairman, Department of Social Science, 1980-88, President, University Senate, 1975-78, Assistant Provost, 1983-, Dean, 1984, Director of Graduate Programs, Associate Director, School of History, Politics and International Studies, 1995-, Director, Language Graduate Studies, President, Academy Senate, 1996-, Honors College, Rutherford, New Jersey; Vice Chairman, Board of Directors, WLC Inc, Highland Park, 1990-; Treasurer, Casitas De Monte Corp, California, 2005-09, Vice President, 2009-; Vice Chairman, 2000-04, Treasurer, 2005, Casitas De Monte Associates, Palm Springs, California; Participant, Board of Trustees, FDU; Speaker, NJ Committee on Humanities. Publications: Numerous articles in professional journals. Honours: Woman of the Year Award; American Businesswomen's Association, 1980; Meritorious Service Award, NJ Credit Union League, 1997; Certificate of Special Congressional Recognition, 2000; NJ Division, Military and Veterans Affairs Award, 2004. Memberships: American Judicature Society; American Historical Society; Academy of Political Science; Director, Raritan-Millstone Heritage Alliance Inc; Phi Alpha Theta; Phi Sigma Alpha. E-mail: hhmts@att.net

BRUNDA Daniel Donald, b. 22 October 1930, Lansford, Pennsylvania, USA. Mechanical Engineer; Aerospace Engineer; Electromagnetics Scientist; Electromagnetic Powerline Radiation Engineer and Founder; Inventor; Author. Education: BSME, Lehigh University, 1952; MSME, 1953; Postgraduate, Johns Hopkins University, 1955; Princeton University, 1958-65, Drexel University, 1983. Appointments: Aerodynamicist, Bell Aircraft; Performance Engineer, Glenn L Martin, Baltimore; Aerospace Engineer, US Naval Air Propulsion Centre, Ewing, New Jersey, 1957-72; Local Manager, Independent Research and Development (IRAD), 1972-83; Consultant, Electromagnetic Radiation Engineer, Ewing, New Jersey, 1978-. Publications: Over 20 articles to professional journals; 1 patent; Powerline Radiation, Your Genes, copyrighted report, 2001, book published (by Xlibris) 2004; Control System for Adjusting the Amount of Low Frequency Electromagnetic Radiation of Power Transmission Lines, copyrighted report, 2001; The Design of Safe Electric Transmission and Distribution Lines, copyrighted book, 2001, published (by Xlibris), 2003; The Design of Safe Electric Transmission and Distribution Lines; The Universal Plague. Honours: Lifetime Deputy Governor American Biographical Institute; Lifetime Deputy Director General in the Americas, International Biographical Centre; Member of Order of International Fellowship, 2001; Included in International Order of Merit, 2002; Certificate of Commendation for Services Rendered Since 1978, Mayor of Ewing Township, 2001; Work exhibited in IBA Gallery of Excellence, 2001; Scientific Faculty Member of the IBC, 2002; IBC On-Line Hall of Fame, 2002, (http://www.internationalbiographicalcentre.com); Scientific Advisor to the Director General, IBC, 2002; 2000 Outstanding Scientists of the 21st Century; The Lifetime of Achievement 100; Ambassador of Goodwill , 1000 Greats, Living Science; Living Legends, 1000 Great Americans, IBC, 2003; Great Minds of the 21st Century, ABI, 2003; Hall of Fame and Inner Circle, Order of Distinction, Da Vinci Diamond Award, Greatest Living Legends, IBC, 2004; Genius Elite in Engineering and Science, Einsteinian Chair of Science, World Academy of Letters, ABI, 2004; Top 100 Scientists of 2005, First Five Hundred, IBC, 2005; Expert in Electromagnetic Radiation Engineering, 21st Century Genius Medal, ABI, 2005; 500 Greatest Geniuses of the 21st Century, Genius Laureate, Man of Science, ABI, 2006; Archimedes Award, Global Year of Science Medal, IBC, 2006; President's Citation in Electromagnetic Radiation Science, ABI, 2007; World Record for Achievement in Electromagnetics, Radiation, Engineering and Science, ABI, 2007; Pinnacle of Achievement Award, IBC, 2007; Lifetime Achievement Award, IBC, 2008; Dedication, Great Minds of the 21st Century, 2007/08; ABI Medal for Distinguished Service Order and Cross, 2008; International Einstein Award, IBC, 2009; IBC Medal of Wisdom, 2010. Memberships: Associate Fellow, Bioelectromagnetic Society; Life Member, ASME; Senior Member, AIAA; Ambassador of Grand Eminence, ABI, 2002; Founding Cabinet Member, World Peace and Diplomacy Forum, IBC, 2003; ABI President's Citation, Electromagnetic Radiation Science, August 2007; IBC Pinnacle of Achievement Award in Electromagnetic Radiation Engineering, November 2007; Certificate of Fellowship Enrolment, World Congress Headquarters, IBC, 2013. Address: 106 West Upper Ferry Road, Ewing, NJ 08628, USA.

BRUNETTA Gian Piero, b. 20 May 1942, Cesena, Italy. University Professor. m. Agostini Giuliana, 1 son, 1 daughter. Education: Degree (Hons), Humanities, 1966. Appointments: Lecturer, History and Criticism of Cinema, University of Padua, 1970-; Professor, History and Criticism of Cinema, 1980-2011; Professor Emeritus. Publications: Storia del cinema Italiano, 1979-82; Buio in Sala, 1988; Cent'Anni di Cinema Italiano, 1993; Il Viaggio dell'Icononauta, 1997; Storia del Cinema Mondiale, 1999-2001; The History of Italian Cinema, 2009. Honours: Premio Empoli Luigi Russo, 1983; Premio Jean Mitry, 2000; Special Prize, Krazna Kraus, 2002; Premio Flaiano per la Critica, 2002. Memberships: Istituto Veneto di Scienze Lettere E Arti of Venice; Accademia delle Scienze of Turin. Address: via Belzoni 180, 35121 Padova, Italy. E-mail: gianpiero.brunetta@unipd.it

DICTIONARY OF INTERNATIONAL BIOGRAPHY 36th EDITION

BRUNO Franklin Roy (Frank), b. 16 November 1961, London, England. Boxer. m. Laura Frances Mooney, 1990, divorced, 2001, 1 son, 2 daughters, 1 daughter with Yvonne Clydesdale. Education: Oak Hall School, Sussex. Appointments: Began boxing with Wandsworth Boys' Club, London, 1970; Member, Sir Philip Game Amateur Boxing Club, 1977-80; Won 20 out of 21 contests as amateur; Professional Career, 1982-96; Won 38 out of 42 contests as professional, 1982-89; European Heavyweight Champion, 1985-86 (relinquished title); World heavyweight title challenges against Tim Witherspoon, 1986, Mike Tyson, 1989; Staged comeback, won 1st contest, 1991; Lost 4th World Title Challenge against Lennox Lewis, 1993; World Heavyweight Boxing Champion, 1995-96, lost title to Mike Tyson, 1996; Appearances in Pantomimes, 1990, 1991, 1996, 1997, 1999; Former presenter, BBC TV. Publication: Personality: From Zero to Hero (with Norman Giller), 1996. Honours: SOS Sports Personality of the Year, 1990; TV Times Sports Personality of the Year, 1990; Lifetime Achievement Award, BBC Sports Personality of the Year Awards, 1996. Address: c/o PO Box 2266, Brentwood, Essex CM15 0AQ, England.

BRUNTON Paul Anthony, b. 1 October 1960, Sale, Cheshire, England. Professor of Restorative Dentistry. Education: BChD, University of Leeds, 1984; MSc, 1992, PhD, 1996, University of Manchester; FDS RCS Edinburgh, 1995; FDS (Rest Dent) RCS Edinburgh, 2001; FADM, 2003; FFGDP RCS England, 2006; FDS RCS, England, 2009. Appointments: House Officer, 1985, Resident Senior House Officer, Oral Surgry, 1986, Leeds Dental Hospital; General Dental Practitioner, Manchester, 1987; Dental Officer, North Staffordshire Health Authority, 1987-93; Senior Dental Officer, North Staffordshire Health Authority, 1993-94; Clinical Director of Dental Services, 1994-96; Senior Registrar in Dental Public Health, Birmingham Health Authority and NHS Executive, 1996-97; Clinical Lecturer, 1997-2001, Clinical Senior Lecturer, 2002-04, Restorative Dentistry, University of Manchester; Honorary Senior Registrar in Restorative Dentistry, Central Manchester Healthcare Trust, 1997-2001, 2002-04; Professor of Restorative Dentistry, University of Leeds, 2004-. Publications: Numerous articles in professional journals. Honours: Leeds Dental School Prosthetic Prize, 1984; Leeds Dental School Rogerson Prize in Oral Surgery, 1984; Alan Hilton Medal, Manchester Medical Society, 1994; Dental Postgraduate Society of Manchester Award, 1994; The Fletcher Exhibition in Dental Surgery, Turner Dental School, University of Manchester, 1998; British Society for Restorative Dentistry Research Award, 1999; Membership, Institute of Teaching and Learning, 2000; Fellowship, Academy of Dental Materials, 2004; Fellowship, Faculty of General Dental Practice, 2005; Fellowship, Faculty of Dental Surgery, 2009. Memberships: Academy of Operative Dentistry; Academy of Dental Materials; Association of Consultants and Specialists in Restorative Dentistry; British Association of Teachers of Conservative Dentistry; British Dental Association; British Society for Dental Research; British Society for Endodontology; British Society for Restorative Dentistry; British Society for the Study of Prosthetic Dentisry; International Association for Dental Research; Institute of Learning and Teaching; Fellow, Royal Society of Medicine. Address: Leeds Dental Institute, Clarendon Way, Leeds, West Yorkshire, LS2 9LU, England.

BRUSLOV Andrey Yurievich, b. 2 July 1954, Moscow, Russia. Reservoir Engineer. m. Irina, 1 daughter. Education: Diploma, Reservoir Engineer, 1976; PhD Diploma, Reservoir Engineering, 1986. Appointments: Scientist, Moscow Gubkin Oil & Gas Institute, 1977-88; Senior, Lead Scientist, Krylov All Russian Scientific Research Oil & Gas Institute, 1989-93; Chief Engineer, AGIO Oil & Gas Corp, 1994-97; Director, Business Development, ROSDI Corp, 1997-98; Co-ordinator, Sakhalin Energy Investment Co Ltd, 1998-2006; Advisor, Shell Exploration and Production Services RF (BV), 2006-09; Advisor, Saipem SpA, 2009-. Publications: About 60 articles and patents on enhanced oil recovery, well stimulation, Russian (local) content maximization, intra-corporate effective business interactions through business focused interaction approach, diversity & inclusion optimization through relevant diversity dimension level approach. Honours: Honourable Diploma of SPE; Listed in international biographical dictionaries. Memberships: Society of Petroleum Engineers; American Society for Training and Development. Address: Flat 187, Leninsky prospect, 45, Moscow 119334, Russia. Address: hibfi@mail.ru

BRUST Peter Herbert, b. 30 April 1955, Leipzig, Germany. Biologist. m. Monika Schneemilsch, 1 son. Education: Diploma, Animal Physiology, Neurobiology and Immunology, 1981, Doctoral thesis, 1986, Postdoctorate, 1986-90, University of Leipzig; Teaching thesis, Dresden University of Technology, 1994. Appointments: Postdoctorate, Montreal Neurological Institute, 1990; Postdoctorate, Johns Hopkins University, Baltimore, 1991; Senior Scientist, 1992-94; Head, Department of Biochemistry, Research Center, Rossendorf, 1994-2001; Head, Department of Radiopharmacy, Institute of Interdisciplinary Isotope Research, Leipzig, 2002-09; Professor, University of Leipzig, 2010-; Head, Division of Neuroradiopharmaceuticals, Helmholtz-Zentrum, Dresden-Rossendorf, 2010-. Publications: More than 100 peer-reviewed original articles; Around 40 reviews and monographs; 6 patents; 42 invited lectures. Honours: Karl Marx Award, 1979; Fellowship Award, Montreal Neurological Institute, 1990. Memberships: International Brain Research Organization; German Neuroscience Society; German Society for Nuclear Medicine; European Society for Neurochemistry; International College of Neuropsychopharmacology.

BRUTIAN Lilit, b. 7 August 1953, Yerevan, Armenia. Professor of Linguistics and English. m. Leonid Zilfugarian, 1 son, 1 daughter. Education: MA with distinction, English Language and Literature, 1970-75, PhD, Philology, 1975-80, Yerevan State University, Yerevan, Armenia; Certificate, International Summer Institute on Argumentation, University of Amsterdam, 1990; Doctor of Sciences in Philology, Institute of Linguistics, National Academy of Sciences, Yerevan, Armenia, 1984-92. Appointments: Assistant Professor, Chair of Foreign Languages, 1979-84, Associate Professor of English, Chair of English Philology and Chair of Foreign Languages, 1984-94, Professor of Linguistics and English, Chair of Linguistics, Chair of English Philology, 1994-2006, Yerevan State University; Senior Researcher, 1984-93, Principal Researcher, 1993-95, Institute of Linguistics, Head of Chair of Foreign Languages, 1994-96, National Academy of Sciences of Armenia; Visiting Professor, Institute for the Advancement of Philosophy for Children, Montclair State University, New Jersey, USA, 1994-95; Chairperson, Chair of Russian Linguistics, Typology and Theory of Communication, Yerevan State University, 2006-. Publications: 89 scientific publications, including 8 monographs include most recently: A Window into the World, or a Path to Myself, 2011. Honours: Leading Educator of the World, 2005; Republic of Armenia Ministry of Science and Education Diploma, 2009. Memberships include: International Society for the Study of Argumentation, The Netherlands; International Pragmatics Association, Belgium; Research Board of Advisors, ABI; Council, Department of Russian Philology, Council,

Department of Romance and Germanic Philology, Yerevan State University; Scientific Council, Institute of Linguistics, National Academy of Sciences of Armenia. Address: The 9th Street of Aigestan, 69, Apt 61, Yerevan 0025, Armenia. E-mail: lilit.brutian@gmail.com

BRUTUS Dennis, b. 28 November 1924, Salisbury, Rhodesia. Educationist; Poet; Writer. m. May Jaggers, 14 May 1950, 4 sons, 4 daughters. Education: BA, University of the Witwatersrand, Johannesburg, South Africa, 1947. Appointments: Director, World Campaign for Release of South African Political Prisons; International Defence and Aid Fund, formerly UN Representative; Director, Program on African and African-American Writing in Africa and the Diaspora, 1989-; Visiting Professor at universities in Amherst, Austin, Boston, Dartmouth, Denver, Evanstown, Pittsburgh. Publications: Sirens, Knuckles, Boots, 1963; Letters to Martha and Other Poems from a South African Prison, 1968; Poems from Algiers, 1970; Thoughts Abroad, 1970; A Simple Lust: Selected Poems, 1973; China Poems, 1975; Stubborn Hope, 1978; Strains, 1982; Salutes and Censures, 1984; Airs and Tributes, 1988; Still the Sirens, 1993; Remembering Soweto, 2004; Leafdrift, 2005; Poetry and Protest, 2006. Contributions to: Periodicals. Honours: Mbari Prize for Poetry in Africa; Freedom Writers' Award, Kenneth David Kaunda Humanism Award; Academic Excellence Award, National Council for Black Studies, 1982; UN Human Rights Day Award, 1983; Paul Robeson Award; Langston Hughes Award. Memberships: President, South African Non-Racial Olympic Committee (SAN-ROC); Chair, International Campaign Against Racisim in Sport (ICARIS), Africa Network, 1984-; ARENA (Institute for Study of Sport and Social Issues); African Literature Association; American Civil Liberties Union; Amnesty International; PEN; Union of Writers of African Peoples.

BRYANT Diana, b. 13 October 1947, Perth, Australia. Chief Justice. m. Richard Notwotny. Education: LLB, University of Melbourne; LLM, Monash University. Appointments: Partner, Phillips Fox, 1979-90; Victoria Bar, 1990-2000; Chief Federal Magistrate, Federal Magistrates Court, 2000-04; Chief Justice, Family Court of Australia, 2004-. Publications: The Role of the Family Court in Promoting Child-Centered Practice, 2006; Evidence of a Different Nature, 2008. Honours: Centenary Award. Memberships: Victorian Legal Aid; Australian Airlines; Royal Perth Hospital; Legal Aid, WA. Address: Chief Justice Chambers, Family Court of Australia, GPO Box 9991, Melbourne, VIC 3000, Australia.

BRYDEN Alan, b. 27 August 1945, Folkestone, England. Ingénieur général du Corps des Mines. m. Laurence, 1 son, 2 daughters. Education: Ecole Polytechnique, Paris, France; Ecole des Mines, Paris; University d'Orsay, France; Diploma in Nuclear Physics. Appointments: Began working in Metrology, USA, National Bureau of Standards (now The National Institute of Standards and Technology); Chair, Laboratories Committee, ILAC (International Laboratory Accreditation Co-operation); Founder, Eurolab (European Federation of Measurement, Testing and Analytical Laboratories), President, 1990-96; Director General, French National Metrology and Testing Laboratory (LNE), 1981-99; Director General, French National Standards Body (AFNOR), 1999-2002; Secretary-General, International Organisation for Standardisation (ISO), 2003-09; Ingénieur général, High Council for Industry, Energy & Technologies, France, 2009-. Honours: Chevalier de la Legion d'Honneur; Ordre National du Mérite, France. Address: CGIET, 120, Rue de Berg, F-75572, Paris, Cedex 12, France. E-mail: alanbryden@orange.fr

BRYMER Timothy, b. 7 November 1951, London, England. Lawyer. m. Helen, 1 son, 1 daughter. Education: Dulwich College, London; Commercial Pilot, College of Air Training, 1970; Private Pilot's Licence and Instrument Rating; Solicitor, College of Law, Lancaster Gate, London, 1977. Appointments: Solicitor, Barlow Lyde & Gilbert, 1977-79; Director, International Insurance Services/Airclaims Ltd, 1979-85; Senior Partner, Brymer Marland & Co, 1986-90; Head of Aviation Department, Cameron McKenna, 1990-2004; Head of Aviation Group, Clyde & Co, 2004-; Consultant, Eurocontrol. Publications: Numerous articles in professional journals; Paper presented to Flight International Crew Management Conference, Dubai, 2008 (later published on Eurocontrol website). Memberships: Founder Member, Lawyers' Flying Association; Member, Guild of Pilots and Air Navigators; Chairman of Panel of Speakers, Royal Aeronautical Society Conference in relation to Criminalisation of air accidents, 2010. E-mail: tim.brymer@clydeco.com

BRYSON Bill, b. 1951, Des Moines, Iowa, USA. Writer. m. 4 children. Education: Drake University. Appointments: Orderly, mental hospital in England, 1973; Journalist, The Times and The Independent newspapers; Returned to USA, 1993; Author. Publications: Penguin Dictionary of Troublesome Words (Bryson's Dictionary of Troublesome Words), 1985; The Lost Continent, 1987; The Mother Tongue: English and How It Got That Way, 1994; Made in America, 1994; Neither Here Nor There: Travels in Europe, 1995; Notes from a Small Island, 1995; A Walk in the Woods, 1998; I'm a Stranger Here Myself (aka Notes from a Big Country), 1999; In a Sunburned Country (aka Down Under), 2000; The Best American Travel Writing, 2002; African Diary, 2002; A Short History of Nearly Everything, 2003; The Life and Times of the Thunderbolt Kid, 2006; A Really Short History of Nearly Everything, 2008; Bryson's Dictionary for Writers and Editors, 2008; On the Shoulders of Giants, 2009. Honours: Member of Selection Panel, Book of the Month Club, 2001; Commissioner for English Heritage; Chancellor, University of Durham, 2005-; Aventis Prize, 2004; Honorary DCL, Durham, 2004; Honorary OBE, 2006; James Joyce Award, 2007; Schwartz Visiting Fellow, Pomfret School, Connecticut, 2007; President, Campaign to Protect Rural England, 2007. Address: The Marsh Agency, 11 Dover Street, London W1S 4LJ, England. Website: www.marsh-agency.co.uk

BRYSON James Graeme, b. 4 February 1913, Caerleon, Monmouthshire, England (now Gwent, Wales). Judge (Retired). m. Jean Glendinning, 3 sons (1 deceased), 4 daughters. Education: St Edwards College, Liverpool; LLM, Liverpool University, 1935; BSc, Open University, 1984. Appointments: Solicitor, 1935-47; Commissioned Officer to Royal Artillery, 1936; War Service, 1939-45, Lieutenant Colonel, now Colonel; Commanded Artillery Regiments, 1947-55; Registrar and Deputy Judge and District Judge to High Court of Justice and Admiralty Registrar, 1947-79; Northwest Cancer Research Fund: Trustee, 1950-80, President, 1985-2001, Life President, 2001-; HM General Commision of Taxes, 1968-88; Honorary General, 33 Signal Regiment, 1975-82; Chairman, Medical Appeal Tribunal, 1978-86. Publications: Books: Contributor to Halsbury's Laws of England, 1976; Shakespeare in Lancashire and the Gunpowder Plot, 1997; A Cathedral in my Time, 2003; A Century of Liverpool Lawyers, 2003; Poetry in My Veins, 2004, Contributor to New Oxford DNB, 2006; James Conway, a Victorian Poet-Policeman, 2009. Honours: Territorial Decoration and two bars, 1952; OBE (Military), 1955; Queen's Commendation for Bravery, 1961; Her Majesty's Vice Lord Lieutenant of the County of Merseyside, 1979-89;

County Life President, Royal British Legion; Fellow, Royal Society of Arts; Knight Commander, Order of St Gregory; Knight Commander, Knights of the Holy Sepulchre; Citizen of Honour, Liverpool City Council, 2009. Memberships: Life Member, Royal British Legion; Past President, Athenaeum (Liverpool); Honourable Society of Knights of the Round Table; Liverpool Law Society, President, 1970;Vice-Patron, Regular Forces Employment Association. Address: 36 Hillary Court, Formby, Merseyside L37 3PS, England.

BUBKA Sergey Nazarovich, b. 4 December 1963, Voroshilovgrad, Ukraine. Athlete. m. Lilya Tioutiounik, 1983, 2 sons. Appointments: World Champion Pole Vaulter, 1983; 16 World Records from 5-85m 1984 to 6.13m 1992, including world's first 6m jump, Paris, 1985; 18 World Indoor Records, from 5.81 1984 to 6.15 1993; Holder of indoors and outdoors world records, 2002; Now represents OSC Berlin. Publications: An Attempt is Reserved, 1987. Honours include: Olympic Gold Medal, 1988. Memberships include: Member, IOC Executive Board, IOC Evaluation Commission for 2008; IOC Athletes' Commission; IAAF Council, 2001-; National Olympic Committee Board; Chairman, EOC Athletes; Commission; President, S Bubka Sports Club; Elected to Parliament, United Union Faction, 2002-. Address: c/o State Committee of Physical Culture & Sport, 42 Esplanadnaya, 252023 Kiev, Ukraine.

BUCHANAN Colin Ogilvie, b. 9 August 1934, Croydon, Surrey, England. Church of England Clerk in Holy Orders. Education: BA, 1959, MA, 1962, Lincoln College, Oxford; Tyndale Hall, Bristol, 1959-61; DD, 1993. Appointments: Assistant Curate, Cheadle, Cheshire, 1961-64; Member of Staff, 1964-85, Principal, 1979-85, London College of Divinity (since 1970, St John's College, Nottingham); Bishop of Aston, Diocese of Birmingham, 1985-89; Assistant Bishop of Rochester, 1989-96; Bishop of Woolwich, Diocese of Southwark, 1996-2004; Retired, 2004; Honorary Assistant Bishop, Diocese of Bradford, 2004-. Publications: Modern Anglican Liturgies, 1958-68, 1968; Further Anglican Liturgies, 1968-75, 1975; Editor, News of Liturgy Monthly, 1975-2003; Latest Anglican Liturgies, 1976-84, 1985; Modern Anglican Ordination Rites, 1987; The Bishop in Liturgy, 1988; Editor, Justin Martyr on Baptism and Eucharist, 2007; Joint Author: Growing into Union, 1970; Anglican Worship Today, 1980; Reforming Infant Baptism, 1990; Sole Author: Open to Others, 1992; Infant Baptism and the Gospel, 1993; Cut the Connection: Disestablishment and the Church of England, 1994; Is the Church of England Biblical? 1998; Consultant Editor: Common Worship Today, 2001; Consultant Editor, Oxford Guide to the Book of Common Prayer, 2006; Editor, Savoy Conference Revisited, 2002; Author, Historical Dictionary of Anglicanism, 2006; Taking the Long View: Three and a half decades of General Synod, 2006; An Evangelical Among the Anglican Liturgists, 2009. Membership: Church of England Liturgical Commission, 1964-86; House of Clergy of General Synod of C/E, 1970-85; C/E Doctrine Commission, 1986-91; House of Bishops of General Synod of the Church of England, 1990-2004; Church of England General Synod Council for Christian Unity, 1991-2001; Vice President, President, 2005-, Electoral Reform Society. Address: c/o Bradford Diocesan Office, Kadugli House, Elmsley Street, Steeton, Keighley, BD20 6SE, England. E-mail: colinbuchanan101@btinternet.com

BUCHANAN Pat(rick Joseph), b. 2 November 1938, Washington, District of Columbia, USA. American Government Official; Journalist. m. Shelley Ann Scarney, 1971. Education: AB, English, cum laude, Georgetown University, 1961; MS, Journalism, Columbia University, 1962. Appointments: Editorial Writer, 1962-64, Assistant Editorial Editor, 1964-66, St Louis Globe Democrat; Executive Assistant to Richard M Nixon, 1966-69; Special Assistant to President Richard M Nixon, 1969-73; Consultant to Presidents Richard M Nixon and Gerald R Ford, 1973-74; Syndicated Columnist, 1975-; Various radio and television broadcasts as commentator, panellist, moderator, etc, 1978-; Assistant to President Ronald Reagan and Director of Communications, White House, Washington DC, 1985-87; Candidate for the Republican Party Nomination for President of the US, 1992, 1996; Chairman, The American Cause, 1993-95, 1997-; Chairman, Pat Buchanan & Co, Mutual Broadcasting System, 1993-95. Publications: The New Majority, 1973; Conservative Votes, Liberal Victories, 1975; Right from the Beginning, 1988; Barry Goldwater, The Conscience of A Conservative, 1990; The Great Betrayal, 1998; A Republic, Not an Empire, 2000; The Death of the West, 2002; Where the Right Went Wrong, 2004; State of Emergency: The Third World Invasion and Conquest of America, 2006. Contributions to: Newspapers and periodicals. Honour: Knight of Malta, 1987. Memberships: Republican Party; Roman Catholic Church. Address: 1017 Savile Lane, McLean, VA 22101, USA.

BUCHHOLZ Noor Niels-Peter, b. 26 August 1957, Muenster, Germany. Consultant Urologist. m. Saima Salahuddin. Education: Registered Nurse, 1980; MBBS, 1987; General Practitioners Certificate, 1987; MD, University of Berne, Switzerland, 1990. Appointments: Intern, 1986-87, Resident, 1988-90, Cantonal Hospital, Switzerland; Registrar, Urology, University Hospital, Basel, Switzerland, 1991-94; Registrar, 1994-97, Visiting Academic, 1995, Urodynamics and Research Fellow in Urology, Flinders Medical Centre, Adelaide, Australia; Freelance Translator, ABC Translations, Switzerland, 1996-97; Visiting Lecturer, Urology, The Aga Khan University, Karachi, Pakistan, 1997-98; Consultant Urologist and Clinical Leader of Stone Research & Stone Treatment, Erasmus University, Rotterdam, The Netherlands, 1998-2000; Consultant Urologist, United Lincolnshire Hospitals, 2000-02; Honorary Consultant Urologist, Newham General Hospital, London, 2002; Consultant Urologist and Director fo Lithotripsy and Stone Services, Barts and the London Hospital, 2002-; Honorary Senior Clinical Lecturer, Queen Mary's School of Medicine, London, 2002-. Publications: Numerous articles in professional journals. Honours include most recently: Best Poster Award, XXth Congress of the European Association of Urology, Istanbul, 2005; Merit Award, Surgery Team of the Year, 2005; Corrie/Caitlin Prize for Medical Research, 2006; Outstanding Poster Award, World Congress of Endourology, 2006; Nominee, Excellence in Teamwork Award, Barts & The London NHS Trust, 2007; Visiting Professor, Syrian Association of Urology, 2007. Memberships: Swiss Medical Association; German Society of Urology; European Urological Association; Swiss Society for Research in Surgery; New York Academy of Sciences; Swiss Society of Urology; British Medical Association; Society of Laparoscopic Surgeons; many others. Address: St Bartholomew's Hospital, London EC1A 5BE, England. E-mail: nielspeter@yahoo.com

BUCKINGHAMSHIRE Earl of, Sir (George) Miles Hobart-Hampden, b 15 December 1944, Madras, India. m. (1) Susan Jennifer Adams, dissolved, (2) Alison Wightman Wishart (nee Forrest), 2 stepsons. Education: Clifton College, Bristol, 1958-63; BA, Honours, History, Exeter University, 1963-67; MA, Area Studies, History and Politics of the Commonwealth, Birkbeck College, London University, 1967-68. Appointments: Noble Lowndes & Partners Ltd, latterly Director of Scottish Pension Trustees, 1970-81; Director, HSBC Gibbs, 1981-86; Wardley Investment Services International (subsidiary of HSBC), 1986-91, Marketing Director and Managing Director, 1988-91; The Wyatt Company, 1991-95; Partner, Watson Wyatt LLP, Watson Wyatt Worldwide, 1996-2004; BESTrustees Plc, 2004-, Director, 2005; Sat in House of Lords, 1984-99; Member All Party Groups on Occupational Pensions and on ageing issues; Member of Select Committee of EC sub-committees on Social and Consumer Affairs, 1985-90, on Finance, Trade and External Relations, 1990-92; Honorary Trustee, Illinois Wesleyan University, USA, 1991-; President, Old Cliftonian Society, 2000-2003 and Governor of Clifton College, 1994-; Member of Council, 2000-09, Honorary Fellow, 2009, Buckinghamshire New University. Memberships: Associate Member, Institute of Actuaries; Hatfield Real Tennis Club; Hobart Real Tennis Club; Leamington Tennis Court Club; Bristol & Bath Tennis Court Club; Freeman, Cities of Glasgow and Geneva (Upper New York State USA); Britain-Australia Society (Chairman, 2008-); The Cook Society (Chairman, 2007); Friends of the Vale of Aylesbury, 2009; Downend Police and Community Amateur Boxing Club; President, Buckingham Conservative Constituency Association, 1989; Aylesbury Vale Community Trust; Patron: Sleep Apnoea Trust, Hobart Town (1804) Early Settlers Association (Tasmania); Goodwill Ambassador for the City of Hobart, 2009; John Hampden Society; Chilterns MS Centre, 2006. Address: The Old Rectory, Church Lane, Edgcott, Aylesbury, Buckinghamshire HP18 0TU, England.

BUCKLAND-WRIGHT (John) Christopher, b. 19 November 1945, London, England. Retired University Professor. m. Rosalin, 2 daughters. Education: BSc, AKC, PhD, King's College, University of London, 1967-73; DSc, University of London, 1995. Appointments: Assistant Head, Department of Comparative Osteology, Centre for Prehistory and Paleontology, Nariobi, 1966-67; Zoology Teacher, Lycée Français de Londres, 1971-72; Anatomy Lecturer, St Mary's Hospital Medical School, London, 1973-76; Anatomy Lecturer, 1976-80, Senior Lecturer, 1980-89, Reader, 1989-97, Guy's Hospital Medical School, London; Professor, Radiological Anatomy, King's College, London, 1997-2008; Head, Macroradiographic Research Unit, Guy's Hospital, 1981-88; Head, Arthology Unit, Guy's Hospital, 1988-96; Chairman, Applied Clinical Anatomy, 1996-2008; Lecturer, Medical Artists Association, 2007-. Publications: Author of over 200 scientific publications; Books: Cockerel Cavalcade, 1988; The Engravings of John Buckland Wright, 1990; Bathers and Dancers, 1993; Baigneuses, 1995; Surreal Times, 2000; Endeavours and Experiments, 2004; To Beauty, 2007. Honours: King's College Award of an SRC Research Studentship, Department of Anatomy, 1970-73; First Jessie Dobson Lecturer, 1984, Vicary Lecturer, 1999, Royal College of Surgeons; Immation-Mayneord Memorial Lecturer, British Institute of Radiology. Memberships: Freeman, City of London, 1980; Liveryman, 1980-, Master, 2007-08, Worshipful Company of Barbers, 1980; Fellow, British Association of Clinical Anatomists; Honorary Fellow, Medical Artists Association. Address: Acer House, Vicarage Road, East Budleigh, Budleigh Salterton, Devon EX9 7EF, England.

BUCKLEY Richard Anthony, b. 16 April 1947, Leicester, England. Legal Scholar. m. Alison Jones, 1 daughter. Education: BA (Oxford), Jurisprudence, 1968, Doctor of Philosophy, 1973, Merton College, Oxford; Doctor of Civil Law, Oxford, 2006. Appointments: Lecturer in Law, King's College, London, 1970-75; Fellow and Tutor in Law, Mansfield College, Oxford, 1975-93; Professor of Law, University of Reading, 1993-2008; Emeritus Professor, 2008-. Publications: The Law of Nuisance, 1st edition, 1981, 2nd edition, 1996; The Modern Law of Negligence, 1st edition, 1988, 3rd edition, 1999; Illegality and Public Policy, 2002, 2nd edition, 2009; The Law of Negligence, 2005; The Law of Negligence and Nuisance, 2011; Articles in legal periodicals. Honours: Leverhulme Research Fellow, 2001. Address: School of Law, Foxhill House, University of Reading, Whiteknights Road, Reading RG6 7BA, England.

BUCUR Constantin I, b. 19 March 1923, Gura Vaii, Racovą, Bacau, Romania. m. Brigitte Iorgovan, 1 son. Education: Ferdinand Boarding College, Bacau; D A Sturza Military College for Officers, Craiova, Romania; Cavalry College for Officers, Targoviste, Romania; MSc with Distinction, ANEF Bucharest, 1947-51; PhD, Université Libre de Bruxelles, Belgium, 1968; Dr honoris causa, University of Craiova, 1998. Appointments: Higher Education Inspector, Bucharest, 1951-53; Assistant Lecturer, Part-time, IEFS, Bucharest, 1951-53; Lecturer, 1953, Consultant, 1962, Professor, 1984, Traian Vuia Polytechnic and University of Timisoara-Romania; Organiser, Principal Researcher, Physical Education Research Centre, 1953-84; Director, Sportforschung Zentrum, Mannheim, Germany, 1986-. Publications: 71 books and 400 booklets about sport research; Created own system in sport; Organised 70 conferences in field. Honours: Wounded, WWII, awarded medals for bravery, Retired General. Membership: Full Member, Professor Emeritus, American Romanian Academy of Arts and Sciences; Academia Română, Filiala Timişoara; Brigadier General at Cavalry. Address: Brandenburger Str 30, D-68309, Mannheim, Germany.

BUCUR Romulus Vasile, b. 19 March 1928, Padova, Italy. Chemistry Researcher (Retired). m. Doina Rodica Motiu, 1 daughter. Education: Graduate, Chemistry, University of Cluj, Romania, 1955; PhD, Electrochemistry, University of Bucharest, Romania, 1970. Appointments: Head Laboratory, Solvay Plant, Ocna Mures, Romania, 1955-56; Scientific Researcher, Institute of Atomic Physics, Cluj, Romania, 1956-58; Principal Scientific Researcher, 1958-87, Head Laboratory, 1974-87, Institute of Isotopic and Molecular Technology, Cluj, Romania; Scientific Researcher, Inorganic Chemistry, Uppsala University, Sweden, 1988-93; Scientific Research Associate, Materials Chemistry Department, Ångström Laboratory, Uppsala University, Sweden, 1993-98. Publications: About 120 scientific papers in the field of analysis and separation of heavy water, solid state electrochemistry (metallic hydrides and sulphides), materials for hydrogen storage, and piezoelectric quartz crystal microbalance. Membership: Honorary Member, The International Association for Hydrogen Energy, USA, 1983-; American Chemical Society. Address: Näktergalsv 5, SE-35242 Växjö, Sweden. E-mail: romulus.bucur@telia.com

BUDENHOLZER Frank Edward, b. 21 August 1945. Catholic Priest; Educator; Chemist. Education: BA, Divine Word College, Epworth, Iowa, 1967; BS, DePaul University, Chicago, Illinois, 1969; MA, Catholic Theological Union, Chicago, Illinois, 1974; PhD, University of Illinois, Chicago, 1977. Appointments: Teaching Assistant, University of Illinois, Chicago, 1972-76; Chinese Language Training, Hsinchu, Taiwan, 1978-80; Associate Professor, Chemistry, Fu Jen University, 1978-83; Professor, Chemistry, 1983-; Director, Graduate Institute of Chemistry, 1980-84; Dean, College of Science and Engineering, 1984-90; Vice-President, 1990-97; Visiting Scholar, Center for Theology and the Natural Sciences; 1997-98; Visiting Scholar, University of

California, 1997-98; Member, Board of Trustees, Fu Jen University, 1999-; Resident Trustee, Fu Jen University, 2001-, Academic Co-ordinator, Centre for the Study of Religion and Science, 2002-07. Publications: Religion and Science in Taiwan: Rethinking the Connection; Some Comments on the Problem of Reductionism; Classical Trajectory Study of the HFCO-HF+CO Reaction. Memberships: American Chemical Society; American Physical Society; Chinese Chemical Society; Chinese Physical Society; Institute for Religion in an Age of Science; Hastings Center; Institute for Theological Encounter with Science and Technology. Address: Department of Chemistry, Fu Jen Catholic University, Hsinchuang 242, Taiwan. E-mail: 001898@mail.fju.edu.tw

BUJAKIEWICZ-KORONSKA Renata, b. 10 August 1961, Nowy Tomysl, Poland. Physicist; Astronomer. m. Jan, 2 sons, 2 daughters. Education: MSc, Astronomy, 1985, MSc, Physics, 1989, The Jagiellonian University, Krakow; Doctorate in Physics, 1997. Appointments: Assistant, Institute of Physics, Krakow University of Technology, Krakow, 1989-90; Research, 1997-, Vice Director, 2008-, Institute of Physics, Pedagogical University, Krakow. Publications: Numerous articles in professional journals. Memberships: Polish Physical Society. Address: Pedagogical University, Institute of Physics, Podchorazych 2, 30-081 Krakow, Poland. E-mail: rbk@up.krakow.pl

BULL Deborah Clare, b. 22 March 1963, Derby, England. Ballerina; Writer; Broadcaster; Artistic Director. Education: Royal Ballet School. Career: Dancer, 1981-, Principal Dancer, 1992-2001, Royal Ballet; Appearances with Royal Ballet include leading roles in La Bayadère, Swan Lake, The Sleeping Beauty, Don Quixote, Steptext; Appeared in Harrogate International Festival, 1993, 1995; An Evening of British Ballet, Sintra Festival, Portugal, 1994, 1995; Diamonds of World Ballet Gala, Kremlin Palace, Moscow, 1996; Rite of Spring, Teatro dell'Opera, Rome, 2001-02; Teacher of Nutrition, Royal Ballet School, 1996-99; Director, Clore Studio Upstairs, Royal Opera House, 1999-2001; Creative Director, ROH2, Royal Opera House, 2002-; Regular contributor to BBC Radio 4 including Breaking the Law, 2001; Law in Order, 2002; A Dance Through Time, 2002; TV: Writer and Presenter, Dance Ballerina Dance, 1998; Writer and Presenter, Travels with my Tutu, 2000; Coppelia, Royal Ballet (live broadcast); Rambert Dance Company, Sadler's Wells (live broadcast); Writer and Presenter, The Dancer's Body, 2002. Memberships: Dance Panel, Arts Council, 1996-98; Arts Council, 1999-2005; Governor, South Bank Centre, 1997-2003; BBC, 2003-06; Columnist, The Telegraph, 1999-2002; Patron, National Osteoporosis Society; Patron, Foundation for Community Dance. Publications: The Vitality Plan, 1998; Dancing Away, 1998; The Faber Guide to Classical Ballets (with Luke Jennings), 2004; numerous articles and reviews in newspapers and dance magazines. Honours: Dr hc (Derby), 1998, (Sheffield), 2001; Prix de Lausanne, 1980; Dancer of the Year, Sunday Express and The Independent on Sunday, 1996; CBE, 1999; Overall Prize, Dancescreen Monaco, 2002; Honorary Degree, Open University, 2005; Carl Alan Award. Address: Royal Opera House, Covent Garden, London WC2E 9DD, England. Website: www.deborahbull.com

BULL Sir George, b. 16 July 1936, London, England. Retired. m. J Fleur Therese, 4 sons, 1 daughter. Education: Ampleforth College, York. Appointments: Military Service with Coldstream Guards; Worked in advertising industry; Joined Wines & Spirits Trade, 1957; Joined International Distillers and Vintners (IDV), 1961; Chairman, Wines & Spirits Association of Great Britain, 1974-75; Deputy Managing Director, 1982, Chief Executive, 1984, Chairman, 1987, IDV Ltd; Appointed to the Board, Grand Metropolitan plc, 1985; Chairman and Chief Executive, GrandMet's Food Sector, 1992; Group Chief Executive, 1993, Chair, 1995-97, Grand Metropolitan plc; Joint Chair, Diageo plc, 1997, 1998; Retired, 1998; Chair, J Sainsbury plc, 1998-2004; Non-Executive Director, BNP Paribas UK Holdings Ltd, 2000-04; Non-Executive Director, The Maersk Company Ltd, 2001-2006; Member, Advisory Board of Marakon Associates, 2002-2006. Honours: Marketing Hall of Fame Award, 1998; Publicity Club of London Cup, 1999; Elected Grand Master of the Keeper of the Quaich, 1994-95, Patron, 1998; Vice President, Honorary Fellow, Chartered Institute of Marketing; Honorary Fellow, Marketing Society; Vice President, Marketing Council; President, Advertising Association, 1996-2000; Chevalier de l'Ordre National de la Legion d'Honneur, 1994; Freedom of the City of London, 1996; Knighted, 1998; Chevalier du Tastevin, 2005; Honorary President, Perkins Bull Collection, 2007; Listed in national and international biographical dictionaries. Memberships: Chair, Mencap Jubilee Appeal, 1996-98; President, Wine & Spirit Trade Benevolent Society, 2000; Chair, Ampleforth Abbey & College Bi-Centenary Appeal, 2000,The Pilgrims, The Cavalry and Guards Club, The Royal Worlington Golf Club. Address: The Old Vicarage, Arkesden, Saffron Walden, Essex CB11 4HB, England.

BULL Peter, b. 24 April 1949, Exeter, Devon, England. University Lecturer. m. Ann Rose Gore, 1 son. Education: MA, Modern History, University of Oxford, 1970; BA, 1973, PhD, 1978, Psychology, University of Exeter. Appointments: Lecturer, 1977-93, Senior Lecturer, 1993-, Reader, 2009-, Psychology, University of York. Publications: Numerous articles in professional journals; 5 books. Honours: Listed in international biographical dictionaries. Memberships: Elected Fellow, British Psychological Society; European Association of Social Psychology; International Association of Language and Social Psychology; International Society for Political Psychology. Address: Department of Psychology, University of York, Heslington, York YO10 5DD, England. Website: http://drbull.nfshost.com

BULLOCK Sandra, b. 26 July 1964, USA. Actress. m. Jesse James, 2005-10, 1 adopted son. Education: East Carolina University. Creative Works: Off-Broadway Productions include: No Time Flat (WPA Theatre). TV Roles: The Preppy Murder (film); Lucky Chances (mini series); Working Girl (NBC series). Films include: Love Potion 9, When The Party's Over, 1992; The Thing Called Love, The Vanishing, Demolition Man, Wrestling Ernest Hemingway, 1993; Speed, 1994; While You Were Sleeping, 1995; Two If By Sea, A Time To Kill, In Love and War, 1996; Speed 2: Cruise Control, 1997; Hope Floats, Making Sandwiches, Practical Magic, The Prince of Egypt (voice), 1998; Forces of Nature, 1999; Gun Shy, 28 Days, Miss Congeniality, 2000; Murder by Numbers, Divine Secrets of the Ya-Ya Sisterhood, Two Weeks' Notice, 2002; Crash, 2004; Loverboy, Miss Congeniality 2: Armed and Fabulous, 2005; The Lake House, Infamous, 2006; Premonition, 2007; The Proposal, All About Steve, The Blind Side, 2009; Extremely Loud and Incredibly Close, 2011; The Heat, 2013. Honours: Star on Hollywood Walk of Fame, 2005; Best Actress, Golden Globes, 2010. Address: CAA, 9830 Wilshire Boulevard, Beverly Hills, CA 90212, USA.

BULYCHEV Nikolay, b. 23 April 1980, Moscow, Russia. Chemist. Education: MS (Hons), 2003, PhD, 2006, Chemistry, Moscow State Academy of Fine Chemical Technology.

Appointments: Scientific Employee, Department of Chemical Technology of High-Molecular Compounds, Moscow State Academy of Fine Chemical Technology, Moscow, 2002-04; Scientific Employee and Postdoctoral Research Assistant, Institute for Polymer Chemistry, University of Stuttgart, Germany, 2004-07; Senior Researcher, NS Kurnakov Institute of General and Inorganic Chemistry of Russian Academy of Sciences, 2007-. Publications: 120 scientific proceedings in Russian and international scientific journals, conference proceedings. Honours: Research Award, Ministry of Education and Science of Russia; Mikhail Lomonosov Program scholarship, German Academic Exchange Service DAAD; Research Grant, Russian Foundation of Basic Research and Government of Flanders, Belgium. Membership: Russian Nanotechnology Society. Address: Ryazansky pr-t, 69, app 27, Moscow 109456, Russia.

BUNBURY Judith Mervyn, b. 7 February 1967, England. Geologist. m. Jonathan Collis, 2 daughters. Education: Bruton School for Girls, 1977-85; BSc (1st Class Hons), Durham University, 1989; PhD, Cambridge University, 1993. Appointments: Accounts Clerk, IBM UK Laboratories Ltd, 1985-86; Research Assistant, British Institute of Archaeology, Ankara, 1993-94; Buyer's Clerk, John Lewis Partnership, 1994; Postdoctoral Researcher, Earth Sciences, 1994-2000; Fellow, 1997-, Admissions Tutor, 2002-, Tutor, 2001-09, Deputy Senior Tutor, 2007-09, Graduate Admissions Tutor, 2010-, Director of Studies, 2002-, St Edmund's College, Director of Studies, Homerton College, 2004-09, Director of Studies, Corpus Christi College, 2003-, Teaching Fellow, Department of Earth Sciences, 2002-, Member, McDonald Institute of Archaeology (Cambridge), 2009-, Cambridge University; Conference Manager, Cambridge Publications, 2000-01. Publications: Numerous articles in professional journals. Memberships: Department of Earth Sciences, University of Cambridge; Teaching Fellow, Honorary Senior Research Assistant, Institute of Archaeology, University College, London; Member, McDonald Institute, Cambridge. Address: Department of Earth Sciences, Downing Street, University of Cambridge, Cambridge CB2 3EQ, England. E-mail: jmb21@cam.ac.uk

BUNTON Emma Lee, (Baby Spice), b. 21 January 1978, London, England. Vocalist. 1 son with Jade Jones. Career: Actress, including appearances in Eastenders; Member, Spice Girls; Numerous TV and radio appearances, many magazine interviews; Films: Spiceworld: The Movie, 1997; Yes You Can, 2001; Chocolate, 2005; World tour including dates in UK, Europe, India and USA; Presenter on TV and radio including Radio 1 and satellite TV show; Solo date on Breast Cancer Awareness concert; Solo career, 1999-. Recordings: Albums with The Spice Girls: Spice, 1996; Spiceworld, 1997; Forever, 2000; Solo albums: A Girl Like Me, 2001; Free Me, 2004; Life in Mono, 2006; Singles with The Spice Girls: Wannabe, Say You'll Be There, 2 Become 1, 1996; Mama/ Who Do You Think You Are, Step To Me, Spice Up Your Life, Too Much, 1997; Stop, (How Does It Feel To Be) On Top Of The World, Move Over/Generation Next, Viva Forever, Goodbye, 1998; Holler/Let Love Lead The Way, 2000; Solo singles: What I Am, 1999; What Took You So Long?, Take My Breath Away, We're Not Gonna Sleep Tonight, 2001; Free Me, Maybe, 2003; Crickets For Anamaria, 2004; Downtown, 2006; All I Need to Know, 2007. Honours: BRIT Award, Best Single, 1997; BRIT Award, Best Video, 1997; 2 Ivor Novello songwriting awards, 1997; Smash Hits Award for Best Band, 1997; 3 American Music Awards, 1998; Special BRIT Award for International Sales, 1998. Address: c/o Virgin Records Ltd, 553-79 Harrow Road, London W10 4RH, England. Website: www.emmabuntonofficial.com

BURACAS Antanas, b. 17 June 1939, Kaunas, Lithuania. Political and Financial Economist. m. Marija Regina Jovaisaite, 2 sons, 1 daughter. Education: Magister of Political Economy, 1962; Dr Political Economy, Institute of World Economy and International Relations, USSR Academy of Sciences, 1967; Dr hab in Political Economy, 1971; Centre for Central Banking Studies, Bank of England, 1992. Appointments: Senior Researcher and Head, Departments of Social Infrastructure and Mathematical Modelling, Lithuanian Academy of Sciences 1967-91; Founding Vice Director, Scientific Center, Bank of Lithuania, 1991-92; Professor of Banking and Macroeconomics, Vytauti Magnus University 1991-2005; Intellectual Paradigmatics, 2000-2005; Professor of Banking and Macroeconomics, M Romeris Law University, 2005-; Head of Banking and Investment Department, 2006-10; Chairman, State Nostrificat Commission in Social Sciences, 1994-2002; Associate Professor and Professor of Political Economy and Banking, Kaunas Polytechnic Institute and Vilnius University, 1962-75, 1995-99; Vice-Chairman, Editing Board, Lithuan Universal Encyclopedia – (now 18/22 vol); Professor, Economics of Intellectual Resources, Vilnius Pedagogical University, 2010-. Publications: 32 books including: Reference Dictionary of Banking and Commerce in 6 volumes, 1997-2011; Dictionary of Statistical Terms (in 5 languages), 2007; Sacred Arts in Lithuania, 1999; The Old Types of the Grand Duchy of Lithuania, 2004; Finance & Investment Information DB on Web, 2006; Editor-in-Chief, Journal Intellectual Economics, 2007-. Honours: Elected Academician, Lithuanian Academy of Sciences, 1976-; Lithuanian Independence Medal, 2000; Honorary Member, Lithuanian Human Rights Association, 2010; Fellow, World Innovation Foundation, 2001; Listed in international, national biographical and encyclopedic publications. Memberships: Founding President, Lithuanian Association for Protection of Human Rights, 1989-94; Co-founding Member, Lithuanian Independence Movement Sajudis, 1988-94; Deputy of its I-II Seimas and Councils; President, Lithuanian Association of History and Philosophy of Science, 1986-92; International Sociological Association, 1982-86; Member of the Board and Presidium Lithuanian Cultural Foundation, 1995-. Address: Lūkesčių 15, Vilnius 2043, Lithuania 04125. E-mail: antanas.buracas@gmail.com Website: www.buracas.com

BURBIDGE Geoffrey, b. 24 September 1925. Astrophysicist. m. Margaret Peachey, 1948, 1 daughter. Education: Graduated, Physics, Bristol University, 1946; PhD, University College, London; Agassiz Fellow, Harvard University. Appointments: Research Fellow, University of Chicago, 1952-53; Research Fellow, Cavendish Laboratories, Cambridge; Carnegie Fellow, Mount Wilson and Palomar University, Caltech, 1955-57; Assistant Professor, Department of Astronomy, University of Chicago, 1957; Associate Professor, 1962-63, Professor of Physics, 1963-88, Professor Emeritus, 1988, University of California at San Diego -; Director, Kitt Peak National Observatory, Arizona, 1978-84; Scientific editor, Astrophysics Journal, 1996-2002. Publications: Quasi-Stellar Objects, with Margaret Burbidge, 1967; A Different Approach to Cosmology, with F Moyle and J Narlikar, 2000; More than 400 astrophysics papers in scientific journals. Honours: Bruce Medal, 1999; Gold Medal, Royal Astronomical Society, 2005; National Academy of Sciences Award for Scientific Reviewing, 2007. Address: Department of Physics, Center for Astrophysics and Space Sciences, University of California, San Diego, La Jolla, CA 92093, USA.

DICTIONARY OF INTERNATIONAL BIOGRAPHY 36th EDITION

BURDA Renate Margarete, b. 14 January 1960, Munich, Germany. Biologist. Education: Abitur, 1980; Diploma, Biology, Ludwig-Maximilian University, Munich, 1993. Appointments: Science Worker, Fluid Engineering, Technology University, Munich, 1985-2000; Laboratory Worker, Medical Care of Urology, Munich, 1995, 1998, 2000; Chief Assistant, Venomous Spider Working Group, Weissenburg, 1995-; Lector, Journal, Latrodecta, 1995-; Scientist, ABiTec, Munich, 2000-; Medical Information, Smith Kline Beecham, Munich, 1996-97, 2000; Medical Customer Care Center, GlaxoSmith Kline, 2001-; Medical Client Service, Bayer Diagnostics, Munich, 1999-2000. Publications: The Role of Web-Building Spiders; New Results Supporting the Theory that Cribra Orbitalia can be caused by iron deficiency anaemia; Electrophoresis of Scorpion Venoms; Die Rolle Radnetzbauender Spinnen in der Biologischen Schädlingsbekämpfung. Honours: Many exhibitions. Memberships: Judge of Trampoline Sports; Venomous Spider Working Group. Address: Eichenstr 17, 82054 Sauerlach, Germany.

BURINSKII Alexander, b. 6 October 1939, Moscow, Russia. Physicist. m. Lubov Zhamnova, 1969, 1 son, 1 daughter. Education: Student, 1957, Postgraduate, 1964, PhD, 1969, Moscow Physics and Technical University; Doctor of Physical and Mathematical Sciences, 2003. Appointments: Engineer Physicist, 1963; Senior Scientific Researcher, 1969; Chief, Laboratory in Computer Centre, 1974; Senior Scientific Researcher in Pedagogical University, 1987; Senior Scientific Researcher, Theoretical Physics Laboratory, Nuclear Safety Institute, Russian Academy of Sciences, 1989-. Publications: About 100 articles in numerous journals. Honours: First Award, Gravity Research Foundation, 2009. Membership: Russian Gravitational Society.

BURKE John Frederick, (Owen Burke, Harriet Esmond, Jonathan George, Joanna Jones, Robert Miall, Sara Morris, Martin Sands), b. 8 March 1922, Rye, England. Author. m. (1) Joan Morris, 1940, 5 daughters, (2) Jean Williams, 1963, 2 sons. Appointments: Production Manager, Museum Press; Editorial Manager, Paul Hamlyn Books for Pleasure Group; European Story Editor, 20th Century Fox Productions. Publications: Swift Summer, 1949; An Illustrated History of England, 1974; Dr Caspian Trilogy, 1976-78; Musical Landscapes, 1983; Illustrated Dictionary of Music, 1988; A Travellers History of Scotland, 1990; Bareback, 1998; Death by Marzipan, 1999; We've Been Waiting for You, 2000; Stalking Widow, 2000; The Second Strain, 2002; Wrong Turnings, 2004; Hang Time, 2007; The Merciless Dead, 2008; Also many short science-fiction and weird tales in magazines and anthologies. Film and TV Novelisations. Contributions to: The Bookseller; Country Life; Denmark. Honour: Atlantic Award in Literature, 1948-49. Memberships: Society of Authors; Danish Club. Address: 5 Castle Gardens, Kirkcudbright, Dumfries & Galloway DG6 4JE, Scotland.

BURKE Kathy, b. 13 June 1964, London, England. Actress; Playwright; Theatre Director. Education: Anna Scher's Theatre School, London. Creative Works: TV include: Harry Enfield and Chums; Absolutely Fabulous; Common as Muck; Mr Wroes' Virgins; Tom Jones; Gimme Gimme Gimme; Ted & Ralph; The F-Word; Dawn French's Girls Who Do Comedy, 2006; The F-Word, 2006; The Catherine Tate Show, The Eejits, 2007; Al Murray's Multiple Personality Disorder (co-writer/director); Horne & Corden (director), 2009; Films: Scrubbers; Nil By Mouth; Elizabeth, 1998; This Year's Love, 1999; Love, Honour and Obey, 2000; The Martins, 2001; Once Upon a Time in the Midlands, 2002; Anita and Me, 2002; Flushed Away (voice), The Rav Doe Show, 2008. Theatre includes: Mr Thomas, London; It's a Great Big Shame!, 1993; Boom Bang-a-Bang, London (director); Out in the Open (director); Kosher Harry (director), 2002; Born Bad (director), 2003. Honours: Royal TV Society Award; Best Actress, Cannes Film Festival, 1997.

BURKE Philip George, b. 18 October 1932, London, England. Physicist. m. Valerie Mona Martin, 1959, 4 daughters. Education: BSc (1st Class Honours), Physics, University College, Exeter, 1953; PhD, Theoretical Nuclear Physics, University College, London, 1956. Appointments: Postdoctoral Research Fellow, UCL, 1956-57; Lecturer, University of London Computer Unit, 1957-59; Postdoctoral Research Physicist, Lawrence Berkeley Laboratory, California, USA, 1959-62; Research Fellow, Senior Principal Scientific Officer, Theory Division, AERE Harwell, 1962-67; Head, Theory & Computational Science Division, Daresbury Laboratory, joint app with QUB, 1977-82; Professor, Mathematical Physics, 1967-98, Emeritus Professor, 1998-, Queen's University, Belfast. Publications: Many research publications in learned journals; 7 books. Honours: DSc, honoris causa, University of Exeter, 1981; Fellow, University College, London, 1986; CBE, 1993; DSs, honoris causa, Queen's University, Belfast, 1999; Guthrie Medal and Prize, Institute of Physics, 1994; David Bates Prize, Institute of Physics, 2000. Memberships: Fellow, Royal Society; Member, Royal Irish Academy; Fellow, Institute of Physics; Fellow, American Physical Society; Member, European Physical Society; Fellow, Royal Astronomical Society. E-mail: p.burke@qub.ac.uk

BURKETT Mary Elizabeth, b. 7 October 1924, Northumberland, England. Teacher; Museum Director. Education: BA, University of Durham. Appointments: Art Teacher, The Laurels School, Wroxall Abbey, 1949-53; Teacher of Art and Craft, Charlotte Mason College, Ambleside, 1954-62; Assistant then Director, Abbot Hall Art Gallery and Museums, Kendal, 1962-86; Director, Border TV, 1982-93; Member: North Western Area Museums and Art Gallery Services Area Council, 1975-86; Arts Council Fine Arts Committee, 1978-80; National Trust North Western Region Executive Committee, 1978-85; Judge: Scottish Museum of the Year Award, 1977-2000, English Museum of the Year Award, 1986-2000; Member, British Tourist Authority Museums Mission to USA, 1981. Publications: The Art of the Felt Maker, 1979; Kurt Schwitters (in the Lake District), 1979; William Green of Ambleside (with David Sloss), 1984; Monograph on Christopher Steele, 1987; Read's Point of View (with David Sloss), 1995; Percy Kelly, A Cumbrian Artist (with V M Rickerby), 1996; Monograph of George Senhouse of Mayport, 1997; Christopher's Steele 1733-1767 of Acre Walls, Egremont: George Romney's Teacher, 2003; The Beckoning East (with Genette Malet de Carteret), Journey Through Persia & Turkey 1962, 2006; Jenny Cowern, A Softer Landscape, monograph (with V M Rickerby), 2007. Honours: OBE, 1978; FMA, 1980; Leverhulme Fellowship for studies in Cumbrian portrait painting, 1986; Honorary MA, Lancaster University, 1997; Honorary Fellow, Cumbria Institute of the Arts, 2005; Fellowship, Cumbria Institute of the Arts, 2005. Memberships: Friends of Abbot Hall Art Gallery Committee, 2000-; Trustee: Carlisle Cathedral Appeal, 1981-86, Armitt Trust, 1982-86, Senhouse Trust, 1985-; President: International Feltmakers Association, 1984-, Executive Committee Lake District Art Gallery Trust, 1993-98, Carlisle Cathedral Fabric Committee, 1993-2001, Blencathra Appeal Committee, 1993-95; President Romney Society, 1999-;

President, NADFAS, North Cumbria, 2003-08. Address: Isel Hall, Cockermouth, Cumbria CA13 0QG, England. E-mail: m.e.burkett@amserve.net

BURN (John) Ian, b. 19 February 1927, London, England. Retired Consultant Surgeon. m. Fiona May Allan, 2 sons, 2 daughters. Educations: St Bartholomew's Medical College, 1944-50; London University. Appointments: RAF Medical Service, 1952-54; Anatomy Department, University of Cambridge, 1954-55; Consultant Surgeon, Hammersmith Hospital, 1965-72; Consultant Surgeon, Charing Cross Hospital, 1973-87; Harley Street Clinic, 1973-91; King Edward VII Hospital, Midhurst, 1988-97. Publications: 9 books. Honours: MBBS, London, 1951; FRCS, England, 1956; Hunterian Professor, Royal College of Surgeons, 1967; President, British Association of Surgical Oncology, 1980-83; Freeman, City of London, 1986; President, European Society of Surgical Oncology, 1987-90; Vice President, Royal Society of Medicine, 1989-91; President, World Federation of Surgical Oncology, 1992-95; BA, Opera Studies, Manchester, 2001. Memberships: British Association of Surgical Oncology; Association of Surgeons of Great Britain and Ireland; Royal Society of Medicine; The Worshipful Company of Barbers; The MCC; The British Croquet Association; Friends of the Welsh National Opera. Address: 17 Catkins Close, Faringdon, Oxfordshire, SN7 7FA, England.

BURNETT Alfred David, b. 15 August 1937, Edinburgh, Scotland. University Librarian; Poet. Education: MA, Honours, English Language and Literature, University of Edinburgh, 1959; ALA, University of Strathclyde, 1964. Appointments: Library Assistant, Glasgow University Library, 1959-64; Assistant Librarian, Durham University Library, England, 1964-90. Publications: Mandala, 1967; Diversities, 1968; A Ballad Upon a Wedding, 1969; Columbaria, 1971; Shimabara, 1972; Fescennines, 1973; Thirty Snow Poems, 1973; Hero and Leander, 1975; The True Vine, 1975; He and She, 1976; The Heart's Undesign, 1977; Figures and Spaces, 1978; Jackdaw, 1980; Thais, 1981; Romans, 1983; Vines, 1984; Autolycus, 1987; Kantharos, 1989; Lesbos, 1990; Root and Flower, 1990; Mirror and Pool, translations from Chinese (with John Cayley), 1992; Nine Poets, 1993; The Island, 1994, 2nd edition, 1996; Twelve Poems, 1994; Something of Myself, 1994; Six Poems, 1995; Transfusions, translations from French, 1995; Hokusai, 1996; Marina Tsvetaeva, 1997; Chesil Beach, 1997; Akhmatova, 1998; Cinara, 2001; Evergreens, 2002; Quoins for the Chase, 2003; Twelve Women, 2004; Despatches, 2006; Snowfalls, 2010; Editor, anthologies. Contributions to: Poetry Durham; Numerous professional and critical periodical contributions and monographs. Honours: Essay Prize, 1956, Patterson Bursary in Anglo-Saxon, 1958, University of Edinburgh; Kelso Memorial Prize, University of Strathclyde, 1964; Essay Prize, Library Association, 1966; Sevensma Prize, International Federation of Library Associations, 1971; Hawthornden Fellowships, 1988, 1992 and 2002; Panizzi Medal, British Library, 1991; Fellow, British Centre for Literary Translation, Norwich, 1994. Memberships: Poetry Book Society; Fine Press Book Association; Private Libraries Association. Address: 6 Bramdean Place, Edinburgh, EH10 6JS, Scotland.

BURNS Jim, b. 19 February 1936, Preston, Lancashire, England. Writer; Part-time Teacher. Education: BA Honours, Bolton Institute of Technology, 1980. Appointments: Editor, Move, 1964-68; Editor, Palantir, 1976-83; Jazz Editor, Beat Scene, 1990-. Publications: A Single Flower, 1972; The Goldfish Speaks from beyond the Grave, 1976; Fred Engels bei Woolworth, 1977; Internal Memorandum, 1982; Out of the Past: Selected Poems 1961-1986, 1987; Confessions of an Old Believer, 1996; The Five Senses, 1999; As Good a Reason As Any, 1999; Beats, Bohemians and Intellectuals, 2000; Take it Easy, 2003; Bopper, 2003; Germany and all that Jazz, 2005; Short Statements, 2006; Laying Something Down, 2007; Cool Kerouac, 2008; Streetsinger, 2010; Contributions to: London Magazine; Stand; Ambit; Jazz Journal; Critical Survey; The Guardian; New Statesman; Tribune; New Society; Penniless Press; Prop; Verse; Others. Address: 11 Gatley Green, Gatley, Cheadle, Cheshire SK8 4NF, England.

BURNS Marjorie Ruth, b. 16 August 1929, Adelaide, South Australia. Librarian. Education: BA, University of Adelaide, 1952; Associate Australian Library and Information Association, 1968; Supervision Certificate, South Australian Institute of Technology, 1968; Non-Graduating Student Elder Conservatorium of Music, University of Adelaide, Pianoforte, 1947-49; Tertiary and Further Education, Music School, Adelaide, Pianoforte, 1990-91; Voice Private Teacher, 1955-56, 1991. Appointments: Library Assistant, Barr Smith Library, University of Adelaide, 1952-62; Librarian, Commonwealth of Australia, Public Service, 1962-67; Librarian to Parliamentary Librarian, Technical Services, South Australia Parliament Library, 1967-88; Reference research, administrative and personnel management to help with community projects, 1988-. Publications: Scottish in South Australia, 1995; Articles in Caledonian paper of Royal Caledonian Society of South Australia; Various journal articles. Honours: Australian Ambassador to World Forum, ABI & IBC, 2006, 2008, 2009, 2010, 2011; American Hall of Fame, ABI, 2007; IBC Hall of Fame, 2008; ABI Intellectual of the Year, 2008; Lifetime of Public Service Achievement, IBC, 2009; World Forum Concert Evening, San Francisco, California, USA, 2011; Director General's Leadership Award, 2011; Plaque for peak performance before an international audience; Listed in World Who's Who of Women; Dictionary of International Biography; Who's Who in the Commonwealth; International Book of Honor; Great Minds of the 21st Century. Memberships: Associate, Library Association of Australia; Recitals Australia; Royal Caledonian Society of South Australia; Alumni, University of Adelaide; Lyceum Club, Adelaide Inc, South Australia; Public Service Association (Commonwealth); MOIF; IOM; OM. Address: Unit 3, 1 Elliot St, Toorak Gardens, 5065 South Australia.

BURRELL Michael Philip, b. 12 May 1937, Harrow, England. Actor; Playwright. Education: BA, MA (Cantab), Peterhouse, Cambridge, 1958-61. Career: Freelance actor since 1961, appearing in major British companies including, the Royal Shakespeare Company, the Chichester Festival Company and Stratford East; Numerous TV appearances; Over 25 feature films; Directing career since 1964, posts include, Associate Director, Royal Lyceum Theatre, Edinburgh 1966-68; Director, Angles Theatre, Wisbech, 1995-2001; Serves on various arts boards, including the Drama Panel of the Eastern Arts Association, 1981-86; King's Lynn Festival and Arts Centre, 1992-95; Theatre Royal, Bury St Edmunds, 1994-2000; Company Secretary, Tiebreak Touring Theatre Ltd, 1987-2004; Chairman, Wisbech Events Forum, 1998-2009; Chairman, Huntingdon Branch Liberal Democrats, 2003-2006, 2008-; Chairman, Natural High Experience Ltd, 2004-; Most recent London appearances in The Mousetrap, 2005-2006 and The Woman in Black, 2007. Publications: Over 17 plays including the multi-award winning Hess, 1978, 5 London productions, including one by the RSC at the Almeida; Borrowing Time; My Sister Next Door; The Man Who Lost America; Love Among the Butterflies; Lord of the Fens; Several articles; A current weekly column, In My View, in the Fenland Citizen newspaper. Honours: Obie Award, for Hess, 1980; Best Actor, Best Show, Edmonton Journal Awards, 1984, 1985; Capital Critics Award for Best Actor, Ottawa, 1986; Bronze Award, New York Film Festival, 1988; Edmonton Journal Award for Best Show, for My Sister Next Door, 1989; Honorary President, Peterhouse Heywood Society, 2002-; American Order of Merit, 2010. Memberships: National Liberal Club, London; National Liberal Club. Address: c/o Richard Stone Partnership, 2 Henrietta Street, London WC2E 8PS, England. Website: www.michaelburrell.net

BURRILL Timothy, b. 8 June 1931, St Asaph, North Wales, UK. m. (1) Philippa Hare, deceased, 1 daughter (2) Santa Raymond, divorced, 1 son, 2 daughters. Education: Eton College; Sorbonne, Paris, France. Appointments: Entered film industry 1956; Joined Brookfield Productions, 1965; Managing Director, Burrill Productions, 1966-; Director, World Film Services, 1967-69; First Production Administrator, National Film and TV School, 1972; Managing Director: Allied Stars, responsible for Chariots of Fire, 1980-81, Pathé Productions Ltd, 1994-99; Director: Artistry Ltd, responsible for Superman and Supergirl films, 1982, Central Casting, 1988-92; Consultant: National Film Development Fund, 1980-81, The Really Useful Group, 1989-90; UK Film Industry Representative on Eurimages, 1994-96; Vice-Chairman, 1979-81 Chairman, 1980-83, BAFTA, Film Asset Development plc, 1987-94, First Film Foundation, 1989-98, Production Training Fund, 1993-2001; Executive Committee, 1990-2001, Vice-Chairman, 1993-94, The Producers' Association; Director, British Film Commission, 1997-99; Producer Member: Cinematograph Films Council, 1980-83; General Council ACTT, 1975-76; Executive Committee, British Film and TV Producers' Association, 1981-90; Governor, National Film and TV School, 1981-92, Royal National Theatre, 1982-88; Member, UK Government's Middleton Committee on Film Finance, 1996; Le Club de Producteurs Européens; Board Member, International Federation of Film Producers Association, 1997-2001, UK Government's Film Policy Review, 1997-98, European Film Academy, 1997-. Films as Co-Producer include most recently: The Pianist, 2001-2002; Swimming Pool, 2002-2003; Two Brothers, 2002; Les Anges de l'Apocalypse, 2003; Double Zero, 2003; Oliver Twist, 2004; Renaissance, 2004; La Vie en Rose, 2006; The Ghost, 2009. Address: 19 Cranbury Road, London SW6 2NS, England. E-mail: timothy@timothyburrill.co.uk

BURROWAY Janet (Gay), b. 21 September 1936, Tucson, Arizona, USA. Professor; Writer; Poet. m. (1) Walter Eysselinck, 1961, divorced 1973, 2 sons, (2) William Dean Humphries, 1978, divorced 1981, (3) Peter Ruppert, 1993, 1 stepdaughter. Education: University of Arizona, 1954-55; AB, Barnard College, 1958; BA, 1960, MA, 1965, Cambridge University; Yale School of Drama, 1960-61. Appointments: Instructor, Harpur College, Binghamton, New York, 1961-62; Lecturer, University of Sussex, 1965-70; Associate Professor, 1972-77, Professor, 1977-, MacKenzie Professor of English, 1989-95, Robert O Lawson Distinguished Professor, 1995-2002, Emerita, 2002-, Florida State University; Fiction Reviewer, Philadelphia Enquirer, 1986-90; Reviewer, New York Times Book Review, 1991-; Essay-Columnist, New Letters: A Magazine of Writing and Art, 1994-. Publications: Fiction: Descend Again, 1960; The Dancer From the Dance, 1965; Eyes, 1966; The Buzzards, 1969; The Truck on the Track, children's book, 1970; The Giant Jam Sandwich, children's book, 1972; Raw Silk, 1977; Opening Nights, 1985; Cutting Stone, 1992; Bridge of Sand, 2009. Poetry: But to the Season, 1961; Material Goods, 1980; Essays: Embalming Mom, 2002. Other: Writing Fiction: A Guide to Narrative Craft, 1982, 8th edition, 2010; Imaginative Writing, 3rd edition, 2010; Editor, From Where You Dream: The Process of Writing Fiction, by Robert Olen Butler, 2005; Play: Medea With Child, 2010. Contributions to: Numerous journals and periodicals. Honours: National Endowment for the Arts Fellowship, 1976; Yaddo Residency Fellowships, 1985, 1987; Lila Wallace-Reader's Digest Fellow, 1993-94; Carolyn Benton Cockefaire Distinguished Writer-in-Residence, University of Missouri, 1995; Woodrow Wilson Visiting Fellow, Furman University, Greenville, South Carolina, 1995; Erskine College, Due West, South Carolina, 1997; Drury College, Springfield, Illinois, 1999. Memberships: Associated Writing Programs, vice president, 1988-89; Authors Guild; PEN; ASCAP; Dramatists Guild. Address: N2484 Elgin Club Dr, Lake Geneva, WI 53147-3744, USA. E-mail: jburroway@fsu.edu

BURTON Anthony George Graham, b. 24 December 1934, Thornaby, England. Writer; Broadcaster. m. 28 March 1959, 2 sons, 1 daughter. Publications: A Programmed Guide to Office Warfare, 1969; The Jones Report, 1970; The Canal Builders, 1972, 4th edition, 2005; The Reluctant Musketeer, 1973; Canals in Colour, 1974; Remains of a Revolution, 1975, 2001; The Master Idol, 1975; The Miners, The Navigators, Josiah Wedgwood, Canal, 1976; Back Door Britain, A Place to Stand, Industrial Archaeological Sites of Britain, 1977; The Green Bag Travellers, 1978; The Past At Work, The Rainhill Story, 1980; The Past Afloat, The Changing River, The Shell Book of Curious Britain, 1982; The National Trust Guide to Our Industrial Past, The Waterways of Britain, 1983; The Rise and Fall of King Cotton, 1984; Walking the Line, Wilderness Britain, Britain's Light Railways, 1985; The Shell Book of Undiscovered Britain and Ireland, Britain Revisited, Landscape Detective, 1986; Opening Time, Steaming Through Britain, 1987; Walk the South Downs, Walking Through History, 1988; The Great Days of the Canals, 1989; Cityscapes, Astonishing Britain, 1990; Slow Roads, 1991; The Railway Builders, 1992; Canal Mania, The Grand Union Canal Walk, 1993; The Railway Empire, The Rise and Fall of British Shipbuilding, 1994; The Cotswold Way, The Dales Way, 1995; The West Highland Way, 1996; The Southern Upland Way, William Cobbett: Englishman, 1997; The Wye Valley Walk, The Caledonian Canal, Best Foot Forward, 1998; The Cumbria Way, The Wessex Ridgeway, Thomas Telford, 1999; Weekend Walks: Dartmoor and Exmoor, Weekend Walks: The Yorkshire Dales, Traction Engines, Richard Trevithick, 2000; The Orient Express, Weekend Walks: The Peak District, The Anatomy of Canals: The Early Years, The Daily Telegraph Guide to Britain's Working Past, 2001; The Anatomy of Canals: The Mania Years, 2002; Hadrian's Wall Path, The Daily Telegraph Guide to Britain's Maritime Past, The Anatomy of Canals: Decline and Renewal, 2003; On the Rails, 2004; The Ridgeway, 2005; The Cotswold Way, 2007; Tracing Your Shipbuilding Ancestors, 2010. Address: c/o Sara Menguc, 58 Thork Hill Road, Thames Ditton, Surrey, KT7 0UG, England.

BURTON David Michael, b. 13 January 1961, Leicester, England. Artist. Education: Bosworth College, Desford, Leicestershire; Southfield College, Leicester. Appointments: Self-taught Artist, Painter & Sculptor. Publications: From Now to Zero: The Work of David Burton; Numerous articles in professional and popular journals; Works held in the library collections of the Tate Gallery, National Library of Wales and the Kohler Art Library, Madison, Wisconsin, USA. Honours: 1st Prize, 1984, 2nd Prize, 1985, Landscape Painting, Nuneaton

Festival of the Arts; Several merits for various categories; Works in many public collections in the UK; The David Burton Collection and Archive, Scolton Manor Museum, Haverfordwest, Pembrokeshire. Memberships: National Acrylic Painters Association, 2004. Address: Glan Preseli, Efailwen, Clynderwen, Pembrokeshire SA66 7UY, Wales.

BURTON Gregory Keith, b. 12 February 1956, Sydney, New South Wales, Australia. Barrister-at-Law; Senior Counsel; FCIArb. m. Penelope Josephine Whitehead, 2 sons, 3 daughters. Education: BCL, Oxon; BA Honours, LLB Honours, University of Sydney; Diploma, International Arbitration (CIArb); Graded Arbitrator, Accredited Mediator; Listed Expert Determiner; Associate, Institute Arbitrators and Mediators, Australia; Barrister, New South Wales, High Court and Federal Courts, Queensland, Ireland; Barrister and Solicitor, Victoria, Western Australia, ACT, Northern Territory. Appointments: Solicitor, Freehill Hollingdale and Page, 1980-83; Associate to Hon Justice Sir William Deane, High Court of Australia, 1984-85; Senior Adviser to Federal MP, 1986; Lecturer, Law, Australian National University, 1987-88; Bar, 1989-; Senior Counsel, 2004-. Publications: Australian Financial Transactions Law, 1991; Chapters and articles in, and editor of, journals, book and legal encyclopaedias, including founding and current editor, Journal of Banking and Finance Law and Practice, 1990-; Directions in Finance Law, 1990; Weaver and Craigie's Banker and Customer in Australia (co-author). Honours: Dux, Trinity Grammar School, Sydney, 1968-73; University Medal, History, University of Sydney, 1978; Prizes in Equity, Commercial Law, Public Law, English, History, Government; Editorial Committee, Sydney Law Review, 1978-79. Memberships: NSW Bar Association; Business Law Section, Law Council of Australia; Banking and Financial Services Law Association; Commercial Law Association; Australian Institute Administrative Law; Various ADR Organizations; Centre International Legal Studies, Vienna; Centre Independent Studies; Institute of Public Affairs; Sydney Institute; Director, Australian Elizabethan Theatre Trust; Procurator, Presbyterian Church of Australia. Address: 5th Floor, Wentworth Chambers, 180 Phillip Street, Sydney, NSW, Australia 2000.

BURTON, Hon Mr Justice; Hon Sir Michael John, b. 12 November 1946, Manchester, England. High Court Judge. m. Corinne Ruth Cowan, deceased, 1992, 4 daughters. Education: Kings Scholar, Captain of School, Eton College, 1959-64; MA, Balliol College, Oxford, 1965-69 (JCR President of Balliol, First President, Oxford University Student Council). Appointments: Called to Bar, Gray's Inn, 1970; Barrister, 1970-98; Lecturer in Law, Balliol College, Oxford, 1970-73; Candidate (Labour), Kensington Council, 1971; Parliamentary Candidate (Labour), Stratford-on-Avon, 1974; Candidate (Social Democrat), GLC Putney, 1981; Queen's Counsel, 1984; Recorder of the Crown Court, 1989-98; Head of Chambers, 1991-98; Deputy Judge of the High Court, 1993-98; Judge of the High Court of Justice (Queen's Bench Division), 1998-; Judge of the Employment Appeal Tribunal, 2000-, President, 2002-05; Chairman, Central Arbitration Committee, 2000-; President, Interception of Communications Tribunal, 2000-2001; Vice-President, Investigatory Powers Tribunal, 2000-; Member, Bar Council Legal Services Commission, 1995; Publication: Civil Appeals (editor) 2002. Honours: Queen's Counsel, 1984; Bencher of Gray's Inn, 1993, Vice Treasurer, 2011; Knighted, 1998; Chairman, High Court Judges Association, 2010. Memberships: Honorary Fellow, 1999-, Member of Council, 2003-05, Goldsmith's College London University; Fellow, Eton College, 2004-. Address: c/o Royal Courts of Justice, Strand, London WC2A 2RR, England.

BURTON Tim, b. 25 August 1958, Burbank, California, USA. Film Director. Partner, Helena Bonham-Carter, 1 son, 1 daughter. Education: California Arts Institute. Appointments: Animator, Walt Disney Studios, projects include: The Fox and the Hound, The Black Cauldron; Animator, Director, Vincent (short length film). Creative Works: Films directed: Vincent (also animator), Luau, Hansel and Gretel (TV), 1982; Frankenweenie, 1984; Aladdin, Pee-wee's Big Adventure, Alfred Hitchcock Presents (TV episode, The Jar), 1985; Beetlejuice, 1988; Batman, 1989; Edward Scissorhands (also producer), 1991; Batman Returns (also producer), 1992; Ed Wood (also producer), 1994; Mars Attacks! (also producer), 1996; Sleepy Hollow, 1999; Planet of the Apes, 2001; Big Fish, 2003; Charlie and the Chocolate Factory, Corpse Bride (also producer), 2005; Sweeney Todd: The Demon Barber of Fleet Street, 2007; Alice in Wonderland, 2010; Producer: Beetlejuice (TV series), Family Dog (TV series), The Nightmare Before Christmas, 1993; Cabin Boy, 1994; Batman Forever, James and the Giant Peach, 1996; 9, 2009; Film screenplays: The Island of Dr Agor, 1971; Stalk of the Celery, 1979; Vincent, Luau, 1982; Beetlejuice (story), 1988; Edward Scissorhands (story), 1990; The Nightmare Before Christmas (story), 1993; Lost in Oz (TV pilot episode story), 2000; Point Blank (TV series), 2002. Publications: My Art and Films, 1993; Burton on Burton, 1995, 2005; The Melancholy Death of Oyster Boy and Other Stories, 1997; The Art of Tim Burton, 2009; various film tie-in books. Honours include: Golden Lion for Lifetime Achievement, 2007; Best Director, National Board of Review Awards, 2008; Scream Immortal Award, 64th Venice International Film Festival 2008. Address: Chapman, Bird & Grey, 1990 South Bundy Drive, Suite 200, Los Angeles, CA 90025, USA. Website: www.timburton.com

BUSCEMI Steve, b. 13 December 1957, Brooklyn, New York, USA. m. Jo Andres, 1987, 1 son. Education: Graduated, Valley Stream Central High School, Valley Stream, New York, 1975; Career: Bartender; Ice-cream truck driver; Stand-up comedian; Firefighter; Actor. Films include: The Way It Is, 1984; Tommy's, 1985; Sleepwalk, Parting Glances, 1986; Heart, 1987; Kiss Daddy Goodnight, Vibes, 1988; New York Stories, Slaves of New York, Mystery Train, Coffee & Cigarettes II, Borders, 1989; King of New York, 1990; Barton Fink, Zandalee, Billy Bathgate, 1991; In the Soup, CrissCross, Reservoir Dogs, Who Do I Gotta Kill? 1992; Claude, Rising Sun, Twenty Bucks, Ed and His Dead Mother, 1993; Floundering, The Hudsucker Proxy, Airheads, Somebody to Love, Pulp Fiction, 1994; Living in Oblivion, Dead Man, Things to Do in Denver When You're Dead, 1995; Fargo, Trees Lounge, Kansas City, Escape from LA, 1996; Con Air, The Real Blonde, 1997; The Wedding Singer, The Big Lebowski, The Imposters, Armageddon, Louis & Frank, 1998; Animal Factory, 28 Days, Ghost World, 2000; Final Fantasy: The Spirits Within, The Grey Zone, Monster Inc, 2001; The Laramie Project, Love in the Time of Money, 13 Moons, Mr Deeds, Spy Kids 2: Island of Lost Dreams, Deadrockstar, 2002; Spy-Kids 3-D: Game Over, Coffee and Cigarettes, Big Fish, 2003; Home on The Range, voice, The Sky is Green, Art School Confidential, 2004; Romance & Cigarettes, The Island, A Licence to Steel, Cordless, Delirious, 2005; Charlotte's Web, (Voice), 2006; Interview, I Think I Love My Wife, I Now Pronounce You Chuck and Larry, Delirious, Romance & Cigarettes, 2007; Igor (voice), 2008; Rage, John Rabe, G-Force, The Messenger, 2009; Director/Producer/Writer: What Happened to Pete? 1992; Trees

Lounge, 1996; Animal Factory, 2000; Lonesome Jim, 2004; Interview, 2007; TV includes: Saturday Night Live, 1975; Miami Vice, 1984; The Equaliser, 1985; Crossbow, 1986; The Simpsons, 1989; In The Life, 1992; Mad About You, 1992; The Drew Carey Show, 1995; The Sopranos, 2004; 30 Rock, 2007; ER, 2008; Honours include: Independent Spirit Award, Best Supporting Male, 1993; Chicago Film Critics Association Award, Best Supporting Actor, 2002; Independent Spirit Award, Best Supporting Male, 2002; Kansas City Film Critics Circle Award, Best Supporting Actor, 2002; Las Vegas Film Critics Society Award, Best Supporting Actor, 2002; San Diego Film Critics Society Award, 1997. Address: c/o Artists Management Group, 9465 Wilshire Blvd, #419, Beverly Hills, CA 90212, USA.

BUSH George W, b. 6 July 1946, USA. 43rd President of the United States of America. m. Laura Lane Welch, twin daughters. Education: Bachelor's Degree, History, Yale University; Master of Business Administration, Harvard University. Appointments: F-102 Pilot, Texas Air National Guard; Founder and Manager, Spectrum 7 Energy Corporation (merged with Harken Energy Corporation, 1986), Midland Texas; Director, Harken Energy Corporation; Professional Baseball Team Executive with Texas Rangers, 1989-94; Elected Governor of Texas, 1994; Re-elected, 1998; Elected President of the United States, 2001-2004, 2004-09.

BUSH Kate (Catherine), b. 30 July 1958, Bexleyheath, Kent, England. Singer; Songwriter. m. Danny McIntosh, 1 son. Education: Voice, dance and mime lessons. Career: Limited live performances include: Tour Of Life, Europe, 1979; Secret Policeman's Third Ball, London, 1987; Television appearances include: Bringing It All Back Home documentary, 1991; Writer, director, actress, film The Line, The Cross And The Curve, 1994. Recordings (mostly self-composed): Albums: The Kick Inside, 1978; Lionheart, 1978; Never For Ever (Number 1, UK), 1980; The Dreaming, 1982; Hounds Of Love (Number 1, UK), 1985; The Whole Story (Number 1, UK), 1987; The Sensual World (Number 2, UK), 1989; This Woman's Work, 1990; The Red Shoes (Number 2, UK), 1993; Aerial, 2005; Contributor, Games Without Frontiers, Peter Gabriel, 1980; Two Rooms - Celebrating The Songs Of Elton John And Bernie Taupin, 1991; Singles include: Wuthering Heights (Number 1, UK), 1978; The Man With The Child In His Eyes, 1978; Wow, 1979; Breathing, 1980; Babooshka, 1980; Army Dreamers, 1980; Sat In Your Lap, 1981; Running Up That Hill, 1985; Cloudbusting, 1985; Hounds Of Love, 1986; Experiment IV, 1986; Don't Give Up, duet with Peter Gabriel, 1986; This Woman's Work (from film soundtrack She's Having A Baby), 1988; The Sensual World, 1989; Moments Of Pleasure, 1993; Rubberband Girl, 1993; Man I Love, 1994; The Red Shoes, 1994; Honours: Ivor Novello Awards, Outstanding British Lyric, 1979; BRIT Award, Best British Female Artist, 1987; Q Magazine Award for Best Classic Songwriter, 2001; Ivor Novello Award for Outstanding Contribution to British Music by a Songwriter, 2002. Address: c/o KBC, PO Box 120, Welling, Kent DA16 3DS, England.

BUSH Ronald, b. 16 June 1946, Philadelphia, Pennsylvania, USA. Professor of American Literature; Writer. m. Marilyn Wolin, 1969, 1 son. Education: BA, University of Pennsylvania, 1968; BA, Cambridge University, 1970; PhD, Princeton University, 1974. Appointments: Assistant to Associate Professor, Harvard University, 1974-82; Associate Professor, 1982-85, Professor, 1985-97, California Institute of Technology; Visiting Fellow, Exeter College, Oxford, 1994-95; Drue Heinz Professor of American Literature, Oxford University, 1997-; Visiting Fellow, American Civilization Program, Harvard University, 2004. Publications: The Genesis of Ezra Pound's Cantos, 1976; T S Eliot: A Study in Character and Style, 1983; T S Eliot: The Modernist in History (editor), 1991; Prehistories of the Future: The Primitivist Project and the Culture of Modernism (co-editor), 1995; Claiming the Stones/Naming the Bones: Cultural Property and the Negotiation of National and Ethnic Identity (co-editor), 2002. Contributions to: Scholarly books and journals. Honours: National Endowment for the Humanities fellowships, 1977-78, 1992-93; AHRB Research Grant, 2003-04. Address: St John's College, Oxford OX1 3JP, England.

BUSH Stephen Frederick, b. 6 May 1939, Bath, England. University Professor; Entrepreneur. m. Gillian Mary Layton, 1 son, 1 daughter. Education: Isleworth Grammar School, 1954-57; Trinity College Cambridge Senior Scholar, 1958, Starred First Class Honours in Engineering, 1960, Research Scholar, 1961, MA, PhD, 1965; NATO Research Studentship, 1960-63, SM, Control Engineering, Massachusetts Institute of Technology, USA, 1960-61; MSc, University of Manchester, 1979. Appointments: Successively, Technical Officer, Section Manager and Manager of Process Technology Group, ICI Corporate Laboratory, 1963-71; Head, Systems Technology Department, ICI Europa Ltd, 1971-79; Professor of Polymer Engineering, 1979-2003, Head of Centre for Manufacture, 2000-05, Professor of Process Manufacture, 2004-05, Professor Emeritus, 2006-, University of Manchester (Institute of Science and Technology) (UMIST); Consultant to many companies including: ICI, Cookson Group (USA), United Biscuits, Terrys-Suchard, Lucas, Camac Inc (USA), Ametex AG (Switzerland), Curver Ltd, Everite (Pty) Ltd (South Africa); Founder and Managing Director, Prosyma Research, 1987-; Executive Chairman and Co-founder, North of England Plastics Processing Consortium, 1990-2000; Chairman, NEPPCO Ltd, 2000-06; Director, Surgiplas Ltd, 2001-08; Advisory Board Member, Business Innovation Center, University of Massachusetts, USA, 2007-; Policy Advisor, UK Independence Party, 2007-; Founder and Editor, www.britain-watch.com, 2009. Publications: (Technical) Around 180 papers and 20 patents on the science and economics of process manufacture including: Measurement and Prediction of Temperature Oscillations in a Chemical Reactor, 1969; Analysis and Control of Variability in the Polyester Fibres Process, 1991; Long Glass Fibre Reinforcement of Thermoplastics, 1999; Technoeconomic Models for New Products and Processes, 2005; (Political) Around 90 articles and letters in the national press and 5 pamphlets including: Britain's Future – No Middle Way, 1990; The Importance of Manufacture to the Economy, 2000. Honours include: Sir George Nelson Prize for Applied Mechanics, Cambridge, 1960; Senior Moulton Medal, Institution of Chemical Engineers, 1969; Sir George Beilby Medal and Prize, Royal Society of Chemistry and the Institute of Materials, 1979; Fellowships: Institution of Mechanical Engineers, 1993 (Council, 1978-81); Institution of Chemical Engineers, 1993; Plastics and Rubber Institute, 1985 (Council, 1985-87); Institute of Materials, Minerals and Mining, 1993; Royal Society of Arts and Manufactures, 1998; ABI Man of the Year for England, 2009. Memberships: Council, Manchester Statistical Society, 2001-07; Editorial Board, International Journal Industrial Systems Engineering, 2005-; Royal Economic Society, 2006-. Address: Alfred House, Pokeriage Gardens, Thurston, Suffolk IP31 3TS, England.

BUSQUETS-MONGE Sergio, b. 14 February 1974, Barcelona, Spain. Associate Professor. Education: BS, MS, 1999, PhD, 2006, Electrical Engineering, Technical University of Catalonia, Spain; MS, Electrical Engineering,

Virginia Polytechnic Institute & State University, USA, 2001. Appointments: Graduate Research Assistant, Virginia Polytechnic Institute & State University, 1999-2001; Electrical Engineer, Crown Audio Inc, USA, 2001-02; Graduate Research Assistant, 2003-04, Assistant Professor, 2005-07, Associate Professor, 2007-, Technical University of Catalonia. Publications: Optimization in Power Electronics; Pulse width modulation for multilevel converters; 1 patent in power supply for an audio amplifier. Honours: Outstanding dissertation award from the Technical University of Catalonia, 2008. Memberships: IEEE: Phi Kappa Phi. Address: Av Diagonal 647, 9th floor, 08028 Barcelona, Spain. E-mail: sergio.busquets@upc.edu

BUSSELL Darcy, b. 27 April 1969, London, England. Ballerina. m. Angus Forbes, 1997, 2 daughters. Education: Royal Ballet School. Career: Birmingham Royal Ballet, then Sadlers Wells, 1987; Soloist; Royal Ballet, 1988, first solo, 1989; Principal, 1989-2006; Retired, 2007; Board of Directors, Sydney Dance Company; Patron, International Dance Teachers Association. Appearances include: The Spirit of Fugue, created for her by David Bintley; Swan Lake; The Nutcracker; The Prince of the Pagodas; Cinderella; Sleeping Beauty; Bloodlines; Romeo and Juliet; Giselle; Raymonda; Numerous appearances on TV; Guest with other ballet companies in Paris, St Petersburg and New York. Publications: My Life in Dance, 1998; Favourite Ballet Stories; The Young Dancer; Pilates for Life, 2005; The Magic Ballerina, 2008. Honours: Prix de Lausanne, 1989; Dancer of the Year, Dance and Dancers Magazine, 1990; Sir James Garreras Award, Variety Club of Great Britain, 1991; Evening Standard Ballet Award, 1991; Joint winner, Cosmopolitan Achievement in the Performing Arts Award, 1991; Olivier Award, 1992; OBE, 1995; Carl Alan Award; Honorary DLitt, University of Oxford, 2009.

BUSTREO Flavia, b. 17 August 1961, Campo Sampiero, Italy. Assistant Director-General. Education: Graduate (Honours), Medicine & Surgery, 1987; Postgraduate, Sports Medicine & Rehabilitation, University of Padova, 1990; Graduate, CUAMM College, Padova, Italy, 1993; Graduate, Communicable Disease Epidemiology, London School of Hygiene & Tropical Medicine, 1994. Appointments: Public Health Specialist, World Bank Headquarters, Washington; Director, Partnership for Maternal, Newborn & Child Health, Geneva; Assistant Director-General, Family, Women's & Children's Health, World Health Organization, Geneva. Publications: Tackling health inequities in Chile: maternal, newborn, infant, and child mortality between 1990 and 2004; Recent trends in maternal, newborn, and child health in Brazil: progress toward Millennium Development Goals 4 and 5, 2010; The World Health Organization policy on global women's health: new frontiers, 2010; Improving global maternal health: progress, challenges, and promise, 2011; Recent trends in maternal, newborn, and child health in Brazil: progress toward Millennium Development Goals 4 and 5, 2010; The World Health Organization policy on global women's health: new frontiers, 2010; Improving global maternal health: progress, challenges, and promise. Honours: Bank Award for Capacity Building for Senior WHO & Bank Staff, 2000; Bank Award for Preparation of the Healthy Start in Life Conference, 2002; Bank Award for Contribution toGlobal Monitoring Report, 2005. Address: 7 rue de Pestalozzi, 1202 Geneva, Switzerland.

BUTCHER David John, b. 19 September 1948, Brighton, England. Economic Consultant. m. Mary Georgina Hall, 1980, 2 daughters. Education: BA, Economics, 1970; BA (Hons), Economics, 1971. Appointments: Minister of Commerce, Trade & Industry, Energy, Regional Development, Postmaster General, Associate Research Economist, Department of Labour, Wellington, 1972-74; Field Officer, Joint Union Services Ltd, Hawke's Bay, 1976-78; Member of Parliament, Legislative Department, Wellington, 1978-84; Under-Secretary to the Ministers of Agriculture, Lands and Forests, Civil List, Wellington, 1984-87; Minister of Finance, Civil List, Wellington, 1987-90; Consultant, David Butcher & Associates Ltd, Wellington, 1991-; Senior Manager, Ernst & Young, Wellington, 1995-96. Publication: Numerous articles in professional journals including: The Forum Island Countries and the Single European Market, 1992; Privatisation Yearbook, 1993, 1994, 1995, 1999; Electricity Sectors in CAREC Member Countries, 2005; Parliamentary Committees in Westminster Systems, 2006; Open the Way to Competition, 2007. Honours: Title of Honour, 1987; Commemorative Medal, 1990. Memberships: NZ Institute of Management Consultants; Institute of Public Administration, New Zealand; New Zealand Association of Economists; New Zealand Association of Former MPs; New Zealand Institute of Management; Telecom Users Association of New Zealand. Address: Box 5279, Wellington, New Zealand. E-mail: david@dba.org.nz

BUTENANDT Otfrid Kurd Walter, b. 31 March 1933, Goettingen, Germany. Professor. m. Dagmar, 2 sons, 2 daughters. Education: State Board, Medicine, 1958; Medical Doctor, 1959; Internship, Surgery, Internal Medicine, Obstetrics & Gynaecology, Pediatrics, 1959-61; Fellow, Pathology, 1961; Fellowship, Cancer Research, University of Chicago; Fellowship, Pediatrics, Johns Hopkins and University of Munich, 1961-64. Appointments: Assistant Physician, Pediatrics, 1964-70, Assistant Professor, Privat Docent, 1970, Associate Professor, Pediatrics, 1976, Full Professor, Pediatrics (Auxology), Medical Faculty, Professor Emeritus, 1998, University of Munich. Publications: More than 300 articles and reviews; Books: Evaluation of Growth Hormone; Clinical Use of Growth Hormone; Growth Hormone Replacement Therapy in Adults – Pros and Cons. Honours: Founding Member, Growth Hormone Research Society. Memberships: Deutsche Gesellschaft für Kinderheilkunde; Deutsche Gesellschaft für Endokrinologie; European Society for Paediatric Endocrinology. Address: N See Str 35, 82541 Ammerland, Germany. E-mail: otfrid@butenandt.de

BUTEVICH Anatol, b. 15 June 1948, Boyary, Republic of Belarus. Journalist. m. Taisa, 1 søn, 2 daughters. Education: Philologist, Belorussian State University, 1966-71; PhD, Information Technologies, 1996. Appointments: Editor, Belorussian Telegraph Agency, 1971-73; Work at Youth Organisations, 1973-75, 1979-80; Deputy Editor-in-chief, Chyrvonaya Zmena newspaper, 1975-79; Work at Public Organisations, 1979-80, 1987-90; Director, Mastatskaya Litaratura Publishing House, 1986-87; Chairman, State Press Committee, BSSR, 1990-92; Minister of Information of the Republic of Belarus, 1992-94; Minister of Culture and Press of the Republic of Belarus, 1994-96; Consul General of the Republic of Belarus in Gdansk, Poland, 1996-98; Ambassador Extraordinary and Plenipotentiary of the Republic of Belarus in Romania, 1998-2001; Counsellor to the Chairman of the International Trade and Investment Bank, 2001-; Counsellor to the Chairman, International Trade and Investment Bank, 2001-09; Chief Specialist, Ministry of Culture, Republic of Belarus, 2009-10. Publications: Approximately 30 fiction books including books for children, historical prose, literary and critical stories; Numerous translations. Honours: Medal for Development of Virgin Lands, 1969; Charter of the Supreme Council of the Belorussian Soviet Socialist Republic,

DICTIONARY OF INTERNATIONAL BIOGRAPHY 36th EDITION

1979; Honour Diploma, Council of Minister of the Republic of Belarus, 1998; Prize Winner, Golden Pen, Belorussian Union of Journalists, 2001; Award for Contribution to Polish Literature Translation, ZAiKS Association of Polish Writers, 2004; Order of the Holy Kiril Turovskiy, Belarusian Orthodox Church, Minsk, 2008. Memberships: Union of Belorussian Writers; Belorussian Union of Journalists; Deputy Chairman, Belarusian Fund of Culture; Chairman, Belarus-Poland Association; Deputy Chairman, Republican Society Council on Cutlure and Art, Council of Ministers, Republic of Belarus, 2010-; Chairman, Observal Society Commission on Keeping Historical-Cultural Heritage under the Ministry of Culture, Republic of Belarus, 2010-. E-mail: anatolbut@mail.ru

BUTLER Manley Caldwell, b. 2 June 1925, Roanoke, Virginia, USA. Lawyer. m. June Parker Nolde, 4 sons. Education: Richmond College, The University of Richmond, Virginia, 1948; Law School, University of Virginia, 1950. Appointments: Private Practice of Law, Roanoke, Virginia, 1950-72; Member, Virginia House of Delegates, Richmond, Virginia, 1963-73; Member, United States House of Representatives, 1972-83; Partner, Wood Rogers Law Firm, Roanoke, Virginia, 1983-98; Retired, 1998. Publications: Co-Author, Abolition of Diversity Jurisdiction, 1983; University of Virginia Miller Center for Public Affairs: The 25th Amendment, 1988; Selection of Vice Presidents, 1992. Honours: Distinguished Eagle Scout Award of Blue Ridge Virginia Council of Boy Scouts of America, 1973; Phi Beta Kappa, Omicron Delta Kappa, Pi Delta Epsilon and Tau Kappa Alpha, University of Richmond; University of Virginia, Editorial Board, Virginia Law Review, Raven Society, Order of the Coif; Silver Hope Award of Multiple Sclerosis Society of Virginia, 1999; Business Hall of Fame Junior Achievement of Roanoke Valley, 1998; The Main United States Post Office Building, Roanoke, Virginia, named The M. Caldwell Butler Building, 2002; Commended for many years of service to the Commonwealth of Virginia, General Assembly of Virginia, 2001; Roger Groot Professionalism Award, Ted Dalton American Inn of Court, 2007. Memberships: Roanoke Bar Association; Virginia State Bar Association; Virginia Bar Foundation;, District of Columbia Bar, American Bar Association; American Bar Foundation; American College of Bankruptcy; American Bankruptcy Institute; Board of Roanoke City Library Foundation; Board of Trustees of Virginia Theological Seminary; Board of Virginia Historical Society, Richmond, Virginia. Address: 200 The Glebe Blvd, unit 1024, Daleville, VA 24083, USA. E-mail: nuniepapa@gleberes.net

BUTLIN Ron, b. 17 November 1949, Edinburgh, Scotland; Poet. Writer. m. Regula Staub (the writer Regi Claire), 1993. Education: MA, Dip CDAE, Edinburgh University. Appointments: Writer-in-Residence, Edinburgh University, 1983, 1985, Midlothian Region, 1990-91, Stirling University, 1993; Writer-in-Residence, The Craigmillar Literacy Trust, 1997-98; Examiner in Creative Writing, Stirling University, 1997-, University of Glasgow, 2004-; Writer in Residence, St Andrews University, 1998-; Edinburgh Poet Laureate (Makar), 2008-. Publications: Creatures Tamed by Cruelty, 1979; The Exquisite Instrument, 1982; The Tilting Room, 1984; Ragtime in Unfamiliar Bars, 1985; The Sound of My Voice, 1987; Histories of Desire, 1995; Night Visits, 1997; When We Jump We Jump High! (editor), 1998; Faber Book of Twentieth Century Scottish Poetry; Our Piece of Good Fortune, 2003; Vivaldi and the Number 3, 2004; Without a Backward Glance: New and Selected Poems 2005; Good Angel, Bad Angel (opera), 2005; Coming on Strong, 2005; Belonging, 2006; No More Angels, 2007; The Perfect Woman (opera), 2008; The Money Man (opera), 2010; The Magicians of Edinburgh (poetry), 2011. Contributions to: Sunday Herald; Scotsman; Edinburgh Review; Poetry Review; Times Literary Supplement. Honours: Writing Bursaries, 1977, 1987, 1990, 1994, 2003, 2007; Scottish Arts Council Book Awards, 1982, 1984, 1985; Scottish Canadian Writing Fellow, 1984; Poetry Book Society Recommendation, 1985; Prix Millepages, 2004 (Best Foreign Novel); Prix Lucioles, 2005 (Best Foreign Novel); Honorary Writing Fellow, University of Edinburgh, 2009; Royal Literary Fund Fellow, OLL (University of Edinburgh), 2010-11. Membership: Scottish Arts Council Literature Committee, 1995-96; Society of Authors. Address: 7W Newington Place, Edinburgh EH9 1QT, Scotland.

BUTTERWORTH Arthur Eckersley, b. 4 August 1923, Manchester, England. Composer; Conductor. m. Diana Stewart, 2 daughters. Education: Royal Manchester College of Music. Career: Member Scottish National Orchestra, 1949-54; Member, Hallé Orchestra, 1955-61; Conductor, Huddersfield Philharmonic Orchestra, 1962-93; Teacher, Huddersfield School of Music. Compositions include: Symphony No 1 op 15, Cheltenham Festival, 1957 and BBC Proms, 1958; Symphony No 2 op 25, Bradford, 1965; Organ Concerto, 1973; Violin Concerto, 1978, Symphony No 3 op 52, Manchester, 1979; Piano Trio, Cheltenham Festival Commission, 1983; Symphony No 4 op 72, Manchester, 1986; Odin Symphony for Brass op 76, National Brass Band Festival London, 1989; Northern Light op 88, Leeds, 1991; Concerto alla Veneziana op 93, York, 1992; Viola Concerto op 82, Manchester, 1993; Mancunians op 96, Hallé Orchestra Commission, Manchester, 1995; 'Cello Concerto op 98, Huddersfield, 1994; Guitar Concerto op 109, Leeds, 2000; Symphony No 5 op 115, Manchester, 2003; Mill Town op 116, for large orchestra; Piano Trio No 2 in E flat op 121; Symphony No 6, 2006 op 124; Capriccio Pastorale op 125 – small orchestra. Honour: MBE, 1995. Membership: Vice-President, British Music Society. Address: Pohjola, Dales Avenue, Embsay, Skipton, North Yorkshire, BD23 6PE, England.

BUTTON Jenson, b. 19 January 1980, Frome, Somerset, England. Professional Racing Driver. Education: Frome Community College. Career: Haywood Racing (9 race wins), 1998; Promatecme (3 race wins), 1999; Williams, 2000; Benetton, 2001; Renault F1, 2002; BAR, 2003-05; Honda Racing F1 Team (first Grand Prix win, Hungary, 2006), 2006-08; Brawn GP (6 race wins), 2009; McLaren, 2010-. Publications: My Championship Year, 2009. Honours: McLaren Autosport BRDC Young Driver Award, 1998.

BUXTON Jennifer Mary, b. 12 April 1937, London, England. Portrait Painter. m. G V Buxton, 2 sons. Education: Northfield School, Watford; Byam Shaw School of Art, London; Part-time, Central School. Appointments: Painter, people and animals, 1954-; Painted miniatures, mostly portraits, 1967-86; Painter, Wild Tigers in India (proceeds of sales to fund school in India and help save the tiger in the wild), 2004-; Teacher of portrait and still life painting to three groups of mostly retired people, Ulverston. Honours: Inaugural Gold Bowl Award, 1985; Royal Society of Miniature Painters, Sculptors and Gravers; Bell Cup for Best Portrait, The Hilliard Society. Memberships: Honorary Member, RMS; Member, Ulverston Society of Artists. Address: Windy Ash Barn, Ulverston, Cumbria LA12 7PB, England. E-mail: jen@windyashbarn.com Website: www.tigertigerburningbright.com

BYATT Antonia Susan (Dame), b. 24 August 1936, England. Author. m. (1) Ian C R Byatt, 1959, dissolved 1969, 1 son (deceased), 1 daughter, (2) Peter J Duffy, 1969, 2 daughters. Education: The Mount School, York, Newnham College, Cambridge; Bryn Mawr College, USA; Somerville College, Oxford. Appointments: Westminster Tutors, 1962-65, Extra-Mural Lecturer, University of London, 1962-71; Part-time Lecturer, Department of Liberal Studies, Central School of Art and Design, 1965-69, Lecturer, 1972-81, Tutor of Admissions, 1980-82, Assistant Tutor, 1977-80, Senior Lecturer, 1981-83, Department of English, University College London; Associate, Newnham College, Cambridge, 1977-82; Full time writer, 1983-; External Assessor in Literature, Central School of Art and Design, External Examiner, UEA; Regular Reviewer and contributor to press, radio and TV. Publications: Shadow of the Sun, 1964, 1991; Degrees of Freedom, 1965, 1994; The Game, 1967; Wordsworth and Coleridge in Their Time, 1970; The Virgin in the Garden, 1978; Still Life, 1985; Sugar and Other Stories, 1987; Unruly Times, 1989; Possession: A Romance, George Eliot: The Mill on the Floss (editor), George Eliot: Selected Essays and Other Writings (editor), 1990; Passions of the Mind (essays), 1991; Angels and Insects, 1992; The Matisse Stories, 1993; The Djinn in the Nightingale's Eye: Five Fairy Stories, 1994; Imagining Characters (with Ignès Sodré), 1995; Babel Tower, 1996; The Oxford Book of English Short Stories (editor), Elementals: Stories of Fire and Ice, 1998; The Biographer's Tale, On Histories and Stories, 2000; Portraits in Fiction, Bird Hand Book (jointly), 2001; A Whistling Woman, 2002; Little Black Book of Stories (short stories), O Henry Prize Stories (contributed short story, The Thing in the Forest), 2003; The Children's Book, 2009; Author of varied literary criticism, articles, reviews and broadcasts. Honours: PEN Macmillan Silver Pen of Fiction, 1985; Booker Prize for Fiction, 1990; Irish Times-Aer Lingus Literature Prize, 1990; CBE, 1990; Premio Malaparte Award, Capri, 1995; Mythopoeic Fantasy Award for Adult Literature, 1998; DBE, 1999; Toepfer Foundation Shakespeare Prize for contributions to British Culture, 2002; Chevalier de l'Ordre des Arts et des Lettres, France, 2003; Fellow, English Association, 2004; Blue Metropolis, 2009; Man Booker Prize, 2009; Hon DLitt: University of Bradford, 1987; University of Durham, 1991; University of York, 1991; University of Nottingham, 1992; University of Liverpool, 1993; University of Portsmouth, 1994; University of London, 1995; University of Cambridge, 1999; University of Sheffield, 2000; Honorary Fellow: Newnham College, Cambridge, 1999; London Institute, 2000; UCL, 2004; University of Kent, 2004. Memberships: Panel of Judges, Hawthornden Prize, BBC's Social Effects of TV Advisory Group, 1974-77; Communications and Cultural Studies Board, CNAA, 1978-84; Committee of Management, Society of Authors, 1984-88 (Chair, 1986-88); Creative and Performing Arts Board, 1985-87; Kingman Committee on English Language, 1987-88; Advisory Board, Harold Hyam Wingate Fellowship, 1988-92; Member, Literary Advisory Panel British Council, 1990-98; London Library Committee, 1990-; Board British Council, 1993-98. Address: c/o Rogers, Coleridge & White, 20 Powis Mews, London W11 1JN, England. Website: www.asbyatt.com

BYE Erik, b. 13 September 1945, Oslo, Norway. Senior Scientist. m. Kirsten Offenberg, 2 daughters. Education: Cand real, Chemistry, 1972, Dr philos, 1976, University of Oslo. Appointments: Scientific Assistant in Chemistry, University of Oslo, 1972-78; Postdoctoral studies, ETH, Zurich, 1977; Scientist, Occupational Hygiene, National Institute of Occupational Health, 1979-2012; Guest Researcher, SINTEF, Oslo, 1987. Publications: Scientific publications in international journals of chemistry and occupational hygiene. E-mail: eri-by@online.no

BYEON Jong Heon, b. 16 January 1966, Chongwon, Chungbuk, Republic of Korea. Professor. m. Yon Mi Kim, 2 daughters. Education: BA, Ethics Education, 1987, ME (Hons), Political Thought, 1989, PhD (Hons), Political Theory, 1995, Seoul National University. Appointments: Teaching Assistant, Seoul National University, 1987-88; Teacher, Ethics and Social Studies, Muhak Girls' High School, and Gochuck High School, Seoul, 1989-95; Part time Instructor, Seowon University, Cheongju, Myungji University, Seoul, and Seoul National University, 1995-97; Professor, Jeju National University, Jeju City, 1997-. Publications: 11 books; Numerous articles in professional journals. Memberships: International Society for the Systems Sciences; Korean Society for the Systems Sciences; Korean Ethics Studies Association; Korean Elementary Moral Education Society; Korean Society for Moral and Ethics Education; Korean Ethics Education Association; Institute for Peace Studies Jeju National University; Jeju Peace Unification Forum; Jeju International Association. Address: Jeju National University Teachers College, 61 Iljudongro, Jeju City, Juju-do, 690-781, Korea. E-mail: byeon@jejunu.ac.kr

BYRNE Gabriel, b. 1950, Dublin, Ireland. Actor. m. Ellen Barkin, 1988, divorced 1999, 1 son, 1 daughter. Education: University College, Dublin. Appointments: Archaeologist; Teacher; Actor. Creative Works: Films include: Hanna K Gothic; Julia and Julia; Siesta; Miller's Crossing; Hakon Hakenson; Dark Obsession; Cool World; A Dangerous Woman; Little Women; Usual Suspects; Frankie Starlight; Dead Man; Last of the High Kings; Mad Dog Time; Somebody is Waiting; The End of Violence (director); Tony's Story; Polish Wedding; This is the Dead; The Man in the Iron Mask; Quest for Camelot; An Ideal Husband; Enemy of the State; Stigmata; End of Days; Spider; Ghost Ship; Shade, 2003; Vanity Fair, 2004; PS, 2004; The Bridge of San Luis Rey, 2004; Assault on Precinct 13, 2005; Wah-Wah, 2005; Leningrad, 2006; Played, 2006; Jindabyne, 2006; Leningrad, Emotional Arithmetic, 2007; In Treatment, 2008; Butte, America, 2009; Co-Producer, In the Name of the Father; Theatre: A Moon for the Misbegotten, 2000; The Exonerated, 2003; A Touch of the Poet, 2005; Camelot, 2008; TV includes: The Riordans, 1978; Bracken, 1978; Madigan Men, 2000; In Treatment, 2008; Honours: Jacob's Award, 1979; Fantasporto, 1987; National Board of Review of Motion Pictures, 1995; Cinequest Film Festival, 1999; Theatre World Award, 2000; Outer Critics Circle Award, 2006; Jameson Dublin International Film Festival, 2007; Dingle Film Festival, 2008; Golden Globe Award, 2009. Address: c/o ICM, 8942 Wilshire Boulevard, Beverly Hills, CA 96211, USA.

BYRNE HILL Elizabeth Mary Stafford, b. 10 January 1941. University Lecturer. m. Graham Byrne Hill, 1 son, 3 daughters. Education: St Leonards-Mayfield School, Mayfield, 1950-59; BA, French and Drama, University of Bristol, 1962; PGCE, Institute of Education, 1963; MA, Anthropology, SOAS, University of London, 2002. Appointments: Government Officer, Grade 2, East Africa, 1963-65; Lecturer, 1966-68, Senior Lecturer, Drama, 1968-2006, St Mary's University College, Twickenham; Governor, 2003, Chair of Education, 2007-, St Leonards-Mayfield School; Trustee, Strawberry Hill Overseas and Community Concern; Education Guide, Walpole House, Twickenham, 2010-. Publications: Articles on drama, 1985-95; Director, 3 films on educational drama, 1987-90; Theatrical adaptions for St Mary's University

College, 1996-98; Cordelia's Pig Day, 2011. Honours: Civilization Prize, Sorbonnne, Paris, 1960; Fellow, Higher Education Academy, 2003. E-mail: byrnehie@smuc.ac.uk

BYUN Jae Ho, b. 26 September 1968, Daegu, Republic of Korea. Radiologist; Associate Professor. Education: MD, 1993, MS, 2000, PhD, 2006, Kyungpook National University, Daegu, Korea. Appointments: Clinical Instructor, Department of Radiology, St Vincent Hospital, 2002-03; Assistant Professor, 2003-08, Associate Professor, 2008-, Department of Radiology, Asan Medical Center, University of Ulsan College of Medicine. Publications: Numerous articles in professional journals. Honours: Certificate of Merit, RSNA, 2003 and 2006; Cum laude, RSNA, 2006; Cum laude with Excellence in Design, RSNA, 2007. Memberships: Korean Medical Association; Korean Radiological Society; Korean Society of Abdominal Radiology; Korean Society of Magnetic Resonance in Medicine. Address: Department of Radiology, Asan Medical Center, 388-1 Pungnap-2 dong, Songpa-gu, Seoul 138-736, Korea. E-mail: jhbyun@amc.seoul.kr

C

CAAN James, b. 26 March 1940, Bronx, New York, USA. Actor; Director. m. (1) DeeJay Mathis, 1961-66, 1 daughter, (2) Sheila Ryan, 1976-77, 1 son, (3) Ingrid Hajek, 1990-95, 1 son, (4) Linda Stokes, 1995, 2 sons. Creative Works: Films include: Irma La Douce, 1963; Lady in a Cage, 1964; The Glory Guys, 1965; Countdown, Games, Eldorado, 1967; Journey to Shiloh, Submarine XI, 1968; Man Without Mercy, The Rain People, 1969; Rabbit Run, 1970; T R Baskin, 1971; The Godfather, 1972; Slither, 1973; Cinderella Liberty, Freebie and the Bean, The Gambler, Funny Lady, Rollerball, The Killer Elite, 1975; Harry and Walter Go to New York, Silent Movie, 1976; A Bridge Too Far, Another Man, Another Chance, 1977; Comes a Horseman, 1978; Chapter Two, 1980; Thief, 1982; Kiss Me Goodbye, Bolero, 1983; Gardens of Stone, 1985; Alien Nation, Dad, 1989; Dick Tracy, 1990; Misery, For the Boys, Dark Backward, 1991; Honeymoon in Vegas, 1992; Flesh and Bone, 1993; The Program, 1994; North Star, Boy Called Hate, 1995; Eraser, Bulletproof, Bottle Rocket, 1996; This Is My Father, Poodle Springs, 1997; Blue Eyes, 1998; The Yards, The Way of the Gun, 1999; In the Boom Boom Room, Luckytown, Viva Las Nowhere, 2000; In the Shadows, 2001; Night at the Golden Eagle, City of Ghosts, 2002; Dogville, Dallas 362, This Thing of Ours, Jericho Mansions, Elf, 2003; Get Smart, 2008; New York, I Love You, Middle Men, Cloudy with a Chance of Meatballs (voice), 2009; Director, Actor, Hide in Plain Sight, 1980; Director, Violent Streets, 1981; Starred in television movie, Brian's Song, 1971; The Warden, 2000; Numerous other TV appearances. Address: c/o Fred Specktor, Endeavor, 9701 Wilshire Boulevard, 10th Floor, Beverly Hills, CA 90212, USA.

CABALLÉ Monserrat, b. 12 April 1933, Barcelona, Spain. Soprano Opera Singer. m. Bernabé Marti, 1 son, 1 daughter. Education: Conservatorio del Liceo; Private studies. Appointments: North American Debut, Manon, Mexico City, 1964; US Debut, Carnegie Hall, 1965; Appearances in several opera houses and at numerous festivals. Creative Works: Lucrezia Borgia; La Traviata; Salomé; Aida. Honours: Most Excellent and Illustrious Dobna and Cross of Isabella the Catholic; Commandeur des Arts et des Lettres, 1986; UNESCO Goodwill Ambassador in her semi-retirement; Numerous honorary degrees, awards and medals. Address: c/o Columbia Artists Management Inc, 165 West 57th Street, New York, NY 10019, USA.

CACKOVIC Hinko, b. Zagreb, Croatia. Resident in Berlin, Germany 1970-. Scientist; Research Physicist; Artist; Photoartist; Painter; Author; Sculptor working in metal. m. Jasna Loboda-Cackovic. Education: Diploma in Science, Physics, University of Zagreb, Croatia, 1962; MSc, Solid State Physics, University of Zagreb, 1964; PhD, Fritz-Haber Institut der Max-Planck-Gesellschaft, Berlin-Dahlem, Germany, and University of Zagreb, and Technical University Berlin, Germany, 1970. Appointments: Scientist, Institute of Physics, University of Zagreb, 1962-65; Scientist, Atom Institute Ruder Boskovic, Zagreb, 1967-71; Postdoctoral 1970-72, Scientist, 1965-67, 1970-80, Fritz-Haber Institut der Max-Planck-Gesellschaft, Berlin-Dahlem, Germany; Scientist, Technical University, Berlin, Germany, 1980-95; Freelance in multidisciplinary fields concerning new developments of art and new fields in science and technology, different aspects of human living and activity, 1995-; Always searching for new ways. Publications: Over 55 scientific articles to professional journals, including: Physics of polymers; Synthetic and biological molecules; Polymer liquid crystals; Memory in Nature, 1971; Self-ordering of the matter; Memory of solid and fluid matter; Order/disorder phenomena in the atomic, molecular and colloidal dimensions; Mutual dependence of order between atomic and colloidal entities; Theoretical and experimental development of small and wide angle x-rays scattering analysis, magnetic susceptibility and of broad line nuclear magnetic resonance analysis; Development of physical instruments; Works of Art in professional journals and books; Photoart-pictures cutting out parts of reality to change it; Photoart revealing hidden worlds; Creative activity in Photoart/sculpturing and science (physics, chemistry) is influenced by literature music, astrophysics; Harmony is the driving force for changes and processes everywhere and is also the cause for the self-organisation in nature, and disharmony is only a temporary state, to prepare the self-ordering to a higher state of order; Work concerning Creative Interaction of Science, Art, various fields of Human Activity; Photoart-pictures presented at numerous exhibitions in Germany, Austria, France, Switzerland, 1991- and in Internet galleries, 1998-; Innovative works, two-artist cooperation JASHIN, with Jasna Loboda-Cackovic from 1997; Permanent art representations: Gallery Kleiner Prinz, Baden-Baden, Germany, 1991-; Cyber Museum at wwwARTchannel, www.art-channel.net, 1999-; Virtual Gallery of Jean-Gebser-Akademie eV, Germany, www.artgala.de, 1999-. Honours: Awards for career achievements, accomplishments and contributions to society: Distinguished Leadership Award, 2000; 21st Century Achievement Awards, 2003; Gold Medal for Germany for Success, Passion, Courage, Spirit, Commitment, Excellence, Virtue, Germany, 2006; Legion of Honour, ABI, 2007; Legendary Leaders Hall of Fame, ABI, 2008; For outstanding contributions to the field of Physics: Hall of Fame, 1000 World Leaders of Scientific Influence, 2002; Distinguished Service to Science Award, for Various Aspects of Physical Science, 2007; Decree of Excellence in Science, 2007; Awards for Art, Science and their Creative Interaction: Da Vinci Diamond, 2004; IBC Lifetime Achievement Award, 2006; Dedication, Dictionary of International Biography, 33rd Edition, 2007; Salute to Greatness Award, 2007; The Roll of Honour, 2007-; World Medal of Freedom, ABI, 2008; Albert Einstein Genius Dedication, ABI, 2009; Award for Science and Art, ABI, 2008; Art awards include: Two Euro Art Prizes, Exhibitions, Germany: Dresden and Baden-Baden, 1994, 1995; Prize for Photoart, 5th Open Art Prize, Bad Nauheim, Germany, 1995 and prize Phoenix, International Virtual Internet Art Competitions, Forschungs-Instituts Bildender Kunste, Germany, 1998, 1999/2000, 2001; Prize and magna cum laude for the oeuvre, Virtual Internet Art Competitions, Jean-Gebser-Akademie, Germany, 2002-03, 2004-05; Grants: Technical University Berlin, Germany, 1965-67; Alexander von Humboldt Stiftung, Bad Godesberg, Germany, 1970-72; Max-Planck-Gesellschaft, Fritz-Haber-Institut, Berlin-Dahlem, Germany, 1972-73. Memberships: Deutsche Physikalische Gesellschaft, 1972-95; Member, Cyber Museum Euro art channel, 1998-; Fellow, International Biographical Association, 1998-2001; Virtual Gallery artgala.de, Forschungs-Institut Bildender Künste and Jean-Gebser-Akademie eV, Germany, 1999-; Europäischer Kulturkreis Baden-Baden, 2002-; Active member, various organisations working against child poverty, sponsoring their education, 2006-; International Order of Merit, 2007-; Sovereign Ambassador, Order of American Ambassadors, 2007-; Vice President, Recognition Board, World Congress of Arts, Sciences and Communication, 2007-; Secretary-General, United Cultural Convention, 2007-09; Digital Art Lexikon, lex-art eu, 2006-; The Order of International Fellowship, for Services to Art, Science and their Mutual Interaction, 2009-. Address: Im Dol 60, 14195 Berlin, Germany.

DICTIONARY OF INTERNATIONAL BIOGRAPHY 36th EDITION

CAESAR Anthony Douglass, b. 3 April 1924, Southampton, England. Clerk in Holy Orders. Education: MA, MusB, FRCO, Magdalene College, Cambridge; St Stephen's House, Oxford. Appointments: RAF, 1943-46; Assistant Music Master, Eton College, 1948-51; Precentor, Radley College, 1952-59; Assistant Curate, St Mary Abbots, Kensington, 1961-65; Priest-in-Ordinary to The Queen, 1968-70; Chaplain, Royal School of Church Music, 1965-70; Assistant Secretary, Advisory Council for the Church's Ministry, 1965-70; Resident Priest, St Stephen's Church, Bournemouth, 1970-73; Precentor and Sacrist, 1974-79, Honorary Canon, 1975-76, 1979-91, Residentiary Canon, 1976-79, Winchester Cathedral; Sub-Dean of HM Chapels Royal, Deputy Clerk of The Closet, Sub-Almoner and Domestic Chaplain to The Queen, 1979-91; Chaplain, St Cross Hospital, Winchester, 1991-93. Publications: Co-Editor, New English Hymnal 1986, Church Music. Honours: John Stewart of Rannoch Scholar in Sacred Music, 1943; LVO, 1987; CVO, 1991; Extra Chaplain to The Queen, Canon Emeritus, Winchester Cathedral, 1991-; Honorary Fellow, Guild of Church Musicians, 2007. Address: 26 Capel Court, The Burgage, Prestbury, Cheltenham, Gloucestershire GL52 3EL, England.

CAGE Nicolas (Nicholas Coppola), b. 7 January 1964, Long Beach, California, USA. Actor. m. 1 son with Kristina Fulton, (1) Patricia Arquette, 1995, divorced 2000, (2) Lisa Marie Presley, 2002, divorced 2002, (3) Alice Kim, 2004, 1 son. Creative Works: Films include: Valley Girl, 1983; Rumble Fish; Racing With the Moon; The Cotton Club; Birdy; The Boy in Blue; Raising Arizona; Peggy Sue Got Married; Moonstruck; Vampire's Kiss; Killing Time; The Short Cut; Queens Logic; Wild of Heart; Wings of the Apache; Zandalee; Red Rock West; Guarding Tess; Honeymoon in Vegas; It Could Happen to You; Kiss of Death; Leaving Las Vegas; The Rock, The Funeral, 1996; Con Air, Face Off, 1997; Eight Millimeter, Bringing Out the Dead, 1999; Gone in 60 Seconds, 2000; The Family Man, Captain Corelli's Mandolin, Christmas Carol: The Movie (voice), 2001; Windtalkers, Sonny, Adaptation, 2002; Matchstick Men, Producer, The Life of David Gale, 2003; National Treasure, 2004; Lord of War, The Weather Man, 2005; The Ant Bull (voice), World Trade Center, The Wicker Man, 2006; Ghost Rider, Grindhouse, Next, National Treasure: Book of Secrets, 2007; Bangkok Dangerous, 2008; Knowing, G-Force (voice), Bad Lieutenant: Port of Call New Orleans, Astro Boy (voice), 2009. Honours include: Golden Globe Award, Best Actor, 1996; Academy Award, Best Actor, 1996; Lifetime Achievement Award, 1996; 4 Blockbuster Entertainment Awards, 1997-2001; P J Owens Award, 1998; Charles A Crain Desert Palm Award, 2001. Address: Saturn Films, 9000 West Sunset Boulevard, Suite 911, West Hollywood, CA 90069, USA.

CAGLAR Mine, b. 14 November 1967, Turkey. Applied Probabilist. m. Mehmet Caglar, 1 son, 1 daughter. Education: BS, Middle East Technical University, 1989; MS, Bilkent University, 1991; PhD, Princeton University, 1997. Appointments: Assistant in Instruction, Princeton University, USA, 1992-97; Research Scientist, Bellcore, 1997-98; Assistant Professor, 1999-2006, Associate Professor, 2006-, Mathematics, Koc University, Istanbul, Turkey. Publications: Articles in scientific journals. Honour: Mustafa Parlor Research Award, 2005. Memberships: Sigma Xi; Informs; ISI Bernoulli Society. Address: Koc University, College of Sciences, Sariyer, Istanbul, Turkey 34450. Website: http://home.ku.edu.tr/~mcaglar

CAHILL George F, b. 7 July 1927, New York City, USA. Medical Science. m. Sarah duPont, 2 sons, 4 daughters. Education: BS, Yale University, 1949; MD, Columbia University, College of Physicians and Surgeons, 1953; MA, Harvard University, 1966. Appointments: Pharmacist Mate 2/c, USNR, American Theater, 1945-47; Research Fellow, National Science Foundation, Department of Biological Chemistry, Harvard Medical School, 1955-57; House Officer and Residencies, 1953-58; Director of Endocrine-Metabolic Unit, Peter Bent Brigham Hospital and Fellow to Director, Joslin Diabetes Research Laboratories, Boston, 1952-76; Member and Chairman, many committees of the National Institutes of Health, Veteran's Administration, National Commission on Diabetes, American Diabetes Association (President, 1975), Science Advisory Board (Chairman, Merck, Sandoz, Johnson and Johnson); Investigator to Director of Research, 1962-89, Vice President, 1985-89, Howard Hughes Medical Institute; Instructor to Professor of Medicine, Emeritus, 1957-, Harvard Medical School; Professor of Biological Sciences, Dartmouth College, Hanover NH, 1990-96. Publications: Over 350 publications in professional journals, chapters in medical texts, etc. Honours: Oppenheimer Award, 1962; Lilly Award, 1965; Banting Award, 1974, 1976; JP Hoet Award, 1973; Joseph Mather Smith Award, 1975; Fellow, American Association for the Advancement of Science, 1975; President, American Diabetes Association, 1975; Charaka Award and Lecture, 1976; Goldberger Award in Nutrition, 1977; Banting Lecture, 1977; Gairdner International Award, 1979; Director's Award, NIH, 1989; Gold Medal, Columbia College of P&S, 1991; Medical Foundation, Boston, Annual Award, 1991; Hotchkiss School Outstanding Alumnus of the Year, 1995; Renold Award, 1996. Memberships: American Diabetes Association; American Academy of Arts and Sciences; American Physiological Society; Endocrine Society; Clinical and Climatological Association; American Society of Clinical Investigation; Association of American Physicians; Historical Society of Cheshire County, New Hampshire; Trustee, Village of Stoddard, NH; Trustee, Monadnock Conservancy; Member, New Hampshire US Agricultural Association; Various forestry state and national organisations.

CAIACOB Elizabeth Anne, b. 11 December 1937, London, England. Actress. m. Paul, 3 sons. Education: St Catherine's Convent, Twickenham, England; Frances Whitton RADA, London. Appointments: Actress; Theatre: various plays over 40 years; Tours throughout Eastern Australian states and overseas; Theatres include The Playhouse, Hole in the Wall, New Fortune, Dolphin and Regal; Film and television: The Proposal; Falcon Island; Daisy & Simon; Christmas Garden; Commericals: Doug & Barry series, 2 years; Bathroom Plus – International. Publications: Book in progress. Honours: Founder, Artistic Director, Effie Crump Theatre, 1999-99; Citizen of the Year (Arts, Culture & Entertainment), 1997; Sixth Excellence in Management Award, Community Based Organisations Association, 1997; Equity Award, Equity Benevolent Guild of WA, 2003; Centenary Medal, 2003; Best Actress Award, Tropfest, 2007. Memberships: Save The Children. Address: 11 Hawkins Avenue, Sorrento, WA 6020, Australia. E-mail: ecaiacob@bigpond.net.au

CAIMBEUL Maoilios MacAonghais, b. 23 March 1944, Isle of Skye, Scotland. Writer; Poet. m. (1) Margaret Hutchison, 1971, divorced 1992, 1 son, (2) Margaret Goodall, 2002. Education: BA, Edinburgh University; Teaching Diploma, Jordanhill College, Glasgow, 1978. Appointments: Gaelic Teacher, Tobermory High School, 1978-84; Gaelic Development Officer, Highlands and Islands Development

Board, 1984-87; Writer, 1987-. Publications: Eileanan, 1980; Bailtean, 1987; A Càradh an Rathaid, 1988; An Aghaidh na Siorraidheachd, (anthology with 7 other Gaelic poets), 1991; Saoghal Ùr, 2003; Gràmar na Gàidhlig (workbook for schools), 2005; Inbhir Ásdal Nam Buadh (songs and poems by Iain Cameron), Editor with Roy Wentworth, 2006; Breac-A'-Mhuiltein, 2007; The Two Sides of the Pass/Dà Thaobhà Blealaich (poetry collection), 2009; Teas (Gaelic novel), 2010. Contributions to: Gairm; Lines Review; Chapman; Cencrastus; Orbis; Poetry Ireland Review; Comhar; Gairfish; Baragab; Weekend Scotsman; West Highland Free Press; An Guth; Gath; Northwords Now; Poetry Scotland; Contributor to Taking You Home, poems and conversations, 2006; Anthologies: Air Ghleus 2, 1989; Twenty of the Best, 1990; The Patched Fool, 1991; Somhairle, Dàin is Deilbh, 1991; An Tuil, 1999; An Leabhar Mòr, PNE, 2002; Scotlands, Poets and The Nation, 2004. Honours: Award, Gaelic Books Council Poetry Competition, 1978-79; Poetry/Fiction Prize, Gaelic Books Council, 1982-83; Poetry Prize Scottish Gaelic Section, Dunleary International Poetry Competition, 1998; Royal National Mod Bardic Crown, 2002; 2nd, BBC Alba Poetry Competition Prize, 2006; Wigtown Poetry Competition Gaelic Prize, 2007. Membership: Scottish PEN. Address: 12 Flodigarry, Staffin, Isle of Skye, IV51 9HZ, Scotland.

CAINE Sir Michael (Maurice Joseph Micklewhite), b. 14 March 1933, London, England. m. (1) Patricia Haines, divorced, 1 daughter; (2) Shakira Khatoon Baksh, 1 daughter. Career: British Army service in Berlin and Korea, 1951-53; Repertory theatres, Horsham and Lowestoft, 1953-55; Theatre Workshop, London, 1955; Acted in: Over 100 TV plays 1957-63; Films include: A Hill in Korea, 1956; Zulu, 1964; The Ipcress File, 1965; Alfie, The Wrong Box, Gambit, 1966; Funeral in Berlin, 1966; Billion Dollar Brain, Woman Times Seven, Deadfall, 1967; The Magus, Battle of Britain, Play Dirty, 1968; The Italian Job, 1969; Too Late the Hero, The Last Valley, 1970; Kidnapped, Pulp, Get Carter, 1971; Zee and Co, 1972; Sleuth, 1973; The Wilby Conspiracy, 1974; The Eagle Has Landed, The Man Who Would be King, 1975; A Bridge Too Far, The Silver Bears, 1976; The Swarm, California Suite, 1977; Ashanti, 1978; Beyond the Poseidon Adventure, The Island, 1979; Deathtrap, The Hand, 1981; Educating Rita, Jigsaw Man, The Honorary Consul, 1982; Blame it on Rio, 1983; Water, The Holcroft Covenant, 1984; Sweet Liberty, Mona Lisa, The Whistle Blower, 1985; Half Moon Street, The Fourth Protocol, Hannah and Her Sisters (Academy Award), 1986; Surrender, 1987; Without a Clue, Jack the Ripper (TV, Golden Globe Award), Dirty Rotten Scoundrels, 1988; A Shock to the System, Bullseye, 1989; Noises Off, 1991; Blue Ice, The Muppet Christmas Carol, 1992; On Deadly Ground, 1993; World War II Then There Were Giants, 1994; Bullet to Beijing, 1995; Blood and Wine, Mandela and de Klerk, 1996; 20,000 Leagues Under the Sea, Shadowrun, 1997; Little Voice, 1998; The Debtors, The Cider House Rules; Curtain Call, Quills, 1999; Get Carter, Shiner, 2000; Last Orders, Quick Sands, 2001; The Quiet American, 2002; The Actors, Secondhand Lions, The Statement, 2003; Around the Bend, 2004; The Weather Man, Batman Begins, Bewitched, The Weather Man, 2005; Children of Men, The Prestige, 2006; Flawless, Sleuth, 2007; The Dark Knight, Is Anybody There? 2008; Harry Brown, 2009. Publications: Michael Caine's File of Facts, 1987; Not Many People Know This, 1988; What's It All About, 1992; Acting in Film, 1993. Honours: CBE, 1992; Oscar, Actor in a Supporting Role, 1999; Knighted by HM Queen Elizabeth II, 2000; Outstanding Contribution to Showbusiness, Variety Club Awards, 2008; Numerous awards, nominations and citations from film and TV industry institutes, including several Golden Globe and Academy awards. Address: International Creative Management, Oxford House, 76 Oxford Road, London W1R 1RB, England.

CAIRNS David (Adam), b. 8 June 1926, Loughton, Essex, England. Music Critic; Writer. m. Rosemary Goodwin, 19 December 1959, 3 sons. Education: Trinity College, Oxford. Appointments: Music Critic, Evening Standard, and Spectator, 1958-62, Financial Times, 1963-67, New Statesman, 1967-70, Sunday Times, 1973-; Classical Programme Co-ordinator, Philips Records, 1967-73; Distinguished Visiting Scholar, Getty Center for the History of Art and Humanities, 1992; Visiting Resident Fellow, Merton College, Oxford, 1993. Publications: The Memoirs of Hector Berlioz (editor and translator), 1969, 4th edition, 1990; Responses: Musical Essays and Reviews, 1973; The Magic Flute, 1980; Falstaff, 1982; Berlioz, 2 volumes, 1989, 2000; Berlioz Volume II: Servitude and Greatness, 1832-1869, 1999. Honours: Chevalier, 1975, Officier, 1991, de l'Ordre des Arts des Lettres, France; Derek Allen Memorial Prize, British Academy, 1990; Royal Philharmonic Society Award, 1990; Yorkshire Post Prize, 1990; Commander of the Order of the British Empire, 1997; Whitbread Biography Prize, 1999; Royal Philharmonic Society Award, 1999; Samuel Johnson Non-Fiction Prize, 2000. Address: 49 Amerland Road, London SW18 1QA, England.

CAIRNS Hugh John Forster, b. 21 November 1922. Professor of Microbiology. m. Elspeth Mary Forster, 1948, 2 sons, 1 daughter. Education: Medical Degree, Balliol College, Oxford, 1943. Appointments: Surgical Resident, Radcliffe Infirmary, Oxford, 1945; Various appointments in London, Newcastle, Oxford; Virologist, Hall Institute, Melbourne, Australia, 1950-51; Viruses Research Institute, Entebbe, Uganda, 1952-54; Director, Cold Spring Harbor Laboratory of Quantative Biology, New York, 1963-68; Professor, State University of New York, American Cancer Society; Head, Mill Hill Laboratories, Imperial Cancer Research Fund, London, 1973-81; Department of Microbiology, Harvard School of Public Health, Boston, 1982-91; Research work into penicillin-resistant staphylococci, influenza virus, E.coli and DNA replication in mammals. Address: Holly Grove House, Wilcote, Chipping Norton, Exon, OX7 3EA, England.

CAITHNESS Peter Westmacott, b. 25 May 1932, Cricklewood, London, England. Security Technologies Marketing Consultant. m. Claude-Noële Gauthier, divorced 1994, 1 son, 2 daughters. Appointments: National Service, 2nd Lieutenant, Royal Artillery, 1950-52; Overseas Management Trainee, Hong Kong & Shanghai Banking Corporation, 1953-54; Overseas Sales Manager, Bradbury Wilkinson, 1954-70; Sales and Marketing Director, Aeroprint, 1970-85; Consultant, British American Banknote Corporation, 1986-96; Director, SATS (UK) Ltd, 1996-. Publications: Numerous articles about security printing in popular and professional journals. Honours: National Marketing Award, 1972; Queen's Award for Export, 1980. Memberships: Institute of Marketing; Councillor, Wooburn and Bourne End Parish Council, 2001-04; Wycombe Talking Newspaper Committee, 1997-07; Trustee, Wooburn Resident's Association, 2010-. Address: Berriedale, 26 Baker's Orchard, Wooburn Green, Buckinghamshire, HP10 0LS, England.

CAJLER Bartosz Tomasz, b. 2 July 1980, Warsaw, Poland. Violinist; Chamber Musician; Teacher. Education: MA, F Chopin Academy of Music, Warsaw, 2004; Postgraduate Diploma, Violin, The Royal College of Music, Stockholm, Sweden, 2007. Appointments: Concert engagements: First

Violinist, Dahlkvist Quartet, 2007; Violin Teacher, Royal Coll of Music, Stockholm, Sweden, 2007; Violin and Chamber Music Teacher, Mälardalen University, Sweden, 2007; CD recording for Polish label, DUX. Honours: Fourth Prize, T Wronski International Solo Violin Competition, Warsaw, 2000; Second Prize, A Postocchini Violin Competition, Fermo, Italy, 2003; Finalist, Yamaha Competition, Gothenburg, 2004; Third Prize, Ljunggrenska Tärlingen competition, Gothenburg, Sweden, 2004; Chamber music scholarship, Royal Swedish Academy of Music, 2009; First Prize, Young and Promising chamber music competition, Västerås, Sweden, 2009. Memberships: Association of Polish Artist Musicians. Website: www.bartoszcajler.com

CALAME Claude, b. 10 September 1943, Lausanne, Switzerland. University Professor. m. Noelle Descoeudres, 2 sons. Education: Graduate studies in Paris and London; PhD, Lausanne, 1977. Appointments: Scientific Assistant, Hamburg; Lecturer and Professor, Ancient Languages, University of Urbino, 1970s; Ordinary Professor, Greek Language and Literature, University of Lausanne; Research at the universities of Lille III, Cornell, Harvard and Princeton; Director of Studies at l'Ecole des Hautes Etudes en Sciences Sociales, Paris, 2001-. Publications: Author, numerous books including The Poetics of Eros in Ancient Greece, 1999; Greek Mythology, Poetics, Pragmatics and Fiction, 2009; Articles for publication in professional journals and magazines. Honours: Visiting scholar, Harvard University; Visiting professor, Yale University. Memberships: Solidarites; SOS-Asile; Ligue des Droits de l'Homme; Nouveau Parti Anticapitaliste; Cimade; ATTAC-France; GISTI. Address: Av Verdeil 7, CH-1005, Lausanne, Switzerland. E-mail: claude.calame@unil.ch

CALDER Alexander Charles, b. 30 August 1948, Aberdeen, Scotland. University Lecturer. m. Alexandria M J Robertson. Education: MA, Aberdeen, 1970; MA, Liverpool, 1974; BA, London, 1976, PhD, Aberdeen, 1989. Appointments: Tutor in English, 1990-92, Fellow in English, 1992-93, Lecturer in English, 1993-95, Aberdeen University, Scotland; Visiting Lecturer, Naples, Italy, 1996; Senior Lecturer, University of Zambia, 1997-. Publications: 27 papers on Shakespearean and rhetorical topics including chapters in: The Literature of Place, 1993 and Literature of Region and Nation, 1998. Honours: Visiting Fellow, Centre for Rhetoric Studies, University of Cape Town, South Africa; Vice-President, Association for Rhetoric and Communication in Southern Africa (ARCSA), 1998-2002. Membership: ARCSA. Department of Literature and Languages, University of Zambia, PO Box 32379, Lusaka, Zambia.

CALDER Nigel (David Ritchie), b. 2 December 1931, London, England. Writer. m. Elisabeth Palmer, 22 May 1954, 2 sons, 3 daughters. Education: BA, 1954, MA, 1957, Sidney Sussex College, Cambridge. Appointments: Research Physicist, Mullard Research Laboratories, Redhill, Surrey, 1954-56; Staff Writer, 1956-60, Science Editor, 1960-62, Editor, 1962-66, New Scientist; Science Correspondent, New Statesman, 1959-62, 1966-71. Publications: The Environment Game, 1967, US edition as Eden Was No Garden: An Inquiry Into the Environment of Man, 1967; Technopolis: Social Control of the Uses of Science, 1969; Violent Universe: An Eyewitness Account of the New Astronomy, 1970; The Mind of Man: An Investigation into Current Research on the Brain and Human Nature, 1970; Restless Earth: A Report on the New Geology, 1972; The Life Game: Evolution and the New Biology, 1974; The Weather Machine: How Our Weather Works and Why It Is Changing, 1975; The Human Conspiracy, 1976; The Key to the Universe: A Report on the New Physics, 1977; Spaceships of the Mind, 1978; Einstein's Universe, 1979, updated 2005; Nuclear Nightmares: An Investigation into Possible Wars, 1980; The Comet is Coming!: The Feverish Legacy of Mr Halley, 1981; Timescale: An Atlas of the Fourth Dimension, 1984; 1984 and Beyond: Nigel Calder Talks to His Computer About the Future, 1984; The English Channel, 1986; The Green Machines, 1986; Future Earth: Exploring the Frontiers of Science (editor with John Newell), 1989; Scientific Europe, 1990; Spaceship Earth, 1991; Giotto to the Comets, 1992; Beyond this World, 1995; The Manic Sun, 1997; Magic Universe: The Oxford Guide to Modern Science, 2003; Einstein's Universe (updated), 2005; Einstein: Relativity (introduction), 2006; The Chilling Stars: A New Theory of Climate Change (co-author with Henrik Svensmark), 2007, updated 2008; Contributions to: Television documentaries; Numerous periodicals. Honours: UNESCO Kalinga Prize, 1972; AAAS, honorary fellow, 1986; Listed in national and international biographical dictionaries. Memberships: Association of British Science Writers, Chairman, 1960-62; Cruising Association, London, Vice President, 1982-85; Fellow, Royal Astronomical Society, Council, 2001-04; Fellow, American Association for the Advancement of Science. Address: 26 Boundary Road, Crawley, West Sussex RH10 8BT, England. E-mail: nc@windstream.demon.co.uk

CALE J J (John Weldon), b. 5 December 1938, Oklahoma City, Oklahoma, USA. Singer; Songwriter; Musician (guitar). Career: Singer, songwriter, pioneer of "Tulsa sound"; Leader, Johnny Cale and the Valentines; Toured briefly with Grand Ole Opry road company; Backing musician to Red Sovine, Little Jimmy Dickens; Studio engineer, guitarist, Los Angeles, 1964; Played with artists including: Leon Russell; Delaney and Bonnie. Compositions include: Crazy Mama; Cajun Moon; Travelin' Light; Don't Cry Sister; Don't Go To Strangers; Songs covered by other artists include: After Midnight; Cocaine; I'll Make Love To You Anytime (all recorded by Eric Clapton); Call Me The Breeze (Johnny Cash, Lynyrd Skynyrd, The Allman Brothers); Clyde (Waylon Jennings); Bringing It Back (Kansas, Lynyrd Skynyrd); Same Old Blues (Bryan Ferry, Captain Beefheart); Magnolia (Deep Purple, Poco, Chris Smither, Jose Feliciano); The Sensitive Kind (John Mayall, Santana); Film scores include: at least 32 television and film score credits including: The Knight Rider, 1982; La Femme De Mon Pote, 1984; Rain Man, 1988; The Wonder Years, 1989; Phenomenon, 1996; That '70s Show, 1999; Eric Clapton: One More Car, One More Rider – Live on Tour 2001, Sunshine State, 2002; Fahrenheit 9/11, Starsky & Hutch, 2004; Lord of War, The Dukes of Hazzard, Bad News Bears, 2005; Wild Hogs, 2007; Men in Trees, 2008; Watchmen, Breaking Bad, 2009; Recordings: Albums: A Trip Down Sunset Strip (recorded under the name The Leathercoated Minds), 1967; Naturally, 1972; Really, 1973; Okie, 1973; Troubadour, 1976; #5, 1979; Shades, 1981; Grasshopper, 1982; #8, 1983; Travel Log, 1989; #10, 1992; Closer To You, 1994; Guitar Man, 1996; Anyway the Wind Blows: The Anthology, 1997; The Very Best of JJ Cale, 1998; Live 2001; To Tulsa And Back, 2004; The Road to Escondido with Eric Clapton, 2006; Rewind, 2007; Roll On, 2009; DVD: To Tulsa And Back – On Tour with J J Cale, 2005; Producer, albums by: Leon Russell: Hank Wilson's Back!; John Hammond: Got Love If You Want It; Trouble No More; Contributor, Will o' the Wisp, Leon Russell, 1975; Rhythm Of The Saints, Paul Simon, 1986; The Tractors, The Tractors, 1994; Fish Tree Water Blues, 1999; Clapton, Eric Clapton (collaborating on 3 songs), 2010. Honours: Grammy Award

Winner, 2008; RIAA Certified Gold Award, 2008. Current Management: Mike Kappus. Address: The Rosebud Agency, PO Box 170429, San Francisco, CA 94117, USA.

CALLOW Simon Philip Hugh, b. 15 June 1949, England. Actor; Director; Writer. Education: Queen's University, Belfast; Drama Centre. Creative Works: Stage appearances include: Kiss of the Spider Woman, 1985; Faust, 1988; Single Spies, 1988, 1989; The Destiny of Me, 1993; The Alchemist, 1996; The Importance of Being Oscar, Chimes at Midnight, 1997; The Mystery of Charles Dickens, 2001-04; The Holy Terror, 2004; There Reigns Love, 2008; Equus, 2008; Waiting for Godot, 2009; Films include: Four Weddings and A Funeral, 1994; Ace Ventura: When Nature Calls, 1995; James and the Giant Peach (voice), The Scarlet Tunic, 1996; Woman In White, Bedrooms and Hallways, Shakespeare in Love, Interview with a Dead Man, 1997; No Man's Land, 2000; Thunderpants, A Christmas Carol, 2001; Bright Young Things, 2003; George and the Dragon, Phantom of the Opera, 2004; Bob the Butler, Rag Tale, The Civilisation of Maxwell Bright, 2005; Sabina, 2006; Chemical Wedding, Arn – The Knight Templar, 2007; TV: Patriot Witness, 1989; Trial of Oz, 1991; Bye Bye Columbus, 1992; Femme Fatale, 1993; Little Napoleons, 1994; An Audience with Charles Dickens, 1996; A Christmas Dickens, 1997; The Woman in White, 1998; Trial-Retribution, 1999, 2000; Galileo's Daughter; The Mystery of Charles Dickens, 2002; Dr Who, Rome, 2005; Midsomer Murders, 2006; The Company, 2007; The Mr Men Show, 2008; Director: Carmen Jones, 1994; Il Trittico, 1995; Les Enfants du Paradis, Stephen Oliver Trilogy, La Calisto, 1996; Il Turco in Italia, HRH, 1997; The Pajama Game, 1998; The Consul, Tomorrow Week (play for radio), 1999; Le Roi Malgré Lui, 2003; Jus' Like That, 2004; Several other radio broadcasts. Publications: Being An Actor, 1984; A Difficult Actor: Charles Laughton, 1987; Shooting the Actor, or the Choreography of Confusion, 1990; Acting in Restoration Comedy, 1991; Orson Wells: The Road to Xanadu, 1995; Les Enfants du Paradis, Snowdon - On Stage, 1996; The National, 1997; Love is Where it Falls, 1999; Shakespeare on Love, Charles Laughton's the Night of the Hunter, Oscar Wilde and His Circle, 2000; The Nights of the Hunter, 2001; Dicken's Christmas, Henry IV Part One, 2002; Henry IV Part Two, 2003; Hello Americans, 2006; Several translations; Weekly columns in professional newspapers; Contributions to The Guardian, The Times, The Sunday Times, The Observer, Evening Standard and others. Honours: Laurence Olivier Theatre Award, 1992; Patricia Rothermere Award, 1999; CBE, 1999. Address: c/o BAT, 180 Wardour Street, London, W1V 3AA, England.

CALNE Roy (Yorke) (Sir), b. 30 December 1930. Professor of Surgery; Consultant Surgeon. m. Patricia Doreen Whelan, 1956, 2 sons, 4 daughters. Education: Guy's Hospital Medical School; MB, BS, Hons, London, 1953. Appointments: Guy's Hospital, 1953-54; RAMC, 1954-56; Departmental Anatomy Demonstrator, Oxford University, 1957-58; Senior House Officer, Nuffield Orthopaedic Centre, Oxford, 1958; Surgical Registrar, Royal Free Hospital, 1958-60; Harkness Fellow in Surgery, Peter Bent Brigham Hospital, Harvard Medical School, 1960-61; Lecturer in Surgery, St Mary's Hospital, London, 1961-62; Senior Lecturer and Consultant Surgeon, Westminster Hospital, 1962-65; Professor of Surgery, 1965-98, Emeritus Professor, 1998, University of Cambridge; Ghim Seng Professor of Surgery, National University of Singapore, 1998-. Publications include: Renal Transplantation, co-author, 1963; Lecture Notes in Surgery, 1965; A Gift of Life, 1970; Clinical Organ Transplantation, editor and contributor, 1971; Immunological Aspects of Transplantation Surgery, editor and contributor, 1973; Transplantation Immunology, 1984; Surgical Anatomy of the Abdomen in the Living Subject, 1988; Too Many People, 1994; Art Surgery and Transplantation, 1996; The Ultimate Gift, 1998; Numerous papers and book chapters. Honours include: Hallet Prize, 1957, Jacksonian Prize, 1961, Hunterian Professor, 1962, Cecil Joll Prize, 1966, Hunterian Orator, 1989, Royal College of Surgeons; Honorary MD, Oslo, 1986, Athens, 1990, Hanover, 1991, Thailand, 1993, Belfast, 1994, Edinburgh, 2001; Prix de la Société Internationale de Chirurgie, 1969; Fastin Medal, Finnish Surgical Society, 1977; Lister Medal, 1984; Knighted, 1986; Cameron Prize, Edinburgh University, 1990; Ellison-Cliffe Medal, 1990; The Medawar Prize, Transplantation Society, 1992; Honorary Fellow, Royal College of Surgeons of Thailand, 1992; Ernst Jung Prize, 1996; Gold Medal of the Catalan Transplantation Society, 1996; Grand Officer of the Republic of Italy, 2000; King Faisal International Prize for Medicine, 2001; Prince Mahidol Prize for Medicine, 2002; Thomas E Starzl Prize in Surgery & Immunology, 2002. Memberships include: Fellow, Royal College of Surgeons; Fellow, Royal Society; Fellow, Association of Surgeons of Great Britain; European Society for Organ Transplantation, 1983-84; Corresponding Fellow, American Surgical Association. Address: 22 Barrow Road, Cambridge CB2 2AS, England.

CALOGERO Francesco, b. 6 February 1935, Fiesole, Italy. Retired University Professor. m. Luisa La Malfa. 1 son, 1 daughter. Education: Laurea in Fisica, cum laude, Rome University, 1958. Appointments: Various positions, Rome University, 1958-; Professor of Theoretical Physics, Rome University La Sapienza, 1976-; Military service, 1959-60; two years in USA, 1961-63; three months in India, 1967; one year in Moscow, 1969-70; one year in London, 1979-80; Visiting Professor in Groningen, London, Montpellier, Hefei, Paris, Cuernavaca. Publications: Over 350 scientific papers published in international journals; 4 written books; 2 edited books; Over 430 publications on science and society (mainly arms control), including written and edited books and a regular column in the oldest popular science magazine in Italy; Member of several editorial boards. Honour: Accepted 1995 Nobel Peace Prize on behalf of the Pugwash Conferences on Science and World Affairs. Memberships: Member, 1987-90, Scientific Secretary, 1990-93, Chairman, 1993-96, Mathematical Physics Commission, International Union of Pure and Applied Physics; Secretary General, Pugwash Conferences, 1989-97; Chairman, Pugwash Council, 1997-2002; Scientific Council, Italian Union of Scientists for Disarmament; Committee on International Security and Arms Control of the Accademia dei Lincei. Address: c/o Physics Department, University of Roma la Sapienza, P Aldo Moro, 00185 Rome, Italy. E-mail: francesco.calogero@roma1.infn.it

CAMERON Rt Hon David William Donald, b. 9 October 1966. Prime Minister and Conservative Party Leader; First Lord of the Treasury. m. Samantha Gwendoline Sheffield, 2 sons (1 deceased), 2 daughters. Education: BA, Brasenose College, Oxford. Appointments: Conservative Research Department, 1988-92; Director of Corporate Affairs, Carlton Communications, 1994-2001; Special Advisor, HM Treasury, then Home Office; MP (Conservative), Witney, 2001-; Member, Home Affairs Select Committee, 2001-; Shadow Deputy Leader, House of Commons, 2003; Deputy Chairman, Conservative Party, 2003; Front Bench Spokesman on Local Government Finance, 2004; Head of Policy Co-ordination (member of shadow cabinet), 2004-; Head, Corporate Affairs, Carlton Communications plc; Head of Policy Co-ordination, 2005; Shadow Secretary of State for Education and Skills,

2005; Leader, Conservative Party, 2005-; Prime Minister, 2010-. Address: 10 Downing Street, London SW1A 2AA, England. Website: www.conservatives.co m

CAMERON James, b. 16 August 1954, Kapuskasing, Ontario, Canada. Director; Screenwriter. m. (1) Sharon Williams, 1978-84, (2) Gale Anne Hurd, 1985-89, (3) Kathryn Bigelow, 1989-91, (4) Linda Hamilton, 1 daughter, (5) Suzy Amiss, 2000, 1 son, 2 daughters. Education: Fullerton Junior College. Appointments: Founder, Lightstorm Entertainment, 1990, Head, 1992-; Chief Executive Officer, Digital Domain, 1993-. Creative Works: Films: Piranha II - The Spawning (director); The Terminator (director, and screenplay), 1984; The Abyss (director and screenplay), 1994; Terminator 2: Judgement Day (co-screenwriter, director, producer), 1994; Point Break (executive producer), 1994; True Lies; Strange Days; Titanic, 1996; Solaris (producer), 2002; Terminator 3: Rise of the Machines (writer), 2003; Ghosts of the Abyss (director and producer), 2003; Volcanoes of the Deep Sea (executive producer), 2003; Aliens of the Deep (director and producer), 2005; Avatar (writer, director and producer), 2009. Honours include: Academy Award, Best Director; 11 Academy Awards; Best Motion Picture (Drama) for Avatar, 2010. Address: Lightstorm Entertainment, 919 Santa Monica Boulevard, Santa Monica, CA 90401, USA.

CAMPBELL Alastair John, b. 25 May 1957, England; Civil Servant; Journalist. Partner, Fiona Millar, 2 sons, 1 daughter. Education: Gonville & Caius College, Cambridge. Appointments: Trainee Reporter, Tavistock Times, Sunday Independent, 1980-82; Freelance Reporter, 1982-83; Reporter, Daily Mirror, 1982-86, Political Editor, 1989-93; News Editor, Sunday Today, 1985-86; Political Correspondent, Sunday Mirror, 1986-87, Political Editor, 1987-89, Columnist, 1989-91; Assistant Editor, Columnist, Today, 1993-95; Press Secretary to Leader of the Opposition, 1994-97; Press Secretary to Prime Minister, 1997-2001; Director of Communications and Strategy, 2001-03; Member, election campaign team, 2005; Visiting Fellow, Institute of Politics, Harvard University, 2004. Publications: The Blair Years, 2007. Membership: President, Keighley Branch, Burnley Football Supporters' Club. Address: Prime Minister's Office, 10 Downing Street, London SW1A 2AA, England.

CAMPBELL Luke, b. 27 September 1987, Hull, England. Amateur Boxer. Career: Winner, English Senior ABA Bantamweight, 2007 and 2008; Winner, European Amateur Boxing Championships, Liverpool, 2008; Gold, Four Nations Challenge, Sheffield, 2010; Silver, World Amateur Boxing Championships, Baku, Azerbaijan, 2012; Gold (56kg Bantamweight), London Olympics, 2012.

CAMPBELL Margaret, b. London, England. Author; Lecturer on Musical Subjects. m. Richard Barrington Beare, deceased, 2 sons, 1 daughter. Education: Art Scholarship, London. Career: Talks and Interviews on BBC Radio; Cleveland Radio; Voice of America; USA; CBC Canada; BBC and Southern Television; Lectures at Cornell; Oberlin; Indiana; Oklahoma and Southern Methodist Universities; Manhattan School of Music, New York; Rice University; University of Texas at Austin; University of Southern California USA; Cambridge, Guildford and Bath Universities; Guildhall School of Music and Drama; Purcell School, England; Festivals at Bergen and Utrecht, Holland; Editor, Journal of British Music Therapy, 1974-90; Member of Jury, International Cello Competition at Spring Festival, Prague, Czech Republic, 1994; Lectures at the Conservatoire and University of Sofia, Bulgaria, 1996; Member of Council (ESTA), 1996-2002; Lectures at Sibelius Academy of Music, Helsinki, Finland, 1998. Publications: Dolmetsch: The Man and His Work, London and USA in 1975; The Great Violinists, London and USA in 1981, Germany 1982; Japan 1983 and China, 1999; The Great Cellists, London and USA, 1988, Japan, 1996, China, 1999; Henry Purcell: Glory of His Age, London 1993, paperback 1995; Married to Music. A Biography of Julian Lloyd Webber, 2001; The Great Violinists and The Great Cellists revised 2nd editions, London, 2004. Contributions: The New Grove Dictionary of Music, 6th edition, 1980; The Independent; The Strad; Cambridge Companion to the Cello, 1999; The New Grove Dictionary of Music & Musicians, 7th edition, 2000. Honours: Winston Churchill Memorial Travelling Fellowship, 1971; Fellow of the Royal Society of Arts, 1991; Board of Governors, The Dolmetsch Foundation; Freeman, Worshipful Company of Musicians, 2005; Freedom of the City of London, 2006. Memberships: Society of Authors; Royal Society of Literature; Royal Society of Arts; English Speaking Union. Address: 8 Kingfisher Court, Woodfield Road, Droitwich Spa, Worcs. WR9 8UU, England.

CAMPBELL Rt Hon Sir (Walter) Menzies, b. 22 May 1941. Member of Parliament. m. Elspeth Mary Grant-Suttie, 1970. Education: MA, LLB, University of Glasgow; Stanford University. Appointments: Competed in 1964 Olympic & 1966 Commonwealth Games; Captain, UK athletics team, 1965-66; Holder, UK 100 metres record, 1967-74; Called to Bar (Scotland), 1968; Chair, Scottish Liberals 1975-77; General Election Candidate 1974-83; Advocate Depute in the Crown Office, 1977-80; Appointed Queen's Counsel (Scotland), 1982; Elected to Parliament, North East Fife, 1987; Members' Interests Select Committee, 1988-90; Trade & Industry Select Committee, 1990-92; Chief Liberal Democrat Foreign Affairs & Defence Spokesperson 1992-97; Defence Select Committee, 1992-97 & 1997-99; Joint Cabinet Select Committee, 1997-2001; Liberal Democrat Shadow Foreign Secretary 1997-2003; Deputy Leader, Liberal Democrats, 2003-2006; Shadow Secretary of State for Foreign & Commonwealth Affairs, 2003-2006; Elected Leader of the Liberal Democrats, 2006-07. Honours: QC (Scot), 1982; CBE, 1987; PC, 1999; Knight, 2004. Memberships: President, Glasgow University Union 1964-65; Scottish Sports Council 1971-81; Chair, Royal Lyceum Theatre Company, Edinburgh 1984-87; Broadcasting Council for Scotland 1984-87; Clayson Committee on Liquor Licensing Reform in Scotland; Trustee, Scottish International Education Trust; Part-time Chair, Medical Appeal Tribunal; Part-time Chair, VAT Tribunal (Scotland); Board of the British Council; UK Delegation to the North Atlantic Assembly 1989-; UK Delegation to the Parliamentary Assembly of the CSCE 1992-. Address: House of Commons, London SW1A 0AA, England.

CAMPBELL Neve, b. 3 October 1973, Guelph, Ontario, Canada. Actress. m. (1) Jeff Colt, 1995, divorced 1998, (2) John Light, 2007. Education: National Ballet School, Canada. Career: Dance: The Phantom of the Opera; The Nutcracker; Sleeping Beauty; Films include: Paint Cans, 1994; The Dark, 1994; Love Child, 1995; The Craft, 1996; Scream, 1996; A Time to Kill, 1996; Simba's Pride, 1997; Scream 2, 1997; Wild Things, 1998; Hairshirt, 1998; 54, 1998; Three to Tango, 1999; Scream 3, 2000; Investigating Sex, 2001; Last Call, 2002; The Company, 2003; Lost Junction, 2003; Blind Horizon, 2004; When Will I Be Loved, 2004; Churchill: The Hollywood Years, 2004; Reefer Madness, 2005; Partition, 2007; Scream 4, 2010; TV includes: Catwalk, 1992-93; Web of Deceit, 1993; Baree, 1994; The Forget-Me-Not Murders, 1994; Party of Five, 1994-98; The Canterville Ghost, 1996; Reefer Madness:

The Movie Musical, 2005; Relative Strangers, 2006; Partition, 2007; I Really Hate My Job, 2007; Closing The Ring, Medium, 2007; Burn Up, 2008; The Philanthropist, The Simpson, 2009. Honours: Saturn Award for Best Actress, 1996; MTV Movie Award for Best Female Performance, 1996; Blockbuster Entertainment Award for Favourite Actress – Horror, 1997. Address: Creative Artists Agency, 9830 Wilshire Boulevard, Beverly Hills, CA 90212, USA.

CAMPBELL OF ALLOWAY, Baron of Ayr in the District of Kyle and Carrick, Alan Robertson Campbell, b. 24 May 1917, United Kingdom. Queen's Counsel. m. (1) Diana Watson-Smyth, 1947, divorced 1953, 1 daughter, (2) Vivien de Kantzow, 1957. Education: Trinity Hall Cambridge; Ecole des Sciences Politiques, Paris. Appointments: Sits as Conservative Peer in the House of Lords; Commissioned 2 Lt RA Supplementary Reserve, 1939, served in BEF France and Belgium, 1939-40, POW, 1940-45; Called to the Bar, Inner Temple, 1939, Bencher, 1972; Western Circuit, Recorder, Crown Court, 1976-89; Head of Chambers; Consultant to Sub-Committee of Legal Committee of Council of Europe on Industrial Espionage, 1965-74; Chairman, Legal Research Committee, Society of Conservative Lawyers, 1968-80; Member of House of Lords Select Committees on: Murder and Life Imprisonment, 1988-89, Privileges, 1982-2000, Personal Bills, 1987-88, Joint Consolidation Bills, 2000; Member: House of Lords Ecclesiastical Committee, 2003-; Joint Committee on Human Rights; All Party Committees on Defence, and on Children. Honours: MA (Cantab); Emergency Reserve Decoration; QC, 1965; Life Peer, 1981; Emergency Reserve Decoration, 1996. Memberships: Scottish Peers' Association; Carlton; Pratt's; Beefsteak Clubs; Perennial Guest of Third Guards Club. Address: House of Lords, London SW1A 0PW, England.

CAMPION Jane, b. 30 April 1954, Wellington, New Zealand. Film Director; Writer. m. Colin Englert, 1992, divorced, 1 daughter. Education: BA, Anthropology, Victoria University, Wellington; Diploma of Fine Arts, Chelsea School of Arts, London, completed at Sydney College of the Arts; Diploma in Direction, Australian Film & TV School, 1981-84. Career: Writer/Director, films: Peel, 1981-82; Passionless Moments, 1984; Mishaps of Seduction and Conquest, 1984-85; Girls Own Story, 1983-84; After Hours, 1984; Producer: I episode ABC TV drama series, Dancing Daze, 1986; Director, Two Friends, for ABC TV Drama, 1985-86; An Angel at My Table, 1989-90; Sweetie, 1988; Writer/Director, The Piano, 1993; Director, The Portrait of a Lady, 1997; Holy Smoke, 1999; In the Cut, 2003; Executive Producer, Abduction: The Megumi Yokota Story, 2006; Bright Star, 2009. Honours: Numerous awards include: for the Piano: Best Picture, 66th Academy Awards Nomination, Best Director, 66th Academy Awards Nomination, LA Film Critics Association, New York Film Critics Circle, Australia Film Critics, Director's Guild of America Nomination, BAFTA Nomination, AFI Awards, Producer, Producer's Guild of America, Best Screenplay, 66th Academy Awards, BAFTA Nomination, AFI Awards; For The Portrait of a Lady: Francesco Pasinetti Award, National Union of Film Journalists, 1996. Address: HLA Management Pty Ltd, 87 Pitt Street, Redfern, NSW 2016, Australia.

CAMPIONE Francesco, b. 4 March 1949, Leonforte, Italy. University Teacher. 1 daughter. Education: Medical degree, 1974, Medical Psychology Specialization, 1978, Bologna University. Appointments: University Assistant, 1978-85, Associate Professor, Clinical Psychology, 1985-2010, Director of Crisis Intervention Service, 1989-2010, Bologna University; Director of Thanatology Institute, Bologna, 1993-2010; Director, Progetto Rivivere, Bologna, 2000-10. Publications: 10 books. Memberships: IATS; IWG; Address: Associazione Rivivere, via Giorgio Ercolani N3, 40122, Bologna, Italy. E-mail: camplone@clinicacrisi.it Website: www.clinicacrisi.it

CAMROSE (Viscount), Sir Adrian Michael Berry. b. 15 June 1937, London, England. Writer; Journalist. Education: Christ Church, Oxford, 1959. Appointments: Correspondent, Time Magazine, New York City, 1965-67; Science Correspondent, 1977-96, Consulting Editor (Science), 1996-, Daily Telegraph, London. Publications: The Next Ten Thousand Years: A Vision of Man's Future in the Universe, 1974; The Iron Sun: Crossing the Universe Through Black Holes, 1977; From Apes to Astronauts, 1981; The Super Intelligent Machine, 1983; High Skies and Yellow Rain, 1983; Koyama's Diamond (fiction), 1984; Labyrinth of Lies (fiction), 1985; Ice With Your Evolution, 1986; Computer Software: The Kings and Queens of England, 1985; Harrap's Book of Scientific Anecdotes, 1989; The Next 500 Years, 1995; Galileo and the Dolphins, 1996; The Giant Leap, 1999. Honour: Royal Geographic Society, fellow, 1984-. Memberships: Royal Astronomical Society, London, Fellow, 1973-; British Interplanetary Society, Fellow, 1986-. Address: 11 Cottesmore Gardens, Kensington, London W8, England.

CANGEMI Joseph P, b. 26 June 1936, Syracuse, New York, USA. Professor; International Consultant. m. Amelia Eléna Santaló, 2 daughters. Education: BS, SUNY; MS, Syracuse University; Doctorate, Indiana University. Appointments include: Supervisor of Education, United States Steel Corporation, Orinoco Mining Division, Ciudad Piar, Venezuela, 1965-66; Supervisor of Training and Development, United States Steel Corporation, Orinoco Mining Division, 1966-68; Project Director, Inter American Development Bank and Universidad de Los Andes, Merida, Venezuela, 1975-77; Teaching Associate, Indiana University, Bloomington, Indiana, 1972-73; Assistant Professor to Associate Professor, Western Kentucky University, Bowling Green, Kentucky, 1968-79; Professor of Psychology and Full Member, Graduate Faculty, Western Kentucky University, 1979; Editorial Board Member, Journal of Foreign Psychology, Chinese Journal of Applied Psychology. Publications include: Leadership for the Twenty-First Century, Russian Academy of Sciences, 1997; Leadership Behaviour, 1998; Heroes of Solidarity, 2010; Developing Trust in Organizations, 2003; Heroes of Solidarity, 2011; Past editor, Organization Development Journal, Journal of Human Behaviour and Learning; Editor, Psychology and Education, An Interdisciplinary Journal; over 300 published articles world-wide. Honours include: Excellence in Productive Teaching Award, 1979, 1991, 1999; Travel Grant to Siberia, Western Kentucky University, 1993; Award, Standard Products Company, Goldsboro, North Carolina, 1995; Outstanding Contribution Award, 1996; Honorary Doctorate (LL.D), William Woods University, 1996; Honorary Doctorate (Doctor honoris causa) sponsored by Russian Academy of Sciences, awarded by Moscow State University, Russia, 2001; Nominee for Carnegie Foundation's Professor of the Year Award, 1999, 2000. Memberships include: American Psychological Association; American Association for Counseling and Development, Life Member; Panamanian Psychological Association (Honorary); Society of Psychologists in Management; Inter-American Society of Psychology; Kentucky Counseling Association; Society of Industrial and Organisational Psychologists (APA). Address: Department of Psychology, Western Kentucky University, Bowling Green, KY 42101, USA. Website: www.creativeleadershipandchange.com

DICTIONARY OF INTERNATIONAL BIOGRAPHY 36th EDITION

CANTER Jean Mary, b. 18 March 1943, Epsom, Surrey. Artist. Education: 13+ Art Award, Epsom School of Art, 1956-61; Major Art Award, Wimbledon School of Art, 1961-63. Career: Colourist, Baynton Williams Antique Prints; Part-time Tutor, Mid-Surrey Adult Education, 1972-2007; Freelance Artist; Exhibitions: London Royal Institute of Painters in Watercolours; Royal Watercolour Society; Society of Graphic Fine Art and many other society exhibitions; Medici Gallery; Llewellyn Alexander Gallery, London and many provincial galleries. Publications: Work reproduced and many demonstration for "How-to-do-it" Art Books; Several features for Artists and Illustrators Magazine; Regular contributor with The Drawing Class to Painting World Magazine, 1999-2001; Occasional Art Tutor, West Dean College, West Sussex, 2008-. Publications: Main Demonstration feature for Painting with Watercolours, 2004. Honours: Prizes: Society of Graphic Fine Art Exhibitions, Frisk Ltd, 1983, 1985, Rexel Ltd, 1984, 1996, Daler-Rowney, 1990, Liquitex, 1993, 1997, Winsor and Newton, 1996; Commendation of Excellence, Llewellyn Alexander Gallery, 2004, 2007; Society of Graphic Fine Art for work on Theme of 'Reflection' 2006; Faber-Castell Prize UK Coloured Pencil Society 2006; Honorary Member, Society of Graphic Fine Art, 2006; Highly Commended, Society of Graphic Fine Art, 2007; Chairman's Award, UK Coloured Pencil Society Exhibition, 2007, 2010; Gold Memorial Bowl, Honourable Mention, Royal Miniature Society, 2008; Listed in national and international biographical dictionaries. Memberships: Society of Graphic Fine Art; Silver Signature Membership, UK Coloured Pencil Society; Associate, Royal Society of Miniature Painters, Sculptors and Gravers. Address: 7 Cox Lane, Ewell, Epsom, Surrey KT19 9LR, England.

CANTLIFFE Daniel J, b. 31 October 1943, New York, USA. Professor of Horticulture. m. Elizabeth, 4 daughters. Education: BS, Delaware Valley College, 1965; MS, 1967, PhD, 1971, Purdue University. Appointments: Research Assistant, Purdue University, 1965-69; Research Associate, Cornell University, 1969-70; Research Scientist, Horticulture Research Institute of Ontario, 1970-74; Visiting Professor, Department of Horticulture, University of Hawaii, 1979-80; Assistant Professor, Assistant Horticulturist, 1974-76, Associate Professor, Associate Horticulturist, 1976-81, Professor, 1981-92, Vegetable Crops Department, Professor and Chairman, 1992-2007, Distinguished Professor and Chairman, 2007-, Horticultural Sciences Department, University of Florida. Publications: 7 book editorships; 1 monograph; 1 bulletin; 20 book chapters; 740 publications in total. Honours include: Distinguished Agricultural Alumni Award, Purdue University, 1999; Best and Most Meritorious Paper, Vegetable Section, Florida State Horticultural Society, 1990, 1992, 1998, 2000-02, 2004; Honorary Membership, Florida State Horticultural Society, 2006; Southern Region, American Society for Horticultural Science Leadership and Administration Award, 2000; Professorial Salary Adjustment Program Award, 2001 and University of Florida Research Foundation Professorship, 2005-07, Distinguished International Educator, 2005, UF/IFAS International Fellow, 2005, University of Florida; Outstanding Graduate Educator, 1991, Outstanding Researcher, 1997, Outstanding International Horticulturist, 2001, American Society for Horticultural Science; International Society for Horticultural Science Fellow Award, 2006. Memberships include: American Society for Horticultural Science; American Society of Plant Biology; American Society of Agronomy; Crop Science Society of America; Florida State Horticultural Society; International Seed Science Society; International Society for Horticultural Science; Listed in national and international biographical dictionaries. Address: Horticultural Sciences Department, University of Florida, IFAS, PO Box 110690, Gainesville, FL 32611-0690, USA. E-mail: djcant@ufl.edu

CANTOR Brian, b. 11 January 1948, Manchester, England. Vice-Chancellor. Widowed, 2 sons. Education: BA, MA, PhD, Christ's College, Cambridge, 1965-72. Appointments: Research Fellow then Lecturer, Sussex University, 1972-81; Lecturer, then Reader, then Professor, Oxford University, 1981-2002; Senior Research Fellow, Jesus College, Oxford, 1985-95; Professorial Fellow, St Catherine's College, Oxford, 1995-2002; Vice-Chancellor, University of York, 2002-; Consultancies: Alcan, 1986-94; Rolls-Royce, 1996-; Board Member: White Rose, Worldwide Universities Network, National Science Learning Centre, Yorkshire Innovation; Royal Academy of Engineering; Former Board Member: Isis Innovation, Kobe Institute; Amaethon, York Science Park; Adviser (at different times) to agencies including: EPSRC, NASA, the EU, Singapore-British Business Council, Dutch, Spanish and German Governments. Publications: Published over 300 papers, books and patents, given over 100 invited talks in more than 15 countries and on the ISI Most Cited Researchers list. Honours: Rosenhain Medal, Institute of Materials, 1993; Ismanam Prize, 1999; Platinum Medal, Institute of Metals, 2002. Memberships: Fellow, Royal Academy of Engineering; Fellow, Institute of Physics; Fellow, Institute of Materials; Companion, Member, Chartered Management Institute; Member, Academia Europaea; Member, World Technology Network; Member, Indian Institute of Metals. Address: Vice-Chancellor's Office, University of York, Heslington, York YO10 5DD, England. E-mail: vc@york.ac.uk Website: www.york.ac.uk

CAPARROS-LERA José María, b. 28 December 1943, Barcelona, Spain. Film Historian. Education: Master of History, PhD, University of Barcelona. Appointments: Full Professor, Contemporary History and Cinema, Director, Centre for Research, Film-Historia, University of Barcelona. Publications: Art y Política en el cine de le República, 1981; 100 película, sobre Historia Contemporánea, 1987; Historia del Cine Español, 2007; Historia del Cine Mundial, 2009. Honours: Award, Best Work Literary, 2007. Memberships: Academia de los Artes y los Ciencia; Cinematoqueficas de España; Académia del Cinema Català. Address: Montalegre, 6, 4a, 08004 Barcelona, Spain. E-mail: jmcaparros@ub.edu

CAPE Donald Paul Montagu Stewart, b. 6 January 1923, Kildare, Ireland. Diplomat. m. Cathune Johnston, 4 sons, 1 daughter. Education: Ampleforth College; Brasenose College, Oxford. Appointments: Scots Guards, 1942-45; Entered Foreign Service, 1946, Belgrade, 1946-48, Foreign Office, 1949-51, Lisbon, 1952-55, Singapore, 1955-57, Bogota, 1960-61, Holy See, 1962-67, Foreign Office, 1968-70, Washington, 1970-73, Brasilia, 1973-75; Ambassador to Laos, 1976-78; Ambassador and UK Permanent Representative to Council of Europe, Strasbourg, 1978-83; Retired, 1983; Administrator of Anglo-Irish Encounter, 1983-98; Chairman of the Anglo-Portuguese Society, 1988-91. Publications: A Lucky Life, 2003. Honours: CMG, 1977; CBE, 1998. Address: Hilltop, Cranleigh Road, Wonersh, Guildford, GU5 0QT, England.

CAPORALE Guglielmo Maria, b. 25 January 1963, Naples, Italy. Professor. Education: Degree in Political Science, LUISS, Rome, Italy, 1984; MSc, 1987, PhD, 1990, Economics, LSE. Appointments: International Economist, Oxford Economic Forecasting, Oxford, 1990-91; Research Officer, National Institute of Economic and Social Research, London, 1991-93; Research Fellow, 1993-95, Senior Research Fellow,

1996-98, Centre for Economic Forecasting, London Business School; Professor of Economics, University of East London, 1998-2000; Professor of Economics and Finance, Director, Centre for Monetary and Financial Economics, currently Visiting Professor, London South Bank University, 2000-; Visiting Professor, London Metropolitan University, 2002-; Visiting Professor, Institute for Advanced Studies, Vienna, Austria, 2004; Professor of Economics and Finance, Brunel University, 2004-; CESifo Research Network Fellow, 2006-; Director, Centre for Empirical Finance, Brunel University, 2007-; Research Professor, DIW Berlin, 2008-. Publications: Numerous articles in books and leading international academic journals. Honours: Foreign and Commonwealth Office and Economic and Social Research Council PhD Scholarships; ESRC and Leverhulme Trust research grants; Citation of Excellence, Highest Quality Rating, ANBAR Electronic Intelligence; Dae-Ying Prize for best publication, Journal of Economic Integration, 2005; Best Paper in Economy, Annual Conference of the American Academy of Economics & Finance, Texas, USA, 2006; Listed in national and international biographical dictionaries. Memberships: Royal Economic Society; Econometric Society; American Economic Association; European Economic Association; Latin American and Caribbean Economic Association; Money, Macro and Finance Research Group Committee. Address: Department of Economics & Finance, Brunel University, West London, UB8 3PH, England. E-mail: guglielmo-maria.caporale@brunel.ac.uk

CARDIN Pierre, b. 2 July 1922, San Biagio di Callatla, Italy. Couturier. Appointments: Worker, Christian Dior; Founder, own fashion houses, 1949; Founder, Espace Pierre Cardin (Theatre Group); Director, Ambassadeurs-Pierre Cardin Theatre (now Espace Pierre Cardin Theatre), 1970-; Manager, Société Pierre Cardin, 1973; Chair, Maxims, 1982-; Honorary UNESCO Ambassador, 1991. Creative Works: Exhibition at Victoria & Albert Museum, 1990. Publications: Fernand Léger, Sa vie, Son oeuvre, Son reve, 1971; Le Conte du Ver a Soie, 1992. Honours include: Grand Officer of Merit, Italy, 1988; Order of the Sacred Treasure (Gold & Silver Star), 1991; UNESCO Goodwill Ambassador, 1991; Goodwill Ambassador, Food and Agriculture Organization, UN, 2009. Address: 27 Avenue Marigny, 75008 Paris, France.

CARDOSO Boaventura, b. 26 July 1944, Luanda, Angola. Governor. m. Maria Laura, 3 sons. Education: 2nd year, Complementary Course, Salvador C Sa'High School, Luanda, 1970-71; BA, Social Sciences, Party School of Higher Education, Luanda, 1989; BA, Social Sciences, University of San Thomas Aquinas, Rome, 2002. Appointments: Director, National Institute BD, 1977-81; Secretary of State of Culture, 1981-90; Minister of Information, 1990-91; Ambassador Extraordinary and Plenipotentiary of Angola (AEPA) in France, 1992-99; AEPA in Italy and Malta, 2000-02; AEPA in Malta, 2001-02; Minister of Culture, 2002-08; Governor, Malanje Province, 2008-. Publications: Narratives: Dizanga don't include address Muenhu, 1977; Ofogo da Fala, 1980; A Morte do Velho Kipacaca, 1987; Novels: O Signo do Fogo, 1992; Maio mês de Maria, 1997; Mâe, Materno Mar, 2001. Honours: Listed in international biographical dictionaries; National Prize for Culture and Arts, 2001; Cultural Merit in the Class of Commendatory, 2006; Subject of essays: Boaventura Cardoso, a escrita em processo, 2005; A Alegórica Mãe, Materno Mar angolana, 2008; Boaventura Cardoso UM (RE) Inventor de Palavras e Tradições, 2009. Mmemberships: Member/Co-founder, Union of Angolan Writers; Militant of MPLA; Honorary member, Palmense Academy of Letters (Arts) in Brazil. Address: Rua Cdte Dangereux No 159, Bairro Alvalade, Malanga, Luanda, Angola. E-mail: lussala@hotmail.com

CAREY Mariah, b. 22 March 1970, Long Island, New York, USA. Singer; Songwriter. m. (1) Tommy Mottola, 1993, divorced 1998, (2) Nick Cannon, 2008, 1 son, 1 daughter. Career: Backing singer, Brenda K Starr, New York, 1988; Solo recording artiste, 1988-; 80 million albums sold to date; Concerts worldwide; Founder, Crave record label, 1997; Founder, Camp Mariah holiday project for inner-city children; Recordings: Albums: Mariah Carey, 1990; Emotions, 1991; MTV Unplugged EP, 1992; Music Box, 1993; Merry Christmas, 1994; Daydream, 1995; Butterfly, 1997; #1s, 1998; Rainbow, 1999; Glitter, 2001; Greatest Hits, 2001; Charmbracelet, 2002; The Remixes, 2003; The Emancipation of Mimi, 2005; E=MC^2, 2008; Memoirs of an Imperfect Angel, 2009; Singles: Vision Of Love,Love Takes Time, 1990; Someday, I Don't Wanna Cry, Emotions, 1991; Can't Let You Go, Make It Happen, I'll Be There, 1992; Dreamlover, Hero, 1993; Without You, Anytime You Need a Friend, Endless Love (with Luther Vandross), All I Want for Christmas Is You, 1994; Fantasy, One Sweet Day (with Boyz II Men), Always Be My Baby, 1995; Open Arms, 1996; Honey, Butterfly, Breakdown, 1997; My All, When You Believe (with Whitney Houston, in film The Prince of Egypt), 1998; I Still Believe, Heartbreaker, 1999; Thank God I Found You, Can't Take That Away, Against All Odds (with Westlife), 2000; Loverboy, Never Too Far, 2001; Through the Rain, Boy I Need You, 2002; Bringin' On The Heartbreak, 2003; Breaking All The Rules, 2004; Film: Glitter, 2001; Wise Girls, 2002; State Property 2, 2005; You Don't Mess with the Zohan, 2008; Tennessee, Precious, 2009. Honours include: Grammy Awards for Best New Artist, Best New Pop Vocal by a Female Artist, 1990; Soul Train Awards for Best New Artist, Best Single by a Female Artist, 1990; Rolling Stone Award for Best Female Singer, 1991; 8 World Music Awards, 1991-95; 7 Billboard Awards, 1991-96; 4 American Music Awards, 1991-95; International Dance Music Award for Best Solo Artist, 1996; American Music Awards Special Award for Achievement, 2000; World's Best Selling Female Artist of the Millennium. Address: The Agency Group Ltd, 361-373 City Road, London, EC1V 1PQ, England. Website: www.mariahcarey.com

CAREY Peter, b. 7 May 1943, Bacchus March, Victoria, Australia. Author. m. (2) Alison Summers, 1985, 2 sons. Education: Monash University. Appointments: Partner, McSpedden Carey Advertising Consultants, Sydney; Teacher, Columbia University, Princeton University. Publications: The Fat Man in History (short stories), 1974; War Crimes (short stories), 1979; Bliss (novel), 1981; Illywhacker (novel), 1985; Oscar and Lucinda, 1988; The Tax Inspector (novel), 1991; The Unusual Life of Tristan Smith (novel), 1994; Collected Stories, 1995; The Big Bazoohley (children's novel), 1995; Jack Maggs, 1997; The True History of the Kelly Gang, 2000; 30 Days in Sydney: A Wildly Distorted Account, 2001; My Life as a Fake, 2003; Wrong About Japan, 2005; Theft: A Love Story (novel), 2006; His Illegal Self, 2008; Screenplays: Bliss; Until the End of the World; Film: Oscar and Lucinda, 1998. Honours include: The Booker Prize (twice); Miles Franklin Award (3 times); National Council Award; Age Book of the Year Award; 3 honorary degrees. Memberships: Fellow, Royal Society of Literature; Fellow, Australian Academy of Humanities; Fellow, American Academy of Arts and Sciences. Address: c/o Amanda Urban, ICM, 40 West 57th Street, New York, NY 10019, USA.

CAREY OF CLIFTON Baron of Clifton in the City and County of Bristol (George Leonard Carey), b. 13 November 1935, London, England. Ecclesiastic; University chancellor. m. Eileen Harmsworth, 1960, 2 sons, 2 daughters. Education: Bifrons Secondary Modern School, Barking, Essex; King's College, London University; University studies and theological training, 1957-62. Appointments: National Service, RAF, 1954-56; Curate, St Mary's, Islington, 1962-66; Lecturer, Oak Hill Theological College, 1966-70; St John's College, Nottingham, 1970-75; Vicar, St Nicholas' Church, Durham, 1975-82; Principal, Trinity Theological College, Bristol, 1982-87; Bishop of Bath and Wells, 1987-91; Archbishop of Canterbury, 1991-2002; Chancellor, University of Gloucestershire, 2003-. Publications: I Believe in Man, 1978; The Great Acquittal, 1981; The Church in the Market Place, 1983; The Meeting of the Waters, 1985; The Gate of Glory, 1986; The Great God Robbery, 1988; I Believe, 1991; Spiritual Journey, 1994; My Journey, Your Journey, 1996; Canterbury – Letters to the Future, 1998; Jesus, 2000; Know the Truth, 2004. Honours: Honorary Bencher, Inner Temple; Freeman, cities of London and of Wells, 1990; Hon DLitt, Polytechnic of East London, 1991; Hon DD (Kent) 1991, (Nottingham) 1992, (Bristol) 1992, (Durham) 1994; Hon LLD, (Bath) 1992; Several honorary degrees from American universities; Greek, Hebrew and theological prizes. Memberships: Patron or president of 300 organisations; Fellow, King's College, London. Address: House of Lords, Westminster, London SW1A 0PW, England.

CARINE James, b. 14 September 1934, Isle of Man, United Kingdom. Retired. m. Carolyn Sally Taylor, 5 sons, 2 deceased, 1 daughter. Education: King William's College, Isle of Man, 1945-51; Royal Naval College, Dartmouth, 1951-52; Qualified Company Secretary (FCIS), 1970. Appointments: Royal Navy, 1951-91; Captain, Executive Assistant to Deputy Supreme Allied Command Atlantic, 1982-95; Captain, Chief Staff Officer (Personnel and Logistics), 1985-88; Commodore in Command of HMS Drake, Devonport Naval Barracks, 1988-89; Rear Admiral, Chief of Staff to Commander-in-Chief, 1989-91; Chief Executive of The Arab Horse Society, 1992-2000; Member, Copyright Tribunal, 1999-2009; Chairman, Wiltshire Ambulance Service NHS Trust, 2002-06; Chairman, Royal United Hospital, Bath, 2006-10. Honours: Freedom of City of London, 1988; Master, Worshipful Company of Chartered Secretaries, 1997-98; Knight of the Order of St Gregory the Great, 1983. Memberships: Fellow Chartered Institute of Secretaries and Administrators, 1970; Admiralty Board nominated Trustee/Director and Executive and Investment Committees of the United Services Trustee (Quoted Unit Trusts), 1995-2005; Trustee/Director and Management and Financial Committees of the Ex-Services Mental Welfare Society (Combat Stress), 1997-2002; Governor St Antony's – Lewiston School, 1997-2005; Wiltshire Committee of the National Art Collections Fund, 2001-; Independent Chairman, Wiltshire and Swindon Fire Authority Standards Committee, 2001-09; Independent Chairman, North Wiltshire District Council Standards Committee, 2002-09; Chairman, Age Concern, Swindon, 2002-05; Chairman Royal United Hospital Bath, 2006-. Address: 5 Little Sands, Yatton Keynell, Chippenham, Wiltshire SN14 7BA, England. E-mail: j.carine@btinternet.com

CARL XVI GUSTAF, (King of Sweden), b. 30 April 1946. m. Silvia Sommerlath, 1976, 1 son, 2 daughters. Education: Sigtuna; University of Uppsala; University of Stockholm. Appointments: Created Duke of Jämtland; Became Crown Prince, 1950; Succeeded to the throne on death of his grandfather, King Gustaf VI Adolf, 1973. Honours: Dr hc, Swedish University of Agricultural Sciences, Stockholm Institute of Technology, Abo Academy, Finland. Memberships: Chair, Swedish Branch, World Wide Fund for Nature; Honorary President, World Scout Foundation. Address: Royal Palace, 111 30 Stockholm, Sweden.

CARLYLE Robert, b. 14 April 1961, Glasgow, Scotland. Actor. m. Anastasia Shirley, 1997, 2 sons, 1 daughter. Education: Royal Scottish Academy of Music & Drama. Appointments: Director, Rain Dog Theatre Company. Creative Works: Productions include: Wasted; One Flew Over the Cuckoo's Nest; Conquest of the South Pole; Macbeth; Stage appearances include: Twelfth Night; Dead Dad Dog; Nae Problem; City; No Mean City; Cuttin' a Rug; Othello; TV includes: Face; Go on Byrne'; Taggart; The Bill; Looking After Jo Jo, 1998; Hitler: The Rise of Evil, 2003; Gunpowder, Treason and Plot, 2004; Human Trafficking, Class of '76, Born Equal, 2006; The Last Enemy, 24: Redemption, 2008; The Unloved, Stargate Universe, 2009; Films include: The Full Monty; Carla's Song; Trainspotting; Priest; Marooned; Being Human; Riff Raff; Silent Scream; Apprentices; Plunkett and Macleane, 1999; The World is Not Enough, 1999; Angela's Ashes, 2000; The Beach, 2000; There's Only One Jimmy Grimble, 2000; To End All Wars, 2000; 51st State, 2001; Once Upon a Time in the Midlands, 2002; Black and White, 2002; Dead Fish, 2004; Marilyn Hotchkiss' Ballroom Dancing and Charm School, 2005; The Mighty Celt, 2005; Eragon, 2006; 28 Weeks Later, Flood, 2007; Stone of Destiny, Summer, I Know You Know, 2008; The Tournament, 2009. Honours include: Paper Boat Award, 1992; BAFTA Award, Best Actor; Salerno Film Festival Award, 1997; Evening Standard Outstanding British Actor Award, 1998; Bowmore Whiskey/Scottish Screen Award for Best Actor, 2001; David Puttnam Patrons Award. Address: c/o ICM, Oxford House, 76 Oxford Street, London, W1D 1BS, England.

ČARNOGURSKÝ Ján, b. 1 January 1944, Bratislava, Slovakia. Lawyer. m. Marta Stachová, 2 sons, 2 daughters. Education: High school, Bratislava, 1961; Faculty of Law, Charles University, Prague, 1969; Doctor of Law (JUDr), Comenius University, Bratislava, 1971. Appointments: Advocate in Bratislava, 1970-81; Various employments, 1981-89; Fired from Bar for defence of dissident, 1981; Deputy PM of Czechoslovakia, 1989-90; PM of Slovakia, 1991-92; Minister of Justice of Slovakia, 1998-2002. Publications: Seen from the Danube, 1997; On the Road of KDH, 2007; Articles in Slovak, Russian and European press. Honours: Armenian State Award, Mechitar Gosh, 2008; Polish State Award, Grand Cross of Merits, 2008; Russian State Award, Orden Druzhby, 2010. Memberships: Teutonic Order; Familiare Slovac-Russian Society. E-mail: jancarnogursky@slovanet.sk Website: www.jancarnogursky.sk

CARON Leslie Claire Margaret, b. 1 July 1931, Boulogne-Billancourt, France. Actress; Ballet Dancer. m. (1) George Hormel, (2) Peter Reginald Frederick Hall, 1956, divorced 1965, 1 son, 1 daughter, (3) Michael Laughlin, 1969, divorced. Education: Convent of the Assumption, Paris; Conservatoire de Danse. Career: with Ballet des Champs Elysées, 1947-50; Ballet de Paris, 1954; Actress, films include: An American in Paris; Man with a Cloak; Glory Alley; Story of Three Loves; Lili; Glass Slipper; Daddy Long Legs; Gaby; Gigi; The Doctor's Dilemma; The Man Who Understood Women; The Subterranean; Fanny; Guns of Darkness; The L-Shaped Room; Father Goose; A Very Special Favor; Promise Her Anything; Is Paris Burning?, Head of the Family; Madron; The Contract; The Unapproachable,

1982; Deathly Moves, 1983; Génie du Faux, 1984; The Train, 1987; Guerriers et Captives, 1988; Courage Mountain, 1988; Damage, 1992; Funny Bones, 1995; Let It Be Me, 1995; The Reef, 1996; The Last of the Blonde Bombshells, 1999; Chocolat, 2000; Murder on the Orient Express, 2001; Le Divorce, 2003; Plays: Orvet; La Sauvage; Gigi; 13 rue de l'Amour; Ondine; Carola; La Répétition; On Your Toes; Apprends-moi Céline; Grand Hotel; George Sand; Le Martyre de Saint; Nocturne for Lovers; Babar the Elephant; stage appearances in Paris, London, USA, Germany and Australia. Honours: Chevalier Légion d'honneur; Officier Ordre nationale du Mérite. Address: PFD, Drury House, 34-43 Russell Street, London WC2B 5HA, England.

CARPENTER Charles John, b. 30 April 1927, Ilford, Essex, England. Electrical Engineer; Consultant. m. Rita Nellie Porter, 2 sons, 2 daughters. Education: BSc, Engineering, London University, 1948; MSc, Engineering, 1951; DSc, Engineering, 1978. Appointments: Engineering Research Engineer Crompton Parkinson Ltd, Chelmsford, England, 1942-46, 1949-53; Lecturer, Imperial College, London, 1953-61, Senior Lecturer, 1964-79; Professor, Head, Department of Electrical Engineering, University of West Indies, Trinidad, 1961-64; Consultant, CA Parsons Ltd, Newcastle, England (and other companies), 1969-79; Senior Lecturer, Gwent College of Higher Education, Newport, Gwent, Wales, 1980-87; Visiting Fellow, University of Bristol, 1987-. Publications: Numerous articles in professional journals. Honours: IEE/IET Institution Premium, 1978; Maxwell Premium, 1993 (and other Premiums); Achievement Medal, 1995. Memberships: Institution of Engineering and Technology; Chartered Engineer; Various committees. Address: Bristol University, Department of Electrical Engineering, Woodland Road, Bristol BS8 1UB, England.

CARPENTER John Randell, b. 14 April 1936, Cambridge, Massachusetts, USA. Writer; Poet; Translator; Editor; Teacher. m. Bogdana Maria-Magdalena Chetkowska, 1963, 1 son, 1 daughter. Education: BA, Harvard College, 1958; Sorbonne, University of Paris, 1962-66. Appointments: Poet in Residence, Writer in Residence, Teacher, 1975-83; Assistant Professor and Lecturer, 1984-87; Freelance Translator and Writer, 1987-. Publications: Gathering Water; Egret; Pebble, Cedar, Star; Translation of poetry. Contributions to: New York Times; The New Yorker; The New York Review of Books; Quarterly Review of Literature; Southwest Review; Minnesota Review; Epoch; Perspective; Mister Cogito; Penny Dreadful; Cafe Solo; Slant; Embers; Poet Lore; The Humanist. Honours: Writter Bynner Poetry Award; Islands and Continents Translation Award; Andrew Mellon Foundation Award; National Endowment for the Arts Fellowships. Memberships: Academy of American Poets; PEN; Poets and Writers. Address: 1606 Granger Avenue, Ann Arbor, MI 48104, USA.

CARPENTER Lucas, b. 23 April 1947, Elberton, Georgia, USA. Professor of English; Writer; Poet; Editor. m. Judith Leidner, 1972, 1 daughter. Education: BS, College of Charleston, 1968; MA, University of North Carolina at Chapel Hill, 1973; PhD, State University of New York at Stony Brook, 1982. Appointments: Instructor, State University of New York at Stony Brook, 1973-78; Instructor, 1978-80, Associate Professor of English, 1980-85, Suffolk Community College; Editorial Consultant, Prentice-Hall Inc, 1981-; Associate Professor of English, 1985-94, Professor of English, 1994-, Oxford College of Emory University. Publications: A Year for the Spider (poems), 1972; The Selected Poems of John Gould Fletcher (editor with E Leighton Rudolph), 1988; The Selected Essays of John Gould Fletcher (editor), 1989; John Gould Fletcher and Southern Modernism, 1990; The Selected Correspondence of John Gould Fletcher (editor with E Leighton Rudolph), 1996; Peril of the Affect (Poetry), 2002. Contributions to: Anthologies, scholarly journals, and periodicals. Honours: Resident Fellow in Poetry and Fiction Writing, Hambidge Center for the Creative Arts, 1991; Oxford College Professor of the Year Awards, 1994, 1996; Emory University Teacher-Scholar of the Year, 2003; Emory University Williams Award for Excellence in Teaching, 2004. Memberships: National Council of Teachers of English; Poetry Atlanta; Poetry Society of America; Southeast Modern Language Association. Address: c/o Department of English, Oxford College of Emory University, Oxford, GA 30267, USA.

CARPINTERI Alberto, b. 23 December 1952, Bologna, Italy. Structural Engineer. Education: PhD, Nuclear Engineering cum laude, University of Bologna, Bologna, Italy, 1976; PhD, Mathematics cum laude, University of Bologna, 1981. Appointments include: Researcher, Consiglio Nazionale delle Ricerche, Bologna, Italy, 1978-80; Assistant Professor, University of Bologna, 1981-86; Professor of Structural Mechanics, Politecnico di Torino, Italy, 1986-; Founding Member and Director, Post-graduate School in Structural Engineering, Politecnico di Torino, Italy, 1990-; Director, Department Structural Engineering, Politecnico di Torino, 1989-95. Publications include: Localized Damage: Computer-Aided Assessment and Control, 1994; Advanced Technology for Design and Fabrication of Composite Materials and Structures, 1995; Structural Mechanics, 1997; Fractals and Fractional Calculus in Continuum Mechanics, 1998; Computational Fracture Mechanics in Concrete Technology, 1999. Honours include: Robert l'Hermite International Prize, 1982; JSME Medal, 1993; Doctor of Physics Honoris Causa, 1994; International Cultural Diploma of Honor, 1995; Honorary Professor, Nanjing Architectural and Civil Engineering Institute, Nanjing, China, 1996; Honorary Professor, Albert Schweitzer University, Geneva, Switzerland, 2000; Griffith Medal, ESIS, 2008; Top 100 Scientists, IBC, 2009; Swedlow Memorial Lecture, ASTM, 2011. Memberships: Fellow: International Congress on Fracture, 1981-, President, 2009-13; International Association of Fracture Mechanics for Concrete and Concrete Structures, 1992-, President, 2004-2007; Réunion Internationale des Laboratoires d'Essais et de Recherches sur les Matériaux et les Constructions, 1982-; American Society of Civil Engineers, 1985-; European Structural Integrity Society, 1991-, President, 2002-2006; European Mechanics Society, 1994-. Address: Chair of Structural Mechanics, Politecnico di Torino, 10129 Torino, Italy.

CARR Pat (Moore), b. 13 March 1932, Grass Creek, Wyoming, USA. Writer; University Teacher. m. (1) Jack Esslinger, 1955, divorced 1970, (2) Duane Carr, 1971, 1 son, 3 daughters. Education: BA, MA, Rice University; PhD, Tulane University. Appointments: Teacher, Texas Southern University, 1956-58, University of New Orleans, 1961, 1965-69, 1987-88, University of Texas at El Paso, 1969-79, University of Arkansas at Little Rock, 1983, 1986-87, Western Kentucky University, 1988-96. Publications: Novels: The Grass Creek Chronicle, 1976, 2nd edition, 1993, 3rd edition, 2012; Bluebirds, 1993; Beneath the Hill, 1999; If We Must Die, 2003; Border Ransom, 2006; The Death of a Confederate Colonel, 2007; Short Story Collections: The Women in the Mirror, 1977; Night of the Luminarias, 1986; Sonahchi, 1988, 2nd edition, 1994; Our Brothers' War, 1993; The Radiance of Fossils, 2012; Lincoln, Booth, and Me, 2013. Criticism: Bernard Shaw, 1976; Mimbres Mythology, 1979; In Fine Spirits, 1986; Non-fiction: Writing Fiction with Pat Carr, 2010; One Page at a Time: On a Writing Life, 2010. Contributions to articles and short stories in numerous publications. Honours: South and West Fiction Award, 1969; Library of Congress Marc IV Award for Short Fiction, 1970; National Endowment for the Humanities Award, 1973; IOWA Fiction Award, 1977; Texas Institute of Letters Short Story Award, 1978; Arkansas Endowment for the Humanities Award, 1985; Green Mountain Short Fiction Award, 1986; First Stage Drama Award, 1990; Al Smith Fellowship in Fiction, 1995; Chateau de Lavigny Writing Fellowship, 1999; Green Literary Award, 2000; PEN Southwest Fiction Award, 2008; John Esten Cooke Civil War Fiction Award, 2008; Finalist, Willa Cather Non-Fiction Award, 2011. Memberships: Board Member, International Women's Writing Guild, 1996-; Texas Institute of Letters; Board Member, Dairy Hollow Writers' Colony; Authors' Guild. Address: 10695 Venice Road, Elkins, AR 72727, USA.

CARR Peter Derek, Sir, b. 12 July 1930, Mexborough, Yorkshire, England. Chairman. m. Geraldine Pamela, 1 son, 1 daughter. Education: Ruskin College, Oxford; Fircroft College, Birmingham; London University. Appointments: Director, Commission on Industrial Relations, 1969-74; Labour, Social Affairs Counsellor, British Embassy, Washington, 1978-83; Regional Director, Department of Employment, 1984-89; Chairman, Occupational Pensions Board, 1993-98; Chairman and Founder, Northern Screen Commission, 1992-2000; Chairman, County Durham Development Company, 1990-99; Company Chairman, Durham County Waste Management, 1990-; Chairman, Northumberland and Tyne & Wear Strategic Health Authority, 2002-2006; Chairman, Northern Assembly Health Forum, 2003-07; Chairman, Northern Advisory Committee on Clinical Excellence Awards, 2003-07; Chairman, NHS North East SHA, 2006-; Chairman, Commission on Rural Health, 2008-. Publications: Industrial Relations in the National Newspapers; Worker Participation in Europe; It Occurred To Me, 2004; Various articles on Management Issues in several journals. Honours: CBE, 1989; Knighthood, 2007; Deputy Lieutenant; Honorary Degree, University of Northumbria; Member of Council, University of Newcastle, 2005-; Honorary Doctor of Science, Sunderland University, 2009. Membership: Royal Overseas League; Royal Society of Medicine. Address: 4 Corchester Towers; Corbridge, Northumberland, NE45 5NP, England. E-mail: petercarr@aol.com

CARREY Jim, b. 17 January 1962, Newmarket, Canada (US citizenship, 2004). Actor. m. (1) Melissa Womer, 1987, divorced 1995, 1 daughter, (2) Lauren Holly, 1995, divorced 1996. Appointments: Performed, Comedy Clubs, Toronto. Creative Works: Films include: Peggy Sue Got Married, 1986; The Dead Pool, 1988; Earth Girls Are Easy, 1989; Ace Ventura! Pet Detective; The Mask; Ace Ventura: When Nature Calls, 1995; Dumb and Dumber; Liar Liar, 1996; Batman Forever; The Cable Guy; The Truman Show, 1997; Man on the Moon; How the Grinch Stole Christmas, 2000; Me, Myself and Irene, 2000; The Majestic, 2001; Bruce Almighty, 2003; Pecan Pie, 2003; Eternal Sunshine of the Spotless Mind, 2004; Lemony Snicket's A Series of Unfortunate Events, 2004; Fun with Dick and Jane, 2005; The Number 23, 2007; Horton Hears a Who!, Yes Man, 2008; A Christmas Carol, I Love You Phillip Morris, 2009; Mr Popper's Penguins, 2011; Several TV appearances. Honours: 2 Golden Globe Awards; 9 MTV Awards; Star on Hollywood Walk of Fame, 2000; American Film Industry Star Award, 2005. Address: UTA, 9560 Wilshire Boulevard, 5th Floor, Beverly Hills, CA 90212, USA.

CARRINGTON 6th Baron (Peter Alexander Rupert Carrington), b. 6 June 1919. m. Iona, 1 son, 2 daughters. Education: Eton; RMC Sandhurst. Appointments: Major, Grenadier Guards, Northwest Europe; Justice of the Peace, Buckinghamshire, 1948, DL, 1951; Parliamentary Secretary, Ministry of Agriculture and Fisheries, 1951-54; MOD, 1954-56; High Commissioner, Australia, 1956-59; First Lord of Admiralty, 1959-63; Minister without portfolio and leader of House of Lords, 1963-64; Leader of Opposition, House of Lords, 1964-70, 1974-79; Secretary of State for Defence, 1970-74, Department of Energy, 1974; Minister of Aviation Supply, 1971-74; Secretary of State for Foreign and Commonwealth Affairs, and Minister of Overseas Development, 1979-82; Chairman, Conservative Party, 1972-74; Secretary General, NATO, 1984-88; Chariman, EC Peace Conference, Yugoslavia, 1991-92; Chairman, GEC, 1983-84 (director, 1982-84); Director, Christie's International plc, 1988-98 (chairman, 1988-93); Director, The Telegraph plc, 1990-2003; Non-Executive Director, Chime Communications, 1993-99; Non-Executive Director, Christie's Fine Art Ltd, 1998-. Publications: Reflect on Things Past: The Memoirs of Lord Carrington, 1988. Honours: Honorary Fellow, St Antony's College, Oxford, 1982; Honorary Bencher, Middle Temple, 1983; Honorary Elder, Brother Trinity House, 1984; Honorary LLD, universities of Leeds (1981), Cambridge (1981), Philippines (1982), South Carolina (1983), Aberdeen (1985), Harvard (1986), Sussex (1989), Reading (1989), Nottingham (1993), Birmingham (1993); Honorary DSc, Cranfield, 1993; Honorary DCL, Oxford, 2003; Honorary DUniv, Essex; Liveryman, Worshipful Company of Clothworkers. Memberships: Fellow, Eton, 1966-81; Member, International Board, United World Colleges, 1982-84; Chairman, Board of Trustees V&A Museum, 1983-88; Chancellor: Order of St Michael and St George (1984-94), University of Reading (1992-), Order of the Garter (1994-); President: Pilgrims (1983-2002), VSO (1993-98). Address: 32A Ovington Square, London SW3 1LR, England.

CARRINGTON Simon Robert, b. 23 October 1942, Salisbury, UK. Conductor; University Professor; Freelance Choral Consultant. m. Hilary Stott, 1 son, 1 daughter. Education: MA, Cantab; Choral Scholar, King's College, Cambridge; Teaching Certificate, New College, Oxford. Appointments: Founder and Co-Director, The King's Singers, 1968-2001; Director, Choral Activities, University of Kansas, Lawrence, 1994-2001; Director, Choral Activities, New England Conservatory, Boston, 2001-03; Professor of Choral Conducting, Conductor of the Yale Schola Cantorum, Yale School of Music, New Haven, 2005-; With the King's Singers: 3,000 concerts; 72 recordings, television and radio performances worldwide. Publications: Various choral arrangements. Honours: Grammy Nomination, 1986; Numerous awards and citations at choral festivals worldwide. Memberships: American Choral Directors Association; Association of British Choral Directors; Chorus America. Address: Yale School of Music, Yale Institute of Sacred Music, 409 Prospect Street, New Haven, CT 06511, USA. E-mail: simon.carrington@yale.edu Website: www.simoncarrington.com

CARRINGTON-SMITH Lynette, b. 9 October 1946, Bath, Somerset, England. Artist. m. Tim Arnold Smith, 2 sons, 1 daughter. Education: Wycliffe School for Girls; Art Foundation and Textile Diploma Course, West of England College of Art, Bristol. Appointments: Textile Designer, several textile and design studios; Freelance Textile Designer working on collections for international clients; Artist for greetings card market; Art Teacher for adults; Exhibited at, and member of, Society of Botanical Artists, London. Publications: Numerous articles in professional and popular journals. Honours: 3 Silver Medals and Silver Lindley Medal,

Royal Horticultural Society's Botanical Art Exhibitions. Address: Mas de Montbaix, Cami de les Planes Romandra, 43746 Tivissa, Tarragona, Spain.

CARSON Sol Kent, b. 6 July 1917, Philadelphia, Pennsylvania, USA. Professor of Fine Arts and Art Education. m. Thelma Clearfield, 1 son. Education: BFA, Temple University Tyler School of Fine Arts, 1944; BSc (Honours), 1945, Education, MEd (Distinction), 1946, Fine Arts, Temple University Teachers College; PhD, Fine Arts & Art Education, Minerva University Graduate School, Italy, 1960. Appointments: Assistantship, Temple University, 1940-45; Director, Department of Visual Education, Temple University, 1944-47; Museum Consultant, University of Pennsylvania, 1945-46; Director, Department of Art, Visual Education, Temple University, Prof Schools, 1946-55; Art Teacher, Philadelphia Board of Education, 1947-58; Art Consultant, Bristol Township School District, Pennsylvania, 1956-66; Summer Faculty Art Department, Wisconsin State University, 1966-67; Associate Professor, Art Department, Millersville University, Pennsylvania, 1966-68; Also museum restoration of paintings and frames; Seminars/lectures on drawing, painting and printmaking. Memberships: National Educational Association; Pennsylvania State Educational Association; Association for Higher Education; American Association of University Professors; Phi Delta Kappa; Artists' Equity; others. Address: 447 Alberto Way C128, Los Gatos, CA 95032, USA.

CARTER Jimmy (James Earl Jr), b. 1 October 1924, Plains, Georgia, USA. Politician; Farmer. m. Rosalynn Smith, 1946, 3 sons, 1 daughter. Education: Georgia Southwest College; Georgia Institute of Technology; US Naval Academy. Appointments: US Navy, 1946-53; Peanut Farmer, Warehouseman, 1953-77; Busman, Carter Farms, Carter Warehouses, Georgia; State Senator, Georgia, 1962-66; Governor of Georgia, 1971-74; President of USA, 1977-81; Distinguished Professor, Emory University, Atlanta, 1982-; Leader, International Observer Teams, Panama, 1989, Nicaragua, 1990, Dominican Republic, 1990, Haiti, 1990; Host, Peace Negotiations, Ethiopia, 1989; Visitor, Korea, 1994; Negotiator, Haitian Crisis, 1994; Visitor, Bosnia, 1994. Publications: Why Not The Best?, 1975; A Government as Good as its People, 1977; Keeping Faith: Memoirs of a President, 1982; The Blood of Abraham: Insights into the Middle East, 1985; Everything to Gain: Making the Most of the Rest of Your Life, 1987; An Outdoor Journal, 1988; Turning Point: A Candidate, a State and a Nation Come of Age, 1992; Always a Reckoning (poems), 1995; Sources of Strength, 1997; The Virtues of Ageing, 1998; An Hour Before Daylight, 2001; The Hornet's Nest, 2003; Sharing Good Times, 2004; Our Endangered Values: America's Moral Crisis, 2005; Faith and Freedom: The Christian Challenge for the World, 2005; Palestine Peace Not Apartheid, 2006. Honours include: Onassis Foundation Award, 1991; Notre Dame University Award, 1992; Matsunaga Medal of Peace, 1993; J William Fulbright Prize for International Understanding, 1994; Shared Houphouët Boigny Peace Prize, UNESCO, 1995; UNICEF International Child Survival Award (with Rosalynn Carter), 1999; Presidential Medal of Freedom, 1999; Eisenhower Medallion, 2000; Nobel Peace Prize, 2002. Address: The Carter Center, 453 Freedom Parkway, 1 Copenhill Avenue, North East Atlanta, GA 30307, USA.

CARVALHO Paulo de, b. 25 August 1960, Luanda, Angola. Sociologist. m. Anabela Cunha, 2 sons, 1 daughter. Education: MA, Sociology, University of Warsaw, Poland, 1990; PhD, Sociology, ISCTE, Lisbon, Portugal, 2004. Appointments: Director of Press Centre, Luanda, Angola, 1991-92; Manager of Consulteste Ltd, 1994-; Lecturer in Sociology and Statistics, 1996-99, Assistant Professor, 1999-2004, Associate Professor, 2004-11, Full Professor, 2011-, University Agostinho Neto, Luanda, Angola; Rector, University Katyavala Bwila, Benguela, Angola, 2009-11. Publications: Most important books: Social Structure in Colonial Angola, 1989; Students from Overseas in Poland, 1990; Media Audience in Luanda, Angola, How Much Time is Left until Tomorrow? 2002; You are Even Nothing..., 2007; Social Exclusion in Angola, 2008; The 2008 Electoral Campaign in the Press of Luanda, 2010; Numerous newspaper articles about social and economic subjects, Luanda and Lisbon. Honours: Kianda Award on Economic Journalism, Luanda, Angola, 1998; Angolan Cultural Award on Social Research, 2002. Memberships: International Sociological Association; World Association for Public Opinion Research; American Sociological Association; British Sociological Association; American Statistical Association; Angolan Sociological Association. Address: Caixa Postal 420, Luanda, Angola. E-mail: paulodecarvalho@sociologist.com

CARWARDINE Richard John, b. 12 January 1947, Cardiff, Wales. University Professor. m. Linda Margaret Kirk, 1975. Education: BA, Oxford University, 1968; MA, 1972; DPhil, 1975. Appointments: Lecturer, Senior Lecturer, Reader, Professor, University of Sheffield, 1971-2002; Rhodes Professor of American History and Fellow of St Catherine's College, Oxford University, 2002-09; Visiting Professor, Syracuse University, New York, 1974-75; Visiting Fellow, University of North Carolina, Chapel Hill, 1989; President, Corpus Christi College, Oxford, 2010-. Publications: Transatlantic Revivalism: Popular Evangelicalism in Britain and America 1790-1865, 1978; Evangelicals and Politics in Antebellum America, 1993; Lincoln, 2003; Lincoln: A Life of Purpose and Power, 2006. Honours: Order of Lincoln, State of Illinois; Lincoln Prize, 2004. Memberships: Fellow, Royal Historical Society; Fellow, British Academy; Founding Fellow, Learned Society of Wales. Address: c/o Corpus Christi College, Oxford OX1 4JF, England.

CARY Phillip Scott, b. 10 June 1958, USA. Professor. m. Nancy Hazle, 3 sons. Education: BA, English Literature and Philosophy, Washington University, St Louis, 1980; MA, Philosophy, 1989, PhD, Philosophy and Religious Studies, 1994, Yale University. Appointments: Teaching Assistant, Philosophy Department, Yale University, 1988-92; Adjunct Faculty, Philosophy Department, University of Connecticut, 1993; Adjunct Faculty, Hillier College, University of Hartford, 1993-94; Arthur J Ennis Postdoctoral Fellow, 1994-97, Rocco A and Gloria C Postdoctoral Fellow, 1997-98, Core Humanities Programme, Villanova University; Assistant Professor of Philosophy, 1998-2001, Associate Professor of Philosophy, 2001-06, Professor of Philosophy, 2006-, Scholar in Residence, Templeton Honors College, 1999-, Eastern University, St Davids. Publications: 6 books; 13 articles in professional journals; 5 taped lecture series. Honours: University Fellowship, Yale University; Mylonas Scholarship, Phi Beta Kappa, Washington University; Lindback Teaching Award, 2003; Listed in national and international biographical dictionaries. Memberships: APA; AAR; SCP; NAPS. Address: Eastern University, 1300 Eagle Road, St Davids, PA 19087-3696, USA. E-mail: pcary@eastern.edu

CASTILLO Enrique Francisco, b. 17 October 1946, Santiago de Compostela, Spain. Civil Engineer; Mathematician. m. María Carmen Sánchez, 2 sons, 3 daughters. Education: Civil Engineer, 1969, PhD, Civil

Engineer, 1973, University Polytechnic, Madrid; PhD, Civil Engineer, Northwestern University, 1972; MS, Mathematics, University Complutensis, Madrid, 1973. Appointments: Full Professor, Applied Mathematics, University of Cantabria, 1976-. Publications: 210 papers in 106 different journals; 165 papers at congresses; 14 books in English; 16 books in Spanish; More than 6,000 citations in Google-Scholar and 2,400 in ISI. Honours: Founding Member, Spanish Royal Academy of Engineering, 1994; Member, Spanish Academy of Sciences, 2011; Leonardo Torres Quevedo National Prize, 2010; Medal, University of Cantabria & University Castilla-la Mancha. Memberships: Real Sociedad Matematica Espanola; Sociedad Española de Mecanica del Suelo; Sociedad Espanola de Estadistica e Investigacion Operativa; AMS; and others. Address: Departamento de Matemática Aplicada y Ciencias de la Computación, University of Cantabria, 39005 Santander, Spain. Website: http://personales.unican.es/castie

CASTLEDEN Rodney, b. 23 March 1945, Worthing, Sussex, England. Archaeologist; Geographer; Writer; Composer. m. Sarah Dee, 29 July 1987. Education: BA, Geography, Hertford College, 1967, Dip Ed, 1968, MA, 1972, MSc, Geomorphology, 1980, Oxford University. Appointments: Assistant Geography Teacher, Wellingborough High School, 1968-74 and Wellingborough School, 1974-75; Acting Head of Geography, Overstone School, 1975-76; Assistant Geography Teacher, North London Collegiate School, 1976-79; Head of Geography Department, 1979-90, Head of Humanities Faculty, 1990-2001, Head of Social Science Faculty, 2001-04, Roedean School; Freelance Writer, 2004-. Publications include: Classic Landforms of the Sussex Coast, 1982; The Wilmington Giant: The Quest for a Lost Myth, 1983; The Stonehenge People: An Exploration of Life in Neolithic Britain, 1987; The Knossos Labyrinth, 1989; Minoans: Life in Bronze Age Crete, 1990; Book of British Dates, 1991; Neolithic Britain, 1992; The Making of Stonehenge, 1993; World History: a Chronological Dictionary of Dates, 1994; British History: A Chronological Dictionary of Dates, 1994; The Cerne Giant, 1996; Classic Landforms of the Sussex Coast, 2nd edition, 1996; Knossos, Temple of the Goddess, 1997; Atlantis Destroyed, Out in the Cold, The English Lake District, 1998; King Arthur: the Truth Behind the Legend, The Little Book of Kings and Queens, 1999; Ancient British Hill Figures, 2000; The History of World Events, Britain 3000 BC, 2003; The World's Most Evil People, 2004; Infamous Murderers, Serial Killers, Mycenaeans, People Who Changed the World, Events That Changed the World, 2005; English Castles, Castles of the Celtic Lands, The Attack on Troy, The Book of Saints, Assassinations and Conspiracies, 2006; Natural Disasters that Changed the World, Inventions that Changed the World, Great Unsolved Crimes, 2007; Discoveries that Changed the World, 2008; Witness to History, 2008; Encounters that Changed the World, 2009. Listed in national and international biographical dictionaries. Music: Fanfare for Prince Charles, 1994; Cuckmere Suite, a suite for string orchestra, 1999; Winfrith, a chamber opera, 2000; String Sextet, 2007. Memberships: Society of Authors; Sussex Archaeological Society. Address: Rookery Cottage, Blatchington Hill, Seaford, East Sussex BN25 2AJ, England.

CASTRO Francisco Ferreira de, b. 28 June 1923, Floriano-Piaui, Brazil. Lawyer; Educator. m. Iracema da Costas Silva Castro, 1 son, 2 daughters. Education: BS, Economics, 1941; LLB, Minas Gerais Federal University, Belo-Horizonte, Brazil, 1948; LLD, Brasilia University, 1967. Appointments: State Representative of the Legislative Assembly, 1950-54; Vice Governor and Substitute Governor, State Government of Piaui, 1954-58; State Lawyer, Teresina, 1960-62; Federal Deputy, National Congress, Brasilia, 1958-62; Advisor of Juridical Affairs of Presidency, Federal Government, Brasilia, 1962-64; Professor, Constitutional Law, 1962-70, Professor of Political Science, 1989-93, University of Brasilia; Attorney NOVACAP Co, Brasilia, 1961-64; 1st Class Attorney, Federal District Government, Brasilia, 1964-86; Lawyer, Supreme Tribunal and Superior Federal Appeals Tribunal, Brasilia, 1964-. Publications: Author: The State's Aim – Main Doctrines, 1956; Modernization and Democracy, 1967; Articles in professional journals. Honours: Juridical Medal of the Centenary Clovis Bevilaqua, Brazilian Government, 1959; Medal, District Federal Government, 1984; Grand Cross Medal, Piaui State Renascenca Merit Order, 1997; The Global 100, ABI, 2011. Memberships: Past President, Brazil Lawyers Order; Congress Club; Honorary Member, Brazilian Tennis Academy; Planetary Society. Address: SMl MI 09, Conj 05 Casa 16, 7150095 Brasilia Distrito Federal, Brazil. E-mail: ffcastro@nuctecnet.com.br

CATALÁ RODRÍGUEZ Myriam, b. 4 March 1970, Madrid, Spain. Associate Professor. m. Jon San Sebastian Sauto. Education: MSc, Chemistry, 1993, PhD, Biochemistry and Molecular Biology, 2002, Complutense University; Vaccines Diploma, Autonomous University of Madrid, 2001. Appointments: Assistant, International Rel Vicerector, 1998-2001; Research Fellow, Faculty of Health Science, 2001, Assistant Professor, Histology, 2001-03, Associate Professor, Cell Biology, 2003-, Rey Juan Carlos University. Publications: 18 articles in international indexed journals; 3 international book chapters; 2 patents. Honours: Honorary Collaborator, Biochemistry & Molecular Biology Department, Complutense University, 1994-96. Memberships: SETAC. Address: Room 212, Departmental I Building, ESCET – Campus of Mostoles, c/ Tulipan s/n, 28933 Móstoles, Madrid, Spain.

CATALANO Elena Maria, b. 22 January 1970, Lecco, Italy. Law Educator. Education: Degree in Law, Summa Cum Laude, 1993, PhD, Comparative Law, 1997, University of Milan. Appointments: Assistant Professor, Criminal Procedure, University of Milan, 1993-99; Acting Professor, Criminal Procedure, Researcher, University Milano Bicocca, 1999-2002; Associate Professor, Law Faculty, Criminal Procedure, University Insubria Como Varese, 2002-; Professor, Law School, University of Parma, 2006-07; Lawyer, admitted practice, supreme court, Milan Bar, 2007; Board Member, University of Milan, 1999-2004; Scientific Board member, Archivio Penale Review. Publications: Contributor of articles to professional publications. Honours: Criminal Procedure Award, Examination Board, LUM University, Casamassima BARI. Memberships: Association Tra Gli Studiosi Del Processo Penale. Address: via Bossi 5, Como 22100, Italy. E-mail: elena.catalano@unisubria.it

CATIC Igor, b. 14 March 1936, Zagreb, Croatia. Professor (retired). m. Ranka, 1963. Education: Dipl ing, Mechanical Engineering Faculty, 1960; MSc, Faculty of Mechanical Engineering, 1972; Dr Ingm, University of Technology, Aachen, Germany, 1972. Appointments: Mould Designer, Stanca, 1954-60; Production Manager, ME-GA, 1960-63; Research and Development, 1963-65, TOZ; Assistant Professor, 1974, Associate Professor, 1980, Professor, 1986-, Faculty of Mechical Engineering and Naval Architecture. Publications: Several hundred articles in professional journals; 23 books. Honours: Science Award, Nikola Tesla, 1977; Golden Wreath, President of Yugoslavia, 1983; Award, Contribution to Society of Plastics and Rubber Engineering, 1983; Science Award, Society of Plastics and Rubber Engineering, 1987; International Education Award, Society of Plastic Engineering, USA, 1998; Technical Scientists Award for popularisation of technical sciences, Parliament of Croatia, 2000; Award, Contribution to science, education and society, Town of Zagreb, 2002; Life Work Award, Faust Vrancic, Technical Culture, 2004; The Order of the Croatian Star with Effigy of Rudjer Boskovic, 2007. Memberships: Fellow, Institute of Materials, Metallurgy and Mining; Society of Plastics and Rubber Engineers; VDI-K. Address: Fancevljev Prilaz 9, HR-10010 Zagreb, Croatia.

CATON-JONES Michael, b. 15 October 1957, Broxburn, Scotland. Film Director. m. (1) Beverley Caton, 2 daughters, (2) Laura Viederman, 1 son, 1 daughter. Education: National Film School. Appointments: Stagehand, London West End Theatres. Creative Works: Films: Liebe Mutter; The Making of Absolute Beginners; Scandal, 1989; Memphis Belle, 1990; Doc Hollywood, 1991; This Boy's Life, 1993; Rob Roy, 1994; The Jackal, 1997; City By The Sea, 2002; Shooting Dogs, 2005; Basic Instinct 2, 2006. Honours: 1st Prize, European Film School Competition.

CAVENDISH Mark, b. 21 May 1985, Douglas, Isle of Man. Racing Cyclist. Career: Joined British Track Cycling Team; Won Gold, Madison, Los Angeles World Track Championships; Winner, European Championship Points Race, 2005; Tour of Berlin, 2005; Tour of Britain, 2005; Team Sparkasse, 2006; Gold Medal, Sprint, Commonwealth Games, Australia, 2006; Stagiare, T-Mobile, 2006; Stages winner, Four Days of Dunkirk, and Volta a Catalunya, 2007; Selected, Tour de France, 2007; Winner, Madison World Championships, Manchester, 2008; 2 victories, Giro d'Italia, 2008; Stages winner, Tour de France, 2008; 3 wins, Tour of Ireland, 2008; Tour of Missouri, 2008; Tour De Romandie, 2008; Winner, Tour of Qatar, 2009; Stages winner, Tour of California, 2009; Competitor, UCI Track Cycling World Championships, 2009; Winner, Milan-San Remo classic race, 2009; Maglia Rosa leaders jersey, Giro d'Italia, 2009; Stage winner, Tour de France, 2009; Winner, Sparksassen Giro Bochum, 2009; Stage winner, Tour of Ireland, 2009; Winner, Tour of Missouri, 2009; Stage winner, Tour of California, 2010; Stage winner, Tour de France, 2010. Publications: Autobiography, Boy Racer, 2009. Honours: First British rider to wear Maglia Rosa leaders jersey, 2009; First Briton to hold green jersey for two days in a row, Tour de France, 2009.

CAWS Ian, b. 19 March 1945, Bramshott, Hants, England. Poet. m. Hilary Walsh, 20 June 1970, 3 sons, 2 daughters. Education: Churcher's College, Petersfield; North-Western Polytechnic. Publications: Looking for Bonfires, 1975; Bruised Madonna, 1979; Boy with a Kite, 1981; The Ragman Totts, 1990; Chamomile, 1994; The Feast of Fools, 1994; The Playing of the Easter Music (with Martin C Caseley and B L Pearce), 1996; Herrick's Women, 1996; Dialogues in Mask, 2000; Taro Fair, 2003; The Blind Fiddler, 2004; The Canterbury Road, 2007. Contributions to: Acumen Magazine; London Magazine; New Welsh Review; Observer; Poetry Review; Scotsman; Spectator; Stand Magazine; Swansea Review. Honours: Eric Gregory Award, 1973; Poetry Book Society Recommendation, 1990. Membership: Poetry Society. Address: 9 Tennyson Avenue, Rustington, West Sussex BN16 2PB, England.

CAZEAUX Isabelle Anne-Marie, b. 24 February 1926, New York, USA. Professor Emeritus of Musicology. Education: BA, magna cum laude, Hunter College, 1945; MA, Smith College, 1946; Ecole normale de musique, Paris, Licence d'enseignement, 1950; Première médaille, Conservatoire National de Musique, Paris, 1950; MS in Library Science, Columbia University, 1959, PhD, Musicology, 1961, Columbia University. Appointments: Music and phonorecords catalteguer, New York Public Library, 1957-63; Faculty of Musicology, Bryn Mawr College, 1963-92; Faculty of Musicology, Manhattan School of Music, 1969-82; A C Dickerman Professor and Chairman, Music Department, Bryn Mawr College; Visiting Professor, Douglass College, Rutgers University, 1978. Publications: Translations: The Memoirs of Philippe de Commynes, 2 vols, 1969-73; Editor: Claudin de Sermisy, Chansons, 2 vols, 1974; Author: French Music in the Fifteenth and Sixteenth Centuries, 1975; Articles. Honours: Libby van Arsdale Prize for Music, Hunter College, 1945; Fellowships and scholarships from Smith College, Columbia University, Institute of International Education, 1941-59; Grants from Martha Baird Rockefeller Fund for Music, 1971-72, Herman Goldman Foundation, 1980; Listed in New Grove Dictionary of Music and Musicians, 1980; Festschrift, Liber amicorum Isabelle Cazeaux, 2005. Memberships: American Musicological Society; International Musicological Society; Société française de musicologie; National Opera Association. Address: 415 East 72nd Street, Apt 5FE, New York, NY 10021, USA.

CECCANTI Stefano, b. 27 January 1961, Pisa, Italy. State Senator; Comparative Public Law Professor. m. Anna Chiara Giorio, 1 son, 1 daughter. Education: Degree, Political Science, University of Pisa, 1985; Certificate, Comparative Public Law, University of Pisa. Appointments: University Teacher, Department of Political Science, University of Rome La Sapienza, 2006; Legislative Head Officer, Ministry of Equal Opportunities, Rome, 2006-08; Senator, Democratic Party, Senate of the Republic, Rome, 2008-. Publications: Numerous articles in professional journals. Honours: il Mulino, Bologna, 1997, 2001, 2006; Giappicchelli, Torino, 2004; Senate of the Republic, 2005-; Editor, Borla, Al Cattolico Perplesso, Rome, 2010. Memberships: Democratic Party. Address: Senate of the Republic, Piazza Madama, Rome 00186, Italy. E-mail: stefano.ceccanti@libero.it Website: www.ceccanti.ilcannocchiale.it

CEDIDI Can C, b. 15 November 1963, Istanbul, Turkey. Plastic Surgeon; Director. m. Yelda Yigittuerk, 2 children. Appointments: Attending, University Witten, Herdecke, 1982-; Certified Professor, Plastic Surgery, University of Heidelberg, Germany, 1990; Clinical Researcher, University Hospital, Bremen, Germany, 1999-, 2006-09; Clinical Director, Klinik Bremen-Mitte, 2006-. Memberships: German Society of Plastic Surgeons. Address: Klinikum Bremen-Mitte, Klinik Plastische Rekonstruktive University, St Juergenstr 1, Bremen 28177, Germany. E-mail: can.cedidi@klinikum-bremen-mitte.de

CERCE Danica, b. 19 February 1953, Crna na Koroskem, Slovenia. Assistant Professor Literature in English. 1 son, 1 daughter. Education: BA, English and Italian Literatures, 1977; MA, Australian Literature, 1995, PhD, Literary Sciences, 2002, Faculty of Arts, University of Ljubljana, Slovenia; London Chamber of Commerce and Industry Certificate in Teaching English for Business, London Guildhall University, 1996. Appointments: Teacher, High School in Velenje, Slovenia, -1995; Assistant Professor of American Literature and English Teacher, Faculty of Economics, University of Ljubljana, 1995-. Publications: Several articles on American and Australian literature in various Slovene and American academic journals, conference proceedings and literary magazines; Contributor of several papers on American and Australian literature at several international conferences in Europe, the United States, Japan and Australia; Book: Pripovednistvo Johna Steinbecka:

druzbenokriticna misel v tradiciji mitov in legend, 2005; Translator, John Steinbeck's Of Mice and Men,and To a God Unknown. Memberships: New Steinbeck Society of America; Steinbeck Society; American Literature Association; Southern Comparative Literature Association; European Association of Australian Studies; International Association of Teachers of English as a Foreign Language. Address: Partizanska 3, 2380 Slovenj Gradec, Slovenia. E-mail: danica.cerce@ef.uni-lj.si

CERIONI Luca, b. 24 June 1969, Jesi (AN), Italy. Lecturer. Education: Degree, Economics and Commerce, University of Ancona, Italy, 1994; LLM, European Community Law, 1996, PhD, Law, 2004, University of Essex, England. Appointments: Academic Research Fellow, Corporate Governance, University of Leeds, England, 2006-07; Law Lecturer, Brunel Law School, Brunel University, 2007-08, 2010-11; Visiting Lecturer, International Tax Law, University of Essex, 2009-10, 2010-11; Lecturer, EU and International Tax Law, Universita Politecnica delle Marche, Italy, 2011-. Publications: Numerous articles in professional journals. Honours: Research grant, 2010. Address: Viale Italia, 8 – 60018 Montemarciano (AN), Italy. E-mail: ricer.r@libero.it

CERWENKA Herwig R, b. 18 June 1964, Leoben, Austria. Surgeon; Researcher. m. Wilma Zinke-Cerwenka, 1 son, 2 daughters. Education: Matura Examination, 1982; Doctor of Medicine, 1988; ECFMG/FMGEMS, 1989; Ius practicandi, 1993; Diploma in Emergency Medicine; Diploma in Surgery. Appointment: Professor of Surgery, Researcher, Department of Visceral Surgery, Medical University, Graz, Austria. Publications: Numerous publications in scientific journals and contributions to books. Honours: Performance Grant, Karl-Franzens University; Numerous other grants and awards for congress contributions and publications. Memberships: International Society of Surgery; International Association of Surgeons and Gastroenterologists; Austrian Society of Surgery; Austrian Society of Surgical Research. Address: Department of Visceral Surgery, Medical University, Auenbruggerplatz 29, A-8036 Graz, Austria. E-mail: herwig.cerwenka@medunigraz.at

CHA Hyouk-Kyu, b. 30 November 1979, Seoul, Korea. Electrical Engineer. Education: BS, 2003, PhD, 2009, Korea Advanced Institute of Science and Technology. Appointments: Senior Research Engineer, Institute of Microelectronics, Singapore, 2009-. Publications: Numerous articles in professional journals. Honours: Listed in international biographical dictionaries. Memberships: IEEE; IEICE. Address: 11 Science Park Road, Singapore Science Park II, Singapore 117685. E-mail: hkcha98@gmail.com

CHA Ji Hoon, b. 6 February 1972, Seoul, Republic of Korea. Electronics Engineer. m. Youn Ju Han, 2 daughters. Education: BS, Sung Kyun Kwan University, Seoul, 1997; MS, Pohang University of Science and Technology, Gyungbuk, 1999. Appointments: Senior Engineer, Daeduk R&D Centre, Honam Petrochemical Co, Daejeon, Chungnam, 1999-2004; Senior Research Engineer, Semiconductor Business, Samsung Electronics Co Ltd, Hwasung-City, Gyenggi-Do, 2004-; Research Assistant, Research institute for Industrial Science and Technology, Pohang, 1997-99. Publications: Numerous articles in professional journals. Honours: Listed in international biographical dictionaries. Address: Samsung Electronics Co Ltd, San #16 Banwol-Dong, Hwasung-City, Gyenggi-Do, 445-701, Republic of Korea. E-mail: jh.cha@samsung.com

CHADWICK Peter, b. 23 March 1931, Huddersfield, England. Retired. m. Sheila Salter, deceased 2004, 2 daughters. Education: Huddersfield College; BSc, University of Manchester, 1952; PhD, 1957, ScD, 1973, Pembroke College, Cambridge. Appointments: Scientific Officer, then Senior Scientific Officer, AWRE, Aldermaston, 1955-59; Lecturer, then Senior Lecturer in Applied Mathematics, University of Sheffield, 1959-65; Professor of Mathematics, 1965-91, Emeritus Professor of Mathematics, 1991-, Leverhulme Emeritus Fellow, 1991-93, University of East Anglia. Publications: Numerous papers and articles in learned journals and books; Continuum Mechanics, Concise Theory and Problems, 1976, 1999. Honours: FRS, 1977; Honorary DSc, University of Glasgow, 1991. Memberships: Fellow, Cambridge Philosophical Society; Honorary Member, British Society of Rheology. Address: 8 Stratford Crescent, Cringleford, Norwich NR4 7SF, England.

CHADWICK Peter Kenneth, b. 10 July 1946, Manchester, England. Writer; Psychologist. m. Rosemary Jill McMahon, 1983. Education: BSc, Geology, University College of Wales, Aberystwyth, 1967; BSc, Psychology, University of Bristol, 1975; MSc, DIC, Structural Geology and Rock Mechanics, Imperial College, London University, 1968; PhD, Structural Geology, University of Liverpool, 1971; PhD, Cognitive and Abnormal Psychology, Royal Holloway and Bedford New College, University of London, 1989; DSc, Psychology, University of Bristol, 2007 (careers in geology, psychology and literature). Appointments: Royal Society European Programme Research Fellow, Geology and Psychology, University of Uppsala, Sweden, 1972-73; Senior Demonstrator in Psychology, University of Liverpool, 1975-76; Lecturer in Psychology, University of Strathclyde, 1976-78; Lecturer in Motivation Psychology, Goldsmiths College, University of London, 1984-85; Professor of Community Psychology, Boston University, 1991-94; Lecturer in Psychology, Birkbeck College, Faculty of Continuing Education, 1982-2009; Associate Lecturer in Psychology, Open University, London Region, 1982-98; Lecturer in Psychology, City Literary Institute, London, 1982-98; Associate Lecturer in Psychology, Open University, East of England Region, 1994-2006. Publications: The psychology of Geological Observations, 1975; Visual Illusions in Geology, 1976; Peak Preference and Waveform Perception, 1983; Borderline, 1992; Understanding Paranoia, 1995; Schizophrenia – The Positive Perspective, 1997, 2nd edition, 2008; Personality as Art, 2001; Paranormal, Spiritual and Metaphysical Aspects of Psychosis, 2004; Beyond the Machine Metaphor, 2004; The psychology of Writing, 2005; The Playwright as psychologist, 2006; Freud meets Wilde: A playlet, 2007. Honours: Royal Society European Programme Research Fellowship, 1972-73; Bristol University Postgraduate Scholarship, 1975; British Medical Association Exhibition, 1985; Postdoctoral Award, British Gas Social Affairs Unit, 1991; Royal Literary Fund Award, 1995. Memberships: Fellow, Geological Society of London, 1972-77; Honorary Member, Mizar Society for Social Responsibility in Science, University of Mississippi, 1975-; Associate Fellow, British Psychological Society, 1989-2005; Member, Psychology and Psychotherapy Association, 1995-2005; Oscar Wilde Society, 2005-; Society for Psychical Research, 2005-; Society of Authors, 2005-; Royal Society of Literature, 2005-. Address: c/o Watson-Little Ltd, Author's Agents, 48-56 Bayham Place, London NW1 0EU, England.

CHAGOYA-CORTES Hector Elias, b. 8 October 1974, Mexico City, Mexico. Chemical Engineer. Education: Chemical Engineering, 1997, Diploma in College Teaching Skills, 2005, Universidad La Salle; Diploma in Management

Skills, ITESM, 2000. Appointments: Manager of Technology Analysis and Transfer, Becerril, Coca & Becerril, S C, 1997-; Consultant in IP matters for Mexican and foreign companies in the fields of polymers, biotechnology, pharmaceuticals, chemical industry and electronics/communications, including trade secrets protection, patent strategies, patent litigation and licensing; Professor, Chemical Engineering program, La Salle University, 1999-; Teacher of diploma programs of Intellectual Property and Technology Transfer in several institutions, including the National Autonomous University of Mexico; Partner, IP Value Extraction Director, Becemil, Coca & Becemil, SC, 2010. Publications: Variety of articles in specialised international magazines of Intellectual Property and Technology Licensing; Co-author of the chapter for Mexico in the publication Licensing Best Practices: Strategic, Territorial, and Technology Issues, 2006; Annual revision of the Chapter for Mexico for the manual, Trade Secrets Throughout the World, 2005-; Co-author, Technology Transfer Offices, ADIAT, 2010. Honours: Scholarship to Excellence, ULSA-P&G, 1995; Hermano Miguel Medal for best academic record; Expert in Engineering Economy (Industrial Property and Technology Transfer), National College of Chemical Engineers and Chemists; Listed in international biographical dictionaries. Memberships: Mexican Institute of Chemical Engineers; Licensing Executives Society; International Association for the Protection of Intellectual Property; Mexican Association of Directors for Applied Research and Technology Development. E-mail: hchagoya@bcb.com.mx

CHAKRABORTY Bhaskar, b. 14 March 1968, Siliguri, Darjeeling, India. Professor. m. Malini, 2 sons. Education: BSc (Hons), 1989; MSc, 1991, Chemistry; PhD, Synthetic Organic Chemistry, 1996. Appointments: Assistant Professor, Chemistry, 1994-2000, Head, Department of Chemistry, 1999-, Senior Assistant Professor, 2000-05, Associate Professor, Chemistry, 2005-11, Professor, Chemistry, 2011-, Sikkim Government College. Publications: 37 international and national research publications. Honours: Best Research Teacher, Chemical Research Society of India, 2011. Memberships: Indian Chemical Society; Indian Science Congress Association. Address: Department of Chemistry, Sikkim Government College, PO Tadong, Gangtok, Sikkim, PIN 737102, India. E-mail: bhaskargtk@yahoo.com

CHALFONT Baron, (Alun Arthur Gwynne Jones), b. 5 December 1919, Llantarnam, Wales. Member, House of Lords; Writer. m. Mona Mitchell, 1948, 1 daughter, deceased. Education: West Monmouth, Wales. Appointments: Regular Officer, British Army, 1940-61; Broadcaster and Consultant on Foreign Affairs, BBC, 1961-64; Minister of State, Foreign and Commonwealth Office, 1964-70; Minister for Disarmament, 1964-67, 1969-70; Minister in charge of day-to-day negotiations for Britain's entry into Common Market, 1967-69; Permanent Representative, Western European Union, 1969-70; Foreign Editor, New Statesman, 1970-71; Chairman, Industrial Cleaning Papers, 1979-86, All Party Defence Group of the House of Lords, 1980-96, Peter Hamilton Security Consultants Ltd, 1984-86, VSEL Consortium, later VSEL plc, 1987-95, Radio Authority, 1991-94, Marlborough Stirling Group, 1994-; Director, W S Atkins International, 1979-83, IBM UK Ltd, 1973-90, Lazard Brothers & Company Ltd, 1983-90, Shandwick plc, 1985-95, Triangle Holdings, 1986-90, TV Corporation plc, 1996-201; President, Abington Corporation Ltd, 1981-, Nottingham Building Society, 1983-90; All Party Defence Group House of Lords, 1996-. Publications: The Sword and the Spirit, 1963; The Great Commanders (editor), 1973; Montgomery of Alamein, 1976; Waterloo: Battle of Three Armies (editor), 1979; Star Wars: Suicide or Survival, 1985; Defence of the Realm, 1987; By God's Will: A Portrait of the Sultan of Brunei, 1989; The Shadow of My Hand, 2000; Contributions to: Periodicals and journals. Honours: Officer of the Order of the British Empire, 1961; Created a Life Peer, 1964; Honorary Fellow, University College of Wales, 1974; Liveryman, Worshipful Company of Paviors; Freeman of the City of London. Memberships: International Institute for Strategic Studies; Royal Institute of International Affairs; Royal Society of the Arts, fellow; United Nations Association, chairman, 1972-73. Address: House of Lords, London SW1A 0PW, England.

CHALKLIN Christopher William, b. 3 April 1933, London, England. University Teacher (Retired). m. Mavis, 1 son, 2 daughters. Education: BA, University of New Zealand, 1953; BA, 1955, MA, University of Oxford; B Litt, University of Oxford, 1960; Litt D, University of Canterbury, 1986. Appointments: Assistant Archivist, Kent County Council, 1958-62; Senior Fellow, University of Wales, 1963-65; Lecturer in History, 1965-75, Reader in History, 1975-93, University of Reading. Publications: Seventeenth century Kent: A Social and Economic History, 1965; The Provincial Towns of Georgian England: A Study of the Building Process, 1974; English Counties and Public Building 1650-1830, 1998. Address: Grantley Lodge, Chinthurst Lane, Shalford, Surrey GU4 8JS, England.

CHALLAMEL Noël, b. 8 December 1971, Paris, France. Professor. Education: Civil Engineer, Master in Mechanics and Civil Engineering, CUT (Clermont-Ferrand), France, 1995; PhD, Paris School of Mines, 1999. Appointments: Research Engineer, Gaz de France, 2000; Associate Professor, INSA of Rennes, 2001; Habilitation to conduct Researches, Philosophical Degree, 2007; Professor, University of South Brittany, 2011. Publications: More than 70 articles in international journals. Honours: Chairman, Stability Committee, ASCE; Member of Scientific Committee, MIM, Hermes Levoisier, ISTE-Wiley; Associate Editor, Journal of Engineering Mechanics (ASCE). Memberships: ASCE; IPACS; AUM; AUGC. Address: University of South Brittany UBS, rue de Saint Maudé, BP 92116, 56321 Lorient cedex, France.

CHAMBERLAIN Douglas Anthony, b. 4 April 1931, Cardiff, Wales. Professor. m. Jennifer Ann, 2 sons, 2 daughters. Education: Ratcliffe College, Leicester, 1944-50; Queens' College, Cambridge, 1950-53; MB BChir (Cantab), 1956; MRCP (London), 1959; MD (Cantab), 1967. Appointments: House appointments, 1956-57, Research Fellow, Department of Cardiology, 1962-63, Registrar in General Medicine, 1964-65, Senior Registrar in General Medicine, 1966-67, 1969-70, St Bartholomew's Hospital; Senior House Officer, Medicine, Royal United Hospital, Bath, 1957-58; Resident Medical Officer, National Heart Hospital, Country Branch, 1958; National Service, Junior Medical Specialist in Charge of Medical Division, British Military Hospital, Hostert, BAOR, 1959-60; Medical Registrar, Brompton Hospital, 1961; Research Assistant, Harvard Medical School, Cardiac Catheterisation Unit, Massachusetts General Hospital, Boston, USA, 1968; Consultant Cardiologist, Royal Sussex County Hospital, Brighton, 1969-2000; Honorary Medical Adviser, South East Coast Ambulance Service; Honorary Medical Adviser, London Ambulance Service, 2009-; Honorary Professor, Cardiology, Brighton & Sussex Medical School, 2009-14. Publications: Over 280 articles in national and international journals. Honours: CBE, 1988; Knight on St Gregory (Papal Award), 1987; Asmund S Laerdal Award, 1987; Officer of the Order of St John, 1989; Paul Harris Fellowship,

DICTIONARY OF INTERNATIONAL BIOGRAPHY 36th EDITION

1989; DSc (Honoris Causa), University of Sussex, 1989, University of Hertford, 2003, University of Coventry, 2008; Honorary member, Association of Anaesthetists, 1992; Life Member, Resusitation Council, UK, 1995; Honorary Member, Ambulance Service Association, 1997; Year 2000 ECC Honoree, American Heart Association; Honorary Life Member, European Resuscitation Council, 2000; Mackenzie Medal, British Cardiac Society, 2002; Lifetime Achievement Award in Cardiac Resuscitation Science, American Heart Association, 2008. Memberships: FRCP (London), 1974; FRCA, 1994; FESC, 1988; FACC, 1992; FERC, 2010. Address: 25 Woodland Drive, Hove, East Sussex, BN3 6DH, England.

CHAMBERS Aidan, b. 27 December 1934, Chester-le-Street, County Durham, England. Author; Publisher. m. Nancy Harris Lockwood, 30 March 1968. Education: Borough Road College, Isleworth, London University. Publications: The Reluctant Reader, 1969; Introducing Books to Children, 1973; Breaktime, 1978; Seal Secret, 1980; The Dream Cage, 1981; Dance on My Grave, 1982; The Present Takers, 1983; Booktalk, 1985; Now I Know, 1987; The Reading Environment, 1991; The Toll Bridge, 1992; Tell Me: Children, Reading and Talk, 1993; Only Once, 1998; Postcards From No Man's Land, 1999; Reading Talk, 2001; This Is All: The Pillow Book of Cordelia Kenn, 2005; The Kissing Game: Short Stories, 2011; Tell Me with the Reading Environment, 2011; Contributions to: Numerous magazines and journals. Honours: Children's Literature Award for Outstanding Criticism, 1978; Eleanor Farjeon Award, 1982; Silver Pencil Awards, 1985, 1986, 1994; Carnegie Medal, 1999; Stockport School Book Award KS4, 2000; Hans Christian Andersen Award, 2002; Michael L Printz Award, 2002; J Hunt Award, 2002; Honorary Doctorate, University of Umeå, Sweden, 2003; Honorary President, School Library Association, 2003-06; Honorary Doctorate of Letters, University of Gloucestershire, 2008; Elected Fellow, Royal Society of Literature, 2009; Lifetime Achievement Award for Services to English Education, National Association for the Teaching of English. Membership: Society of Authors. Address: Lockwood, Station Road, Woodchester, Stroud, Gloucestershire, GL5 5EQ, England.

CHAMBERS Guy, b. 12 January 1963. Producer; Writer; Musician (Keyboards). Career: Jimmy Nail, Robbie Williams, World Party, The Waterboys, Julian Cope, Lemon Trees. Recordings: with Robbie Williams, Cathy Dennis, World Party, Holly Johnson: Blast; Julian Cope: Fried; Lemon Trees. Honours: Musicians' Union; PRS; 3 Ivor Novello Awards, 3 Brit Awards; Q Classic Songwriter Award; MMF Best Produced Record Award. Current Management: One Management, 43 St Alban's Avenue, London W4 5JS, England.

CHAMPION Margrét Gunnarsdóttir, b. 30 January 1953, Reykjavik, Iceland. Senior Lecturer. Divorced. Education: English, Trinity College, Dublin, 1975-77; BA (magna cum laude), 1980, MA, 1985, PhD, 1991, English, University of Georgia. Appointments: Teaching Assistant, Department of English, University of Georgia, 1985-90; Lecturer, Department of Comparative Literature, University of Iceland, 1992-94; Research Fellow, 1995-98, Lecturer, 1999, Visiting Teacher, 2006-08, Part time Teacher, 2003-05, Department of English, University of Uppsala; Lecturer, Department of English, University of Stockholm, 1999; Senior Lecturer, Department of English, University of Gothenburg, 2000-. Publications: Numerous articles in professional journals. Honours: Exchange Scholarship, Trinity College, Dublin, 1975-76; Phi Beta Kappa (academic honours society), University of Georgia, 1980; Research Grant, University of Iceland, 1993; Research Grant, Icelandic Council of Sciences, 1993; Research Fellowship, University of Uppsala, 1995-98; Research Grant, Swedish Council of Sciences, 2000; Research Grant, Humanities Faculty, University of Gothenburg, 2002. Address: Geijersgatan 50A, 75231, Uppsala, Sweden. E-mail: margret.gunnarsdottir.champi@eng.gu.se

CHAN Alan Hoi Shou, b. 9 January 1960, Dongguan, Guandong, China. Ergonomics Educator. m. Cindy Ip, 2 sons. Education: BSc, Industrial Engineering, 1982, MPhil, 1985, PhD, Ergonomics, 1995, University of Hong Kong. Appointments: Certified Engineer, Research Staff, Hong Kong University, 1982-85; Manager, Technical Services, YHY Food Products Ltd, 1988-89; Associate Professor, Ergonomics, City University of Hong Kong, 1989-; Council Member, Pan Pacific Council of Occupational Ergonomics, Japan, 1997-; Editor, Industrial and Occupational Ergonomics: Users Encyclopaedia, 1997; Member, Editorial Board, Asian Journal of Ergonomics, 1997-, and International Journal of Industrial Ergonomics, 1998-; Associate Editor, Industrial Engineering Research, 1997-; Regional Vice-President, Institute of Industrial Engineering, 2001-02. Publications: More than 120 papers in refereed journals and conference proceedings. Honour: Fellow, Ergonomics Society, UK; Fellow, Hong Kong Ergonomics Society; Listed in Who's Who publications. Memberships: Institute of Electrical Engineering; Institute of Industrial Engineers; Ergonomics Society; Hong Kong Ergonomics Society; International Ergonomics Association. Address: MEEM Department, City University of Hong Kong, Tat Chee Avenue, Kowloon Tong, Hong Kong, China. E-mail: alan.chan@cityu.edu.hk

CHAN Jackie, b. 7 April 1954, Hong Kong. Actor; Producer; Director. m. Feng-Jiao Lin, 1 December 1982, 1 son; 1 daughter with Elaine Ng. Education: China Drama Academy. Career: Actor; Producer; Director; Films include: The Big Brawl, 1980; Cannonball Run, 1981, 1984; Project A, 1983 and 1987; Wheels on Wheels, 1984; The Protector, 1985; Armor of God, 1986, 1991; Police Story, 1987, 1989; Dragons Forever, 1988; Miracles, 1990; Twin Dragons, 1992; Policy Story 3 – Supercop, 1992; Crime Story, 1993; Rush Hour, 1998; Rush Hour 2, 2001; Shanghai Knights, 2003; Around the World in 80 Days, 2004; Enter the Phoenix, 2004; New Police Story, 2004; Rice Rhapsody, 2005; Rush Hour 3, 2007; Kung Fu Panda (voice), 2008; Little Big Soldier, 2009; Ambassador, Hong Kong Tourism Board, 2003-; Ambassador, Beijing Olympics, 2003-; UN Goodwill Ambassador, 2004-. Honours: Best Picture Award, Hong Kong Film, 1989; Best Actor, Golden Horse Awards, Taiwan, 1992, 1993; MTV Lifetime Achievement Award, 1995; Best Action Choreography, Hong Kong Film, 1996, 1999; Maverick Tribute Award Cinequest San Jose Film Festival, 1998; Third Hollywood Film Festival Actor of the Year, 1999; Silver Bauhinia Star, 1999; Indian Film Awards International Achievement Award, 2000; Montreal World Film Festival Grand Prix of the Americas, 2001; MTV Movie Awards Best Fight Scene, 2002; Golden Horse Best Action Choreography, Taiwan, 2004; Hong Kong Film Award for Professional Achievement, 2005; Member, Most Excellent Order of the British Empire, British Government for Hong Kong/ Commonwealth; Chevalier des Arts et des Lettres, French Minister of Culture and Communication; Honorary Doctor of Social Science, Hong Kong Baptist University; Honorary Fellow, Hong Kong Academy of Performing Arts. Address: The Jackie Chan Group, 145 Waterloo Road, Kowloon-Tong, Kowloon, Hong Kong. E-mail: jcgroup@jackiechan.com Website: www.jackiechan.com

CHANDLER Daniel Ross, b. 22 July 1937, Wellston, Oklahoma, USA. Minister; Professor; Author. Education: BS, University of Oklahoma, 1959; MA, Purdue University, West Lafayette, Indiana, 1965; BD, Garrett Theological Seminary, Evanston, Illinois, 1968; PhD, Ohio University, Athens, Ohio, 1969; Masland Fellow (postdoctoral research), Union Theological Seminary, New York, 1975-76; Ordained Deacon, 1960, elder, 1968, United Methodist Church. Appointments: Assistant Debate Coach, Duke University, 1959-62; Graduate Assistant, Purdue University, 1962-64; Instructor, Augustana College, Illinois, 1965-66; Assistant Pastor, Peoples Church, Chicago, 1965-66; Graduate Assistant, University of Southern California, 1966-67; Graduate Assistant, Ohio University, 1968-69; Assistant Professor, Central Michigan University, Mt Pleasant, 1969-70; Assistant Professor, SUNY, New Paltz, 1970-71; Assistant Professor, CUNY, 1971-75; Assistant Professor, Rutgers University, New Brunswick, NJ, 1976-83; Adjunct Assistant Professor to Adjunct Associate Professor, CUNY, 1983-90; Adjunct Professor, Hofstra University, Hempstead, NY, 1985-90; Adjunct Professor, New York Institute of Technology, Old Westbury, 1985-89; Lecturer, Loyola University, Chicago, 1991-93; Adjunct Professor, Northeastern Illinois University, Chicago, 1994-95; Visiting Scholar, Garrett Theological Seminary, Northwestern University, 1996-; Adyar Library, International Headquarters, Theosophical Society, Chennai, India, 1998; World Buddhist University and World Fellowship of Buddhists, Bangkok, 2001-04; Lecturer, Harold Washington College, Chicago, 2002-03. Publications: Author: The Reverend Dr Preston Bradley, 1971; The Rhetorical Tradition, 1978; The History of Rhetoric, 1990; Toward Universal Religion, 1996; The 1993 Parliament of the World's Religions, 1995; Book review editor, Religious Humanism, 1988-2006; Contributor of chapters to books and numerous articles in professional journals. Honours: Financial Research grants: W Clement and Jessie V Stone Foundation, 1965-66; Kern Foundation, 1967, 1997, 1998; Highest Civilian Commendation for Heroism, New York City Police Department, 1981; Plandome Veatch Fund, 1983-84; Fulbright Scholar, India, 1986; Outstanding Teacher of the Year, Golden Key Honor Society, 1988; Planning Board Committee, Parliament of the World's Religions, 1993; many others. Memberships: National Communication Association; Religious Speech Communication Association; Fulbright Association; Pi Kappa Delta; Tau Kappa Alpha-Delta Sigma Rho. Address: 1929 Sherman Ave, WI, Evanston, IL 60201, USA; 83/226 Soi Sathorn 12, North Sathorn Road, Bangrak, Bangkok 10500, Thailand.

CHANG Chip Hong, b. 7 September 1964, Singapore. Professor. m. Gek King Heng. Education: B Eng (Hons), National University of Singapore, 1989; M Eng, 1993, PhD, 1998, Postgraduate Diploma of Teaching in Higher Education, 2001, Nanyang Technological University, Singapore. Appointments: Supplier Quality Engineer, General Motor Singapore Ltd, 1989-90; Research Assistant, 1990-91, Assistant Professor, 1999-2005, Associate Professor, 2005-, Programme Director, Centre for Integrated Circuits and Systems, 2003-2010, Nanyang Technological University; Lecturer, French-Singapore Institute, 1995-98; Technical Consultant, Flextech Electronics, 1998-99; Deputy Director, Centre for High Performance Embedded Systems, 2000-; Assistant Chair of Alumni, School of EEE, Nanyang Technological University, 2008-. Publications: 53 refereed international journals; 110 refereed international conference papers; 3 book chapters; 1 edited volume of lecture notes in computer science. Honours: Finalist, Best Paper Award, VLSI '95; Charter Fellow of Advisory Directorate International, 2008; Gold and Silver Leaf Certificates of Prime Asia, 2010; Listed in international biographical dictionaries. Memberships: Senior Member, Institute of Electrical and Electronics Engineers; Fellow, Institution of Engineering and Technology. Address: Block 52, School of EEE, Nanyang Technological University, 50, Nanyang Avenue, Singapore 639798.

CHANG Dae-Ig, b. 10 August 1959, South Korea. Research Engineer; Professor. m. Hye-Ran Kim, 2 sons. Education: BS, 1985, MS, 1989, Electronics & Telecommunications Engineering, Hanyang University, Seoul; PhD, Electronics Engineering, Chungnam National University, Daejeon, 1999. Appointments: Teaching Assistant, Hanyang University, Seoul, 1988-89; Research Engineer, VSAT team, MPR Teltech Ltd, Vancouver, Canada, 1991-93; Team Leader, Satellite Broadcasting & Telecommunications Convergence Research Team, ETRI, Daejeon, 1990-; Professor, Department of Mobile Communications & Digital Broadcasting Engineering, UST, Daejeon, 2005-; Vice Chair, Korea TTA, 2006-. Honours: Minister's Award, Ministry of Information & Communications, 1996; President's Award, ETRI, 2001; Government Administrator's Award, Small and Medium Business Administration, 2008; Superior Paper Award, JCCI, 2008. Memberships: Korea Information & Communications Society; Institute of Electronics Engineers of Korea; Korea Information Processing Society. Address: 105-1303 Mugigae Apt, Weolpyung-dong, Sur-gu, Daejeon, 302-750, South Korea. E-mail: dchang@etri.re.kr Website: www.etri.re.kr

CHANG Hae Choon, b. 20 December 1961, Seoul, Korea. Professor. m. In Cheol Kim, 1 daughter. Education: Post-graduate course, Microbiology, Department of Applied Microbiological Biotechnology, University of Tokyo, Japan, 1990; MS, 1986, PhD, 1991, Department of Food Science & Technology, Seoul National University. Appointments: Postdoctoral, Department of Microbiology, Michigan State University, East Lansing, USA, 1992-94; Director, Kimichi Research Center, Chosun University, Republic of Korea, 1992-; Professor, Department of Food & Nutrition, Gwangju, Republic of Korea, 1996-; Director, Human Resources Development Center for Traditional Food Innovation, 2004-09. Publications: Numerous articles in professional journals. Honours: Seoul International Invention Fair, Korea Invention Promotion Association; Silver Prize, 2008. Memberships: IFT. Address: #375 Seosuck-dong, Donggu, Department of Food & Nutrition, Chosun University, Gwanggu 501-759, Republic of Korea. E-mail: hcchang@chosun.ac.kr

CHANG Hyo Sik, b. 13 May 1975, Yesan, Chungnam, South Korea. Research Scientist. m. Sun-Young Lee, 1 son, 1 daughter. Education: MA, 2000, PhD, 2004, Department of Materials Science & Engineering, Gwangju Institute of Science and Technology. Appointments: Researcher, Korea Research Institute of Standards & Science, 1998-2004; Senior Researcher, HYNIX Semiconductor Inc, 2004-07; Senior Researcher, Korea Institute of Ceramic Engineering & Technology, 2007-. Honours: MRS Graduate Student Awards, 2004. Memberships: KRS, Korea. Address: 30 Gyeongchung Road, Shindunmyeon, Icheon, Gyeonggido, 467-843, Republic of Korea.

CHANG Michael, b. 22 February 1972, Hoboken, New Jersey, USA. Former Tennis Player. m. Amber Liu, 2008. Appointments: Aged 15 was youngest player since 1918 to compete in men's singles at US Open, 1987; Turned Professional, 1988; Played Wimbledon, 1988; Winner, French Open, 1989; Davis Cup Debut, 1989; Winner, Canadian Open, 1990; Semi-Finalist, US Open, 1992, Finalist, 1996; Finalist, French Open, 1995; Semi-Finalist, Australian Open, 1995,

Finalist, 1996; Winner of 34 singles titles by end of 2002; Retired, 2003; USA Tennis High Performance Committee, US Tennis Association, 2005-06; Joined Jim Courier's Senior Tour, Naples, Florida, 2006. Honours: Inducted into Tennis Hall of Fame, 2008; Chinese Historical Society of Southern California, 2009. Address: Advantage International, 1751 Pinnacle Drive, Suite 1500, McLean, VA 22102, USA. Website: www.highperformance.usta.com/home.default.sps

CHANG Shuenn-Yih, b. 12 June 1958, Taiwan. Professor. m. Chiu-Li Huang, 2 daughters. Education: BS, 1977-81, MS, 1981-83, National Taiwan University; M Eng, University of California, Berkeley, California, USA, 1988-92; PhD, University of Illinois, Urbana-Champaign, USA, 1992-94. Appointments: Engineer, Eastern International Engineers, 1985-87; Associate Research Fellow, National Center for Research on Earthquake Engineering, 1995-2002; Associate Professor, 2002-04, Professor, 2005-, Professor and Head, 2007-, National Taipei University of Technology. Publications include most recently: Bi-Directional Pseudodynamic Testing, 2009; Experimental Studies of Reinforced Concrete Bridge Columns under Axial Load plus Biaxial Bending, 2010; Explicit Pseudodynamic Algorithm with Improved Stability Properties, 2010; A New Family of Explicit Method for Linear Structural Dynamics, 2010; An explicit structure-dependent algorithm for pseudodynamics testing, 2013. Honours: Research Award, National Science Council, Taiwan, Republic of China; Research Award, Chinese Institute of Civil and Hydraulic Engineering; Distinguished Research Award, National Taipei University of Technology, 2006; Distinguished Professor, National Taipei University of Technology. Memberships: Senior Member, Chinese Institute of Civil and Hydraulic Engineering; Chinese Institute of Earthquake Engineering. Address: National Taipei University of Technology, Department of Civil Engineering, #1 Section 3 Jungshiau East Road, Taipei, Taiwan, Republic of China. E-mail: changsy@ntut.edu.tw

CHANG Ta-Yuan, b. 19 December 1973, Taichung, Taiwan, Republic of China. Medical Professor. m. Hsiu-Mei Tang. Education: PhD, Occupational Medicine and Industrial Hygiene, National Taiwan University, Taipei, 2004. Appointments: Assistant Professor, 2004-09, Associate Professor, 2009-, Department of Occupational Safety and Health, China Medical University. Honours: 14th Outstanding Research Award, Taiwan Public Health Association, 2008. Memberships: International Society of Environmental Epidemiology; International Commission on Occupational Health. Address: No 91, Hsueh-Shih Road, Taichung 40402, Taiwan, ROC. E-mail: tychang@mail.cmu.edu.tw

CHANG Wei-Tien, b. 23 July 1968, Taipei, Taiwan. Physician. m. Yi-Hui Chiu, 2 sons. Education: MD, Department of Medicine, 1994, PhD, Graduate Institute of Clinical Medicine, 2007, National Taiwan University College of Medicine. Appointments: Attending Physician, 2000-, Lecturer, 2003-07, Assistant Professor, 2007-, National Taiwan University College of Medicine; Visiting Research Associate, University of Chicago, USA, 2004-06. Publications: 75 peer-reviewed articles in medical journals; 73 conference papers; 14 book chapters or textbooks; One encyclopaedia chapter. Honours: Listed in biographical dictionaries. Memberships: American Heart Association; American Chemical Society; American Society of Cell Biology; Society of Internal Medicine, Taiwan; Society of Cardiology, Taiwan; Society of Critical Care Medicine, Taiwan. Address: No 7 Chang-Shan South Road, Taipei 100, Taiwan. E-mail: wtchang@ntu.edu.tw

CHANG Yoon-Suk, b. 27 July 1965, Seoul, Republic of Korea. Research Professor. Education: BS, 1991, MS, 1993, PhD, 1996, Mechanical Engineering, Sungkyunkwan University, Republic of Korea. Appointments: Senior Researcher, 1996-99, Principal Researcher, 1999-2002, Power Engineering Research Institute, Korea Power Engineering Company, Republic of Korea; Fellow Researcher, Materialprufungsanstalt, University of Stuttgart, Germany, 2002; Fellow Researcher, Institute of Industrial Science, University of Tokyo, Japan, 2002-03; Research Professor, Department of Mechanical Engineering, Sungkyunkwan University, 2004-10; Assistant Professor, Department of Nuclear Engineering, Kyung Hee University, 2010-. Publications include most recently: Numerical Simulation of Cylinder Oscillation by Using a Direct Forcing Technique, 2010; Effect of Residual Stress of Dissimilar Metal Welding on Stress Corrosion Cracking of Bottom-Mounted Instrumentation Penetration Mockup, 2010; Probabilistic Fracture Mechanics Round Robin Analysis on Reactor Pressure Vessels during Pressurized Thermal Shock, 2010. Honours: President's Award, Korea Power Engineering Company, 2002; Co-author, 2nd Prize of Student Paper Competition on PVP Conference, ASME, 2005; Award for Best Research Team, Korean Ministry of Education and Human Resources Development, 2005. Memberships: Korean Society of Mechanical Engineers, 1992-; Korean Nuclear Society, 1996-; Korean Society for Precision Engineering, 2005-; Korean Society of Pressure Vessel and Piping, 2005-; ASME, 2005-. Address: 656-1041, Sungsu 1-Ga 2-Dong, Sungdong-Gu, Seoul, 133-823, Republic of Korea. E-mail: yschang7@khu.ac.kr

CHANG Yuan-Chieh, b. 1 January 1968, Taiwan. Professor. m. Ming-Huei Chen, 1 son, 1 daughter. Education: Bachelor, National Changhua University of Education, Taiwan, 1990; MBA, Asian Institute of Technology, Thailand, 1996; PhD, University of Manchester, England, 2001. Appointments: Assistant Professor, Yuan-Ze University, Taiwan, 2001-04; Assistant Professor, 2004-06, Associate Professor, 2006-11, Professor, 2011-, National Tsing Hua University; Deputy General Secretary, 2008-, International Co-operation Chair, 2012-, Chinese Society for Management of Technology; Editorial Advisory Board, R&D Management, 2008-. Publications: More than 20 international journal papers. Honours: AIT Scholar, 1994; Manchester Best Doctoral Thesis Award, 2001; CSMOT Best Papers, 2004, 2005, 2006, 2007, 2008. Memberships: R&D Management Association; Chinese Society for Management of Technology. Address: Institute of Technology Management, National Tsing Hua University, 101, Sec 2, Kuang-Fu Road, Hsinchu, Taiwan 300. E-mail: yucchang@mx.nthu.edu.tw

CHANG Yun Seok, b. 20 March 1965, Pusan, Korea. Professor. m. Bo Yeon Kim, 2 daughters. Education: BS, Physics, 1988, MS, 1990, PhD, 1998, Computer Engineering, Seoul National University. Appointments: Professor, Department of Computer Engineering, Daejin University, 1998-; Committee of Public Procurement Service (Government Institute), Korea, 2008-10; Editor of international journals, 2010-11; Visiting Scholar, Department of Electronic Engineering Systems, University of Southern California, 2000-01. Publications: Nonlinear Analysis on 3-Channel Arterial Pulse for Fast Heart Algorithm, 2006; Improved RAID5 Controller using load-balanced destage algorithm, 1998; A design of Authentication Protocol for Multi-key RFID Tag, 2007. Honours: Best Award, National IT Industry Promotion Agency, 2003; Research Award, National Research Foundation, 2006; Listed in international biographical dictionaries. Memberships: IEEE Computer Society; ACM;

AICIT; KIPS; KSII. Address: Department of Computer Engineering, Daejin University, Mt 11-1, Sundan-dong, Pocheon, 487-711, Korea. E-mail: cosmos@daejin.ac.kr Website: http://mess.daejin.ac.kr/cosmos

CHANNING Stockard, b. 13 February 1944, New York, USA. Actress. m. (1) Walter Channing, 1963-67, (2) Paul Schmidt, 1970-76, (3) David Debin, 1976-80, (4) David Rawle, 1980-88. Education: Harvard University. Career: Actress; Films include: Comforts of the Home, 1970; The Fortune, Sweet Revenge, 1975; The Big Bus, 1976; Grease, The Cheap Detective, Boys Life, 1978; Without A Trace, 1983; Heartburn, Men's Club, 1986; Staying Together, Meet the Applegates, 1987; Married to It, Six Degrees of Separation, 1993; Bitter Moon, 1994; Smoke, 1995; Up Close and Personal, Moll Flanders, Edie and Pen, The First Wives Club, 1996; Practical Magic, Twilight, Lulu on the Bridge (voice), 1998; The Red Door, Other Voices, 1999; The Business of Strangers, 2001; Life of Something Like IT, Behind the Red Door, 2002; Bright Young Things, Le Divorce, Anything Else, 2003; Red Mercury, Must Love Dogs, 3 Needles, 2005; Sparkle, 2007; Theatre includes: Two Gentlemen of Verona, 1972-73; No Hard Feelings, 1973; Vanities, 1976; As You Like It, 1978; They're Playing Out Song, Lady and the Clarinet, The Golden Age, 1983; A Day in the Death of Joe Egg, 1985; House of Blue Leaves, 1986; Woman in Mind, 1988; Love Letters, 1989; Six Degrees of Separation, 1990; Four Baboons Adoring the Sun, 1992; TV includes: The Stockard Channing Show, 1979-80; The West Wing, 1999-2006; Batman Beyond, 1999; The Truth About Jane, The Piano Man's Daughter, 2000; Confessions of an Ugly Stepsister, 2002; Hitler: The Rise of Evil, 2003; Jack, 2004; Out of Practice, 2005-06. Honours: Tony Award, Best Actress, 1985. Address: ICM, c/o Andrea Eastman, 40 W 57th Street, New York, NY 10019, USA.

CHANNON Merlin George Charles, b. 14 September 1924, St Johns Wood, London, England. Retired HM Inspector of Schools; Community Musician; Handelian. m. Ann Carew Robinson, 1951, 1 daughter. Education: Guildhall School of Music, College of St Mark and St John, 1943-45; BMus (London), Trinity College of Music, 1950-55; MA, Birmingham University, 1981-84; PhD, Open University, 1986-95. Appointments: Teacher, Middlesex and London schools, 1945-54; Director of Music, Woolverstone Hall School, Suffolk, 1955-62; Director of Music and Senior Lecturer, St Paul's College, Cheltenham, 1962-65; HM Inspector of Schools, Department of Education and Science, Midland and Eastern Divisions successively, 1965-84; Conductor of various amateur orchestral and choral societies including: Ipswich Orchestral Society, 1956-62; Ipswich Bach Choir, 1957-62, 1975-87; Dudley Choral Society, 1966-72; Clent Hills Choral Society and Clent Cantata Choir, 1968-72; Kidderminster Choral Society, 1970-72; Suffolk Singers, 1972-78; Stowmarket Choral Society, 1973-75; Eye Bach Choir, 1974-94. Publications: Handel's 'Judas Maccabaeus' in Music and Letters and in the New Novello Choral Edition; Handel's 'Occasional Oratorio' for Halle Handel Edition. Honours: Hon FTCL, 1984; Conductor Emeritus, Eye Bach Choir, 1994; President, Ipswich Bach Choir, 2008. Memberships: Royal Music Association; Incorporated Society of Musicians; MCC; Royal Overseas League. Address: 42 Church Street, Eye, Suffolk, IP23 7BD, England.

CHAPMAN Barry Lloyd, b. 6 June 1936, Werris Creek, New South Wales, Australia. Consultant Cardiologist; Educator; Military Officer (Retired). m. 1961, divorced 1988, 2 sons, 2 daughters. Education: Tamworth High School, New South Wales; MB, BS, Sydney University, 1960; Member, 1966, Fellow, 1972, Royal Australasian College of Physicians; Associate Member, 1980, Member 1981, Fellow, 2004, Cardiac Society of Australia and New Zealand. Appointments: Resident Medical Officer, 1960-62, Medical Registrar, 1963-66, Fellow in Medicine, 1967-70, Foundation Director of Coronary Care, 1968-70, Royal Newcastle Hospital, New South Wales, Australia; Believed to be first person in Australia, outside of a capital city, to insert a temporary transvenous cardiac pacemaker; Research Fellow, Senior Registrar, West Middlesex Hospital, Isleworth, England, with attachment to Hammersmith Hospital, London, 1971-73; Staff Specialist in Medicine, 1973-91, Consultant Cardiologist, 1984-87, Senior Consultant Cardiologist, 1988-91, Royal Newcastle Hospital, New South Wales; Senior Consultant Cardiologist, Foundation Director, Electrocardiography Services, John Hunter Hospital, Newcastle, New South Wales, 1991-2001; Clinical, and later Conjoint, Lecturer in Medicine, Faculty of Medicine and Health Sciences, University of Newcastle, New South Wales, 1979-2001; Retired, 2001. Publications: Numerous original papers on subjects including: Liver cirrhosis, peptic ulcer - particularly risk factors especially aspirin, coeliac disease, dermatitis herpetiformis, polymyalgia rheumatica, acute myocardial infarction - particularly prognostic factors, a new coronary prognostic index, effects of coronary care on myocardial infarction mortality, medical history (coronary artery disease in antiquity and prehistoric times), medical audit and quality control; Papers published in medical journals which include: Medical Journal of Australia; Australasian Annals of Medicine; Gut; Proceedings of the Third Asian Pacific Congress of Gastroenterology; Lancet; Proceedings of the Royal Society of Medicine; British Heart Journal; Papers also read before learned societies. Honours: Rususcitation Certificate, Intermediate Certificate, Bronze Medallion and Instructor's Certificate, Royal Life Saving Soc of Australia, 1949-53; Australian Defence Medal; Efficiency Decoration; Medal, Anniversary of National Service, 1951-72; Award "in recognition of a long-term and substantive contribution to the Faculty of Medicine and Health Sciences", University of Newcastle, New South Wales, Australia, 2000; Testamur in "Sincere Appreciation for Support given in the Cause of Postgraduate and Continuing Education of Medical Practitioners in the Hunter Region", Board of the Hunter Postgraduate Medical Institute, Newcastle, New South Wales, 2008, 2009, 2010, 2011, 2012, 2013; Long Service Awards: Royal Newcastle Hospital, John Hunter Hospital, Hunter Area Health Service, New South Wales, Australia; American Medal of Honor, American Biographical Institute, Raleigh, North Carolina, USA; Da Vinci Diamond, IBC; Lifetime Achievement Award, World Congress of Arts, Sciences and Communications; Man of the Year, ABI, 2008; 500 Great Leaders, ABI, 2010; World Forum, Cambridge, 2010; Lifetime Achievement Award, IBC; Lifetime Achievement Award, United Cultural Convention; Life Fellow, International Biographical Association; Ambassador of Australia, World Forum St John's College, University of Cambridge, 2010, and World Forum, St Catherine's College, University of Oxford, 2012. Memberships include: Retired Fellow, Cardiac Society of Australia and New Zealand; Life Fellow, Royal Australasian College of Physicians; Retired Member; World Federation for Ultrasound in Medicine and Biology; American Institute of Ultrasound in Medicine; Australian Society for Medical Research; International Society for Heart Research; Australasian Society of Ultrasound in Medicine; Gastroenterological Society of Australia; The Gut Foundation; Emeritus Member, American Association for the Advancement of Science; Emeritus Fellow, International College of Angiology; Life Member, Australian and New

Zealand Society of the History of Medicine, New South Wales Branch; Life Fellow, Royal Society of Medicine; Active Member, New York Academy of Sciences; Society Affiliate, American Chemical Society. Address: 31 Elbrook Drive, Rankin Park, NSW 2287, Australia.

CHAPMAN Jean, b. 30 October 1939, England. Writer. m. Lionel Alan Chapman, 1 son, 2 daughters. Education: BA (Hons), Open University, 1989. Appointments: Freelance Creative Writing Tutor and Speaker. Publications: The Unreasoning Earth, 1981; Tangled Dynasty, 1984; Forbidden Path, 1986; Savage Legacy, 1987; The Bellmakers, 1990; Fortune's Woman, 1992; A World Apart, 1993; The Red Pavilion, 1995; The Soldier's Girl, 1997; This Time Last Year, 1999; A New Beginning, 2001; And a Golden Pear, 2002; Danced Over The Sea, 2004; Both Sides of the Fence, 2009; A Watery Grave, 2011. Other: Many short stories. Honours: Shortlisted, Romantic Novel of Year, 1982, 1996, and Kathleen Fidler Award, 1990. Memberships: Society of Authors; Chairman, Romantic Novelists Association, 2002-03; Member, Crime Writers Association. Address: 3 Arnesby Lane, Peatling Magna, Leicester LE8 5UN, England.

CHAPMAN Mark, b. 30 January 1958, Cuckfield, Sussex, England. Artist. Education: BA (Hons), Fine Art, 1st Class, 1982, MA, Fine Art, 1983, Birmingham. Appointments: Artist in watercolour, metal and wood construction; Teacher of Art, Sherborne School for Girls, Dorset; Exhibitions: Leicestershire Schools Exhibition, 1983-90; Sculpture in the Garden, Deans Court, Wimborne, 1991, 1993, 1995. Address: Marnel Cottage, Church Lane, Osmington, Dorset DT3 6EW, England.

CHAPMAN Stanley D(avid), b. 31 January 1935, Nottingham, England. Professor; Writer. Education: BSc, London School of Economics and Political Science, 1956; MA, University of Nottingham, 1960; PhD, University of London, 1966. Appointments: Lecturer, 1968-73, Pasold Reader in Business History, 1973-, Professor, 1993-97, Emeritus Professor, 1997- University of Nottingham; Editor, Textile History Bi Annual, 1982-2002. Publications: The Early Factory Masters, 1967; The Beginnings of Industrial Britain, 1970; The History of Working Class Housing, 1971; The Cotton Industry in the Industrial Revolution, 1972, new edition, 1987; Jesse Boot of Boots the Chemists, 1974; The Devon Cloth Industry in the 18th Century, 1978; Stanton and Staveley, 1981; European Textile Printers in the 18th Century (with Serge Chassagne), 1981; The Rise of Merchant Banking, 1984; Merchant Enterprise in Britain from the Industrial Revolution to World War I, 1992; Hosiery and Knitwear: Four Centuries of Small-Scale Industry in Britain, 2002; Southwell Town and People (with Derek Walker), 2006; Minister People (with Derek Walker), 2009. Address: Rochester House, Halam Road, Southwell, Nottinghamshire NG25 0AD, England.

CHARLIER Roger Henri Liévin Constance Louise, b. 10 November 1924, Antwerp, Belgium. University Professor. m. Patricia Simonet, 1 son, 1 daughter. Education: Certificate of Political and Adm Sci, Colonial University of Belgium, 1940; MPolSci, Brussels, 1942; MS (Earth and Oceans), Brussels, 1945; PhD, Erlangen (high honours), 1947; Postgraduate study, Arctic and Soviet Studies, McGill University, 1953; LitD, Paris (high honours), 1956; Diploma, Industrial College of the Armed Forces, 1956; DSc (highest honours), Paris, 1958; Education Curriculum Diploma, Parsons College, 1962. Appointments include: Major (Intelligence), Major (Resistance Movement), 1941-45, Political Prisoner, 1943-44, World War II; Deputy Director, United Nations Relief & Rehabilitation Administration, 1945-46; Vice-Chair, id Belgian ORI-OIC Newspaper Correspondent, various US, Belgian, Swiss papers, 1945-60, 1983-99; Research Analyst, International War Crimes Tribunal, Nürnberg, 1946-47; Writer, Consultant, 20th Century Fox Corporation, Hollywood, California, USA, 1948; Professor, Polycultural University, Washington, DC, 1950-54; Professor, Finch College, USA, 1954-56; Special Lecturer, Chairman, Department of Geology and Geography, Hempstead NY, Hofstra University, USA, 1956-59; Visiting Professor, University of Minnesota, USA, 1959-61; Professor of Geology, Parsons College (now University), 1961-62; Professor of Geology, Geography and Oceanography, 1961-87, Special Research Scholar, 1962-64, Northeastern Illinois University, Chicago; Visiting Professor, De Paul University, Chicago, 1968-70; Professor Extraordinary, 1970-86, Professor Emeritus, 1986-, Vrije Universiteit Brussels, Belgium; Professeur associé, 1970-74, hon, 1986-, Université de Bordeaux I, France; Fulbright Fellow, 1974-76; Kellogg Fellow, 1980-82; Scientific Advisor to CEO HAECON, 1984-88, 1989-2000; Scientific Advisor to CEO SOPEX, 1988-89; Professor Emeritus, Northeastern Illinois University, USA, 1988-; Chair, Task Force Environment and Sustainability, European Federation Consulting Engineers Association, 1998-2002; Research Professor, Florida Atlantic University, 2006-. Publications include: Books: I Was a Male War Bride, 1948; For the Love of Kate, 1958; Pensées, 1962; Economic Oceanography, 1980; Study of Rocks, 1980; Tidal Power, 1982; Ocean Energies, 1993; Coastal Erosion, 1999; Tools for the Black Sea, 2000; Ocean Tidal Energy, 2009; Co-editor, Proc 6th Int Congr Hist Oceanog, [UNESCO] Ocean Sciences Bridging the Millennium, 2004; Black Sea Seminar, 2002; Articles include: Small Sources of Methane; The Atmospheric Methane Cycle: Sources, Sinks, Distribution and Role in Global Change; Tourism and the Coastal Zone: The Case of Belgium: Ocean and Coastal Management; I was a Male War Bride. Honours include: Prix François Frank, 1939; Belgian Government Awards, 1939, 1975; Chicago Public Schools Award, 1975, 1987, 1992; Outstanding Achievement Presidential Award, 1980; Paul-Henri Spaak Memorial Lecture Award, 1992; Coastal Research and Education Foundation bursary, 2005, id 2006; Knight Order of Leopold (Belgium); Knight Order of Academic Palms; and many others. Memberships include: Fellow, Geological Society of America; Charter Member, International Association for the History of Oceanography; Charter Member and Fellow, New Jersey Academy of Science, President, 1954-57, Past President, 1957-58; Fellow, American Association for the Advancement of Science; Fellow, Royal Belgian Society for Geographical Studies; Education Committee, Marine Technology Society; Association of American University Professors; Académie Nationale des Arts, Sciences et Belles-Lettres, France, 1970-; Romanian Society for Marine Studies. Address: 2 Ave du Congo, Box 23, Brussels 1050, Belgium.

CHARLTON Alan, b. Nottingham, England. Diplomat. m. Judith Angela, 2 sons, 1 daughter. Education: MA, Cambridge University, 1974; PGCE, Leicester University, 1975; B Ling, Manchester University, 1978. Appointments: Joined FCO, 1978, West Africa Department, 1978-79, Arabic Language Training, 1979-80, First Secretary, Amman, 1981-84, Near East North Africa Department, 1984-86, Head, Eastern Adriatic Unit, 1993-96, FCO; Deputy Political Adviser, British Military Government, Berlin, 1986-90; Deputy Chief of Assessments Staff, Cabinet Office, 1991-92; Political Counsellor, Bonn, 1996-98; Deputy Head of Mission, Bonn, Berlin, 1998-2000; Director, South East Europe, 2000-01,

Human Resources Director, 2001-04, FCO; Deputy Head of Mission, Washington, 2004-08; Ambassador, Brasilia, 2008-. Honours: CMG, 1996; CVO, 2007. Memberships: FRSA.

CHARLTON John (Jack), b. 8 May 1935. Former Football Player; Broadcaster; Football Manager. m. Patricia, 1958, 2 sons, 1 daughter. Appointments: Professional footballer, Leeds Utd FC, 1952-73; Manager, Middlesbrough FC, 1973-77, Sheffield Wednesday FC, 1977-83, Newcastle Utd FC, 1984-85, Republic of Ireland Football Team, 1986-95; Played with winning teams in League Championship, 1969, Football Association Cup, 1972, League Cup, 1968, Fairs Cup, 1968, 1971, World Cup (England v Germany), 1966. Publication: Jack Charlton's American World Cup Diary, 1994. Honours: Football Writers Association Footballer of the Year, 1967; OBE. Membership: Sports Council, 1977-82.

CHARLTON Robert (Bobby) (Sir), b. 11 October 1937. Former Football Player. m. Norma, 1961, 2 daughters. Career: Footballer with Manchester Utd, 1954-73; Played 751 games scoring 245 goals; FA Cup Winners' Medal, 1963; First Division Championship Medals, 1956-57, 1964-65, 1966-67; World Cup Winners' Medal (England team), 1966; European Cup Winners' Medal, 1968; 106 appearances for England, scoring 49 goals, 1957-73; Manager, Preston North End, 1973-75; Chairman, NW Council for Sport and Recreation, 1982-; Director, Manchester Utd Football Club, 1984-. Publications: My Soccer Life, 1965; Forward for England, 1967; This Game of Soccer, 1967; Book of European Football, Books 1-4, 1969-72. Honours: Honorary Fellow, Manchester Polytechnic, 1979; Honorary MA, Manchester University; Knighthood; CBE. Address: 17 The Square, Hale Barns, Cheshire WA15 8ST, England.

CHASE Chevy (Cornelius Crane), b. 8 October 1943, New York, USA. Comedian; Actor; Writer. m. (1) Jacqueline Carlin, 1976, divorced 1980, (2) Jayni Luke, 3 daughters. Education: Bar College; Institute of Audio Research, MIT. Career: Writer, Mad magazine, 1969; Actor: Channel One; The Great American Dream Machine; Lemmings; National Lampoon Radio Hour; Saturday Night Live; Films include: Tunnelvision, 1976; Foul Play, 1978; Oh Heavenly Dog, 1980; Caddyshack, 1980; Seems Like Old Times, Under the Rainbow, 1981; Modern Problems, 1981; Vacation, 1983; Deal of the Century, 1983; European Vacation, 1984; Fletch, 1985; Spies Like Us, 1985; Follow that Bird, 1985; The Three Amigos, 1986; Caddyshack II, 1988; Funny Farm, 1988; Christmas Vacation, 1989; Fletch Lives, 1989; Memoirs of an Invisible Man, 1992; Hero, 1992; Last Action Hero, 1993; Cops and Robbersons, 1994; Man of the House, 1995; National Lampoon's Vegas Vacation, 1997; Snow Day, 1999; Orange County, 2002; Bad Meat, 2003; Karate Dog (voice), 2004; Goose! 2004; Ellie Parker, 2005; Funny Money, 2005; Zoom, 2006; Jack and the Beanstalk, 2008; Stay Cool, Not Another Not Another Movie, Help, 2009; TV includes: The Great American Machine; Smothers Brothers Show; Saturday Night Live; The Secret Policeman's Ball, 2006; Law and Order, 2006. Honours: 3 Emmy Awards; Writers Guild of America Award; Man of the Year, Harvard University Theatrical Group, 1992. Memberships: American Federation of Musicians; Stage Actors Guild; Actors Equity; American Federation of TV and Radio Artists. Address: Cornelius Productions, Box 257, Bedford, NY 10506, USA.

CHASSAING Stefan Jean-Philippe, b. 2 August 1975, Haguenau, France. Assistant Professor. m. Pauline Gendrot, 2 sons. Education: Master, 2002, PhD, 2006, Organic Chemistry, Université de Strasbourg, France. Appointments: Teacher, Physical Sciences, secondary school level, 1997-2000; Assistant Professor, Paul Sabatier University, Toulouse, France, 2008-; Leader of Research Group, ITAV, Toulouse, 2013-. Publications: Around 30 publications in international journals of organic chemistry; 3 chapter books. E-mail: chassaing@chimie.ups-tlse.fr

CHATTERJEE Margaret, b. 13 September 1925, London, England. Professor. m. Nripendranath Chatterjee (deceased), 1 son, 2 daughters. Education: BA, 1946, MA, 1956, Oxford University; PhD, Delhi, 1960; Postdoctoral Research, London University, 1961. Appointments: Chair of Philosophy, Delhi University; Professor of Comparative Religion, Visva Bharati, Santiniketan; Professor of Philosophy, Westminster College, Oxford; Lady Davis Visiting Professor, Department of Indian, Iranian and Armenian Studies, Hebrew University, Jerusalem; Visiting Professor, Department of Philosophy, Bryn Mawr College, USA; Spalding Visiting Fellow in Indian Philosophy and Ethics, Wolfson College, Oxford; Visiting Professor, Drew University; Commonwealth Visiting Fellow, Calgary University; Director, Indian Institute of Advanced Study, Simla. Publications: Numerous articles in professional journals; Books include: Gandhi's Religious Thought, 1983; The Concept of Spirituality, 1989; Gandhi and His Jewish Friends, 1992; Studies in Modern Jewish and Hindu Thought, 1997; Between Friends, 2011; Modalities of Otherness, 2011. Memberships: Former President, International Society for Metaphysics; Governing Body, National Gandhi Museum, New Delhi. Address: 49 Kala Kunj, A O Shalimar Bagh, Delhi 110088, India.

CHATTERJEE Tathagata, b. 22 November 1961, Poona, India. Medical Practitoner. m. Sonali Jha, 2 daughters. Education: MBBS; MD, Pathology; Postdoctoral Fellow, Oncopathology; DM, Haematopathology. Appointments: Assistant Professor, AFMC Poona; Assistant Professor, Base Hospital, Delhi Cantt 10; Classified Specialist, Pathology & Hematology, and Associate Professor, Command Hospital, Kolkata, India; Senior Adviser and Professor, Pathology & Hematology, Army Hospital R&R, Delhi Cantt. Publications: 44 arricles in national and international journals; 10 book chapters. Honours: Distinction in Pathology, MBBS, AFMC, Poona; 1st DM in Haematology, AIIMS, New Delhi, and also in India; Fellow, UICC, USA; Fellow, International Outreach Programme, St Jude Cancer Research Hospital, USA; Fellow, India Society of Haematology. Memberships: Senior Specialist, Armed Forces Medical Services, India. E-mail: Department of Pathology, Army Hospital R&R, Delhi Cantt, New Delhi 110010, India. E-mail: catahagat@hotmail.com

CHATTOPADHYAY Ajit Kumar, b. 29 February 1936, West Bengal, India. Engineering Teacher and Researcher. m. Sumitra Ganguly, 1 son, 1 daughter. Education: BE, Electrical Engineering, Calcutta University, 1958; MTech, Elect Machines, IIT, Kharagpur, 1963; PhD, Power Electronics, UMIST, Manchester, England, 1971. Appointments: Lecturer, Electrical Engineering, KGEI, Bishnupur, 1959-60; Associate Lecturer, 1960-62, Lecturer, 1962-68, Assistant Professor, 1968-76; Professor, 1976-96, IIT Kharagpur; Visiting Professor, UOT, Baghdad, Iraq, 1980-81; Head, Electrical Engineering, IIT, Kharagpur, 1992-95; AICTE Emeritus Fellow, BE College (DU), Howrah, India, 1996-99; CSIR Emeritus Scientist, BE College, 1999-2001; UGC Emeritus Fellow, 2001-03; Honorary Emeritus Professor, BESU, Shibpur. Publications: Over 140 in international and national journals, conference records in the area of power electronics and drives. Honours: Colombo Plan Study Fellow, 1969-71; Bimal Bose Award from IETE (I), 1986; Bhartia Cutler Hammer Prize, 1986; Tata Rao Prize, 1993; Distinguished Alumnus Award, BESU, Shibpur, 2006.

Memberships: Life Fellow, IEEE (USA); Fellow, Institution of Engineers (India); Fellow, Indian Academy of Engineering; Fellow, Institute of Electronics and Telecommunications Engineers; Fellow, West Bengal Academy of Scientists and Technologists. Address: Flat 3B, 48/1 Laxmi Narayan Tala Road, Howrah - 711103, India.

CHATTOPADHYAY Madhab Kumar, b. 19 April 1956, Chandernagore, West Bengal, India. Scientist. Education: B Pharm, M Pharm, PhD, Jadavpur University, Kolkata, India. Appointments: Visiting Scientist, Leibniz Institute of Freshwater Ecology and Inland Fisheries, Department of Limnology of Stratified Lakes, Alte Fischerhuette, Stechlin-Neuglobsow, Germany; Post Doctoral Fellow, Institut Jacques Monod, Paris University, France; Lecturer, Department of Pharmaceutical Sciences, Dibrugarh University, Assam, India; Student Worker, Indian Institute of Chemical Biology, Kolkata, India; Reviewer, several science journals; Examiner, Kakatiya University, Warangal, AP, India; Examiner, Jadavpur University, India; Scientist, Centre for Cellular and Molecular Biology (CCMB), India. Publications: 12 research papers; 16 review articles; 30 popular science articles. Honours: National Scholarship, 1974. Memberships: Society of Biological Chemists, India. Address: CCMB, Hyderabad 500 007, AP, India. E-mail: mkc@ccmb.res.in

CHATURVEDI Mahashweta, b. 2 February 1950, Etawah, UP, India. College Associate Professor. m. Uma Kant Chaturvedi, 2 sons, 1 daughter. Education: MA (English), 1966, MA, Sanskrit, 1969, Agra University; MA, Hindi, RU, 1978; Sangeet Prabhakar (Sitar), 1975, Vocal Music, 1976, Tabla, 1977, Sahitya Charya, 1977, Diploma, Journalism, 1980, PhD, RU, 1984, DLitt, RU, 1991; LLB, RU, 1993. Appointments: Reader in Hindi, Dept RPPG College, Meerganj, Bly, UP, currently; Principal, Vishal Kanya Degree College, Bareilly, UP, India. Publications: Vedayan; Voice of Agony; Throbbing Lyre; Roaming Aroma; Way of Melody; Eternal Pilgrim; Waves of Joy; Immortal Wings; Stone-God; Back to the Vedas; Mother-Earth; 3 books (English articles), The Streams of Supraconsciousness, On the Sands of Time and Horizon of Thoughts; Manthachala, 2010; Kavyamritum, 2010; 12 books in English; 48 books in Hindi; Founder, Editor, Mandakini (bilingual English/Hindi, International Journal). Honours: Saint Ravidas Award, 2005; Jan Kavi Bhoop Ram Bhoop Award, 2005; Subhadra Kumari Chauhan Award, 2005; Voice of Kolkata Award, 2006; Saraswat Sanstavan Award, 2007; Maheeyasee Maha Deviverma Award, 2007; Hazari Prasad Dwivedi Award, 2007; Rising Personality of India Award, 2008; Award of Honour, Malaysia, 2008; Award of Honour, Singapore, 2008; Award of Honour, Bangkok, 2008; Michael Madhusudan Award, Kolkata, 2008; Decree of Merit, 2008; Best Poetess Award, 2009; Sitapur Bala Sahitya Kara Shiromani Award, Khatima, 2009; Rabindra Nath Tagore Award, Kolkata, 2009; Excellence in World Poetry Award, 2009; Bharat Gaurav Award, 2010 and 2012; Hoshangabad (MP) Kabir Award, Hyderabad, 2010; Best Poetess Award, Gauwahati, Assam, 2010; Sankeet Sanstha Award, 2011; Sahitya Surabhi Award, 2011; Shan-e-Bareilly, 2011; Shikshak Shree Award, 2011; Poetry Award, 2011; Award in Journalism, 2012; Sriyan Award, 2012; Mauritius, Letter of Honour, 2013; M S D Bala Sahitya Ratna Award, 2013; Listed in many biographical dictionaries. Memberships: International Writers Association, USA; International Poetry Society; Chennai Authors Guild of India, Hindi SSUP; Hindi SS Prayag; Advisor, Indian Institute of Management and Education, Kapurthala; Patron, Photo Today and many others. Address: 24 Aanchal Colony, Shyam Ganj, Bareilly 243005, UP, India.

CHAUHAN Rajesh, b. 25 June 1961, Mainpuri, India. Physician. m. Sandeep, 1 son, 1 daughter. Education: MBBS (AFMC), 1983; Advance Diploma, Hospital Administration, 1996; FCGP, 1997; Diploma, Family Medicine, 2003; Fellow, Indian Society of Malaria & Other Communicable Diseases, 2000. Appointments: Medical Officer, 1983-93, Senior Medical Officer, 1993-96, Senior Medical Officer, 1997-2005, Commanding Officer, 2005-08, Retired, 2008, Botswana Defence Force; Medical Director, Tertiary Care Hospital, Surat, India. Publications: Over 100 publications; Reviewer of professional journals. Honours: 10 service medals from Indian Army; Certificate of Merit, Botswana Defense Force. Memberships: Indian Medical Association; Indian Society of Malaria & Other Communicable Diseases; Quality & Safety in Healthcare; Peer View Institute; StopTB; Solution Exchange. Address: Family Healthcare Centre, 154 Sector 6B, AV Colony, Sikandra, AGRA 282002, India.

CHAVADAR Mahesh S, b. 7 June 1983, Bedag (MS), India. Lecturer. Education: BSc, Microbiology, 2004; MSc, Microbiology, 2006; PhD (Regd), 2008. Appointments: Lecturer, Microbiology, PG and UG Department of Microbiology, YCCS Kara (MS), India. Publications: Magnetotactic bacteria from Lonar Lake, 2009. Honours: Young Scientist Award, ISEPEHH-09, 2007. Memberships: International Society for Salt Lake Research, California, USA. Address: Shri Ram Niwas, Main Road, BEDAG, Tal Miraj Dist, Sangli (MS), Pin 416 421, India. E-mail: maheshchavadar@yahoo.co.in

CHE Hui-Chung (Charlie), b. 11 November 1966, Taipei city, Taiwan. Patent Engineering. m. Lan-Chu Lee, 2 sons. Education: Bachelor, 1989, Master, 1991, Mechanical Engineering, Cheng Kung University, Tainan, Taiwan; PhD, Management, Chung Hua University, Hsinchu, Taiwan, 2009. Appointments: Engineer, 1991-2000, Project Manager, 2000-03, Industrial Technology Research Institute, Taiwan; Assistant Professor, Yuan Ze University, Chungli, 2003-04; Assistant Professor, Chung Hua University, Hsinchu, 2009-10; Chief Technology Officer, Gainia Intellectual Assest Services Inc, 2004-; Vice President, II Union IP Consulting Ltd, Beijing, China, 2010. Publications: Numerous articles in professional journals. Honours: Excellent Work, Promotion Service Award, Industrial Technology Research Institute, 2004; Masterpiece Paper in Practical Application, Annual Conference of Chinese Institute of Industrial Engineers, 2004; Outstanding Speaker, ITRI College; Excellent Work, IPR Thesis Award, Asia Pacific Intellectual Property Association, 2009; Listed in international biographical dictionaries. Memberships: American Chemical Society; Phi Tau Phi Scholastic Honor Society; Chinese Society of Mechanical Engineering; Taiwan TRIZ Association; Society of Systematic Innovation; Rotary E-Club of Taiwan. Address: R219, B53, 195 Sec 4, Chung-Hsing Road, Chutung, Hsinchu, 30040, Taiwan.

CHEAL MaryLou, b. 5 November 1926, Michigan, USA. Research Psychologist. m. James Cheal, 2 sons, 1 daughter. Education: BA, Oakland University, Rochester, Michigan, USA, 1969; PhD, Psychology, University of Michigan, 1973. Appointments include: Assistant to Associate Psychologist, McLean Hospital, Harvard Medical School, 1977-83; Faculty Research Associate, Arizona State University, 1983-87; Visiting Professor, Air Force Systems Command University Resident Research Program Appointment, Williams Air Force Base, Arizona, USA, 1986-88; Research Psychologist, University of Dayton Research Institute at Williams Air Force Base, 1986-94; Adjunct Associate Professor, Professor, Department of Psychology, Arizona State University, USA,

1987-; Senior Research Psychologist, University of Dayton Research Institute at the Air Force Armstrong Laboratory, Mesa, Arizona, USA, 1994-95. Publications: 70 publications including: Timing of facilitatory and inhibitory effects of visual attention, 2002; Inappropriate capture by diversionary dynamic elements, 2002; Efficiency of visual selective attention is related to the type of target, 2002. Honours include: Society of Sigma Xi, 1972; Fellow, American Association for Advancement of Science, 1987; Fellow, American Psychological Association, 1986; Charter Fellow, Association for Psychological Science, 1988; World Intellectual of 1993; Commemorative Medal of Honor, American Biographical Institute, 1993; Professional Women's Advisory Board, 1998; The C T Morgan Distinguished Service to Division 6 Award, American Psychological Association, 1999; Listed in national and international biographical dictionaries. Memberships include: American Association for Advancement of Science, 1969-87, Fellow, 1987-; Sigma Xi, 1972-; Society for Neuroscience, 1974-; American Psychological Association, member, 1980-86, fellow, 1986-; President, Division 6, 1997-98, Committee on Division/APA Relation, member, 1997-98, chair, 1999, Representative to Council, 2000-05, division 6; Committee on Structure and Function of Council Member, 2004-05, Chair, 2006, Membership Committee, Member, 2007-08, Membership Board, Chair Elect, 2008, Chair, 2009; Division 1: Awards Coordinator 2008-2011; Coalition for Academic Scientific and Applied Research; Member, 2000, Secretary, 2001-2004, President, 2005, Past President, 2006; The Psychonomic Society, 1988-; Association for Psychological Science, charter fellow, 1988-; International Brain Research Organization. Address: 127 Loma Vista Drive, Tempe, AZ 85282-3574, USA.

CHEATHAM Wallace McClain, b. 3 October 1945, Cleveland, Tennessee, USA. Musician. m. Willie Faye Watson, 2 daughters. Education: BS, Knoxville College, 1967; MS, University of Wisconsin-Milwaukee, 1972; PhD, Columbia Pacific University, 1982; DFA (honoris causa), University of Wisconsin-Milwaukee, 2002. Appointments: Involvement as a church musician since 12 years of age for various denominations; Music Teacher, Knoxville (Tennessee) City School System, 1967-68; Music Teacher, Unified School District, Racine, Wisconsin, 1968-71; Music Teacher, Milwaukee (Wisconsin) Public Schools, 1971-2003; Composer; Conductor; Researcher; Interviewed for podcast series, Centre for Black Music Research, Columbia College, Chicago, 2010; Profiled composer in doctoral research of Jennifer Ciobanu, The Wider View: Engaging a New Generation of Singers Through African American Art Song, University of North Texas, 2010. Publications: Choral compositions and works for solo voice, piano, organ, and orchestra; Contributing author, Challenges in Music Education, 1976; Just Tell the Story of Troubled Island, 2004; Editor, Dialogues on Opera and the African American Experience, 1997; Contributing Author, African American National Biography, 2008; Contributor of articles to professional journals; Contributing author, Weyward Macbeth, 2010; Contributing author, Composition in Africa and the Diaspora, 2010. Honours: Listed in international biographical dictionaries; Lecturer, Shakespeare in Color, Rhodes College, 2008; Organist, Fiftieth Anniversary Operation Crossroads Africa Service of Thanksgiving, Remembrance and Hope, 2008; International performances of compositions; Lecturer and Panelist, William Grant Still Tribute Conference, 2009; Featured Composer, New York State School Music Association, Zone 8 Area, All-State Festival, 2010; Outstanding Citizen's Community Service Award, Wisconsin Council of Deliberation, PHA, 2010; Featured Composer and Collaborative Artist, African American Art Song Alliance, 2012; Featured Composer, World Saxophone Congress, 2012; Knoxville College Alumni Hall of Fame Inductee, 2012. Memberships: Lyrica Society; National Association of Negro Musicians; Wisconsin Alliance of Composers; American Choral Directors Association; Music Educators National Conference; American Guild of Organists; African Methodist Episcopal Church; Phi Beta Sigma Fraternity; Association for the Study of African American Life and History; Center for Black Music Research Associate. Address: 2961 North Fifth Street, Milwaukee, WI 53212, USA. E-mail: fchea44172@aol.com

CHEDEA Veronica Sanda, b. 12 August 1974, Curgir, Alba, Romania. Researcher. Education: Engineer, Agriculture, 1997, Dr, Biotechnology, 2009, University of Agricultural Sciences & Veterinary Medicine, Cluj-Napoca; MSc, DSPU, Mediterranean Agronomic Institute of Chania, Greece, 2000. Appointments: Researcher, University of Agricultural Sciences & Veterinary Medicine, Cluj-Napoca, 2009-10; JSPS Postdoctoral Fellow, Simane University, Japan, 2010-12; Researcher, Laboratory of Animal Nutrition, National Research Development Institute for Animal Biology and Nutrition, Balotesti, Romania, 2010-. Publications: Numerous articles in professional journals. Honours: Intensive Course, School of Modern Greek Language, Aristotle University, Thessaloniki, 2002; Research Fellowship, Venetian Institute of Molecular Medicine, Italy, 2003-04; Research Fellowship, Institute of Biochemistry and Biophysics, Russian Academy of Sciences, 2005-06; Research Fellowship, University of Science, Vietnam, 2008-09; Research Postdoctoral Fellowship, Romanian Ministry of Education, 2009-10; Research mobility, University of the West of England, Faculty of Health and Life Sciences, Bristol, 2010; Postdoctoral Fellowship, Japan Society for the Promotion of Science, 2010-12. Memberships: International Society of Organic Agriculture Research; Romanian Society of Biochemistry and Molecular Biology; European Society for New Methods in Agricultural Research. Address: Str Alex Sahia Nr 19, Sc D, Ap 2, 515600 Cugir, Jud Alba, Romania. E-mail: chedeaveronica@hotmail.com

CHEDID Andrée, b. 20 March 1920, Cairo, Egypt. Poet; Novelist; Dramatist. m. Louis A Chedid, 23 August 1942, 1 son, 1 daughter. Education: Graduated, American University of Cairo, 1942. Publications: Poetry Collections: Textes pour un poème (1949-1970), 1987; Poèmes pour un texte (1970-91), 1991; Par delà les mots, 1995; Fugitive Suns: Selected Poetry, 1999; Novels: Le Sommeil délivré, 1952, English translation as From Sleep Unbound, 1983; Jonathon, 1955; Le Sixième Jour, 1960, English translation as The Sixth Day, 1988; L'Autre, 1969; La Cité fertile, 1972; Nefertiti et le reve d'Akhnaton, 1974; Les Marches de sable, 1981; La Maison sans racines, 1985, English translation as The Return to Beirut, 1989; L'Enfant multiple, 1989; Lucy: La Femme Verticle, 1998; Le Message, 2000; Plays: Bérénice d'Egypte, Les Nombres, Les Montreur, 1981; Echec à la Reine, 1984; Les saisons de passage, 1996; Other: The Prose and Poetry of Andrée Chedid: Selected Poems, Short Stories, and Essays (Renée Linkhorn, translator), 1990; A la Mort, A la Vie, 1992; La Femme de Job, 1993; Les Saisons de passage, 1996; Le Jardin perdue, 1997; Territoires du Souffle, 1999; Le Cœur demeure, 1999; Essays; Children's books. Honours: Prix Louise Labe, 1966; Grand Prix des Lettres Francaise, l'Académie Royale de Belgique, 1975; Prix de l'Académie Mallarmé, 1976; Prix Goncourt de la nouvelle, 1979; Prix de Poésie, Société des Gens de Lettres, 1991; Prix de PEN Club International, 1992; Prix Albert Camus, 1996; Prix Poésie de la SALEH, 1999; Légion d'honneur, Commandeur des Arts et des Lettres. Membership: PEN Club International. Address: c/o Flammarion, 26 rue Racine, Paris 75006, France.

CHELTSOV Vladislav, b. 24 June 1934, Moscow, Russia. Professor of Physics; Theorist in quantum electrodynamics of emission from microstructures. Divorced, 2 sons. Education: MS Diploma, Moscow Engineering Physical University, 1958; PhD, Kahzan University, 1969; Associate Professor of Physics, Textile Academy, 1972. Appointments: Assistant Professor, 1958-62, Researcher, 1962-69, Department of Theoretical Nuclear Physics of Moscow Engineering Physics University; Senior Instructor, Associate Professor, Higher School, 1969-88; Associate Professor, Department of Physics, Moscow State Mining University, 1988-. Publications: Effect of phase mixing of co-operative quantum states in the system of two level atoms and lasing without inversion, 1965, 1969, 1970, 1989; Theory of co-operative resonance fluorescence of two-level atoms, 1981-86; Theory of spontaneous and stimulated emission in semiconductor, Bose-Einstein distribution for photons with non-zero chemical potential, 1969 (thesis), 1971, 1997; New theory (without series expansions and intermediate virtual states but with using the novel algorithm in operating the causal functions) has been elaborated to describe spontaneous emission of resonance photons from atoms trapped in micro-cavities, 1993-95, 2003; Optical Mössbauer effect on the AC Stark-sublevels, 1998-99, 2001; Storage of light by two two-level atoms, 2001; New non-linear optical effects in emission and absorption of resonance photons by two-level atoms, trapped in damped microcavity, 2001; Cavity-controlled spontaneous emission spectral lineshape, 2003; Fundamentals of the theory of co-operative spontaneous emission from two level atoms trapped in micro-cavity, 2006; Non-linear optical effects in spontaneous and stimulated emission from two band intrinsic semi-conductor, 2007; Spectral properties and non-linear dynamics of a spontaneous photon emitted by two level atoms trapped in a damped nanocavity with a single resonance mode, 2008; Nonperturbative quantum theory of nonlinear effects in spontaneous emission by two level atoms trapped in damped nanocavity with a single resonance mode, 2009. Honour: Nominee for the Peter Kahpitza Grant from the Royal Society, 1991. Memberships: Senior Member, IEEE/LEOS; Individual Member, European Physical Society; Member of the Institute of Physics, UK. Address: Post Box 31, 119313 Moscow V313, Russia. E-mail: vcheltsov@hotmail.com

CHEN Andrea Ya-Huei, b. 25 October 1957, Tainan, Taiwan. Attorney-at-Law. Education: LLB, Law School, National Taiwan University, 1979; LLM, Law School, University of Pennsylvania, USA, 1983; LLM, Law School, Harvard University, 1984. Appointments: Attorney-at-Law, World Patent & Trademark Law Office, 1996-2010; Dacheng Law Offices, 2011-; Associate Professor of Law, School of Law, Soochow University, 1987-95; Lecturer at Law, School of Law, Cultural University, 1988-93; Committee Member, Board of Appeal, Environmental Protection Administration of the ROC, 1993-99; Committee Member, Board of Petition, Directorate General of Telecommunications of the ROC, 1995-97; Committee Member, Board of Regulations, Taipei Municipal Government, 1995-98; Committee of Law, Biotechnical and Pharmaceutical Industrial Program Office, 1998-2000, Mediator, Mediation Office for Dispute on Shipment Inspection and Supervision, 1999-2000, Ministry of Economic Affairs of the ROC. Publications: Numerous articles in professional journals. Memberships: Taiwan Bar Association; Taipei Bar Association; Taiwan Law Society. E-mail: andrea@dachenglaw.com.tw

CHEN Bin-Hao, b. 17 November 1975, Taipei, Taiwan. Scientist. Education: BS, 1998, MS, 2000, PhD, 2005, Mechanical Engineering, National Cheng Kung University, Tainan city. Appointments: Researcher, Industrial Technology Research Institute, 2005-10; Visiting Scholar, Angonne National Laboratory, 2007; Assistant Professor, Far East University, 2011-. Publications: Atomic Force Microscopy Tip Noise induced by Adhesion, Nanoindentation and Fracture, 2004; Molecular Dynamics Simulations of Cu Thin Film Growth on a Giant-Magnetoresistance Corrugated Structure, 2007; Thermal Loading Induced Tunable Flattening Dynamics of Flexible Single-Walled Carbon Nanotubes, 2008; Thermal-Mechanical Properties of Carbon Nanotube: A Molecular Dynamics Simulation, 2009; Numerical simulation of hydrogen atom transport in thick nickel membrane using semi-empirical quantum model, 2009. Honours: Listed in international biographical dictionaries. Memberships: American Chemistry Society; Optical Society of America. Address: IIF-1, No 33, Wenhua Road, East District, Tainan City 701, Taiwan. E-mail: bhcho@cc.feu.edu.tw

CHEN Bing-Huei, b. 30 January 1954, Taichung, Taiwan. Professor. m. Wen-Huei Wang, 1 son, 1 daughter. Education: BS, Food Science, Fu Jen University, 1977; MS, Agricultural Chemistry, California State University, Fresno, 1983; PhD, Food Science, Texas A and M University, 1988. Appointments: Associate Professor, 1988-93, Professor and Chair, 1994-2001, Chair Professor in Food Science and Technology, 2004-, Department of Nutrition and Food Science, Director, Graduate Institute of Medicine, 2006-09, Fu Jen University, Taipei. Publications: More than 140 research articles have been published in internationally renowned journals. Honours: Outstanding Research Awards, National Science Council of Taiwan and Chinese Institute of Food Science and Technology. Memberships: Institute of Food Technologists; New York Academy of Science; AOAC International; American Chemical Society. Address: Department of Nutrition and Food Science, Fu Jen University, Taipei, Taiwan 242, ROC. E-mail: 002622@mail.fju.edu.tw

CHEN Chen-Peng, b. 26 December 1965, Taipei, Taiwan. University Teacher. m. Mei-Chih Lee. Education: BS, Environmental Science, Tunghai University, Taiwan, 1988; MS, 1993, PhD, 1999, Environmental Toxicology, University of Wisconsin-Madison, USA. Appointments: Acting Director, National Occupational Research Agenda Dermal Exposure Research Program, National Institute for Occupational Safety and Health, Centers for Disease Control and Prevention, Cincinnati, USA, 2005-06; Assistant Professor, 2006-11, Associate Professor, 2011-, Department of Occupational Safety and Health, China Medical University, Taichung, Taiwan. Publications: Effects of temperature steps on human skin physiology and thermal sensation response, 2011; Efficacy of predictive modeling as a scientific criterion in dermal hazard identification for assignment of skin notations, 2011. Honours: Best Risk Assessment Award, American Industrial Hygiene Conference and Expo, 2003; Honorable Mention, NIOSH Alice Hamilton Award, 2010. Memberships: American Chemical Society; Society of Environmental Toxicology and Chemistry; American Industrial Hygiene Association. Address: Department of Occupational Safety and Health, China Medical University, 91 Hsueh-Shih Road, Taichung 40402, Taiwan. E-mail: chencp@mail.cmu.edu.tw

CHEN Christopher, b. 27 December 1939, Singapore. Infertility Specialist; Senior Obstetrician; Gynaecologist. m. Stella Yfantidis, 1 son. Education: MBBS, Bachelor of Medicine and Bachelor of Surgery, 1964; Fellow of the Royal

College of Obstetricians and Gynaecologists (FRCOG), 1969; Fellow of the Royal Australian and New Zealand College of Obstetricians and Gynaecologists (FRANZCOG), 1978; Fellow of the American College of Surgeons (FACS), 1979; Fellow of the International College of Surgeons (FICS), 1978; Fellow of the Academy of Medicine, Singapore (FAMS), 1971; Master off Business Administration (MBA) 2000; Doctor of Management, 2000. Appointments: Numerous academic and hospital postings, including Examiner for the Master of Medicine (Obstetrics and Gynaecology), Examiner for the MBBS, National University of Singapore; Member, Expert Committee on Medical Sciences, National Science and Technology Board; Professor, National University of Singapore; Head, Department of Reproductive Medicine, Kandang Kerbau Hospital, Singapore; Director, Gleneagles IVF Centre, Gleneagles Hospital, Singapore; Head, Centre for Reproductive Medicine, Gleneagles Hospital, Singapore. Main research interests: In vitro fertilization; Assisted reproduction; Human egg freezing; Immunological aspects of seminal plasma. Publications: Over 120 papers and 5 books; Titles include Long Term Low Dose Pulsatile GnRH for the Treatment of Anovulatory Infertility; Sperm-Oocyte Membrane fusion in the Human during Monospermic Fertilization. Honours: include, Lord of Stokes, Buckinghamshire, England; William Blair-Bell Memorial Lectureship, Royal College of Obstetricians and Gynaecologists; World Treasurer, International College of Surgeons; Council Member, Academy of Medicine, Singapore. Memberships: Numerous professional and scientific affiliations, including Guest Editor, Annals, Academy of Medicine, Singapore; British Medical Association (BMA); Singapore Medical Association; Founder Member, Australian Gynaecological Endoscopy Society. Address: Christopher Chen Centre for Reproductive medicince Pte Ltd, Gelneagles Hospital, 6a Napier Road, Annexe Blk,04-38, Singapore, 258200. E-mail: secretary@cccm.com

CHEN Hong-Ying, b. 13 July 1973, Taiwan. Associate Professor. m. Huei-Ting Tang. Education: MS, 1996, PhD, 2003, National Chung-Hsing University, Taiwan. Appointments: Assistant Professor, Asia University, Taiwan, 2005-06; Assistant Professor, 2006-08, Associate Professor, 2008-, National Kaohsiung University of Applied Sciences. Publications: 27. Honours: Dorothy & Earl S Hoffman Student Travel Grant, American Vacuum Society, 2002. Memberships: American Vacuum Society; Taiwan Association for Coating and Thin Film Technology. Address: 415 Chien Kung Road, Kaohsiung 807, Taiwan, ROC. E-mail: hychen@cc.kuas.edu.tw

CHEN Hui-Jye, b. 6 January 1967, Yunlin County, Taiwan. Professor. Education: PhD, Biochemistry, Graduate Institute of Biochemistry, National Yang-Ming University. Appointments: Assistant Professor, China Medical University, Taiwan, 2007. Publications: The role of Microtubule Actin Crosslinking Factor I (MACFI) in the Wnt signaling pathway, 2006. Memberships: American Society for Cell Biology; Chinese Society of Cell and Molecular Biology, Taiwan. Address: No 222, 5F-1, Wu Chung St, North 404, Taichung, Taiwan.

CHEN Jeng-Fung, b. 20 April 1958, Miaoli, Taiwan. Professor. m. Chien-Hui Chu, 1 son. Education: BS, Tunghai University, 1981; MS, Clemson University, 1987; PhD, Texas A&M University, 1991. Appointments: Associated Professor, 1992-2005, Professor, 2005-, Department of Industrial Engineering & Systems Management, Feng Chia University. Publications: Numerous articles in professional journals. Honours: Research Awards, 1995-98, 2003, 2007; Outstanding Research Award, 2004-06. Memberships: Phi Tau Phi. Address: Department of Industrial Engineering & Systems Management, Feng Chia University, No 100 Wenhwa Road, Seatwen, Taichung, Taiwan, 40724, ROC. E-mail: jfchen@fcu.edu.tw

CHEN Po-Han, b. 4 June 1972, Taipei, Taiwan. College Professor. m. Stella C Chia. Education: BSc, Civil Engineering, National Taiwan University, 1994; MSc, Civil Engineering, 1999, PhD, 2001, Purdue University, USA. Appointments: Research Assistant, Hydrotech Research Institute, National Taiwan University, 1992-94; Assistant Researcher, Taiwan Construction Research Institute, 1996-97; Research Assistant, School of Civil Engineering, Purdue University, 1999-2001; Assistant Professor, 2001-09, Program Director, MSc in Maritime Studies Program, 2006-09, Nanyang Technological University, Singapore; Associate Professor, Department of Civil Engineering, National Taiwan University, 2009-. Publications: More than 60 publications in refereed journals and conference proceedings, book chapters, reports, etc. Honours: Best Paper Award, ISARC, 2007; Excellent Paper Award, ICCEM-ICCPM, 2009; Listed in international biographical dictionaries. Memberships: Associate Member, American Society of Civil Engineers; Member, Construction Institute, ASCE; Invited Member, Asian Institute of Intelligent Buildings, Singapore Chapter. Address: Department of Civil Engineering, National Taiwan University, No 1, Sec 4, Roosevelt Rd, Taipei, Taiwan. E-mail: pohanchen@ntu.edu.tw

CHEN Shen-Ming, b. 8 July 1957, Chunghua (Lukang), Taiwan. Professor. m. Mei-Lin Lu, 1 son, 1 daughter. Education: BSc, Chemistry, National Kaohsiung Normal University, Taiwan, 1980; MSc, 1983, PhD, 1991, National Taiwan University, Taiwan. Appointments: Associate Professor, Department of Chemical Engineering, 1991-97, Director of Extracurricular Activity, Office of Student Affairs, 1995-2000, Library Dean, 2000-06, National Taipei University of Technology, Taipei; Visiting Postdoctoral Fellow, Institute of Inorganic Chemistry, Friedrich-Alexander University, Erlangen-Nuremberg, Germany, 1997; Professor, 1997-, Distinguished Professor, 2010-, Department of Chemical Engineering and Biotechnology, National Taipei University of Technology, Taipei. Publications: Above 270 research papers in internationally peer-reviewed journals. Honours: Outstanding Research Awards, National Taipei University of Technology, 2005, 2009; 6 Academic Honours, National Taipei University of Technology, 2005, 2006, 2007, 2008, 2009, 2010; 3 Outstanding Research Awards, Engineering College, National Taipei University of Technology, 2004, 2005 & 2006. Memberships: International Society of Electrochemistry; Electrochemical Society; Chemical Society of Taipei; American Chemical Society. Address: Department of Chemical Engineering and Biotechnology, National Taipei University of Technology, No 1, Section 3, Chung-Hsiao East Road, Taipei, Taiwan 106 (ROC). E-mail: smchen78@ms15.hinet.net

CHEN Shilu, b. 24 September 1920, Dong Yang, Zhejiang, China. Professor. m. Xiaosu Gong, 2 sons, 1 daughter. Education: BSc, Aeronautics, Tsinghua University, China, 1945; PhD, Aeronautics, Moscow Aeronautical Institute, Russia, 1958. Appointments: Honorary Dean, College of Astronautics, Northwestern Polytechnical University, China, 1987-; Foreign Academician, Russian Academy of Astronautics, 1994-; Academician, Chinese Academy of Engineering, 1997-. Publications: Dynamic Stability Coupling and Active Control of Elastic Vehicles with

Unsteady Aerodynamic Forces Considered; Longitudinal Stability of Elastic Vehicles; Progress and Development of Space Technology in China, 2000. Honours: Recipient of First Grade Award for Progress in Science and Technology on "Dynamics and Control of Elastic Vehicles", Chinese National Education Committee, 1991; Honoured as "Excellent Postgraduate Supervisor", "Distinguished Specialist", Ministry of Aeronautics and Astronautics, 1992. Memberships: Director, Chinese Society of Aeronautics and Astronautics, 1964-92; Chairman, Session of Aeronautics and Astronautics, China Advisory Committee for Academic Degrees, 1985-91; Honorary President, Shanxi Provincial Society of Astronautics, 1994-; Associate Fellow, AIAA, 1996-. Address: Northwestern Polytechnical University, South Apt 17-1-301, Xian 710072, People's Republic of China. E-mail: s.l.chen@nwpu.edu.cn

CHEN Wei Yeu, b. 25 October 1936, Wu Chuan, Kwangtung, China. Physics Professor. m. Ming Ju Chou. Education: BS, National Taiwan University, 1959; PhD, University of Southern California, 1970. Appointments: Associate Professor, Department of Physics, TamKang University, Taipei, Taiwan, 1971-74; Chairman, Department of Physics, 1972-73, Professor, Department of Physics, 1974-; Consultative Committee Member, National Science Council, Taipei, 1992-93; Advisory Committee Member, Physics Ext Ctr, 1993-94; Editor, Bentham Science Publications, 2008-. Publications: Effects of collective Pinning on topological order-disorder phase transition, 2005; Apply the full Hamiltian quantum theory for vortice lattice developed by the author to solve the problem of peak effects in type-II superconductor, 2006; Superconducting cuprate, 2009; Magnesium Diboride (MgBr) superconductor research, 2009; Theory of thermally activated vortex bundles flow over the directional-dependent potential barriers in type-II superconductors, 2010; Theory of anomalous Hall effect in type-II superconductors, 2011. Honours: Research Awards, 1989-92, Research Grants, 1993-2005, National Science Council, Republic of China; TamKang University, 1997-2004; Listed in international biographical dictionaries. Memberships: Phi Tau Phi Scholastic Honor Society. Address: 7F No 205-3, Sec 7, Chuan Sun North Road, Taipei 11151, Taiwan. E-mail: wychen@mail.tku.edu.tw

CHEN Yuanshan, b. 2 June 1966, Taipei, Taiwan. Teacher. m. Chien-Chung Chang, 1 son. Education: PhD, Graduate Institute of English, National Taiwan Normal University, 2007. Appointments: Associate Professor, Department of Applied English, National Chin-Yi University of Technology. Publications: American and Chinese complaints: Strategy use from a cross-cultural perspective, 2011; Investigating the complimenting behaviours of Chinese Speakers of American English, 2011; Evaluation of American and Taiwanese English speakers' apologies, 2011; What constitutes an appropriate email request? 2011; The effect of explicit teaching of American compliment exchanges to Chinese learners of English, 2011; A genre-based approach to teaching EFL summary writing, 2012; Symposium – The Contextualization of Teaching and Learning English as an International Language, 2012. Honours: The Language Training and Testing Service Prizes for Outstanding Masters and/or Doctoral Theses, 2007; Outstanding Adviser Award, 2010; Outstanding Research Award, 2011. Address: Department of Applied English, National Chin-Yi University of Technology, No 57, Sec 2, Zhongshan Road, Taiping District, Taichung 41170, Taiwan ROC. E-mail: yuanshan@ncut.edu.tw

CHEN Zhe, b. 16 June 1976, Hepu, China. Research Scientist. Education: PhD, 2005. Appointments: Research Scientist, MIT; Instructor, Massachusetts General Hospital, Harvard Medical School. Publications: 1 book; 4 book chapters; Over 50 papers. Memberships: Senior Member, IEEE. Address: 43 Vassar Street, Bldg 46-6057, Massachusetts Institute of Technology, Cambridge, MA 02139, USA. E-mail: zhechen@mit.edu

CHEN Zhong-Mou, b. 23 October 1937, Wuxi, China. Engineer. m. (1) Fu-Ru Tan, deceased 1972, (2) Hai-Hong Qian, 1974, 1 son, 2 daughters. Education: MB, Moscow Engineering Institute, 1962; Postdoctoral Fellow, Norwegian University of Science and Technology, Trondheim, Norway, 1991. Appointments: Research Group Leader, Beijing Vacuum Tubes Institute, 1962-71; Chief Engineer, Office of Rear Territory, Beijing Vacuum Tubes Institute, 1968-69; Department Head, Xin-Xang 824 Factory, Honan, China, 1972-75; Vice Director, Division of Microwave Propagation Institute, Honan, 1976-78; Vice Director, Division of Night Vision Tubes, Nanjing Electronics Devices Institute, 1979-83; Director, Professor, Division of Night Vision Tubes, 1983-; Visiting Researcher, Applied Optics Group Division of Physics, Norwegian University of Science and Technology, Trondheim, 1990-91. Publications: Inventor in field/author: A Si Wide Barrier Photodetector and Application in Color Sensor, 1987-97; A Thermo photovoltaic cell, 2000; Contributions to development of new theory of regenerative amplifier in microwave bands and design of a magnetron regenerative amplifier; Contributions to improve EBS-CCD characteristics; Invention of a new principle for colometric measurements; Invention of a new thermoionic photodetector. Memberships: Chinese Institute of Electrons. Address: 524 Zhong Shan E Road, 210016 Nanjing, China.

CHENG Fai Chut, b. 15 July 1933, Shanghai, China. Researcher in Electrical Engineering. Education: BSc, Electric Engineering, Tsing Hua University, Beijing, 1957; MPhil, Electric Engineering, University of Hong Kong, 1990. Appointments: Engineer, North East Power Administration, Central Laboratory, Harbin, 1957-73; Technician, Tomoe Electrons Company, Hong Kong, 1973-76; Lecturer, School of Science and Technology, Hong Kong, 1976-80; Part-time Demonstrator, University of Hong Kong, 1980-88; Temporary Teacher, Haking Wong Technical Institute, Hong Kong, 1987-88; Evening Visiting Lecturer, 1988-89, 1990-93, Research Assistant, 1989-92, Teaching Assistant, 1992-93, Honourable Research Associate, 1993-94, Part-time Research Assistant, 1994-95, Hong Kong Polytechnic (now Hong Kong Polytech University); Part-time Research Assistant, 1995-97, Honorary Research Fellow, 1998-99, Honorary Fellow, 2000-02, Hong Kong Polytech University; Unemployed Researcher, 2003-. Publications: Insulation Thickness Determination of Polymeric Power Cables, 1994; Discussion on Insulation Thickness Determination of Polymeric Power Cables, in journal IEEE Transactions on Dielectrics and Electrical Insulation, 1995. Honours: Decree of Merit Award; Outstanding Achievement Medal, Gold Star Award, Silver Medal, IBC, 1997; Distinguished Leadership Award, 20th Century Achievement Award, Most Admired Man of the Decade, 1997, Man of the Year Commemorative Medal, ABI, 1997; 2000 Millennium Medal of Honour, ABI, 1998; Listed in specialist biographical directories. Memberships: IEEE, US. Address: 2-019 Lotus Tower 1, Garden Estate, 297 Ngau Tau Kok Rd, Kowloon, Hong Kong.

CHENG Joseph Yu-Shek, 11 November 1949, Hong Kong, China. University Professor. m. Grace Yin-Ting Cheng, 1 son, 1 daughter. Education: BSocl Scis (Honours), University of Hong Kong, 1972; BA (Honours), Victoria University of Wellington, New Zealand, 1973; PhD, Flinders University of South Australia, 1979. Appointments: Assistant Lecturer, 1977-79, Lecturer, 1979-85, Senior Lecturer, 1985-89, Department of Government and Public Administration, Chinese University of Hong Kong; Dean, School of Arts and Humanities, Open University of Hong Kong, 1989-90; Member, Central Policy Unit, Hong Kong Government Secretariat, 1991-92; Dean, Faculty of Humanities and Social Sciences, 1992-95, Chair Professor of Political Science, Contemporary China Research Project, City University of Hong Kong. Publications: Over 20 books and 100 book chapters and journal articles in English; Over 20 books and 100 articles in Chinese including most recently: Preface and Epilogue in China – A New Stage of Development for an Emerging Superpower, 2012; China – A New Stage of Development for an Emerging Superpower, 2012. Honours: JP, 1992-; Outstanding Australian Alumnus of Hong Kong Award, 1993; Inaugural Distinguished Alumni Award, Flinders University of South Australia, 2006. Memberships: Guest Professor, Beijing University, People's University, Wuhan University, Zhongshan University; Founding Editor, Hong Kong Journal of Social Sciences; The Journal of Comparative Asian Development; Founding President, The Asian Studies Association of Hong Kong. Address: Contemporary China Research Project, City University of Hong Kong, Tat Chee Avenue, Kowloon, Hong Kong, China. E-mail: rcccrc@cityu.edu.hk

CHENG Yuan-Kai, b. 16 August 1967, Taichung, Taiwan, Republic of China. Physician; Otorhinolaryngologist. m. Li-Hua Chang, 1 son, 2 daughters. Education: MD, 1992, MSc, 2002, China Medical University, Taichung; PhD, Tung-Hai University, Taichung, 2006. Appointments: Attending Physician, Department of Otolaryngology, National Taiwan University Hospital, 1996-98; Attending Physician, Department of Otolaryngology, China Medical University Hospital, 1998-2006; Chief & Attending Physician, Department of Otolaryngology, Buddhist Tzu Chi General Hospital, Taichung, 2006-07; President, Dr Cheng's OtoRhinoLaryngological Clinic, Taichung, 2007-. Publications: Numerous articles in professional journals. Honours: Grant, National Science Constitution, 2003; Listed in international biographical dictionaries. Memberships: Taiwan Otolaryngologic Society; Taiwan Society of Sleep Medicine. Address: No 376, Sec 4, Henan Road, Nantun Dist, Taichung City 408-74, Taiwan, Republic of China. E-mail: keiko56@ms25.hinet.net.

CHEON Samuel, b. 15 March 1960, Kwangju, Korea. Professor. m. Sung Sook Kim, 2 sons. Education: B Th, 1983, Th M, 1985, Yonsei University; M Div, Presbyterian Theological Seminary, 1988; STM, Yale University, USA, 1990; PhD, Graduate Theological Union, 1994. Appointments: Professor of the Old Testament, Hannam University, 1995-. Publications: The Exodus Story in the Wisdom of Solomon, 1997; B S Childs' Debate with Scholars about his Canonical Approach, 1997; Anonymity in the Wisdom of Solomon, 1998; Three Characters in the Wisdom of Solomon, 2001; Filling the Gap in the Story of Lot's Wife (Genesis 19:1-29), 2001; Reconsidering Jephthah's Story in Asian Perspective, 2003-04; Josephus and the Story of Plagues: An Appraisal of a Moralising Interpretation, 2004; Biblical Interpretation in Korea: History and Issues, 2006; The Old Testament Apochrypha and its Studies in Korea, 2006. Honours: Course Award Winner, CTNS, 2002. Memberships: Society of Biblical Literature; Korea Old Testament Society; Catholic Biblical Association of America. Address: Expo Apt 502-701, Jeonmin-dong, Yousung-gu, Daejeon, South Korea. E-mail: samuel@hnu.kr

CHEONG Seong Kyun, b. 25 July 1959, Young Kwang, Korea. Professor. m. Oh Nam Kwon. Education: BS, Seoul National University, 1982; MS, 1984, PhD, 1988, Korea Advanced Institute of Science and Technology. Appointments: Professor, Seoul National University of Science and Technology, 1993-; Visiting Professor, Ohio State University, 2000-01; International Scientific Committee Member for Shot Peening, 2005-; Visiting Professor, University of California, San Diego, 2007-08. Publications: Static Behavior Characteristics of Hybrid Composites with Nonwoven Carbon Tissue, 2003; An area-average approach to peening residual stress under multi-impacts using a three-dimensional symmetry-cell finite element model with plastic shots, 2010. Honours: Outstanding Presentation Award, full conference of Korean Society of Machine Tool Engineers, 2008; Best Paper, full conference of Korean Society for Precision Engineering, 2009; Outstanding Presentation Award, full conference of Korean Society of Machine Tool Engineers, 2009. Memberships: International Scientific Committee for Shot Peening.

CHER (Cherilyn Sarkisian LaPierre), 20 May 1946, El Centro, California, USA. Singer; Actress; Entertainer. m. (1) Sonny Bono, 1964, divorced, deceased, 1 daughter, (2) Gregg Allman, 1975, divorced, 1 son. Career: Worked with Sonny Bono in duo Sonny and Cher, 1964-74; Also solo artiste, 1964-; Performances include: Hollywood Bowl, 1966; Newport Pop Festival, 1968; Television includes: Sonny And Cher Comedy Hour, CBS, 1971; Cher, CBS, 1975-76; Sonny And Cher Show, CBS, 1976-77; Vocalist with rock group Black Rose, including US tour supporting Hall & Oates, 1980; Actress, films: Good Times, 1967; Chastity, 1969; Come Back To The Five And Dime, Jimmy Dean Jimmy Dean, 1982; Silkwood, 1984; Mask, 1985; The Witches Of Eastwick, 1987; Moonstruck, 1987; Suspect, 1987; Mermaids, 1989; The Player, 1992; Prêt-à-Porter, 1994; Faithful, 1996; Tea with Mussolini, 1999; Stuck on You, 2003; Recordings include: Singles: with Sonny And Cher: I Got You Babe (Number 1, UK and US), 1975; Baby Don't Go, 1965; Just You, 1965; But You're Mine, 1965; What Now My Love, 1966; Little Man, 1966; The Beat Goes On, 1967; All I Ever Need Is You, 1971; A Cowboy's Work Is Never Done, 1972; Solo hit singles include: All I Really Want To Do, 1965; Bang Bang, 1966; Gypsies Tramps And Thieves (Number 1, US), 1971; The Way Of Love, 1972; Half Breed (Number 1, US), 1973; Dark Lady (Number 1, US), 1974; Take Me Home, 1979; Dead Ringer For Love, duet with Meatloaf, 1982; I Found Someone, 1987; We All Sleep Alone, 1988; After All, duet with Peter Cetera (for film soundtrack Chances Are), 1989; If I Could Turn Back Time, 1989; Jesse James, 1989; Heart Of Stone, 1990; The Shoop Shoop Song (from film soundtrack Mermaids) (Number 1, UK), 1991; Love And Understanding, 1991; Oh No Not My Baby, 1992; Walking In Memphis, 1995; One By One, 1996; Paradise Is Here, 1996; Believe, 1998; Strong Enough, 1999; Albums: with Sonny and Cher: Look At Us, 1965; All I Really Want To Do, 1965; The Wondrous World Of Sonny And Cher, 1966; Sonny And Cher Live, 1972; Solo albums include: All I Really Want To Do, 1965; The Sonny Side Of Cher, 1966; With Love, 1967; Backstage, 1968; Jackson Highway, 1969; Gypsies Tramps And Thieves, 1972; Foxy Lady, 1972; Greatest Hits, 1974; Stars, 1975; I'd Rather Believe In You, 1976; Take Me Home, 1979; I Paralyze, 1984; Cher, 1988; Heart Of Stone, 1989; Love Hurts, 1991; Cher's Greatest Hits 1965-1992, 1992;

It's A Man's World, 1995; Believe, 1999; Black Rose, 1999. Honours include: Oscar, Best Actress, Moonstruck, 1988; Oscar Nomination, Best Supporting Actress, Silkwood, 1984. Current Management: Bill Sammeth Organisation, PO Box 960, Beverly Hills, CA 90213, USA.

CHERPAK Evelyn, b. 3 April 1941, New Britain, Connecticut, USA. Archivist. Education: BA, Connecticut College; MA, University of Pennsylvania; PhD, University of the North Carolina. Appointments: Archivist, Naval War College, Newport, Rhode Island; Graduate Extension Studies, Adjunct Faculty, Salve Regina University, Newport. Publications: A Diplomat's Lady in Brazil: Selections from the Diary of Mary Robinson Hunter, 2001; The Memoirs of Admiral H K Hewitt, 2004; The Redwood Library, 2005; Timothy Murphy's Civil War: The Letters of a Bounty Solder and Sailor, 1864-1865, 2006; Three Splendid Little Wars: The Diary of Joseph K Taussig 1898-1901, 2009. Honours: NDEA Fellowship in Latin American History; Lampadia Foundation Grant. Memberships: Newport Historical Society; Redwood Library; John Carter Brown Library; Association of Documentary Editors; New England Archivists; Manuscript Society; New England Council of Latin American Studies; Oral History Association; Hakluyt Society; North American Society of Oceanic History. Address: 36D Glen Meade Drive, Portsmouth, RI 02871-3403, USA. E-mail: evelyn.cherpak@usnwc.edu

CHERRY Kelly, b. Baton Rouge, Louisiana, USA. Professor; Writer; Poet. m. (1) Jonathan B Silver, 1966, divorced 1969, (2) Burke Davis III, 2000. Education: Du Pont Fellow, University of Virginia, 1961-63; MFA, University of North Carolina, 1967. Appointments: Visiting Lecturer, 1977-78, Assistant Professor, 1978-79, Associate Professor, 1979-82, Professor 1982-, Romnes Professor of English, 1983-88, Evjue-Bascom Professor in the Humanities, 1993-99, Eudora Welty Professor of English, 1997-99, Professor Emerita, 1999-, University of Wisconsin at Madison; Writer-in-Residence, Southwest State University, Marshall, Minnesota, 1974, 1975; Visiting Professor and Distinguished Writer-in-Residence, Western Washington University, 1981; Faculty, MFA Program, Vermont College, 1982, 1983; Distinguished Visiting Professor, Rhodes College, Tennessee, 1985. Publications: Fiction: Sick and Full of Burning, 1974; Augusta Played, 1979; Conversion, 1979; In the Wink of an Eye, 1983; The Lost Traveller's Dream, 1984; My Life and Dr Joyce Brothers, 1990; The Society of Friends, 1999; We Can Still Be Friends, 2003. Poetry: Lovers and Agnostics, 1975, revised edition, 1995; Relativity: A Point of View, 1977; Songs for a Soviet Composer, 1980; Natural Theology, 1988; Benjamin John, 1993; God's Loud Hand, 1993; Time out of Mind, 1994; Death and Transfiguration, 1997; Rising Venus, 2002; Hazard and Prospect: New and Selected Poems, 2007; The Retreats of Thought, 2009; The Woman Who, 2010. Other: The Exiled Heart: A Meditative Autobiography, 1991; Writing the World (essays and criticism), 1995; The Poem: An Essay, 1999; History, Passion, Freedom, Death and Hope: Prose about Poetry, 2005; The Globe and the Brain, 2006; Girl in a Library: On Women Writers & the Writing Life, 2009. Translations: Octavia, by Seneca; Antigone, by Sophocles. Contributions to: Anthologies and periodicals. Honours: Canaras Award, 1974; Bread Loaf Fellow, 1975; Yaddo Fellow, 1979, 1989; National Endowment for the Arts Fellowship, 1979; Romnes Fellowship, 1983; Wisconsin Arts Board Fellowships, 1984, 1989, 1994; Hanes Prize for Poetry, Fellowship of Southern Writers, 1989; Wisconsin Notable Author, 1991; Arts America Speaker Award, 1992; Hawthornden Fellowship, Scotland, 1994; E B Coker Visiting Writer, Converse, 1996; Leidig Lectureship in Poetry, 1999; Bradley Major Achievement Award, 2000; Rockefeller Foundation Fellowship, 2009; Director's Visitor, Institute for Advanced Study in Princeton, 2010. Membership: Associated Writing Programs, board of directors, 1990-93; Elector, Poets Corner, Cathedral Church of St John the Divine, 2009.

CHERUBIM Victor Emmanuel, b. 29 October 1934, Colombo, Ceylon, Sri Lanka. Business Executive; Shipbroker. m. Vasanthi Josephine Sandrasagra, 1 child. Education: BA (Hons), St Patrick's College, Jaffna, Ceylon, 1953; Student, Aquinas University College, Colombo, 1957, Albion College, Michigan, 1958, City London College, 1968; Diploma, Counselling, Tower Hamlets College, London, 2005. Appointments: College Visitor Staff, World University Services, New York, 1958-62; Founder, Secretary, Jaffna District Co-operative Harbour Services Union Ltd, Jaffna, Ceylon, 1962-64; Shipping Assistant, Campbel, Booker Carter Ltd, London, 1966-73; Freight Bookings Officer, Booker Export Services Ltd, London, 1966-73; Manager of Shipping, Permutit Ltd, Isleworth, 1973-74; Shipping Operations Executive, Polish Ocean Lines, London, 1974-85; Management Trainee, Manpower Services Commission, London, 1985-86; Management Consultant, English Folk Song & Dance Society, London, 1985-86; Chairman, Tamil Refugee Action Group, 1988-; Co-secretary, Tamil Refugee Housing Association Ltd, London, 1989-98; Director, Tamil Community Housing Association Ltd, London, 1989-2003; Royal Mail, London, 1987-99; General Secretary, Commission for Cultural Affairs of Tamils, UK, 1993-; Consultant in shipping, chartering and realty, Senior Partner, Cargo & Ship Agency, Essex, 1995-; CEO, Victor Lettings Management, London, 2006-12; Speaker in field. Publications: Contributor of articles to newspapers in Sri Lanka and UK. Honours: Travel grantee, US scholarship, Asia Foundation, 1957; US State Department Scholar, Institute of International Educational Exchange, 1957-58; Honorary Citizen of Albion, Michigan, 1958; David Savage Memorial Prize, City of London College, 1967; Freeman, City of London, 2003; Honorary Associate, Company of Master Mariners, 2004; Director, Sevai Society, London, UK, 2007-09. Memberships: Fellow, Institute of Chartered Shipbrokers. Address: 35 Crystal Way, Dagenham, RM8 1UE, England. E-mail: victorcherubim@aol.com

CHESHER Andrew Douglas, b. 21 December 1948, Croydon, England. Professor. m. Valérie Lechene, 2 sons, 2 daughters. Education: B Soc Sc, University of Birmingham, 1970. Appointments: Research Associate, The Acton Society, 1970-71; Lecturer, Econometrics, Department of Economics, University of Birmingham, 1971-83; Head, 1987-90, 1996-98, Professor of Econometrics, 1984-99, Department of Economics, Visiting Professor, 2000-, University of Bristol; Professor of Economics, Department of Economics, University College London, 1999-; Research Fellow, Institute for Fiscal Studies, 1999-; Director, Centre for Microdata Methods and Practice, 2001-. Publications: Numerous articles in professional journals. Honours: Elected Fellow, British Academy; Elected Fellow, Econometric Society, 1999. Memberships: Fellow, Royal Statistical Society; Fellow, Econometric Society. E-mail: andrew.chesher@ucl.ac.uk

CHEUN Hyeng Il, b. 15 January 1968, Seoul, Republic of Korea. Government Official. m. Ji-Hyeun Kim, 2 daughters. Education: Master of Agriculture, Department of Bioresources Chemistry, Obihiro University, 1996; PhD, Agricultural Science, United Graduate School of Agricultural Science, Iwate, 1999. Appointments: Researcher, Department of Veterinary Microbiology, Obihiro University, 1999-2000;

Researcher, Japan Health Sciences Foundation, 1999-2001; Postdoctoral Researcher, Department of Molecular and Cell Biology, University of California at Berkeley, USA, 2001-02; Assistant Professor, National Research Center for Protozoan Diseases, Japan, 2003. Publications: Numerous articles in professional journals. Address: Division of Malaria & Parasitic Diseases, Korea National Institute of Health, 187 OsongSaengmyeong2-ro, Gangoe-myeon, Cheongnom-gun, Chungbuk 363-951, Korea.

CHEUNG Johnny Ka Wai, b. 24 March 1966, Hong Kong. Lawyer; Business Manager. Education: BA, Economics, University of Toronto, Canada, 1987; BA, Jurisprudence, University of Oxford, England, 1989; Bachelor of Laws, Dalhousie University, Canada, 1990; Master of Laws (with Merit), London School of Economics & Political Science, University of London, 1992-93; Master of Business Administration, INSEAD, France, 2002. Appointments: Associate, Clifford Chance International Law Firm; Associate, Linklaters & Paines, International Law Firm; Legal Counsel, Intercontinental Hotel Group plc; Legal Counsel, Exxonmobil Corporation; Management Consultant, Boston Consulting Group; Counselor to the Chairman, American International Group Companies in China; Regional General Counsel, AXA Asia Pacific. Publications: Reorganzing Chinese State-Owned Companies into Joint Stock Companies, 1995; Basic Law of Hong Kong and Business Investors After 1997, 1996; Selected Shareholdings in China, 1997; Corporate Governance Challenges in the USA and Asia, 2006; Shortcomings in China's Corporate Governance Regime, 2007. Honours: Judicial Pupil to Rt Hon Lord Justice Sir Martin Nourse & Rt Hon Lord Justice Sir Ralph Gibson of the Court of Appeal, England & Wales, 1992-93; Honorary Fellow, Center for International Legal Studies, Salzburg, Austria, 1995; Chairperson, Asia Pacific In-House Legal Counsel Summit on Improving Corporate Governance, 2006; Listed in international biographical dictionaries. Memberships: Oxford Society; Oxford & Cambridge Club; Law Society of England & Wales; Law Society of British Columbia, Canada; Law Society of Hong Kong; Hong Kong Junior Chamber of Commerce; Supreme Court of British Columbia, Canada; Supreme Court of England & Wales; High Court of Hong Kong. E-mail: johnnykwcheung@yahoo.com.hk

CHEUNG Kingman, b. 8 June 1965, Hong Kong. Professor. m. Soo Hing Maria Ng, 1 daughter. Education: PhD, Wisconsin, 1992. Appointments: Postdoctoral Fellow, UC-Davis, UT-Austin, Northwestern University, 1992-2000; Staff Scientist, 2000-03, Scientist, 2006-, National Center for Theoretical Sciences; Professor, National Tsing Hua University, 2004-. Publications: More than 130 articles in particles & fields journals. Honours: Fellow, Chinese Physical Society; NSC Outstanding Research Award, 2009. Memberships: American Physical Society; Chinese Physical Society. Address: Department of Physics, National Tsing Hua University, 101 Sec 2 Kuang Fu Road, Hsinchu, Taiwan. E-mail: cheung@phys.nthu.edu.tw

CHEUNG Kwok-Leung, b. 5 February 1963, Hong Kong. Surgeon. m. Loretta Po-Yin Fung, 1 son, 1 daughter. Education: MB BS, University of Hong Kong, 1987; DM, University of Nottingham, 2001. Appointments: House Officer, 1987-88, Honorary Clinical Lecturer, Surgery, Senior Medical Officer and Medical Officer, 1988-98, University of Hong Kong at Queen Mary Hospital, Tung Wah Hospital and the Grantham Hospital, Hong Kong; Medical Research Fellow, Division of Breast Surgery, University of Nottingham, Nottingham City Hospital, 1999-2001; Consultant Breast Surgeon, Nottingham City Hospital, 2001-04; Clinical Associate Professor, Division of Breast Surgery, University of Nottingham, 2004-; Honorary Consultant Breast Surgeon, 2004-, Head of Service, Breast Services, 2007-10, Cancer Lead Clinician for Breast Cancer, 2007-11, Nottingham University Hospitals. Publications: Numerous articles in professional journals. Honours: Clinical Excellence Award, Nottingham University Hospitals, 2004-; International Guest Scholar, American College of Surgeons, 2007; Nominee, National Teaching Fellowship for institutes of higher education, 2007; Nominee, Lord Dearing Award, University of Nottingham, 2007. Memberships: Fellow, Royal College of Surgeons of Edinburgh; Fellow, College of Surgeons of Hong Kong; Fellow, Hong Kong Academy of Medicine; Fellow, American College of Surgeons; European Society of Mastology; European Study Grou for Serum Tumour Markers in Breast Cancer; American Society of Clinical Oncology; British Association for Cancer Surgery; Association of Breast Surgery, BASO; European Society of Surgical Oncology; International Society of Geriatric Oncology; British Breast Group. Address: Nottingham University Hospitals City Hospital Campus, Hucknall Road, Nottingham, NG5 1PB, England. E-mail: kl.cheung@nottingham.ac.uk

CHEVALIER Tracy Rose, b. 19 October 1962, Washington, DC, USA. Writer. m. 1 son. Education: BA, Oberlin College, Ohio, 1984; MA, University of East Anglia, Norwich, England, 1994. Appointments: Former Reference Book Editor; Writer, 1997-. Publications: Novels: The Virgin Blue, 1997; Girl With a Pearl Earring, 1999; Falling Angels, 2001; The Lady and the Unicorn, 2003; Burning Bright, 2007; Remarkable Creatures, 2009. Honours: Barnes & Nobel Discover Award, 2000. Memberships: Fellow, Royal Society of Literature. Address: c/o Curtis Brown, 28-29 Haymarket, London SW1Y 4SP, England. E-mail: hello@tchevalier.com

CHEW Fong Peng, b. 21 November 1971, Malaysia. Lecturer. m. Lam Yook Woh, 2 daughters. Education: BA, 1996, MA, 1997, Diploma of Education, 1998, PhD, 2004, National University of Malaysia. Appointments: Teacher, Assunta National Secondary School, Petaling Jaya, Selongor, Malaysia, 1998-2000; Teacher, Taman Sri Muda National Secondary School, Shah Alam, Selangor, Malaysia, 2001-06; Senior Lecturer, University of Malaya, Kuala Lumpur, 2006-. Publications: 30 articles in international journals and local journals; 22 articles in conference proceedings; 10 book chapters; 6 translation works; 4 books. Honours: Excellent Service Award, University of Malaya, 2008; Silver Medal, International Invention, Innovation & Technology Exhibition, 2009; Bronze Medal, International Exposition of Research & Invention of Higher Learning, 2009; Silver Medal, Malaysia Technology Expo, 2010; Silver Medal, UM Expo, 2010. Memberships: International Association of Intercultural Communication Studies; Association of Translation & Creative Writing; Association of National Writer; Association of Social Science, Malaysia. Address: Department of Language & Literacy Education, Faculty of Education, University of Malaya, Lembah Pantai Road, 50603 Kuala Lumpur, Malaysia. E-mail: fpchew@um.edu.my, fpchew@yahoo.com

CHEYNET DE BEAUPRE Bertrand Rene Constantin, b. 7 November 1948, Lyon, France. Research Engineer. Education: MA; PhD, Thermodynamics. Appointments: Research Engineer, Thermodata; Administrator, SGTE. Publications: More than 100 scientific papers. Memberships: Cincinnati. Address: 131 rue des Marquis du Gresivandan, 38920 Crolles, France.

CHHABRA Jitender Kumar, b. 13 January 1972, Kurukshetra, India. Educator; Software Collaborator and Consultant; Researcher. m. Alka, 1 daughter. Education: B Tech, Computer Engineering, 2nd Rank Holder; M Tech, Computer Engineering, 1998; PhD, Software Engineering. Appointments: Software Engineer, Softek Limited, New Delhi, 1993; Teaching Faculty, Department of Computer Engineering, National Institute of Technology (formerly REC), Kurukshetra, Institution of National Importance, India, 1994-; Guide and Coach, ACM ICPC International Programming Contest, 2006-10; Guide of project selected among Best 20 Projects in IEEE-ICSE-SCORE contest, 2011. Publications: More than 60 publications in international and national journals and conferences including IEEE, Elsevier, ACM, Springer; Research paper accepted as a chapter in an international book published from the USA; Author, international book on Programming with C; Tricky Programming Problems, 2010. Honours: M Tech Gold Medal; B Tech, 2nd Topper; Open Debate Winner; Scholarship from Vth Class onwards until end of education; Best Project Award; Best Teacher's Honour, 2002-08; Honorary Master's Recognition Award; Best Presentation Award; Technical Session Chair Honour in USA, 2006; Honour of HP-Chair; Honour of Reviewer for World's most reputed journals; More than 40 keynote speeches; Invited expert at international and national conferences, universities and institutes. Memberships: Member, Board of Governors, ISTK & SMB Gita Society; Member, BOS and many other technical committees; Member, International Program & Advisory Boards of international bodies; Organizing Secretary of International Conference; Technical Expert for many universities and institutes; Consultant and collaboratory for software companies such as Hewlett Packard and Tata Consultancy Services; Computer Society of India; Indian Society of Technical Education; Haryana Vigyan Bharti. Address: Department of Computer Engineering, National Institute of Technology, Kurukshetra 136119, India. E-mail: jitenderchhabra@nitkkr.ac.in

CHHABRA Tarlok Singh, b. 1 February 1942, Shikhupura, India. Bank Executive. m. S Kaur, 1 son, 1 daughter. Education: MA; LLB; CAIIB; MBA; MIAM; MAIMA. Appointments: Bank Executive, largest bank on India, 36 years; Retired. Publications: Presented at annual conferences of the academies and professional associations. Honours: Fellow, Indian Academy of Social Sciences; Life Fellow, Indian Academy of Forensic Sciences; Member, All India Management Association; Fellow, Punjab Academy of Sciences; many others. Memberships: Life Member, Indian Institute of Banking & Finance, Bombay; Fellow, Indian Institute of Administrative Management. Address: 889 Sector 60, Phase 3/B2, Mohali, SAS Nagar, Chandigarh 160 059, India. E-mail: singhtarlok91@yahoo.com

CHHAJLANI Prakash, b. 18 May 1956, Indore, India.Consultant Cosmetic Plastic Surgeon. m. Asha, 1 son. Education: MBBS, MS, General Surgery; MCh, Plastic Surgery. Appointments: Consultant Cosmetic Plastic Surgeon. Publications: Papers published in various plastic surgery international journals; Chapter in Grab's Encyclopaedia of Flaps; Chapters in textbook for dental surgery. Honours: Glaxo Award for Original Research in Plastic Surgery, 1986; UICC (Geneva) Visiting Fellowship, Detroit, USA; Millard Visiting Fellowship, Miami, USA. Memberships: Interplast; Surgeons; Plastic Surgeons; Asthetic Surgeons; Burns; Cleft Lip & Palate Associations; Founder, School of Plastic Surgery & Cleft Lip & Palate Foundation. Address: Naidunia Campus, BLC Chhajlani Marg, Indore, 452009, MP, India. E-mail: pchhajlani@hotmail.com Website: www.cosmetic-plastic-surgeon.com

CHI Mijung, b. 5 July 1976, Korea. Ophthalmologist; Assistant Professor. m. Jinsung Moon, 1 daughter. Education: Master in Medicine, 2008; Doctor in Medicine, 2010; PhD, Gachon University, 2010. Appointments: Resident, 2001-05, Full time Instructor, 2006-08, Assistant Professor, 2008-, Ophthalmologic Department, Gachon University, Gil Hospital; Fellowship, Oculoplastic Department, Korea University, Ansan Hospital, 2005-06. Publications: Clinical analysis of benign eyelid and conjunctival tumors, 2006; Eyelid splitting with follicular ertivpation using a monopolar cautery for the treatment of trichiasis and distichiasis, 2007; Temporary unilateral neurogenic blephanoptosis after orbital medial wall reconstruction: 3 cases, 2008; A case of orbital lipom with exophthalmes and visual disturbance, 2009; An analysis of 733 surgically treated blowout fractures, 2010; Clinical study of single-suture inferior retractor repair for involutional entropian, 2009; Clinical study of endoscopic endonasal conjunctivary pcystorphinestomy with Jones tube placement, 2009; Effectiveness of canalicular laceration repair using monocanalicular intubation with monoka tubes, 2009; Efficacy of dye disappearance test and tear meniscus height in diagnosis and postoperative assessment of nasolacrimal duct obstruction, 2010. Memberships: Korean Ophthalmological Society; Korean Oculoplastic Society. Address: Department of Ophthalmology, Gachon University of Medicine and Science, 1198, Guwol-dong, Namdong-gu #1198, Incheon, 405-760, Korea. E-mail: cmj@gilhospital.com

CHIANG Chii-Chung Akcell, b. 18 September 1960, Taipei, Taiwan. Pioneer Scientist. m. Hui-Mei Liu, 1 son, 1 daughter. Education: BSc, Applied Mathematics, Chinese Culture University, Taiwan; MSc, Applied Mathematics/ Computer Option, University of Massachusetts, USA; PhD, Faculty of Computer Science & Information Technology, University of Malaya, Malaysia. Appointments: Assistant Professor, Tung Nun University; Executive Chair, MALES Abrain PBL Agent System Research Society; Executive Chair, Emotional Problem Diagnostical Center; Creator, AK-cell. Publications: Developing an intelligent system to acquire meeting knowledge in problem-based learning environment, 2006; Redesigning chat forum for critical thinking in a problem-based learning environment, 2004; Problem-Based e-Learning with Agents, 2010. Honours: Listed in international biographical dictionaries. Address: 2 Floor, No 19, Lane 117, Chung-Chen Road, Xin Dian City, Taipei 231, Taiwan, ROC. E-mail: akcellchiang@yahoo.com Website: http://akcell.no-ip.org

CHIANG Cheng-Wen, b. 24 October 1943, I-Lan, Taiwan. Cardiologist. m. Mei-Yu Yang, 2 sons. Education: Department of Medicine, College of Medicine, National Taiwan University, 1971. Appointments: Councilor, World Federation of Ultrasound in Medicine and Biology; President, Asian Federation of Societies of Ultrasound in Medicine and Biology; President, Asian Pacific Society of Cardiology; Immediate Past President, Taiwan Society of Cardiology; Professor, Department of Internal Medicine, Cathay General Hospital. Publications: 130 articles in peer-reviewed medical journals. Honours: Best Medical Physician Award, Chang Gung Memorial Hospital, 1977; Cheng-Shin Medical Award, Medical Association of Taiwan, 1979; Long Ting Award, Taiwan Society of Cardiology, 2001. Memberships: Fellow, American College of Cardiology; American Society of Echocardiography; Asian Pacific Society of Cardiology;

Taiwan Society of Internal Medicine; Taiwan Society of Cardiology; Taiwan Heart Foundation; Taiwan Society of Ultrasound in Medicine; Asian Federation of Society of Ultrasound in Medicine & Biology; World Federation of Society of Ultrasound in Medicine & Biology; Western Pacific Association of Critical Care Medicine, Taiwan; Formosan Medical Association. Address: 1st Fl, No 23, Lane 165, Kuang-Fu N Road, Taipei 10579, Taiwan. E-mail: cwchiang@cgh.org.tw

CHIDAN KUMAR C S, b. 31 August 1982, Mandya, India. Teacher; Researcher. Education: MSc; MPhil. Appointments: Lecturer. Publications: 40 articles in professional journals. Memberships: Life Member, Indian Crystallographic Association; Life Member, Indian Science Congress Association. Address: Bharathi College, Bharathi Nagar 571422, Mandya, Karnataka, India. E-mail: chidankumar@gmail.com

CHIKUSE Yasuko, b. 11 May 1943, Taiwan. Professor Emeritus. Education: BS, 1966, MS, 1968, Tsuda College; M Philosophy, 1972, PhD, 1974, Yale University, USA; DSc, Kyushu University, 1986. Appointments: Professor 1979-2007, Professor Emeritus, 2007, Kagawa University; Visiting Professor or Researcher: University of Pittsburgh, 1979-80; University of California at Santa Barbara, 1980-81; York University, University of Toronto, 1987-88; McGill University, 1990-91; Princeton University, 1991; University of St Andrews, England, 1996. Publications: Statistics on Special Manifolds, 2003; Many articles published in the international journals in mathematics and statistics. Memberships: Institute of Mathematical Statistics; Japan Statistical Society; Mathematical Society of Japan. Address: 2-9-1-1401, Fukuoka-cho, Takamatsu-shi, 760-0066, Kagawa-ken, Japan.

CHILD Dennis, b. 10 July 1932, Ulverston, England. Emeritus Professor of Educational Psychology; Author. m. Eveline Barton, 1 son, 1 daughter. Education: teachers' Certificate, St John's College, York, 1957; BSc, London, 1962; M Ed, Leeds, 1968; PhD, Bradford, 1973. Appointments: Teacher of General Science, Easingwold Comprehensive School, near York, 1957-59; Teacher of Physics and Chemistry, Bootham School, York, 1959-62; Lecturer in Physics, 1962-65, Senior Lecturer in Education, 1965-67, City of Leeds College of Education; Lecturer, 1967-73, Senior Lecturer, 1973-76, Psychology of Education, Postgraduate School of Studies of Research on Education, University of Bradford; Visiting Professorships: University of Illinois, USA, 1972, 1973; University of Yucatan, Merida, Mexico, (annually) 1979-89; Botswana and Malawi Teacher Training Colleges, 1980; University of Lisbon, Portugal, 1983; East China Normal University, Shanghai, 1987; Beijing Foreign Studies University, 1988; Professor and Head of School of Education, University of Newcastle upon Tyne, 1976-81; Professor of Educational Psychology, School of Education, 1981-92, Head of School, 1984-87, Emeritus Professor of Educational Psychology, School of Education, 1992-, University of Leeds; Author. Publications include: Some technical problems in the use of personality measures in occupational settings illustrated using the "Big Five" (book chapter), 1998; Painters of the Northern Counties of England and Wales, 1994, 2nd edition, 2002; The Yorkshire Union of Artists 1888-1922, 2001; Psychology and the Teacher, 7th edition (major revision), 2004, 8th edition, 2007; The Yorkshire Union of Artists 1888-1922 in Antique Collecting, 2004; Entry for James Lonsdale (1777-1839) in Dictionary of National Biography, 2004; Essentials of Factor Analysis, 3rd edition, 2006. Honours: OBE, 1997; Directions in Educational Psychology edited by Dianne Shorrocks-Taylor. An appreciation of the works of Dennis Child, 1998; Biography for Dennis Child in European Revue of Applied Psychology, 1999. Memberships: FBPsS; FCST; C Psychol; Past member of government and related bodies, as well as numerous organisations in the areas of medicine, education of the deaf and the performing arts. Address: The Cottage, Main Street, Scholes, Leeds LS15 4DP, England.

CHIN Yoong Kheong, b. 13 April 1958, Ipoh, Perak, Malaysia. Accountant. m. Yap Siew Pin, 2 sons, 1 daughter. Education: BA Hons 1st Class, Economics/Accounting, University of Leeds, England, 1979; Doctor of Business Administration, American University of Hawaii, USA, 1996. Appointments: Auditor assistant/Audit Senior, KPMG Leeds, England, 1979-82; Auditor Assistant, KPMG Kuala Lumpur, 1983; Tax Consultant/Partner, KPMG Tax, Kuala Lumpur, 1983-97; Joint General Director, KPMG Vietnam, 1992-97; Partner-in-charge, KPMG Consulting, Malaysia, 1997-2004; Director, KPMG Business Advisory, Malaysia, 2004-. Publications: ASEAN: A Link in Your Global Strategy; Malaysian Taxation 4th Edition; Malaysian Taxation Practice; The Water Tablet: Malaysian Water Reforms. Honours: Crabtree Prize for Top Economic Students, University of Leeds, 1977; Gerald Veale Prize for Top Accounting Graduate, University of Leeds, 1979; Merit Award Winner, Professional Examination of the Institute of Chartered Accountants in England and Wales, 1980. Memberships: Fellow of Institute of Chartered Accountants in England and Wales; Member of Malaysian Institute of Certified Public Accountants; Malaysian Institute of Taxation; Malaysian Institute of Arbitrators; Institute of Financial Consultants. Address: 73 Jalan Semarak Api, Sierramas Resort Homes, 47000 Sungai Bhloh, Selangor, Malaysia. E-mail: cyk@kpmg.com.my

CHINN Yuen Yuey, b. 24 December 1922, Canton, China. Art Educator; Painter. m. Theres Chow, 2 sons. Education: BFA, 1953, MFA, 1954, Studies with William Hayter, 1958, Columbia University. Appointments: Teacher, Art Study Abroad, Paris, France, 1968-69; Director, Recreation City of New York, 1974-93; Teacher, Art, Brooklyn College, 1974-2003. Publications: Creative works held in private and public collections and displayed in solo and group exhibitions around the world, 1953-. Numerous articles in professional journals. Honours: Brevoort Eickmeyer, 1952 and 1953; Fulbright, Italy, 1954-55; John Hay Whitney, 1956-57; Listed in international biographical dictionaries. Address: 80 North Moore St, Apt 15J, New York, NY 10013-2731, USA. E-mail: bbigyuen@yahoo.com

CHIRAC Jacques René, b. 29 November 1932, Paris, France. Politician. m. Bernadette Chodron de Courcel, 1956, 2 children. Education: Lycée Carnot; Lycée Louis-le-Grand, Paris; Institute of Political Science, Paris; Harvard University Summer School, USA. Appointments: Military Service, Algeria; Auditor, Cour des Comptes, 1959-62; Special Assistant, Government Secretariat General, 1962 Counsellor, Cour des Comptes, 1965-94; Secretary of State for Employment Problems, 1967-68; Secretary of State for Economy and Finance, 1968-71; Minister for Parliamentary Relations, 1971-72, for Agriculture and Rural Development, 1972-74, of the Interior, 1974; Prime Minister of France, 1974-76, 1986-88; Secretary General, Union des Démocrates pour la République (UDR), 1975, Honorary Secretary General, 1975-76; President, Rassemblement pour la République (formerly UDR), 1976-94, Honorary Secretary General, 1977-80; Mayor of Paris, 1977-95; President of France, 1995-2002; Re-elected President of France, 2002-2007. Publications: Discours pour la France a l'heure du choix; La lueur de l'espérance: Réflexion du soir pour le matin, 1978; Une Nouvelle France, Reflexion 1, 1994; La France pour tous, 1995. Honours include: Prix Louis Michel, 1986; Grand-Croix de la Légion d'Honneur; Grand Croix de l'Ordre National du Mérite; Chevalier du Mérite. Address: Palais de l'Eysée, 55-57 rue du Faubourg Saint-Honoré, 75008 Paris, France.

CHIRINO ARGENTA Marta, b. 12 June 1963, Madrid, Spain. Artist. m. Eduardo Rodríguez Pérez, 2 daughters. Education: Degree (Honours), Biology, Universidad Autónoma de Madrid, Spain; Postgraduate studies, Fine Arts Faculty, Madrid, 4 years; Further studies at drawing academies and Centre for Video and Image Studies, 3 years; Graphic Design, Professional School of New Technologies (CICE). Appointments: Royal Botanical Gardens, Madrid, 1987-; Artist and Graphic Designer; Solo and group exhibitions in Spain and England. Publications: Drawings published in numerous books and magazines; Illustrator of science and childrens books; Botanical illustrations for books and posters. Honours: Royal Horticultural Society Gold Medal, 1999; Certificate of Botanical Merit, 2010. Memberships: Member, Society of Botanical Artists, England. Address: Calle Reyes Magos 18, 28009 Madrid, Spain. E-mail: martachirino@hotmail.com Website: www.martachirino.com

CHISTOLINI Sandra, b. 2 November 1951, Italy. Professor. Education: Master's degree, Sociology, 1974, Doctor's degree, Sociology and Social Research, 1977, Master's degree, Psychology, 1981, La Sapienza University of Rome; Teacher Education, University of Edinburgh, 1984-85. Appointments: School teacher, Italy, 1970; Researcher in multidisciplinary equipe working in various institutions, 1976-92; Teacher training in several courses aimed to school innovation, 1977-80; School teacher in Scotland, UK, 1982-85; University appointment, Pedagogy, La Sapienza University of Rome, 1988; Co-operation in higher education distance-teaching and learning course, La Sapienza University of Rome, 1988-90; Associate Professor, School Pedagogy, University of Macerata, 1992-94; Associate Professor, Comparative Education and Experimental Pedagogy, University of Perugia, 1995-2001; Full Professor, General and Social Pedagogy, University of Roma Tre, 2001-12. Publications: Numerous books and articles in scientific and professional journals. Memberships: National Association of Teachers; CiCe, Children's Identity and Citizenship in Europe, Erasmus Academic Network and Cicea, Children's Identity and Citizenship European Association, London Metropolitan University. Address: via Manin 53, 00185 Roma, Italy. E-mail: schistolini@uniroma3.it

CHITESCU Ion, b. 19 July 1947, Bucharest, Romania. Professor of Mathematics. m. Rodica Chitescu, 2 daughters. Education: Licencié, Maths, 1970, PhD, Maths, 1975, University of Bucharest. Appointments: Assistant Professor, 1970-80, Lecturer, 1980-91, Associate Professor, 1991-2000, Professor, 2000-, Dean-, Faculty of Mathematics, University of Bucharest. Publications: Main books: Monograph: Function Spaces; Mathematical Analysis Dictionary (in collaboration); Measure Theory (in collaboration); 50 papers (research); Fields of interest: Vector Measures and Integration; Function Spaces; Random Sequences; Probability and Statistics; Optimization; Fractal Theory. Honours: Romanian National Academy Prize, for "Function Spaces", 1985. Memberships: American Mathematical Society; Mathematical Reviews Referee; Mathematical Reports Advisory Board. Address: Str Henri Coanda 44, Sector 1, Bucharest 010668, Romania.

CHITHAM Edward Harry Gordon, b. 16 May 1932, Harborne, Birmingham, England. Education Consultant. m. Mary Patricia Tilley, 1962, 1 son, 2 daughters. Education: BA, MA (Classics), Jesus College, Cambridge, 1952-55; PGCE, University of Birmingham, 1955-56; MA, English, University of Warwick, 1973-77; PhD, University of Sheffield, 1983. Publications: The Black Country, 1972, second expanded edition 2009; Ghost in the Water, 1973; The Poems of Anne Brontë, 1979; Brontë Facts and Brontë Problems (with T J Winnifrith), 1983; Selected Brontë Poems (with T J Winnifrith), 1985; The Brontës' Irish Background, 1986; A Life of Emily Brontë, 1987, revised edition 2010; Charlotte and Emily Brontë (with T J Winnifrith), 1989; A Life of Anne Brontë, 1991; A Bright Start, 1995; The Poems of Emily Brontë (with Derek Roper), 1996; The Birth of Wuthering Heights: Emily Brontë at work, 1998; A Brontë Family Chronology, 2003; Harborne: A History, 2004; Rowley Regis: A History, 2006; West Bromwich: A History, 2009. Contributions to: Byron Journal; Gaskell Society Journal; ISIS Magazine; Brontë Society Transactions. Memberships: Fellow, Royal Society of Arts, 1997. Joint Association of Classics Teachers; Gaskell Society; Brontë Society. Address: 25 Fugelmere Close, Harborne, Birmingham B17 8SE, England.

CHITU Cristian Ovidiu, b. 22 May 1969, Ploiesti, Romania. Electrical Engineering; Researcher. m. Marcela, 1 son. Education: Diploma, Electrical Engineering, Polytechnic University of Bucharest, Romania, 1993; MS, Electrical Engineering, Technical University of Montpellier, France, 1997; PhD, Science, Institute of Computer Science, Germany, 2000. Appointments: Design Engineer, ASIC Laboratory, Heidelberg, Germany, 1997-2000; MTS Research Scientist, Rockwell Science Center, Thousand Oaks, California, USA, 2000-01; Postdoctoral, University of California at Los Angeles, USA, 2001-02; Scientific Management, Institute of Microelectronic Systems, Darmstadt, Germany, 2002-03; Senior Design Engineer, Infineon Technologies Austria AG, Villach, Austria, 2004-. Publications: Numerous articles in professional journals; 1 book chapter. Honours: 1st Prize, Scientific Student Research Competition, Faculty of Electronics and Telecommunications, Bucharest, 1993; Fellowship, Scientific Research, Austrian Government, 1996; Fellowship, MS degree, French Government, 1996-97; Fellowship, PhD degree, Max-Planck-Institute, Heidelberg, 1997-2000; Top 10 Hottest Article, Microelectronics Journal, 2005; Scientific achievements announced in professional press; Listed in international biographical dictionaries. Memberships: IEEE; World Scientific and Engineering Society. Address: Villacher Schechtestrasse 2/3, A-9500 Villach, Austria. E-mail: cochitu@ieee.org

CHIU Tzu-Chien, b. July 1976, Taipei, Taiwan. Researcher; Geologist. Education: BSc, 1998, MSc, 2000, National Taiwan University, Taipei; Master of Philosophy, Doctor of Philosophy, Columbia University, New York, USA, 2005. Appointments: Columbia Science Fellow & Lecturer in Earth and Environmental Sciences, Columbia University, New York, USA, 2005-06; Postdoctoral Research Scientist, Lamont-Doherty Earth Observatory, New York, USA, 2005-07; Research Assistant Professor, Earth Dynamic System Research Center, National Cheng Kung University, Tainan, Taiwan, 2007; Assistant Research Fellow, Institute of Earth Sciences, Academia Sinica, Taipei, 2008-. Publications: Numerous articles in professional journals. Honours: Geological Scholarship, Ministry of Economic Affairs, Taiwan, 1995, 1996; Presidential Award, 1994-97, Director Honor, College of Science, 1998, National Taiwan University; Research Creativity Award for College Students, National

Science Council, Taiwan, 1998; Student Poster Competition Winner and Scholarship, Geological Society of China, Taiwan, 1999; International Student Travel Award for AGU Fall Meeting, American Geophysical Union, USA, 1999; Faculty Fellowship, Graduate School of Arts and Sciences, Columbia University, USA, 2000-05; Best Teaching Assistant Award, Department of Earth and Environmental Sciences, Columbia University, 2002-03; Columbia Postdoctoral Science Fellowship, Columbia University, 2005; Abrupt Climate Change Fellowship, Comer Science and Education Foundation, 2006; Listed in international biographical dictionaries. E-mail: tc423@columbia.edu

CHIZHOV Vladimir A, b. 3 December 1953, Moscow, Russia. Ambassador. m. Elena, 1 son, 1 daughter. Education: Graduated with honours, Moscow State Institute of International Relations, 1976. Appointments: Director, 3rd European Department, Ministry of Foreign Affairs, 1997-99; Russian Special Representative for Cyprus, 1997-2000; Director, European Co-operation Department, Ministry of Foreign Affairs, 1999-2002; Russian Special Representative for the Balkans, 2000-02; Deputy Minister, Foreign Affairs, 2002-05; Permanent Representative of the Russian Federation to the European Communities, Brussels, Belgium, 2005-10; Permanent Representative of the Russian Federation to the European Union and Euratom, Brussels, 2010-. Publications: Conducted analytical research work on European security, OSCE, Russia-EU and Russia-NATO relations, Mediterranean, Balkans, problems of Cyprus and Northern Ireland, UN peace-keeping operations. Honours: Order of Friendship, Russia; Commander of the Order of Merit, Grand Duchy of Luxembourg. Address: Boulevard du Regent 31-33, 1000 Bruxelles. E-mail: misrusce@numericable.be Website: www.russiamission.eu

CHKHARTISHVILI Levan S, b. 13 June 1957, Tbilisi, Georgia. Physicist. Education: MSc, Theoretical Physics, 1980; PhD, Solid State Physics, 1989; Dr Sci, Physics & Mathematics, Solid State Physics, 2006. Appointments: Professor, Department of Physics, Faculty of Informatics & Control Systems, Georgian Technical University; Researcher, Laboratory for Boron, Borides and Related Compounds, Ferdinand Tavadze Institute of Metallurgy & Materials Sciences. Publications: More than 120 scientific publications including: Quasi-Classical Theory of Substance Ground-State, Tbilisi, 2004; Iterative Solution of the Secular Equation, 2005; Boron nitride nanosystems of regular geometry, 2009. Honours: The Albert Einstein Award of Excellence, 2011. Memberships: Euro Science; American Chemical Society. Address: 11 Alexander Kazbegi Avenue, Tbilisi, 0160, Georgia. E-mail: chkharti2003@yahoo.com

CHO Byeong-Ok, b. 21 July 1968, Seoul, South Korea. Engineer; Researcher. m. Ji-Young Gho, 1 son. Education: BS, 1991, PhD, 1999, Seoul National University; Postdoctorate, University of California, Los Angeles, USA, 2003. Appointments: R&D Division, Semiconductor Business, Principal Engineer, Memory Division, Samsung Electronics, 2003-. Publications: Expression of the Si Etch Rate in a CF_4 Plasma with Four Internal Process Variables, 1999; Tuning the electrical properties of zirconium oxide thin films, 2002; Thermally Robust Multi-layer Non-Volatile Polymer Resistive Memory, 2006. Honours: MRS General Poster Session Award, 1997; Great Achievement, Samsung Electronics Memory Division Presidential Award, 2011. Memberships: AIP; AVS; ECS; MRS; IEEE. Address: Jugong-APT 211-306, Goduk-Dong, Gangdong-Gu, Seoul 134-757, South Korea. E-mail: byeongok.cho@samsung.com

CHO Chungho, b. 27 December 1967, Namwon-gun, Jeonbuk, Republic of Korea. Mechanical Engineer; Researcher. m. Dongeun Lee, 1 daughter. Education: BS, 1992, MS, 1994, PhD, 2002, Chungnam National University, Daejeon, Republic of Korea. Appointments: Assistant Teacher, Chungnam National University, Daejeon, Republic of Korea, 1996-98; Lecturer, Cheongyang College, Chungnam, Republic of Korea, 1998-2002; Lecturer, Chungnam National University, Daejeon, Republic of Korea, 1999-2002; Postdoctoral Researcher, 2002-2004, Senior Researcher, 2004-, Korea Atomic Energy Research Institute, Daejeon, Republic of Korea. Publications: Articles in scientific journals. Honours: Listed in international biographical dictionaries. Memberships: Research Board of Advisors, ABI. Address: Korea Atomic Energy Research Institute, 1045 Daedeok-daero, Yuseong-Gu, Daejeon 305-353, Republic of Korea. E-mail: chcho@kaeri.re.kr

CHO Ho-Chan, b. 13 June 1973, Daegu, Korea. Professor; Doctor. m. Ji-Eun Park. Education: MD, School of Medicine, 1998, MS, 2006, PhD, 2008, Graduate School, Keimyung University, Daegu. Appointments: Assistant Professor, Keimyung University School of Medicine, Keimyung University Dongsan Hospital. Publications: 7 articles in professional journals. Honours: Award of Excellent Presentation in annual spring scientific meeting, Korean Endocrine Society, 2007. Memberships: The Endocrine Society; Korean Association of Internal Medicine; Korean Endocrine Society; Korean Diabetes Association; Korean Thyroid Association; Korean Society of Bone Metabolism. Address: 56 Dalsung-Ro, Jung-Gu, Daegu, 700-712, South Korea. E-mail: ho3632@naver.com

CHO Ilkwon, b. 21 January 1974, Republic of Korea. Researcher. m. Yeonhee Park, 1 daughter. Education: BS, 1996, MS, 1998, Electronic Engineering, Hanyang University, Korea; PhD, Computer Science and Communication Engineering, Kyushu University, Japan, 2010. Appointments: Senior Research Scientist, LG Cable Co, Seoul, 1998-2001; Research Scientist, Ringnet and Fowiz Co, Seoul, 2001-03; Principal Reseracher, National Information Society Agency, Seoul, 2003-. Honours: Commendation from Chairman of Korea Communication Commission, 2010. Address: 101-409 Banghwa Hyundai Apt, Gangseo, Seoul 157-855, Korea.

CHO Jae Hwan, b. 10 February 1977, Seoul, South Korea. Professor. Education: Radiological License; Master of Engineering; Professor, Department of Radiologic Technology, 2010. Appointments: Radiological Technologist, Department of Radiology, Soonchunhyang University, Bucheon Hospital; Professor, Department of Radiologic Technology, Gyeongsan University College. Publications: Korean Journal of Medical Physics; Journal of Digital Contents Society; Journal of the Korean Society of MR Technology. Honours: Listed in international biographical dictionaries. Address: Department of Radiological Science, Hallym University of Graduate Studies, 427, Yeoksam-ro, Gangnampgu, Seoul 135-841, Republic of Korea. E-mail: 8452404@hanmail.net

CHO Jinsung, b. 10 November 1969, Seoul, Korea. Professor. m. Eunjung Han, 2 sons. Education: BS, 1992, MS, 1994, PhD, 2000, Computer Engineering, Seoul National University. Appointments: Visiting Scholar, IMB T J Watson Research Center, 1998; Senior Engineer, Samsung Electronics Ltd, 1999-2003; Associate Professor, Kyung Hee University, 2003-; Visiting Professor, Oregon State University, 2009. Publications: 68 international journal/conference papers including: A dynamic CFP allocation and opportunity contention-based WBAN MAC protocol; 16 international patents including: Method and system for fast handover of Mobile IP between different networks. Honours: Summa cum laude, Seoul National University, 1992. Memberships: IEEE: IEICE; KIISE; KIPS; KICS. Address: Daewoo Worldmark 101-1801, Yeongtong-dong, Yeongtong-gu, Suwon-si, Gyeonggi-do 443-851, Korea. E-mail: chojs@khu.ac.kr

CHO Yong-Baik, b. 10 November 1960, Seoul, Korea. New Drug Research Scientist. m. Ji-Hey Kim, 1 son, 1 daughter. Education: BS, Pharmacy, 1982, MS, 1984, PhD, 1997, Pharmacology, Chung Ang University, Seoul. Appointments: Researcher, Chongkundang Pharma, Seoul, 1984-88; Researcher, Vice President, SK Chemicals, Suwon, 1989-2007; CTO, Whan In Pharmaceuticals, Suwon, 2008-. Publications: Over 30 articles in professional journals. Honours: Best Inventor, Korea Intellectual Property Office, 1996; Best Researcher, Korea Health Industrial Development Institute, 2005; Listed in international biographical dictionaries. Memberships: Pharmaceutical Society of Korea; Korean Society of Applied Pharmacology; Korean Society of Toxicology; Korean Society of Pharmacognosy. Address: Central Research Institute, Whan In Pharmaceuticals, 906-5, Iui-Dong, Yeongton-Gu, Suwon-Si, Gyeonggi-Do, 443-766, Korea. E-mail: ybcho59@naver.com

CHO Young Bok, b. 6 August 1959, Incheon city, Korea. Entomological Researcher. m. Hyun Joo Jung, 1 son, 1 daughter. Education: BA, Biology, Hannam University, 1982; MSc, Biology, Graduate School, Hannam University, 1984; PhD, Graduate School, Kyungpook National University, 1989; Postdoctoral Fellow, Entomology, Manitoba University, Canada, 1992-94. Appointments: Researcher, Natural History Museum, Hannam University, 1998-; Additional Professor, Department of Biology, Kyungsan University, 1998-2000; Additional Professor, Department of Biology, Chunnam National University, 2007-09; Editor-in-Chief, Journal of Korean Nature, 2008-09. Publications: Numerous articles in professional journals. Honours: Listed in international biographical dictionaries. Memberships: Entomological Society of Korea; Korean Society of Systematic Zoology; Korean Society of Integrative Biology; Korean Society of Applied Entomology. Address: Natural History Museum, Hannam University, 133 Ojeong-dong, Daedeok-gu, Daejeon 306-791, Korea. E-mail: youngcho@hnu.kr

CHO YoungJun, b. 21 April 1963, Jinju City, Korea. Professor. m. MiMi, 2 daughters. Education: Bachelor, 1986, Master, 1991, Seoul National University; Doctor, University of Seoul, 2002. Appointments: Researcher, KICT, CCC, CN and Sungchang Patent. Publications: Construction Management & Engineering, Kimoondang, Seoul, 2003; Characteristics of Contractor's Liabilities for defect and defective work in Korean Public Projects, 2004; Construction Contract Management, 2010. Memberships: AIK; KICEM; KIC. Address: 129-41, Chowondong, Jangangu, Suwon, Kyeongkido, 440-220, Republic of Korea. E-mail: claimz@hanmail.net

CHOI Hwan-Suk Chris, b. 3 September 1967, WonJu, Republic of Korea. Professor. 1 son, 1 daughter. Education: BA, Chung-Ang University, Seoul, 1991; MTA, George Washington University, USA, 1995; PhD, Texas A&M University, USA, 2003. Appointments: Assistant Project Manager, Lowe Engineering, Seoul, 1990-91; Professional Tour Conductor, Miju Travel Inc, Washington DC, USA, 1994; Marketing Director, International Marketing Development Inc, Laurel, Maryland, 1994-96; Research Assistant, 1999, 2001-03, Graduate Teaching Assistant, 1998-2001, Department of Recreation, Park & Tourism Sciences, Texas A&M University; US Branch Representative, Pacific Amusements Inc, Seoul, 1997-2003; Assistant Professor, School of Hospitality and Tourism Management, University of Guelph, Canada, 2003-08; Associate Professor, 2008-, Visiting Professor, 2009-10, Korea Culture and Tourism Institute, Seoul. Publications: Numerous articles in professional journals; 2 books. Honours: Certificate of Commendation, Secretary of Department of Education, Republic of Korea, 1988; Gamma Sigma Delta, 2000; Gene Phillips Scholarship in Tourism Management, Texas Travel Industry Association and Department of Recreation, Park & Tourism Sciences, 2000; New Opportunities Fund Award, Canadian Foundation for Innovation, 2005; TOSOK Excellent Research Paper Award, 2010; Best Paper Award, iHITA 2011 Conference. Memberships: Tourism Sciences Society of Korea; Travel and Tourism Research Association International; TTRA Canada Chapter; International Society of Six Sigma Professionals; Asian Pacific Tourism Association.

CHOI Jae Seok, b. 1 May 1975, Incheon, Korea. Postdoctoral Researcher. Education: BS, 2002, MS, 2005, PhD, 2009, Department of Mechanical Engineering, Yonsei University. Appointments: Researcher, Center for Information Storage Device, Yonsei University; Postdoctoral Researcher, Kyoto University, 2009-. Publications: Design of Halbach magnet array based on optimization techniques, 2008; Topology optimization using a reaction-diffusion equation, 2011. Honours: JSPS Postdoctoral Fellowship for Foreign Researchers, Japan Society for the Promotion of Science, 2009. Memberships: Korean Society of Mechanical Engineers; International Society for Structural and Multidisciplinary Optimization. Address: Department of Mechanical Engineering and Science, Kyoto University, Yoshida-honmachi, Sakyo-ku, Kyoto 606-8501, Japan. E-mail: jschoi.ok@gmail.com

CHOI Jeong Ryeol, b. 21 March 1963, Kyeongju, Republic of Korea. Professor in Physics. Education: BS, Hankuk University of Foreign Studies, Yongin, Republic of Korea, 1989-93; MS, 1993-95, PhD, 1996-2001, Korea University, Seoul, Republic of Korea. Appointment: Professor, Department of Physics and Advanced Materials Science, Sun Moon University, Asan, Republic of Korea, 2003-08; Researcher, National Institute for Mathematical Sciences, Daejeon, Republic of Korea, 2008-09. Publications: Quantum analysis for the evolution of the cosmological constant via unitary transformation, 2007; Articles in scientific journals: Invariant operator theory for the single-photon energy in time-varying media, 2010; Interpreting quantum states of electromagnetic field in time-dependent linear media, 2010. Address: Department of Radiologic Technology, Daegu Health College, Taejeon 1-dong, Buk-gu, Daegu 702-722, Republic of Korea. E-mail: choiardor@hanmail.net

CHOI Kyoung-Kyu, b. 26 February 1971, Jinju, Kyoungnam, Republic of Korea. Professor. m. Eun-Kyoung Hong, 1 son, 1 daughter. Education: BS, 1999, MS, 2001, PhD, 2004, Seoul National University. Appointments: Postdoctoral Research Associate, University of Michigan, USA, 2004-05; Research Assistant Professor, University of New Mexico, USA, 2006-07; Professor, Civil Engineering, WongKwang University, Republic of Korea, 2009; Professor, School of Architecture, Soongsil University, Seoul, 2009-. Publications: Over 40 peer-reviewed papers including: Evaluation of Inelastic Deformation Capacity of Beams Subjected to Cyclic Loading, 2010. Honours: Young Researchers Award,

Korean Concrete Institute, 2001; Chester Paul Siess Awards, American Concrete Institute, 2009 and 2012. Memberships: Korean Concrete Institute; American Concrete Institute. Address: School of Architecture, Soongsil University, 369 Sangdo-Ro, Dongjak-gu, Seoul 156-743, Republic of Korea. E-mail: kkchoi@ssu.ac.kr

CHOI Suk Soon, b. 8 July 1963, Seoul, Republic of Korea. Associate Professor. m. Yeon Hee Park, 2 sons. Education: PhD, Seoul National University, 1999. Appointments: Researcher, Oriental Chemical Industry Research Centre, 1990-91; Assistant Professor, Youngin Songdam College, 1995-2001; Associate Professor, Semyung University, 2001-. Publications: 1 patent; Article in professional journal; Book, Calculation of Chemical and Environmental Process. Honours: Paper Presentation of Conference, Korean Society of Environmental Engineers, 2004, 2005; Contribution to Korean Society of Organic Resource Association, 2007. Memberships: Korean Society of Industrial & Engineering Chemistry; Journal of Korean Industrial & Engineering Chemistry; Listed in international biographical dictionaries. Address: Department of Biological and Environmental Engineering, Semyung University, Jecheon 390-711, Republic of Korea. E-mail: sschoi@semyung.ac.kr

CHOI Tae-Ji, b. 23 September 1959, Kyoto, Japan. Director; Artistic Director. 2 daughters. Education: Graduate, Dongmuhak High School, Japan, 1977; Graduate, Department of French Language & Literature, Bunka Gakuin University, Japan, 1981; Franchetti Ballet Academy, France, 1981-82; Joffrey Ballet School, USA, 1985-87; Graduate, Department of Japanese Studies, Seoul Digital University, 2006; CEO programme, Graduate School of Business, Dankook University, 2006; Honorary Doctorate, Pedgogy, Irkutsk State University, Russia, 2012. Appointments: Dancer, Gaitani Ballet Academy, Japan, 1968-80; Principal, 1987-92, Ballet Mistress, 1993-95, Director and Artistic Director, 1996-2001, 2008-10, 2011-, Principal of Ballet Academy, 2000-01, 2008-, Korean National Ballet; Chief Instructor, Cultural School, Korean National Ballet, 1993-95; Adjunct Professor, Department of Dance, Sungkyunkwan University, 2001-08; General Director, Chongdong Theater, 2004-07; Board Member, Jung-gu Cultural Foundation, 2004-06; Member, Presidential Committee, Government Innovation & Decentralization, 2005-06; Permanent Member, National Unification Advisory Council, 2005-07; Member, Council of Management, Construction Fund for Nodeul Island Cultural Center, Seoul, 2006; Member, Committee on Promotion of the Value of Basic Art, Arts Council Korea, 2007; Member, Dance Committee, Arts Council Korea, 2007. Publications: Book, Ballet, How Enjoyable It Is!, 2005; Numerous articles in professional journals. Honours: Prima Ballerina Prize, Korea Ballet Association, 1996; Achievement Award, 2002; Arts, Culture and Sports Prize, Seoul, 2005; Award, National Unification Advisory Council, 2006; Paradise Prize, Department of Arts & Culture, 2008; Achievement Award, Dankook University, 2008; Cultural Prize, Federation of Korean Arts and Culture Association, 2009; Best Leader Prize, Perm Arabesque Competition, Russia, 2010; Letter of Appreciation, 2010; Okgwan Order of Cultural Merits, 2011. Memberships: World Dance Alliance, Korea; Korea Ballet Association; Dance Association of Korea; Seoul Foundation for Arts and Culture; and many others. Address: Korea National Ballet, 4th Fl, Seoul Calligraphy Art Centre, Nambu Loop Line 2406, Seocho-Gu, Seoul, Korea. E-mail: taejichoi3@hotmail.com

CHOI Woon-Seop, b. 24 December 1959, Seoul, Korea. Professor. m. Eunok Kim, 1 daughter. Education: BS, 1982, MS, 1984, Seoul National University; PhD, University of Akron, USA, 1997. Appointments: Research Associate, University of Arizona, USA, 1997-2000; Principle Researcher, R&D Center, Samsung SDI, 2000-05; Professor, Hoseo University, 2005-. Publications: Numerous articles in professional journals. Honours: Academic Award, KIEEME, 2010; Listed in international biographical dictionaries. Memberships: Material Research Society; Society for Information Displays; Displays; KIDS; Polymer Society of Korea; KIEEME; Korea Physical Society; SPIE; ECS. Address: Department of Display Engineering (NewIT, Rm506), 165 Sechul-ri, Babang, Hoseo University, Asan-city, Chungnam 336-795, Republic of Korea. E-mail: wschoi@hoseo.edu

CHOMSKY (Avram) Noam, b. 7 December 1928, Philadelphia, Pennsylvania, USA. Linguist; Philosopher; Professor; Author. m. Carol Doris Schatz, 24 December 1949, 1 son, 2 daughters. Education: BA, 1949, MA, 1951, PhD, 1955, University of Pennsylvania. Appointments: Assistant Professor, 1955-58, Associate Professor, 1958-61, Professor of Modern Languages, 1961-66, Ferrari P Ward Professor of Modern Languages and Linguistics, 1966-76, Institute Professor, 1976-, Massachusetts Institute of Technology; Visiting Professor, Columbia University, 1957-58; National Science Foundation Fellow, Institute for Advanced Study, Princeton, New Jersey, 1958-59; Resident Fellow, Harvard Cognitive Studies Center, 1964-65; Linguistics Society of America Professor, University of California at Los Angeles, 1966; Beckman Professor, University of California at Berkeley, 1966-67; John Locke Lecturer, Oxford University, 1969; Shearman Lecturer, University College, London, 1969; Bertrand Russell Memorial Lecturer, Cambridge University, 1971; Nehru Memorial Lecturer, University of New Delhi, 1972; Whidden Lecturer, McMaster University, 1975; Huizinga Memorial Lecturer, University of Leiden, 1977; Woodbridge Lecturer, Columbia University, 1978; Kant Lecturer, Stanford University, 1979; Jeanette K Watson Distinguished Visiting Professor, Syracuse University, 1982; Pauling Memorial Lecturer, Oregon State University, 1995. Publications: Syntactic Structures, 1957; Current Issues in Linguistic Theory, 1964; Aspects of the Theory of Syntax, 1965; Cartesian Linguistics, Topics in the Theory of Generative Grammar, 1966; Language and Mind, Sound Patterns of English (with Morris Halle), 1968; American Power and the New Mandarins, 1969; At War with Asia, 1970; Problems of Knowledge and Freedom, 1971; Studies on Semantics in Generative Grammar, 1972; For Reasons of State, The Backroom Boys, Counterrevolutionary Violence (with Edward Herman), 1973; Peace in the Middle East?, Bains de Sang (with Edward Herman), 1974; Reflections on Language, The Logical Structure of Linguistic Theory, 1975; Essays on Form and Interpretation, 1977; Human Rights and American Foreign Policy, 1978; Language and Responsibility, The Political Economy of Human Rights (with Edward Herman), 2 volumes, 1979; Rules and Representations, 1980; Radical Priorities, Lectures on Government and Binding, 1981; Towards a New Cold War, Some Concepts and Consequences of the Theory of Government and Binding, 1982; Fateful Triangle: The United States, Israel and the Palestinians, 1983; Modular Approaches to the Study of the Mind, 1984; Turning the Tide, 1985; Barriers, Pirates and Emperors, Knowledge of Language: Its Nature, Origin and Use, 1986; Generative Grammar: Its Basis, Development and Prospects, On Power and Ideology, Language in a Psychological Setting, Language and Problems of Knowledge, The Chomsky Reader, 1987; The Culture of Terrorism, Manufacturing Consent (with

Edward Herman), Language and Politics, 1988; Necessary Illusions, 1989; Deterring Democracy, 1991; Chronicles of Dissent, What Uncle Sam Really Wants, 1992; Year 501: The Conquest Continues, Rethinking Camelot: JFK, the Vietnam War, and US Political Culture, Letters from Lexington: Reflections on Propaganda, The Prosperous Few and the Restless Many, 1993; Language and Thought, World Orders, Old and New, 1994; The Minimalist Program, 1995; Powers and Prospects, 1996; The Common Good, Profit over People, 1998; The New Military Humanism, 1999; New Horizons in the Study of Language and Mind, Rogue States: The Rule of Force in World Affairs, A New Generation Draws the Line, Architecture of Language, 2000; 9-11, 2001; Understanding Power, On Nature and Language, 2002; Middle East Illusions, Hegemony or Survival: America's Quest for Global Dominance, 2003; Contributions to: Scholarly journals. Honours: Distinguished Scientific Contribution Award, American Psychological Association, 1984; George Orwell Awards, National Council of Teachers of English, 1987, 1989; Kyoto Prize in Basic Science, Inamori Foundation, 1988; James Killian Faculty Award, Massachusetts Institute of Technology, 1992; Lannan Literary Award, 1992; Joel Selden Peace Award, Psychologists for Social Responsibility, 1993; Homer Smith Award, New York University School of Medicine, 1994; Loyola Mellon Humanities Award, Loyola University, Chicago, 1994; Helmholtz Medal, Akademie der Wissenschaft, Berlin-Brandenburg, 1996; Benjamin Franklin Medal, Franklin Institute, Philadelphia, 1999; Rabinranath Tagore Centenary Award, Asiatic Society, 2000; Peace Award, Turkish Publishers Association, 2002; Many honorary doctorates. Memberships: American Academy of Arts and Sciences; American Association for the Advancement of Science, fellow; American Philosophical Association; Bertrand Russell Peace Foundation; British Academy, corresponding member; Deutsche Akademie der Naturforscher Leopoldina; Linguistics Society of America; National Academy of Sciences; Royal Anthropological Institute; Utrecht Society of Arts and Sciences. Address: 15 Suzanne Road, Lexington, MA 02420, USA.

CHON Heesoo, b. 4 May 1967, Seoul, Korea. Researcher. m. Munhwan Kim. Education: BA, Agriculture, Chung-Ang University, Seoul, 1990; MSc, Botany, Biological Science, Auckland University, New Zealand, 1996; PhD, Immunology, Seoul National University, Seoul, 2009. Appointments: Senior Researcher, R&D Department, Microbia Co Ltd, 2000-05; Chief Researcher, R&D Department, Milae Resources ML Co Ltd, 2005-11; Project Manager, Bio Business Department, Dongbu Hannong, 2011-. Publications: Avian Pathology, Vol 37, 2008; Journal of Applied Microbiology, Vol 107, 2009; Comparative Immunology, Microbiology and Infectious Diseases, Vol 33, 2010; Microbiology and Immunology, 2010; Natural Product Communications, Vol 5, 2010; Studies in Natural Products Chemistry, 2012. Honours: Listed in biographical dictionaries. Memberships: Microbiological Society of Korea; Korean Society of Food Science & Technology; Korean Society of Pharmacy; Korean Society of Microbiology and Biotechnology. Address: 135-840, Dongbu Hannong Co Ltd, 4F Nobel Building, 891-44, Daechi-dong Gangnam-gu, Seoul, Korea. E-mail: kini132@dongbu.com

CHONG Nak Young, b. 19 April 1965, Wonju, Korea. Professor. m. Dou Hee Oh, 2 daughters. Education: BS, 1987, MS, 1989, PhD, 1994, Hanyang University, Korea. Appointments: Senior Researcher, Daewoo Heavy Industries Limited, Korea, 1994-98; Postdoctoral Fellow, MEL, Japan, 1995-96; Research Associate, KIST, Korea, 1998; Research Fellow, AIST, Japan, 1998-2003; Researcher, MSTC, Japan, 2000; Senior Researcher, Hanyang University, 1998-2005; Visiting Scholar, Northwestern University, America, 2001-02; Associate Professor, Japan Advanced Institute of Science and Technology, 2003-; Visiting Professor, Georgia Institute of Technology, USA, 2008-09; Visiting Professor, University of Genoa, Italy, 2010; Director, JAIST Center for Intelligent Robotics, 2011-. Publications include: A Collaborative Multi-site Teleoperation over an ISDN, 2003; Multioperator Teleoperation of Multirobot Systems with Time Delay, Part I, Part II; Presence: Teleoperators and Virtual Environments, 2002; Direction Sensing RFID Reader for Mobile Robot Navigation, 2009; Biologically Inspired Robotic Systems Control: Multi-DOF Robotic Arm Control, 2010; Handbook of Research on Ambient Intelligence and Smart Environments: Trends and Perspectives, IGI Global, 2011. Honours: Co-Chair, IEEE Robotics and Automation Society's Technical Committee on Networked Robots; Co-Chair, Fujitsu Scientific System Colloquium Robotics WG; Most Active Technical Committee Award, IEEE Robotics and Automation Society, 2005; 2008 Award for Excellence in Physical Sciences and Mathematics, Association of American Publishers, 2009; IEEE Technical Expert, 2009-; Associate Editor, IEEE Transactions on Robotics, 2009-; Associate Editor, International Journal of Assistive Robotics and Systems, 2009-; Editor, IEEE Conference on Automation Science & Engineering, 2010-; Best Paper Award, URAI, 2010; Best Paper Award, IRIS, 2010; Associate Editor, Springer Journal of Intelligent Service Robotics, 2011-; Editor, IEEE International Conference on Robotics & Automation, 2012-; Best Paper Award, SICE, 2012. Memberships: IEEE; RSJ; SICE; KROS; KSME; KIEE; ICASE; Steering Committee Member, IEEE CASE. Address: School of Information Science, Japan Advanced Institute of Science and Technology, 1-1 Asahidai, Nomi, Ishikawa 923-1292, Japan. E-mail: nychong@ieee.org; Web: http://www.jaist.ac.jp/robot

CHOPE John Norman, b. 27 June 1948, Birmingham, England. Dental Surgeon. m. Susan Mary Le Page, 1 daughter. Education: BSc (Hons), Physiology, 1969, BDS (Hons) Bristol University Faculty of Medicine, Department of Physiology and Dental School, 1966-72; LDS RCS Eng, Royal College of Surgeons of England, 1972; MFGDP (UK) RCS Eng, Royal College of Surgeons of England, 1992. Appointments include: Trainee Dental Technician, 1965, Dental Pathology Research Technician, University of Birmingham, 1966; Neurophysiologist, USA, Sudan, 1969, 1973; Senior House Officer, Oral Surgery, United Bristol Hospitals, 1973; Associate Dental Surgeon, Backwell, Somerset, 1973, Stockwood, Bristol and Shepton Mallet, Somerset, 1973-74; Principal Dental Surgeon and Dental Practice Owner, Holsworthy, Devon, 1974-, Hartland, Devon, 1975-, Bude, Cornwall, 1981-90, Okehampton, Devon, 1983-98; Consultant, VDC plc (Veterinary Drug Company), 1996-98; Member, British Dental Association Research Foundation Committee, 1997-2000; National Council Member, 1989-2004, Chairman, 1995-2004, Confederation of Dental Employers; National Council Member, Dental Practitioners Association, 2004-08; Elected Member, 1996-2009, Chairman of Standards Committee, 2005-08, Investigating Committee Member, 2003-, General Dental Council; Member, Dental Technologists Association Education Committee, 2003-09; Editorial Board Member, Dentistry, 2000-; Justice of the Peace, 1993-; Expert Professional Panel Member, Family Health Services Appeal Authority, 2001-10; Expert Professional Member, Health Education and Social Care Chamber of the First Tier Tribunal, 2010-. Publications: Recording from taste receptors stimulated by vascular route, 1969; Dental Practice Guide to the Therapeutic Laser, 1995;

A Look at Bodies Corporate, 1997; Numerous articles in dental journals, 1974-. Honours: Duke of Edinburgh's Gold Award; Associate Dental Company Scholarships, University of Bristol, 1966-67, 1969-72; Medical Research Council Award, Bristol University, 1967-69 L E Attenborough Medal, 1972, The George Fawn Prize, 1972, Bristol University. Memberships include: British Dental Association; Medical Protection Society; Magistrates Association; Country Landowners Association; Fellow, Royal Society of Medicine; Faculty of General Dental Practitioners(UK) Royal College of Surgeons of England. Address: Penroses Dental Practice, Bodmin Street, Holsworthy, Devon EX22 6BB, England.

CHOPRA Ramesh, b. 8 April 1946, Lahore, Pakistan. Publishing Director. m. Neena, 1973, 2 sons. Education: BSc, Delhi University, 1966; B Tech, IIT, Madras, 1969. Appointments: Editor, Electronics For You, New Delhi, 1969-; Managing Director, EFY Enterprises Pvt Ltd, New Delhi, 1979-. Publications: Numerous articles in professional journals; Publisher of several magazines, books and directories. Honours: Kohinoor of India Award, All India Achievers Conference, 2006; Bhartiya Udyog Ratna Award, Council for Economic Growth and Research, 2008. Memberships: Fellow, Institute of Electronics and Telecommunication Engineers. Address: D 87/1, Okhla Industrial Area, Phase-I, New Delhi – 110020, India. E-mail: efymd@efyindia.com

CHOU Hsiu-Jung, b. 24 July 1969, Taiwan. Associate Professor. Education: BS (magna cum laude), 1992, MBA (High Honours), 1993, Oklahoma City University, USA; PhD, Management, National Yunlin University of Science and Technology, 2008. Appointments: International Marketing Co-ordinator, Accton Technology Corporation, Hsinchu, Taiwan, 1993-94; Instructor, Cheng Shiu University, Kaohsiung, Taiwan, 1995-2009; Associate Professor, Cheng Shiu University, Kaohsiung, Taiwan, 2009-. Publications: 12 Taiwan Utility Model Patents, 2010-. Honours: 2 Great Masters Awards, Taiwan Project Management Association, 2009, 2010; Listed in international biographical dictionaries. Memberships: Project Management Institute. E-mail: chou724@yahoo.com

CHOU Pao-Nan, b. 4 June 1979, Hsinchu City, Taiwan ROC. Professor. m. Ya-Ling Wu, 1 daughter. Education: BS, Electronic Engineering, 2001, BS, Teacher Education, 2003, MED, Vocational and Technological Education, 2003, National Taipei University of Technology, Taiwan; MED, 2007, PhD, 2009, Instructional Systems, Pennsylvania State University, USA. Appointments: Post-doctoral Researcher, Cheng Shiu University, Taiwan, 2009-10; Assistant Professor, National University of Tainan, Taiwan, 2010-. Honours: Outstanding Research Fellowship, National Science Council, Taiwan, 2010-12; Listed in biographical dictionaries. Memberships: American Society of Engineering Education; Association of Taiwan Engineering Education and Management; Informing Science Institute. E-mail: pnchou@mail.nutn.edu.tw

CHOUDHARY Mahendra Pratap, b. 5 November 1974, Kosana, Jodhpur, Rajasthan, India. Engineer. m. Manisha, 1 son, 1 daughter. Education: BE (Hons), Civil Engineering, 1996; ME, Environmental Engineering, 2002; PhD, Civil Engineering, 2006; MA, Sociology, 2008. Appointments: Assistant Engineer, Public Health Engineering Department, Government of Rajasthan, India. Publications: More than 12 research papers published in engineering journals; Author, Water Hyacinth Treatment of Industrial Wastewater, 2011. Honours: Listed in international biographical dictionaries; Gold Medalist, MA Sociology; Marquis Who's Who in the World, 2009, 2010; Top 100 Engineers, 2009; Top 100 Educators, 2009; International Engineer of the Year, 2010; International Educator of the Year, 2010; International Plato Award for Educational Achievement, IBC; Man of the Year, India, 2009; Gold Medal for India; International Peace Prize, American Order of Merit, 2010, ABI, USA; Man of Achievement, 2011. Address: 9A Panchwati Colony, Ratanada, Jodhpur, Rajasthan, PIN – 342001, India. E-mail: choudhary_mp@yahoo.co.in

CHOUGH Chungkee, b. 5 November 1965, Seoul, Republic of Korea. Neurosurgeon; Educator. m. Youngah Choi, 1992, 2 children. Education: MD, Catholic University of Korea, Seoul, 1990; PhD, 2002; Licence in Korean Medicine, certified Korean Board of Medical Examiners, 1990; Korean Board of Neurological Surgey, 1995. Appointments: Internship & Neurosurgical Resident, Seoul St Mary's Hospital, Republic of Korea, 1990-95; Captain, Korean Army, 1995-98; Instructor, Assistant Professor, Associate Professor, 1998-, Department of Neurosurgery, Catholic University of Korea; Visiting Scholar, Department of Neurosurgery, University of Pittsburgh, USA, 2005-07; Expert Adviser, Auto Insurance Med Fee Rev Coun Korea, 2009-. Publications: Numerous articles in professional journals. Memberships: Congress of Neurological Surgeons; International Society for the Advancement of Spine Surgery; Korean Spinal Neurosurgery Society; Korean Neurosurgical Society. Address: Yeouido St Mary's Hospital, Department of Neurosurgery, #62 Yeouido-dong, Yeongdeungpo-gu, Seoul 150-173, Republic of Korea. E-mail: chough@catholic.ac.kr

CHOUGULE Mahavir, b. 31 March 1979, India. Professor. m. Priya Patil. Education: Diploma, Institute of Pharmacy, Bombay Technical Education, Mumbai, 1998; Bachelor (1st class), Pharmacy, Pataldhamal Wadhwani College of Pharmacy, Amravati University, 2001; Master, Pharmacy, 2004, PhD, 2007, Maharaja Sayajirao University of Baroda. Appointments: Formulation Officer, Ajit Laboratories Ltd, Miraj, 2001; Formulation Officer, Shehat Pharm Pvt Ltd, Himmatnager, 2001-02; Lecturer, Maharaja Sayajirao University of Baroda, 2004; Research Scientist, Wockhardt Ltd, Aurangabad, 2006-07; Postdoctoral Research Fellow, Florida A&M University, 2007-10; Assistant Professor, College of Pharmacy, University of Hawaii, 2010-. Publications: Numerous articles in professional journals. Honours: Junior Research Fellowship, Lady Tata Memorial Trust, Mumbai; Senior Research Fellowship, Indian Council of Medical Research, Delhi; Postdoctoral Fellow, National Institute of Health Sciences, USA; Best Student Award, 2001, Gold Medallist, Pataldhamal Wadhwani College of Pharmacy, Amravati University. Memberships: American Association of Cancer Research; American Association of Pharmaceutical Scientists. Address: Department of Pharmaceutical Sciences, College of Pharmacy, University of Hawaii at Hilo, 34 Rainbow Drive, Room 59, Hilo, HI 96720, USA. E-mail: mahavir@hawaii.edu

CHOW YUN-FAT, b. 18 May 1955, Lamma Island, China. Film Actor. m. (1) Candice Yu, 1983, divorced, (2) Jasmine Chow, 1986. Appointments: Actor, TV Station, TVB, Hong Kong, 1973, appearing in over 1,000 TV series. Creative Works: Films include: The Story of Woo Viet; A Better Tomorrow, 1986; God of Gamblers, 1989; The Killer; Eighth Happiness; Once a Thief, 1991; Full Contact, 1992; Hard Boiled, 1992; Peace Hotel, 1995; Broken Arrow, 1999; Anna and the King, 1999; Crouching Tiger, Hidden Dragon, 2000; King's Ransom, 2001; Bulletproof Monk, 2003; Hua Mulan, 2004; Pirates of the Caribbean: At Worlds End, Stranglehold, 2007; The Children of Huang Shi, 2008; Dragonball Evolution,

Confucius, The Founding of a Republic, 2009. Publications: Collection of photos, 2008. Honours: Numerous awards and nominations. Address: c/o William Morris Agency, 151 El Camino Drive, Beverly Hills, CA 90212, USA.

CHRISTENSEN Allan Robert, b. 5 January 1953, Newton, Kansas, USA. Electronics Engineer; Enrolled Agent; Social Services Advisor; Financial Services Advisor. Education: BSc, Electrical Engineering, Wichita State University, 1976; MSc, Electrical Engineering, Southern Methodist University, Texas, 1981; Texas Notarial Law, Notary Public, Eastfield College, Mesquite, 1991; Special Agent Training Program, Enrolled Agent License, United States Department of Treasury, Dallas, 1992; Certificate of Completion, Montano Securities School, Dallas, 1995; Accreditation, Chartered Mutual Fund Counselor Program, 1998, Accredited Asset Management Specialist Program, 1999, College for Financial Planning, Denver; State Certification, Texas Agency on Aging, Dallas, 2005; State Certification, Texas Department of Insurance, Austin, 2005. Appointments include: Enrolled Agent/Tax Advisor, self employed, Garland, Texas, 1990-; Social Worker, Volunteer Co-ordinator, Board Member, Community Restoration Services, Dallas, 1998-2000; Senior Electrical Test Engineer, Montgomery Elevators Inc, Illinois, 2000-01; Senior Electrical Test Engineer, KONE Inc, Texas, 2001-; Social Worker/State Certified Benefits Counselor, Texas Department of Aging and Disability Services, and Texas Department of Insurance, Dallas, 2005-. Publications: Numerous articles in professional journals. Honours include: J C Penney Golden Rule Award, Dallas, 1995; Defense Systems and Deign Group Stretch Award, Defense Systems and Design Group Take a Shot Award, Texas Instruments Inc, Dallas, 1996; Defense Superior Management Award, United State Navy Group Award, Dallas, 1996-97; Silver Medalist Award, 2000, Gold Medalist Award, 2001, for Educational Achievement, NATP Inc, Wisconsin. Memberships: National Association of Tax Professionals; Eta Kappa Knu; Tau Beta Phi; American MENSA; Accreditation Council for Accountancy and Taxation; Mysterium Society, USA; Texas State Board of Registered Professional Engineers. Address: 2629 Emberwood Drive, Garland, TX 75043-6047, USA. E-mail: allanchris@yahoo.com

CHRISTENSEN Helena, b. 25 December 1968, Copenhagen, Denmark. Model. 1 son. Appointments: Former child model; Adult modelling career, 1988-99; Front cover model, major magazine covers; Major contracts with: Versace; Chanel; Lagerfeld; Revlon; Rykiel; Dior; Prada and others; Magazine Photographer, 1999-. Address: c/o Marilyn's Agency, 4 Rue de la Paix, 75003 Paris, France.

CHRISTIE Julie Frances, b. 14 April 1940, Assam, India. Actress. m. Duncan Campbell, 2007. Education: Brighton Technical College; Central School of Speech & Drama. Creative Works: Films: Crooks Anonymous, 1962; The Fast Lady, 1962; Billy Liar, 1963; Young Cassidy, 1964; Darling, 1964; Doctor Zhivago, 1965; Fahrenheit 451, 1966; Far From the Madding Crowd, 1966; Petulia, 1967; In Search of Gregory, 1969; The Go-Between, 1971; McCabe & Mrs Miller, 1972; Don't Look Now, 1973; Shampoo, 1974; Demon Seed, Heaven Can Wait, 1978; Memoirs of a Survivor, 1980; Gold, 1980; The Return of the Soldier, 1981; Les Quarantiemes rugissants, 1981; Heat and Dust, 1982; The Gold Diggers, 1984; Miss Mary, 1986; The Tattooed Memory, 1986; Power, 1987; Fathers and Sons, 1988; Dadah is Death (tv), 1988; Fools of Fortune, 1989; McCabe and Mrs Miller, 1990; The Railway Station, 1992; Hamlet, 1995; Afterglow, 1998; The Miracle Maker (voice), 2000; No Such Thing, 2001; Snapshots, 2001; I'm With Lucy, 2002; Troy, 2004; Harry Potter and the Prisoner of Azkaban, 2004; Finding Neverland, 2004; The Secret Life of Words, 2005; Away From Her, 2006; New York, I Love You, Glorious 39, 2009; Plays: The Comedy of Errors, 1964; Uncle Vanya, 1973; Old Times, 1995, 2007; Suzanna Andler, 1997; Afterglow, 1998; Cries From The Heart, 2007. Honours include: Motion Picture Laurel Award, Best Dramatic Actress, 1967; Motion Picture Herald Award, 1967. Address: c/o International Creative Management, 76 Oxford Street, London W1D 1BS, England.

CHRISTODOULOU Christodoulos, b. 13 April 1939, Avgorou, Cyprus. Business Consultant. m. Maria, 1 daughter. Education: Diploma in Pedagogical Studies, Pedagogical Academy of Cyprus, 1962; Bachelor's Degree in Political Sciences, Pantios High School of Political Sciences, Athens, Greece, 1968; Bachelor's Degree in Law, Aristotelian University of Salonica, Greece, 1972; PhD, Labour Law, University of Wales, Wales, UK, 1992. Appointments: Director of the Government Printing Office, 1972-85; Permanent Secretary at the Ministry of Labour and Social Insurance, 1985-89; Permanent Secretary at the Ministry of Agriculture and Natural Resources, 1989-94; Minister of Finance, 1994-99; Minister of Interior, 1999-2002; Governor of the Central Bank of Cyprus, 2002-07; Business Consultant. Publications: Numerous books, studies and articles on legal, social, economic and political matters. Honours: Numerous honorary prizes and awards for national, social, economic and other contributions. Address: 12 Pnitagora Street, 2406 Engomi, Nicosia, Cyprus. E-mail: a.c.consultants@cytanet.com.cy

CHU Ka Hou, b. 22 February 1954, Macau, China. Professor. m. Sok Ching Mabel Chan, 2 sons. Education: AB, University of California at Berkeley, 1976; PhD, Massachusetts Institute of Technology, 1984. Appointments: Teaching Fellow, Harvard University, 1979; Research Assistant, Harvard Medical School, 1979-80; Postdoctoral Fellow, University of Pennsylvania Medical School, 1984; Lecturer, Associate Professor, Professor, 1984-, Director, School of Life Sciences, 2010-12, Chinese University of Hong Kong. Publications: Around 120 papers in professional journals; More than 10 book chapters. Honours: Exemplary Teaching Award, Faculty of Science, 2005, Research Excellence Award, 2007-08, Chinese University of Hong Kong; Higher Education Outstanding Scientific Research Award, (Science & Technology) in the category of Natural Sciences (Second Class), Ministry of Education, People's Republic of China. Memberships: Society of Integrative and Comparative Biology; The Crustacean Society; Chinese Crustacean Society; World Aquaculture Society; Asia Pacific Society for Marine Biotechnology. Address: School of Life Sciences, The Chinese University of Hong Kong, Shatin, NT, Hong Kong. E-mail: kahouchu@cuhk.edu.hk

CHUKOVA Yulia, b. 5 May 1935, Vladimir region, USSR. Physicist. Education: MSc Diploma (with honours), Lomonosov State University, Moscow, 1959; PhD, Lebedev Physical Institute, Russian Academy of Science, 1965; Diploma of Senior Research Scientist, 1968. Appointments: Senior Research Scientist, National Illuminating Engineering Institute, 1959-75; Senior Research Scents, Natural Diamond Research Laboratory, 1975-85; Senior Research Scents, Academy of Medical Science, USSR, 1985-86; People's Deputy of Moscow, 1990-93; Head, Bioelectromagnetics Laboratory, Institute of Human Ecology, 1995-2000; Director, Krasnopresnenskiy Ecological Fund, Moscow, 1991-. Publications: Over 300 publications; 10 patents; 20 books including: Anti-Stokes luminescence and new possibility for its application, 1980; Advances in nonequilibrium thermodynamics of systems under electromagnetic radiation, 2001; Low-level influence effects, 2002; The Weber-Fechner law, to the 150th Anniversary of the publication of the book, Elemente der Psychophysik, by G T Fechner, 2010. Honours: Grant, J D and C T MacArthur Foundation, 2001; Diploma and Medal, Best Persons in Russia, 2005; Silver Order for outstanding service to society, 2005; 2nd prize, All Russian Competition, Medicine: methods of health preservation in the 3rd millennium, 2005; Diploma of the Moscow Society of Nature Scientists, 2007; International Association of Writers, 2010. Memberships: Academician, Russian People's Academy of Science; Head of Department, Public Health and Ecological Safety of RPAS; Moscow Society of Nature Scientists; Popov Russian Scientific & Technological Society of Radio Engineering, Electronic Engineering and Communication; International Association of Writers. Address: Malaya Gruzinskaya St 6-42, Moscow 123242, Russian Federation. E-mail: y.chukova@mtu-net.ru

CHUKWUNYERE Njoku Paul, b. 25 December 1962, Calabarcross, River State, Nigeria. M. Achana Swati, 1 son, 1 daughter. Education: BA, Panjab; MA, JNU New Delhi; M Phil, Delhi; PhD, IIT Delhi. Appointments: Engineering, Medicine, Biomedical Engineer, Health Systems. Publications: More than 120 articles in professional journals. Honours: Listed in biographical dictionaries. Memberships: Biomedical Engineering Society; Cardiothoracic Surgery; Electrical Engineering, IIT, Delhi; Mechanical Engineering, MMME, India. Address: Department of Environmental Technology, School of Engineering, Technical Federal University, Owerri, Imo State, Nigeria.

CHUN Byung Suk, b. 1 September 1937, Hongseong, Korea. Publisher. m. 24 March 1963, 3 sons. Education: BA Economics, Korea University, 1960. Appointments: Chief Editor, Jinmyung Publishing Company, 1960-66; President, Moonye Publishing Company Ltd, 1966-; Director, 1975-2003, Vice President, 1985-87, Korean Publishers Association; Director, Korean Publishers Co-operative, 1982-98; Director, Korean Publishing Research Institute, 1991-2002; Director, Korean Publishing Fund, 1994-2003; Chief Editor, Korean Publishing Journal, 1994-99; Adviser, Korean Publishers Society, 1999-2002. Honours: Order of Cultural Merit, Government of Korea; Commendation, Prime Minister; Commendation, Minister of Culture and Public Information; Award, Korean Publishing Science Society; Publication Ethics Award, Korean Publication Ethics Commission; Korea Publishing Culture Award, Hankook Ilbo; Korean Translation Publishing Award, Korean Society of Translators; Chungang Journalism Culture Award, President of Chungang University; Seoul City Culture Award, Seoul Metropolitan Government; Korea Culture Art Prize, Government of Korea; The Publications Ethics Greatest Award, Korea Publication Ethics Commission; Catholic Masscommunication Award of Korea. Address: 108-201 Hyundai noblesse Villa 85, Gumi-dong, Bundang-gu, Seongnam-si, Gyeonggi-do 463-809, Republic of Korea. E-mail: info@moonye.com

CHUN Hoon Jai, b. 17 September 1959, Seoul, Korea. Medical Doctor; Professor. m. Jung Sook Choi, 1 son, 1 daughter. Education: MD, 1985, MSc, 1988, PhD, 1994, Korea University College of Medicine. Appointments: Clinical Instructor, 1992-94, Assistant Professor, 1996-2000, Associate Professor, 2000-04, Professor, 2004-, Korea University College of Medicine, Seoul; Guest Doctor, Munchen, Germany, 1994-95; Guest Doctor, Dusseldorf, Germany, 1995-96; Editor, Korean Society of Gastroenterology, Seoul, 2000-03; Technical Committee Member, Korean Society of Gastroenterology, Seoul, 2000-03; Chief of Endoscopy Unit, Korea University Medical Center, Seoul, 2005-; Consultant Committee Member, Ministry of Health & Welfare, Republic of Korea, 2005; Consultation Committee Member, Korea Food and Drug Administration, Seoul; Central Review Committee Member, Health Insurance Review Agency, Seoul, 2005. Publications: Over 30 articles in professional journals. Memberships: Korean Medical Association; Korean Association of Internal Medicine; Korean Society of Gastrointestinal Endoscopy; Korean Society of Gastroenterology; Korean College of Helicobacter and Upper Gastrointestinal Research; Korean Gastric Cancer Association; Korean Society of Gastrointestinal Cancer; Die Sektion Gastroenterologische Endoskopie der DGVS; Japan Gastroenterological Endoscopy Society; American Gastroenterological Association. Address: 126-1, 5-Ga Anam-Dong, Seongbuk-Gu, Seoul 136-705, Korea. E-mail: drchunhj@chol.com

CHUN Jang Ho, b. 23 November 1948, Koyang, Kyunggido, Korea. Professor; Researcher. m. Kyung Won Hong, 1 son, 1 daughter. Education: Bachelor of Electronic Engineering, Kwangwoon University, Seoul, Korea, 1968-75; Master of Electronic Engineering, Yonsei University, Seoul, Korea, 1976-78; PhD, Electrophysics, Stevens Institute of Technology, New Jersey, USA, 1980-84; Professor and Researcher, Kwangwoon University, 1984-; Technical Advisor, Mission Telecom Company, Seoul, Korea, 2004-09; Visiting Scientist, Princeton University, New Jersey, USA, 1988-89; Visiting Scientist, University of Tokyo, Tokyo, Japan, 1994. Publications include: The phase-shift method for determining adsorption isotherms of hydrogen at electrified interfaces; Methods for determining adsorption isotherms in electrochemical systems; Correlation constants between adsorption isotherms of intermediates in electrochemical systems; A negative value of the interaction parameter for OPDH at platinum and iridium electrode interfaces; Determination of adsorption isotherms of hydrogen and deuterium isotopes at interfaces using the phase-shift method and correlation constants. Honours: Commendation for Excellent Teaching and Research, Korea Government, 1997, 2006; Fellowships for Visiting Scientists, Korea Science and Engineering Foundation, 1988-1989, 1994; Studying Abroad Scholarship, Korea Government, 1980-84; The Most Excellent Graduation, Kwangwoon University, 1975; Award of Excellent Papers, Korean Federation of Science and Technology Societies, 2006; Scientific Award of Excellence, 2011; Listed in Who's who publications and biographical dictionaries; Listed in Top 25 Hottest Articles of International Journal of Hydrogen Energy, 2008. Memberships: The Electrochemical Society; International Association for Hydrogen Energy; The Korean Electrochemical Society. Address: Department of Electronic Engineering, Kwangwoon University, Seoul 139-701, Korea. E-mail: jhchun@kw.ac.kr

CHUN Young Nam, b. 3 July 1961, Paju, Gyeonggi, Republic of Korea. Professor. m. Eum Mi Kang, 2 daughters. Education: BA, 1983, PhD, 1993, Inha University; Postdoctoral, University of Illinois at Chicago, 1999. Appointments: Visiting Researcher, Institute of IVD, Stuttgart University, Germany, 1990; Research, Development Institute of Korea Gas Corporation, 1990-92; Visiting Researcher, Institute of IVD, Stuttgart University, 1992-93; Visiting Researcher, Russian Academy of Sciences, 1993-94; Full Time Lecturer, 1994-96, Assistant Professor, 1996-2000, Associate Professor, 2000-05, Visiting Professor, 2004-05,

Professor, 2005-, McMaster University; Chosun University, Korea; Head, Environmental Institute, Chosun University, 2007-08; Technology Planning Committee Member, Korea Institute of Energy and Resources Technology Evaluation and Planning, 2008-; Editor, The Open Process Chemistry Journal, 2008-; Publisher, Science and Technology Group (STG). Publications: Air Pollution Engineering, 2000; Incineration and Air Pollution Control, 2002; Environmental Design and CAD, 2004; Environmental and Pollution, 2004. Honours: Best Teacher, Chosun University, 2001; Paper Award, Korea Society of Environmental Engineers, 2003; Paper Award, Korean Society of Waste Management, 2008; Listed in Who's Who publications and biographical dictionaries. Memberships: Korean Society of Environmental Engineers; Korean Society of Mechanical Engineers; Korean Society of Combustion. Address: Chosun University, #375 Seosuk-dong, Dong-gu, Gwangju 501-759, Republic of Korea. E-mail: ynchun@chosun.ac.kr

CHUN OAKLAND Suzanne, b. Hawaii, USA. State Senator. m. Michael Sands Chun Oakland, 1 son, 2 daughters. Education: Bachelor of Arts Degree in Communications and Psychology, University of Hawaii. Appointments: Administrative Assistant, Au's Plumbing and Metal Works, 1979-90; Community Services Specialist to Hawaii State Senate under Senator Anthony Chang, 1984; Administrative Assistant for Smolenski and Woodell, Attorneys at Law, 1984-86; Research Assistant and Office Manager to City Council Member Gary Gill, 1987-90; State Representative for House District 27, 1990-96; State Senator for Senate District 13, 1996-; Senate Committee Member: Chair Human Services; Vice-Chair, Health; Education and Military Affairs; Higher Education; Judiciary and Hawaiian Affairs. Honours: Numerous honours and awards include: Hawaii Medical Association 1996 Outstanding Legislator Award; Mental Health Association 1999 Legislator of the Year Award; Certificate of Appreciation, Department of Health and Human Services, 2000; Hawaii Breastfeeding Advocacy Award, 2001; Public Service Champion, Coalition for a Tobacco Free Hawaii, 2004. Memberships include: Chinese Chamber of Commerce; Hawaii Chinese Civic Association; Children's Trust Advisory Council; Elder Abuse and Neglect Task Force; Hawaii Women's Legal Foundation; US-China People's Friendship Association of Honolulu; Hawaii Council on Economic Education Board. Address: Hawaii State Capitol, Room 226, 415 South Beretania Street, Honolulu, HI 96813, USA.

CHUNG Bongkil, b. 20 May 1936, Yeonggwang, South Korea. Education. m. Shin O, 2 sons. Education: BA, Wonkwang University, 1959; MA, Roosevelt University, 1970; MA, Ohio State University, 1972; PhD, Michigan State University, 1979. Appointments: Instructor, 1979-80, Assistant Professor, 1981-86, Associate Professor, 1981-86, Professor, 1999-2009, Emeritus Professor, 2009-, Philosophy, Florida International University; Lecturer, Towson State University, 1980-81. Publications: 3 books: The Dharma Words of Master Chongsan, 2000; The Scriptures of Won Buddhism, A Translation of Wonbulgyo, 2003; The Dharma Words of Won Buddhism, 2012; 3 book chapters; 5 articles in professional journals. Honours: Research Excellence Awards, Florida International University, 2003. Memberships: American Philosophical Association; International Society for Chinese Philosophy; International Society for Asian and Comparative Philosophy. Address: Department of Philosophy, Florida International University, Miami, FL 33199, USA. E-mail: chungbongkil143@gmail.com

CHUNG Bum-Jin, b. 9 February 1965, Seoul, Korea. Professor. m. Il Sun, 1 son. Education: Bachelor's degree, 1987, Master's degree, 1989, PhD, 1994, Seoul National University, Korea. Appointments: Deputy Director, Ministry of Science and Technology, 1995-2002; Lecturer, Kyunghee University, 1996-99; Visiting Researcher, Manchester University, England, 1999-2001; Professor, Jeju National University, 2002-; Exchange Professor, University of Florida, USA, 2007-08; Policy Advisory Board Member, Korean Ministry of Education, Science and Technology, National Electricity Demand and Supply Planning Committee; Member, Korean Ministry of Knowledge and Economy. Publications: Numerous articles in professional journals regarding condensation heat transfer, nuclear manpower issue, and mixed convection. Honours: Best Presentation Award, International Youth Nuclear Congress, 2004; Listed in international biographical directories. Memberships: Life Member, Korean Energy Engineering Society; Editor, Korean Nuclear Society; Editor, Korean Radioactive Waste Society; Editor, Journal of Nuclear Engineering Technology. Address: Jeju National University; Department of Nuclear & Energy Engineering, 66 Jejudaehakno, Jeju-Si, Jeju-Do, Korea. E-mail: bjchung@jejunu.ac.kr

CHUNG Kang-Sup, b. 11 August 1960, Busan, Korea. Research Scientist. m. Sun-Ja Kang, 1 son. Education: BS, Chemistry, 1986, MS, 1991, PhD, 1995, Inorganic Chemistry, Sung Kyun Kwan University. Appointments: General Affairs Secretary, Korea Society of Analytical Science, 1988-92; Professor, Department of Resources Recycling, University of Science and Technology, 2004-; Principal Researcher, 1986-, Head, Seawater-Dissolved Resources Research Division, 2011-, Korea Institute of Geoscience and Mineral Resources. Publications: Inorganic adsorbant containing polymeric membrane reservoir for the recovery of lithium from seawater, 2008; Synthesis of highly concentrated TiO_2 nanocolloids and coating on boron nitride powders, 2008. Honours: Testimonial of Prime Minister, Korean Government, 2007; Order of Industrial Service Merit, Korean Government, 2010; Grand Prize of ISTK Chairman Aard, Korea Research Council Industrial Science and Technology, 2010. Memberships: Korean Chemical Society; Korea Society of Analytical Science. Address: Korea Institute of Geoscience and Mineral Resources, 92 Gwahang-no, Yuseong-gu, Daejeon 305-350, Korea.

CHUNG Kyung-Nam, b. 28 March 1955, Seoul, Korea. Researcher. m. Sung-Won Lee, 1 son. Education: Bachelor, 1978, Master, 1980, Naval Architecture, Seoul National University; PhD, Mechanical Engineering, University of Iowa, 1993. Appointments: Researcher, Hyundai Heavy Industries, 1983-. Publications: A Study of NPSH required Performance Improvement for an Industrial Vertical Pump, 2009; A Study of Performance Improvement of Vertical Diffuser Pumps, 2009. Memberships: ASME; KSME; KFMA. Address: 21-3 Mipo Apt, Seobudong, Dongku, Ulsan 682-030, Republic of Korea. E-mail: kuchung@hhi.co.kr

CHUNG Sang Yong, b. 20 April 1952, Seoul, Korea. Professor. m. Jea Suk, 1 son, 1 daughter. Education: BSc, Geology, 1975, MSc, Geophysics, 1982, Seoul National University; PhD, Hydrogeology, University of Nevada at Reno, USA, 1992. Appointments: Professor, Department of Earth Environment Sciences, Pukyong National University, 1982-; President, Korean Society of Soil & Groundwater Environment, 2002-05; Director, Korea Water Forum, 2006-; Chairman, Groundwater Management Committee, Busan Metropolitan City, 2007-10. Publications: 60 articles; 3 books; 125 conference proceedings; 3 patents. Honours: Achievement

Award, Mayor of Busan Metropolitan City, 2005; Academic Award, Korean Federation of Science & Technology, 2005; Achievement Award, Ministry of Education, Korea, 2006. Memberships: American Geophysical Union; Korean Society of Soil & Groundwater Environment; National Groundwater Association, USA. Address: 599-1 Dayeon-dong, Nam-gu, Busan 608-737, Korea. E-mail: chungsy@pknu.ac.kr

CHUNG Tae-Young, b. 10 October 1973, Seoul, South Korea. Medical Doctor. m. Hye-Ryung Lee, 1 son, 1 daughter. Education: MD, 1998, PhD, Postgraduate School, 2007, Seoul National University College of Medicine. Appointments: Intern, Residency, Fellowship, Seoul National University Hospital; Fellowship, Department of Ophthalmology, Massachusetts Eye and Ear Infirmary, Schepens Eye Research Institute, Harvard Medical School; Assistant Professor, Department of Ophthalmology, Samsung Medical Center, Sungkyunkwan University School of Medicine. Address: Department of Ophthalmology, Samsung Medical Centre, #50 Ilwon-dong, Kangnam-ku, Seoul 135-710, South Korea. E-mail: tychung@skku.edu

CHUNG Yoonsik, b. 25 March 1956, Korea. Professor. m. Younghae Song, 1 son, 1 daughter. Education: PhD, Mass Communication, Korea University, 1988. Appointments: Senior Researcher, Korea Information Society Development Institute, 1986-95; Professor, Kangwon National University, 1995-; Member, KBS Board of Governors, 2009-12. Publications: Media & Law Policy. Honours: Ministry of Information & Communication Award, 1988; Ministry of Korea Broadcasting Commission, 1989; Listed in international biographical dictionaries. Memberships: Academy of Korea Mass Media; Academy of Korea Broadcasting. Address: Kangnamgu Ilwondong Woosung, 7th 107-401, Seoul 135-230, Korea. E-mail: ysjung@kangwon.ac.kr

CHUNTRASAKUL Chomchark, b. 22 January 1937, Trang, Thailand. Medical Doctor. m. Patchaneepan. Education: Bangkok Christian College, 1955-57; Chulalongkorn University, Bangkok, 1957-59; Faculty of Medicine, Siriraj Hospital, Mahidol University, 1959-63. Appointments: Adviser, Faculty of Medicine, Siriraj Hospital, Mahidol University, 1998-; Ethical Committee Member, Human Research Projects, Ministry of Public Health, Thailand, 1999-; Adviser of several associations, 1998-; Adviser, Royal College of Surgeons of Thailand, 2003-; Executive Director, Parental and Enteral Nutrition Society of Asia, 2005-12. Honours include: Distinguished Award for Excellent People of Trang Province, 2003; Honorary Director General, IBC, 2009; Vice President, World Congress of Arts, Sciences and Communications, Cambridge, 2009; Honorary Doctorate Degree, Mahidol University, Thailand, 2009; Medal of Noble Distinction, ABI, 2010; Hall of Fame for Outstanding Achievement, 2010. Memberships include: Medical Association of Thailand; Royal College of Surgeons of Thailand; American Burn Association; International Society of Burn Injuries; International Association for Surgery of Trauma and Surgical Intensive Care; Asian Surgical Association. Address: Department of Surgery, Faculty of Medicine, Siriraj Hospital, Mahidol University, Bangkok 10700. E-mail: chomchark@loxinfo.co.th

CHURCH Charlotte Maria, b. 21 February 1986, Llandaff, Cardiff, Wales. Singer. 1 son and 1 daughter with Gavin Henson. Career: Albums include: Voice of an Angel, 1998; Charlotte Church, 1999; Christmas Offering, 2000; Dream a Dream, 2000; Enchantment, 2001; Tissues and Issues, 2005; Back to Scratch, 2010; Singles: Crazy Chick, 2005; Call My Name, 2005; Performances include: Charlotte Church: Voice of an Angel in Concert, 1999; Dream a Dream: Charlotte Church in the Holy Land, 2000; The Royal Variety Performance 2001, 2001; The 43rd Annual Grammy Awards, 2001; Concerts include: Hollywood Bowl; Hyde Park. Preludes include: Pie Jesu; Panis Anjulicus; Dream a Dream; The Prayer (duet with Josh Groban); It's the Heart that Matters; TV Appearances include: Heartbeat, 1999; Touched by an Angel, 1999; Have I Got News For You, 2002; The Kumars at No. 42, 2002; Parkinson, 2002, 2005; Friday Night with Jonathon Ross, 2003, 2005; This Morning, 2005; The Paul O'Grady Show, 2005, 2006; The Charlotte Church Show, 2006; Numerous others; Film: I'll Be There, 2003. Publications: Voice of An Angel – My Life (So Far), autobiography, 2001; Keep Smiling, autobiography, 2007. Honours include: British Artist of the Year, Classical BRIT Awards, 2000; Rear of the Year, 2002; Woman of the Year, GQ Awards, 2005; Funniest TV Personality, Loaded Magazine, 2006; Solo Artist of the Year, Glamour Awards, 2006; Readers Favourite TV Personality, Glamour Awrads, 2007.

CHURCHILL Caryl, b. 3 September 1938, London, England. Dramatist. m. David Harter, 1961, 3 sons. Education: BA, Lady Margaret Hall, Oxford, 1960. Career: Playwright: Stage plays: Having a Wonderful Time, 1960; Owners, 1972; Objections to Sex and Violence, 1975; Vinegar Tom, 1976; Light Shining in Buckinghamshire, 1976; Traps, 1977; Cloud Nine, 1979; Top Girls, 1982; Fen, 1983; Softcops, 1984; A Mouthful of Birds, 1986; Serious Money, 1987; Ice Cream, 1989; Lives of the Great Poisoners, 1991; The Skriker, 1994; Thyestes, 1994; Hotel, 1997; This is a Chair, 1997; Blue Heart, 1997; Faraway, 2000; A Number, 2002; Drunk Enough to Say I Love You, 2006; Radio: The Ants; Not…not…not…not enough Oxygen; Abortive; Schreiber's Nervous Illness; Identical Twins; Perfect Happiness; Henry's Past; Television: The Judge's Wife; The After Dinner Joke; The Legion Hall Bombing; Fugue. Publications: Owners, 1973; Light Shining, 1976; Traps, 1977; Vinegar Tom, 1978; Cloud Nine, 1979; Top Girls, 1982; Fen, 1983; Softcops, 1984; A Mouthful of Birds, 1986; Serious Money, 1987; Plays I, 1985; Plays II, 1988; Objections to Sex and Violence in Plays by Women Vol 4, 1985; Ice Cream, 1989; Mad Forest, 1990; Lives of the Great Poisoners, 1992; The Striker, 1994; Thyestes, 1994; Blue Heart, 1997; This is a Chair, 1999; Far Away, 2000; A Number, 2002; A Dream Play, 2005; Drunk Enough to Say I Love You? 2006; Seven Jewish Children, 2009; anthologies. Address: c/o Casarotto Ramsay Ltd, National House, 60-66 Wardour Street, London W1V 3HP, England.

CHURCHILL Martin, b. 18 November 1954, Glasgow, Scotland. Artist. Education: DA (with distinction), Edinburgh College of Art, 1976; Postgraduate Diploma in Fine Art (with distinction), Painting, 1977: Fellow, Painting, Gloucester College of Art, 1981-82. Appointments: Artist; Group and solo exhibitions throughout Scotland; Works held in public and private collections; Commissions include University of Edinburgh. Honours: Guthrie Award, RSA; 1st Prize, Hunting Group Art Prize; Elizabeth Greenshields Award, Canada; 2nd Prize, BP Portrait Award; Winner, Morrison Scottish Portrait Award; David Cargill Award, RGI. Memberships: The Fine Art Society, London; RA; RSA; RGI; NPG; RP Society; RCA, London. Address: 69 Fillebrook Road, Leytonstone, London E11 4AU, England.

CHUTISANT Kerdvibulvech, b. 19 August 1983, Bangkok, Thailand. University Lecturer. Education: B Eng (Hons), Computer Engineering, Chulalongkorn University, Thailand, 2005; MSc, 2007, PhD, 2009, Computer Engineering, Keio

University, Japan. Appointments: Lecturer, Department Head of Information and Communication Technology, Rangsit University, Thailand, 2009-. Publications: Papers published in several refereed international journal papers; Invited speaker at various international conferences in North America, South America, Europe and Asia. Honours: Scholarship from Keio University (Fujiwara Foundation); Keio Leading-edge Laboratory of Science and Technology; Adjunct Lecturer, Stenden-Rangsit University; Guest Lecturer, Sripatum University; 2nd Best Presenter Award from International Workshop on Electronic & Information Engineering at Xian Jiaotong University, China. 2008; Dissertation Committee Member and Board of Examiners, Chulalongkorn University, Faculty of Engineering, 2010. Memberships: IEEE. E-mail: dr-chutisan@hotmail.com Website: www.dr-chutisan.tk

CHVOJKA Ludovít Rudolf, b. 7 March 1928, Nandraž, Slovakia. Retired Scientific Worker. m. Vladislava Vyskočilová, 1 son, 1 daughter. Education: Chemické inž Bratislava, 1948-50; Zemědělské inž Leningrad, 1950-55; BRNO Ing Agronomy, Mendel University, 1955-56; Doctorate, Biology, Czechoslovak Academy of Sciences, Prague, 1956-61; PhD, Institute of Experimental Botany, 1961. Appointments: Head, Department of Growth and Development of Plants, 1961-91. Publications: Numerous articles in professional journals. Honours: Memory Medal of Slovak Uprising, Governance of State, 1974; Silver Medal of Mendel, Presidium of Czechoslovak Academy of Sciences, 1978; Honour of Institute of Experimental Botany for meritorious scientific and organizing work since 1956, 1988. Address: Praha 9, 190 00, Sluknovska 313, Czech Republic.

CHWA Dongkyoung, b. 23 December 1971, Tokyo, Japan. Professor. Education: Master's degree, 1995, Bachelor's degree, 1997, Department of Control and Instrumentation Engineering, PhD, 2001, School of Electrical and Computer Engineering, Seoul National University. Appointments: Postdoctoral Researcher, 2001-04, BK21 Assistant Professor, 2004-05, Seoul National University; Associate Professor, Ajou University, 2005-. Publications: Missile Guidance and Control; Robot Control; Numerous articles in professional journals. Honours: Listed in international biographical dictionaries. Address: Electrical Engineering, Anjou University, San 5 Wonchun-Dong, Yeongtong-gu, Suwon 443-749, Republic of Korea.

CIAMPI Sara, b. 24 January 1976, Genova, Italy. Writer; Journalist; Literary Critic. Education: Leaving Certificate, Linguistics School; Laurea Honoris Causa, Literature; Laurea Honoris Causa, Philosophy; Certificate, Ordre Docteurs Cee; Master Diploma, Literature and Philosophy. Career: Literary activity began at 14 years of age stimulated initially by significant health problems and later by serious illness (tuberculosis, malaria and scoliosis). Publications: Momenti, 1995; Malinconia di Un'anima, 1999; La Maschera Delle Illusioni, 1999; Rassegna di Novelle e Canti, 2000; Giacomo Leopardi, degree thesis, 2000; La Mia Vita, 2003; I Giorni dei Cristalli, 2006; L'Orizzonte e la Pietra (into Voci del Verso), 2008; Il Crepuscolo Oltre la Luce – The Dusk Before the Light, 2009; Gocce di Tristezza, 2009; Nostalgie e Rimpianti (into Olimpo Lirico), 2010; Canti di Mestizia – Chants de Tristesse, 2010; Il Vento dei Sentimenti, 2010. Honours: Over 300 national and international honours and awards; Included in important anthologies and in prestigious Italian and foreign dictionaries and encyclopaedias as Utet and Treccani; Premio della Cultura della Presidenza del Consiglio dei Ministri, 2001; Silver Medal, President of the Italian Republic, 2003; International Peace Prize, 2002; American Medal of Honor, 2002; International Writer of the Year, 2003; World Medal of Freedom, 2004; Legion of Honor, 2005; Gold Medal for Italy, 2006; Congressional Medal of Excellence, 2007; American Hall of Fame, 2007; Distinguished Service Order & Cross, 2008; Presidential Inaugural Certificate, 2009; Lifetime Achievement Award, 2009; Oscar for Arts and Letters, 2009; Title of Countess of San Diego Tower, Baroness von Derneck and Dame St Lukas, with Royal Order; Candidate, Nobel Prize in Literature, 2001, 2002, 2007, 2010; Oscar for Arts and Letters, 2009; San Giorgio d'Oro career prize, 2010. Memberships: Pontzen Academy; Giosuè Carducci Academy; Micenei Academy; Paestum Academy; Costantiniana Academy; Gentium Pro Pace Academy; Etruscan Academy; Marzocco Academy; CONVIVIO Academy; Federico II Academy; Giacomo Leopardi Academy; International Biographical Centre; American Biographical Institute; International Writers and Artists Association; San Giorgio Academy. Address: Via San Fruttuoso 7/4, I 16143 Genova, Italy.

CIDON Esther Una, b. 19 October 1975, Zamora, Spain. Medical Oncologist; Professor. Education: Medicine and Surgery degree, University of Salamanca, 1999; Medical Oncologist, Central University Hospital of Oviedo, 2000-04; Advanced Studies Certificate, Research in Cancer, University of Oviedo, 2004; Master in Palliative Medicine, University of Valladolid, 2004-06; Professor, Oncology and Palliative Medicine, 2007-11, PhD, 2009, University of Valladolid; Master in Molecular Oncology, National Center of Research in Cancer, Madrid, 2008-10; Research Training Certificate, NIH Office of Clinical Research Training and Medical, 2009; Master in Clinical Management, Financial Studies Center, Madrid, 2010-11; Politics Sciences degree, University of Distance Education, in progress. Appointments: Medical Oncologist, Oncology Department, 2004-, Secretary, Digestive Tumours Committee, 2008-, Member, Tumours Committee, 2010-, Clinical University Hospital of Valladolid; Associate Professor, Oncology and Palliative Medicine, Faculty of Medicine, Valladolid, 2007-; Associated Editor, Global Journey of Surgery and US-China Medical Science; Editor in Chief of book, The Challenge of Colorectal Cancer: A review book; Senior Editor, Jounral of Solid Tumours. Publications: Several chapters in different books; Numerous articles in professional journals. Honours: Driver Education, Institutional Prize of Editorial Awards, 1988; Professor Barea National Awards, 2009, 2010; Listed in international biographical dictionaries. Memberships: Spanish Society of Medical Oncology; American Society of Clinical Oncology; Society for Translational Oncology; European Association for Cancer Research; International Society for Gastrointestinal Oncology. Address: Medical Oncology Department, Clinical University Hospital, c/Ramon y Cajal s/n, 47005 Valladolid, Spain. E-mail: aunacid@hotmail.com

CIMBALA Stephen Joseph, b. 4 November 1943, Pittsburgh, PA, USA. College Professor. m. Elizabeth Ann Harder, 2 sons. Education: BA, Pennsylvania State University, 1965; MA, 1967, PhD, 1969, University of Wisconsin, Madison. Appointments: Assistant Professor of Political Science, State University of New York, Stony Brook, New Brook, 1969-73; Associate Professor, 1973-86, Professor, 1986-, Distinguished Professor, 2000-, Political Science, Pennsylvania State University, Delaware County; Consultant to various US Government Agencies and Defense Contractors. Publications: Books include: The Past and Future of Nuclear Deterrence, 1998; Coercive Military Strategy, 1998; Nuclear Strategy in the Twenty-First Century, 2000; Clausewitz and Chaos, 2001; Through a Glass Darkly: Looking at Conflict Prevention, Management and Termination, 2001; Russian and

Armed Persuasion, 2001; A New Nuclear Century: Strategic Stability and Arms Control, 2002; The Dead Volcano: The Background and Effects of Nuclear War Complacency, 2002; US National Security: Policymakers, Processes and Politics, 2002; Military Persuasion: The Power of Soft, 2002; The US, NATO and Military Burden Sharing, 2005; Nuclear Weapons and Strategy: US Nuclear Policy for the Twenty-First Century, 2005; Russia and Postmodern Deterrence, 2007; Shield of Dream, 2008; Nuclear Weapons and Cooperative Security in the 21st Century, 2010; Contributing editor, various works; Numerous articles and chapters. Honours: Milton S Eisenhower Award for Distinguished Teaching, Pennsylvania State University, 1995; Distinguished Professor of Political Science, 2000. Address: 118 Vairo Library, Penn State Brandywine, 25 Yearsley Mill Road, Media, PA 19063-5596, USA. E-mail: chacal@psu.edu

CIMINO Lorenzo, b. 26 May 1938, Trani, Italy. Psychologist; Writer. m. Maria Peduzzi, 1975. Education: Piano Diploma, 1957; PhD, 1966. Appointment: Psychologist in public administration, 1972-92; Freelance Psychologist, 1992-2006; Writer; Musician. Publications: Scientific papers on: work psychology and family therapy, 1971-92; history of psychology and art psychology, 1993-2000; Music: Reviews in Magazines, 1979-91; A CD, 1998; Poetry: 5 books and numerous collective books, 1979-2010 (3 books reprinted 2008); 1 book of essays. Honours: Formal appreciation of paper from Psychological Service Director, Rome; Honours as piano player, 1996-98; Prized in literary competitions in Leonforte, Turin, Florence, Rome, Forte dei Marmi and so on; Gold Medal for Italy, ABI; Lifetime Award, IBC; Listed in international biographical dictionaries. Memberships: Italian Society of Psychology, Promoter of Italian Society of Arts Psychology; FWLA; Italian Authors' and Publishers' Association. Address: via Nosee 4, 22020 Schignano, Italy.

CIOFFI Ugo, b. 26 November 1955, San Paolo, Brazil. Doctor. m. Sara de Pascalis, 2 sons. Education: MD, University of Naples, Italy, 1981; General Surgery, 1988, PhD, Cardiovascular Pathophysiology, 1996, University of Milan, Italy. Appointments: Fellow, Department of General Surgery, 1983-84, Visiting Scientist, Department of General Surgery, 2000, Albany Medical Center, University of New York at Albany; Fellow, Department of Cardiothoracic Surgery, Albert Einstein College of Medicine, University of New York, 1993, 1998; Surgeon, Researcher, Ospedale Maggiore Policlinico, Milan; Professor of Surgery, University of Milan. Publications: Numerous articles and papers in scientific journals; Reviewer and member, editorial board of scientific journals. Honours: Yearbook of Diagnostic Radiology, 1999; Ospedale Maggiore Policlinico Milano, Ministry of Public Health, 2003, 2005, 2007, 2008; Listed in international biographical dictionaries. Memberships: Italian Society of Surgery; Italian Society of Ambulatory and Day Surgery; CTS Net; American Association for the Advancement of Science. Address: Fondazione Ospedale Maggiore Policlinico, Department of Surgery, via F Sforza 35, 20122 Milano, Italy. Website: www.dsc.unimi.it

CIRIC Rade, b. 22 June 1962, Zagreb, Croatia. Power Engineer. m. Konstandina Simic, 1 son, 1 daughter. Education: Dipl-Ing, 1987, Dr-Ing (PhD), 2000, Electrical Power Engineering, University of Novi Sad, Serbia; MSc, Electrical Power Engineering, University of Belgrade, Serbia, 1992; Post-doctorate, Electrical Power Engineering, UNESP ILHA Solteira, Brazil, 2002. Appointments: EPS, Elektrovojvodina Novi Sad, 1987-2001; UNESP ILHA Solteira, Brazil, 2001-02; UWE Bristol, UK, 2004; Deputy Secretary for Science & Technological Development, The Government of AP Vojvodina, Serbia, 2005-12; Associated Professor, University of Belgrade, 2007; Professor, The School of Higher Technical Professional Education, Novi Sad, 2012. Publications: More than 100 scientific and technical papers. Honours: Distributech Europe Innovation Award, Penn Well Global Energy Group and Utility Automation, Madrid, 1999. Memberships: CIRED; World Scientific and Engineering Academy Society. E-mail: rciric@aol.com

CLAIRE Regi, (Yvonne Regula Butlin-Staub), b. 8 June 1962, Münchwilen/TG, Switzerland. m. Ron Butlin. Fiction Writer; Translator. Education: Matura, Frauenfeld, Switzerland, 1981; lic. phil. 1, English and German, Zurich University, Switzerland, 1992. Appointment: Research Assistant, Department of English, Zurich University, 1992-93. Publications: Inside-Outside (short stories), 1998; The Beauty Room (novel), 2002; Fighting It (short stories), 2009. Honours: Winner of Exchange Scholarship with Aberdeen University, 1983-84; Winner, Semester Prize, Zurich University, 1986; Winner, Edinburgh Review 10th Anniversary Short Story Competition, 1995; Scottish Arts Council Writer's Bursary, 1997; Inside-Outside shortlisted for Saltire Society Scottish Book of the Year Award, 1999; Writer's Bursary from Thurgau Canton, Switzerland, 2002; The Beauty Room longlisted for Allen Lane/MIND Book of the Year Award, 2003; Writer's Bursary from Pro Helvetia (Swiss Arts Council), 2003; UBS Cultural Foundation Award, 2004; Scottish Arts Council Writer's Bursary, 2009; Fighting It, shortlisted for Saltire Society Scottish Book of the Year Award, 2009, and longlisted for Edge Hill Short Story Prize, 2010. Memberships: Scottish PEN (Executive Committee); Autorinnen und Autoren der Schweiz; Society of Authors. Address: 7 West Newington Place, Edinburgh EH9 1QT, Scotland. Website: www.regiclaire.com

CLAPTON Eric (Eric Patrick Clapp), b. 30 March 1945, Ripley, Surrey, England. Musician (guitar); Singer; Songwriter. m. (1) Patti Boyd, 1979, divorced; 1 son, deceased, 1 daughter, (2) Melia McEnery, 2002, 3 children. Career: Guitarist with groups: The Roosters, 1963; The Yardbirds, 1963-65; John Mayall's Bluebreakers, 1965-66; Cream, 1966-68; Blind Faith, 1969; Derek and the Dominoes, 1970; Delaney And Bonnie, 1970-72; Solo artiste, 1972-; Concerts include: Concert for Bangla Desh, 1971; Last Waltz concert, The Band's farewell concert, 1976; Live Aid, 1985; Record series of 24 concerts, Royal Albert Hall, 1991; Japanese tour with George Harrison, 1991; Film appearance: Tommy, 1974; Blues Brothers 2000, 1998. Compositions include: Presence Of The Lord; Layla; Badge (with George Harrison). Recordings include: Albums: Disraeli Gears, 1967; Wheels Of Fire, 1968; Goodbye Cream, 1969; Layla, 1970; Blind Faith, 1971; Concert For Bangladesh, 1971; Eric Clapton's Rainbow Concert, 1973; 461 Ocean Boulevard, 1974; E C Was Here, 1975; No Reason To Cry, 1976; Slowhand, 1977; Backless, 1978; Just One Night, 1980; Money And Cigarettes, 1983; Behind The Sun, 1985; August, 1986; Journeyman, 1989; 24 Nights, 1992; MTV Unplugged, 1992; From The Cradle, 1994; Rainbow Concert, 1995; Crossroads 2, 1996; Live In Montreux, 1997; Pilgrim, 1998; One More Car One More Rider, 2002; Me and Mr Johnson, 2004; She's So Respectable, 2004; Sessions for Robert J, 2004; Soundtracks include: Tommy; The Color Of Money; Lethal Weapon; Rush; Starskey and Hutch; School of Rock; Friends; Hit singles include: I Shot The Sheriff; Layla; Lay Down Sally; Wonderful Tonight; Cocaine; Behind The Mask; Tears In Heaven; Contributed to numerous albums by artists including: Phil Collins; Bob Dylan; Aretha Franklin; Joe Cocker; Roger Daltrey; Dr John;

Rick Danko; Ringo Starr; Roger Waters; Christine McVie; Howlin' Wolf; Sonny Boy Williamson; The Beatles: The White Album (listed as L'Angelo Mysterioso). Honours include: 6 Grammy Awards, 1993; Q Magazine Merit Award, 1995; Grammy Award for best pop instrumental performance, 2002; CBE, 2004; Grammy Lifetime Achievement Award, 2006. Address: c/o Michael Eaton, 22 Blades Court, Deodar Road, London, SW15 2NU, England.

CLARK Alan George, b. 2 July 1965, Melbourne, Australia. Engineering and Business Consulting. m. Sian Lloyd, 3 children. Education: Bachelor of Applied Science, Metallurgy, University of South Australia, 1986; Master of Business Administration, Technology, Melbourne University Business School, 1994. Appointments: Research Engineer, Comalco Ltd (RioTinto), 1987-92; Specialist, Business Analyst, Rio Tinto, 1992-95; Director, Camora Glen Engineering Consulting, 1995-2000; Director, Clark & Marron Business Consulting, 1999-2010. Publications: Numerous articles in professional journals. Honours: Leading Engineers and Scientists of the World, IBC. Memberships: Institution of Engineers, Australia. Address: PO Box 789 Glenelg, South Australia 5045, Australia. Website: www.clarkandmarron.com.au

CLARK Bruce Michael, b. 17 July 1937, Bedfont, Middlesex, England. Artist; Teacher. m. Jill Wilkinson, 2 sons. Education: Bath Academy of Art, Corsham, 1958-60; Christchurch College, Canterbury, 1980-84. Appointments: Teacher, Bagshot C S School, Surrey, 1960-65; Teacher, Pershore School, Worcester, 1965-72; Head of Art, Barton Court School, Canterbury, 1972-89; Art & Design Inspector for Ofsted, 1993-96; Exhibiting Artist with 14 solo exhibitions; Part-time Lecturer in Art History and Art Education. Publications: Listed in international biographical dictionaries. Honours: Certificate in Education, University of Bristol, 1960; Diploma in Art Education, 1981; MA, University of Kent, 1985. Address: 11 Charles Graven Court, Ely, Cambridgeshire CB7 4FN, England.

CLARK David, Lord Clark of Windermere, b. 19 October 1939, Castle Douglas, Scotland. Member of Parliament. m. Christine, 1 daughter. Education: BA (Econ), MSc, 1963-65, University of Manchester; PhD, University of Sheffield, 1974-78. Appointments: House of Commons, 1970-2001; House of Lords, 2001-. Publications: Books: The Industrial Manager, 1966; Radicalism to Socialism, 1981; Labours Lost Leader, 1985; We Do Not Want The Earth, 1992. Honours: Privy Councillor, 1997; Freedom of South Tyneside, 1998. Memberships: North Atlantic Assembly; Forestry Commission; Vindolanda Trust; History of Parliament Trust; Gravetye Trust; UK Defence Forum. Address: House of Lords, London SW1A 0PW, England.

CLARK Eric, b. 29 July 1937, Birmingham, England. Author; Journalist. m. Marcelle Bernstein, 12 April 1972, 1 son, 2 daughters. Appointments: Reporter, The Exchange Telegraph news agency, London, 1958-60; Reporter, The Daily Mail, 1960-62; Staff Writer, The Guardian, 1962-64; Home Affairs Correspondent, Investigations Editor, The Observer, London, 1964-72; Author and journalist, 1972-. Publications: Len Deighton's London Dossier, Part-author, 1967; Everybody's Guide to Survival, 1969; Corps Diplomatique, 1973, US edition as Diplomat, 1973; Black Gambit, 1978; The Sleeper, 1979; Send in the Lions, 1981; Chinese Burn, 1984, US edition as China Run, 1984; The Want Makers (Inside the Hidden World of Advertising), 1988; Hide and Seek, 1994; The Advertising Age Encyclopedia of Advertising, 2003; The Secret Enemy; The Real Toy Story, 2007; Numerous newspaper articles. Honours: Fellow, English Centre, International PEN. Memberships: Society of Authors; Authors Guild; Mystery Writers of America; National Union of Journalist. Address: c/o A M Heath Agency, 6 Warwick Court, London WC1R 5DJ, England.

CLARK Graham Ronald, b. 10 November 1941, Littleborough, Lancashire, England. Opera Singer. m. Joan, 1 step-daughter. Education: Loughborough College of Education, Leicestershire, 1961-64; MSc, Recreation Management, Loughborough University, Leicestershire, 1969-70; Singing studies with Bruce Boyce in London. Career: Teacher, Head of Physical Education Departments in 3 schools, 1964-69; Senior Regional Officer, The Sports Council, 1971-75; Operatic début with Scottish Opera, 1975; Principal, English National Opera, 1978-85; Performances with The Royal Opera Covent Garden, Glyndebourne Festival Opera, Opera North and Welsh National Opera in the UK; International performances include: 16 seasons and over 100 performances, Bayreuth Festspiele, 1981-2004; 15 seasons, Metropolitan Opera, New York, 1985-2010; Performances in Aix-en-Provence, Amsterdam, Barcelona, Berlin, Bilbao, Biwako, Bonn, Brussels, Catania, Chicago, Dallas, Frankfurt, Geneva, Hamamatsu, Hamburg, Los Angeles, Madrid, Matsumoto, Milan, Munich, Nagoya, Nice, Paris, Rome, Salzburg, San Francisco, Stockholm, Tokyo, Toronto, Toulouse, Turin, Vancouver, Vienna, Yokohama, Zurich, 1976-2011; Over 385 Wagner performances including over 275 performances of Der Ring des Nibelungen, 1977-2010; International festivals include, Amsterdam, Antwerp, Bamberg, Berlin, Brussels, Canaries, Chicago, Cologne, Copenhagen, Edinburgh, Lucerne, Milan, Paris, Rome, Tel Aviv, Washington and the London Proms. Recordings with the BBC, BMG, Chandos, Decca, Deutsche Grammophon, EMI, Erato, Etcetera, EuroArts, Oehms Classics, Opera Rara, Opus Arte, Philips, Profil, Sony, Teldec, The Met, United Artists and Warner Classics; Videos include: The Makropulos Case, Canadian Opera, Toronto; The Ghosts of Versailles, The Met, New York; Die Meistersinger, Der fliegende Holländer, Der Ring des Nibelungen, Bayreuther Festspiele; Wozzeck, Deutsche Staatsoper, Berlin; Ariadne auf Naxos, Opéra National de Paris; Der Ring des Nibelungen, Gran Teatre del Liceu, Barcelona; Der Ring des Nibelungen, De Nederlandse Opera, Amsterdam; Videos and DVDs. Honours: 3 nominations for Outstanding Individual Achievement in Opera, including an American Emmy, 1983, 1986, 1993; Sir Laurence Olivier Award, 1986; Honorary Doctor of Letters, Loughborough University, 1999; Sir Reginald Goodall Memorial Award, 2001; Sherwin Award, 2009; Honorary Bachelor of Science, Loughborough University, 2009. Membership: The Garrick Club. Address: c/o Ingpen & Williams, 7 St George's Court, 131 Putney Bridge Road, London, SW15 2PA, England.

CLARK Patricia Denise (Claire Lorrimer, Patricia Robins, Susan Patrick), b. 1921, England. Writer; Poet. Publications: As Claire Lorrimer: A Voice in the Dark, 1967; The Shadow Falls, 1974; Relentless Storm, 1975; The Secret of Quarry House, Mavreen, 1976; Tamarisk, 1978; Chantal, The Garden (a cameo), 1980; The Chatelaine, 1981; The Wilderling, 1982; Last Year's Nightingale, 1984; Frost in the Sun, 1986; House of Tomorrow (biography), 1987; Ortolans, 1990; The Spinning Wheel, Variations (short stories), 1991; The Silver Link, 1993; Fool's Curtain, 1994; Beneath the Sun, 1996; Connie's Daughter, The Reunion, 1997; The Woven Thread, The Reckoning, Second Chance, 1998; An Open Door, 1999; Never Say Goodbye, Search for Love, 2000; For Always, 2001; The Faithful Heart, 2002;

Over My Dead Body, Deception, 2003; Troubled Waters, 2004; Dead Centre, 2005; Autobiography, You Never Know, 2006; Infatuation, 2007; Truth to Tell, 2008; Emotions (short stories), 2008; Dead Reckoning, 2009. As Patricia Robins: To the Stars, 1944; See No Evil, 1945; Three Loves, 1949; Awake My Heart, 1950; Beneath the Moon, Leave My Heart Alone, 1951; The Fair Deal, 1952; Heart's Desire, So This is Love, 1953; Heaven in Our Hearts, One Who Cares, 1954; Love Cannot Die, 1955; The Foolish Heart, Give All to Love, 1956; Where Duty Lies, He Is Mine, 1957; Love Must Wait, 1958; Lonely Quest, 1959; Lady Chatterley's Daughter, The Last Chance, 1961; The Long Wait, The Runaways, Seven Loves, 1962; With All My Love, 1963; The Constant Heart, Second Love, The Night is Thine, 1964; There Is But One, No More Loving, Topaz Island, 1965; Love Me Tomorrow, The Uncertain Joy, 1966; The Man Behind the Mask, Forbidden, 1967; Sapphire in the Sand, Return to Love, 1968; Laugh on Friday, No Stone Unturned, 1969; Cinnabar House, Under the Sky, 1970; The Crimson Tapestry, Play Fair with Love, 1972; None But He, 1973; Fulfilment, Forsaken, Forever, 1993; The Legend, 1997; Memberships: Society of Authors; Romantic Novelists Association. Address: Chiswell Barn, Marsh Green, Edenbridge, Kent TN8 5PR, England.

CLARK Petula (Sally Olwen), b. 15 November 1934, Epsom, Surrey, England. Singer; Actress. m. Claude Wolff, 1961, 1 son, 2 daughters. Musical Education: Taught to sing by mother. Career: Stage and screen actress, aged 7; Own radio programme, 1943; Numerous film appearances, 1944-; Films include: Medal For The General, 1944; Here Come The Huggetts, 1948; Finian's Rainbow, 1968; Goodbye Mr Chips, 1969; Stage appearances include: Sound Of Music, 1981; Someone Like You (also writer), 1989; Blood Brothers, Broadway, 1993; Sunset Boulevard, 1995-96; national tour 1994-95, Sunset Boulevard, 1995, 1996, New York, 1998, US tour, 1998-2000; Host, own BBC television series; US television special Petula, NBC, 1968; Solo singing career, 1964-; Sold over 30 million records to date. Recordings: Hit singles include: Ya-Ya Twist, 1960; Downtown (Number 1, US and throughout Europe), 1964; The Other Man's Grass; My Love; I Know A Place; Downtown; Oxygen; Albums: Petula Clark Sings, A Date With Pet, 1956; You Are My Lucky Star, 1957; Pet Clark, Petula Clark In Hollywood, 1959; In Other Words, Petula, Les James Dean, 1962; Downtown, 1964; I Know A Place, The New Petula Clark Album, Uptown With Petula Clark, 1965; In Love, Hello Paris, Vols I and II, I Couldn't Live Without Your Love, 1966; Hit Parade, 1967; The Other Man's Grass Is Always Greener, Petula, 1968; Portrait Of Petula, Just Pet, 1969; Memphis, 1970; The Song Of My Life, Warm And Tender, 1971; Live At The Royal Albert Hall, Now, 1972; Live In London, Come On Home, 1974; I'm the Woman You Need, 1975; Don't Sleep on the Subway, 1995; Wind of Change, 1998; The Ultimate Collection, 2002. Honours include: 2 Grammy Awards; Grand Prix Du Disque, 1960; More Gold discs than any other UK female artist. Address: c/o John Ashby, PO Box 288, Woking, Surrey GU22 0YN, England.

CLARK Rodney Jeremy, b. 7 September 1944, Andover, England. Voluntary Sector Executive. Civil partnership: Peter Bailey. Education: University College, London. Appointments: Various posts, 1965-69; Administrative Assistant, Welfare Department, London Borough of Camden, 1969-71; Administrator, Capital Projects Manager, London Borough of Islington, then Camden and Islington Area Health Authority, 1971-78; Capital Projects Director, The Royal National Institute for the Deaf, 1978-81; Chief Executive, Sense, The National Deafblind & Rubella Association, 1981-2001; Chairman, Signhealth; Chairman, The Woodford Foundation; Chairman, Christopher Brock Trust. Publications: Numerous articles in professional and popular journals. Honours: OBE. Address: 31 Sutton Road, Shrewsbury, Shropshire SY2 6DL, England.

CLARKE Ann Margaret, b. 3 November 1928, Madras, India. Psychologist. m. ADB Clarke, 2 sons. Education: BA, Psychology, University of Reading, 1948; PhD, Psychology, University of London, 1950. Appointments: Clinical Psychologist then Principal Psychologist, The Manor Hospital NHS, Epsom, 1951-62; Research Fellow, 1963-71, Lecturer, 1973-76, Reader,1976-85, Professor, 1985-87, Professor Emeritus, 1987-, Department of Educational Studies, University of Hull. Publications with Alan Clarke: Mental Deficiency: the Changing Outlook, 1958, 1964, 1974, 1985; Early Experience: Myth and Evidence, 1976; Mental Retardation and Behavioural Research, 1973; Early Experience and the Life Path, 2000; Human Resilience: a Fifty Year Quest, 2003; numerous articles in Psychological and Medical journals. Honours: B A Priestly Prize as Best Female Undergraduate, University of Reading; Research Award, American Association on Mental Deficiency, 1977; Distinguished Achievement Award for Scientific Literature, International Association for Scientific Study of Mental Deficiency, 1982; Honorary Fellow, British Psychological Society, 2007. Membership: British Psychological Society. Address: 109 Meadway, Barnet, Hertfordshire EN5 5JZ, England.

CLARKE Anthony Peter (Lord Clarke of Stone-cum-Ebony), b. 13 May 1943, Ayr, Scotland. Judge. m. Rosemary, 2 sons, 1 daughter. Education: MA, Economics Part I, Law Part II, King's College, Cambridge. Appointments: Called to Bar, Middle Temple, 1965; QC, 1979; Judge of the High Court QBD, 1993-8; Admiralty Judge, 1993-98; Lord Justice of Appeal, 1998-2005; Master of the Rolls, 2005-09; Justice of the Supreme Court of the United Kingdom, 2009-. Honours: Knight, 1993; PC, 1998; Lord, 2009. Memberships: Garrick Club; Rye Golf Club. Address: Supreme Court of the United Kingdom, Parliament Square, London SW1P 3BD, England.

CLARKE Hilda Margery, b. 10 June 1926, Monton, Eccles, Manchester, England. Artist; Gallery Director. Widowed, 2 sons. Education: Studied privately in Manchester with L S Lowry, and in Hamburg; Drawing, Printmaking and Sculpture, Southampton College of Art, part-time, 1960-88; Ruskin School of Art Workshops under Tom Piper, Chris Orr and Norman Ackroyd, 4 weeks, 1975; BA (Honours), Open University, 1975-82. Career: Founder and Director, "The First" Gallery, Southampton, 1984-; Curator, long running national touring exhibitions, 1988-; Exhibitions: Southampton City Art Gallery; FPS Gallery, Buckingham Gate, London; Mall Galleries, London; Chalk Farm Gallery, London; Ditchling, Sussex; Bettles Gallery, Ringwood; New Ashgate Gallery, Farnham; Tib Lane Gallery, Manchester; St Barbe Gallery, Lymington; Mottisfont Abbey, Romsey, National Trust, 2010; John Martin of Chelsea, 2005; John Martin of London, Albemarle Street, 2006; Edgar Modern Gallery, Bath, 2008/09; One man exhibitions: Hamwic Gallery, Southampton, 1970; Westgate Gallery, Winchester, 1973; University of Southampton, 1975; Hiscock Gallery, Southsea, 1977; "The First" Gallery, Southampton, 1989, 1998, 2004; Turner Sims Concert Hall, Southampton (by invitation) for the Inauguration of the Foyer, 1994; Ramsgate Library Gallery, 2001; Southampton City Art Gallery, 2006; Works in public collections: Southampton University; Southern Arts Association; St Mary's Hospital, Isle of Wight; Works in private collections: Felder Fine Art, London; Michael Hurd, Liss; Mrs B Hunt, Southampton; Dr C Williams, Bristol; Lady Lucas, Stockbridge; Professor and Mrs David Brown, Braishfield. Publications: Catalogues: Two Memorable Men: Crispin Eurich (1936-76) photographs, LS Lowry (1887-1976) drawings; The Animated Eye; Paintings and Moving Machines by Peter Markey; Showman-Shaman- Showman: Paintings and Prints by Stephen Powell; Architect at Leisure: Watercolours and Drawings by Arthur Mattinson (1853-1932); Passage from India, Jacqueline Mair. Membership: FRSA, elected 1996. Address: "The First" Gallery, 1 Burnham Chase, Bitterne, Southampton SO18 5DG, England.

CLARKE Karen Ann, b. 21 January 1969, Freeport, Bahamas. Doctor of Medicine. Education: BSc Chemistry, 1989; MSc Microbiology and Immunology, 1993; Master of Public Health, Environmental Health, 1994; MD, 1996. Career: Internal Medicine Department, Catskill Regional Medical Center, Harris, New York, 2000-05; Internal Medicine Department, Tucson Medical Center, St Joseph's Hospital, and St Mary's Hospital, Tucson, Arizona, 2005-06; Internal Medicine Department, Christus St Michael Hospital, Texarkana, Texas, 2007-08; Clinical Instructor, Division of Hospital Medicine, Emory University, Atlanta, Georgia, 2008-. Publications: Characterization of Anergy to the Superantigen SEB, 1993; A Stimulatory Mls-1 Superantigen is Destroyed by UV Light While Other MTV Antigens Remain Intact. Significance for Mls-1 Unresponsiveness, 1992; CD4 Engagement Induces Fas Antigen – Dependent Apoptosis of T Cells in vivo, 1994; What is the best empirical therapy for community-acquired cellulitis? 2009; What is the Appropriate Evaluation and Treatment of Funguria? 2010; Reduction of Catheter-Associated Urinary Tract Infections through a Bundled Intervention in a Community Hospital, 2010; Conference highlights growing healthcare-associated infection (HAI) concerns, 2010. Honours: Outstanding Senior Chemistry Student, American Institute of Chemistry Foundation, 1989; Dean's List, NE Wesleyan University (twice); Fellow, American College of Physicians, 2009; Emory Hospital Medicine Director's Award, 2009. Memberships: Cardinal Key; American College of Physicians; Fellow, American Biographical Institute, 1995; Life Patron, IBA, 2001; Lifetime Achievement Award, IBC, 2001; America's Registry of Outstanding Professionals, 2002-; International Order of Merit, IBA, 2004. Listed in includes: Who's Who Among Students in American Universities and Colleges, 1988-89; The World Who's Who of Women 1994/5; 2000 Outstanding People of the 20th Century, 2001; Dictionary of International Biography. Address: 8 Misty Creek Cove, Newnan, GA 30265, USA.

CLARKE Kay Knight, b. 22 November 1938, USA. Company Director; Artist. m. Logan Clarke Jr, 1 son, 1 daughter. Education: BA (Hons), English Literature and Music, University of North Carolina, 1960; MS, 1962, PhD (ABD), 1963, Statistics-Mathematics, North Carolina State University; Residency, VT Studio Center, 2004; BFA, Painting, Lyme Academy College of Fine Arts, 2005; MFA, Visual Arts, Massachusetts College of Art, 2007. Appointments: TTI/Citigroup, Polaroid, Arthur D Little, Research Triangle Institute, 1960-73; Senior Vice President, Shawmut Corporation and Shawmut Bank of Boston, 1973-78; Director, McGraw-Hill, 1976-88; Vice President, Arthur D Little, 1978-79; Vice President, Connecticut General Life Insurance Co, 1979-81; President, CIGNA Corporation, CIGNA Securities, 1981-85; President, Templeton Ltd, 1985-; Executive Vice President, 1988-90, McGraw-Hill Inc; Director, Guardian Life Insurance Company, 1989-2010; Lead Director, 2006-10, President, 1990-95, Micromarketing Division, ADVO Inc; Director, The Providence Journal Company, 1995-; Director, Berkshire Life Insurance Company, 2001-09; Many non-profit boards; Artist, group and solo exhibitions, Massachusetts, Connecticut and Maine, 2001-; Works held in permanent collections. Publications: Numerous articles in professional journals. Honours: Business Hall of Fame; Junior Achievement of Southwestern New England; Executive Women of New Jersey Salute to Policy Makers Award; Distinguished Alumni Award, University of North Carolina; Women '76 Award for Singular Achievement in Business, Boston; Executive in Residence, Dartmouth, Amos Tuck, Wheaton; Phi Beta Kappa; Phi Kappa Phi. Memberships: International Women's Forum. E-mail: kclarke3@mindspring.com

CLARKE Keith Edward, b. 1940, United Kingdom. Consultant. m. Barbara, 1 son, 1 daughter. Education: B Eng, Electrical Engineering, University of Bradford; Diploma, Computing Science, Imperial College of Science and Medicine; M Phil, Computing Science, University of London; Management, London Business School. Appointments: Adviser, Ministry of Technology, 1969-70; Various management posts, BT Research, 1972-83; Deputy Director of Research, BT, 1985-89; Director, Applications and Services Development, BT Laboratories, Martlesham, Suffolk, 1989-92; Senior Vice-President Engineering, BT North America, San Jose, California, 1992; Director, Group Systems Engineering, BT plc, 1992-95; Director of Engineering Collaboration and Business Planning, BT Global Engineering, 1995-97; Director, Technology External Affairs, BT plc, 1997-2000; Executive Director (part-time), British Approvals Board for Telecommunications; Consultant in ITC with clients in UK and Europe, 2000-; Company Directorships: BT (CBP) Limited, 1989-95; Cellnet Limited, 1989-92; British Approvals Board for telecommunications, 1992-2000; BPS Inc, 2000; BABT Holdings, 2000; Hermont (Holdings, 2000-2002. Publications: Over 60 publications in the field of telecommunications include: How Viewdata Works (editor, R Winsbury), 1981; The Immediate Past and Likely Future of Videotext Display Technology, 1982; On the Road to Worldwide Communication (jointly with J Chidley), 1987; Royal Academy of Engineering Seminar on the Public Perception of Risk-Lessons from the Mobile Phone Industry, 2000. Memberships: Guild of Freeman; The City Livery Yacht Club; The Windsor Yacht Club (Past Commodore); Fellowships: Institution of Engineering and Technology, British Computer Society, Chartered Management Institute, Royal Academy of Engineering, RSA; Liveryman of the Worshipful Company of Information Technologists; Liveryman of the Worshipful Company of Engineers; Freeman of the City of London. E-mail: kclarke@totalonline.net

CLARKE Kenneth Harry (Rt Hon), b. 2 July 1940, Nottingham, England. MP. Education: Gonville and Caius College, Cambridge; BA, LLB, Cambridge University; Called to Bar, Grays Inn, London, 1963. Appointments: MP for Rushcliffe, Nottinghamshire, 1970; Parliamentary Private Secretary to Solicitor General, 1971-72; Assistant Government Whip, 1972-74; Lord Commissioner, HM Treasury, 1974; Member, Parliamentary Delegate to Council of Europe and Western European Union, 1973-74; Opposition Spokesman on Social Services, 1974-76; Opposition Spokesman on Industry, 1976-79; Parliamentary Under-Secretary of State, Department of Transport, 1979-82; Mininistry of State, Health, 1982-85; Paymaster General, 1985-87; Chancellor, Duchy of Lancaster, 1987-88; Ministry of Trade and Industry, Ministry for Inner Cities, 1987-88; Secretary of State for Health, 1988-90;

Secretary of State for Education, 1990-92; Secretary of State for Home Department, 1992-93; Chancellor of the Exchequer, HM Treasury, London, 1993-97; Lord Chancellor and Secretary of State for Justice, 2010-. Publications: New Hope for the Regions, 1979; The Free Market and the Inner Cities, 1987. Honours: QC; MP; Liveryman, Clockmakers' Co, 2001-; Hon LLD, Nottingham, 1989, Huddersfield, 1993; D University, Nottingham Trent, 1996. Address: House of Commons, London SW1A 0AA, England.

CLARKE William Malpas, b. 5 June 1922, Ashton-under-Lyne, England. Author. m. Faith Elizabeth Dawson, 2 daughters. Education: BA Hons, Econ, University of Manchester, England, 1948; Hon DLitt, London Guildhall University, 1992. Appointments: Financial Editor, The Times, 1956-66; Director-General, British Invisible Exports Council, 1967-87; Chairman, ANZ Merchant Bank, 1987-91; Chairman, Central Banking Publications, 1991-2008. Publications: City's Invisible Earnings, 1958; City in the World Economy, 1965; Private Enterprise in Developing Countries, 1966; The World's Money, 1970; Inside the City, 1979; How the City of London Works, 1986; Secret Life of Wilkie Collins, 1988; Planning for Europe, 1989; Lost Fortune of the Tsars, 1994; Letters of Wilkie Collins, 1999; The Golden Thread, 2000; Hidden Treasures of the Romanovs, 2009. Contributions to: The Banker; Central Banking; Euromoney; Wilkie Collins Society Journal. Honour: CBE, 1976. Memberships: Thackeray Society; Wilkie Collins Society; Reform Club. Address: 37 Park Vista, Greenwich, London SE10 9LZ, England.

CLARKSON Jeremy Charles Robert, b. 11 April 1960, Doncaster, England. Broadcaster; Writer, m. (1) Alexandra James (divorced), (2) Frances Cain, 1993, 3 children. Career: Presenter of various TV programmes and radio shows, including: Top Gear (Original Format), 1988–2000; Jeremy Clarkson's Motorworld, 1995–1996; Jeremy Clarkson's Extreme Machines, 1997; Robot Wars, 1998; Jeremy Clarkson's Car Years, 2000; Jeremy Clarkson's Speed, 2001; You Don't Want To Do That, 2001; Top Gear (Current Format), 2002-; Jeremy Clarkson: Meets the Neighbours, 2002; The Victoria Cross: For Valour, 2003; Inventions That Changed the World, 2004; Jeremy Clarkson: The Greatest Raid of All Time, 2007; Newspaper columnist. Publications: Jeremy Clarkson's Motorworld, 1996; Clarkson on Cars, 1996; Clarkson's Hot 100, 1997; Planet Dagenham, 1998; Born To Be Riled, 1999; Jeremy Clarkson On Ferrari, 2000; The World According To Clarkson, 2004; I Know You Got Soul, 2005; And Another Thing.., 2006; Don't Stop Me Now!!, 2007; For Crying Out Loud!, 2008; Driven To Distraction, 2009; How Hard Can It Be?, 2010; Round The Bend, 2011. Honours: Honorary D Eng, Oxford Brookes University, 2005.

CLASSEN Carl Joachim, b. 15 August 1928, Hamburg, Germany. University Professor. m. Roswitha Rabl, 3 sons. Education: PhD, University of Hamburg, Germany, 1952; BLitt, 1957, DLitt, 1988, University of Oxford, England; Habilitation, University of Göttingen, Germany, 1961. Appointments: Assessor, Christianeum Hamburg, 1956; Lecturer, Classics, University of Ibadan, Nigeria, 1956-59; Lecturer, 1960-63, Dozent, 1961-66, University of Göttingen, Germany; Professor, Technical University, Berlin, Germany, 1966-69; Professor, University of Würzburg, 1969-73; Professor, 1973-93, Emeritus Professor, 1993-, University of Göttingen, Germany; Visiting Professor: University of Tübingen, Germany, 1964-65; University of Texas, Austin, USA, 1967-68; Changchun, China, 1992, 1993, Tartu, Estonia, 1994, 1996, Rome, 1995, 1997; Member, Institute for Advanced Study, Princeton, USA, 1975; Visiting Fellow: All Souls College, Oxford, 1980, Merton College, Oxford, 1995. Publications: Sprachliche Deutung, 1959; Laudes Urbium, 1980; Recht Rhetorik Politik, 1985, Italian translation, 1998; Ansätze, 1986; Welt der Römer, 1993; Zur Literatur und Gesellschaft der Römer, 1998; Rhetorical Criticism of the New Testament, 2000; Antike Rhetorik im Zeitalter des Humanismus, 2003; Vorbilder, Weste, Norman, 2008; Aretai I virtutes, 2008; Herrscher, Burger und Erzicher, 2010; Aretai und Virtutes, 2010. Memberships: Mommsen Gesellschaft, President, 1983-87; International Society for the History of Rhetoric, President, 1987-89; International Federation of the Association of Classical Studies, Vice-President, 1994-97, President, 1997-2002; Akademie der Wissenschaften, Göttingen; Honorary Member, Polish Philological Association and Greek Philological Association; Foreign Member, Accademia di Archeologia, Lettere e Belle Arti Napoli; Corresponding Member, Akadimia Athinon. Address: Aes König Stift, Feldbergstrasse 13-15, A001, 61476 Kronberg, Germany. E-mail: cclasse@gwdg.de

CLAUDEL Bernard Michel, b. 20 May 1932, Strasbourg, France. Professor (retired). 3 sons. Education: Ecole Normale Superieure, Paris, France, 1952-56; Agregation des Sciences Physiques, 1956; Doctorat es Sciences, 1962. Appointments: Professor, National Institute of Applied Science (INSA), Lyon, France, 1963-97; NSF Senior Foreign Scientist, University Missouri, Columbia, Missouri, USA, 1969-70. Visiting Associate Professor, University Missouri, Columbia, Missouri, USA, 1970-71. Publications: Books: La Catalyse au Laboratoire et Dans l'Industrie, 1967; Elements of Chemical Kinetics, 1970; Bases du Genie Chimique, 1977; Numerous scientific articles in various journals. Honour: Herpin Prize, Academy of Lyon, 1994. Memberships: Member, scientific staff, Research Institute on Catalysis, 1960-79; Board of Administrators, INSA, 1976-82; Head, Department of Energetics, INSA, 1979-82.

CLAYTON Peter Arthur, b. 27 April 1937, London, England. Publishing Consultant; Archaeological Lecturer. m. Janet Frances Manning, 5 September 1964, 2 sons. Education: School of Librarianship; North West Polytechnic, London, 1958; Institute of Archaeology, London University, 1958-62; University College, London, 1968-72. Appointments: Librarian, 1953-63; Archaeological Editor, Thames & Hudson, 1963-73; Humanities Publisher, Longmans, 1973; Managing Editor, British Museum Publications, 1974-79; Publications Director, BA Seaby, 1980-87; Writer, Lecturer, 1987-; Consulting Editor, Minerva Magazine, 1990-; Expert Advisor (coins and antiquities), Department for Culture Media and Sport (Treasure Committee), 1992-2007; Member, The Treasure Valuation Committee, 2007-. Publications: The Rediscovery of Ancient Egypt; Archaeological Sites of Britain; Seven Wonders of the Ancient World; Treasures of Ancient Rome; Companion to Roman Britain; Great Figures of Mythology; Gods and Symbols of Ancient Egypt; Chronicle of the Pharaohs; Family Life in Ancient Egypt; The Valley of the Kings; Egyptian Mythology. Contributions to: Journal of Egyptian Archaeology; Numismatic Chronicle; Coin & Medal Bulletin; Minerva. Honours: Liveryman of the Honourable Company of Farriers of the City of London, 2000; Freeman of the City of London, 2000; Court of Assistants and Freeman of the Company of Arts Scholars, Dealers and Collectors, City of London, 2004. Memberships: Chartered Institute of Library and Information Professionals, fellow; Society of Antiquaries of London, fellow; Royal Numismatic Society, fellow. Address: 41 Cardy Road, Boxmoor, Hemel Hempstead, Hertfordshire HP1 1RL, England.

DICTIONARY OF INTERNATIONAL BIOGRAPHY 36th EDITION

CLEARE John Silvey, b. 2 May 1936, London, England. Photographer; Writer. m. (2) Jo Jackson, 12 May 1980, 1 daughter. Education: Wycliffe College, 1945-54; Guildford School of Photography, 1957-60. Appointments: Joint Editor, Mountain Life magazine, 1973-75; Editorial Board, Climber and Rambler magazine, 1975-85. Publications: Rock Climbers in Action in Snowdonia, 1966; Sea-Cliff Climbing in Britain, 1973; Mountains, 1975; World Guide to Mountains, 1979; Mountaineering, 1980; Scrambles Among the Alps, 1986; John Cleare's Best 50 Hill Walks in Britain, 1988; Trekking: Great Walks in the World, 1988; Walking the Great Views, 1991; Discovering the English Lowlands, 1991; On Foot in the Pennines, 1994; On Foot in the Yorkshire Dales, 1996; Mountains of the World, 1997; Distant Mountains, 1999; Britain Then and Now, 2000; On Top of the World, 2000; Pembrokeshire – The Official National Park Guide, 2001; The Tao Te Ching, 2002; Moods of Pembrokeshire & its Coast, 2004; Portrait of Bath, 2004; Books of Songs, 2004; Tales from the Tao, 2005; Classic Haiku, 2007; Mountains – A Panoramic Vision, 2007; Chinese Wisdom, 2009; Buddhist Wisdom, 2009; Contributions to: Times; Sunday Times; Independent; Observer; World; Country Living; Boat International; Intercontinental; Alpine Journal; High; Climber; Great Outdoors; The Pembrokeshire Coast Path, 2010; The Ridgeway, 2011. Honours: 35mm Prize, Trento Film Festival, for film The Climbers (as Cameraman), 1971; Golden Eagle Award, Outdoor Writers Guild for Services to the Outdoors; Honorary Membership, Outdoor Writers Guild; Honorary Membership, BAPLA. Membership: Outdoor Writers Guild, executive committee; British Association of Picture Libraries; Alpine Club. Address: Hill Cottage, Fonthill Gifford, Salisbury, Wiltshire SP3 6QW, England.

CLEESE John (Marwood), b. 27 October 1939, Weston-Super-Mare, Somerset, England. Author; Actor. m. (1) Connie Booth, 1968, dissolved 1978, 1 daughter, (2) Barbara Trentham, 1981, dissolved 1990, 1 daughter, (3) Alyce Faye Eichelberger, 1993, divorced 2008. Education: MA, Downing College, Cambridge. Career: Began writing and making jokes professionally, 1963; Appeared in and co-wrote TV Series: The Frost Report; At Last the 1948 Show; Monty Python's Flying Circus; Fawlty Towers; The Human Face; Founder and Director, Video Arts Ltd, 1972-89; Films include: Interlude; The Magic Christian; And Now For Something Completely Different; Monty Python and the Holy Grail; Life of Brian; Yellowbeard, 1982; The Meaning of Life, 1983; Silverado, 1985; A Fish Called Wanda, 1988; Mary Shelley's Frankenstein, 1993; The Jungle Book, 1994; Fierce Creatures, 1996; The World Is Not Enough, 1999; The Quantum Project, Rat Race, Pluto Nash, 2000; Harry Potter and the Philosopher's Stone, 2001; Die Another Day, Harry Potter and the Chamber of Secrets, 2002; Charlie's Angels: Full Throttle, 2003; Around the World in 80 Days, 2004; Valiant (voice), Jade Empire (voice), 2005; Man About Town, Complete Guide to Guys', Entente cordiale, L, 2006; Charlotte's Webb (voice), 2006; Skrek the Third (voice), 2007. Publications: Families and How to Survive Them, (with Robin Skynner), 1983; The Golden Skits of Wing Commander Muriel Volestrangler FRHS and Bar, 1984; The Complete Fawlty Towers (with Connie Booth), 1989; Life and How to Survive It (with Robin Skynner), 1993; The Human Face (with Brian Bates), 2003; The Pythons Autobiography (co-author), 2003. Honour: Honorary LLD, St Andrews; 7 Awards, 12 nominations. Address: c/o David Wilkinson, 115 Hazlebury Road, London SW6 2LX, England.

CLEGG The Rt Hon Nick (Nicholas William Peter), b. 7 January 1967, Chalfont St Giles, Buckinghamshire, England. Member of Parliament for Sheffield Hallam; Leader of the Liberal Democrats; Deputy Prime Minister; Lord President of the Council. m. Miriam Gonzalex Durantez, 3 sons. Education: Master's degree, Archaeology and Anthropology, Robinson College, Cambridge; Political Philosophy scholarship, University of Minnesota, USA; Master's degree, College of Europe, Bruges. Appointments: Intern, Christopher Hitchens, The Nation magazine, New York; Trainee, G24 Co-ordination Unit, Brussels; TACIS aid programme, European Commission, 1994-96; European Union Policy Adviser and Speech Writer for Leon Brittan; Member, European Parliament, 1999-2004; Member of Parliament for Sheffield Hallam, 2005-; Leader, Liberal Democrats, 2007-; Deputy Prime Minister and Lord President of the Council in a coalition with the Conservative Party, 2010-. Honours: Financial Times' David Thomas Prize, 1993.

CLÉMENT Alain Claude, b. 16 April 1973, Vevey, Vaud, Switzerland. Mathematician. Education: PhD, Mathematics, University of Lausanne, 2002. Appointments: Captain, Intelligence, Swiss Air Force; Deputy Director, University of Lausanne. Publications: Integral cohomology of finite postnikov towers, 2002; Integral Cohomology of 2-Local Hopf Spaces with at Most Two Non-Trivial Finite Homotopy Groups, 2004; Homology expondents for H-spaces, 2008. Honours: Prix de la Faculté des Sciences de l'Université de Lausanne, 1998; Prix de la Ville de Lausanne, 2002; United Nations Medal in the Service of Peace, 2005; Swiss Military Medal, 2005. Memberships: Association of Swiss Military Observers; Fédération Suisse de Krav Maga; Ecole de Parachutisme de Château d'Oex; Para-Club de la Gruyère; Fédération Suisse Parachutisme; Aéro Club de Suisse. Address: University of Lausanne, Direction, CH-1015 Lausanne, Switzerland. E-mail: alain.clement@unil.ch

CLEMENTS-CROOME Derek John, b. England. Architectural Engineering. Education: BSc; MSc; PhD; C Eng; C Phys; FICE; FCIBSE; FIOA; FRSA; FASHRAE; F Institute P. Appointments: Trainee Engineer, 1955-60, Research and Development Officer, 1960-66, Brightside Heating and Engineering Co Ltd, Birmingham; Research Fellow, Institute of Sound and Vibration, Southampton University, 1966-67; Lecturer/Senior Lecturer, Department of Ergonomics and Cybernetics, then Department of Civil Engineering, Loughborough University, 1967-78; Senior Lecturer/Reader, School of Architecture and Building Engineering, Bath University, 1978-88; Honorary Visiting Professor: Chongqing Jianzhu University, China, 1994; Tianjin University, 2000; Benxi University, 2002; Shenyang Jianzhu University, 2002; Shenyang Ligong University, 2002; Hong Kong Polytechnic University, 2006-; Xian University, 2007; Professor, Construction Engineering, Department of Construction Management & Engineering, University of Reading, 1988-2007, and Director of Research, 2002-07; Director, Intelligent Buildings Research Group, 2005-; Emeritus Professor and Research Project Advisor, 2008-; Editor/Founder, Intelligent Buildings International Journal, 2006-; Adviser on sustainability and intelligent buildings, Middlesex and Dundee Universities, 2009-. Publications: Books, papers and articles in professional journals. Honours: Bronze medallist, Chartered Institution of Building Services Engineers, 1970; Northcroft Silver medallist, Institute of Hospital Engineering, 1990; Ove Arup Partnership Award, 1993; Freedom of the City of London, 1996; Fellowship, American Society of Heating, Refrigeration and Air-conditioning Engineers, 1997; Lifetime Membership,

International Academy of Indoor Air Sciences, 2000; UK Ambassador for Clima 2000, 7th World Congress, Naples, 2001; Silver Medal, Chartered Institution of Building Services Engineers, 2005; Commissioner for Ministry of Construction, Beijing and Member of Editorial Board for Proceedings for Conferences, 2005-09; Appointed Member, Taiwan Government Science and Technology Advisory Group, 2005-07; President, National Conference of University Professors, 2005-07; Vice President, CIBSE, 2007-09; Special Award, Building Controls Industry Awards, 2009. Memberships include: Board of British Council of Offices; Federation of European Heating and Air-conditioning Associations; Council of Building Services Research and Information Association, 2002-05; Association of Parliamentary Engineering Group; Chairman, UK-Green Building Council, CIBSE; Intelligent Buildings Group; National Ventilation Group. E-mail: d.j.clements-croome@reading.ac.uk

CLEOBURY Stephen John, b. 31 December 1948, Bromley, Kent, England. Conductor. m. Emma Sian Disley, 3 daughters. Education: MA, Mus B, St John's College, Cambridge; FRCO; FRCM. Appointments: Director of Music, St Matthew's, Northampton. 1971-74; Sub-organist, Westminster Abbey, 1974-78; Master of Music, Westminster Cathedral, 1979-82; Director of Music, King's College, Cambridge, 1982-; Conductor, Cambridge University Music Society, 1983-; Chief Conductor, BBC Singers, 1995-. Publications: Sundry arrangements and short compositions. Honour: Hon D Mus, Anglia Polytechnic University, 2001. Memberships: ISM; Vice-President, RCO; Member of Advisory Board, RSCM. Address: King's College, Cambridge CB2 1ST, England. E-mail: sjc1001@cam.ac.uk

CLETO Fabio, b. 6 July 1967, Bergamo, Italy. University Professor. Education: MA, University of Bergamo, 1992; PhD, University of Genoa, 1997. Appointments: Lecturer, University of Genoa, 1999-2003; Lecturer, 2003-06, Professor, 2006-, University of Bergamo. Publications: 6 academic books published, including Camp: Queer Aesthetics and the Performing Subject, 1999. Address: University of Bergamo, Room 201, Piazza Rosate 2, 24129 Bergamo, Italy. E-mail: fabio.cleto@unibg.it

CLIFF Ian Cameron, b. 11 September 1952, Twickenham, England. Diplomat. m. Caroline Redman, 1 son, 2 daughters. Education: 1st Class Honours, Modern History, Magdalen College, Oxford, 1971-74. Appointments: History Master, Dr Challoner's Grammar School, Amersham, 1975-79; 2nd Secretary, Foreign and Commonwealth Office, 1979-80; Arabic Language Training, Damascus and St Andrews University, 1980-82; 1st Secretary, British Embassy, Khartoum, 1982-85; 1st Secretary, Foreign and Commonwealth Office, 1985-89; 1st Secretary, UK Mission to UN, New York, 1989-93; Director, Exports to the Middle East, Near East and North Africa, Department of Trade and Industry, 1993-96; Deputy Head of Mission, British Embassy, Vienna, 1996-2001; HM Ambassador to Bosnia and Herzegovina, 2001-05; HM Ambassador to the Sudan, 2005-07; Ambassador to the Organisation for Security and Co-operation in Europe (OSCE), Vienna, 2007-11; HM Ambassador to Kosovo, 2011-. Publications: Occasional articles in Railway Magazines. Honour: OBE, 1992. Address: c/o Foreign and Commonwealth Office, London SW1A 2AH, England.

CLIFFORD Max, b. April 1943, Kingston-upon-Thames, England. Public Relations Executive. m. Elizabeth, deceased, 1 daughter. Appointments: Worker, Department Store; Former Junior Reporter, Merton & Morden News; Former Press Officer, EMI Records (promoted the Beatles); Founder, Max Clifford Associates, clients have included Muhammad Ali, Marlon Brando, David Copperfield, O J Simpson, Frank Sinatra, Simon Cowell, SEAT, Laing Homes, Mohamed Al-Fayed, Michael Watson, Derek Hatton, Richard Tomlinson, Tony Martin, Rebecca Loos, Shilpa Shetty, Jade Goody. Address: Max Clifford Associates Ltd, 109 New Bond Street, London, W1Y 9AA, England.

CLIFT Roland, b. 19 November 1942, Epsom, Surrey, England. Emeritus Professor of Environmental Technology. m. Diana Helen Manning, 2 sons (1 deceased), 1 daughter. Education: BA, 1963, MA, 1966, Trinity College, Cambridge; PhD, McGill University, Montreal, Canada, 1970. Appointments: Head, Department of Chemical Engineering, 1981-91, Professor of Chemical Engineering, 1981-92, Professor of Environmental Technology, 1992-2008, Emeritus Professor, 2008-, University of Surrey; Editor-in-Chief, Powder Technology, 1987-95; Member, UK Ecolabelling Board, 1992-98; Director, Centre for Environmental Strategy, 1992-2005; Member, Royal Commission on Environmental Pollution, 1996-2005; Visiting Professor, Chalmers University, Göteborg, Sweden, 1999-; Adjunct Professor, University of British Columbia, Canada, 2009-; Director: ClifMar Associates Ltd, 1996-2007; Merrill Lynch New Energy Technologies Ltd, 1999-2010; Industrial Ecology Solutions Ltd, 2001-07; Member, Research Advisory Committee, Forest Research and Forestry Commission, 2004-09; Member, Science Advisory Committee of Department of Environment, Food and Rural Affairs, 2006-11; President, 2009-10, Executive Director, 2011-, International Society for Industrial Ecology. Publications: Bubble, Drops and Particles, 1978, reprint 2006; Slurry Transport using Centrifugal Pumps, 1996, 3rd edition 2005; Processing of Particulate Solids, 1997; Sustainable Development in Practice: Case Studies for Engineers and Scientists, 2004; Numerous edited books and articles in professional journals. Honours: Henry Marion Howe Medal, American Society for Metals, 1976; Frank Moulton Medal, Institution of Chemical Engineers, 1978; Officer of the Order of the British Empire, 1994; Sir Frank Whittle Medal, Royal Academy of Engineering, 2003; Commander of the Order of the British Empire, 2006; Hansen Medal, Institution of Chemical Engineers, 2008. Memberships: Fellow, Royal Academy of Engineering; Fellow, Institution of Chemical Engineers; Honorary Fellow, Chartered Institute of Waste and Environmental Management; Fellow, Royal Society of Arts. Address: Centre for Environmental Strategy, University of Surrey, Guildford, Surrey GU2 7XH, England. E-mail: r.clift@surrey.ac.uk

CLINTON Hilary Rodham, b. 26 October 1947, Chicago, Illinois, USA. Secretary of State; Lawyer and Former First Lady of USA. m. Bill Clinton, 1 daughter. Education: Wellesley College; Yale University. Career: Rose Law Firm, 1977-, currently Senior Partner; Legal Counsel, Nixon Impeachment Staff, 1974; Assistant Professor of Law, Fayetteville and Director, Legal Aid Clinic, 1974-77; Lecturer in Law, University of Arkansas, Little Rock, 1979-80; Chair, Commission on Women in the Profession, ABA, 1987-91; Head, President's Task Force on National Health Reform, 1993-94; Newspaper Columnist, 1995-; Senator from New York, 2001-; Secretary of State, 2009-; Various teaching positions, committee places, public & private ventures. Publications include: It Takes a Village, 1996; Dear Socks, Dear Buddy, 1998; An Invitation to the White House, 2000; Living History (memoirs), 2003; numerous magazine articles. Honours include: Hon LLD (Little Rock, Arkansas) 1985, (Arkansas College) 1988, (Hendrix College) 1992; Hon DHL

(Drew) 1996; One of Most Influential Lawyers in America, 1988, 1991; Outstanding Lawyer-Citizen Award, Arkansas Bar Association, 1992; Lewis Hine Award, National Child Labor Law Commission, 1993; Friend of Family Award, American Home Economics Foundation, 1993; Humanitarian Award, Alheimer's Association, 1994; Elie Wiesel Foundation, 1994; AIDS Awareness Award, 1994; Grammy Award, 1996; numerous other awards and prizes. Address: US Senate, 476 Russell Senate Office Building, Washington, DC 20510, USA. Website: www.clinton.senate.gov

CLINTON William Jefferson (Bill), b. 19 August 1946, Hope, Arkansas, USA. Former President, USA. m. Hillary Rodham, 1975, 1 daughter. Education: BS, International Affairs, Georgetown University, 1964-68; Rhodes Scholar, University College, Oxford, 1968-70; JD, Yale University Law School, 1970-73. Appointments: Professor, University of Arkansas Law School, 1974-76; Democrat Nominee, Arkansas, 1974; Attorney-General, Arkansas, 1977-79; State Governor of Arkansas, 1979-81, 1983-92; Member, Wright, Lindsey & Jennings, law firm, 1981-83; Chairman, Southern Growth Policies Board, 1985-86; Chairman, Education Commissioner of the States, 1986-87; Chairman, National Governor's Association, 1986-87; Vice-Chairman, Democrat Governor's Association, 1987-88, Chairman elect, 1988-89, Chairman, 1989-90; Co-Chairman, Task Force on Education, 1990-91; Chairman, Democrat Leadership Council, 1990-91; President, USA, 1993-2001; Impeached by House of Representatives for perjury and obstruction of justice, 1988; Aquitted in the Senate on both counts, 1999; Suspended from practising law in Supreme Court, 2001-06; UN Special Envoy for Tsunami Relief, 2005-. Publications: Between Hope and History, 1996; My Life (memoir), 2004; Recordings: Peter and the Wolf: Wolf Tracks, 2003; My Life, 2005. Honours: National Council of State Human Service Administrators Association Award; Award, Leadership on Welfare Reform; National Energy Efficiency Advocate Award; Honorary Degree, Northeastern University, Boston, 1993; Honorary Fellow, University College, Oxford, 1993; Honorary DCL, Oxford, 1994; Honorary DLitt, Ulster University, 1995; Hon Co-Chair, Club of Madrid; Grammy Award, Best Spoken Word Album for Children, 2004, Best Spoken Word Album, 2005; British Book Award for Biography of the Year, 2005. Address: 55 West 125th Street, New York, NY 10027, USA. Website: www.clintonpresidentialcenter.org

CLODIUS Leo, b. 29 April 1930, Osnabruck, Germany. Retired Plastic Reconstructive Surgeon. m. Martha Tobler. Education: Resident, Boston City Hospital, Massachusetts Memorial Hospital, 1957-60. Appointments: Plastic Reconstructive Surgeon, St Barnabas Medical Centre, 1960-63, Roswell Park Memorial Institute, 1963; Military service, Swiss Army Medical Corps; Head, Plastic Surgery, University of Zurich, Switzerland, 1964-87; Docent, Plastic Surgery University, 1983. Publications: Around 200 articles in professional journals. Honours: Grantee, Swiss National Research, 1973-82; Recipient, Asellius Ring, Tucson, 1973; Scudo D'Oro Award, 1979; Purkinje Medal, 1982; Dieffenbach Medal, 1990; Golden Question Mark, American Ignorance Society, 2006. Memberships: Diplomate, American Board of Plastic Reconstructive Surgery; Swiss Board of Plastic Reconstructive Surgery; Swiss Medical Association; Swiss Society for Plastic Reconstructive Surgery; Swiss Society of Aesthetic Surgery; International Society of Lymphology; Swiss Society of Lymphology; British Association of Plastic Surgeons; German Association of Plastic Surgeons; University Catolica Argentina. Address: Weid 17, 8126 Zumikon, Switzerland.

CLOONEY George, b. 6 May 1961, Kentucky, USA. Actor. m. Talia Blasam, 1989, divorced 1993. Appointments: TV series: E/R, 1984-85; The Facts of Life, 1985-86; Roseanne, 1988-89; Sunset Beat, 1990; Baby Talk, 1991; Sister, 1992-94; ER, 1994-99; Films include: Return of the Killer Tomatoes, 1988; Red Surf, 1990; Unbecoming Age, 1993; From Dusk Till Dawn, 1996; Batman and Robin, The Peacemaker, 1997; Three Kings, 1999; O Brother, Where Art Thou?, Perfect Storm, 2000; Spy Kids, Ocean's Eleven, 2001; Welcome to Collinwood, Solaris, Confessions of a Dangerous Mind, 2002; Spy Kids 3-D: Game Over, Intolerable Cruelty, 2003; Ocean's Twelve, 2004; Good Night and Good Luck, Syriana, Good Night and Good Luck, 2005; The Good German, 2006; Ocean's Thirteen, Michael Clayton, 2007; Leatherheads, Burn After Reading, 2008; Fantastic Mr Fox, The Men Who Stare at Goats, Up in the Air, 2009; The Descendants, 2011. Honours: Golden Globe Award, Best Supporting Actor, 2006; Oscar, Best Supporting Actor, 2006. Address: William Morris Agency, 151 El Camino, Beverly Hills, CA 90212, USA.

CLOSE Glenn, b. 19 March 1947, Greenwich, Connecticut, USA. Actress. m. (1) C Wade, divorced, (2) J Marlas, 1984, divorced, 1 daughter (with J Starke). Education: William and Mary College. Career: Co-owner, The Leaf and Bean Coffee House, 1991-; Films include: The World According to Garp, 1982; The Big Chill, 1983; The Stone Boy, 1984; Jagged Edge, 1985; Fatal Attraction, 1987; Dangerous Liaisons, Hamlet, 1989; The House of Spirits, Hamlet, 1990; 101 Dalmatians, Mars Attacks! 1996; Air Force One, Paradise Road, 1997; Tarzan, Cookie's Fortune, 1999; 102 Dalmatians, 2000; The Safety of Objects, 2001; Pinocchio (voice), 2002; Le Divorce, 2003; The Stepford Wives, Heights, 2004; Hoodwinked (voice), 2005; Nine Lives, The Chumscrubber, Tarzan II (voice), 2005; Evening, 2007; HOME, 2009; Albert Nobbs, 2011; Theatre includes: The Rules of the Game; A Streetcar Named Desire; King Lear; The Rose Tattoo; Death and the Maiden; Sunset Boulevard; TV: The Lion in Winter, 2003; The West Wing, 2004; The Shield, 2005; Damages, 2007-. Honours: Golden Globe Award, Best Actress in a Miniseries or TV Movie, 2005; Screen Actors Guild Awards, 2005; Common Wealth Award of Distinguished Service, 2008; Star on Hollywood Walk of Fame, 2009; Emmy Award, Outstanding Lead Actress in a Drama Series, 2009. Address: Creative Artists Agency, 9830 Wilshire Boulevard, Beverly Hills, CA 90212, USA.

CLOSE Seamus Anthony, b. 12 August 1947. Financial Director. m. Deirdre McCann, 3 sons, 1 daughter. Education: St Malachy's College, Belfast; Belfast College of Business Studies. Appointments: Member, 1973-2011, Mayor, 1993-94, Lisburn (Borough) City Council; Chairman, Alliance Party, 1981-82, Deputy Leader, 1991-2001, Member, Northern Ireland Assembly, 1982-86; Financial Director, S D Bell & Co Ltd, 1986-; Negotiator, Brooke/Mayhew Talks, 1991-92; Good Friday Agreement, 1996-98; Forum for Peace and Reconciliation, Dublin, 1994-95; Northern Ireland Forum for Political Dialogue, 1996-98; Member, Northern Ireland Legislative Assembly, 1998-2007. Honours: Officer of the Most Excellent Order of the British Empire (OBE), 1996; Honorary Burgess (Freeman), Lisburn City Council, 2010. Address: 123 Moira Road, Lisburn, BT28 1RJ, Northern Ireland.

CLOSSICK Peter, b. 18 May 1948, London. Artist. m. Joyce, 1 daughter. Education: Shoe Design, Leicester Polytechnic, 1969; BA, Fine Art, Camberwell College of Art, 1978; Post-grad, Goldsmiths London University, 1979. Appointments: Visiting Lecturer: Oxford-Brookes University; Open College of the Arts; Greenwich Community College;

Ulster University; Woodlands Gallery Exhibitions Adviser, 1995-2004; Art Consultant, Blackheath Conservatoire of Music and Art, 2003-06; Exhibiting Artist, solo and group exhibitions around the UK; Work held in public and private collections. Publications: Dictionary of Artists in Britain Since 1945, Art Dictionaries Ltd; Who's Who in Art Since 1927, Art Trade Press Ltd; Painting Without A Brush, Studio Vista; The London Group – 90th Anniversary, Tate Britain. Honours: Elected London Group President, 2000-05; Elected Vice President, The London Group, 2008; Elected President, Blackheath Art Society, 2008-10; Prize, Lynn Painter-Stainers Exhibition, 2008. Memberships: The London Group; New English Art Club. Address: 358 Lee High Road, Lee Green, London SE12 8RS, England. E-mail: j.clossick@ntlworld.com Website: www.peterclossick.com

CLOUDSLEY Peter Leslie, b. 27 July 1952, Esher, Surrey, England. Musicologist. Education: Pembroke College, Cambridge, 1971-74. Appointments: Harpsichord maker with own workshop, Clerkenwell Workshops, London, 1976-82; Courses taught at City Literary Institute and elsewhere in Popular and Traditional Music, Peru, Brazil, South America, lectures at Canning House, Globe, Latin American Music Seminar, etc; Research through sound recording of traditional music in the Peruvian Andes, in collaboration with the National Sound Archive, British Museum and collecting instruments for the Museum of Mankind, British Museum, 1980-2000; Research of Shamanism and plant medicine, Peruvian Andes and Amazon, recording icaros, chants and interviews with shamans and patients, 1988-; Manager and Owner, Amazon Retreat Centre, Mishana, Loreto, Peru, 2003-. Publications: The Ayahuasca Visions of Pablo Amaringo, 2011; Numerous articles in professional journals; Programmes and interviews on national radio. Address: 44 Alconbury Road, London E5 8RH, England.

CLOUDSLEY Anne, (Jessie Anne Cloudsley-Thompson), b. 20 March 1915, Reigate, Surrey, England. Physiotherapist; Artist. m. Professor JL Cloudsley-Thompson, 3 sons. Education: MCSP, ME, LET, 1937, University College Hospital, London, England; LCAD, 1976, DipBS Hons, 1977, Byam Shaw School of Art, University of the Arts, London. Appointments: Established Physiotherapy Department, Hatfield Military Hospital, Hertfordshire, England, 1940-42; Superintendent Physiotherapist, Peripheral Nerve Injuries Centre, Wingfield Orthopaedic Hospital, Oxford, England, 1942-44; Superintendent Physiotherapist, Omdurman General Hospital, Sudan, 1960-71; Founder and Honorary Gallery Curator, Africa Centre, London, 1978-82; Visiting Lecturer, Fine Art, University of Nigeria, Nsukka, 1981; Lecturer, Lithography, Working Men's College, London NW1, 1982-91. Publications: Women of Omdurman: life, love and the cult of virginity, 1983, reprinted 1983, 1984, 1987; Articles and reviews; Numerous exhibitions: Individual: AFD Gallery, 1977; Mandeer Gallery, 1981; Ecology Centre, 1990; Budapest, 1990; Walk Gallery, 2004; Little Known Aspects of Sudanese Life (throughout Europe 1982-84); SOAS and Brunei Gallery, 2006; Highgate Gallery, 2010; Group: The Royal Academy Summer Exhibition, 1992, 1993; Fresh Art, 2001, 2002, 2003; Cork Street, 2003; Discerning Eye, Mall Galleries, 2004; Menier, 2004, 2007, 2008, 2009; Bankside, 2005, 2006; Pastel Society, Mall Galleries, 2006; Royal Society of British Artists, Mall Galleries, 2008, 2009, 2010. Honours: Listed in national and international biographical directories. Memberships: Chartered Society of Physiotherapy, 1935-; Print Makers Council, 1996-2010; Elected to The London Group, 2002-. Address: 10 Battishill Street, London N1 1TE, England.

CLOUDSLEY-THOMPSON John Leonard, b. 23 May 1921, Murree, India. Professor of Zoology. m. Jessie Anne Cloudsley, 3 sons. Education: BA, 1947, MA, 1949, PhD, 1950, Pembroke College, Cambridge; DSc, University of London, 1960. Appointments: War Service, 1940-44; Lecturer in Zoology, King's College, University of London, 1950-60; Professor of Zoology, University of Khartoum and Keeper, Sudan Natural History Museum, 1960-71; Professor of Zoology, Birkbeck College, University of London, 1972-86; Professor Emeritus, 1986-. Publications: Over 55 books, including: Ecophysiology of Desert Arthropods and Reptiles, 1991; The Nile Quest, novel, 1994; Biotic Interactions in Arid Lands, 1996; Teach Yourself Ecology, 1998; The Diversity of Amphibians and Reptiles, 1999; Ecology and Behaviour of Mesozoic Reptiles, 2005; Sharpshooter: Memories of Armoured Warfare 1939-45, 2006; Monographs, 11 Children's natural history books: Contributions to Encyclopaedia Britannica, Encyclopedia Americana; Articles in professional journals. Honours: Honorary Captain, 1944; Royal African Society Medal, 1969; Institute of Biology KSS Charter Award, 1981; Honorary DSc, Khartoum and Silver Jubilee Gold Medal, 1981; Biological Council Medal, 1985; J H Grundy Memorial Medal, Royal Army Medical College, 1987; Peter Scott Memorial Award, British Naturalists' Association, 1993, Honorary Fellow, 2007; Fellow Honoris Causa, Linnean Society, 1997; Honorary Fellow, British Herpetological Society, 2008; Listed in national and international biographical publications. Memberships: Liveryman, Worshipful Company of Skinners; C Biol, FBS; FWAAS; FRES; FLS; FZS. Address: 10 Battishill Street, Islington, London N1 1TE, England.

COAKLEY Sarah Anne, b. 10 September 1951, London, England. Professor; Anglican Priest. m. James Farwell Coakley, 1973, 2 daughters. Education: BA (1st class Hons), 1970-73, PhD, 1983, MA, 1983, New Hall, Cambridge; ThM (distinction), Harvard Divinity School, USA, 1973-75. Appointments: Lecturer, Senior Lecturer, Religious Studies, University of Lancaster, 1976-91; Tutorial Fellow, University Lecturer in Theology, Oriel College, Oxford, 1991-93; Mallinckrodt Professor of Divinity, 1995-2007, Professor, Christian Theology, 1993-95, Harvard University; Norris-Hulse Professor of Divinity, University of Cambridge, 2007-. Publications: Theological monographs and numerous articles in professional journals. Honours include: Dr Theol (honoris causa), Lund University, Sweden, 2006; DD (honoris causa), General Theology Seminary, New York, 2007; Honorary Canon, Ely Cathedral, 2011. Memberships: Society for the Study of Theology; Society of Christian Philosophers; American Academy of Religion; North American Patristics Society; American Theological Society; British Society for the Philosophy of Religion; Professorial Fellow, New Hall/ Murray Edwards, Cambridge. Address: Faculty of Divinity, West Road, Cambridge, CB3 9BS, England.

COBB David Jeffery, b. 12 March 1926, Harrow, Middlesex, England. Freelance Writer; Poet. Widowed, 2 sons, 3 daughters. Education: BA, Bristol, 1954; PGCE, 1955. Appointments: German Teacher, Nottinghamshire, 1955-58; Programme Officer, UNESCO Institute of Education, Hamburg, 1958-62; English Teacher, British Council, Bangkok, 1962-68; Assistant Professor, Asian Institute of Technology, Bangkok, 1968-72; Manager, RDU, Longman Group Ltd, 1972-84; Freelance, 1985-. Publications: A Leap in the Light; Mounting Shadows; Jumping From Kiyomizu; Chips off the Old Great Wall; The Spring Journey to the Saxon Shore; The Iron Book of British Haiku; A Bowl of Sloes; The Genius of Haiku, Readings From R H Blyth;

DICTIONARY OF INTERNATIONAL BIOGRAPHY 36th EDITION

Forefathers; Palm; The British Museum Haiku; The Dead Poets' Cabaret; Business in Eden; Im Zeichen des Janus; Veter se obrne (A Shift in the Wind); Spitting Pips,2009; Lap Stone, 2011; Contributions to: Rialto; Blithe Spirit; Modern Haiku; Frogpond; HQ; Snapshots; Chimera. Honours: 1st Prize, Cardiff International Haiku Competition, 1991; 2nd Prize, HSA Merit Book Awards, 1997 and 2002; The Sasakawa Prize for Innovation in the Field of Haikai, 2004; Takahama Kyoshi Prize, 2006; Oi Ocha Haiku First Prize, 2010. Memberships: British Haiku Society, president, 1997-2002; Haiku Society of America; Royal Bangkok Sports Club; Suffolk Poetry Society. Address: Sinodun, Shalford, Braintree, Essex CM7 5HN, England. E-mail: email:@davidcobb.co.uk Website: www.davidcobb.co.uk

COCKER Jarvis Branson, b. 19 September, 1963, England. Singer. m. Camille Bidault-Waddington, divorced, 1 son. Education: St Martin's College of Art & Design. Appointments: Singer with Pulp (formerly named Arabacus Pulp), 1981-; Made Videos for Pulp, Aphex Twin, Tindersticks; Co-Producer, Do You Remember The First Time? (TV); Singer with Relaxed Muscle, 2002-. Creative Works: Singles include: My Legendary Girlfriend, 1991; Razzmatazz, 1992; O U, 1992; Babies, 1992; Common People, 1995; Disco 2000, 1996; Running the World, 2006; Don't Let Him Waste Your Time, 2007; Fat Children, 2007; Temptation (Live), 2008; Angela, 2009; Albums include: It, 1983; Freaks, 1987; Separations, 1992; His 'N' Hers, 1994; Different Class, 1995; This is Hardcore, 1998; We Love Life, 2001; A Heavy Nite With ..., 2003; Jarvis, 2006; Further Complications, 2009; Compositions for films: Do You Remember the First Time? 1994; Wild Side, 1995; Harry Potter and the Goblet of Fire, 2005; Children of Men, 2006. Address: Rough Trade Management, 66 Golborne Road, London W10 5PS, England. Website: www.pulponline.com

COCKER Joe, b. 20 May 1944, Sheffield, South Yorkshire, England. Singer; Songwriter. Career: Singer, Northern club circuit with group The Grease Band, 1965-69; Solo artiste, 1968-; Regular worldwide tours; Major concert appearances include: National Jazz And Blues Festival, 1968; Denver Pop Festival, 1969; Newport '69 Festival, 1969; Woodstock Festival (filmed), 1969; Isle Of Wight Festival, 1969; Co-headliner with Beach Boys, Crystal Palace Garden Party, 1972; Prince's Trust Rock Gala, 1988; Nelson Mandela's 70th Birthday Tribute, Wembley Stadium, 1988; Rock In Rio II Festival, 1991; Guitar Legends, Seville, Spain, 1991; Montreux Jazz Festival, filmed for MTV's Unplugged series, 1992; Blues Music Festival, with B.B.King, 1992; Numerous television and radio broadcasts worldwide. Recordings: Hit singles include: With A Little Help From My Friends (Number 1, UK), 1968; Delta Lady, 1969; The Letter, 1970; Cry Me A River, 1970; You Are So Beautiful, 1975; Unchain My Heart, 1987; When The Night Comes, 1990; Night Calls, 1993; Simple Things, 1994; Could You Be Loved, 1998; with Jennifer Warnes: Up Where We Belong (Number 1, US), theme to film An Officer And A Gentleman, 1982; Contributions to film soundtracks include: Edge Of A Dream, for film Teachers, 1984; You Can Leave Your Hat On, for film 9« Weeks, 1986; Love Lives On, for film Bigfoot And The Hendersons, 1987; (All I Know) Feels Like Forever, for film The Cutting Edge, 1992; Trust In Me, duet with Sass Jordan, for film The Bodyguard, 1992; Albums include: With A Little Help From My Friends, 1969; Joe Cocker, 1970; Mad Dogs And Englishmen, 1970; Cocker Happy, 1971; Something To Say, 1972; I Can Stand A Little Rain, 1974; Jamaica Say You Will, 1975; Live In Los Angeles, 1976; Stingray, 1976; Joe Cocker's Greatest Hits, 1977; Luxury You Can Afford, 1978; Sheffield Steel, 1982; Civilized Man, 1984; Cocker, 1986; Unchain My Heart, 1987; Nightriding, 1988; One Night Of Sin, 1989; Joe Cocker Live, 1990; Night Calls, 1992; The Legend - The Essential Collection, 1992; Have A Little Faith, 1994; Organic, 1996; Across from Midnight, 1997; Contributor, Two Rooms (tribute album to Elton John and Bernie Taupin), 1991. Honours: Grammy, Best Pop Vocal Performance, Up Where We Belong, 1983; Academy Award, Best Film Song, Up Where We Belong, 1983; Grammy Nomination, One Night Of Sin, 1989. Current Management: Roger Davies Management, 15030 Ventura Blvd #772, Sherman Oaks, CA 91403, USA.

COE, Baron of Ranmore in the County of Surrey, Sebastian Newbold, b. 29 September 1956. Athelete. m. Nicola Susan Elliott, 1990, divorced 2002, 2 sons, 2 daughters. Education: BSc Hons, Economics, Social History, Loughborough University. Career: Winner, Gold Medal for running 1500m and silver medal for 800m, Moscow Olympics, 1980; Gold medal for 1500m and silver medal for 800m, Los Angeles Olympics, 1984; European 800m Champion, Stuttgart, 1986; World Record Holder at 800m, 1000m and mile, 1981; Research Assistant, Loughborough University, 1981-84; Member, 1983-89, Vice Chairman, 1986-89, Chairman, Olympic Review Group, 1984-85, Sports Council; Member, HEA, 1987-92; Olympic Committee, Medical Commission, 1987-; Conservative MP for Falmouth and Camborne, 1992-97; PPS to Deputy PM, 1995-96; Assistant Government Whip, 1996-97; Private Secretary to Leader of the Opposition, The Rt Hon William Hague, MP, 1997-2001; Global Advisor, NIKE, 2000-; Council Member, International Association of Athletic Federations, 2003-; Vice Chair, 2003-04, Chair and President, 2004-, London 2012 Olympic and Paralympic Games Bid; Chairman, FIFA's Ethics Commission, 2006; Committee Member, bid to bring 2018 World Cup to England. Publications: Running Free, with David Miller, 1981; Running for Fitness, with Peter Coe, 1983; The Olympians, 1984, 1996; More Than a Game, 1992; Born to Run (autobiography), 1992. Honours: Prince of Asturias Awad, 1987; MBE, 1982; OBE, 1990; Life Peer, 2000; BBC Sports Personality of the Year, Special Award, 2005; Knight Commander of the Order of the British Empire, 2006. Memberships: Associate Member, Academie des Sports, France; Athletes Commission, IOC; IOC Medical Commission, 1988-94; Member, Sport For All Commission, 1998-; IOC Commission 2000, 1999.

COEN Ethan, b. 21 September 1958, St Louis Park, Minnesota, USA. Film Producer; Screenwriter. m. Tricia Cooke. Education: Princeton University. Appointments: Screenwriter with Joel Coen, Crime Wave (formerly XYZ Murders); Producer, Screenplay, Editor, Blood Simple, 1984. Creative Works: Films: Raising Arizona, 1987; Miller's Crossing, 1990; Barton Fink, 1991; The Hudsucker Proxy, 1994; Fargo, 1996; The Naked Man; The Big Lebowski, 1998; O Brother, Where Art Thou? 2000; The Man Who Wasn't There, 2001; Fever in the Blood, 2002; Intolerable Cruelty, Bad Santa, 2003; The Ladykillers, 2004; Paris I Love You, Romance & Cigarettes, 2006; No Country for Old Men (Producer), 2007; Burn After Reading, 2008; A Serious Man, Suburbicon, 2009; True Grit, 2010. Honours: 12 Awards, 32 nominations. Publication: Gates of Eden, 1998. Address: c/o UTA, 9560 Wilshire Boulevard, Beverly Hills, CA 90212, USA.

COEN Joel, b. 29 November 1955, St Louis Park, Minnesota, USA. Film Director; Screenwriter. m. Frances McDormand, 1984, 1 adopted son. Education: Simon's Rock College; New York University. Appointments: Assistant Editor, Fear No

Evil, Evil Dead; Worked with Rock Video Crews; Screenwriter with Ethan Coen, Crime Wave (formerly XYZ Murders). Creative Works: Films: Blood Simple, 1984; Raising Arizona, 1987; Miller's Crossing, 1990; Barton Fink, 1991; The Hudsucker Proxy, 1994; Fargo, 1996; The Big Lebowski; O Brother, Where Art Thou? 2000; The Man Who Wasn't There, 2001; Intolerable Cruelty, Santa, 2003; The Ladykillers, 2004; Paris I Love You, Romance & Cigarettes, 2006; No Country For Old Men, 2007; Burn After Reading, 2008; Suburbicon, A Serious Man, 2009; True Grit, 2010. Honours include: Best Director Award, Cannes International Film Festival, 1996; 31 Awards, 44 Nominations. Address: c/o UTA, 9560 Wilshire Boulevard, Beverly Hills, CA 90212, USA.

COERPER Milo George, b. 8 May 1925, Milwaukee, Wisconsin, USA. Naval Officer; Lawyer; Episcopal Priest. m. Wendy Hicks, 1 son, 2 daughters. Education: BS, US Naval Academy, 1946; LLB, University of Michigan Law School, 1954; MA, 1957, PhD, 1960, Georgetown University; Certificate, Theology (by extension), University of the South, 1980. Appointments: Ensign, Lieutenant (jg), Lieutenant (sg), US Navy; Aide to Admiral in charge of battleships during the Korean War; Associate Law Firm, 1954-60; Part-time Professor, Catholic University Law School and George Washington University Law School, 1960; Associate, 1961-64, Partner, 1964-95, Retired Partner,1996-, Coudert Brothers International Law Firm; Expert Geographical Indications – World Intellectual Property Organization (WIPO), 1991; Ordained Episcopal Priest in the Diocese of Maryland, 1979; Voluntary Chaplain, Washington National Cathedral, 1986-; Trustee, The Friends of Canterbury Cathedral in the United States, 1999-. Publications: The Use of Public International Law by Municipal Courts in Cases Arising out of the Taking of Alien Property (PhD dissertation), 1960; A Deeper Dimension, 1995; Certification Marks as a Means of Protecting Wine Appellations in the US, 1998. Honour: Cross of the Order of Merit of the Federal Republic of Germany, 1993. Memberships: American Society of International Law; International Law Association; American Bar Association; Metropolitan Club; Army and Navy Club. Address: 7315 Brookville Road, Chevy Chase, MD 20815, USA.

COETZEE Liza (Elizabeth Susanna Maria), b. 7 April 1971, Durban, South Africa. University Lecturer. m. Anton, 3 sons, 1 daughter. Education: B Com, Accounting; B Com (Hons), Accounting; H Dip, Tax Law; M Com, Taxation. Appointments: Deloitte Taxation Services, Johannesburg, South Africa, 1997-99; Lecturer, University of South Africa, 2000-06; Lecturer, University of Pretoria, South Africa, 2007-. Memberships: South African Institute of Chartered Accountants; South African Institute of Tax Practitioners. Address: University of Pretoria, Department of Taxation, Private Bag X20, Hatfield 0028, South Africa. E-mail: liza.coetzee@up.ac.za

COGGON David Noel Murray, b. 25 December 1950, Sutton Coldfield, England. Doctor. m. Sarah, 1 son, 4 daughters. Education: BA, 1972, MA, 1976, Cambridge University; BM BCh, 1976, DM, 1993, Oxford University Medical School; PhD, Southampton, 1984. Appointments: House Physician, Royal South Hants Hospital, Southampton, 1976; House Surgeon, North Staffs Royal Infirmary, Stoke-on-Trent, 1976-77; SHO, 1977-78, Registrar, 1978-80, Medicine, Nottingham; Clinical Scientist, 1980-97, Reader in Occupational and Environmental Medicine, 1992-97, MRC Environmental Epidemiology Unit, University of Southampton; Director, Occupational Health, Southampton University Hospitals Trust, 1992-96; Professor, Occupational and Environmental Medicine, MRC Lifecourse Epidemiology Unit, University of Southampton, 1997-; President, Faculty of Occupational Medicine, Royal College of Physicians, 2008-11. Publications: Numerous articles in professional journals. Honours: OBE, 2002. Memberships: FRCP; FFOM; FFPH; FMedSci. E-mail: dnc@mrc.soton.ac.uk

COHEN Leonard, b. 21 September 1934, Montreal, Quebec, Canada. Singer; Songwriter. 1 son and 1 daughter with Suzanne Elrod. Education: McGill University. Career: Founder, Country and Western group, The Buckskin Boys, 1951; Novelist; Poet; Solo singer; Zen Buddhist monk, 1994-99. Compositions include: Suzanne; Priests (both recorded by Judy Collins); Sisters Of Mercy; Hey, That's No Way To Say Goodbye; Story Of Isaac; Bird On A Wire. Recordings: Albums: The Songs Of Leonard Cohen, 1968; Songs From A Room, 1969; Songs Of Love And Hate, 1971; Live Songs, 1973; New Skin For The Old Ceremony, 1974; Greatest Hits, 1975; The Best Of Leonard Cohen, 1976; Death Of A Ladies Man, 1977; Recent Songs, 1979; Various Positions, 1985; I'm Your Man, 1988; The Future, 1992; Ten New Songs, 2001; Dear Heather, 2004. Publications: Poetry: Let Us Compare Mythologies, 1956; The Spice-Box of Earth, 1961; Flowers for Hitler, 1964; Parasites of Heaven, 1966; Selected Poems 1956-1968, 1968; The Energy of Slaves, 1972; Death of a Lady's man, 1978; Book of Mercy, 1984; Stranger Music, 1993; Book of Longing, 2006; Novels: The Favourite Game, 1963; Beautiful Losers, 1966. Honours include: McGill Literary Award for Let Us Compare Mythologies; Governor General's Award, 1968; Canadian Music Hall of Fame, 1991; 2 Juno Awards, 1993, 1994; SNEP Award, 2002; Companion of the Order of Canada, 2003; Canadian Songwriters Hall of Fame, 2006; Grammy, Album of the Year, 2007; Rock and Roll Hall of Fame, 2008; Grand Officer, National Order of Quebec, 2008. Address: Suite 91, 419 N Larchmont Blvd, Los Angeles, CA 90004, USA.

COHN-SHERBOK Dan, b. 1 February 1945, Denver, Colorado, USA. Emeritus Professor of Judaism. m. Lavinia Cohn-Sherbok. Education: BA, Williams College, 1962-66; BHL, MAHL, Hebrew Union College, 1966-71; PhD, Cambridge University, 1971-74. Appointments: Lecturer, Theology, University of Kent, Canterbury, 1975-97; Emeritus Professor of Judaism, University of Wales, Lampeter; Visiting Professor, York St John University, St Mary's University College. Publications: The Jewish Heritage; Dictionary of Judaism and Christianity; Atlas of Jewish History; The Jewish Faith; The Hebrew Bible; Fifty Key Jewish Thinkers; Judaism; Judaism: History, Belief and Practice; Understanding the Holocaust; Holocaust Theology; Interfaith Theology; A Concise Encyclopaedia of Judaism; Jewish Mysticism: An Anthology; Judaism and Other Faiths; Jewish Petitionary Prayers; Modern Judaism; Dictionary of Jewish Biography; The Paradox of Antisemitism; Politics of Apocalypse; Kabbalah and Jewish Mysticism; Dictionary of Jewish Biography; Judaism Today. Honours: Honorary DD, Hebrew Union College; Honorary Professor, University of Aberystwyth; Honorary Research Fellow, Heythrop College, University of London; Listed in numerous Who's Who and biographical publications. Memberships: London Society for the Study of Religion; Cymmrodian Society; Athenaeum; Williams Club; Lansdowne Club; AHRC Peer Review College. Address: Department of Theology and Religious Studies, University of Wales, Lampeter SA48 7ED, Wales.

COLE B J, b. 17 June 1946, North London, England. Musician (pedal steel guitar); Producer. Career: Musician, Country Music circuit, London, 1964-; Pedal steel guitar player, Cochise; Founder member, producer, Hank Wangford Band; Leading exponent of instrument in UK; Currently prolific session musician and solo artiste; Leader, own group Transparent Music Ensemble; Replacement guitarist for the Verve, 1998-. Recordings: Albums: New Hovering Dog, 1972; Transparent Music, 1989; The Heart Of The Moment, 1995; As session musician: Tiny Dancer, Elton John, 1970; Wide Eyed And Legless, Andy Fairweather-Low, 1975; No Regrets, Walker Brothers, 1976; City To City, Gerry Rafferty, 1978; Everything Must Change, Paul Young, 1984; Silver Moon, David Sylvian, 1986; Diet Of Strange Places, k d lang, 1987; Montagne D'Or, The Orb, 1995; Possibly Maybe, Björk, 1995; Drum 'n' Bass 'n' Steel, 1999; Stop the Panic, 2000; Spring Collection, 2000; A Virtual Landslide, 2008; with Hank Wangford: Hank Wangford, 1980; Live, 1982; Other recordings with: Johnny Nash; Deacon Blue; Level 42; Danny Thompson; Alan Parsons Project; Shakin' Stevens; Beautiful South; John Cale; Echobelly; Elton John; R.E.M; The Verve; Depeche Mode; David Gilmour.

COLE Cheryl, b. 30 June 1983, Newcastle upon Tyne, England. Singer; TV Personality. m. Ashley Cole, 2006. Career: Singer; Albums with Girls Aloud: Sound of the Underground, 2003; What Will the Neighbours Say? 2004; Chemistry, 2005; Tangled Up, 2007; Out of Control, 2008; Singles with Girls Aloud: Sound of the Underground, 2002; No Good Advice, Life Got Cold, Jump, 2003; The Show, Love Machine, I'll Stand by You, 2004; Wake Me Up, Long Hot Summer, Biology, See the Day, 2005; Whole Lotta History, Something Kinda Ooooh, I Think We're Alone Now, 2006; Walk This Way, Sexy! No No No, Call the Shots, 2007; Can't Speak French, The Promise, 2008; The Loving Kind, Untouchable, 2009; Solo Album: 3 Words, 2009; Solo Singles: Heartbreaker, 2008; Fight For This Love, 2009; Judge, The X Factor, 2008-. Publications: Dreams that Glitter – Our Story (autobiography of Girls Aloud), 2008.

COLE Lily, b. 19 May 1988, Torquay, Devon, England. Model; Actress. Education: St Marylebone Girls School; Latymer Upper School; Cambridge University. Career: Model: Signed to Storm Models, 2002; Appeared in: Vogue, Citizen K, V; Advertising campaigns for: Chanel, DKNY, Jean Paul Gautier, Versace; Alexander McQueen, John Galliano, Louis Vuitton, Marks & Spencer, Rimmel London; Actress: Films: St Trinian's, 2007; Rage, 2009; The Imaginarium of Doctor Parnassus, 2009; Phantasmagoria: The Visions of Lewis Carroll, 2010. Honours: Model of the Year, British Fashion Awards, 2004.

COLE Natalie Maria, b. 6 February 1950, Los Angeles, California, USA. Singer. m. (1) Marvin J Yancy, 1976, divorced 1980, 1 son, (2) Andre Fischer, 1989, divorced 1995, (3) Kenneth Dupree, 2001, divorced, 2004. Education: BA, Child Psychology, University of Massachusetts, 1972. Career: Stage debut, 1962; Solo recording artist, 1975-; Major concerts worldwide include: Tokyo Music Festival, 1979; Nelson Mandela 70th Birthday Concert, Wembley, 1988; Nelson Mandela tribute, Wembley, 1990; John Lennon Tribute Concert, Liverpool, 1990; Homeless benefit concert with Quincy Jones, Pasadena, 1992; Rainforest benefit concert, Carnegie Hall, 1992; Commitment To Life VI, (AIDs benefit concert), Los Angeles, 1992; Television appearances include: Sinatra And Friends, 1977; Host, Big Break, 1990; Motown 30, 1990; Tonight Show, 1991; Entertainers '91, 1991; Recordings: Hit singles: This Will Be, 1975; Sophisticated Lady, 1976; I've Got Love On My Mind, 1977; Our Love (Number 1, US R&B chart), 1977; Gimme Some Time (duet with Peabo Bryson), 1980; What You Won't Do For Love (duet with Peabo Bryson), 1980; Jump Start, 1987; I Live For Your Love, 1988; Pink Cadillac, 1988; Miss You Like Crazy (Number 1, US R&B charts), 1989; Wild Women Do, from film Pretty Woman, 1990; Unforgettable (duet with father Nat "King" Cole), 1991; Smile Like Yours, 1997; Say You Love Me, Snowfall on the Sahara, 1999; Livin' for Love, Angel on My Shoulder, 2000; Day Dreaming, 2006; Albums: Inseparable, 1975; Natalie, 1976; Unpredictable, 1977; Thankful, 1978; Natalie...Live!, 1978; I Love You So, 1979; Don't Look Back, 1980; Happy Love, 1981; Natalie Cole Collection, 1981; I'm Ready, 1982; Dangerous, 1985; Everlasting, 1987; Good To Be Back, 1989; Unforgettable...With Love (Number 1, US), 1991; The Soul Of Natalie Cole, 1991; Take A Look, 1993; Holly and Ivy, 1994; Stardust, 1996; This Will Be, 1997; Snowfall on the Sahara, 1999; Love Songs (compilation), 2000; Ask a Woman Who Knows, 2002; Leavin' 2006; Still Unforgettable, 2008; with Peabo Bryson: We're The Best Of Friends, 1980. Publications: Angel on My Shoulder (autobiography), 2000. Honours: Numerous Grammy Awards include: Best New Artist, 1976; Best Female R&B Vocal Performance, 1976, 1977; 5 Grammy Awards for Unforgettable, including Best Song, Best Album, 1992; 5 NAACP Image Awards, 1976, 1988, 1992; American Music Awards: Favourite Female R&B Artist, 1978; Favourite Artist, Favourite Album, 1992; Soul Train Award, Best Single, 1988; Various Gold discs. Memberships: AFTRA; NARAS. Address: c/o Jennifer Allen, PMK, 8500 Wilshire Boulevard, Suite 700, Beverly Hills, CA 90211, USA.

CÖLFEN Helmut, b. 24 July 1965, Krefeld, Germany. Scientist; Chemist. m. Stefanie Sender, 2 daughters, 1 son. Education: Chemistry Studies, Gerhard-Mercator University, Duisburg, 1985-91; PhD, Chemistry, 1993; Postdoctoral Studies, National Centre for Macromolecular Hydrodynamics, Nottingham, England, 1993-95; Habilitation, Max-Planck-Institute for Colloids and Interfaces, 1995-2001. Appointments: Research Assistant, University of Duisburg, 1991-93; Postdoctoral Studies, 1993-95; Scientist, Head of Analytical Services in Colloid Chemistry, Head of Biominetic Mineralisation Group, Max-Planck-Institute for Colloids and Interfaces, 1995-2010; Private Dozent, Potsdam University, 2004-; Full Professor, University of Konstanz, Physical Chemistry, 2010-. Publications: More than 180 papers as co-author and first author in scientific journals. Honours: Graduate Scholarship, University of Duisburg, 1991-93; Hochschulabsolventenpreis, University of Duisburg, 1991; Studienabschlussstipendium, Fonds der chemischen Industrie, 1993; Dr Hermann Schnell Award, German Chemical Society; Travel Award, Macromolecular Chemistry Division, German Chemical Society; Steinhofer Lecture, Steinhofer Foundation, University of Freiburg, 2006. Membership: German Chemical Society. Address: University of Konstanz, Physical Chemistry, Universitätsstr 10, D-78457, Germany. E-mail: helmut.coelfen@uni-konstanz.de

COLGAN Michael Anthony, b. 17 July 1950, Dublin, Ireland. Theatre Artistic Director. Education: BA, Trinity College, Dublin. Appointments: Director, Abbey Theatre, Dublin, 1974-78; Co-Manager, Irish Theatre Company, 1977-78; Manager, 1978-80, Artistic Director, 1981-83, Member Board of Directors, 1983-, Dublin Theatre Festival; Artistic Director and Board Member, Gate Theatre Dublin, 1983-; Executive Director, Little Bird Films, 1986-; Co-Founder, Blue Angel Film Company, 1999 (producers of The Beckett Film Project with RTÉ and Channel 4, 2000, commissioned by Channel 4 and RTÉ to film all 19 of Beckett's plays, and Celebration by Harold Pinter with Channel 4, 2006); Artistic Director Parma Film Festival, 1982; Chairman, St Patrick's Festival, 1996-99; Board Member: Millennium Festivals Ltd, Laura

Pels Foundation, New York, 2000-04; Theatre productions include: Faith Healer, Dublin and New York; No Man's Land, Dublin and London; I'll Go On; Juno and the Paycock; Salomé; 6 Beckett Festivals, Dublin, New York and London; All 19 Samuel Beckett stage plays; 4 Pinter Festivals: Dublin and New York; World premieres include: The Birds, Molly Sweeney, Afterplay, Shining City, The Home Place; Director: First Love, Faith Healer and Krapp's Last Tape; Producer: TV drama, Troubles, 1986; Two Lives, 1993. Honours: LLD TCD; Sunday Independent Arts Awards, 1985, 1987; National Entertainment Award, 1996; People of the Year Award, 1999; Best Drama Award, South Bank Show, 2002; Peabody Award, 2002; Irish Times Theatre Lifetime Achievement Award, 2006; Chevalier dans l'Ordre des Arts et des Lettres, 2007; OBE, 2010. Memberships: Governing Authority Dublin City University. Address: The Gate Theatre, 1 Cavendish Road, Dublin 1, Ireland. E-mail: info@gate-theatre.ie

COLLETTE Toni, b. 1 November 1972, Sydney, Australia. Actor. m. Dave Galafassi, 2003, 1 daughter. Education: National Institute of Dramatic Art, Sydney. Career: Actor: Theatre: Uncle Vanya; Away; Summer of the Aliens; King Lear; A Little Night Music; Blue Murder; The Wild Party; Films include: Muriel's Wedding, 1994; Emma, 1996; Velvet Goldmine, 1998; 8 ½ Women, The Sixth Sense, 1999; Shaft, 2000; Changing Lanes, About a Boy, The Hours, 2002; In Her Shoes, 2005; The Night Listener, Little Miss Sunshine, The Dead Girl, 2006; Evening, Nothing is Private, Towelhead, 2007; The Black Balloon, Hey, Hey, It's Esther Blueburger, 2008; Mary and Max (voice), 2009; Jesus Henry Christ, Fright Night, Foster, 2011; Hitchcock, Mental, 2012; TV: A Country Practice, 1990; Dinner with Friends, 2001; Tsunami: the Aftermath, 2006; United States of Tara, 2009. Honours: Best Newcomer in a Play or Musical, 16th Annual Sydney Critic's Circle Award, 1992; Australian Film and Television Award for Best Actress, 1994; Australian Film Institute, Best Actress, 1994; Film Critic's Circle of Australia, Best Actress, 1994; Best Supporting Actress, 2008; Australian Film Institute, Best Supporting Actress, 1996; Australian Film Institute, Best Supporting Actress, 1998, 2008, Best International Actress, 2009; The Blockbuster Film Awards, Best Supporting Actress (Suspense), 2000; Primetime Emmy, 2009; Golden Globe, 2010.

COLLINGBOURNE Stephen, b. 15 August 1943, Dartington, Devon, England. Artist. 1 son, 1 daughter. Appointments: Lecturer, Dartington College of Art, 1965-70; Worked at Serpentine Gallery, London, 1971; Assistant to Robert Adams, sculptor, 1972; Lived and worked in Malaya, 1972-73; Fellow in Sculpture, University College of Wales, 1974; Lecturer in Sculpture, Edinburgh College of Art, 1976-99; Early retirement, 1999-; One man exhibitions include: Bluecoat Gallery, Liverpool, 1972; British Council, Kuala Lumpur, Malaysia, 1973; Plymouth City Art Gallery, 1977; Southampton City Art Gallery, 1977; Informal Works on Paper, Edinburgh Festival, 1990; High Cross House, Dartington, Devon, 1997; Galleri Viktor, Nykarleby, Finland, 1998; Group exhibitions include: Serpentine Gallery, London, 1972; Kettles Yard, Cambridge, 1973; Built in Scotland Touring Show, Camden Arts Centre, London, 1983; Renlands Konstmuseum, Karleby, Finland, 1998. Honours: Commissions include: Leicester University, 1974; Collections include: Welsh Arts Council; Leicester City Art Centre; Edinburgh City Art Gallery; Awards and prizes from: Arts Council of Great Britain, 1972; John Moore's Liverpool, 1972; The British Council, 1973; Welsh Arts Council, 1975; Arts Council of Great Britain, 1975; Welsh Arts Council, 1976; Royal Scottish Academy, 1977, 1978; Scottish Arts Council, 1985. Address: Tofts, Blyth Bridge, West Linton, EH46 7AJ, Scotland.

COLLINS Jackie, b. England. Novelist; Short Story Writer; Actress. m. (1) Wallace Austin, 1959, divorced, 1963, 1 daughter, (2) Oscar Lerman, 1965, deceased 1992, 2 daughters. Creative Works: Screenplays: Yesterday's Hero; The World in Full of Married Men; The Stud. Publications: The World is Full of Married Men, 1968; The Stud, 1969; Sunday Simmons and Charlie Brick, 1971; Sinners, 1981; Lovehead, 1974; The World is Full of Divorced Women, 1975; The Love Killers, Lovers & Gamblers, 1977; The Bitch, 1979; Chances, 1981; Hollywood Wives, 1983; Lucky, 1985; Hollywood Husbands, 1986; Rock Star, 1988; Lady Boss, 1990; American Star, The World is Full of Married Men, 1993; Hollywood Kids, 1994; Dangerous Kiss, 1999; Hollywood Wives: The New Generation, Lethal Seduction, 2001; Deadly Embrace, 2002; Hollywood Divorces, 2003; Lovers & Players, 2006; Drop Dead Beautiful, 2007; Married Lovers, 2008; Poor Little Bitch Girl, 2009. Address: c/o Simon & Schuster, 1230 Avenue of the Americas, New York, NY 10020, USA.

COLLINS Joan, b. 23 May 1933, London, England. Actress. m. (1) Maxwell Reed, 1954, divorced, 1957, (2) Anthony Newley, 1963, divorced, 1970, 1 son, 1 daughter, (3) Ronald Kass, 1972, divorced, 1983, 1 daughter, (4) Peter Holm, 1985, divorced, 1987, (5) Percy Gibson, 2002. Career: Films include: I Believe in You, 1952; Girl in Red Velvet Swing, Land of the Pharaohs, 1955; The Opposite Sex, 1956; Rally Round Flag Boys, Sea Wife, 1957; Warning Shot, 1966; The Executioner, 1969; Revenge, 1971; The Big Sleep, Tales of the Unexpected, 1977; Stud, 1979; The Bitch, 1980; Nutcracker, 1982; Decadence, 1994; Hart to Hart, Annie: A Royal Adventure, In the Bleak Midwinter, 1995; The Clandestine Marriage, The Flintstones-Viva Rock Vegas, Joseph and the Amazing Technicolor Dreamcoat (voice), 1999; Ozzie, 2001; Alice in Glamourland, 2004; Plays include: The Last of Mrs Cheyne, 1979-80; Private Lives, 1990, 1991; Love Letters, 2000; Over the Moon, 2001; Full Circle, 2004; Numerous TV appearances include: Dynasty, 1981-89; Cartier Affair, 1984; Sins, 1986; Monte Carlo, 1986; Tonight at 8.30, 1991; Pacific Palisades (serial), 1997; These Old Broads, Will and Grace (USA), Guiding Light, 2002; Footballers' Wives, Hotel Babylon, 2006; Marple, 2009. Publications: J C Beauty Book, 1980; Katy: A Fight for Life, 1981; Past Imperfect, 1984; Prime Time, 1988; Love and Desire and Hate, 1990; My Secrets, 1994; Too Damn Famous, 1995; Second Act, 1996; My Friends' Secrets, 1999; Star Quality, 2002; Joan's Way, 2003; Misfortune's Daughters, 2004; The Art of Living Well: Looking Good, Feeling Great, 2007. Honours: Golden Globe, Best TV Actress, 1982; People's Choice, Favourite TV Performer, 1985; OBE, 1997; Lifetime Achievement Award, San Diego Film Festival, 2005. Address: c/o Paul Keylock, 16 Bulbecks Walk, South Woodham Ferrers, Essex, CM3 5ZN, England.

COLLINS John Alexander, b. 10 December 1941, Zimbabwe. Businessman. m. Sue, 1 son, 1 daughter. Education: BSc, Agriculture, Honorary Doctorate, Reading University. Appointments: Chairman & CEO, Shell UK, 1990-93; CEO, Vestey Group, 1993-2001; Chairman, National Power, 1998-2000; Chairman, DSGi Group, 2001-09; Non-Executive Director, 3i Infrastructure. Honours: Knighted, 1993. Memberships: Royal Yacht Squadron; Energy Institute. Address: Le Repos au Coin, La Fosse, St Martin, Guernsey GY4 6EB, Channel Islands. E-mail: john.collins@cwgsy.net

DICTIONARY OF INTERNATIONAL BIOGRAPHY 36th EDITION

COLLINS Neil Adam, b. 20 January 1947, England. Journalist/Consultant. m. Julia, 1 son, 2 daughters. Education: Selwyn College, Cambridge. Appointments: City Editor, Daily Telegraph, 1986-2005; Columnist, Evening Standard, 2005-09; Director, Templeton Emerging Markets Investment Trust plc, 2006-; Director, Finsbury Growth & Income Trust plc, 2008-; Columnist, Reuters Breaking Views, 2009-10. Address: 12 Gertrude Street, London, SW10 0JN, England. E-mail: neilcollins10@gmail.com

COLLINS Pauline, b. 3 September 1940, Exmouth, Devon, England. Actress. m. John Alderton, 2 sons, 1 daughter. Education: Central School of Speech & Drama. Creative Works: Stage Appearances: A Gazelle in Park Lane (stage debut, Windsor 1962); Passion Flower Hotel; The Erpingham Camp; The Happy Apple; The Importance of Being Ernest; The Night I Chased the Women with an Eel; Come as You Are; Judies; Engaged; Confusions; Romantic Comedy; Woman in Mind; Shirley Valentine; Films: Shirley Valentine, 1989; City of Joy, 1992; My Mother's Courage, 1997; Paradise Road, 1997; Mrs Caldicott's Cabbage War, 2002; Albert Nobbs, 2011; Quartet, 2012; TV appearances: Upstairs Downstairs; Thomas and Sarah; Forever Green; No-Honestly; Tales of the Unexpected; Knockback, 1984; Tropical Moon Over Dorking; The Ambassador, 1998; Man and Boy, 2002; Sparkling Cyanide, 2003; Bleak House, 2005; Doctor Who, 2006; What We Did on Our Holiday, 2006; From Time to Time, 2009; Agatha Christie's Marple, 2010; Merlin, 2010. Publication: Letter to Louise, 1992. Honours include: Laurence Olivier Award, Best Actress; Tony Award; Theatre World Award; Drama Desk Award; Outer Critics' Circle Award; BAFTA Award; OBE, 2001.

COLLINS Phil, b. 30 January 1951, Chiswick, London, England. Pop Singer; Drummer; Composer. m. (1) 1976, 1 son, 1 daughter, (2) Jill Tavelman, 1984, divorced, 1 daughter, (3) Orianne Cevey, 1999, divorced 2008, 2 sons. Education: Barbara Speake Stage School. Appointments: Former Actor, Artful Dodger in London Production of Oliver; Joined Rock Group, Genesis as Drummer, 1970, Lead Singer, 1975-96. Creative Works: Albums with Genesis: Selling England by the Pound, 1973; Invisible Touch, 1986; We Can't Dance, 1991; Solo Albums include: Face Value, 1981; Hello I Must Be Going, 1982; No Jacket Required, 1985; 12"Ers, 1987; But Seriously, 1989; Serivous Hits Live, 1990; Dance into the Light, 1996; Hits, 1998; A Hot Night in Paris, 1999; Testify, 2002; The Platinum Collection, 2004; Love Songs: A Compilation ... Old and New, 2004; Solo Singles include: In the Air Tonight, 1981; You Can't Hurry Love, 1982; Against All Odds, 1984; One More Night, 1985; Easy Lover, 1985; Separate Lives, 1985; Groovy Kind of Love, 1988; Two Hearts, 1988; Another Day in Paradise, 1989; I Wish It Would Rain Down, 1990; Both Sides of the Story, 1993; Dance Into the Light, 1996; Soundtrack Albums: Against All Odds, 1984; White Nights, 1985; Buster, 1988; Tarzan, 1999; Brother Bear, 2003. Films include: Buster, 1988; Frauds, 1993. Honours include: 7 Grammy's; 6 Ivor Novello Awards; 4 Brits; 2 Awards, Variety Club of Great Britain; 2 Silver Clef's; 2 Elvis Awards; Academy Award for You'll be in my Heart from Tarzan film, 1999; Oscar for Best Original Song, You'll be in my Heart, 2000. Membership: Trustee, Prince of Wales Trust, 1983-97. Address: Hit and Run Music, 30 Ives Street, London SW3 2ND, England. Website: www.philcollins.co.uk

COLLIS Louise Edith, b. 29 January 1925, Arakan, Burma. Writer. Education: BA, History, Reading University, England, 1945. Publications: Without a Voice, 1951; A Year Passed, 1952; After the Holiday, 1954; The Angel's Name, 1955; Seven in the Tower, 1958; The Apprentice Saint, 1964; Solider in Paradise, 1965; The Great Flood, 1966; A Private View of Stanley Spencer, 1972; Maurice Collis Diaries (editor), 1976; Impetuous Heart: The story of Ethel Smyth, 1984. Contributions to: Books and Bookmen; Connoisseur; Art and Artists; Arts Review; Collectors Guide; Art and Antiques. Memberships: Society of Authors; International Association of Art Critics. Address: 65 Cornwall Gardens, London SW7 4BD, England.

COLMENARES QUINTERO Juan Carlos, b. 23 February 1973, Aguachica, Colombia. Research Scientist. m. Justyna, 1 son. Education: BSc, 1995; MSc, Catalysis, 1997; PhD, Chemical Sciences, 2004. Appointments: Researcher, Professor, University of America, Colombia, 2004; Postdoctorate, University of Cordoba, Spain, 2005-06; Postdoctorate, assistance for graduate students, UOPLLC-USC Research Partnership, University of Southern California, USA, 2006-09; Research Scientist, Institute of Physical Chemistry, Polish Academy of Sciences, 2009-; Visiting Professor, University of Southern California, LA, USA, 2012. Publications: More than 20 publications in international journals; Over 25 papers at conferences, seminars and symposia; Chapter in Catalysis: Principles, Types and Applications, 2011; Book chapter, Tunable biomass transformations by means of photocatalytic materials; Book, Producing Fules and Fine Chemicals from Biomass Using Nanomaterials. Honours: Warsaw University of Technology Scholarship for PhD studies; Polish Government Scholarship for MSc studies and BSc studies; Andrés Bello Prize, State Examination, Colombia; EC Marie Curie Grant; Best Publication, 2009. Memberships: Polish Chemical Society; Polish Club of Catalysis; International Advisory Board of Revista Ingenium; Reviewer for many international journals; Green Chemistry; FA COST Action TD 1203; Biowaste Industrial Symbiosis network; American Nano Society; American Chemical Society; and others. Address: ul Kaprzaka 44/52, 01-224 Warsaw, Poland. E-mail: jcarloscolmenares@ichf.edu.pl Website: http://www.photo-catalysis.org/

COLSTON Freddie C, b. 28 March 1936, Gretna, Florida, USA. Professor of Political Science. m. Doris Suggs, 1 daughter. Education: BA, Morehouse College, 1959; MA, Atlanta University, 1966; PhD, Ohio State University, 1972. Appointments: Instructor, Social Studies, Attucks High School, Hollywood, Florida, 1959-65, The Fort Valley State College, Georgia, 1966-68; Teaching Associate, Political Science, Ohio State University, 1968-71; Lecturer, Political Science, Ohio Dominican College, 1970; Associate Professor, Political Science, Benedict College, Columbia, South Carolina, 1971-72; Lecturer, Black Politics, Franklin University, Colombus, Ohio, 1972; Associate Professor, Political Science, Southern University, Baton Rouge, 1972-73; Associate Professor, Political Science and Black Studies, University of Detroit, 1973-76; Associate Professor, Political Science, Chairman, Division of Social Science, Dillard University, New Orleans, 1976-78; Assistant Professor, Department of Political Science, Delta College, University Center, Michigan, 1978-79; Associate Director, Executive Seminar Center, US Office of Personnel Management, Oak Ridge, 1980-87; Professor of Public Administration and Coordinator of Graduate Studies, Institute of Government, Tennessee State University, 1987-88; Director, Public Administration Program, North Carolina Central University, Durham, 1988-91; Professor, Political Science, Georgia Southwestern State University, Americus, 1992-97. Publications: Articles in professional journals; Dr Benjamin E Mays Speaks: Representative Speeches of a Great American Orator, 2002;

A Long Journey: Dr Benjamin E Mays Speaks on the Struggle for Social Justice in America. Honours include: Scholarships, University of Illinois, Summer 1964, Atlanta University, 1965. Memberships: American Political Science Association; Center for the Study of Presidency. Address: 116 Downing Drive, Oak Ridge, TN 37830-8790, USA.

COLTRANE Robbie, b. 31 March 1950, Glasgow, Scotland. Actor. m. Rhona Irene Gemmel, 2000, 1 son, 1 daughter. Education: Glasgow School. Appointments: Director, Producer, Young Mental Health (documentary), 1973. Creative Works: Stage appearances include: Waiting for God; End Game; The Bug; Mr Joyce is Leaving; The Slab Boys; The Transfiguration of Benno Blimpie; The Loveliest Night of the Year; Snobs and Yobs; Your Obedient Servant (one-man show), 1987; Mistero Buffo; TV: The Comic Strip Presents...; Five Go Mad In Dorset; The Beat Generation; War; Summer School; Five Go Mad in Mescalin; Susie; Gino; Dirty Movie; The Miner's Strike; The Supergrass (feature film); The Ebb-tide; Alice in Wonderland; Guest Roles: The Yong Ones; Kick Up the Eighties; The Tube; Saturday Night Live; Lenny Henry Show; Blackadder; Tutti Frutti; Coltrane in a Cadillac; Cracker; The Plan Man; Frasier; Still Game; Cracker: Nine Eleven; Murderland; TV film: Boswell and Johnson's Tour of the Western Isles; Films include: Mona Lisa; Subway Riders; Britannia Hospital; Defence of the Realm; Caravaggio; Eat The Rich; Absolute Beginners; The Fruit Machine; Slipstream; Nuns on the Run; Huckleberry Finn; Bert Rigby, You're A Fool; Danny Champion of the World; Henry V; Let It Ride; The Adventures of Huckleberry Finn; Goldeneye; Buddy; Montana; Frogs for Snakes; Message in a Bottle; The World is Not Enough, 1999; On the Nose, 2000; From Hell, 2000; Harry Potter and the Philosopher's Stone, 2001; Harry Potter and the Chamber of Secrets, 2002; Van Helsing, 2004; Harry Potter and the Prisoner of Azkaban, 2004; Ocean's 12, 2005; Harry Potter and the Goblet of Fire, 2005; Provoked: A True Story, 2006; Cracker, 2006; Stormbreaker, 2006; Harry Potter and the Order of the Pheonix, 2007; The Tale of Despereaux, The Brothers Bloom, 2008; Harry Potter and the Half-Blood Prince, 2009. Publications: Coltrane in a Cadillac, 1992; Coltrane's Planes and Automobiles, 1999. Honours: OBE, 2006. Address: c/o CDA, 125 Gloucester Rd, London SW7 4TE, England.

COLUMBUS Chris, b. 10 September 1958, Spangler, Pennsylvania, USA. Film Director; Screenplay Writer. m. Monica Devereux, 1983, 2 daughters. Education: New York University Film School. Career: Wrote for and developed TV cartoon series, Galaxy High School; Founder of own production company, 1942 Productions; Screenplays include: Reckless, 1983; Gremlins, 1984; The Goonies, 1985; The Young Sherlock Holmes, 1985; Only the Lonely, 1991; Little Nemo: Adventures in Slumberland, 1992; Nine Months, 1995; Films directed include: Adventures in Babysitting, 1987; Heartbreak Hotel, 1988; Home Alone, 1990; Only the Lonely, 1991; Home Alone 2: Lost in New York, 1992; Mrs Doubtfire, 1993; Nine Months (also producer), 1995; Jingle All the Way (also producer), 1996; Stepmom (also producer), 1998; Monkey Bone (producer), 1999; Bicentennial Man (also producer), 1999; Harry Potter and the Philosopher's Stone (also producer), 2001; Harry Potter and the Chamber of Secrets (also producer), 2002; Harry Potter and the Prisoner of Azkaban (producer), 2004; Christmas with the Kranks (producer), 2004; 3- D Rocks (producer), 2005; Fantastic Four (executive producer), 2005; Rent (producer), 2005; Night at the Museum (producer), 2006; Fantastic Four: Rise of the Silver Surfer, 2007; Night at the Museum: Battle of the Smithsonian, I Love You, Beth Cooper, 2009. TV directed includes: Amazing Stories; Twilight Zone; Alfred Hitchcock Presents (series). Address: c/o Beth Swofford, CAA, 9830 Wilshire Boulevard, Beverly Hills, CA 90212, USA.

COMANECI Nadia, b. 12 November 1961, Oneşti, Bacău County, Romania. Former Gymnast. m. Bart Connor, 1996. 1 son. Education: College of Physical Education and Sports, Bucharest. Career: Overall European Champion, Skien 1975, Prague 1977, Copenhagen 1979; Overall Olympic Champion, Montreal, 1976; First gymnast to be awarded a 10; Overall World Universal Games Champion, Bucharest, 1981; Gold medals: European Championships, Skien 1975 (vault, asymmetric bars, beam); Prague 1977 (bars); Copenhagen 1979 (vault, floor exercises); World Championships, Strasbourg 1978 (beam); Fort Worth 1979 (team title); Olympic Games, Montreal 1976 (bars, beam); Moscow (beam, floor); World Cup, Tokyo 1979 (vault, floor); World Universal Games, Bucharest 1981 (vault, bars, floor and team title); Silver medals: European Championships, Skien 1975 (floor); Prague 1977 (vault); World Championships, Strasbourg 1978 (vault); Olympic Games, Montreal 1976 (team title); Moscow (individual all-round, team title); World Cup, Tokyo 1979 (beam); Bronze medals: Olympic Games, Montreal 1976 (floor); Retired, May 1984; Junior Team Coach, 1984-89; Granted refugee status, USA, 1989; Currently with Bart Connor Gymnastics Academy, Oklahoma, USA; Performs as dancer, gymnastics entertainer and promotes commercial products; Contributing Editor, International Gymnast magazine; UN Spokesman for International Year of Volunteers, 2001; Founder, Nadia Comaneci Children's Clinic, Bucharest, 2004. Publications: Letters to a Young Gymnast, 2004. Honours: Sportswomen of the Century Prize, Athletic Sports Category, 1999; Government Excellence Diploma, 2001. Address: c/o Bart Conner Gymnastics Academy, 3206 Bart Conner Drive, POB 72017, Norman, OK 73070-4166, USA. Website: www.bartconnergymnastics.com

COMBS Sean (Diddy), b. 4 November 1969, Harlem, New York, USA. Rap Artist; Producer; Fashion designer. 1 son with Misa Hylton-Brim, 1 son and 2 daughters with Kim Porter, 1 daughter with Sarah Chapman. Career: R&B label, Uptown; Talent spotter; Producer for Ma$e, Sting, MC Lyte, Faith Evans, The Lox, Mariah Carey, Aretha Franklin, Notorious BIG; Founder, Bad Boy Entertainment label, 1994-; Remixed and reworked songs by various artists; Co-producer, soundtrack to film Godzilla; Creator, fashion collection Sean John, 2001 (flagship stored opened 2002); Charged with gun possession, 1999; Acquitted of gun possession and bribery, 2001. Films: Made, 2001; Monster's Ball, 2001; Death of a Dynestry, 2003. Recordings include: I'll Be Missing You; Been Around the World, 1997; Roxanne, Can't Nobody Hold Me Down, 1997; Victory, 1998; Come With Me, 1998; It's All About the Benjamins, 1998; PE, 2000; Albums include: No Way Out, 1997; Forever, 1999; The Saga Continues, 2001; We Invented the Remix, 2002; Press Play, 2006; Last Train to Paris, 2010; Albums produced include: Honey (Mariah Carey); Life After Death and Mo Money Mo Problems (Notorious BIG); Cold Rock a Party (MC Lyte); Cupid (112); Feel So Good (Ma$e); Plays: A Raisin in the Sun, 2004. Honours: MTV Video Music Awards, 1997, 1998; Grammy Award, Best Rap Performance by a Duo or Group, 1998; Grammy Award, Best Rap Album, 1998; Grammy Award, Best Rap Performance by a Duo or Group, 2004; Council of Fashion Designers of America menswear designer of the year award, 2004; Concert for Diana, 2007; MOBO Awards, 2007; BET Awards, 2007; NAACP Image Awards, 2009. Address: Sean John Clothing Inc, 525 Seventh Avenue, Suite 1009, New York, NY 10018, USA. Website: www.seanjohn.com

COMFORT Nicholas Alfred Fenner, b. 4 August 1946, London, England. Writer and Government Adviser. 2 sons, 1 daughter. Education: Scholar, Highgate School; MA (Exhibitioner), History, Trinity College, Cambridge. Appointments: Municipal Correspondent, Sheffield Morning Telegraph, 1968-74; Midlands Correspondent, Washington Bureau, Political Staff, Leader Writer, The Daily Telegraph, 1974-89; Political Editor, Independent on Sunday, 1989-90; Political Editor, The European, 1990-92; Political Editor, Daily Record, 1992-95; Obituarist, Daily Telegraph, 1995-; Consultant, Politics International, 1996-97; Freelance Lobby Correspondent, 1997-2000; Consultant on European Presentation, DTI, 2000-01; Special Adviser to Secretary of State for Scotland, 2001-02; Government Adviser, QinetiQ, 2003-06; Government Advisor, Unisys, 2008-09. Publications: Books: Olympic Report, 1976; The Tunnel: The Channel and Beyond, 1987; Brewer's Politics, 1993; The Lost City of Dunwich, 1994; The Mid-Suffolk Light Railway, 1997; How to Handle the Media, 2003; The Politics Book, 2005; The Channel Tunnel and its High Speed Links, 2006; Numerous articles. Memberships: The Athenaeum; Essex CCC. Address: 129 Croydon Road, London SE20 7TT, England. E-mail: nc65464@yahoo.com

ČOMIĆ Irena, b. 29 March 1938, Subotica, Yugoslavia. Professor of Mathematics. m. Ljubomir, 2 daughters. Education: BSc, 1960; MA, 1966; PhD, 1974. Appointments: Faculty of Technical Sciences, University of Novi Sad, Serbia. Publications include: Various papers on Finsler geometry and its generalisation appearing in mathematical journals and proceedings of conferences. Address: Department of Mathematics, Faculty of Technical Sciences, University of Novi Sad, 21000 Novi Sad, Serbia. E-mail: comirena@uns.ac.rs Website: http://imft.ftn.uns.ac.rs/~irena/

COMPSTON Christopher Dean, b. 5 May 1940, Ryde, Isle of Wight, England. Circuit Judge. m. (1) Bronwen Henniker-Gotley, 2 sons (deceased), 1 daughter, (2) Caroline Odgers, 2 sons, 1 daughter. Education: Epsom College, 1953-59; MA, Magdalen College, Oxford, 1960; Called to the Bar, Middle Temple, 1965. Appointments: Barrister, 1965-86; Circuit Judge, 1986-. Publications: Recovering from Divorce, 1993; Breaking Up Without Cracking Up, 1999; Articles and appearances on radio and TV. Honours: Bencher, Middle Temple, 2006. Memberships: Seaview Yacht Club.

CONLON James, b. 18 March 1950, New York, USA. Conductor. m. Jennifer Ringo, 2 daughters. Education: Bachelor of Music, Juilliard School of Music, New York, 1972. Appointments: Professional conducting debut, Spoleto Festival, 1971; New York debut, La Boheme, Juilliard School of Music, 1972; Member of orchestral conducting faculty, Juilliard School of Music, 1972-75; Debuts: New York Philharmonic, 1974, Metropolitan Opera, 1976, Covent Garden, 1979, Paris Opera, 1982, Maggio Musicale, Florence, 1985, Lyric Opera of Chicago, 1988, La Scala, Milan, 1993, Kirov Opera, 1994; Music Director: Cincinnati May Festival, 1979-; Berlin Philharmonic Orchestra, 1979-; Rotterdam Philharmonic Orchestra, 1983-91; Ravinia Festival, 2005-; Musical Advisor to Director, 1995-, Principal Conductor, 1996-, Paris Opera; Conducted opening of Maggio Musicale, Florence, 1985; Chief Conductor, Cologne Opera, 1989; General Music Director, City of Cologne, Germany, 1990-; Frequent guest conductor at leading music festivals; Conducted virtually all leading orchestras in North America; Numerous television appearances. Honours: Grand Prix du Disque, Cannes Classical Award and ECHO Classical Award; Officier de l'Ordre des Arts et des Lettres, 1996; Zemlinsky Prize, 1999; Legion d'Honneur, 2001. Address: c/o Shuman Associates, 120 West 58th Street, 8D, New York, NY 10019, USA. E-mail: shumanpr@cs.com

CONNELLY Jennifer, b. 12 December 1970, Catskill Mountains, New York, USA. m. Paul Bettany, 2003, 1 son, 1 daughter, 1 son with David Duggan. Education: Career: Actress; Films include: Once Upon a Time in America, 1984; Phenomena, Seven Minutes in Heaven, 1985; Labyrinth, 1986; Etoiler, Some Girls, 1988; The Hot Spot, 1990; The Rocketeer, 1991; Of Love and Shadows, 1994; Higher Learning, 1995; Mulholland Falls, Far Harbor, 1996; Inventing the Abbotts, 1997; Dark City, 1998; Waking the Dead, Requiem for a Dream, Pollock, 2000; A Beautiful Mind, 2001; Hulk, House of Sand and Fog, 2003; Dark Water, 2005; Little Children, Blood Diamond, 2006; Reservation Road, 2007; The Day the Earth Stood Still, Inkheart, 2008; He's Just Not That Into You, 9, Creation, 2009; Virginia, 2010; The Dilemma, Salvation Boulevard, 2011; Stuck in Love, Winter's Tale, 2013. Honours: Golden Globe, 2001; BAFTA, 2001; AFI, 2001; Oscar for Best Supporting Actress, 2001. Address: c/o International Creative Management, 8942 Wilshire Boulevard, Beverly Hills, CA 90211, USA.

CONNERY Sean (Thomas Connery), b. 25 August 1930. Actor. m. (1) Diane Cilento, 1962, dissolved 1974, 1 son, (2) Micheline Roquebrune, 1975, 2 stepsons, 1 stepdaughter. Creative Works: Appeared in Films: No Road Back, 1956; Action of the Tiger, Another Time, Another Place, 1957; Hell Drivers, 1958; Tarzan's Greatest Adventure, Darby O'Gill and the Little People, 1959; On the Fiddle, 1961; The Longest Day, The Frightened City, 1962; Woman of Straw, 1964; The Hill, 1965; A Fine Madness, 1966; Shalako, The Molly Maguires, 1968; The Red Tent, 1969; The Anderson Tapes, 1970; The Offence, Zardoz, 1973; Ransom, Murder on the Orient Express, 1974; The Wind and the Lion, The Man Who Would Be King, 1975; Robin and Marian, 1976; The First Great Train robbery, Cuba, 1978; Meteor, 1979; Outland, 1981; The Man with the Deadly Lens, Wrong is Right, Five Days One Summer, 1982; Highlander, 1986; The Name of the Rose, The Untouchables, 1987; The Presido, Indiana Jones and the Last Crusade, 1989; Family Business, the Hunt for Red October, 1990; The Russia House, Highlander II - The Quickening, 1991; Medicine Man, 1992; Rising Sun, 1993; A Good Man in Africa, 1994; First Knight, Just Cause, 1995; The Rock, Dragonheart, 1996; The Avengers, 1998; Entrapment, Playing By Heart, 1999; Finding Forrester, 2000; The League of Extraordinary Gentlemen, 2003; Sir Billi the Vet (voice), 2006; James Bond in: Dr No, 1963; From Russia with Love, 1964; Goldfinger, 1965; Thunderball, 1965; You Only Live Twice, 1967; Diamonds are Forever, 1971; Never Say Never Again, 1983. Publication: Neither Shaken Nor Stirred, 1994. Honours include: BAFTA Lifetime Achievement Award, 1990; Man of Culture Award, 1990; Rudolph Valentino Award, 1992; Golden Globe Cecil B De Mille Award, 1996 BAFTA Fellowship, 1998; AFI Life Achievement Award, 2006. Address: c/o Creative Artists Agency Inc, 9830 Wilshire Boulevard, Beverly Hills, CA 90212, USA.

CONNICK Harry Jr, b. 1968, New Orleans, USA. Jazz Musician; Actor; Singer. m. Jill Goodacre, 1994, 3 daughters. Education: New Orleans Centre for the Creative Arts; Hunter College; Manhattan School of Music; Studies with Ellis Marsalis. Creative Works: Band Leader, Harry Connick's Big Band; Albums include: Harry Connick Jr, 1987; 20, When Harry Met Sally, 1989; We Are In Love, Lofty's Roach Soufflé, Blue Light, Red Light, 1991; Eleven, 25, 1992; When My Heart Finds Christmas, 1993; She, 1994; Star Turtle,

1996; To See You, 1997; Come By Me, 1999; 30, Songs I Heard, 2001; Other Hours: Connick on Piano, Vol I, Harry for the Holidays, 2003; Only You, 2004; Occasion: Connick on Piano, Vol II, 2005; Harry on Broadway, Act I, 2006; Oh, My NOLA, 2007; Chanson du Vieux Carre: Connick On Piano, Vol III, 2007; What a Night! A Christmas Album, 2008; Your Songs, 2009; Contribution to music for films: Memphis Belle, 1990; Little Man Tate, 1991; Actor: Films: Memphis Belle, 1990; Little Man Tate, 1991; Copycat, 1995; Independence Day, 1996; Excess Baggage, Action League Now!! (voice), 1997; Hope Floats, 1998; The Iron Giant (voice), Wayward Son, 1999; My Dog Skip (voice), The Simian Line, 2000; Life Without Dick, 2001; Basic, 2003; Mickey, 2004; The Happy Elf (voice), 2005; Bug, 2006; PS I Love You, 2007; Living Proof, 2008; New In Town, 2009; TV includes: South Pacific, 2001; Will & Grace, 2002-; Theatre: Thou Shalt Not (composer), 2001; The Pajama Game (actor), 2005. Honours include: Grammy Award, Male Jazz Vocal Performance, 1990. Address: Columbia Records, 51/12, 550 Madison Avenue, PO Box 4450, New York, NY 10101, USA. Website: www.hconnickjr.com

CONNOLLY Billy, b. 24 November 1942. Comedian; Actor; Playwright; Presenter. m. (1) Iris Pressagh, divorced 1985, 1 son, 1 daughter, (2) Pamela Stephenson, 1990, 3 daughters. Appointments: Apprentice Welder; Performed originally with Gerry Rafferty and The Humblebums; 1st Play, The Red Runner, staged at Edinburgh fringe, 1979. Creative Works: Theatre: The Great Northern Welly Boot Show; The Beastly Beatitudes of Balthazar B, 1982; TV include: Androcles and the Lion, 1984; Return to Nose and Beak (Comic Relief); South Bank Show Special (25th Anniversary Commemoration), 1992; Billy; Billy Connolly's World Tour of Scotland (6 part documentary), 1994; The Big Picture, 1995; Billy Connolly's World Tour of Australia, 1996; Erect for 30 Years, 1998; Billy Connolly's World Tour of England, Ireland and Wales, 2002; Gentleman's Relish; World Tour of New Zealand, 2004; The X-Files: I Want to Believe, 2008; Journey to the Edge of the World, 2009; Films include: Absolution, 1979; Bullshot, Water, 1984; The Big Man, 1989; Pocahontas, 1995; Treasure Island (Muppet Movie), Deacon Brodie (BBC Film), 1996; Mrs Brown, Ship of Fools, 1997; Still Crazy, Debt Collector, 1998; Boon Docksaints, 1998; Beautiful Joe, An Everlasting Piece, 2000; The Man Who Sued God, White Oleander, Gabriel and Me, 2002; The Last Samurai, Timeline, 2003; Lemony Snicket's A Series of Unfortunate Events, 2004; Garfield: A Tail of Two Kitties, Fido, Open Season (voice), 2006; Numerous video releases of live performances include: Bite Your Bum, 1981; An Audience with Billy Connolly, 1982; Numerous albums include: The Great Northern Welly Boot Show (contains No 1 hit DIVORCE); Pick of Billy Connolly. Publications include: Gullible's Travels, 1982. Honours include: Gold Disc, 1982; CBE, 2003. Address: c/o Tickety-boo Ltd, 94 Charity Street, Victoria, Gozo VCT 105, Malta. E-mail: tickety-boo@tickety-boo.com Website: www.billyconnolly.com

CONRAN Jasper Alexander Thirlby, b. 12 December 1959, London, England. Fashion Designer. Education: Bryanston School, Dorset; Parsons School of Art & Design, New York. Appointments: Fashion Designer, Managing Director, Jasper Conran Ltd, 1978-. Creative Works: Theatre Costumes: Jean Anouilh's The Rehearsal, Almeida Theatre, 1990; My Fair Lady, 1992; Sleeping Beauty, Scottish Ballet, 1994; The Nutcracker Sweeties, Birmingham Royal Ballet, 1996; Edward II, 1997; Arthur, 2000; TV Costume Designer, Nutcracker Sweeties, 2006; The Shakespear Sweet; Arthur, Part I; Arthur, Part II; Maria Stuarda. Honours include: Fil d'Or (International Linen Award), 1982, 1983; British Fashion Council Designer of the Year Award, 1986-87; Fashion Group of America Award, 1987; Laurence Olivier Award for Costume Designer of the Year, 1991; British Collections Award (in British Fashions Awards), 1991; Honorary Doctor of Letters, Heriot-Watt University; Visiting Professor, University of the Arts, London; Honorary Doctor of Civil Law, University of East Anglia; OBE, 2008. Memberships: Governor, Bryanston School; Patron, Work-Life Balance Trust; Trustee, Wallace Collection. Address: Jasper Conran Ltd, 6 Burnsall Street, London SW3, England.

CONRAN Sir Terence (Orby), b. 4 October 1931, Esher, Surrey, England. Designer; Retail Executive. m. (1) Brenda Davison, divorced, (2) Shirley Conran, divorced 1962, 2 sons, (3) Caroline Herbert, 1963, divorced 1996, 2 sons, 1 daughter, (4) Vicki Davis, 2000. Education: Bryanston School, Dorset; Central School of Art and Design, London. Appointments include: Joint Chairman, Ryman Conran Ltd, 1968-71; Chairman, Habitat Group Ltd, 1971-88; RSCG Conran Design, 1971-92; Habitat France SA, 1973-88; Conran Stores Inc, 1977-88; J Hepworth & Son Ltd, 1981-83; Habitat Mothercare Ltd, 1982-88; Jasper Conran Ltd, 1982-; Heal & Sons Ltd, 1983-87; Richard Shops Ltd, 1983-87; Storehouse plc, 1986-90; Butlers Wharf Ltd, 1984-90; Bibendum Restaurant Ltd, 1986-; Benchmark Woodworking Ltd, 1989-; Blue Print Cafe Ltd, 1989-; Conran Shop Holdings Ltd, 1990-; Terence Conran Ltd, 1990-; Le Pont de La Tour Ltd, 1991-; Quaglino's Restaurant Ltd, 1991-; Conran Shop SA, 1991-; Cantina Del Ponte, 1992; Butlers Wharf Chop House Ltd, 1993-; Conran & Partners, 1993-; Chairman, Conran Holdings Ltd, 1993-; Bluebird Store Ltd, 1994-; Mezzo Ltd, 1995-; Conran Shop: Paris, 1992, 1999, Tokyo, 1994, (Marylebone) Ltd, 1995-, (Germany) Ltd, 1996, Fukuoka, 1996; Coq d'Argent Ltd, 1997-; Zinc Bar & Grill, 1997; Orrery, 1997; Sartoria Ltd, 1998; Accazar Ltd, (Paris), 1998; Conran Collection, 1998; Berns Ltd (Stockholm), 1999; Great Eastern Hotel, 1999; The Terence Conran Shop, (New York), 1999; Giastavino's (New York), 2000; Content by Conran, furniture for Christie Tyler, 2003. Publications: The House Book, 1974; The Kitchen Book, 1977; The Bedroom & Bathroom Book, 1978; The Cook Book (revised as The Conran Cookbook, 1996), 1980; The New House Book, 1985; Conran Directory of Design, 1985; Plants at Home, 1986; The Soft Furnishings Book, 1986; Terence Conran's France, 1987; Terence Conran's DIY by Design, 1989; Terence Conran's Garden DIY, 1990; Toys and Children's Furniture, 1992; Terence Conran's Kitchen Book, 1993; Terence Conran's DIY Book, 1994; The Essential House Book, 1994; Terence Conran on Design, 1996; The Essential Garden Book, 1998; Easy Living, 1999; Chef's Garden, 1999; Terence Conran on Restaurants, 1999; Terence Conran on London, 2000; Q and A: A Sort of Autobiography, 2001; Terence Conran on Small Spaces, 2001. Honours include: RSA Bicentenary Medal, 1982; Presidential Award, D&AD, 1989; Commandeur de l'Ordre des Arts et des Lettres, France, 1991; Minerva Medal; Prince Philip Designers Prize, 2003; Provost, Royal College of Art, 2003; Honorary Degree, London South Bank University, 2007. Memberships: Council, Royal College of Art, 1979-81, 1986-; Trustee, 1989-, Chair, 1992-, Design Museum; Creative Leaders' Network; Fellow, Chartered Society of Designers. Address: 22 Shad Thames, London SE1 2YU, England. Website: www.conran.com

CONROY (Donald) Pat(rick), b. 26 October 1945, Atlanta, Georgia, USA. Writer. m. (1) Barbara Bolling, 1969, divorced 1977, 3 daughters, (2) Lenore Guerewitz, 1981, divorced 1995, 1 son, 2 daughter, (3) Cassandra King, 1997. Education:

BA in English, The Citadel, 1967. Publications: The Boo, 1970; The Water is Wide, 1972; The Great Santini, 1976; The Lords of Discipline, 1980; The Prince of Tides, 1986; Beach Music, 1995; The Pat Conroy Cookbook: Recipes of My Life, 1999; My Losing Season, 2002; South of Broad, 2009. Honours: Ford Foundation Leadership Development Grant, 1971; Anisfield-Wolf Award, Cleveland Foundation, 1972; National Endowment for the Arts Award for Achievement in Education, 1974; Governor's Award for the Arts, Georgia, 1978; Lillian Smith Award for Fiction, Southern Regional Council, 1981; SC Hall of Fame, Academy of Authors, 1988; Golden Plate Award, American Academy of Achievement, 1992; Georgia Commission on the Holocaust Humanitarian Award, 1996; Lotos Medal of Merit for Outstanding Literary Achievement, 1993; South Carolina Hall of Fame, 2009; Many others. Memberships: Authors Guild of America; PEN; Writers Guild. Address: c/o Houghton Mifflin Co, 222 Berkeley Street, Boston, MA 02116, USA.

CONTI Matteo, b. 2 October 1971, Faenza, Italy. Researcher. m. Barbara, 1 son. Education: Laurea, Chemistry; PhD, Medical Sciences; Specialist Master, Analytical Chemistry. Appointments: Researcher, Biochemistry; Researcher, Nanomaterials; Researcher, Anticancer Research and Pharmacology. Publications: The Selfish Cell, 2008; various papers. Honours: Listed in biographical dictionaries. Address: via Albergone 23/A, 48012 Bagnacavacco, Italy.

CONTI Tom, b. 22 November 1941, Paisley, Scotland. Actor; Director; Novelist. m. Kara Wilson, 1967, 1 daughter. Education: Royal Scottish Academy of Music. Creative Works: London Theatre include: Savages (Christopher Hampton), 1973; The Devil's Disciple (Shaw), 1976; Whose Life is it Anyway? (Brian Clarke), 1978; They're Playing Our Song (Neil Simon/Marvin Hamlisch), 1980; Romantic Comedy (Bernard Salde); An Italian Straw Hat, 1986; Two Into One; Treats, 1989; Jeffrey Bernard is Unwell, 1990; The Ride Down Mt Morgan, 1991; Present Laughter (also director), 1993; Chapter Two, 1996; Jesus My Boy, 1998, 2009; Barrymore, 2002; The Real Thing, 2005; Films include: Dreamer; Saving Grace; Miracles; Heavenly Pursuits; Beyond Therapy; Roman Holiday; Two Brothers Running; White Roses; Shirley Valentine; Chapter Two; Someone Else's America; Crush Depth; Something to Believe In, 1996; Out of Control, 1997; The Enemy, 2000; Derailed, 2005; Paid, 2006; Rabbit Fever, 2006; Almost Heaven, 2006; O Jerusalem, 2006; Dangerous Parking, 2007; TV works include: Madame Bovary; Treats; The Glittering Prizes; The Norman Conquests; The Beate Klarsfield Story; Fatal Dosage; The Quick and the Dead; Blade on the Feather; The Wright Verdicts; Deadline; Donovan; Director: Last Licks; Broadway, 1979; Before the Party, 1980; The Housekeeper, 1982; Treats, 1989; Present Laughter, 1993; Last of the Red Hot Lovers, 1999. Publications: The Doctor, 2004. Honours: West End Theatre Managers Award; Royal TV Society Award; Variety Club of Great Britain Award, 1978; Tony Award, New York, 1979; Academy Award, Best Actor Nominee. Address: Finch & Partners, 4-8 Heddon Street, London W1B 4BS, England.

COOK Colin Burford, b. 20 January 1927, London, England. Doctor of Medicine. Education: Stainsby Hall Boarding School, Derbyshire, England; St Aloyisius College, London, 1943; MBBS, London University, Middlesex Hospital, London, 1944-51; Rotating Internship, Bridgeport Hospital, Connecticut, USA, 1952-53; Ships Surgeon, British Navy, 1953-55; Resident, Psychiatry, Marquette School of Medicine, Milwaukee, Wisconsin; Resident, Psychiatry, Cornell University, White Plains, New York; Post Graduate Fellowship, National Hospital for Nervous Diseases, Queen Square, London, England. Appointments: Psychiatrist, Psycho-analytically orientated psychotherapy, private practice, Stamford, Connecticut, over 30 years; Professor, Psychiatry, Columbia University, New York City, 1992-95. Publications: Author (as Alan Phillips), Jazz Improvisation & Harmony, 1965, 4th edition, 1998. Honours: Diplomate, American Board of Psychiatry & Neurology, 1979. Memberships: American Medical Association; American Society of Psychoanalytic Physicians; Authors League; Masons 32°. Address: 373 Strawberry Hill Ave, Stamford, CT 06902, USA. E-mail: ccookie3210@aol.com

COOK John Barry, b. 9 May 1940, Gloucester, England. Educator. m. Vivien Lamb, 2 sons, 1 daughter. Education: BSc, Physics and Mathematics,1961, Associate, Diploma in Theology, 1961 King's College, University of London, 1958-61; PhD, Biophysics, 1965, Guy's Hospital Medical School, University of London, 1961-65. Appointments: Lecturer (part-time), Physics, Royal Veterinary College, 1962-64; Lecturer, Physics, Guy's Hospital Medical School, 1964-65; Physics Teacher, Senior Science Master, Head of Physics Department, Haileybury, Hertford, 1965-72; Headmaster, Christ College, Brecon, 1973-82; Headmaster, Epsom College, 1982-92; Director, Inner Cities Young Peoples Project, 1992-95, Principal, King George VI & Queen Elizabeth Foundation of St Catharine's at Cumberland Lodge, 1995-2000, Educational Consultant, 2000-; OFSTED Inspector of Schools, 1993-2005; Inspecting, Consultancy and Advisory work for a wide range of schools in UK, Kenya, Egypt, Malaysia, Argentina, Abu Dhabi, France and Austria; Chairman, Academic Policy Committee, Headmasters' Conference; Chairman, South Wales Branch, Independent Schools' Information Service; Member, Curriculum Committee of the Schools' Council, the Council of the Midlands Examining Group, the Oxford and Cambridge Schools' Examination Board and of the Examination Committees of the Universities of Oxford and Cambridge; At various times Governor of 15 schools in Hertfordshire, Wales, Surrey, Staffordshire, Kent, Worcestershire; Chairman of Governors at The Royal School. Publications: Books as joint author: Solid State Biophysics; Multiple Choice Questions in A-level Physics; Multiple Choice Questions in O-level Physics; Papers and articles in: Nature, International Journal of Radiation Biology; Molecular Physics; Journal of Scientific Instruments; School Science Review. Memberships: College of Episcopal Electors and Governing Body of the Church in Wales; Chairman, Children's Hospice Association of the South East. Address: 6 Chantry Road, Bagshot, Surrey GU19 5DB, England.

COOK Manuela, b. 29 March 1941, Lisbon, Portugal. Professor. m. Ronald Cook, 1 daughter. Education: BA, Universidade Clássica de Lisboa, Portugal; MA, Universidade de Coimbra, Portugal; PhD, University of Birmingham, England; PGCE, University of Wolverhampton, England. Appointments: Teacher/Lecturer, Modern Languages, numerous institutions, 1960s-1970s; Portuguese Studies, School of Languages and European Studies, University of Wolverhampton, 1970s-1990s; Examiner, Principal, Chief Examiner, Moderator and Assessor for national and international boards, 1970s-; Book Reviewer for various publications including: The Times Higher Education Supplement, Contemporary Portuguese Politics & History Research Centre, Journal of the Association for Contemporary Iberian Studies, and Vida Hispánica, 1970s-; Committee chairmanships, course director, etc, 1990s-; Reviews Editor, International Journal of Iberian Studies, 1994-2004;

Editor (by correspondence), Lusotopie, France, 2001-. Publications: Author, N-V-T Theory on Forms of Address; Author, Portuguese tuition materials for native speakers of English, French and German (Complete Portuguese, 2010); Numerous papers and articles in scholarly journals. Honours: Fellowship, Linguist of Distinction, Institute of Linguistics, England, 1987-; Listed in international biographical dictionaries. Memberships: Society of Authors; Chartered Institute of Linguists; Association of Hispanists of Great Britain and Ireland; Association for Contemporary Iberian Studies; International Conference Group on Portugal; Women in Spanish, Portuguese and Latin American Studies; Anglo-Portuguese Society; Association for Language Learning; Associação Internacional de Lusitanistas; Founding Member, Association of British and Irish Lusitanists, 2006. E-mail: mcook.ac@btinternet.com

COOKE Fred C, b. 3 December 1915, Winchester, Tennessee, USA; Realtor Emeritus; Lt Col USAF (Ret). m. Pamela B Cooke, 4 children. Education: BA, 4 year pre-med; Realtor's Graduate Institute; Rated Senior Aerial Navigator, Kelly Field, 1942; Research and Development Engineer; Real Estate Counsellor and Exchanger, San Diego; Command School, USAF. Appointments: Realtor: Local Board President, 3 terms; State Director, 8 years; National Director, 4 years; Civitan International Club, Local President, District Vice-President. Honours: Distinguished Flying Cross, 1942; Veteran, Battle of Midway, 1942; Air Medal with Oak Leaf Clusters, 1943; The first study from the air of Gulf Stream current velocities by Doeppler radar, 1952; Founder, Emerald Coast Sailing Association; Lincoln Memorial University Athletic Hall of Fame, 1980; Professional Hall of Fame, 1993. Memberships: Vestry Member, St Simon's on the Sound Episcopal Church, 1957; State of Florida Waterways Committee, 1976; Commander, Fort Walton, Power Squadron; Commodore, Fort Walton Yacht Club, 1990. Address: PO Drawer 4070, Ft Walton Beach, FL 32549, USA.

COOKE Jonathan Gervaise Fitzpatrick, b. 26 March 1943, London, England. Sailor; Administrator. m. Henrietta Chamier, 1 son, 2 daughters. Education: Marlborough College, 1956-61; Dartmouth 1961-64; Joint Services Defence College, 1984; Royal College of Defence Studies, 1993. Appointments: Royal Navy, 1961-96; Navigation and Submarine Specialist; Commanded HMS Rorqual, HMS Churchill, HMS Warspite, 1980-84; 3rd Submarine Squadron, 1988-89; Naval Attaché, Paris, 1990-93; Commodore, 1993; Director Intelligence, Ministry of Defence; Chief Executive to Leathersellers Company, 1996-2009; Director AngloSiberian Oil, 1998-2003; Chairman, Leathersellers Federation of Schools, 2008-; Chairman, Leather Conservation Centre, 2009-. Honours: OBE; Commandeur de L'Ordre Nationale de Merité, France. Memberships: Naval and Military Club; Queen's Club. Address: Downstead House, Morestead, Winchester, Hampshire, SO21 1LF, England. E-mail: jgfcooke@tiscali.co.uk

COOLAHAN Catherine Anne, b. 2 November 1929. Artist; Designer. m. Maxwell Dominic Coolahan, 5 March 1951. Education: Associate, Sydney Technical College, 1950. Appointments: Advertising and Publicity Design, Farmer and Co, Sydney, 1950-52; Advertising and Publicity Design, J Inglis Wright, New Zealand Ltd, 1952-53; Advertising and Publicity Design, Carlton Carruthers du Chateau and King, 1954-57; Assistant Education Officer, Dominion Museum, 1957-58; Fashion Illustrator, James Smith Ltd, 1959-60; Publicity Design, Carlton Carruthers, 1960-62; James Smith and Tutor, Wellington Polytechnic School of Design, 1962-64; Self-Employed Graphic Design, Fine Arts, Curriculum Development and Teaching for School of Design, 1964-66; Wellington Polytechnic, 1966-71, 1972-83, 1984, 1985, 1995; Travelling Scholarship, QE II Arts Council, 1971-72. Creative Works include: Flight, Fabric Sculpture, 1984; Predator, Predator, Paper Wood, Flax Ties, Sculpture, 1984; Hunter, Paper Sculpture, 1984; Appropriations, Aquatint, 1986; Lifeguard, 3 Dimensional Etching and Hand Made Paper, 1987; Map of the Sounds, Etching, 1988; Isis and Rangi, Lithograph, 1988; Art Sees, Etching, 1989; New Zealand Portraits, 1990; Winged Victories and Clipped Wings, 1992; Anima, Etching, 1994; Topiary, Multimedia Assemblage, 1998; Foxy, Artists' Book, 1999; Dawn, Artists' Book; 2000; Noah's Ark, Metal and Glass Diorama, 2000; Animus, Etching, 2000. Publications: New Zealand Dictionary of Biography, Vol. 5 (Contributor); 8 pages in full colour in PRO Design, 2009. Honours include: Represented New Zealand at 36th Venice Bienalle, 1972; Japanese cultural ex as Printmaker to learn papermaking, 1977; QE II Purchase Grant for Retrospective Exhibition at Dowse Art Museum, 1984; QE II Grant to attend National Paper Conference, Tasmanian University Research Co, Hobart, Australia, 1987; Appointed Life Member, New Zealand Crafts Council for work on Education Committee with Craft Design Courses, 1989; Funding Support/Sufferage Centennial Year Trust and QE II Arts Council, Dowse Art Museum, 1992; Doctor of Literature (honoris causa), Massey University, 2003; Listed in: Artists and Galleries of Australia and New Zealand, 1979; Numerous national and international biographical publications; Encyclopaedia of New Zealand, 1986; Concise Dictionary of New Zealand Artists, 2000; The Order of New Zealand – Merit, 2007. Memberships: Board, New Zealand Print Council, 1968-76; Board, New Zealand Design Council, 1977-84; Board, Queen Elizabeth II Arts Council, 1979; Board, Wellington Community Arts Council, 1981; Board, Central Region Arts Council, 1982-85; Design Council Representative, New Zealand Industrial Design Council, 1984; Board, New Zealand Craft Council, 1984-85; Board, Humanz, New Zealand Society of the Humanities, 1995-2002; Chair International Committee, Zonta International, 1969-2009; Wellington Club, 1998-99; Board, New Pacific Studios, Berkley, California and Masterton, New Zealand, 2000-01. Address: Flat 3, Rutherford Flats, 5 Levy Street, Mount Victoria, Wellington 6011, New Zealand.

COOMBES Gaz (Gareth), b. 8 March 1976, Oxford, England. Singer; Musician (guitar). Partner, Jools Poore, 2 daughters. Career: Member, The Jennifers; Lead singer, guitarist, Supergrass, 1994-; Major concerts include: Support to Blur, Alexandra Palace, 1994; UK tour with Shed Seven, 1994; T In The Park Festival, Glasgow, 1995. Recordings: Albums: I Should Coco (Number 1, UK), 1995; In It for the Money, 1997; Supergrass, 1999; Life On Other Planets, 2002; Road to Rouen, 2005; Diamond Hoo Ha, 2008. Honours: Q Award, Best New Act, 1995; BRIT Award Nominations: Best British Newcomer, Best Single, Best Video, 1996. Address: c/o Courtyard Management, 22 The Nursery, Sutton Courtenay, Abingdon, Oxon OX14 4UA, England.

COONEY Muriel Sharon Taylor, b. 12 October 1947, Edenton, North Carolina, USA. Nurse. 2 sons. Education: BSN, East Carolina University, Greenville, North Carolina, 1969; MSN, St Louis University, St Louis, Missouri, USA, 1972; Orthopaedic Nurse Certificate. Appointments: Occupational: Staff Nurse, Johns Hopkins Hospital, Baltimore, Maryland, 1969-71; Staff Nurse, Barnes Hospital, St Louis, Missouri, 1971-72; Cardiovascular Clinical Nurse Specialist, Jackson Memorial Hospital, Miami, Florida, 1973-74; Home Healthcare Supervisor, Manager, Co-ordinator Council for

Senior Citizens, Durham, North Carolina, 1985; Staff Nurse, Person County Memorial Hospital, Roxboro, North Carolina, 1989-98; Staff Nurse, Specialty Hospital, Durham, North Carolina, 2002-04; Teaching: Clinical Instructor, Shepherd College, Shepherdstown, West Virginia, 1983; Lecturer, Clinical Instructor, Shepherd College, 1984; Instructor, Piedmont Community College, Roxboro, North Carolina, 1989-90; Instructor, Watts School of Nursing, Durham, North Carolina, 1990-2004; Independent Education Consultant, 2005-09; Instructor, North Carolina Central University, Durham, NC, 2006-2007; Instructor, Brunswick Community College, Supply, NC, 2007-09; Curriculum Developer, Kaplan, Test Prep and Admissions, 2009-. Publications: The Effects of Selected Teaching on the Recognition of Digitalis Toxicity, research thesis. Honours: Life Fellow, IBA; Distinguished Leadership Award for Service to Nursing Profession, 1994; The Great 100 of North Carolina, 2002. Memberships: American Nurses Association; North Carolina Nurses Association; NCNA Council of Nurse Educators, Chairperson, 1994-97, Vice Chairperson, 1992-93; NCNA Council of Medical Surgical Nursing; NCNA Cabinet of Education and Resource Development; NCNA Council of Clinical Nurse Specialists; National League of Nursing; Academy of Medical Surgery Nursing, Bylaw Committee, 1994; Watts School of Nursing Association of Nursing, Student Advisors, 1993-2004; National Association of Orthopaedic Nurses, Parliamentarian, 2006; Triangle Chapter, Treasurer, 1995-2008, NAON; North Carolina Association of Nursing Students, Parliamentarian, 1997-2003, 2008-; NCANS North Carolina Nurses Association Consultant, 2004-. Address: 105 NW 8th Street, Oak Island, NC 28465, USA.

COONEY Thomas, b. 21 January 1942, Drogheda, Ireland. Catholic Priest; Augustinian. Education: Philosophical Studies, Good Counsel, House of Studies, Ballyboden, Dublin, Ireland, 1960-62; STB, Theological Studies, Gregorian University, Rome Italy, 1963-67; Dip.Catechtics, Corpus Christi College, London, 1968-69; MA, St Louis University, St Louis, Missouri, USA, 1973-75; Dip. Communications, Communication Centre, Hatch End, London, 1989; CPE, Holy Family Hospital and Medical Center, Methuen, Massachusetts, USA, 1990; Dip. Spiritual Direction, Center for Religious Development, Cambridge, Massachusetts, USA, 1990-91; Masters, Clinical Pastoral Counselling, Emmanuel College, Boston, Massachusetts, 1991-93. Appointments: Entered Augustinian Order, Dublin, 1959; Ordained, Rome, 1967; Teaching Chaplain, Vocational School, Dublin, 1967-68; Housemaster and Teacher, St Augustine's College, Dungarvan, 1969-72; Teacher, Good Counsel College, New Ross, 1972-73; Master of Students, Good Counsel, Dublin, 1974-81; Provincial, Irish Province of the Augustinian Order, 1981-89; Executive, CMRS, 1983-89; President, Conference of Major Superiors of Ireland, 1986-89; Prior, St John's Priory, Dublin, 1993-95; Assistant General of the Augustinian Order, North West Europe and Canada, 1995-2001; Director of Pastoral Studies, Milltown Institute of Theology and Philosophy, Dublin, 2001-10. Publications: Articles in religious and theological journals. Memberships: Honorary Treasurer and Member of the Executive, National Conference of Priests of Ireland, 1994-95; Theological Faculty, Milltown Institute, 2001-; Member of the Executive and Treasurer, All Ireland Spiritual Guidance Association, 2005; Honorary President, Seapoint, Pitch and Putt Golf Club, Termonfeckin, Ireland; Founding Member, Supervisors Association of Ireland. Address: St John's Priory, Thomas Street, Dublin 8, Ireland. E-mail: tcooney@milltown-intitute.ie

COOPER Alice (Vincent Furnier), b. 4 February 1948, Detroit, Michigan, USA. Singer. m Sheryl Goddard, 1 sons, 2 daughters. Career: First to stage theatrical rock concert tours; Among first to film conceptual rock promo videos (pre-MTV); Considered among originators and greatest hard rock artists; Known as King of Shock Rock; Many film, television appearances including: Sextette, 1978; Sgt Pepper's Lonely Hearts Club Band, 1978; Leviatán, 1984; Prince of Darkness, 1987; Freddy's Dead: The Final Nightmare, 1991; The Attic Expeditions, 2001; Sound Off, 2005. Recordings: Singles include: I'm Eighteen; Poison; No More Mr Nice Guy; I Never Cry; Only Women Bleed; You And Me; Under My Wheels; Bed Of Nails; Albums include: School's Out, 1972; Billion Dollar Babies, 1973; Welcome To My Nightmare, 1976; From The Inside, 1978; Constrictor, 1986; Raise Your Fist And Yell, 1987; Trash, 1988; Hey Stoopid, 1991; Last Temptation, 1994; He's Back, 1997; Science Fictino, 2000; Brutal Planet, 2000; Alice Cooper Live, 2001; Take 2, 2001; Dragontown, 2001; Eyes of Alice Cooper, 2003; Hell Is, 2003; Dirty Diamonds, 2005; Vengence is Mine, 2007; Along Came a Spider, 2008; Keepin' Halloween Alive, 2009. Publications: Wrote foreword to short story book: Shock Rock; Alice Cooper, Golf Monster (autobiography), 2007. Honour: Foundations Forum, Lifetime Achievement Award, 1994. Memberships: BMI; NARAS; SAG; AFTRA; AFofM. Address: Alive Enterprises, PO Box 5542, Beverly Hills, CA 90211, USA. Website: www.alicecooper.com

COOPER (Brenda) Clare, b. 21 January 1935, Falmouth, Cornwall, England. Writer. m. Bill Cooper, 6 April 1953, 2 sons, 1 daughter. Publications: David's Ghost; The Black Horn; Earthchange; Ashar of Qarius; The Skyrifters; Andrews and the Gargoyle; A Wizard Called Jones; Kings of the Mountain; Children of the Camps; The Settlement on Planet B; Miracles and Rubies; Timeloft; Marya's Emmets; Cat of Morfa, 1998; Stonehead, 2000; One Day on Morfa, 2001; Time Ball, 2003. Honour: Runner Up, Tir Na Nog Award. Memberships: PEN; Society of Authors; Welsh Academy. Address: Tyrhibin Newydd, Morfa, Newport, Pembrokeshire SA42 0NT, Wales.

COOPER Chris, b. 9 July 1951, Kansas City, Missouri, USA. Actor. m. Marianne Leone, 1983, 1 son. Education: University of Missouri; Ballet, Stephens College, Missouri. Career: US Coast Guard Reserves; Studied theatre acting, New York, 1976; Films include: Bad Timing, 1980; Matewan, Non date da mangiare agli animali, 1987; Guilty by Suspicion, Thousand Pieces of Gold, City of Hope, 1991; This Boy's Life, 1993; Money Train, Pharaoh's Army, 1995; Boys, Lone Star, A Time to Kill, 1996; Great Expectations, The Horse Whisperer, 1998; The 24 Hour Woman, October Sky, American Beauty, 1999; Me, Myself & Irene,The Patriot, 2000; Interstate 60, The Bourne Identity, Adaptation, 2002; My House in Umbria, Seabiscuit, 2003; Silver City, The Bourne Supremacy, 2004; Capote, Jarhead, Syriana, 2005; Breach, The Kingdom, Married Life, 2007; American Experience, 2008; New York, I Love You, Where the Wild Things Are, 2009; Stage appearances include: Of the Fields Lately, 1980; The Ballad of Soapy Smith, A Different Moon, 1983; Cobb; The Grapes of Wrath; Sweet Bird of Youth; Love Letters. Honours: Best Actor Award, Cowboy Hall of Fame, 1991; Screen Actors Guild Award, 2000; Golden Globe Award, 2003; Best Supporting Actor: Academy Awards, 2004, National Board of Review, San Francisco Film Critics, Toronto Film Critics, San Diego Film Critics, Broadcast Film Association, LA Critics Association. Address: Paradigm Talent Agency, 10100 Santa Monica Boulevard, Suite 2500, Los Angeles, CA 90067, USA.

DICTIONARY OF INTERNATIONAL BIOGRAPHY 36th EDITION

COOPER David J, b. 4 July 1951, London, England. Business Development and Coporate Finance. Education: B Ed, Chemistry, London University Certificate in Education, 1974. Appointments: Founder and Principal, David Cooper Associates, 1974-; Director, European Corporate Business Development, Pfizer Inc, 1984-87; Corporate Financier, Robert Fleming & Co Ltd, 1987-89; Co-founder and Partner, Quantum Capital Partners, 2004-. Memberships: Fellow: The Chartered Securities Institute; Royal Society of Chemistry; Chartered Institute of Marketing. Address: 15 Bedford Square, London WC1B 3JA, England. E-mail: davidcooper@dca-uk.com

COOPER Jessica Harriet, b. 28 January 1967, Bristol, England. Artist. m. Benjamin Yarwood, 1 son, 1 daughter. Education: Foundation Course Diploma, Falmouth College of Art, 1986; BA (Hons), Textiles/Fine Art, Goldsmiths College, London, 1989. Appointments: Artist. Publications: 22 Painters Who Happen to be Women, 1993; Drawings Towards the End of a Century, 1996; Artnsa, 2002; Behind the Canvas, 2002; Catching the Wave, 2003; Reading Between the Lines, 2004; Art Now Cornwall, 2007; New Paintings, 2008; Who's Who in Art, 2008. Honours: High Commended Award, Open Painting Exhibition, RWA, 2005; Drawing Quaters Award, University of the West of England, 2005. Memberships: Newlyn Society of Artists; Penwith Society of Artists; Council of Mangement, Newlyn Art Gallery and the Exchange; RWA Academician. Website: www.jessicacooper.co.uk

COOPER Jilly (Sallitt), b. 21 February 1937, Hornchurch, Essex, England. Writer; Journalist. m. Leo Cooper, 1961, 1 son, 1 daughter. Appointments: Reporter, Middlesex Independent Newspaper, Brentford, 1957-59; Columnist, The Sunday Times, 1969-82, The Mail on Sunday, 1982-87. Publications: How to Stay Married, 1969; How to Survive from Nine to Five, 1970; Jolly Super, 1971; Men and Super Men, 1972; Jolly Super Too, 1973; Women and Super Women, 1974; Jolly Superlative, 1975; Emily (romance novel), 1975; Super Men and Super Women (omnibus), 1976; Bella (romance novel), 1976; Harriet (romance novel), 1976; Octavia (romance novel), 1977; Work and Wedlock (omnibus), 1977; Superjilly, 1977; Imogen (romance novel), 1978; Prudence (romance novel), 1978; Class: A View from Middle England, 1979; Supercooper, 1980; Little Mabel series, juvenile, 4 volumes, 1980-85; Violets and Vinegar: An Anthology of Women's Writings and Sayings (editor with Tom Hartman), 1980; The British in Love (editor), 1980; Love and Other Heartaches, 1981 (re-named Lisa & Co, 1982); Jolly Marsupial, 1982; Animals in War, 1983; The Common Years, 1984; Leo and Jilly Cooper on Rugby, 1984; Riders, 1985; Hotfoot to Zabriskie Point, 1985; Turn Right at The Spotted Dog, 1987; Rivals, 1988; Angels Rush In, 1990; Polo, 1991; The Man Who Made Husbands Jealous, 1993; Araminta's Wedding, 1993; Appassionata, 1996; How to Survive Christmas, 1996; Score! 1999; Pandora, 2002; Wicked, 2006. Honours: Publishing News Lifetime Achievement Award, 1998; OBE, 2004; Honorary Doctorate of Letters, University of Gloucestershire, 2009. Membership: NUJ. Address: c/o Vivienne Schuster, Curtis Brown, 4th Floor, Haymarket House, 28-29 Haymarket, London, SW1Y 4SP, England. E-mail: cb@curtisbrown.co.uk

COOPER Leon N, b. 28 February 1930, New York, USA. Physicist. m. Kay Anne Allard, 1969, 2 daughters. Education: BA, 1951, MA, 1953, PhD, 1954, Columbia University. Appointments: Institute for Advanced Study, Princeton, 1954-55; Research Associate, University of Illinois, 1955-57; Assistant Professor, Ohio State University, 157-58; Associate Professor, Brown University, Rhode Island, 1958-62; Professor, 1974, Thomas J Watson, Senior Professor of Science , 1974-, Director, Center for Neural Science, 1978-90, Institute for Brain and Neural Systems, 1991-, Brain Science Program, 2000-. Publications: An Introduction to the Meaning and Structure of Physics, 1968; Structure and Meaning, 1992; How We Learn, How We Remember, 1995. Honour: Comstock Prize, NAS, 1968; Joint Winner, Nobel Prize, Physics, 1972; Honorary DSc, Columbia, Sussex, 1973, Illinois, Brown, 1974, Gustavus Adolphus College, 1975, Ohio State University, 1976, Pierre and Marie Curie University, Paris, 1977; Award in Excellence, Columbia University, 1974; Descartes Medal, Academy de Paris, University Rene Descartes, 1977; John Jay Award, Columbia College, 1985. Memberships: National Science Foundation Post-doctoral Fellow, 1954-55; Alfred P Sloan Foundation Research Fellow, 1959-66; John Simon Guggenheim Memorial Foundation Fellow, 1965-66; Fellow, American Physical Society, American Academy of Arts and Sciences; American Federation of Scientists; Member, NAS, American Philosophical Society. Address: Box 1843, Physics Department, Brown University, Providence, RI 02912, USA.

COOPER Ross Gordon, b. 23 September 1970, Harare, Zimbabwe. Senior Lecturer. Education: BSc (Hon), Biological Sciences, 1993; Diploma, Management, 1997; MBA, 1999; D Phil, Medical Physiology, 2000; PGCE, 2001; PGC & DE, 2005, 2006; MA, 2010. Appointments: Research Associate, 1995-98, Lecturer, Physiology, 1999-2001, University of Zimbabwe; Research Associate, St Thomas Hospital, London, 2001-04; Research Associate & Demonstrator, University of Bristol, 2003-04; Senior Lecturer, 2004-; Physiology Subject Quality Co-ordinator, 2006-; Acting Programme Director of Health Studies, 2008. Publications: 78 renowned journals; 37 review articles; 57 abstracts/congress posters; 39 non-peer reviewed articles; 18 letters; 3 symposium lectures; 7 newsletters; 5 magazine; 33 dissertations/books/chapters; 7 discursive articles; 6 poems; 5 radio interviews; 7 newspaper articles; 1 in-flight magazine; 1 website. Honours: 2nd best essay submission, Allied Arts Award, Chipinge Junior School, Zimbabwe, 1975; Academic Award, Avondale Junior School, Harare, Zimbabwe, 1981; Licentiate Award, London C of C and Industry, 1982; Allied Arts Literary Award Grade B, Zimbabwe; British Korum Challenge Roach Fishing Competition Medal, 2006; Delta Force Paintball Challenge Champion, UK, 2008; Excellent Paper Award, Animal Science Journal, 2009; Poster Award, Runner up, 2010, Winner, 2011; Mathematics Olympiad International; Allied Arts Literary Award, Zimbabwe; Staff & Development Association, UK; Listed in international biographical dictionaries; Citation in Marquis Who's Who for outstanding research in Physiological Sciences, 2005-; Staff and Educational Development Association (SEDA), UK; Accreditation as a Teacher in Higher Education, 2006; National Poetry Anthology, 2011; Mayor's Civic Award, 2011. Memberships: Zimbabwean Physiology Society; MInst Professional Managers. Address: 5 Eurohouse, Dog Kennel lane, Walsall, Ws1 2BU, England. E-mail: rgcooperuk@yahoo.com

COOTE John Haven, b. 5 January 1937, London, England. Medical Scientist. m. Susan Mary Hylton, 1 son, 2 daughters. Education: BSc, 1961, PhD, 1964, Royal Free Hospital School of Medicine, University of London; DSc, University of Birmingham, 1980. Appointments: International Res App, Caracas, 1971-72, Warsaw, 1976, Chicago, 1988, Shanghai, 1984, Tianjin, 2005; Bowman Professor, Physiology, University of Birmingham, 1983-2003; Head, School of Basic Medical Sciences, 1988-91; Chair, Editorial Board, Experimental Physiology, 1999-2006; Chair, Human Sciences

Ethics Committee, Qinetiq, 1999-2009; Chair, Grants Committee, British Heart Foundation, 2001-06; Member, Defence Science Advisory Council, 2001-11; Consultant, Applied Physiology, RAF Centre, Aviation Medicine, 2002-; Visiting Professor, University of Warwick, 2003-05; Visiting Professor, Cardiology, Glenfield Hospital, Leicester, 2003-; Professor Emeritus, University of Birmingham, 2003-. Publications: Over 300 original research publications; Many review chapters in books. Honours: Design Council, Orthotic Appliances, 1981; Carl Ludwig Distinguished Lecturer, APS, USA, 2003; Paton Lecturer, 2004, Honorary Member, 2005, Physiology Society, UK; Dip Med, Krakow, Poland, 1995; C Biol, FiBiol, 1988; FRGS, 2004; FSB, 2010. Memberships: The Physiology Society; the Pharmacological Society; British Neuroscience Association; Society of Experimental Biology; New York Academy of Sciences. Address: School of Clinical and Experimental Medicine, College of Medical and Dental Sciences, University of Birmingham, B15 2TT, England. E-mail: j.h.coote@bham.ac.uk

COPE Jonathan, b. 1963, England. Ballet Dancer. m. Maria Almeida, 1 son, 1 daughter. Education: Royal Ballet School. Career: Dancer, 1982-, Soloist, 1985-86, Principal, 1987-90, 1992-, Royal Ballet; Property development business, 1990-92; Leading roles (with Royal Ballet): Swan Lake; The Sleeping Beauty; The Nutcracker; Romeo and Juliet; La Bayadère; Giselle; Le Baiser de la Fée; The Prince of the Pagodas; Cinderella; Ondine; Serenade; Agon; Apollo; Opus 19/The Dreamer; The Sons of Horus; Young Apollo; Galanteries; The Planets; Still Life at the Penguin Café; The Spirit of Fugue; Concerto; Gloria; Requiem; A Broken Set of Rules; Pursuit; Piano; Grand Pas Classique; Monotones; Mayerling; Different Drummer; The Judas Tree; A Month in the Country; Birthday Offering; La Valise; Air Monotones II; Renard; Fearful Symmetries; Symphony in C; Duo Concertant; If This Is Still A Problem; Manon; Illuminations. Honours: CBE, 2003. Address: The Royal Ballet, Royal Opera House, Covent Garden, London WC2E 9DD, England.

COPLEY Paul, b. 25 November 1944, Denby Dale, Yorkshire, England. Actor; Writer. m. Natasha Pyne, 1972. Education: Teachers Certificate, Northern Counties College of Education. Appointments: Freelance Actor/Writer; Extensive work in theatre, TV, radio and film: As an Actor: Theatre: For King and Country, Mermaid Theatre, 1976; Billy Liar, Ambassador Theatre Group National Tour; Ghosts Gate Theatre, 2007; King Lear, Shakespeare's Globe, 2008; Lulu, Gate Theatre, 2010; Winterlong, Royal Exchange, Soho, 2011; TV: Messiah 3: The Promise; Best Friends; Life on Mars; The Street; Waking the Dead; Shameless; Hornblower; Dalziel and Pascoe; The Lakes; This Life; Heartbeat; Clocking Off; Cracker; Torchwood; George Gently; The Royal; Survivors; Downtown Abbey; Radio: Serjeant Musgrave's Dance; A Sunset Touch; Everyone Quite Likes Justin; Once More with Feeling; Film: The Remains of the Day; Jude; Blow Dry; A Bridge Too Far; Zulu Dawn; A Distant Marriage; Recorded over 200 hundred radio plays and TV works; As a Writer: Pillion, Bush Theatre, London, 1977; Viaduct, Bush Theatre, London, 1979; Tapster, Stephen Joseph Theatre, Scarborough, 1981; Fire-Eaters, Tricycle Theatre, London, 1984; Calling, Stephen Joseph Theatre, Scarborough, 1986; Plays for children: Odysseus and the Cyclops, 1998; The Pardoner's Tale, 1999; Loki the Mischief Maker, 2000; Jennifer Jenks and Her Excellent Day Out, 2000; Radio: On May-Day, 1986; Tipperary Smith, 1994; Words Alive, 1996-2003. Honours: Olivier Award, Actor of the Year in a New Play, 1976; Plays and Players Award for Most Promising Actor (King and Country), 1976; Best Actor in a Supporting Role (The Servant), Martini/TMA British Regional Theatre Awards, 1995. Membership: Writers Guild. Address: Literary Agent: Casarotto Ramsey Ltd, 60 Wardour Street, London W1V 4ND, England.

COPPEN Luke Benjamin Edward, b. 8 February 1976, Basingstoke, Hampshire. Journalist. m. Marlena Marciniszyn, 2 daughters. Education: Testbourne Community School, Whitchurch, 1988-92; Cricklade Tertiary College, Andover, 1992-94; BA (1st class honours), Religion and Politics, School of Oriental and African Studies, London, 1997; Diploma, Journalism Studies, Cardiff, 1998. Appointments: Film Editor, The London Student, 1996-97; Reporter, 1998-2000, Deputy Editor, 2000-04, Editor, 2004-, The Catholic Herald. Address: The Catholic Herald, Lambs Passage, Bunhill Road, London EC19 8TQ, England. E-mail: editorial@catholicherald.co.uk

COPPOLA Francis Ford, b. 7 April 1939, Detroit, Michigan, USA. Film writer and director. m. Eleanor Neil, 2 sons (1 deceased), 1 daughter. Education: Hofstra University; University of California. Career: Films include: Dementia 13, 1963; This Property is Condemned, 1965; Is Paris Burning?, 1966; You're A Big Boy Now, 1967; Finian's Rainbow, 1968; The Rain People, 1969; Patton, 1971; The Great Gatsby, 1974; The Godfather Part II, 1975; The Black Stallion (produced), 1977; Apocalypse Now, 1979; One From the Heart, Hammett (produced), The Escape Artist, The Return of the Black Stallion, 1982; Rumble Fish, The Outsiders, 1983; The Cotton Club, 1984; Peggy Sue Got Married, Gardens of Stone, 1986; Life Without Zoe, Tucker: the Man and His Dream, 1988; The Godfather Part III, 1990; Dracula, 1991; My Family/Mia Familia, Don Huan de Marco, 1995; Jack, 1996; The Rainmaker, 1997; The Florentine, The Virgin Suicides, 1999; Grapefruit Moon, 2000; Assassination Tango; Supernova; Megalopolis; Executive producer: The Secret Garden, 1993; Mary Shelley's Frankenstein, 1994; Buddy, 1997; The Third Miracle, Goosed, Sleepy Hollow, 1999; Monster; Jeepers Creepers No Such Thing; Pumpkin; Lost in Translation, 2003; Kinsey, 2004; Marie Antoinette, The Good Shepherd, 2006; Youth Without Youth, 2007; Tetro, 2009. Theatre direction includes: Private Lives, The Visit of the Old Lady (San Francisco Opera Co); 1972; Artistic Director, Zoetrope Studios, 1969-; Owner, Niebaum-Coppola Estate, Napa Valley. Honours: 5 Oscars, 36 awards including, Cannes Film Award for The Conversation, 1974; Director's Guild Award for The Godfather; Academy Award for Best Screenplay for Patton, Golden Palm (Cannes), for Apocalypse Now, 1979; Also awarded Best Screenplay, Best Director and Best Picture Oscars for the Godfather Part II; US Army Civilian Service Award; Commandeur, Ordre des Arts et des Lettres; Irving Thalberg Memorial Award (Lifetime Achievement Oscar), 2010. Address: Zoetrope Studios, 916 Kearny Street, San Francisco, CA 94133, USA.

COPPOLA Sofia, b. 14 May 1971, New York, USA. Film Director; Screenwriter; Producer; Photographer. m. Spike Jonze, divorced, 2003; Partner, Thomas Mars, 1 daughter. Career: Creator, Pop-culture magazine show, Hi-Octane, 1994; Former designer, Milkfed fashon label; Photography work appeared in Interview, Paris Vogue and Allure; Films include: The Godfather: Part III, 1990; Lick the Star (director, producer and writer), 1998; Star Wars: Episode 1 – The Phantom Menace, 1999; The Virgin Suicides (director and writer); CQ, 2001; Lost in Translation (director, producer and writer), 2004; Cut Shorts, 2006; Marie Antoinette (producer), 2006; Honours: Academy Award, Best Original Screenplay, 2004; Golden Globe Award, Best Picture, and Best Screenplay, 2004; Independent Spirit Awards for Best Screenplay, Best Director, and Best Picture, 2004; Cesar

Award for Best Foreign Feature, 2005. Memberships: Writers Guild of America. Address: c/o Focus Features, 65 Bleeker Street, Second Floor, New York, NY 10012, USA.

CORBET Christian Cardell, Portrait Sculptor; Portrait, Landscape and Abstract Painter; Forensic Artist; Designer; Lecturer; Art Historian; Curator. Education: University of Guelph, 1991-95; McMaster University, 1996; Private tutelage under Dr Elizabeth Bradford Holbrook, CM, RCA, 1998-2004. Appointments: President, 1996-2001, Director, 2001-, Canadian Portrait Academy; Patron Artist, International Dyslexia Association, British Columbia Region, Vancouver, 1998-99; Patron Artist, Women's International League for Peace and Freedom, British Columbia Region, Vancouver, 1998-2000; Patron Artist, Jane Goodall Institute, 1999-2000; Forensic Artist-in-Residence, University of Western Ontario, 2003-; Patron Artist, Churchill Society for the Advancement of Parliamentary Democracy, 2008-; Patron Artist, Guernsey Channel Islands Corbet-Brock Medallion, 2010-; Numerous group and solo exhibitions in North America and Europe; Represented in over 60 permanent collections worldwide to include: British Museum; Imperial War Museum; Rijksmuseum; Guernsey Museum and Art Gallery and others, also corporate and private collections worldwide; Authorized portrait paintings and sculptures, especially of the late HM Queen Elizabeth the Queen Mother, Dame Jane Goodall, the late Sir Winston Churchill, Countess Mountbatten of Burma and Margaret Atwood among other famous world figures; Forensic sculpture, Sulman Project, for facial reconstruction of Egyptian mummy first ever reconstruction based on CT and laser scans. Publications: Several articles in professional journals and encyclopaedias. Honours: Honourable Mention, Canadian Portrait Academy, 1998; Creative Achievement Award, Canadian Portrait Academy, 1999; 1900-2000 100 Years of Canada's Best Portrait Artists, 2000; 21st Century Award for Achievement, 2001; PPCPA; CGAM; FIDEM; BAMS; FA; FRSA. Memberships: Founder, Canadian Portrait Academy; Founder, Canadian Group of Art Medallists; Fellow, Royal Society of Arts; Member, Federation of International Medallists; Member, British Art Medal Society; Official Protégé: Benjamin Trickett Mercer, CPA appointed, 2010. Address: "Vallaettes", 77 West Valley Road, Corner Brook, Newfoundland, A2H 2X4, Canada. E-mail: contact@christiancardellcorbet.com Website: www.christiancorbet.com

CORBETT Peter George, b. 13 April 1952, Rossett, North Wales. Artist. Education: Liverpool College of Art & Design; BA Hons, Manchester Regional College of Art & Design. Appointments: Hooker, 1 XV Waterloo Rugby Union Football Club, 1973-74; Speaker, Art Gallery and Senate House Gallery, University of Liverpool, 2004; Founder Member, Chairman, Merseyside Visual Arts Festival, 1989/90; Liverpool Biennial of Contemporary Art Independent, A Transformative Vision, 2008; Solo art exhibitions include: Paintings and Open Studio, Bluecoat Arts Centre, Liverpool, 2002; Retrospective of paintings 1987-2002, University of Liverpool, 2004; Liverpool Biennial of Contemporary Art, 2008, 2010; Group art exhibitions include: Influences and Innovations, Agora Gallery, New York, 2000; Mixed Exhibition, Liverpool University Art Gallery, 2002; Lexmark European Art Prize, Air Gallery, London, 2004; Florence Biennale of Contemporary Art, Italy, 2007; Public collections: Liverpool Hope University; Atkinson Gallery, Southport; Private collections in America, Netherlands, Australia, Germany, Britain, Spain, Nigeria and France. Publications include most recently: Anthologies: Memories of the Millennium, 2000; Tales from Erewhon, 2001; The Pool of Life, 2003; 180th Edition Ambit Magazine (Apple City), 2005; Poems from North and Northwest England (Below Midnight), 2005; Songs of Honour, 2006; Public Art Catalogue, London, 2011. Honours include most recently: Best Poems and Poets of 2002; International Poet of Merit Award, 2002, 2003; Poet of the Year, International Society of Poets, USA, 2003; Outstanding Professional Award for Achievement, ABI, 2003; 21st Century Achievement Award, ABI, 2003; Great Minds of the 21st Century Hall of Fame, ABI, 2004; Lexmark European Art Prize, London, 2004; Research Fellow, ABI, 2006; Greatest Minds of the 21st Century Diploma, 2006; International Who's Who in Poetry, 2007; Peter G Corbett Award Foundation, ABI, 2007; Genius Laureate of the United Kingdom, ABI. Memberships: Maison Internationale Des Intellectuals, Paris; Honorary Professor of the Academie Des Sciences Universelles, Paris; Lifelong Fellow and Honorary Professor in Fine Arts, University of Co-ordinated Research, State of Victoria, Australia; Life Member, Design & Artist's Copyright Society. Address: Flat 4, 7 Gambier Terrace, Hope Street, Liverpool L1 7BG, England. Website: www.axisweb.org/artist/petercorbett

CORBETT Robin, (Lord Corbett of Castle Vale), b. 22 December 1933, Fremantle, Australia. Parliamentarian. m. Valerie, 1 son, 2 daughters. Appointments: Trainee, Birmingham Evening Mail; Reporter, Daily Mirror; Deputy Editor, Farmer's Weekly; Editorial Staff Development Executive, IPC Magazines; Labour Relations Executive, IPC; National Executive Committee Member, Honorary Secretary Magazine and Book Branch, National Union of Journalists; Elected Member of Parliament for Hemel Hempstead, 1974-79; Elected Member of Parliament for Birmingham Erdington, 1983-2001; Opposition Front Bench Spokesman on Broadcasting and Media, 1987-94 and Disabled People's Rights, 1994-95; Chairman, House of Commons Home Affairs Select Committee, 1999-2001; Appointed to House of Lords, 2001; Member, Select Committee on the EU (SCF). Honours: Dr of Laws, Birmingham University, 2005. Memberships: Vice Chairman Indo-British Parliamentary Group; Chairman, Friends of Cyprus; Vice-Chairman, All Party Motor Group, sustainable development, renewable energy; Member, Wilton Park Academic Council, 1995-2005; Vice-President, Lotteries Council; Treasurer, ANZAC Group, 1946-2006; Member, Friends of Eden Project; Patron, Hope for Children; Director, Rehab UK; Chairman, Castle Vale Neighbourhood Management Board, 2001-04; President, Josiah Mason College, Erdington, 2001-; Chairman, Castle Vale Neighbourhood Partnership, 2004-; Chairman, Parliamentary Labour Peers' Group, 2005-; Member, Lords PLP Co-ordination Committee, 2004-05. Address: House of Lords, London, SW1A 0PW, England. E-mail: castlevale@corbetts.plus.com

CORBLUTH Elsa, b. 2 August 1928, Beckenham, Kent, England. Writer; Photographer. m. David Boadella, divorced 1987, 1 son, 1 daughter, deceased 1980. Education: BA, Combined Creative Arts, 1st Class Honours, Alsager College, 1982; MA, Creative Writing, Lancaster University, 1984. Publications: St Patrick's Night, poems on daughter's death in charity hostel fire while working there, 1988; The Planet Iceland, 2002; The Hill Speaks, 2008; Out There; Various booklets; Wilds, travelling exhibition of poems illustrated by her photographs, accompanied by poetry readings; Group of 7 poems in SW Arts Proof Series of small books, 1998; Contributions to: Poetry Review; Outposts; The Rialto; Times Literary Supplement, etc; Anthologies: Green Book; Arts Council of Great Britain; PEN, etc. Honours: 1st Prizes, South-West Arts Competition, Bridport, 1979 and 1981; Joint

1st, Cheltenham Festival Competition, 1981; 1st, Sheffield Competition, 1981; 1st, ORBIS Rhyme Revival, 1986, 1993, 1995; 1st Prize Yorkshire Poetry Competition, 1997; 1st Prize, Poetry on the Lake, Formal Class, Italy, 2007; and others. Membership: Harbour Poets Weymouth; CND. Address: Hawthorn Cottage, Rodden, Near Weymouth, Dorset DT3 4JE, England.

CORBY Peter John Siddons, b. 8 July 1924, Leamington Spa, England. Businessman. m. (1) Gail Susan Clifford-Marshall, 2 sons, (2) Inés Rosemary Mandow, 1 son. Education: Private Grammar School (Boarding). Appointments: Engineering Apprentice, Coventry Gauge & Tool Co Ltd, 1940-42; Wartime Service: Flight Engineer (Halifax and Lancaster), 78 Squadron, 4 Group, Bomber Command Royal Airforce, 1943-48; Managing Director of family business, Corbys Ltd and John Corby Ltd; Created manufactured and marketed the Corby Electric Trouser Press, also served on the boards of various other manufacturing and service companies, 1949-74; Sold Corby companies to Thomas Jourdan plc, 1974; Various non-executive directorships, including Thomas Jourdan plc, 1974-2006; Company Memberships: Cordeal Limited (family company); SaveTower Ltd (property company). Honours: Freeman of the City of London, 1977; Liveryman (Marketors), 1978. Memberships: Ocean Cruising Club; Island Sailing Club; Honorary Member, Yacht Club de France; Fellow of the Institute of Directors, 1955; Lloyd's of London, 1974. Address: The Sloop, 89 High Street, Cowes, Isle of Wight PO31 7AW, England.

CORDA Christian, b. 3 July 1969, Nuoro, Italy. Professor. m. Maria Nasti, 1 son. Education: Graduate degree, PhD, Physics, University of Pisa, Italy. Appointments: Full Professor, Theoretical Physics, Institute for Basic Research, Palm Harbor, Florida, USA. Publications: Numerous articles in professional journals. Honours: World's Most Cited Author, Astroparticle Publication Review of Aspera, 2007; World's Youngest Editor in Chief of an astrophysics journal, 2008; Honorable Mention Winner, Gravity Research Foundation Awards, 2009. Memberships: International Institute for Theoretical Physics and Mathematics, Einstein Galiley, Prato, Italy; IBR, Palm Harbor, USA. Address: via B Buozzi 47, 59100 Prato, Italy.

CORDINGLY David, b. 5 December 1938, London, England. Writer. m. Shirley, 1 son, 1 daughter. Education: Honours Degree Modern History, MA, Oriel College, Oxford; D Phil, University of Sussex. Appointments: Graphic Designer with various design groups and publishing firms in London; Exhibition Designer, The British Museum; Keeper, Art Gallery and Museum, Brighton; Assistant Director, Museum of London; Keeper of Pictures and then Head of Exhibitions, National Maritime Museum, Greenwich. Publications: Books: Marine Painting in England 1700-1900, 1974; Painters of the Sea, 1979; Nicholas Pocock, Marine Artist, 1986; Life among the Pirates: the romance and the reality, 1995; Pirates: an illustrated history; Ships and Seascapes: an introduction to marine prints, drawings and watercolours, 1997; Heroines and Harlots: women at sea in the great age of sail, 2001; Billy Ruffian: the Bellerophon and the downfall of Napoleon, 2003; Cochrane the Dauntless, 2007. Address: 2 Vine Place, Brighton, Sussex BN1 3HE, England.

CORLUY Walter Josephus, b. 8 April 1938, Borgerhout, Belgium. Education: MA, Economics, PhD, Law, Catholic University, Louvain, Belgium. Appointments: Ex-Regional General Manager, Generale Bank (now BNP Paribas Fortis); Retired University Senior Teaching Professor, University of Antwerp; Publications: Finance and Risk Management in International Trade, 1990, 2nd edition 1995; Co-author, Practical Guide for Financial Management, 1995; Different articles in professional papers. Honours: Knight, Order of Leopold, Belgium; Knight, Order of the Crown, Belgium; Senator, Jaycees International; Paul Harris Fellow, Sapphire, Rotary International; Diocesan Order of Merit with Silver (Diocese Antwerp); Honorary Inhabitant of Antwerp, 1993. Memberships: Rotary Club, Antwerpen Voorkempen; Formerly Chairman, Asociacion-Belgo-Ibero-Americana; Treasurer, Dante Alighieri; Director, NGO Trias; Chairman, Church Council, Saint Anthony, Antwerp. Address: Prins Albertlei, 5 Box 1, 2600 Antwerp, Belgium. E-mail: walter.corluy@skynet.be

CORP Ronald Geoffrey, b. 4 January 1951, Wells, Somerset, England. Musician; Cleric. Education: MA, Christ Church, Oxford; Dip. Theol., University of Southampton. Appointments: Librarian, Producer and Presenter, BBC Radio 3, 1973-87; Musical Director, Highgate Choral Society, 1984; Musical Director, The London Chorus, 1985; Founder, New London Orchestra, 1988; Founder, New London Children's Choir, 1991; Non-stipendiary Minister, St Mary's Kilburn with St James' West End Lane, 1998-2002; Non-stipendiary Assistant Curate, Christ Church, Hendon, 2002-07; Non-Stipendiary Assistant Curate, St Alban's, Holban; Compositions include: And All the Trumpets Sounded, 1989; Laudamus, 1994 Cornucopia, 1997; Piano Concerto, 1997; A New Song, 1999; Adonai Echad, 2001; Missa San Marco, 2002; Dover Beach, 2003; String Quartet No 1, The Bustard, 2007; String Quartet No 2, 2009; Symphony, 2009; The Hound of Heaven, 2009; String Quartet No 3, 2010; Dhammapada, 2010; The Ice Mountain, 2010. Publications: 20 recordings with New London Orchestra; CD of own choral music, Forever Child; Book: The Choral Singer's Companion, 1987, revised edition, 2000; Symphony and Piano Concerto on Dutton. Memberships: Trustee, 2000-, Chairman, Education Committee, Musician's Benevolent Fund; Vice-President, The Sullivan Society; President, Bracknell Choral Society; Freeman, Worshipful Company of Musicians, 2007. Address: Bulford Mill, Bulford Mill Lane, Cressing, Essex, CM77 8NS, England. E-mail: ronald.corp@btconnect.com

CORREIA Alexandre C M, b. Lisbon, Portugal. Associate Professor. m. Edite. Education: PhD, Astrophysics and Spacial Techniques, University of Paris VIII. Appointments: Associate Professor, University of Aveiro. Publications: Numerous articles in professional journals. Address: Physics Department, University of Aveiro, Campus de Santiago, 3810-193 Aveiro, Portugal.

CORTES Joaquin, b. 1970, Madrid, Spain. Appointments: Joined Spanish National Ballet, 1985; Principal Dancer, 1987-90; Now appears in own shows, blending gypsy dancing, jazz blues and classical ballet; De Amor y Odio, international tour, 2004; Mi Soledad, 2007; Dancing with the Stars, USA, 2007. Films: Pedro Almodóvar's, The Flower Of My Secret; Gitano, 2000; Vaniglia e cioccolato, 2004; Unleashed, 2009.

CORTES DURAN Gabriel, b. 4 January 1976, Veracruz, Mexico. Obstetric-Gynaecologist; Reproductive Medicine Specialist. m. Maria Angelica Estrada Tapia, 2 daughters. Education: Medical Genetics, National Institute for Nutrition and Medical Science, 2002; Obstetrics and Gynaecology, 2007, Reproductive Medicine, 2009, Hospital Angeles Pedregal, Mexico. Appointments: Obstetric-Gynaecologist and Reproductive Medicine Specialist, Women's Hospital, Hermosillo, Sonora, Mexico. Publications: Numerous articles related to Recurrent Pregnancy Loss, Thrombophilia and Immunologic Factor, in professional journals. Honours: First Place, The Cytogenetic in recurrent pregnancy loss patients, the Preimplanation Genetic Diagnosis, could help prevent abortion?, 2003; First Place, Recurrent Pregnancy Loss related to Thrombophilia Genes Mutations, 2005; Listed in international biographical dictionaries. Address: Juarez y Ld, Colosio Consultorio, 204 Hermosillo, Sonora 83200, Mexico. E-mail: doctorgen@hotmail.com

CORTI Christopher Winston, b. 30 July 1940, London, England. Consultant. m. Shirley Anne Mack, 3 sons. Education: Bishopshalt School, Hillingdon, Middlesex, 1951-59; BSc, Metallurgy, Battersea College of Advanced Technology, London, 1959-63; PhD, Metallurgy, University of Surrey, Guildford, 1968-72. Appointments: Student, UK Atomic Energy Authority, Lancashire, 1961-62; Research Officer, Central Electricity Research Laboratories, Leatherhead, Surrey, 1963-68; Scientific Officer, Department of Materials Science & Engineering, University of Surrey, 1968-72; Project Leader, Brown Boveri Research Centre, Baden, Switzerland, 1973-77; Research Manager, Materials Technology, Johnston Matthey Technology Centre, Reading, 1978-88; Technical Director, Colour & Print Division, Johnson Matthey plc, Stoke on Trent, 1988-92; SPT Officer, Department of Trade & Industry, UK Government, 1993-94; Managing Director, International Technology, World Gold Council, London, 1994-2004; Managing Director, COReGOLD Technology Consultancy, 2004-. Publications: Over 70 scientific articles and conference papers in refereed scientific journals. Honours: Chartered Engineer; Chartered Scientist; Fellow, Institute of Materials, Minerals and Mining; Fellow, City & Guilds Institute, London; Sir Andrew Bryan Medal, 2010. Memberships: Institute of Materials, Minerals and Mining, London; City & Guilds Institute, London; Engineering Council, UK; Science Council, UK; Royal Horticultural Society, UK; National Trust, UK. Address: 21 Marchwood Avenue, Emmer Green, Reading, Berkshire RG4 8UH, England. E-mail: chris@corti.force9.co.uk

COSBY Bill, b. 12 July 1937, Philadelphia, USA. Actor. m. Camille Hanks, 1964, 5 children (1 son deceased). Education: Temple University; University of Massachusetts. Appointments: Served USNR, 1959-60; President, Rhythm and Blues Hall of Fame, 1968-; TV appearances include: The Bill Cosby Show, 1969, 1972-73, I Spy, The Cosby Show, 1984-92, Cosby Mystery Series, 1994-; "Cosby" 1996-2000; Touched by an Angel, 1997-99; Becker, 1999; Everybody Loves Raymond, 1999; Sylvia's Path (voice), 2002; Recitals include: Revenge, To Russell, My Brother With Whom I Slept, To Secret, 200 MPH, Why Is There Air, Wonderfulness, It's True, It's True, Bill Cosby is a Very Funny Fellow: Right, I Started Out as a Child, 8:15, 12:15, Hungry, Reunion 1982, Bill Cosby... Himself, 1983, Those of You With or Without Children, You'll Understand; Numerous night club appearances; Executive Producer: A Different Kind of World (TV series), 1987-; I Spy Returns (TV), 1994; "Cosby" (TV), 1996; Little Bill (TV), 1999; Men of Honor, 2000; The Cosby Show: A Look Back (TV), 2002; Fatherhood (TV), 2004; Fat Albert, 2004; Films include: Hickey and Boggs, 1972; Man and Boy, 1972; Uptown Saturday Night, 1974; Let's Do It Again, 1975; Mother, Jugs and Speed, 1976; Aesop's Fables, A Piece of the Action, 1977; California Suite, 1978; Devil and Max Devlin, 1979; Leonard: Part IV, 1987; Ghost Dad, 1990; The Meteor Man, 1993; Jack, 1996; 4 Little Girls. Publications: The Wit and Wisdom of Fat Albert, 1973; Bill Cosby's Personal Guide to Power Tennis, Fatherhood, 1986; Time Flies, 1988; Love and Marriage, 1989; Childhood, 1991; Little Bill Series, 1999; Congratulations! Now What? 1999; Cosbyology: Essays and Observations from the Doctor of Comedy, 2001; I am what I Ate---and I'm Frightened!!!, 2003; Friends of a Feather, 2003. Honours: 4 Emmy Awards and 8 Grammy Awards. Address: c/o The Brokaw Co, 9255 Sunset Boulevard, Los Angeles, CA 90069, USA.

COSH (Ethel Eleanor) Mary, b. Bristol, England. Historian. Education: MA, St Anne's College Oxford, 1946-49. Appointments: Employment Clerk/Officer, Ministry of Labour, 5 years; WRNS, Londonderry and Alexandria, Egypt, 1942-45; Worked for Design Review, Council of Industrial Design, 1951-52; Free-lance part-time employment includes: Transcriber for Hansard (for Standing Committees); Re-cataloguing Library, Order of St John; Artist's Model at leading London art schools. Publications: The Real World (fiction), 1961; Inveraray and the Dukes of Argyll (with the late Ian G Lindsay), 1973; Edinburgh: The Golden Age, 2003; A History of Islington, 2005; 53 Cross Street (with Martin King), 2008; Numerous local publications including: The Squares of Islington (in 2 parts); Contributions to: The Times, Times Educational Supplement, The Spectator, Country Life. Honours: MA; FSA. Memberships: Conservation societies including: Society of Architectural Historians of Great Britain; National Trust; NACF; Georgian Group; Victorian Society; Architectural Heritage Society of Scotland; Cockburn Association; Islington (Civic) Society; Islington Archeology & History Society. Address: 10 Albion Mews, Islington, London N1 1JX, England.

COŞKUN Ömer, b. 5 March 1970, Adana, Turkey. Doctor. m. Mine, 2 daughters. Education: BSc, Faculty of Medicine, Istanbul University, Capa; PhD, Aksaray Medicinal Faculty, Erciyes University. Appointments: Officer, Turkish General Staff, Gulhane Military Medicine; Commandership, Department of History & Embriology and Tube Baby Central (IVF Centre), 2001-03; Getinkaya Medical Centre/Yildiz Policlinic Ambulatorium (temp), Zonguldak and Trakya Universities Medicinal Faculties, 2001-05; Dr Omer Coskun Healthy Living Centre, Tonsalp Herbal Medicine Research Institute, 2005-11. Publications: BIOTEST Cancer Archive. Honours: 24th International Consumer Summit Awards, Halic Congress Centre, 2011. Memberships: Turkish Doctoral Association; Kentucky University Diabetes Investigation Center; Antaly Doctoral Chamber; Research Hospital Diagnostics Commission and Consultation. Address: Basin Ekspress Yolu Uzeri, Merkez Mh Cevdet Ulusay Cd No 43, Istanbul, Turkey.

COSTA CABRAL E GIL Luis Manuel, b. 30 March 1960, Lisbon, Portugal. Researcher; Consultant; Translator. m. Maria Dulce, 1 son. Education: Graduate, Chemical Engineering, 1985; MSc, Technological Organic Chemistry, 1989; Specialisation, Science and Technology Management, 1994. Appointments: Research Engineer, ICTM, 1985-87; Researcher, INETI, 1987-2009; Patent Translator, AGCF, JPC, CM, RCF, 1990-2013; Technical Advisor, ART/Belgium, 1990-94; Researcher, ITIME, 1994-97; Consultant, ZILTCH, 1998-2005; Consultant, AIEC, BETACORK, JPC, 2004-2008; Senior Researcher, LNEG, 2009-13. Publications: 135 technical and scientific papers in national and international journals; 145 presentations in international meetings; 8 technical books on cork; 5 chapters on books/encyclopaedia; 16 patents. Honours: 6 patent awards; 11 R&D awards; 4 IBC awards; Listed in national and international biographical dictionaries. Memberships: Portuguese Engineer Association, 1987; New York Academy of Sciences, 1994; Creativity Portuguese Association, 1996; Portuguese Materials Society,

1997; CSC, 2008; Board of Portuguese Materials Society. Address: LNEG, Estrada do Paco Do Lumiar, 1649-038 Lisboa, Portugal. E-mail: luis.gil@lneg.pt

COSTELLO Elvis (Declan McManus), b. 25 August 1955, London, England. Singer; Songwriter; Musician; Record Producer. m. (1) 1 child, (2) Cait O'Riordan, divorced, (3) Diana Krall, 2004, twin sons. Career: Lead singer, Elvis Costello And The Attractions, 1977-; Appearances include: UK tour, 1977; US tour, 1978; Grand Ole Opry, 1981; Royal Albert Hall, with Royal Philharmonic, 1982; Cambridge Folk Festival, 1995; Television includes: Appearance in Scully, ITV drama, 1985; Films: Americathon, 1979; No Surrender, 1985; Straight to Hell, 1987; Prison Song, 2001; De-Lovely, 2004; Also worked with The Specials; Paul McCartney; Aimee Mann; George Jones; Roy Orbison; Wendy James; Robert Wyatt; Jimmy Cliff; Co-organiser, annual Meltdown festival, South Bank Centre, London. Compositions include: Alison, Watching The Detectives, 1977; Crawling To The USA, Radio Radio, Stranger In The House, 1978; (I Don't Want To Go To) Chelsea, Girls Talk, Oliver's Army, 1979; Boy With A Problem, 1982; Every Day I Write The Book, 1983; Music for television series (with Richard Harvey): G.B.H., 1991; Jake's Progress, 1995; Other songs for artists including Johnny Cash; June Tabor. Recordings: Albums include: My Aim Is True, 1977; This Years Model, 1978; Armed Forces, 1979; Get Happy, Trust, 1980; Almost Blue, 1981; Taking Liberties, Imperial Bedroom, 1982; Goodbye Cruel World, Punch The Clock, 1984; The Best Of, 1985; Blood And Chocolate, King Of America, 1986; Spike, 1989; Mighty Like A Rose, My Aim Is True, 1991; The Juliet Letters, with the Brodksy Quartet, 1993; Brutal Youth, 1994; The Very Best Of Elvis Costello And The Attractions, Kojak Variety, Deep Dead Blue, Live At Meltdown (with Bill Frisell), 1995; All The Useless Beauty, 1996; Terror & Magnificence, 1997; Painted From Memory, 1998; The Sweetest Punch: The Songs of Costello, Best of Elvis Costello, 1999; For the Stars (with Anne Sofie von Otter), 2001; When I Was Cruel, 2002; North, Scarlet Tide, 2003, The Delivery Man, 2004; The River in Reverse, 2006. Honours include: BAFTA Award, Best Original Television Music, G.B.H., 1992; MTV Video, Best Male Video, 1989; Rolling Stone Award, Best Songwriter, 1990; 2 Ivor Novello Awards; Nordoff-Robbins Silver Clef Award; ASCAP Founders Award, 2003; Rock and Roll Hall of Fame, 2003.

COSTIN Claudia, b. 19 April 1964, Falticeni, Romania. Associate Professor. m. Ioan Costin, 1 son. Education: Nicu Gane National College, Falticeni, 1982; Philology licence, 1988; Doctor in Philology, 2003, Al i Cuza University, Iasy. Appointments: Teacher, Mihai Busuioc high school, Pascany, 1988-93; Teacher, Miron Costin high school, Pascany, 1993-98; Lecturer, 1998-2007, Associate Professor, 2007-, Stefan cel Mare University, Suceava; Head, Department of Romanian Language and Literature, 2008-. Publications: Books: Mythical structures and dominant symbols in Lucian Blaga's drama, 2003; References in the history of medieval Romanian literature, 2006; Romanian literary folklore, 2007; Article, The feminine hypostasis of the malefic in Romanian Mythology, 2008. Memberships: Dante Alighieri Society; North-East Pascany XXI Local Action Group. Address: Nicolae Iorga Street, No 11, Bl V6-7, Sc 1, Ap 7, Pascany City, Iasy, Postal Code 705200, Romania. E-mail: claudiacostin@litere.usv.ro

COSTNER Kevin, b. 18 January 1955. Actor. m. (1) Cindy Silva, 1978, divorced 1994, 1 son, 2 daughters, 1 son with Bridget Rooney (2) Christine Baumgartner, 2004. Education: California State University. Appointments: Directing debut in Dances With Wolves, 1990; Films include: Frances, 1982; The Big Chill, 1983; Testament, 1983; Silverado, 1985; The Untouchables, 1987; No Way Out, 1987; Bull Durham, 1988; Field of Dreams, 1989; Revenge, 1989; Robin Hood: Prince of Thieves, 1990; JFK, 1991; The Bodyguard, 1992; A Perfect World, 1993; Wyatt Earp, 1994; Waterworld, 1995; Tin Cup, 1996; Message in a Bottle, 1998; For Love of the Game, 1999; Thirteen Days, 2000; 3000 Miles to Graceland, 2001; Dragonfly, 2002; Open Range, 2003; Upside of Anger, 2005; Rumor Has It, 2005; The Guardian, 2006; Mr Brooks, 2007; Swing Vote, 2008; Co-producer, Rapa Nui; Co-producer, China Moon. Honours include: Academy Award for Best Picture, 1991; 2 Oscars, 26 Awards, 30 nominations. Address: TIG Productions, Producers Building 5, 4000 Warner Boulevard, Burbank, CA 91523, USA.

COTTELL Michael Norman Tizard, b. 25 July 1931, Southampton, England. Retired Civil Engineer. m. Joan Florence, 2 sons. Education: Southampton University; Birmingham University. Appointments: Assistant County Surveyor, East Suffolk County Council, 1965-73; Deputy County Surveyor, East Sussex County Council, 1973-76; County Surveyor, Northants County Council, 1976-84; County Surveyor, Kent County Council, 1984-91; Executive Consultant, Travers Morgan Consultants, 1991-95; Chairman, Aspen Consultancy Group, 1995-2002. Honour: OBE, 1988.Memberships: F R ENG; FICE; FCIHT; MCIM. Address: Salcey Lawn, Harrow Court, Stockbury, Sittingbourne, Kent, ME9 7UQ, England.

COTTRELL Alan Howard, b. 17 July 1919, Birmingham, England. Scientist; Academic. m. Jean Elizabeth Harber, 1 son. Education: Moseley Grammar School, Birmingham; BSc, PhD, University of Birmingham; Sc D, University of Cambridge. Appointments: Lecturer, 1943-49, Professor, 1949-55, Physical Metallurgy, University of Birmingham; Atomic Energy Research Establishment Harwell, 1955-58; Goldsmith's Professor, University of Cambridge, 1958-65; Deputy Chief Scientific Adviser, 1965-67, Chief Adviser, 1967, MOD, Deputy Chief Scientific Adviser, 1968-71, Chief Scientific Adviser, 1971-74, Her Majesty's Government; Vice Chancellor, University of Cambridge, 1977-79; Master, Jesus College, Cambridge, 1974-86. Publications: Several scientific books; Many papers in scientific journals. Honours: FRS, 1955; Knighted, 1971; Honorary LLD, University of Cambridge, 1996; Various honorary DScs; Honorary membership of various scientific institutions and medals. Memberships: American Academy of Arts & Sciences, USA; National Academy of Science, USA; National Academy of Engineering, USA; Royal Swedish Academy of Sciences; Jesus College & Christ's College, Cambridge. E-mail: ah.cottrell@virgin.net

COULOMB René Paul, b. 20 November 1932, Clermont-Ferrand, France. Retired. m. Francoise Laval, 4 sons, 1 daughter. Education: Ecole Polytechnique, 1953; Ecole Nationale des Ponts et Chaussées, 1956. Appointments: Engineer des Ponts et Chaussées, 1956-58; Engineer, Chief, Barrages-Réservoirs, Paris, 1958-67, Lyonnaise-des-Eaux, then Suez, 1967-2003; Founding Member, World Water Council, 1996-; President, Société Hydro Technique de France, 1997-2007. Publications: Bilingual books: The World Water Council. From its origin through the World Water Forum in the Hague, 2011; The World Water Council: From the Forum in the Hague through the Forum in Marseille, 2012; Numerous articles in professional journals. Honours: Honorary President, Société Hydro Technique de France; Honorary Member, International Water Association; Member, Académie de l'Eau.

Memberships: IWA; French Water Academy; Prospective 2010. Address: Résidence Gallia, 15 rue Sarrette, 75014 Paris, France. E-mail: rene-coulomb@orange.fr

COULSON-THOMAS Colin Joseph, b. 26 April 1949, Mullion, Cornwall, England. Professor; Author; Chairman. 1 son, 2 daughters. Education: MSc, London Business School, 1975; DPA, 1977, MSc (Econ), 1980, LSE/London University; PCL, MA, CNAA, 1981, AM, 1982, University of Southern California; UNISA, MPA, 1985, PhD, 1988, University of Aston. Appointments: Consultant, Coopers & Lybrand, 1975-78; Editor, Publisher, Head of Public Relations, ICSA, 1978-81; Publishing Director, Longman Group, 1981-84; Corporate Affairs, Xerox, Rank Xerox, 1984-93; Founder, Chairman of companies including: Adaptation, ASK Europe, Cotoco, Policy Publications, 1987-; Trustee, Community Network, 1989-; Willmot Dixon Professor, Dean of Faculty, Head of Patteridge Bury Campus, 1994-97, Visiting Professor, 1998-99 and 2006-, University of Luton; Professor, Head, Centre for Competitiveness, 2000-06; Professor of Direction and Leadership, University of Lincoln, 2005-09; Member, Institute of Directors, Board of Examiners, 1998-2010, Professional Accreditation Committee, 2003-08; Member, Governance and Risk Management Committee, ACCA, 2006-; Chairman, Bryok Systems, 2008-; Chair, Audit Committee, Peterborough PCT, 2009-; Professor, Direction and Leadership, University of Greenwich, 2009-. Publications: Author of over 30 books and reports including: The Future of the Organisation, 1997/98; Individuals and Enterprise, 1999; Shaping Things to Come, 2001; Transforming the Company, 2002, 2004; The Knowledge Entrepreneur, 2003; Winning Companies, Winning People, 2007; Developing Directors, 2007; Reports include: Pricing for Profit, 2002; Winning New Business, 2003. Honours: First place prizes in final examinations of these professions. Memberships: Chartered Accountant; FCA; FCCA; FCIS; FMS; FCIPR; FCIPD; FCIM; FCMI, Hon FAIA, FRGS; FSCA; Has served on regional and national public sector boards; Trustee, Community Network, 1989-; Association of Chartered Certified Accountants, 2006-; Representative Governor, Peterborough and Stamford Hospitals NHS Foundation Trust, 2010-. Address: Mill Reach, Mill Lane, Water Newton, Cambridgeshire PE8 6LY, England. E-mail: colinct@tiscali.co.uk Website: www.coulson-thomas.com

COUPLES Fred, b. 3 October 1959, Seattle, Washington, USA. Professional Golfer. m. (1) Deborah, divorced 1993, 1 son, 1 daughter, (2) Thais Baker, deceased 2009. Education: University of Houston. Appointments: Member, Rider Cup Team, 1989, 1991, 1993; Named All-American, 1979, 1980; Winner, numerous tournaments including Kemper Open, 1983; Tournament Players Championship, 1984, Byron Nelson Golf Classic, 1987, French PGA, 1988, Nissan LA Open, 1990, 1992, Tournai Perrier de Paris, 1991, BC Open, 1991, Federal Express St Jude Classic, 1991, Johnnie Walker World Championship, 1991, 1995, Nestle Invitational, 1992, The Masters, 1992, with Jan Stephenson J C Penney Classic, 1983, with Mike Donald, Sazale Classic, 1990, with Raymond Floyd, RMCC Invitational, 1990, Buick Open, 1994, Dubai Desert Classic, 1995, Players Championship, 1996, Skins Game, 1996, Australian Skins Game, 1997; Member, US Team, Presidents Cup, 1997; Champion, Bob Hope Chrysler Classic, 1998; Champion, Memorial Tournament, 1998; Houston Open, 2004; Merrill Lynch Skins Game, 2004; ING Par-3 Shootout, 2006; Member, President Cup Team, 1998, 2005. Honours: Vardon Trophy, 1991, 1992; Named PGA Player of Year, Golf World magazine, 1991, 1992. Address: c/o PGA Tour, 100 Avenue of the Champions, PO Box 109601, Palm Beach Gardens, FL 33410, USA.

COURANT Ernest David, b. 26 March 1920, Goettingen, Germany. Physicist. m. Sara Paul, 1944, 2 sons. Education: BA, Swarthmore, 1940; MS, 1942, PhD, 1943, Rochester. Appointments: Scientist, NRC, Montral, 1943-46; Research Associate, Cornell, 1946-48; Physicist, Brookhaven National Laboratory, 1948-89; Distinguished Scientist Emeritus, 1990-. Publications: Numerous articles in professional journals. Honours: Fermi Award, DOE, 1986; Wilson Prize, APS, 1987. Memberships: American Physics Society; US National Academy of Sciences. Address: 40 W 72, Apt 41, New York, NY 10023, USA. E-mail: ecourant@msn.com

COURIER Jim (James Spencer), b. 17 August 1970, Sanford, Florida, USA. Tennis Player. Career: Professional Tennis Player, 1989-; Winner of tournaments including: Orange Bowl, 1986, 1987, Basel, 1989, French Open, 1991, 1992, Indian Wells, 1991, 1993, Key Biscayne, 1991, 1993, Australian Open, 1992-93, Italian Open, 93; Finalist US Open, 1991; Quarterfinalist, Wimbledon, 1991; Runner-up French Open, 1993, Wimbledon, 1993; Semifinalist, Australian Open, 1994, French Open, 1994; Winner of 23 singles titles and six doubles titles and over $16 million dollars in prize money; Retired, 2000; Founded InsideOut Sport and Entertainment, 2004; Now plays in the Outback Series was No 1, 2006. Address: IGM, Suite 300, 1 Erieview Place, Cleveland, OH 44114, USA. Website: www.atptennis.com/championstour/default.asp

COURTENAY Sir Thomas (Tom) Daniel, b. 25 February 1937. Actor. m. (1) Cheryl Kennedy, 1973, divorced 1982, (2) Isabel Crossley, 1988. Education: Kingston High School, Hull; University College, London; Royal Academy of Dramatic Art. Career: Actor, 1960-; Films include: The Loneliness of the Long Distance Runner, Private Potter, 1962; Billy Liar, 1963; King and Country, Operation Crossbow, King Rat, Doctor Zhivago, 1965; The Night of the Generals, The Day the Fish Came Out, 1967; A Dandy in Aspic, 1968; Otley, 1969; One Day in the Life of Ivan Denisovitch, 1970; Catch Me A Spy, 1971; The Dresser, 1983; The Last Butterfly, 1990; Redemption (TV), Let Him Have It, 1991; Old Curiosity Shop (TV), 1995; The Boy from Mercury, 1996; A Rather English Marriage (TV), 1998; Whatever Happened to Harold Smith, 1999; Last Orders, Nicholas Nickleby, 2002; Ready When You Are Mr McGill (TV), 2003; Flood, The Golden Compass, 2007; Little Dorrit (TV), 2008; Plays include: Billy Liar, 1961-62; The Cherry Orchard, Macbeth, 1966; Hamlet, 1968; She Stoops to Conquer, 1969; Charley's Aunt, 1971; Time and Time Again, 1972; Table Manners, 1974; The Norman Conquests, 1974-75; The Fool, 1975; The Rivals, 1976; Clouds, Crime and Punishment, 1978; The Dresser, 1980, 1983; The Misanthrope, 1981; Andy Capp, 1982; Jumpers, 1984; Rookery Nook, 1986; The Hypochondriac, 1987; Dealing with Clair, 1988; The Miser, 1992; Moscow Stations, Edinburgh, Poison Pen, Manchester 1993; London 1994, New York 1995; Uncle Vanya, New York 1995; Art, London 1996; King Lear, Manchester 1999. Publications: Dear Tom: Letters from Home (memoirs), 2000. Honours: Fellow, University College London; Hon DLitt (Hull); Best Actor Award, Prague Festival, 1968; TV Drama Award, 1968; Variety Club of Great Britain Stage Actor Award, 1972; Golden Globe Award, Best Actor, 1983; Drama Critics' Award and Evening Standard Award, 1980, 1983; BAFTA Award, Best Actor, 1999; KBE, 2001. Address: c/o Jonathan Altaras Associates, 13 Shorts Gardens, London WC2H 9AT, England.

COURTILLOT Vincent Emmanuel, b. 6 March 1948, Neuilly, France. Professor of Geophysics. m. Michèle Consolo, 1 son, 1 daughter. Education: Civil Engineer, Paris School of Mines, 1971; MS, Geophysics, Stanford University, 1972; PhD, Geophysics, University of Paris VI, 1974; DSc, Geophysics, University of Paris VII, 1977. Appointments: Assistant, University of Paris VII, 1973-77; Maitre-Assistant, 1977-78; Maitre de Conférences, 1978-83; Professor, 1983-89; Physicien classe exceptionnelle, 1989-94; Director, Ministry of Education, 1989-93; Professor classe exceptionnelle, University of Paris VII, 1994-; Director, Graduate School of Earth Sciences, 1995-98; President, European Union of Geosciences, 1995-97; Professor, Institut Universitaire de France, 1996-2010; Director, Institut de Physique du Globe de Paris, 1996-98, 2004-10; Special Adviser to the Minister of Education, Research and Technology, 1997-98; Director, Ministry of Research, 1999-2001; President, Scientific Council of the City of Paris, 2002-2009; Chief Editor, Earth and Planetary Science Letters, 2003-05; President, American Geophysical Union, Geomagnetism and Paleomagnetism section, 2006-2008. Publications: Several articles in professional journals, two books. Honours: Prix Gay, French Academy of Sciences, 1981; 1st Franco-British Prize, 1985; Fellow, AGU, 1990; Chevalier, Ordre national du Mérite, 1990, Officier, 1997; Silver Medal, Centre National de la Recherche Scientifique, 1993; Fairchild Distinguished Scholar, 1994; Chevalier, Legion of Honour, 1994; Member, Academia Europea, 1994; Gerald Stanton Ford Lecturer, University of Minnesota, 1996; Associate, Royal Astronomical Society; Commandeur, Ordre National des Palmes Académiques, 1997; Prix Dolomieu, French Academy of Sciences, Moore Distinguished Fellow, CalTech, 2002; Commencement Speaker, University of Lausanne; Member, Paris Academy of Sciences, 2003; Member, Chinese Academy of Sciences, 2008. Address: IPG, 4 Place Jussieu, 75230 Paris Cedex 5, France.

COUSIN-DESJOBERT Jacqueline Marie Antoinette, b. 5 September 1928, La Chartre sur le Loir, Sarthe, France. Doctor; Retired. m. Michel Cousin, 2 sons, 2 daughters. Education: Lycée Charles de Gaulle, London, 1951-52; Fulbright grant, Mount Holyoke College, USA, 1952; Licence es Lettres d'Anglais, 1984; Maitrise, 1985; DEA d'Anglais de la Renaissance, 1987; Erasmus grant, Warwick University, 1987. Appointments: Professor, Technical Instruction, Rennes, 1949-51; Assistant, French, Mount Holyoke College, USA, 1952-53; Principal Assistant, Graham Parker's Office, Paris, 1953-58. Publications: Les chevaux de Shakespeare, 2003; La théorie et la pratique d'un éducateur élisabéthain: Richard Mulcaster (c.1531-1611), 2003; Dictionnaire Shakespeare, Ellipses, Paris, 2005; Articles on Shakespeare and Renaissance culture in Dictionnaire Shakespeare, 2005; A l'exigeante école de l'évasion, in 1916: La Grande-Bretagne en guerre, 2007; Richard Mulcaster, in The Literary Encyclopedia, 2007; Over 20 contributions to professional journals. Honours: Docteur de l'Université de Paris-Sorbonne (Paris IV), 1996. Memberships: Societé Francaise Shakespeare; Episteme; SIRIR; Society for Renaissance Studies; Tudor Symposium. Address: 7 rue Margueritte, 75017 Paris, France.

COWELL Simon, b. 7 October 1959, Brighton, England. A&R Executive; TV Producer; TV Personality. Education: Dover College. Career: EMI Music Publishing; Co-owner, E&S Music, 1980s; Fanfare Records; A&R Consultant, BMG; Owner, Syco Records, 2002; TV programmes include: Pop Idol; American Idol; American Inventor; The X Factor; Grease is the Word; America's Got Talent; Britain's Got Talent; Rock Rivals; Films: Scary Movie 3; Shrek 2. Publications: I Don't Mean to be Rude, but... (autobiography), 2003.

COX Brian, b. 1 June 1946, Dundee, Scotland. Actor. m. (1) Caroline Burt, 1 son, 1 daughter, (2) Nicole Ansari, 2 sons. Career: Actor; Films include: Braveheart; Rob Roy; The Long Kiss Goodnight; The Glimmer Man; Kiss The Girls; Strictly Sinatra; LIE; Bourne Identity; Adaption; The Rookie; The Ring; The 25th Hour; Sin; X-Men 2; Troy; The Bourne Supremacy; A Woman in Winter; Match Point; Red-Eye; The Ringer; Burns; Running With Scissors; The Bourne Ultimatum, Trick 'r Treat, The Secret of the Nutcracker, Zodiac, Battle for Terra, The Water Horse, 2007; Red, The Escapist, Agent Crush, Shoot on Sight, 2008; Tell-Tale, Fantastic Mr Fox, 2009; Theatre includes: As You Like It; Peer Gynt; Othello; Romeo and Juliet; Hedda Gabler; Julius Caesar; Macbeth; Rat in the Skull; Titus Andronicus; The Taming of the Shrew; Frankie and Johnny; Richard III; King Lear; The Master Builder; The Music Man; St Nicholas; Skylight; Art; Dublin Carol; Desire Under the Elms; Uncle Varick; Rock 'n Roll; TV includes: The Cloning of Joanna May; Inspector Morse; Sharpe's Rifles; The Negotiator; Picasso; Witness Against Hitler; Red Dwarf; Food For Ravens; Family Brood; Longitude; Nuremburg; The Cup; The Bench; Frasier; Blue/Orange; Deadwood; The Colour of Magic; Kings; The Take; Producer: I Love My Love; The Philanderer; The Master Builder; Richard III; Oz. Publications: 2 books: The Lear Diaries; From Salem to Moscow. Honours: Winner, BSFC Award for Best Actor, 2001; Nominated AFI Film Award, Featured Actor of the Year (Male), 2002; Winner, Golden Satellite Award, Best Performance by an Actor in a Motion Picture (Drama), 2002; CBE, 2003. Address: c/o Conway Van Gelder, 18-21 Jermyn Street, London SW1Y 6HP, England.

COX Courteney, b. 15 June 1964, Birmingham, Alabama, USA. Actress. m. David Arquette, 1999, 1 daughter. Appointments: Modelling career, New York; Appeared in Bruce Springsteen music video, Dancing in the Dark, 1984; Films: Down Twisted, 1986; Masters of the Universe, 1987; Cocoon: The Return, 1988; Mr Destiny, Blue Desert, 1990; Shaking the Tree, 1992; The Opposite Sex, 1993; Ace Ventura, Pet Detective, 1994; Scream, Commandments, 1996; Scream 2, 1997; The Runner, Scream 3, 1999; The Shrink Is In, 2000; 3000 Miles to Graceland, Get Well Soon, 2001; Alien Love Triangle, 2002; November, 2004; The Longest Yard, 2005; Barnyard (voice), Zoom, The Tripper, 2006; Bedtime Stories, 2008; TV series: Misfits of Science, 1985-86; Family Ties, 1987-88; The Trouble With Larry, 1993; Friends, 1994-2004; Dirt, 2007-08; Scrubs, Cougar Town, 2009; TV films include: Roxanne: The Prize Pulitzer, 1989; Till We Meet Again, 1989; Curiosity Kills, 1990; Morton and Hays, 1991, Tobber, 1992; Sketch Artist II: Hands That See, 1995. Address: c/o Creative Artists Agency, 9830 Wilshire Boulevard, Beverly Hills, CA 90212, USA.

COX Richard, b. 8 March 1931, Winchester, Hampshire, England. Writer. m. 1963, 2 sons, 1 daughter. Education: MA degree in English, St Catherine's College, Oxford, 1955. Publications: Operation Sealion, 1974; Sam 7, 1976; Auction, 1978; The Time it Takes, 1980; KGB Directive, 1981; Ground Zero, 1985; The Columbus Option, 1986; An Agent of Influence, 1988; Park Plaza, 1991; Eclipse, 1996; Murder at Wittenham Park, 1998 (as R W Heber, 1997); How to Meet a Puffin (for children), 2005; Island of Ghosts, 2007. Contributions to: Daily Telegraph (Staff Correspondent, 1966-72); Travel & Leisure; Traveller; Orient Express Magazine. Honours: Territorial Decoration, 1966; General Service Medal, 1967; Australian Bicentennial Award, 2009. Membership: Army and Navy Club; CARE International UK Board, 1985-97, (Council of Patrons, 2006); Member, States of Alderney, 2001-08; Representative States of Guernsey,

2003-06; Member, Guernsey Overseas Aid Commission, 2004-08; Postgraduate, Kings College London, 2008-11. Address: The Mews, Salisbury Road, Coombe Bissett, Wiltshire SP5 4JT, England.

COX Robert Ashley, b. 25 August 1928, Rhymney, Monmouthshire, England. m. Isobel Terry Pepper, 1957, 3 sons, 1 daughter. Education: BSc, 1952, PhD, 1955, DSc, 1971, University of Birmingham. Appointments: Research Scientist, Central Research Laboratories, Tube Investments, Cambridge, 1955-58; Weizmann Research Fellow, Weizmann Institute of Science, Israel, 1958-59; Research Fellow, Chemistry, Harvard University, USA, 1959-60; Research Scientist (Professorial Grade), 1960-93, Sabbatical Year, Department of Molecular Biology, University of Edinburgh, Scotland, 1976-77, Attached worker, Division of Mycobacterial Research, 1993-, National Institute for Medical Research, Mill Hill, London. Publications: Over 100 articles in professional journals; 2 books. Memberships: Society of Harvard Chemists; Biochemical Society; American Society of Microbiology; Fellow, Royal Society of Medicine; Fellow, Royal Society of Chemistry. Address: 8 Gills Hill Lane, Radlett, Hertfordshire WD7 8DF, England.

CRACKNELL James, b. 5 May 1972, Sutton, Surrey, England. Oarsman. m. Beverley Turner, 2002, 1 son, 1 daughter. Education: Kingston Grammar School. Career: International debut in coxed pair, 10th at Junior World Championships, 1989; Winner, gold medal in coxless four Junior World Championships, 1990; Senior international debut in coxless four, 7th in World Championships, 1991; Winner, silver medal in the Eight at World Student Games, 1993; Part of British coxless four tea, 1997-; Gold medals, World Championships, 1997-99; Gold medals, Federation Internationale des Societes d'Aviron World Cup, 1997, 1999, 2000; Gold medals, Olympic Games, Sydney, 2000, Athens, 2004; with Matthew Pinsent won gold medals in the pair at World Championships, 2001 and 2002, also gold medal in coxed pair; qualified geography teacher; took 12 month break from rowing, November 2004-; 2nd Pairs Division of the Atlantic Rowing Race with Ben Fogle, 2005-06; Retired from competitive rowing, 2006; Amundsen Omega3 South Pole Race, with Ben Fogle and Dr Ed Coats, 2008. Publications: Race to the Pole, 2008. Honours: MBE. Address: c/o British International Rowing Office, 6 Lower Mall, London W6 9DJ, England. Website: www.ara-rowing.org

CRAGGS Stewart Roger, b. 27 July 1943, Ilkley, West Yorkshire, England. Academic Librarian. m. Valerie J Gibson, 28 Sept 1968, 1 son, 1 daughter. Education: ALA, Leeds Polytechnic, 1968; FLA, 1974; MA, University of Strathclyde, Glasgow, 1978; PhD, University of Strathclyde, 1982. Appointments: Teesside Polytechnic, 1968-69; JA Jobling, 1970-72; Sunderland Polytechnic, later University, 1973-95; Consultant to the William Walton Edition, Oxford University Press, 1995-. Publications: William Walton: A Thematic Catalogue, 1977; Arthur Bliss: A Bio-Bibliography, 1988; Richard Rodney Bennett: A Bio-Bibliography, 1990; William Walton: A Catalogue, Second Edition, 1990; John McCabe: A Bio-Bibliography, 1991; William Walton: A Source Book, 1993; John Ireland: A Catalogue, Discography and Bibliography, 1993; Alun Hoddinott: A Bio-Bibliography, 1993; Edward Elgar: A Source Book, 1995; William Mathias: A Bio-Bibliography, 1995; Arthur Bliss: A Source Book, 1996; Soundtracks: An International Dictionary of Composers for Films, 1998; Malcolm Arnold: A Bio-Bibliography, 1998; William Walton: Music and Literature, 1999; Lennox Berkeley: A Source Book, 2000; Benjamin Britten: A Bio-Bibliography, 2001; Arthur Bliss: Music and Literature, 2002; Peter Maxwell Davies: A Source Book, 2002; Alan Bush: A Source Book, 2007; Alun Hoddinott: A Source Book, 2007; John Ireland: A Catalogue, Discography and Bibliography: Second Edition, 2007. Honour: Professor of Music Bibliography, University of Sunderland, 1993; Library Association McColvin Medal for Best Reference Book, 1990. Address: 106 Mount Road, High Barnes, Sunderland, SR4 7NN, England.

CRAIG Daniel, b. 2 March 1968, Chester, England. Actor. m. (1) Fiona Loudon, divorced 1994, 1 daughter, (2) Rachel Weisz, 2011. Education: National Youth Theatre; Guildhall School of Music and Drama. Career: Actor: TV includes: Between the Lines, 1993; Drop the Dead Donkey, 1993; Sharpe's Eagle, 1993; Our Friends in the North, 1996; The Fortunes and Misfortunes of Moll Flanders, 1996; The Ice House, 1997; Sword of Honour, 2001; Copenhagen, 2002; Archangel, 2005; Films include: The Power of One, 1992; Elizabeth, 1998; The Trench, 1999; I Dreamed of Africa, 2000; Some Voices, 2000; Hotel Splendide, 2000; Lara Croft: Tomb Raider, 2001; Road to Perdition, 2002; The Mother, 2003; Sylvia, 2003; Layer Cake, 2004; Casino Royale, 2006; The Invasion, 2007; His Dark Materials: The Golden Compass, 2007; Quantum of Solace, Defiance 2008: The Adventures of Tintin; The Girl with the Dragon Tattoo, 2011: Skyfall, 2012. Honours: One of European films Shooting Stars, European Film Promotion, 2000; Nominated London Evening Standard Theatre Award, 2002.

CRAIK Katharine Anne, b. 5 August 1972, Dundee, Scotland. Academic; Writer. m. Stephen James Chapman, 1 son, 1 daughter. Education: BA (Hons), 1993, M Phil, 1995, PhD, 1999, University of Cambridge. Appointments: Research Associate, University of Leeds, 1999-2000; Lecturer, Renaissance Literature, University College London, 2000-04; Lecturer and Junior Research Fellow, Worcester College, Oxford, 2004-06; Senior Lecturer, Early Modern Literature (1500-1700), Oxford Brookes University, 2006-. Publications: Books: An Essay on the Art of Ingeniously Tormenting, 2006; Reading Sensations in Early Modern England, 2007. Memberships: Executive Secretary, Malone Society; Shakespeare Association of America. Address: Department of English, Oxford Brookes University, Headington Campus, Gipsy Lane, Oxford OX3 0BP, England. E-mail: kcraik@brookes.ac.uk

CRANHAM Kenneth Raymond, b. 12 December 1944, Dunfermline, Scotland. Actor. m. Fiona Victory, 2 daughters. Education: Tulse Hill School, London; Royal Academy of Dramatic Art; National Youth Theatre; Films: Two Men Went to War; Born Romantic; Shiner; Gangster No 1; Women Talking Dirty; The Last Yellow; Under Suspicion; Chocolat; The Clot; Oliver; Brother Sun Sister Moon; Joseph Andrews; The Rising; Layer Cake; Trauma; Mandancin; A Good Year; Hot Fuzz; Valkyrie; Running in Traffic; Plays include: RSC: School for Scandal; Ivanov; The Iceman Cometh; National Theatre: Flight; An Inspector Calls; Kick for Touch; Cardiff East; From Kipling to Vietnam; The Caretaker; Strawberry Fields; Love Letters on Blue Paper; The Passion; The Country Wife; Old Movies; Madras House; Royal Court; Saved; Ruffian on the Stair; Samuel Beckett's Play; Cascando; The London Cuckolds; Tibetan in Roads; Magnificance; Cheek; Owners; Geography of a Horse Dreamer; West End: Loot; Comedians; Entertaining Mr Sloane; The Novice; Doctor's Dilemma; Paul Bunyan (Royal Opera House); Broadway: Loot; An Inspector Calls; Radio: The Barchester Chronicles; New Grub Street; Sons and Lovers; Hard Times; Answered Prayers; Earthly Powers; TV includes: Night Flight; Orange are Not the Only Fruit; Rules of Engagement; The Contractor; The Birthday Party; Lady Windemere's Fan; Thérèse Raquin; 'Tis Pity She's A Whore; Merchant of Venice; The Caretaker; The Dumb Waiter; La Ronde; The Sound of Guns; Sling Your Hook; Shine on Harvey Moon; The Genius of Mozart; Rome; The Party; Polyanna; Hustle; New Tricks; Afterlife; Doc Martin; Lilies; The Last Detective; Spanish Flu, 2009. Honours: Bancroft Gold Medal, RADA, 1966. Address: c/o Markham & Froggatt Ltd, 4 Windmill Street, London W1P 1HF, England.

CRAPON de CAPRONA Noël François Marie, (Comte), b. 1928, Savoie, France. Lawyer; UN Senior Official, retired. m. Barbro Sigrid Wenne, 2 sons. Education: Diploma, Institute of Comparative Law, 1951; LLB, University of Paris, 1952; Postgraduate Studies, School of Political Science, 1952-54. Appointments: Assistant Manager, Sta Catalina Estancias, Argentina, 1947-48; Trilingual Editor, Food and Agriculture Organization of the United Nations, 1954-57; Liaison Officer, UN and Other Organisations, Director General's Office, 1957-65; Chief, Reports and Records, 1966-72; Chief, Conference Operations, 1972-74; Secretary General, Conference and Council, 1974-78; Director, FAO Conference, Council and Protocol Affairs, 1974-83. Publication: The Longobards, a tentative explanation, 1995. Honours: Served with French Army, 1944; FAO Silver Medal, 25 Years of Service; Medal of Honour, City of Salon de Provence, 1992; Who's Who Medal, 2000; World Medal of Honour, American Biographical Institute, 2003; Fellow, ABI; American Order of Merit. Memberships: Society in France of the Sons of the American Revolution; Alumni Associations, College St Martin de France and Ecole des Sciences Politiques, Paris. Address: Lojovägen 73-75, S-18147 Lidingö, Sweden; Palais Hadrien, Place dei Tres Mast, 83600 Port-Frejus, France.

CRAVEN Wes, b. 2 August 1939, Cleveland, Ohio, USA. Director; Screenplay writer; Actor. m. (1) Bonnie Broecker, divorced, 2 children, (2) Mimi, divorced, (3) Iya Labunka, 2004. Education: Wheaton College, Johns Hopkins University. Career: Former Professor of Humanities; Assistant to Company President, film production house; Assistant Editor to Sena Cunningham; Screenplay writer; Editor; Writer; Films include: The Last House on the Left, 1972; The Hills Have Eyes, 1976; You've Got to Walk It Like You Talk It or You'll Lose That Beat, Deadly Blessing, 1979; Swamp Thing, 1980; The Hills Have Eyes II, 1983; Invitation to Hell, A Nightmare on Elm Street, 1984; Deadly Friend, A Nightmare on Elm Street III, 1986; The Serpent and the Rainbow, 1988; Shocker, 1989; The People Under the Stairs, 1991; Vampire in Brooklyn, 1995; The Fear, Scream, 1998; Scream 2, Music of the Heart, 1999; Scream 3; Carnival of Souls; Alice; Cursed, Red Eye, 2005; Paris, je t'aime, 2006; My Soul to Take, 2010; TV includes: A Stranger in our House, 1978; Invitation to Hell, 1982; Chiller, 1983; Casebusters, 1985; A Little Peace and Quiet, Wordplay, Chameleon, Her Pilgrim Soul, Shatterday, Dealer's Choice, 1987; The Road Not Taken, 1988; Night Vision, 1990; Nightmare Café, 1991; Laurel Canyon; Body Bags; Twilight Zone; Crimebusters. Memberships: Directors Guild of America. Address: c/o Joe Quenqua, PMK, 1775 Broadway, Suite 701, New York, NY 10019, USA.

CRAWFORD Alistair, b. 25 January 1945, Fraserburgh, Aberdeenshire, Scotland. Artist; Writer. m. Joan Martin. Education: Diploma in Art, Glasgow School of Art, 1966; Art Teachers Certificate, Aberdeen College of Education, 1968. Career: Painter; Printmaker; Photographer; Art Historian; Performer; Lecturer, Department of Textile Industries University of Leeds, 1968-71; Senior Lecturer, Graphic Design, Coventry Polytechnic, 1971-73; Lecturer in Graphic Art, 1974-83, Senior Lecturer, 1983, Reader, 1987, Head of Department, 1986-95; Professor of Art, 1990, Head of the new University of Wales, School of Art, Aberystwyth, 1994; Research Professor of Art, University of Wales, Aberystwyth, 1995-2010; Balsdon Senior Fellow, 1995-96, First Archive Research Fellow, 1997-2001, British School at Rome; Exhibitions: Over 55 solo exhibitions and over 200 selected exhibitions in Britain and Europe and USA; 457 works represented in over 60 public and corporate collections including British Museum, Ashmolean Museum and over 2,800 in private collections world-wide; Recent solo exhibitions include: Landscape Capriccios, University of Wales, Aberystwyth, 2004-05, Martin's Gallery, Cheltenham, Denbighshire Arts Tour; North by Northwest, Jersey Arts Centre, 2006, Oriel Cambria Gallery, Tregaron, 2008; Made from Wales, Brecknock Museum, Brecon, 2007; Some Thoughts and Feelings, National Library of Wales, 2009; Curator of several major exhibitions of photography in Europe and USA; Performances: Brief Exposure, 2001-; A Little Bit More Brief Exposure, 2004-; Brief Exposure, Let's Get Worse, 2005-; Brief Exposure, the Farewell Tour, 2008-. Publications: Over 145 publications; Books and catalogues include: Made of Wales; Father P P Mackey (1851-1935) Photographer, 2000; Mario Giacomelli, 2001, 2002, 2004, 2006; Erich Lessing Vom Festhalten der Zeit. Reportage – Fotografie 1948-73, 2002, 2003, 2005; Contributor to Routledge Encyclopaedia of Nineteenth-Century Photography, volumes I & II, 2008; Column "Brief Exposure", Inscape Magazine, 1999-; Co-editor, Photoresearcher, Vienna, 2004-08. Honours include: Arts Council of Wales; British Council; British Academy; Goethe Institute; Winston Churchill Fellow, 1982; Gold Medal in Fine Art, Royal National Eisteddfod of Wales, 1985; Invited Fellow, Royal Photographic Society, 1991; Invited Academician, Royal Cambrian Academy, 1994; Elected Honorary Fellow, Royal Society of Painter-Printmakers, 2000; Honorary Member, European Society for the History of Photography, 2009. Memberships: The Picturemakers; Gainsborough' House Printmakers. E-mail: information@alistaircrawford.co.uk Website: www.alistaircrawford.co.uk

CRAWFORD Cindy, b. 1966, USA. Model. m. (1) Richard Gere, 1991, divorced, (2) Rande Gerber, 1998, 1 son, 1 daughter. Career: Major contracts with Revlon & Pepsi Cola; Presenter on own MTV fashion show; Appearances on numerous magazine covers, model for various designers; Face of Kelloggs Special K, 2000; Film: Fair Game, 1995; Released several exercise videos; Several TV appearances. Publications: Cindy Crawford's Basic Face, 1996; About Face (for children), 2001. Address: c/o Wolf-Kasteler, 231 South Rodeo Drive, Suite 300, Beverly Hills, CA 90212, USA.

CRAWFORD John William, b. 9 February 1936, Ashdown, Arkansas, USA. College Professor Emeritus. m. Kathryn Bizzell, 1962, 1 son, 1 daughter. Education: AA, Texarkana College, 1956; BA, BSE, Ouachita Baptist University, 1959; MSE, Drake University, 1962; EdD, Oklahoma University, 1968. Appointments: Instructor, English, Clinton College, 1962-66; Instructor, English, Oklahoma University, 1966-67; Associate Professor, English, 1967-73, Director of Freshman English, 1970-76, Chairman, Department of English, 1976-86, Professor, English, 1973-2006, Professor Emeritus, Henderson State University. Publications: Making The Connection, 1989; Just Off Highway 71, 1992; I Have Become Familiar With The Rain, 1995; The Learning, Wit and Wisdom of Shakespeare's Renaissance Women, 1997. Contributions to: Rendezvous; Theology Today; ELF; Inlet; Lucidity; Voices

International; Rivers Edge; Black Buzzard Review; Another Small Magazine; Potpourri; Independent Review; Soundings; Zephyr. Honours: 1st in Childrens Poetry, Deep South Writers Conference, 1975; Sybil Nash Abrams Awards, Arkansas Poets Roundtable Poetry Day, 1982, 1995; Byron Reece Narrative Award, Georgia Poetry Society, 1985; Merit Award for Service, Arkansas Poets Roundtable Poetry Day, 1988. Memberships: Arkansas Poets Roundtable; Arkansas Writers Conference; Arkansas Philological Association; Mississippi Philological Association; Philological Association of Louisiana; South Central Modern Language Association. Address: 1813 Walnut Street, Arkadelphia, AR 71923, USA.

CRAWFORD Michael, b. 19 January 1942. Actor; Singer. Appointments: Actor, 1955-; Films for Children's Film Foundation; 100's radio broadcasts; Appeared in original productions of Noyess Fludde and Let's Make an Opera, by Benjamin Britten; Tours, UK, USA, Australia. Stage roles include: Travelling Light, 1965; The Anniversary, 1966; No Sex Please, We're British, 1971; Billy, 1974; Same Time, Next Year, 1976; Flowers for Algernon, 1979; Barnum, 1981-83, 1984-86; Phantom of the Opera, London, 1986-87; Broadway, 1988, Los Angeles, 1989; The Music of Andrew Lloyd Webber (concert tour), USA, Australia, UK, 1992-92; EFX, Las Vegas, 1995-96; Dance of the Vampires, Broadway, 2003; The Woman in White, 2004-05; Performed at Harrah's Casino, Stateline, Nevada, 2007; Films include: Soap Box Derby, 1950; Blow Your Own Trumpet, 1954; Two Living One Dead, 1962; The War Lover, 1963; Two Left Feet, 1963; The Knack, 1965; A Funny Thing Happened on the Way to the Forum, 1966; The Jokers, 1966; How I Won the War, 1967; Hello Dolly, 1969; The Games, 1969; Hello Goodbye, 1970; Alice's Adventures in Wonderland, 1972; Condor Man, 1980; TV appearances include: Sir Francis Drake (series), 1962; Some Mothers Do 'Ave 'Em (several series); Chalk and Cheese (series), 1979; Sorry (play), 1979. Publication: Parcel Arrived Safely: Tied with String (autobiography), 2000. Honours: OBE; Tony Award, 1988. Address: c/o ICM Ltd, Oxford House, 76 Oxford Street, London W1D 1BS, England.

CREQUIE Guy, b. 2 November 1943, Villefranche, Saone, France. Former Human Resources Consultant; Writer and Singer. m. Madeleine Rougies, 1 son. Education: University Diploma. Appointments: Human Resources Consultant; Writer and singer for peace and human rights. Publications: 22 books, 1981-. Honours: Messager de la culture de la apix et de la non violence par l'UNESCO; Member, L'Association Mondiale des Artistes et Auteurs; French Representative, ONG International of Peace and Harmony; Medal, Vermei de la Société Académique Française; Arts-Sciences-Letters Award, l'Academie Europeenne des Arts; Docteur honoris causa de l'Academie Mondiale de la Cultur et des Arts; Many other significant awards. Memberships: Academic writers' companies; ONG. Address: Hameu des Ecrins, 53 rue Auguste Renoir, 69200 Venissieux, France. E-mail: guy.crequie@wanadoo.fr Website: http://guycrequie.blogspot.com

CRESSON Edith, b. 27 January 1934, Boulogne-sur-Seine, France. Politician. m. J Cresson, 1959, deceased 2001, 2 daughters. Education: Hautes Etudes Commerciales, Doctorat de Démographie. Appointments: Economist, Conventions des Institutions Republicans, 1965; Socialist Party National Secretary, 1974; Mayor of Thure, 1977; Member, Eurpean Assembly, 1979; Ministry of Agriculture,1981-83; Mayor of Chatellerault, 1983-97; Adjoint au maire, 1997-; Minister, for Foreign Trade and Tourism, 1983-84, Minister, for Industrial Redeployment and Foreign Trade, 1984-86, Minister for European Affairs, 1988-90; PM, 1990-92; President of Schneider International Services Industries et Environnement, 1990-91, 1992-95; Commissaire européen chargé de la recherche et de l'éducation, 1995-99; Presidente de la Fondation pour les Ecoles de la Deuxième Chance. Publications: Avec le Soleil, 1976; Innover ou subir, 1998; Docteur Honoris Causa de l'Open University, UK and l'Institut Weisman, Israel, 1999; Présidente de la Fondation pour les Écoles de la Deuxième Chance, 2002-; President, Institut d'Etudes Européennes University de Seine St Denis; Chevalier de la Légion d'honneur; Dr hc, Weizmann Institute, and Open University, England. Address: 10 Av. George V, Paris, France.

CRIPPS Joy Beaudette, b. 13 June 1923, Melbourne, Australia. Poet; Writer. m. Charles John Cripps, deceased, 2 sons. Education: Lit, D hon, Marquis Giuseppe Scicluna International University, Valleta, Malta, 1986; Litt, D hon, World Academy of Arts & Culture, Taipei, Taiwan, 1986; Professor, AUPAC Attache Recherche, Member, ACTIF, Paris-Bruxelles, 1993. Appointments: President, Board of Governors, Ansted University, 2000-03; Founder, Diplomatic Counsellor, London Diplomatic Academy, 2000; Professional Women's Advisory Board, American Biographical Institute, 2000; World Peace & Diplomacy Forum, June 2003; Founding Cabinet Member, WPDF. Honours: Poet of the Millennium, International Poets Academy, 2000; Lifetime Deputy Governor, ABI, 1990; International Order of Merit, IBC, 1990; First Five Hundred, 1985, 2003-04; Token of Appreciation for Contribution to Ansted University; Recommended and Nominated to World Peace Academy of Geneva; 5 certificate issued by President Professor Dr Francis Dessart, 2000; Certificate of Academician, World Peace Academy; Certificate of Honour, Institute of International Affairs; Doctor of Philosophy in Political Sciences, International Academy of Culture and Political Science; Diploma D'honneur, International Association of Education for World Peace; Diploma in International Relations, Institute for International Relations and Intercultural Studies, Alabama A&M University, USA. Memberships: Oceania Regent and Parnassian Jurist POET Intercontinental, 1986-2004; Founder, President, Melbourne Poetry Society, 1982; Founder, Poetry Day; Founder, Dove in Peace Award Medallions for Excellence in Peace Poetry, 1993. Address: 3 Mill Street, Aspendale 3195, Australia.

CRISTEA Valentin Gabriel, b. 7 June 1968, Targoviste, Romania. Mathematician. Education: Bachelor Degree, Mathematics, University of Bucharest, Romania, 1987-91; Grant Holder, International Congress of Mathematicians, ICM '98, Technische Universität Berlin, Germany, 1998; Arbeitstagung, Max-Planck-Institut fuer Mathematik, Bonn Germany, 1999. Appointments: Assistant Professor of Mathematics "Valahia" University, Targoviste, Romania, 1995-; Assistant Professor of Mathematics, Politechnic University of Bucharest, 1995-96; Mathematician, Instituto de Fisica Aplicada, CSIC, Madrid, Spain, 1994-95 (6 months); Mathematician, CIMAT, Guanajuato, Mexico, 1998 (1 month); Mathematician Max-Planck-Institut fuer Mathematik, Bonn, Germany, 1999 (7 months). Publications: Considerations sur les paires de superconnexions sur des supervarietes, 1991; Remarks about the Supermanifolds, 1992; Totally geodesic graded Riemannian submanifolds of the (4,4)-dimensional graded Riemannian manifold, 1995; Existence and uniqueness theorem for Frenet frames supercurves, 1999; The reduced bundle of the principal superfibre bundle, 2001; Euler's superequations, 2001; Curvilinear Integral I(C) for problems of variations calculus on supermanifolds, 2002. Honours: Distinguished Leadership

Award, American Biographical Institute; Nominated as inaugural member of the Leading Scientists of the World, 2005; Listed in biographical dictionaries. Membership: Romanian Society of Mathematical Sciences. Address: Str G-ral Matei Vladescu, BL 30 Sc A, Ap 6 Targoviste, 0200 Jud Dambovita, Romania. E-mail: valentin_cristea@yahoo.com

CRONENBERG David, b. 15 March 1943, Toronto, Canada. Film Director. Education: University of Toronto. Appointments: Directed fillers and short dramas for TV; Films include: Stereo, 1969; Crimes of the Future, 1970; The Parasite Murders/Shivers, 1974; Rabid, 1976; Fast Company, 1979; The Brood, 1979; Scanners, 1980; Videodrome, 1982; The Dead Zone, 1983; The Fly, 1986; Dead Ringers, 1988; The Naked Lunch, 1991; Crash, 1996; eXistenZ, 1998; Camera, 2000; Spider, 2002; A History of Violence, 2005; To Each His Camera, 2007; Eastern Promises, 2007, Sisters, 2007, William Burroughs: A Man Within, 2010; Director: Transfer, 1966; From the Drain, 1967; Acted in: Nightbreed, 1990; The Naked Lunch (wrote screenplay); Trial by Jury; Henry and Verlin; To Die For, 1995; Extreme Measures, 1996; The Stupids, 1996; Director, writer, producer, actor, Crash, 1996. Publications: Crash 1996; Cronenberg on Cronenberg, 1996. Honours: Cannes Jury Special Prize, 1997; Silver Berlin Bear, 1999; 43 Awards, 25 nominations. Address: David Cronenberg Productions Ltd, 217 Avenue Road, Toronto, Ontario, M5R 2J3, Canada.

CRONIN James Watson, b. 29 September 1931, Chicago, Illinois, USA. Physicist. m. Annette Martin, 1954, 1 son, 2 daughters. Education: BS, Southern Methodist University, 1951; MS, 1953, PhD, Physics, 1955, University of Chicago. Appointments: National Science Foundation Fellow, 1952-55; Assistant Physicist, Brookhaven National Laboratory, 1955-58; Assistant Professor of Physics, 1958-62, Associate Professor, 1962-64, Professor, 1964-71, Princeton University; Professor of Physics, University of Chicago, 1971-; Loeb Lecturer in Physics, Harvard University, 1976. Honours: Research Corporation Award, 1968; Ernest O Lawrence Award, 1977; John Price Wetherill Medal, Franklin Institute, 1975; Joint Winner, Nobel Prize for Physics, 1980; Honorary DSc, Leeds, 1996; National Medal of Science, 1999. Memberships: NAS; American Academy of Arts and Sciences; American Physical Society. Address: Enrico Fermi Institute, University of Chicago, 5630 South Ellis Avenue, Chicago, IL 60637, USA.

CROSLAND Margaret (McQueen), b. 17 June 1920, Bridgnorth, Shropshire, England. Writer; Translator. m. Max Denis, 1950, divorced 1959, 1 son. Education: BA, University of London, 1941. Appointments: Civil Service, London; Marks & Spencer Head Office, London. Publications: Strange Tempe (poems), 1946; Madame Colette: A Provincial in Paris, 1953; Jean Cocteau, 1955; Ballet Carnival: A Companion to Ballet, 1955, new edition, 1957; Home Book of Opera, 1957; Ballet Lover's Dictionary, 1962; Louise of Stolberg, Countess of Albany, 1962; The Young Ballet Lover's Companion, 1962; Philosophy Pocket Crammer, 1964; Colette-The Difficulty of Loving: A Biography, 1973; Raymond Radiguet: A Biographical Study with Selections from His Work, 1976; Women of Iron and Velvet: French Women Writers after George Sand, 1976; Beyond the Lighthouse: English Women Novelists in the Twentieth Century, 1981; Piaf, 1985; The Passionate Philosopher: The Marquis de Sade Reader, 1991; Simone de Beauvoir, The Woman and Her Work, 1992; Sade's Wife, 1995; The Enigma of Giorgio de Chirico, 1999; Madame de Pompadour, 2000; The Mysterious Mistress: The Life and Legend of Jane Shore, 2006. Editor: Marquis de Sade: Selected Letters, 1965; A Traveller's Guide to Literary Europe, 1965; Jean Cocteau: My Contemporaries, 1967; Cocteau's World: An Anthology of Major Writings by Jean Cocteau, 1972. Translator: Over 30 books. Honours: Prix de Bourgogne, France, 1973-74; Enid McLeod Prize, Franco-British Society, 1992-93. Membership: Society of Authors. E-mail: crosland.denis@virgin.net

CROSSLEY Gordon Thomas, b. 6 December 1929, Surrey, England. Designer; Senior Lecturer; Painter. m. Jo Glosby (deceased), 1 son, 3 daughters. Education: Art & Design, Wimbledon School of Art; College Diploma in Design. Appointments: Advertising, 17 years; Teacher, College of Art and Design, London, 26 years; Retired; Full time artist; Group and solo exhibitions in various London and provincial galleries including Madden, Phoenix, RA Summershow, 17 paintings; One-man show, Aubrey Art Gallery; New English, The National, RBA and Thompson's Gallery, Aldeburgh; Private collections in UK and abroad. Honours: Listed in international biographical dictionaries. Address: The Sanctuary, Sheering, Nr Bishops Stortford, CM22 7LN, England.

CROUCH Colin, b. 1 March 1944, Isleworth, Middlesex, England. University Professor. m. Joan Ann Freedman, 2 sons. Education: BA, first class, Sociology, London School of Economics, 1969; DPhil, Nuffield College, Oxford, 1975. Appointments: Temporary Lecturer in Sociology, London School of Economics, 1969-70; Research Student, Nuffield College, Oxford, 1970-72; Lecturer in Sociology, University of Bath, 1972-73; Lecturer, 1973-79, Senior Lecturer, 1979-80, Reader, 1980-85, Sociology, London School of Economics and Political Science; Professor of Sociology, Fellow of Trinity College, University of Oxford, 1985-95; Chairman, Department of Social and Political Sciences, Professor of Comparative Social Institutions, European University Institute, Florence, Italy; External Scientific Member, Max-Planck-Institut für Gesellschaftsforschung, Cologne, Germany; Chairman, The Political Quarterly Ltd. Publications: 8 books; Editor, 18 books; 108 other articles and chapters. Honours: Hobhouse Memorial Prize, 1969. Memberships: President of Society for the Advancement of Socio-Economics; Max-Planck-Gesellschaft. E-mail: colin.crouch@wbs.ac.uk

CROUCH Peter, b. 30 January 1981, Macclesfield, England. Footballer. 1 daughter with Abigail Clancy. Education: Drayton Manor High School, Hanwell. Career: Trainee, Tottenham Hotspur, 1998-2000; Played for several teams including Portsmouth, Aston Villa, Southampton and Liverpool, 2000-09; Member of England squad, World Cup, 2006, 2010; Senior Tottenham debut, 2009; Debut for Stoke City, 2011. Website: www.stokecityfc.com

CROW Jonathan Rupert, b. 25 June 1958, London, England. Barrister. m. Claudia Jane Turner, 3 sons, 1 daughter. Education: St Paul's School; Oxford University. Appointments: Called to the Bar (LI), 1981; Treasury Counsel, 1994-98; First Treasury Counsel, 1998-2006; Deputy High Court Judge, 2001-; Queen's Counsel, 2006; Attorney General to HRH the Prince of Wales, 2006-. Publications: Contributing Author, Annotated Companies Act. Memberships: Commercial Bar Association; Chancery Bar Association; Administrative Law Bar Association. Address: 4 Stone Buildings, Lincoln's Inn, London WC2A 3XT, England. E-mail: clerks@4stonebuildings.com

CROW Sheryl, b. 11 February 1962, Kennett, Missouri, USA. Singer; Songwriter; Musician (guitar). 1 adopted son. Musical Education: Classical Music degree, Missouri State University; Organ and piano lessons; Self-taught guitar. Career: Backing singer, Michael Jackson tour, 18 months; Also backing singer for Joe Cocker; Rod Stewart; Don Henley; Songwriter, solo performer, mid 1980s-; International concerts and tours with John Hiatt; Crowded House; Big Head Todd; Support tours to Bob Dylan; Eagles, 1994; Joe Cocker, Wembley Arena, 1994; Performed at Woodstock II, 1994. Recordings: Solo album: Tuesday Night Music Club, 1993; Sheryl Crow, 1996; The Globe Sessions, 1998; Sheryl Crow and Friends: Live in Central Park, 1999; C'mon C'mon, 2002; Sheryl Crow: Life At Budokan, 2003; The Very Best of Sheryl Crow, The Videos, 2004, Wildflower, 2005, Detours, 2008; Singles include: All I Wanna Do, 1994; Leaving Las Vegas, 1994; Strong Enough, 1994; Can't Cry Anymore, 1995; If It Makes You Happy, 1996; Everyday Is A Winding Road, 1996; My Favorite Mistake, 1998; There Goes The Neighbourhood, 1998; Anything But Down, 1999; Sweet Child O' Mine, 1999; Soak Up The Sun, 2002; Steve McQueen, 2002; First Cut is the Deepest, 2003; It's So Easy, 2004; Light In Your Eyes, 2004; Contributor, albums: The End Of Innocence, Don Henley, 1989; Late Night, Neal Schon, 1989; Other recordings by Eric Clapton; Wynnona Judd; Contributor, film soundtracks: Kalifornia, 1994; Leaving Las Vegas, 1995; Cars, 2006. Honours: 3 Grammy Awards, Tuesday Night Music Club, 1995; BRIT Award, Best International Female Artist, 1997; American Music Awards, Best Female Pop/Rock Artist, 2003, 2004. Address: Helter Skelter, The Plaza, 535 Kings Road, London SW10 0SZ, England. Website: www.sherylcrow.com

CROWE Russell, b. 7 April 1964, New Zealand. Actor. m. Danielle Spencer, 2003, 1 son. Career: Films include: The Crossing, 1993; The Quick and the Dead, Romper Stomper, Rough Magic, Virtuosity, Under the Gun, 1995; Heaven's Burning, Breaking Up, LA Confidential, 1997; Mystery Alaska, The Insider, 1999; Gladiator, Proof of Life, 2000; A Beautiful Mind, 2001; Master and Commander: The Far Side of the World, 2003; Cinderella Man, 2005; A Good Year, 2006; 3:10 to Yuma, Tenderness, American Gangster, 2007, State of Play, 2009, Body of Lies, 2009. Honours: Variety Club Award (Australia), 1993; Film Critics Circle Award, 1993; Best Actor, Seattle International Film Festival, 1993; Management Film and TV Awards, Motion Pictures Exhibitors Association, 1993; LA Film Critics Association, 1999; National Board of Review, 1999; National Society of Film Critics, 1999; Academy Award for Best Actor, 2000; Oscar, 2000; Golden Globe, 2001; BAFTA Award, 2001; Screen Actors' Guild Award for Best Actor, 2001. Address: ICM, 8942 Wilshire Blvd, Beverly Hills, CA, 90211, USA.

CRUISE Tom (Thomas Cruise Mapother IV), b. 3 July 1962, Syracuse, New York, USA. Actor. m. (1) Mimi Rogers, 1987, divorced 1990, (2) Nicole Kidman, 1990, divorced 2001, 1 adopted son, 1 adopted daughter, (3) Katie Holmes, 2006, divorced 2012, 1 daughter. Career: Actor, films include: Endless Love, Taps, 1981; All The Right Moves, Losin' It, The Outsiders, Risky Business, 1983; Legend, 1984; Top Gun, 1985; The Color of Money, 1986; Rain Man, 1988; Cocktail, Born on the Fourth of July, 1989; Daytona, Rush, Days of Thunder, 1990; Sure as the Moon, 1991; Far and Away, A Few Good Men, 1992; The Firm, 1993; Interview with the Vampire, 1994; Jerry Maguire, Mission Impossible, 1996; Eyes Wide Shut, 1997; Mission Impossible 2, Magnolia, 1999; Vanilla Sky, 2001; Minority Report, Space Station 3D, voice, 2002; The Last Samurai, 2003; Collateral, 2004; War of the Worlds, 2005; Mission Impossible 3, Lions for Lambs, 2007, Valkyrie, 2008; Producer: Without Limits, Vanilla Sky, Narc, Hitting It Hard, Shattered Glass, The Last Samurai, Suspect Zero, Elizabeth Town, Ask the Dust, Elizabethtown, Ask the Dust, Mission Impossible 3. Honours: Golden Globe, 2000; David di Donatello lifetime achievement award, 2005. Address: Creative Artists Agency, 9830 Wilshire Boulevard, Beverly Hills, CA 90212-1825, USA. Website: www.caa.com

CRULL Jan Jr, b. The Netherlands. Lawyer. Education: Lake Forest Academy; Northwestern University; BA (Hons), Dalhousie University; MA, Purdue University; MA, University of Chicago; JD, Tulane University. Appointments: Intern, GGvA, New York City, 1973-74; Teaching Assistant, Graduate Instructor, Purdue University, 1975-76; Assistant to OOTC, New York City, 1978; Assistant to Chapter President, Ramah Navajo Reservation, Pinehill New Mexico, 1979-80; Professional Staff Member, US House of Representatives, Washington DC, 1981; Assistant Money Manager, 1982, 1985-86, 1989, Counsel, Advisor, 1990-91, Gulf and Occidental Investment Co SA, Geneva; Counsel, Co-Principal, SandCru Inc, Chicago, 1992-; President, General Counsel, Vigil Film Production Co, Los Angeles and Sacramento, California, 1993-97; Director, Counsel, Von Quesar Holdings OHG, Vienna, 1994-98; Director, Counsel, Beeltsnijder KG, Berlin, 1994-97; Advisor, Infrastructure Bond Development, Carioccа Capital Partners, Rio de Janeiro, 1999; Advisor, LFFE Ltd, Heibei, China, 2004-08; Outside Director and Advisor, Shang Bat T&H, Shanghai, Luxembourg, and United Arab Emirates, 2004-. Publications: Provisions for First Reauthorization of Tribally Controlled Community College Assistance Act, 97th US Congress (author); Special Provisions for Native Americans in Library Services Construction Act, 97th-98th US Congress (author). Films: Developer: What About My Friend's Children, 1973; Not in Fiction Only: There and Here Also, 1974; A Free People, Free to Choose, 1992-93; AIDDS: American Indian's Devastating Dilemma Soon, 1993; To Mute Them Once Again, 1994; Indian Buckaroos, 1996. Honour: Nominee, Rockefeller Public Service Award, 1981. Memberships: American Bar Association; Chicago Council on Foreign Relations; Chicago Bar Association; Illinois State Bar Association; Calumet Country Club; Quadrangle Club, Chicago; 1781 Club, Netherlands Antilles; Phi Kappa Psi, Northwestern University. Address: c/o Shang Bat T&H, PO Box 0492, Chicago, IL 60690-0492, USA.

CRUYFF Johan, b. 25 April 1947, Amsterdam, Netherlands. Footballer. m. Danny Coster, 1968, 3 children. Appointments: Played for Ajax, 1964-73; Top scorer in Dutch league, with 33 goals, 1967; Moved to Barcelona, now Coach of Barcelona; Captained Netherlands, 1974 World Cup Final, 1974; Retired, 1978; Started playing again and signed for Los Angeles Aztecs; Played for Washington Diplomats, 1979-80; Levante, Spain, 1981; Ajax and Feyenoord, 1982; Manager, Ajax, 1987-87, winning European Cup-Winners Cup, 1987; Manager, Barcelona, winning Cup-Winners Cup, 1989, European Cup, 1992, Spanish League, 1991, 1992, 1993, Spanish Super Cup, 1992; Formed Cruyff Foundation for disabled sportspeople and Johan Cruyff University to assist retired sportspeople, 1998, Head Coach of Catalonia football team, 2009. Honour: European Footballer of the Year, 1971, 1973-74.

CRUZ Penelope, b. 28 April 1974, Madrid, Spain. Actor. m. Javier Bardem, 2010, 1 son. Education: National Conservatory, Spain. Career: Actor: Several roles on Spanish TV and music videos; Films include: Live Flesh, Belle Epoque, Jamón Jamón, 1992; La Celestina, 1996; Open Your Eyes, 1997; The Hi-Lo Country, Talk of Angels, The Girl of Your Dreams,

1998; All About My Mother, 1999; Woman on Top, All the Pretty Horses, 2000; Captain Corelli's Mandolin, Blow, Vanilla Sky, 2001; Fanfan La Tulipe, Gothika, 2003; Noel, Head in the Clouds, Don't Move, 2004; Sahara, Chromophobia, 2005; Bandidas, Volver, 2006; The Good Night, Manolete, Elegy, 2007; Vicky Christina Barcelona, 2008. Honours: Goya for Best Actress, 1998; 17 awards, 27 nominations. Address: c/o Kuranda Management International, 8626 Skyline Drive, Los Angeles, CA 90046, USA.

CRYSTAL Billy, b. 14 March 1948, Long Beach, NY, USA. Actor; Comedian. m. Janice Goldfinger, 2 daughters. Education: Marshall University. Appointments: Member of group, 3's Company; Solo appearances as stand-up comedian; TV appearances include: Soap, 1977-81; The Billy Crystal Hour, 1982; Saturday Night Live, 1984-85; The Love Boat; The Tonight Show; TV films include: Breaking Up is Hard to Do, 1979; Enola Gay; The Men; The Mission; The Atomic Bomb, 1980; Death Flight; Feature films include: The Rabbit Test, 1978; This is Spinal Tap, 1984; Running Scared, 1986; The Princess Bridge, Throw Momma From the Train, 1987; When Harry Met Sally..., 1989; City Slickers, 1991; Mr Saturday Night (Director, Producer, co-screenplay writer), 1993; City Slickers II: The Legend of Curly's Gold, 1994; Forget Paris, 1995; Hamlet; Father's Day; Deconstructing Harry; My Grant, Analyse This, 1998; The Adventures of Rocky and Bullwinkle, 2000; Monsters Inc (voice), 2001; America's Sweethearts, 2001; Mike's New Car (voice), 2002, 2006; Analyze That, 2002; Howl's Moving Castle (voice), 2004. Publication: Absolutely Mahvelous, 1986; My Giant, 1998; America's Sweethearts, 2001; I already Know I Love You, 2004; 700 Sundays, 2005; Grandpa's Little One, 2006..

CSABA György, b. 31 May 1929, Törökszentmiklos. Physician. m. (1) 1954, (2) Katalin Kallay, 1970, 2 sons, 2 daughters. Education: MD, 1953; PhD, 1957; DSc, 1969. Appointments: Assistant Professor, 1953-59, 1st Assistant, 1959-63, Associate Professor, 1963-70, Professor, 1970-, Director, Department of Biology, Semmelweis University of Medicine, 1971-94; Professor, 1970-99; Professor Emeritus, 2000-. Publications: 25 books, 24 chapters and over 800 scientific publications in peer-reviewed journals. Honours: Huzella Prize, 1983; Pal Bugat Award, Scientific Educational Society, 1989; Hung Higher Education Medal, Ministry of Education, 1994; Golden Signet, Semmelweis University of Medicine, 1994; 5 Prizes for High Level Books; Khwarizmi International Award; Comsats Award; Pro Universitate, 2009. Memberships: President, General and Theoretical Section, Hung Biological Society, 1978-87; Chairman, Book Committee, Scientific Press Council, Budapest, 1980-88; Chairman, Editorial Committee, Semmelweis Publisher, 1989-2001. Address: PO Box 370, H-1445 Budapest, Hungary.

CSIKAI Gyula, b. 31 October 1930, Tiszaladány, Hungary. Professor in Physics. m. Margit Buczkó, 2 sons. Education: University Diploma in Mathematics and Physics, 1953, Candidate, 1957, DSc, 1966, Corresponding, 1973, and Ordinary Member, 1985, Hungarian Academy of Sciences. Appointments: Head, Neutron Physics Department, ATOMKI, Debrecen, Hungary, 1956-67; Head Institute of Experimental Physics, Debrecen, 1967-95; Deputy Minister of Culture and Education of Hungary, 1987; Professor, 1967, Dean, 1972-75, Rector, 1981-86, Kossuth University, Debrecen, Hungary; Professor Emeritus, 2001-. Publications: More than 290 papers in scientific journals; Handbook of Fast Neutron Generators I-II, 1987; Handbook on Nuclear Data, 1987, 2003; Nuclear Chemistry, chapter 9, Applications of Neutron Generators, 2003, 2010; 2 patents. Honours: Brody Prize, 1957; First Prize of Hungarian Academy of Sciences, 1967; Eötvös Medal, 1980, Golden Medal of Hungary, 1980; State Award, 1983; Named Honorary Freeman of Tiszaladány, 2000-; Honorary Doctor, Kiev National University, 2001; Leo Szilard Prize, 2004; Wigner Prize, 2005; Diamond Chair Prize, Debrecen University, 2007; Medal and Certificate of Merit, ENPA, Egypt, 2008; Medal of Honor, Debrecen University, 2010; Listed in international biographical dictionaries.. Memberships: The New York Academy of Sciences; Hungarian Academy of Sciences; Academia Europea; IUPAP Commission, Nuclear Physics; Physics Society of Hungary; Editor of international journals. Address: Institute of Experimental Physics, University of Debrecen, H-4010 Debrecen-10, P O Box 105, Hungary.

CUERDA RIEZU Antonio, b. 24 October 1956, Madrid, Spain. Professor in Criminal Law. m. Paz Iglesias, 1 son, 1 daughter. Education: Doctor of Law, 1983; PhD (Distinction), 1983. Appointments: Lecturer, 1982-84, Adjunct Professor, 1984-89, Universidad de Alcala; Professor, Universidad de Leon, 1989-96; Assistant, Tribunal Constitutional, 1996-2001; Professor, Universidad Rey Juan Carlos, Madrid, 2001-. Publications: Numerous articles in professional journals. Honours: Prize of the Instituto de Criminologia de Barcelona, 1991. Memberships: Association Internationale de Droit Penale, Group de Estudios de Politica Criminal; Association de Letrados del Tribunal Constitutional. Address: Facultad de Ciencias Juridicas y Sociales, Universidad Rey Juan Carlos, Paseo de los Artilleros s/n, 28032 Madrid, Spain. E-mail: Antonio.cuerda@urjc.es

ÇUHADAR Cem, b. 1974, Istanbul, Turkey. m. Selmin, 1 son. Education: BA, Firat University, 1997; MS, Trakya University, 2000; PhD, Anadolu University, 2008. Appointments: Research Assistant, 1997-2002, Assistant Professor, 2008-, Computer Education and Instructional Technologies Department, Faculty of Education, Trakya University, Edirne; Research Assistant, Computer Education and Instructional Technologies Department, Faculty of Education, Anadolu University, Eskisehir, 2002-08. Publications: Numerous articles in professional journals, books, book chapters and scientific projects. Honours: Listed in biographical dictionaries. Address: Computer Education and Instructional Technologies Department, Faculty of Education, Trakya University, Aysekadin Campus, Edirne, Turkey.

CULKIN Macauley, b. 26 August 1980, New York, USA. Actor. m. Rachel Miner, 1998, divorced 2000. Education: George Balanchine's School of Ballet, NY. Appointments: Actor, films: Rocket Gibralter, 1988; Uncle Buck, 1989; See You in the Morning, 1989; Jacob's Ladder, 1990; Home Alone, 1990; My Girl, 1991; Only the Lonely, 1991; Home Alone 2: Lost in New York, 1992; The Nutcracker; The Good Son, 1993; The Pagemaster, 1995; Getting Even with Dad, 1995; Body Piercer, 1998; Party Monster, 2003; Saved! 2004; Richie Rich, 2004; Jerusalemski Sindrom, 2004; TV: Will & Grace, 2003; Frasier, 2004; Robot Chicken, 2005-06; Play: Madame Melville, Vaudeville Theatre, London, 2001. Address: c/o Brian Gersh, William Morris Agency, 151 S El Camino Drive, Beverley Hills, CA 90212, USA.

CULL-CANDY Stuart G, b. 2 November 1946. Professor of Neuroscience; Gaddum Professor of Pharmacology. m. Barbara Paterson Fulton, 1 daughter. Education: BSc (Hons), Biology, University of London, 1969; MSc, Physiology, University College London, 1970; PhD, Synaptic Physiology, University of Glasgow, 1974; Postdoctoral Fellow, Institute of Pharmacology, University of Lund, Sweden, 1974-75.

Appointments: Beit Memorial Research Fellow and Associate Research Staff, Department of Biophysics, 1975-82, Wellcome Trust Reader in Pharmacology, 1982-90, Professor of Neuroscience, Personal Chair, 1990-, Gaddum Chair of Pharmacology, Professor of Neuroscience, 2006-, University College London; Medical Research Council Neuroscience Committee, 1987-91; Wellcome Trust International Interest Group Grants Committee, 1991-97; International Research Scholar, Howard Hughes Medical Institute, 1993-98; Royal Society – Wolfson Position, 2003-; Royal Society University Research Fellow Grants Committee, 2003-; Leverhulme Trust Research Fellowship Committee, 2006; Royal Society Research Grants Board, 2007-. Publications: Numerous articles on synaptic transmission and glutamate receptors in the brain and peripheral nervous system in the scientific journals: Nature, Neuron, Nature Neurosciences, Journal of Neuroscience, Journal of Physiology; Various book chapters; Editor of scientific journals: Reviewing Editor, Journal of Neuroscience, 2000-; Editor, Neuron, 1994-98; External Editorial Adviser in Neuroscience, Nature, 1993-97; Editor, Journal of Physiology, 1987-95; European Journal of Neuroscience, 1988-; Guest Editor, Current Opinions in Neurobiology, 2007. Honours: Appointed International Scholar, Howard Hughes Medical Institute, USA, 1993-98; GL Brown Prize, Physiological Society, 1996; Elected Fellow of the Royal Society, 2002; Wolfson Award, Royal Society, 2003; Elected Fellow of the Academy of Medical Sciences, 2004; Elected Fellow, British Pharmacological Society, 2005; Listed in Who's Who and other biographical publications. Memberships: Royal Society; Academy of Medical Sciences; Society for Neuroscience, USA; Physiological Society, UK; British Neuroscience Association; International Brain Research Organisation; Pharmacological Society, UK. Address: Department of Pharmacology, University College London, Gower Street, London WC1E 6BT, England. E-mail: s.cull-candy@ucl.ac.uk

CURIO Eberhard Otto Eugen, b. 22 October 1932, Berlin, Germany. Professor of Biology. m. Dorothea Curio, 1 son, 1 daughter. Education: Doctor rer. nat., Free University of Berlin, 1957; Professor of Biology, Ruhr University Bochum, 1970. Appointments: Research Associate, Max-Planck-Institute for Behavioural Physiology, 1957-64; Assistant Professor, 1964-68, Lecturer, 1968-70, Professor, 1970-, Ruhr University Bochum, Germany. Publications: The Ethology of Predation, 1976; Behavior as a Tool for Management Intervention in Birds (book chapter), 1998. Honours: Ornithologists Award, German Ornithologists' Society, 1994; Honorary Member, Ethological Society, 2000; Chair for Biodiversity, ASEAN Regional Center for Biodiversity Conservation, 2001-04; Hall of Fame, ABI; Gold Medal for Germany, ABI. Memberships: Society for Conservation Biology; International Society for Behavioral Ecology; Ethological Society; Founding President, Philippine Association for Conservation and Development, 2005-07; Association for the Study of Animal Behaviour; Frankfurt Zoological Society; German Zoological Society; German Ornithologists' Society; American Society of Naturalists; Society for Conservation Biology. Address: Conservation Biology Unit, Faculty of Biology, Ruhr-University Bochum, Postfach 102148, 44801 Bochum, Germany. E-mail: eberhard.curio@rub.de Website: www.pescp.org

CURL James Stevens, b. 26 March 1937, Belfast, Northern Ireland. Architect; Architectural Historian. m. (1) 2 daughters, (2) Stanisława Dorota Iwaniec, 1993. Education: Queen's University, School of Architecture, Belfast, 1954-58; DiplArch, Oxford School of Architecture, 1961-63; Dip TP, Oxford Department of Land Use Studies, 1963-67; PhD, University College London, 1978-81. Appointment: Professor Emeritus of Architectural History, having held Chairs at two British universities; Visiting Professor, University of Ulster, 2010-. Publications include: The Londonderry Plantation 1609-1914, 1986; English Architecture: An Illustrated Glossary, 1987; Encyclopaedia of Architectural Terms, 1993; A Celebration of Death, 1993; Egyptomania, 1994; Victorian Churches, 1995; The Oxford Dictionary of Architecture, 1999, 2000; The Honourable The Irish Society and the Plantation of Ulster 1608-2000: The City of London and the Colonisation of County Londonderry in the Province of Ulster in Ireland – A History and Critique, 2000; The Victorian Celebration of Death, 2000, 2004; The Art and Architecture of Freemasonry, 2002; Georgian Architecture, 2002; Classical Architecture, 2002; Death and Architecture, 2002; The Egyptian Revival, 2005; The Oxford Dictionary of Architecture and Landscape Architecture, 2006; Victorian Architecture; Diversity and Invention, 2007; Spas, Wells & Pleasure – Gardens of London, 2010; Freemasonry & The Enlightenment: Architecture, Symbols & Influences, 2011. Honours: British Academy Research Awards, 1982, 1983. 1992, 1994, 1998; Sir Banister Fletcher Award for Best Book of Year (1991) 1992; Building Centre Trust Award, 1992; Interbuild Fund Award, 1992 Royal Institute of British Architects Research Award, 1993; Marc Fitch Fund Award, 2003; Authors Foundation Fund Award, 2004. Memberships: Royal Irish Academy; Society of Authors; Royal Institute of British Architects; Royal Institute of the Architects of Ireland; Royal Incorporation of Architects in Scotland; Society of Antiquaries of Scotland; Society of Antiquaries of London; Oxford and Cambridge Club. Address: 15 Torgrange, Holywood, County Down BT18 0NG, Northern Ireland. E-mail: jscurl@btinternet.com

CURRIE JONES Edwina, b. 13 October 1946. Politician; Broadcaster; Writer. m. (1) R F Currie, 1972, dissolved 2001, 2 daughters, (2) John Jones, 2001. Education: St Anne's College, Oxford, London School of Economics. Appointments: Lecturer in Economics, Economics History and Business Studies, 1972-81; Elected: Birmingham City Council, 1975-86, Conservative MP Derbyshire South, 1983-97; Appointed: Junior Minister, Department of Health, 1985-86 and 1986-88; Chair, Conservative Group for Europe, 1995-97; Vice Chair, European Movement, 1995-99; Host of Radio Programme, Late Night Currie, BBC Radio 5 Live, 1998-2003; Presenter TV Programmes for BBC and others; Winner, Celebrity Mastermind, 2004; Appeared in numerous reality TV Programmes. Publications: Six novels, including, A Parliamentary Affair, 1994; A Woman's Place, 1996; She's Leaving Home, 1997; The Ambassador, 1999; Chasing Men, 2000; This Honourable House, 2001; Diaries (1987-92) 2002; Diaries (1992-97) 2004; Several non-fiction works, Life Lines, 1989; What Women Want, 1990; Three Line Quips, 1992, Diaries: v (2010). Honours: Speaker of the Year, 1990; Campaigner of the Year, Spectator, 1994. Address: c/o Little Brown, Brettenham House, Lancaster Place, London WC2E 7EN, England.

CURTIS David Roderick, b. 3 June 1927, Melbourne, Australia. Neuropharmacologist. m. Lauri Sewell, 1 son, 1 daughter. Education: MB BS, University of Melbourne, 1950; PhD, Australian National University, 1957. Appointments: Research Scholar, 1954-56, Research Fellow, 1956-57, Fellow, 1957-59, Senior Fellow, 1959-62, Professorial Fellow, 1962-66, Professor of Pharmacology, 1966-73, Department of Physiology, John Curtin School; Professor and Head, Department of Pharmacology, 1973-88, Chairman, Division of Physiological Sciences, 1988-89, Howard Florey Professor of Medical Research, Director of School, 1989-92, University Fellow, 1993-95, Emeritus Professor, 1993, John Curtin School of Medical Research, Australian National University. Publications: Numerous articles in professional journals; Co-author, The John Curtin School of Medical Research. The First Fifty Years, 1948-1998. Honours: FAA, 1965; FRS, 1974; Burnet Medal, Australian Academy of Science, 1983; President, Australian Academy of Science, 1986-92; FRACP, 1987; AC, 1992; Centenary Medal, 2003. Memberships: Honorary Fellow, The British Pharmacological Society; Honorary Member Emeritus, The Australian Association of Neurologists; Honorary Member: The Neurosurgical Society of Australasia; The Australian Neuroscience Society; The Australian Physiological and Pharmacological Society. Address: 7 Patey Street, Campbell, ACT 2612, Australia.

CURTIS Jamie Lee (Lady Haden-Guest), b. 22 November 1958, Los Angeles, California, USA. m. Christopher Guest, 1 son, 1 daughter. Education: University of the Pacific, California, USA. Career: Films include: Halloween; The Fog; Halloween 2; Prom Night; Trading Places; The Adventures of Buckaroo Banzai: Across the 8th Dimension; 8 Million Ways to Die; A Fish Called Wanda; Blue Steel; My Girl; Forever Young; My Girl 2; True Lies, 1994; House Arrest, 1996; Fierce Creatures, 1996; Halloween H20, 1998; Virus, 1999; The Tailor of Panama (also director), 2000; Daddy and Them; Halloween H2K: Evil Never Dies; True Lies 2, 2003; Freaky Friday, 2003; Christmas with the Kranks, 2004; Molly & Roni's Dance Party, 2005; The Kid & I, 2005; TV includes: Dorothy Stratten: Death of a Centrefold; The Love Boat; Columbo Quincy; Charlie's Angels; Mother's Boys; Drowning Mona (director), 2000; A Home for the Holidays, 2005. Publications: When I Was Little, 1993; Today I Feel Silly and Other Moods That Make My Day, 1999; Where Do Balloons Go? An Uplifting Mystery, 2000; I'm Gonna Like Me Letting Off a Little Self-Esteem, 2002; It's Hard to be Five, Learning How to Work my Control Panel, 2004. Address: c/o Rick Kurtzmann, CAA, 9830 Wilshire Boulevard, Beverly Hills, CA 90212, USA.

CUSACK John, b. 28 June 1966, Evanston, Illinois, USA. Actor. Appointments: Piven Theatre Workshop, Evanston, from age 9-19; New Criminals Theatrical Company, Chicago; Films include: Class, 1983; Sixteen Candles, Grandview USA, 1984; The Sure Thing, 1985; One Crazy Summer, 1986; Broadcast News, Hot Pursuit, 1987; Eight Men Out, Tapeheads, 1988; Say Anything, Fatman and Little Boy, The Thin Red Line, 1989; The Grifters, 1990; True Colors, 1991; Shadows and Fog, Roadside Prophets, The Player, Map of the Human Heart, Bob Roberts, 1992; Money for Nothing, 1993; Bullets Over Broadway, The Road to Wellville, 1994; City Hall, 1995; Anastasia, Con Air, Hellcab, Midnight in the Garden of Good and Evil, 1997; This is My Father, Pushing Tin, 1998; Being John Malkovich, 1999; Live of the Party, 2000; America's Sweethearts, Serendipity, 2001; Max, Adaptation, 2002; Identity, Runaway Jury, 2003; Ice Harvest, 2005; The Ice Harvest: Alternate Endings, The Contract, 2006; 1408, Grace is Gone, Summerhood, Martian Child, War, Inc, 2007; Igor (voice), 2008; Actor, director, writer: Grosse Pointe Blank, 1997; Arigo (producer, actor), 1998; High Fidelity (actor, writer), 1997; The Cradle Will Rock, 1999. Address: 1325 Avenue of the Americas, New York, NY 10019, USA,

CUSACK Sinead Mary, b. 1948. Actress. m. Jeremy Irons, 1977, 2 sons. Appointments: Appearances with RSC include: Lady Amaranth in Wild Oats, Lisa in Children of the Sun, Isabella in Measure for Measure, Celia in As You Like It, Evadne in the Maid's Tragedy, Lady Anne in Richard III, Portia in the Merchant of Venice, Ingrid in Peer Gynt, Kate in the Taming of the Shrew, Beatrice in Much Ado About Nothing, Lady MacBeth in MacBeth, Roxanne in Cyrano de Bergerac, Virago in A Lie of the Mind, 2001, The Mercy Seat, 2003; Other stage appearances at Oxford Festival, Gate Theatre, Dublin, Royal Court and others; numerous appearances in TV drama; Films include: Alfred the Great; Tamlyn; Hoffman; David Copperfield; Revenge; The Devil's Widow; Horowitz in Dublin Castle; The Last Remake of Beau Geste; Rocket Gibralter; Venus Peter; Waterland; God on the Rocks; Bad Behaviour; The Cement Garden; The Sparrow; Flemish Board; Stealing Beauty; I Capture the Castle; V for Vendetta, 2005; The Tiger's Tail, 2006; Eastern Promises, 2007. Address: c/o Curtis Brown Group, 4th Floor, Haymarket House, 28-29 Haymarket, London, SW1Y 4SP, England.

CUSCOLECA Christoph, b. 11 June 1968, Vienna, Austria. Professor. Appointments: Academic Initiative Ambassador. Honours: Common Award, 2001. Memberships: COMMON Europe. Address: Kaeferkreuzgasse 33/7, A-3400 Klosterneuburg, Austria. E-mail: cuscoleca@isso.co.at

CUSSLER Clive (Eric), b. 15 July 1931, Aurora, Illinois, USA. Author; Advertising Executive. m. Barbara Knight, 1955, 3 children. Education: Pasadena City College, 1949-51; Orange Coast College; California State University. Appointments: Advertising Directorships; Author. Owner, Bestgen and Cussler Advertising, Newport Beach, California, 1961-65; Copy Director, Darcy Advertising, Hollywood, California and Instructor in Advertising Communications, Orange Coast College, 1965-67; Advertising Director, Aquatic Marine Corporation, Newport Beach, California, 1967-79; Vice President and Creative Director of Broadcast, Meffon, Wolff and Weir Advertising, Denver, Colorado, 1970-73; Chair, National Underwater and Marine Agency. Publications: The Mediterranean Caper, 1973; Iceberg, 1975; Raise the Titanic, 1976; Vixen O-Three, 1978; Night Probe, 1981; Pacific Vortex, 1982; Deep Six, 1984; Cyclops, 1986; Treasure, 1988; Dragon, 1990; Sahara, 1992; Inca Gold, 1994; Shock Wave, 1996; Flood Tide, 1997; Serpent, 1999; Atlantis Found, 1999; Blue Gold, 2000; Valhalla Rising, 2001; Fire Ice, 2002; Sea Hunters II, 2002; The Golden Buddha, 2003; White Death, 2003; Trojan Odyssey, 2003; Black Wind, 2004; Treasure of Khan, 2006; The Chase, 2007; The Aventures of Hotsy Totsy, 2010. Honours: Numerous advertising awards; Lowell Thomas Award, New York Explorers Club. Memberships: Fellow, New York Explorers Club; Royal Geographical Society. Address: c/o Putnam Publishing Group, 2000 Madison Avenue, New York, NY 10016, USA.

CWUDZINSKI Adam, b. 10 May 1980, Czestochowa, Poland. Assistant Professor; Metallurgist. m. 1 son. Education: MSc, 2004, PhD, 2008, Czestochowa University of Technology. Appointments: Research Staff, 2004-08, Assistant Professor, 2008-, Czestochowa University of Technology. Publications: Numerous articles in professional journals. Honours: Stipends for Young Researchers, Start Programme, Foundation for Polish Science, 2010; Stipend for Young Distinguished Researchers, Ministry of Science and Higher Education, 2011. Memberships: Polish Association of Metallurgical Engineers and Technicians; French Society for Metallurgy and Materials. Address: Czestocholia University of Technology, Armii Krajowej 19 Ave, 42-200 Czestochowa, Poland. E-mail: cwudzinski@wip.pcz.pl

CYRUS Miley, b. 23 November 1992, Nashville, Tennessee, USA. Singer; Actress. Career: Actress: Films: Big Fish, 2003; High School Musical 2, 2007; Hannah Montana & Miley

Cyrus: Best of Both Worlds Concert, Bolt (voice), 2008; Hannah Montana: The Movie, 2009; The Last Song, 2010; Wings, 2011; TV: Doc, 2003; The Suite Life of Zack & Cody, 2006; Hannah Montana, 2006-10; The Emperor's New School, 2007 Disney Channel Games, 2007; The Replacements, 2007-08; Studio DC: Almost Live, 2008; The Suite Life on Deck, 2009; Singer: Albums: Hannah Montana, 2006; Meet Miley Cyrus, 2007; Hannah Montana 2, 2007; Breakout, 2008; Hannah Montana: The Movie, 2009; Hannah Montana 3, 2009; The Time of Our Lives, 2009. Honours: 4 Kids' Choice Awards, 2007, 2008, 2009; 8 Teen Choice Awards, 2007, 2008, 2009; Young Artist Award, 2008; Gracie Allen Award, 2008; MTV Movie Award, 2009; BMI Award, 2009.

CZECZUGA Bazyli, b. 30 October 1930, Plutycze. Scientist. m. Ada Matusewicz, deceased, 1 daughter. Education: National Faculty, University of Minsk, USSR; MSc, 1956, Degree of Science Doctor, 1960; Degree Assistant Professor, Docent, Academy A Techn in Olsztyn, Poland, 1963. Appointments: Assistant, Medical Academy Bialystok, 1956-61; Assistant Professor, Head of Department of Biology, Medical Academy, Bialystok, 1962-71; Professor, Head of Department, General Biological Medical Academy, Bialystok, Poland, 1972-2001. Publications: Ecological-Physiological Aspects of Chironomidae, monograph, 1962; The Nature of North-East of Poland, 1973; The Wigry Lake, 1979; Over 440 scientific papers and articles. Honours: Gold Order of Merit, 1976; Order Polonia Restituta, 1977; Order of Merit Teacher, 1978; Prize, Polish Academy of Sciences, Health Ministry, 1975. Memberships include: New York Academy of Sciences, Belarus Academy of Sciences; Honourable Member, Slavobaltiska Sallskapet Vid Lunds University, Sweden, 1972; Advisor, University of Wales Icelandic Expedition, 1970; Correspondent, Centre for Short-Lived Phenomena Smithsonian Institute, Washington, 1970-73; Paleolimnological Working Group, Kyoto, Japan, 1975-90; Expert, University of La Laguna, Canary Islands, Spain, 1983; Mangalore University, India, 1987; Complutense University, Madrid, Spain, 1992; Federal University of Parana, Brazil, 1994; Israel Academy of Sciences and Humanities, 1996; Chairman, Bialystok Committee of Defenders of Peace, 1984-89; National Geographic Society; American Association for the Advancement of Science. Address: Ul Szpitalna 35a m 50, 15 295 Bialystok, Poland.

CZECZUGA-SEMENIUK Ewa, b. 13 April 1957, Mińsk, Belarus. Physician. m. Janusz Włodzimierz Semeniuk, 1 daughter. Education: PhD, Medicine, Medical University, Department of Reproduction and Gynaecological Endocrinology, Białystok, Poland, 1986. Appointments: Junior Researcher in Microbiology, 1982-83, Lecturer in Microbiology, 1983-85, Lecturer, 1985-2003, Senior Lecturer, Gynaecological Department, 2003-05, Senior Lecturer, Department of Reproduction and Gynaecological Endocrinology, 2005-, Medical University, Białystok, Poland. Publications: Numerous articles in professional scientific journals. Honours: Award I degree, 2000, Award II degree, 2005, Award I degree, 2006, Award III degree, 2008, Award II degree, 2010, Medical University, Białystok, Poland; Listed in international biographical dictionaries. Memberships: Polish Society of Gynaecology; Polish Society of Endocrinology; Polish Society of Andropause and Menopause. Address: Legionowa 9/54, 15-281, Białystok, Poland.

CZIGNER Jenô, b. 1 March 1937, Bedeg, Hungary. Otorhinolaryngologist. m. Irene Vass, 2 daughters. Education: Diploma, Medical Faculty, University of Pécs, Hungary, 1961; DSc med, 1995; Doctor of Hungarian Academy of Sciences, 1996. Appointments: Chairman, Department of Otolaryngology, Budapest Uzsoki University Teaching Hospital, 1978-85; Visiting Professor, Germany, England, Scotland, Japan, USA, Finland, Australia and Romania; Professor and Chairman, 1986-2002, Professor, Otolaryngology, 2002-, Department of Otolaryngology, Head & Neck Surgery, University of Szeged, Hungary. Publications: 186 articles and book chapters; 476 papers presentations or referates. Honours: Outstanding Specialist of Education, 1977; Outstanding Specialist of Health, 1983; Krompecher Award, 1992; Award of Japan Otolaryngology Head-Neck Surgery Society, 1992; Réthi and Cseresnyés S awards, 2001; Bárczi Gusztáv award, 2002; Admiral Award, 2003. Memberships: European Laryngological Society; German, Polish, Slovakian and Austrian Otolaryngological, Head & Neck Societies; American Academy of Otolaryngological Head and Neck Surgery; European Association for Cancer Research; Neurootological and Equilibriometry Society; Journal of Diagnostic and Therapeutic Endoscopy. Address: Kolcsey u 10, Szeged H-6720, Hungary.

D

DADIC Miroslav, b. 28 May 1932, Split, Croatia (Yugoslavia). Chemist (retired). Education: BSc, Chemistry, University of Zagreb, Croatia (Yugoslavia), 1955; PhD, Organic Chemistry, 1961; Postdoctoral work, MIT, Cambridge, Massachusetts, USA, 1964-67 and McGill University, Montreal, Canada, 1967-69. Appointments: Lecturer, University of Zagreb, 1956-64; External Associate, Institute Rudjer Boskovic, Zagreb, 1956-61; Research Associate, Department of Chemistry, MIT, Cambridge, Massachusetts, 1964-67; Postdoctoral Fellow, Chemical Department, McGill University, Montreal, Canada, 1967-69; Senior Research Chemist, R&D, Molson Co, Montreal & Toronto, 1969-90. Publications: 108 publications and patents since 1959, including: The Synthesis Of Oxygen Analogs Of Cepham. A New Bicyclic System, 1968; Phenolic Antioxidants as Potential Carcinostatic Agents, 1971; Beer Stability – A Key to Success in Brewing, 1984. Honours: Master Brewers Association of America Award of Merit, 1983. Past Memberships: American Chemical Society; Chemical Institute of Canada; Order of Chemists of Quebec; Association of Chemical Profession of Ontario; American Society of Brewing Chemists; New York Academy of Sciences. Address: 77 Gerard Street West #1204, Toronto, ON M5G 2A1, Canada.

DAEHNE Siegfried, b. 13 October 1929, Meissen, Saxony, Germany. Chemist. m. Anneliese Daehne Koelling, 2 sons, 1 daughter. Education: Study of Chemistry, 1949-57, Doctor's Degree, 1961, Habilitation, 1968, Humboldt University, Berlin; Venia Legendi, Technical University, Dresden, 1977. Appointments: Head of Laboratory, Institute of Optics and Spectroscopy, Berlin, 1957-62; Head of Department, 1963-84, Staff Member, 1985-87, Central Institute of Optics and Spectroscopy, Berlin; Head of Department, Analytical Centre, Academy of Sciences of the GDR, Berlin, 1988-91; Head of Laboratory, Federal Institute for Materials Research and Testing, Berlin, 1992-95; Head of Project, DFG Sonderforschungsbereich 337, Free University, Berlin, 1992-98; Consultant, Federal Institute for Materials Research and Testing, Berlin, 1996-2001. Publications: Over 270 research publications in professional journals; 9 patents in field of molecular spectroscopy, colour chemistry and supramolecular chemistry, with basic contributions to the mechanisms of spectral sensitization and desensitization in photography, 1965, 1967, theory of the ideal polymethine state, 1966, history of colour and constitution theories, 1970, 1978, structural principles of conjugated organic compounds (triad theory), 1977, 1985, 1990; Microstructural model of Solvatochromism, 1977; Spontaneous and enantioselective generation of chiral J-aggregate helices from achiral cyanine dye molecules, 1996, 1997; Artificial light harvesting systems for photo-induced electron transfer reactions, 2003, 2006; Initiator, main author, Prognosis of Time-Resolved Spectroscopy, Berlin, 1968; Initiator and organiser, Annual Application Schools of Laser Pulse Spectrometry, Berlin, 1982-86; Fifth Symposium of Photochemistry, Reinhardsbrunn, 1986; NATO Advanced Research Workshop on Syntheses, Optical Properties and Applications of Near-Infrared Dyes in High Technology Fields, Trest, Czech Republic, 1997. Honours: Leibniz Medal of the Academy of Sciences of the GDR, 1976; Lieven Gevaert Medal, Society of Photographic Scientists and Engineers, USA, 1997. Memberships include: Society for German Chemists; European Photochemistry Association; German Bunsen Society of Physical Chemistry. Address: Kastanienallee 6, D-12587, Berlin, Germany.

DAESCU Constantin, b. 21 May 1943, Bucharest, Romania. Chemist; Professor. m. Ana-Elena, 1967, 1 son, 1 daughter. Education: Engineer, 1966, Doctorate Degree, 1977, Polytechnical University, Timisoara. Appointments: Assistant, 1966-77, Assistant Professor, 1977-89, Professor, 1990-2008, Polytech University, Timisoara. Publications include: Biosynthetic and Semisynthetic Products, 1982, 2006; Drugs Chemistry and Technology, 1994, 2008; Natural Fibrous Materials, 1996; Drug Industry, 1999, 2005; Print History, 2002; Dyeing and Printing, 2002; Basics of Typographical Style, 2004; Textile Chemical Technology, 2009. Honours: Listed in international biographical directories. Memberships: Romanian Chemical Society; New York Academy of Sciences, London Diplomatic Academy. Address: 11-13 Take Ionescu, 300062 Timisoara, Romania.

DAFOE Willem, b. 22 July 1955, Appleton, Wisconsin, USA. Actor. m. Giada Colagrande, 2005, 1 son from previous relationship. Education: Wisconsin University. Appointments: Actor, films include: The Loveless, New York Nights, 1981; The Hunger, 1982; Communists are Comfortable (and 3 other stories), Roadhouse 66, Streets of Fire, 1984; To Live and Die in LA, 1985; Platoon, 1986; The Last Temptation of Christ, Saigon, 1988; Mississippi Burning, Triumph of the Spirit, 1989; Born on the Fourth of July, Flight of the Intruder, Wild at Heart, 1990; The Light Sleeper, 1991; Body of Evidence, 1992; Far Away, So Close, Tom and Viv, The Night and the Moment, Clear and Present Danger, 1994; The English Patient, Basquiat, 1996; Speed 2: Cruise Control, Affliction, 1997; Lulu on the Bridge, Existenz, 1998; American Psycho, 1999; Shadow of the Vampire, Bullfighter, The Animal Factory, 2000; Edges of the Lord, 2001; Spider-Man, Auto Focus, 2002; Once Upon a Time in Mexico, 2003; The Clearing, The Reckoning, The Life Aquatic with Steve Zissou, The Aviator, 2004; xXx: State of the Union, Ripley Under Ground, Manderlay, Before It Had a Name, Ripley Under Ground, 2005; American Dreamz, Inside Man, Paris, je t'aime, 2006; The Walker, Mr Bean's Holiday, Spider-Man 3, Go Go Tales, Anamorph, 2007; Adam Resurrected, 2008; Fire Flies in the Garden, 2008; Antichrist, 2009; Cirque Du Freak: The Vampire's Assistant, 2009; Fantastic Mr. Fox, 2009; Daybreakers, 2010. Address: c/o William Morris Agency, 1325 Avenue of the Americas, New York, NY 10019, USA.

DAHL Sophie, b. 1978. Fashion Model. m. Jamie Cullum, 1 daughter. Appointments: Discovered by Isabella Blow; Worked with fashion photographers: Nick Knight, David La Chapelle, Karl Lagerfeld, David Bailey, Enrique Badulescu, Herb Ritts and Ellen Von Unwerth; Appeared in: ID, The Face, Elle, Esquire, Scene magazines; Advertising campaigns for Lainey, Keogh, Bella Freud, Printemps, Nina Ricci, Karl Lagerfeld, Oil of Ulay, Hennes; Music videos for U2, Elton John, Duran Duran; Cameo appearances in films: Mad Cows, Best, 1999; Stage appearance in The Vagina Monologues, Old Vic Theatre, 1999; Judge, Orange Prize for Fiction, 2003. Publication: The Man with the Dancing Eyes, 2003, Playing with the Grown-ups, Miss Dahl's Voluptous Delights, 2009. Address: c/o Storm Model Management, 5 Jubilee Place, London SW3 3TD, England.

DAILYUDENKO Victor F, b. 1959. Senior Scientific Researcher. Education: Graduated with excellence, Department of Radiophysics and Electronics, Belarussian State University, 1981; PhD, 1997. Appointments: Senior Scientific Researcher in Mathematical and Computational Physics regarding Self-organization Systems Analysis, Institute of Informatics Problems, National Academy of Sciences of Belarus, 1982-. Publications: 48 articles in scientific journals and proceedings.

Honours: Listed in international biographical dictionaries. Address: PO Box 195, Minsk 15, 220015, Belarus. E-mail: selforg@newman.bas-net.by

DALAI LAMA The (Tenzin Gyatso), b. 6 July 1935, Taktser, Amdo Province, North East Tibet. Temporal and Spiritual Head of Tibet 14th Incarnation. Appointments: Enthroned at Lhasa, 1940; Rights exercised by regency, 1934-50; Assumed political power, 1950; Fled to Chumbi in South Tibet, 1950; Agreement with China, 1951; Vice-Chair, Standing Committee, Member, National Committee, CPPCC, 1951-59; Honorary Chairman, Chinese Buddhist Association, 1953-59; Delegate to National People's Congress, 1954-59; Chairman, Preparatory Committee for Autonomous Region of Tibet, 1955-59; Fled to India after suppression of Tibetan national uprising, 1959. Publications: My Land and People, 1962; The Opening of the Wisdom Eye, 1963; The Buddhism of Tibet and the Key to The Middle Way, 1975; Kindness, Charity and Insight, 1984; A Human Approach to World Peace, 1984; Freedom in Exile (autobiography), 1990; The Good Heart, 1996; Ethics for the New Millennium, 1998; Art of Happiness, (co-author), 1999; A Simple Path: basic Buddhist Teachings by His Holiness the Dalai Lama, 2000; Stages of Meditation: training the Mind for Wisdom, 2002; The Spirit of Peace, 2002. Honours: Dr Buddhist Philos (Monasteries of Sera, Drepung and Gaden, Lhasa), 1959; Supreme Head of all Buddhist sections in Tibet; Memory Prize, 1989; Congressional Human Rights Award, 1989; Nobel Prize, 1989; The Freedom Award (USA), 1991. Address: Thekchen Choeling, McLeod Ganj 176219, Dharamsala, Himachal Pradesh, India.

DALAL Prafulchandra, b. 29 January 1932, Ahmedabad, India. Consultant Neurophysician. Education: MBBS, 1955, MD, 1958, Mumbai University. Appointments: Professor, Head of Medicine, Neurologist, 1965-69; Professor, Head of Neurosciences, 1963-90; Director of Research, Sir H N H Medical Research Society, Mumbai, 1983-87; Chief of Neurosciences, Consultant Neurophysician, Research Director, Lilavati Hospital & Research Centre, Mumbai; Guest Professor, Neurology: Wayne State University, Detroit, USA, 1967-68; Wake Forest University, W Salem, USA, 1978; Visiting Scientist, National Institute of Health, NIH, USA, 1983. Publications: Numerous articles in professional journals. Honours: Rockefeller Fellow, Harvard Medical School, Boston, 1960-62; Senior Commonwealth Fellow, Oxford, UK, 1967; Wellcome Foundation Research Fellow, Oxford, UK, 1968-69; Fellow, Royal Society of Medicine, London; American College of Chest Physicians, USA; International College of Angiology, USA, 1969; National Academy of Medical Sciences, India, 1975; Expert Member, WHO International Panel on Neurosciences, Geneva, 1980-86; Honorary Fellow: Stroke Council; American Heart Association; ICMR Consultant on Neuroepidemiological Studies; Founder Fellow: Indian College of Physicians, 1988; President, Association of Physicians of India; Dr B C Roy National Award, 1995; Visiting Professor, La Sapienza, University of Rome, Italy, 1999; President, Indian Stroke Association, 2008. Memberships: World Federation on Neurology; WHO Commission on Application of Advances in Neurosciences; ICMR; IMA Academy of Medical Specialties; American Neurological Association.

DALBY John Mark Meredith, b. 3 January 1938, Southport, Lancashire, England. Clergyman. Education: MA, Exeter College, Oxford; Ripon Hall, Oxford; PhD, University of Nottingham. Appointments: Ordained Deacon, 1963, Priest, 1964, Oxford; Curate of the Hambledon Valley Group, 1963-68; Vicar of St Peter, Spring Hill, Birmingham, 1968-75; Rural Dean of Birmingham City, 1973-75; Secretary of the Committee for Theological Education, Advisory Council for the Church's Ministry, also Honorary Curate of All Hallows, Tottenham, 1975-80; Vicar, later Team Rector of Worsley, 1980-91; Rural Dean of Eccles, 1987-91; Archdeacon of Rochdale, 1991-2000; Chaplain of the Beauchamp Community, Newland, 2000-07. Publications: Open Communion in the Church of England, 1959; The Gospel and the Priest, 1975; Tottenham: Church and Parish, 1979; The Cocker Connection, 1989; Open Baptism, 1989; Anglican Missals and their Canons, 1998; Infant Communion: The New Testament to the Reformation, 2003; Infant Communion: Post-Reformation to Present Day, 2009; Victorian Wesleyan Sermons Preached by Benjamin Cocker and Charles Horsfield, 2010. Address: St Christopher's, The Beauchamp Community, Newland, Malvern, Worcestershire WR13 5AX, England. E-mail: jmmdalby@btinternet.com

DALE Jim (James Smith), b. 15 August 1935. Actor. m. 3 sons, 1 daughter. Education: Kettering Grammar School; Musical Hall Comedian, 1951; Singing, compering, directing, 1951-61; First film appearance, 1965; Theatre: The Card, 1973; The Taming of the Shrew, 1974; Scapino, 1974; Barnum, 1980; Joe Egg, 1985; Me and My Girl, 1987-88; Candide, 1997; Privates on Parade; Travels with My Aunt, 1995; Fagin in Oliver! 1995-97; Host, Sunday Night at the London Palladium, TV show, 1994; Lyricist for film, Georgy Girl; Films include: Lock Up Your Daughters; The Winter's Tale; The Biggest Dog in the World; National Health; Adolf Hitler – My Part in his Downfall; Joseph Andrews; Pete's Dragon; Hot Lead Cold Feet; Bloodshy; The Spaceman and King Arthur; Scandalous; Carry On Cabby; Carry On Cleo; Carry On Jack; Carry On Cowboy; Carry On Screaming; Carry On Spying; Carry On Constable; Carry On Doctor; Carry On Don't Lose Your Head; Carry On Follow That Camel; Carry On Columbus, 1992; Hunchback of Notre Dame, 1997, Pushing Daisies, Narrator, 2008. Honours: Tony Award, 1980. Address: c/o Sharon Bierut, CED, 257 Park Avenue South, New York, NY 10010, USA.

DALEY Tom (Thomas Robert), b. 21 May 1994, Plymouth, England. Diver. Education: Plymouth College. Career: Winner, 10m, Australian Junior Elite Diving Championships, 2005; Winner, Junior 10m, 2005, 2006, 2007, Winner, Synchro 10m, 2008, Winner, 10m, 2008, 2009, British Championships; Winner, 1m, 3m, 10m, ASA Elite Junior National Championships, 2006; Winner, Synchro 10m, CAMO Invitational Meet, 2007; Winner, 10m, 2007, Winner, Synchro 10m, 2007, Winner, Junior 10m, 2007, Winner, Junior 3m, 2005, 2006, 2007, ASA National Championships; Winner, 10m, European Championships, 2008; Winner, Synchro 10m, FINA Diving World Series, Sheffield, 2008; Winner, 10m, FINA Diving Grand Prix, Fort Lauderdale, 2009; Winner, 10m, FINA World Championships, 2009. Honours: Youngster of the Year, BBC South West, 2005; BBC South West Sports Personality of the Year, and Young Sports Personality of the Year, 2009; BBC Young Sports Personality of the Year, 2007 and 2009; Athlete of the Year, LEN Magazine, 2009.

DALGLISH Kenneth (Kenny) Mathieson, b. 4 March 1951, Glasgow, Scotland. Football Manager. m. Marina, 4 children. Appointments: Played for Celtic, Scottish League Champions, 1972-74, 1977; Scottish Cup Winners, 1972, 1974, 1975, 1977; Scottish Cup Winners, 1972, 1974, 1975, 1977; Scottish league Cup winners, 1975; Played for Liverpool, European Cup Winners, 1978, 1981, 1984; FA Cup Winners, 1986, 1989; League Cup winners, 1981-84; Manager, 1986-91; Manager Blackburn Rovers, 1991-97; Newcastle United, 1997-98;

Director of Football Operations, Celtic, 1999-2000; 102 full caps for Scotland scoring 30 goals. Honours: Footballer of the Year, 1979, 1983; MBE; Freeman of Glasgow; 3 times Manager of the Year; Scottish Sports Hall of Fame, 2001; Scottish Football Hall of Fame, 2004. Address: c/o Celtic Football Club, Celtic Park, Glasgow, G40 3RE, Scotland.

DALTON Ann, b. 28 October 1933, East Sussex, England. BBC Studio Manager; Volunteer Trainer in Broadcast Communications and Coloratura Soprano Soloist for classical, folk and operatic concerts; BBC Programme Producer, Programme Operator and simultaneous Voluntary Radio and TV Communications Trainer to benefit mainly Third World Needs; Accredited Chaperone for children performing on stage (Glyndebourne Opera House and Talisman Film Company). Education: BBC Programme and Engineering Training Colleges, Evesham & Marylebone Road; Guildhall School of Music and Drama Performance Certificate (singing); Piano & Cello Grade V, Royal Academy of Music; City & Guilds Teaching Certificate. Appointments: Producer and Studio Manager, British Broadcasting Corporation, London, 1955-89; Seconded via BBC International Relations Department to be Head of Training and Operations (later Director, External Affairs) for the International Radio and TV Training Centre at Hatch End, Middlesex, to assist Third World and other communicators, 1972-89; Voluntary vocational assistance as Co-Founder and Manager of this centre (while off-duty from the BBC), 1955-72; Lecturer, Loyola University Summer Communications Courses, USA, 1973-76; Organiser, British Radio & TV UNDA Festivals and competitions to encourage the pursuit of excellence and to provide a forum for debate; Jury Member, Prix d'Italia UNDA-TV Awards, 1978; Jury Member, Sandford St Martin TV awards, 1987; Selected as Mass Media Commission Representative to present Loyal Address at Buckingham Palace, 1981; Broadcasters' Liaison Assistant, Rome, 1980-85; Various appearances on radio and television broadcasts; Selected singing candidate in the English National Opera TV series, "Operatunity", 2002; First solo singing broadcast 'live' from BBC Concert Hall, accompanied by Dr George Thalben-Ball; Selected Classical Soloist for Gala Re-Opening of the De La Warr Pavilion, Bexhill, Sussex, 2005 and 2009. Honours: Woman of the Year Award, 1987; Pro Ecclesia Cross, 1981; Nine Championship Awards from Sussex Singing Contests, 2000-2009; Two Gold Medals for Singing, Eastbourne, 2001, 2005; Concert in Sussex won audience vote for their most enjoyable performance of the summer season, 2002; Highest Achiever Award, Eastbourne Music Festival, 2003; Recital Soloist, Oxford University, 2008, and Cambrige University, 2010; Listed in: Great Women of the 21st Century; Women of Achievement; International Peace Prize, Secretary-General of the United Cultural Convention; Cambridge Blue Book, 2007. Memberships: Fellow, Royal Society of Arts; Royal Television Society; Radio Academy; Association of Independent Producers; Advisory Council for Local Broadcasting; UNDA-World Association for Broadcast Communicators; Consultative Council for Animal Welfare. Address: 13 Warrior Square, St Leonards-on-Sea, East Sussex, TN37 6BA, England.

DALTON Michael Neale, b. 15 November 1946, Purley, Surrey, England. Retired. m. Kathryn Mary Shrimpton, 1972, 1 son, 1 daughter. Education: BA, 1968, MA, 1971, Mathematics & Economics, Trinity College, Cambridge. Appointments: Various sales, support and marketing roles, ICL, 1968-86; Founder and Chairman, 1970-, Honorary Life President, 1993-, Dalton Genealogical Society; Marketing Services Manager, 1986-87, Communications Strategy Manager, 1987-91, ICL (UK) Limited; Partner, Dalton Marketing Services, 1991-2001; Vice-Chairman of Council, National Bursars Association, 1997-2001; Bursar & Clerk to the Governors, de Stafford School, Caterham, Surrey, 1992-2005; Trustee & Honorary Secretary, London Stained Glass Repository, 2007-. Publications: Editor, Journal of the Dalton Genealogical Society, 1970-92; Numerous articles on Dalton family history in various publications, 1975-; Various papers on school administration and funding matters, 1992-2005. Honours: Freeman of the City of London, 2005; Liveryman, Worshipful Company of Glaziers & Painters of Glass, 2006. Memberships: Society of Genealogists; Oxford & Cambridge Club; Rotary Club of Caterham; Glyndebourne Festival Society; Founder Member, Guild of One Name Studies. Address: 2 Harewood Close, Reigate, Surrey RH2 0HE, England. E-mail: michaelndalton@aol.com

DALTON Timothy, b. 21 March 1946. Actor. Education: Royal Academy of Dramatic Art. Career includes: National Youth Theatre; Theatre includes: Toured with Prospect Theatre Company; Guest Artist, RSC; Co-starred with Vivien Merchant in Noel Coward's The Vortex; Anthony and Cleopatra, The Taming of the Shrew, 1986; A Touch of the Poet, Young Vic, 1988; Lord Asriel in Philip Pullman's His Dark Materials, National Theatre, 2003-04; Films include: The Lion in Winter, 1968; Cromwell, 1970; Wuthering Heights; Mary, Queen of Scots, 1972; Permission to Kill, 1975; The Man Who Knew Love; Sextette, 1977; Agatha, 1978; Flash Gordon, 1979; James Bond in The Living Daylights, 1987 and Licence to Kill, 1989; The Rocketeer, 1991; The Reef, The Beautician and the Beast, 1996; Made Men, Cleopatra, 1998; Possessed, 1999; American Outlaws, 2001; Looney Tunes – Back in Action, 2002; Hot Fuzz, 2007; TV roles include: Mr Rochester in Jane Eyre, BBC TV, 1983; Master of Ballentrae, HTV, 1983; Mistral's Daughter, TV mini-series, 1984; Florence Nightingale, TV mini-series; Sins, TV mini-series, 1985; Philip von Joel in Framed, mini-series, Anglia TV, 1992; Jack in Red Eagle; Rhett Butler in Scarlett, Sky, 1994; Salt Water Moose, comedy, 1995; The Informant, 1996; Cleopatra, 1998; Possessed, 1999; Time Share, 2000; Hercules, 2004; Dunkirk, 2005; Marple, Dr Who, 2009-2010: The Sittaford Mystery, 2006. Membership: Actors' Equity. Address: c/o ICM, Oxford House, 76 Oxford Street, London W1D 1BS, England.

DALYELL Tam, b. 9 August 1932, Edinburgh, Scotland. Member of Parliament; Writer. m. Kathleen Wheatley, 26 December 1963, 1 son, 1 daughter. Education: Harecroft Hall, Eton; King's College, Cambridge, 1952-56. Appointments: Elected to House of Commons, 1962-2005; Father of the House of Commons, 2001-05. Publications: The Case for Ship Schools, 1958; Ship School Dunera, 1961; One Man's Falklands, 1982; A Science Policy for Britain, 1983; Misrule: How Mrs Thatcher Deceived Parliament, 1987; Dick Crossman: A Portrait, 1988; The Importance of Being Awkward, 2011. Contributions to: Weekly Columnist, New Scientist, 1967-; Many Obituaries, Independent Newspaper. Honours: Various Awards of Science; Honorary Doctor of Science, University of Edinburgh, 1994; Honorary Degree, City University, London, 1998; Trustee, History of Parliament, 1999-2005; Chairman, All-Party Latin America Group, 1999-2004; St Andrew's University, 2003; Napier University, Edinburgh, 2004; Northumbria University, 2005; Honorary Doctorate: Stirling University, 2006, Open University, 2006. Address: Binns, Linlithgow, EH44 7NA, Scotland.

DAMACEANU Romulus-Catalin, b. 14 March 1975, Iasi, Romania. Lecturer. m. Mariana-Dana, 1 son. Education: Advanced Studies in Economic Sciences, Intraeuropean Trade, Faculty of Economics and Business Administration, 1994-99, Doctorate, 1999-2005, Alexandru Ioan Cuza University of Iasi. Appointments: Assistant, Researcher, Lecturer, Faculty of Economics, Petre Andrei University of Iasi, 2000-. Publications: The exchange rate regime and the international trade, 2007; Implementation of simulation model of world economy using LSD, 2007; An agent-based computational study of wealth distribution in function of resource growth interval using Netlogo, 2008; Applied Computational Mathematics in Social Sciences, 2010; The exchange rate regime and the international trade. Address: Ghica Voda 13, Iasi 700400, Romania.

DAMON Matt, b. 8 October 1970, Cambridge, Massachusetts, USA. Actor. m. Luciana Barroso, 3 daughters, 1 step daughter. Appointments: Film actor, Films include: Mystic Pizza, 1988; School Ties, 1992; Geronimo: An American Legend, 1993; Courage Under Fire, Glory Daze, 1996; Chasing Amy, The Rainmaker, Good Will Hunting (also co-writer), 1997; Saving Private Ryan, Rounders, 1998; Dogma, The Talented Mr Ripley, Titan AE (voice), All The Pretty Horses, 1999; The Legend of Bagger Vance, Finding Forrester, 2000; Ocean's Eleven, The Majestic (voice), 2001; Gerry (also writer), Spirit: Stallion of the Cimarron (voice), The Third Wheel, The Bourne Identity, 2002; Confessions of a Dangerous Mind, Stuck on You, 2003; Eurotrip, Jersey Girl,The Bourne Supremacy, Ocean's Twelve, 2004; The Brothers Grimm, Syriana, 2005; The Good Shepherd, 2006; Ocean's Thirteen, Margaret, The Bourne Ultimatum, The Departed, 2006; Youth Without Youth, 2007; The Informant, 2009; Ponyo, 2009: Invictus, 2009; The Adjustment Bureau, 2010; Hereafter, 2010; Green Zone, 2010; TV: Rising Son, 1990; The Good Old Boys, 1995. Honours: Empire Film Award for Best Actor, 2005. Address: Creative Artists Agency, 9830 Wilshire Boulevard, Beverly Hills, CA 90212, USA.

DANCE Charles, b. 10 October 1946, Rednal, Worcestershire, England. Actor. m. Joanna Haythorn, 1970, 1 son, 1 daughter. Appointments: Formerly employed in industry; with RSC, 1975-80, 1980-85; TV appearances include: The Fatal Spring; Nancy Astor; Frost in May; Saigon - The Last Day; Thunder Rock (drama); Rainy Day Women; The Jewel in the Crown (nominated for Best Actor BAFTA Award); The Secret Servant; The McGuffin; The Phantom of the Opera, 1989; Rebecca, 1996; In the Presence of Mine Enemies; The Ends of the Earth, Bleak House, 2004; Fingersmith, Last Rights, 2005; Consulting Adults, 2007; Films include: For Your Eyes Only; Plenty; The Golden Child; White Mischief; Good Morning Babylon; Hidden City; Pascali's Island, 1988; China Moon, 1990; Alien III, Limestone, 1991; Kabloonak; Century; Last Action Hero; Exquisite Tenderness, Short Cut to Paradise, 1993; Undertow; Michael Collins; Space Trucker, 1996; Goldeneye; The Blood Oranges; What Rats Won't Do; Hilary and Jackie, 1998; Don't Go Breaking My Heart, Jurij, 1999; Dark Blue World, 2000; Gosford Park, Ali G in da House, 2001; Black and White, 2002; Swimming Pool, Labyrinth, 2003; Ladies in Lavender (writer/director), 2005; Dolls, Scoop, Twice Upon a Time, 2006; Intervention, 2007; Starter for Ten, 2007; Theatre: Coriolanus (title role), RSC, 1989; Irma La Douce; Turning Over; Henry V; Three Sisters, 1998; Good, 1999; Long Day's Journey Into Night, Radio: The Heart of the Matter, The Charge of the Light Brigade, 2001; The Play What I Wrote, 2002; Honours: OBE. Address: c/o ICM, Oxford House, 76 Oxford Street, London, W1D 1BS, England.

DANDY Gillian Margaret (Gill), b. 17 August 1957, Ely, Cambridgeshire, England. Public Relations Consultant. Education: Birmingham College of Food and Domestic Arts, 1976-79. Appointments: Harrison Cowley Public Relations Ltd, Birmingham, 1980-83; Associate Director, Leslie Bishop Company, 1983-90; Director, Shandwick Communications, 1990-96; Director of Development and PR, London Bible College, 1990-2002; Communications Director, Evangelical Alliance, 2002-04; Non-Executive Director, Shared Interest Society Limited, 2004-; Senior Consultant, Centre for Strategy and Communications, 2004-. Memberships: Fellow, Chartered Institute of Public Relations; Fellow, Royal Society for the Encouragement of the Arts. E-mail: gill.dandy@the-centre.co.uk

DANES Claire, b. 12 April 1979, New York, USA. Film Actress. m. Hugh Dancy. Education: Performing arts school, New York; Lee Strasburg Studio. Appointments: 1st acting roles in off-Broadway theatre productions: Happiness; Punk Ballet; Kids on Stage; Films: Dreams of Love (debut), 1992; Thirty (short), 1993; The Pesky Suitor (short); Little Women, 1994; Romeo and Juliet, To Gillian on Her 37th Birthday, 1996; Polish Wedding, U Turn, The Rainmaker, 1997; Les Misérables, 1998; The Mod Squad, Brokedown Place, 1999; Monteret Pop, Dr T and the Women, Flora Plum, 2000; The Cherry Orchard, Igby Goes Down, The Hours, 2002; Terminator 3: Rise of the Machines, 2003; Stage Beauty, 2004; Shopgirl, The Family Stone, 2005; Evening, The Flock, Stardust, 2007; Evening, 2007; Me and Orson Welles, 2009. TV: My So-Called Life (series); No Room for Opal (Film); The Coming Out of Heidi Leiter.

DANG Mohinder Singh, b. 13 December 1946, Amritsar, India. Medical. m. Sona, 2 daughters. Education: MBBS, 1968; DOMS, 1970; MS (Ophth), 1973; DO (London), 1975; FRCS (Edin), 1979; FRCOphth, England, 1988. Appointments: Research Fellow, ICMR, India, 1970-73; SHO, Ophthalmology, London, 1974-75; Registrar, Ophthalmology, Wirral and Birmingham, 1976-80; Senior Registrar, Ophthalmology, Manchester, 1980-83; Senior Consultant, Ophthalmology, 1983-. Publications: Numerous articles in professional journals; Many presentations to national and international conventions. Honours: 1st Class First in MS (Ophthalmology); Award of Excellence, NRI's, London. Memberships: Fellow, Royal College of Ophthalmologists, England; Member, European Society of Cataract & Refractive Surgeons; Member, UK & Ireland Society of Cataract & Refractive Surgeons. Address: Mussoorie House, Compton Grove, Darlington, DL3 9AZ, England. E-mail: m.dang@02.co.uk

DANIELS Harvey, b. 17 June 1936, London, England. Artist; Lecturer. m. Judith Stapleton, 2 daughters. Education: National Diploma in Design, Willesden School of Art, 1956; Diploma, Fine Art, London University, Slade, 1958; ATD, Brighton College of Art, University of Brighton, 1959. Appointments: Principal Lecturer, Printmaking, University of Brighton, 1970-89; Artist; Solo exhibitions in USA, Norway, France, Germany, England and Scotland; Work held in public collections in USA, England and Norway. Publications: Printmaking, 1970; Exploring Printmaking for Young People, 1971; Simple Printmaking for Children, 1971; Printing, 1974; Catalogue of Peacock Printmakers, 1986; The Day Book, 1988; Exhibition, 1989; Article in Printmaking Today, 1993 Collection, 1999; Summer Psalms, 1999. Honours: Painting Purchase Prize, Open Field Exhibition, 1972; Chichester Open Prize, 1998; Judge, 64th Aberdeen Artists Society Exhibition, 1998; Honorary RE, 1998; Watercolour in 21st

Century, Royal Watercolour Society, 1999; Prize Winner, Freshfields Award in Watercolour, 21st Century Bankside, 1999; Prize Winner, Royal Watercolour Society Awards, Bankside, 2003. Memberships: London Group. E-mail: harveymdaniels@gmail.com Website: www.harveydaniels.eu

DANIELS Jeff, b. 19 February 1955, Athens, Georgia, USA. Actor. m. Kathleen Treado, 1979, 3 children. Education: Central Michigan University. Appointments: Apprentice Circle Repertory Theatre, New York; Founder, Purple Rose Theatre Company, Chelsea, Michigan; Theatre: The Farm, 1976; Brontosaurus, My Life, Feedlot, 1977; Lulu, Slugger, The Fifth of July, 1978; Johnny Got His Gun (Obie Award), 1982; The Three Sisters, 1982-83; The Golden Age, 1984; Redwood Curtain, Short-Changed Review, 1993; Lemon Sky; Films: Ragtime, 1981; Terms of Endearment, 1983; The Purple Rose of Cairo, Marie, 1985; Heartburn, Something Wild, 1986; Radio Days, 1987; The House on Carroll Street, Sweet Hearts Dance, 1988; Grand Tour, Checking Out, 1989; Arachnophobia, Welcome Home, Roxy Carmichael, Love Hurts, 1990; The Butcher's Wife, 1992; Gettysburg, 1993; Speed, Dumb and Dumber, 1994; Fly Away Home, Two Days in the Valley, 101 Dalmatians, 1996; Trial and Error, 1997; Pleasantville, All the Rage, My Favourite Martian, 1999; Chasing Sleep, Escanaba in da Moonlight, 2000; Super Sucker, Blood Work, The Hours, Gods and Generals, 2002; I Witness, 2003; Imaginary Heroes, 2004; The Squid and the Whale, Because of Winn-Dixie, The Squid and the Whale, Good Night, and Good luck, 2005; RV, Infamous, 2006; The Lookout, Mama's Boy, A Plumm Summer, 2007; Space Chimps, 2008; Traitor, 2008; State of Play, 2009; Away We Go, 2009; Arlen Faber, 2009. TV films: A Rumor of War, 1980; Invasion of Privacy, 1983; The Caine Mutiny Court Martial, 1988; No Place Like Home, 1989; Disaster in Time, 1992; Redwood Curtain, 1995; Teamster Boss: The Jackie Presser Story; (specials) Fifth of July; The Visit (Trying Times). Publications: Author, Plays: Shoeman, 1991; The Tropical Pickle, 1992; The Vast Difference, 1993; Thy Kingdom's Coming, 1994; Escanaba in da Moonlight, 1995; The Goodbye Girl, The Five People You Meet in Heaven, 2004. Address: Purple Rose Theatre, 137 Park Street, Chelsea, MI 48118, USA. Website: www.purplerosetheatre.org

DANIELSEN Lis, b. 29 April 1930, Holbæk, Denmark. Medical Doctor. m. Jan Danielsen, 2 sons. Education: Medical Doctor, 1958; Speciality in Dermato-Venerology, 1967; Doctor of Medical Science, 1979. Appointments: Physician, Department of Dermato-Venerology, Rigshospitalet, Copenhagen, 1963-74; Consultant, Municipal Hospital of Copenhagen, 1974-83; Bispebjerg Hospital, Copenhagen, 1983-2000; Retired, 2000; Chairman, Scientific Committee, Rehabilitation and Research Centre for Torture Victims, Copenhagen, 1998-2002; Senior External Medical Consultant, International Rehabilitation Council for Torture Victims, Copenhagen. Publications: Co-author: The Medical Documentation of Torture; Istanbul Protocol; Articles in medical journals. on Pseudoxanthoma Elasticum, leg ulcers and signs of torture on the skin. Memberships: Danish Medical Association; Danish Dermatological Society; Danish Wound Healing Society; Amnesty International. Address: Skjoldagervej 22, 2820 Gentofte, Denmark. E-mail: janda@mail.dk

DANILOV Gennady Stepanovich, b. 26 March 1935, St Petersburg, Russia. Physicist. m. Kotova Lidya Michajlovna, 1 son, 1 daughter. Education: PhD, 1964, DSc, 1976, Institute of Theoretical and Experimental Physics, Moscow. Appointments: Researcher, 1959-66, Senior Researcher, 1966-71, Physics Technical Institute, St Petersburg; Senior Researcher, 1971-86, Leading Researcher, 1986-, Head of Group, St Petersburg Nuclear Physics Institute. Publications: Several articles for professional journals. Address: St Petersburg Nuclear Physics Institute, 188350 Gatchina, Leningrad district, Russia. E-mail: danilov@thd.pnpi.spb.ru

DANN Colin Michael, b. 10 March 1943, Richmond, Surrey, England. Author. m. (1) Janet Elizabeth Stratton, 1977, deceased 2007, (2) Susanne Elizabeth Stanbury, 2010. Publications: The Animals of Farthing Wood, 1979; In the Grip of Winter, 1981; Fox's Feud, 1982; The Fox Cub Bold, 1983; The Siege of White Deer Park, 1985; The Ram of Sweetriver, 1986; King of the Vagabonds, 1987; The Beach Dogs, 1988; The Flight from Farthing Wood, 1988; Just Nuffin, 1989; In the Path of the Storm, 1989; A Great Escape, 1990; A Legacy of Ghosts, 1991; The City Cats, 1991; Battle for the Park, 1992; The Adventure Begins, 1994; Copycat, 1997; Nobody's Dog, 1999; Journey to Freedom, 1999; Lion Country, 2000; Pride of The Plains, 2002. Honour: Arts Council National Award for Children's Literature, 1980. Membership: Society of Authors. Address: Castle Oast, Ewhurst Green, East Sussex, England.

DANNER Karl Heinz (né Roeckel von Huebner), b. 25 February 1940, Rodalben, Rhineland-Palatinate, Germany. Author; Poet; Cultural Mediator; Educator. m. Ingrid Karola Danner-Jekel, 1972. Education: German and Canadian Junior and Senior Matriculation, 1957, 1962, 1964, 1967 (Abitur), Pirmasens, Sudbury, Saarbruecken; BA, Laurentian University, Canada, 1982; Diplomas, Universities of Madrid, Salamanca, Strasbourg and Toulouse, 1978-84; Master of Arts, University of the Saarland, Germany, 1976; State Teaching Certificates, Universities of Mainz and Trier, 1978, 1979, 1981, 1984; Licence/Maîtrise ès Lettres, University of Toulouse, France, 1984-86; Secondary School Honour Diploma, Diplôme d'études secondaires supérieures, Toronto, Canada, 1986; Master and Doctor of Education, PW University, Los Angeles, California, 1986, 1988; PhD (Doctor of Literature), American University, 1990, 1994; Professor h.c.; Doctor of Philosophy, University of London, 2007; Professor for Educational Sciences; Aesthetical, Philosophical and Spiritual Education by Roberto Walser, Gabriel Marcel, Albert Schweitzer, Swami Ragagopalan, Doris Zoells; Willigis Jaeger, Clemens Kuby, P Saint John, Alain Guy, Mantak Chia, Ernst Schoenwiese, Dalai Lama, Ioannes Paulus II, Benedictus XVI, Martin Luther King, Brigitte Fassbaender, Gundula Janowitz; Rita Streich; Dietrich Fischer-Dieskau; András Schiff, Sabine Meyer, Menahem Pressler, Claude Frank, Manfred Henninger, Fritz Wotruba, Annette Dasch, Anne-Sophie Mutter, Ignazio Silone, Hermann Kesten, Friedrich Torberg, Arthur Rubinstein. Appointments include: Teacher, Modern Languages and Literature, Canada and West Germany; Research Assistant, Associate and Lecturer, University of the Saarland, Germany, 1965-76; Lecturer and Senior Lecturer, Modern Languages, Education Authority, Palatinate, Germany, 1978-2002; Student Exchange Organiser and Liaison Teacher, Exchanges in France and England; Adviser Partner for Cultural Exchange/Relations, 1989-; Founding Member, Member of the Board, General Secretary, International Robert Musil Society, Austria; Founder, President of German-Latin American Friendship Associations, 1989-; Doctor of Literature hc, World University of America, 1994; Member, Accademia Culturale d'Europa, Italy, 1989; Counsellor on German Culture in Europe and Overseas, 1991-; Extensive travelling and lecturing in Europe & the Americas, 1965-2009; Honorary Member, Société de Philosophie, France, 1994; Member of Pontificia Academia, Vaticana, Rome, 1996-; Member, Jury of National Foreign Language Competition; Curator of Literature exhibitions, 1965-77; Humanities Educator (Philologist). Publications:

Prose and poetry in English, French, German and German translations from Catalan, English, French, Portuguese and Spanish; Essays, reviews and studies on modern German, English, French, Portuguese/ Brazilian and Spanish literature; Over 1,300 articles in periodicals in Europe and the Americas; Research Publications; Didactics of Modern Languages; Emigration of German-speaking Europeans; 25 papers, dissertations, treatises in Humanities, documentations; Large correspondence over 50 years with contemporary personalities. Honours include: Various official decorations of Austria, Canada, Germany, Italy, Spain, USA; Founder, Chairman of German-French Friendship Circle, 2004; Doctor of Philosophy, honoris causa, International Christian University, 1999; Certificates, diplomas, awards from IBC, UK and ABI, USA; Listed in national and international biographical directories. Memberships: German Schiller Society; German-Indian Children's Fund; Modern Language Association; Sponsor of Cultural, Literary & Academic Institutions in Europe and the Americas; Research Advisor, Cambridge, North & South America, Europe; German Folklore Federation; Patron, Palatines to America, National Society, USA. Address: Casa Carola, D 66953 Pirmasens, Germany.

DANSON Ted, b. 29 December 1947, San Diego, California, USA. Actor. m. (1) Randell L Gosch, divorced, (2) Cassandra Coates, 1977, divorced, 2 daughters, (3) Mary Steenburgen, 1995, 1 stepdaughter, 1 stepson. Education: Stanford University; Carnegie-Mellon University. Appointments: Teacher, The Actor's Institute, Los Angeles, 1978; Star, NBC-TV series Cheers, 1982-93; CEO Anasazi Productions (Formerly Danson/Fauci Productions); Off-Broadway plays include: The Real Inspector Hound, 1972; Comedy of Errors; Actor, producer TV films including: When the Bough Breaks, 1986; We Are The Children, 1987; Executive Producer TV films: Walk Me to the Distance, 1989; Down Home, 1989; Mercy Mission: The Rescue of Flight 771, 1993; On Promised Land, 1994; Other appearances in TV drama; Films include: The Onion Field, 1979; Body Heat, 1981; Creepshow, 1983; A Little Treasure, 1985; A Fine Mess, 1986; Just Between Friends, 1986; Three Men and a Little Lady, 1990; Made in America, 1992; Getting Even With Dad, 1993; Pontiac Moon, 1993; Gulliver's Travels (TV), 1995; Loch Ness, 1996; Homegrown, 1998; Thanks of a Grateful Nation, 1998; Saving Private Ryan, 1998; Becker, 1998; Mumford, 1999; Fronterz, 2004; Our Fathers, 2005; The Moguls, 2005; Bye Bye Benjamin, 2006; Nobel Son, 2007; Mad Money, 2008; The Human Contract, 2009; The End of the Line, 2009. Address: c/o Josh Liberman, Creative Artists Agency, 9830 Wilshire Boulevard, Beverly Hills, CA 90212, USA.

DAR Imran Ahmad, b. 6 April 1983, Sopore Town, Kashmir State, India. Research Scholar. Education: MSc, Environmental Sciences, Grade 1, University of Kashmir, 2008. Appointments: Researcher, PhD in Environmental Sciences; Editorial Board member of 6 international journals; Referee to many international journals of repute. Publications: 15 articles in professional journals. Honours: Invited talk, Environmental Remote Sensing: Geomatic Based Natural Resources Disaster Mitigation and Management, 2010; Listed in international biographical dictionaries. Address: Department of Industries and Earth Sciences, The Tamil University, Thanjavur 613010, Tamilnadu, India. E-mail: wonder_env@yahoo.com

DAS Niranjan, b. 22 January 1945, Bhomradaha, Bangladesh. Teacher. m. Shila, 1 son, 1 daughter. Education: BSc, 1964; MSc, 1968; BEd, 1977; Puppetry in Education, Certificate Course, 1985; PhD, 2005. Appointments: Mathematics Teacher, Haldibari H S School, 1968-85; Assistant Headmaster, 1985-2002, Headmaster, 2002-03, Phansidewa H S School; Retired, 2005; Visiting Lecturer, Mathematics, Siliguri Institute of Technology, Siliguri, Darjeeling, West Bengal, 2005, 2006; Principal, Community College, Itanagar, Arunachal Pradesh, 2010; Professor, IMPS College of Engineering & Technology, Malda, West Bengal, 2011. Publications: Papers and articles in professional scientific journals. Honours: President, Bharatiya Jawnata Party, Haldibari, Cooch Behar, West Bengal; Established Ram Krishna Temple in rural Haldibari; Writer, Bengali textbooks. Address: Melarmath, PO Haldibari Dt, Cooch Behar, West Bengal, 735122, India. E-mail: biplab28@rediffmail.com

DASHDAMIROVA Asmar, b. 17 September 1981, Baku, Azerbaijan. Business & Marketing Manager. Education: BSc, Computational Mathematics and Cybernetics, Lomonosov Moscow State University. Appointments: BP pls, 2006-10; Microsoft Corp, 2010-12. Publications: Numerous interviews in key Azerbaijani media. Honours: Azerbaijan Medial Alliance State National Flag Award; Best Customer of Partner Subsidiary Cup, Microsoft; Annual Best Intellectual Gameshow Player.

DAŠIĆ Pedrag, b. 16 September 1958, Peć, Serbia. Professor of Information Scientific and Technical Systems. 1 son. Education: Graduate, Faculty of Mechanical Engineering, Priština, 1982; Master of Science, Faculty of Mechanical Engineering, Belgrade; ECDL Tester, 2005; ECDL Expert Tester, 2006. Appointments: Technological Designer of CNC Machines, 1982-1985, Research Assistant, 1985-88, Institute Industry "14 October", Kruševac, Serbia and Montenegro; Professor of Information Science and Technological Systems, High Mechanical School, Trstenik and High Technological School, Kruševac, Serbia and Montenegro 1988-; President of Organising Committee of the International Conference of RaDMI, 2001-2008. Publications: 300 scientific papers, 150 of them published abroad; 1 monograph; 7 books; 2 scripts; Editor of 18 proceedings; Over 10 scientific and research projects; 14 scientific software and 2 Web presentations. Honours: 2 innovations for improving production, Industry "14 October", Kruševac; 2nd Award, for scientific and technical creative work and innovations in Kruševac community, 1987; Editorial Board in 6 international journals. Memberships include: International Neural Network Society; European Neural Network Society; International Association for Statistic Computing; International Association for Management of Technology; European Association for Programming Languages and Systems; European Association of Software Science and Technology. Address: Ratka Pešića No 59, 37208 Čitluk-Kruševac, Serbia. E-mail: dasicp@yahoo.com Website: www.RaDMI.org/

DASTAGIRI Madiga Bala, b. 3 May 1963, Kurnool district, India. Senior Scientist. Education: BSc, Agriculture, 1985, MSc, Agricultural Economics, 1987, APAU, Hyderabad; PhD, Agricultural Economics, IARI, New Delhi, 1992. Appointments: Assistant Farm Management Specialist, 1995-96, Assistant Professor of Agricultural Economics, 1996-97, UAS, Dharwad Karnataka; Scientist, Agricultural Economics, 1997-99, Scientist (Senior Scale), 1999-2004, Senior Scientist, 2004-, NCAP, New Delhi. Publications: Numerous articles in professional journals including: Innovative Models in Horticulture Marketing in India, 2009; Investment, Value of output and Trade in Livestock Sector in India: Pre and Post WTO Era, 2010; Government Expenditure, Growth and Its Effect on Promoting Livestock GDP and Rural Poverty in India, 2010. Honours: Rashtriya Gaurav Award, 2010; Best Citizens of India Award, 2010; International Gold Star Award,

2010; India-International Achievers Award, 2010; Rajiv Gandhi Excellence Award, 2010; Vikas Rattan Award, 2010; Excellence in Economic Development Awards, 2011; Qualified, IUNUS Award, 2011; Listed in international biographical dictionaries. Memberships: Indian Society of Agricultural Economics; Agricultural Economics Research Association; Journal of Global Economy. Address: National Centre for Agricultural Economics and Policy Research, Library Avenue, Pusa, New Delhi 12, India. E-mail: dgiri_mb@yahoo.in

DATTA Dipankar, b. 30 January 1933, India. Physician. m. Jean Bronwen, 1 son, 1 daughter. Education: MBBS, Calcutta University, 1958; MRCP (UK), 1970; FRCP, Royal College of Physicians and Surgeons of Glasgow, 1980; FRCP, Royal College of Physicians of London, 1996. Appointments: Consultant Physician with special interest in Gastroenterology, 1975-97; Honorary Senior Clinical Lecturer in Medicine, 1984-97, Honorary Clinical Sub-Dean, Faculty of Medicine, 1989-97, Member of the Faculty of Medicine, 1989-95, Member of the Senate, 1991-94, Glasgow University; Member of the Lanarkshire Health Board, 1983-87; President, BMA, Lanarkshire, 1993-95; Chairman, Overseas Doctor's Association, Scotland, 1989-95; Member, General Medical Council, UK, 1994-99; Chairman, South Asia Voluntary Enterprise, 1994-; Director, British Overseas NGO's for Development, 1993-96. Memberships: Royal College of Physicians and Surgeons of Glasgow; Royal College of Physicians of London; Chairman, Scotland India Foundation. Address: 9 Kirkvale Crescent, Newton Mearns, Glasgow G77 5HB, Scotland.

DATTA Pran Gopal, b. 1 October 1953, Comilla, Bangladesh. Otolaryngologist. m. Joya Sree Roy, 1 son, 1 daughter. Education: MBBS, Chittagong Medical College; MCPS, FCPS,Bangladesh College of Physicians & Surgeons; MS, Odessa State Medical Institute, USSR; PhD, Kiev Scientific & Research Institute, USSR; MSc, University of Manchester, UK; FRCS, Royal College of Physicians and Surgeons, Glasgow. Appointments: Vice-Chancellor, Bangabandhu Sheikh Mujib Medical University, Dhaka. Publications: More than 50 publications in different journals of Pakistan, India, Russia & Bangladesh. Honours: Chandina Gold Award, Chandina Jubokalyan Samity; Bangabandhu Gold Award, Hamdard Foundation; Gold Award, Comilla Foundation; Gold Award, Bangladesh Medical Association, 2011. Memberships: Bangladesh Diabetic Association; Society of Assistance to Hearing Impaired Children; Bangladesh National Society for the Blind; many others. Address: Road 10/A, House 35, Dhanmondi Residential Area, Dhaka 1207, Bangladesh. E-mail: prangopal@gmail.com Website: www.prangopaldatta.com

DAUNTON Martin James, b. 7 February 1949, Cardiff, Wales. University Professor of History. m. Claire Gobbi, 7 January 1984. Education: BA, University of Nottingham, 1970; PhD, University of Kent, 1974; Litt D, Cambridge, 2005. Appointments: Lecturer, University of Durham, 1973-79; Lecturer, 1979-85, Reader, 1985-89, Professor of History, 1989-97, University College London; Convenor, Studies in History series, Royal Historical Society, 1995-2000; Professor Economic History, University of Cambridge, 1997-; Trustee, National Maritime Museum, 2002-10; Master, Trinity Hall, Cambridge, 2004-; President, Royal Historical Society, 2004-08; Syndic, 2006-, Chairman, 2008-, Fitzwilliam Museum; Member, Research Awards Committee, Leverhulme Trust. Publications: Coal Metropolis: Cardiff; House and Home in the Victorian City, 1850-1914; Royal Mail: The Post Office since 1840; A Property Owning Democracy?; Progress and Poverty; Trusting Leviathan; Just Taxes; Wealth and Welfare; State, Market and Society. Contributions to: Economic History Review; Past & Present; Business History; Historical Research; Charity, Self-Interest and Welfare in the English Past; English Historical Review; Twentieth Century British History; Empire and Others; Politics of Consumption; Organisation of Knowledge. Honour: Fellow of the British Academy, 1997; Honorary D. Lit (UCL), 2006; D Litt (Nottingham), 2010. Membership: Royal Historical Society. Address: Trinity Hall, Cambridge, CB2 1TJ, England.

DAVAAKHUU Sambuu, b. 2 June 1943, Govi-Altai province, Mongolia. Chemist; Pharmacist. m. Bazar, 2 sons, 1 daughter. Education: Education: Bachelor, Pharmacy, National Medical University of Mongolia, 1966. Appointments: Director, Pharmacy of Ulaanbaatar, 1966-75; Professor, Biochemistry, National Medical University of Mongolia, 1975-2004; Retired, 2004-. Publications: Precious Stone World, 2002; Bioenergy I, 2003; Miracles of Pyramids, 2005; Brain and Science, 2007; Bioenergy II, 2010; Bioenergy, III, 2010. Honours: Best Educator Award of Mongolia; Best Book of Mongolia, 2002 and 2007; Honorary Professor, National Medical University of Mongolia, 2004. Memberships: Academic Council Member, Mongolian Academy. E-mail: bazaramarsaikhan@yahoo.com

DAVEY-SMITH George, b. 9 May 1959. Professor of Clinical Epidemiology. Education: BA (Hons), Psychology, Philosophy, Physiology, 1981, MA, 1984, DSc, Epidemiology, 2000, Oxford University; MB BChir (distinction), 1983, MD, Epidemiology, 1991, Cambridge University; MSc (distinction), Epidemiology, London School of Hygiene & Tropical Medicine, 1988. Appointments: Clinical Research Fellow, Welsh Heart Programme, 1985-86; Wellcome Research Fellow, Clinical Epidemiology, University College and Middlesex School of Medicine, 1986-89; Lecturer, Epidemiology, London School of Hygiene & Tropical Medicine, 1989-92; Senior Lecturer, Public Health & Epidemiology, Honorary Senior Registrar, then Consultant in Public Health Medicine, Department of Public Health, University of Glasgow, 1992-94; Professor of Clinical Epidemiology, University of Bristol, Honorary Consultant, North Bristol NHS Trust, 1994-. Publications: Over 700 peer reviewed journal publications; Numerous editorials, commentaries, book chapters and reports, letters, abstracts and others. Honours: Honorary Professor, Department of Public Health, University of Glasgow; Visiting Professor, Department of Epidemiology and Population Health, London School of Hygiene & Tropical Medicine. Memberships: MFPHM, 1992, FFPHM, 1996, Faculty of Public Health Medicine; FRCP, Royal College of Physicians, 2005; FMedSci, Academy of Medical Sciences, 2006; Foreign Associate, Institute of Medicine, 2008. E-mail: zetkin@bristol.ac.uk

DAVID Arlette, b. 25 August 1964, Brussels, Belgium. Egyptologist; Lecturer; Researcher. 1 son, 1 daughter. Education: LLB, LLM, Université Libre de Bruxelles, Belgium, 1982-87; PhD, Egyptology (summa cum laude), Hebrew University of Jerusalem, Israel, 2000-03. Publications: Books and numerous articles in professional journals. Honours: Prize of the Red Cross, International Humanitarian Law Contest, 1986; Red Cross Max Schlomiuk Prize of the Authority for Research Students for PhD, 2003. Memberships: International Association of Egyptologists; Association Internationale pour l'Etude du Droit de l'Egypte Ancienne, Paris. Address: POB 3807, Qadima 60920, Israel. E-mail: msarlett@mscc.huji.ac.il

DAVID Joanna Elizabeth, b. 17 January 1947, Lancaster, England. Actress. m. Edward Fox, 1 son, 1 daughter. Education: Elmhurst Ballet School; Royal Academy of Dance; Webber Douglas Academy of Dramatic Art. Career: Theatre includes: The Family Reunion, The Royal Exchange, 1973; Uncle Vanya, Royal Exchange Manchester, 1977; The Cherry Orchard, 1983 and Breaking the Code, 1986, Theatre Royal Haymarket; Stages, Royal National Theatre, 1992; The Deep Blue Sea, Royal Theatre Northampton, 1997; Ghost Train Tattoo, Royal Exchange Theatre, 2000; Copenhagen, Salisbury Playhouse, 2003; The Importance of Being Earnest, Royal Exchange Theatre, 2004, A Voyage Round My Father, 2006; Television includes: War and Peace; Sense and Sensibility, Last of the Mohicans, Duchess of Duke Street, Rebecca, Carrington and Strachey; Fame is the Spur, First Among Equals; Paying Guests; Unexplained Laughter; Hannay; Children of the North; Secret Friends; Inspector Morse; Maigret; Rumpole of the Bailey; Darling Buds of May; The Good Guys; Sherlock Holmes; The Cardboard Box; Pride and Prejudice; A Touch of Frost; Bramwell; A Dance to the Music of Time; Midsummer Murders; Written in Blood; Dalziel and Pascoe; Blind Date; Heartbeat; The Mill on the Floss; The Dark Room; The Glass; The Way We Live Now; The Forsyte Saga; He Knew He Was Right; Brides in the Bath; Foyles War; Heartbeat; Monarch of the Glen; Falling; Bleak House; Films: Secret Friends; Rogue Trader; Cotton Mary, 1999; My Name was Sabina Spielrein; The Soul Keeper; The Tulse Hill Suitcase; These Foolish Things. Memberships: Trustee, Ralph and Meriel Richardson Foundation; Committee Member, The Theatrical Guild; Council Member, King George V Pension Fund; Board Member, Unicorn Children's Centre. Address: 25 Maida Avenue, London W2 1ST, England.

DAVIE Ronald, b. 25 November 1929, Birmingham, England. Child Psychologist. m. Kathleen, 1 son, 1 daughter. Education: BA Psychology (Hons), University of Reading, 1954; PGCE, University of Manchester, 1955; Diploma in Educational Psychology, University of Birmingham, 1961; PhD, University of London, 1970. Appointments: Various teaching, psychology and research posts, 1955-67; Co-Director, National Child Development Study and Deputy Director, National Children's Bureau, 1968-74; Director, NCB, 1982-90; Professor, Educational Psychology, University of Cardiff, 1974-81; Consulting and Forensic Psychologist, 1990-99; Member, SEN Tribunal, 1994-2003; Visiting Professor, University of Gloucestershire, 1997-2006. Publications include; Living With Handicap, 1970; From Birth to Seven, 1972; Children Appearing Before Juvenile Courts, 1977; The Home and The School, 1979; Street Violence and Schools, 1981; Children and Adversity, 1982; Understanding Behaviour Problems, 1986; Child Sexual Abuse, 1989; Childhood Disability and Parental Appeals, 2001; The Voice of the Child, 1996; Mobile Phone Usage in Pre-Adolescence, 2004. Honours: Hon DEd, CNAA, 1991; Visiting Professor, Oxford Polytechnic (later Oxford Brookes University), 1991-97; Hon Fellow, RCPCH, 1996; Hon DEd, University of West of England, 1998; Hon DLitt, University of Birmingham, 1999. Memberships: Fellow, British Psychological Society; Former President, National Association for SEN; Former Chairman, Association for Child Psychology and Psychiatry; Vice President, Young Minds. Address: Bridge House, Upton, Caldbeck, Wigton, Cumbria, CA7 8EU, England.

DAVIES Alan Roger, b. 6 March 1966, Chingford, Essex, England. Actor; Comedian; Writer. Education: BA (Hons), Drama, University of Kent, 1984-88. Career: Television: Jonathan Creek, BBC, 1996-; A Many Splintered Thing, BBC, 1998-2000; Bob and Rose, ITV, 2001; QI, BBC, 2003-; The Brief, ITV, 2004-; Roman Road, 2004; Marple: Towards Zero, 2006; The Good Housekeeping Guide, 2006; Radio: Alan's Big One, Radio 1, 1994-95; The Alan Davies Show, Radio 4, 1998. Publications: Regular contributor to The Times Sports Section; Urban Trauma, DVD/Audio Cassette; Live at the Lyric, DVD/Audio Cassette. Honours: Critics Award for Comedy, Edinburgh Festival, 1994; BAFTA Award for Best Drama for Jonathan Creek, 1997; Best Actor for Bob and Rose, Monte Carlo TV Festival, 2002; DLitt, University of Kent, 2003. Membership: Arsenal Season Ticket Holder. Address: c/o ARG, 4 Great Portland Street, London W1W 8PA, England.

DAVIES Andrew, b. 5 March 1949, London, England. Pianist; Brass Player; Consultant; Adjudicator. 1 adopted son. Education: Studied piano with Harry Isaacs, trombone and bass trumpet with Sidney Langston, Royal Academy of Music, London; Further piano study with Noel Lee, Paris. Career: Documentaries for Hong Kong Radio, Singapore Radio; Musical editor, Film on Liszt; Solo pianist; Piano Duo with the late David Branson; Ensemble recitals; Orchestral (brass) Early music ensembles, freelance orchestral player; Adjudicator, international competitions in Singapore, Hong Kong, Macau, China; BBC Young Musician of the Year; International Examiner until 1994; Masterclasses and private teaching throughout Taiwan, Hong Kong, Malaysia, Sabah, Sarawak, Indonesia, Sri Lanka, Thailand and India. Recordings: RCA, Gold Seal; Hummel, Spohr piano duets; Solo Spanish piano music, 1995; French repertoire piano duets on Nisus, 2005. Honours: Hon LCM, 1997; ARAM, 2001; Conferred HH Prince Regent Asmiruddin of Sulu by HRH Sultan Muhammad Yahcub S Alimuddin V, Sultan of Sulu & North Borneo Territories, 2010. E-mail: andrewdavi@yahoo.com

DAVIES James Atterbury, b. 25 February 1939, Llandeilo, Dyfed, Wales. Former Senior Lecturer; Writer. m. Jennifer Hicks, 1 January 1966, 1 son, 1 daughter. Education: BA, 1965; PhD, 1969. Appointments: Visiting Professor, Baylor University, Texas, 1981; Senior Lecturer, University College of Swansea, 1990-; Mellon Research Fellow, University of Texas, 1993; Senior Lecturer, UWS, 1990-98; Part-time Senior Lecturer, UWS, 1998-2001. Publications: John Forster: A Literary Life, 1983; Dylan Thomas's Places, 1987; The Textual Life of Dickens's Characters, 1989; Dannie Abse, The View from Row B: Three Plays (editor), 1990; Leslie Norris, 1991; The Heart of Wales (editor), 1995; A Swansea Anthology (editor), 1996; A Reference Companion to Dylan Thomas, 1998; Dylan Thomas's Swansea, 2000; A Swansea Anthology (editor) expanded edition 2006. Honours: Fellow, Welsh Academy, 1999. Address: 93, Rhyd-y-Defaid Drive, Sketty, Swansea SA2 8AW, Wales

DAVIES Jonathan, b. 24 October 1962. Rugby Player. m. (1) Karen Marie, 1984, deceased 1997, 2 sons, 1 daughter, (2) Helen Jones, 2002. Appointments: Rugby Union outside-half; Played for following rugby clubs: Trimsaran, Neath, Llanelli; Turned professional, 1989; with Cardiff, 1995-97; Played for Welsh national team (v England), 1985; World cup Squad (6 appearances), 1987; Triple Crown winning team, 1988; Tour New Zealand (2 test appearances), 1988; 29 caps, sometimes Captain; Also played for Barbarians Rugby Football Club; Rugby League career; Played at three-quarters; Widnes (world record transfer fee), 1989; Warrington (free transfer), 1993-95; Reverted to rugby union, 1995; Welsh national team; British national team; Tour New Zealand, 1990; 6 caps, former Captain; Hosts Rugby themed Chatshow, Jonathan,

2004. Publication: Jonathan, 1989. Honours: MBE, 1996. Address: C/o Cardiff Rugby Football Club, Cardiff Arms Park, Westgate Street, Cardiff, Wales.

DAVIES Laura, b. 5 October 1963, Coventry, England. Golfer. Appointments: Turned professional, 1985; Won Belgian Open, 1985; British Women's Open, 1986; US Women's Open, 1987; AGF Biarritz Open, 1990; Wilkinson Sword English Open, 1995; Irish Open, 1994, 1995; French Masters, 1995; LPGA Championship, 1996; Danish Open, 1997; Chrysler Open, 1998, 1999; WPGA Championship, 1999; Compaq Open, 1999; TSN Ladies World Cup of Golf (Individual), 2000; WPGA International Matchplay, 2001; Norwegian Masters, 2002; 2006. Represented, England, World Team Championship, Taiwan, 1992; Europe in Solheim Cup, 1990, 1992, 1994, 1996, 1998, 2000, 2002, 2003.; Women's World Cup of Golf, 2005, 2006, 2007. Publication: Carefree Golf, 1991. Honours: Rookie of the Year, 1985; Order of Merit Winner, 1985, 1986, 1992, 1996, 1999, 2004; MBE, 1988; Rolex Player of the Year, 1996; CBE, 2000. Address: c/o Women's Professional Golf European Tour, The Tytherington Club, Dorchester Way, Tytherington, Macclesfield, SK10 2JP, England.

DAVIES Mark Alexander Phillip, b. 25 May 1957, Hereford, England. Senior Lecturer. m. Isabel M Nunes-Oliveira, 1 son. Education: PhD, University of Leeds, 2003. Appointments: Lecturer, Marketing, Loughborough University, 1989-2000; Senior Lecturer, Marketing, School of Management and Languages, Heriot-Watt University, 2001-. Publications: More than 30 articles in refereed journals; 6 books and monographs; Numerous contributions to other edited works, conferences, workshops and official reports. Memberships: British Academy of Management; Chartered Institute of Marketing. E-mail: m.a.p.davies@hw.ac.uk

DAVIES Ryland, b. 9 February 1943, Cwym, Ebbw Vale, Wales. Opera and Concert Singer (Tenor). m. (1) Anne Howells (divorced 1981); (2) Deborah Rees, 1983, 1 daughter. Education: FRMCM, Royal Manchester College of Music, 1971. Debut: Almaviva, Barber of Seville, Welsh National Opera, 1964. Career: Glyndebourne Chorus, 1964-66; Soloist and Freelance, Glyndebourne and Sadler's Wells, Royal Opera House, Covent Garden, Welsh National Opera, Scottish Opera, Opera North; Performances in Salzburg, San Francisco, Chicago, New York, Hollywood Bowl, Paris, Geneva, Brussels, Vienna, Lyon, Amsterdam, Mannheim, Rome, Israel, Buenos Aires, Stuttgart, Berlin, Hamburg, Nice, Nancy, Philadelphia; Sang Lysander in A Midsummer Night's Dream at Glyndebourne, 1989, Tichon in Katya Kabanova at the 1990 Festival; Other roles have included Mozart's Ferrando and Don Ottavio, Ernesto, Fenton, Nemorino, Pelléas, (Berlin 1984), Oberon, (Montpellier, 1987); Tamino, Lensky, Belmonte and Enéas in Esclarmonde; Sang Podestà in Mozart's Finta Giardiniera for Welsh National Opera, 1994; Arbace in Idomeneo at Garsington, 1996; Season 1998 with Mozart's Basilio at Chicago; Concert appearances at home and abroad; Radio and TV Broadcasts; Appeared in films including: Capriccio, Entführung, A Midsummer Night's Dream; Trial by Jury, Don Pasquale; Die Entfuhrung aus dem Serail; Love of Three Oranges; Katya Kabanova; Recordings include: Die Entführung; Les Troyens; Saul; Così fan tutte; Monteverdi Madrigals, Messiah, Idomeneo, Il Matrimonio Segreto, L'Oracolo (Leoni), Lucia di Lammermoor, Thérèse, Judas Maccabeus, Mozart Requiem, Credo Mass, Mozart Coronation Mass and Vêspres Solenelle; Oedipus Rex; Il Trovatore; Don Carlo; Le nozze di Figaro; Esclarmonde. Honours include: Boise and Mendelssohn Foundation Scholarship, 1964; Ricordi Prize, 1964; Imperial League of Opera Prize, 1964; John Christie Award, 1965; Honorary Fellow, Royal Manchester College of Music, 1971; Fellow, Welsh College of Music and Drama, 1996. Address: c/o Hazard Chase Ltd, 25 City Road, Cambridge CB1 1DP, England.

DAVIS Andrew (Frank) (Sir), b. 2 February 1944, Ashridge, Hertfordshire, England. Conductor. m. Gianna, 1 son. Education: DMusB (Organ Scholar), King's College, Cambridge; MA (Cantab), 1967; With Franco Ferrara, Rome, 1967-68; DLitt (Hons), York University, Toronto, 1984. Debut: BBC Symphony Orchestra, 1970. Career: Pianist, Harpsichordist, Organist, St Martin-in-the-Fields Academy, London, 1966-70; Assistant Conductor, BBC Scottish Symphony Orchestra, Glasgow, 1970-72; Appearances, major orchestras and festivals internationally including Berlin, Edinburgh, Flanders; Conductor, Glyndebourne Opera Festival, 1973-; Music Director, 1975-88, Conductor Laureate, 1988-, Toronto Symphony; Conductor, China, USA, Japan and Europe tours, 1983, 1986; Principal Guest Conductor, Royal Liverpool Philharmonic Orchestra, 1974-77; Associate Conductor, New Philharmonic Orchestra, London, 1973-77; Conducted: La Scala Milan, Metropolitan Opera, Covent Garden, Paris Opera; Music Director, Glyndebourne, 1988-; Chief Conductor, 1989-2000, Conductor Laureate, 2000-, BBC Symphony Orchestra; Musical Director, Chicago Lyric Opera, 2000-; Conducted La Clemenza di Tito, Chicago, Oct 1989; Szymanowski King Roger, Festival Hall, London, 1990; Katya Kabanova and Tippett's New Year, (1990) Glyndebourne Festival; Opened 1991 Promenade Concerts, London, with Dream of Gerontius; Glyndebourne, 1992, Gala and The Queen of Spades; Conducted Elektra, at First Night, 1993 London Proms; Berg's Lulu, Festival Hall, 1994, returned 1997, for Stravinsky's Oedipus Rex, Persephone and The Rakes's Progress; Hansel and Gretel, 1996-97, and Capriccio, 1997-98, for the Met; Philadelphia, Chicago and Boston Orchestras, New York Philharmonic, and other leading American and European orchestras; Contracted to become Music Director and Principal Conductor of the Chicago Lyric Opera, 2000; Season 1999 with a new production of Pelléas et Mélisande at Glyndebourne and Tippett's The Mask of Time at the London Prom concerts. Compositions: La Serenissima (Inventions on a Theme by Claudio Monteverdi); Chansons Innocentes. Recordings include: All Dvorák Symphonies, Mendelssohn Symphonies, Borodin Cycle; Enigma Variations, Falstaff, Elgar; Overtures: Coriolan, Leonore No 3, Egmont, Fidelio Beethoven; Symphony No 10, Shostakovich, and violin concertos; Canon and other digital delights, Pachelbel; Cinderella excerpts; The Young Person's Guide to the Orchestra; Concerto No 2, Rachmaninov; The Planets, Gustav Holst; Symphony No 5, Horn Concerto, Piano Concerto No 2, Hoddinott; Brahms piano concertos; Nielsen Symphonies nos 4 and 5; Currently working on The British Line series with the BBC SO including the Elgar Symphonies and Enigma Variations, Vaughan Williams, Delius, Britten and Tippett; Operatic releases including Glyndebourne productions of Katya Kabanova, Jenufa, Queen of Spades, Lulu and Le Comte Ory. Honours: 2 Grand Prix du Disque Awards, Duruflé's Requiem recording with Philharmonic Orchestra; Gramophone of Year Award, 1987, Grand Prix du Disque, 1988, Tippett's Mask of Time; Royal Philharmonic Society/Charles Heidsieck Award, 1991; CBE, 1992; Royal Phiharmonic Society Award, Best musical opera performance of 1994, Eugene Onegin, on behalf of Glyndebourne Festival Opera, 1995; Gramophone Award for Best Video for Lulu; 1998 Award for Best Contemporary recording of Birtwistle's Mask of Orpheus; Critics Choice Award for Elgar/Payne

Symphony No 3; Knight Bachelor, New Years Honours List, 1999. Address: c/o Askonas Holt Ltd, Lonsdale Chambers, 27 Chancery Lane, London WC2A 1PF, England.

DAVIS Bryn Derby, b. 22 March 1938, Thurnscoe, Yorkshire, England. Professor Emeritus of Nursing Education. m. (1) Valerie, 1962, 2 sons, divorced, 1979, (2) Catherine, 1979, 1 son, 1 daughter. Education: RMN, 1961; SRN, 1965; RNT, 1969; BSc (Hons), Psychology, 1973; PhD, Social Psychology, 1983. Appointments: Principal Tutor, Holloway Sanatorium, Virginia Water, Surrey, 1970-73; DHSS, Research Fellow, London School of Economics, 1973-76; Deputy Director, Nursing Research Unit, University of Edinburgh, 1976-84; Principal Lecturer, Head of Nursing Research, Brighton Polytechnic, 1984-89; Professor and Dean, School of Nursing, 1989-99, Professor Emeritus of Nursing Education, 1999-, University of Wales College of Medicine, Cardiff; Elected Member, UKCC, 1998-2003; Academic and Professional Nursing Consultant, 1999-; Editor, Journal of Psychiatric and Mental Health Nursing, 1998-2004; Non-Executive Director, Pontypridd and Rhondda NHS Trust, 2001-2003. Publications: Research into Nursing Education (editor), 1983; Nurse Education: research and developments (editor), 1987; Caring for People in Pain, 2000; Various articles in nursing journals and many chapters in books by others on pain, culture, relationships and mental health. Honours: Visiting Professor of Nursing, NEWI, Wrexham; Visiting Professor of Psychology, University of Wales, Bangor; Lifetime Achievement Award, Mental Healtcare, 2008. Memberships: Royal College of Nursing; Fellow, Royal Astronomical Society. Address: 108 New Road, Brading, Sandown, Isle of Wight, PO36 0AB, England. E-mail: davisbryn3@aol.com

DAVIS Carl, b. 1936, New York, USA. Composer; Conductor. m. Jean Boht, 1971, 2 daughters. Education: Studied composition with Hugo Kauder and with Per Norgaard in Copenhagen. Career: Assistant Conductor, New York City Opera, 1958; Associate Conductor, London Philharmonic Orchestra, 1987-88; Principal Conductor, Bournemouth Pops, 1984-87; Principal Guest Conductor, Munich Symphony Orchestra, 1990-; Artistic Director and Conductor, Royal Liverpool Philharmonic Orchestra, Summer Pops, 1993-; Musical theatre: Diversions, 1958; Twists, 1962; The Projector and Cranford; Pilgrim; The Wind in the Willows, 1985; Alice in Wonderland, The Vackees; Incidental music for theatre includes: Prospect Theatre Co; The National Theatre; RSC. Ballet: A Simple Man, 1987; Lipizzaner, Liaisons Amoureuses, 1988; Madly, Badly, Sadly, Gladly; David and Goliath; Dances of Love and Death; The Picture of Dorian Grey; A Christmas Carol, 1992; The Savoy Suite, 1993; Alice in Wonderland, 1995; Aladdin, 2000; Pride and Prejudice: First Impressions, 2002. Music for TV includes: The Snow Goose, 1971; The World at War, 1972; The Naked Civil Servant, 1975; Our Mutual Friend, 1978; Hollywood, 1980; Churchill: The Wilderness Years, 1981; Silas Marner, 1985; Hotel du Lac, 1986; The Accountant, The Secret Life of Ian Fleming, 1989; Separate But Equal, The Royal Collection, 1991; A Year in Provence, Fame in the 20th Century: Clive James, 1992; Ghengis Cohn, Thatcher: The Downing Street Years, 1993; Pride and Prejudice, Oliver's Travels, Eurocinema: The Other Hollywood, 1995; Cold War, 1998-99; Goodnight, Mr Tom, 1998; The Great Gatsby, 2000; The Queen's Nose; An Angel for May; Book of Eve, Promoted to Glory, 2003; Mothers and Daughters, 2004; Garbo, I'm King Kong! The Exploits of Merian C Cooper, 2005; The Understudy, 2008. Operas for TV: The Arrangement; Who Takes You to the Party?; Orpheus in the Underground; Peace. Film music: The Bofors Gun, 1969; The French Lieutenant's Woman, 1981; Champions, 1984; The Girl on a Swing, Rainbow, Scandal, 1988; Frankenstein Unbound, 1989; The Raft of the Medusa, 1991; The Trial, 1992; Voyage, 1993; Widow's Peak, 1994; Topsy Turvy, 2000; series of Thames Silents including Napoleon, 1980, 2000; The Wind; The Big Parade; Greed; The General; Ben Hur; Intolerance; Safety Last; The Four Horsemen of the Apocalypse, 1992; Wings, 1993; Waterloo, 1995; Phantom of the Opera, 1996; 6 Mutuals (Chaplin Shorts), 2004; Cranford Chronicles, 2007. Concert works: Music for the Royal Wedding; Variations on a Bus Route; Overture on Australian Themes, Clarinet Concerto, Lines on London Symphony, 1984; Fantasy for Flute and Harpsichord, 1985; The Searle Suite for Wind Ensemble; Fanfare for Jerusalem, 1987; The Glenlivet Fireworks Music, Norwegian Brass Music, Variations for a Polish Beggar's Theme, Pigeons Progress, 1988; Jazz Age Fanfare, Everest, 1989; Landscapes, The Town Fox, A Duck's Diary, 1990; Paul McCartney's Liverpool Oratorio, 1991. Recordings: Christmas with Kiri, Beautiful Dreamer, 1986; The Silents, 1987; Ben Hur, A Simple Man, 1989; The Town Fox and Other Musical Tales, 1990; Leeds Castle Classics, Liverpool Pops at Home, 1995. Honours: Obie Prize Best Review, 1958; Emmy Award, 1972; BAFTA Awards, 1981, 1989; Chevalier des Arts et des Lettres, 1983; Honorary Fellowship, Liverpool University, 1992; Honorary DA, Bard, New York, 1994; Honorary DMus, Liverpool, 2002; Special Achievement Award for Music for Television and Film, 2003; CBE, 2005. Address: c/o Paul Wing, 3 Deermead, Little Kings Hill, Great Missenden, Buckinghamshire, HP16 0EY, England.

DAVIS Colin (Rex) (Sir), b. 25 September 1927, Weybridge, Surrey, England. Conductor. m. (1) April Cantelo, 1949, 1 son, 1 daughter, (2) Ashraf Naini, 1964, 3 sons, 2 daughters. Education: Royal College of Music. Career: Conductor Associate, Kalmar Orchestra and Chelsea Opera Group; Assistant Conductor, BBC Scottish Orchestra, 1957-59; Conductor, Sadler's Wells Opera House (ENO), 1959, Principal Conductor, 1960-65, Musical Director, 1961-65; Artistic Director, Bath Festival, 1969; Chief Conductor, BBC Symphony Orchestra, 1967-71, Chief Guest Conductor, 1971-75; Musical Director, Royal Opera House, Covent Garden, 1971-86; Guest Conductor, Metropolitan Opera, New York, 1969 (Peter Grimes), 1970, 1972; Principal Guest Conductor, Boston Symphony Orchestra, 1972-84; Principal Guest Conductor, London Symphony Orchestra, 1975-95; Bayreuth Festival, first British conductor, 1977 (Tannhäuser); Vienna State Opera, debut, 1986; Music Director and Principal Conductor, Bavarian State Radio Orchestra, 1983-92; Honorary Conductor, Dresden Staatskapelle, 1990-; Principal Conductor, London Symphony Orchestra, 1995; Principal Guest Conductor, New York Philharmonic Orchestra, 1998-2003; Has worked regularly with many orchestras in Europe and America; Season 1999 with the Choral Symphony at the London Prom concerts and Benvenuto Cellini and Les Troyens at the Barbican Hall, both with the London Symphony Orchestra. Recordings: Extensive recording with Boston Symphony Orchestra, London Symphony Orchestra, Dresden Staatskapelle, Bavarian Radio Symphony Orchestra. Honours: Officier dans L'Ordre National de Legion d'Honneur, 1999; Maximiliansorden, Bavaria, 2000; Best Classical Album and Best Opera Recording (for Les Troyens), Grammy Awards, 2002; Honorary DMus, Keele, 2002, RAM, 2002; South Bank Show Award, 2004. Address: c/o Alison Glaister, 39 Huntingdon Street, London N1 1BP, England.

DAVIS Geena, b. 21 January 1957, Wareham, Massachusetts, USA. Actress. m. (1) Richard Emmolo, 1981, divorced 1983, (2) Jeff Goldblum, divorced 1990, (3) Renny Harlin,

1993, divorced, (4) Reza Jarrahy, 2001, 2 sons, 1 daughter. Education: Boston University. Appointments: Member, Mt Washington Repertory Theatre Company; Worked as model; TV appearances incude: Buffalo Bill, 1983; Sara, 1985; The Hit List; Family Ties; Remington Steele; Secret Weapons, TV film; The Geena Davis Show, 2000; Commander in Chief, 2006; Films include: Tootsie, 1982; Fletch, 1984; Transylvania 6-5000, 1985; The Fly, 1986; The Accidental Tourist; Earth Girls Are Easy, 1989; Quick Change; The Grifters; Thelma and Louise; A League of Their Own; Hero; Angie; Speechless (also producer); Cutthroat Island; The Long Kiss Goodnight, 1996; Stuart Little, 1999; Stuart Little 2, 2002; Stuart Little 3: Call of the Wild (voice), 2005; Accidents Happen, 2009. Honours: Academy Award, Best Supporting Actress, 1989; Golden Globe Award, Best Actress in a TV Series, 2006. Address: C/o ICM, 8942 Wilshire Boulevard, Beverly Hills, CA 90211, USA.

DAVIS Steve, b. 22 August 1957, Plumstead, London, England. Snooker Player. m. Judith Lyn Greig, 1990, (divorced), 2 sons. Appointments: Professional snooker player, 1978; Has won 73 titles; In 99 tournament finals, as at 2002; Major titles include: UK Professional Champion, 1980, 1981, 1984, 1985, 1986, 1987; Masters Champion, 1981, 1982, 1988, 1997; International Champion, 1981, 1983, 1984; World Professional Champion, 1981, 1983, 1984, 1987, 1988, 1989; Winner, Asian Open, 1992, European Open, 1993, Welsh Open, 1994; Member, Board World Professional Billiards and Snooker Association, 1993-; TV: Steve Davis and Friends (chat show); They Think It's All Over (presenter), 2003-. Honours: BBC Sports Personality of Year, 1989; BBC TV Snooker Personality of Year, 1997; OBE, 2001. Publications: Steve Davis, World Champion, 1981; Frame and Fortune, 1982; Successful, 1982; How to Be Really Interesting, 1988; Steve Davis Plays Chess, 1996. Address: 10 Western Road, Romford, Essex, England.

DAWE (Donald) Bruce, b. 15 February 1930, Fitzroy, Victoria, Australia. Associate Professor; Poet; Writer. m. (1) Gloria Desley Blain, 27 January 1964, deceased 30 December 1997, 2 sons, 2 daughters, (2) Ann Elizabeth Qualtiough, 9 October 1999. Education: BA, 1969, MLitt, 1973, MA, 1975, PhD, 1980, University of Queensland; Hon. DLitt (USQ), 1995; Hon.DLitt (UNSW), 1997. Appointments: Lecturer, 1971-78, Senior Lecturer, 1978-83, DDIAE; Writer-in-Residence, University of Queensland, 1984; Senior Lecturer, 1985-90, Associate Professor, 1990-93, School of Arts, Darling Heights, Toowoomba. Publications: No Fixed Address, 1962; A Need of Similar Name, 1964; Beyond the Subdivisions, 1968; An Eye for a Tooth, 1969; Heat-Wave, 1970; Condolences of the Season: Selected Poems, 1971; Just a Dugong at Twilight, 1974; Sometimes Gladness: Collected Poems, 1978, 5th edition, 1993; Over Here Harv! and Other Stories, 1983; Towards Sunrise, 1986; This Side of Silence, 1990; Bruce Dawe: Essays and Opinions, 1990; Mortal Instruments: Poems 1990-1995, 1995; A Poets' People, 1999; The Chewing-Gum Kid, 2002; No Cat – and That's That!, 2002; Show and Tell, 2003; Luke and Lulu, 2004. Contributions to: Various periodicals. Honours: Myer Poetry Prizes, 1966, 1969; Ampol Arts Award for Creative Literature, 1967; Dame Mary Gilmore Medal, Australian Literary Society, 1973; Braille Book of the Year, 1978; Grace Leven Prize for Poetry, 1978; Patrick White Literary Award, 1980; Christopher Brennan Award, 1984; Philip Hodgins Medal for Literary Excellence, 1997; Order of Australia, 1992; Distinguished Alumni Award, UNE, 1996; Australian Arts Council Emeritus Writers Award, 2000. Memberships: Australian Association for Teaching English, honorary life member; Centre for Australian Studies in Literature; Victorian Association for Teaching of English, honorary life member; Patron, Speech and Drama Teachers' Association of Queensland; Patron, PEN (Sydney). Address: c/o Pearson Education, 95 Coventry St, South Melbourne, Australia, 3205.

DAWKINS (Clinton) Richard, b. 26 March 1941, Nairobi, Kenya. Zoologist; Professor of the Public Understanding of Science. m. (1) Marian Stamp, 19 August 1967, divorced 1984, (2) Eve Barham, 1 June 1984, deceased, 1 daughter, (3) Lalla Ward, 15 September 1992. Education: BA, 1962, MA, 1966, DPhil, 1966, Balliol College, Oxford. Appointments: Assistant Professor of Zoology, University of California at Berkeley, 1967-69; Fellow, New College, Oxford, 1970-; Lecturer, 1970-89, Reader in Zoology, 1989-95, Charles Simonyi, Professor of the Public Understanding of Science, 1996-, Oxford University; Editor, Animal Behaviour, 1974-78, Oxford Surveys in Evolutionary Biology, 1983-86; Gifford Lecturer, University of Glasgow, 1988; Sidgwick Memorial Lecturer, Newnham College, Cambridge, 1988; Kovler Visiting Fellow, University of Chicago, 1990; Nelson Lecturer, University of California at Davis, 1990. Publications: The Selfish Gene, 1976, 2nd edition, 1989; The Extended Phenotype, 1982; The Blind Watchmaker, 1986; River Out of Eden, 1995; Climbing Mount Improbable, 1996; Unweaving the Rainbow, 1998; A Devil's Chaplain, 2003; The Ancestor's Tale: A Pilgrimage to the Dawn of Life, 2004; The Greatest Show on Earth; The God Delusion; The Oxford Book of Modern Science Writing. Contributions to: Scholarly journals. Honours: FRS; Royal Society of Literature Prize, 1987; Los Angeles Times Literature Prize, 1987; Honorary Fellow, Regent's College, London, 1988; Silver Medal, Zoological Society, 1989; Michael Faraday Award, Royal Society, 1990; Nakayama Prize, Nakayama Foundation for Human Sciences, 1994; Honorary DLitt, St Andrews University, 1995; Honorary DLitt, Canberra, 1996; International Cosmos Prize, 1997; Honorary DSc, University of Westminster, 1997; Honorary DSc, University of Hull, 2001; Kistler Prize, 2001; Honorary DUniv, Open University, 2003; Honorary DSc, Sussex, 2005; Honorary DSc, Durham, 2005; Honorary DSc, Brussels, 2005; Shakespeare Prize, 2005. Address: c/o Oxford University Museum, Parks Road, Oxford, OX1 3PW, England.

DAWSON Patricia Vaughan, b. 23 January 1925, Liverpool, England. Artist; Poet. m. James N Dawson, 25 September 1948, 1 son, 2 daughters. Education: Croydon School of Art, 1941-45; Diploma, Industrial Design. Appointments: Ashfold School, 1947-48; Lecturer, Tate Gallery, London, 1963-66; Making relief paintings and preparing a film. Creative Works: Etchings in: La Bibliotheque Nationale, Paris, France; British Museum, and many UK museums. Publications: Poems and works represented in: New Education; Pictorial Knowledge; Still, New Knowledge; Observer; Guardian; Times Educational Supplement; The Artist Looks At Life; La Lanterne Des Morts; The Kiln; The Forge; Reliquaries; Wet Leaves; Relief Paintings from 1998; Films from 2009. Address: 701 Dolphin Square, London SW1V 3NP, England.

DAY Doris, b. 3 April 1924, Cincinnati, Ohio, USA. Singer; Actress. m. (1) Al Jorden, March 1941, divorced 1943, 1 son, (2) George Weilder divorced 1949, (3) Marty Melcher, 3 April 1951, deceased 1968. Career: Former dancer, Cincinnati; Singer, shows including: Karlin's Karnival, WCPO-Radio; Bob Hope NBC Radio Show, 1948-50; Doris Day CBS Show, 1952-53; Solo recording artist, 1950-; Actress, numerous films including: Tea For Two, 1950; Lullaby Of Broadway, 1951; April In Paris, 1952; Pajama Game, 1957; Teacher's

Pet, 1958; Pillow Talk, 1959; Midnight Lace, 1960; Jumbo, 1962; That Touch Of Mink, 1962; The Thrill Of It All, 1963; Send Me No Flowers, 1964; Do Not Disturb, 1965; The Glass Bottom Boat, 1966; Caprice, 1967; The Ballad Of Josie, 1968; Where Were You When The Lights Went Out, 1968; With Six You Get Eggroll, 1968; Own television series, The Doris Day Show, 1970-73; Doris Day And Friends, 1985-86; Doris Day's Best, 1985-86; TV special, The Pet Set, 1972. Honours: Winner (with Jerry Doherty), Best Dance Team, Cincinnati; Laurel Award, Leading New Female Personality In Motion Picture Industry, 1950; Top audience attractor, 1962; American Comedy Lifetime Achievement Award, 1991. Address: c/o Doris Day Animal League, 227 Massachusetts Avenue NE, Washington, DC 20002, USA.

DAY Elaine, b. 30 June 1954, Hendon, North London, England. Freelance Writer. m. David John Day, 1994, 1 daughter. Publications include: Natural Tranquillity, Crystal Pillars/Fossil Seas Poetry Book, A Celebration of Poets, The Star-Laden Sky, anthology, 1997; Light of the World, anthology, 1997; Beyond the Horizon, anthology, 1997; Poetry Now East Anglia, Acorn Magazine, The Secret of Twilight, A Quiet Storm, anthology, 1998; A Celebration of Friendship (anthology), A Celebration of Poets (anthology), 1999; Prayer for Jesus and other poems, People Who Counted, Praying in Poems, Let's Shout About It, 2000; Praise Poetry Book, Praise the Lord, 2001; Heaven & Earth, 2003; Poetry Comes Like Waves, 2005; History of Havering in Essex, 2007; 29 Short Stories, 2008; All Year Long, 2008; Rhyme and Reason (humour verse), 2009. Contributions to: Dogs Monthly Magazine; Old Yorkshire Magazine; Acorn Magazine; One Magazine; Day By Day Magazine; Forward Press; Freehand Magazine; Poetic Hour Magazine; Citizen Newspaper; Faith in Focus anthology; Gentle Reader Magazine; Animal Crackers Magazine; Science Friction anthology; Monomyth Magazine; Superfluity Magazine; The Snoring Cat Magazine; Linkway Magazine, International Poetry Institute of South Africa; BBC Children in Need Pamphlet, Rainstorms & Rainstorms Anthology, Small Press Poets Anthology, Roobooth Publications; Poetry Church, 2000; Book of Christian poetry, Knocking on Heaven's Door, Book of Christian poetry, Closer to Heaven, 2005. Honours: 7 Editors Choice Awards for Poetry; MENSA Certificate. Memberships: Imagine Writing Group; British Academy of Songwriters, Composers and Authors. Address: 141 Turpin Avenue, Collier Row, Romford, Essex RM5 2LU, England.

DAY William, b. 28 August 1946, Hove, England. Music Teacher. m. Education: Bassoon and flute studies, Royal College of Music, London, 1963-66. Appointments: Part time flute and bassoon teacher, Drayton Manor Grammar School, 1964-66; Principal bassoon, D'Oyly Carte Opera Company, 1966-70; Principal bassoon, London Festival Ballet, 1968; Freelance engagements as principal and sub-principal bassoon, New Cantata Chamber Orchestra, 1966-70; Bassoon, BBC Training Orchestra, Bristol, 1970; Flute and bassoon teacher, Wolverhampton Education Authority, 1970-71; Woodwind teacher, Darlington Education Authority, 1971-73; Principal flute, Mid-Sussex Sinfonia, 1973-74; Woodwind coach, Brighton Youth Orchestra, 1973-75; Part time teacher of student teachers, Brighton Teacher Training College, 1973-77; Woodwind teacher, many schools and sixth form colleges, Brighton area, 1973-86; Solo flute, Music Room, Royal Pavilion, Brighton, 1974; Flute teacher, Roedean School, 1976; Various concerts, New Cantata Soloists, 1977-79; Solo flute and bassoon, Cantilena Soloists Ensemble, 1975; Teacher, Oriel School, Ludlow and Grange House School, Leominster, 1987-89; Woodwind tutor, Llandovery College, South Wales, 1999-2001; Education Network, 2001-; Unaccompanied Solo Flautist (Hereford Cathedral, Ludlow Castle, Shrewsbury Flower Show, Ludlow Feathers Hotel, Malvern Garden Fair, and many other venues), 2004-. Memberships: Incorporated Society of Musicians. Address: 24 Llwynu Close, Abergavenny, Gwent, NP7 6BS, United Kingdom.

DAY-LEWIS Daniel, b. 20 April 1957, London, England. Actor. m. Rebecca Miller, 1996; 2 sons (1 by Isabelle Adjani). Education: Bristol Old Vic Theatre School. Career: Plays: Class Enemy, Funny Peculiar, Bristol Old Vic; Look Back in Anger, Dracula, Little Theatre, Bristol and Half Moon Theatre, London; Another Country, Queen's Theatre; Futurists, National Theatre; Romeo, Thisbe, Royal Shakespeare Company Hamlet, 1989; TV: A Frost in May; How Many Miles to Babylon?; My Brother Jonathan; Insurance Man; Films: My Beautiful Launderette; A Room with a View; Stars and Bars; The Unbearable Lightness of Being; My Left Foot, 1989; The Last of the Mohicans, 1991; The Age of Innocence, 1992; In the Name of the Father, 1993; The Crucible, 1995; The Boxer, 1997; Gangs of New York, 2002; The Ballad of Jack and Rose, 2005; There Will Be Blood, 2007; Nine, 2009; Lincoln, 2012. Honours: Academy Award for Best Actor, 1989, 2007, 2013; Screen Actors' Guild Award for Best Actor, 2003, 2012; BAFTA Awards, 1989, 2003, 2012. Address: c/o Julian Belfrage Associates, 46 Albemarle Street, London W1S 4DF, England.

DE Ashis Kumar, b. 3 December 1935, Calcutta, India. Medical Practitioner; Senior Consultant Physician. m. Nirmala. Education: MBBS, Calcutta University, 1959; MD (Medicine), Calcutta University, 1970; MRCP (UK), Royal College of Physician, 1978. Appointments: Resident House Officer, NRS Medical College, Kolkata, 1959-60; Medical Officer, E Railway, B R Singh Hospital, Kolkata, 1960-74, 1978-80; Senior House Officer and Registrar, various hospitals in England, 1974-78; Voluntary retirement from railways, 1981; Own practice as Physician and Cardiologist, 1981-88; Senior Consultant Cardiologist, KFS Hospital, Buraidah, Saudi Arabia, 1988-91; Senior Consultant Physician, General Medicine, Seven Hills Hospital, Visakhapatnam, India, 1992-. Publications: Several papers in different Indian medical journals. Memberships: Fellow, American College of Chest Physicians. Address: Flat 303, Kurupam Castle, Beach Road, Pedda Waltair, Visakhapatnam – 530 017, Andhra Pradesh, India.

DE BERNIÈRES Louis, b. 8 December 1954, Woolwich, London, England. Novelist. Education: Bradfield College, Berkshire; BA, Manchester University; MA, Leicester Polytechnic and University of London. Appointments: Landscape gardener, 1972-73; Teacher and rancher, Columbia, 1974; Philosophy tutor, 1977-79; Car mechanic, 1980; English teacher, 1981-84; Bookshop assistant, 1985-86; Supply teacher, 1986-93. Publications: The War of Don Emmanuel's Nether Parts, 1990; Señor Vivo and the Coca Lord, 1991; The Troublesome Offspring of Cardinal Guzman, 1992; Captain Corelli's Mandolin, 1994; Labels, 1997; The Book of Job, 1999; Gunter Weber's Confessino, 2001; Sunday Morning at the Centre of the World, 2001; Red Dog, 2001; Birds Without Wings, 2004; Notwithstanding: Stories from an English Village; A Partisan's Daughter. Contributions to: Second Thoughts and Granta. Honours: Commonwealth Writers Prizes, 1991, 1992, 1995; Best of Young British Novelists, 1993; Lannan Award, 1995. Membership: PEN. Address: c/o Secker and Warburg, Michelin House, 81 Fulham Road, London SW3 6RB, England.

DICTIONARY OF INTERNATIONAL BIOGRAPHY 36th EDITION

DE BHALDRAITHE Eoin, b. 28 May 1938, Cloonbook, Co Mayo, Ireland. Cistercian Monk. Education: St Jarlath's College, Tuam, Co Galway; Mount St Joseph Abbey, Roscrea, Co Tipperary; Sant' Anselmo, Rome, 1963-65. Appointments: Prior, 1994-2000, Abbot, 2000-06, Bolton. Publications: The High Crosses of Moone and Castledermot; Articles on interchurch marriage in Ireland; Several studies on The Rule of Saint Benedict; Mainly historical studies of Eucharist and Divine Office. Memberships: Irish Theological Association; Association of Irish Liturgists; The Patristic Symposium; Association Internationale d'Etudes Patristiques; English Language Consultation on the Liturgy. Address: Bolton Abbey, Moone, Co Kildare, Eire. E-mail: eoin@boltonabbey.ie

DE BONO Edward (Francis Publius Charles), b. 19 May 1933, Malta. Author; Physician; Inventor; Lecturer. m. Josephine Hall-White, 1971, 2 sons. Education: St Edward's College, Malta; BSc, 1953, MD, 1955, Royal University of Malta; MA, 1957, DPhil, 1961, Oxford University; PhD, Cambridge University, 1963. Appointments: Research Assistant, 1957-60, Lecturer, 1960-61, Oxford University; Assistant Director of Research, 1963-76, Lecturer in Medicine, 1976-83, Cambridge University; Honorary Director and Founding Member, Cognitive Research Trust, 1971-; Secretary-General, Supranational Independent Thinking Organisation, 1983-; Lecturer. Publications: The Use of Lateral Thinking, The Five-Day Course in Thinking, 1967; The Mechanism of Mind, 1969; Lateral Thinking: A Textbook of Creativity, The Dog Exercising Machine, 1970; Lateral Thinking for Management: A Handbook of Creativity, Practical Thinking: Four Ways to Be Right, Five Ways to Be Wrong, 1971; Children Solve Problems, PO: A Device for Successful Thinking, 1972; Think Tank, 1973; Eureka: A History of Inventions (editor), 1974; Teaching Thinking, The Greatest Thinkers, 1976; Wordpower: An Illustrated Dictionary of Vital Words, 1977; Opportunities: A Handbook of Business Opportunity Search, The Happiness Purpose, 1978; Future Positive, 1979; Atlas of Management Thinking, 1981; De Bono's Thinking Course, Learn to Think, 1982; Tactics: The Art and Science of Success, 1984; Conflicts: A Better Way to Resolve Them, Six Thinking Hats: An Essential Approach to Business Management from the Creator of Lateral Thinking, 1985; CoRT Thinking Program: CoRT 1-Breadth, Letters to Thinkers: Further Thoughts on Lateral Thinking, 1987; Masterthinker II: Six Thinking Hats, 1988; Masterthinker, Masterthinker's Handbook, Thinking Skills for Success, I Am Right, You Are Wrong: From This to the New Renaissance: From Rock Logic to Water Logic, 1990; Handbook for the Positive Revolution, Six Action Shoes, 1991; Serious Creativity: Using the Power of Lateral Thinking to Create New Ideas, Surpetition: Creating Value Monopolies When Everyone Else is Merely Competing, 1992; Teach Your Child How to Think, Water Logic, 1993; Parallel Thinking, 1994; Teach Yourself to Think, Mind Pack, 1995; Edward do Bono's Textbook of Wisdom, 1996; How to be More Interesting, 1997; Simplicity, 1998; New Thinking for the New Millennium, Why I Want to be King of Australia, 1999; The Book of Wisdom, The de Bono Code, 2000; How to Have a Beautiful Mind, 2004; Six Value Medals, 2005; H+ (plus): A New Religion, 2006; How to Have Creative Ideas; 2007; Think!: Before It's Too Late. Contributions to: Television series, professional journals, and periodicals. Honour: Rhodes Scholar; Honorary Registrar, St Thomas' Hospital Medical School, Harvard Medical School. Membership: Medical Research Society. Address: 12 Albany, Piccadilly, London W1V 9RR, England.

DE BONT Jan, b. 22 October 1943, Netherlands. Cinematographer and Director. Education: Amsterdam Film Academy. Appointments: Cinematographer: Turkish Delight; Keetje Tippel; Max Heulaar; Soldier of Orange; Private Lessons (American debut), 1981; Roar; I'm Dancing as Fast As I Can; Cujo; All The Right Moves; Bad Manners; The Fourth Man; Mischief; The Jewel of the Nile; Flesh and Blood; The Clan of the Cave Bear; Ruthless People; Who's That Girl; Leonard Part 6; Die Hard, Bert Rigby - You're A Fool; Black Rain; The Hunt for Red October; Flatliners; Shining Through; Basic Instinct; Lethal Weapon 3, 1992; TV Photography: The Ray Mancini Story; Split Personality (episode of Tales From the Crypt); Director, films: Speed (debut), 1994; Twister; Speed 2: Cruise Control (also screenplay and story); The Haunting; Lara Croft Tomb Raider: The Cradle of Life, 2003. Address: C/o David Gersh, The Gersh Agency, 232 North Canon Drive, Beverly Hills, CA 90210, USA.

DE BURGH Chris (Christopher Davison), b. 15 October 1948, Argentina. Singer; Songwriter. m. Diane Patricia Morley, 2 sons, 1 daughter. Education: Trinity College, Dublin. Career: Irish tour with Horslips, 1973; Solo artiste, 1974-; Album sales, 40 million to date; Sell-out concerts world-wide; Performances include: Carol Aid, London, 1985; The Simple Truth, benefit concert for Kurdish refugees, Wembley, 1991; Royal Albert Hall, London. Recordings: Singles include: Flying, 1975; Patricia The Stripper, 1976; A Spaceman Came Travelling, 1976; Don't Pay The Ferryman, 1982; High On Emotion, 1984; Lady In Red (Number 1, UK), 1984; Love Is My Decision, theme from film Arthur 2, 1988; Missing You, 1988; Albums: Far Beyond These Castle Walls, 1975; Spanish Train And Other Stories, 1975; At The End Of A Perfect Day, 1977; Crusader, 1979; Eastern Wind, 1980; Best Moves, 1981; The Getaway, 1982; Man On The Line, 1984; The Very Best Of Chris De Burgh, 1985; Into The Light, 1986; Flying Colours, 1988; From A Spark To A Flame - The Very Best Of Chris De Burgh, 1989; High On Emotion - Live From Dublin, 1990; Power Of Ten, 1992; This Way Up, 1994; Beautiful Dreams, 1995; The Love Songs, 1997; Quiet Revolution, 1999; Notes from Planet Earth – The Ultimate Collection, 2001; Timing is Everything, 2002; The Road to Freedom, 2004, Storyman, 2006; Footsteps, 2008. Honours: ASCAP Award, The Lady In Red, 1985, 1987, 1988, 1990, 1991, 1997; IRMA Awards, Ireland, 1985-90; Beroliner Award, Germany; BAMBI Award, Germany; Midem Trophy, France. Current Management: Kenny Thomson, 754 Fulham Road, London SW6 5SH, England.

DE CRESPIGNY (Richard) Rafe (Champion), b. 16 March 1936, Adelaide, South Australia, Australia. m. Christa Charlotte Boltz, 1 son, 1 daughter. Education: BA, 1957, MA, 1961, Cambridge University; BA, University of Melbourne, 1961; BA, 1962, MA, 1964, PhD, 1968, Australian National University. Appointments: Lecturer, 1965-70, Senior Lecturer, 1970-73, Secretary-General, 28th International Congress of Orientalists, 1971, Reader in Chinese, 1973-1999, Dean of Asian Studies, 1979-1982, Australian National University, Canberra; Master, University House, 1991-2001; Adjunct Professor of Asian Studies, 1999-. Publications: The Biography of Sun Chien, 1966; Official Titles of the Former Han Dynasty (with H H Dubs), 1967; The Last of the Han, 1969; The Records of the Three Kingdoms, 1970; China: The Land and Its People, 1971; China This Century: A History of Modern China, 1975, 2nd edition, 1992; Portents of Protest, 1976; Northern Frontier, 1984; Emperor Huan and Emperor Ling, 1989; Generals of the South, 1990; To Establish Peace, 1996; A Biographical Dictionary of Later Han to the Three Kingdoms, 2007; Imperial Warlord: a biography of Cao Cao,

2010. Membership: Australian Academy of the Humanities, fellow; Chinese Studies Association of Australia, President, 1999-2001. Address: Faculty of Asian Studies, Australian National University, Canberra 0200, Australia.

DE DUVE Christian René, b. 2 October 1917, Thames Ditton, Surrey, England (Belgian Citizen). Biochemist. m. Janine Herman, 1943, 1 son. Education: Graduated in Medicine, University of Louvain, Belgium, 1941. Appointments: Professor of Physiological Chemistry, 1947-85, Emeritus Professor, 1985-, University of Louvain Medical School, Belgium; Professor of Biochemical Cytology, 1962-88, Emeritus Professor, 1988-, Rockefeller University, New York City. Publications: A Guided Tour of the Living Cell, 1984; Blueprint for a Cell, 1991; Vital Dust, 1995. Honours: Prix des Alumni, 1949; Prix Pfizer, 1957; Prix Francqui, 1960; Prix Quinquennal Belge des Sciences Médicales, 1967; Gairdner Foundation International Award of Merit, Canada, 1967; Dr H P Heineken Prijs, Netherlands, 1973; Nobel Prize for Medicine, 1974; Honorary DSc, Keele University, 1981; Doctor honoris causa, Rockefeller University, 1997; Numerous other honorary degrees. Memberships: Royal Academy of Medicine, Belgium; Royal Academy of Belgium; American Chemical Society, Biochemical Society; American Society of Biological Chemistry; Pontifical Academy of Sciences; American Society of Cell Biology; Deutsche Akademie der Naturforschung, Leopoldina; Koninklijke Akademie voor Geneeskunde van België; American Academy of Arts and Sciences; Royal Society, London; Royal Society of Canada. Address: c/o Rockefeller University, 1230 York Avenue, New York, NY 10021, USA.

DE GIOVANNI-DONNELLY Rosalie Frances, b. 22 November 1926, Brooklyn, New York, USA. m. Edward F, 2 sons. Education: BA, Brooklyn College, 1947; MA, 1953; PhD, Columbia University, 1961. Appointments: Chief, Microbial Genetics Laboratory, 1962-67; Research Biologist, Food and Drug Administration, 1968-88; Professor, George Washington University Medical School, 1968-94. Publications: Articles to Scientific Journals. Honours: Food and Drug Award of Merit, 1970. Memberships: American Association for the Advancement of Science; American Society of Microbiology; Sigma Xi; Sigma Delta; Environmental Mutagen Society. Address: 1712 Strine Dr, McLean, VA 22101, USA.

DE HAMEL Christopher Francis Rivers, b. 20 November 1950. Fellow, Corpus Christi College, Cambridge. Education: BA, Otago University, New Zealand; DPhil, Oxford University. Appointments: Cataloguer, later Director, Western Manuscripts, Sotheby's, 1975-2000; Visiting Fellow, All Souls College, Oxford, 1999-2000; Donnelley Fellow Librarian, Corpus Christi College, Cambridge, 2000-. Publications include: A History of Illuminated Manuscripts, 1986, 2nd edition, 1994; Syon Abbey, The Library of the Bridgettine Nuns and their Peregrinations after the Reformation, 1991; Scribes and Illuminators, 1992; The Book: A History of the Bible, 2001. Honours: FSA; FRHistS; Hon LittD, St John's Minnesota, 1994; Hon LittD, Otago University, 2002; PhD, Cambridge, 2002. Membership: Roxburghe Club; Athenaeum; Grolier Club; Chairman, Association for Manuscripts and Archives in Research Collections. Address: Corpus Christi College, Trumpington Street, Cambridge CB2 1RH, England.

DE HAVILLAND Olivia Mary, b. 1 July 1916, Tokyo, Japan. Actress. m. (1) Marcus Aurelius Goodrich, 1 sons, (2) Pierre Paul Galante, 1955, divorced 1979, 1 daughter. Appointments: Actress, films including: Captain Blood, 1935; Anthony Adverse, 1936; The Adventures of Robin Hood, 1938; Gone With The Wind, 1939; Hold Back the Dawn, 1941; Princess O'Rourke, 1942; To Each His Own (Academy Award), 1946; The Dark Mirror, 1946; The Snake Pit, 1947; The Heiress (Academy Award), 1949; My Cousin Rachel, 1952; Not as a Stranger, 1954; The Proud Rebel, 1957; The Light in the Piazza, 1961; Lady in a Cage, 1963; Hush Hush Sweet Charlotte, 1964; The Adventurers, 1968; Airport '77, 1976; The Swarm, 1978; The Fifth Musketeer; Plays: Romeo and Juliet, 1951; Candida, 1951-52; A Gift of Time, 1962; TV: Noon Wine, 1966; Screaming Women, 1972; Roots, The Next Generations, 1979; Murder is Easy, 1981; Charles and Diana: A Royal Romance, 1982; North and South II, 1986; Anastasia (Golden Globe award), 1986; The Woman He Loved, 1987. Publications: Every Frenchman Has One, 1962; Contributor, Mother and Child, 1975. Honours: Numerous awards include: Academy awards, 1946, 1949; New York Critics Award, 1948, 1949; Look Magazine Award, 1941, 1946, 1949; Venice Film Festival Award, 1948; Filmex Tribute, 1978; American Academy of Achievement Award, 1978; American Exemplar Medal, 1980; Golden Globe, 1988; DRhc, American University of Paris, 1994. Address: BP 156-16, 75764 Paris, Cedex 16 France.

DE JAGER Cornelis, b. 29 April 1921, Den Burg, Netherlands. Professor, Space Research and Astrophysics. m. Duotje Rienks, 2 sons, 2 daughters. Education: Doctoral Degree, 1945, Doctor Degree, cum laude, 1952, University of Utrecht. Appointments: Assistant, 1946, Senior Scientist, 1955, Lecturer, 1957, Professor, 1960, University of Utrecht; Professor, University of Brussels, 1961-86. Publications: 35 books, 400 scientific publications, 200 popular publications. Honours: Gold Medal, RAS, London; Hale Medal, AAS; Dr Hon Causa, Paris, Wroclaw. Memberships: Several. Address: Molenstraat 22, 1791 DL Den Burg, Texel, The Netherlands. E-mail: cdej@kpnplanet.nl

DE KLERK Frederik Willem, b. 18 March 1936, Johannesburg, South Africa. Politician. m. (1) Marike Willemse, 1959, 2 sons, 1 daughter, (2) Elita Georgiadis, 1998. Education: Potchefstrom University. Appointments: In law practice, 1961-72; Member, House of Assembly, 1972; Information Officer, National Party, Transvaal, 1975; Minister, Posts, Telecommunications and Social Welfare and Pensions, 1978; Minister, Posts, Telecommunications and Sport and Recreation, 1978-79; Minister, Mines, Energy and Environmental Planning, 1979-80; Mineral and Energy Affairs, 1980-82; Internal Affairs, 1982-85; National Education and Planning, 1984-89; Acting State President South Africa, August-September, 1989; State President, South Africa, 1989-94; Executive Deputy President, Government of National Party, 1994-96; Leader of Official Opposition, 1996-97; Founder, F W De Klerk Foundation, 2000; Founding Member of GLF, Global Leadership Foundation, 2004; Former, Chairman, Cabinet and Commander-in-Chief of the Armed Forces; Former, Chairman, Council of Ministers. Publications: The Last Trek: A New Beginning (autobiography), 1999; Various articles and brochures for the National Party Information Service. Honours: Joint winner, Houphouet Boigny Prize (UNESCO), 1991; Asturias Prize, 1992; Liberty Medal (SA), 1993; Shared Nobel Prize for Peace with Nelson Mandela, 1993; Order of Mapungubwe, Gold, 2000. Address: PO Box 15785, Panorama, 7506, Cape Town, South Africa.

DE LA BILLIÈRE Peter (Sir), b. 29 April 1934, Plymouth, Devon, England. Retired Army Officer. m. Bridget Constance Muriel Goode, 1965, 1 son, 2 daughters. Education: Royal

College of Defence Studies, Staff College. Appointments: Joined King's Shropshire Light Infantry, 1952; Commissioned Durham Light Infantry; Served Japan, Korea, Malaya, Jordan, Borneo, Egypt, Aden, Gulf States, Sudan, Oman, Falklands; Commanding Officer 22 Special Air Service Regiment (SAS), 1972-74; General Staff Officer 1 (Directing Staff) Staff College, 1974-77; Commander, British Army Training Team, Sudan, 1977-78; Director, SAS, Commander, SAS Group, 1978-83; Commander, British Forces, Falklands and Military Commissioner, 1984-85; General Officer Commanding, Wales, 1985-87; General Officer Commanding South East District and Permanent Peace Time Commander, Joint Forces Operations Staff, 1987-90; Commander, British Forces, Middle East, 1990-91; Adviser to HM Government on Middle East Affairs; Current appointments: Director, Robert Fleming Holdings Ltd, 1977-99; Chairman, FARM Africa; Chairman, Meadowland Meats Ltd, 1994-2002; President, Army Cadet Force, 1992-99. Publications: Storm Command: A Personal Story, 1992; Looking For Trouble (autobiography), 1994; Supreme Courage: Heroic Stories from 150 Years of the Victoria Cross, 2004. Honours include: Several honorary doctorates; Order of Bahrain, 1st class, 1991; Chief Commander, Legion of Merit, USA, 1992; Meritorious Service Cross, Canada, 1992; Order of Abdul Aziz, 2nd class, Saudi Arabia, 1992; Kuwait Decoration, 1st class, 1992; Qatar Sash of Merit, 1992; KCB; KBE; DSO; MC and Bar; MSC DL. Address: c/o Naval and Military Club, 4 St James's Square, London SW1Y 4JU, England.

DE LA MARE Walter Giles Ingpen, b. 21 October 1934, London, England. Publisher. m. Ursula Steward, 1 son, 1 daughter. Education: MA (Oxon), Trinity College, Oxford, 1955-59. Appointments: National Service, Royal Navy, 1953-55; Midshipman, RNVR, 1954, Sub-lieutenant, 1955; Director, Faber and Faber Ltd, 1969-98; Director, Faber Music Ltd, 1977-87; Director, Geoffrey Faber Holdings Ltd, 1990-; Chairman, Giles de la Mare Publishers Ltd, 1995-; Literary Trustee of Walter de la Mare, 1982-; Founder Walter de la Mare Society, 1997. Publications include: The Complete Poems of Walter de la Mare (editor), 1969; Motley and Other Poems by Walter de la Mare (editor with introduction for Folio Society), 1991; Publishing Now (contributor of general chapter), 1993; Short Stories 1895-1926 by Walter de la Mare (editor), 1996; Short Stories 1927-1956 by Walter de la Mare (editor), 2001; Richard de la Mare at 75 (editor with Tilly de la Mare), 2004; Short Stories for Children by Walter de la Mare (editor), 2006; The Walter de la Mare Library, 2007. Memberships: Publishers Association: Chairman, University, College and Professional Publishers Council, 1982-84, Member of PA Council, 1982-85, Chairman of Copyright Committee, 1988, Chairman, Freedom to Publish Committee, 1992-95, 1998-2000; International Publishers Association Freedom to Publish Committee, 1993-96; Stefan Zweig Committee, British Library, 1986-95; Executive Committee, Patrons of British Art, Tate Gallery, 1998-2001; Translation Advisory Group, Arts Council of England, 1995-98; Club: Garrick. Address: PO Box 25351, London NW5 1ZT, England. E-mail: gilesdelamare@dial.pipex.com; www.gilesdelamare.co.uk

DE LA RENTA Oscar, b. 22 July 1932, Santo Domingo. Fashion Designer. (1) Françoise de Langlade, 1967, deceased 1983, (2) Anne de la Renta, 1989. Education: Santo Domingo University; Academia de San Fernando, Madrid. Appointments: Staff designer, under Cristobel Balenciaga, AISA couture house, Madrid; Assistant to Antonio Castillo, Lanvin-Castillo, Paris, 1961-63; Designer, Elizabeth Arden couture and ready-to-wear collection, New York, 1963-65; Designer and partner, Jane Deby Inc, New York, 1965; After her retirement, firm became Oscar de la Renta Inc, purchased by Richton International, 1969; Chief Executive, Richton's Oscar de la Renta Couture, Oscar de la Renta II, Oscar de la Renta Furs, Oscar de la Renta Jewelry, Member of Board of Directors, Richton Inc, 1969-73; Oscar de la Renta Ltd, 1973; Chief Executive Officer, 1973--; Couturier for Balmain, Paris, Nov, 1992-; Producer, 80 different lines including high-fashion clothing, household linens, accessories and perfumes for shops in USA, Canada, Mexico and Japan; Owner, Oscar de la Renta Shop, Santo Domingo, 1968-. Honours: Recipient, numerous fashion awards; Caballero, Order of San Pablo Duarte, Order of Cristobal Colon. Address: Oscar de la Renta Ltd, 550 7th Avenue, 8th Floor, New York, NY 10018, USA.

DE LA TOUR Frances, b. 30 July 1944, Bovingdon, Hertfordshire, England. Actress. m. Tom Kempinski, 1972, divorced 1982, 1 son, 1 daughter. Education: Lycée français de Londres, Drama Centre, London; With the Royal Shakespeare Company, 1965-71. Appointments: Stage appearances include: As You Like It, 1967; The Relapse, 1969; A Midsummer Night's Dream, 1971; The Man of Mode, 1971; Small Craft Warnings, 1973; The Banana Box, 1973; The White Devil, 1976; Hamlet (title role), 1979; Duet for One, 1980; Skirmishes, 1981; Uncle Vanya, 1982; Moon for the Misbegotten , 1983; St Joan, 1984; Dance of Death, 1985; Brighton Beach Memoirs, 1986; Lillian, 1986; Facades, 1988; King Lear, 1989; When She Danced (Olivier Award), 1991; The Pope and the Witch, 1992; Greasepaint, 1993; Les Parents Terrible (Royal National Theatre), 1994; Three Tall Women, 1994-95; Blinded by the Sun (Royal National Theatre), 1996; The Play About the Baby (Almedia Theatre), 1998; The Forest (Royal National Theatre), 1998-99; Antony and Cleopatra (RSC), 1999; Fallen Angels (Apollo), 2000-01; The Good Hope and Sketches by Harold Pinter, (Royal National Theatre), 2001-02; Dance of Death (Lyric), 2003; Films include: Our Miss Fred, 1972; To The Devil a Daughter, 1976; Rising Damp, 1980; The Cherry Orchard, 1998; Harry Potter and the Goblet of Fire, 2005; The History Boys, 2006. TV appearances include: Crimes of Passion, 1973; Rising Damp, 1974, 1976; Cottage to Let, 1976; Flickers, 1980; Skirmishes, 1982; Duet for One, 1985; Partners, 1986; Clem, 1986; A Kind of Living (series), 1987, 1988; Downwardly Mobile (series), 1994; Cold Lazarus, 1996; Tom Jones, 1997; Heartbeat, 1998; Born & Bread, 2003; Poirot, 2004; Waking the Dead, 2004; Sensitive Skin, 2005; New Tricks, 2006. Honours: Best Supporting Actress Plays and Players Award, 1973; 3 Best Actress Awards, 1980; Best Actress Standard Film Award, 1980; Best Actress SWET Award, 1983; Honorary Fellow, Goldsmiths College, University of London, 1999; Best Actress, Royal Variety Club, 2000; Tony Award for Best Actress in a Supporting Role, 2006. Address: c/o Kate Feast Management, 10 Primrose Hill Studios, Fitzroy Road, London, NW1 8TR, England.

DE MASSIS Alfredo, b. 16 June 1978, Atri, Italy. Assistant Professor. Education: MSc, Management Engineering, 2003; PhD, Management Engineering, 2007. Appointments: Deputy Director, Centre for Young & Family Enterprise (CYFE), Assistant Professor, Family Business & Entrepreneurship, University of Bergamo; Manager, SCS Consulting; Strategy Consultant, Accenture; Financial Analyst, Borsa Italiana (Italian Stock Exchange). Publications: Author, 3 books; More than 60 scientific publications in the field of family business and entrepreneurship. Honours: Several academic awards. Memberships: Several scientific associations including: Italian Family Enterprise Research Academy; European Council for Small Business & Entrepreneurship; EIASM;

IAMOT; and others. Address: University of Bergamo, Department of Economics & Technology Management, via G Marconi 5, 24044 Dalmine (BG), Italy. E-mail: alfredo.demassis@unibg.it Website: www.cyfe.unibg.it

DE MORNAY Rebecca, b. 29 August 1959, Santa Rosa, California, USA. Actress. m. Bruce Wagner, 1989, divorced 1991. Patrick O'Neal, 2 daughters. Education: in Austria; Lee Strasberg Institute, Los Angeles. Appointments: Film and television actress: Theatre includes: Born Yesterday, 1988; Marat/Sade, 1990; Films include: One from the Heart, 1982; Risky Business, 1983; Testament, 1983; The Slugger's Wife, 1985; Runaway Train, 1985; The Trip to Bountiful, 1985; Beauty and The Beast, 1987; And God Created Woman, 1988; Feds, 1988; Dealers, 1989; Backdraft, 1991; The Hand that Rocks the Cradle, 1992; Guilty as Sin, 1993; The Three Muskateers, 1993; Never Talk to Strangers, 1995; The Winner, 1996; Thick as Thieves, 1998; Table for One, 1998; The Right Temptation, 2000; Identity, 2003; Raise Your Voice, 2004; Lords of Dogtown, 2005; Wedding Crashers, 2005; Music Within, 2007; American Venus, 2007; Flipped, 2010. TV includes: The Murders in the Rue Morgue, 1986; By Dawn's Early Light, 1990; An Inconvenient Woman, 1992; Blind Side, 1993; Getting Out, 1994; The Shining, 1996; The Con, 1997; Night Ride Home, 1999; The Conversion (director), 1996; ER, 1999; Range of Motion, 2000; A Girl Thing, 2001; Salem Witch Trials, 2002; Manipulated, 2006; John from Cincinnati, 2007. Honours: Best Actress, Cognac Crime Film Festival, 1992.

DE NIRO Robert, b. 17 August 1943, New York, USA. Actor. m. Diahnne Abbott, 1976-88 (divorced) 1 son, 1 daughter, 2 children by Toukie Smith, Grace Hightower, 1997, 1 child. Career: Actor; Producer; Director; Films include: Trois chambres à Manhattan, 1965; Greetings, 1968; The Wedding Party, 1969; Sam's Song, 1969; Bloody Mama, 1970; Jennifer On My Mind, Born To Win, The Gang That Couldn't Shoot Straight, 1971; Bang the Drum Slowly, Mean Streets, 1973; The Godfather Part II, 1974; The Last Tycoon, Taxi Driver, 1900, 1976; New York, New York, 1977; The Deer Hunter, 1978; Raging Bull, 1980; True Confessions, 1981; The King of Comedy, 1983; Once Upon a Time in America, 1984; Falling in Love, 1984; Brazil, 1985; The Mission, 1986; Angel Heart, The Untouchables, 1987; Midnight Run, 1988; We're No Angels, Jacknife, 1989; Stanley and Iris, Goodfellas, Awakenings, 1990; Backdraft, Cape Fear, Guilty of Suspicion, 1991; Mistress, Night and the City, Mistress, The Godfather Trilogy: 1901-1980, 1992; Mad Dog and Glory, This Boy's Life, A Bronx Tale, 1993; Mary Shelley's Frankenstein, 1994; Heat, Casino, Le Cent et une nuits de Simon Cinéma, 1995; The Fan, Marvin's Room, Sleepers, 1996; Jackie Brown, Wag The Dog, Cop Land, 1997; Great Expectations, Ronin, 1998; Analyze This, Flawless, 1999; Men of Honor, Meet the Parents, The Adventures of Rocky & Bullwinkle, 2000; 15 Minutes, The Score, 2001; Showtime, City by the Sea, Analyze That, 2002; Godsend, Shark Tale (voice), Meet the Fockers, The Bridge of San Luis Rey, 2004; Hide and Seek, 2005; The Good Shepherd, Chaos, King Arthur and the Invisibles (voice), 2006; Stardust, 2007; What Just Happened, 2008, Righteous Kill, 2008; Everybody's Fine, 2009. Honours include: Commander, Ordre des Arts et des Lettres; Academy Award, Best Supporting Actor, 1974; Academy Award, Best Actor, 1980. Address: CAA, 9830 Wilshire Boulevard, Beverly Hills, CA 90212, USA.

DE PALMA Brian, b. 11 September 1940, Newark, New Jersey, USA. Film Director. m. Nancy Allan 1979 (divorced), Gale Ann Hurd, 1991, (divorced) 1 daughter, Darnell Gregoria De Palma, 1995 (divorced), 1 child. Education: Sarah Lawrence College, Bronxville; Columbia University. Appointments: Director: (short films) Icarus, 1960; 660124: The Story of an IBM Card, 1961; Wotan's Wake, 1962; (feature length) The Wedding Party, 1964; The Responsive Eye (documentary), 1966; Murder à la Mod, 1967; Greetings, 1968; Dionysus in '69 (co-director), 1969; Hi Mom!, 1970; Get to Know Your Rabbit, 1970; Sisters, 1972; Phantom of the Paradise, 1974; Obsession, 1975; Carrie, 1976; The Fury, 1978; Home Movies, 1979; Dressed to Kill, 1980; Blow Out, 1981; Scarface, 1983; Body Double, 1984; Wise Guys, 1985; The Untouchables, 1987; Casualties of War, 1989; Bonfire of the Vanities, 1990; Raising Cain, 1992; Carlito's Way, 1993; Mission Impossible, 1996; Snake Eyes, 1998; Mission to Mars, 2000; Femme Fatale, 2002; The Black Dahlia, 2006; Redacted, 2007; Sisters, 2007; Capone Rising, 2008. Address: Paramount Pictures, Lubitsch Annex #119, 555 Melrose Avenue #119, W Hollywood, CA 90038, USA.

DE SARAM Rohan, b. 9 March 1939, Sheffield, Yorkshire, England. Cellist. m. Rosemary, 1 son, 1 daughter. Education: Studied in Ceylon, with Gaspar Cassado in Florence and with Casals in Puerto Rico; Further study with John Barbirolli. Career: Gave recitals and concerts in Europe; US debut with New York Philharmonic, Carnegie Hall, 1960; Further concerts in Canada, USSR, Australia and Asia; As a soloist in addition to standard repertoire has worked personally with Kodály, Walton, Shostakovich; Premieres of works by Pousseur and composers of the younger generation; Has taught at Trinity College of Music; Member, Arditti Quartet (repertoire includes works by Boulez, Carter, Ferneyhough, Henze, Ligeti and many other living composers); Has also premiered works by Böse, Britten, Bussotti, Cage, Davies, Glass, Gubaidulina, Hindemith, Kagel, Nancarrow, Rihm and Schnittke, with Arditti Quartet; As soloist has premiered Kottos for solo cello by Xenakis, Ligeti's Racine 19 and Berio's Il Ritorno degli Snovidenia for cello and orchestra; Played in the Russian Spring series at South Bank, May 1991, Quartets by Rozlavets, Schnittke and Firsova; Founder, de Saram Clarinet Trio and a duo with his brother Druvi; Interested in the music of his native Sri Lanka and plays the Kandyan drum. Honours: Suggia Award, 1957; Ernst von Siemens Prize, 1999. Address: 20 St Georges Avenue, London N7 0HD, England. E-mail: rosiedesaram@hotmail.com

DE SAVORGNANI Adriane Aldrich, b. 17 December 1940, Boston, Massachusetts, USA. Nurse; Naval Medical Administrator. m. Luciano de Savorgnani, deceased, 1 son, 2 daughters. Education: AB, 1962, Radcliffe College, Cambridge, Massachusetts; Diploma, Coordinated Program, Radcliffe College and Massachusetts General Hospital General Hospital School of Nursing, Boston, Massachusetts, 1965; MPH, University of Hawaii School of Public Health, Honolulu, Hawaii, 1974; DBA, Nova University, Fort Lauderdale, Florida, USA, 1992. Appointments: Numerous nursing and executive medicine appointments in the USA and Europe, including, Charge Nurse Emergency Room, Outpatient Care Co-ordinator, Inpatient Care Co-ordinator, US Naval Hospital, Naples, Italy, 1979-83; Head, Health Care Plans, Special Projects, Head, Preventive Medicine and Health Promotion, Bureau of Medicine and Surgery, Washington, DC, 1989-92; Executive Officer, Naval Hospital, Lemoore, California, USA, 1995-98; Commanding Officer, US Naval Medical Clinics, United Kingdom, 1998-2001; Head, Clinical Plans and Management Division, and Assistant Deputy Chief, BUMED Medical Operations Support (Acting), Bureau of Medicine and Surgery, Washington, DC, 2001-03; Retired from Navy, 2003; Administrative Assistant,

US Defense Attache Office, American Embassy, London. Publications: Numerous papers and articles in nursing and health care administration journals, such as Midwest Business Administration Association Proceedings; Military Medicine; Navy Medicine; The Nursing Spectrum; Caring; Journal of Nursing Administration; The Case Manager. Honours: Legion of Merit; Meritorious Service Medal (5 times awarded); Navy Commendation Medal (twice awarded); National Defense Service Medal (one star); Global War on Terrorism Service Medal; Volunteer Service Medal; Navy and Marine Corps Overseas Service Ribbon (7 stars); Incentive Award, 2007, 2009, 2010; Quality Step Increase Award, 2008, 2010. Memberships: Life Member, Association of Military Surgeons of the United States; Fellow, American College of Healthcare Executives; Member: American Nurses Association; American Public Health Association; Academy of Management; Sigma Theta Tau International; Vice President, The Scholarship Society for Nurses, Midwives and Allied Health Professionals; Recertified in Advanced Nursing Administration; Vice President, England Honour Society (Nursing). Address: 14 Bardsley Lane, Greenwich, London SE10 9RF, United Kingdom.

DE SILVA JAYASURIYA Shihan, b. 8 September 1953, Colombo, Sri Lanka. Economist; Linguist; Ethnomusicologist. m. Hemal Jayasuriya, 1 son. Education: BSc (Hons), Economics, 1993, MSc, Finance, 1995, University of London; PhD, Linguistics, University of Westminster, 2004. Appointments: Research Associate, King's College, London, University of London, 2002-; Senior Fellow, Institute of Commonwealth Studies, University of London, 2007-; Adviser, International Scientific Committee, Member of Bureau, UNESCO Slave Route Project, 2009-; Rapporteur, UNESCO Slave Route Project (Paris), 2009-11. Publications: Tagus to Taprobane: Portuguese Impact on the Socioculture of Sri Lanka for 1505 AD, 2001; Indo-Portuguese of Ceylon: A Contact Language, 2001; An Anthology of Indo-Portuguese Verse, 2001; African Diaspora in the Indian Ocean, 2003; Uncovering the History of Africans in Asia, 2008; The Portuguese in the East: A Cultural History of a Maritime Trading Empire, 2008; African Identity in Asia: Cultural Effects of Forced Migration, 2008; The African Diaspora in Asian Trade Routes and Cultural Memories, 2010. Honours: Elected Fellow, Royal Asiatic Society of Great Britain and Ireland, 2005-; Nominated Key Figure in Creole Studies, University of Warwick, UK; Adviser, Editorial Board, African Diasporas and Transnationalism, Brill, Netherlands; Adviser, Editorial Board, An Encyclopaedia of the African Diaspora, ABC-CLIO, USA; Member, Editorial Board, Information, Society and Justice, London Metropolitan University, UK. Memberships: Co-founder, The African Diaspora in Asia; International Advisory Board, Centre for Research on Slavery and Indenture, Mauritius; Examiner, Commonwealth Essay Competition. Address: Institute of Commonwealth Studies, Senate House, Malet Street, London WC1E 7HU, England. E-mail: shihan.desilva@sas.ac.uk

DE SOUSA Alice, b. 11 January 1966, Portugal. Actress; Producer; Artistic Director. Education: BA, Honours, EEC Law, 1st Class, 1995; MA, Portuguese Studies, 1997. Career: Numerous roles in television, radio and film productions; Lead roles in over 30 productions, including Hermione, The Winter's Tale; Millamant, The Way of the World; Elvira, Blithe Spirit; Producer of more than 60 theatre productions, including: Never Nothing From No One, Hamlet, Company, Pymaglion, Richard III, You're Gonna Love Tomorrow, Hedda Gabler, Peep Show, Cousin Basillio; Shadows on the Sun; The Importance of Being Earnest, Three Sisters, The White Devil, 'Tis Pity She's a Whore, The Ruffian on the Stair and The Erpingham Camp, The Maias, Ines de Castro, King Lear, Absent Friends, A Doll's House, and The Heiress of the Cane Fields. Address: Greenwich Playhouse, 189 Greenwich High Road, London, SE10 8JA, England.

DE VILLIERS François Pierre Rousseau, b. 10 May 1950, Namibia. Professor of Paediatrics. m. (1) J Gai, deceased 2001, 1 son, 1 daughter (2) Mariana Catharina, 2004. Education: MBChB, 1974; BA, 1983; MMed, 1987; PhD, 1990; Lic Mus (UNISA), 2000; FACP, 2000; FCPaed (SA), 2001; FCFP (SA), 2007. Appointments: Professor and Chair, Paediatrics, 1994, Deputy Dean (Research), 1997-2001, Deputy Dean (Academic Matters), 2004-06, Medical University of South Africa; Director, School of Medicine, 2010; Curriculum Guardian, 2010-. Publications: Book: Practical Management of Paediatric Emergencies, 4th Edition, 2004; Practical Management of Paediatric Emergences, 2008; Numerous articles in professional journals. Honour: Research Excellence Award, Medunsa, 1998; Research Excellence Award for Senior Researcher, Medunsa, 2001. Memberships: New York Academy of Sciences; International Society for the Study of Paediatric and Adolescent Diabetes; American College of Physicians. Address: PO Box 480, Medunsa 0204, South Africa.

DEAN Christopher, b. 27 July 1958, Nottingham, England. Ice Skater. m. (1) Isabelle Duchesnay, 1991, divorced, 1993, (2) Jill Ann Trenary, 1994, 2 sons. Appointments: Police Constable, 1974-80; British Ice Dance Champion (with Jayne Torvill), 1978-83, 1993; European Ice Dance Champion (with Jayne Torvill), 1981, 1982, 1984, 1994; World Ice Dance Champion (with Jayne Torvill), 1981-84; World professional Champions, 1984-85, 1990, 1995-96; Choreographed Encounters for English National Ballet, 1996; Stars on Ice, USA, 1998-99, 1999-2000; Ice Dance: World tours with own and international companies of skaters, 1985, 1988, 1994, 1997, tours of Australia and New Zealand, 1984, 1991, UK, 1992, Japan, 1996, USA and Canada, 1997-98. Publications: Torvill and Dean's Face the Music and Dance (with Jayne Torvill), 1993; Torvill and Dean: An Autobiography (with Jayne Torvill), 1994; Facing the Music (with Jayne Torvill), 1996. Honours: BBC Sportsview Personality of the Year (with Jayne Torvill), 1983-84; Honorary MA, 1994; OBE, 1999. Address: c/o Sue Young, PO Box 32, Heathfield, East Sussex, TN21 0BW, England.

DEANE Seamus (Francis), b. 9 February 1940, Derry City, Northern Ireland. Professor of Irish Studies; Writer; Poet. m. Marion Treacy, 19 August 1963, 3 sons, 1 daughter. Education: BA, Honours, 1st Class, 1961, MA, 1st Class, 1963, Queen's University, Belfast; PhD, Cambridge University, 1968. Appointments: Visiting Fulbright and Woodrow Wilson Scholar, Reed College, Oregon, 1966-67; Visiting Lecturer, 1967-68, Visiting Professor, 1978, University of California at Berkeley; Professor of Modern English and American Literature, University College, Dublin, 1980-93; Walker Ames Professor, University of Washington, Seattle, 1987; Julius Benedict Distinguished Visiting Professor, Carleton College, Minnesota, 1988; Keough Professor of Irish Studies, University of Notre Dame, Indiana, 1993-. Publications: Fiction: Reading in the Dark, 1996. Poetry: Gradual Wars, 1972; Rumours, 1977; History Lessons, 1983; Selected, 1988. Non-Fiction: Celtic Revivals: Essays in Modern Irish Literature, 1880-1980, 1985; A Short History of Irish Literature, 1986, reissued, 1994; The French Revolution and Enlightenment in England, 1789-1832, 1988; Strange Country: Ireland, Modernity and Nationhood, 1790-1970, 1997; Foreign Affections: Essays on Edmund Burke, 2005.

Editor: The Adventures of Hugh Trevor by Thomas Holcroft, 1972; The Sale Catalogues of the Libraries of Eminent Persons, Vol IX, 1973; Nationalism, Colonialism and Literature, 1990; The Field Day Anthology of Irish Writing, 3 volumes, 1991; Penguin Twentieth Century Classics: James Joyce, 5 volumes, 1993; Field Day Review 1, 2005. Honours: AE Memorial for Literature, 1973; American-Irish Fund, Literature, 1989; Guardian Fiction Prize, 1997; Irish Times International Fiction Award, 1997; Irish Times Fiction Award, 1997; London Weekend Television South Bank Award for Literature, 1997; Ruffino Antico-Fattore International Literature Award, Florence, 1998; Honorary DLitt, Ulster, 1999. Memberships: Aosdana (Irish Artists' Council); Field Day Theatre and Publishing Company, director; Royal Irish Academy. Address: Institute of Irish Studies, 1145 Flanner Hall, University of Notre Dame, IN 46556, USA.

DEARDEN James Shackley, b. 9 August 1931, Barrow-in-Furness, England. Appointment: Curator, Ruskin Galleries, Bembridge School, Isle of Wight and Brantwood, Coniston, 1957-96. Publications: The Professor: Arthur Severn's Memoir of Ruskin, 1967; A Short History of Brantwood, 1967; Iteriad by John Ruskin (editor), 1969; Facets of Ruskin, 1970, Japanese edition, 2001; Ruskin and Coniston (with K G Thorne), 1971; John Ruskin, 1973, 2nd edition, 1981, Japanese edition, 1991, enlarged edition, 2004; Turner's Isle of Wight Sketch Book, 1979; John Ruskin and Les Alpi, 1989; John Ruskin's Camberwell, 1990; A Tour to the Lakes in Cumberland: John Ruskin's Diary for 1830 (editor), 1990; John Ruskin and Victorian Art, 1993; Ruskin, Bembridge and Brantwood, 1994; Hare Hunting on the Isle of Wight, 1996; John Ruskin, a life in pictures, 1999; King of the Golden River by John Ruskin (editor), 1999; Brantwood: The Story of John Ruskin's Coniston Home, 2009; Further Facets of Ruskin, 2009. Contributions to: Book Collector; Connoisseur; Apollo; Burlington; Bulletin of John Rylands Library; Country Life; Ruskin Newsletter (editor); Ruskin Research Series (general editor); Journal of Pre-Raphaelite Studies; The Companion; Ruskin Programme Bulletin; Turner Society News; Whitehouse Edition of Ruskin's Works (joint general editor); John Ruskin's Guild of St George, 2010; Contributions to Ruskin Review & Bulletin. Honour: Hon D Litt (University of Lancaster), 1998. Memberships: Ruskin Society; Turner Society; Companion of the Guild of St George, Past Master and Past Director for Ruskin Affairs; Old Bembridgians Association, past president; Isle of Wight Foot Beagles, former Master and President; Friends of Ruskin's Brantwood, vice president. Address: 4 Woodlands, Foreland Road, Bembridge, Isle of Wight, England.

DEARLOVE Richard Billing (Sir), b. 23 January 1945, Cornwall, England. Master, Pembroke College, Cambridge. m. Rosalind, 2 sons, 1 daughter. Education: MA, Queens' College Cambridge. Appointments: Entered Foreign Office, 1966; Nairobi, 1968-71; Prague, 1973-76; Foreign and Commonwealth Office, 1976-80; First Secretary Paris, 1980-84; Foreign and Commonwealth Office, 1984-87; Counsellor, UKMIS Geneva, 1987-91; Washington, 1991-93; Director, Personnel and Administration, 1993-94, Director, Operations, 1994-99, Assistant Chief, 1998-99, Chief, 1999-2004, Secret Intelligence Service; Master of Pembroke College, Cambridge, 2004-; Trustee, Kent School, Connecticut, USA, 2001-; Advisor to The Monitor Group, 2004-; International Advisory Board, AIG, 2005-10; Chairman of Ascot Underwriting, 2006-; Chairman of Trustees, Cambridge Union Society. Honours: OBE, 1984; KCMG, 2001; Honorary Dr of Law, Exeter. Address: Master's Lodge, Pembroke College, Cambridge, CB2 1RF, England.

DEB Suash, b. 26 October 1960, Karimganj, Assam, India. Researcher; Educator. Education: BE, Mechanical Engineering, Jadavpur University, Calcutta, 1984; MTech, Computer Science, University of Calcutta, 1987; Postgraduate, Computer Science, Stanford University, USA, 1991. Appointments: Trainee Engineer, CESC Ltd, Calcutta, 1984-85; Systems Executive, Webel Computer Ltd, Calcutta, 1987-88; Research Scientist, National Centre for Knowledge Based Computing, Calcutta, 1988-1997; Director, Global Vision, 1998-2002; Associate Professor, Asia-Pacific International University, Calcutta, 2003-06; Professor, National Institute of Science and Technology, Berhampore, 2004-08, CV Raman College of Engineering, Bhubaneswar, 2008-. Honours: Asian Expert Consultant, ARPA, Department of Defense, Federal Government of USA, 1996; Guest of Honour, International Conference on Advanced Robotics, Intelligent Automation, Vienna, Austria, 1996; Outstanding Achievement Medal, IBC, 1998; Certificate of Appreciation, IBC, 2001; General Chair, World Congress on Nature & Biologically Inspired Computing, Coimbatore, 2009; General Chair, International Conference on Natural Computing, Cochin, 2009; Bharat Excellence Award, 2009; Jewel of India Gold Award, 2010; Rising Personalities of India Award, 2010; General Chair, International Conference on Information Technology & Business Intelligence, Nagpur, General Chair, International Conference on Nano Science, Technology & Societal Implications, Bhubaneswar, 2011, Program Chair, 3rd International Conference on Data Mining and Intelligent Information Technology Applications, Macau, 2011, General Chair, International Conference on Computer Modeling & Simulations, Mumbai, 2011, Conference Chair, International Conference on Computer Technology & Science, New Delhi, 2012; Conference Chair, International Conference on Intelligent Network and Computing, New Delhi, 2012; Conference Chair, International Conference on Future Information Technology, Cochin, 2012; Conference Chair, 5th International Conference on Computer & Electrical Engineering, Cochin, 2012; President, International Neural Network Society (INNS) India Regional Chapter, 2010-, Secretary IEEE Computational Intelligence Society, Calcutta chapter, 2012-, Chair, Task Force on Business Intelligence & Knowledge Management, IEEE Computational Intelligence Society, 2010-; Program Chair, 8th International Conference on Computer Information Systems & Industrial Management Application, Coimbatore, 2012; Many advisory roles and contributions to professional international journals. Memberships: Senior Member, Institute of Electrical and Electronics Engineers, USA; Honorary Member, Advisory Council, IBC; Research Board of Advisers, ABI; Adviser to Director General, IBC. E-mail: suashdeb@gmail.com

DEBAKEY Lois, b. Lake Charles, Louisiana, USA. Professor of Scientific Communication; Writer; Editor; Lecturer. Education: BA, Mathematics, Newcomb College, Tulane University; MA, PhD, English and Linguistics, Tulane University; Postgraduate Courses in Biostatistics, Medical School, Tulane University. Appointments include: Professor of Scientific Communications, Baylor College of Medicine, 1968-; Consultant, National Library of Medicine, Bethesda, Maryland, 1986-; Member, National Advisory Committee, University of Southern California Development and Demonstration Center in Continuing Education for Health Professionals; Consultant, American Bar Association Legal Writing Committee; Advisory Committee, Society for the Advancement of Good English; Trustee, DeBakey Medical Foundation; Member, Advisory Council, University of Texas at Austin School of Nursing Foundation, 1993-; Member, Usage Panel, American Heritage Dictionary; Team Leader Consultant,

DICTIONARY OF INTERNATIONAL BIOGRAPHY 36th EDITION

Health and Medical Data Base, Encyclopaedia Britannica; Consultant, Friends of the Texas Medical Center Library Advisory Committee, 2008-; Consultant, Methodist DeBakey Heart & Vascular Center Community Council, 2008-; Board of Directors, Friends of the National Library of Medicine, 2009; Current Editorial Board Member, CV Network, 2003-; Journal of the Methodist DeBakey Heart & Vascular Center, 2008-; Advisory Committee, Methodist Hospital Educaiton Institute Annual Creative Writing Competition: On Being a Doctor, 2010-; Internationally renowned course developer and authority in the field of medical writing; Acclaimed for use of cartoons and humour as teaching aids. Publications: Editor and author of numerous medical and scientific articles, chapters and books; Senior author, The Scientific Journal: Editorial Policies and Practices, 1976; Co-author, Medicine: Preserving the Passion, 1987; Co-author, Medicine: Preserving the Passion in the 21st Century, 2004. Honours include: Phi Beta Kappa; Golden Key National Honor Society; Harold Swanberg Distinguished Service Award, American Medical Writers Society, 1970; Inaugural John P McGovern Award, Medical Library Association, 1983; Life Honorary Member, Medical Library Association, 1989; 50 Outstanding Women of Houston, 1990; Service Recognition Award, Baylor College of Medicine, 2008; Award, Greater Houston Women's Chamber of Commerce, 2008; Michael E DeBakey, Selma DeBakey, and Lois DeBakey Endowed Scholarship in Medical Humanities, Baylor University at Waco, Texas, 2009; Selma and Lois DeBakey Lectures in Biomedical Communication, The Methodist DeBakey Heart & Vascular Center, 2009; Proclamation, Lois and Selma DeBakey Family Day, City of Houston, 2008. Memberships include: Founding Board of Directors, Friends of the National Library of Medicine; Fellow, American College of Medical Informatics; Fellow, Royal Society for the Encouragement of Arts, Manufactures and Commerce, UK; Medical Library Association; National Association of Science Writers; Foundation for Advanced Education in the Sciences; Plain English Forum. Address: Baylor College of Medicine, 1 Baylor Plaza, Houston TX 77030 3411, USA.

DEBAKEY Selma, b. Lake Charles, Louisiana, USA. Professor of Scientific Communication. Education: BA, Languages, Newcomb College; Postgraduate studies, French and Philosophy, Tulane University. Appointments: Director, Department of Medical Communications, Ochsner Clinic and Alton Ochsner Medical Foundation, New Orleans, 1942-68; Medical Writer and Editor; Consultant Editor; Internationally renowned course developer; Served on numerous committees, 1955-; Co-editor, Quarterly Bulletin, American Medical Writers' Association, 1961-64; Methodist DeBakey Heart & Vascular Center Community Council, 2008-; Advisory Committee, Friends of the Texas Medical Center Library, 2008-; Board of Directors, Friends of the National Library of Medicine, 2009-; Editorial Board, Methodist DeBakey Cardiovascular Journal, 2008-; Advisory Committee, Methodist Hospital Education Institute Annual Creative Writing Competition: On Being a Doctor, 2010-. Publications: A huge body of work, as writer, editor, consultant, course developer; Co-author, Current Concepts in Breast Cancer, 1967; Numerous articles and papers contributed to specialist peer-reviewed journals; Over 1000 articles as Editor; Judge for several prestigious medical writing awards, including Modern Medical Monographs Awards, AORN DuPuy Writer's Awards. Honours: Exhibit of 50 Outstanding Women of Houston, 1990; Friends of the Texas Medical Center Library Advisory Committee, 2008; Proclamation, Lois and Selma DeBakey Family Day, 2008; Service Recognition Award for 40 years service, Baylor College of Medicine, 2008; Recognition, Greater Houston Women's Chamber of Commerce, 2008; Editorial Board, Methodist DeBakey Cardiovascular Journal Center, 2008-; Selma and Lois DeBakey Lectures in Biomedical Communication, The Methodist DeBakey Heart & Vascular Center, 2009; Michael E DeBakey, Selma DeBakey and Lois DeBakey Endowed Scholarship in Medical Humanities, Baylor University, Waco, Texas, 2009; Listed in numerous international and specialist biographical directories; Profiled in numerous newspapers and magazines. Memberships: American Association for the Advancement of Science; Fellow, American Medical Writers' Association; Association of Teachers of Technical Writing; Council of Biology Editors; Society for Health and Human Values; Society for Technical Communication. Address: Fondren-Brown Building, The Methodist Hospital, 6565 Fannin Street, A975, Houston, TX 77030, USA.

DEEKEN Alfons Theodor, b. 3 August 1932, Emstek, Niedersachsen, Germany. Philosopher; Writer. Education: MA, Berchmanskolleg, Munich, Germany, 1958; MA, Sophia University, Tokyo, 1966; PhD, Fordham University, New York, 1973. Appointments: Assistant Professor to Professor, 1973-82, Professor of Philosophy, 1982-2003, Professor Emeritus, 2003-, Sophia University, Tokyo, Japan; President, Japanese Association of Death Education & Grief Counselling, 1974-2003; President, Japanese Society of Clinical Thanatology, 2001-02. Publications: Growing Old and How to Cope With It, 1972; Process and Permanence in Ethics: Max Scheler's Moral Philosophy, 1974; Kirisutokyoo to Watakushi (Christianity), 1995; Humor wa Oi to Shi no Myooyaku (Humour), 1995; Confronting Death, 1996; Death Education, 2001; Hikari no dialogue (Words of the Bible), 2002; Yoku Iki, Yoku Warai, Yoki Shi to Deau (Good living, good humour, good death), 2003; Anata no jinsei o ashrunote, 2007; Inochi o Kataru, 2009; Confronting Death, 2011. Honours: Best Ethics Book of 1974, Catholic Press Association, America, 1975; Kikuchi Kan Literary Award, Literary Association of Japan, 1991; Cross of the Order of Merit of the German Federal Republic, President of Germany, 1998; Cultural Award, City of Tokyo, 1999. Memberships: Japanese Society of Clinical Thanatology; Japanese Association for Clinical Research on Death and Dying; International Work Group on Death, Dying and Bereavement. Address: Sophia University, S J House, Kioicho 7-1, Chiyoda-ku, 102-8571 Tokyo, Japan.

DEERING Anne-Lise, b. Norway. Clay Artist; Medallic Sculptor; Former Potter. Education: Science Degree, Norway, 1954; Oil Painting, Southern Illinois University, Carbondale, Illinois, 1958; Ceramics, Foothill College, Los Altos, California, 1975; BA, Art, Penn State University, University Park, Pennsylvania, 1977; Computer Graphic Design and Medallic Art, Penn State University, 1990-91; Residential Real Estate Appraisal Courses, Marketing Strategy, Sales and Promotion Courses, PA Realtors Institute, 1994-96. Career: Middle Eastern Dance Teacher, 1975-80; Self-employed Clay Artist and Potter, 1977-98; Member, 1977-2000, Juried Member, 1981-2000, Board of Directors, 1984-97, Pennsylvania Guild of Craftsmen (PGC); Participant in PGC Craft Fairs for 10 years; Artist Member, Art Alliance of Central Pennsylvania, 1978-99; Participant in Art Alliance Gallery Shop, 1989-99; Licensed Real Estate Sales Person, 1991-99; Exhibits include: American Medallic Sculpture Association juried exhibit, Newark Museum, New Jersey, 1990; Invitational, Mountain Top Gallery, Cresson, Pennsylvania, 1998; The Pen and Brush Gallery juried exhibit, New York City, 1998, 1999, 2000, 2001; American Numismatic Association, Colorado Springs, 2001; Penn State University, 2002, Wroclav, Poland, 2002; AMSA juried exhibit, Ornamental Metal Museum, Memphis, Tennessee,

2003; Co-ordinator and chair of AMSA members juried exhibit, Nordic Heritage Museum, Seattle, Washington, 2004; In charge of AMSA medals displays at numerous libraries throughout the greater Seattle area, 2004; Participated in AMSA members exhibit, Forest Lawn Museum, Glendale, California, 2005; Medal in private collections and the permanent collection of the Museum of Medallic Art, Wroclav, Poland; Exhibited in FIDEM shows: Weimar, Germany, 2000; Paris, France, 2002; Seixal, Portugal, 2004; Colorado Springs, USA, 2007; FIDEM exhibit, Tampere, Finland, 2010; AMSA members exhibit, Birmingham Museum, Birmingham, Michigan, 2007; MASC exhibitions, Ottawa, 2002 and 2005; The Best of MASC, 2008. Memberships: Pennsylvania Guild of Craftsmen and Central Pennsylvania Chapter, 1977-2000; Member of American Medallic Sculpture Association (AMSA), 1990-, Newsletter Editor, 2000-09, Secretary, 2001-08; Charter Member, National Museum of Women in the Arts, 1998-; Board of Directors, Washington Clay Art (previously Washington Potters Association), 2000-; Member, Federation International de la Medaille (FIDEM); Member, Pacific Northwest Sculptors, 2006-; Associate Member, National Sculpture Society; Member, Medallic Art Society of Canada (MASC); Listed in Who's Who publications and biographical dictionaries. Address: 24229 92nd Ave W, Edmonds, WA 98020, USA.

DEERING Richard John, b. 15 July 1947, London, England. Concert Pianist. m. Emma Caroline Budgen, 2 sons, 2 daughters. Education: Studied with Frank Merrick, Trinity College of Music, 1965-69; Private studies with Peter Wallfisch. Appointments: Senior Examiner, Trinity College, London; Concerts worldwide in over 90 countries, 1975-. Publications: Several recordings made in both UK and Japan; Numerous articles for Classical Music, Piano, Music Teacher and Business Traveller magazines. Honours: Award for Distinguished Service to British Music, Royal Philharmonic Society, 1981; Trinity College London Chairman's Award 2006. Memberships: Incorporated Society of Musicians; British Music Society; Royal Philharmonic Society; British & International Federation of Festivals; British MENSA. Address: 55 Dalmally Road, Croydon, Surrey CR0 6LW, England. E-mail: richard@malacca.demon.co.uk

DEGENHARDT Richard, b. 1 April 1965, Rosenberg, Germany. Scientist; Professor. m. Alice, 2 sons, 1 daughter. Education: Master, Civil Engineering, 1990, PhD, Applied Mechanics, 1996, TU, Braunschweig; Structural Engineering, 1996-2000; Professor, University of Applied Sciences, Göttingen, 2008-. Appointments: Structural Engineer in industry, 1996-2000; Scientist, DLR German Aerospace Centre, Institute of Composite Structures, 2000-. Publications: Over 40 articles in professional journals. Memberships: American Institute of Aeronautics and Astronautics; German Society for Aeronautics and Astronautics. Address: Dorothea-Erxleben str 23, 38116 Braunschweig, Germany.

DEIGHTON Len, b. 18 February 1929, London, England. Writer. m. Publications: The Ipcress File, 1962; Horse Under Water, 1963; Funeral in Berlin, 1964; Ou Est Le Garlic/ Basic French Cooking, 1965, 1979; Action Cook Book, 1965; Cookstrip Cook Book, Billion Dollar Brain, 1966; An Expensive Place to Die, Len Leighton's London Dossier, The Assassination of President Kennedy, co-author, 1967; Only When I Larf, 1968; Bomber, 1970; Declarations of War, 1971; Close-up, 1972; Spy Story, 1974; Eleven Declarations of War, Yesterday's Spy, 1975; Twinkle, Twinkle, Little Spy, Catch a Falling Spy, 1976; Fighter, 1977; SS-GB, Airshipwreck, co-author, 1978; Blitzkreig, 1979; Battle of Britain, co-author, 1980, 1990; XPD, 1981; Goodbye Mickey Mouse, 1982; Berlin Game, 1983; Mexico Set, 1984; London Match, 1985; Game, Set and Match, 13 part TV series; Winter: A Berlin Family 1899-1945, 1987; Spy Hook, 1988; Spy line, ABC of French Food, 1989; Spy Sinker, Basic French Cookery Course, 1990; Mamista, 1991; City of Gold, 1992; Violent Ward, Blood, Tears and Folly, 1993; Faith, 1994; Hope, 1995; Charity, Midnight in Saint Petersburg, 1996; . Address: c/o Jonathan Clowes Ltd, 10 Iron Bridge House, Bridge House, Bridge Approach, London NW1 8BD, England.

DE LA HOUSSAYE Brette Angelo-Pepe, b. 20 August 1960, Los Angeles, California, USA. Researcher; Engineer; Educator. Education: BSEET, DeVry Institute, City of Industry, California, 1989. Appointments: Engineer Researcher, private practice, 1990-2003; Calcgate (Software), 2003-; Mathematics Teacher, Los Angeles Unified School District, 2007-; Discovered alternate method for calculating energy using Newton's Second Law of Motion and Work Energy Theorem, applications also include integral calculus. Memberships: IEEE; American Physical Society; American Museum of Natural History. Address: 7719 Goodland Ave, North Hollywood, CA 91605, USA. E-mail: brette@calcgate.com

DELAPALME Bernard, b. 23 May 1923, Paris, France. Engineer. m. Evelyne Balay, 3 sons, 2 daughters. Education: Bacalaureat Scientifique, 1940; Ingénieur Ecole Polytechnique, 1943; Ingénieur du Génie Maritime, 1947. Appointments: Director, Electronic War Research Department; Professor, Electronics, Ecole du Génie Martime, 1951-; Director of Project, Technology University of Compiégne, 1978; Founder and Manager, The Electronic Commission at French Plan, 1961; Vice President for Scientific Research and Innovation, ELF Aquitaine, 1964-82; Founder and Chairman, ELF Technologies Inc, USA, 1985. Publications: Microelectronics applications in oil industry, 1963; Technologic Change and Economic Policy, 1980; Materials for the Future, 1982; Without Innovation, No Survival, 1982; Science, Technology and Society, 1994; Numerous articles in professional journals. Honours: Officier de la legion d'Honneur; Commandeur de l'Ordre du Mérite; Officier des Palmes Academiques; Grand Prix Technique de la Ville de Paris; President, EIRMA; President, Mission à l'Innovation, Industry Minister, France. Memberships: Fellow, AAS; Past memberships: Club du Siecle; Grant Council for Audiovisual, France; Advisory Committee of United Nations for the Application of Science and Technology to development; Honorary President, Association Nationale pour la Recherche Techniques. E-mail: justiniendelapalme@gmail.com

DELBOURGO Roger, b. 21 February 1937, Alexandria, Egypt. Retired University Lecturer. m. (1) Françoise Valois, deceased, 1 son, (2) Maria Gloria Bernal. Education: BSc, Electrical Engineering, Battersea Polytechnic, London University, 1959; DIC, Imperial College, 1960; BSc, Pure Mathematics (part-time study), Birkbeck College, London University, 1974; MSc, Mathematics/Numerical Analysis (part-time study), 1980, PhD, Mathematics/Numerical Analysis (part-time study), 1984, Brunel University, Uxbridge. Appointments: Tutor in Mathematics, University Tutorial College, London, 1960-62; Teacher of Mathematics, Ealing Grammar School for Boys, 1963-64; Lecturer, Mathematics, Electrical Engineering Department, Hendon College of Technology, Hendon, London, 1964-72; Lecturer, then Senior Lecturer, Mathematics, Faculty of Engineering, Science and Mathematics, Middlesex Polytechnic (later University), Bounds Green, London, 1972-98, Retired, 1998. Publications:

Pure Mathematics – A revision course for A-level (with R G Meadows), 1971; Articles published in the Journal of the Institute of Mathematics and Applications (jointly with J A Gregory), 1982-88; Articles in the Society for Industrial and Applied Mathematics, 1993. Honours: Certificate of Merit for Distinguished Service, 1996; Decree of Merit Plaque for an Outstanding Contribution to Mathematics, International Biographical Centre, 1996; American Medal of Honor, ABI, 2006; Honorary Member, Research Board of Advisors and Research Fellow, American Biographical Institute, 2005; Listed in Who's Who publications and biographical dictionaries. Memberships: New York Academy of Sciences, 1994-2003; Society for Industrial and Applied Mathematics, 1994-2002; American Association for the Advancement of Science, 1995-2002. Address: 10 Flanders Mansions, Flanders Road, Chiswick, London W4 1NE, England.

DELILLO Don, b. 20 November 1936, New York, New York, USA. Author. Education: BA in Communication Arts, Fordham University, 1958. Publications: Americana, 1971; End Zone, 1972; Great Jones Street, 1973; Ratner's Star, 1976; Players, 1977; Running Dog, 1978; Amazons, 1980; The Names, 1982; White Noise, 1985; The Day Room, 1987; Libra, 1988; Mao II, 1991; Underworld, 1997; Valparaiso, 1999; The Body Artist, 2001; Cosmopolis, 2003; Game 6, 2005; The Rapture of the Athlete Assumed Into Heaven, 2007; Falling Man. Contributions to: Periodicals. Honours: National Book Award, 1985; Irish Times-Aer Lingus International Fiction Prize, 1989; PEN/Faulkner Award, 1992; Jerusalem Prize, 1999; William Dean Howells Medal, 2000. Address: c/o Wallace Literary Agency, 177 East 70th Street, New York, NY 10021, USA.

DELOCHE Bernard, b. 27 May 1944, Lyon, France. Highly skilled professor. m. Chantal Drillien, 1 daughter. Education: Diploma, Institut d'Etudes Politiques, 1965; Degree, Philosophy, 1974; PhD, Université Jean Moulin-Lyon 3, 1979. Appointments: Professor, Lycée Julien-Wittmer, Charolles, France, 1967-70; Professor, Lycée Jean-Moulin, Lyon, 1971-74; Professor, Lycée du Parc, Lyon, 1975-80; Lecturer, 1980-91, Professor, 1991-2009, Université Lyon 3. Publications: L'art du meuble, 1980; Museologica, 1985; Le musée virtuel, 2007; La nouvelle culture, 2007; Mythologie du musée, 2010; and many other books; 100 articles. Honours: Chevalier, Ordre des Palmes académiques. Memberships: International Council of Museums. Address: 36 rue Raulin, 69007 Lyon, France. E-mail: bernard.deloche@univ-lyon3.fr

DELONG Lukasz Michal, b. 28 August 1980, Radom, Poland. Assistant Professor. Education: MD, Economics, Warsaw School of Economics, 2003; Actuarial Licence, Polish Financial Supervisory Authority, 2003; PhD, Mathematics, Institute of Mathematics, Polish Academy of Sciences, 2007. Appointments: Teaching Assistant, 2002-04, Assistant, 2004-07, Assistant Professor, 2007-, Warsaw School of Economics; Life Pricing Actuary, PZU Zycie SA, 2007-09. Publications: Numerous articles in professional journals. Honours: Best PhD thesis in Actuarial Science, PZU Insurance Group, 2007; Award for PhD Thesis, Polish Prime Minister, 2008; Scholarship for Young Outstanding Researcher, The Foundation for Polish Science, 2010 and 2011. Memberships: Polish Society of Actuaries; Board Member, Polish Society of Actuaries; Associate Editor, European Actuarial Journal. E-mail: lukasz.delong@sgh.waw.pl Website: akson.sgh.waw.pl/delong

DELPY Julie, b. 21 December 1969, Paris, France. Film Actress. Education: New York University Film School. Appointments: Actress, films include: Detective, 1985; Mauvais Sang, 1986; La Passion Béatrice, 1987; L'Autre Nuit, 1988; La Noche Oscura, 1989; Europa Europa, Voyager, 1991; Warszawa, 1992; Young and Younger, The Three Musketeers, When Pigs Fly, 1993; The Myth of the White Wolf, Killing Zoe, Mesmer, Trois Couleurs Blanc, Trois Couleurs Rouge, 1994; Before Sunrise, 1995; An American Werewolf in Paris, 1997; The Treat; LA without a Map; Blah, Blah, Blah (director); The Passion of Ayn Rand, But I'm A Cheerleader, Beginner's Luck, 1999; Tell Me, Sand, 2000; Waking Life, MacArthur Park, 2001; Looking for Jimmy, Cinemagique, 2002; Notting Hill Anxiety Festival, 2003; Before Sunset, 2004; Broken Flowers, 3 & 3, 2005; The Legend of Lucy Keyes, The Hoax, The Air I Breathe, 2006; 2 Days in Paris, 2007; The Countess, 2009. TV: ER, 2001; Frankenstein, 2004. Honours: Empire Film Award for Best Actress, 2005. Address: c/o William Morris Agency, 151 El Camino Drive, Beverley Hills, CA 90212, USA.

DEMERJIAN Jacques, b. 18 April 1975, Lebanon. IT Security Expert. m. Karine, 1 daughter. Education: PhD, Computer Sciences, Ecole Nationale Superieure des Telecommunications, Paris. Appointments: Software Development Engineer, Levant Net and Technosoft, 1998-2000; Security Engineer, Telecom Paristech, 2001-04; Security Engineer, France Telecom R&D, 2005; IT Security Expert, Altran Group, 2006-07; IT Security Expert, Communication & Sytems, 2008-11; Associate Professor, Antonine University, 2012-. Publications: Co-author of more than 30 scientific papers in IETF, journals and international conferences on computer and network security. Honours: IEEE Senior Member Award. Memberships: ACM; PhD Group; ESR Groups; IEEE France Section; Telecom ParisTech Alumni; EDITE of Paris. Address: 4 rue Aristide Briand, 94410 Saint Maurice, France.

DEMETGUL Mustafa, b. 22 May 1978, Duzce, Turkey. Assistant Professor. m. Sangul, 1 daughter. Education: BS, MS, PhD, Marmara University. Appointments: Research Assistant, 2002-11, Assistant Professor, Technology Faculty, Mechatronics Engineering, 2011-, Marmara University; Visiting Scholar, Florida International University, USA, 2007-09. Publications: Design and testing of an efficient and compact pieroelectric energy harvester, 2011. Honours: Post-doc Scholarship from Tubitak to Florida International University, 2007-09; Research Project from Scientific and Technological Research Council of Turkey, 2010-12; Listed in biographical dictionaries. Address: Marmara University, Teknik Epitim Faculty, Mechanical Department, Istanbul, Kadikoy, Goztepe, 34722, Turkey.

DEMETRIOU Andreas, b. 15 August 1950, Strongylo, Famagusta, Cyprus. Professor; Minister of Education & Culture. m. Julia Tsakalea, 2 sons. Education: BA, Psychology and Education, PhD, Psychology, 1983, Aristotle University, Thessaloniki; DSc (honoris causa), Middlesex University, 2010; Honorary President, Cyprus Psychological Association, 2011. Appointments: Professor, Developmental Psychology, Aristotle University, 1975-96; Professor, Psychology, 1996-, Chairman, Department of Educational Sciences, 1996-98, Vice Rector, Acting Rector, 1999-2002, Dean, School of Humanities and Social Sciences, 2003-04, Dean, School of Social Sciences and Sciences of Education, 2004-06, University of Cyprus; Founding President, Interim Governing Board, Cyprus University of Technology, 2004-08; President, Conference of Rectors, Cyprus Universities, 2006-08; Minister of Education and Culture, Republic of Culture, 2008-. Publications: More than 150 books and articles in professional journals. Honours: Distinguished Visiting

Professor, University of Fribourg, Switzerland, 2001; Fellow, International Academy of Education, 2004; Honorary Visiting Professor, Northeastern Normal University, China, 2009; Doctor Honoris Causa, Middlesex University, London. Address: Kimonos & Thoukididou, 1434 Nicosia, Cyprus. E-mail: ademetriou@ucy.ac.cy

DEMIRCI Mustafa, b. 30 August 1964, Ispir, Erzurum, Turkey. Professor; Doctor of Dentistry. m. Oya, 1 daughter. Education: PhD, Faculty of Dentistry, Institute of Health Sciences, Istanbul University, 1996. Appointments: Associate Professor Doctor of Dentistry, 2003; Professor Doctor, Dentistry, 2009. Publications: Numerous articles in professional journals. Memberships: International Association for Dental Research; Conservative Dentistry European Federation. Address: Istanbul University, Faculty of Dentistry, Capa 34093, Istanbul, Turkey.

DEMIRTÜRK (Emine) Lale, b. 5 October 1956, Canakkale, Turkey. Associate Professor. Education: BA, English Language & Literature, Hacettepe University, Turkey; MA, English, 1982, PhD, American Studies, 1986, University of Iowa, USA. Appointments: Assistant Professor, 1990-94, Associate Professor, 1994-, Department of American Culture & Literature, Bilkent University, Turkey. Publications: Numerous articles in professional journals. Honours: Listed in international biographical dictionaries. Memberships: John Edgar Wideman Society; African American Literature & Culture Society; American Studies Association. Address: Bilkent University, Faculty of Humanities & Letters, 06800 Bilkent, Ankara, Turkey. E-mail: dturk@bilkent.edu.tr

DENCH Dame Judith (Judi), b. 9 December 1934, York, Yorkshire, England. Actress. m. Michael Williams, 1971, deceased, 1 daughter. Education: Central School of Speech Training and Dramatic Art. Career: Appeared Old Vic, leading roles, 1957-61; Royal Shakespeare Company, 1961-62; Leading roles include: Anya (The Cherry Tree); Titania (A Midsummer Dream); Isabella (Measure for Measure); West African Tour with Nottingham Playhouse, 1963; Subsequent roles include: Irina (The Three Sisters, Oxford Playhouse, 1964); Title role, St Joan and Barbara (Nottingham Playhouse, 1965); Lika (The Promise, 1967); Sally Bowles (Cabaret, 1968); Numerous appearances in lead roles and tours to Japan, 1970, 1972, and Australia, 1970 as Associate Member Royal Shakespeare Company, 1969-, these include: Viola (Twelfth Night); Beatrice (Much Ado About Nothing); Duchess (Duchess of Malfi); Other Performances include: Miss Trant (The Good Companions, 1974); Nurse (Too Good to Be True, 1975, 1976); Cymbeline, 1979; Lady Bracknell (The Importance of Being Ernest, 1982); Pack of Lies, 1983; Waste, 1985; Antony and Cleopatra, 1987; Hamlet, 1989; The Seagull (Royal National Theatre, 1994); The Convent, 1995; Absolute Hell, 1995; A Little Night Music, 1995; Amy's View, 1997, 1999; Filumena, 1998; The Royal Family, 2001; The Breath of Life, 2002; All's Well That Ends Well, 2003-04; Plays Directed: Much Ado About Nothing, 1988; Look Back in Anger, 1989; The Boys from Syracuse, 1991; Absolute Hell (Royal National Theatre, 1995); A Little Night Music, 1995; Amy's View, 1997; Filumena, 1998. Films include: A Study in Terror, 1965; Four in the Morning, 1966; A Midsummer Night's Dream (RSC, 1968); Dead Cert, Wetherby, 1985; A Room with a View, 1986; 84 Charing Cross Road, 1987; Henry V, 1989; Goldeneye, 1995; Tomorrow Never Dies, 1996; Mrs Brown, 1997, Shakespeare in Love, 1998; Tea with Mussolini, 1998; The World is Not Enough, 1999; Chocolat, 2000; Iris, 2001; The Shipping News, 2001; The Importance of Being Earnest, 2002; Die Another Day, 2002; Ladies in Lavender, 2004; The Chronicles of Riddick, 2004; Mrs Henderson Presents, 2005; Casino Royale, 2006; Notes on a Scandel, 2006; Doogal, 2006; Quantum of Solace, 2008; Nine, 2009; My Week with Marilyn, 2011; The Best Exotic Marigold Hotel, 2012; Skyfall, 2012; TV includes: Major Barbara; Talking to a Stranger; The Funambulists; Age of Kings; Jackanory; Neighbours; Marching Song; On Approval; Langrishe Go Down; Love in a Cold Climate; A Fine Romance; Going Gently; Saigon-Year of the Cat, 1982; Ghosts, 1986; Behaving Badly, 1989; Absolute Hell; Can You Hear Me Thinking?; As Time Goes By; Last of the Blonde Bombshells; Cranford Chronicles, 2007. Publications: Judi Dench: A Great Deal of Laughter (biography); Judi Dench - With a Crack in Her Voice (biography), 1998. Honours include: Numerous Honorary degrees and Honorary Fellowship (Royal Holloway College); Best Actress: Variety London Critic's (Lika, The Promise, 1967); Guild of Directors (Talking to a Stranger, 1967); Society West End Theatre (Lady MacBeth, 1977); New Standard Drama Awards: Juno and the Paycock, 1980; Lady Bracknell (The Importance of Being Ernest, 1983); Deborah (A Kind of Alaska, 1983); Variety Club Award for Best Actress, Filumena, 1998; Academy Award, Best Supporting Actress (Shakespeare in Love), 1999; BAFTA Award for Best Actress (Last of the Blonde Bombshells); BAFTA Award for Best Actress (Iris), 2002; BAFTA Tribute for Lifetime Achievement, 2002; Olivier Award for Lifetime Achievement, Society of London Theatres, 2004; The William Shakespeare Award, The Shakespeare Theatre in Washington, 2004; Evening Standard Special Award for Outstanding Contribution to British Theatre, 2004; Honorary Doctorate, Mary Baldwin College, Staunton, Virginia, 2004; Honorary Doctorate, The Juilliard Academy, New York, 2004; Theatregoers' Award for Best Supporting Actress, 2005. Address: c/o Julian Belfrage Associates, 46 Albermarle Street, London, W1X 4PP, England.

DENEUVE Catherine (Catherine Dorléac), b. 22 October 1943, Paris, France. Actress. m. David Bailey (divorced), 1 son (by Roger Vadim), 1 daughter (by Marcello Mastroianni). Appointments: Film debut in: Les petitis chats, 1959; President, Director-General, Films de la Citrouille, 1971-79; Films include: Les portes claquent, 1960; L'homme à femmes, le Vice et la Vertu, Et Satan conduit le bal, 1962; Vacances portugaises, Les parapluies de Cherbourg (Palme D'Or, Cannes Festival), Les plus belles escroqueries du monde, 1963; La chasses à l'homme, Un monsieur de compagnie, La Costanza della Ragione, Repulsion, 1964; Le chant du monde, La Vie de chateau, Liebes Karusell, Les créatures, 1965; Les demoiselles de Rochfort, 1966; La chamade, 1966; Belle de jour (Golden Lion, Venice Festival), Benjamin, Manon 70, 1967; Mayerling, 1968; Folies d'avril, Belles d'un soir, La sirène du Mississippi, 1969; Tristana, 1970; Peau d'âne, Ça n'arrive qu'aux autres, Liza, 1971; Un flic, 1972; Touche pas la femme blanche, 1974; Hustle, 1976; March or Die, Coup de foudre, 1977; Ecoute voir... L'argent des autres, 1978; A nous deux, Ils sont grandes ces petits, 1979; Le dernier métro, Je vous aime, 1980; Hotel des Americaines, 1981; L'africain, The Hunger, 1983; Le bon plaisir, Paroles et musiques, 1984; Le lieu du crime, 1986; La reine blanche, 1991; Indochine (César Award), 1992; Ma saison préférée, 1993; La Partie d'Echecs, 1994; The Convent, Les cent et une nuits, Les Voleurs, 1995; Genéalogie d'un crime, 1997; Le Vent de la nuit, Belle-Maman, Pola x, Time Regained, 1999; Dancer in the Dark, 2000; Je centre a la maison, Absolument fabuleux, 2001; 8 Femmes, Au plus près du paradis, 2002; Un film parle, 2003; Kings and Queen, Changing Times, 2004; Palais royal !, 2005; The Stone Council, Family Hero, 2006; After Him, Persepolis (voice), Je veux voir, 2007; Un conte de

Noël, 2008; Bancs publics, 2009; Potiche, 2010; L homme qui voulait vivre sa vie, 2010; The Girl on the Train, 2010. Honours: Honorary Golden Bear, Berlin Film Festival, Arts de l'Alliance française de New York Trophy, 1998. Memberships include: Co-Chairman, UNESCO Campaign to protect World's Film Heritage, 1994-. Address: c/o Artmedia, 20 avenue Rapp, 75007 Paris, France.

DENISOV Evgenii, b. 19 June 1930, Kaluga, Russia. Researcher. m. Taissa, 2 sons. Education: Graduate, Moscow State University, 1953; PhD, Chemistry, 1957; Doctor of Science, Chemistry, 1965. Appointments: Postgraduate Student, Moscow State University, 1953-56; Junior Senior Researcher, 1956-67, Head of Laboratory, 1967-2000, Principal Researcher, 2001-, Institute of Problems of Chemical Physics. Publications: 20 monographs, Kinetics, Physical Chemistry; Over 500 papers on oxidation, antioxidants and free radical kinetics. Honours: Award from Printing House Nauka for papers published, 1997; Diploma, Russian Academy of Science, 1999; S Arrhenius Medal, Academy of Endeavors; Honoured Scientist of Russia, 2001; Honoured Doctor of Bashkin State University, 2009; Order of Glory of Academy of Engravers, 2011. Memberships: Academy of Endeavors; International Academy of Sciences. Address: Chernogolovka Central St 4A/39, Moscow Region 142432, Russia.

DENISOV Sergey, b. 4 May 1937, Moscow, Russia. Physicist. m. Dina Stoyanova, 2 sons. Education: Department of Physics, Moscow State University, 1955-61. Appointments: Senior Scientist, 1964-70, Group Leader, 1970-77, 2007-, Head, Neutrino Department, 1977-2007, Institute for High Energy Physics; Professor, Moscow Physical and Technical Institute, 1977-87; Professor, Department of Physics, Moscow State University, 1987-. Publications: 560 articles. Honours: Lenin Prize in Science, 1986; Fellow, Indiana University Institute for Advanced Study, USA, 1994; Cherenkov Prize, Russian Academy of Science, 2001; Order of Honour, Russia, 2003. Memberships: Correspondent Member, Russian Academy of Science. Address: 17-1 Stroiteley Street, Protvino, Moscow Region, 142280, Russia. E-mail: denisov@ihep.ru

DENNEHY Brian, b. 9 July 1939, Bridgeport, Connecticut, USA. Actor. m. (1) 3 children, (2) Jennifer. Education: Chaminade High School, Columbia; Yale University. Career: US Marine Corps, 5 years; Numerous stage appearances; Films include: Looking for Mr Goodbar, Semi-Tough, 1977; FIST, Foul Place, 1978; Butch and Sundance: the Early Days, 10, 1979; Little Miss Market, 1980; Split Image, First Blood, 1982; Never Cry Wolf, Gorky Park, 1983; Finders Keepers, The River Rat, 1984; Twice in a Lifetime, Silverado, Cocoon, 1985; The Check is in the Mail, F/X, Legal Eagles, 1986; Best Seller, The Belly of an Architect, 1987; Return to Snowy River, Miles from Home, Cocoon: The Return, 1988; Indio, Georg Elser – Einer aus Deutschland, 1989; The Last of the Finest, Presumed Innocent, 1990; FX2, 1991; Gladiator, 1992; Tommy Boy, The Stars Fell on Henrietta, 1995; Romeo + Juliet, 1996; Out of the Cold, Silicon Towers, 1999; Summer Catch, 2001; Stolen Summer, 2002; She Hate Me, 2004; Our Fathers, Assault on Precinct 13, 2005; 10th & Wolf, Everyone's Hero (voice), The Ultimate Gift, Welcome to Paradise, 2006; Ratatouille (voice), 2007; Tumbo, 2008; Righteous Kill, 2008; Miss January, 2008; War Eagle, Arkansas, 2009; Cat City, 2009; TV includes: Big Shamus, Little Shamus; Star of the Family, Birdland, The Exonerated; Our Fathers; Marco Polo; Just Shoot Me. Honours: Tony Award, Best Actor in a Drama, 1999. Address: c/o Susan Smith & Associates, 121 North San Vicente Boulevard, Beverly Hills, CA 90211, USA.

DENT Ann Langford, b. Kensington, London, England. m. Anthony Rubinstein, divorced, 1 son, 2 daughters. Education: Coventry Art School, 1940-42; St Martin's Art School, 1942-43. Appointments: Bletchley Codes and Cyphers, 1943-46; Professional Artist. Publications: Commissions include: Sir Angus Johnson Wilson (of Bletchley Codes & Cyphers). Honours: Veteran Status, Bletchley Park Recommendation; Certificate and Medal from Rt Hon Gordon Brown PM, Bletchley Park, 2009. Memberships: Chelsea Art Society. Address: 12 Smith Street, Chelsea, London SW3 4EE, England.

DENTON Derek Ashworth, b. 27 May 1924, Launceston, Tasmania. Medical Research Scientist. m. Margaret Scott, 2 sons. Education: MMB, BS, University of Melbourne, Australia, 1947. Appointments: Haley Research Fellow, Walter & Eliza Hall Institute, Melbourne, 1947; Formed Ionic Research Unit, 1948-; Overseas National Health and Medical Research Council Fellow with Professor E B Verney, FRS, Cambridge, England, 1952-53; Principal Research Fellow, National Health and Medical Research Council, Head and Chief Scientist, Howard Florey Laboratories of Experimental Physiology and Medicine, University of Melbourne, 1962-70; Member, Medical Research Advisory Committee, National Health and Medical Research Council, 1976-81; Founding Director and Originating Board Member, Howard Florey institute of Experimental Physiology and Medicine, 1971-89; Appointed Research Professor, 1977-90, Emeritus Research Professor, 1990-, Experimental Physiology and Medicine, University of Melbourne; Adjunct Scientist, South West Foundation for Biomedical Research, San Antonio, Texas, 1991-2009; Vice President, Howard Florey Biomedical Research Foundation, 1997; Honorary Senior Research Fellow, Department of Anatomy and Human Development, University College, London, 1997-. Publications: Approximately 400 papers in scientific journals and as chapters of books; 3 books. Honours include: Elected Foreign Medical Member, Royal Swedish Academy of Sciences, 1974; Honorary Fellow, Royal College of Physicians, London, 1988-; Elected Foreign Fellow, American Academy of Arts and Sciences, 1986; Foreign Associate, National Academy of Sciences, USA, 1995-; Elected Fellow, Royal Society, London, 1999-; Foreign Associate, Académie des Sciences, 2000-; Centenary Medal, 2001; Companion of the Order of Australia, 2005; Doctorate of Laws (honoris causa), University of Melbourne, 2006. Memberships: Physiological Society of Great Britain; Endocrine Society of US; Endocrine Society of Australia; Australian High Blood Pressure Research Council; International Society of Ingestive Behaviour; European Brain Research Society; Australian Physiological Society; American Association for Advancement of Science. Address: 816 Orrong Road, Toorak, Melbourne, VIC 3142, Australia.

DEPARDIEU Gerard, b. 27 December 1948, Chateauroux, France. Actor; Vineyard Owner. m. Elisabeth Guignot, 1970 (divorced), 1 son, 1 daughter. Education: Cours d'art dramatique de Charles Dullin and Ecole d'art dramatique de Jean Laurent Cochet. Appointments: President, Jury, 45th Cannes International Film Festival, 1992; Appeared in several short films. Creative Works: Feature Films include: Les gaspards, Les valseuses, 1973; Pas si mechant que ca, 1974; 1900, La derniere femme, Sept morts sur ordonnance, Maîtresse, 1975; Barocco, René la Canne, Les plages de l'Atlantique, Baxter vera Baxter, 1976; Dites-lui que je l'aime, Le camion, Reve de singe, 1977; Le sucre, 1978; Buffet froid, Loulou, 1979; Le dernier metro, 1980 (César award Best Actor, France); Le choix des armes, La femme d'à côté, La chèvre, Le retour de Martin Guerre, (Best Actor Award, American Society of Film Critics); Danton, 1981; Le grand frère, 1982 La lune dans le carniveau, Les compères, Fort Saganne, 1983; Tartuffe (also Director), Rive Droit, Rive Gauche, Police, 1984; One Woman or Two, Jean de Florette, Tenue de soirée, 1985; Rue de départ, Les fugitifs, 1986; Cyrano de Bergerac, 1989 (César award Best Actor); Uranus, 1990; Green Card (Golden Globe for Best Comedy Actor), Mon Pere Ce Heros, 1492: Conquest of Paradise, Tous les matins due monde, 1991; Germinal, 1992 A Pure Formality, Le Colonel Chabert, 1993; La Machine, Elisa, Les Cents et Une Nuits, Les Anges Gardiens, Le Garçu, all 1994; Bogus, Unhook the Stars, Secret Agent, 1995; Vatel, The Man in the Iron Mask, 1997; Les Portes du Ciel, Astérix et Obélix, Un pont entre deux rives (also Director), Vatel, 1999; Les Acteurs, Chicken Run, 2000; Le Placard, 102 Dalmatians, 2001; Astérix et Obélix: Mission Cleopatra, 2002; Nathalie, Tais-toi, Les Clefs de bagnole, 2003; San Antonio, Nouvelle France, 36 quai des orfevres, Bon Voyage, Changing Times, 2004; How Much Do You Love Me, 2005; Last Holiday, Paris, I Love You, The Singer, 2006; Bastardi, Disco, 2007; Asterix at the Olympic Games, Babylon A.D. 2008; Public Enemy Number One, 2009; Diamond 13, 2009; Death Instinct, 2009; Coco; 2009; Bellamy, 2009; Potiche, 2010; Mammouth, 2010; Several plays and television productions. Publication: Lettres volées, 1988. Honours: Numerous national and international awards. Address: Art Media, 10 Avenue George V, 75008 Paris, France.

DEPP Johnny, b. 9 June 1963, Owensboro, Kentucky, USA. Actor. m. (1) Lori Anne Allison (divorced), (2) Vanessa Paradis, 1 son, 1 daughter. Appointments: Former rock musician; TV appearances include 21 Jump Street; Films include: A Nightmare on Elm Street; Platoon; Slow Burn; Cry Baby; Edward Scissorhands, 1990; Benny and Joon, 1993; What's Eating Gilbert Grape, 1991; Arizona Dream; Ed Wood; Don Juan de Marco, 1994; Dead Man; Nick of Time; Divine Rapture; The Brave (also writer and director), Donnie Brasco, 1997; Fear and Loathing in Las Vegas, The Astronaut's Wife, 1998; The Source, The Ninth Gate, The Libertine, Just to Be Together, Sleepy Hollow, 1999; Before Night Falls, The Man Who Cried, Chocolat, 2000; Blow, From Hell, 2001; Lost in La Mancha, Once Upon a Time in Mexico, 2002; Pirates of the Caribbean: The Curse of the Black Pearl, 2003; Secret Window, Finding Neverland, 2004; The Corpse Bride, The Libertine, Charlie and the Chocolate Factory, 2005; Pirates of the Caribbean: Dead Man's Chest, 2006; Pirates of the Caribbean: At World's End, Sweeney Todd: The Demon Barber of Fleet Street, 2007; Gypsy Caravan, 2007; Gonzo: The Life and Work of Dr. Hunter S. Thompson, 2008; The Imaginarium of Doctor Parnassus, 2009; Public Enemies, 2009; The Rum Diary, 2010; Alice in Wonderland, The Tourist, 2010; Rango, Pirates of the Caribbean: On Stranger Tides, The Rum Diary, Jack and Jill, 2011; 21 Jump Street, Dark Shadows, 2012; The Lone Ranger, 2013. Honours: Screen Actors Guild Award, Best Actor, 2004.

DERBYSHIRE Eileen, b. 6 October 1931, Urmston, Manchester, England. Actress. m. Thomas Wilfrid Holt, 1 son. Education: Northern School of Music. Career: First broadcast, 1948; Appeared in numerous radio productions; First repertory appearance, 1952; Numerous repertory jobs including Manchester Library Theatre, Farnham, Harrogate Festival, Scarborough (Stephen Joseph Theatre in the Round); Touring with the Century Theatre; Played Emily Bishop in Coronation Street since 1961. Honour: LRAM. Membership: Life Member, British Actors' Equity. Address: c/o Granada Television Ltd, Quay Street, Manchester, M60 9EA, England.

DERN Laura, b. 10 February 1967, Los Angeles, USA. Actor. m. Ben Harper, 2005, divorced, 1 son, 1 daughter with. Appointments: Film debut aged 11 in Foxes, 1980; TV appearances include: Happy Endings; Three Wishes of Billy Greer; Afterburn; Down Came a Blackbird; Director, The Gift, 1999; Within These Walls, 2001; Damaged Care, 2002; King of the Hill, 2002-03; Recount, 2008; Enlightened, 2011-; Films: Teachers; Mask; Smooth Talk; Blue Velvet; Haunted Summer; Wild of Heart; Rambling Rose; Jurassic Park; A Perfect World; Devil Inside; Citizen Ruth, Bastard Out of Carolina, Ruby Ridge, 1996; October Sky, 1999; Dr T and the Women, 2000; Daddy and Them, Focus, Novocaine, Jurassic Park III, I Am Sam, 2001; We Don't Live Here Anymore, 2004; Happy Endings, The Prize Winner of Defiance, Ohio, 2005; Lonely Hearts, 2007; Inland Empire, 2006; Year of the Dog, 2007; Tenderness, 2009; Little Fockers, 2010; Everthing Must Go, 2011; The Master, 2012. Honours: Montréal World Film Festival Award for Best Actress, 1991, 1996; Golden Globe Award for Best Actress – Miniseries or Television Film, 992; Boston Society of Film Critics Award for Best Supporting Actress, 2004; Independent Spirit Awards - Special Distinction Award, 2006; Golden Globe Award for Best Supporting Actress – Series, Miniseries or Television Film, 2008; Golden Globe Award for Best Actress – Television Series Musical or Comedy, 2011.

DERSHOWITZ Alan (Morton), b. 1 September 1938, New York, New York, USA. Lawyer; Professor of Law; Writer. m. Carolyn Cohen, 2 sons, 1 daughter. Education: BA, Brooklyn College, 1959; LLB, Yale University, 1962. Appointments: Called to the Bar, Washington, DC, 1963, Massachusetts, 1968, US Supreme Court, 1968; Law Clerk to Chief Judge David L Bazelon, US Court of Appeals, 1962-63, to Justice Arthur J Goldberg, US Supreme Court; Faculty, 1964-, Professor of Law, 1967-, Fellow, Center for Advanced Study of Behavioural Sciences, 1971-72, Felix Frankfurter Professor of Law, 1993-, Harvard University. Publications: Psychoanalysis, Psychiatry and the Law (with others), 1967; Criminal Law: Theory and Process, 1974; The Best Defense, 1982; Reversal of Fortune: Inside the von Bulow Case, 1986; Taking Liberties: A Decade of Hard Cases, Bad Laws and Bum Raps, 1988; Chutzpah, 1991; Contrary to Popular Opinion, 1992; The Abuse Excuse, 1994; The Advocate's Devil, 1994; Reasonable Doubt, 1996; The Vanishing American Jew, 1997; Sexual McCarthyism, 1998; Just Revenge, 1999; The Genesis of Justice, 2000; Supreme Injustice, 2001; Letters to a Young Lawyer, 2001; Shouting Fire: Civil Liberties in a Turbulent Age, 2002; Why Terrorism Works, 2002; America Declares Independence, 2003; The Case for Israel, 2003; America on Trial, 2004; Rights from Wrongs: A Secular Theory of the Origins of Rights, 2004; The Case for Peace: How the Arab-Israeli Conflict Can be Resolved, 2005; Preemption: A Knife That Cuts Both Ways, 2006; The Case for Moral Clarity: Israel, Hamas and Gaza. Contributions to: Periodicals. Honours: Guggenheim Fellowship, 1978-79; Honorary doctorates. Memberships: Order of the Coif; Phi Beta Kappa. Address: c/o Harvard University Law School, Cambridge, MA 02138, USA.

DERWENT Richard Austin, b. 28 September 1953. Chartered Accountant. Education: BA Hons (1st Class), History, MSc, American Politics, London University. Appointments: Chartered Accountant, Deloitte, Haskins and Sells, Southampton, 1972-81; Audit Manager, Brooking Knowles and Lawrence, 1981-82; Audit Manager, Rawlinson and Hunter, 1982-84; Senior Technical Manager, Pannell Kerr Forster, 1984-86; Senior Technical Manager, Clark Whitehill, 1986-91; Self-employed Consultant, 1991-. Publications:

Charities: An Industry Accounting and Auditing Guide, 1995, 1997; Contributions to: Financial Reporting: A Survey of UK Published Accounts; The Times; Charity World; Accountancy; Certified Accountant; Corporate Money; True and Fair; The Small Practitioner. Memberships: Secretary and Chairman, London Society Financial Reporting Discussion Group, 1989-91; Financial Reporting Committee, ICAEW, 1990-97. Address: Flat 7, Foxlea, 70 Northlands Road, Southampton SO15 2LH, England.

DESAI Anita, b. 24 June 1937, Mussoorie, India. Writer. m. Ashvin Desai, 13 December 1958, 2 sons, 2 daughters. Education: BA, Honours, Miranda House, University of Delhi. Publications: Cry, The Peacock; Voices in the City; Fire on the Mountain; Clear Light of Day; In Custody, (also filmed, 1994); Baumgartner's Bombay; Where Shall We Go This Summer?; Bye Bye Blackbird; The Peacock Garden; Cat on a Houseboat; The Village by the Sea, (also BBC TV Serial, 1992); Games at Twilight; Journey to Ithaca, 1995; Fasting, Feasting, 1999; Diamond Dust and Other Stories, 2000; The Zig Zag Way, 2004; . Honours: Winifred Holtby Award, Royal Society of Literature, 1978; Sahitya Akademi Award for English, 1978; Federation of Indian Publishers Award, 1978; Padma Shri Award, India, 1989; Hadassah Magazine Award, 1989; Guardian Prize for Children's Fiction, 1993; Literary Lion, New York Public Library, 1993; Neil Gunn International Writers Fellowship, Scotland, 1994; Alberto Moravia Prize for Literature, Italy, 2000. Memberships: Royal Society of Literature; Sahitya Akademi of India; PEN; Fellow, American Academy of Arts and Letters, 1992; Fellow, Girton College and Clare Hall, Cambridge. Address: c/o Rogers, Coleridge and White Ltd, 20 Powis Mews, London W11 1JN, England.

DESAI Rajendrakumar, b. 17 February 1949, Talodh, Bilimora, India. Consultant; Civil and Structural Engineer. m. Uma, 1 son, 1 daughter. Education: BE Civil, Gold Medalist; MIE, India; MASCE, USA; MS (Struct); EI, USA; MACI, USA; FIV, India. Appointments: Self-employed, Proprietor (formerly Chief Engineer), Sarjan Consultants, 1972-; Sarabhai Technological Syndicate Pvt Ltd. Publications: Numerous articles in professional journals. Honours: 3 Gold Medals, Governor of Gujarat; Gold Medal, Chief Justice High Court; Pridarshini Award, President of India; Award, Bramsamaj of India; Award of Excellence, Chief Minister of Gujarat State. Memberships: Institution of Engineers (India); American Society of Civil Engineers, USA; American Concrete Institute, USA; Gujarat Institute of Civil Engineers & Architects; Institute of Valuers (India); Institute and Association of Structural Engineers (India); Gujarat Chambers of Commerce and Industry. Address: 47 Ashwamegh Bungalows Part 3, 132 ft Ring Road, Behind Bileshwal Mahadev Temple, India. E-mail: garjan001@yahoo.com

DESAI Subhash Jagdish Kumar, b. 2 January 1937, Vadodara, Gujarat, India. Retired Professor. m. Shruti, 2 daughters. Education: M Tech, University of Saugor, Madhya Pradeshi, India; PhD, M S University of Baroda, India; Diploma, Imperial College, London, UK. Appointments: Professor & Head, Geology, M S University of Baroda; Retired. Publications: About 15 articles in national and international journals. Honours: Fellow, Gujarat Science Academy. Memberships: Life Member (Fellow), Geological Society of India.

DESLIPPE Richard Joseph, b. 5 September 1962, Windsor, Ontario, Canada. Associate Professor of Ecology. Education: BSc, Biology, Department of Zoology, University of Guelph, 1981-85; MSc, Biology, Department of Biology, University of Windsor, 1987-1989; PhD, Zoology, Department of Zoology, University of Alberta, 1990-94. Appointments: Postdoctoral Fellow, Cornell University, 1994-96; Visiting Assistant Professor, Texas Tech University, 1996-97; Adjunct Professor, The Institute of Environmental and Human Health; Assistant Professor of Ecology, 1997-, Associate Professor, 2003-, Texas Tech University. Publications: Numerous papers and articles. Honours: Recipient of various awards. Address: Department of Biological Sciences, Texas Tech University, Lubbock, TX 79409-3131, USA. E-mail: richard.deslippe@ttu.edu

DETJEN David Wheeler, b. 25 January 1948, St Louis, Missouri, USA. Lawyer. m. Barbara Morgan Detjen, 2 daughters. Education: AB Magna Cum Laude, Washington University, 1970; History and Law, Eberhard-Karls Universität, Tübingen, Germany, 1969-70; JD with Honours, Washington University School of Law, 1973. Appointments: Law Clerk to the Honorable M C Matthes, Chief Judge and later Senior Judge of the United States Court of Appeals for the Eighth Circuit, St Louis, Missouri, 1973-1975; Adjunct Lecturer in Law, Washington University School of Law, 1975-80; Admitted to the Missouri Bar, 1973, the New York Bar, 1981; Associate, Lewis, Rice, Tucker, Allen and Chubb, St Louis, Missouri, 1975-80; Associate, 1980-82, Partner, 1983-2000, Walter, Conston, Alexander & Green, PC, New York, New York; Partner, Alston & Bird LLP, New York, New York, 2001-. Publications include: Distributorship Agreements in the United States, 1983, 2nd edition, 1989; The Germans in Missouri 1900-1918, Prohibition, Neutrality and Assimilation, 1985; Establishing a US Joint Venture with a Foreign Partner, 1988, 2nd edition, 1989, 3rd edition, 1993; Licensing Technology and Trademarks in the United States, 1988, 2nd edition, 1997; US Joint Ventures with International Partners, 2000; Executive Editor, 1988-, Editor-in-Chief, 2004-, International Law Practicum. Honours: Delta Phi Alpha (German Language Honorary); Order of the Coif (Law Honorary); Distinguished Alumnus, Washington University School of Law, 1998; Regional Distinguished Leadership Award, Washington University, 2003; Distinguished Alumnus, Washington University, College of Arts & Sciences, 2010; Distinguished Alumnus, Washington University, 2010; Honorable Order of Kentucky Colonels, 2009; Recipient, Officer's Cross, First Class, of the Order of Merit of the Federal Republic of Germany, 2007; Political Offices: Member, Republican Central Committee of St Louis County, Missouri, 1976-83; Member, Representative Town Meeting (Municipal Legislature) of Greenwich, Connecticut, 2000-. Memberships: American Council on Germany, New York City; Atlantic-Bruecke eV, Berlin; Board Membership, Washington University Board of Trustees, 2004-08; Deutscher Verein, New York (Vice-President-Secretary, 2000-03); NY Regional Cabinet of Washington University (Chairman, 2004-10); Washington School of Law National Council; Sam Fox School of Design and Visual Arts at Washington University; American Institute for Contemporary German Studies, Johns Hopkins University (Corporate Secretary, 2000-, Vice-Chairman, 2004-); German Forum (Secretary, 1988-2005, Chairman, 2005-), New York; German American Chamber of Commerce, New York (Vice-Chairman, 2006-); Friends of Goethe, New York Inc (Chairman, 2009-); Arthur M Burns Fellowship; Friends of Atlantik-Bruecke eV Foundation Inc, New York (Treasurer, 2008-10, President, 2010-); Bucerius Kunst Forum, Hamburg, Germany; American Bar Association; American Friends of Bucerius; Leo Baeck Institute; New York State Bar Association (Vice-Chairman, International Section, 2004-); Missouri Bar; Association of the Bar of the City of New York (Member, Council on International Affairs, 2008-; Member,

Committee on International Legal Practice, 2010-); Bar Association of Metropolitan St Louis; German American Law Association. Address: 90 Park Avenue, 14th Floor, New York, NY 10016, USA.

DETTORI Lanfranco (Frankie), b. 15 December 1970, Milan, Italy. Flat Race Jockey. m. Catherine Allen, 1997, 2 sons, 3 daughters. Appointments: Ridden races in England, France, Germany, Italy, USA, Dubai, Australia, Hong Kong and other countries in Far East, 1992-; 1000 rides and 215 wins in UK, 1995; Horses ridden include Lamtarra, Barathea, Vettori, Mark of Distinction, Balanchine, Moonshell, Lochsong, Classic Cliché, Dubai Millennium, Daylami; Sakhee; Authorized, Ouija Board; major race victories include: St Leger (twice), The Oaks (twice); The Breeders Cup Mile; Arc de Triomphe (three times); French 2000 Guineas (twice); English 1000 Guineas (twice); Queen Elizabeth II Stakes; Prix L'Abbaye; The Japan Cup (three time); The Dubai World Cup (three times); Rode winner of all 7 races at Ascot, 28 October 1996; Epsom Derby, 2007. Publication: A Year in the Life of Frankie Dettori, 1996; Frankie: The Autobiography, 2004. Honours: Jockey of the Year, 1994, 1995, 2004; BBC Sports Personality of the Year, 1996; International Sports Personality of the Year, Variety Club, 2000, MBE. Address: c/o Peter Burrell Classic Management, 53 Stewarts Grove, London, SW3 6PH, England. E-mail: pburrell@classicmanagement.com

DEUCHAR Stephen John, b. 11 March 1957, United Kingdom. Director, Tate Britain. m. Katie Scott, 1 son, 3 daughters. Education: BA, History 1st Class Honours, University of Southampton; PhD, History of Art, Westfield College, University of London, 1986; Andrew W Mellon Fellow in British Art, Yale University, 1981-82. Appointments: Curator of Paintings, 1985-87, Curator, Armada Exhibition, 1987-88, Corporate Planning Manager, 1988-90; Head of Exhibitions and Displays, 1990-95, Director, Neptune Court Project, 1995-97, National Maritime Museum; Director, Tate Britain, 1998-, Director of the Art Fund, 2010-. Publications: Noble Exercise: the Sporting Ideal in 18th Century British Art, 1982; Paintings, Politics and Porter, Samuel Whitbread and British Art, 1984; Concise Catalogue of Oil Paintings in the National Maritime Museum (jointly), 1988; Sporting Art in 18th Century England: A Social and Political History, 1988; Nelson: An Illustrated History (jointly), 1995; Articles on British Art. Memberships: Visual Arts Committee, British Council; Advisory Council, Paul Mellon Centre for Studies in British Art; Council, University of Southampton; Trustee, Metropole Arts Centre Trust. Address: Tate Britain, Millbank, London SW1P 4RG, England.

DEUTSCH Claude, b. 20 July 1936, Paris, France. Professor of Physics. m. Nimet El Abed, 2 sons. Education: Engineer, ENSCP, Paris, 1959; Master of Theoretical Physics, Orsay, 1961; Doctor of Science, University Paris XI, 1969. Appointments: Visiting Scientist, Research Laboratory of Electronic, MIT, 1976-78; Visiting Physicist, Applied Physics Department, Stanford University, 1980; Director, Paris Sud Informatique, University Paris XI, Orsay, 1985-93; Director GDR-918, CNRS, Ion-plasma Interaction, 1989-96; Director, Physics Laboratory, University Paris XI, 1994-98; Invited Professor, Tokyo Institute of Technology, Japan, 1999-2000; Professor, Physics, Exceptional Class, 1995-. Publications: Numerous articles in professional journals; Co-editor, Laser Particle Beams. Honours: Bronze Medal, 1973, Silver Medal, 1980, CNRS; Bronze Medal, Madrid Polytechnic, 1995; Fellow, American Physical Society, 1996. Memberships: Societé Francaise de Physique; American Physical Society; Scientific Adviser, CEA-DAM, France; Al Faroubi Reform Consultant, University Almaty, Kazakhstan. Address: Laboratoire de Physique des Gaz et Plasmas, Bat 210, UPS, 91405-Orsay, France. E-mail: claude.deutsch@lpgp.u-psud.fr

DEVANARAYANAN Sankaranarayanan, b. 11 November 1940, Thiruvananthapuram, India. University Professor; Physicist. m. Chitra, 1 son, 1 daughter. Education: BSc, University of Kerala, 1961; MSc, University of Kerala, 1963; PhD, Indian Institute of Science, Bangalore, 1969; Diploma, Uppsala University, Sweden, 1971; DSc, International University, USA, 1999. Appointments: Research Fellow, Indian Institute of Science, 1963-69; Senior Research Assistant, Indian Institute of Science, 1969-70; SIDA Fellow, Institute of Physics, Uppsala, Sweden, 1970-71; Lecturer, 1971-75, Reader, 1975-84, Professor, 1984-2000, Professor and Head, 1993-2000, Physics Department, University of Kerala; Professor, Physics, University of Puerto Rico, Rio Piedras, USA, 1989-91; Principal, KVVS Institute of Technology, Via Adur, 2003-04; Computer Software Languages known: FORTRAN; JAVA; JAVASCRIPT; HTML; SERVELETS. Publications: Over 84 research articles in standard scientific journals in science in solid state physics, spectroscopy, crystal growth and atmospheric physics; Thermal Expansion of Crystals, monograph, 1979; Report on working of University of Kerala, Commission set up by Government of Kerala, 2000; Quantum Mechanics, book, 2005; Quantum Chemistry, book; in press; Physics in Nutshell for Competitive Tests, book, in press; A Course Book on Nuclear Physics, to be published. Honours: Merit Scholar, University of Kerala, 1961-63; SIDA Fellowship, Sweden, 1970-71; Associate Professor, University of Puerto Rico, 1989-91; Member, Commission of Enquiry into Working of University of Kerala 1985-2000, 2000; Over 20 biographies in national and international publications. Memberships: American Physical Society; Indian Vacuum Society; American Chemical Society; Senate, Academic Council, Board of Studies in Physics, Doctoral Committeein Physics, and Faculty of Science, University of Kerala; Indian Physics Association; Indian Meteorological Society; United Writers' Association; Indian Association Physics Teachers; Indian Institute of Science Alumni Association; Elite Indian. Address: Apt 2C, SFS Fairmont, TC15/1494(5), MP Appan Road, Vazhuthacaud, Thiruvananthapuram – 695014, India. E-mail: sdevanarayanan@yahoo.com

DEVLIN Dean, b. 27 August 1962. Actor; Screenplay Writer; Producer. Creative Works: Film produced: The Patriot, 2000; Eight Legged Freaks, 2002; Cellular, 2004; Who Killed the Electric Car? 2006; Fly Boys, 2006; Isobar, 2007; Films written and produced; Stargate, 1994; Independence Day, 1996; Godzilla, 1998; Universal Soldier: The Return, 1999; Isobar, 2007; Film screenplay: Universal Solider, 1992; Actor: My Bodyguard, 1980; The Wild Life, 1984; Real Genius, 1985; City Limits, 1985; Martians Go Home, 1990; Moon 44, 1990; Total Exposure, 1991; TV series: The Visitor (creator, executive producer), 1997; TV appearances in: North Beach, 1985; Rawhide, 1985; Hard Copy, 1987; Generations, 1989; Guest appearances in: LA Law; Happy Days; Misfits of Science. Address: c/o Creative Artists Agency, 9830 Wilshire Boulevard, Beverly Hills, CA 90212, USA.

DEWEY David Lewis, b. 17 November 1927, Scotland. Research Scientist. m. Jacqueline, 1 son, 2 daughters. Education: BA, 1948, MA, 1950, Cambridge; PhD, 1953, London. Appointments: Research Staff, University College Hospital Medical School, London, 1950; Research Staff, University College, London, 1953; Head of Biochemistry and Microbiology, The Gray Institute, 1956-90; Retired, 1990. Publications in the scientific journal, Nature, as author and co-author include: Diaminopimelic acid and lysine, 1952; Modification of the oxygen effect when bacteria are given large pulses of radiation, 1959; Effects of oxygen and nitric oxide on the radiosensitivity of human cells, 1960; X-ray inactivation of inducible enzyme synthesis, 1962; 6-Amino-nicotinamide and the radiosensitivity of human liver cells, 1963; Interconvertion of cystine and cysteine induced by X-rays, 1965; Action of atomic hydrogen on aqueous bacteriophage, 1968; Major publications in other journals include: The use of the Hersch Cell for the measurement of oxygen in biological material, 1961; Cell dynamics in the bean root tip, 1963; The X-ray sensitivity of Serratia marcescens, 1963; The mechanism of radiosensitisation by iodacetamide, 1965; The survival of Micrococcus radiodurans irradiated at high LET., 1969; The viability of bateriophage T4 after irradiation of only the head component or the tail component, 1973; Treatment of malignant melanoma by intravascular 4-hydroxyanisole, 1981. Honours: Rockefeller Fund Grant, 1950; Damon Runyon Memorial Fellowship, 1965. Memberships: Biochemical Society (Emeritus); British Association; Radiation Research Society (Emeritus); British Institution of Radiology. Address: Happs Edge, Box Lane, Bovingdon, Herts HP3 0DJ, England.

DEWHIRST Ian, b. 17 October 1936, Keighley, Yorkshire, England. Retired Librarian; Writer; Poet. Education: BA Honours, Victoria University of Manchester, 1958. Appointment: Staff, Keighley Public Library, 1960-91. Publications: The Handloom Weaver and Other Poems, 1965; Scar Top and Other Poems, 1968; Gleanings From Victorian Yorkshire, 1972; A History of Keighley, 1974; Yorkshire Through the Years, 1975; Gleanings from Edwardian Yorkshire, 1975; The Story of a Nobody, 1980; You Don't Remember Bananas, 1985; Keighley in Old Picture Postcards, 1987; In the Reign of the Peacemaker, 1993; Down Memory Lane, 1993; Images of Keighley, 1996; Co-editor, A Century of Yorkshire Dialect, 1997; Keighley in the Second World War, 2005; Nah Then! A Treasury of Yorkshire Dialect Quotations, 2010. Contributions to: Yorkshire Ridings Magazine; Lancashire Magazine; Dalesman; Cumbria; Pennine Magazine; Transactions of the Yorkshire Dialect Society; Yorkshire Journal; Down Your Way; Northern Life. Honour: Honorary Doctor of Letters, University of Bradford, 1996; MBE, 1999. Memberships: Yorkshire Dialect Society; Edward Thomas Fellowship. Address: 14 Raglan Avenue, Fell Lane, Keighley, West Yorkshire BD22 6BJ, England.

DEXTER Colin, b. 29 September 1930, Stamford, Lincolnshire, England. Author; Educationist. m. Dorothy, 1 son, 1 daughter. Education: Christ's College, Cambridge; MA (Cantab); MA (Oxon). Appointments: National Service, Royal Signals, 1948-50; Assistant Classics Master, Wyggeston School for Boys, 1953-57; Sixth Form Classics Master, Loughborough Grammar School, 1957-59; Senior Classics Master, Corby Grammar School, 1959-66; Senior Assistant Secretary, Oxford University Delegacy of Local Examinations, 1966-88. Publications: Co-author, 3 General Studies textbooks, 1960s; Last Bus to Woodstock, 1975; Last Seen Wearing, 1976; The Silent World of Nicholas Quinn, 1977; Service of All the Dead, 1979; The Dead of Jericho, 1981; The Riddle of the Third Mile, 1983; The Secret of Annexe 3, 1986; The Wench is Dead, 1989; The Jewel That Was Ours, 1991; The Way Through the Woods, 1992; Morse's Greatest Mystery, 1993; The Daughters of Cain, 1994; Death is Now My Neighbour, 1996; The Remorseful Day, 1999; Chambers Book of Morse Crosswords, 2006; Cracking Cryptic Crosswords, 2009. Honours: MA (Cantab); MA (Oxon); Hon MA (Leicester University); Hon D Litt (Oxford Brookes University); Crime Writers' Silver Dagger, 1979, 1981; Crime Writers' Gold Dagger, 1989, 1992; Crime Writers' Diamond Dagger, 1997; Officer of the Order of the British Empire, 2000; Freedom of the City of Oxford, 2001; Honorary Fellow, St Cross College, Oxford. Memberships: Housman Society; Crime Writers' Association; Detection Club. Address: 456 Banbury Road, Oxford OX2 7RG, England.

DHALL Dharam Pal, b. 8 December 1937, Kenya. Vascular Surgeon. m. Tehseen, 1 son, 1 daughter. Education: MBChB, 1961; FRCS, 1965; PhD, 1967; MD, 1968; FRACS, 1994, MACE, 2002. Appointments: Senior Registrar, Lecturer, Surgery, Aberdeen University; Professor of Surgery, University of Nairobi; Senior Consultant Surgeon, Canberra Hospital; Visiting Fellow, John Curtin School of Medical Research, Canberra; Director, Institute of Sathya Sai Education, Canberra, Director, Educare International Ltd; Academic Adviser, University of Central Queensland for Master of Learning Management in Human Values, University of Queensland; Adjunct Professor of Bioethics, University of Canberra. Publications: Approximately 200 articles in Scientific Medical Journals; 15 books on the teachings of Sri Sathya Sai Baba including Human Values, The Heart of Dynamic Parenting; Workshops on Dynamic Parenting; Stepping Stones to Peace; Dynamic Dharma; Over one hundred articles in professional journals. Honours include: Hallett Award, 1963; National Heart Foundation; NH and MRC, Australia; Pharmacia Uppsala, Sweden. Memberships: World Education Federation; Associate Member, Australian Counselling Association; Member, Australian College of Educators; Past Chairman, Education Committee, Prashanti Council, Puttaparthi, India; Member, Education Committee, Sr Sathya Sai World Foundation; Member, Expert's Panel in Education in Human Values, UN Habitat. Address: PO Box 697, Queanbeyan, NSW 2620, Australia. E-mail: paldhall@aol.com

DHANA RAJU Reddy, b. 10 December 1942, Rajahmundry, AP, India. Geologist. m. Manikyamba, 2 sons, 1 daughter. Education: MSc, Geology, 1965, PhD, Mineralogy and Petrology, 1970, Andhra University, Visakhapatnam. Appointments: Junior Research Fellow, University Grants Commission, 1965-67; Senior/Postdoctoral Research Fellow, 1967-70, Pool Officer, 1971-73, CSIR; Scientific Officer, 1973-2000, Associate Director, 2000-02, Department of Atomic Energy; Honorary Visiting Professor, Department of Applied Geochemistry, Osmania University, 2005-08; Adviser, Taurian Resources Niger SA, 2010-11. Publications: Over 140 research papers in peer-reviewed journals; 3 books. Honours: Society's Medal, 1974; National Mineral Award, 2002; S Narayanaswamy Award, 2003; Professor P R J Naidu Gold Medal, 2005; Bharat Excellence Award, 2011. Memberships: Research Advisory Committee, Wadia of Institute of Himalayan Geology; Department of Science and Technology's Deep Continental Studies; Life Fellow: Geological Society of India; Geological, Mining & Metallurgical Society of India; Indian Society of Applied Geochemists; South Asian Association of Economic Geologists; Andhra Pradesh Akademi of Sciences; Life Member: Indian Science Congress Association; Indian Nuclear Society; Indian Physics Association. Address: 1-10-284/1, Begumpet, Brahmanwadi Lane no 5, Hyderabad – 500 016, India. E-mail: dhanaraju.reddi@gmail.com

DHARIWAL Kewal Singh, b. 17 March 1950, Chack Vendal, India. Mechanical Engineer. m. Balwinder Kaur. Education: HND, 1974, T Cert, 1984, University of Wolverhampton; BSc, University of Central England, 1981; MSc, University of Aston, 1983; DPTM, University of Greenwich, 1985; Fellowship, University of Sussex, 1990. Appointments: Various employment, 1968-70; Part-time Engineering Trainee, 1970-73; Designer, 1974-81; Education Officer (Technical), 1983-84; Employment Officer, 1984-87, late Chief Officer. Publications: Various research reports, educational and work related. Honours: Fellow, American Biographical Institute; Biographical Honour Award, IBC, 1993; Distinguished Leadership Award, ABI; World Lifetime Achievement Award, ABI, 1993; Gold Medal for England, ABI, 2007; The World Medal of Freedom, ABI, 2007; American Medal of Honor, ABI, 2007; International Peace Prize, United Cultural Convention, 2008; Order of Merit, ABI, 2008; Distinguished Service Order, ABI, 2010. Memberships: Member, Chartered Management Institute; Late Chartered Engineer; Late Member, Institute of Training and Development; Chairman and Executive Committee Member, Croydon Race E Council, 1987-93; Member, Croydon Ethnic Minority Forum, 1989-93; Croydon Police Consultative Committee, 1989-93; Croydon Career & Training Advice Committee, 1984-87; Served on various projects locally and internationally; Member, Siri Guru Singh Sabha and Sutton Race Equality Council. Address: 4 Clarice Way, Wallington, Surrey SM6 9LD, England.

D'HEURLE Adma, b. 21 June 1924, Lebanon. Professor. m. Francois, 3 sons. Education: AB (distinction), University of Beirut, 1947; MA, Smith College, 1948; PhD, University of Chicago, 1953. Appointments: Lecturer, Social Thought, Slanford University, 1972-73; Adjunct Professor, Long Island University, 1975-80; Visiting Professor, University of Uppsala, Sweden, 1980-81; Visiting Adjunct Professor, University of Turku, Finland, 1987, 1989-96; Professor of Psychology, Mercy College, New York. Publications: Numerous articles in professional journals. Honours: Honoured Nominee for Professor of the Year, 1987; Fulbright Grant, 1987; Research Grant, Finnish Peace Institute, 1990; Outstanding Education of America, 1992; Special Recognition of Extraordinary Service to the Commission of Higher Education, 1994; Mercy College Teaching Excellence Award, 1995; Gold Medal for Distinguished Accomplishments in Psychology, Mercy College, 1998. Memberships: American Psychological Association; American Psychological Society; American Association of University Professors; Ibsen Association of America; Psychiatrists for Social Responsibility. Address: 1695 Spring Valley Road, Ossining, NY 10562, USA. E-mail: adamdh@gmail.com

DHOLAKIA Navnit, The Right Honourable Lord Navnit, Baron Dholakia of Waltham Brooks. m. 2 daughters. Appointments: Deputy Lieutenant, County of West Sussex, 1999; President, National Association for the Care and Resettlement of Offenders; Chair, NACRO Race Issues Advisory Committee; Vice President, Mental Health Foundation; Vice Chairman, Policy Research Institute on Ageing and Ethnicity; Sits on House of Lords Appointment Commission; Trustee, Pallant House Gallery, Chichester; Trustee, British Empire and Commonwealth Museum, Bristol; Previously with Commission for Racial Equality; Previously with Police Complaints Authority; Served on Council of Save the Children Fund; Served on Howard League of Penal Reform; Serves on Editorial Board of Howard Journal; Member, Ethnic Minority Advisory Committee of the Judicial Studies Board; Served on Lord Carlisle's Committee on Parole Systems Review; Magistrate and Member, Board of Visitors for HM Prison Lewes; Elected President, Liberal Democrats, 2000-04; Deputy Leader, Liberal Democrats, 2004. Honours: Asian of the Year, 2000; Pravasi Bharatiya Samman Award, 2003; OBE; Member of HGL Appointment Commission. Address: House of Lords, London SW1A 0PW, England.

DI FALCO Gerard Anthony, b. 26 September 1952, Camden, New Jersey, USA. Visual Artist; Independent Curator; Writer. Education: BA, Rutgers University, Camden, New Jersey, 1974; MS, Drexel University, Philadelphia, USA, 1985. Appointments: Self-employed Visual Artist, 1979-; Self-employed Curatorial Consultant, 1984-; Solo exhibitions: Retrospective (Twenty Year), University of Pennsylvania, 2002; Holy Family University, Philadelphia, 2009; Philadelphia Open Studio Tours, 2010. Publications: Novel, Waiting for the Countdown, 2006; Over 250 solo and juried group exhibitions, 1984-. Honours: Alumni Association Award in Creative Writing, Rutgers University, 1974; Individual Artist's Grant, Pennsylvania Council on the Arts, 1992; Individual Artist's Grant, Pollock-Krasher Foundation, New York City, 2002; Resident Artist Award in Education, Philadelphia Museum of Art, 2003; City of Philadelphia's Humanitarian Award in Art and Culture for 30 years of Social Service to the Community of Arts, 2009. Memberships: DaVinci Art Alliance, Philadelphia; Episcopal Church and Visual Artists; The Print Center, Philadelphia; The Fleisher Art Memorial, Philadelphia. Address: 2201 Cherry Street, Unit 902, Philadelphia, PA 19103, USA. Website: www.absolutearts.com/gerarddifalco/

DI MELCHIORRE Silvio, b. 23 May 1972, Buenos Aires, Argentina. Airline Consultant; Political Scientist; Private Investor. Education: Participant, Jornadas Nietzsche, 1994, 1998; Political Scientist with speciality, International Relations, University of Buenos Aires, 1997; Graduate, IATA-UFTAA Basic Course, IATA Learning Centre, 1998; Participant, Quinto Programa de Simulación Búrsatil, University of Buenos Aires, 1999. Appointments: Managing Director, BII Worldwide, Buenos Aires, 1991-92; President, SDM Internacional, Buenos Aires, 1993-95; Consulting in field, Buenos Aires, 1993-95; Banking Mediator, Buenos Aires, 1995-96; Founder Director, Biblioteca Silvio Di Melchiorre, Buenos Aires, 1996-97; Airline Consultant, Buenos Aires, 1996; Airways Policy Adviser, Buenos Aires, 1997-2000; Private Investor, Buenos Aires, 2000-. Publications: Editor, Director, TAIN Magazine, Buenos Aires, 1987-88; Boletín Informativo Internacional, Buenos Aires, 1989-90; Author: Information Service, IO Club, 1992; TV Novel, Ramsés II, 1995; Political Expression, Airways Policy, 1998; Banking Publication, La Banque, 1998. Memberships: Donor countries information service to Fundación Poder Ciudadano, Buenos Aires, 1994; Donor publications to Library of University Del Salvador, Buenos Aires, 1996-97; Instituto del Servicio Exterior de la Nación, Buenos Aires, 1997-98; Bolsa de Comercio de Buenos Aires, 1997-2001. Address: Bartolome Mitre 1676, Piso 3, Dpto 11, Cuerpo 2, C1037ABF Buenos Aires, Argentina. E-mail: sdimelchiorre@hotmail.com Website: www.ukshares.com.ar

DIAMOND Neil Leslie, b. 24 January 1941, Brooklyn, New York, USA. Singer; Composer. m. Marcia Murphey, 1975, 4 children. Education: Pre-med student, New York University. Career: Songwriter for publishing company; Formerly with Bang and MCA Records, 1973-, with Columbia; Record 20 show run at Winter Garden Theatre, 1972; Tours worldwide, include: 2 year, Love In The Round, world tour; Television and radio specials, numerous including: Christmas specials, 1992, 1993; Acted with Sir Laurence Olivier in The Jazz

Singer, 1980; Set major box office records world wide; 92 million albums sold. Compositions include: I'm A Believer (number 1 for Monkees); Film scores: Jonathan Livingston Seagull, 1973; Every Which Way But Loose, 1978; The Jazz Singer, 1980. Recordings: Albums include: The Feel Of Neil Diamond, 1966; Just For You, 1967; Shilo, 1970; Velvet Gloves and Spit, 1968; Touching You Touching Me; Stones, 1971; Hot August Nights; Moods, 1972; Jonathan Livingston Seagull, 1973; Serenade, 1974; Beautiful Noise, 1976; Live At The Greek, 1977; I'm Glad You're Here Tonight, 1977; You Don't Bring Me Flowers, 1978; September Morn, 1980; Jazz Singer, 1980; Song Sung Blue, 1982; Headed For The Future, 1986; Hot August Night II, 1987; The Best Years of Our Lives, 1989; Christmas Album, 1992; Greatest Hits 1966-1992, 1992; Up On the Roof - Songs From The Brill Building, 1993; Live In America, 1994; Christmas Album, Vol II, 1994; Tennessee Moon, 1996; Live in Concert, 1997; The Movie Album, 1998; Singles include: Sweet Caroline, 1969; Song Sung Blue; Cracklin' Rosie; I Am... I Said; Love on the Rocks; As Time Goes By. Honours: Platinum, Gold Records; Globe Awards; Grammy, 1973 for: Jonathan Livingston Seagull. Membership: SESAC. Address: c/o Columbia Records, Media Department, 550 Madison Avenue, New York, NY 1002-3211, USA.

DIAS PEREIRA FILHO Antonio, b. 5 October 1970, Leopoldina, MG, Brazil. Professor; Researcher. m. Neusa Faria, 3 daughters. Education: Accounting degree, Pontificia Universidade Católicade Minas Gerais, 1993; MBA, Universidade Federal de Minas Gerais, 1997; Postgraduate, Universidad Carlos III de Madrid, 2003; PhD, Sciences de gestion, Université de Grenoble II, 2007. Appointments: Assistant Professor, Pontificia Universidade Católicade Minas Gerais, 1996-98; Professor and Researcher, Universidade Federal de Minas Gerais, 1997-; Consultant Ad hoc, Ministério da Educação e Cultura do Brasil, 2000-02; Vice Chief, Department of Management, Universidade Federal de Minas Gerais, 2000-02; Co-ordinator MBA Program, UFMG, 2008; Head, Research Group Finance and Strategy Area, 2008-. Publications: Um Olhar Sobre a Governança das Empresas, 2010; Co-author, Relationship Between the Capital Structure and the Asset Structure in the Electrical Energy and Telecommunications Brazilian Branches, 2010; Structure du Capital, Dynamisme Envionnemental et Performance, 2012. Honours: Honored Professor by graduate students for many years; Best Student in Accounting, PUC, 1990-93; International Award, Conselho Regional de Contabilidade de Minas Gerais, 2009; Fourth Best Article presented at Convibra, 2010. Memberships: Academia Leopoldinense de Letras e Artes; Sociedade Brasileira de Finanças; Association Française de Finance; Instituto dos Auditores Independentes do Brasil.

DIAZ Cameron, b. 30 August 1972, Long Beach, California, USA. Actress. Appointments: Films include: The Mask, 1994; The Last Supper, 1995; Feeling Minnesota, 1996; She's the One, 1996; A Life Less Ordinary, 1997; There's Something About Mary, 1998; Very Bad Things, 1998; Being John Malkovich, 1999; Invisible Circus, 1999; Any Given Sunday, 1999; Charlie's Angels, 2000; Things You Can Tell Just by Looking at Her, 2000; Shrek (voice), 2001; Vanilla Sky, 2001; The Sweetest Thing, 2002; Gangs of New York, 2002; Minority Report, 2002; Charlie's Angels: Full Throttle, 2003; Shrek 2 (voice), 2004; In Her Shoes, 2005; The Holiday, 2006; The Who is Norman Lloyd?, 2007; Shrek the Third (voice), 2007; What Happens in Vegas, 2008; The Box, 2009; My Sister's Keeper, 2009; Shrek Forever After (voice), 2010; Knight and Day, 2010; The Green Hornet, 2011; Bad Teacher, 2011; What to Expect When You're Expecting, 2012; Gambit, 2012; The Counselor, 2013. Honours: Boston Society of Film Critics Best Supporting Actress, 2001; Chicago Film Critics Best Supporting Actress, 2002. Address: c/o International Creative Management, 8942 Wilshire Boulevard, Beverly Hills, CA 90211, USA.

DiCAPRIO Leonardo, b. 11 November 1974, Hollywood, USA. Actor. Films include: Critters III, 1991; Poison Ivy, 1992; This Boy's Life, 1993; What's Eating Gilbert Grape, 1993; The Quick and the Dead, 1995; The Basketball Diaries, 1995; William Shakespeare's Romeo and Juliet, 1996; Titanic, 1996; Man in the Iron Mask, 1997; The Beach, 1999; Don's Plum, 2001; Gangs of New York, 2002; Catch Me If You Can, 2002; The Aviator, 2004; The Departed, 2006; Blood Diamond, 2006; The 11th Hour 2007; Revolutionary Road, 2008; Body of Lies, 2008; Shutter Island, 2010; Inception, 2010; J Edgar, 2011; Django Unchained, 2012; The Great Gatsby, 2013; TV series include: Parenthood, 1990; Growing Pains, 1991; Honours: Commandeur de l'Ordre des Arts et Lettres; Platinum Award, Santa Barbara International Film Festival, 2005. Address: c/o Birken Productions Inc, PO Box 291958, Los Angeles, CA 90029, USA. Website: www.leonardodicaprio.com

DICKINSON Angie (pseudonym of Angeline Brown), b. 30 September 1931, Kulm, North Dakota, USA. Actress. Education: Glendale College. Appointments: Actress in films: Lucky Me, 1954; Man With the Gun; The Return of Jack Slade; Tennessee's Partner; The Black Whip; Hidden Guns; Tension at Table Rock; Gun the Man Down; Calypso Joe; China Gate; Shoot Out at Medicine Bend; Cry Terror; I Married a Woman; Rio Bravo; The Bramble Bush; Ocean's 11; A Fever in the Blood; The Sins of Rachel Cade; Jessica; Rome Adventure; Captain Newman MD; The Killers; The Art of Love; Cast a Giant Shadow; The Chase; Poppy is Also a Flower; The Last Challenge; Point Blank; Sam Whiskey; Some Kind of Nut; Young Billy Young; Pretty Maids All in A Row; The Resurrection of Zachery Wheeler; The Outside Man; Big Bad Mama; Klondike Fever; Dressed to Kill; Charlie Chan and the Curse of the Dragon Queen; Death Hunt; Big Bad Mama II; Even Cowgirls Get The Blues; The Maddening; Sabrina; The Sun - The Moon and the Stars; Sealed with a Kiss, 1999; The Last Producer, 2000; Duets, 2000; Pay It Forward, 2000; Big Bad Love, 2001; Ocean's Eleven, 2001; Elvis Has Left the Building, 2004; 3055 Jean Leon, 2006; TV series: Police Woman; Cassie & Co; TV films: The Love War; Thief; See the Man Run; The Norliss Tapes; Pray for the Wildcats; A Sensitive Passionate Man; Overboard; The Suicide's Wife; Dial M for Murder; One Shoe Makes it Murder; Jealousy; A Touch of Scandal; Still Watch; Police Story: The Freeway Killings; Once Upon a Texas Train; Prime Target; Treacherous Crossing; Danielle Steel's Remembrance; Mini-series: Pearl; Hollywood Wives; Wild Palms. Address: 1715 Carla Ridge, Beverly Hills, CA 90120-1911, USA.

DICKINSON David Robert, b. 10 April 1933, Styford, Northumberland, England. Salesman. m. Mona Mackenzie, 1 son, 1 daughter. Education: Greshams School, Norfolk. Appointments: Shell International Petroleum Co; Guinness Overseas Ltd; Arthur Guinness (Park Royal) Ltd; Chairman, East Midlands Museums Service, 1997; Chairman, North Kesteven District Council, 2000; Chairman, Lincolnshire County Council, 2007; Chairman, Evedon Enterprises. Memberships: Marylebone Cricket Club; Conservative Party; Vice President, Sleaford & North Hykeham. Address: Manor House, Evedon, Sleaford, Lincolnshire NG34 9PA, England.

DIDO (Dido Florian Cloud de Bounevialle Armstrong), b. 25 December 1971, London, England. m. Rohan Gavin, 1 son. Singer; Musician; Songwriter. Education: Guildhall School of Music, London. Career: Toured UK with classical music ensemble before joining pop groups aged 16; Toured with brother Rollo's band, Faithless; Signed solo deal with Arista Records, New York; Recordings: Albums: No Angel, 1999; Life for Rent, 2003; Safe Trip Home, 2008; Girl Who Got Away, 2013; Singles: The Highbury Fields (EP), 1999; Here With Me, 2001; Thank You, 2001; Hunter, 2001; All You Want, 2002; Life for Rent, 2003; White Flag, 2003; Don't Leave Home, 2004; Don't Believe in Love, 2008; Quiet Times, 2009; Everything to Lose, 2010; If I Rise, 2011; Let Us Move On, 2012; No Freedom, 2013; TV: Numerous appearances. Honours: BRIT Award, Best Album, 2002; BRIT Award, Best Female Solo Artist, 2002, 2004; Ivor Novello Songwriter of the Year Award, 2002; BAMBI Award for Best International Pop Act, 2003; BRIT Awards, 2004, 2010; International Dance Music Awards, 2005; Grammy Award, 2007; Academy Award, 2010. Address: c/o Arista, 423 New King's Road, London SW6, England. Website: www.didomusic.com

DIEMER Emma Lou, b. 24 November 1927, Kansas City, Missouri, USA. Composer; Professor; Musician. Education: BM, 1949, MM, 1950, Yale School of Music; PhD, Eastman School of Music, 1960. Appointments: Composer-in-Residence, Arlington Virginia Schools; Professor of Composition, University of Maryland, 1965-70; Professor of Composition, 1971-91, Professor Emeritus, 1991-, University of California. Publications: Over 200 publications, 1957-2009; Orchestra, chamber works, choral works, vocal works and solo instrumental works; Several articles on music; Listed in national and international biographical dictionaries. Honours include: Fulbright Scholarship in composition and piano, 1952-53; NEA Fellowship in electronic music, 1980; ASCAP Award annually since 1962; AGO Composer of the Year, 1995; Honorary Doctorate, University of Central Missouri, 1999; Guest Composer, Eastman School of Music Women in Music Festival, 2010. Memberships: ASCAP; Mu Phi Epsilon; American Guild of Organists; American Music Center; International Alliance for Women in Music. Address: 2249 Vista del Campo, Santa Barbara, CA 93101, USA. E-mail: eldiemer@cox.net

DIERINGER Gregg, b. 18 October 1956, Athens, Ohio, USA. Plant Ecologist. m. Leticia Cabrera, 2 sons. Education: BS cum laude, 1979, MS, 1981, University of Akron; PhD, University of Texas at Austin, 1988. Appointments: Teaching Assistant, University of Akron, 1979-81; Teaching Assistant, 1983, Research Assistant, 1983-84, Teaching Assistant, 1984-88, Instructor, 1990-92, University of Texas at Austin; Instructor, Austin Community College, 1988, 1989-92; Assistant Professor, Southwest Texas State University, 1989; Visiting Professor, Instituto de Ecologia, Veracruz, Mexico, 1992-93; Assistant Professor, 1993-97, Associate Professor, 1997-99, Western Illinois University; Lecturer, University of Texas at Brownsville, 1999-2002; Associate Professor 2003-2006; Professor and Chair, 2006-, Department of Biological Sciences, Northwest Missouri State University. Publications: Numerous articles in professional journals; Presentations at scientific meetings; General reports and book reviews. Honours: Eagle Scout, 1973; Phi Sigma Alpha, University of Akron, 1978; Scholarship to attend Rocky Mountain Biological Station, 1983; Several research grants. Memberships: Botanical Society of America. Address: Department of Biological Sciences, Northwest Missouri State University, 800 University Dr, Maryville, MO 64468, USA. E-mail: greggd@nwmissouri.edu

DIGBY-BELL Christopher, b. 21 June 1948, Aberdeen, Scotland. Lawyer. 2 sons, 1 daughter. Education: Marlborough College, 1961-65; College of Law. Appointments: Articled at Taylor & Humbert, 1966-71; Taylor Garrett (now Taylor Wessing), 1972-89, Managing Partner, Taylor Garrett, 1987-89; Frere Cholmeley Bischoff, 1989-98, International Managing Partner, 1995-97; Chief Executive and General Counsel, 1998-2009, Vice Chairman, 2009, Palmer Capital Partners. Publications: Regular contributor to Times, Lawyer and other legal journals. Honours: Special Award, UNICEF Child Rights Lawyer of the Year Awards, 2002; Judges Award, Liberty/Justice Human Rights Lawyer of the Year Awards, 2002. Memberships: Law Society; Cambridgeshire and District Law Society; City of London Law Society; Honorary Legal Advisor, Down's Syndrome Association; City of London Member of Law Society Ruling Council, 2001-03 and 2010; Bedfordshire & Cambridgeshire Member of Law Society Ruling Council, 2005-08. Address: Palmer Capital Partners, Time & Life Building, 1 Bruton Street, Mayfair, London W1J 6TL, England. E-mail: chdb@palmercapital.co.uk

DIGUMARTI Bhaskara Rao, b. 9 June 1957. Principal; Professor. Education: BSc, Zoology, Botany, Chemistry, Andhra University, 1977; MSc, Zoology, 1980, MA, Political Science, 1982, Bhopal University; B Ed, Biological Science, English, 1981, M Ed, Education, 1982, MA, Sociology, 1993, Nagarjuna University; PhD, Education, Osmania University, 1990. Appointments: Academic Adviser, Ravindra Bharathi Public School, Vijayawada, 1983-; Counsellor, Indira Gandhi National Open University, 1993-; Adviser, Krosur Mandal Co-operative Junior College, 1994-; Secretary, Academy of Culture Communication Education Science and Service, 1997-; President, Programme Advisory Committee, 2000-03, President, Grievance/Vigilance Committee, 2001-03, Jan Shikshan Sansthan, Guntur; Principal, 2001-02, 2009-10, 2011-, Reader, 2002-11, Professor, 2011-, RVR College of Education, Guntur; Counsellor, MS University, 2003-; Research Director, Education, Nagarjuna University, 2003-; Academic Co-ordinator, Sri Nagarjuna Publishers, Guntur, 2003-. Publications: Numerous articles in professional journals. Honours: Seva Ratna, 1996, 1998; Vidya Seva Vibhushan, 2000; Bharat Gaurav Award, 2000; Best Citizen of India Award, 2001; Jewel of India Award, 2001, 2004; Best Educationist Award, 2004; Chakarapani Kolasani Award, 2009; Global Achievers Award, 2010; Indira Gandhi Sadbhavana Award, 2011; Lifetime Education Achievement Award, 2011. Memberships: UNESCO Club of Repalle; UNESCO Club of Guntur; SITU Council of Educational Research, Madras; District Research Advisory Board, Government of AP; European Peace Research Association; International Peace Research Association; Peace Education Commission, USA. Address: D-43 (277) SVN Colony, Guntur – 522 006, Andhra Pradesh, India. E-mail: digumartibhaskararao@rediffmail.com

DILLON Doris, b. 1 December 1929, Kansas City, Missouri, USA. Artist; Lecturer; Professor. m. Louis Kenofer, 1 son, 1 daughter. Education: BA, Art and Interior Design, 1951, MA, Art History, 1965, University of Denver. Appointments: Deputy Director General (IBC); Continental Governor of the ABI; Advisory Panel, Colorado Council of the Arts and Humanities; Member of the Board, Asian Art Association, Denver Art Museum; Life Fellow, IBC; Consular Representative of the United Cultural Council; Founding Curator, Van Vechten/Lineberry Art Museum (now The Taos Art Museum), Taos, New Mexico; Consultant, Sarkisian's Oriental Imports, Denver, Colorado; Lecturer, Arapantoe Junior College, Littleton, Colorado; Chairperson,

Department of Fine Arts, Regis College, Denver, Colorado; Board of Directors, Asian Art Association, Denver Art Museum. Art Exhibits include: By invitation: Dublin, Ireland; St John's College, Cambridge, England; University of Oxford, England; Honolulu, Hawaii; 26th Congress on the Arts and Communications, Lisbon, Portugal; Aerospace: Century XXI, University of Colorado, Boulder, Colorado, USA; One Person Show, Colburn Earth/Science Museum, Asheville, North Carolina, USA; International Platform Association, Washington DC; Nelson Rockefeller Collection Gallery, New York; St John's College, Cambridge University, England; Denver Art Museum Group Show; Colorado State Centennial; Denver Museum of Natural History; Vancouver, BC, Canada; Group show, Merriman Galleries, Asheville, NC, 2008; One person show, Margo Fish Gallery, New York, 2009. Honours: Art 1st place, Western States Rocky Mountain Conference Center, USA; Best of Show by Vote, International Platform Association, Washington, DC; International Woman of the Year, IBC; Excellence in the Arts, Key Award, ABI; AAUW Salute to Women Award; Congress Medallion of Distinctive Participation, 30th Congress on Science Art and Communication, Dublin, Ireland, 2004; International Visual Artist, 2004; Permanent Appointment to the United Cultural Council World Forums; Ambassador for US to the World Forum; Merriman Galleries, Asheville, NC, 2009. Memberships: International Governors' Club (ABI); National League of Pen Arts Women; International Platform Association; Mensa International Scholarship Juror. Address: 315 Delphia Drive, Brevard, NC 28712, USA.

DILLON Matt, b. 18 February 1964, New Rochelle, New York, USA. Actor. Appointments: Films include: Over the Edge, 1979; Little Darlings, 1980; My Bodyguard, 1980; Liar's Moon, 1982; Tex, 1982; The Outsiders, 1983; Rumble Fish, 1983; The Flamingo Kid, 1984; Target, 1985; Rebel, 1985; Native Son, 1986; The Big Town (The Arm), 1987; Kansas, 1988; Drugstore Cowboy, 1989; A Kiss Before Dying, 1991; Singles, 1992; The Saint of Fort Washington, 1993; Mr Wonderful, 1993; Golden Gate, 1994; To Die For; Frankie Starlight; Beautiful Girls; Grace of My Heart; Albino Alligator; In and Out, 1997; There's Something About Mary, 1998; One Night at McCool's, 2000; Deuces Wild, 2000; City of Ghosts, 2002; Employee of the Month, 2004; Loverboy, 2005; Factotum, 2005; Herbie Fully Loaded, 2005; You, Me and Dupree, 2006; Nothing But the Truth, 2008; Old Dogs, 2009; Amored, 2009; Takers, 2010. Address: William Morris Agency, ICM 151 S El Camino Drive, Beverly Hills, CA 90212, USA.

DIMACOPOULOS Jordan E, b. 1 January 1940, Lebadeia, Boeotia, Central Greece. Retired High-Rank Civil Clerk. Education: Diploma, Athens Technical University, School of Architecture, 1964; PhD, Polytechnic School, Aristotle University of Thessaloniki, 1977; Diploma in Conservation Studies, University of York, UK, 1975. Appointments: Architect, Ioannis Despotopoulos' Architectural Studio, Athens, 1964-65; Architect, Directorate for Monument Restoration, 1965-76; Director, Directorate for Monument Restoration, 1976-80; Director, Directorate for the Restoration of Post 1830 Historic Monuments, 1980-82; Director, Directorate for the Restoration of Ancient Monuments, 1982-98; Director General, 1998-2000, Honorary Director General, 2001-, Directorate General for Monument Restoration, Museums and Construction Works; Member, Greek Central Archaeological Council, 1976-80, 1982-2000, 2002-05; Major works of tenure: Designed and built the museums of Poros, Kilkis, Lavrion and Setia, 1965-73; Much work on saving and restoring the Houses of Plaka, the area around the Acropolis, 1980-82; Conceived and supervised the erection of a tumulus-like shelter for the Vergina Royal Tombs, 1991-93; Constructed a system of walkways for visitors to the Knossos Minoan Palace, 1996-97. Publications: Books: The Houses of Rethymnon, 1977, reprinted 2001; An Anthology of Greek Architecture 15th –20th Centuries, 1981; George Whitmore on Corfu, 1994; Scripta Minora: Architectural Investigations and Monument-Conservation Projects, 2005; Articles in various learned periodicals and journals including: The Archaeologhikon Deltion; The Archaeologhike Ephemeris; Athens Annals of Archaeology; Bulletin of the Christian Archaeological Society; Castellum, Rome, The Architectural Review, London; Architectura, Berlin-Munich; Revue Archéologique, Paris; Arkos, Scienza e Restauro, Milan; ICOMOS Information, The Monumentum, Europa Nostra Bulletin. Honours: Athens Academy Award, 1982; Europa Nostra Medal, 1982; Greek State "Prize of Satisfaction", 1997. Memberships: Member of the Board, 2000, 2002-, Athens Archaeological Society; Korrespondierendes Mitglied des Deutschen Archäologischen Instituts, 1999. Address: 12 St George Karytsis Square, Athens 10561, Greece.

DIMBLEBY David, b. 28 October 1938, London, England. Broadcaster; Newspaper Proprietor. m. (1) Joceline Gaskell, 1967, dissolved, 1 son, 2 daughters, (2) Belinda Giles, 2000, 1 son. Education: Christ Church, Oxford; University of Paris; University of Perugia. Appointments: Presenter and interviewer, BBC Bristol, 1960-61; Broadcasts include: Quest; What's New?; People and Power, 1982-83; General Election Results Programmes, 1979, 1983, 1987; various programmes for the Budget, by-elections, local elections; Presenter, Question Time BBC, 1993-; Documentary films include: Ku-Klux-Klan; The Forgotten Million; Cyprus: The Thin Blue Line, 1964-65; South Africa: The White Tribe, 1979; The Struggle for South Africa, 1990; US-UK Relations: An Ocean Apart, 1988; David Dimbleby's India, 1997; A Picture of Britain, 2005; How We Built Britain, 2007; The Seven Ages of Britain; 2010; Live commentary on many public occasions including: State Opening of Parliament; Trooping the Colour; Wedding of HRH Prince Andrew and Sarah Ferguson; H M The Queen Mother's 90th Birthday Parade; Funeral of Diana, Princess of Wales, 1997; Memorial Services including Lord Olivier. Publication: An Ocean Apart (with David Reynolds), 1988. Honours: Supreme Documentary Award, Royal TV Society; US Emmy Award, Monte Carlo Golden Nymph; Royal TV Society, Outstanding Documentary Award, 1990, 1997; Honorary Graduate of the University of Essex, 2005; The President of the Institute for Citizenship. Address: c/o Coutts & Co, 440 Strand, London WC1R 0QS, England.

DIMBLEBY Jonathan, b. 31 July 1944. Broadcaster; Journalist; Author. m. (1) Bel Mooney, 1968, divorced, 1 son, 1 daughter. (2) Jessica Ray, 2007, 1 daughter. Education: University College, London. Appointments: Reporter, BBC Bristol, 1969-70; BBC Radio, World at One, 1970-71; Reporter, This Week, Thames TV, 1972-78, 1986-88, TV Eye, 1979; Reporter, Yorkshire TV, Jonathan Dimbleby in Evidence: The Police (series); The Bomb, 1980; The Eagle and the Bear, 1981; The Cold War Game, 1982; The American Dream, 1984; Four Years On - The Bomb, 1984; Associate Ed/Presenter, First Tuesday, 1982-86; Presenter/Ed, Jonathan Dimbleby on Sunday, TV AM, 1985-86; On the Record, BBC TV, 1988-93; Charles: The Private Man, The Public Role, Central TV, 1994; Jonathan Dimbleby, London Weekend TV, 1995-; Presenter, Any Questions?, BBC Radio 4, 1987-; Any Answers?, 1989-; Writer/Presenter, The Last

Governor, Central TV, 1997; An Ethiopian Journey, LWT, 1998; A Kosovo Journey, LWT, 2000; Michael Heseltine – A Life in the Political Jungle, LWT, 2000. Publications: Richard Dimbleby, 1975; The Palestinians, 1979; The Prince of Wales: A Biography, 1994; The Last Governor, 1997. Honours: Richard Dimbleby Award, 1974. Memberships: VP, Council for Protection of Rural England, 1997-; Soil Association, 1997-; President, Voluntary Service Overseas, 1999-; Bath Festivals Trust, 2003. Address: c/o David Higham Associates Ltd, 5 Lower John Street, W1R 4HA, England.

DINI Luciana, b. 19 January 1955, Rome, Italy. Full Professor. Education: MD, Biology, University of Rome "La Sapienza", 1977. Appointments: Researcher, University of Rome "Tor Vergata", Department of Biology, 1982-92; Associate Professor of Comparative Anatomy and Cytology, Department of Biology, 1992-2000, Full Professor of Comparative Anatomy and Cytology, Department of Biological and Environmental Science Technology, 2000-, University of Lecce, Lecce, Italy. Publications: Articles in scientific journals including: Journal of Clinical Investigation, 1994; Blood, 1994; Hepatology, 1995; Microscopy Research Technology, 2002; Cell and Tissue Research, 2003. Honour: Award Winner for best work in the field of cellular biology, Societa Nazionale di Scienza, Lettere ed Arti, 1987. Memberships: European Microscopy Society; European Cell Death Organisation. Address: Department of Biological and Environmental Science Technology, University of Lecce, Via Per Monteroni, Lecce 73100, Italy. E-mail: luciana.dini@unile.it

DINSDALE Reece, b. 6 August 1959, Normanton, West Yorkshire, England. Actor. m. Zara Turner, 1 son, 1 daughter. Education: Normanton Grammar, 1970-77; Guildhall School of Music and Drama, 1977-80. Career: Films include: Rabbit on the Moon; Hamlet; Romance and Rejection; ID; A Private Function; Television includes: Conviction; Ahead of the Class; The Trouble with George; Spooks; Murder in Mind; Thief Takers; Young Catherine; Take Me Home; Coppers; Home to Roost; Threads; Winter Flight; Love Lies Bleeding; The Chase; Coronation Street; Theatre includes: Visiting Mr Green; Love You Too; A Going Concern; Racing Demon; Wild Oats; Observe the Sons of Ulster Marching Towards the Somme. Honours: International Press Award for Best Actor at the Geneva Film Festival for the film ID, 1996; Honorary Vice-President of Huddersfield Town Football Club Patrons Association. Membership: Huddersfield Town Football Club. Address: c/o Jonathan Artaras Associates Ltd, 11 Garrick Street, London WC2E 9AR, England.

DINWIDDY Bruce Harry, b. 1 February 1946, Epsom, England. Diplomat. m. Emma Victoria Dinwiddy, 1 son, 1 daughter. Education: MA, Philosophy, Politics and Economics, New College, Oxford, 1964-67. Appointments: ODI Fellow, Swaziland, 1967-69; Research Officer, ODI, 1970-73; FCO, 1973; First Secretary, UK Delegation (MBFR) Vienna, 1975-77; FCO, 1977-81; Head of Chancery, British Embassy, Cairo, 1981-83; FCO, 1983-86, Cabinet Office, 1986-88; Counsellor, British Embassy, Bonn, 1989-91; Deputy High Commissioner, Ottawa, 1992-95; Head, African Department (Southern), FCO, 1995-98; Commissioner, British Indian Ocean Territory, 1996-98; High Commissioner, Dar Es Salaam, 1998-2001; Seconded to Standard Chartered Bank, 2001-2002; Governor, Cayman Islands, 2002-05; Trustee, Cayman Islands National Recovery Fund, 2004-; Council Member and Chairman, Wider Caribbean Working Group, UK Overseas Territories Conservation Forum, 2006-; Consultant, UK Trade and Investment, 2007-09. Publication: Promoting African Enterprise, 1974. Honour: CMG, 2003. Memberships: Vincent's Club, Oxford; Aldeburgh Golf Club; Royal Wimbledon Golf Club. Address: 8 Connaught Avenue, London, SW14 7RH, England.

DION Celine, b. 1968, Charlemagne, Quebec, Canada. Singer. m. Rene Angelil, 17 Dec 1994. Career: Began singing in father's restaurant; Recording artiste, 1979-; Winner, Eurovision Song Contest for Switzerland, 1988; Recorded in French until 1990; 35 million albums sold to date. Recordings: Albums: 9 albums recorded in French (including Tellement J'ai D'Amour; Dion Chante Plamondon; Incognito); Unison, 1990; Celine Dion, 1991; The Colour Of My Love, 1994; D'Eux, 1995; Falling Into You, 1996; Live a Paris, 1996; Let's Talk About Love, 1997; A l'Olympia, 1998; Chansons en Or, 1998; These Are Special Times, 1998; Let's Talk About Love, 1999; Singles: Les Chemins De Ma Maison, 1984; Melanie, 1985; Une Colombe, 1985; Incognito, 1988; Where Does My Heart Beat Now, 1991; The Power Of Love; Think Twice, 1995; Pour Que Tu M'Aimes Encore, 1995; Misled, 1995; Falling Into Love, 1996; Beauty And The Beast, duet with Peabo Bryson; When I Feel In Love, from film soundtrack Sleepless In Seattle; My Heart Will Go On, from film soundtrack of Titanic, 1998; I'm Your Angel, 1998; Treat Her Like a Lady, 1999. Honours: Gala de L'Adisq Awards: Pop Album of Year, 1983; Best Selling Record, 1984, 1985; Best Selling Single, 1985; Pop Song of the Year, 1985, 1988; Female Artist of Year, 1983-85, 1988; Discovery of the Year, 1983; Best Quebec Artist Outside Quebec, 1983, 1988; JUNO Awards: Album of the Year, 1991; Single of the Year, 1993; Female Vocalist of the Year, 1991-93; Journal de Quebec Trophy, 1985; Spectrel Video Award, Best Stage Performance, 1988. Current Management: c/o Rene Angelil, Feeling Productions Inc., 755- 2540 Daniel-Johnson, Laval, Quebec H7T 2S3, Canada.

DIVAN Gautam Ramanlal, b. 22 July 1940, Bombay, India. Chartered Accountant. m. Bapsy, 1 son, 1 daughter. Education: B Com, University of Bombay, 1959; Associate Member, 1964, Fellow Member, 1969, Institute of Chartered Accountants of India. Appointments: Practising Chartered Accountant, 1964-; Former Chairman, Midsnell Group International, Indo-Swiss Business Committee; Director, Asian Hotels (North) Ltd, Brady & Morris Engineering Co Ltd, HDFC Standard Life Insurance Co Ltd; Past Grand Master, Grand Lodge of India; Trustee, Madgavkar Trust; Representative in India: Murli Laj Chugani Charitable Trust; Royal Overseas League; Former Visiting Lecturer, Sydenham College of Commerce and Economics; Former Member, Board of Governors, N M Institute of Management Studies. Publications: Co-author, Business Opportunities and Taxation – An Overview; Co-author, Business Operations in India. Honours: Arjuna Award, 1964; Maharashtra Gaurav Puraskar. Memberships: All India Management Association; International Fiscal Association. Address: 134 Mittal Tower C Wing, Nariman Point, Mumbai 400 021, India.

DIXON Alan (Michael), b. 15 July 1936, Waterloo, Lancashire, England. m. Josephine Stapleton, 1960. Education: Studied Art, Goldsmiths' College, University of London, 1956-63; University of London Diploma in Visual Arts. Appointments: Teacher of Art, Schools in London and Peterborough, England, 1959-87. Poetry collections: Snails and Reliquaries, 1964; The Upright Position, 1970; The Egotistical Decline, 1978; The Immaculate Magpies, 1982; The Hogweed Lass, 1991; A Far-Off Sound, 1994; Transports, 1996; The Ogling of Lady Luck, 2005; The Seaweed's Secret (versions of poems by Max Jacob), 2011. Contributions to: Poetry; Partisan Review; The

Observer; The Times Literary Supplement; The Listener; New Statesman; London Review of Books; The Nation; London Magazine; Encounter; The Spectator; Prairie Schooner; Salmagundi; The Scotsman. Address: 51 Cherry Garden Road, Eastbourne, BN20 8HG, England.

DIYUNUGE Chandranandana, b. 9 February 1971, Devinuwara, Sri Lanka. Electrical Engineer. m. Meenu, 2 daughters. Education: BSc (Hons), Engineering, University of Moratuwa, 1998; CNC Turret Punching, Amada India (Pvt) Ltd, Bangalore, India & Yokohama, Japan; Designing & Manufacturing Panel Enclosure & Cable Management Systems, VNS (India) (Pvt) Ltd, Mumbai, India; Powder Coating Pretreatment of Metal Product, Anand Impex Powder Coating Plants, Pune, India; CNC Engraving, Tubing & Labeling Machine, Singapore. Appointments: Design Electrical Engineering, Zeus Engineering (Pvt) Ltd, Colombo, 1998-2001; Electrical Engineer, Malco Engineering (Pvt) Ltd, Engineering Contracting Co, 2001-02; Design Electrical Engineer, S TEAM (Pvt) Ltd, Singapore, 2002-03; Engineering Manager, Pubudu Engineers (Pvt) Ltd, 2003; Chairman, Electro Metal Pressings (Pvt) Ltd, 2003-; Chairman, EMP Group of Companies. Honours: 2 Merit Awards, Sri Lanka Entrepreneur of the Year, 2008, 2010; Gold Category International Star Award for World Quality Commitment, Business Initiative Directions, 2011; Prestigious Award, CNCI Achiever Award, Ceylon National Chamber of Industries, 2011; Man of the Year, ABI, 2011. Memberships: institute of Engineering & Technology, UK; Engineers Guild, Sri Lanka; Institute of Engineers, Sri Lanka; Templeburg Industrialist Association; Chamber of Small & Medium Industries Association; National Chamber of Commerce, Sri Lanka; Federation of Chambers of Commerce and Industry of Sri Lanka; Sri Lanka Institute of Directors; Sri Lanka Institute of Builders. Address: c/o Electro Metal Pressings (Pvt) Ltd, Lot No 86, Templeburge Industrial Estate, Panagoda, Sri Lanka. E-mail: empsales@sltnet.lk Website: www.emp.lk

DJOKICH Danka (Danica), b. Belgrade, Serbia. Applied Linguist; Author. Divorced. Education: French Primary School; State High School; Mokranjac High School of Music; History of Art course, 1 year; BA, English Language and Literature, Belgrade University; Postgraduate Diploma, Applied Linguistics, Edinburgh University, Scotland, 1962; Diploma, International Phonetics Association, 1962; MA, Applied Phonetics, 1974, PhD, Philology, Belgrade University, 1984; Grants, Pisa University, Italy, 1970, 1972. Appointments: Teacher of English, Higher School of Foreign Trade; Teacher of English, Centre for Foreign Languages, Secretariat for Foreign Affairs, 10 years; Teacher of English, School for Foreign Languages, Kolarac People's University; Volunteer, Belgrade Orphanage; Volunteer, Children's Tiršova Surgical Hospital; Volunteer, Belgrade Refugee Camp, 1995-97. Publications: Numerous articles in professional journals; Papers in Error Analysis and Linguistic Communication; Several textbooks for learning English including: An English-Serbian Dictionary of English Phrasal Verbs, 2002; A Serbian-English Dictionary of English Phrasal Verbs, 2005; Translations from Serbian into English of history of arts texts; Active participation in the work of symposia and conferences on applied linguistics, psycholinguistics and phonetics. Honours: Life Award, Kolarac People's University, 1995; Nominee, Woman of the Year. Memberships: Honorary Life Member, IWAB; Vice President, Canadian Society; International Association of Applied Linguistics; AILA Commission of Language Methodology and Foreign Language Teaching; Contrastive Linguistics and Error Analysis; International Association of Applied Psycholinguistics; Balkan Association of Teachers of English. Address: Hilandarska 13, 11000 Belgrade, Serbia.

DJORIC Dejan, b. 24 May 1959, Belgrade, Serbia. Art Critic. m. Vera, 1 daughter. Education: Belgrade University, Faculty of Philosophy, History of Art Department, 4 years. Appointments: Professional Writer, prefaces, articles, reviews, studies and books, 1985-; Author/Co-Author, Serbian books on art; Curator/Adviser, two Belgrade galleries; Organiser of numerous art exhibitions. Publications: Author/Co-Author, 44 multilingual monographs and thematic publications, Belgrade and Zurich; Co-Author, Belgrade, City of Secrets; Co-Author, Mediala, book and movie. Honours: ULUPUDS Annual Award, 1991. Memberships: International Association of Art Critics; Association of Fine, Applied Artists and Designers of Serbia. Address: Dr Riharda Burijana 2, 11060 Beograd 38, PAK 139705, Serbia. E-mail: devoluta@gmail.com Website: www.dejandjoric.com

DOBBS Michael John, b. 14 November 1948. Author. m. Amanda L Collingridge, 1981, 2 sons. Education: Christ Church, Oxford; Fletcher School of Law & Diplomacy, USA. Appointments: UK Special Adviser, 1981-87; Chief of Staff, UK Conservative Party, 1986-87; Joint Deputy Chairman, 1994-95; Deputy Chairman, Saatchi & Saatchi, 1983-91; Deputy Chairman, Conservative Party, 1994-95; Chairman, Spirit Advertising, 1998-; BBC TV Presenter, 1999-2001. Publications: House of Cards, 1989; Wall Games, 1990; Last Man to Die, 1991; To Play the King, 1993; The Touch of Innocents, 1994; The Final Cut, 1995; Goodfellowe MP, 1997; The Buddha of Brewer Street, 1998; Whispers of Betrayal, 2000; Winston's War, 2002; Never Surrender, 2003; Churchill's Hour, 2004; Saboteurs: The Nazi Raid on America, 2004; Churchill's Triumph, 2005; First Lady, 2006; The Lords Day, 2007; The Edge of Madness, 2008; The Reluctant Hero, 2010. Address: Newton House, Wylye, Wiltshire BA12 0QS, England. E-mail: michldobbs@aol.com

DÖBEREINER Jürgen, b. 1 November 1923, Königsberg Pr, Germany. Veterinarian. m. Johanna Kubelka, deceased 2000, 2 sons, 1 deceased 1996, 1 daughter. Education: DMV, Rio de Janeiro, 1954; MSc, University Wisconsin-Madison, USA, 1963; Dr med vet hc, Justus-Liebig-University Giessen, Germany, 1977. Appointment: Research Worker in Animal Pathology, Ministry Agriculture-Embrapa, Rio de Janeiro, Brazil, 1955-2009. Publications: More than 170 scientific papers; Co-author, Plantas Tóxicas da Amazonia a Bovinos e outros Herbivoros, 1979, 2007; Co-author, Plantas Tóxicas do Brasil, 2000; Co-author, Deficiências Minerais em Animais de Produção, 2010; Editor-in-Chief, Pesquisa Agropecuaria Brasileira (Brazilian Journal of Agricultural Research), 1966-76; Editor, Pesquisa Veterinária Brasileira (Brazilian Journal of Veterinary Research), 1981-. Honours: Frederico Menezes Veiga Prize, 2005. Membership: President, Brazilian College of Animal Pathology, 1978-; President, Brazilian Association of Science Editors, 2000-2004; President, The Johanna Döbereiner Research Society, 2002-10. Address: Caixa Postal 74 591, Km 47, Seropédica, Rio de Janeiro 23890-000, Brazil.

DOBRESCU Mircea Virgil, b. 27 October 1952, Turnu-Magurele, Romania. (German citizen; arrived in Germany, 1983). Veterinary Surgeon; High Level Expert; Veterinary Dentist and Periodontist; Consultant; Scientist; Researcher; Writer. Education: DVM, summa cum laude, 1976; PhD Veterinary Medicine, Dentistry Science and Periodontology, 1993, University of Bucharest; Master in

Veterinary Dentistry and Periodontology, Munich, Germany, 1992; Studies throughout Europe and Israel. Appointments: Assistant Professor, Pathology, Diagnostics and Clinics, State Veterinary Institute, Beit-Dagan, Ministry of Agriculture of State of Israel, University of Tel Aviv's Weizmann Institute of Sciences, University of Jerusalem, 1978; Specialist in Microbiology, Virology, Pathology and Leukaemia, Central Laboratories for Diagnosis, Ministry of Agriculture, Bucharest, 1978-82; Studies in Germany for Specialist in Veterinary Dentistry and Periodontology, 1983-89; Private practice for Veterinary Dentistry and Peridontology for small animals, Augsburg, Germany, 1989-; Owner and Senior Lecturer, School of Veterinary Dentistry and Periodontology for medical postgraduate training in Germany, 1992-; Presenter, numerous animal and veterinary conferences, seminars and workshops. Publications include: Odonton Therapy: A new human and animal Periodontology therapy; First Periodontal Status and First Dentistry Reference Cards in Veterinary Medicine for Cat and Dog; Use of Periodontal Status in Veterinary Dentistry Science; First Vade-mecum stomatologicum in Veterinary Medicine; Cast crown restorative dentistry of canini in dogs and cats with gold and porcelain, two new methods; Corrective orthodontics of common malocclusions in dogs with acrylic intraorale plates with expansion screw; Corrective Protrusion (corrective orthodontic) of Incisivi in a Rottweiler with chrome-cobalt intraorale plate with expansion screw – a premiere; Books: Da grinst selbst das Pferd (Even the Horse Would Grin); Joyful Stories of a Veterinary Surgeon, edited in Germany, 1996; The Last Secret of the Red Stone, fiction-adventure-novel, forthcoming; 38 articles in professional journals on veterinary dentistry and Periodontology and on animal and human cancer. Honours: International Personality of the Year 2001 in recognition of service to Education; International Scientist of the Year 2001 and of the Year 2003; 2000 Eminent Scientists of Today, 2003; Great Minds of the 21st Century; Man of the Year, 2001-02; Living Legends; American Medal of Honor, 2002; World Medal of Honour, ABI, 2003; Nominated, International Peace Prize, United Cultural Convention, ABI, USA, 2003; Worldwide Honours List, IBC, 2003; Contemporary Hall of Fame, ABI, 2003; Leading Intellectuals of the World, ABI, 2004; The Contemporary Who's Who of Professionals, ABI, 2005; Listed in several international directories of biography. Memberships: Research Board of Advisors, American Biographical Institute; New York Academy of Sciences; American Association for the Advancement of Science; Federation of European Microbiological Societies; International Union of Microbiological Societies; Romanian Oncological Society. Address: Stettenstr 28, 86150 Augsburg, Bayern, Germany.

DOBRZYNSKI Leonard, b. 12 October 1941, Lodz, Poland, France. Director of Research. m. Marie-Françoise Brisoux, 1 son, 3 daughters. Education: Doctorat de 3 cycle, Paris, 1968; Diploma, Institut Superieur d'Electronique du Nord, Lille, 1968; Diploma d'Etudes Approfondies de Physique, Paris, 1968; Doctorat d'Etat, Paris, 1969. Appointments: Professeur à l'Universite de Lille, Nord de France, 1966-; Directeur de recherche émerite du Centre National de la Recherche Scientifique, 1970-. Publications: Handbook of Surfaces and Interfaces, Volume I and 2, 1978, Volume 3, 1980; Author, Surface Phenons and Polaritons, 1980; Co-editor, Surface Science Reports journal, 1981-; Dynamics of Interfaces, 1984. Honours: Prix Spécial de la Societé des Sciences de Lille, 1981. Memberships: Societé Française de Physique; Societé Européene de Physique. Address: CNRS Université de Lille 1, Unite de Formation et de Recherche de Physique, F-59655 Villeneuve d'Ascq, France. E-mail: leonard.dobrzynski@univ-lille1.fr

DODD Seetal, b. 6 May 1964, Geel, Belgium (Australian citizen). Research Co-ordinator. Education: BSc, 1991, Dip Ed, 1992, University of New England, Australia; MS, 1995, PhD, 2000, University of Melbourne, Australia. Appointments: Vice President, Inter-Campus Liaison Officer and Delegate, National Union of Students for the Students' Representative Council, University of New England, NSW, Australia, 1985-87; Technician, Department of Radiology, Austin & Repatriation Medical Centre, Melbourne, 1990-97 (full time), 1997-2001 (part time); Research Assistant, Department of Psychiatry, University of Melbourne, 2000-01; Research Fellow Level A, Department of Pharmaceutics, Monash University, Melbourne, 2001-03; Research Co-ordinator, The Geelong Hospital, 2003-; Senior Fellow, 2003-, Honours Co-ordinator, 2006-09, Department of Clinical and Biomedical Sciences, Barwon Health, University of Melbourne, The Geelong Hospital; Member, Editor-in-Chief, Current Drug Safety, 2005-; Department of Psychiatry, University of Melbourne, 2011-; School of Medicine, Deakin University, 2011. Publications: Numerous articles in professional journals, editorials, comments and letters. Honours: Ten Years of Service Award, 2001; Project of the Year Award, 2001; Samuel Gershon Award, 2009; 3rd Place, Poster Award, Australasian Society for Bipolar Disorder Conference, 2009. Memberships: Royal Australian Chemical Institute; Australian Society for Biological Psychiatry; Australasian Society for Psychiatric Research; International Society for Bipolar Disorders; Collegium Internationale Neuropsychopharmacologicum, 2005. Address: Swanston Centre, PO Box 281, Geelong, VIC 3220, Australia. E-mail: seetald@barwonhealth.org.au

DOERRIES Chantal-Aimée, b. 26 August 1968, Germany. Barrister. Education: University of Pennsylvania, USA, 1986-87; Cambridge University, New Hall, 1987-91. Appointments: Leading practitioner in commercial dispute resolution; Areas include construction, engineering and infrastructure projects, energy and natural resources, professional negligence, shipbuilding, IT and telecommunications and general commercial. Honours: Fellow, American Bar Association; Queen's Counsel, 2008; Gertrude de Gallaix Achievement Award for Study of Law, FAWCO; Diplock Scholarship, Middle Temple; Major Harmsworth Entrance Exhibition, Middle Temple; TECBAR accredited adjudicator; Co-chairman of Forum for Barristers and Advocates, International Bar Association, 2009-; Appointed Bencher of Middle Temple, 2010. Memberships: Chairman, 2009, Bar Branded Arbitration Working Group of the Bar Council; Commercial Bar Association; International Bar Association; Chairman, International Committee of the Bar of England and Wales, 2011; Chairman, Technology and Construction Bar Association, 2010-. Address: 1 Atkin Building, Gray's Inn, London WC1R 5AT, England.

DOHLE Rainer G, b. 4 June 1956, Dresden, Germany. Education: Dr Ing (PhD). Appointments: Master's, Electrical Engineering; Dr Ing (PhD), TU Dresden; Postdoctorate, Georgia Institute of Technology in Atlanta, Georgia; Senior Principal Electro/Optics Engineer, Lightpoint Europe GMBH; Dr Ing, Assembly and Test, MSE. Publications: 36 patents; 42 publications. Honours: Postdoctoral Research Fellowship, German Academic Exchange Service, 1996; Best Paper Award,

IMAPS Symposium, 2009 and 2011. Memberships: Senior Member, IEEE; IMAPS. Address: MSE, Schlegelweg 17, 95180 Berg/Bavaria, Germany. E-mail: rainer.dohle@ieee.org

DOI Etsuo, b. Tokyo, Japan. Attorney-at-Law. Education: LLB, Department of Law, Tokyo University, 1988; LLM, Columbia University School of Law, 1996. Appointments: Adjunct Professor of Law, Temple University Law School, Japan Campus, over 10 years; Practicing Lawyer, Japan and New York, over 10 years. Publications: Numerous articles in professional journals. Honours: Best Lawyers, 2009, 2010; Legal 500, 2010, 2011; Leading Lawyer 100 Asia Pacific, 2011; World's Leading Patents & Technology License Lawyer, 2010, 2011; and others. Memberships: Tokyo Bar Association; American Bar Association; New York Bar Association.

DOIG John, b. 2 August 1958, Helensburgh, Scotland. Violinist; Conductor. Education: First enrolled pupil, St Mary's Music School, Edinburgh, 1972. Appointments: BBC Symphony Orchestra, 1975-78; Principal Violin, BBC Philharmonic Orchestra, 1979-81; Co-Leader, Orchestra of Scottish Opera, 1981-83; Co-Leader and Guest Leader, Scottish Chamber Orchestra, 1986-90; Leader, Orchestra of Scottish Opera, 1991-98; Founder and Artistic Director, Scottish Bach Consort, 1994-. Honour: Honorary President, Scottish Bach Society. Membership: Society of Musicians. Address: Endrick Mews, Killearn, Stirlingshire G63 9ND, Scotland.

DOJCINOVIC Uros, b. 15 May 1959, Belgrade, Yugoslavia (Serbia). Guitarist; Composer; Pedagogue. 1 son. Education: University of Philology, Belgrade, 1979; Music Academy, Zagreb, 1979-83; Graduated in Classical Guitar, 1984; Pedagogic Licence Examination, Music University of Belgrade, 1985; Postgraduate work (PhD) done interdisciplinary in Musicology and Philology, University of Philology, Belgrade, 1988-2006; Second doctorate, University of Philosophy, Belgrade (History Department), 2007-09. Debut: Belgrade Concert Hall, Cultural Centre Stari Grad, 1976. Career: Over 2500 concerts worldwide; Over 500 radio and television appearances; Numerous masterclasses, lecturers and presentations; Worldwide adjudications; Professor of Classical Guitar, Chamber Music, theoretical subjects, various music schools in Belgrade and Zagreb; Professor of Classical Guitar and Music Theory, University of Fine Arts, Belgrade, 2007-, and Music Conservatory J Slavenski, Belgrade, 1984-. Compositions: Solo Guitar works, opus 1-15, 17-25, 28-30, 41-43, 45-47, 50-52, 57, 58; Chamber Music with Guitar, opus 16, 26, 27, 31, 33, 34, 35, 36, 37, 39, 40, 48, 49, 53-56, 59 includes 10 suites, themes with variations, fantasias, cycle-form compositions, some for different guitar orchestras and chamber groups including classical guitar; Music Works (published) include altogether 60 opus in Yugoslavia, Italy, Germany, France, Switzerland, Poland, Sweden, Belarus, Czech, Belgium, Bulgaria, England and USA. Recordings: South American Guitar; Exotic Guitar; Characteristic Guitar; Guitar Recital; Classical and Romantic Music for two guitars; Danza Caracteristica; Chamber Music for Guitar; Exotic Guitar Music. Publications: Magic World of the Guitar, 1984; Yugoslav Guitar History, 1992; The Guitar Triumph, 1994; The First Guitarist Steps, 1995; Anthology of Guitar Music in Serbia, 1996; Anthology of Guitar Music in Montenegro, 1996; Bibliography of the Serbian Guitar Literature, 2009; Numerous articles in journals. Honours: Over 50 National and International medals, diplomas and prizes; First Republic and Federal Prizes in Guitar Composition, 1975, 1977; First Prize, Cultural Olympiad, Belgrade, 1978; Jeunesses Musicales of Serbia Charter, 1984; Golden Badge from Cultural and Educational Bureau of Serbia, 1995; Golden Marker of Cultural and Educational Bureau of Belgrade, 2005; Vuk's Prize, National Award of Serbia, 2007; Listed in national and international biographical dictionaries, lexicons and music encyclopaedias. Memberships: Society for Music Artists of Serbia; Society of Composers of Montenegro; Matica Srpska-Novi Sad; Founder, President, Yugoslav Guitar Society and Foundation, 2000-. Address: str Lička 3/V, ap 25, 11000 Belgrade, Serbia. E-mail: urosdojcinovic@eunet.rs

DOKULIL Milos, b. 23 July 1928, Brno, Czech Republic. University Professor. m. Anna Chudoba, 1 daughter. Education: BA, 1949, MA, 1951, University of Political and Social Sciences, Prague, 1947-51; Charles University, Faculty of Arts, 1948-50; MA, University of Russian Language and Literature, 1954-57; PhD, Czechoslovak Academy of Sciences, 1963; DSc, Charles University, 1993. Appointments: Lecturer, Senior Lecturer, Technical University, 1956-63; Senior Lecturer, Faculty of Pedagogy, 1963-69; For political reasons prevented from academic activity, including publishing of 3 books, 1970-89; Associate Professor, Department Head, 1990; Professor, Masaryk University, 1992-. Publications: A Primer of Logic for Teachers, 1967; Through the Philosophy of History to the History of Philosophy, 1970, enlarged, 1992; The Formation of a Philosopher: Through Toleration Towards the Epistemology of John Locke, 1972; On the Issue over Toleration: Lockean Contemplations, 1995; Ethics, 3 vols (Co-author, co-editor), 1998; Masaryk as a Rear-view Mirror? 2005; Masarykian Comebacks, 2006; Numerous professional articles. Honours: Nominations to Man of Year, International Biographical Centre, American Biographical Institute; Nomination for Ministry of Education Prize (Czech Republic), 1999; Nominations: IBC Top 100 Educators, 2006; International Educator, 2006; International Peace Prize, United Cultural Convention, 2005, 2006. Address: Faculty of Informatics, Masaryk University, Botanicka 68a, CZ 602 00 Brno, Czech Republic.

DOLE Elizabeth Hanford, b. 29 July 1936, Salisbury, North Carolina, USA. Administrator. m. Robert J Dole, 1975. Education: Duke University; Harvard University; University of Oxford. Appointments: Called to Bar, District of Columbia, 1966; Staff Assistant to Assistant Secretary for Education, Department of Health, Education & Welfare, 1966-67; Practising lawyer, Washington DC, 1967-68; Associate Director Legislative Affairs, then Executive Director Presidents Commission for Consumer Interests, 1968-71; Deputy Assistant, Office of Consumer Affairs, The White House, Washington DC, 1971-73; Commissioner, Federal Trade Commission, 1973-79; Assistant to President for Public Liaison, 1981-83; Secretary of Transport, 1983-87; Candidate for Republican presidential nomination, 1999; Senator for North Carolina, 2003-2008. Publications: A Leader in Washington, 1998; The Doles: Unlimited Partners, 1988; Hearts toughed by Fire: My 500 Most Inspirational Quotations, 2004. Memberships: Trustee, Duke University, 1974-88; Member, Visiting Committee, John F Kennedy School of Government, 1988-; Secretary of Labour, 1989-90; President, American Red Cross, 1991-98; Member, Commission, Harvard School of Public Health, 1992-; Board of Overseers, Harvard University, 1989-95. Address: Office of the Senator from North Carolina, Suite B34, Dirksen Building, US Senate, Washington, DC 20510, USA.

DOLE Bob (Robert J), b. 22 July 1923, Russell, Kansas, USA. Politician. m. (2) Elizabeth Hanford Dole, 1975, 1 daughter. Education: University of Kansas; Washburn Municipal University. Appointments: Member, Kansas

Legislature, 1951-53; Russell County Attorney, 1953-61; Member, House of Representatives, 1960-68; US Senator from Kansas, 1969-96, Senate Majority Leader, 1995-96; Senate Republic Leader, 1987-96; House Majority Leader, 1985-87; Minority Leader, 1987; Chairman, Republic National Committee, 1971-72; Vice-Presidential Candidate, 1976; Presidential Candidate, 1996; Member of Counsel, Verner, Liipfert, Bernhard, McPherson and Hand, Alston and Bird, 2003-. Publications: Great Political Wit (co-ed), 1999; Great Presidential Wits, 2001; One Soldier's Story: A Memoir, 2005. Memberships: Chairman, Senate Finance Committee, Dole Foundation, 1981-84; Director, Mainstream Inc; Advisor, US Delegate to FAO Conference, Rome, 1965, 1974, 1977; Member, Congressional delegate to India, 1966, Mid E, 1967; Member, US Helsinki Commission; Delegate to Belgrade Conference, 1977; Trustee, William Allen White Foundation, University of Kansas; Member, National Advisory Committee, The John Wesley Colleges; American Bar Association; National Advisory Committee, on Scouting for the Handicapped, Kansas Association for Retarded Children; Advisory Board of Utd Cerebral Plasy, Kansas; Honorary Member, Advisory Board of Kidney Patients Inc; Presidential Medal of Freedom, 1997; Distinguished Service Award, 1997. Address: Alston & Bird LLP, 10th Floor, North Building, 601 Pennsylvania Avenue, NW, Washington DC 20004-2601, USA. E-mail: bdole@alston.com Website: www.alston.com

DOLEZAL Urszula Marta, b. 8 September 1933, Krakow, Poland. Microbiologist, Scientific Worker. m. Marian Dolezal. Education: Manager, 1956, Doctor, PhD, 1959, Faculty Biology and Science of Earl Jagiellonian University; Associate Professor, Medical Academy in Cracow, 1965; Professor, sc.title, 1977; Professor ordinary Academy of Physical Education, 1990. Appointments: Head, Department of Mycology Medicine, Medical Academy Institute of Microbiology, 1970, Head of Chair, Department of Hygiene and Health Protection, later Health Promotion of Cracow Academy of Physical Education 1975; Retired, 2003-. Publications: 243 publications of topics: mycological pollution of air, mycology of the human environment and the influence of fungi, mould, yeast on the health of the population, mycoflora of flats and buildings, hygiene and different topics of preventive medicine, new aspect of health promotion, HIV/AIDS. Honours: Zloty Krzyz Zaslugi, 1980; Medal Komisji Edukacji Narodowej, 1983; Krzyz kawalerski Orderu Odrodzenia Polski, 1987. Memberships: Polish Academy of Science Commission of Biology; Commission of Public Health; International Scientific Forum on Home Hygiene, delegate of Poland in ERNA/RECS; Inter. Red Cross and Red Crescent Societies; Jagiellonian University Graduates' Association. Address: Daszynskiego 32 app 6, 31534 Cracow, Poland.

DOLGUI Alexandre, Professor. Education: MSc, 1983, Certificate of doctoral study, 1986, Minsk Radioengineering Institute, Belarus, USSR; PhD, Engineering Cybernetics and Computer Aided Production Management, Academy of Sciences of Belarus, Institute of Engineering Cybernetics, Minsk, 1990; Docent Diploma, Computational Methods and Programming, Ministry of Research and Education, Russia, 1992; Dr Hab, University of Technology of Compiègne, France, 2000. Appointments: Researcher, 1986-88, Assistant Professor, 1988-91, Associate Professor, 1991-97, Belarusian State University of Informatics and Radioelectronics, Minsk; Guest Professor, France and Canada, 1992-2005; Assistant Professor, 1994-96, Associate Professor, 1996-2001, Full Professor, 2001-03, University of Technology of Troyes, Industrial Engineering Department, Troyes, France; Full Professor, Department Head, Centre Director, Ecole Nationale Supérieure de Saint-Etienne, Centre for Industrial Engineering and Computer Sciences, France, 2003-. Publications: Over 400 refereed journal and conference papers, book chapters and research reports; 3 books. Honours: Listed in international biographical dictionaries. Memberships: Institute of Industrial Engineers; Institute for Operations Research and the Management Sciences; French Operational Research Society; International Foundation for Production Research; International Institute for Innovation, Industrial Engineering and Entrepreneurship. Address: Ecole Nationale Supérieure des Mines de Saint-Etienne, 158, cours Fauriel, 42023 Saint-Etienne, Cedex 2, France. E-mail: dolgui@emse.fr

DOLLFUS Audouin Charles, b. 12 November 1924, Paris, France. Physicist; Astronomer. m. Catherine Browne, 1959, 4 children. Education: Doctor of Mathematics, Faculty of Sciences, University of Paris. Appointments: Astronomer, Astrophysical Section, Meudon Observatory, Paris, 1946-; Head of Laboratory for Physics of the Solar System; Astronomer, Observatoire de Paris, 1965; Discovered Janus, innermost moon of Saturn, 1966; Emeritus President, Observatoire de Triel, 1994-; Research into polarisation of light. Publications: 7 books; 350 scientific publications on astrophysics. Honours: Grand Prix of Academie des Sciences; International Award Galabert for Astronautics; Diploma Tissandier, International Federation of Astronautics. Memberships: International Academy of Astronautics; Société Astronomique de France; Aéro-club de France; French Association for the Advancement of Science; Royal Astronomical Society, London; Society of French Explorers; Explorers Club, USA; Société Philomatique de Paris; Honorary member, Royal Astronomical Society of Canada. Address: 77 rue Albert Perdreaux, 92370 Chaville, France.

DOMEIKA Povilas, b. 20 November 1938, Radviliskis Region, Lithuania. Economist; Professor. m. Audrone Zilnyte, 2 sons. Education: Economist, Lithuanian Academy of Agriculture (now University), 1963; Dr of Economics, Leningrad Institute of Agriculture (now St Petersburg State Agrarian University), 1970; Dr Habil of Economics, Lithuanian Institute of Agrarian Economics, 1991; Professor, Lithuanian Academy of Agriculture (now University), 1993. Appointments: Senior Assistant of Economics and Accounting Department, 1964-67, Dr Senior Assistant, 1970, Dr Associate Professor, 1976, Economical Cybernetics Department, Dr Associate Professor, Vice-Dean of Faculty of Economics, 1971-80; Dr Associate Professor, Head of Department of Economical Cybernetics, 1980-91, Dr Habil Professor, Department of Economical Cybernetics, 1993; Professor Dr Habil, Informatics Department, 1996-2005, Professor Dr Habil, Accounting and Finance Department, 2005-09, Lithuanian University of Agriculture. Publications: Author of monographs: Mechanization of Accounting in Agricultural Enterprises, 1977, 1978; Monograph, Accounting Information System, 2008; Monograph, The Journeys of Life, 2012; Co-author of textbooks: Accounting in Agriculture (with Essentials of Computerized Technology), 1974, 1980, 1987; Computerization of Accounting in Agricultural Enterprises, 1984; Author, over 130 published scientific articles. Honours include: Academician, International Academy of Informatization of the United Nations, 1999; Order of Merit, Lithuanian University of Agriculture, 2004. Memberships: Member, Professors' Club "Scientia", Lithuanian University of Agriculture; Member, Lithuanian Scientific Society, 2006; Association of Lithuanian Agrarian Economists; Lithuanian

Association of Ignotas Domeika. Address: Pilenu 7-52, Akademicku m, LT-53351 Kauno rajonas, Lithuania. E-mail: povilas.domeika@asu.lt

DOMIN Jan, b. 1 June 1947, Bzianka, dist Krosno, Poland. Physicist. m. Urszula, 1 daughter. Education: MS, Physics, Pedagogical College, Rzeszow, 1969; PhD, Physics, University of Gdansk, 1981. Appointments: Assistant, Pedagogical College, Rzeszow, 1970-80; Post-Doctoral Position, Pedagogical College, Rzeszow, 1981-84; Lecturer, Polish Institute of Science, Chicago, USA, 1985-88; Lecturer, Geodesy College, Rzeszow, 1989-93; Vice President, Rzeszow City Council, 1991-94; Stage for local authorities in Leicester University of Technology, England, 1992; Vice Director, Methodology Center, Rzeszow, 1994-96; Studious stage of French Educational System, France, 1995; Studious stage of Norwegian Educational System, Norway, 1996; Lecturer, University of Technology, Rzeszow, 1996-. Publications: Research work reports in professional international journals. Honours: Golden Medal of Polish Commission of National Educaiton, 2012; Listed in international biographical dictionaries. Memberships: Polish Physical Association. E-mail: spjanusz@prz.edu.pl

DOMINGO Placido, b. 21 January 1941, Madrid, Spain. Singer; Conductor; Administrator. m. Marta Ornelas, 3 sons. Education: Studies in Piano, Conducting and Voice, National Conservatory of Music, Mexico City. Appointments: Operatic debut as Alfredo in La Traviata, Monterrey, Mexico, 1961; 12 roles, 280 performances, Israel National Opera, 2½ years; Title role, Ginastera's Don Rodrigo, New York City Opera, 1966; Debut as Maurizio in Adriana Lecouvreur, Metropolitan Opera, NY, 1968; 41 roles, over 400 performances, Metropolitan Opera, 36 years; Regularly appears at: Milan's La Scala, the Vienna State Opera, London's Covent Garden, Paris' Bastille Opera, the San Francisco Opera, Chicago's Lyric Opera, the Washington National Opera, the Los Angeles Opera, the Lyceo in Barcelona, the Colon in Buenos Aires, the Real in Madrid, and at the Bayreuth and Salzburg Festivals; Conductor of opera performances at the Metropolitan, London's Covent Garden and Vienna State Opera, etc; Conductor of symphonic concerts with the Berlin Philharmonic, London Symphony and Chicago Symphony, etc; Music Director, Seville World's Fair; General Director, Washington National Opera, 1994-; General Director, Los Angeles Opera, 2000-; Over 120 different roles including: Wagner's "Parsifal", "Lohengrin" and Seigmund in "Walkure"; "Meistersinger", "Tannhauser"; "Flying Dutchman"; Richard Strauss's "Die Frau Ohne Schattern"; Weber's "Oberon"; Beethoven's "Fidelio"; Gherman in Tchaikovsky's "Queen of Spades" (in Russian); the Spanish opera "Margarita la Tornera" by Roberto Chapi; Verdi's "La Battaglia di Legnano"; Anton Garcia Abril's "Divinas Palabras"; Rasputin in Deborah Drattell's "Nicholas and Alexandra"; Breton's "La Dolores"; Albeniz's "Merlin"; Founder, yearly competition for young singers, "Operalia"; Inaugurated Domingo Cafritz Young Artists Program of the Washington Opera, 2002; Special benefit concerts to help 1985 Mexican earthquake, AIDS charities, Armenian earthquake, mudslides in Acapulco, and others. Publications: Over 100 recordings; More than 50 videos; 3 theatrically released films; Double CD of every Verdi aria for the tenor voice; CD of excerpts from Wagner's "Siegfried" and "Gotterdaemmerung"; My First Forty Years (autobiography), 1983; My Operatic Roles, 2000. Honours: Dr hc, Royal College of Music, 1982; Dr hc, University Complutense de Madrid, 1989; Hon Dmus, University of Oxford, 2003; Commander, Legion d'honneur, 2002; Honorary KBE, 2002; Medal of Freedom; 9 Grammy Awards; European Culture Foundation Prize, 2003. Address: c/o Vincent and Farrell Associates, Suite 740, 481 8th Avenue, New York, NY 10001, USA.

DOMINIAN Jack, b. 25 August 1929, Athens, Greece. Doctor. m. Eddith Mary, 4 daughters. Education: MA; FRCPEd; FRCPsy; DSc (Hons); MBE. Appointments: Qualified as doctor, 1955; Qualified as psychiatrist, 1961; Consultant Psychiatrist, 1964-88; Private Practice, 1988-2003; Retired, 2003-. Publications: 32 books including: Christian Marriage, 1967; Marriage, Faith & Love, 1981; Marital Breakdown, 1968; Authority, 1976; Cycles of Affirmation, 1975; One Like Us, 1998; Let's Make Love, 2001; Living Love, 2004; Over 100 articles in leading Catholic journal, Tablet; Numerous articles in BMJ, Lancet and other scientific journals. Honours: DSc (Hon), Lancaster University, 1976; MBE, 1994. Memberships: Royal College of Psychiatry; Royal College of Physicians, Edinburgh; Fellow, Royal Society of Medicine, London. Address: 19 Clements Road, Chorleywood, Hertfordshire, England.

DOMINICZAK Anna Felicja, b. 26 August 1954, Gdansk, Poland. Professor. m. Marek Dominiczak, 1 son. Education: MD (Hons), Medical School, Gdansk, 1978; MRCP (UK), 1986; MD, University of Glasgow, 1989; FRCP (Glasgow), 1995. Appointments: British-American Research Fellow, University of Michigan, USA, 1990-91; Clinical Lecturer and Honorary Senior Registrar in Medicine and Endocrinology, Department of Medicine and Therapeutics, 1992-93, Senior Lecturer, Reader in Medicine and Honorary Consultant Physician and Endocrinologist, 1993-96, University of Glasgow; British Heart Foundation Senior Research Fellow, Honorary Consultant Physician and Endocrinologist, 1993-; Regius Professor of Medicine, Vice Principal and Head of College of Medical Veterinary & Life Sciences. Publications: Over 300 articles in professional medical journals. Honours most recently include: R D Wright Award & Lecture, High Blood Pressure Research Council of Australia, 2005; OBE, 2005; The Lord Provost's Special Award for 2006; Scotswoman of the Year, 2006; Bjorn Folkow Award and Lecture, European Society of Hypertension, 2008; The Graham Lecture and Medal, The Royal Philosophical Society of Glasgow, 2009. Memberships include: British Medical Association; Scottish Society of Experimental Medicine; British Hypertension Society; British Endocrine Society; Association of Physicians of Great Britain and Northern Ireland; American Physiological Society; British Atherosclerosis Society; Honorary Life Member, High Blood Pressure Research Council of Australia; Honorary Life Member, Polish Hypertension Society; British Cardiovascular Society; European Society of Cardiology. Address: College of Medical, Veterinary & Life Sciences, University of Glasgow, University Avenue, Glasgow G12 8QQ, Scotland.

DOMINIK William John, b. 29 December 1953, Cleveland, Ohio, USA. Professor. Education: Cert IES, University of Durham, UK, 1974; BA, University of the Pacific, Stockton, California, USA, 1975; California Teaching Credential, 1975; MA, Texas Tech University, Lubbock, Texas 1982; PhD, Monash University, Melbourne, Australia, 1989. Appointments: Teacher, Administrator, Ministry of Education, Melbourne, Australia, 1976-90; Teaching and Research Assistant, 1981-82, Assistant Professor, 1990-91, Texas Tech University, Lubbock, USA; Tutor, Research Assistant, Monash University, 1985-88; Tutor, Council of Adult Education, Victoria, Australia, 1989; Lecturer, 1991-94, Associate Professor, 1994-97, 1998-2000, Professor, Chair, 2001, Classics, University of Natal, Durban, South Africa;

Visiting Professor, Classics, University of Leeds, England, 1997-98; Visiting Teaching Fellow, Christ's College and Newnham College, University of Cambridge, England, 2000; Research Fellow, Clare Hall, University of Cambridge, England, 2000-01; Professor, Chair, Department of Classics, University of Otago, New Zealand, 2002-; Visiting Professor, Classics, Visiting Research Fellow, Institute for Advanced Studies in the Humanities, University of Edinburgh, Scotland, 2006-07; Visiting Foreign Professor, Classics, Federal University of Bahia, Brazil, 2010. Publications: 254 publications, including 16 books. Honours: Recipient of 169 grants and awards, including: Commonwealth Research Award, Australia, 1987-88; Commonwealth Fellowship, UK, 1997-98; Fellow and Life Member, Clare Hall, University of Cambridge, UK, 2001-; Ministry of Education Visiting Foreign Professorship and Fellowship, Brazil, 2010. Memberships: American Philological Association; Classical Association of South Africa; Australasian Society of Classical Studies; Brazilian Society for Classical Studies; New Zealand Association of Classical Teachers; Classical Association of Otago. Address: Department of Classics, University of Otago, PO Box 56, Dunedin 9054, New Zealand. E-mail: william.dominik@otago.ac.nz

DONALDSON Antony, b. 2 September 1939, Godalming, Surrey, England. Artist. m. Patricia, 2 sons. Education: Slade School of Fine Art, London, 1958-62; Postgraduate, Fine Art, University College London, 1963. Appointments: Artist; Group and solo exhibitions around the world; Work held in public collections in UK, Northern Ireland, Australia, Portugal, Germany, Holland, Brazil, Italy and USA; Selected commissions: 9 sculptures for the entrance hall of Parr Hyatt, Tokyo, 1992-2004; Giant Head of the Master of Suspense, Gainsborough Studios, London, 1999-2002. Publications: Numerous articles in professional journals. Honours: 2nd Prize, Guiness Award, 1962; 2nd Prize, John Moores Open Competition, Liverpool, 1963; Harkness Foundation Fellowship, USA, 1968; Field & Sons Co Ltd Prize, Bradford Print Biennale, 1970.

DONALDSON WALTERS Sheila, b. 17 October 1920, London, England. Artist; Designer. m. Nigel Vincent Walters (deceased 1988), 1 son (deceased 1978). Education: Drawing & Pictorial Design, Bromley School of Art; Lithography, Beckenham School of Art; Etching, Chelsea School of Art; Royal College of Art. Appointments: Calligrapher, Historical Section, War Cabinet Offices; Part-time Lecturer, V&A Museum, 1970s and 1980s, and Bethnal Green Museum of Childhood; Artist; Exhibitions in London, Belfast, Sussex and Portugal; Designer, Joseph's first shop in King's Road, Salon 33 and Hairline in Gloucester Road, London; Consultant Designer, World Congress of Anaesthesiologists, London, 1968; Graphic design, costume design & textile design; Former Chairman, Kensington & Chelsea Arts Council (Festival of Arts, 1972-77); Member, GLAA Council; Member, Datec & BTEC Design Council.

DONG Kyung-Rae, b. 11 March 1972, SeongnamSi, Korea. Professor. m. Eun-Jin Choi, 1 daughter. Education: Master, Department of Public Health, Yonsei University, 2002; PhD, Department of Nuclear Engineering, Chosun University, 2006. Appointments: Radiological Technologist, Asan Medical Center, 1996-2003; Assistant Professor, Gwangyang Health College University, 2004-07; Assistant Professor, Gwangju Health College University, 2008-. Publications: 25 articles in professional journals. Honours: Excellent Paper Award, Korean Radiological Technologists Association, 2010; Excellent Paper Award, Korean Association for Radiation Protection, 2010; Young Medical Physicist Award, Korean Society of Medical Physics, 2010; Excellent Paper Award, Yonsei University, 2011; Honorable Mention Submissions, American Society of Radiologic Technologists, 2011; Listed in biographical dictionaries. Memberships: Korean Society of Radiology; Korean Society for Digital Imaging in Medicine; Korean Association for Radiation Protection; Korean Society of Radiological Science. Address: Department of Radiology, Gwangju Health College University, 683 Shinchang-Dong, Gwangju, Republic of Korea. E-mail: krdong@hanmail.net

DONG Yuning, b. 16 June 1955, Nanjing, China. Professor. Education: B Eng, 1982, M Eng, 1984, Nanjing University of Posts and Telecommunications; PhD, South East University, Nanjing, China, 1988; M Phil, Queen's University, Belfast, Northern Ireland, 1998. Appointments: Lecturer, 1988-92, Associate Professor, 1992-1999, Professor, Information Engineering Department, 1999-, Nanjing University of Posts and Telecommunications; Visiting Scholar, Imperial College, London, England, 1992-93; Postdoctoral Fellow, University of Texas, Galveston, Texas, 1993-95; Research Fellow, Queen's University, Belfast, Northern Ireland and University of Birmingham, England, 1995-98. Publications: 3D reconstruction of irregular shapes, 2001; Fast computation of various templates, 2003; Technical papers in Chinese Journal of Electronics, Chinese Journal of Computers and others, 2000-2003. Honours: Best University Teacher, Jiangsu Province, China, 1992; Best Researcher, Ministry of Posts and Telecommunications, China, 1993. Memberships: Senior Member, China Communications Institute; Senior Member, Chinese Institute of Electronics; Member, IEEE. Address: PO Box 166, Nanjing University of Posts and Telecommunications, Nanjing, Jiangsu 210003, China. E-mail: dongyn@njupt.edu.cn

DONIN Valery Il'yich, b. 11 March 1941, Nerchinsk, Eastern Siberia, Russia. Physicist. m. Tamara Kurtz, 1 daughter. Education: MSc, 1963, Tomsk State University; PhD (CPMSc), 1972; Doctorate in Phys and Math Sc, 1989, Russian Academy of Sciences. Appointments: Engineer, Research Scientist, Head of Laboratory, quantum electronics, Siberian Branch of Russian Academy of Sciences, 1963-. Publications: Over 110 research papers in field of laser and plasma physics; book, High-Power Gas Ion Lasers, 1991. Honours: First degree diploma, Siberian Branch of Russian Academy of Sciences, 1973; Honorary diplomas, Russian Academy of Sciences, 1974 and 1999; Medal, Exhibition of National Economic Achievements, USSR, 1979; Honorary professor, Albert Schweitzer International University, 2000; 21st Century Achievement Award and American Medal of Honor, ABI, 2001; Inducted into 500 Leaders of World Influence Hall of Fame, ABI, and 500 Founders of 21st Century Honours List, IBC, 2002. Memberships: Rozhdestvensky Optical Society; New York Academy of Sciences; European Optical Society. Address: Institute of Automation and Electrometry, Siberian Branch of Russian Academy of Sciences, Acad Koptyuga pr. 1, Novosibirsk 630090, Russia. E-mail: donin@iae.nsk.su

Donnelly Declan Joseph Oliver, b. 25 September, 1975, Newcastle, England. TV Presenter. Career: Presenter: SMTV Live; Friends Like These; Pop Idol; I'm a Celebrity...Get Me Out of Here!; Ant & Dec's Saturday Night Takeaway; Britain's Got Talent; Pokerface; Push the Button; Red or Black?; Actor: Byker Grove; A Tribute to The Likely Lads, 2002; Alien Autopsy, 2006; Singer (as PJ and Duncan): Let's

Get Ready to Rumble ; Stepping Stone; Shout; and others. Honours: 16 National Television Awards; 6 British Comedy Award; BAFTA; many others.

DONNELLY Dervilla M X, b. 25 April 1930, Dublin, Ireland. Chemist. Education: BSc (1st class honours) Chemistry, 1948, PhD, 1954, DSc (on published work), 1978, University College Dublin; ScD, (honoris causa), Dublin University, 1992, DSc (hc), Queen University Belfast, 1994, DSc (hc), University of Nottingham, 1995; LLD (honoris causa), National University of Ireland, 2002. Appointments: Emeritus Professor, Organic Chemistry, University College Dublin Society; Honorary Member, Council Royal Dublin; Member, Austrian Council for Science and Technology and Innovation, Vienna, Austria, 2000-; Chairman of Council, Dublin Institute for Advanced Studies; Board Member, National Museum of Ireland and Chairman of the Audit Committee of NMI; Member of Council, Royal Irish Academy. Honours: Honorary Fellow, Hiberian Academy, 1999; Institute of Chemistry of Ireland Boyle Medallist, 1999; Charter Day Medallist, University College Dublin, 2000. Memberships: Royal Irish Academy; Fellow, Royal Society of Chemistry; Fellow, Institute of Chemistry of Ireland; Fellow, Society of Chemical Industry; Osterreichische Ehrenkreuz fur Wissenschaft und Kunst I Klasse, 2010. Address: 27 St Kevin's Park, Dublin 6, Ireland. E-mail: donnellydmx@eirecom.net

DONNER Richard, b. 24th April 1930, New York, USA. Director; Producer. Appointments: Actor off-Broadway; Collaborated with director Martin Ritt on TV adaption of Somerset Maugham's Of Human Bondage; Moved to California and began commercials, industrial films and documentaries; Films: X 15, 1961; Salt and Pepper, 1968; Twinky, 1969; The Omen, 1976; Superman, 1978; Inside Moves, 1981; The Toy, 1982 Ladyhawke, 1985; The Goonies, 1985; Lethal Weapon, 1987; Scrooged, 1988; Lethal Weapon 2, 1989; Radio Flyer, 1991; The Final Conflict (executive producer), 1991; Lethal Weapon 3, 1992; Free Willy (co-executive producer), 1993; Maverick, 1994; Assassins, 1995; Conspiracy Theory 1997; Free Willy 3: The Rescue; Lethal Weapon 4, 1998; Blackheart (producer), 1999; Timeline (producer), 2003; 16 Blocks, 2006; X-Men Origins: Wolverine, 2009. TV films: Portrait of a Teenage Alcoholic; Senior Year; A Shadow in the Streets; Tales From the Crypt presents Demon Knight (co-executive producer); Any Given Sunday, 1999; X-Men (executive producer), 2000; Series episodes of: Have Gun Will Travel; Perry Mason; Cannon; Get Smart; The Fugitive; Kojak; Bronk; Twilight Zone; The Banana Splits; Combat; Two Fisted Tales; Conspiracy Theory. Address: The Donners Company, 9465 Wilshire Boulevard, #420, Beverly Hills, CA 90212, USA.

DONOVAN Marie-Andrée, b. 1947, Timmins, Ontario, Canada. Writer. 1 daughter. Education: BA, University of Ottawa, Canada. Publications: Books: Nouvelles volantes (short stories), 1994; L'Envers de toi (novel), 1997, 2000; Mademoiselle Cassie (novel), 1999, 2003; L'Harmonica (novel), 2000; Les Bernaches en voyage (story for children), 2001; Les soleils incendiés (novel), 2004; Fantômier (short stories), 2005; La Couleur des Voyages (story for children), 2008. Honours: Finalist, Prix littéraire Le Droit, 1998; Prix littéraire Le Droit, 2000; Finalist, Prix des lecteurs de Radio-Canada, 2001; Prix littéraire de la Fondation franco-ontarienne, 2002; Prix des lecteurs de Radio-Canada, 2005; Prix Émile-Ollivier, 2006; Prix Champlain, 2006; Listed in Who's Who publications and biographical dictionaries. E-mail: marieandree.donovan@gmail.com

DONOVAN Paul Anthony, b. 13 December 1956, London, England. Principal Chaplain, Royal Navy. Education: Venerable English College, Rome, 1975-82; PhB, 1977, STB, 1980, STL, 1982, Pontifical Gregorian University, Rome; MBA, Open University, 2002. Appointments: Ordained Priest, Farnham Royal, Slough, 1981; Assistant Priest, Kettering, 1982; Joined Royal Navy as a Chaplain, 1985; Exchange with USN, Great Lakes Training Center, Illinois, 2001; Director (RN) Armed Forces Chaplaincy Centre, 2003; Chaplain, HMS Illustrious, 2005; Director, Naval Chaplaincy Service, Principal Roman Catholic Chaplain (Naval) & Vicar General, Bishopric of the Forces, 2007; Returned to Diocese of Northampton, 2012. Honours: Prelate of Honour, 2006; Queen's Honorary Chaplain, 2007. Memberships: Fellow, Chartered Management Institute; Fellow, Royal Society of Arts. Address: c/o Bishop's House, Marriott Street, Northampton NN2 6AW, England. E-mail: paul@pauldonovan.co.uk

DONTAS Ismene, b. 15 April 1954, Ann Arbor, Michigan, USA. Veterinarian. m. Miltiades Andriopoulos, 1 daughter. Education: DVM, Aristotellian University of Thessaloniki, Greece, 1977; PhD, School of Medicine, University of Athens, Greece, 1981. Appointments: Lecturer, 1982, Assistant Professor, 1990, Associate Professor, 1999, School of Medicine, University of Athens, Greece. Publications: 102 articles in professional journals, cited Donta (s). Honours: 29 national and international scientific awards: Listed in various international biographical dictionaries. Memberships: International Society of Musculoskeletal and Neuronal Interactions; European Society of Laboratory Animal Veterinarians; Laboratory Animal Science Association. E-mail: idontas@med.uoa.gr

DORFF Stephen, b. 29 July 1973, Atlanta, Georgia, USA. Actor. Appointments: Started acting aged 9; Films: The Gate; The Power of One; An Ambush of Ghosts; Judgement Night; Rescue Me; Backbeat; SFW; Reckless; Innocent Lies; I Shot Andy Warhol; City of Industry, Blood and Wine, 1997; Blade, 1998; Entropy, 1999; Quantum Project, Cecil B Demented, 2000; The Last Minute, Zoolander, 2001; All For Nothin', Deuces Wild, Riders, FearDotCom, 2002; Den of Lions, Cold Creek Manor, 2003; Alone in the Dark, Tennis, Anyone?, Shadowboxer, 2005; World Trade Center, 45, 2006; Botched, The Passage, 2007; Felon, 2008; Public Enemies, 2009; Somewhere, 2010; Born to Be a Star,2010. TV films: I Know My First Name is Steven, Always Remember I Love You, Do You Know the Muffin Man? 1989; A Son's Promise, 1990; Earthly Possessions, 1999; Skip Tracer, Covert One: The Hades Factor, 2007. TV series: What a Dummy, 1990. Address: 9350 Wilshire Boulevard, Suite 4, Beverly Hills, CA 90212, USA.

DORFMAN Ariel, b. 6 May 1942, Buenos Aires, Argentina (Chilean citizen). Research Professor of Literature and Latin; Author; Dramatist; Poet. Education: Graduated, University of Chile, Santiago, 1967. Appointment: Walter Hines Page Research Professor of Literature and Latin, Centre for International Studies, Duke University, Durham, North Carolina, 1984-. Publications: Fiction: Hard Rain, 1973; My House is On Fire, 1979; Widows, 1983; Dorando la pildora, 1985; Travesia, 1986; The Last Song of Manuel Sendero, 1986; Mascara, 1988; Konfidenz, 1996. Poetry: Last Waltz in Santiago and Other Poems of Exile and Disappearance, 1988. Plays: Widows, 1988; Death and the Maiden, 1991; Reader, 1992; Who's Who (with Rodrigo Dorfman), 1997, The Other Side, 2006, Purgatorio, 2006. Films: Death and the Maiden, 1994; Prisoners in Time, 1995; My House is on Fire, 1997. Non-Fiction: How to Read Donald Duck (with Armand

Mattelart), 1971; The Empire's Old Clothes, 1983; Some Write to the Future, 1991; Heading South, Looking North: A Bilingual Journey, 1998; The Nanny and Iceberg, 1999. Honours: Olivier Award, London 1991; Time Out Award, 1991; Literary Lion, New York Public Library, 1992; Dora Award, 1994; Charity Randall Citation, International Poetry Forum, 1994; Best Film for Television, Writers Guild of Great Britain, 1996. Address: c/o Centre for International Studies, Duke University, Durham, NC 27708, USA.

DOROFTEI Mugur Gideon, b. 11 October 1943, Bucharest, Romania. Music Educator; Conductor; Composer; Musician. m. Cornelia Mesinschi, 1969, 2 sons, 1 daughter. Education: MusM, Ciprian Porumbescu Conservatory of Music, Bucharest, 1970; PhD, Music Academy of Bucharest, 1994. Appointments: Violinist, Opera and Operetta, Constanza, Romania, 1960-61; Violinist, Philharmonic Orchestra, Ploiesti, Romania, 1961-62; Violinist, Ciocirlia Opera Radio Orchestra Operetta, Bucharest, Romania, 1962-70; Violin Teacher, School of Arts No 1, Suceava, Romania, 1977-80; Artist in Residence, Strings & Orchestra, Southwestern University, Keene, Texas, USA, 1981-; Dallas Independent School District, 2001-04. Publications: Music Theory Made Clear; Music Theory Made Clear Workbook; Music Theory for the Young Musician; Music Theory for the Young Musician Workbook; Ear Trining Intervals & Chords; Solfeggio Sight Singing; Violin Method for Beginners Book One, with CD; Violin Method for Beginners Book Two, with CD. Honours: Personalities of the South, ABI, 1983; Presidential Citation of Excellence, 1987; Listed in international biographical dictionaries. Address: PO Box 711, Keene, TX 76059, USA.

DOSHI Rupak, b. 22 November 1984, Kolkata, India. Academic; Researcher. m. Kinnary. Education: BSc, Biotechnology, Vellore Institute of Technology University, India, 2006; M Res, Translation Medicine, University of Manchester, 2008; PhD, Pharmacology, University of Cambridge, 2011. Appointments: PhD student, in progress. Publications: Numerous articles in professional journals. Honours: Two Academic Merit scholarships, 2004-06; AstraZeneca and Cancer Research bursary, 2007-08; British Library Best Poster Prize, 2008; Overseas Research Studentship, Cambridge Commonwealth Trust-Dharam Hinduja Cambridge Scholarship, 2008-11; Charter Studentship, 2008-11, Tutorial Award, 2009, American Alumni Award, 2010, St Edmund's College, Cambridge; Bursary, The Faraday Institute, 2010; Bursary, MRC and WORD, 2010; Best Oral Presentation prize, Wellcome Trust Conference Centre, 2010. Address: Department of Pharmacology, University of Cambridge, Tennis Court Road, Cambridge, CB2 1PD, England. E-mail: rupakdoshi@gmail.com

DOTRICE Roy, b. 26 May 1925, Guernsey, Channel Islands. Actor. m. Kay Newman, 1946, 3 daughters. Education: Dayton and Intermediate Schools, Guernsey; Air Gunner, RAF, 1940; POW, 1942-45; Acted in repertory, 1945-55; Formed and directed Guernsey Theatre Co, 1955; Films include: The Heroes of Telemark, 1965; A Twist of Sand, 1968; Lock up Your Daughters, 1969; Buttercup Chain; Tomorrow; One of Those Things, 1971; Nicholas and Alexandra, 1971; Amadeus; The Corsican Brothers, 1983; The Eliminators, 1985; Shaka Zulu, 1985; Young Harry Houdini, 1986; Camila; L-Dopa; The Lady Forgets; The Cutting Edge; The Scarlet Letter; Swimming with Sharks; Alien Hunter; These Foolish Things; Played; Go Go Tales; Stage appearances throughout England and tours of Canada and USA; TV includes: Dear Liar, Brief Lives; The Caretaker; Imperial Palace; Misleading Cases; Clochemerle; Dickens of London; Stargazy on Zummerdown; Life Begins; Just Shoot Me; numerous appearances on US TV. Honours: TV Actor of the Year Award, 1968; Emmy Award; Tony Award, 2000. Address: 98 St Martin's Lane, London WC2, England.

DOUGLAS Brian David, b. 8 July 1948, Scotland. Painter. Education: York School of Art, 1963-67; Maidstone College of Art, 1967-70; Royal Academy Schools, London, 1970-73; Leeds Polytechnic, 1973-74. Career: Teacher, 1974-83; Technician, York University, 1984-89; Painter, 1970-2004. Honours: RAS (Painting and Engraving); NEAC; RBA. Memberships: Royal Society of British Artists; New English Art Club. Address: 26 Whitestone Drive, York YO31 9HZ, England.

DOUGLAS James, b. 4 July 1932, Dumbarton, Scotland. Composer. m. Helen Torrance Fairweather, 2 sons, 1 daughter. Education: Edinburgh, Paris, Salzburg & Munich, Germany; LRAM, ARCM, London. Appointments: Composer; Accompanist; Organist; Recording Artist; Proprietor, Eschenbach Editions (distributed by Caritas Music Publishing), 1986-; Compositions include: orchestral works, chamber music, piano music, organ music, choral music, songs to texts by David Adam and G R D Maclean; The Christ Church Sequence, The Glorious Sequence, The Highlands and Islands Sequence, 15 CDs by Caritas Records and 1 DVD: "A Musical Journey", Broadcasts on local and international stations over the years; Performances in Edinburgh, Europe and America. Membership: Music Publishers Association, London; Licensing: PRS/MCPS Ltd, London. Address: c/o Eschenbach Editions, Achmore, Moss Road, Ullapool, IV26 2TF, Scotland. E-mail: eschenbach@caritas-music.co.uk. Web: www.caritas-music.co.uk

DOUGLAS Kirk, b. 9 December 1916, Amsterdam, New York, USA. Actor. m. (1) Diana Dill, 2 sons, (2) Anne Buydens, 2 sons. Education: St Lawrence University; American Academy of Dramatic Arts. Appointments: President, Bryna Productions, 1955-; Director, Los Angeles Chapt, UN Association. Stage appearances: Spring Again; Three Sisters; Kiss and Tell; The Wind is Ninety; Alice in Arms; Man Bites Dog; The Boys of Autumn; Films include: The Strange Love of Martha Ivers; Letters to Three Wives; Ace in the Hole; The Bad and the Beautiful; 20,000 Leagues under the Sea; Ulysses; Lust for Life; Gunfight at Ok Corral; Paths of Glory; the Vikings; Last Train from Gun Hill; The Devil's Disciple; Spartacus; Strangers When We meet; Seven Days in May; Town Without Pity; The List of Adran Messenger; In Harms Way; Cast a Giant Shadow; The Way West; War Waggon; The Brotherhood; The Arrangement; There Was a Crooked Man; Gunfight, 1971; Light at the Edge of the World; Catch Me a Spy; A Man to Respect, 1972; Cat and Mouse; Scalawag (director), 1973; Once is Not Enough, 1975; Posse (producer, actor), 1975; The Moneychangers (TV), 1976; Holocaust 2000, 1977; The Fury, 1977; Villain, 1978; Saturn 3, 1979; The Final Countdown, 1980; The Man From Snowy River, 1986; Tough Guys, 1986; Queenie (TV mini series), 1987; Oscar, Welcome to Veraz, Greedy, 1994; Diamonds, 1999; Family Jewels, 2002; Eddie Macon's Run; Tough Guys; Oscar; Greedy; Diamonds; It Runs in the Family; Illusion.; Trumbo, 2008; Empire State Building Murders, 2008; Publications: The Ragman's Son: an Autobiography, 1988; Novels: Dance With The Devil, 1990; The Secret, 1992; The Gift, 1992; Last Tango in Brooklyn, 1994; Climbing the Mountain: My Search for Meaning, 1997; The Broken Mirror (novel), 1997; My Stroke of Luck, 2002. Honours: Academy awards, critics awards; Commandeur, Ordre des Arts et Lettres, 1979; Légion d'honneur, 1985; Presidential Medal of Freedom, 1981; American Film Industries Lifetime Achievement, 1991; Kennedy Center Honors, 1994; Lifetime

DICTIONARY OF INTERNATIONAL BIOGRAPHY 36th EDITION

Achievement Award, Screen Actors' Guild, 1999; Golden Bear, Berlin Film Festival, 2000; National Medal of Arts, 2002. Address: The Bryna Company, 141 S El Camino Drive, Beverly Hills, CA 90212, USA.

DOUGLAS Michael Kirk, b. 25 September 1944, New Brunswick, NJ, USA. m. (1) Diandra Mornell Luker (divorced), 1 son, (2) Catherine Zeta Jones, 2000, 1 son, 1 daughter. Appointments: Actor in films: It's My Turn; Hail Heroll, 1969; Summertime, 1971; Napoleon and Samantha, 1972; Coma, 1978; Running, 1979; Star Chamber, 1983; Romancing the Stone, 1984; A Chorus Line, 1985; Jewel of the Nile, 1985; Fatal Attraction, 1987; Wall Street, 1987; Heidi, 1989; Black Rain, 1989; The War of the Roses, 1990; Shining Through, 1990; Basic Instinct, 1992; Falling Down, 1993; The American President, 1995; The Ghost and the Darkness, 1996; The Game, 1997; A Perfect Murder, 1998; Traffic, 2000; Wonder Boys, 2000; One Night at McCool's, 2000; Don't Say a Word, 2001; A Few Good Years, 2002; It Runs in the Family, 2003; Monkeyface, 2003; The In-Laws, 2003; Producer, films including: One Flew Over the Cuckoo's Nest, 1975; The China Syndrome; Sarman (executive producer); Romancing the Stone; Jewel of the Nile, Flatliners, 1990; Made in America (co-executive, producer); Disclosure, 1994; A Perfect Murder, 1998; One Night at McCool's, 2000; Godspeed; Lawrence Mann, 2002; It Runs in the Family, 2003; The In-Laws, 2003; The Sentinel, 2006; You, Me and Dupree, 2006; Kings of California, 2007; Actor in TV series: Streets of San Francisco. Honours include: Academy Award for Best Actor for Wall Street, 1988; Spencer Tracey Award, 1999; UN Messenger of Peace, 2000. Address: C/o Creative Artists Agency Inc, 9830 Wilshire Boulevard, Beverly Hills, CA 90212, USA. Website: www.michaeldouglas.com

DOWEL Terence, b. 7 April 1941, Kerang, Australia. Entrepreneur; Managing Director; Chief Executive Officer; Inventor. m. Kaye, 2 sons, 2 daughters. Education: Year 10; Dux Year 8; Dux Year 10. Appointments: Inventor and entrepreneur: Introduced Australia's first modern hair conditioner for retail sale, 1963; Designed and built first fully Australian aerosol filling machine, 1967; The first in Australia to commercially extract aloe vera gel, 1979; Formulated Australia's first two-in-one shampoo and conditioner, 1987; Built the first camera in wheel tyre test laboratory in the world, 2002; Discovered the cause of the mysterious scuff mark on tyres and rims, 2003; Formulated the world's first non-latex tyre puncture sealant to flow through the valve core, 2007; Owner/Managing Director, Trydel Research Pty Ltd; Owner, Chief Executive Officer, Natures Organics Pty Ltd; Innovation through environmentally sustainable packaging using bioplastic that reduces C02 emissons by 90%. Honours: Outstanding Chapter Jaycee of the Year, 1976; Car Racing Hill Climb Vic (State) Champion (Historic Class), 2001, 2002, 2003; Car Racing Hill Climb Australian Champion (Historic Class), 2004; Natures Organics won the AGE/D&B Victorian Manufacturing Business of the Year Award, 2011; Natures Organics was a finalist in the AGE/D&B Victorian Business of the Year Award, 2011. Memberships: Member, 1973-82, Chapter President, 1981, Jaycees; Art Deco Society; Classic and Historic Automobile Club; ACD (Auburn Cord Duesenburg) Club, Australia; ACD (Auburn Cord Duesenburg) Club, USA; Cruelty Free; Kosher certified on various products. Address: 31 Cornhill Street, Ferntree Gully, Victoria 3156, Australia. E-mail: terry@trydel.com.au

DOWER-GOLD Catherine, b. 19 May 1924, South Hadley, Massachusetts, USA. Professor of Music History. m. Arthur Gold, 1994, deceased 1998. Education: Full Scholarship, Pius X School of Liturgical Music, Manhattanville College, 1945-46; Dean's Scholarship, AB, Music Composition, Hamline University, 1945; B. of Liturgical Music, University of Montreal & Gregorian Institute of America; MA, Musicology, Smith College, 1948; Musicology, Boston University School of Fine Arts, 1956-62; Visiting Scholar, University of Southern California, 1969; Dean's Scholarship, PhD, Catholic University of America, 1968; Public Speaking, Dale Carnegie, 1973; Poet Laureate Course, International Society of Poets, 2002. Career: Organist, St Theresa Church, South Hadley, Massachusetts, 1937-42; Organist, St Matthew, New York City, 1945-46; New England Representative, Gregorian Institute of America, 1948-49; School Music Teacher, Church Organist, Saint Rose School & Church, 1949-53; Elementary School Music Supervisor, Holyoke, Massachusetts, 1953-55; Instructor, University of Massachusetts, 1955; Visiting Associate Professor of Music, Herbert Lehman College, CUNY, 1970-71; Assistant Professor, 1956-68, Associate Professor, 1970, Professor, 1956-90, Westfield State University; Columnist & Feature Writer, Holyoke Daily Transcript, 1991-93. Publications: Books: 18th Century Sistina Capella Codices, 1968; Puerto Rican Music Following the Spanish American War, 1983; Alfred Einstein on Music, 1991; Yella Pessl, First Lady of the Harpsichord, 1992; Fifty Years of Marching Together, A Social History of the St Patrick's Committee of Holyoke, Massachusetts, Parade, 2001; Actividades Musicales en Puerto Rico, después de la guerra hispanoamericana, 1898-1910, 2006; Monographs: And Suddenly It Is Evening, 1979; Yella Pessl, First Lady of the Harpsichord: A Life of Fire and Conviction, 1986; Numerous articles in scholarly journals. Honours: Professor of the Year Award, Westfield State College, 1975; Installed as member of the Academia des Artes y Ciencias de Puerto Rico, 1977; Distinguished Service Awards, Westfield State College, 1979, 1981, 1983, 1985; Citation Academia Interamericana de Puerto Rico, 1979; Plaque, Springfield Symphony Orchestra, 1982; Citation, Holyoke Public Library, 1983; Human Relations Award, Massachusetts Teachers Association 1984; Invested in Papal Equestrian Order, 1984, Lady Commander, 1987, Lady Commander with Star, 1990, Order of the Holy Sepulchre of Jerusalem; Tolerance Medal, Council for Human Understanding, Holyoke, 1985; Career Woman of the Year, Quota International - Holyoke Chapter, 1988; Pride in Performance Award, Governor Michael Dukakis, 1988; US Congressional Certificate of Merit, 1990; Commonwealth of Massachusetts Citation, 1990; WSC concert series named Catherine A Dower Performing Arts Series, 1991; WSC seniors yearbook dedicated to Catherine Dower, 1991; Fellow, International Biographical Association, 1991; Professor Emerita conferred at WSC graduation, 1991; Award, Puerto Rican Revista Al Margen, 1992; Appointed to Westfield State College Foundation, 1994; Human Relations Award, Council for Human Understanding, Holyoke, 1994; Certificate of Honor, WSC, 1994; Honorary Member, Westfield State College Foundation & Scholarship in the name of Catherine Dower, 1994-; First Prize, Survivors of the Holocaust: A Legacy of Hope, Florida Atlantic University, 1996; Phi Beta Kappa, Hamline University, 2000; Distinguished Member, International Society of Poets, 2002; Silver Bowl & Medal, International Poet of Merit Award, 2002; Outstanding Achievement in Poetry Award, 2003; Silver Bowl, Editor's Choice Award, 2004, 2005, 2006, 2007; Editor's Published Poet Ribbon Award Pin, 2007, 2008; Westfield State College Honorary Marshal, Holyoke St Patrick's Parade, 2007; Distinguished Service Award, Holyoke Community College, 2010. Memberships: American Musicological Society; College Music Society; Church Music Association of America; Consociatio Internationalis Musicae Sacrae, Rome;

Equestrian Order of the Holy Sepulchre of Jerusalem; Phi Beta Kappa; Life Member, Lifelong Learning Society Florida Atlantic University; American Friends of the Vatican Library; Life Member, Friends of the Conservatory of Music, Lynn University; International Society of Poetry; Board Member, Council for Human Understanding of Holyoke; St Patrick's Committee of Holyoke; Smith College Club of Hampshire County; Honorary Member, Westfield State University Foundation; President, 1980-81, 1990-91, Quota International Holyoke Chapter; Life Member, Irish Cultural Center at Elms College; Holyoke Public Library Corporator, 2007-; Secretary, Parish Pastoral Council, Holy Cross Church, Holyoke; Board Member, President, 2008-09, Friends of the Holyoke Public Library; Board Member, Holyoke Cultural Council, 2008-. Address: 60 Madison Avenue, Holyoke, Massachusetts 01040-2041, USA. E-mail: cdowergold@comcast.net

DOWNES Andrew, b. 20 August 1950, Handsworth, Birmingham, England. Composer. m. Cynthia Cooper, 9 August 1975, 2 daughters. Education: Choral Scholar, 1969-72, BA Hons, 1972, St John's College, Cambridge; MA (Cantab), 1975; Royal College of Music, 1972-74; Singing with Gordon Clinton; Composition with Herbert Howells. Debut: Wigmore Hall, 1969. Career includes: Established Faculty of Composition, 1975, Head of School, 1990, Professor, School of Composition and Creative Studies, 1992-2005, Birmingham Conservatoire, England; Chaired Symposium on Music Criticism, Indian Music Congress, University of Burdwan, 1994; Performances of own works include: Berlin, Kaiser Willhelm Gedächtniskirche, 1980; Vienna, 1983, 1998, 2001, 2002; Israel Philharmonic Guest House, Tel Aviv, 1989; New York, 1993, 1996, 2003; Calcutta School of Music, 1994; Paris, 1995-2007; University of New Mexico, 1995, 1997, 1999; Bombay, Delhi, Calcutta, 1996; Barletta, Italy, 1996; Eugene, Oregon, 1996; Chicago, 1997; Caracas, Venezuela, 1997; Symphony Hall, Birmingham, 1997, 2003-05; Phoenix, Arizona, 1998, 2001; Rudolfinum, Prague, 1998, 2001, 2002, 2005, 2008; Lichtenstein Palace, Prague, 1999; James Madison University, Virginia, 2000; Boston, Massachusetts, 2000, 2005-09; Genoa, 2002; Washington, DC, 2002-04; Colorado, Michigan, Las Vegas, 2003; Dublin, 2003; North Carolina, California, Indiana, Columbia and Nashville, Tennessee, 2004; Mexico City, 2004; Mozarteum, Prague, 2005-08; Cambridge, Massachusetts, 2005, 2007-08; New Jersey, 2006; Harvard University, 2005, 2007-08; Podebrady Castle, Czech Republic, 2009; Melbourne, Australia, 2009; BBC Radio 2, 3 and 4; French Radio (France Musique); Austrian, Czech, Dutch, USA and Beijing Radios; Italian TV. Compositions include: Sonata for 8 Horns Opus 54, University of New Mexico commission, 1994, performed by the horns of the Czech Philharmonic Orchestra, 1998, 2000, 2005, 2008-09; Sonata for 8 Flutes (premiered New York, 1996, subsequent performances worldwide); Songs From Spoon River, performed at Tanglewood Festival and on BBC Radio 3; Towards A New Age, premièred by the Royal Philharmonic Orchestra in Symphony Hall, Birmingham, 1997; New Dawn, oratorio based on American Indian texts, Adrian Boult Hall, Birmingham, 2000, King's College Chapel, Cambridge, 2001; Sonata for 8 Pianists, Birmingham, 2000, Genoa, 2002; Sonata for Horn and Piano for Roland Horvath of Vienna Philharmonic Orchestra; Concerto for 4 Horns and Orchestra for the Czech Philharmonic Orchestra, Prague, 2002, Czech radio, 2003; Songs of Autumn and Songs of the Skies, performed by massed children's choirs, Symphony Hall, Birmingham, 2003-05, Lichfield Cathedral, 2004; 5 dramatic pieces for 8 Wagner Tubas for Czech Philharmonic Horns, premiered Dvorak Hall, Prague, 2005; Opera, Far From The Madding Crowd for The Thomas Hardy Society, 2006. Recordings include: The Marshes of Glynn, cantata, commission for Royal opening of Adrian Boult Hall, Birmingham, 1986; O Vos Omnes, motet, Cantamus commission (published by Faber Music in anthology, "30 Sacred Masterworks for Upper Voice Choir"); Sonata for 2 Pianos; Fanfare for a Ceremony, commission for Open University; Centenary Firedances, commissioned by City of Birmingham for its centenary celebrations; Shepherd's Carol; 3 Song Cycles on CD entitled "Old Loves Domain", 2000; The Souls of the Righteous, anthem, 1997; Sacred Choral Music on CD entitled "The Lord is My Shepherd", 2001; Sonata for Oboe and Piano, 1998; Sonata for 8 Horns by Horns of Czech Philharmonic Orchestra; Suite for 6 Horns, Sonata for Horn and Piano, Sontata for 4 Horns, Piano Sonata No 1 on 2 CDs on the Aricord label (Vienna); Concerto for 2 Guitars and Strings; Flute Choir Music by James Madison University Flute Choir and Massachusetts Flute Choir, 2000; Sonatina for Piano, Piano Sonatas 1 & 2 performed by Duncan Honeybourne, 2005; Sonata for Violin, Horn and Piano performed by The Brahms Trio, Prague, 2008; Music for Horns and Wagner Tubas, performed by the Horns of the Czech Philharmonic Orchestra, 2008; Concerto for Piano and Symphony Orchestra, 2009; Songs from Spoon River (film), 2010. Publications (by Lynwood Music and Faber Music): 100 works including 5 symphonies, 4 large-scale choral works, 6 concertos, 3 string quartets, 2 brass quintets, flute octet, Sonata for 8 pianists, horn octet, horn sextet and horn quartet, 9 song cycles, 2 operas and many sacred works. Honours include: Prizewinner, Stroud International Composers' Competition, 1980; Trees planted in Israel in name of Andrew Downes in recognition of composition, Sonata for 2 pianos, 1987; Invited by Crane Concert Choir, University of New York, to conduct his choral work A St Luke Passion, 1993; Leather bound presentation copy of Fanfare for a Ceremony given to HRH Prince Edward on his visit to Birmingham Conservatoire, 1995; Bound presentation copy of Fanfare for Madam Speaker given to Rt Hon Betty Boothroyd MP at her installation as Chancellor of Open University, 1995; Awarded Gold Medal by Institution of Mechanical Engineers for composition for their 150th Anniversary, 1997; Honorary Fellowship, Birmingham Conservatoire, 2010. Memberships include: Representing Birmingham Conservatoire, Indian Music Congress; President, Central Composers' Alliance; PRS; MCPS; Life Fellow, Royal Society of Arts. Address: c/o Lynwood Music, 2 Church Street, West Hagley, West Midlands DY9 0NA, England.

DOWNEY Robert Jr, b. 4 April 1965, New York, USA. Actor. m. (1) Deborah Falconer, (divorced) 1 son, (2) Susan Levin, 2005, 1 son. Career: Actor; Sentenced to probation for possession of cocaine; imprisoned for further drugs offence breaching terms of probation, 1997; released for rehabilitation, 1998; imprisoned again, 1999, freed, 2000, charged with drugs possession, 2000; Singing career, 2005-. Films include: Pound, 1970; Firstborn; Weird Science; To Live and Die in LA; Back to School; The Pick-Up Artist; Johnny B Good; True Believer; Chances Are; Air America; Soapdish; Chaplin; Heart and Souls; Short Cuts; The Last Party; Natural Born Killers; Only You; Restoration; Restoration; Danger Zone; Home for the Holidays; Richard III; Bliss Vision, The Gingerbread Man, 1997; Two Girls and a Guy, 1998; In Dreams, Friends and Lovers, 1999; Wonder Boys, Automotives, 2000; Lethargy, 2002; Whatever We Do, The Singing Detective, Gothika, 2003; Eros, 2004; Game 6, Kiss Kiss, Bang Bang, The Shaggy Dog, 2005; A Scanner Darkly, Good Night and Good Luck, 2006; Zodiac, Lucky You, Charlie Bartlett, 2007; Iron Man, 2008; The Soloist, 2009; Sherlock Holmes, 2009; Iron Man 2, Love & Distrust,

Due Date, 2010; Sherlock Holmes: A Game of Shadows, 2011; The Avengers, 2012; Iron Man 3, 2013; Television includes: Mussolini: The Untold Story (TV mini-series), 1985; Mr Willoughby's Christmas Tree, 1995; Ally McBeal, 2000-01; Black and White, 2000. Honours: BAFTA Award. Address: c/o Sony Classical, 550 Madison Avenue, New York, NY 10022, USA. Website: www.robertdowneyjrmusic.com

DOWNING Richard, b. 8 February 1951, Stourbridge, West Midlands, England. Consultant Vascular Surgeon. m. Stella Elizabeth, 2 sons, 2 daughters. Education: BSc (Hons), Physiology, 1972, MB ChB (Distinction in Pharmacology and Therapeutics), 1975, MD, 1983, University of Birmingham; Fellow, Royal College of Surgeons of England, 1980. Appointments: Lecturer in Anatomy, University of Birmingham, 1976-77; Research Associate, Washington University, St Louis, Missouri, USA, 1977-78; Registrar in Surgery, United Birmingham Hospitals, 1979-83; Lecturer in Surgery, 1983-86, Senior Lecturer in Surgery, 1986-90, University of Birmingham; Consultant Vascular Surgeon, 1990-, Director, Islet Research Laboratory, Worcestershire Royal Hospital; Honorary Senior Clinical Lecturer, University of Birmingham, 2010-. Publications: Publications on pancreatic islet transplantation, peripheral vascular disease. Honours: Examiner, Faculty of Dental Surgery, Royal College of Surgeons of England, 1989-95; Member of the Editorial Board: Journal of the Care of the Injured, 1989-96 and British Journal of Diabetes and Vascular Disease, 2002-. Memberships: Vascular Society of Great Britain and Ireland; European Society of Vascular and Endovascular Surgery; International Pancreas and Islet Transplant Society. Address: Worcestershire Royal Hospital, Charles Hastings Way, Worcester WR5 1DD, England.

DOYLE Roddy, b. 1958, Dublin Ireland. Writer. m. Bellinda, 2 sons. Publications: The Commitments, 1987, filmed 1991; The Snapper, 1990, filmed, 1992; The Van, 1991; Paddy Clarke Ha Ha Ha, 1993; The Women Who Walked Into Doors, 1996; Two Lives: Hell for Leather, 1999; Not Just for Christmas, 1999; A Star Called Henry, 1999; The Giggler Treatment, 2000; When Brendon Met Trudy, 2000; Rover Saves Christmas, 2001; Rory and Ita, 2002; Oh, Play That Thing, 2004; The Meanwhile Adventures, 2004; Paula Spencer, 2006; Wilderness, 2007; Her Mother's Face, 2008; The Dead Republic, 2010. Honour: Booker Prize for Paddy Clarke Ha Ha Ha, 1993. Address: c/o Patti Kelly, Viking Books, 375 Hudson Street, New York, NY 10014, USA.

DRABBLE Dame Margaret, b. 5 June 1939, Sheffield, England. Author. m. (1) Clive Swift, divorced 1975, 2 sons, 1 daughter, (2) Michael Holroyd, 1982. Education; Newnham College, Cambridge. Appointments: Editor, The Oxford Companion to England Literature, 1979-84; Chairman, National Book League, 1980-82; Vice-Patron, Child Psychotherapy Trust, 1987-. Publications: A Summer Bird-Cage, 1963; The Garrick Year, 1964; The Millstone, 1965 Jerusalem the Golden, 1967; The Waterfall, 1969; The Needle's Eye, 1972; Arnold Bennett: A Biography, 1974; The Realms of Gold, 1975; The Genius of Thomas Hardy (editor), 1976; The Ice Age, 1977; For Queen and Country: Britain in the Victorian Age, 1978; A Writer's Britain, 1979; The Middle Ground (novel), 1980; The Oxford Companion to English Literature (editor), 1985; The Radiant Way (novel), 1987; A Natural Curiosity, 1989; Safe as Houses, 1990; The Gates of Ivory, 1991; Angus Wilson: A Biography, 1995; The Witch of Exmoor (novel), 1996; The Peppered Moth (novel), 2001; The Seven Sisters (novel), 2002; The Red Queen, 2004; The Sea Lady, 2006; The Pattern on the Carpet (memoir), 2009.

Honours include: John Llewelyn Rhys Memorial Prize, 1966; E M Forster Award, American Academy of Arts and Letters, 1973; Hon D Litt, Sheffield, 1976, Bradford, 1988, Hull, 1992; Honorary Fellow, Sheffield City Polytechnic, 1989; Honorary member, American Academy of Arts and Letters, 2002; St Louis Literary Award, 2003; Queen's Birthday Honours, 2008. Address: c/o PFD, Drury House, 34-43 Russell Street, London, WC2B 5HA, England.

DRAGIĆ KIJUK Predrag R, b. 8 December 1945, Kragujevac, Serbia, Yugoslavia. Writer; Lexicographer. m. Dragoslava, 1 son, 1 daughter. Education: MA, Faculty of Philology, University of Belgrade, 1968. Appointments: Librarian, University Cultural Centre, Belgrade, 1970-93; Founder, The Christian Thought, 1993-; Special Adviser, Government of RSK, Knin, 1993-95; Executive Editor, Serbian Literary Magazine, 1993-2001; President, Serbian Diaspora Edition, 2000-08; Editor in Chief, Journal of Literature, 2001-04; Member, Advisory Board, Philosophy School, Krusevac, 2001-04; General Secretary, Serbian Literary Foundation, 2004-. Publications: Mediaeval and Renaissance Serbian Poetry 1200-1700, 1987; The Ordeal Maker and the Redeemer, 1990; Coming Out for a Game, 1990; Catena Mundi I-II, 1992; The Art and the Evil, 2005; Europe Versus Europe, 2006; Atlantocracy, 2006; The Eristics' Essays, 2007; Treatise of Homiletics, 2008. Honours: The Slobodan Jovanovic Award, Politika's Yearly Award, 1992; Diploma of National Library of Serbia, 2004; Freedom Charter, Dveri Srpske, 2008. Memberships: Foundation of the Truth; Centre for The Christian Studies; Liberty and Freedom of Rights Committee. Address: Bojanska 15, Belgrade 11118, Serbia. E-mail: rankodragickijuk@gmail.com

DRAGOUN Otokar, b. 15 March 1937, Sedlec, Czech Republic. Physicist. m. Nadezda Novotná, 5 July 1961, 2 daughters. Education: Diploma in Engineering, Czech Technical University, Prague, 1962; PhD, Physics, 1967, DSc, Physics, 1985, Charles University, Prague. Appointments: Researcher, Nuclear Physics Institute, Czech Academy of Science, 1962-; Head of Research Group, 1971-2005; Postdoctoral Fellow, Max-Planck Institute for Nuclear Physics, Heidelberg, Germany, 1966-69; Visiting Professor, Faculty of Physics Technical University, Munich, Spring 1992, Summer 1994; External Lecturer, Charles University, Prague, 1986-2005; External Lecturer, Czech Technical University, Prague, 1999-2006; Member of the Karlsruhe Tritium Neutrino Experiment, 2001-. Publications: Contributor of reviews and science papers on nuclear, nuclear atomic and neutrino experimental physics in international journals; Patentee in field. Honours: Medal Science Achievement, Union Czech Mathematicians and Physicists, 1988. Membership: Czech Physical Society. Address: Nuclear Physics Institute of the Academy of Sciences of Czech Republic, CZ-25068, Rez near Prague, Czech Republic.

DRAŽANČIĆ Ante, b. 28 November 1928, Šibenik, Croatia. Physician. m. (1) Jakica, divorced, 1 son, 1 daughter, (2) Liliana, 1 daughter. Education: Medical Doctor, 1953; Specialist in Obstetrics & Gynaecology, 1961; PhD, University of Zagreb, 1966; Associate Professor, Obstetrics & Gynaecology, 1970; Professor of Obstetrics & Gynaecology, 1980. Appointments: Resident Physician, General Hospital Varaždin, 1953-57; Assistant Physician, Department of Obstetrics & Gynaecology, University Medical School of Zagreb, 1958-73; Head of Division of Perinatal Medicine, 1974-94; Retired, 1994. Publications: 4 books; 423 scientific and professional papers and reviews. Honours: Medal of Work, President of Yugoslavia; Past President, Croatian Medical

Association; Past President, Croatian Society of Perinatal Medicine; Croatian Society of Obstetrics & Gynaecology. Address: Jakova Gotovca 7, 10000 Zagreb, Croatia. E-mail: ante.drazancic@zg.t-com.hr

DRCHAL Vaclav, b. 21 May 1945, Prague, Czech Republic. Physicist. m. Jaroslava, 2 sons. Education: Faculty of Mathematics and Physics, 1968, Doctorate, 1974, Charles University; Candidate of Science, 1974. Appointments: Academy of Sciences, Institute of Solid State Physics, 1968-80; Institute of Physics, 1980-. Publications: 229 original scientific articles, 1 monograph. Honours: State Prize, 1982; Prize, Academy of Sciences, 1989, 1998. Membership: Union of Czech Mathematicians and Physicists. Address: Academy of Sciences, Institute of Physics, Na Slovance 2, CZ-182 21, Prague 8, Czech Republic.

DREIMANIS Aleksis, b. 13 August 1914, Valmiera, Latvia. Geologist. m. Anita Kana, 2 daughters. Education: Mag.rer.nat, University of Latvia, 1938; Habilitation, 1941. Appointments: Assistant/Privatdocent, University of Latvia, 1937-44; Military Geologist, Latvian Legion, 1944-45; Associate Professor, Baltic University, 1946-48; Lecturer/Professor Emeritus, University of Western Ontario, 1948-. Publications: Over 200 articles in professional journals. Honours include: Teaching Award, Ontario Confederation of University Faculty Associations, 1978; Fellow, Royal Society of Canada, 1979; Doctor honoris causa, University of Waterloo, 1969, University of Western Ontario, 1980; Distinguished Career Award, Quaternary Geology and Geomorphology Division of the Geological Society of America, 1987; Foreign Member, Latvian Academy of Sciences, 1990; Doctor geographiae honoris causa Univeritatis Latviensis, 1991; Distinguished Fellow, Geological Association of Canada, 1995; Three Star Order of Latvia, 2003; Honorary Member, several geological, geographical and social associations. Address: 287 Neville Drive, London, Ontario, N6G 1C2, Canada.

DREYFUSS Richard Stephen, b. 29 October 1947, New York, USA. Actor. m. Jeramie, 1983, 2 sons, 1 daughter. Education: San Fernando Valley State College. Appointments: Alternative military service, Los Angeles County General Hospital, 1969-71; Actor, stage appearances include: Julius Caesar, The Big Fix (also producer), 1978; Othello, 1979; Death and the Maiden, 1992; The Prison of Second Avenue, 1999; Films include: American Graffiti, 1972; Dillinger, 1973; The Apprenticeship of Duddy Kravitz, 1974; Jaws, Inserts, 1975; Close Encounters of the Third Kind, 1976; The Goodbye Girl, 1977; The Competition, 1980; Whose Life Is It Anyway?, 1981; Down and Out in Beverly Hills, 1986; Stakeout, 1988; Moon over Parador, Let It Ride, Always, 1989; Rosencrantz and Guildenstern are Dead, Postcards from the Edge, Once Around, Randall and Juliet, 1990; Prisoners of Honor, What About Bob?, 1991; Lost in Yonkers, Another Stakeout, 1993; The American President, Mr Holland's Opus, 1995; Mad Dog Time, James and the Giant Peach, 1996; Night Falls on Manhattan, The Call of the Wild, 1997; Krippendorf's Tribe, A Fine and Private Place, 1998; The Crew, The Old Man Who Read Love Stories, 2000; Who is Cletis Tout? 2001; Silver City, 2004; Unsung (voice), Poseidon, 2006; Suburban Girl, 2007; My Life in Ruins, 2009; Leaves of Grass, 2009; The Lightkeepers, 2009; TV includes: Oliver Twist, 1997; Fail Safe, 2000; Education of Max Bickford, Day Reagan Was Shot, 2001; Coast to Coast, Copshop, 2004; Tin Man, 2007; Happiness Isn't Everything, 2009; Family Guy, 2009; Director, producer, Nuts, 1987; Hamlet (Birmingham), 1994. Publication: The Two Georges (with Harry Turtledove), 1996. Honours: Golden Globe Award, 1978; Academy Award for Best Actor in the Goodbye Girl, 1978. Memberships: American Civil Liberties Union Screen Actors Guild; Equity Association; American Federation of TV and Radio Artists; Motion Picture Academy of Arts and Sciences. Address: William Morris Agency, 151 S El Camino Drive, Beverly Hills, CA 90212, USA.

DRIVER Minnie (Amelia), b. 21 January 1970. Actress. 1 son. Appointments: Actress, TV appearances include: God on the Rocks; Mr Wroe's Virgins; The Politician's Wife; Will & Grace; The Riches; Mallory; Modern Family; The Deep; Film appearances include: Circle of Friends; Goldeneye; Baggage; Big Night; Sleepers; Grosse Point Blank; Good Will Hunting; The Governess; Hard Rain; An Ideal Husband, South Park: Bigger, Longer and Uncut, 1999; Slow Burn, Beautiful, Return to Me, The Upgrade, 2000; High Heels and Lowlifes, D.C. Smalls, 2001; Owning Mahoney, Hope Springs, 2003; The Phantom of the Opera, Ella Enchanted, Portrait, 2004; The Virgin of Juarez, Delirious, 2006; Ripple Effect, Take, The Simpsons Movie, (voice), 2007; Motherhood, Betty Anne Waters, 2009; Barney's Version, Hunky Dory, 2010; I Give It a Year, 2013; Play: Sexual Perversity in Chicago, Comedy Theatre, London, 2003; Recording: Albums: Everything I've Got In My Pocket, 2004; Seastories, 2007. Honours: Best Newcomer, 1997, Best Actress, 1988, London Circle of Film Critics. Address: c/o Lou Coulson, 1st Floor, 37 Berwick Street, London, W1V 3LF, England.

DRIVER Paul William, b. 14 August 1954, Manchester, England. Music Critic; Writer. Education: MA, Honours, Oxford University, 1979. Appointments: Music Critic, The Boston Globe, 1983-84, Sunday Times, 1985-; Member, Editorial Board, Contemporary Music Review; Patron, Manchester Musical Heritage Trust. Publications: A Diversity of Creatures (editor), 1987; Music and Text (editor), 1989; Manchester Pieces, 1996; Penguin Popular Poetry (editor), 1996; Ear to the Ground (series of conversations with British composers), BBC Radio 4, 2004; Four Elegies (verse), 2009; A Metropolitan Recluse (novel), 2010. Contributions to: Sunday Times; Financial Times; Tempo; Gramophone; London Review of Books; New York Times; Numerous others; Frequent broadcaster. Membership: Critics Circle. Address: 15 Victoria Road, London NW6 6SX, England.

DROUIN Herbert Rudolf Ludwig, b. 23 January 1936, Offenbach am Main, Germany. Educator; Researcher. Education: Diploma in Engineering, Chemistry, Technische Hochschule Darmstadt, Germany, 1962; Dr Ing, Physical Chemistry, Rheinisch-Westfälische Technische Hochschule Aachen, Germany, 1967; Privatdozent, Physiology, Universität des Saarlandes, Germany, 1979. Appointments: Visiting Professor: Boston University, USA, 1981; Universität Konstanz, Germany, 1984; Medizinische Universität zu Lübeck, Germany, 1989; Max-Planck-Institut für Biophysik, Frankfurt am Main, Germany, 1993. Publications: Numerous articles in chemistry, physiology, pharmacology and biophysics in professional scientific journals. Honours: Charter Member, Leading Intellectuals of the World for Biophysics and Physiology in the Fields: Nonlinear Electro-osmosis, Surface Charges at Nerve Membranes, Polyamines and Activities of the Nerve Cells, ABI, 2010; Listed in international biographical dictionaries. Memberships: Deutsche Gesellschaft für Biophysik; Deutsche Physiologische Gesellschaft; The New York Academy of Sciences. Address: Taunusstrasse 95, D-63263, Neu-Isenburg, Germany.

DROZDZ Wiktor, b. 6 April 1965, Stalowa Wola, Poland. Academic Teacher; Researcher; Clinician. m. Beata, 2 daughters. Education: Medical Doctor, Warsaw Medical University, 1990; PhD, University Medical School of Bydgoszcz, Poland, 2000. Appointments: Post-doctoral thesis, Collegium Medicum Bydogozscz, 2010. Publications: Low dose Ripseridone in the treatment of Schizophrenia-like symptoms in high-risk subjects, 2007; Chronic paranoid psychosis and dementia following interferon-alpha treatment of hepatitic C: A Case Report, 2007; The Wisconsin Card Sorting Test and N-Back Test in Mild Cognitive Impairment and Elderly Depression, 2009; Polish Validation of the Temps-A: The Profile of Affective Temperaments in a College Student Population, 2010. Honours: Best Poster Award, 3rd Conference of the International Society for Bipolar Disorders, 2008. Memberships: Polish Psychiatric Association. Address: Clinical Neuropsychology Unit, 9 Sklodowskiej St, 85-094 Bydgoszcz, Poland. E-mail: wikdr@cm.umk.pl

DRUYANOV Boris, b. 1 October 1930, Charkov, Ukraine. Lecturer; Scientific Worker. m. Yulia, 1 son, 1 daughter (deceased). Education: Candidate in Physics and Mathematics, 1961, Doctor in Physics and Mathematics, 1970, Professor of Theoretical Mechanics, 1971, Moscow State University. Appointments: Assistant, Docent, Professor, Head of the Department of Theoretical Mechanics, Moscow Institute for Industrial Devices, 1971-90; Research Professor, Hebrew University of Jerusalem, Israel, 1990-2005; Retired, 2005. Publications: Books: Technological Mechanics of Porous Bodies, 1993; Problems of Technological Plasticity, 1994; Direct Safe Design, in press. E-mail: borisu@bezeqint.net

DRYDAKIS Nick, b. 14 October 1980, Athens, Greece. Economist; Educator. Education: BA, 2003, PhD, 2008, Economics, University of Crete, Gallus Campus, Greece; MSc, Economics, Athens University of Economics and Business, 2005. Appointments: Researcher, Business Economics laboratory, University of Crete, 2005-10; Director, Scientific Center of the Study of Discrimination, 2005-; Academic Staff, University of Piraeus, Greece, 2008-; Academic Staff, University of Central Greece, Livadia, 2008-; Academic Staff, Panteion University of Social and Political Sciences, Athens, 2008-; Academic Staff, Athens University of Economics and Business, Athens, 2009-10; Academic Staff, University of Patras, Greece; Lecturer, Labour Economics, University of Patras, Greece; Research Fellow, Institute for the Study of Labor (IZA), Bonn, Germany. Publications: Numerous articles in professional journals. Honours: Design of field experiments on ethnic, race, health, sexual orientation, discrimination in the labour and housing market, construction data bases on ethnic, race, health, and sexual orientation in the labour market. Address: Department of Economics, University Campus Patra, Rio, 26504, Greece. E-mail: ndrydakis@econ.society.uoc.gr

DU Yuzhou, b. 2 February 1942, China. Businessman. m. Meiqi Gu, 1 son. Education: Bachelor's degree, School of Architecture, Tsinghua University, 1966. Appointments: Deputy Director, Deputy President, President, Architecture, China Textile Industrial Engineering Institute, 1973-85; Vice President, Ministry of Textile Industry of China, 1985-93; Vice President, China Textile Council (former Ministry of Textile Industry of China), 1993-98; President, China National Textile Council (former China Textile Council), 1998-2001; President, 2001-11, Honorary Director, 2012-, China National Textile & Apparel Council (former China National Textile Council); PhD Supervisor, Tianjin Polytechnic University, 2004-; Chairman, China National Garment Association; Chairman, China Fashion Color Association. Publications: Photography and Drawing Capricio, 2005; Exhibition of personal art works in New York UN Headquarters, China and Hong Kong, 2005-07; Over 20 articles in China Textile News and China Textile Industry Development Report. Honours: Officier, Ordre des Arts et des Lettres, Ministry of Culture of France, 2011. Memberships: Communist Party of China. Address: No 12, East Chang'an Street, Beijing, 100742, China. E-mail: foreignaffairs@ctei.gov.cn

DUBONOSOV Alexander, b. 7 July 1954, Rostov on Don, Russia. Chemistry. m. Irina, 1 son, 1 daughter. Education: Postgraduate, 1977-80, Candidate of Science, 1985, Doctor of Science, 2004, Professor, 2009, Rostov State University. Appointments: Junior Scientist, 1980, Senior Scientist, 1985, Institute of Physical and Organic Chemistry of RSU; Leading Scientist, 2005, Chief Research Scientist, Deputy Head of Department of Physical and Organic Chemistry, 2008, Southern Scientific Centre of Russian Academy of Sciences. Publications: About 250 publications in chemical books, journals and conference materials. Honours: Science/ Interperiodica Award, International Academic Publishing Company, 2009. Memberships: European Academy of Natural History; American Chemical Society; Russian Academy of Natural History. Address: Mechnikov st 146A/75, Rostov on Don 344000, Russia. E-mail: aled54@mail.ru

DUBROVIN Valeriy Ivanovich, b. 25 January 1945, Omsk, Russia. Computer Scientist; Educator. m. Nina Efimovna, 2 daughters. Education: Electrician, Kharkov Technical School of Radio Engineering, Kharkov, 1960-64; Radio Engineer, Zaporizhian Machine-Building Institute, Zaporozhye, 1965-70; Postgraduate Study, Institute of Control Sciences of Academy of Sciences of USSR, 1971-74. Appointments: Electrician, Relay-Plant, Kharkov, 1963-64; Technician, Radiopribor plant, Zaporozhye, 1965; Engineer, Design Office of Electro-Instrument-Making, 1970; Soldier in Army, Moscow Command, Moscow, 1970-71; Research Staff, 1975-77, Senior Teacher, 1977-79, Deputy Dean, 1977-81, Senior Lecturer, 1979-, Zaporizhye Machine-Building Institute (now Zaporizhian National Technical University); Deputy Chief Editor, Radio Electronics, Computer Science, Control journal, 1999-; Expert, State Accreditation Committee, Ukrainian Ministry of Education and Science, 1999-; Deputy Chief, Department of Software Systems, 2001-. Publications: 13 articles in English; 3 books and 250 articles in Russian; 8 patents. Honours: Laureate of Best Work, 1973, Laureate of Best Work among Young Scientists, 1974, Institute of Control Sciences, Academy of Sciences of USSR; Ukrainian Ministry of Education, 1997; Progress in the Field of Quality, Zaporizhian Regional Public Administration, 2000; Excel of Ukrainian Education, 2000; Diploma for Data Base Creation, Book of Memory of Ukraine, Zaporizhian Regional Public Administration, 2000. Memberships: Member, Academic Council, Scientific Council, Zaporizhian National Technical University; Academy Secretary, Scientific Council, Department of Informatics and Radio Electronics, National Technical University of Zaporozhye; Member, Academic Council, Department of Informatics and Radio Electronics, Zaporizhian National Technical University. Address: Gudimenko, 40/113 Zaporizhian, Zaporozhye 69114, Ukraine. E-mail: vdubrovin@gmail.com Website: http://gw-zntu.zntu.edu.ua/dubrovin

DUBURS Gunars, b. 12 June 1934, Riga, Latvia. Chemist. m. Renate, 1 daughter. Education: Chemist, Latvian University, 1957; PhD, 1961; Dr chem habil, 1979; Professor, 1988. Appointments: Research Scientist, 1957-64, Head of

Laboratory, 1964-, Scientific Director, 1980-2004, Institute of Organic Synthesis. Publications: 535 science papers; 177 patents. Honours include: D Grindel's Award, 1996; Award of the Latvian Cabinet of Ministers, 1999; Award of the Latvian Academy of Science and Patent Office, 2000; O Schmiedeberg's Medal, 2001; WIPO (World Intellectual Property Organization) Award, 2006; Diploma of Gratitude from the Prime Minister of Latvia, 2007; Gold Owl Medal, Grindex Fund for Science and Latvian Academy of Science, 2008; The Latvian State Three-Star Order, The Cross of Officer, 2009; Listed in numerous biographical publications. Memberships: Latvian Academy of Science; International Society of Heterocyclic Chemistry; Albert Schweitzer International University; Latvian Chemical Society; UNESCO Molecular and Cell Biology Network; Latvian Society of Medicinal Chemistry. Address: 21 Aizkraukles Street, Latvian Institute of Organic Synthesis, Riga, LV 1006, Latvia.

DUCHOVNY David, b. 7 August 1960, New York, USA. Actor. m. Tea Leoni, 1997, separated 2011, 1 son, 1 daughter. Education: Yale University; Princeton University. Appointments: Stage appearances include: Off-Broadway plays, The Copulating Machine of Venice, California and Green Cuckatoo; TV series: The X Files; Films include: New Year's Day, 1989; Julia Has Two Lovers, 1990; The Rapture, 1991; Don't Tell Mom The Babysitter's Dead, 1991; Chaplin, 1992; Red Shoe Diaries, 1992; Ruby, 1992; Kalifornia, 1993; Venice, Venice, Apartment Zero; Close Enemy; Loan; Independence Day; Playing God; The X Files, 1998; Return To Me, 2000; Evolution, 2001; Zoolander, 2001; Full Frontal, 2002; XIII, 2003; Connie and Carla, 2004; House of D, 2004; The X Files: Resist or Serve (voice), 2004; Area 51 (voice), 2005; Trust the Man, 2005; The TV Set, 2006; The Secret, 2007; Things We Lost in the Fire, 2007; The X Files: I Want to Believe, 2008; The Joneses, 2009; Goats, 2012; Phantom, After the Fall, Relative Insanity, 2013; Television includes: Twin Peaks, 1990; The X-Files, 1993-; Life With Bonnie, 2002; Sex and the City, 2003; Californication, 2007-. Address: 20th Century Fox Film Corporation, PO Box 900, Beverly Hills, CA 90213, USA.

DUCORNET Erica Lynn, (Rikki Ducornet), b. 19 April 1943, New York, New York, USA. Writer; Artist; Teacher. 1 son. Education: Bard College, 1964. Appointments: Novelist-in-Residence, University of Denver, 1988-; Visiting Professor, University of Trento, Italy, 1994. Publications: The Stain, 1984; Entering Fire, 1986; The Fountains of Neptune, 1989; Eben Demarst, 1990; The Jade Cabinet, 1993; The Butcher's Tales, 1994; Phosphor in Dreamland, 1995; The Word "Desire", 1997; The Fan-Maker's Inquisition, 1999; Gazelle, 2003; Contributions to: Periodicals. Honours: National Book Critics Circle Award Finalist, 1987, 1990, 1993; Critics Choice Award, 1995; Charles Flint Kellogg Award in Arts and Letters, 1998. Membership: PEN. Address: c/o Department of English, University of Denver, Denver, CO 80208, USA.

DUCOURTHIAL Guy, b. 7 December 1931, Paris, France. Manager. Education: Licence Geography, Sorbonne, Paris; Master, Geography, Institut de Geographie, Sorbonne; Doctorate in Sciences, Museum National d'Histoire Naturelle. Appointments: Section Head, SCET, 1958-64; Secretary General, SEAH, 1964-69; Manager, SOPREC, 1969-71; Manager, SCIC, 1971-89. Publications: Books: La Pomme, 1996; Flore magique et astrologique de l'Antiquite, 2003; Recueil de naltes pour remedes et autres secrets, 2007; La Botanique, 2009. Address: 4 Passage des Fours a Chaux, 75019 Paris, France.

DUERDEN Brian Ion, b. 21 June 1948, Nelson, Lancashire, England. Medical Practitioner. m. Marjorie Hudson. Education: BSc, Honours, Medical Science, 1970, MB ChB, 1972, MD, 1979, Edinburgh University Medical School; MRCPath, 1978; FRCPath, 1990; FRCP Edin, 2005. Appointments: House Officer, Thoracic Surgery and Infectious Diseases, Edinburgh City Hospital, 1972-73; Lecturer in Bacteriology, Edinburgh University, 1973-76; Lecturer, 1976-79, Senior Lecturer, 1979-83, Professor, 1983-90, Medical Microbiology, Sheffield University; Honorary Consultant, Microbiology, Sheffield Children's Hospital, 1979-90; Professor of Medical Microbiology, 1991-2008, Emeritus Professor, 2009-, University of Wales College of Medicine/Cardiff University; Medical Director and Deputy Director of Service, 1995-2002, Director of Service, 2002-2003, Public Health Laboratory Service; Director for Clinical Governance and Quality, Health Protection Agency, 2003; Inspector of Microbiology and Infection Control, Department of Health, 2004-10. Publications: 150 articles in scientific journals; Contributions to text books for undergraduate and postgraduate use; Editor-in-Chief, Journal of Medical Microbiology, 1982-2002; Articles on anaerobic microbiology, antibiotics, healthcare associated infection and public health. Honours: CBE, 2008. Memberships: Society for Anaerobic Microbiology; Fellow, Infectious Diseases Society of America; Society for General Microbiology; Anaerobe Society of the Americas. Address: Department of Medical Microbiology, Cardiff University Medical School, University Hospital of Wales, Heath Park, Cardiff CF14 4XN, Wales. E-mail: duerden@cf.ac.uk

DUFFY Kaye Lynette, b. 14 April 1942, Newcastle, Australia. Journalist; Businesswoman. m. (1) Terence Alan Farrelly, 1962, dissolved 1974, 3 sons, (2) Kenneth Roy Duffy. Education: Newcastle Girls' High School. Appointments: Newcastle Herald and various media outlets, 1958-83; Journalist NBN3 TV, Newcastle, 1974-83; Company Director, Kary Pty Ltd, 1976-; Franchisor/Owner, Australian Spit Roast Professionals, 1985-92; Business Consultant, Rightnow Solutions, 1990-; Palliative Care Volunteer, Mercy Hospice, Newcastle, 1990-2007; Co-ordinator of Volunteers, Life Without Barriers, 1998-99; Advisory Board, Salvation Army, Newcastle Division, 1996-2002; Minister's Health Participation Cl, NSW, 2001-04; NSW State Palliative Care Advisory Group, 2002-; Yallarwah Advisory Board, John Hunter Hospital, Newcastle, 2003-04; Consumer Representative, Cancer Institute of NSW, 2004-; Establishing Chair, Greater Newcastle Community Health Forum, Hunter New England Area Health Service, 2005; Co-founder and Co-convenor White Ribbon Day Breakfast, Newcastle, 2005, 2006; NSW Neuro-oncology Group, 2005-08; National Chair, Brain Tumour Australia Inc, 2005-08; Consumer Advice Group Cancer Australia, 2006-; Member, Steering Committee, Health Direct NSW Health, 2007-; Board Member, WEA Hunter, 2009-. Honours: City of Newcastle Medal, 2004; Order of Australia Medal, 2006. Memberships: Newcastle Club. Address: 1/104 Memorial Drive, Bar Beach, Newcastle, NSW, Australia. E-mail: kduffy@hunterlink.net.au

DUFFY Lawrence Kevin, b. 1 February 1948, Brooklyn, New York, USA. Biochemist; Educator. m. Geraldine, 2 sons, 1 daughter. Education: BS, Chemistry, Fordham University, 1969; MS, Chemistry, University of Alaska, 1972; PhD, Biochemistry, 1977. Appointments: Laboratory Instructor, University of Alaska, 1969-71; Research Assistant, University of Alaska Fairbanks, 1974-76; Post-doctoral Fellow, Boston University, 1977-78; Post-doctoral Fellow, Roche Institute of Molecular Biology, 1978-80; James W

McLaughlin Fellow, University of Texas, 1980-81; Research Assistant Professor, University of Texas Medical Branch, 1982-83; Instructor, Middlesex Community College, 1983-84; Assistant Biochemist, McLean Hospital, Belmont, 1983-85; Assistant Professor, Biochemistry, Harvard Medical School, 1983-87; Science and Organic Chemistry Instructor, Roxbury Community College, 1984-87; Associate Biochemist, Brigham and Women's Hospital, 1985-87; Research Associate, Duke University Centre, 1986-87; Professor, Chemistry and Biochemistry, University of Alaska Fairbanks, 1987-; Co-ordinator, Program in Biochemistry and Molecular Biology, 1987-90, 1992-93; Adjunct Researcher, Brigham and Women's Hospital, 1987-90; Affiliate Professor, Centre for Alcohol Addiction Studies, 1995-98; Head, Department of Chemistry and Biochemistry, 1994-99; Co-ordinator, RSI Scientist in Residence Programme, 1996-2003; President, UAF Faculty Senate, 2000; President American Institute of Chemists 2005-2006; Associate Dean for Graduate Studies and Outreach, 2001-07; Graduate Dean, 2007-11; Co-lead, UARCTIC Graduate Studies. Publications: 300 scientific papers and abstracts. Honours: Fiest Outstanding Advisor Award; ACS Analytical Chemistry Award; Phi Lambda Upsilon; NIDCD Minority Research Mentoring Award, 1996; University of Alaska Alumni Award for Professional Achievement, 1999; Usibelli Award for Research, 2002; Sven Ebbesson Award; University of Alaska Fairbanks Contributions to Diversity Award, 2011. Memberships: American Chemical Society; New York Academy of Sciences; Member of Editorial Board, The Science of the Total Environment, 1999; President, American Institute of Chemists, 2005-06; Member, Metals Working Groups, Arctic Monitoring and Assessment Program, 2003; Society for Neuroscience; AmnSoc for Circumpolar Health. Address: 2712 Tall Spruce, Fairbanks, Box 80986, Alaska 99708-0986, USA.

DUFFY Maureen Patricia, b. 21 October 1933, Worthing, Sussex, England. Writer; Poet. Education: BA, Honours, English, King's College, University of London, 1956. Appointments: President of Honour, British Copyright Council; President of Honour, Authors Licensing & Collecting Society; Royal Society of Literature Council. Publications: Novels: That's How It Was, 1962; The Single Eye, 1964; The Microcosm, 1966; The Paradox Players, 1967; Wounds, 1969; Love Child, 1971; I Want to Go to Moscow, 1973; All Heaven in a Rage, 1973; Capital, 1975; Housespy, 1978; Gor Saga, 1981; Londoners, 1983; Change, 1987; Illuminations, 1992; Restitution, 1998; Alchemy, 2004; The Orpheus Trail, 2009; Poetry: Lyrics for the Dog Hour, 1968; New Short Plays: No 2, 1969; The Venus Touch, 1971; Evesong, 1975; Memorials for the Quick and the Dead, 1979; Collected Poems, 1949-84, 1985; Pool: New Fiction from Liverpool John Moores University, 2001; Family Values, 2008; Non-fiction: The Erotic World of Faery, 1972; The Passionate Shepherdess: Aphra Behn, 1640-89, 1977; Inherit the Earth, 1980; Men and Beasts: Animal Rights Handbook, 1984; A Thousand Capricious Chances: History of the Methuen List, 1889-1989, 1989; Henry Purcell (1659-95) 1994; England: The Making of the Myth from Stonehenge to Albert, 2001. Honours: Fellow, King's College; Fellow, Royal Society of Literature; CISAC Gold Medal; Benson Silver Medal; Vice President, Royal Society of Literature, 2010-. Memberships: Fabian Society; Labour Party; Poetry Society; Writer's Guild of Great Britain; Honorary Life Member, Society of Authors; Society of Genealogists. Address: 18 Fabian Road, London SW6 7TZ, England.

DUJARDIN Charlotte, b. 13 July 1985, Enfield, England. Dressage Rider. Career: Four times winner, Horse of the Year Show; Three times winner, Hickstead; Gold, European Dressage Championship, Rotterdam, 2011; Winner, FEI World Cup Grand Prix, London Olympia, 2011; 2 gold medals (team dressage and individual dressage), London Olympics, 2012.

DUKAKIS Olympia, b. 20 June 1931. Actress. m. Louis Zorich, 3 sons. Education: Boston University. Appointments: Teacher of Drama, New York University graduate programme for 15 years; Founding member, The Charles Playhouse, Boston, Whole Theatre, Montclair, New Jersey; Appeared in over 100 regional theatre productions; Off-Broadway shows including: Mann Ish Mann; The Marriage of Bette and Boo; Titus Andronicus; Peer Gynt; The Memorandum; The Curse of the Starving Class; Electra; Appearances in Broadway productions of Abraham Cochrane; The Aspern Papers; The Night of the Iguana; Who's Who in Hell; Mike Nichol's Social Security; Numerous TV appearances, TV include: Tales of the City (series); Films include: The Idolmaker; John Loves Mary; Death Wish; Rich Kids; Made for Each Other; Working Girl; Moonstruck; Dad; Look Who's Talking; Steel Magnolias; In the Spirit; Look Who's Talking Too; The Cemetery Club; Digger; Over the Hill; Look Who's Talking Now; Naked Gun 331/3; The Final Insult (Cameo); I Love Trouble; Jeffrey; Mighty Aphrodite; Mr Holland's Opus; Picture Perfect; My Beautiful Son, Ladies and The Champ, And Never Let Her Go, 2001; The Event, Charlie's War, 2003; The Intended, 2004; The Great New Wonderful, The Thing About My Folks, 3 Needles, Whiskey School, Jesus, Mary and Joey, 2005; Away from Her, Day on Fire, 2006; In the Land of Women, 2007; Hove (The Wind), 2009; Dottie's Thanksgiving Pickle, 2010. Honours: Academy Award for Best Supporting Actress for Moonstruck, 1988; 2 Obie awards. Membership: Board, National Museum of Women in the Arts, Washington DC. Address: William Morris Agency, 151 S El Camino Drive, Beverly Hills, CA 90212, USA.

DUKANOVIĆ Milo, b. 15 February 1962, Niksic, Montenegro. Economist. m. Lidjia, 1 son. Education: Faculty of Economics. Appointments: Prime Minister, 1992-2010 (6 terms); President of the Republic, 1998-2002; Chairman, Democratic Party of Socialists. Honours: Award, Crans Montana Forum Foundation, 1999; Award for Democracy, international campaign experts; Great Charter for Peace and Medal for Peace, International Association of Educators for World Peace, 2004; Personality of the Year, Dnevni Avaz, 2007; Award, European Centre for Peace and Development, 2007; Listed in international biographical dictionaries. Memberships: International Raoul Wallenberg Foundation; European Academy of Sciences and Arts. Address: DPS CG, 20000 Podgorica, Jovana Tomaševića 2, Montenegro.

DUKE Chris, b. 4 October 1938. London. England. Professor; Scholar. m. Elizabeth Sommerlad, 3 sons, 2 daughters. Education: BA, 1st Class Honours, 1960, PGCE, 1961, MA, 1963, Jesus College, Cambridge, England; PhD, King's College, London, England, 1966. Appointments: Woolwich Polytechnic, England, 1961-66; University of Leeds, 1966-69; Director (Founding), Continuing Education, Australian National University, 1969-85; Professor, Continuing Education, 1985-96, Pro-Vice-Chancellor, 1991-95, University of Warwick, England; President, UWS Nepean, Sydney, Australia and Professor of Lifelong Learning, 1996-2000; Director and Professor of Continuing Education, University of Auckland, New Zealand, 2000-2002; Professor and Director of Community and Regional Partnerships, RMIT University, Melbourne, Australia, 2002-. Publications: Many books, edited volumes, chapters and journal articles in the fields of higher education, adult, continuing and non-formal education and lifelong learning and in policy and management of higher education; Recent books include: The Learning University, 1992, reprinted 1996; The Adult University, 1999; Managing the Learning University, 2002. Honours: Hon. DLitt. Keimyung University, Republic of Korea; Fellow, Australian College of Education. Memberships: Leadership and membership of international and national professional bodies in the fields of adult and continuing education. Address: 26 Nepean Street, Emu Plains, NSW 2750, Australia. E-mail: chris.duke@rmit.edu.au

DUNAWAY (Dorothy) Faye, b. 14 January 1941, Bascom, Florida, USA. Actress. m. (1) Peter Wolf, 1974, (2) Terry O'Neill, 1981, (divorced), 1 son. Education: Florida University; Boston University. Appointments: Lincoln Center Repertory Company, New York, 3 years, appearances in: A Man For All Seasons; After the Fall; Tartuffe; Off-Broadway in Hogan's Goat, 1965; Old Times, Los Angeles; Blanche du Bois in A Streetcar Named Desire, 1973; The Curse of an Aching Heart, 1982; Films include: Hurry Sundown; The Happening; Bonnie and Clyde, 1967; The Thomas Crown Affair, 1968; A Place For Lovers, The Arrangement, 1969; Little Big Man, 1970, Doc, 1971; The Getaway, 1972; Oklahoma Crude, The Three Musketeers, 1973; Chinatown, 1974; Damned, Network, 1976; The Eyes of Laura Mars, 1978; The Camp, 1979; The First Deadly Sin, Mommie Dearest, 1981; The Wicked Lady, 1982; Supergirl, 1984; Barfly, 1987; Burning Secret, 1988; The Handmaid's Tale, On A Moonlit Night; Up to Date, 1989; Scorchers; Faithful; Three Weeks in Jerusalem; The Arrowtooth Waltz, 1991; Double Edge; Arizona Dream; The Temp; Dun Juan DeMarco, 1995; Drunks; Dunston Checks In; Albino Alligator; The Chamber; Fanny Hill, 1998; Love Lies Bleeding, The Yards, Joan of Arc, The Thomas Crown Affair, 1999; The Yards, Stanley's Gig, 2000; Yellow Bird, 2001; Changing Hearts, Rules of Attraction, Mid-Century, The Calling, 2002; Blind Horizon, 2003; Last Goodbye, El Padrino, Jennifer's Shadow, 2004; Ghosts Never Sleep, Love Hollywood Style, 2005; Rain, 2006; Cougar Club, Say It in Russian, Dr Fugazzi, The Gene Generation, 2007; The Bait, Flick, La rabbia, 2008; The Magic Stone, The Seduction of Dr Fugazzi, 21 and a Wake-Up, 2009; TV includes: After the Fall, 1974; The Disappearance of Aimee, 1976; Hogan's Goat; Mommie Dearest, Evita! - First Lady, 1981; 13 at Dinner, 1985; Beverly Hills Madame, 1986; The Country Girl; Casanova; The Raspberry Ripple; Cold Sassy Tree; Silhouette; Rebecca; Gia, 1998; Running Mates, 2000; The Biographer, 2002; Anonymous Rex, Back When We Where Grownups, 2004; Pandemic, 2007; Grey's Anatomy, 2009; Midnight Bayou, 2009. Publications: Looking for Gatsby (Autobiography with Betsy Sharkey), 1995. Honours include: Academy Award for Best Actress for Network. Address: c/o Ed Limato, ICM, 8942 Wilshire Boulevard, Beverly Hills, CA 90211, USA.

DUNBAR Adrian, b.1 August 1958, Enniskillen, Northern Ireland. Actor. m. Anna Nygh, 1 stepson, 1 daughter. Education: Guildhall School of Music and Drama, London, UK. Career: Films include: The Fear; A World Apart; Dealers; My Left Foot; Hear My Song, 1992; The Crying Game, 1993; Widow's Peak, 1994; Richard III, 1995; The Near Room, 1996; The General, 1998; Wild About Harry, 2000; Shooters, 2000; The Wedding Tackle, 2000; How Harry Became a Tree, 2001; Triggerman, 2002; Darkness, 2002; The Measure of My Days, 2003; Mickybo and Me, 2004; Tma, 2005; Against Nature, 2005; Eye of the Dolphin, 2006; Stage appearances include: Ourselves Alone, Royal Court Theatre, 1985; King Lear, Royal Court; TV appearances include: Reasonable Force; Cracker; Murphy's Law; Suspicion; Kidnapped; The Quatermass Experiment; Child of Mine; Whistleblower; Ashes to Ashes; A Touch of Frost; Mo.

DUNCAN Doris Gottschalk, b. 19 November 1944, Seattle, Washington, USA. Professor of Computer Information Systems. Divorced. Education: BA 1967, MBA 1968, University of Washington, Seattle; PhD, Golden Gate University, San Francisco, 1978; Certified Data Processor, 1980; Certified Data Educator, 1984; Certified Systems Professional, 1985; Certified Computer Professional, 1994, 2006. Appointments: Director of Company Analysis and Monitoring programme, Input, Palo Alto, 1975-76; Lecturer, Associate Professor, Professor, Computer Information Systems, California State University, East Bay, 1976-; Co-ordinator, Computer Information Systems, 1994-97; Co-adviser, MS graduate program in Computer Information Systems, 2005-09; Graduate Advisor for Electronic Business program, 1999-2009; Director of MBA Programs, 2006-08; Independent Consultant, Computer Information Systems, part time, 1976-; Director, Information Systems programme, Golden Gate University, San Francisco, 1982-83; Visiting Professor, Information Systems, University of Washington, Seattle, 1997-98. Publications: 1 book; Over 70 research papers and journal articles; Frequent speaker before professional groups. Honours include: Computer Educator of the Year, International Association for Computer Information Systems, 1997; Distinguished research award for "Comicstand.com: an E-Commerce Start-Up", Allied Academies, 1999; Fulbright Senior Specialist/Scholar, 2009; Service awards from International Association of Technology Professionals: bronze, silver, gold, emerald, diamond, double diamond, triple diamond, 2000; Meritorious service award as faculty advisor of student chapter, CSUH and grant recipient; Winner of beautiful home awards and decorating, Foster City, 1994, 1995, 1996, 2003. Memberships include: Board member: Institute for Certification of Computer Professionals, Education Foundation Board; AITP Special Interest Group in Education Board; Advisory Board, Ximnet Corp; Editorial Review Board member: Journal of Informatics Education Research (Associate Editor): Journal of Information Systems Technology Education; Journal of Information Systems Education; Member: International Association of Information Technology Professionals and past President of San Francisco Chapter; Association of Computing Machinery; International Academy of Information Management; International Association of Computer Information Systems; Academy of Business Education; Decision Sciences Institute; Beta Gamma Sigma; Volunteer Docent, Computer History Museum, Mountain View, California, 2003-. Address: California State University, East Bay, Hayward, CA 94542, USA.

DUNN Charleta J, b. 18 January 1927, Clarendon, Texas, USA. Clinical Psychologist. m. Roy E Dunn Jr, 2 sons, 1 daughter. Education: BS, 1951, MEd, 1954, West Texas University at Canyon; EdD, University of Houston, Houston, Texas, 1966; Postdoctorate in Clinical Psychology, University of Texas Medical Branch, Galveston, Texas, 1971. Appointments: Teacher, Amarillo Public Schools, 1951-62; Assistant Professor, University of Houston, 1966-70; Director Pupil Appraisal, Goose Creek, ISD, Baytown, Texas, 1971-73, Full Professor, 1974-90, Professor Emeritus, 1990-, Texas Women's University. Publications: 6 research-based monographs (Funded Research Grants); Over 36 articles in professional journals; 4 books: World of Work, 1971; Sisk: Book of Ages, 1998; Burcham and Allied Families, 2000; For the Pearl Fisher, 2005; 35 Family Trees with Colonial

DICTIONARY OF INTERNATIONAL BIOGRAPHY 36th EDITION

Roots, 2010. Honours: Woman of the Year, 1996-99, 2001. Memberships: National Registrar of Mental Health; American Medical Psycho-Therapy Association; American Psychological Association.

DUNN Douglas (Eaglesham), b. 23 October 1942, Inchinnan, Scotland. Professor of English; Writer; Poet. m. Lesley Jane Bathgate, 10 August 1985, 1 son, 1 daughter. Education: BA, University of Hull, 1969. Appointments: Writer-in-Residence, University of Hull, 1974-75, Duncan of Jordanstone College of Art, Dundee District Library, 1986-88; Writer-in-Residence, 1981-82, Honorary Visiting Professor, 1987-88, University of Dundee; Fellow in Creative Writing, 1989-91, Professor of English, 1991-, Head, School of English, 1994-99, University of St Andrews; Director, St Andrews Scottish Studies Institute, 1993-. Publications: Terry Street, 1969; The Happier Life, 1972; Love or Nothing, 1974; Barbarians, 1979; St Kilda's Parliament, 1981; Europea's Lover, 1982; Elegies, 1985; Secret Villages, 1985; Selected Poems, 1986; Northlight, 1988; New and Selected Poems, 1989; Poll Tax: The Fiscal Fake, 1990; Andromache, 1990; Scotland: An Anthology (editor), 1991; The Faber Book of 20th Century Scottish Poetry (editor), 1992; Dante's Drum-Kit, 1993; Boyfriends and Girlfriends, 1994; The Oxford Book of Scottish Short Stories (editor), 1995; Norman MacCaig: Selected Poems (editor), 1997; The Donkey's Ears, 2000; 20th Century Scottish Poems (editor), 2000; The Year's Afternoon, 2000; New Selected Poems, 2002; Contributions to: Newspapers, reviews, and journals. Honours: Somerset Maugham Award, 1972; Geoffrey Faber Memorial Prize, 1975; Hawthornden Prize, 1982; Whitbread Poetry Award, 1985; Whitbread Book of the Year Award, 1985; Honorary LLD, University of Dundee, 1987; Cholmondeley Award, 1989; Honorary DLitt, University of Hull, 1995. Membership: Scottish PEN. Address: c/o School of English, University of St Andrews, St Andrews, Fife KY16 9AL, Scotland.

DUNNING Patricia Lynette (Trisha), b. 19 December 1946, Inverell, New South Wales, Australia. Nurse. m. John Hayward Dunning, 1 son, 2 daughters. Education: Diploma of Health Education, Victoria College, Melbourne, 1991; MEd, 1993, PhD, 1998, Graduate Diploma, Professional Writing, 1999, Deakin University, Melbourne. Appointments: Registered Nurse, Inverell District Hospital, New South Wales, 1968-69; Registered Nurse, Neonatal Nursery, The Bankstown Hospital, 1969-70; Registered Nurse, Isolation Unit, Royal Alexandra Hospital for Children, Sydney, 1971; Nursing Refresher Education Program, 1981, Registered Nurse, Cardiothoracic Surgical Ward, 1982-84, St Vincent's Hospital, Melbourne; Registered Nurse, 1981-82, Clinical Nurse Consultant, Diabetes Education, 1985-2001, Director, Diabetes Education Services and Clinical Nurse Consultant, Diabetes Education, 2001-07, St Vincent's Health, Melbourne; Nurse Adviser, Education and Practice Department, 1998-99, Manager, Nurse Practitioner Project, 2000, Nurses Board of Victoria; Professor, Endocrinology and Diabetes Nursing Research, St Vincent's Health and The University of Melbourne, 2001-07; Chair in Nursing, Deakin University and Barwon Health, Geelong, Victoria, Australia, 2007-. Publications: Over 100 refereed journals; Over 100 other journals; Invited papers; 19 book chapters. Honours: Outstanding Achievement Award, Diabetes Australia, 2010; Grants from many professional organisations; Invited keynote speaker on numerous occasions. Memberships: Australian Diabetes Educators Association; Australian Diabetes Society; Australian Nursing Federation; Australasian Integrative Medicine Association; Diabetes Australia, Victoria; Fellow, Royal College of Nursing, Australia; International Diabetes Federation; Life Member, Order of Australia Association; Australian Society of Authors; Sigma Theta Tau Omicron Chapter; many others. E-mail: trisha.dunning@barwonhealth.org.au

DUNST Kirsten Caroline, b. 30 April 1982, Point Pleasant, New Jersey, USA. Actor. Career: Over 70 commercials, 1985-; Films include: New York Stories, 1989; Darkness Before Dawn, 1993; Greedy, 1994; Interview with the Vampire: The Vampire Chronicles, 1994; Little Women, 1994; Jumanji, 1995; Small Soldiers, 1998; Dick, 1999; Drop Dead Gorgeous, 1999; The Virgin Suicides, 1999; Deeply, 2000; Bring It On, 2000; Crazy/Beautiful, 2001; The Cat's Meow, 2001; Get Over It, 2001; Spider-Man, 2002; Levity, 2003; Mona Lisa Smile, 2003; Eternal Sunshine of the Spotless Mind, 2004; Spider-Man 2, 2004; Wimbledon, 2004; Elizabethtown, 2005; Marie Antoinette, 2006; Spider-Man 3, 2007; Be Kind Rewind, 2008; House to Lose Friends & Alienate People, 2008; All Good Things, 2010; Melancholia, 2011; On the Road, 2012; Upside Down, 2013; TV appearances include: The Tonight Show with Jay Leno, 1992; Rank, 2001; Gun, 1997; Sisters, 1991. Honours include: Academy of Science Fiction, Fantasy & Horror Films, Best Performance by a Young Actor in Interview with the Vampire: The Vampire Chronicles, 1995; Boston Society of Film Critics Award, Supporting Actress, Interview with the Vampire: The Vampire Chronicles,1994; Empire Awards, Best Actress, Spider-Man, 2003; MTV Movie Awards, Best Female Performance, Spider-Man, 2003; MTV Movie Awards, Best Breakthrough Performance, Interview with the Vampire: The Vampire Chronicles, 1995; Young Star Award, Best Performance by a Young Actress in a Drama Film, 1995.

DUNWOODY Richard, b. 18 January 1964, Belfast, North Ireland. Ex-Jockey. Appointments: Rode winner of: Grand National (West Tip), 1986, (Minnehoma), 1994; Cheltenham Gold Cup (Charter Party), 1988; Champion Hurdle (Kribensis), 1990; Champion National Hunt Jockey, 1992-93, 1993-94, 1994-95; Held record for most wins at retirement in 1999; Group Manager, Partner, Dunwoody Sports Marketing, 2002; Motivational speaker. Publications: Hell For Leather (with Marcus Armytage); Dual (with Sean Magee); Hands and Heels (with Marcus Armytage); Obsessed. Honours: National Hunt Jockey of the Year 1990, 1992-95; Lester Award, Jump Jockey of the Year, 1990, 1992-95; Champion of Champions, 2001. Memberships: Patron/Trustee: Sparks; Spinal Research; Racing Welfare. Address: c/o Dunwoody Sports Marketing, The Litten, Newtown Road, Newbury, Berkshire, RG14 7BB, England. E-mail: richard.d@du-mc.co.uk

DURDEN-SMITH Neil, b. 18 August 1933, Richmond, Surrey, England. Co-Director; Broadcaster. m. Judith Chalmers, 1 son, 1 daughter. Education: Aldenham and Royal Naval College. Appointments: Royal Navy, 1952-63; ADC to Governor General of New Zealand, 1957-59; Commanded HMS Rampart, 1960-62; Cricket and Hockey for Royal Navy and Combined Services; Producer, BBC Outside Broadcasts (special responsibility for 1966 World Cup), 1963-66; Radio and television broadcaster, Test Match and County Cricket, Olympic Games (1968 and 1972), International Hockey, Trooping the Colour, Royal Tournament, Money Matters, Sports Special, 1967-74; Director, The Anglo-American Sporting Clubs, 1969-74; Chairman and Managing Director, Durden-Smith Communications, 1974-81; Trustee, The Lord's Taverner's, 1976-2004; Chairman, The Lord's Taverners, 1980-82; Chairman, Sports Sponsorship International, 1982-87; Chairman, The Altro Group, 1982-94; Director, Ruben Sedgwick, 1987-95; Chairman, Woodside Communications, 1992-99; Director, BCM

Grandstand, 1993-2006; President, Middlesex Region, The Lord's Taverners, 1993-; Chairman, Brian Johnston Memorial Trust, 1994-2000; Consultant, AON, 1995-2007; Trustee, Charlie Walker Memorial Trust, 1997-; Consultant, Tangible Securities, 2003-; Patron, Motor Neurone Disease Association, 1993-; Aspire Trust, 2004-; Westminster Society for the Disabled, 2006-. Publications: Forward for England: Bobby Charlton's Life Story, 1967; World Cup '66, 1967. Honours: OBE, 1997; Freeman of the City of London. Memberships: MCC; The Lord's Taverners; Sparks; I Zingari; Cricket Writers; Free Foresters; Lords & Commons Cricket; County Cricketers Golf; Saints & Sinners; Home House; Ritz; 50 St James's; Highgate, Archerfield and Vale Do Lobo Golf Clubs; FAGS; Ladykillers and Surbiton Hockey Clubs. Address: 28 Hillway, Highgate, London N6 6HH, England.

DURKAN Mark, b. 26 June 1960, Derry, Northern Ireland. Social Democratic and Labour Party Member. m. Jackie, 1 daughter. Education: Politics at Queen's University Belfast; Public Policy Management at University of Ulster. Appointments: Assistant and Advisor to John Hume, 1984-1998; SDLP Chairperson, 1990-95; Elected to Northern Ireland Assembly for Foyle, 1998; Minister of Finance and Personnel, 1999-2001; SDLP Leader, 2001-10; Deputy First Minister, 2001-2002; Elected to Northern Ireland Assembly for Foyle, 2003; Elected to Westminster as MP for Foyle, 2005, 2010; Re-Elected to Northern Ireland Assembly for Foyle, 2007, Resigned, 2010; Chair, Committee for Enterprise, Trade and Investment, 2007-09. Address: 23 Bishop Street, Derry, BT48 6PR, UK. E-mail: m.durkan@sdlp.ie

DURNOVO Eugenia Alexandrovna, b. 17 August 1970, Gorkiy, Russia. Maxillofacial Surgery. 1 daughter. Education: Diploma, 1993, PhD, 1998, Nizhny Novgotrod Medical Academy. Appointments: Chair, Maxillofacial Surgery Department, Nizhny Novgorod Medical Academy, 2000-. Publications: Over 200 articles in professional journals including, Morphological efficiency criteria for treatment of patients with acute purulent-inflammatory diseases of maxillofacial zone. Memberships: Scientific Council on Dentistry, Russian Academy of Sciences; Maxillofacial Surgery section, Ministry of Health, Nizhny Novgorod region; Nizhny Novgorod State Medical Academy; Nizhny Novgorod Association of Dentists; European Association of Maxillofacial Surgeons. Address: 20a Minina str, Nizhny Novgorod, 603000, Russia. E-mail: star@gma.nnov.ru Website: www.nizhgma.ru

DURRANT Steven Frederick, b. 4 April 1959, London, England. Physicist. Education: BSc (Hons), Physics, University of Birmingham, England, 1981; MSc, Medical Physics, 1986, PhD, Analytical Chemistry, 1989, University of Surrey, England. Appointments: Researcher, Unicamp, Campinas, Brazil, 1990-91, 1994-96, 1998-2001; Postdoctoral Associate, University of Massachusetts, USA, 1992-93; Assistant Professor, UEL, Londrina, Brazil, 1997; Researcher, CENA, USP, Piracicaba, 2001; Professor, UNIVAP, Sao Jose dos Campos, 2002-03; Assistant Professor, 2003-10, Associate Professor, 2010-, UNESP, Sorocaba. Publications: Over 90 articles in professional journals. Memberships: New York Academy of Sciences. Address: Laboratório de Plasmas Tecnológicos, Campus Experimental de Sorocaba, UNESP, Av Três de Marco 511, Alto de Boa Vista, 18087-180 Sorocaba – SP, Brazil.

DURUP Jean, b. 8 July 1932, Paris, France. Professor Emeritus. 1 son, 3 daughters. Baccalaureat, 1947, Licence, 1952, Doctorat, 1959, Paris, France. Appointments: Research Fellow, CNRS, Paris, 1952-61; Research Fellow, CNRS, Orsay, 1961-68; Professor, Université de Paris-Sud, Orsay, 1968-85; Professor, Université Paul Sabatier, Toulouse, 1985-97; Professor Emeritus, 1997-2005. Publications: Book, Positive ion-molecule reactions in gas phase; Over 100 papers in high-level journals, on physics, biology and chemistry. Honours: Silver Medal of CNRS, 1968; Fellow, American Physical Society, 1980. Address: 16 rue Romain Rolland, F-34200 Sète, France.

DUTTA Anjan Kumar, b. 20 October 1966, Calcutta, India. Consulting Structural Engineer. m. Manisha Dutta, 2 daughters. Education: PhD, Fibre Reinforced Concrete; M Phil, Environmental Science; M Phil, Management; MBA, Financial Management. Appointments: Senior Structural Engineer, CEC Eastern, 1990-92; CEO, A K Dutta & Associates, 1992-. Publications: 33 published articles in national and international technical journals. Honours include: Netaji Subhan Chandra Bose National Award, Approved by Ministry of Forest, Government of India and UNESCO; Scientist of the Year, National Environmental Science Academy, 2002; Albert Schweitzer Medal for Science, Peace and Engineering, 2007; Ultratech Excellence Award for Structural Excellence, 2010. Memberships: Institution of Engineers; Chartered Engineer; American Society of Civil Engineers; Indian Roads Congress; American Concrete Institute. Address: HA-333, Flat-1, Sector III, Salt Lake, Kolkata 700097, West Bengal, India. E-mail: anjandutta1@rediffmail.com

DUTTA Paramartha, b. 14 June 1966, Calcutta, India. Professor. m. Paramita, 1 son. Education: B Stat (Hons), 1988, M Stat, 1990, M Tech, Computer Science, 1993, Indian Statistical Institute, Calcutta; PhD, Engineering, Bengal Engineering and Science University, Shibpur. Appointments: Research Fellow, Indian Statistical Institute, Calcutta; Research Fellow, Bengal Engineering and Science University, Shibpur; Assistant Professor, College of Engineering and Management, Kalaghat; Assistant Professor, Professor, Kalyani Government Engineering College; Professor, Visva Bharati University. Publications: About 100 articles in professional journals and in various national and international conference proceedings. Honours: Member of board of studies of different universities; Member of academic/research boards of various Government appointed bodies; Member of selection boards for recruitments for relevant areas. Memberships: IEEE, USA; Computer Society, USA; ACM; CSI; Fellow, IETE; Fellow, OSI; Life Member, IUPRAI; ISTE; ISCA; ACCS. Address: C4M1/221, CMDA Nagar Barrackpore Housing Complex, 24 Parganas (North), West Bengal, PIN 700212, India.

DUURSMA Egbert Klaas, b. 27 March 1929, Smallingerland, Netherlands. Professor of Oceanology; Director. m. Caroline Bosch, 3 sons, 1 daughter. Education: Graduated, Organic Chemistry, Free University, Amsterdam; PhD, 1960. Appointments: Research Scientist, dairy industry, Leeuwarden, Netherlands, 1953-56; Senior Scientist, Marine Radioactivity, NIOZ, Den Helder, 1960-65; Chief of Section, Sedimentology, International Laboratory of Marine Radioactivity, IAEA, Monaco, 1965-76; Expert FAO, Jepara, Indonesia, 1975; Director, Delta Institute for Hydrobiological Research, Royal Netherlands Academy of Sciences, Yerseke, Netherlands, 1976-86; Chairman, Dutch Council for Ocean Research and Antarctic Commission, 1985-93; First Scientific, later General, Director, NIOZ, Texel, Netherlands, 1986-89; Professor of Oceanology, University of Groningen, 1986-91; Many Guest Professorships. Publications include: The dissolved organic constituents of sea water, chapter in Chemical Oceanography, 1965; Theoretical, experimental and field studies concerning reactions of radioisotopes with sediments and suspended particles of the sea, 1967; Geochemical aspects and applications of (all) radionuclides in the sea, chapter, 1972; Role of pollution and pesticides in brackish water aquaculture in Indonesia, 1976; Pollution of the North Sea, co-author, 1988; Are tropical estuaries environmental sinks or sources?, 1995; Environmental compartments, equilibria and assessment of processes (of radioactive, metal and organic contaminants), between air, sediments and water, 1996; Stratospheric ozone chemistry: A literature review and synthesis, 1997, 2000; Dumped chemical weapons in the sea, options, Synopsis on the state of the art, emergency actions, first aid and state responsibilities, Editor and co-author, 1999; Global and regional rainfall, river-flow and temperature profile records; consequences for water resources, 2002; Energy and environment; irreversible events, 2005; Global energy and environment conflicts, facts and consequences, 2009; Numerous book chapters, articles in scientific journals and conference proceedings. Honour: Medal, Royal Netherlands Academy of Art and Sciences, 1986. Memberships: Academia Europaea. Address: 302 Av du Semaphore, 06190 Roquebrune/Cap Martin, France. E-mail: duursma@orange.fr

DUVALL Robert, b. 5 January 1931, San Diego, USA. Actor. m. (1) Barbara Benjamin, (2) Gail Youngs, divorced, (3) Sharon Brophy, 1991, divorced, (4) Luciana Pedraza, 2004. Education: Principia College, Illinois, USA; Student, Neighbourhood Playhouse, New York. Appointments: Actor, stage appearances include: A View From the Bridge (Obie Award), 1965; Wait Until Dark, 1966; American Buffalo; Films include: To Kill a Mockingbird, 1963; Captain Newman, MD, 1964; The Chase, 1965; Countdown, The Detective, Bullitt, 1968; True Grit, The Rain People, 1969; M*A*S*H, The Revolutionary, 1970; The Godfather, Tomorrow, The Great Northfield; Minnesota Raid, Joe Kidd, 1972; Lady Ice, 1973; The Outfit, The Conversation, The Godfather Part II, 1974; Breakout, The Killer Elite, 1975; Network, 1976; The Eagle Has Landed, The Greatest, 1977; The Betsy, 1978; Apocalypse Now, 1979; The Great Santini, 1980; True Confessions, 1981; Angelo My Love (actor and director), Tender Mercies, 1983; The Stone Boy, The Natural, 1984; The Lightship, Let's Get Harry, Belizaire the Cajun, 1986; Colors, 1988; Convicts; Roots in Parched Ground; The Handmaid's Tale, A Show of Force, Days of Thunder, 1990; Rambling Rose, 1991; Newsies, The New Boys, Stalin, 1992; The Plague; Geronimo; Falling Down, 1993; The Paper, Wrestling Ernest Hemingway, 1994; Something to Talk About: The Stars Fell On Henrietta; The Scarlet Letter; A Family Thing (also co-producer); Phenomenon, 1996; The Apostle, Gingerbread Man, 1997; A Civil Action, 1999; Gone In Sixty Seconds, A Shot at Glory (also producer), The 6th Day, 2000; Apocalypse Now: Redux, 2001; John Q, Assassination Tango (also producer), 2002; Secondhand Lions, Gods and Generals, Open Range, 2003; Kicking & Screaming, Thank You for Smoking, 2005; The Godfather: The Game, Broken Trail, 2006, (TV); Lucky You, We Own the Night, 2007; Four Christmases, 2008; The Godfather II (voice), The Road, Get Low, Crazy Heart, 2009; Director, We're Not the Jet Set; Assassination Tango, 2002; Several TV films and appearances. Address: c/o William Morris Agency, 151 S El Camino Drive, Beverly Hills, CA 90212, USA.

DVORKOVICH Arkady, b. 26 March 1972, Moscow, Russian Federation. Aide to the President of Russian Federation. m. Zumrud Rustamova, 2 sons. Education: Degree, Economic Cybernetics, Moscow State University, 1994; Master, Economics, New Economic School in Moscow; Master, Economics, Duke University, USA, 1997. Appointments: Adviser and Head, Economic Expert Group, Russia's Ministry of Finance, 1994-2000; Expert, Strategic Development Center, Adviser to Minister of Economic Development and Trade, 2000-01; Deputy Minister, Ministry of Economic Development and Trade, 2001-04; Head, Presidential Experts' Directorate, 2004-08; Aide to the President of Russian Federation and Russian Sherpa in the G8, 2008-; Board Chairman, Russian Chess Federation, 2010-. Honours: Gratitude of the President of the Russian Federation, Medal for the Merits of the Fatherland; Honour Award, 2010; Award for the Merits of the Italian Republic. Address: 4 Staraya Square, Moscow, 103132, Russian Federation. E-mail: dvorkovich_av@gov.ru

DWIVEDI Yogesh Kumar, b. 13 June 1975, Pratapgarh, India. Lecturer. m. Anju, 1 daughter. Education: BSc, University of Allahabad, 1996; MSc, Indian Agricultural Research Institute, 2000; MSc, 2002, PhD, 2005, Brunel University, England. Appointments: Lecturer, 2006-09, Senior Lecturer 2009-, Information Systems, School of Business and Economics, Swansea University, Wales. Publications: Books: Consumer Adoption and Usage of Broadband, 2007; Proliferation of the Internet Economy: E-Commerce for Global Adoption, Resistance and Cultural Evolution, 2009; Numerous articles in professional journals. Honours: Contribution Award, Swansea University, 2007-08; EFMD/Emerald 2007 Highly Commended Award; Best Paper Award, 5th International Conference on E-Governance, 2007; Best Paper Nomination, European Conference on Information Systems, 2008; Listed in international biographical dictionaries. Memberships: Association of Information Systems; IFIP WG 8.6; Global Institute of Flexible Systems Management, New Delhi; Indian Society of Plant Genetic Resources; Biotechnological Society of India. Address: 57 Pen Y Garn, Pentrechwyth, Swansea, SA1 7ET, United Kingdom. E-mail: ykdwivedi@gmail.com

DYBKAER René, b. 7 February 1926, Copenhagen. Physician. m. Nanna Gjoel, deceased. Education: MD, 1951, Dr Med Sci, 2004, University of Copenhagen; Specialist Clinical Chemistry, 1957. Appointments: Various medical residencies, 1951-55; Reader, Copenhagen University Institute of Medical Microbiology, 1956-70; Head, Department of Medical Microbiology, Royal Dental School of Copenhagen, 1959-70; Head, Department of Clinical Chemistry at De Gamles By, 1970-77, at Frederiksberg Hospital, 1977-96, at Department of Standardization in Laboratory Medicine, H S Kommunehositalet, 1997-99, H:S Frederiksberg Hospital, 2000-. Publications: Books: Quantities and units in clinical chemistry, 1967; Good practice in decentralised analytical clinical measurement, 1992; Continuous quality improvement in clinical laboratories, 1994; Compendium on terminology and nomenclature in clinical laboratory sciences, 1995; An Ontology on Property for physical, chemical and biological systems, thesis, 2004, updated 2009; numerous articles to professional journals. Honours: Commemorative Lecture Enrique Concustell Bas, 1988; Henry Wishinsky Distinguished International Services Award, 1993; Honorary member of various national clinical laboratory societies; Professor James D Westgard Quality Award, 1998. Memberships: Vice President, 1973-78, President, 1979-84, Past President, 1985-90, International Federation of Clinical Chemistry; President, European Confederation of Laboratory Medicine, 1994-97; Chairman, Danish Society of Clinical Chemistry, 1991-93. Address: Region H Frederiksberg Hospital, Department of Standardization in Laboratory Medicine, Nordre Fasanvej 57, DK-2000 Frederiksberg, Denmark.

DYER Charles, b. 17 July 1928, Shrewsbury, England. Playwright. m. Fiona, 20 February 1960, 3 sons. Publications: Turtle in the Soup, 1948; Who On Earth, 1950; Poison in Jest, 1952; Jovial Parasite, 1955; Red Cabbage and Kings, 1958; Rattle of a Simple Man, novel, play, film, 1962; Staircase, novel, play, film, 1966; Mother Adam, 1970; Lovers Dancing, 1982; Those Old Trombones, 2005; Various screenplays. Address: Old Wob, Gerrards Cross, Buckinghamshire SL9 8SF, England.

DYER James Frederick, b. 23 February 1934, Luton, England. Archaeological Writer. Education: MA, Leicester University, 1964. Appointment: Editor, Shire Archaeology, 1974-. Publications: Southern England: An Archaeological Guide, 1973; Penguin Guide to Prehistoric England and Wales, 1981; Discovering Archaeology in England and Wales, 1985, 6th enlarged edition, 1997; Ancient Britain, 1990; Discovering Prehistoric England, 1993, 2nd edition, 2001; The Stopsley Book, 1998; Luton Modern School History, 2004; Hillforts of England and Wales, 4th edition, 2009. Contributions to: Bedfordshire Magazine; Illustrated London News; Archaeological Journal. Honours: Honorary Doctor of Arts, University of Luton, 1999. Memberships: Society of Authors; Royal Archaeological Institute; Society of Antiquaries. Address: 6 Rogate Road, Luton, Bedfordshire LU2 8HR, England.

DYER Pamela Kay, b. 6 September 1943, Mt Isa, Australia. Dean. m. Michael Dyer, 4 sons, 1 daughter. Education: BA, 1987, BA (1st Class Honours), 1988, Graduate Certificate, Environmental Management, 2000, PhD, 1992, The University of Queensland. Appointments: Research Support Officer, 1993-94, Senior Administrative Officer, 1994-95, The University of Queensland; Administration Officer (Research), Queensland University of Technology, 1995-96; Lecturer, 1996-2000, Area of Study Co-ordinator, 1996-2005, Senior Lecturer, 2000-, Environmental and Planning Studies, Associate to the Dean, 2002-04, Associate Dean, 2004, Acting Dean, 2004-05, Dean, 2005-, Faculty of Arts and Social Science, University of the Sunshine Coast. Publications: Numerous articles in professional journals. Memberships: Planning Institute Australia; Australian Federation of University Women Qld Inc; Ecotourism Association of Australia; Australian Bird Study Association; Sunshine Coast Environment Council; many others.

DYKE Greg, b. 20 May 1947. Journalist; Broadcaster. 1 son, 1 stepson, 1 daughter, 1 stepdaughter. Education: York University; Harvard Business School. Appointments: Management Trainee, Marks & Spencer; Reporter, local paper; Campaigner for Community Relations Council, Wandsworth; Researcher, The London Programme; London Weekend TV (LWT); Later, Founding Producer, The Six O'Clock Show; Joined TV-AM, 1983; Director of Programmes, LWT, 1987-91; Group Chief Executive, LWT (Holdings) PLC, 1991-94; Chairman, GMTV, 1993-94; Chairman, Chief Executive Officer, Pearson TV, 1995-99; Chairman, Channel 5 Broadcasting, 1997-99; Former TVB Hong Kong; Director, BSkyB, 1995; Phoenix Pictures Inc, New York, Pearson PLC, 1996-99 and others; Director (non-executive) Manchester Utd, 1997-99; Director General, BBC, 2000-04; Supervisory Board Member, ProSiebenSat.1 Media, 2004-; Chairman, Brentford Football Club; Chairman, British Film Institute. Publications: Memoirs, 2004. Honours: Royal TV Society Lifetime Achievement Award, Broadcasting Press Guild, 2004. Memberships: Trustee Science Museum, 1996-; English National Stadium Trust, 1997-99. Address: ProSiebenSat.1 Media AG, Medienhallee 7, 85774 Unterfoehring, Germany. Website: www.prosieben.com

DYKES David Wilmer, b. 18 December 1933, Swansea, Wales. Retired; Independent Scholar. m. Margaret Anne George, 2 daughters. Education: MA, Corpus Christi College, Oxford, 1952-55; PhD, University of Wales. Appointments: Commissioned Service, RN and RNR, 1955-62; Civil Servant, 1958-59; Administrative Appointments, University of Bristol and University College of Swansea, 1959-63; Deputy Registrar, University College of Swansea, 1963-69; Registrar, University of Warwick, 1969-72; Secretary, 1972-86, Acting Director, 1985-86, Director, 1986-89, National Museum of Wales; Treasure Valuation Committee, DCMS, 2010-. Publications: Anglo-Saxon Coins in the National Museum of Wales, 1977; Alan Sorrell: Early Wales Recreated, 1980; Wales in Vanity Fair, 1989; The University College of Swansea, 1992; Coinage & Currency in Eighteenth-Century Britain, 2011; Articles and reviews in numismatic, historical and other journals. Honours: Parkes-Weber Prize and Medal, Royal Numismatic Society, 1954; K St J, 1993; Honorary Member, President, 1998-2003, Vice President, British Numismatic Society, 2009-. Memberships: Liveryman, Worshipful Company of Tin Plate Workers; Freeman City of London; Foundation Member, Welsh Livery Guild, 1993; United Kingdom Numismatic Trust, 1999-; Treasure Valuation Committee, DCMS, 2010-; FSA; FRHistS; FRNS; FRSAI. Address: 3 Peverell Avenue East, Poundbury, Dorchester, Dorset, DT1 3RH, England.

DYLAN Bob (Robert Allen Zimmerman), b. 24 May 1941, Duluth, Minnesota, USA. Singer; Musician (guitar, piano, harmonica, autoharp); Poet; Composer. Musical Education: Self-taught. Career: Solo folk/rock artist, also performed with The Band; The Traveling Wilburys; Grateful Dead; Songs recorded by estimated 3000 artists, including U2, Bruce Springsteen, Rod Stewart, Jimi Hendrix, Eric Clapton, Neil Young; Numerous tours: USA, Europe, Australia, 1961-; Film appearances include: Pat Garrett and Billy The Kid; Concert For Bangladesh; Hearts Of Fire; Catchfire; Paradise Cove; Masked and Anonymous; Compositions include: Blowin' In The Wind; Like A Rolling Stone; Mr Tambourine Man; Lay Lady Lay; Forever Young; Tangled Up In Blue; Gotta Serve Somebody; Don't Think Twice; It's Alright; A Hard Rain's Gonna Fall; The Times They Are A-Changin'; Just Like A Woman; I'll Be Your Baby Tonight; I Shall Be Released; Simple Twist Of Fate; Paths Of Victory; Dignity. Recordings: Over 40 albums include: The Freewheelin' Bob Dylan, 1964; Bringing It All Back Home, 1965; Highway 61 Revisited, 1965; Blonde On Blonde, 1966; John Wesley Harding, 1968; Nashville Skyline, 1969; Self Portrait, 1970; New Morning, 1970; Before The Flood, 1974; Hard Rain, 1976; Desire, 1976; Street Legal, 1978; Slow Train Coming, 1979; Infidels, 1983; Empire Burlesque, 1985; Knocked Out Loaded, 1986; Down In The Groove, 1988; Biograph (5 record set), 1988; Oh Mercy, 1989; Under The Red Sky, 1990; MTV Unplugged, 1995; Time Out of Mind, 1997; with The Band: Planet Waves, 1974; Blood On The Tracks, 1975; with Traveling Wilburys: Traveling Wilburys, 1988; Vol 3, 1990; with Grateful Dead, Dylan And The Dead, 1989; Singles include: One Too Many Mornings, 1965; Mr Tambourine Man, 1966; Love Sick, 1997. Publications: Tarantula, 1966; Writings And Drawings, 1973; The Songs Of Bob Dylan 1966-75, 1976; Lyrics 1962-85, 1986. Honours include: Honorary D Mus, Princeton University, 1970; Inducted, Rock and Roll Hall of Fame, 1988; Grammy, 1990. Current Management: Jeff Rosen, PO Box 870, Cooper Station, New York, NY 10276, USA.

DYRENFORTH Noel, b. 17 June 1936, London, England. Artist. 1 son. Education: St Clement Danes Grammar School, 1944-54; Central School of Art; Goldsmiths College of Art, University of London. Appointments: Visiting Lecturer/Artist; International lectures and workshops. Publications: Batik with Noel Dyrenforth, 1975; The Technique of Batik, 1989, 1997; Batik, Modern Concepts and Techniques, 2003; Art Textiles of the World, 2006. Honours: British Council Awards; Craft Council Grant; 133 exhibitions worldwide; Collections held in: Victoria & Albert Museum; National Gallery, Melbourne, Australia; Crafts Council, London; Guizhon Museum, China. Memberships: President, Batik Guild; Member, Contemporary Applied Arts. Address: 11 Shepherds Hill, London, N6 4QJ, England.

DYSON Freeman J(ohn), b. 15 December 1923, Crowthorne, England (US citizen, 1957). Professor of Physics Emeritus. m. (1) Verena Haefeli-Huber, 1950, divorced 1958, 1 son, 1 daughter, (2) Imme Jung, 1958, 4 daughters. Education: BA, Cambridge University, 1945; Graduate Studies, Cornell University, 1947-48, Institute for Advanced Study, Princeton, New Jersey, 1948-49. Appointments: Research Fellow, Trinity College, Cambridge, 1946-49; Warren Research Fellow, University of Birmingham, England, 1949-51; Professor of Physics, Cornell University, 1951-53; Professor of Physics, 1953-94, Professor Emeritus, 1994-, Institute for Advanced Study. Publications: Symmetry Groups in Nuclear and Particle Physics, 1966; Neutron Stars and Pulsars, 1971; Disturbing the Universe, 1979; Values at War, 1983; Weapons and Hope, 1984; Origins of Life, 1986; Infinite in All Directions, 1988; From Eros to Gaia, 1992; Imagined Worlds, 1997; The Sun The Genome and the Internet, 1999; The Scientist as Rebel, 2006; Advanced Quantum Mechanics, World Scientific, 2007. Honours: Heineman Prize, American Institute of Physics, 1966; Lorentz Medal, Royal Netherlands Academy of Sciences, 1966; Hughes Medal, Royal Society, 1968; Max Planck Medal, German Physical Society, 1969; J Robert Oppenheimer Memorial Prize, Center for Theoretical Studies, 1970; Harvey Prize, Israel Institute of Technology, 1977; Wolf Prize, Wolf Foundation, 1981; National Book Critics Circle Award, 1984; Templeton Prize for Progress in Religion, 2000; Pomeranchuk Prize, 2003; Honorary doctorates. Memberships: American Physical Society; National Academy of Sciences; Royal Society, fellow. Address: 105 Battle Road Circle, Princeton, NJ 08540, USA.

DYSON James, b. 2 May 1947, Cromer, Norfolk, Designer. m. Deidre Hindmarsh, 1967, 2 sons, 1 daughter. Education: Royal College of Art. Appointments: Director, Rotork Marine, 1970-74; Managing Director, Kirk Dyson, 1974-79; Developed and designed, Dyson Dual Cyclone vacuum cleaner, 1979-93; Founder, Chairman Prototypes Ltd, 1979-; Dyson Appliances Ltd, 1992-; Hon DLitt (Staffordshire), 1996; Hon DSc, Oxford Brookes, 1997, Huddersfield, 1997, Bradford, 1998. Publications include: Doing a Dyson, 1996; Against the Odds (autobiography), 1997; History of Great Inventions, 2001. Honours: Numerous design awards and trophies; Knight Bachelor, 2006. Address: Dyson Ltd, Tetbury Hill, Malmesbury, Wiltshire SN16 0RP, England.

DZOKIC Gjorgje, b. 14 January 1957, Skopje, Macedonia. Plastic and Reconstructive Surgeon. m. Tatyana, 2 sons. Education: MD, 1980; PhD (Dr.Sci.), 1999; Docent of Surgery, 2000-2004; Professor of Surgery, 2005-. Appointments: University Clinic for Plastic and Reconstructive Surgery, 1983-; Past Secretary, Macedonian Association of Plastic Surgeons, 1997-99; Past Head of Clinic, 2000-2002, Head of Division for Ambulance and Daily Hospital; Professor of Surgery, Trainer and Mentor in National Plastic Surgery Education; Member, National Commission for Doctor's Licence, Doctors Chamber of Macedonia; President, Scientific Committee and Moderator of Vth BAPRAS Congress, 2009; Member, Editorial Board for publishing Macedonian Book of Surgery. Publications: Author and co-author of over 100 articles in national and international medical journals and congress proceedings; Author of Scripta of Plastic Surgery for students; Author of chapters in forthcoming Macedonian Book of Surgery for students; Main author, Thermal Injuries, 2008; Co-author, Chapter in Albanian Book of Surgery for Students of Medicine, Tirana, 2009. Honours: Executive Plaque, Macedonian Doctors Association, 2001; Certificate for successfully finished Second Workshop for Medical Education, 2002; 10th Oxford European Wound Healing Summer School, 2005; Man of the Year, ABI, 2005; Research Board of Advisors, ABI; Charter Fellow, Advisory Board, ABI, 2008; First International Workshops of Wound Technology, Paris, France, 2009; Listed in international biographical dictionaries. Memberships: National and International Associations of Plastic Surgeons (BAPRAS, ESPRAS, ISPRAS); Cathedra in Surgery, Medical Faculty, Skopje; Board for Postgraduate Study, Medical Faculty, Skopje; Doctors Chamber of Macedonia; Macedonian Doctors Association; National Commission for Doctors Licence; European Wound Management Association; Medical Faculty Board Member for Surgical Specialisation; Medical Faculty Board Member for Book Publishing; EWMA; ERTS. Address: University of Sts Cyril and Methodius, Clinic for Plastic and Reconstructive Surgery, Medical Faculty, Str Vodnjanska 17, Skopje 1000, Republic of Macedonia.

E

E Dongchen, b. 15 July 1939, Jiangxi Province, China. Teacher. m. Ziyun Wang, 2 sons, 1 daughter. Education: BSc, Geodesy, Wuhan Surveying and Mapping College, China, 1965. Appointments: Wuhan Surveying & Mapping College, 1965-86; Vice President, Wuhan Technical University of Surveying & Mapping, 1986-99; Director, Chinese Antarctic Center of Surveying & Mapping, Wuhan University, 2000-; Director, Key Laboratory of Polar Surveying and Mapping, State Bureau of Surveying & Mapping, 2005-. Publications: Numerous articles in professional journals. Honours: 2nd class award, National Science and Technology Progress, 1998; Ho Leung Ho Lee Prize, Science and Technology Progress, 2002. Memberships: Chinese Standing Delegate, GSSC of Scientific Committee on Antarctic Research; Academician, International Eurasian Academy of Sciences. Address: Chinese Antarctic Center of Surveying & Mapping, Wuhan University, 129 Luoyu Road, Wuhan 430079, P R China. E-mail: edc@whu.edu.cn

EASTERLY Susan, b. 2 February 1963, St Petersburg, Florida, USA. Independent Accompanist; Independent Piano Teacher. Partner, Sylvia Kay Fisher, 1 daughter. Education: AA, 1983, BA, Magna cum Laude, 1985, M Mus, 1987, University of South Florida; BA, Excelsior College, 1990; MA, Humanities, California State University, 1991. Appointments: Independent Piano Teacher; Independent Accompanist; Religious Education Teacher, Cedar Lane Unitarian Universalist Church; Previously: Advisory Review Panellist for Arts and Humanities Council, Montgomery County; Adjunct Instructor: Pasco-Hernando Community College; Stratford University; Polk Community College; Hillsborough Community College; Miami-Dade Community College; Piano Instructor: Travelling Teachers Inc; Performers' Music Institute; Accompanist: City of Gaithersburg Children's Chorus; Crescendo – The Tampa Bay Women's Chorus; Classical Ballet Center of Tampa; Montgomery County Chamber Music Society; University of South Florida and others; Accompanist for Children's Choir, Member of Bell Canto, Member of Music Committee, Cedar Lane Unitarian Universalist Church. Publications: Biography of Naum Gabo, Dictionary of American Biography, 1995; Biography of Nicholas Nabokov, Dictionary of American Biography, 1995; Hey Sugar, What Do You Know About Type 2 Diabetes?, 2005; LGBT Families and their Children (book chapter title), second author, 2008. Honours: FSMTA State Community Service Award for Florida; Listed in Who's Who publications and biographical dictionaries. Memberships: National Workgroup for the Needs of LGBTQI-2S Youth within Systems of Care; Newport Mill Middle School PTSA. Address: 10425 Haywood Drive, Silver Spring, Maryland, USA.

EASTON Sheena (Sheena Shirley Orr), b. 27 April 1959, Bellshill, Glasgow, Scotland. Singer; Actress. m. (1) Sandi Easton, 1979, divorced, (2) Rob Light, 1984, divorced, (3) Timothy Delarm, 1997 divorced, (4) John Minoli, 2002 divorced. 2 adopted children. Education: Speech and Drama, Royal Scottish Academy of Music and Drama. Career: Singer, Glasgow club circuit, 1979; Featured in television series; Concerts and tours worldwide; Television appearances include: TV special, Sheena Easton ...Act 1, NBC, 1983; Actress, Miami Vice, NBC, 1987; Stage debut, Man Of La Mancha, Chicago, then Broadway, 1991-92; Launched own Seven Minute Flat Stomach fitness video. Recordings: Albums: Sheena Easton, You Could Have Been With Me, 1981; Madness Money And Music, 1982; Best Kept Secret, 1983; A Private Heaven, Do You, 1985; The Lover In Me, For Your Eyes Only - The Best Of Sheena Easton, The Collection, 1989; What Comes Naturally, 1991; No Strings, 1993; My Cherie, 1995; Body and Soul, 1997; Freedom, Fabulous, 2000; Hit singles include: Modern Girl, 1980; Morning Train (9 To 5) (Number 1, US), One Man Woman, When He Shines, For Your Eyes Only, theme music to James Bond film, 1981; We've Got Tonight, duet with Kenny Rogers, Telefone, 1983; Strut, 1984; Sugar Walls, 1985; U Got The Look, duet with Prince, 1987; The Lover In Me (Number 2, US), 1989; What Comes Naturally, You Can Swing It, To Anyone, Contributor, Voices That Care charity record, 1991; Contributor, film soundtracks: Santa Claus - The Movie, 1985; About Last Night, 1986; Ferngully...The Last Rainforest, 1992. Honours include: Grammy Awards: Best New Artist, 1982; Best Mexican/American Performance, with Luis Miguel, 1985; First artist in history to have Top 5 hits in all major US charts (Pop, R&B, Country, Dance, Adult Contemporary), 1985; Emmy Award, Sheena Easton...Act 1, 1983. Current Management: Harriet Wasserman Management, 15250 Ventura Blvd, Suite 1215, Sherman Oaks, CA 91403-3201, USA.

EASTWOOD Clint, b. 31 May 1930, San Francisco, USA. Actor; Film Director. m. (1) Maggie Johnson, 1 son, 1 daughter; 1 daughter by Frances Fisher; m. (2) Dina Ruiz, 1996, 1 daughter. Education: Los Angeles City College. Appointments: Lumberjack, Oregon; Army service; Actor, TV series, Rawhide, 1959-65; Owner, Malposo Productions, 1969-; Mayor, Carmel, 1986-88. Films include: The First Travelling Saleslady; Star in the Dust; Escapade in Japan; Ambush at Cimarron Pass; Lafayette Escadrille; A Fistful of Dollars, 1964; For a Few Dollars More, 1965; The Good, the Bad and the Ugly, 1966; The Witches, 1967; Hang 'Em High, Coogan's Bluff, Paint Your Wagon, 1968; Where Eagles Dare, 1969; Kelly's Heroes, Two Mules for Sister Sara, 1970; Dirty Harry, 1971; Joe Kidd, 1972; High Plains Drifter (also director), Magnum Force, 1973; Thunderbolt and Lightfoot, 1974; The Eiger Sanction (also director), 1975; The Outlaw Josey Wales (also director), The Enforcer, 1976; The Gauntlet (also director), Every Which Way But Loose, 1978; Escape From Alcatraz, 1979; Bronco Billy (also director), Any Which Way We Can, 1980; Firefox (also director), Honky Tonk Man (also director), 1982; Sudden Impact (also director), 1983; Tightrope, City Heat, 1984; Pale Rider (also director), 1985; Heartbreak Ridge (also director); Director, Breezy, 1973; Bird, The Dead Pool, 1988; Pink Cadillac, White Hunter, Black Heart (also director), 1989; The Rookie (also director), 1990; Unforgiven (also director), 1992; In the Line of Fire, A Perfect World (also director), 1993; The Bridges of Madison County (also director, producer), 1995; The Stars Fell on Henrietta (co-producer); Absolute Power (also director), Midnight in the Garden of Good and Evil, (director), 1997; True Crime, 1998; Space Cowboys (also director), 2000; Blood Work (also director, producer), 2002; Mystic River (director), 2003; Million Dollar Baby (also director, composer), 2004; Gran Torino (director), 2008. Honours: Academy Awards, 1993; Fellow, BFI, 1993; Irving G Thalberg Award, 1995; Legion d'honneur, Commander, Ordre des Arts et Lettres, American Film Institute's Life Achievement Award, 1996; Screen Actors Guild, 2003; Special Filmmaking Achievement Award, National Board of Review, 2005; Best Director, Golden Globe Awards, 2005; Directors Guild of America Awards, 2005; Best Film, Best Director, Academy Awards, 2005. Address: c/o Leonard Hirshan, William Morris Agency, 151 S El Camino Drive, Beverly Hills, CA 90212, USA.

EBELING Norbert, b. 8 June 1956, Bochum, Germany. m. Walburga, 1 daughter. Professor. Education: Dr Ing, RWTH, Aachen. Appointments: Professor, Chemical Engineering Plant Design, FH Münster, 1995-. Publications: Abluft und

Abgas, 1999. Honours: Professor Adalbert-Seifrith-Preis, 2008. Address: FH Münster FB1, Stegerwaldstr 39, 48565 Steinfurt, Germany. E-mail: ebeling@fh-muenster.de

EBRÍ Bernardo Torné, b. 26 October 1949, Zaragoza, Spain. Internist; Medical Researcher. m. Immaculada, 3 sons, 2 daughter. Education: BSc, 1985, MD, 1972, PhD, 1978, University of Zaragoza; Studies in biological medicine and complementary therapies; Music Diploma, Specialist in Piano, 1984; Theological studies, Institute of Theological Studies, Zaragoza, 1989-92. Appointments: Research Fellow, Education & Science Ministry, Madrid, 1973-76; Assistant Professor, University of Zaragoza, 1973-86; Consultant, International Medicine, Miguel Servet Hospital, 1974; Director of Thesis and Advisor to Medical Residents, 1977-; Lecturer at Conferences of Bioethical and Medical-Social Issues, 1980-; Medical Resident, Miguel Servet Hospital, Zaragoza, 1986; Associate Professor, Faculty of Medicine, Zaragoza, 1987; Medical Homeopathic-Naturist, Zaragoza, 1993; Director and Professor of Post-graduate Courses in Biological Medicine, 1999-; National Group of Researchers of Cardiovascular Risk, Member of Spanish Society of Internal Medicine, 2002-. Publications: Author, 15 books on medical and humanities issues; More than 500 participations as lecturer and speaker in conferences on medical, ethical and humanities issues; More than 200 articles in professional journals. Honours: End of Degree Award, Zaragoza, 1971-72; Award of General Military Academy, Zaragoza, 1972; Award for Best Academy Record, Zaragoza City Council, 1973; Prince Ferdinand Award, 1973; Zaragoza City Hall Award, 1973; Extraordinary Degree Award, 1973; National Award Degree, 1975, PhD Award, 1979, Royal National Academy, Madrid; Best Doctoral Thesis Award, Government of Aragon, 1976-77; First Award, Medical Surgical Research, Official College of Medicine Doctors, Zaragoza, 1988-89; Award for Best Communication of Internal Medical Resident, Semergen Congress of General Practitioners, Spain, 2004. Memberships: Life Protection Association, Zaragoza; Academic of Medicine, Zaragoza; Spanish Society of Internal Medicine; Association of Naturist Doctors, Zaragoza; New York Academy of Sciences; Hypertension Society of Aragon; Spanish and Aragon Federation of Homeopathic Doctors; Writers Association of Aragon; Spanish Society of Doctors, Writers and Artists. Address: Viñedo Viejo 2, 13-1D, 50009, Zaragoza, Spain. E-mail: b.ebri@yahoo.es

ECCLESTON Christopher, b. 16 February 1964, Salford, England. Actor. Appointments: Actor, films: Let Him Have It, 1991; Shallow Grave, 1995; Jude, 1996; Elizabeth, 1998; A Price Above Rubies, 1998; Heart, 1999; Old New Borrowed Blue, 1999; Existenz, 1999; Gone in 60 Seconds, 2000; The Invisible Circus, 2001; The Others, 2001; I am Dina, 2002; 28 Days Later, 2002; The Dark Is Rising, 2007; New Orleans, Mon Amour, 2007; TV appearances: Cracker, 1993-94; Hearts and Minds, 1995; Our Friends in the North, 1996; Hillsborough, 1996; Strumpet, 2001; Flesh and Blood, 2002; Dr Who, 2005; Heroes, 2007; The Seeker: The Dark Is Rising, 2007; New Orleans: Mon Amour, 2008; The Sarah Silverman Program, 2008; The Happiness Salesman, 2009; GI Joe: The Rise of Cobra, 2009; Amelia, 2009; Lennon Naked, 2010. Theatre includes: Miss June, 2000. Address: Hamilton Asper Management, Ground Floor, 24 Hanway Street, London W1P 9DD, England.

ECCLESTONE Bernie, b. October 1930, Bungay, Suffolk, Business Executive. m. (1) 1 daughter, (2) Slavica, 2 daughters, 1 son. Education: Woolwich Polytechnic, London. Appointments: Established car and motorcycle dealership, Bexley, Kent; Racing-car driver for short period; Set up Brabham racing team, 1970; Owner, Formula One Holdings, now controls Formula One Constructors Association, representing all top racing-car teams; Vice-President in charge of Promotional Affairs, Federal Institute de l'Automobile (FIA), racing's international governing body. Address: Formula One Administration Limited, 6 Prince's Gate, London SW7 1QJ, England. Website: www.formula1.com

ECO Umberto, b. 5 January 1932, Alessandria, Italy. Professor of Semiotics; Author. m. Renate Ramge, 24 September 1962, 1 son, 1 daughter. Education: PhD, University of Turin, 1954. Appointments: Assistant Lecturer, 1956-63, Lecturer 1963-64, University of Turin; Lecturer, University of Milan, 1964-65; Professor, University of Florence, 1966-69; Visiting Professor, New York University, 1969-70, 1976, Northwestern University, 1972, Yale University, 1977, 1980, 1981, Columbia University, 1978, 1984; Professor of Semiotics, Milan Polytechnic, 1970-71, University of Bologna, 1971-, UCLA Medal, 2005. Publications: Il Problema Estetico in San Tommaso, 1956, English translation as The Aethetics of Thomas Aquinas, 1988; Sviluppo dell'Estetica Medioevale, 1959, English translation as Art and Beauty in the Middle Ages, 1986; Diario Minimo, 1963; La Struttura Assente, 1968; Il Costume di Casa, 1973; Trattato di Semiotica Generale, 1976; Il Nome della Rosa (novel), 1981, English translation as The Name of the Rose; Sette anni di desiderio 1977-83, 1984; Il Pendolo di Foucault, 1988; L'isola del giorno prima (novel), 1995, English translation as The Island of the Day Before; The Search for the Perfect Language, 1995; Serendipities, 1997; Kant and the Platypus, 1999; Baudolino (novel), 2000; Experiences in Translation, 2000; Five Moral Pieces, 2001; Mouse or Rat?: Translation as Negotiation, 2003; On Beauty: A History of a Western Idea (editor), 2004; The Mysterious Flame of Queen Loana (novel), 2005; On Ugliness, 2007; Turning Back The Clock, 2008; The Infinity Of Lists, 2009. Contributions to: various publications. Honours: Medici Prize, 1982; McLuhan Teleglobe Prize, 1985; Honorary DLitt, University of Glasgow, 1990, University of Kent, 1992; Crystal Award, World Economic Forum, 2000; Prince of Asturias Prize for Communications and the Humanities, 2000; Transcendent Satrape du College de Pataphysique, 2001; Austrian State Award for European Literature, 2002; Prix Mediterranee Etranger, 2002; Officier de la Legion d'Honneur, 2003; Gran Gagliaudo d'Oro della Citta di Alessandria, 2004; Kenyon Review Award, 2005; Prize 2007 of the City of Budapest, 2007; Premio Internazionale Diritti Umani Città di Orvieto, 2007; Premio Letterario Giorgio Calcagno, Almese, 2007; McKim Medal of The American Academy in Rome, 2007. Membership: International Association for Semiotic Studies; Aspen Institute, Italy. Address: Scuola Superiore Studi Umanistici, Via Marsala 26, Bologna, Italy. E-mail: sssub@dsc.unibo.it

ECONOMOPOULOS Konstantinos, b. 11 February 1984, Athens, Greece. Physician. m. Sousanna Choussein. Education: MD, Medicine, 2008, PhD, Molecular Biology, in progress, University of Athens. Appointments: Clinical Elective Student, Surgery, Ben Taub General Hospital, 2006; Airman Physician, Surgery, 251 Airforce General Hospital, Hellenic Airforce, 2008-09; Clinical & Research Fellow, Surgery, Athens Medical Center, 2009-10; Clinical Research Fellow, Surgery, Ptolepsis Medical Group, 2010-11; Postdoctoral Research Fellow, Surgery, Massachusetts General Hospital, 2011-; Research Fellow, Surgery, Harvard Medical School, 2011-. Publications: 50 scientific articles in peer-reviewed medical journals. Honours: 2 travel grants, European Society for Medical Oncology Conference, Lugano; Travel grants for two oral presentations; Instructor Potential Award, Advanced Trauma Life Support in Greece, 2009. Memberships: American College of Surgeons; American Association for the Advancement of Science; Hellenic-American Medical Society; Society of Junior Doctors. Address: 2 Hawthorne Place, Boston, MA 02114, USA.

EDBERG Stefan, b. 19 January 1966, Vastervik, Sweden. Tennis Player. m. Annette, 1 son, 1 daughter. Appointments: Tennis player, winner of: Junior Grand Slam, 1983; Milan Open, 1984; San Francisco, Basle and Memphis Opens, 1985; Gstaad, Basle and Stockholm Opens, 1986; Australian Open, 1986, 1987; Wimbledon, 1988, 1990, finalist, 1989; US Open, 1991; Masters, 1989; German Open, 1992; US Open, 1992; Winner (with Anders Jarryd) Masters and French Open, 1986, Australian and US Opens, 1987; Member, Swedish Davis Cup Team, 1984, 1987; Semi-finalist, numerous tournaments; Retired in 1996 having won 60 professional titles and more than 20 million dollars in prize money; Founded the Stefan Edberg Foundation to assist young Swedish tennis players. Honour: Adidas Sportsmanship Award (four times); United Press International Athlete of the Year Award, 1990; Inducted into International Tennis Hall of Fame, 2004. Address: c/o ATP Tour 200, ATP Tour Boulevard, Ponte Vedra Beach, FL 32082, USA.

EDER Andrew Howard Eric, b. 21 April 1964, London England. Dental Surgeon. m. Rosina Jayne Saideman, 2 sons, 1 daughter. Education: BDS (Hons), KCHMDS, University of London, 1986; LDS, Royal College of Surgeons of England; MSc, Conservative Dentistry, Eastman Dental Institute, University of London, 1990; Elected to MFGDP, Royal College of Surgeons of England, 1993; Membership in Restorative Dentistry, Royal College of Surgeons of England and Glasgow, 1994; Fellowship in Dental Surgery (Ad Eundum), Royal College of Surgeons of Edinburgh, 2003; Elected to FHEA, Higher Education Academy, 2002. Appointments: Professor of Restorative Dentistry and Dental Education, Honorary Consultant in Restorative Dentistry, UCL Eastman Dental Institute; Specialist in Restorative Dentistry and Prosthodontics, Director of London Tooth Wear Centre ®, Private Practice; Currently: Director of Education and Continuing Professional Development, UCL Eastman Dental Institute, Associate Dean, UCL School of Life and Medical Sciences. Publications: 40, single and multi-author papers, edited articles posters and abstracts; Textbook: Tooth Surface Loss (with R Ibbetson), 2000; Editorial Advisory Board: The European Journal of Restorative Dentistry, 1995-; Clinical Adviser, Editorial Advisory Board: Private Dentistry, 1997-; Board of Advisors, British Dental Journal, 2005-; Premium Practice Dentistry, 2010-. Memberships: President, 1994-95, Chairman of Trustees, 2003-, Alpha Omega; Fellowship, 1997, President, 2005-2006, British Society for Restorative Dentistry; President, 2001-2002, Odontological Section, Royal Society of Medicine. Address: UCL Eastman CPD, 123 Gray's Inn Road, London WC1X 8WD, England. E-mail: aeder@eastman.ucl.ac.uk

EDINBURGH HRH Duke of, Philip Mountbatten, b. 10 June 1921. Education: Salem School, Baden; Gordonstoun; RNC Dartmouth. m. Princess Elizabeth (later HM The Queen), 3 sons, 1 daughter. Appointments: Midshipman, HMS Ramillies Indian Ocean and Valiant Mediterranean Fleet, 1940; Sub-Lieutenant, 1941, Lieutenant, 1942, 1st Lieutenant (HMS Wallace, then HMS Whelp); 1st Lieutenant, HMS Chequers, 1949; Lieutenant-Commander, 1950, Commander, 1952, HMS Magpie; Personal ADC to HM King George VI, 1948; Admiral of the Fleet: RN, RAN, RNZN, Royal Canadian Sea Cadets; Captain-General RM; Field Marshal: UK, 1953, Australian Military Forces, 1954; New Zealand Army, 1977; Colonel-in-Chief (UK); Queen's Royal Hussars, 2002-, The Rifles, 2007-, REME, 1969-, Intelligence Corps, 1977-, ACF, 1953-; Colonel-in-Chief (Commonwealth): Royal Canadian Regiment, 1953-, Royal Hamilton LI, 1978-, Cameron Highlanders, Ottawa, 1967-, Queen's Own Cameron Highlanders, Canada, 1967-, Seaforth Highlanders, Canada, 1967-, Royal Canadian Army Cadets, 1953-, Royal Australian Corps Electrical and Mechanical Engineers, 1959-, Australian Army Cadet Corps, 1963-; Col, Grenadier Guards, 1975-; Royal Colonel, Highlanders 4th Battalion, Royal Regiment of Scotland; Royal Honorary Colonel: City of Edinburgh Universities, OTC, 1965-, Trinidad and Tobago Regiment, 1964-; Marshal: RAF, RAAF, RNZF; Air Commodore-in-Chief: ATC, Royal Canadian Air Cadets; Royal Honorary Air Commodore, RAF Kinloss: Admiral, Royal Yacht Squadron; Chancellor: University of Wales, 1948-76, University of Edinburgh, 1952-, University of Salford, 1967-91, University of Cambridge, 1976-; Life Governor, KCL; President: CCPR, 1951-, BAAS, 1952, FEI, 1964-86; Competed in six FEI World Championships; Patron: Duke of Edinburgh's Award, 1956-, Industrial Society, London Guildhall University. Honours: 1939-45, Atlantic, Africa, Burma and Italy Stars; War Medal, 1939-45; French Croix de Guerre; King George VI 1937 and Queen Elizabeth II 1953 Coronation Medals; Grand Master and First or Prince Knight Order of the British Empire, 1953; FRS, 1951; Grand Master, Guild of Air Pilots and Air Navigators; Master, Trinity House, 1969-; Equestrian Hall of Fame, 2007; British Horse Society Queen's Award for Equestrianism, 2008. Memberships: Founder Member, British Equestrian Centre; Horse Driving Trials Association; Honorary member: BHS, USA Equestrian Association; Canadian Horse Cutting Association; Founder, WWF.

EDMONDS Dean Stockett Jr, b. 24 December 1924. Professor of Physics. Education: BS, Physics, Massachusetts Institute of Technology (MIT), 1950; MA, Physics, Princeton University, 1952; PhD, MIT, 1958. Appointments: Co-founder, Vice President, Director, Nuclide Corporation, 1958-65; Research Fellow, Harvard University, Guest of Physics Department, MIT for work on Cambridge Electron Accelerator, 1959-61; Assistant Professor, 1961-67, Associate Professor, 1967-83, Physics, Boston University, College of Liberal Arts; Co-founder, Director, past President and past Chairman, Tachisto Laser Systems Inc, 1971-85; Visiting Professor of Physics, University of Western Ontario, Faculty of Science, London, Ontario, Canada, 1972-74; Director, Spectrametrics Inc, 1972-80; Honorary Professor of Physics, University of Western Ontario, Faculty of Science, Canada, 1974-; Director, Chief of Science Advisory Board, General Ionex Inc, 1974-85; Professor of Physics, Boston University, College of Liberal Arts, 1983-91; Professor of Physics Emeritus, Boston University, College of Arts and Sciences, 1991-. Publications: Numerous (as co-author) in professional journals and conferences; Cioffari's Experiments in College Physics. Honours: Special Merit Award, American Association of Physics Teachers, 1971; Sigma Xi, 1950-, President, Boston University Chapter, 1984-86. Memberships: American Physical Society, 1951-; American Association of Physics Teachers, 1962-; Institute of Electrical and Electronic Engineers (formerly Radio Engineers). Address: 1019 Spyglass Lane, Naples, FL 34102-7734, USA.

EDMONDSON Christopher Paul, b. 25 June 1950, Carlisle, Cumbria. Bishop of Bolton. m. Susan, 2 sons. Education: BA, 1971, MA, 1981, University of Durham; Diploma in Theology, Cranmer Hall, St John's College, Durham, 1972.

Appointments: Curate/Team Vicar, Kirkheaton, Huddersfield, 1973-79; Vicar, St George's, Ovenden, Halifax, 1979-86; Diocesan Missioner, Carlisle Diocese, and Priest in Charge, Bampton with Mardale, 1986-92; Vicar, St Peter's, Shipley, Bradford, 1992-2002; Warden of Lee Abbey, Devon, 2002-08; Bishop of Bolton, Manchester Diocese, 2008-. Publications: Strategies for Rural Evangelism, 1989; How Shall They Hear?, 1994; Minister, Love Thyself, 2000; Fit to Lead, 2002, 2007/09; Celebrating Community, 2006; Leaders Learning to Listen, 2010. Address: Bishop's Lodge, Walkden Road, Worsley, M28 2WH, England. E-mail: bishopchris@manchester.anglican.org

EDWARDS Anthony, b. 19 July 1962, Santa Barbara, California, USA. Actor. m. Jeanine Lobell, 1994, 4 children. Education: RADA, London. Appointments: Member, Santa Barbara Youth Theatre in 30 productions, aged 12-17; Commercials aged 16; Stage appearance: Ten Below, New York, 1993. Actor, films: Fast Times at Ridgemont High, 1982; Heart Like a Wheel, 1982; Revenge of the Nerds, 1984; The Sure Thing, 1985; Gotcha!, 1985; Top Gun, 1985; Summer Heat, 1987; Revenge of the Nerds II, 1987; Mr North, 1988; Miracle Mile, 1989; How I Got Into College, 1989; Hawks, 1989; Downtown, 1990; Delta Heat, 1994; The Client, 1994; Us Begins with You, 1998; Don't Go Breaking My Heart, 1999; Jackpot, 2001; Northfork, 2003; Thunderbirds, 2004; The Forgotten, 2004; Zodiac, 2007; Motherhood, 2009. TV series: It Takes Two, 1982-83; Northern Exposure, 1992-93; ER, 1994-2008; Soul Man; TV films: The Killing of Randy Webster, 1981; High School USA, 1983; Going for Gold: The Bill Johnson Story, 1985; El Diablo, 1990; Hometown Boy Makes Good, 1990; In Cold Blood, 1996; TV specials: Unpublished Letters; Sexual Healing. Honours: People's Choice Award, 1995; SAG Award, 1996, 1997, 1998, 1999; Golden Globe, 1998; Andrew Carnegie Medal, 2002; Daytime Emmy, 2002; TV Land Icon Award, 2009;   Address: c/o United Talent Agency, 9560 Wilshire Boulevard, Suite 500, Beverly Hills, CA 90212, USA.

EDWARDS Brigid O'Neil (née Segrave), b. 16 February 1940, London, England. Artist. m. Robert Edwards. Education: Central School of Art, London, 1960-63; BSc (Hons), University College London, 1971-75. Career: Television Researcher, 1964-66; Television Documentary Film Producer/Director, 1966-76; Artist, 1980-. Publication: Illustrator of Primula by J Richards, 1993 revised edition, 2003. Honour: Special Jury Award for Documentary, San Francisco International Film Festival, 1973. Address: Tregeseal House, St Just, Penzance, Cornwall TR19 7PW, England. E-mail: brigedwards@aol.com

EDWARDS (Frederick) Gary, b. 3 August 1943, Melbourne, Australia. Company Director; Architect; Health Facility Planner. m. Kathryn Winford, 1979, 1 stepson, 1 stepdaughter, 1 daughter. Education: Certificate in Architectural Draftsmanship, Royal Melbourne Institute of Technology, 1967; Diploma in Architectural Design, University of Melbourne, 1974; Architectural Registration, Architects' Registration Board of Victoria, 1975; Diploma in Architecture, Royal Melbourne Institute of Technology, 1976; Accreditation Certificate, Architects' Accreditation Council of Australia, 1991; Certificate, Computer Aided Drafting, Box Hill College of Technical and Further Education, Victoria, 1993. Appointments: Draftsman, then Architect, Stephenson and Turner Architects, Melbourne, 1961-83; Associate and Senior Health Facility Planner, Stephenson and Turner Architects, Australasia, 1983-91; Co-founding Principal, Health Facilities Consultant Architects, 1991-; Co-founding Director, Health Planners Australia Pty Ltd, 1993-98, Newpolis Pty Ltd, 1996-98, and ArcHealth Pty Ltd, 2000-; Honorary Practice Board Member, Lecturer, Awards Assessor, and Contracts, Fees and Complaints Committees Convenor, The Royal Australian Institute of Architects, 1978-; Honorary Councillor, RAIA Victorian Chapter, 1990-94; Architectural Practice Examiner, Architects' Registration Board of Victoria, 1980-; Honorary Committee Member, and Former Vice President, Bestchance-Child and Family Care, 1981-; Honorary Life Governor, Burwood Children's Homes-CFCN, 1986-; Senior Lecturer, Architectural Practice, RMIT University, 1995-97. Publications: Papers and articles in professional journals; numerous architectural practice guidenotes, health facility planning guidelines and Standard Building Contracts. Honours: Applied Art Prize, Scotch College, Melbourne, 1960; Inaugural Art Prize, Stephenson and Turner, Melbourne, 1971; Recognition for Design Thesis (on Facilities for Care of Aged and Disabled), University of Melbourne, 1973; Honorary Life Governor, Burwood Children's Homes, 1986; Planning of Freemason's Hospital Day Procedure and Women's Health Centre, Melbourne, which received the BOMA Award for Excellence, 1993; Certificate of Recognition for Contribution and Commitment to the Advancement of Architecture, Royal Australian Institute of Architects, 1994; Inaugural President's Award for Outstanding Contribution to the Profession of Architecture and the Royal Australian Institute of Architects, RAIA, Victorian Chapter, 1995; Certificate of Appreciation for Voluntary Service to the Community, Premier of Victoria, 2001; Certificate of Appreciation in Recognition of over 35 years Voluntary Service to the Liberal Party of Australia and the Highfield Park Branch, 2005; A number of certificates of appreciation for his support of various sporting clubs and charities; International Health Professional of the Year Award for Innovative Health Facilities Architecture, IBC, 2007; Lifetime Achievement Award, for contributions to Health Architecture, Community and Business, The World Congress of Arts, Sciences and Communications, 2007; UCC International Peace Prize, 2009; American Order of Merit, ABI, 2009. Memberships: Fellow, Royal Australian Institute of Architects; Chartered Member, Royal Institute of British Architects; Member, Association of Consulting Architects of Australia; Member, Institute of Hospital Engineering Australia; Member, Australian Institute of Company Directors; Associate Member, Royal Melbourne Institute of Technology; Member, Order of International Fellowship. Address: Health Facilities Consultant Architects, 10 Cochran Ave, Camberwell, VIC 3124, Australia. E-mail: hfca@bigpond.com

EDWARDS Gareth Owen, b. 12 July 1947. Rugby Union Player (retired); Businessman. m. Maureen Edwards, 1972, 2 sons. Education: Cardiff College of Education. Appointments: Welsh Secondary Schools Rugby international, 1965-66; English Schools 200 yards Champion (UK under 19 record holder), 1966; Welsh national team: 53 caps, 1967-78; Captain 13 times, youngest captain (aged 20), 1968; Played with clubs: Cardiff, 1966-78; Barbarians, 1967-78; British Lions, 1968, 1971, 1974; Joint Director, Euro-Commercials (South Wales) Ltd, 1982-; Players (UK) Ltd, 1983-889 Chairman, Hamdden Ltd, 1991-; Chairman, Regional Fisheries Advisory Committee, Welsh Water Authority, 1983-89; Commentator for BBC and S4C. Publications: Gareth - An Autobiography, 1978; Rugby Skills, 1979; Gareth Edwards on Rugby, 1986; Gareth Edwards' 100 Great Rugby Players, 1987. Address: Hamdden Ltd, Plas y Ffynnon, Cambrian Way, Brecon, Powys, LD3 7HP, Wales.

EDWARDS Jonathan, b. 10 May 1966, London, England. Athlete. m. Alison Joy Briggs, 2 sons. Career: Athlete, Bronze Medal, World Championships, 1993; Gold Medal, Fifth Athletics World Championships, Gothenburg, twice breaking own record for triple jump, clearing 18.29m, 1995, Edmonton, 2001; Silver Medal, Olympic Games, Atlanta, 1996; World Championships, 1997, 1999; Gold Medal, European Championships, 1998; European Indoor Championships, 1998; Goodwill Games, 1998; Sports Fellowship, University of Durham, 1999; Olympic Games, 2000; World Championships, 2001; Commonwealth Games, 2002; Retired from athletics after 2003 World Championships; Currently working mainly for the BBC as a sports commentator and presenter of programmes including Songs of Praise; Member London Organising Committee for the Olympic Games, 2012. Publication: A Time to Jump, 2000. Honours: BBC Sportsman of the Year, 1995; IAAF Athlete of the Year, 1995; BBC Sports Personality of the Year, 1995; British Male Athlete of the Year, 1995, 2000, 2001; CBE; Honorary Doctorate, University of Exeter, 2006; Duniv, University of Ulster, 2006. Address: c/o Jonathan Marks, MTC, 20 York Street, London W1U 6PU, England. E-mail: info@mtc-uk.com Website: www.mtc-uk.com

EDWARDS Philip Walter, b. 7 February 1923, Cumbria, England. Retired Professor of English; Writer. m. Sheila Mary Wilkes, 8 May 1952, 3 sons, 1 daughter. Education: BA, 1942, MA, 1946, PhD, 1960, University of Birmingham. Appointments: Lecturer, University of Birmingham, 1946-60; Professor, Trinity College, Dublin, 1960-66, University of Essex, 1966-74, University of Liverpool, 1974-90. Publications: Sir Walter Raleigh, 1953; Kyd, The Spanish Tragedy, 1959; Shakespeare and the Confines of Art, 1968; Massinger: Plays and Poems, 1976; Shakespeare's Pericles, 1976; Threshold of a Nation, 1979; Hamlet, 1985; Shakespeare: A Writers Progress, 1986; Last Voyages, 1988; The Story of the Voyage, 1994; Sea-Mark, 1997; The Journals of Captain Cook, 1999; Pilgrimage and Literary Tradition, 2005. Membership: British Academy, fellow, 1986-. Address: High Gillinggrove, Gillinggate, Kendal, Cumbria LA9 4JB, England.

EDWARDS Sir Robert, b. 27 September 1925. Physiologist. m. Ruth E Fowler, 1956, 5 daughters. Education: University of Wales; University of Edinburgh. Appointments: Research Fellow, California Institute of Technology, 1957-58; Scientist, National Institute of Medical Research, Mill Hill, 1958-62; Glasgow University, 1962-63; Department of Physiology, University of Cambridge, 1963-89; Ford Foundation Reader in Physiology, 1969-85; Professor of Human Reproduction, 1985-89, Professor Emeritus, 1989-, University of Cambridge. Publications: A Matter of Life, with P C Steptoe, 1980; Conception in the Human Female, 1980; Mechanisms of Sex Differentiation in Animals and Man, with C R Austin, 1982; Human Conception in Vitro, with J M Purdy, 1982; Implantation of the Human Embryo, with J M Purdy and P C Steptoe, 1985; In Vitro Fertilisation and Embryo Transfer, with M Seppala, 1985; Life Before Birth, 1989; Numerous articles in scientific and medical journals. Honours: Honorary Member, French Society for Infertility; Honorary Citizen of Bordeaux; Hon FRCOG; Hon MRCP; Hon DSc (Hull, York, Free University Brussels); Gold Medal, Spanish Fertility Society, 1985; King Faisal Award, 1989. Memberships: Fellow, Churchill College, Cambridge, now Extraordinary Fellow; Scientific Director, Bourn Hall Clinics, Cambridge and London; Chair, European Society of Human Reproduction and Embryology, 1984-86; Visiting Scientist, Johns Hopkins University, 1965, University of North Carolina, 1966, Free University of Brussels, 1984; Honorary President, British Fertility Society, 1988-; Life Fellow, Australian Fertility Society; Chief Editor, Human Reproduction, 1986-; Albert Lasker Clinical Medical Research Award, 2001; Knighted, 2011. Address: Duck End Farm, Dry Drayton, Cambridge, CB3 8DB, England.

EDWARDS Robert John, b. 25 October 1925, Farnham, Surrey, England. Journalist. m. Brigid, 2 sons, 2 daughters. Education: Marlborough House, Reading, Berkshire; Ranelagh School, Bracknell, Berkshire. Appointments: Editor, Tribune, 1951-54; Feature Writer, London Evening Standard, 1955-57; Deputy Editor, Sunday Express, 1957-59; Managing Editor, Daily Express, 1959-61; Editor, Daily Express, 1961, 1963-65; Editor, Evening Citizen, Glasgow, 1962-63; Editor, Sunday People, 1966-72; Editor, Sunday Mirror, 1972-84; Director, Mirror Group Newspapers, 1976-88; Senior Group Editor, 1984-85, Deputy Chairman, 1985-86, Mirror Group Newspapers; Chairman, Scoop of the Year Awards Panel, London Press Club, 1988, 2003; Ombudsman to Today newspaper, 1990-95. Publications: Goodbye Fleet Street (autobiography), 1988. Honours: CBE, 1986. Appointments: Tregeseal House, Nancherrow, St Just, Penzance, Cornwall, TR19 7PW, England. E-mail: edwardsrj@aol.com

EDWARDS Steven, b. 9 March 1948, Solihull, England. Veterinarian. m. Virginia E M L Evans, 2 sons. Education: BA, 1969, VetMB, 1972, MA, 1973, Trinity Hall, University of Cambridge; MSc, 1977, DVM & S, 1989, University of Edinburgh. Appointments: Private Veterinary Practice, Montgomery, Wales, 1972-76; Veterinary Investigation Officer, British Veterinary Team, San Salvador, El Salvador, 1978-80; Veterinary Research Officer, Central Veterinary Laboratory, Weybridge, Surrey, 1980-92; Head of Virology, 1992-98, Director of Surveillance & Laboratory Services, 1998-2000, Veterinary Laboratories Agency (MAFF), Weybridge; Chief Executive, Veterinary Laboratories Agency (DEFRA), UK, 2000-08; Interim Chief Executive, Animal Health Agency (DEFRA), UK, 2008; Part Time Consultant to World Organisation for Animal Health (OIE), Paris, France, 2009-; Chairman, FAO/OIE network on animal influenza (OFFLU), 2005-. Publications: Over 60 papers in peer-reviewed scientific journals; Conference proceedings, magazines, etc; Various scientific and genealogical editorial works. Honours: CBE, 2009; Gold Medal, World Organisation for Animal Health (OIE). Memberships: Royal College of Veterinary Surgeons; British Veterinary Associations; Various specialist veterinary and scientific societies; Trustee: Foundation for Medieval Genealogy; APT, overseas enterprise development charity.

EDWARDS-NIXON Jennifer Veronica, b. 21 October 1956, Grenada. Certified Assistant Audiologist Speech Language Pathologist. m. Jude V Nixon, 2 sons, 1 daughter. Education: Cambridge University, England; Truett McConnell College, Cleveland, USA; Baylor University, Texas; California Colleges for Health Sciences, California; MA, Counseling (Mental Health and Wellness); Certificate in Complementary Medicine. Appointments: Clinician, Laboratory Assistant, Electroneurodiagnostic & Intraoperative Monitoring; Assistant Audiologist Speech Language Pathologist, Immunopathology and Histology; Science Teacher/Supervisor Research Project Leader, Kiddy College; Co-ordinator Psychiatric Nursing; Tutor Supervisor, Oakland University College Prep Academy. Publications: Composer, Move On (music lyrics on CD); 15 poems. Honours: Academic Rotary Scholarship; Principal's Prize, St George's University School of Medicine; Golden Key National Honor Society Academic Scholarship; William Beaumont Hospital Service Excellence Profession, WBH; Certificate in Complementary Medicine. Memberships:

American Baptist Churches of Michigan Diversity Council; William Beaumont Hospital Center for Integrating Body, Mind & Spirit; American Journal of Electroneurodiagnostic Technology; Advance Medical Laboratory Professionals Interactive Communicating. Address: Oakland University, PUB College Club Tutor Supervisor, 261 South Foundation Hall, Rochester, MI 48309-4401, USA. E-mail: jvedward@oakland.edu

EFFAT Baher Abd El-Khalik Mahmoud, b. 11 October 1954, Cairo, Egypt. Professor. m. Manal Aly El-Sherbiny, 1 son, 2 daughters. Education: PhD, Faculty of Agriculture, Ain Shams University, 1990. Appointments: Technical Specialist, Food and Dairy Science Department, National Research Centre, 1979-84; Professor of Food and Dairy Microbiology, Food and Dairy Science Department, National Research Centre, 2001-. Publications: Over 45 research papers in field of Dairy Microbiology, Food Microbiology Pathogenic Bacteria; Lactic and Bacteria, Probiotics and Propionic Acid Bacteria in Food and Dairy Products. Honours: CAS-TWAS Visiting Scholar Fellowship, Institute of Microbiology, Biosynthesis and Function of Microbial Polysaccharide Laboratory, China, 2006. Memberships: Association of Official Analytical Chemistry (AOAC), USA.

EFIMOV Alexander Vasilievich, b. 12 May 1954, Lugovaya, Orenburg Region, Russia. Chemist. Widower, 1 daughter. Education: Bachelor's Degree, Moscow State University, 1976; Candidate of Science (PhD), 1983; Doctor of Science, Chemistry, 1995. Appointments: Probationer, 1976-79, Junior Researcher, 1979-87; Senior Researcher, 1987-96, Leading Researcher, 1996-1998, Principal Researcher, 1998-, Deputy Director, 2002-, Institute of Protein Research, Russian Academy of Sciences. Publications: Articles in scientific journals including: Journal of Molecular Biology, 1979, 1995; FEBS Letters, 1984, 1987, 1991, 1992, 1993, 1994, 1996, 1997, 1998, 2003; Structure, 1994; Proteins, 1997. Membership: Scientific Secretary, 1989-2000; Deputy Director, 2002-, Institute of Protein Research. Address: Institute of Protein Research, RAS, 142290 Pushchino, Moscow Region, Russia. E-mail: efimov@protres.ru

EFRON Zac, b. 18 October 1987, San Luis Obispo, California, USA. Actor; Singer. Education: Arroyo Grande High School; Pacific Conservatory of the Performing Arts, Santa Maria, California. Career: TV: Firefly, 2002; The Guardian, ER, 2003; Summerland, CSI: Miami, The Replacements, 2005; Heist, The Suite Life of Zack & Cody, NCIS, 2006; Robot Chicken, 2008; Saturday Night Live, Entourage, 2009; Film: Melinda's World, The Big Wide World of Carl Laernke, 2003; Miracle Run, Triple Play, 2004; The Derby Stallion, 2005; If You Lived Here, You'd be Home Now, High School Musical, 2006; Hairspray, High School Musical 2, 2007; High School Musical 3: Senior Year, 2008; 17 Again, Me and Orson Welles, 2009; The Death and Life of Charlie St Cloud, 2010; Jonny Quest, 2011; Singer: Hairspray, 2007; High School Musical 2, 2007; High School Musical 3: Senior Year, 2008. Honours: 6 Teen Choice Awards, 2006, 2007, 2009; Kids' Choice Award, 2007; Hollywood Film Award, 2007; Young Hollywood Award, 2007; 2 MTV Movie Awards, 2008, 2009.

EGGERS Klaus Wilhelm Heinrich, b. 14 January 1922, Hammoor, Germany. Retired Professor. m. Dagmar Ortmann, 1 son. Education: Naval Architecture, Techn Hochschule Berlin, 1941-43; Diploma in Mathematics, 1952, Dr rer nat, 1960, University of Hamburg. Appointments: Research Assistant, 1953-61, Professor of Applied Mechanics, 1961-85, Institute of Schiffbau, Hamburg University; Research Assistant, University of Notre Dame, Indiana, USA, 1963-64; Research Assistant, Stevens Institute of Technology, Hoboken, USA, 1967-68. Publications: Numerous articles in professional journals. Honours: Foreign Senior Fellowship, Notre Dame University, Indiana, 1963; Japanese Society for the Promotion of Science, 1976; Honorary Professor, Harbin Institute of Technology, China, 1985. Address: Horstlooge 16, 22359 Hamburg-Volksdorf, Germany. E-mail: kwheggers@web.de

EGOROV Mikhail Alekseevich, b. 1 November 1975, Astrakhan, Russia. University Professor. m. Olga, 1 son. Education: Master, Water Bioresources and Aquaculture, 1997; PhD, Ecology, Astrakhan State Technical University, 1999; PhD, Biological Sciences, Astrakhan State University, 2002. Appointments: Laboratory Assistant, 1996-97, Senior Project Engineer, 1997-99, Postgraduate Researcher, 1997-99, Assistant Lecturer, 1999-2001, Associate Professor, 2001-03, Post-PhD Researcher, 1999-2002, Astrakhan State Technical University; Head of Laboratory of Biotechnologies, Head of Department of Biotechnology and Bioecology, Astrakhan State University, 2003-. Publications: Numerous articles in professional journals. Honours: Diploma, International Exhibition, Cryogen Expo, Moscow, 2005; Silver Medal, Arkhimed Innovation Forum, Moscow, 2009. Memberships: Reginal State Academic Dissertation Council in Physiology; Academic and Advisory Council for Fish Genetics and Selection, Moscow. Address: Astrakhan State University, 20a Tatischev Street, 414056 Astrakhan, Russian Federation. E-mail: egorov@astranet.ru Website: www.aspu.ru

EGTESADI Shahryar, b. 6 November 1952, Sanandaj, Iran. Professor of Clinical Nutrition. m. Akhtar Afshari, 3 daughters. Education: BS, Nutrition Science and Food Chemistry, Shahid Beheshti University, 1975, Tehran; MSPH, Nutrition Science, Tehran University, Teheran, 1977; PhD, Nutrition, University of California, Davis, USA, 1986. Appointments: Instructor, Tabriz University, Tabriz, Iran, 1978-86; Assistant Professor, 1986-90, Associate Professor, 1990-95, Professor, 1995-2002, Associate Dean for Education and Research Affairs, School of Public Health and Nutrition, 2002, Tabriz University of Medical Sciences; Chair, Department of Biochemistry and Nutrition, Tabriz, Iran, 1986-93; Visiting Scientist, Human Nutrition Research Center on Aging, Tufts University, USA, 1995; Chair, Department of Biochemistry and Clinical Nutrition, 1996-98; Head of Research Department, School of Public Health and Nutrition, Tabriz, Iran, 1996-2002; Professor, Iran University of Medical Sciences, School of Public Health, Tehran, 2002-10; Chair, Department of Nutrition, Iran University of Medical Sciences, 2004-; Dean of School of Public Health, Iran University of Medical Sciences, 2010; Professor, Tehran University of Medical Sciences, School of Public Health, Tehran, 2010-. Publications: Over 140 articles presented or published in Iranian and international journals and congresses mainly on the topics of regulation of metabolism, nutrition assessments of infants and children, growth pattern and nutrition status of adolescents, nutrition behaviour and food choice of adolescents, food insecurity; Trace Elements and antioxidants nutrition and metabolism, gene nutrition interactions, nutritional pharmacology, nutritional immunology, diabetes, obesity and issues of clinical nutrition. Honours: Distinguished Editor of Article presented in the Iranian Research Forum, National Research Centre of Iran, Iranian Ministry of Science, 1999; Distinguished Scientist of Tabriz University of Medical Sciences, School of Public Health and Nutrition, 2000; Listed in Great Minds of 21st Century, ABI, 2001; Distinguished Scientist, Iran University of Medical Sciences, School of Public Health,

2002, 2010; Honoured Professor, Iranian Ministry of Health and Medical Education, 2006 and 2007; Distinguished Department Chair, Iran University of Medical Sciences, 2007, 2010. Memberships: Iranian Society of Nutrition; Iranian Society of Physiology and Pharmacology; Iranian Board of Nutrition; Ministry of Health and Medical Education of Iran, 2000-. Address: Tehran University of Medical Sciences, School of Public Health, Dept of Nutrition, Argentina Square, Alvand Street, Tehran, Iran. E-mail: sh_egtesadi@tums.ac.ir

EHLE Jennifer, b. 29 December 1969, Winston-Salem, North Carolina, USA. Actress. m. Michael Ryan, 2001, 1 son. Education: Central School of Speech and Drama. Career: Theatre includes: Summerfolk; The Relapse; The Painter of Dishonour; Richard III, 1996; Tartuffe; The Real Thing, 1999, 2000; The Philadelphia Story, 2005; TV includes: the Camomile Lawn, 1992; Micky Love, The Maitlands, 1993; Self Catering, Pleasure, La Récréation, 1994; Beyond Reason, Pride and Prejudice, 1995; Melissa, 1997; Films: Backbeat, 1994; Paradise Road, Wilde, 1997; Bedrooms and Hallways, 1998; This Year's Love, Sunshine, 1999; Possession, 2002; The River King, 2005; Alpha Male, 2006; Before the Rains, 2007; Pride and Glory, 2008; The Greatest, 2009. Honours: Tony Award, Best Actress, 2000; BAFTA Award, Best Actress, 1995. Address: c/o ICM, 76 Oxford Street, London W1N 0AX, England.

EIDERMAN Boris, b. 23 February 1934, Kharkov, Ukraine, USSR. Mechanics Researcher. m. Susanna Nuger, 1 son. Education: MSc, Engineer-Mechanic, Mining Institute, Kharkov, 1957; PhD, 1968, Dr Sci, 1986, Professorship, 1989, Academy, Mining Institute, Moscow. Appointments: Engineer and Designer of Mining Machinery, Machine Build Works, Kharkov, 1957-61; Head, Mechanics Section, Mining Institute, Kharkov, 1961-66; Senior Scientist, Leading Scientist, Professor, Mechanisation Section, Academy Mining Institute, Moscow, 1967-91; Scientist, Researcher, College of Technology, Jerusalem, Israel, 1992-93; Chief Scientist, Sortech Separation Technologies Ltd, Jerusalem, Israel, 1997-2003; Consultant, 2004-. Publications: Mechanisms for Formation of Traffic and Energy Expenditure of Conveyors, 1984; Parameters and Calculation Methods for Conveyors, 1987; Scraper Conveyors, 1993; Triboclassification Technology for Minerals and Fly Ash, 2000; Triboclassification Technology for Bulk Powder, 2001; Development of a high productivity Tribo-Classifier for mining 2003. Honours: Prize Winner, USSR Council of Ministers, 1983; Grantee, Ministry of Industry and Trade of Israel, 1992, 1997. Memberships: Forum for Bulk Solids Handling. Address: Home: Gvirtsman Moshe str 6/4, 97793 Jerusalem, Israel. E-mail: boris@eiderman.com

EIGEN Manfred, b. 9 May 1927, Ruhr, Germany. Physical Chemist. m. Elfriede Müller, 1 son, 1 daughter. Education: Doctorate, Göttingen University, 1951. Appointments: Assistant, Professor, Head of Department, 1953-, Director, 1964, Max-Planck Institute of Physical Chemistry, Göttingen; Honorary Professor, Technical University, Göttingen, 1971-; President, Studienstiftung des Deutschen Volkes, 1983-. Honours: Hon Dr, University of Washington, St Louis University, Harvard University, Cambridge University; Numerous other honorary degrees; Foreign Honorary Member, American Academy of Arts and Sciences; Otto Hahn Prize, 1967; Joint Winner, Nobel Prize for Chemistry, 1967. Memberships: Akademie der Wissenschaften, Göttingen; Foreign Associate Member, National Academy of Sciences, USA; Foreign Member, Royal Society, UK; Academie Française, 1978. Address: Georg-Dehio-Weg 14, 37075, Germany.

EISELIN Rolf, b. 6 November 1925, Zurich, Switzerland. Architect; Artist. Education: Architect's Diploma, Swiss Federal Institute of Technology, Zurich; Registered Architect, State of Illinois, USA and Switzerland. Appointments: Architect, Skidmore, Owings & Merrill, Chicago and other firms in New York, Boston, Paris, Zurich; Producer, Prints USA world tour exhibition, 1984-87; Represented San Francisco Museum of Modern Art; Cabo Frio CIPB collection, Brazil; Grafik Sammlung ETH, Zürich. Publications: Numerous articles in professional journals. Honours: Outstanding Photography Award, National Exhibition, USA, 1989; Medal of Honor, Jersey City Museum, USA (prints); Listed in international biographical dictionaries. Memberships: Former President, California Society of Printmakers; Visarte Visual Arts Association, Switzerland; Swiss Architects and Engineers Association. Address: Rés La Côte 60, 1110 Morges, Switzerland.

EISENREICH Günther, b. 12 April 1933, Leipzig, Germany. Retired Professor of Mathematics. m. Gisela Busse. Education: Studies in Mathematics, Physics and Biology, 1951-56; Degree in Mathematics, 1956; Doctor of Natural Sciences, 1963; Habilitation in Natural sciences, 1968. Appointments: Scientific Worker, Saxon Academy of Sciences, Leipzig, 1957-58; Scientific Assistant, 1959-67; Senior Assistant, 1967-69; University Docent, Mathematical Section, 1969-70, Professor of Theoretical Mathematics, 1970-98, (appointments delayed for political reasons), University of Leipzig. Publications: Books: Vorlesungen über Vektor–und Tensorrechnung; Lineare Algebra und Analytische Geometrie; Vorlesung über Funktionentheorie mehrerer Variabler; Lexikon der Algebra; Fachwörterbuch Mathematik Englisch/Deutsch/Französisch/Russisch; Fachwörterbuch Physik Englisch/Deutsch/ Französisch/Russisch; Articles on mathematics, biology, philosophy, linguistics and biographies which include: Untersuchungen über Ideale in Stellenringen; Eine Dualitätsbeziehung zwischen s-Moduln; Zur Syzygientheorie und Theorie des inversen Systems perfekter Ideale und Vektormoduln in Polynomringen und Stellenringen; Zum Wahrheitsproblem in der Mathematik; Numerous reviews, translations of Scientific books from the English, French, Russian and Hungarian. Honour: General Honouring for Scientific Success, Education of students and Democratizing the University. Memberships: Deutsche Mathematiker-Vereinigung, 1990-98; Mathematische Gesellschaft der DDR; Deutscher Hochschulverband, Speaker of the Saxons; Federation of Trade Unions. Address: Gartenbogen 7, D-04288 Leipzig, Germany.

EISNER Michael Dammann, b. 7 March 1942, Mt Kisco, New York, USA. Entertainment Executive. m. Jane Breckenridge, 1967, 3 sons. Education: Denison University. Appointments: Senior Vice President, prime-time production and development, ABC Entertainment Corporation, 1973-76; President, COO, Paramount Pictures Corporation, 1976-84; Chairman and Chief Executive Officer, 1984-2004, CEO, 2004-05, Member of Board of Directors, 2005-06, The Walt Disney Company; Established Eisner Foundation.. Publications: The Keys to the Kingdom; Disney War. Honour: Légion d'honneur. Memberships: Board of Directors, California Institute of the Arts, Denison University; American Hospital of Paris Foundation; UCLA Executive Board for Medical Sciences; National Hockey League (ice hockey); Business Steering Committee of the Global Business

Dialogue on Electronic Commerce; The Business Council. Address: Walt Disney Company, 500 South Buena Vista Street, Burbank, CA 91521, USA.

EISSA Fawzy Ismail Ismail, b. 8 January 1974, Kafr El Sheikh, Egypt. Associate Professor. m. Nour El-Hoda, 1 son, 2 daughters. Education: BSc, 1995, MSc, 1999, Agricultural Science, Tanta University; PhD, Agricultural Science, Al Azhar University, 2005. Appointments: Associate Professor, Environmental Pollution, Environment & Bio-agriculture Department, Al Azhar University, Cairo. Publications: Numerous articles in professional journals. Honours: Listed in biographical dictionaries. Memberships: Agricultural Chemistry & Environment Protection Society; Egyptian Society of Pest Control and Environmental Protection; Nature Friends Society; Egyptian Society of Environmental and Agricultural Sciences. Address: Environment & Bio Agriculture Department, Faculty of Agriculture, Al Azhar University, 11884 Nasr City, Cairo, Egypt. E-mail: fawzy.eissa@yahoo.com

EL CHAHAL Ghassan, b. 13 January 1980, Tripoli, Lebanon. Marine Coastal Engineer; Researcher. Education: Diploma, 2002, MSc, 2003, Mechanical Engineering, Faculty of Engineering, Lebanese University, Lebanon; PhD, Design Optimization of Floating Breakwaters, University of Technology of Troyes, France, 2007. Appointments: Postdoctoral Research, University of Technology of Troyes, France, 2007-08; Marine Coastal Engineer, COWI (Engineering and Consultancy), Doha, Qatar, 2008-. Publications: Author, Reply to Discussion on paper, Design Optimization of Floating Breakwaters with an Interdisciplinary Fluid-Solid Structural Problem; Numerous articles in professional journals. Honours: Listed in international biographical dictionaries. Memberships: International Society of Polar Engineers, USA. Address: COWI A/S, Marine Department, Al Mana Tower, 8th Floor, Suhaim Bin Hamed St, C-Ring Road, Bin Mahmoud Area, PO Box 23800, Doha, Qatar. E-mail: ghel@cowi.com

EL KINAWY Omayma Sayed, b 7 September 1963, Cairo, Egypt. Professor; Researcher. m. Ahmed El Maghraby, 1 son, 2 daughters. Education: BSc, 1985, MSc, 1990, PhD, 1996, Chemical Engineering Department, Faculty of Engineering, Cairo University. Appointments: Research Assistant, 1989-90, Assistant Researcher, 1990-96, Researcher, 1996-2003, Assistant Professor, 2003-10, Research Professor, 2010-, National Research Center, Cairo. Publications: About 30 publications in different fields. Honours: Award in Engineering Science, Academic of Scientific Research and Technology, Egypt, 2004. Memberships: Egyptian Society for Industry Development; Scientific Egyptian Society. Address: National Research Center, El Tahrir Street, Dokki, Cairo, Egypt. E-mail: am_am_ar@yahoo.com

EL-ALFY El-Sayed M, b. 20 February 1968, Egypt. University Professor; Researcher. m. O El-Ghandor, 3 sons, 3 daughters. Education: BSc, Electronics Engineering, Egypt, 1991; MSc, Automatic Control Engineering, Egypt, 1994; MSc, Computer Science, USA, 2001; PhD, Computer Engineering, USA, 2001. Appointments: Research Assistant, College of Engineering, El-Mansoura University, Egypt, 1991-92; Graduate Assistant and Affiliated Instructor, 1992-97, Assistant Professor, 2002-04, College of Engineering, Tanta University, Egypt; Web Editor Assistant, Elsevier Engineering Information Inc, New Jersey, USA, 1997-98; Teaching Assistant, 1998-99, Affiliated Instructor, 1999-2001, Postdoctoral Fellow, 2001-02, Stevens Institute of Technology, NJ, USA; Member of Technical Staff, Bell Labs Innovations, Network Planning Solutions, Lucent Technologies, USA, 2001; Adjunct Assistant Professor, Delta Academy for Science, El-Mansoura, Egypt, 2003-04; Assistant Professor, 2004-10, Associate Professor, 2010-, College of Computer Sciences and Engineering, King Fahd University of Petroleum & Minerals. Publications: Numerous articles in professional journals. Honours: Outstanding Student Certificate of Honour, El-Mansoura Governorate, 1985; 5 times winner, Outstanding Student Certificate, El-Mansoura University, 1986-91; Mansoura University Scholarship for Master's degree, 1991; Distinguished Graduate Award, Egyptian Syndicate of Engineers, 1991; Distinguished Student Certificate, El-Mansoura University, 1992; Certificate of Appreciation, TOEFL Computer Familiarity Study Summer, 1996; Egyptian Governmental Scholarship for PhD, 1997-2001; Letter of Appreciation for Distinguished Performance, 2004-07, Development Program certificate, 2007, King Fahd University of Petroleum & Minerals; Excellence in Teaching Award, King Fahd University of Petroleum & Minerals, 2011; Listed in international biographical dictionaries. Memberships: IEEE; ACM; ACS; ARISE; ICST; CISTC; ADPRL; IJAST; IJCI; IJCSE. Address: College of Computer Sciences & Engineering, King Fahd University of Petroleum & Minerals, PO Box 371, Dhahran 31261, Saudi Arabia. E-mail: alfy@ieee.org Website: http://faculty.kfupm.edu.sa/ics/alfy/

EL-ALFY Taha, b. 7 May 1941, Kaliobia, Egypt. Professor. m. Ekhlass Youssef Ibrahiam, 1 son, 1 daughter. Education: BSc, Pharmaceutical Chemistry, 1962, MSc, Pharmacognosy, 1968, PhD, Phytochemistry, 1971, Faculty of Pharmacy, Cairo University, Egypt. Appointments: Professor, Pharmacognosy, Faculty of Pharmacy, Cairo University, Egypt; Scientific Consultant, Ottoman Royal for Herbs, Sekem Company, El Kahira Company & Misr Company for Pharmaceutical Products; Head, Pharmaceutical Chemistry Department, Jordan University for Women. Publications: Over 120 publications including: Anti-hepatotoxic activity of aqueous extract of Capparis Planta Medica, 1988; Quaternary ammonium compounds in intact plants & cell suspension cultures of Atriplex semibaccata & A halimus during osmotic stress phytochemistry, 1992-; Two novel acylated flavonol glycosides from platanus orientalis, NPC, 2008; Formulation and evaluation of leaf ext of Zizyphus Spina-christi Pharmazie, 2009; Phytochemical & biological investigation of the extracts of Nigella satira seed waste Drug Testing & Analysis, 2010. Honours: Hifny Saber Prize; Listed in international biographical dictionaries. Address: Ali Abd El-Razek st, No 31, Nozha, Heliopolis, Cairo, Egypt. E-mail: tahaelalfy@yahoo.com

EL-BAHRAWY Mona Ahmed, b. 25 February 1967, Egypt. Consultant; Senior Lecturer. m. 2 sons. Education: MBBCh, 1989, MSc, Pathology, 1995, University of Alexandria, Egypt; PhD, Imperial College, University of London, England, 2002. Appointments: House Officer, Alexandria University Hospitals, 1990-91; Registrar, Demonstrator, 1991-96, Assistant Lecturer, 1996-97, Department of Pathology, University of Alexandria; Specialist Registrar, North Thames Region, London, 2001-04; Locum Consultant, Department of Histopathology, Charing Cross Hospital, 2004-05; Locum Consultant, Department of Histopathology, Whipps Cross University Hospital, 2005; Consultant Histopathologist and Honorary Clinical Senior Lecturer, Department of Histopathology, Imperial College, London, 2005-. Publications: Numerous articles in professional journals. Honours: Professor Abdel Wahab Sorour Award,

1985; Professor Ahmed Abdel Razek Saad Award, 1989; Professor Nabil Amin Ragheb Award, 1989; Professor Wedad Mohammed Reyad Award, 1995; Best Presentation, Meeting of British Association of Dermatopathologists, 2002; President's Prize, Royal Society of Medicine, 2002; Listed in international biographical dictionaries. Memberships: Member, 2003, Fellow, 2008, Royal College of Pathologists. Address: Department of Histopathology, Hammersmith Hospital, DuCane Road, London W12 0NN, England. E-mail: m.elbahrawy@imperial.ac.uk

EL-FAR Mohamed, b. 15 January 1953, Mansoura, Egypt. Professor; Head of Division. m. Hala Etman, 1 son, 2 daughters. Appointments: Demonstrator, 1974-77, Assistant Lecturer, 1977-81, Lecturer, Biochemistry, 1981-87, Associate Professor, 1987-94, Professor and Head, Biochemistry Division, 1994-, Faculty of Science, Mansoura University. Publications: More than 50 articles in professional journals. Honours: Visiting Professor: University of California, USA; Munchen, Germany; Cardiff University, UK. Memberships: International Photodynamic Association; Royal Society of Chemistry, England; New York Academy of Science, USA. Address: Faculty of Science, Chemistry Department, Mansoura University, Mansoura, Egypt.

EL-GOHARY Mohammed, b. 10 May 1968, Zifta, El-Gharbia, Egypt. Professor. m. M A Mervat, 3 sons. Education: BA, Conservation of Archaeological Materials, 1990, MSc, Conservation of Stones & Archaeological Sites, 1996, Cairo University; PhD, Conservation of Stones & Archaeological Sites, Cairo University and Rome University, 2000. Appointments: Demonstrator, 1992-96, Assistant Lecturer, 1996-2000, Conservation Department, Assiute University, Egypt; Lecturer, 2005-10, Assistant Professor, 2005-10, Director, Archaeological & Conservation Sciences, 2008-, Full Professor, 2010-, Conservation Department, Sohag University, Egypt. Publications: 5 books; 20 articles. Honous: Listed in biographical dictionaries. Memberships: Postgraduate Studies & Researches Board, Sohag University; Conservation Plan of Sammad Village, Jordan; Association of the Arabian Archaeologists; Conservation Project of Red Monastery; Egypt and Greece Civilizations Committee. Address: Sohag University, El-Nile St, Postal Code 82524, Sohag, Egypt. E-mail: m_1968_algohary@yahoo.com

EL-SHARKAWY Mabrouk A, b. 7 April 1937, Shobratana, Gharbia Governate, Egypt. Scientist. m. Stella Navarro, 1 daughter. Education: BSc honours, Agriculture, Alexandria University, Egypt, 1958; Research Assistant, National Research Centre, Dokki, Cairo, 1958-60; Graduate Student, Louisiana State University and University of Arizona, 1960-65; MSc, Agronomy, Louisiana State University, 1962; PhD, Agronomy, University of Arizona, 1965. Appointments: Associate Plant Physiologist, University of California at Davis, 1965-66; Crop Physiologist, Ministry of Agriculture, Cairo, 1966-68; Professor, University of Tripoli, Libya, 1968-78; Head, Agronomy Division, Faculty of Agriculture, 1972-75; Head, Plant Production, Arab Organization of Agricultural Development, 1978-80; Crop Physiologist, Centro Internacional de Agric Tropical, Cali, Colombia, 1980-97; Co-ordinator and Manager of Integrated Cassava Production Project, 1988-96; Discovered C3/C4 Syndrome in plant photosynthesis, farming sandy soil; Discovery leaf Kranz anatomy and photorespiration reassimilation in C4 photosynthesis species including maize, tropical grasses, amaranthus species; Physiological characteristics cassava productivity in tropics; Discovered mechanisms underlying resistance of cassava to atmospheric and edaphic water-stress; Selection of cassava cultivars drought and poor soils resistant; Integrated cassava production systems in hillside and marginal lands; Characterisation of cassava germ plasm for leaf photosynthesis in relation to crop productivity in humid, seasonally dry and semi-arid environment; Characterisation of cotton germ plasm for leaf photosynthesis; Genetic inheritance of fibre traits in upland cotton; Selection of wheat and barley cultivars for desert conditions; Research on cropping systems, irrigation and plant-soil relationships in Libyan Sahara Desert; Developed method to measure plant photorespiration in CO_2-free air now in use; Developed photosynthesis-based biochemical assay for drought tolerance in Cassava; Scientific advisor, centro de investigacion en Palma de Aceite, Cenipalma, Bogota, Colombia, 1997-2001. Publications: Over 150 in professional journals. Honours: University of Alexandria fellow, 1955-58; University of California fellow, 1965-66; Egyptian Government Scholar, 1959-65; Recipient, Citation Classic Award, Institute of Scientific Information, PA, USA, 1986; Over 1,000 citations in literature, Citation Index ISI; Recognition awards: Universidad Nacional, Palmira,Valle, Colombia, 2005; Universidad del Valle, Cali, Valle, Colombia, 2005; Centro Investigacion, Palmira CORPOICA, Valle, Cali, Colombia, 2005. Memberships: Sigma Xi; New York Academy of Sciences; American Society of Agronomy; Crop Science Society of America; AAAS; American Institute of Biological Sciences, Alpha Zeta. Address: A A 26360 Cali Valle, Colombia, South America. E-mail: mabrouk99@hotmail.com

ELAD-BOUSKILA Ami, b. 7 February 1950, Israel. Professor of Arabic Literature. m. Osnat, 2 sons, 1 daughter. Education: BA, Arabic Language and Literature and Middle East Studies, 1976, MA, Arabic Language and Literature, 1981, PhD, Arabic Literature, 1986, The Hebrew University of Jerusalem. Appointments: Teacher, primary and secondary schools, 1977-79; Lecturer, Modern Arabic Literature, The Hebrew University of Jerusalem, 1979-86; Chair, Arabic Department, 1993-96, 1998-2003, Chair Arabic Translation Track, 1994-96, Beit Berl College. Publications: Numerous books, book chapters and articles in professional journals. Honours: Michael Landou Scholarship, 1981; The Jerusalem Institute for Israel Studies, 1993-94; The Israeli Junior Visiting Fellow, St Antony's College, England, 1997-98; The Research Committee of Beit Berl College, 1999-2002; The Tami Steinmetz Centre for Peace Research, Tel Aviv University, 2001-03; Skirball Visiting Fellowship, Oxford Centre for Hebrew and Jewish Studies, Oxford, England, 2002. Memberships: Beit Berl Senate; Academic Institute for Training Arab Teacher, Beit Berl College. Address: 3 Ein Rogel Street, Abu-Tor, Jerusalem, 93543, Israel. E-mail: amibous@hotmail.com

ELBERN Victor H, b. 9 June 1918, Düren, Germany. Art Historian. m. Theresia Schager, 2 sons, 1 daughter. Education: University of Bonn; Bacc Phil, Rome Gregorian University; Dr phil, Zurich University; Studies in Philosophy, History, Classical Archaeology, Roman Languages, History of Art. Appointments: Chief Curator, State Museums of Berlin, Early Christian and Byzantine Department; International Exhibitions: Essen, 1956, Brussels Expo, 1958; Honorary Professor, History of Art, Free University, Berlin, 1970; Chairman, Görres-Gesellschaft, 1982-93; Director, Jerusalem Institute Görres-Gesellschaft, 1987-93; Visiting Professor: Tel-Aviv University, 1979, Zurich University, 1983, Jerusalem Hebrew University, 1983. Publications: Der Goldaltar von Mailand, 1952; Das erste Jahrtausend, 3 volumes, 1962-64; Der eucharistische Kelch in frühen Mittelalter, 1964; St Liudger und die Abtei Werden, 1962; Dom und Domschatz in Hildesheim, 1979; Die Goldschmiedekunst in frühen Mittelalter, 1988; Fructus Operis, Gesammelte Aufsätze, 1998; Fructus Operis II, Beiträge liturgische Kunst, 2003; Fructus Operis III, Ausgewählte kunsthistorische Schriften aus den Jahren 1961-2007, 2008; About 500 articles. Honours: Chevalier Couronne de Belgique, 1958; Cavaliere San Silvestro, 1958; Commendatore S Gregorio Magno, 1981; Bundesverdienstkreuz Deutschland, 1983; Grand Officer, Holy Sepulchre, 1990; Silver Palm of Jerusalem, 1998. Memberships: Société des Antiquaires, Poitiers, 1961; Deutsches Archäologisches Institut, 1980; Braunschweig Wiss Gesellschaft, 1984; Accademia Nazionale dei Lincei Roma, 1988. Address: Ilsensteinweg 42, D-14129 Berlin, Germany.

ELDRIDGE Colin Clifford, b. 16 May 1942, Walthamstow, England. Professor of History; Writer. m. Ruth Margaret Evans, 1970, deceased 2003, 1 daughter. Education: BA, 1963, PhD, 1966, Nottingham University. Appointments: Arts & Social Science Research Fellow, 1966-68, Lecturer, 1968-75, Senior Lecturer in History, 1975-92, Reader, 1992-98, Professor, 1998-, University of Wales. Publications: England's Mission: The Imperial Idea in the Age of Gladstone and Disraeli, 1973; Victorian Imperialism, 1978; Essays in Honour of C D Chandaman, 1980; British Imperialism in the 19th Century, 1984; Empire, Politics and Popular Culture, 1989; From Rebellion to Patriation: Canada & Britain in the Nineteenth & Twentieth Centuries, 1989; Disraeli and the Rise of a New Imperialism, 1996; The Imperial Experience: From Carlyle to Forster, 1996; The Zulu War, 1879, 1996; Kith and Kin: Canada, Britain and the United States form the Revolution to the Cold War, 1997. Contributions to: Various learned journals. Honour: Fellow, Royal Historical Society. Memberships: Historical Association; Association of History Teachers in Wales; British Association of Canadian Studies; British Australian Studies Association. Address: Tanerdy, Ciliau Aeron, Lampeter, Ceredigion, SA48 8DL, Wales.

ELFMAN Danny, b. 29 May 1953, USA. Composer; Musician (guitar); Vocalist. Career: Lead singer, songwriter, guitarist, band Oingo Boingo; Compositions: Film scores: Pee-Wee's Big Adventure; Beetlejuice; Batman; Batman Returns; Dick Tracy; Darkman; Edward Scissorhands; Sommersby; Other music for films includes: Weird Science; Ghostbusters II; Something Wild; Television series score: The Simpsons. Recordings: Albums: with Oingo Boingo: Only A Lad, 1981; Nothing To Fear, 1982; Good For Your Soul, 1983; Dead Man's Party, 1985; Boingo, 1986; Skeletons In The Closet, 1989; Dark At The End Of The Tunnel, 1990; Article 99, 1992; Batman Returns, 1992; Dolores Claiborne, 1995; Mission Impossible, 1996. Honour: BMI Film and TV Awards, 1987, 1989, 1990-91, 1993, 1996-98, 2000-5, 2008-9; Emmy Award, 2005. Address: c/o L A Personal Development, 950 N. Kings Road, Suite 266, West Hollywood, CA 90069, USA.

ELIAS Kenneth Stuart, b. 9 November 1944, Glynneath, West Glamorgan, Wales. Artist. Education: Cardiff College of Art, 1965-66; BA (Hons), Fine Art, Newport College of Art and Design, 1969; PGCE, University of Wales, Cardiff, 1970; MA, Fine Art, University of Wales, Institute College, Cardiff, 1987. Appointments: Artist; Solo and group exhibitions in UK, Belgium, France, Germany, Lithuania and USA, 1970-; Work represented in private and public collections including: National Museum of Wales; The National Library of Wales; The Arts Council of Wales; Contemporary Art Society of Wales; Editions Alecto; Newport Museum and Art Gallery; University of Glamorgan; University of Wales, Aberystwyth; Bangor College, Normal; Carmarthen County Museum; West Wales Arts Association; Brecknock Musem and Art Gallery.

Publications: Numerous articles in professional journals; Monograph, Ken Elisas: Thin Partitions, 2009. Honours: Welsh Arts Council Award, 1978; Welsh Arts Council Editions Alecto Award, 1978; Second Prizewinner, Wales Open, 1989; Prizewinner, The Watercolour Society of Wales Open, 1996; Prizewinner, Aspects of Wales. Memberships: Royal Cambrian Academician; Member, Welsh Group; Member, 56 Group Wales. Address: 29 Park Avenue, Glynneath, West Glamorgan SA11 5DP, Wales.

ELIASSON Jan, b. 1940, Göteborg, Sweden. Ambassador; Minister for Foreign Affairs in Sweden; President of the 60th session by the General Assembly of the UN. m. Kerstin, 1 son, 2 daughters. Education: Exchange Student, Indiana, USA, 1957-58; Graduate, Swedish Naval Academy, 1962; Master's degree, Economics, 1965. Appointments: Part of UN mission mediating in the war between Iran and Iraq, 1980-86; Diplomatic Advisor to Swedish Prime Minister, 1982-83; Director General for Political Affairs, Ministry for Foreign Affairs, 1983-87; Secretary-General's Personal Representative on Iran/Iraq, 1988-92; Sweden's Ambassador to the UN in New York, 1988-92; Chairman, UN Trust Fund for South Africa, 1988-92; Chairman, UN General Assembly's working group on emergency relief, 1991; Vice President of ECOSOC, 1991-92; Appointed first Under-Secretary-General for Humanitarian Affairs of the UN, 1992; Mediator, Nagorno Karabakh conflict for the OSCE; Visiting professor, Uppsala University, Sweden; State Secretary for Foreign Affairs, 1994-2000; Sweden's Ambassador to the US, 2000-05; Elected President of the 60th session by the General Assembly of the UN, 2005; Minister for Foreign Affairs in Sweden, 2006; Special Envoy of the UN for Darfur, 2007-08; International Adviser, ICRC, 2008-11; Chairman, Water Aid, Sweden, 2009-. Publications: Author and co-author of numerous books, articles and frequent lecturer on foreign policy and diplomacy. Honours: Honorary Doctorate degrees: American University of Washington DC; Göteborg University, Uppsala University, Sweden; Bethany College, Kansas; California Lutheran University, California; Decorated by numerous governments. Address: Stockbyvagen 15, 18278 Stocksund, Sweden.

ELIZABETH II (Elizabeth Alexandra Mary), Queen of Great Britain and Northern Ireland and of Her other Realms and Territories, Head of the Commonwealth, Defender of the Faith, b. 21 April 1926, London, England. m. HRH The Prince Philip, Duke of Edinburgh, 3 sons, 1 daughter. Education: Private. Appointments: Subaltern then Junior Commander ATS, LG 1947, Lord High Admiral of the United Kingdom; Proclaimed Queen, 8 February 1952, crowned Westminster Abbey, 2 June 1953; Colonel-in-Chief (UK): Life Guards, 1952-, Blues and Royals, 1969-, Royal Scots Dragoon Guards, 1971-, Queen's Royal Lancers, 1993-, Royal Tank Regiment, 1953-, RE, 1952-, Grenadier Guards, 1952-, Coldstream Guards, 1952-, Scots Guards, 1952-, Irish Guards, 1952-, Welsh Guards, 1952-, Royal Welsh Fusiliers, 1953, The Royal Welsh, 2006-, The Royal Regiment of Scotland, 2006-, The Duke of Lancasters Regiment, 2006-, Adj General's Corps, 1992-, Royal mercian and Lancastrian Yeomanry, 1994-; Colonel-in Chief (Commonwealth): Governor General's Horse Guards (Canada), 1953-, Canadian Forces Military Engineers Branch, 1977-, King's Own Calgary Regiment, 1953-, Royal 22e Regiment (Canada), 1953-, Governor-General's Foot Guards (Canada), 1953-, Canadian Grenadier Guards, 1953-, Le Régiment de la Chaudière (Canada), 1947-, Royal New Brunswick Regiment, 1956-, 48 Highlanders Canada, 1947-, Argyll and Sutherland Highlanders Canada (Princess Louise's), 1950-, Royal

Canadian Ordnance Corps, 1958-, Calgary Highlanders, 1981-, Royal Australian Engineers, 1953-, Royal Australian Infantry Corps, 1953-, Royal Australian Army Ordnance Corps, 1953-, Royal Australian Army Nursing Corps, 1953-, Corps of Royal New Zealand Engineers, 1953-, Royal New Zealand Infantry Regiment, 1964-, Malawi Rifles, 1964-; Affiliated Colonel-in-Chief Queen's Gurkha Engineers; Royal Colonel The Argyll and Sutherland Highlanders 8th Battalion, Royal Regiment of Scotland, 2006-; Captain-General: RA, 1952-, HAC, 1952-, CCF, 1953-, Royal Regiment of Canadian Artillery, 1952-, Royal Regiment of Australian Artillery, 1953- , Royal Regiment of New Zealand Artillery, 1953-, Royal New Zealand Armoured Corps, 1953-; Patron, Royal Army Chaplains' Department; Air Commandore-in-Chief: RAuxAF, RAF Regiment, Air Reserve Canada, RAAF Reserve, Territorial Air Force (New Zealand); Commander-in-Chief, RAF College Cranwell; Royal Honorary Air Commodore: RAF Marham, 603 Squadron RAuxAF; Sovereign of all British Order of Knighthood, Order of Merit, Royal Order of Victoria and Albert, Order of Crown of India, Order of Companions of Honour, Order of Canada, Distinguished Service Order and Imperial Service Order; Sovereign Head of Order of Hospital of St John of Jerusalem, Order of Australia and Queen's Service Order of New Zealand; Freedom: City of London, Edinburgh, 1947; FRS, 1947; Racehorse owner; Cartier Millennium Award, 2000. Address: Buckingham Palace, London SW1A 1AA, England.

ELKANZI Nadia Ali Ahmed, b. 20 November 1972, Aswan, Egypt. Lecturer. m. Magdy Mohamed Hussein, 1 son. Education: PhD, Organic Chemistry, South Vally University, Aswan, 2003. Appointments: Lecturer, Organic Chemistry, South Vally University. Publications: Studies on fused azoles: synthesis of several poly functionally. Address: Faculty of Science, Chemistry Department, South Vally University, Aswan, Egypt. E-mail: kanzi2nour@yahoo.com

ELLIOTT Sir John Huxtable, b. 23 June 1930, Reading, Berkshire, England. Historian. m. Oonah Sophia Butler. Education: BA, 1952, MA, 1955, PhD, 1955, Cambridge University. Appointments: Lecturer in History and Fellow, Trinity College, Cambridge, 1957-67; Professor of History, King's College, London, 1968-73; Professor, School of Historical Studies, Institute for Advanced Study, Princeton, USA, 1973-90; Regius Professor of Modern History and Fellow of Oriel College, Oxford University, 1990-97. Publications include: The Revolt of the Catalans, 1963; Imperial Spain, 1963; Europe Divided, 1968; The Old World and the New, 1970; A Palace for a King (with Jonathan Brown), 1980; Richelieu and Olivares, 1984; The Count-Duke of Olivares, 1986; Spain and Its World, 1989; Empires of the Atlantic World, 2006; Spain, Europe and the Wider World, 2009. Honours: Grand Cross Order of Alfonso X, 1988; FBA, 1992; Kt, 1994; Prince of Asturias Prize, 1996; Grand Cross Order of Isabel la Católica, 1996; Wolfson Prize, 1986; Balzan Prize for History, 1999; Francis Parkman Prize, 2007; Honorary Doctorates: Madrid (Autónoma); Madrid (Complutense); Genoa; Barcelona; Portsmouth; Valencia; Lleida; Warwick; Brown; College of William and Mary, London; Honorary Fellow: Trinity College, Cambridge; Oriel College, Oxford. Memberships: British Academy; American Philosophical Society; American Academy of Arts and Sciences; Accademia dei Lincei. Address: Oriel College, Oxford OX1 4EW, England.

ELLIS Royston, b. 10 February 1941, Pinner, England. Author. 1 son. Career: Author; Poet; Travel Writer. Publications: Fiction: (as Royston Ellis) Myself for Fame, 1963; The Flesh Merchants, 1966; The Rush at the End, 1967; A Hero in Time, 2000; (as Richard Tresillian) The Bondmaster, 1977; Blood of the Bondmaster, 1978; The Bondmaster Breed, 1979; Fleur, 1979; Bondmaster Fury, 1982; Bondmaster Revenge, 1983; Bondmaster Buck, 1984; Bloodheart, 1985; Bloodheart Royal, 1986; Bloodheart Feud, 1987; Giselle, 1988; (as Raynard Devine) Master of Black River, 1984; Black River Affair, 1985; Black River Breed, 1985; Biographies: Driftin' with Cliff Richard, 1960; Rebel, the story of James Dean, 1961; The Big Beat Scene, 1961; The Shadows by Themselves, 1961; A Man for All Islands – President Gayoom of Maldives, 1998; Toni, the Maldives Lady, 1999; Travel: India by Rail, 1989, 1992, 1995; Bradt Guide to Mauritius, 1988-2008; History of the Grand Hotel, 1991; History of the Tea Factory Hotel, 1993; Sri Lanka by Rail, 1994; Bradt Guide to Maldives, 1995, 2000, 2005, 2008, 2011; A Maldives Celebration, 1998; Festivals of the World: Trinidad, 1999; Festivals of the World: Madagascar, 1999; The Sri Lanka Story, 1998, 2002; Bradt Guide to Sri Lanka, 2000, 2005, 2008; Story of Full Moon, 2003; Story of Baros, 2004; The Growing Years – History of the Ceylon Planters' Association, 2004; Indian Railways Handbook, 2008; Berlitz Pocket Guide to Maldives, 2007; Sri Lanka Step By Step, 2010; Beat: The Collected Poems, 2011; Poetry: Jiving to Gyp, 1959; Rave, 1960; The Rainbow Walking Stick, 1961; A Seaman's Suitcase, 1963; The Cherry Boy, 1966; Contributions to UK newspapers and magazines, and world's inflight magazines. Honours: Dukedom of Gypino y Tintinabulation de Redonda; Warden, British High Commission, Southern Province of Sri Lanka. Address: Horizon Cottage, Kaikawala, Induruwa, Sri Lanka.

ELLIS Harold, b. 13 January 1926, London, England. Professor of Surgery. m. Wendy Levine, 1 son, 1 daughter. Education: BM BCh, University of Oxford, 1948; FRCS, 1951; MCh, 1956; DM, 1962. Appointments: Resident appointments in: Oxford, Sheffield, Northampton and London, 1948-60; RAMC (Graded Surgical Specialist), 1950-51; Senior Lecturer in Surgery, 1960-62, Professor of Surgery, 1962-89, Westminster Medical School; Professor Emeritus, University of London, 1989; Clinical Anatomist, University of Cambridge, 1989-93; Clinical Anatomist, United Medical and Dental School, Guy's Campus (now School of Biomedical Sciences, King's College, Guy's Campus), 1993-. Publications: 25 books include most recently: Clinical Anatomy for Laparoscopic and Thoracoscopic Surgery, 1995; Gray's Anatomy (38th edition) Section Editor, 1995; Operations That Made History, 1996; Index to Differential Diagnosis, 1996; Index of Surgical Differential Diagnosis, 1999; Applied Radiological Anatomy, 1999; A History of Surgery, 2000; Numerous book chapters and articles in medical journals. Honours include: CBE, 1987; Honorary, FACS, 1989; Honorary Fellow, Royal Society of Medicine, 1996; Honorary Gold Medal, Royal College of Surgeons of England. Memberships: President, Armed Services Combined Assessment Board in Surgery; Honorary Freeman, Company of Barbers. Address: 16 Bancroft Avenue, London N2 0AS, England.

ELLIS John Norman, b. 22 February 1939, Leeds, England. Employment Law Consultant. m. 1 son, 2 stepsons, 1 daughter. Appointments: Civil Servant, 1954-68; Trade Union Full Time Officer, 1968-95; Deputy General Secretary, 1982-86, General Secretary, 1986-92, CPSA: Secretary General Council of Civil Service Unions, 1992-1995; Panel Member, Employment Tribunal, 1992; Associate Consultant & Chairman, Talking People, an ACS Company. Publications: Published 36 editions of the National Whitley Bulletin, 1992-95; Articles in the Public Policy and Administration

Journal. Honours: OBE for services to industrial relations, 1995. Memberships: Labour Party; Civil Service Pensioners' Alliance; Institute of Employment Right; Chairman, Tandridge Leisure Ltd. Address: 26 Harestone Valley Road, Caterham, Surrey CR3 6HD, England. E-mail: johnellis60@aol.com

ELLIS Richard Mackay, b. 9 July 1941, Chalfont St Peter, England. Consultant Physician. m. Gillian Ann Cole, 1 son, 1 daughter. Education: Wellington College; MB BChir, Clare College, Cambridge, 1965; St Thomas's Hospital Medical School, London; MD, New York, 1982. Appointments: Senior Lecturer in Rheumatology, University of Southampton, 1980; Consultant in Rheumatology and Rehabilitation, Salisbury District Hospital, 1980; Director, Wessex Rehabilitation Unit, Salisbury, 1989; Editor-in-Chief, International Musculoskeletal Medicine, 2008. Publications: Co-editor, Textbook of Musculoskeletal Medicine, 2005. Memberships: Fellow, Royal College of Surgeons, London, 1971; Editor, Journal of Orthopaedic Medicine, 1985; Fellow, Royal College of Physicians, London, 1988; Council Member, British Institute of Musculoskeletal Medicine, 1990; Convenor, Examining Board for Diploma in Musculoskeletal Medicine, Society of Apothecaries of London, 1998; Honorary President, Society of Orthopaedic Medicine, 2000. Address: 161 Bouverie Avenue, Salisbury, Wiltshire SP2 8EB, England.

ELS Ernie, b. 17 October 1969, Johannesburg, South Africa. Professional Golfer. m. Leizl, 1 son, 1 daughter. Career: Professional, 1989-; Winner, US Open, 1994, 1997; Toyota World Matchplay Championships, 1994, 1995, 1996; South Africa PGA Championship, 1995; Byron Nelson Classic, 1995; Buick Classic, 1996, 1997; Johnny Walker Classic, 1997; Bay Hill Invitational, 1998; Nissan Open, 1999; Int presented by Quest 2000; Standard Life Loch Lomond, 2000; Open Championship, 2002; Genuity Championship, 2002; British Open, 2002; Sixth World Match Play title, 2004; Mercedes Championship, 2003; Member, Dunhill Cup Team, 1992-2000; World Cup Team, 1992, 1993, 1996, 1997, 2001; Member, President's Cup, 1996, 1998, 2000; Founder, Ernie Els & Fancourt Foundation, 1999; Founder, The Els for Autism Foundation, 2009. Honour: South African Sportsman of Year, 1995. Address: 46 Chapman Road, Klippoortjie 1401, South Africa.

ELSAYED Khairy, b. 20 October 1975, Cairo, Egypt. Researcher. m. Rania Abd Elati, 2 sons. Education: PhD, Mechanical Engineering, Vrije Universiteit Brussel, 2011. Appointments: Postdoctoral Researcher, Vrije Universiteit Brussel. Publications: Numerous articles in professional journals. Honours: Listed in biographical dictionaries. Address: Department of Mechanical Engineering, Faculty of Engineering, Vrije Universiteit Brussel, Pleinlaan 2, 1050 Brussels, Belgium. E-mail: kelsayed@vub.ac.be

ELSTEIN Cecile Hoberman, b. 8 February 1938, Cape Town, South Africa. Sculptor; Printmaker; Environmental Artist. m. Max Elstein, 1 son (deceased), 1 daughter. Education: Self-directed part-time study in Cape Town: portrait sculpture with Nel Kaye, sculpture with Mitford-Barbaton and Lippy Lipshitz, Michaelis School of Art, Cape Town, 1956-61; Self-directed part-time study in London: painting with Hans Swartz, colour with Tom Hudson, Royal College of Art, drawing with Beatrice Lyssy, 1961-69; Studied ceramics with Catherine Yarrow, 1965-69; Studied sculpture, West Surrey College of Art, 1975-77, tutor Ian Walters. Career: Constructed sculpture for landscape, in wood designed for disabled children; Screen prints with Kip Gresham, 1979-91; Exhibition titled "A Printmaking Partnership", Whitworth Art Gallery, Manchester, 1991; Sculpture, "Song of the Pine's Sun", 1991; MA, Art as Environment, Manchester Metropolitan University, 1994-96; Sculpture, "Together with Tangents", for landscape of Wimpole Hall Gardens, Cambridge, 1996; Video direction and DVD production, "Tangents, a mindscape in a landscape", 2004; Solo and group exhibitions of prints, drawing and sculpture in UK and abroad, 1965-2010; Commissions: Portrait Bronzes, 1959-2009; Michael Kennedy, author and music critic, 2005; Memory of Paul, 2008; Portrait bronze, Max Elstein, 2009; Sundial project in collaboration with Tam Giles for the Marie Louise Gardens, Manchester, 2010; "House of Light and Air", screen print in process. Publications: Co-production Cecile Elstein and Maureen Kendal "Tangents, a mindscape in a landscape" DVD with companion booklet, 2004; Included in, A Colourful Canvas, 12 Women Artists in the North West, Judy Rose and Wendy J Levy, 2006. Awards: Bursary, North West Arts, 1984; Sericol Colour Prize, 9th British International Print Biennale, 1986. Memberships: Elected Member, MAFA; Elected Fellow, RSA, 1997; Member, Public Monument and Sculpture Association, Landscape and Arts Network. Address: 25 Spath Road, Didsbury, Manchester M20 2QT, England. E-mail: cecile@cecileelstein.com. Website: www.cecileelstein.com

ELTIS Walter (Alfred), b. 23 May 1933, Warnsdorf, Czechoslovakia. Economist. m. Shelagh Mary Owen, 5 September 1959, 1 son, 2 daughters. Education: Emmanuel College, Cambridge; BA, Cambridge University; MA, Nuffield College, 1960; DLitt, Oxford University, 1990. Appointments: Fellow, Tutor, Economics, 1963-88, Emeritus Fellow, 1988-, Exeter College, Oxford; Director General, National Economic Development Office, London, 1988-92; Chief Economic Adviser to the President of the Board of Trade, 1992-95; Visiting Professor, 1992-2004, University of Reading. Publications: Growth and Distribution, 1973; Britain's Economic Problem: Too Few Producers (with Robert Bacon), 1976; The Classical Theory of Economic Growth, 1984 (2nd Edition, Palgrave 2000); Keynes and Economic Policy (with Peter Sinclair), 1988; Classical Economics, Public Expenditure and Growth, 1993; Britain's Economic Problem Revisited, 1996; Condillac, Commerce and Government (editor, with Shelagh M Eltis), 1997; Britain, Europe and EMU, 2000. Contributions to: Economic journals and bank reviews. Memberships: Reform Club, chairman, 1994-95; Political Economy Club; Vice President, European Society for the History of Economic Thought, 2000-04. Address: Danesway, Jarn Way, Boars Hill, Oxford OX1 5JF, England.

ELTON Ben(jamin Charles), b. 3 May 1959, England. Writer; Comedian. m. Sophie Gare, 3 children. Education: BA, Drama, University of Manchester. Appointments: Writer, TV series and for British Comedians; Stand-up Comedian: Tours, 1986, 1987, 1989, 1993, 1996, 1997; Host, Friday Night Live, TV Comedy Showcase, 1986-88; Co-writer, Presenter, South of Watford (documentary TV series), 1982; Writer/Director, Inconceivable, film, 2000. Publications: Bachelor Boys, 1984; Stark, 1989; Gridlock, 1991; This Other Eden, 1993; Popcorn, 1996; Blast from the Past, 1998; Inconceivable, 1999; Dead Famous, 2001; High Society, 2002; Past Mortem, 2004; The First Casualty, 2005; Chart Throb, 2006; Plays: Gasping, 1990; Silly Cow, 1991; Popcorn, 1996; Blast from the Past, 1998; The Beautiful Game, musical, book and lyrics, 2000; Maybe Baby, writer/director, feature film, 2000; High Society, 2002; We Will Rock You, musical, 2002; Tonight's the Night, 2003; Other: Recordings, The Young Ones, 1982; Happy Families, 1985; Blackadder, 1985, 1987, 1989; Filthy Rich and Catflap, 1986; Motormouth, 1987; Motovation (album), 1988; The Man From Auntie, 1990, 1994; The Very Best of Ben Elton Live, 1990; A Farties Guide to the Man From Auntie, 1990; Ben Elton Live, 1993; Stark, 1993; The Thin Blue Line (sitcom); 1995, 1996; Ben Elton Live, 1997; The Ben Elton Show, 1999. Honours: Best Comedy Show Awards, Brit Academy, 1984, 1987; BAFTA Award, 1990; Gold Dagger Award, 1996; TMA Award, 1997; Lawrence Olivier Award, 1998. Address: c/o Phil McIntyre, 2nd Floor, 35 Soho Square, London, W1D 3QX, England.

EMANOV Alexander, b. 31 October 1958, Tyumen, Russia. Historian. m. Tatiana, 1 son, 2 daughters. Education: Diploma, 1982, Candidate, Historical Sciences, 1986, S Petersburg University, Russia; Docent's Attestation, 1992, Doctor, Historical Sciences, 1997, Urals University, Ekaterinburg, Russia; Professor's Attestation, 1999. Appointments: Assistant, 1986-89, Docent, 1989-97, Department of General History, Head, Department of Ancient and Middle Ages History, 1998-2009, Director, Information Library Center, 2009-, Tyumen State University. Publications: North and South in the History of Trade, 1995; History of World Civilization, Vol 1-2, 2001; History of World Civilization (pre-Industrial Epoch), DVD-ROM, 2004; Culturology, 2008. Honours: American Medal of Honor, 2003; Distinguished Leadership Award, 2004; Man of the Year, 2005. Memberships: Medieval Academy of America. Address: 10 Semakov St, Tyumen University, 625003 Tyumen, Russia. E-mail: a_emanov@mail.ru

EMANUEL Elizabeth Florence, b. 5 July 1953, London, England. Fashion Designer. m. David Leslie Emanuel, 1975, separated 1990, 1 son, 1 daughter. Education: Harrow College of Art. Appointments: Opened London salon, 1978; Designer, wedding gown for HRH Princess of Wales, 1981; Costumes for Andrew Lloyd Webber's Song and dance, 1982; Sets and costumes for ballet, Frankenstein, The Modern Prometheus, Roy Opera House, London, La Scala Milan, 1985; Costumes for Stoll Moss production of Cinderella, 1985; Costumes for films: Diamond Skulls, 1990; The Changeling, 1995; Uniforms for Virgin Atlantic Airways, 1990; Britannia Airways, 1995; Launched international fashion label Elizabeth Emanuel, 1991; Launched Bridal Collection for Berkertex Brides UK Ltd, 1994; Launched bridal collection in Japan, 1994; Opened new shop and design studio, 1996; Launched own brand label (with Richard Thompson), 1999. Publications: Style for All Seasons (with David Emanuel), 1982. Address: Ground Floor Studio, 23 Warrington Crescent, London, W9 1ED, England.

EMBERSON Ian McDonald, b. 29 July 1936, Hove, Sussex, England. Retired Librarian; Writer and Artist. Publications: Doodles in the Margins of My Life, 1981; Swallows Return, 1986; Pirouette of Earth, a novel in verse, 1995; Natural Light, 1998; The Comet of 1811, 2001; The Snake and the Star, 2003; Pilgrims from Loneliness, an interpretation of Charlotte Brontë's Jane Eyre and Villette, 2005; Messages from Distant Shores, 2006; Yorkshire Lives and Landscapes, 2006; Mourning Ring, 2008; The Zig Zag Path (ebook), 2010; Contributions to: Pennine Platform; Envoi; Orbis; New Hope International; Bradford Poetry Quarterly; Dalesman; Countryman; Acumen; Poetry Scotland; Brontë Studies; IOTA; Poets Voice; Aireings; Pennine Ink. Honour: William Alwyn International Poetry Society Award, 1981. Memberships: Pennine Poets; Brontë Society; Gaskell Society. Address: Eastroyd, 1 Highcroft Road, Todmorden, Lancashire OL14 5LZ, England. Website: www.ianemberson.co.uk

EMERY Alan E H, b. 21 August 1928, Manchester, England. Physician. m. Marcia Lynn Maler, 3 sons, 3 daughters. Education: University of Manchester, England; PhD, Johns Hopkins University, USA. Appointments: Reader, Medicine, Manchester University, 1964-68; Foundation Professor, Human Genetics, Edinburgh University, 1968-83; Research Professor and Fellow, Edinburgh University, 1983-90; Research Director, 1990-2000, Chief Scientific Adviser, 2000-, European Neuro-Muscular Centre; Visiting Professor, Peninsula Medical School, Exeter, 2002-. Publications: Around 300 medical science papers; 21 books. Honours: Various visiting professorships and named lectures; Honorary MD, University of Naples and University of Wurzburg; National Foundation USA, International Award; Gaetano Gold Medal; Honorary Membership or Fellowship: Dutch Society of Human Genetics; Association of British Neurologists; Royal Society of South Africa; Hon MD, Naples, Wurzburg; International Award for Genetic Research, USA; Gaetano Conte Prize for Clinical Research, 2000; Pro Finlandiae Gold Medal for contributions to Neuroscience, 2000; Lifetime Achievement Award, WFN, 2002. Memberships: FRCP; FRCPE; FLS; FRSE. Address: Peninsula Medical School, Department of Neurology, Royal Devon and Exeter Hospital, Exeter EX2 5DW, England.

EMERY Lin, b. New York, USA. Sculptor. m. S Braselman, deceased, 1 son. Education: Sorbonne: Cours de la civilisation française, 1949; Atelier of Ossip Zadkine, Paris, 1950; New York Sculpture Centre, 1952. Appointments: Solo Exhibitions: Retrospective, New Orleans Museum of Art, LA, 1996; Mitsuhashi Gallery & Honen-In Temple, Kyoto, Japan, 1999; Tour, Five Museums in Louisiana State, 2001-03; Arthur Roger Gallery, LA, 2005; Kouros Gallery, NY, 2006; Retrospective, Leepa-Ratner Museum, Tarpon Springs, FL, 2010-11; Arthur Roger Gallery, New Orlean, 2010; Kouros Gallery, New York, 2011; Public Sculptures: G E, Wall Street, NY, 1994; Osaka Dome, Japan, 1997; Izumisano Hospital, Japan, 1997; Sterling Co, Dallas, TX, 1999; Schiffer Publishing, PA, 2000; Federal Aviation Authority, DC, 2001; Renaissance Arts Hotel, LA, 2004; Knight Oil Tool Co, LA, 2006; Terminus, Atlanta, GA, 2009; University of Houston, TX, 2010; Performing Center, Virginia Beach, VA, 2011; LSU Business Center, Baton Rouge, LA, 2012-13; International Kinetic Art Symposium, Boynton Beach, Florida, 2013. Publications: Book, Lin Emery, 2012; Articles in Museums and Art Centres worldwide. Honours include: Mayor's Award for Achievement in the Arts, 1980; Louisiana Women of Achievement Award, 1984; NOCCA Distinguished Louisiana Artist Award, 1988; YWCA Role Model Award, 1989; Lazlo Aranyi Award of Honour for Public Art, 1990; Delgado Society Award for Artistic Excellence, 1997; Osaka Prefecture, Japan, Grand Prix for Public Sculpture, 1998; Governor's Arts Award, 2001; Young Leadership Council, Role Model, New Orleans, 2003; Honorary Doctorate, Loyola University of the South, 2004; Opus Award, Ogden Museum of Southern Art, 2012; Honorary Chair, Art Against Aids Gala, 2012. Memberships: Honorary Associations include: Century Association, New York; National Academy; Royal Society of British Sculptors (International member) Sculptors Guild, New York; International Women's Forum. Address: 7520 Dominican Street, New Orleans, LA 70118-3738 USA. E-mail:lin@linemery.com

EMIN Tracey, b. 3 July 1963, Margate, England. Artist. Education: John Cass School of Art, London; Maidstone College of Art; Royal College of Art. Career: Founder, Tracey Emin Museum, London, 1996; Artist, exhibitions include: White Cube Gallery, London, 1992; Minky Manky, 1995; My Major Retrospective, Part of What Made Me What I Am, Loose Ends, 1998; Personal Effects, 1998; Made in London, 1998; Sweetie, 1999; Temple of Diana, 1999; Now It's My Turn

DICTIONARY OF INTERNATIONAL BIOGRAPHY 36th EDITION

to Scream, 1999; Art in Sacred Places, 2000; What Do You Know About Love, 2000; Commissions: The Roman Standard, BBC for Art05 Festival, London, 2005; Films: Why I Never Became a Dancer; Top Spot, 2004. Publications: Exploration of the Soul, 1995; Always Glad to See You, 1997; Tracey Emin: Holiday Inn, 1998; Tracey Emin on Pandaemonium, 1998; Absolute Tracey, 1998. Honours: International Award for Video Art, Baden-Baden, 1997; Video Art Prize, Suedwest Bank, Stuttgart, 1997; Royal Academician, Royal Academy of Arts, 2007. Address: The Tracey Emin Museum, 221 Waterloo Road, London SE1, England.

EMINEM (Slim Shady) (Marshall Bruce Mathers III), b. 17 October 1972, St Joseph, Missouri, USA. Rap Artist; Musician. m. Kim, 1999, divorced, 1 daughter. Career: Founder and Owner, Slim Shady record label, 1999-; Recordings: Albums: The Infinite, 1997; The Slim Shady LP, 1999; The Marshall Mathers LP, 2000; The Eminem Show, 2002; Eminem is Back, 2004; Encore, 2004; King Mathers, 2007; Relapse, 2009; Relapse 2, 2009; Singles: The Slim Shady EP, 1998; Just Don't Give a F***, 1999; My Name Is, 1999; Guilty Conscience, 1999; The Real Slim Shady, 2000; The Way I Am, 2000; Stan, 2000; Without Me, 2002; Lose Yourself, 2003; Business, 2003; Just Lose It, 2004. Honours: MTV Annual American Music Awards, Best Hip Hop Artist, 2000, 2002; MTV Award, Best Album, 2000; 3 Grammy Awards, 2001; Best Pop/Rock Male Artist, 2002; MTV Awards, Best Album, 2002; MTV Europe Music Awards, Best Male Act, Best Hip Hop Act, 2002; BRIT Award for Best International Male Solo Artist, 2002, 2005; Grammy Award, Best Rap Album, 2003; BRIT Award, Best International Album, 2003; American Music Awards for Best Male Pop/Rock Artist; Best Male Hip Hop/R&B Artist, 2003; Academy Award, Best Music (song in film, 8 Mile), 2004; Grammy Awards, Best Male Rap Solo Performance and Best Rap Song, 2004; Echo Award for Best International Hip Hop Artist, Germany, 2005. Address: c/o William Morris Agency, 1325 Avenue of the Americas, New York, NY 10019, USA. Website: www.eminem.com

EMMERICH Roland, b. 10 November 1955, Stuttgart, Germany. Director; Screenplay Writer; Executive Producer. Education: Film School in Munich. Appointments: Producer (as student) The Noah's Ark Principle, shown at Berlin Film Festival (sold to over 20 countries), 1984; Founder, Centropolis Film Productions; Films: Making Moon 44; Universal Soldier; Stargate; Independence Day; The Thirteenth Floor (producer); The Patriot; Eight Legged Freaks (executive producer), 2002; The Day After Tomorrow (producer), 2004; Trade (producer), 2007; Isobar (writer), 2007; 10,000 BC (producer), 2008; TV series: The Visitor (producer), 1997. Honours: Academy of Science Fiction, Fantasy & Horror Films, Best Director, Godzilla, 1998 and Independence Day, 1996; Address: c/o Creative Artists Agency, 9830 Wilshire Boulevard, Beverly Hills, CA 90212, USA.

EMORI Hideyo, b. 17 September 1959, Tokyo, Japan. Professor. m. Junko Higuchi, 1 son, 1 daughter. Education: Graduate School of Education, 1989-94, PhD, 2003, University of Tsukuba. Appointments: Assistant Professor, 1994-97, Associate Professor, 1997-2000, Kanto Gakuin University, Yokohama; Associate Professor, Utsunomiya University, Tochigi, 2000-05; Visiting Professor, Khon Kaen University, Thailand, 2004-; Associate Professor, 2005-09; Professor, 2009-, Gunma University, Maebashi, Gunma. Publications: The mechanism of communication chain in learning mathematics, 2006. Honours: 1st Best Teacher of Gunma University, 2007; Listed in international biographical dictionaries. E-mail: emori@edu.gunma-u.ac.jp

EMSBACH Michael, b. 26 March 1949, Braunschweig, Germany. Psychologist. Education: PhD, 1979, Diploma, Psychologist, Organizational Scientist, 1982, University of Hamburg; Graduate, Insurance Business Economist, Chamber of Commerce, Hanover, Germany, 1988; 2nd doctoral degree, University of Cologne, 2007. Appointments: Trainer, Allianz Insurance Co, Hamburg, 1983-86; Unternehmensgruppe Gauselmann, Espelkamp, Germany, 1986-88; Christliches Jugenddorfwerk, Hanover, Germany, 1989-92; Federal Traffic Authority, Flensburg, 1993-95; Lecturer, University of Flensburg, 1995-97; Federal Traffic Research Institute, Berg Gladbach, 1997-2001; University of Flensburg, 2001-. Publications: The Sophists' Enlightenment, 1980; Evaluation of a traffic safety campaign, 1998; Contribution of articles to professional journals including: Sozialpaedagogik; Journal for Gerontology and Geriatrics; Perspectives of Traffic Safety Training for Senior Citizens, 2001; Coaching for Children, 2005; Coaching of Women to Avoid Dequalification, 2008; Coaching during vocational orientation, 2008; Marketing of Non-Profit Organizations, 2008; Evaluation of Hospice Movement, 2008; Marketing of Non-Profit-Organizations, 2010; Learning people in learning organizations, 2012. Address: Rheinpromenade 42, 46446 Emmerich, Germany. E-mail: michael.emsbach@imail.de

ENDERBY John Edwin (Sir), b. 16 January 1931, Grimsby, Lincolnshire, England. Physicist. m. Susan, 1 son, 3 daughters. Education: Westminster College, London; BSc, PhD, Birkbeck College, London. Appointments: Professor of Physics and Head of Department, University of Bristol, 1976-96; Vice President, Royal Society, 1999-2004; Chief Scientific Advisor, Institute of Physics Publishing, 2002-; Chairman, Melys Diagnostics Ltd, 2004-; President, Institute of Physics, 2004-06. Publications: Numerous papers and articles in professional journals. Honours: Westminster College Wright Prize, 1953; College Award, 1956; Guthrie Medal, 1995; Hon DSc, Loughborough University, 1996; CBE, 1997; Honorary Fellowship, Birkbeck College, 2000; Knight Bachelor, 2004; Hon DSc, Leicester, 2006; Hon DSc, Bristol, 2006; Hon DSc, Sheffield, 2007; Hon DSc, East Anglia, 2008; Hon DSc, Kent, 2009; Hon D Univ (Huddersfield), 2011. Memberships: Fellow, Institute of Physics; Fellow, Royal Society; Member, Academia Europaea; Athenaeum Club. Address: 7 Cotham Lawn Road, Bristol, BS6 6DU, England.

ENDO Akira, b. 14 November 1933, Japan. Company President. m. Orie Taga, 1 son, 1 daughter. Education: BS, 1957, PhD, 1966, Tohoku University. Appointments: President, Biopharm Research Laboratories Inc, Tokyo, Japan. Publications: The Discovery and Development of HMG-CoA Reductase Inhibitors, 1992. Honours: Japan Prize, 2006; Lasker Clinical Medical Research Award, 2008; Person of Cultural Merit, Japan, 2011. Membership: National Academy of Sciences, USA, 2011. Address: CIIP Building Room 215, TUAT, 2-24-16 Naka-cho, Koganei, Tokyo 184-8588, Japan.

ENDO Hiroshi, b. 29 September 1948, Tokyo, Japan. Professor. m. Seiko, 1 daughter. Education: Master Degree, Tokyo University of Science, 1974; PhD, Mathematics (Differential Geometry), Al I Cuza University, Iasi, 1997. Appointments: Senior High School Teacher, Chiba Prefecture, 1975-97; Associate Professor, Kurashiki City College, 1997-2000; Associate Professor, Tokoha Gakuen University, 2000-02; Professor, Utsunomiya University,

2002-. Publications: On invariant submanifolds of contact metric manifolds, 1985; The part of Bochner curvature tensors, Encyclopaedia of Mathematics, Supplement Vol I, 1997. Memberships: Mathematical Society of Japan; Tensor Society; Society of Finsler Geometry, Japan. E-mail: hsk-endo@cc.utsunomiya-u.ac.jp

ENGLISH Terence Alexander Hawthorne, b. 3 October 1932, Pietermaritzburg, South Africa. Cardiac Surgeon (Retired). m. (1) Ann Margaret Dicey, 2 sons, 2 daughters, (2) Judith Francis Milne. Education: BSc, Engineering, Witwatersrand University, South Africa, 1951-54; MB BS, Guy's Hospital Medical School, 1955-62; FRCS (England and Edinburgh), 1967. Appointments: Surgical training at Brompton and National Heart Hospitals, Senior Registrar; Consultant Cardiothoracic Surgeon, Papworth and Addenbrooke's Hospitals, 1972-95; Performed Britain's first successful heart transplant, 1979; President, Royal College of Surgeons of England, 1989-92; Master, St Catharine's College, Cambridge, 1993-2000; President, British Medical Association, 1995-96. Publications: Principles of Cardiac Diagnosis and Treatment, 2nd edition, 1992; 23 contributions to chapters in books; 118 peer-reviewed articles mainly on surgery and cardiac transplantation. Honours: KBE, 1991; Honorary DSc, Universities of Sussex and Hull; Honorary MD, Universities of Nantes and Mahidol, Thailand and Witwatersrand; Honorary Fellow, Worcester College, Oxford, St Catharine's College and Hughes Hall, Cambridge, King's College, London, American College of Surgeons, Royal College of Physicians and Surgeons of Canada, College of Medicine of South Africa, College of Physicians and Surgeons of Pakistan, Royal College of Anaesthetists, Royal College of Surgeons of Ireland; Royal Society of Medicine; Lifetime Achievement Award, Society for Cardiothoracic Surgery in Great Britain and Ireland. Memberships: 20 national and international professional societies; Clubs: The Athenaeum; The Hawk's Club, Cambridge, Chairman, 1997-2001. Address: 28 Tree Lane, Oxford, OX4 4EY, England. E-mail: tenglish@doctors.org.uk

ENGLY Piphal, b. 28 January 1944, Kam Pong-Cham, Cambodia (Australian citizen). Librarian. m. Sayaratt Thannorak, 1963, 1 son, 1 daughter. Education: BA, University of Phnom Penh, 1965; Diploma, Applied Social Science, Swinburne University, 1990; Graduate Diploma, Asian Studies (Political Sciences), Australian National University, 1998; Graduate diploma, Library & Information Management, University of Canberra, 2000; PhD, Montash University, 2009; 16 other certificates in different fields. Appointments include: Minister-Counselor; Librarian; Library Manager, International Public Relation Officer; Teacher; Midwifery Teacher. Publication: The Royal Family of Cambodia; The Connection Between SEA Countries: Java and Cambodia; The Kingdom of Cambodia: Culture and Tradition. Honours: Nominee, Local Hero, Australian of the Year Award, 2007, 2008, 2009; Finalist, Australian Capital Territory Senior Awards, Nominee for the Australian of the Year Award, 2008. Memberships: Australian Library and Information Association. Address: ACT 2602, Australia.

ENKHDAVAA Dambii, b. 3 April 1961, TUV province, Mongolia. Graphic Artist. m. Munkhtsetseg Ts, 1 son, 1 daughter. Education: Fine Art College, Ulaanbaatar, 1977-81; MA, Ukrainian Academy of Fine Arts, Kiev, Ukraine, 1991; MA, State University of Pedagogy, Ulaanbaatar, 1996; Central Academy of Arts & Design, Beijing, China, 1997-99; PhD, Mongolian University of Art & Culture, Ulaanbaatar, 2011. Appointments: Graphic Artist; Solo exhibition, Blue Angel, Mongolian Embassy, Beijing, 1999; Group exhibitions in Mongolia, Ukraine, Russia, Finland, USA, England, Korea and China; Art work collections displayed: Gallery of Contemporary Art, Ulaanbaatar; Committee of the Union of Mongolian Artists, Ulaanbaatar; Mongolian Presidential Palace, Ulaanbaatar; Other galleries around the world. Publications: 7 books; 30 scientific articles; 20 articles in magazines and newspapers; Over 120 art creations; 45 displayed art exhibitions; 60 book illustrations. Honours: Prize, exhibition on book illustration, Ukraine, 1987; 1st place, book design and illustration, 750th anniversary of the secret history of the Mongols, 1989; Medal, Distinguished Artist of Mongolia, 1995; Prize, Union of Mongolian Artists, 2001; 1st place, children's book illustration competition, 2002; Labour Medal of Distinguished Worker, 2004; 1st place, medal artwork competition, 800th anniversary of Mongol State Establishment, 2006. Memberships: Mongolian Art Union; Teachers of Art Association. Address: Mongolian University of Art & Culture, Chinggis avenue 1, 20A Ulaanbaatar, Mongolia.

ENKHJIN Tsultem, b. 18 January 1953, Ulaanbaatar, Mongolia. Painter. m. L Altantsetseg, 1 son, 1 daughter. Education: Fachschule fuer Angewandte Kunst, Berlin, Germany, 1972-73; Hochschule fuer Bildende Kuenste, Dresden, Germany, 1973-78. Appointments: Chairman, Union of Mongolian Artists, 1995-2001, 2007-. Publications: Union of Mongolian Artists, 2000 and 2010. Honours: UMA Prize, 1982; Pole Start State Award, 1992; State Prize of Mongolia, 2002. Memberships: Union of Mongolian Artists. Address: Union of Mongolian Artists, Chinggis avenue 1, Ulaanbaatar, Mongolia. E-mail: enjee25@yahoo.com Website: www.uma.mn

ENNIS Jessica, b. 28 January 1986, Sheffield, England. Athlete. Education: King Ecgbert School, Dore; Psychology, University of Sheffield, 2007. Career: Multi-eventing disciplines and 100m hurdles; Bronze Medal, Heptathlon, Summer Universidade, Izmir, 2005; Bronze Medal, Heptathlon, Melbourne, 2006; Gold Medal, Heptathlon, World Championships, Berlin, 2009; Gold Medal, Heptathlon, World Indoor Championships, Doha, 2010; Gold Medal, Heptathlon, European Championships, Barcelona, 2010; Silver Medal, Heptathlon, World Championships, Daegu, 2011; Silver Medal, Pentathlon, World Indoor Championships, Istanbul, 2012; Gold Medal, Heptathlon, London Olympics, 2012. Honours: Sportswoman of the Year, Sports Journalists' Association, 2009; Sportswoman of the Year, Ultimate Woman of the Year Award, Cosmopolitan magazine, 2009; Honorary D Litt, University of Sheffield, 2010; MBE, 2011; CBE, 2013.

ENO Brian Peter George, b. 15 May 1948, Melton, Suffolk, England. Recording Artist; Record Producer; Musician (keyboards). Career: Founder Member, Roxy Music, 1971-73; Invented Ambient Music, 1975; Visiting Professor, RCA, 1995-; Founder, Long Now Foundation, 1996; Co-founder (with Peter Gabriel), The Magnificent Union of Digitally Downloading Artists, 2004; Recordings: Solo Albums include: Here Come the Warmjets, 1973; Taking Tiger Mountain (by Strategy), 1974; Another Green World, 1975; Music for Films, 1976; Before and After Science, 1977; Ambient 1/Music for Airports, 1978; Nerve Net, 1992; The Drop, 1996; Albums as producer include: with John Cale: Fear, 1974; with Robert Calvert, Lucky Lief And The Longships, 1975; with Michael Nyman: Decay Music, 1976; with Penguin Café Orchestra: Music From The Penguin Café, 1976; with Ultravox: Ultravox, 1977; with Talking Heads: More Songs About Buildings And Food, 1978; Remain In Light, 1980; with Devo: Q- Are We

DICTIONARY OF INTERNATIONAL BIOGRAPHY 36th EDITION

Not Men? A- We Are Devo, 1978; with U2: The Unforgettable Fire, 1984; The Joshua Tree, 1987; Achtung Baby, 1991; Zooropa, 1993; Passengers (film soundtrack), 1995; All That You Can't Leave Behind, 2000; with Carmel: The Falling, 1986; with Geoffrey Oryema: Exile, 1990; with James: Laid, 1993; Wah Wah, 1994; Pleased to Meet You, 2001; with Laurie Anderson: Bright Red, 1994; Collaborations include: with Roxy Music: Virginia Plain, 1972; Roxy Music, 1972; For Your Pleasure, 1973; Pyjamarama, 1973; with David Bowie: Low, 1977; Heroes, 1977; Lodger, 1979; with J Peter Schwalm: Music for Onmyo-ji, 2000; Drawn From Life, 2001; As guest musician: Captain Lockheed And The Starfighters, Robert Calvert, 1974; The End, Nico, 1974; The Lamb Lies Down On Broadway, Genesis, 1974; with Phil Mazanera: Diamond Head, 1975; Listen Now, 1977; with John Cale: Slow Dazzle, 1975; Helen Of Troy, 1975; Rain Dances, Camel, 1977; Exposure, Robert Fripp, 1979; Yellow Rain, The Neville Brothers, 1989; Rattle And Hum, U2, 1989; Mamouna, Bryan Ferry, 1994; with Jah Wobble: Spinner, 1995. Remix productions include: Unbelieveable, EMF, 1992; I Feel You, Depeche Mode, 1993; The River, Geoffrey Oryema, 1993; I'm Only Looking, INXS, 1993; In Your Room, Depeche Mode, 1993; Brian Eno: Box I & Box II, 1993; Introducing The Band, Suede, 1994; 39 Steps, Bryan Ferry, 1994; Protection, Massive Attack, 1994; Numerous film soundtracks. Honours: Doctor, Technology, University of Plymouth; Ivor Novello Award; 3 Grammy Awards; BRIT Awards: Best Producer, 1994, 1996; Q Magazine Awards: Best Producer (with Flood, The Edge), 1993; Inspiration Award (with David Bowie), 1995; Montblanc Arts Patronage Award, 2000; Grammy Award, Producer of Best Record of the Year, 2000. Memberships: PRS; BASCA; ICA; Long Now Foundation; Global Business Network. Current Management: Opal Ltd. Address: 4 Pembridge Mews, London W11 3EQ, England.

ENYA (Eithne Ni Bhraonain), b. 17 May 1961, Gweedore, County Donegal, Ireland. Singer; Musician (piano, keyboards); Composer. Musical Education: Clasical piano; Career: Member, folk group Clannad, 1980-82; Solo artiste, 1988-; 25 million albums sold to date. Compositions: Music for film and television scores: The Frog Prince, 1985; The Celts, BBC, 1987; LA Story, 1990; Green Card, 1990. Recordings: Albums: with Clannad: Crann Ull, 1980; Fuaim, 1982; Solo albums: Watermark, 1988; Shepherd's Moon, 1991; Enya, 1992; The Celts (reissued), 1992; The Book Of Trees, 1996; On My Way Home, 1998; Storms in Africa, 1998; Amarantine, 2000. Singles include: Orinoco Flow (Number 1, UK), 1988; Evening Falls, 1988; Storms In Africa (Part II), 1989; Caribbean Blue, 1991; How Can I Keep From Singing, 1991; Book Of Days, 1992; Anywhere Is, 1995; Only If, 1997; Oiche Chiun, 1998; Orinoco Flow, 1998. Honours: Grammy Award, Best New Age Album, Shepherd's Moon, 1993 and The Memory of Trees, 1997 and A Day Without Rain, 2002 and Amarantine, 2007; IRMA Award, Best Irish Female Artist, 1993. Current Management: Aigle Music, 6 Danieli Drive, Artane, Dublin 5, Ireland.

EO Eunkyung, b. 26 October 1968, Gwangju Metropolitan City, Korea. Professor; Physician. m. Hyunho Lee, 1 daughter. Education: MD and Bachelor's degree, School of Medicine, Ewha Womans University, Seoul, 1987-94; Master's degree, 2002, PhD, 2006, Thoracic Surgery, College of Medicine, Chung-Ang University, Seoul. Appointments: Emergency Medicine Residency, 1994-99, Director, Emergency Department, 2007-09, Ewha University Medical Center, Seoul; Associate Professor, 1999-, Director, Ewha Basic-Life-Support Training Site & Ewha Medical Simulation Center, 2006-, School of Medicine, Ewha Womans University, Seoul. Publications: Numerous articles in professional journals. Memberships: Korean Society of Emergency Medicine; Korean Society of Traumatology; Korean Society of Clinical Toxicology; Korean Society of Medical Education; Korean Society of Medical Ethics; Korean Society of Critical Care Medicine. Address: Department of Medical Education, School of Medicine, Ewha Womans University, 911-1 Mokdong, Yangcheongu, Seoul 158-710, Korea. E-mail: liz0803@ewha.ac.kr

EOM Joo Beom, b. 23 February 1975, Ulsan, Republic of Korea. Researcher. m. Soo-Hee Kim, 2 daughters. Education: BS, Physics, 2000; MS, 2002, PhD, 2011, Information and Communications. Appointments: Researcher, 2003-05, Senior Researcher, 2005-, Korea Photonics Technology Institute. Publications: Numerous articles in professional journals. Honours: Best Paper Award, 10th Photonics Conference, Korea, 2001. Memberships: Optical Society of Korea. Address: 5 Cheomdan 5 gil, Buk-gu, Gwangin, 500-779, Republic of Korea. E-mail: jbeom@kopti.re.kr

EÖSZE László, b. 17 November 1923, Budapest, Hungary. Musicologist. m. (1) 1 son, 1 daughter, (2) Margit Szilléry, 1983. Education: PhD, Aesthetics and Literature. Appointments: Music Teacher and Pianist; Concerts in Hungary and Europe, 1946-51; Editor, 1955-57, Chief Editor, 1957-61, Art Director, 1961-87, Editio Musica, Budapest. Publications: 16 books including: Life and Work of Zoltán Kodály, 1956; Zoltán Kodály's Life in Pictures, 1957; History of Opera, 1960; Giuseppe Verdi, 1961, 2nd edition, 1966, enlarged, 1975; Zoltán Kodály, His Life and Work, in English, 1962, in German, 1965; Zoltán Kodály, 1967; Kodály, His Life in Pictures and Documents, in English and German, 1971; Richard Wagner, 1969; Richard Wagner, Eine Chronik seines Lebens und Schaffens, 1969; Zoltán Kodály, életének krónikája, 1977; 2nd , enlarged edition, 2007; 119 római Liszt dokumentum, 1980; Selected studies on Z Kodály, 2000; The Family Tree of Zoltán Kodály, 2007; Essays and articles in various languages; Contributions to numerous professional publications. Honours: Erkel Prize, 1977; Gramma Award, 1978; Medium Cross of the Order of the Hungarian Republic, 1998; Medal for Merit of the President of the Republic, 2003; Grand Prize of the National Society of Creative Artists, 2003. Memberships: Honorary Co-president, F Liszt Society; Executive Secretary, 1975-95, International Kodály Society; Hungarian Musicological Society, 1996-. Address: Attila ut 133, 1012 Budapest, Hungary.

EPPERT Günter J, b. 2 August 1933, Friedland, Czechia, Germany. Chemist. m. Christa Traubach, 2 sons, 1 daughter. Education: Diploma, 1958; Dr rer nat, 1961; Dr habil, 1980. Appointments: University Lecturer in Analytical Chemistry, 1982; Collaborator of UNIDO, 1984-89; Founder of the firm SEPSERV Separation Service Berlin, Germany, 1990-. Publications: About 70 publications and patents; Books: Einführung in die Schnelle Flüssigchromatographie; Leitfaden ausgewählter Trennmethoden; HPLC Trouble Shooting; Flüssigchromatographie HPLC - Theorie und Praxis; Fiction and poetry: Gedanken im Morgengrauen; Iffi und die Energys; Iffi und der Planet Erde; Das Kuckucksei; Die Stimmen des Teufels; Trimmers Mäuse; Die Zeit Vergeht (poems and compositions for piano). Membership: Gesellschaft Deutscher Chemiker. Address: Dovestr 1B, 10587 Berlin, Germany. E-mail: sepserv.berlin@t-online.de Website: www.sepserv.com

EPPSTEIN Ury, b. 3 February 1925, Saarbrücken, Germany. Israeli Musicologist. m. Kikue lguchi, 2 sons. Education: MA, Hebrew University of Jerusalem, 1949; Diploma in Japanese Language, Tokyo University of Foreign Studies, 1959; Diploma in Japanese Music, Tokyo University of Fine Arts and Music, 1963; PhD, Tel Aviv University, 1984. Appointments: Academic Assistant, Music Research Centre, Hebrew University, 1966-1972; Lecturer, Musicology and Theatre Departments, Tel Aviv University, 1972-1977; Lecturer, Departments of Musicology, Theatre, East Asian St, Hebrew University, 1972-; Guest Lecturer, Copenhagen University; East Asian Institute and Musicology Department, Lund University, 1986; Guest Lecturer, Dokkyō University, Japan; Tokyo University of Fine Arts and Music, 1997; Guest Professor, Vienna University, 2009. Publications: Kanjinchō, translation of Kabuki play from Japanese, 1993; The Beginnings of Western Music in Meiji Era Japan, 1994; Musical Means to Political Ends - Japanese School Songs in Manchuria, 1996; Governmental Policy and Controversy - The Beginnings of Western Music in Japan, 1998; Changing Western Attitudes to Japanese Music in: Collected Articles and Essays in Honour of His Imperial Highness Prince Mikasa on the Occasion of His 88th Birthday, 2004; Schools Songs, the (Russo-Japanese) War and Nationalist Indoctrination, 2007; From Torture to Fascination – Changing Western Attitudes to Japanese Music, 2007; Eine neue japanische Oper, ein japanischer Diplomat und der Holocaust Minikomi 78, Vienna, 2009. Honours: Order of the Rising Sun conferred by the Emperor of Japan, 1989; Israel Ministry of Education and Culture Prize for translation of Kabuki drama from Japanese, 1996. Memberships: European Association for Japanese Studies, Israel Musicological Society; International Council for Traditional Music. Address: 80 Tchernihovsky St, Jerusalem, Israel.

EPSTEIN (Michael) Anthony (Sir), b. 18 May 1921, London, England. Medical Scientist; University Teacher. 2 sons, 1 daughter. Education: Trinity College, Cambridge; Middlesex Hospital Medical School, London. Appointments: House Surgeon, Middlesex Hospital, London and Addenbrooke's Hospital, Cambridge, 1944; Lieutenant and Captain, Royal Army Medical Corps, 1945-47; Assistant Pathologist, Middlesex Hospital Medical School, 1948-65; Berkeley Travelling Fellow, 1952-53; French Government Scholar, Institut Pasteur, Paris, 1952-53; Visiting Investigator, Rockefeller Institute, New York, 1956; Honorary Consultant Virologist, Middlesex Hospital, 1965-68; Reader in Experimental Pathology, Middlesex Hospital Medical School, 1965-68; Honorary Consultant Pathologist, Bristol Hospitals, 1968-82; Professor of Pathology, 1968-85, Head of Department, 1968-82, University of Bristol; Emeritus Professor of Pathology, University of Bristol and Fellow, Wolfson College, Oxford, 1986-. Publications: Over 240 original contributions to major scientific journals; Joint Founder Editor, International Review of Experimental Pathology, volumes 1-28, 1962-86; Joint Editor, 5 scientific books including The Epstein-Barr Virus 1979; The Epstein-Barr Virus: Recent Advances, 1986; Oncogenic γ-herpesviruses: An Expanding Family, 2001. Honours include: Paul Ehrlich and Ludwig Darmstaedter Prize and Medal, West Germany, 1973; Fellow, Royal Society, 1979; Honorary Professor, Sun Yat Sen University, China, 1981; Bristol Myers Award for Cancer Research, USA, 1982; Honorary Fellow, Queensland Institute of Medical Research, 1983; CBE, 1985; Prix Grifuel, France, 1986; Honorary Fellow, Royal College of Physicians of London, 1986; Extraordinary Governing Body Fellow, Wolfson College, Oxford, 1986-2001; Honorary MD, University of Edinburgh, 1986; Honorary Professor, Chinese Academy of Preventive Medicine, 1988; Gairdner International Award, Canada, 1988; Honorary Fellow, Royal Medical Society of Edinburgh, 1988; Member, Academia Europea, 1988; Honorary Fellow, Royal Society of Edinburgh, 1991; Knight Bachelor, 1991; Royal Medal, The Royal Society of London, 1992; Fellow, University College London, 1992; Honorary Fellow, Royal College of Pathologists of Australasia, 1995; Honorary DSc, University of Birmingham, 1996; Honorary MD, Charles University of Prague, 1998; Founder Fellow, Academy of Medical Sciences, 1998; Honorary Fellow, Wolfson College Oxford, 2001. Address: Nuffield Department of Clinical Medicine, University of Oxford, John Radcliffe Hospital, Oxford, OX3 9DU, England.

EREJUWA Omotayo Owomofoyon, b. 2 May 1981, Erunna-Ero, Malaysia. PhD student. Education: BSc (Hons), Pharmacology, University of Lagos, 2004; PhD, Pharmacology, Universiti Sains Malaysia, 2012. Appointments: Assistant Pharmacist, 2004-05. Publications: Numerous articles in professional journals. Honours: Universiti Sains Malaysia Doctoral Fellowship, 2007-12; DNSG Travel Award, Diabetes and Nutrition Study Group, 2009; Young Investigator Support by Society for Free Radical Research Europe, 2011. Memberships: Society for Free Radical Biology and Medicine; Society for Free Radical Research – Africa; American Society for Pharmacology and Experimental Therapeutics. Address: Department of Pharmacology, School of Medical Sciences, Universiti Sains Malaysia, 16150 Kubang Kerian, Kelantan, Malaysia. E-mail: erejuwa@gmail.com

ERICKSON Ray Charles, b. 30 January 1918, St Peter, Minnesota, USA. Wildlife Biology. m. (1) Patricia Katherine Miles, 1950, divorced 1951, 1 daughter, (2) Helen Josephine Haworth, 1953, deceased 1996, 2 sons, 1 daughter, (3) Grace M Hayes, 2001. Education: AB, Gustavus Adolphus College, St Peter College; MS, Iowa State University, 1943; Ibid, PhD, 1948. Appointments: Officer, US Navy, 1943-46; Wildlife Management Biologist, Malheur National Wildlife Refuge, Burns, Oregon, 1948-55; Chief, Section of Habitat Management, Division of Wildlife Refuges, Washington, DC, 1955-57; Research Staff Specialist, Division of Wildlife Research, US Fish & Wildlife Service, US Department of the Interior, Washington, DC, 1958-65; Assistant Chief in charge, Endangered Wildlife Research Program, Patuxent Wildlife Research Center, Laurel, Maryland, US Fish & Wildlife Service, USDI, 1965-80; Retired, 1980-. Publications: Chapter, Planting and Misplanting, in Waterfowl Tomorrow, 1964; A Federal Research Program for Endangered Wildlife, 1968; Many other scientific and popular articles. Honours: Distinguished Alumnus, Gustavus Adolphus College, 1991; Distinguished Service Award, US Department of the Interior, 1968; President, 1967-70, Washington Biologist's Field Club; Special Conservation Award, National Wildlife Federation, 1975; Wildlife Conservation Award, San Diego Zoological Society, 1979; Listed in international biographical directories. Memberships: Ecological Society of America; Society of Range Management; Wilson Ornithological Club; American Ornithologists' Union; The Wildlife Society. Address: 3010 Twin Oak Place NW, Salem, OR 97304, USA.

ERITJA Ramon, b. 9 August 1955, Lleida, Spain. Chemist. m. Elisenda Olivella, 2 sons. Education: BSc, Chemistry, BSc Pharmacy, PhD, Chemistry, 1984, University of Barcelona, Spain. Appointments: Postdoctoral Fellow, Department of Molecular Genetics, Beckman Research Institute of the City of Hope, Duarte, California, USA, 1984-86; Research Associate,

Department of Chemistry and Biochemistry, University of Colorado, Boulder, Colorado, USA, 1986-87; Postdoctoral Fellow, Department of Organic Chemistry, University of Barcelona, Spain, 1987-89; Research Associate, Group Leader, Centre for Research and Development, CSIC Barcelona, Spain, 1989-94; Group Leader, European Molecular Biology Laboratory, Heidelberg, Germany, 1994-99; Group Leader, Consejo Superior de Investigaciones Cientificas, Barcelona, Spain, 1999-. Publications: 200 publications on synthesis and study of properties of oligonucleotides and peptides in scientific journals. Memberships: American Peptide Society; International Society for Nucleosides, Nucleotides and Nucleic Acids. Address: Tarragona 106, 1, 1, E-08015, Barcelona, Spain. E-mail: recgma@cid.csic.es

ERKAN Husnu, b. 1 April 1947, Alanya, Turkey. Academic. m. Canan, 1 son, 1 daughter. Education: Antalya High School, 1965; Undergraduate, Faculty of Political Science, Ankara University, 1969; Doctor of Philosophy & Master of Arts (Magna cum laude/High honour), Freiburg Albert Ludwings University, 1976. Appointments: Lecturer, Economics Department, Hacettepe University, 1977-80; Lecturer, Ege University, 1980-82; Associate Professor, 1982-88, Department Professor, 1988-, Economics Department, Faculty of Economics and Administrative Sciences, Dokuz Eylul University. Publications: Numerous articles in professional journals, newpapers and conferences; Over 30 books including most recently, Economic Transformation Processes and Development for the Future in terms of Integrated Systems, 2010. Honours: Turkish Industrialists' and Businessmens' Association Research Award, 1991; Society and Human Sciences Gross Award, Turkey Isbank, 1992; Serket Bilgin Award, Yeni Asir Newspaper, 1993. Memberships: Gozlem Newspaper; Turkish Democracy Foundation; Philosophical Society of Turkey; Regional Science Association; Political Science Graduates' Association, Ankara University; National Unity and Strategy Association. Address: Dokuz Eylul University, Faculty of Economics and Administrative Sciences, Economics Department, Dokuz Cesmeler, Buca, Izmir, Turkey. E-mail: husnu.erkan@deu.edu.tr

ERMOLENKO Alexander, b. 1 March 1942, Gorlivka, Ukraine. Radiologist. m. Nadezhda Lagushkina, 3 daughters. Education: Doctor of General Practice, Medical State Institute, Donetsk, 1967; PhD, A V Vishnevsky Institute of Surgery, Moscow, 1978. Appointments: Physician of General Practice, hospital, Summa, Ukraine, 1967-69; Research Fellow, 1969-76, Scientific Employee, 1976-80, AV Vishnevsky Institute of Surgery, Moscow; Radiologist, 1980-85, Chief, Nuclear Medicine Department, 1985-, Institute of Transplantology, Moscow. Publications: The General Plan of Human Structural Organisation, 1996; The use of human structure principle in transplantology, 1998; Symmetry in the development of human cardiovascular system, 1999; Two-plane Symmetry in the Structural Organisation of Man, 2005; The Biocrystalloid Structure of Man (an Extracellular Theory), 2006; Origin of Segmentation in the Human Structure, 2006; Origin of Vertebrates, 2007; Symmetry and Segmentation in the Human Limb Structure, 2007. Honours: Medal of Moscow by President of Russia, B Eltsin, 1997; Outstanding Scientists of the 21st Century, 2007; Medal for Professionalism and Business Reputation, Public Awards Council of Russia, 2008; Certificate of Merit and the Gold Commemorative Medal of Distinguished Service to Humankind Award, England, 2009; Patents for Two-plane Symmetry in the Structural Organisation of Man; Origin of Segmentation in the Human Structure; The Biocrystalloid Structure of Man (an Extracellular Theory); Origin of Vertebrates. Address: Fl 19, 13, B, Sukharevskiy Lane, Moscow 127051, Russia. E-mail: alex-ermol@yandex.ru Website: http://ww.zivert.rii/people/ermolenko.php

ESAKI Leo, b. 12 March 1925, Osaka, Japan. Physicist. m. (1) Masako Araki, 1959, 1 son, 2 daughters, (2) Masako Kondo, 1986. Education: Graduated, University of Tokyo, 1947, PhD. Appointments: With Sony Corporation, 1956-60; IBM Fellow, 1967-92, IBM T J Watson Research Center, New York, 1960-92, Manager, Device Research, 1962-92, IBM Corporation, USA; Director, IBM Japan, 1976-92, Yamada Science Foundation, 1976-; President, University of Tsukuba, Ibaraki, Japan, 1992-98; Chair, Science and Technology Promotion Foundation of Ibaraki, 1998-; Director General, Tsukuba International Congress Center, 1999-; President, Shibaura Institute of Technology, 2000-2006; President, Yokohama College of Pharmacy, 2006-. Publications: Numerous articles in professional journals. Honours: Nishina Memorial Award, 1959; Asahi Press Award, 1960; Toyo Rayon Foundation Award, 1961; Morris N Liebmann Memorial Prize, 1961; Stuart Ballantine Medal, Franklin Institute, 1961; Japan Academy Award, 1965; IBM Fellow, 1967; Joint Winner, Nobel Prize for Physics, 1973; Order of Culture, Japanese Government, 1974; Sir John Cass Senior Visiting Research Fellow, London Polytechnic, 1981; US-Asia Institute, Science Achievement Award, 1983; American Physical Society, Institute Prize for New Materials, 1985; IEEE Medal of Honour, 1991; Japan Prize, 1998; Grand Cordon Order of Rising Sun, First Class, 1998. Memberships: Japan Academy; American Philosophical Society; Max-Planck Gesellschaft; Foreign Associate, NAS; American National Academy of Engineering. Address: Shibaura Institute of Technology, 3-9-14 Shibaura, Minato-ku, Tokyo 108, Japan.

ESILABA Anthony Obutiatia, b. 26 September 1956, Maseno, Vihiga District, Kenya. Research Scientist; Consultant. m. Rosemary Nyambura Ngotho, 2 sons. Education: BSc, Agriculture, 1978, MSc, Soil Science, 1984, University of Nairobi, Kenya; PhD, Agronomy-Soil Chemistry/Fertility, University of Nebraska, Lincoln, USA, 1986. Appointments: Research Officer, Kenya, 1978-81; Senior Research Scientist, Kenya Agricultural Research Institute, 1981-95; Regional Research Fellow, International Centre for Maize and Wheat Improvement (CIMMYT), Addis Ababa, Ethiopia, 1995-98; Regional Research Fellow, International Centre for Tropical Agriculture (CIAT), Kampala, Uganda, 1999-2002; Programme Officer, Land and Water Management Research Programme and Assistant National Co-ordinator, Desert Margins Programme, Kenya Agricultural Research Institute, 2003-. Publications: Articles in professional scientific journals. Honours: Regional Research Fellow, CIAT, 1999-2002; Regional Research Fellow, African Highlands Initiative (AHI), CIMMYT/ICRAF, 1995-98; Listed in biographical dictionaries. Memberships: World Association for Soil and Water Conservation; Soil and Water Management Network; African Network for Soil Biology and Fertility; Agriculture Research and Extension Network; Trees on Farm Network. Address: PO Box 72504, City Square, 00200, Nairobi, Kenya. E-mail: aoesilaba@kari.org or aesilaba@yahoo.co.uk.

ESSLEMONT Iain, b. 2 September 1932, Aberdeen, Scotland. General Medical Practitioner (Retired). m. Mary Gibb Mars, 1 son, 2 daughters. Education: MB ChB, 1956; D ObstRCOG, 1960; MRCGP, 1973; Dip Aust COG, 1980; FRACGP, 1981; MCGP (Malaysia), 1982; FAFP (Malaysia), 1997; FRCGP, 2006. Appointments: House Surgeon, Ayr County Hospital, Scotland, 1956-57; House Physician,

Paediatrician, General Hospital, Dewsbury, England, 1957; RAMC, 1957-60; House Surgeon, Obstetrics, Ayrshire Central Hospital, Scotland, 1960; General Practitioner, Cha'ah, Johore, Malaya, 1960-62; General Practitioner, Drs Allan and Gunstensen, Penang, Malaysia, 1962-77; MO, Kununurra, Western Australia, 1977-78; Southside After-Hours Medical Service, Perth, Western Australia, 1978-82; General Practitioner, Huntingdale Family Medical Practice, Gosnells, Western Australia, 1979-99; General Practitioner, Gosnells Health Care Practice, Gosnells, Western Australia, 1999; Examiner, Royal Australian College of General Practitioners, 1985-2010; President, The Dalton Society, 1994; External Clinical Teacher, Royal Australian College of General Practitioners, 2001-02. Publications: Articles in the Australian Family Physician: Non surgical treatment for Meibomian Cysts, 1995; Sick doctors – a personal story, Why use soap?, What is a GP?, The clue was in the ingots, Birth, death and life, 2001; Where is general practice heading?, Dying, 2002; Life is what you make it, 2009. Honour: Paul Harris Fellowship (Rotary), 1998; Examiner, Royal Australian College of General Practitioners, 1985-2010; Listed in national and international biographical dictionaries. Memberships: Royal College of General Practitioners, UK; Royal Australian College of General Practitioners; Academy of Family Physicians Malaysia; Rotary Club of Margaret River; Probus Club of Margaret River. Address: 2, Chardonnay Avenue, Margaret River, Western Australia, 6285 Australia. E-mail: esslemont@wn.com.au

ESTEFAN Gloria (Fajado), b. 1 September 1957, Havana, Cuba. Singer; Songwriter. m. Emilio Estefan, 1978, 1 son, 1 daughter. Education: BA, Psychology, University of Miami, 1978. Career: Singer, backed by Miami Sound Machine, 1974-; Billed as Gloria Estefan, 1989-; Appearances include: Tokyo Music Festival, Japan, 1985; World tour, The Simple Truth, benefit concert for Kurdish refugees, Wembley, White House State Dinner, for President of Brazil, 1991; South American tour, Royal Variety Performance, London, before Prince and Princess of Wales, Co-organiser, benefit concert for victims of Hurricane Andrew, Florida, 1992; 45 million albums sold to date. Compositions include: Anything For You; Don't Wanna Lose You; Oye Mi Canto (co-written with Jorge Casas and Clay Ostwald); Cuts Both Ways; Coming Out Of The Dark (co-written with Emilio Estefan and Jon Secada); Always Tomorrow; Christmas Through Their Eyes (co-written with Dianne Warren). Recordings: Albums: Renacer, 1976; Eyes Of Innocence, 1984; Primitive Love, 1986; Let It Loose, 1988; Anything For You (Number 1, UK), Cuts Both Ways, 1989; Exitos De Gloria Estefan, 1990; Into The Light, 1991; Greatest Hits, 1992; Mi Tierra, Christmas Through Your Eyes, 1993; Hold Me, Thrill Me, Kiss Me, 1994; Abriendo Puertas, 1995; Destiny, 1996; Gloria!; Santo Santo, 1999; Alma Caribeño: Caribbean Soul, 2000; Also featured on: Jon Secada, Jon Secada (also co-producer), 1991; Til Their Eyes Shine (The Lullaby Album), 1992; Hit singles include: Dr Beat, 1984; Conga, Hot Summer Nights, used in film soundtrack Top Gun, Bad Boy, Words Get In The Way, 1986; Rhythm Is Gonna Get You, 1987; Can't Stay Away From You, Anything For You (Number 1, US), 1-2-3, 1988; Oye Mi Canto (Hear My Voice), Here We Are, Don't Wanna Lose You, Get On Your Feet, 1989; Coming Out of The Dark (Number 1, US), Remember Me With Love, 1991; Always Tomorrow, 1992; Cuts Both Ways, Go Away, Mi Tierra, 1993; Turn the Beat Around, 1994; Abrienda Puertos; Tres Deseos; Mas Alla. Publications: The Magically Mysterious Adventures of Noelle the Bulldog, 2005; Noelle's Treasure Tale: A New Mysterious Adventure, 2006. Honours: Grand Prize, Tokyo Music Festival, 1985; Numerous Billboard awards, 1986-; American Music Award, Favourite Pop/Rock Duo or Group, 1989; Crystal Globe Award, 21 Club, New York, 1990; Latin Music Award, Crossover Artist Of Year, 1990; Humanitarian Award, B'Nai B'rith, 1992; Desi Entertainment Awards, Performer of Year, Song of Year, 1992; Humanitarian Award, National Music Foundation (for helping victims of Hurricane Andrew), 1993. Address: c/o Estefan Enterprises, 6205 Bird Road, Miami Beach, FL 33155, USA.

ESTEVES Sandro Cassiano, b. 19 July 1967, Tupa, Brazil. Physician. m. Fabiola, 1 son, 1 daughter. Education: MD, 1990, Master degree, 1996, University of Campinas Medical School, Brazil; PhD, Federal University of Sao Paulo, Brazil, 1998; Post-residency, Andrology and Male Infertility, Cleveland Clinic Foundation International Center, Center for Reproductive Medicine, Glickman Urological & Kidney Institute, Cleveland, USA, 1995-96. Appointments: Founder, Director, ANDROFERT, Referral Center for Male Reproduction, Brazil, 1997-. Publications: Over 60 published articles in peer-reviewed journals; Several book chapters. Honours: Thomas S Chang Award, American Society of Andrology, 1998; Reproductive Research Center's Alumni of the Year Award, 2006; Listed in international biographical dictionaries. Memberships: Brazilian Society of Urology; American Society for Reproductive Medicine; Brazilian Society for Assisted Reproduction; Society for Male Reproduction and Urology.

ESTEVEZ Emilio, b. 12 May 1962, New York, USA. Actor. m. Paula Abdul, 1992, divorced 1994, 1 son, 1 daughter. Appointments: Actor, films include: Tex, 1982; Nightmares, 1983; The Outsiders, 1983; The Breakfast Club, 1984; Repo Man, 1984; St Elmo's Fire, 1984; That Was Then...This is Now, 1985; Maximum Overdrive, 1986; Wisdom (also writer and director), 1986; Stakeout, 1987; Men at Work, 1989; Freejack, 1992; Loaded Weapon, 1993; Another Stakeout, 1993; Champions II, 1993; Judgement Night, 1993; D2: The Mighty Ducks, 1994; The Jerky Boys (co-executive, producer); Mighty Ducks 3; Mission Impossible, 1996; The War at Home, 1996; The Bang Bang Club, 1998; Killer's Head, 1999; Sand, 2000; Rated X, 2000; The LA Riot Spectacular, 2005; Bobby, 2006; Arthur and the Invisibles (voice), 2006. Address: c/o UTA, 5th Floor, 9560 Wilshire Boulevard, Beverly Hills, CA 90212, USA.

ESTÉVEZ RADÍO Hernán, b. 5 August 1950, Montevideo, Uruguay. Physicist. m. Eva Fernández Roqueiro, 1 daughter. Education: 2nd Class Deck Officer, 1972, 1st Class Deck Officer, 1974, Captain, 1978, Merchant Marine; BS, Physics, 1986; MS, Physics, 1987; PhD, Physics, 1992. Appointments: 3rd Officer, 2nd Officer, 1972, Chief Officer, 1973, Professor, 1978, Atlantic Polytechnic Institute; Professor, National University of Distance Education, Pontevedra, Spain, 1990-. Publications: IEEE Transactions on Microware Theory and Techniques; IEEE Transactions on Antennas and Propagation, Microwave and Optical Technology Letters; IJEEE; Anales de Fisica; Revisita Espanola de Fisica. Memberships: IEEE; Spanish Royal Society of Physics. Address: Torrente Ballester 4-1ºF, 36204 Vigo, Pontevedra, Spain. E-mail: hernanestevezradio@hotmail.com

ETHERIDGE Melissa Lou, b. 29 May, 1961 Leavenworth, Kansas, USA. Singer; Songwriter; Musician (guitar). 4 children. Musical Education: Berklee College of Music, Boston. Career: Musician, Los Angeles bars, 5 years; Recording artiste, 1988-. Recordings: Albums: Melissa Etheridge, 1988; Brave And Crazy, 1989; Never Enough, 1992; Yes I Am, 1993; Your Little Secret, 1995; Breakdown, 1999; Skin, 2001; Lucky, 2004; Greatest Hits: The Road Less

Travelled, 2005; The Awakening, 2007; Singles: I'm the Only One, 1994; Come to My Window, 1994; If I Wanted To, 1995; Nowhere to Go, 1996; Angels Would Fall, 1999; Enough of Me, 2000; Breathe, 2004; This Moment, 2004; Cry Baby, 2005; Refugee, 2005; I Run for Life, 2005; I Need to Wake Up, 2006; The Awakening, 2007; A New Thought for Christmas, 2008; Fearless Love, 2010. Honours: Grammy Nomination, Bring Me Some Water, 1988. Current Management: Bill Leopold, W F Leopold Management, 4425 Riverside Drive, Ste 102, Burbank, CA 91505, USA.

ETORKI Abdunnaser, b. 26 September 1970, Tripoli, Libya. Chemistry. m. Faiza Enammi, 1 son, 3 daughters. Education: BSc, Chemistry, 1994; M Phil, Electroanalytical Chemistry, 2005; PhD, Electroanalytical Chemistry, University of Leicester, England, 2006. Appointments: Electroanalytical Chemistry. Publications: 12. Honours: 3. Memberships: RSC; ACS; AOAC; ECS; IEEE; SETC; GCS; CCS; IOP; IOM; SEAC. Address: Department of Chemistry, University of Tripoli, PO Box 13340, Tripoli, Libya. E-mail: ae32@le.ac.uk

EUBANK Chris, b. 8 August 1966, Dulwich, England. Middleweight Boxer. m. 4 children. Career: WBC International Middleweight Boxing Champion, 2 defences, March-November, 1990; WBO Middleweight Boxing Champion, 3 defences, November 1990-August 1991; WBO World Super-Middleweight Boxing Champion, 14 defences, September 1991-March 1995; Lost title to Steve Collins, Cork, Sept 1995; Failed to regain title against Joe Calzaghe, Sheffield, October 1997; Unsuccessful fights for WBO Cruiserweight title against Carl Thompson, Manchester, April 1998, Sheffield, July 1998; Patron Breakthrough; Ambassador, International Fund for Animal Welfare; Spokesperson, National Society for the Prevention of Cruelty to Children. Address: 9 The Upper Drive, Hove, East Sussex, BN3 6GR, England.

EUN Duk-Soo, b. 20 June 1978, Daegu, Republic of Korea. Postdoctoral Fellow; Research Scientist. Education: Bachelor, Keimyung University, Daegu, 2001; Master, 2003, PhD, 2009, Kyungpook National University, Daegu. Appointments: Researcher, Kyungpook National University, 2003-08; Postdoctoral Fellow, Research Scientist, Toyohashi University of Technology, 2009-. Publications: Numerous articles in professional journals; Patents pending. Honours: Various scholarships, 2003-07; Most Impressive Poster Award, 2006; Listed in international biographical dictionaries. Address: Toyohashi University of Technology, 1-1 Hibarigaoka Tempaku-cho, Toyohashi Aichi 444-8580, Japan. E-mail: beast22@unitel.co.kr

EVANGELISTA Linda, b. 10 May, 1965, St Catherines, Toronto, Ontario, Canada. Model. m. Gerald Marie (divorced 1993). 1 son previous relationship. Career: Face of Yardley Cosmetics; Numerous catwalk appearances. Address: c/o Elite Model Management, 40 Parker Street, London WC2B 5PH, England.

EVANS Chris, b. 1 April 1966, Warrington, England. Broadcaster. m. (1) Carol McGiffin, 1991, divorced, (2) Billie Piper, 2000, divorced, (3) Natasha Shishmanian, 2007. 1 daughter from previous girlfriend. Career: Numerous sundry jobs; Joined Piccadilly Radio, Manchester; Producer, GLR Radio, London; Presenter of numerous television programmes including Don't Forget Your Toothbrush, co-presenter, The Big Breakfast; Presenter, Radio 1 Breakfast Show, 1995-97, Virgin Radio Breakfast Show, 1997-2001; Established Ginger Productions, media production company; Presenter and Executive Producer, TFI Friday, Channel 4; Saturday Afternoon Show, 2005, Drive Time, 2006-, BBC Radio 2. Presenter BRIT Awards 2005, 2006. Honours: British Comedy Award Prizes, Best Entertainment Series, Top Channel 4 Entertainment Presenter, 1995; Sony music radio personality of the Year, 2006. Address: Ginger Productions, 131-151 Great Titchfield Street, London W1P 8DP, England.

EVANS (Daniel) John (Owen), b. 17 November 1953, Morriston, Swansea, South Wales. Broadcaster, Academic, Writer. Education: BMus, 1975; MA, 1976; PhD, University of Cardiff, Wales. Appointments: First Research Scholar, Britten-Pears Library and Archive, Aldeburgh, England, 1980-84; Music Producer, BBC Radio 3, 1985-89; Senior Producer, BBC Singers, 1989-92; Chief Producer, Series, BBC Radio 3, 1992-93; Head of Music Department, BBC Radio 3, 1993-97; Head of Classical Music, BBC Radio, 1997-2000; Head of Music Programming, BBC Radio 3, 2000-2006; President and Executive Director, Oregon Bach Festival, 2007. Publications: Author with Donald Mitchell, Benjamin Britten: Pictures from a Life 1913-1976, 1978; Editor, Benjamin Britten: His Life and Operas, by Eric Walter White, revised 2nd edition, 1982; Journeying Boy: The early diaries of the young Benjamin Britten, 2009. Contributions include: A Britten Companion, 1984; A Britten Source Book, 1987; ENO, Royal Opera House and Cambridge Opera Guides on Britten's Peter Grimes, Gloriana, The Turn of the Screw, Death in Venice. Honours: Prix Italia Award and Charles Heidsieck Award, 1989; Royal Philharmonic Society Award, 1994; Sony Radio Award, 1997; Outstanding Achievement in Classical Music, Portland Music Awards, 2011; Listed in Who's Who publications and biographical dictionaries. Memberships: Chair, Opera Jury for RPS Awards and Sony Radio Awards; Juror, BBC Singer of the World Competition; Tosti International Singing Competition, BBC Choir of the Year, Prix Italia 2005; Vice-President, Welsh Music Guild; Trustee, The Britten-Pears Will Trust; Trustee, The Britten Family and Charitable Settlement; Chorus America; All Classical FM, Portland. Address: Oregon Bach Festival, 1257 University of Oregon, Eugene OR97403-1257, USA. E-mail: bachfest@uoregon-edu

EVANS Donald, (Onwy), b. 12 June 1940, Cardiganshire, Wales. Retired Welsh Teacher. m. Pat Thomas, 29 December 1972, 1 son. Education: Honours Degree, Welsh, 1962, Diploma, Education, 1963, University College of Wales Aberystwyth; PhD, University of Wales Lampeter, 2006. Appointments: Welsh Master, Ardwyn Grammar School, Aberystwyth, 1963-73, Penglais Comprehensive School, Aberystwyth, 1973-84; Welsh Specialist, Cardigan Junior School, 1984-91; Welsh Supply Teacher in Ceredigion, Primary and Comprehensive Schools, 1991-2002. Publications: Egin (Shoots), 1976; Parsel Persain (Sweet Parcel) (editor), 1976; Haidd (Barley), 1977; Grawn (Seeds), 1979; Blodeugerdd o Gywyddau (Anthology of Alliterative Poems) (editor), 1981; Eden, 1981; Gwenoliaid (Swallows), 1982; Machlud Canrif (Century's Sunset), 1983; Eisiau Byw (Needing to Live), 1984; Cread Crist (Christ's Creation), 1986; O'r Bannau Duon (From the Black Hills), 1987; Iasau (Thrills), 1988; Seren Poets 2 (with others), 1990; The Life and Work of Rhydwen Williams, 1991; Wrth Reddf (By Instinct), 1994; Asgwrn Cefen (Backbone), 1997; Y Cyntefig Cyfoes (The Contemporary Primitive), 2000; Awdlau'r Brifwyl 1950-99 (The National Eisteddfod Odes 1950-1999), PhD thesis, 2008; Cartre'n y Cread (Home in the Universe), 2010; Sut i Greu Cywydd (How to Write an Alliterative Poem), 2011; Contributions to: Several publications. Honours: National Eisteddfod Crown and Chair, 1977, 1980; Welsh Arts

Council Literary Prizes, 1977, 1983, 1989; Welsh Academy Literary Award, 1989. Memberships: Welsh Academy; Welsh Poetry Society; Gorsedd of Bards, National Eisteddfod of Wales. Address: Y Plas, Talgarreg, Llandysul, Ceredigion SA44 4XA, West Wales.

EVANS Karen Marilyn, b. 22 January 1949, London, England. University Professor. m. Peter Evans, 1 son, 1 daughter. Education: BSc, University of Bristol, 1971; PhD, University of Surrey, 1982. Appointments: Professor, Post-Compulsory Education, Director, Postgraduate Centre for Professional and Adult Education, University of Surrey, Guildford, 1995-2000; Professor, Chair in Education (Lifelong Learning), 2001-, Head, School of Lifelong Education and International Development, 2001-05, University of London, Institute of Education. Publications: Numerous articles in academic and professional journals; Editor, international journal COMPARE, 2004-09; 9 books. Honours: Academician, Academy of Social Sciences; Visiting Fellowships/ Professorships, Commonwealth of Learning, Vancouver and the University of Melbourne; Economic and Social Research Council Major Awards, 1990-2010. Memberships: Fellow, Royal Society of Arts; British Association of International and Comparative Education; British Educational Research Association; American Educational Research Association; Society of Educational Studies.

EVANS Louise, b. 6 September, San Antonio, Texas, USA. Investor; Clinical Psychologist (retired); Philanthropist. m. Thomas Ross Gambrell. Education: BS, Psychology, Northwestern University, 1949; MS, Clinical Psychology, Purdue University, 1952; Intern, Clinical Psychology, Menninger Foundation, 1953; PhD, Clinical Psychology, Purdue University, 1955; Post-doctoral Fellowship, Clinical Child Psychology, Department of Child Psychiatry, Menninger Clinic, 1956; Diploma, American Board of Examiners in Professional Psychology, 1966. Appointments: Teaching Assistant, Psychology Department, Purdue University, 1950-51; Intern, Menninger Foundation, 1952-53; Staff Psychologist, Kankakee State Hospital, Illinois, 1954-55; Postdoctoral Fellow Child Psychology, Menninger Clinic, US Public Health Service, 1955-56; Head Staff Psychologist, Child Guidance Clinic, Kings County Hospital, Brooklyn, New York, 1957-58; Clinical Research Consultant, Episcopal Diocese, St Louis, Missouri, 1959-60; Director, Psychology Clinic, Barnes-Renard Hospitals, Instructor, Medical Psychology, Washington University School of Medicine, St Louis, 1959-60; Private Practice, Fullerton, California, 1960-93. Publications: Articles in professional journals. Honours include: Citizenship Award for contributions to mental health (1 of first 5 ever given), Purdue University, 1975; Silver Goblet, World's Leading Biographee of 1987, IBC; World Biographical Hall of Fame, ABI, 1987; 25 Year Silver Achievement Award, ABI, 1993; World Lifetime Achievement Award, ABI, 1995; Distinguished Alumni Award, Purdue University, 1993; Old Master Award, Purdue University, 1993; Northwestern University College of Arts and Sciences, Merit Award (one of two given), 1997; International Woman of the Year, Medal of Honour, 1996-97; 2000 Outstanding Scientists of the 20th Century Medal; 2000 Outstanding Scientists of the 21st Century Medal, IBC; Scientific Achievement Award, ABI; American Psychological Association, International Award for Lifelong Contributions to the Advancement of Psychology Internationally, 2002; Plaque for Pioneering Leadership in International Psychology, 2003, Certificate as Ambassador in recognition of outstanding leadership and enduring commitment, 2003, International Council of Psychologists;

Marie Curie Award and Gold Medal, IBC, 2006; ABI International Women's Review Board, Founding Member; Corann Okorodudu International Women's Advocacy Award, awarded by Society for the Psychology of Women (Division) of the American Psychological Association, 2009; Listed in numerous Who's Who publications and national and international biographical dictionaries. Memberships include Fellow of 15 professional organisations and societies, including: Life Fellow, IBA; Fellow: Academy of Clinical Psychology, American Psychological Association, Royal Society of Health, UK; Fellow, American Association for the Advancement of Science. Address: PO Box 6067, Beverly Hills, CA 90212-1067, USA.

EVE Trevor, b. 1 July 1951. Actor. m. Sharon Patricia Maughn, 1980, 2 sons, 1 daughter. Education: Kingston Art College; RADA. Career: Actor, Theatre includes: Children of a Lesser God, 1981; The Genius, 1983; High Society, 1986; Man Beast and Virtue, 1989; The Winter's Tale, 1991; Inadmissible Evidence, 1993; Uncle Vanya, 1996; TV includes: Shoestring, 1980; Jamaica Inn, A Sense of Guilt, 1990; Parnell and the Englishwoman, A Doll's House, 1991; The Politician's Wife, Black Easter, 1995; Under the Sun, 1997; Evilstreak, David Copperfield, 1999; Waking The Dead, 2000-08; Films include: Hindle Wakes; Dracula; A Wreath of Roses; The Corsican Brothers; Aspen Extreme; Psychotherapy; The Knight's Tale; The Tribe; Appetite; Possession; Troy; Producer for Projector Productions: Alice Through the Looking Glass, 1998; Cinderella; Twelfth Night, 2002, She's Out of My League, 2010. Honours include: Olivier Award for Best Supporting Actor, 1997. Address: c/o ICM Ltd, Oxford House, 76 Oxford Street, London, W1N 0AX, England.

EVERETT Lorne Gordon, b. 1 January 1943, Thunder Bay, Ontario, Canada. Hydrologist. m. Jennifer, 1 son, 1 daughter. Education: BSc, 1966; BSc H, 1968; MS, 1969; DSc, 1996; PhD, 1972. Appointments: Chief Scientist, Senior Vice President, Haley & Aldrich, The Shaw Group, The IT Group, Metcalf & Eddy; President & CEO, L E Everitt & Associates LLC. Publications: More than 15 books and 200 papers and reports. Honours: Kapitsa Gold Medal, Russian Academy of Natural Sciences; Gold Medal, Governor General of Canada; C U Theis Award, Medal of Excellence, US Navy. Memberships: FASTM; NGWA; AIH; IAH; FASCE; FAWRA. Address: 1312 Portcsuello Ave, Bel Air, Santa Barbara, CA 93105, USA.

EVERETT Rupert, b. 29 May 1959, Norfolk, England. Actor. Education: Central School for Speech and Drama, London. Appointments: Apprentice, Glasgow Citizen's Theatre, 1979-82; Model, Versace, Milan; Image of Opium perfume for Yves Saint Laurent; Stage appearances include: Another Country, 1982; The Vortex, 1989; Private Lives; The Milk Train Doesn't Stop Here Anymore; The Picture of Dorian Gray; The Importance of Being Earnest; Films include: Another Country, 1984; Dance With a Stranger, The Right Hand Man, 1985; Duet for One; Chronicle of Death Foretold, Hearts of Fire, 1987; Haunted Summer, 1988; The Comfort of Strangers, 1989; Inside Monkey Zetterland; Pret à Porter, The Madness of King George, 1995; Dunstan Checks In; My Best Friend's Wedding, 1997; A Midsummer's Night's Dream, B Monkey, 1998; An Ideal Husband, Inspector Gadget, 1999; The Next Best thing, 2000; Unconditional Love, The Importance of Being Earnest, The Wild Thornberrys Movie (voice), 2002; To Kill A King, 2003; Stage Beauty, People, Shrek 2 (voice), A Different Loyalty, 2004; Separate Lies, The Chronicles of Narnia: The Lion, the Witch and the Wardrobe (voice), 2005; Quiet Flows the Don,

2006; Shrek the Third(voice), Stardust, 2007; St Trinian's, 2007; St Trinian's 2: The Legend of Fritton's Gold, 2009; TV includes: Arthur the King; The Far Pavilions, 1982; Princess Daisy, 1983. Publications: Hello Darling, Are You Working?, 1992; The Hairdressers of San Tropez, 1995. Honours: American Comedy Awards, My Best Friends Wedding. Address: c/o ICM, 8942 Wilshire Boulevard, Beverly Hills, CA 90211, USA.

EVERT Chris(tine) Marie, b. 21 December 1954, Fort Lauderdale, Florida, USA. Former Lawn Tennis Player. m. (1) J Lloyd, 1979, divorced 1987, (2) A Mill, 1988, divorced 2006, 3 sons, (3) Greg Norman, 2009, divorced 2009. Education: High School, Ft Lauderdale. Career: Amateur, 1970-72; Professional, 1972-. Winner of: French Championship, 1974, 1975, 1979, 1980, 1982, 1985, 1986; Wimbledon Singles: 1974, 1976, 1981; Italian Championship: 1974, 1975, 1980; South African Championship: 1973; US Open: 1975, 1976, 1977, 1979, 1980, 1982 (record 100 victories); Colgate Series, 1977, 1978; World Championship, 1979; Played Wightman Cup, 1971-73, 1975-82; Federation Cup, 1977-82; Ranked No 1 in the world for seven years; Won 1309 matches in her career; Holds 157 singles titles and 18 Grand Slam titles. Appointments: President, Women's Tennis Association, 1975-76, 1983-91; Director, President's Council on Physical Fitness & Sports, 1991-; NBC TV sports commentator and host for numerous TV shows; Other: Established Chris Evert Charities, 1989; Owner, Evert Enterprises/IMG, 1989-; Chris Evert Pro-celebrity Tennis Classic, 1989-. Publications: Chrissie (autobiography), 1982; Lloyd on Lloyd (with J Lloyd) 1985. Honours include: International Tennis Hall of Fame, 1995; International Tennis Federation Chartrier Award, 1997; Named by ESPN as One of Top 50 Athletes of the 20th Century, 1999. Address: Evert Enterprises, 7200 W Camino Real, Suite 310 Boca Raton, FL 33433, USA.

EVTIMOVA Zdravka, b. 24 July 1959, Pernik, Bulgaria. Literary Translator; Author. m. Todor Georgiev, 2 sons, 1 daughter. Education: BA, American Studies, MA, English and American Studies, St Kiril and Methodius University, Bulgaria. Appointments: Translator, Interpreter, National Institute of Scientific Information, Sofia; Chief of Interpreters Section, Rare Earth Elements Institute, Bulgarian Academy of Sciences; Chief Expert, English and American Sector Translations, Ministry of Defence. Publications: Books published in Bulgaria: Your Shadow Was My Home (novel), 2000; Thursday (novel), 2003; 3 short story collections; Bitter Sky (short story collection) published in the UK, 2003. Honours: Chudomir Short Story National Award; Anna Kamenova National Literary Award, 1995; Gencho Stoev Short Story Award for a Short Story by a Balkan Author; Best Novel of the Year 2003 for the novel, Thursday; Best Short Story Collection by an established author; Award, MAG Press, San Diego, California; BBC Short Story Contest Award, 2005; Short Story Award, International Short Story Competition, Nantes, France, 2005; Golden Chain Short Story Award, Bulgaria, 2005. Membership: Bulgarian Writers' Union; Bulgarian PEN; International Organisation of Artists without Frontiers. Address: 36/61 Gagarin Street, 2304 Pernik, Bulgaria. E-mail: zevtimova@yahoo.com

EWINGTON John, b. 14 May 1936, Goodmayes, Essex, England. Lloyd's Broker; Church Musician. m. Helene Mary Leach, 2 sons. Education: County Technical School, Dagenham, South East Essex; ACertCM, 1968; Diploma, Church Music, Goldsmiths' College, 1988. Appointments: Administrative Assistant, Institute of London Underwriters, 1953-67; RN National Service, 1954-56; Underwriting Assistant, PCW Agencies, Lloyd's, 1967-86; Senior Broker, 1986-97, Consultant, 1997-2000, HSBC Gibbs; Director of Music and Organist: Blechingley Parish Church, 1966-97, St Mary Woolnoth, 1970-93 (also Senior Church Warden, 1973-93), St Katharine Cree, 1998-; Director, City Singers, 1976-; Vice Chairman of Governors, Oxted School, 1984-2005. Publications: Joint author (with Canon A Dobb), Landmarks in Christian Worship and Church Music; Articles on church music in professional journals. Honours: Knight, Order of St Lazarus of Jerusalem; Hon RSCM, 2002; MA, Lambeth Degree, 2003; Freeman, City of London, 1980; FGCM, 1988; Hon FCSM, 1990; Hon FFCM, 1998; OBE, 1996; Hon Fellow, University of Newcastle, NSW, 2004. Address: Hillbrow, Godstone Road, Blechingley, Surrey RH1 4PJ, England. E-mail: johnmusicsure@aol.com

EZAKI Shoichi, b. 27 September 1970, Kobe, Hyogo, Japan. Medical Doctor; Pediatrician. m. Yuko Hayase. Education: Medical Doctor, Japan, 1995; PhD, Saitama Medical University, Kawagae, Japan, 2009. Appointments: Instructor, Division of Neonatal Medicine, Centre for Maternal, Fetal and Neonatal Medicine, Saitama Medical Centre, Saitama Medical University, 2010-. Publications: Levels of catecholamines, arginine vasopressin and atrial natriuretic peptide in hypotensive extremely low birth infants in the first 24 hours after birth; Resuscitation of preterm infants with reduced oxygen results in less oxidative stress than resuscitation with 100% oxygen; Association between total antioxidant capacity in breast milk and postnatal age in days in premature infants; Successful treatment by probiotic enema of necrotizing enterocolitis. Memberships: Japan Pediatric Society; Japanese Society of Allergology; Japan Society of Perinatal and Neonatal Medicine; Japanese Society of Antiaging Medicine; Japan Society for Oriental Medicine; Society for Free Radical Research, Japan. Address: 3-20-2 Ochiai Tama, Tokyo 206-0033, Japan. E-mail: allergy@aol.jp

F

FABIAN Tibor Karoly, b. 14 January 1967, Budapest, Hungary. Dentist. m. Elisabeth Jung. Education: DMD, Semmelweis University, 1990; PhD, Hungarian Academy of Sciences, 1999; Teacher of Religion, Eger College of Religion, 2002. Appointments: Clinical Dentist Fellow, 1990-91, Adjunct Professor, 1999-2007, Associate Professor, 2007-, Semmelweis University, Budapest; Research Scholar, Hungarian Academy of Sciences, Budapest, 1991-92; Max-Planck Research Scholar, Max-Planck-Institut für Biophysik, Germany, 1992-93; PhD Research Scholar, Hungarian Academy of Sciences, 1993-95. Publications: Psychosomatic Dentistry, 2007; Religion, Faith and Healing, 2008; Psychogenic Denture Intolerance, 2010; Mind-Body Connections, 2011; Dentures: Types, Benefits and Potential Complications, in press. Honours: Two Zoltan Kormoczi Awards, Degree III, 1995, Degree II, 1996, Hungarian Dental Association. Memberships: Hungarian Association of Hypnosis; German Speaking Hypnosis Societies.

FAHMI Wael Salah, b. 10 October 1962, Cairo, Egypt. Architect; Professor. Education: BSc, Architectural Engineering, Cairo University, 1985; PhD, Department of Planning and Landscape, University of Manchester, 1994. Appointments: Site Manager and Architectural Supervisor, The Arab Bureau for Design and Technical Consultations, Cairo, 1985-88; Visiting Academic, University of Manchester, England, 2000-08; Principal, Urban Design Experimental Research Studio, Cairo, 2001-; Professor, Architecture and Urban Design, Helwan University, Cairo, 2001-. Publications: Numerous articles in professional journals. Honours: Listed in international biographical dictionaries; Scholarship, city of Amsterdam, 1999; Leverhulme Visiting Fellowship, 2001; Scholarship, International Institute for Urban Environment, 2002; Grant, Bauhaus Dessau Foundation, 2003; J William Fulbright Research Fellowship, USA, 2003; Travel Grant, University of Salford, 2007; INTAS grant, New Independent States of the Former Soviet Union, 2008; IHS grant, Institute for Housing and Urban Development Studies, 2009. Memberships: Royal Geographical Society; International Society for City and Regional Planners; Syndicate of Egyptian Engineers; Architectural Humanities Research Association. Address: 34 Abd El Hamid Lotfi Street, Mohandessein, Giza 12311, Egypt. E-mail: uders2003@yahoo.co.uk

FAHMY Tamer Y A, Associate Professor. Education: BSc (Hons), Chemistry, 1997, MSc, 2002, PhD, 2004, Physical Chemistry, Faculty of Science, Cairo University. Appointments: Researcher, 1998-2009, Associate Professor, 2009-, National Research Center, Cairo; Achievements include introducing nanotechnology of natural fibres, and its manipulations in the cellulose & paper discipline, for the first time worldwide. Publications: Numerous articles in professional journals. Honours: Top 100 Scientists, 2010; Listed in international biographical dictionaries. Memberships: American Chemical Society. Address: National Research Center, Cellulose & Paper Department, Sh El-Tahrir, Dokki, Cairo, Egypt. E-mail: drtamer_y_a@yahoo.com

FAINLIGHT Ruth (Esther), b. 2 May 1931, New York, New York, USA. Writer; Poet; Translator; Librettist. m. Alan Sillitoe, 19 November 1959, 1 son, 1 daughter. Education: Colleges of Arts and Crafts, Birmingham, Brighton, UK. Appointment: Poet-in-Residence, Vanderbilt University, USA, 1985, 1990. Publications: Poetry: Cages, 1966; To See the Matter Clearly, 1968; The Region's Violence, 1973; Another Full Moon, 1976; Sibyls and Others, 1980, 2nd edition 2007; Climates, 1983; Fifteen to Infinity, 1983; Selected Poems, 1987, 2nd edition, revised, 1995; The Knot, 1990; Twelve Sibyls, 1991; This Time of Year, 1994; Sugar-Paper Blue, 1997; Burning Wire, 2002; Moon Wheels, 2006; Visitação: Selected Poems in Portuguese translation, 1995; Encore La Pleine Lune, Selected Poems in French translation, 1997; Poemas, translation of selected poems in Spanish, 2000; Bleue Papier-Sucre, 2000; La Verita Sulla Sibilla, selected poems in Italian translation, 2003; Plumas, selected poems in Spanish translation published in Mexico, 2005; Autoral la Rampă, selected poems in Romanian translation, 2007; La Nueva Ciencia de los Materiales Fuertes, 2009; New & Collected Poems, 2010. Translations: All Citizens Are Soldiers, from Lope de Vega, 1969; Navigations, 1983; Marine Rose: Selected Poems of Sophia de Mello Breyner, 1988; Sophocles' Theban Plays (with Robert Littman), 2009. Short Stories: Daylife and Nightlife, 1971; Dr Clock's Last Case, 1994; Libretti: The Dancer Hotoke, 1991; The European Story, 1993; Bedlam Britannica, 1995. Contributions to: Atlantic Monthly; Critical Quarterly; English; Hudson Review; Lettre Internationale; London Magazine; London Review of Books; New Yorker; Poetry Review; Threepenny Review; Times Literary Supplement. Honours: Cholmondeley Award for Poetry, 1994; Hawthornden Award for Poetry, 1994; Fellow, Royal Society of Literature, 2008. Memberships: Society of Authors; PEN Writers in Prison Committee. Address: 14 Ladbroke Terrace, London W11 3PG, England.

FAIRBRASS Graham John, b. 14 January 1953, Meopham, Kent, England. Traveller; Writer; Poet; Painter. Education: BA, Arts, Open University, 1991; Coleg Harlech, 1995-96; Diploma, University of Wales, 1996; Norwich School of Art and Design, 1996-99. Publication: Conquistadors Shuffle Moon, 1989; Moon on its Back, 2004; Ashes at the Moon, 2005; Twentyone Poems, 2006; Evolution, 2007; Ciao, 2008; Revolution, 2009; Anthology Poems, 2010. Contributions to: Poetry Now, 1994; Anthology South East; Parnassus of World Poets, 1994, 1995, 1997; Poetry Club Anthology, vol l, 1995; Birdsuit, 1997-99. Honours: BA Hons, Cultural Studies. Address: 136A High Street, Deal, Kent CT14 6BE, England.

FAIRBURN Eleanor M, (Catherine Carfax, Emma Gayle, Elena Lyons), b. 23 February 1928, Ireland. Author. m. Brian Fairburn, 1 daughter. Appointments: Past Member, Literary Panel for Northern Arts; Tutor, Practical Writing, University of Leeds Adult Education Centre. Publications: The Green Popinjays, 1962; New edition, 1998; The White Seahorse, 1964, 3rd edition, 1996; translated into German, 1997. The Golden Hive, 1966; Crowned Ermine, 1968; The Rose in Spring, 1971; White Rose, Dark Summer, 1972; The Sleeping Salamander, 1973, 3rd edition, 1986; The Rose at Harvest End, 1975; Winter's Rose, 1976. As Catherine Carfax: A Silence with Voices, 1969; The Semper Inheritance, 1972; To Die a Little, 1972. As Emma Gayle: Cousin Caroline, 1980; Frenchman's Harvest, 1980. As Elena Lyons: The Haunting of Abbotsgarth, 1980; A Scent of Lilacs, 1982. Biographies (as Eleanor Fairburn): Edith Cavell, 1985; Mary Hornbeck Glyn, 1987; Grace Darling, 1988. Membership: Middlesbrough Writers Group, president, 1988, 1989, 1990. Address: 27 Minsterley Drive, Acklam, Middlesbrough, Cleveland TS5 8QU, England.

FAITHFULL Marianne, b. 29 December 1946, Hampstead, London, England. Singer. 1 son. Career: Recording artist, 1964-; Tours, appearances include: UK tour with Roy Orbison, 1965; US tour with Gene Pitney, 1965; Uxbridge Blues and Folk Festival, 1965; Montreux, Golden Rose Festival, 1966; Roger Water's The Wall, Berlin, 1990; Chieftains Music Festival, London, 1991; Acting roles include: I'll Never Forget Whatisname, 1967; Three Sisters, Chekkov, London, 1967; Hamlet, 1970; Kurt Weill's Seven Deadly Sins, St Ann's Cathedral, New York, 1990; Film appearance, Girl On A Motorcycle, 1968. Recordings: Singles include: As Tears Go By; Come And Stay With Me; This Little Bird; Summer Nights; Something Better/ Sister Morphine; The Ballad Of Lucy Jordan; Dreaming My Dreams; Electra, 1999; Albums: Come My Way, 1965; Marianne Faithfull, 1965; Go Away From My World, 1966; Faithfull Forever, 1966; Marianne Faithfull's Greatest Hits, 1969; Faithless, with the Grease Band, 1978; Broken English, 1979; Dangerous Acquaintances, 1981; A Child's Adventure, 1983; Strange Weather, 1987; Blazing Away, 1990; A Secret Life, 1995; 20th Century Blues, 1997; The Seven Deadly Sins, 1998; Vagabond Ways, 1999; Contributor, Lost In The Stars - The Music Of Kurt Weill, 1984; The Bells Of Dublin, The Chieftains, 1992. Publications: Faithfull (ghost written by David Dalton). Honours include: Grammy Nomination, Broken English, 1979. Current Management: Art Collins Management, PO Box 561, Pine Bush, NY 12566, USA.

FALCK (Adrian) Colin, b. 14 July 1934, London, England. Poet; Critic; Educator. (1) 1 daughter, (2) 2 sons. Education: BA, Philosophy, Politics and Economics, 1957, BA, Philosophy, Psychology and Physiology, 1959, MA, 1986, Magdalen College, Oxford; PhD, Literary Theory, University of London, 1988. Appointments: Military Service: British Army, Royal Artillery, 1952-54, Royal Air Force (Volunteer Reserve), 1954-65; Lecturer in Sociology, London School of Economics and Political Science, 1961-62; Part-time Lecturer in Philosophy and Education, University of Maryland, European Division, London, 1962-64; Lecturer in Modern Literature, Chelsea/King's College, University of London, 1964-84 Adjunct Professor in Literature, Syracuse University, London Program, Antioch University, London Program, 1985-89; Associate Professor in Literature, York College, Pennsylvania, 1989-99; Editorial: Co-Founder, 1962, Associate Editor, 1965-72, The Review; Poetry Editor, The New Review, 1974-78. Publications: The Garden in the Evening: Poems from the Spanish of Antonio Machado, 1964; Promises (poems), 1969; Backwards into the Smoke (poems), 1973; Poems Since 1900: An Anthology (editor with Ian Hamilton), 1975; In This Dark Light (poems), 1978; Robinson Jeffers: Selected Poems (editor), 1987; Myth, Truth and Literature: Towards a True Post-Modernism, 1989, 2nd edition, 1994; Edna St Vincent Millay: Selected Poems (editor), 1991; Memorabilia (poems), 1992; Post-Modern Love: An Unreliable Narration (poems), 1997; American and British Verse in the Twentieth Century: The Poetry that Matters (critical history), 2003. Address: Johnson & Alcock Ltd, 45-47 Clerkenwell Green, London EC1R 0HT, England. E-mail: falck.colin@gmail.com

FALDO Nick, b. 18 July 1957, Welwyn Garden City, England. Professional Golfer. m. (1) Melanie, divorced, (2) Gill, divorced, 1 son, 2 daughters, (3) Valerie Bercher, 1 daughter. Career: Professional, 1976-; Winner numerous tournaments including: Skol Lager Individual, 1977; Colgate PGA Championship, 1978; Sun Alliance PGA Championship, 1980, 1981; Haig Whisky TPC, 1982; Paco Rabanne Open de France, 1983; Martini International, 1983; Car Care Plan International, 1983, 1984; Lawrence Batley International, 1983; Ebel Euro Masters Swiss Open, 1983; Heritage Classic, US, 1984; Peugeot Spanish Open, 1987; 116th Open Gold Championship, 1987; Peugeot Open de France, 1988, 1989; Volvo Masters, 1988; 2nd, US Open Championships, 1988; Masters Tournament, US, 1989; Volvo PGA Championship, 1989; Dunhill British Masters, 1989; Suntory World Match Play, 1989; 119th Open Golf Championship, 1990; Masters Tournament, US, 1991, 1996; Carroll's Irish Open, 1991, 1992, 1993; 121st Open Golf Championship, 1992; Scandinavian Masters, 1992; 2nd, USPGA Championship, 1992; GA European Masters, 1992; Toyota World Match Play, 1992; Volvo Bonus Pool, 1992; Johnnie Walker Classic, 1993; 2nd, 122nd Open Golf Championship, 1993; Alfred Dunhill Open, 1994; Doral-Ryder Open, US, 1995; Nissan Open, US, 1997; World Cup of Golf, 1998; 5th, US Open (including third round record 66), 2002; 8th 132nd Open Golf Championship, 2003; Team Member: Ryder Cup, 1977, 1979, 1981, 1983, 1985 (winners), 1987 (winners), 1989, 1991, 1993, 1995 (winners), 1997 (winners); Alfred Dunhill Cup, 1985, 1986, 1987 (winning team), 1988, 1991, 1993; World Cup of Golf, 1977, 1991, 1998 (winners). In 2006 signed with CBS as the networks leading golf analyst. Publications: In Search of Perfection, (with Bruce Critchley), 1995; Faldo - A Swing for Life, 1995. E-mail: nfdo@faldodesign.com

FALK Heinz, b. 29 April 1939, St Pölten. Emeritus Professor of Organic Chemistry. m. Rotraud, 1 son. Education: Dr Phil, University of Vienna. Appointments: Assistant, University Vienna, 1966; Post-Doctoral ETH, Zurich, 1971; Habilitation, University of Vienna, 1972; Assistant Professor, Physical Organic Chemistry, 1975; University Professor, Organic Chemistry, University Linz, 1979; Guest Professor, University of Barcelona, 1982; Dean, Science Technical Faculty, University of Linz, 1989-91. Publications: 300 papers in refereed journals; 2 books; Several patents. Honours include: Loschmidt Medal, 1998, and others. Memberships include: Austrian Academy of Science; Austrian Chemical Society; German Chemical Society; American Chemical Society; New York Academy of Science; European Academy of Sciences. Address: Institute for Organic Chemistry, Johannes Kepler University Linz, Altenbergerstr 66, A 4040 Linz, Austria. E-mail: heinz@falk.net

FALLOWELL Duncan Richard, b. 26 September 1948, London, England. Writer. Education: Magdalen College, Oxford. Publications: Drug Tales, 1979; April Ashley's Odyssey, 1982; Satyrday, 1986; The Underbelly, 1987; To Noto, 1989; Twentieth Century Characters, 1994; One Hot Summer in St Petersburg, 1994; Gormenghast (opera libretto), 1998; A History of Facelifting, 2003; Going As Far As I Can, 2008; How To Disappear, 2011. Address: c/o Aitken Alexander Associates, 18-21 Cavaye Place, London SW10 9PT, England.

FANG Jin-Qing, b. 11 July 1939, Fu-jian, China. Scientific Researcher. m. 1 son, 1 daughter. Education: Graduate, Department of Physics, Tsing-Hua University, Beijing, China, 1958-64; Postdoctoral Fellow, Australian National University and University of Texas at Austin, USA, 1988-90. Appointments: Researcher into atomic energy science and technology, non-linear science, nonlinear complex networks and complexity science with applications including chaos control and synchronisation, China Institute of Atomic Energy, 1964; Research Professor (Fellow), 1987-; Vice Chair, Chinese National Complex System and Complex Network; Head of the Key Program Projects of the National Natural Science Foundation of China, 2005-08; Visiting Professor in about 20 universities world-wide, 1987-. Publications include: More than 200 articles and more than 60 Science and EI recorded scientific papers; 10 monographs and textbooks from 1976 including most recently: Taming Chaos and Developing High Technology, 2002; Mastering Beam Halo and Exploring Network Science, 2008; Co-author: Chaos Control-Theory and Applications, 2003; Network Science and Statistical Physical Methods, 2011. Honours: 12 Awards and

Prizes, China include: National Science Conference Prize, 1978; 2nd Prizes of Progress in Science and Technology in National Defence of China, 1998, 2000, 2002, 2004, 2005, 2008; And the Best Paper Award, China Association for Science and Technology, 2008. Memberships: China Institute of Physics; Chinese Institute of Applied Mathematics and Industry; Chinese Institute of System Science. Address: China Institute of Atomic Energy, PO Box 275-68, Beijing 102413, China. E-mail: fjq96@126.com

FANG Yanjun, b. 10 July 1957, Fuzhou, Fujian, China. Control Science and Engineering. m. Ying Cheng, 1 daughter. Education: BA, 1982, MA, 1985, PhD, 1988, Wuhan University of Hydraulic and Electrical Engineering. Appointments: Associate Professor, 1991, Professor, 1995, Wuhan University of Hydraulic and Electrical Engineering; Research Fellow, Holland, 1992-93; Professor and PhD Supervisor, Wuhan University, 2000-; Distinguished Professor, Nanjing Normal University, 2001-06. Publications: Intelligent Instrument and Application, 2005; Measurement Technology and Systems, 2006; Measurement Technology and System Design, 2007; Principles and Application of Embedded System, 2010; More than 200 academic papers published in journals or collected in conference proceedings. Honours: Cross-Century Talent Prize, Ministry of Electrical Power of PR China, 1997. Address: Department Automation, Wuhan University, No 8 South Donghu Road, Wuhan Hubei 430072, China. E-mail: yjfang@whu.edu.cn

FANNING Fred, b. 8 December 1956, Valdosta, Georgia, USA. Public Administrator. m. Tammy Hanson, 2 sons. Education: BSc, Excelsior College, 1993; M Ed, National Louis University, 1996; MA, Webster University, 2005. Appointments: Safety Specialist, Fort Riley, Kansas, USA, 1986-89; Safety Specialist, 8th Infantry Division, Bad Kreuznach, Germany, 1989-90; Safety Manager, US Army Berlin, Germany, 1990-94; Safety Specialist, US Army Europe, Heidelberg, Germany, 1994-95; Safety Director, US Army V Corps, Heidelberg, Germany, 1995-98; Safety Director, Fort Leonard Wood, Missouri, USA, 1999-2004; Senior Safety Manager, Army Safety Office, Arlington, Virginia, USA, 2004-05; Safety Manager, 2005-06, Director for Administrative Services, 2005-09, Department of Commerce, Washington, DC; Director of Program Integration and Logistics Operations, US Department of Energy, Washington, DC, 2009-. Publications: Basic Safety Administration: A Handbook for the New Safety Specialist, 2003; Chapter, Safety Training and Documentation Principles. Honours: Appointed to Senior Executive Service; Department of Commerce Bronze Medal; NATO Medal. Memberships: American Society of Safety Engineers; Missouri Writers Guild. Address: 3 Chandler Court, Fredericksburg, VA 22405, USA. E-mail: fanningf@verizon.net

FARAG Radwan Sedkey, b. 27 November 1941, Cairo, Egypt. Professor of Biochemistry. m. Fatma Mahmoud El-Shishi, 1 son. Education: BSc, 1963, MSc, 1967, Faculty of Agriculture, Cairo University, Egypt; PhD, St Bartholomew's Hospital Medical College, London University, 1974. Appointments: Demonstrator, 1963-67, Associate Lecturer, 1967-74, Lecturer, 1974-79, Associate Professor, 1979-84, Professor of Biochemistry, 1984-, Head of Biochemistry Department, 1988-94, Faculty of Agriculture, Cairo University; Director of Central Lab, 1975-95; Over 45 MSc and 56 PhD students obtained their degrees under his direct supervision. Publications: Author; Chromatographic Analysis, 1990; Lipids, 1991; Physical and Chemical Analysis of Fats and Oils, 1995; Principles of Biochemistry, 1999; Modern Methods of Amino Acid Analysis and Assessment of Protein Quality, 2003. Publications: Over 150 papers in prominent journals; Referee of some national and international journals. Honours: Egyptian State Award, Egyptian Academy of Scientific Research and Technology, 1978, 1984; 20th Century Award Achievement, IBC, 1997; Decree of Merit, Cairo University, 2008; Honorary Doctorate, International Yorker University, Italy, 2008. Memberships: National Encyclopedia, Egypt; American Oil Chemists Society; International Association for Cereal Science and Technology; New York Academy of Sciences; American Association for the Advancement of Science; National Committee of Biochemistry and Molecular Biology; Advisory Board of J Drug Res. Address: Biochemistry Department, Faculty of Agriculture, Cairo University, PO 12613, El-Gamma St, Giza, Egypt.

FARAH Mo (Mohamed), b. 23 March 1983, Somalia (British citizen). Track and Field Athlete. m. Tania Nell, 1 stepdaughter, 2 daughters. Education: Feltham Community College, London; Isleworth and Syon School; St Mary's University College, Twickenham. Career: 5000m, European Athletics Junior Championship, 2001; Silver medal (5000m), European Championship, Gothenburg, 2006; Winner, Euorpean Cross Country Championship, San Giorgio su Legnano, Italy, 2006; 6th (5000m), World Championships, Osaka, Japan, 2007; Gold medal (3000m), European Indoor Championships, Turin, 2009; 7th (5000m), World Championships in Athletics, 2009; Winner, Great South Run, 2009; Silver medal, European Cross Country Championships, 2009; Winner, London 10,000m, 2010; Winner, European Cup 10,000m, 2010; 2 Gold medals (10,000m and 5,000m) European Athletics Championships, 2010; Winner, Edinburgh Cross Country, 2011; Gold medal (3,000m), European Indoor Championships, 2011; Winner, NYC Half Marathon, 2011; Winner, Prefontaine Classic 10,000m, Diamond League, Oregon, USA, 2011; Winner (5,000m), Diamond League, Monaco, 2011; Silver medal (10,000m) and Gold medal (5,000m), World Championships in Athletics, Daegu, South Korea, 2011; Gold medal (10,000m), London Olympics, 2012. Honours: Track and Field Athlete of the Year, British Olympic Association, 2010; British Athletics Writers Association Award, 2010 and 2011; European Athlete of the Year, 2011; CBE, 2013.

FARHI Nicole, b. 25 July 1946. Fashion Designer. m. David Hare, 1992; 1 daughter with Stephen Marks. Education: Cours Berçot Art School, Paris. Appointments: Designer, Pierre d'Albi, 1968; Founder, French Connection with Stephen Marks, 1973; Former designer, Stephen Marks; Founder and designer, Nicole Farhi, 1983-; Nicole Farhi For Men, 1989-; Opened Nicole's Restaurant, 1994. Honours: British Fashion Award for Best Contemporary Design, 1995, 1996, 1997; FHM Awards Menswear Designer of the Year, 2000; Maxim Awards, British Designer of the Year, 2001. Address: 16 Foubert's Place, London W1F 7PJ, England.

FARICY Robert, b. 29 August 1926, St Paul, Minnesota, USA. Theology Educator. Education: BS, US Naval Academy, 1949; MA, 1954, PhL, 1955, St Louis University; STL, Lyon-Fourviere, Lyons, France, 1963; STD, Catholic University of America, Washington, District of Columbia, 1966. Appointments: Ensign, US Navy, 1944-50; Entered Society of Jesus, 1950; Teacher, Marquette University High School, Milwaukee, 1955-59; Professor, Catholic University of America, Washington, 1966-71; Professor of Spiritual Theology, Pontifical Gregorian University, Rome, Italy, 1971-; Visiting Professor, Sogang University, Seoul, Korea, 1992-93; Visiting Professor, Pontifical Urbanian University,

2000-2002; Professor of Spiritual Theology, Pontifical Institute Regina Mundi, 2003-; Professor, Regina Mundi Institute, 1998-. Publications: All Things in Christ, 1981; Wind and Sea, 1982, 2nd edition, 1988; Discernment and Contemplation, 1983, 3rd edition, 1989; Lord's Dealing, 1988; "Your Wounds I Will Heal", 1999; 30 other books, translated into various languages. Address: Piazza della Pilotta 4, Rome 00187, Italy.

FARKAS Árpád, b. 27 January 1974, Gheorgheni, Romania. Physicist. m. Júlia Konyicska-Egresi, 2 sons. Education: MSc, 1996; PhD, 2008. Appointments: IPCMS, Strasbourg, France, 1999; MTA KFKI Atomic Energy Research Institute, Hungary, 2001-; University of Salzburg, Austria, 2005. Publications: 1 book chapters; 21 papers in international peer reviewed journals; 65 abstracts and proceedings papers; 13 scientific reports. Honours: Junior Prize, Hungarian Academy of Sciences, 2005-; Fermi Young Scientist Award, 2008-. Memberships: Eurados, the European Radiation Dosimetry Group; Aerosol Society, UK; Hungarian Nuclear Society. Address: MTA KFKI Atomic Energy Research Institute, Konkoly Thege M 29-33, 1121 Budapest, Hungary. E-mail: farkasa@aeki.kfki.hu Website: www.kfki.hu/~farkasa/index.html

FARMAN Allan George, b. 26 July 1949, Birmingham, England. Professor of Radiology and Imaging Science. m. Taeko Takemori. Education: BDS, 1971; LDSRCS, 1972; PhD, 1977; Dip ABOMR, 1982; EdS, 1983; MBA, 1987; DSc, 1996; Dip JBOMR, 1997. Appointments: Professor, Radiology and Imaging Science, School of Dentistry, University Louisville; Clinical Professor, Diagnostic Radiology, University Louisville School of Medicine, 1980-; Adjunct Professor, Anatomical Sciences & Neurobiology. Publications: More than 350 science articles, numerous texts and contributions to textbooks; Oral and Maxillofacial Diagnostic Imaging; Editor: Panoramic Imaging News, 2001-08; Deputy Editor, International Journal of Computer Assisted Radiology and Surgery, 2006-. Honours: President of Honour, First Latin-American Regional Meeting on Dentomaxillofacial Radiology, 1996; Honoured Guest Professor, University of Buenos Aires, Argentina, 1996-; Honoured Guest Professor, Peking University, 2006-; Distinguished Service Medal, University of Louisville, 2006-. Memberships: International Association of Dentomaxillofacial Radiology, President, 1994-97; American Academy of Oral and Maxillofacial Radiology, Editor, 1988-95 and 2005-09; President Elect, 2007-09, President, 2009-11; American Dental Association, Representative to International DICOM Committee, 2001-10; Founder, Organiser, International Congress Computed Maxillofacial Imaging, 1995-. Address: c/o School of Dentistry, University of Louisville, Louisville, KY 40292, USA.

FARR Marie L (Lennie), b. 6 September 1927, Vienna, Austria. Mycologist (retired). Widow. Education: BS, Agriculture and Soil Science, Michigan State University, 1948; MS, Botany, Michigan State University, 1950; PhD, Mycology, University of Iowa, 1957. Appointments: Assistant Botanist (temporary position), Institute of Jamaica, Kingston, 1954-55; Assistant Botanist (temporary position), Mycological Institute, University of Recife, Brazil, 1958; Research Mycologist, USDA, Agricultural Research Service, 1958-87; Retired. Publications: 95 papers and articles in professional scientific journals; Identification key to slime moulds; Co-author, advanced textbook on slime moulds; Translation of an elementary mycology textbook, English to German. Honours: President, Mycological Society of America, 1981-82. Memberships: MSA. Address: 241 Courtyards Blvd, Apt 107, Sun City Center, FL 33573-5781, USA.

FARRELL Colin James, b. 31 May 1976, Castleknock, Dublin, Ireland. Actor. m. Amelia Warner, divorced, 1 son with Kim Bordenave. Education: Gaiety School of Drama. Career: TV: Ballykissangel, 1996; Falling for a Dancer, 1998; Scrubs, 2005; The War Zone, 1999; Ordinary Decent Criminal, 2000; Tigerland, 2000; Hart's War, 2002; Minority Report, 2002; Phone Booth, 2002; SWAT, 2003; The Recruit, 2003; Alexander, 2004; Miami Vice, 2006; Cassandra's Dream, 2007; In Bruges, 2008; Pride and Glory, 2008; The Imaginarium of Doctor Parnassus, 2009; Triage, 2009; Ondine, 2009; Crazy Heart, 2009. Honours: Golden Globes, Best Actor in Comedy or Musical, In Bruges, 2009.

FARROW Mia Villiers, b. 9 February 1945, California, USA. Actress. m. (1) Frank Sinatra, 1966, divorced 1968, (2) André Previn, 1970, divorced 1979, 14 children, 1 deceased, including 1 son with Woody Allen. Career: Stage debut in The Importance of Being Ernest, New York, 1963; other stage appearances include: The Three Sisters, House of Bernard Alba, 1972-73; The Marrying of Ann Leete, Ivanov, RSC, London, 1976; Romantic Comedy, Broadway, 1979; Films include: Guns at Batasi, 1964; Rosemary's Baby, 1968; John and Mary, Secret Ceremony, 1969; The Great Gatsby, 1973; Full Circle, A Wedding, Death on the Nile, 1978; A Midsummer Night's Sex Comedy, 1982; Broadway Danny Rose, 1984; Hannah and Her Sisters, 1986; Radio Days, 1987; Another Woman, 1988; Oedipus Wrecks, 1989; Alice, Crimes and Misdemeanours, 1990; Husband and Wives, Shadows and Fog, 1992; Widow's Peak, 1994; Miami Rhapsody, 1995; Reckless, 1995; Private Parts, 1997; Coming Soon, 2000; Purpose, 2002; The Omen, 2006; Arthur and the Invisibles, 2006; Fast Track, 2006; Be Kind Rewind, 2007; Arthur and the Revenge of Maltazard, 2009; TV appearances include: Peyton Place, 1964-66; Peter Pan, 1975. Publication: What Falls Away (autobiography), 1996. Honours: Academy Award; Best Actress, 1969; David Donatello, 1969; Film Festival Award, 1969; San Sebastian Award. Address: International Creative Management, c/o Sam Cohn, 40 West 57th Street, New York, NY 10019, USA. Website: www.mia-farrow.com

FARRUGIA Charles John, b. 17 January 1946, Marsa, Malta. Research Professor. m. Maria Dolores. Education: BS, University of Malta, 1966; MSc, 1979, D Phil (PhD), 1984, University of Berne, Switzerland; Dip Educ, University of London, UK, 1982; GDSD, University of Munich, Germany, 1987. Appointments: Teacher of Physics and Mathematics, later Head of Physics, Naxxar Technical School, Malta, 1966-74; Research Associate, Imperial College of Science and Technology, London, 1984-90; Research Scientist, NASA-Goddard Space Flight Center, Maryland, USA, 1990-93; Senior Lecturer, Pedagogy of Science, University of Malta, 1993-96; Scientist III, later Research Professor, Space Science Center and Department of Physics, University of New Hampshire, Durham, USA, 1996-. Publications: Around 320 scientific papers; Articles for general public and schools on science topics; Convenor and co-convenor, International Scientific Meetings. Honours: NATO Essay Prizewinner, 1962; European Space Agency Fellow, 1984-86. Memberships: American Geophysical Union; European Geophysical Union. Address: Space Science Center, College Road, Morse Hall, Rm 414, University of New Hampshire, Durham, NH 03824, USA. E-mail: charlie.farrugia@unh.edu

DICTIONARY OF INTERNATIONAL BIOGRAPHY 36th EDITION

FARRUGIA Edward George, b. 1 October 1947, Marsa, Malta. Teacher; Celibate Priest and Religious Member of the Jesuit Order. Education: AB (Classical), 1968, MA, PhL (Philosophy), 1969, PhD (Philosophy), 1972, St Louis University, USA; Mag Theol, Innsbruck University, Austria, 1976; Dr Theol, Tübingen University, Germany, 1985. Appointments: Ordained Roman Catholic Priest, 1976; Philosophy Teacher, St Louis University, USA, 1968-70; English Language Teacher, Istituto Leone XIII, Milan, Italy, 1972; Teacher of Religion, Walter Erben Technical School, Tübingen, Germany, 1977-80; Teacher, 1981-85, Extraordinary Professor, 1986-92, Full Professor, 1993-, Eastern Theology and Patristics, Pontifical Institute of Oriental Studies, Rome; Teacher of Eastern Theology, Pontificio Ateneo Antonianum, Rome, 1984-86; Chaplain, Church of the Sisters of the Eucharist, Rome, 1984-87; Teacher of Eastern Theology, Pontifical Gregorian University, Rome, 1992-2007; Malta University, 1992-2009; Member, Administrative Counsel, Association Culturelle Mediterranées, Paris-La Rochelle, 1997-; St Thomas Institute of History, Philosophy and Theology, Moscow, 2001-04; Teacher of Eastern Theology, Innsbruck University, 2003-04. Publications: Del Pensiero Religioso Russo, 1909-2009, 2012; Dies Amalphitana II: Amalfi nel Medioevo; Dies Amalphitana III: Le Amalfitanie nel Mediterraneo, 2012. Honours: Listed in international biographical dictionaries. Address: Pontificio Istituto Orientale, Piazza Sta Maria Maggiore 7, 00185 Rome, Italy. E-mail: farrugia1947@gmail.com

FATHELRAHMAN Ahmed Ibrahim, b. 1970, Khartoum, Sudan. Pharmacist. m. Khadeja, 3 sons, 1 daughter. Education: B Pharm, Assiut University, Egypt, 1996; Postgraduate diploma, Communication, Omdurman Islamic University, 2001; MSc, Clinical Pharmacology, 2005, PhD, 2010, Universiti Sains Malaysia, Malaysia. Appointments: Pharmacist, Quality Control, Central Medical Supplies, Sudan, 1997-2000; Inspection & Supervision, Revolving Drug Fund, Ministry of Health, Khartoum, 2000-02; Head, Department of Pharmaceutical Services and Drug Information Centre, Directorate of Pharmacy, Ministry of Health, Khartoum, 2004-06; Research Fellow, Universiti Sains Malaysia, 2006-09. Publications: 9 publications in international peer-reviewed journals. Honours: Young Investigator Scholarship of APACT Conference, 2007. Memberships: Society for Research on Nicotine & Tobacco; Asia Life Sciences Council. Address: Directorate of Pharmacy, Ministry of Health, Khartoum State, Khartoum Post Office Box 1517, Sudan. E-mail: afathelrahman@yahoo.com

FAULKS Sebastian, b. 20 April 1953, Newbury, Berkshire, England. Author; Journalist. m. Veronica Youlten, 1989, 2 sons, 1 daughter. Education: Wellington College; Emmanuel College, Cambridge. Appointments: Reporter, Daily Telegraph newspaper, 1979-83; Feature Writer, Sunday Telegraph, 1983-86; Literary Editor, The Independent, 1986-89; Deputy Editor, The Independent on Sunday, 1989-90, Associate Editor, 1990-91; Columnist, The Guardian, 1992-, Evening Standard, 1997-99; Mail on Sunday, 1999-2000. Television: Churchill's Secret Army, 2000. Publications: The Girl at the Lion d'Or, 1989; A Fool's Alphabet, 1992; Birdsong, 1993; The Fatal Englishman, 1996; Charlotte Gray, 1998; On Green Dolphin Street, 2001; Human Traces, 2005; The Footprints on Mount Low, 2005; Pistache (an essay collection), 2006; Engleby, 2007; Devil May Care, 2008; A Week in December, 2009; Faulks on Fiction: Great British Characters and the Secret Life of the Novel, 2011; A Possible Life, 2012. Honours: British Book Awards, Author of the Year, 1995; James Tait Black Memorial Prize (for fiction) Charlotte Gray, 1998; CBE, 2002; British Book Awards Galaxy Popular Fiction Title, Devil May Care, 2009. Address: c/o Aitken and Stone, 29 Fernshaw Road, London, SW10 0TG, England.

FAULSTICH-WIELAND Hannelore Hilde, b. 10 December 1948, Hannoversch Muenden, Germany. University Professor. m. Peter Faulstich, 2 sons. Education: Diploma, Psychology, 1972, Habilitation, Education, 1980, Technical University, Berlin; Phd, Social Sciences, University of Bremen, 1975. Appointments: Assistant Professor, Technical University, Berlin, 1973-77; Researcher, Sociological Research Institute, Goettingen, 1977-79; Researcher, University of Dortmund, 1980-82; Deputy Head, Women's Research Centre, Hannover, 1982-84; Professor, Fachhochschule, Frankfurt/Main, 1984-92; Professor, Women's Studies, Westfaelische Wilhelms University, Muenster, 1992-96; Professor, Education, University of Hamburg, 1997-. Publications: Numerous articles in professional journals. Memberships: Deutsche Gesellschaft fuer Erziehungswissenschaft. Address: Querenburg 32, 34346 Hann Muenden, Germany. E-mail: h.faulstich-wieland@uni-hamburg.de Website: http://www.epb.uni-hamburg.de/Personal/faulstich-wieland

FAUR Antonio Viorel, b. 9 September 1969, Oradea, Bihor County, Romania. Professor. Education: Bachelor's degree, History, 1995, Postgraduate degree, 1996, PhD, Contemporary History, 2001, Babes-Bolyai University, Cluj Napoca. Appointments: Assistant Professor, 1996-2000, Lecturer, 2000-04, Associate Professor, 2004-09, Head of History Department, 2008-, Professor PhD, 2009-, University of Oradea. Publications: 11 books; Numerous articles in professional journals. Honours: Certificate of Merit, University of Oradea, 2008; Certificate of Excellence, Ministry of Culture and National Heritage, 2010. Memberships: Society for Historical Sciences; Cultural Association Crisana, Oradea; Cultural Association ASTRA, Oradea branch. Address: Str Aluminei nr 39, Bl A 1, Sc C, Et IV, Ap 58, Jud Bihor, Oradea, 410313, Romania. E-mail: afaur@uoradea.ro

FAURE Sabine, b. 22 October 1963, Labastide-Rouairoux, France. Fashion, Beauty & Advertising Photographer. Education: Master's degree, English Literature, University of Avignon, 1986. Appointments: Photographer (fashion, advertising, beauty, children, landscape, architecture and food), 1989-. Publications: Hermes Menswear; BIBA magazine; Paris Chamber of Notaries; French Federation of Cardiology; FHM magazine, UK; Cosmopolitan magazine, Italy; DNR magazine, New York; Vogue Hommes International; Conde Nast Publications (Paris); Vogue Homes (Paris). Address: 46 Chemin des Falaises, 30 400 Villeneuve les Avignon, France. E-mail: mail@sabinefaure.com Website: www.sabinefaure.com

FAVRET Eduardo Alfredo, b. 5 May 1962, Moron, Argentina. Physicist. Education: Licentiate, Physical Sciences, University of Buenos Aires, 1992; PhD, Physical Sciences, Faculty of Sciences, University of Buenos Aires, 1998. Appointments: Researcher, Conicet; Researcher, Institute of Soils, INTA; Assistant Professor and Researcher, Institute of Technology, University of San Martin, National Commission on Atomic Energy; Researcher, Fellowships, National Council on Scientific and Technological Research, Argentina; Postdoctoral Fellowship, German Science Foundation, Saarland University, Germany, 2001-02; Researcher at Institute of Soils, National Institute of Agricultural Technology (INTA), 2005-; Researcher, Conicet. Publications: Materials Characterization, 1990, 1991, 2003; Practical Metallography, 1996, 1997, 1999, 2003; Optics and Laser Technology, 1997; Microstructural Science, 1999; Kerntechnik, 2000; Journal of Archaeological Science, 2001; Microscopy and Analysis, 2001, 2002; Microscopy Research and Technique, 2001; Journal of Microscopy, 2002; Microscopy and Microanalysis, 2002, 2003, 2004, 2006, 2007; 2008; Applied Surface Science, 2004; Microscopy Today, 2004, 2007; Microscopy Research and Technique, 2006; Microscopy and Analysis, 2007; International Journal of Plant Science, 2008; Microscopy and Microanalysis, 2009; Micron, 2008; Book, Functional Properties of Bio-Inspired Surfaces: Characterization and Technological Applications, 2009; Microscopy and Microanalysis, 2010, 2011; Acta Microscopia, 2009; Microscopy and Microanalysis, 2010; Book chapter, Rimaps and Variogram Characterization of Micro-Nanotopography. Honours: 2nd Prize, International Metallographic Contest, 1995; Prize, Metallographic Photography, 1988; Honorable Mention Award, International Metallographic Contest, 2001. Memberships: Argentine Society of Microscopy; American Society for Metals; International Metallographic Society; Microscopy Society of America; American Chemical Society. Address: Lincoln 831, (1712) Castelar, Argentina. E-mail: eafavret@cnia.inta.gov.ar

FAZEKAS Kalman, b. 4 November 1938, Budapest, Hungary. Professor. m. Elisabeth. Education: MSc, EE, MSc, Teacher Engineering, PhD, EE, Budapest University of Technology and Economics. Appointments: University Teacher; Professor. Publications: More than 160 journal papers and conference paper; Textbooks; Book chapters. Honours: Minister of Education Award; Rector of BME Award; 3 times winner, Pollak-Virag Award for best journal paper. Memberships: IEEE: EURASIP; HTE. Address: Vinceller u 47, Budapest, H-1113, Hungary.

FEARON Daniel, b. 14 October 1944, Beaconsfield, Buckinghamshire, England. Numismatist. m. Karen Dawn Wark, 1971, 1 son, 1 daughter. Education: Canford School, 1958-63. Appointments: Sotheby & Co, 1963-69; Sotheby Parke Bernet, New York, 1969-70; Spink & Son, 1970-86; Managing Director, Glendining's, 1986-93; Manager, Coin & Medal Department, Bonhams, 1993-2000; Consultant, Independent Numismatic Consultant, 2000-. Publications: Catalogue of British Commemorative Medals, 1558 to the present day, 1984; Victorian Souvenir Medals, 1986; Numerous articles of numismatic interest and specialist auction sale catalogues including: Out of the Barbed Wire – A Newly Discovered Medal Design by Arnold Zadikow, 2009. Memberships: Liveryman, Drapers' Company; British Numismatic Society; British Numismatic Trade Association. Address: PO Box 492, New Malden, Surrey, KT3 9EY, England. E-mail: info@danielfearon.com

FEBLAND Harriet, b. New York City, New York, USA. Artist. 2 sons. Education includes: Pratt Institute; New York University; The American Artists School; Art Students League: Studies abroad in England and France, 11 years. Career: Pioneer Constructionist Sculptor and Painter; Exhibitions in European art circles including Museé d'Art Moderne, Paris and Alwin Galleries, the Drian Gallery in London and the Lessedra Gallery in Sofia, Bulgaria; On return to USA opened a studio in New York and Westchester; Founded, 1962, Director until 1993, Harriet FeBland Art Workshop for advanced painters; Gave workshops in New York, Vermont, New Mexico and England; Lecturer and Instructor, New York University, 1960-61; Faculty Member, Westchester Art Workshop, 1965-72; Numerous group exhibitions includes: MOMA; Carnegie Institute; Brooklyn Museum; 52 solo exhibitions include most recently: Zimmerli Art Museum, Rutgers, New Brunswick, New Jersey; Works in collections including: Grounds for Sculpture Museum, Hamilton, New Jersey; Library of Congress, Washington, DC; Cincinnati Art Museu, Cincinnati, Ohio; Pepsico Corporation, Somers, New York; Metromedia Corp, Los Angeles, California; Sealy Corp, Chicago, Illinois; Hempstead Bank of LI, Hempstead, New York; The State of Hawaii Art and Cultural Foundation, Hilo, Hawaii; The Hudson River Museum, Yonkers, New York; Tweed Art Museum, University of Minnesota, Duluth, Minnesota; Mercy College, Dobbs Ferry, New York; Haverly Collection, The Agnes K Haverly Foundation, Guildford, Connecticut; Westchester County, County Court House Plaza, White Plains, New York; Westisle Art Center, Prince Edward Isle, Canada. Publications: Works included in 37 books on art; Book, Harriet FeBland (& DVD). Honours include: Various awards in painting, sculpture and printmaking, National Association of Women Artists, 1966-2002; Awards in painting and printmaking, American Society of Contemporary Artists, 1977-2008; Awards in painting and sculpture, Hudson River Museum, 1976-87; Robert Conover Memorial Award in Graphics, Society of American Graphic Artists, 1999; American Medal of Honor, ABI, 2002, 2005; Archives of American Art, Smithsonian Institution; International Art Biography, Germany; Agnes K Haverly Foundation Lifetime Achievement Award, 2009; Painting Award and Acquisition, Lessedra Gallery, Sofia, Bulgaria, 2010; Listed in Who's Who publications and biographical dictionaries. Memberships: American Society of Contemporary Artists (President, 1981-83, 2005-07); ABI International Women's Review Board. Address: 245 East 63rd Street, 1803, New York, NY 10065, USA. E-mail: harrietfebland@aol.com Website: www.harrietfebland.com

FEDERER Roger, b. 8 August 1981, Basel, Switzerland. m. Mirka Vavrinec, 2 daughters. Professional Tennis Player. Career: Started playing as junior in 1995, turned professional 1998. Career Titles/Finals: 12/8. Current ATP Rank: 1. Numerous television appearances and interviews. Honours: Winner of the Allianz Suisse Open Singles, Gstaad Singles, Halle Singles, Hamburg Singles, Australian Open Singles, Dubai Singles, Indian Wells Singles, 2004; Winner of the Marseille Singles, Dubai Singles, Munich Singles, Halle Singles, Wimbledon Singles (5 consecutive years, 2003-07), Vienna Singles, Tennis Masters Cup Singles, Miami Doubles (Max Mirny), Vienna Doubles (Yves Allegro), 2003. Address: Oberwil, Switzerland.

FEDRIGOTTI Lanfranco Vigilio Maria, b. 23 June 1949, Tiarno di Sotto, Trento, Italy. Catholic Priest; Teacher. Education: Diploma, Academy of Philosophy for the Far East Salesians of Don Bosco, 1969; BA, University of London, 1973; STB, Pontificia Universitas Urbaniana, 1977; SSL, 1984, SSD, 2004, Pontificium Insititutum Biblicum; Certificate in Psychological Approaches to Correctional Treatment, Hong Kong University, Extramural Studies, 1990. Appointments: Teacher of Sacred Scripture, St Pius X Seminary, Tainan, Taiwan, 1984-85; Teacher of Philosophy, Holy Spirit Seminary College, Hong Kong, 1985-98, 2006-; Teacher of Sacred Scripture, Holy Spirit Seminary College, Hong Kong, 1987-98, 2002-; Teacher of Philosophy & Sacred Scripture, Sheshan Regional Seminary, Shanghai & Hebei Regional Seminary, Shijiazhuang, 1994-98. Publications: Book, An Exegetical Study of the Nuptial Symbolism in Matthew 9:15: Jesus of Nazareth, The Bridegroom Who is Present and Will Depart, 2006; Numerous articles in professional journals in English, Chinese and Italian. Memberships: Associazione Biblica

Salesiana; Catholic Biblical Association of America; Society of Biblical Literature. Address: Salesian House of Studies, 18, Chai Wan Road, Shau Kei Wan, Hong Kong, China.

FEHR Manfred, b. 25 March 1936, Jena, Germany. Chemical Engineer. m. Giomar Yemaíl, 1971, 1 son, 1 daughter. Education: BSc, Université Laval, Québec, 1967; MSc, University of Alberta, Edmonton, 1969; PhD, Université Laval, Québec, 1978; Postdoctoral Fellow, Kungliga Tekniska Högskolan, Sweden, 1990; fluent in 5 languages. Appointments: Professional handball player, 2 clubs; International consultant, 34 clients; Marketing administrator 3 companies; Research and process engineer, 4 companies; Lecturer and professor, 6 universities; Professional activities in 29 countries on all continents; Registered engineer, 2 countries; Citizen of 3 countries; Presently retired collaborating professor, Federal University at Uberlândia, Brazil. Publications: 166 journal and newspaper articles; 110 research reports; 128 conference and symposium presentations; 53 invited speaking engagements; 6 books; 439 literature citations. Honours: 4 scholarships in Canada, 1963-75; 34 TV, radio and newspapers interviews in Argentina and Brazil, 1992-2011; Consular Warden in Brazil, 1991-2008; 82 international biographical reference listings, 1981-2011, 151 awards, 1963-2011; Editor and reviewer of 28 scientific journals. Memberships (past and present): 38 professional associations in various countries; Former President of Environmental Foundation; Former Local Chapter President, Engineering Association; Former President, University Staff Evaluation Commission. Address: PO Box 811, 38400974 Uberlândia, Brazil. E-mail: prosec22@yahoo.com Website: www.manfredfehr.com.br

FEI Juntao, b. 1 October 1969, Hefei, China. Research Associate. m. Yunmei Fang, 2 sons. Education: BS, Hefei University of Technology, 1991; MS, University of Science & Technology, China, 1998; MS, 2003, PhD, 2007, University of Akron, USA. Appointments: Graduate Assistant, University of Akron, 2000-07; Research Assistant, University of Virginia, 2002-03; Research Associate, University of Louisiana at Lafayette, 2008-. Publications: Book, Adaptive Vibration Control of Flexible Structure, 2008; Book, Adaptive Sliching mode control of MEMS gyroscope, 2008; Article, Robust adaptive control for a MEMS gyroscope, 2008. Honours: Graduate Scholarship, University of Akron; Listed in international biographical dictionaries. Memberships: IEEE; ASME; Sigma Xi. E-mail: jtfei@yahoo.com

FEICHTINGER Dietmar, b. 18 November 1961, Bruck, Austria. Architect. m. Barbara Felber, 3 sons. Appointments: Student Lecturer, Technical University of Graz, Austria, 1981-88; Founder, Feichtinger Architectes, Paris, France, 1994; Visiting Professor, Construction Institut, University of Innsbruck, Austria, 1995; Teacher, University Paris La Villette, UP6, Paris, France, 1999-; Visiting Professor, RWTH, Aachen, Germany, 1999-2000; Founder, second office of Feichtinger Architects, Vienna, Austria, 2002; Architect Advisory Board, Salzburg, Austria, 2006-. Honours: Architecture of Academy of Fine Arts, Berlin, 1998; Equerre d'Argent, 2005, 2006; Architecture Award, Land of Styria, Geramb-Rose, 2006; Architecture Award, Land of Lower Austria, Austrian Construction Prize, 2005, 2006; Award for Best Building, 2006; European Steel Design Award, 2007; Twice winner, ZV Bauherrenpreis, Austria, 2007, 2009; Renault Future Traffic Award, 2007; German Bridge and Footbridge Award, 2008; 2 Footbridge Awards, 2008; Hayden Medal, 2008; ECCS Award, 2008; Wood Award, Land of Upper Austria, 2009; DETAIL Award, 2009. Address: 11 rue des Vignoles, 75020, Paris, France.

FEILITZEN Maria Cecilia von, b. 26 September 1945, Stockholm, Sweden. Scientific Co-ordinator; Professor. Education: BA, 1969, PhD, 1971, Stockholm University. Appointments: Researcher, Swedish Broadcasting Corporation, 1964-96; Senior Researcher, Department of Journalism, Media and Communication, Stockholm University, 1981-2002; Senior Researcher and Lecturer, 2002-09, Professor, 2009-, Head of Department, 2003-06, Media and Communication Studies, University of Södertörn; Scientific Co-Ordinator, The International Clearinghouse on Children, Youth and Media, Nordicom, Göteborg University, 1997-; President, Member Board of Directors, Association for Swedish Media and Communication Science; Examiner, Board of Films for Children and Young People, Swedish Film Institute, 1983-88; Head of Centre for Mass Communication Research, Stockholm University, 1990-93; Expert Member, The Media Council, The Swedish Ministry of Education and Culture, 1991-2006; Member, Board of Directors, Swedish National Board of Film Classifications, 2000-06; Co-Editor, several international journals on media and communication. Publications: About 225 scientific articles, reports and books in the field of media and communications. Memberships: International Association for Media and Communication Science; Association For Swedish Media And Communication Science; Amnesty International. Address: Media and Communication Studies, University of Södertörn, 14189 Huddinge, Sweden.

FEKETE John, b. 7 August 1946, Budapest, Hungary. Professor of English and Cultural Studies; Writer. Education: BA, Honours, English Literature, 1968, MA, English Literature, 1969, McGill University; PhD, Cambridge University, 1973. Appointments: Visiting Assistant Professor, English, McGill University, Montreal, Quebec, 1973-74; Associate Editor, Telos, 1974-84; Visiting Assistant Professor, Humanities, York University, Toronto, Ontario, 1975-76; Assistant Professor, 1976-78, Associate Professor, 1978-84, Professor, English, Cultural Studies, 1984-, Trent University, Peterborough, Ontario; Distinguished Research Professor, 1990-; Director, PhD Program in Cultural Studies, 2009-. Publications: The Critical Twilight: Explorations in the Ideology of Anglo-American Literary Theory from Eliot to McLuhan, 1978; The Structural Allegory: Reconstructive Encounters With the New French Thought, 1984; Life After Postmodernism: Essays on Culture and Value, 1987; Moral Panic: Biopolitics Rising, 1994. Contributions to: Canadian Journal of Political and Social Theory; Canadian Journal of Communications; Science-Fiction Studies. Address: 1818 Cherryhill Road, Peterborough, Ontario K9K 1S6, Canada.

FELBER Ewald, b. 24 March 1947, Vienna, Austria. Professor, Musician, Composer. m. Elfriede Halmschlager, 1 son. Education: Music Teacher, University of Music, Vienna, 1976; Primary School Teacher, State College, Vienna, 1983; Doctor Phil, Musicology, University of Vienna, 1993; Diploma, Summer Course, University of Santiago de Compostela, Spain, 1980. Appointments: Concert Activities, 1970-; Guitar Teacher, High School, Vienna, 1973-81; Professor, State College of Teacher Education, Vienna, 1981-2007; Professor, 2007-12, Lectureship, 2013-, University of Education, Vienna; Visiting Professor at various foreign universities. Publications: Book: Klangfarben zur Musik von Ewald Felber, 1998; Musical Notes (own compositions), 2004; Gesellschoftliche Standortbestimmung durch Analyse des gitarrebegleitoten Kunstliedes der

Biedermeierzeit Journal fur Bildungsforschung, Wien, 2005; Records and CDs. Honours: Professor, 1983; Oberstudienrat, 1998; Winner, Composing Competition, 2003; Jury Member, European Doctorate, University of Granada, Spain, 2005, 2009. Memberships: Scientific and editorial board, DEDICA. Address: Rosentalgasse 5-7/2/6, A-1140 Vienna, Austria. E-mail: ewald.felber@ewaldfelber.com

FÉLIX François, b. 26 January 1961, Fribourg, Switzerland. Professor. Education: MA, 1986, PhD, 2005, University of Lausanne. Appointments: President, Revue de théologie et de philosophie, 2003; Replacement Professor, University of Lausanne, 2007; Publication Director, Editions l'Age d'Homme, 2007; Member, Scientific Committee, Revue Corps, CNRS, France, 2010. Publications: Numerous articles in professional journals in the field of Schopenhauer, philosophy and music, phenomenology, aesthetics, philosophy and psychology. Honours: Named one of 100 Conspicuous Personalities in Western Switzerland; Listed in international biographical dictionaries. Memberships: Société Frank Martin; Société Suisse de Philosophie. Address: Rue du Village 8, CH 1121, Bremblens, Switzerland. E-mail: francoisfelix@bluewin.ch

FELLS Ian, b. 5 September 1932, Sheffield, England. Professor of Energy Conversion. m. Hazel Denton Scott, 4 sons. Education: MA, PhD, Trinity College, Cambridge, 1952-58. Appointments: Lecturer, Chemical Engineering, Sheffield University, 1958-62; Reader, Fuel Science, Durham University, 1962-75; Professor of Energy Conversion, Newcastle University, 1975-88; Chairman, New and Renewable Energy Centre, Blyth, Northumberland, 2002-05; Former Science Adviser, World Energy Council; Special adviser to select committees in House of Lords and House of Commons; Served on several Cabinet and Research Council committees; Former Energy Adviser to the European Union and European Parliament; Principal, Fells Associates; Director and Trustee, International Centre for Life, Newcastle upon Tyne, 1995-2009; Life President, 2009-; Made over 500 radio and TV programmes including: The Great Egg Race, Take Nobody's World for It (with Carol Vorderman) and Murphy's Law; What If… The Lights Go Out? 2004. Publications include: UK Energy Policy Post Privatisation, 1991; World Energy 1923-1998 and beyond; Turning Point. Independent Review of UK Energy Policy; A Pragmatic Energy Policy for the UK, 2008; More than 200 articles. Honours: Royal Society Faraday Medal and Prize, 1993; Melchett Medal, Energy Institute, 1999; Collier Memorial Medal, Institute of Chemical Engineers and Royal Society, 1999; CBE, 2000; Kelvin Medal, 2002; Listed in national and international biographical directories. Memberships: Fellow, Royal Academy of Engineering; Fellow, Royal Society of Edinburgh; Fellow, Energy Institute; Fellow, Institution of Chemical Engineers. Address: 29 Rectory Terrace, Newcastle upon Tyne, NE3 1YB, England.

FENG Lanrui, b. 16 September 1920, Guiyang, Guizhou, China. Economics. m. Li Chang, 1946, 2 sons, 2 daughters. Education: Political Economy, Central Party School, Beijing, 1954-56. Appointments: Director of Propaganda Bureau, New Democratic Youth League, Municipal Committee of Shanghai; Director and Editor-in-Chief, Youth Daily; Standing Member, Editorial Committee, China Youth Daily; Editor-in-Chief, Harbin Daily; Director, Teaching and Research Department of Political Economy, Polytechnic University of Harbin; Deputy Director, Provincial Economic Institute of Heilongjiang; Deputy Director, Provincial Bureau of Statistics of Heilongjiang; Member, State Council's Political Research Department; Deputy Director, Party Secretary, Senior Research Fellow, and Advisor, Institute of Marxism-Leninism Mao Zedong Thought, Chinese Academy of Social Sciences; Professor, Postgraduate School, Chinese Academy of Social Sciences, -1986; Retired, 1986-. Publications include: How was the idea of the initial stage of socialism raised? – A historical retrospection, 2001; A suggestion for amending the PRC Constitution: Restore the citizen's freedom of residence and the freedom to change it, 2002; Improve the way to help the migrant laborers get their back pays through legal means, 2003; Memories Picked Up and Collected in the Study of Bamboos, 2003; Taking the Other Torturous Path in the World, 2005; Let democratic constitutionalism escort the reform, 2006; Five questions put to Mr Deng Liqun, 2006; Who is to supervise the supervisor? 2007; Friendship through half a century – in memory of Liu Binyan, 2007; How chaos was swept away and order restored among the theoreticians in the initial days of the reform, 2008; Who was it, after all, that set off the December 9th Movement?, 2009; The CPC Resolution on Spiritual Civilization of 1986 – the great opportunity brushed past, 2009; The founding, transformation and re-establishment of the Youth League, 2010. Honours: Sun Yefang Prize for Best Economic Articles, 1984; CASS Prize for Continuing Contributions from the Elderly, 1988; Marxism-Leninism Institute's Prize for Excellent Research Results, 1993; Xinhua Digest's Prize for Most Impressive Article of the Year, 1997. Memberships: Kaida Economist Consultation Center, Beijing; China Council of Economic Associations; Economics Weekly; Chinese People's Association for Friendship with Foreign Countries. E-mail: fenglanrui@sohu.com

FERGUSON Alexander Chapman (Sir), b. 31 December 1941, Glasgow, Scotland. Football Club Manager. m. Catherine Holding, 1966, 3 sons. Appointments: Footballer, Queen's Park, 1958-60, St Johnstone, 1960-64, Dunfermline Athletic, 1964-67, Glasgow Rangers, 1967-69, Falkirk, 1969-73, Ayr Utd, 1973-74; Manager, East Stirling, 1974, St Mirren, 1974-78, Aberdeen, 1978-86, Scottish National Team (assistant manager), 1985-86, Manchester Utd, 1986- (winners FA Cup 1990, 1994, 1996, 1999, 2004; European Cup Winners' Cup, Super Cup, 1991; FA Premier League Championship 1992/93, 1993/94, 1995/94, 1996/97, 1998/99, 1999/2000, 2000/01, 2002/03; 2006/07. League and FA Cup double 1994 and 1996 (new record); Champions League European Cup, 1999. Publications: A Light in the North, 1984; Six Years at United, 1992; Just Champion, 1993; A Year in the Life, 1995; A Will to Win, 1997; Managing My Life: My Autobiography, 1999; The Unique Treble, 2000. Honours include: KBE, 1999; CBE; Voted Best Coach in Europe, UEFA Football Gala, 1999; Freeman, Cities of Aberdeen, Glasgow and Manchester. Address: c/o Manchester United Football Club, Old Trafford, Manchester M16 0RA, England.

FERGUSON Ian Forster, b. 11 September 1931, Blundellsands, Crosby, Lancashire, England. Inorganic Chemist. m. Margot Y Scott, 2 daughters. Education: Andover Grammar School, 1942-45; King Edward VI School, Southampton, 1945-50; University of Southampton, 1950-53. Appointments: UKAEA, 1953-90; AERE, Harwell, 1953-59; Capenhurst, 1960; SNL, Springfields, 1960-1990. Publications: Scanning Auger Microprobe Analysis, Bristol, 1989; Numerous papers and articles for professional journals include Proc. Roy Soc; J Chem Soc; J Applied Cryst; La Vide; Computer Physics Communications. Honours: BSc (Special Chemistry) Southampton, 1953; BSc (Special Chemistry), 1954, MSc, 1956, PhD, 1961, all External London; British Crystallographic Society Industrial Group Prize.

Memberships: Member, Royal Society of Chemistry; Fellow, Institute of Physics; Chartered Physicist; British Astronomical Association. Address: 1 Ingle Head, Fulwood, Preston, PR2 3NR, England. E-mail: Inglehead @aol.com

FERNANDEZ Mary Joe, b. 19 August 1971, Dominican Republic. Tennis Player. m. Tony Godsick, 2000, 1 daughter, 1 son. Career: Ranked No 1 USA, 1984; Turned professional, 1986; Reached quarter-finals of French open, 1986, quarter-finals, Geneva, 1987, semi-finals Eastbourne, 1988, semi-finals, French Open, 1989, runner up to Graf in singles and runner up with Fendick in doubles, Australian Open, 1990; Reached semi-finals at Wimbledon and Australian Open, Italian Open, 1991; Runner-up Australian open, 1992; Won Bronze Medal in singles and Gold in doubles with G Fernandez, Olympic Games, 1992; Reached semi-finals US Open, 1992; Reached semi-finals Italian Open, quarter-finals Australian Open, 1993; Won singles title, Strasbourg, 1994; Winner, (with Davenport) French Open Doubles, 1996; Winner doubles, Hilton Head, Carolina, 1997, Madrid, 1997, won singles title German Open, 1997; Member, US Federal Cup Team, Atlantic City, 1991, 1994-99; Spokesperson for Will to Win Scholarship Programme, 1998; Retired, 2000. Publication: Mary Joe Fernandez (with Melanie Cole).

FERNANDEZ-GUASTI Manuel, b. 2 May 1956, Manchester, England. Physicist. Education: BSc, Universidad Autonoma Metropolitana, Mexico City, 1978; D Phil, Clarendon Laboratory, Oxford, England, 1983. Appointments: Founder, Quantum Optics Laboratory; Research Lecturer, Universidad Autonoma Metropolitana, Iztapalapa. Publications: 74 research articles; 11 articles in proceedings; 134 citations; 5 internal reports; 1 patent; 70 conferences. Honours: SNI; PROMEP. Address: Rafael Atlixco 186, Col Vicentina, Iztapatapa, 09340 DF, Mexico city, Mexico.

FERNANDO Joseph Basil, b. 14 October 1944, Colombo, Sri Lanka. Attorney-at-Law; Human Rights Advocate; Poet. m. Jasinta Peiris, 1 daughter. Education: Graduate, Faculty of Law, University of Colombo, 1972; Final Law College Exams, 1979. Appointments: English Instructor, University of Srijayawardanapura, 1973-79; Attorney-at-Law, 1980-89; Legal Counsel for Vietnamese refugees in Hong Kong, UNHCR Project, 1989-92; Senior Human Rights Officer, UN Transitional Authority in Cambodia, 1992-93; Senior UN Officer attached to UN Human Rights Office, in charge of Legal Assistance to Cambodian Government, 1993-94; Executive Director, Asian Human Rights Commission and Asian Legal Resource Centre, 1994-2010; Director, Policy & Programs, AHRC & ALRC, 2010-. Publications: Problems facing the legal system of Cambodia; Demoralisation and Hope: A comparative study of B R Ambedkar; Recovering the Authority of Public Institutions in Sri Lanka; and many others. Honours: KWANJU (South Korea) Human Rights Award, 200. Memberships: Bar Association of Sri Lanka; English Writers' Cooperative, Sri Lanka. Address: 25 G/F, Tai Wai New Village, Tai Wai Sha Tin, NT, Hong Kong. E-mail: basil.fernando@ahrc.asia

FERRARIS Giovanni, b. 20 March 1937, Prarolo, Italy. Crystallographer. m. Margherita, 2 sons. Education: Laurea in Physics, 1960, Libera Docenza, DSc equivalent, in Crystallography, 1969, University of Turin. Appointments include: Currently Emeritus Professor of Crystallography, Faculty of Sciences, University of Turin; Doctor Honoris Causa, University of Bucharest, Romania and Darmstadt, Germany. Publications: More than 200 articles in mineralogical crystallography and crystal chemistry; 3 monographs, 2004, 2005, 2008. Honours: Plinius Medal, SIMP; Tartufari Prize, Accademia dei Lincei. Membership: Russian Academy of Natural Sciences; Accademia delle Scienze di Torino and Accademia Nazionale dei Lincei. Address: Dipartimento di Scienze Mineralogiche e Petrologiche, Università di Torino, Via Valperga Caluso 35, I-10125 Torino, Italy. E-mail: giovanni.ferraris@unito.it

FERREIRA Danton Diego, b. 15 June 1982, Lavras, Minas Gerais, Brazil. Professor. Education: Electrical Engineer, Federal University of São João del Rei; Master of Science degree, Electrical Engineering, Federal University of Juiz de Fora; Doctor of Science degree, Electrical Engineering, Federal University of Rio de Janeiro. Appointments: Adjunct Professor, Federal University of Lavras. Publications include: Automatic System for Classification of Isolated and Multiple Disturbances in Electric Signals, 2011; Exploiting Higher-Order Statistics Information for Power Quality Monitoring, 2011. Memberships: Collegiate Course in Control and Automation Engineering, Federal University of Lavras; Informatic Assessor of the Engineering Department, Federal University of Lavras. Address: Neca Firmiano, 93, Marciolândia, Nepomuceno, Minas Gerais, CEP 37250-000, Brazil.

FERRERAS Antonio, b. 1 August 1972, León, Spain. m. Ana Belén, 3 sons. Education: MD, 1996, PhD, Medicine, University of Zaragoza; Eye Surgery Training, Ophthalmology Residency, Miguel Servet University Hospital, 1999-2003. Appointments: Consultant Surgeon, Ophthalmology, Miguel Servet University Hospital, Zaragoza; Associate Professor, Health Sciences, University of Zaragoza; Researcher, Glaucoma Diagnosis Techniques and Retina Diseases. Publications: Numerous articles in scientific journals. Honours: Grants from Carlos III Health Institute and Aragon Health Sciences Institute; Doctorate Award, University of Zaragoza, 2003-04; Arruga Award, 2010. Memberships: American Academy of Ophthalmology; Association for Research in Vision and Ophthalmology; European Glaucoma Society; European Association for Vision and Eye Research; International Society of Dacryology and Dry Eye; Spanish Society of Ophthalmology; Spanish Society of Glaucoma. Address: Breton 12, 3A, 50005 Zaragoza, Spain.

FERRIGNO (Ferry) Pietro Camillo (John Bailey) (King Ferry of London), b. 10 December 1961, London, England (adopted 6 February 1962, Treviglio, Italy). Therapist; Adventurous Scientist. Partner, Jenny. Education: Black belt of Karate, Milan, 1972; Diploma of Pianoforte, Bergamo, 1979; Diploma of mental Dynamics and Applied psychology, Rome, 1981; Diploma di Liceo Classico, Treviglio, 1982; University of London, 1983; Faculty of Medicine, University of Milan; Studies in Parapsychology and Alchemy; Masseur's Certificate (Classical Massage-Shiatsu), Milan, 1995. Appointments: Secret Intelligence Service (MI6); The Duke of Burlington; Chevalier, Order of Malta, 1989. Honours: Nominations for various awards, American Biographical Institute including The American Medal of Honor 2004-2005, 2006; The Da Vinci Diamond; International Medal of Honour; The Marie Curie Award, 2006; 21st Century Award for Achievement, MM-MMC; Honorary Director General, IBC; Medical Advisor to the Director General, IBC; The Order of International Fellowship; IBC Lifetime Achievement Award; IBC Hall of Fame, 2007; Ambassador of the International Order of Merit, 2007; Director General's Roll of Honour, IBC, 2008; Salute to Greatness Award, IBC, 2011; Olympian Achiever Medal, IBC, 2011; Lifetime Achievement Award, World Congress of Arts, 2011; Olympian Gold Medal, World Congress of Arts, 2012; Listed in Who's Who publications and biographical dictionaries. Memberships: International Order of Merit; Order of International Ambassadors; Sovereign Ambassador of the Order of American Ambassadors; IBC Leading Health Professionals of the World; Deputy Director General, IBC, 2006; Vice President, Recognition Board of the World Congress of Arts, Sciences and Communications; Legion of Honor, United Cultural Convention, 2006; Legion of Honour, 2008; Life Member, Order of Distinction, IBC, 2009; Ambassador to the World Congress of Arts, Sciences and Communications, 2009; World Medal of Freedom, ABI, 2009; Inner Circle, IBC, 2009; The Final Honours List, IBC, 2010; Member, World Congress of Arts, Sciences and Communications, Order of International Merit, 2010; The Director General's Leadership Award, IBC, 2011; The International Hippocrates Award, IBC, 2011; Charter Fellow, World Congress of Arts, 2013; Leading Scientists of the World, IBC, 2012. Address: Via Ing Grossi 5, 24047 Treviglio (BG), Italy.

FERRY Bryan, b. 26 September 1945, Washington, County Durham, England. Singer; Songwriter; Musician. 4 sons. Education: Fine Art, Newcastle University. Career: Formed Roxy Music, 1971; Solo artiste, 1973-; Worked with: Brian Eno; Phil Manzanera; Andy Mackay; Steve Ferrone; David Williams; Robin Trower; Pino Palladino; Nile Rodgers; Carleen Anderson; Shara Nelson; Jhelisa; Numerous worldwide tours; Major concerts include: Crystal Palace, 1972; Live Aid, Wembley, 1985; Radio City, New York, 1988; Wembley, 1989; Support tours, Alice Cooper, David Bowie; Television appearances include: Subject of Without Walls documentary, 1992; Videos: New Town (live), 1990; Total Recall (documentary), 1990. Recordings: Singles include: Love Is The Drug, 1975; Dance Away, 1979; Angel Eyes, 1979; Over You, 1980; Jealous Guy, 1981; Slave To Love, 1985; The Right Stuff, 1987; I Put A Spell On You, 1993; Albums: Solo: These Foolish Things, 1973; Another Time Another Place, 1974; Let's Stick Together, 1976; In Your Mind, 1977; The Bride Stripped Bare, 1978; Boys And Girls, 1985; Bete Noire, 1987; The Ultimate Collection, 1988; Taxi, 1993; Mamounia, 1994; As Time Goes By, 1999; with Roxy Music: Roxy Music, 1972; For Your Pleasure, 1973; Stranded, 1973; Country Life, 1974; Siren, 1975; Viva Roxy Music, 1976; Manifesto, 1979; Flesh And Blood (Number 1, UK), 1980; Avalon, (Number 1, UK), 1982; The High Road (live mini-album), 1983; The Atlantic Years, 1983; Street Life, 1987; Recent compilations include: The Thrill Of It All, 1995; More Than This - The Best Of Roxy Music and Bryan Ferry, 1995. Honours include: Grand Prix Du Disque, Best Album, Montreux Golden Rose Festival, 1973; CBE, 2011. Current Management: IE Management, 59a Chesson Road, London W14 9QS, England.

FETHERSTON Brian, b. 26 January 1955, Milwaukee, Wisconsin, USA. Artist; Sculptor; Painter. m. Marianne, 1 son. Education: Ontario College of Art, Canada. Appointments: Commissions and Creative Works: Solo exhibitions of Fetherston & Fetherston (Brian & Marianne): Galerie Cluny, Geneva, Switzerland, 1986; Switzerland Gallery Jaime III, Palma de Mallorca, Spain, 1987; In permanence, Galerie Cluny, Geneva, 1989-90; Gallery Montserrat, New York, 1996; Six Tech SA, Geneva, Switzerland, 1997; Ballard-Fetherston Gallery, Seattle, Washington, 1998; DWT Gallery, Geneva, 2000-01; Fetherston Gallery Designer Work Team, 2005; Group exhibitions of Fetherston & Fetherston (Brian & Marianne) in Spain, Switzerland, Turkey, France, include: Gallery Ramko, Istanbul, Turkey, 1991; Gallerie du Vieux-Chêne, Geneva, 1991; Museum International Art, Carnac, France, 1996; Finansbank SA, Geneva, 1991; United Nations, Geneva, 1995, 1996; Red Cross, Geneva, 1996; Biennale du Japon Grand Prix de Sapporo, Japan, 1997; Société Générale & Trust, Zurich, 1997; Art EXPO 99, New York, 1999; Barcelona Art Expo, 1999; Mural, Trompe l'Oeil, BPI Investments, Geneva; Mural, Gallay-Jufer, SA; Designer Work Team Gallery, Switzerland, 2000. Mural (Trompe L'Oeil BPI Investments, Geneva; Mural, Gallay-Jufer SA, Geneva. Publications: Gallery Guide Paris, 12th, 13th editions; Business Guide to Switzerland, 1992; Art News Magazine, USA, 1996; Gallery Guide, New York, 1996; Epoch Times Int, 2005-06. Honours: Accademical Knight, Greci Marino, Italy. Membership: Professor of Fine Arts, Greci Marino, Italy. Address: 8 rue de Fribourg, 1201 Geneva, Switzerland. Website: www.ffetherston.com

FETHERSTON Marianne, b. 14 August 1959, Alexandria, Egypt (Swiss citizen). Artist Painter. m. Brian, 1 son. Education: Ontario College of Art, Toronto, Canada. Honour: Gallery Art et Vie, Jury Prize, Paris, 1987. Commissions and Creative Works: Solo Exhibitions of Fetherston & Fetherston (Brian & Marianne): Galerie Cluny, Geneva, 1986; (permanent), Circulo Bellas Artes, Salon de Otono, Palma de Mallorca, Spain, 1987; Gallery Bearn, Palma de Mallorca, Spain, 1988; Galerie Cluny, Geneva, 1989-90; Gallery Montserrat, New York, 1996; Six Tech SA, Geneva, 1997; Ballard-Fetherston Gallery, Seattle, Washington, 1998; DWT Gallery, Geneva, 2000-01, 2005; Group exhibitions of Fetherston & Fetherston (Brian & Marianne) in Switzerland, Spain, France, Japan, USA, include: Finansbank SA, Geneva, 1991; Museum International Art, Carnac, France, 1996; United Nations, Switzerland, 1995-96; Red Cross, Geneva, 1996; Biennale du Japan Grand Prix de Sapporo, 1997; Société Générale & Trust, Zurich, 1997; Art Expo 99 New York, 1999; Barcelona Art Expo, 1999; Mural (Trompe l'oeil) BPI Investments, Geneva; Mural, Gallay-Jufer, SA; Solo exhibition of Fetherston & Fetherston Gallery Designer Work Team, Geneva, 2005. Publications: Gallery Guide, Paris, 12th, 13th edition; Art News Magazine, 1996; Gallery Guide, New York, 1996; Epoch Times International, 2005, 2006. Honours: Accademical Knight, Creamarino, Italy. Membership: Professor of Fine Arts, Greci Marino, Italy. Address: 8 rue de Fribourg, 1201 Geneva, Switzerland. Website: www.ffetherston.com

FETTWEIS Günter B L, b. 17 November 1924, Düsseldorf, Germany. Mining Engineer; Professor Emeritus. m. Alice, 1 son, 3 daughters. Education: Diploma in Mining, Technical University of Aachen, 1950; Dr Ing, 1953; Assessor des Bergfachs, 1955. Appointments: Junior Mining Inspector, State of North Rhine-Westphalia, 1953-55; Mining Engineer, 1955-57, Production Manager, 1957-59, Mining Co Neue Hoffnung, Oberhausen; Professor of Mining, 1959-93, Rector, 1968-70, Emeritus Professor, 1993-, University of Leoben, Leoben, Austria. Publications: About 270 articles and 14 books in the fields of mining and mineral economics. Honours: Dr hc: University of Aachen, 1980; Dr hc, University of Miskolc, Hungary, 1987; Dr hc, Petrosani University, Romania, 1996; Dr hc, Mining University of Moskwa, Russia, 1999; Dr hc, University of Kosice, Slovakia, 2003; Several awards, Austria, Germany, Poland, Vatican; Honorary Member, Austrian Mining Association (BVÖ); German Mining Association (GDMB); International Committee of World Mining Congress; Lions Club, Germany. Memberships: Several Academies of Science, Austria, Hungary, Poland, Russia and International. Address: Gasteigergasse 5, A-8700 Leoben, Austria.

FIECHTER Jean Jacques, b. 25 May 1927, Alexandria, Egypt. Historian; Novelist. 2 sons. Education: MA, History, 1950; PhD, History, Cum Laude, 1965. Appointments: CEO President, Blancpain Watches, 1950-80; General Manager,

Swiss Watch Industrial Corporation, 1960-80; Independent Historian specialising in Egyptology, 1981-. Publications: More than 15 biographies and historical works including: Gouvernor Morris; Baron de Besenval; The Harvest of Gods; Mykerinos, le dieu englouti; Faux et Faussaires en Art Egyptien; 4 novels: Death by Publication; A Masterpiece of Revenge; Egyptian Fakes, 2009; A le Recherche du Sarcophage de Mykerinos; Immortelle, Egyptian Fakes. Honours: Grand Prize, Literature, Bern State; General History Prize, French Academy; French Grand Prize for detective novel. Memberships: Société de Belles-Lettres, Switzerland; PEN International (Swiss French Section). Address: 80 Rte Geneve, 1028 Preverenges, Switzerland.

FIELD Brian Orlando, b. 27 October 1932, Blackburn, Lancashire, England. University Senior Lecturer, retired. Education: Blackburn Technical High School and College, 1943-53; University of Durham, 1953-57. Appointments: Research Chemist, United Kingdom Atomic Energy Authority, Harwell, Berkshire, 1957-64; Lecturer in Inorganic Chemistry, Mid-Essex Technical College, Chelmsford, 1964-66; Senior Lecturer in Chemistry and Senior Halls Warden, City University, London, 1966-89; Publications: Numerous Research Papers in Professional Journals. Honours: The Gold Carrot Award from the Student Body of the City University. Membership: MRSC; FRSA. Address: 65 Woodnook Road, Appley Bridge, Wigan, Lancs WN6 9JR, UK. E-mail: brianfield@blueyonder.co.uk

FIELDS Stuart H, b. 15 December 1943, Chicago, Illinois, USA. Human Resources Specialist. m. Birgit Fields, 1 son, 1 daughter. Education: BSc, Business Administration, University of California, Los Angeles, 1965; MS, Business Administration, California State University at Northridge, 1968. Appointments: Employee Relations Specialist, US Department of Commerce, 1989-97; Paralegal Specialist, Gagliardo and Zipin, 1997; Lead Labour Relations Specialist, Internal Revenue Service, 1997-2004; Federal Election Commission, 2004-06; Chief, Employee and Labor Relations Branch, National Capital Region, General Services Administration, 2007-09; Human Resources Specialist, Labor Relations Division, Human Resources Department, Pension Benefit Guaranty Coporation, 2009-10; Human Resources Specialist, US Department of Labor, 2010-11; Contract Human Resources Specialist, 2011-. Publications: An Analytical Study of Educational Requirements for Top Positions in Personnel Administration, Master's thesis, 1968. Honours: Numerous performance based cash awards; Letters of commendation and recognition; Debating and public speaking awards. Memberships: Society of Federal Labor and Employee Relations Professionals; Industrial Relations Research Association; National Employment Law Institute. Address: 9449 Reach Road, Potomac, MD 20854, USA.

FIENNES Ranulph (Twisleton-Wykeham), b. 7 Mar 1944, Windsor, Eng. Explorer; Writer. m. Virginia Pepper, 9 Sept 1970. Appointments: Brit Army, 1965-70; Specl Air Serv, 1966; Sultan of Muscat's Armed Forces, 1968-70; Led Brit Expdns to White Nile, 1969, Jostedalsbre Glacier, 1970, Headless Vall, BC, 1970; Transglobal expdn, first circumpolar journey round the world, 1979-82, N Pole (5 expeditions), 1985-90, Ubar Expdn (discovered lost cty of Ubar, Oman), 1992, Pentland first unsupported crossing of Antarctic Continent, 1993; Lects; TV and film documentary appearances. Publications: A Talent for Trouble, 1970; Ice Fall on Norway, 1972; The Headless Valley, 1973; Where Soldiers Fear to Tread, 1975; Hell on Ice, 1979; To the Ends of the Earth: The Transglobe Expedition - The First Pole-to-Pole Circumnavigation of the Globe, 1983; Bothie the Polar Dog (with Virginia Fiennes), 1984; Living Dangerously (autobiog), 1988; The Feather Men, 1991; Atlantis of the Sands, 1992; Mind Over Matter: The Epic Crossing of the Antarctic Continent, 1994; The Sett, 1996; Fit for Life, 1998. Honours: Dhofar Campaign Medal, 1969; Sultan of Muscat Bravery Medal, 1970; Krug Awd for Ex, 1980; Gold Medal and Hon Life Mbrshp, Explorer's Club of NY, 1983; Livingstone's Gold Medal, Roy Scottish Geog Soc, 1983; Fndr's Medal, Roy Geog Soc, 1984; Hon DSc, Loughborough Univ, 1986; Guiness Hall of Fame, 1987; Polar Medal and bar, 1987; ITN Awd, 1990; OBE, 1993; Polar Medal and bar, 1994; Hon Deg of Dr of Univ, Cntrl Eng, Birmingham, 1995; Hon MRIN. Address: Greenlands, Exford, Somerset TA24 7NU, England.

FIGES Eva, b. 15 April 1932, Berlin, Germany. Writer. 1 son, 1 daughter. Education: BA, Honours, English Language and Literature, University of London, 1953. Publications: Winter Journey, 1967; Patriarchal Attitudes, 1970; B, 1972; Nelly's Version, 1977; Little Eden, 1978; Waking, 1981; Sex and Subterfuge, 1982; Light, 1983; The Seven Ages, 1986; Ghosts, 1988; The Tree of Knowledge, 1990; The Tenancy, 1993; The Knot, 1996; Tales of Innocence and Experience, 2003. Honour: Guardian Fiction Prize, 1967. Membership: Society of Authors. Address: c/o Rogers, Coleridge & White Ltd, 20 Powis Mews, London W11 1JN, England.

FIGGIS Mike, b. 28 February 1948, Kenya. Film Director; Writer; Musician. Career: Came to England, 1957; Studied music, performing in band, Gas Board; Musician, experimental theatre group, The People Show, early 1970s; Maker of independent films including: Redheugh; Slow Fade; Animals of the City; TV film, The House, Channel 4; Films include: Stormy Monday (also screenplay and music), 1988; Internal Affairs (also music), 1990; Liebestraum (also screenplay and music), 1991; Mr Jones, 1993; The Browning Version, 1994; Leaving Las Vegas (also screenplay and music), 1995; One Night Stand, 1997; Flamenco Women, 1997; Miss Julie, 1999; The Loss of Sexual Innocence, 1999; Time Code, 1999; Hotel, 2001; The Battle of Orgreave, 2001; Ten Minutes Older: The Cello, 2002; Cold Creek Manor, 2003; Co/Ma, 2004; The Four Dreams of Miss X, 2007; Love Live Long, 2008. Honours: IFP Independent Spirit Award, 1996; National Society of Film Critics Award. Address: c/o ICM, 8942 Wilshire Boulevard, Beverly Hills, CA 90211, USA.

FILA John Charles, b. Boston, USA. Psychoanalyst. Education: AB, Harvard University, 1992; PhD, University of Berkeley, Michigan, 1995; Diplomate, American College of Professional Mental Health Practitioners. Appointments: Volunteer mentor of disadvantaged, 1995-; Private Practice, Wellesley, Massachusetts, 1997-2000, Santa Monica, California, 2000-; National Board of Directors, International Academy of Philosophy, North Hollywood, California. Publications: Contributed articles to professional journals. Honours: Affiliate: Sigma XI. Memberships: Ombudsman/ Officer, The Prometheus Society International; Member, National Commission on American Foreign Policy, New York City; National Campaign for Tolerance, Montgomery, Alabama; AAAS; New York Academy of Sciences; Menninger Society; Harvard Club (Boston, South California and Palm Beach); The International Neuro-Psychoanalysis Society (London). Address: 2928 4th St, Apt 40, Santa Monica, CA 90405, USA. E-mail: psychdr721@hotmail.com

FINDIK Serhat, b. 8 March 1969, Izmit, Turkey. Medical Doctor. m. 1 son. Education: MD, 1993, Pulmonary Medicine, 1997, Hacettepe University.- Appointments: Associate

Professor, Department of Pulmonary Medicine, Ondokuz Mayis University, 2005. Publications: 80-90 articles in national and international professional journals. Honours: Fellow, American College of Chest Physicians, 2004; Listed in international biographical dictionaries. Memberships: American Thoracic Society; European Respiratory Society; International Association for the Study of Lung Cancer. Address: Ondokuz Mayis University, Faculty of Medicine, Department of Pulmonary Medicine, Kurupelit, Atakum, Samsun, 55139, Turkey. E-mail: serhatfindik1@yahoo.com

FINER Stephen Alan, b. 27 January 1949, London, England. Artist. Career: Solo Exhibitions: Four Vine Lane, London, 1981, 1982, 1985; Anthony Reynolds Gallery, London, 1986, 1988; Berkeley Square Gallery, London, 1989; Bernard Jacobson Gallery, London, 1992, 1995; Woodlands Art Gallery, 1994; Agnew's, London, 1998; Pallant House Gallery, Chichester, Sussex, 2001, Charleston, Sussex, 2002; Art Space Gallery, London, 2004; Art Space Gallery, 2010; Selected Mixed Exhibitions: British Art, 1940-80, from the Arts Council Collection, Hayward Gallery, London, 1980; Collazione Inglese II, Venice Biennale, Italy, 1984; Academicians' Choice, Stephen Finer invited by Kitaj, Mall Galleries, London; The Portrait Now, National Portrait Gallery, London, 1993-94, 1990; The Discerning Eye, Stephen Finer invited by Martin Gayford, Mall Gallery, London, 1996; Men on Women, Touring Exhibition Stephen Finer invited by Peter Edwards, Wales, 1997-98; 50 Contemporary Self-Portraits, Six Chapel Row, Bath, 1998; British Art, 1900-98, Agnew's, London, 1998; About the Figure, Six Chapel Row, Bath, 1999; Painting the Century, 101 Portrait Masterpieces, 1900-2000, National Portrait Gallery, London, 2000-01; The National Portrait Gallery Collects, Bodelwyddan Castle, Wales, 2003; Fusion Gallery, Spain, 2005-07; View Gallery, 2006; Winter Journey, 2008-09; Public Collections: Arts Council; Southport Art Gallery; The British Council; Contemporary Art Society; Los Angeles County Museum of Art; National Portrait Gallery, "David Bowie", London; Pallant House Gallery, "Sir Morris Finer", Chichester, Sussex and Towner Gallery; Tullie House Museum & Art Gallery; University of Sussex. Selected publications: Allgemeines Kunstlerlexikon; Dictionary of British Artists Since 1945; Handbook of Modern British Painting and Printmaking, 1900-2000; The Portrait Now, Robin Gibson, National Portrait Gallery, 1993; Painting the Century 101 Portrait Masterpieces, 1900-2000, Robin Gibson, National Portrait Gallery, London, 2000; Stephen Finer: Presence and Identity, Martin Golding, Modern Painters, Spring, 2000; Intimacy and Mortality, Finer's People, Robin Gibson, Charleston Trust, 2002; Who's Who in Art. Address: 20 Kipling Street, London SE1 3RU, England. Websites: www.stephenfiner.com

FINN Neil, b. 27 May 1958, Te Awamutu, New Zealand. Singer; Musician (guitar); Songwriter. Career: Member, Split Enz, 1977-85; Founder member, Crowded House, 1985-; Duo with brother Tim, 1995; International concerts include: A Concert For Life, Centennial Park, Sydney, 1992; WOMAD Festival, 1993; Television appearances include: Late Night With David Letterman, NBC; The Tonight Show, NBC; In Concert '91, ABC; Return To The Dome, Ch4; MTV Unplugged; Top Of The Pops, BBC1. Recordings: Albums: with Split Enz: Frenzy, 1978; True Colours, 1979; Beginning Of The Enz, 1980; Waita, 1981; Time And Tide, 1982; Conflicting Emotions, 1984; See Ya Round, 1985; History Never Repeats Itself - The Best Of Split Enz, 1993; Oddz & Endz, 1993; Rear Enz, 1993; with Crowded House: Crowded House, 1986; Temple Of Low Men, 1988; Woodface, 1991; Together Alone, 1993; Seductive & Emotional, 1994; Unplugged in the Byrdhouse, 1995; Recurring Dream, 1996; Originals, 1998; with Tim Finn: Finn, 1995; Solo Albums: Try Whistling This, 1998; Encore!, 1999; Singles: with Split Enz include: I See Red; I Got You; History Never Repeats; Six Months In A Leaky Boat; with Crowded House include: Don't Dream It's Over; Something So Strong; Better Be Home Soon; Chocolate Cake; Fall At Your Feet; Four Seasons In One Day; Distant Sun; Nails In My Feet; Solo Singles: Sinner, 1998; She Will Have Her Way, 1998; Last One Standing, 1999; Can You Hear Us, 1999. Honours: Q Awards: Best Live Act (with Crowded House), 1992; Best Songwriter, 1993; OBE, for services to New Zealand, 1993. Current Management: Grant Thomas Management, 3 Mitchell Road, Rose Bay, NSW 2029, Australia.

FINNEY Albert, b. 9 May 1936. Actor. m. (1) Jane Wenham, divorced, 1 son; (2) Anouk Aimée, 1970, divorced, 1978. Education: Royal Academy of Dramatic Art. Appointments: Birmingham Repertory Company, 1956-58; Shakespeare Memorial Theatre Company, 1959; National Theatre, 1965, 1975; Formed Memorial Enterprises, 1966; Associate Artistic Director, English Stage Company, 1972-75; Director, United British Artists, 1983-86; Plays include: Julius Caesar; Macbeth; Henry V; The Beaux Strategem; The Alchemist; The Lizard on the Rock; The Party, 1958; King Lear; Othello, 1959; A Midsummer Night's Dream; The Lily-White Boys, Billy Liar, 1960; Luther, 1961, 1963; Much Ado About About Nothing; Armstrong's Last Goodnight, Miss Julie, Black Comedy, Love for Love, 1965; A Flea in Her Ear, 1966; A Day in the Death of Joe Egg, 1968; Alpha Beta, 1972; Krapp's Last Tape, Cromwell, 1973; Chez Nous, 1974; Loot (Director), 1975; Hamlet, Tamburlaine the Great, 1976; Uncle Vanya, Present Laughter, 1977; The Country Wife, 1977-78; The Cherry Orchard, Macbeth, 1978; Has 'Washington' Legs?; The Biko Inquest (director), Sergeant Musgrave's Dance (director), 1984; Orphans, 1986; J J Farr, 1987; Another Time, 1989; Reflected Glory, 1992; Art, 1996; Films include: The Entertainer; Saturday Night and Sunday Morning, 1960; Tom Jones, Night Must Fall, 1963; Two For the Road, 1967; Scrooge, 1970; Gumshoe, 1971; Murder on the Orient Express, 1974; Wolfen, 1979; Looker, 1980; Shoot the Moon, 1981; Annie, 1982; Life of John Paul II, The Dresser, Under the Volcano, 1983; Miller's Crossing, The Image, 1989; The Run of the Country, 1995; Washington Square, Breakfast of Champions, Simpatico, Delivering Milo, 1999; Erin Brokovich, Traffic, 2000; Hemingway, The Hunter of Death, 2001; Big Fish, 2003; Corpse bride (voice), 2005; A Good Year, Amazing Grace, 2006; The Bourne Ultimatum, Before the Devil Knows You're Dead, 2007; Munich The Documentary, 2008; TV appearances include: My Uncle Silas, 2001, 2003; The Gathering Storm, 2002. Honours: Hon DLitt (Sussex), 1966; Lawrence Olivier Award, 1986; London Standard Drama Award for Best Actor, 1986; Dilys Powell Award, London Film Critics Circle, 1999; BAFTA Fellowship, 2001; Emmy Award, 2002; BAFTA Award for Best Actor, 2003; Golden Globe, 2003. Address: c/o Michael Simkins, 45/51 Whitfield Street, London W1T 4HB, England.

FIORENTINO Linda, b. 9 March 1958, Philadelphia, Pennsylvania, USA. Actress. m. John Byrum, 1992, divorced, 1993. Education: Rosemont College; Circle in the Square Theatre School. Career: Member, Circle in the Square Performing Workshops; Films: Vision Quest, Gotcha, After Hours, 1985; The Moderns, 1988; Queens Logic, Shout, 1991; Wildfire, 1992; Chain of Desire, 1993; The Desperate Trail, The Last Seduction, 1994; Bodily Harm, Jade, 1995; Unforgettable, The Split, Men in Black, Kicked in the Head, 1997; Dogma, 1998; Ordinary Decent Criminal, Where the Money Is, 1999; What Planet Are You From? 2000; Liberty

Stands Still, 2002; Once More With Feeling, 2009. Films for TV include: The Neon Empire, 1989; The Last Game, 1992; Acting on Impulse, 1993; Beyond the Law, 1994; The Desperate Trail. Address: c/o United Talent Agency, 9560 Wilshire Boulevard, Floor 5, Beverly Hills, CA 90212, USA.

FIRTH Colin, b. 10 September 1960. Actor. m. Livia Giuggioli, 1997, 3 children, 1 child from previous relationship. Education: Drama Center, London. Career: Theatre includes: Another Country, 1983; Doctor's Dilemma, 1984; The Lonely Road, 1985; Desire Under the Elms, 1987; The Caretaker, 1991; Chatsky, 1993; Three Days of Rain, 1999; TV appearances: Dutch Girls, 1984; Lost Empires (series), 1985-86; Robert Lawrence in Tumbledown, 1987; Out of the Blue, 1990; Hostages, 1992; Master of the Moor, 1993; The Deep Blue Sea, Pride and Prejudice (Mr Darcy), 1994; Nostromo, 1997; The Turn of the Screw, Donovan Quick, 1999; Radio: Richard II in Two Planks and a Passion, 1986; The One Before the Last (Rupert Brooke), 1987; Films: Another Country, 1983; Camille, 1984; A Month in the Country, 1986; Femme Fatale, 1990; The Hour of the Pig, 1992; Good Girls, 1994; Circle of Friends, 1995; The English Patient, Fever Pitch, 1996; Shakespeare in Love, 1998; The Secret Laughter of Women, My Life So Far, Relative Values, 1999; Londinium, Bridget Jones's Diary, 2000; The Importance of Being Earnest, 2002; Hope Springs, Girl With a Pearl Earring, Love Actually, 2003; Trauma, 2004; Where The Truth Lies, Nanny McPhee, 2005; The Last Legion, And When Did You Last See Your Father?, Then She Found Me, The Accidental Husband, St Trinian's, Genova, 2007; Mamma Mia!, Easy Virtue, 2008; Dorian Gray, A Single Man, A Christmas Carol, St. Trinian's: The Legend of Fritton's Gold, 2009; The King's Speech, Main Street, 2010. Honours: Radio Times Actor Award for Tumbledown, 1996; Best Actor Award, Broadcasting Press Guild for Pride and Prejudice; BAFTA Award, Best Actor for A Single Man, 2010; BAFTA Award, The King's Speech, 2011; CBE, 2011. Address: c/o ICM Ltd, Oxford House, 76 Oxford Street, London, W1N 0AX, England.

FISCH Jörg, b. 28 April 1947, St Gallen, Switzerland. Professor of General Modern History. Education: PhD, University of Heidelberg, Germany, 1976; Habilitation, University of Bielefeld, Germany, 1983. Appointments: Professor, University of Bielefeld, Germany, 1986; Professor, University of Mainz, Germany, 1986-87; Professor, University of Zürich, Switzerland, 1987-. Publications: Krieg und Frieden im Friedensvertrag, 1979; Cheap Lives and Dear Limbs: The British Transformation of the Bengal Criminal Law 1769-1817, 1983. Die europäische Expansion und das Völkerrecht, 1984; Hollands Ruhm in Asien: François Valentyns Vision des niederländischen Imperiums im 18 Jahrhundert, 1986; Geschichte Südafrikas, 1990; Reparationen nach dem Zweiten Weltkrieg, 1992; Tödliche Rituale. Die indische Witwenverbrennung und andere Formen der Totenfolge, 1998 (English translation: Immolating Women, 2005; Burning Women, 2006); Europa zwischen Wachstum und Gleichheit 1850-1914, 2002; Das Selbstbestimmungsrecht der Völker, 2010. Honours: Corresponding Member, Jungius Gesellschaft der Wissenschaften, Hamburg, 1998-; Member, Academia Europaea, 2010. Address: Hammerstrasse 91, CH-8032 Zürich, Switzerland. E-mail: joerg_fisch@uzh.ch

FISCHER-MÜNSTER Gerhard, b. 17 November 1952, Münster- Sarmsheim, Germany. Composer, Soloist, Lecturer, Conductor. m. Bettina, 1 son, 1 daughter. Education: Peter Cornelius Konservatorium Mainz, Staatliche Musikhochschule und Johannes-Gutenberg- Universität Mainz, Staatsexamen, 1974; Seminar for conducting, Bingen, Exam. Career: First Compositions in 1965. Concerts as Soloist, Piano and Clarinet; Concerts as Conductor of different orchestras and ensembles. TV records, Radio records/performances in Germany, Italy, Austria, Switzerland, France, Belgium, USA, Columbia, Japan; Guest Conductor European Symphony Orchestra, Luxembourg 1993; Performances at International Festivals. Guest Lecturer at various Institutes; Founder of Symphonic Wind Orchestra of Conservatory Mainz 1991; Founder of Wind Chamber Ensemble 1981; Lecturer Peter-Cornelius Konservatorium (composition, improvisation, clarinet, chamber music, orchestra), 1975-. Publications: Over 600 compositions (main: 5 Symphonies, Psalm 99, Schizophonie, Sonatas, Haiku-Lieder words by Sigrid Genzken-Dragendorff, Sonnet words by Shakespeare, Symphonic Lieder words by Brigitte Pulley-Grein, Piano Concertino, Daliphonie); Harmonie aus dem Einklang (historical/physical work)' Lehrplan Klarinette; Publications in Music Journals; Publications about Fischer-Münster at different Universities; Editor, Komponisten-Atelier, Loosmann publisher for promotion to young composers, 2011; Jury member at numerous music contests; Guest Lecturer, University Mainz. Honours: Award, Adv. Ministry of Culture 1984, 1989, 1992, 2000; Award, Adv. Management of International Music Festival of Switzerland, 1985; Adv Ecole du Musique et Ballet, France, 2008; Honorary Member, IBC Advisory Council; St. Rochus Cup (Bingen) for cultural achievement; Honorary Member, ABI Research Board of Advisers and Research Fellow. Memberships: Deutscher Komponisten-Interessenverband; World Association for Symphonic Bands and Ensemble (WASBE), GEMA, Association for German Lecturers and Artists; Fördergesellschaft Peter-Cornelius-Konservatorium. Address: Auf den Zeilen 11, D-55424 Münster-Sarmsheim, Germany. E-mail: Fischer-Muenster@gmx.de Website: www.fischer-muenster.de

FISCHLER Ben-Zion, b. 24 May 1925, Vienna, Austria. Educator; Teacher; Lecturer. m. Bracha Dalmatzky, 2 sons. Appointments: Hebrew Teacher, detention camps in Cyprus, 1947-49; Teacher, Ulpanim in Pardess Chana & Motzkin, Haifa, 1949-58; Lecturer in Hebrew, Sir George Williams College (now Concordia University), Montreal, Canada, 1958-61; Lecturer in Hebrew, New School for Social Research (now New School University), New York, USA, 1961-64; Director, Hebrew Language Division, Department of Education & Culture, WZO, Jerusalem. Memberships: Founding Member, Executive Vice-President, Council on the Teaching of Hebrew (Hamoatza Lehanchalat Halashon); Founding Member, Acting Director, Committee on Hebrew Studies at Universities Abroad; Founding Member, Israel Association for Applied Linguistics; Member, Board of the (Hebrew University) Jerusalem Examination. Publications: Editor, Bulletins of The Council on the Teaching of Hebrew; Editor, From the Workshop (Studies & Research on Hebrew as a Second Language); Co-editor: Rosen Memorial Volume; Kodesh Jubilee Volume; Rabin Jubilee Volume; numerous other publications (see Bibliography in Studies in Hebrew, and Language Teaching in Honor of Ben-Zion Fischler, Israel 2001) & articles on Hebrew, Linguistics and (the) Sayings of the Sages (Talmud). Address: 5, Mendele St, Jerusalem 92147, Israel.

FISH Michael, b. 27 April 1944, Eastbourne, England. Semi-retired Broadcast Meteorologist. m. Susan, 2 daughters. Education: Eastbourne College; Sandwich course in Applied Physics, City University. Appointments: Joined Meteorological Office, Gatwick Airport, 1962; Research projects, Met Office Headquarters, Bracknell, 1965; London Weather Centre; Broadcast Meteorologist, BBC Radio, 1971,

BBC TV, 1974; Retired, 2004; Numerous other television and radio appearances on light entertainment and factual programmes; Involved in training of television weathermen in various African countries. Publications: Numerous articles in professional journals; Consultant for several meteorological books. Honours: Honorary DSc, City University, London, 1996; Freedom of the City of London, 1997; MBE, 2004; Honorary DSc, Exeter University, 2005; TRIC Award of TV Presenter of the Year, 2004; Named a National Treasure, Sunday Times, 2004. Memberships: Fellow, Royal Meteorological Society; Patron, Age Concern; many other organisations and charities. E-mail: michael@michaelfish.org Website: www.michael-fish.com

FISHBURNE Laurence, b. 30 July 1961, Augusta, Georgia, USA. Actor. m. (1) Hanja Moss, 1985, divorced 1 son, 1 daughter, (2) Gina Torres, 2002. Career: Stage appearances include: Short Eyes; Two Trains Running; Riff Raff (also writer and director); TV appearances include: One Life to Live (series, debut age 11); Pee-wee's Playhouse; Tribeca; A Rumour of War; I Take These Men; Father Clements Story; Decoration Day; The Tuskagee Airmen; Miss Ever's Boys; Always Outnumbered; Films include: Cornbread Earl and Me, 1975; Fast Break; Apocalypse Now; Willie and Phil; Death Wish II; Rumble Fish; The Cotton Club; The Colour Purple; Quicksilver; Band of the Hand; A Nightmare on Elm Street 3; Dream Warriors; Gardens of Stone; School Daze; Red Heat; King of New York; Cadence; Class Action; Boyz N the Hood; Deep Cover; What's Love Got to Do With It?; Searching for Bobby Fischer; Higher Learning; Bad Company; Just Cause; Othello; Fled; Hoodlums (also exec producer); Event Horizon; Welcome to Hollywood; Once in the Life (also writer); The Matrix, 1999; Michael Jordan to the Max, Once in the Life, 2000; Osmosis Jones, 2001; The Matrix Reloaded, The Matrix Revolutions, Mystic River, 2003; Assault on Precinct 13, 2005; Akeelah and the Bee, Mission: Impossible III, Five Fingers, Bobby, 2006; The Death and Life of Bobby Z, 4: Rise of the Silver Surfer (voice), 2007; Days of Wrath, 21, Tortured, 2008; Black Water Transit, Armored, 2009. Honours: Emmy Award, Tribeca, 1993, Miss Evers' Boys, 1997. Address: c/o Paradigm, 10100 Santa Monica Boulevard, 25th Floor, Los Angeles, CA 90067, USA.

FISHER Allen, b. 1 November 1944, Norbury, Surrey, England. Painter; Poet; Art Historian. Education: BA, University of London; MA, University of Essex. Appointment: Head of Contemporary Arts, Professor of Poetry and Art, Emeritus Professor, 2010, Manchester Metropolitan University. Publications: Over 140 single-author publications including: Place Book One, 1974; Brixton Fractals, 1985; Unpolished Mirrors, 1985; Stepping Out, 1989; Future Exiles, 1991; Fizz, 1994; Civic Crime, 1994; Breadboard, 1994; Now's the Time, 1995; The Topological Shovel (essays), Canada, 1999; Gravity, 2004; Entanglement, 2004, Canada; Place (collected books), 2005; Leans, 2007; Proposals, 2010. Contributions to: Various magazines and journals. Honour: Co-Winner, Alice Hunt Bartlett Award, 1975. Address: 14 Hopton Road, Hereford HR1 1BE, England.

FISHER Carrie, b. 21 October 1956, Beverly Hill, Los Angeles, CA. Actress and Author. m. Paul Simon, 1983, divorced, 1984, 1 daughter with Bryan Lourd. Education: Central School of Speech & Drama, London. Career: First appearances: at a nightclub, with mother, aged 13, Broadway chorus in Irene, aged 15; Stage appearances: Censored Scenes from Hong Kong, Agnes of God, both Broadway; Films include: Star Wars; The Empire Strikes Back; Return of the Jedi; The Blues Brothers; Garbo Talks; The Man With One Red Shoe; When Harry Met Sally; Hannah and Her Sisters; The 'Burbs; Sibling Rivalry; Drop Dead Fred; Soapdish; This is My Life; Austin Powers: International Man of Mystery; Scream 3; Famous; Heartbreakers, 2001; Jay and Silent Bob Strike Back, 2001; A Midsummer Night's Rave, 2002; Charlie's Angels: Full Throttle, 2003; Wonderland, 2003; Stateside, 2004; Undiscovered, 2005; Suffering Man's Charity, 2007; Cougar Club, 2007; Fanboys, The Women, 2008; White Lightnin', Sorority Row, 2009. Several TV appearances. Publications: Postcards from the Edge, also screenplay, 1987; Surrender the Pink, 1990; Delusions of Grandma, 1994; Several short stories. Honours: Photoplay Best Newcomer of the Year, 1974; PEN for first novel (Postcards from the Edge, 1987). Address: Creative Artists Agency, 9830 Wilshire Boulevard, Beverly Hills, CA 90212, USA.

FISHER John William, b. 15 February 1931, Ancell, Missouri, USA. Professor Emeritus; Structural Engineer. m. Nelda Rae Adams, 3 sons, 1 daughter. Education: BScE, Washington University, St Louis, Missouri, USA, 1956; MS, 1958, PhD, 1964, Lehigh University, Bethlehem, Pennsylvania, USA. Appointments: US Army, 1951-53; Assistant Bridge Research Engineer, National Academy of Sciences, AASHO Road Test, Ottawa, Illinois, 1958-61; Research Instructor, 1961-64; Assistant and Associate Professor of Civil Engineering, 1966-69; Professor of Civil and Environmental Engineering, 1969-2002; Associate Director, Fritz Engineering Laboratory, 1971-85; Director, ATLSS, 1986-99; Joseph T Stuart Chair in Civil Engineering, 1988-2002; Co-Director, ATLSS Engineering Research Center (Center for Advanced Technology for Large Structural Systems), 1999-2001; Professor Emeritus, 2002. Publications: Co-author: 275 articles in professional journals; 4 books. Honours include: The John Fritz Medal awarded by the five engineering societies of the United Engineering Foundation, 2000; Roy W Crum Distinguished Service in 2000 Award by the Transportation Research Board, 2001; Achievement Educator Award, American Institute of Steel Construction, 2001; Laureate of the International Award of Merit in Structural Engineering, International Association for Bridge and Structural Engineering, 2001; Chairman's Lecture Award American Association of State Highway Officials Subcommittee on Bridges and Structures, 2004; Geerhard Haaijer Award for Excellence in Education, American Institute of Steel Construction, 2006; Outstanding Projects and Leaders (OPAL) Lifetime Achievement Award in Education, American Society of Civil Engineers, 2007; T Y Lin Medal, International Association for Bridge Maintenance and Safety, Seoul, Korea, 2008; Listed in national and international biographical dictionaries. Memberships: National Academy of Engineers; Corresponding Member, Swiss Academy of Engineering Sciences; Transportation Research Board Executive Committee, 1997-2000; Committee A2CO2 Steel Bridge Committee; Specification Committee, American Institute of Steel Construction; Honorary Member of American Society of Civil Engineers; Specifications Committee, American Railroad Engineering and Maintenance-of-Way Association; American Welding Society; American Society for Engineering Education. Address: ATLSS Center, Lehigh University, 117 ATLSS Drive, Bethlehem, PA 18015, USA. E-mail: jwf2@lehigh.edu

FISHER Lynn Helen, b. 2 June 1943, Red Wing, Minnesota, USA. Writer; Mathematician; Inventor; Poet. Education: College Studies; Doctor of Genius Degree, 1986. Appointments: Editor, Genius Newsletter, 1990-98, A Welcome Neighbor Newsletter, 1995-2000, Genius Newsletter Renewed, 2003-. Publications: The 1, 2, 4 Theory:

A Synthesis, Sexual Equations of Electricity, Magnetism and Gravitation, Human Sexual Evolution, 1971; Middle Concept Theory, A Revised Meaning of Paradox, 1972; Unitary Theory, 1973; An Introduction to Circular or Fischerian Geometry, Two Four Eight Theory, 1976; Fischer's Brief Dictionary of Sound Meanings, 1977; Introducing the Magnetic Sleeve: A Novel Sexual Organ, 1983; The Expansion of Duality, 1984; The Inger Poems, 1985; Circular Geometry, The Four Inventions, The Expansion of Dualism: A 2 4 8 System, The Early Poems of Musical Lynn, 1990; The Musical Lynn Song Lyrics, 1991; The Musical Lynn Essays, Caveman Talk, The Three in One Ring (and) The Magnetic Woman, 1992; Music that Sings, Apple Skies, 1993; Math of Poetry, 1994; A Triversal Woman, 1997; Feature: 8.4.2 Unified Theory at hellominnesotalynn.8m.com; A Visit to a Friend, 2006. Membership: The Loft Literary Center. Address: 2728 East Franklin Avenue, Apt 1907, Minneapolis, MN 55406-1164, USA. Website: http://minnesotalynn.mysite.com

FISHER Yael, b. 26 November 1953, Jerusalem, Israel. College Professor. m. Rafi Fisher, 2 daughters. Education: B Mus, Academy of Music and Dance, Jerusalem, 1978; MA, Educational Administration, 1991, PhD, 1998, Hebrew University, Jerusalem. Appointments: Acting Director, MA Program in Educational Administration, Head of Principals' Training Program, Senior Lecturer, Department of School Administration, Achva Academic College, Israel; Senior Lecturer, Department of Educational Administration, Hemdat Hadarom College, Israel; Expert in parental involvement and evaluation and Educational Administration, Ministry of Education; Educational Adviser to Minister of Minority Issues; Secretary and Tresurer, Facet Theory Association; Member, Movement for Quality Government in Israel. Publications: 3 books; Numerous articles in professional journals. Honours: Certificate of Distinction, Excellence in Teaching, Achva Academic College of Education, 2010; Certificate of Special Contribution Appreciation, President of Academic College of Education, 2011; Listed in biographical dictionaries. Memberships: Facet Theory Association. Address: 3 Barazani Street, Tel-Aviv, 69121, Israel. E-mail: yael@fisher.co.il Website: http://yoter.macam.ac.il/

FITCH Val Lodgson, b. 10 March 1923, Nebraska, USA. Physicist. m. (1) Elise Cunningham, 1949, died 1972, 2 sons, 1 deceased, (2) Daisy Harper Sharp, 1976. Education: BEng, McGill University, 1948; PhD, Physics, Columbia University, 1954. Appointments: US Army, 1943-46; Instructor, Columbia University, 1953-54; Instructor, 1954-60, Professor of Physics, 1960-, Chair, Department of Physics, 1976, Cyrus Fogg Bracket Professor of Physics, 1976-84, Princeton University; James S McDonald Distinguished University Professor of Physics, 1984-. Honour: Research Corporation Award, 1968; Ernest Orlando Laurence Award, 1968; John Witherill Medal, Franklin Institute, 1976; Joint Winner, Nobel Prize for Physics, 1980. Membership: Sloan Fellow, 1960-64; Member, NAS, American Academy of Arts and Sciences, President's Science Advisory Committee, 1970-73; American Philosophical Society. Address: PO Box 708, Princeton University, Department of Physics, Princeton, NJ 08544, USA.

FITTI Charles J(ohn), b. 9 September 1929, Bryn Mawr, Pennsylvania, USA. Education: University of Pennsylvania; Temple University; George Washington University; Dunbarton College of the Holy Cross, Washington DC. Appointments: Volunteer Teacher, Sisters of Most Blessed Sacrament, Philadelphia; Volunteer, Suburban Hospital, Bethesda, Maryland; Lector, St Jane Frances de Chantal Church, Bethesda; CCD Teacher; Eucharistic Minister, St John Neumann Church, Bryn Mawr; Various positions at: the University of Penna; The Franklin Institute; The Budd Co, 1947-64; United States Atomic Energy Commission; United States Nuclear Regulatory Commission, 1964-89; Retired, 1989; Volunteer Processor of Papers of 20th Century Scientists, American Philosophical Society, Philadelphia. Publications: A Philosophy of Creation; A Poetry Series; Between God and Man; Death Comes to Fernwood; 50 poems in various publications. Honours: Distinguished Service Award, US Nuclear Regulatory Commission, 1987; Named in National Library Poetry Hall of Fame, 1997; Poetry Prize, 1997-98, International Biographical Association, World Literary Academy, World Federation of Successful Women; Christmas Card Artwork to Berman Museum, Ursinus College, Collegeville, Pennsylvania. Memberships: Health Physics Society; Union League of Philadelphia; Undine Barge Club of Philadelphia; Former Member: Potomac Boat Club, Washington DC, Capital Hill Club, Washington DC, Peerless Rockville Preservation Society, Board of Directors, American Management Society, American Nuclear Society, Philadelphia Chapter Membership Chairman, Special Library Association of Philadelphia. Address: Dunwoody Village, Apt E-310, 3500 West Chester Pike, Newtown Square, PA 19073, USA.

FITZGERALD Tara, b. 18 September 1967, Cuckfield, Sussex. Actress. m. John Sharian, 2001 (separated). Career: Stage debut in Our Song, London; Ophelia in Hamlet, London, 1995; Antigone, 1999; TV appearances include: The Black Candle; The Camomile Lawn; Anglo-Saxon Attitudes; Six Characters in Search of An Author; Fall From Grace; The Tenant of Wildfell Hall; The Student Prince; Women in White; Frenchman's Creek; In the Name of Love; Like Father Like Son; The Virgin Queen; Jane Eyre; Waking the Dead; Theatre includes: Our Song (London); Hamlet (New York); Films: Sirens, 1994; The Englishman Who Went up a Hill but Came Down a Mountain, 1995; Brassed Off, 1996; Childhood, 1997; Conquest, 1998; New World Disorder, 1998; The Cherry Orchard, 1999; Rancid Aluminium, 1999; Dark Blue World, 2000; I Capture the Castle, 2003; Secret Passage, 2004; Five Children and It, 2004; In A Dark Place, 2006. Address: c/o Caroline Dawson Associates, 19 Sydney Mews, London, SW3 6HL, England.

FITZPATRICK, Horace, the Rt Hon the Earl of Upper Ossory & Castletown, b. 1934, Louisville, Kentucky, USA, British subject. University Research Professor; Musician; internationally recognised authority on history of musical instruments and performance; pioneer in use of music (mainly Classical period 1740-1830), according to Greek philosophical principles, as a form of healing support. Education: BA, 1956, MMus, 1958, Yale University; Diploma (1st Honours), State Academy of Music and Drama, Vienna, 1959; Studied horn with Reginald Morley-Pegge, London, Philip Farkas, Chicago, John Barrows, Yale, Gottfried v. Freiberg, Vienna; Teenage conducting studies with uncle, Glenn Welty, leading free-lance conductor, Chicago Radio; later with Paul Hindemith (Yale), Hans Swarowsky (Vienna), and Robert Heger (Munich); Doctor of Philosophy, Oxford University, 1965. Career includes: various orchestral posts as principal horn, 1958-66, including: Metropolitan Opera, Radio Symphony of the Air (New York under Leonard Bernstein), Vienna Philharmonic and State Opera (deputy for Gottfried v Frieberg as principal horn); Orchestra da Camera di Palazzo Pitti, Florence; Cairo State Opera; Hamburg Kammerorchester; Royal Opera House Covent Garden; London Mozart Players; Deputy Curator, Yale Collection of Musical Instruments, 1956-58; First ever Lecturer in European Music, American University, Cairo, 1959-60;

DICTIONARY OF INTERNATIONAL BIOGRAPHY 36ᵗʰ EDITION

First ever solo recording on 18th century horn, Golden Crest Records, 1959; Solo Debut on Natural Horn, Wigmore Hall, London, 1964; International appearances as soloist on Natural Horn including: Salzburg, City of London, Flanders (Bruges), Edinburgh and Vienna Festivals, 1964-88; Tutoring in Music History, Wadham College, Oxford University, 1961-64; Principal Music Critic, Oxford Mail, 1961-65; Series of Annual Public University Lectures, Faculty of Music, Cambridge University, 1961-71; BBC Artist (Natural Horn); University Music Critic (under William Mann), The Times, 1962-65; Stipendiary Lecturer, St Catherine's College, Oxford University, Member of Faculty of Music, History of Instruments, 1963-71; Co-founder, Music Therapy Charity, 1966; Director, International Summer Academy for Historic Performance, Austria, 1971-80; Secured Philip Bate Collection for Oxford University, set up Oxford Foundation for Historic Musical Instruments, 1964-71; Secured funding for permanent endowment, and established study of History of Instruments in University curriculum; Founded and directed Atelier for Historic Wind Instruments, Oxford, 1971-80; Historic Musical Instrument Assessor, Philips Son & Neale Fine Art Auctioneers, 1971-80; Professor of Natural Horn, Guildhall School of Music and Drama, 1972-79; Founded Hanover Band, 1974 and the Florilegium, 1975; Leverhulme Visiting Professor, Johannes Gutenberg-Universität, Mainz, 1981-85; Leverhulme Visiting Research Professor, Music University "Mozarteum", Salzburg, 1985-; Research Unit and Laboratory Orchestra (historic instruments) at Salzburg in dialogue with the Royal Swedish Academy of Music and the Royal Technical Institute, Stockholm, 1985-; Chairman, Aula Classica Salisburgensis, charitable research, education and performance network to study the music of the Mozartean Era through its related disciplines, 1988-2001; Patronage of the Secretary General of the Council of Europe, 1989; Professorial Research Fellow, Institute of Musicology, University of Vienna, 1994-2000. Publications include: The Horn and Horn-Playing and the Austro-Bohemian Tradition 1680-1830, 1970; Telemann, 1973; 17 articles in The New Grove; Articles in German, French and Spanish music encyclopaedias; Concert and book reviews for The Times, Times Literary Supplement and Oxford Mail. Honours: Numerous research grants and scholarships; Medaglia d'Oro per la Cultura, Italy, 1959; Order of St Martin, Austria, 1977; Listed in biographical dictionaries, including Cambridge Blue Book and 2000 Outstanding Musicians of the 20th Century. Memberships: Athenaeum, 1981-97; Country Club UK, Founding Member; Irish Georgian Society; Jaguar Enthusiasts Club; Daimler Enthusiasts Club. Address: c/o Wadham College, Oxford OX1 3PN, England.

FITZPATRICK Nicholas David, b. 23 January 1947, Leicester, England. Consulting Actuary. m. Jill Brotherton, 1 son, 1 daughter. Education: Industrial Economics, Nottingham University. Appointments: Investment Analyst, Friends Provident, 1969-72; Portfolio Manager, Abbey Life, 1972-76; Equity Manager and Director of Investments, British Rail Pension Fund, 1976-86; Partner, 1986-92, Head of Investment Consulting, 1992-2001, Bacon & Woodrow; Head of Global Investment Consulting, Hewitt, 2001-05; Associate, BESTrustees plc. Memberships: FSIP; FIA; FRSA. Address: Sommarlek, Woodhurst Park, Oxted, Surrey, RH8 9HA, England. E-mail: ndfitz@gmail.com

FITZWANGA Nashon (H.E.Hon.Dr), b. 26 July 1947, Kenya. International Lawyer; Ad Hoc Judge; International Judicial Arbitrator; Land Economist; Architectural Surveyor. Education: BA Honours, Architectural Surveying, Faculty of Architecture and Engineering; BL, Faculty of Laws; LLM, International Law; PhD, International Law, Matriculation; Alumnus of University of Nairobi, University of London, University of Nottingham, University of Knightsbridge, City University of Hong Kong. Appointments: Ad Hoc Judge, Permanent Court of Arbitration, Mauritius; Ad Hoc Judge, Arbitral Commercial Side, Supreme Court of Egypt; Emeritus Representative, United Nations in East Africa for International Law Association; President, The Fitzwanga United Nations Foundation; President, East African Institute of International Law and Foreign Policy Analysis; President, African Institute of International and Comparative Law; Regional Director, Martin Heyman Group of Companies, Uganda; Chief Estate & Rating Surveyor, East African Community, Tanzania; Chairman, Board of Directors of Urban Associated Surveyors Ltd, Kenya; Chairman, Board of Directors, Forensic Advisory Services Ltd, Kenya. Publications: Numerous articles in professional journals. Honours: Leading International Achiever, Certificate and Plaque, Who's Who in the World; Certificate, Who's Who of Professionals; Certificate, Stanley Mathews International Lawyers Directory of Leading International Lawyers; Certificate of Merit, Rotary International; Crystal Globe Prize for Outstanding Global Achiever in the 21st Century; People-to-People Ambassador of 2007 Trial Lawyers Delegation to China of the People-to-People Ambassador Incorporated Program under the Honorary Chairmanship of emeritus US President George W Bush; Laureate, World Forum Medal and Order of International Fellowship, 2008; Medal of Honour, Noble Order of International Ambassadors, 2008; Medal of Honour, American Hall of Fame, 2009; Sovereign Ambassador Medal of Honour, Order of American Ambassadors, 2009; Presidential Inaugural Certificate of the 44th President of the United States of America, Barrack Obama, 2009; Medal of Outstanding Intellectuals of the 21st Century, 2010; Special Commemorative Momento, Malaysian Institute of Arbitrators, Inter-Pacific Bar Association and the Malaysian Bar Association, International Dispute Resolution and RAIF Conference, 2010; University of Cambridge Ambassador of Knowledge Medallion of Honour, 2010; Listed in international biographical dictionaries. Memberships: International Law Association; International Bar Association; Inter-Pacific Bar Association; East African Law Society; Commonwealth Lawyers Association; Association of Trial Lawyers of America; American Society of International Law; Asian Society of International Law; European Society of International Law; Netherlands Society of International Law; Chartered Institute of Arbitrators; London Court of International Arbitration; Commonwealth Magistrates and Judges Association; International Council of Jurists; London Maritime Arbitrators Association; Commonwealth Association of Surveying and Land Economy; European Real Estate Society. Address: 4th Floor, Southern House, Moi Avenue, PO Box 99845, Mombasa 80107, Kenya. E-mail: drfitzwanga@gmail.com

FLAMM Christoph Alexander, b. 20 July 1968, Ilshofen, Germany. Musicologist. m. Michaela Hell, 2 sons. Education: PhD, University of Heidelberg, 1996; Habilitation, University of Saarland, Saarbrücken, 2007. Appointments: Editorial Staff Member, Die Musik in Geschichte und Gegenwart (music encyclopaedia), 1994-2001; Scientific Assistant, Music History Department, German Historical Institute, Rome, Italy, 2001-04; Lecturer, Frankfurt Musikhochschule, 2003-07; 2-year Research Grant, 2005-07; Lecturer, Department of Musicology, Saarland University, 2007-. Publications: Numerous articles and reveiws in professional journals. Honours: Scheffel-Treis of the Deutsche Literische Gesellschaft, 1987; Listed in international biographical dictionaries. Memberships: International Musicological Society; Societa Italiana di Musicologia; Gesellschaft für Musikfurschung. Address: University of Saarland, Institute of Musicology, Geb C 5 2, 66123 Saarbrücken, Germany.

FLECK Marcelo Pio de Almeida, b. 25 February 1960, Porto Alegre, Brazil. Psychiatrist. m. Valkiria Alberti Fleck, 1 son, 1 daughter. Education: MD, 1983; Master, Medical Sciences, 1991; PhD, Medical Sciences, 1997. Appointments: Associate Professor, Psychiatry, Universidade Federal do Rio Grande do Sul, Porto Alegre, Brazil; Editor, Revista Brasileira de Psiquiatria, Brazilian Psychiatric Association; Co-ordinator Member, Pos Graduate Course in Psychiatry, Universidade Federal do Rio Grande do Sul; Co-ordinator, Affective Disorder Programme, Hospital de Clinicas de Porto Alegre; Co-ordinator, WHOQOL Group, Brazilian Center; Temporary Consultant, WHO. Publications: More than 100 scientific papers; 15 book chapters; Editor, Quality of Life. Honours: Distinct Professor in Psychiatry, Residence Hospital de Clinicas de Porto Alegre, 2002, 2004, 2008, 2010; Best Physicians Award, Brazil, 2009 and 2010; Several awards for best poster at scientific congresses. Memberships: Brazilian Psychiatric Association; American Psychiatric Association; International Society of Quality of Life. Address: Rua Miguel Tostes 533 cj 302, 90430-61, Porto Alegre, Brazil. E-mail: mfleck.voy@terra.com.br

FLENSMARK Jarl Gustav Vincent, b. 16 June 1938, Klippan, Sweden. Retired. Education: M Ed kand, Lund University, 1973. Appointments: Assistant Physician, Östersund Hospital, 1977; Assistant Physician, Sundsvall Hospital, 1978; Assistant Physician, Visby Hospital, 1978; Assistant Physician, Helsingborg Hospital, 1978-79; Assistant Surgeon, Eskilstuna Hospital, 1979-80; Assistant Physician, Malmö General Hospital, 1980-81. Publications: Is there an association between the use of heeled footwear and schizophrenia? 2004; Physical Activity, Eccentric Contractions of Plantar Flexons and Neurogenesis: Therapeutic Potential of Flat Shoes in Psychiatric and Neurological Disorders, 2009. Address: Grönkullagatan 41, S-254 57 Helsingborg, Sweden. E-mail: j_flensmark@yahoo.se

FLESSEL Klaus, b. 5 December 1940, Recklinghausen, Germany. University Professor. m. Michiko Flessel-Takayanagi, 2 daughters. Education: PhD, Sinology, 1971, Habilitation, Sinology, 1983, Tübingen University, Germany. Appointments: Assistant Professor, 1971, Lecturer, 1979-84, Tübingen University; Professor, Erlangen-Nürnberg University, 1984-. Publications: Der Huang-Ho und die Historische Hydrotechnik in China (author); Lexikon Alte Kulturen, 3 volumes (author/editor), 1990-93; Frühe Hochkulturen in Fernost – Brockhaus Weltgeschichte Volume 1, 3, (author) 1997-98. Address: Ringstr 5, 91475 Lonnerstadt, Germany. E-mail: kflessel@phil.uni-erlangen.de

FLETCHER Philip, b. 2 May 1946. Director General of OFWAT. m. Margaret Anne Boys, 2 daughters, 1 deceased. Education: MA, Trinity College, Oxford. Appointments: Joined Civil Service, 1968, Director, Central Finance, 1986-89, Director (grade 3), Planning & Development Control, 1990-93, Chief Executive, PSA Services and Property Holdings, 1993-94, Deputy Secretary (grade 2), Cities and Countryside, 1994-95, Department of Environment; Receiver, Metropolitan Police District, 1996-2000; Director General, Water Services, 2000-2006, Chairman, Water Services, 2006-. Address: OFWAT, Centre City Tower, 7 Hill Street, Birmingham B5 4UA, England. E-mail: philip.fletcher@ofwat.gsi.gov.uk

FLIGGE Jörg, b. 1 December 1940, Königsberg, East Prussia. Librarian. m. Gabriele Edner, 2 daughters. Education: PhD, University of Bonn, Germany, 1972; Cert Sci Libr, 1974. Appointments: Junior Librarian, University Library, Bonn, 1972-74; Head Librarian, Administrator, 1978-79, Deputy Director, 1983-90, University Librarian, Duisburg; Deputy Director, City Library, Duisburg, 1983-90; Librarian, Director, Bibliothek de Hansestadt Lübeck, Germany, 1990-2005. Publications: Author, Herzog Albrecht von Preussen und der Osiandrismus, 1972; Grossherzog Carl August von Sachsen-Weimar-Eisenach, Lübeck, 2007; Numerous articles in professional journals. Honours: Proceedings of Fourth International Symposium Bibliotheca Baltica dedicated to Dr Jörg Fligge, Stockholm, 1998; Festschrift for Dr Jörg Fligge, Lübeck, 2005. Memberships: German-Russian Librarian Commission, Berlin; Many local librarian commissons and local cultural associations; Verein Deutscher Bibliothekare; Rotary. Address: Hermann-Löns-Weg 24, 23562 Lübeck, Germany. E-mail: jrfligge@aol.com

FLINTOFF Freddie (Andrew), b. 6 December 1977, Preston, England. Cricketer. m. Rachael Wools, 2005, 2 sons, 1 daughter. Career: Played in Lancashire Leagues for Preston; Played for Lancashire County Cricket Club; International debut, played for England against South Africa, 1998; Played for England, Ashes, 2005. Honours: NBC Dennis Compton Award, 1997; Walter Lawrence Trophy, 1999; Wisden Cricketer of the Year, 2004; ICC One-Day Player of the Year, 2004; ICC Player of the Year, 2005; BBC Sports Personality of the Year, 2005; MBE, 2005; Man of Series, 2005 England Ashes.

FLÖCKINGER Gerda, b. 8 December 1927, Innsbruck, Austria (naturalised British citizen, 1946). Designer Maker Jewellery; Photographer; Lecturer. Education: Painting, St Martin's School of Art, 1945-50; Etching, Jewellery Techniques and Enamelling, Central School of Arts and Crafts, 1950-56. Appointments: Creator and Teacher, Modern Jewellery Course, Hornsey College of Art, 1962-68; Invited to be first living woman to have a solo show at the V&A, 1971; Seven solo shows and numerous group shows throughout the UK and internationally. Publications: Introduction to "Vintage Jewellery" by Caroline Cox, 2010. Honours: CBE, 1991; Freeman of the Goldsmiths' Company, 1998; Honorary Fellow, University of the Arts, 2006; Entries in many biographical dictionaries and in numerous books and magazines. Address: c/o Catherine Williams, The Crafts Council, 44a Pentonville Road, London N1 1BY, England. Goldsmiths' Company Website: www.whoswhoingoldandsilver.com

FLOROS Constantin, b. 4 January 1930, Salonica, Greece. Professor of Musicology. Education: Composition and Conducting, Vienna Music Academy, 1953; Doctorate, Musicology, Art History, Philosophy and Psychology, Vienna University, 1955. Appointments: Habilitation, Musicology, Hamburg University, 1961; Supernumerary Professor, 1967, Professor of Musicology, 1972, Professor Emeritus, 1995, University of Hamburg. Publications: 30 books (many books translated in other languages); Numerous papers; Monographs on Mozart, Beethoven, Joh Brahms, Bruckner, Mahler (4 volumes), Alban Berg, G Ligeti and Tchaikovsky; Translated oldest Byzantine and Slavic notations and developed new method of semantic analysis. Honours: President, Gustav Mahler Vereinigung, Hamburg, 1988; Honorary Doctorate, University of Athens, 1999; Member, European Academy of Sciences and Arts, 2002; Honorary Doctorate, University of Salonica, 2004; Golden Honorary

Diploma, University of Vienna, 2005; Mahler Gold Medal, International Mahler Society, 2010. Address: c/o Mac Lean, Loehrsweg 1, 20249 Hamburg, Germany.

FLOURNOY Dayl Jean II, b. 17 December 1944, San Antonio, Texas, USA. Clinical Microbiologist. m. 2 sons, 1 daughter. Education: BS, Southwest Texas State University, San Marcos, Texas, 1965; AS, San Antonio College, Texas, 1966; MT, ASCP, Santa Rosa Medical Center, Texas, 1966; MA, Incarnate Word College, San Antonio, Texas, 1968; PhD, University of Houston, Texas, 1973; Postdoctoral, St Luke's Episcopal Hospital, Houston Texas, 1975; Fellow, Oklahoma Geriatric Education Center, Oklahoma City, 1991. Appointments include: Director of Clinical Microbiology/ Serology, Veterans Affairs Medical Center, Oklahoma City, 1975-; Professor of Pathology, OUHSC, 1987-. Publications: Over 200 articles in peer reviewed journals. Honours: Fellowships, awards include: Charlotte S Leebron Memorial Trust Award, Oklahoma State Medical Association, 1993; Advanced Toastmaster Silver Certification, Toastmasters International, 2000; Fellow, American Academy of Microbiology, 1986-; Fellow, Society for Hospital Epidemiology of America, 2004. Listed in national and international biographical dictionaries. Memberships include: American Society for Microbiology; Society for Hospital Epidemiology of America. Address: Dir Micro, VAMC (113) 921 13th Street, Oklahoma City, OK 73104, USA.

FLOWER David John Colin, b. 7 June 1956, London, England. Occupational Physician. m. Harriett Ann Sinclair, 1 son, 1 daughter. Education: BSc (Eng), Chemical Engineering, 1977; MB BS, 1982; MD, 1996; Diploma, Royal College of Obstetricians & Gynaecologists, 1986; Member, Royal College of General Practitioners, 1987; Associate, 1993, Member, 1996, Fellow, 2002, Faculty of Occupational Medicine RCP; Diploma in Aviation Medicine, 1999; Fellow, American College of Occupational and Environmental Medicine, 2007. Appointments: House Surgeon, Professorial Surgical Unit, University College Hospital, London; Principal in General Practice, Wantage, Oxfordshire; Occupational Physician, UK Atomic Energy Authority; Consultant and Senior Consultant, Occupational Physician, British Airways plc; Group Head of Occupational Health, Centrica plc; Senior Health Director, BP plc; Part-time Consultant, Adviser, UK Sport. Publications: Scientific and popular articles on alertness, performance and the management of jet lag; Contributing author, British Olympic Association Athlete Publications, Sydney 2000, Athens 2004, Beijing, 2008; Battelle, US Department of Transportation, Handbook on Fatigue in Transportation; Kushida Editor, Sleep Deprivation: Clinical Issues, Pharmacology and Sleep Loss Effects. Memberships: Past President, Section of Occupational Medicine; Royal Society of Medicine; Member, Society of Occupational Medicine. Address: BP plc, Chertsey Road, Sunbury on Thames, Middlesex TW16 7LN, England.

FLOWER Roderick John, b. 29 November 1945, Southampton, England. Pharmacologist. m. Lindsay Joyce Riddell. Education: BSc, University of Sheffield, 1971; PhD, University of London, 1974; DSc, 1985. Appointments: Senior Scientist, Wellcome Foundation, 1973-84; Professor of Pharmacology, University of Bath, 1984-89; Lilly Professor, Biochemical Pharmacology, St Bart's Hospital Medical School, London, 1989-94; Wellcome Trust Principal Fellow, 1994-2008; Professor of Pharmacology, 1994-2008; Head of William Harvey Research Institute, 1998-2002; Consultant in field; Co-editor, Glucocorticoids, 2000. Publications: Co-author, Rang and Dale's Pharmacology, 2007 and 2011; More than 300 peer reviewed papers; More than 200 other publications including reviews, books, book chapters, abstracts, conference proceedings, editorials and published correspondence. Honours: Sandoz Prize, 1978; Gaddum Medal, 1986; William Withering Prize, 2003; Lifetime Achievement Award, International Association of Inflammation Societies, 2005; Baylis-Starling Prize, 2006; LLD (Hon), University of Bath, 2011. Memberships: British Pharmacological Society; Biochemical Society; Fellow, Academy of Medical Sciences, 1999; Fellow, Academia Europea, 2001; Fellow, Royal Society, 2003; Honorary Fellow, School of Pharmacy, 2008.

FO Dario, b. 24 March 1926, Leggiuno-Sangiamo, Italy. Dramatist; Actor. m. Franca Rame, 1954, 1 child. Education: Academy of Fine Arts, Milan. Appointments: Dramatist and Actor in agitprog theatre and television; Co-Founder (with Franca Rame), Dramatist, Actor, Nuova Scena acting groupe, 1968, Collettivo Teatrale la Comune, 1970. Publications: Numerous plays, including: Le commedie, I-IX, 1966-91, 1992; Morte accidentale di un anarchico (Accidental Death of an Anarchist), 1974; Non si paga, non si paga! (We Can't Pay? We Won't Pay!), 1974; Tutta casa, letto e chiesa (Adult Orgasm Escapes From the Zoo), 1978; Female Parts (with Franca Rame), 1981; Manuale et minimo dell attore, 1987; Mistero Buffo, 1977; Coming Home; History of Masks; Archangels Don't Play Pinball; Hooters, Trumpets and Raspberries; The Tricks of the Trade, 1991; Il papa e la stega (The Pope and the Witch), 1989; L'Eroina-Grassa e'Bello, 1991; Johan Padan a la Descoverta de le Americhe, 1991; Dario Fo Recita Ruzzante, 1993; Il diavolo con le zinne, 1997; Pareja abierta Una, 2002; Matka Reimsiin, 2003. Honour: Hon DLitt, Westminster, 1997; Nobel Prize for Literature, 1997.

FOCSA Mircea, b. 13 October 1967, Timisoara, Romania. Senior Medical Analyst. Education: General Medicine Licence, University of Medicine and Pharmacy Victor Babes, Timisoara. Appointments: Internal Physician, 1995-96; Assistant Professor, Lecturer, Department of Medical Informatics, UMF Victor Babes, 2001-; Senior Medical Analyst, Medicogenes SA, Belgium, 2008-. Publications: Numerous articles in professional journals. Memberships: Eurorec Board of Directors; Vice President, Purec, Romania; Romanian Society of Medical Informatics. Address: Str IOM VIDU Mr 16, 300576 Timisoara, Romania.

FODOR László, b. 25 November 1961, Budapest, Hungary. Geologist. m. Judit Fodor, 1 daughter. Education: Master of Geology, Eötvös University, Budapest, Hungary, 1987; PhD, Université P et M Curie, Paris, France, 1991. Appointments: Assistant Lecturer, Department of Applied and Environmental Geology, 1993-98, Assistant Professor, Department of Applied Geology, 1998-2000, Eötvös University; Senior Scientist, Geological Institute of Hungary, 2000-. Publications: Articles in scientific journals as co-author include: Miocene-Pliocene tectonic evolution of the Slovenian Periadriatic line and surrounding area, 1998; Tectonics 17, 690-709; Tertiary tectonic evolution of the Pannonian basin system and neighbouring origins: a new synthesis of paleostress data, Geol Soc, London, Spec Publ. 156, 1999; An outline of neotectonic structures and morphotectonics of the western and central Pannonian basin, 2005. Honours include: Széchenyi Professorial Scholarship, Ministry of Education of Hungary, 1997-2000; Bolyai Janos Scholarship for Research, Hungarian Academy of Sciences, 2001-04, 2006-09. Memberships: American Geophysical Union; Geological Society of America; International Association of Sedimentologists;

Hungarian Geological Society. Address: Geological Institute of Hungary; Stefania ut 14, H-1143 Budapest, Hungary. E-mail: fodor@mafi.hu

FONDA Bridget, b. 27 January 1964, Los Angeles, CA, USA. Actress. m. Danny Elfman, 2003. Education: NY University theatre programme; Studied acting at Lee Strasburg Institute and with Harold Guskin. Career: Workshop stage performances include Confession and Pastels; Films: Aria (Tristan and Isolde sequence), 1987; You Can't Hurry Love, Shag, 1988; Scandal, Strapless, 1989; Frankenstein Unbound, The Godfather: Part III, 1990; Doc Hollywood, Out of the Rain, 1991; Single White Female, Singles, 1992; Bodies Rest and Motion, Point of No Return, 1993; Little Buddha, It Could Happen To You, Camilla, The Road to Welville, 1994; Rough Magic, Balto (voice), 1995; Grace of My Heart, City Hall, 1996; Drop Dead Fred; Light Years (voice); Iron Maze; Army of Darkness; Little Buddha; Touch; Jackie Brown; Finding Graceland; The Break Up; South of Heaven West of Hell; Monkey Bone; Lake Placid; Delivering Milo; Monkeybone; Kiss of the Dragon; The Whole Shebang. TV series: 21 Jump Street; Jacob Have I Loved; WonderWorks (episode), 1989; The Edge (The Professional Man); After Amy; The Chris Isaak Show; Snow Queen. TV film: Leather Jackets, 1991; In the Gloaming, 1997. Address: c/o IFA, 8730 West Sunset Boulevard, Suite 490, Los Angeles, CA 90069, USA.

FONDA Jane, b. 21 December 1937. Actress. m. (1) Roger Vadim, 1967, divorced 1973, deceased 2000, 1 daughter, (2) Tom Hayden, 1973, divorced 1989, 1 son, (3) Ted Turner, 1991, divorced. Education: Vassar College. Films include: Tall Story, 1960; A Walk on the Wild Side, 1962; Sunday in New York, 1963; La Ronde, 1964; Barbarella, 1968; They Shoot Horses Don't They? 1969; Steelyard Blues, Tout va Bien, 1972; The Blue Bird, 1975; Fun with Dick and Jane, 1976; Coming Home, California Suite, 1978; The China Syndrome, 1979; Nine to Five, 1980; On Golden Pond, 1981; Agnes of God, 1985; Stanley and Iris, 1990; Lakota Woman, Producer, 1994; Monster-in-Law, 2005; Georgia Rule, 2007; Stage Work includes: Invitation to a March; The Fun Couple; Strange Interlude; TV: The Dollmaker, 1984. Publications: Jane Fonda's Workout Book, 1982; Women Coming of Age, 1984; Jane Fonda's Workout and Weightloss Program, 1986; Jane Fonda's New Pregnancy Workout and Total Birth Program, 1989; Jane Fonda Workout Video; Jane Fonda Cooking for Healthy Living, 1996. Honours: Academy Award Best Actress, 1972, 1979; Emmy Award, The Dollmaker, 1984. Address: c/o Kim Hodgert, CAA, 9830 Wilshire Boulevard, Beverly Hills, CA 90212, USA.

FONDA Peter, b. 23 February 1940, NY, USA. Film Actor, Director and Producer. m. Susan Brewer, divorced 1974, 2 children. Education: University of Omaha. Career: Tammy and the Doctor, The Victors, 1963; Lilith, The Young Lovers, 1964; The Wild Angels, 1966; The Trip, 1967; Easy Rider (also co-screenplay writer, co-producer), 1969; The Last Movie, The Hired Hand (also director), 1971; Two People (also director), 1973; Dirty Mary, Crazy Harry, 1974; Race With the Devil, 92 in the Shade, Killer Force, 1975; Fighting Mad, Future World, 1976; Outlaw Blues, 1977; High Ballin', 1978; Wanda Nevada (also director), 1979; Open Season; Smokey and the Bandit II, 1980; Split Image, 1982; Certain Fury, 1985; Dead Fall, 1993; Nadja, Love and a 45, 1994; Painted Hero, Escape From LA, 1996; Idaho Transfer (also director); Ulee's Gold, 1997; Spasm; Fatal Mission; Reckless; Cannonball Run (cameo); Dance of the Dwarfs; Mercenary Fighters; Jungle Heat; Diajobu My Friend; Peppermint Frieden; The Rose Garden; Family Spirit; South Beach; Bodies Rest and Motion; Deadfall; Molly and Gina; South of Heaven West of Hell; The Limey; South of Heaven, West of Hell; Thomas and the Magic Railroad; Second Skin; Wooly Boys; The Laramie Project; El Cobrador: In God We Trust; Ghost Rider, Wild Hogs; Japan; 3:10 to Yuma, 2007; Japan, Journey to the Center of the Earth, Grindhouse Universe, 2008; The Perfect Age of Rock 'n' Roll, The Boondock Saints II: All Saints Day, 2009; TV films: The Hostage Tower, 1980; Don't Look Back, 1996; A Reason to Live; A Time of Indifference; Sound; Certain Honorable Men; Montana; The Maldonado Miracle; Capital City. Address: IFA Talent Agency, 8730 West Sunset Boulevard, Suite 490, Los Angeles, CA 90069, USA.

FONF Vladimir, b. 13 August 1949, Michurinsk, Russia. Mathematician. Divorced, 1 daughter. Education: MSc, Mathematics, 1971; PhD, Mathematics, 1979; DSc Mathematics, 1991. Appointments: Docent, Professor, Kharkov Railroad Institute, Ukraine, 1983-93; Associate Professor, Ben-Gurion University, Israel, 1993-97, Professor, Ben-Gurion University of the Negev, 1997-. Publications: More than 70 articles in mathematical journals in: Bulgaria, Canada, England, Germany, Israel, Poland, Spain, USA, USSR; Co-author, Handbook of Banach Spaces, 2001. Honour: Guastella Fellowship, 1993-96. Membership: Israel Mathematical Union. Address: Department of Mathematics, Ben-Gurion University of the Negev, PO Box 653, Beer-Sheva 84105, Israel. E-mail: fonf@math.bgu.ac.il

FOOTE Russell, b. 1955, Trinidad and Tobago. Social Scientist. m. Gemma, 1 son, 2 daughters. Education: BSc, Sociology; Postgraduate Diploma, Educational Administration; PhD, Sociology of Education, 2002. Appointments: Primary School Teacher, 12 years; Secondary School Teacher, 12 years; Part-time Lecturer, Sociology, Sociological Theory, Research Methods, and Education courses, University of the West Indies, St Augustine Campus; Director, Social Investigations Unit, Ministry of Social Development; Deputy Director, Academic Affairs, Cipriani College of Labour and Co-operative Studies; Associate Provost and Associate Professor, Teacher Education, School for Studies in Learning, Cognition and Education. Publications: Numerous articles in professional journals. Honours: Excellence in Teaching Award, Cowen Hamilton Secondary School; Award for Contribution to the University of Trinidad and Tobago. Memberships: American Sociological Association; Sociology Without Borders. Address: 16 Jarvis Street, San Fernando, Trinidad and Tobago, West Indies. E-mail: russelljfoote@yahoo.com

FORBES Bryan, b. 22 July 1926, Stratford, London, England. Film Executive; Director; Screenwriter; Author. m. Nanette Newman, 1955, 2 daughters. Education: West Ham Secondary School; Royal Academy of Dramatic Art. Appointments: Writer, Producer, Director of numerous films and TV programmes. Publications: Truth Lies Sleeping, 1951; The Distant Laughter, 1972; Notes for a Life, 1974; The Slipper and the Rose, 1976; Ned's Girl, 1977; International Velvet, 1978; Familiar Strangers, 1979; That Despicable Race, 1980; The Rewrite Man, 1983; The Endless Game, 1986; A Song at Twilight, 1989; A Divided Life, 1992; The Twisted Playground, 1993; Partly Cloudy, 1995; Quicksand, 1996; The Memory of all That, 1999. Honours: Best Screenplay Awards; UN Award; Many Film Festival Prizes; Honorary DL, London, 1987; Honorary Doctor of Literature, Sussex University, 1999; CBE. Memberships: Ex-President, Writers Guild of Great Britain; Ex-President, Beatrix Potter Society; President, National Youth Theatre of Great Britain. Address: Pinewood Studies, Iver Heath, Buckinghamshire, England.

FORD Anna, b. 2 October 1943, Tewkesbury, Gloucestershire, England. Broadcaster. m. (1) Alan Holland Bittles, (2) Charles Mark Edward Boxer, deceased 1988, 2 daughters. Education: Manchester University. Appointments: Work for student interests, Manchester University, 1966-69; Lecturer, Rupert Stanley College of Further Education, Belfast, 1970-72; Staff Tutor, Social sciences, North Ireland Region, Open University, 1972-74; Presenter and Reporter, Granada TV, 1974-76, Man Alive, BBC, 1976-77, Tomorrow's World, BBC, 1977-78; Newscaster, ITN, 1978-80; W TV am, 1980-82; Freelance broadcasting and writing, 1982-86; BBC news and current affairs, 1989-; Non-executive director, J Sainsbury plc, 2006. Publication: Men: A Documentary, 1985. Honour: Hon LLD (Manchester), 1998; Honourable Bencher Middle Temple, 2002. Membership: Trustee, Royal Botanic Gardens, Kew. Address: BBC Television Centre, Wood Lane, London, W12 7RJ, England.

FORD Harrison, b. 13 July 1942, Chicago, USA. Actor. m. (1) Mary Marquardt, 2 sons, (2) Melissa Mathison, divorced 2004, 1 son, 1 daughter, (3) Calista Flockhart, 1 adopted son, 2010. Education: Ripon College. Career: Numerous TV appearances; Films include: Dead Heat on a Merry-Go-Round, 1966; Luv, The Long Ride Home, 1967; Getting Straight, Zabriskie Point, 1970; The Conversation, American Graffiti, 1974; Star Wars, Heroes, 1977; Force 10 from Navarone, 1978; Hanover Street, Frisco Kid, 1979; The Empire Strikes Back, 1980; Raiders of the Lost Ark, 1981; Blade Runner; Return of the Jedi, 1983; Indiana Jones and the Temple of Doom; Witness; The Mosquito Coast, 1986; Working Girl, Frantic, 1988; Indiana Jones and the Last Crusade, 1989; Presumed Innocent, 1990; Regarding Henry, 1991; The Fugitive, Patriot Games, 1992; Clear and Present Danger, 1994; Sabrina, 1995; Air Force One, 1996; Six Days and Seven Nights, 1998; Random Hearts, 1999; What Lies Beneath, 2000; K-19: The Widowmaker (also executive producer), 2002; Hollywood Homocide, 2003; Firewall, 2006; Indiana Jones and the Kingdom of the Crystal Skull, 2008; Crossing Over, 2009; Extraordinary Measures, 2010. Address: 10279 Century Woods Drive, Los Angeles, CA 90067, USA.

FORDE Walter Patrick, b. 17 June 1943, Bunclody, County Wexford, Ireland. Roman Catholic Priest. Education: Maynooth College, Ireland, BA, 1964; BD, 1967; H Dip Ed, 1969; Diploma in Social Science, London University, 1972; Ordained, 1968. Appointments: Teacher, St Peter's College, Wexford, 1969-73; General Secretary, National Youth Federation, 1973-74; Director of Social Services and Press Officer, The Diocese of Ferns, 1974-96; Parish Priest, Castlebridge, Co Wexford. Publications: Books include: Adventuring in Priesthood, 1993; The Christian in the Market Place, 1994; Changing Social Needs, 1995; Changing Christian Concerns, 1999; Joan's People, 2003. Honours: County Wexford Person of the Year, 1988; Honorary Life Member, National Youth Federation; Lifetime Achievement Award, Religious Press Association of Ireland, 1998. Address: The Presbytery, Castlebridge, Co Wexford, Ireland.

FOREMAN Alfred G, b. 19 March 1960, Sulfur, Louisiana, USA. Theologian; Philosopher; Scientist. Education: BA, University of Louisiana, Louisiana, 1987; MA, Liberty University, Lynchburg, Virginia, 1991. Appointments: Pastor, Church of God, 1986-2002; Al-Ruh-Al-Amin Masjid (Spirit of Faith and Truth Mosque), 2003-09; Louisiana Philosophical Institute of Humanities, 1992-2004; Lecturer, Islamic Center of Lafayette, Louisiana, 1983-84; Founder, South Louisiana Weather Station, 1986-. Publications: Exposition of Theoretic & Applied Meta-Epistemic Sciences Book I-II: Book I Precedence Exposition of Islamic Philosophy and Science: Level I-II-III Epistemic and Metaphysical History with Classification and Detailing; Book II: Axiosophy as Axioms of Being to Theorems as Levels I-III Opus Middle Part I-Aggregation from Original Notion to Essential Being, Opus Middle Part II – Philosophy of Centricity and Algorithms, Opus Middle Part III – Theory and Proofs; Expanded from Book II is System Documentation Part I-II, System Impetus Theorem 1 Phases 1-5, System Impetus Theorem 2 Phase Σ-Efficient Summation, Extensionality: Symbolica Metaphysica (Fields & Formulae); Book of Curricula: The Epitome; Book III: Christian Thesis in History as Antecedent & Contemporary Issuing. Honours: Listed in Who's Who Publications. Address: 130 Palms Road, Crowley, LA 70526, USA.

FORMAN Milos, b. 18 February 1932, Caslav, Czech Republic. Producer, Director. m. (1) Jane Brejchova, divorced, (2) Vera Kresadlova, divorced, 2 children, (3) Martina Zhorilova, 1999, 2 children. Education: Film Faculty, Academy of Music and Dramatic Art, Prague. Appointments: Director, Film presentations, Czech TV, 1954-56; of Laterna Magika, Prague, 1958-62; Member, artistic committee, Sebor-Bor Film Producing Group; Director, films including: Talent Competition; Peter and Pavla, 1964; The Knave of Spades; A Blonde in Love, 1965; Episode in Zruc; Like a House on Fire (A Fireman's Ball), 1968; Taking Off, 1971; Co-Director, Visions of Eight, 1973; One Flew Over the Cuckoo's Nest, 1975; Hair, 1979; Ragtime, 1980; Amadeus, 1983; Valmont, 1988; The People Vs Larry Flint, 1995; Man on the Moon, 1999; Goya's Ghosts, 2006; Appeared in New Year's Day, 1989; Keeping the Faith, 2000. Publications: Turnaround: A Memoir (with Jan Novak), 1993. Honours: Czech Film Critics' award for Peter and Pavla, 1963, Grand Prix 17th International Film Festival, Locarno, for Peter and Pavla, 1964; Prize Venice Festival, 1965; Grand Prix, French Film Academy for a Blonde in Love, 1966; Klement Gottwald State Prize, 1967; Academy Award (Best Director) for One Flew Over the Cuckoo's Nest, 1976; Academy Award, César Award, 1985; Golden Globe for Best Director, 1996; Silver Bear for Best Director, Berlin Film Festival, 2000.

FORREST Sir (Andrew) Patrick (McEwen), b. 25 March 1923, Mount Vernon, Lanarkshire, Scotland. Surgeon (retired). m. (1) Margaret Beryl Hall, 1955, deceased 1961, (2) Margaret Anne Steward, 1964, 1 son, 2 daughters. Education: BSc, 1942, MB ChB, 1945, University of St Andrews; ChM (Honours), 1954; MD (Honours), 1958; Fellow, Royal Colleges of Surgeons of Edinburgh, 1948, London, 1950, and Glasgow, 1962; Fellow, Royal Society of Edinburgh, 1976; Fellow, Institute of Biology, 1986; Fellow, Royal College of Physicians of Edinburgh, 2000. Appointments: House Surgeon, Dundee Royal Infirmary, 1945; Service with Royal Navy, 1946-48; House Physician, North General Hospital, Edinburgh, 1948; Junior surgical training posts, Dundee, 1948-54; Mayo Foundation Fellow, Mayo Clinic, Rochester, Minnesota, USA, 1951-52; Lecturer, Senior Lecturer in Surgery, University of Glasgow, 1954-62; Professor of Surgery, Welsh National School of Medicine, University of Wales, 1962-71; Regius Professor of Clinical Surgery, 1971-88, Honorary Fellow, Faculty of Medicine, 1988-93, Professor Emeritus, 1988-,University of Edinburgh; Civil Consultant to Royal Navy for Surgical Research, 1977-88; Chief Scientist (part time), Department of Home and Health, Scotland, 1981-87; Visiting Scientist, National Cancer Institute, Bethesda, Maryland, USA, 1989-90; Associate Dean of Clinical Studies, International Medical University, Kuala Lumpur, 1993-95. Publications: 5 books; Numerous articles in professional medical journals. Honours: Knight Bachelor,

1986; University Gold Medal, 1954; Rutherford Gold Medal, 1988; Hon DSc: University of Wales, 1981, Chinese University of Hong Kong, 1986; Hon LLD, University of Dundee, 1986; Hon MD, International Medical University, 2007. Memberships: Honorary Fellow: American Surgical Association; Royal Australian College of Surgeons; Royal College of Radiologists; Royal College of Physicians and Surgeons of Canada; Faculty of Public Health Medicine; Member: Scottish Society of Experimental Medicine; Surgical Research Society; Association of Surgeons of Great Britain and Ireland; British Breast Group; James IV Association of Surgeons; International Surgical Group; British Society of Gastroenterology; British Association of Surgical Association; European Surgical Association. Address: 19 St Thomas Road, Edinburgh EH9 2LR, Scotland. E-mail: patrickforrest@blueyonder.co.uk

FORSCHNER Maximilian, b. 19 April 1943, Reichling, Bavaria, Germany. Professor. m. Adelheid, 2 sons. Education: Diploma of Theology, 1967; Dr phil, 1972; Dr phil habil, 1980. Appointments: Assistant Professor, Universities of Augsburg and Erlangen, 1972-82; Full Professor, University of Osnabrück, 1982-85; Full Professor, 1985-2008, Emeritus, 2008-, University of Erlangen-Nuremberg. Publications: 7 books; More than 100 articles. Honours: Award for best habilitation of the year, 1980. Memberships: German Society for Philosophy; Mommsen Society; Goerres Society; Rotary Club Nueremberg. Address: Institut für Philosophie, Universität Erlangen-Nuremberg, 91054 Erlangen, Germany. E-mail: mnforsch@philmail.uni-erlangen.de

FORSLING Mary Louise, b. 25 March 1942, Rugby, England. University Professor. m. Jonathan Townley-Smith, 2 daughters. Education: BSc, 1963, PhD, 1967, Bedford College, University of London. Appointments: Research Lecturer, Chemical Pathology, St Bartholomew's Hospital, 1969-73; Lecturer, 1975-78, Senior Lecturer, 1979-88, Department of Physiology, Middlesex Hospital Medical School; Reader, Physiology, University College of Middlesex School of Medicine, 1988-89; Reader, Reproductive Physiology, United Medical & Dental School of Guys & St Thomas Hospitals (UMDS), 1989-95; Professor, Neuroendocrinology, GKT School of Medicine (formerly UMDS), 1995-. Publications: 16 books; 300 papers and reviews in professional medical journals. Honours: DSc, 1995; Edkins Memorial Prize; Numerous other awards for research. Memberships: Physiological Society; Society for Endocrinology; Honorary Member, British Society Neuroendocrinology; Trustee, British Society for Neuroendocrinology; Trustee, Martyn Jones Memorial Fund; Senior Member, Society for Endocrinology. Address: 15 Woodland Rise, Muswell Hill, London N10 3UP, England.

FORSTER Gordon Colin Fawcett, b. 30 August 1928, Tadcaster, Yorkshire, England. Academic. m. Judith Mary Duffus Passey. Education: BA, University of Leeds, 1949; Institute of Historical Research, University of London, 1950-52. Appointments: Douglas Knoop Research Fellow, University of Sheffield, 1952-55; Assistant Lecturer, Lecturer, Senior Lecturer, School of History, 1955-93; Chairman, School of History, 1982-85, Life Fellow, 1993-, University of Leeds. Publications: Chapters in Victoria County History volumes: York; Hull; Beverley; Chester; The East Riding Justices of the Peace in the Seventeenth Century; Catalogue of the Records of the Borough of Scarborough; Articles in Northern History and county historical journals; Founder-Editor, Northern History, 1966-; Joint Author, Leeds in the Seventeenth Century, 2008. Honours: Fellow of the Royal Historical Society; Fellow of the Society of Antiquaries; Silver Medal, Yorkshire Archaeological Society. Memberships: Committee, Historic Towns Atlas, 1968-; President, Yorkshire Archaeological Society, 1974-79; Chairman, Yorkshire Archaeological Society Record Series, 1978-; President, Thoresby Society, 1983-87; President, Conference of Regional and Local Historians; Vice President, Surtees Society, 1986-; Council, Chetham Society, 1988-; Historical Advisory Committee, York Archaeological Trust, 1996-. Address: School of History, University of Leeds, Leeds LS2 9JT, England.

FORSYTH Frederick, b. 25 August 1938, Ashford, Kent, England. Writer. m. (1) Carole Cunningham, 1973, 2 sons, (2) Sandy Molloy. Education: University of Granada. Appointments: Reporter, Eastern Daily Press, 1958-61, Reuters News Agency, 1961-65; Reporter, 1965-67, Assistant Diplomatic Correspondent, BBC, 1967-68; Freelance journalist, Nigeria and Biafra, 1968-69; Narrated Soldiers (TV), 1985; Several TV appearances. Publications: Novels: The Day of the Jackal, 1971; The Odessa File, 1972; The Dogs of War, 1974; The Shepherd, 1975; The Devil's Alternative, 1979; The Fourth Protocol, 1984; The Negotiator, 1989; The Deceiver, 1991; Great Flying Stories, 1991; The Fist of God, 1993; Icon, 1996; The Phantom of Manhattan, 1999; Quintet, 2000; The Veteran and Other Stories, 2001; Avenger, 2003; The Afghan, 2006. Other: The Biafra Story, 1969, revised edition as The Making of an African Legend: The Biafra Story, 1977; Emeka, 1982; No Comebacks: Collected Short Stories, 1982; The Fourth Protocol (screenplay), 1987. Honour: Edgar Allan Poetry Award, Mystery Writers of America, 1971; CBE. Address: c/o Bantam Books, 62-63 Uxbridge Road, London, W5 5SA, England.

FORTEY Richard Alan, b. 15 February 1946, London, England. Writer; Palaeontologist. m. Jacqueline, 1 son, 2 daughters. Education: Ealing Grammar School for Boys, 1960-65; BA, 1968, PhD, 1971, Cambridge University. Appointments: Senior Scientific Officer, Principal Scientific Officer, 1970-86, Merit Researcher, 1986-2006, Natural History Museum; Visiting Professor, Palaeobiology, Oxford University, 2000-; Collier Professor, Public Understanding of Science and Technology, Bristol University, 2002-03. Publications: 200 scientific papers, 1968-2008; Fossils: The Key to the Past, 1982; The Hidden Landscape, 1993; Life: An Unauthorised Biography, 1997; Trilobite! Eyewitness to Evolution, 2000; The Earth, An Intimate History, 2004; Dry Store Room No 1, 2008. Honours: SCD, Cambridge, 1986; Lyell Medal, Geological Society of London, 1996; FRS, 1997; Frink Medal, Zoological Society of London, 2001; Lewis Thomas Prize, Rockefeller University, New York, 2003; Zoological Medal, Linnean Society of London, 2006; Michael Faraday Prize, Royal Society, 2006; Honorary DSc, Open University, St Andrew's University, 2007; Honorary F BAA Sc, RC Moore Medal, SEPM, 2008; Hon DSc, University of Birmingham, 2010. Memberships: Geological Society of London; Linnean Society of London; British Mycological Society. Address: Natural History Museum, Cromwell Road, London, SW7 5BD, England. E-mail: r.fortey@nhm.ac.uk

FOSTER Brendan, b. 12 January 1948, Hebburn, County Durham, England. Athlete. m. Susan Margaret Foster, 1972, 1 son, 1 daughter. Education: Sussex University; Carnegie College, Leeds. Career: Competed: Olympic Games, Munich, 5th in 1500 m, 1972; Montreal, bronze medal in 10,000m, 5th in 5000m, 1976; Moscow, 11th in 10, 000m, 1980; Commonwealth Games, Edinburgh, bronze medal at 1500m, 1970; Christchurch, silver medal at 5,000m, 1974; Edmonton, gold medal at 10,000m, bronze medal at 5000m,

1978; European champion at 5000m, 1974 and bronze medallist at 1500m, 1974; World record holder at 3000m and 2 miles; European record holder at 10,000m Olympic record holder at 5000m; Director, Recreation, Gateshead, March, 1982; Managing Director, Nike International, 1982-86; Vice President, Marketing (Worldwide), Vice President (Europe), 1986-87; Chairman and Managing Director, Nova International; BBC TV Commentator, 1980-. Publications: Brendan Foster with Cliff Temple, 1978; Olympic Heroes 1896-1984, 1984. Honours: Hon MEd, Newcastle University; Hon DLitt, Sussex University, 1982; BBC Sports Personality of the Year, 1974; MBE, 1976. Address: Nova International, Newcastle House, Albany Court, Monarch Road, Newcastle upon Tyne, NE4 7YB, England.

FOSTER David (Manning), b. 15 May 1944, Sydney, New South Wales, Australia. Novelist. Education: BSc, Chemistry, University of Sydney, 1967; PhD, Australian National University, Canberra, 1970. Publications: Novels: The Pure Land, 1974; The Empathy Experiment, 1977; Moonlite, 1981; Plumbum, 1983; Dog Rock: A Postal Pastoral, 1985; The Adventures of Christian Rosy Cross, 1986; Testostero, 1987; The Pale Blue Crochet Coathanger Cover, 1988; Mates of Mars, 1991; Self Portraits (editor), 1991; A Slab of Fosters, 1994; The Glade Within the Grove, 1996; The Ballad of Erinungarah, 1997; Crossing the Blue Montain (contributor), 1997; In the New Country, 1999; The Land Where Stories End, 2001; Sons of the Rumour, 2009. Short Stories: North South West: Three Novellas, 1973; Escape to Reality, 1977; Hitting the Wall: Two Novellas, 1989. Honours: The Age Award, 1974; Australian National Book Council Award, 1981; New South Wales Premier's Fellowship, 1986; Keating Fellowship, 1991-94; James Joyce Foundation Award, 1996; Miles Franklin Award, 1997; Courier Mail Award, 1999; Shortlisted, International Dublin IMPAC Award, 1998; Patrick White Award, 2010. Address: PO Box 57, Bundanoon, New South Wales 2578, Australia.

FOSTER Giles Henry, b. 30 June 1948, Winchester, England. Film and TV Director. m. Nicole Anne Coates, 2 sons. Education: BA Honours, English, University of York, 1969-72; MA (RCA), Film and TV, Royal College of Art, 1972-75. Career: Film and Television Director and Writer; TV include: Starting Over; The Four Seasons; Summer Solstice; Foyle's War; Bertie and Elizabeth; The Prince and the Pauper; Coming Home; Oliver's Travels; The Rector's Wife; Adam Bede; Monster Maker; Northanger Abbey; Dutch Girls; The Aerodrome; The Obelisk; 5 Alan Bennett scripts; Hotel du Lac; Silas Marner; A Lady of Letters; Devices and Desires; Shades of Love, 2010-11; Films: Consuming Passions; Tree of Hands (Innocent Victim, USA); The Lilac Bus. Honours: BAFTA Nominations for: Silas Marner, A Lady of Letters, BAFTA Award for: Hotel du Lac; Grierson Award for Best Short Film for: Devices and Desires; BAFTA Nomination, Foyle's War. Memberships: British Academy of Film and Television Arts; Groucho Club; Directors' Guild of Great Britain. Address: c/o ITG, Laura Rouke, 76 Oxford Street, London, W1D 1BS. E-mail: ghf@clara.co.uk

FOSTER Jodie (Alicia Christian), b. 19 November 1962, Los Angeles, USA. Actress; Film Director and Producer. 2 sons. Education: Yale University. Career: Acting debut in TV programme, Mayberry, 1969; Films include: Napoleon and Samantha, Kansas City Bomber, 1972; Menace of the Mountain; One Little Indian, Tom Sawyer, 1973; Alice Doesn't Live Here Any More, 1975; Taxi Driver, Echoes of a Summer, Bugsy Malone, Freaky Friday, 1976; The Girl Who Lives Down the Lane, Candleshoe, 1977; Foxes, Carny, 1980; Hotel New Hampshire, The Blood of Others, 1984; Siesta, Five Corners, 1986; The Accused, Stealing Home, 1988; Catchfire, The Silence of the Lambs, 1990; Little Man Tate (also director), 1991; Shadows and Fog, 1992; Sommersby, 1993; Maverick, Nell, 1994; Home for the Holidays (director, co-producer only), 1996; Contact, The Baby Dance (executive producer only), 1997; Waking the Dead (executive producer only), Contact, 1998; Anna and the King, 1999; Panic Room, The Dangerous Lives of Altar Boys (also producer), 2002; Flightplan, 2005; Inside Man, 2006; The Brave One, 2007, Nim's Island, 2008; The Simpsons, 2009; The Beaver, 2011; Carnage, 2011; Elysium, 2013. Honours: BAFTA Film Awards, 1977, 1992; Golden Globe Awards, 1989, 1992; Academy Award for Best Actress, 1989, 1992; Independent Spirit Award, 1989; People's Choice Award, 1995; Screen Actors Guild Award, 1995; Hon DFA, Yale, 1997; Saturn Award, 1998; Cecil B DeMille Award, 2013. Address: E G G Pictures Production Co, 7920 Sunset Boulevard, Suite 200, Los Angeles, CA 90046, USA.

FOTADAR Ramesh Kumar, b. 20 February 1954, Srinagar, Kashmir, India. Scientist. m. Santosh, 1 son, 1 daughter. Education: PhD. Appointments: Scientist D. Publications: 79 articles in professional journals; 3 books; 6 chapters in books. Honours: Participated in 13th Shanti Swarup Batnagar Memorial Tournament. Memberships: Indian Journal of Genetics; Indian Society of Secricultural Science; Indian Journal of Secriculture. Address: Central Secricultural Research and Training Institute, Pampore, Central Sigk Board, Government of India, Ministry of Textiles, Pampore 194121, India.

FOTOPOULOS Takis, b. 14 October 1940, Greece. Political Philosopher; Writer; Editor; Senior Lecturer. m. Sia Mamareli, 1966, 1 son. Education: LLB, 1962, BA, Economics & Politics, 1965, University of Athens; MSc, Economics, London School of Economics, 1968. Appointments: Lecturer Grade I, Economics, 1969-70, Lecturer, Grade II, 1970-72, North Western Polytechnic; Senior Lecturer, Economics, University of North London, 1973-89; Editor, Society and Nature, 1992-98, Democracy and Nature, 1999-2003; Editor, International Journal of Inclusive Democracy, 2004-. Publications: Towards An Inclusive Democracy, 1997; Per Una Democrazia Globale, 1999; Vers une democratie generale, 2002; Hacia Una Democracia Inclusiva, 2002; Umfassende Demokratie, 2003; The multi-dimensional crisis and Inclusive Democracy (in Chinese), 2007; Published in Athens: Dependent Development, 1985; The War in the Gulf, 1991; The Neoliberal Consensus, 1993; The New World Order and Greece, 1997; Inclusive Democracy, 1999; Drugs, liberalisation vs penalisation, 1999; The New Order in the Balkans, 1999; Religion, Autonomy and Democracy, 2000; From Athenian Democracy to Inclusive Democracy, 2000; Globalisation, Left and Inclusive Democracy, 2002; The war against "terrorism", 2003; Chomsky's capitalism, Albert's post-capitalism and inclusive democracy, 2004; Inclusive Democracy – 10 Years Afterwards, 2008; The pink revolution in Iran and the "left", 2009; Global Crisis, Greece and the Antisystemic Movement, 2009; Greece as a protectorate of the transnational elite, 2010; Contributions to: Education, Culture and Modernization, 1995; Routledge Encyclopedia of International Political Economy, 2001; Defending Public Schools, 2004; Complessita sistemica e sviluppo eco-sostenibil, 2001; Studies on the contemporary Greek Economy, 1978; Environment, Growth and Quality of Life, 1983; Globalisation and Social Economy, 2001; Psyche, Logos Polis – in memory of Castoriadis, 2007; Critical Perspectives on Globalisation, 2006; Globalised Capitalism, the Eclipse of the Left and Inclusive Democracy,

DICTIONARY OF INTERNATIONAL BIOGRAPHY 36th EDITION

2008; Over 900 articles to scholarly journals, magazines and newspapers around the world. Memberships: Theomai Editorial Board; Alternatives Journal Editorial Board; Inclusive Democracy (in Greek) Advisory Board. Address: 20 Woodberry Way, London N12 OHG, England. Website: www.inclusivedemocracy.org/fotopoulos/

FOUCHE Gerda, b. 10 February 1961, Pretoria, South Africa. Researcher. m. Frikkie Fouche, 1 son, 2 daughters. Education: BSc, Chemistry and Mathematics, 1981; BSc (Hons), Chemistry, 1982; MSc, Organic Chemistry, 1985; PhD, Organic Chemistry, 1991; DTE, UNISA, 1994. Appointments: Senior Researcher, CSIR, 1998-; Lecturer, TUT, 1994-98; Senior Researcher, UNIVEN, 1991-94; Assistant Researcher, UNISA, 1988-90; Researcher, CSIR, 1983-88. Publications: 3 international patents in the area of drug discovery; 17 peer-reviewed publications in international journals. Memberships: SACI; Professional Scientist, SACNSP. Address: Mulberry Str 485, Moreleta Park, 0044, Republic of South Africa. E-mail: gfouche@csir.co.za

FOULKES OF CUMNOCK George (Rt Hon Lord Foulkes of Cumnock), b. 21 January 1942, Oswestry, England. Director of Voluntary Organisations; Former Member of Parliament. m. Elizabeth Anna Hope, 1970, 2 sons, 1 daughter. Education: BSc, Psychology, Edinburgh University, 1964. Appointments: President, Scottish Union of Students, 1964-66; Director, ELEC, 1966-68; Scottish Organiser, European Youth Movement, 1968-69; Director, Enterprise Youth, 1969-73; Director, Age Concern Scotland, 1973-79; Member of Parliament for Carrick Cumnock & Doon Valley, 1979-2005; Parliamentary Under-Secretary of State, Department of International Development, 1997-2001; Minister of State, Scotland Office, 2001-02; Elected, Member of Scottish Parliament, 2007 Publications: Editor, 80 Years On (History of Edinburgh University SRC); Chapters in: Scotland – A Claim of Right and Football and the Commons People. Honours: Privy Counsellor, 2000; Justice of the Peace; Wilberforce Medal, 1998. Memberships: Commonwealth Parliamentary Association; President, Caribbean Britain Business Council; Chair, Dominican Republic and Belize All-Party Parliamentary Group; Vice Chair, Trinidad & Tobago and British – Central American All Party Parliamentary Group. Address: House of Lords London SW1A 0WP, England. E-mail: foulkesg@parliament.uk

FOULKES Roland Alexander, b. 6 February 1956, Fort Lauderdale, Florida, USA. Medical Anthropologist; Consultant. Education: BA, Medical Anthropology, Cornell University, Ithaca, New York, 1982; Certificate, Health Care in Developing Countries, Boston University School of Public Health, 1984; MA, Anthropology, University of California at Berkeley, USA, 1985; PhD, Medical Anthropology, University of California at San Francisco Medical Center, 1989. Appointments: Undergraduate Teaching Assistant, Cornell University, New York, 1975-78; Special Assistant, United States Department of Health, Education and Welfare, Washington, DC, 1978-79; Research Associate & Staff Assistant, World Health Organization, Switzerland, 1979-84; Field Co-ordinator/Peace Corps Volunteer, West Africa, 1982-84; Instructor and Tutor, Boston University, 1985; Graduate Student Instructor, 1985-91, Instructor, 1991, University of California at Berkeley; Assistant Professor, Department of Anthropology, University of Florida at Gainesville, 1991-94; Consultant, Researcher, Life Coach, and Substance Abuse Counselor, Gainesville Drug Treatment Center, Florida, 1994-95; Director/ Investor, Equinox International Nevada and Gainesville, Florida, 1995-97; Director/ Investor, Global Solutions, Florida, 1997-2000; Founder, President and CEO, Roland A Foulkes & Associates, 1980-2000; Founder and Chief Strategist, One Broward: A Vision of Our Future and the one May for One Broward Coalition, Fort Lauderdale, 2001-; Behavioral & Social Science Volunteer, American Psychological Association, Washington, DC, 2005-; Consultant/Trainer, National Center for Training, Support and Technical Assistance, New Jersey, 2006-; Consultant/Trainer, National Center for Cultural Competence, Washington, DC, 2006-; Director, Public Relations and Governmental & Corporate Affairs, Florida Inter-Cultural Academy, Florida, 2010-. Publications: Numerous articles in professional journals. Honours include: Grand Prize Winner, National Essay Contest, 1994; Member, Vision Broward, 2003-07; Winner, Franklin H Williams National Prize, 2005; Winner, John F Kennedy Public Service Award, 2006; Winner, Civil Rights Award, 2009; Charter Member, South Florida DiversityAlliance, 2009. Memberships: Broward Republican Executive Committee; Broward 2020 Cultural Plan; Council for Diversity and Equal Opportunity; South Florida Diversity Alliance; Racism and Health Workgroup. Address: Post Office Box 101492, Fort Lauderdale, FL 33310-1492, USA. E-mail: rolandafoulkes@gmail.com

FOX Edward, b. 13 April 1937. Actor. m. (1) Tracy Pelissier, 1958, divorced 1961, 1 daughter, (2) Joanna David, 2 children. Education: Royal Academy of Dramatic Art. Career: Actor, 1957-; Provincial repertory theatre, 1958; Worked widely in films, stage plays and TV; Stage appearances include: Knuckle, 1973; The Family Reunion, 1979; Anyone for Denis, 1981; Quartermaine's Terms, 1981; Hamlet, 1982; The Dance of Death, 1983; Interpreters, 1986; The Admirable Crichton, 1988; Another Love Story, 1990; The Philanthropist, 1991; My Fair Lady; Father, 1995; A Letter of Resignation, 1997; The Chiltern Hundreds, 1999; The Browning Version, 2000; The Twelve Pound Look, 2000; Films include: The Go-Between, 1971; The Day of the Jackal; A Doll's House, 1973; Galileo, 1976; A Bridge Too far; The Duellists; The Cat and the Canary, 1977; Force Ten from Navarone, 1978; The Mirror Crack'd, 1980; Gandhi, 1982; Never Say Never Again, 1983; Wild Geese; The Bounty, 1984; The Shooting Party; Return from the River Kwai, 1989; Circles of Deceit (TV), 1989; Prince of Thieves, 1990; They Never Slept, 1991; A Month by the Lake, 1996; Prince Valiant, 1997; Lost in Space, 1998; All the Queen's Men, 2001; The Importance of Being Earnest, 2002; Nicholas Nickleby, 2002; The Republic of Love, 2003; Stage Beauty, 2004; Lassie, 2005; Television includes: I Was a Rat, 2001; Daniel Deronda, 2002; Foyle's War, 2002; Poirot, 2004; Oliver Twist, 2007. Honours: Several awards for TV performance as Edward VIII in Edward and Mrs Simpson.

FOX James, b. 19 May 1939, London, England. Actor. m. Mary Elizabeth Piper, 1973, 4 sons, 1 daughter. Career: Actor, films include: Mrs Miniver, 1952; The Servant, 1963; King Rat, 1965; Those Magnificent Man in Their Flying Machines, 1965; Thoroughly Modern Millie, 1966; Isadora, 1967; Performance, 1969; Passage to India, 1984; Runners, 1984; Farewell to the King, 1987; Finding Mawbee (video film as the Mighty Quinn), 1988; She's Been Away, 1989; The Russia House, 1990; Afraid of the Dark, 1991; Patriot Games, 1991; As You Like It, 1992; The Remains of the Day, 1993; The Old Curiosity Shop, 1994; Gulliver's Travels, 1995; Elgar's Tenth Muse, 1995; Uncle Vanya, 1995; Anna Karenina, 1997; Mickey Blue Eyes, 1998; Jinnah, 1998; Up at the Villa, 1998; The Golden Bowl, 1999; Sexy Beast, 2000; The Lost World, 2001; The Prince and Me, 2004; The Freediver, 2004; Charlie and the Chocolate Factory, 2005; Goodbye Mr Snuggles, 2006;

Mister Lonely, 2007; Margaret, 2009; Red Riding: In the Year of Our Lord 1980, 2009; Sherlock Holmes, 2009. Publication: Comeback: An Actor's Direction, 1983. Address: c/o ICM Oxford House, 76 Oxford Street, London, W1D 1BS, England.

FOX Matthew, b. 14 July 1966, Wyoming, USA. Actor; Former Model. m. Margherita Ronchi, 1991, 1 son, 1 daughter. Education: Economics, Columbia University; The School for Film and Television, New York City. Career: TV: Freshman Dorm, 1992; Party of Five, 1994-2000; Haunted, 2002; Lost, 2004-; Film: A Token for Your Thoughts, 2003; We Are Marshall, 2006; Vantage Point, 2008; Speed Racer, 2008.

FOX Michael J, b. 9 June 1961, Edmonton, Alberta, Canada. Actor. m. Tracy Pollan, 1988, 1 son, 2 daughters. Career: TV appearances include: Leo and Me, 1976; Palmerstown USA, 1980; Family Ties, 1982-89; Spin City, 1996-2000; Scrubs, 2004; Boston Legal, 2006; The Magic 7 (voice), 2008; Rescue Me, 2009; TV films include: Letters from Frank, 1979; Poison Ivy, 1985; High School USA, 1985; Films include: Midnight Madness, 1980; Class of '84, 1981; Back to the Future, 1985; Teen Wolf, 1985; Light of Day, 1986; The Secret of My Success, 1987; Bright Lights, Big City, 1988; Back to the Future II, 1989; Back to the Future III, 1989; The Hard Way, 1991; Doc Hollywood, 1991; The Concierge, 1993; Give Me a Break, 1994; Greedy, 1994; The American President, 1995; Mars Attacks!, 1996; The Frighteners, 1996; Stuart Little (voice), 1999; Atlantis: The Lost Empire (voice), 2001; Interstate 60, 2002; Stuart Little 2 (voice), 2002; Stuart Little 3: Call of the Wild (voice), 2005. Address: c/o Kevin Huvane, CAA, 9830 Wilshire Blvd, Beverly Hills, CA 90212, USA.

FOXX Jamie, b. 13 December, 1967, Texas, USA. Actor; Singer; Standup Comic. Career: TV: Roc, 1991; In Living Color, 1991; The Jamie Foxx Show, 1996; Film: Any Given Sunday, 1999; Ali, 2001; Collateral, 2004; Ray, 2004; Jarhead, 2005; Miami Vice, 2006; Dreamgirls, 2006; The Kingdom, 2007; The Soloist, 2009; Law Abiding Citizen, 2009; Valentine's Day, 2010; Album: Peep This, 1994; Featured on Slow Jamz, 2004; Featured on Gold Digger, 2004; Featured on Georgia, 2005; Unpredictable, 2005. Honours: Academy Award for Best Actor, 2004; Academy of Motion Picture Arts and Sciences, 2005; Best Duet/Collaboration, BET Awards, 2006; Video of the Year, 2006; Hollywood Walk of Fame, 2007.

FRAGA Mariana Amorim, b. 11 May 1980, Bom Jesus da Lapa, Bahia, Brazil. Researcher. m. Leandro Koberstein. Education: Master's degree, Microelectronics and Electrical Engineering, University of Sao Paulo, 2005; PhD, Aeronautics and Mechanical Engineering, Technological Institute of Aeronautics, 2009. Appointments: Researcher, Plasma and Processes Laboratory, Technological Institute of Aeronautics, 2005-; Researcher, Institute for Advanced Studies, 2010-. Publications: 12 papers in journals; 1 book; 2 book chapters; More than 30 papers at conference. Honours: IEEE Women in Engineering Poster, 2011; Listed in biographical dictionaries. Memberships: IEEE; SPIE; ECS. Address; Praça Marechal Eduardo Gomes, 50, Sao José dos Campos – SP, 12232-380, Brazil. E-mail: mafraga@ita.br

FRAGOMENI James Mark, b. 24 September 1962, Columbus, Ohio, USA. Engineer; Educator. Education: Bachelor of Science (BS) in Metallurgical Engineering, University of Pittsburgh, Pennsylvania, 1981-85; Master of Science in Engineering (MSE), 1987-89, Doctor of Philosophy (PhD), Mechanical Engineering, 1990-94, Purdue University, College of Engineering, West Lafayette, Indiana. Appointments: Purdue Engineering Research Center, 1987-94; Purdue CINDAS, 1995; Assistant Professor, University of Alabama, 1995-97; NASA Faculty Research Fellow, summers, 1996, 1997; AFOSR/Airforce Faculty Research Fellow, summer, 1998; Assistant Professor, Ohio University, 1997-2000; Assistant Professor, University of Detroit Mercy, 2000-2005; Instructor at Ford Training Center, 2001-2005; Instructor at Focus Hope (part-time), Detroit, Michigan, 2001-2003; Senior Metallurgical Technician, Volt Technical Services, 2006; Metallurgical Engineering Consultant, Westmoreland Mechanical Testing and Research Inc, 2007-09. Publications: Over 60 technical articles in conference proceedings and scientific journals including: Acta Mechanica, 1999; Aluminum Transactions, 2000; Journal of Advanced Materials, 2001, 2002, 2005; Acta Astronautica, 2002, 2004; Aerospace Science and Technology, 2002; Computer Assisted Mechanics and Engineering Sciences, 2004; Journal of Materials Engineering and Performance, 2005. Honours: University of Pittsburgh Merit Scholarship, 1981-85; Carpenter Technology Scholarship, 1982; Order of Engineer, 1989; Tau Beta Pi; Phi Eta Sigma; Omicron Delta Kappa; Sigma Xi The Scientific Research Society, 1996-; Pi Tau Sigma, Mechanical Engineering Honor Society, 1998-; Certified Quality Technician, 2005; ABI: Lifetime Deputy Governor, 2005; Life Fellow, 2005; Ambassador of Grand Eminence, AGE, 2005; International Directory of Experts and Expertise, 2006; American Hall of Fame, 2006; Great Minds of the 21st Century, 2006; 500 Greatest Geniuses of the 21st Century, 2006, 2009; Great Minds of the 21st Century Hall of Fame, 2006; Outstanding Professional Award, 2006; Man of the Year, 2005, 2006; International Peace Prize, 2006; Ambassador-General of the United Cultural Convention, 2006; Prestigious National Honor Society, 2010-11. Memberships: The Materials Society Titanium Committee; The American Society for Engineering Education; The American Society for Mechanical Engineers; The American Society for Quality; The American Society for Materials; Michigan Education Association, 2001-; Engineering Society of Detroit, 2002-; Society of Manufacturing Engineers, 2002-; Motown Writers Network, 2006. Address: 25105 Biarritz Circle, #C Oak Park, MI 48237, USA. E-mail: jamesfrag@yahoo.com Website: www.jamesmatsci.org, www.jamesfrag.net

FRAILE Medardo, b. 21 March 1925, Madrid, Spain. Writer; Emeritus Professor in Spanish. Education: DPh, DLitt, University of Madrid, 1968. Publications: Cuentos con Algun Amor, 1954; A La Luz Cambian las Cosas, 1959; Cuentos de Verdad, 1964; Descubridor de Nada y Otros Cuentos, 1970; Con Los Dias Contados, 1972; Samuel Ros Hacia una Generacion Sin Critica, 1972; La Penultima Inglaterra, 1973; Poesia y Teatro Espanoles Contemporaneos, 1974; Ejemplario, 1979; Autobiografia, 1986; Cuento Espanol de Posguerra, 1986; El gallo puesto en hora, 1987; Entre parentesis, 1988; Santa Engracia, numero dos o tres, 1989; Teatro Espanol en un Acto, 1989; El rey y el pais con granos, 1991; Cuentos Completos, 1991; Claudina y los cacos, 1992; La Familia irreal inglesa, 1993; Los brazos invisibles, 1994; Documento Nacional, 1997; Contrasombras, 1998; Ladrones del Paraiso, 1999; Cuentos de Verdad (anthology), 2000; Descontar y Contar, 2000; Años de Aprendizaje, 2001; Escritura y Verdad, 2004; Palabra en el tiempo, 2005; En Madrid Tambien Se Vive En Oruro, 2007; Entradas de cine, 2008; El Cuento de Siempre Acabar (Mémoires), 2009; Antes del Futuro Imperfecto, 2010. Translation: El Weir de Hermiston by R L Stevenson, 1995; Contributions to: Many publications. Honours: Sesamo Prize, 1956; Literary Grant, Fundacion Juan March, 1960; Critics Book of the Year, 1965; La Estafeta literaria Prize, 1970; Hucha de Oro Prize, 1971; Research Grant, Carnegie Trust for Universities of Scotland, 1975; Colegiado de Honor del

Colegio heraldico de España y de las Indias, 1995; Comendador con Placa de la Orden Civil de Alfonso X El Sabio, 1999; Orden venezolana de Primera Clase de Don Balthazar de Leon. Memberships: General Society of Spanish Authors; Working Community of Book Writers, Spain; Association of University Teachers. Address: 24 Etive Crescent, Bishopbriggs, Glasgow G64 1ES, Scotland.

FRANCHI Giuseppe, b. 16 November 1924, Siena, Italy. University Professor. m. Rampazzo Rosana, 1 son. Education: Laurea Pharmacy, University of Siena, 1948; Libera Docenza, Pharmaceutical Technology and Legislation, 1958; Libera Docenza, Pharmaceutical Chemistry, 1962. Appointments: Lecturer and Professor, Pharmaceutical Technology and Legislation, 1958-75; Dean Faculty of Pharmacy, University of Siena, Italy, 1976-88; Pharmaceutical Chemistry Department, University of Siena, Director, 1976-81, 1995-97; Retired, 1997. Publications: 92 papers on pharmaceutical chemistry and pharmaceutical techniques, 1951-97; 1 book on analytical chemistry; 2 patents on pharmaceutical technological equipment. Honours: Gold Medal for services to school, culture and art, 1984; Commendatore al merito della Repubblica Italiana, 1997. Memberships: Accademia delle Scienze di Siena, detta dei Fisiocritici, 1954, President, 1990-98; Association of Italian Teachers and Researchers in Pharmaceutical Technology and Legislation, 1971, President, 1981-97; Italian Society of Pharmaceutical Sciences, 1966-2004; Pharmaceutical Society of Latin Mediterranean Countries, 1963; Rotary Club 2070 District, 1980. Address: Via della Sapienza 39, 53100 Siena, Italy.

FRANCO BRANAS Jose Ramon, b. 4 July 1948, Santiago de Compostela, Spain. University Professor. m. Soledad Villa, 1 son, 1 daughter. Education: Graduate, Mathematics, University La Laguna; Doctor, Mathematics, University Las Palmas de Gran Canaria. Publications: Introduccion al Calculo; Manual de Combinatoria; Calculo I; Iniciacion a la Programacion Basic; Introduccion a la Matematica Aplicada; Numerous articles in professional journals. Honours: Listed in international biographical dictionaries. Memberships: Mathematical Association of America; Isaac Newton Society of Teachers. Address: C/Fray Diego, 73, Tacoronte, Santa Cruz de Tenerife, 38350, Spain.

FRANKLAND (Anthony) Noble, b. 4 July 1922, Ravenstonedale, England. Historian; Biographer. m. (1) Diana Madeline Fovargue Tavernor, 28 February 1944, deceased 1981, 1 son, 1 daughter, (2) Sarah Katharine Davies, 7 May 1982. Education: Open Scholar, MA, 1948, DPhil, 1951, Trinity College, Oxford. Appointments: Served Royal Air Force, 1941-45, Bomber Command, 1943-45; DFC, 1944; Official British Military Historian, 1951-60; Deputy Director of Studies, Royal Institute of International Affairs, 1956-60; Director, Imperial War Museum, 1960-82. Publications: Crown of Tragedy: Nicholas II, 1960; The Strategic Air Offensive Against Germany (co-author), 4 volumes, 1961; The Bombing Offensive Against Germany: Outlines and Perspectives, 1965; Bomber Offensive: The Devastation of Europe, 1970; Prince Henry, Duke of Gloucester, 1980; Witness of a Century: Prince Arthur, Duke of Connaught, 1850-1942, 1993; History at War: The Campaigns of an Historian, 1998; The Unseen War (novel), 2007; Belling's War (novel), 2008; Encyclopaedia of Twentieth Century Warfare (general editor and contributor), 1989; The Politics and Strategy of the Second World War (joint editor), 9 volumes. Contributions to: Encyclopaedia Britannica; Times Literary Supplement; The Times; Daily Telegraph; Observer; Spectator; Military journals. Honours: Companion of the Order of the Bath; Commander of the Order of the British Empire; Holder of the Distinguished Flying Cross. Address: 26/27 River View Terrace, Abingdon, Oxon, OX14 5AE, England.

FRANKLIN Aretha, b. 25 March 1942, Memphis, Tennessee, USA. Singer; Songwriter. m. Glynn Turman, 1978. Career: Recording artist, 1960-; European tour, 1968; Appearances include: Inaugural Eve Gala, Jimmy Carter, Washington DC; Jamaica World Music Festival, 1982; Budweiser Superfest, 1982; Presidential Inauguration, Barack Obama. Actress, film The Blues Brothers, 1980; Subject, TV specials: Aretha Franklin - The Queen Of Soul, 1988; Aretha Franklin - Duets, 1993. Recordings: Albums include: The Great Aretha Franklin, 1960; The Electrifying Aretha Franklin, 1962; The Tender, The Moving, The Swinging, 1962; Unforgettable - A Tribute To Dinah Washington, 1964; Runnin' Out Of Fools, 1965; Yeah!!!, 1965; Soul Sister, 1966; I Never Loved A Man (The Way I Loved You), 1967; Aretha Arrives, 1967; Aretha: Lady Soul, 1968; Aretha In Paris, 1968; This Girl's In Love With You, 1969; Spirit In The Dark, 1970; Aretha Live At Fillmore West, 1971; Amazing Grace, 1972; Hey Now Hey (The Other Side Of The Sky), 1973; Let Me In Your Life, 1974; With Everything I Feel In Me, 1975; You, 1975; Sweet Passion, 1977; Almighty Fire, 1978; La Diva, 1979; Aretha, 1980; Love All The Hurt Away, 1981; Jump To It, 1982; Get It Right, 1983; Who's Zoomin' Who?, 1985; The First Lady Of Soul, 1986; Aretha, 1987; One Lord, One Faith, One Baptism, 1988; Through The Storm, 1989; What You See Is What You Sweat, 1991; Queen Of Soul, 1993; Greatest Hits 1980-1994, 1994; A Rose Is Still A Rose, 1998; You Grow Closer, 1998; Hit singles include: I Never Loved A Man (The Way I Loved You), 1967; Respect (Number 1, US), 1967; Baby I Love You, 1967; (You Make Me Feel Like A) Natural Woman, 1967; Chain Of Fools, 1968; (Sweet Sweet Baby) Since You've Been Gone, 1968; Think, 1968; I Say A Little Prayer, 1968; Call Me, 1970; Don't Play That Song, 1970; You're All I Need To Get By, 1971; Rock Steady, 1972; Young Gifted And Black, 1972; Day Dreaming, 1972; Until You Come Back To Me, 1974; Sisters Are Doin' It For Themselves, duet with Annie Lennox, 1985; I Knew You Were Waiting For Me, duet with George Michael (Number 1, UK and US), 1987; Through The Storm, duet with Elton John, 1989; Contributor, film soundtracks including: Sparkle, 1976; Jumpin' Jack Flash, 1986; White Men Can't Jump, 1992. Honours include: Aretha Franklin Day, Detroit, 1967; Numerous Grammy Awards, 1968-; American Music Awards; Inducted into Rock'n'Roll Hall Of Fame, 1987; Living Legend Award, NARAS, 1990; Rhythm & Blues Foundation Lifetime Achievement Award, 1992. Current Management: Aretha Franklin Management, 30150 Telegraph Road, Suite 444, Birmingham, MI 48025, USA.

FRANZ Gerhard, b. 3 April 1953, Korbach, Hesse, Germany. Professor. m. Elli Schaeder. Education: MSc, 1977; PhD, 1980. Appointments: Group Leader, 1992, Project Manager, 1995; Professor, 2002; Speaker, The Competence Center, Nanostructuring Technology, 2005. Publications: Books: Kalte Plasmen, 1990; Oberflaechen-Technologie mit Niederdruckplasmen, 1994; Niederdruckplasmen und Mikrostruktur-Technik, 2004; Fluktuationen – Schoenheit in Kunst und Wissenschaft, 1st edition, 2001, 2nd edition, 2007; Low Pressure Plasmas and Microstructuring Technology, 2009; More than 40 peer-reviewed articles, more than 60 external talks, 5 review articles and 1 book chapter. Membership: American Vacuum Society. Address: 17A Luetzowstreet, 81245 Munich Bavaria, Germany. E-mail: gerhard.franz@hm.edu Website: www.gerhard-franz.org

FRASER (John) Malcolm (Rt Hon), b. 21 May 1930, Melbourne, Australia. Past Prime Minister of Australia. m. Tamara Beggs, 1956, 2 sons, 2 daughters. Education: MA, 1952, Honorary Fellow, 1982, Oxford University. Appointments: Prime Minister of Australia, 1975-83; Chairman, UN Secretary General's Expert Group on African Commodity Problems, 1983-86; Co-Chairman, Commonwealth Eminent Persons Group on South Africa, 1986; Member, 1983-, Chairman, 1996-2005, Honorary Chairman, 2005-, Interaction Council for Former Heads of Government; Chairman, Care Australia, 1987-2001; President, 1990-95, Vice President, 1995-99, Care International. Publications: Common Ground – Issues That Bind & Divide Us, 2002, 2003; Malcolm Fraser The Political Memoirs (co-author with Margaret Simons), 2010. Honours: PC, 1976; CH, 1977; B'nai B'rith Gold Medal, 1980; Hon LLD, SC, USA, 1981; AC, 1988; Hon Dr Letters, Deakin University, 1989; Australian Human Rights Medal, The Human Rights and Equal Opportunity Commission, 2000; Grand Cordon, Order of the Rising Sun, Japan, 2006; Medal of Gratitude, Polish Embassy Canberra, 2011; Grand Companion of the Order of Logohu, PNG High Commission Canberra, 2011. Membership: Melbourne Club. Address: 32nd Floor, 101 Collins Street, Melbourne, VIC 3000, Australia.

FRASER Lady Antonia, (Lady Antonia Pinter), b. 27 August 1932, London, England. Author. m. (1) Sir Hugh Fraser, 1956, dissolved 1977, 3 sons, 3 daughters, (2) Harold Pinter, 1980. Education: MA, Lady Margaret Hall, Oxford. Appointment: General Editor, Kings and Queens of England series. Publications: King Arthur and the Knights of the Round Table, 1954; Robin Hood, 1955; Dolls, 1963; A History of Toys, 1966; Mary Queen of Scots, 1969; Cromwell, Our Chief of Men, 1973; King James: VI of Scotland, I of England, 1974; Kings and Queens of England (editor), 1975; Scottish Love Poems: A Personal Anthology (editor), 1975; Love Letters: An Anthology (editor), 1976, revised edition, 1989; Quiet as a Nun, 1977; The Wild Island, 1978; King Charles II, 1979; Heroes and Heroines (editor), 1980; A Splash of Red, 1981; Mary Queen of Scots: Poetry Anthology (editor), 1981; Oxford and Oxfordshire in Verse: An Anthology (editor), 1982; Cool Repentance, 1982; The Weaker Vessel: Woman's Lot in Seventeenth Century England, 1984; Oxford Blood, 1985; Jemima Shore's First Case, 1986; Your Royal Hostage, 1987; Boadicea's Chariot: The Warrior Queens, 1988; The Cavalier Case, 1990; Jemima Shore at the Sunny Grave, 1991; The Six Wives of Henry VIII, 1992; The Pleasure of Reading (editor), 1992; Political Death, 1994; The Gunpowder Plot, 1996; The Lives of the Kings and Queens of England, 1998; Marie Antoinette: the Journey, 2001; Love and Louis XIV: The Women in the Life of the Sun King, 2006; Must You Go? My Life with Harold Pinter, 2010; Other: Several books adapted for television. Contributions to: Anthologies. Honours: James Tait Black Memorial Prize, 1969; Wolfson History Award, 1984; Prix Caumont-La Force, 1985; Honorary DLitt, Universities of Hull, 1986, Sussex, 1990, Nottingham, 1993 and St Andrews, 1994; St Louis Literary Award, 1996; CWA Non Fiction Gold Dagger, 1996; Shortlisted for NCR Award, 1997; Norten Medlicott Medal, Historical Association, 2000. Memberships: Society of Authors, chairman, 1974-75; Crimewriters' Association, chairman, 1985-86; Writers in Prison Committee, chairman, 1985-88, 1990; English PEN, vice president, 1990-. Address: c/o Curtis Brown Ltd, 162-168 Regent Street, London W1R 5TB, England.

FRASER Ian Masson, b. 15 December 1917, Forres, Moray, Scotland. Ordained Minister. m. Margaret D D Stewart, deceased, 2 sons, 1 daughter. Education: MA, BD (New College for Theology), with distinction in Systematic Theology, 1936-42; PhD, 1955, Edinburgh University, Scotland. Appointments: Manual Working Industrial Chaplain, Fife, Scotland, 1942-44; Interim appointment, Hopemouth Church, Arbroath, Scotland, 1944-45; Scottish Secretary, Student Christian Movement, 1945-48; Parish Minister, Rosyth, Fife, Scotland, 1948-60; Warden of Scottish Churches House, Dunblane, Scotland, 1960-69; Executive Secretary, Consultant and Programme Co-ordinator, 1969-75, World Council of Churches; Dean and Head of the Department of Mission, Selly Oak Colleges, Birmingham, England, 1973-82; Voluntary Research Consultant, Scottish Churches' Council, 1982-90, Action of Churches Together in Scotland, 1990-2010. Publications: Numerous articles and books including: Strange Fire, a book of life stories and prayers, 1994; A Celebration of Saints, 1997; Signs of Fire (audio cassette), 1998; Salted with Fire, more stories, reflections, prayers, 1999; Caring for Planet Earth, children's stories and prayers, 2002; R B Cunninghame Graham – Fighter for Justice, 2002; ACTS, Ecumenical Adventure, beginnings in the 1960s of the work of Scottish Churches House and Council, 2002; Many Cells One Body, 2003; The Way Ahead – grown-up Christians in integrated community serving the world God loves, 2006; A Storehouse of Kingdom Things, 2010; Pieces for the Smith, 2012; Which Way for the World? 2012. Honours: Cobb Scholarship, Cunningham Fellowship, Gunning Prize, New College, Edinburgh. Address: Ferndale, Gargunnock, by Stirling FK8 3BW, Scotland.

FREDERIKSEN Jens Mejer, b. 25 March 1963, Copenhagen, Denmark. Consulting Engineer. m. Helle Hjelm, 1 son, 2 daughters. Education: BSc Eng (Hon), Civil Engineer, The Engineering Academy, Technical University of Denmark, 1986. Appointments: Consulting Engineer, Expert, 2012-. Publications: More than 40 papers in professional publications. Memberships: RILEM; The Danish Society of Engineer; Danish Concrete Association; The Danish Society for Materials Testing and Research. Address: Alectia a/s, Teknikerbyen 34, DK-2830 Virum, Denmark. E-mail: jmf@alectia.com

FREEMAN Cathy, b. 16 February 1973, Mackay, Australia. Athlete. m. (1) Alexander Bodecker, divorced, 2003; (2) James Murch, 2009. Career: Public Relations Adviser; Winner, Australian 200m, 1990-91, 1994, 1996; Australian 100m, 1996; Amateur Athletics Federation 400m, 1992, 200m, 1993; Gold Medallist 4x100m, Commonwealth Games, 1990; Gold Medallist 200m, 400m, Silver Medallist 4x100m, Commonwealth Games, 1994; Silver Medallist 400m, Olympic Games, Atlanta, 1996; Winner, World Championships 400m, Athens (first Aboriginal winner at World Championships), 1997; Set 2 Australian 200m records, 5 Australian 400m records, 1994-96; 1st, World Championships, Seville, 400m, 1999; Gold Medallist, Sydney Olympic Games 400m, 2000; took break from athletics in 2001; returned to international competition, Gold Medal 4x400m relay, Commonwealth Games, Manchester, 2002; Retired from competition, 2003; Media and Communications Officer, Australia Post. Honours: Numerous national awards include: Australian of the Year, 1998; OAM, 2001. Address: c/o Melbourne International Track Club, 43 Fletcher Street, Essendon, Vic 3040, Australia.

FREEMAN David Franklin, b. 13 April 1925, Raleigh, North Carolina, USA. Adult and Child Psychiatrist and Psychoanalyst. m. Constance Covell Freeman, 1 son, 2 daughters. Education: BS, Wake Forest College, North Carolina, 1948; MD, Bowman Gray School of Medicine,

Winston-Salem, 1951; Internship, Philadelphia General Hospital, 1951-52; Resident, Adult and Child Psychiatry, Boston Psychopathic Hospital, Massachusetts, 1952-55; Research Fellow, Psychiatry, Harvard University, 1952-55; 2nd Year Child Psychiatry, Worcester Youth Guidance Center, Massachusetts, 1955-56; Candidate, Adult and Child Psychoanalysis, Boston, Washington, UNC-Duke University Psychoanalytic Institutes, 1955-66. Appointments: Private Practice, Adult and Child Psychiatry, Lincoln, Massachusetts, 1956-61; Director, North Central Mental Health Consultation Service, Fitchburg, Massachusetts, 1956-57; Staff Psychiatrist, Douglas A Thom Clinic for Children, Boston, Massachusetts, 1957-61; Assistant in Child Psychiatry, Boston University School of Medicine, 1960-61; Consultant, several child psychiatry clinics, 1956-66; Clinical Faculty, Assistant Professor to Clinical Professor, University of North Carolina, 1961-95; Adjunct Professor, University of North Carolina at Chapel Hill, 1995-; Training and Supervising Psychoanalyst, UNC-Duke University Psychoanalytic Education Program, 1972-; Psychiatric Consultant, NE Home for Little Wanderers, Boston, Massachusetts, 1959-61; Director, Child Psychiatry Outpatient Clinic, North Carolina Memorial Hospital, Chapel Hill, 1961-63; Private Practice, Adult and Child Psychiatry and Psychoanalysis, Chapel Hill, North Carolina, 1963-2009. Publications: Several articles in professional medical journals. Honours include: Alpha Omega Alpha, 1950; Herman Lineberger Award, 1997; NC Psychoanalytic Foundation, 2003. Memberships include: Life member: American Psychiatric Association; International Psychoanalytical Association; North Carolina Psychiatric Association; American Academy of Child and Adolescent Psychiatry; North Carolina Medical Society; American Psychoanalytic Association; Association for Child Psychoanalysis; Life Member and Past President: North Carolina Psychoanalytic Society; North Carolina Council of Child Psychiatry; Founder and Chair: North Carolina Psychoanalytic Foundation, 1995-2000; Chair, Carolina Psychoanalytic Consortium, 2006-. Address: 374 Carolina Meadows Villa, Chapel Hill, NC 27517, USA.

FREEMAN Jennifer Margaret, b. 28 October 1944, Sale, Cheshire, England. Architectural Writer; Specialist in Building Conservation; Director; Chairman. m. Rt Hon Lord Freeman, 1 son, 1 daughter. Education: BA (Honours), University of Manchester, 1963-66; Postgraduate Diploma in Building Conservation, Architectural Association, London, 1979-81. Appointments: Economic Intelligence Department, Bank of England, London, 1966-68; Eurobond Dealer, N H Rothschild & Sons, London, 1968-69; International Banking Department, Bankers Trust Company, New York City, 1969-70; Consultant Researcher, New York City Landmarks Preservation Commission, 1970-72; Assistant to Architect, European Architectural Heritage Year 1975, Civic Trust, 1972-74; Co-author, Project Co-ordinator, Save the City: A Conservation Study of the City of London, 1974-80; Secretary, The Victorian Society, 1982-85; Founding Member, London Advisory Committee, English Heritage, 1986-2001; Member, Council for the Care of Churches, 1991-2001; Leading organiser of national efforts to save and refurbish 23 historic buildings in the City of London including Mansion House/No 1 Poultry, 1980's and 1990's; Chairman, Freeman Historic Properties Ltd, 1991-; First Director, Historic Chapels Trust, 1993-2012. Publications include: Save the City: a Conservation Study of the City of London (co-author), 1976, reprinted, 1977, revised, 1979; Billingsgate Market (co-author) 1981; W D Caroe: His Architectural Achievement, 1991; Kensal Green Cemetery (co-author), 2001; Don't Butcher Smithfield (contributor),

2004; Numerous articles in architectural and conservation journals. Honours: Honorary Doctorate of Arts, De Montfort University, 1997; Freedom of the City of London, 1998; FRSA, 2003; FSA, 2005; OBE, 2012. Memberships include: Institute of Historic Buildings and Conservation; President, Friends of Kensal Green Cemetery; Vice-President, Friends of the City Churches; Committee Member, Save Britain's Heritage, 1977-; Founding Trustee, Heritage Link, 2002-08; Trustee, Constable Trust, 2004-10; Vice President, National Churches Trust, 2005-; Bodleian Library Development Board, 2003-10; President, Kettering Civic Society, 2004. E-mail: jmfhproperties@gmail.com

FREUD Anthony Peter, b. 30 October 1957, London, England; Opera Administrator; Barrister. Education: LLB (Hons), King's College, London, 1975-78; Inns of Court School of Law, 1978-79. Appointments: Trained as Barrister; Theatre Manager, Sadler's Wells Theatre, 1980-84; Company Secretary, Director of Opera Planning, Welsh National Opera, 1984-91; Executive Producer Opera, Philips Classics, 1992-94; General Director, Welsh National Opera, 1994-. Honour: Honorary Fellowship of Cardiff University, 2002. Memberships: Member, Honorary Secretary of Gray's Inn, 1979; Chairman of Jury, Cardiff Singer of the World, 1995-; Chairman, Opera Europa, 2002-2005; Trustee, National Endowment for Science, Technology and the Arts (NESTA), 2004-2005; OBE, 2006. Address: Welsh National Opera, Wales Millennium Centre, Bute Place, Cardiff Bay CF10 5AL, Wales. E-mail: anthony.freud@wno.org.uk

FREUD Bella, b. 17 April 1961, London, England. m. James Fox. Fashion Designer. Education: Accademia di Costuma e di Moda, Rome; Institutto Mariotti, Rome. Appointments: Assistant to Vivienne Westwood on her designer collections, 1986-89; Launched own label presenting autumn/winter collection of tailored knitwear and accessories, 1990; Exhibited, London Designer Show, 1991, London Fashion Week, 1993. Honours: Winner, Innovative Design - the New Generation Category (British Fashion Awards), 1991. Address: 21 St Charles Square, London, W10 6EF, England.

FREUND Hans-Joachim, b. 4 March 1951, Solingen, Germany. Institute Director. m. Tatiana, 3 sons, 1 daughter. Education: BS, 1972, MSc, 1975, Chemistry and Physics, PhD, 1978, Private Docent, 1983, Universität zu Köln. Appointments: Teacher, Gymnasium Solingen, 1975-78; Scientific Assistant, 1978-79, Scientific Assistant, 1981-83, Private Docent, 1983, Universität zu Köln; Postdoctoral Fellow, University of Pennsylvania and Xerox Corporation, Webster, 1979-81; Associate Professor, Universitat Erlangen, 1983-87; Professor, Ruhr-Universitat Bochum, 1987-96; Director and Scientific Member, Fritz-Haber-Institut der Max-Planck Gesellschaft, 1996-. Publications: 600 articles in professional journals; 1 book. Honours: Leibnitz Award, German Research Foundation, 1995; Centenary Lecturer in Chemistry, 2006, 2007; Gabor Somorjai Award for Creative Research in Catalysis, American Chemical Society, 2007; G B Kistiakowsky Lecturer, Harvard Department of Chemistry and Chemical Biology, 2011; Arthur D Little Lecturer in Physical Chemistry, Massachusetts Institute of Technology, 2011. Memberships: American Chemical Society; American Physical Society; Bunsengesellschaft für Physikalische Chemie; Deutsche Physikalische Gesellschaft; Gesellschaft Deutscher Chemiker; Institute of Physics, UK; Academia Europaea, London; Berlin-Brandenburg Academy of Sciences, Berlin; Academia Brasileira, Rio de Janeiro;

German National Academy of Sciences Leopoldina, Halle, Germany. E-mail: freund@fhi-berlin.mpg.de Website: http://fhi-berlin.mpg.de/ep/hjf.epi

FREWER Glyn Mervyn Louis, (Mervyn Lewis), b. 4 September 1931, Oxford, England. Author; Scriptwriter. m. Lorna Townsend, 11 August 1956, 2 sons, 1 daughter. Education: MA, English Language and Literature, St Catherine's College, Oxford, 1955. Publications: The Hitch-Hikers (BBC Radio Play), 1957; Adventure in Forgotten Valley, 1962; Adventure in the Barren Lands, 1964; The Last of the Wispies, 1965; Death of Gold (as Mervyn Lewis), 1970; The Token of Elkin, 1970; Crossroad, 1970; The Square Peg, 1972; The Raid, 1976; The Trackers, 1976; Tyto: The Odyssey of an Owl, 1978; Bryn of Brockle Hanger, 1980; Fox, 1984; The Call of the Raven, 1987. Other scripts for children's television series, industrial films, etc. Contributions to: Birds; Imagery; The Countryman. Honours: Junior Literary Guild of America Choice, for Adventure in Forgotten Valley, 1964; Freeman of the City of Oxford, 1967. Address: Ascott House, Wychwood Close, Charlbury, Chipping Norton, Oxfordshire, OX7 3TB, England.

FRIDMANN Andre, b. 10 April 1952. Dental Surgeon. 2 daughters. Education: Doctor of Dental Surgery, Lund's University, Sweden, 1986; Masters level, Aesthetic Dentistry, New York University, USA, 2009; Diploma, Oral Implants, Branemark Institute, Gothenberg, Sweden, 1990; Masterclass, Facial Aesthetics, RCS, London, England, 2011. Appointments: Junior DDS, Maloerten, Trelleborg, Sweden, 1986-89; Partner, Soendermarken Tandlage Praxis, Copenhagen, Denmark, 1989-99; Associate Dentist, Nottingham, 1999-2000; Owner, Kingswood Dental, Hailsham, UK, 2000-. Memberships: American Academy of Cosmetic Dentistry; British Academy of Cosmetic Dentistry; International Academy of Advanced Facial Aesthetics. E-mail: info@drfridmann.com

FRIEDLANDER John B, b. 4 October 1941, Toronto, Canada. Mathematician. m. Cherryl, 2 sons, 2 daughters. Education: BSc, University of Toronto, 1965; MA, University of Waterloo, 1966; PhD, The Pennsylvania State University, 1972. Appointments: Assistant to A Selberg, 1972-73; Member, 1973-74, Institute for Advanced Study, Princeton, New Jersey; Lecturer, Massachusetts Institute of Technology, 1974-76; Visiting Professor, Scuola Normale Superiore, Pisa, Italy, 1976-77; Assistant Professor, 1977-79, Associate Professor, 1980-82, Scarborough College, University of Toronto; Lecturer, University of Illinois, Urbana, 1979-80; Appointed to School of Graduate Studies, 1980; Professor, 1982-; Member, School of Mathematics, Institute for Advanced Study, 1983-84; Chair, Department of Mathematics, University of Toronto, 1987-91; Visitor, 1990-91, Member, 1995-96, 1999-2000, 2004, 2009, School of Mathematics, Institute for Advanced Study, Princeton; Research Professor, Mathematical Science Research Institute, Berkeley, California, 1991-92; Visiting Professor, Macquarie University, Sydney, 1996. Publications: Over 120 articles and papers in professional journals; Numerous lectures at conferences and workshops. Honours: Fellow, Royal Society of Canada, 1988; Invited Lecture, ICM Zurich, 1994; Participant, Taniguchi Symposium in Analytic Number Theory, Kyoto, 1996; Jeffery-Williams Prize Lecturer, Canadian Mathematical Society, 1999; Principal's Research Award, University of Toronto at Scarborough, 1999-2000; CRM-Fields Prize, 2002; University Professor, University of Toronto, 2002-; Killam Research Fellowship, 2003-05. Memberships: Royal Society of Canada; Canadian Mathematical Society; American Mathematical Society; Mathematical Association of America. Address: Computer and Mathematical Sciences, University of Toronto at Scarborough, Toronto ON M1C 1A4, Canada.

FRIEDMAN (Eve) Rosemary, (Robert Tibber, Rosemary Tibber, Rosemary Friedman), b. 5 February 1929, London, England. Writer. m. Dennis Friedman, 1949, 4 daughters. Education: Queen's College, Harley Street, London; Law Faculty, University College, London University. Publications: No White Coat, 1957; Love on My List, 1959; We All Fall Down, 1960; Patients of a Saint, 1961; The Fraternity, 1963; The Commonplace Day, 1964; Aristide, 1966; The General Practice, 1967; Practice Makes Perfect, 1969; The Life Situation, 1977; The Long Hot Summer, 1980; Proofs of Affection, 1982; A Loving Mistress, 1983; Rose of Jericho, 1984; A Second Wife, 1986; Aristide in Paris, 1987; An Eligible Man, 1989; Golden Boy, 1994; Vintage, 1996; The Writing Game, 1999; Intensive Care, 2001; Paris Summer, 2004; A Writer's Commonplace Book, 2006; Stage plays: Home Truths, 1997; Change of Heart, 2004; An Eligible Man, 2008; Life Is A Joke – A Writer's Memoir, 2010; Commissioned screenplays and television drama; Contributions to and reviewer for: Sunday Times; Times Literary Supplement; Guardian; Jewish Quarterly. Memberships: Royal Society of Literature; Society of Authors; Writers' Guild of Great Britain; British Academy of Film and Television Arts; Fellow, English PEN. Address: Apt 5, 3 Cambridge Gate, London NW1 4JX, England. E-mail: rosemaryfriedman@hotmail.com Website: www.rosemaryfriedman.co.uk

FRIEDMAN Isaiah, b. 28 April 1921, Luck, Poland. University Professor Emeritus; Historian. m. Barbara Joan Braham, 1 son. Education: MA, 1945, Jewish History, Hebrew University, Jerusalem; PhD, International History, London School of Economics and Political Science, University of London, 1964. Appointments: Research Fellow, Hebrew University, 1965-68; Fellow, Deutsche Forschungsgemeinschaft, 1968-71; Associate Professor, Modern Jewish History and Political Science, Dropsie University, Philadelphia, 1971-77; Professor of History, Ben-Gurion University, Beersheba, Israel, 1977-91; Professor Emeritus of History, 1991-. Publications: Books: The Question of Palestine, 1914-1918, British-Jewish-Arab Relations, 1973, 2nd and expanded edition, 1992 (also in Hebrew); Germany, Turkey and Zionism, 1897-1918, 1977, 2nd edition, 1998 (also in Hebrew); The Rise of Israel: A Documentary Record, 12 volumes, 1987; Palestine: A Twice Promised Land? (also in Hebrew), 2000; Editor, Sefer Luck (Hebrew), 2007; Co-editor, Encyclopaedia Judaica, 2007; British Pan-Arab Policy, 1915-1922: A Critical Appraisal, 2009; Contributed numerous articles and entries. Honour: Recipient Theodor Körner Foundation Prize, University of Vienna, 1964. Memberships: Fellow, American Philosophical Society, 1971-76; Fellow, American Council Learned Society, 1972; Fellow, The Lucius Littauer Foundation, 1972; Fellow, American Academy for Jewish Research, 1975; Member, World Jewish Studies; Oriental Society of Israel. Address: 39 Sigalon Street, Omer 84-965, Israel.

FRIEDRICH Fabian, b. 2 May 1965, Blumenau, Santa Catarina, Brazil. Biochemist; Molecular Biologist. Education: Graduation, Biochemistry, Universidade Federal de Santa Catarina, Brazil, 1988; Postgraduate Specialisation, Biotechnology, Universidade Federal do Rio Grande do Sul, Brazil, 1988; Master Degree, Parasitology, Molecular Biology, Institute Oswaldo Cruz, Fiocruz, Brazil, 1993; Doctorate (PhD), Cell and Molecular Biology, Instituto Oswaldo Cruz, Fiocruz, Brazil, 1996. Appointments:

Working with molecular biology and biotechnology, for past 20 years. Publications: Images of UFOs; UFOs: The Search for Unidentified Flying Objects and Unknown Civilizations Continues ... (exobiology and ufology); Articles in professional biomedical journals and nucleotide sequences published in the gene bank. Honours: Listed in numerous biographical directories. Membership: Brazilian Society of Virology, 1993-2000. Address: Rua Vasco da Gama, 69, Blumenau- Santa Catarina, Cep 89.065-080, Brazil.

FRIER Brian Murray, Consultant Physician; Honorary Professor of Diabetes. m. Isobel Wilson, 1 daughter. Education: BSc (Honours Class 1), Physiology, 1969, MB ChB, 1972, MD, 1981, University of Edinburgh. Appointments: Junior medical appointments in Edinburgh and Dundee, 1972-76; Clinical Research Fellow, Cornell University Medical Center, The New York Hospital, New York, USA, 1976-77; Senior Medical Registrar, Edinburgh, 1978-82; Consultant Physician, Western Infirmary and Gartnavel General Hospital, Glasgow, 1982-87; Consultant Physician, Royal Infirmary of Edinburgh, 1987-, and Honorary Professor of Diabetes, University of Edinburgh, 2001-. Publications: Books co-edited with B M Fisher: Hypoglycaemia and Diabetes, Clinical and Physiological Aspects, 1993; Hypoglycaemia in Clinical Diabetes, 1999; Hypoglycaemia in Clinical Diabetes, Second Edition, 2007; Original publications in peer reviewed journals, review articles, editorials and book chapters on hypoglycaemia, insulin therapy, complications of diabetes, driving and diabetes etc. Honours: R D Lawrence Lecturer of British Diabetic Association, 1986; Somogyi Award of the Hungarian Diabetes Association for hypoglycaemia research, 2004; Banting Memorial Lecturer, Diabetes UK, 2009. Memberships: MRCP (UK), 1974; FRCP (Edin), 1984; FRCP (Glas), 1986; Chairman of Honorary Medical Advisory Committee on Driving and Diabetes to Secretary of State for Transport, 2001-; Council Member 2002-08, Vice President, 2008-, Royal College of Physicians of Edinburgh; Chairman, Chief Scientist Office committee on Diabetes Research in Scotland 2003-2006. Address: Department of Diabetes, Royal Infirmary, Edinburgh EH16 4SA, Scotland.

FRIGGIERI Oliver, b. 27 March 1947, Furjana, Malta. Professor; Poet; Novelist; Critic. m. Eileen, 1 daughter. Education: BA, cum laude, 1968; MA, 1975; PhD, 1978. Appointments: Full Professor; Ex-Head of Department of Maltese, University of Malta, 1987-2005; Presenter of radio programmes; Guest Speaker at numerous academic and literary international congresses in Europe. Publications: Numerous books in Maltese, most of which have been translated and published in numerous languages; History of Maltese Literature; Dictionary of Literary Terms; Numerous scholarly articles in Maltese, English, Italian, published in major international magazines; Translator, various works from Latin, English, Italian into Maltese; Guest Poet in various international poetry recitals throughout Europe; Books: Storia della Letteratura Maltese; Rituel du Crepuscule; Nous Sommes un Desir; La Menzogna; Storie per una Sera; La cultura italiana a Malta – Dun Karm; It-Tfal Jigu Bil-Vapuri; Fil-Parlament ma Jikbrux Fjuri; Koranta and other Short Stories from Malta; A Mentira; Author of various oratorios and cantatas. Honours: Holder of various international literary awards including Premio Mediterraneo Internazionale, Palermo and Premio Internazionale Trieste Poesia, 2002; Holder of the Maltese Government Prize for Literature; Guest Lecturer in various foreign Universities; Member of the Order of Merit, Maltese Government, 1999; Officer, Al Merito Delle Republica Italiane, 2012. Memberships: Association International des Critiques Litteraire, Paris; Member PEN Club Switzerland. Address: Department of Maltese, University of Malta, Msida, Malta.

FRITZE Lothar, b. 5 April 1954, Karl-Marx-Stadt. Researcher; Political analyst. m. Ulrike Fritze Otto, 2 sons. Education: Dipl-Ing oec, Betriebswirtschaft, 1978; Dr phil, Promotion in Philosophie, 1988; Dr phil habil, Habilitation in Politikwissenschaft, 1998. Appointments: Scientific collaborator, Forschungsinstitut fuer Textiltechnologie, Karl-Marx-Stadt, 1978-90; Institut fuer Wirtschafts u Sozialforschung, Chemnitz, 1992-93; Hannah-Arendt-Institut fuer Totalitarismusforschung, Dresden, 1993-. Publications: Books: Innenansicht eines Ruins: Gedanken zum Untergang der DDR, 1993; Panoptikum DDR-Wirtschaft: Machtverhaeltnisse, Organisationsstrukturen, Funktionsmechanismen, 1993; Die Gegenwart des Vergangenen: Ueber das Weiterleben der DDR nach ihrem Ende, 1997; Taeter mit gutem Gewissen: Ueber menschliches Versagen im diktatorischen Sozialismus, 1998; Die Toetung Unschuldiger. Ein Dogma auf dem Pruefstand, 2004; Verfuehrung und Anpassung. Zur Logik der Weltanschauungsdiktatur, 2004; Die Moral des Bombenterrors. Alliierte Flaechenbombardements im Zweiten Weltkrieg: Legitimer Widerstand? Der Fall Elser; Numerous articles to professional journals. Honours: Außerplanmaßiger Professor, Technical University, Chemnitz; Award, Gesellschaft fuer Deutschlandforschung, 1998. Address: Georgistrasse 2, D-09127 Chemnitz, Germany.

FROHNE Vincent Sauter, b. 26 October 1936, LaPorte, Indiana, USA. Composer; Organist; Pianist; Educator. m. Joan E Ruebush, 3 daughters. Education: Studies at Hochschule fuer Musik, Berlin; Summer schools at Aspen & Tanglewood Music Festivals, 1957, 1959, USA; Bachelor of Music (cum laude), DePauw University, 1958; MM, Eastman School of Music, 1959; Certificate, Goethe Institut, Lueneburg, 1961; Technische University, Berlin, 1961-65; PhD, University of Rochester, 1963. Appointments: Director, Kammermusik des 20th Jahrhunderts, Berling, 1968-71; Dozent, Berlin Volkshochschulen, 1967-70; Founder/Director/Professor, Schiller College, Berlin Music Program, 1970-74; Associate Professor, University of Tulsa, 1975-78; Associate Professor, Tulsa Junior College, 1979; Guest Professor, Western Illinois University, 1979-80; Organist, St Paul RC Church, Macomb, Illinois, 1984-; Lecturer, Spoon River College, Macomb branch, 1988; Sandburg College, Galesburg, Illinois, 1989; Colorado Mountain College, 2002. Publications in Europe and USA: Adam's Chains for soprano and orchestra; Antinomy for orchestra; String Quartet; Pendulum; Study for Clarinet Solo; Various radio recordings, disc and CD recordings; Author, Aesthetics & Creativity in the 20th Century, in progress; Numerous articles in professional journals. Honours: Guggenheim Fellow, 1966; Three times winner, Rome Prize, 1963-66; Rockefeller Orchestra Prize, 1967; Benjamin Award, 1959; Koussevitsky Commission in Library of Congress, 1965; Commissions from Gazzeloni, Mancinelli, Kuhnert, Williams College, DePauw University; UCC Church; Presbyterian Church; Kaiser Friedrich Memorial Church, Berlin; WFMT Radio, Chicago; Sandwich Opera; Music Teachers National Association; Fullbright Grant, 1961; BBC Radio inteview; Various other print & media honours. Memberships: Fellow, American Academy in Rome; GEMA, Berlin & Munich; Phi Mu Alpha; Pi Kappa Lambda; Lambda Chi Alpha; Macomb Philosophy Club; Music Teachers National Association; Various political and church organisations. Address: 12965 E 900th St, Macomb, IL 61455-8907, USA. E-mail: vcompfro@yahoo.com

FROIMOWICZ Pablo, b. 24 August 1974, Alta Gracia, Cordoba, Argentina. Scientist; Researcher. Education: Tech Chemist, El Obraje Institute, Alta Gracia, Cordoba, 1993; Lic, Chemical Sciences, 1999, PhD, Chemical Sciences, Organic and Polymer Synthesis, 2005, National University of Cordoba; PhD, Materials Science and Engineering, National Polytechnic Institute of Grenoble, France, 2005. Appointments: Post-doctoral Fellow, University of Toronto, Canada, 2006-08; Visiting Scientist, Max Planck Institute for Polymer Research, Mainz, Germany, 2008-. Publications: 2 doctoral thesis; Author and co-author of numerous peer-reviewed research articles in international journals; 2 books in progress. Honours: 2 Scholarships for Outstanding Undergraduate Students, National University of Cordoba, 1998, 1999; Student Fellow, University of Bahia Blanca, Argentina, 1999; Scholarship from FOMEC, 2001; Student Fellow, University of Basque Country, Spain, 2004; Finalist, Ten Outstanding Young Persons of the Year, 2005; Listed in international biographical dictionaries. Address: Max Planck Institute for Polymer Research, Ackermannweg 10, D-55128 Mainz, Germany. E-mail: pablo.froimowicz@mpip-mainx.mpg.de

FROST David Paradine (Sir), b. 7 Apr 1939. Auth; Prodr; Writer; TV Presenter and interviewer. m. Lady Carina Fitzalan-Howard, 1983, 3 s. Education: MA, Gonville and Caius Coll, Cambridge; LLD, Emerson Cooll, USA. Appointments include: Jt Fndr, Dir, TV-am, 1981-93; BBC TV series, That Was The Week That Was, 1962-63, USA, 1964-65; A Degree of Frost, 1963, 1973; Not So Much a Programme, More a Way of Life, 1964-65; The Frost report, 1966-67; Frost Over England, 1967; Frost Over America, 1970; Frost's Weekly, 1973; The Frost Interview, 1974; We British, 1975-76; Forty Years of Television, 1976; The Frost Programme, 1977; Breakfast with Frost, 1993-; BBC Radio incls David Frost at the Phonograph, 1966; Pull the Other One, series, 1987, 1988, 1990; ITV series and progs incl: Frost on Friday, 1968-69; The Sir Harold Wilson Interviews, 1976; A Prime Minister on Prime Ministers, 1977-78; The BAFTA Awards and Onward Christian Soldiers, 1981; A Night of Knights: a Royal Gala, 1982; The End of the Year Show, 1982, 1983; Frost on Sunday, TV-am, 19183-92; Through the Keyhole, 1987; Num other progs. Publications include: That Was The Week That Was, 1963; David Frost: an autobiography: part one: From Congregations to Audiences, 1993. Honours include: Richard Dimbleby Awd, 1967; Emmy Awd, USA, 1970, 1971; Albert Einstein Awd, Comms Arts, 1971; OBE, 1970; Kt, 1993. Memberships include: Brit/USA Bicentennial Liaison Cttee, 1973-76; Pres, Lord's Taverners, 1985, 1986. Address: David Paradine Ltd, 5 St Mary Abbots Place, London W8 6LS, England.

FRY Stephen John, b. 24 August 1957. Actor; Writer. Education: Queen's College, Cambridge, England. Appointments: Columnist, The Listener, 1988-89; Daily Telegraph, 1990-; Appeared with Cambridge Footlights in revue, The Cellar Tapes, Edinburgh Festival, 1981; Re-wrote script: Me and My Girl, London, Broadway, Sydney, 1984; Plays: Forty Years On, Chichester Festival and London, 1984; The Common Pursuit, London, 1988 (TV, 1992); TV series: Alfresco, 1982-84; The Young Ones, 1983; Happy Families, 1984; Saturday Night Live, 1986-87; A Bit of Fry and Laurie, 1989-95; Blackadder's Christmas Carol, 1988; Blackadder Goes Forth, 1989; Jeeves and Wooster, 1990-92; Stalag Luft, 1993; Laughter and Loathing, 1995; Gormenghast, 2000; Fortysomething, 2003; A Bear Named Winnie, 2004; Tom Brown's Schooldays, 2005; Absolute Power, 2003-05; Bones, 2007; Kingdom, 2007; Radio: Loose Ends, 1986-87; Whose Line Is It Anyway?, 1987; Saturday Night Fry, 1987; Harry Potter and the Chamber of Secrets (Narrator, CD), 2002; Harry Potter and the Prisoner of Azkaban (Narrator, CD), 2004; Films: The Good Father; A Fish Called Wanda; A Handful of Dust; Peter's Friends, 1992; IQ, 1995; Wind in the Willows, 1997; Wilde, 1997; A Civil Action, 1997; Whatever Happened to Harold Smith? 2000; Relatives Values, 2000; Discovery of Heaven, 2001; Gosford Park, 2001; Thunderpants, 2002; Bright Young Things, 2003; Tooth, 2004; The Life and Death of Peter Sellers, 2004; MirrorMask, 2005; The Hitchhiker's Guide to the Galaxy (voice), 2005; A Cock and Bull Story, 2005; V for Vendetta, 2005; Stormbreaker, 2006; Eichmann, 2007; St Trinian's, 2007; Tales of the Riverbank, Fable 2 (voice), LittleBigPlanet, 2008; LittleBigPlanet PSP (voice), House of Boys, Alice in Wonderland (voice), 2009. Publications: Paperweight (collected essays), 1992; The Liar (novel); The Hippopotamus, 1994; Fry and Laurie 4 (with Hugh Laurie), 1994; Paperweight, 1995; Making History, 1996; Moab is My Washpot (autobiography), 1997; The Star's Tennis Balls (novel), 2000. Honour: Hon LLD (Dundee), 1995. Memberships: Patron, Studio 3 (arts for young people); Freeze (nuclear disarmament charity); Amnesty International; Comic Relief. Address: c/o Hamilton Asper Management, Ground Floor, 24 Hanway Street, London, W1P 9DD, England.

FRYBA Ladislav, b. 30 May 1929, Studenec. Professor. m. Dagmar Frybova. Education: Ing, 1953, DSc, 1959, Docent, 1966, Professor, 1993, Czech Technical University; Doctor honoris causa, University of Pardubice, 2004. Appointments: Head, Bridge Department, Railway Research Institute, 1972-84; Professor, Institute of Theoretical and Applied Mechanics, Academy of Sciences of the Czech Republic, 1984-. Publications: 6 books; Co-author, 6 books; Over 200 papers in 9 world languages; Best known world-wide: Dynamics of Railway Bridges, 3rd edition, 1996; Vibration of Solids and Structures Under Moving Loads, 3rd edition, 1999. Honours: Medals, Czechoslovak Academy of Sciences, Czech Society for Mechanics; 5 medals from Japanese Universities and Society of Japanese Association of Mechanical Engineering; Diploma, European Association for Structural Dynamics; Listed in international biographical dictionaries. Memberships: Chairman, Committees of Experts of the European Rail Research Institute, Utrecht, 1967-2001; President, Czech Society for Mechanics, 1991-2007; President, European Association for Structural Dynamics, 1996-99; Member, Engineering Academy of the Czech Republic, 1996-; Research Board of Advisors, American Biographical Institute, 1999; Member, Editorial Board of the Journal of Sound and Vibration, 2001-09.

FRYDRYCH Angieszka, b. 13 March 1976, Krosno, Poland. Specialist in Oral Medicine. m. Clement Wong. Education: BDSc (Hons), 1999; MDSc, Oral Medicine and Oral Pathology, 2005; FRACDS, Oral Medicine, 2009. Appointments: Associate Professor, Oral Medicine, University of Western Australia. Publications: Numerous articles in professional journals. Honours: Pierre Fouchard Academy Undergraduate Certificate of Merit, 1999; Dental Study group of West Australia, KJG Southerland Award for Lecturer of the Year, 2005; University of West Australia, Excellence in Teaching Award, 2005; University of Western Australia, Faculty of Medicine & Dentistry, Excellence in Teaching Award, 2005; University of Western Australia, Teaching & Learning Committee Award for Outstanding Contribution to Improving Student Learning, 2005. Memberships: Australian Dental Association; Dental Board of Western Australia Study Group YWAA; International Association of Oral Pathologists; Australian Academy of Oral Medicine; Fellow, RACDS; NA

Center & Palliative Care Network; Tumour Collaboration for Head & Neck. Address: 25 Jutland Parade, Dalkeith, WA 6009, Western Australia. E-mail: agnieszka.frydrych@uwa.edu.au

FUCIKOVA Terezie Svobodova, b. 25 April 1936, Eger, Czech Republic. Medical Doctor. m. Zdenek Fucik, 1 son, 1 daughter. Education: Baccallaureat, 1954, MUDr, 1960, Faculty of Medicine, Postgraduate diplomas, Internal Medicine I grade, 1965, Internal Medicine II grade, 1968, PhD, Internal Medicine, 1974, Postgraduate diploma, Clinical Immunology, 1988, Docent, Internal Medicinae, 1987, Professor, Clinical Immunology and Allergology, 1996, Charles University, Prague; DrSc, Immunology, Academy of Science, Prague, 1995. Appointments: Head, Department of Clinical Immunology, Medical Faculty, 1989-2002, Vice-Head, Institute of Clinical Immunology and Microbiology, 2002-09, Professor, 2009, Charles University, Prague. Publications: Monographs: Clinical Immunology in Practice, 1995, 1997; Immune-Mediated Diseases in Rorejsi, 2006; Laboratory Methods in Immunology and Allergology, 2007. Honours: Award for Monography Clinical Immunology, 1996; Nummum Magnum Universitae Carolinae, 1998; Award, Monograph Laboratory Diagnostic in Medicine, 2003; Golg Medal for Medicine, Slovak Medical Society, 2007; Purkyn Medal, Czech Medical Society, 2008. Memberships: Czech Society for Allergology and Clinical Immunology; Czech Immunological Society; EAACI; Society of Internal Medicine.

FUENTES Carlos, b. 11 November 1928, Panama City, Panama. Professor of Latin American Studies; Writer. m. (1) Rita Macedo, 1957, 1 daughter, (2) Sylvia Lemus, 1973, 1 son, 1 daughter. Education: Law School, National University of Mexico; Institute de Hautes Études Internationales, Geneva. Appointments: Head, Cultural Relations Department, Ministry of Foreign Affairs, Mexico, 1955-58; Mexican Ambassador to France, 1975-77; Professor of English and Romance Languages, University of Pennsylvania, 1978-83; Professor of Comparative Literature, 1984-86, Robert F Kennedy Professor of Latin American Studies, 1987-, Harvard University; Simon Bolivar Professor, Cambridge University, 1986-87; Professor-at-Large, Brown University, 1995-. Publications: La Region Mas Transparente, 1958; Las Buenas Conciencias, 1959; Aura, 1962; La Muerte de Artemio Cruz, 1962; Cantar de Ciegos, 1964; Cambio de Piel, 1967; Zona Sagrada, 1967; Terra Nostra, 1975; Una Familia Lejana, 1980; Agua Quemada, 1983; Gringo Viejo, 1985; Cristóbal Nonato, 1987; Myself with Others (essays), 1987; Orchids in the Moonlight (play), 1987; The Campaign, 1991; The Buried Mirror, 1992; El Naranjo, 1993; Geography of the Novel: Essays, 1993; La frontera de cristal (stories), 1995; Los Años con Laura Diaz (novel), 1999; Los Cincosoles de Mexico (anthology), 2000; Inez, 2000; Ce que je crois, 2002; La Silla de Aguila, 2003; Contra Bush, 2004; Todas las Familias Felices, 2006; La Voluntad y la Fortuna, 2008. Contributions to: Periodicals. Honours: Biblioteca Breva Prize, Barcelona, 1967; Rómulo Gallegos Prize, Caracas, 1975; National Prize for Literature, Mexico, 1984; Miguel de Cervantes Prize for Literature, Madrid, 1988; Légion d'Honneur, France, 1992; Principe de Asturias Prize, 1992; Latin Civilisation Prize, French and Brazilian Academies, 1999; DLL, Ghent, 2000, Madrid, 2000; Mexican Senate Medal, 2000; Los Angeles Public Library Award, 2001; Commonwealth Award Delaware, 2002. Memberships: American Academy and Institute of Arts and Letters; El Colegio Nacional, Mexico; Mexican National Commission on Human Rights. Address: c/o Brandt & Brandt, 1501 Park Avenue, New York, NY 10036, USA.

FUJISAWA Shinsuke, b. 31 May 1947, Tokyo, Japan. Psychology Researcher. Education: BA, 1971, MA, Psychology, 1983, Keio University, Tokyo; PhD, Psychology, Nagoya University, Aichi, 2004. Appointments: Director, Learning Development Center, Tokyo, 1975-2001; Assistant Professor, 1977-80, Associate Professor, 1980-86, Professor, 1986-, Atomi University, Tokyo; Director, Japan Juku Association, Tokyo, 2007-. Publications: Books: Fake Scholarly Skills, 2002; The Process of Development of Teaching Ability in Teachers Regarded as Reflective Practitioners, 2005; The Faculty of Language: Psychology of Cognition and Meaning, 2011. Memberships: Japanese Association of Educational Psychology; Japanese Psychological Academy for Human Care; Japanese Association of Psychology in Teaching and Learning. E-mail: fujisawa@atomi.ac.jp

FUJITA Hagino, b. 1 November 1969, Yokohama, Japan. Electrical Engineer. m. Kenichiro, 1 son. Education: Graduate, Musashi Institute of Technology, 1995; PhD, Tokai University, 2009. Appointments: Facility Design of Manufacturing Lines and Inspection Apparatus for Image Processing, and Computer Simulation of Electromagnetic Field and Applications of Electromagnetic Force to Magnetic Levitation of Thin Metal Plate, Toyo Seikan Ltd, 1995-. Publications: Numerous articles in professional journals. Honours: Incentive Award, 2008; Best Technical Contribution Award, 2010. Memberships: IEEE; Institute of Electrical Engineers of Japan; Japan Society of Applied Electromagnetics and Mechanics. Address: 3-1 Uchisiwaicho I-chome, Chiyoda-ku, Tokyo 100-8522, Japan.

FUJITA Masayuki, b. 15 August 1956, Takamatsu, Kagawa, Japan. Biologist; Educator. m. Tomoko, 1 son. Education: BS, Chemistry, Shizuoka University, Faculty of Science, 1975-79; Doctor of Agriculture, Biochemistry, Nagoya University, Graduate School of Bioagricultural Sciences, 1979-83. Appointments: Assistant Professor, 1983-91, Associate Professor, 1991-99, Professor, 1999-, Kagawa University; Serving concurrently as Professor, Ehime University and The United Graduate School of Agricultural Sciences, 1999-; Researcher, Institute of Biological Chemistry, Washington State University, USA, 1996-97. Publications: Plant Infection, 1982; Handbook of Phytoalexin Metabolism and Action, 1995; Lignin and Lignan Biosynthesis, 1998; Biochemistry and Molecular Biology of Plant Stress, 2001; Floriculture, Ornamental and Plant Biotechnology, Vol III, 2006; Current Topics in Plant Biology, 2008; Abiotic Stress, 2011; Selenium Sources, Functions and Health Effects, 2012; Onion Consumption and Health, 2012; Crop Stress and its Management, 2012; Oxidative Stress in Plants: Causes, Consequences and Tolerance, 2012; Reactive Oxygen Species in Plants, 2012; Remediation of Environmental Contaminants, 2012; Photosynthetic Pigments – Chemical Structures, Biological Function and Ecology, 2013; Abiotic Stress, 2013; Salt Stress in Plants: Signaling, Omics and Adaptions, 2013; Plant Acclimation to Environmental Stress, 2013; Ecophysiology and Responses of Plants under Salt Stress, 2013. Honour: Fellow, Co-operative Research Programme: Biological Resource Management for Sustainable Agricultural Systems, Organisation for Economic Co-operation and Development (OECD). Memberships: American Chemical Society; American Society of Plant Biologists; Phytochemical Society of North America; International Society for Horticultural Science. Address: Kagawa University; 2393 Ikenobe Miki-cho, Kagawa 761-0795, Japan. E-mail: fujita@ag.kagawa-u.ac.jp

DICTIONARY OF INTERNATIONAL BIOGRAPHY 36th EDITION

FUJIWARA Hidenori, b. 22 April 1946, Okayama, Japan. Professor. m. Tomoko Hongo, 1 son, 1 daughter. Education: MSc, 1974, DSc, 1977, Tokyo University. Appointments: Assistant, 1976-87, Associate Professor, 1987, Kyushu University; Researcher, CNRS, Paris, France, 1982-83; Professor, Kinki University, 1987-. Publications: Numerous articles in professional journals. Honours: Analysis Prize, Mathematical Society of Japan, 2005; Prize, Faculty of Sciences, Sfax, Tunisia, 2006; Prize, Association of Mathematics and Application, Tunisia, 2006. Memberships: Mathematical Society of Japan; American Mathematical Society; Society of Mathematics, France; Mathematical Association of America. Address: 13-27-402 Minamisho 6, Sawara-ku, Fukuoka-shi, 814-0031, Japan. E-mail: fujiwara@fuk.kindai.ac.jp

FUKASAWA Suguru, b. 1 November 1934, Tokyo, Japan. Professor Emeritus. m. Kazuko Yoshida, 2 sons. Education: BA, 1960, MA, 1963, University of Tokyo, Japan. Appointments: Lecturer, English, Ibaraki University, 1963-66; Lecturer, English, 1966-68, Associate Professor, 1968-74, Professor, 1974-2005, Director, Institute of Cultural Science, 1997-2000, Professor Emeritus, 2005-, Chuo University; Principal, Chuo University High School, 1993-97. Publications: Hardy, 1971; T Hardy, 1978; A Preface to English Novel Studies, 1981; Virginia Woolf, 1982; Thomas Hardy: A Little Dictionary, 1993; Comedy of Manners: Drama and Fiction, 1996; From Sense of Loss to Awakening, 2001; The Consolation of Literature, 2002; The Age of "Modernism" Reappraisal, 2007. Honours: Translation Award, 1984. Memberships: Thomas Hardy Society, UK; Thomas Hardy Society of Japan; Jane Austen Society of Japan. Address: 4-4-18, Utsukushigaoka, Aoba-ku, Yokohama, 225-0002, Japan.

FUKUDA Hideaki, b. 11 May 1962, Japan. Professor. Education: Master of Education, Chiba University, 1989; Doctor of Agriculture, Kyushu University, Fukuoka, 2006. Appointments: Associate Professor, 1994-2010, Professor, 2010-, University of the Ryukyus, Okinawa. Publications: Change in Feelings by Perfume of Essential Oils, 2003; Corrosive Wear of Woodcutting Tools, 2006; Effect of Electrical Potentials on Tool Wear and Measurement of Electrostatic Voltage in Machining of Air-dried Douglas-fir, 2006; Examination of School Furniture by Three-dimensional Motion Analysis, 2009. Memberships: The Japan Wood Research Society; The Japan Society of Technology Education; The Japanese Society of Environmental Education; International Technology Education Association. Address: Faculty of Education, University of the Ryukyus, Senbaru 1, Nishihara, Okinawa, 903-0213, Japan. E-mail: fukudah@edu.u-ryukyu.ac.jp

FUKUDA Mahito, b. 19 September 1957, Kyoto, Japan. Professor. m. Tomoe Matsuzawa, 1 son, 1 daughter. Education: BA, MA, Engineering, Kyoto University; MA, Letters, 1983, PhD, Comparative Literature & Culture, 1993, University of Tokyo. Appointments: Visiting Research Fellow, Wellcome Unit, University of Oxford, 1983-85, 1989, 2004-05; Visiting Fellow, Harvard University, 1992-93; Visiting Professor, University of Delhi, 2000; Senior Programme Officer, Japan Society for the Promotion of Science, 2010-13. Publications: A History of Tuberculosis, 1995; Tuberculosis as Culture, 2001; A Cultural History of Syphilis in Japan, 2005; Dr Shiabasaburo Kitasato, 2008; A History of Medicine, 2009; Diseases and Hospitals, 2010. Honours: Mainichi Book Award, 1995. Memberships: Oxbridge Club, Japan. Address: 1201-2-33 Yamadatamachi, Kita-ku, Nagoya 402-0811, Japan.

FUKUSHIMA Akiko, b. 25 October 1951, Kyoto, Japan. Researcher. m. Takeo Takuma. Education: MA, Paul H Nitze School of Advanced International Studies, Johns Hopkins University; PhD, Osaka University. Appointments: Director, Policy Studies, National Institute for Research Advancement, Tokyo, Japan; Senior Fellow, Japan Foundation. Publications: Japan Foreign Policy: A Logic of Multilateralism, 1999; The Uses of Institution: The United Nations for Legitimacy, 2007. Address: Joint Research Institute for International Peace & Culture, Aoyama Gakuin University, 4-4-25, Shibuya, Shibuya-ku, Tokyo 150-8366, Japan. E-mail: kikifuushima@gmail.com

FULLER Cynthia Dorothy, b. 13 February 1948, Isle of Sheppey, England. Poet; Adult Education Tutor. Divorced, 2 sons. Education: BA Honours, English, Sheffield University, 1969; Postgraduate Certificate of Education, Oxford University, 1970; MLitt, Aberdeen University, 1979. Appointments: Teacher of English, Redborne School, 1970-72; Freelance in Adult Education, University Departments at Durham and Newcastle Universities, also Open University and Workers Education Association. Publications: Moving towards Light, 1992; Instructions for the Desert, 1996; Only a Small Boat, 2001; Jack's Letters Home 1917-18, 2006; Background Music, 2009. Contributions to: Poems in various magazines including: Other Poetry; Iron; Poetry Durham; Literary Review. Honour: Northern Arts Financial Assistance. Address: 28 South Terrace, Esh Winning, Co Durham DH7 9PR, England.

FULLER Peter Frederic, b. 10 April 1929, Ramsgate, Kent, England. Artist. m. Rosemary Blaker, 1 daughter. Education: John Haslet School; Maidstone College of Art. Appointments: Watercolour Artist; Exhibitions include: The Royal Academy; Royal Watercolour Society; Royal Institute of Painters in Watercolour; Royal Society of Portrait Painters; New English Art Club; Royal Society of Marine Artists; Discerning Eye Exhibition; Works held in many private collections in UK, USA, Australia, Canada and Europe. Honours: Finalist, Laing Watercolour Competition; Winner, Whatman Prize; Numerous articles in professional journals; Listed in international biographical dictionaries. Address: 29 Sandling Lane, Maidstone, Kent ME14 2HS, England.

FUNDA Otakar, b. 13 September 1943, Prague, Czechoslovakia. Professor. m. Jarmila, 1 son, 1 daughter. Education: Mgr degree, Protestant Theology, Comenius Protestant Theological Faculty, Charles University, Prague, 1965; ThD, Faculty of Theology and Philosophy, University of Basel, 1971; ThD, Faculty of Philosophy and Arts, Charles University, 1981; Habilitation, 1990; PhD, 2003. Appointments: Associate Professor, Hussite Theological Faculty, 1990, Associate Professor, Philosophy and Religious Studies, 1994-, Vice Dean, 2000-03, Faculty of Education, Charles University. Publications: Numerous articles in professional journals. Memberships: International Seminary, Birmingham, England; Albert Schweitzer Wissenschaftliche Gesellschaft; Redaction Philosophical Journal of Academy of Sciences, Prague. Address: Chrpová 43, Praha 10, CZ 106 00, Czech Republic. E-mail: jofundovi@seznam.cz

FUNDAL Karsten, b. 27 April 1966, Copenhagen, Denmark. Composer. 1 son, 1 daughter. Education: Composition studies, Royal Conservatory, Copenhagen, 1986-88; Master degree, Jutland Conservatory, 1991. Appointments: Teacher, Orchestration and Musical Form Analysis, Royal Conservatory of Music, 1997-; Freelance Composer. Publications: Orchestral scores include: Piano concerto, 1993; Violin concerto, 1997; Percussion concerto, 1998;

Entropia, 2001; Hush, 2003; Viola concerto, 2008; Double concerto English horn/flute, 2010; Orchestral score for 10 films, 2003-11. Honours: Wilhelm Hansen Composer award, 1994; Danish Composers Society Award, 1995; Hass Fond Grand, 1995; Carl Nielsen Award, 2005; Queen Ingrids Memorial Award, 2005; Work Grant, Danish National Art Council, 2005; Robert Award, Danish Film Academy, 2007; Haakon Boerresen Award, 2009; Nominatee, Flame and Citron, Danish Film Academy, 2009; Nominatee, Jernanger, Kanon prisen, Norway, 2010. Memberships: Federation of Audiovisual Composers, EU; Danish Composers Society; Danish Film Composers.

FUNG Wye-Poh, b. 9 January 1937, Telok-Anson, Malaysia. Consultant Physician; Gastroenterologist. m. Saw-Lin Fung, 1 son, 1 daughter. Education: MB, BS, University of Malaya, Singapore, 1961; MRACP, Melbourne, 1965; FRACP, 1972; FACG, 1972; MD, University of Singapore, 1972; FAMS, 1978. Appointments: Assistant Lecturer, Clinical Medicine, University of Singapore, 1964-65; Research Fellow, Gastroenterology, A W Morrow, Department of Gastroenterology, Royal Prince Alfred Hospital, Camperdown, Sydney, 1965-66; Lecturer, Clinical Medicine, 1965-70, Senior Lecturer, Medicine, 1970-74, Associate Professor, Medicine, 1975, University of Singapore, Singapore General Hospital; Associate Physician, Department of General Medicine, Royal Perth Hospital, 1975-76; Senior Lecturer, Medicine, University of Western Australia, Royal Perth Hospital, 1976-85; Visiting Associate Professor, Department of Medicine and GI Unit, University of California, San Francisco, 1981-82; Consultant Physician, Gastroenterologist, Private Practice, 1985-; Gastroenterologist, Swan District Hospital, 1985-; St John of God Hospital, Wembly, Australia, 1986-; Osborne Park Hospital, 1986-; Armadale-Kelmscott Hospital, 1987-, Perth, Western Australia. Publications: Numerous articles in professional journals. Memberships: Foundation Secretary, Treasurer, Gastroenterological Society of Singapore, 1967-75; Gastroenterological Society of Australia, 1975-. Address: Mount Claremont, WA 6010, Australia.

FURÅKER Bengt, b. 25 October 1943, Mariestad, Sweden. Professor Emeritus. m. Carina, 1 son, 1 daughter. Education: BA, 1968, PhD, Sociology, 1977, Lund University; MA, Sociology, University of California, Santa Barbara, 1970. Appointments: Assistant Professor, 1979-84, Associate Professor, 1984-90, Umeå University; Lecturer, Teaching Assistant, 1970-79, Professor, 1990-2011, Professor Emeritus, 2011-, University of Gothenburg; Visiting Fellow, Yale University, 2002-03. Publications: Most recent books: Sociological Perspectives on Labor Markets, 2005; Flexibility and Stability in Working Life, 2007; Commitment to Work and Job Satisfaction, 2012. Address: Department of Sociology & Work Science, University of Gothenberg, Box 720, 40530 Gothenburg, Sweden. E-mail: bengt.furaker@gu.se

FURUYA Daniela Tomie, b. 5 May 1976, São Paulo, Brazil. Scientist; Biomedical Researcher. m. Raphael de Carvalho Aranha. Education: B Pharm, 2000, MSc, 2002, PhD, 2008, University of São Paulo. Appointments: Researcher, Hokkaido University, Japan, 2002-04; Researcher, University of São Paulo, 2009-. Publications: Numerous articles in professional journals. Honours: Award, Congress Diabetes and Metabolism; Listed in biographical dictionaries. Memberships: Brazilian Society of Physiology. Address: Institute of Biomedical Sciences (University of São Paulo), Av Professor Lineu Prestes 1524, Sala 126, São Paulo, SP, 05508-900, Brazil. E-mail: danifuruya@yahoo.com

FUSHIMI Masahito, b. 4 May 1964, Hokkaido, Japan. Psychiatrist. m. Hiromi, 1 son, 2 daughters. Education: MD, 1990, PhD, 1997, Akita University School of Medicine, Japan. Appointments: Medical Staff, Department of Neuropsychiatry, Akita University School of Medicine, 1990-91, 2000-03; Director, Akita Prefectural Mental Health & Welfare Centre, Akita city, 2003-. Publications: PLEDs in Creutzfeldt-Jakob disease following a cadaveric dural graft, 2002; Benign bilateral independent periodic lateralized epileptiform discharges, 2003; Progression of P300 in a patient with bilateral hippocampal lesions, 2005; Suicide patterns and characteristics in Akita, Japan, 2005. Memberships: Japan Medical Association; Japanese Society of Psychiatry and Neurology; Japanese Society of Clinical Neurophysiology; Japanese Society of Biofeedback Research; International Association for Suicide Prevention. Address: 2-1-51 Nakadori, Akita city, Akita prefecture, 010-0001, Japan.

FYODOROV Nikolai Vasilyevich, b. 9 May 1958, Chuvash Republic. Politician. m. Svetlana Yuryevna Fyodorova, 1 son, 1 daughter. Education: Graduate, Law Faculty, Kazan State University, 1980; Cand. Sc. (Law), Moscow Institute of State and Law, 1985; Appointments: Teacher, Chuvash State University, 1980-82, 1986-89; Member, USSR Supreme Soviet, 1989-91; Minister of Justice of Russia, 1990-93; President of Chuvash Republic, 1994-, re-elected, 1997 and 2001; Member, Council of Federation, 1996-2002; Representative of Russia in the Parliamentary Assembly of Council of Europe. Publications: More than 100 books and articles in economy, law and national relations. Honours: State Counsellor of Justice of Russia; The Russian Federation State Prize in the field of science and technology for restoration of the historical part of Cheboxary, 1999; Order, For Merits in Fatherland IV class; The highest All-Russian Femida Prize, 1997; Peter the Great National Prize; Honorary Construction Worker of Russia; Order of the Saint Duke Daniil Moskovskii 1 class and Order of Reverend Sergii Radonezhskii, Russian Orthodox Church. Address: 1 Republic Square, House of Government, 428004 Cheboxary, Chuvash Republic, Russia. E-mail: president@cap.ru

G

GABITSINASHVILI George, b. 1 April 1963, Tbilisi, Georgia. Hydrologist. m. M Lordkipaidze, 1 son, 1 daughter. Education: BA, River Constructions and Hydrotechnical Building of Hydroelectric Power Station, Georgian Polytechnic Institute, Tbilisi, 1985; MSc, Water Resources, Lund Institute of Technology, Lund University, Sweden, 2004; PhD, Hydraulic and Engineering Hydrology, Georgian Research Institute of Power Engineering and Power Structures, the Board of Academic Experts of Georgia, 2006. Appointments: Researcher, Department of Hydro Machines, Georgian Technical University, 2001-03; Senior Hydrologist, Consultant Company Basiani-93, 2005; National Technical Expert, UNDP/Sida Project, 2005-06; Researcher, Georgian Technical University, 2006-; Senior Consultant, Envco-Environmental Consultancy, 2006-. Publications: Numerous articles in professional journals. Memberships: International Association of Hydrological Sciences. Address: Noordendorpstraat 31, 8922JJ, Leeuwarden, The Netherlands. E-mail: georgegabi@hotmail.com

GABRIEL Peter, b. 13 February 1950, Cobham, Surrey, England. Singer; Songwriter. Career: Founder member, Genesis, 1969-1975; Appearances include: with Genesis: Reading Festival, 1971, 1972, 1973; UK and US tours; Solo artiste, 1975-; Solo appearances include: Worldwide tours; Knebworth II, 1978; Reading Festival, 1979; Inaugurator, WOMAD Festival Bath, 1982-; Amnesty International benefit tour, 1987; Hurricane Irene Benefit, Japan, 1987; Prince's Trust Rock Gala, 1988; Nelson Mandela tribute concerts, Wembley, 1988, 1990; Senegal (with Youssou N'Dour), 1991; The Simple Truth concert for Kurdish refugees, Wembley, 1991. Compositions include: Co-writer: Bully For You, Tom Robinson; Listen To The Radio, Tom Robinson; Animals Have More Fun, Jimmy Pursey; Film scores: Birdy, 1985; Last Temptation Of Christ, 1989. Recordings: Albums with Genesis: From Genesis To Revelation, 1969; Foxtrot, 1972; Genesis Live, 1973; Selling England By The Pound, 1973; Nursery Crime, 1974; The Lamb Lies Down On Broadway, 1974; Solo albums include: 4 albums all entitled Peter Gabriel, 1977-82; Peter Gabriel Plays Live, 1983; So, 1986; Passion, 1989; Shaking The Tree - Sixteen Golden Greats, 1990; Us, 1992; Revisited, 1992; Secret World (interactive CD), 1995; Come Home to Me Snow, 1998; OVO, 2000; Long Walk Home, 2002; Up, 2002 Featured on: All This And World War II, 1975; Exposure, Robert Fripp, 1979; Conspiracy Of Hope (Amnesty International), 1986; Set, Youssou N'Dour, 1989; Exile, Geoffrey Oryema, 1990; It's About Time, Manu Katche, 1992; Until The End Of The World, (soundtrack), 1992; Tower Of Song (Leonard Cohen tribute), 1995; Compiler, Plus From Us, 1993; Singles include: Solsbury Hill; Games Without Frontiers; Shock The Monkey; Sledgehammer; In Your Eyes; Don't Give Up (duet with Kate Bush); Biko; Big Time; Red Rain; Digging In The Dirt; Steam; Blood Of Eden; Kiss That Frog; Come Talk to Me, 1993; Lovetown, 1994; Snow Flake, 1994; Contributor, Sun City, Artists United Against Apartheid, 1985; Rainbow Warriors, 1989; Until The End Of The World (soundtrack), 1991; Give Peace A Chance, the Peace Choir, 1991. Honours: Ivor Novello Awards: Outstanding Contribution To British Music, 1983; Best Song, 1987; BRIT Awards: Best British Male Artist, Best British Music Video, Sledgehammer, 1987; Best Producer, 1993; 9 Music Video Awards for Sledgehammer, and Video Vanguard Trophy, 1987; Grammy Awards: Best New Age Performance, 1990; Best Short Form Video, 1993. Address: c/o Real World Inc., Real World Studios, Box, Wiltshire SN13 8PL, England.

GADA Manilal Talakshi, b. 12 January 1947, Gujarat, India. Psychiatrist. m. Manjula, 2 daughters. Education: MBBS, University of Bombay, 1971; DPM, College of Physicians and Surgeons of Bombay, 1975; MD, University of Bombay, 1976. Appointments: Hon Professor of Psychiatry, Padamashree Dr D Y Patil Medical College (deemed University); Head, Department of Psychiatry and Psychiatrist, Rajawadi Municipal General Hospital; Retired; Senior Specialist (Psychiatrist), Panel Consultant, Oil and Natural Gas Commission, Bombay Region; Honorary Psychiatrist, Sulabha School for Mentally Retarded Children; Post Graduate Teacher and Examiner for DPM, DNB; Conducts continuing medical education programmes for family physicians. Publications include: Stress Management: Holistic Approach, 2001, reprint 2002, revised 2nd edition, 2006, 3rd revised edition, 2008; Khinnata Nakoj (Defeat Depression, book in local Marathi language), 2003; Co-editor, Essentials of Post-graduate Psychiatry, 2005; Chitabraham, book on schizophrenia in local Gujarati language, 2005; Essential information on schizophrenia, 2004, reprint 2006; Panic Disorder, in English, 2007, revised 2008, in Gujarati, 2nd edition, 2008; Manobhrahm (Schizophrenia), 2011; 8 book chapters; More than 60 papers in scientific journals, newspaper article on Psychiatry every fortnight. Honours include: West Zone President's Award, 1984, 1997; Tilak Venkoba Rao Oration, Indian Psychiatric Society, 1987; Dr R K Menda Oration, Indian Medical Association, Nagpur Branch, 1995; District Committee Chairman, Lions District 323A2 of Lions Club International, 1998-; Dr S M Lulla Oration: Bombay Psychiatric Society, 2000; Lions International President's Appreciation Certificate, 2003; Essential Information on Schizophrenia, 2004, reprint 2006; Chitabraham (book on schizophrenia in local Gujarati language), 2005; Dr L P Shah Oration Award, Indian Psychiatric Society West Zone, 2006. Memberships include: Life Fellow, Indian Psychiatric Society; Chair, Biological Psychiatry Section, 1997-99; Chair, Ethics Committee, 2001-03, 2003-05; Chairman, Organising Committee of 58th Annual Conference of Indian Psychiatric Society, 2006; Life Fellow, Indian Psychiatric Society - West Zone, President, 1994-95; Life Fellow, Bombay Psychiatric Society, President, 1989-90; Life Fellow, Indian Association of Private Psychiatry; Founder Life Fellow, Indian Association for Child and Adolescent Mental Health; Life Member, Kutchi Medicos Association, President, 1992-94; Life Member Indian Medical Association; Member, Editorial Board of Archives of Indian Psychiatry, journal of Indian Psychiatric Society West Zone; Chairman, Awards Committee, Indian Psychiatric Society, West Zone, 2009. Address: 201 Kumudini, Above Andhra Bank, 7th Road, Rajawadi, Ghatkopar (East), Bombay 400 077, India.

GADSBY Roger, b. 2 March 1950, Coventry, England. General Practitioner. m. Pamela Joy, 1 son, 1 daughter. Education: BSc (Hons), Medical Biochemical Studies, 1971, MB ChB (Hons), Obstetrics and Gynaecology, 1974, Birmingham University Medical School; Post qualification experience in hospitals in Birmingham and Stoke-on-Trent, GP training in Stoke. Appointments: Full-time General Practitioner, later Senior Partner, Redroofs Practice, Nuneaton Warwickshire, 1979-2010; Part-time Associate Clinical Professor, University of Warwick, 1992-; Co-Founder, Warwick Diabetes Care, 2000. Publications: Over 150 papers and articles on diabetes and pregnancy sickness symptoms; 4 textbooks on diabetes; 8 chapters on diabetes issues in primary care in major diabetes textbooks. Honours: DCH, 1978; DRCOG, 1978; MRCGP (by examination), 1978; FRCGP (by election), 1992; MBE, 2009. Memberships: Fellow, Royal College of General

Practitioners; Diabetes (UK); Primary Care Diabetes Society; American Diabetes Association; British Medical Association; Chairman of Trustees, Pregnancy Sickness Support Charity. Address: Rivendell, School Lane, Exhall, Coventry, CV7 9GF, England. E-mail: rgadsby@doctors.org.uk

GADZHIEVA Nushaba Nubarak, b. 6 May 1950, Altiagac, Absheron, Azerbaijan. Leading Research Scientist. m. Mahmudov Mayis Mikayil, 1980, 1 daughter. Education: Honours higher diploma, Department of Physics, Baku State University, 1967-72; Department of Physics, Moscow State University, 1971; Doctorate Thesis, Institute of Chemical Physics of Academic Science of USSR, Moscow, 1972; DSc, Physics (Optics), Institute of Spectroscopy Academy of Sciences of USSR, Troitsk, 1981; Diploma of Assistant Professor in Optics, Moscow, USSR, 1989. Appointments: Engineer, 1972-74, Junior Scientific Researcher, 1974-76, Department of Radiation Investigations of Azerbaijan Academic Sciences, Baku, Azerbaijan; Postgraduate Student, Institute of Spectroscopy Academic Sciences of USSR, Troitsk, 1976-79; Scientific Researcher, 1979-85, Senior Scientific Researcher, 1985-2003, Head of Laboratory of Molecular Spectroscopy of Irradiated Materials, 2003-08; Leading Research Scientist, Institute of Radiation Problems, National Academy of Sciences of Azerbaijan, Baku, 2009-. Publications: 225 scientific papers in professional journals; 10 patents and inventions. Honours: Diploma for achievements in spectroscopy research, 1978-79; Gold Medal, VDNX, Moscow, 1981; Z Tagiev Medal, Baku, 1992. Memberships: Science and Life Journals; Institute of Physics NAS of Azerbaijan, Baku State University; Knowledge Society; Repression Fictions Society. Address: Yeni Yasamal 1, bl4, fl80, Baku, AZ 1012, Azerbaijan.

GAFOOR Adam Abdul, b. 8 February 1968, Singapore. Principal Scientist. m. Liz Diani Misrudin Anwar. Education: Hakim-ul-Akbar of Medicine, Science and Philosophy, 1992. Appointments: Principal Scientist, Adam Science Technology and Research International. Honours: Leading Scientists of the World, 2008. Memberships: Direct Member, World Organization of Family Doctors; Member, European Federation of Biotechnology. Address: Adam Science Technology and Research International, 2 Joo Chiat Road, #02-1127 Joo Chiat Complex, 420002 Singapore. E-mail: professor.adamgafoor@gmail.com

GAFUROV Ravil Gabdrakhmanovich, b. 18 April 1930, Chistopol, Republic of Tatarstan, Russia. Chemist; Investigator. m. Margarita Pavlovna, 1 son. Education: Engineer, Chemist-Technologist, Technology Organic Synthesis (1st class honours), 1948-53, Candidate of Chemical Science (the first higher science degree in USSR and Russia), 1964, Kazan State Technological University, Kazan, Republic of Tartarstan, Russia; PhD, Chemical Science, Zelinski Institute of Organic Chemistry, Russian Academy of Science (RAS), Moscow, 1978, Professor on Organic Chemistry, 1982, and Bioorganic Chemistry, 1990, Institute of Physiologically Active Compounds RAS, Chernoglovka, Moscow, Russia; Engineer, Telecomputer Science, Moscow Aviation Institute, Moscow, 1989-90. Appointments: Student, 1948-53, Senior Laboratory Assistant, 1953-56, Post Graduate Student, 1956-59, Assistant Lecturer, 1959-65, Kazan State Technological University, Kazan, Republic of Tartarstan, Russia; Senior Scientific Worker, Institute of Chemical Physics Problems RAS, Chernogolovka, Moscow area, Russia, 1965-80; Scientific Deputy Director, 1980-86, Head of Laboratory of Chemistry of Low-Molecular Bioregulators, 1986-93, Chief Scientific Worker, 1993-, Institute of Physiologically Active Compounds RAS, Chernogolovka; Director and Supervisor of Studies, Innovation Centre, Chernogolovka, 1993-. Publications: Numerous articles on Bio-organic Chemistry and Physico-Chemical Biology of Low-Molecular Bioregulators in professional journals. Honours (Russian government): Medal, for valorous work in commemoration of the 100th anniversary of V I Lenin's birthday, 1970; Medal, Veteran of Labour, 1988; Medal of Order for merits before Fatherland II degrees, 1999; Man of the Year, ABI, 2007; Honoured Science Worker of Russian Federation, 2008; N I Vavilov Medal, Russian Academy of Natural Sciences, 2010; Award for Merits, European Academy of Natural Sciences, 2010; Listed in international biographical dictionaries. Memberships: Honoured Member, Russian and European academies of Natural Sciences. Address: Centralnaya, 4-A, Apartment 24, Chernogolovka, Moscow, 142432, Russia. E-mail: ravig@icp.ac.ru

GAHERY Yves, b. 18 August 1940, Masserac, France. Retired Neuroscientist. Education: BS, Chemistry and Physiology, 1962, Diploma in Higher Education, 1964, Faculty of Sciences, Rennes; Doctor en Sciences, Neurosciences, University of Paris VI, 1972. Appointments: Head of Research, 1966, Director of Research, 1984-2003, National Centre for Scientific Research, Paris; Part-time Lecturer in Neurosciences, University of Aix-Marseille I and II, 1989-2003. Publications: Contributed to 160 scientific papers; Patent, 1985. Honours: Prix de l'Académie des Sciences, Paris, 1988. Memberships: Groupement des Retraités Educateurs sans Frontières. Address: 83 Bd du Redon, Bât B5, 13009 Marseille, France. E-mail: gahery.yves@yahoo.fr

GAHUKAR Ruparao Tulashiramji, b. 3 December 1942, Mohpa, India. Consultant. m. Hemlata, 2 sons. Education: BSc, 1964, MSc, 1966, Nagpur University, India; DSc, Orsay Centre, Paris University, France, 1976. Appointments: Senior Technical Assistant, Government of India, 1967-71; Principal Entomologist, ICRISAT, Africa, 1976-81; Entomologist, 1981-87, Chief Technical Adviser, 1988-89, FAO of UN, Africa; Pest Control Consultant, self employed, 1989-95; Chairman, Arag Biotech Pvt Ltd, India, 1995-; Consultant, Sir Ratan Tata Trust. Publications: 9 books/bulletins; 10 book chapters; 110 research/technical papers; 21 conference papers; 15 project reports; 250 popular/extension articles. Honours: Maharashtra Krishak Samaj, 2000; Marathi Vidnyan Parishad, 2001; Naik Agricultural Research Trust, 2001. Memberships: Fellow of 3 Indian and 1 USA societies; Member, 20 scientific and educational organisations. Address: Plot 220, Reshimbag, Opp. Reshimbag Ground, Nagpur 440009, India. E-mail: rtgahukar@gmail.com

GAIER Ulrich, b. 18 June 1935, Stuttgart, Germany. Professor. m. Anke Winter, 3 sons, 1 daughter. Education: German, English and French Language & Literature studies, Tübingen, 1954-59, Paris, 1955-56; State Exams for High School Teachers, 1959 and 1962; Doctorate, 1961, Habilitation, 1966, Tübingen. Appointments: Lecturer, German, University College of Swansea, Wales, 1960-61; Assistant Professor, Leibniz Kolleg, Tübingen, 1962-63; Assistant Professor, 1963, Associate Professor, 1966, University of California/ Davis, USA; Full Professor, 1968-2000, Emeritus Professor, 2000-, University of Konstanz; Guest Professor: Rice University, Houston, Texas; Pisa; Zürich; Lawrence, Kansas; Madison, Wisconsin; Gainesville, Florida. Publications: 22 books; 200 articles in professional journals. Honours: Max Kade Distinguished Professorship in Lawrence, Kansas and Gainesville, Florida; Honorary Professor, Al I Cuza University, Iasi, Romania; President, Hölderlin Gesellschaft, 2006-10;

DICTIONARY OF INTERNATIONAL BIOGRAPHY 36th EDITION

Honorary Member, Goethe Society of North America, International Herder Society and Hölderlin Gesellschaft. Memberships: Hölderlin Gesellschaft, International Herder Society; Goethe Society of North America. Address: Haydnstrasse 17, 78464 Konstanz, Germany.

GAIKWAD Ravindra, b. 27 September 1965, Mehkar, India. Teacher. m. Rekha, 1 son, 1 daughter. Education: B Tech (Chemical); PhD. Appointments: Trainee Engineer, 1989-90; Lecturer, Chemical Engineering, 1990; Assistant Professor, Chemical Engineering, 2002-. Publications: 5 books; 110 research papers. Honours: Best Participant Award, AICTE, ISTE, STTP course on Industrial Solid Waste Treatment and Disposal Practices, MACT; Promising Engineer Award, Institution of Engineers, India; Elected Chairman, Board of Studies in Chemical Engineering, University of Pune, 2005-10. Memberships: AIChE. Address: Chemical Engineering, Pravara Rural Engineering College, Loni, Dist: Ahmednagar (MS), India. E-mail: rwgaikwad@yahoo.com

GAILLARD Mary K, b. 1 April 1939, New Brunswick, New Jersey, USA. m. Bruno Zumino, 2 sons, 1 daughter. Education: BA, Hollins University, 1960; MA, Columbia University, 1961; Doctorat de Troisième Cycle, 1964, Doctorat d'Etat, 1968, University of Paris, Orsay. Appointments: Attaché de recherche, 1964-66, Chargé de recherche, 1968-73, Maître de recherche, 1973-79 CNRS; Visiting Scientist, Fermilab, 1973-74, 1983; Scientific Associate, Theory Division, CERN, 1964-81; Theory Group Leader, LAPP; Directeur de recherche, CNRS, 1980-81; Professor of Physics, University of California, Berkeley, Faculty Senior Staff, Lawrence Berkeley Laboratory, 1981-2009; Professor, Graduate School, UCB and Guest Scientist, LBNL, 2009-. Publications: 200 articles in scientific journals and conference proceedings; Co-editor: Weak Interactions, 1977; Gauge Theories in High Energy Physics, 1982. Honours: Woodrow Wilson Scholarship, 1960; Prix Thibaud, 1977; Loeb Lecturer in Physics, Harvard University, 1980; Chancellor's Distinguished Lecturer, University of California, Berkeley, 1981; Warner-Lambert Lecturer, University of Michigan, 1984; Fellow, American Physical Society, 1985; Miller Research Professorship, University of California, Berkeley, 1987-88, Fall 1996; E O Lawrence Memorial Award, 1988; Guggenheim Fellow, 1989-90; Fellow, American Academy of Arts and Sciences, 1989; Member, National Academy of Arts and Sciences, 1991; J J Sakurai Prize, 1993; Trustee, Council of Penn Women Lecturers, University of Pennsylvania, 1994; APS Centennial Lecturer, 1998-99; Member, American Philosophical Society, 2000. Memberships: American Physical Society; French Physical Society; European Physical Society; American Association for the Advancement of Science; American Civil Liberties Union; Arms Control Association; Union of Concerned Scientists. Address: Department of Physics, University of California, Berkeley, CA 94720, USA

GAIT Judith Diane, b. 4 December 1948, Monroe, Michigan, USA. Artist; Teacher. m. P D Gait (annulled 1994), 2 sons, 3 daughters. Education: BFA, California College of Arts & Crafts; MA, Fine Art, University of the West of England, 2007. Appointments: Non-Executive Director, Avon & Wiltshire NHS Trust, 1997-2001; Artist in Residence, Bradford-on-Avon Arts Festival, 2005-; Visiting Lecturer, University of the West of England, 2006-; Tutor, Pupil Referral Unit, 1999-2007; Associate Lecturer, City of Bristol College, 2000-. Publications: The Sunday Times: A Life in the Day, 2003. Honours: Lottery Award; Esmeé Fairbairn grant, 2009; Nominated Star Award for Teaching; Various personal grants to improve arts access in NHS Hospitals; Listed in international biographical dictionaries. Memberships: Institute for Learning. E-mail: judithgait@hotmail.com Website: www.judithgait.co.uk

GAL Tomas, b. 11 July 1926, Zilina, Czechoslovakia. Professor Emeritus. m. (1) Dagmar, deceased 1983, 1 son, 1 daughter, (2) Gisela, 1986. Education: PhD, Physical Chemistry, 1953; PhD, Operations Research, 1966; Dr habil, Operations Research, 1969. Appointments: Lecturer, Department of Physical Chemistry, Charles University, Prague, 1950-53; Researcher, Institute of Cardiovascular Diseases, Prague, 1952-54; Research Associate, Research Institute, Prague, 1951-52; Assistant Professor, Department of Mathematics, 1954-64, Associate Professor, Department of Linear Programming, 1964-69, University of Agriculture, Prague; IMS Research Fellow, CORE, Louvain, Belgium, 1969-70; Associate Professor, Technical University of Aachen, Germany, 1970-77; Full Professor, Chairman, Department of Mathematics and Operations Research, University of Hagen, Germany, 1977-. Publications: Over 100 refereed articles in professional journals; 14 books; Visiting Professor at several universities throughout the world; Several talks and lectures at universities and conferences. Honours: Cantor Award in Gold; Listed in international biographical dictionaries. Memberships: Numerous professional scientific organisations. Address: Falkenstrasse 6, 76530 Baden-Baden, Germany. E-mail: tomas.gal@fernuni-hagen.de

GALASKO Charles Samuel Bernard, b. 29 June 1939, Johannesburg, South Africa. Orthopaedic Surgeon. m. Carol, 1967, 1 son, 1 daughter. Education: MB, BCh, 1st Class Honours, 1962, ChM, 1970, Witwatersrand; FRCS, Edinburgh, 1966; FRCS, England, 1966; Honorary MSc, Manchester, 1980; FCMSA (Honorary Fellow, College of Medicine of South Africa), 2003; FFSEM, Ireland, 2002; (UK), 2006. F Med Sci. Appointments include: House positions, Johannesburg and London; Nuffield Scholar, Nuffield Orthopaedic Centre, Oxford, 1969; Registrar, 1970, Senior Orthopaedic Registrar, 1970-73, Radcliffe Infirmary and Nuffield Orthopaedic Centre, Oxford; Director, Orthopaedic Surgery, Assistant Director, Division of Surgery, Royal Postgraduate Medical School, Director, Orthopaedic Surgery, Consultant, Hammersmith Hospital, 1973-76; Member, Unit Management, Royal Manchester Children's Hospital, Clinical Director, Department of Orthopaedic Surgery, Salford General Hospitals, 1989-92; Member, Unit Management Board, 1989-96, Medical Director, 1993-96, Salford Royal Hospitals NHS Trust; Professor, Orthopaedic Surgery, University of Manchester, 1976-2004; Consultant Orthopaedic Surgeon, Hope Hospital and Royal Manchester Children's Hospital, 1976-2004; Director of Education and Training, Salford Royal Hospitals NHS Trust, 2002-05. Publications: Numerous articles and papers in the field of orthopaedics; 9 books include: Skeletal Metatases, author, 1986; Competing for the Disabled, co-author, 1989; Editor: Principles of Fracture Management, 1984; Neuromuscular Problems in Orthopaedics, 1987. Honours include: Moynihan Prize, Association of Surgeons of Great Britain and Ireland, 1969; Hunterian Professor, Royal College of Surgeons of England, 1971; AO Fellowship; Australian Commonwealth Fellowship, 1982; Sir Arthur Sims Commonwealth Professor, 1998; Scholarships; Academic prizes; Numerous lectureships, UK and abroad. Memberships include: International Orthopaedic Research Society, Programme Chairman, 1984-87, Membership Committee Chairman, 1987-90, President, 1990-93; International Association Olympic Medical Officers, Treasurer, 1988-2000; British Orthopaedic Association, Council, 1988-91, 1998-2003, Vice President,

1999-2000, Chairman, Hospital Recognition Committee, 1992-95, President, 2000-2001; Royal College of Surgeons, England, Council, 1991-2003, Vice-President, 1999-2001, Chairman, Training Board, 1995-99, Chairman, Head Injury Working Party, 1997-99; Chairman, Joint Committee on Higher Surgical Training of the United Kingdom and Ireland, 1997-2000; Chairman, Intercollegiate Academic Board for Sport and Exercise Medicine, 2002-05; President, Faculty of Sport and Exercise Medicine, 2006-09. Address: 72 Gatley Road, Gatley, Cheshire, SK8 4AA, England.

GALATOPOULOS Stelios Emille, b. 2 August 1932, Nicosia, Cyprus. Civil & Structural Engineer; Music Critic; Journalist; Author. Education: Hellenion School, Nicosia; The English School, Nicosia; BSc Eng (Lond), University of Southampton, England, 1950; Also studied Musicology and History of Opera. Appointments: Civil and Structural Engineer: Designer, T C Jones Co, 1954-55; Kellogg Int Corp, 1956-60; Designer and head of Civil and Structural Department, Tripe & Wakeham (Chartered Architects), London and in Cyprus Akrotiri Strategic Base, 1960-66; Freelance Engineer, 1967-72; Designer, Pell Frischmann, 1973-75; Freelance Engineer, intermittently, 1976-83. Opera and Music Critic/Journalist/Broadcaster/Lecturer/Concert presenter and compere, 1966-. Publications: Reviews and articles in music magazines and for recording companies; Author of books published worldwide: Callas La Divina, 1966, Italian Opera, 1971, Callas Prima Donna Assoluta, 1976, Maria Callas: Sacred Monster, 1998, Bellini: Life, Times, Music, 2002. Honours: Nominated for literary awards: Whitbread and Samuel Johnson, 1998 and 2002. Memberships: The Society of Authors, 1971-; Vice President, Opera Italiana, 1985-. Address: Flat 4, 47 Sheen Road, Richmond, Surrey TW9 1AJ, England.

GALL Henderson Alexander (Sandy), b. 1 October 1927, Penang, Malaysia. Writer; Broadcaster. m. Eleanor Mary Patricia Anne, 1 son, 3 daughters. Education: MA, Aberdeen University, Scotland, 1952. Appointments: National Service, RAF, 1945-48; Foreign Correspondent: Reuters, 1953-63, Independent Television News, 1963-92; Co-presenter, News At Ten, 1970-90; Writer, Presenter, Producer of numerous documentaries including: Cresta Run, 1970, 1985; King Hussein, 1972; Afghanistan, 1982, 1984, 1986; George Adamson, 1989; Richard Leakey, 1995; Empty Quarter, 1996; Imran's Final Test, 1997; Afghanistan: War Without End, 2004. Publications: Books: Gold Scoop, 1977; Chasing the Dragon, 1981; Don't Worry about the Money Now, 1983; Behind Russian Lines: An Afghan Journal, 1983; Afghanistan: Agony of a Nation, 1988; Salang, 1989; George Adamson: Lord of the Lions, 1991; News From the Front: The Life of a Television Reporter, 1994; The Bushmen of Southern Africa: Slaughter of the Innocent, 2001; War Against the Taliban: Why It All Went Wrong in Afghanistan, 2012. Honours: Rector, 1978-81, Honorary LLD, 1981, Aberdeen University; Sitara-i-Pakistan, 1986; Chairman, Sandy Gall's Afghanistan Appeal, 1986-; Lawrence of Arabia Memorial Medal; RSAA, 1987; Commander of the Order of the British Empire, 1988; Companion of the Order of St Michael & St George, 2011. Memberships: Turf; Rye Golf Club; Honorary Member, St Moritz Tobogganing; Saints' & Sinners' Club of London. Address: Doubleton Oast House, Penshurst, Tonbridge, Kent TN11 8JA, England. E-mail: sgaa@btinternet.com Website: www.sandygallsafghanistanappeal.org

GALLAGHER Jessica, b. 14 March 1986, Geelong, Australia. Atheelete; Osteopath. Education: Bachelor of Applied Science, 2006, Master, 2009, Osteopathy, RMIT University, Melbourne. Appointments: 1st Australian athelete in history to medal at a summer & winter Paralympics &/or World Championships; 1st Australian woman in Paralympic history to win a winter Paralympic medal (Bronze) in the women's vision impaired Slalom, Vancouver, 2010; Winter Paralympics, Silver (Long Jump) & Bronze (Javelin), IPC World Atheletics Championships, 2011. Honours: Australian Female Paralympian of the Year, 2010; Australian institute of Sport, Sport Achievement Award, 2010; Victorian Institute of Sport, Gatorade Spirit Award, 2011; Listed in biographical dictionaries. Memberships: Australian & Victorian Institute of Sport Scholarship Holder; Global Ambassador for Vision 2020, Australia; Ambassador, Vision Australia; Ambassador, Australian Paralympic Committee.

GALLAGHER Liam, b. 21 September, 1972, Burnage, Manchester, England. Vocalist; Musician (guitar, keyboards). m. Patsy Kensit, 1 son. Career: Founder member, Oasis, 1991-; Support tours with Verve; Concerts include: Glastonbury Festival, 1994; US debut, Wetlands, New York; Earls Court, London (UK's largest-ever indoor concert), 1995; Glastonbury, headlining, 1995; Knebworth (largest-ever outdoor concert), 1996; Regular tours, UK, Europe, US; Left Creation Records to set up own label, 1999. Recordings: Albums: Definitely Maybe, 1994; What's The Story (Morning Glory)?, 1995; Be Here Now, 1997; Masterplan, 1998; Standing on the Shoulder of Giants, forthcoming. Singles: Supersonic, 1994; Shakermaker, 1994; Cigarettes And Alcohol, 1994; Live Forever, 1994; Whatever, (Number 3, UK), 1994; Some Might Say (Number 1, UK), 1995; Wonderwall (Number 2, UK), 1995; Roll With It (Number 2, UK), 1995; Don't Look Back In Anger (Number 1, UK), 1996; D'You Know What I Mean, (Number 1, UK), 1997; All Around the World, 1998; Go Let It Out, 2000. Honours: BRIT Awards: Best Newcomers, 1995; Best Album, Best Single, Best Video, Best British Group, 1996; BRIT Nominations: Best Group, Best Album; Q Awards: Best New Act, 1994; Best Live Act, 1995. 2 Multi-Platinum albums. Current Management: Ignition, 54 Linhope Street, London NW1 6HL, England.

GAMAL M Nour Abdalla, b. 9 April 1934, Cairo, Egypt. Pharmacist. m. Aida M Elbadry, 2 sons, 1 daughter. Education: B Pharm, 1956, Higher Diploma of Drug Analysis & Biological Standardisation, 1961, MSc, Pharmaceutical Sciences (Pharmacognosy), 1970, Cairo University. Appointments: Expert on Drug Analysis and Director of Central Labs, General Pharmaceutical Industry Co, Samaraa, Iraq, 1971-74; Director, Research & Control, Misr Pharmaceutical Co, 1980-86; Chairman, CEO, Kahira Pharmaceutical Co, 1986-89; Deputy Chairman, Egyptian Drug Organisation, 1989-92; Deputy Chairman, Member of the Board, 1992-96, Counsellor, Member of the Board, 1996-2000, Egyptian Drug Holding Co; Member of the Board, Egyptian Drug Holding Co, 2000-. Publications: More than 18 original research papers and survey studies in international and local pharmaceutical periodicals; Main contributor to Case Study of Egyptian Pharma Industry in the Nineties; Main editor, Guide for Training on Quality Assurance and Good Manufacturing Practices for Pharmaceutical Manufacturers, 2000. Honours: Several medals and awards. Memberships: Egyptian Pharmaceutical Society; Drug Research Section, Medical Research Assembly; Academy of Scientific Research and Technology. E-mail: mgnour2007@yahoo.com

GAMBLE Cynthia Joan, b. 20 December 1941, Much Wenlock, Shropshire, England. University Lecturer. Education: L ès L, Université de Grenoble, Grenoble, France, 1971; BA (Hons), 1971; Diploma in Education,

1974, PhD, 1997, Birkbeck College, University of London. Appointments: Assistante d'Anglais, Lycée de Jeunes Filles, Quimperlé, 1963-64; Assistante d'Anglais, Lycée Stendhal, Grenoble, 1964-65; Head of French Department, Lanfranc School, Croydon, 1965-69; Teacher of French, Ealing Girls' Grammar School, London, 1969-71; Lecturer in French, City of Leeds and Carnegie College of Education, Leeds, 1971-76; Senior Lecturer in French, Director of International Exchanges, Department of International Relations, 1976-86, Head of European Secretariat, Senior Lecturer in French, Leeds Metropolitan University 1986-89; Head of European Relations, University of East London, 1989-97; Honorary Research Fellow, The Ruskin Programme, Lancaster University, 1997-2001; Honorary Research Fellow, Birkbeck College, London University, 2001-2002; Visiting Fellow, The Ruskin Programme, Lancaster University, 2001-. Publications: Author, Proust as Interpreter of Ruskin: The Seven Lamps of Translation, 2002; Insights into Ruskin's Northern French Gothic: Abbeville, Amiens and Rouen, 2002; A Perpetual Paradise: Ruskin's Northern France (co-author with S Wildman), 2002; Ruskin-Turner: Dessins et Voyages en Picardie romantique (co-author with M Pinette and S Wildman), 2003; L'Oeil de Ruskin (co-author with M Pinette), 2011; Contributor, Dictionnaire Marcel Proust, 2004; John Ruskin, Henry James and the Shropshire Lads, 2008; Au seuil de la modernè: Proust, Literature and the Arts, 2011; Numerous conference papers and invited lectures. Honours: Vice Chairman, Ruskin Society. Memberships: Société des Amis de Marcel Proust et de Combray; Franco-British Society. Address: Flat 89, 49 Hallam Street, London W1W 6JP, England.

GAMBON Sir Michael John, b. 19 October 1940, Dublin, Ireland. Actor. m. Anne Miller, 1962, 1 son. Appointments: Former, Mechanical Engineer; Actor with Edwards/Macliammoir Co, Dublin, 1962, National Theatre, Old Vic, 1963-67, Birmingham Repertory and other provincial theatres, 1967-69; Title roles include: Othello; Macbeth, Coriolanus, King Lear, Anthony and Cleopatra, Old Times; RSC, Aldwych, 1970-71; The Norman Conquests, 1974; Otherwise Engaged, 1976; Just Between Ourselves, 1977; Alice's Boys, 1978; with National Theatre, 1980; with RSC, Stratford and London, 1982-83; TV appearances include: Ghosts; Oscar Wilde; The Holy Experiment; Absurd Person Singular; The Borderers; The Singing Detective; The Heat of the Day; Maigret; The Entertainer, Truth; Joe's Palace, Cranford, Emma. Films: The Beast Must Die; Turtle Diary; Paris by Night; The Cook, the thief, his wife and her lover; A Dry White Season; The Rachel Papers; State of Grace; The Heat of the Day; Mobsters; Toys; Clean Slate; Indian Warrior; The Browning Version; Mary Reilly; Two Deaths; Midnight in Moscow; A Man of No Importance; The Innocent Sleep; All Our Fault; Two Deaths; Nothing Personal; The Gambler; Dancing at Lughnasa; Plunket and McClean; The Last September; Sleepy Hollow; The Insider, End Game; Charlotte Gray; Gosford Park; Ali G Indahouse; Path to War; The Actors; Open Range; Harry Potter, The Prisoner of Azkaban; Being Julia; Sky Captain and the World of Tomorrow; Layer Cake; The Life Aquatic with Steve Zissou; Stories of Lost Souls; Harry Potter and the Goblet of Fire; Celebration; The Omen; Amazing Grace; John Duffy's Brother; The Good Shepherd; Cranford Chronicles; The Good Night; The Baker; The Alps; Harry Potter and the Order of the Phoenix, Brideshead Revisited, Harry Potter and The Half Blood Prince, Fantastic Mr. Fox (voice), The Book of Eli. Honours include: London Theatre Critics Award for Best Actor; Olivier Award for Best Comedy Performance; Evening Stand Drama Award. Membership: Trustee, Roy Armouries, 1995-. Address: c/o ICM, Oxford House, 76 Oxford Street, London, W1N 0AX, England.

GAMMON Philip Greenway, b. 17 May 1940, Chippenham, Wiltshire, England. Pianist; Conductor. m. Floretta Volovini, 2 sons. Education: Royal Academy of London, London, 1956-61; Badische Müsikhochschule, Karlsruhe, Germany, 1961-64. Appointments: Deputy Piano Teacher, RAM and RSAM, 1964; Pianist, Royal Ballet, Covent Garden, 1964-68; Principal Pianist, Ballet for All, 1968-71; Pianist, Royal Ballet, 1971-99; Principal Pianist, Royal Ballet, 1999-2005; Also Conductor with Royal Ballet and as Guest Conductor with the English National Ballet, Hong Kong Ballet and National Ballet of Portugal; Guest Pianist, Royal Ballet, 2005-. Honours: The Recital Diploma, 1960; MacFarren Gold Medal, 1961; Karlsruhe Kultür Preis, 1962; ARCM, 1968; ARAM, 1991; FRAM, 2002. Address: 19 Downs Avenue, Pinner, Middlesex HA5 5AQ, England.

GAN Anthony Eng Keong, b. 3 June 1938, Malaysia. Architect. m. Alexandra Desnica, 2 sons, 2 daughters. Education: Overseas School Certificate A, University of Cambridge, 1956; B Arch (Hons), NSWIT, 1974. Appointments: Director, Arena Gan Associates Pty Ltd, 1976-83; Sole practitioner, Anthony Gan Architects Pty Ltd, 1984-. Honours: B Arch (Hons). Memberships: Custodian, State Library; Museum of Contemporary Arts; Listed in international biographical dictionaries. Address: 1 Taunton Street, Pymble, NSW 2073, Australia. E-mail: anthony@aganarchitects.com.au

GAN Woon Siong, b. 6 March 1943, Singapore. Acoustician. m. Siu Hui Chiong, 2 sons, 1 daughter. Education: BSc, Physics, 1965, DIC, Acoustics and Vibration Science, 1967, PhD, Acoustics, 1969, Postdoctoral research, 1969-70, Imperial College, London; Postdoctoral research, 1968-69, Chelsea College, London. Appointments: Postdoctoral Research Assistant, Chelsea College, London, 1969; Postdoctoral Research, Imperial College, London, 1969-70; Conducted research at International Centre for Theoretical Physics, Trieste, Italy, 1970, 1973; Associate Professor, Nanyang University, Singapore, 1970-79; Director, Acoustical Services Pte Ltd, Singapore, 1976-89; Chairman, Chief Scientist, Acoustical Technologies Singapore Pte Ltd, 1989-; First to apply gauge theory to acoustics; Founder of the new field of New Acoustics, based on metamaterials. Publications: About 150 papers on active noise cancellation, acoustical imaging and application of gauge theory to acoustics and turbulence; First paper, Application of Acoustical Holography to Noise Source Identification, 1974; Application of Negative Refraction to Acoustical Imaging, 2007; Application of Gauge Theory to Acoustic Fields, 2007; Gauge Invariance Approach to Acoustic Fields, 2007; Major contributions to acoustics by publication of papers on Application of Gauge Theory to Acoustic Fields – Revolutionizing and Rewriting the Whole Field of Acoustics; Book, Acoustical Imaging: Techniques and Applications for Engineers, 2012; Several patents. Honours: UNESCO Postdoctoral Research Fellowship, 1970, 1973; Introduced gauge theory to acoustics; Started field of New Acoustics, based on metamaterials. Memberships: Fellow, Institution of Engineering & Technology, UK; Fellow, Institute of Acoustics, UK; Fellow, Institution of Engineers, Singapore; Fellow, Southern African Acoustics Institute; Life Senior Member, Institute of Electrical and Electronics Engineers, USA; Senior Member, American Institute of Ultrasound in Medicine; Member, Acoustical Society of America. Address: Acoustical Technologies Singapore Pte Ltd, 5 Derbyshire Road, #04-05, Singapore 309461, Singapore. E-mail: wsgan@acousticaltechnologies.com Website: www.acousticaltechnologies.com

GANAPATHY Pattukandan, b. 2 June 1976, India. Teacher; Researcher. m. N Shanmugapriya, 1 daughter. Education: PhD, Disaster Management. Appointments: Teacher and Researcher, 1999-. Publications: 35 articles in international and national journals and conferences. Honours: Best Researcher Award, VIT University; Special Member, Working Group on Landslides; Managing Editor and Editorial Board Member, 12 international journals. Memberships: 12 professional organisations. Address: Centre for Disaster Mitigation and Management, VIT University, Vellore 632014, Tamil Nadu, India. E-mail: seismogans@yahoo.com

GANCHEV Ivan, b. 30 June 1964, Shumen, Bulgaria. University Lecturer. m. Petya, 2 sons. Education: Dip Eng, Leningrad Electro-technical Institute of Telecommunications, 1989; PhD, St Petersburg State University of Telecommunications, 1994. Appointments: Telecom Expert, Bulgarian Telecom, 1995; Visiting Lecturer, ECE Department, University of Limerick, 1997, 1998, 1999; Part-time Senior Lecturer, Department of Informatics, University of Shumen, 1999-2000; Junior Lecturer, 1996, Lecturer, 1997, Senior Lecturer, 1998, Associate Professor, 2004, Department of Computer Systems, Plovdiv University, Bulgaria; Lecturer, Department of Electronic and Computer Engineering, University of Limerick, 2000-; Deputy Director, Telecommunications Research Centre, University of Limerick, 2004-. Publications: 3 books; 23 chapters and contributions to books; 25 papers in refereed journals; 111 papers published in international conferences and workshops proceedings; More than 20 technical reports; 1 newspaper article. Honours: Research Seed Funding Award, University of Limerick, 2001; Grant Award, Teaching & Research Innovation Programme Funding, General Electric & University of Limerick Foundation, 2001-04; Grant Award, Targeted Funding for Strategic Initiatives, Higher Education Authority, Ireland, 2002-06; Basic Research Grant Award, Science Foundation, Ireland, 2004-07; Travel Grant Award, Higher Education Authority/Department of Education and Science, Ireland, 2005; Best Research Paper Award, 2005. Memberships: IEEE; Senior Member, IEEE Communication Society; Bulgarian Mathematical Society. Address: TRC, ECE Department, University of Limerick, Ireland. E-mail: ivan.ganchev@ul.ie

GANELLIN Charon Robin, b. 25 January 1934, London, England. Medicinal Chemist. m. Tamara Green, deceased, 1 son, 1 daughter. Education: BSc, 1955, PhD, 1958, Queen Mary College, London University; Fellow of the Royal Society of Chemistry, 1968; Chartered Chemist, 1976; DSc, London University, 1986; FRS, 1986. Appointments: Medicinal Chemist, Smith Kline & French, 1958; Research Associate, Massachusetts Institute of Technology, 1960; Medicinal Chemist, 1961-62, Head of Chemistry, 1962-78, Director, 1978-86, Vice-President Research, 1980-84, Vice-President, 1984-86, Smith Kline & French Research Ltd; Smith Kline & French Professor of Medicinal Chemistry, 1986-2002, Emeritus Professor of Medicinal Chemistry, 2002-, University College London. Publications: Books as co-editor: Pharmacology of Histamine Receptors, 1982; Frontiers in Histamine Research (a tribute to Heinz Schild), 1985; Dictionary of Drugs, 1990; Medicinal Chemistry, 1993; Dictionary of Pharmacological Agents, 1997; Analogue-based Drug Discovery, 2006; Practical Studies in Medicinal Chemistry, 2007; Analogue-Based Drug Discovery II, 2010; 270 papers and articles as author or co-author in learned scientific journals or books. Honours include: UK Chemical Society Medallion in Medicinal Chemistry, 1977; Prix Charles Mentzer, 1978; Medicinal Chemistry Award, American Chemical Society, 1980; RSC Tilden Medal and Lecture, 1982; SCI Messel Medal and Lecture, 1988; Society for Drug Research Award for Drug Discovery (jointly), 1989; USA National Inventors Hall of Fame, 1990; Fellow, Queen Mary and Westfield College, London, 1992; DSc, Honoris Causa, Aston University, 1995; RSC Adrien Albert Lectureship and Medal, 1999; Nauta Prize for Medicinal Chemistry, European Federation for Medicinal Chemistry, 2004; Foreign Corresponding Academician of the Spanish Royal Academy of Pharmacy, 2006; Pratesi Medal from the Medicinal Chemistry Division of the Italian Chemical Society, 2006; Honorary Member, European Histamine Research Society, 2007; ACS Division of Medicinal Chemistry Hall of Fame, 2007. Memberships: American Chemical Society; British Pharmacological Society; European Histamine Research Society; International Union of Pure and Applied Chemistry; The Royal Society; The Royal Society of Chemistry; Save British Science Society; Society of Chemical Industry; Society for Medicines Research; Chair, IUPAC Subcommittee on Medicinal Chemistry and Drug Development, 2002-. Address: Department of Chemistry, University College London, 20 Gordon Street, London WC1H 0AJ, England. E-mail: c-r.ganellin@ucl.ac.uk

GANEV Margarit, b. 13 May 1959, Popovo, Bulgaria. Education: Master degree, Law, Sofia University St Climent Ohridski, 1985; PhD, Law, 1991. Appointments: Professor, International Public Law, Diplomatic and Consular Law, International Organizations and International Humanitarian Law, 1991-2008; Vice Dean, Faculty for Law Studies, 1997-2004; Visiting Professor, 1991-93, 1996-97, Sofia University St Kliment Ohridski; Visiting Professor, University for National and International Economy, Sofia, 1999-2000; Professor, International Public Law, Free University of Varna, 2007; Deputy Minister, Ministry of Justice, 2004-07. Publications: The Specialized Agencies in the System of the United Nations Organization, 2005; Contemporary International Jurisdiction, 2010. Memberships: International Law Association, Bulgarian branch; Institute of International Law, Sofia; International Law Association, London; Permanent Court of Arbitration in Hague. Address: Ap 31, fl 9, bl 6, Belite brezi, Sofia 1680, Bulgaria. E-mail: m.ganev@mail.bg

GANGADHARAN Siva Kumar, b. 10 June 1965, Kanyakumari, India. Professor. m. Sathi, 1 son, 1 daughter. Education: MSc, 1990, M Phil, 1991, Madurai Kamarai University, India; PhD, University of Madras, India, 2010. Appointments: Assistant Professor, Professor of Chemistry, Panimalan Engineering College. Publications: High Performance Polymer, 2009, 2010; Indian Journal of Science and Technology, 2009; Journal of Polymer Materials, 2010. Honours: Listed in international biographical dictionaries. Memberships: American Chemical Society; American Nano Society. Address: Panimalan Engineering College, Poonamalle, Chennai, Tamil Nadu, PIN 600123, India. gsivakumarchemistry@yahoo.com

GANI Joseph Mark, b. 15 December 1924, Cairo, Egypt. Statistician; Educator. m. Ruth Stephens, 1955, deceased 1997, 2 sons, 2 daughters. Education: BSc, 1947, DIC, 1948, Imperial College, London; PhD, Australian National University, Canberra, 1955; DSc, London University, 1970. Appointments: Lecturer, Department of Mathematics, University of Melbourne, Victoria, 1948-50; Lecturer, Senior Lecturer, Reader, Department of Mathematics, University of West Australia, 1953-60; Senior Fellow, Department of Statistics, Australian National University, 1961-64;

DICTIONARY OF INTERNATIONAL BIOGRAPHY 36th EDITION

Professor, Department of Statistics and Probability, Michigan State University, USA, 1964-65; Professor, Department of Probability and Statistics, University of Sheffield, England, 1965-74; Director, Manchester-Sheffield School of Probability and Statistics, 1967-74; Chief, Division of Mathematics and Statistics, CSIRO, Australia, 1974-81; Chairman, Department of Stats, University of Kentucky, USA, 1981-85; Chairman and Professor, 1985-89, Professor, 1989-94, Statistics and Applied Probability Program, University of California, Santa Barbara; Visiting Fellow, Australian National University, 1995-; University Fellow, 1998-2000. Publications: Author of over 300 papers; 2 books: The Condition of Science in Australian Universities, 1963; Epidemic Modelling: An Introduction (with D J Daley), 1999. Honours: Fellow, Australian Academy of Science, 1976; Member, Order of Australia, 2000. Memberships include: 15 professional societies including: Australian Academy of Science; Australian Mathematical Society; Statistical Society of Australia; Royal Statistical Society. Address: Mathematical Sciences Institute, Bldg 26B, Australian National University, Canberra, ACT 0200, Australia.

GANT Diana Jillian (nee Scutt), b. 25 April 1948, Wembley, Middlesex, England. Retired Headmistress. m. Brian Gant, 2 daughters. Education: Harrow County Grammar School for Girls, 1959-66; BD (Hons), King's College, London, 1970; PGCE, Christ Church College, Canterbury, 1973. Appointments: Various posts as Head/Teacher of Religious Education, -1984; Head of Religious Studies, The King's School, Worcester, 1984-89; Head of Careers and Assistant Head of Sixth Form, Tonbridge Grammar School for Girls, Kent, 1989-95; Deputy Headmistress, Norwich High School for Girls, GDST, 1995-2000; Headmistress, The Mount School, York, 2001-09; Retired, 2009. Address: 7 Slessor Road, York, YO24 3JJ, England. E-mail: dianajgant@aol.com

GANTI Prasada Rao, b. 25 August 1942, Seethanagaram (AP), India. Educator. m. Meenakshi Vedula, 1 son, 2 daughters. Education: BE, (Hons), Electrical Engineering, Andhra University, Waltair, India, 1963; M Tech, Control Systems Engineering, 1965, PhD, Electrical Engineering, 1970, Indian Institute of Technology, Kharagpur, India. Appointments: Assistant Professor, Department of Electrical Engineering, PSG College of Technology, Coimbatore, India, 1969-71; Assistant Professor, 1971-78, Professor, 1978-97, Chairman, Curriculum Development Cell, Electrical Engineering, 1978-80, Indian Institute of Technology, Kharagpur, India; Commonwealth Postdoctoral Research Fellow, Control Systems Centre, University of Manchester Institute of Science and Technology, Manchester, England, 1975-76; Alexander von Humboldt Foundation Research Fellow, Ruhr University, Bochum, Germany, 1981-83, 1985, 1991, 2003, 2004, 2007, 2009; Scientific Advisor, Directorate of Power and Desalination Plants, Water and Electricity Department, Government of Abu Dhabi, 1992-; Visiting Professor, Henri Poincare University, Nancy, France, 2003; Fraunhofer Institut für Rechnerarchitektur und Software Technik (FIRST), Berlin, 2007, 2007; Royal Society Visiting Professor, Brunel University, England, 2007; Member, UNESCO-EOLSS Joint Committee. Publications: Author and Co-author of 4 books and over 150 research papers; Co-editor of 1 book. Honours include: IIT Kharagpur Silver Jubilee Research Award, 1985; The Systems Society of India Award, 1989; International Desalination Association Best Paper award, 1995; Honorary Professor, East China University for Science and Technology. Memberships: Life Fellow, Institution of Engineers, India; Fellow, Institution of Electronic and Telecommunications Engineers, India; Fellow, IEEE, USA; Fellow Indian National Academy of Engineering; Member of numerous editorial boards. Address: PO Box 2623, Abu Dhabi, United Arab Emirates. E-mail: gantirao@emi.ae

GANTS Oded, b. 26 October 1971, Rehovot, Israel. Lecturer. m. Malka, 3 sons, 5 daughters. Education: B Technology, Applied Science, Jerusalem College of Technology, 1993; MSc, Systems Engineering, Tel Aviv University, 2007. Appointments: Team Leader, Video Algorithms, Polycom Israel, 1999-2006; Expert, Video Systems, Harmonic Israel, 2006-; Lecturer, Video Compression, Logtel, 2009-. Publications: US Patent, Methods & systems for providing continuous presence video in cascading. Memberships: IEEE. Address: Harmonic Inc, Ha'amal 10, Rosh Ha'agin, 48092, Israel.

GANTZ Benny, b. 9 June 1959, Kfar Ahim, Israel. Military Officer. m. 4 children. Education: Graduate, Staff and Command College, National Security College; BA, History, Tel Aviv University; Master's, Political Science, Haifa University, Israel; Master's, Management of National Resources, National Defence University, USA. Appointments: Paratroopers Brigade, 1977-79, Platoon Commander to Deputy Company Commander, 1979-87, Commander, Ef'a battalion, 1987-89, Commander, Shaldag Unit, Israeli Air Force, Commander, Operation Shlomo, 1989-92, Commander, Reserve Paratroopers Brigade, 1992-94, Commander, Judea Brigade, 1994-95, Commander, Paratroopers Brigade, 1995-97, Brigadier General, 1998-2001, Commander, Reserves Division in the Northern Command, 1998-99, Commander, Liaison Unit with Lebanon, 1999-2000, Commander, Judea and Samara Division, 2000-02, Major General, 2001-11, Commander, Northern Command Reserve core, 2001, Commander, Northern Command, 2002-05, Commander, Ground Forces Command, 2005-07, Military Attaché to the US, 2007-09, Deputy Chief General Staff, 2009-10, Lt General, 2011-, Chief, General Staff, 2011-, Israeli Defence Force. Address: IDF Home Front Headquarters, Ha-Kirya, Yitzak Rabin Base, 67659 Tel Aviv, Israel.

GARAB Gyözö, b. 1 January 1948, Szomód, Hungary. Research Scientist. m. Anikó, 27 October 1979, 2 sons, 2 daughters. Education: Physics, University of Szeged, 1971; PhD, Biophysics, 1974; DSc, 1992. Appointments: Research Scientist, Head of Laboratory, 1987-, Deputy Director, 1999-2000, Biology Research Centre, Szeged; Visiting Scientist, University of Illinois, University of New Mexico, CEA Saclay, Brookhaven National Laboratory; Director, Biofotonika Ltd, 2004-. Publications: Photosynthesis: Mechanisms and Effects; More than 150 articles in professional journals. Honours: J Ernst Award, Hungarian Biophysical Society, 1994; Straub Medal, Biology Research Centre, 2001; Knight of the International Order of Merit of Inventors, 2009. Memberships: Hungarian Biophysical Society; International Society of Photosynthesis Research. Address: Dózsa György u 7, H-6720 Szeged, Hungary.

GARCIA MIRA Ricardo, b. 19 August 1956, A Coruna, Spain. Professor. 1 son, 2 daughters. Education: BS, PhD, Psychology, University of Santiago de Compostela. Appointments: Subdirector, Computer Network, 1987-91, Research Fellow, 1991-94, University of Santiago de Compostela; Head, Human Resources, 1991-95, Professor, Social and Environmental Psychology, 1995-, Director of People-Environment Research Group, 1995-, University of Corunna, Spain; Professor, Data Analysis and Research Methods, UNED, 1999-; International Visiting Scholar, Texas State University, USA, 2001; Visiting Reader, University of

- 355 -

Surrey, England, 2003-12; Visiting Professor, University of Tallinn, Estonia, 2002, University of Timisoara, Romania, 2004, University of Mexico, 2006. Publications: The Perceived City, 1997; Psychology and the Environment, 2002; Environment – Behaviour Studies in Spain, 2002; Culture, Environmental Action and Sustainability, 2003; Housing, Space and Quality of Life, 2005; Sustainability, Values and Environmental Culture, 2009. Memberships: International Association for People-Environment Studies; Institute of Psychosocial Studies and Research; International Association of Applied Psychology. Address: Department of Psychology, University of Corunna, Campus de Elvina, s/n 15071 – A Coruna, Spain. E-mail: ricardo.garcia.mira@udc.es

GARCIA Y GARCIA Ernesto Luis, b. 23 August 1946, Cogolludo, Spain. Doctor in Medicine and Surgery; Rehabilitation and Physical Medicine Specialist; Phoniatry. m. María Soledad Vicente, 1971, 2 sons, 1 daughter. Education: Degree in Medicine and Surgery, Medical Faculty Zaragoza, Spain, 1970; Certified in Puericulture, 1975; Certified in Medicine of the Work, 1976; Resident in Rehabilitation and Physical Medicine Specialist, University Hospital Miguel Servet, 1974-77; Doctor in Medicine and Surgery, 1991. Appointments: General Physician and General Health Management in autonomous communities of Guadalajara, Aragon and Catalonia, Spain, 1970-73; Emergency in Medicine Officer, Royal and Provincial Hospital, Saragossa, Spain, 1973-88; Specialist, Rehabilitation Department, Chief of Unit of Phoniatry and Logotherapy, University Hospital Miguel Servet, Saragossa, 1977-; Vicarial-Consultant, Company Derfonia SL, 1997-; Director, Centre of Phoniatric and Logotherapy Aragon; Specialist, Rehabilitation, Cerebral Palsy Centre, ASPACE, Aragon 1980-92; Lecturer on medical rehabilitation, phoniatry and the handicapped at scientific sessions and congresses; Lecturer tutor, MIR of Rehabilitation, 1992-2003, Co-ordinator, Improvement of Assistance Quality, Department of Rehabilitation, 2003-, Chief of Service, Physical Medicine and Rehabilitation, 2004-, University Hospital Miguel Servet. Publications: Articles in professional journals on human communication disorders; Editor of book chapters and magazines. Honours include: Premium FAMI Aragon, 1995; Aragon Man of 2002; Recognition as team member for Choclear Implant, School of Doctors of Zaragoza, 2002. Memberships: President, Founding Manager, Spanish Phoniatry Magazine; Chairman, Spanish Medical Society of Phoniatry, 1992-97; Aragon Society of Rehabilitation and Physical Medicine; Spanish Society of Medical Physicians and rehabilitation; Aragon Society of Otorinolaryngology; Member numerous investigative commissions; Collaborative Associate, NGO's and humanitarian associations; First Vice-Chairman, Civil International Committee; Chairman, Civil International Committee, 2006-. Address: University Hospital Miguel Servet, Physical Medicine and Rehabilitation Service, Isabel la Catolica 1-3, 50007 Saragossa, Spain. E-mail: elgarcia@salud.aragon.es

GARCIA-SOTO Carlos, b. 19 February 1965, Bilbao, Spain. Oceanographer. Education: First Degree, Ecology, 1988; MSc, Estuarine Ecology, 1989; Diploma, University of Dundee, 1990; PhD, Oceanography, University of Southampton, 1994; Diploma, University of Hamburg, 2006; Diploma, University of Western Australia, 2006. Appointments: Visiting Researcher, Plymouth Marine Laboratory, UK, 1990-97; Senior Researcher, National Institute of Oceanography, 1998-2011; Government Panel of Experts, 2004-11; Principal Investigator, European Space Agency, 2004-11. Publications: More than 50 scientific works; Editor, 3 books and special issues. Honours: Joint Award, The National Foundation of Science and Technology, The Royal Society of Physics and The Royal Society of Mathematics, 2005. Memberships: American Geophysical Union, USA; Challenger Society of Ocean Science, UK; Marine Biological Association, UK. Address: National Institute of Oceanography, Promontorio S Martin S/N, 39004 Santander, Spain. E-mail: carlos.soto@st.ieo.es

GARDNER Hall, b. 10 January 1954, North Carolina, USA. Professor; Consultant. m. Isabel Sanz, 2 daughters. Education: High school degree, Tower Hill School, 1972; BA, Colgate University, 1977; MA, 1982, PhD, 1987, Johns Hopkins University, School of Advanced International Studies. Appointments: Visiting Professor, Johns Hopkins, Nanjing Center for Chinese and American Studies, Nanjing, China, 1988-89; Visiting Professor, Johns Hopkins University, Nitze School of Advanced International Studies, Washington, USA, 1989-90; Chair, International Affairs Department, 1992-2005, Full Professor, 1998-, Chair, 2008-, Department of International and Comparative Politics, American University of Paris, France. Publications: Author, 4 books; Numerous articles in professional journals. Honours: Invited speaker, World Political Forum, 2003, 2006, 2008; Participant: Doha Forum on Democracy, Development and Free Trade, 2005, 2007, 2008; Doha Forum, 2009; Invited speaker, Assemblée Nationale France, 2007; Member, Russia, Europe and US Policy Study Group, 2008; Lecturer, NATO School, Oberammergau, 2008, 2009, 2010. Memberships: Cicero Foundation; Geostratégiques; Institute for Euro-Atlantic Integration, Kosovo. Address: Department of International and Comparative Politics, American University of Paris, 6 rue du Colonel Combes, 75007 Paris, France. E-mail: hgardner@aup.edu Website: www.epsilen.com/hgardner

GARDNER Mariana Carmen Zavati, b. 20 January 1952, Bacau, Romania. Poet. m. John Edward Gardner, 8 August 1980, 1 son, 1 daughter. Education: Baccalauréat with distinction, Vasile Alecsandri Boarding College for Girls, 1971; MSc, Philology, 1st class honours, Alexandru Ioan Cuza University of Iasi, 1975; PGCE, University of Leeds, 1987; Postgraduate Courses: Goethe Institut Rosenheim, Germany, 1991; L'Ecole Normale Supérieure, Auxerre, France, 1991. Appointments: Teacher, Modern Languages (English, French, German, Latin, Spanish, Italian), various high schools in Romania and England, 1975-99; Part-time Assistant Lecturer, University of Iasi, 1975, 1976; Full-time Assistant Lecturer, University of Bacau, 1979. Publications include: Volumes of verse: Whispers; The Journey; Watermarks; Travellers/ Calatori; The Spinning Top; Pilgrims/Pelerini; The Remains of the Dream Catcher; Bequests/Mosteniri Seasons; Sketches; Soapte; Vise la Minut; Poems included in anthologies: Between a Laugh and a Tear; Light of the World; The Sounds of Silence; The Secret of Twilight; A Blossom of Dreams; The Lyre's Song; Honoured Poets of 1988; Last Good-Byes; A Celebration of Poets; The Definitive Version; A Celebration of Poets; Sunrise and Soft Mist; Memories of the Millennium; Nature's Orchard; Lifelines; Antologia Poezia Padurii V; International Notebook of Poetry 2000-08; Journal of the American Academy of Arts and Sciences; Eastern Voices; Family Ties; Sunkissed; Reflections of Time; Spotlight Poets Anthologies; Science Friction, The Best Poets and Poems of 2002; Pictured Visions; Searching for Paradise; Poetical Reflections; Waters of the Heart; Translations; Short Stories: New Fiction Collection; 2 novels. Honours: Editor's Choice Award, International Society of Poets, UK, 1996; Editor's Choice Award, International Library of Poetry, UK, 1997; Editor's Choice Award, National Library of Poetry, UK, 1998; Bronze Medal, North American Poetry Competition, USA,

1998; The American Romanian Academy Award, The Ionel Jianu Award for Arts, American Romanian Academy of Arts and Sciences, Canada, 2001; The Provincia Corvina Diploma of Excellence RO, 2007; Outstanding Commendation, International Competition of Romanian Poetry, RO, USA, 2008; The Novalis Prize, Germany, 2008; Listed in national and international biographical dictionaries. Memberships: American Romanian Academy of Arts and Sciences; National Geographic Society, USA; Royal Society of Literature, UK; Uniunea Scriitorilor RO. Address: 14 Andrew Goodall Close, East Dereham, Norfolk NR19 1SR, England.

GARDNER-THORPE Christopher, b. 22 August 1941. Consultant Neurologist. Education: St Philip's School, London, 1948-54; Beaumont College, Old Windsor, Berkshire, 1954-59; MB BS, 1964, MD, 1973, University of London, St Thomas' Hospital; FRCP; FACP. Appointments: House Surgeon, Peace Memorial, Watford, 1964; House Physician, Royal South Hants Hospital, Southampton, 1964-65; Senior House Officer in Neurology, 1965-66, Registrar in Neurology, 1967-69, Wessex Neurological Centre, Southampton General Hospital; Medical Registrar, North Staffordshire Infirmary and City General Hospital, Stoke on Trent, 1966-67; Registrar in Neurology, Southampton General Hospital, 1969; Neurological Research Registrar, 1969-71, Neurological Registrar, Special Centre for Epilepsy, 1969-71, Bootham Park Hospital, York and General Infirmary, Leeds; Senior Registrar in Neurology, Newcastle General Hospital and Royal Victoria Infirmary, Newcastle-upon-Tyne, 1971-74; Physician in Charge, Newcourt Hospital, Exeter, 1974-88; Consultant Neurologist, South Western Regional Health Authority, 1974-93; Consultant Neurologist, North Devon District Hospital, Barnstable, 1974-95; Consultant Neurologist, Mardon House Neurorehabilitation Centre, 1997-2006; Consultant Neurologist, Royal Devon and Exeter Hospital, Exeter and Plymouth General Hospital, 1993-2006, Lead Clinician in Neurology, 1997-2006, Exeter Healthcare NHS Trust; Independent Consultant Neurologist, 2006-. Publications: Numerous articles in professional and popular journals; Editor, Journal of Medical Biography. Honours: Freeman of the City of London, 1979; Her Majesty's Lieutenant for the City of London, 1981-; Freeman, 1979-, Liveryman, 1980-, Worshipful Company of Barbers; Esquire, Order of St John, 1980-; Fellow, Linnean Society; Invited Fellow, Royal Society of Arts, 1997. Memberships include: World Federation of Neurology; European Federation of Neurological Societies; Association of British Neurologists; International League Against Epilepsy; British Epilepsy Association; Irish Neurological Association; British Medical Association; Royal Society of Medicine; Royal College of Physicians; Society of Expert Witnesses; Institute for Learning and Teaching. Address: The Coach House, 1a College Road, Exeter, Devon, EX1 1TE, England. E-mail: cgardnerthorpe@doctors.org.uk

GARGANAS Nicholas C(hristos), b. 20 January 1937, Soufli Evrou, Greece. Economist. m. Maria Kokka, 1 daughter. Education: BSc Economics, Athens School of Economics and Business Studies, 1959; MSc Economics, London School of Economics and Political Science, London, 1963; PhD Economics, University College London, 1971. Appointments: Head, Economic Research Unit, Agricultural Bank of Greece, Athens, 1964-66; Research Officer, National Institute of Economic and Social Research, London, 1968-75; Senior Economist, Director/Advisor, Economic Research Department, Bank of Greece, Athens, 1975-85, 1987-93; Chief Economic Advisor, Ministry of National Economy, Athens, 1985-87; Member, EU Monetary Committee, 1985-87, 1994-98; Economic Counsellor (Chief Economist), Bank of Greece, 1993-96; Deputy Governor, Bank of Greece, 1996-; Alternate Governor for Greece, IMF, 1996-; Member, EU Economic and Financial Committee, 1999-. Publications: Books; Articles in professional journals. Honours: Honorary Fellow, LSE, London, 1998. Memberships: European Economic Association; American Economic Association; Royal Economic Society. Address: Bank of Greece, 21 El Venizelos Ave, GR 10250 Athens, Greece. E-mail: garganas@otenet.gr

GARIGLIO Bartolomeo, b. 10 February 1947, Raceonigi, Italy. Professor. m. Maria Teresa Chiurato, 2 sons. Education: Degree, Philosophy, Catholic University of Milan, 1970. Appointments: Researcher, 1982; Associate Professor, Political History, 1992; Full Professor, Contemporary History, 1999. Publications: Cattolico-democratici e cleric-faseisti, 1976; Stampa e opinone pubblica nil Risorgimento, 1987; Cattolica, ebrei ed evangelica nella guerro 1939-1945, 1999; L'autunno delli liberta, 2009. Honours: Piero Gobetti Research Centre; National Executive Committee, St Giuseppe Caffasso's; Italia Contemporanea. Memberships: President of the Historians, Faculty of Political Sciences, University of Turin. Address: via Sant Ottavio 20, 10124 Turin, Italy. E-mail: bartolo.gariglio@unito.it

GARMANOV Maksim E, b. 29 May 1961, Moscow, Russia. Chemist; Electrochemist; Researcher; Scientist. Education: Highest Degree with honours, Chemical Faculty, Moscow State University, Russia, 1983; Postgraduate Course, The Karpov's Physico-Chemical Research Institute, Moscow, Russia, 1990. Appointments: Special Researcher, Institute of Physical Chemistry, Academy of Sciences, Moscow, 1983-86; Junior Scientist, 1986-87, Postgraduate Student, 1987-90, The Karpov's Physico-Chemical Research Institute, Moscow; Junior Scientist, 1990-92, Scientist, 1992-, Institute of Physical Chemistry, Academy of Sciences, Moscow. Publications: Numerous articles in professional scientific journals. Honours: Highest degree with honours, Moscow State University, 1983; All-Russia Exhibition Centre Award, Moscow, 2003; Listed in national and international biographical honours and grand editions. Memberships: Honorary Research Consultant, IBC; Distinguished Research Board of Advisors, ABI, USA; Australasian Corrosion Association Inc; Electrocheical Society of Japan; International Society of Electrochemistry; Electrochemical Society, USA. Address: The Institute of Physical Chemistry and Electrochemistry of RAS, Leninsky Prospect 31, Moscow 119991, Russia. E-mail: maxsuperrrr@rambler.ru

GARNER James (James Baumgardner), b. 7 April 1928, Norman, Oklahoma, USA. Actor. m. Lois Clarke, 1995, 1 son, 2 daughters. Appointments: Former travelling salesman, oil field worker, carpet layer, bathing suit model; Toured with road companies; Actor, TV appearances include: Cheyenne, Maverick, 1957-62; Nichols, 1971-72; The Rockford Files, 1974-79; Space, 1985; The New Maverick; The Long Summer of George Adams; The Glitter Dome; Heartsounds; Promise (also executive producer); Obsessive Love; My Name is Bill (also executive producer); Decoration Day; Barbarians at the Gate; The Rockford Files; A Blessing in Disguise; Dead Silence; First Monday (series), 2002; Films include: Toward the Unknown; Shoot-Out at Medicine Bend, 1957; Darby's Rangers, 1958; Sayonara; Up Periscope, 1959; The Americanization of Emily, 1964; 36 Hours; The Art Of Love, 1965; A Man Could Get Killed, 1966; Duel at Diablo, 1966; Master Buddwing, 1966; Grand Prix, 1966; Hour of the Gun, 1967; Marlowe, 1969; Support Your Local Sheriff,

1971; Support Your Local Gunfighter, 1971; Skin Game, 1971; They Only Kill Their Masters, 1972; One Little Indian, 1973; Health, 1979; The Fan, 1980; Victor/Victoria, 1982; Murphy's Romance, 1985; Promise (made for TV), 1986; Sunset, 1987; Decoration Day (TV film), 1990; Fire in the Sky, 1993; Maverick (TV), 1994; My Fellow Americans, 1996; Twilight, 1998; Space Cowboys, 2000; Atlantis: The Lost Empire, 2001; Roughing It (TV), 2002; Divine Secrets of the Ya-Ya Sisterhood, 2002; First Monday (TV), 2002; The Land Before Time X: The Great Longneck Migration, 2003; The Notebook, 2004; Al Roach: Private Insectigator, 2004; 8 Simple Rules...for Dating My Teenage Daughter (TV), 2003/05; The Ultimate Gift, 2006; Terra, 2008. Honours: Emmy Award; Purple Heart.

GARNETT Richard (Duncan Carey), b. 8 January 1923, London, England. Writer; Publisher; Translator. Education: BA, King's College, Cambridge, 1948; MA, 1987. Appointments: Production Manager, 1955-59, Director, 1957-66, Rupert Hart-Davis Ltd; Director, Adlard Coles Ltd, 1963-66; Editor, 1966-82, Director, 1972-82, Macmillan London; Director, Macmillan Publishers, 1982-87. Publications: Goldsmith: Selected Works (editor), 1950; Robert Gruss: The Art of the Aqualung (translator), 1955; The Silver Kingdom (in US as The Undersea Treasure), 1956; Bernard Heuvelmans: On the Track of Unknown Animals (translator), 1958; The White Dragon, 1963; Jack of Dover, 1966; Bernard Heuvelmans: In the Wake of the Sea-Serpents (translator), 1968; Joyce (editor with Reggie Grenfell), 1980; Constance Garnett: A Heroic Life, 1991; Sylvia and David, The Townsend Warner/Garnett Letters (editor), 1994; Rupert Hart-Davis Limited: A Brief History, 2004. Address: 28 Albany Road, Salisbury, Wiltshire SP1 3YH, England.

GARRETT Godfrey John, b. 24 July 1937, Beckenham, Kent, England. Former Diplomat; Consultant. m. Elisabeth Margaret Hall, 4 sons, 1 daughter. Education: Degree in Modern Languages, Sidney Sussex College, Cambridge, 1958-61. Appointments: Foreign and Commonwealth Office, 1961-93; Head of International Peace Keeping Missions in Croatia and Ukraine, 1993-95; Consultant to Control Risk Company, 1996-98; Consultant on Eastern Europe, 1998-2011; Consultant for HMG in Global Conflict Prevention Policy, 2004-06. Honours: OBE, 1982; Swedish Order of the North Star, 1983. Address: White Cottage, Henley, Haslemere, Surrey GU27 3HQ, England.

GARRETT Lesley, b. 10 April 1955. Opera Singer. m. 1991, 1 son, 1 daughter. Education: Royal Academy of Music; National Opera Studio. Career: Winner, Kathleen Ferrier Memorial Competition, 1979; Performed with Welsh National Opera; Opera North; At Wexford and Buxton Festivals and at Glyndebourne; Joined ENO (Principal Soprano), 1984; Major roles includes: Susanna, Marriage of Figaro; Despina, Cosi Fan Tutte; Musetta, La Bohème; Jenny, Rise and Fall of the City of Mahaggony; Atalanta, Xerxes; Zerlinda, Don Giovanni; Yum-Yum, The Mikado; Adèle, Die Fledermaus; Oscar, A Masked Ball; Dalinda, Ariodante; Rose, Street Scene; Bella, A Midsummer Marriage; Eurydice, Orpheus and Eurydice; Title roles in the The Cunning Little Vixen and La Belle Vivette; Numerous concert hall performances in UK and abroad (including Last Night of the Proms); TV and radio appearances. CDs include: Prima Donna; Soprano in Red; Travelling Night; The Best of Lesley Garrett; When I Fall In Love. Honours: Hon DArts (Plymouth), 1995; Best selling Classical Artist, Gramophone Award, 1996. Address: The Music Partnership Ltd, 41 Aldebert Terrace, London, SW8 1BH, England.

GARRO Ibrahim, b. 11 May 1946, Aleppo, Syria. Mathematical Logician; Engineer. Education: BS, Electrical Engineering, University of Florida, 1966; MS, Engineering, University of California, Berkeley, 1967; Dr rer nat, University of Bonn. Appointments: Teaching and Research, Catholic University of Louvain, Belgium; Assistant Professor, University of Jordan, Amman; Researcher, universities of Berkeley and Toronto. Publications: 20-30 publications in English and Arabic in the fields of epistemology and history of science, mathematical logic and applications in mathematics and systems science. Honours: Listed in international biographical dictionaries. Memberships: AMS; ASL; DVMLG. Address: Nayyal, Amira Str, Aleppo, Syria. E-mail: ab_garro@hotmail.com

GASCH Bernd Carl, b. 5 February 1941, Karlsbad, Czechoslovak Republic. Professor. m. Angela, 1991, 1 son, 1 daughter. Education: Diploma in Psychology, 1965; Doctors Degree, 1970. Appointments: Research Assistant, University of Erlangen-Nuremberg, 1965-66; Founder and Head, Team for Psychological Management, 1972; Head, Centre for the Advancement of Tertiary Learning and Teaching, University of Augsburg, Germany, 1973-77; Head, Central Research Group for the Evaluation of Models of Legal Education, Mannheim, 1977-78; Visiting Fellow, Australian National University, Australia, 1978; Professor of Psychology, University of Dortmund, Germany, 1979; Special Commissioner, Organizational Psychology, University of Dortmund, 1980-90; Visiting Professor, University of Wollongong, Australia, 1984-85; Dean, Faculty of Social Sciences, 1987-90, Dean, Faculty of Human Science and Theology, 2001-05, University of Dortmund; Vice Rector, University of Dortmund, 1990-94; Visiting Professor, Universita Luigi Bocconi, Milano, 1992; Visiting Scholar, Obermann Centre for Advanced Studies, University of Iowa, USA, 1999; Retired, 2007. Publications: 7 books; Numerous articles; Several television productions. Memberships: German Association for Psychology; International Association of Applied Psychology; Association for Tertiary Education. Address: University of Dortmund, Fakultaet 14, Postfach 500500, D-44221 Dortmund, Germany. E-mail: bernd.gasch@t-online.de

GASCOIGNE Paul John, b. 26 May 1967, Gateshead, England. Footballer. m. Sheryl Failes, divorced, 1 son. Career: Played for Newcastle United, 1985-88; Tottenham Hotspur, 1988-92, Lazio, Italy, 1992-95, Glasgow Rangers, 1995-98; Middlesbrough, 1998-2000; Everton, 2000-02; Burnley, 2002; Signed as player/coach, Gansu Tianma (Gansu Sky Horses), Chinese B-League, 2003; Played for England, 13 under 21 caps, 57 full caps, World Cup Italy, 1990. Publication: Paul Gascoigne, autobiography with Paul Simpson, 2001; Gazza: My Story, 2004; Gazza: Tackling My Demons, 2006. Honours: BBC Sports Personality of the Year, 1990; FA Cup Winners Medal, 1991. Address: c/o Robertson Craig & Co, Clairmont Gardens, Glasgow, G3 7LW, Scotland.

GASIMOV Balakishi, b. 20 October 1978, Baku, Azerbaijan. Economist. m. Narmin Isgandarova, 2 sons. Education: Bachelor, Faculty of Business Management, Azerbaijan State Economic Institute, 1999; Master's degree, Faculty of Business Management, Azerbaijan State Economic University, 2001. Appointments: Financial Consultant, United Nations Development Programme, 2001-04; Head, Procurement Department, Azpetrol Group, 2003-04; Head, Procurement Department, Amorgo Management & Consulting, 2004-05; Business Consultant, 2005-06; Owner/General Director, Game TV.az production company, 2006-. Publications: Numerous interviews in key Azerbaijan media.

Honours: First prize, Brain-Ring intellectual game World Cup, 2002; First prize, 2008, Main prize, 2010, What? Where? When? intellectual TV show.

GASTON Kevin John, b. 5 November 1964, Pembury, England. Professor. m. Sian Roberts, 1 daughter. Education: BSc, University of Sheffield, 1986; D Phil, University of York, 1989. Appointments: Junior, Senior and Principal Research Fellow, The Natural History Museum, London, 1989-94; Royal Society University Research Fellow, Imperial College, 1994; Royal Society University Research Fellow, 1995-2002, Professor of Biodiversity and Conservation, 2002-, University of Sheffield. Publications: Author: Rarity, 1994; Physiological Diversity and Its Ecological Implications, 1999; Pattern and Process in Macroecology, 2000; The Structure and Dynamics of Geographic Ranges, 2003; Biodiversity: An Introduction, 2nd edition, 2004; Gough Island: A Natural History, 2005; Endemic Plants of the Altai Mountain Country, 2008; Over 400 peer-reviewed papers. Honours: Ecology Institute IRPE Prize, 1999; Professor Extraordinary in Zoology, University of Stellenbosch, 2002-; Royal Society – Wolfson Research Merit Award, 2006-11. Address: Department of Animal and Plant Sciences, University of Sheffield, Western Bank, Sheffield S10 2TN, England. E-mail: k.j.gaston@sheffield.ac.uk

GATES William Henry (Bill), b. 28 October 1955, Seattle, USA. Computer Software Executive. m. Melinda French, 1994, 1 son, 2 daughters. Education: Harvard University. Appointments: Joined MITS, 1975; Programmer, Honeywell, 1975; Founder, Chairman, Board, Microsoft Corporation, 1976-, CEO, 1976-99; Software Architect, 1999-2008; Founder, Bill & Melinda Gates Foundation. Publications: The Future, 1994; The Road Ahead, 1996; Business at the Speed of Thought, 1999. Honours: Howard Vollum Award, Reed College, Portland, Oregon, 1984; Named CEO of Year, Chief Executive Magazine. Address: Microsoft Corporation, 1 Microsoft Way, Redmond, WA 98052, USA.

GATHORNE-HARDY Jonathan, b. 17 May 1933, Edinburgh, Scotland. Author. m. (1) Sabrina Tennant, 1962, 1 son, 1 daughter, (2) Nicolette Sinclair-Loutit, 12 September 1985. Education: BA, Arts, Trinity College, Cambridge, 1957. Publications: One Foot in the Clouds (novel), 1961; Chameleon (novel), 1967; The Office (novel), 1970; The Rise and Fall of the British Nanny, 1972; The Public School Phenomenon, 1977; Love, Sex, Marriage and Divorce, 1981; Doctors, 1983; The Centre of the Universe is 18 Baedeker Strasse (short stories), 1985; The City Beneath the Skin (novel), 1986; The Interior Castle: A Life of Gerald Brenan (biography), 1992; Particle Theory (novel), 1996; Alfred C. Kinsey - Sex The Measure of All Things, A Biography, 1998; Half An Arch (autobiographical memoir), 2004. Other: 12 novels for children. Contributions to: Numerous magazines and journals. Honours: J R Ackerley Prize for Autobiography, 2005. Address: 31 Blacksmith's Yard, Binham, Fakenham, Norfolk NR21 0AL, England.

GATTING Michael William (Mike), b. 6 June 1957, Kingsbury, Middlesex, England. Cricketer. m. Elaine Mabbott, 1980, 2 sons. Career: Right-hand batsman and right-arm medium bowler, played for Middlesex, 1975-98, Captain, 1983-97; 79 Tests for England, 1977-95, 23 as Captain; Scoring 4,409 runs (average 35.5) including 10 hundreds; Scored 36,549 first-class runs (94 hundreds); Toured Australia (Captain), 1986-87; Captain, rebel cricket tour to South Africa, 1989-90; 92 limited-overs internationals, 37 as Captain; Member, England Selection Committee, 1997-; Director of Coaching, Middlesex Cricket Club, 1999-2000; Director, Ashwell Leisure, 2001-. Publications: Limited Overs, 1986; Triumph in Australia, 1987; Leading From the Front (autobiography), 1988. Honour: OBE; Wisden Cricketer of The Year, 1984; President, Lord's Taverners, 2005/2006. Address: c/o Middlesex County Cricket Club, Lord's Cricket Ground, St John's Wood Road, London, NW8 8QN, England.

GAUGHAN John Anthony, b. 19 August 1932, Listowel, Co Kerry, Ireland. Catholic Priest. Education: BA, University College, Dublin, 1953; BD, St Patrick's College, Maynooth, Ireland, 1956; MA, University College, Dublin, 1965; PhD, 1992; DLitt, 1996. Appointments: Chaplain and Vocational School Teacher, Presentation College, Bray, 1957-60; Reader, Most Precious Blood, Cabra West, 1960-62; Curate, Most Sacred Heart: Aughrim-Greenane, 1962-64; Chaplain and University Tutor, University College Dublin, St Mary's Convent, Donnybrook, 1964-65; Curate, St Joseph's, Eastwall, 1965-67, Our Lady of Good Counsel, Drimnagh, 1967-70, St Patrick's, Monkstown, 1970-77, St Thérèse, Mount Merrion, 1977-83, University Church, St Stephen's Green, 1983-88; Parish Priest, Guardian Angels, Blackrock, 1988-2009; Pastor Emeritus, 2009-. Publications: Contributor of over 95 articles to professional journals; Author of 25 books including most recently: Olivia Mary Taaffe (1832-1918): Foundress of St Joseph's Young Priests Society, 1995; Memoirs of Senator Joseph Connolly: A Founder of Modern Ireland (editor), 1996; Newmans's University Church: A History and Guide, 1997; Memoirs of Senator James G Douglas: Concerned Citizen (editor), 1998; At the Coal Face: Recollections of a City & Country Priest 1950-2000, 2000; Scouting in Ireland, 2006; The Archbishops, Bishops & Priest of the Archdiocese of Dublin in the Seventeenth Century, 2010; Articles and book reviews to various periodicals and newspapers. Memberships: National Library of Ireland Society, Chairman, 2000-; Kerry Archaeological and History Society, Committee Member, 1976-89; Writers Week, Founding Member, 1971, President, 1983-90, Vice-President, 1991-; Irish PEN, Committee Member, 1976-, Chairman, 1981-2004. Address: 56 Newtownpark Ave, Blackrock, Co Dublin, Ireland. Website: www.janthonygaughan.com

GAULTIER Jean-Paul, b. 24 April 1952, Arcueil, Paris, France. Fashion Designer. Career: Launched first collection with his Japanese partner, 1978; Since then known on international scale for his men's and women's collections; First junior collection, 1988; Costume designs for film The Cook, The Thief, His Wife and Her Lover, 1989, for ballet le Défilé de Régine Chopinot, 1985; Madonna's World Tour, 1990; My Life Is Hell, 1991; The City of Lost Children, 1995; The Fifth Element, 1997; Absolutely Fabulous, 2001; Dangerous Liaisons, 2003; Bad Education, 2004; Madonna: The Confessions Tour Live from London (TV), 2006; Released record, How to Do That (in collaboration with Tony Mansfield), 1989; Launched own perfume, 1993; Designer of costume for Victoria Abril in Pedro Almodóvar's film Koka, 1994. Launched perfume brands Jean-Paul Gaultier, 1993, La Mâle, 1995, Fragile, 1999. Honours: Fashion Oscar, 1987; Progetto Leonardo Award for How to Do That, 1989; Chevalier des Arts et des Lettres. Address: Jean-Paul Gaultier SA, 30 rue du Faubourg-Saint-Antoine, 75012 Paris, France.

GE Yucheng, b. 25 August 1965, Fenghua, Zhejiang Province, China. Teacher. m. Haiping He, 1 daughter. Education: Bachelor, Defense University of Science and Technology, 1987; Master, Institute of Modern Physics, Chinese Academy of Sciences, 1990; PhD, Peking University, 2003. Appointments: Engineer, GYC Digital Machines Laboratory, 1991-2000; Post Doctor, Tsinghua University,

2003-05; Researcher, Professor, Peking University, 2005-. Publications: 2 articles in professional journals. Honours: Discovery of transfer equations used to precisely measure the intensity and the chirp of an attosecond or a femtosecond x-ray pulse with laser-assisted photo-ionizations. Address: School of Physics, Peking University, Beijing 100871, China. E-mail: gyc@pku.edu.cn

GÉBLER Carlo, b. 21 August 1954, Dublin, Ireland. Writer; Film-Maker. m. Tyga Thomason, 23 August 1990, 3 sons, 2 daughters. Education: BA, English and Related Literature, University of York, 1976; Graduate, National Film and Television School, 1979; PhD, Queen's University, Belfast, 2009. Appointments: Part-time Teacher, Creative Writing, HMP Maze, Co Antrim, 1993-95; Appointed Writer-in-Residence, HMP Maghaberry, Co Antrim, 1997; International Writing Fellow, 2004, Arts Council Writing Fellow, 2006, Lecturer, 2010, Trinity College, Dublin; Temporary Lectureship in Creative Writing, Queen's University, Belfast, 2007; Royal Literary Fund Fellow, 2008 and 2009, Lecturer, 2011, Queen's University, Belfast. Publications: The Eleventh Summer, 1985; August in July, 1986; Work & Play, 1987; Driving through Cuba, 1988; Malachy and His Family, 1990; The Glass Curtain: Inside an Ulster Community, 1991; Life of a Drum, 1991; The Cure, 1994; W9 and Other Lives, 1998 (re-issue, expanded edition, 2011); How to Murder a Man, 1998; Frozen Out, 1998; The Base, 1999; Father & I, 2000; Dance of Death, 2000; Caught on a Train, 2001; 10 Rounds, 2002; August' 44, 2003; The Siege of Derry, A History, 2005; The Bull Raid, 2005; Silhouette, 2007; Henry & Harriet and Other Plays, 2007; A Good Day for a Dog, 2008; My Father's Watch (co-author with Patrick Maguire), 2008; Charles & Mary, 2011; The Dead Eight, 2011. Membership: Elected to Aosdána, Ireland, 1990. Address: c/o Antony Harwood, 103 Walton Street, Oxford, OX2 6EB, England.

GEETHA Kannappan, b. 5 March 1971, Vellore, India. Professor. m. R Senthil Kumar, 1 daughter. Education: BSc, Chemistry, DKM College for Women, Vellore, 1991; MSc, Chemistry, MGA College, Vellore, 1993; PhD, Inorganic Chemistry, IISc, Bangalore, 2000. Appointments: Lecturer, Chemistry, Government Arts College, Ariyalur, 1998-2000; Assistant Professor, Chemistry, MGA College, Vellore, 2000-. Publications: 13 papers in international journals with good impact factor; Presented papers in 19 conferences. Honours: Best Paper presentations, international conference; MSc Gold Medal; Best PhD Thesis Award, Gold Medal; BOYSCAST Fellowship, 2002; Tamil Nadu Young Women Scientist Award, 2003; National Best Teacher Award, 2011. Memberships: CRSI; TNSF; RUSAC. Address: HOD of Chemistry, MGA College, Otteri, Vellore, Tamil Nadu, 632002, India. E-mail: senthil_geetha@redeffmail.com

GEFFEN David, b. 21 February 1943, Brooklyn, New York, USA. Film, Recording and Theatre Executive. Career: Worked at William Morris talent agency, 1964; Launched new film studio with Steven Spielberg, Jeffrey Katzenberg; Co-founder (with Laura Nyro), Tunafish Music Publishing; Joined Ashley Famous Agency; Executive Vice-President, Creative Man, 1968; Co-founder (with Elliot Roberts), Asylum Records and Geffen-Roberts Manufacturing Company, 1970 (later merged with Elektra Records); Vice Chairman, Warner Brothers Pictures, 1975-76; Founder, Geffen Records, Geffen Film Company; Films produced include Little Shop Of Horrors; Beetlejuice; Men Don't Leave; Defending Your Life; Co-producer, musicals: Dreamgirls; Little Shop Of Horrors; Cats; Chess; Founder, DGC record label. Address: c/o Geffen Film Company, 9130 Sunset Boulevard, Los Angeles, CA 90069, USA.

GENEL (Guenel) Leonid Samooilovitch, b. 11 August 1946, Moscow, Russia. Materials Scientist. m. Galkina Valentina Vassilyevna. 2 sons. Education: Moscow Steels and Alloys Institute, 1964-69; Magistre Diploma, 1969; Moscow D I Mendeleev Chemical Processing Institute; Postgraduate Studies, 1976-79; DrPhil, 1980. Appointments: Engineer, Institute for Sources of Electrical Energy, 1972; Senior Engineer, Research Worker, Institute for Metal Protection from Corrosion, 1982; Chief of Sector, Chief of Department, NPO Polymerbyt, 1991; General Director, Spectroplast Ltd, 1991-. Publications: More than 100 publications including patents in the following fields: Mechanochemistry of gluing and treatment of surface of articles, for development of polymer based materials with new properties; Wave approach to the control strength and durability of solids and to making new materials; Formulations for heatmassexchange; Secondary cooling media (Antifreezes); Concentrates of additives: anti-corrosion, anti-scaling, controlling viscosity, decreasing foaming and freezing point; Compositions and packaging materials for keeping food stuffs fresh during more extended storage; The control cryoprotective and anticryoprotective properties of water in the temperature range from -60°C to +80°C. Philosophy and chemical physics of live matter as doctrines concerning: bioquanta and biozones, explaining some aspects of behaviour of living organisms' associations, including people's; origin of the alive from the lifeless; interdependence mass and space through acceleration of the Universe's expansion; language, creating the Universe, in which explanation of possibility of effect of expressions, being emitted by human, on the biozones and cosmic vacuum has been given. All main kinds of sounds (and corresponding to them letters) form 5 positions of tongue in larynx. Each position of the tongue generates signal of excitation in a concrete area of cerebral cortex. The excited area of cerebral cortex consists of hundred millions of cells with 46 (45) the alike DNA with chromosomes. At the excitation they sound as orchestra with electromagnetic (but not acoustic) instruments – DNA-bioquantum generators. Such electromagnetic waves as 'electromagnetic symphonies' being coherent and chiral are capable to reach the biozones and go out into the cosmic space and in certain way to structure it; Analogously (but not identically) sounds and the accumulation of nerve cells near the heart; The same approach is being used for the development a common language of biomagnetic nature, clear not only to each person on the Earth, but to all breathing creatures (maintaining the uniqueness of each creature in the biological, cultural, linguistic and world-outlook level). The opposing directed helix of DNA of life on the Earth is being considered as the derivative from DNA of the Universe, which is the idea and tool of development of the Universe. Honours: The Outstanding Scholar of the 20th Century Medal, IBC, 2000; The Leading Intellectual of the World Medal, IBC, 2004; The Top 100 Scientists Medal, IBC, 2005; The World Medal of Freedom, ABI, USA, 2005; The Laureate of All-Russian Exhibition Centre Medal; Title of Honorary Chemical Industry Worker, Russia. Memberships: Academician of Russian Academy of Sciences and Arts (RooAN); Academician of International Academy of Refrigeration (IAR). Address: 11, 2nd Vladimirskaya str, Moscow 111123, Russia. E-mail: lg@splast.ru Website: www.splast.ru

GENTIL MARTINS António, b. 10 July 1930, Lisbon, Portugal. Paediatric Surgeon; Plastic, Reconstructive and Aesthetic Surgeon. m. Maria Guilhermina Ivens Ferraz

Jardim, 3 sons, 5 daughters. Education: Medicine and Surgery, Lisbon's Medical Faculty, 1953; Pedagogical Sciences, Lisbon's Humanities Faculty, 1955; British Council Scholar for Paediatric Surgery, London and Liverpool, 1956/1959. Appointments: Head, Department of Surgery, Children's Hospital, D Estefania; Associate Professor, Paediatric Surgery, Faculty of Medical Sciences, New Lisbon's University; Temporary Counselor of WHO for Paediatric Oncology, 1976; Consultant Paediatric Surgeon, Dr Alfredo da Costa Maternity Hospital, Lisbon; Consultant Paediatric Surgeon, Paediatric Oncology Department, Portuguese Cancer Institute of Francisco Gentil, Lisbon. Publications: Co-author, 5 books; Invited Lecturer in 18 countries; More than 200 papers presented in 23 countries. Honours: Great Cross of the Order of Henry the Navigator; Grand Oficial da Ordem do Infante D Henrique, 1984; Gold Medal, Portuguese Ministry of Health, 2001; Medal of Honour, Ordem dos Médicos; Medal of Merit, King's Order of Our Lady of Vila Viçosa; Merit Award for Cancer Prevention; Honorary Member, SIOP and IPSO; Honorary Member, Intl Society of Aesthetic Plastic Surgery; Member Emeritus, Portuguese Academy of Medicine; Honorary Member, AMI; Honorary Member, CNAF; Honorary Member, MIL; Keys of Miami and Dale County, 1983; Professional of the Year, 2005; Medal of FEDRA. Memberships: National League Against Prostitution; Parents Association of Marqueza de Alorna Secondary School; IAC; League of Friends of the Hospital D Estefania; Acreditar; ICCCPO; President/Founder, Portuguese Society of Paediatric Surgeons; many others. Address: Av Almirante Reis 242, 4 Dto, 1000-057, Lisbon, Portugal. E-mail: agentilmartins@gmail.com

GEORGE Andrew Robert, b. 3 July 1955, Haslemere, Surrey, England. University Professor. m. Junko, 3 sons. Education: BA (1st Class Honours), University of Birmingham, 1976; PhD, 1985. Appointments: Teaching Assistant, 1983-85, Lecturer, Ancient Near Eastern Studies, 1985-94, Reader, Assyriology, 1994-2000, Professor, Babylonian, 2000-, Head, Department of Near and Middle East, 2001-04, School of Oriental and African Studies (SOAS), London; Honorary Research Fellow, Institute of Archaeology, University College, London, 1995-98; Honorary Lecturer, Institute of Archaeology, University College, London, 1998-2002; Visiting Professor, Seminar für Sprachen und Kulturen des vorderen Orients, Ruprecht-Karls-Universität, Heidelberg, Germany, 2000; Honorary Professor, Institute of Archaeology, University College, London, 2002-; Visiting Scholar, School of Historical Studies, Institute for Advanced Study, Princeton, New Jersey, 2004-05; Fellow, British Academy, 2006-. Publications: Babylonian Topographical Texts, 1992; House Most High. The Temples of Ancient Mesopotamia, 1993; The Epic of Gilgamesh, A Concise Dictionary of Akkadian, Wisdom, Gods and Literature. Studies in Assyriology in Honour of W G Lambert, 2000; The Babylonian Gilgamesh Epic. Introduction, Critical Edition and Cuneiform Texts, 2003; La epopeya de Gilgamesh (Spanish translation), 2004; Nineveh: Papers of the 49e Rencontre Assyriologique Internationale, London, 7-11 July 2003, 2005; Babylonian Literary Texts in the Schøyen Collection, 2009; Many articles in academic journals. Honours: Kuwait-British Fellowship Society Prize for Middle Eastern Studies, 2000. Memberships: Vice Chair, Treasurer, London Centre for the Ancient Near East, 2001-; Board, Norwegian Institute for Palaeography and Historical Philology, Oslo, 2003-; Patron, Enheduanna Society, 2003-; Kommission für das Akademie prokjekt Edition der Literarischen Keilschrifttexte aus Assur, Heidelberger Akademie der Wissenschaften, 2004-; Council, British Institute for the Study of Iraq, 2009-. Address: SOAS, University of London, Russell Square, London WC1H 0XG, England. E-mail: ag5@soas.ac.uk

GEORGE Porbeni, b. 3 March 1973, Oshogbo, Osun State, Nigeria. Maritime Transport. m. Elizabeth Buratu, 1 son, 1 daughter. Education: HND, Accountancy; Fellow, Certified Institute of Shipping of Nigeria; Master, Maritime Transport Management. Appointments: Group CEO, Porgeo Nig Ltd and Bulo Chartering & Marine Logistics Ltd, 2000-. Publications: Chartering Oil Tankers; New IMO Rule for Ship to Ship Operations; Ominous Challenges in Ship Chartering; A Guide to Accounting in the Current Shipping Market. Honours: Awards of Excellence in Shipping, 2011. Memberships: Full Gospel Businessman's Fellowship International; International Who's Who. Address: Suite 133, Block A2, Sura Complex, Simpson Street, Lagos Island, Lagos, Nigeria. E-mail: bullocharteringandmarine@gmail.com Website: www.bulocharteringandmarine.com

GEORGE Sanju, b. 9 February 1973. Consultant; Senior Research Fellow. m. Education: MBBS, MRCPscyh, St Johns Medical College, Bangalore, India, 1996; Specialist Training in Psychiatry, West Midlands Rotational Training Scheme, England, 1999-2005. Appointments: Consultant, Addiction Psychiatry, Birmingham and Solihull Mental Health NHS Foundation Trust, 2006-; Senior Research Fellow, Addiction Psychiatry, Birmingham and Solihull Mental Health NHS Trust, 2007-; Honorary Senior Lecturer, Addiction Psychiatry, University of Birmingham, 2008-. Publications: Over 80 scientific papers in international, peer-reviewed journals; Published poet. Honours: Hospital Doctor Award, 2007; Winner, National Guardian Public Services Award, 2008; Excellence Network Award, Community Care, 2008; BUPA Foundation Award for Patient Safety, 2008; 2 Health and Social Care Awards, 2008. Address: The Bridge, Larch Croft, Chelmsley Wood, Birmingham, B37 7UR, England. E-mail: sanju.george@bsmhft.nhs.uk

GEORGIEV Georgi Nikolov, b. 17 January 1957, Polikraishte, Bulgaria. Professor. Education: MS (Hons), Physics, University of Sofia "St Clement Okhridski", Sofia, Bulgaria, 1979; PhD, Microwave Physics, Institute of Electronics, Bulgarian Academy of Sciences, Sofia, 1987; Specialization, Institute of Communication and Computer Systems, National Technical University of Athens, Greece, 1996. Appointments: Assistant Professor, 1988-94, Associate Professor, 1994 -, Physics, University of Veliko Tirnovo "St St Cyril and Methodius", Veliko Tirnovo, Bulgaria; Visiting Professor, Democritus University of Thrace, Xanthi, Greece, 2004; Invited lecturer: Hungary, 1986; People's Republic of China, 1994; Greece, 1995, 1996, 2001, 2004, 2005, 2006, 2010, 2011; Belarus, 1995; Turkey 2001; Poland, 2003, 2004; UK, 2006; Georgia, 2009, 2010; Lithuania, 2010; Germany, 2010; Ukraine, 2010; Bulgaria, 2010; Member, Organizing Committees, First and Second Trans Black Sea Region Symposia on Applied Electromagnetism, Metsovo, Epirus, Greece, 1996 and Xanthi, Greece, 2000; Member of the Editorial Board, Journal of Applied Electromagnetism, Athens, Greece, 1997-; Member, Technical Programme Committee, European Conference on Antennas and Propagation Series, 2007 -, Edinburgh, Scotland, 2007, Berlin, Germany, 2009, Barcelona, Spain, 2010, Rome, Italy, 2011; Associate Editor, Journal of Applied Electromagnetism, Athens, Greece, 2009-; Member, Technical Committee, International Scientific Conference on Advanced Lightweight Structures and Reflector Antennas, Tbilisi, Georgia, 2009; Guest Editor, Special Issue, Journal of Applied Electromagnetism,

December 2010, Guest Editor, Special Issue, Journal of Applied Electromagnetism, June 2011; Member, DIPED, Lvov, Ukraine, 2011; Chairman, Member & invited Plenary Speaker, Scientific Symposium, Veliko Tirnovo, Bulgaria, 2011; Co-organiser, ICEAA, Turin, Italy, 2011; Co-organiser, IEEE APWC, Turin, Italy, 2011. Publications: More than 120 articles in professional journals and scientific conferences in physics; 1 book chapter; 2 invited plenary papers; 13 invited papers; Reviewer for several international scientific journals in USA, UK and Greece; Reviewer for international scientific conferences around the world. Honours: Winner, National Olympiade in Physics, Sofia, Bulgaria, 1974; Member, Bulgarian National Olympic Team, VIIth International Olympiade in Physics, Warsaw, Poland, 1974; Golden Medal and G Dimitrov's Stipendium, First Gymnasium "St St Cyril and Methodius", Veliko Tirnovo, 1974; Award, Minister of Education of Republic of Bulgaria, 1974; Honorary Speaker, Goce Delchev School for Reserve Officers, 1979; Honorary Speaker, University of Sofia St Clement Okhridski, 1980; Bulgarian Representative, East-West Workshop on Advanced Techniques in Electromagnets, Poland, 2004; Golden Medal, University of Veliko Tirnovo "St St Cyril and Methodius", 2006; Award for Contribution in the field of Science, 2011; Nomiated Honorary Citizen of the Municipality of Gorna Oriakhovitsa, 2011; Listed in international biographical dictionaries. Memberships: IEEE, MTT-S, AP-S, ED-S, Communications-Society; Trans Black Sea Region Union of Applied Electromagnetism, Athens, Greece; Chinese Institute of Electronics; Society of Photo-Optical Instrumentation Engineers; American Chemical Society; Electromagnetic Academy; IEEE Student Branches at University of Veliko Tirnovo and National Military University Vasil Levski, Veliko Tirnovo. Address: University Veliko Tirnovo "St St Cyril and Methodius", 2, St Theodosiy Tirnovski Str, Veliko Tirnovo, BG-5000 Bulgaria. E–mail: gngeorgiev@yahoo.com.

GEORGIEV Svetlin Georgiev, b. 5 April 1974, Rousse, Bulgaria. Mathematics; Researcher. 1 son. Education: Mathematics diplomate, 1997; PhD, Velino Tarnovo University, 2002; DSc, Germany, 2005. Appointments: Assistant Professor, Velino Tarnovo University, 1997-2002; Professor, Sofia University, 2002-. Publications: On the non autonomous n-competing species problem, 2001; On the uniformly continuity of the solution map for two dimensional wave maps, 2003; Blow up of the solutions of nonlinear wave equation, 2004; Blow-up of the solutions on nonlinear wave equation in Reissner-Nordstrom metric, 2006; Blow-up of the solutions of nonlinear wave equation, 2007; Positive periodic solutions of the nonlinear parabolic equation, 2007. Honours: Listed in international biographical dictionaries. Memberships: American Mathematical Society; Reviewer of mathematical reviews. Address: Str Iondola 2, Entrance 2, Floor 4, Rousse 7005, Bulgaria. E-mail: sgg2000bg@yahoo.com

GEORGIEV Viden, b. 1 February 1925, Gintsi, Sofia Region, Bulgaria. Physician. m. Elena Kisselkova, 1 son, 1 daughter. Education: Doctor of Medicine, Medical University, Sofia, Bulgaria, 1954; Doctor of Philosophy, Institute of Experimental Medicine, Saint Petersburg, Russia, 1962. Appointments: Assistant, 1955-58, Senior Assistant, 1959-63, Associate Professor, 1967-75, Professor of Physiology, 1975-, National Sports Academy, Sofia, Bulgaria; Researcher, Sorbonne, Paris, France, 1964-66. Publications: Author: Proprioceptors and Circulation, (monograph), 1965; Vascular Reactions in Sportsmen after Physical Efforts (monograph), 1973; Nervous System and Sport (book), 1975; Peripheral and Brain Circulation at Physical Efforts (monograph), 1991. Memberships: Bulgarian Society of Physiological Sciences; Bulgarian Society of Sports Medicine; New York Academy of Sciences; National movement for development and protections of the science and higher education. Address: 14 Tsar Peter Street, Sofia 1463, Bulgaria.

GEORGIEVA-TRIFONOVA Tsvetanka, b. 29 June 1974, Gorna Oryahovitsa, Bulgaria. Assistant Professor. m. Tihomir Trifonov, 1 son. Education: MSc, Mathematics and Informatics, 1997; PhD, Computer Science, 2009, St Cyril and St Methodius, University of Veliko Tarnovo. Appointments: Assistant Professor, Department of Information Technologies, St Cyril and St Methodius, University of Veliko Tarnovo, 1999-. Publications: Numerous articles in professional journals. Honours: Editorial Board Member, International Journal of Knowledge-Based Organisations; Listed in international biographical dictionaries. Memberships: Bulgarian Union of Automation and Informatics; Union of Bulgarian Mathematicians; Ithea International Scientific Society; International Association of Engineers; International Society for Environmental Information Sciences; Institute of Advanced Scientific Research. Address: St Cyril and St Methodius, University of Veliko Tarnovo, 3 Arc Georgi Kozarev Str, Veliko Tarnovo, Bulgaria. E-mail: cv.georgieva@uni-vt.bg

GERSTENKORN Tadeusz, b. 7 February 1927, Łódź, Poland. Professor of Mathematics. m. Zofia Szwalm, 1 son, 2 daughters. Education: Master of Philosophy, 1951, Master of Mathematics, 1952, University of Łódź; Doctorate in Mathematics, 1961; Doctor Habil of Mathematics with specialisation in probability theory, 1983. Appointments: Teacher, Mathematics, vocational schools, Łódź, 1949-51; Lecturer, Logic, State Higher Pedagogical School, Łódź, 1951-52; Assistant, Mathematics, Technical University of Łódź, 1952-61; Assistant Professor, Institute of Mathematics, 1961-84, Associate Professor, Institute/Faculty of Mathematics, 1984-97, Łódź University; Member, Group of Mathematical Applications in Basic and Clinical Researches of the Committee of the Basic Sciences in Medicine, Polish Academy of Sciences, 1987-90; Supervisor of scientific grant, Application of the Fuzzy Set Theory to Medical Diagnostics and Therapy, Polish State Committee of Scientific Researches, Warsaw, 1996-2002; Professor, Mathematics, Academy of Management, Łódź, 1997-2001; Professor, Mathematics, University of Trade, Łódź, 2001-07; Professor, Mathematics, Demography and Statistics, Toruń Academy of Social and Media Culture, Toruń, 2004-10. Publications: 10 editions of academic handbooks; 120 papers on Probability Theory, Statistics and Fuzzy Set Theory with Applications in Medicine; 2 books translated; Around 200 articles in Polish social and culture journals. Honours: Golden Cross of Merit, 1973; Golden Award of Łódź University, 1979; Medal of Łódź University in Service of Society and Science, 1982; Knight Cross of Order of Revival of Poland, 1983; Listed in international biographical dictionaries. Memberships: Polish Mathematical Society; Polish Statistical Society; Polish Philosophical Society; Catholic Association of Journalists. Address: ul Inżynierska 8, Łódź, PL 93-569, Poland. E-mail: tadger@math.uni.lodz.pl

GHIMIRE Jhamak, b. 5 July 1980, Kachide, Dhankuta, Nepal. Writer. Education: Self study. Appointments: Writer. Publications: 11 books including: Jiwan Kanda Ki Phool; Several articles in key newspapers and magazines. Honours: Madan Puraskar Award; Padma Shree Award, Shankar Lamichhane Essay Award; Uttam Peace Award; Gorkha Dakshin Bahu; Several other renowned awards. Memberships: Patron, Jhamak Ghimire Literary Foundation; Honorary member, Gunjan Literary Agency and Disabled Service Organisation. Address: Kachide, Dhankuta Municipality, Ward No 3, Nepal. E-mail: ghimirejhamak@gmail.com

GHIYA Bhanulal, b. 18 May 1934, Dhoraji (Gujarat State), India. Professor of Organic Chemistry. m. Usha Dhabalia, 1 daughter (deceased). Education: BSc, 1956, PhD, 1964, MSc, Organic Chemistry, 1958, Nagpur University. Appointments: Lecturer in Chemistry, V M V Amravati, 1958-83; Reader, Organic Chemistry, Institute of Science, 1983-94; Principal, S M Science College, Nagpur, 1994-95; Emeritus Professor, 1995-. Publications: Over 70 research papers in Indian and foreign journals; Text Book of Chemistry for Standard XI, XII, BSc I, II, III; Guided 24 PhD students. Honour: Nagpur University Gold Medal, 1958; DSVC Gold Medal, 1964. Memberships: Life Member, Indian Science Congress Association; Indian Cancer Society. Address; 23, B-1, Vrindavan Apts, 173, Civil Lines, Nagpur 440001, India.

GHODS Ahad J, b. 30 May 1941, Tabriz, Iran. Professor. m. Rouhangiz Sayed, 1 son, 1 daughter. Education: Tabriz University School of Medicine, 1960-67; Residency in Internal Medicine, and Fellowship in Nephrology, USA, 1972-77. Appointments: Medical & Public Health Service in Rural Areas of East Azerbaijan, Iran, 1967-71; Attending Nephrologist, Beh Avar Kidney Center, Tehran, 1977-79; Chief, Division of Nephrology, Department of Internal Medicine, Iran University of Medical Sciences, Tehran, 1979-; Program Director for Nephrology Fellowship, 1989-, Professor and Chairman, Division of Nephrology & Transplantation Unit, Hashemi Nejad Kidney Hospital, Iran University of Medical Sciences. Publications: Numerous articles in professional journals. Honours: Ranked first among all high school graduates of the State, 1960; Ranked first in all academic years of medical school, 1967; Ranked first as investigator of the year, Ministry of Health and Medical Education, Iran, 2001; 3rd prize, Avicena Research Festival, 2006; Listed in international biographical dictionaries. Memberships: Iranian Society of Nephrology; Iranian Society of Internal Medicine; Iranian Society of Organ Transplantation; European Renal Association; International Society of Nephrology; American College of Physicians; American Society of Internal Medicine; Middle East Society for Organ Transplantation; The Transplantation Society. Address: Hashemi Nejad Kidney Hospital, Iran University of Medical Sciences, Vanak Square, 19697, Tehran, Iran. E-mail: ahad.ghods@gmail.com

GIACCONI Riccardo, b. 6 October 1931, Genoa, Italy (US Citizen). Astrophysicist. m. Mirella Manaira, 1957, 1 son, 2 daughters. Education: Doctorate, University of Milan, 1954. Appointments: Assistant Professor of Physics, University of Milan, 1954-56; Research Associate, Indiana University, 1956-58; Research Associate, Princeton University, 1958-59; American Science and Engineering Inc, 1958-73; Associate, Harvard College Observatory, 1970-72; Associate Director, Center for Astrophysics, 1973-81; Professor of Astrophysics, Harvard University, 1973-81; Professor of Astrophysics, 1981-99, Research Professor, 1999-, Johns Hopkins University; Director, Space Telescope Science Institute, Baltimore, 1981-92; Professor of Astrophysics, Milan University, Italy, 1991-99; Director General, European Southern Observatory, Garching, Germany, 1993-99; President, Associated Universities Inc, 1999-; Carried out fundamental investigations in the development of x-ray astronomy. Publications X-Ray Astronomy (co-editor), 1974; Physics and Astrophysics of Neutron Stars and Black Holes (co-editor), 1978; A Face of Extremes; The X-ray Universe (co-editor), 1985; Numerous articles in professional journals. Honours: Space Science Award, AIAA, 1976; NASA Medal for Exceptional Scientific Achievement, 1980; Gold Medal, Royal Astronomical Society, 1982; A Cressy Morrison Award in Natural Sciences, New York Academy of Sciences, 1982; Wolf Prize, 1987; Laurea hc in Physics, Rome, 1998; Nobel Prize in Physics, 2002; National Medal of Science, 2003; Numerous other awards. Memberships: American Academy of Arts and Sciences; American Astronomical Society; American Physical Society; Italian Physical Society; International Astronomical Union; Max Planck Society; Foreign member, Accademia Nazionale dei Lincei. Address: Associated Universities Inc, 1400 16th Street, NW, Suite 730, Washington, DC 20036, USA.

GIAMALAKI Melpomeni, b. 18 March 1976, Athens, Greece. Researcher. Education: Physics Department, University of Crete, 2001; PhD, School of Electrical and Computer Engineering, National Technical University of Athens, 2009. Appointments: Researcher, Microwave and Fibre Optics Laboratory, School of Electrical and Computer Engineering, National Technical University of Athens, 2002-; Researcher, PENED 2003, 2006-09. Publications: 10 articles in international journals and international conference proceedings. Honours: Listed in international biographical dictionaries. Address: 6 Rimini str, Filothei 15237, Athens, Greece. E-mail: melina@esd.ece.ntua.gr Website: http://mfol.ece.ntua.gr/cvs/melpomeni_giamalaki.pdf

GIANNINI Mirella, b. 1 March 1948, Bari, Italy. Sociologist. Education: Degree, Political Sciences, ThD, Political Sciences, University of Bari, 1971. Appointments: Junior Research Assistant, Sociology, University di Bari, 1972; Senior Research Assistant, Sociology, 1974-81; Adjunct Professor, Sociology, 1978-89; Lecturer, Sociology, 1981-94; Associate Professor, University of Paris X Nanterre, 1990-91; Maison de Science de l'Homme, Paris, 1992; Lecturer, Sociology of Public Administration, University di Napoli Federico II, 1994-2000; Professor, Sociology of Post-Industrial Work, Gender Statistics and Communication d'Entreprise, 2001-, University de Napoli Federico II; Visiting Professor, University of California at Berkeley, 1998; Visiting Researcher, University of Califonia, Riverside, and Gotenborg, Sweden. Publications: Editorial Board, Economia & Lavoro, Knowledge, Work & Soc/Savoirs, Travail et Société; Editor, Edizioni Dedalo. Memberships: Fondazione Brodolini; Italian Sociological Association; International Sociology Association. Address: University of Naples Federico II, Department of Sociology, Vico Monte della Pietà 1, Naples, 80138, Italy. E-mail: migianni@unina.it Website: www.dipsociologia.unina.it/docenti/giannini.htm

GIBB Barry Alan Crompton, b. 1 September 1946, Douglas, Isle Of Man, England. Singer; Songwriter. m. Linda Gray, 1 Sept 1970, 4 sons, 1 daughter. Career: Formed The Bee Gees, with brothers Robin and Maurice, 1958-69; Reformed group, 1971; Appeared on own weekly television show, Australia; Returned to England; Signed with NEMS Enterprises, 1967; Performed live with Barbra Streisand, One Voice Concert/Video, 1987; Compositions: Co-writer (with brothers), Saturday Night Fever soundtrack, 1977 (40 million copies sold); Producer, co-writer, albums for: Andy Gibb; Barbra Streisand: Guilty; Dionne Warwick: Heartbreaker; Diana Ross: Eaten Alive; Kenny Rogers: Eyes That See In The Dark; Second most Top Ten hits written (after Lennon and McCartney); 5 simultaneous US Top Ten hits written by the Gibb brothers, 1978; Only artists to write and produce 6 consecutive Number 1 singles, 1979;

Producer, writer, Grease, for Frankie Valli; Bee Gees songs recorded by artists including: Boyzone, Take That, Steps, 911, Tina Turner, Celine Dion, Elton John, Eric Clapton, Elvis Presley; Janis Joplin; Andy Williams; Glen Campbell; Rod Stewart; Roberta Flack; Frankie Valli; Michael Bolton; Saturday Night Fever musical stage show opens at London Palladium 1998, Broadway (October 1999), Sydney (March 2000), as well as Cologne, Germany and Japan. Sell-out stadium concerts in Dublin, Wembley Stadium, London, Buenos Aires, South Africa, 1998; Stadium concerts, New Zealand, new Olympic stadium in Sydney, 1999; Millennium Eve concert, South Florida, 1999; 6 shows in Europe planned for 2000. Recordings: Albums include: Bee Gees 1st, 1967; Horizontal And Idea, 1968; Odessa, 1969; Cucumber Castle, 1971; Two Years On, 1971; Trafalgar, 1972; Life In A Tin Can, 1973; Mr Natural, 1974; Main Course, 1975; Children Of The World, 1976; Here At Last...Live, 1976; Saturday Night Fever, 1977; Spirits Having Flown, 1978; Greatest Hits, 1979; Living Eyes, 1980; ESP, 1988; One, 1989; The Very Best Of The Bee Gees, 1990; Tales From The Brothers Gibb (A History In Song 1967-90), 1990; High Civilisation, 1991; You Wouldn't Know, 1992; Size Isn't Everything, 1993; Solo: Now Voyager, 1984; Hawks, 1988; Still Waters, 1997; One Night Only, live album 1998. Singles include: Alone. Honours include: 7 Grammy Awards; Inducted into Songwriters Hall Of Fame; Inducted in Rock and Roll Hall of Fame, Cleveland; Lifetime Achievement Award, Brit Awards, London; International Artist Award, American Music Awards, Los Angeles. Memberships: Musicians' Union; Equity. Current Management: Left Bank Organization, 9255 Sunset Boulevard, 2nd Floor, Los Angeles, CA 90069, USA. Address: c/o 1801 Bay Road, Miami Beach, FL 33139, USA.

GIBSON Mel, b. 3 January 1956, Peekshill, New York, USA. Actor; Producer. m. Robyn Moore, divorced, 5 sons, 1 daughter, 1 daughter with Oksana Grigorieva. Education: National Institute for Dramatic Art, Sydney. Career: Founder, ICONS Productions; Actor, films include: Summer City; Mad Max, Tim, 1979; Attack Force Z; Gallipoli, 1981; The Road Warrior (Mad Max II), 1982; The Year of Living Dangerously, 1983; The Bounty, The River, Mrs Soffel, 1984; Mad Max Beyond the Thunderdome, 1985; Lethal Weapon; Tequila Sunrise; Lethal Weapon II; Bird on a Wire, 1989; Hamlet, 1990; Air America, 1990; Lethal Weapon III, 1991; Man Without a Face (also director), 1992; Maverick, 1994; Braveheart (also director, co-producer), 1995; Ransom, 1996; Conspiracy Theory, Payback, 1997; Lethal Weapon 4, 1998; The Million Dollar Hotel, 1999; The Patriot, What Women Want, 2000; We Were Soldiers, Signs, 2002; The Singing Detective, 2003; Paparazzi, 2004; Payback: Straight Up – The Director's Cut, 2006; Edge of Darkness, 2010. Plays include: Romeo and Juliet; Waiting for Godot; No Names No Pack Drill; Death of a Salesman. Honours include: Commandeur, Ordre des Arts et des Lettres; 2 Academy Awards, Best Director and Best Actor, Braveheart, 1996; Golden Globe Award, Best Director, Braveheart, 1996. Address: c/o ICONS Productions, 4000 Warner Boulevard, Room 17, Burbank, CA 91522, USA.

GIBSON OF MARKET RASEN, Baroness of Market Rasen in the County of Lincolnshire, Anne Gibson, b. 10 December 1940, United Kingdom. m. (1) John Donald Gibson, 1 daughter, (2) John Bartell, 1 stepdaughter. Education: BA, University of Essex. Appointments: Full-time Organiser, Labour Party, Saffron Walden, 1965-70; Researcher, House Magazine (journal of Houses of Parliament), 1975-77; Party Candidate, Labour, Bury St Edmunds, 1979; Assistant, Assistant Secretary and Deputy Head of Organisation and Industrial Relations Department, TUC, 1977-87; National Officer Amicus, with special responsibility for voluntary sector and equal rights sections, 1987-96, policy and political work, 1996-2000; Member: General Council, TUC, 1989-2000; Trade Union Sustainable Development Committee; Department of Employment Advisory Group on Older Workers, 1993-96; Board, Bilbao Agency, 1996-2000; Parliamentary and Scientific Committee; Labour Party: NEC Women's Committee, 1990-98, National Constitutional Committee, 1997-2000, Labour Party Policy Reform, 1998-2000; Subcommittees in the House of Lords: Foreign and Commonwealth Affairs Group, Home Affairs Group, Defence Group; Member, BBC Charter Review Group; Equal Opportunities Commissioner, 1991-98, Health and Safety Commissioner, 1996-2000; Member All-Party Parliamentary Groups: Adoption, Brazil, Bullying at Work, Arts and Heritage, Asbestos Sub-Committee, Asthma, BBC, Breast Cancer, Children, Countryside, Fibromualgia, Insurance and Financial Services, Latin America, Rail Freight, Safety and Health, Sex Equality, TU(nion) Group of MP's, Wildlife Protection, World Government. Publications: Numerous TUC and MSF equal opportunities booklets including: Disability and Employer – A Trade Union Guide, 1989; Charter of Equal Opportunities for 1990's, 1990; Lesbian and gay Rights in Employment, 1990; recruitment of Women Workers, 1990; Part-time Workers Rights, 1991; Sexual Harassment at Work, 1993; Caring – A Union Issue, 1993; Women in MSF, 1991. Honours: OBE, 1998; Life Peer, 2000. Memberships: Chair, Andrea Adams Trust, 2002-2004; President, RoSPA; Chair, DTI Dignity at Work Group; Fawcett Society; Fabian Society. Address: House of Lords, London SW1A 0PW, England.

GIDDENS Anthony, Baron Giddens of Southgate in the London Borough of Enfield, b. 18 January 1938. University Administrator; Sociologist. m. Jane M Ellwood, 1963. Education: Hull University; London School of Economics; Cambridge University. Appointments: Lecturer, late Reader, Sociology, University of Cambridge, 1969-85; Professor of Sociology, 1985-97; Fellow, King's College, 1969-96; Director, London School of Education, 1997-2003. Publications: Over 34 books and 200 articles including: Capitalism and Modern Social Theory, 1971; Ed, Sociology of Suicide, 1972; Politics and Sociology in the Thought of Max Weber, 1972; Editor and translator, Emile Durkheim: Selected Writings, 1972; Ed, Positivism and Sociology, 1974; New Rules of Sociological Method, 1976; Studies in Social and Political Theory, 1976; Central Problems in Social Theory, 1979; Class Structure of the Advanced Societies (2nd editor), 1981; Contemporary Critique of Historical Materialism (vol 1), Power, Property and State, 1981, (vol 2) Nation, State and Violence, 1985; Jointly, Classes, Power and Conflict, 1982; Profiles and Critiques in Social Theory, 1983; Joint editor, Social Class and the Division of Labour, 1983; Constitution of Society, 1984; Social Theory and Modern Sociology, 1987; Joint editor, Social Theory Today, 1987; Sociology, 1989; The Consequences of Modernity, 1990; Modernity and Self-Identity, 1991; The Transformation of Intimacy, 1992; Beyond Right and Left, 1994; In Defence of Sociology, 1996; Third Way, 1998; Over to You, Mr Brown – How Labour Can Win Again, 2007. Honours include: Prince of Asturias Award, Spain, 2002; Life Peerage, 2004; Member, House of Lords. Address: London School of Economics, Houghton Street, London, WC2A 2AE, England.

GIELEN Uwe Peter, b. 15 August 1940, Berlin, Germany. Professor of Psychology. Education: MA, Psychology, Wake Forest University, 1968; PhD, Social Psychology, Harvard University, USA, 1976. Appointments: Assistant Professor of Psychology, City University of New York,

1977-80; Associate Professor, 1980-87, Professor, 1987-, Chairman, 1980-90, Director, Institute for International and Cross-Cultural Psychology, 1998-, St Francis College, New York, USA. Publications: 18 books; 170 other publications; Editor-in-Chief, World Psychology, 1995-97, International Journal of Group Tensions, 1997-2002; Co-editor, Psychology in the Arab Countries; International Perspectives on Human Development; The Family and Family Therapy in International Perspective; Cross-Cultural Topics in Psychology; Migration: Immigration and Emigration in International Perspective; Handbook of Culture, Therapy and Healing; Families in Global Perspective; Childhood and Adolescence; Violence in Schools: Cross-National and Cross-Cultural Perspectives, 2005; Toward a Global Psychology: Theory, Research, Intervention and Pedagogy, 2007; Principles of Multicultural Counseling and Therapy, 2008. Honours: Kurt Lewin Award, 1993, Wilhelm Wundt Award, 1999, New York State Psychological Association; Distinguished International Psychologist Award, International Psychology Division, American Psychological Association, 2005. Memberships: Fellow, American Psychological Association; Fellow, American Psychological Society; Fellow, New York Academy of Sciences; Fellow, Eastern Psychological Association; President, International Council of Psychologists, 1994-95; President, Society for Cross-Cultural Research, 1998-99; President, International Psychology Division, American Psychological Association, 2008. Address: Department of Psychology, St Francis College, Brooklyn, NY 11201, USA. E-mail: ugielen@hotmail.com

GIFFORD Zerbanoo, b. 11 May 1950, India. Foundation Director. m. Richard Gifford, 2 sons. Education: Roedean School; Watford College of Technology; London School of Journalism; BA Honours, Open University. Appointments: Director ASHA Foundation; National Endowment of Science, Technology and Arts Fellowship; Adviser to Rt. Hon. Jack Straw on Community Relations at the Home Office; Director Anti-Slavery International. Publications: The Golden Thread – Asian Experiences in Post Raj Britain; Thomas Clarkson and the Campaign Against Slavery; Dadabhai Naoroji – The 1st Asian MP; Celebrating India; Asian Presence in Europe; Confessions to a Serial Womaniser – the Secrets of the World's Inspirational Women. Honours: Nehru Centenary Award for international work championing the cause of women and children; Freedom of City of Lincoln, Nebraska for work against all forms of slavery and racism; International Woman of the Year for Humanitarian Work, 2006; The Splendour Award, celebrating India's 60th anniversary of Independence. Address: 4 Dean Rise, Dean Road, Newnham on Severn, Gloucestershire, GL14 1AB, England. E-mail: zerbanoogifford@hotmail.com www.zerbanoogifford.org

GIGGS Ryan, b. 29 November 1973, Cardiff, Wales. Footballer. m. Stacey Cooke, 2007, 1 son, 1 daughter. Career: Professional football player, Manchester United. Honours include: First player to win two consecutive PFA Young Player of the Year Awards, 1992, 1993; Only player to have played and scored in every single season of the Premier League; OBE, 2007; Honorary Master of Arts, Salford University, 2008; First footballer to collect 11 top division English league title medals, 2009; BBC Sports Personality of the Year, 2009; PFA Player of the Year, 2009; Freedom of the City of Salford, 2010.

GIL David Georg, b. 16 March 1924, Vienna, Austria. Emeritus Professor; Author. m. Eva Breslauer, 2 August 1947, 2 sons. Education: Certificate in Psychotherapy with Children, Israeli Society for Child Psychiatry, 1952; Diploma in Social Work, School of Social Work, 1953, BA, 1957, Hebrew University, Jerusalem, Israel; MSW, 1958, DSW, 1963, University of Pennsylvania. Appointment: Professor, Emeritus Professor, 2011-, Social Policy, Brandeis University. Publications: Violence Against Children, 1970; Unravelling Social Policy, 1973, 5th edition, 1992; The Challenge of Social Equality, 1976; Beyond the Jungle, 1979; Child Abuse and Violence (editor), 1979; Toward Social and Economic Justice (editor with Eva Gil), 1985; The Future of Work (editor with Eva Gil), 1987; Confronting Injustice and Oppression, 1998, Korean translation, 2007; Confronting Injustice and Oppression (German translation), 2006; Contributions to: Over 50 articles to professional journals, book chapters, book reviews. Honours: Leadership in Human Services, Brandeis University, Heller School, 1999; Social Worker of the Year, National Association of Social Workers, Massachusetts, 2000; Mentoring Award, Brandeis University, Heller School, 2005; Presidential Award, Council on Social Work Education, 2006; Noam Chomsky Award, Justice Studies Association, 2008. Memberships: National Association of Social Workers; American Orthopsychiatric Association; Association of Humanist Sociology; Justice Studies Association. Address: 1010 Waltham St Apt B445, Lexington, MA 02421-8044, USA.

GILBERT Anthony, b. 26 July 1934, London, England. 2 sons, 1 daughter. Composer. Education: MA, DMus, University of Leeds; Composition with Anthony Milner, Mátyás Seiber, Alexander Goehr and Gunther Schuller; Conducting with Lawrence Leonard, Morley College, London. Career: Lecturer in Composition, Goldsmiths College, 1968-73; Composer in Residence, University of Lancaster, 1970-71; Lecturer in Composition, Morley College, 1972-75; Senior Lecturer in Composition, Sydney Conservatorium, Australia, 1978-79; Composer in Residence, City of Bendigo, Victoria, 1981; Senior Tutor in Composition, Royal Northern College of Music, 1973-96; Head of School of Composition and Contemporary Music, Royal Northern College of Music, 1996-99. Compositions: Operas: The Scene-Machine, The Chakravaka-Bird; Orchestra: Symphony; Sinfonia; Ghost and Dream Dancing; Crow Cry; Towards Asávari; On Beholding a Rainbow; Sheer; Dance Concerto; Wind orchestra: Dream Carousels; Chamber: 5 string quartets; Saxophone Quartet; Quartet of Beasts; Nine or Ten Osannas; Vasanta With Dancing; Palace of the Winds; Instrumental: Ziggurat; Reflexions, Rose Nord; Moonfaring; Dawnfaring; 3 Piano Sonatas; Spell Respell; The Incredible Flute Music; Treatment of Silence; Osanna for Lady O; Farings; Stars; Rose luisante; Vocal: Certain Lights Reflecting; Love Poems; Inscapes; Long White Moonlight; Beastly Jingles; Vers de Lune; Encantos; Music Theatre: Upstream River Rewa. Recordings: Os; Moonfaring; Beastly Jingles; Nine or Ten Osannas; Towards Asávari; Dream Carousels; Igorochki; Quartet of Beasts; Six of the Bestiary; Another Dream Carousel; Quartets Number 3 and 4; Farings; On Beholding a Rainbow; Certain Lights Reflecting; … into the Gyre of a Madder Dance; Unrise; Those Fenny Bells; Doubles; Ondine; En Bateau; all piano works; Reflexions; Rose Nord. Honours: Fellow of Royal Northern College of Music, 1981; Listed in national and international biographical dictionaries. Memberships: Performing Right Society; Mechanical Copyright Protection Society; British Academy of Songwriters, Composers and Authors; Incorporated Society of Musicians. Address: 4 Oak Brow Cottages, Altrincham Road, Styal, Wilmslow, Cheshire SK9 4JE, England.

GILBERT Robert Andrew, b. 6 October 1942, Bristol, England. Antiquarian Bookseller; Editor; Writer. m. Patricia Kathleen Linnell, 1970, 3 sons, 2 daughters. Education: BA, Honours, Philosophy, Psychology, University of Bristol,

1964; PhD, School of Advanced Study, Institute of English Studies, University of London, 2009. Appointment: Editor, Ars Quatuor Coronatorum, 1994-2000; Editor, The Christian Parapsychologist, 2009-. Publications: The Golden Dawn: Twilight of the Magicians, 1983; A E Waite: A Bibliography, 1983; The Golden Dawn Companion, 1986; A E Waite: Magician of Many Parts, 1987; The Treasure of Montsegur (with W N Birks), 1987; Elements of Mysticism, 1991; World Freemasonry: An Illustrated History, 1992; Freemasonry: A Celebration of the Craft (J M Hamill), 1992; Casting the First Stone, 1993; Editor with M A Cox: The Oxford Book of English Ghost Stories, 1986; Victorian Ghost Stories: An Oxford Anthology, 1991; The Golden Dawn Scrapbook, 1997; Editor, The House of the Hidden Light, 2003. Contributions to: Ars Quatuor Coronatorum; Avallaunius; Christian Parapsychologist; Dictionary of National Biography; Dictionary of 19th Century British Scientists; Dictionary of Gnosis and Western Esotericism; Gnosis; Hermetic Journal; Cauda Pavonis; Yeats Annual. Memberships: Society of Authors; Librarian, Supreme Council for England and Wales (A&A Rite); Prestonian Lecturer, United Grand Lodge of England, 1997. Address: 215 Clevedon Road, Tickenham, Clevedon, North Somerset, BS21 6RX.

GILBERT Virginia, b. 19 December 1946, Elgin, Illinois, USA. Associate Professor of English; Poet; Writer. Education: BA, English, Iowa Wesleyan College, 1969; MFA, Creative Writing and Poetry, University of Iowa, 1971; PhD, Creative Writing, Poetry and English, University of Nebraska, 1991. Appointments: Instructor, College of Lake County, Illinois, 1979; Teaching Fellow, Creative Writing, University of Nebraska, 1984-87; Assistant Professor, 1990-92, Associate Professor, 1992-2001, Professor, 2001-07, Department of English, Alabama A&M University; Retired, 2007. Publications: To Keep at Bay the Hounds, 1985; The Earth Above, 1993. That Other Brightness, 1996. Contributions to: Anthologies: Wordlens, Ordinary and Sacred as Blood, Claiming the Spirit Within: A Source Book of Women's Poetry; Journals, reviews, and quarterlies. Honours: National Endowment for the Arts Fellowship, 1976-77; 2nd Place, Hackney Awards, 1990; 1st Place, Sakura Festival Haiku Contest, 1992; Fulbright Fellow to China, 1993; Nominated Book of the Year, Alabama Poetry Society, 1995 1st Place Alabama State Poetry Society's Poetry Slam, 1998; Alabama Poet of the Year, 2001; Alumni Achievement Award, 2006; Alabama State Council on the Arts Individual Artist Grant in Literature, 2009-10. Memberships: Modern Language Association; Association of Writers and Writing Programs; Poets & Writers Inc; Poetry Society of America; Academy of American Poets; International Women's Writing Guild; International League of American Pen Women; Huntsville Photographic Society; Huntsville Literary Association. Address: 125 Horseshoe Bend S, Madison, AL 35758, USA E-mail: vgpoet@aol.com

GILBERT Walter, b. 21 March 1932, Boston, Massachusetts, USA. Molecular Biologist. m. Celia Stone, 1953, 1 son, 1 daughter. Education: Graduated, Physics, Harvard University, 1954; Doctorate in Mathematics, Cambridge University, 1957. Appointments: National Science Foundation Fellow, 1957-58; Lecturer, Research Fellow, 1958-59, Professor of Biophysics, 1964-68, Professor of Molecular Biology, 1969-72, American Cancer Society Professor of Molecular Biology, 1972, Harvard University; Devised techniques for determining the sequence of bases in DNA. Honours: US Steel Foundation Award in Molecular Biology (NAS), 1968; Joint Winner, Ledlie Prize, Harvard University, 1969; Joint winner, Warren Triennial Prize, Massachusetts General Hospital, 1977; Louis and Bert Freedman Award, New York Academy of Sciences, 1977; Joint winner, Prix Charles-Léopold Mayer, Académie des Sciences, Institute de France, 1977; Harrison Howe Award of the Rochester branch of the American Chemical Society, 1978; Joint winner, Louisa Gross Horowitz Prize, Columbia University, 1979; Gairdner Foundation Annual Award 1979; Joint winner, Albert Lasker Basic Medical Research Award, 1979; Joint winner, Prize for Biochemical Analysis, German Society for Clinical Chemistry, 1980; Sober Award, American Society of Biological Chemists, 1980; Joint Winner, Nobel Prize for Chemistry, 1980; New England Entrepreneur of the Year Award, 1991; Ninth National Biotechnology Ventures Award, 1997. Memberships: Foreign member, Royal Society; NAS; American Physical Society; American Society of Biological Chemists; American Academy of Arts and Sciences. Address: Biological Laboratories, 16 Divinity Avenue, Cambridge, MA 02138, USA.

GILFANOV Marat, b. 18 July 1962, Kazan, USSR. Astrophysicist. m. Marina Gilfanova, 1 daughter. Education: Diploma Physics, Moscow Physical-Technical Institute, 1985; PhD, Physics, Space Research Institute, Moscow, 1989; Doctor of Physics and Mathematics, Space Research Institute, Moscow, 1996. Appointments: Junior Scientist, Space Research Institute, Moscow, 1985-88; Scientist, 1988-91; Senior Scientist, 1991-; Leading Scientist, 1996-; Max-Planck-Institut für Astrophysik, Garching, Germany, 1996-. Publications: Over 300 in international scientific journals. Honours: COSPAR, Commission E Zeldovich medal, 1992; Professor of Astrophysics, High Commission of the Ministry of Science and Education of Russian Federation, 2010. Memberships: COSPAR, Commission E; International Astronomical Union, 1994-; Scientific Council of Space Research Institute, 1997-; Wissenschaftlicher Institutsrat, Max-Planck-Institut für Astrophysik. Address: Max-Planck-Institut für Astrophysik, Karl-Schwarzschild-Str 1, 85741 Garching, Germany.

GILL Sir Ben, b. 1 January 1950. Company Director. m. Carolyn Davis, 4 sons. Education: Barnard Castle School, Co Durham, 1960-67; General Agriculture degree, St John's College, Cambridge, 1968-71. Appointments: Worked on family farm, North Yorkshire, 1971; Teacher of science and agriculture, Namasagali College, Uganda, East Africa, 1972-75; Ran 200 sow pig unit, Holderness, East Yorkshire, 1975-77; Family farming business, North Yorkshire, 1978-; Chairman, English Apples & Pears Ltd, 2007-; Managing Director, The Hawk Creative Business Park Ltd, 2007-; Non-Executive Director, 2008-, Chairman, 2009, Eden Research plc; Trustee, John Innes Foundation, 2010-; Chairman, Meriton Developments Ltd, 2011-; Chairman, Visit Herefordshire, 2011-. Honours: CBE, 1996; Visiting Professorship, Department of Biology, Leeds University, 1996; Fellow, Royal Agricultural Society, 1997; Honorary DSc, Leeds University, 1997; Fellow, Institute of Grocery Distribution, 1998; Honorary DSc, Cranfield University, 2000; Honorary DSc, University of West England, 2002; Honorary D, Civil Law University of East Anglia, 2003. Memberships: Parent Governor, Easingwold County Primary School, 1982-88; Member, Vice Chairman, 1985-86, NFU National Marketing Committee, 1984-87; Member, NFU National Council, 1985-2004; Member, Vice Chairman, 1986-87, Chairman, 1987-2001, National Livestock and Wool Committee, 1985-1991; Vice President, NFU, 1991-92; Deputy President, NFU, 1992-98; President, NFU, 1998-2004; Member, Agriculture and Food Research Council, 1991-94; Member, Chairman of Agricultural Systems Directorate, Biotechnology and Biological Sciences Research

Council, 1994-97; Founder and Chairman, Alternative Crops Technology Interaction Network, 1994-2004; OST Technology Foresight, 1994-99; Director of FARM Africa, 1991-98; Executive Member, International Federation of Agricultural Producers, 1998-2004; Member, Council of Food from Britain, 1999-2005; Vice President, Comitee des Organisations Professionelles des Agriculteurs, 1999-2003; President, Confederation of European Agriculture, 2000-04; Non-Executive Director, Countrywide Farmers plc, 2004-; Governor, University of Lincoln, 2004-09; Chairman, Governing Body, Harrogate International Business School, 2010-; President, Cambridge University Potato Growers Research Association, 2004-; Director, Hawkhills Consultancy Ltd, 2004-; Member, Governing Council of the John Innes Centre, Norwich, 2002-; Patron: Pentalk, Farmers Overseas Action Group, Plants & Us, Rural Stress Information Network, St John's Ambulance Bricks and Wheels Appeal. Address: Prospect Farm, Upper Dormington, Hereford, HR1 4ED, England. E-mail: sirbengill@hawkcreative.com

GILL Wonpyong, b. 2 February 1956, Busan, Korea. Professor. m. Moung Sook Kim, 2 daughters. Education: BS, 1978, MS, 1980, Department of Physics, Seoul National University; PhD, Department of Physics, University of California, Santa Barbara, 1986. Appointments: Full-time Lecturer, 1986, Assistant Professor, 1989, Associate Professor, 1997, Department of Physics, Pusan National University. Publications: Ground-State properties of the Periodic-Anderson model, 1987; Monte Carlo Study of a one-dimensional degenerate Hubbard model, 1987. Honours: The Scientific Award of Excellence, ABI, 2011. Memberships: American Physical Society; Korean Physical Society; Korea Association for Creation Research. Address: 1808 Hyundae 2 Apt, Jangjun1-dong, Kumjung-gu, Busan 609-768, Korea. E-mail: wpgill@pusan.ac.kr

GILLARD David Owen, b. 8 February 1947, Croydon, Surrey, England. Writer; Critic. m. Valerie Ann. Education: Tavistock School, Croydon, Surrey. Appointments: Scriptwriter and Assistant Director, Associated British Pathé, 1967-70; Film and Theatre Critic, Daily Sketch, 1970-71; Ballet Critic, Daily Mail, 1971-88; Instituted drama preview pages, The Listener, 1982; Founder-Editor, English National Opera Friends Magazine, 1983-92; Radio Correspondent, Radio Times, 1984-91; Classical Music Editor, Radio Times, 2001-2003; Opera Critic, Daily Mail, 1971-. Publications: Play: Oh Brothers! 1971; Beryl Grey: A Biography, 1977. Honours: MBE, 2008. Memberships: National Union of Journalists; Critics Circle; Broadcasting Press Guild. Address: 1 Hambledon Court, 18 Arundel Way, Highcliffe, Christchurch, Dorset, BH23 5DX, England.

GILLARD The Hon Julia, b. 29 September 1961, Barry Island, Wales. Prime Minister of Australia; Minister of Employment and Workplace Relations; Minister for Education; Minister of Social Inclusion. Education: Mitcham Demonstration School; Unley High School; University of Adelaide; B Laws, 1987, BA, 1990, University of Melbourne. Appointments: Lawyer, 1987, Partner, 1990, Slater & Gordon, Werribee; Chief-of-Staff to Victorian Opposition Leader, John Brumby, 1996-98; Member of the Australian Parliament for Lalor, 1998-; Population and Immigration, 2001, Reconciliation and Indigenous Affairs, 2003, Shadow Cabinet; Shadow Minister for Health, 2003-06; Deputy Prime Minister of Australia, 2007-10; Prime Minister of Australia, 2010-. Memberships: Australian Labour Party. Address: PO Box 6022, House of Representatives, Parliament House, Canberra, ACT 2600, Australia. E-mail: julia.gillard.mp@aph.gov.au

GILLES Herbert Michael, b. 10 September 1921. Emeritus Professor of Tropical Medicine. m. (1) Wilhelmina Caruana, 1955, deceased, 3 sons, 1 daughter; (2) Mejra Kacic-Dimitri, 1979, deceased. Education: St Edward's College, Malta; Royal University of Malta, Rhodes Scholar, 1943; MSc Oxon; MD (Malta); FRCP; FFPH; FMCPH (Nig); DTM&H. Appointments: Alfred Jones and Warrington Yorke Professor of Tropical Medicine, 1972-86, Emeritus Professor, 1986-, University of Liverpool; Served in World War II, 1939-45; Member of Scientific Staff, MRC Laboratory, Gambia, 1954-58; University of Ibadan Lecturer, Tropical Medicine, 1958-63; Professor of Preventive and Social Medicine, 1963-65; Senior Lecturer, Tropical Medicine, Liverpool University, 1965-70; Professor of Tropical Medicine (Personal Chair), 1970; Visiting Professor, University of Lagos, 1965-68; Royal Society Overseas Visiting Professor, University of Khartoum, Sudan, 1979-80; Honorary Professor of Tropical Medicine, Sun-Yat-Sen Medical College, Guangzhou, People's Republic of China, 1984; Visiting Professor of Public Health, University of Malta, 1989-; Consultant in Malariology to the Army, 1974-86; Consultant in Tropical Medicine to the RAF, 1978-86, to the DHSS, 1980-86; President, RSTM&H, 1985-87; Vice President, International Federation of Tropical Medicine, 1988-92; Liverpool School of Tropical Medicine, 1991-; Visiting Professor of Tropical Medicine, Royal College of Surgeons in Ireland, Dublin, 1994-; Visiting Professor of Tropical Medicine, Mahidol University, Bangkok, 1980-; Member, Malta Association of Physicians, 2000-; Honorary President, Malta Association of Public Health Physicians, 2003-. Publications: Over 150 papers in peer-reviewed journals including: Tropical Medicine for Nurses, 1955, 4th edition, 1975; Pathology in the Tropics, 1969, 2nd edition, 1976; Management and Treatment of Tropical Diseases, 1971; A Short Textbook of Public Health Medicine for the Tropics, 1973, 4th edition, 2003; Atlas of Tropical Medicine and Parasitology, 1976, 4th edition, 1996; First Prize, BMA Medical Book Competition, 1996; Recent Advances in Tropical Medicine, 1984; Human Antiparasitic Drugs, Pharmacology and Usage, 1985; The Epidemiology and Control of Tropical Diseases, 1987; Management of Severe and Complicated Malaria, 1991; Hookworm Infections, 1991; Editor, Essential Malariology, 4th edition, 2002; Highly Commended, BMA Medical Book Competition, 2003; Tropical Medicine: A Clinical Text, 5th edition, 2006; Protozoal Diseases, 2001. Honours: 1939-45 Star; Africa Star; VM; Honorary MD, Karolinska Institute, 1979; Honorary DSc, Malta, 1984; Darling Foundation Medal and Prize, WHO, 1990; Mary Kingsley Medal, 1996; Officer of the Order of Merit (Malta), 2003; CMG, 2005; Manson Medal, Royal Society of Tropical Medicine & Hygiene, 2007; Knight of Justice, Sovereign Order of St John of Jerusalem, 2007; Companion of the Exalted Order of the White Elephant of the Kingdom of Thailand, 2008. Memberships: Royal Society of Tropical Medicine & Hygiene; Royal Society of Medicine; International Epidemiological Association. Address: 3 Conyers Avenue, Birkdale, Southport PR8 4SZ, England.

GILLHAM Paul Maurice, b. 26 November 1931, Carshalton, Surrey, England. Company Director. m. Jane Pickering, 2 sons, 1 daughter. Education: Royal College of Music, 1950-52; Guildhall School of Music, 1954-55; BA, MA, Christ's College, Cambridge. Appointments: Chairman, St Giles Properties Ltd; 1984: Chairman, Patent Developments International Ltd; 1986; Chairman, AccuSphyg LLC, New York, USA; Chairman, Gillham Hayward Ltd, 1994; Chairman, London Philharmonic Orchestra Council, 1994-1999; Director, Cathedral Capital Plc, 1997-2007. Honours: MA (Cantab); LGSM. Address: 3 Broadhatch Cottages, Bentley, Farnham, Surrey, GU10 5JL, England.

GILLIAM Terry Vance, b. 22 November 1940, Minnesota, USA. Animator; Film Director; Actor; Illustrator; Writer. m. Margaret Weston, 1 son, 2 daughters. Education: BA, Occidental College. Appointments: Associate Editor, HELP! magazine, 1962-64; Freelance illustrator, 1964-65; Advertising copywriter/art director, 1966-67; with Monty Python's Flying Circus (UK), 1969-76; Animator: And Now For Something Completely Different (film); Co-director, actor, Monty Python and the Holy Grail; Director, Jabberwocky; Designer, actor, animator, Monty Python's Meaning of Life (film), 1983; Co-writer, director, Brazil, 1985; The Adventures of Baron Munchausen, 1988; Director, The Fisher King (film), 1991; Twelve Monkeys, 1996; Presenter, TV series: The Last Machine, 1995; Executive Producer, Monty Python's Complete Waste of Time, 1995; Director and co-writer, Fear and Loathing in Las Vegas, 1998; Executive Producer, Monty Python's Complete Waste of time (CD-Rom), 1995; Appeared in Lost in La Mancha, documentary, 2002; Director and co-writer, The Brothers Grimm (film), 2005; Director and co-writer, Tideland (film), 2005. Publications: Monty Python's Big Red Book; Monty Python's Paperback, 1977; Monty Python's Scrapbook, 1979; Animations of Mortality, 1979; Monty Python's The Meaning of Life; Monty Python's Flying Circus - Just the Words (co-ed), 1989; DFA (hon), Occidental College, 1987; The Adventures of Baron Munchausen, 1989; Not the Screenplay or Fear and Loathing in Las Vegas, 1998; Gilliam on Gilliam, 1999; Dark Knights and Holy Fools, 1999; The Pythons Autobiography by the Pythons, 2003. Honour: Hon DFA, Occidental College, 1987; Hon DFA, Royal College of Art, London, 1988; Honorary Dr of Arts, Wimbledon School of Art, 2004. Address: c/o Jenne Casarotto, National House, 60-66 Wardour Street, London, W1V 4ND, England.

GILLIARD Allen Fletcher Jr, b. 27 June 1943, Morgantown, West Virginia, USA. Attorney. 1 son. Education: BA, Political Science and Economics, Yale University, New Haven, Connecticut, 1965; JD, University of Pennsylvania Law School, Philadelphia, Pennsylvania, 1968; BS, Electrical Engineering, Southern Illinois University at Edwardsville, 1995. Appointments: Attorney in Private Practice, Madison, Illinois; Abstract and title work for Madison County Title Co Inc. Honours: Admitted to Illinois Bar, 1971; Passed Engineer in Training Examination, 1995; Listed in Who's Who publications and biographical dictionaries; Professional of the Year, Law/Insurance, 2007. Memberships: Madison County Bar Association, Illinois; Chairman, Real Estate Committee; Illinois State Bar Association; Class Council, Yale University, Class of 1965; American Bar Association; Member, ABA Advisory Panel. Address: 801 Greenwood Street, Madison, IL 62060 1329, USA.

GILLIS Richard, b. 22 April 1950, Dundee, Scotland. Solicitor; Managing Director. m. Ruth J P Garden. Education: Admitted as a Solicitor, 1975; Kenya Advocate, 1978. Appointments: Solicitor, Greater London Council, 1975-77; Archer & Wilcock, Nairobi, Kenya, 1977-80; Shoosmiths, 1980-81; Assistant to the Secretary, TI Group plc, 1981-85; Secretary, ABB Transportation Holdings Ltd (British Rail Engineering Ltd until privatisation), Trustee, Company Pension Schemes, 1985-95; Clerk to the Council and Company Secretary, University of Derby, 1995-2002; Managing Director, family investment companies, 2001-; Secretary, Justice report on perjury; Director then Vice-Chairman, Crewe Development Agency, 1992-95; The Order of St John: Chairman, Property Committee, Derbyshire Council of the Order of St John, 1994-2003; Trustee, Priory of England and the Islands of the Order of St John and Trustee, St John Ambulance, 1999-2003; Chairman, Audit Committee and Priory Regulations Committee, Regional Member of Priory Chapter, 1999-2005; Court of Assistants, Worshipful Company of Basketmakers, 2004-, Prime Warden, 2013-14. Honours: OStJ, 1999; Honorary Life Member, Court of the University of Derby, 2003. Memberships: CBI East Midlands Regional Council, 1993-95; Stakeholders' Forum, Derby City Challenge, 1993-98; Guild of Freemen of the City of London; Provincial Grand Lodge of Warwickshire; Maccabæans; FRSA; Clubs: Athenæum; City Livery; New (Edinburgh); New Golf (St Andrews). Address: Nether Kinfauns, Church Road, Kinfauns, Perth, PH2 7LD, Scotland.

GILLMOR Robert, b. 6 July 1936, Reading, England. Artist. m. Susan Norman, 1 son, 1 daughter. Education: Leighton Park School, 1949-54; Fine Art Department, Reading University, 1954-59; National Diploma in Design, 1958; Art Teaching Diploma, 1959. Appointments: Director of Art and Craft, Leighton Park School, 1959-65; Freelance Artist, Illustrator, 1965-. Publications: Editor: Sketches of Bird Life, 1981; Shorelands Winter Diary, 1982; The Peregrine Sketchbook, 1996; Author: Cutting Away, 2006; Art Editor, Birds of the Western Palearctic, 1966-96; Joint author, Art of the New Naturalists, 2009; Designer of 24 bird stamps for Royal Mail's Post & Go, 2010-11; Illustrator of over 100 books and numerous dust jacket designs. Honours: Jubilee Medal, British Trust for Ornithology, 1984; Natural World Art Award, 1990; Medal, British Ornithologists Union, 1996; President's Medal, Royal Society for the Protection of Birds, 2000. Memberships: Reading Ornithological Club; Reading Guild of Artists; Cape Clear Bird Observatory; BTO; RSPB; BOU; Society of Wildlife Artists. Address: Norfolk.

GINGRICH Newt (Newton Leroy), b. 17 June 1943, Harrisburg, USA. American Politician. m.(1) Jackie Battley, 2 daughters (divorced), (2) Marianne Ginther, 1981-99 (divorced), Callista Bisek, 2000. Education: Emory and Tulane Universities. Appointments: Member, Faculty, West Georgia College, Carrollton, 1970-78, Professor of History, 1978; Member, 96-103rd Congresses from 6th District of Georgia, 1979-92; Chair, GOPAC, now Chair Emeritus; House Republican Whip, 1989; Speaker, House of Representatives, 1994-99; Adjunct Professor, Reinhardt College, Waleska, Georgia, 1994-95; Co-founder, Congressional Military Reform Caucus, Congressional Space Caucus; Chief Executive Officer, The Gingrich Group, Atlanta, 1999-; Board of Directors, Internet Policy Institute; Advisory Board, Museum of the Rockies. Publications: Window of Opportunity, 1945, 1995; To Renew America, 1995; Winning the Future, 2005; Rediscovering God in America, 2006; A Contract with the Earth, 2007; Real Change: From The World That Fails To The World That Works, 2008; Drill Here, Drill Now, Pay Less, 2008; To Save America: Abolishing Obama's Socialist State and Restoring Our Unique American Way, 2010. Honour: Distinguished Visiting Scholar, National Defense University, 2001. Membership: AAAS. Address: The Committee for New American Leadership, 1800 K Street #714, Washington, DC 20006, USA.

GINOLA David, b. 25 January 1967, Gassin, Var, France. Professional Footballer; Sportsman. m. Coraline Delphin, 1990, 2 daughters. Career: Football clubs: 1st division Toulon clubs, 1986-87; Matraracing, Paris, 1987-88; Racing Paris 1, 1988-89; Brest-Armorique, 1989-90; Paris-Saint-Germain (French national champions, 1993-94, winners Coupe de France, 1993, 1995, winners coupe de la ligue, 1995) 1991-95; Newcastle Utd, England, 1995-97; Tottenham Hotspur, 1997-2000; Aston Villa, 2000-02; Everton, 2002; 17

International caps; Anti-landmine campaigner for Red Cross, 1998-. Honours: Football Writers' Association, Player of the Year, 1999; Professional Football Association Player of the Year, 1999. Publication: David Ginola: The Autobiography (with Niel Silver), 2000. Website: www.ginola14.com

GIRHAMMAR Ulf Arne, b. 13 October 1948, Skelleftea, Sweden. Professor. m. Gudrun, 2 sons. Education: MSc, Civil Engineering, Lund Institute of Technology, 1973; D Eng, Structural Engineering, Lulea University of Technology, 1980. Appointments: Research Professor, Research Department, Royal Swedish Fortification Administration, 1981; Adjunct Professor, Department of Lightweight Structures, Royal Institute of Technology, 1989; Professor, Building Engineering, Umea University, 2010-; Professor, Timber Engineering, Lulea University of Technology, 2010-. Address: Umea University, Department of TFE, Building Engineering, SE-90187 Umea, Sweden. E-mail: ulfarne.girhammar@tfe.umu.se

GIRMA Woldegiorgis Lutcha, b. December 1925, Addis Ababa, Ethiopia. President of the Federal Democratic Republic of Ethiopia. m. 2 sons, 3 daughters. Education: Air Traffic Control Management, Canada, 1952; School of Social Science, Holland, 1952-53; Air Traffic Management School, Sweden, 1953. Appointments: Soldier (later Sergeant, then Second Lieutenant), Ethiopian Army Communications, 1941-46; Transferred to Ethiopian Air Force, 1946; Assistant Instructor in air navigation and air traffic control, 1948; Chief of Technical Services, Civil Aviation Authority, 1949; Head, Civil Aviation Department, Federal Government of Eritrea, 1955; Director General, Ethiopian Civil Aviation, and Board Member of Ethiopian Air Lines, 1958; Director General, Ministry of Commerce, Industry and Planning, 1959; Member, House of Representatives and three-times elected President, 1961; Elected Member, Board of Ethiopian Chamber of Commerce, 1967; Elected Member (later Manager of Import and Export Enterprise), Civil Advisory Consul, 1974; First Vice-Commissioner, Peace Commission, 1976; Head of Logistics, Section of ICRC pertaining to Demobilized Ex-Army persons, Addis Ababa, 1990; Founded LEM Ethiopia (later Vice President), 1992; Elected member, House of People's Representatives and Member, Economic Standing Committee of the House, 2000; Elected President, Federal Democratic Republic of Ethiopia, 2001, re-elected, 2008. Honours: World Peace & Love, 2004; Honorary Degree, Doctor of Management, 2005; Order of Peter the Great 1st Degree, 2007; Effort to Improve the Environment Award, 2008; Outstanding Green Leadership Award, 2008; Environmental Protection Award, 2009; Honor Degree, Top Leaders of the World; Life Long Leadership Award, 2009. Address: POB 577, Addis Ababa, Ethiopia.

GISTELINCK Peter H, Executive Director. Education: BA, History of Arts, 1981, MA, Musicology, 1984, Universiteit Gent; MA, Music Theory & History, Composition, Orchestrating & Arranging, Hogeschool Gent, 1985. Appointments: Pianist and Musical Co-ordinator, Arena Musical Theatre, Gent, 1981-86; In House Arranger and Orchestrator, Belgian National Radio and Television, 1984-95; Music Director, Royal Ballet of Flanders, Musical Division, 1986-89; Professor, Royal Music Conservatory, Antwerpen, 1989-92; Music Education and Publishing Manager, Roland Central Europe, 1991-97; General Manager, I Fiamminghi, Gent, 1997-99; General Manager of Business Affairs, Le Concert Spirituel, Paris, 1999-2004; Director of Sales and Marketing, Brussels Philharmonic (Flemish Radio Symphony Orchestra) and Flemish Radio Choir, 2004-06; Executive Director, Chamber Orchestra of Philadelphia, 2006-. Honours: International Who's Who in Music Certificate, 1987; SABAM/BAP Award for Best Belgian Composition, 1987, 1990; Laureate Golden Orpheus Festival, 1988; Arranger's Prize, UNICEF Danny Kaye Award, 1989; Laureate Benelux International Song Festival, 1990; Arranger's Prize, Golden Orpheus Festival, 1990; Arranger's Prize, Makfest Festival, 1992; ABI Distinguished Leadership Award, 1993; ABI Men's Inner Circle of Achievement, 1993; Grammy Nomination Award, 2002; Cambridge Who's Who Honouree, 2009. Memberships: Kimmel Center Inc, Philadelphia; League of American Orchestras, New York; The Recording Academy ®, Santa Monica, California; American Film Institute, Los Angeles; Musical Fund Society, Philadelphia; Arts & Business Council, Philadelphia; International Society for Performing Arts, New York City; International Academy of Jazz, Pittsburgh; Union League, Philadelphia; Vesper Club, Philadelphia; SABAM, Brussels, Belgium; URADEX, Brussels; Universal Music Publishing, Brussels. Address: The Chamber Orchestra of Philadelphia, 1520 Locust Street, Suite 500, Philadelphia, PA 19102, USA. Website: www.chamberorchestra.org

GIUGGIOLI Pier Filippo, b. 29 March 1968, Milan, Italy. Lawyer. Education: Visiting Scholar, Law School, University of Pennsylvania, USA, 2000; Visiting Professor, Cambridge University, England, 2001; Visiting Professor, Pilzen University, 2006-07; PhD, Italian Private Law, University of Turin; Associate Professor, Private Comparative Law, University of Milan; Community Law Course, Centro Internazionale di Studi & Documentazion delle Comunita Europee, Milan. Appointments: Member, Non-Executive Directors Community; President, Associazion Amici dell'Accademia dei Giusprivatisti Europei Advisor, Italian Ministry of Justice in Relation to Class Action, 2007-08. Publications: La Protezione delle Informazioni Segrete, Esperizena Francese e Italiana a Contronto; Multiproprieta in Trattato di Diritto Privato dell'Unione Europea, Torino, 2008; L'Azione Collettiva Risarcitoria, Una Prima Lettura in Corriere Giuidico, 2008; La Nuova Azione Collettiva Risarcitoria, Padova, 2008. Memberships: Italian Member, Task Force on Criminal Law and Arbitration of the Commission on Arbitration, International Chamber of Commerce. Address: via Serbelloni 14, 20122 Milan, Italy. Website: www.agnoli-giouggioli.it

GIVENCHY Hubert de, b. 21 February 1927, Beauvais, France. Fashion Designer. Education: Ecole Nat Supérieure des Beaux-Arts, Paris; Faculté de Droit, Univ de Paris. Appointments: Apprentice, Paris fashion houses of Lucien Lelong, 1945-46, Robert Piguet, 1946-48, Jacques Fath, 1948-49, Elsa Shiaparelli, 1949-51; Established own fashion house in Parc Morceau, Paris, 1952-56, Avenue George V, 1956; President, Director-General Society Givenchy-Couture and Society des Parfums Givenchy, Paris, 1954; Honorary President, Administrative Council Givenchy SA, 1988-; President, Christie's France, 1997-; Work included in Fashion: An Anthology, Victoria & Albert Museum, London, 1971; Costume designer for films: Breakfast at Tiffany's, 1961; Charade, 1963; The VIPs, 1963; Paris When It Sizzles, 1964; How to Steal a Million, 1966; Love Among Thieves, 1987. Honour: Chevalier, Légion d'honneur. Address: 3 Avenue George V, 75008 Paris, France.

GLÄSER Albrecht, b. 27 July 1928, Chemnitz, Saxony, Germany. Professor of Surgery. m. Hannelore Gläser, 1 daughter. Education: Studies of Medicine, 1947-53; Dr. med., 1953; Dr. med. habil., 1961; Dozent (Assistant

Professor), 1961-66; Professor of Surgery, 1966; Chair, 1969. Appointments: Assistant, Pathological Institute University of Leipzig, Germany, 1956; Assistant, 1961, Deputy Director, 1962-83, Surgical Clinic, Leipzig, Germany; Director, Surgical Clinic, Martin Luther University, Halle, Germany, 1983-95; Retired 1995. Publications: Klinische Pathologie der Geschwülste (4 volumes), 1974-83; Students textbook on Oncology, 2nd edition, 1975, 1980; Krebsoperationen, 1993; Many articles and chapters in monographs. Honours: Honorary Member of several medical associations. Memberships: EACR; Deutsche Gesellschaft Chirurgie; Deutsche Krebsgesellschaft; Sächsische Akademie der Wissenschaften; Mitteldeutsche Chirugenvereinigung; International Society of Surgery; Deutsche Vribsfesellschaft. Address: Surgical Clinic, Martin Luther University, Ernst-Gruber-Str 40, D 06420 Halle, Germany.

GLASSMAN George M, b. 7 September 1935, New York City, USA. Physician; Dermatologist. m. Carol Frankford, 1 son, 1 daughter. Education: BA, Brown University, Providence, Rhode Island, 1957; MD, New York University School of Medicine, New York, 1962; Rotating Internship, Greenwich Hospital, Greenwich, Connecticut, 1962-63; Dermatology Residency, New York University Medical Centre (including Bellevue Hospital, University Hospital, Skin and Cancer Unit and Manhattan VA Hospital), 1963-66. Appointments: Chief of Dermatology, LCDR, MC, US Naval Hospital, St Albans, New York, 1966-68; Private Practice in Dermatology, White Plains, New York, 1968-96; Clinical Assistant Professor, Albert Einstein College of Medicine, 1970-75; Clinical Assistant Professor, New York Medical College, 1975-87; Associate Attending, Westchester County Medical Centre, 1974-87; Attending, White Plains Hospital, 1969-96 (Associate attending, 1969-77) (Honorary, 1996-); Associate Attending, St Agnes Hospital, White Plains, 1978-96 (Assistant attending, 1969-78) (Honorary, 1996-). Publications: 1 article, New York State Journal of Medicine. Honours: Continuing Medical Education Award of American Academy of Dermatology 1980-; Physician's Recognition Award of the American Medical Association, 1980-; Who's Who in Science and Engineering; Who's Who in the World; Who's Who in America; Who's Who in the East. Memberships: American Academy of Dermatology; New York State Society of Dermatology; Westchester County Medical Society; Westchester Academy of Medicine; AMA; Society for Paediatric Dermatology. Address: 268 Stuart Dr, New Rochelle, NY 10804-1423, USA.

GLATTRE Eystein Junker, b. 16 April 1934, Kristiansand, Norway. Epidemiologist. m. Ruth Lillian Jordal, 3 daughters. Education: MD, University of Oslo, 1962; Fellowship in Medical Statistics, Medical Statistics Institute, Oslo, 1965-67, Mayo Graduate School of Medicine, Rochester, USA, 1967-68; PhD, History of Ideas (Bio-temporal Structures), University of Aarhus, Denmark, 1980. Appointments: Assistant Professor, Nordic School of Public Health, Sweden, 1968-69; Consultant, Statistics Norway, 1969-70, Amanuensis, Institute of Preventive Medicine, University of Oslo, 1970-79; Senior Epidemiologist, 1980-91, Head of Department, 1992-2002, Cancer Registry of Norway; Leader of Norwegian Thyroid Cancer Project, 1985-2003; Board Member, Norwegian Canine Cancer Registry, 1990-2000; Professor in Epidemiology, Norwegian Veterinary College, 1992-2002; Developed fractal epidemiology 1997-2007; from 2008 hypo-mathematical analysis of cortical networks. Publications: Around 160 papers and books on cancer research, trace element research, disease classification, cartography, vital statistics, theory of science and mathematics including: A Temporal Quantum Model, 1972; (co-author) Atlas of Cancer Incidence in Norway 1970-79, 1985; Pre-diagnostic s-Selenium in a Case-Control Study of Thyroid Cancer, 1989; Case-control study Testing the Hypothesis that Seafood Increases the Risk of Thyroid Cancer, 1993; Human Papillomavirus Infection as a Risk Factor for Squamous Cell Carcinoma of the Head and Neck, 2001; Norwegian Thyroid Cancer Project: History, Achievements and Present View on Carcinogenesis, 2003; The Fractal Meta-Analysis and 'Causality' Embedded in Complexity: Advanced Understanding of Disease Aetiology, 2004; Fundamental Aspects of Fractal Epidemiology, Oslo, 2008. Honour: H M King Olav's Award for Young Mathematicians, 1953; Listed in various international biographical dictionaries. Memberships: Norwegian Medical Association; Czech Society for Experimental and Clinical Pharmacology and Toxicology; Society for Chaos Theory in Psychology and Life Sciences. Address: Dron Ingeborgs v 14 N-3530 Royse, Norway.

GLENN John Herschel, b. 18 July 1921, Cambridge, Ohio, USA. US Senator. m. Anna Margaret Castor, 1943, 1 son, 1 daughter. Education: Muskingum College; Naval Aviation Cadet program. Appointments: Marine Corps, 1943; Test Pilot, USN and Marine Corps; 1 of 1st 7 Astronauts in US Space Program, 1959; 1st American to orbit Earth, 1962; Resigned, US Marine Corps, 1965; Director, Roy Crown Cola Company, 1965-74; Consultant, NASA; US Senator, Ohio, 1975-99; Announced return as astronaut, 1997, on board Discovery shuttle, 1998. Publications: We Seven, co-author, 1962; P.S., I Listened to Your Heart Beat. Honours include: DFC 6 times; Air Medal with 18 Clusters; Set environmental speed record for 1st flight to average supersonic speeds from Los Angeles to New York, 1957; Space Congressional Medal of Honour; 1st Senator to win 4 consecutive terms in office. Address: Ohio State University, John Glenn Institute, 100 Bricker Hall, 190 North Oval Mall, Columbus, OH 43210, USA.

GLENNIE Evelyn, b. 19 July 1965, Aberdeen, Scotland. Musician. m. Gregorio Malcangi, 1993, (divorced). Education: Ellon Academy, Aberdeenshire; Royal Academy of Music; Furthered studies in Japan on a Munster Trust Scholarship, 1986. Appointments: Solo debut Wigmore Hall, 1986; Concerts with major orchestras world-wide; Tours UK, Europe, USA, Canada, Australia, New Zealand, Far East, Japan, Middle East, South America, China; Performs many works written for her including Bennett, Bourgeois, Heath, Macmillan, McLeod, Muldowney and Musgrave; First solo percussionist to perform at the Proms, London, 1989, subsequent appearances, 1992, 1994, 1996, 1997. Creative work: Recordings include: Rebounds; Light in Darkness; Dancin'; Rhythm Song; Veni, Veni, Emmanuel; Wind in the Bamboo Grove; Drumming; Sonata for two pianos and percussion – Bela Bartok; Last Night of the Proms – 100th Season; Her Greatest Hits; The Music of Joseph Schwantner; Street Songs, Reflected in Brass; Shadow Behind the Iron Sun. Publications: Good Vibrations (autobiography), 1990; Great Journeys of the World, Beat It! Honours: Honorary Doctorates include: Honorary DMus from the Universities of Aberdeen, 1991, Bristol, 1995, Portsmouth, 1995, Surrey, 1997; Queens University, Belfast, 1998, Exeter, Southampton, 2000; Hon DLitt from Universities of Warwick, 1993, Loughborough, 1995; Numerous prizes include Queen's Commendation Prize (RAM); Gold Medal Shell/LSO Music Scholarship, 1984; Charles Heidsieck Soloist of the Year Award, Royal Philharmonic Society, 1991; OBE, 1993; Personality of the Year, International Classical Music Awards, 1993; Young Deaf Achievers Special Award, 1993; Best studio percussionist, Rhythm Magazine, 1998, 2000, 2002, 2003, 2004; Best Live Percussionist, Rhythm Magazine, 2000; Classic FM

Outstanding Contribution to Classical Music, 2002; Walpole Medal of Excellence, 2002; Musical America, 2003; 2 Grammy Awards; Sabian Lifetime Achievement Award, 2006; Hall of Fame PAS, 2008. Address: IMG Artists Europe, Lovell House, 616 Chiswick High Road, London W4 5RX, England. Website: www.evelyn.co.uk

GLIKIN Arkady, b. 20 June 1943, Kostroma, Russia. Crystallographer. m. Elena Kotelnikova, 1 son. Education: Dipl Specialist, Geology, Geochemistry and Crystallography, 1965, PhD, 1978, Senior Scientist, 1985, Crystallography and Crystallophysics, Dr Sci, 1997, Professor, 1999, Mineralogy and Crystallography, Crystallography Department, Geological Faculty, St Petersburg State University. Appointments: Engineer, 1965-74, Scientific Researcher, 1974-84, Senior Scientist, 1984-97, Head, Crystal Genesis Laboratory, 1991-95, Leading Scientist, 1997-98, General Scientist, 1998-, Crystallography Department, Geological Faculty, St Petersburg State University. Publications: 2 issued monographs; About 100 papers; More than 200 presentations at various conferences. Honours: Inventor of the USSR, 1976; Honorary Diploma, Ministry of Education of Russian Federation, 1996; Jubilee Medal, 275 Anniversary of St Petersburg University, 1999; Honorary diplomas of St Petersburg State University, 1983, 1999, 2003; Honorary diplomas, Russian Mineralogical Society, 2003, 2004; High Achiever in Mineral Prospecting, 2006; Honorary Employment of Higher Professional Education of Russian Federation, 2007; 1st Degree Diploma, Russian Mineralogical Society, 2010; Numerous grants. Memberships: Russian Mineralogical Society; International Mineralogical Association; International Union of Crystallography; St Petersburg Society of Naturalists. Address: Liteiny prospect, 34 apt 44, 191028, St Petersburg, Russia. E-mail: glikin43@mail.ru

GLINKA Elena, b. 27 September 1958, Tjumen, USSR. Biologist. 2 sons. Education: Diploma, Physiology, Lomonosov Moscow State University, 1981; PhD, Biochemistry, A N Bach Institute of Biochemistry, RAS, 1993. Appointments: Senior Scientist, Laboratory of Plant Immunity, A N Bach Institute of Biochemistry, 1996-2001; Senior Scientist, Laboratory of Molecular Immunology, IBCh, RAS, 2002-07; Senior Scientist, Laboratory of Structural Biochemistry, Institute of Bioorganic Chemistry, RAS, 2007-. Publications: Numerous articles in professional journals. Honours: Medal In Memory of 850 Years of Moscow, 1997.

GLOAG Julian, b. 2 July 1930, London, England. Novelist. 1 son, 1 daughter. Education: Rugby School; Exhibitioner, BA, 1953, MA, 1957, Magdalene College, Cambridge. Publications: Our Mother's House, 1963; A Sentence of Life, 1966; Maundy, 1969; A Woman of Character, 1973; Sleeping Dogs Lie, 1980; Lost and Found, 1981; Blood for Blood, 1985; Only Yesterday, 1986; Love as a Foreign Language, 1991; Le passeur de la nuit, 1996; Chambre d'ombre, 1996. Teleplays: Only Yesterday, 1986; The Dark Room, 1988. Memberships: Fellow, Royal Society of Literature; Fellow, Royal Society of Arts. Address: 36 rue Gabrielle, 75018 Paris, France

GLOVER Danny, b. 22 July 1946, Georgia, USA. Actor. m. Asake Bomani, 1 daughter. Education: San Francisco State University. Appointments: Researcher, Office of Mayor, San Francisco, 1971-75; Member, American Conservatory Theatre's Black Actor Workshop; Broadway debut, Master Harold...and the Boys, 1982; Other stage appearances include: The Blood Knot, 1982; The Island; Sizwe Banzi is Dead; Macbeth; Suicide in B Flat; Nevis Mountain Dew; Jukebox; Appearances in TV films and series; Founder, with wife, Bomani Gallery, San Francisco; Actor films: Escape From Alacatraz, 1979; Chu Chu and the Philly Flash, 1981; Out, 1982; Iceman, Places in the Heart, Birdy, The Color Purple, 1984; Silverado, Witness, 1985; Lethal Weapon, 1987; Bat 21, 1988; Lethal Weapon II, 1989; To Sleep With Anger, Predator 2, 1990; Flight of the Intruder, A Rage in Harlem, Pure Luck, 1991; Grand Canyon, Lethal Weapon II, 1992; The Saint of Fort Washington, Bopha, 1993; Angles in the Outfield, 1994; Operation Dumbo Drop, 1995; America's Dream, 1996; The Rainmaker, 1997; Wings Against the Wind, Beloved, Lethal Weapon IV, Prince of Egypt (voice), Antz (voice), 1998; The Monster, 1999; Bàttu, Boseman and Lena, Wings Against the Wind, Freedom Song, 2000; 3 A M, The Royal Tenebaums, 2001; The Real Eve (TV series), 2002; Good Fences (TV), The Henry Lee Project (TV), 2003; Saw, The Cookout, Legend of Earthsea (TV), 2004; The Exonerated (TV), Missing in America, Manderlay, 2005; The Shaggy Dog, The Adventures of Brer Rabbit, Bamako, Dreamgirls, 2006; Poor Boy's Game, Shooter, Honeydripper, Be Kind Rewind, 2007; Terra, This Life, Gospel Hill, Blindness, Unstable Fables (voice), Prana, 2008; Night Train, The Harimaya Bridge, Down for Life, 2012, 2009; Death At A Funeral, 2010. Honours: Chair's Award, National Association for the Advancement of Colored People, 2003. Address: c/o Cary Productions Inc, PMB 352, 6114 LaSalle Avenue, Oakland, CA 9461, USA.

GLOVER Judith, b. 31 March 1943, Wolverhampton, England. Author. 2 daughters. Education: Wolverhampton High School for Girls, 1954-59; Aston Polytechnic, 1960. Publications: Place Names of Sussex (non-fiction), 1975; Place Names of Kent (non-fiction), 1976. Drink Your Own Garden (non-fiction), 1979; The Sussex Quartet: The Stallion Man, 1982, Sisters and Brothers, 1984, To Everything a Season, 1986; Birds in a Gilded Cage, 1987; The Imagination of the Heart, 1989; Tiger Lilies, 1991; Mirabelle, 1992; Minerva Lane, 1994; Pride of Place, 1995; Sussex Place-Names (non-fiction), 1997. Address: c/o Artellus Ltd, 30 Dorset House, Gloucester Place, London NW1 5AD, England.

GNANALINGHAM (Mo) Muhuntha Giritharalingham, b. 1 February 1971, Colombo, Sri Lanka. Consultant. Education: MBChB (Hons), Manchester Medical School, 1995; FRCPCH (UK); PhD, University of Nottingham, 2006; NLP (Diploma), 2011. Appointments: PRHO, Preston, 1995-96; PRHO, Wythenshawe, 1996; SHO, Paediatric Surgery, 1996-97; Paediatric Medicine, 1997, Booth Hall Children's Hospital; SHO, Neonates, St Mary's Manchester, 1997-98; SHO, Paediatrics/Neonates, Trafford, 1998; Senior SHO, Paediatrics/Neonates, Bolton, 1998-99; Senior SHO, Paediatrics/Neonates, New Cross, 1999; LATS SpR, Paediatrics/Neonates, Peterborough, 1999; SpR, Paediatrics/Neonates, Warrington, 1999-2000; SpR, Paediatric Intensive Care, Alder Hey Children's Hospital, Liverpool, 2000-01, 2005-06, 2007-08; SpR, Neonates, Liverpool Women's Hospital, 2001; Clinical Lecturer, Child Health, Queen's Medical Centre, 2001-05; SpR, Community Paediatrics, Nottingham, 2005; SHO, Anaesthetics, Glan Clwyd, Denbighshire, 2006-07; PICU Fellow, Paediatric Intensive Care, Royal Melbourne Children's Hospital, Australia, 2008-09; PICU Consultant, Paediatric Intensive Care, Royal Manchester Children's Hospital, 2009-. Publications: Numerous articles in professional journals. Honours: R&D Award, 2000; Special Trustees for Nottingham University Hospitals, 2002, 2004; 3rd Poster Prize, Institute of Clinical Research, Nottingham University, 2005. Memberships: Fellow, Royal College of Paediatrics and Child Health; Paediatric Intensive Care Society; European Society of

Intensive Care Medicine; European Society of Paediatric & Neonatal Intensive Care; Resuscitation Council (UK); Paediatric Research Society; Physiological Society. E-mail: molingham@doctors.org.uk

GÖKER Ali Ihsan, b. 28 January 1980, Akşehir, Turkey. Assistant Professor. Education: BS, Physics, Koc University, 2001; MS, 2004, PhD, 2007, Physics, Rice University. Appointments: Postdoctoral Fellow, Universite de Montreal, 2007-08; Instructor, Fatih University, 2008-09; Researcher, Tübitak and King Abdullah University of Science & Technology, 2009-10; Assistant Professor, Bilecik University, 2010-. Publications: Numerous articles in professional journals. Honours: Welch Foundation Fellowship; NSERC Postdoctoral Fellowship; Vehbi Koq Scholar. Memberships: American Physical Society. Address: Department of Physics, Bilecik University, 11210, Gülümbe, Bilecik, Turkey.

GOLABEK Tomasz, b. 12 March 1974, Pulawy, Poland. Urologist. Education: MD, 2000, PhD, 2004, Medical University of Bialystock, Poland. Appointments: Junior Lecturer, Department of Urology, Teaching University Hospital, Bialystock, Poland, 2001-05; Postdoctoral Urology Researcher, Harvard Medical School & Boston University School of Medicine, 2005-06; Basic Surgical Training, Royal College of Surgeons, Ireland, 2006-08; Senior House Officer, Department of Urology, Cork University Hospital, and Mercy University Hospital, Cork, 2008-09; Registrar, Department of Urology, Cork University Hospital & Mercy University Hospital, 2009-. Honours: Fellow, Robert J Krane Fellowship, Harvard Medical School & Boston University School of Medicine. Memberships: RCS (Ireland); Irish Society of Urology; Polish Urological Association; European Association of Urology. Address: Mercy University Hospital, Department of Urology, Grenville Place, Cork, Ireland. E-mail: mrtomaszgolabek@gmail.com

GOLAN Shammai, b. 5 April 1933, Poland. Emigrated to Israel, 1947. Holocaust Survivor; Hebrew Writer; Diplomat. m. Arna Ben-Dror, 2 sons, 2 daughters. Education: BA, Literature and History, Hebrew University of Jerusalem, 1961. Appointments: Director, Writers' House, Jerusalem, 1971-78; Head, Department of Jewish Education and Culture for the Diaspora, Buenos Aires, Argentina, 1978-81; Chairman, Hebrew Writers' Association, 1981-84, 1989-91; Counsellor, Cultural Affairs, Embassy of Israel, Mexico, 1984-87, Moscow, 1994-99; Director and Secretary, Board of Directors, Society of Authors, Composers and Music Publishers in Israel, 2000-08. Publications: Novels and short stories: The Last Watch; Guilt Offerings; The Death of Uri Peled; Escape for Short Distances; Canopy: The Ambush; Holocaust: Anthology; My Travels with Books: Essays; And If You Must Love, novel, 2008; Scenarios; Radio plays; Numerous articles. Honours: Literary Awards: Barash, 1962; Acum, 1965; Ramat-Gan, 1973; The Agnon Jerusalem, 1976; Walenrod Prize, 1979; Prime Minister's Prize, 1992; Laureate of Light (Khattan Haor), Zionist Council, Israel, Jerusalem, 2006; Laureate of the Hebrew Writers Association, 2010; Award of Honour, ACUM, 2010. Memberships: Hebrew Writers' Association; PEN Centre; ACUM; Cultural Academy of Mexico; Council, Yad Vashem Museum Memorial. Address: 1 Haamoraim Str, Tel Aviv 69207, Israel. E-mail: golan-sa@barak.net.il

GOLDADE Victor Antonovich, b. 19 September 1947, Altai Region, Russia. Physicist. m. Svetlana Neronskaja, 1 son. Education: Diploma of Engineer, Physics, Leningrad Polytechnical Institute, Russia, 1971; PhD, 1980, Dr Sci Eng, 1989, Institute of Polymer Mechanics, Riga, Latvia; Full Professor, Physics, Belarus State Transport University, Gomel, Belarus, 1998. Appointments: Engineer, Postgraduate Student, Scientific Researcher, Laboratory Head, 1972-, Department Head, 2009-, Metal-Polymer Research Institute, National Academy of Sciences of Belarus. Publications: 285 scientific publications including 18 monographs; 202 patents of USSR, Russia, Belarus, USA, UK, Germany, Italy and others. Honours: Diploma of Honour, 20th Century Award for Achievement, 2000; Member, Research Board of Advisors, ABI, 2001. Memberships: International Eurasian Academy of Science; Belarusian Engineering Academy. Address: 32a Kirov str, 246050 Gomel, Belarus. E-mail: victor.goldade@gmail.com

GOLDBERG Whoopi, b. 13 November 1955, New York, USA. Actress. m.(1) Alvin Martin 1973-79, divorced, 1 daughter, (2) David Claessen, 1986-88, divorced, (3) Lyle Trachtenberg, 1994-95 divorced. Career: First appearance aged 8, Hudson Guild Theatre, New York; Helen Rubenstein Children's Theatre, San Diego, moved 1974; Co-founder, San Diego Repertory Theatre, appeared in 2 productions, Brecht's Mother Courage and Marsha Norman's Getting Out; Moved to San Francisco, Jointed Blake Street Hawkeyes Theatre, appeared in The Spook Show and Moms, co-wrote, a one-woman show in US Tours, debut, The Lyceum Theatre, Broadway, 1984; Films include: The Color Purple, 1985; Jumpin' Jack Flash, Ghost, 1990; Sister Act; Made in America, 1992; Sister Act II; Corrina Corrina, 1993; Star Trek Generation 5; Moonlight and Valentino; Bogus; Eddie; The Associate, The Ghost of Mississippi, 1996; How Stella Got Her Groove Back, 1998; Deep End of the Ocean, Jackie's Back! Girl Interrupted, 1999; Rat Race, Call Me Claus, Kingdom Come, Monkeybone, Golden Dreams, 2001; Star Trek: Nemesis, Blizzard (voice), More Dogs Than Bones, 2002; Good Fences, 2003; Pinocchio 2000 (voice), Jiminy Glick in La La Wood, 2004; Racing Stripes (voice), The Magic Roundabout (voice), 2005; Farce of the Penguins (voice), Doogal (voice), Everyone's Hero (voice), 2006; If I Had Known I Was a Genius, Homie Spumoni, 2007; Snow Buddies (voice), Descendents (voice), 2008; Stream, 2009. TV: Moonlighting, 1985-86; own TV show, 1992-93; What Makes a Family, 2001; It's a Very Merry Muppet Christmas Movie, 2002; Whoopi (series), 2003; Littleburg (series), 2004; Everybody Hates Chris (series), 2006; A Muppets Christmas: Letters to Santa, 2008. Honours: Several nominations as best actress for The Color Purple including Academy Award, Golden Globe; Emmy Nomination for Moonlighting; Grammy for Best Comedy Album, 1985; Hans Christian Andersen Award for Outstanding Achievement by a Dyslexic; Academy Award, Best Supporting Actress, Ghost, 1990; Mark Twain Prize for Humor, Kennedy Centre of Arts, 2001. Address: 4000 Warner Boulevard, #404, Burbank, CA 90068, USA.

GOLDBLUM Jeff, b. 22 October 1952, Pittsburgh, USA. Actor. m. (1) Patricia Gaul, 1980-1986, divorced (2) Geena Davis, 1987-1990, divorced. Education: Studied at New York Neighbourhood Playhouse. Career: Actor, films include: California Split, Death Wish, 1974; Nashville, 1975; Next Stop Greenwich Village, 1976; Annie Hall, Between the Lines, The Sentinel, 1977; Invasion of the Body Snatchers, Remember My Name, Thank God it's Friday, 1978; Escape From Athena, 1979; The Big Chill, The Right Stuff, Threshold, 1983; The Adventures of Buckaroo Banzai, 1984; Silverado, Into the Night, Transylvania 6-5000, 1985; The Fly, 1986; Beyond Therapy, 1987; The Tall Guy, Earth Girls Are Easy, First Born (TV), 1989; The Mad Monkey, 1990; Mister Frost, 1991; Deep Cover, The Favour, The Watch and the Very Big Fish,

1992; Father and Sons, Jurassic Park, 1993; Lushlife (TV); Future Quest (TV), 1994; Hideaway, Nine Months, 1995; Independence Day, 1996; The Lost World, 1997; Holy Man, 1998; Popcorn, 1999; Chain of Fools, Angie Rose, 2000; Cats and Dogs, 2001; Igby Goes Down, 2002; Dallas 362, Spinning Boris, 2003; Incident at Loch Ness, The Life Aquatic with Steve Zissou, 2004; Mini's First Time, Fay Grim, Man of the Year, 2006; Raines (TV), 2007; Adam Resurrected, 2008, Law & Order: Criminal Intent (TV), 2009-2010. Producer: Little Surprises, 1995; Holy Man, 1999. Address: c/o Peter Lemie, William Morris Agency, 151 El Camino Drive, Beverly Hills, CA 90212, USA.

GOLDENBERG Iosif Sukharovich, b. 1 May 1927, Ukraine. School Teacher. Education: PhD, Philology Department, Kharkov State University, 1949. Publications: Tavolga, English translation as Meadow-sweet; Nad Propast'yu v Tishi, English translation as On the Verge of Abyss in the Silence; Zalozhniki Zaveta, English translation as Hostages of Behest; Izbrannoe, English translation as Selected Rhymes; Stikhi dlya Detei (Rhymes for Children); Serdoliki (Sards); Kashtanovye Svechi (Chestnut Candlelights); Na Kazhdy Den' (Everyday Reading); Ten' I Svet (Shade and Light); 1996 God (The Year of 1996); Iz Pushchino s Lyubov'yu (From Pushchino with Love); Sto Stikhotvorenyi (A Hundred Rhymes); Predvaritelnye Itogi (Preliminary Outcomes); Posle Vosmidesyati (After My Eighty). Contributions to: Periodicals. Address: Building AB-1, Apt 43, 142290 Pushchino, Moscow Region, Russia.

GOLDING Allan Peter, b. 26 March 1960, Jamestown, South Australia. Physician. m. Dymphna, 2 sons, 1 daughter. Education: MBBS, University of Adelaide, Australia, 1984; Diploma in Obstetrics, Gynaecology and Neonatal Care, Royal Australian and New Zealand College of Obstetrics and Gynaecology, 1987; Registered Medical Board of South Australia; Certificate, Civil Aviation Medicine, Australia, 2001. Appointments include: Intern, Royal Adelaide Hospital, Adelaide, 1984; Resident Medical Officer, Lyell McEwin Health Service, Elizabeth Vale, 1985-86; Resident Medical Officer, Modbury Hospital, Modbury, South Australia, 1987; Rural General Practice, Medicine, Surgery and Obstetrics, Port Pirie, South Australia, 1988-; Clinical Lecturer, University of Adelaide, Department of General Practice, 1993-; Designated Aviation Medical Examiner, 2000-06; Steering Committee, Mid-North Rural South Australia Division General Practice, 1994-; Chairman, Drug and Therapeutics Committee, Port Pirie Regional Health Service Inc, 1994-2000; Mental Health Advisory Committee, Mid-North Regional Health Service Inc, 1996-2000; Medical Officer, Port Pirie Abattoir, 1991-2002; Club Doctor, Port Pirie Racing and Harness Club, 1993-; Club Doctor, Port Pirie Power Boat Club, 1990-2003; Clinical Lecturer, Adelaide University, School of Nursing, 2008-. Publications: Articles in medical journals as co-author: South Australian Hypertension Survey. General Practitioner Knowledge and Reported Management Practices – A Cause for Concern? 1992; A Comparison of Outcomes with Angiotensin-Converting Enzyme Inhibitors and Diuretics for Hypertension in the Elderly. Honours: Order of International Fellowship, 2004; International Health Professional of the Year, 2004, 2005; Fellow, ABI, 2005; ABI, Man of the Year, 2004, 2005; Legion of Honour, UCC, 2005; International Peace Prize, UCC, 2006. Memberships include: Fellow, Royal Australian College of General Practitioners; Fellow, Australian College of Rural and Remote Medicine; Port Pirie Medical Practitioners Society; Australian Medical Association; Sports Medicine Australia; International Federation of Sports Medicine; Arthritis Foundation of Australia; Rural Doctors Association of Australia; Australasian Society of Aerospace Medicine; Port Pirie Asthma Support Group; Life Member, Asthma Foundation; Leader Member, Lord Baden-Powell Society; Patron, Member of Lord Baden Powell Society, 2005. Address: Central Clinic, 101 Florence Street, Port Pirie, SA 5540, Australia. E-mail: supadocs@westnet.com.au

GOLDING Anthony Mark Barrington, b. 21 August 1928, London, England. Medical Practitioner. m. Olwen Valery Bridgeman, 1 son, 3 daughters. Education: Marlborough College, 1942-46; Cambridge University, 1946-49; Middlesex Hospital, 1949-52. Appointments: Consultant, Public Health Medicine, Redbridge & Waltham Forest, 1989-96; Senior Consultant, Community Medicine, Camberwell Health Authority, 1986-88; Chairman, 2002-06, Governor, 2001-, Portman early Childhood Centre; Trustee, Honorary Secretary, Sir John Golding Fund, 1986-. Publications: Editor, Water and Public Health, 1994; Editor, Violence as a Public Health Issue, 1997; Editor, Health & Hygiene journal, 1988-97; Author, Numerous articles in professional journals. Honours: MB B Chir, Cantab, 1952; MA (Hons), Cantab, 1954; MFCM, 1972; FFCM, 1979; FFPHM, 1989; FFPH, 2003; Fellow, Member of Council, 1987-2007, Chairman, Council, 1997, Vice President, 1999-2007, RIPH; Honorary FRSPH, 2007-; President, 1990-92, Vice President, 1994-2005, Section of Epidemiology and Public Health, Royal Society of Medicine. Memberships: Royal College of Ophthalmologists. Address: 12 Clifton Hill, London, NW8 0Q9, England. E-mail: amb.golding@btinternet.com

GOLDMAN William, b. 12 August 1931, Chicago, Illinois, USA. Author. m. Ilene Jones, 1961-91 (divorced), 2 daughters. Education: Columbia University. Publications: Novels: The Temple of Gold, 1957; Your Turn to Curtsey, My Turn to Bow, 1958; Soldier in the Rain, 1960; Boys and Girls Together, 1964; The Thing of It Is, 1964; No Way to Treat a Lady (as Harry Longbaugh); Father's Day, 1971; Marathon Man, 1974; Wigger, 1974; Magic, 1976; Tinsel, 1979; Control, 1982; The Silent Gondoliers, 1983; The Color of Light, 1984; Play: Blood Sweat and Stanley Poole (with James Goldman), 1961; Musical comedy: A Family Affair (with James Goldman and John Kander), 1962; Non-fiction: Adventures in the Screen Trade, 1983; Hype and Glory, 1990; Four Screenplays, 1995; Five Screenplays, 1997; Screenplays: Harper, 1966; Butch Cassidy and the Sundance Kid, 1969; The Princess Bride, 1973; Marathon Man, 1976; All the President's Men, 1976; A Bridge Too Far, 1977; Magic, 1978; Heat, 1985; Brothers, 1987; Year of the Comet, 1992; Memoirs of an Invisible Man, 1992; Chaplin, 1992; Indecent Proposal, 1993; Maverick, 1994; Ghost and the Darkness, 1996; Absolute Power, 1997; Hearts in Atlantis, 2001; Dreamcatcher, 2003; The Monkey Wrench Gang, 2008. Honours: Academy Awards, 1970, 1977. Address: c/o William Morris, 151 El Camino Drive, Beverly Hills, CA 90212, USA.

GOLDSMITH Harvey, b. 4 March 1946, London, England. Chief Executive; Impresario. m. Diana Gorman, 1971, 1 son. Education: Christ's College; Brighton College of Technology. Career: Partner, Big O Posters, 1966-67; Organised first free open-air concert in Parliament Hill Fields with Michael Alfandary, 1968; Opened Round House, Camden Town, 1968, Crystal Palace Garden Party series of concerts, 1969-72; Merged with John Smith Entertainments, 1970; Formed Harvey Goldsmith Entertainments (rock tours promotion company), 1976; Acquired Allied Entertainments Group (rock concert promotions company), 1984; Formed Classical Productions with Mark McCormack, 1986; Promoter and Producer of pop, rock and classical musical events including:

Concerts: Bruce Springsteen; The Rolling Stones; Elton John; The Who; Pink Floyd; Opera: Aïda, 1988, Carmen, 1989, Tosca, 1991, Earls Court; Pavarotti at Wembley, 1986; Pavarotti in the Park, 1991; The Three Tenors, 1996; Lord of the Dance, 1996-97; Cirque du Soleil, 1996-97; Mastercard Masters of Music, 1996; Music for Montserrat at the Royal Albert Hall, 1997; The Bee Gees, 1998; Ozzfest, 1998; Paul Weller, 1998. Honour: CBE, 1996. Memberships include: Chairman, Concert Promoters Association, 1986; Chairman, National Music Festival, 1991; Co-Chairman, President's Club, 1994; Vice Chairman, Prince's Trust Action Management Board, 1993; Vice President, REACT, 1989; Vice President, Music Users Council, 1994; Trustee, Band Aid, 1985; Trustee, Life Aid Foundation, 1985; Trustee, Royal Opera House, 1995; Trustee, CST, 1995; British Red Cross Communications Panel, 1992; Prague Heritage Fund, 1994; London Tourist Board, 1994. Address: Greenland Place, 115-123 Bayham Street, London NW1 0AG, England.

GOLDSTEIN Myrna, b. 5 August 1948, Rochester, New York, USA. Journalist; Writer. Education: Master's Degree, Teaching English as a Second/Foreign Language, St Michael's College, Vermont, USA; BSJ, Journalism, Northwestern University, Illinois, USA; Diploma, Italian Language and Culture; Certification to Teach Italian, University for Foreigners, Perguia, Italy. Appointments: Journalism includes: Feature Writer, Gannett Co, Rochester New York and Harrison, Westchester County, New York, 1986-89; Cross-Cultural Journalist, Editor, Copywriter, Publicist, Perugia, Italy, 1990-2005; Teaching includes: Professor, Tourism English, 1997-98, Professor, Business Communications and International Marketing, 1997-98, Institute for Commercial Services, Gualdo Tadino; Professor of Journalism, Spoleto and Norcia, 2000; Professor, Italian Army Officers Language Training Centre (SLEE), Perugia, 1998-2003; Lecturer, 2001-2002, Contract Professor, 2002-04, Program for Interpreters and Translators, Faculty of Philosophy and Letters, University of Perugia; Founder, Director, Chief Researcher, Are You in Your English File?®, Second Language Learning Research Center; Adjunct Expert, TESOL, Politecnico, Milan, Italy 2006-; Adjunct Expert, North American English and Culture, Catholic University of the Sacred Heart, Milan 2007-. Publications: Numerous articles in newspapers; Linguistics articles in Cognitive Linguistics, Issues in Applied Linguistics, and TESOL Quarterly; Unpublished texts, books, presentations; Are You in Your English File? Decoding Listening Comprehension Through Pre-Listening Strategies: A Pilot Case Study, 2002; ESL/EFL Study Frameworks, A personal language trainer's study manual for language atheletes, 2010-2011; Creating Autonomous, Plurilingual L2 Learners Through Contrual and Code Switching, 2011; Drama & Literary Texts: Sensing Worlds of Worlds – Poem-Songs on Loving and the World, 2004; Stealing Vesuvius, 2004-09; For Love of Monday, 2008; The Termite in the Violin, 2011; Works in progress: The One-Breasted Titan; Concorso; Casini's Cure; Etruscans. Honours: Pulitzer Prize Nominee, 1980; Reader's Digest Magazine Writing Award; Summer Intern, Magazine Publishers Association, 1969. Memberships: TESOL, USA; Linguistic Society of America; FAI; American Association for Applied Linguistics; Society of Children's Book Writers & Illustrators, Los Angeles; Dramatists Guild of New York. E-mail: myrnaedithgoldstein@gmail.com

GOLDSTEIN-JACKSON Kevin Grierson, b. 1946, Windsor, Berkshire, England. Writer; Artist; Poet. m. Mei Leng Ng, 1975, 2 daughters. Education: BA, Reading University; MPhil, Southampton University; FRSA. Appointments: Programme Organizer, Southern TV, 1970-73; Assistant Producer, HK-TVB, Hong Kong, 1973; Freelance Writer, TV Producer, 1974-75; Head of Film, Dhofar Region TV Service, Sultanate of Oman, 1975-76; Assistant to Head of Drama, Anglia TV, 1977-81; Founder, Chief Executive and Programme Controller, Television South West, 1981-85; Freelance Writer, 1985-. Contributions to numerous magazines and newspapers including: Sunday Times; Financial Times; Author of 19 published books; Writer of film and TV screen plays; Poetry published in US, UK, Australia, Canada, etc. Memberships: Writers' Guild; Society of Authors; Poetry Society. Address: c/o Alcazar, 18 Martello Road, Branksome Park, Poole, Dorset BH13 7DH, England.

GOLDTHORPE (John) Michael, b. 7 February 1942, York, England. Singer (Tenor). Education: MA, Trinity College, Cambridge, 1964; Certificate of Education, King's College, London, 1965; Guildhall School of Music and Drama, London, 1966-67. Debut: Purcell Room, London, January 1970. Career includes: Paris debut, 1972; Opera Royal, Versailles, 1977; Royal Opera, Covent Garden and BBC Television, 1980; Regular Broadcaster, BBC Radio; US debut, Miami Festival, 1986; Appearances in Singapore, Iceland, most countries Western Europe; Concertgebouw, Amsterdam, 1986, Directed Medieval Concert in Rome, 1987; Noted Bach Evangelist and exponent of French Baroquer; Lucerne Festival's performance of Frank Martin's Golgotha, 1990; Series of concerts for the Sorbonne, Paris, 1992; London performances Verdi Requiem, Janácek's Glagolitic Mass, Britten's Cantata Misericordium Beethoven's Missa Solemnis; Former Teacher, Royal Holloway College, Egham, London College of Music, Great Marlborough Street, Trinity College of Music, London; Lecturer and Adjudicator; Currently Singing Tutor at Priestlands School, Lymington; Founder and Artistic Director of the specialist Victorian music group and charity, The Bold Balladiers, 1995; Musical Director, Lymington Choral Society, 2006. Recordings include: Rameau: Hippolyte et Aricie, La Princesse de Navarre and Pygmalion; Charpentier Missa Assumpta est Maria; Mondonville Motets; Cavalli Ercole Amante; 100 Years of Italian Opera; Delius Irmelin; L'Incoronazione di Poppea; Monteverdi Madrigali Libri Primo, Secondo, Sesto; Blanchard Cantatas; The Snowy Breasted Pearl (Victorian and Edwardian Ballads); St Cuthbert of Lindisfarne and other Songs by Stuart Ward. Honours: Lieder Prize GSM, 1967; Choral Exhibition, Cambridge, 1961; GLAA Young Musicians Award, ISM Young Musicians Award, Park Lane Group's Young Musician Award, early 1970's; Wingate Scholarship, 1994. Memberships: Hon Fellow, Cambridge Society of Musicians, 1993; Member of the Royal Society of Musicians of Great Britain, 1999. Address: 77 Southampton Road, Lymington, Hants, SO41 9GH, England.

GOLLAPUDI Sastry V R S, b. 1 July 1962, Vijayawada, India. Lecturer. m. G Chandra Kumari, 1 son, 1 daughter. Education: B Technology, Electronics & Communicatino Engineering, 1983; ME, Computer Science & Engineering, 2001; PhD, Computer Science, 2011. Appointments: Lecturer, Department of Technical Education, Government of Andhra Pradesh, India. Publications: Velocity Modulated BFO; Bacterial Foraging Optimization Technique to Calculate Resonant Frequency; Intelligent Bacterial Foraging Optimization Technique. Honours: Listed in biographical dictionaries. Memberships: Indian Society for Technical Education. E-mail: sastry_gollapudi@rediffmail.com

GOLOVCHENKO Alexander Volodymyrovich, b. 3 February 1978, Kamyarika, Churkassy region, Ukraine. Senior Researcher. m. Oksana Ivanovna Lozko, 1 daughter. Education: Chemical Department, Kyiv State University, 2000. Appointments: Senior Researcher, Institute of Biochemistry and Petrochemistry, NAS of Ukraine. Publications: Synthesis of C-heteryl-sustituted aminomethyl phosphonic acids derivatives, 2010. Address: Murmanskaya 1, Kyiv, 02660, Ukraine.

GOLU Mihai, b. 4 March 1934, Poienari, Gorj, Romania. Psychologist; University Professor. m. Elena, 2 sons. Education: Diploma, Primary School Teacher, Educational College, 1952; Psychologist's Diploma, Master of Arts, Psychology, University of Moscow, 1958; Doctoral Studies, 1962-66, PhD, 1968, University of Bucharest; Postdoctoral Advanced Research in Human Information Processing, Carnegie-Mellon University, Pittsburgh, USA, 1973-74. Appointments: Assistant, 1958-62, Lecturer, 1962-70, Assistant Professor, 1970-82, Senior Researcher, Anthropological Center, 1982-90, Full Professor, 1990-2001, Department of Psychology, University of Bucharest; Minister of Education, Minister of Culture, 1991-93; Professor and Head, Department of Psychology, University Spiru Havet, Bucharest, 2001-. Publications: Over 150 articles; Books: Sensory Processes, 1970; General Cybernetics applied to psychology, 1970; Perception and Activity, 1971; Introduction to Psychology, 1972; Colour and Behaviour, 1974; Psychophysiology, 1976; Principles of Psychocybernetics, 1978; Psychoneurology, 1983; The Neurophysiological Bases of Mind, 1981; Handbook of General Psychology, 2003; Dynamics of Personality, 2005; Handbook of Neuropsychology, 2006; Fundamentals in Psychology, 2007-. Honours: National Order for Merit; UNESCO Medal, Pablo Picasso; Medal Ian Amos Comeius, Tcheck Academy; Doctor Honoris Causa, 2006, 2010; American Order of Excellence, 2007; Listed in international biographical dictionaries. Memberships: Romanian Academy of Scientists; Academy of Natural Sciences of Russian Federation; Romanian Association of Psychologists; International Association of Cybernetics. Address: Bd Libertatii 22, bloc 102, sc 5, apt 89, sector 5, Bucharest, Romania.

GOLUBYATNIKOV Leonid Leonidovich, b. 22 January 1962, Obraztsovo, Russia. Mathematician; Researcher. 2 daughters. Education: Diploma, Department of Mechanics and Mathematics, M V Lomonosov Moscow State University, 1984; Postgraduate Research Fellow, Computer Centre of the USSR Academy of Sciences, Moscow, 1988-91; Candidate of Physical-Mathematical Sciences (PhD), 1994. Appointments: Mathematician, Research Institute of Precise Apparatus, Moscow, 1984-88; Postgraduate Research Fellow, Computer Centre, USSR Academy of Sciences, Moscow, 1988-91; Junior Researcher, Institute of Atmospheric Physics, Russian Academy of Sciences, 1991-94; Head, Laboratory of Mathematical Ecology, Institute of Atmospheric Physics, 1994-2002; Senior Researcher, A M Obukhov Institute of Atmospheric Physics, Russian Academy of Sciences, 2002-. Publications: Numerous articles in professional journals. Honours: Eco-Frontier Fellowship Award, Environmental Agency of Japan, 2000; Listed in various international biographical dictionaries. Address: A M Obukhov Institute of Atmospheric Physics, 3 Pyzhevsky Lane, Moscow, 119017, Russia. E-mail: golub@ifaran.ru Website: www.ifaran.ru

GOMES DE MATOS Francisco Cardoso, b. 3 September 1933, Crato, Brazil. University Professor. m. Helen Herta Bruning, 1 son, 2 daughters. Education: Bachelor in Law and Languages, Federal University, Pernambuco, 1958; Master's in Linguistics, University of Michigan, 1960; PhD in Applied Linguistics, Catholic University of Sao Paulo, 1973. Appointments: Visiting Professor, Catholic University of Sao Paulo, 1966-79; Fulbright Visiting Professor, University of Georgia, Athens Georgia, USA, 1985-1986; Professor Emeritus, Federal University of Pernambuco; Co-founder, Brazil-America Association; Retired 2003 from the Federal University of Pernamuco, Consultant (Language & Culture) to Brazil America Association, Recife. Publications: Plea for Universal Declaration of Linguistic Rights, 1984; Plea for Communicative Peace, 1993; Chapter on Using Peaceful Language, from Principles to Practices in EOLSS, 2005; Chapter on Language, Peace and Conflict Resolution in the Handbook of Conflict Resolution (2nd Edition), 2006; Nurturing Nonkilling: a Poetic Plantation, 2009. Honours: Benefactor Member, International Society for the Teaching of Portuguese as a Foreign Language; Received Tribute at the 30th Anniversary of the Graduate Program in Letters/ Linguistics, Federal University of Pernambuco, 2006; Listed in 2000 Outstanding Intellectuals of the 21st Century. Memberships: Brazilian Linguistics Association; Brazilian Academy of Philology; Brazilian Association for Applied Linguistics; Columbia University-based research group www.humiliationstudies.org. Address: Rua Setubal 860-B, Apto 604, 51030-010 Recife, Brazil. E-mail: fcgm@hotlink.com.br Website: http://nonkilling.org/node/18

GOMEZ Rajan Gaetan, b. 21 November 1938, Kalutara, Sri Lanka. Consultant and Researcher in Parliamentary and Commonwealth Affairs. m. Rosanne Pinto, 2 daughters. Education: BSc (Hons), University of Sri Lanka, 1961; DIC (Diploma of Imperial College), 1973, MSc, Management Studies (with Distinction) Imperial College, 1973. Appointments: Directorates in the Commonwealth Secretariat and the Sri Lanka Administrative Service; Director of Development and Planning, Commonwealth Parliamentary Association, 1992-2003; Senior Research Fellow, University College London. Publications: Several publications in management operations research, human resource development, parliamentary and public administration; Member of Editorial Boards including Journal of Public Administration and Development. Honours: Nominee for Smith-Mundt Fulbright Award, 1961-62; Kluwer-Harrap Award, University of London, 1973. Memberships include: Fellow Royal Society of Chemistry; Fellow Royal Society of Arts; Member, Institute of Management Services; Treasurer and Trustee, Emmaus UK Federation. Address: 51 Linkway, London SW20 9AT, England.

GOMI Harumi, b. 14 January 1968, Kurashiki, Japan. Medical Doctor. m. Shuji Yano. Education: MD, Okayama University Medical School, 1993; DTM&H, London School of Hygiene & Tropical Medicine, 2000; MPH, Johns Hopkins Bloomberg School of Public Health, 2003. Appointments: Associate Professor, Jichi Medical University, 2005-. Memberships: Infectious Diseases Society of America; American College of Physicians; American Society for Microbiology.

GÖNCZ Árpád, b. 10 February 1922, Budapest, Hungary. Politician; Writer; Dramatist; Translator. m. Maria Zsuzsanna Göntér, 1947, 2 sons, 2 daughters. Education: DJ, Pázmány Péter University, 1944; University of Agricultural Sciences. Appointments: Active with Independent Smallholders' Party, 1947-48; Imprisoned for political activities, 1957-63; Founding Member, Free Initiative Network, Free Democratic Federation, Historic Justice Committee; Member and Speaker of Parliament, 1990; Acting President, 1990, President,

1990-2000, Republic of Hungary. Publications: Men of God (novel), 1974; Hungarian Medea (play), 1979; Iron Bars (play), 1979; Encounters (short stories), 1980; 6 plays, 1990; Homecoming (short stories), 1991; Shavings (essays), 1991. Honours: Honorary Knight Commander of the Order of St Michael and St George, England, 1991; Dr hc, Butler, 1990, Connecticut, 1991, Oxford, 1995, Sorbonne, 1996, Bologna, 1997; George Washington Prize, 2000; Pro Humanitate Award, 2001; Polish Business Oscar Award, 2002. Membership: Hungarian Writers' Union, President, 1989-90.

GONDA Takehiko, b. 14 July 1937, Toyokawa, Aichi, Japan. Meteorologist. m. Ikuko, 1969, 1 child. Education: BS, Tokyo University of Science, 1962; MS, 1965, DSc, 1968, Nagoya University. Appointments: Research Assistant, 1968, Instructor, 1971, Associate Professor, 1978, Secretary, 1980, Professor, 1991, Department of Physics, Tokyo University of Science, Chiba; Professor, 1992, Visiting Professor, 2008, Aichi Gakuin University; Editor: Meterological Society of Japan, 1988; Japanese Association of Crystal Growth, 1991; Japanese Society of Snow and Ice, 1996. Honours: Academy Award, Meterological Society of Japan, 1984. Memberships: Japanese Society of Cryobiology and Cryotechnology. Address: Aichi Gakuin University, Araike 12, Iwasaki, Nisshin, Aichi 470-0195, Japan. E-mail: t.-gonda@nifty.com

GONZÁLEZ PÉREZ Juan Antonio, b. 9 January 1963, Valencia, Spain. Architect. Education: Architecture & Urban Design (Hons), University of Las Palmas de Gran Canaria, ULPGC, Spain, 1990. Appointments: Professor, Architectural Design, School of Architecture, ETSA, ULPGC, 1993-; Principal Architect, GPY Arquitectos, 1997-; Cultural Delegate, Official Architects' Association, Canary Islands, Tenerife, 2000-10. Publications: Inner Landscapes, Biennale di Venezia, 2002; 100 Architects, 10 Critics, Phaidon, 2005; On Site: New Architecture in Spain, Moma, 2006; 1000 x European Architecture, Braun, 2006; Phaidon Atlas of 21st Century World Architecture, 2008. Honours: AR Award for Emerging Architects, 2003; Silver and Bronze Medals, Bienal, Miami Beach, Florida International University, AIA Miami Chapter; Nominee, European Union Prize, Mies Van Der Rohe Award, 2003; Nominee, Iakov Chernikhov International Prize, Iakov Chernikov Foundation, 2008; International Architecture Award, The Chicago Athenaeum, 2010. Memberships: Official Architects' Association of the Canary Islands, Spain. Address: c/Castillo 56 – 2d, Santa Cruz de Tenerife, 38003, Spain. E-mail: jgonzalez@gpyarquitectos.com

GONZALEZ-GONZALEZ Jesus Maria, b. 25 January 1961, Herreros de Suso, Avila, Spain. Stomatologist. m. Maria Teresa Rubio Hortells, separated 2003, 2 children. Education: BMed, University of Salamanca, 1985; Programmer Basic, Pontificia University of Salamanca, 1988; Specialist in Stomatology, University of Murcia, 1992; DMed, University of Alicante, 1992. Appointments: Medical Practitioner, State Health Service, Salamanca and Provence, 1987-88, La Manga, Murcia, 1990; Dentist, State Health Service, Cartagena, Murcia, 1990, 1991, Bejar and Ciudad Rodrigo, Salamanca, 1992; Private Practice in Stomatology, Murcia, 1991, Salamanca, 1991-; Speaker in field, 18 reports in congress. Publications: Several books in Spanish; Articles in professional journals and magazines; 2 patents. Honours: Honorable Mention, Children's Meeting of Painting, Town House of Salamanca, 1974 and Military Service, Lerida, 1986; Listed in numerous Who's Who publications and biographical dictionaries. Memberships: Professional Association of Dentists, Spain; Ski Club of Salamanca; New York Academy of Sciences; Founder President, Asociacion de Padres de Familia Separados de Salamanca y Pro-Derechos de Nuestros Hijos. Address: c/ Avila, No 4, lo A, 37004 Salamanca, Spain.

GONZALEZ-MARINA Jacqueline, b. 19 February 1935, Madrid, Spain. Lecturer; Translator and Official Interpreter in 7 Languages; Poet; Writer; Publisher; Journalist; Editor; Artist. m. (1) 2 sons, 1 daughter, (2) Desmond Savage, 1982. Education: BA, Modern Philology, 1959, MA, Modern Philology, 1962, University of Barcelona. Appointments: Lecturer, University of Barcelona, 1960-68, St Godrics College, London, 1970-91; Founder and Editor, Dandelion Arts Magazine (International), 1979-; Editor, Fern Publications, 1979-; Editor, The Student Magazine (International), 2000-08; Lecturer in Modern Languages, American Intercontinental University, London, 1994-2000; More than 60 art exhibitions, one person and collective in England and Spain; Arts Societies Lecturer in the UK and Spain. Publications: Dieciocho Segundos, 1953; Tijeras Sin Filo, 1955; Antología de Temas, 1961; Short Stories, 1972; Brian Patten, 1975; A Survival Course, 1975; Once Poemas a Malaga, 1977; Poesía Andaluza, 1977; Adrian Henri, 1980; Historias y Conversaciones, 1995; Mediterranean Poetry, bilingual anthology, 1997; Conversaciones en Español, 1998; Drawing and Painting for Fun, 1998; The Millennium Anthology, poetry and prose, Vol 1, 1999, Vol II, 2000; The International Book of Short Stories, 2002; Cats in the Palm Tree and Other Stories (co-writer), 2002; Dali & I, poems, 2003; Contributions to: Countless anthologies and international magazines; Writer and broadcaster for the BBC, London, 1975-78. Honours: Royal Academician, Royal Academy of St Telmo, Malaga, Spain, 1975; Honorary Member of the Atheneum in Alicante, Spain, 1999. Memberships: Society of Women Writers and Journalists, London; The Historical Association Saxoferreo, Cordoba, Spain; The Poetry Society; Listed in national and international biographical dictionaries. Address: "Casa Alba", 24 Frosty Hollow, East Hunsbury, Northants NN4 0SY, England.

GONZINI Ornella, b. 20 June 1980, Foggia, Italy. Environmental Scientist. Education: B Eng, Chemical Engineering, University of Naples, Italy, 2006; PhD, Chemical Engineering for Safety and Environment, University of Rome, Italy, 2010. Appointments: Internship, Centre of Research ENEA (Italian National agency for new technologies); Researcher, IMIDRA (Instituto Madrileño Desarrollo Rural y); Researcher, ISPRA (Institute for Environmental Protection and Research); Environmental Scientist, Gardline. Publications: Enhancement of biomass speciation in step sludge recirculation activated sludge system by the use of submerged membranes, 2010; Electro-bioremediation of gasoil contaminated soil, 2010; Effect of acidification and modified Fenton treatment on a contaminated harbor sediment, 2011; Use of different chelating agents for heavy metal extraction from contaminated harbor sediment, 2011. Honours: Listed in biographical dictionaries. Memberships: Engineering Association of Rome; Assoicated Member, IChemE; Associate Member, IEMA. Address: 219 Queensbridge Road, London E8 4LA, England.

GOOCH Graham Alan, OBE, b. 23 July 1953, Leytonstone, London. Cricketer. m. Brenda Daniels, 3 daughters. Career: Right-hand opening batsman, right-arm medium bowler; Played for Essex 1973-97, (captain, 1986-87, 1989-94), West Prov, 1982-83,1983-84; Played in 118 tests for England, 1975 to 1994-95, 34 as captain, scoring 8900 runs (England record, average 42.5) including 20 hundreds (highest score 333 and Test match aggregate of 456 v India, Lord's 1990, becoming only batsman to score triple century and century in a first-class match and holding 103 catches; scored 44,841 runs (128 hundreds) and held 555 catches in first-class cricket; Toured Australia 1978-79, 1979-80, 1990-91 (captain) and 1994-95; 125 limited-overs internationals, including 50 as captain (both England records); Member, England Selection Committee, 1996-; Manager, England Tour to Australia, 1998-99; Head Coach, Essex, 2001-2005. Publications: Testing Times, 1991; Gooch: My Autobiography, 1995. Honours include: OBE; Wisden Cricketer of the Year, 1980. Address: c/o Essex County Cricket Club, The County Ground, New Writtle Street, Chelmsford, Essex, CM2 0PG, England.

GOODALL Sir (Arthur) David (Saunders), b. 9 October 1931, Blackpool, England. Diplomatist (retired). m. Morwenna Peecock, 1962, 2 sons, 1 daughter. Education: Ampleforth College; Trinity College, Oxford. Appointments: Army service in Kenya, Aden, Cyprus, 1954-56; Joined Foreign (now Diplomatic) Service, 1956, served at Nicosia, Jakarta, Bonn, Nairobi, Vienna, 1956-75; Head, Western European Department, FCO, 1975-79; Minister, Bonn, 1979-82, Deputy Secretary, Cabinet Office, 1982-84, Deputy Under-Secretary of State, FCO, 1984-87; High Commissioner in India, 1987-91; Joint Chair, Anglo-Irish Encounter, 1992-97; President, Irish Genealogical Research Society, 1992-2009; Chair, Leonard Cheshire Foundation, 1995-2000 (Chair International Committee, 1992-95); Chair, British-Irish Association, 1997-2002; Chair, Advisory Governors, Ampleforth College, 2004-10; Chair, Governing Body, Heythrop College, University of London, 2000-06; Visiting Professor in Irish Studies, University of Liverpool, 1996-; Member of Council, University of Durham, 1992-2000 (Vice Chair, 1997-2000); One-man exhibitions: (watercolours): Berlin, 1979; Bonn, 1982; London, 1987, 1994; New Delhi, 1991; Durham, 1996; Hull, 1998; Helmsley (York), 2004, 2006, 2008. Publications: Remembering India, 1997; Rydale Pilgramage, 2000; Contributions to The Tablet, The Ampleforth Journal; The Past; The Irish Genealogist. Honours: GCMG 1991 (KCMG 1987); KSG, 2007; Honorary Fellow, Trinity College, Oxford; Distinguished Friend of the University of Oxford, 2001; Honorary LLD (Hull), 1994. Address: Greystones, Ampleforth, North Yorkshire, YO62 4DU, England.

GOOD-BLACK Edith Elissa, b. 10 January 1945, Hollywood, California, USA. Writer. m. Michael Lawrence Black, deceased. Education: BA, English, California State University, Northridge, 1974; Student, University of California, Los Angeles and University of California, Berkeley, 1962-92; Explorer, Mayan ruins, Mexico, 1963; Music student, Ballet Folklorico, Mexico, 1963. Appointments: Participant, numerous dance, art, music, literature, mathematics and science classes; Dancer, Hajde Dance Troop, Berkeley, California, 1962-66; One-woman art shows, Los Angeles, 1962-95; Singer in various languages, coffee houses, cafés, nightclubs, half-way houses, libraries, picnics, churches, temples and others, Los Angeles, 1986-; Sole Proprietor, Gull Press. Publications include: (pseudonym, Pearl Williams) The Trickster of Tarzana, 1992; Short Stories, 1995; Mad in Craft, 1995; Missives, 1995; Dictionary of Erudition, 1995; American Poetry Anthology; International Library of Poetry. Contributed poetry to CDs, radio and ipod broadcasts, internet broadcasts, publications; American Poetry Anthology; International Library of Poetry; and others. Honours: Summa Cum Laude, California State University; Writing chosen by a jury of experts for permanent collection in the Library of Congress, USA; Leonardo da Vinci Prize, Shakespeare Prize, International Biographical Centre; 25 Years Award, MENSA; Listed in numerous Who's Who and biographical publications. Memberships: MENSA; American Society of Composers, Authors and Publishers; Plummer Park Writers; Westside Writers; Beyond Baroque Literary Foundation; Songwriters' Resources and Services; Democratic clubs, California and Mexico, 1962-; Supporter, mental health organisations, 1962-; Delegate to local Democratic conventions, fundraiser, canvasser, office worker, driver and participant in consciousness raising groups in support of civil rights; CORE, San Francisco, Berkeley, Los Angeles, and Oakland, 1965; Peace in Alliance for Survival, Berkeley, Oakland, Los Angeles, 1964-80; Women's rights, Westside Women's Center, Woman's Building, Los Angeles, 1974-80; Environment in Earth Day, Los Angeles, 1977; Literary Consultant, tutor and book reviewer; Supporter of Residential Collective, 1985-; Member, Advisory Board, American Biographical Institute; Member, Research Academy, IBC. Address: 1470 South Robertson Blvd, Apt 210, Los Angeles, CA 90035-3402, USA.

GOODBODY Michael Ivan Andrew, b. 23 January 1942, Wicklow, Ireland. m. Susannah Elizabeth Pearce, 1 son, 2 daughters. Education: Kingstown School, Dublin, Ireland. Appointments: J & L F Goodbody Ltd, Jute Manufacturers, 1960-62; Member of the Stock Exchange, 1968-87; Member of the Securities Institute, 1987-2006; Stockbroker, Smith Rice & Hill, 1962-74; Stockbroker, 1974-82, Partner/Director, 1982-89, Divisional Director, 1989-2000, Capel-Cure Myers Ltd; Private Client Fund Manager, Carr Sheppards Crosthwaite, 2000-06-. Publications: The Goodbody Family of Ireland, 1979; A Quaker Wedding at Lisburn; Occasional articles on family history. Memberships: Territorial Army – 289 Parachute Regiment RHA, 1964-75; Society of Genealogists; Treasurer, Colne and Stour Countryside Association; Member, Irish Genealogical Research Society; Quaker Family History Society. Address: The Old Rectory, Wickham St Paul's, Essex CO9 2PJ, England.

GOODENOUGH Frederick Roger, b. 21 December 1927, Broadwell, Oxfordshire, England. Retired Director: Farmer. m. Marguerite June, 1 son, 2 daughters. Education: MA (Cantab), 1955; MA (Oxon), 1975; FCIB; FLS; FRSA. Appointments: RN, 1946-48; Joined Barclays Bank Ltd, 1950; Local Director, Birmingham, 1958-60, Reading, 1960-69, Oxford, 1969-87, Director Barclays, Bank UK, Ltd, 1971-87, Barclays Bank International Ltd, 1977-87, Barclays PLC, 1985-89, Barclays Bank PLC, 1979-89; Advisory Director, Barclays Bank Thames Valley Region, 1988-89; Member, London Committee Barclays Bank DCO, 1966-71, Barclays Bank International Ltd, 1971-80; Senior Partner, Broadwell Manor Farm, 1968-; Curator, Oxford University Chest, 1974-93; President, Oxfordshire Rural Community Council, 1993-98; Trustee: Nuffield Medical Benefaction, 1968-2002 (Chairman, 1987-2002), Nuffield Dominions Trust, 1968-2002 (Chairman, 1987-2002); Nuffield Oxford Hospitals Fund, 1968-2003 (Chairman, 1982-88), Nuffield Orthopaedic Centre Trust, 1978-2003 (Chairman, 1981-2003), Oxford Preservation Trust, 1980-89, Radcliffe Medical Foundation, 1987-98; Governor: Shiplake College, 1963-74 (Chairman, 1966-70),Wellington College, 1968-74, Goodenough College, 1985-2006; Patron, Anglo Ghanaian Society, 1991-. Publication: Co-author, Britain's Future in Farming (edited by Sir Frank Engledow and Leonard Amey, 1980. Honours: High Sheriff, Oxfordshire, 1987-88; Deputy Lieutenant, Oxfordshire, 1989-; Supernumerary Fellow, 1989-95, Honorary Fellow, 1995, Wolfson College, Oxford. Memberships: Fellow, Linnean Society (Member of Council 1968-75, Treasurer, 1970-75, Finance Committee,

1968-2008); Brooks's, London. Address: Broadwell Manor, Nr Lechlade, Gloucestershire, GL7 3QS, England. E-mail: f.r.goodenough@broadwellmanor.co.uk

GOODING Cuba Jr, b. 2 January, 1968, Bronx, New York, USA. Actor. m. Sara Kapfer, 1994, 3 children. Career: TV appearances include: Kill or Be Killed, 1990; Murder with Motive: The Edmund Perry Story, 1992; Daybreak, 1993; The Tuskagee Airmen; Film appearances include: Coming to America, 1988; Sing, 1989; Boyz N the Hood, 1991; Gladiator, A Few Good Men, Hitz, 1992; Judgement Night, 1993; Lightning Jack, 1994; Losing Isiah, Outbreak, 1995; Jerry Maguire, The Audition, 1996; Old Friends, As Good As It Gets, 1997; What Dreams May Come, 1998; A Murder of Crows, Instinct, Chill Factor, 1999; Men of Honor, 2000; Pearl Harbor, Rat Race, In the Shadows, 2001; Snow Dogs, Boat Trip, 2002; Psychic, The Fighting Temptations, Radio, 2003; Home on the Range (voice), A Dairy Tale (voice), 2004; Shadowboxer, Dirty, 2005; Lightfield's Home Videos, End Game, 2006; Norbit, What Love Is; Daddy Day Camp, American Gangster, Hero Wanted, 2007; Harold, Linewatch, The Way of War, 2008; Gifted Hands: The Ben Carson Story, Lies & Illusions, The Devil's Tomb, Wrong Turn at Tahoe, Hardwired, 2009; Red Tails, 2010. Honours: 2 NAACP Awards; Academy Award; Best Supporting Actor (for Jerry Maguire), 1997; Chicago Film Critics Award; Screen Actor Guild Award. Address: c/o Rogers and Cowan, 1888 Century Park East, Suite 500, Los Angeles, CA 90067, USA.

GOODISON Sir Nicholas, b. 16 May 1934, Radlett, England. Former Chairman, London Stock Exchange. m. Judith Abel Smith, 1960, 1 son, 2 daughters. Education: BA Classics, 1958, MA, PhD, Architecture and History of Art, 1981, King's College, Cambridge. Appointments: H E Goodison & Co (now Quilter & Co Ltd), 1958-86, Chairman, 1975-86; Member of Council, 1968-88, Chairman, 1976-88, Stock Exchange, London; President, International Federation of Stock Exchanges, 1985-86; Member, Panel on Takeovers and Mergers, 1976-88; Member, Council for the Securities Industry, 1978-85; Member, Securities Association, 1986-88; Director, Ottoman Bank, 1986-92; Director, Banque Paribas Capital Markets, 1986-88; Director, General Accident plc, 1987-95; Director, 1989-2002, Deputy Chairman, 1993-99, British Steel plc (from 1999, Corus plc); Chairman, TSB Group plc, 1989-95; Deputy Chairman, Lloyds TSB Group plc, 1995-2000; President, British Bankers' Association, 1991-96; Member, Executive Committee, 1976-2002, Chairman, 1986-2002 National Art Collections Fund; Trustee, 1975-, Director, 1975-2007, Chairman, 2002-07, Burlington Magazine; Director, 1977-98, Vice-Chairman, 1980-88, English National Opera; Chairman, 1982-2002, Member of Governing Board, 2002-09, Courtauld Institute of Art, London University; Trustee, Kathleen Ferrier Memorial Scholarship Fund, 1987-; Trustee, National Heritage Memorial Fund, 1988-97; Member of Council ABSA (now Arts and Business), 1990-99; Chairman, Crafts Council, 1997-2005; Member of Council, 1965-, President, 1990-, Furniture History Society; Trustee, 2001-, President, 2007-, Walpole Society; Chairman, National Life Story Collection, 2003-; Governor Marlborough College, 1981-97; Trustee, Harewood House Trust; Chairman of Review Steering Group, National Record of Achievement, (Department for Education and Science) 1996-97; Member, Royal Commission on Long Term Care for the Elderly, 1997-99; Chairman, Goodison Group on Lifelong Learning, 1999-2006; Member, Further Education Funding Council, 2000-2001; Leader and author, Goodison Review "Securing the Best for our Museums: Private Giving and Government Support" (HM Treasury), 2003. Publications: English Barometers 1680-1860, 1968, 2nd edition, 1977; Ormolu: the Work of Matthew Boulton, 1974, revised as Matthew Boulton: Ormolu, 2003; Hotspur, Eighty Years of Antiques dealing (with Robin Kern), 2004; These Fragments, 2005; Articles and lectures on stock exchange, banking, financial regulation, etc; Articles and lectures on arts, history of decorative arts, museums, etc. Honours: KB, 1982; Chevalier, Legion d'Honneur, 1990; Victoria and Albert Museum, Robinson Medal, 2007; Hon DLitt, City University, 1985; Hon LLD, Exeter University, 1989; Hon DSc, Aston University, 1994; Hon DArt, deMontfort University, 1998; Hon DCL, University of Northumbria, 1999; Hon DLitt, University of London, 2003; Honorary Fellow, King's College, Cambridge, 2002; Honorary Fellow, Courtauld Institute of Art, 2003; Honorary Fellow, British Academy, 2004; Honorary Fellow, Royal Academy of Arts; Senior Fellow, Royal College of Art; Honorary Fellow, RIBA; Honorary Fellow, City and Guilds, 2007. Memberships: Fellow, Society of Antiquaries; Fellow, Royal Society of Arts. Address: PO Box 2512, London W1A 5ZP, England.

GOODMAN John, b. 20 June 1952, St Louis, USA. Film Actor. m. Annabeth Hartzog, 1989, 1 daughter. Education: South West Missouri State University. Career: Broadway appearances in: Loose Ends, 1979; Big River, 1985; TV appearances include: The Mystery of Moro Castle; The Face of Rage; Heart of Steel; Moonlighting, Chiefs (min-series); The Paper Chase; Murder Ordained; The Equalizer; Roseanne (series); Normal, Ohio, Pigs Next Door, 2000, The Emperor's New School, 2008; Films include: The Survivors, Eddie Macon's Run, 1983; Revenge of the Nerds, CHUD, 1984; Maria's Lovers, Sweet Dreams, 1985; True Stories, 1986; The Big Easy, Burglar, Raising Arizona, 1987; The Wrong Guys, Everybody's All-American, Punchline, 1988; Sea of Love, Always, 1989; Stella, Arachnophobia, King Ralph, 1990; Barton Fink, 1991; The Babe, 1992; Born Yesterday, 1993; The Flintstones, 1994; Kingfish: A Story of Huey P Long, 1995; Pie in the Sky, Mother Night, 1996; Fallen, Combat!, The Borrowers, 1997; The Big Lebowski, Blues Brothers 2000, Dirty Work, 1998; The Runner, 1999; Coyote Ugly, One Night at McCool's, 2000; Happy Birthday, My First Mister, Storytelling, Monsters Inc (voice), 2001; Dirty Deeds, 2002; Masked and Anonymous, The Jungle Book 2 (voice), 2003; Home of Phobia, Clifford's Really Big Movie (voice), Beyond the Sea, 2004; Marilyn Hotchkiss Ballroom Dancing & Charm School, The Emperor's New Groove 2: Kronk's New Groove (voice), 2005; Cars (voice), 2006; Evan Almighty, Drunkboat, Death Sentence, Bee Movie, In the Electric Mist, 2007; Speed Racer, 2008; Gigantic, Confessions of a Shopaholic, In the Electric Mist, Alabama Moon, Beyond All Boundries (voice), The Princess and The Frog (voice), 2009; Spring Break '83, You Don't Know Jack, 2010. Honours: Golden Globe Award, 1988; People's Choice Awards, 1989 & 2001; Emmy Award, 2006; Address: c/o Fred Spektor, CAA 9830 Wilshire Boulevard, Beverly Hills, CA 90212, USA.

GOODSON Ivor, b. 30 September 1943, Reading, England. Professor of Learning Theory. m. Mary Nuttall, 1 son. Education: BSc (Econ), University College, London, 1965; Teachers Certificate (Distinction), 1970, Academic Diploma, 1974, London Institute of Education; DPhil, University of Sussex, 1979. Appointments: Lecturer, BA General, University of Kingston, 1966-69; Specialist in History and Social Studies, Countesthorpe College, Leicestershire, 1970-73; Head of Humanities Faculty, Stantonbury Campus, Milton Keynes, 1973-75; Research Fellow, 1975-78, Director, The Schools Unit, 1978-85, University of Sussex; Full Professor, Faculty of Education, Faculty of Graduate Studies and Centre for Theory and Criticism, 1986-96, Director of

DICTIONARY OF INTERNATIONAL BIOGRAPHY 36th EDITION

Educational Research Unit, 1989-96, Honorary Professor of Sociology, 1993-98, University of Western Ontario, Canada; Frederica Warner Scholar, Scholar in Residence and Professor of Education, Margaret Warner Graduate School, University of Rochester, 1996-2002; Chair of Education, Centre for Applied Research in Education, School of Education and Professional Development, University of East Anglia, England, 1996-2004; Professor of Learning Theory, Education Research Centre, University of Brighton, 2004-; Research Associate, Von Hugel Institute, St Edmunds College, University of Cambridge, 2004-. Publications: Numerous books, and articles published in professional journals. Honours: Visiting Professor, University of Sussex, University of Exeter, Institute of Political Science in Paris, France; Stint Foundation Professor, Sweden, 2003-08; Catalan Research Professor, Spain, 2005; Michael Huberman Award, USA, 2006; Laureate Chapter of Kappa Delta Pi, USA, 2007; Joss Owen Professor (Chair of Education), University of Plymouth, 2007-10; Honorary Doctorate, Göteborg University, Sweden, 2008; Life Fellow, Royal Society of Arts, 2009; Listed in international biographical dictionaries. Memberships: Executive Member, Centre for Theory and Criticism. E-mail: i.f.goodson@brighton.ac.uk

GOODSON-WICKES Charles, b. 7 November 1945, London, England. Consulting Physician; Company Director; Business Consultant; Charity Executive. m. Judith Hopkinson, 2 sons. Education: MB BS, St Bartholomew's Hospital, 1970; Barrister-at-Law, Inner Temple, 1972. Appointments: Consulting Physician, BUPA, 1976-86; Principal, Private Occupational Health Practice, 1980-94; Member of Parliament, Parliamentary Private Secretary, The Treasury, Departments of Environment and Transport, 1987-97; Surgeon Lieutenant Colonel, The Life Guards, 1990-91 (Gulf War); Director, Nestor Healthcare Group, 1993-99; Chairman, British Field Sports Society, 1994-97; Founder Chairman, Countryside Alliance, 1997-99; Currently: Chief Executive, Medarc Ltd; Director, Chairman, 2010-, Thomas Greg & Son Ltd; Director Gyrus Group plc; Chief Executive, London Playing Fields Society; Chairman, The Rural Trust; London Sports Board; Director General, Canning House, 2010-; Member, Advisory Council, Institute for the Study of the Americas, University of London, 2010-; Director, Royal Institution & Chartered Surveyors (RICS), Business Development Board, 2010-. Publications: The New Corruption, 1984; Another Country (contributor), 1999. Honour: Deputy Lieutenant, Greater London, 1999; Representative Deputy Lieutenant, London Borough of Islington, 2011-. Memberships: Boodle's; Pratt's; MCC. Address: Watergate House, Bulford, Wiltshire SP4 9DY, England.

GOOT Roman, b. 1 December 1937, Leningrad, USSR. Lecturer. m. Galina, 1 daughter. Education: MSc, State Electrotechnical Institute, Leningrad, 1961; PhD, State Institute of Communication Engineers, Leningrad, 1970. Appointments: Engineer-Developer, Radiotechnical Factory, Leningrad; Senior Scientific Fellow, Investigative Radiotechnical Institute, Leningrad; Head of Biometric Laboratory, Institute of Roentyenology, Leningrad; Lecturer, Technical Institute, Holon, Israel. Publications: Approximately 180 scientific and technical publications; 87 patents. Address: Har Hatzofim St 38, Apt 39, Holon 58492, Israel.

GOPALAN Rama, b. 14 September 1951, New Delhi, India. Education: MBBS, 1973, MD, Pathology, 1980, University of Madras, Jipmer, Pondicherry. Appointments: Assistant Research Officer, 1982, Research Officer, 1983, RRIUM, Chennai; Lecturer, Reader, Professor and Head, Department of Pathology, Taramani, Chennai, 1983-. Publications: Numerous articles in professional journals. Honours: Secretary/Treasurer, Indian Division of International Academy of Pathology, 1992-94; Fellow, Indian College of Pathologists, 2008; President, Indian Society for Atherosclerosis Research, 2010-11. Memberships: Indian Association of Pathologists and Microbiologists; ISAR; International Academy of Pathology; International Atherosclerosis Society. Address: Department of Pathology, University of Madras, Taramani, Chennai 600113, India. E-mail: rama_gopalan@rediffmail.com

GOPAUL-MCNICOL Sharon-ann, b. 6 October 1958, Trinidad, West Indies. Professor. m. Ulric McNicol, 1 daughter. Education: BA, Psychology, New York University, 1981; MA, Developmental Psychology, Columbia University, New York, 1982; MA, General Psychology, 1984, Masters of Education/Certification, School Psychology, 1985, PhD, Clinical/School Psychology, 1986, Hofstra University, Hempstead, New York. Appointments: Psychologist/Special Need Co-ordinator, Community Life Headstart, 1984-85; Psychologist, Nassau County Department of Drug and Alcohol Addiction, 1985-86; Psychologist, Creedmoor Psychiatric Center, 1986-87; Executive Director, Multicultural Educational & Psychological Services, 1987-93; Director, Bilingual Program/Assistant Professor, St John's University, 1993-96; Associate Professor, 1997-98, Director of School Psychology/Professor, 1998-2000, Howard University; Assistant Director of Accreditation, American Psychological Association, 2000-01; Psychological/Educational Consultant, NYC Board of Education, 1987-2001; International Consultant (Political, Educational & Clinical), 2001-; Board Director, TIDCO, 2002-03; Board Director, TSTT, 2004-05; Adviser to Minister Valley, Minister of Trade and Industry and Minister in the Ministry of Finance, 2002-04; Director, Secretariat for the Implementation of Spanish, 2004-09; Senator, Member of Parliament, 2009-10; Professor, University of the West Indies, 2009-. Publications: Numerous articles in professional journals; Author/co-author, 13 books.

GOPHEN Moshe, b. 18 December 1936, Israel. Professor. m. Eva, 1 son, 3 daughters. Education: BSc, 1960-63, MSc, 1964-67, PhD, 1971-76, Hebrew University, Jerusalem. Appointments: Senior Scientist, 1969-2001, Director, 1980-86, Kinneret Limnological Laboratory, Israel; Visiting Professor, University of Oklahoma, USA, 1992-95; Consultant for Reservoir Management, Brazil, on behalf of Tahal, Israel, 1995; Scientific Co-ordinator, Hula Project, Israel, 1995-; External Full Professor, Tel Hai Academic College, Israel, 1996-; Chairman, Hula Committee, Israel, 1997; Senior Scientist, Migal, Israel, 2002-; Consultant for Reservoir Management, China, on behalf of Tahal, Israel, 2005; Visiting Professor in Limnology, Valldivia University, Chile, 2007 and UNAM University, Mexico, 2009. Publications: Lake Kinneret, Jerusalem, 1992; 70 Research reports; 160 papers in reviewed international journals; 50 articles in non-reviewed magazines. Honours: Fellowship, Eshkol Foundation, Ministry of Science, Israel, 1969-; Fellowship, Limnology, UNESCO, Israel, 1970; Fellowship, Carlsberg Institute, Denmark, Ministry of Science, Israel, 1974; Fellowship, Oceanographic Institute, Plymouth, England, 1978; Fellowship, DAAD, Germany, Konstanz; Fellowship, MINERVA, Konstanz, Germany; Fellowship, University of Western Australia, Perth, Australia. Memberships: International Association of Theoretical and Applied Limnology, SIL; American Society of Limnology and Oceanography, ASLO; Israel Zoological Society; Israel Malacological Society, Chairman, 1977-8; Israel Ecological Society, ISEEQ; Freshwater Biological Association, FBA,

England, Life Member; North American Lake Management Society, NALMS; The National Geographic Society. Address: Migal-Galilee Technology Center, POB 831 Kiryat Schmone, Israel, 11016. E-mail: Gophen@Migal.Org.IL

GORAIN Ganesh Chandra, b.6 December 1969, Purulia, India. Associate Professor; Researcher. m. Munmun, 1 son. Education: BSc (Hons), Mathematics, 1990, MSc, Applied Mathematics, 1992, Burdwan University; PhD, Mathematics, Jadavpur University, 2000. Appointments: Lecturer, 1997-2001, Senior Lecturer, 2001-06, Reader, 2006-09, Associate Professor, 2009-, Mathematics, J K College, Purulia. Publications: 20 articles in professional journals. Honours: Gold Medal, University of Burdwan, 1993; National scholarships. Memberships: Indian Statistical Institute; Listed in international biographical dictionaries. Address: Department of Mathematics, UG & PG, J K College, Purulia, Pin 723101, WB, India. E-mail: goraing@gmail.com

GORARD David, b. 23 December 1960, London, England. Doctor. m. Philippa, 1 son, 2 daughters. Education: St Benedicts School, London, 1979; St Mary's Hospital, University of London, 1979-84. Appointments: Research Fellow, St Batholomew's Hospital, 1990-94; Senior Registrar, Royal London Hospital and Oldchurch Hospital, 1994-96; Consultant Physician & Gastroenterologist, Wycombe Hospital, 1996-. Publications: Various publications related to clinical medicine and clinical gastroenterology. Honours: MB BS; MD; MRCP; FRCP. Memberships: Royal College of Physicians; British Society of Gastroenterology. Address: Wycombe Hospital, Queen Alexandra Road, High Wycombe, Buckinghamshire HP11 2TT, England. E-mail: david.gorard@buckshealthcare.nhs.uk

GORBACHEV Mikhail Sergeyevich, b. 2 March 1931, Privolnoye, Krasnogvardeisky, Stavropol, Russia. Politician. m. Raisa Titarenko, 25 September 1953, 1 daughter. Education: Faculty of Law, Moscow State University, 1955; Stavropol Agricultural Institute, 1967. Appointments: Machine Operator, 1946; Joined CPSU, 1952; Deputy Head, Department of Propaganda Stavropol Komsomol Territorial Committee, 1955-56; First Secretary, Stavropol Komsomol City Committee, 1956-58; Second, then First Secretary Komsomol Territorial Committee, 1958-62; Party Organizer, Stavropol Territorial Production Board of Collective and State Farms, 1962; Head Department of Party Bodies of CPSU Territorial Committee, 1963-66; First Secretary, Stavropol City Party Committee, 1966-68; Second Secretary, Stavropol Territorial CPSU Committee, 1968-70, First Secretary, 1970-78; CPSU Central Secretary for Agricultural, 1978-85; General Secretary, CPSU Central Committee, 1985-91; Chairman, Supreme Soviet, 1989-90; President, USSR, 1990-91; Head, International Foundation for Socio-Econ and Political Studies, 1992-; Head, International Green Cross, 1993-; Co-founder, Social Democratic Party of Russia, 2000-04. Publications: A Time for Peace, 1985; The Coming Century of Peace, 1986; Speeches and Writings, 1986-90; Peace Has No Alternative, 1986; Moratorium, 1986; Perestroika: New Thinking for Our Country and the World, 1987; The August Coup (Its Cause and Results), 1991; December-91, My Stand, 1992; The Years of Hard Decisions, 1993; Life and Reforms, 1995. Honours: Indira Gandhi Award, 1987; Nobel Peace Prize, 1990; Peace Award World Methodist Council, 1990; Albert Schweitzer Leadership Award, Ronald Reagan Freedom Award, 1992; Honorary Citizen, Berlin, 1992; Freeman of Aberdeen, 1993; Urania-Medaille, Berlin, 1996; Honorary Degrees: University of Alaska, 1990; University of Bristol, 1993; University of Durnham, 1995; Order of Lenin, 3 times; Orders of Red Banner of Labour, Badge of Honour and other medals. Address: International Foundation for Socio-Economic and Political Studies, Leningradsky Prosp 49, 125468 Moscow, Russia.

GORBACHEV Mikhail Yurievich, b. 14 October 1959, Kishinev, Moldova. Chemist. m. V V Gorbacheva, 3 sons, 1 daughter. Education: MSc, Chemistry, Kishinev State University, 1981; PhD, Chemistry, Rostov-on-Don State University, 1986. Appointments: Post Graduate, 1982-85, Scientific Researcher, 1986-95, Senior Scientific Researcher, 1995-, Institute of Chemistry, Academy of Sciences of Moldova. Publications: Over 60 scientific publications including articles in the journal Physics and Chemistry of Liquids, 2000, 2001, 2002, 2003, 2004, 2006, 2009. Honour: Diploma, Russian Mendeleev's Society of Chemistry, Odessa, 1983. Memberships: Russian Mendeleev's Society of Chemistry; International Association of Water Quality; Moldavian Chemical Society. Address: Drumul Viilor Str. 42, Ap 77, Kishinev MD-2021, Republic of Moldova. E-mail: myugorbachev@yahoo.com

GORDON Irwin Glenn (Yashad), b. 7 December 1965, Brooklyn, New York, USA. Genealogist; Archivist; Stand-up Comedian. Education: BA, Judaic Studies, Brooklyn College, 1989; MLS, Information and Library Science, Pratt Institute, 1993. Appointments: Amateur Stand-up Comedian, New York Comedy Club, Pips Comedy Club, Gotham Comedy Club, Stand-Up New York Comedy Club, Laugh-In Comedy Club, Broadway (Improv) Comedy Club, Comic Strip Live, Gladys' At Hamburger Harry's, Boston Comedy Club, HA! Comedy Club, Caroline's, Comix, New York City, 1997-; Recording Secretary, Chmielniker Sick and Benevolent Society of Kielce-Guberniye, Poland, Arbeiter Ring/ Workmen's Circle, New York City, 1999-2000; Member, Board of Directors, Beta Phi Mu, Theta Chapter, New York City, 2005-08; Lecturer and Speaker, Steamship Passenger Lists & Naturalization Records, Westchester County Genealogical Society, Dobbs Ferry, NY, 2002; Irvington Public Library, Irvington-On-Hudson, NY, 2003; I Want My Daddy's (& Mommy's) Work Records! – Social Security Employment Earnings Statements, International Association of Jewish Genealogical Societies Annual Conference, Las Vegas, NV, 2005 and Philadelphia, PA, 2009; Independent Scholar, Local History Panel, Researching New York Annual Conference - Perspectives on Empire State History, State University of New York, Albany, NY, 2007; Sensational Archives and Collections: A Pecha Kucha (Chatter) Panel Session, Mid-Atlantic Regional Archives Spring Conference, Alexandra, VA, 2011. Publications: Articles include most recently: Hadassah HaMalkah – Hilda Cutler on Her 7th Yahrzeit, 2002; Cream of Wheat Cents, 2003-05, 2009; Mommy Matil – Lynn Gordon, on Her 22nd Yahrtzeit, 2006; Daddy Dave – David Gordon, on His 28th Yahrtzeit, 2006; Narriockh Narrows, 2007-08; News Around the Metropolitan Archivists Round Table – Social Security Records Lecture, 2010; Elusive Ocean Parkway Sepia Photograph, forthcoming; Official Family Historian and Compiler, Baris (Barishansky) Family Circle, 1985-; Part-time Shaliach Tzibur (prayer leader), Warbasse Jewish Heritage Association Synagogue, 1996; Book Review Contributor, National Genealogical Society Quarterly, 1997-98; Observations/ Tatzpiyos (editorial column), Hatikvah newspaper, 1988-89; Artwork: Coney Island Street Maps, 1973-77; Zesty & Crunchy Mazes/Labyrinths, 1973-77; Gan Eden, 1981; Tevas No'ach, 1982; Mem, 1988; Chai, 1988; Zachor, 1989; Har Sinai, 1989; BiVrachas Chanukah!, 1991; Alef-Tidom, 1992; Tikvah, 1993. Honours: General Organization Raffle Winner, Wilson Wilt Chamberlain basketball, Junior High School

303, 1978; Homeroom Class Spelling Bee Champion, JHS 303, 1979; Brooklyn College Dean's List, 1986; Beta Phi Mu, Theta Chapter 1994. Memberships: Assistant Editor, Editor-in-Chief and Editor Emeritus, Hatikvah newspaper, 1987-89; President, School of Information and Library Science Student Association, 1992-93. Address: 13 Livonia Drive, Patterson, NY 12563-8912, USA.

GORDON John William, b. 19 November 1925, Jarrow-on-Tyne, England. Writer. m. Sylvia Young, 9 January 1954, 1 son, 1 daughter. Publications: The Giant Under the Snow, 1968, reissue, 2006, sequel, Ride the Wind, 1989; The House on the Brink, 1970; The Ghost on the Hill, 1976; The Waterfall Box, 1978; The Spitfire Grave, 1979; The Edge of the World, 1983; Catch Your Death, 1984; The Quelling Eye, 1986; The Grasshopper, 1987; Secret Corridor, 1990; Blood Brothers, 1991; Ordinary Seaman (autobiography), 1992; The Burning Baby, 1992; Gilray's Ghost, 1995; The Flesh Eater, 1998; The Midwinter Watch, 1998; Skinners, 1999; The Ghosts of Blacklode, 2002; Left in the Dark (short story collection) 2006; Fen Runners, 2009; Contributions to: Beginnings (Signal 1989); Ghosts & Scholars 21. Membership: Society of Authors. Address: 99 George Borrow Road, Norwich, NR4 7HU, England.

GORDON Lyndall, b. 1941, Capetown, South Africa. Biographer. m. Siamon, 2 daughters. Education: BA (Hons), University of Cape Town, 1960-63; PhD (distinction), Columbia University, New York, 1973. Appointments: Assistant Professor, Columbia University, 1975-76; Lecturer, Jesus College, Oxford, 1977-84; CUF Lecturer in English, Oxford University and Tutorial Fellow (Dame Helen Gardner Fellow), St Hilda's College, 1984-95; Senior Research Fellow, St Hilda's College, 1995-. Publications: Books: Charlotte Bronte: A Passionate Life, 1994, revised 2008; T S Eliot: An Imperfect Life, 1998; A Private Life of Henry James, 1998; Shared Lives, 1992; Vindication: A Life of Mary Wollstonecraft, 2005; Revised edition of Virginia Woolf: A Writers Life, 2006; Lives Like Loaded Guns: Emily Dickinson and her Family's Feuds, 2010. Honours: British Academy's Rose Mary Crawshaw prize; James Tait Black prize for biography; Cheltenham prize for literature. Memberships: Fellow, Royal Society of Literature; PEN. Address: St Hilda's College, Oxford, OX4 1DY, England.

GORDON Philip H, b. 13 September 1942, Saskatoon, Saskatchewan, Canada. Physician. m. Rosalie, 1 son, 1 daughter. Education: MD, University of Saskatchewan, 1966; LMCC, 1966; Diplomate, National Board of Medical Examiners, 1968; Certifications: Royal College of Surgeons of Canada, 1972, General Surgery, Province of Quebec, 1972; Diplomate, American Board of Surgery, 1973: Diplomate, American Board of Colon and Rectal Surgery, 1974, Recertification, 1994; Training in medicine and surgery, Jewish General Hospital, Montreal, Canada, 1966-74; McGill University, Montreal, Montefiore Hospital Pittsburgh, USA, University of Minnesota, USA, St Mark's Hospital, London, England. Appointments: Clinical Assistant, 1974-77, Assistant Surgeon, 1977-79, Associate Surgeon, 1979-87, Senior Surgeon, Director, Division of Colon and Rectal Surgery, 1987-, Director Clinical Teaching Unit II, 1989-, Vice-Chairman, Department of Surgery, 1993-, Department of Surgery, Sir Mortimer B Davis, Jewish General Hospital, Montreal, Canada; Lecturer, 1978-79, Assistant Professor of Surgery, 1979-84, Associate Professor of Surgery, 1984-89, Professor of Surgery, 1989-, Director, Section of Colorectal Surgery, 1996-, Department of Surgery, Professor of Oncology, Department of Oncology, 1992-, McGill University, Montreal, Canada; Advisory Council, American Board of Colon and Rectal Surgery, 2001-. Publications: Author and co-author of over 146 peer reviewed articles in medical journals; 6 textbooks; 39 textbook chapters; numerous abstracts, editorials, book reviews and papers presented at national and international conferences and symposia. Honours include: William & Mary Diefenbaker Fellowship, 1962; Agora Award "Ambassador by Appointment", Palais de Congress, City of Montreal, 1988; American Medical Illustrators Best Illustrated Medical Textbook of the Year 1992; Award of Appreciation, American Society of Colon and Rectal Surgeons, 1999; Dr Carl Arthur Goresky Memorial Award, McGill Inflammatory Bowel Disease Research Group, 2002; Honorary Fellow, Canadian Society of Colon and Rectal Surgeons, 2008; Master in Colorectal Surgery, 2011; Listed in numerous Who's Who publications and biographical dictionaries. Memberships include: Fellow, Royal College of Surgeons of Canada, Royal Society of Medicine, American College of Surgeons, American and Canadian Society of Colon and Rectal Surgeons; Founding President, Canadian Society of Colon and Rectal Surgeons; Past President, American Society of Colon and Rectal Surgeons; Past President, American Board of Colon and Rectal Surgery. Address: 3755 Cote Ste, Catherine Road, Suite G-314, Montreal, Quebec, Canada H3T 1E2. E-mail: philip.gordon@mcgill.ca

GORDON Robert Patterson, b. 9 November 1945, Belfast, Northern Ireland. University Teacher. m. Helen Ruth, 2 sons, 1 daughter. Education: St Catharine's College, Cambridge, 1964-69: BA, 1968, MA, 1972, PhD, 1973, Litt. D, 2001 (all Cambridge). Appointments: Assistant Lecturer, Hebrew and the Old Testament, 1969-70, Lecturer in Hebrew and Semitic Languages, 1970-79, University of Glasgow; Lecturer in Divinity, 1979-95, Regius Professor of Hebrew, 1995-, University of Cambridge. Publications: 1 and 2 Samuel: Introduction, 1984; 1 and 2 Samuel: A Commentary, 1986; The Targum of the Minor Prophets (jointly), 1989; Studies in the Targum to the Twelve Prophets, 1994; The Place is Too Small for Us (editor), 1995; Wisdom in Ancient Israel (joint editor), 1995; The Old Testament in Syriac: Chronicles, 1998; Hebrews: Commentary, 2000; Holy Land, Holy City, 2004; The Old Testament in its World (jointly), 2005; Hebrew Bible and Ancient Versions, 2006; The God of Israel (editor), 2007. Honours: Jarrett Scholarship, 1966; Rannoch Hebrew Scholarship, 1966; Senior Scholarship, 1968; Bender Prize, 1968; Tyrwhitt Scholarship, 1969; Mason Prize, 1969. Memberships: Society for Old Testament Studies; British Association of Jewish Studies; Society of Biblical Literature; National Club. Address: Faculty of Asian and Middle Eastern Studies, Sidgwick Avenue, Cambridge, CB3 9DA.

GORE Albert Jr, b. 31 March 1948. Politician. m. Mary 'Tipper' Aitcheson, 1970, 1 son, 3 daughters. Education: Harvard University; Vanderbilt University. Appointments: Investigative reporter, editorial writer, The Tennessean, 1971-76; Home-builder and land developer, Tanglewood Home Builders Co, 1971-76; Livestock and tobacco farmer, 1973-; Head, Community Enterprise Board, 1993-; Member, House of Representatives, 1977-79; Senator, from Tennessee, 1985-93; Vice President, USA, 1993-2001; Democrat candidate in Presidential Elections, 2000; Lecturer, Middle Tennessee State, Fisk, Columbia Universities, 2001-; Vice-Chairman, Metropolitan West Financial, 2001-; Senior Advisor, Google Inc, 2001-; Chair, Newsworld International network, 2004-; Co-founder and Chair, Generation Investment Management, Washington, DC and London, England, 2004-; President, Current TV; Director, Apple Inc; Chairman, Alliance for Climate Protection. Films: An Inconvenient Truth.

Publications include: Earth in the Balance, 1992; The Spirit of Family, 2002; Joined at the Heart: The Transformation of the American Family, 2002; An Inconvenient Truth, 2006; The Assault on Reason, 2007. Honours: Nobel Peace Prize, 2007; Emmy Award, Current TV, 2007; Prince of Asturias Award, 2007; Academy Award, Best Documentary, An Inconvenient Truth, 2007; Grammy, Best Spoken Album, 2009. Address: Metwest Financial, 11440 San Vicente Boulevard, 3rd Floor, Los Angeles, CA 90049, USA.

GORMLEY Antony Mark David, b. 30 August 1950, London, England. Sculptor. m. Vicken Parsons, 2 sons, 1 daughter. Education: BA, Archaeology, Anthropology and History of Art, Trinity College, Cambridge, 1968-71; Central School of Art, London, 1974-75; BA, Fine Art, Goldsmiths School of Art, London, 1975-77; Postgraduate Studies, Slade School of Fine Art, London, 1977-79. Career: Artist and Sculptor; Solo exhibitions include: Whitechapel Art Gallery, London, 1981; Coracle Press, London, 1983; Riverside Studios, Cardiff, Wales, 1984; Drawings, 1981-1985, Salvatore Ala Gallery, New York, USA, 1985; Five Works, Serpentine Gallery, London, England, 1987; The Holbeck Sculpture, Leeds City Art Gallery, Leeds, England, 1988; Drawings, Mcquarrie Gallery, Sydney, Australia, 1989; Bearing Light, Burnett Miller Gallery, Los Angeles, USA, 1990; Drawings and Etchings, Frith Street Gallery, London, England, 1991; American Field (touring), USA, 1992; Antony Gormley (touring), Konsthall, Malmo, Sweden, Tate Gallery, Liverpool, England, Irish Museum of Modern Art, Ireland, 1993; Field for the British Isles (touring) UK, 1994; Critical Mass, Remise, Vienna, Austria, 1995; Total Strangers, Koelnischer Kunstverein, Cologne, Germany, 1997; Angel of the North, The Gallery, Central Library, Gateshead, England, 1998; Quantum Cloud (part of North Meadow Sculpture Project), Millennium Dome, London, England, 2000; New Works, Galerie Nordenhake, Berlin, Germany, 2001; Gormley Drawing, The British Museum, London, England, 2003; Asian Field (touring) China, 2003; Domain Field, The Great Hall, Winchester, England, 2004; Antony Gormley Display, Tate Britain, London, England, 2004; Antony Gormley: New Works, Sean Gallery, New York, USA, 2005; Antony Gormley, Glyndebourne Opera House, England, 2005; Another Place, Crosby Beach, Merseyside, England; Field for the British Isles, Longside Gallery, Yorkshire Sculpture Park, England, 2005; Certain Made Places, Koyanagi Gallery, Tokyo, Japan, 2005; Asian Field, ICA, Singapore, 2005; Inside Australia, Anna Schwartz Gallery, Melbourne, Australia, 2005; Numerous group exhibitions, including: British Sculpture in the Twentieth Century, Whitechapel Art Gallery, London, England, 1982; Aperto '82, Biennale de Venezia, Venice, Italy; An International Survey of Recent Painting and Sculpture, The Museum of Modern Art, New York, USA, 1984; Turner Prize, Tate Gallery, London, England, 1994; A Secret History of Clay: From Gauguin to Gormley, Tate Liverpool, Liverpool, England, 2004; Space: Now and Then, Art and Architecture, Fundament Foundation, AaBé Fabrieken, Tilburg, Netherlands, 2005; Making a Mark, Newcastle upon Tyne, 2006; Turner Prize: A Retrospective 1984-2006, Tate Britain, London, 2007; Sutra, London, 2008; Innovations in the Third Dimension: Sculpture of Our Time, 2009; Visceral Bodies, Vancouver, 2010; Summer Exhibition, Royal Academy of Arts, London, 2011. Works in collections including: Arts Council of Great Britain; Tate Gallery; British Council; Walker Arts Center Minneapolis; Leeds City Art Gallery; Irish Museum of Modern Art; Major commissions include: The Angel of the North, Gateshead, 1998; Quantum Cloud, London, 2000. Honours: Turner Prize, 1994; OBE, 1998; South Bank Art Award, 1999; Civic trust Award (for The Angel of the North), 2000; Honorary Fellow, RIBA, 2001; Honorary Doctorates: University of Sunderland, 1998, University of Central England, Birmingham, 1998, Open University, 2001, Cambridge University, 2003, Newcastle University, 2004, Teeside University, 2004; Honorary Fellowships: Goldsmith's College, University of London, 1998, Jesus College, Cambridge, 2003, Trinity College, Cambridge, 2003; Fellow, RSA, 2000; RA, 2003; Trustee, Baltic Centre for Contemporary Art; Trustee, British Museum, 2007. Website: www.antonygormley.com

GORODSKY Sergey Nikolaevich, b. 13 April 1959, Moscow, Russia. Chemist; Researcher. Education: BSc, Organic Synthesis and Biotechnology, 1995, MS, Technique and Technology, 1997, PhD, Chemistry, 2001, Moscow State Academy of Fine Chemical Technology (MITHT), Moscow. Appointments: Junior Research Scientist, 2001-02, Research Scientist, 2002-04, Senior Staff Researcher, 2004-11, MITHT; Co-Chairman, ICC14 Pre-Simposium Section, Kyoto, 2008; Visiting Member of Staff, Newcastle University, England, 2010; Reviewer of scientific journals. Publications: Contributions to 11 Russian and 26 international conferences, 1999-2010; Numerous articles in professional journals, 2000-10. Honours: Grants, RFBR, Russia, 1995-2011; Financial support of Org Com 5th Int Conf, Osaka, 2006; MITHT Award for excellent study, 2000-01; Scientific Committee, 11th International Conference on Physical Chemistry, Belgrade, 2012; Listed in international biographical dictionaries. Memberships: Russian Chemical Society; American Chemical Society. Address: Lomonosow's MITHT, Vernadsky Avenue 86, Moscow 119571, Russian Federation. E-mail: gorodsky@yandex.ru

GOROKHOV Igor M, b. 6 April 1932, Leningrad, Russia. Professor of Geochemistry. m. Irina A Ostrovskaya, 1 daughter. Education: Certificate of Research Chemist (honours), Leningrad State University, 1954; PhD, Chemical Sciences, Leningrad Technology Institute, 1965; Senior Research Officer, Geochemistry, Higher Education Board of the USSR, Moscow, 1979; DSc, Geology and Mineralogical Sciences, Institute of Geochemistry, Kiev, Ukraine, 1981. Appointments: Junior Research Fellow, USSR Academy of Science, V G Khlopin Radium Institute, Leningrad, 1954-61; Junior Research Fellow, USSR Academy of Science, Laboratory of Precambrian Geology, Leningrad, 1961-67; Junior Research Fellow to Head of Laboratory, Russian Academy of Science, Institute of Precambrian Geology and Geochronology, St Petersburg, 1967-. Publications: 2 books; Over 100 articles in scientific journals. Honours: Medal for scientific service, Geological Survey, Prague, 1986; Medal for scientific service, Geological Survey, Bratislava, 1986; State Scientific Grants, 1994, 1997, 2000; Awards, Nauka/Interperiodica Publishing House, 1996, 2003; Academician A.P. Karpinsky medal for scientific achievements, Russian Academy of Sciences and St Petersburg City Administration, 2007. Memberships: Board, Council on Isotope Geology and Geochronology, USSR Academy of Sciences, 1973-91, 1999-, Commission on the Upper Precambrian, Moscow, 1988-; Editorial Board, Chemical Geology, 1987-99; New York Academy of Sciences, 1995. Address: Institute of Precambrian Geology and Geochronology, Russian Academy of Sciences, nab Makarova 2, 199034 St Petersburg, Russia. E-mail: gorokhov@ig1405.spb.edu

GORRARA Sir Richard, b. 29 May 1964, Metz, France. Magistrate. Education: MA, English, 2004; PhD, Political Science, 2005; LLM, Criminal Justice, 2006; LLD (Doctorate), Law, 2006; Professor of Law, 2006; Doctor of

Music, 2006. Appointments: Investment Advisor; Business Consultant; Magistrate; Judge. Honours: Knighthood; Lord of the Manor; Baron; Chevalier Legion d'honneur; Sir (Knight), Order of St John. Memberships: Labour Party; Conservative Party; Irish Green Party. Address: 196 High Road, London, N22 8HH, England. E-mail: mailcom@inbox.com

GORRIE Donald Cameron Easterbrook, b. 2 April 1933, Dehra Dun, India. m. Astrid Salvesen, 2 sons. Education: MA, Modern History, Corpus Christi College, Oxford, 1953-57. Appointments: School Master: Gordonstoun School, 1957-60, Marlborough College, 1960-66; Director of Research then Administration, Scottish Liberal Party, 1968-75; Liberal Councillor, Edinburgh Town Council, 1971-75, Councillor and Liberal Democrat Group Leader, Lothian Regional Council, 1974-96, City of Edinburgh District Council, 1980-96, City of Edinburgh Council, 1995-97; MP, Liberal Democrat, Edinburgh West, 1997-2001; Member Liberal Democrat Scotland Team, 1997-99; MSP, Liberal Democrat, Central Scotland, 1999-2007; Spokesman on Local Government, 1999-2000, Finance, 2000-01; Justice, 2001-03; Procedures, 1999-2003, 2005-2007; Communities, Culture, Sport, Voluntary Sector, Older People, 2003-05; Convenor, Procedures Committee, 2005-2007. Honours: Former holder of Scottish Native Record 880 yards, 1955; OBE; DL; Backbencher of the Year, 1999; Free Spirit of the Year, 2001. Publications: Party manifestos and political pamphlets including Planning: Beyond the White Paper. Memberships: Former Chairman, Edinburgh Youth Orchestra; Sometime Board/Committee: Royal Lyceum Theatre; Queen's Hall, Edinburgh; Edinburgh Festival; Scottish Chamber Orchestra; Castle Rock Housing Association; Lothian Association of Youth Clubs; Edinburgh City Youth Café; Diverse Attractions; Edinburgh Zoo; Chairman, Corstorphine Dementia Project, Secretary, Friends of Corstorphine Hill; President, Lothian Association of Youth Clubs, Edinburgh City Youth Café; Edinburgh Athletic Club, Corstorphine AAC; Vice President, Achilles Club; Trustee, Nancy Ovens Trust. Address: 9 Garscube Terrace, Edinburgh EH12 6BW, Scotland.

GORSHKOV Oleg, b. 8 December 1959, Permskaya Region, Russia. Physicist; Educator. m. Elena Rolandovna, 1 son. Education: Honorary School Certificate, 1977; Honorary Engineer's Diploma, Moscow Aviation Institute, 1983; PhD, 1990, DSc, 2006, Keldysh Research Center. Appointments: Engineer, 1983-88, Section Manager, 1988-89, Research Assistant, 1989-90, Senior Staff Scientist, 1990-91, Head, Department of Electrophysics, 1991-, Chief Designer, Electric Propulsion, 2002-, Keldysh Research Centre, Moscow; Lecturer, 1997-2000, Associate Professor, 2000-08, Professor, 2008-, Institute of Physics and Technology, Moscow. Publications: Numerous articles in professional journals; Monograph, Hall and Ion Plasma Propulsion for Spacecraft, 2008. Honours: Prize, Russian Academy of Sciences, 2001; Honoured Worker of Rocket-Space Industry of the Russian Federation, Government of the Russian Federation, 2003; Grants, ISTC, 1997, 1999, 2000, 2002, 2003 and 2004. Memberships: Scientific Council, Russian Academy of Sciences; International Astronautical Federation. Address: Keldysh Research Centre, 8 Onezhskaya, Moscow 125438, Russia. E-mail: kercgor@dol.ru

GORYAEVA Elena Mikhailovna, b. 11 November 1944, Leningrad, Russia. Research Scientist; Physicist. m. Mikhail Alexandrovich Goryaev, 1976, 1 daughter. Education: MS, Opto-Electronics, Leningrad Institute of Optics and Exact Mechanics, 1967. Appointments: Engineer, 1967-72, Junior Research Specialist, 1972-82, Research Specialist, 1982-2008, Retired 2008, Laboratory of Luminescence and Photochemistry, S I Vavilov State Optical Institute, St Petersburg. Publications: Over 40 scientific publications, patents and reports presented. Honours: Labour Veteran Medal, Leningrad City Council of People's Deps, 1988; Listed in national and international biographical dictionaries. Memberships: Member, All Russian Inventors Society. Address: S I Vavilov State Optical Institute, Birzhevaya liniya 12, 199034 St Petersburg, Russia. E-mail: goryaeva@yahoo.com or ogoryaev@og2172.spb.edu

GOTO Taichiro, b. 8 October 1971, Osaka, Japan. Medical Doctor; Thoracic Surgeon. m. Miwa, 1 daughter. Education: MD, 1997, PhD, 2005, School of Medicine, Keio University. Appointments: Thoracic Surgeon, Keio University Hospital, 1997-. Address: Division of General Thoracic Surgery, Department of Surgery, School of Medicine, Keio University, 35 Shinanomachi, Shinjuku-ku, Tokyo 160-8582, Japan. E-mail: taichiro@1997.jukuin.keio.ac.jp

GOUGH Douglas Owen, b. 8 February 1941, Stourport, Worcestershire, England. Astrophysicist. m. Rosanne Penelope, 2 sons, 2 daughters. Education: BA, 1962, MA, PhD, 1966, St John's College, University of Cambridge; DSc, University of Sydney, 1987. Appointments: Research Associate, Joint Institute for Laboratory Astrophysics, and Department of Physics and Astrophysics, University of Colorado, 1966-67; Visiting Member, Courant Institute of Mathematical Sciences, New York University, 1967-69; National Academy of Sciences Senior Postdoctoral Resident/ Research Associate, Goddard Institute for Space Studies, New York, 1967-69; Member, Graduate Staff, Institute of Theoretical Astronomy, 1969-73; Lecturer, Astronomy and Applied Mathematics, 1973-85, Reader in Astrophysics, 1985-93 Institute of Astronomy and Department of Applied Mathematics and Theoretical Physics, Professor of Theoretical Astrophysics, 1993-, Deputy Director, 1993-99, Director, 1999-2004, Institute of Astronomy, University of Cambridge; Associate Professor, University of Toulouse, 1984-85; Honorary Professor of Astronomy, Queen Mary and Westfield College, University of London, 1986-2005; Fellow Adjoint, Joint Institute for Laboratory Astrophysics, Boulder, Colorado, 1986-; Scientific Co-ordinator, Institute for Theoretical Physics, University of California, Santa Barbara, 1990; Professor, Theoretical Astrophysics, 1993-2008; Visiting Professor, Department of Physics, Stanford University, 1996-; Visiting Fellow, South African Astronomical Observatory, 2004-; Visiting Fellow, Japan Society for the Promotion of Science, 2005; Chercher Associé du Centre National de la Recherche Scientifique, Observatoire de Paris-Meudon, France, 2005-06; Visiting Professor, Department of Physics and Astronomy, Aarhus University, 2006; Leverhulme Emeritus Fellow, 2009-; Research Associate, Department of Applied Mathematics and Statistics, University of California, Santa Cruz, 2010. Publications: About 300 papers in scientific literature; Books edited include: Problems of solar and stellar oscillations, 1983; Seismology of the Sun and the distant stars, 1986; Challenges to theories of the structure of moderate-mass stars, 1991; Equation-of-state and phase-transition issues in models of ordinary astrophysical matter, 2004; The Scientific Legacy of Fred Hoyle, 2005. Honours: Gravity Research Foundation Prize (shared with F W W Dilke), 1973; James Arthur Prize, Harvard University, 1982; William Hopkins Prize, Cambridge Philosophical Society, 1984; George Ellery Hale Prize, American Astronomical Society, 1994; Mousquetaire d'Armagnac, 2001; Eddington Medal, Royal Astronomical Society, 2002; Gold Medal, Royal Astronomical Society,

2010. Memberships: Fellow, Royal Astronomical Society; American Astronomical Society; International Astronomical Union; Astronomical Society of India; Fellow, Royal Society; Fellow, Institute of Physics; Foreign Member, Royal Danish Academy of Sciences and Letters. Address: Institute of Astronomy, Madingley Road, Cambridge CB3 0HA, England. E-mail: douglas@ast.cam.ac.uk

GOULD Elliott, b. 29 August 1938, Brooklyn, New York, USA. Actor. m. (1) Barbra Streisand, 1963, divorced 1971, 1 son, (2) Jenny Bogart, divorced, 1 son, 1 daughter. Career: Actor, theatre appearances include: Say Darling, 1958; Irma La Douce, 1960; I Can Get It For You Wholesale, 1962; Drat! The Cat, 1965; Alfred in Little Murders, 1967; Toured in the Fantastiks with Liza Minelli; National tour with Deathtrap; Films include: The Confession, 1966; The Night They Raided Minsky's, 1968; Bob and Carol and Ted and Alice, 1969; Getting Straight, 1970; M*A*S*H, 1970; The Touch, 1971; Little Murders, 1971; The Long Good-Bye, 1972; Nashville, 1974; I Will...I Will...For Now, 1976; Harry and Walter Go to New York, 1976; A Bridge Too Far, 1977; The Silent Partner, 1979; The Lady Vanishes, 1979; Escape to Athens, 1979; The Muppet Movie, 1979; Falling in Love Again, 1980; The Devil and Max Devlin, 1981; Over the Brooklyn Bridge, 1984; The Naked Face, 1984; Act of Betrayal, 1988; Dead Men Don't Die, 1989; Secret Scandal, 1990; Strawanser, The Player, Exchange Lifeguards, Wet and Wild Summer, Naked Gun 331/3, the Final Insult (cameo), White Man's Burden, The Glass Shield, Kicking and Screaming, A Boy Called Hate, Johns, The Big Hit, American History, X, Bugsy, Hoffman's Hunger, Capricorn One; Boys Life 3, 2000; Ocean's Eleven, 2001; Puckoon, 2002; The Cat Returns (voice), 2002; Ocean's Twelve, 2004; Open Window, 2006; Ocean's Thirteen, 2007; Little Hercules in 3-D, 2007; The Ten Commandments (voice), 2007; The Redemption of Sarah Cain, 2007; Ocean's Thirteen, 2007; Saving Sarah Cain, 2007; The Deal, 2008; The Caller, 2008; Uncorked, 2009; Numerous TV appearances including Doggin' Around; Once Upon a Mattress; Friends; Kim Possible. Website: www.elliottgould.net

GOURGUES Michel, b. 22 August 1942, Saint-Michel, Québec, Canada. University Professor. Education: Bachelor of Arts, Université Laval, Québec, 1963; Bachelor in Philosophy, 1966, Bachelor in Theology, 1969, Licence in Theology, MA in Theology, 1971, Dominican University College, Ottawa; Diplôme d'Élève titulaire, Ecole Biblique et Archéologique Française, Jerusalem, 1974; Doctorate in Theology, Institut Catholique de Paris, 1976. Appointments: Assistant Professor, 1971-73, Professor, 1978-, Dean, 1978-87, Faculty of Theology, President, 1988-2004, Dominican University College; Guest Professor, Institut dominican de pastorale, Montreal, 1976-; Visiting Professor, Ecole Biblique et Archéologique Française, Jerusalem, 1997-. Publications: 15 books; Numerous articles in professional journals. Honours: Master in Sacred Theology, Rome, 1988; President, Association Catholique des Études Bibliques au Canada, 1998-2004; Member, International Academy of Religious Sciences, Bruxelles, 1999; Doctorate Honoris Causa in Theology, Université de Sudbury, 2000; Member, Direction Committee, Studiorum Novi Testamenti Societas, Oxford, 2001-04. Memberships: Association Catholique Française pour l'étude de la Bible, Paris; Society of Biblical Literature; SNTS; ACÉBAC; Société canadienne de théologie; Catholic Biblical Association; Director, Reduction Committee, Science et Esprit. Address: Dominican University College, 96 avenue Empress, Ottawa, ON – K1R 7G3, Canada. E-mail: michel.gourgues@collegedominicain.ca

GOURLAY Caroline, b. 10 August 1939, London, England. Poet. m. Simon Gourlay, 17 May 1967, 3 sons. Education: Royal Academy of Music, 1957-60; LRAM, 1960. Appointment: Editor, Blithe Spirit, Journal of the British Haiku Society, 1998-2000. Publications: Crossing the Field, 1995; Through the Café Door, 1999; Reading All Night, 1999; Against the Odds, 2000; This Country, 2005; Lull Before Dark, 2005. Contributions to: Envoi; Poetry Wales; New Welsh Review; Iron; Haiku Quarterly; Outposts; Blithe Spirit; Journal of the British Haiku Society; Planet; Modern Haiku; Frogpond; Tanka Splendor; American Tanka; Presence. Honour: James Hackett Award, 1996. Address: Hill House Farm, Knighton, Powys LD7 1NA, Wales.

GOVRIN Nurit, b. 6 November 1935, Israel. Scholar and Researcher; Writer. m. Shlomo Govrin, deceased, 3 sons. Education: BA, Hebrew Literature, Bible Studies; MA, Hebrew Literature; PhD, Hebrew Literature; Tel-Aviv University; Harvard University, USA; University of Oxford, England. Appointments: Administrative positions, Tel-Aviv University; Teaching, University of California at Los Angeles, Columbia University, New York, Hebrew Union College; Assistant, 1965-68, Teacher, 1968-72, Lecturer, 1972-74, Senior Lecturer, 1974-78, Associate Professor 1978-90, Full Professor, 1990-, Tel-Aviv University; Public Council for Culture and Art, Ministry of Education; Judge, Selection Committees for many literary prizes. Publications: 19 books including: G Shoffman: His Life and Work, 2 volumes, 1982; The Brenner Affair - The Fight for Free Speech, 1985; The Literature of Eretz - Israel in the Early Days of the Settlements, 1985; The First Half - The Life and Work of Dvora Baron 1888-1923, 1988; Honey from the Rock, 1989; Brenner - Nonplussed and Mentor, 1991; Burning - Poetry About Brenner, 1995; Literary Geography - Lands and Landmarks on the Map of Hebrew Literature, 1998; Reading the Generations – Contextual Studies in Hebrew Literature, 2 Volumes, 2002; Nurit Govrin: Bibliography: 1950-2004 by Joseph Galrom-Goldshlayer; Nurit Govrin: The Forgotten Traveler: Shlomith F Flaum – Her Life and Work, 2005; Prescriptives on Modern Hebrew Literature – In Honor of Professor Nurit Govrin, edited by Avner Holzman, 2005; Reading the Generations – Contextual Studies in Hebrew Literature, Volumes 3, 4, 2008; Editor of 14 books. Honours: Postgraduate Scholarship, Rothschild Fund, 1973-74; Research Grants: Israel National Academy for Sciences, 1975-78, Jewish Memorial Fund, 1982, Israel Matz Fund, 1982, 1984-86, 1989, American Academy for Jewish Studies, 1984-85, 1989; Haifa Municipality Prize, 1993; Shalom Aleichem Prize, 1996; Creative Woman Prize, Wizo Prize, 1998; Bialik Prize, 1998; Israel Efros Prize, 2001; Honourable Citizen of Tel-Aviv, 2010; Ramat-Gam Municipality Prize, 2010. Memberships: Katz Institute for Research of Hebrew Literature; Literature Committee, Israel National Academy of Sciences and Humanities. Address: 149 Jobotinsky St, Tel-Aviv 62150, Israel.

GOWANS James, b. 7 May 1924, Sheffield, England. Medical Scientist. m. Moyra, 1 son, 2 daughters. Education: Kings College, London; Kings College Medical School, London; Lincoln College, Oxford. Appointments: Research Professor, Royal Society, Oxford University, 1962-77; Secretary, UK Medical Research Council, 1977-87; Secretary General, Human Frontier Science Program, Strasbourg, France, 1989-93. Publications: Numerous articles in scientific journals. Honours: FRS; FRCP; Kt; CBE; Royal Medal, Royal Society; Foreign Associate, US National Academy of Sciences; Gairdner Foundation Award, Toronto; Wolf Prize in Medicine, Israel; Honorary Degrees at Yale, Chicago,

DICTIONARY OF INTERNATIONAL BIOGRAPHY 36th EDITION

Rochester (NY), Birmingham, Edinburgh, Glasgow, Southampton and Sheffield. Memberships: Honorary Fellow at Lincoln, Exeter and St Catherine's Colleges, Oxford. Address: 75 Cumnor Hill, Oxford, OX2 9HX, England.

GOWER David Ivon, b. 1 April 1957, Tunbridge Wells, Kent, England. Cricketer. m. Thorunn Ruth Nash, 1992, 2 daughters. Education: University College, London. Career: Left-hand batsman; Played for Leicestershire, 1975-89, captain, 1984-86, Hampshire, 1990-93; Played in 117 Tests for England, 1978-92, 32 as captain, scoring then England record 8,231 runs (average 44.2) with 18 hundreds; Toured Australia, 1978-79, 1979-80, 1982-83, 1986-87, 1990-91; Scored 26,339 first-class runs with 53 hundreds; 114 limited-overs internationals; Sunday Express Cricket Correspondent, 1993-95; Public Relations Consultant for cricket sponsorship National Westminster Bank, 1993-; Commentator, Sky TV, 1993-; Commentator and presenter, BBC TV, 1994-99; Columnist, Sunday Telegraph, 1995-98; Presenter, Sky TV cricket, 1999-; Columnist, The Sun, 2000-04; Columnist, The Sunday Times, 2004-; Television: They Think It's All Over, 1995-2003. Publications: A Right Ambition, 1986; On The Rack, 1990; The Autobiography, 1992; Articles in Wisden Cricket Monthly. Address: SFX Sports Group, 35/36 Grosvenor Street, London W1K 4QX, England.

GRACE Sherrill Elizabeth, b. Ormstown, Quebec, Canada. University Professor. 2 children. Education: BA, University of Western Ontario, 1962-65; MA, 1968-70, PhD, 1970-74, McGill University. Appointments: Teacher, Netherhall Secondary Girls School, Cambridge, England, 1967-68; Teaching Assistant, 1970-73, Special Lecturer, 1974-75, Assistant Professor, 1975-77, McGill University; Assistant Professor, 1977, Associate Professor, 1981, Professor, 1987-, Departmental Head, 1997-2002, University of British Columbia. Publications include: Violent Duality: A Study of Margaret Atwood, 1980; The Voyage That Never Ends: Malcolm Lowry's Fiction, 1982; Regression and Apocalypse: Studies in North American Literary Expressionism, 1989; Sursum Corda: The Collected Letters of Malcolm Lowry, 1995, 1996; Staging the North: 12 Canadian Plays, 1999; Canada and the Idea of North, 2002; Performing National Identities: Essays on contemporary Canadian Theatre, 2003; New annotated edition, A Woman's Way Through Unknown Labrador, 2004; Inventing Tom Thomson: From Biographical Fictions to Fictional Autobiographies, 2004. Honours include: University of British Columbia President Killam Research Prize, 1990; FEL Priestley Award, 1993; University of British Columbia Jacob Biely Research Prize, 1998; Fellow, Royal Society of Canada; Richard Plant Prize, 2003; Canada Council Killam Fellowship, 2003-05; Brenda and David McLean Chair in Canadian Studies, 2003-05; UBC Distinguished University Scholar, 2003-. Memberships: International Association of University Professors of English; Modern Language Association; Association of Canadian University Teachers of English. Address: Department of English, University of British Columbia, #397-1873 East Mall, BC V6T 1Z1, Canada.

GRADE Michael Ian, b. 8 March 1943, London, England. Broadcasting Executive. m. (1) Penelope Jane Levinson, 1967, divorced 1981, 1 son, 1 daughter, (2) Hon Sarah Lawson, 1982, divorced, (3) Francesca Mary Leahy, 1998, 1 son. Education: St Dunstan's College, London, UK. Appointments: Trainee Journalist, Daily Mirror, 1960, Sports Columnist, 1964-66; Theatrical Agent, Grade Organisation, 1966; Joint Managing Director, London Management and Representation, 1969-73; Deputy Controller of Programmes (Entertainment), London Weekend TV, 1973-77; Director of Programmes and Member Board, 1977-81; President, Embassy TV, 1981-84; Controller, BBC 1, 1984-86; Director of Programmes BBC TV, 1986-87; Chief Executive Officer, Channel Four, 1988-87; Chairman, VCI PLC, 1995-98; Director, 1991-2000, non-executive Chairman, 1995-97, Chairman, 1997-98, First Leisure Corp; Vice President, Children's Film Unit, 1993-; Delfont Macintosh Theatres Ltd, 1994-99; Entertainment Charities Fund, 1994-; Deputy Chairman, Society of Stars, 1995-; RADA, 1996-; Royal Albert Hall, 1997-; Charlton Athletic Football Club, 1997-; Camelot Group, 2000-04; Digitaloctopus, 2000-; Chair, Octopus, 2000-; Pinewood Studio Ltd, 2000-; Hemscott.NET, 2000-; BBC, 2004-06; ITV, 2007-. Publications: It Seemed Like a Good Idea at the Time, 1999. Honours: Honorary Professor, Thames Valley University, 1994; Honorary Treasurer, Stars Organisation for Spastics, 1986-92; CBE, Hon LLD (Nottingham), 1997; Royal TV Society Gold Medal, 1997. Memberships: International Council National Academy of TV Arts and Sciences, 1991-97; Council, London Academy of Music and Dramatic Art, 1981-93; BAFTA, 1981-82, 1986-88 (Fellow, 1994); Gate Theatre, Dublin, 1990-; Cities in Schools, 1991-95; Cinema and TV Benevolent Fund, 1993-; Royal Academy of Dramatic Art, 1996-; Royal Albert Hall, 1997; 300 Group; Milton Committee; British Screen Advisory Council, 1986-97; National Commission of Inquiry into Prevention of Child Abuse, 1994-96; Board of Governors, BANFF TV Festival, 1997-; Trustee, Band Aid; National Film and TV School; Virgin Health Care Foundation. Address: BBC, Broadcasting House, London W1A 1AA, England. Website: www.bbc.co.uk

GRADWELL David Peter, b. 5 July 1953, Salisbury, England. Doctor. m. Jane Risdall. Education: Callington Grammar School, Cornwall; BSc (Hons), Physiology, University of Dundee Faculty of Science, 1976; MB ChB, University of Dundee Faculty of Medicine, 1976-81; Diploma in Aviation Medicine, 1988; PhD, Physiology, United Medical & Dental Schools of Guy's and St Thomas's, London, 1993. Appointments: Consultant, Aviation Medicine, 1993; Head, Altitude Life Support Division, RAF Institute of Aviation Medicine, Farnborough, -1998; Officer Commanding, Aviation Medicine Wing, RAF Centre of Aviation Medicine, Henlow; Visiting Professor, Aviation Medicine, King's College, London and Whittingham Professor of Aviation Medicine, Royal College of Physicians of London; Chief Examiner, Diploma in Aviation Medicine, Faculty of Occupational Medicine, RCP London; Director and Chair, Scientific Committee, International Academy of Aviation & Space Medicine; Chairman, Specialty Advisory Committee in Aviation Medicine, Royal College of Physicians. Publications: Human Factors for Pilots, 1991; Human Physiological Responses to Positive Pressure Breathing for High Altitude Protection, 1993; Ernsting's Aviation Medicine, 2006; Fundamentals in Aerospace Medicine, 2007; Hunter's Diseases of Occupation, 2010. Honours: Richard Fox-Linton Memorial Award, 1996; Stewart Memorial Lecturer, Royal Aeronautical Society, 1999; Lady Cade Medal, Royal College of Surgeons, 2000; Louis H Bauer Founders Award for Outstanding Contributions to Aerospace Medicine, 2005; Eric Liljencrantz Award for Excellence in Education, 2006. Memberships: Royal College of Physicians, London; Faculty of Occupational Medicine, London; Aerospace Medical Association, Alexandria, USA; Royal Aeronautical Society, London; International Academy of Aviation & Space Medicine; The Physiological Society; Editorial Board, Aviation, Space & Environmental Medicine.

GRAF Steffi, b. 14 June 1969, Bruehl, Germany. Tennis Player. m. Andre Agassi, 2001, 1 son, 1 daughter. Career: Won Orange Bowl 12s, 1981; European 14 and under and European Circuit Masters, 1982, Olympic demonstration event, Los Angeles; Winner, German Open, 1986, French Open, 1987, 1988, 1993, 1995, 1996; Australian open, 1988, 1989, 1990, 1994; Wimbledon, 1988, 1989, 1991, 1992, 1993, 1995, 1996; US Open, 1988, 1989, 1993, 1995, 1996; Ranked No 1, 1987; Official World Champion, 1988; Grand Slam winner, 1988, 1989; Olympic Champion, 1988; German Open, 1989; Youngest player to win 500 Singles victories as professional, 1991; 118 tournament wins, 23 Grand Slam titles, 1996; Won ATP Tour World Championship, 1996; Numerous Women's Doubles Championships with Gabriela Sabatini, Federation Cup, 1992; Retired, 1999. Publication: Wege Zum Erfolg, 1999. Honours: Olympic Order, 1999; German Medal of Honour, 2002; International Tennis Hall of Fame, 2004. Memberships: Ambassador, World Wildlife Fund, 1984-; Founder and Chair, Children for Tomorrow; Ambassador, EXPO 2000. Address: Stefanie Graf Marketing GmbH, Mallaustrasse 75, 68219 Mannheim, Germany. E-mail: kontakt@stefanie-graf.com Website: stefanie.graf.com

GRAHAM Ross King, b. 15 August 1947, London, England. Chartered Accountant. m. Jillie, 3 daughters. Education: Loretto School. Appointments: ACA, 1969, Manager, 1973, Corporate Recovery, 1975, Partner, 1981-2003, Arthur Young McClelland Moores & Co, London; Finance Director, 1987-98, Corporate Development Director, 1998-2003, Misys plc; Non Executive Director, Chairman of Audit Committee, Patientline plc, 2005-06; Non Executive Director, Chairman of Audit Committee Acambis plc, 2004-08; Non Executive Director, Chairman of Audit Committee and Senior Independent Director, Wolfson Microelectronics plc, 2003; Non Executive Director, Chairman of Audit Committee and Senior Independent Director, Psion plc, 2006-. Memberships: Institute of Chartered Accountants in England & Wales; Insolvency Practitioners Association; Sunningdale Golf Club; Blackwell Golf Club; Queens Club. Address: c/o Mail Boxes etc, Unit 180, 61 Praed Street, London W2 1NS, England. E-mail: ross.graham@virgin.net

GRAHAM-DIXON Anthony Philip, b. 5 November 1929, Woodford, England. Retired Queen's Counsel. m. Suzanne Villar, 1 son, 1 daughter. Education: Westminster School; MA, Christ Church, Oxford, 1948-52; CS Russian Interpreter Examination, 1955. Appointments: Lieutenant, Special Branch RNVR, 1955; Called to the Bar, Inner Temple, 1956, Bencher, 1982; QC, 1973; Retired from the Bar, 1986; Governor, Bedales School, 1988-96; Deputy Chairman, Public Health Laboratory Service, 1988-95; Chairman of the Trustees, London Jupiter Orchestra, 1999-2003; Chairman of the Trustees, Society for the Promotion of New Music, 1990-95; Chair, External Advisory Panel to Oxford University Faculty of Music, 2008-. Publications: Consulting Editor, Competition Law in Western Europe and the USA, 1973. Honours: Scholar, Westminster School and Christ Church Oxford; QC, 1973. Membership: Member of the Livery, Goldsmiths Company. Address: Masketts Manor, Nutley, East Sussex TN22 3HD, England. E-mail: anthony@graham-dixon.com

GRAHAM-SMITH Francis (Sir), b. 25 April 1923, Roehampton, Surrey, England. Astronomer. m. Elizabeth Palmer, 3 sons, 1 daughter. Education: Natural Sciences Tripos, Downing College Cambridge, 1941-43, 1946-47; PhD (Cantab), 1952. Appointments: Telecommunications Research Establishment, Malvern, 1943-46; Research into Radio Astronomy Cavendish Laboratory, Cambridge, 1946-64, Jodrell Bank, 1964-74 and 1981-; Director, Royal Greenwich Observatory, 1976-81; Responsible for establishing the Isaac Newton Group of telescopes on La Palma, Canary Islands; Professor of Radio Astronomy, 1964-74, 1981-90, Langworthy Professor of Physics, 1987-90, Pro-Vice-Chancellor, 1988-90, Emeritus Professor, 1990-, University of Manchester; Director, Nuffield Radio Astronomy Laboratories, Jodrell Bank, 1981-88; 13th Astronomer Royal, 1982-90. Publications: Books: Radio Astronomy, 1960; Optics (with J H Thomson), 1971, 2nd edition, 1988; Pulsars, 1977; Pathways to the Universe (with Sir ACB Lovell), 1988; Pulsar Astronomy (with A G Lyne), 1989, 2nd edition, 1998; Optics and Photonics (with T King), 2000; Introduction to Radio Astronomy (with B F Burke), 1997, 2nd edition, 2002. Honours: Fellow, 1953-64, Honorary Fellow, 1970, Downing College, Cambridge; Kt Bachelor, 1986; Royal Medal, Royal Society, 1987; DSc: Queens University Belfast, 1986, Keele University 1987, Birmingham University, 1989, Dublin University, 1990; Nottingham University, 1990, Manchester University, 1993; Salford University, 2003, Liverpool, 2003; Glazebrook Medal, Institute of Physics, 1991. Memberships: Fellow of the Royal Society, Physical Secretary and Vice-President, 1988-94; Fellow of the Royal Astronomical Society, Secretary, 1964-71, President, 1975-77; Foreign Associate, Royal Society of South Africa, 1988; Chairman of the Governors, Manchester Grammar School, 1987-98. Address: Old School House, Henbury, Macclesfield, Cheshire SK11 9PH, England. E-mail: fgsegs@ukonline.co.uk

GRAMATIKOV Georgi, b. 14 February 1943, Pokrovan, Bulgaria. Historian. m. Dimitiya Ivanova, 2 sons. Education: Degree in History, University of Sofia, 1968; PhD, History, 1991; Senior Research Scientist, 2005. Appointments: Curator, 1969-85, Director, 1985-, Regional Historical Museum, Haskovo; Retired. Publications: 90 monographs and scientific publications in professional journals. E-mail: gramatik43@abv.bg

GRANOV Anatoly Mikhaylovich, b. 21 April 1932, Donetsk, Russia. Surgeon; Physician. m. Svetlana Vashetina, 1 son. Education: Diploma, Donetsk Medical Institute, 1956; PhD, 1963; Doctoral thesis, 1970; Professor of Medical Sciences, 1974. Appointments: Physician, Department Head, Donetsk Medical Institute, 1956-69; Assistant Faculty Head, Donetsk Medical Institute, 1964-65; Junior Researcher, N N Petrov Institute of Oncology, Leningrad, 1965-66; Assistant Professor, N I Pavlov First Medical Institute, Leningrad, 1966-77; Faculty Head, Odessa Medical Institute, 1977-80; Head of Operative Surgery Department, 1980-93, Director, 1993-, Central Research Institute of Roentgenology and Radiology. Publications: Author, 11 books; Over 350 articles published in domestic and western medical journals. Honours: Medal "For Labour Activity", 1984; State Prize Winner, 1993; Order "For Services to Motherland", 2001; Medal "For Services to Domestic Health Care", 2001; Pirogov Gold Medal, IV grade, 2003; N N Blokhin Gold Medal "For Development in Domestic Oncology", 2003; Order of Andrey Pervozvanny, 2004; Russian Federation Government Prizewinner, 2006. Memberships: Member, Russian Academy of Medical Sciences; Honoured Member of N N Pirogov Association of Surgeons; Member, Association of Oncologists; Member, Association of Radiologists. Address: 197758 Leningradskaya st, 70/, Pesochny, St Petersburg, Russia.

GRANT Hugh John Mungo, b. 9 September 1960, London, England. Actor. 1 son, 1 daughter with Tinglan Hong. Education: BA, New College, Oxford. Career: Actor in theatre, TV and films, producer for Simian Films; Began career in the

Jockeys of Norfolk (writer with Chris Lang and Andy Taylor); Films include: White Mischief, Maurice, 1987; Lair of the White Worm, La Nuit Bengali, 1988; Impromptu, 1989; Bitter Moon, 1992; Remains of the Day, 1993; Four Weddings and a Funeral, Sirens, 1994; The Englishman who went up a hill but came down a mountain, Nine Months, An Awfully Big Adventure, Sense and Sensibility, 1995; Restoration, Extreme Measures, 1996; Mickey Blue Eyes, Notting Hill, 1998; Small Time Crooks, 2000; Bridget Jones' Diary, 2001; About a Boy, Two Weeks' Notice, 2002; Love Actually, 2003; Bridget Jones: The Edge of Reason, 2004; Travaux, on sait quand ça commence..., 2005; American Dreamz, 2006; Music and Lyrics, 2007; Did You Hear About the Morgans? 2009; The Pirates! In an Adventure with Scientists, 2012; Cloud Atlas, 2012. Honours include: Golden Globe Award, BAFTA Award for Best Actor, Four Weddings and a Funeral, 1995; Peter Sellers Award for Comedy; Evening Standard British Film Awards, 2002; London Critics Circle Film Awards, Best British Actor, 2003; BAFTA/LA Stanley Kubrick Britannia Awad, 2003. Address: c/o Simian Films, 3 Cromwell Place, London SW7 2JE, England.

GRANT Richard E, b.5 May 1957, Mbabane, Swaziland. Actor. m. Joan Washington, 1 daughter. Career: Actor, Theatre appearances include: Man of Mode, 1988; The Importance of Being Earnest, 1993; A Midsummer Night's Dream, 1994; TV appearances include: Honest, Decent, Legal and True, 1986; Here is the News, 1989; Suddenly Last Summer, 1992; Hard Times, 1993; Karaoke, A Royal Scandal, 1996; The Scarlet Pimpernel, 1998; Hound of the Baskervilles, 2002; Posh Nosh, 2003; Patrick Hamilton: Words, Whisky and Women, 2005; Films: Withnail and I, 1986; How to Get Ahead in Advertising, Warlock, 1989; Henry and June, Mountains of the Moon, 1990; LA Story, Hudson Hawk, 1991; Bram Stoker's Dracula, 1992; The Player, The Age of Innocence, 1993; Prêt à Porter, Jack and Sarah, Portrait of a Lady, Twelfth Night, 1995; The Serpent's Kiss, 1996; The Match, 1998; A Christmas Carol, Trial and Retribution, Little Vampires, 1999; Hildegarde, 2000; Gosford Park, 2001; Monsieur 'N', 2002; Bright Young Things, 2003; Tooth, 2004; The Story of an African Farm, Corpse Bride (voice), Colour Me Kubrick: A True...ish Story, 2005; Garfield: A Tail of Two Kitties (voice), Penelope, 2006; Always Crashing in the Same Car; 2007; Jackboots on Whitehall, The Garden of Eden, 2008; Cuckoo, Love Hurts, 2009; The Man Who Married Himself, 2010. Publications: With Nails: The Film Diaries of Richard E Grant, 1995; Twelfth Night, 1996; By Design - A Hollywood Novel. Address: c/o ICM, Oxford House, 76 Oxford Street, London W1N 0AX, England. Website: www.richard-e-grant.com

GRATTON Guy Brian, b. 16 July 1970, Kirkcaldy, Scotland. Engineer; Writer; Test Pilot. Education: BEng (Hons), Aeronautics and Astronautics, 1992, PhD, Aerospace Engineering, 2005, University of Southampton. Appointments: Flight Test Engineer, 1993-96, Manager, Environmental Test Facilities, 1996-97, Ministry of Defence, Boscombe Down; Chief Technical Officer, British Microlight Aircraft Association, 1997-2005; Lecturer, Aeronautics, Brunel University, 2005-08; Head, Brunel Flight Safety Laboratory, 2006-; Head, Facility for Airborne Atmospheric Measurements, 2008-. Publications: Articles in professional journals including: International Journal of Aerospace Management, 2002; Journal of Aerospace Engineering, 2003; Aeronautical Journal, 2006, 2007, 2008; SETP Cockpit, 2003, 2006; Microlight Flyers Handbook, 2008. Honours: D G Astridge Prize for Aerospace Safety, 2003; Safety in Mechanical Engineering Award, 2003; Herman R Salmon Technical Publications Award, 2006. Memberships: Fellow, Institution of Mechanical Engineers; Fellow, Royal Aeronautical Society; Society of Experimental Test Pilots; Society of Flight Test Engineers. Address: School of Engineering and Design, Brunel University, Uxbridge, Middlesex UB8 3PH, England. E-mail: guy.gratton@brunel.ac.uk

GRAUER Gay Sherrard, b. 20 February, Toronto, Ontario, Canada. Visual Artist. m. John W Keith-King, 3 sons. Education: Art History, Wellesley College, 1958; Ecole du Louvre and Atelier Ziegler, Paris, 1958-59; San Francisco Art Institute, 1959-60, 1962-65. Career: Honorary Secretary, Member of the Board of Directors, 1975-76, Member of Acquisition Committee, 1993-94, Vancouver Art Gallery; Member, B-Grant jury, Visual Arts Grants, Canada Council, 1978-79; Founding Member, Arts, Sciences, and Technology Centre (now Science World), 1980; Jury member, BC Arts Council 13th Annual Regional Exhibition, 1994; Jury member, Royal Canadian Academy, Arts 2000, 1999-2000; Visiting Artist Scholar, Churchill College, Cambridge University, England, 2001; Council Member, Royal Canadian Academy of the Arts, 2002-05; Member, Inaugural jury, Joseph Plaskett Foundation Award, 2004; Artist in Residence, The Artist Project, Island Mountain Arts, Wells, BC, 2006; Solo and group exhibitions throughout Canada; Numerous commissions; Work held in public collections. Memberships: Royal Canadian Academy; CARFAC. E-mail: sherrard@shaw.ca

GRAVES Rupert, b. 30 June 1963, Weston-Super-Mare, England. Actor. m. Susie Lewis, 2 children. Career: Theatre: Killing Mr Toad; Sufficient Carbohydrates; Torch Song Trilogy; The Importance of Being Earnest; A Midsummer Night's Dream; Madhouse in Goa; The Elephant Man, 2002; Films: A Room With a View, 1986; Maurice, 1987; A Handful of Dust, 1988; The Children, The Plot to Kill Hitler, 1990; Where Angels Fear to Tread, 1991; Damage, 1992; Royal Celebration, 1993; The Madness of King George, Sheltering Desert, 1994; The Innocent Sleep, 1995; Intimate Relations, Different for Girls, 1996; The Revenger's Comedies, Mrs Dalloway, 1997; Dreaming of Joseph Lees, 1998; Room to Rent, 2000; The Extremists, 2002; Rag Tale, V for Vendetta, 2005; Death at a Funeral, The Waiting Room, Intervention, 2007. TV: Fortunes of War, 1987; Open Fire, Doomsday Gun, 1994; The Tenant of Wildfell Hall, 1996; Blonde Bombshell, Cleopatra, 1999; The Forsyte Saga, 2002; Charles II: The Power and the Passion, 2003; Pride (voice), 2004; Son of the Dragon, 2006; To Be First, Clapham Junction, 2007; Midnight Man, Marple: A Pocket Full of Rye, God on Trial, 2008; The Good Times Are Killing Me, 2009. Honours: Best Actor, Montreal Film Festival, 1996. Website: www.rupert-graves.com

GRAY Douglas, b. 17 February 1930, Melbourne, Victoria, Australia. Professor of English; Writer. m. 3 September 1959, 1 son. Education: MA, Victoria University of Wellington, New Zealand, 1952; BA, 1956, MA, 1960, Merton College, Oxford. Appointment: J R R Tolkien Professor of English, Oxford, 1980-97, Emeritus, 1997-. Publications: Themes and Images in the Medieval English Religious Lyric, 1972; Robert Henryson, 1979; The Oxford Book of Late Medieval Verse and Prose (editor), 1985; Selected Poems of Robert Henryson and William Dunbar (editor), 1998; The Oxford Companion to Chaucer (editor), 2003. Contributions to: Scholarly journals. Honours: British Academy, fellow, 1989; Honorary LitD, Victoria University of Wellington, 1995. Memberships: Early English Text Society; Society for the Study of Medieval Languages and Literatures, president, 1982-86. Address: Lady Margaret Hall, Oxford OX2 6QA, England.

GRAY Dulcie (Winifred Catherine), b. 20 November 1919, Kuala Lumpur, Malaya. Actress; Dramatist; Writer. m. Michael Denison, 1939, (deceased 1998). Education: England and Malaysia. Appointments: Numerous stage, film, radio, and television appearances. Publications: Murder on the Stairs, 1957; Baby Face, 1959; For Richer, for Richer, 1970; Ride on a Tiger, 1975; Butterflies on My Mind, 1978; Dark Calypso, 1979; The Glanville Women, 1982; Mirror Image, 1987; Looking Forward, Looking Backward (autobiography), 1991; J B Priestley, biography, 2000. Contributions to: Periodicals. Honours: Queen's Silver Jubilee Medal, 1977; Times Educational Supplement Senior Information Book Prize, 1978; Commander of the Order of the British Empire, 1983; CBE. Memberships: British Actors Equity; Linnean Society, fellow; Royal Society of Arts, fellow; Society of Authors. Address: Shardeloes, Amersham, Buckinghamshire HP7 0RL, England.

GRAY (Edna) Eileen Mary, b. 25 April 1920, United Kingdom. Cyclist. m. Walter Herbert Gray, deceased 2001, 1 son. Education: St Saviour's; St Olave's Grammar School for Girls, London. Appointments: Inspectorate, Fighting Vehicles, 1940-45; Invited to ride abroad, British Women's Cycling Team, 1946; International Delegation, Paris, 1957; Organiser first international competition for women in UK, 1957; Campaigner for international recognition of women in cycling; Team Manager, inaugural women's world championship, 1958; Member, Executive Committee, 1958-87, President, 1976, British Cycling Federation; Elected to Federation International Amateur de Cyclism, 1977; Vice-President, British Olympic Association, 1992-, Vice-Chairman, 1988-92; Chairman, British Sports Forum, 1991; Member, Manchester & Birmingham Olympic Bid Committee, 1991; Deputy Commandant, British Olympic Team, 1992; International Official, Commonwealth Games, Edmonton and Brisbane; Trustee, London Marathon Trust. Councillor, 1982-98, President, Kingston Sport Council, Mayor, 1990-91, Royal Borough of Kingston upon Thames. Honours: Special Gold Award, Ministry of Education, Taiwan; OBE, 1978; Freeman of the City of London, 1987; Olympic Order, International Olympic Committee, 1993; Grandmaster, Hon Fraternity of Ancient Freemasons (women); CBE, 1997. Memberships: Chairman, 1990-2007, President, 2007-, London Youth Games; Vice-President: Cyclists Touring Club, 2000; British School Cycling Association, 2001. Address: 129 Grand Avenue, Surbiton, Surrey KT5 9HY, England.

GRAY Jane Campbell, b. 8 February 1931, Lincoln, England. Stained Glass Designer/Craftsman. m. Kiril Gray (deceased), 2 daughters. Education: NDD, Kingston School of Art, National Diploma of Design; Associate, Royal College of Art, London. Appointments: Stained Glass Designer and Craftsman, 1955-; Over 80 commissions for churches including two in Shrewsbury Abbey; Commissions for libraries, private houses, hospitals, shopping centres, funeral parlours, Livery Company Halls, marriage rooms and a castle in Ireland; Worked for Lawrence Lee, assisting him in Coventry Cathedral nave windows and in his own studio. Publications: Book, Playing with Rainbows, 2011; Numerous articles in professional journals. Honours: Silver Medal, for work of Special Distinction, RCA, 1955. Memberships: Fellow, British Society of Master Glass Painters; Liveryman, Worshipful Company of Glaziers; Associate Member, Guild of Freemen of Shrewsbury; Council Member, Artists' General Benevolent Society; Royal College of Art Society. Address: Ferry Cottage, Shrawardine, Shrewsbury, Shropshire, SY4 1AJ, England.

GRAY John Clinton, b. 9 April 1946, Ripon, Yorkshire, England. University Professor. m. Julia Hodgetts, 1 son, 1 daughter. Education: BSc, Biochemistry, 1967, PhD, 1970, University of Birmingham; MA, University of Cambridge, 1977. Appointments: University Research Fellow, University of Birmingham, 1970-73; Research Biochemist, University of California, Los Angeles, 1973-75; Science Research Council Research Fellow, 1975-76, University Demonstrator, 1976-80, University Lecturer, 1980-90, Reader in Plant Molecular Biology, 1990-96, Professor of Plant Molecular Biology, 1996-, Head of Department of Plant Sciences, 2003-09, University of Cambridge. Publications: Numerous articles in scientific journals; Ribulose Bisphosphate Carboxylase-Oxygenase (editor with R J Ellis), 1986; Plant Trichomes (editor with D L Hallahan), 2000. Honours: Nuffield Foundation Science Research Fellowship, 1984-85; Royal Society Leverhulme Trust Senior Research Fellowship, 1990-91; European Molecular Biology Organisation Member, 1994; Listed in national and international biographical dictionaries. Membership: Midlands Association of Mountaineers. Address: 47 Barrons Way, Comberton, Cambridge CB23 7EQ, England. E-mail: jcg2@mole.bio.cam.ac.uk

GREEFF Minrie, b. 15 February 1954, Pretoria, South Africa. Professor. Education: BA (Cur), University of South Africa, 1984; M Cur, 1986, PhD (Psychiatric Nursing), 1991, Rand Afrikaans University. Appointments: Student Nurse, HF Verwoerd Hospital, 1972-73; Paarl Hospital, 1974-75; Professional Nurse, 1 Military Hospital, 1975-78; Professional Nurse and Senior Professional Nurse, Sterkfontein Hospital, 1978-80; Chief Professional Nurse and Vice-Principal, Sterkfontein College of Psychiatric Nursing, 1981-88; Lecturer, 1988-91, Senior Lecturer, 1991-93, Rand Afrikaans University; Head, Department of Nursing Science, 1994-98, Director, School of Nursing Science, 1999-2004, Potchefstroom University for Christian Higher Education; Professor in Research, School for Nursing Science, 2005-08, Professor in Research, AUTHeR, 2008-, North-West University, Potchefstroom Campus. Publications: Numerous articles in professional journals. Honours: Several research and project grants; Verka Financial Awards, 1996-; Special awards; Rated Researcher, National Research Foundation Award for Leadership in international research. Memberships: Institutional Health and Wellness Committee, North-West University; Research Ethics Committee, NWU; Education Committee and Research Committee, Faculty of Health Science; FLAGH forum; Chair of the Health and Wellness Advisory Committee, NWU. Address: P O Box 20981, Noordburg, 2522, South Africa. E-mail: minrie.greeff@nwu.ac.za

GREEN Lorna, b. Manchester, England. Sculptor; Environmental Artist. m. David Rose, 2 daughters. Education: BA, Honours, Fine Art, Manchester Polytechnic, 1982; MPhil, Fine Art, University of Leeds, 1991. Appointments: Site specific public and Environmental Artist; Visiting Lecturer; Commissions throughout the UK, Canada, China, Korea, Australia, New Zealand, Israel, Germany, Austria, France, Ireland, Bosnia, Holland and Lithuania; Many exhibitions and installations; Earthworks and landscape sculpture and public art. Appointments: Visiting Lecturer: universities throughout UK and abroad, 1985-, Manchester University, 1989-95, Leeds University, 1990-97, Leeds Metropolitan University, 2003-. Creative works: Most recent public commissions: Look, Reflect and Recover, 1 and 2, Queen Elizabeth Hospital, Gateshead, 2005; Spring, Summer and Autumn, 1, 2 and 3, Something Beautiful, Tatton Park,

Cheshire, 2007/08; Timescale, Kelloe, Durham, 2008; Saver>Screens, CIS Building, Manchester, 2008; The Festival Labyrinth with Jeff Teasdale, Bollington, Cheshire, 2009; River Darwen Leisure Centre, Lancashire, 2011; Most recent solo installations: Pool, Bonington Gallery, Nottingham Trent University, 1992; Power Flowers, Stockport Art Gallery, 1998; The Sword and the Stone, Heaton Park, Manchester, 2006; Homage to Fantin-Latour, York Art Gallery, 2007; Most recent selected residencies and group exhibitions: Verso l'Inizio – Towards the Beginning, Italy, 2008; Une Rivière pour l'Arc Mosellan, France, 2008; Solar Light, Lithuania, 2008; Sculpture and Snowdrops, Scotland, 2009; Blooming Branches, NSW, Australia, 2010; Blue Bird, Vale of Belvoir, 2011; Liber Plantarum, University of Leicester, 2011. Honours: Architecture 2000, Leeds City Council, 2000; Many travel bursaries. Memberships: Fellow, Royal Society of British Sculptors; Landscape and Art Network; Art and Architecture; Artists in Nature International Network; Manchester Academy of Fine Art; Cheshire Artists Network; Greenmuseum. Address: Mount Pleasant Farm, 105 Moss Lane, Bramhall, Cheshire, SK7 1EG, England. Website: www.lornagreen.com

GREEN Malcolm, b. 25 January 1942, London, England. Physician. m. Julieta Caroline Preston, 2 sons, 3 daughters (1 deceased). Education: Charterhouse, 1955-60; BA, MA,Trinity College, Oxford, 1960-65; MB, B Ch, BSc, DM, St Thomas's Hospital Medical School, 1965-68; Harvard School of Public Health, 1971-73. Appointments: Consultant Physician, St Bartholomew's Hospital, London, 1975-86; Chairman and President, British Lung Foundation, 1985-2001; Dean, National Heart & Lung Institute, 1988-90; Director, British Postgraduate Medical Federation, London, 1991-96; Campus Dean, St Mary's Hospital, 1997-2001; Consultant Physician, Royal Brompton Hospital, London, 1975-2006; Head, National Heart and Lung Institute, 2001-06, Vice Principal, Faculty of Medicine, Imperial College, 1997-2006. Publications: Numerous articles in professional journals. Honours: Knight Bachelor, 2007; British Thoracic Society Achievement Medal, 2008; Honorary Life Membership, European Respiratory Society, 2010. Memberships: Academy of Medical Science; Royal College of Physicians; British Thoracic Society; European Respiratory Society; Medical Research Society. Address: 38 Lansdowne Gardens, London SW8 2EF, England. E-mail: malcolm@malcolmgreen.net

GREEN Michael Frederick, b. 2 January 1927, Leicester, England. Writer. Education: BA, Honours, Open University. Publications: The Art of Coarse Rugby, 1960; The Art of Coarse Sailing, 1962; Even Coarser Rugby, 1963; Don't Print my Name Upside Down, 1963; The Art of Coarse Acting, 1964; The Art of Coarse Golf, 1967; The Art of Coarse Moving, 1969 (TV serial, 1977); The Art of Coarse Drinking, 1973; Squire Haggard's Journal, 1976 (TV serial, 1990 and 1992); Four Plays For Coarse Actors, 1978; The Coarse Acting Show Two, 1980; Tonight Josephine, 1981; The Art of Coarse Sex, 1981; Don't Swing from the Balcony Romeo, 1983; The Art of Coarse Office Life, 1985; The Third Great Coarse Acting Show, 1985; The Boy Who Shot Down an Airship, 1988; Nobody Hurt in Small Earthquake, 1990; Coarse Acting Strikes Back, 2000. Memberships: Society of Authors; Equity; National Union of Journalists. Address: 31 Clive Road, Twickenham, Middlesex, TW1 4SQ, England.

GREEN Timothy (Seton), b. 29 May 1936, Beccles, England. Writer. m. Maureen Snowball, October 1959, 1 daughter. Education: BA, Christ's College, Cambridge, 1957; Graduate Diploma in Journalism, University of Western Ontario, 1958. Appointments: London Correspondent, Horizon, and American Heritage, 1959-62; Life, 1962-64; Editor, Illustrated London News, 1964-66. Publications: The World of God, 1968; The Smugglers, 1969; Restless Spirit, UK edition as The Adventurers, 1970; The Universal Eye, 1972; World of Gold Today, 1973; How to Buy Gold, 1975; The Smuggling Business, 1977; The World of Diamonds, 1981; The New World of Gold, 1982, 2nd edition, 1985; The Prospect for Gold, 1987; The World of Gold, 1993; The Good Water Guide, 1994; New Frontiers in Diamonds: The Mining Revolution, 1996; The Gold Companion, 1997; The Millennium in Gold, 1999; The Millennium in Silver, 1999; The Ages of Gold, 2007; The London Good Delivery List: Building a Global Brand, 1750-2010. Address: Flat 3, Aura House, 39 Meliss Avenue, Richmond, TW9 4BX, England.

GREENBLATT Hellen, b. 15 May 1947, Frankfurt, Germany. Scientist; Educator. Education: PhD. Appointments: Senior Research Immunoparasitologist, Merck, Sharp & Dohme, Rahway, New Jersey, 1980-81; Member, Department of Microbiology and Immunology, Associate, Department of Medicine, Albert Einstein College of Medicine, Bronx, New York, 1981-84; Director, Research and New Business Development, Clinical Sciences Inc. Whippany, New Jersey, 1984-87; Senior Scientist, E I Dupont de Nemours & Company, Wilmington, Delaware, 1998-99; President, Managing Director, M-Cap Technologies International, 1990-93, Director, Technical Affairs, BTR Separations, 1993-94, Vice-president, Research and Development, 1994-97, Vice President, Product Development, 1998-2000, DuPont ConAgra Visions (DCV Inc), Wilmington, Delaware; Executive Vice President, 2000-04, Chief Science Officer, 2004-, Legacy for Life. Publications: Book chapters, articles in scientific journals and papers presented at conferences: Performance Improvement Caused by Feeding Broilers Egg Yolk Antibodies to Cholecystokinin is Correlated with the Specific Antibody Dose Not the Mass of Egg Yolk, 1997; The Inhibitory Effect of Nutrient Drink on the Serum Cholesterol Levels and Total Cholesterol: HDL Ratios of US Army Sergeants Major Academy Students, 1997; Effects of an Egg protein Nutrient Drink on Serum Lipid and Apolipoprotein Values, 1998; Method of Preventing, Countering or Reducing NSAID-Induced Gastrointestinal Damage by Administering Milk or Egg Products from Hyperimmunized Animals, 1998; Administration to Arthritis Patients of a Dietary Supplement Containing Immune Egg: An Open-Label Pilot Study, 1998; Anti-diarrheal and method for using the same, 2004; Holds a number of patents in the area of hyperimmune egg. Honours: NRC Research Associateship Program Awardee; The Amanda Cox Spirit of Life Award for Service to Others. Memberships: New York Academy of Sciences; Inflammation Research Association; American Academy of Anti-Aging Medicine; American Society for Nutrition; International Society of Exercise and Immunology. E-mail: hgreenblatt@legacyforlife.net

GREENFIELD, Baroness of Ot Moor in the County of Oxfordshire, Susan Adele Greenfield, b. 1 October 1950, London, England. Professor of Pharmacology. Education: BA (Hons) Oxon, 1973, MA Oxon,1974, DPhil, Oxon, 1974, St Hilda's College, Oxford University. Appointments: Travelling Scholarship to Israel, 1970; MRC Research Scholarship, Department of Pharmacology, 1973-76, Dame Catherine Fulford Senior Scholarship, St Hughes College, 1974, J H Burn Trust Scholarship, Department of Pharmacology, 1977, MRC Training Fellowship, Laboratory of Physiology, 1977-81, Oxford University; Royal Society Study Visit Award, 1978, MRC-INSERM French Exchange Fellow,

1979-80, College de France, Paris; Junior Research Fellow, Green College, 1981-84, Tutorial Fellow in Medicine, Lincoln College, 1985-, University Lecturer in Synaptic Pharmacology, 1985-, Professor of Pharmacology, 1996-, Oxford University; Deputy Director, Squibb Projects, 1988-95; Gresham Chair of Physic, Gresham College, London, 1995-98; Director, Royal Institution of Great Britain, 1998-, Fullerian Professor of Physiology, 1998-; Visiting Fellow in Neurosciences, Institute of La Jolla, USA, 1995; Distinguished Visiting Scholar, Queen's University, Belfast, 1996; Royal Institution Christmas Lecturer (first woman to present series), 1994; Columnist, Independent on Sunday, 1996-98; Brain Story (series BBC 2), 2000; Trustee, Science Museum, 1998-; World Economic Forum Fellow, 2001. Publications: Books: Mindwaves (co-editor with C B Blackmore), 1987; Journey to the Centres of the Brain (with G Ferry), 1994; Journey to the Centres of the Mind, 1995; The Human Mind Explained (editor) 1996, The Human Brain: A Guided Tour, 1997; Brain Power (editor), 2000; The Private Life of the Brain, 2000; Tomorrow's People, 2003; ID: The Quest for Identity in the 21st Century, 2008; Numerous published research papers and articles to journals. Honours: Woman of Distinction of the Year, Jewish Care, 1998; Michael Faraday Award, The Royal Society, 1998; Woman of the Year, The Observer, 2000; CBE, 2000; Life Peerage, 2001; Golden Plate Award, Academy of Achievement, USA, 2003; L'Ordre National de la Légion d'Honneur, France, 2003; Honorary Australian of the Year, 2006; The British Inspiration Awards – Science and Technology, 2010; Australian Society for Medical Research Medal, 2010; Fellow, Science Museum, 2010. Memberships: Royal Society of Edinburgh; Australian Davos Connection; Science Museum; many others. Address: Department of Pharmacology, University of Oxford, Mansfield Road, Oxford OX1 3QT, England. E-mail: susan.greenfield@pharm.ox.ac.uk

GREENSTOCK Sir Jeremy Quentin, b. 27 July 1943, Harrow, Middlesex, England. Diplomat. m. Anne Ashford Hodges, 1 son, 2 daughters. Education: Worcester College, Oxford. Appointments: Assistant Master, Eton College, 1966-69; Diplomatic Postings in Lebanon, Dubai, Washington, Saudi Arabia, Paris, 1969-90; Assistant Under Secretary for Western and Southern Europe, 1990-93; Minister, Washington, 1994-95; Political Director, Foreign and Commonwealth Office, 1996-98; UK Permanent Representative at the United Nations, 1998-2003; UK Special Representative for Iraq, 2003-2004; Director, The Ditchley Foundation, 2004-10; Chairman, UN Association, UK, 2011-. Honours: CMG, 1991; KCMG, 1998; GCMG, 2003. Membership: Oxford and Cambridge Club. Address: 3 Cornwall Gardens, London SW7 4AJ, England.

GREENWOOD Norman Neill, b. 19 January 1925, Melbourne, Australia. Emeritus Professor of Chemistry. m. Kirsten Rydland, 3 daughters. Education: BSc, 1st Class, 1946, MSc, 1st Class, 1948, DSc, 1966, University of Melbourne, Australia; PhD, 1951, ScD, 1961, Cambridge University. Appointments: Laboratory Cadet, CSIR(O), Melbourne, 1942-46; Resident Tutor and Lecturer in Chemistry, Trinity College, Melbourne, 1946-48; Exhibition of 1851 Overseas Scholar, 1948-51; Senior Harwell Research Fellow, Atomic Energy Research Establishment, Harwell, 1951-53; Lecturer, then Senior Lecturer, Inorganic Chemistry, University of Nottingham, 1953-61; Professor and Head of Department of Inorganic Chemistry, University of Newcastle upon Tyne, 1961-71; Professor and Head of Department of Inorganic and Structural Chemistry, 1971-90, Head of the School of Chemistry, 1971-74, 1983-86, Dean of the Faculty of Science, 1986-88, Emeritus Professor of Chemistry, 1990-, University of Leeds; Numerous visiting professorships, 1966-93. Publications: Some 480 research papers and reviews; 10 books. Honours include: Masson Memorial Medal, Royal Australian Chemical Institute, 1946; Tilden Lectureship and Medal, Chemical Society, London, 1966; Main Group Element Chemistry Award and Medal, 1974, Liversidge Lectureship and Medal, 1984, Ludwig Mond Lectureship and Medal, 1991, Tertiary Education Award and Medal, 1993, Royal Society of Chemistry; A W von Hofmann, Lectureship, Gesellschaft Deutscher Chemiker, 1983; Foreign Member, l'Académie des Sciences, Institut de France, 1992; Fellow of the Royal Society, 1987; Royal Society Humphry Davy Lectureship, 2000; D de l'Université, honoris causa, Université de Nancy I, France, 1977; Gold Medal and Honorary Citizenship of the City of Nancy, France, 1977; DSc, honoris causa, Toho University, Tokyo, Japan, 2000. Memberships: FRSC; MRI; FRS. Address: University of Leeds School of Chemistry, Leeds, LS2 9JT, England.

GREER Germaine, b. 29 January 1939, Melbourne, Victoria, Australia. Writer; Broadcaster. Education: BA, Honours, Melbourne University, 1959; MA, Honours, Sydney University, 1962; PhD, Cambridge University, 1967. Appointments: Senior English Tutor, Sydney University, 1963-64; Assistant Lecturer and Lecturer, English, University of Warwick, 1967-72; Broadcaster, journalist, columnist and reviewer, 1972-; Lecturer, American Program Bureau, 1973-78; Visiting Professor, Graduate Faculty of Modern Letters, 1979, Professor of Modern Letters, 1980-83, University of Tulsa; Founder-Director, Tulsa Centre for Studies in Women's Literature, 1981; Proprietor, Stump Cross Books, 1988-; Special Lecturer and Unofficial Fellow, Newnham College, Cambridge, 1989-98. Publications: The Female Eunuch, 1969; The Obstacle Race: The Fortunes of Women Painters and Their Work, 1979; Sex and Destiny: The Politics of Human Fertility, 1984; Shakespeare (editor), 1986; The Madwoman's Underclothes (selected journalism), 1986; Daddy, We Hardly Knew You, 1989; The Change: Women, Ageing and the Menopause, 1991; Slip-Shod Sybils: Recognition, Rejection and the Woman Poet, 1995; The Whole Woman, 1999. Editor: The Uncollected Verse of Aphra Behn, 1989. Co-Editor: Kissing the Rod: An Anthology of Seventeenth Century Verse, 1988; Surviving Works of Anne Wharton (co-editor), 1997; The Whole Woman, 1999; John Wilmot, Earl of Rochester, 1999; 101 Poems by 101 Women (editor), 2001; The Boy, 2003; Poems for Gardeners (editor), 2003; Whitefella Jump Up, 2004. Contributions to: Numerous articles in Listener, Spectator, Esquire, Harper's Magazine, Playboy, Private Eye and other journals. Honours: Scholarships, 1952, 1956; Commonwealth Scholarship, 1964; J R Ackerly Prize and Premio Internazionale Mondello, 1989. Address: c/o Aitken and Stone Associates Ltd, 29 Fernshaw Road, London SW10 0TG, England.

GRESSER Sy, b. 9 May 1926, Baltimore, Maryland, USA. Stone Sculptor; Writer; Poet. 4 sons, 1 daughter. Education: BS, 1949, MA, 1972, Zoological Sciences, English and American Literature, University of Maryland; Institute of Contemporary Arts, Washington, DC, 1949-50. Appointments: Publications Consultant for various firms, 1960-; Teacher, 1965-70; Private Students; Exhibitions include: University of Maryland, University College (20 sculptures, Stone & Wood), 2009; Slifka Center, Yale University, 26 sculptures, Stone & Wood), 2009. Publications: Stone Elegies, 1955; Coming of the Atom, 1957; Poems From Mexico, 1964; Voyages, 1969; A Garland for Stephen, 1971; A Departure for Sons, 1973; Fragments and Others, 1982; Hagar and Her Elders, 1989; Stone, Wood and Words, 2006. Contributions to: Poetry Quarterly; Stand; Antioch Review; Western Humanities Review; Johns Hopkins Review; Atavist Magazine; New York Times Book Review; California Quarterly. Address: 1015 Ruatan Street, Silver Spring, MD 20903, USA.

GRETZKY Wayne, b. 26 January 1961, Brantford, Canada. Ice Hockey Player. m. Janet Jones, 1988, 3 sons, 2 daughters. Career: Former player with Edmonton; Played with Los Angeles Kings, 1988-96, St Louis Blues, 1996, New York Rangers, 1996-99; Retired, 1999; Director Canadian National Men's Hockey Team, 2002. Part-owner Phoenix Coyotes, 2000; Head Coach Peoenix Coyotes, 2005-. Most prolific scorer in National Hockey League history; Most Valuable Player (9 times). Publication: Gretzky: An Autobiography (with Rick Reilly). Honour: Hockey Hall of Fame, 1999. Address: New York Rangers, Madison Square Garden, 2 Pennsylvania Plaza, New York, NY 10121, USA.

GREY Dame Beryl, b. 11 June 1927, London, England. Prima Ballerina. m. Sven G Svenson, 1950, 1 son. Education: Sherborne Preparatory School; Dame Alice Owen's Grammar School; Sadlers Wells Ballet School. Appointments: Prima Ballerina, Royal Ballet, 1942-57; International Guest Artist, Europe, USA, Canada, Latin and South America, Australia, Russia and China, 1957-66; Director, Arts Educational Schools and Teacher Training College, 1966-68; International Guest Producer/Director, Sleeping Beauty, Giselle and Swan Lake, 1966-; Artistic Director, London Festival Ballet (now English National Ballet), 1968-79; Governor, Royal Ballet, 1982-2002; Director, Royal Opera House, Covent Garden, 1999-2003; Chairman, Royal Ballet Benevolent Fund, 1992-; Life President, Imperial Society of Dancing, 2002-; Vice President, Royal Academy of Dancing, 1948-; President, British Ballet Organisation. Publications: Author of several books and lectures internationally. Honours: DBE; CBE; Honorary degrees: D Mus, Leicester, 1970; D Litt, City of London, 1974; D Ed, CNNA, 1989; D Litt, Buckingham, 1993; D Mus, University of London, 1996; D Art, Bedford, 2010; Many other prestigious awards. Memberships: Patron of several charities and societies related to dance, music, the visual arts and medicine. Address: Pen-Bre, Beaconsfield Road, Chelwood Gate, East Sussex RH17 7LF, England.

GREY-THOMPSON Dame Tanni (Carys Davina), b. 26 July 1969, Cardiff, Wales. Athlete. m. Ian Thompson, 1999, 1 daughter. Education: Loughborough University of Technology. Career: Bronze Medal, 400m wheelchair races, Seoul Paralympics, 1988; Gold Medals, 100m, 200m, 400m and 800m wheelchair races, Barcelona Paralympics, 1992; Gold Medal, 800m, Silver Medals for 100m, 200m and 400m wheelchair races, Atlanta Paralympics, 1996; Gold Medals, 100m, 200m, 400m and 800m wheelchair races, Sydney Paralympics, 2000; Gold Medals, 100m and 400m wheelchair races, Athens Paralympics, 2004; Gold Medals, women's wheelchair race, London Marathon, 1992, 1994, 1996, 1998, 2001, 2002, Bronze Medal, 1993, Silver Medals, 1997, 1999, 2000, 2003; 3 Gold Medals and 1 Silver Medal, European Championships, 2003; Broke over 20 world records; Development Officer, UK Athletics, 1996-2001; TV and radio presenter, conference and motivational speaker, numerous guest appearances; President, Welsh Association of Cricketers with a Disability; Vice-president, Women's Sports Foundation, South Wales Region of Riding for the Disabled, Get Kids Going; Deputy Chair, UK Lottery Awards Panel (Sport). Publications: Seize the Day: My Autobiography, 2001; Articles in popular press. Honours: Hon Fellow: University of Wales College, Cardiff, 1997; University of Wales Institute, Cardiff, 2001; University of Swansea, 2001; College of Ripon and York St John, 2001; Institute of Leisure and Amenity, Manchester, 2001; University of Wales College, Newport, 2003; Freeman, City of Cardiff, 2003; Hon DUniv (Staffordshire) 1998, (Southampton) 1998; Hon LLD (Exeter) 2003; Dr hc (Surrey) 2000, (Leeds Metropolitan) 2001, (Wales) 2002, (Loughborough) 2002, (Heriot-Watt) 2004; Hon Masters degree (Loughborough) 1994, (Teeside) 2001; Hon MSc (Manchester Metropolitan) 1998; BBC Wales Sports Personality of the Year; Sunday Times Sportswoman of the Year 1992, 2000, (3rd place) 2004; Royal Mail Best Female Performance of the Paralympic Games, 1992; Panasonic Special Award, 1992; Variety Club Disabled Sportwoman of the Year, 1992; Welsh Sports Hall of Fame, 1993; Sports Writers' Association Female Disabled Athlete of the Year, 1994; Sporting Ambassador, 1998; Sportswriters Award, 2000; 3rd place, BBC Sports Personality of the Year, 2000; Helen Rollason Award for Inspiration, BBC Sports Personality of the Year, 2000; Helen Rollason Award, Sunday Times Sports Woman of the Year, 2000; Welsh Woman of the Year, 2001; Pride of Britain Special Award, 2001; UK Sporting Hero, Sport UK, 2001; Chancellor's Medal, University of Glamorgan, 2001; Appears in 50 British Sporting Greats, 2002; Walpole Best British Sporting Achievement Award, 2002; Commonwealth Games Sports Award for Best Female Disabled Athlete, 2002; 3rd Greatest Briton of all time; 47th, 100 Greatest Sporting Moments, 2002; BBC Ouch disability website, 2003; UK Sport Fair Play Award, 2004; Sports Journalist UK Sport Award, 2004; Numerous appearances on radio and TV. Memberships: The Sports Council for Wales's National Excellence Panel; Sports Council for Wales Sportlot Panel; Minister of Sport Implementation Group for the Development of Sport; Welsh Hall of Fame Roll of Honour, 1992-; English Sports Council Lottery Awards Panel, 1995-99; Sports Council for Wales, 1996-2002, for UK Sport, 1998-2003; National Disability Council, 1997-2000; Manchester Commonwealth Games Organising Council Association, 2002; Member Elect, 2001, Member, 2002-, Laureus World Sports Academy; Patron: British Sports Leaders; British Sport Trust; Durham Sport Millennium Youth Games; Regain; Youth Sport Trust; The National Sports Medicine Institute of the United Kingdom; Shelter Cymru; 2003 London Marathon; Lady Taverners; The National Blood Service; Vice-patron, The Helen Rollason Cancer Care Appeal; The Jubilee Sailing Trust, 2002-. Address: c/o Helen Williams, Creating Excellence, Equity House, 1st Floor, Knight Street, South Woodham Ferrers, Chelmsford, Essex CM3 5ZL, England. Website: www.creatingexcellence.co.uk

GRIER Pam, b. 26 May 1949, Winston-Salem, North Carolina, USA. Actress; Writer; Singer. Career: Actress, films: The Big Doll House, Women in Cages, 1971; Big Bird Cage, Black Mama, White Mama, Cool Breeze, Hit Man, Twilight People, 1972; Coffy, Scream, Blacula, Scream!, The Arena, 1973; Foxy Brown, 1974; Bucktown, Friday Foster, Sheba Baby, 1975; Drum, 1976; Greased Lightning, 1977; Fort Apache: The Bronx, 1981; Something Wicked This Way Comes, 1983; Stand Alone, 1985; The Vindicator, On the Edge, 1986; The Allnighter, 1987; Above the Law, 1988; The Package, 1989; Class of 1999, Bill and Ted's Bogus Journey, 1991; Tough Enough, Posse, 1993; Serial Killer, 1995; Original Gangstas, Escape from LA, Mars Attacks!, 1996; Strip Search, Fakin' Da Funk, Jackie Brown, 1997; Holy Smoke, In Too Deep, Fortress 2, 1999; Snow Day, Wilder, 2000; 3 A.M., Love the Hard Way, Bones, John Carpenter's Ghosts of Mars, 2001; Undercover Brother, The Adventures of Pluto Nash, Baby of the Family, 2002; TV: Roots: The Next Generation; Badge of the Assassin, 1985; A Mothers

Right: The Elizabeth Morgan Story; 1st to Die; The L word. Stage appearances: Fool for Love; Frankie and Johnnie; In the Claire de Lune. Honour: Best Actress NAACP, 1986.

GRIEVES John Kerr, b. 7 November 1935, England. Business Consultant. m. Ann, 1 son, 1 daughter. Education: MA, Keble College, Oxford, 1955-58; Harvard Business School, USA, 1979. Appointments: Joined, 1963, Partner, 1964-74, Departmental Managing Partner, Company Department, 1974-78, Managing Partner, 1979-85, Head of Corporate Finance Group, 1985-89, Senior Partner, 1990-96, Freshfields; Subsequently Non-Executive Director: Northern Electric, Enterprise Oil, Hillsdown Holdings, First Leisure Corporation plc (Chairman), New Look Group plc, (Chairman), Esporta plc (Chairman). Membership: The Athenaeum. Address: 7 Putney Park Avenue, London SW15 5QN, England.

GRIFFIN James Patrick, b. 8 July 1933, Wallingford, Connecticut, USA. White's Emeritus Professor of Moral Philosophy. m. Catherine Maulde Von Halban, deceased, 1 son, 1 daughter. Education: BA, Yale University, USA, 1955; D Phil, 1960, MA, 1963, University of Oxford, England. Appointments: Tutorial Lecturer, Christ Church, Oxford, 1960-66; Lecturer in Philosophy, University of Oxford, 1964-90; Fellow and Tutor in Philosophy, Keble College, University of Oxford, 1966-96; Reader in Philosophy, 1990-96, White's Professor of Moral Philosophy, 1996-2000, University of Oxford; Fellow, 1996-2000, Emeritus Fellow, 2000-, Corpus Christi College, Oxford; Adjunct Professor, Centre for Applied Philosophy and Public Ethics, Canberra, Australia, 2002-; Distinguished Visiting Professor, Rutgers University, USA, 2002-. Publications: Books: Wittgenstein's Logical Atomism, 1964; Well-Being, 1986; Value Judgement, 1996; Values, Conflict and the Environment (with others), 1996; On Human Rights, 2008. Honours: Medal, National Education Commission, Poland; Order of Diego de Lusada Venezuela; Doctor, honoris causa, University of Santiago de Compostela, Spain. Memberships: Brooks's; Oxford and Cambridge Club; Honorary Fellow, Keble College, Oxford, 2002-. Address: 10 Northmoor Road, Oxford OX2 6UP, England.

GRIFFITH Melanie, b. 9 August 1957, New York, USA. Actress. m. (1) Don Johnson, 1975, divorced 1976, remarried 1989, divorced 1993, 1 daughter, (2) Steve Bauer, divorced, 1 daughter (3) Antonio Banderas, 1996, 1 daughter. Education: Hollywood Professional School. Career: Films include: Night Moves, 1975; One On One, 1977; Roar, Body Double, 1984; Stormy Monday, 1987; Working Girl, 1988; Bonfire of the Vanities, 1991; Close to Eden, 1993; Nobody's Fool, 1994; Mulholland Falls, 1996; Lolita, 1996; Shadow of Doubt, 1998; Celebrity, 1998; Another Day in Paradise, 1998; Crazy in Alabama, 1999; Cecil B. Demented, 2000; Forever Lulu, 2000; Life with Big Cats, 2000; Tart, 2001; Stuart Little 2 (voice), 2002; The Night We Called It a Day, 2003; Shade, 2003; Tempo, 2003; Have Mercy, 2006; TV Includes: Once an Eagle (mini-series); Carter Country (series); Steel Cowboy; She's in the Army Now; Heartless; Twins. Address: Creative Artists Agency, 9830 Wilshire Boulevard, Beverly Hills, CA 90212, USA.

GRIFFITHS Anthony Edward, b. 29 November 1948, Stafford, England. Private Investor. Divorced, 1 son, 1 daughter. Education: Gnosall Secondary Modern School. Honours: Listed in international biographical dictionaries. Address: Holly Byre, Audmore, Gnosall, Stafford, ST20 0HF, England. E-mail: anthony.griffiths@hemscott.net

GRIGORYAN Karine, b. 28 March 1958, Yerevan, Armenia. Chemist; Educator. m. Artashes Aslanyan, 2 daughters. Education: IHE, YSU, 1984; Candidate, Chemical Sciences, 1991; Doctor, Chemical Sciences, 2010. Appointments: Laboratory Assistant, 1981-88; Laboratory Senior Assistant, 1988-2000; Associate professor, 2000-04; Chemist, 2004-. Publications: 47 articles; 3 patents; 1 book. Honours: The Best Scientific Research Work, YSU, 1988; Grants, ISTC, 1999-2002; USA Civil Research, 2003-04. Address: Yerevan State University, Alek Manukyan, 1 Yerevan, 0025, Armenia. E-mail: kara@ysu.am

GRIMSBY Bishop of, The Rt Rev David Douglas James Rossdale, b. 22 May 1953, London, England. Bishop. m. Karen, 2 sons. Education: Westminster College, Oxford; Roehampton Institute; King's College, London. Appointments: Curate of Upminster, 1981-86; Vicar of St Luke's Moulsham, 1986-90; Vicar of Cookham, 1990-2000; Area Dean of Maidenhead, 1994-2000; Honorary Canon, Christ Church, Oxford, 1990-2000; Canon and Prebendary, Lincoln Cathedral, 2000-; Suffragan Bishop of Grimsby, 2000-. Honours: Diploma in Applied Theology, 1990; MA in Applied Theology, 1991; MSc, Management of Ministry, 2001; MSc, Ministerial and Theological Research, 2002. Memberships: Chairman of the Board of Education for the Diocese of Lincoln; Trustee, Corporation for the Sons of Clergy; The Friends of the Clergy; Governor, Wellington College, 2004-. Address: Bishop's House, Church Lane, Irby, Grimsby, North East Lincolnshire DN37 7JR, England. E-mail: rossdale@btinternet.com

GRINDE Kjell, b. 1 August 1929, Bergen, Norway. Civil and Structural Engineer. m. (1) Heidi, divorced, 1 son, 1 daughter, (2) Anneliv, 2 step-daughters. Education: BSc, 1954, MSc, 1956, Technical University of Norway; Diploma, Total Quality Management, Lausanne, Switzerland. Appointments: Scientific Assistant to Professor, Technical University of Norway, 1954-56; Site Engineer, Snowy Mountains Hydro-Electric Authority, Australia, 1956-58; Site Engineer, Norconsult Ethiopia, Koka Power Plant, 1958-60; Site Engineer, Assab Harbour and Water Supply, 1960-62; Chief Engineer and Resident Manager, Norconsult Nigeria, 1962-64; Marketing Director, 1964-68, Managing Director, 1968-81, Norconsult International, Oslo; Projects for World Bank, UN Agencies, Regional Banks, Developing Countries' Governments; Saga Petroleum, Oslo; Corporate Management Technical Director, projects in North Sea, Benin, Caribia, USA, 1981-91; Working Chairman, Senior Expert Group, 1991-2007. Publications: Professional articles; Conference papers. Honours: Honours Award for Technical Assistance to Developing Countries, Norwegian Natural Sciences Research Council, 1976. Memberships: Director, President, Federation International des Ingenieurs Conseil, 1973-80; Chairman of the Board, Norwegian Petroleum Consultants, 1975-80; Member, Executive Committee Royal Polytechnical Society, 1979-84; Director, Norwegian Export Council, 1975-80; Elected Member, The Norwegian Academy of Technological Sciences, 1976-; Chairman, Drammen Technical Society, 1996-2004. Address: Hanna Winsnesgate 1, 3014 Drammen, Norway. E-mail: kjellgrinde@online.no

GRINT Rupert, b. 24 August 1988, Watton-at-Stone, Hertfordshire, England. Actor. Education: Richard Hale School. Career: Films: Harry Potter and the Philosopher's Stone, 2001; Harry Potter and the Chamber of Secrets, Thunderpants, 2002; Harry Potter and the Prisoner of Azkaban, 2004; Harry Potter and the Goblet of Fire, 2005; Driving Lessons, 2006; Harry Potter and the Order of the Phoenix, 2007; Harry Potter and the Half-Blood Prince,

Cherrybomb, Wild Target, 2009; Harry Potter and the Deathly Hallows: Part 1, 2010; Harry Potter and the Deathly Hallows: Part 2, 2011. Honours: Special Achievement Award, Outstanding New Talent, 2002; Supporting Young Actor, Young Artists Awards, 2002;

GRISEZ Germain, b. 30 September 1929, University Heights, Ohio, USA. Professor of Christian Ethics; Writer. m. Jeannette Selby, 1951, 4 sons. Education: BA, John Carroll University, University Heights, Ohio, 1951; MA and PhL, Dominican College of St Thomas Aquinas, River Forest, Illinois, 1951; PhD, University of Chicago, 1959. Appointments: Assistant Professor to Professor, Georgetown University, 1957-72; Lecturer in Medieval Philosophy, University of Virginia at Charlottesville, 1961-62; Special Assistant to Patrick Cardinal O'Boyle, Archbishop of Washington, DC, 1968-69; Consultant, Archdiocese of Washington, DC, 1969-72; Professor of Philosophy, Campion College, University of Regina, Saskatchewan, Canada, 1972-79; Archbishop Harry J Flynn Professor of Christian Ethics, Mount Saint Mary's College, Emmitsburg, Maryland, 1979-. Publications: Contraception and the Natural Law, 1964; Abortion: The Myths, the Realities, and the Arguments, 1970; Beyond the New Morality: The Responsibilities of Freedom (with Russell Shaw), 1974, 3rd edition, 1988; Beyond the New Theism: A Philosophy of Religion, 1975; Free Choice: A Self-Referential Argument (with Joseph M Boyle Jr and Olaf Tollefsen), 1976; Life and Death with Liberty and Justice: A Contribution to the Euthanasia Debate (with Joseph M Boyle Jr), 1979; The Way of the Lord Jesus, Vol I, Christian Moral Principles (with others), 1983, Vol II, Living a Christian Life (with others), 1993, Vol III, Difficult Moral Questions (with others), 1997; Nuclear Deterrence, Morality and Realism (with John Finnis and Joseph M Boyle Jr), 1987; Fulfilment in Christ: A Summary of Christian Moral Principles (with Russell Shaw), 1991; Personal Vocation: God Calls Everyone by Name (with Russell Shaw), 2003. Contributions to: Many scholarly journals. Honours: Pro ecclesia et pontifice Medal, 1972; Special Award for Scholarly Work, 1981, Cardinal Wright Award for Service to the Church, 1983, Fellowship of Catholic Scholars; Various other fellowships and grants. Memberships: American Catholic Philosophical Association, president, 1983-84; Catholic Theological Society of America. Address: Mount Saint Mary's College, Emmitsburg, MD 21727, USA.

GRISHAM John, b. 8 February 1955, Jonesboro, Arkansas, USA. Author; Lawyer. m. Renée, 1 son, 1 daughter. Education: Mississippi State University; University of Mississippi Law School. Appointment: Ran one-man criminal defence practice in Southaven, Mississippi, 1981-90. Publications: The Pelican Brief; A Time to Kill; Stand in Line at a Super Crown; The Firm; The Client; The Chamber; The Rainmaker; The Runaway Jury; The Partner; The Street Lawyer; The Testament; The Brethren; A Painted House, 2001; Skipping Christmas, 2001; The Summons, 2002; The King of Torts, 2003; Bleachers, 2003; The Last Juror, 2004; The Broker, 2005; The Innocent Man, 2006; Playing For Pizza, 2007; The Appeal, 2008; The Associate, 2009; Ford County, 2009. Address: Doubleday & Co Inc, 1540 Broadway, New York, NY 10036, USA.

GROBBELAAR Nicolaas Johannes, b. 27 July 1942, Villiers, Freestate, South Africa. General Surgeon. Education: MB Ch B, Medicine, 1966, M Med, Medicine, 1973, MD, Surgery, 1977, University of Pretoria; FRCS (Surgery), Royal College of Surgeons of Edinburgh, 1973; FCS (Surgery), College of Medicine of South Africa, 1973. Appointments: Part time Lecturer, University of Pretoria, 1974-2007; Gull time General Surgeon in private practice, Pretoria, 1974-. Honours: Honorary Life Member, Medical Association of South Africa. Memberships: South African Medical Association; Surgical Society of South Africa; Endoscopic Surgical Society of South Africa; Vascular Society of South Africa; Paediatric Surgical Society of South Africa. Address: 36 Guineafowl Street, Silver Lakes, Pretoria, 0054, South Africa. E-mail: njgrobbelaar@telkomsa.net

GROENING Matthew, b. 15 February 1954, Portland, Oregon, USA. Writer; Cartoonist. m. Deborah Lee Caplan (divorced), 2 children. Education: Evergreen State College. Appointments: Cartoonist, Life in Hell syndicated weekly comic strip, Sheridan, Oregon, 1980-; President, Matt Groening Productions Inc, Los Angeles, 1988-, Bongo Entertainment Inc, Los Angeles, 1993-; Creator, The Simpsons interludes, The Tracey Ullman Show, 1987-89; Creator, Executive Producer, The Simpsons TV show, 1989-; Founder and Publisher, Bongo Comics Group; Founder and Publisher, Zongo Comics, including Jimbo, 1995, Fleener, 1996. Publications: Love is Hell, 1985; Work is Hell, 1986; School is Hell, 1987; Childhood is Hell, 1988; Akbar and Jeff's Guide to Life, Greetings From Hell, 1989; The Postcards That Ate My Brain, The Big Book of Hell, The Simpsons Xmas Book, Greetings From the Simpsons, 1990; With Love From Hell, The Simpsons' Rainy Day Fun Book, The Simpsons' Uncensored Family Album, The Alphabet Book, Maggie Simpson's Counting Book, Maggie Simpson's Book of Colors and Shapes, Maggie Simpson's Book of Animals, 1991; The Road to Hell, The Simpson's Fun in Sun Book, Making Faces with the Simpsons, 1992; Bart Simpson's Guide to Life, The Simpsons Ultra-Jumbo Rain-Or-Shine Fun Book, 1993; Binky's Guide to Love, Love is Hell 10th Anniversary Edition, Simpsons Comics Extravaganza, Simpsons Comic Spectacular, Bartman: The Best of the Best, 1994; Simpson Comics Simps-O-Rama, Simpsons Comics Strike Back, 1995; Simpsons Comics Wing Ding, The Huge Book of Hell, 1997; Bongo Comics.

GROSS Johann, b. 5 May 1939, Klosdorf, Romania. Physician. m. Margaretha Görgner, 1 son, 1 daughter. Education: State Examination in Medicine, 1965; Dr med, 1966; Dr med habil, 1973; Specialization in Biochemistry/Laboratory Medicine, Facharzt, 1970; Professor, Pathological Biochemistry, Charite Hospital, Humboldt University, Berlin, Germany, 1980. Publications: Around 300 articles in international journals; Book editor. Honours: International Federal Clinical Chemistry Grantee, Mexico City, 1978; WHO Grantee, Milton Keynes, England, 1979; National Prize, Science and Technology, GDR, 1984. Memberships: German Society of Clinical Chemistry and Laboratory Medicine; German Society of Biochemistry and Molecular Biology. Address: Dolgenseestrasse 14, Berlin 10319, Germany. E-mail: johann.gross@charite.de

GROSSMAN Margaret Rosso, b. 17 October 1947, Illinois, USA. Professor. m. Michael, 2 sons. Education: BMus, highest honours, University of Illinois, 1969; AM, Stanford University, 1970; PhD, Musicology, 1977, JD, summa cum laude, 1979, University of Illinois. Appointments: Bock Chair and Professor, Agricultural Law, Department of Agricultural and Consumer Economics, University of Illinois at Urbana-Champaign; Frequent Visiting Professor, Wageningen University, The Netherlands; Visiting Professor, University of Copenhagen, Denmark; Newcastle Law School, UK, 2008. Publications: Numerous law review articles, book chapters, books. Honours: Fulbright Research Fellow (3 awards); German Marshall Fund Research Fellow; Distinguished Service Award, American Agricultural Law Association,

1993; Silver Medal, European Council for Agricultural Law, 1999; Professional Scholarship Award, American Agricultural Law Association, 2006, 2008. Memberships: American Agricultural Law Association; American Veterinary Medical Law Association; European Council for Agricultural Law; Dutch Society for Agrarian Law; Unione Mondiale degli Agraristi Universitari; European Union Studies Association. Address: 333 Mumford Hall, 1301 W Gregory Dr, Urbana, IL 61801, USA.

GROVES Paul Raymond, b. 28 July 1947, Gloucester, England. m. Annette Kelsall, 1972, 2 daughters. Education: Monmouth School, 1958-65; Caerleon College of Education, 1966-69. Appointments: Teacher, 1970-87; Creative Writing Lecturer, 1989-2009; Freelance Reviewer. Publications: Poetry Introduction 3, 1975; Academe, 1988; Ménage à Trois, 1995; Eros and Thanatos, 1999; Wowsers, 2002; Country Boy, 2007; Qwerty, 2008. Honours: Eric Gregory Award, 1976. Address: 4 Cornford Close, Osbaston, Monmouth NP25 3NT, Wales.

GROVES Philip Denys Baker, b. 9 January 1928, Watford, Hertfordshire, England. Architect. m. Yvonne Joyce Chapman, 2 sons, 1 daughter. Education: Watford Grammar School, 1939-44; Regent Street Polytechnic School of Architecture, 1948-55. Appointments: RAF, 1945-48: Served in UK, Palestine, Egypt; Architects Co-Partnership: Joined 1955, Partner, 1965, Chairman, 1983-95; Architect for education and health projects, UK, Middle East, Far East and Caribbean; Royal Institute of British Architects; Member of Council, 1962-81, Vice President, 1972-75, 1978-80, Chairman, Board of Education, 1974-75, 1979-80; ARCUK Council, 1962-80; Chairman, 1971-74; Chairman, University of York Centre for Continuing Education, 1978-81; Chairman, CPD in Construction Gp, 1990-96; Construction Industry Council, 1993-96; Comité de Liaison des Architects du Marché Commun, 1986-92; Examiner at Schools of Architecture UK and overseas; Chairman, HCCI, 1985-88; President, 1989, Herts Community Foundation; Chairman, 1988-97, Vice President, 1998-; Chairman, Herts TEC, 1992-97; Business Link Herts, 1993-2003, TEC National Council, 1996-99. Publications: Design for Health Care (jointly); Hospitals and Health Care Facilities (jointly); Various articles in professional journals. Honours: Associate, 1955, Fellow, 1968, Royal Institute of British Architects; FRSA, 1989; Deputy Lieutenant of Hertfordshire, 1988-. Memberships: Fellow, Royal Institute of British Architects; Registered Architect ARB; Fellow Royal Society of Arts. Address: The Dingle, Whisper Wood, Loudwater, Rickmansworth, Hertfordshire WD3 4JU, England.

GRUBB George Darlington Wilson, b. 5 December 1935, Edinburgh, Scotland. Lord Lieutenant and Lord Provost of the City of Edinburgh. m. Elizabeth Grant, 1 son, 1 daughter. Education: MA, 1974, B Phil, 1983, Open University; BD, University of Edinburgh, 1978; D Ministry, San Francisco Theological Seminary, 1993. Appointments: Ordained, Church of Scotland, 1962; RAF Squadron Leader Chaplain, 1962-70; Parish Minister, Edinburgh, 1971-2001; Liberal Democrat Member, City of Edinburgh Council, 1999-; Chair, Liberal Democrat Group, 1999-2007; President, Edinburgh International Science Festival; Director and Chair, Edinburgh International Festival Society, Edinburgh Military Tattoo Ltd, Edinburgh Military Tattoo (Charities) Ltd; Director, Dynamic Earth Charitable Trust. Address: City Chambers, High Street, Edinburgh, EH1 1YJ, Scotland. E-mail: lord.provost@edinburgh.gov.uk

GRUBERG Martin, b. 28 January 1935, New York, USA. Professor. 1 son, 1 daughter. Education: BA, City College, New York City, 1955; PhD, Columbia University, New York City, 1963. Appointments: Agent Adjudicator, US State Department, NY Passport Agency, 1960-61; Social Studies Instructor, Pelham, New York and New York City High Schools, 1961-63, Hunter College, 1961-62, Wisconsin State University, 1965; Professor, Political Science Department, University of Wisconsin, Oshkosh, 1963-. Publications: Around over 30 articles in professional journals; 4 book chapters; Books: Women in American Politics, 1968; A Case Study in US Urban Leadership: The Incumbancy of Milwaukee Mayor Henry Maier, 1996; A History of Winnebago County Government, 1998; Introduction to Law, 2003; A Record of Natural and Social Disasters and Their Political Implications: A New Issue for Public Policy Planners, 2009. Honours: Book, Women in American Politics, twice cited by US Supreme Court; Senior Editor, Encyclopedia of American Government. Memberships: American Political Science Association; International Political Science Association; Midwest Political Science Association; Wisconsin Political Science Association; Academy of Criminal Justice Sciences; American Civil Liberties Union. Address: 2121 Oregon Street, Oshkosh, WI 54902, USA. E-mail: gruberg@uwosh.edu

GRUDEN POKUPEC Josipa Sanja, b. 11 December 1973, Zagreb, Croatia. Specialist in Oral Medicine. m. Damir, 1 son, 1 daughter. Education: Doctor of Stomatology; Magistre of Science, 2000; Doctor of Science, 2003; Appointments: High Assistant of Oral Medicine, 2009; Cooperate of Science in Institution of Oral Medicine, 2009; Master of Autogenous Training; Lecturer, High Business School; Participation in many international congresses. Publications: 7 articles in professional journals. Memberships: Croatian Society of Oral Medicine; Croatian Medical Meeting; Croatian Society of Autogenous Training; Croatian Society of Medical Hypnosis. Address: Dedici 76, 10 000 Zagreb, Croatia. E-mail: jspokupec@net.ur

GRYBAUSKAITE Dalia, b. 1 March 1956, Vilnius, Lithuania. President of the Republic of Lithuania; Member of the European Commission. Education: Economist, Leningrad University, 1983; PhD, Economics, Moscow Academy of Public Sciences, 1988; Special Program for Senior Executives, Georgetown University, Washington DC, School of Foreign Service, 1991. Appointments: Head, Department for Science, Institute of Economics, 1990-91; Program Director, Prime Minister's Office, 1991; Director, European Department, Ministry of International Economic Relations, Republic of Lithuania, 1991-93; Director, Economic Relations Department, Ministry of Foreign Affairs, Republic of Lithuania, 1993-94; Chair, Aid-Co-ordination Committee (PHARE and G-24), Chief Negotiator for the Free Trade Agreement with the EU; Extraordinary Envoy and Plenipotentiary Minister, Lithuanian Mission to the EU, 1994-95; Deputy Chief Negotiator, Europe Agreement with the EU; Representative, National Aid Co-ordinator in Brussels; Plenipotentiary Minister, Lithuanian Embassy in the USA, 1996-99; Deputy Minister of Finance, Republic of Lithuania, 1999-2000; Chief Negotiator with IMF and WB; Deputy Minister of Foreign Affairs, Republic of Lithuania, 2000-01; Deputy Head, Lithuanian Delegation for the EU Accession Negotiations; Minister of Finance of the Republic of Lithuania, 2001-04; National Aid Co-ordinator; European Commissioner for Financial Programming and Budget, 2004-; President of the Republic of Lithuania, 2009-. Honours: Commander's Cross Order of Grand Duke Gediminas, 2003; The Commissioner of the Year, 2005;

Leader of a Partnership, 2005; Special Award, LTU TV3, 2006; Wladislva Grabski Award, 2006. Address: S Daukanto a 3, LT 01122 Vilnius, Lithuania.

GRYNING Sven-Erik, b. 9 June 1948, Naestved, Denmark. Scientist. m. Susanne, 2 sons. Education: MS, Technical University of Denmark, 1972; PhD, 1982; DSc, 2006. Appointments: Scientific Staff, Health Physics Department, Riso National Laboratory, 1974-77; Scientific Staff, Physics Department, 1977-84; Scientific Staff, Meteorology and Wind Energy, 1984-; Senior Scientist, 1992-; Adjoint Director, Research, Swedish Defence Research Establishment, 1992-96; Chairman, Convenor, NATO/CCMS International Technical Conference Series on Air Pollution Modelling and its Application, 1992-2000; Project Leader, Oresund Experiment, 1982-90; Chairman, Executive Committee, NOPEX, 1992-2000; Member, Scientific Panel on Atmospheric Chemistry European Commission, 1995-2000. Publications: Editor, Air Pollution Modelling and Its Application. XI, XII, XIII, XIV, XV; Guest Editor, Atmospheric Environment; Agricultural and Forest Meteorology; Theoretical and Applied Meteorology. Honours: Grantee, Nordic Council of Ministry; NATO/CCMS ITM Scientific Committee award for providing outstanding leadership in arranging and conduction 5 NATO/CCMS Conferences on Air Pollution Modelling and its Application, 2000. Memberships: Danish Meteorological Society; Honorary Secretary, European Association for the Science of Air Pollution. Address: Haraldsborgvej 120, DK-4000 Roskilde, Denmark.

GU Yinian, b. 22 March 1963, Beijing, China. Librarian. Education: B Eng (Hons), School of Electronic Engineering, Union University, Beijing, 1986; Master, Library and Information Science, Faculty of Computer Science and Information Technology, University of Malaya, Kuala Lumpur, 2000. Appointments: Reference Librarian, Tsinghua University Library, 1986-94; Instructor, Beijing Inti Management College, 1994-95; Information Manager, Beijing Concord Consulting Company, 1996-98; Senior Reference Librarian, 1998-2000; Principal Reference Librarian, 2000-03, Associate University Librarian (Public Services), 2003-07, Standing Associate University Librarian, 2008-11, Capital Engineering and Science University Library; Visiting Reference Librarian and Secretary to the University Library's Management Committee, Macau University of Science and Technology, 2007-08. Publications: Numerous articles in professional journals. Honours: BIRG Grant, 8th International Conference on Scientometrics and Informetrics, The University of New South Wales, Australia, 2001; Science Citation Index Outstanding Scholarly Article Prize, 2002, 2004; Teaching/Training Excellence Award, 2003, Research Excellence Award, 2004, Capital Engineering and Science University, China; Medal of Wisdom; The Da Vinci Diamond; The International President's Award for Iconic Achievement; The International Plato Award for Educational Achievement – Iconic Achievers; Top 100 Professionals; Top 100 Educators, 2010; Scholarship, 9th International Conference on Scientometrics and Informetrics, Chinese Association for Science of Science and Science and Technology Policy, China, 2003; International Postgraduate Research Scholarship, The Australia Commonwealth Department of Education, Science and Training, Australia, 2003; Charles Sturt University Postgraduate Research Studentship, Centre for Research & Graduate Training, Charles Sturt University, 2003; Listed in international biographical dictionaries. Memberships: Chinese Western Returned Scholars Association; Chinese Overseas-Educated Scholars Association; Chartered Institute of Library and Information Professionals, UK; China Society for Library Science; China Society for Scientific and Technical Information. Address: East 4-2-402, Tsinghua University, Beijing 100084, China. E-mail: gyn@tsinghua.org.cn

GUAN Dagao, b. 20 December 1932, Guangfeng, Jianxi, China. Metallurgical Engineer. m. Yuexian Fang, 3 sons. Education: Graduate, Central South University of Technology, Changsha, China, 1956. Appointments: Technician, Section Chief, Technology Section, Shanghai Nonferrous Metals Company, 1956-59; Technician, Group Chief No.1 Department of Shanghai Nonferrous Metals Research Institute, Shanghai, 1960-77; Engineer, Department Chief, 1978-82; Senior Engineer, Department Chief, No.8 Department of Shanghai Nonferrous Metals Research Institute, Shanghai, 1983-86; Professor, Chief editor Shanghai Metals, 1986-93; Professor, Adviser, Shanghai Nonferrous Metals, 1994-; Member, Precious Metals Branch, New Materials Plan Group, National Science and Technology Committee of China, Beijing, 1976-; Member, Precious Metals Plan Group, China National Nonferrous Metals Industry Corporation, Beijing, 1978-; Consulting Specialist, Chongqing Instrument Materials Research Institute of Machine Industry, Ministry of China, 1987-; Corresponding Committeeman, Editing and Screening, Committee of Journal of Functional Materials, Chongqing, 1997-. Publications: Study on the Preparation of Ultrapure Germanium by Chemical Process, 1958; Study on High Precision Resistor Material used in Wide Temperature, 1973; Study on the Longevous Material used in the Recorder Motors, 1987; Chief editor, Shanghai Metals, 1986-. Awards: Science and Technology Award, Shanghai City Government, 1959; Award, China Countrywide Scientific Conference, 1978; 3rd Award, Electronic Industry, Ministry of China, 1989; Award of Excellent Grade, 1992. Memberships: People's Political Conference, Shanghai, 1959; People's Congress, 1959; National Science and Technology Conference, 1959; Shanghai Science and Technology Conference, 1963; Board of Directors, Shanghai Society of Nonferrous Metals, 1986; Board of Directors, China Society of Instrument Materials, 1990-. Address: 403 Rm No 102 Guyang Rd N, 201600 Songjiang, Shanghai, China.

GUDIVOK Petro Mikhajlovich, b. 12 April 1936, Lavki, Transcarpathia, Ukraine. Mathematician. m. Hanna Chukhno. Education: Physics and Mathematics Faculty, Uzhgorod University, 1958; Candidate, 1963, Doctor, 1975, Physical and Mathematical Sciences, Leningrad University; Professor, 1978. Appointments: Assistant, 1958-59, Postgraduate Student, 1959-62, Senior Lecturer, 1962-75, Professor, 1975-2009, Head of Department of Algebra, 1968-75, 1980-2009, Dean, Mathematical Faculty, 1986-92, Uzhgorod University. Publications: More than 120 scientific papers; 4 monographs. Honours: Honoured Worker of the National Education of Ukraine, 1991; Academician, Academy of Sciences for Higher Education of Ukraine, 1992; Soros Professor, 1997. Memberships: American Mathematical Society; Shevchenko Scientific Society. Address: Ukrainska str, 23/2, 88000 Uzhgorod, Transcarpathia, Ukraine. E-mail: algebra@tn.uz.ua

GUESGEN Hans Werner, b. 24 April 1959, Bonn, Germany. Professor. m. Gaby, 1984, 3 daughters. Education: Dipl-Inform, University of Bonn, 1983; Dr rer nat, University of Kaiserlautern, 1988; Dr habil, University of Hamburg, 1993. Appointments: Post Doctoral Fellow, ICSI, Berkeley, California, 1989-90; Scientific Researcher, GMD St Augustin, Germany, 1983-92; Associate Professor, Computer Science Department, University of Auckland, 1992-2007; Professor, School of Engineering and Advanced

Technology, Massey University, Palmerston North, New Zealand, 2007-. Publications: 2 monographs; 8 edited books, journals and reports; Over 100 refereed articles in journals, books, conference proceedings and workshop notes; Over 30 technical reports. Memberships: Association for the Advancement of Artificial Intelligence. Address: School of Engineering and Advanced Technology, Massey University, Private Bag 11222, Palmerston North, New Zealand. E-mail: h.w.guesgen@massey.ac.nz

GUEST Harry, (Henry Bayly Guest), b. 6 October 1932, Glamorganshire, Wales. Poet; Writer. m. Lynn Doremus Dunbar, 28 December 1963, 1 son, 1 daughter. Education: BA, Trinity Hall, Cambridge, 1954, DES, Sorbonne, University of Paris, 1955. Appointments: Lecturer, Yokohama National University, 1966-72; Head of Modern Languages, Exeter School, 1972-91; Teacher of Japanese, Exeter University, 1979-96. Publications: Arrangements, 1968; The Cutting-Room, 1970; Post-War Japanese Poetry, (editor and translator), 1972; A House Against the Night, 1976; Days, 1978; The Distance, the Shadows, 1981; Lost and Found, 1983; The Emperor of Outer Space (radio play), 1983; Mastering Japanese, 1989; Lost Pictures, 1991; Coming to Terms, 1994; Traveller's Literary Companion to Japan, 1994; So Far, 1998; The Artist on the Artist, 2000; A Puzzling Harvest, Collected Poems, 2002; Time After Time, 2005; From a Condemned Cell ,2008; Comparison & Conversions, 2009; Some Times, 2010; Contributions to: Reviews, quarterlies, and journals. Honours: Hawthornden Fellow, 1993; Honorary Research Fellow, Exeter University, 1994-; Honorary Doctor of Letters, Plymouth University, 1998; Elected to the Welsh Academy, 2001. Membership: Poetry Society, General Council, 1972-76. Address: 1 Alexandra Terrace, Exeter, Devon EX4 6SY, England.

GUEST Hazel Skelsey (née Rider), b. 23 January 1929, London, England. Mathematics Lecturer. m. Kenneth George Guest, divorced. Education: BA, 1949, MA, 1953, Mathematics, Newnham College, Cambridge; BSc (1st class honours), Mathematics, London, 1954; Teacher's Certificate, Dress-making & Design, 1961; FIMA, 1966; Certificate, 1980, Diploma, 1992, ADVDip, 1996, Transpersonal Psychotherapy; C Math, 1991; C Sci, 2005. Appointments: Mathematics Lecturer, SW Essex Technical College, 1949-52; Mathematics Lecturer, Borough Polytechnic, London, 1954-55; Mathematics Lecturer, Senior Lecturer, Woolwich Polytechnic, London, 1955-66; Mathematics Lecturer, City University, London, 1966-84; Examiner, Associated Examination Board, 1984-87; Private Psychotherapist, 1984-98; Part time Occasional Tutor, Cambridge University, 1990-. Publications: 1 paper in mathematics; 5 papers on psychotherapy; 2 papers on low frequency noise. Memberships: Fellow, Institute of Mathematics & Its Applications; Centre for Transpersonal Psychology; Association for Humanistic Psychology (Emerita); Cambridge Jungian Circle; Newnham College (Cambridge) Alumnae; UK Noise Association; Scientific & Medical Network; Mensa; Fellow, Cambridge Philosophical Society. Address: 44 Beaufort Place, Thompson's Lane, Cambridge, CB5 8AG, England.

GUEUDET Edouard Philippe, b. 20 January 1976, Paris, France. Banker. Education: JD, Université Paris II Panthéon – Assas, 1999; MS, Institut Supérieur du Commerce de Paris, 2000; LLM, American University, Washington, DC, 2002; MBA, Kogod School of Business, American University, Washington DC, 2006. Appointments: Project Manager, Procar SA, 2000-01; Compagnie Financière d'Organisation et de Gestion (CFOG), 2002-05; Gueudet Frères SA, 2004-05; Consultant, 2006-07; Private Banker, Hottinger & Cie Geneva, 2007-; Vice President, 2008-09, First Vice President, Head of Private Banking, 2009-10, Hottinger Bank & Trust Limited, Nassau, The Bahamas; Vice President & Partner, Hottinger & Cie SA, 2010. Memberships: Lyford Cay Club; Old Fort Bay Club, Bahamas; Automobile Club de France; The Travellers, Paris; Cercle MBC; Societé Nautique de Genève. Address: Hottinger & Cie SA, 3 Place des Bergues, CH-1201, Geneva.

GUFFANTI Fabio Paolo, b. 31 July 1965, Milan, Italy. Consultant; Director. Education: Degree, Political Science, University of Milan, 1990; Certificate in EU International Affairs, SIOI, Milan, 1991; Diploma in EU Law and Politics, SIOI, Rome, 1993; Certificate of International Trade, IUIL Luxembourg, 1994; Certificate in Human Rights and International Humanitarian Law, Strasbourg Institute R Cassin, 1995; Certificate in Political Affairs, Milan, 1998; ISPI – The Enlargement of the European Union, 2000; ASERI, Postgraduate Course on International relations, High School of International Relations, 2001; ASERI, Equilibri.net Course in Political Analysis of International Politics/Relations, Milan, 2005; Diploma, ISPI-UNICEF, 2008. Appointments: Military service in the secretariat of the General Commander of the Italian First Air Region, Milan, 1991-92; Consultant of the Vice President, European Parliament, 1996-; Consultant, Nyrae Group, 1997-99; Consultant, Electoral Committee of Mr Pecorella, MP of Italian Parliament; Consultant, ETCETERA Ltd, Milan, Nairobi, 1999-; Private Brokerage of Commodities, 2000-; Consultant, Electoral Campaign of Mrs C Muscardini for re-election at EU Parliament, 2004; UN Volunteer Service (on-line) Consulting Service, 2005-; Consultant, Brokerage of Commodities, MP Enterprise, India, 2007-. Publications: Some publications written for the Vice President of the European Parliament. Honours: Distinguished Deputy Governor and Continental Governor, American Biographical Institute; Life Fellow, International Biographical Institute; Order of International Merit, IBC, 2001; Knight of the World Order of Education, Science and Culture, Euro-Academy, Brussels, 2000; Researcher of the Year, ABI, 2001; Eminent Personalities of India, 2005. Memberships: Experts Board, EU Consultants Affairs; Press and Publicity International; Secretary General, United Cultural Convention; International Directory and Distinguished Leadership; 2000 Leaders of Influence; Outstanding People of the 20th Century; International Diplomatic Academy; World Council for Peace and Diplomacy, 2003; International Association of Business Leaders, 2003; Federation of UN Associations, 2004; IBRF Governor, Nagpur, India, 2005. Address: Viale Umbria 109, I-20135, Milan, Italy.

GUHA Kamal Kumar, b. 25 September 1928, Dhaka, Bangladesh. Writer and Retired Banker. m. Sujaya Basu, deceased, 1970. Education: BA (Hons); MA; LLB. Appointments: Management Staff, Anz Grindlays Bank, Retired. Publications: Co author of best Bengali Film Story, Bigolito Koruna, 1972; Editor, Himavanta: India's only Mountaineering Monthly for 43 Years Since 1968, judged as one of four World's Best Mountaineering Journals by UIAA. Honours: Civic Reception by Kolkata Corporation for promotion of mountaineering in 1969. Memberships: Himalayan Mountaineering Institute, Darjeeling, Nehru Institute of Mountaineering; Jawahar Institute of Mountaineering; Honorary Member, Himalayan Club, Mumbai. Address: 63E Mahanirban Road, Kolkata 700 029, India.

GUI Gerald P H, b. 8 June 1962, Kuala Lumpur, Malaysia. Consultant Surgeon. m. Corina Espinosa, 2 sons. Education: MB BS, University College and Middlesex Hospital Medical

School, London, 1981-86; FRCS Edinburgh, 1990; FRCS England, 1991; Master of Surgery, University of London, 1996. Appointments: Previously: Senior Registrar and Lecturer in Surgery, St George's Hospital Medical School; Registrar in Surgery, St Bartholomew's Hospital, London; Currently: Consultant Surgeon, Royal Marsden NHS Trust and Honorary Senior Lecturer, Institute of Cancer Research, London. Publications: Many peer-reviewed original manuscripts in surgery and breast cancer management, tumour biology of breast cancer. Honours: University of London Laurels, 1986; Royal College of Surgeons of England Travelling Fellowship, 1997; Surgeon in Training Medal, Royal College of Surgeons, Edinburgh, 1994. Memberships: British Association of Surgical Oncology; British Breast Group; British Oncological Association; Society of Academic and Research Surgeons; Fellow, Association of Surgeons of Great Britain and Ireland. Address: Academic Surgery (Breast Unit), Royal Marsden NHS Trust, Fulham Road, London SW3 6JJ, England. E-mail: gerald.gui@rmh.nhs.uk

GUILLEMIN Roger Charles Louis, b. 11 January 1924, Dijon, France (US Citizen). Endocrinologist. m. Lucienne Jeanne Billard, 1951, 1 son, 5 daughters. Education: BA, 1941, BSc, 1942, University of Dijon; Medicine, University of Lyons, medical degree, 1949; PhD, Institute of Experimental Medicine and Surgery, Montreal, 1950. Appointments: Resident Intern, University Hospital, Dijon, 1949-51; Professor, Institute of Experimental Medicine and Surgery, Montreal; Baylor College of Medicine, Houston, Texas, 1953; Associate Director, Department of Experimental Endocrinology, Collège de France, Paris, 1960-63; Resident Fellow and Research Professor, 1970-89, Dean, 1972-73, 1976-77, Distinguished Professor, 1997-, The Salk Institute for Biological Studies, San Diego, California; Distinguished Scientist, 1989-93, Medical and Scientific Director, Director, 1993-94, 1995-97, Whittier Institute for Diabetes and Endocrinology, La Jolla; Adjunct Professor of Medicine, University of California, San Diego, 1995-97. Honours: Bonneau and La Caze Awards in Physiology, 1957, 1960; Gairdner Award, 1974; Officier, Legion d'honneur, Lasker Foundation Award, 1975; Nobel Prize for Physiology or Medicine, 1977; National Medal of Science, 1977; Barren Gold Medal, 1979; Dale Medallist, UK Society for Endocrinology, 1980. Memberships: NAS; American Academy of Arts and Sciences; American Physiological Society; Society for Experimental Biology and Medicine; International Brain Research Organisation; International Society for Research in Biology and Reproduction; Swedish Society of Medical Sciences; Academie Nacionale de Medecine; Academie des Sciences; Academie Royale de Medecine de Belgique; The Endocrine Society. Address: The Salk Institute, 10010 North Torrey Pines Road, La Jolla, CA 92037, USA.

GUIMARAES Romeu Cardoso, b. 29 July 1943, Belo Horizonte MG, Brazil. m. Alexandrina M Guimaraes. Education: MD, 1965; PhD, Pathology, 1970; Full Professor, Genetics, 1987. Appointments: University Federal Minas Gerais, 1966-75, 1993-; University Estadual Paulista, 1976-93; Currently working on: Origin of Life, Philosophy of Biology. Publications: A self-referential model for the formation of the genetic code, 2008; Metabolic Basis for the Self-Referential Genetic Code, 2010. Honour: Illustrious Son of Belo Horizonte. Memberships: Sao Paulo Academy of Sciences; Minas Gerais Academy of Medicine. Address: Dpto Biologia Geral, Instituto Ciencias Biologicas, UFMG, 31270-901 Belo Horizonte MG, Brazil. E-mail: romeucg@icb.ufmg.br

GUINNESS (Cecil) Edward, b. 1924, Great Britain. Brewery Director. m. Elizabeth Mary Fossett Thompson, 3 daughters, 1 deceased. Education: Stowe School, 1938-42; Army Course, University of Belfast, 1942-43; Ex-Serviceman's Course, School of Brewing, Birmingham, 1946-47. Appointments: WWII: Officer Cadet, Royal Artillery (invalided out due to Battle Course injury), 1942-45; Former Vice-Chairman, Guinness Brewing Worldwide; Joined Guinness as Junior Brewer, 1945; Director: Wolverhampton and Dudley Breweries, 1964-87, Guinness plc, 1971-89; Chairman and Managing Director, Harp Lager Consortium, 1971-87; Chairman: Brewer's Society, 1985-86, Fulmer Parish Council, 1973-81, UK Trustees Duke of Edinburgh's Commonwealth Study Conferences, 1972-86; Licensed Trade Charities Trust, 1981-92, Governing Body, Dame Alice Owen's School, Potters Bar, 1981-92, Scottish Licensed Trade Association, 1972, Wine and Spirit Trade Benevolent Society, 1989-90, Chairman, Executive Committee, Fulmer Sports and Community Association, 2003-2004; President, 2004-, Chairman, Development Trust, 1993-96, Governor and Member of Executive Committee, 1996-, Queen Elizabeth Foundation for Disabled People; President: Performing Arts Centre Campaign, Dame Alice Owen's School, 1997-2002, Fulmer Recreation Ground Campaign, 2000-2003; Former President and Vice-President, 1980 and 1991, Licensed Victuallers National Homes; Member, Governing Body, Lister Institute of Preventive Medicine, 1968-2001, Gerrards Cross with Fulmer Parochial Church Council, 2002-2005. Publication: The Guinness Book of Guinness, 1988; Co-author, Fulmer's Fallen, 2009. Honours: CVO, 1986; Master, Worshipful Company of Brewers, 1977-78; Order of the League of Mercy at Mansion House, London, 2010. Membership: Life Member, Industrial Society. Address: Huyton Fold, Fulmer Village, Buckinghamshire SL3 6HD, England.

GULIK Elisabeth Thecla Maria van der, b. 19 December 1947, Amsterdam, Netherlands. Occupational Health Physician. Education: Analytical Chemist, Westeinde Hospital, The Hague, 1967-69; MD, Catholic University, Nijmegen, 1969-80; Course in General and Experimental Oncology, Institute ARC, Villejuif, France, 1985-86; Assessment Medicine, SMI course, School of Public Health, Utrecht, 1999; Counseling and Coaching, Benelux University Centre, Eindhoven, 2002-05. Appointments: Assurance Physician, General Administration Office, GAK, Amsterdam, 1992-96; Assurance Physician, Joint Executive Organization GUO, Zoetermeer, Netherlands, 1996-98; Cure Supplies, Netherlands, ZVN BV, Amsterdam, 1998-99; Occupational Health Physician, AGG Arbo Service, Amstelveen, 1999, 2000; Arbo Unie, Delft, 2001, Commit Arbo, De Meern, 2001, 2002; Arbo Unie BV 21731, 2002-04; AGW, 2005-06, Hoorn; Maetis Ardyn, Amsterdam, 2006-. Publications: The Applicability of Several Stress Models and the Relation to Change and Stress Management in the Working Situation, 2005; The Absenteeism Conversation, 2005. Honours: Grantee, Association Naturalia et Biologia, 1985; Decree of Merit, The World Who's Who of Women, IBC, 1997; Achievement Award, Five Hundred Leaders of Influence, ABI, 1997; International Woman of the Year, 1997-98, IBC; Award of Excellence, ABI-IBC International Congress, 1998; World Laureate, ABI, 1999; Continental Governor and Member of the International Governors Club, ABI Research Association, 1999; Lifetime Deputy Governor, ABI Research Association, 1999; Member, Research Board of Advisors, ABI, 1999; 2000 Millennium Medal of Honor, 1999; Hall of Fame, International Who's Who of Professional and Business Women, 6th edition, ABI, 1999; International Book of Honor, 6th world edition, ABI, 1999; Research Council Member,

IBC, 2000; Award for Outstanding Artistic Performance, ABI-IBC International Congress, 2000, 2001, 2002, 2004, 2005, 2006, 2007, 2008; ABI-IBC Congress Medal, 2000; Life Patron, IBA, 2001; Medical Advisor to the Director General, IBC, 2001; Secretary General, United Cultural Convention, 2001; Diploma of the Greatest Minds of the 21st Century, 2001; International Directory of Distinguished Leadership, 10th Edition, 2001; Hall of Fame, IBC, 2007; American Medal of Honor, ABI, 2007. Memberships: Dutch Royal Academy of Medicine, Utrecht, 1979. Address: Smedemanstraat 2, NL 1182 HT Amstelveen, Netherlands. E-mail: etm.vander.gulik@12move.nl

GUMBS Pamela Yancy (Dr Pam), b. 6 August 1946, Andover, Massachusetts, USA. Clinical Pharmacy. m. John J Gumbs. Education: Doctorate-in-Pharmacy, UCSF School of Pharmacy, 1975; Geriatric Residency, UCSF Geriatric Institute, 1991. Appointments: CEO Clinical Affairs, Clinical Pharmacist, Royal Medical Inc United Pharmacy, 1996-. Publications: Editor, Pills & Potions Newsletter Alameda Country Pharmacists Association. Honours: Pharmacy Leader, Presidential Tour, 1987; Northern California Forensics Association Award for Communication Excellence, 1987; US Ambassador to World Forum, Cambridge, England, 2010; Listed in international biographical dictionaries. Memberships: California Pharmacists' Association; American Society of Consultant Pharmacists'; Christian Pharmacists Fellowship International; American Pharmacists Association; National Association of Female Executives. Address: Royal Medical Ltd, 2929 Telegraph Ave, Berkeley, CA 94705, USA. E-mail: drpam@consultingwithdrpam.com

GUMLEY-MASON Frances Jane Miriah Katrina, b. 28 January 1955, London, England. Headmistress. m. Andrew Samuel Mason, 1 son, 1 daughter. Education: MA, Newnham College, Cambridge. Appointments: Parliamentary Researcher, 1974; Braille Transcriber, 1975; Editorial Assistant, 1975-76, Staff Reporter and Literary Editor, 1976-79, Editor, 1979-81, Catholic Herald; Senior Producer, Religious Broadcasting, BBC, 1981-88; Series Editor, Channel 4, 1988-89; Acting Executive Producer, Religion, BBC World Service, 1989; Guest Producer and Scriptwriter, BBC Radio 4, 1989-95; Headmistress, St Augustine's Priory, Ealing, 1995-. Publications: Books: The Good Book; The Christian Centuries; The Pillars of Islam; Protestors for Paradise; Discovering Turkey (jointly). Honour: MA, Newnham College, Cambridge. Membership: Mistress of the Keys, Catholic Writers' Guild, 1982-87. Address: St Augustine's Priory, Hillcrest Road, Ealing, London W5 2JL, England. E-mail: registrar@saintaugustinespriory.org.uk

GUMPERTZ Werner H, b. 26 December 1917, Berlin, Germany. Consulting Engineer. Education: BCE Swiss Federal Institute of Technology, 1939; Sanitary Engineering, New York University, 1941; SB in Civil Engineering, MIT, 1948; SM in Building Engineering and Construction, MIT, 1950; Advanced Professional degree of Building Engineer, MIT, 1954; Appointments: Office and Field Engineer, United Engineers and Constructors, 1948-49; Assistant Professor of Building Technology, Massachusetts Institute of Technology, 1949-1957; Senior Principal, Simpson Gumpertz & Heger Inc, 1956-. Publications: Numerous publications, presentations and lectures on field of building and building materials, 1948-. Honours: Sigma Xi; 1st Prize, paper contest, American Society of Civil Engineers, 1948; Citation for Good Citizenship, Freedom Inc, 1957; Award of Merit, Boston Arts Festival, 1958; Commendation for Public Service, member of Engineering Board, City of Newton, Massachusetts, 1961; Honour Award for Design in Urban Transportation, US Department of Housing and Urban Development, 1968; Award of Appreciation, American Society for Testing and Materials, 1980-85; Award of Merit, American Society for Testing and Materials, 1986; ASTM Walter C Voss Award to Engineer for Outstanding Contribution to Advancement of Building Technology, 1987; William C Cullen Award, ASTM, 2004; Dudley Award, Award of Merit, ASTM, 2008; Carl Cash Award, ASTM, 2008. Memberships: Fellow, ASCE; Fellow, ASTM; ACI; AAA; NFPA; Midwest Roofing Contractors Association. Address: c/o Simpson Gumpertz & Heger Inc, 41 Seyon Street, Waltham, MA 02453, USA.

GUNEPIN Mathieu, b. 12 June 1975, Angers, France. Military Dentist. m. Florence Derache, 1 son, 1 daughter. Education: PhD, Dentistry, 2000. Appointments: 26th Marines Battalion, Libreville, Gabon, 2000-02; Inter-Army School of Language Studies and Intelligence, Strasbourg, France, 2002-06; Inter-Army Training Center of Intelligence, 2006-08; Military School of Artillery, Draguigan, 2008-10; Military Medical Center of Draguigan, 2011-. Publications: 47 articles in French and international journals; 17 congress communications. Honours: NATO medal for Yugoslavia; French medal for Yugoslavia; Medal for overseas deployments (TCHAD); Medal for Technical and Scientific work; Medal of National Recognition. Memberships: International Association for Aerospace Dentistry. Address: Military Medical Center of Draguigan, BP 400, 83007 Draguigan Cedex, France. E-mail: mgunepin@yahoo.fr

GÜNEY Kamil Rifat Irfan, b. 12 April 1957, Istanbul, Turkey. Professor. m. Aysegül, 2 daughters. Education: Electrical Engineer, Istanbul State Academy of Architecture and Engineering, 1980; MSc, Electrical & Electronic Engineering, Istanbul Technical University, 1983; PhD, Electrical Engineering, Marmara University, 1987. Appointments: Assistant Professor, 1988, Associate Professor, 1989, Professor, 1994, Vice Dean, 1995-2000, Dean, 2000-03, Vice Rector, 2002-06, Electrical Engineering, Marmara University; Dean, Faculty of Engineering, 2007-08, Vice Rector, 2007-08, Okan University; Dean, Faculty of Engineering, Vice Rector, Acibadem University, 2008-. Publications: 25 research articles; 89 (national and international) conference presentations; 2 books; 1 chapter in international book. Honours: Industrial Education Project; Visiting Lecturer, Glasgow University, 1992; Marmara University Award of Exceptional Success; Visiting Lecturer, Arizona State University, 1995; Mechatronics Project awarded for Success in Profession, Rotary Club. Memberships: Advanced Modelling and Simulation Enterprises; Turkish Electrical Engineering Chamber Member; International Electrical Electronic Engineering. Address: Acibadem University, Inönü Caddesi, Divon Sokak No 1, Gülsuyu/Maltepe, Istanbul 34848, Turkey. E-mail: irfan.guney@acibaden.edu.tr

GUNNELL Sally, b. 29 July 1966, Chigwell, Essex, England. Sport Commentator; Former Professional Athlete. m. Jonathan Bigg, 1992, 3 sons. Education: Chigwell High School; Trained by Bruce Longdon. Career: Specialised in hurdles; 400m hurdles, Olympic Games, Seoul, 1988; 2nd, 400m hurdles World Championship, Tokyo, 1991; Bronze Medal, 400m relay, Olympic Games, Barcelona, 1992; Women's Team Captain, Olympic Games, 1992-97; Gold Medal, 400m hurdles, Olympic Games, Barcelona, 1992; Gold Medal (world record), 400m hurdles, World Championships, 1993; Gold Medal, 400m hurdles, European Championships, Helsinki, 1994; Gold Medal, 400m hurdles, Commonwealth Games, Canada, 1994; Retired, 1997; Sport

Commentator, BBC,1999-2006; Fitness Consultant, Crown Sports, 2001-. Publication: Running Tall (with Christopher Priest), 1994; Be Your Best, 2001. Honour: OBE, 1999; Only woman in history to have held four gold medals concurrently as at end of 2002. Membership: Essex Ladies Athletic Club. Address: Old School Cottage, School Lane, Pyecombe, West Sussex, BN45 7FQ, England.

GUNSTON Bill, (William Tudor Gunston), b. 1 March 1927, London, England. Author. m. Margaret Anne, 1964, 2 daughters. Education: University College, Durham, 1945-46; City University, London, 1948-51. Appointments: Pilot, Royal Air Force, 1946-48; Editorial Staff, 1951-55, Technical Editor, 1955-64, Flight; Technology Editor, Science Journal, 1964-70; Compiler, Jane's All the World's Aircraft, 1968-; Compiler/Editor, 1996-2008, Assistant Editor, 2008-, Jane's Aero-Engines; Freelance author, 1970-; Director, So Few Ltd. Publications: Over 370 books including: Aircraft of The Soviet Union, 1983; Jane's Aerospace Dictionary, 1980, 4th edition, 1998; Encyclopaedia of World Aero Engines, 1986, 3rd edition, 1995; 5th edition, 2006; Encyclopaedia of Aircraft Armament, 1987; Airbus, 1988, 2nd edition 2009; Avionics, 1990; Giants of the Sky, 1991; Faster Than Sound, 1992, 2nd edition, 2008; Jet Bombers, 1993; Piston Aero Engines, 1994, 2nd edition, 1998; Encyclopaedia of Russian Aircraft, 1995; Jet and Turbine Aero Engines, 1995, 2nd edition, 1997, 4th edition, 2006; Night Fighters, 2nd edition, 2004; The Cambridge Aerospace Dictionary, 2004, new edition 2009; Nimrod, 2009; World Encyclopaedia of Aircraft Manufacturers, 2nd edition, 2005; Contributions to: 188 periodicals; 18 partworks; 75 video scripts; Member Association of British Science Writers. Honours: Fellow, Royal Aeronautical Society; Officer of the Order of the British Empire. Address: High Beech, Kingsley Green, Haslemere, Surrey GU27 3LL, England.

GUO Gong-Yi, b. 16 June 1940, Shanghai, China. Professor. m. Yu-Li Chen, 2 daughters. Education: BS, Rare Metals, East China University of Science and Technology, 1963. Appointments: Associate Professor, Shanghai Jiao Tong University, 1988-96, Professor, Shanghai Jiao Tong University, 1996-. Publications: Book, Fuel Cells, 1984; New Research on Solid State Chemistry, Chapter 3, 2007; Numerous articles in national and international scientific journals include most recently: Optical and Thermal Properties of Some Chemically Durable Lead Phosphate Glasses, 1998; Structural Study of a Lead-Barium-Aluminium Phosphate Glass by MAS-NMR Spectroscopy, 1998; ^{31}P-and ^{27}Al-MAS-NMR Investigations of Some Lead Phosphate Glasses, 1999; Achieving Practically Zero Discharge for an Acrylic Acid Plant by a Metalorganic Precipitation Process, 2000; High-Quality Zirconia Powder Resulting from the Attempted Separation of Acetic Acid from Acrylic Acid with Zirconium Oxychloride, 2001; A Nearly Pure Monoclinic Nanocrystalline Zirconia, 2005. Honours: Progress in Science and Technology on Extraction and Purification of Scandium Oxide, State Ministry of Education, 1991; Shanghai Excellent Invention on Yttria-stabilised Zirconia Ultrafine Powder, Shanghai Scientific and Technological Commission, 1996. Memberships: TMS, USA; The American Ceramic Society; The Chinese Society of Rare Earth. Address: Department of Materials Science Engineering, Shanghai Jiao Tong University, 1954 Hua Shan Road, 200030 Shanghai, China. E-mail: guo_gongyi@hotmail.com

GUO Lan-Yuen (Timothy), b. 22 June 1970, Taiwan. Professor. m. Meng-Chun Hsieh, 2 sons, 1 daughter. Education: BS, National Yang-Ming University, Taiwan, 1992; MS, 1996, PhD, 2003, Biomedical Engineering, National Cheng-Kung University, Taiwan. Appointments: Physical Therapist (Military Service), Hsin-Chu Base, Chinese Air Force, Hsin Chu, Taiwan, 1992-94; Special Project Associate, Orthopedic Biomechanics Laboratory, Mayo Clinic, Rochester, USA, 2001-03; Instructor, 1996-2003, Associate Professor, 2003-04, Department of Physical Therapy, Tzu-Chi College of Technology, Hualien, Taiwan; Assistant Professor, 2004-06, Associate Professor, 2006-, Director, 2010-, Department of Sports Medicine, College of Medicine, Kaohsiung Medical University, Kaohsiung, Taiwan. Publications: Numerous articles in professional journals. Honours: Many awards including most recently: 2008 Outstanding Merit Awards Annual Academic Co-operation, 2009 Technology Transfer Award for Outstanding Contribution, 2010, Kaohsiung Medical University; Best Poster Paper, The 2nd Asia-Oceanian Conference of Physical and Rehabiliation Medicine, 2010; Oral Paper Award, Annual Meeting of Taiwanese Society of Biomechanics, 2010; Poster Paper Competition Winner, Annual Meeting of Taiwanese Society of Biomechanics in Sports, 2010; Listed in biographical dictionaries. Memberships: Taiwan Sports Technology Association; Physical Therapy Association of the ROC; Taiwanese Society of Biomedical Engineering; Taiwanese Society of Biomechanics; Taiwanese Society of Biomechanics in Sports; International Society of Biomechanics; International Society of Electromyography and Kinesiology; International Association for the Study of Pain; American College of Sports Medicine. Address:

GUPTA Himanshu, b. 21 July 1982, India. Senior Research Fellow. Education: D Pharm, Delhi University, 2001; B Pharm, UP Technical University, Lucknow, 2004; M Pharm, VMRF, 2006; Post Graduate Diploma in International Business, SCDL, 2009; PhD, Pharmaceutics, Hamdard University, 2011. Appointments: Dispensing Pharmacist, Hindu Rao Hospital, Delhi, 2001; Trainee Production Pharmacist, UNICHEM Labs Ltd, Ghaziabad, India, 2003; Research Student, Institute of Nuclear Medicine and Allied Sciences, Ministry of Defence, Delhi, 2005-06; Research Student, Ocular Pharmacology Lab, Dr R P Centre for Ophthalmic Sciences, AIIMS, 2006; Lecturer, Bharat Institute of Technology, UPTU, 2006-07; Research Associate, Shri Ram Institute for Industrial Research, 2007-08; Senior Research Fellow, Council of Scientific and Industrial Research, Government of India, 2009; Managing Editor, Journal of Pharmacy & Bioallied Sciences (www.jpbsonline.org), 2009; Assistant Editor, Chronicles of Young Scientists (www.cysonline.org), 2010; Team Member, Organization of Pharmaceutical Unity with Bioallied Sciences. Publications: Numerous articles in professional journals. Memberships: Association of Pharmaceutical Teachers of India; Registered Pharmacist, Delhi Pharmacy Council; Society of Nuclear Medicine; Organization of Pharmaceutical Unity with BioAllied Sciences (OPUBS) www.opubs.com. Address: H No 21, Jaina Building, Roshanara Road, Delhi 110007, India. E-mail: dr.hgupta@yahoo.com

GUPTA Pawan K, b. 14 February 1943, Moga, Punjab, India. Veterinary Teacher; Research Expert Consultant. m. Smt Rakesh Gupta, 2 sons. Education: BVSc and AH, 1965; MSc (VM and AH), 1967; PhD, 1971; FACVT (USA), 1977. Appointments: Senior Lecturer, Punjab University, Chandigarh, 1970-73; Scientist-in-Charge, Safety Evaluation, Industrial Toxicology Research Centre, Lucknow, 1973-80; University Professor, Indian Veterinary Research Institute, 1980-; Chief of the Division of Pharmacology and Toxicology, 1982-85, 1987-90, 1994-95. Publications: Author and editor of several books; Over 400 research papers, monographs, book chapters, technical reports and review articles; Editor, three-volume set on Modern Toxicology. Honours: Gold

Medals; Best Teachers Award; Alarsin Gold Medal Award and Scroll of Honour; Listed in numerous Who's Who publications. Memberships include: Director and Councillor, International Union of Toxicology; Founder, Convenor, Society of Toxicology, India, 1979, General Secretary, 1980-83, President, 1984-87; President, Bareilly Mahaan, (Rotary International) District 3110; Executive Committee Member, All India Veterinary Scientists Association; Editorial Board, Clinical Toxicology, Indian Journal of Pharmacology; Editor-in-Chief, Indian Journal of Toxicology. Address: Dr P K Gupta, C-44 Rajinder Nagar, Bareilly 243 122, India.

GUPTA Shanti Swaroop, b. 2 July 1962, Kalinjer, Banda, UP, India. Senior Development Officer. m. Meera, 1 son, 2 daughters. Education: BE, Electrical, ME, Electrical, PhD, Electronics & Communication Engineering. Appointments: Lecturer, EED, MNR Engineering College, Allahabad, India, 1984-85; Design Engineer, BHEL, Jhansi, India, 1985-87; Assistant Development Officer, 1988-2000, Development Officer, Senior Development Officer, 2005-, Ministry of Commerce & Industry, Government of India; Assistant Professor, ECE, Netaji Subhas Institute of Technology, New Delhi, 2000-05. Publications: 27 research papers in reputed international journals; 1 book chapter. Honours: Letter of Appreciation, Prime Minister of India; Commendation for Industrial Policy and Promotion. Memberships: Fellow, IETE, India; IE (India); Life Member, ISTE, India. Address: B-119, Kendriya Vihar, Sectar 56, Gugaon 122011 (Haryana), India.

GURDON John Bertrand, b. 2 October 1933, Dippenhall, Hampshire, England. Molecular Biologist. m. Jean Elizabeth Margaret Curtis, 1964, 1 son, 1 daughter. Education: Eton College; Graduated, Zoology, Christ Church College, Oxford, 1956; Doctorate, Embryology, Zoology Department, 1960. Appointments: Beit Memorial Fellow, 1958-61; Gosney Research Fellow, California Institute of Technology, 1961-62; Research Fellow, 1962-72, Departmental Demonstrator, 1963-64, Lecturer, Department of Zoology, 1966-72, Christ Church, Oxford; Visiting Research Fellow, Carnegie Institute, Baltimore, 1965; Scientific Staff, 1973-83, Head of Cell Biology Division, 1979-83, John Humphrey Plummer Professor of Cell Biology, 1983-2001, Medical Research Council, Molecular Biology Laboratory, University of Cambridge; Fellow, Churchill College, Cambridge, 1973-95; Dunham Lecturer, Harvard Medical School, 1974; Croonian Lecturer, Royal Society, 1976; Carter-Wallace Lecturer, Princeton University, 1978; Fellow, Eton College, 1978-93; Master, Magdalene College, Cambridge, 1995-2002; Group Leader, Wellcome CR UK Institute (Wellcome Trust/Cancer Research UK Gurdon Institute, 2004-), Cambridge, 2001-; Chair, Company of Biologists, Cambrige, UK, 2001-11. Publications: Control of Gene Expression in Animal Development, 1974. Honours include most recently: Foreign Associate, US National Academy of Sciences, Institute of Medicine, 2003; Pioneer in Stem Cell Award, Frontiers in Human Embryonic Stem Cell Organizing Committee, 2004; Charles M and Martha Hitchcock Professorship, University of California, Berkeley, 2005-06; DSc, Honoris causa, University of Cambridge, 2007; Honorary Foreign Member, Anatomical Society of Great Britain, 2007; Saxen and Toivonen Memorial Medal and Prize, Finland, 2007; Honorary Fellowship, Churchill College, Cambridge, 2007; Lewis S Rosenstiel Award for Distinguished Work in Basic Medical Sciences, Brandeis, USA, 2009; Albert Lasker Award for Basic Medical Research, USA, 2009; DSc, Honoris causa, Vrije Universiteit Brussel, Belgium, 2009; DSc, Honoris causa, Université Libre de Bruxelles, Belgium, 2009; Honorary Fellowship, Cambridge Philosophical Society, 2010. Memberships: Honorary Foreign Member, American Academy of Arts and Sciences, 1978; Honorary Student, Christ Church, Oxford, 1985; Fullerian Professor of Physiology and Comparative Anatomy, Royal Institute, 1985-91; President, International Society for Developmental Biology, 1990-94; Foreign Associate, NAS, 1980, Belgian Royal Academy of Science, Letters and Fine Arts, 1984, French Academy of Science, 1990; Foreign Member, American Philosophical Society, 1983; Chair, Wellcome Cancer Campaign Institute, University of Cambridge, 1990-2001; Governor, The Wellcome Trust, 1995-2000; Chair, Company of Biologists, 2001-. Address: Whittlesford Grove, Whittlesford, Cambridge CB2 4NZ, England.

GURNEY A(lbert) R(amsdell), b. 1 November 1930, Buffalo, New York, USA. Professor of Literature; Dramatist; Writer. m. Mary Goodyear, 1957, 2 sons, 2 daughters. Education: BA, Williams College, 1952; MFA, Yale University School of Drama, 1958. Appointments: Faculty, 1960-, Professor of Literature, 1970-, Massachusetts Institute of Technology. Publications: Plays: Children, 1974; The Dining Room, 1982; The Perfect Party, Another Antigone, Sweet Sue, 1986; The Cocktail Hour, 1988; Love Letters, 1989; The Old Boy, 1991; The Fourth Wall, 1992; Later Life, 1993; A Cheever Evening, 1994; Sylvia, Overtime, 1995; Labor Day, 1998; The Guest Lecturer, Far East, Ancestral Voices, 1999; Human Events, 2000; Buffalo Gal, 2001; O Jerusalem, Big Bill, 2003; Mrs Farnsworth, 2004; Screen Play, 2005; Novels: The Gospel According to Joe, 1974; The Snow Ball, 1985. Screenplay: The House of Mirth, 1972. Television: O Youth and Beauty (from a story by John Cheever), 1979; Kinder; The Dining Room; My Brother's Wife; Love Letters; Far East; Silvia. Opera libretto: Strawberry Fields. Honours: Drama Desk Award, 1971; Rockefeller Foundation Grant, 1977; National Endowment for the Arts Award, 1982; Theatre Award, American Academy of Arts and Sciences, 1990; Lucille Lortel Award, 1992; William Inge Award, 2000; Theatre Hall of Fame, 2005; Honorary doctorates. Address: 40 Wellers Bridge Road, Roxbury, CT 06783, USA.

GUSTAVSSON Anders, b. 7 December 1970, Orust Island, Sweden. Professor. m. Kristina, 1 son. Education: Teol Kand, 1964, Phil lic, 1969, Phil doctor, 1972, University of Lund. Appointments: Associate Professor, Ethnology, University of Lund, 1973; Professor, Ethnology, University of Uppsala, 1987; Professor, Ethnology, University of Oslo, Norway, 1997. Publications: Cultural studies on death and dying, 2011; The folk-life artist Carl Gustaf Bernhardson, 2011; Cultural Studies on Folk Religion in Scandinavia, 2012; Resident Population and Summer Holiday Visitors, 2012. Memberships: Royal Gustav Adolph Academy; Society International of Ethnology and Folklore; Nordic Network of Thanatology. Address: Tegneby-Hogen 140, S-47397 Henan, Sweden. E-mail: anders.gustavsson@ikos.uio.no

GUTERSON David, b. 4 May 1956, Seattle, Washington, USA. Writer. m. Robin Ann Radwick, 1979, 5 children. Education: BA, 1978, MA, 1982, University of Washington. Appointment: High School Teacher of English, Bainbridge Island, Washington, 1984-94. Publications: The Country Ahead of Us, The Country Behind, 1989; Family Matters: Why Home Schooling Makes Sense, 1992; Snow Falling on Cedars, 1994; The Drowned Son, 1996; East of the Mountains, 1999; Our Lady of the Forest, 2003; The Other, 2008. Honour: PEN/Faulkner Award for Fiction, 1995; Barnes and Noble Discovery Award, 1995; Pacific NW Booksellers Award, 1995. Address: c/o Georges Borchardt Inc, 136 East 57th Street, New York, NY 10022, USA.

GUTHRIE OF CRAIGIEBANK, Gen. Charles Ronald Llewelyn Guthrie, b. 17 November 1938, London, England. Company Director. m. Catherine Worrall, 2 sons. Education: Royal Military Academy, Sandhurst. Appointments: Command, Welsh Guards, 1979; Served BAOR and Aden 22 SAS Regiment, 1965-69; Staff College Graduate, 1972; Military Assistant to Chief of General Staff, Ministry of Defence, 1973-74; Brigade Major, Household Division, 1976-77; Commanding Officer, 1 Battalion Welsh Guards, served Berlin and Northern Ireland, 1977-80; Colonel General Staff Military Operations, Ministry of Defence, 1980-82; Command British Forces New Hebrides, 1980, 4 Armed Brigade, 1982-84; Chief of Staff, 1 (British) Corps, 1984-86; General Officer Commanding, North East District Command 2 Infantry Division, 1986-87; Assistant Chief to the General Staff, Ministry of Defence, 1987-89; Command 1 British Corps, 1990-91; Commander in Chief, BAOR, 1992-94; Command, Northern Army Group, 1992-93 (now disbanded); Chief of the General Staff, 1994-97; Chief of the Defence Staff, 1997-2001; Colonel Commandant, Intelligence Corps, 1986-95; Colonel Life Guards (Gold Stick; ADC General to HM The Queen, 1993-2001; Colonel Commandant, SAS Regiment, 2000-; Non-Executive Director: N M Rothschild & Sons; Advanced Interactive Systems Inc; Ashley Gardens Block 2 Limited; BICE Chileconsult; Colt Defence LLC; N M Rothschild & Sons (Brazil) Limitada; N M Rothschild & Sons (Mexico) SA de CV; Rothschilds Continuation Holding AG; Member of Council, Institute of International Strategic Studies. Honours: LVO, 1977, OBE, 1980; KCB, 1990; GCB, 1994; Kt SMO Malta, 1999; Commander, Legion of Merit, USA, 2001; Life Peer, 2001; Freeman City of London, 1988; Liveryman, Painter Stainers Co, 1989. Memberships include: President: Federation of London Youth Clubs, Action Research, Army Benevolent Fund; Chairman of the Advisory Board, King's Centre for Military Health Research; Patron: Canning House Library Appeal, Cardinal Hume Centre, Household Cavalry Museum Appeal, Order of Malta's Care Trust, Second World War Experience Centre, UK Defence Forum. Address: New Court, St Swithin's Lane, London EC4P 4DU, England. E-mail: lordguthrie@rothschild.co.uk

GUZMAN-GERONIMO Rosa Isela, b. 9 May 1972, Las Choapas, Veracruz, Mexico. Food Scientist. Education: BS, Industrial Chemistry, University of Veracruz, 1995; MS, Food Science, National School of Biological Science, 1998, PhD, 2003, National Polytechnic Institute, Mexico. Appointments: Research Associate, Research & Assistance Technology, Design State Jalisco, Merida, Yucatan, Mexico, 2004-05; Research Professor, Institute of Technology, University of Mixteca, Huajuapan de Leon, Oaxcica, Mexico, 2006-08; Research Professor, Basic Science Institute, University of Veracruz, Xalapa, Veracruz, Mexico, 2008-. Publications: Numerous articles in professional journals. Honours: Recipient, Excellent in Teaching from Mexico, 2010-13; Distinguished Citizen, Las Choapas, Veracruz, 2003; Visiting Professor, Interdisciplinary Research Center, Integral Regional Development Campus, Oaxaca, Mexico, 2008-. Memberships: National Council for Science and Technology, Mexico. Address: Lafragua 103, Las Choapas, Veracruz 96980, Mexico. E-mail: raguzman@uv.mx

GYÖRY Kálmán, b. 23 February 1940, Òzd, Hungary. Mathematics Professor. m. Sàra Beregszàszi, 2 sons. Education: MSc, PhD, 1966, Mathematics, Kossuth Lajos University, Debrecen, Hungary. Appointments: Doctor of Mathematical Sciences, Hungarian Academy of Sciences, 1984; Supervisor of 13 PhD students, 1968-2005; Leader, Number Theory Research Group, Debrecen, 1968-; Head of Department of Algebra and Number Theory, 1985-2005, Professor, Mathematics, 1985-2010, Dean of Faculty of Sciences, 1993-98, Vice-rector, 2000-01, Rector, 2001-02, Pro-rector, 2002-03, Professor Emeritus, 2010-, University of Debrecen; Visiting and guest professor in universities around the world. Publications: 1 book; 160 research papers in professional journals. Memberships: Bolyai Janos Mathematical Society; Hungarian Academy of Sciences; American Mathematical Society; New York Academy of Sciences. Address: Institute of Mathematics, University of Debrecen, 4010 Debrecen, Pf 12, Hungary.

H

HA Hong-Youl, b. 17 April 1970, Seoul, Korea. Professor. m. Eun-Joo Kang, 2 daughters. Education: Bachelor, Business, 1996, Master, Marketing, 1999, Dongguk University, Korea; PhD, Marketing, Swinburne University of Technology, Australia, 2008. Appointments: Professor, Marketing, Kangwon National University, Korea, 2009-. Publications: Numerous articles in professional journals. Memberships: Academy of Marketing Science. Address: College of Business Administration, Kangwon National University, 192-1 Hyoja-dong, Chuncheon-si, Kangwon-do, 200-701, South Korea. E-mail: ha.h@kangwon.ac.kr

HA Seoyong, b. 30 January 1969, Seoul, Korea. Material Scientist. m. Jungeun Kim. Education: BSc, 1991, MSc, 1993, Seoul National University, South Korea; MSc, 1998, PhD, 2002, Carnegie Mellon University, Pittsburgh, Pennsylvania, USA. Appointments: Senior Researcher, LG Cable and Machinery, 1994-97; Research Associate, Carnegie Mellon University, 2002-04; Senior Research Engineer, 2004-07, Principal Research Engineer, 2007, Samsung Corning Precision Glass; Principal Research Engineer, Neosemitech Corporation, 2007-10; Principal Research Engineer, LG Innotek Co Ltd, 2010-. Publications: Contributed articles to professional journals. Honours: Sejong Institute Scholarship, Seongnam, 1997-2001; Graduate Seminar Award for Excellence, Carnegie Mellon University, 2002. E-mail: seoyong@gmail.com

HA Tae Kyung, b. 21 August 1973, Seoul, Korea. General Surgeon. m. Youn Kyoung Seo, 1 son, 2 daughters. Education: Diplomate, Ministry of Health, Welfare and Family Affairs, 1998; PhD, Hanyang University College of Medicine, 2007. Appointments: Clinical Assistant Professor, Hanyang University Medical Center, 2008-09; Assistant Professor, Hanyang University College of Medicine, 2010. Publications: Annals of Surgical Oncology, 2008; Numerous articles in professional journals. Honours: Best Poster Award, Korean Gastric Cancer Association, 2007; Clinical Research Grant, Korean Society of Clinical Oncology, 2008; Roche Academic Award, 2010. Memberships: Korean Gastric Cancer Association; Korean Society of Clinical Oncology; Korean Surgical Society; Korean Cancer Association; Korean Society of Endoscopic & Laparoscopic Surgeons. Address: Hanyang University College of Medicine, 17 Haengdang-dong, Seongdong-ku, Seoul 133-787, Republic of Korea. E-mail: missurgeon@hanyang.ac.kr

HA Tae-Sun, b. 6 February 1962, Seoul, Korea. Medical Doctor; Professor. m. Sun-Min Kim, 1 son, 1 daughter. Education: MD, Bachelor of Science, 1987, Master of Medical Science, 1992; Medical Doctorship of Medicinal Science, 1995, Seoul National University, Seoul, Korea. Appointments: Residency, Seoul National University Hospital, 1988-91, Instructor, 1992-94, Assistant Professor, 1994-98, Associate Professor, 1998-2003, Professor, 2003-, Chungbuk National University, Korea. Publications: Articles in scientific journals as author and first author include most recently: Regulation of glomerular endothelial cell proteoglycans by glucose, 2004; Effects of advanced glycosylation end products on perlecan core protein of glomerular epithelium, 2004; The role of tumour necrosis factor-a in Henoch-Schönlein purpura, 2005; Delay of renal progression in methylmalonyl acidemia using angiotensim II inhibition, 2008. Honour: Research Award, Chungbuk National University College of Medicine, 2005; AGE inhibition can improve orthostatic proteinuria associated with nutcracker syndrome, 2006; High glucose and AGE affect the expression of a-actinin-4 in glomerular epithelial cells, 2006; Scrotal involvement in childhood Henoch-Schonlein purpura, 2007; Regulation of type IV collagen α chains of glomerular epithelial cells in diabetic conditions, 2009; High glucose and advanced glycosylation endproducts increased podocytes permeability via PI3K/Akt signalling, 2010. Honours: Research Award, Korean Paediatric Society, 2006. Memberships: Korean Society of Nephrology; Korean Paediatric Society; Korean Society of Paediatric Nephrology; International Paediatric Nephrology Association; American Society of Nephrology; European Renal Association; International Society of Nephrology. Address: Sannam-dong, Gyeryong Richeville 104-1302, Heungdeok-gu, Cheongju, Chungbuk, Republic of Korea. E-mail: tsha@chungbuk.ac.kr

HAAPAKOSKI Pekka Olavi, b. 14 November 1946, Oulu, Finland. Physicist. Divorced, 1 daughter. Education: MA, 1969, PhLic, 1971, University of Helsinki, Finland; PhD, University of Oulu, Finland, 1987. Appointments: Researcher, Research Institute of Theoretical Physics, University of Helsinki, 1971-73; Research Fellow, Nordita, Copenhagen, 1973-75; Senior Assistant, University of Jvaskyla, Finland, 1974-77; Senior Lecturer, Hame University of Applied Sciences, Finland, 1990-. Publications: eBook, Field theoretic approach that forms a bijection between wave mechanics and a system obeying classical mechanics, 2010; Scientific articles on nuclear collective motion, nuclear force, neutron matter, nucleon-antinucleon physics and high temperature superconductivity. Memberships: American Chemical Society. Address: HAMK, Kaartokatu 2, 11100 Riihimäki, Finland. E-mail: pekka.haapakoski@hamk.fi

HABGOOD John Stapylton, Baron of Habgood Calverton, b. 23 June 1927. Retired Archbishop of York; Author. m. Rosalie Mary Ann Boston, 7 June 1961, 2 sons, 2 daughters. Education: BA, 1948, MA, 1951, PhD, 1952, King's College, Cambridge; Cuddesdon College, Oxford. Appointments: Demonstrator in Pharmacology, Cambridge, 1950-53; Fellow, King's College, Cambridge, 1952-55; Curate, St Mary Abbots, Kensington, 1954-56; Vice Principal, Westcott House, Cambridge, 1956-62; Rector, St John's Church, Jedburgh, 1962-67; Principal, Queen's College, Birmingham, 1967-73; Bishop of Durham, 1973-83; Archbishop of York, 1983-95; Pro Chancellor, University of York, 1985-90; Hulsean Preacher, University of Cambridge, 1987-88; Bampton Lecturer, University of Oxford, 1999; Gifford Lecturer, University of Aberdeen, 2000. Publications: Religion and Science, 1964; A Working Faith: Essays and Addresses on Science, Medicine and Ethics, 1980; Church and Nation in a Secular Age, 1983; Confessions of a Conservative Liberal, 1988; Making Sense, 1993; Faith and Uncertainty, 1997; Being a Person: Where Faith and Science Meet, 1998; Varieties of Unbelief, 2000; The Concept of Nature, 2002. Contributions: Theology and the Sciences, Interdisciplinary Science Reviews, 2000. Honours: Honorary DD, Universities of Durham, 1975, Cambridge, 1984, Aberdeen, 1988, Huron, 1990, Hull, 1991, Oxford, 1996, Manchester, 1996; Honorary DU, York, 1996; Privy Counsellor, 1983; Honorary Fellow, King's College, Cambridge, 1986; Life Peer, 1995. Address: 18 The Mount, Malton, North Yorkshire YO17 7ND, England.

HACKMAN Gene, b. 30 January 1930, San Bernardino, California, USA. Actor. m. 1. Fay Maltese 1956, divorced 1985, 1 son, 2 daughters; 2. Betsy Arakawa, 1991. Education: Studied Acting, Pasadena Playhouse. Career: Films include: Lilith, 1964; Hawaii, 1966; Banning, 1967; Lucky Lady, 1975; Night Moves, 1976; Domino Principle, 1977; Superman, 1978; Superman II, 1980; Bat 21, 1987; The Package, The

Von Metz Incident, Loose Connections, Full Moon in Blue Water, Postcards From the Edge, Cass Action, 1989; Loose Canons, Narrow Margin, 1990; Necessary Roughness, The William Munny Killings, 1991; The Unforgiven, The Firm, 1992; Geronimo, Wyatt Earp, 1994; Crimson Tide, The Quick and the Dead, 1995; Get Shorty, Birds of a Feather, Extreme Measures, The Chamber, Absolute Power, 1996; Twilight, Enemy of the State, 1998; Under Suspicion, 2000; Heist, The Royal Tenenbaums, 2001; Runaway Jury, 2003; Welcome to Mooseport, 2004; Numerous TV appearances and stage plays. Publication: Co-author, Wake of the Perdido Star, 2000. Honours: Academy Award, Best Actor; New York Film Critics Award; Golden Globe Award; British Academy Awards; Cannes Film Festival Award; National Review Board Award; Berlin Film Award; Golden Globe for Best Actor in a Musical or Comedy, 2001; Cecil B DeMille Award, Golden Globes, 2003. Address: c/o Barry Haldeman, 1900 Avenue of the Stars, 2000 Los Angeles, CA 90067, USA.

HADDAD Ghassan, b. 1926, Lattaquia, Syria. Educationist; Academic. Education: Bachelor and Master in Military Sciences, Military Academy, Damascus, Syria; PhD in Economic Sciences, DSc in International Economic Sciences, University of Humboldt-Berlin, Germany. Appointments: Several important military positions before reaching the rank of Staff Major General, Syria, 1963; Planning Minister, Syria, 1963-66; Researcher then Visiting Professor, Germany, 1966-75; Economic Advisor and Chief of Experts, Ministry of Planning, Baghdad, Iraq, 1975-85; Professor of Postgraduate Studies in Economic Science, Baghdad University, 1975-85; Professor of Postgraduate Studies in Economic Science, Al Mustansyriah, Iraq, 1985-2002; Researcher and Visiting Professor of Postgraduate Studies in Economic Science, Paris, France, 2002-. Publications: Books and researches in Arabic, French and German. Honours: Many distinguished medals and honours include: Syrian Medal of Merit (Excellent Degree); Syrian Medal of Fidelity; Certificate of Honour, Iraqi Union of Writers; Listed in Who's Who publications and biographical dictionaries; Participation in many regional, national and international conferences. Memberships: Union of Arab Writers; Union of Arab Historians; Union of Arab Economists; Editorial committees of several academic periodicals. Address: 7 Allée du Bosquet, 92310 Sèvres, France. E-mail: grhaddad@ymail.com

HADFIELD Andrew David, b. 25 April 1962, Kendal, Cumbria, England. Professor of English. m. Alison Sarah Yarnold, 1 son, 2 daughters. Education: BA, 1st Class Honours, University of Leeds, England, 1984; DPhil, University of Ulster, Northern Ireland, 1988. Appointments: British Academy Postdoctoral Fellow, University of Leeds, 1989-92; Lecturer in English, 1992-96, Senior Lecturer in English, 1996-98, Professor of English, 1998-2003, University of Wales, Aberystwyth; Visiting Professor in English, Columbia University, New York, USA, 2002-2003; Professor of English, University of Sussex, England, 2003-. Publications: Literature, Politics and National Identity, 1994; Spenser's Irish Experience, 1997; Literature Travel and Colonial Writing, 1998; The English Renaissance, 2000; Shakespeare, Spenser and the Matter of Britain, 2003; Shakespeare and Renaissance Politics, 2003; Shakespeare and Republicanism, 2005. Honours: Fellow of the English Association; Leverhulme Major Award, 2001-2004; Chatterton Lecture at the British Academy, 2003. Memberships: English Association; Spenser Society of America. Address: Department of English, University of Sussex, Falmer, Brighton BN1 9QN, England.

HAGBERG Anders Erik, b. 11 September 1958, Uppsala, Sweden. Musician. m. Anna Wennerbeck, 1 son, 1 daughter. Education: BA, Music and Music Education, Academy of Music, Gothenburg University, 1983. Appointments: Musician, Music Pedagogue, Composer, Senior Lecturer, Improvisation for Flute and Saxophone, Göteborg University; Freelance Jazz Musician, various venues around the world, 1983-. Publications: CDs and books with original compositions, including: Earthsongs; Winduo; Mynta; Yggdrasil; Commissioned compositions, 1985-2010. Honours: Swedish Arts Grants Committee, 1989, 1997, 2004; Municipality of Gothenburg, 1990; The Swedish Performing Rights Society, 1997, 1999. Address: Sveag 5, S-41314 Goteborg, Sweden. Website: www.andershagberg.se

HAGGAG Rim Said Mahmoud, Analytical Chemist; Educator. m. Walid Hussein Gemea, 1996, 2 sons. Education: PhD, Faculty of Pharmacy, Alexandria University, Egypt, 1991. Appointments: Assistant Lecturer, Faculty Faculty of Pharmacy, 1996-2002, Lecturer, 2002-, Assistant Professor, 2009-, Analytical Chemistry, Alexandria University, Egypt. Address: Faculty of Pharmacy, Alexandria University, Khartoum Square, Azarita, Alexandria 21521, Egypt. E-mail: haggag@tecmina.com

HAGGER Nicholas Osborne, b. 22 May 1939, London, England. British Poet; Verse Dramatist; Short Story Writer; Lecturer; Author; Man of Letters; Philosopher; Cultural Historian. m. (1) Caroline Virginia Mary Nixon, 1961, 1 daughter, (2) Madeline Ann Johnson, 1974, 2 sons. Education: MA English Literature, Worcester College, Oxford, 1958-61. Appointments: Lecturer in English, University of Baghdad, 1961-62; Professor of English Literature, Tokyo University of Education and Keio University, Tokyo, 1963-67, Tokyo University, 1964-65; Lecturer in English, University of Libya, Tripoli, 1968-70; Freelance Features for Times, 1970-72. Publications: The Fire and the Stones: A Grand Unified Theory of World History and Religion, 1991; Selected Poems: A Metaphysical's Way of Fire, 1991; The Universe and the Light: A New View of the Universe and Reality, 1993; A White Radiance: The Collected Poems 1958-93, 1994; A Mystic Way: A Spiritual Autobiography, 1994; Awakening to the Light: Diaries, Vol 1, 1958-67, 1994; A Spade Fresh with Mud: Collected Stories, Vol 1, 1995; The Warlords: From D-Day to Berlin, A Verse Drama, 1995; A Smell of Leaves and Summer: Collected Stories, Vol 2, 1995; Overlord, The Triumph of Light 1944-1945: An Epic Poem, Books 1 & 2, 1995, Books 3-6, 1996, Books 7-9, 10-12, 1997; The One and the Many, 1999; Wheeling Bats and a Harvest Moon: Collected Stories, Vol 3, 1999; Prince Tudor, A Verse Drama, 1999; The Warm Glow of the Monastery Courtyard: Collected Stories, Vol 4, 1999; The Syndicate: The Story of the Coming World Government, 2004; The Secret History of the West: The Influence of Secret Organisations on Western History from the Renaissance to the 20th Century, 2005; Classical Odes: Poems on England, Europe and a Global Theme, and of Everyday Life in the One, 2006; The Light of Civilization, 2006; Overlord, one-volume edition, 2006; Collected Poems, 1958-2005, 2006; Collected Verse Plays, 2007; Collected Short Stories: A Thousand and One Mini-Stories or Verbal Paintings, 2007; The Secret Founding of America, 2007; The Rise and Fall of Civilizations: Why Civilizations Rise and Fall and What Happens When They End, 2008; The Last Tourist in Iran, 2008; The New Philosophy of Universalism, 2009; The Libyan Revolution, Its Origins and Legacy, A Memoir and Assessment, 2009; Armageddon, The Triumph of Universal Order, An Epic Poem on the War on Terror and of Holy-War Crusaders, 2010; The World Government, A Blueprint for a

Universal World State, 2010; The Secret American Dream: The Creation of a New World Order with the Power to Abolish War, Poverty and Disease, 2011; A New Philosophy of Literature: The Fundamental Theme of World Literature, The Vision of the Infinite and the Universalist Literary Tradition, 2011. Membership: Society of Authors. E-mail: info @nicholashagger.co.uk Website: www.nicholashagger.co.uk

HAGIWARA Motoaki, b. 7 January 1932, Gunma-Ken, Japan. University Professor. m. Teruko. Education: MEd, Tokyo University of Education, 1957. Appointments: Professor, Gunma University, 1979-97; Professor, Open University, 1989-92; Dean, Humanity Faculty, Saitamagakuen University, 2005-09; Dean, Social Work Faculty, University of Creation, Art, Design, Music & Social Work, 2009-. Publications: On Early Childhood Education in Multi-Culture Society, 2008; An Attempt on Possibility to Children's Active Participation in the Life Environment, 2008; Children's Participation: The Method of Facilitating Activities of Sustainable Development in Communities, 2010. Honours: Award for Adult & Youth Activity, Japan Government of Science & Education. Memberships: Councilor, Japan Society of Research on Early Childhood Care and Education. Address: 5-11-11-8 Hachioji, Chuo-ku, Saitama-shi, 338-0006, Japan. E-mail: m.hagiwara@souzou.ac.jp

HAGUE William Jefferson, b. 26 March 1961, Rotherham, Yorkshire, England. Politician; Management Consultant. m. Ffion Jenkins, 1997, 1 son. Education: BA, Honours, Magdalen College, Oxford, England; MBA, Insead Business School, France, 1986. Appointments: Management Consultant, McKinsey & Co, 1983-88; Elected to Parliament, Richmond, Yorkshire, England, 1989; Parliamentary Private Secretary to Chancellor of Exchequer, 1990-93; Parliamentary Under-Secretary of State, Department Social Security, 1993-94; Ministry of State, Department of Social Security, 1994-95; Secretary of State for Wales, 1995-97; Leader, Conservative Party, 1997-2001; Chair, International Democratic Union, 1999-2001; Political Adviser, JCB PLC, 2001-; Non-Executive Director, AES Eng PLC, 2001-; Member, Political Council of Terra Firma Capital Partners, 2001-; Shadow Foreign Secretary, 2005-. Publications: William Pitt the Young, 2004. Honours: British Book Award for History Book of the Year, 2005. Honour: Privy Councillor, 1995. Address: House of Commons, London SW1A 0AA, England.

HAHN Doug-Woong, b. 5 March 1942, Incheon city, Republic of Korea. Emeritus Professor. m. Soon-Hee Cho, 1 son, 1 daughter. Education: Bachelor of Arts, 1964, MA, 1970, PhD, 1978, Department of Psychology, Sungkyunkwan University. Appointments include: Assistant Professor, 1979-81, Associate Professor, 1981-88, Professor, 1989-2007, Director, 1992-93, Department of Industrial & Organizational Psychology, Dean, College of Business and Commerce, 1998, Director, Institute of Applied Psychology, 2001-02, Director, Department of Psychology, 2003-05, Dean, College of Social Sciences, 2005-07, SKKU, Seoul; Adjunct Associate Professor, Department of Psychology, University of Massachusetts, USA, 1988-89; President: Korean Social and Personality Psychological Association, 1984-86; Korean Association of Psychologicaland Social Issues, 1993-94; Korean Health Psychologist Association, 1995-97; Korean Psychological Association, 2000-01; Editor-in-Chief: Korean Journal of Social and Personality Psychology, 1983-84; Korean Journal of Psychology General, 1985-86; Korean Journal of Psychological and Social Issues, 1992-93; Consulting Professional Psychologist of Forensic Psychology, Seoul Metropolitan Police Bureau, 2006-11; Lecturer, Korean National Police University, 2007-09. Publications: Numerous articles in professional journals; Book Awards: Toegye Psychology, 1993; Far-Eastern Psychology, 2000; Korean Confucian Psychology, 2003; Psychology of Social Motivation, 2004; Social Psychology, 2005. Honours: 2nd grade, Army, 1972-73; Outstanding Scholastic Performance Award, Korean Association of Science and Technology Organizations, 1992; Distinguished International Achievement Award, Toegye Studies, 1995; Distinguished Scholastic Performance Award, SKKU, 1998, 1999, 2000-07; Distinguished Scholastic Achievement Award, Korean Psychological Association, 2002; Distinguished Teaching Professor Award, Vice-Prime Minister of Korea, 2005; 60th Anniversary Special Distinguished Contribution Award, Korean Psychological Association, 2006; Distinguished Life-long Contribution Award, Korean Psychological Association, 2007; Distinguished Life-long Educational Contribution Award, President of Korea, 2007. Memberships: Korean Psychological Association; Korean Society of Social and Personality; Korean Society of Health Psychology; Korean Society of Counseling Psychology; Korean Association of Psychological and Social Issues. Address: Hongwoo Psychologial Research Institute, Ui-dong 73-48, Kangbug-gu, Seoul, 142-892, Republic of Korea. E-mail: dwhahn@skku.edu

HAHN Frank Horace, b. 26 April 1925, Berlin, Germany. Emeritus Professor of Economics. m. Dorothy Salter. Education: Bournemouth Grammar School; BSc (Econ), 1945, PhD, 1951, London School of Economics; MA, University of Cambridge, 1960. Appointments: Lecturer in Economics, University of Birmingham, 1948-58; Reader in Mathematical Economics, University of Birmingham, 1958-60; Fellow, Churchill College, Cambridge, 1960-; Lecturer in Economics, University of Cambridge, 1960-66; Professor of Economics, London School of Economics, 1967-72; Professor of Economics, 1972-92, Professor Emeritus, 1992-, University of Cambridge; Professor Ordinario, 1989-2000, Emeritus Professor, 2000-, University of Siena. Publications: 135 publications including books written and edited. Honours: D Soc Sci, Birmingham, 1981; Doctor Honoris Causa, Strasbourg, 1984; D Litt, East Anglia, 1984; DSc (Econ), London, 1985; Doctor of the University, York, 1991; Doctor of Letters, Leicester, 1993; Doctor of Philosophy, Athens, 1993; Doctcur Honoris Causa de l'Universite Paris X, Nanterre, 1999. Memberships: Fellow, British Academy; Corresponding Fellow, American Academy of Arts and Sciences; Foreign Associate, US National Academy of Sciences; Honorary Member, American Economic Association; Honorary Fellow, London School of Economics; Member, Academia Europaea; Palacky Gold Medal, Czechoslovak Academy of Sciences; Honorary Member, Italian Association for the History of Political Economy; President, Econometric Society, 1968-69; President, Royal Economic Society, 1986-89; President, Section F, British Association for the Advancement of Science, 1990. Address: Churchill College, Cambridge, CB3 0DS, England.

HAILPARN Diana F, b. 25 January 1949, Newark, New Jersey, USA. Psychotherapist. m. Michael Hailparn. Education: BA, William Paterson University, 1971; MA, Fairleigh Dickinson University, 1973; MS, Columbia University, 1975. Appointments: Private practice; Bonnie Brae Residential Treatment Center, 1973-75; Clifton Mental Health Clinic, 1975-79. Publications: Fear No More: A Psychotherapist's Guide to Overcoming Anxiety and Panic Forever, 2000; Numerous articles in professional journals. Honours: Diplomate, Clinical Social Work; Listed in international

DICTIONARY OF INTERNATIONAL BIOGRAPHY 36th EDITION

biographical dictionaries. Memberships: National Association of Social Workers; Columbia University Alumni Association; New Jersey Association of Social Workers; Academy of Certified Social Workers; State of New Jersey, Licensed Clinical Social Worker; National Association of Professional Women. Address: 19 North Bayard Lane, Mahwah, New Jersey 07430, USA. E-mail: leaurore@yahoo.com Website: www.overcominganxieties.com

HAINES John Francis, b. 30 November 1947, Chelmsford, Essex, England. Retired; Poet. m. Margaret Rosemary Davies, 1977. Education: Padgate College of Education, 1966-69; ONC in Public Administration, Millbank College of Commerce, 1972. Appointments: General Assistant; Payments Assistant. Publications: Other Places, Other Times, 1981; Spacewain, 1989; After the Android Wars, 1992; Orders from the Bridge, 1996; Pennine Triangle (with Steve Sneyd & J C Hartley), 2002; A Case Without Gravity (translation), 2005; The Bards 14: Overdrawn at the Memory Bank, 2006; Bus Stop (with Dainis Bisenieks 'The Long Trip') 2006; Three Medieval Tales & a Prologue by Robert Mannyng of Brunne (translation with L A Hood), 2007; Contributions to: Dark Horizons; Fantasy Commentator; First Time; Folio; Idomo, Iota; Macabre; New Hope International; Not To Be Named; Overspace; Purple Patch; Sandor; The Scanner; Simply Thrilled Honey; Spokes; Star Line; Stride; Third Half; Yellow Dwarf; A Child's Garden of Olaf; A Northern Chorus; Ammonite; Boggers All; Eldritch Science; Foolscap; Heliocentric Net; Lines of Light; Ore; Pablo Lennis; Pleiade; Premonitions; Mentor; Rampant Guinea Pig; Zone; Positively Poetry; What Poets Eat; Mexicon 6 - The Party; Terrible Work; Xenophilia; Literae; XUENSē; Dreaming Scryers True Deceivers; Yesterday & Today, Tomorrow; Old Rossum's Book of Practical Robots; 1969 And All That; Boys Own Rocket Science. Memberships: Science Fiction Poetry Association; The Eight Hand Gang, founder-member. Address: 5 Cross Farm, Station Road North, Fearnhead,, Warrington WA2 0QG, England.

HAINS Gaétan Joseph Daniel Robert, b. 9 May 1963, Montreal, Canada. Computer Scientist. Education: BSc, honours, Concordia University, 1985; MSc, 1987, DPhil, 1990, Oxford University. Appointments: Researcher, CRIM Montreal, 1989; Assistant Professor, Associate Professor, University of Montreal, 1989-95; Visiting Professor, ENS Lyon, 1994; Visiting Researcher, Fujitsu-ISIS, Japan, 1994-95; Professor, 1995-, Director, 2000-05, 1st Class Professor, 2004-, Laboratoire d'informatique fondamentale d'Orleans, University of Orleans; Program Officer, Software Research Programs at Agence Nationale de la Recherche (ANR), 2005-06; Professor, 2006-, Director, 2007-08, Laboratoire d'Algorithmique Complexité et Logique, Université Paris-Est; Visiting Professor, SAP Labs, France, 2008; Research Engineer, EXQIM SAS, 2009-. Honours: Commonwealth Scholar, 1986-89; IISF Visiting Scholarship, Japan, 1992. Memberships: ACM; IEEE. Address: LACL, UPEC, 94000 Créteil, France. Website: http://hains.org

HAKIM Alan James, b. 4 March 1968, London, England. Doctor. Education: MB BChir, MA, Fitzwilliam College, Cambridge University, 1991. Appointments: House Officer, 1992-93, Senior House Officer, 1993-94, Addenbrooke's Hospital, Cambridge; Specialist Registrar, North Thames Deanery, 1994-2000; Clinical Research Fellow, Arthritis Research Campaign, St Thomas' Hospital, London, 2000-03; Consultant Rheumatologist and Physician, Whipps Cross University Hospital, 2001-; Honorary Consultant Rheumatologist, University College London Hospitals, 2003-08; Associate Clinical Director for Accident and Emergency, 2007-09, Director of Strategy and Business Development, 2009-, Whipps Cross. Publications: 78 papers, reviews, chapters and abstracts; Textbook, The Oxford Handbook of Rheumatology, 2003, 2nd edition, 2006, 3rd edition, 2011; The American Handbook of Rheumatology, 2009; Textbook, Hypermobility Fibromyalgia and Chronic Pain, 1st edition, 2010. Honours: Highly Commended, British Medical Association Book Competition, 2003. Memberships: Fellow, Royal College of Physicians, London; Vice President, Section for Rheumatology and Rehabilitation, The Royal Society of Medicine; British Society of Rheumatology; British Medical Association; Hunterian Society; Advanced Medical Leader, British Association of Medical Managers, 2007. Address: Department of Rheumatology, Whipps Cross University Hospital NHS Trust, Leytonstone, London E11 1NR, England.

HAKKANEN Matti Klaus, b. 21 July 1936, Helsinki, Finland. Retired Ambassador. m. Pirkko Hentola, 2 sons. Education: Master of Laws, Helsinki University, 1960. Appointments: Ambassador of Finland to Bucharest, 1976-80; Under Secretary of State, 1980-83; Ambassador to the Hague, 1983-87; Ambassador to Buenos Aires, 1987-88; Ambassdor to Paris, 1988-93; Ambassador to Rome, 1993-97; Ambassador to Lisbon, 1997-2001. Publications: Marshal Mannerheim in Portugal, 1975; Finnish Diplomats – Johan Nykopp, 2003; Mannerheimiana, 2004. Honours: Grand Officer, Lion of Finland; Grand Cross, Oranje-Nassau of the Netherlands; Grand Cross, National Merit of Italy; Grand Cross, Infante Dom Henrique of Portugal; Grand Officer, National Merit of France. Memberships: Finnish Club of Helsinki. Address: Toolonkatu 9, 00100 Helsinki, Finland. E-mail: matti-hakkanen@welho.com

HAKKINEN Mika, b. 28 September 1968, Helsinki, Finland. Racing Driver. m. Erja Honkanen, 1 son, 1 daughter. Appointments: Formerly, go-kart driver, Formula Ford 1600 driver, Finnish, Swedish and Nordic Champion, 1987; Formula 3 driver, British Champion with West Surrey racing, 1990; Formula 1 driver Lotus, 1991-93; McLaren, 1993-2001; Grand Prix wins: European, 1997, Australia, 1998, Brazil, 1998, 1999, Spain, 1998, 1999, 2000, Monaco, 1998, Austria, 1998, 2000, Germany, 1998, Luxembourg, 1998, Japan, 1998, 1999, Malaysia, 1999, Hungary, 1999, 2000, Belgium, 2000; Formula One Driver's Championship Winner, 1998, 1999; Sabbatical, 2001; Retirement from Formula One, 2002; FIA European Rally Championship, Finland, 2003. Publication: Mika Hakkinen: Doing What Comes Naturally.

HALADAPPA Manjula, b. 18 March 1967, Hassan, India. Educaton: BE, ME, PhD, Computer Science & Engineering. Appointments: Chairperson, Department of Computer Science & Engineering, University of Visvesvarya College of Engineering, Bangalore. Publications: 20 technical papers in international journals and conferences. Honours: Best Paper Award for Technical Paper, ICIP Conference, 2009. Memberships: IEEE (USA); MISTE. Address: 141 Ground Floor, 14 Cross, Vyalikaval, Bangalore 560003, India.

HALATSCH Marc-Eric, b. 25 October 1967, Hannover, Germany. Academic Neurosurgeon. m. Ursula Smidt, 1996, 2 sons. Education: MD, 1993, Board-Certified neurosurgeon, 2003, Georg August University Medical School, Göttingen, Germany; PhD, Experimental Neuro-oncology, 2004. Appointments: Research Fellow, 1993, Post-doctoral Research Fellow, 1996-98, Mount Sinai School of Medicine, NYC; Attending Neurosurgeon, Ruprecht-Karls University

- 405 -

Medical School, Heidelberg, Germany, 2005-09; Vice Chairman and Professor of Neurosurgery, University of Ulm Medical School, 2009-. Publications: Numerous articles and invited reviews in professional journals. Honours: Merit Scholar, German National Scholarship Foundation, 1987-93; Samuel Bronfman Medical Research Award, New York City, 1997. Memberships: European Association of Neurosurgical Societies; German Society of Neurosurgery; Händel Music Society; American Association of Cancer Research. Address: Department of Neurosurgery, University of Ulm Medical School, Steinhövelstrasse 9, D-89075, Ulm, Germany. E-mail: halatsch@aol.com

HALE Andrew Richard, b. 7 August 1944, Tonbridge, Kent, England. Professor. Education: Tonbridge School, 1958-62; MA, Trinity Hall, Cambridge University, 1966; PhD, Aston University, Birmingham, 1978. Appointments: Scientific Staff, National Institute of Industrial Psychology, London, 1966-72; Lecturer, Senior Lecturer, Occupational & Environmental Health & Safety, University of Aston, Birmingham, 1972-84; Co-ordinator, Human Resources, Calcosearch Inc, Algeria, 1980-81; Professor, Safety Science, Delft University of Technology, Netherlands, 1984-2009; Director, 2006, Chairman, 2009, Hastam. Publications: Author/co-author: 6 books; Over 35 book chapters; More than 85 refereed scientific papers; Over 350 other publications on risk and safety management, safe behaviour, design and risk control. Honours: Distinguished Service Awards: Institution of Occupational Safety & Health, UK, 1987; Dutch Association of Safety Science, 2006; Royal Society for the Prevention of Accidents, UK, 2007; Knight in the Order of the Dutch Lion, 2006. Memberships: Fellow, Instititution of Occuaptional Safety & Health; Fellow, Dutch Association of Safety Science; Registered Member (retired), Institute of Ergonomics & Human Factors; Chartered Psychologist (retired), Associate of British Psychological Society. E-mail: andrew_hale@yahoo.com

HALE-BARRETT Lori, b. 15 February 1960, St Louis, Missouri, USA. Realtor. Education: Degrees in Psychology, Education and Business, Washington University, St Louis, 1982. Appointments: Optical Specialist, Marketing, Trans America Optical Co Inc, 1991-92; Realtor, 1992- Research Advisor, IBC, ABI, 1991-. Publications: Several professional publications including: Tips on a Good Direct Mail Marketing Program, 1990. Honours: Participant in Miss Missouri Pageant and Judge, 1980's; First Place Ribbons in Public Speaking; First Place regional Awards in Marketing and Sales; The Key of Success Award, 1991; The Most Admired Woman of the Decade, ABI; International Woman of the Year, 1991-98; Delta Gamma Sorority; Outstanding Woman of the 20th Century; Outstanding Woman of the 21st Century; International Woman of the Millennium, 2000; International Ambassador of Goodwill to England, IBC, 2003; 100 of the Most Intriguing People, IBA, 2003; Inducted into Hall of Fame for Real Estate, IBC, 2004; International Peace Prize, IBA, 2004; Living Legends, IBC; Great Minds of the 21st Century, ABI; Genius Laureate of the United States of America, ABI, 2005; Established Lori Hale Barrett Award Foundation, 2007; Elite Portfolio, 2010. Address: PO Box 491, Chesterfield, MO 63006, USA.

HALIDE Halmar, b. 15 March 1963, Makassar, Indonesia. Lecturer. m. Ita Idrus, 3 sons. Education: BSc, Physics, Institute Tek Bandung, Indonesia, 1987; MSc, Physics, Memorial University, Newfoundland, Canada, 1992; PhD, Physics, James Cook University, Australia, 2002; Postdoctorate, Australian Institute of Marine Science, 2005-08. Appointments: Head, Marine & Geophysics Laboratory, 1995-97, Chairman, Study Program Geophysics, 1995-97, Physics Department, Member, Planning & Development Team, 2003-05, Head, Physics Department, 2008-, University of Hasanuddin; Research Scientist, Australian Institute of Marine Science, 2005-08. Publications: Numerous articles in professional journals. Honours: Fellow, Graduate School, Memorial University, Newfoundland, Canada; Augmentative Research Grants, Great Barrier Reef Marine Park, Australia. Address: Jurusan Fisika FMIPA UNHAS, JL Perintis Kemerdekaan, KM10, Makassar 90245, Indonesia. E-mail: halmarh@yahoo.com

HALL Christopher Sandford, b. 9 March 1936, Tunbridge Wells, Kent, England. Solicitor. m. Susanna Bott, 3 sons. Education: MA, Trinity College, Cambridge. Appointments: National Service and Reserve TAVR, 5 Royal Inniskilling Dragoon Guards, 1954-56, 1956-70; Solicitor, 1963, Partner, Senior Partner, 1964-96, Cripps, Harries, Hall, Tunbridge Wells; Consultant, Knights Solicitors; Chairman, A Burslem & Son Ltd, Stonemasons; Director, Brighton Race Course Ltd, 2000-08; Chairman, World Horse Welfare, 2006-12; Racing Welfare, retired 2006. Honours: Territorial Decoration (TD), 1970; Deputy Lieutenant, East Sussex, 1986. Memberships: Tunbridge Wells and Tonbridge District Law Society, President, 1987; Jockey Club, 1990-, Chairman Disciplinary Committee and Steward, 1996-2000; Member, Jockey Club Appeal Board, 2006-11; Chairman, Jockey Club Arab Horse Racing Committee, 2000-08; South of England Agricultural Society, Chairman, 1984-90; Worshipful Company of Broderers, Master, 1980; Member County Committee for Sussex, Country Landowners Association (retired 2007); Southdown and Eridge Hunt, Chairman, 1978-84; Olympia Show Jumping, Chairman, 2000; Hackney Horse Society, President, 2007-2009. Address: Great Danegate Farm, Eridge, Tunbridge Wells TN3 9HU, England. E-mail: cshall.danegate@virgin.net

HALL David M, b. 21 June 1928, Gary, Indiana, USA. Professor. m. Jacqueline V Branch, 2 sons. Education: BA, Howard University, 1951; MS, North Carolina Agricultural & Technical State University, 1966; PhD, Kennedy Western University, 2002. Appointments: Financial Management, United State Air Force; Director, Data Processing, General Motor Corporation; Regional Manager, Electronic Data Systems; Associate Professor, Northwood University; Executive in Residence, Saginaw Valley State University. Publications: The ABC's of Leadership; Dare to be Different. Honours: USAF Distinguished Service Medal; Key to City of Gary, Indiana; Honorary Citizen of East Saint Louis; Key to Scott AFB, Illinois; Silver Beaver Boy Scouts of America, Award of Merit Boy Scouts; Spirit of Saginaw Award. Address: 49 W Hannum Bl, Saginaw, MI 48602-1938, USA. Website: www.dhall.biz

HALL Graham Stanley, b. 5 September 1946, Warrington, England. Professor of Mathematics. 1 son, 1 daughter. Education: BSc in Mathematics (1st class honours), 1968, PhD, Relativity Theory, 1971, University of Newcastle Upon Tyne. Appointments: Earl Grey Memorial Fellow, University of Newcastle Upon Tyne, 1971-73; Lecturer, 1973-82, Senior Lecturer, 1982-90, Reader, 1990-96, Professor, 1996-, Department of Mathematical Sciences, University of Aberdeen. Publications: Over 150 research articles in various journals; Author, Symmetries and Curvature Structure in General Relativity, 2004; Editor, General Relativity, 1996; Nearly 200 invited research lectures in Europe, North and South America, Asia, Australasia and the Middle East.

DICTIONARY OF INTERNATIONAL BIOGRAPHY 36th EDITION

Honours: Elected Fellow, The Royal Society of Edinburgh, 1995; Elected Fellow, Royal Astronomical Society, 2004. Memberships: Royal Society of Edinburgh; Edinburgh Mathematical Society; European Mathematical Society; Society for General Relativity and Gravitation; Royal Astronomical Society. E-mail: g.hall@abdn.ac.uk

HALL Jerry, b. 2 July 1956, Texas, USA. Model; Actress. m. Mick Jagger, 1990, divorced 1999, 2 sons, 2 daughters. Education: Trained at the Actors Studio in New York and the National Theatre, London; 2 years Humanities, Open University. Career: Began modelling, Paris, 1970s; Numerous TV appearances including David Letterman Show, USA; Own TV series, Jerry Hall's Gurus, BBC, 2003; Contributing editor, Tatler, 1999-; Stage debut in William Inge's Bus Stop, Lyric Theatre, London, 1990; Films: Merci Docteur Rey, Willie and Phil, 1980; Urban Cowboy, 1980; Topo Galileo, 1987; Let's Spend the Night Together, Running Out of Luck, 1987; Hysteria! 2 (TV), 1989; The Emperor and the Nightingale, Batman, 1989; 25 x 5: The Continuing Adventures of the Rolling Stones, 1989; The Wall: Live in Berlin (TV), 1990; Bejewelled (TV), 1991; Freejack, 1992; Princess Caraboo, 1994; Savage Hearts, 1995; Vampire in Brooklyn, 1995; Diana and Me, 1997; RPM, 1997; Being Mick (TV), 2001; Comic Relief, 2001; Tooth, 2004; Plays: The Graduate, 2000, 2003; Picasso's Women, 2001; The Play What I Wrote, 2002; The Vagina Monologues, 2002, 2003; Benchmark, 2003; Bus Stop. Publications: Tell Tales, 1985; Jerry Hall's Gurus, 2004. Address: c/o Artists International Network, 32 Tavistock Street, London WC2E 7PB, England.

HALL J(ohn) C(live), b. 12 September 1920, London, England. Poet. Education: Oriel College, Oxford. Appointments: Staff, Encounter Magazine, 1955-91; Editor, Literary Executor of Keith Douglas. Publications: Poetry: Selected Poems, 1943; The Summer Dance and Other Poems, 1951; The Burning Hare, 1966; A House of Voices, 1973; Selected and New Poems 1939-84, 1985; Long Shadows: Poems 1938-2002, 2003. Other: Collected Poems of Edwin Muir, 1921-51 (editor), 1952; New Poems (co-editor), 1955; Edwin Muir, 1956. Address: 25 Chancellor House, Mount Ephraim, Tunbridge Wells, Kent, TN4 8BT, England.

HALL Nigel John, b. 30 August 1943, Bristol, England. Sculptor. m. Manijeh Yadegar. Education: NDD, West of England College of Art; MA, Royal College of Art; Harkness Fellowship to USA, 1967-69. Career: Tutor, Royal College of Art, 1971-74; Principal Lecturer, Chelsea School of Art, 1974-81; Solo exhibitions include: Robert Elkon Gallery, New York, 1974, 1977, 1979, 1983; Annely Juda Fine Art, London, 1978, 1981, 1985, 1987, 1991, 1996, 2000, 2003, 2005; Galerie Maeght, Paris, 1981, 1983; Staatliche Kunsthalle, Baden-Baden, 1982; Nishimura Gallery, Tokyo, 1980, 1984, 1988; Garry Anderson Gallery, Sydney, 1987, 1990; Gallery Hans Mayer, Dusseldorf, 1989, 1999; Galerie Scheffel, Bad Homburg, 2004, 2007; Kunsthalle, Mannheim, 2004; Park Ryu Sook Gallery, Seoul, 1997, 2000, 2005, 2008; Galerie Lutz und Thalman, Zurich, 2006; Yorkshire Sculpture Park, 2008; Oklahoma City Arts Center, 2010; Galerie Andres Thalmann, 2010; Galerie Scheffel, Bad Homburg, 2010; Annely Juda Fine Art, 2011; Group Exhibitions include: Documenta Kassel, 1977; Whitechapel Gallery, 1981; Tokyo Metropolitan Museum, 1982; Le Havre Museum of Fine Art, 1988; MOMA, New York, 1993; Fogg Art Museum, Harvard University, 1994; Schloss Ambras, Innsbruck, 1998; British Council Touring Exhibition, Pakistan, South Africa, Zimbabwe, 1997-99; Bad Homburg, 2001, 2003; Work in public collections include: Tate Gallery; National Museum of Modern Art, Paris; National Gallery, Berlin; MOMA, New York; Australian National Gallery, Canberra; Art Institute of Chicago; Kunsthaus, Zurich; Tokyo Metropolitan Museum; Museum of Modern Art, Brussels; Louisiana Museum, Denmark; National Museum of Art, Osaka; Museum of Contemporary Art, Sydney; Dallas Museum of Fine Art; Tel Aviv Museum; Los Angeles County Museum; National Museum of Contemporary Art, Seoul; Commissions include: Australian National Gallery, Canberra, 1982; IBM London, 1983; Airbus Industries, Toulouse, 1984; Museum of Contemporary Art, Hiroshima, 1985; Olympic Park, Seoul, 1988; Clifford Chance, London, 1992; Glaxo Wellcome Research, Stevenage, 1994; NTT, Tokyo, 1996; Bank of America, London, 2003; Said Business School, University of Oxford, 2005; Bank for International Settlements, Basel, 2006; Sparkasse, Lörrach, 2006; Energiedienst AG, Laufenburg, 2008. Honour: Elected, Royal Academy, 2003. Address: 11 Kensington Park Gardens, London, W11 3HD, England.

HALL Sir Peter (Geoffrey), b. 19 March 1932, London, England. Professor of Planning; Writer. m. (1) Carla Maria Wartenberg, 1962, divorced 1966, (2) Magdalena Mróz, 1967. Education: MA, PhD, St Catharine's College, Cambridge. Appointments: Assistant Lecturer, 1957-60, Lecturer, 1960-65, Birkbeck College, University of London; Reader in Geography, London School of Economics and Political Science, 1966-67; Professor of Geography, 1968-89, Professor Emeritus, 1989-, University of Reading; Professor of City and Regional Planning, University of California at Berkeley, 1980-92; Director, Institute of Urban and Regional Development, 1989-92, Professor Emeritus, 1992-, University of California; Special Adviser, Secretary of State for the Environment, 1991-94; Bartlett Professor of Planning, 1992-2005, Bartlet Professor of Planning and Regeneration, 2005-, University College, London; Chair, ReBlackpool Urban Regeneration Company, 2004-08. Publications: The Industries of London, 1962; London 2000, 1963, revised edition, 1969; Labour's New Frontiers, 1964; Land Values (editor), 1965; The World Cities, 1966, 3rd edition, 1984; Von Thunen's Isolated State (editor), 1966; An Advanced Geography of North West Europe (co-author), 1967; Theory and Practice of Regional Planning, 1970; Containment of Urban England: Urban and Metropolitan Growth Processes or Megapolis Denied (co-author), 1973; Containment of Urban England: The Planning System: Objectives, Operations, Impacts (co-author), 1973; Planning and Urban Growth: An Anglo-American Comparison (with M Clawson), 1973; Urban and Regional Planning: An Introduction, 1974, 2nd edition, 1982; Europe 2000, 1977; Great Planning Disasters, 1980; Growth Centres in the European Urban System, 1980; Transport and Public Policy Planning (editor with D Banister), 1980; The Inner City in Context (editor), 1981; Silicon Landscapes (editor), 1985; Can Rail Save the City? (co-author), 1985; High-Tech America (co-author), 1986; Western Sunrise (co-author), 1987; The Carrier Wave (co-author), 1988; Cities of Tomorrow, 1988; London 2001, 1989; The Rise of the Gunbelt, 1991; Technopoles of the World, 1994; Sociable Cities (co-author), 1998; Cities in Civilisation, 1998; Urban Future 21 (co-author), 2000; Working Capital co-author), 2002; To-Morrow: A Peaceful Path to Real Reform (co-author), 2003; The Polycentric Metropolis (co-author), 2006; London Voices London Lives, 2007. Honours: Gill Memorial Prize, 1968; Honorary Member, Royal Town Planning Institute, 1975; Adolph Bentinck Prize, 1979; Fellow, British Academy, 1983; Founder's Medal, Royal Geographical Society, 1988; Member of the Academia Europea, 1989; 6 honorary degrees; Knight Bachelor, 1998; Ebenezer Howard Memorial Medal, Town and Country Planning Association, 1999; Degree of Doctor of Law (honoris causa), University of Reading, 1999; Degree of Doctor of

Science (honoris causa), University of the West of England, 2000; Degree of Doctor of Laws (honoris causa), University of Manchester, 2001; Prix Vautrin Lud (Nobel de Géographie), 2001; Degree of Doctor of Letters (honoris causa), Heriot Watt University, Edinburgh, 2002; Doctor of Letters (honoris causa), London Guildhall University, 2002; Gold Medal, Royal Town Planning Institute, 2003; Degree of Doctor of Social Sciences (honoris causa), Queen Mary University of London, 2004; Degree of Doctor of Technology (honoris causa), University of Greenwich, 2004; Honorary Professor, Tongji University, Shanghai, China, 2004; Deputy Prime Minister's Lifetime Achievement Award, Urban Summit, Manchester, 2005; Degree of Doctor of Science (honoris causa), Loughborough University, 2005; Balzan International Prize for Social and Cultural History of Cities since the Beginning of the 16th Century, 2005; Sir Patrick Abercrombie Prize, International Union of Architects, 2008. Memberships: SSRC Committee on Urban Underclass; Town and Country Planning Association; Regional Studies Association. Address: c/o Bartlett School, University College, London, Wates House, 22 Gordon Street, London WC1H 0QB, England.

HALL Sir Peter (Reginald Frederick), b. 22 November 1930, Bury St Edmunds, Suffolk, England. Director and Producer for Stage, Film, Television, and Opera; Associate Professor of Drama. m. 1) Leslie Caron, 1956, divorced 1965, 1 son, 1 daughter, (2) Jacqueline Taylor, 1965, divorced 1981, 1 son, 1 daughter, (3) Maria Ewing, 1982, divorced 1990, 1 daughter, (4) Nicola Frei, 1990, 1 daughter. Education: BA, Honours, St Catharine's College, Cambridge. Appointments: Director, Arts Theatre, London, 1955-56, Royal Shakespeare Theatre, 1960, National Theatre, 1973-88; Founder-Director-Producer, International Playwright's Theatre, 1957, Peter Hall Co, 1988; Managing Director, Stratford-on-Avon and Aldwych Theatre, London, 1960-68; Associate Professor of Drama, Warwick University, 1966-; Co-Director, Royal Shakespeare Co, 1968-73; Artistic Director, Glyndebourne Festival, 1984-90; Artistic Director, Old Vic, 1997; Wortham Chair in Performing Arts, Houston University, Texas, 1999; Chancellor, Kingston University, 2000-; Theatre, opera and film productions. Publications: The Wars of the Roses, adaptation after Shakespeare (with John Barton), 1970; John Gabriel Borkman, by Ibsen (translator with Inga-Stina Ewbank), 1975; Peter Hall's Diaries: The Story of a Dramatic Battle (edited by John Goodwin), 1983; Animal Farm, adaptation after Orwell, 1986; The Wild Duck, by Ibsen (translator with Inga-Stina Ewbank), 1990; Making an Exhibition of Myself (autobiography), 1993; An Absolute Turkey, by Feydeau (translator with Nicola Frei), 1994; The Master Builder (with Inga-Stina Ewbank), 1995; Mind Millie For Me (new translation of Feydeau's Occupe-toi d'Amélie, with Nicola Frei), 1999; Cities in Civilization, 1999; The Necessary Theatre, 1999; Exposed by the Mask, 2000; Shakespeare's Advice to the Players, 2003. Honours: Commander of the Order of the British Empire, 1963; Honorary Fellow, St Catharine's College, Cambridge, 1964; Chevalier de l'Ordre des Arts et Des Lettres, France, 1965; Tony Award, USA, 1966; Shakespeare Prize, University of Hamburg, 1967; Knighted, 1977; Standard Special Award, 1979; Special Award for Outstanding Achievement in Opera, 1981, and Awards for Best Director, 1981, 1987; Several honorary doctorates. Membership: Theatre Directors' Guild of Great Britain, founder-member, 1983-.

HALL Sean Michael, b. 8 August 1969, Australia. Chief Executive Officer. m. Larah, 1 son. Education: Leadership, Corporate Governance, Harvard Business School; Negotiations, Harvard Law School; Innovation, Sloan School of Management, Massachusetts Institute of Technology; HSC, St Aloysius College; Finance, University of New South Wales. Appointments: Sales Manager, 1998-2001, Sales and Innovation Manager, 2001-04, COO, 2004-08, CEO, 2008-, FIT BioCeuticals; Owner, Breach Pty Ltd, 2001-03. Honours: Valued Contribution, Institute of Function Medicine, 1997; Listed in biographical dictionaries. Memberships: Behavioral Economics Group; Harvard Business School; MIT Sloan School of Management Alumni. Address: FIT, BioCeuticals Pty Ltd, 16/37-41 O'Riordan St, Alexandria, NSW 2015, Australia.

HALLIDAY Esther Dawn, b. 6 November 1933, Brisbane, Australia. Company Director. m. Kenneth Halliday, 1 son, 4 daughters. Education: BA, University of New England, New South Wales, Australia; Tamworth TAFE, Receptionist/Typist; JP. Appointments: Part time Literacy Tutor, Teacher, Intellectually and Physically Disabled Adults, 1986-92; Chairman, Tamworth District Training, 1992-96; Chairman, 1996-2010, Director (Board), Joblinkplus Limited. Honours: Federal and State Award Certificates Member Family Committees, 1989; Chamber of Commerce Award for Continuing Service to the Business Community, 1999; Local Government Association NSW Medal for over 20 years as an ALD/Cr with Tamworth City Council, 2000; Centenary of Federation Medal, 2003; OAM, 2010. Memberships: MAICD; Lions Lady; Reader, Local News-on-Wheels Programme; Tamworth Sister City Com; Tamworth View Club; Tamworth Historical Society; Tamworth Arts Council; Patron, Tamworth Musical Society; Volunteer, Tamworth City Art Gallery. Address: 149 Crown Street; Tamworth, NSW 2340, Australia. E-mail: estherh@joblinkplus.com.au

HALLIER Bernd Otto, b. 28 July 1947, Hamburg, Germany. Managing Director. m. Ingeborg, 2 sons, 1 daughter. Education: MA, 1974, PhD, 1983, University of Hamburg. Appointments: Managing Director, EHI Retail Institute, 1985-; President, European Retail Academy, 2005-; President, Euro Shop exhibition. Publications: 9 books; More than 300 articles. Honours: Professor hc, Moscow, 2003; Dr h c, 2007; Dr hc, 2011. Memberships: Association of the Eurasian Economic Club of Scientists, Kazakhstan. Address: Veilchenweg 8, 51503 Rosrath, Germany. E-mail: hallier@ehl.org

HALLIWELL Geri Estelle, b. 6 August 1972, Watford, England. Singer. 1 daughter. Career: Member, Spice Girls, 1994-1998; Started as Touch, renamed as Spice Girls; Found manager and obtained major label recording deal; Numerous TV appearances, radio play and press interviews; UK, European and US tours; Nominated United Nations Ambassador, 1998; Solo career, 1998-; Video and book releases. Recordings: Singles with Spice Girls: Wannabe, 1996; Say You'll Be There, 1996; 2 Become 1, 1996; Mama/Who Do You Think You Are, 1993; Spice Up Your Life, 1997; Too Much, 1997; Stop, 1998; (How Does It Feel to Be) On Top of the World, as part of England United, 1998; Move Over/Generation Next, 1998; Viva Forever, 1998; Albums: Spice, 1996; Spiceworld, 1997; Solo Singles: Look At Me, 1999; Mi Chico Latino, 1999; Lift Me Up, 1999; Bag It Up, 2000; It's Raining Men, 2001; Scream If You Want to Go Faster, 2001; Calling, 2002; Ride It, 2004; Desire, 2005. Albums: Schizophonic, 1999; Scream If You Want to Go Faster, 2001;Passion, 2005. Films: Spiceworld The Movie, 1997; Fat Slags, 2004. Publications: If Only, 1999; Just for the Record, 2002; Ugenia Lavendar, 2008. Honours: With Spice Girls, numerous music awards in polls. Address: Hackford Jones PR, Third Floor, 16 Manette Street, London W1D 4AR, England. Website: www.geri-halliwell.com

HALLWORTH Grace Norma Leonie Byam, b. 4 January 1928, Trinidad, West Indies. Ex-Librarian; Author; Storyteller. m. Trevor David Hallworth, 1964. Education: Exemptions from Matriculation, 1946; Associate of Library Association, 1956; Diploma in Education, London University, 1976. Publications: Listen to this Story, 1977; Mouth Open Story Jump Out, 1984; Web of Stories, 1990; Cric Crac, 1990; Buy a Penny Ginger, 1994; Poor-Me-One, 1995; Rhythm and Rhyme, 1995; Down By The River, 1997 Contributions to: Books and journals. Honours: Runner-up for Greenaway Medal. 1997. Membership: Society for Storytelling, patron, 1993-94. Address: 34 Birtchnell Close, Berkhamsted, Hertfordshire HP4 1FE, England.

HALPERN Daniel, b. 11 September 1945, Syracuse, New York, USA. Associate Professor; Poet; Writer; Editor. m. Jeanne Catherine Carter, 31 December 1982, 1 daughter. Education: San Francisco State College, 1963-64; BA, California State University at Northridge, 1969; MFA, Columbia University, 1972. Appointments: Founder-Editor, Antaeus literary magazine, 1969-95; Instructor, New School for Social Research, New York City, 1971-76; Editor-in-Chief, Ecco Press, 1971-; Visiting Professor, Princeton University, 1975-76, 1987-88, 1995-96; Associate Professor, Columbia University, 1976-. Publications: Poetry: Traveling on Credit, 1978; Seasonal Rights, 1982; Tango, 1987; Foreign Neon, 1991; Selected Poems, 1994. Other: The Keeper of Height, 1974; Treble Poets, 1975; Our Private Lives: Journals, Notebooks and Diaries, 1990; Not for Bread Alone: Writers on Food, Wine, and the Art of Eating, 1993; The Autobiographical Eye, 1993; Holy Fire: Nine Visionary Poets and the Quest for Enlightenment, 1994; Something Shining, 1998. Editor: Borges on Writing (co-editor), 1973; The American Poetry Anthology, 1975; The Antaeus Anthology, 1986; The Art of the Tale: An International Anthology of Short Stories, 1986; On Nature, 1987; Writers on Artists, 1988; Reading the Fights (with Joyce Carol Oates), 1988; Plays in One Act, 1990; The Sophisticated Cat (with Joyce Carol Oates), 1992; On Music (co-editor), 1994. Contributions to: Various anthologies, reviews, journals, and magazines. Honours: Jesse Rehder Poetry Award, Southern Poetry Review, 1971; YMHA Discovery Award, 1971; Great Lakes Colleges National Book Award, 1973; Borestone Mountain Poetry Award, 1974; Robert Frost Fellowship, Bread Loaf, 1974; National Endowment for the Arts Fellowships, 1974, 1975, 1987; Pushcaft Press Prizes, 1980, 1987, 1988; Carey Thomas Award for Creative Publishing, Publishers Weekly, 1987; Guggenheim Fellowship, 1988; PEN Publisher Citation, 1993. Address: c/o The Ecco Press, 100 West Broad Street, Hopewell, NJ 08525, USA.

HALSE Sharanappa Vaijinath, b. 5 June 1962. Professor. Education: BSc, 1985, MSc, Applied Electronics, 1987, M Phil, 1997, PhD, 2003, Gulbarga University; EDP and Comp Management, Bharatiya Vidya Bhavan, Bombay, 1988. Appointments: Teacher, PG & UG, 21 years; Guest Lecturer, PGDCA, 14 years; Guest Lecturer, MCA, 2 years; Lecturer, Electronics, BE, 1 year; Researcher, 15 years; Executive Council Member, ISOI IISC Bangalore, 2004-. Publications: Numerous articles in professional journals. Address: Department of MSc Electronics, City Campus, Karnataka State Women's University, Bijapur – 586 101, Karnataka, India.

HALSEY Alan, b. 22 September 1949, Croydon, Surrey, England. Bookseller; Poet. Education: BA, Honours, London. Publications: Yearspace, 1979; Another Loop in Our Days, 1980; Present State, 1981; Perspectives on the Reach, 1981; The Book of Coming Forth in Official Secrecy, 1981; Auto Dada Cafe, 1987; A Book of Changes, 1988; Five Years Out, 1989; Reasonable Distance, 1992; The Text of Shelley's Death, 1995; A Robin Hood Book, 1996; Fit to Print (with Karen McCormack), 1998; Days of '49 , with Gavin Selerie, 1999; Wittgenstein's Devil: Selected Writing 1978-98, 2000; Sonatas and Preliminary Sketches, 2000; Marginalien (Poems, Prose & Graphics 1988-2004), 2005; Not Everything Remotely: Selected Poems 1978-2005, 2006; Lives of the Poets, 2009; Term as in Aftermath, 2009; Contributions to: Critical Quarterly; Conjunctions; North Dakota Quarterly; Writing; Ninth Decade; Poetica; South West Review; Poetry Wales; Poesie Europe; O Ars; Figs; Interstate; Prospice; Reality Studios; Fragmente; Screens and Tasted Parallels; Avec; Purge; Grille; Acumen; Shearsman; Oasis; New American Writing; Agenda; Colorado Review; Talisman; PN Review; Resurgence; West Coast Line; The Gig; Boxkite. Membership: Thomas Lovell Beddoes Society; David Jones Society. Address: 40 Crescent Road, Nether Edge, Sheffield S7 1HN, England.

HALTON Charles Christopher, b. 4 March 1932. Commissioner. m. Shirley Harden, 1956, 2 sons, 1 daughter. Education: BSc (Hons), 1953, MSc, 1955, Mathematics, University of London. Appointments: Head, Advanced Systems and Research, British Aircraft Corp, Bristol, 1967; Director, Science and Technol Research Branch, Canadian Transport Commission, 1969-70; Senior Minister, Executive Policy Planning and Major Projects, Canadian Transport Ministry, 1970-73; Secretary, Australian Department of Transport, 1973-82; Secretary, Department of Defense Support, 1982-84; Member, Australian Cl of Defence, 1982-84; Chairman, Commonwealth Review of Youth Allowance Administration, 1985-86; Australian Trustee, International Institute of Communications, 1986-; Secretary, Department of Communications, Australia, 1986-87; Director, AUSSAT and Commissioner, Australian Telecommunications Commission, 1986-87; Chairman, Commonwealth Task Force on Training and Education, 1987-88; Commissioner, Overseas Telecommunications Commission, 1987-89; Commissioner, Snowy Mountains Hydro-electric Authority, 1987-93; Chairman, Employment and Skills Formation Council of Australia, 1988-91; Chairman, Development Allowance Authority, 1992-95; Member, National Investment Council of Australia, 1993-96; Chairman, Commonwealth Review of Fire Policy, 1997; Director, Hydromet Pty Ltd, 1997-; Co-Convenor, Balanced State Development Working Group, 1997-; Chairman, First Regional IIF Management Pty Ltd, 1997-; Director, Sky Station Australia Pty Ltd, 1998-; Member of Council, Southern NSW Local Health Network, 2011-. Honour: CBE, 1983; Centenary Medal, 2003. Memberships: FRAeS; FCIT; FIE (Aust); FAIE, CPEng; Life Member, Australian Elizabethan Theatre Trust, 1982-; Member, National Board of Employment, Education and Training, 1988-91. Address: PO Box 234, Curtin, ACT 2605, Australia.

HAM Sang-Hyun, b. 25 April 1973, Seoul, Republic of Korea. Reliability Engineer; Manager. m. In Sook Choi, 2006, 2 sons. Education: BS, 1997, MS, 1999, DS, 2011, University of Incheon, Republic of Korea. Publications: Vibration analysis of gyro sensors by using ESPI technique, 2005; A friction induced impulse noise detection of a PDP TV by using the double pulse ESPI, 2005; Analysis of Engineering – Plastic Behaviors in Thermal Stress Condition, 2006. Honours: Six Sigma Black Belt, Samsung Electronics, 2007; Listed in international biographical dictionaries. Memberships: Optical

Society of Korea. Address: 155 Changhu-ri, Hajeom-myeon, Ganghwa-gun, Incheon, 417-873, Republic of Korea. E-mail: togoone@hanmail.net

HAMA Yukihiro, b. 5 May 1972, Hakodate, Japan. Researcher. m. Junko, 1 son, 2 daughters. Education: MD, National Defense Medical College, 1997; PhD, Saitama Medical School, 2003. Appointments: Resident, 1997-99, Fellow, Department of Radiology, 2000-04, Docent, 2007-09, National Defense Medical College, Tokorozawa; Chief Medical Officer, Iwo-Jima ASS, JMSDF, 1999-2000; Clinical Fellow, NCI/NIH, Bethesda, USA, 2005-06; Lecturer, Nihon University School of Medicine, 2009-; Chairman, Department of Radiology, Tokyo-Edogawa Cancer Center, Edogawa Hospital, Tokyo, 2010-. Honours: Certificate of Merit, 1999, Molecular Imaging Research Award Winner, 2006, Certificate of Merit, 2007, Research in Molecular Imaging, 2007, Excellence in Design Award, 2010, Radiological Society of North America; Research Award Winner, Japan-US Radiological Exchange Association, 2004; International Exchange Award, Japan Society of Interventional Radiology, 2005; Research Fellowship Award, Japan Radiological Society, 2005; Visiting Fellowship Award, NIH, USA, 2005-06. Memberships: Radiological Society of North America; American Association for Cancer Research; American Society for Therapeutic Radiology and Oncology; European Congress of Radiology.

HAMANDAWANA Hamisai, b. 3 August 1959, Zimbabwe. Remote Sensing/GIS Scientist. Education: BA, 1983, Dip Ed, 1983, Post-grad Diploma, Rural Development Planning, 1987, PhD, 2006, University of Botswana. Appointments: Secondary School Teacher, Assisi Secondary School, Zimbabwe, 1983-84; Secondary School Teacher, Makumbe Secondary School, Zimbabwe, 1985-87; Senior Lecturer & Principal Lecturer, Morgenster Teacher Training College, Zimbabwe, 1992-97; Lecturer, Gweru Teacher Training College, Zimbabwe, 1989-91; Lecturer, University of Botswana, 2006-07; Senior Lecturer and Head, North West University, South Africa, 2007-09; GeoInformatics Programme Manager, Agricultural Research Council, Institute for Soil, Water & Climate, Pretoria, South Africa, 2009-. Publications: Numerous articles in professional journals. Honours: Undergraduate Scholarship, 1979, Post-Grad Scholarship, 1987, German Academic Exchange Service; MIOMBO Network, GIS/Remote Sensing workshop, 2000; Graduate Research Grant, Canon Collins Educational Trust for Southern Africa, 2000, 2001; Graduate Research Grant, Southern Africa Science Regional Initiative, 2001; International Conference Funding, International Human Dimension Program, 2000, 2006, 2008, 2009; Doctoral Fellowship, 2003, Remote Sensing/GIS course, 2005, Pan African START Secretariat; International Conference Funding, Canadian International Development Agency, 2004; Academic Exchange Visit, University of Glasgow, 2008; International Conference Funding, University of East Anglia, Tyndall Centre for Climate Change Research, 2009. Memberships: International Science Advisory Board; Applied Centre for Climate and Earth System Studies; Research Co-operative for Researchers, Science Writers, Research Editors, Translators and Publishers. Address: Agricultural Research Council, Institute for Soil, Water & Climate, PB X79, Pretoria 0001, South Africa. E-mail: hamandawanah@yahoo.com

HAMILTON Linda, b. 26 September 1956, Salisbury, Maryland, USA. Actress. m. (1) Bruce Abbott, divorced, 1 son (2) James Cameron, 1996, divorced, 1 daughter. Career: Stage appearances: Looice, 1975; Richard III, 1977; Films include: TAG: The Assassination Game, 1982; Children of the Corn, 1984; The Stone Boy, 1984; The Terminator, 1984; Black Moon Rising, 1986; King Kong Lives! 1986; Mr Destiny, 1990; Terminator 2: Judgement Day, 1991; Silent Fall, 1994; The Shadow Conspiracy, 1997; Dante's Peak, 1997; Skeletons in the Closet, 2001; Wholey Moses, 2003; Jonah, 2004; Smile, 2005; Missing in America, 2005; The Kid and I, 2005; In Your Dreams, 2006; Broken, 2006. TV: The Secrets of Midland Heights, 1980-81; King's Crossing, 1982; Beauty and the Beast, 1987-90; Country Gold, 1982; Secrets of a Mother and Daughter, 1983; Secret Weapons, 1985; Club Med, 1986; Go Toward the Light, 1988; On the Line, 1998; Point Last Seen, 1998; The Color of Courage, 1999; The Secret Life of Girls, 1999; Sex & Mrs X, 2000; A Girl Thing, 2001; Bailey's Mistake, 2001; Silent Night, 2004; According to Jim, 2005; Thief, 2006; Home by Christmas, 2006; In Your Dreams, 2007; Jeremiah Wright Painting a Picture of US Aggression, 2008. Address: United Talent Agency, 5th Floor, 9560 Wilshire Boulevard, Beverly Hills, CA 90212, USA.

HAMMAD Talaat, b. 10 December 1957, Gaza, Palestine. Physicist. m. Sadya Yessen Taha, 4 sons, 2 daughters. Education: BSc, Physics, 1980, MSc, Solid State Physics, 1983, Cairo, Egypt; PhD, Solid State Physics, Moscow State University, Moscow, Russia, 1998. Appointments: Assistant Professor of Solid State Physics, Head of Physics Department, Al-Azhar University, Palestine. Publications: 22 articles in professional journals. Honours: DAAD Scholarship; Listed in Who's Who publications and biographical dictionaries. Address: Physics department, Faculty of Science, Al-Azhar University, PO Box 1277, Gaza, Palestine. E-mail: talaath55@yahoo.com

HAMMETT Louise B (Biddy), b. 18 September 1929, Columbus, Georgia, USA. Community Service Volunteer; Artist; Writer; Playwright; Historian; Publisher. m. Paul Lane Hammett Jr (deceased), 2 daughters. Education: BA, Auburn University, Alabama, 1950; Postgraduate Studies, Audited Art Studies, LaGrange College, Georgia, 1962-69; Certified equivalent MA in Art, University of Georgia, 1982. Appointments: School Teacher, LaGrange Public Schools, Georgia, 1950-51; Founder of Art Division, 1970, Volunteer, 1970-71, LaGrange Academy; Co-founder and Art Instructor, Chattahoochee Valley Art Museum Association, LaGrange; Founder and Chair, Chattahoochee Valley Art Association's Sidewalk Art Show; Artist in Residence, Instructor, Chattahoochee Valley Community College; Private Studio Art Instructor, LaGrange, 1963-80; Exhibited Power Crossroads, Coweta Counter, Georgia, 1971; Private Studio Art Instructor, Columbus, 1980-; Oil painting demonstrations; Represented in group shows and in permanent art collections. Publications: Articles in professional and popular journals and magazines; Oil painting, Georgia to Georgia, gifted to Zugdidi, Republic of Georgia; Oil painting, Peach Trees, gifted to Kiryu City, Japan; I Must Sing! The Era with Carrie Fall Benson, 2007; The Pen of Carrie Fall Benson, 2009; Books: A Hammett Family in Georgia History; Louise Calhoun Barfield's Tablet; Campaigns of the Wise Guards with Pinckney Barfield Walking Away from Death. Honours include: Award for Excellence in Community Service, NSDAR, 1990; Chattahoochee Valley Art Museum, 1994; 6 separate awards under the Seals of two Mayors and Councils of Columbus, Georgia for Meritorious Civic Service; NSSAR Gold Medal, 2007; NSSAR Certificate of Appreciation, 2008; NSDAR Oglethorpe Chapter Certificate of Appreciation, 2009; Nominated Georgia State NSDAR Vice-Chair Education, Georgia Day, 2009; Le Grange College, 13 December, 2009, author, for book The Pen of Carrie Fall Benson; Paintings: What Shall I Give Him,

Vapor of Praise, and His Eye is on the Sparrows,, permanently hanging in First Presbyterian Church, Columbus, GA; Resolution from Georgia House of Representatives, 2011; Wrote & produced program in Spanish, History of Georgia, WHINSEC, Ft Benning, Georgia, 2011; 1st Place Award, DAR Georgia Day Chairman, GA Society, DAR, 2011; Spoke at Erskine Caldwell Museum, 2011; Received National DAR Medal in Historic Preservation, 2011; Program, Oglethorpe Chapter, DAR, 2011; Featured Speaker, Hammett Reunion, Newman, Georgia, 2011. Memberships: National Daughters of the American Revolution, Home Chapter Oglethorpe, Associate Chapters, Kettle Creek and La Grange; United Daughters of the Confederacy; Georgia Poetry Society; Friends of Columbus State University Swobe Library; American Author's Guild. Address: Cherith Creek Designs, P O Box 123, Columbus, GA 31902-0123, USA.

HAMMOND Peter, b. 13 July 1942. Mining Supervisor. m. Diane Ivy, 1989. Education: Modules Diploma of Higher Education, 1985. Appointments: Environmental and Mining Supervisor; Public Speaker on Poetry and Literature Black Country in Colleges and Universities, Schools and Art Societies nationwide. Publications: Two in Staffordshire with Graham Metcalf, 1979; Love Poems, 1982. Contributions to: New Age Poetry; Outposts; Charter Poetry; Chase Post; Swansea Festival, 1982. Honour: School Poetry Prize, 1956. Memberships: Rugeley Literary Society; Co-Founder, Cannock Poetry Group; Poetry Society Readings. Address: 6 Gorstey Lea, Burntwood, Staffordshire WS7 9BG, England.

HAMMONS Thomas James, b. England. Chartered Engineer; Power Engineer; Consultant, University Teacher. Education: ACGI, City and Guilds College, London, 1957; BSc (1st class honours), Engineering, 1957, DIC, 1961, PhD, 1961, Imperial College, London University. Appointments: Engineer, System Engineering Department, Associated Electrical Industries, Manchester, 1961-62; Professor, Electrical and Computer Engineering, McMaster University, Canada, 1978-79; Visiting Professor, Silesian Polytechnic University, 1978; Visiting Academic, Czechoslovakian Academy of Sciences, Prague, 1982, 1985, 1988; Visiting Professor, Polytechnic University Grenoble, France, 1984; Teacher, Faculty of Engineering, University of Glasgow, Scotland; Lectured in North America, Africa, Asia and throughout Europe. Publications: Over 400 scientific papers and articles; Editor, Renewable Energy, 2009; Electricity Infrastructure in the Global Marketplace, 2011. Honours: IEEE Power Engineering Society Energy Development and Power Generation Award in Recognition of Distinguished Service to the Committee, 1996; IEEE Power Engineering Society 2003 Outstanding Large Chapter Award; 2 higher honorary Doctorates in Engineering. Memberships: Fellow, IEEE; UK Parliamentary Renewable and Sustainable Energy Group; Founder Member, International Universities Power Engineering Conference; Past Permanent Secretary of UPEC; Registered European Engineer, Federation of National Engineering Associations in Europe. Address: Clairmont, 11c Winton Drive, Kelvinside, Glasgow G12 0PZ, Scotland. E-mail: T.Hammons@ieee.org

HAMNETT Katharine, b. 16 August 1947. Designer. 2 sons. Education: St Martin's School of Art. Appointments: Tuttabankem, 1969-74; Designed freelance in New York, Paris, Rome and London, 1974-76; Founder, Katherine Hamnett Ltd, 1979; Launched Choose Life T-shirt collection, 1983; Involved in Fashion Aid, 1985; Opened first Katherine Hamnett shop, London, 1986, 2 more shops, 1988; Production moved to Italy, 1989; Visiting Professor, London Institute, 1997-; International Institute of Cotton Designer of the Year, 1982; British Fashion Industry Designer of the Year, 1984; Bath Costume Museum Menswear Designer of the Year Award, 1984; British Knitting and Clothing Export Council Award for Export, 1988. Publications: Various publications in major fashion magazines and newspapers. Address: Katherine Hamnett Ltd, 202 New North Road, London N1 7BJ, England.

HAMPE Michael H, b. 3 June 1935, Heidelberg, Germany. Stage Director. m. Sibylle, 1 daughter. Education: Studied Acting Literature, Musicology, Philosophy, D Phil, Universities of Munch, Heidelberg and Vienna. Appointments: Deputy Director, Schauspielhaus, Zurich, 1965-70; Intendant, National Theatre, Mannheim, 1972-75; Intendant, Cologne Opera and Ballet, 1975-95; approximately 250 productions in opera and drama. Member, Board of Directors, Salzberg Festival, 1984-90; Intendant, Dresden Music Festival, 1992-2000; Stage Director, opera, drama, television, 2000-. Publications: Articles, books, features on various subjects concerning opera and theatre, theatre administration, theatre construction. Honours: Großes Bundesverdienstkreuz, Germany; Commendatore della Repubblica Italiana; Goldenes Ehrenzeichen des Landes, Salzburg; Olivier Award, London. Membership: Board member, European Music Theatre Academy, Vienna. Address: Carl Spitteler Straße 105, CH 8053 Zurich, Switzerland. E-mail: mhampe@bluewin.ch

HAMPSHIRE Susan, b. 12 May 1937, London, England. Actress; Writer. m. (1) Pierre Granier-Deferre, 1967, divorced 1974, 1 son, (2) Eddie Kulukundis, 1981. Education: Knightsbridge, England. Appointments: Actress on the London stage, 1959-; Film and television appearances; Writer. Publications: Susan's Story: An Autobiographical Account of My Struggle with Dyslexia, 1982; The Maternal Instinct, 1985; Lucy Jane at the Ballet, 1987; Trouble Free Gardening, 1989; Lucy Jane on Television, 1989; Every Letter Counts, 1990; Lucy Jane and the Dancing Competition, 1990; Easy Gardening, 1992; Lucy Jane and the Russian Ballet, 1993; Rosie's First Ballet Lesson, 1995. Honours: Emmy Awards, 1970, 1971, 1973; Honorary doctorates, London University, 1984, St Andrew's University, 1986, Kingston University, 1994, Pine Manor College, Boston, Massachusetts, 1994; Officer of the Order of the British Empire, 1995. Memberships: Dyslexia Institute; Royal Society of Authors. Address: c/o Chatto and Linnit Ltd, 123a Kings Road, London SW3 4PL, England.

HAMPTON Christopher (James), b. 26 January 1946, Fayal, The Azores. Playwright. m. Laura de Holesch, 1971, 2 daughters. Education: Lancing College, Sussex, 1959-63; BA, Modern Languages, 1968, MA, New College, Oxford. Career: Resident Dramatist, Royal Court Theatre, London, 1968-70; Freelance Writer, 1970-. Publications: Tales from Hollywood, 1983; Tartuffe or The Imposter (adaptation of Moliére's play), 1984; Les Liaisons Dangereuses (adaptation of C de Laclos's novel), 1985; Hedda Gabler and A Doll's House (translations of Ibsen's plays), 1989; Faith, Hope and Charity (translator), 1989; The Ginger Tree (adaptation of Oscar Wynd's novel), 1989; White Chameleon, 1991; The Philanthropist and Other Plays, 1991; Sunset Boulevard, 1993; Alice's Adventures Underground, 1994; Carrington, 1995; Mary Reilly, 1996; The Secret Agent, 1996; Art (translator), 1996; Nostromo, 1997; An Enemy of the People (translator), 1997; The Unexpected Man (translator), 1998; Conversations After a Burial (translator), 2000; Life x Three, 2001; Three Sisters, 2003. Screenwriter: The Quiet American, 2002; Imagining Argentina, 2003; Atonement, 2007; Tokyo Rose, 2008. Other: Screenplays, radio and television plays. Honours: Evening Standard Award, 1970, 1983, 1986; Plays and Players London

Critics' Award, 1970, 1973, 1985; Los Angeles Drama Critics Circle Award, 1974; Laurence Olivier Award, 1986; New York Drama Critics' Award, 1987; Prix Italia, 1988; Writers Guild of America Screenplay Award, 1989; Oscar, 1989; BAFTA, 1990; Special Jury Award, Cannes Film Festival, 1995; 2 Tony Awards, 1995; Scott Moncrieff Prize, 1997; Officier, Ordre des Arts et des Lettres, 1998. Membership: Royal Society of Literature, fellow. Address: National House, 60-66 Wardour Street, London W1V 3HP, England.

HAN Cheon-Goo, b. 22 August 1953, Cheong Ju City, Korea. Professor. m. He-Soon Park, 1 son, 1 daughter. Education: Bachelor's degree, Department of Architectural Engineering, Cheong Ju University, 1975; Master's degree, Department of Architectural Engineering, Dankook University, 1980; Doctor's degree, Department of Architectural Engineering, Chung Nam University, 1989. Appointments: Engineer Officer, 1975-77; POSCO Co Ltd, 1977-78; Full time Lecturer, Department of Architectural Engineering, In Cheon University, 1978-81; Professor, Department of Architectural Engineering, Cheong Ju University, 1981-. Publications: Quality Control of Remicon (I), (II), (III); Use of maturity methods to estimate the setting time of concrete containing super retarding agent; Synergistic effect of combined fiber for spalling protection of concrete in fire. Honours: Science Technology Best Thesis Award, 3 times; Thesis Awards, Architectural Institute of Korea, Korea Institute of Building Construction; The Minister of Education's Award; The Minister of Construction and Transportation Award. Memberships: Korea Recycled Construction Resource Institute; Korea Concrete Institute; Korea Association of Professional Construction Quality Engineering. Address: Bang Seo-Dong 58-1, Sang Dang-Gu, Cheong Ju, 360-183, Korea. E-mail: cghan@cju.ac.kr Website: www.cju.ac.kr

HAN Heechul, b. 12 July 1973, Jinju city, South Korea. Senior Research Engineer. m. Juhee Seo, 1 son. Education: BS, Computer Engineering, 1999, MS, Multimedia Engineering, 2001, Kyungsung University, South Korea; PhD, Electronic-Electrical Engineering, Yonsei University, South Korea, 2010. Appointments: Adjunct Professor, Dongju College, South Korea, 2000; CTO & Founder, Hanizone, 2000-01; Research Engineer, Samsung Electronics, 2001-. Publications: Face relighting based on virtual irradiance sphere and reflection coefficient, 2008; Automatic Illumination and color compensation using mean shift and sigma filter, 2009; Numerous articles in professional journals and at conference. Honours: Designated Technology Business Incubator, Korea Institute of Industrial Technology Evaluation and Planning, 2000; Proud Samsung Employee Award, 2004; Bronze Medal, Samsung Best Paper Awards, 2009. Memberships: IEEE. Address: 625-1301, Hanhwa-2cha-Apt, Dongtan, Hwasung City, 445-757, Republic of Korea. E-mail: leonhan@samsung.com Website: www.leonhan.com

HAN Heesup, b. 19 September 1975, Cheonan, Korea. Professor. m. Yunhi Kim, 1 daughter. Education: MSc, PhD, Kansas State University. Appointments: Assistant Manager, Kansas Housing & Dining Center; Adjunct Professor, Research Associate, Kansas State University; Assistant Professor, Dong-A University. Publications: Numerous articles in professional journals. Honours: Martin Oppermann JTTM Best Article of the Year, 2007; Best Teaching Award, 2009; Best Teaching Award, 2010. Memberships: Director of Information & Technology, Asia-Pacific Tourism Association. Address: BB1209, Dong-A University, Tourism Management, 2-1 Bumin-dong, Seo-gu, Busan 602-760, Korea. E-mail: heesup.han@gmail.com

HAN Kihwan, b 7 April 1954, Daegu, Korea. Medical Doctor; Professor. m. Shinhyang Kim, 2 daughters. Education: MD, 1978, MSc, Medicine, 1981, PhD, 1989, Kyungpook National University, Korea. Certified Plastic Surgeon, Korean Board of Plastic and Reconstructive Surgery. Appointments: Intern, 1978-79, Resident, 1979-83, Chief, Department of Plastic and Reconstructive Surgery, 1994-, Dongsan Medical Centre, Daegu, Republic of Korea; Captain, Daegu Military Medical Centre, 1983-86; Professor, Keimyung University School of Medicine, 1986-; Visiting Professor, Harvard Medical School, Boston, USA, 1990-91; Visiting Professor, Chang Gung Memorial Hospital, Taiwan, 2006; CEO, Gyeongjoo Dongsan Hospital, 2010-11; CEO, Daegu Dongsan Hospital, 2011-. Publications: Plastic and Reconstructive Surgery, 1994; Aesthetic Plastic Surgery, 1998; Plastic Surgery for Students, 1999; Translation of Plastic Surgery chapter in Sabiston's General Surgery, 2003; Translation of Daniel's Rhinoplasty, 2005; Cleft Lip and Palate, 2005; Translation of The Art of Aesthetic Surgery, 2007; Clinical Photography, 2008; Cosmetic and Reconstructive Oculoplastic Surgery, 2009. Memberships: Asian Pacific Cranio-Facial Association; American Cleft Palate-Craniofacial Association; American Society of Plastic and Reconstructive Surgeons; Board of Directors, Korean Society for Aesthetic Plastic Surgery, 2008; President, The Korean Cleft-Palate-Craniofacial Surgery Association, 2009-. Address: Department of Plastic and Reconstructive Surgery, Keimyung University School of Medicine, Dongsan Medical Centre, 194, Dongsan-dong, Daegu 700-712 Korea. E-mail: kihwanhan54@gmail.com

HAN Man-Joo, b. 2 August 1954, Cheongju, Chungbuk, Korea. Law Professor. m. Wha-Shin Park, 2 sons. Education: LLB, 1977, LLM, 1986, PhD, 1989, Kangwon National University, Republic of Korea. Appointments: Professor, Law School, 1991-, Dean, College of Law, 1998-2000, Dean, Law School, 2000, Director, Institute of Legal Studies, 2009-11, Kangwon National University. Publications: Books: Minority Protection Law, 2005; Cases on Martime Law, 2006; Cases on Insurance Law, 2006; Law in Practice, 2007; Jurisprudence, 2007; Cases on Anti-Trust Law; Insurance Law, 2007; Maritime Law, 2007; Environmental Law and Policy, 2008; Introducton to the Law, 2008; Gender Discrimination and Law, 2009; Consumer Protection Law, 2009; Fair Trade Law, 2011; Anti-Trust Law, 2011. Honours: Abroad Research Professor, Seongkok Foundation, Asann Foundation and Yeonam Foundation. Memberships: Labor Relations Commission. Address: Kangwon National University, Law School, Hyoja-2-dong, 192-1, Chunchon, 200-701, South Korea. E-mail: mihan@kangwon.ac.kr

HAN Myeong-Sook, b. 24 March 1944. Prime Minister of the Republic of Korea. Education: BA, French Literature & Language, 1967, MA, Women's Studies, 1986, Ewha Womans University. Appointments: Member of Staff, Korea Christian Academy, 1974-79; Jailed as a prisoner of conscience, Christian Academy Case, 1979-81; Lecturer, Department of Women's Studies, Ewha Womans University, 1986-87; Lecturer, Department of Women's Studies, Sungsim Womans University, 1988-94; Chair, Special Committee on Revision of Family Law, Korea Women's Associations United (KWAU), 1989; President, Korean Womenlink, 1990-94; Chief Director, Korea Institute for Environmental and Social Policies, 1992; Member of Executive Committee, Seoul and Pyungyang Symposium, Peace of Asian and Women's Role, 1992-96; Co-representative, Viewers Alliance for Fair Broadcasting Policy Advisor, Committee for Interchange and Co-operation, Ministry of Unification, 1993-94; Member, Environmental Reservation Committee, Ministry of Environment, Member of Anti-Corruption Committee, The Board of Audit and Inspection of the Republic of Korea, 1993-95; Co-Representative, KWAU, 1993-96; Co-Representative, Citizens Association for Broadcasting Reform, 1994-95; Visiting Researcher, Asian Center for Women's Studies, Ewha Womans University, 1996-2003; Member, 16th National Assembly, Republic of Korea, 2000-01; Minister of Gender Equality, 2001-03; Minister of Environment, 2003-04; Elected Member, 17th National Assembly, Republic of Korea, 2004; Member, National Assembly, Unification, Foreign Affairs and Trade Committee, 2004-; President, Korean Parliamentary League on Children, Population and Environment, 2004-06; President, Executive Committee, Asia-Pacific Parliamentarians Conference on Environment and Development, 2004-06; Member, Central Standing Committee, Uri Party, 2005; President, Korea-Singapore Parliamentarians' Friendship Association, 2004-; Vice President, Korea-Japan Parliamentary League, 2006-; Member, National Assembly, Environment and Labor Committee, 2006-; 37th Prime Minister of the Republic of Korea, 2006-2007. Honours: Civil Merit Medal, 1998; Order of Service Merit Medal (Blue Stripes), 2005. Address: Prime Minister's Office, Seoul, Republic of Korea.

HAN Seungoh, b. 14 June 1973, Korea. Professor. Education: B Eng, 1996, M Eng, 1998, PhD, 2006, Korea University. Appointments: Assistant Manager, Jasontech, 2000-01; Assistant Manager, Daou Xilicon Inc, 2001-06; Assistant Professor, Department of Robotics Engineering, Hoseo University, 2007-. Honours: Listed in biographical dictionaries. Address: Hoseo University, 165 Sechul-Ri, Baebang-Myun, Asan-City, Chungnam 336-795, Korea. E-mail: sohan@hoseo.edu

HAN Tae Hee, b. 20 April 1966, Incheon, South Korea. Medical Doctor; Professor. m. Yun Seon Lee, 1 son, 1 daughter. Education: Doctor of Medicine, 1991, PhD, Medical Science, 2005, Seoul National University. Appointments: Resident, Department of Laboratory Medicine, Seoul National University Hospital, 1996-2000; Clinical Fellow, 2000-02, Assistant Professor, 2002-08, Associate Professor, 2008-, Inje University, Sanggye Paik Hospital. Publications: Numerous articles in professional journals. Honours: Mir Award, Korean Society of Blood Transfusion. Memberships: Korean Society of Blood Transfusion; Korean Society for Laboratory Medicine. Address: Inje University, Sanggyepaik Hospital, 761-1 Sanggye7-Dong, Nowon-Gu, Seoul 139-7017, South Korea. E-mail: taeheehan@paik.ac.kr

HAN Youngmo, b. 22 June 1969, Republic of Korea. Professor. Education: BSc, Department of Physics Education, Seoul National University, 1992; BE, Department of Control and Instrumentation, Seoul National University, 1995; ME, Department of Electric Engineering, Seoul National University, 1998; PhD, Department of Mechanical and Aerospace Engineering, Seoul National University, Seoul, Republic of Korea, 2002. Appointments: Researcher, 2002-03, Research Professor, 2003, UAV group of Sejong-Rockheed Martin Aerospace Research Center, Seoul; Part time Lecturer, Department of Mechanical Engineering, Dankook University, Seoul, 2002-04; Full time Research Lecturer, 2004-05, Research Professor, 2005-06, Department of Information Electronics, Ewha Womans University, Seoul; Full time Lecturer, Assistant Professor, Department of Computer Engineering, Hanyang Cyber University, Seoul, 2006-; Deputy Director General and Honorary Director General, IBC, 2007-; Vice President, World Congress of Arts, Science and Communications, 2007-; Deputy Governor, ABI Research Association, USA, 2009-; Vice Chancellor, World Academy of Letters, USA, 2010-. Publications: Numerous papers and articles in professional journals. Honours: Graduated 2nd, 1995, Department Control and Instrumentation, Graduated 4th, Department of Physics Education, 1992, Seoul National University; Lifetime Achievement Award, World Congress of Arts, Science and Communications, UK, 2007; IBC Hall of Fame, 2007; Top Two Hundred, 2007; Top 100 Engineers, 2008, 2011; Top 100 Scientists, 2008; ABI Hall of Fame, 2009; Listed in international biographical directories. Memberships: IEE; Korean Information Science Society; Institute of Electronics Engineers. Address: Department of Computer Engineering, Hanyang Cyber University, HIT 2F, 17 Haengdang-Dong, Seongdong-Gu, Seoul 133-791, Republic of Korea. E-mail: ymhan123@hanmail.net

HANDRA-LUCA Adriana-Alina, b. 4 April 1970, Cluj-Napoca, Romania. Medical Doctor; Associate Professor. Education: MD, Universitatea de Medicina Cluj, Romania, 1994; PhD, Université Paris 6, France, 2004. Appointments: Assistant Professor, APHP-Hôpitaux Beaujon, Pitie-Salpetriere, Jean Verdier and Universités Paris, 5, 6 and 13, 2000-05; Associate Professor, APHP-Hôpitaux Jean Verdier and Avicenne and Université Paris 13 Nord, 2005-. Publications: Research on Tumour Pathology; Articles in professional journals. Honours: UEGW, 2004, 2005, 2010; ESCOP, 2001, 2002, 2003. Memberships: Societé Nationale Francaise de Gastroenterologie; Societe Nationale Francaise de Gastroenterologie; College Universitaire Francais de Pathologistes. Address: Department of Pathology, APHP-Hôpital Avicenne, Université Paris 13/Nord UFRSMBH, 125 rue de Stalingrad, 93000 Bobigny, France. E-mail: adriana.handra-luca@avc.aphp.fr

HANDS Timothy Roderick, b. 30 March 1956, London, England. Master, Magdalen College School, Oxford. m. Jane Smart, 2 sons. Education: Emanuel School, Battersea; Guildhall School of Music and Drama; BA (1st class), English Language and Literature, King's College London; Senior Scholar, St Catherine's College, Oxford; D Phil (RWB Burton Senior Scholar), Oriel College, Oxford, 1984. Appointments: Stipendiary Lecturer, Oriel College, Oxford, 1985-86; Assistant Master, 1986-94, Housemaster Galpin's, 1990-94, King's School, Canterbury; Second Master, Whitgift School, 1994-97; Headmaster, The Portsmouth Grammar School, 1997-2007; Master, Magdalen College School, Oxford, 2008-. Publications: A George Eliot Chronology, 1989; Thomas Hardy: Distracted Preacher, 1989; A Hardy Chronology, 1992; Thomas Hardy: Writers in Their Time, 1995; Ideas to Assemble, 2006; Contributions to: New Perspectives on Thomas Hardy, 1994; The Achievement of Thomas Hardy, 2000; Ashgate Research Companion to Thomas Hardy, 2010; Oxford Reader's Companion to Hardy, 2000; Miscellaneous literary and musical articles, editions and reviews. Honours: William Stebbing Prize, 1976, JS Brewer Prize, 1977, Early English Text Society and LM Faithfull Prizes, 1978, AKC, with Credit, 1st Leathes Prizeman, 1978, Jelf Medalist, King's College London. Memberships: Editorial Board, Conference and Common Room; HMC GSA Universities Committee; Schola Cantorum of Oxford; External Advisory Board, Oxford University Faculty of English; Governor, Our Lady's Abingdon, Bedale School and St Mary's Calne. Address: Magdalen College School, Oxford, OX4 1DZ, England.

HANEMANN Clemens Oliver, b. 23 January 1962. Professor; Consultant; Academic Head of Department of Neurology. Education: MD, PhD, Institute of Molecular Neurology, Medical School, University of Hamburg,

1985. Appointments: DFG Research Fellow, Molecular Neurological Laboratory, Department of Neurology, University of Düsseldorf, 1988-90; Department of Paediatric Neurology, University of Michigan, USA, 1994; Laboratory of Neuromorphology, Department of Neurology, University Nijmegen, 1996; Neurology Resident, 1990-96, Neurology Fellow, 1996, Assistant Professor, 1998, Department of Neurology, Psychiatry Resident, Department of Psychiatry, 1994, University of Düsseldorf; Assistant Professor (Neurobiology/Neurology), University Ulm, 2000-15. Publications: Numerous articles in professional journals. Honours: DFG Scholarship, 1988-90; Bennigsen-Foerder Award; Numerous invited lectures; Research grants. Memberships: German Neuromuscular Society; NFA-UK; NCRI; DenDroN Network; CTF + Lord Dowdy scientific councils. Address: Peninsular Medical School, The John Bull Building, Tamar Science Park, Research Way, Plymouth, PL6 8BU, England. E-mail: oliver.hanemann@pms.ac.uk

HANKE Hans-Joachim, b. 25 November 1966, Ochtrup, Germany. Engineer. Education: Dipl. Ing (equivalent to Master's Degree), General Electrical Sciences, RWTH, Aachen, Germany, 1986-93. Appointments: Project Engineer, SICOWA, Aachen, 1993-98; Project Manager, Voith Siemens Hydro Power Generation GmbH & Co KG, Heidenheim, Germany, 1999-2004; Department Manager, AREVA NP GmbH, Erlangen, Germany. Publications: Articles in professional journals: Modernising the control system at two German plants, 2003; Automation Solutions for power plants of SWU Energie GmbH; Book chapter: Hydro Energy in The International Directory of Power Generation and Distribution, 2003. Membership: Verein Deutsche Ingenieure (Association of German Engineers). Address: Tillypark 202, Nuremberg 90431, Germany.

HANKS Tom, b. 9 July 1956, California, USA. Actor. m. (1) Samantha Lewes, 1977, divorced 1987, 2 children, (2) Rita Wilson, 1988, 2 sons. Career: Began acting with Great Lakes Shakespeare Festival; Appeared in Bosom Buddies, ABC TV, 1980; Films include: Splash; Bachelor Party; The Man with One Red Shoe; Volunteers; The Money Pit; Dragnet; Big; Punch Line; The Burbs; Nothing in Common; Every Time We Say Goodbye; Joe Versus the Volcano, The Bonfire of the Vanities, 1990; A League of Their Own, 1991; Sleepless in Seattle, Philadelphia, 1993; Forrest Gump, 1994; Apollo 13, 1995; That Thing You Do (also directed), Turner & Hooch, 1997; Saving Private Ryan, You've Got Mail, 1998; Cast Away, The Green Mile, Toy Story 2 (voice), From the Earth to the Moon, 1999; Road to Perdition, 2002; Catch Me If You Can, 2003; The Ladykillers, The Terminal, Elvis Has Left the Building, The Polar Express, 2004; The Da Vinci Code, 2006; Charlie Wilson's War, 2007; The Great Buck Howard, 2008; Angels and Demons, 2009; Toy Story 3, 2010. Honours: Academy Award, 1994, 1995. Membership: Board of Governors, Academy of Motion Picture Arts and Sciences, 2001-. Address: c/o CAA, 9830 Wilshire Boulevard, Beverly Hills, CA 90212, USA.

HANNAH Daryl, b. 3 December, 1960, Chicago, Illinois, USA. Actress. Education: University of Southern California at Los Angeles; Professional Training: Ballet tuition with Marjorie Tallchief, also studied with Stella Adler. Career: Film appearances include: The Fury; The Final Terror; Hard Country; Blade Runner; Summer Lovers; Splash; The Pope of Greenwich Village; Reckless; Clan of the Cave Bear; Legal Eagles; Roxanne; Wall Street; High Spirits; Steel Magnolias; Crazy People; At Play in the Fields of the Lord; Memoirs of an Invisible Man; Grumpy Old Men; Attack of the 50ft Woman; The Tie That Binds; Grumpier Old Men; Two Much; The Last Days of Frankie the Fly; Wild Flowers, My Favorite Martian, 1999; Dancing at the Blue Iguana, Cord, 2000; Speedway Junky, Jackpot, 2001; A Walk to Remember, Hard Cash, 2002; Northfork, Kill Bill Vol 1, Casa de Los Babys, 2003; Yo puta, Kill Bill Vol 2, Silver City, Careful What You Wish For, 2004; Lucky 13, Supercross, 2005; Love Is The Drug, Keeping up with the Steins, Olé, 2006; The Poet, Vice, Dark Honeymoon, 2007; Shannon's Rainbow, 2009; A Closed Book, 2010. Play: The Seven Year Itch, 2000; Directed: The Last Supper, 1994; A Hundred and One Nights, 1995. Address: Columbia Plaza Producers, Building 8-153, Burbank, CA 91505, USA.

HANNAH John, b. 23 April 1962, Glasgow, Scotland. Actor. m. Joanna Roth, 1 son, 1 daughter. Education: Royal Scottish Academy of Music and Drama. Career: Formerly electrician, formerly with Worker's Theatre Company; TV appearances include: McCallum; Joan; Faith; Rebus; Dr Jekyll and Mr Hyde, MDs, Amnesia, Marple: 4.50 from Paddington; Sea of Souls; Cold Blood; New Street Law; Agatha Christie's Poirot: Appointment with Death, 2008; Spartacus: Blood and Sand, 2010; Spartacus: Gods of the Arena, 2011. Film appearances include: Four Weddings and a Funeral, 1994; Sliding Doors, 1998; The James Gang, 1999; The Mummy, 1999; The Mummy Returns, 2001; Pandaemonium, 2001; Before You Go, 2002; I'm with Lucy, 2002; I Accuse, 2003; Male Mail, 2004; Ghost Son, 2006; The Last Legion, 2007; The Mummy: Tomb of the Dragon Emperor, 2008; Zip 'n Zoo, 2008.

HANRAHAN Brian, b. 22 March 1949, London, England. Journalist. m. 1 daughter. Education: BA, Essex University. Appointments: Far East Correspondent, Hong Kong, 1983-85; Moscow Correspondent, 1986-88; Foreign Affairs Correspondent, working in Middle East, Balkans and Eastern Europe, 1987-97; Diplomatic Editor, BBC TV News, 1997-. Publications: "I counted them all out and I counted them all back": The Battle for the Falklands (with Robert Fox), 1982; The Day That Shook the World (Essays on 9/11 by BBC journalists), 2002. Honours: Reporter of the Year, Royal Television Society, 1982; Richard Dimbleby Award, British Academy of Film and Television Arts (BAFTA), 1982; Honorary Doctorates, Essex University, Middlesex University. Memberships: Chicken Shed Theatre Trust; Royal Institute of International Affairs; Royal United Services Institute; Frontline Club. Address: c/o BBC TV News, Television Centre, Wood Lane, London W12 7RJ, England.

HANS-ADAM II (His Serene Highness Prince Hans-Adam II of Liechtenstein), b. 14 February 1945, Vaduz, Liechtenstein. m. Marie Kinsky von Wchinitz und Tettau, 3 sons, 1 daughter. Education: Advanced Level Diploma and Abitur Certificate, Grammar School, Zuoz, 1960-65; Licentiate Degree, Management and Economics, University of St Gallen, 1965-69. Appointments: Bank trainee, London, England; Undertook reorganisation of management and administration of assets belonging to the Princely House, 1970; Appointed permanent deputy to Prince Franz Joseph II, 1984; Assumed regency, 1989; Transferred executive power to Hereditary Prince Alois, 2004. Address: Schloss Vaduz, FL-9490 Vaduz, Fürstentum, Liechtenstein.

HANSON Albert L, b. 9 July 1952, Gainesville, Florida, USA. Physicist; Engineer. m. Anta LoPiccolo, 2 sons. Education: BS with Honors, Engineering Honors Program, North Carolina State University, 1974; MSE, 1976, PhD, 1979, University of Michigan. Appointments: Research Associate, 1979-81, from Assistant Physicist to Physicist, 1981-, Brookhaven National Laboratory, Upton, New York,

USA. Publications: Contributed more than 60 articles to professional journals; 10 Reports for the US Government. Honour: Co-recipient, Research and Development 100 Award, 1988. Memberships: American Nuclear Society; American Association for the Advancement of Science; International Radiation Physics Society. Address: Brookhaven National Laboratory, Department of Energy Sciences and Technology, Building 130, Upton, NY 11973, USA. E-mail: alh@bnl.gov

HANSON Curtis, b. 24 March 1945, Los Angeles, USA. Film Director; Screenplay Writer. Partner: Rebecca Yeldham, 1 son. Career: Editor, Cinema magazine; Began film career as screenplay writer; Director, films: The Arousers, 1970; Sweet Kill (also screenplay), 1972; Little Dragons (also co-producer), 1977; Losin' It, 1983; The Bedroom Window (also screenplay), 1988; Bad Influence, 1990; The Hand That Rocks the Cradle, 1992; The River Wild, 1994; LA Confidential, 1998; The Children of Times Square (TV film); Wonder Boys, 1999; 8 Mile, 2002; In Her Shoes, 2005; Lucky You, 2007. Screenplays: The Dunwich Horror, 1970; The Silent Partner, 1978; White Dog, 1982; Never Cry Wolf, 1983; Television: Hitchcock: Shadow of A Genius, 1999. Honours: Academy Award, LA Confidential, 1998. Address: United Talent Agency, 9560 Wilshire Boulevard, Floor 5, Beverly Hills, CA 90212, USA.

HARA Keishiro, b. 4 August 1975, Kumamoto, Japan. Associate Professor. Education: BS, Engineering, 1999, MS, 2001, PhD, 2004, Environmental Studies, University of Tokyo. Appointments: Researcher, Institute for Global Environmental Strategies, 2004-06; Assistant Professor, 2006-09, Associate Professor, 2009-10, RISS, Osaka University; Associate Professor, CEIDS, Osaka University, 2010-. Publications: Numerous articles in professional journals including: Book chapter, Establishing a Resource-Circulating Society in Asia, 2010. Honours: Fellowship, Academic Frontiers Student Exchange Promotion Program, 2003; Top Reviewer Award, Waste Management Journal, 2009; others. Memberships: Public Policy Studies Association, Japan; Center for Environmental Information Science, Japan. Address: Osaka University, Research Institute for Sustainability Science, Centre for Advanced Science and Innovation, 6F, 2-1 Yamada-oka, Saita, Osaka, 565-0871, Japan. E-mail: hara@riss.osaka-u.ac.jp

HARADA Julio, b. 12 June 1948, São Paulo, Brazil. Mechanical Engineer. m. Fatima Regina, 1 son, 1 daughter. Education: Degree in Engineering, Faculty of Technology, Universidade Estadual Paulista, 1972; Specialisation in Industrial Management, University of São Paulo, 1982; Plastics Specialisation, Osaka Municipal Technical Research Institute, 1982; Specialisation in Foreign Trade, Universidade Paulista, São Paulo, 1988. Appointments: Production Manager, Dixie SA; Technical Services Manager, Monsanto SA; Technical Service & Development Manager, BASF SA. Publications: Book, Injection Moulding: Projects and Basic Principles. Honours: Best Project Award for Latin America, Monsanto Co; Polymers Technology Award, Brazilian Polymers Association (ABPol), 2007. Memberships: ABPol; Society of Plastic Engineers. Address: Avenida Brigadeiro Faria Lima, 3600, São Paulo, SP, CEP: 04538-132, Brazil. E-mail: julio.harada@basf.com

HARAGUCHI Takashi, b. 8 May 1969, Tamano city, Okayama, Japan. Physician; Researcher of Clinical Science. m. Yuko, 2 sons, 1 daughter. Education: Medical Diplomate, Tokushima University, 1995; PhD, Okayama University, 2001. Appointments: Head Physician, Onomichi Municipal Hospital, Onomichi, Hiroshima, 2001-06; Head Physician, Minami-Okayama Medical Center, Tsukubo-gun, Okayama, 2006-. Publications: An autopsy case of postencephalitic parkinsonism of von Economo type: some new observations concerning neurofibrillary tangles and astrocytic tangles, 2000; Diffuse neurofibrillary tangles with calcification (a form of dementia): X-ray spectrometric evidence of lead accumulation in calcified regions, 2001; Lead content of brain tissue in diffuse neurofibrillary tangles with calcification (DNTC): the possibility of lead neurotoxicity, 2001; Coexistance of Creutzfeldt-Jakob disease, Lewy body disease, and Alzheimer's disease pathology: an autopsy case showing typical clinical features of Creutzfeldt-Jakob disease, 2009; Coexistance of TDP-43 and tau pathology in neurodegeneration with brain iron accumulation type 1 (NBIA-1, formerly Hallervorden-Spatz syndrome), 2011. Memberships: Japanese Society of Neuropathology; Japan Society for Dementia Research; Japanese Society of Neurology. Address: Department of Neurology, Minami-Okayama Medical Center, 4066 Hayashima-cho, Tsukubo-gun, Okayama 701-0304, Japan. E-mail: haraguchit@s-okayama.hosp.go.jp

HARARY Keith, b. 9 February 1953, New York, USA. Research Scientist; Writer; Science Journalist. Education: BA, Psychology, Duke University, 1975; PhD, Union Institute, 1986. Appointments: Research Consultant, American Society for Psychical Research, 1971-72; Crisis Counselor, Durham Mental Health Centre, 1972-76; Research Associate, Psychical Research Foundation, 1972-76; Research Associate, Department of Psychiatry, Maimonides Medical Centre, Brooklyn, 1976-79; Director of Counseling, Human Freedom Center, Berkeley, California, 1979; Research Consultant, SRI International, Menlo Park, California, 1980-82; Visiting Researcher, USSR Academy of Sciences, 1983; Design Consultant, Atari Corp, Sunnyvale, California, 1983-85; Lecturer in field; Adjunct Professor, Antioch University, San Francisco, 1985-86; Guest Lecturer, Lyceum School for Gifted Children, 1985-89; President, Research/Executive Director, Institute for Advanced Psychology, 1986-; Freelance Science Journalist, 1988-; Science Applications International Corp, 1991-93; Invited Lecturer, Duke University, 1995; Editor at Large, Omni Magazine, 1996-98; Senior Vice President, Research Director, Capital Access, 1996-2001; Psychological Consultant, National Media Spokesperson for Budget Rent A Car Corp, 1997-99; Psychological Consultant, Microsoft Corp, 1998-99; Executive Vice President, Owl's Pals, 2003-; Editorial Director, Netsplorer, 2004-. Publications: Author: Owl Pals Children's Book Series 2007-; Co-author, The Mind Race, 1984, 1985; 30-Day Altered States of Consciousness Series, 1989-91, revised edition 1999; Co-author, Who Do You Think You Are? Explore Your Many Sided Self with the Berkeley Personality Profile, 1994, revised edition, 2005, CD-ROM edition 1996; Monthly Columnist, Omni Mind Brain Lab in Omni Magazine, 1995-98; Contributor of over 100 articles to professional journals and other publications. Memberships: American Psychological Association; Association for Media Psychology; American Society for Psychical Research. Address: PO Box 4601, Portland, OR 97208, USA.

HARBOUR Malcolm John Charles, b. 19 February 1947, Woking, Surrey, England. Member of the European Parliament. m. Penny Johnson, 2 daughters. Education: MA, Mechanical Engineering, Trinity College, Cambridge; Diploma in Management Studies, University of Aston in Birmingham. Appointments: Engineering Apprentice, 1967; Designer and Development Engineer, 1969-72, Product Planning Manager, Rover-Triumph, 1972-76, Project Manager, Medium Cars, 1976-80, Director, Business Planning, Austin

Rover, 1980-82, Director Marketing, 1982-84, Director, Sales UK and Ireland, 1984-86, Director, Overseas Sales, 1986-89, BMC, Longbridge; Established Harbour Wade Brown, Motor Industry Consultants, 1989-; Jointly founded ICDP (International Car Distribution Programme), 1993; Co-Founder and Project Director, 3 Day Car Programme, 1998-99; Conservative Member of the European Parliament for the West Midlands, 1999-, Re-elected 2004-09; Committee Chairman: Internal Market and Consumer Protection, 2009; Co-Chairman, European Forum for the Automobile and Society, 1999-2009; Chairman, European Ceramics Industry Forum; Governor, European Internet Foundation; Chairman, Conservative Technology Forum, 2003-11; Leader of European Parliament Delegation to the World Summit on the Information Society, 2003; Member, EP delegation, 2005; Global Internet Governance Forums, 2006-07; EPP-ED Group Co-ordinator, International Market and Consumer Protection Committee, 2004-09; Vice President, Science and Technology Options Assessment (STOA), 2004-; Member, Lisbon Strategy Co-ordinating Committee, 2004-09; Member, High Level Working Group on the Car Industry. Publications: Winning Tomorrow's Customers, 1997; Many car industry reports. Honours: Honorary DSc, Aston University, 2008. Memberships: FRSA; CEng; MIMechE; FIMI; Solihull Conservative Association, 1972-, Former Chairman, Solihull Constituency; Guardian, Birmingham Assay Office. Address: 285 Kenilworth Road, Balsall Common, Coventry, CV7 7EL, England. E-mail: malcolm.harbour@europal.europa.eu

HARCOURT Geoffrey (Colin), b. 27 June 1931, Melbourne, Australia. Academic; Professor Emeritus; Economist; Writer. m. Joan Margaret Bartrop, 30 July 1955, 2 sons, 2 daughters. Education: BCom, Honours, 1954, MCom, 1956, University of Melbourne; PhD, 1960, LittD, 1988, Cambridge University. Appointments: Professor Emeritus, University of Adelaide, 1988; President, Jesus College, Cambridge, 1988-89, 1990-92; Reader in the History of Economic Theory, Cambridge University, 1990-98; Emeritus Reader, History of Economic Theory, Cambridge, 1998-; Emeritus Fellow, Jesus College, Cambridge, 1998-. Publications: Economic Activity (with P H Karmel and R H Wallace), 1967; Readings in the Concept and Measurement of Income (editor with R H Parker), 1969; Some Cambridge Controversies in the Theory of Capital, 1972; Theoretical Controversy and Social Significance: An Evaluation of the Cambridge Controversies, 1975; The Microeconomic Foundations of Macroeconomics (editor), 1977; The Social Science Imperialists (selected essays), 1982; Keynes and His Contemporaries: The Sixth and Centennial Keynes Seminar Held in the University of Kent at Canterbury (editor), 1985; Controversies in Political Economy (selected essays), 1986; International Monetary Problems and Supply-Side Economics: Essays in Honour of Lorie Tarshis (editor with Jon S Cohen), 1986; On Political Economists and Modern Political Economy (selected essays), 1992; The Dynamics of the Wealth of Nations. Growth, Distribution and Structural Change. Essays in Honour of Luigi Pasinetti (co-editor with Mauro Baranzini), 1993; Post-Keynesian Essays in Biography: Portraits of Twentieth Century Political Economists, 1993; Income and Employment in Theory and Practice (editor with Alessandro Roncaglia and Robin Rowley), 1994; Capitalism, Socialism and Post-Keynesianism: Selected Essays, 1995; A "Second Edition" of The General Theory (editor, with P A Riach), 2 volumes, 1997; 50 Years a Keynesian and Other Essays, 2001; Selected Essays on Economic Policy, 2001; L'Economie rebelle de Joan Robinson, editor, 2001; Joan Robinson: Critical Assessments of Leading Economists, 5 volumes (editor with Prue Kerr), 2002; Editing Economics: Essays in Honour of Mark Perlman (co-editor), 2002; Joan Robinson (co-author), 2009. Contributions to: Many books and scholarly journals. Honours: Fellow, Academy of the Social Sciences in Australia (FASSA), 1971; President, Economic Society of Australia and New Zealand, 1974-77; Officer in the General Division of the Order of Australia (AO), 1994; Economic Society of Australia, Distinguished Fellow, 1996; Honorary DLitt, De Montfort University, 1997; Honorary Fellow, Queen's College, University of Melbourne, 1998; Honorary DComm, Melbourne, 2003; Hon D.h.c.rer.pol., University of Fribourg, Switzerland, 2003; Academician of the Academy of Learned Societies for the Social Sciences (AcSS), 2003; Distinguished Fellow, History of Economics Society, USA, 2004; Honorary Member, European Society for the History of Economic Thought, 2004. Memberships: Royal Economic Society. Address: Jesus College, Cambridge CB5 8BL, England.

HARCOURT Richard David, b. 17 September 1931, Melbourne, Australia. Quantum Chemist. m. Alison Grant Doig, 1 son, 1 daughter. Education: Ripponlea State School, Melbourne, 1938-42; Wesley College, Melbourne, 1943-48; BSc, 1949-51, Dip Ed, 1952, MSc, 1958-60, Melbourne University; PhD, Monash University, 1961-62. Appointments: Victorian Education Department, Box Hill and Sale Technical Schools, 1953-55; Overseas Travel, 1957; Postdoctoral Research Fellow, 1963-64, Lecturer/Senior Lecturer, 1965-93, Research Fellow, 1994-96, Honorary Research Fellow, 1997-2011, School of Chemistry, University of Melbourne. Publications: Book: Qualitative Valence Bond Descriptions of Electron-Rich Molecules: Pauling "3-Electron Bonds" and "Increased-Valence" Theory, 1982; 170 papers and articles including: Bohr Circular Orbit Diagrams for some Fluorine Containing Molecules, 2006; Atomic Shell Structure People Identity: Pauli + Schrödinger = Heisenberg + Bohr, (online comment) 2007; Increased-Valence or Electronic Hypervalence for Symmetrical Three-Centre Molecular Orbital Configurations, 2007; Pauling Three-Electron Bonds and Increased-Valence Structures as Components of the "Intellectual Heritage" of Qualitative Valence Bond Theory, 2008; Quantum Chemistry Formulae for Atomic Shell Structure, Separation of Variables, Valence, Hartree-Fock/ Hückel Orbitals and Electron Transfer Matrix Element, 2008. Memberships: Royal Australian Chemical Institute. Address: School of Chemistry, The University of Melbourne, Victoria 3010, Australia. E-mail: r.harcourt@unimelb.edu.au

HARDAS Anant Prabhakar, b. 18 August 1948, Nagpur, India. Pharmacist; Educationalist; Editor; Writer & Publisher. m. Lalita, 1 son, 1 daughter. Education: M Pharm, DBM, AIC (PhD), Nagpur University. Appointments: Founder/ Director, Indian Pharma Guidance Academy, Nagpur. Publications: 5 books; 1 bibliography; 1 directory; 10 research papers; 35 educational articles, view points and reviews; Editor, Pharmacists Times. Honours: Government Nominee, CPCSCA Body, Government of India, Ministry of Environment & Forest for AHF & IAEC activities; 1st pharmacist to offer to donate body posthumously for nearest medical college; 1st pharmacist deputed to attend CYPMC meeting, London, 2000; First Indian pharmacist who offered body donation; Pioneer of Slide Show on History of Indian Pharmacy; M Fule Fellowship Award, New Delhi, 2009; Listed in various international biographical dictionaries. Memberships: Indian Pharma Association; Association of Pharmacy Teachers of India; Indian Pharmacy Graduates Association; Indian Science Teachers Association; IHPA; IPS; ISP; ISTE; ISEC; ISCA; AIC; British Society for History of Pharmacy; Commonwealth Pharma Association; Drug Information Association; American Society of Health System Pharmacist; Canadian Society of Hospital Pharmacist;

Recipient, Mahatma Jyotiba Phule Scholarship Award, Dalit Sahitya Academy, New Delhi, 2009. Address: Indian Pharma Guidance Academy, 52 Madhav Nagar, Nagpur 440010 (MS), India. E-mail: profaphardas@rediffmail.com Website: www.nagpurpharmaguidance.com

HARDINGHAM Michael, b. 16 October 1939, Birmingham, England. Ear Nose & Throat Specialist. m. Ellen, 1 son, 1 daughter. Education: West House School, Edgbaston, 1953; Solihull School, Warwickshire, 1958; MB BS, University of London, St Mary's Hospital, 1963. Appointments: St Mary's, Paddington; Royal Marsden Hospital, South Kensington; Royal Hospital for Sick Children, Edinburgh; Childrens Hospital, Gothenburg, Sweden; Consultant Ear Nose & Throat Specialist, Cheltenham & Gloucester, 1974-. Publications: Numerous articles on wide variety of ENT conditions in British and American journals; Chapters in Otolaryngological Clinics of North America. Honours: Fellow, Royal Colleges of Surgeons, Edinburgh and England; Life Fellow, Royal Society of Medicine; Honorary Fellow, British Medical Association. Memberships: British Association of Head & Neck Oncologists; Nurses Association of Midland Institute of Otorhinolaryngology; South Western Laryngological Association; Midland Institute of Otorhinolaryngology; Gloucester Division of BMA. Address: Little Ashley, Ashley Road, Cheltenham, GL52 6QE, England.

HARDISH Patrick, b. Perth Amboy, New Jersey, USA. Librarian; Composer. Education: BA, Queens College, CUNY, 1976; MS, Pratt Institute, 1981; Juilliard School, 1969-72; Columbia University, graduate work, 1978-80; Bennington College composition seminar, 1980. Appointments: Library Assistant V, Columbia University, 1978-84; Co-Director and Co-Founder, Composers Concordance and its New Music Now Series, 1983-; Senior Librarian, New York Public Library, 1984-2007; Editorial Board, New Music Connoisseur, 1994-2008; Virginia Center for Creative Arts: Fellowships, 1981, 1982, 1986, 1988; Guest Composer Lectures, New York University, 2000. Publications: Reviews in music journal, Notes, 1985, 1994; Accordioclusterville (for Accordian), 1985; Article on-line, 1999; Music: Sonorities VI (for Vibraphone), 2004; Sonorities VII (for Clarinet), 2004; Duo (for Piano and Percussion), 2005; Sonorities VIII (for Timpani), 2008; Recording: Solo for Pete (for drum set), on the CD Ballets & Solos, 2010. Honours: Meet the Composer awards, 1978, 1982 (2x), 1983, 1991, 1997; Margaret Fairbank-Jory Copying Assistance Program from the American Music Center; Eucharistic Minister, Holy Spirit Church, Perth Amboy, New Jersey, 2008-; Lectures: Many radio and television interviews. Memberships: American Music Center; Music Library Association (and its New York Chapter); International Big Band Society; New York Library Club; North American Guild of Change Ringers; New York Public Library Retirees Association; North American British Music Association. Address: PO Box 3620548, New York, NY 10129, USA. E-mail: pathardish@hotmail.com

HARDWICK David Francis, b. 24 January 1934, Vancouver, Canada. Pathologist; Professor. m. Margaret M, 1 son, 2 daughters. Education: MD, University of British Columbia, 1950-57. Appointments: Research Associate, Paediatrics, University of Southern California, 1960-62; Clinical Instructor, Pathology, 1963-65, Assistant Professor, Pathology, 1965-69, Associate Professor, Pathology, 1969-74, Professor, Pathology, 1974-99, Professor and Head, Pathology, 1976-90, Honorary Associate Professor, Paediatrics, 1972-87, Honorary Professor, Paediatrics, 1974-99, Special Advisor Planning, Medicine, 1997-, Professor Emeritus, Pathology and Paediatrics, 1999-, University of British Columbia; Secretary, International Academy of Pathology, 2006. Publications: Author and co-author of numerous refereed journals; books; chapters; abstracts; reports. Honours include: Certificate of Merit, Master Teacher Awards; University of British Columbia Teaching Excellence Award; Canadian Silver Jubilee Medal, 1978; President's Award for service to the University of British Columbia; LLD honoris causa, University of British Columbia, 2001; Senior Member, Canadian Medical Association, 2002; Gold Medal, International Academy of Pathology, 2002; President's Award, US and Canadian Academy of Pathology, 2004; Bartholomew Mosse Memorial Lecturer, Dublin, 2004; Lifetime Achievement Award, UBC Alumni Association, 2007; Award of Excellence, British Columbia College of Physicians and Surgeons, 2008. Memberships include: BC Association of Pathologists; Canadian Association of Pathologists; Society for Paediatric Pathology; Secretary, International Academy of Pathology, 2006. Address: Dean's Office, Faculty of Medicine, University of British Columbia, #317-2194 Health Sciences Mall, Vancouver, British Columbia, Canada V6T 1Z3. E-mail: david.f.hardwick@ubc.ca

HARDY Alan William, b. 10 March 1951, Luton, Bedfordshire, England. Teacher; Poet. m. Sibylle Mory, 1985, 1 daughter. Education: BA, English and Italian Literature, 1973, MA, Comparative Literature, 1976, Warwick University; Dip TEFL, Christ Church College, Kent University, 1983. Appointments: English Teacher, Sir Joseph Williamson's Mathematical School, Rochester, Kent; English Language Teacher, Whitehill Estate School of English, Flamstead, Hertfordshire. Publications: Wasted Leaves, 1996; I Went With Her, 2007. Contributions to: Orbis; Envoi; Iota; Poetry Nottingham; The Interpreter's House; South; Poetic Licence; Braquemard; Fire; Borderlines. Honour: 2nd Prize, Hastings National Poetry Competition, 1994. Address: Whitehill Estate School of English, Flamstead, St Albans, Hertfordshire AL3 8EY, England.

HARDY John Philips, b. 1 January 1933, Brisbane, Queensland, Australia. Retired Professor. m. Patricia, 3 sons, 1 daughter. Education: BA (Hons), Latin Language and Literature, University of Queensland, 1955; BA (Hons), English Language and Literature, University of Oxford, 1959; MA, D Phil (Oxon), 1965. Appointments: Assistant Professor, University of Toronto, 1965-66; Professor, English, University of New England, 1966-72; Professor, English, Australian National University, 1972-85; Honorary Secretary, Australian Academy of the Humanities, 1981-88; Dean, Humanities and Social Sciences, 1988-89, Professor, Humanities, 1989-95, Bond University. Publications: Reinterpretations, 1971; Samuel Johnson: A Critical Study, 1979; Jane Austen's Heroines, 1985; Editions of Johnson's Political Writings, Rasselas, and Lives of the Poets; Stories of Australian Migration, 1988. Honours: Queensland Rhodes Scholar, 1957; Senior Demy, Magdalen College, 1961-62; Fellow by Examination, Magdalen College, 1962-65; Australian Centenary Medal, 2001. Memberships: Johnson Society of London. Address: PO Box 9593, Deakin, ACT 2600, Australia.

HARDY Robert, b. 29 October 1925. Actor; Author. m. (1) Elizabeth Fox, 1952-1956 (divorced) 1 son, (2) Sally Pearson, 1961-1986 (divorced), 2 daughters. Career: Theatre appearances include: 4 seasons of Shakespeare, Stratford-on-Avon, 2 at Old Vic; World tours include Henry V and Hamlet, USA; Numerous appearances London and Broadway theatres, 1952-; Winston Churchill in Celui qui a dit Non, Palais des Congres, Paris,

1999-2000; Writer and/or presenter numerous TV programmes including The Picardy Affair, The History of the Longbow, Heritage, Horses in Our Blood, Gordon of Khartoum; Other TV appearances include; Prince Hal and Henry V in Age of Kings; Prince Albert in Edward VII; Malcolm Campbell in Speed King; Winston Churchill in the Wilderness Years; Siegfried Farnon in All Creatures Great and Small; Twiggy Rathbone and Russell Spam in Hot Metal; The Commandant in the Far Pavilions; Sherlock Holmes; Inspector Morse; Middlemarch; Castle Ghosts; Gulliver's Travels; Grand Charles, Le; Murder on the Orient Express, 2008. Films include: How I Won the War; Yellow Dog; Dark Places; Young Winston; Ten Rillington Place; Le Silencieux; Gawain and the Green Knight; The Spy Who Came in From the Cold; La Gifle; Robin Hood; The Shooting Party; Paris By Night; War and Remembrance; Mary Shelley's Frankenstein; Sense and Sensibility; Mrs Dalloway; The Tichborne Claimant, 1998; An Ideal Husband, 1999; The Gathering, 2001; Harry Potter and the Chamber of Secrets, 2002; Harry Potter and the Prisoner of Azkaban, 2004; Harry Potter and the Goblet of Fire, 2005; Lassie, 2005; Grand Charles. Le, 2005; Goodbye Mr Snuggles, 2006; Harry Potter and the Order of the Phoenix, 2007; Framed, 2008. Publications: Longbow, 1976; The Great War Bow, 2005. Honours: Hon DLitt (Reading), 1990; CBE; FSA. Memberships: Consultant, Mary Rose Trust, 1979-, Trustee, WWF, 1991-; Trustee, Royal Armouries, 1984-96; Master of Worshipful Company of Bowyers, 1988-90. Address: c/o Chatto & Linnit, 123A King's Road, London, SW3 4PL, England.

HARE David, b. 5 June 1947, St Leonards, Sussex, England. Dramatist; Director. m. (1) Margaret Matheson, 1970, divorced 1980, 2 sons, 1 daughter, (2) Nicole Farhi, 1992. Education: Lancing College; MA, Honours, Jesus College, Cambridge. Appointments: Founder, Portable Theatre, 1968, Joint Stock Theatre Group, 1975, Greenpoint Films, 1982; Literary Manager and Resident Dramatist, Royal Court, 1969-71; Resident Dramatist, Nottingham Playhouse, 1973; Associate Director, National Theatre, 1984-88, 1989-. Plays: Slag, 1970; The Great Exhibition, 1972; Knuckle, Brassneck, 1974; Fanshen, Teeth 'n' Smiles, 1976; Plenty, Licking Hitler, 1978; Dreams of Leaving, 1980; A Map of the World, 1982; Saigon, 1983; The History Plays, 1984; Pravda, Wetherby, 1985; The Asian Plays, The Bay at Nice and Wrecked Eggs, 1986; The Secret Rapture, 1988; Paris by Night, 1989; Straples, Racing Demon, 1990; Writing Lefthanded, Heading Home, The Early Plays, Murmuring Judges, 1991; The Absence of War, Asking Around, 1993; Skylight, Mother Courage, Skylight, 1995; Ivanov, 1996; Amy's View, 1997; The Judas Kiss, The Blue Room, Via Dolorosa, 1998; My Zinc Bed, Royal Court, Via Dolorosa, 2000; The Hours, Lee Miller, 2001; The Breath of Life, 2002; The Permanent Way, 2003; Stuff Happens, 2004; The Corrections, 2005; My Zinc Bed, The Reader, 2008. Honours: John Llewellyn Rhys Award, 1974; BAFTA Award, 1978; New York Drama Critics' Circle Award, 1983; London Standard Award, 1985; Plays and Players Awards, 1985, 1990; Drama Award, 1988; Olivier Award, 1990; Critic's Circle Best Play of the Year, 1990; Time Out Award, 1990. Membership: Royal Society of Literature, fellow.

HARE John Neville, b. 11 December 1934, Bexhill, England. Explorer; Writer. m. Philippa, 3 daughters. Education: ABU, University of Zaria, Nigeria, 1957; Diploma, Administration/Law. Appointments: District Officer, Colonial Service, Northern Nigeria, 1957-64; Director, Macmillan Publishers, 1965-75; Consultant, Hodder and Stoughton Publishers, 1975-89; United National Environment Programme, 1989-96; Founder, Wild Camel Protection Foundation, 1996-. Publications: The Lost Camels of Tartary, 1998; Shadows Across the Sahara, 2003; Mysteries of the Gobi, 2009; 32 books for children on environmental issues; Over 50 articles on the wild camel and expeditions in the Gobi and Saharan Deserts. Honours: Ness Award, Royal Geographical Society, 2004; Lawrence of Arabia Memorial Medal, Royal Society of Asian Affairs, 2004; Mungo Park Medal, Royal Scottish Geographical Society, 2006; Lowell Thomas Award, Explorers Club, 2010. Memberships: Reform Club. Address: School Farm, Benenden, Kent TN17 4EU, England. E-mail: harecamel@aol.com Website: www.wildcamels.com

HARFOUSH Adel, b. 2 December 1947, Chahba, Syria. Lecturer. m. Samira Alzughayar, 1 son, 2 daughters. Education: BSc, Damascus University, Syria, 1973; DEA, 1976, Doctorat 3rd Cycle, 1978, PhD, 1981, Louis Pasteur University, France. Appointments: Teacher, Physics and Chemistry, secondary schools, Syria, 1970-74; Part time Lecturer, Technology of Chemistry, 1978-79, General Chemistry, 1979-80, University Institute for Technology, France; Part time Supervisor, General Diploma in Biology, Louis Pasteur University, 1976-81; Part time Lecturer, Spectroscopy, 1982-83, Inorganic Chemistry, 1984-85, Damascus University, Syria; Officer in Charge, Mass Spectrometry Laboratory, 1985-88, Deputy Head, Chemistry Department, 1987-88, Head, Microanalysis Division, 1988-92, Translator, Aalam Al-Zarra journal, 1992-94, Syrian Atomic Energy Commission, Syria; Head, Chemical Synthesis Division, 1994-98, Head, Physical Chemistry Division, 1998-2003, Head, Translation, Authorship and Publication Office, 2003-10, Editor-in-Chief, Aalam Al-Zarra journal, 2004-10, Research Director, Chemistry Department, 2005-10, Atomic Energy Commission of Syria; Part time Lecturer, Organic Chemistry, Syrian International Private University for Science and Technology, Damascus, 2008-10. Publications: More than 50 articles in professional journals. Honours: Member, World Forum of Researchers and Inventors; IFIA Scientific Gold Medal, 2009. Address: PO Box 6091, Damascus, Syria. E-mail: aharfoush2@yahoo.com

HARIHAR Abdulazizkhan, b. 25 July 1966, Shiralkoppa, Karnatak, India. Professor. 1 son, 1 daughter. Education: MSc, Chemistry, 1989; PhD, Chemistry, 2001. Appointments: Lecturer, degree college, 1991; Senior Lecturer, 2004; Professor, 2007; Professor, Chemistry, Kittel Science College, Dharwad. Publications: 30 research papers; 3 research projects. Honours: Listed in international biographical dictionaries. Memberships: Journal of Indian Chemical Society; Journal of Biotechniques; Research guide for MPhil and PhD degree. Address: Department of Chemistry, Kittel Science College, Dharwad – 580001, Karnatak, India. E-mail: harihar_al@yahoo.co.in

HARJO Joy, b. 9 May 1951, Tulsa, Oklahoma, USA. 1 son, 1 daughter. Education: BA, University of New Mexico 1976; MFA, University of Iowa, 1978; Non-degree, Film-making, Anthropology, Film Centre, 1982; Native Screenwriters Workshop, Sundance Institute, 1998; Summer Songwriting Workshop, Berklee School of Music, 1998. Appointments: Assistant Professor, Department of English, University of Colorado, 1985-88; Associate Professor, Department of English, University of Arizona, 1988-90; Professor, Department of English, University of New Mexico, 1991-97; President, Mekko Production Inc, 1992-; Visiting Writer, UCLA Department of English, 1998; Professor, UCLA, 2001-; Joseph M Russo Professor of Creative Writing, University of New Mexico, 2005-. Publications: She Had Some Horses, 1985; Secrets from the Centre of the World, 1989; In Mad Love & War, 1990; The Woman Who Fell From the Sky, 1994; Reinventing the Enemy's Language; A Map To The Next World, poems and tales, 2000; The Good Luck Cat, children's book, 2000; How We Became Human, New and Selected Poems, W W Norton, 2002; Co-author, A Thousand Roads (signature film of The National Museum of The American Indian), 2005; CDs: Native Joy for Real, Joy Harjo, Mekko Prod; Letter from the End of the 20th Century, music and poetry with her band Joy Harjo and Poetic Justice, 1997; Native Joy for Real, 2006; She Had Some Horses, 2006; Winding Through the Milky Way, 2008; For a Girl Becoming, 2009; CD: Red Dreams, A Trail Beyond Tears, 2010. Honours: National Council on the Arts; The London Observer Best Book of 1997 (Reinventing the Enemy's Language); Lila Wallace Reader's Digest Writers Award, 1998-2000; Honorary Doctorate, St Mary-in-the-Woods College, 1998; First American in the Arts, Outstanding Medal of Achievement, 1998; Lifetime Achievement in the Arts, National Writers Circle of America; Western Literature Distinguished Achievement Award, 2000; Oklahoma Book Arts Lifetime Achievement, 2002; US Artists Award Rasmusm, 2008; New Mexico Music Award, 2008. Membership: Board of Directors, Russell Moore Foundation; Board of Directors, Arts Research; Board of Directors, Native Arts & Cultures Foundation. Address: Mekko Productions Inc, 3939 Rio Grande Blvd NW #7, Albuquerque, New Mexico 87107, USA.

HARMAN Nigel, b. 11 August 1973, Purley, England. Actor. Education: Dulwich College, London; Rosslyn School of Drama, London. Career: Theatre: Mamma Mia; Three Sisters; A Midsummer Night's Dream; Guys and Dolls; The Caretaker; TV: Eastenders, 2003-05; The Outsiders, 2006; Blood Diamond, 2006; City of Vice, 2008; Lark Rise to Candleford, 2008; The Friday Night Club, 2009; Plus One, 2009; Hotel Babylon, 2009. Honours: Best Newcomer at the National Television Awards, 2003.

HARNICK Sheldon Mayer, b. 30 April 1924, Chicago, Illinois, USA. Lyricist. m. (1) Mary Boatner, 1950, (2) Elaine May, 1962, (3) Margery Gray, 1965, 1 son, 1 daughter. Education: Northwestern University. Career: Contributor to revues: New Faces of 1952; Two's Company, 1953; John Murray Anderson's Almanac, 1954; The Shoestring Revue, 1955; The Littlest Revue, 1956; Shoestring 1957, 1957; with composer Jerry Bock: Body Beautiful, 1958; Fiorello, 1959; Tenderloin, 1960; Smiling The Boy Fell Dead (with David Baker), 1961; She Loves Me, 1963; Fiddler On The Roof, 1964; The Apple Tree, 1966; The Rothschilds, 1970; Captain Jinks Of The Horse Marines (opera with Jack Beeson), 1975; Rex (with Richard Rodgers), 1976; Dr Heidegger's Fountain Of Youth (opera with Jack Beeson), 1978; Gold (cantata with Joe Raposo), 1980; Translations: The Merry Widow, 1977; The Umbrellas Of Cherbourg, 1979; Carmen, 1981; A Christmas Carol, 1981; Songs Of The Auvergne (musical; book; lyrics), 1982; The Appeasement of Aeolus, 1990; Cyrano, 1994. Address: Kraft, Haiken & Bell, 551 Fifth Avenue, 9th Floor, New York, NY 10176, USA.

HAROON Abdullah Hussain Saeed, b. 21 October 1950, Karachi, Pakistan. Businessman. Education: BA, Karachi University, 1970. Appointments: Co-ordinator, Pakistan Muslim League, 1970; Councillor, Karachi Metropolitan Corporation (KMC), 1979-85; Trustee, Karachi Port Trust, 1980-82; Speaker, Provincial Assembly of Sindh, 1985-86; Member, Sindh Provincial Assembly, 1985-88; Leader of Opposition, Sindh Assembly, 1986-88; Consultant, Pakistan Herald Publication, 1988-89; Delegate, UN General Assembly; Member, Board of Governors, Institute of Business Administration, Karachi, 1996-99; Director, Board of Directors, Karachi Electric Supply Corporation, 1997-99; President, Pakistan-China Business Forum, 1999-2004; Chairman, Griffith College, Karachi, 1999-2005; Permanent Representative of Pakistan to the United Nations, New York, 2008. Honours: International Order of Fellowship; World Lifetime Achievement Award. Memberships: General Secretary of the Sir Abdullah Haroon Association, Chief Organizer of the 27th Pakistan National Football Championships; Member of the Estate Committee, Karachi Port Trust; Vice President, Karachi Golf Club; Executive Board, English Speaking Union of Pakistan; Vice President, Pakistan Environmental Protection Council. Address: Seafield, Abdullah Haroon Road, Karachi, Pakistan.

HARPER Alison, b. 25 February 1964, Glasgow, Scotland. Artist. m. Andrew T Wamae, 1 son. Education: BA (1st class Hons), Fine Art, Glasgow School of Art, 1985; Postgraduate studies, Kunstakademie, Oslo, 1986; Post-Diploma in Fine Art (1st class), MS University, Baroda, India, 1993-95. Career: Artist; Selected solo and group shows; Royal Academy; Royal Scottish Academy; National Portrait Gallery; Collin's Gallery; Leicester City Art Gallery; Nairobi Museum; Shetland Museum; Stirling Museum; India Today Gallery, New Delhi; Iwate Arts Festival, Kyoto, Japan; National Autumn Exhibition, Oslo; City Arts Centre, Edinburgh; Compass Gallery; Sahmet, New Delhi; 400 Women, London; Works held in public collections; Strathclyde University; Museum & Arts Loans Service; BBC Scotland; Glasgow School of Art; Book cover commissions; Lecturer, Glasgow School of Art, 1995-2001. Publications: Scottish Painting: 1837 to Present, 1990; Angels Wear Silver, 1995; Restoring Female Identity, Strategies by Scottish Female Artists, 1997; Introducing Scottish Culture & the Environment of Iwate, 1998; Tongues of Diamond, 1999; The Core of Attraction, 2002. Honours: John and Anna Laurie Bequest Travelling Scholarship, 1985; Norwegian Government Scholarship, 1985; Lady Artists' Trust Award, 1988; Commonwealth Scholarship, 1993-95; Cheltenham National Drawing Competition Prize, 1998; Ruth Davidson Memorial Award, 1998; The Prince of Wales Drawing Studio Bursary, 2001. Address: 47 Radborne Crescent, London E17 3RR, England.

HARRAN Don, b. 22 April 1936, Cambridge, USA. Professor. 1 son, 1 daughter. Education: BA, magna cum laude, French Literature, Yale University; MA, PhD, Musicology, University California, Berkeley, USA. Appointments: Faculty of Hebrew University, Jerusalem, Faculty of Humanities, Department of Musicology, 1966-; Artur Rubinstein Professor of Musicology, 1980-2003; Artur Rubinstein Professor Emeritus of Musicology, 2004-; 3 times Chairman, Department of Musicology; Chairman, Israel Musicological Society, 1978-80; Board of Directors, International Musicological Society, 1987-92; VP, International Musicological Society, 1992-97; Acting Director, Jewish Music Research Centre, Hebrew University, 1996-2000. Publications: The Anthologies of Black-Note Madrigals, 5 volumes in 6, 1978-81; Maniera e il madrigale, 1980; Hubert Naich: Collected Works, 1983; Word-Tone Relations in Musical Thought: From Antiquity to the 17th Century, 1986; In Search of Harmony: Hebrew and Humanist Elements in 16th-Century Musical Thought, 1988; In Defense of Music: The Case for Music as Argued by a Singer and Scholar of the Late 15th Century, 1989; Salamone Rossi, Jewish Musician in Late Renaissance Mantua, 1999, softcover reprint, 2003; Salamone Rossi: Complete Works, first 12 volumes, 1995, Volumes 13a-13b, 2003; Sarra Copia Sulam, Jewish Poet and Intellectual in 17th-Century Venice, 2009; more than 120 articles in professional journals and anthologies. Honours: Grants: Edmond de Rothschild Foundation; Israel National Academy of Sciences, 3 times;

American Philosophical Society; French Ministry of Culture; National Endowment Fund for the Humanities; Fellowships: American Council Learned Societies; Memorial Foundation Jewish Culture, 3 times; Newberry Library; Folger Institute; Institute for Advanced Study, Princeton, twice. Prizes: Tovey Memorial Prize, Oxford University, 1977; Medal, City of Tours, 1997; Guest Lecturer, Salzburg Seminar, 1997; Michael Landau Prize for Scholarly Achievement, 1999; Honorary Foreign Member of the American Academy of Arts and Sciences, 2005; Knight (Cavaliere) of the Order of the Star of Italian Solidarity, 2006; Corresponding (Honorary Foreign) Member, American Musicological Society, 2006; Honorary Member, AISG, 2009; Visiting Scholar, Centre for Medieval and Renaissance Studies, UCLA, twice. Address: PO Box 3154, Savyon 56540, Israel.

HARRELSON Woody, b. 23 July 1961, Midland, Texas, USA. Actor. m. (1) Nancy Simon, 1985 (divorced), (2) Laura Louie, 2008, 3 children. Education: Hanover College. Career: Theatre includes: The Boys Next Door; 2 on 2 (author, producer, actor); The Zoo Story (author, actor); Brooklyn Laundry; Furthest from the Sun; On An Average Day; TV includes: Cheers; Bay Coven; Killer Instinct; Films include: Wildcats; Cool Blue; LA Story; Doc Hollywood; Ted and Venus; White Men Can't Jump; Indecent Proposal; I'll Do Anything; The Cowboy Way; Natural Born Killers; Money Train; The Sunchaser; The People vs Larry Flint; Kingpin; Wag the Dog; The Thin Red Line; After the Sunset; The Big White; North Country; The Prize Winner of Defiance, Ohio; A Prairie Home Companion; Free Jimmy (voice); A Scanner Darkly; The Walker; No Country for Old Men; The Grand; Transsiberian; Sleepwalking; Battle in Seattle; Semi-Pro; EdTV; Play It to the Bone; American Saint; Scorched; Anger Management; She Hate Me; Seven Pounds; Zombieland; 2012. Address: c/o Creative Artists Agency, 9830 Wilshire Boulevard, Beverly Hills, CA 90212, USA.

HARRIES The Rt Revd Richard Douglas, Lord Harries of Pentregarth, b. 2 June 1936. Ecclesiastic. m. Josephine Bottomley, 1963, 1 son, 1 daughter. Education: Wellington College; Royal Military Academy, Sandhurst; Selwyn College, Cambridge; Cuddesdon College, Oxford. Appointments: Lieutenant, Royal Corps of Signals, 1955-58; Curate, Hampstead Parish Church, 1963-69; Chaplain, Westfield College, 1966-69; Lecturer, Wells Theological College, 1969-72; Warden of Wells, Salisbury and Wells Theological College, 1971-72; Vicar, All Saints, Fulham, London, 1972-81; Dean, King's College, London, 1981-87; Bishop of Oxford, 1987-2006; Vice-chair, Council of Christian Action, 1979-87; Council for Arms Control, 1982-87; Chair, Southwark Ordination Course, 1982-87; Shalom, End Loans to South Africa (ELSTA), 1982-87; Christian Evidence Society; Chair, Church of England Board of Social Responsibility, 1996-2001; Consultant to Archbishops on Jewish-Christian Relations, 1986-92; Chair, Council of Christians and Jews, 1993-2001; House of Lords Select Committee on Stem Cell Research, 2001-02; Visiting Professor, Liverpool Hope College, 2002; Member, Home Office Advisory Committee for Reform of Law on Sexual Offences, 1981-85; Board of Christian Aid, 1994-2001; Royal Commission on Lords Reform, 1999-; Nuffield Council of Bioethics, 2002-; Human Fertilisation and Embryology Authority, 2003-. Publications: Prayers of Hope, 1975; Turning to Prayer, 1978; Prayers of Grief and Glory, 1979; Being a Christian, 1981; Should Christians Support Guerrillas?, 1982; The Authority of Divine Love, 1983; Praying Around the Clock, 1983; Seasons of the Spirit (co-editor), 1984; Prayers and the Pursuit of Happiness, 1985; Reinhold Niebuhr and the Issues of Our Time (editor), 1986; Morning has Broken, 1985; Christianity and War in a Nuclear Age, 1986; C S Lewis: The Man and his God, 1987; Christ is Risen, 1988; Is There a Gospel for the Rich? 1992; Art and the Beauty of God, 1993; The Value of Business and its Values (co-author), 1993; The Read God, 1994; Questioning Faith, 1995; The Gallery of Reflections, 1995; In the Gladness of Today, 2000; Christianity: Two Thousand Years (co-editor), 2000; God Outside the Box: Why Spiritual People Object to Christianity, 2002; After the Evil: Christianity and Judaism in the Shadow of the Holocaust, 2003; Praying the Eucharist, 2004; The Passion in Art, 2004; Abraham's Children, 2005. Contributions to several books; Numerous articles. Honours: Fellow, Kings College, London, 1983; Sir Sigmund Sternberg Award, 1989; Honorary Fellow, Selwyn College, Cambridge; St Annes College, Oxford; Honorary Fellow, Academy of Medical Sciences, 2004; Fellow, Royal Society of Literature, 1996; Hon DD (London), 1996; Hon DUniv (Oxford Brookes), 2001; Hon DUniv, Open University; Life Peer, 2006; Honorary Professor of Theology, Kings College, London, 2006-. Address: The House of Lords, London SW1A 0PW, England.

HARRIS Angela Felicity (Baroness Harris of Richmond), b. 4 January 1944, St Annes-on-Sea, Lancashire, England. Member of the House of Lords. m. John Philip Roger Harris, 1 son from previous marriage. Education: Ealing Hotel and Catering College. Appointments: Member, Richmond Town Council, 1978-81, 1991-99, Mayor of Richmond, 1993-94; Member, 1979-89, Chairman, 1987-88, Richmondshire District Council; Member, 1981-2001, First Woman Chair, 1991-92, North Yorkshire County Council; Deputy Chair, Association of Police Authorities, 1997-2001; Chair, North Yorkshire Police Authority, 1994-2001; Appointed to House of Lords, 1999; Member, Refreshment Select Committee, 2000-, Member, EU Select Committee, 2000-04, Chair, EU Select Sub-Committee, 2000-04, House of Lords. Honours: Deputy Lieutenant of North Yorkshire, 1994; Created Liberal Democrat Life Peer, 1999. Memberships: Member, Court of the University of York, 1996-; Former Member: Service Authority, national Crime Squad, 1997-2000, Police Negotiating Board, 1995-2001; Former Justice of the Peace, 1982-98; Former, NHS Trust Non-Executive Director, 1990-97; President, National Association of Chaplains to the Police. Address: House of Lords, London, SW1A 0PW. E mail: harrisa@parliament.uk

HARRIS Edward Allen (Ed), b. 28 November 1950, Englewood, New Jersey, USA. Actor. m. Amy Madigan, 1983, 1 daughter. Education: Columbia University; University of Oklahoma, Norman; California Institute of Arts. Career: Stage appearances include: A Streetcar Named Desire; Sweetbird of Youth; Julius Caesar; Hamlet; Camelot; Time of Your Life; Grapes of Wrath; Present Laughter; Fool for Love; Prairie Avenue; Scar, 1985; Precious Sons, 1986; Simpatico, 1994; Taking Sides, 1996; Films include: Come, Borderline, 1978; Knightriders, 1980; Creepshow, 1981; The Right Stuff, Swing Shift, Under Fire, 1982; A Flash of Green, Places in the Heart, 1983; Alamo Bay, 1984; Sweet Dreams, Code Name: Emerald, 1985; Walker, 1987; To Kill a Priest, 1988; Jacknife, The Abyss, 1989; State of Grace, 1990; Paris Trout, 1991; Glengarry Glen Ross, 1992; Needful Things, The Firm, 1993; China Moon, Milk Money, 1994; Apollo 13, Just Cause, Eye for an Eye, 1995; The Rock, Riders of the Purple Sage, 1996; Absolute Power, 1997; Stepmom, The Truman Show, 1998; The Third Miracles, 1999; Enemy at the Gates, A Beautiful Mind, 2001; The Hours, 2002; Buffalo Soldiers, Masked and Anonymous, The Human Stain, Radio, 2003; Winter Passing, 2005; Dirt Nap, Copying Beethoven, 2006;

Gone Baby Gone, Cleaner, Winston, National Treasure: Book of Secrets, 2007; Touching Home, Appaloosa, 2008. TV films include: The Amazing Howard Hughes, 1977; The Seekers, 1979; The Aliens are Coming, 1980; The Last Innocent Man, 1987; Running Mates, 1992; The Stand, 1994. Address: 22031 Carbon Mesa Road, Malibu, CA 90265, USA.

HARRIS Emmylou, b. 2 April 1947, Birmingham, Alabama, USA. Singer. m. Tom Slocum, 1969 (divorced) 1 daughter, Brian Ahern, 1977-84 (divorced) 1 daughter, Paul Kennerley, 1985 (divorced). Education: UNC, Greensboro. Career: Toured with Fallen Angel Band; Performed across Europe, USA; Recording artist; Appeared in rock documentary, The Last Waltz. Compositions: Songs; Co-writer, co-producer, Ballad Of Sally Rose with Paul Kennerley, 1985. Recordings: Singles include: Together Again, 1975; Two More Bottles of Wine, 1978; Beneath Still Waters, 1979; (Lost His Love) On Our Last date, 1982; To Know Him is to Love Him (Trio), 1987; We believe in Happy Endings (duet with Earl Thomas Conley), 1988; Wheels of Love, 1990; Never Be Anyone, 1990; High Powered Love, 1993; Albums include: Gliding Bird, 1969; Pieces Of The Sky, 1975; Elite Hotel, 1976; Luxury Liner, 1977; Quarter Moon In A Ten-Cent Town, 1978; Blue Kentucky Girl, 1979; Roses in the Snow, 1980; Evangeline, 1981; Cimarron, 1981; Last Date, 1982; White Shoes, 1983; Profile: Best Of Emmylou Harris, 1984; The Ballad Of Sally Rose, 1985; Thirteen, 1986; Trio (with Dolly Parton, Linda Ronstadt), 1987; Angel Band, 1987; Bluebird, 1989; Brand New Dance, 1990; Duets (with Nash Ramblers), 1990; At The Ryman, 1992; Cowgirls Prayer, 1993; Wrecking Ball, 1995; Portraits, 1996; Nashville, 1996; Spyboy, 1998; Light of the Stable, 1999; Red Dirt Girl, 2000; Singin' with Emmylou Harris, 2000; Anthology, 2001; Stumble into Grace, 2003; All I Intended To Be, 2008; Assisted Gram Parsons on album GP, Grievous Angel, 1973. Honours: 12 Grammy Awards, 1976-2005; 27 Grammy Nominations; Female Vocalist of the Year, Country Music Association, 1980; Academy Country Music Award, Album of the Year, 1987. Membership: President, Country Music Foundation, 1983. Address: Monty Hitchcock Management, PO Box 159007, Nashville, TN 37215, USA.

HARRIS Ian Edsel, b. 21 March 1941, Montreal, Quebec, Canada. Retired Lawyer; Astronomer. m. Mireille Chassay, 1 son. Education: BA, 1962, BCL, 1965, McGill University; Bar of Province of Quebec, 1967. Appointment: Practice of law in the Courts of Quebec, 1967-99; House Counsel with Federal Commerce and Navigation, 1968-72; Nominal Partner, Cerini Salmon Watson Souaid and Harris, 1974-86; City Councillor, St Bruno de Montarville, 1974-78; Junior Associate Partner, Gamache Godin and Doyle, 1987-89. Publications: Papers in journals and conference proceedings in advanced astronomy, physics, chemistry of minerals and rocks include: Geology in Practice, 1998; Origin of Moon and Earth, 1998; Forming Outer Planets and Timing of Formation, 2001; Identification of elements and molecular combinations of atmosphere of Jupiter from measurements of magnetic field induced in atmosphere of planet by passage of moons Ganymede and Europa, 2002; Some 50 papers remain unpublished due to restrictions on classified material. Memberships: Royal Astronomical Society of Canada (Montreal Centre); Mineralogical Society of America. Address: 536 Crescent Street, St Lambert, Quebec J4P 1Z2, Canada. E-mail: ieharris_374@sympatico.ca

HARRIS Robert Sidney, b. 30 March 1951, London, England. Engineer. m. Beverley, 1 son, 2 daughters. Education: BSc (Eng) 1st Class Honours, Electrical Engineering, Imperial College, London, 1969-72. Appointments include: Spacecraft AOCS Designer, 1972-74, Project Leader on ESTEC AOCS Contracts, 1975-79, BAC Bristol, UK; AOCS Group Leader on ESTEC AOCS Contracts, 1980, AOCS Systems Engineer responsible for design and analysis of L-SAT AOCS, 1981-82, Design Manager for HIPPARCOS power subsystem, harness subsystem and AOCS, 1982-87, Proposal preparation for STSP missions, 1987-89, Design Manager for STSP activities (SOHO AOCS, CLUSTER AOCS, CLUSTER reaction control subsystem), 1989-94, BAe, Bristol, UK; Design Manager for INTEGRAL AOCS, 1997-99, Design Manager of XMM AOCS, 1994-99, Member of SOHO recovery team following the temporary loss of the spacecraft, 1998, Member of SOHO "tiger team", 1998, part of recovery team at NASA leading to a successful transition back to full operations, 1998-99, MMS Bristol, UK; Senior Principal Consultant, working on systems, AOCMS, RCS and operations activities for the Rosetta spacecraft, 1999-2003, supporting launch campaign and post-launch activities for the Rosetta spacecraft at ESOC, design and operations for the drag-free attitude control system of the GOCE spacecraft, Phase A design for the GAIA spacecraft, proposal preparation for the BepiColombo spacecraft, AOCS architect responsible for the design and development of the AOCS for the BepiColombo spacecraft, 2003-, RHEA Systems SA, Louvain-La-Neuve, Belgium (located at Astrium GmbH, Friedrichshafen, Germany). Publications: Numerous technical reports supporting the design development and operations of the various spacecraft attitude and orbit control systems. Honours: Sylvanus P Thompson Award for achieving the top degree in electrical engineering and electronics, 1972; MBE for contribution to the recovery of the SOHO spacecraft, 2000; Laurels for Team Achievement Award (jointly), International Academy of Astronautics, 2003. Memberships: Associate, City and Guilds Institute; Institution of Engineering and Technology. Address: Hoher Weg 60, 88048 Friedrichshafen, Germany. E-mail: family.harris@t-online.de

HARRIS Rolf, b. 30 March 1930, Perth, Australia. TV Entertainer; Singer; Musician; Artist. m. Alwen Myfanwy Wiseman Hughes, 1958, 1 daughter. Education: University of Washington; Claremount Teachers College, Washington. Appointments: TV Entertainer, Australia and England; Host of English TV programmes including, Hey Presto, It's Rolf, Rolf Harris Show, Rolf on Saturday OK!, Rolf's Walkabout, Cartoon Time, Rolf's Amazing World of Animals, Animal Hospital; Rolf On Art; Rolf Harris Star Portraits. Appearances include, Opening Ceremony, Commonwealth Games, Brisbane, 1982, Olympic Gala, Los Angeles, 1984, Bicentennial Command Performance, Sydney, 1988. Creative Works: Numerous hit recordings include: Tie Me Kangaroo Down Sport; Sun Arise; Jake the Peg; Two Little Boys; Stairway to Heaven. Publications: How to Write Your Own Pop Song, 1968; Rolf Goes Bush, 1975; Your Cartoon Time, 1986; Catalogue of Comic Verse, 1988; Every Picture Tells a Story, 1989; Win or Die: The Making of a King, 1989; Your Animation Time, 1991; Personality Cats, 1992; Me and You and Poems Too, 1993; Beastly Behaviour, 1997; Draw Your Own Cartoons with Rolf Harris, 1998; Can You Tell What It Is Yet? (autobiography), 2001; Rolf on Art, 2002. Honours: MBE, 1968; OBE, 1978; AM, 1989; 3 times winner, National TV Awards; 2 times winner, TV Quick Award; CBE, 2006. Memberships: President, PHAB; Equity. Address: c/o Jan Kennedy, Billy Marsh Associates, 174-178 North Gower Street, London NW1 2NB, England.

HARRIS Rosemary, b. Ashby, Suffolk, England. Actor. m. John Ehle, 1 daughter. Education: Bancroft Gold Medal, Royal Academy of Dramatic Art, 1952. Career: Bristol Old Vic; London Old Vic; Chichester Festival Theatre; National Theatre at the Old Vic; West End: Seven Year Itch; Plaza Suite; All My Sons; Heartbreak House; The Petition; Best of Friends; Steel Magnolias; National Theatre: Women of Troy; Broadway: Lion in Winter; A Street Car Named Desire; Hay Fever; An Inspector Calls; A Delicate Balance; Waiting in the Wings; The Royal Family; The Road to Mecca; Films: Tom & Viv; Sunshine; Spiderman; Spiderman Two; Spiderman Three; When the Devil Knows You Are Dead. Honours: Evening Standard Award; Golden Globe Award; Emmy Award; Tony Award; Academy Award Nomination. Address: c/o Independent Talent Ltd; 76 Oxford Street, London W1N 0AX, England.

HARRIS Thomas, b. 11 April, 1940, Jackson, Tennessee, USA. Writer. m. divorced, 1 daughter. Education: Baylor University, Texas, USA. Appointments: Worked on newsdesk Waco News-Tribune; Member, Staff, Associated Press, New York. Publications: Black Sunday; Red Dragon (filmed as Manhunter); The Silence of the Lambs (filmed); Hannibal; Hannibal Rising. Address: St Martin's Press, 175 Fifth Avenue, New York, NY 10010, USA.

HARRISON Sir David, b. 3 May 1930, Clacton-on-Sea, Essex, England. Retired University Vice-Chancellor. m. Sheila Rachel Debes, 2 sons, 1 deceased, 1 daughter. Education: BA, 1953, PhD, 1956, MA, 1957, ScD, 1979, FREng, FRSC, FIChemE, FRSA, FRSCM, CCMI, Selwyn College, Cambridge. Appointments: Senior Tutor, 1967-79, Master, 1994-2000, Fellow, Selwyn College, Cambridge; Vice-Chancellor, University of Keele, 1979-84; Chairman, Board of Trustees, Homerton College, Cambridge, 1979-2010; Vice-Chancellor, University of Exeter, 1984-94; Chairman, Governing Body, Shrewsbury School, 1989-2003; President, IChemE, 1991-92; Chairman, Committee of Vice-Chancellors and Principals, 1991-93; Deputy Vice-Chancellor, University of Cambridge, 1995-2000; Chairman, Council Royal School of Church Music, 1996-2005; Director, Salters Institute of Industrial Chemistry; Liveryman, Salters' Company; Chairman, Ely Cathedral Council. Publications: Fluidised Particles (with J F Davidson), 1963; Fluidization (with J F Davidson and R Clift), 1971, 1985. Honours: CBE, 1990; Hon DUniv, Keele University, 1992; Hon DSc, Exeter University, 1995; Kt, 1997; George E Davis Medal, IChemE, 2001; Hon DUniv, York University, 2008. Memberships: Athenaeum; Oxford and Cambridge; Federation House, Stoke-on-Trent. Address: 7 Gough Way, Cambridge, CB3 9LN, England. E-mail: sirdavidharrison@yahoo.co.uk

HARRISON John, b. 12 November 1944, Stockton-on-Tees, England. Chartered Accountant. m. Patricia Alice Bridget, 1 son, 2 daughters. Education: BA Honours, Economics, Sheffield University; FCA. Appointments: Articled Clerk, Coopers & Lybrand, 1963-67; Corporate Planner, Tillotson, 1967-70; Partner, DeLoitte & Touche, 1970-2001; Chairman, Portal Ltd, 2001-08; Chairman, Spring Grove plc, 2002-07; Non-executive Director, Dere Holdings plc, 2005-09; Non-executive Director, Crown Northcorp Inc, 2007-10; Crown Northcorp Ltd, 2010-; Administrator, Ely Cathedral, 2010-. Membership: FRSA. Address: Goodwin Manor, Swaffham Prior, Cambridge CB25 0LG, England. E-mail: john.harrison@swaffham.demon.co.uk

HARRY Deborah Ann, b. 1 July 1945, Miami, Florida, USA. Singer; Songwriter; Actress. Career: Former Playboy bunny waitress; Singer, groups: Wind In The Willows; The Stilettos; Founder, Blondie, 1974-83; Appearances include: New York punk club, CBGBs, 1974; Support to Iggy Pop, US, 1977; Solo recording career, 1981-; Actress, films including: Blank Generation, 1978; The Foreigner, 1978; Union City, 1979; Roadie, 1980; Videodrome; Hairspray; The Killbillies; Tales from the Darkside: The Movie, 1990; Intimate Stranger, 1991; Joe's Day, 1999; 200, 1999; Six Ways to Sunday, 1999; Ghost Light, 2000; Dueces Wild, 2000; Red Lipstick, 2000; The Curse of Blondie, 2003; Honey Trap; 2005; Patch, 2005; I Remember You Now; 2005; Full Grown Men; 2006; Anamorph, 2007; Elegy, 2007. TV appearances: Saturday Night Life; The Muppet Show; Tales from the Darkside; Wiseguys; Theatre: Teaneck Tanzi; The Venus Flytrap; Recordings: Hit singles: with Blondie: Denis (Denee), 1978; (I'm Always Touched By Your) Presence Dear, 1978; Picture This, 1978; Hanging On The Telephone, 1978; Heart Of Glass, 1979; Sunday Girl, 1979; Dreaming, 1979; Union City Blue, 1979; Call Me, 1980; Atomic, 1980; The Tide Is High (Number 1, UK and US), 1980; Rapture (Number 1, US), 1981; Island Of Lost Souls, 1982; Solo: Backfired, 1981; French Kissin' (In The USA), 1986; I Want That Man, 1989; I Can See Clearly, 1993; Albums with Blondie: Blondie, 1976; Plastic Letters, 1978; Parallel Lines, 1978; Eat To The Beat, 1979; Autoamerican, 1980; The Best Of Blondie, 1981; The Hunter, 1982; Solo albums: Koo Koo, 1981; Rockbird, 1986; Def, Dumb And Blonde, 1989; Debravation, 1993; Compilations: Once More Into The Bleach, 1988; The Complete Picture, 1991; Blonde And Beyond, 1993; Rapture, 1994; Virtuosity, 1995; Rockbird, 1996; Der Einziger Weg, 1999; No Exit, 1999; Livid, 2000; Contributor, film soundtracks: American Gigolo, 1980; Roadie, 1980; Scarface; Krush Groove, 1984. Publications: Making Tracks - The Rise Of Blondie (co-written with Chris Stein), 1982. Memberships: ASCAP; AFTRA; Equity; Screen Actors Guild. Current Management: Overland Productions, 156 W 56th Street, 5th Floor, New York, NY 10019, USA.

HART David, b. 6 September 1950, Darlington, England. Radiation Protection Scientist. m. Doreen Carter. Education: BSc, University College London; PhD, University of Edinburgh. Appointments: Research Fellow, Imperial College London, 1978-80; Lecturer, University of East Anglia, Norwich, 1980-87; Principal Radiation Scientist, Health Protection Agency and National Radiological Protection Board, 1987-. Publications: The Volta River Project, 1980; Nuclear Power in India, 1983; Articles in Nature, New Scientist, British Journal of Radiology, Nuclear Medicine Communications, European Journal of Radiology. Membership: Institute of Physics and Engineering in Medicine. Address: Health Protection Agency, Chilton, Didcot, Oxfordshire OX11 0RQ, England.

HART Margie Ruth, b. 28 October 1943, Chesterfield, South Carolina, USA. Board Member, Niangua Senior Citizen Complex. m. Leonard Monty Hart, 3 sons, 1 daughter. Education: Barstow Junior College, 1985-87. Appointments: Choir Member, 2003-08, Teacher, Special Education Sunday School Class, 2007-08, Fellowship of Leaders Wives, 2007-08, Co-ordinator for Bus Ministry, 2008, Van Driver, 2008, Co-ordinator for Gardening, 2008, Temple Baptist Church. Publications: The Girl That Never Was. Honours: Certificates from TBC; Certificate for Candidate State Assembly, California. Memberships: Silver Haired Legislator (Senator); Pen & Ink Society; Smithsonian Member; Temple Baptist Church; Temple Baptist Church Choir; Bikers Against Child Abuse; Webster County Art Guild; Ladies Fellowship, Temple Baptist Church. Address: PO Box 76, 172 S Spruce, Niangua, MO 65713, USA. E-mail: margie4278@hotmail.com

HART Raymond Kenneth, b. 15 February 1928, Newcastle, New South Wales, Australia. Forensic Metallurgist. m. Betty Joyce Hart, 1 son, 1 daughter. Education: ASTC, Sydney Technical College, 1949; DIC, Imperial College, London, 1952; PhD, Metallurgy, University of Cambridge, 1955; JD, Kennedy Western University, 1991. Appointments: Scientific Officer, Aeronautical Research Laboratories, Melbourne, Victoria, 1955-58; Senior Scientist, Argonne National Laboratory, Illinois, USA, 1958-70; Manager, ANL-AMU High Voltage Program, 1966-70; Principal Research Scientist, Georgia Institute of Technology, 1970-74; President, Pasat Research Association Inc, 1974-90; Contracted with California Institute of Technology/Jet Propulsion Laboratory to design/build a space vehicle compatible Scanning Electron Microprobe Analyzer (SEMPA), 1976-82; Consultant Metallurgist, Raymond K Hart Ltd, Atlanta, Georgia, 1991. Publications: 22 refereed scientific texts; 5 chapters in technical books; 41 presentations at professional meetings; 400 sworn depositions; 100 trial testimonies. Honours include: NASA Certificate of Recognition, 1976; President's Award, Midwest Society of Electronic Microscopy, 1986; Distinguished Scientist Award, Southeastern Microscopy Society, 1993; Morton D Maser Distinguished Service Award, Microscopy Society of America, 1995; Elected to Guild of Benefactors, Corpus Christi College, Cambridge, 1996; International Order of Merit, IBC, 2000; IBC Millennium Time Capsule Book, 2000; American Medal of Honor, ABI, 2001; Engineering Sciences Section's Founders Award, American Academy of Forensic Sciences, 2002; Companion of the 1209 Society, University of Cambridge, 2003; Founding Member, 1352 Foundation Society, Corpus Christi College, Cambridge, 2005; Eminent Fellow, ABI, 2006. Memberships: Fellow, American Academy of Forensic Science; Honorary Life Fellow, Royal Australian Chemistry Institute; American Society of Metals, International Branch; American Physical Society; Fellow, Microscopy Society of America; Sigma Xi; Oxford and Cambridge Club, London, 1991; Diplomate, International Institute of Forensice Engineering Sciences, 2002-. Address: 145 Grogan's Lake Dr, Sandy Springs, GA 30350-3115, USA. E-mail: rayhart@comcast.net

HARTAL Paul, b. 25 April 1936, Hungary. Visual Artist; Writer. 2 sons, 1 daughter. Education: MA, Concordia University, Montreal, 1977; PhD, Diversity of Montreal, Columbia Pacific University, San Rafael, 1986. Appointments include: Director, Centre for Art, Science & Technology, 1987-; Educator, Explorations Program, McGill University, 1994; Consultant, McGill University; Project Director, Culture and Eco-System, Shijavi University, India; Originator of Lycoism (Lyrical Conceptualism, Art Trend); Exhibitions in France, USA, Canada, Switzerland, Spain, Japan, Korea and Hungary. Publications: Books include: A History of Architecture, 1972; Painted Melodies (essay), 1983; Black and White (images), 1984; The Brush and the Compass: The Interface Dynamics of Art and Science, 1988; Rain Drop, 1994; The Kidnapping of the Painter Miro (The Butterfly Kite), novel illustrated by author, 1997, 2001; Selected Visual Poems of the 20th Century, 1998; Visions: Moment in Frame, poems, 1998; Love Poems, 2004; Postmodern Light: A Collection of Poetry, 2006; Mathematics and Reality, 2010. Honours include: Rubens Award and Prix de Paris, 1978; Academia Italia Award, 1984; American National Medal for Poetry; Hanseo University Visiting Artist, 2004; Poetry Canada; Canadian Federation of Poets Award; British Library Award, 2010. Memberships: YLEM; New York Academy of Sciences; International Association of the Astronomical Arts; Canadian Federation of Poets; Writers' Union of Canada. E-mail: pzhartal@hotmail.com

HART-DAVIS Duff, b. 3 June 1936, London, England. Author. Education: BA, Oxford University, 1960. Appointments: Feature Writer, 1972-76, Literary Editor, 1976-77, Assistant Editor, 1977-78, Sunday Telegraph, London; Country Columnist, Independent, 1986-2001. Publications: The Megacull, 1968; The Gold of St Matthew (in USA as The Gold Trackers), 1968; Spider in the Morning, 1972; Ascension: The Story of a South Atlantic Island, 1972; Peter Fleming (biography), 1974; Monarchs of the Glen, 1978; The Heights of Rimring, 1980; Fighter Pilot (with C Strong), 1981; Level Five, 1982; Fire Falcon, 1984; The Man-Eater of Jassapur, 1985; Hitler's Games, 1986; Armada, 1988; The House the Berrys Built, 1990; Horses of War, 1991; Country Matters, 1991; Wildings: The Secret Garden of Eileen Soper, 1992; Further Country Matters, 1993; When the Country Went to Town, 1997; Raoul Millais, 1998; Fauna Britannica, 2003; Audubon's Elephant, 2004; Honorary Tiger, 2005; Philip de László, 2010. Address: Owlpen Farm, Uley, Dursley, Gloucestershire GL11 5BZ, England.

HART-DYKE David, b. 3 October 1938, Havant, Hampshire, England. Retired Naval Officer. m. Diana Luce, 1967, 2 daughters. Education: St Lawrence College, Ramsgate, 1952-57; Britannia Royal Naval College, Dartmouth, 1959-61; Staff Course, Royal Naval College, Greenwich, 1974-75. Appointments: Royal Navy, 1958-90; National Service, Commissioned Midshipman RNVR, 1958-59; Sub-Lieutenant RN, HMS Eastbourne, Far East Fleet, 1961-62; Lieutenant, HM Coastal Forces, 1962; Served in HM Ships Lanton, Palliser and Gurkha; Specialist Navigation Course, HMS Dryad, 1967; Navigating Officer, Promoted to Lieutenant Commander, Frigates HMS Tenby, HMS Scylla, 1968-71; Divisional Officer and Head of Navigation, Britannia Royal Naval College, Dartmouth, 1971-73; Promoted to Commander, 1974, Executive Officer, Guided Missile Destroyer, HMS Hampshire, 1974; Staff, Royal Naval Staff College, Greenwich, 1976; Commander of the Royal Yacht Britannia, 1978; Captain, 1980; Captain, HMS Coventry, 1981-82 when sunk by enemy action in the Falklands War; Assistant Chief of Staff to the Commander of the Chief Fleet, Northwood, 1982-84; Assistant Naval Attaché and Chief of Staff to the Commander British Naval Staff, Washington DC, 1985-87; Director of Naval Recruiting, Ministry of Defence, 1987; Retired from Royal Navy, 1990; Clerk to the Worshipful Company of Skinners, City of London, 1990-2003. Publications: Four Weeks In May (The story of HMS Coventry in the Falklands War 1982) 2007. Articles on experiences in the Falklands War and on Combat Stress published in Naval Review and other related journals. Honours: LVO, 1979; ADC to Her Majesty the Queen, 1988-90; CBE, 1990. Address: Hambledon House, Hambledon, Hants PO7 4RU, England. E-mail: dhartdyke@tiscali.co.uk

HARTILL Brenda, b. London, England. Artist. Education: FA (Hons), Auckland University, New Zealand; Graduate Student, Central School of Art and Design, London. Appointments: Theatre Design; Lecturer and Designer, North Carolina State University, USA; Designer, National Theatre, British Arts Council, 1970s; Freelance Designer: National Theatre, Young Vic, Criterion Theatre, Piccadilly, Royal Shakespeare Company, Birmingham Rep, Traverse Theatre, Edinburgh and Theatre Royal, York; Printmaker: Solo and group exhibitions in UK, New Zealand, Australia, USA and Europe; Work held in public and private collections worldwide. Publicatons: Collagraphs and mixed media printmaking, 2004. Memberships: Royal Society of Painter

Printmakers. Address: Pound House, Udimore, Rye, East Sussex TN31 6BA, England. E-mail: brenda@gmail.com Website: www.brendahartill.com

HARTILL Edward Theodore, b. 23 January 1943, United Kingdom. Consultant. m. Gillian Ruth Todd, 2 sons, 2 sons from previous marriage. Education: BSc, Estate Management, College of Estate Management, London University; FRICS. Appointments: Joined Burd and Evans, Land Agents, Shrewsbury, 1963; Estates Department, Legal and General Assurance Company, 1964-73; Visiting Lecturer in Law of Town Planning and Compulsory Purchase, Hammersmith and West London College of Advanced Business Studies, 1968-78; Property Investment Department, Guardian Royal Exchange Assurance Group, 1973-85, Head Office Manager, 1980-85; City Surveyor, City of London Corporation, 1985-2008; Member, Government appointed Study team on Professional Liability, 1988-99; Member, 1985-2007, National Council, 1988-2007, President, 1996-97, Honorary Member, 2007, Association of Chief Estates Surveyors and Property Managers in Local Government (formerly Local Authority Valuers' Association); Member, General Practice Divisional Council, 1989-97, President, 1992-93, General Council, 1990-2004, Honorary Treasurer, 2000-04, Royal Institution of Chartered Surveyors; Member, Steering Group, 1992-99, Chairman Property Services Sub-Group, 1992-99, Construction Industry Standing Conference; Founder Member, Chairman, Property Services NTO, 1999-2005; Chair, 2003, Vice Chair, 2004-2007, Assets Skills (a sector Skills Council); Member of Council, 2004-08, Member, Estates Committee, 2004-08, Deputy Chairman, 2006-08, Member, Investments Committee, 2008-, Deputy Chairman, 2009-, Member, College Hall Project Board, 2006-09, Chairman, 2006-, Chairman, Senate House Project Board, 2006-, Member, Board of Management, 2008-, Deputy Chairman, 2009, Member and Chairman, Safety Committee, 2009-, University Marine Biological Station, University of London; Governor and Trustee, 2006-, Vice Chairman 2007-08, Chairman, 2008-, Thomas Coram Foundation for Children; Consultant, Corderoy (International Chartered Quantity Surveyors and Cost Consultants), 2008. Publications: Occasional lectures and articles on professional topics. Honours: Honorary Associate, Czech Chamber of Appraisers, 1992; Honorary Member Investment Property Forum, 1995; OBE, 2004. Memberships: British Schools Exploring Society; FRSA, 1993; Liveryman, 1985-; Court of Assistants, 1991-2009, Master, 2003-2004, Chairman, Fundraising Committee, 2009-, Worshipful Company of Chartered Surveyors. Address: 215 Sheen Lane, East Sheen, London SW14 8LE, England.

HARTLAND Michael, b. 7 February 1941. Writer and Broadcaster. m. 1975, 2 daughters. Education: Christ's College, Cambridge, 1960-63. Appointments: British Diplomatic and Civil Service, 1963-78; United Nations, 1978-83; Full-time Writer, 1983-; Book Reviewer and Feature Writer, The Sunday Times, The Times, Guardian and Daily Telegraph; Thriller Critic, The Times, 1989-90; Daily Telegraph, 1993-2003; Travel Correspondent: The Times, 1993-2003; Television and Radio include: Sonia's Report, ITV documentary, 1990; Masterspy, interviews with KGB defector Oleg Gordievsky, Radio 4, 1991. Publications: Down Among the Dead Men; Seven Steps to Treason (dramatised for BBC Radio 4, 1990); The Third Betrayal; Frontier of Fear; The Year of the Scorpion; The Verdict of Us All (jointly, short stories); Masters of Crime: Lionel Davidson & Dick Francis; As Ruth Carrington: Dead Fish. Honours: Fellow, Royal Society of Arts; Honorary Fellow, University of Exeter; South West Arts Literary Award. Memberships: Executive Committee of PEN, 1997-2001; Detection Club; Mystery Writers of America. Address: Cotte Barton, Branscombe, Devon, EX12 3BH, England.

HARTLEY Frank Robinson, b. 29 January 1942, Epsom, Surrey, England. Retired University Vice-Chancellor. m. (1) Valerie, 1964, deceased 2005, 3 daughters, (2) Charmaine, 2009. Education: Sambrooke Scholar, Kings College School, Wimbledon; BA, MA, DPhil, DSc, Magdalen College, Oxford. Appointments: Post-doctoral Fellow, Commonwealth Scientific and Industrial Research Organisation, Melbourne, Australia, 1966-69; ICI Research Fellow and Tutor, Physical Chemistry, University College, London, 1969-70; Lecturer, Inorganic Chemistry, Southampton University, 1970-71; Professor of Chemistry, Head of Department of Chemistry and Metallurgy, Royal Military College of Science, 1975-82; Principal, Royal Miltiary College of Science, Shrivenham, 1982-89; Vice-Chancellor, Cranfield University, 1989-2006; Chairman, Senior Council for Devon, Teignmouth Branch; Chairman, Teignmouth and Dawlish Ramblers. Publications: The Chemistry of Platinum and Palladium, 1973; Elements of Organometallic Chemistry, 1974 (Japanese edition 1981, Chinese edition 1989); Solution Equilibria, 1980 (Russian edition 1983); The Chemistry of the Metal-Carbon Bond (Vols 1-5), 1983-89; The Chemistry of the Phosphorus-Carbon Bond (Vols 10-4), 1990-94; Chemistry of the Platinum Group Metals, 1991. Honours: Deputy Lieutenant, Bedfordshire. Memberships: Fellow, Royal Society of Chemistry; Fellow, Royal Society of Arts; Member, Shrivenham Club. E-mail: f.r.hartley@cranfield.ac.uk

HARTMANN Reinhard R K, b. 8 April 1938. Education: Translator's Diploma, University of Vienna, 1956-60; BSc, Economics, 1956-60, Doctorate, 1960-65, Vienna School of Economics; MA, International Economics, Southern Illinois University, USA, 1961-62. Appointments: Lecturer, Modern Languages, University of Manchester Institute of Science and Technology, 1964-68; Lecturer, Applied Linguistics, University of Nottingham, 1968-74; Director, Language Centre and Head of Linguistics, University of Exeter, 1974-92; Reader, Applied Linguistics, 1991-, Head, Department of Applied Linguistics, 1992-96, in School of English, 1996-2001, University of Exeter; Honorary Professor of Lexicography, Department of English, University of Birmingham, 2000-11; Honorary University Fellow, School of English, University of Exeter, 2001-09. Publications: Author/editor of 19 books on lexicography and related subjects; Articles in national and international scholarly journals; Papers presented at conferences; Numerous invited contributions. Honours: Fellow, Royal Society of Arts; Fellow, Chartered Institute of Linguists (London); Honorary Life Member, European Association for Lexicography; MCB UP/Literati Club award for best specialist reference work, 1998. Memberships include: British Association for Applied Linguistics; European Association for Lexicography; Dictionary Society of North America. Address: 40 Velwell Road, Exeter, Devon EX4 4LD, England. E-mail: r.r.k.hartmann@exeter.ac.uk

HARUTYUNIAN Gagik, b. 23 March 1948, Geghashen, Kotayk Region, Armenia. President of the Constitutional Court of the Republic of Armenia. Education: Graduate, Faculty of Economics, 1970, Postgraduate Student, Yerevan State University. Appointments: Lecturer, Yerevan State University, 1973; Chief Lecturer, Institute of National Economics; Economist-Lecturer, Central Committee of Communistic Party of the Armenian Republic, 1982-87; Head, Social-Economic Department, Central Committee,

1987; Elected Deputy, Supreme Council of the Republic of Armenia, 1990; Elected Vice Chairman, Supreme Council of the Republic of Armenia, 1990; Elected Vice President, Republic of Armenia 1991-1996; Prime Minister of the Republic of Armenia, 1991-92; President, Constitutional Court of the Republic of Armenia, 1996; President, Center of Constitutional Law, Republic of Armenia, 1996-. Publications: Author: 23 monographs; 150 scientific works. Honours: High Judicial Qualification of Judge, Decree of the President of the Republic of Armenia, 1998; Scientific Degree of Doctor of Law, 1999. Memberships: Member, International Academy of Information, 1997; Member, Council of International Association of Constitutional Law, 1998; Co-ordinator of Mandatory Acting, Conference on Constitutional Review bodies of New Independent Countries and President of Editorial Council of International Bulletin on Constitutional Justice (published in 2 languages), 1997; Member, European Commission for Democracy through Law, Council of Europe, 1997; Head of Project, Almanac; Constitutional Justice in the New Millennium (published in 4 languages), 2002. Address: The Constitutional Court of the Republic of Armenia, 10 Marshal Bagramyan Avenue, Yerevan 0019, Republic of Armenia 375019. E-mail: mma@athgo.org

HARVEY Barbara Fitzgerald, b. 21 January 1928, Teignmouth, Devon, England. University Teacher. Education: BA (Oxon) 1949, MA (Oxon), 1953, B Litt (Oxon), 1953, Somerville College, Oxford. Appointments: Assistant, Department of Scottish History, University of Edinburgh, 1951-52; Assistant Lecturer then Lecturer, Department of History, Queen Mary College, University of London, 1952-55; Tutor in Medieval History, 1955-56, Fellow and Tutor in Medieval History, 1956-93, Emeritus Fellow, 1993-, Somerville College, Oxford. Publications: Books: Westminster Abbey and its Estates in the Middle Ages, 1977; The Westminster Chronicle, 1381-94 (editor with L C Hector), 1982; Living and Dying in England 1100-1540: The monastic experience, 1993; The Twelfth and Thirteenth Centuries, 1066-c.1280 (editor) in Short Oxford History of the British Isles, 2001; Articles in: Transactions of the Royal Historical Society; Bulletin of the Institute of Historical Research; Economic History Review; Journal of Ecclesiastical History and other learned journals and similar works. Honours: FBA, 1982; Ford's Lecturer in English History, University of Oxford, 1989; Joint Winner, Wolfson Foundation Prize for History, 1993; CBE, 1997. Memberships: Fellow, Society of Antiquaries, London, 1964-; President, Henry Bradshaw Society, 1997-2007; Honorary Vice-President, Royal Historical Society, 2003-. Address: Flat 6, Ritchie Court, 380 Banbury Road, Oxford OX2 7PW, England. E-mail: barbara.harvey@some.ox.ac.uk

HARVEY John Robert, b. 25 June 1942, Bishops Stortford, Hertfordshire, England. University Lecturer; Writer. m. Julietta Chloe Papadopoulou, 1968, 1 daughter. Education: BA, Honours Class 1, English, 1964, MA, 1967, PhD, 1969, Litt D, University of Cambridge. Appointments: English Faculty, Emmanuel College, Cambridge; Editor, Cambridge Quarterly, 1978-86; University Reader, Cambridge; Vice-Master, Emmanuel College, Cambridge, 2004-06. Publications: Victorian Novelists and Their Illustrators, 1970; Men in Black, 1995; Clothes, 2008. Novels: The Plate Shop, 1979; Coup d'Etat, 1985; The Legend of Captain Space, 1990; Bathmedon/Stairs, 2011. Contributions to: London Review of Books; Sunday Times; Sunday Telegraph; Listener; Encounter; Cambridge Quarterley; Essays in Criticism. Honour: David Higham Prize, 1979. Address: Emmanuel College, Cambridge, England.

HARVEY Jonathan Dean, b. 3 May 1939, Sutton Coldfield, England. Composer. m. Rosaleen Marie Harvey, 1 son, 1 daughter. Education: Major Scholar, MA, St John's College Cambridge, 1957-61; PhD, Glasgow University, 1961-63; DMus, Cambridge University, 1970. Appointments: Lecturer, Senior Lecturer, Southampton University, 1964-77; Senior Lecturer, Professor, Sussex University, 1977-92; Full Professor, Stanford University, 1995-2000; Visiting Professor, Imperial College, 1999-2002; About 200 performances per annum. Publications: Books: The Music of Stockhausen, 1975; Music and Inspiration, 1999; In Quest of Spirit, 1999; About 40 articles; About 200 compositions for orchestra, choir, chamber and electronic combinations; 3 operas. Honours: Britten Award, 1993; 2 Koussevitsky Awards; British Academy Composer Award, 2004; Gigahertz Prize for Lifetime Achievement in Electronic Music, 2008; Grand Prix du Président de la Republique (Charles Cros Academy) for Lifetime Achievement, 2010; Honorary Doctorates: Bristol, Southampton and Sussex Universities; FRCM; Honorary RAM; FRSCM; Honorary Fellow, St John's College, Cambridge; Honorary Doctorates, Huddersfield, Birmingham City. Memberships: British Academy; European Academy; Fellow, Institute for Advanced Study, Berlin, 2009. Address: c/o Faber Music, 74-77 Gt Russell Street, London WC1B 3DA, England.

HARVEY Pamela Ann, b. 15 October 1934, Bush Hill Park, Edmonton, London, England. Writer; Poet. Education: 6 GCEs, Edmonton County Grammar; RSA Diploma, Shorthand & Typing, A level French Oral, Pitman's Business College. Appointments: Secretarial Work, London; Library Work, Southgate Library. Publications: Poetry, 1994; Quiet Lines, 1996; The Wellspring (co-author with Anna Franklin), 2000; Children's Fun Fiction (story), 2006; The Jovian System (booklet), 1990; Grail (4 short stories); Monomyth (5 short stories); Garbaj; Contributions to: The People's Poetry; Romantic Heir; Rubies in the Darkness; Cadmium Blue Literary Journal; Pendragon (stories, articles, poems); Keltria, USA; Celtic Connections; Silver Wheel (articles and poems); Sharkti Laureate; Time Haiku; Azami, Japan; The Lady magazine (short story); Avalon magazine (articles); Poetry Now (new fiction) included: Hold That Thought (story), Timeless Tales (story) and Share Our Worlds Anthology (poem); 'Night of Midsummer' (new fiction) in Fabrication & Imagination, 2009; 'Cave of the Dragon' (new fiction) in Fairy Tales for Little Imps, 2009; Contributor to poems on an All About War theme; Littoral magazine (articles and poems), 2005-2006; Celebrations (Poetry Now), 2006. Honours: 1st prize Poetry (Rubies in Darkness Award, editor Peter G P Thompson), 2004; 3rd prize, Poetry (Rubies in Darkness), 2005; 2nd Prize, Poetry (Rubies in Darkness), 2010. Memberships: Enfield Writers Group; New Renaissance Poets Society; Metverse Muse (poetry magazine).

HARVIE Christopher Thomas, b. 21 September 1944, Motherwell, Scotland. Historian; Professor. m. Virginia Roundell (deceased 2005), 1 daughter. Education: MA (1st class honours), History, 1966, PhD, History, 1972, Edinburgh University. Appointments: Shaw Macfie Lang Fellowship, Edinburgh University, 1966-69; Lecturer, 1969-78, Acting Head of History, 1975, 1978-80, Senior Lecturer, 1978-80, History, Open University; Professor, British and Irish Studies, English Seminar, Eberhard-Karls University, Germany, 1980-2007; Deputy Director, English Seminar, 1981-82, Director, 1982-83, 1986-87, 1989, 1992-93, 2001-02; Academic Visitor, Nuffield College, Oxford, Michaelmas Term, 1983, Hilary Term, 1984; Visiting Professor, History, Strathclyde University, Glasgow, 1988-89; Honorary Research Fellow, University College, Lampeter, 1994; Regional

Member, Scottish National Party, 2007-11. Publications: Over 50 full academic articles published on history, politics and literature; Short articles/reviews in numerous publications; Journalist work for a variety of newspapers, including many broadcasts for BBC and others; Books include: Scotland and Nationalism, 1977, 2004; Scotland since 1914, 1981, 2000; The Centre of Things: British Political Fiction since Disraeli, 1991; The Rise of Regional Europe, 1993; Fool's Gold: the Story of North Sea Oil, 1994; Deep-Fried Hillman Imp: Scotland's Transport, 2001; Scotland, a Short History, 2002; Floating Commonwealth: Politics, Technology and Culture on Britain's Atlantic Coast, 1860-1930, 2008; Broonland: the Last Days of Gordon Brown, 2010. Honours: Honorary Professor of Politics, University of Wales, 1996-; Honorary Professor of History, Strathclyde University, 1999-; Honorary President, Scottish Association for Public Transport, 2000-; Honorary Vice President, Scottish Centre for Social and Economic Research; Floating Commonwealth finalist for Research Book of the Year, Saltire Society/Scottish Arts Council, 2008-09. Memberships: Scottish National Party; Plaid Cymru; German Democratic Party; UK Labour Party; Association of Scottish Library Studies; National Trust; Saltire Society; Scottish Railway Preservation Society; many others. E-mail: christopher.harvie@uni-tuebingen.de

HASANOV Alakbar, b. 25 June 1961, Govlar, Azerbaijan. Pediatrist. m. Mehriban Gavadova, 2 sons, 2 daughters. Education: N Narimanov Azerbaijan State Medical Institute, 1978-84; Diploma of Candidate of Medical Sciences, 1993; Doctor of Medical Sciences, 2009. Appointments: Pediatrist, Siyazan Children's Hospital, 1984-89; Assistant Professor, Azerbaijan Medical University, 1992-2002; Pediatrist, Saudi Arabia's Prince Sultan Hospital, 2002-06; Pediatrist, Scientific Center of Children's Health, Moscow, 2006-09; Pediatrist, Azerbaijan Medical University, 2009-. Publications: 47 publications; 27 articles. Memberships: Union of Russian Pediatrists; Azerbaijan Pediatrists Association. Address: Flat 59, Building 8, Chingizkhan Street, Baku, AZ 1123, Azerbaijan. E-mail: doctorhasanov@yahoo.com

HASELHURST Alan Gordon Barraclough (Rt Hon Sir), b. 23 June 1937, South Elmsall, Yorkshire, England. Member of Parliament. m. Angela Margaret Bailey, 2 sons, 1 daughter. Education: Oriel College, Oxford, 1956-60. Appointments: Member of Parliament for Middleton and Prestwich, 1970-74; MP for Saffron Walden, 1977-; Parliamentary Private Secretary to the Home Secretary, 1973-74; Parliamentary Private Secretary to Education Secretary, 1979-81; Chairman of Ways and Means and Deputy Speaker, 1997-; Member of Committee of Essex County Cricket Club, 1996-. Publications: Occasionally Cricket, 1999; Eventually Cricket, 2001; Incidentally Cricket, 2003; Accidentally Cricket, 2009. Honours: Knight Bachelor, 1995; Privy Counsellor, 1999. Memberships: MCC; Essex County Cricket Club; Yorkshire County Cricket Club. Address: House of Commons, London SW1A 0AA, England. E-mail: haselhursta@parliament.uk Website: www.siralanhaselhurst.net

HASHIGUCHI Yasuo, b. 31 July 1924, Sasebo, Japan. Professor of English (retired). m. Eiko Uchida, 1 son, 1 daughter. Education: BA, University of Tokyo, 1948; MEd, Ohio University, USA, 1951. Appointments: Associate Professor, English, Kagoshima University, 1951-64, 1964-68, Professor, 1968-82, Kyushu University; Fukuoka University, 1982-88; President, Fukuoka Jo Gakuin Junior College, 1988-93; Professor, Yasuda Women's University, 1993-96. Publications: Editor, Complete Works of John Steinbeck, 20 vols, 1985. Honours: Dick A Renner Prize, 1977; Special Recognition for Outstanding Publication, 1988; Recognition for Many Years of Outstanding Leadership in American Literature and Steinbeck Studies, 1991; Richard W and Dorothy Burkhardt Award, 1994; John J and Angeline R Pruis Award, 1996; John J and Angeline R Pruis Award for the Outstanding Steinbeck Translator in Honour of John Steinbeck's Centennial, 2002. Memberships: President, 1977-89, Advisor, 1989-, Kyushu American Literature Society; President, 1977-91, Honorary President, 1991-, Steinbeck Society of Japan; International Association of University Professors of English, 1999-. Address: 7-29-31-105 Iikura, Sawara-ku, Fukuoka 814-0161 Japan.

HASHIMOTO Tohru, b. 3 February 1930, Kumamoto, Japan. Professor. m. Yoshiko Sakamoto, 1 son, deceased, 1 daughter. Education: Tokyo Gakugei University, 1951-53; BSc, Institute of Biology, Tohoku University, Sendai, 1955; MSc, 1957, DSc, 1961, University of Tokyo; Postdoctoral work, University of California at Davis, 1962-63. Appointments: Lecturer of Biology, Musashi University, Tokyo, 1960-63; Assistant, Department of Agricultural Chemistry, University of Tokyo, 1963-70; Senior Research Scientist, Institute of Physical and Chemical Research, Wako, 1970-86; Professor of Plant Physiology, Department of Biology, Kobe University, Kobe, 1986-93; Professor of Biochemistry, 1993-2003, Emeritus Professor, 2003-, Department of Life Sciences, Kobe Women's University, Kobe; Director, Uozaki Life Science Laboratory, 2005-; Member, Research Project Evaluation Committee, Ministry of Environment of Japan, 1990-99. Publications: 80original articles and books on plant photomorphogenesis, including: Harmful and beneficial effects of solar UV light on plant growth, 1993; Phytochrome elicits the cryptic red-light signal which results in amplification of anthocyanin biosynthesis in sorghum, 1999; Photoregulation of seed germination, in Handbook of Seed Science and Technology, 2006. Honours: University Faculty Exchange Grant, Royal Society, 1992. Memberships: Botanical Society of Japan; Japanese Society of Plant Physiology; American Society of Plant Biologists. Address: Uozakiminami 5-chome, 9-45-101, Kobe 6580025, Japan. E-mail: hashimt@hotmail.com

HASHMI (Aurangzeb) Alamgir, b. 15 November 1951, Lahore, Pakistan. Professor; Poet; Writer; Editor; Broadcaster. Education: Doctorate. Appointments: Lecturer to Professor of English and Comparative Literature, 1971-2000: Government College, Lahore; Punjab University, Lahore; Forman Christian College, Lahore; University of Berne; University of Basel; University of North Carolina; Harvard University; Fribourg University; University of Louisville; University of Zürich and Volkshochschule, Zürich; University of Bahawalpur, Pakistan; Universities of Geneva, Azad Jammu & Kashmir; Iceland; International Islamic University, Islamabad; Pakistan Futuristics Institute, Islamabad; Quaid-i-Azam University, Islamabad. Publications: Books: The Oath and Amen, 1976; Pakistani Literature, 1978; America is a Punjabi Word, 1979; An Old Chair, 1979; My Second in Kentucky, 1981; Ezra Pound, 1983; This Time in Lahore, 1983; Commonwealth Literature, 1983; Neither This Time/Nor That Place, 1984; The Worlds of Muslim Imagination, 1986; Inland and Other Poems, 1988; The Commonwealth, Comparative Literature and the World, 1988; Pakistani Short Stories in English, 1992; The Poems of Alamgir Hashmi, 1992; Sun and Moon and Other Poems, 1992; A Choice of Hashmi's Verse, 1997; Postindependence Voices in South Asian Writings, 2001; The Ramazan Libation, 2003; Numerous other publications in collections, festschrifts, anthologies and periodicals. Honours: Poetry Prize, All Pakistan Creative Writing Contest, 1972; The Academic Roll of Honour, Government College, Lahore, 1972; Certificate of Academic Merit, University of the Punjab, Lahore, 1973; National Literature Prize, Pakistan Academy of Letters, 1985; Roberto Celli Memorial Award, 1994; Rockefeller Fellow, 1994; President's Award for Pride of Performance, Pakistan, 2004. Memberships: Modern Language Association of America; Council on National Literatures; Association for Commonwealth Studies; International Conference Committee on English in South Asia (Chair); Pakistan Academy of Letters (Life Fellow); Pakistan Academy of Letters (Board of Governors); International Association of University Professors of English; International Centre for Asian Studies; PEN (Fellow); Founding President, The Literature Podium, Islamabad; New York Academy of Sciences. Address: 1542 Service Road West, G-11/2 Islamabad, Pakistan.

HASKINS Christopher (The Rt Hon The Lord Haskins), b. 1937, Dublin, Ireland. Businessman; Member of House of Lords. m. Gilda Horsley, 5 children. Education: History (Hons), Trinity College, Dublin. Appointments: De La Rue Trainee, 1959-60; Ford Motors Dagenham Personnel, 1960-62; Manager, Belfast, 1962-68, Pioneered foods in Marks & Spencer, 1968-2002; Director, 1974, Deputy Chair, 1974, Chairman, 1980, Northern Dairies (later Northern Foods); Chairman, Express Dairies (merged with Northern Foods), 1998-2002; Member, MAFF Review of CAP, 1995; Chairman, Better Regulation Task Force, 1997-2002; Member, New Deal Task Force, 1998-2001; Member, Britain in Europe Campaign, 1998-; Non Executive Director, Yorkshire Regional Development Agency, 1998-; Advisor to the Prime Minister on Foot and Mouth "Recovery", 2001; Heading Review of Defra, 2002-2003; Chair, Selby Coalfields Task Force (Managing the impact of closure), 2002-2003; Member, CBI President's Committee, 1995-98; Member, Hampel Committee on Corporate Governance, 1996-98; Member, Irish Economic Policy Review Group, 1998; Member, Commission for Social Justice, 1992-94; Member, UK Round Table on Sustainable Development, 1995-98; Trustee, Runnymede Trust, 1989-98; Chairman, Demos Trustees, 1993-2000; Trustee, Civil Liberties, 1997-99; Trustee, Legal Assistance Trust, 1998-2004; Trustee, Lawes Agricultural Trust, 1999-; Director, Yorkshire TV, 2002-; Trustee, Business Dynamics, 2002; Chair, DEFRA Review Group, 2002-03; Chair, European Movement, 2004-; Chair of Council and Pro-Chancellor, Open University, 2005-; Regular speaker and writer about Europe, agriculture, regulation, corporate governance. Honours: Labour Peer, 1998; Honorary Degrees: Dublin, Hull, Essex, Nottingham, Leeds, Metropolitan, Cranfield, Huddersfield. Address: Quarryside Farm, Main Street, Skidby, Nr Cottingham, East Yorkshire HU16 5SG, England.

HASLAM Michael Trevor, b. 7 February 1934, Leeds, England. Retired Medical Director. m. Shirley Dunstan, 1 son, 2 daughters. Education: Sedbergh School; Exhibitioner to St John's College, Cambridge, MA, MD, BChir, 1947-52; LMSSA, LRCP, MRCS, St Bartholomew's Hospital, London, 1955-59; MRCP (G), 1967, F, 1979; MA, Theology, St John's College, York, 2003; Diploma in Psychological Medicine, 1962; Diploma in Medical Jurisprudence, 1972; MRCPsych, 1972, F, 1980; Certificate in Hypnotherapy, BSMDH, 1982. Appointments: Captain, RAMC, Military Service, 1960-62; Senior Registrar to Sir Martin Roth, Newcastle upon Tyne, 1964-67; Consultant in Psychological Medicine, Doncaster, 1967-70; Consultant in Psychological Medicine, York, 1970-89; Medical Director, Harrogate Clinic, 1989-91; Medical Director, South Durham, NHS Trust, 1994-98; Retired 1999. Publications: Books: Psychiatric Illness in Adolescence, 1975; Sexual Disorders, 1978; Psychosexual Disorders, 1979; Psychiatry Made Simple, 1982; Clifton Hospital an era, 1996; Close to the Wind, 2006; Shrink in the Clink, 2008; Alzheimer, 2009; Editor: Transvestism, 1996; Psychiatry in the New Millennium, 2002; Editor of the Celtic Times, 1953-56. Honours: TD (National Service Decoration); Retired Fellow, Royal College of Physicians, Glasgow, 2001-; Retired Fellow, Royal College of Psychiatrists, 2001; Freeman of London; Liveryman of the Society of Apothecaries; Retired, Warden of North, Association of Freeman of England and Wales; Honorary Secretary, Society of Clinical Psychiatrists; Listed in national and international biographical dictionaries. Memberships: Chairman retired, Society of Clinical Psychiatrists; Author's Club to 1999; Royal Society of Medicine to 2004. Address: Chapel Garth, Crayke, York, YO61 4TE, England.

HASLUCK Sally Anne, b. 2 January 1945, Birmingham, England. Museum Consultant. m. Nicholas Paul Hasluck, 2 sons. Education: Alcester Grammar School, Warwickshire; Furzedown Teacher Training College, London. Appointments: Maths Teacher, Perth Girls School, Australia, 1968; Law Museum Management Committee, 1973-83; Honorary Curator, Claremont Museum, Perth, 1974-94; Vice President, 1978-82, President, 1982-86, Museums Association, WA Branch; WA State Task Force Museums Policy, 1991; Museum Consultant, 1994-; Trustee/Deputy Chair, Western Australian Museum, 1994-2001; Councillor, National Museum of Australia, 2004-. Publications: Numerous articles for professional magazines; Contributions to Australian Dictionary of Biography. Honours: Community Scholarship for Executive Management Course AIM, 1991; ANZAC Fellowship, 1991; Honorary Certificate for contribution to advancement of Museums Association & Museum Community, 1993; Honorary Life Member, Friends of Claremont Museum, 1993; Citizen of the Year, 1993, Freeman of the Town, 1994, Claremont Town Council; Fellow, WA Museum, 2002; Merit Award, Federation of Australian Historical Societies, 2009. Memberships: International Council of Museums; Museums of Australia; Friends of National Museum of Australia; Friends of Western Australian Museum; Friends of Claremont Museum, WA; Royal WA Historical Society; National Trust WA; Friends of New Norcia, WA. E-mail: hasluck@iinet.net.au

HASSAN IBN TALAL H R H, b. 20 March 1947, Amman, Jordan. Crown Prince of Jordan. m. Sarrath Khujista Akhter Banu, 1968, 1 son, 3 daughters. Education: Christ Church, Oxford University. Appointments: Regent to the throne of Jordan in absence of King Hussein; Ombudsman for National Development, 1971-; Founder, Royal Science Society of Jordan, 1970; Royal Academy of Islamic Civilization Research (AlAlbait), 1980; Arab Thought Forum, 1981; Forum Humanum (now Arab Youth Forum), 1982; Co-Chairman, Independent Commission on International Council for Science and Technology; Honorary General of Jordan Armed Forces. Publications: A Study on Jerusalem, 1979; Palestinian Self-Determination, 1981; Search for Peace, 1984; Christianity in the Arab World, 1994; Continuity, Innovation and Change, 2001; To be a Muslim, 2003; In Memory of Faisal I: The Iraqi Question, 2003. Honours: Honorary degrees from universities of Yarmouk, 1980, Bogazici (Turkey), 1982, Jordan, 1987, Durham, 1990, Ulster, 1996; Medal, President, Italian Republic, 1982; Knight of Grand Cross of Order of Self-Merit (Italy), 1983. Address: The Royal Palace, Amman, Jordan.

HASSAN Khadiga Abdel Hamid, b. 23 August 1941, Dondate, Egypt. Professor. m. Kamal Youssef, 1 son, 2 daughters. Education: BSc, Chemistry & Entomology, 1963, Aishams University, Cairo, 1963; MSc, 1968, PhD, 1973, Animal Physiology, Assiut University. Appointments: Demonstrator, Zoology, 1963, Lecturer, 1973, Associate Professor, 1978, Professor, 1988, Animal Physiology, Faculty of Science, Assiut University. Publications: Over 60 articles in animal physiology. Honours: Assiut University Award, 2009. Memberships: Egyptian-German Society of Zoology. Address: Zoology Department, Faculty of Science, Assiut University, Assiut, Egypt.

HASTE Cate (Catherine Mary), b. 6 August 1945, Leeds, England. Writer; Television Documentary Producer/Director. m. Melvyn Bragg (Rt Hon The Lord Bragg), 18 December 1973, 1 son, 1 daughter. Education: BA Honours, English, University of Sussex, 1963-66; Postgraduate Diploma Adult Education, Manchester University, 1967. Appointments: Television: The Secret War (BBC); End of Empire (Granada TV); Writing on the Wall (Channel 4) Munich – The Peace of Paper (Thames); Secret History – Death of a Democrat (Channel 4); The Churchills (ITV); Cold War (Jeremy Isaacs Productions/BBC/CNN); Millennium (Jeremy Isaacs Productions/BBC/CNN); Hitler's Brides (Flashback TV/ Channel 4); Married to the Prime Minister (Flashback TV/ Channel 4). Publications: Keep the Home Fires Burning: Propaganda to the Home Front in the First World War, 1977; Rules of Desire: Sex in Britain World War I to the Present, 1992; Nazi Women – Hitler's Seduction of a Nation, 2001; The Goldfish Bowl – Married to the Prime Minister 1955-97, co-authored with Cherie Booth, 2004; Editor, Clarissa Eden: A Memoir from Churchill to Eden, 2007; Sheila Fell: A Passion for Paint, 2010. Memberships: British PEN; British Academy of Film and Television Arts. Address: 12 Hampstead Hill Gardens, London NW3 2PL, England. E-mail: cate.haste@virgin.net

HASTINGS Max Macdonald, (Sir) b. 28 December 1945, London, England. Author; Broadcaster; Journalist. m. (1) Patricia Edmondson, 1972, dissolved, 1994, 2 sons, 1 deceased, 1 daughter, (2) Penny Grade, 1999. Education: Exhibitioner, University College, Oxford, 1964-65; Fellow, World Press Institute, St Paul, Minnesota, USA, 1967-68. Appointments: Researcher, BBC TV, 1963-64; Reporter, London Evening Standard, 1965-67; Reporter, BBC TV Current Affairs, 1970-73; Editor, Evening Standard Londoner's Diary, 1976-77; Editor, Daily Telegraph, 1986-95; Editor, Evening Standard, 1996-2002; Columnist, Daily Express, 1981-83, Sunday Times, 1985-86; Editor-in-Chief and a Director, Daily Telegraph Plc, 1989-96. Publications: The Fire This Time, 1968; The Struggle for Civil Rights in Northern Ireland, 1970; Montrose: The King's Champion, 1977; Yoni: The Hero of Entebbe, 1979; Bomber Command, 1979; The Battle of Britain (with Lee Deighton), 1980; Das Reich, 1981; Battle for the Falklands (with Simon Jenkins), 1983; Overlord: D-Day and the Battle for Normandy, 1984; Oxford Book of Military Anecdotes (editor), 1985; Victory in Europe, 1985; The Korean War, 1987; Outside Days, 1989; Outside Days, 1989; Scattered Shots, 1999; Going to the Wars, 2000; Editor, 2002; Armageddon, 2004; Warriors, 2005; Country Fair, 2005; Nemesis, 2007; Finest Years: Churchill as Warlord 1940-45, 2009; Did You Really Shoot the Television? 2010; Inferno: The World at War 1939-45, 2011. Honours: Somerset Maugham Prize, 1979; British Press Awards, Journalist of the Year, 1982; Granada TV Reporter of the Year, 1982; Editor of the Year, 1988; Yorkshire Post Book of the Year Award, 1983, 1984; London Press Club Edgar Wallace Trophy, 2009; Honorary DLitt, Leicester University, 1992; Royal Society of Literature, Fellow, 1996; KBE, 2002; Honorary Fellow of King's College, London; Doctorate, Nottingham University, Nottingham; Knighthood; Doctorate, Leicester University; Westminster Medal, RUSI for lifetime contribution to Military Literature. Address: c/o PFD, Drury House, 34-43 Russell Street, London WC2B 5HA, England.

HATADA Koichi, b. 15 December 1934, Osaka, Japan. Chemistry Professor. m. Michiko Sawada, 1961, 3 sons. Education: BSc, Chemistry, 1957, MSc, Polymer Chemistry, 1960, DSc, 1965, Osaka University. Appointments: Research Associate, Daicel Co, Japan, 1957-64; Assistant Professor, 1964-67, Associate Professor, 1967-83, Professor, 1983-98, Senator, 1994-96, Vice President, 1997-98, Professor Emeritus, 1998-, Faculty of Engineering Science, Osaka University; Postdoctoral Fellow, University of Massachusetts, Amherst, 1973-74; Professor, Fukui University of Technology, 1998-2007; Visiting Professor, University of Air, 1998-2006. Publications: Macromolecular Design of Polymeric Materials (with Kitayama and Vogl), 1997; NMR Spectroscopy of Polymers (with Kitayama), 2004. Honours: Herman F Mark Medal, Austrian Research Institute for Chemistry and Technology, 2002; Paul J Flory Polymer Research Prize, World Forum on Advanced Materials, 2006. Memberships: Society of Polymer Science, Japan; American Chemical Society; Chemical Society of Japan; Osaka Owners' Association Registered Tangible Cultural Properties of Japan.

HATEGAN Cornel, b. 17 August 1940, Ohaba-Matnic Romania. Physicist. 1 daughter. Education: University Diplomat Physics, University Bucharest, 1964; Dr, Physics, Institute of Atomic Physics, Bucharest, 1973. Appointments: Assistant Researcher, Researcher, Senior Researcher, Institute of Atomic Physics, 1964-70, 1972-; Humboldt Researcher, University Erlangen Nuernberg, 1970-71; Humboldt Researcher, University Munich (Summer Semesters 2002, 2004, 2006, 2008). Publications: Science Papers on Atomic and Nuclear Physics. Honours: Urkunde of Humboldt Foundation; Physics Prize of Romanian Academy; Corresponding Member Romanian Academy, elected, 1992; Fellow, Institute Physics, London, elected 2000; Honorary citizen of the city of Caranebes, conferred 2003. Memberships: Humboldt Club; Nuclear Physics Division of Romanian Physical Society. Address: Institute of Atomic Physics, CP MG 6, 76900 Bucharest, Magurele, Romania.

HATJIYIANNAKIS Constantine, b. 23 May 1948, Athens, Greece. Mechanical and Electrical Engineer. Divorced, 3 daughters. Education: Mechanical and Electrical Engineering, School of Mechanical and Electrical Engineering, 1971, Doctor's degree, School of Chemical Engineering, 1993, National Technical University, Athens. Appointments: Mechanical and Electrical Engineer, Head of Technical Service, Loumidis Coffee-Kakao-Chocolate Industry, 1973-76; Officer and Director, Directorates for Energy Policies and Electricity Production, and Directorates for Industrial Matters and Petroleum Installations; General Director of Energy, Ministry of the Environment, Energy and Climate Change, 1976-. Publications: Numerous articles on biomass-energy systems sustainability in scientific and professional journals; Wide experience in European Union and international energy and climate change matters, also as representative to EU and international fora, meetings or conferences, including OECD, IEA and UNFCCC. Honours: Plaque of Honour, Greek Centre of Scientific Research Journal Ihor. Memberships: Association of Greek Mechanical and Electrical Engineers; Technical Chamber of Greece; Greek Geographical Society; Society of

Friends of Ancient Greek Names; Organisation of the Greek Language; Greek Centre of Scientific Research; Association for the Promotion of Ancient Greek Mathematics; International Foundation of the Greek Language and Greek Civilization; Greek Language Inheritance Society.

HATTERSLEY OF SPARKBROOK, Baron Roy Sydney George, b. 28 December 1932, Sheffield, England. Politician; Writer. m. Molly Loughran, 1956. Education: BSc, Economics, University of Hull. Appointments: Journalist and Health Service Executive, 1956-64; Member, City Council, Sheffield, 1957-65; Member of Parliament, Labour Party, Sparkbrook Division, Birmingham, 1964-97; Parliamentary Private Secretary, Minister of Pensions and National Insurance, 1964-67; Director, Campaign for a European Political Community, 1966-67; Joint Parliamentary Secretary, Ministry of Labour, 1967-69, Minister of Defence for Administration, 1969-70; Visiting Fellow, Harvard University, 1971, 1972, Nuffield College, Oxford, 1984-; Labour Party Spokesman on Defence, 1972, and on Education and Science, 1972-74; Minister of State, Foreign and Commonwealth Office, 1974-76; Secretary of State for Prices and Consumer Protection, 1976-79; Principal Opposition Spokesman on the Environment, 1979-80, Home Affairs, 1980-83, Treasury and Economics Affairs, 1983-87, Home Affairs, 1987-92; Deputy Leader, Labour Party, 1983-92. Publications: Nelson: A Biography, 1974; Goodbye to Yorkshire (essays), 1976; Politics Apart, 1982; Press Gang, 1983; A Yorkshire Boyhood, 1983; Choose Freedom: The Future for Democratic Socialism, 1987; Economic Priorities for a Labour Government, 1987; The Maker's Mark (novel), 1990; In That Quiet Earth (novel), 1991; Skylark Song (novel), 1994; Between Ourselves (novel), 1994; Who Goes Home? 1995; 50 Years On, 1997; Buster's Diaries: As Told to Roy Hattersley, 1998; Blood and Fire: The Story of William and Catherine Booth and their Salvation Army, 1999; A Brand from the Burning: The Life of John Wesley, 2002; The Edwardians, 2004. Contributions to: Newspapers and journals. Honours: Privy Counsellor, 1975; Columnist of the Year, Granada, 1982; Honorary doctorates; Life Peer, 1997. Address: House of Lords, London SW1A 0PW, England.

HATTERSLEY-SMITH Geoffrey Francis, b. 22 April 1923, London, England. Glaciologist; Toponymist. m. Maria Kefallinou, 2 daughters. Education: Scholar, Winchester College; BA Geology (Hons), 1948, MA, 1951, D Phil, 1956, New College, Oxford. Appointments: Sub-Lieutenant, (Russian Convoys, D-day 6 June 1944, Relief of Singapore 12 September 1945) RNVR, 1942-46; Falklands Dependencies Survey (Base Leader, Admiralty Bay, King George Island, 1948-50); Defence Scientific Staff Officer, Canadian Defence Research Board (I/c field operations in northern Ellesmere Island from 1953 and established first camp on Ward Hunt Island, and stations at Lake Hazen (Leader, Canadian IGY Expedition) and Tanquary Fiord, 1951-73; Secretary, Antarctic Place-Names Committee, FCO London, 1974-89; Commemorated in Cape Hattersley-Smith, Black Coast, Graham Land, as proposed by the Americans in 1986. Publications: Present Arctic Ice Cover, 1974; North of Latitude Eighty, 1974; The History of Place-Names in the Falkland Islands Dependencies, 1980; Editor, The Norwegian with Scott, 1984; The History of Place-Names in the British Antarctic Territory (2 vols), 1991; Geographical Names in the Ellesmere Island National Park Reserve, 1998; numerous papers. Honours: 4 UK, 2 USSR Clasp Campaign Medals, 2006; Founders Gold Medal, Royal Geographical Society, 1966; Polar Medal – Antarctic & Arctic; Elected Fellow, Royal Society of Canada, Academy of Sciences, 1971.

Memberships: Royal Society of Canada; Royal Geographical Society; Editorial Committee, Polar Record, Cambridge; UK Polar Medal Assessment Committee.

HAUER Rutger, b. 23 January 1944, Amsterdam, Holland. Actor. m. (1) Heidi Merz (divorced), 1 daughter, (2) Ieneke, 1985. Career: Turkish Delight, 1973; The Wilby Conspiracy, Keetje Tippel, 1975; Max Havelaar, 1976; Mysteries, Solider of Orange, 1978; Woman Between Dog and Wolf, 1979; Spetters, 1980; Nighthawks, Chanel Solitaire, 1981; Blade Runner, Eureka, 1982; Outsider in Amsterdam, The Osterman Weekend, 1983; A Breed Apart, Ladyhawke, 1984; Flesh and Blood, 1985; The Hitcher, Wanted Dead or Alive, 1986; The Legend of the Holy Drinker, 1989; Salute of the Juggler, Ocean Point, On a Moonlit Night, Split Second, Buffy the Vampire Slayer, Past Midnight, Nostradamus, Surviving the Game, The Beans of Egypt Maine, Angel of Death, New World Disorder, 1999; Wilder, Lying in Wait, Partners in Crime, 2000; Jungle Juice, Flying Virus, 2001; I Banchieri di Dio, Scorcher, Warrior Angels, Confessions of a Dangerous Mind, 2002; In the Shadow of the Cobra, Tempesta, Camera ascunsa, 2004; Sin City, Batman Begins, 2005; Minotaur, Mentor, 2006; Goal II: Living the Dream, 7eventy 5ive, Moving McAllister, Magic Flute Diaries, Tonight at Noon, Spoon, 2007; Magic Flute Diaries, Bride Flight, The Rhapsody, 2008; Oogverblindend, Barbarossa, 2009; Happiness Runs, 2010. TV: commercials for Guinness, 1989; TV films: Angel of Death, 1994; Menin, 1998; The 10th Kingdom, 2000. Address: c/o William Morris Agency, 151 El Camino Drive, Beverly Hills, CA 90212, USA.

HAUTCOEUR Pierre Cyrille, b. 9 October 1964, Paris, France. Professor. m. Guiomar Perez-Espejo, 2 sons, 1 daughter. Education: Ecole normale supérieure, Paris, 1983-88; Master, History, Paris X, Nanterre, 1985; Master, Economics, EHESS, 1986; Agrégation, Social Sciences, 1986; PhD, Economics, Paris I, Sorbonne, 1994; Agrégation de sciences économiques, 1998. Appointments: Assistant Professor, Ecole normale supérieure, Paris, 1989-96; Visiting Scholar, Rutgers University, USA, 1996-97; Researcher, CNRS, 1997-98; Professor, Economics, Orleans University, 1998-2002; Professor, Economics, Paris I, Sorbonne, 2002-06; Director, Social Sciences, Ministry of Research, 2001-03; Professor, Social Sciences, EHESS, 2006-; Professor, Economic History, Paris School of Economics, 2006-. Publications: Le Marché Financier Français au 19 siecle, 2007; Monnaie, banque et marchés Financiers, 2007; La Crise de 1929, 2009. Honours: Fulbright Grant, 1997; Best PhD, International Economic History Association, 1998; Best Young Economist, Cercle des Economists, Le Monde, 2003. Address: PSE-EHESS, 48 bd Jourdan, 75014 Paris, France. E-mail: hautcoeur@pse.eus.fr Website: www.pse.eus.fr/hautcoeur/

HAVEL Jean Eugène Martial, b. 1928, Le Havre, France. Writer. m. Anne Marie Luhr, 1955, deceased, 2 sons (1 deceased), 2 daughters. Education: Lic, Faculté de Droit, Université de Paris, 1950; Diploma, Institut des Etudes Politiques, 1952; Institut des Etudes Scandinaves, 1953; School of Law, University of Oslo, 1953-54; Dr es L (dissertation: Le socialisme en Norvège), Faculté des Lettres, Université de Paris, 1956. Appointments: Part time Teacher of French, University of Stockholm, 1956-59; Assistant Professor of Political Science, University of Montréal, 1959-62; Assistant Professor of Political Science, 1962, Associate Professor, 1964, Acting Head of Department, 1967-70, Professor of Political Science, 1969-93, Professor Emeritus, 1995-, Laurentian University. Publications: Author: Cours de journalisme: la rédaction, 1956; La fabrication du journal, 1957; La politique suédoise du logement de 1940 à 1957, 1957; Habitat et Logement, 1957, 1964, 1967, 1974, 1985; Le mouvement socialiste norvégien, 1958; Le socialisme réformiste modéré en Suède, 1958; Le socialisme danois, 1958; La question du pastoret féminin en Suède, in Archives de sociologie des religions, 1959; Le séparatisme dans le grand Montréal opinion poll: in Montreal media, 1961; La condition de la femme, 1961; Les citoyens de Sudbury et la politique, 1966; Les états scandinaves et l'intégration européenne, 1970; Some effects of the introduction of a policy of bilingualism in the polyglot community of Sudbury in Canadian Review of Sociology and Anthropology, 1972; Grandes villes, nations et empires: une carte politique de la nouvelle société industrielle avancée in Revue canadienne de science politique, 1972; La Finlande et la Suède, 1978; Kalaallit Nunaat/Groënland in Europa Ethnica, 1992; The Franco-Ontarians' in Canadian Diversity, 1995; Effacement de la Normandie, 1998; La politique de l'Eglise Catholique Romaine, in Italian Politics and Society, 1998 & 1999; Brooks, 2002; Le fédéralisme (samizdat), 2007; The Five Sisters, 2011; A Young Norman in the Second World War and other publications; Numerous articles and reviews for learned journals. Honours: Research Scholarships from Norwegian and Finnish governments, Swedish Institute; Council of Europe; Canada Council; Carnegie Endowment for International Peace Award, 1958; Canada Centennial Medal, 1967; Canada Council Fellowship Award, 1968, 1975. Memberships: Canadian Political Science Association; Association for the Advancement of Scandinavian Studies in Canada. Address: 175 Boland Ave, Sudbury, Ontario P3E 1Y1, Canada.

HAVRÁNEK Antonin, b. 16 January 1934, Prague, Czech Republic. Physicist. m. Eva Hollasová, 2 sons, 1 daughter. Education: Magister of Science, Physics, 1957, Cert RNDr, 1966, PhD, 1967, Faculty of Mathematics and Physics, Charles University, Prague. Appointments: Assistant, 1957-72, Researcher, 1972-91, Head of Department of Polymer Physics, 1990-94, Assistant Professor, 1992-, Faculty of Mathematics and Physics, Charles University. Publications: Several textbooks on mechanics and polymer physics including Introduction to Biorheology, 2007; Around 100 articles and scientific contributions. Memberships: Union of Czech Mathematicians and Physicists; Czech Physical Society; Czech Chemical Society. Address: MFF UK, V Holesovickach 2, Prague 8, CZ 180 00, Czech Republic. E-mail: antonin.havranek@mff.cuni.cz

HAWK Tony, b. 12 May 1968, San Diego, California, USA. Professional Skateboarder. m.(1) Cindy Dunbar, 1990-95 (divorced) 1 son (2) Erin Lee, 1996-2004 (divorced), 2 sons, (3) Lhotse Merriam, 2006. Career: Started skateboarding 1978; Turned Professional for Dogtown, 1982; Created own company, Birdhouse skateboards, 1992; Film appearances including: Police Academy 4, 1987; Sight Unseen, Transworld skateboarding, 2001; Tony Hawk's Gigantic Skatepark Tour, 2001; Haggard, 2002; End, 2002; Tony Hawk's Boom Boom Huck Jam, 2004; TV Appearances including: Tony Hawk's Gigantic Skatepark Tour; Various "X-Games" Vert Competitions (televised); Various "Gravity Games" Vert Competitions (televised); Jackass, 2000; Max Steel, 2000; Viva la Bam, 2003. Publications: Tony Hawk, Occupation: Skateboarder, autobiography, 2002; The Tony Hawk Pro Skater series, 1999-2004. Honours include: 16 X Games Medals, all Gold, 1995-2004; Various awards for his games, including best game, 2000; Best sports game, 2003; Transworld, best Vert skater, 2000; Slam City Jam, Best Vert trick, 2003. Address: Carlsbad, California, USA.

HAWKE Ethan, b. 6 November 1970, Austin, Texas, USA. Actor. m. (1) Uma Thurman, 1998-2004 (divorced) 1 son, 1 daughter, (2) Ryan Shawhughes, 2008, 1 daughter. Career: Co-founder, Malaparte Theatre Company; Theatre appearances include: Casanova, 1991; A Joke, The Seagull, 1992; Sophistry; Films include: Explorers, 1985; Dead Poets Society, Dad, 1989; White Fang, Mystery Date, 1991; A Midnight Clear, Waterland, 1992; Alive, Rich in Love, Straight to One (director), 1993; Reality Bites, Quiz Show, Floundering, 1994; Before Sunrise, 1995; Great Expectations, Gattaca, Joe the King, 1999; Hamlet, 2000; Tape, Waking Life, Training Day, The Jimmy Show, 2001; Before Sunset, Taking Lives, 2004; Assault on Precinct 13, Lord of War, 2005; Fast Food Nation, The Hottest State, 2006; Tonight at Noon, Before the Devil Knows You're Dead, 2007; Welcome to Gattaca, Do Not Alter, What Doesn't Kill You, 2008; Staten Island, New York, I Love You, Brooklyn's Finest, Day Breakers, 2009; Moby Dick (TV), 2010. Publications: Ash Wednesday, 2002. Address: Creative Artists Agency, 9830 Wilshire Boulevard, Beverly Hills, CA 90212, USA.

HAWKESWORTH Pauline Mary, b. 28 April 1943, Portsmouth, England. Secretary. m. Rex Hawkesworth, 1961, 2 daughters. Appointments: Secretarial Manager, Administrator, Ladies Athletic Club; Track and Field Judge. Publications: 3 books of poetry: Dust and Dew, 1969; Developing Green Films, 1998; Bracken Women in Lime Trees, 2009; Anthologies: Parents Enitharmon, 2000; Spirit of Wilfred Owen, 2001. Contributions to: Envoi; South; Interpreters House; Script; Iota; Poetry Nottingham International; Frogmore Press; Others. Honours: 1st Prize, Short Story, Portsmouth Polytechnic, 1981; 1st Prize, South Wales Miners Eisteddfod, 1990; 1st Prize, Hastings Open Poetry Competition, 1993; Runner-Up, Redbeck Competition, 1996; 1st Prize Tavistock and North Dartmoor, 2000; 1st Prize Newark and Sherwood Millennium Project, 2001; 2nd Prize Richmond Adult CC; Winner, Indigo Dreams Book Competition, 2008. Membership: President, Portsmouth Poetry Society. Address: 4 Rampart Gardens, Hilsea, Portsmouth PO3 5LR, England.

HAWKING Stephen (William), b. 8 January 1942, Oxford, England. Professor of Mathematics; Writer. m. (1) Jane Wilde, 1965 (divorced), 2 sons, 1 daughter, (2) Elaine Mason, 1995 (divorced). Education: BA, University College, Oxford; PhD, Trinity Hall, Cambridge. Appointments: Research Fellow, 1965-69, Fellow for Distinction in Science, 1969-, Gonville and Caius College, Cambridge; Member, Institute of Theoretical Astronomy, Cambridge, 1968-72; Research Assistant, Institute of Astronomy, Cambridge, 1972-73; Research Assistant, Department of Applied Mathematics and Theoretical Physics, 1973-75, Reader in Gravitational Physics, 1975-77, Professor, 1977-79, Lucasian Professor of Mathematics, 1979-2009, Cambridge University. Publications: The Large Scale Structure of Space-Time (with G F R Ellis), 1973; General Relativity: An Einstein Centenary Survey (editor with W W Israel), 1979; Is the End in Sight for Theoretical Physics?: An Inaugural Lecture, 1980; Superspace and Supergravity: Proceedings of the Nuffield Workshop (editor with M Rocek), 1981; The Very Early Universe: Proceedings of the Nuffield Workshop (co-editor), 1983; Three Hundred Years of Gravitation (with W W Israel), 1987; A Brief History of Time: From the Big Bang to Black Holes, 1988; Black Holes and Baby Universes and Other Essays, 1993; The Nature of Space and Time (with Roger Penrose), 1996 and other essays; The Universe in a Nutshell, 2001; The Theory of Everything: The Origin and Fate of the Universe, 2002; The Future of Space Time, co-editor, 2001; On the Shoulders of Giants, 2002; Information Loss in Black

Holes, 2005; A Briefer History of Time, 2005. Contributions to: Scholarly journals. Honours: Eddington Medal, 1975; Gold Medal, 1985, Royal Academy of Science; Pius XI Gold Medal, Pontifical Academy of Sciences, 1975; William Hopkins Prize, Cambridge Philosophical Society, 1976; Maxwell Medal, Institute of Physics, 1976; Dannie Heineman Prize for Mathematical Physics, American Physical Society and American Institute of Physics, 1976; Honorary fellow, University College, Oxford, 1977; Trinity Hall, Cambridge, 1984; Commander of the Order of the British Empire, 1982; Paul Dirac Medal and Prize, Institute of Physics, 1987; Wolf Foundation Prize for Physics, 1988; Companion of Honour, 1989; Britannica Award, 1989; Albert Medal, Royal Society of Arts, 1999; Presidential Medal Of Freedom, 2009; Honorary doctorates. Memberships: American Academy of Arts and Sciences; American Philosophical Society; Pontifical Academy of Sciences; Royal Society, fellow. Address: c/o Department of Applied Mathematics and Theoretical Physics, Cambridge University, Silver Street, Cambridge CB3 9EW, England.

HAWKINS Peter John, b. 20 June 1944, Old Welwyn, Hertfordshire, England. Art and Antiques Consultant. Education: Eton; MA, Modern Languages, Oxford University. Appointments: Director of Christie's (Auctioneers), 1973-2003; Managing Director of Christie's, Monte Carlo, 1987-89. Publication: The Price Guide to Antique Guns and Pistols, 1973. Honours: Freedom of the City of London; Liveryman of the Worshipful Company of Gunmakers, 1978-. Memberships: Turf Club, 1973-. Address: 20 Ennismore Gardens, London SW7 1AA, England.

HAWKINS Sally, b. 27 April 1976, London, England. Actress. Education: Royal Academy of Dramatic Arts, London, 1998. Career: Film: Never Let Me Go; It's a Wonderful Afterlife; Happy Ever Afters; Desert Flower; An Education; Happy-Go-Lucky; Cassandra's Dream; Waz; The Painted Veil; Vera Drake; Layer Cake; All or Nothing; Made in Dagenham; Submarine; Television: Persuasion; Man to Man with Dean Learner; Shiny Shiny Bright New Hole in My Heart; 20,000 Streets Under the Sky; Fingersmith; Dinos After Dark; Little Britain; The Young Visiters; Bunk Bed Boys; Byron; Promoted to Glory; Tipping the Velvet; Jane Eyre; Love Birds; Theatre: The Winterling; House of Bernarda Alba; Country Music; The Way of the World; Misconceptions; A Midsummer Night's Dream; Much Ado About Nothing; Perapalas; The Cherry Orchard; Romeo & Juliet; The Dybbuk; Svejk; Accidental Death of An Anarchist; The Whore of Babylon; As You Like It; Mrs Warren's Profession. Honours: Golden Nymph Award, Best Actress, Monte Carlo Television Festival, 2007; RTS Award for Best Actress, 2008; Silver Bear Award for Best Actress, Berlin Film Festival; Breakthrough Award, 12th Annual Hollywood Film Festival; Nominated for Best Actress, BIFA; Nominated for European Actress Award for European Film Awards; LA Film Critics Award for Best Actress; New York Film Critics Award for Best Actress; Nominated for Best Actress in a British Film, London Film Critics Awards; Best Actress, NYFC Online; Best Actress, Boston Critics Awards; Best Actress, American National Society of Film Critics Awards; Golden Globe for Best Actress in a Comedy or Musical. Address: c/o Conway van Gelder Grant Ltd, 8-12 Broadwick Street, London W1F 8HW, England.

HAWN Goldie, b. 21 November 1945, Washington, USA. Actress. m. (1) Gus Trikonis, 1969 (divorced), (2) Bill Hudson, 1976 (divorced), 1 son, 1 daughter, 1 son with partner Kurt Russell. Career: debut, Good Morning, World, 1967-68; TV includes: Rowan and Martin's Laugh-In, 1968-70; Pure Goldie, Natural history documentary, 1996; Films include: Cactus Flower; There's a Girl in my Soup; Dollars; The Sugarland Express; The Girl from Petrovka; Shampoo; The Duchess and the Dirtwater Fox; Foul Play; Seems Like Old Times; Private Benjamin; Best Friends; Protocol; Swing Shift; Overboard; Bird on a Wire; Housesitter; Deceived; Death Becomes Her; The First Wives Club, 1996; Everybody Says I Love You, 1996; The Out of Towners, 1999; Town and Country, 2001; The Banger Sisters, 2003; Star and Executive Producer: Goldie Hawn Special, 1978, Private Benjamin, 1980; Executive Producer, Something To Talk About; Co-Executive Producer, My Blue Heaven, 1990. Honours: Academy Award, Best Supporting Actress, 1970; Golden Globe Award, Best Supporting Actress, 1970. Address: Creative Artists Agency, 9830 Wilshire Boulevard, Beverly Hills, CA 90212, USA.

HAWRYLYSHYN Bohdan, b. 19 October 1926, Koropec, Ukraine. Professor. m. Leonida Hayovska, 1 son, 2 daughters. Education: BA Sc, Mechanical Engineering, University of Toronto; MBA, IMI (now IMD), Geneva, Switzerland; PhD, Social and Economic Studies, University of Geneva, Switzerland. Appointments: Adviser to 3 prime ministers, 4 chairmen of Parliament and 1st President of Ukraine; Chairman, International Management Institute (IMI), Kyiv. Publications: 2 books; Over 100 articles in professional journals. Honours: Honorary Doctorates: University of York, Toronto; University of Alberta, Edmonton; Ternopil Academy of National Economy; V Stefanyk University; Y Fedlovsky University, Ukraine. Memberships: 2 medals from two Presidents of Ukraine; Gold Medal, President of the Republic of Italy; Club of Rome; International Management Academy; Jean Monet Foundation; World Academy of Art and Science; National Academy of Science of Ukraine; Baden Powell Fellowship.

HAY David Colin, b. 27 August 1973, Dunfermline, Scotland. Scientist. m. Chantal Geoghegan, 1 daughter. Education: BSc, 1996, PhD, 2000, University of St Andrews. Appointments: Research Fellow, University of St Andrews, 1999-2002; Research Fellow, Roslin Institute, 2000-06; Senior Research Fellow, University of Edinburgh, 2006-07; Chairman, Co-ordinating Committee, Stem Cells for Safer Medicine, 2008-09; Editor, RESCUE Society, 2008-09; RCUK Senior Research Fellow, University of Edinburgh, 2008-12; Principal Investigator, MRC Centre for Regenerative Medicine, 2008; Lead Guest Editor, Journal of Biomedicine and Biotechnology, 2009; Managing Editor, Frontiers of Bioscience, 2009; Editorial Board Member, World Journal of Stem Cells, 2009; Faculty Member, 1000 Medicine, 2009; Editorial Board Member, Journal of Biochips & Tissue Chips; Editorial Board Member, World Journal of Gastrointestinal Pathophysiology. Publications: Numerous articles in professional journals. Honours: Listed in international biographical dictionaries; Several research and travel grants. Memberships: Associate Member, Royal Society Medicine; International Society for Stem Cell Research; British Association for the Study of the Liver. E-mail: davehay@talktalk.net

HAY Jocelyn, b. 30 July 1927, Wales, United Kingdom. Writer. m. Andrew Hay, 2 daughters. Education BA (Hons), Open University. Appointments: Freelance Writer and Broadcaster, 1954-83; Work included: Forces Broadcasting Service, Woman's Hour, BBC Radio 2 and 4, World Service; Head, Press and PR Department, Girl Guides Association, Commonwealth Headquarters, 1973-78; Founder and Director, London Media Workshops (training agency), 1978-94; Founder and Honorary Chairman, 1983-2008, Honorary President, 2008-, Voice of the Listener and Viewer(the leading advocate of the citizen and consumer in broadcasting in the UK); Honorary Chair of

Trustees, The Voice of the Listener Trust, 1987-; Honorary Trustee, Presswise, 2003-10; President Emeritus, The European Association of Listeners' and Viewers' Associations, Euralva. Publications: Numerous articles, speeches and broadcasts on broadcasting and cultural issues. Honours: MBE, 1999; Commonwealth Broadcasting Association's Elizabeth R Award for services to public service broadcasting, 1999; CBE, 2005; European Woman of Achievement Award (Humanitarian Category), European Union of Women, British Section, 2007. Memberships: Fellow, Royal Society of Arts; Society of Authors. Address: 48 St James' Oaks, Trafalgar Road, Gravesend, Kent DA11 0QT, England.

HAYE David, b. 13 October 1980, Bermondsey, South London, England. Heavyweight Boxer. m. Natasha, 1 son. Career: Silver Medal, World Amateur Championships, Belfast, 2001; WBC Cruiserweight Champion, 2007-08; WBA Cruiserweight Super Champion, 2007-08; The Ring Cruiserweight Champion, 2007-08; WBO Cruiserweight Champion, 2008; WBA Heavyweight Champion, 2009-.

HAYEK Salma, b. 2 September 1966, Coatzacoalcos, Veracruz, Mexico. Actress. m. Francois-Henri Pinault, 2009, 1 daughter. Career: Films: Mi vida loca, 1993; Desparado, Four Rooms, Fair Game, 1995; From Dusk Till Dawn, Fled, 1996; Fools Rush In, Breaking Up, Follow Me Home, 1997; The Velocity of Gary, 54, 1998; Wild Wild West, Dogma, 1999; Frida, Death to Smoochy, 2002; Once Upon A Time in Mexico, Hotel, 2003; After the Sunset, 2004; Sian Ka'an (voice), 2005; Bandidas, Ask the Dust, Lonely Hearts, 2006; Across the Universe, 2007; Cirque du Freak: The Vampire's Assistant, 2009. TV: NYPD Blue; Dream On; Nurses; Action; Ugly Betty, 30 Rock. Address: c/o William Morris Agency, 1325 Avenue of the Americas, New York, NY 10019-4701, USA.

HAYMAN, Rt Hon Baroness Helene Valerie, b. 26 March 1949, Wolverhampton, England. Peer. m. Martin Hayman, 4 sons. Education: BA Law, Newnham College, Cambridge, 1969. Appointments: MP, Labour, Welwyn and Hatfield, 1974-79; Founder Member, Maternity Alliance, Broadcaster, 1979-85; Vice-Chairman, Bloomsbury Health Authority, 1985-92; Chairman, Bloomsbury and Islington District Health Authority, 1992; Chairman, Whittington Hospital National Health Trust, 1992-97; Sits as Labour Peer in The House of Lords, 1995-; Parliamentary Under Secretary for State, Department of Environment, Transport and the Regions, 1997; Parliamentary Under Secretary of State, Department of Health, 1998; Minister of State, Ministry of Agriculture Fisheries and Food, 1999-2001; Chair, Cancer Research UK, 2001-2004; Lord Speaker, House of Lords, 2006. Member, Committee of Privy Counsellors reviewing the Anti-Terrorism, Crime and Security Act, 2001; Trustee, Royal Botanic Gardens, Kew, 2002; Member, Board of Road Safe, 2003; Chair, Specialised Health Care Alliance, Member, Select Committee on the Assisted Dying for the Terminally Ill Bill, 2004; Member, Constitution Committee, 2004; Chair, Human Tissue Authority, 2005; Member, Human Fertilisation and Embryology Authority. Honours: Life Peerage, 1995; Privy Counsellor, 2000. Address: The House of Lords, Westminster, London SW1A 0PW, England.

HAYMAN Walter Kurt, b. 6 January 1926, Cologne, Germany. Mathematician. m. (1) Margaret Riley Crann, 1947, deceased 1994, 3 daughters, (2) Waficka Katifi, 1995, deceased 2001; (3) Marie Jennings, MBE, 2007. Education: Gordonstoun school, 1938-43; St John's College, Cambridge, 1943-46; MA ScD Fellow, 1947-50. Appointments: Lecturer, King's College, Newcastle, 1947, Exeter, 1947-53; Reader, 1953-56; First Professor of Pure Mathematics, Imperial College, University of London, 1956-85; Dean of RCS, 1978-81; FIC, 1989; Part time Professor, University of York, 1985-93; Professor Emeritus, Universities of London and York, Senior Research Fellow, Imperial College, 1995-. Publications: Multivalent Functions, Cambridge, 1958, 2nd edition, 1994; Meromorphic Functions, Oxford, 1964; Research Problems in Function Theory, 1967; Subharmonic Functions, Vol I 1976, Vol II 1989; Papers in various journals. Honours: 1st Smith's Prize, 1948, shared Adam's Prize, 1949, Cambridge University; Junior Berwick Prize, 1955, Senior Berwick Prize, 1964, de Morgan Medal, 1995, Vice President, 1982-84, London Mathematical Society; Co-founder with Mrs Hayman, British Mathematical Olympiad. Memberships: London Mathematical Society, 1947-; Visiting Lecturer, Brown University, USA, 1949-50; American Mathematics Society, 1961; Fellow, 1956-, Council, 1962-63, Royal Society; Foreign Member, Finnish Academy of Science and Letters; Accademia Nazionale dei Lincei (Rome); Corresponding Member, Bavarian Academy of Science; Hon DSc, Exeter, 1981, Birmingham, 1985, University of Ireland, 1997; Hon Dr rer nat, Giessen, 1992; Hon DPhil, Uppsala, 1992. Address: Department of Mathematics, Imperial College London, London SW7 2AZ, England.

HAYS Joe Martin, b. 11 December 1954, Phoenix, Arizona, USA. Professor. m. Anicca, 3 sons, 1 daughter. Education: BA, Psychology and Sociology, University of Maryland, USA, 1982; M Ed, Human Services Delivery, 1984, D Ed, Administration, Training and Policy Studies, 1991, Boston University, USA. Appointments: Technical and Secure Communications Technician, Army Communications Command, 1975-82; Student Administration and Training Officer, Command and General Staff College, Munich, Germany, 1984-88; Intelligence Operations Specialist, US Department of Defense, Europe, 1982-89; President and Founder, Metaforce Organisational Consulting and Development, Boston, USA, 1990-92; Director, Professional Practice Program, Boston University, USA, 1992-95; Organisational Development Specialist, Department of Transportation, Research & Special Programs Administration, Change Management Division, Cambridge, Massachusetts, USA, 1995-96; Technology Transfer Consultant, Peritus Software Services Inc, Boston, USA, 1996-97; Process Consultant, 1997-98, Director, 1998-2000, CSC Australia, Canberra and Sydney; National Practice Leader, Coolong Consulting, Canberra, 2000-02; President and Director, Synapsis, Canberra, 2002-05; Senior Lecturer, Lecturer in Management, The Australian National University, Canberra, 2003-10; Academic Director, Swinburne University of Technology, Melbourne, 2010-. Publications: Numerous articles in professional journals. Honours: Listed in biographical dictionaries. Address: Higher Education Division, Swinburne University of Technology, 3122 Hawthorne, Victoria, Australia. E-mail: jhays@swin.edu.au

HAYTHORNTHWAITE Richard Neil, b. 17 December 1956, Chatham, Kent, England. Businessman. m. Janeen, 1 son, 1 daughter. Education: Colstons School, Bristol, UK, 1963-74; MA, Geology, The Queen's College, Oxford, 1978; SM Business Management, Sloan Fellowship, Massachusetts Institute of Technology, 1991. Appointments: British Petroleum plc, 1978-95; Director, Corporate & Commercial, Premier Oil plc, 1995-97; Chief Executive, Europe & Asia, 1997-99, Group Chief Executive, 1999-2001, Blue Circle Industries plc; Chief Executive Officer, Invensys plc, 2001-05; Board and advisory positions with Cookson Group plc, Lafarge SA, ICI plc, Land Securities plc; Chairman,

MasterCard Inc; Chairman, Network Rail; President, PetroSaudi International (UK) Ltd; Advisor, STAR Capital Partners. E-mail: rh@rhaythornthwaite.com

HE Xu-Chang, b. 12 November 1941, Shanghai, China. Medicinal Chemist. m. Xing Chen, 1 son. Education: BS, Department of Chemistry, Fudan University, 1964; Postdoctoral, Dr E L Eliel group, Department of Chemistry, University of North Carolina, USA, 1988; Postdoctoral, Research Triangle Institute, USA, 1989. Appointments: Research Associate, Synthesis of Natural Products, Shanghai Institute of Organic Chemistry, CAS, 1964-85; Research Professor, Department of Medicinal Synthesis, Shanghai Institute of Materia Medica, CAS, 1989-2006; Retired, 2006. Publications: Over 40 scientific papers in scientific journals. Honours: Secondary Award for Significant Achievements in Science & Technology, Chinese Academy of Sciences, 1984, 1985; First Award in Science-Technology for New Products, Shanghai Administration, 1988. E-mail: hexuchan@yahoo.com

HEAD Brian William, Professor. Education: MA, Monash University, 1974; PhD, London University, 1980. Appointments: Public Service Commissioner, Queensland, 1998; Professor of Governance, Griffith University, 2003; Professor of Public Policy, University of Queensland, 2007-. Publications: Intellectual Movements, 1988; Ideology and Social Science, 1985; State, Economy & Public Policy, 1994; Promoting Integrity, 2008. Honours: Fellow, Australian Institute of Management; Fellow, Australian Institute of Company Directors; Fellow, Institute of Public Administration, Australia. Memberships: International Research Society for Public Administration; Australian Political Studies Association; Australian Social Policy Association. Address: Institute for Social Science Research, University of Queensland, St Lucia, Q4072, Australia. E-mail: brian.head@uq.edu.au

HEALD Tim(othy Villiers), (David Lancaster), b. 28 January 1944, Dorset, England. Journalist; Writer. m. (1) Alison Martina Leslie, 30 March 1968, dissolved, 2 sons, 2 daughters, (2) Penelope Byrne, 1999. Education: MA, Honours, Balliol College, Oxford, 1965. Appointments: Reporter, Sunday Times, 1965-67; Feature Editor, Town magazine, 1967; Feature Writer, Daily Express, 1967-72; Associate Editor, Weekend Magazine, Toronto, 1977-78; Columnist, Observer, 1990; Visiting Fellow, Jane Franklin Hall, University of Tasmania, 1997, 1999; University Tutor, Creative Writing, 1999, 2000; FRSL, 2000; Writer-in-Residence, University of South Australia, 2001. Publications: It's a Dog's Life, 1971; Unbecoming Habits, 1973; Blue Book Will Out, 1974; Deadline, 1975; Let Sleeping Dogs Lie, 1976; The Making of Space, 1999, 1976; John Steed: An Authorised Biography, 1977; Just Desserts, 1977; H.R.H: The Man Who Will be King, with M Mohs, 1977; Murder at Moose Jaw, 1981; Caroline R, 1981; Masterstroke, 1982; Networks, 1983; Class Distinctions, 1984; Red Herrings, 1985; The Character of Cricket, 1986; Brought to Book, 1988; Editor, The Newest London Spy, 1988; Business Unusual, 1989; By Appointments: 150 Years of the Royal Warrant, 1989; Editor, A Classic English Crime, 1990; Editor, My Lord's, 1990; The Duke: A Portrait of Prince Philip, 1991; Honourable Estates, 1992; Barbara Cartland: A Life of Love, 1994; Denis: The Authorised Biography of the Incomparable Compton, 1994; Brian Johnston: The Authorised Biography, 1995; Editor, A Classic Christmas Crime, 1995; Beating Retreat: Hong Kong Under the Last Governor, 1997; Stop Press, 1998; A Peerage for Trade, 2001;

Village Cricket, 2004; Death and the Visiting Fellow, 2004; Death and the d'Urbervilles, 2005; Princess Margaret – A Life Unravelled, 2007. Contributions: Short stories: EQMM; Strand magazine; Tatler; Mail on Sunday. Memberships: Crime Writers Association, Chairman, 1987-88; PEN; Society of Authors. Address: 66 The Esplanade, Fowey, Cornwall PL23 1JA, England. E-mail: timheald@compuserve.com

HEALEY Denis (Lord Healey of Riddlesden), b. 30 August 1917, Keighley, Yorkshire, England. Politician; Writer. m. Edna May Edmunds, 1945, 1 son, 2 daughters. Education: BA, 1940, MA, 1945, Balliol College, Oxford. Appointments include: Served, World War II, 1939-45; Contested, (Labour) Pudsey and Otley Division, 1945; Secretary, International Department, Labour Party, 1945-52; Member of Parliament, South East Leeds, 1952-55, Leeds East, 1955-92; Shadow Cabinet, 1959-64, 1970-74, 1979-87; Secretary of State for Defence, 1964-70; Chancellor of the Exchequer, 1974-79; Opposition Spokesman on Foreign and Commonwealth Affairs, 1980-87; Deputy Leader, Labour Party, 1980-83; Member House of Lords. Publications: The Curtain Falls, 1951; New Fabian Essays, 1952; Neutralism, 1955; Fabian International Essays, 1956; A Neutral Belt in Europe, 1958; NATO and American Security, 1959; The Race Against the H Bomb, 1960; Labour Britain and the World, 1964; Healey's Eye, 1980; Labour and a World Society, 1985; Beyond Nuclear Deterrence, 1986; The Time of My Life (autobiography), 1989; When Shrimps Learn to Whistle (essays), 1990; My Secret Planet, 1992; Denis Healey's Yorkshire Dales, 1995; Healey's World, photographs, 2002. Honours include: Grand Cross of Order of Merit, Germany, 1979; Freeman, City of Leeds, 1992; FRSL, 1993. Membership: President, Birkbeck College, 1992-98. Address: House of Lords, London SW1A 0PQ, England.

HEALEY Robin Michael, b. 16 February 1952, London, England. Historian; Biographer. Education: BA, 1974, MA, 1976, University of Birmingham. Appointments: Documentation Officer, Tamworth Castle and Cambridge Museum of Archaeology and Anthropology, 1977-80; Museum Assistant, Saffron Walden Museum, 1983-84; Research Assistant, History of Parliament, 1985-92; Visiting Research Fellow, Manchester University, 1997-2003, Editor, Lewisletter, 2000-; Judge, HASSRA Literary Competition, 2003-07; Co-editor, Also, 2006-09. Publications: Books: Hertfordshire (A Shell County Guide), 1982; Diary of George Mushet (1805-13), 1982; Grigson at Eighty, 1985; A History of Barley School, 1995; My Rebellious and Imperfect Eye: Observing Geoffrey Grigson, 2002; Contributions to: Biographical Dictionary of Modern British Radicals, 1984; Domesday Book, 1985; Secret Britain, 1986; Dictionary of Literary Biography, 1991; Encyclopaedia of Romanticism, 1992; Consumer Magazines of the British Isles, 1993; Postwar Literatures in English, 1998-; I Remember When I Was Young, 2003; Oxford Dictionary of National Biography, 2004; History of Parliament (1820-32), 2009; Blogger, Bookride Website, 2009-. Also: Country Life; Hertfordshire Countryside; Guardian; Literary Review; Private Eye; Book and Magazine Collector; Rare Book Review; Independent; Times Literary Supplement; Bristol Review of Books; Local History Magazine; Art Newspaper; B M Insight; Mensa Magazine; Wyndham Lewis Annual; Charles Lamb Bulletin; Cobbett's New Political Register. Honour: 1st Prize, Birmingham Post Poetry Contest, 1974. Memberships: Executive, Charles Lamb Society, 1987-; MENSA, 1988-; Press Officer, Alliance of Literary Societies, 1997-2005; Wyndham Lewis Society, 2000-. Address: 80 Hall Lane, Great Chishill, Royston, Herts SG8 8SH, England.

HEALY Mark, b. 27 May 1975, Castlebar, Co Mayo, Republic of Ireland. University Lecturer. Education: BE, Civil Engineering, 1998, M Eng Sc, Engineering Hydrology, 2000, PhD, Civil Engineering, 2004, National University of Ireland, Galway. Appointments: Project Engineer, MarCon Computations International Ltd, 2003-04; Fixed-Term Lecturer, 2004-07, Lecturer (above the bar), 2007-, Department of Civil Engineering, Programme Director, BE (Environmental) degree, National University of Ireland. Publications: 2 book chapters; Numerous articles in peer-reviewed journals, published reports and other publications. Memberships: Engineers Ireland – Chartered Engineer; Federation Internationale d'Associations Nationales d'Ingenieurs; Soil Science Society of America.

HEANEY Seamus (Justin), b. 13 April 1939, County Londonderry, Northern Ireland. Poet; Writer; Professor. m. Marie Devlin, 1965, 2 sons, 1 daughter. Education: St Columb's College, Derry; BA 1st Class, Queen's University, Belfast, 1961. Appointments: Teacher, St Thomas's Secondary School, Belfast, 1962-63; Lecturer, St Joseph's College of Education, Belfast, 1963-66, Queen's University, Belfast, 1966-72, Carysfort College, 1975-81; Senior Visiting Lecturer, 1982-85, Boylston Professor of Rhetoric and Oratory, 1985-97, Harvard University; Professor of Poetry, Oxford University, 1989-94. Publications: Eleven Poems, 1965; Death of a Naturalist, 1966; Door Into the Dark, 1969; Wintering Out, 1972; North, 1975; Field Work, 1979; Selected Poems, 1965-1975, 1980; Sweeney Astray, 1984, revised edition as Sweeney's Flight, 1992; Station Island, 1984; The Haw Lantern, 1987; New Selected Poems, 1966-1987, 1990; Seeing Things, 1991; The Spirit Level, 1996; Opened Ground: Selected Poems, 1966-1996, 1998; Electric Light, 2000; The Testament of Cresseid, 2005; District & Circle, 2006. Prose: Preoccupations: Selected Prose, 1968-1978, 1980; The Government of the Tongue, 1988; The Place of Writing, 1989; The Redress of Poetry: Oxford Lectures, 1995; Beowulf: A New Verse Translation and Introduction, 1999; Finders Keepers: Selected Prose, 1971-2001. Honours: Somerset Maugham Award, 1967; Cholmondeley Award, 1968; W H Smith Award, 1975; Duff Cooper Prize, 1975; Whitbread Awards, 1987, 1996; Nobel Prize for Literature, 1995; Whitbread Book of the Year Award, 1997, 1999; Honorary DLitt, Oxford, 1997, Birmingham, 2000. Memberships: Royal Irish Academy; British Academy, American Academy of Arts and Letters. Address: c/o Faber & Faber, 3 Queen Square, London WC1N 3RU, England.

HEARN Jeff, b. 5 August 1947, London, England. Professor. Education: BA, Geography, Mansfield College, Oxford University, 1968; PG Dip TP, Urban Planning, Oxford Polytechnic (Oxford Brookes University), 1970; MA, Organisation Studies, University of Leeds, 1974; PhD, Social Sciences, University of Bradford, 1986. Appointments: Lecturer, Senior Lecturer, Reader, University of Bradford, 1974-95; Professorial Research Fellow, University of Manchester, 1995-2003; Professor II, University of Oslo, 1998-2001; Professor, Hanken School of Economics, 2003-; Professor, Sociology, University of Huddersfield, 2003-; Professor, Gender Studies, Critical Studies on Men, University of Linköping, 2006-; Co-Director, GEXcel Centre of Gender Excellence, Linköping and Örebro Universities. Publications: The Gender of Oppression, 1987; Sex at Work, 1987/1995; Men in the Public Eye, 1992; The Violences of Men, 1998; Gender, Sexuality and Violence in Organizations, 2001; Men and Masculinities in Europe, 2006; European Perspectives on Men and Masculinities, 2006; The Limits of Gendered Citizenship, 2011; Co-editor, Men and Masculinities; Co-managing editor, Routledge Advances in Feminist Studies and Intersectionality; Many other editorships; Around 500 publications. Honours: First Honorary College Scholar, 1966; First Professorial Research Fellow, Faculty of Social Sciences & Law, University of Manchester, 1995; Hallsworth Research Fellow, University of Manchester, 1988-89; Academy of Finland Research Fellow, 2000-05; Academician in Social Sciences, UK, 2006; National Award for Men and Gender Equality, Finland, 2009; Visiting Professor of 9 universities in 5 countries. Memberships: British Sociological Association; International Sociological Association. Address: FLO, Hanken School of Economics, PO Box 479, Arkadiankatu 22, FIN-00101, Helsinki, Finland. E-mail: hearn@hanken.fi

HEBERGER Karoly, b. 16 August 1953, Budapest, Hungary. Scientist. m. Eva Maria Bekesi, 2 sons. Education: PhD (summa cum laude), 1981; Cand Sci, 1990; D Sc, 2000. Appointments: Technical University of Budapest; Polytechnic University of Tallinn. Publications: More than 120 scientific papers; More than 250 lectures (posters); More than 1400 independent citations. Honours: Prize for Excellent Work; High Standard Prize (twice). Memberships: Hungarian Chemical Society; QSAR & Modeling Society. Address: Sasadi ut 169, 1112 Budapest, Hungary.

HECHE Anne, b. 25 May 1969, Aurora, Ohio, USA. Actress. m. Coleman Lafoon, 2001 (divorced) 1 son, 1 son with boyfriend James Tupper. Career: Films: An Ambush of Ghosts, 1993; The Adventures of Huck Finn, 1993; A Simple Twist of Fate, 1994; Milk Money, 1994; I'll Do Anything, 1994; The Wild Side, 1995; Pie in the Sky, 1995; The Juror, 1996; Walking and Talking, 1996; Donnie Brasco, 1997; Volcano, 1997; Subway Stories, Wag the Dog, 1997; Six Days and Seven Nights, 1998; A Cool Dry Place, 1998; Psycho, 1998; The Third Miracle, 1999; Auggie Rose, 2001; John Q, 2002; Prozac Nation, 2003; Birth, 2004; Sexual Life, 2005; Suffering Man's Charity, 2007; What Love Is, 2007; Superman/Doomsday (voice), 2007; Toxic Skies, 2008; Spread, 2009. TV: Another World; O Pioneers! 1992; Against the Wall, 1994; Girls in Prison, 1994; Kingfish: A Story of Huey P Long, 1995; If These Walls Could Talk, 1996; If These Walls Could Talk 2, One Kill, 2000; Gracie's Choice, 2004; The Dead Will Tell, 2004; Silver Bells, 2006; Fatal Desire, 2006; Men in Trees, 2006-07; Hung, 2009. Address: c/o CAA, 9830 Wilshire Boulevard, Beverly Hills, CA 90212, USA.

HEFNER Hugh Marston, b. 9 April 1926, Chicago, Illinois, USA. Publisher. m. (1) Mildred Williams, 1949 (divorced) 1 son, 1 daughter, (2) Kimberley Conrad, 1989 (divorced) 2 sons. Education: BS, University of Illinois. Appointments: Editor-in-Chief, Playboy magazine, 1953-, Oui magazine, 1972-81; Chairman Emeritus, Playboy Enterprises, 1988-; President, Playboy Club International Inc, 1959-86; TV shows Honour: International Press Directory International Publisher Award, 1997. Address: Playboy Enterprises Inc, 9242 Beverly Boulevard, Beverly Hills, CA 90210, USA.

HEGGLAND Roar, b. 25 May 1954, Vikebygd, Norway. Geoscientist. m. Lindis Åslid, 2 daughters. Education: Cand Real (MSc), Physics, University of Bergen, Norway, 1982. Appointment: Geophysicist, Statoil, 1984-. Publications include as author and co-author most recently: Chimneys in the Gulf of Mexico, 2000; Detection of Seismic Chimneys by Neural Networks a New Prospect Evaluation Tool, 2000; Detection of Seismic Objects, the Fastest Way to do Prospect and Geohazard Evaluations, 2001; Identifying gas chimneys and associated features in 3D seismic data by the use of various attributes and special processing, 2001; Mud volcanoes and gas hydrates on the Niger Delta front, 2001; Seismic Evidence of Vertical Fluid Migration Through Faults, Applications of Chimney and Fault Detection, 2002; Method of Seismic Signal Processing including Detection of objects in seismic data like gas chimneys and faults; More than 10 invited papers and articles including Using gas chimneys in seal integrity analysis, 2005. Memberships: American Association of Petroleum Geologists; Society of Exploration Geophysicists. Address: Statoil ASA, N-4035 Stavanger, Norway. E-mail: rohe@statoil.com

HEINONEN Reijo Eljas, b. 3 October 1938, Helsinki, Finland. Professor Emeritus. m. Essi Vatanen, deceased 2008, 2 sons. Education: Master of Theology, 1965, Master of Arts, 1986, University of Helsinki; Doctor of Theology, University of Tübingen, 1972. Appointments: Acting Senior Lecturer, Teacher Training School, University of Helsinki, 1975-81; Senior Lecturer, Teacher Training Institute, University of Turku, 1981-94; Acting Associate Professor, Church History, University of Helsinki, 1987-88; Adviser on interreligious issues to President M Ahtisaari, 1994-; Acting Professor, Historical Theology, 1994-, Professor Ordinarius, 1995-2003, Dean, Faculty of Theology, 2002-03, University of Joensuu; Retired, 2003-. Publications: 7 monographs; Around 130 scientific articles on religious education, church history and ethics. Honours: Corresponding Member, Collegium Europaeum Jenense, University of Jena; Knight First Class of the Order of the Holy Lamb, Finnish Orthodox Church; Knight First Class of the Order of the White Rose of Finland; Golden Rule Award, United Religions Initiative and Faith without Borders, 2009. Memberships: European Forum for Teachers of Religious Education; Intercultural counselling programme, Project Islam and the West; Crisis Management Center, Kuopio, Finland; UNIPID. Address: Haapakatu 4, FIN-21110 Naantali, Finland. E-mail: reijo.e.heinonen@jippii.fi

HEINTZ Monica, b. 31 October 1974, Bucharest, Romania. Social Anthropologist. Divorced, 3 sons, 1 daughter. Education: Bachelor, 1996, Master, 1997, Philosophy, University of Paris IV (Sorbonne), France; Master, Studies in Social Anthropology, University of Oxford, England, 1998; PhD, Social Anthropology, University of Cambridge, England, 2002. Appointments: Postdoctoral Fellow, Max Planck Institute for Social Anthropology, Halle, Germany, 2002-05; Associate Professor (Lecturer), Social Anthropology, University of Paris, Oust Nanterre, France, 2005-. Publications: Be European, Recycle Yourself, 2006; Weak State, Uncertain Citizenship, 2008; The Anthropology of Moralities, 2009; many others. Honours: First Book Award, Romania Literara, 2006; Laureate, Institut Universitaire de France, 2009-14. Memberships: European Association for Social Anthropology; Association of Social Anthropologies of Britain and the Commonwealth. Address: 78 rue Taitbout, 75009 Paris, France. E-mail: monica.heintz@free.fr

HEISS Wolf-Dieter, b. 31 December 1939, Zell am See, Salzburg, Austria. Physician; Researcher. m. Brigitte Kroiss, 1940, 1 son, 1 daughter. Education: MD, Medical School, Vienna, 1965. Appointments: Assistant, 1965-70, Assistant Professor, 1970-76, Associate Professor, 1976-78, Professor and Chairman, 1985-2005, University Neurology Department, Cologne, Germany; Director, Max Planck Institute for Neurological Research, Cologne, 1978-2005; Professor Emeritus, MPI for Neurological Research, Cologne, 2005-; Visiting Professor, Danube University, Krems, Austria, 2006-; Adjunct Professor, McGill University, Montreal, Canada, 2009-. Publications: More than 500 original publications in international journals. Honours: Eiselsberg Award, Vienna, 1969; Federal Cross of Merit, FRG, 1989; Zülch Award, Reemtsma Foundation, 1994; Mihara Award, Mihara Foundation, 1995; Bergmann Plague, German Medical Association, 1999; Berson Yalow Award, Society of Nuclear Medicine, 2002; Von-Hevesy Medal, German Society of Nuclear Medicine, 2005; Kuhl-Lassen-Award, Society of Nuclear Medicine, 2008; Leadership in Stroke Medicine, World Stroke Organization, 2008; Wepfer Award, European Stroke Organization, 2011. Address: Max Planck Institute for Neurological Research, Gleueler Str 50, 50931 Cologne, Germany. E-mail: wdh@uf.mpg.de

HELLAWELL Keith, b. 18 May 1942, Yorkshire, England. Anti-Drugs Co-ordinator; Police Officer. m. Brenda Hey, 1963, 2 daughters. Education: Dewsbury Technology College; Cranfield Institute of Technology; London University. Appointments: Miner, 5 years; Joined Huddersfield Borough Police, progressed through every rank within West Yorkshire Police to Assistant Chief Constable; Deputy Chief Constable of Humberside, 1985-90; Chief Constable of Cleveland Police, 1990-93; Chief Constable of West Yorkshire Police, 1993-98; First UK Anti Drugs Co-ordinator, 1998-2001; Adviser to Home Secretary on International Drug Issues, 2001-. Publications: The Outsider, autobiography, 2002. Memberships include: Association of Police Officers Spokesman on Drugs; Advisory Council on the Misuse of Drugs; Board, Community Action Trust; Trustee, National Society for the Prevention of Cruelty to Children; Editorial Advisory Board, Journal of Forensic Medicine. Address: Government Offices, George Street, London SW1A 2AL, England.

HELLSTEN Sirkku Kristiina, b. 16 June 1962, Helsinki, Finland. Professor. m. Joseph A L Blais. Education: MA, Social Sciences, 1992, Licenciate, 1994, PhD, 1997, Social and Political Philosophy, University of Helsinki. Appointments: Manager, Professor and Civic Education Project, Tanzania, 2001-04; Philosophy Programme Co-ordinator, University of Dar es Salaam, Tanzania, 2000-04; Director/Reader, Development Ethics, Centre for the Study of Global Ethics, University of Birmingham, UK, 2002-; Adjunct Professor, University of Helsinki; Counsellor, Good Governance and Human Rights, Embassy of Finland in Nairobi, Kenya, 2004-10 and Embassy of Finland in Maputo, Mozambique, 2011-13; Visiting Professor, University of South Florida, USA, 2011; Professor, Philosophy, University of Dar es Salaam, 2012-. Publications: Numerous articles in professional journals; 5 books. Memberships: International Development Ethics Association; Finnish Society for Philosophy of Law; Finnish Science Studies Association; American Philosophical Association; Finnish Philosophical Association; Editor, Journal of Global Ethics.

HELLWIG Birgitta Öman, b. 11 June 1932, Borås, Sweden. Mathematician. m. Professor Günter Hellwig, 1 son, 3 daughters. Education: Filosofie Kandidat, Uppsala University, Sweden, 1954. Appointments: Technical Officer, Imperial Chemical Industries Ltd, Birmingham, England, 1957; Assistant, Mathematics Department, Uppsala University, 1958; Teaching Fellow, Harvard University Cambridge, Massachusetts, 1959; Senior Mathematician, Republic Aviation, Farmingdale, New York, 1960; Member, Research Staff, Systems Research Center, Lockheed Electrons Co, Bedminster, New Jersey, 1960-61; Translator Maths Textbooks, Addison-Wesley Publishing Co, Reading, Massachusetts, 1964; Reviewer Mathematics Reviews, Ann Arbor, Michigan, 1968-; Assistant to applicants' lawyers by proceedings European Court Human Rights, Strasbourg, France, 1989-. Publications: Contribution articles on differential operators to scientific journals: Math Zeitschrift 86, 1964; Math Zeitschrift 89, 1965; Journal of Mathematical Analysis and Applications 26, 1969; Wissenschaftliche Zeitschrift der Technischen Hochschule Karl-Marx-Stadt, 1969. Honour: Grantee, University Zürich, Switzerland, 1955-56. Memberships: President, Foreign Students Association, Zürich, 1955-56; Secretary, Swedish Students Association, Zürich, 1955-56; Nordiska Komitten för Mänskliga Rättigheter, 1998-. Listed in: Several Biographical Publications. Address: Pommerotter Weg 37, D-52076 Aachen, Germany.

HELYAR Jane Penelope Josephine, (Josephine Poole), b. 12 February 1933, London, England. Writer. m. (1) T R Poole, 1956, (2) V J H Helyar, 1975, 1 son, 5 daughters. Publications: A Dream in the House, 1961; Moon Eyes, 1965; The Lilywhite Boys, 1967; Catch as Catch Can, 1969; Yokeham, 1970; Billy Buck, 1972; Touch and Go, 1976; When Fishes Flew, 1978; The Open Grave, The Forbidden Room (remedial readers), 1979; Hannah Chance, 1980; Diamond Jack, 1983; The Country Diary Companion (to accompany Central TV series), 1983; Three For Luck, 1985; Wildlife Tales, 1986; The Loving Ghosts, 1988; Angel, 1989; This is Me Speaking, 1990; Paul Loves Amy Loves Christo, 1992; Scared to Death, 1994; Deadly Inheritance, 1995; Hero, 1997; Run Rabbit, 1999; Fair Game, 2000; Scorched, 2003. Television scripts: The Harbourer, 1975; The Sabbatical, 1981; The Breakdown, 1981; Miss Constantine, 1981; Ring a Ring a Rosie, 1983; With Love, Belinda, 1983; The Wit to Woo, 1983; Fox, 1984; Buzzard, 1984; Dartmoor Pony, 1984; Snow White (picture book), 1991; Pinocchio (re-written), 1994; Joan of Arc (picture book), 1998; The Water Babies (re-written), 1996; Anne Frank (picture book), 2005. Address: Poundisford Lodge, Poundisford, Taunton, Somerset TA3 7AE, England.

HEMINGWAY Wayne, b. 19 January 1961, England. Designer. m. Gerardine, 2 sons, 2 daughters. Education: BSc, Honours, Geography and Town Planning, 1979-82, University College, London; MA, Surrey. Appointments: Joint business, market stall, Camden, London; Creator and Co-founder with Geraldine Hemingway of footwear, clothing and accessory label, Red or Dead, 1992; Collection retailed through 8 Red or Dead shops in England, 3 Red or Dead shops in Japan and wholesaled to international network of retailers; Business sold, 1999; Joint venture with Pentland Group PLC, 1996-; Founder, Hemingway Design, 1999; Designer, new wing for Institute of Directors, Pall Mall, 2001; Current design and consultancy projects include Staiths South Bank, Tyneside (800-unit housing estate), carpet design, wall covering and menswear; Projects with local councils including: Lancashire, Copeland Borough Council and the North West Development Agency, Newcastle and Gateshead; Chair, Prince's Trust Fashion Initiative; Patron, Morecambe Winter Gardens; Judge, Stirling Prize; Professor, Development and Planning Department, Northumbria University, Newcastle upon Tyne. Publications: The Good, the Bad and the Ugly, with Geraldine Hemingway, 1998; Kitsch Icons, 1999; Just Above the Mantelpiece, 2000; Mass Market Classics The Home, 2003. Honours: Second Place, Young Business Person of the Year, 1990; Street Designers of the Year, British Fashion Awards, 1995, 1996, 1997, 1998; MBE, 2006. Address: Hemingway Design, 15 Wembley Park Drive, Wembley, Middlesex HA9 8HD, England.

HEMMERT Martin, b. 5 March 1964, Oberhausen, Germany. Professor. m. Mi Jung, 1 son. Education: Diploma, 1989, Doctoral Degree, 1993, Business Administration, University of Cologne; Habilitation (professorial qualification), Business Administration, University of Essen, 2001. Appointments: Research Assistant, University of Cologne, 1989-90; Visiting Research Fellow, Hitotsubashi University, 1990-93; Research Associate, DIJ Tokyo, 1993-98; Assistant Professor, 1998-2001, Associate Professor, 2001-04, University of Essen; Associate Professor, 2004-09, Professor, 2009-, Korea University Business School. Publications: 5 books including: Technology and Innovation in Japan: Policy and Management for the 21st Century, 1998; Over 50 articles in peer reviewed journals and book chapters. Honours: First Foreign Business Professor appointed for a permanent position in Korea; DFG Research Fellowship, 1998-2001. Memberships: Academy of Management; Academy of International Business; Euro-Asia Management Studies Association. E-mail: mhemmert@korea.ac.kr

HEMMING John Henry, b. 5 January 1935, Vancouver, British Columbia, Canada. Author; Publisher. m. Sukie Babington-Smith, 1979, 1 son, 1 daughter. Education: McGill and Oxford Universities; MA; D.Litt. Appointments: Explorations in Peru and Brazil, 1960, 1961, 1971, 1972, 1986-87; Director and Secretary, Royal Geographical Society, 1975-96; Joint Chairman, Hemming Group Ltd, 1976-; Chair, Brintex Ltd., Newman Books Ltd. Publications: The Conquest of the Incas, 1970; Tribes of the Amazon Basin in Brazil (with others), 1973; Red Gold: The Conquest of the Brazilian Indians, 1978; The Search for El Dorado, 1978; Machu Picchu, 1982; Monuments of the Incas, 1983, rewritten 2010; Change in the Amazon Basin, (editor), 2 volumes, 1985; Amazon Frontier: The Defeat of the Brazilian Indians, 1987; Maracá, 1988; Roraima: Brazil's Northernmost Frontier, 1990; The Rainforest Edge (editor), 1994; The Golden Age of Discovery, 1998; Die If You Must, Brazilian Indians in the 20th Century, 2003; Tree of Rivers: The Story of the Amazon, 2008. Honours: CMG; Pitman Literary Prize, 1970; Christopher Award, New York, 1971; Order of Merit (Peru) 1991; Order of the Southern Cross (Brazil), 1998; Grand Cross, Peruvian Order of Merit, 2008; El Sol del Peru, 2010; Honorary doctorates, University of Warwick, University of Stirling; Honorary Fellow, Magdalen College, Oxford; Medals from Royal Geographical Society, Boston Museum of Science, Royal Scottish Geographical Society; Citation of Merit, New York Explorers' Club. Address: Hemming Group Ltd, 32 Vauxhall Bridge Road, London SW1V 2SS, England. E-mail: j.hemming@hgluk.com

HEN Yitzhak, b. 5 November 1963, Israel. Historian. m. Rachel Shalomi, 1 son, 2 daughters. Education: BA, Psychology/History, 1988, MA, History, 1991, Hebrew University of Jerusalem; PhD, Medieval History, University of Cambridge, England, 1994. Appointments: Senior Lecturer, Haifa University, 1994-2002; Professor of History, Ben-Gurion University of the Negev, 2002-. Publications: Culture & Religion in Merovingian Gaul, 1995; The Sacramentary of Echternach, 1997; The Royal Patronage of Liturgy in Frankish Gaul, 2001; Roman Barbarians, 2007. Honours: Life Member, Clare Hall Cambridge. Memberships: Medieval Academy of America; The Henry Bradshaw Society. Address: Department of General History, Ben-Gurion University of the Negev, PO Box 653, Beer-Sheva 84105, Israel. E-mail: yhen@bgu.ac.il Website: www.bgu.ac.il/~yhen

HENDERSON Douglas James, b. 28 July 1934, Calgary, Alberta, Canada. Theoretical Physicist. m. Rose-Marie Steen-Nielssen, 3 daughters. Education: BA, 1st Class Honours, 1st place, Mathematics, University of British Columbia, 1956; PhD, Physics, University of Utah, USA, 1961. Appointments include: Assistant Professor, Associate Professor, Professor, Physics, Arizona State University, USA, 1962-69; Associate Professor, Physics, 1964-67, Professor,

Applied Mathematics, Physics, 1967-69, Adjunct Professor, Applied Mathematics, 1969-85, University of Waterloo, Canada; Research Scientist, 1969-90, Research Scientist Emeritus, 1992-, IBM Almaden Research Center, San Jose, California; Research Scientist, IBM Corporation, Salt Lake City, Utah, 1990-92; Adjunct Professor, Physics, 1990-93, Adjunct Professor, Chemistry, Mathematics, 1990-95, Research Scientist, Center for High Performance Computing, 1990-95, University of Utah; Manuel Sandoral Vallarta Professor, Physics, 1988; Juan de Oyarzabal Professor, Physics, 1993-95, Juan de Oyarzabal Honorary Professor, 1996-, Universidad Autonoma Metropolitana, Mexico; Honorary Professor of Chemistry, University of Hong Kong, 1993-, Rush Medical University, 2002-; Professor, Chemistry, Brigham Young University, 1995-; Many visiting positions. Publications: Over 500 research papers in scientific journals; Co-author, Statistical Mechanics and Dynamics, 1964, 2nd edition, 1982; Co-editor, Physical Chemistry: An Advanced Treatise, 15 volumes, 1966-75; Co-author, Chemical Dynamics, 1971; Co-editor, Advances and Perspectives, 6 volumes, 1973-81; Editor, Fundamentals of Inhomogeneous Fluids, 1992; Co-author, Stochastic Differential Equations in Science and Engineering, 2006. Honours include: Alfred P Sloan Foundation Fellowship, 1964, 1966; Ian Potter Foundation Fellowship, 1966; Outstanding Research Contribution Award, 1973, Outstanding Innovation Award, 1987, IBM; Corresponding Member, National Academy of Sciences of Mexico, 1990-; Catedra Patrimoniales de Excelencia, Mexico, 1993-95; Premio a las Areas de Investigacion, Universidad Autonoma Metropolitana, 1996; John Simon Guggenheim Memorial Foundation Fellow, 1997; Joel Henry Hildebrand National American Chemical Society Award in Theoretical and Experimental Chemistry of Liquids, 1999; American Chemical Society Utah Award, 2005; Listed in Who's Who publications and biographical dictionaries. Memberships include: Fellow, American Physical Society, 1963-; Fellow, Institute of Physics, UK, 1965-; Fellow, American Institute of Chemists, 1971-; Fellow, Royal Society of Chemistry, UK, 2009-; American Chemical Society; Biophysical Society; Canadian Association of Physicists; Mathematical Association of America; New York Academy of Sciences; Phi Kappa Phi; Sigma Xi; Sigma Pi Sigma. Address: Department of Chemistry, Brigham Young University, Provo, UT 84602, USA. E-mail: doug@chem.byu.edu

HENDERSON Neil Keir, b. 7 March 1956, Glasgow, Scotland. Education: MA, English Language, English Literature, Scottish Literature, University of Glasgow, 1977. Appointments: Assistant Lexicographer, University of Glasgow, 1983-86; Freelance Creative Writer, 1987-. Publications include: Maldehyde's Discomfiture, 1997; Fish-Worshipping – As We Know It, 2001; Labyrinths 6 (showcased), 2002; An English Summer In Scotland, 2005; Hormones A-Go-Go, 2007. Memberships: Scottish Area Secretary, International Syd Barrett Appreciation Society, circa 1974. Address: 46 Revoch Drive, Knightswood, Glasgow G13 4SB, Scotland.

HENDERSON William James Carlaw, b. 26 September 1948, Galashiels, Selkirkshire, Scotland. Lawyer; Writer to the Signet. Education: George Heriot's School, Edinburgh; Old College, Faculty of Law, University of Edinburgh. Appointments: Trainee Solicitor, Patrick and James WS, 1971-73; Solicitor, Wallace and Guthrie, 1973-74; Solicitor, 1974-76, Partner, 1976-83, Allan McDougall and Co; Partner, Brodies WS, 1983-2003. Publications: 2 seminar papers, Moscow School of Political Studies, 1996, 1997; 1 monograph, 2001. Honours: Bachelor of Laws, LLB, 1971; Notary Public, 1975; Writer to the Signet, 1981. Memberships: Society of HM Writers to the Signet; Fellow, Royal Geographical Society; Royal Scottish Geographical Society; Secretary, 1980-83, Society of Scottish Artists, Honorary Life Member, 2005; Governor, Edinburgh College of Art, 1996-99; Director, Edinburgh Printmakers Workshop, 2001-; Trustee, Mendelssohn on Mull Music Festival, 2003-; Director, Family Mediation, Lothian, 2005-; Member, Royal Highland Yacht Club; Member, Edinburgh Sports Club. Address: 11 Inverleith Place, Edinburgh EH3 5QE, Scotland. E-mail: wjchenderson@suhamet.com

HENDRY Diana (Lois), b. 2 October 1941, Meols, Wirral, Cheshire, England. Poet; Children's Writer. Divorced, 1 son, 1 daughter. Education: BA, Honours, 1984, MLitt, 1986, University of Bristol, England. Appointments: Reporter and Feature Writer, Western Mail, Cardiff, 1960-65; Scriptwriter/broadcaster, Radio Merseyside, 1965-67; Freelance journalist, 1967-80; Tutor, University of Bristol, 1984-87; Part-time English Teacher, Clifton College, 1984-87; Part-time Lecturer, University of the West of England, Bristol, 1987-93; Tutor, Open University, 1991-92; Tutor, Creative Writing, University of Bristol, 1995-97; Tutor, Creative Writing, North Cornwall, 1996; Writer-in-Residence, Dumfries and Galloway Royal Infirmary, 1997-98; Tutor, University of Bristol, 1999; Writer-in-Residence, Edinburgh Royal Infirmary, 2000; Book Reviewer, The Spectator, 2000-; Tutor, Poetry Course, Ty Newydd, 2001; Tutor, Poetry, Fiction and Children's Writing, 2001, Pushkin Prize Students, 2005, 2006, Moniack Mhor; Assistant Editor, Mariscat Press, 2004-; Royal Literary Fund Fellow, Edinburgh University, 2008-10. Publications: Children's books include: The Crazy Collector, 2001; You Can't Kiss It Better, 2003; No Homework Tomorrow, 2003; Swan Boy, 2004; The Very Snowy Christmas, 2005; Catch a Gran, 2006; Poetry books: Making Blue, 1995; Strange Goings-on, 1995; Borderers, 2001; Twelve Lilts: Psalms & Responses, 2003; No Homework Tomorrow, 2003; Sparks! 2005; Late Love and Other Whodunnits, 2008; Numerous contributions to anthologies and periodicals; Poems and books broadcast on radio and television. Honours: Stroud Festival International Poetry Competition, 1976; 3rd Prize, 1991, 2nd Prize, 1993, Peterloo Poetry Competition; Whitbread Award, 1991; 1st Prize, Housman Poetry Society, 1996; Commended, Phras Open Poetry Competition, 1997, 1998; Commended, Blue Nose Rivers Competition, 2000; Scottish Arts Council Children's Book Award, 2001. Memberships: Society of Authors; PEN; The Poetry Society; Shore Poets, Edinburgh. Address: 23 Dunrobin Place, Stockbridge, Edinburgh EH3 5HZ, Scotland.

HENDRY Stephen Gordon, b. 13 January 1969, Edinburgh, Scotland. Snooker Player. m. Amanda Elizabeth Teresa Tart, 1995, 2 sons. Appointments: Professional Player, 1985; Scottish Champion, 1986, 1987, 1988; Winner, Rothmans Grand Prix, 1987; World Doubles Champion, 1987; Australian Masters Champion, 1987; British Open Champion, 1988, 1991, 1999; New Zealand Masters Champion, 1988; Benson and Hedges Master Champion, 1989, 1990, 1991, 1992, 1993, 1996; UK Professional Champion, 1989, 1990, 1994, 1995, 1996; Asian Champion, 1989; Regal Masters Champion, 1989; Dubai Classic Champion, 1989; Embassy World Champion, 1990, 1992, 1993, 1994, 1995, 1996, 1999; 2006. Irish Masters, 1992; International Open, 1993; Malta Cup, 2004. Publication: Snooker Masterclass, 1994. Honours: MBE, 1994; Dr hc (Stirling), 2000; MacRoberts Trophy, 2001. Address: Stephen Hendry Snooker Ltd, Kerse Road, Stirling FK7 7SG, Scotland.

HENLEY Elizabeth Becker, b. 8 May 1952, Jackson, Mississippi, USA. Playwright. Education: BFA, Southern Methodist University. Publications: Crimes of the Heart, 1981; The Wake of Jamey Foster, 1982; Am I Blue, 1982; The Miss Firecracker Contest, 1984; The Debutante Ball, 1985, 1991; The Lucky Spot, 1987; Abundance, 1989; Beth Henley: Monologues for Women, 1992; Screenplays: Nobody's Fool, 1986; Crimes of the Heart, 1986; Miss Firecracker, 1989; Signatures, 1990; Control Freaks, 1993; Revelers, 1994; L-Play, 1996; Impossible Marriage, 1998; Family Week, 2000; Ridiculous Fraud, 2006. Honours: Pulitzer Prize for Drama, 1981; New York Drama Critics Circle Best Play Award, 1981; George Oppenheimer/Newsday Playwriting Award, 1981. Address: c/o The William Morris Agency, 1350 Avenue of the Americas, New York, NY 10019, USA.

HÉNON Susan Patricia, b. 8 January 1961, Hayes, Middlesex, England. Botanical Artist. m. Sylvain Hénon. Education: Courses, seminars, etc with Colin Radcliffe, NDD ATD DA Manchester; and Trudy Friend, NDD ATD, 1987-96; Open College of Arts, Barnsley, 1996-2001. Appointments: Art Teacher, Atelier Hénon, Dieburg, 1998-; Exhibitions include: Say It With Flowers, Schloss und Museum Fechenbach, 2008; The Botanical Palette, Westminster, London, 2008; Regular exhibit (and demonstration) with Palmengarten, Frankfurt, Germany. Publications: Say It With Flowers; Mariannes Garden; Contributor of articles to newspapers and magazines. Honours: Prize Winner, EMAP Newspapers, 1986. Memberships: Association of Advancing Artists; Reinheimer Kunst and Kulturvereins; Kunst Archive, Darmstadt; The Society of Botanical Artists; Gesellschaft zur Forderung der Gartenkultur ev; Committee Member, Museums Society, Dieburg, Germany. Address: Atelier Hénon, Steinstrasse 23, 64807 Dieburg, Germany.

HENRY Lenny, b. 29 August 1958, England. m. Dawn French, 1 daughter. Appointments: Numerous tours including Loud!, 1994; Australia, 1995. Creative Works: TV includes: New Faces (debut), Tiswas, Three of a Kind, 1981-83; The Lenny Henry Show, Alive and Kicking, 1991; Bernard and the Genie, 1991; In Dreams, 1992; The Real McCoy, 1992; Chef (title role) (3 series), Lenny Hunts the Funk, New Soul Nation, White Goods, 1994; Funky Black Shorts, 1994; Comic Relief, Lenny Go Home, 1996; Lenny's Big Amazon Adventure, 1997; Lenny Goes to Town, 1998; The Man, 1998; Hope and Glory, 1999, 2000; Lenny's Big Atlantic Adventure, 2000; Lenny in Pieces, 2000, 2001; Lenny Henry – This is My Life, 2003; The Lenny Henry Show, 2004; Films include: True Identity, 1991; Harry Potter and the Prisoner of Azkaban (voice), 2004; Video: Lenny Henry Live and Unleashed, 1989; Lenny Henry Live and Loud, 1994; Toured Australia with Large! Show, 1998; Live performances: Have You Seen This Man tour, 2001; So Many Things to Say, 2003, tour 2004; Othello, Northern Broadsides, 2009. Publications: The Quest for the Big Woof (autobiography), 1991; Charlie and the Big Chill (childrens book), 1995; Berry's Way, 2006. Honours include: Monaco Red Cross Award; The Golden Nymph Award; BBC personality of the Year, Radio and TV Industry Club, 1993; Golden Rose of Montreux Award for Lenny in Pieces, 2000; CBE, 1999; Lifetime Achievement Award for Ongoing Performance, UK Comedy Awards, 2003. Address: c/o PBJ Management Ltd, 5 Soho Square, London W1V 5DE, England.

HENSON Gavin Lloyd, b. 1 February 1982, Bridgend, Wales. Rugby Player. 1 son and 1 daughter with Charlotte Church. Education: Brynteg Comprehensive, Bridgend, South Wales. Career: Joined Swansea RFC, 2000; International debut for Wales against Japan, 2001; Joined Ospreys, 2003; Grand Slam in the Six Nations Championship, 2005. Publications: My Grand Slam Year, 2005. Honours: International Rugby Board's Young Player Of The Year award, 2001; Named Man of the Match, EDF cup Semi Final, 2008.

HER Moon, b. 14 February 1969, Damyang, Jeonnam, South Korea. m. Ae-Suk Park, 1 son, 2 daughters. Education: DVM, College of Veterinary Medicine, Jeonnam National University, 1987-91; MS, Veterinary Public Health, Konkuk University, 1995; PhD, Veterinary Microbiology, Seoul National University, 2010. Appointments: Researcher, Veterinary Research Department, 1992-2004; Senior Researcher, Veterinary Research Department, 2005-, National Veterinary Research and Quarantine Service; Member, OIE Reference Laboratory for Burcellosis, 2009-. Publications: 21 papers on animal disease in peer-reviewed journals; 2 patents. Honours: Award Certificate, Minister of Agriculture and Forestry, 1999. Memberships: Korean Society of Veterinary Science; Korean Society of Veterinary Public Health; Korean Society of Zoomoses. Address: #175 Anyang-ro, Manan-gu, Hayang-city, Gyeonggi-do, 430-757, South Korea.

HERBERT (Edward) Ivor (Montgomery), b. 20 August 1925, Johannesburg, South Africa. Author; Journalist; Scriptwriter. Education: Eton College; MA, Trinity College, Cambridge, 1949. Appointments: Travel Editor, Racing Editor, The Mail on Sunday, 1982-2002; Chairman, Bradenhamm Parish Council, 1970-; Chairman, Friends of St Botolph's Church, 1970-. Publications: Eastern Windows, 1953; Point to Point, 1964; Arkle: The Story of a Champion, 1966, further editions, 1975, 2003; The Great St Trinian's Train Robbery (screenplay), 1966; The Queen Mother's Horses, 1967; The Winter Kings (co- author), 1968, enlarged edition, 1989; The Way to the Top, 1969; Night of the Blue Demands, play (co-author), 1971; Over Our Dead Bodies, 1972; The Diamond Diggers, 1972; Scarlet Fever (co-author), 1972; Winter's Tale, 1974; Red Rum: Story of a Horse of Courage, 1974, further editions, 1974, 1977, 1995, 2005; The Filly (n, 1977; Six at the Top, 1977; Classic Touch (TV documentary), 1985; Spot the Winner, 1978, updated, 1990; Longacre, 1978; Horse Racing, 1980; Vincent O'Brien's Great Horses, 1984; Revolting Behaviour, 1987; Herbert's Travels, 1987; Reflections on Racing (co-author), 1990; Riding Through My Life (with HRH The Princess Royal), 1991; Vincent O'Brien (official biography), 2005. Memberships: Society of Authors; Writers' Guild: Turf Club. Address: The Old Rectory, Bradenham, Buckinghamshire HP14 4HD, England. E-mail: ivorherbert@tiscali.co.uk

HERCENBERG Dov Bernard, b. 1949, Paris, France. Professor. Education: BA, History of Art and Archaeology, 1971, MA, Art History, Institute d'Histoire de l'Art, 1974, University of Paris IV, France; PhD, Philosophy, University of Paris I, France, 1978. Appointments: Intern, Académie de France à Rome, Villa Medicis, 1973-75; Thesis, Ecole du Louvre, 1974; Assistant Lecturer, 1978-83, Senior Lecturer, 1983-96, Professor, 1996-, Department of Philosophy, University of Bar-Ilan, Israel. Publications: 5 books; Numerous articles in professional journals. Honours: Keren Beracha Foundation Grant, Jerusalem, 1979-81; Daria Borghese Prize, Rome, 1976; Memorial Foundation for Jewish Culture Grant, New York, 1975-76; Fondation Paul Cailleux Prize, Paris, 1975. Memberships: Israeli Association of Philosophy. Address: Department of Philosophy, Bar-Ilan University, 52900 Ramat-Gan, Israel. E-mail: dovberg1@smile.net.il

HERCZEG Márton, b. 1976, Budapest, Hungary. Senior Consultant. m. Katalin Szántó, 2008, 1 son. Education: MSc, Bioengineering, 2000; PhD, Environmental Economics and Management, 2008. Appointments: Project Officer, 2003-04, Project Manager, 2004-07, The Regional Environmental Center for Central and Eastern Europe; Environmental Expert, GeoLogika, 2007-08; University Lecturer and Research Fellow, Budapest University of Technology and Economics, 2003-08; Senior Consultant, Copenhagen Resource Institute, 2008-. Publications: Author and co-author of more than 40 publications including several books, research reports and articles in professional journals. Honours: Award, Hungarian Ministry for Education and Culture, 2007; Ferenc Deák Scholarship Award; Environmental Science Award, Hungarian Minister for Environment. Memberships: Senior Expert, European Topic Centre on SCP; Environmental Management and Law Association; European Topic Centre on Resources and Waste Management. Address: Copenhagen Resource Institute, Børsgade 4, 1215 Copenhagen K, Denmark. E-mail: marhe@etc.mim.dk Website: www.cri.dk

HERDMAN John Macmillan, b. 20 July 1941, Edinburgh, Scotland. Writer. m. (1) Dolina Maclennan, divorced, (2) Mary Ellen Watson, 17 August 2002. Education: BA, 1963, MA, 1967, PhD, 1988, Magdalene College, Cambridge, England. Appointments: Creative Writing Fellow, Edinburgh University, Scotland, 1977-79; William Soutar Fellow, Perth, Scotland, 1990-91. Publications: Descent, 1968; A Truth Lover, 1973; Memoirs of My Aunt Minnie/Clapperton, 1974; Pagan's Pilgrimage, 1978; Stories Short and Tall, 1979; Voice Without Restraint: Bob Dylan's Lyrics, 1982; Three Novellas, 1987; The Double in Nineteenth-Century Fiction, 1990; Imelda and Other Stories, 1993; Ghostwriting, 1996; Cruising (play), 1997; Poets, Pubs, Polls and Pillarboxes, 1999; Four Tales, 2000; The Sinister Cabaret, 2001; Triptych, 2004; My Wife's Lovers, 2007. Honours: Scottish Arts Council Book Awards, 1978, 1993. Listed in national biographical dictionaries. Address: 5A Barossa Place, Perth, PH1 5HG, Scotland.

HERLEA Alexandre, b. 11 October 1942, Brasov, Romania (French and Romanian Citizen). Professor. Married, 1 daughter. Education: Mechanical Engineer, Institutul Politechnic, Brasov, Romania, 1965; PhD, History of Science and Technology, Ecole des Hautes Etudes en Sciences Sociales and Conservatoire National des Arts et Métiers (CNAM), 1977; Habilitation, Sciences, Université de Paris Sud – Orsay, Sorbonne, France, 1993. Appointments: Engineer, IRGU Company, Bucharest, Romania, 1966-69; Lecturer, Scoala Technica "23 August", Bucharest, Romania, 1969-72; University Researcher, History of Technology, CNAM, Paris, 1972-77; Visiting Researcher, Smithsonian Institution and Harvard, Princeton and Pennsylvania Universities, 1978-79; Research Engineer, CNAM, Paris, 1980-88; Associated Professor, Ecole Centrale des Arts et Manufactures, 1980-88; Senior Lecturer, History of Technology, 1988-94, Member of Teaching Staff, PhD Programmes, 1988-2000, CNAM, Paris; Visiting Professor, Michigan Technological University, USA, 1990, Universitatea Bucuresti, Romania, 1994; Professor with tenure, History of Technology, 1995-, Director of Social Science Department, 1995-97, Director of International Relations, 2001-, Université de Technologie, Belfort-Montbeliard, France; Minister for European Integration, Romanian Government, 1996-99; Ambassador, Head of the Romanian Mission to the European Union, 2000-2005. Publications: Author, co-author and editor of 12 books published in France, Italy, United States, United Kingdom including: Histoire générale des techniques. Les techniques de la civilisation industrielle, 1978; Les moteurs, 1985; Over 40 scientific studies and numerous political articles. Honours: Silver Medal, Société d'Encouragement au Progrés, France; The Prize "Soziale Marktwirtschaft, Wirtschaftspolitischer Club, Berlin, Germany; Chevalier, Palmes Académiques, France; Chevalier, Merite de l'Invention, Chambre Belge des Inventeurs, Belgium; Commandeur, Légion d'Honneur, France; Mare Ofiter (High Officer) Serviciul Credincios, Romania; Doctor Honoris Causa, University Transilvania Brasov, Romania. Memberships include: Comité das Traveaux Historiques et Scientifiques, France; International Committee for the History of Technology (Member of the Executive Committee, former President); International Academy of the History of Science; Romanian Christian Democrat Party (PNT-CD, Vice-President); Christian Democratic International (Member of the Executive Committee, former Vice-President). Address: 4, rue H. Fragonard, 92130 Issy-les-Moulineaux, France. E-mail: alexandre.herlea@wanadoo.fr

HERLIN Gunnar, b. 8 February 1951, Stockholm, Sweden. Medical Doctor. m. Gudrun Ekman, 1 son, 1 daughter. Education: Medical Examination, 1977; Licensed Doctor, 1979; Specialist in Clinical Chemistry, 1985; Specialist in Medical Radiology, 1992. Appointments: Senior Doctor, Medical Radiology, Karolinska University Hospital, Huddinge, Stockholm, Sweden. Publications: Quantitative assessment of 99mTc-depreotide uptake in patients with non-small-cell lung cancer, immunohistochemicals correlations; Role of scintigraphy with Tc-99m depreotide in the diagnosis and management of patients with suspected lung cancer; IIC-harmine as a potential PET tracer for ductal pancreas cancer: In vitro studies. Honours: Listed in international biographical dictionaries. Address: Skånegatan 71, Stockholm, S-11637, Sweden. E-mail: gunnar.herlin@karolinska.se

HERMAN Witold Walenty, b. 14 February 1932, Toruń, Poland. Cellist; Academic; Professor. m. Catherine Bromboszcz, 1970, 1 son, 1 daughter. Education: Diploma, distinction, Szymanowski Conservatory, Toruń, 1950-51; MA, Academy of Music, Cracow, 1956; Diploma, Ecole Normale de Musique, Paris, France, 1960; Doctor of Philosophy of Music, World University, Tucson, Arizona, 1984. Appointments: Concert Debut, State Philhamonia Cracow, 1954; Cello concerts with orchestra and cello recitals in Poland and other European countries; Professor, Music Academy, Cracow; Guest Professor, Franz Liszt Musik Akademie, Weimar, Germany; Jury Member, International Pablo Casals Cello International Competition, Budapest, 1968; Honorary Guest, International Tschajkowski Competition, Moscow and International J S Bach Competition, Leipzig; Jury Member, Cello Competition in Markneukirchen, Germany, 2001; Director, Cello and Double Bass Chair, State Academy of Music, Cracow; Expert, Polish Ministry of Culture and Art. Creative Works: Recordings for radio and TV in Poland and European countries. Honours: Special Prize, 2nd Class, 1972, 1st Class, 1982, Polish Ministry of Culture and Arts; Golden Cross of Merit, Polish Government, 1977; Chevalier Cross of the Order Polonia Restituta, 1986; Ray Robinson's Excellence in Teaching Award, Palm Beach University, Florida, USA, 2001. Membership: International Jeunesse Musicale, Paris, 1960. Address: ul Friedleina 49 m 5, 30-009 Cracow, Poland.

HERMANN Armin Daniel, b. 26 November 1937, Neu-Sarata, Moldavia. Nuclear Chemistry Engineer. m. Christine Seidel Hermann, 1970, divorced 1981, 1 son. Education: Diploma in Engineering, 1961, DSc, 1984, Technical University Dresden; PhD, Lomonossow University,

Moscow, 1965. Appointments: Scientist, 1965-66, Group Leader, 1966-75, Head of Department, 1975-87, German Academy of Sciences; Project Manager, Paul Scherrer Institute, Switzerland, 1990-2005; Adviser, Nuclear Fuel Industry Research Group, Palo Alto, 1994-2004; Member, Co-ordination Council, Council of Mutual Economic Aid, Moscow, 1971-87; Nuclear Chemistry Educator, German Academy of Sciences, Technical High School, Zittau, Technical University, Dresden. Publications: Radiochemical Methods, textbook; 100 articles in scientific publications; Patentee in field of nuclear reactors. Honour: Recipient, Order Banner of Labour, governmental award. Memberships: German Chemical Society; Working Group, Nuclear Chemistry; German Society of Nuclear Technology; Swiss Nuclear Forum; Christian Parish Control Commission. Address: Sommerhaldenstr 5A, 5200 Brugg, Aargau, Switzerland. E-mail: armin.hermann@bluewin.ch.

HERMANN Edward Robert, b. 9 October 1920, Newport, Kentucky, USA. Professor Emeritus; Consultant. m. Eleanor Marie Hill, 1946, 3 sons, 4 daughters. Education: BSCE, University of Kentucky, 1942; SM, Sanitary Engineering, MIT, 1949; CE, University of Kentucky, 1953; PhD, University of Texas, 1957; Licensed Industrial Hygienist, Illinois, 1994-. Appointments: Professor of Environmental and Occupational Health Sciences, School of Public Health, University of Illinois at Chicago; Director of Industrial Hygiene Graduate Programmes, University of Illinois Medical Centre; Professor & Acting Director, Occupational and Environmental Medicine, University of Illinois School of Public Health; Professor, Environmental Engineering, Department of Civil Engineering, Mechanics and Metallurgy, University of Illinois at Chicago; Professor, Environmental Health Engineering, Northwestern University; Industrial Health Engineer, Humble Oil and Refining Company, (now Exxon Mobil); Founding President, Board of Trustees, Bayshore Municipal Utilities District, Harris County, Texas; Chief Sanitary Engineer and Chief of Public Health, US Atomic Energy Commission, Los Alamos, New Mexico; President Kennedy's Energy Study Group; Consultant to various industries, government agencies, law offices and universities. Publications: Over 100 articles, monographs and book chapters in reviewed scientific, engineering and medical journals. Honours: Sigma Xi, 1956; Harrison Prescott Eddy Medal, 1959; Resources Division Award, American Water Works Association, 1960; Michigan Industrial Hygiene Society Award, 1964; Tau Beta Pi, 1973; Radebaugh Award, 1976; Award of Merit, Chicago Technical Societies Council, 1978; Borden Foundation Award, 1988; Outstanding Civil Engineering Alumnus Award, University of Kentucky, 1995; Donald Eddy Cummings Memorial Award, 1999; Outstanding Publications Award, American Industrial Hygiene Association, 2000. Memberships include: Fellow, American Association for the Advancement of Science; American Academy of Environmental Engineers; Fellow, American Public Health Association; Fellow, Life Member, American Society of Civil Engineers. Address: 117 Church Road, Winnetka, IL 60093, USA. E-mail: hygieology@aol.com

HERNÁNDEZ MARCOS Maximiliano, b. 14 April 1963, Alba de Tormes, Salamanca, Spain. University Teacher. m. Rosario Pozo Garciá, 1 daughter. Education: Philosophy degree, 1986, PhD, 1993, University of Salamanca. Appointments: Public Scholarship, Research Training, 1987-91, Assistant Lecturer, 1991-96, Contracted Teacher, 1996-2007, Professor, Lecturer, 2007-, University of Salamanca. Publications: Numerous articles in professional journals; Book, La Crítica de la Razón pura como Proceso Civil, 1994. Memberships: Deutsche Gesellschaft für die Erforschung des 18 Jahrhunderts; ISECS (Voltaire Foundation). Address: Facultad de Filosofia – Edificio FES Campus Unamuno, E-37007 Salamanca, Spain. E-mail: marcos@usal.es

HERNANDEZ-GOMEZ Luis Hector, b. 15 April 1956, Mexico. Researcher; Lecturer. m. Laura Leticia Mendoza Carpio, 1986, 2 sons. Education: BSc, ESIME, Mexico, 1977; MSc, Mexico, 1986; PhD, Oxford University, 1992. Appointments: Stress Analyst, Bufete Industrial SA Mexico City, 1977-78; Analyst, Mexican Petroleum Institute, Mexico City, 1978-86; Researcher, Institute de Investigaciones Electricas, Mexico, 1986-95; Lecturer Researcher, Seccion De Estudios De Posgrado ESIME IPN, 1986-. Publications: 40 papers in international journals; 100 papers in international congresses; 20 papers in Mexican magazines; 40 papers in Mexican symposiums. Honours: Ciudad Capital Heberto Castillo Martinez, 2009; Engineering Award, Mexico City, 2010. Memberships: Mexican Academy of Science; American Society of Mechanical Engineering. Address: Miraflores 94, Colonia Industrial, Gustavo A Madero, 07800 Mexico, DF Mexico.

HERRING Horace Jean-Pierre, b. 13 July 1950, London, England. Freelance Writer; Researcher. Divorced, 1 son, 1 daughter. Education: BSc (Hons), Engineering with Social Studies, Sussex University, 1971-74; PhD, Open University, 1994-2003. Appointments: Conservation Officer, National Union of Students, London, 1974-75; Editor, Whole Earth magazine, Brighton, 1975-78; Senior Research Associate, Energy Analysis Group, Lawrence Berkeley Lab, University of California at Berkeley, USA, 1980-81; Principal Energy Conservation Officer, Department of Energy, Government of Fiji, 1982-84; Research Fellow, Chief Scientist's Group, Energy Technology Support Unit, Harwell Lab, Oxfordshire, 1985-88; Energy Economist, Business Planning Branch, PowerGen plc, 1988-92; Research Fellow, Faculty of Technology, Open University, 1999-2001; Freelance Consultant, Writer, specialising in energy economics, energy efficiency policy and environmental history, 1992-. Publications: Alternative Technology Directory, 1978; Energy Use in UK Commercial and Public Buildings, 1988; Energy Use in the UK Domestic Sector up to Year 2010, 1990; Energy Savings in Domestic Electrical Appliances, 1992; Is Britain a Third World Country? The case of German refrigerators, 1994; Electricity Use in Minor Appliances in the UK, 1995; Is Energy Efficiency Good for the Environment: some conflicts and confusions, 1996; Does energy efficiency save energy? The debate and its consequences, 1999; Editorial: How Green is Energy Efficiency?, 2000; The Conservation Society: harbinger of the 1970s environment movement in the UK, 2001; The Rebound Effect, Sustainable Consumption and electronic appliances, 2001; Sustainable Services, Electronic Education and the Rebound Effect, 2002; The Rebound Effect and Energy Conservation, 2004; Energy Efficiency and Consumption, 2004; Energy Efficiency: A Critical View?, 2005; From Energy Dreams to Nuclear Nightmares: Lessons for the 21st century from a previous nuclear era, 2005; Energy Efficiency and Sustainable Consumption, 2008. Honours: Best Paper Award, 15th International Symposium, Informatics for Environmental Protection, Zurich, 2001. Memberships: Chair, Interdisciplinary Research Network of Environmental Researchers, UK, 2000-05; Referee, Energy – the International Journal, and Ecological Economics. Address: EERU, DDEM, The Open University, Milton Keynes, MK7 6AA, England. E-mail: h.herring@open.ac.uk

HERSHEY Barbara, b. 5 February 1948, Hollywood, California, USA. Actress. m. (1) 1 son, (2) Stephen Douglas, 1992, divorced 1995. Career: Films: With Six You Get Eggroll, 1968; Heaven with a Gun, The Last Summer, 1969; The Liberation of L B Jones, The Baby Maker, 1970; The Pursuit of Happiness, 1971; Dealing: Or the Berkeley-to-Boston Forty-Brick Lost-Bag Blues, Boxcar Bertha, 1972; Love Comes Quietly, 1973; The Crazy World of Julius Vrooder, 1974; You and Me, Diamonds, 1975; Trial by Combat, The Last Hard Men, 1976; The Stuntman, 1980; The Entity, Americana, Take This Job and Shove It, 1981; The Right Stuff, 1983; The Natural, 1984; Hoosiers, 1986; Tin Men, Shy People, 1987; T Hannah and Her Sisters, The Last Temptation of Christ, A World Apart, Beaches, 1988; Tune in Tomorrow..., Paris Trout, 1990; The Public Eye, Defenseless, 1991; Swing Kids, Splitting Heirs, Falling Down, 1993; A Dangerous Woman, 1994; Last of the Dogmen, 1995; Portrait of a Lady, The Pallbearer, 1996; A Soldier's Daughter Never Cries, 1998; Frogs for Snakes, Drowning on Dry Land, Breakfast of Champions, 1999; Lantana, 2001; 11:14, 2003; Riding the Bullet, 2004; The Bird Can't Fly, Love Comes Lately, Childless, 2007; Vacuuming the Cat, 2008; Albert Schweitzer, 2009. Many TV shows and series. Honours: Best Actress, Cannes Film Festival, 1987, 1988; Emmy and Golden Globe Awards, 1990. Address: c/o Suzan Bymel, Bymel O'Neill Management, N Vista, Los Angeles, CA 90046, USA.

HERTFORD, 9th Marquess of, Henry Jocelyn Seymour, b. 6 July 1958, Birmingham, England. Landowner. m. Beatriz Karam, 2 sons, 2 daughters. Education: Royal Agricultural College, Cirencester. Appointments: Estate Owner; Farm Manager; Flock Master; Shepherd. Memberships: Country Land and Business Association; National Farmers Union. Address: Ragley Hall, Alcester, Warwickshire B49 5NJ, England. E-mail: info@ragleyhall.com

HERVIK Jill Angela Brook, b. 25 March 1958, Yorkshire, England. Physiotherapist. m. Håvard, 2 sons, 1 daughter. Education: BSc, Physiotherapy, Sheffield Polytechnic, 1981; Acupuncture Study, Norwegian Acupuncture College, 1985-88, 2000-03; Research Diploma, Høuskolen Agder, 2005-06. Appointments: Physiotherapist, Stafford Hospital, England, 1981-82; Physiotherapist, 1982-90, 1992-94, Acupuncturist and Researcher, Pain Clinic, 1994-2011, Vestfold Hospital, Norway; Acupuncturist private practice, Grancanari, Spain, 1991-92. Publications: Acupuncture for the treatment of hot flashes in breast cancer patients, a randomized, controlled trial, 2009; Quality of Life of breast cancer patients medicated with anti-estrogens, 2 years after acupuncture treatment: a qualitative study, 2010. Memberships: Norwegian Acupuncture Association. Address: Husvikveien 143, 3124 Tønsberg, Norway.

HESELTINE Michael (Rt Hon Michael Ray Dibdin Heseltine), b. 21 March 1933, Swansea, Wales. Politician. m. Anne Edna Harding Williams, 1962, 1 son, 2 daughters. Education: Pembroke College, Oxford. Appointments: Chair, Haymarket Press, 1965-70, 1999-; MP for Tavistock, 1966-74, for Henley, 1974-2001; Parliamentary Sectretary, Ministry of Transport, 1970; Parliamentary Under Secretary of State, Department of the Environment, 1970-72; Minister of Aerospace and Shipping, 1972-74; Opposition Spokesman for Industry, 1974-76, for the Environment, 1976-79; Secretary of State for the Environment, 1979-83, 1990-92, for Defence, 1983-86; Secretary of State for Industry and President of the Board of Trade, 1992-95; Deputy Prime Minister and First Secretary of State, 1995-97; Director, Haymarket Publishing Group, 1997-, Chair, 2001-; President, Association of Conservative Clubs, 1982-83, Chair, Conservative Mainstream, 1998-; President, Quoted Companies Alliance International Advisory Council, 2000-, Federation of Korean Industries, Anglo-China Forum, 1998-; President, Conservative Group for Europe, 2001-; Development Patron, Trinity College of Music, Institute of Marketing. Publications: Reviving the Inner Cities, 1983; Where There's A Will, 1987; The Challenge of Europe: Can Britain Win? 1988; Life in the Jungle (memoirs), 2000. Honorary Fellow, Pembroke College, Oxford, 1986, University of Wales (Swansea); Bentinck Prize, 1989; Honorary Fellow, Chartered Institute of Management, 1998; Hon FRIBA; Hon LLD (Liverpool) 1990; Hon DBA (Luton), 2003. Address: House of Lords, London SW1A 0PW, England.

HESKETH Ronald David, b. 16 June 1947, Broughty Ferry, Angus, Scotland. Chaplain. m. Vera, 1 son, 1 daughter. Education: BA Hons, Geography, University of Durham, 1968; Theology, University of Cambridge, 1969; Diploma, Pastoral Studies, St Michael's College, Cardiff, 1971; Diploma, Reformation Studies, Open University, 1977. Appointments: Ordained Deacon, 1971; Priest, 1972; Curate, Holy Trinity Church, Southport, 1971-73; Assistant Chaplain, Mersey Mission to Seamen, 1973-75; RAF Chaplain, 1975-98; Command Chaplain, 1998-2001; Chaplain-in-Chief, 2001-2006; Vocations Officer Diocese of Worcester, 2006-. Honours: Honorary Chaplain to HM The Queen, 2001-2006; Fellow, Royal Geographical Society; Companion of the Most Honourable Order of the Bath; CB; BA; DPS; RAF; Listed in national biographical dictionaries. Membership: Royal Air Force Club; Fellow of the Chartered Management Institute, 2006-; Chairman of the Naval, Military and Airforce Bible Society, 2006-; Vice President, Friends of St Clement Danes. Address: The Old Police Station, Bredon Road, Tewkesbury Gloucestershire, GL20 5BZ, England. E-mail: ron@hesketh.org.uk

HESS Peter Otto, b. 13 December 1953, Konigstein, Germany. Professor. m. Andrea, 3 sons. Education: Physics diploma, 1978, PhD, 1980, Habilitation, 1985, University of Frankfurt am Main. Appointments: Assistant, GSI-Darmstadt, 1982; Senior Lecturer, University of Cape Town, South Africa, 1983-85; Associate Professor, 1985-90, Full Professor, 1990-, Instituto de Ciencias Nucleares, UNAM. Publications: Around 150 articles in professional journals, 50 proceedings and contributions, and 10 popular science and short notes. Honours: Distinction, Universidad Nacional, 1993; Premio a la Investigacion Cientifica-Mexican Academy of Science, 1993; Marcos Moshinsky Medal, 2001; Premio a la Investigacion Cientifica-Mexican Physical Society, 2004; Scopus Award, 2010; Mercator Professor, University Giotsen, Germany, 1992-93; Mercator Professor, University Frankfurt am Main, Germany, 2006-07. Memberships: Sociedad Mexican de Fisica; APS; New York Academy of Sciences; Mexican Academy of Sciences; Deutsche Gesellschaft für Luft und Raumfahrt. Address: Instituto de Ciencias Nuclear, Universidad Nacional Autonomos de Mexico, Ciudad Universitaria Circuito Exterior S/N, Ap 70-543, 04510 Mexico DF, Mexico. E-mail: hess@nucleares.unam.mx

HESSE Reinhard, b. 9 March 1936, Halle/Saale, Germany. Geologist. m. Ellenmarie Von Sydow, deceased. Education: MSc, 1961, PhD, 1964, DSc, 1969, Technical University, Munich, Germany. Appointments: Assistant Professor, Associate Professor, Full Professor, 1969-96, Professor Emeritus, McGill University, Montreal, Canada; Honorary Professor, Ludwig-Maximillian University, Munich. Publications: Numerous articles in professional journals. Honours: Credner Award, German Geological Society;

Keen Award, Geological Association of Canada, 2009. Memberships: American Geophysical Union; Geological Society of America; Society for Sedimentary Geology; International Association of GeoChemistry; Deutsche Gesellschaft fuer Geowissenschaften. Address: Earth & Planetary Sciences, McGill University, Montreal, QC H3A 2A7, Canada. E-mail: reinhard.hesse@mcgill.ca

HESTERWERTH Kathleen Ann (Kathy), b. 8 June 1948, McCook, Nebraska, USA. Business Owner. Education: Associate of Arts Degree, McCook University, 1968; BSc, Home Economics/Business Administration, University of Nebraska, Kearney, 1971. Appointments: Federal Service Career: Washington DC Area – HQ COMD USAF; US Army Military Personnel Center; Naval Telecommunications Unit; HQ US Army Computer Systems Command; HQ Military Traffic Management Command; US Government Printing Office; US Small Business Administration, Jacksonville, Florida; US National Park Service, Yellowstone National Park, Wyoming; Air Force Flight Test Center, Edwards Air Force Base, California; Established Flat Rock Oil, LLC, 2001. Honours: Cambridge Who's Who Empowering Executives, Professionals and Entrepreneurs Executive of the Year, 2006-2007 representing Crude Oil Production; Eminent Fellow, ABI; International Peace Prize and Ambassador General, United Cultural Convention. Memberships: American Home Economics Association; Appaloosa Horse Club; American Paint Horse Association; Arabian Horse Association. E-mail: flatrockoil@earthlink.net

HETZEL Basil Stuart, b. 13 June 1922, London, England. Medical Scientist. m. Anne Gilmour Fisher, 3 sons, 2 daughters. Education: MBBS, University of Adelaide, 1944; Registrar, Royal Adelaide Hospital, 1946-49; MD, 1949; Member, Royal Australasian College of Physicians, 1949; Research Fellowships, Adelaide, New York, London, 1949-55. Appointments: Reader, Professor of Medicine, Adelaide University, 1956-68; Honorary Physician, Royal Adelaide Hospital and Queen Elizabeth Hospital; Foundation Professor, Social & Preventive Medicine, Monash University, Melbourne, 1968-75; Visiting Commonwealth Professor, University of Glasgow, 1972-73; First Chief, CSIRO Division of Human Nutrition, Adelaide, 1976-85; Executive Director, Chairman, International Council for Control of Iodine Deficiency Disorders, 1985-95, Chairman, 1986-2001; Lieutenant Governor of South Australia, 1992-2000. Publications include: Health & Australian Society, 1974; Lifestyle & Health, 1987; The Story of Iodine Deficiency, 1989; SOS for a Billion, 1994; Towards the Global Elimination of Brain Damage due to Iodine Deficiency, 2004; Chance and Commitment, Memoirs of a Medical Scientist, 2005. Honours: Companion of Order of Australia, 1990; Honorary Professor, Tianjin Medical University, China, 1989; Alwyn Smith Medal, Royal Colleges of Physicians, UK, 1993; Anzac Peace Prize, Australia, 1997; Prince Mahidol Award, Thailand, 2007; Pollin Prize, New York, 2009. Memberships: President, Endocrine Society of Australia, 1964-66; Life Member, Public Health Association of Australia; Fellow, Nutrition Society, Australia, 1991; Honorary Member, International Epidemiology Association, 1993; Chancellor, University of South Australia, 1992-98. E-mail: iccidd@a011.aone.net.au

HEUN Werner, b. 25 September 1953, Frankfurt/Main, Germany. Professor of Law. m. Sarah J Weaver, 2 sons. Education: Degree in Law, University of Würzburg, Germany; Dr jur utr, 1983; Habil, University of Bonn, 1988; Dr hc, Eötvös Lorand University, Budapest, 2008. Appointments: Research Assistant, 1980-83, Assistant, 1983-88, University of Bonn; Counselor-at-Law, 1980-83; Substitute Professor, University of Cologne, 1988-89; University of Bielefeld, 1989, University of Hamburg, 1989-90; Professor of Law, University of Göttingen, 1990-. Publications: Das Mehrheitsprinzip in der Demokratie, 1983; Staatshaushalt und Staatsleitung, 1989; Das Budgetrecht im Regierungssystem der USA, 1989; Funktionell-rechtliche Schranken der Verfassungsgerichtsbarkeit, 1992; Co-author, Grundgesetz-Kommentar, 3 vols, 1996-2000, 2nd edition 2004-08; Editor, Deutsche Verfassungsdokumente 1806-1849, 6 vols, 2006-08; Co-editor, Evangelisches Staatslexikon, 2006; The Constitution of Germany and Contextual Analysis, 2011. Memberships: Vereinigung der deutschen Staatsrechtslehrer; Deutsche Gesellschaft zur Erforschung des politischen Denkens; Gesellschaft für Rechtsvergleichung; Deutsche Vereinigung für Parlamentsfragen. Address: Institut für Allgemeine Staatslehre, Goßlerstr 11, 37073 Goettingen, Germany. E-mail: staatsl@gwdg.de

HEWISH Antony, b. 11 May 1924, Fowey, Cornwall, England. Astronomer; Physicist. m. Marjorie E C Richards, 1950, 1 son and 1 daughter. Education: Graduated, Gonville and Caius College, Cambridge, 1948. Appointments: War Service, 1943-46; Research Fellow, Gonville and Caius College, 1951-54; Supernumerary Fellow, 1956-61; University Assistant Director of Research, 1953-61, Lecturer, 1961-69; Fellow, Churchill College, Cambridge, 1962-; Reader in Radio Astronomy, University of Cambridge, 1969-71, Professor, 1971-89, Professor Emeritus, 1989; Professor, Royal Institute, 1977; Director, Mullard Radio Astronomy Observatory, Cambridge, 1982-88; Vikram Sarabhai Professor, Ahmedabad, 1988. Publications: The First, Second, Third and Fourth Cambridge Catalogues; Seeing Beyond the Invisible, Pulsars and physics laboratories. Honours: Hamilton Prize, 1951; Eddington Medal, Royal Astronomical Society, 1968; Boys Prize, Institute of Physics, 1970; Dellinger Medal, International Union of Radio Science, Hopkins Prize, Cambridge Medal and Prize, Society Francaise de Physique, 1974; Nobel Prize for Physics, 1974; Hughes Medal, Royal Society, 1977; Vainu Bappu Prize, Indian National Science Academy, 1998. Memberships: Foreign Member, American Academy of Arts and Sciences, 1970; Member, Belgian Royal Academy of Arts and Sciences, 1989; Member, Emeritus Academia Europea, 1996; Foreign Fellow, Indian National Science Academy; 6 Honorary ScD. Address: Cavendish Laboratory, Madingley Road, Cambridge, CB3 7NQ, England.

HEWITT Patricia Hope, b. 2 December 1948. Politician. m. William Birtles, 1981, 1 son, 1 daughter. Education: Cambridge University. Appointments: Public Relations Officer, Age Concern, 1971-73; Women's Rights Officer, 1973-74, General Secretary, 1974-83, National Council for Civil Liberties (now Liberty); Labour Party candidate, Leicester East general election, 1983; Press and Broadcasting Secretary to Leader of Opposition, 1983-88; Policy Co-ordinator, 1988-89; Senior Research Fellow, 1989, Deputy Director, 1989-94, Institute for Public Policy Research; Visiting Fellow, Nuffield College, Oxford, 1992-; Head, then Director of Research, Andersen Consulting (now Accenture), 1994-97; Labour MP for Leicester West, 1997-; Member, Select Committee on Social Security, 1997-98; Economic Secretary to the Treasury, 1998-99; Minister of State, Department of Trade and Industry, 1999-2001; Secretary of State for Trade and Industry, 2001-05; Minister for Women, 2001-05; Secretary of State for Health, 2005-07. Publications: Civil Liberties, the NCCL Guide, 1977; The Privacy Report, 1977; Your Rights at Work, 1981; The Abuse of Power, 1981; Your Second Baby, 1990; About Time: The Revolution in Work and Family Life, 1993; Pebbles in the Sand, 1998; Unfinished Business, 2004. Honours: Hon Fellow, London Business School, 2004. Address: Department of Health, Richmond House, 79 Whitehall, London SW1A 2NS, England. Website: www.doh.gov.uk

HIBBERD Alan Ronald, b. 25 October 1931, Bendigo, Australia. Clinical Ecologist; Toxicologist. m. (1) Doreen Imilda Collier, 2 sons, 2 daughters, (2) Lois Stratton. Education: Ridley College, Melbourne; PhC, Victorian College of Pharmacy; DCC, PhD, Chelsea College, University of London. Appointments: Community Pharmacy Practice, Melbourne, 1953-73; Director: ARH Pharmaceuticals, 1959-74, Pressels Laboratories, 1959-74; Part-time Demonstrator, Practical Pharmaceutics, Victorian College of Pharmacy, 1961-64; Lecturer to Postgraduate Students in Pharmacology and Therapeutics and Consultant in Dental Therapeutics and Prescribing, Victorian Branch, Australian Dental Association, 1966-74; In Charge of Drug Information Department and Ward Pharmacy Services, Hackney Hospital, London, 1975; Research Fellow, Pharmacy Department, Chelsea College, University of London, 1976-79; Lecturer, School of Pharmacy, University of London, 1980-81; Tutor and in charge of Clinical Pharmacy Services, Northwick Park Hospital, Harrow, 1980-81; First Course Organiser and Supervisor MSc Course in Clinical Pharmacy, University of London, 1980-81; Director, Hibbro Research, Hereford, 1981-84; Private Practice in Clinical Ecology, London, 1985-; Consultant, Clinical Pharmacology and Toxicology, Biocare Ltd, 1989-; Consultant in Clinical Biochemistry/Pharmacology, Society for Promotion of Nutritional Therapy (UK), 1992-97; Scientific Adviser to Register of Nutritional Therapists (UK), 1993-. Publications: Author of numerous articles and scientific papers on drug metabolism and relating to specialist field; Contributor to numerous learned publications. Memberships: Vice-president, International Academy of Oral Medicine and Toxicology (UK), 1994; Fellow (by examination), Pharmaceutical Society of Victoria, 1961; Royal Society of Victoria, 1968; British Dental Society for Clinical Nutrition, 1985; Nutrition Association, 1987; Environmental Dental Association, USA, 1991; British Society for Allergy, Environmental and Nutritional Medicine, 1993; FRSH, 1971; MRPharmS, 1974; Life Fellow, Pharmaceutical Society of Australia, 1991; British Association for Nutritional Therapy, 2001; Fellow, The Royal Society of Medicine, 2003; The British Society for Ecological Medicine, 2005. Address: c/o 42 Kendal St, London W2 2BU, England.

HICK Graeme Ashley, b. 23 May 1966, Salisbury, Zimbabwe. Cricketer. Appointments: Right-Hand Batsman, Off-Break Bowler, Slip Fielder; Teams: Zimbabwe, 1983-86, Worcestershire, 1984-, Northern Districts, 1987-89, Queensland, 1990-91; Scored 100 aged 6 years; Youngest player to appear in 1983 World Cup and youngest to represent Zimbabwe; 65 tests for England, 1991-97, scoring 3,383 runs (average 31.32), including 6 hundreds; Scored 30,189 1st class runs (average 55.2), with 104 hundreds (including 9 doubles, 1 triple, 1 quadruple (405 not out) to 1 April 1999); Youngest to score 2,000 1st class runs in a season, 1986; Scored 1,019 runs before June 1988, including a record 410 runs in April; Fewest innings for 10,000 runs in county cricket (179); Youngest (24) to score 50 1st class hundreds; Toured Australia, 1994-95; 120 limited-overs ints for 3,846 runs (average 37.33) by December 2002; Scored 315 not out v Durham, June 2002- (highest championship innings of the season); Played 65 tests and 120 one-day Internationals for England. Publication: My Early Life (autobiography), 1992. Honours: Wisden Cricketer of the Year, 1987. Membership: England World Cup Squad, 1996. Address: c/o Worcestershire County Cricket Club, New Road, Worcester WR2 4QQ, England.

HICKS Jerry (Gerald Anthony William), b. 12 June 1927, London, England. Artist. m. Anne Hayward, 1 son, 1 daughter. Education: Slade School of Art, 1944-45; Sandhurst, 1946-; Diploma, Slade School of Art, 1948-50; Department of Education, London University, 1950-51; Judo, 1949-. Appointments: Head of Art, Cotham Grammar School, 1951-81; Freelance Artist, 1981-; Exhibitions at: Royal Academy, London, 1952; Royal West of England Academy, 1950-2007; Annual exhibition and 2 person retrospective, 2008; Chairman and Executive Vice President; Portraits of: G Kulzumi; HM The Queen (for RWA); University Scientists include: Charles Frank and N Mott (Nobel Prize Winner); John Woodvine (Actor); Numerous headmasters; Paul Chad QC; Public art with Anne Hayward including: SS Great Britain Mural. Publications: A Place for People, 1976; Judo Through the Looking Glass; Numerous articles for Bristol Civil Society; RWA Friends; The World of Judo; Environmental Broadcaster with Keith Warmington; Numerous articles on environment for Bristol Civic Society. Honours: Queen's Silver Jubilee Award, 1977; MBE for Services to Sport & Community in South West, 1994; Bristol 600 Prize, 1997; Hon MA, Bristol University, 2004; Building a Better Bristol Award; 7th Dan Judo; Vice President, British Judo Association; Chairman, BJA Coaching. Memberships: Local Agenda 21 Land Use Group; South West Council for Sport & Recreation; Old Cothamians; SS Great Britain Project; Bristol Civic Society; Dodo Environmental Group. Address: Goldrush, Great George Street, Bristol BS1 5QT, England.

HICKS Philip, b. 11 October 1928, Leamington Spa, England. Artist; Painter. m. Jill Doreen Tweed, 1 son, 1 daughter. Education: Royal Military Academy, Sandhurst; Chelsea School of Art and Royal Academy Schools, 1949-54. Career: Part-time teacher, various schools of art, London area, 1960-86; Full-time painting, over 40 solo exhibitions, UK and abroad; Work appears in many public and corporate collections, including Tate Britain, Victoria and Albert Museum, Imperial War Museum, Contemporary Art Society, Royal College of Music, Nuffield Foundation; Represented by Messum's Fine Art, Cork Street, London. Publications: Mentioned in numerous journals, magazines and newspapers. Honours: British Council Award, 1977. Memberships: Royal Overseas League, St James's, London; Chelsea Arts Club, London; Past Chairman and Vice President, The Artists General Benevolent Institution. Address: Radcot House, Buckland Road, Bampton, Oxfordshire OX18 2AA, England.

HIDDLESTON James Andrew, b. 20 October 1935, Edinburgh, Scotland. Professor of French. m. (1) Janet Taylor, deceased 2000, 2 daughters, (2) Alison Coates, 2008. Education: MA, 1957, PhD, 1961, Edinburgh University; D Litt (Oxon), 2006. Appointments: Lecturer in French, University of Leeds, 1960-66; Fellow, Exeter College, Oxford, 1966-, Professor of French, University of Oxford, 1996-2003; Retired, 2003. Publications: Books: L'Univers de Jules Supervielle, 1965; Malraux: "La Condition humaine", 1973; Poems: Jules Laforgue, edition with introduction and notes, 1975; Essai sur Laforgue et les derniers vers, suivi de Laforgue et Baudelaire, 1980; Baudelaire and "Le Spleen de Paris", 1987, Japanese translation, 1989; Laforgue aujourd'hui (contributing editor), 1988; Collaboration with Michel Collot in edition of Jules Supervielle, Oeuvres poétiques complètes, 1996; Baudelaire and the Art of Memory, 1999; Victor Hugo, romancier de l'abîme (contributing editor),

2002; A wide variety of articles. Honour: Officier de l'ordre des arts et des lettres. Memberships: Society of French Studies; Nineteenth-Century French Studies. Address: 16 Dean Terrace, Edinburgh EH4 1NL, Scotland. E-mail: james.hiddleston@exeter.ox.ac.uk

HIGGINS Huntly Gordon, b. 8 January 1917, Perth, Western Australia. Research Scientist. m. Irena, 2 sons, 1 daughter. Education: Bachelor of Science (Hons), 1939; Doctor of Applied Science, 1962. Appointments: Geologist, Oil Co, Mining Co, WA School of Mines, 1938-40; Meteorologist, Flight Lieutenant, RAAF, 1941-45; Research Scientist, Forest Products, CSIRO, 1945-82; Assistant Chief, 1973-79, Chief, 1979-82, Honorary Research Fellow, 1982-2003, Division of Chemical Technology, CSIRO. Publications: Around 180 research papers, reports, book chapters, etc; Books: A Commonplace Book, 1996; Paper Physics in Australia, 1996. Honours: Hackett Post-Graduate Scholarship, 1939; Benjamin Medal, 1977; Centenary Medal, 2003; Minor Scholarships. Memberships: Fellow: Australian Academy of Technological Sciences and Engineering; International Academy of Wood Science; Institute of Physics; Royal Australian Chemical Institute; Appita; International Association of Scientific Papermakers. Address: 59 Fellows Street, Kew, VIC 3101, Australia. E-mail: huntlyhiggins@hotmail.com

HIGGS Peter Ware, b. 29 May 1929, Newcastle upon Tyne, England. University Teacher (retired). m. JoAnn Williamson, 2 sons. Education: Halesowen Grammar School, 1940-41; Cotham Grammar School, Bristol, 1941-46; City of London School, 1946-47; BSc, 1950, MSc, 1951, PhD, 1954, King's College London. Appointments: Senior Student, Royal Commission for the Exhibition of 1851, King's College London, 1953-54, University of Edinburgh, 1954-55; Senior Research Fellow, University of Edinburgh, 1955-56; ICI Fellow, University of London, 1956-58; Lecturer in Mathematics, University College London, 1959-60; Sabbatical Leave, University of North Carolina, USA, 1965-66; Lecturer in Mathematical Physics, 1960-70, Reader in Mathematical Physics, 1970-80, Professor of Theoretical Physics, 1980-96, University of Edinburgh. Publications: Papers in professional journals. Honours: Hughes Medal, Royal Society, 1981; Rutherford Medal, Institute of Physics, 1984; Scottish Science Award, Saltire Society, 1990; James Scott Prize Lectureship, Royal Society of Edinburgh, 1993; Paul Dirac Medal & Prize, Institute of Physics, 1994; Hon DSc, Bristol, 1997; High Energy & Particle Physics Prize, European Physical Society, 1997; Hon DSc, Edinburgh, 1998; Honorary Fellow, Institute of Physics, 1998; Fellow, King's College London, 1998; Royal Medal, Royal Society of Edinburgh, 2000; Hon DSc, Glasgow, 2002; Wolf Prize in Physics, 2004; Honorary Fellow, Swansea, 2008; Hon DSc, King's College London, 2009; Oskar Klein Medal, Swedish Royal Academy of Sciences, 2009; DSc, University College London, 2010; Sakurai Prize, American Physical Society, 2010. Memberships: Fellow, Royal Society of Edinburgh, 1974; Fellow, Royal Society, 1983. Address: 2 Darnaway Street, Edinburgh EH3 6BG, Scotland.

HIGHMORE Freddie, b. 14 February 1992, London, England. Actor. Education: Currently studying for GCSE's. Appointments: Lead roles in the following, Finding Neverland, 2004; Two Brothers, 2004; Five Children and IT, 2004; Charlie and the Chocolate Factory, 2005; A Good Year, 2006; Arthur and the Invisibles, 2006; The Golden Compass (voice), 2007; Spiderwick Chronicles, 2008; August Rush, 2008; Kis Vuk (voice), 2008; Astro Boy (voice), 2009; Honours: BFCAA, Best Young Actor, 2005, 2006; Empire Award, Best Newcomer, 2005; Golden Satellite Award, Outstanding New Talent, 2005; Young Artist Award, Best Leading Young Actor, 2005; Nominated for Screen Actors Guild, Outstanding Supportive Male Actor and Outstanding Cast, 2005. Membership: Screen Actors Guild. Address: C/o Artists Rights Group Limited, 4 Great Portland Street, London W1W 8PA, England.

HIGUCHI Takayoshi, b. 29 October 1927, Agematsu, Nagano, Japan. Professor Emeritus. m. Sachiko, 1 daughter. Education: BSc, Nagoya University, 1950; D Agric Science, University of Tokyo, 1959; Dr honoris causa, University of Science, Technology & Medicine, Grenoble, France, 1987. Appointments: Instructor, 1950-53, Lecturer, 1953-59, Associate Professor, 1960-67, Professor, 1967-68, Faculty of Agriculture, Gifu University, Japan; Professor, 1968-91, Director, 1978-84, 1988-91, Wood Research Institute, Professor Emeritus, 1991-, Kyoto University, Japan; Professor, Nihon University, College of Agriculture and Veterinary Medicine, Tokyo, 1991-94; Research Fellow, Prairie Regional Laboratory, Saskatoon, Canada, 1960-62; Associate Professor, Faculty of Science, Grenoble University, France, 1963-64; Concurrent Professor, Beijing Institute of Forestry, and Nanjing Institute of Forestry, People's Republic of China, 1985-86. Publications: Biosynthesis and Biodegradation of Wood Components, Academic Press, 1985; Biochemistry and Molecular Biology of Wood, Springer, 1997; Over 300 scientific papers. Honours: Japan Forestry Prize, 1959; Japan TAPPI Prize, 1959; Japan Forestry Science & Technology Prize, 1968; Japan Agricultural Science Prize, 1985; Anselme Payen Award, American Chemical Society, 1987; International Academy of Wood Science Award, 1988; Purple Ribbon Medal for outstanding contribution, 1990; Foreign Associate, US National Academy of Science, 1991; Fujiwara Award, 1992; The Second Order of the Sacred Treasure, 2000; Japan Academy Award, 2001. Memberships: Editorial Board Member, Cellulose Chemistry and Technology, Romania; Editorial Advisory Board Member, Journal of Wood Chemistry and Technology, USA; Holzforschung, Federal Republic of Germany. Address: Fushimiku, Momoyamacho, Yosai 22-8, Kyoto-shi 612-8016, Japan.

HILDEBRANDT Sabine, b. 5 August 1978, Bremerhaven, Germany. R&D Officer; Food Scientist. m. Frank Hildebrandt. Education: MSc, 2003, PhD, 2007, University of Hamburg. Appointments: Scientific Researcher, US FDA, Maryland, USA, 2007-10; Scientific Officer, Federal Office of Consumer Protection & Food Safety, Germany, 2010-11; R&D Officer, Stern-Wywiol Group, Germany, 2011-. Publications: Numerous articles in professional journals including: Effects of processing on detection and quantification of the parvalbumin gene in Atlantic salmon (Salmo salar), 2010; Multiplexed identification of different fish species by detection of parvalbumin, a common fish allergen gene: a DNA application of multi-analyte profiling (xMAP™) technology, 2010. Memberships: Executive Editor, Journal of Analytical & Bioanalytical Techniques; Food & Drug Law Institute, USA; GDCh; LChG.

HILFIGER Tommy, b. 24 March 1951, Elmira, New York, USA. Men's Fashion Designer. m. Susie 1980-2000 (divorced), 4 children. Appointments: Opened 1st store, People's Place, Elmira, 1969; Owned 10 clothes shops, New York State, 1978; Full-time Designer, 1979; Launched own sportswear label, 1984; Acquired fashion business from Mohan Muranji; Founder, Tommy Hilfiger Corporation, 1989. Honours include: Winner, From the Catwalk to the Sidewalk Award, VH-1 Fashion and Music Awards, 1995; Menswear

Designer of the Year, Council of Fashion Designers of America, 1995. Memberships: Board, Fresh Air Fund, Race to Erase Multiple Sclerosis.

HILL Colin Arnold Clifford, b. 13 February 1929, Cambridge, England. Clerk in Holy Orders. m. (1) Shirley Randall, deceased 1963, (2) Irene Florence Chamberlain, 1 son, 1 stepson. Education: Bristol University, 1952; Ripon Hall Theological College, Oxford, 1955; M Phil, University of Wales, Bangor, 2003; Ordained, Sheffield Cathedral, 1957. Appointments: Curate, Rotherham Parish Church, 1957; Vicar of Brightside, 1961; Rector of Easthampstead, 1964; Chaplain, RAF Staff College, Bracknell Berkshire, 1968-73; Vicar of Croydon, 1973-94; Honorary Canon, Canterbury Cathedral, Canterbury, 1974; Honorary Canon, Southwark Cathedral, 1984; Chaplain to The Queen, 1990-99. Publication: Unpublished thesis: Archbishop John Whitgift: Free School and Hospital 1596-1604. Honour: OBE, 1995. Memberships: General Synod and Convocation of Canterbury, 1969-73, 1984-86; Leander Club. Address: Silver Birches, Preston Crowmarsh, Wallingford, Oxfordshire OX10 6SL, England. E-mail: colinatSB@clara.co.uk

HILL Damon Graham Devereux, b. 17 September 1960, Hamstead, London, England. Motor Racing Driver. m. Georgie Hill, 1988, 2 sons, 2 daughters. Appointments: Began motorcycle racing, 1979; Driver, Canon Williams Team, 1993; Driver, Rothmans Williams Renault Team, 1994-96; Driver, Arrows Yamaha Team, 1997; Benson and Hedges Jordan Team, 1998-99. Honours: First motor racing victory in Formula Ford 1600, Brands Hatch, 1984; First Formula One Grand Prix, Silverstone, 1992; Winner, Hungarian Grand Prix, 1993; Winner, Belgian and Italian Grand Prix, 1993, 1994; 3rd Place, Drivers' World Championship, 1993; Winner, Spanish Grand Prix, Barcelona, 1994; Winner, British Grand Prix , Silverstone, 1994; Winner, Portuguese Grand Prix, 1994; Winner, Japanese Grand Prix, 1994, 1996;French Grand Prix, 1996; Spanish Grand Prix, 1995, 1996; San Marino Grand Prix, 1995, 1996; Hungarian Grand Prix, 1995; Brazilian Grand Prix, 1996; German Grand Prix, 1996; Australian Grand Prix, 1995, 1996; Canadian Grand Prix, 1998; Belgian Grand Prix, 1998; 2nd place, Drivers' World Championship, 1994-95; World Champion, 1996; British Competition Driver of the Year, Autosport Awards, 1995; 122 Grand Prix starts; 22 wins; 20 pole positions; 19 fastest laps; 42 podium finishes; numerous racing and sports personality awards; OBE; President, British Racing Driver's Club, 2006. Publications: Damon Hill Grand Prix Year, 1994; Damon Hill: My Championship Year, 1996; F1 Through the Eyes of Damon Hill.

HIMMELFARB Gertrude, b. 8 August 1922, New York, USA. Professor of History Emerita; Writer. m. Irving Kristol, 18 January 1942, 1 son, 1 daughter. Education: Jewish Theological Seminary, 1939-42; BA, Brooklyn College, 1942; MA, 1944, PhD, 1950, University of Chicago; Girton College, Cambridge, 1946-47. Appointments: Professor, 1965-78, Distinguished Professor of History, 1978-88, Professor Emerita, 1988-, Graduate School of the City University of New York. Publications: Lord Acton: A Study in Conscience and Politics, 1952; Darwin and the Darwinian Revolution, 1959, revised edition, 1968; Victorian Minds: Essays on Nineteenth Century Intellectuals, 1968; On Liberty and Liberalism: The Case of John Stuart Mill, 1974; The Idea of Poverty: England in the Industrial Age, 1984; Marriage and Morals Among the Victorians and Other Essays, 1986; The New History and the Old, 1987; Poverty and Compassion: The Moral Imagination of the Late Victorians, 1991; On Looking Into the Abyss: Untimely Thoughts on Culture and Society, 1994; The De-Moralization of Society: From Victorian Virtues to Modern Values, 1995; One Nation, Two Cultures, 1999; The Roads to Modernity: The British, French and American Enlightenments, 2004; The Moral Imagination: From Edmund Burke to Lionel Trilling, 2006; The Jewish Odyssey of George Eliot, 2009. Contributions to: Scholarly books and journals. Honours: American Association of University Women Fellowship, 1951-52; American Philosophical Society Fellowship, 1953-54; Guggenheim Fellowships, 1955-56, 1957-58; National Endowment for the Humanities Senior Fellowship, 1968-69; American Council of Learned Societies Fellowship, 1972-73; Phi Beta Kappa Visiting Scholarship, 1972-73; Woodrow Wilson Center Fellowship, 1976-77; Rockefeller Humanities Fellowship, 1980-81; Jefferson Lectureship, National Endowment for the Humanities, 1991; Templeton Foundation Award, 1997; Professional Achievement Citation, University of Chicago Alumni Association, 1998; National Humanities Medal, 2004. Memberships: American Academy of Arts and Sciences; American Historical Association; American Philosophical Society; British Academy, fellow; Royal Historical Society, fellow; Society of American Historians. Address: 2510 Virginia Avenue, NW, Washington, DC 20037, USA.

HINDE Robert Aubrey, b. 26 October 1923, Norwich, England. Biologist; Psychologist. m. (1) Hester Cecily Coutts, dissolved 1971, 2 sons, 2 daughters, (2) Joan Stevenson, 2 daughters. Education: BA, 1948, St John's College, University of Cambridge; BSc, London University, 1948; DPhil, Oxford University, 1950; ScD, University of Cambridge, 1961. Appointments: RAF Pilot, Coastal Command, 1940-45; Research Assistant, Edward Grey Institute, Oxford University, 1948-50; Curator, Ornithological Field Station, University of Cambridge, 1950-64; Research Fellow, 1951-54, Steward, 1956-58, Fellow, 1958-89, 1994-, Tutor, 1958-63, St John's College, Cambridge; Royal Society Research Professor, 1963-89; Honorary Director, Medical Research Council Unit on the Development and Integration of Behaviour, 1970-89; Master, St John's College, Cambridge, 1989-94; Chair, British Pugwash Group, 2001-08; President, Movement for the Abolition of War, 2005. Publications: Over 300 journal articles and book chapters; 9 books. Honours: Fellow, Royal Society; Foreign Honorary Member, American Academy of Arts & Science; Honorary Foreign Associate, US National Academy of Sciences; Honorary Fellow, Royal College of Psychiatry; Zoological Society's Scientific Medal; Osman Hill Medal; Leonard Cammer Award; Albert Einstein Award for Psychiatry; Commander of the British Empire; Huxley Medal; Distinguished Scientific Contribution Award, Society for Research in Child Development; Frink Medal; Distinguished Career Award; G Stanley Hall Medal; Royal Society Medal; Association for the Study of Animal Behaviour Society's Medal; Honorary DSc, Oxford University; Numerous honorary doctorates, memberships and fellowships committees. Memberships: British Psychological Society; British Trust for Ornithology; President, British Pugwash Group; President, Movement for the Abolition of War. Address: St John's College, Cambridge, CB2 1TP, England. E-mail: rah15@cam.ac.uk

HINE Patrick, b. 14 July 1932, Chandlers Ford, Hampshire, England. Air Force Officer. m. Jill Adèle Gardner, 1956, 3 sons. Career: Fighter Pilot and Member, RAF Black Arrows and Blue Diamonds Formation Aerobatic Teams, 1957-62; Commander, No 92 Squadron, 1962-64 and 17 Squadron, 1970-71; RAF Germany Harrier Force, 1974-75; Director, RAF Public Relations, 1975-77; Assistant Chief of Air Staff for Policy, 1979-83; Commander in Chief, RAF

Germany and Commander, NATO's 2nd Allied Tactical Air Force, 1983-85; Vice Chief of the Defence Staff, 1985-87; Air Member for Supply and Organisation, Air Force Board, 1987-88; Air Officer Commanding in Chief, Strike Command, Commander in Chief, UK Air Forces, 1988-91; Joint Commander, British Forces in Gulf Conflict, 1990-91; with reserve force, rank of Flying Officer, 1991-; Military Adviser to British Aerospace, 1992-99. Honours: King of Arms, Order of the British Empire, 1997.

HINGIS Martina, b. 30 September 1980, Košice, Czech Republic. Tennis Player. Appointments: 1st Tennis Tournament, 1985; Winner, French Open Junior Championship, 1993, Wimbledon Junior Championship, 1994; Competed in the Italian Open, US Open, Chase Championship (New York) and Wimbledon; Won 1st Professional Tournament, Filderstadt, Germany, 1996; Winner, Australian Open, 1997 (youngest winner of a Grand Slam title in 20th Century), 1998, 1999; Beaten Finalist, Australian Open, 2000, 2001, 2002; Winner, US Open, 1997; Beaten Finalist, US Open, 1998, 1999; Wimbledon Singles Champion, 1997; Winner, Australian Open, 1998; Won US Open, 1997, beaten finalist, 1998, 1999; Wimbledon singles champion, 1997; Swiss Federation Cup Team, 1996-98; Semi-finalist, US Open, 2001; By end of 2002 had won 76 tournament titles including five Grand Slam singles and nine doubles titles; Elected to WTA Tour Players' Council, 2002; After injury returned to WTA tour, 2005. Honours: WTA Tour Most Impressive Newcomer, 1995; Most Improved Player, 1996; Player of the Year, 1997. Address: c/o AM Seidenbaum 17, 9377 Truebbach, Switzerland.

HINTON Alistair, b. Dunfermline, Scotland. Composer; Archivist. m. Terry Piers-Smith. Education: Royal College of Music, London; Composition with Humphrey Searle, Piano with Stephen Savage. Career: Numerous broadcasts and performances worldwide; Founder and Curator of The Sorabji Archive. Compositions include: String Quintet, 1969-77; Violin Concerto, 1980; Pansophiæ for John Ogdon (organ), 1990; Sequentia Claviensis, 1993-94; Vocalise-Reminiscenza (piano), 1994; 5 Piano Sonatas, 1962-95; Variations for piano and orchestra, 1996; Szymanowski-Étude (18 wind instruments), 1992-96; In Solitude, In Plenitude (bass, piano), 1996; Sinfonietta, 1997; Cadenza to Medtner's Piano Concerto No 3, 1998; Conte Fantastique (euphonium, piano), 1999; Sonata for 'cello and piano, 1999, String quartet, 1999; Concerto for 22 instruments, 1969 & 2000-05; Piano Quintet, 1980-81 & 2005-10. Recordings: Variations and Fugue on a Theme of Grieg, 1970-78; Pansophiæ for John Ogdon, 1990; String Quintet, 1999. Publications: Sorabji: A Critical Celebration, 1992, reprinted, 1994. Contributions to: Grove's Dictionary of Music and Musicians; Tempo; The Organ; The Godowsky Society Newsletter; Notes (USA). Address: The Sorabji Archive, Warlow Farm House, Eaton Bishop, Hereford, HR2 9QF, England.

HINZ Vinko, b. 19 March 1968, Hannover, Germany. Classicist. m. Cristina Corradetti. Education: MA, Classics, MA, History, University of Heidelberg, 1996; PhD, Classics, University of Cologne, 2000. Appointments: Postdoctoral Researcher, University of Dresden, 2000; Lecturer, University of Halle, 2000-05; Visiting Research Fellow, CNRS Paris, 2006-07; Senior Lecturer, University of Göttingen, 2007-; Erasmus Lecturer, University of Bologna, 2011. Publications: Nunc Phalaris Doctum Protulit Ecce Caput, 2001; Numerous articles in professional journals, chapters in books and book reviews. Honours: Scholarship, Studienstiftung des Deutschen Volkes, 1997-2000; Research Fellowship, Deutsche Forschungsgemeinschaft, 2006-07; Late Professor Heinimann Prize, Basel, 2009; Listed in international biographical dictionaries. Memberships: Göttinger Freunde der Antiken Literatur; Mommsen-Gesellschaft, Oxford University Society; Studienstiftung des Deutschen Volkes. Address: Georg-August-Universität Göttingen, Humboldtallee 19, D-37073 Göttingen, Germany. E-mail: vhinz@uni-goettingen.de

HIRASAWA Nobuyasu, b. 27 February 1955, Maebashi, Gumma, Japan. Professor. Education: BS, 1978, MS, 1981, University of Tokyo. Appointments: Lecturer, Minami-Kyushu University, 1988-; Associate Professor, 1991-, Professor, 2000-, NIFS. Publications: Gomusai and Education in Shinshu – Life of a Great Educator Hyakusuke Hoshina, 2001. Memberships: Gakushi-kai; Kobinata-kai; International House of Japan. Address: #893-0014, Kotobuki 8-17-44-10, Kanoya, Kagoshima, Japan. E-mail: hirasawa@nifs-k.ac.jp

HIRATA Hayato, b. 4 May 1957, Marugame-city, Kagawa, Japan. Law Educator. m. Kyoko. Education: LLB, Chuo University, Hachioji-city, 1980; LLM, Hiroshima University Graduate School, 1983; Accomplished credits for doctral programme, Nagoya University Graduate School, 2006; Visiting Scholar, Cambridge University, 1990, 2009. Appointments: Civil Conciliator appointed by Japanese Supreme Court, 2001-; Professor of Law, Aichi Sangyo University, Okazaki-city, Japan, 2002-06; Professor of Law, Asahi University Faculty of Law and Graduate School of Law, Mizuho-city, Gifu, Japan, 2006-; Vice Dean, Faculty of Law, Asahi University, 2009-11. Publications: Author, The Good Faith and What Underlies the Principles; Editor, Access to Business Judicial Affairs; Numerous articles in professional journals. Honours: Listed in international biographical dictionaries. Memberships: Japan Association of the Law of Civil Procedure. Address: Asahi University Graduate School of Law, 1851-1 Hozumi, Mizuho-city, Gifu-pref, #501-0296, Japan. E-mail: hirahaya@alice.asahi-u.ac.jp Website: http://scw.asahi-u.ac.jp/~hirahaya/

HIRATA Tatsuya, b. 26 June 1943, Tokyo, Japan. Painter; Ceramic Artist. m. Saeko, 2 sons (1 deceased). Education: Bachelor, French Language, French Language Department, Sophia University; Professor, Art Department, Accademia del Verbano, Italy. Creative works: Paintings; Ceramic art; Exhibitions include: France: Art Impact, Paris, 1994; Espace Branly Société Nationale des Beaux Arts, Paris 1997; Salon International de Peintures et de sculpture, Nancy, 1997; Salon de la Nationale des Beaux Arts, Paris, 2001, 2002; Triennale de Paris, 2002; Japan: Salon de l'Automne Franco-Japonais, Tokyo, 1994; USA; Galerie Montserrat, New York, 1994; Italy: Accademia Italiana "Gli Etruschi" – L'Aquila della Liberta, Florence, 2002; Accademia Internazionale d'Arte Moderna, Rome, 2002. Publications: Oil-Water color-Etching, Japan, 1987, France, 1996. Publications: Bosco Hirata, 1987; Tatsuya Hirata, 1996. Honours: Accademicien del Verbano Italia, 1995; Chevalier de l'Ordre Templier, France, 1997; Academical Official Knight, Arts Department, Greci-Marino, 1998; Honorary Member, Foundation Marabello, Spain; Honorary Professor, Accademia Italiana, Gli Etruschi, 2000; Diploma di Mérite, Chevalier de la Paix, Accademia Internazionale "Il Marzocco, 2002; Médalle de la République Française, Fédération National de la Culture Française at Conours International, Fréjus, France, 2005; Diploma di Merito, Fondation Federico II Eventi, Bali Italy by Principessa Yasmine von Hohenstaufen, 2005. Memberships: Société Nationale des Beaux Arts; Society of Arts, Sciences, Lettres, Paris; Société des Artistes Français; Le Mérite et Dévoument Français; Accademia del Verbeno; Association Galleria

Centro Storico, Italy; Accademia Araldia Internazionale "Il Marzocco", Italy; Accademia Italiana "Gli Etruschi", Italy; Japan International Artists Society; La Société Franco-Japonaise d'Art et d'Archéologie, Japan. Address: 2 Banchi, 2 Bancho, Chiyoda-ku, Tokyo 102-0084, Japan.

HIROHATA Atsufumi, b. 16 March 1971, Tokyo, Japan. Lecturer. Education: BSc, 1995, MSc, 1997, Physics, Keio University, Japan; PhD, Cavendish Laboratory, Department of Physics, University of Cambridge, England, 2001. Appointments: Research Associate, Cavendish Laboratory, University of Cambridge, 2001-02; Postdoctoral Associate, Francis Bitter Magnet Laboratory, MIT, USA, 2002-03; Researcher, Department of Materials Science, Tohoku University, 2003-05; Researcher, Quantum Nano-Scale Magnetics Laboratory, Frontier Research System, Riken, 2005-2007; Lecturer, Department of Electronics, University of York, 2007-. Publications: Approximately 75 scientific articles in international journals; 3 book chapters; 1 patent. Honours: Materials Research Society Graduate Student Silver Award, 1999; Finalists of the Best Student Presentation Award, MMM-Intermag Conference, 2001; Magnetics Society of Japan Young Scientist Award, 2005; Magnetics Society of Japan Oustanding Presentation Award, 2006. Memberships: Magnetics Society of Japan; Physical Society of Japan; Institute of Physics; Cambridge Philosophical Society; Materials Research Society; Institute of Electrical and Electronics Engineers; American Physical Society; American Association for the Advancement of Science; Senior Member, Institute of Electrical and Electronics Engineers; Technical Committee, IEEE. Address: Department of Electronics, University of York, Heslington, York, YO10 5DD, England.

HIROWATARI Yuji, b. 27 October 1963, Yokohama, Japan. Medical Researcher. m. Shimakawa Tokuko, 3 sons. Education: Faculty of Science and Engineering, 1982-86, Doctor of Philosophy, 1996, Waseda University. Appointments: National Cancer Centre Research Institute, 1992-94; Tosoh Corporation, 1986-91, 1995-. Honours: Young Investigator Award, 22nd World Congress of Pathology and Laboratory Medicine, 2003. Address: 1890-14 Minamiyama Hadamo-shi, Kamagawa, 257-0003, Japan.

HIRSCH Judd, b. 15 March 1935, New York, USA. Actor. m. (1) Elissa 1956-58 (divorced), (2) Bonni Chalkin, 1992-2005 (divorced), 2 children. Career: Theatre: Barefoot in the Park, 1966; Knock Knock, 1976; Scuba Duba, 1967-69; King of the United States, 1972; Mystery Play, 1972; Hot L Baltimore, 1972-73; Prodigal, 1973; Chapter Two, 1977-78; Talley's Folly, 1979; The Seagul, 1983; I'm Not Rappaport, 1985-86, revival 2002; Conversations with My Father, 1992; A Thousand Clowns, 1996; Below the Belt, 1996; Death of a Salesman, 1997; Art, 1998; Sixteen Wounded, 2004; TV: Devecchio, 1976-77; Taxi, 1978-83; Dear John, 1988-92; George and Leo, 1997; Welcome to New York, 2000; The Law, 2001; Philly, 2001; Law and Order, 2002; Regular Joe, 2003; NUMB3RS, 2005-07; many TV movies; Films: King of the Gypsies, 1978; Ordinary People, 1980; Without A Trace, 1983; Teachers, 1984; The Goodbye People, 1984; Running on Empty, 1988; Independence Day, 1996; Man on the Moon, 1999; A Beautiful Mind, 2002; Zeyda and the Hitman, 2004; Brother's Shadow, 2006. Honours: Drama Desk Award, 1976; Obie Award, 1979; Tony Award, 1986, 1992; Emmy Award; Golden Globe Award. Memberships: Screen Actors Guild; AEA; AFTRA. Address: c/o J Wolfe Provident Financial Management, POB 4084, Santa Monica, CA 90411-9910, USA.

HIRST Damien, b. 7 June, 1965, Bristol, England. Artist. 3 sons. Education: Goldsmiths College, London. Creative Works: One-man exhibitions include: Institute of Contemporary Arts (ICA), London, 1991; Emmanuel Perrotin, Paris, 1991; Cohen Gallery, New York, 1992; Regen Projects, Los Angeles, 1993; Galerie Jablonka, Cologne, 1993; Milwaukee Art Museum, 1994; Dallas Museum, 1994; Kukje Gallery, Seoul, 1995; White Cube/Jay Jopling, London, 1995; Prix Eliette von Karajan, 1995; Max Gandolph-Bibliothek, Salzburg, Germany, Gasogian Gallery, New York, 1996; Bruno Bischofberger, Zurich, 1997; Astrup Fearnley, Oslo, 1997; Southampton City Art Gallery, 1998; Pharmacy, Tate Gallery, London, 1999; Sadler's Wells, London, 2000; Damian Hurst, The Saatchi Gallery, 2003; The Agony and The Ecstasy: Selected Works from 1989-2004, Archaeological Museum, Naples, 2004; MFA, Boston, 2005; Numerous group exhibitions world-wide. Television: Channel 4 documentary about Damien Hirst and exhibition at Gagosian Gallery, directed by Roger Pomphrey, 2000. Publications: I Want to Spend the Rest of My Life Everywhere, One to One, Always, Forever, 1997; Theories, Models, Methods, Approaches, Assumptions, Results and Findings, 2000. Honour: Turner Prize, 1995.

HIRST Paul Heywood, b. 10 November 1927, Huddersfield, England. Academic. Education: BA, 1948, MA, Trinity College, Cambridge, 1945-48, 1951-52; Academic Diploma in Education, University of London, 1954; MA, Christ Church Oxford, 1955. Appointments: Lecturer and Tutor, University of Oxford, Department of Education, 1955-59; Lecturer in Philosophy of Education, London University, Institute of Education, 1959-65; Professor of Education, King's College, University of London, 1965-71; Professor of Education and Head, Department of Education, University of Cambridge, Fellow of Wolfson College, Cambridge, 1971-88; Emeritus Professor of Education, University of Cambridge, 1988-; Emeritus Fellow of Wolfson College, Cambridge, 1988-; Visiting Professor, Universities of British Columbia, Malawi, Otago, Melbourne, Puerto Rico, Alberta, Sydney; Visiting Professor or Visiting Professorial Fellow, University of London, Institute of Education; Member, Swann Committee on Education of Children of Ethnic Minorities, 1981-85; Chair, Universities Council for the Education of Teachers, 1985-88; Chair, Committee for Research, CNAA, 1988-92. Publications: Logic of Education (with R S Peters), 1970; Knowledge and the Curriculum, 1974; Moral Education in a Secular Society, 1974; Educational Theory and Its Foundation Disciplines (editor), 1983; Initial Teacher Training and the Role of the School (with others), 1988; Philosophy of Education: Major Themes in the Analytic Tradition, 4 volumes (co-editor), 1998; 87 papers published in collections and philosophical and educational journals. Honours: Member, Royal Norwegian Society of Sciences and Letters; Honorary DEd, CNAA; Honorary DPhil, Cheltenham and Gloucester College of Higher Education, now University of Gloucestershire; Honorary DLitt, University of Huddersfield. Listed in national and international biographical dictionaries. Memberships: Honorary Vice-President, Philosophy of Education Society; Athenaeum Club. Address: Flat 3, 6 Royal Crescent, Brighton BN2 1AL, England.

HISLOP Ian David, b. 13 July 1960. Writer; Broadcaster. m. Victoria Hamson, 1988, 1 son, 1 daughter. Education: Ardingly College; BA Honours, English Language and Literature, Magdalen College, Oxford. Appointments: Joined staff, 1981-, Deputy Editor, 1985-86, Editor, 1986-, Private Eye, satirical magazine; Columnist, The Listener magazine, 1985-89; TV Critic, The Spectator magazine, 1994-96; Columnist, Sunday Telegraph, 1996-2003; Radio: Newsquiz,

1985-90; Fourth Column, 1992-96; Lent Talk, 1994; Gush (with Nicholas Newman), 1994; Words on Words, 1999; The Hislop Vote, 2000; A Revolution in 5 Acts, 2001; The Patron Saints, 2002; A Brief History of Tax, 2003; The Choir Invisible, 2003; There'll be Bluebirds Over the White Cliffs of Dover, 2004; Are We Being Offensive Enough? 2004; Television scriptwriting: Spitting Image, 1984-89 (with Nick Newman) The Stone Age, 1989; Briefcase Encounter, 1990; The Case of the Missing, 1991; He Died a Death, 1991; Harry Enfield's Television Programme, 1990-92; Harry Enfield and Chums, 1994-97; Mangez Merveillac, 1994; Dead on Time, 1995; Gobble, 1996; Sermon from St Albion's, 1998; Confessions of a Murderer, BBC2, 1999; My Dad is the Prime Minister, 2003, 2004; Performer: Have I Got News For You, 1990-; Great Railway Journeys, 1999; Documentaries: Canterbury Tales, 1996; School Rules, 1997; Pennies from Bevan, 1998; East to West, 1999; Who Do You Think You Are? 2004. Publications: various Private Eye collections, 1985-; Contributor to newspapers and magazines on books, current affairs, arts and entertainment. Honours: BAFTA Award for Have I Got News for You, 1991; Editors' Editor, British Society of Magazine Editors, 1991; Magazine of the Year, What the Papers Say, 1991; Editor of the Year, British Society of Magazine Editors, 1998; Award for Political Satire, Channel 4 Political Awards, 2004. Address: c/o Private Eye, 6 Carlisle Street, London W1V 5RG, England.

HITZAZIS Iasonas, b. 11 January 1978, Thessaloniki, Greece. Mathematician; Researcher. Education: BSc, Mathematics, 1999; MSc, 2009, PhD, 2010, Applied Mathematics, Department of Mathematics, University of Patras, Greece. Appointments: Instructor of Mathematics, Technological Educational Institution, 2010-11; Research Scientist, Computational Fluid Mechanics Laboratory, Department of Chemical Engineering, University of Patras, 2011-. Publications: Riemann-Hilbert formulation for the KdV equation on a finite interval, 2009; Initial-boundary value problems for nonlinear evolution partial differential equations, 2009; The KdV equation on a finite interval, 2010. Honours: Listed in biographical dictionaries; Honorary Distinction, Hellenic Mathematical Society, 1995; Aristeion Prize, Hellenic SSF, 1997; Full PhD Fellowship, SSF; Ranked 1st (Highest Honors), graduates, University of Patras, 1999; Ranked 1st, MSc graduates, Department of Mathematics, 2009. Memberships: Hellenic Mathematical Society. E-mail: hitzazis@math.upatras.gr

HLAVÁČ Libor Metoděj, b. 19 January 1958, Karviná 4, Czech Republic. Professor. m. Irena, 3 sons, 4 daughters. Education: Physical Engineer Diploma, Physical Electronics, Faculty of Nuclear and Physical Engineering, Czech Technical University, Prague, 1982; PhD degree, Automation of Technological Processes, Faculty of Mining and Geology, VŠB Technical University, Ostrava, 2001; Inception at Applied Physics, Palacki University, Olomouc, 2003. Appointments: Research Worker, Electronics and Optics, Research Institute of Civil Engineering, Ostrava, 1982-86; Research Worker, Problem of Liquid Jets, Mining Institute of Czechoslovak Academy of Sciences, Ostrava, 1986-93; Scientific Worker, Physical Problems of Liquid Jet Interactions with Materials, Institute of Geonics, Czech Academy of Sciences, Ostrava, 1993-97; Lecturer of Physics, Scientific Worker on Interactions of Liquid and Laser Jets with Solid-State Materials, Institute of Physics, VŠB-Technical University, Ostrava, 1997-2003; Assistant Professor, Professor 2006, Scientific Worker in Physical Problems of Liquid and Laser Jet Interactions, Institute of Physics, VŠB-Technical University, Ostrava, 2006-. Publications: Over 200 publications including: Physical description of high energy liquid jet interaction with material, 1992; JETCUT – software for prediciton of high-energy waterjet efficiency, 1998; Investigation of the Abrasive Water Jet Trajectory Curvature inside the Kerf, 2009; Material Grinding by Water Jets – Feasibility and Limits, 2010; Listed in national and international biographical publications. Memberships: Union of Czech Mathematicians and Physicists; Waterjet Technology Association; Czech Engineering Association; Czech Society for New Materials and Technologies, 2008-. Address: Proskovická 37/679, 70030 Ostrava-Výškovice, Czech Republic. E-mail: libor.hlavac@vsb.cz

HO Feng-Chi (Frank), b. 10 December 1942, Taiwan. Administrator. m. Wei-Chu Yang, 2 sons. Education: PhD, Cytological Study of Genetics, The Research institute of Evolutionary Biology, Tokyo University of Agriculture, 1986-90; Postdoctoral Course, Prevention and Cure to Fight Anti-Cancer of Clinical Oncology, Institute of Oriental Medicine, 1988-91. Appointments: Honorary Consultant, China Herbal Society, Taipei, Taiwan, 1990-; National Cancer Institute, USA, 1991-96; Professor, Institute of Oriental Medicine, Japan, 1991-; Co-work, Germany Research Institute for Chinese Medicine, Germany, 1996-; Honorary Consultant, Consulting Physician, Singapore Chinese Medical College, 2000-; President, International Canceriatry Academy of Chinese Medicine (now Global Oncology Academy), Canada, 2001-08; First International College of Chinese Medicine, Germany; Director, Canceriatry Institute of Chinese Medicine. Publications: Editor Member of Commission, The Executive Yuan, The Department of Public Health, Pharmacopoeia of Chinese & Herbal Medicine, Taipei, 1981-91; Screening Study on Chemically Compounds and Combinations of Medical Plants, Department of Pharmacognosy, Teikyo University, 1983-; Screening Study on Effectual Compounds of Medical Plants, Department of Pharmacognosy, Tokyo University, 1983-; Screening Study on Plant of Anti-Cancer, Gifu Pharmaceutical University, 1987-; Analysis Study on Tanin and relative Compounds, Department of Pharmacognosy, Kyushu University, 1987-; Author, 3-prenyylindoles from Murraya paniculata and their biogenetic significance, 1989; Author, Tanins and related Compounds, 1990; Author, Chemical Studies on Sophora tomentosa: The Isolation of a New class of flavoid, 1990; 8 special projects on Anti-Cancer or AIDS including Study on Botanical List of Anti-Cancer in Korea and Taiwan, Institute of Oriental Botanical Resources, Seoul, Korea and Institute of Tropics Botanical Resources, Kenting, Taiwan, 1998-; Author, New Flavoid Compounds in the Roots of Euchresta formosana, in press. Honours: National Science Council Grant, Taiwan, 1970-80; Honoree, Pacific Science Association; Honoree, International Plant Taxonomist; Carnegie-Mellon University, 1980; Merit Award for Research, Research Society of Chinese Medicine, Japan, 1983; Top 100 Health Professionals, IBC, 2000; Distinguished Service Order & Cross, ABI, 2000; 500 Great Leaders, ABI, 2000; Great Minds of the 21st Century, ABI, 2007/2008; 2000 Outstanding Intellectuals of the 21st Century, IBC, 2009; Order of International Ambassadors, ABI, 2009; Honorary Director General for Asia, IBC, 2010. Memberships: Life Member, Kowloon Chinese Herbalists Association Limited; World Society for Practising Physician of Chinese Medicine & Herbal; UICC, Global Cancer Control Community; American Chemical Society; American Association of Acupuncture and Oriental Medicine; AACR Foundation for the Prevention and Cure of Cancer; Global Cancer Leadership; World Natural Medicine Foundation, Canada; China Herbal Society; Honorary Member, Research

Society of Chinese & Herbal Medicine in Japan. Address: 860-999 West Broadway, Vancouver, BC V5Z 1K5, Canada. E-mail: ezoma@live.com Website: www.goa.med.pro

HOAGLAND Edward, b. 21 December 1932, New York, USA. Author; Teacher. m. (1) Amy J Ferrara, 196l, divorced 1964, (2) Marion Magid, 28 March 1968, died 1993, 1 daughter. Education: AB, Harvard University, 1954. Appointments: Faculty: New School for Social Research, New York City, 1963-64, Rutgers University, 1966, Sarah Lawrence College, 1967, 1971, City University of New York, 1967, 1968, University of Iowa, 1978, 1982, Columbia University, 1980, 1981, Bennington College, 1987-2001, Brown University, 1988, University of California at Davis, 1990, 1992, Beloit College, Wisconsin, 1995; General Editor, Penguin Nature Library, 1985-2004. Publications: Cat Man, 1956; The Circle Home, 1960; The Peacock's Tail, 1965; Notes from the Century Before: A Journal from British Columbia, 1969; The Courage of Turtles, 1971; Walking the Dead Diamond River, 1973; The Moose on the Wall: Field Notes from the Vermont Wilderness, 1974; Red Wolves and Black Bears, 1976; African Calliope: A Journey to the Sudan, 1979; The Edward Hoagland Reader, 1979; The Tugman's Passage, 1982; City Tales, 1986; Seven Rivers West, 1986; Heart's Desire, 1988; The Final Fate of the Alligators, 1992; Balancing Acts, 1992; Tigers and Ice, 1999; Compass Points, 2000; Hoagland on Nature, 2003; Early in the Season, 2008; Numerous essays and short stories. Honours: Houghton Mifflin Literary Fellowship, 1954; Longview Foundation Award, 1961; Prix de Rome, 1964; Guggenheim Fellowships, 1964, 1975; O Henry Award, 1971; New York State Council on the Arts Award, 1972; National Book Critics Circle Award, 1980; Harold D Vursell Award, 1981; National Endowment for the Arts Award, 1982; Literary Lion Award, New York Public Library, 1988; National Magazine Award, 1989; Lannon Foundation Literary Award, 1993; Literary Lights Award, Boston Public Library, 1995; American Academy of Arts and Letters, 1982. Address: PO Box 51, Barton, VT 05822, USA.

HOBBS Lewis Mankin, b. 16 May 1937, Upper Darby, Pennsylvania, USA. Astronomer. m. Jo Ann Hagele Hobbs, 2 sons, 1 daughter. Education: BEP, Engineering Physics, Cornell University, Ithaca, New York, 1960; MS, Physics, 1962, PhD, Physics, 1966, University of Wisconsin, Madison, Wisconsin. Appointments: Junior Astronomer, Lick Observatory, University of California, 1965-66; Assistant Professor, 1966-72, Associate Professor, 1972-76, University of Chicago; Director, Yerkes Observatory, University of Chicago, 1974-82; Professor of Astronomy and Astrophysics, University of Chicago, 1976-; Emeritus Professor, 2002. Publications: About 150 articles in professional journals. Honours: Alfred P Sloan Scholar, 1956-60. Memberships: International Astronomical Union; American Astronomical Society; American Physical Society; National Advisory Committees, NASA and NSF, USA. Address: University of Chicago, Yerkes Observatory, Williams Bay, WI 53191, USA.

HOBBS Peter Thomas Goddard, b. 19 March 1938, Gloucester, England. Director. m. Victoria Christabel Matheson, 1 daughter. Education: Waugh Scholar, MA, Exeter College, Oxford; CCIPD, 1988; F Inst D, 1989; FRSA, 1992. Appointments: Manager, ICI Ltd, 1962-79; Director, Wellcome Foundation and Wellcome plc, 1979-92; Founder Chairman, Employers Forum on Disability, 1986-93; HM First Non-Police Inspector of Constabulary, 1993-98; Non-Executive Director, Forensic Science Service, 1996-2006; Chairman, Learning From Experience Trust, 1992-93, 1998-2008. Publications: Miscellaneous human resource and organisation matters; Old St Albans Court Archaeologia Cantia, 2005. Honour: Dr hc, IMC, 2000. Memberships: Confederation of British Industry, Education and Training Committee, 1990-94; Institute of Directors, Employment Committee, 1989-93; Chemical Industries Association, Training Committee, Employment Board, Council, 1979-92. Address: Blenheim Crescent, London W11 2EQ, England.

HOBHOUSE Penelope, (Penelope Malins), b. 20 November 1929, Castledawson, Northern Ireland. Writer; Designer. m. (1) Paul Hobhouse, 1952, 2 sons, 1 daughter, (2) John Malins, 1 November 1983. Education: Honours, Economics, University of Cambridge, 1951. Publications: The Country Gardener; Colour in Your Garden; Garden Style; Flower Gardens; Guide to the Gardens of Europe; The Smaller Garden; Painted Gardens; Private Gardens of England; Borders; Flower Gardens; Plants in Garden History; Garden Style; The Story of Gardening; The Gardens of Persia. Contributions to: The Garden; Horticulture; Vogue; Antiques; Plants and Gardens. Honour: Awarded Royal Horticultural Society Victoria Medal of Honour, 1996; Lifetime Achievement Award, Guild of Garden Writers, 1999; MA; Hon DLitt. Address: The Clock House, Hadspen House, Castle Cary, Somerset, BA7 7NG, England.

HOBSON Fred Colby Jr, b. 23 April 1943, Winston-Salem, North Carolina, USA. Professor of Literature; Writer. m. 17 June 1967, divorced, 1 daughter. Education: AB, English, University of North Carolina, 1965; MA, History, Duke University, 1967; PhD, English, University of North Carolina, 1972. Appointments: Professor of English, University of Alabama, 1972-86; Professor of English and Co-Editor, Southern Review, Louisiana State University, 1986-89; Professor of English, Lineberger Professor in the Humanities and Co-Editor, Southern Literary Journal, University of North Carolina at Chapel Hill, 1989-. Publications: Serpent in Eden: H L Mencken and the South, 1974; Literature at the Barricades: The American Writer in the 1930's (co-editor), 1983; Tell About the South: The Southern Rage to Explain, 1984; South-Watching: Selected Essays of Gerald W Johnson (editor), 1984; The Southern Writer in the Post-Modern World, 1990; Mencken: A Life, 1994; Thirty-Five Years of Newspaper Work by H L Mencken (co-editor), 1994; The Literature of the American South: A Norton Anthology (co-editor), 1998; But Now I See: The Southern White Racial Conversion Narrative, 1999; Faulkner's Absalom, Absalom!: Selected Essays (editor), 2002; South to the Future: An American Region in the Twenty-First Century (editor), 2002; The Silencing of Emily Mullen and Other Essays, 2005; Off the Rim: Basketball and Other Religions in a Carolina Childhood, 2006; A Southern Enigma: Essays on the US South, 2008. Contributions to: Virginia Quarterly Review; Sewanee Review; Atlantic Monthly; Kenyon Review; New York Times Book Review; American Literature; Times Literary Supplement. Honours: Lillian Smith Award, 1984; Jules F Landry Award, 1984, 1999; Cecil Woods Award for Creative Non-Fiction, 2009. Address: Department of English, University of North Carolina at Chapel Hill, NC 27599-3520, USA.

HOCHBERG Kenneth J, b. 26 July 1950, New York, USA. Professor. m. Shifra Stollman, 4 daughters. Education: BA, Summa cum Laude, Yeshiva University, 1971; MS, 1973, PhD, Mathematics, 1976, New York University. Appointments: Assistant Professor, Mathematics, Carleton University, Canada, 1976-78; Associate Professor, Mathematics, Case Western Reserve University, USA, 1978-86; Professor and Chairman of Mathematics and Computer Science, 1986-, Dean, Faculty of Exact Sciences, 2003-07, Bar-Ilan University, Israel. Publications: Numerous papers and articles in professional national and international journals. Honours: Fulbright Senior Scholar Award, 1986-87; Research Grants, National Science Foundation; National Institutes of Health, National Security Agency, USA, 1978-88. Memberships: American Mathematical Society; Institute of Mathematical Statistics; Israel Mathematical Union; Israel Statistical Association. Address: Department of Mathematics, Bar-Ilan University, 52900 Ramat-Gan, Israel. E-mail: hochberg@macs.biu.ac.il

HOCKNEY David, b. 9 July 1937, Bradford, England. Artist. Education: Bradford College of Art; Royal College of Art. Appointments: Teacher, Maidstone College of Art, 1962, University of Iowa, 1964, University of Colorado, 1965, University of California, Los Angeles, 1966, University of California, Berkeley, 1967. Creative Works: First one-man exhibition, Kasmin Galley, London, 1963; Subsequent one-man exhibitions include: Nicholas Wilder, Los Angeles, 1976; Galerie Neundorf, Hamburg, 1977; Warehouse Gallery, 1979; Knoedler Gallery, 1979, 1981, 1982, 1983, 1984, 1986; Tate Gallery, 1980, 1986, 1988; Hayward Gallery, 1983, 1985; Los Angeles County Museum, 1988; The Metro Museum of Art, New York, 1988; Knoedler Gallery, London, 1988; A Emmerich Gallery, New York, 1988, 1989; Los Angeles Louvre Gallery, Venice, 1982, 1983, 1985, 1988; Nishimura Gallery, Tokyo, Japan, 1988; Manchester City Art Galleries, 1996; National Museum of American Art, Washington DC, 1997, 1998; Museum Ludwig, Cologne, 1997; Museum of Fine Arts, Boston, 1998; Centre Georges Pompidou, Paris, 1999; Musee Picasso, Paris, 1999; Annely Juda Fine Art, 2003; National Portrait Gallery, 2003. Publications: Hockney by Hockney, 1976; David Hockney, Travel with Pen, Pencil and Ink, 1978; Photographs, 1982; China Diary (with Stephen Spender), 1982; Hockney Paints the Stage, 1983; David Hockney: Cameraworks, 1984; Hockney on Photography: Conversations with Paul Joyce, 1988; David Hockney: A Retrospective, 1988; Hockney's Alphabet, 1991; That's the Way I See It, 1993; Off the Wall: Hockney Posters, 1994; David Hockney's Dog Days, 1998; Hockney on Art: Photography, Painting and Perspective, 1998; Hockney on "Art": Conversation with Paul Joyce, 2000; Secret Knowledge: Rediscovering the Lost Techniques of the Old Masters, 2001; Hockney's Pictures, 2004. Honours: Numerous; Companion of Honour, 1997. Memberships include: Royal Academy, 1985. Address: c/o 7508 Santa Monica Boulevard, Los Angeles, CA 90046, USA.

HOCQUETTE Jean-François, b. 30 June 1962, Chamalieres, France. Research Director. m. Christine, 3 daughters. Education: Engineer, Agronomy, 1985; Master, Animal Nutrition, 1985; PhD, Endocrinology, Paris XI University. Appointments: Director, Herbivore Research Unit, 2007-10; Head, Muscle Growth and Metabolism Group, 1999-2006. Publications: More than 150 publications including about 100 original papers in refereed international journals and review papers; 15 conferences in international meetings; 1 patent. Honours: Member, French Meat Academy. Address: INRA Herbivore Research Unit, Theix 63122 Saint Genes Champanelle, France.

HODDLE Glenn, b. 27 October 1957, England. Footballer; Football Manager. m. Christine Anne Stirling, divorced, 1 son, 2 daughters. Appointments: Player with Tottenham Hotspur, 1976-86, AS Monaco, France, 1986; (12 under 21 caps, 53 full caps on England National Team 1980-88, played in World Cup 1982, 1986); Player/Manager, Swindon Town, 1991-93 (promoted to FA Premier League 1993); Player/Manager, Chelsea, 1993-96; Coach, English National Team, 1996-99; Manager, Southampton, 2000-01; Manager, Tottenham Hotspur, 2001-03; Wolverhampton Wanderers, 2004-06; Skysports, 2006-. Publication: Spurred to Success (autobiography); Glenn Hoddle: The 1998 World Cup Story, 1998. Honours: FA Cup Winners Medal (Tottenham Hotspur), 1984; French Championship Winners Medal (Monaco), 1988.

HODGE Ian David, b. 15 February 1952, Chelmsford, Essex, England. Professor of Rural Economy. m. Bridget Anne, 1 son, 3 daughters. Education: BSc, Agricultural Economics, University of Reading, 1973; PhD, Countryside Planning Unit, Wye College, University of London, 1977. Appointments: Temporary Lecturer and Research Associate in Agricultural Economics, University of Newcastle upon Tyne, 1976-78; Visiting Research Associate, Department of Agricultural Economics, University of Idaho, USA, 1982; Lecturer in Agricultural Economics, University of Queensland, Australia, 1979-83; Gilbey Lecturer in the History and Economics of Agriculture, 1983-2000, Acting Head, Department of Land Economy, 1998, University Senior Lecturer, 2000-2001, University Reader in Rural Economy, 2001-05, Head of Department of Land Economy, 2002-, Professor of Rural Economy, 2005-, University of Cambridge; Visiting Professor, Department of Agricultural Economics, University of Wisconsin, 1994; Governor: Macaulay Land Use Research Institute, 1998-2003, Cambridge International Land Institute, 2003-11; Visiting Scholar, University of Califorani, Berkeley, 2005; Distinguished Visiting Scholar, Vermont Law School, 2006. Publications include: Rural Employment: Trends, Options, Choices (with Martin Whitby), 1981; Environmental Economics: Individual Incentives and Public Choices, 1995; Countryside in Trust, Land management by Conservation, Amenity and recreation Organisations (with Janet Dwyer), 1996; Numerous article in academic journals. Honours: BSc, University of Reading, 1973; PhD, University of London, 1977; Fellow Royal Institution of Chartered Surveyors, 2004; President, Agricultural Economics Society, 2007-08. Memberships include: Fellow Hughes Hall Cambridge, 2004; Socio Economic Advisory Group, English Nature, 1994-2006, Broads Research Advisory Panel, 1999-2003, MAFF/DEFRA Academic Economist Panel, 1999-; MAFF Task Force for the Hills, 2000-2001; Resource Policy Research Consortium, 1989-98; Cambridge International Land Institute, 2002-11. Address: Department of Land Economy, University of Cambridge, 19 Silver Street, Cambridge CB3 9EP, England. E-mail: idh3@cam.ac.uk

HODGE Patricia, b. 29 September 1946, Grimsby, England. Actress. m. Peter Owen, 2 sons. Education: London Academy of Music and Dramatic Art. Creative Works: Stage appearances include: No-one Was Saved; All My Sons; Say Who You Are; The Birthday Party; The Anniversary; Popkiss; Two Gentlemen of Verona; Pippin; Maudie; Hair; The Beggar's Opera; Pal Joey; Look Back in Anger; Dick Whittington; Happy Yellow; The Brian Cant Children's Show; Then and Now; The Mitford Girls; As You Like It; Benefactors; Noel and Gertie; Separate Tables; The Prime of Miss Jean Brodie; A Little Night Music; Heartbreak House, 1997; Money, 1999; Noises Off, 2000-01; His Dark Materials, 2004. Film appearances: The Disappearance; Rose Dixon - Night Nurse; The Waterloo Bridge Handicap; The Elephant Man; Heavy Metal; Betrayal; Sunset; Just Ask for Diamond; The Secret Life of Ian Fleming; The Leading Man, 1996; Prague Duet, 1996; Jilting Joe, 1997; Before You Go, 2002. TV appearances: Valentine; The Girls of Slender Means; Night of the Father; Great Big Groovy Horse; The Naked Civil Servant; Softly, Softly; Jackanory Playhouse; Act of Rape; Crimewriters; Target; Rumpole of the Bailey; The One and

Only Mrs Phyllis Dixey; Edward and Mrs Simpson; Disraeli; The Professionals; Holding the Fort; The Other 'Arf; Jemima Shore Investigates; Hayfever; The Death of the Heart; Robin of Sherwood; OSS; Sherlock Holmes; Time for Murder; Hotel du Lac; The Life and Loves of a She Devil; Rich Tea and Sympathy, 1991; The Cloning of Joanna May, 1991; The Legacy of Reginald Perrin, 1996; The Moonstone, 1996; The Falklands Play, 2002; Sweet Medicine, 2003; Maxwell, 2007; Miranda, 2009. Honours: Eveline Evans Award for Best Acrtress; Olivier Award for Best Supporting Actress, 1999; Hon D Litt (Hull) 1996, (Brunel) 2001, (Leicester) 2003; The Olivier Award, 2000. Address: c/o ICM, Oxford House, 76 Oxford Street, London W1R 1RB, England.

HODGSON Peter Barrie, b. 12 March 1942, Gosforth, England. Market Research Director. m. Audrone Grudzinskas, 1 son. Education: BA, St Peter's College, Oxford, England. Appointments: Senior Research Executive, Marplan Ltd, 1967-69; Senior Research Planner, Garland Compton Ltd, 1970-72; Director, Opinion Research Centre Ltd, 1973-75; Managing Director, Professional Studies Ltd, 1975-77; Director, Professional Studies Ireland Ltd, 1977-78; Managing Director, Action Research Ltd, 1977-78; Director, City Research Associates, Ltd, 1981-89; Managing Director, Travel and Tourism Research Ltd, 1978-. Publications: Articles published in: Espaces (Paris); Marketing; Journal of the Market Research Society; Journal of the Professional Marketing Research Society of Canada; Tourism Management; Journal of Travel Research; BMRA Bulletin; Synergie. Honours: Fellow, Tourism Society; Fellow, Institute of Travel and Tourism. Memberships: Council Member, Market Research Society, 1978-81; Council Member Tourism Society, 1981-84; Chairman, Association of British Market Research Companies, 1987-89; Chairman, Association of European Market Research Institutes, 1991-93; Deputy Chairman/Honorary Secretary, British Market Research Association, 1998-2004. Address: Travel and Tourism Research Ltd, 4 Cochrane House, Admirals Way, London E14 9UD, England. E-mail: pb.hodgson@virgin.net

HOE Susanna Leonie, b. 14 April 1945, Southampton, England. Writer. m. Derek Roebuck, 1981. Education: London School of Economics, 1980-82; BA, University of Papua New Guinea, 1983-84. Appointments: Campaign Co-ordinator, British Section Amnesty International, 1977-80; TEFL Teacher, Women's Centre, Hong Kong, 1991-97. Publications: Lady in the Chamber, 1971; God Save the Tsar, 1978; The Man Who Gave His Company Away, 1978; The Private Life of Old Hong Kong, 1991; Chinese Footprints, 1996; Stories for Eva: A Reader for Chinese Women Learning English, 1997; The Taking of Hong Kong, with Derek Roebuck, 1999; Women at the Siege, Peking 1900 (history), 2000; At Home in Paradise (Papua New Guinea, travel), 2003; Madeira: Women, History, Books & Places, 2004; Crete: Women, History, Books and Places, 2005; Watching the Flag Come Down: An Englishwoman in Hong Kong 1987-97, 2007; Tasmania: Women, History, Books and Places, 2010; Contributions to: Times (Papua New Guinea); Liverpool Post; Women's Feature Service. Honours: Te Rangi Hiroa Pacific History Prize, 1984. Membership: Honorary Research Fellow, Centre of Asian Studies, University of Hong Kong, 1991-. Address: 20A Plantation Road, Oxford OX2 6JD, England.

HOFFMAN Dustin Lee, b. 8 August 1937, Los Angeles, California, USA. Actor. m. (1) Anne Byrne, 1969, divorced, 2 daughters, (2) Lisa Gottsegen, 1980, 2 sons, 2 daughters. Education: Santa Monica City College. Appointments: Attendant, Psychiatric Institute; Demonstrator, Macy's Toy Department. Creative Works: Stage appearances include: Harry, Noon and Night, 1964; Journey of the Fifth Horse, Star Wagon, Fragments, 1966; Eh?, 1967; Jimmy Shine, 1968; Death of a Salesman, 1984; The Merchant of Venice, 1989; Films include: The Tiger Makes Out, Madigan's Millions, 1966; The Graduate, 1967; Midnight Cowboy, John and Mary, 1969; Little Big Man, 1970; Who is Harry Kellerman..?, Straw Dogs, 1971; Alfredo Alfredo, Papillon, 1973; Lenny, 1974; All the President's Men, 1975; Marathon Man, 1976; Straight Time, 1978; Agatha, Kramer vs Kramer, 1979; Tootsie, 1982; Ishtar, 1987; Rain Man, 1988; Family Business, 1989; Dick Tracy, 1990; Hook, Billy Bathgate, 1991; Hero, 1992; Outbreak, 1995; American Buffalo, Sleeper, 1996; Wag the Dog, Mad City, Sphere, 1997; Joan of Arc, The Messenger: the Story of Joan of Arc, Being John Malkovich, 1999; Moonlight Mile, 2002; Confidence, Runaway Jury, 2003; Finding Neverland, I Heart Huckabees, Meet the Fockers, 2004; Racing Stripes (voice), The Lost City, 2005; Prefume: The Story of a Murderer, Stranger Than Fiction, 2006; Mr Magorium's Wonder Emporium, 2007; Kung Fu Panda, Last Chance Harvey, The Tale of Despereaux (voice), 2008. TV appearances in: Death of a Salesman, 1985. Honours include: Obie Award, 1966; Vernon Rice Award, 1967; Academy Award, 1980, 1989; New York Film Critics Award, 1980, 1988; Golden Globe Award, 1988; BAFTA Award, 1997. Address: Punch Productions, 1926 Broadway, Suite 305, NY 10023, USA.

HOFFMAN Patricia A, Professor. Education: BA, Education, 1976, MA, Early Childhood Education, 1983, Concordia University River Forest; PhD, Family Studies, University of Wisconsin-Madison, 1997. Appointments: Teacher of elementary classes in preschool and third grades, 13 years; Assistant Professor of Education, Chair, Early Childhood Education, Concordia University, WI, 1989-93; Associate Professor of Education, Program Director, Early Childhood Education, Concordia University, Irvine, 1993-2000; Orange County, CA, Institute for Leadership Development, 2001-06; Professor of Family Studies Director, MA in Family Studies, Concordia University, Irvine, 2001-. Memberships: National Council on Family Relations; Listed in international biographical dictionaries. Address: 2517 Great Auk Ave, N Las Vegas, NV 89084, USA. E-mail: hoffmanpa@cox.net

HOGWOOD Christopher (Jarvis Haley), b. 10 September 1941, Nottingham, England. Harpischordist; Conductor; Musicologist; Writer; Editor; Broadcaster. Education: BA, Pembroke College, Cambridge, 1964; Charles University, Prague; Academy of Music, Prague. Appointments: Founder-Member, Early Music Consort of London, 1967-76; Founder-Director, The Academy of Ancient Music, 1973-; Faculty, Cambridge University, 1975-; Artistic Director, 1986-2001, Conductor Laureate, 2001-, Handel and Haydn Society, Boston; Honorary Professor of Music, University of Keele, 1986-89; Music Director, 1988-92, Principal Guest Conductor, 1992-98, St Paul Chamber Orchestra, Minnesota; International Professor of Early Music Performance, Royal Academy of Music, London, 1992-; Visiting Professor, King's College, London, 1992-96; Principal Guest Conductor, Kammerorchester Basel, 2000-; Principal Guest Conductor, Orquesta Ciudad de Granada, 2001-04. Publications: Music at Court, 1977; The Trio Sonata, 1979; Haydn's Visits to England, 1980; Music in Eighteenth-Century England (editor), 1983; Handel, 1984; Holme's Life of Mozart (editor), 1991; The Keyboard in Baroque Europe, 2003. Contributions to: The New Grove Dictionary of Music and Musicians, 1980, 2000. Honours: Walter Wilson Cobbett Medal, 1986; Commander of the Order of the British Empire, 1989; Honorary Fellow, Jesus

College, Cambridge, 1989, Pembroke College, Cambridge, 1992; Freeman, Worshipful Company of Musicians, 1989; Incorporated Society of Musicians Distinguished Musician Award, 1997; Martinu Medal, Bohuslav Martinu Foundation, Prague, 1999; Honorary Professor of Music, Cambridge University, 2002-. Membership: Royal Society of Authors, fellow. Address: 10 Brookside, Cambridge CB2 1JE, England.

HOLBROOK David (Kenneth), b. 9 January 1923, Norwich, England. Author. m. 23 April 1949, 2 sons, 2 daughters. Education: BA, Honours, English, 1946, MA, 1951, Downing College, Cambridge. Appointments: Fellow, King's College, Cambridge, 1961-65; Senior Leverhulme Research Fellow, 1965, Leverhulme Emeritus Research Fellow, 1988-90; Writer-in-Residence, Dartington Hall, 1972-73; Fellow and Director of English Studies, 1981-88, Emeritus Fellow, 1988, Downing College; Publications: English for Maturity, 1961; Imaginings, 1961; Against the Cruel Frost, 1963; English for the Rejected, 1964; The Secret Places, 1964; Flesh Wounds, 1966; Children's Writing, 1967; The Exploring Word, 1967; Object Relations, 1967; Old World New World, 1969; English in Australia Now, 1972; Gustav Mahler and the Courage to Be, 1975; Chance of a Lifetime, 1978; A Play of Passion, 1978, 2004; English for Meaning, 1980; Selected Poems, 1980; Nothing Larger than Life, 1987; The Novel and Authenticity, 1987; A Little Athens, 1990; Edith Wharton and the Unsatisfactory Man, 1991; Jennifer, 1991; The Gold in Father's Heart, 1992; Where D H Lawrence Was Wrong About Women, 1992; Creativity and Popular Culture, 1994; Even If They Fail, 1994; Tolstoy, Women and Death, 1996; Wuthering Heights: a Drama of Being, 1997; Getting it Wrong with Uncle Tom, 1998; Bringing Everything Home (poems), 1999; A Study of George MacDonald and the Image of Woman, 2000; Lewis Carroll: Nonsense Against Sorrow, 2001; Going Off The Rails, 2003. Contributions to: Numerous professional journals. Honour: Festschrift, 1996. Honours: Founding Fellow, English Association, 2000. Membership: Society of Authors. Address: 1 Tennis Court Terrace, Cambridge CB2 1QX, England.

HOLBROOKE Richard C, b. 24 April 1941, New York, USA. Diplomat. m. (1) 2 sons, (2) Kati Morton, 1995. Education: Brown University; Woodrow Wilson School; Princeton University. Appointments: Foreign Service Officer, Vietnam and Related Posts, 1962-66; White House Vietnam Staff, 1966-67; Special Assistant to Under-Secretaries of State, Katzenbac and Richardson, Member, US Delegate to Paris Peace Talks on Vietnam, 1967-69; Director, Peace Corporations, Morocco, 1970-72; Managing Director, Foreign Policy (quarterly magazine), 1972-76; Consultant, President's Commission on Organisation of Government for Conduct of Foreign Policy, Contributing Editor, Newsweek, 1974-75; Co-ordinator, National Security Affairs, Carter-Mondale Campaign, 1976; Assistant Secretary of State for East Asian and Pacific Affairs, 1977-81; Vice President of Public Strategies, 1981-85; Managing Director, Lehman Brothers, 1985-93; Ambassador to Germany, 1993-94; Assistant Secretary of State for European and Canadian Affairs, 1994-96; Vice Chair, Credit Suisse First Boston Corporation, 1996-98; Adviser, Baltic Sea Council, 1996-98; Special Presidential Envoy for Cyprus, 1997-98, to Yugoslavia (on Kosovo crisis); Permanent Representative to UN, 1999-2000; Ambassador to UN, 1999-2001; Director, Human Sciences Inc, 2001-04; Chairman, Asia Society, 2002; United States Special Envoy for Afghanistan and Pakistan, 2009. Publications: Counsel to the President, 1991; To End a War, 1998; Several articles and essays. Honours: 12 honorary degrees; Distinguished Public Service Award, Department of Defense, 1994, 1996; Humanitarian of the Year Award,

American Jewish Congress, 1998; Dr Bernard Heller, Prize, Hebrew Union College, 1999; Grand Cross of the Order of Merit (Germany), 2002. Address: c/o Department of State, 2201 C Street NW, Washington, DC 20520, USA.

HOLDER Stanley John, b. 21 September 1928, London, England. Nursing Educator. Education: South East Essex Technical College and School of Art Day School; Battersea College (University of Surrey); Sister Tutor Diploma, Advanced Diploma in Education, Master's Level, Adult Education, London University; Institute of Education; Registered General Nurse, Oldchurch Hospital, Romford, Essex. Appointments include: Charge Nurse, Surgical Unit, 1950-54, Tutor, 1956-60, Oldchurch Hospital; Principal Tutor, Hackney Hospital, London, 1960-65; Assistant Editor, Nursing Times, 1965-67; Principal Tutor, St Mary's Hospital, London, 1967-70; Director of Education, St Mary's Hospital and Parkside Health Authority, 1970-90; Chief Nursing Advisor, BRCS, 1988-93; Consultant: Curriculum Design, Middlesex University, 1991, BBC Nursing Education Series, 1991, Tayside Health Board, Scotland, 1991; Government and Official Appointments: Secretary of State appointments: East London Hospital Management Committee, 1966-74, Tower Hamlets Health Authority, 1980-90; Education Consultant, Rampton Inquiry, 1979; DHSS Working Party, Extended Role of the Nurse, 1974-77; Chairman, King's Fund Working Party overseas recruitment, The Language Barrier, 1973-74; Member of Council Royal College of Nursing, Chairman, Representative Body, 1969-74; Chief Assessor, University of London Extra Mural Department, 1965-89; Founding Member, 1978-83, Vice-Chairman, 1981-83, Linacre Centre for Health Care Ethics; Vice-Chairman, Mildmay Mission Hospital (HIV/AIDS), 1983-91; Chairman, Mental Health Act Managers, Tower Hamlets, 1980-98; Elected Member, Chairman, Adult Nursing Committee, English National Board for Nursing, Midwifery and Health Visiting, 1983-90; Member, UK Council for Nursing and Midwifery, 1983-90. Publications: Founding Editor, Nurse Education Today; UK Editor, Nursing Series, McGraw Hill; Co-author, Programmed Learning text of Physiology of Respiration; Numerous articles on health matters and nursing education. Honours: OBE; Fellow, Royal College of Nursing; Florence Nightingale Scholar, USA and Canada, Florence Nightingale Foundation; Freeman City of London; Badge of Honour for Distinguished Service, BRC Society. Memberships: Freeman of City of London, Freeman's Guild; Rotary International, President, Epping, 2003-2004; University of the Third Age. Address: 155 Theydon Grove, Epping, Essex CM16 4QB, England.

HOLDERNESS William (Bill) Leslie, b. 10 October 1947, Harare, Zimbabwe. Professor. m. Rosalind, 3 daughters. Education: BA, 1969, UED, 1971, B Ed (Hons), 1973, Rhodes University, Grahamstown; MA (Educ), 1975, Advanced Course in Curriculum Planning, 1983, PhD, 1990, London University, England. Appointments: Secondary School Educator, St Andrew's College, Grahamstown, 1970-74; Lecturer, Senior Lecturer, English, Johannesburg College of Education, South Africa, 1976-80; Senior Lecturer, English, 1981-87, Associate Professor, Head of Educational Projects, 1987-96, University of the North West; Full Professor, Education and English, University of Port Elizabeth/Nelson Mandela Metropolitan University, 1996-. Publications: 12 books; Over 45 articles and conference papers; 5 chapters in books; 5 co-authored commissioned evaluation reports. Honours: Major Teacher Scholarship for Overseas Study; DAAD (German Academic Exchange) Research Study Awards, 2001, 2006; International Educator of the Year, 2006; Listed in international biographical directories. Memberships:

Life Member, Association for the Study of Evaluation of Education in Southern Africa; National Association of Distance Educators of Southern Africa; Wildlife and Environment Society of Southern Africa. Address: Faculty of Education, PO Box 77000, Nelson Mandela Metropolitan University, Port Elizabeth, 6031, South Africa. E-mail: bill.holderness@nmmu.ac.za

HOLE Derek Norman, b. 5 December 1933, Plymouth, Devon, England. Provost Emeritus of Leicester. Education: Public Central School, Plymouth; Lincoln Theological College, 1957-60. Appointments include: National Service Royal Air Force, 1952-54; Assistant Librarian, Codrington Library, Oxford, 1954-56; Ordained Deacon, 1960, Ordained Priest, 1961, Leicester Cathedral; Assistant Curate, St Mary Magdalene, Knighton, Leicester, 1960-62; Domestic Chaplain to the Archbishop of Cape Town, 1962-64; Assistant Curate, St Nicholas, Kenilworth, Warwickshire, 1964-67; Rector of St Mary the Virgin, Burton Latimer, Kettering, Northants, 1967-73; Independent Member, Burton Latimer Urban District Council, 1971-73; Vicar of St James the Greater, Leicester, 1973-92; Chaplain, Lord Mayor of Leicester, 1976-77, 1994-95, 1996-97; Chaplain, Leicester Branch of the Royal Air Forces Association, 1978-92; Chaplain, Haymarket Theatre, Leicester, 1980-83, 1993-95; Member, Actors' Church Union, 1980-95; Chaplain, High Sheriffs' of Leicestershire, 1980-85, 1987-88, 1995-96, 1999-2000, 2001-02, 2007-08; Honorary Canon, Leicester Cathedral, 1983-92; Rural Dean of Christianity South in the City of Leicester, 1983-92; Chaplain, Leicester High School, 1983-92; Chaplain to the Queen, 1985-92; Chairman, House of Clergy for the Diocese of Leicester, 1986-94; Vice-President, Leicester Diocesan Synod, 1986-94; President, Leicester Rotary Club, 1987-88; Member, Association of English Cathedrals, 1992-99; Provost of Leicester, 1992-99; Governor, Leicester Grammar School, 1992-99; Governor, Leicester High School, 1992-2004; Vice-President, The English Clergy Association, 1993-; Priest Associate, Actors' Church Union, 1995-; Chaplain, Merchant Taylors' Company, 1995-96; Chaplain, Guild of Freemen of the City of Leicester, 1996-99; Commissary to the Bishop of Wellington, New Zealand, 1998-; Senior Fellow, De Montford University, Leicester, 1998-; Trustee Leicester Grammar School, 1999-2007, Patron, 2007-; Provost Emeritus of Leicester, 1999-; Chairman of the Leicestershire Branch of the Britain-Australia Society, 2000-05; Chaplain, The Royal Society of St George, 2000-2006; Chaplain to the Master of the Worshipful Company of Framework Knitters, 2004-10; Chaplain to the Mayor of Oadby & Wigston Borough Council, 2005-06; Chaplain, Leicestershire Branch, Royal Society of St George, 2006-08; Chaplain, British Korean Veterans Association, Leicestershire Branch, 2006-. Publications: Contributions to: The History of St James The Greater, Leicester, edited by Dr Alan C McWhirr; Century to Millennium St James the Greater Leicester 1899-1999. Honours: Honorary D Litt, De Montford University, 1999; Freeman of the City of London, 2003-; Liveryman of the Worshipful Company of Framework Knitters, 2003-; Honorary LLD, Leicester University, 2005; President, Leicester Probus Club, 2010-11; President, Leicestershire Book Society, 2011-12. Memberships: Patron, Leicestershire Victoria County History Trust, 2008-. Address: 25 Southernhay Close, Leicester LE2 3TW, England. E-mail: derek.hole@talktalk.net

HOLLAND Jools (Julian), b. 24 January 1958, London, England. Musician (keyboards); Television Presenter. 1 son, 2 daughters. Career: Founder member, pianist, Squeeze, 1974-81, 1985-90; Solo artiste and bandleader: Jools Holland and his Big Band, 1982-84; Jools Holland and his Rhythm And Blues Orchestra, 1991-; Television presenter, music shows: The Tube, C4, 1981-86; Juke Box Jury, 1989; Sunday Night (with David Sanborn), 1990; The Happening, 1990; Hootenanny, 1992-; Later With Jools Holland, BBC2, 1993-; Various other television specials, including Sunday Night, NBC, 1989; Beat Route, BBC2, 1998-99; Jools Meets the Saint, 1999. Recordings: Albums: with Squeeze: Squeeze, 1978; Cool For Cats, 1979; Argy Bargy, 1980; Cosi Fan Tutti Frutti, 1985; Babylon And On, 1987; Frank, 1989; Solo albums: A World Of His Own, 1990; The Full Complement, 1991; A To Z Of The Piano, 1992; Live Performance, 1994; Solo Piano, 1994; Sex and Jazz and Rock and Roll, 1996; Lift up the Lid, 1997; The Best of Jools Holland, 1998; Sunset Over London, 1999; Hop the Wag, 2000; Small World Big Band – Friends, 2001; Small World Big Band Vol 2 – More Friends, 2002; Small World, Big Band Vol 3, 2003; Beatroute, 2005; Swinging the Blues, Dancing the Ska, 2005; Moving Out To The Country, 2006; Best of Friends, 2007; The Informer, 2008. Hit singles include: with Squeeze: Take Me I'm Yours, 1978; Cool For Cats, 1979; Up The Junction, 1979; Slap And Tickle, 1979; Another Nail In My Heart, 1980; Pulling Mussels From A Shell, 1980; Hourglass, 1987; 853 5937, 1988. Honours: OBE, 2003; Deputy Lieutenant for Kent, 2006; Music Industry Trusts' Award, 2011. Memberships: Musicians' Union; Equity; Writer's Guild.

HOLLEBEEK Linda, b. 26 November 1979, Netherlands. Lecturer; Researcher. Education: PhD, Master of Commerce (Hons), University of Auckland. Appointments: Lecturer, Research Fellow, University of Auckland; Lecturer, Auckland University of Technology; Consultant, Cap Gemini/HP. Publications: Numerous articles in professional journals including, Demystifying Customer Engagement: Exploring the Loyalty Nexus, 2010. Honours: University of Auckland Business School PhD Scholarship; Highly Commended Award, Emerald Literati Network Awards for Excellence, 2010. Address: University of Auckland Business School, Owen G Glenn Building, 12 Grafton Road, Department of Marketing, Auckland 1142, New Zealand. E-mail: l.hollebeek@auckland.ac.nz

HOLLINGHURST Alan, b. 26 May 1954, Stroud, Gloucestershire, England. Novelist. Education: BA, 1975, MLitt, 1979, Magdalen College, Oxford. Appointments: Assistant Editor, 1982-84, Deputy Editor, 1985-90, Poetry Editor, 1991-95, Times Literary Supplement, London; Old Dominion Fellow, Princeton University, 2004. Publications: Novels: The Swimming-Pool Library, 1988; The Folding Star, 1994; The Spell, 1998; The Line of Beauty, 2004; The Stranger's Child, 2011. Translator: Bajazet, by Jean Racine, 1991. Honours: Somerset Maugham Award, 1988, E M Forster Award of the American Academy of Arts and Letters, 1989; James Tait Black Memorial Prize, 1995; Man Booker Prize, 2004. Memberships: Fellow, The Royal Society of Literature. Address: c/o Antony Harwood, 103 Walton Street, Oxford, OX2 6EB, England.

HOLLOWAY Gill Margaret, b. 24 April 1928, London, England. Artist. m. (1) Alec Harman, 1 son, 2 daughters, (2) Ted Holloway. Education: Roedean School; BA (Hons), Fine Arts, University of Durham, 1950. Appointments: Lecturer, Arts Council; Part time Teacher, Durham Prison; Tutor, Art, Extra Mural Department, Durham University, 1952-67; Head, Art and Art History, Cheltenham Ladies' College, 1969-88; Part time Teacher and Lecturer, 1988-; Freelance Painter, Writer, and Art Historian. Publications: A Bevin Boy Remembers: The Drawings and Memories of

Ted Holloway and many other Bevin Boys, 1993; Numerous articles for various art publications; Reviews for newspapers; Art programmes for Tyne Tees TV and BBC Radio. Honours: Honorary Bevin Boy; Many solo exhibitions around Britain; Paintings bought by galleries and private collectors in UK and abroad. Memberships: RA; Founder Member, Helios Group of Artists. Address: Henge Barn, Manor Farm, Condicote, Stow on the Wold, Gloucestershire GL54 1ES, England.

HOLLOWAY James, b. 24 November 1948. Gallery Director. Education: Courtauld Institute of Art, London University, 1969-71. Appointments: Research Assistant, National Gallery of Scotland, 1972-80; Assistant Keeper of Art, National Museum of Wales, 1980-83; Deputy Keeper, Scottish National Portrait Gallery, 1983-97; Director, Scottish National Portrait Gallery, 1997-. Publications: Editor, Scottish Masters booklets for National Gallery of Scotland; Several articles; Frequent lectures on Scottish art and collections. Memberships: Curatorial Committee, National Trust for Scotland; Committee Member, Scottish Sculpture Trust; Committee Member, Scottish-Indian Arts Forum. Address: Scottish National Portrait Gallery, 1 Queen Street, Edinburgh, EH2 1JD, Scotland.

HOLLOWAY Julian Robert Stanley, b. 24 June 1944, Watlington, Oxford, England. Actor; Director; Writer; Producer. m. (1) Zena Cecilia Walker, dissolved 1977, 1 daughter, (2) Deborah Jane Wheeler, dissolved 1996. Education: Ludgrove Preparatory School; Harrow School; Royal Academy of Dramatic Art. Career: Actor: Theatre includes: My Fair Lady; Arsenic & Old Lace; The Norman Conquests; Charley's Aunt; Pygmalion; Spitting Image; Films include: Ryan's Daughter; Carry on Up The Khyber; Carry on Loving; Carry on Henry; Carry on Camping; Carry on England; Carry on Doctor; Hostile Witness; Rough Cut; TV includes: The Importance of Being Earnest; An Adventure in Bed; Rebecca; The Scarlet and The Black; Ellis Island; The Endless Game; Michelangelo; Grass Roots; Torch Song; The Vet; Dan Dare; Remember Wenn; My Uncle Silas; Doctor Who; The Chief; Where's Wally (voice); My Uncle Silas II; Father of the Pride; Director: Play It Again Sam; When Did You Last See My Mother; Actor/Producer: Carry on Films; The Spy's Wife; The Chairman's Wife; Loophole. Address: c/o Michelle Braidman Associates, Suite 10, 11 Lower John Street, London W1R 3PE, England.

HOLLOWAY Laurence, b. 31 March 1938, Oldham, Lancashire, England. Musician (Piano); Composer; Musical Director. m. Marion Montgomery, deceased, 2 daughters. Career: Touring Dance Band Pianist, 1950s; Cyril Stapleton Showband; Joe Daniels Hotshots, 1950s; Cunard Line, 1956-57; London Weekend Television, regular pianist, 1967-80; Musical Director, Engelbert Humperdinck, 1970-75; Played at studios in London, 1975-85; Musical Director for many top artistes such as Judy Garland, Cleo Lane, Sacha Distel, Dame Edna Everage, Liza Minelli, Rolf Harris, Frankie Howerd, Mel Torme, Elaine Paige in "Piaf"; Featured pianist on Dame Kiri Te Kanawa's popular music albums; Musical Director for Michael Parkinson on the "Parkinson" series; Musical Director of Strictly Come Dancing, BBC, 2004. Compositions: several saxophone quartets, clarinet quartets, pieces for flute and piano and clarinet and piano; Numerous TV signature tunes including Blind Date, Beadle's About; Walking Fingers selected by Associated Board of the Royal Schools of Music for 2001/2002 Grade 1 Examinations;. Recordings: Solo albums: Blue Skies; Showtime; Cumulus; About Time; Laurie Holloway, Live at Abbey Road, 2000; The Piano Player, 2004; Also recorded with many artists including Kiri Te Kanawa, Marion Montgomery, Robert Farnon, Rolf Harris. Honour: Gold Badge of Merit, BASCA. Membership: Temple Golf Club. Address: Elgin, Fishery Road, Bray, Nr Maidenhead, Berkshire SL6 1UP, England.

HOLM Ian, Sir, b. 12 September 1931, Ilford, England. Actor. m. (1) Lynn Mary Shaw, 1955, 2 daughters, (2) Bee Gilbert, 1 son, 1 daughter, (3) Sophie Baker, 1982, 1 son, (4) Penelope Wilton, 1991, 1 step-daughter, (5) Sophie de Stempel, 2003-. Education: Royal Academy of Dramatic Arts. Creative Works: Roles include: Lennie in The Homecoming, Moonlight, 1993;Puck, Ariel, Lorenzo, Henry V, Richard III, the Fool (in King Lear), King Lear, 1997; Max in The Homecoming, 2001; Films include: Young Winston; Oh!; What a Lovely War; Alien; All Quiet on the Western Front; Chariots of Fire; The Return of the Soldier; Greystoke, Laughterhouse, 1984; Brazil, Wetherby, Dance with a Stranger, Dreamchild, 1985; Henry V, Another Woman, 1989; Hamlet, 1990; Kafka, 1991; The Hour of the Pig, Blue Ice, The Naked Lunch, 1992; Frankenstein, 1993; The Madness of King George, Loch Ness, 1994; Big Night, Night Falls on Manhattan, 1995; The Fifth Element, A Life Less Ordinary, 1996; The Sweet Hereafter, 1997; Existence, Simon Magus, 1998; Esther Kahn, Joe Gould's Secret, Beautiful Joe, 1999; From Hell, The Emperor's New Clothes, 2000; The Lord of the Rings: The Fellowship of the Ring, 2001; The Lord of the Ring: The Return of the King, 2003; Garden State, The Day After Tomorrow, The Aviator, 2004; Strangers with Candy, Chromophobia, Lord of War, 2005; Renaissance, The Treatment, O Jerusalem, Ratatouille (voice), 2006. TV appearances include: The Lost Boys, 1979; We, the Accused, 1980; The Bell, Strike, 1981; Inside the Third Reich, 1982; Mr and Mrs Edgehill, 1985; The Browning Version, 1986; Game, Set and Match, 1988; The Endless Game, 1989; The Last Romantics, 1992; The Borrowers, 1993; The Deep Blue Sea, 1994; Landscape, 1995; Little Red Riding Hood, 1996; King Lear, 1997; Alice Through the Looking Glass, 1998; Animal Farm (voice), The Miracle Maker (voice), The Last of the Blonde Bombshells, 2000; D-Day 6.6.1944 (voice), 2004. Publications: Acting My Life, 2004. Honour: CBE, 1990; Laurence Olivier Award, 1998; Knighted, 1998. Address: c/o Julian Belfrage Associates, 46 Albemarle Street, London W1X 4PP, England.

HOLMES Bryan John, (Charles Langley Hayes, Ethan Wall, Jack Darby, Sean Kennedy, J William Allen), b. 18 May 1939, Birmingham, England. Lecturer (retired); Writer. m. 1962, 2 sons. Education: BA, University of Keele, 1968. Publications: The Avenging Four, 1978; Hazard, 1979; Blood, Sweat and Gold, Gunfall, 1980; A Noose for Yanqui, 1981; Shard, Bad Times at Backwheel, 1982; Guns of the Reaper, On the Spin of a Dollar, 1983; Another Day, Another Dollar, 1984; Dark Rider, 1987; I Rode with Wyatt, 1989; Dollars for the Reaper, A Legend Called Shatterhand, 1990; Loco, 1991; Shatterhand and the People, The Last Days of Billy Patch, Blood on the Reaper, 1992; All Trails Leads to Dodge, Montana Hit, 1993; A Coffin for the Reaper, 1994; Comes the Reaper, Utah Hit, Dakota Hit, 1995; Viva Reaper, The Shard Brand, 1996; High Plains Death, Smoking Star, 1997; Crowfeeders, 1999; North of the Bravo, 2000; Pocket Crossword Dictionary, 2001; The Guide to Solving Crosswords, Jake's Women, 2002; Solving Cryptic Crosswords, 2003; Rio Grande Shoot-Out, Trail of the Reaper, Three Graves to Fargo, The Expediter, 2004; Trouble in Tucson, Shotgun, 2005; Pocket Crossword Dictionary, 2006; Catfootr, 2007; Gunsmoke in Vegas, 2006; Yuma Breakout (with estate of Jeff Sadler), 2008; Short stories, contributions to professional journals and peer-reviewed papers in academic journals. Address: c/o Robert Hale Ltd, Clerkenwell Green, London EC1R 0HT, England.

HOLMES James Christopher (Jim), b. 21 November 1948, London, England. Musician; Opera Conductor and Coach. m. Jean Wilkinson, 2 sons. Education: BA (Hons), University of Sheffield; Repetiteurs Diploma, London Opera Centre. Appointments: Principal Coach, Conductor, English National Opera, 1973-96; Numerous productions including: Pacific Overtures, London premiere; Street Scene, also BBC TV; La Belle Vivette, premiere of new version with Michael Frayn; Dr Ox's Experiment, world premiere; Arranger, National Youth Orchestra, BBC Proms; Musical Assistant to Simon Rattle, Glyndebourne Festival Opera, 1986-94; Associate Music Director, Carousel, Royal National Theatre; Conductor, BBC Concert Orchestra, London Sinfonietta, Montreal Symphony Orchestra, City of Birmingham Symphony Orchestra, Sinfonia Viva; Head of Music, Opera North, 1996-; Conductor: Gloriana, Tannhäuser, Sweeney Todd, Of Thee I Sing, Katya Kabanova, Péllèas and Melisande, Genoveva, Paradise Moscow, Cunning Little Vixen, Albert Herring; Arranger: Something Wonderful and If Ever I Would Leave You for Bryn Terfel; Guest Lecturer/Coach: National Opera Studio, Royal Northern College of Music. Publications: Numerous articles for programmes especially relating to American musical theatre; Arrangements of American musical songs for singers including: Bryn Terfel, Sally Burgess, Lesley Garrett; TV Programmes: I'm a Stranger Here Myself, Kurt Weill in America, BBC/HR; Street Scene BBC and WDR. Honours: USA Grammy Nomination for recording of Pacific Overtures; Gramophone Award for recording of Lesley Garrett, Soprano in Red. Memberships: Member, Advisory Board, Kurt Weill Complete Edition; Joint Artistic Advisor, Kurt Weill Festival, Dessau. Address: c/o Opera North, Grand Theatre, New Briggate, Leeds, W Yorkshire LS1 6NU, England.

HOLMES John Eaton (Sir), b. 29 April 1951, Preston, England. Diplomat. m. Margaret Penelope Morris, 3 daughters. Education: BA, 1st Class Honours, Literae Humaniores (Greats), 1973, MA, 1975, Balliol College, Oxford. Appointments: Joined Foreign and Commonwealth Office, 1973: Second Secretary, British Embassy, Moscow, 1976-78; Near East and North Africa Department, 1978-82; Assistant Private Secretary to the Foreign Secretary, 1982-84; First Secretary (Economic), British Embassy, Paris, 1984-87; Deputy Head, Soviet Department, Foreign and Commonwealth Office, 1987-89; Seconded to Thomas de la Rue & Co, 1989-91; Economic and Commercial Counsellor, New Delhi, 1991-95; Head of the European Union Department, Foreign and Commonwealth Office, 1995; Private Secretary then Principal Private Secretary to the Prime Minister, 1996-99; British Ambassador to Portugal, 1999-2001; British Ambassador to France, 2001-. Honours: CMG, 1997; CVO, 1998; KBE, 1999; GCVO, 2004. Address: 35 rue du Faubourg St-Honoré, 75383 Paris Cedex 08, France. Website: www.amb-grandebretagne.fr

HOLMES-WALKER William Anthony, b. 26 January 1926, Horwich, Lancashire, England. Scientist. m. Marie-Anne Russ, 2 daughters. Education: BSc (Hons) Chemistry, 1950, PhD, Chemistry, 1953, Queen's University, Belfast, Northern Ireland; DIC, Chemical Engineering, Imperial College, London, 1954. Appointments: Technical Officer, ICI Limited, 1954-59; Head of Plastics R&D, The Metal Box Company, 1959-66; Professor of Polymer Science and Technology, Chairman of School of Materials, Brunel University, 1966-74; Director, The British Plastics Federation, 1974-81; Visiting Professor, The City University, 1981-83; Secretary General, European Brewers' Trade Association, CBMC, Brussels, 1983-87; Director, Industrial Liaison, University of Reading, 1987-90; Director, International Technology and Innovation, 1990-94; Chairman of Working Group, The Executive Committee, 1995-96; Chairman, BioInteractions Ltd, 1991-. Publications: Many articles in scientific journals and business publications; Chapter in Thermoplastics, 1969; Polymer Conversion, 1975; Best Foote Forward, 1995; Life-Enhancing Plastics, forthcoming. Honours: ERD, 1972, TD, 1980; Member, Army Emergency Reserve and TAVR, with rank of Lieutenant Colonel. Memberships: Royal Institution, 1953; FRSC, 1966; FPRI, 1969; FIM, 1972; FSA, 1989; Past Master, Skinners' Company. Address: 7 Alston Road, Boxmoor, Herts HP1 1QT, England. E-mail: anthonyhw@ntl.com.uk

HOLROYD Michael (de Courcy Fraser), Sir, b. 27 August 1935, London, England. Biographer; Writer. m. Margaret Drabble, 17 September 1982. Appointment: Visiting Fellow, Pennsylvania State University, 1979. Publications: Hugh Kingsmill: A Critical Biography, 1964; Lytton Strachey: A Critical Biography, 2 volumes, 1967, 1968, revised edition, 1994; A Dog's Life (novel), 1969; The Best of Hugh Kingsmill (editor), 1970; Lytton Strachey by Himself: A Self-Portrait (editor), 1971, new edition, 1994; Unreceived Opinions (essays), 1973; Augustus John, 2 volumes, 1974, 1975, revised edition, 1996; The Art of Augustus John (with Malcolm Easton), 1974; The Genius of Shaw (editor), 1979; The Shorter Strachey (editor with Paul Levy), 1980; William Gerhardie's God Fifth Column (editor with Robert Skidelsky), 1981; Essays by Diverse Hands (editor), Vol XLII, 1982; Peterley Harvest: The Private Diary of David Peterley (editor), 1985; Bernard Shaw: Vol I, The Search for Love 1856-1898, 1988, Vol II, The Pursuit of Power 1898-1918, 1989, Vol III, The Lure of Fantasy 1918-1950, 1991, Vol IV, The Last Laugh 1950-1991, 1992, Vol V, The Shaw Companion, 1992, one-volume abridged edition, 1997; Basil Street Blues, 1999; Works on Paper, 2002; Mosaic, 2004; A Strange Eventful History, 2008; A Book of Secrets, 2010; Contributions to: Radio, television, and periodicals. Honours: Saxton Memorial Fellowship, 1964; Bollingen Fellowship, 1966; Winston Churchill Fellowship, 1971; Irish Life Arts Award, 1988; Commander of the Order of the British Empire, 1989; Prix du Meilleur Live Etranger, 1995; Heywood Hill Prize, 2001; Companion of Literature, 2004; David Cohen British Literature Prize, 2005; Golden Pen Award, 2006; Knighted, 2007; James Tait Black Memorial Prize, 2009; Honorary DLitts, Universities of Ulster, 1992, Sheffield, 1993, Warwick, 1994, and East Anglia, 1994, London School of Economics, 1998; Honorary D Litt, University of Sussex, 2008; Sheridan Morley Prize, 2008. Memberships: Arts Council, chairman, literature panel, 1992-95; National Book League, chairman, 1976-78; PEN, president, British branch, 1985-88; Royal Historical Society, fellow; Royal Society of Literature, chairman, 1998-2001, President, 2003-; Society of Authors, chairman, 1973-74; Royal Society of Arts, fellow; Strachey Trust, chairman, 1990-95; Public Lending Right Advisory Committee, chairman, 1997-2000; Royal Literary Fund, vice-president, 1997-Royal Society of Literature, President, 2003-10, President Emeritus, 2010-. Address: c/o A P Watt Ltd, 20 John Street, London WC1N 2DR, England.

HOLSTEIN-BECK Maria Danuta, b. 9 September 1923, Warsaw, Poland. Sociologist. m. Marian, 1 son, 3 daughters, 1 deceased. Education: Master of Sociology, University of Warsaw, 1968; Dr of Humanistic Science, Praxeology Department, Polish Academy of Science, 1973; Dr Hab of Economy in Social Policy, Main School of Planning and Statistics, Warsaw, 1979; Professor of Humanistic Science, 1990. Appointments: Social Inspector, Institute of Mathematical Machines, Polish Academy of Science, 1959-63; Sociologist, Warsaw Mechanical Works DELTA, 1967-71; Economist, 1971-73, Adjunct, 1974-80, Docent, 1981-90, Chief of Department of Management Technics, 1982-90, Administration and Management Institute, 1971-90; Lecturer, R Łazarski First Business College, Warsaw, 1994-96; Full-time Professor, P Włodkowic Academy, Plock, 1996-2001; Full-time Professor, L Koźminski Academy of Management, Warsaw, 2001-05; Full-time Professor, Chief of Cathedra of Social-Economical Globalization, First Private School of Business and Administration, Warsaw, 2004-10. Publications: Over 160 reports for conferences, articles, papers, handbooks, monographs; Books: Conflicts, 1978-83; Study on the Work, 1987; To Be or Not To Be a Manager, 1997; Manager Wanted, 2001; Managerial Functions, 2004; The Brilliant Gateway to Heaven, 2000; Studies and Materials of Social Policy, 2007; Modernized Managerial Functions, in The Problems of Management, 2008; Contemporised Managerial Functions, 2009/10. Honours: The Cavalry Cross, Polonia Restituta, 1987; Medal of 55th Anniversary of Married Life, 1998; Listed in international biographical dictionaries. Memberships: ISA, 1973-90; PTS, 1968-; TNOIK, 1973-. Address: ul Boya-Żeleńskiego str No 4/55, 00-621 Warsaw, Poland. E-mail: maria.hosteinbeck@neostrada.pl

HOLYFIELD Evander, b. 19 October 1962, Atlanta, Georgia, USA. Boxer. Career: Founder, Real Deal Record Label, 1999; Founder, Holyfield Foundation to help inner-city youth; Bronze Medal, Olympic Games, 1984; World Boxing Association Cruiserweight Title, 1986; International Boxing Federation Cruiserweight Title, 1987; World Boxing Council Cruiserweight Title, 1988; World Heavyweight Champion, 1990-92, 1993-94, 1996- (following defeat of Mike Tyson, 1996); Defended title against Mike Tyson 1997 (Tyson disqualified for biting off part of Holyfield's ear); Defended IBF Heavyweight Title against Michael Moorer, 1997; Defended WBA and IBF Titles, and Contested WBC Title, against Lennox Lewis, 1999, bout declared a draw; Lost to Lennox Lewis, November 1999; WBA heavyweight champion, 2000-01; WBF heavyweight champion, 2010. Career record 43 wins, 10 defeats, 2 draws; Suspended by NY State Boxing Commission after defeat by Larry Donald, 2004. Honours: Epsy Boxer of the Decade, 1990-2000. Address: Main Events, 390 Murray Hill Parkway, East Rutherford, NJ 07073, USA.

HOMAN Roger Edward, b. 25 June 1944, Brighton, England. University Professor. m. Caroline Baker. Education: BA, Religious Studies, University of Sussex, 1969; MSc, Government, London School of Economics, 1979; PhD, Sociology, University of Lancaster, 1979. Appointments: School teaching posts, 1966-67, 1969-71; Lecturer, Brighton College of Education, 1971-76; Senior Lecturer in Education, Brighton Polytechnic, 1976-92; Principal Lecturer, 1992-98, Professor of Religious Studies, 1998-, University of Brighton. Publications: 90 articles published in academic and professional journals. Honours: Fellow, Victoria College of Music, 1994. Memberships: Victorian Society; National Vice President, Prayer Book Society; Anglo-Catholic Research Society; Ecclesiological Society. Address: University of Brighton, Falmer, East Sussex, BN1 9PH, England. E-mail: r.homan@bton.ac.uk

HOME, Earl of, David Alexander Cospatrick Douglas-Home, b. 20 November 1943, Coldstream, Scotland. Banker. m. Jane Margaret Williams-Wynne, 1 son, 2 daughters. Education: MA, Christ Church, Oxford. Appointments: Director, Morgan Grenfell & Co Ltd, 1974-99; Chairman, Coutts & Co, 1999-; Chairman, Committee for Middle East Trade, 1986-92; Trade Industry and Finance Spokesman, House of Lords, 1997-98. Honours: CVO; CBE; FCIB. Membership: Turf. Address: Coutts & Co, 440 Strand, London WC2R 0QS, England.

HONEYBOURNE Duncan, b. 27 October 1977, Weymouth, Dorset, England. Concert Pianist. Education: Junior Academy, Royal Academy of Music, 1992-96; Birmingham Conservatoire 1996-2000; Studied with Rosemarie Wright, John York, Philip Martin; Leeds with Fanny Waterman and London with Mikhail Kazakevich; BMus, First Class Honours, 2000; HonBC, 2006. Debut: Symphony Hall, Birmingham, and National Concert Hall, Dublin, 1998. Career: Concertos and Recitals throughout UK and Ireland; Has recorded for BBC Radio 3 and RTE, Dublin, Radio and TV; Piano Teacher: Bryanston School, 2003-; Lecturer in Piano and Performance Tutor University of Chichester, 2005-08; Dedicatee and first performer of Sonatas by Andrew Downes and John Joubert; Played world premiere of Andrew Downes Piano Concerto, Birmingham Town Hall, 2009; Recording: Double CD, Piano Music from the Midlands, featuring rare works by Midlands composers, 2008; Piano Music by Moeran and Howells, 2010. Publications: Articles contributed to The Times, The Western Mail, The Birmingham Post, and BMI Insight. Honours include: Sheila Mossman Memorial Prize and Silver Medal, AB London; Iris Dyer Piano Prize, Royal Academy of Music, 1995; Several solo piano and chamber music prizes at Birmingham Conservatoire; Goldenweiser Scholarship; John Ireland Prize, 1999; Honorary Member, Birmingham Conservatoire. Membership: ISM Solo Performers' and Musicians' in Education sections. Address: 77 Monmouth Avenue, Weymouth, Dorset, DT3 5JR, England. E-mail: duncan.honeybourne@btopenworld.com

HONG Eui, b. 14 March 1971, Seoul, Korea. Academic. m. Sunjae Lee, 1 daughter. Education: PhD, Supply Chain Management, Sogang University, Seoul, 2002; MSc, Trade, Finance and Logistics, City University, London, England, 2003. Appointments: Postdoctoral Fellowship, Cass Business School, City University, London, 2003-04; Research Associate, Judge Business School, University of Cambridge, England; Associate Professor, Kwangwon University, Seoul, Korea. Publications: Book, The Changing Face of Korean Management, 2009; Articles include: Exploring the link between IT systems and the outsourcing of logistics activities: A transaction cost perspective, 2010; On risk and cost in global sourcing, 2011. Address: Kwangwoon University, 447-1 Wolgye-Dong, Nowon-Gu, Seoul 139-701, Korea. E-mail: euihong@kw.ac.kr

HONG Jae-Seok, b. 21 May 1974, Seoul, Republic of Korea. Medical Researcher. Education: BS, Soon Chung Hyang University, Asan, 1999; MPH, 2001, PhD, 2004, Yonsei University. Appointments: Assistant, Department of Preventive Medicine & Public Health, College of Medicine, Yonsei University, 2002-04; Fellow, Graduate School of Public Health, 2004-06; Associate Research Fellow, Health Insurance Review & Assessment Service, 2006-; Plural Professor, Graduate School of Public Health, Yonsei University, 2008-11. Publications: Many papers in professional journals. Honours: Listed in international biographical dictionaries. Memberships: Korean Society of Health Policy & Administration; Korean Society of Toxicogenomics & Toxicoproteomics. Address: Health

Ins Rev & Assessment SVC, Peace Bldg (IIF), 1451-34 Seocho-3dong, Seoul, Seocho-gu 137-927, Korea. E-mail: dr_hongjs@hanmail.net

HONG Jiann-Ruey, b. 30 March 1961, Kaohsiung, Taiwan. Science Educator. m. Jing-Yun Lee, 1 son, 2 daughters. Education: BS, Chinese Culture University, Taipei, 1986; MS, Chinese Culture Medical Center, 1991; PhD, Life Science, National Defense University, Taipei, 1999. Appointments: Research Assistant, Zoology, Academy Sinica, Taipei, 1991-94; Postdoctoral Fellow, 1999-2002; Associate Professor, National Cheng Kung University, Tainan, 2003-. Publications: Reviewer of scientific journals; Numerous articles in professional journals. Honours: Listed in international biographical dictionaries. Memberships: Chinese Society of Microbiology; Taiwan Society for Biochemistry and Molecular Biology; Fisheries Society of Taiwan; Member, European Cell Death Organization; Academician, American Biographical Institute. Address: No 1, Ta-Hsueh Road, Tainan 701, Taiwan, ROC. E-mail: jrhong@mail.ncku.edu.tw

HONG Jin Hwa, b. 2 November 1974, Seoul, South Korea. Doctor. m. Gee Yeun Kim. Education: MD, College of Medicine, 1999, Master, 2003, PhD, Graduate School, 2009, Korea University; Board of Korea Medical Association, 1999; Korean Board of Obstetrics & Gynecology, 2004. Appointments: Intern, 1999-2000, Resident, Obstetrics & Gynecology, 2000-04, Clinical Fellowship, 2007-10, Korea University Hospital; Public Health Doctor, Korean Army, 2004-09; Clinical Fellowship, Division of Gynecological Oncology, Kangbuk Samsung Hospital, Sungkyunkwan University, School of Medicine, Seoul, 2010-. Publications: Numerous articles in professional journals including: Association between serum cytokane profiles and clearance or persistance of high-risk human papillomavirus infection: a prospective study, 2010; Laparoscopic incidental appendectomy during laparoscopic surgery for ovarian endometrioma, 2011. Honours: Achievement awards, 25th Annual Meeting, Korean Society of Gynecologic Oncology and Colposcopy; Listed in international biographical dictionaries. Memberships: Korean Society of Obstetrics & Gynecology; Korean Society of Gynecologic Oncology & Colposcopy; American Association of Gynecologic Laparoscopists. Address: Division of Gynecologic Oncology & Minimally Invasive Surgery, Department of Obstetrics & Gynecology, Kangbuk Samsung Hospital, Sungkyunkwan University, School of Medicine, 108 Pyung-dong, Jongro-gu, Seoul, 110-746, Republic of Korea. E-mail: jhblue5@naver.com

HONG Seok Min, b. 1 November 1957, Seoul, South Korea. Principal Researcher. m. Young Hee Hong Lee, 1 son, 1 daughter. Education: Bachelor degree, Kwang Woon University, Seoul, 1979; Master degree, 1991, PhD, 1995, Chung Nam National University, Dae Jeon City. Appointments: Researcher/Senior Researcher, 1979-97; Principal Researcher, 1998-, Agency for Defense Development, Dae Jeon, South Korea. Publications: Articles in professional journals. Honours: Minister of National Defense, South Korea, 1999, 2005; Prime Minister's Award, South Korea, 2001. Address: Agency for Defense Development (3rd R&D Institute-1),Yuseong PO Box 35-3, Dae Jeon City, 305-600, South Korea. E-mail: hongsm@add.re.kr

HONG Soon-Ku, b. 1 October 1966, Seoul, Korea. Associate Professor. m. Soo-Kyung Chae, 1 son. Education: BS, Korea University, 1989; MS, KAIST, 1992; PhD, Tohoku University, Japan, 2001. Appointments: Researcher, SKC, Korea, 1992-94; Senior Researcher, SAIT, Korea, 1994-98; Postdoctoral Researcher, Brown University, USA, 2002-03; Assistant Professor, 2003-07, Associate Professor, 2007-, Chungnam National University, Korea. Publications: Book, Oxide and Nitride Semiconductors, 2009; About 120 articles in professional journals. Address: Department of Materials Science & Engineering, Chungnam National University, 220 Gung-dong, Youseong-gu, Daejeon 305-764, Korea. E-mail: soonku@cnu.ac.kr

HONG Sung Noh, b. 22 April 1973, Republic of Korea. m. Professor. Education: Yonsei University, Wonju Medical College, 1992-98; Master's degree, Sunkyunkwan University School of Medicine, 2004. Appointments: Intern, 1998-99, Resident, 1999-2003, Fellowship, Gastroenterology, 2003-04, Samsung Medical Center, Sunkyunkwan University School of Medicine; Chief Physician, Internal Medicine, Aerospace Medical Center, ROKAF, 2004-07; US Education Commission for Foreign Medical Graduate Certification, 2004; Clinical Full-time Instructor, Department of Gastroenterology, 2007-09, Assistant Professor, Department of Internal Medicine, 2009-, Vice Director, 2011-, Healthcare Center, Konkuk University Medical Center. Publications: Numerous articles in professional journals. Honours: Young Investigators' Bursary, European Association for the Study of the Liver, 2002; 7th KSGM Research Initiative Award, Korean Society of Neurogastroenterology and Motility, 2006. Memberships: Korean Association of Internal Medicine; Korean Society of Gastroenterology; Korean Society of Gastrointestinal Endoscopy; Korean Society of Neurogastroenterology and Motility; Korean Association for the Study of Intestinal Diseases; Multi-Society Task Force for the Guidelines for Colorectal Polyp Screening, Surveillance and Management. Address: Kang Byeon Gudaega Galaxy Apt 203-501, Cheonho2-dong, Gandong-Gu, Seoul 134-022, South Korea.

HONG Sung-Hun, b. 14 August 1973, Busan, Republic of Korea. Public Official. m. Hyun-Jin Kim, 1 son, 1 daughter. Education: BH, MS, PhD, Department of Civil Engineering, Dong-A University, Korea. Appointments: Lecturer, 2001-06, Senior Research Fellow, 2004-06, Dong-A University; K-water, 2006-07; Ministry of Land Transport & Maritime Aff, Nakdong River Flood Control Offic, 2007-. Publications: 18 papers; 30 conference papers; 3 technical and 8 R&D reports; 4 books. Honours: Research award, Korea Society of Civil Engineers, 2005; Research grant, Asia Pacific Association of Hydrology & Water Resources, 2005. Memberships: Korea Water Resources Association; KSCE; KOSSGE; AOGS. Address: 105/2302, Yugok-Prugio Apt, Yugok-dong, Jung-gu, Ulsan, Korea. E-mail: wghsh72@korea.kr

HONG Sung-Jei, b. 11 July 1968, Seoul, Korea. Researcher. Education: BA, 1991, MA, 1993, Sungkyunkwan University; PhD, Tohoku University, 2006. Appointments: Principal Researcher, Korea Electronics Technology Institute, 1993-. Publications: Articles in professional scientific journals: Fabrication of Indium Tin Oxide (ITO) Thin Film with Pre-Treated Sol Coating; Quantum Confined Y_2O_3:Eu^{3+} Nanophosphor Fabricated with Pre-dissipation Treatment; Improvement in the Long-Term Stability of SnO_2 Nanoparticle Surface Modification with Additives; Low Temperature Catalyst Adding (LTCA) for Tin Oxide Nanostructure Gas Sensors; Indium tin oxide (ITO) thin film fabricated by indium-tin-organic sol including ITO nanoparticle; Optimization of solvent condition for highly luminescent Y_2O_3:Eu^{3+} nanophospor; Development of Ultrafine Indium Tin Oxide (ITO) Nanoparticle for Ink-Jet Printing by Low-Temperature Synthetic Method; Effect of Heat-treatment on the Characteristics of the ITO Nanoparticle for Inkjet

Printing; Development of Ultrafine Indium Tin Oxide (ITO) Nanoparticle for Ink-Jet Printing by Low-Temperature Synthetic Method, Effect of Heat-treatment on the Characteristics of the ITO Nanoparticle for Inkjet Printing; Improvement of electrical properties of ITO thin films by heat-treatment conditions; Eco-friendly synthesis of SiO_2 nanoparticles with high purity for digital printing. Honours: Best Oral Presentation Award; Best Poster Presentation Award, 2002. Address: 1122-903, Bakhap LG APT, Sanbon 2 Dong, Gunposi, Gyeonggido, 435-743, Republic of Korea.

HONG Sunghoon, b. 8 December 1967, Busan, Korea. Senior Research Staff. m. Yoonhee Lee, 1 son. Education: BS, Department of Electronics Engineering, Kyungpook National University, 1992; MSc, Department of Electronics Engineering, 1994, PhD, School of Electrical Engineering, 1999, Seoul National University, Korea. Appointments: Senior Research Staff Member, Nsystem Communications, 2000-03; Chief Technology Officer, Winton Haus, 2003-08; Chief Technology Officer and President, Atomm Inc, 2008-10; Senior Research Staff, Electronics and Telecommunications Research Institute, 2010-. Publications: 16 articles in professional journals. Honours: Invited Speaker and Appreciation Award, KSEA, San Diego, 2010; Invited Speaker and Award, IEEE Vehicular Technology Society, San Diego Chapter, 2010; Invited Speaker and Appreciation Award, Kyungpook National University, 2010; Invited Speaker and Appreciation Award, Busan National University, 2010; Invited Speaker, ETRI, 2010. Memberships: IEEE; KSEA, San Diego Chapter. Address: 7047 Chapala Canyon Court, San Diego, CA 92129, USA. E-mail: rapidhong@hotmail.com

HONG Yang-Pyo, b. 27 September 1936, Kangwon-Do, Korea. Professor Emeritus. m. Dung-Ja Hwang, 2 sons. Education: BA, Department of Political Science, Tong-Ah University, Busan, Korea, 1970; MA, 1975, PhD, 1984, Department of Political Science, Graduate School, Kyungpook National University (KNU), Daegu. Appointments: Army Officer, 1960-73, Retired as captain, 1973; Military Training, Huntsville Alabama US for HAWK Maintenance, 1965-66, 1970-71; Councillor, KNU Chorus, 1978-; Director, Korean Association of Middle East Studies, 1980-2002; Full Instructor, Teachers College, 1977-80, Assistant Professor, 1980-84, Associate Professor, 1984-90, Professor, 1990-2003, KNU; Board Member, Daegu YMCA, 1985-2002; Fulbright Senior Scholar for Research, Lecturing and Exchanging Course, Hoover Institute, Stanford University, USA, 1985; Standing Committee of Daegu Citizens Activity for Economy Justice, 1990-96; Vice President, Korean Ethics Association, 1993-; Director, Korean Political Science Association, 1997-; Director, Peace House for Runaway Adolescence, Daegu, 1997-; President, KNU Political Science Association, 2001-02. Publications: Numerous papers on peace research in professional domestic and international journals; 6 books including Causes of War w/Peace Problems, and Life Sciences. Honours: Outstanding Contribution, 80th Anniversary of Daegu YMCA, 1977; Professor Hong's Tenor Concert with Chorus commemoration of 60th birthday, 1986; Yellow Bird Medal, President of Korea, 2002; Another Hong's Concert commemoration of Retirement, KNU University Chorus, 2002; Listed in Who's Who in the World, 1999-; Diploma of Achievement in Education, IBC, 2005; International Peace Prize, United Cultural Convention; International Professional of the Year, IBC, 2005. Memberships: Korean Ethics Studies Association; Korean Political Science Association; Korean Association of Middle East Studies; KNU Political Science Association; Bibliotheque World Wide Society; Daegu Christian Elders' Choir. Address: 107-605 Sharp (#) 1, Esiapolis, 1524 Bongmu-dong, Dong-ku, Daegu 701-170, Korea. E-mail: yphong45@hotmail.com

HONIG Edwin, b. 3 September 1919, New York, New York, USA. Retired Professor of English and of Comparative Literature; Poet; Writer; Dramatist; Translator. m. (1) Charlotte Gilchrist, 1940, deceased 1963, (2) Margot Dennes, 1963, divorced 1978, 2 sons. Education: BA, 1939, MA, 1947, University of Wisconsin at Madison. Appointments: Poetry Editor, New Mexico Quarterly, 1948-52; Instructor, Claremont College, California, 1949; Faculty, 1949-57, Assistant Professor of English, Harvard University; Faculty, 1957-60, Professor of English, 1960-82, Professor of Comparative Literature, 1962-82, Professor Emeritus, 1983-, Brown University; Visiting Professor, University of California at Davis, 1964-65; Mellon Professor, Boston University, 1977. Publications: Poetry: The Moral Circus, 1955; The Gazabos: 41 Poems, 1959; Survivals, 1964; Spring Journal, 1968; Four Springs, 1972; At Sixes, 1974; Shake a Spear with Me, John Berryman, 1974; Selected Poems 1955-1976, 1979; Interrupted Praise, 1983; Gifts of Light, 1983; The Imminence of Love: Poems 1962-1992, 1993; Time and Again: Poems 1940-97, 2000. Stories: Foibles and Fables of an Abstract Man, 1979. Non-Fiction: García Lorca, 1944, revised edition, 1963; Dark Conceit: The Making of Allegory, 1959; Calderón and the Seizures of Honor, 1972; The Poet's Other Voice: Conversations on Literary Translation, 1986. Plays: Ends of the World and Other Plays, 1984. Translations: Over 10 books, 1961-93. Contributions to: books, anthologies, reviews, journals, and periodicals. Honours: Guggenheim Fellowships, 1948, 1962; National Academy of Arts and Letters Grant, 1966; Amy Lowell Traveling Poetry Fellowship, 1968; Rhode Island Governor's Award for Excellence in the Arts, 1970; National Endowment for the Humanities Fellowship, 1975, and Grants, 1977-80; National Endowment for the Arts Fellowship, 1977; Translation Award, Poetry Society of America, 1984; National Award, Columbia University Translation Center, 1985; Decorated by the Portuguese President for translation of Pessoa, 1989; Decorated by the King of Spain for translation of Calderón, 1996. Memberships: Dante Society of America; Poetry Society of America. Address: 229 Medway Street, Apt 305, Providence, RI 02906, USA.

HOOK Andrew Dunnet, b. 21 December 1932, Wick, Caithness, Scotland. m. Judith Ann Hibberd, deceased, 1984, 2 sons, 1 daughter, deceased, 1995. Education: MA, University of Edinburgh, Scotland, 1954; PhD, Princeton University, USA, 1960. Appointments: Assistant Lecturer, 1961-63, Lecturer in American Literature, 1963-71, University of Edinburgh; Senior Lecturer in English, University of Aberdeen, 1971-79; Bradley Professor of English Literature, University of Glasgow, 1979-98; Visiting Fellow, English Department, Princeton University, 1999-2000; Gillespie Visiting Professor, The College of Wooster, Wooster, Ohio, 2001-2002; Visiting Professor, Dartmouth College, Hanover, New Hampshire, 2003. Publications: Scott's Waverley (editor), 1972; Charlotte Brontë's Shirley (co-editor), 1974; John Dos Passos, Twentieth Century Views (editor), 1974; Scotland and America 1750-1835, 1975; American Literature in Context 1865-1900, 1983; History of Scottish Literature, Vol II 1660-1800 (editor), 1987; Scott Fitzgerald, 1992; The Glasgow Enlightenment (co-editor), 1995; From Goosecreek to Gandercleugh: Studies in Scottish-American Literary and Cultural History, 1999; Scott's The Fair Maid of Perth (co-editor), 1999; F Scott Fitzgerald: A Literary Life, 2002. Honours: Fellow, Royal Society of Edinburgh, 2000-; Fellow,

DICTIONARY OF INTERNATIONAL BIOGRAPHY 36th EDITION

British Academy, 2002. Memberships: British Association for American Studies; Eighteenth Century Scottish Studies Society; Modern Languages Association; Institute of Contemporary Scotland. Address: 5 Rosslyn Terrace, Glasgow G12 9NB, Scotland.

HOOKWAY Harry Thurston (Sir), b. 23 July 1921, London, England. Administrator. m. Barbara Butler, deceased, 1 son, 1 daughter. Education: BSc, PhD, London University. Appointments: Assistant Director, National Chemical Laboratory, 1959; Director, United Kingdom Scientific Mission to North America, Scientific Attaché, British Embassy, Washington, Scientific Advisor, High Commission, Ottawa, 1960-64; Head, Information Division, DSIR, 1964-65; Chief Scientific Officer, Department of Education and Science, 1966-69; Under Secretary, Department of Education and Science, 1969-73; Deputy Chairman and Chief Executive, British Library Board, 1973-84; Pro-Chancellor, Loughborough University, 1987-93. Publications: Papers in learned and professional journals. Honours: Hon LLD; Hon D Litt; HON FLA; Hon F I Inst Sci; Gold Medal, International Federation of Library Associations; Knight Bachelor, 1978; President, Institute of Information Scientists, 1973-76; President Library Association, 1985. Memberships: Royal Commission on Historical Monuments (England), 1981-87; Fellow, Royal Society of Arts. Address: 3 St James Green, Thirsk, North Yorkshire YO7 1AF, England.

HOOPER Michael Wrenford, b. 2 May 1941, Gloucester, England. Cleric. m. Rosemary, 2 sons, 2 daughters. Education: St David's College, Lampeter, Dyfed; St Stephen's House, Oxford. Appointments: Curate, Bridgnorth, Shropshire, 1965; Vicar of Minsterley, Rural Dean, Pontesbury, 1970; Rector and Rural Dean, Leonminster, 1981; Archdeacon of Hereford, 1997; Suffragan Bishop of Ludlow, Archdeacon of Ludlow, 2002-2009.

HOOPLE Sally Crosby, b. 23 October 1930, Dansville, New York, USA. Professor. m. Donald G, 2 sons, 2 daughters. Education: BA, English Education, 1952, MA, English Education, 1953, Syracuse University; MA, English, New York University, 1971; PhD, English, Fordham University, 1984. Appointments: English 10, 11 and 12, Teacher Counsellor, 1963-66, White Plains High School, White Plains, New York, 1963-86; Assistant Professor, 1986-89, Associate Professor, 1989-95, Professor of Humanities, 1995-96, Maine Maritime Academy; Foreign Expert, Henan Normal University, China, 1997-98; Honorarium Instructor, China Agricultural University, Beijing, 1999, 2001. Publications include: Rationalism in The Dictionary of Art; Doors and Windows in the Age of Innocence; Chance's White-cane Garden in Jerzy Kosinski's Being There; Tabitha Tenney Humorist of the New Republic; Maine Coon Cat in Encyclopedia of New England Culture, 2005. Honours: Rho Delta Phi, 1951, Phi Beta Kappa, 1952, Syracuse University. Memberships: Melville Society; Hawthorne Society; Exeter Historical Society; Metropolitan Museum of Art; Boston Museum of Fine Art; Metropolitan Opera Guild; Castine Scientific Society; Farnsworth Museum. Address: 80 Matthew Drive, Brunswick, ME 04011, USA. E-mail: sandd@gwi.net

HOPE Ronald Anthony, b. 16 March 1951, London, England. Professor of Medical Ethics. m. Sally Hirsh, 2 daughters. Education: MA, New College, Oxford, 1970-73; PhD, National Institute for Medical Research, 1973-76; BM BCh, University of Oxford Clinical School, 1977-80. Appointments: House Surgeon, Royal United Hospital, Bath, 1980-81; House Physician, John Radcliffe Hospital, Oxford, 1981; Senior House Officer, Registrar rotation in Psychiatry, Oxford Hospital, 1981-85; Wellcome Trust Training Fellow in Psychiatry, 1985-87; Clinical Lecturer in Psychiatry, University of Oxford, 1987-90; Leader, Oxford Practice Skills Project, 1990-95; University Lecturer in Practice Skills, 1995-2000; Reader in Medicine, 1996-2000, Professor of Medical Ethics, 2000-, University of Oxford; Delegate, Oxford University Press; Chairman, Wellcome Trust Medical Humanities Strategy Committee, 2005-08; Chairman, Working Party on Ethics and Dementia, Nuffield Council on Bioethics. Publications: Books: Oxford Handbook of Clinical Medicine, editions, 1, 2, 3, 4 (9 translations), 1985-98; Essential Practice in Patient Centred Care, 1995; Manage Your Mind (4 translations), 1995; Medical Ethics and Law, 2003; A Very Short Introduction to Medical Ethics, 2004; Empirical Ethics in Psychiatry, 2008; Numerous articles and chapters mainly in fields of medical ethics and behavioural disturbance in Alzheimer's Disease. Honours: Rhodes Travel Scholarship, 1969; Bosanquet Open Scholarship, New College, 1970; Wellcome Trust Training Fellowship, 1985-87; Research Prize and Medal, Royal College of Psychiatrists, 1997; Member, through distinction, Faculty of Public Health, 2003; Honorary Fellow (International), The Hastings Centre. Memberships: Fellow, St Cross College, Oxford; Fellow, Royal College of Psychiatrists; Member, Faculty of Public Health. Address: Departments of Public Health and Primary Care, University of Oxford, Old Road Campus, Oxford OX3 7LF, England. E-mail: admin@ethox.ox.ac.uk

HOPE Ronald (Sidney), b. 4 April 1921, London, England. Writer. Education: BA, 1941, MA, 1946, DPhil, New College, Oxford. Appointments: Fellow, Brasenose College, Oxford, 1945-47; Director, Seafarers' Education Service, London, 1947-76; Director, The Marine Society, 1976-86. Publications: Spare Time at Sea, 1954; Economic Geography, 1956; Dick Small in the Half Deck, Ships, 1958; The British Shipping Industry, 1959; The Shoregoer's Guide to World Ports, 1963; Seamen and the Sea, 1965; Introduction to the Merchant Navy, 1965; Retirement from the Sea, 1967; In Cabined Ships at Sea, 1969; Twenty Singing Seamen, 1979; The Seamen's World, 1982; A New History of British Shipping, 1990; Poor Jack, 2001. Address: 2 Park Place, Dollar, FK14 7AA, Scotland.

HOPKINS Anthony (Philip), b. 31 December 1937, Port Talbot, South Wales. Actor. m. (1) Petronella Barker, 1967, divorced 1972, 1 daughter, (2) Jennifer Lynton, 1973, divorced 2002, (3) Stella Arroyave, 2003. Education: Welsh College of Music and Drama. Career: Assistant Stage Manager, Manchester Library Theatre, 1960; Joined Nottingham Repertory Company; Royal Academy of Dramatic Art; Phoenix Theatre, Leicester; Liverpool Playhouse and Hornchurch Repertory Company. Films include: The Lion in Winter, 1967; The Looking Glass War, 1968; Hamlet, 1969; Young Winston, 1971; A Doll's House, 1972; The Girl from Petrovka, 1973; Juggernaut, 1974; Audrey Rose, A Bridge Too Far, 1976; International Velvet, 1977; Magic, 1978; The Elephant Man, 1979; A Change of Seasons, 1980; The Bounty, 1983; The Good Father, 1985; 84 Charing Cross Road, 1986; The Dawning, 1987; A Chorus of Disapproval, 1988; Desperate Hours, 1989; The Silence of the Lambs, Free Jack, One Man's War, Spotswood, 1990; Howard's End, Bram Stoker's Dracula, 1991; Chaplin, The Trial, The Innocent, Remains of the Day, 1992; Shadowlands, Legends of the Fall, The Road to Wellville, 1993; August, 1994; Nixon, Surviving Picasso, 1995; The Edge, 1996; The Mask of Zorro, Amistad, Meet Joe Black, 1997; Instinct, 1998; Titus, 1999; Hannibal, Hearts of Atlantis, 2000; Mission Impossible 2, Hannibal, The Devil and Daniel Webster, 2001; Bad Company, Red

Dragon, 2002; Human Stain, 2003; Alexander, 2004; Proof, The World's Fastest Indian, 2005; Bobby, 2006; Slipstream, Fracture, City of Your Final Destination, Beowulf, 2007; Immutable Dream of Snow Lion, Where I Stand: The Hank Greenspan Story (voice), 2008; Bare Knuckles, 2009; The Wolfman, 2010; You Will Meet a Tall Dark Stranger, 2010; The Rite, 2011; Thor, 2011; 360, 2012; Hitchcock, 2012; RED 2, 2013; Theatre includes: A Flea in Her Ear, 1967; A Woman Killed with Kindness, 1971; Macbeth, 1972; Equus, 1974; The Tempest, USA, 1979; Old Times, USA, 1984; The Lonely Road, 1985; King Lear, 1986. TV includes: A Company of Five, 1968; The Poet Game, 1970; War and Peace, 1971; Lloyd George, 1972; All Creatures Great and Small, 1974; Kean, 1978; The Bunker, 1980; Othello, BBC, 1981; A Married Man, 1982; Blunt, 1985; Across the Lake, Heartland, 1988; To Be the Best, 1990; A Few Selected Exits, Big Cats, 1993. Honours include: Variety Club Film and Stage Actor Awards, 1984, 1985, 1993; BAFTA Best Actor Awards, 1973, 1991, 1994, 1995; Emmy Awards, 1976, 1981; Oscar, 1991; Laurence Olivier Awards 1985; CBE, 1987; KB, 1993; Commandeur dans l'Ordre des Arts et des Lettres, France, 1996; Honorary DLit, University of Wales, 1988; Honorary Fellowship, St David's College, Wales, 1992; 2 Los Angeles Film Critics Association, Best Actor Awards, 1993; Donesta, 1998; Cecil B DeMille Award, 2006; BAFTA Fellowship, 2008; Numerous other awards. Address: c/o CAA, 9830 Wilshire Blvd, Beverly Hills, CA 90212, USA.

HOPKINS Antony, b. 21 March 1921, London, England. Musician; Author. m. Alison Purves, 1947, deceased 1991. Education: Royal College of Music with Cyril Smith and Gordon Jacob. Career: Lecturer, Royal College of Music, 15 years; Director, Intimate Opera Company, 1952-64; Series of radio broadcasts, Talking About Music, 1954-92. Compositions include: Operas: Lady Rohesia; Three's Company; Hands Across the Sky; Dr Musikus; Ten o'Clock Call; The Man from Tuscany; Ballets: Etude; Cafe des Sports; 3 Piano Sonatas; Numerous scores of incidental music including: Oedipus; The Love of Four Colonels; Cast a Dark Shadow; Pickwick Papers; Billy Budd; Decameron Nights. Publications include: Understanding Music, 1979; The Nine Symphonies of Beethoven, 1980; The Concertgoer's Companion, 2 volumes, 1984, 1986. Honours: Gold Medal, Royal College of Music, 1943; Italia Prize for Radio Programme, 1951, 1957; Medal, City of Tokyo for Services to Music, 1973; Commander of the British Empire, 1976. Address: Woodyard, Ashridge, Berkhamsted, Hertfordshire HP4 1PS, England.

HOPKINS Timothy John, b. 7 March 1967, Manchester, England. Roman Catholic Priest. Education: MA, Classics, Christ's College, Cambridge, 1985-88; STL, PhB, Venerable English College and Pontifical Gregorian University, Rome, 1988-94. Appointments: Assistant Priest, St Willibrord's, Clayton, 1994-95; Chaplain, St Gregory's RC High School, Openshaw, 1994-99; Diocesan Chaplain to Italian Community, 1994-; Governor, St Anne's (Ancoats) RC Primary School, 1994-2010: Parish Priest, St Brigid's, Beswick and St Vincent's, Openshaw, 1995-2003; Governor, St Brigid's RC Primary Beacon School, 1995-2010; Secretary, Diocesan Council of Priests, 1997-2003; Chair, East Manchester Education Action Zone, 1999-2004; Vice Chair, University of Manchester Settlement, 1999-; Chaplain, Lord Mayor of Manchester, 2001-02; Governor, St Bede's College and Preparatory School, Manchester, 2001-; Founder and Chair, East Manchester E-Learning Foundation, 2001-08; Chaplain, Commonwealth Games, Manchester, 2002; Manchester LEA Joint Consultative Committee, 2002-10; Manchester City Council Children and Young People Scrutiny Committee, 2002-10; Greater Manchester Area Officer, Salford Diocese Boundaries & Sites Board, 2003-; Parish Priest of St Anne, St Brigid, St Michael and St Vincent, East Manchester, 2003-10; Director, New East Manchester Urban Regeneration Company, 2005-; Governor, St John Fisher RC Primary School, 2010-; Governor, St Mary's Denton RC Primary School, 2010-; Governor, St Thomas More RC College, Denton, 2010-; Parish Priest, St Mary and St John Fisher RC Parish, Denton, 2010-. Publications: The Power of the Holy Spirit in the Sacrament of Reconciliation, 1994; Commonwealth Games Chaplaincy: Going for Gold in Manchester, 2002; Education Action Zone and Microsoft Work Together for a Prosperous Future in East Manchester, 2003. Address: St Mary's Presbytery, Duke Street, Denton, Manchester, M34 2AN, England. E-mail: tim@vincents.fslife.co.uk

HOPWOOD David Alan (Sir), b. 19 August 1933, Kinver, Staffordshire, England. Scientist. m. Joyce Lilian Bloom, 2 sons, 1 daughter. Education: BA 1st class honours, Natural Sciences, 1954, PhD, 1958, University of Cambridge; DSc, University of Glasgow, 1974. Appointments: John Stothert Bye-Fellow, Magdalene College, Cambridge, 1956-58; University Demonstrator, Assistant Lecturer in Botany, University of Cambridge, 1957-61; Research Fellow, St John's College, Cambridge, 1958-61; Lecturer in Genetics, University of Glasgow, 1961-68; John Innes Professor of Genetics, University of East Anglia, Norwich and Head of the Genetics Department, John Innes Institute, 1968-98; John Innes Emeritus Fellow, John Innes Centre, Emeritus Professor of Genetics, University of Eat Anglia, Norwich, 1998-; Visiting Research Fellow, Kosan Biosciences, Inc, 1998-2008. Publications: Over 270 articles on genetics, microbiology and genetic engineering in scientific publications. Honours: 3 honorary memberships; 4 honorary fellowships; Fellow, Royal Society of London; Foreign Fellowship, Indian National Science Academy; 2 honorary Doctorates of Science; Medal of the Kitasato Institute for Research in New Bioactive Compounds; Hoechst-Roussel Award for Research in Antimicrobial Chemotherapy; Chiron Biotechnology Award; Knight Bachelor; Mendel Medal of the Czech Academy of Sciences; Gabor Medal of the Royal Society; Stuart Mudd Prize, International Union of Microbiological Societies; Ernst Chain Prize, Imperial College, London; Andre Lwoff Prize, Federation of European Microbiological Societies; SGM Prize Medal, Society for General Microbiology. Memberships: Genetical Society of Great Britain; Society for General Microbiology; American Society for Microbiology; European Molecular Biology Organisation; Academia Europaea. Address: John Innes Centre, Norwich, Norfolk NR4 7UH, England. E-mail: david.hopwood@bbsrc.ac.uk

HORDER John Plaistowe, b. 9 December 1919, Ealing, London, England. Physician; General practitioner. m. Elizabeth June Wilson, 2 sons, 2 daughters. Education: Classical Scholarship, University College Oxford, 1938-40; Army war service; Medical Student, Oxford and London Hospital, 1943-48; Intern Appointments, London Hospital, 1948-51. Appointments: General Practitioner, North West London, 1951-81; Foundation Member, 1952, various offices including President, 1979-82, Royal College of General Practitioners; Vice-President, Royal Society of Medicine, 1987-89; Visiting Professor, Royal Free Hospital Medical School, 1983-92; Founder, 1st President, Centre for the Advancement of Inter-professional Education, 1983-2003. Publications include: Articles in medical journals: Illness in General Practice, 1954; Physicians and Family Doctors, A New Relationship, 1977; Book: The Future General Practitioner. Learning and

Teaching, (editor and contributor), 1972; Book: General Practice under the National Health Service 1948-1997, (joint editor and contributor), 1998. Honours: OBE, 1971; CBE, 1981; Honorary MD, 1985; Honorary DSc, 2000; FRCGP, 1970; FRCP, 1972; FRCP (Ed), 1981; FRCPsych, 1980; Honorary Fellow, Green College, Oxford, 1985; Honorary Fellow, Queen Mary College University of London, 1997. Memberships: Medical Royal Colleges; Royal Society of Medicine; Past President, Medical Art Society. Address: 98 Regents Park Road, London NW1 8UG, England.

HORI Hidenobu, b. 17 October 1942, Takaoka, Toyama, Japan. Professor Emeritus. m. Masako, 1 daughter. Education: BS, Niigata University, 1964; MS, 1966, PhD, 1972, Osaka University. Appointments: Research Associate, 1971-86, Associate Professor, 1986-92, Osaka University; Professor, 1992-2008, Professor Emeritus, 2008, Japan Advanced Institute of Science and Technology. Publications: Numerous articles in professional journals. Memberships: Physical Society of Japan; Japan Society of Energy and Resources. E-mail: nrp03887@nifty.com

HORIGUCHI Hironori, b. 16 December 1971, Suita, Osaka, Japan. Associate Professor. m. Kazuyo, 2 daughters. Education: Bachelor, 1995, Master, 1997, PhD, 1999, Engineering, Osaka University. Appointments: Research Associate, Faculty of Engineering, Tokushima University, Tokushima, Japan, 1999; Associate Professor, Graduate School of Engineering Science, Osaka University, 2003-. Publications: Numerous articles in professional journals. Honours: Outstanding Paper Award, Japan Society of Mechanical Engineers, 2002; Challenge Award, 2008, Paper Award, 2010, Turbomachinery Society of Japan. Memberships: Japan Society of Mechanical Engineers; Turbomachinery Society of Japan. Address: Graduate School of Engineering Science, Osaka University, 1-3 Machikaneyama, Toyonaka, Osaka 560-8531, Japan. E-mail: horiguti@me.es.osaka-u.ac.jp

HORLOCK John Harold (Sir), b. 19 April 1928, Edmonton, England. University Administrator and Engineer. m Sheila J Stutely, 1 son, 2 daughters. Education: MA, Mechanical Sciences, 1953, PhD, Mechanical Engineering, 1955, ScD, Mechanical Engineering, 1975, Cambridge University. Appointments: Design and Development Engineer, Rolls-Royce Ltd, 1948-51, Research Fellow, St John's College Cambridge, 1954-57; Lecturer, Engineering, 1956-58, Professor of Engineering, Cambridge University, 1967-74; Harrison Professor of Mechanical Engineering, University of Liverpool, 1958-67; Vice-Chancellor, University of Salford, 1974-80; Vice-Chancellor, 1981-90, Fellow, 1991-, Open University; Treasurer and Vice-President, Royal Society, 1992-97; Pro-Chancellor UMIST, 1995-2001; President, Association for Science Education, 1999. Publications: Books: Axial Flow Compressors, 1958; Axial Flow Turbines, 1973; Actuator Disc Theory, 1978; The Thermodynamics and Gas Dynamics of Internal Combustion Engines (co-editor), Volume I, 1982, Volume II, 1986; Cogeneration, Combined Heat and Power, 1987; Combined Power Plants, 1992; Energy for the Future (co-editor), 1995; Advanced Gas Turbine Cycles, 2003. Honours include: James Clayton Prize, 1962, Thomas Hawksley Gold Medal, 1969, Arthur Charles Main Prize, 1997, Institution of Mechanical Engineers; Honorary Doctorates: Heriot-Watt University, 1980, University of Salford, 1981, University of East Asia, 1987, University of Liverpool, 1987, Open University, 1991, CNAA, 1991, De Montford University, 1995, Cranfield University, 1997; Honorary Fellowships: St John's College, Cambridge, 1989, UMIST, 1991, Royal Aeronautical Society, 2003; Knighthood,

1996; R Tom Sawyer Award, ASME, 1997; Sir James Ewing Medal, ICE, 2002; ISABE Achievement Award, 2003. Memberships: Fellow, Royal Society; Fellow, Royal Academy of Engineering; Fellow, Institution of Mechanical Engineers; Fellow, American Society of Mechanical Engineers; Foreign Associate, National Academy of Engineering, USA. Address: 2 The Avenue, Ampthill, Bedford MK45 2NR, England. E-mail: john.horlock1@btinternet.com

HORN Jürgen, b. 21 February 1943, Poznan, Poland. Humanities Scholar. Education: Diploma in Law, 1968; Diploma in Protestant Theology and Religious Studies, 1973; PhD, Oriental Studies and Religious Studies, 1981. Appointments: Scientific Collaborator, University of Goettingen, 1978-85, 1990-91, University of Halle-Wittenberg, 1994-2000; Lecturer, University of Goettingen, 1978-2011. Publications: History of Science and Theoretical Foundations of Egyptology, 1974; Studies in Piety and Literature of Christian Egypt, 1981; Studies Relating to the Martyrs of Northern Upper Egypt, Vol I, 1986, Vol II, 1992. Honours: Visiting Scholar, University of California at Los Angeles, 1997; Corresponding Member, German Archaeological Institute, 2002. Memberships: International Association for Coptic Studies; International Association of Egyptologists; International Association of Papyrologists; German Association for Religious Studies. Address: Foersterweg 22, 22525 Hamburg, Germany. E-mail: dr.j.horn@t-online.de

HORNBY Nick, b. 17 April 1957, London, England. Freelance Journalist; Novelist. m. (1) Virginia Bovell (divorced), 1 son, (2) Amanda Posey, 2 sons. Publications: Contemporary American Fiction, 1992; Fever Pitch, 1992; My Favourite Year: A Collection of New Football Writing, 1993; High Fidelity, 1995; Speaking With the Angel, 2000; About a Boy, 2000; How to be Good, 2001; 31 Songs, 2003; A Long Way Down, 2005;The Polysyllabic Spree, 2004; Housekeeping vs. the Dirt, 2006; Slam, 2007, Juliet, Naked, 2009. Screenplay: Fever Pitch, 1997; About a Boy. Contributions to: Sunday Times; Times Literary Supplement; Literary Review; New Yorker; New York Times. Honours: William Hill Sports Book of the Year Award, 1992; Writers' Guild Best Fiction Book Award, 1995; American Academy of Arts and Letters E M Forster Award, 1999; WHSmith Fiction Award, 2002; London Award, 2003. Address: c/o Peters Fraser and Dunlop, Drury House, 34-43 Russell Street, London WC2B 5HA, England.

HORNE Alistair Allan (Sir), b. 9 November 1925, London, England. Author; Journalist; Lecturer. m. (1) Renira Margaret Hawkins, 3 daughters, (2) The Hon Mrs Sheelin Eccles, 1987. Education: MA, Jesus College, Cambridge. Appointments: Served WWII: RAF, 1943-44; Coldstream Guards, 1944-47; Captain attached Intelligence Service MI-5; Foreign Correspondent, Daily Telegraph, 1952-55; Founded Alistair Horne Research Fellowship in Modern History, 1969, Honorary Fellow, 1988-, St Antony's College, Oxford, 1969; Honorary Fellow, Jesus College Cambridge, 1996-; Fellow Woodrow Wilson Center, Washington DC, 1980-81; Member: Management Committee, Royal Literary Fund, 1969-91; Franco-British Council, 1979-93; Committee of Management, Society of Authors, 1979-82; Trustee, Imperial War Museum, 1975-82. Publications: Back into Power, 1955; The Land is Bright, 1958; Canada and the Canadians, 1961; The Price of Glory: Verdun 1916, 1962; The Fall of Paris 1870-1871, 1965; To Lose a Battle: France 1940, 1969; Death of a Generation, 1970; The Terrible Year: The Paris Commune, 1971, 2005; Kissinger's Year, 1973; A Savage War of Peace: Algeria, 1954-62, 1977, new edition 2006; Small Earthquake in Chile,

1972; Napoleon, Master of Europe 1805-1807, 1979; The French Army and Politics 1870-1970, 1984; Macmillan, Vol I, 1894-1956, 1985; Vol II, 1957-1986, 1989; A Bundle from Britain, 1993; The Lonely Leader: Monty 1944-45, 1994; How Far From Austerlitz: Napoleon 1805-1815, 1996; Telling Lives (editor), 2000; Seven Ages of Paris, 2002; The Age of Napoleon, 2004; Friend or Foe: An Anglo-Saxon History of France, 2004; La Belle France, 2005; Macmillan I & II, 25th Anniversary Edition, 2008; The French Revolution, 2009; Kissinger's Year: 1973, 2009; Numerous contributions to books and periodicals. Honours: Hawthornden Prize, 1963; Yorkshire Post Book of Year Prize, 1978; Wolfson Literary Award, 1978; Enid Macleod Prize, 1985; Commander of the Order of the British Empire, 1992; Chevalier, Legion d'Honneur, 1993; LittD, Cambridge, 1993; Kt, 2003. Memberships: Society of Authors; Fellow, Royal Society of Literature; Garrick Club. Address: The Old Vicarage, Turville, Nr Henley on Thames, Oxon RG9 6QU, England.

HORNE ROBERTS Jennifer, b. 15 February 1949, Harrow, London, England. Barrister; Writer; Artist. m. Keith M P Roberts, 1 son (deceased 2009), 1 daughter. Education: Diploma, Italian, University of Perugia, Italy, 1966; BA, Honours, London University, 1969; Law Diploma CLLE, 1974; Bar Finals, Council of Legal Education, Middle Temple, 1976; Ad eundem Member, Inner Temple. Appointments: In practice at Bar 1976-; Currently, Civil Law, Family Law, Goldsmith Chambers, Temple, London. Publications: Trade Unionists and Law, 1984; New Frontiers in Family Law (co-author), 1994; Labour's True Way Forward, 1998; Labour's Agenda, 2000; Selected Poems, 2002; The MMR10 –Access to Justice (co-author) 2006, The MMR10-Justice in Europe (co-author) 2006; Harry's Story – A Brilliant Boy's Short Life (co-author with Keith Roberts), 2010. Memberships: Founder and First Chair, Association of Women Barristers; Family Law Bar Association; Tate; Royal Academy; Highgate Literary and Scientific Society; Professional Negligence Bar Association; Bar European Group; Personal Injury Bar Association; Highgate Golf Club; Director, Harington Scheme Charity, Highgate, London; Director, Trust for Autism Charity, London. Address: Goldsmith Chambers, Temple, London EC4Y 7BL, England. E-mail: keith@horne-roberts.co.uk. Website: www.Horne-Roberts.co.uk

HOROBIN Richard William, b. 13 May 1939, Britain. m. Rose Evison, 1 daughter. Education: BSc, PhD, Chemistry Department, University of Sheffield, England. Appointments: Science Research Council Research Assistant to Reader, The University of Sheffield, 1964-68; Visiting Professor, University of Connecticut, 1987; Honorary Senior Research Fellow, School of Life Sciences, University of Glasgow, Scotland. Publications: Numerous articles in professional journals, books and booklets. Memberships: Biological Stains Commission; Royal Microscopical Society. Address: School of Life Sciences, University of Glasgow, West Medical Building, Glasgow G12 8QQ, Scotland. E-mail: richardwhorobin@tomcroy.co.uk

HOROVITZ Michael, b. 4 April 1935, Frankfurt am Main, Germany. Writer; Poet; Editor; Publisher; Literary and Arts Journalist; Songwriter; Singer; Musician; Visual Artist; Impresario. Education: BA, 1959, MA, 1964, Brasenose, College, Oxford. Appointments: Editor and Publisher, New Departures International Review, 1959-; Founder, singer-player, director, Jazz Poetry SuperJam bandwagons, 1969-; Founder, Co-ordinator and Torchbearer, Poetry Olympics Festivals, 1980-. Publications: Europa (translator), 1961; Alan Davie, 1963; Declaration, 1963; Strangers: Poems, 1965; Poetry for the People: An Essay in Bop Prosody, 1966; Bank Holiday: A New Testament for the Love Generation, 1967; Children of Albion (editor), 1969; The Wolverhampton Wanderer: An Epic of Football, Fate and Fun, 1971; Love Poems, 1971; A Contemplation, 1978; Growing Up: Selected Poems and Pictures 1951-1979, 1979; The Egghead Republic (translator), 1983; A Celebration of and for Frances Horovitz (editor), 1984; Midsummer Morning Jog Log, 1986; Bop Paintings, Collages and Drawings, 1989; Grandchildren of Albion (editor), 1992; Wordsounds and Sightlines: New and Selected Poems, 1994; Grandchildren of Albion Live (on cassette and CD) (editor), 1996; The POW! Anthology, 1996; The POP! Anthology, 2000; The POM! Anthology, 2001; Jeff Nuttall's Wake on Paper, 2004; Jeff Nuttall's Wake on CD, 2004; Lost Office Campaign Poem, 2005; The POT! Anthology, 2005; A New Waste Land: Timeship Earth at Nillennium, 2007; The POE! Anthology, 2011. Honours: Arts Council of Great Britain Writers Award, 1976; Arts Council Translator's Award, 1983; Poetry Book Society Recommendation, 1986; Creative Britons Award, 2000; Officer of the Order of the British Empire, 2002. Address: c/o New Departures, PO Box 9819, London, W11 2GQ, England.

HOROWITZ Irving (Louis), b. 25 September 1929, New York, USA. Editor; Publisher. m. (1) Ruth Lenore Horowitz, 1950, divorced 1964, 2 sons, (2) Mary Curtis Horowitz, 1979. Education: BSS, City College, New York City, 1951; MA, Columbia University, 1952; PhD, University of Buenos Aires, 1957; Postgraduate Fellow, Brandeis University, 1958-59. Appointments: Associate Professor, University of Buenos Aires, 1955-58; Assistant Professor, Bard College, 1960; Chairman, Department of Sociology, Hobart and William Smith Colleges, 1960-63; Editor-in-Chief, Transaction Society, 1962-94; Associate Professor to Professor of Sociology, Washington University, St Louis, 1963-69; President, Transaction Books, 1966-94; Chairman, Department of Sociology, Rutgers, The State University of New Jersey, 1969-73; Professor of Sociology, Graduate Faculty, 1969-, Hannah Arendt Professor of Social and Political Theory, 1979-, Rutgers University; Bacardi Chair of Cuban Studies, Miami University, 1992-94; Editorial Chairman and President Emeritus, Transaction/USA and Transaction/UK. Publications: Numerous articles in professional journals; Books include: Daydreams and Nightmares: Reflections of a Harlem Childhood, 1990; The Decomposition of Sociology, 1993; Behemoth: Main Currents in the History and Theory of Political Sociology, 1999; Veblen's Century: A Collective Portrait, 2002; Tributes: An Informal History of Twentieth Century Social Science, 2004; The Idea of War and Peace: The Experience of Western Civilization, 2007; The Long Night of Dark Intent: A Half-Century of Cuban Communism, 2008; Radicalism and the Revolt Against Reason, 1961, 1968, 2010. Honours: Best Biography, National Jewish Book Award, 1990; Harold D Lasswell Award; Festschrift, 1994; Lifetime Achievement Award, Inter-University Seminar on Armed Forces and Sco; Gerhart Neimeyer Award, Intercollegiate Studies Association, 2003; International Humanist Award, 2004; Thomas S Szasz Award, Centre for Industrial Thought, 2004; Distinguished Scholarly Lifetime Achievement Award, American Sociological Association, 2006. Memberships: AAAS; AAAS Science and Human Rights Program; AAUP; USIA; American Political Science Association; National Association of Scholars; Authors Guild; Center for Study of the Presidency; Council on Foreign Relations; International Society of Political Psychology; Society for International Development; US General Accounting Office; US Information Agency; National Association of Scholars; Institute for a Free Cuba; Raymond Aron Society; Senior Editorial Advisor,

Spring Scientific. Address: Rutgers University, Transaction Pubs Bldg, 4051 New Brunswick, NJ 08903, USA. E-mail: ihorowitz@transactionpub.com

HORRIDGE G Adrian, b. 12 December 1927. Professor. m. Audrey Lightburne, 1 son, 3 daughters. Education: First Class Honours, Natural Sciences Tripos, St John's College, Cambridge, England. Appointments: Scientific Officer, Senior Scientific Officer, Department of Structures, Royal Aircraft Establishment, Farnborough, England, 1953-54; Research Fellowship, St John's College, Cambridge. 1954-56; Lecturer, Reader in Zoology, St Andrews University, Scotland, 1956-59; Visiting Associate Professor, University of California, Los Angeles, USA, 1959-60; Fellow, Center for Advanced Study in the Behavioural Sciences, Stanford, California, USA, 1959-60; Director, Marine Laboratory, St Andrews University, Scotland, 1960-69; Visiting Full Professor, Yale University, USA, 1965; Fellow, Royal Society of London, 1969; Professor of Behavioural Biology, Australian National University, Canberra, Australia, 1969; Fellow, Australian Academy of Science, 1971; Examiner in Biology, University Sains, Penang and University of Malaya, Kuala Lumpar, Malaysia, 1972, 1976, 1980, 1984; Visiting Fellowship, Balliol College, Oxford, England, 1973-74; Chief Scientist, US Research Ship, Alpha Helix, in the Moluccas, East Indonesia, 1975; Visiting Fellow, Churchill College, Cambridge, England, 1976-77; Executive Director, Centre for Visual Sciences, Australian National University, 1987-1990; Royal Society Visiting Professorship, St Andrews, Scotland, 1992; Visiting Fellow, Churchill College, Cambridge, 1993-94; Appointed University Fellow, Visiting Fellow, Australian National University, 1993. Publications: 250 papers on Sciences; 20 titles on Indonesian traditional boats; 10 titles on other topics, including: The Structure and Function of the Nervous Systems of Invertebrates (co-author), 1965; Interneurons, 1968; The Compound Eye of Insects (editor), 1975; The Prahu, Traditional Sailing Boat of Indonesia, 2nd edition, 1985; Sailing Craft of Indonesia, 1986; Outrigger Canoes of Bali and Madura, Indonesia, 1987; Natural and low-level seeing systems (co-editor), 1993; What Does the Honey Bee See? 2009. Memberships: Fellow, Royal Society of England; Society for Nautical Research; Fellow, Australian Academy of Science; International Society of NeuroEthology. Address: 76 Mueller Street, Yarralumla, ACT 2600, Australia.

HORROCKS Jane, b. 18 January 1964, Lancashire, England. Actress. Partner Nick Vivian, 1 son, 1 daughter. Education: Royal Academy of Dramatic Art. Creative Works: Stage appearances include: The Rise and Fall of Little Voice; TV appearances include: Hunting Venus (film); Red Dwarf (series); Absolutely Fabulous; The Flint Street Nativity; Little Princess; The Amazing Mrs Pritchard. Film appearances: The Dressmaker, 1989; Life is Sweet, 1991; Little Voice, 1998; Born Romantic, 2001; Chicken Run (voice), 2002; Last Rumba in Rochdale (voice), 2003; Wheeling Dealing, 2004; Corpse Bride (voice), 2005; Brothers of the Head, 2005; Garfield: A Tail of Two Kitties (voice), 2006; The Amazing Mrs Pritchard, 2006; No One Gets Off in this Town, 2008; Grace! (TV), 2009; Pixie Hollow Games (voice), 2011; Trollied (TV), 2011; Phineas and Ferb (voice), 2011; True Love (TV), 2012; Secret of the Wings (voice), 2012. Honour: Best Supporting Actress Los Angeles Critics Award, 1992. Address: ICM, Oxford House, 76 Oxford Street, London W1D 1BS, England.

HORTACSU Mahmut Onder, b. 4 January 1943, Izmir, Turkey. Physicist. m. Ayfer Aksit, 1 son, 1 daughter. Education: BS, Electrical Engineering, Robert College Engineering School, Istanbul, 1966; PhD, Physics, University of Pittsburgh, USA. Appointments: Assistant, Associate Professor, Bogazici University, 1972-86; Professor, Istanbul Technical University, 1986-10; Part time Employee, Senior Physicist, Feza Gursey Institute, 2001-06. Publications: Over 60 scientific papers in professional journals. Honours: Junior Scientist, Scientific & Technical Research Council of Turkey, 1981. Memberships: Academy of Sciences of Turkey. Address: ITU, Physics Department, Faculty of Science & Letters, Masiak, Istanbul 34465, Turkey. E-mail: hortascu@itu.edu.fr Website: www.fizik.itu.edu.tr/hortacsum

HORTON Antony Brian, b. 21 August 1933, Edgbaston, Birmingham, England. Artist. m. Sheila, 3 daughters. Education: Shrewsbury School; Exeter College, Oxford; Cheltenham College of Art. Appointments: National Service; Commission, The Lancashire Fusiliers; Employed in commerce, 5 years; Worked in restoring paintings; Freelance artist, 1983-; Solo and group exhibitions in London and the UK; Paintings and drawings in private collections in Europe and USA. Publications: Cover illustrations for Everyman Library of works by Dylan Thomas: Under Milk Wood, The Poems, A Dylan Thomas Treasury, Collected Poems 1934-1953, and The Loud Hills of Wales, 1991. Honours: Exhibited in RA, RWS, David Messum Gallery and National Library of Wales; Listed in international biographical dictionaries. Address: The Old Rectory, Taplow, Buckinghamshire SL6 0ET, England.

HORTON James Victor, b. 24 July 1948, London, England. Artist; Painter. m. Rosalind Lucy, 2 sons. Education: Sir John Cass School of Art, 1964-66; City & Guilds Art School, 1966-70; Royal College of Art, 1971-74. Appointments: Professional Artist; Exhibits widely in London and provincial galleries; Many portrait commissions; Exhibited abroad, mostly in Delhi; Artist in Residence, HRH Prince Charles, Mount Athos; Teacher, Part time Tutor, Sir John Cass, Cambridge Art School and other London Colleges, -1990; Private tutor. Publications: Numerous articles in professional journals; Artist/Illustrator for 9 books. Honours: Prizewinner, BEA Art Awards, 1972; Discerning Eye Prizewinner, 1992; President,k Royal Society of British Artists. Memberships: President, Royal Society of British Artists; Arts Club, Dover Street. Address: 11 Victoria Road, Cambridge, CB4 3BW, England. E-mail: jvhorton@hotmail.co.uk

HORVERAK Sveinung, b. 15 May 1961, Oslo, Norway. Associate Professor. m. Elisabeth, 5 sons, 1 daughter. Education: BEd, Social Work, 1988; Cand Political Science Work (Child Welfare), 1999; PhD, Social Work (Child Welfare, Youth in Family Group Conference), 2006. Appointments: Child Welfare, Social Service and Refugee Service, 1988-98; Researcher and Lecturer, University of Nordland, 1999-2010; State Department of Child Welfare, 1999. Publications: Numerous books and articles in national and international journals. Memberships: Board Member, Norwegian Association of Research in Social Work. Address: Parallellen 44, 8072 Bodø, Norway. E-mail: sveinung.horverak@uin.no

HORWITZ Angela Joan, b. 14 October 1934, London, England. Sculptress; Painter; Professor. 2 sons, 1 daughter. Education: Lycée Francais de Londres; Studied art, Marylebone Institute, 1978-90; Sir John Cass College, 1983-85; Hampstead Institute, 1990-92. Career: Fashion Designer, owner of own company, 1960-80; Exhibitions: Grand Palais, Paris, 1985, 1986; RBA, NS, RAS, SWA, Mall Galleries, Civic Centre, Southend, SEFAS, Guildhall, Ridley Society, City of Westminster Arts Council, Alpine Gallery, Smiths Gallery Covent Garden, Wintershall Gallery; The Orangery, Hyde Park

Gallery, London (Winchester Cathedral, 1992); Exhibition with City of London Polytechnic, Whitechapel, London, 1985; Salon International du Livre et de la Presse à Geneva, 1997; Miramar Hotel, 1998 and Beaux Arts, Cannes, France, 1999; Raymond Gallery, Beaux Arts, 2000; The Atrium Gallery, London, 2000; Gallery le Carre d'or, Paris, 2000; Le Cannet, St Sauveur, 2005, 2006, 2007, 2008; Lansdowne Club, Mayfair, 2005, 2007, 2008; Plaister's Hall in aid of the Red Cross, 2005, 2006; St Catherine's College, Oxford, 2008; St John's College, Cambridge, 2010. Work in permanent collections: Sculpture in stone for Winchester Cathedral; Well Woman Centre, The United Elizabeth Garrett Anderson Hospital for Women, London; Private collection: Zurich, Switzerland; National Society Ridley Arts Society. Honours: Academical Knight, Arts, Academia Internazionale Greci-Marino, 1999; Academical Knight, Department of Arts, Ordine Accademico Internatzionale, Italy; Fellow, American Biographical Institute. Memberships: NS, 1982; RAS, 1983; FABI, 2005; Beaux Arts, Cannes, France, 1997-2007; Landsdown Club; British Red Cross. Address: 6 Wellington House, Aylmer Drive, Stanmore, Middlesex HA7 3ES, England.

HOSHINO Tetsuya, b. 8 May 1968, Osaka, Japan. Chemical Engineer. m. Haruko. Education: BS, Tohoku University, 1991; MS, Kyoto University, 1993; PhD, University of Tsukuba, 2008. Appointments: Researcher, Hitachi Chemical, 1994-. Publications: Articles in professional journals; 1 patent. Memberships: Japan Society of Applied Physics; Society of the Polymer Science, Japan. Address: Amakubo 4-7-54, Tsukuba-shi, Ibaraki-ken 305-0005, Japan. E-mail: qym03533@nifty.ne.jp

HOSKING Geoffrey Alan, b. 28 April 1942, Troon, Scotland. University Teacher. m. Anne Lloyd Hirst, 2 daughters. Education: Kings College, Cambridge, 1960-64; Moscow State University, 1964-65; St Antony's College, Oxford, 1965-66. Appointments: Lecturer in History, University of Essex, 1966-71, 1972-76; Visiting Professor, Department of Political Science, University of Wisconsin-Madison, 1971-72; Gastprofessor, Slavisches Institut, University of Cologne, 1980-81; Senior Lecturer, Reader in Russian History, University of Essex, 1976-80, 1981-84); Professor of Russian History, 1984-99, 2004-07, Emeritus Professor, 2007-, SSEES, University of London; Leverhulme Personal Research Professor in Russian History, SSEES-UCL, 1999-2004; Editor, Rossiiskaia Istoria, 2007-. Publications: Author: The Russian Constitutional Experiment, 1973; Beyond Socialist Realism, 1980; The First Socialist Society: A History of the Soviet Union from Within, 1985, 1990, 1992; The Awakening of the Soviet Union, 1990; The Road to Post-Communism: Independent Political Movements in the Soviet Union 1985-91, 1992; Russia: People and Empire (1552-1917), 1997; Russia and the Russians: A History from Rus to Russian Federation, 2001; Rulers and Victims: the Russians in the Soviet Union, 2006; Editor: Myths and Nationhood, 1997; Russian Nationalism Past and Present, 1998; Reinterpreting Russia, 1999; Trust: money, markets and society, 2010. Honours: Los Angeles Times History Book Prize, 1986; US Independent Publishers History Book Award, 2002; Alec Nove Prize, 2008; Fellow, British Academy, 1993; Fellow, Royal Historical Society; Honorary Doctorate, Russian Academy of Sciences, 2000; Member, Council of the Royal Historical Society, 2002-06. Memberships: Writers and Scholars Educational Trust; Museum of Contemporary History, Moscow; Moscow School of Political Studies; Institute for Advanced Study, Princeton. Address: School of Slavonic and East European Studies, University College London, Gower Street, London WC1E 6BT, England. E-mail: geoffreyhosking@mac.com

HOSKINS Bob (Robert William), b. 26 October 1942, Bury St Edmunds, Suffolk. Actor. m. (1) Jane Livesey, 1970, 1 son, 1 daughter: (2) Linda Barnwell, 1984, 1 son, 1 daughter. Career: Several stage roles at the National Theatre; Films include: National Health, 1973; Royal Flash, 1974; Zulu Dawn, The Long Good Friday, 1980; The Wall, 1982; The Honorary Consul, 1983; Lassiter, The Cotton Club, 1984; Brazil, The Woman Who Married Clark Gable, Sweet Liberty, 1985; Mona Lisa, 1986; A Prayer for the Dying, The Lonely Passion of Judith Hearne, Who Framed Roger Rabbit?, 1987; The Raggedy Rawney (director, actor and writer), 1988; Mermaids, 1989; Shattered, Heart Condition, The Projectionist, The Favour, The Watch and the Very Big Fish, 1990; Hook, 1991, The Inner Circle, Super Mario Brothers, 1992, Nixon, 1995, The Rainbow (also director), Michael, Cousin Bette, 1996; Twenty-four-seven, The Secret Agent, 1998; Felicia's Journey, Parting Shots, 1999; Enemy at the Gates, Last Orders, 2001; Where Eskimos Live, Maid in Manhattan, 2002; Sleeping Dictionary, Den of Lions, 2003; Vanity Fair, Beyond the Sea, 2004; Unleashed, Son of the Mask, Mrs Henderson Presents, Stay, 2005; Paris, I Love You, Garfield: A Tail of Two Kitties (voice), Hollywoodland, 2006; Sparkle, Outlaw, Ruby Blue, Go Go Tales, Doomsday, 2007; A Christmas Carol, 2009. TV appearances include: Omnibus – It Must be Something in the Water, 1971; Villains, Thick as Thieves, 1972; Schmoedipus, Shoulder to Shoulder, 1974; Pennies From Heaven, Peninsular, 1975; Sheppey, Flickers, 1980; Othello, 1981; The Beggers' Opera, 1983; Mussolini and I, 1984; The Changeling, World War Two: Then There Were Giants, 1993; David Copperfield, 1999; The Lost World (film), 2001; The Wind in the Willows, 2006; The Englishman's Boy, 2007. Stage: Old Wicked Songs, 1996. Honours: For Mona Lisa, New York Critics Award, Golden Globe Award, Best Actor Award, Cannes Festival, 1986; Variety Club Best Actor Award, 1997; Richard Harris Award for Outstanding Contribution by an Actor to British Film, British Film Awards, 2004.

HOSKINS Donald, b. 9 June 1932, Abertillery, Wales. Pianist; Conductor. m. Dinah Patricia Stanton, 1972. Education: BMus, including piano studies, Cardiff University, 1950-54; MA, University of Wales, 1974; PhD, University of Wales, 1990. Career: National Service, 1954-56; Directed choral groups, gave lectures and recitals and performed on television; Teacher, Tudor Grange Grammar School, Solihull, 1956-60; Presented music concerts; Adjudicated at school festivals; Founded local arts orchestra; Performed as soloist with Birmingham Philharmonic Orchestra, 1956-60; Guest Conductor on a visit to Wales, 1962; Director of Music, Hayes Grammar School, Middlesex, 1960-64; Founded and conducted local chamber orchestras and ensembles for concerts at major London venues; Solo recital, Paris, 1962; Lecturer, Eastbourne College of Education, East Sussex, 1964-67; Piano Soloist, Hillingdon Festival, 1964; Senior Lecturer, Department of Education, Barking Regional College of Technology, 1967; Song Recital Accompanist, Purcell Room, South Bank, 1972; Researcher, English musical theatre during 18th and early 19th centuries (MA and PhD degrees); Head, North East London Polytechnic Music Centre, 1978; Created wide range of musical teaching, training courses, and conducted many prestigious concerts with international artists; Established annual band courses and festivals by the University of East London concert band, 1980; Guest Conductor, London Mozart Players,

1983; Piano recital, Athens, 1984; Founded and Directed Aminta Chamber Orchestra (of London), 1985; Guest Piano Soloist with combined Desford Dowty, Fodens and Coventry brass bands conducted by Harry Mortimer, 1989; Soloist, inaugural concert, Zweibrucken University, Germany, 1994; Presented concert band performances in Witten, Germany, 1995, University of Kaiserslautern, 1997 and Royal Star and Garter Home, Richmond, 1998-2002; President, Redbridge Music Society; Visiting Professor, University of Provo, Salt Lake City, and Music Conservatorium, University of Cincinnati, 1994; Guest Conductor, Royal Philharmonic Concert Orchestra, 1995 and 1996, BBC Concert Orchestra, 1997 and 1998, London Philharmonic Choir, 1999, 2000 and 2002 (latter two concerts at Queen Elizabeth Hall, South Bank London); Retired, 1996; Continued as Consultant and Director of Concerts, University of East London; Presented 26th annual concert band performance at UEL and 22nd annual concert given by Aminta Chamber Orchestra, Church of St Martin-in-the-Fields, London, 2006; Directed children's concerts including 14 annual open-air events at Barking Abbey, Essex. Honours: Honorary degree, Doctor of Music, University of East London, Barbican Theatre, London, 2003; Guest conductor: Cantus Firmus Chamber Orchestra, Moscow, 2004; Presented with the Freedom of the Borough, London Borough of Barking and Dagenham, 2005; MBE for services to music, 2007; Conducted Aminta Concert Orchestra in 75th birthday concert at Queen Elizabeth Hall, London, 2007; Piano soloist, chamber music concert, Moscow Conservatoire, and conducted the Cantus Firmus chamber orchestra at the Bulgarian Cultural Centre, Moscow, 2007; Oratorio performances of Handel's Messiah and Haydn's "The Creation" with the Aminta Singers, 2009 and 2010; Presented concert of music by Mozart, Mendelssohn and Beethoven, St James's Church, Piccadilly, London, 2010. Address: Aminta, 12 Hurst Park, Midhurst, West Sussex GU29 0BP, England. E-mail: donaldhoskins@btinternet.com

HOTOLEANU Cristina, b. 17 May 1969, Cluj-Napoca, Romania. Medical Specialist. 1 son, 1 daughter. Education: Specialist, Internal Medicine, 1999; Senior Specialist, Internal Medicine, 2004; 2 competences in Ultrasound, 2007, 2006; Specialist in Diabetes and Nutrition Diseases, 2009; PhD, UMF, Cluj-Napoca, 2009. Appointments: Assistant Professor, 1998-2009, Lecturer, 2009-, UMF Cluj-Napoca. Publications: Main author and co-author, 7 books; More than 30 articles in medical journals. Honours: Awards for results of scientific activity; Listed in biographical dictionaries. Memberships: Colegiul Medicilor, Romanian Society of Angiology and Vascular Surgery; Societatea Romana de Semiologie si Medicina Interna. Address: Victor Babes 8, Cluj-Napoca, Romania.

HOTTOVY Tibor C, b. 15 September 1923, Budapest, Hungary. Building Research Scientist. m. Eva Bella, deceased 2004. Education: Master of Architecture, Polytechnic University School of Architecture, Budapest, 1948; Philosophy, Art, Environment, Forecasting, University of Human Sciences, Budapest, Royal Institute of Technology, University of Stockholm, University of Florida. Appointments: Architect, Ministry of Transport and Communication, Budapest, 1949-56; Architect and Planner, Private Town Planning and Structural Engineering Office, 1956-65; Senior Research Scientist, National Swedish Institute for Building Research, 1965-89; President and Owner, Unibell Information & Consult AB, 1989-2005. Publications: Numerous articles in professional journals including: The Role of Technologies in Shaping Regions; Information Cities and Intelligent Buildings, 1998; Intelligent Integrated Systems.

Memberships: Scientific Society; Hungarian Academy of Sciences; Swedish Association of Future Studies; Working Commissions of International Council for Building Research Studies and Documentation; The Swedish Computer Society; World Future Study Federation; Swedish Co-ordinator, World Future Society; The Swedish Society of Parliamentarians and Scientists. Address: Makrillvägen 16, Lidingö 181 30, Sweden. E-mail: t.hottovy@glocalnet.net

HOUGHTON Eric, b. 4 January 1930, West Yorkshire, England. Teacher; Author. m. Cecile Wolffe, 4 June 1954, 1 son, 1 daughter. Education: Bradford Grammar School, 1940-46; Sheffield City College of Education, 1950-52. Publications: The White Wall, 1961; Summer Silver, 1963; They Marched with Spartacus, 1963; A Giant Can Do Anything, 1975; The Mouse and the Magician, 1976; The Remarkable Feat of King Caboodle, 1978; Steps Out of Time, 1979; Time-Piece, 1981; Gates of Glass, 1987; Walter's Wand, 1989; The Magic Cheese, 1991; The Backwards Watch, 1991; Vincent the Invisible, 1993; Rosie and the Robbers, 1997; The Crooked Apple Tree, 1999. Honour: American Junior Book Award, 1964. Memberships: Society of Authors; Childrens Writers Group. Address: The Crest, 42 Collier Road, Hastings, East Sussex TN34 3JR, England.

HOUGHTON Ivan Timothy, b. 23 February 1942, Royal Leamington Spa, England. Physician. m. Teresa Wan. Education: St John's College, Cambridge, 1960-63; St Thomas's Hospital Medical School, 1963-1966, BA (Cantab), 1963; LMSSA (Lond), 1966; BChir (Cantab), 1966; MB (Cantab), 1966; MA (Cantab), 1967; FFARCS (Eng), 1970; LLB (Lond), 1987; MD, Chinese University of Hong Kong, 1993; DMCC, 1995; Dip Med Ed (Dundee), 1996; LLM (Wales), 2000; BSc (Lond Met) 1st Class Honours, 2005. Appointments include: Various positions as House Officer, Senior House Officer and Registrar, 1966-72; RAMC, 1972-2002, Brigadier L/RAMC, 1996-2002; Senior Specialist, Anaesthesia, 23 Parachute Field Ambulance, 1973-75; Regimental Medical Officer, 22 Special Air Service Regiment, 1975-76; Second in Command, 19 Airportable Field Ambulance, 1976-77; Consultant Anaesthetist, 6 Field Ambulance, 1977-78; Second in Command, 5 Field Force Ambulance, Münster, 1978-80; Consultant Anaesthetist and Second in Command, Military Wing, Musgrave Park Hospital, Belfast, 1981-82; Consultant Anaesthetist, British Military Hospital, Hong Kong, 1982-85; Senior Consultant Anaesthetist, British Military Hospital, Münster, 1985-87; Senior Consultant Anaesthetist, British Military Hospital, Hong Kong, 1987-94; Honorary Lecturer, Anaesthesia, 1982-85, Honorary Lecturer, Anaesthesia and Intensive Care, 1987-94, Chinese University of Hong Kong; Senior Consultant Anaesthetist, 1994-97, Commanding Officer, 1996-97, British Military Hospital, Rinteln; Clinical Director of Clinical Care, Royal Hospital Haslar, 1997-98; Regional Educational Adviser (Armed Forces), Royal College of Anaesthetists, 1998-2001; Consultant Adviser in Anaesthesia and Resuscitation to the Surgeon General, 1998-2001; Queen's Honorary Surgeon, 1999-2002; Editor, European Journal of Anaesthesiology, 2002-05; Currently: Visiting Research Fellow, Restoration and Conservation, Sir John Cass Department of Art, Media and Design, London Metropolitan University and Researcher, Paintings and Frames Conservation Section, Tate, London. Publications: Papers on field anaesthesia, ethnic differences in anaesthesia, history of anaesthesia and conservation. Memberships: Liveryman, Society of Apothecaries; Fellow, Royal Society of Medicine; Member, Army and Navy Club; Member, Hong Kong Jockey Club; Member, British Medical Association; Association of Anaesthetists of Great Britain and Ireland; Member, Medico-Legal Society; Member, The Institute of Conservation; Councillor, Medical Society of London. Address: Canary Riverside, Canary Wharf, London E14, England. E-mail: ivanhoughton@doctors.org.uk

HOUSE Michael Charles Clutterbuck, b. 31 May 1927, Weston-super-Mare, Somerset, England. Catholic Priest. Education: Hereford Cathedral School, 1943-45; Officers Training School, Bangalore, India, 1946; Kings College, London, 1948-51; Campion College, Osterley, 1952-53; St Mary's College, Oscott, Birmingham, 1954-60. Appointments: H M Military Commission, 1946; 2nd Battalion Queen's Royal West Surrey Regiment, Poona, India,1946-47, Dortmund, Germany, 1947-48; 2nd Battalion Queen's Royal Regiment, 1945-48; Ordained Priest, 1960; Assistant Priest: St Joseph's, Bristol, 1960-64, St Gerard Majella, Bristol, 1964-69, St Patrick's, Bristol, 1968-69; Financial Secretary to the Bishop of Clifton and Diocesan Trustees, 1969-80; Parish Priest: St George's, Warminster, 1980-87, St Mary's, Bath, 1987-91, St Thomas More, Marlborough, 1991-98; Religious Advisor to HTV West, 1966-98; Chairman of Governors, St Augustine's School, Trowbridge, 1985-87 and St Edward's School, Romsey, 1969-98; Catholic Chaplain to Marlborough College, 1991-98; National Conference of Priests, 1992-98; Retired from Active Ministry, 1998; . Publications: Articles in local papers and magazines. Honours: British Empire War Medal, 1939-45; Associateship of Kings College, London, 1951. Membership: Honorary Member, Portishead Cruising Club, Commodore, 1978-79. Address: Mirthios, Finikas 74060, Rethymnon, Crete, Greece.

HOWARD Anthony Michell, b. 12 February 1934, London, England. Biographer; Reviewer; Writer. m. Carol Anne Gaynor, 1965. Education: BA, Christ Church, Oxford, 1955. Appointments: Called to the Bar, Inner Temple, 1956; Political Correspondent, Reynolds News, 1958-59; Editorial Staff, Manchester Guardian, 1959-61; Political Correspondent, 1961-64, Assistant Editor, 1970-72, Editor, 1972-78, New Statesman; Whitehall Correspondent, 1965, Sunday Times; Washington Correspondent, 1966-69, Deputy Editor, 1981-88, Observer; Editor, The Listener, 1979-81; Reporter, BBC TV News and Current Affairs, 1989-92; Obituaries Editor, The Times, 1993-99. Publications: The Making of the Prime Minister (with Richard West), 1965; The Crossman Diaries: Selections from the Diaries of a Cabinet Minister (editor), 1979; Rab: The Life of R A Butler, 1987; Crossman: The Pursuit of Power, 1990; The Times Lives Remembered (editor with David Heaton), 1993; Basil Hume: The Monk Cardinal, 2005. Contributions to: Books, newspapers, and journals. Honours: Harkness Fellowship, USA, 1960; Commander of the Order of the British Empire, 1997; Hon LLD, Nottingham, 2001; Hon DLitt, Leicester, 2003. Address: 11 Campden House Court, 42 Gloucester Walk, London W8 4HU, England.

HOWARD Catherine Audrey, b. 5 February 1953, Huddersfield, England. Retired Government Officer. m. Leslie Howard, 1987. Education: Elland Grammar School; Harold Pitchforth School of Commerce; Ashlar and Spen Valley Further Education Institute; Royal Society of Arts Diplomas. Appointments: Clerk, Treasury Department, 1969-70, Clerk, Housing Department, 1970-74, Elland Urban District Council; Clerk, Telephonist, Housing Department, Calderdale Metropolitan Borough Council, 1974-83; Social Work Assistant; Social Services Department, Calderdale, 1983-88. Publications: Elland in Old Picture Postcards, 1983; Poetry: Down By the Old Mill Stream, 1993; The Flamborough Longsword Dance, 1994; Sacrifice for Christianity, 1994; My Pennine Roots, 1994; The Old and the New, 1994; Having Faith, 1994; The Might of the Meek, 1995; Tough as Old Boots, 1995; Portrait of All Hallows, 1996; Childhood Memories, 1996; Old Ways in Modern Days, 1996; Northern Cornucopia, 1996; A Glimpse of Spring, 1998; Poetry From Yorkshire, 1999. Contributions to: Mercedes-Benz Gazette, 1996; Commemorative Poem presented to Bridlington Public Library on the centenary of Amy Johnson, titled Wonderful Amy, 2003. Honours: National Poet of the Year Commendations, 1996 (3 times); National Open Competition Commendations, 1996, 1997; Robert Bloomfield Memorial Awards Commendation, 1998. Address: 17 Woodlands Close, Bradley Grange, Bradley, Huddersfield, West Yorkshire HD2 1QS, England.

HOWARD Deborah (Janet), b. 26 February 1946, London, England. Architectural Historian; Writer. m. Malcolm S Longair, 1975, 1 son, 1 daughter. Education: BA, Honours, 1968, MA, 1972, Newnham College, Cambridge; MA, 1969, PhD, 1973, University of London. Appointments: Professor of Architectural History, University of Cambridge, 2001-; Fellow, St John's College, Cambridge; Head of Department of History of Art, University of Cambridge. Publications: Jacopo Sansovino: Architecture and Patronage in Renaissance Venice, 1975, 2nd edition, 1987; The Architectural History of Venice, 1980, 3rd edition, 1987, revised and enlarged edition, 2002; Scottish Architecture from the Reformation to the Restoration, 1560-1660, 1995; Venice and the East: The Impact on the Islamic World on Venetian Architecture 1100-1500, 2000. Contributions to: Professional journals. Honour: Honorary Fellow, Royal Incorporation of Architects of Scotland; Fellow, Royal Society of Edinburgh. Memberships: Fellow, Society of Antiquarians of Scotland; Fellow, Society of Antiquaries. Address: St John's College, Cambridge CB2 1TP, England.

HOWARD Grahame Charles William, b. 15 May 1953, London, England. Consultant Clinical Oncologist. 3 sons. Education: King Edward VI School, Norwich, 1960-70; St Thomas Hospital Medical School, London, 1970-76; London University Degrees: BSc, MBBS, MD. Appointments: Registrar, The Royal Free Hospital, London; Senior Registrar and Research Fellow, Addenbrooke's Hospital Cambridge; Honorary Senior Lecturer, University of Edinburgh; Consultant Clinical Oncologist, 1987-, Clinical Director,The Edinburgh Cancer Centre, 1999-2005; Clinical Director, Cancer Services, 2005-07. Publications: Author, The Tales of Dod; Over 100 publications in scientific journals on various topics related to cancer; several book chapters including oncology chapter in Davidson's Principles and Practice of Medicine; Co-author of several evidence based guidelines for various cancers. Professional qualifications: MRCP; FRCP (Ed); FRCR; Assistant Editor, Clinical Oncology; Previous Chair, Scottish Intercollegiate Guideline Network, Cancer Speciality Subgroup; South East Scotland Urology Oncology Group. Address: 4 Ormelie Terrace, Edinburgh, EH15 2EX, Scotland.

HOWARD John Winston (The Honourable), b. 26 July 1939, Earlwood, New South Wales, Australia. Prime Minister of Australia. m. Alison Janette Parker, 1971, 2 sons, 1 daughter. Education: LLB, University of Sydney, 1961. Appointments: Solicitor, Supreme Court, New South Wales, 1962; Partner, solicitors' firm, 1968-74; MP for Bennelong, New South Wales, Federal Parliament, 1974-; Minister for Business and Consumer Affairs, 1975-77; Minister Assisting Prime Minister, 1977; Minister of State for Special Trade Negotiations, 1977; Federal Treasurer, 1977-83; Minister for Finance, 1979; Deputy Leader of the Opposition, 1983-85; Leader of the Opposition, 1985-89, 1995-96; Leader, Liberal Party, 1985-89; Prime Minister, Government of Australia, 1996-. Memberships: Member State Executive, New South

Wales Liberal Party, 1963-74; Vice President, New South Wales Division, Liberal Party, 1972-74. Honours: Centenary Medal, 2001; Named one of the most influential people, TIME magazine, 2005; Star of the Soloman Islands, 2005. Address: St MG8 Parliament House, Canberra, ACT 2600, Australia.

HOWARD Lord Michael, Baron Howard of Lympne, b. 7 July 1941. m. Sandra, 1 son, 1 stepson, 1 daughter. Education: Llanelli Grammar School; Peterhouse, Cambridge. Appointments: Called to the Bar, 1964; Appointed QC, 1982; Elected Member of Parliament, Folkestone and Hythe, 1983; Parliamentary Private Secretary to the Solicitor General, 1984; Parliamentary Under Secretary of State, Department of Trade and Industry, 1985; Minister of State for Local Government, Minister of State for Water and Planning, Department of Environment, 1987-90; Secretary of State for Employment, Member of Cabinet, 1990-92; Secretary of State for the Environment, 1992-93; Home Secretary, 1993-97; Shadow Foreign Secretary, 1997-99; Shadow Chancellor, 2001-03; Leader of the Conservative Party, 2003-05; Deputy Chairman, Entre Gold Inc; Chairman, Northern Racing Limited; Chairman, Luup Ltd; Member, International Advisory Board, Thorium Inc. Honours: CH, 2011. Address: House of Lords, London, SW1A 0AA, England. E-mail: howardm@parliament.uk

HOWARD Michael Newman, b. 10 June 1947, London, England. Barrister; Arbitrator. Education: Clifton College; MA, BCL, Magdalen College, Oxford. Appointments: Queens Counsel, 1986-; Member, Panel of Lloyd's Salvage Arbitrators, 1987-2009; Recorder of Crown Court, 1993-; Visiting Professor, Maritime Law, University College, London, 1996-99; Bencher, Gray's Inn, 1996-; Leader of Admiralty Bar, 2000-; Visiting Professor of Maritime Law, Tulane University, 2011. Publications: Phipson on Evidence, 1983, 2000; Force Majeure and Frustration of Contract, 1991, 1995; Halsbury's Laws of England: Title – Damages, Commercial Court and Arbitration Pleadings; Title – Time Charters; Contributor, Palmer on Bailment (3rd edition, 2010); Articles, notes, reviews, etc in legal journals. Memberships: Oxford & Cambridge Club; RAC; Garrick Club. Address: Quadrant Chambers, 10 Fleet Street, London EC4Y 1AU, England. E-mail: michael.howard@quadrantchambers.com

HOWARD Norman, b. 25 November 1926, London, England. Medical Practitioner; Consultant Clinical Oncologist. m. Anita, deceased, 2 sons. Education: BM BCh, MA, 1952; DM, 1965, Oxford University; FFR, 1958; FRCR, 1975. Appointments: House Physician and Surgeon, 1953-54, Registrar, 1954-56, University College Hospital; Registrar and Senior Registrar, Royal Marsden Hospital, 1956-63; Consultant, Radiotherapy and Oncology, Charing Cross Hospital, 1963-91, Wembley Hospital, 1964-91; Honorary Consultant, Royal Marsden Hospital, 1970-; Consultant in Clinical Oncology, Cromwell Hospital, 1982-2001; Chairman: Royal College of Radiologists Research Appeal, 1993-2003, Gunnar Nilsson Cancer Research Trust Fund, Medical Staff Committee, Charing Cross Hospital, 1974-79. Publications: Mediastinal Obstruction in Lung Cancer, 1967; Numerous chapters and articles concerning cancer, radiotherapy and radioisotopes. Honour: Commendatore Order of Merit Republic of Italy, 1976. Memberships: Royal College of Radiologists; Royal Society of Medicine; British Medical Association. Address: 5A Clarendon Road, London W11 4JA, England. E-mail: norman.anita@btinternet.com

HOWARD Ron, b. 1 March 1954, Duncan, Oklahoma, USA. Film Actor; Director; Producer. m. Cheryl Alley, 1975, 2 sons, 2 daughters. Education: University of Southern California; Los Angeles Valley College. Appointments: Director, Co-Author, Star, Grand Theft Auto, 1977; Regular TV series The Andy Griffith Show, 1960-68, The Smith Family, 1971-72, Happy Days, 1974, and many other TV appearances. Creative Works: Films directed include: Night Shift, 1982; Splash, 1984; Cocoon, 1985; Gung Ho, 1986; Return to Mayberry, 1986; Willow, 1988; Parenthood, 1989; Backdraft, 1991; Far and Away (also co-producer), 1992; The Paper, 1994; Apollo 13, 1995; A Beautiful Mind, 2001; The Missing, 2003; Cinderella Man, 2005; Film appearances include: The Journey, 1959; Five Minutes to Live, 1959; Music Man, 1962; The Courtship of Eddie's Father, 1963; Village of the Giants, 1965; Wild Country, 1971; Mother's Day, 1974; American Graffiti, 1974; The Spikes Gang, 1976; Eat My Dust, 1976; The Shootist, 1976; More American Graffiti, 1979; Leo and Loree (TV), 1980; Act of Love, 1980; Skyward, 1981; Through the Magic Pyramid (director, executive producer), 1981; When Your Lover Leaves (co-executive producer), 1983; Return to Mayberry, 1986; Ransom, 1996; Osmosis Jones (voice), 2001; Arrested Development (TV) 2003-06. Ed TV, 1999. Honours include: Outstanding Directorial Achievement in Motion Picture Award, Directors Guild of America, 1996; Academy Awards for Best Director and Best Film (producer), 2002; DGA Best Director Award, 2002; National Medal of Arts, 2003. Address: c/o Peter Dekom, Bloom Dekom & Hergott, 150 South Rodeo Drive, Beverly Hills, CA 90212, USA.

HOWARTH Nigel John Graham, b. 12 December 1936, Manchester, England. Circuit Judge. m. Janice Mary Hooper, 2 sons, 1 daughter. Education: LLB, 1957, LLM, 1959, University of Manchester; Bar Finals, 1st class honours, Inns of Court Law School, 1960; Macaskie Scholar, 1960, Atkin Scholar, 1961, Grays Inn. Appointments: Called to the Bar, Grays Inn, 1960; Private practice, Chancery Bar, Manchester, 1961-92; Assistant Recorder, 1983-89; Acting Deemster, Isle of Man, 1985, 1989; Recorder of Crown Court, 1989-92; Circuit Judge, 1992-. Memberships: Vice President, Disabled Living; Manchester Pedestrian Club; Northern Chancery Bar Association, Chairman, 1990-92. Address: c/o Circuit Administrator, Northern Circuit Office, 15 Quay Street, Manchester, M60 9FD, England. E-mail: nhowarth@lix.compulink.co.uk

HOWE Elspeth Rosamund Morton (Baroness Howe of Idlicote), b. 8 February 1932. Member of the House of Lords. m. Lord Howe of Aberavon, 1953, 1 son, 2 daughters. Education: BSc, London School of Economics, 1985. Appointments: Secretary to Principal, A A School of Architecture, 1952-55; Deputy Chairman, Equal Opportunities Commission, Manchester, 1975-79; President, Federation of Recruitment and Employment Services, 1980-94; Non-Executive Director, United Biscuits plc, 1988-94; Non-Executive Director, Kingfisher plc, 1986-2000; Non-Executive Director, Legal and General, 1989-97; Chairman, The BOC Foundation for the Environment, 1990-2003; Chairman, The Broadcasting Standards Commission, 1993-99. Publications: 2 pamphlets; Co-author, Women on the Board, 1990; Articles for newspapers; Lectures, speeches, television and radio broadcasts. Honours: Honorary Doctorates: London University, 1990; The Open University, 1993; Bradford University, 1993; Aberdeen University, 1994; Liverpool University, 1994; Sunderland University, 1995; South Bank University, 1995; Honorary Fellow, London School of Economics, 2001. Memberships: President, the UK Committee of UNICEF, 1993-2002; Vice Chairman,

The Open University, 2001-03; Trustee, The Architectural Association; Trustee, The Ann Driver Trust; Institute of Business Ethics; President, The Peckham Settlement; NCVO Advisory Council. Address: House of Lords, London SW1A 0PW, England. E-mail: howee@parliament.uk

HOWE, 7th Earl, Frederick Richard Curzon, b. 29 January 1951, London, England. Parliamentarian. m. Elizabeth Helen, 1 son, 3 daughters. Education: BA, 1973, MA, 1977, Christ Church College, Oxford. Appointments: Barclays Bank plc, 1973-87; Director, Adam & Co plc, 1987-90; Government Whip, 1991-92; Parliamentary Secretary, Ministry of Agriculture and Fisheries, 1992-95; Parliamentary Under Secretary of State for Defence, 1995-97; Opposition Spokesman for Health and Social Services, 1997-; Chairman, LAPADA, 1999-. Address: House of Lords, London SW1A 0PW, England.

HOWE Geoffrey (Lord Howe of Aberavon), b. 20 December 1926. Politician; Lawyer m. Elspeth Rosamund Morton Shand, 1953, 1 son, 2 daughters. Education: MA, LLB, Trinity Hall, Cambridge. Appointments: Lieutenant, Royal Signals, 1945-48; Chairman, Cambridge University Conservative Association, 1951; Chairman, Bow Group, 1955; Contested Aberavon, 1955, 1959; Managing Director, Crossbow, 1957-60; Editor, 1960-62; Called to the Bar, Middle Temple, 1952, QC, 1965, Bencher, 1969, Reader, 1993; Member, General Council of the Bar, 1957-61; Member, Council of Justice, 1963-70; MP, Bebington, 1964-66, Reigate, 1970-74, Surrey East, 1974-92; Secretary, Conservative Parliamentary Health and Social Security Committee, 1964-65; Opposition Front Bench Spokesman on labour and social services, 1965-66; (Latey) Interdepartmental Committee on Age of Majority, 1965-67; Deputy Chairman, Glamorgan Quarter Sessions, 1966-70; (Street) Committee on Racial Discrimination, 1967; (Cripps) Conservative Committee on Discrimination Against Women, 1968-69; Chair, Ely Hospital, Cardiff, Inquiry, 1969; Solicitor-General, 1970-72; Minister for Trade and Consumer Affairs, Department of Trade and Industry, 1972-74; Opposition front bench spokesman on social services, 1974-75, on Treasury and Economic Affairs, 1975-79; Director, Sun Alliance & London Insurance Co Ltd, 1974-79; AGB Research Ltd, 1974-79; EMI Ltd, 1976-79; Chancellor of the Exchequer, 1979-83; Chair, Interim Committee, IMF, 1982-83; Secretary of State, Foreign and Commonwealth Affairs, 1983-89; Lord President of the Council, Leader of House of Commons, Deputy Prime Minister, 1989-90; Visiting Fellow, John F Kennedy School of Government, Harvard University, 1991-92; Glaxo Holdings, 1991-95; Herman Phleger Visiting Professor, Stanford Law School, California, 1993; Glaxo Wellcome plc, 1995-96; BICC plc, 1991-97; Visitor, SOAS, University of London, 1991-2001; Special Adviser, International Affairs, Jones, Day, Reavis & Pogue, 1991-2001; Advisory Council, Bertelsmann Foundation, 1992-97; J P Morgan International Advisory Council, 1992-2001; Chair, Framlington Russian Investment Fund, 1994-2003; Chair, Steering Committee, Tax Law Rewrite Project, Inland Revenue, 1996-; Fuji Wolfensohn International European Advisory Board, 1996-98; Carlyle Group, European Advisory Board, 1997-2001; Fuji Bank International Advisory Council, 1999-. Publications: Conflict of Loyalty (memoirs), 1994; Various political pamphlets. Honours include: Grand Cross, Order of Merit (Portugal), 1987; Hon LLD, Wales, 1988; Honorary Freeman, Port Talbot, 1992; Grand Cross, Order of Merit, Germany, 1992; Life Peer, 1992; Hon DCL, City, 1993; Joseph Bech Prize, FVS Stifting, Hamburg, 1993; Companion of Honour, 1996; Order of Public Service, Ukraine, 2001. Memberships: International Advisory Council; Member, Council of Management, Private Patients' Plan, 1969-70; Honorary Vice President, 1974-92, President, 1992-, Association for Consumer Research; National Union of Conservative and Unionist Associations, 1983-84; Institute of International Studies, Stanford University, California, 1990-; Patron, Enterprise Europe, 1990-2004; Vice President: RUSI, 1991-; Joint President, Wealth of Nations Foundation, 1991-; Member, Advisory Council, Presidium of Supreme Rada of Ukraine, 1991-97; Member, Steering Committee, Project Liberty, 1991-97; Chair, Advisory Board, English Centre for Legal Studies, Warsaw University, 1992-99; Centre for European Policy Studies, 1992-; English College Foundation in Prague, 1992-; GB China Centre, 1992-; Trustee: Cambridge Commonwealth Trust, 1993-; Cambridge Overseas Trust, 1993-; Paul Harris Fellow, Rotary International, 1995; Thomson Foundation, 1995-, Chair, 2004-; President, Academy of Experts, 1996-; Honorary Fellow: UCW, Swansea, 1996; President: Conservative Political Centre National Advisory Committee, 1997-79; Patron, UK Metric Association, 1999-; UCW, Cardiff, 1999; American Bar Foundation, 2000; Chartered Institute of Taxation, 2000; SOAS, 2003. Address: House of Lords, London SW1A 0PW, England.

HOWELL David Arthur Russell (Lord Howell of Guildford), b. 18 January 1936, London, England. Economist; Journalist; Author. m. Davina Wallace, 1 son, 2 daughters. Education: King's College, Foundation Scholar. Appointments: Member of Parliament for Guildford, 1966-97; Parliamentary Secretary, Civil Service Department, 1970-72; Minister of State, Northern Ireland, 1972-74; Secretary of State for Energy, 1979-81; Secretary of State for Transport, 1981-83; Chairman, House of Commons Foreign Affairs Select Committee, 1987-97; Chairman, UK-Japan 21st Century Group, 1989-2001; Visiting Fellow, Nuffield College, Oxford, 1991-99; Director, Monks Investment Trust, 1993-; Advisory Director, UBS Warburg, 1996-2000; Chairman, Lords European Committee, Sub-Committee, 1998-2000; Director, John Laing plc, 1999-2002; Trustee, Shakespeare Globe Theatre, 2000-; Chief Opposition Spokesman on Foreign Affairs, House of Lords, 2000-. Publications: Columnist: The Japan Times; Wall Street Journal; International Herald Tribune; Books: Freedom and Capital, 1979; Blind Victory, 1986; The Edge of Now, 2000; Numerous pamphlets and articles. Honours: Privy Counsellor, 1979; Created Peer of the Realm, 1997; Grand Cordon of the Order of the Sacred Treasure, Japan, 2001. Memberships: Beefsteak Club; County Club, Guildford. Address: House of Lords, London SW1A 0PW, England. E-mail: howelld@parliament.uk

HOWELL Sister Veronica (formerly known as Sister Mary Aidan), b. 23 May 1924, Woolwich, London, England. Educator. Education: Mount Pleasant Training College, Liverpool; Corpus Christi Theological College, London; Heythrop Theological College, London University; Licentiate of the Royal College of Music. Appointments: Became a member of the Congregation of the Daughters of Jesus, 1944; Teacher, Our Lady of Lourdes Convent School and Sacred Heart Infants School, Colne, Lancashire, 1946-51; Teacher, St Teresa's, Princes Risborough, Buckinghamshire, 1951-56; Teacher, St Stephen's Primary School, Welling, Kent, 1956-60; Teacher, Sts Thomas More and John Fisher Secondary School, Colne, Lancashire, 1960-63; Head Mistress, St Stephen's Primary School, Welling, Kent, 1963-75; Assistant to National Director and Training Officer of Catholic Information Services of England and Wales also helping to produce audio-visual material for spiritual retreats, 1975-79; Vocation's Director for the English Province of the Daughters of Jesus (Religious Congregation), 1979-84; Communications and Press Officer for female and male religious of England and Wales for the Pope's visit to England and Wales, 1982; Parish Assistant of Our Lady of Grace Parish, Governor of St Augustine's First and Middle School, Sister in Charge of Religious Community, High Wycombe, Buckinghamshire, Co-ordinator of Communications for Diocese of Northampton, Co-Editor of Diocesan newspaper, Member of Steering Committee winning the charter for a Christian radio station, 1986-92; Sister in Charge of Community and Parish Sister, Our Lady Help of Christians Parish, Rickmansworth, Hertfordshire, 1993-99; Parish Sister to Sacred Heart Church, Colne, Lancashire, 2000-; Governor of St Thomas More Catholic Humanities College, 2001-. Publication: Founder and former Co-editor, The Vine newspaper, Northampton Diocese. Memberships: Congregation of the Daughters of Jesus; Founder and Chairperson, Association of Christian Education, Welling, Kent, 1970-75; Co-Founder, Day Centre for Elderly Mentally Infirm, High Wycombe, Buckinghamshire, 1988-92; Caring Church Week Groups, 1979-84; Association of Head Teachers, 1963-75. Address: Southworth, 6 Netherheys Close, Colne, Lancashire, BB8 9QY, England. E-mail: vghowell@yahoo.uk.com

HOWLETT Neville Stanley, b. 17 April 1927, Prestatyn, Wales. Retired Air Vice-Marshal. m. Sylvia, 1 son, 1 daughter. Education: Liverpool Institute High School and Peterhouse, Cambridge, England. Appointments: Pilot Training, Royal Air Force, 1945-48; 32 and 64 Fighter Squadrons, 1948-56; RAF Staff College, 1957; Squadron Commander, 229 (Fighter) OCU, 1958-59; OC Flying Wing, RAF Coltishall, 1961-63; Directing staff, RAF Staff College, 1967-69; Station Commander, RAF Leuchars, 1970-72; Royal College of Defence Studies, 1973; Director of Operations, Air Defence and Overseas, 1973-74; Air Attaché, Washington DC, USA, 1975-77; Director, Management Support of Intelligence, 1978-80; Director General, Personal Services, 1980-82; Retired, 1982; Member, Lord Chancellors Panel of Independent Inquiry Inspectors, 1982-95; Member, Pensions Appeal Tribunal, 1988-2001. Honour: CB. Memberships: Royal Air Force Club; Royal Air Forces Association, Vice-President, 1984-, Chairman Executive Committee, 1990-97, Chairman Central Council, 1999-2001; Royal Air Force Benevolent Fund; Officers Association; Phyllis Court Club, Henley; Huntercombe Golf Club. Address: Milverton, Bolney Trevor Drive, Lower Shiplake, Oxon RG9 3PG, England.

HOY Sir Chris (Christopher Andrew), b. 23 March 1976, Edinburgh, Scotland. Track Cyclist. m. Sarra Kemp, 2010. Education: George Watson's College, Edinburgh; University of St Andrews; BSc (Hons), University of Edinburgh, 1999. Career: World Championships: Silver (team sprint), 1999; Silver (team sprint), 2000; Bronze (team sprint), 2001; 2 golds (1km time trial and team sprint), 2002; Bronze (team sprint), 2003; Gold (1km time trial) and Bronze (team sprint), 2004; Gold (team sprint) and Bronze (1km time trial), 2005; Gold (1km time trial) and Silver (team sprint), 2006; 2 golds (keirin and 1km time trial) and Silver (team sprint), 2007; 2 Golds (sprint and keirin) and Silver (team sprint), 2008; Gold (keirin) and Bronze (team sprint), 2010; 3 Silvers (keirin, team sprint and sprint), 2011; Gold (keirin) and Bronze (sprint), 2012; Olympic Games: Silver (team sprint), 2000; Gold (1km track time trial), 2004; Gold (team sprint, keirin and sprint), 2008; 2 Golds (team sprint and keirin), 2012; Commonwealth Games: Gold (1km time trial) and Bronze (team sprint), 2002; Gold (team sprint) and Bronze (1km time trial), 2006. Publications: Chris Hoy: the Autobiography, 2009. Honours: Honorary DSc, University of Edinburgh, 2005; MBE, 2005; Sportsman of the year, 2008; BBC Sports Personality of the Year, 2008; Honorary DSc, University of St Andrews, 2009; Knighted, 2009; University of Edinburgh's Sports Hall of Fame, 2009.

HØYE Gudrun Kristine, b. 25 December 1970, Trondheim, Norway. Physicist. m. Andrei Leonidovich Fridman. Education: MSc, Physics, Norwegian Institute of Technology, 1994; PhD, Astrophysics, Norwegian University of Science and Technology, 1999. Appointments: Technical Student, European Laboratory for Particle Physics, Switzerland, 1993-94; Stipendiat (PhD), Astrophysics, Norwegian University of Science and Technology, 1995-99; Senior Scientist, Forsvarets Forskningsinstitutt, Norway, 1999-. Publications: Numerous articles in professional journals. Honours: Award for Best Paper, International Academy of Astronautics, 2001; Best Technical/Scientific Report, Forsvarets Forskningsinstitutt, 2001, 2003. Address: Forsvarets Forskningsinstitutt, Information Management Division, PO Box 25, NO-2027 Kjeller, Norway. E-mail: gkh@ffi.no

HOZAWA Koji, b. 8 August 1956, Morioka, Japan. Medical Doctor. m. Hiromi Hozawa, 1 son, 2 daughters. Education: MD, Tohoku University School of Medicine, Sendai Japan, 1975-81; Degree of Science, Tohoku University Graduate School of Medicine, Sendai, Japan, 1983-87; Research Fellow, Harvard Medical School, Boston, USA, 1986-88; Visiting Scholar, Washington University, Seattle, USA, 1992. Appointments: Assistant Professor, 1995-2001, Associate Professor, 2001-2002, Department of Otolaryngology, Tohoku University School of Medicine, Sendai, Japan; Chief Director, Department of Otolaryngology, Sendai Shakai Hoken Hospital, Sendai, Japan, 2002-; Visiting Lecturer, Department of Otolaryngology, Chinese Medical School, Shenyang, China, 1997-2000; Lecturer, Japan International Co-operation Agency, Tokyo, Japan, 1997-2000; Authorised Researcher, Ministry of Health and Welfare of Japan, 1999-2001; Secretary General, International Symposium on Recent Advances in Otitis Media, 1998-2000. Publications: Numerous articles in scientific journals include most recently: Hearing and glycoconjugates, 1993; Sympathetic and CGRP-positive nerve supply to the endolymphatic sac of guinea pig, 1993; Pathogenesis of attic cholesteatoma, 1999; Is Cholesteatoma a Cytokine Disease? – in vitro Model of Cholesteatoma, 2002; Editor, Recent Advances in Otitis Media: Proceedings of Otitis Media 2001, 2001. Honours: Silver Prize, Tohoku University School of Medicine Scholarship, 1988; Listed in Who's Who publications and biographical dictionaries. Memberships: International Otopathology Society; Otolaryngological Society of Japan, Member Public Relations Section, 1997-2002, Journal Reviewer, 2004-; Japanese Bronchoesophageal Society, Councillor, 2004-; Otological Society of Japan, Secretary General, 1997-98; Japan Society of Stomato-Pharyngology, Secretary General, 1998-99; Japan Society for Equilibrium Research, Committee, 2001-2003; Japan Society of Laryngology. Address: 2-14-18-303, Kokubun-cho, Aoba-ku, Sendai, 980-0803, Japan.

HOZUMI Motoo, b. 12 March 1933, Fukushima, Japan. Cancer Research. m. Sakiko Wakabayashi, 1 son, 2 daughters. Education: BSc, 1956, MSc, 1958, DSc, 1961, Tokyo University of Education. Appointments: Research Member, National Cancer Center Research Institute, Tokyo, 1962-64; Chief, Central Laboratory, National Cancer Center Research Institute, Tokyo, 1964-75; Research Member, Roswell Park Memorial Institute, Buffalo, New York, 1965-67; Director, Department of Chemotherapy, Saitama Cancer Center Research Institute, Japan, 1975-93; Visiting Professor, Showa University School of Medicine, Tokyo,

1988-2001; Director, Saitama Cancer Center Research Institute, 1990-93. Publications: Over 300 papers and books on cancer research. Honours: Princess Takamatsu Cancer Research Foundation Prize, Tokyo, 1974. Memberships: Japanese Cancer Association; Japanese Haematological Society; American Cancer Association; American Association for the Advancement of Science. Address: 12-288 Fukasaku, Minuma, Saitama, Saitama 337, Japan.

HRH The Duchess of Cambridge, Catherine, Countess of Strathearn, b. 9 January 1982, Berkshire, England. m. HRH Prince William of Wales, The Duke of Cambridge, 2011. Education: St Andrew's Prep School; Marlborough College; Bachelor's degree, History of Art, University of St Andrews, Fife, Scotland, 2005. Appointments: Accessory Buyer, Jigsaw, 2006-08; Marketing Officer, Party Pieces, -2011.

HRH THE PRINCESS ROYAL, Anne Elizabeth Alice Louise, b. 15 August 1950. m. (1) Mark Anthony Peter Phillips, 1973, dissolved 1992, 1 son, 1 daughter, (2) Timothy James Hamilton Laurence, 1992. Education: Benenden. Career: Equestrian: Member, 3-day event team, Olympic Games, Montreal, 1976; Founder and Course Designer, Gatcombe Park One-Day Event, 1995. Appointments: UK Member, IOC, 1988-;Commodore-in-Chief, Portsmouth, 2006-; Colonel-in-Chief (UK): King's Royal Hussars, 1992-, Royal Corps of Signals, 1977-, Royal Logistic Corps, 1993-, Royal Army Veterinary Corps, 2003-; Colonel-in-Chief (Commonwealth): 8 Canadian Hussars (Princess Louise's), 1972-, Canadian Forces Communications and Electronics Branch, 1977-, Grey and Simcoe Foresters, 1972-, Royal Regina Rifle Regiment, 1982-, Canadian Forces Medical Branch, Royal Australian Corps Signals, 1977-, Royal New Zealand Corps of Signals, 1977-, Royal New Zealand Nursing Corps, 1977-, Royal Newfoundland Regiment; Affiliated Colonel-in-Chief: Queen's Gurkha Signals, 1993-, Queen's Own Gurkha Signals, 1993-; Colonel, Blues and Royals, 1998-; Royal Colonel: Scots Borderers 1st Battalion, 2006-; 52nd Lowland 6th Battalion, The Royal Regiment of Scotland, 2006-; Royal Honorary Colonel, University of London OTC, 1989-; Royal Honorary Air Commodore: RAF Lyneham, 1977-, London University Air Squadron, 1993-; Commandant-in-Chief, First Aid Nursing Yeomanry 1981-; Rear Admiral and Chief Commandant Women in the RN, 1993-; Sponsor: HMS Albion, HMS Talent; Presidcnt, National Equine Forum, 2009-; Patron, Save the Children Fund, 1970-, and other charities; Chancellor, University of London, 1981-. Publications: Riding Through My Life, 1991. Honours: Sportswoman of the Year Sports Writers' Association; Daily Express and World Sport; BBC Sports Personality of the Year; GCVO, 1974; Silver Jubilee Medal, 1977; Princess Royal, 1987; New Zealand Commemorative Medal, 1990; CD, 1990; QSO, 1990; KG, 1994; KT, 2000; Golden Jubilee Medal, 2002; GCSt.

HŘIB Jiří Emil, b. 16 September 1942, Frýdek-Místek, Czech Republic. Plant Physiologist. m. Marie Malá, 1970, 1 daughter. Education: Engineer, 1966, PhD, 1973, University of Agriculture, Brno (now Mendel University, Brno). Appointments: Scientist Aspirant, Scientific Film Laboratory, Institute of Scientific Instruments, 1967-73, Scientist, Institute of Vertebrate Zoology, 1973-74, Scientist, Institute of Botany, 1974-83, Scientist, Institute of Experimental Phytotechnics, 1984-87, Scientist, Institute of Systematic and Ecological Biology, 1987-91, Czechoslovak Academy of Sciences, Brno; Scientist, Institute of Plant Genetics, 1991-97, Principal Scientist, Institute of Plant Genetics and Biotechnology, 1997-98, External Scientific Co-worker, Institute of Plant Genetics and Biotechnology, 1999-, Slovak Academy of Sciences, Nitra. Publications: Over 100 articles in professional scientific journals; The Co-Cultivation of Wood-Rotting Fungi with Tissue Cultures of Forest Tree Species, 1990; Research films: (author) Ontogeny of the Alga Scenedesmus quadricauda, 1973; Co-author, Regeneration of the Cap in the Alga Acetabularia mediterranea, 1980; 1 patent. Honours: Research Board of Advisors, American Biographical Institute, 1999; Consulting Editor, Contemporary Who's Who, 2003; FABI, 2005; Consulting Editor, International Directory of Experts and Expertise, 2006; Dr hc, Yorker International University, Milano, 2010. Memberships: Czech Society for Scientific Cinematography, Brno; Czech Botanical Society, Prague; International Association for Plant Biotechnology; International Association of Sexual Plant Reproduction Research; New York Academy of Sciences; Czechoslovak Biological Society, Brno; Czech Phycological Society, Prague. Address: Ukrajinská 17, 625 00 Brno, Czech Republic.

HSU Wen-Ping, b. 13 August 1963, Kaohsiung, Taiwan. Professor. m. Pei-Hua Tsai, 2 daughters. Education: Bachelor, Chemical Engineering, National Taiwan University, Taipei, Taiwan, 1985; Master, Chemical Engineering, 1990, PhD, Chemical Engineering, 1992, Polytechnic University, New York, USA. Appointments: Associate Professor, 1993-99, Professor, 1999-2004, Chairman, 2002-04, Department of Applied Chemistry, Chia-Nan University of Pharmacy & Science, Tainan, Taiwan; Professor, 2004-, Chairman, 2010-, Department of Chemical Engineering, Curator of Library, 2007, Dean of Research and Development, 2007-2008, National United University, Miao-Li, Taiwan. Publications: About 42 scientific papers. Honours: Listed in national and international biographical directories. Memberships: Polymer Society, Taiwan, Republic of China; Taiwan Institute of Chemical Engineers. E-mail: wenping@nuu.edu.tw

HU Bingkun, b. 15 July 1935, Shanghai, China. Qigong Therapist; Qigong Master. m. Linda Susan Weems-Hu, 1 daughter. Education: BA, English and Linguistics, Fudan University, China, 1956; MA, Folklore and Cultural Anthropology, University of California in Berkeley, USA, 1985; PhD, Psychology, Sierra University, Costa Mesa, USA, 1987. Appointments: Associate Professor, Shanghai Science and Technology Institute and Fudan University, 1964-80; Instructor, Monterey Institute of International Study, 1980-84; Qigong therapist, Private practice, San Francisco Bay, 1988-; Adviser, East-West Academy of Healing Arts; Adviser, Qigong Institute; Instructor, San Francisco State University. Publications: Articles on Qigong in magazines and journals; Qigong workshops and lectures, 1991-2011; 13 Qigong DVDs (10 of which are devoted to Wild Goose Qigong). Honours: Listed in Who's Who publications and biographical dictionaries. Memberships: American Qigong Association; World Qigong Federation. Address: 2114 Sacramento Street, Berkeley, CA 94702, USA.

HU May, b. 12 May 1953, Shanghai, China. Broadcaster; Journalist. Partner: Hua Pan, 1 son. Education: Graduate diploma, Interpreting/Translation in English/Chinese, Deakin University, Australia, 1992; Graduate certificate, Multicultural Journalism, Wollongong University, Australia, 1998; Honorary Master Degree, Communication & Media Studies, Monash University, Australia, 2008. Appointments: Interpreter/Translator in Professional Level, NAATI3, 1991-; Executive Producer, Head of Group, Senior Broadcaster/Journalist, Mandarin Program, SBS Radio, Melbourne, Australia, 1992-; Teacher, Interpreting/Translation, 1995-; Trainer of Cross Culture; Justice of the Peace, 1996-.

Publications: Author/editor, Australia Today, 1996; A Series of Australian History, Arts & Sports, 2008; The Journey of SBS Radio 1975-2010, 2010. Honours: Australian National OPSO Media Award, 2002; Honour Roll of Women, 2010; Award for Excellence in Multicultural Affairs, VMC, 2006; Listed in Who's Who of Australian Women, 2011-2012. Memberships: Australian Institute of Interpreters & Translators; National Council for Women in Victoria; Media Entertainment of Arts Alliance. Address: 7 Leigh Street, Huntingdale, VIC 3166, Australia. E-mail: may.hu@sbs.com.au

HUANG Christopher, b. 28 December 1951, Singapore. Professor of Cell Physiology. Education: BA (Oxford), The Queen's College, Oxford, 1971-74; BM BCh (Oxford), Oxford University Clinical School, 1974-76; Medical Research Council Scholar, Physiological Laboratory and Gonville and Caius College, Cambridge, 1978-79; PhD (Cambridge), 1980; DM (Oxford), 1985; MD (Cambridge), 1986; DSc (Oxford), 1995; ScD (Cambridge), 1995; Fellow, Society of the Biology, 2011. Appointments: Pre-registration appointments, Nuffield Department of Medicine, University of Oxford, 1977-78; University Demonstrator in Physiology, 1979-84; Fellow and College Lecturer in Physiology, 1979-2002, Director of Studies in Medical Sciences, 1981-, Professorial Fellow, 2002-, Murray Edwards College (formerly New Hall), Cambridge; University Lecturer in Physiology, 1984-96, University Reader in Cellular Physiology, 1996-2002, University Professor of Cell Physiology, 2002-, Cambridge; Several visiting professorships, 1984-2004; Director, Cambridge Cardiac Systems, 2009-. Publications: Monographs and books: Intramembrane charge movements in striated muscle, 1993; Applied Physiology for Surgery and Critical Care (co-editor), 1995; Research in medicine. A guide to writing a thesis in the medical sciences (co-author), 2010; Nerve and Muscle, 2011; Molecular and cellular biology of bone (co-editor), 1998; Over 250 scientific papers in medical journals. Honours: Florence Heale Open Scholar, The Queen's College, Oxford, 1971-76; President's Scholar, Republic of Singapore, 1971-76; Benefactor's Prize, The Queen's College, Oxford, 1973; Brian Johnson Prize in Pathology, University of Oxford, 1976; LEPRA Award, British Leprosy Relief Association, 1977; Rolleston Memorial Prize for Physiological Research, University of Oxford, 1980; Gedge Prize in Physiology, University of Cambridge, 1981. Memberships: Physiological Society, UK; Research Defence Society, UK; American Society of General Physiologists, USA; Biophysical Society, USA; Association of Bone and Mineral Research, USA; Ordinary Member of Council, 1994-, Biological Secretary, 2000-08, Adjudicator and Convenor, William Bate Hardy Prize, 2008, 2010; Cambridge Philosophical Society; Director, Aw Boon Haw Foundation, 2004-08; Independent Non-Executive Director, Hutchison China Meditech, 2006-. Address: Murray Edwards College, Huntingdon Road, Cambridge CB3 0DF, England.

HUANG Dongzhou, b. 5 November 1949, Ruijin, China. Scientist; Educator, Civil Engineer. m. Yingying Shu, 1 son. Education: BS, Civil Engineering, 1974; MS, Civil Engineering, 1985; PhD, Structural Engineering, 1989. Appointment: Professor, Civil Engineering, Fuzhou University; President, BSD Engineering Inc, USA; Associate Editor, Journal of Bridge Engineering, ASCE; Board Member, Journal of ISRN Civil Engineering; Developed finite element methods for analyzing elastic and inelastic lateral buckling of trussed-arch bridges; Developed methods for analyzing dynamic/impact factors of various types of bridges due to moving vehicles; Found basic relationships between static and dynamic responses as well as between impact factor and lateral distribution factor; Developed a practical method for determining lateral load distribution factors of arch and beam bridges, a load capacity rating method of bridges through field test and a shear reinforcement design method for prestressed concrete beam anchorage zones; Developed a practical analytical method of concrete segmental bridges; Developed a finite element method for static and dynamic analysis of curved box girder bridges. Publications: Over 50 papers in professional journals, 2 books. Honour: 1st Prize, Best Publications. Memberships: ASCE; AISC; IABSE; New York Academy of Sciences; American Association for the Advancement of Science. Address: 2408 Tea Olive Terrace, Valrico, FL 33594, USA.

HUANG Her-Hsiung, b. 10 October 1964, Taiwan. Educator and Researcher. m. Wei-Ho Lo, 1 son, 1 daughter. Education: BS, Mechanical Engineering, 1987, MS, Mechanical Engineering, 1989, National Central University; PhD, Materials Science, National Cheng Kung University, Taiwan, 1995. Appointments: Assistant Professor, Institute of Dental Materials, 1999-2002, Associate Professor, Institute of Oral Materials Science, 2002-05, Chung Shan Medical University, Taiwan; Associate Professor, Department of Chemical and Materials Engineering, National University of Kaohsiung, Kaohsiung, Taiwan, 2005-06; Professor, School of Dentistry, National Yang-Ming University, Taipei, Taiwan, 2006-. Publications: More than 80 articles published in related journals and conference proceedings. Honours: Scholar, Industry of Science and Technology, Ministry of Education, Taiwan, 1989-92; Scholar, Sandwich Programme of NSC, Taiwan/DAAD, Germany, 1991-92; Listed in Who's Who publications and biographical dictionaries. Memberships: National Association of Corrosion Engineers; International Association for Dental Research; Chinese Society for Materials Science; Association for Dental Sciences of the ROC; Corrosion Engineering Society of the ROC. Address: National Yang-Ming University, School of Dentistry, No 155, Sec 2, Li-Nong Street, Bei-Tou District, Taipei City 112, Taiwan. E-mail: hhhuang@ym.edu.tw Website: http://home.educities.edu.tw/biomaterials

HUANG Jian-Sheng, b. 8 February 1980, Yi-Lan County, Taiwan. Thermal and Fluid Engineering. Education: Natural Science Section, National Yi-Lan Senior High School, 1995-98; BE, 2002, MS, 2004, PhD, 2008, Mechanical Engineering, Chung Yuan Christian University, Taiwan. Appointments: Postdoctoral Fellow, National Taiwan University of Science and Technology, Taipei, 2008-11. Publications: 13 journal papers; 35 conference papers; Numerous articles in professional journals. Honours: Excellent Paper Award, 21st AIROC Conference, 2009; Level I Thermographer Certification, The American Society for Nondestructive Testing, 2009; Grant for attending 2010 International Winter School: Beyond Moore's Law, Academia Sinica; Excellent R&D Prize, Ministry of the Interior, 2010; Listed in international biographical dictionaries. Memberships: Phi Tau Phi Scholastic Honor Society of the Republic of China; Chinese Society of Mechanical Engineers; Society of Theoretical and Applied Mechanics; Journal of the Acoustical Society of the Republic of China. Address: 6F, No 1, Ln 206, Huanzhong E Rd, Zhongli City, Taoyuan County 32071, Taiwan, ROC. E-mail: lilysonq@yahoo.com.tw; g1213991@ms3b.hinet.net

HUANG Jui-Chen, b. 8 October 1971, Taiwan. Professor. Education: BS, Nursing, Taipei Medical University, 1994; MS, Public Health, Kaohsiung Medical University, 1997; PhD, Institute of Technical Management, Chung-Hua

University, 2009. Appointments: Commissioner, Division of Research and Development, Department of Planning, Landseed Hospital, 1997-98; Lecturer, Department of Healthcare Administration and Hospital Management, Meiho University, 1998-2004; Associate Researcher, Social Welfare Promotion Committee, Executive Yuan, Republic of Taiwan, 2005-06; Assistant Professor, Department of Health business Administration, Hungkuang University, 2009-. Publications: Numerous articles in professional journals. Honours: Reviewer of many scientific journals; Listed in biographical dictionaries. Memberships: Taiwan College of Healthcare Executives; Taiwan Hospital Association; Taiwan Association of Gerontology and Geriatrics; Taiwan Long-term Care Management Association; Taiwan TRIZ Association; Society of Adaptive Science in Taiwan; Chinese Health Services Management Association; Taiwan Public Health Association. Address: 4F, No 42, Jhuangjing 3rd Rd, Jhubei City, Hsin Chu County 302, Taiwan, ROC.

HUANG Kao-Cheng, b. 7 February 1968, Taiwan. Vice President. m. Hsueh-Man Shen. Education: BSc, Physics, 1991, M Phil, Electrical Engineering, 1993, Tsinghua University, Taiwan; D Phil, Engineering Science, University of Oxford, England, 2000. Appointments: Platoon Leader, Air Force Radar Group, 1993-95; Assistant Professor, Ta-Hwa Institute of Technology, Taiwan, 2000-01; Senior RF Engineer, SONY Technology Centre, Germany, 2001-05; Senior Lecturer, MSc Programme Leader, University of Greenwich, England, 2005-08; Vice President, Dharma Academy, Taiwan, 2008-. Publications: Numerous patents, books and articles in professional journals. Honours: Swire Scholar, University of Oxford, 1997-2000. Memberships: Senior Member, IEEE, USA. Address: No 123, Fucheng Road, Fu-hsin, Changhua, 506, Taiwan. E-mail: k.huang@univ.oxon.org

HUANG Xianya, b. 1 January 1947, Chengdu, Sichuan, China. Scientist; Consultant; Engineer. m. Yang Su, 1 daughter. Education: M Eng, Metal Physics, Beijing University of Iron & Steel Technology, 1981; Dr rer nat fur Metallkunde, University of Stuttgart, Germany, 1989. Appointments: Engineer, Project Manager, HanZhong Steel Works, ShanXi, 1970-78; Research Engineer, Project Manager, General Research Institute of Non-Ferrous Metals, Beijing, 1981-85; Visiting Scientist, 1985-86, Research Scientist, 1986-88, Max-Planck-Institute for Materials Science, Germany; Research Scientist, Special Research Region, 270, German Research Society, MPI and University of Stuttgart, 1989-91; Senior Research Fellow, Principal Scientific Officer, Singapore Institute of Standards and Industrial Research, Singapore, 1991-96; Head & Principal Consultant, 1996-2001, Failure Analysis & Consultation, Singapore Productivity Board, Singapore; Head & Principal Consultant, Failure Analysis & Evaluation, PSB Corporation, Singapore, 2001-06; Vice President & Principal Consultant, Failure Analysis Centre, 2006-, Vice President & Chief Consultant, Inspection & Failure Analysis Centre, 2010-, TUV SUD PSB, Singapore. Publications: Over 30 articles in professional journals; More than 800 technical reports regarding failure investigation and risk assessment of different critical devices for various industries in Singapore and south-east Asia countries. Honours: Innovation Award, 1975; Outstanding Academic Paper of 30 Years Award, 1981; 2nd Prize, National Science Award, 1989; SISIR Innovation Award (Silver), 1995; PSB Star Award, 2001; TUV SUD PSB P^3 Award, 2007; New Immigrant Outstanding Contribution Award, HuaYuan General Association of New Immigrants from China & TKK International Society, 2010; Listed in international biographical dictionaries. Memberships: Chinese Society for Corrosion and Protection; German Society for Materials; Fellow, Institute of Materials, Minerals & Mining (FIMMM), UK; Chartered Engineer, Engineering Council of UK. Address: 1 Science Park Drive, Singapore 118221, Singapore. E-mail: xianya.huang@tuv-sud-psb.sg

HUANG Zheng-Bo, b. 26 December 1949, Xiamen, China. Physician. m. Liya He, 1 daughter. Education: MD, Fujian Medical College, Fujian, 1976; Internal Medicine Residency, 1st Teaching Hospital of Fujian Medical College, 1977-79; Fellowship, Internal Medicine, Peking Union Medical College, Beijing, 1979-82; Resident, Internal Medicine, St Luke's-Roosevelt Hospital Center, USA, 1993-96; Geriatrics Fellowship, Mt Sinai Medical Center, New York, 1996-98. Appointments: Attending Physician, Peking Union Medical College Hospital, Beijing, China, 1982-84; Physician and Medical Consultant, The Chinese Mission to the United Nations, New York, 1984-86; Research Associate, St Luke's-Roosevelt Hospital Center, New York, 1986-93; Assistant Professor of Medicine, New York Medical College, 1998-2003; Director, Geriatrics Consult Service, 1999-2002, Director, Geriatric Medical Education & Research, 2002-03, Department of Medicine, St Vincent's Hospital and Medical Centre, New York; Assistant Professor of Clinical Medicine, Weill Medical College of Cornell University, New York, 2003-; Director, Inpatient Geriatrics, 2003-, Director, Geriatric Fellowship Program, 2005-, New York Hospital Medical Center of Queens, New York. Publications: 15 articles in professional journals; 17 presentations or posters. Memberships: Association of Chinese American Physicians; Geriatrics Research Institute of Fujian Province; American Geriatrics Society; American Society of Internal Medicine; Metropolitan Area Geriatrics Society; Chinese American Medical Society; American Chinese Medical Association. Address: 142-18 38th Ave, #1C, Flushing, NY 11354, USA. E-mail: zhh9003@nyp.org

HUBALEK Zdenek, b. 22 August 1942, Brno, Czech Republic. Research Microbiologist. m. Dagmar, 2 daughters. Education: MS, Biology, 1964, RNDr, 1970, University of Brno; PhD, 1972, DSc, 1987, Academy of Sciences, Prague. Appointments: Research Assistant, Institute of Fodder Research, 1964-66; Research Assistant, Institute of Parasitology, Academy of Sciences, Prague, 1966-83; Principal Research Worker, Institute of Systematic and Ecological Biology, Institute of Landscape Ecology, Institute of Vetrebrate Biology, Academy of Sciences, Brno, 1984-; Associate Professor, Masaryk University, Brno, 1999-2006; Professor, Veterinary Microbiology, Immunology and Parasitology, Veterinary and Pharmaceutical University of Brno, 2007-. Publications: 250 scientific articles on the ecology of pathogenic microorganisms which are arthropod-borne, numerical classifications, medical zoology and ornithology; 2 books: Cryopreservation of Microorganisms, 1996; Microbial Zoonoses and Sapronoses, 2011. Honours: J E Purkyne Medal for Achievements in Biology, Czech Academy of Sciences, Prague; Award, Czech Academy of Sciences, Prague, 2004. Memberships: Czech Scientific Societies of: Biology; Microbiology; Mycology; Zoology. Address: Medical Zoology Laboratory, Institute of Vertebrate Biology, Academy of Sciences, Klasterni 2, CZ-69142 Valtice, Czech Republic. E-mail: zhubalek@brno.cas.cz Website: http://publicationslist.org/zdenek.hubalek

HUBEL David Hunter, b. 27 February 1926, Ontario, Canada. Neurophysiologist. m. S Ruth Izzard, 1953, 3 sons. Education: Graduated, Medicine, McGill University, Montreal, Canada. Appointments: Professor of Neurophysiology, Harvard Medical School, 1965-67; George Packer Berry Professor of Physiology and Chairman, Department of Physiology, 1967-68; George Packer Berry Professor of Neurobiology, 1968-92; John Franklin Enders University Professor, 1982-; George Eastman Professor, University of Oxford, 1991-92; First Annual George A Miller Lecture, Cognitive Neuroscience Society, 1995; Worked on the physiology of vision and the way in which the brain processes visual information. Publications: Eye, Brain and Vision, 1987; Articles in scientific journals. Honours: Lewis S Rosenstiel Award for Basic Medical Research, 1972; Friedenwald Award, 1975; Karl Spencer Lashley Prize, 1977; Louisa Gross Horwitz Prize, 1978; Dickson Prize in Medicine, 1979; Society of Scholars, Johns Hopkins University, 1980; Ledlie Prize, 1980; Joint Winner, Nobel Prize for Physiology or Medicine, 1981; New England Ophthalmological Society Award, 1983; Paul Kayser International Award of Merit in Retina Research, 1989; City of Medicine Award, 1990; Gerald Award, 1993; Charles F Prentice Medal, 1993; Helen Keller Prize, 1995. Memberships: NAS; Leopoldina Academy, Board of Syndics, Harvard University Press; Foreign Member, Royal Society, London; Senior Fellow, Harvard Society of Fellows; Fellow, American Academy of Arts and Sciences. Address: Department of Neurobiology, Harvard Medical School, 220 Longwood Avenue, Boston, MA 02115, USA.

HUČÍN Bohumil, b. 30 March 1934 Velké Popovice, Czech Republic. Cardiac Surgeon. m. Jana Hučínová-Vrbská. 3 sons, 1 daughter. Education: Graduate, Medical School, Charles University, Prague, Czech Republic, 1958; Specialist in General Surgery, 1962; Specialist in Paediatric Surgery, 1967; PhD, 1967; Doctor of Medical Sciences, 1987; Professor of Surgery, 1990; Specialist in Cardiac Surgery, 1998. Appointments: Resident, Department of General Surgery, Regional Hospital Vlašim, Czech Republic, 1958-61; Clinical Assistant in Paediatric Surgery, Prague, 1962-67; Head of Division of Paediatric Cardiac Surgery, Department of Paediatric Surgery, Children's University Hospital, Prague, 1968-76; Surgeon in Chief, Paediatric Cardiac Centre, University Hospital Motol, Prague, Czech Republic, 1977-2004; Retired Professor Emeritus of Paediatric Cardiac Surgery, 2004. Publications: Cardiac Surgery in Newborns and Infants; Cardiac Surgery in Deep Hypothermia and Circulatory Arrest in Infants; Cardiac Surgery in Adults with Congenital Heart Defects; Paediatric Cardiac Surgery (monograph), 2002. Honours: National Prize of Czechoslovak Republic, 1984; Prize of City of Prague; Medal of Charles University Prague; Medal of Czech Medical Society; Medal of Faculty of Paediatrics; Medal of University of Padua, Italy; Jan Evanelista Purkyne Prize, 2010. Memberships: Czech Medical Society; British Association of Paediatric Surgeons; European Association for Cardio-thoracic Surgery; European Society of Cardiovascular Surgery; Society of Thoracic Surgeons (USA), International Society of Cardio-thoracic Surgeons (Japan); Association of Cardiovascular Surgery of Ukraine. Address: Hodkovická 10/64, Prague 4, 142 00 Czech Republic. E-mail: bohumil.hucin@volny.cz

HUCKNALL Mick, 8 June 1960, Manchester, England. Singer; Songwriter. Career: Formed early band, Frantic Elevators, 1979; Formed Simply Red, essentially a solo career with changing band members; Numerous hit singles, television appearances; Numerous tours and festival dates worldwide; Founder, Blood and Fire label, dedicated to vintage reggae tracks. Recordings: Singles: Money's Too Tight to Mention; Come To My Aid; Holding Back the Years; Jericho; Open Up The Red Box; Ev'ry Time We Say Goodbye; The Right Thing; Infidelity; Maybe Some Day; Ev'ry Time We say Goodbye; I Won't Feel Bad; It's Only Love; If You Don't Know Me By Now; A New Flame; You've Got It; Something Got Me Started; Stars; For Your Babies; Thrill Me; Your Mirror; Fairground; Remembering The First Time; Never Never Love; We're In This Together; Angel; Nightnurse; Say You Love Me; The Air That I Breathe; Ghetto Girl; Ain't That a Lot of Love; Your Eyes; Sunrise; Albums: Picture Book, 1985; Early Years, 1987; Men and Women, 1987; A New Flame, 1989; Stars, 1991; 12"ers, 1995; Life, 1995; Fairground, 1995; Greatest Hits, 1996; Blue, 1998; Love and the Russian Winter, 1999; It's Only Love (greatest hits), 2000; Home, 2003. Address: PO Box 20197, London, W10 6YQ, England.

HUDGENS Vanessa, b. 14 December 1988, Salinas, California, USA. Actress; Singer. Career: Actress: Films: Thirteen, 2003; Thunderbirds, 2004; High School Musical 3: Senior Year, 2008; Bandslam, 2009; Beastly, 2010; Sucker Punch, 2011; TV films: High School Musical, 2006; High School Musical 2, 2007; many TV guest appearances; Singer: Albums: V, 2006; Identified, 2008; Concert Tours: High School Musical: The Concert, 2006-07; Identified Summer Tour, 2008. Honours: Teen Choice Awards, 2006, 2007, 2008; Kids Choice Awards, MTV Movie Awards, 2009.

HUDSON Harry Robinson, b. 18 November 1929, Kingston-upon-Hull, England. Emeritus Professor of Chemistry. m. Jacqueline Ruth Feeney, 2 sons, 2 daughters. Education: BSc (Special) Honours, Chemistry, External Student of London University at Hull Municipal Technical College, 1949; ARIC by Examination; PhD, Organic Chemistry, London University, 1960; DSc (London), 1976. Appointments: National Service, Education Branch, Technical Training Command, Royal Air Force, 1949-51; Research and Development Chemist, Distillers Company Ltd, Chemical Division, Hull, 1951-58; Research Assistant, 1958-60, Full-time Member of Academic Staff, 1961-94, Reader in Chemistry, 1969, Professor, 1990-94, Emeritus Professor, 1995-, Northern Polytechnic (subsequently The Polytechnic of North London, University of North London, London Metropolitan University); Consultant: Dermal Laboratories Ltd, 1977-87; KenoGard AB, Stockholm, 1987-91; British Technology Group, 1989-92. Publications: Book: Aminophosphonic and Aminophosphinic Acids: Chemistry and Biological Activity (co-editor), 2000; Author or co-author of 6 book chapters and over 100 research publications and review articles. Honours: Fellow Royal Society of Chemistry, 1964; Honorary Research Fellow, University College, London, 1979-80; Visiting Lecturer, Royal Holloway College, University of London, 1979-82; Medal, Organophosphorus Chemistry, University of Lódz, Poland, 1996. Membership: Royal Society of Chemistry. Address: London Metropolitan University, 166-220 Holloway Road, London N7 8DB, England. E-mail: harryrhudson@aol.com

HUDSON Mark James, b. 10 July 1963, Roade, England. Anthropologist. Education: BA, University of London, 1986; M Phil, University of Cambridge, 1988; PhD, Australian National University, 1996. Appointments: Lecturer, Okayama University, Japan, 1996-98; Foreign Professor, 1998-2002, Adjunct Professor, 2003-05, Associate Professor, 2005-07, University of Tsukuba; Associate Professor, 2007-08, Professor, 2009-, Anthropology, Nishi Kyushu University. Publications: Co-editor, Multicultural Japan: Palaeolithic to Postmodern, 1996; Author, Ruins of Identity: Ethnogenesis in the Japanese Islands, 1999. Honours: J G Crawford Prize, Australian National University, 1996; President's Prize, Asian Studies Association of Australia, 1996. Memberships: Anthropological Society of Nippon;

American Anthropological Association. Address: Department of Occupational Therapy, Nishi Kyushu University, 4490-9 Osaki, Kanzaki, Saga 842-8585, Japan. E-mail: hudsonm@nisikyu-u-ac.jp

HUERTA-ESCUDERO Eliu Antonio, b. 18 May 1982, Mexico City, Mexico. Student. m. Yolanda Gago Sanz-Huerta. Education: BSc, Instituto de Astronomia, Universidad Nacional Autonoma de Mexico, 2006; Master of Advanced Study, Department of Applied Mathematics and Theoretical Physics, University of Cambridge, 2007; PhD, Institute of Astronomy, University of Cambridge, in progress. Publications: A simple accretion model of a rotating gas sphere onto a Schwarzschild black hole, 2007; Influence of conservative corrections on parameter estimation for extreme-mass-ratio inspirals, 2009; Intermediate-mass-ratio-inspirals in the Einstein Telescope: I Signal-to-noise ratio calculations, 2010; Intermediate-mass-ratio-inspirals in the Einstein Telescope: II Parameter estimation errors, 2010; Conference publications, talks and posters. Honours: Gabino Barreda Medal, 2001; UNAM Studentship, 2001-05; CONACyT Studentship, 2006-11; Honorable Mention, Best Undergraduate Thesis in Astrophysics within 2006-07, XXII Mexican Astronomy Meeting, 2008; Travel grants, 2009 and 2010. Address: Churchill College, Cambridge, CB3 0DS, England. E-mail: eliuhe@gmail.com

HUET Denise, b. 2 February 1931, Nancy, France. Professor Emeritus. Education: Agregation de Mathematiques, 1954; Doctorat d'etat en Mathematiques, Paris, 1959. Appointments: Attachee de Recherche, Centre National de la Recherche Scientifique, Paris, 1955-59; Professor, Faculty of Sciences, Dijon, 1959-66; Visiting Professor, Georgetown University, USA, 1966-67; Visiting Professor, Professor, University of Maryland, USA, 1967-72; Professeur à l'Université de Nancy I, France, 1972-94; Professor Emeritus, 1994-. Publications: Many publications. Honours: Woman of the Year, American Biographical Institute, 1996; 2000 Millennium Medal of Honor; Legion of Honor, United Cultural Convention, 2005. Memberships: American Mathematical Society; Societe Mathematique de France. Address: 86 Rue Felix Faure, 54000 Nancy, France.

HUETTEMAN Susan Bice, b. 24 January 1934, Crossville, Illinois, USA. m. Albert, 2 sons. Writer. Education: AA, Colby-Sawyer College, 1953; B Music, New England Conservatory, 1956; MA, Goddard Graduate School, 1979. Appointments: Private Voice and Piano Instruction and Fine Arts Pre-School, Huetteman Studio, 1957-1998; Choir Director, Urbana-Champaign Women's Chorus, 1960-1961, First United Methodist Church, Terre Haute, 1961-1962, First Congregational Church, Terre Haute, 1962-1964, First Congregational Church, Cedar Rapids, 1964-1966; 6th grade music teacher, Forest Park-Greenhills Middle Schools, Cincinnati, 1972-1974; Voice Faculty, Amherst Schools Continuing Education, 1974-1975; Director, Leonard Bernstein Festival of American Music, 1978, Director and Voice Faculty, Performing Arts Division, 1979-1998, Director, American Music Workshops in Jazz, 1981, University of Massachusetts/Amherst; Essayist, Writer/Poet. Publications: Numerous articles in professional journals, poetry and lyrics; Editor and columnist for weekly newspapers and music journals; Web essayist for NCTE and Masterpiece Theatre's American Collection. Memberships: Society of Children's Book Writers and Illustrators; Poetry Society of America; International Women's Writing Guild; Theater Communications Group; International Women's Writing Guild; Florida Writer's Association. Website: www.susanhuetteman.com

HUFFMAN Felicity, b. 9 December 1962, New York, USA. Actress. m. William H Macy, 2 daughters. Education: BFA in Drama, New York University, Tisch School of the Arts, 1988. Career: Films include: Raising Helen, 2004; Christmas with the Kranks, 2004; Transamerica, 2005; Georgia Rule, 2007; Phoebe in Wonderland, 2009. TV includes: The DA; Frasier; Desperate Housewives.

HUGHES Barry Peter, b. 29 August 1932, Wolverhampton, England. Professor. m. Pamela Anne Barker, 1 son, 2 daughters. Education: BSc honours, 1953, PhD, 1956, Civil Engineering, University of Birmingham. Appointments: Assistant Civil Engineer, Concrete Engineer, Berkeley Power Station, 1956-59; Civil Engineer, Planning Engineer, John Laing Construction Ltd, 1959-62; Lecturer, 1962-68, Senior Lecturer, 1968-73, Professor of Civil Engineering, 1974-95, Emeritus Professor, 1995-, University of Birmingham; Private Consulting, Concrete and Concrete Structures, 1989-; Visiting Professor, University of Coventry, 1999-. Publications: Numerous research and technical papers on concrete and concrete structures; 2 books. Honours: Reader in Concrete Technology, 1971, DSc, 1972, DEng, 1990, Emeritus Professor, 1995, University of Birmingham. Memberships: Institution of Civil Engineers; Institution of Structural Engineers; Concrete Society. Address: Long Barn, 8 Parkfields, Arden Drive, Dorridge, Solihull, West Midlands, B93 8LL, England. E-mail: bphughes@onetel.net.uk

HUGHES Christopher Wyndham, b. 22 November 1941, Ipswich, Suffolk. Solicitor. m. Gail, 3 sons. Education: LL B. Honours, University College, London, 1960-63; College of Law, London, 1963-64. Appointments: Solicitor then Partner, 1970, Wragge & Co; Managing Partner, Wragge & Co, 1993-95; Head of International Wragge & Co LLP, 2004-09; Notary Public; Member, Bar of Advocatesof Poland, 2009; Non-executive roles: Board Member, Severn Trent Water Authority, 1982-84; Chairman, Newman Tonks Group PLC, 1995-97; Member, Board of the Pension Protection Fund, 2004-. Publications: Former Member, Editorial Board, The Guide to Professional Conduct of Solicitors. Honour: LL.B. (London), 1963. Membership: Warwickshire County Cricket Club. Address: Cuttle Pool Farm, Cuttle Pool Lane, Knowle, Solihull, West Midlands B93 0AP, England.

HUGHES Henry Goronwy Alun (Alun Gwenffrwd), b. 15 July 1921, Pontlotyn, Glamorgan, Wales. Writer; Editor; Reviewer; Translator. m. (1) Alison M Mair, (2) Brenda Cross (née Stenning), 2 adopted sons, (3) Zuzana Dvořáková (née Kot'átková) 1964, deceased 1996, 1 daughter, deceased. Education: BA (Hons II); LI B; MA; D Phil; CSc; D Ed; D Anthrop; prom fil; Meyricke Exhibitioner in Modern Languages, Jesus College, Oxford, 1939-40, 1944-46; University of London; University of Liverpool; Charles University, Prague; Oriental Institute, Czechoslovak Academy of Sciences, Prague. Appointments: Merchant Seaman in Norwegian, Swedish, Panamanian and British ships, and Naval Counter-intelligence agent, 1940-44; Research Assistant, Tropical Education, I of E, London, 1947-49; Lecturer, Oceanic Languages, SOAS, London, 1949-53; Lecturer, London Co-operative Society, 1953-56; Freelance journalist, international conference interpreter, film critic; International Librarian, Liverpool, 1956-59; Lecturer, Liverpool College of Commerce, 1956-59; Head of Department/Vice Principal, Colwyn Bay Technical College,

1959-63; Editor, ČTK Praha, 1963-66; Senior Lecturer, KU Praha and U 17. eho listopadů, Praha, 1963-66; Krátký Film, Praha, 1963-66; Borough Librarian/Chief Officer, Flint MB, 1966-74; Counsellor, Open University, Wales, 1972-75; Retired, 1975; National Secretary, Cyngres Gweithwyr Cymru (Congress of Welsh Workers); Financial Administrator and Hospital Secretary, St Clare's Convent, Pantasaph; Associate, Swayne, Johnson and Wight Solicitors, Denbigh; Trade Union Representative (MSF), Writer, Editor, Reviewer, Translator; Bookdealer, Bronant Books; Publisher, Gwasg Gwenffrwd; Proprietor, ASTIC Research Associates, A&Z Hughes Ltd, Bronant Books, Gwasg Gwenffrwd, Translations Wales, 1947-2007; Adult Education and Extra-mural Lecturer, Film Critic, Scriptwriter and Commentator, Trade Union Representative, Political Militant and Anti-war Activist, 1947-. Publications: Numerous articles, bibliographies, poems, reviews and translations; 70 books, monographs, pamphlets and CDs. Memberships: Institute of Polynesian Languages and Literatures; Polynesian Society; North Wales Racial Equality Network; Friends of the Clwyd Archives; Friends of the National Library of Wales, Cefnogwyr Y Byd; Friends of the Welsh Books Council; Denbighshire Voluntary Services Council; Institute of Welsh Affairs; Bevan Foundation; Friends of the Earth; CND Cymru; Movement for the Abolition of War; VES/Dignity in Dying; Woodland Trust; Socialist History Society; Cymru Rydd; Senedd '04; Communist Party of Scotland; Connolly Association; UNISON; AMICUS/UNITE; Tenants Defence Union (UAC/TDU); Cynon Valley History Society; Glamorgan History Society; Pentyrch and District Local History Society; Cymdeithas Hanes Gweithwyr Cymru; Friends of the National Museums and Galleries of Wales; Denbighshire Historical Society; Red Poets Society; All 6 family history societies in Wales; Royal British Legion; National Secretary, PGC/CPW (Communist Party of Wales). Address: Alwen, Uwch y Llan, Cerrigydrudion, Corwen LL21 9UD, Wales.

HUH Yungoo, b. 4 June 1974, Pusan, Republic of Korea. Aerospace Scientist; Engineer. m. Yunrim Jung, 1 daughter. Education: BS, 1998, MS, 2000, PhD, 2004, Computer Science and Engineering, POSTECH, Korea. Appointments: Senior Researcher, location management for wireless network, 1998-2004; Senior Engineer, Samsung Electronics Co Ltd (development of smart phone based on simbian and plamos), 2004-07; Senior Researcher, Kompsat 3/5 (development of common ground system), 2008-09. Publications: A Delayed Location Registration Procedure for Wireless Mobile Communication Networks, 2001; Group-based Location Management Scheme in Personal Communications Networks, 2002; Efficient Multicast Support Exploiting Mobility, 2002; Efficient Mobile Multicast Support board on the Mobility of Mobile Hosts, 2006. Memberships: Korean Society for Aeronautical & Space Sciences; Korean Space Science Society. Address: Korea Aerospace Research Institute, 115 Gwahangno, Yuseong Gu, Daejeon 305-333, Korea. E-mail: perfect@postech.ac.kr

HULCE Tom, b. 6 December 1953, Detroit, Michigan, USA. Actor. Education: North Carolina School of Arts. Career: Plays: The Rise and Rise of Daniel Rocket, 1982; Eastern Standard, 1988; A Few Good Men, 1990; Films: September 30th 1955; National Lampoon's Animal House; Those Lips Those Eyes; Amadeus, 1985; Echo Park, 1985; Slam Dance, 1987; Nicky and Gino, 1988; Parenthood, 1989; Shadowman; The Inner Circle; Fearless; Mary Shelley's Frankenstein, 1994; Wings of Courage, 1995; The Hunchback of Notre Dame (voice), 1996; Home at the End of the World (producer), 2004; Stranger Than Fiction, 2006; Jumper, 2008. TV: Emily

Emily; St Elsewhere; Murder in Mississippi, 1990; Black Rainbow; The Heidi Chronicles, 1995. Address: c/o CAA, 9830 Wilshire Boulevard, Beverly Hills, CA 90212, USA.

HULSTAERT Caesar Emmanuel, b. 15 March 1941, Middelburg, The Netherlands. Cell Biologist; University Administrator. m. Yvonne Sylvia Nemmers, divorced 1984, 1 daughter. Education: Master Degree, Biology, University of Utrecht, 1969; PhD, University of Groningen, 1974. Appointments: Researcher, Lecturer, Centre for Medical Electron Microscopy, 1969-92, Student Counsellor, 1992-98, International Liaison Officer, 1992-2005, University Medical Centre, Groningen. Publications: Articles on histochemistry and cytochemistry in books and scientific journals. Memberships: Dutch Society for Microscopy, 1970-96, Secretary, 1986-92. Address: Nieuwe Vlissingseweg 290, 4335 JJ Middelburg, The Netherlands. E-mail: chulstaert@solcon.nl

HULTQVIST Bengt K G, b. 21 August 1927, Hemmesjo, Sweden. Professor; Director. m. Gurli Gustafsson, 2 sons, 1 daughter. Education: Dr Sci Degree, Physics, University of Stockholm, 1956. Appointments: Director, Swedish Institute of Space Physics (and its predecessors). 1957-94; Director, International Space Science Institute, 1995-99; Chairman, Space Science Advisory Committee of ESA, 1998-2000; Secretary General of IAGA, 2001-09. Publications: Some 200 articles in scientific journals and books; 3 books; Editor of 6 scientific books. Honours include: Grand Gold Medal, Royal Swedish Academy of Engineering Science, 1988; Cospar Prize for International Co-operation, 1990; King's Medal, 1991; Bartel's Medal, 1998; Hannes Alfvén Medal, 2002. Memberships include: Royal Astronomical Society (UK); International Academy of Astronautics; Academia Europaea; Royal Swedish Academy of Sciences; Royal Swedish Academy of Engineering Science; Academy of Finland; Royal Norwegian Academy of Sciences. Address: Gronstensv 2, S-98140, Kiruna, Sweden. E-mail: hultqv@irf.se

HUME John, b. 18 January 1937, Londonderry, Northern Ireland. Politician. m. Patricia Hone, 1960, 2 sons, 3 daughters. Education: St Colomb's College, Londonderry; St Patrick's College, Maynooth; National University of Ireland. Appointments: Research Fellow, Trinity College; Associate Fellow, Centre for International Affairs, Harvard; Founder Member, Credit Union, Northern Ireland, President, 1964-68; Non-Violent Civil Rights Leader, 1968-69; Representative, Londonderry, Northern Ireland Parliament, 1969-72, in Northern Ireland Assembly, 1972-73; Minister of Commerce, Powersharing Executive, 1974; Representative, Londonderry in Northern Ireland Convention, 1975-76; Elected to European Parliament, 1979-; Leader, Social Democratic and Labour Party (SDLP), 1979-2001; Member, Northern Ireland Assembly, 1982-86; MP for Foyle, 1983-; Member for Foyle Northern Ireland Assembly, 1998- (Assembly suspended 2002). Publications: Politics, Peace and Reconciliation in Ireland. Honours include: Nobel Peace Prize (shared), 1998; Martin Luther King Award, 1999; Gandhi Peace Prize, 2002; Freedom of the City of Cork, 2004. Numerous honorary doctorates. Address: 5 Bayview Terrace, Derry BT48 7EE, Northern Ireland.

HUME Robert, b. 6 January 1928, Glasgow, Scotland. Consultant Physician. m. Kathleen Anne Ogilvie Hume, 2 sons, 1 daughter. Education: Ayr Academy; Bellahouston Academy; University of Glasgow; MB ChB, 1948-53; MD (Commend), 1967; DSc, 1985. Appointments: National Service, Intelligence Corps; Commissioned, Gordon

Highlanders, India and Germany, 1946-48; Hutcheson Research Scholar, 1955-56, Hall Fellowship, 1956-59, Honorary Clinical Lecturer, 1965, Honorary Sub-Dean, Faculty of Medicine, 1988, University of Glasgow; Consultant Physician, Southern General Hospital Glasgow, 1965-93; Retired, 1993; Member of the Board of Directors, Healthcare International, 1995-2002. Publications: Author of numerous publications on haematological and vascular disorders. Memberships: BMA, 1954; Scottish Society for Experimental Medicine, 1955; British Society for Haematology, 1960; Member, Research Support Group, Greater Glasgow Health Board, 1978-90; Member, Intercollegiate Standing Committee on Nuclear Medicine, UK, 1980-83; Scottish Council, BMA, 1980-83; Chairman, Sub-Committee on Medicine, Greater Glasgow Health Board, 1955-90; RCPS (Glas), Honorary Registrar for Examinations 1971-83, Chairman, Board of Examiners, 1983-88, Visitor and President Elect, 1988, President, 1990-92; Chairman, Conference of Scottish Royal Colleges and Faculties, 1991-92; Chairman, Joint Committee on Higher Medical Training of Royal Colleges of UK, 1990-93; Member, Scottish Society of Physicians, 1965; FRCPS, 1968; FRCPE, 1969; Honorary Member, Association of Physicians of Great Britain and Ireland, 1971; Honorary FACP, 1991; Honorary RACP, 1991; Member, Academy of Medicine of Malaysia, 1991; Honorary FCM(SA); Honorary FRCPS (Canada); FRCPath, 1992; FRCSEd, 1992; FRCPI, 1993; Member, Buchanan Castle Golf Club; The Royal Philosophical Society of Glasgow; Glasgow Antiques and Fine Arts Society; National Trust of Scotland. Address: 6 Rubislaw Drive, Bearsden, Glasgow G61 1PR, Scotland.

HUMPHREYS Emyr Owen, b. 15 April 1919, Clwyd, Wales. Author. m. Elinor Myfanwy, 1946, 3 sons, 1 daughter. Education: University College, Aberystwyth; University College, Bangor. Publications: The Little Kingdom, 1946; The Voice of a Stranger, 1949; A Change of Heart, 1951; Hear and Forgive, 1952; A Man's Estate, 1955; The Italian Wife, 1957; A Toy Epic, 1958; The Gift, 1963; Outside the House of Baal, 1965; Natives, 1968; Ancestor Worship, 1970; National Winner, 1971; Flesh and Blood, 1974; Landscapes, 1976; The Best of Friends, 1978; The Kingdom of Bran, 1979; The Anchor Tree, 1980; Pwyll a Riannon, 1980; Miscellany Two, 1981; The Taliesin Tradition, 1983; Salt of the Earth, 1985; An Absolute Hero, 1986; Open Secrets, 1988; The Triple Net, 1988; Bonds of Attachment, 1990; Outside Time, 1991; Unconditional Surrender, 1996; The Gift of a Daughter, 1998; Collected Poems, 1999; Dal Pen Rheswm, 1999; Ghosts and Strangers, 2000; Conversations and Reflections, 2002; Old People are a Problem, 2003; The Shop, 2005; The Woman at the Window, 2009; Welsh Time, 2009. Honours: Somerset Maugham Award, 1953; Hawthornden Prize, 1959; Society of Authors Travel Award, 1978; Welsh Arts Council Prize, 1983; Honorary DLitt, University of Wales, 1990; Welsh Book of the Year, 1992, 1999; Honorary Professor of English, University College of North Wales, Bangor. Membership: Fellow, The Royal Society of Literature, 1991; Cymmrodorion Medal, 2003. Address: Llinon, Penyberth, Llanfairpwll, Ynys Môn, Gwynedd LL61 5YT, Wales.

HUMPHRIES (John) Barry, b. 17 Feb 1934, Australia. Actor; Writer. m. 2 sons. Education: University of Melbourne. Appointments: Various one-man shows; film appearances. Publications: Bizarre I, 1965; Innocent Australian Verse, 1968; Wonderful World of Barry McKenzie, 1968; Bazza Pulls It Off, 1972; Adventures of Barry McKenzie, 1973; Bazza Holds His Own, 1974; Dame Edna's Coffee Table Book, 1976; Bazza Comes Into His Own, 1978; Les Patterson's Australia, 1979; Barry Humphries' Treasury of Australian Kitsch, 1980; Dame Edna's Bedside Companion, 1982; Les Patterson: The Traveller's Tool, 1985; Dame Edna: My Gorgeous Life, 1989; Women in the Backyard, 1996. Honour: Society of West End Managements Award, 1979.

HUMPHRYS John, b. 17 August 1943. Broadcaster. Divorced, 2 sons, 1 daughter. Appointments: Washington Correspondent, BBC TV, 1971-77, Southern Africa Correspondent, 1977-80, Diplomatic Correspondent, 1981; Presenter, BBC Nine o'Clock News, 1981-87; Presenter, BBC Radio 4 Today Programme, 1987-, On the Record, BBC TV, 1993-, John Humphrys Interview Radio 4, 1995-. Publication: Devil's Advocate, 1999; Great Food Gamble; Lost for Words: The Mangling and Manipulation of the English Language, 2004; Beyond Words, 2006; In God We Doubt, 2007; Blue Skies & Black Olives, 2009. Honours: Fellow, Cardiff University, 1998; Honorary DLitt, Dundee, 1996; Honorary MA, University of Wales, 1998; Honorary LLD, St Andrews, 1999. Address: BBC News Centre, Wood Lane, London W12, England.

HUNEMAN Philippe, b. 10 July 1970, Boulogne, France. Philosopher; Researcher. 1 son, 1 daughter. Education: MD, Pure Mathematics, 1991, DEA, History of Mathematics, 1992, University Paris 7; Agregation, Philosophy, 1993; PhD, Philosophy, University Paris 1, 2001. Appointments: Fellowship, MRT, 1994, 1997; Fellowship, CNRS, 1997-2000; High School Professor, 2000-02; Postdoctoral studies, Institut d'Histoire des Sciences et des Techniques, Paris, 2002-04; Full time Researcher (equivalent of Associate Professor), Institut d'Histoire de la Philosophie des Sciences et des Techniques (CNRS/Universite Paris I Sorbonne), 2004-; Teacher, Philosophy of Science Program, Universite Paris I Sorbonne, 2008-; Affiliated Professor, IHPST, University of Toronto, Canada. Publications: 5 books; Numerous articles in professional journals; Book Series Editor, History, Philosophy and Theory of the Life Sciences. Honours: Pensionnaire de la Fondation Theirs, 1997-2000; Young Research in Humanities Award, European Science Foundation, 2007; Scientific Excellence Prize, CNRS, 2010. Memberships: Philosophy of Science Association; International Society for Philosophy, History and Social Sciences of Biology; European Journal for Philosophy of Science. Address: IHPST, 13 rue du Four, 75006 Paris, France. E-mail: huneman@wanadoo.fr

HUNT Anthony James, b. 22 June 1932, London, England. Structural Engineer. m. (1) Patricia Daniels, 1957, dissolved, 1972, remarried, 1975, dissolved, 1982, 1 son, 1 daughter, (3) Diana Joyce Collett. Education: CEng, Westminster Technical College, 1961; FIStructE, 1973. Appointments: Articled via Founders' Co to J L Wheeler Consulting Engineer, 1948-51; F J Samuely and Partners, Consulting Engineers, 1951-59; Morton Lupton, Architects, 1960-62; Founded Anthony Hunt Associates, Consulting Engineers, 1962, Stood down as Chairman of Anthony Hunt Associates, became a consultant to them in 2002; Acquired by YRM plc, Building Design Consultants, 1988; Became separate limited company, 1997; Major buildings: Sainsbury Centre for the Visual Arts, Norwich, 1978, 1993; Willis Faber Dumas HQ, Ipswich, 1975; Inmos Micro Electronics Factory, Gwent, 1982; Schlumberger Cambridge Research, 1985; Waterloo International Terminal, 1993; Law Faculty, Cambridge, 1995; National Botanic Garden, Wales, 1998; New Museum of Scotland, Edinburgh, 1998; Lloyd's Register of Shipping, London, 2000; Eden Project, Cornwall, 2001; Willis Visiting Professor of Architecture, Sheffield University, 1994-. Publications: Tony Hunt's Structures Notebook, 1997; Tony Hunt's Sketchbook, 1999. Honours: FRSA, 1989; Honorary FRIBA, 1989; Gold Medallist, IStructE, 1995; Honorary DLitt, Sheffield, 1999;

DICTIONARY OF INTERNATIONAL BIOGRAPHY 36th EDITION

Graham Professor of Architecture, Graduate School of Fine Arts, University of Pennsylvania, 2002; Honorary DEng, Leeds, 2003; Visiting Professor, Chinese University of Hong Kong; Visiting Professor, IST, Lisbon. Address: Stancombe Farm, Bisley with Lippiatt, Stroud, Gloucestershire, GL6 7NF, England. E-mail: tony@huntprojects.co.uk

HUNT David Roderic Notley, b. 22 June 1947, Brighton, England. Barrister. m. Alison Connell Jelf, 2 sons. Education: MA Honours, Law, Trinity College, Cambridge, 1968; Inns of Court School of Law, 1968-69. Appointments: Called to the Bar, Gray's Inn, 1969; Queen's Counsel, 1987; Recorder, 1991; Master of the Bench of Gray's Inn, 1995. Publications: Article in the Solicitor's Journal. Address: Blackstone Chambers, Blackstone House, Temple, London EC4Y 9BW, England. E-mail: davidhunt@blackstonechambers.com

HUNT Helen, b. 15 June 1963, Los Angeles, USA. Actress; Director. m. Hank Azaria, 1999 (divorced), 1 daughter with Matthew Carnahan. Creative Works: Stage appearances include: Been Taken; Our Town; The Taming of the Shrew; Methusalem; Films include: Rollercoaster; Girls Just Want to Have Fun; Peggy Sue Got Married; Project X; Miles From Hume; Trancers; Stealing Home; Next of Kin; The Waterdance; Only You; Bob Roberts; Mr Saturday Night; Kiss of Death; Twister; As Good As It Gets; Twelfth Night; Pay It Forward, 2000; Dr T and the Women, 2000; Cast Away, 2000; What Women Want, 2000; The Curse of the Jade Scorpion, 2001; A Good Woman, 2004; Bobby, 2006; Then She Found Me, 2007; Every Day, 2011; Soul Surfer, 2011; Jock of the Bushveld (voice), 2011; The Sessions, 2012; TV includes: Swiss Family Robinson; Mad About You; Empire Falls; Californication. Honours include: Emmy Award, 1996, 1997; Golden Globe Award, 1997; Academy Award, Best Actress, 1998. Address: c/o Connie Tavel, 9171 Wilshire Boulevard, Beverly Hills, CA 90210, USA.

HUNTER Holly, b. 20 March 1958, Atlanta, Georgia, USA. Actress. m. J Kaminski, divorced. Education: Career: Theatre includes: on Broadway: Crimes of the Heart; The Wake of Jamey Foster; The Miss Firecracker Contest; Other Stage Appearances include: The Person I Once Was; Battery, New York; A Lie of the Mind, Los Angeles; By the Bog of Cat, London, 2004; Regional work; Films include: Broadcast News, Raising Arizona, 1987; Once Around, 1990; The Piano and The Firm, 1993; Copycat, 1995; Crash, 1996; Living Out Loud, 1998; Time Code, O Brother Where Art Thou? 2000; When Billie Beat Bobby, Festival in Cannes, 2001; Goodbye Hello, 2002; Levity, Thirteen, 2003; Levity, 2003; The Incredibles (voice), Little Black Book, 2004; Nine Lives, The Big White, 2005; Saving Grace (TV), 2007. Honours: 2 for TV appearances: Best Actress Emmy for Roe vs Wade, 1989; Best Actress Award, American TV Awards, 1993; Best Actress Award, Cannes Film Festival Award, 1993; Academy Award, 1994. Memberships: Director, California Abortion Rights Action League. Address: 41 Stutter Street, #1649, San Francisco, CA 94104, USA.

HUNTER Robert John, b. 26 June 1933. Research Chemist. m. Barbara Robson, 1954, divorced 1995, 1 son, 1 daughter. Education: BSc, 1954, PhD, 1962, Sydney. Appointments: Master, Mathematics/Science, Wolaroi College, Orange, NSW, 1953-54; Technical Officer/Chemist, 1954-57, Research Officer, 1960-64, CSIRO; Lecturer, 1964-67, Associate Professor, 1972-90, Head, School of Chemistry, 1987-90, Research Fellow/Consultant, 1990-2006, University of Sydney. Publications: Zeta Potential in Colloid Science, 1981; Foundations of Colloid Science, Vol I, 1987, Vol II, 1989, 2nd edition 2001; Introduction to Modern Colloid Science, 1993. Honours include: CSIRO Graduate Scholarship from Division of Soils, 1957-60; Foundation for Fundamental Study of Materials, Research Fellowship, Utrecht, Netherlands, 1967; Visiting Professorships: Bristol, 1974; UC Berkeley, 1979; Canterbury, NZ, 1984; EPFL, Lausanne, Switzerland, 1987; Archibald D Ollé Prize, NSW Branch, RACI, 1982; A E Alexander Memorial Lecturer, RACI, 1987; Liversidge Lecturer, Royal Society of NSW, 1988; Archibald D Ollé Prize, 1994. Memberships: Fellow, Royal Australian Chemical Institute; Fellow, Australian Academy of Science; President, International Association of Colloid and Interface Science, 1990-94. Listed in Who's Who in Australia; Who's Who in the World. Address: 26/20A Austin St, Lane Cove, NSW 2066, Australia. E-mail: r.hunter@chem.usyd.edu.au

HUPPERT Herbert E, b. 26 November 1943, Sydney, Australia. m Felicia Ferster, 2 sons. Education: BSc, Honours, Sydney University, 1964; MSc, Australian National University, 1966; MS, University of California at San Diego, 1967; PhD, California, 1968; MA, Cambridge, 1971; ScD, Cambridge, 1985. Appointments: ICI Research Fellow, 1968-69; Assistant Director of Research in DAMTP, 1970-81; University Lecturer in DAMTP, 1981-88; Reader in Geophysical Dynamics, University of Cambridge, 1988-89; Professor of Theoretical Geophysics and Foundation Director of the Institute of Theoretical Geophysics, 1989-; Professor of Mathematics, University of New South Wales, 1991-96; Member, NERC Council, 1993-99; Visiting Scientist, Australian National University, University of California at San Diego, Canterbury University, Caltech, MIT, University of New South Wales, University of Western Australia, the Weizmann Institute, Woods Hole Oceanographic Institute; Chairman, Royal Society Working Group on Bioterrorism, which published a report, Making the UK Safer, 2004, 2002-. Publications: Author or co-author of approximately 230 papers discussing applied mathematics, crystal growth, fluid mechanics, geology, geophysics, oceanography, meteorology and science in general. Honours: Sydney University Medal and Baker Prize in Mathematics, 1964; Fellow, King's College Cambridge, 1970-; Maurice Hill Research Fellow of the Royal Society, 1977; Royal Society Anglo-Australian Research Fellow, 1991, 1995; Evnin Lecturer, Princeton University, 1995; Midwest Mechanics Lecturer, USA, 1996-97; Henry Charnock Distinguished Lecturer, Southampton Oceanography Centre, 1999; Smith Industries Lecturer, Oxford University, 1999; Elected to National Academy of America's Arthur L Day Prize and Lectureship, 2005; Distinguished Israel Pollak Lecturer of the Technion, 2005; William Hopkins Prize, Cambridge Philosophical Society, 2005; Royal Society Wolfson Merit Award, 2006; Murchison Medal London Geological Society, 2007; Balkerian Lecture of the Royal Society, 2011. Memberships: Elected Fellow: Royal Society, 1987, American Geophysical Union, 2002, American Physical Society, 2004; Royal Society Dining Club, 1993. Address: Institute of Theoretical Geophysics, DAMTP, University of Cambridge, Centre for Mathematical Sciences, Wilberforce Road, Cambridge CB3 0WA, England. E-mail: heh1@esc.cam.ac.uk Website: www.itg.cam.ac.uk/people/heh/index.html

HURD Douglas (Richard) (Lord Hurd of Westwell), b. 8 March 1930, Marlborough, England. Politician; Diplomat; Writer. m. (1) Tatiana Elizabeth Michelle, 1960, divorced, 3 sons, (2) Judy Smart, 1982, 1 son, 1 daughter. Education: History (First Class), Trinity College, Cambridge. Appointments: HM Diplomatic Service, 1952-66; Joined Conservative Research Department, 1966, Head, Foreign Affairs Section, 1968; Private Secretary to the Leader of the Opposition, 1968-70; Political Secretary to the Prime Minister, 1970-74; Member of Parliament, Conservative Party, Mid-Oxon, 1974-83, Witney, 1983-97; Opposition Spokesman on European Affairs, 1976-79; Visiting Fellow, Nuffield College, 1978-86; Minister of State, Foreign and Commonwealth Office, 1979-83, Home Office, 1983-84; Secretary of State for Northern Ireland, 1984-85, Home Secretary, 1985-89, Foreign Secretary, 1989-95; Director NatWest Group, 1995-99; Deputy Chairman, NatWest Markets, 1995-98; Deputy Chairman, Coutts & Co, 1998-; Chairman, Centre for Dispute Resolution, 2000-04; Chairman, Hawkpoint Advisory Committee, 1998-2002; Chairman, British Invisibles, 1998-2000; Chairman, then President, Prison Reform Trust, 1998-; Chairman, The Booker Prize Panel, 1998; High Steward, Westminster Abbey, 2002-; President, Royal Institute of International Affairs, 2003-. Publications: The Arrow War, 1967; Send Him Victorious (with Andrew Osmond), 1968; The Smile on the Face of the Tiger (with Andrew Osmond), 1969; Scotch on the Rocks (with Andrew Osmond), 1971; Truth Game, 1972; Vote to Kill, 1975; An End to Promises, 1979; War Without Frontiers (with Andrew Osmond), 1982; Palace of Enchantments (with Stephen Lamport), 1985; The Search for Peace (BBC TV Series), 1997; The Shape of Ice, 1998; Ten Minutes to Turn the Devil, 1999; Image in the Water, 2001; Memoirs, 2003. Honours: Commander of the Order of the British Empire, 1974; Privy Councillor, 1982; Companion of Honour, 1995; Baron Hurd of Westwell, 1997. Address: Freelands, Westwell, Burford, Oxon OX18 4JT, England.

HURLEY Elizabeth, b. 10 June 1965, England. Model; Actress; Producer. m. Arun Nayer, 2007, divorced 2011, 1 son previous relationship. Career: Former model and spokeswoman, Estée Lauder; Head of Development for Simian Films, 1996; Films include: Aria, 1987; The Skipper, 1989; The Orchid House, 1990; Passenger '57, 1992; Mad Dogs and Englishmen, 1994; Dangerous Ground, 1995; Samson and Delilah, Produced Extreme Measures, Austin Powers: International Man of Mystery, 1996; Permanent Midnight, 1997; My Favorite Martian, EdTV, Austin Powers: The Spy Who Shagged Me, 1999; The Weight of Water, Bedazzled, 2000; Serving Sara, The Weight of Water, Double Whammy, 2002; Method, 2004; Gossip Girl, 2011-12. Address: c/o Simian Films, 3 Cromwell Place, London SW7 2SE, England.

HURSTHOUSE Miles Wilson, b. 27 October 1919, Hastings, New Zealand. Medical Practitioner. m. Jillian, 2 sons, 1 daughter. Education: MB, ChB, Auckland University College, Otago University, Sydney University, Australian College of Dermatologists, Sydney, Australia; FACD, Australasian College of Dermatologists. Appointments: Civil Servant; Army Service WW2, 5 years New Zealand Artillery reaching rank of Captain; Hospital Service as House Surgeon, 2 years; Private Medical Practice, 48 years, including 3 years postgraduate study in Australia; Anaesthetist, Nelson Hospital, 16 years; Lecturer, Obstetrics Nelson Hospital, 10 years; Specialist Dermatologist, Nelson Hospital, 10 years; Retired, still registered medical practitioner for emergencies; Managing Director, Private Property Company. Publications: Autobiography, Vintage Doctor: 50 Years of Tears and Laughter, 2001; 10 scientific papers on subjects including: Melanoma incidence in the Nelson-Marlborough region of New Zealand, use of topical Retinoic acid in bullous ichthyosiform erythroderma, confusing rashes and exanthemata, basal cell carcinoma in burn scars. Honours: International Silver C Gliding Award; Member of winning car team, Southland Centennial Car Trial (International); New Zealand University Blue, Shooting, 1950; Otago University Blues, Shooting, 1949, 1950; Navigation Cup, Nelson Aero Club, 1964; Numerous cups and trophies for local motor sport; Honorary Life Member, Nelson Car Club and Nelson Gliding Club; Honorary Life member, Otago University Student Association; Patron, Nelson Lakes Gliding Club. Memberships include: President: Nelson Car Club, Nelson Gliding Club, Nelson Division, New Zealand Medical Association, Nelson Branch New Zealand Cancer Society, Nelson Branch, New Zealand Heart Foundation, New Zealand Dermatological Association, New Zealand Faculty Australasian College of Dermatologists, Stoke Tahunanui Probus Club; Member, Nelson Area Health Board; Inaugural President, Nelson Branch, National Society of Alcoholism; President, Otago University Student Association. Address: 306 Princes Drive, Nelson, New Zealand.

HURT David, b. 7 September 1961, San Francisco, California, USA. Storeworker; Business Owner. 1 foster son. Education: Hillsdale College, External Affairs; BS, Business Management, Liberty University; Open MIT; MBA, Ashford University, in progress. Appointments: Business Owner, 1981-2007; Storeworker, 1985-2007; Consumer Panels Worker, 2005-2006; Processor.com. Publications: Better Home and Garden; money.com; fortune.com; EOP; Techbriefs. Honours: Diploma of Expertise in Computers and Business; Man of the Year; 500 Greatest Geniuses of the 21st Century; American Ambassadors Medal; American Medal of Honor; ABI Man of the Year, 2009; Hall of Fame in Science, Law and Medicine; Pinnacle Achievement in Business and Retail Services. Memberships: Costco Business; ABI Advisory Directorate International; Boys Town; The J Paul Getty Trust; United State Olympic Committee; Slavic Gospel Association; Cooking Club of America; PETA; American Israel Public Affairs Commission. Address: 218 Calle de La Palmoa, Fallbrook, CA 92028, USA. E-mail: dchurt@earthlink.net

HURT John, b. 22 January 1940, Chesterfield, England. m. (1) Annette Robertson, (2) Donna Peacock, 1984, divorced 1990, (3) Jo Dalton, 1990, divorced 1995, 2 sons, (4) Ann Rees Meyers, 2005. Education: Lincoln Academy of Dramatic Art; Royal Academy of Dramatic Art. Appointments: Painter; Actor. Creative Works: Stage appearances include: Chips With Everything, 1962; The Dwarfs, 1963; Hamp, 1964; Inadmissible Evidence, 1965; Little Malcolm and His Struggle Against the Eunuchs, Belcher's Luck, 1966; The Only Street, 1973; Travesties, 1974; The Shadow of a Gunman, 1978; The London Vertigo, 1991; A Month in the Country, 1994; Krapp's Last Tape, 2000, Gate Theatre, 2001; Afterplay, 2002; Films include: The Elephant Man, 1980; King Ralph, Lapse of Memory, 1991; Dark at Noon, 1992; Monolith, Even Cowgirls Get the Blues, Rob Roy, 1994; Wild Bill, 1995; Dead Man, 1996; Contact, 1997; Love and Death on Long Island, 1998; All the Little Animals, You're Dead, The Love Letter, 1999; Lost Souls, Night Train, 2000; Captain Corelli's Mandolin, Harry Potter and the Philosopher's Stone, Tabloid, Bait, Miranda, Owning Mahony, 2001; Crime and Punishment, 2002; Miranda, Dogville (voice), 2003; Hellboy, 2004; Short Order, Valiant (voice), The Proposition, Shooting Dogs, Manderlay (voice), The Skeleton Key, V for Vendetta, 2005, Boxes, Outlander, 2007; Lezione 21, The Oxford Murders, Outlander, Hellboy II, 2008; An Englishman in New York, 2009. TV: The Waste Places, 1968; Nijinsky: God of the Dance, The Naked Civil Servant, 1975; I, Claudius, 1976; Treats, 1977; Crime and Punishment, 1979; Poison Candy, Deadline, 1988; Who Bombed Birmingham? 1990; Journey to Knock, Red Fox, 1991; Six Characters in Search of an Author, 1992; Prisoner in Time, Saigon Baby, 1995; Alan Clark Diaries, 2004. Honours:

Best Television Actor, 1975; British Academy Award, 1975; Emmy Award, 1978; British Academy Award, Best Supporting Actor, 1978; Golden Globe, Best Supporting Actor Award, 1978; Variety Club, Best Actor Award, 1978; British Academy Award, Best Actor, 1980; Variety Club, Best Film Actor Award, 1980; Evening Standard, Best Actor Award, 1984; Cable Ace Award, 1995; Richard Harris Award for Outstanding Contribution to British Film, British Film Industry Awards, 2003. Address: c/o Julian Belfrage & Associates, 46 Albemarle Street, London W1X 4PP, England.

HURT William, b. 20 March 1950, Washington, USA. Actor. m. (1) Mary Beth Hurt, (2) Heidi Henderson, 1989 (divorced), 2 sons. Education: Tufts University; Juilliard School. Creative Works: Stage appearances include: Henry V, 1976; Mary Stuart; My Life; Ulysses in Traction; Lulu; Fifth of July; Childe Byron; The Runner Stumbles; Hamlet, Hurlyburly; Beside Herself, 1989; Ivanov, 1991; Films include: Altered States; Eyewitness; Body Heat; The Big Chill; Corky Park; Kiss of the Spider Woman; Children of a Lesser God; Broadcast News, 1987; A Time of Destiny, 1988; The Accidental Tourist, 1989; The Plastic Nightmare; I Love You to Death, The House of Spirits, 1990; The Doctor, Until the End of the World, 1991; Mr Wonderful, The Plague, 1993; Trial By Jury, Second Best, 1994; Jane Eyre, Secrets Shared With a Stranger; Smoke, 1995; Michael; Loved; Lost in Space, One True Thing, Dark City, 1998; The Miracle Marker, 2000; AI: Artificial Intelligence, The Flamingo Rising, Rare Birds, 2001; Changing Lanes, Nearest to Heaven, Tuck Everlasting, 2002; The Blue Butterfly, The Village, 2004; The King, A History of Violence, Neverwas, Syriana, 2005; The Legend of Sasquatch (voice), Beautiful Ohio, The Good Shepherd, 2006; Mr Brooks, Noise, Into The Wild, 2007; Vantage Point, Yellow Handkerchief, The Incredible Hulk, 2008; The Countess, 2009. Honours include: Theatre World Award, 1978; Best Actor Award, Cannes Film Festival, 1985; Academy Award, Best Actor, 1985; 1st Spencer Tracy Award, 1988. Address: c/o Hilda Quille, William Morris Agency,151 El Camino Drive, Beverly Hills, CA 90212, USA.

HUSBANDS Sir Clifford (Straughn), b. 5 August 1926, Barbados. Governor-General. m. Ruby C D Parris, 1 son, 2 daughters. Education: Parry School; Harrison College, Barbados; Middle Temple, Inns of Court, London, England. Appointments: Called to Bar, Middle Temple, 1952; Private Practice, Barbados, 1952-54; Deputy Registrar (Ag) Barbados, 1954; Legal Assistant to Attorney General, Grenada, 1954-56; Magistrate, Grenada, 1956-57; Magistrate, Antigua, 1957-58; Crown Attorney, Magistrate and Registrar, Montserrat, 1958-60; Crown Attorney (Ag), St Kitts-Nevis-Anguilla, 1959; Attorney General (Ag), St Kitts-Nevis-Anguilla, 1960; Assistant to Attorney-General and Legal Draughtsman, Barbados, 1960-63; Assistant to Attorney General, Barbados, 1960-67; Director of Public Prosecutions, Barbados, 1967-76; Queen's Counsel, 1968; Judge, Supreme Court, Barbados, 1976-91; Justice of Appeal, Barbados, 1991-96; Chairman, Community Legal Services, 1985-96; Member, Judicial and Legal Service Commission, Barbados, 1987-96; Chairman, Penal Reform Committee, Barbados, 1995-96; Governor-General of Barbados, 1996; President of the Privy Council for Barbados, 1996. Honours: Queen's Silver Jubilee Medal, 1977; Gold Crown of Merit, 1989; Companion of Honour of Barbados, 1989; Knight of St Andrew, 1995; Knight of Grand Cross of the Most Distinguished Order of Saint Michael and Saint George, 1996; Paul Harris Fellowship Award, 2001; Knight of Grace in the Most Venerable Order of the Hospital of St John of Jerusalem, 2004. Memberships: Vice President, Barbados Lawn Tennis Association, 1970's; President, Old Harrisonian Society, 1983-87; Council Member, Barbados Family Planning Association, 1960-96. Address: Government House, Government Hill, St Michael, Barbados.

HUSSAIN Altaf, b. 31 July 1944, Kashmir, India. Consultant Orthopaedic Surgeon. m. Khalida Sultan, 1 son, 1 daughter. Education: MBBS, 1966, MS, 1973, Medical College, Kashmir University; MChOrth, Liverpool University, England, 1982. Appointments: Registrar, Lecturer and Assistant Professor, Orthopaedics, Government Medical College & SMHS Hospital, Srinagar, 1970-81; Further Higher Orthopaedic Training, Liverpool, 1979-83; Head, Surgical Division & Department of Orthopaedic Surgery, Al-Zulfi General Hospital, 1983-86; Consultant Orthopaedic Surgeon, Kingdom of Saudi Arabia, 1983-92; Head, Department of Orthopaedic Surgery, 1987-92, Chairman, Scientific Activities, 1987-92, Prince Salman Hospital, Riyadh, Saudi Arabia; Consultant Orthopaedic Surgeon, UK, 1992-; Consultant Editor, JK Practitioner, 1996-; Consultant Orthopaedic Surgeon, 2000-09, Lead Clinician, Clinical Audit & Effectiveness, T&O Department, 2001-09, Supervisor, Research & Development, 2005-09, Prince Charles Hospital, Merthyr Tydfil, Wales; Tutor, Royal College of Surgeons, University Hospital of Wales, Cardiff, 2002-; Examiner (OSCE), MBBS, Cardiff University, 2004-09. Publications: Numerous articles in professional journals. Honours: Best Practice Team Award, 2007; Glory of India Award, 2008; Bharat Gaurav Award, 2009; Lifetime Achievement Award, Global Friendship Day, 2010; Listed in international biographical dictionaries; Fellow, British Orthopaedic Association; Fellow, International College of Orthopaedic Surgeons. Memberships: Indian Orthopaedic Association; American Medical Society; British Medical Association; Welsh Orthopaedic Society; Kashmir Orthopaedic Surgeons Association; Indian Orthopaedic Society. Address: 20 Plas Ty Mawr, Penyfai, Bridgend, Mid Glamorgan, CF31 4NH, Wales. E-mail: altafhussain_uk@hotmail.com

HUSSAR Piret, b. 9 March 1971, Tartu, Estonia. Histologist. Education: MD, 1997; Doctor of Medical Sciences, 2002. Appointments: Laboratory Technician, 1995-97, Assistant, Histology and Embryology, 1997-2004, Senior Assistant, Histology and Embryology, 2004-08, Associate Professor, 2008-, University of Tartu; Associate Professor, Histology, Estonian University of Life Studies, 2007-10. Publications: Co-author of article, Histology of the Post-traumatic Bone Repair, 2009; Co-author of textbooks: Histoloogia, 2005; Erihistoloogia, 2007. Honours: ETF Grants; Monbusho's grant for research in Japan, 1998-2000; JSPS grant for postdoctoral studies in Japan, 2005-06; Listed in international biographical dictionaries. Memberships: Association of Estonian Morphologists; St Petersburg's Society of Ecology and Toxicology; ISVM; Association Anatomici Fenniae; EAVA. Address: Leevikese 1A-12, Tartu 50413, Estonia. E-mail: piretut@gmail.com

HUSSEIN, HM Queen Noor of Jordan, b. Lisa Najeeb Halaby, 23 August 1951. m. King Hussein I of Jordan, 1978, deceased 1999, 2 sons, 2 daughters. Education: Princeton University. Appointments: Architechtural and Urban Planning Projects, Australia, Iran, Jordan, 1974-78; Founder, Royal Endowment for Culture and Education, Jordan, 1979, Annual Arab Childrens Congress, Jordan, 1980, Annual International Jerash Festival for Culture and Arts, Jordan, 1981, Jubilee School, Jordan, 1984, Noor Al-Hussein Foundation, Jordan, 1985, National Music Conservatory, Jordan, 1986; Chair, National Task Force for Children; Advisory Committee, UN University International Leadership Academy, Amman;

Patron, General Federation of Jordanian Women, National Federation of Business and Professional Womens Clubs, Royal Society for Conservation of Nature and various cultural, sporting and national development organisations; WWF International, Aspen International, 2004-; International Alert's Women and Peace-building Campaign, Council of Women World Leaders' Advisory Group, 2004-; Honorary President, Jordan Red Crescent, Birdlife Int, 1996-2004 (Honorary President Emeritus, 2004-). Publication: Leap of Faith: Memoirs of an Unexpected Life, 2002. Honours: Numerous honorary doctorates, international awards and decorations. Memberships include: Honorary President, Jordan Red Crescent; Founding Member, International Commission on Peace and Food, 1992; President, United World Colleges, 1995. Address: Royal Palace, Amman, Jordan.

HUSSIN Sufean, b. 25 March 1956, Malacca, Malaysia. Professor. m. Noraihan Abd Rashid, 3 sons, 1 daughter. Education: BSc Ed (Hons), 1981; M Ed, 1986; PhD, 1994. Appointments: Teacher, 1981-84; Lecturer, 1985-94; Associate Professor, 1995-2003; Professor, 2004-11; Dean of Education, 2004-2005. Publications: Author, 21 academic books; Author, more than 80 papers and journal articles in education, management and leadership. Honours: Ambassador of Peace by Universal Peace Federation, New York; Twice awarded, Excellence of Service. Memberships: Universal Peace Federation; World Youth Institute; Alumni of Salzburg Seminar; Alumni University of Oregon. Address: Faculty of Education, University of Malaya, Lembah Pantai, 50603, Kuala Lumpur, Malaysia. E-mail: drsufean@um.edu.my

HUSTON Anjelica, b. 8 July 1951, Los Angeles, California, USA. Actress. m. Robert Graham, 1992. Creative Works: Stage appearances include: Tamara, Los Angeles, 1985; TV appearances include: The Cowboy and the Ballerina, NBC-TV Film, 1984, Faerie Tale Theatre, A Rose for Miss Emily, PBS Film, Lonesome Dove, CBS Mini-Series; The Mists of Avalon, 2001; Iron Jawed Angels, 2004; Films include: Sinful Davey; A Walk with Love and Death, 1969; The Last Tycoon, 1976; The Postman Always Rings Twice, 1981; Swashbuckler; This is Spinal Tap, The Ice Pirates, 1984; Prizzi's Honor, 1985; Gardens of Stone; Captain Eo; The Dead; Mr North; A Handful of Dust; The Witches; Enemies; A Love Story; The Grifters; The Addams Family; Addams Family Values; The Player; Manhattan Murder Mystery; The Crossing Guard, The Perez Family, 1995; Buffalo '66, Phoenix, 1997; Director, Bastard Out of Carolina, 1995, Phoenix, 1997; Agnes Browne, 1999; The Golden Bowl, 2001; The Royal Tenenbaums, Blood Work, The Man from Elysian Fields, 2002; Daddy Day Care, 2003; The Life Aquatic with Steve Zissou, 2004; These Foolish Things, Art School Confidential, Material Girls, Seraphim Falls, 2006; The Darjeeling Limited, Martian Child, 2007; Choke, The Kreutzer Sonata, Tinker Bell (voice), 2008. Honours include: Academy Award, Best Supporting Actress, 1985; NY & Los Angeles Film Critics Awards, 1985; Best Supporting Actress in a Series, Miniseries or TV Movie, Golden Globe Awards, 2005. Address: c/o International Creative Management, 8942 Wilshire Boulevard, Beverly Hills, CA 90211, USA.

HUSTON Janis Lynne, b. USA. Health Information Manager. Education: BSc (cum laude), Ohio State University, 1975; MEd, Bowling Green State University, 1983; PhD, University of Kentucky, 1997. Appointments: Assistant/Acting Director, Medical Record Department, Providence Hospital, Alaska, 1976-79; Director, Medical Record Administration Program, College of Health and Community Services, Bowling State University, 1979-84; Medical Record Analyst, Wyoming Medical Center, 1985; Director, Medical Record Department, and Utilization Review Coordinator and Quality Assurance Coordinator, Crest View Hospital, Wyoming, 1985-86; Associate Professor, College of Allied Health and Nursing, Eastern Kentucky University, 1987-94; Telemedicine Evaluation Research Associate, University of Kentucky Medical Center, 1995-97; Visiting Assistant Professor, College of Medicine and Public Health, Ohio State University, USA, 1997-98; Health Information Manager, Histopathology Laboratory, Wiesbaden, Germany, 1998-2000; Electronic Patient Record Facilitator, North London Cancer Network, UK, 2001-02; Medical Record and Data Quality Manager, UCLH NHS Trust, London, 2002; Clinical Dataset Researcher, Royal College of Physicians, London, 2002-03; Clinical Coding Advisor and Tutor, Connecting for Health, London, 2003-04; Health Information Management Consultant, 2005-; Clinical Coding Consultant, Salford Royal NHS Foundation Trust, Manchester, 2008; Clinical Coding Services Manager, Royal Marsden NHS Hospital Trust, London, 2009-. Publications: Numerous articles in professional journals. Memberships: International Federation of Health Records Organization; British Computer Society; Royal Society of Medicine; American Health Information Management Association. E-mail: jl.huston@yahoo.com

HUTSON Jeremy Mark, b. 7 May 1957, West Kirby, Cheshire, England. Professor of Chemistry. Education: BA, 1st Class, Chemistry, Wadham College, Oxford University, 1975-79; DPhil, Physical Chemistry, Hertford College, Oxford University, 1979-81. Appointments: NATO/SERC Postdoctoral Research Fellow, University of Waterloo, Canada, 1981-83; Drapers Company Research Fellow, 1983-84, Stokes Research Fellow, 1984-86, Pembroke College, Cambridge and Theoretical Chemistry Department, University of Cambridge; Lecturer, 1987-93, Reader, 1993-96, Professor, 1996-, Head of the Department of Chemistry, 1998-2001, University of Durham; Chair, Gordon Conference on Molecular and Ionic Clusters, Ventura, 2008; Chair, Faraday Discussion 142 on Cold and Ultracold Molecules, 2009; Numerous invited lectures at international conferences include most recently: Coherence in Ultracold Molecular Physics, Vancouver, 2010; 11th International Meeting on Quantum Reactive Scattering, Santa Fe, New Mexico, 2011. Publications: 170 scientific publications with over 6,000 citations; Editor, International Reviews in Physical Chemistry, 2000-. Honours: Corday-Morgan Medal, Royal Society of Chemistry, 1991; Visiting Fellowship, Joint Institute for Laboratory Astrophysics, Boulder, Colorado, USA, 1991; Nuffield Foundation Science Research Fellowship, 1993-94; Visiting Professorship, University of Colorado, 2001-2002; Kołos Medal, University of Warsaw and Polish Chemical Society, 2007; Award in Computational Chemistry, Royal Society of Chemistry, 2007; Tilden Prize, Royal Society of Chemistry, 2011. Memberships: Fellow, Royal Society of Chemistry, UK; Fellow, Institute of Physics, UK; Fellow, Royal Society. Address: Department of Chemistry, University of Durham, Durham DH1 3LE, England.

HUTTON, Baron of Bresagh in the County of Down, (James) Brian Edward Hutton, b. 29 June 1931, United Kingdom. Retired Law Lord. m. (1) Mary Gillian Murland, deceased, 2000, 2 daughters, (2) Rosalind Anne Nickols, 2 stepsons, 1 stepdaughter. Education: BA, Balliol College, Oxford; Queen's University, Belfast. Appointments: Called to the Bar, Northern Ireland, 1954; Junior Counsel to Attorney General of Northern Ireland, 1969; Queen's Counsel, Northern Ireland, 1970; Senior Crown Counsel, Northern Ireland, 1973-79; Judge of the High Court of Justice, Northern

Ireland, 1979-88; Lord Chief Justice of Northern Ireland, 1988-97; a Lord of Appeal in Ordinary, 1997-2004; Chairman, Hutton Inquiry, 2003-2004; Member, Joint Law Enforcement Commission, 1974; Deputy Chairman, Boundary Commission for Northern Ireland, 1985-88. Honours: Kt, 1988; Privy Councillor, 1988; Life Peer, 1997. Memberships: President, Northern Ireland Association for Mental Health, 1983-90; Visitor, University of Ulster, 1999-2004. Address: House of Lords, London SW1A 0PW, England.

HUTTON Ronald Edmund, b. 19 December 1953, Ootacamund, India. Historian. m. Lisa Radulovic, 5 August 1988. Education: BA, Cantab, 1976; MA, 1980; DPhil, 1980. Appointments: Professor of History, Bristol University, 1996-. Publications: The Royalist War Effort, 1981; The Restoration, 1985; Charles II, 1989; The British Republic, 1990; The Pagan Religions of the Ancient British Isles, 1991; The Rise and Fall of Merry England, 1994; The Stations of the Sun, 1996; The Triumph of the Moon: A History of Modern Pagan Witchcraft, 1999; Shamans, 2001; Witches, Druids and King Arthur, 2003; Debates in Stuart History, 2004; The Druids, 2007; Blood and Mistletoe: The History of the Druids in Britain, 2009. Contributions to: Journals. Honour: Benjamin Franklin Prize, 1993. Memberships: Royal Historical Society; Folklore Society; Fellow, Society of Antiquaries. Address: 13 Woodland Road, Bristol BS8 1TB, England.

HUTTON Timothy, b. 16 August 1960, Malibu, California, USA. Actor. m. (1) Debra Winger, 1986, divorced, 1 son. (2) Aurore Giscard d'Estaing, 2000, 1 son. Career: Plays: Prelude to a Kiss, 1990; Babylon Gardens, 1991; TV: Zuma Beach, 1978; Best Place to Be; Baby Makes Six; Sultan and the Rock Star; Young Love; First Love; Friendly Fire, 1979; Nero Wolfe Mystery, 2001; WW3, 2001; 5ive Days to Midnight, 2004; Films: Ordinary People, 1980; Taps, 1981; Daniel, 1983; Iceman, 1984; Turk, The Falcon and the Snowman, 1985; Made in Heaven, 1987; A Time of Destiny, Everybody's All-American, Betrayed, 1988; Torrents of Spring, Q&A, 1990; The Temp, The Dark Half, 1993; French Kiss, City of Industry, Scenes From Everyday Life, 1995; The Substance of Fire, Mr and Mrs Loving, Beautiful Girls, 1996; City of Industry, Playing God, 1997; The General's Daughter, 1999; Just One Night, Deliberate Intent, Deterrence, Lucky Strike, 2000; Sunshine State, 2002; Secret Window, Kinsey, 2004; Turning Green, 2005; Last Holiday, Stephanie Daley, The Kovak Box, Heavens Fall, Falling Objects, Off the Black, The Good Shepherd, 2006; The Last Mimzy, When a Man Falls in the Forest, Lymelife, The Alphabet Killer, Brief Interviews with Hideous Men, Multiple Sarcasms, 2007; Reflections, 2008; The Killing Room, Serious Moonlight, Broken Hill, 2009; The Ghost Writer, 2010. Honours: Oscar, Best Supporting Actor, 1980. Address: CAA, 9830 Wilshire Boulevard, Beverly Hills, CA 90212, USA.

HUXLEY George Leonard, b. 23 September 1932, Leicester, England. Scholar. m. Davina Best, 3 daughters. Education: BA, Magdalen College, Oxford, 1955. Appointments: Fellow, All Souls College, Oxford, 1955-61; Professor of Greek, The Queen's University of Belfast. 1962-83; Director, Gennadius Library, American School of Classical Studies, Athens, Greece, 1986-89; Research Associate, later Honorary Professor, Trinity College, Dublin, 1983-; Adjunct Professor, Ancient Classics & Mathematics, NUI Maynooth, 2008-. Publications: Books and articles on Greek and Byzantine subjects. Honours: Hon DLitt, Belfast; Hon Litt D, Dublin. Memberships: Athenaeum; Fellow of the Society of Antiquaries; Member of the Royal Irish Academy; Member, Academia Europaea. Address: School of Classics, Trinity College, Dublin 2, Ireland.

HUXLEY Hugh Esmor, b. 25 February 1924, Birkenhead, England. Physiologist. m. Frances Frigg, 1966, 2 stepsons, 1 daughter, 1 stepdaughter. Education: Graduated, Christ's College, Cambridge, 1943; PhD, 1952. Appointments: Radar Officer, RAF Bomber Command and Telecommunications Research Establishment, Malvern, 1943-47; Research Student, Medical Research Council Unit for Molecular Biology, Cavendish Laboratory, Cambridge, 1948-52; Commonwealth Fund Fellow, Biology Department, MIT, 1952-54; Research Fellow, Christ's College, Cambridge, 1952-56; Member, External Staff, 1962-87, Joint Head, Structural Studies Division, 1976-87, Deputy Director, 1977-87, Medical Research Council Laboratory of Molecular Biology, Cambridge; Professor of Biology, 1987-97, Director, 1988-94, Professor Emeritus, 1997-, Rosenstiel Basic Medical Sciences Research Center, Brandeis University, Boston, Massachusetts; Fellow, King's College, Cambridge, 1961-67; Fellow, Churchill College, Cambridge, 1967-87; Harvey Society Lecturer, New York, 1964-65; Senior Visiting Lecturer, Physiology Course, Woods Hole, Massachusetts, 1966-71; Wilson Lecturer, University of Texas, 1968; Dunham Lecturer, Harvard Medical School, 1969; Croonian Lecturer, Royal Society of London, 1970; Ziskind Visiting Professor of Biology, Brandeis University, 1971; Penn Lecturer, University of Pennsylvania, 1971; Mayer Lecturer, MIT, 1971; Miller Lecturer, State University of New York, 1973; Carter-Wallace Lecturer, Princeton University, 1973; Pauling Lecturer, Stanford University, 1980; Jesse Beams Lecturer, University of Virginia, 1980; Ida Beam Lecturer, University of Iowa, 1981. Publications: Articles in scientific journals. Honours: Feldberg Award for Experimental Medical Research, 1963; William Bate Hardy Prize of the Cambridge Philosophical Society, 1965; Honorary DSc, 1969, 1974, 1976, 1988; Louis Gross Horwitz Prize, 1971; International Feltrinelli Prize for Medicine, 1974; International Award, Gairdner Foundation, 1975; Baly Medal, Royal College of Physicians, 1975; Royal Medal, Royal Society of London, 1977; E B Wilson Medal, American Society for Cell Biology, 1983; Albert Einstein World Award of Science, 1987; Franklin Medal, 1990; Distinguished Scientist Award, Electron Microscopy Society of America, 1991; Copley Medal, Royal Society of London, 1997. Memberships: Member, Advisory Board, Rosenstiel Basic Medical Sciences Center, Brandeis University, 1971-77; Member, Council of Royal Society of London, 1973-75, 1984-86; Member, Scientific Advisory Committee, European Molecular Biology Laboratory, 1975-81; Member, Board of Trustees, Associated Universities Inc, 1987-90; Member, Germany Academy of Science, Leopoldina, 1964; Foreign Associate, NAS, 1978; American Association of Anatomists, 1981; American Physiologeal Society, 1981; American Society of Zoologists, 1986; Foreign Honorary Member, American Academy of Arts and Sciences, 1965; Danish Academy of Sciences, 1971; American Society of Biological Chemists, 1976; Honorary Fellow, Christ's College, Cambridge, 1981. Address: Rosenstiel Basic Medical Sciences Research Center, Brandeis University, Waltham, MA 02254, USA.

HUXTABLE Ada Louise, b. 14 March 1921, New York, New York, USA. Architecture Critic; Writer. m. L Garth Huxtable. Education: AB, magna cum laude, Hunter College, New York City; Postgraduate Studies, Institute of Fine Arts, New York University. Appointments: Assistant Curator of Architecture and Design, Museum of Modern Art, New York, 1946-50; Contributing Editor, Progressive Architecture and Art in America, 1950-63; Architecture Critic, The New York Times,

1963-82, The Wall Street Journal, 1996-; Cook Lecturer in American Institutions, University of Michigan, 1977; Hitchcock Lecturer, University of California at Berkeley, 1982. Publications: Pier Luigi Nervi, 1960; Classic New York, 1964; Will They Ever Finish Bruckner Boulevard?, 1970; Kicked a Building Lately?, 1976; The Tall Building Artistically Reconsidered: The Search for a Skyscraper Style, 1985; Goodbye History, Hello Hamburger, 1986; Architecture Anyone?, 1986; The Unreal America: Architecture and Illusion, 1997. Contributions to: Various publications. Honours: Many honorary doctorates; Fulbright Fellowship, 1950-52; Guggenheim Fellowship, 1958; Architectural Medal for Criticism, American Institute of Architects, 1969; 1st Pulitzer Prize for Distinguished Criticism, 1970; Medal for Literature, National Arts Club, 1971; Diamond Jubilee Medallion, City of New York, 1973; Secretary's Award for Conservation, US Department of the Interior, 1976; Thomas Jefferson Medal, University of Virginia, 1977; John D and Catharine T MacArthur Foundation Fellowship, 1981-86; Henry Allen Moe Prize in the Humanities, American Philosophical Society, 1992. Memberships: American Academy of Arts and Letters; American Philosophical Society; American Academy of Arts and Sciences, fellow; New York Public Library, director's fellow; Society of Architectural Historians. Address: 969 Park Avenue, New York, NY 10028, USA.

HUYNH My Hang V, b. 30 May 1962, Saigon, Vietnam (Naturalized US citizen). Chemist. Education: BS, Chemistry, BA, Mathematics, State University College of New York at Geneseo, 1987-91; PhD, Co-ordination Chemistry, State University of New York at Buffalo, 1998; Post-Doctoral Research Associate, University of North Carolina, Chapel Hill, North Carolina, 1998-2000; Post-Doctoral Research Associate, 2000, Director-Funded Postdoctoral Fellow, 2001-02, Los Alamos National Laboratory, New Mexico; PhD, Chemistry (Co-ordination Chemistry). Appointments: Tutor, Chemistry and Mathematics, State University College of New York at Geneseo, 1988-90; Lecturer, Chemistry, State University of New York at Buffalo, 1992-1997; Synthetic Organic and Inorganic Chemist in High-Nitrogen Energetic Materials, Dynamic Materials Property and Energetic Materials Science Division, Los Alamos National Laboratory, Los Alamos, 2002-; MacArthur Fellow in Chemistry, 2008-12. Publications: Numerous appearances in national and international media resulting from Green Primary Explosives; 62 articles in scientific journals; 16 patents; 5 books. Honours include: Director-Funded Postdoctoral Fellow, Los Alamos National Laboratory, 2001-02; Postdoctoral Distinguished Performance Award, Los Alamos National Laboratory, 2002; Living Science Award for Services to Research, Application, Healthcare and Education in all Scientific Fields, 2004; Distinguished Licensing Award, Los Alamos National Laboratory, 2005; Individual Distinguished Performance Award, Los Alamos National Laboratory, 2005; 21st Century Award for Achievement, 2005; R&D 100 Award Winner: Combustion Synthesis of Nano-structured Metal Foams, 2005; R&D 100 Award Winner: Green Primaries – Enviro-Friendly Energetic Materials, 2006; National Registry of Environmental Professional (NREP) Awards in Health and Safety, 2006; Ernest Orlando Lawrence Award for Chemistry, 2006; Best-in-class Pollution Prevention, DOE/NNSA Award, Green Primaries – Enviro-Friendly Energetic Materials, 2007; International Medal of Honor, 2007; Geneseo Alumni Association Professional Achievement Award, 2008; Best-in-Class Pollution Prevention DOE/NNSA Award, Ultrapure Carbon and Carbon Nitrides nano-materials; MacArthur Fellowship Genius Award, 2008-12; Pollution Prevention P2 Star Award Honorable Mention, Green Primary-Enviro-Friendly Energetic Materials; Listed in several Who's Who and biographical publications. Address: Los Alamos National Laboratory, High Explosive Science and Technology Group, MS C920 Los Alamos National University, New Mexico 87545, USA. E-mail: huynh@los-alamos.net

HWANG Chang Ho, b. 2 February 1973, Cheon-An City, Republic of Korea. Medical Doctor; Professor. Education: Bachelor, Chung-Han National University, 1997; Master, Medical Science, Ulsan University. Appointments: Intern, 200, Resident, 2001-05, Asan Medical Center, Seoul; Chief Director, Assistant Professor, Department of Physical Medicine & Rehabilitation, 2005-, Adjunct Professor, Department of Biomedical Engineering, 2010-, Ulsan University Hospital. Publications: Numerous articles in professional journals. Honours: Listed in international biographical dictionaries. Memberships: Korean Medical Association; Korean Academy of Rehabilitation Medicine; Korean Society of Neurorehabilitation; Korean Academy of Electrodiagnostic Medicine; Korean Dysphagia Society; Korean Society of Paediatric Rehabilitation & Developmental Medicine. Address: Department of Rehabilitation, Ulsan University Hospital, University of Ulsan College of Medicine, 290-3 Jeonho-dong, Dong-gu, Ukan city 682-714, Republic of Korea. E-mail: chhwang1220ciba@yahoo.co.kr

HWANG Hyosik, b. 20 December 1960, Taebaek, Kangwon-do, Korea. Professor. m. Hyunsook Kim. Education: PhD, University of Nebraska-Lincoln, USA, 2000. Appointments: Chair, Department of English, College of Humanities, Chungbuk National University, 2008-10. Publications: Shakespeare the Political Man: The Second Tetralogy and Its Historical Moment, 2000; What doctrine call you this?: Calvinism and Marlowe's Doctor Faustus, 2006; Hamlet and the English Reformation, 2007. Memberships: The Shakespeare Association of Korea; The Korea Society for Teaching English Literature. Address: Department of English, College of Humanities, Chungbuk National University, 410 Sungbong-ro, Heungduk-gu, Cheongju 361-763, Korea. E-mail: hhwang@chungbuk.ac.kr

HWANG Seung-Hyun, b. 17 December 1973, Seoul, Korea. Senior Researcher. m. Ji-Yeon Kim, 1 son. Educaiton: BS, 1996, MS, 1998, PhD, 2005, Space Science, Kyung Hee University, Suwon. Appointments: Associate Researcher, Satellite Technology Research Center, Korea Advanced Institute of Science & Technology, Daejeon, 1996-99; Senior Researcher, KSLV System Integration Team, KARI, Daejeon, 2000-. Publications: National Point of Contact, SGAC, Vienna, 2007-08. Honours: Best Researcher of the Year, KARI, 2003; Listed in biographical dictionaries. Memberships: Korean Earth Science Society; Korean Society for Aeronautical and Space Sciences; Korean Space Science Society; American Geophysical Union. Address: 45, Eoeun-dong, Yuseong, Daejeon 305-333, Republic of Korea.

HWANG Sungwook, b. 14 February 1975, Daegu, Republic of Korea. Professor. m. Soyeon Kang, 1 son, 1 daughter. Education: BA, Public Administration, Pusan National University, 1997; MA, 2003, PhD, 2008, Journalism, University of Missouri at Columbia, USA. Appointments: Account Executive, Public Relations Team, Cheil Communication, 2004-05; Assistant Professor, Department of Digital Media, Myongji University, 2008-10; Assistant Professor, Department of Communication, Pusan National University, 2010-. Publications: The estimation of a corporate crisis, 2009; The effect of charitable giving by celebrities on the personal public relations, 2010; The strategic use of Twitter to manage personal public relations, 2012. Honours: Professional Presentation Travel Fellowship, University of Missouri at Columbia, 2008; Best Research Paper Award, Korean Association for Advertising & Public Relations, 2009. Memberships: International Communication Association; Association for Education in Journalism & Mass Communication; Korean Association for Advertising & Public Relations. Address: College of Social Sciences, Pusan National University, Korea. E-mail: hsw110@gmail.com

HWANG Tae-Won, b. 26 February 1958, Daejeon, Republic of Korea. Researcher. m. Chan-Boon Park, 1 son, 1 daughter. Education: BA, 1980, MS, 1984, PhD, 2005, Chemical Engineering, Chungnam National University. Appointments: Senior Researcher, Korea Atomic Energy Research Institute, 1988-96; Principal Researcher, 1997-2009, Director, 2010-, Korea Hydro & Nuclear Power Company. Publications: Numerous articles in professional journals. Honours: Meritorious Award, Korea Hydro & Nuclear Power Company, 2002; Meritorious Award, Korea Ministry of Knowledge Economy, 2011. Memberships: Executive Officer of Korean Radioactive Waste Society; R&D Planning Committee, Ministry of Knowledge Economy. Address: NETEC of KHNP, 25-1 Jang-dong, Yuseong-gu, Daejeon 305-343, Republic of Korea. E-mail: twhwang@khnp.co.kr

HWANG Taeyon, b. 22 August 1974, Cheonan, Republic of Korea. Researcher; Educator. m. Yuran Seo, 1 son. Education: B Eng, 2002, M Eng, 2004, Kyung Hee University, Republic of Korea; PhD, Architecture, University of Tokyo, Japan, 2007. Appointments: Senior Researcher, Samsung C&T Corporation, Republic of Korea, 2007; Research Scholar, EETD in Lawrence Berkeley National Laboratory, California, USA, 2011-; Research Fellow, Engineering Research Center, Ministry of Education, Science & Technology of Korea, 2011. Publications: Effects of indoor lighting on occupants' visual comfort and eye health in a green building, 2011; Optimization of the building integrated photovoltaic system in office buildings, 2012; Optimal illuminance of seven major lighting colours in LED, 2012. Honours: Best Paper Awardee, Indoor and Built Environment, 2011. Memberships: Lighting Designer, Korean Institute of Illuminating and Electrical Installation Engineers. Address: Light & Architectural Environment Laboratory, Department of Architectural Engineering, Kyung Hee University, 1732 Deokyeong-daero, Giheung-gu, Yongin-si, Gyeonggi-do 446-701, Republic of Korea. E-mail: hwang@khu.ac.kr

HWANG Tzu-Yang, b. 21 September 1953, Taiwan, Republic of China (nationalised US citizen, 1994). Professor; President; Senior Pastor; Honorary Chair. m. Wei-Chih, 1 adopted son. Education: Humanity Sciences, Tung-Hai University, Taiwan, 1977-78; The Workshop of Pastoral Church Growth and Field Education, 1983-84; International Workshop on Theology and Asian Studies, 1984; Missiology, Fuller Theological Seminary, 1987; Master of Divinity, Systematics and Church History, Tainan Theological Seminary; Masters of Theology, Systematic Theology, The History of Christian Doctrine, Princeton University Theological Seminary; PhD, Religious Philosophy, Theology and Culture, Chinese for Christ Theological Seminary, USA, 1990; Researching Religions, Culture, Philosophy, Theology at Harvard University Divinity School, and Duke University Divinity School, 1991-92; Master Diploma, Religion, Philosophy and Cultural Theology; Missio-History; Education; Culture; History and Missions; Religious Philosophy; Theology. Appointments: President, Sunday School of King-Men Church; Preacher, Ta-Tseng Church, Taiwan; Chair, Erhin District Changhua Union Church; The Bible Study in University Center for University Students for Presbyterians of Chenghua and Taichung; Teaching Assistant, Tainan Theological Seminary; Founder, Youth Fellowship, Kingston Taiwanese American Fellowship Presbyterian Church, USA; Head Pastor, Good Shepherd Presbyterian Church, USA; Chair for Philosophy and Theology, Chinese for Christian Theological Seminary; Adjunct Professor, Holy Light Theological Seminary; President, Supreme Master, Grand Master, Distinguished Professor, CEO, Founder, Honorary Chair, Chair of the Faculty Committee, Chair of the Research Department; Honorary Doctor of Philosophy, American Chichou Theo-Philosophical Institute, El Monte, California, USA; Senior Pastor, Founder, President, Honorary Chair, Light Christ Church, USA; President, Incorporator, CEO, Founder, Chair, Charter Governor, Light Christ Foundation. Publications: Numerous publications; Over 700 items for numerous awards, prizes, orders, laureates, medals, ranks, citations, certificates and diplomas; Over 36 books; Over 1,200 professional and academic articles and papers; Over 100 international biographical dictionaries and books. Honours: Numerous awards and prizes including: International Order of Ambassador; Minister of Culture; Secretary General, UCC, American Registry of Outstanding Professionals; Ambassador-General of the USA, UCC; International Top 100 Scientists; Leading Scientists of the World; International Governor; International Order of Fellowships; International Top 100 Educator; Leading Educators of the World; Diploma of Experts, Leading International Leaders of Achievement; The Certificate of Leading Scientists of the World; Leading Professionals of the World; Senator, World Nations Congress Global Fellowship; World Academy of Letters; Gold Medal, United States; International Medal of Honour (3 times); Sovereign Ambassador of the Order of American Ambassador; Meritorious Decoration (4 times), IBC; International Cultural Diploma of Honor (5 times), ABI; Presidential Seal of Honor; International Sash of Academia; International Directory of Experts and Expertise; The Ambassador of Grand Eminence; Mutual Loyalty Award, IBC; International Expert; Registry of the World's Most Respected Expert; Noble Laureate; Genius Laureate of the United States; World Laureate; International Registry of Profiles; International Ambassador of Goodwill; Greatest Intellectuals; Greatest Living Legends; Grand Master, Supreme Master; Adviser of Arts and Humanities to the Director General; International Medal of Honor; Life Member, Research Council of Biography; International Order of Distinction; Adviser on Arts and Humanities to the Director General, IBC; Greatest Minds; Greatest Lives; Leading Intellectuals of the World (Founding Member, Charter Member, Noble Member, Hall of Fame); Leading Educators of the World; Leading Scientists of the World; The Tzu-Yang Hwang Award Foundation; Vice President, Recognition Board of the World Congress for Arts, Science and Communications; Socratic Chair; Humanities and Philosophy; World Academy of Letters; Board Member, International Order of Merit; Founding Cabinet Member, Presidential Dedication, World Peace and Diplomacy Forum to the United Nations Organisation; Founder, Life Academician, Diplomatic Counsellor, London and International Diplomatic Academy; The Royal Book of Diplomacy and Science; Albert Schweitzer International University to UNO; Prominent Member, Cavalier/Commander, International and The World Order of Sciences, Culture and Education, European and International Academy of Informatization, Belgium and World Distributed Information University to UNO; World Distributed University; International Information Center; Deputy Governor, Continental Governor for the USA, American Biographical Institute; Deputy Director General,

Continental Governor for the USA, Honorary Director General, International Biographical Centre; Founder of the Order; Founder, American Order of Excellence (medal); many others. Memberships: Harvard Co-operative Society; American Chi-Chou Theo-Philosophical Institute; Light Christ Church; Light Christ Foundation; American Academy of Religion; The Society of Biblical Literature; The Scientific Study of Religion, Purdue University; Decree Number 4 of Only One Hundred for Decree of Excellence in Education; Pinnacle Achievement Award for Education; Cogressional Medal of Excellence; Gold Laureates; International Medal of Vision; Man of Achievement; Outstanding Achievement Award, 3 times; Light Christ Church Foundation; National Republican Congressional Committee's Member (Sustaining Member & Gold Member); Register of Congressional Order of Merit (US House); Honorary Chairman, Prestigious House Republican Trust, premier group of Advisors to Republican Leadership, US House of Representatives; Member, National Geography; Member, USA Olympic Team Committee; Member, Harvard Co-operative Society; American Chi Chou Theo-Philosophical Institute recognised and accredited to California Government (CPSVE), Association of Theological Schools (ATS), USA, Canada, Taiwan, and mainland China; World Nations and United Nations Organisations (UNO); Muriel Van Orden Jennings Society, Princeton Theological Seminary; Diamond Leader, Gold Leader, Disabled American Veteran, Commander's Club; Gallery of Excellence; President Award; World Medal of Freedom; World Citizen; World Cup; Noble Prize; Legion of Honor; President's Citation; Gold Laurel; International Expert Elite; World Record Holder; 500 Greatest Genius of 21st Century; Ambassador (Consular) of the International Order of Merit; The Top 200 of the IBC; The Rev Dr Professor Tzu-Yang Hwang, HonDG Foundation; Vice-Chancellor, World Academy of Letters; (Senator; Supreme Master, Vice President, Recognition Board, World Nations Congress); International Profile of the Accomplished Leader; Greatest Intellectuals; Outstanding 2000 Intellectuals of 21st Century Triptych Award & Medal of Inclusion; Dictionary of Greatest Intellectuals Dedication; World Record Holder; International Peace Prize; others. Address: 11768 Roseglen Street, El Monte, CA 91732, USA.

HWANG Yoon-Min, b. 16 January 1980, Incheon, South Korea. Researcher. Education: BA, Management & Economics, BS, Computer Science, Handong Global University, 2002; MA, IT Management, Information & Communications University, 2008; PhD, Management Science, KAIST, in progress. Appointments: Advisory board member, CASTRIZE, Seoul, 2004-05; Researcher, Auto-ID Lab Korea, Daejeon, 2006-; Visiting Researcher, Cambridge Auto-ID Lab, Cambridge University, England, 2007. Publications: Wisdom Management: On Ethical Aspects of Knowledge, 2001; The Situation Dependent Application Areas of EPC Sensor Network in U-Healthcare, 2007; Network Design for Strategic Alliance in Express Courier Services: A Fuzzy Set Approach, 2010. Best Award of Venture Company Club in University, Kyung-Pook Provincial Government in South Korea, 2002; Best Award of Business Strategy Analysis Championship, Korean Academic Society of Business Administration, 2002. Memberships: International Christian Fellowship of Cambridge; International Christian Fellowship of KAIST. Address: Rm 4108, Department of Management Science (N22), KAIST, 335 Gwahak-ro, Yuseong-gu, Daejeon, 305-701, Republic of Korea. E-mail: ymhwang@kaist.ac.kr

HYAM Ronald, b. 16 May 1936, Isleworth, England. Historian. Education: Isleworth Grammar School, 1947-1954; Royal Air Force, 1954-56; St John's College Cambridge, 1956-60; First Class in both parts of the Historical Tripos, 1958-59, BA, 1959, MA, 1963, PhD, 1963. Appointments: Fellow, Magdalene College Cambridge, 1962-; Reader, British Imperial History, University of Cambridge, 1996; Emeritus, 1999-; Sometime Librarian, Archivist, Admissions Tutor and President of Magdalene College, Cambridge. Publications: Books on imperial history including: Empire and Sexuality, 1990, 1991, 1992; Britain's Imperial Century 1915-1914, 3rd edition, 2002; The Lion and the Springbok: Britain and South Africa Since the Boer War (with Peter Henshaw), 2003; Britain's Declining Empire: The Road to Decolonisation 1918-1968, 2006; Understanding the British Empire, 2010. Honour: LittD, University of Cambridge, 1993. Membership: Project Committee, British Documents on the End of Empire Project 1991-2005. Address: Magdalene College, Cambridge CB3 0AG, England.

HYATT Derek James, b. 21 February 1931, Ilkley, Yorkshire, England. Artist; Teacher; Writer. m. Rosamond Joy Rockey, 1 daughter. Education: NDD Illustration, 1st class honours, Leeds College of Art, 1948-52; Part-time studies, Norwich School of Art, 1953; 1st class honours, Royal College of Art, 1954-58; Part-time courses, Film Studies, 1960, Philosophy, 1962, London University. Career: Solo exhibitions annually, throughout UK, 1958-; Visiting Lecturer, Art History and Foundation Course, Kingston School of Art, Surrey, 1959-64; Senior Lecturer, Visual Studies and Illustration Studies, Leeds Polytechnic, 1964-84; Visiting Professor, Cincinnati University, USA, 1980; Full-time artist and writer, 1984-. Publications: Numerous articles in professional art journals and magazines; Author and Illustrator, The Alphabet Stone, 1992; Co-author, Stone Fires-Liquid Clouds, The Shamanic Art of Derek Hyatt, monograph, 2001. Honours: Phil May Drawing Prize, 1954; Royal Scholar Prize, RCA, 1956; Landscape Painting Prize, RCA, 1958; Companion of the Guild of St George, Ruskin Society, 1990; Yorkshire Arts Award, Bradford Art Gallery, Retrospective, 2001. Memberships: Artists for Nature Foundation International, Extremadura, Spain, 1998. Address: Rectory Farmhouse, Collingham, Wetherby, Yorkshire LS22 5AS, England.

HYDON Kenneth John, b. 1944, England. Accountant. m. 1 son, 1 daughter. Education: FCMA; FCCA; FCT. Appointments: Financial Director: Racal SES Ltd, 1979-81; Racal Defence Radar and Avionics Group Ltd, 1981-85; Vodafone Group plc, 1985-2005; Non-Executive Director: Verizon Wireless (USA), 2000-05; Reckitt Benckiser plc, 2003-; Tesco plc, 2004-; Royal Berkshire NHS Trust Foundation, 2005-; Pearson plc, 2006-. Membership: Leander; RAC.

HYMAN Timothy James, b. 17 April 1946, Hove, Sussex, England. Painter; Writer. m. Judith Ravenscroft. Education: Slade School of Fine Art, 1963-67. Career includes: 9 London solo exhibitions including, Austin/Desmond Fine Art, 1990, 2000, 2003, 2006, 2009; Has shown widely in mixed exhibitions including: Royal Academy Summer Exhibition; Hayward Annual; Whitechapel Open; National Portrait Gallery; Works in public collections including: Arts Council Collection; British Museum; Government Art Collection; Los Angeles County Museum; British Council Collection; Contemporary Art Society; Museum of London; Swindon Art Gallery; Deutsche Bank; Artist-in-Residence, Lincoln Cathedral, 1983-84; Artist-in Residence, Sandown Racecourse, 1992; Curated, Narrative Paintings, ICA, London and tour, 1979-80; Curated, Stanley Spencer,

Tate Britain, 2001; Curated, British Vision, Ghent, 2007. Publications include: Bonnard, 1998; Bhupen Khakhar, 1998; Carnivalesque, 2000; Sienese Painting, 2003; Frequent contributions to The Times Literary Supplement, 1990-. Honours: Leverhulme Award, 1992; Wingate Award, 1998; Honorary Research Fellow, University College, London; Beato Angelico Medal, Florence, 2004; BP/NPG Travel Award, 2007-08; Elected RA, 2011. Address: 62 Myddelton Square, London EC1R 1XX, England.

HYND Ronald, b. 22 April 1931, London, England. Choreographer. m. Annette Page, 1 daughter. Education: Holloway County School, London; Ballet Rambert School, Mercury Theatre, Notting Hill Gate. Appointments: Principal Dancer, Ballet Rambert, 1949-51, Royal Ballet, 1951-70; Roles as principal dancer noble: Siegfried in Swan Lake; Florimund in Sleeping Beauty; Albrecht in Giselle; Les Sylphides; Prince of the Pagodas; Lady and the Fool; The Firebird; and a diverse repertoire of classical and dramatic leads; Ballet Director, Bavarian State Ballet, Munich, 1970-73, 1984-86; Freelance Choreographer, Full length ballets include: The Merry Widow, 1975; The Nutcracker, 1976; Rosalinda, 1978; Papillon, 1979; Le Diable a Quatre, 1984; Coppelia, 1985; Ludwig II, 1986; Hunchback of Notre Dame, 1988; The Sleeping Beauty, 1993; One act ballets include: Le baiser de la Fee; Dvorak Variations; Mozartiana; La Chatte; Valses Nobles et Sentimentales; La Valse; Wendekreise; The Seasons; In a Summer Garden; Charlotte Bronte; Scherzo Capricciosso; Performed by international companies including: La Scala, Milan; Deutsche Oper Berlin; Vienna State Opera; Bavarian State Ballet, Munich; Royal Danish Ballet; Australian Ballet; National Ballet of Canada; London Festival Ballet/English National Ballet; Royal Sadler's Wells; American Ballet Theatre; Houston Ballet; Pacific Northwest Ballet; Tokyo Ballet; Grands Ballets Canadiens; Maggio Musicale, Florence; Ballet de Santiago, Chile; Slovenian Ballet; Hong Kong Ballet; Estonian National Ballet; Joffrey Ballet, Chicago; Nice Opera; Tulsa Ballet; Malmo Ballet; Bonn Opera; Dutch National Ballet; TV productions include: The Nutcracker; The Sanguine Fan; Merry Widow; Rosalinda. Honours: Listed in international biographical directories including Who's Who and People of Today.

HYNDE Chrissie, b. 7 September 1951, Akron, Ohio, USA. Singer; Songwriter; Musician. 1 daughter with Ray Davies, m. (1) Jim Kerr, divorced, 1 daughter, (2) Lucho Brieva, 1999, separated. Appointments: Contributor to New Musical Express; Co-Founder, Chrissie Hynde and the Pretenders, 1978, Singer, Songwriter, Guitarist, New Band Formed, 1983; Tours in Britain, Europe & USA. Creative Works: Singles include: Stop Your Sobbing, 1978; Kid; Brass in Pocket; I Go to Sleep, 1982; Back on the Chain Gang, 1982; Middle of the Road, 1984; Thin Line Between Love and Hate; Don't Get Me Wrong; Hymn to Her; Albums include: Pretenders, 1980; Pretenders II, 1981; Extended Play, 1981; Learn to Crawl, 1985; Get Close, 1986; The Singles, 1987. Honours: Platinum and gold discs.

HYNDMAN Robin John, b. 2 May 1967, Melbourne, Victoria, Australia. Professor of Statistics. m. Leanne, 1989, 2 sons, 2 daughters. Education: BSc (Hons), 1988, PhD, 1992; University of Melbourne; A Stat, Statistical Society of Australia, 2000. Appointments: Statistical Consultant, Statistical Consulting Centre, University of Melbourne, 1985-92; Lecturer, Department of Statistics, 1993-94; Lecturer, Department of Mathematics, Monash University, 1995-96; Senior Lecturer, Department of Mathematics and Statistics, 1997-98; Senior Lecturer, Department of Econometrics and Business Statistics, 1998-; Visiting Professor, Department of Statistics, CO State University, 1998; Director of Consulting, 1999-2006, Director, Business & Economic Forecasting Unit, 2001-, Professor of Statistics, 2003-, Department of Econometrics & Business Statistics, Monash University; Editor-in-Chief, International Journal of Forecasting, 2005-; Director, International Institute of Forecasters, 2005-. Publications: 4 books; 72 refereed papers; 8 book chapters; 9 conference proceedings; 13 unrefereed research papers; 12 other statistical publications; 185 statistical consulting reports; 9 non-statistical books. Honours: Second Maurice H Belz Prize in Statistics, 1986, Norma McArthur Prize in Statistics, 1987, Dwights Prize in Statistics, 1988, University of Melbourne; Finalist, Channel Ten Young Achiever Awards, 1990; Award for Excellence in Teaching, Monash Science Society, 1998; Belz Lecturer, Statistical Society of Australia, 2006; Moran Medal for Statistical Science, Australian Academy of Science, 2007; Listed in international biographical dictionaries. Memberships: International Statistical Institute; International Institute of Forecasters; International Association for Statistical Computing; American Statistical Association; Statistical Society of Australia. Address: Department of Econometrics & Business Statistics, Monash University, VIC 3800, Australia. E-mail: rob.hyndman@monash.edu.au Website: www.robjhyndman.com

HYODO Haruo, b. 3 March 1928, Japan. Medical Doctor. m. Keiko Tomita, 1 son, 2 daughters. Education: Dokkyo University School of Medicine, Japan; Tokushima University, Japan. Appointment: Professor, Radiology, Dokkyo University School of Medicine, Tochigi, Japan, 1977-90; Assistant Director, Fukuda Memorial Hospital and Chief of Health Medical Center, Mooka, Tochigi, 1993-. Publications: Encyclopaedia of Clinical Radiology and others; Patent in field of a table of X-ray CT, 1994; Patent pending for method of observation of three-dimensional imaging, 2003. Honours: Gold Medal, 2005, Honorary Member, Japanese Society of Interventional Radiology; Honorary Member, Japan Billiary Association; International Hippocrates Award, 2010; Listed in international biographical publications. Memberships: Japanese Radiological Society; Japan Biliary Association; Japanese Society of Interventional Radiology; Japanese Society of Medical Imaging Technology. Address: 1-9-3 Saiwai-cho, Mibu-machi, Shimotsuga-gun, Tochiki-ken, 321-0203 Japan. E-mail: hyodo283@green.ocn.ne.jp

HYUN In-Taek, b. 27 September 1954, South Korea. Minister; Professor. Education: BA, Political Science & International Relations, 1978, MA, Political Science, 1982, Korea University; PhD, Political Science, University of California, Los Angeles, USA, 1990. Appointments: Professor, Department of Political Science & International Relations, Korea University, 1995-; Director, Ilmin International Relations Institute, Korea University, 2003-09; Member, Presidential Transition Committee for the 17th President of the Republic of Korea, 2008; Member, Presidential Council for Future & Vision, 2008-09; Minister of Unification, 2009-11; Special Advisor to the President for Unification Policy, 2011-. Address: Korea University, 145 Anam-ro, Seongbuk-gu, Seoul 136-701, South Korea.

I

I Yet-Pole, b. 15 October 1963, Chiayi, Taiwan. Professor. m. Chia-Chen Lin, 1 son, 1 daughter. Education: Bachelor of Science, National Central University, Taiwan, 1986; Master of Science, 1988, Doctor of Philosophy, 1995, National Tsing-Hua University, Taiwan. Appointments: Assistant Researcher, Grand Pacific Petrochemical Corp, Taiwan, 1990-91; Researcher, Industrial Technology Research Institute, Taiwan, 1995-96; Post Doctoral Researcher, UC Berkeley, California, USA, 1996-97; Researcher/Manager, 1997-99, Researcher/Assistant Director, 1999-2000, Industrial Technology Research Institute, Taiwan; Assistant Professor, National Yunlin University of Science and Technology, Taiwan, 2000-06. Publications: Articles in professional scientific journals. Honours: Scholarship of Dr Yuan-Iseh Lee, 1995; Award of Promotion and Service, ITRI, Taiwan, 1998; Chevning Scholarship, BTCO, 2000; 1st and 3rd Prize of Paper Competition, 2002; Listed in various international biographical dictionaries. Memberships: Life Fellow, Taiwan Institute of Chemical Engineers; Life Fellow, Biochemical Engineering Society of Taiwan; Life Fellow, Chinese Institute of Environmental Engineers; Life Fellow, Chinese Institute of Mining & Metallurgical Engineers (CIMME) Address: Department of Safety, Health and Environmental Engineering, No 123, Sec 3, University Road, Douliu City, Yunlin, Taiwan 640. E-mail: iyp@yuntech.edu.tw

IBRAHIM Nabil, b. 11 April 1949, El-Mansoura, Egypt. Professor; Doctor. Education: BSc, Applied Chemistry, Faculty of Science, Ain Shams University, 1970; MSc, 1976, PhD, 1979, Applied Organic Chemistry, Faculty of Science, Al-Azhar University. Appointments: Researcher Chemist, National Institute of Industrial Safety Studies, 1970-75; Researcher Chemist, Technical Research Division, Occupational Safety & Health Department, Ministry of Manpower and Vocational Training, 1975-80; Researcher Chemistry, 1980-85, Associate Professor, Dyeing and Finishing, 1985-90, Professor, Textile Chemistry and Technology, 1990-, Head of Textile Engineering, 2005-06, Head, 2001-07, Textile Research Division, National Research Centre. Publications: 206 articles in professional journals; More than 45 R&D and industrial projects; Supervision of over 50 MSc and PhD theses. Honours: NRC Prize in Chemistry, 1996; Professor Dr M K Tolba's Environmental Prize, 1998; State Prize of Distinction for Advanced Technological Science, 2004; One of the leading scientists and engineers OIC (Organisation of Islamic Conference) Member States (COMSTECH's Study 2008); 2 NRC prizes for excellent publications and patent 2009-10; Listed in international biographical dictionaries. Memberships: Egyptian Syndicate for Scientific Professions in Egypt; Egyptian Chemical Society; Egyptian Textile Society; Egyptian Society of Polymer Science and Technology; Several Scientific and Technical Committee in NRC and ASRT; Head, Unit of Special Status of Textile Industries; R&D Council, NRC. Address: National Research Centre, El-Behouth Street, PO Box 12311, Dokki, Cairo, Egypt. E-mail: nabibrahim49@yahoo.co.uk

ICE-T (Tracey Marrow), b. 16 February, 1958, Newark, New Jersey, USA. Rapper; Actor. Career: Innovator of LA Gangsta Rap; Recording artist, 1987-; Rapper, rock group Body Count, 1992; Tours: UK; Europe; US; Canada; South America; Asia; Australia; Middle East; Actor, films include New Jack City; Trespass; Breakin'; Tank Girl; Television includes: Players; Baadasss TV; Law & Order, SVU; Owner, Rhyme Syndicate Records; Lecturer and spokesman, major US universities; Also involved in Hands Across Watts and South Central Love, 2 youth intervention programmes. Recordings: Singles include: Lifestyles of Rich and Infamous, 1991; New Jack Hustler, 1991; What Really Goes On, 1998; Valuable Game, 1999; Albums: Rhyme Pays; Power; The Iceberg...; Freedom Of Speech - Just Watch What You Say; O.G.- Original Gangster; Home Invasion; Ice VI-Return Of The Real; with Body Count: Body Count; Born Dead; Cold as Ever; 7th Deadly Sin; Also featured on film soundtracks: Colors; Dick Tracy. Publication: The Ice Opinion, 1994. Honours: Best Male Rapper, Rolling Stone Readers Poll, 1992; Grammy Award, Best Rap Song for Back on the Block. Current Management: Rhyme Syndicate Management, 4902 Coldwater Canyon Ave, Sherman Oaks, CA 91423, USA.

IDAHOSA Kennedy, b. 26 May 1975, Benin City, Nigeria. Engineer. Education: B Eng, Civil Engineering. Appointments: Project Engineer, Construction Contractor, private practice. Honours: Civil Engineering award. Memberships: American Society of Civil Engineers; Institute of Civil Engineers. Address: via dei Sabbioni 3, 43055 Mezzano, Italy.

IDANG Gabriel Ema, b. 25 May 1962. Lecturer. m. Edidiong, 1 son, 2 daughters. Education: BA (Hons), 1999, MA, 2002, PhD, 2006, Philosophy. Appointments: Auxiliary Teacher, 1980-81; Bank Supervisor, 1981-96; University Lecturer, 1999-. Publications: 3 thesis/dissertations; 2 books; 11 book chapters; 7 articles in journals. Honours: Best Graduating Student in Philosophy. Memberships: Chartered Institute of Bankers; Nigeria Philosophical Association; International Society for African Philosophy and Studies. Address: Department of Philosophy, University of Uyo, PMB 1017, Uyo, Akwa Ibom State, Nigeria. E-mail: gabrielidang@yahoo.com

IDLE Eric, b. 29 March 1943, South Shields, England. Actor; Writer; Comedian; Musician. m. (1) Lyn Ashley, 1969-75, 1 son, (2) Tania Kosevich, 1981-, 1 daughter. Education: Royal Wolverhampton School; English, Pembroke College, Cambridge University, 1965-67. Career: Cambridge Footlights, 1965-67; TV & film: Do Not Adjust Your Set, 1967-69; Monty Python, 1969-83; Rutland Weekend Television; The Rutles; All You Need Is Cash; Transformers: The Movie, 1986; The Mikado, 1987; Nearly Departed, 1989; The Adventures of Baron Munchausen, 1989; Nuns on the Run, 1990; Splitting Heirs, 1993; Casper, 1995; The Wind in the Willows, 1996; Burn Hollywood Burn, 1998; The Simpsons; Suddenly Susan; The Greedy Bastard Tour, 2003; Shrek the Third, 2007; Spamalot. Publications: Fiction and non-fiction: Hello Sailor, 1975; The Rutland Dirty Weekend Book, 1976; Pass the Butler (play), 1982; The Quite Remarkable Adventures of the Owl and the Pussycat, 1996; The Road to Mars, 1998; Eric Idle Exploits Monty Python, 2000; The Greedy Bastard Diary: A Comic Tour of America, 2005; Not the Messiah (He's a Very Naughty Boy) (play); Songs: Eritc the Half-A-Bee; The Philosophers' Song; Galaxy Song; Always Look on the Bright Side of Life. Honours: Tony Award, 2004-05; Drama Desk Award for Outstanding Lyrics, 2005.

IDOWU Phillips, b. 30 December 1978, Hackney, London, England. Triple Jumper. 1 son, 1 daughter. Career: Gold Medal, Triple Jump, Commonwealth Games, Melbourne, 2006; Gold Medal, Triple Jump, European Indoor Championships, Birmingham, 2007; Silver Medal, Triple Jump, Olympic Games, Beijing, 2008; Gold Medal, Triple Jump, World Indoor Championships, Valencia, 2008; Gold Medal, Triple Jump, World Championships, Berlin, 2009; Gold Medal, Triple Jump, European Championships, Barcelona, 2010.

DICTIONARY OF INTERNATIONAL BIOGRAPHY 36th EDITION

IGLESIAS Enrique, b. 8 May 1975, Madrid, Spain. Singer; Songwriter. m. Anna Kournikova, 2004. Career: Sings in English and Spanish; Albums: Enrique Iglesias, 1995; Master Pistas, Vivir, 1997; Cosas Del Amor, 1998; Enrique, 1999; Escape, 2001; Quizas, 2002; 7, 2003; Insomniac, 2007. Singles: Experienca Religiosa, No Llores Por Mi, Bailamos, Rhythm Divine, 1999; Be With You, Solo Me Importas Tu, Sad Eyes, 2000; Hero, 2001; Escape, Don't Turn Off the Lights, Love To See You Cry, Maybe, 2002; Addicted, 2003; Not In Love ..., 2004. Honours: Grammy Award, 1997; 8 Premios Los Nuestro; Billboard Awards for Artist of the Year; Album of the Year, 1997; ASCAP Award for Songwriter of the Year, 1998; American Music Award for Favorite Latin Artist, 2002. Address: c/o Interscope Records, 2220 Colorado Avenue, Santa Monica, CA 90404, USA. Website: www.enriqueiglesias.com

IGLESIAS Julio (Julio Jose Iglesias de la Cueva), b. 23 September 1943, Madrid, Spain. Singer; Songwriter. m. Isabel Preisler, 1971, divorced, 3 sons, Partner: Mirander Rijnsburger, 3 children. Education: Law student, Cambridge University. Musical Education: Learnt to sing in hospital (recovering from car crash). Career: Goalkeeper, Real Madrid junior team; Winner, Spanish Song Festival, Benidorm, 1968; Professional singer, songwriter, 1968-; Winner, Eurovision Song Contest, Netherlands, 1970; Major success in Latin America, 1970s; English Language releases, 1981-; Concerts and television appearances worldwide; In excess of 100 million records sold to date. Compositions include: La Vida Sigue Igual; Mi Amor; Yo Canto; Alguien El Alamo Al Camino; No Ilores. Recordings: Over 70 albums include: Soy, 1973; El Amor, 1975; A Mis 33 Anos, 1977; De Nina A Mujer, 1981; 1100 Bel Air Lace, 1984; Un Hombre Solo, 1987; Starry Night, 1990; La Carretera, 1995; Tango, 1996; Corazon Latino, 1998; Noche de Cuatro Lunas, 2000; Una Donna Puo Cambiar la Vita, 2000; Ao Meu Brasil, 2000; Divorcio, 2003; Love Songs; 2004; l'homme que Je suis, 2005; Romantic Classics, 2006; Quelque chose de France, 2007. Also on: Duets (with Frank Sinatra), 1993; Hit singles include: Manuela, 1975; Hey, 1979; Begin The Beguine, 1981; To All The Girls I've Loved Before, duet with Willie Nelson, 1983; My Love, duet with Stevie Wonder, 1988. Publications: Autobiography: Entre El Cielo y El Infernierno, 1981. Honours: Grammy, Best Latin Pop Performance, 1987; Diamond Disc Award, Guinness Book Of Records (most records in most languages), 1983; Medaile de Vermeil de la Ville de Paris, 1983; Eurovision Song Contest Winner, 1970. Membership: Honorary member, Spanish Foreign Legion. Address: c/o Anchor Marketing, 1885 NE 149th Street, Suite G, North Miami, FL 33181, USA. Website: www.julioiglesias.com

IGNATIEV Sergei, b. 10 January 1948, Leningrad, Soviet Union. Economist. m. Education: Economics Faculty of the M B Lomonosov Moscow State University (MGU); Postgraduate course, MGU Economics Faculty. Appointments: Professor's Assistant, Senior Lecturer, F Engels Leningrad Institute of Soviet Trade, 1978-88; Senior Lecturer, Associate Professor, N A Voznesensky Leningrad Financial and Economic Institute, 1988-91; Deputy Minister of Economics and Finance, 1991-92; Deputy Minister of Finance, 1992; Deputy Chairman, Bank of Russia, 1992-93; Deputy Minister of Economics, 1993-96; Aide on Economic Issues to the President of Russia, 1996-97; First Deputy Minister of Finance, 1997-2002; Chairman, Bank of Russia, Member of the Bank of Russia Board of Directors, 2002-. Publications: Author of more than 20 research papers. Honours: Numerous government awards. Address: 12 Neglinnaya Street, Moscow 107016, Russia. Website: www.cbr.ru

IIDA Yôichi, b. 21 August 1940, Kobe, Japan. Chemist; Molecular Biologist. m. Hiroko Yokoyama, 1 son, 1 daughter. Education: BS, University of Tokyo, 1963; MS, University of Tokyo, 1965; DSc, University of Tokyo, 1969. Appointments: Research Associate, 1965-77, Lecturer, 1977-95, Associate Professor, 1995-, Hokkaido University, Japan. Publications: Author, Seminar Book of Basic Physical Chemistry, 1992; Human Genome Project and Bioinformatics, 1995; Handbook of Multivariate Statistical Analysis and Examples, 2002; Contributor of articles to professional journals. Memberships: Physical Society of Japan; Chemical Society of Japan; Biophysical Society of Japan; Molecular Biological Society of Japan. Address: 5-27-510 Ryodo-cho, Nishinomiya, Hyogo 662-0841, Japan. E-mail: chemjimu@sci.hokudai.ac.jp

IKE Adebimpe Olurinsola, b. 29 June 1933, Ijebu Igbo, Ogun State, Nigeria. Librarian; Administrator; Teacher. m. Chukwuemeka Ike, 1 son. Education: BA (Hons), London, 1960; MA, Ghana, 1974; PG Dip Lib, Ibadan, 1965. Appointments: Sub-Librarian, University of Nigeria, Nsukka, 1962-71; Readers Adviser, Ghana Library Board, Accra, Ghana, 1972-74; Assistant Documentalist, Association of African Universities, Accra, Ghana, 1974-75; Senior Librarian, Principal Librarian, University of Lagos, 1976-81; Pioneer University Librarian, Abubakar Tafawa Balewa University, Bauchi, 1981-93; National Co-Ordinator NADICEST Project, 1988-; Visiting Lecturer, Department of Library Science and Archives, University of Ghana, Legon, Ghana, 1975-76; Professor of Library Science, Nnamdi Azikiwe University, Awka, 1995-. Publications: 60 contributions in monographs, scholarly journals, conferences, seminars, workshops and technical reports. Honours and awards include: Lions Club Merit Award for Professional Excellence; Fellow, Nigerian Library Association; Mothers in Unity, Nigeria; Federal Government Scholarships, Secondary School and University. Memberships include: Life Member, Chartered Institute of Library and Information Professionals, UK; Founding Member, Fellow, Nigerian Library Association; Member, Nigerian Institute of Management; Member, Nigeria National Committee, ICSU, IGBP. Address: PO Box 2, Ndikelionwu, Orumba North LGA, Anambra State, Nigeria.

IKEDA Kiyohiro, b. 19 February 1956, Kumamaoto, Japan. University Professor. m. Tomoko Yasida, 1 son, 1 daughter. Education: BEng, 1978, MEng, 1980, Tokyo University; PhD, University of California, Berkeley, 1984. Appointments: Research Associate, 1984-87, Associate Professor, 1987-93, Nagaoka University of Technology; Associate Professor of Engineering, 1993-96, Professor, 1996-, Tohoku University, Sendai, Japan. Publications: Articles: Echelon Modes in Uniform Materials, 1994; Mode Switching and Recursive Bifurcation in Granular Materials, 1997; Imperfect Bifurcation in Structures and Materials, 2002. Memberships: Japan Society of Civil Engineers; Japan Society for Industrial and Applied Mathematics. Address: Department of Civil Engineering, Tohoku University, Aoba, Sendai 980-8579, Japan. E-mail: ikeda@civil.tohoku.ac.jp

ILLSLEY Eric, b. 9 April 1955, Barnsley, South Yorkshire, England. Member of Parliament. m. Dawn Illsley, 2 daughters. Education: LLB, Law, University of Leeds. Appointments: Head of Administration, Yorkshire National Union of Mineworkers; Member of Parliament, Barnsley Central, 1987-; Member, Select Committee, on Energy, 1987, 1991, on Televising Proceedings of the House of Commons, 1988-91, on Procedure, 1991-; on Foreign Affairs, 1997-; Opposition Whip, 1991-94; Opposition spokesperson, on health, 1994-95, on local government, 1995, on Northern Ireland, 1995-97.

Memberships: Member, Co-operative Party and MSF; Joint Chair, All Party Parliamentary Glass Committee; Treasurer, Yorkshire Labour Group of Members of Parliament; Member, Chairman's Panel; Vice Chair, Parliamentary and Scientific Committee; Vice Chair, Commonwealth Parliamentary Association UK Branch; Executive Committee Member, Inter Parliamentary Union. Address: House of Commons, London SW1A 0AA, England. E-mail: illsleye@parliament.uk

ILYUMZHINOV Kirsan Nikolayevich, b. 5 April 1962, Elista, Kalmykia. President of the Republic of Kalmykia. m. 1 son. Education: Graduate, Moscow State University for International Relations, 1989. Appointments: Elected President of the Republic of Kalmykia, 1993, re-elected, 1995, 2002-. Publications: President's Crown of Thorns (a documentary novel), 1995; Kalmykia at the turn of centuries (research work), 1997; Kalmykia. Heading toward democracy (research work), 1998. Honour: Order of Friendship by the Decree of the Russian President, 1997. Address: House of Government, 35800 Elista, Republic of Kalmykia, Russian Federation. E-mail: 1p@kalm.ru

ILYUSHIN Michael, b. 8 June 1945, Chapaevsk Kuibyshev Region, USSR. Professor; Chemistry. m. Shugalei Irina Vladimirovna, 1983, 1 daughter. Education: Engineer Chemist-Technologist Diploma, Leningrad Liensovet Institute of Technology (LTI), 1969; Candidate of Chemical Sciences (PhD), LTI, 1975; Doctor of Chemical Sciences, State Institute of Technology, St Petersburg, 1995. Appointments: Engineer, 1969-72, Aspirant (post-postgraduate), 1972-75, Researcher, 1975-78, Assistant Professor, 1978-93, LTI, Leningrad; Associate Professor, 1993-97, Professor, 1997-, SPSIT (U), St Petersburg. Publications: 1 textbook; 5 books; Around 350 papers in journals or other professional publications. Honours: Medal, Inventor of the USSR, 1981; Soros Associate Professor, Russia, 1997; Award for Achievement, 1998; 20th Century Award for Achievement, 1999; International Man of the Year, 1997-98, 1999-2000; International Man of the Millennium, 1999; Soros Professor, Russia, 2004. Membership: All-Russian Chemical Society, 1972. Address: St Petersburg State Institute of Technology (Technical University), Moskovsky pr 26, 190013, St Petersburg, Russia.

IM Hana, b. 25 August 1963, Seoul, Korea. Professor. m. Hyeong Jin Kim, 2 sons. Education: BS, Microbiology, Seoul National University, 1986; PhD, Microbiology, University of Texas at Austin, USA, 1993. Appointments: Research Associate, University of Wisconsin at Madison, USA, 1993-95; Senior Research Scientist, Korea Research Institute of Bioscience & Biotechnology, 1996-2000; Professor, 2000-, Chairman, 2005-, Department of Molecular Biology, Sejong University. Publications: Numerous articles in professional scientific journals; 3 patents. Honours: Silla Cultural Foundation Fellowship, Korea, 1984-86; Texas State Fellowship, USA, 1991; Outstanding Scholar of the Year, Daeyang Foundation, Korea, 2001; Who's Who in the World, 2005; Outstanding Publication Award, Journal of Microbiology, 2005. Memberships: Member, Protein Society, USA, 1995; Secretary of Editorial Affairs, Korean Society of Biochemistry and Molecular Biology, 2008-; Editor, Journal of Microbiology, 2002. Address: Department of Molecular Biology, Sejong University, 98 Gunja-dong, Kwangjin-gu, Seoul 143-747, Republic of Korea. E-mail: hanaim@sejong.ac.kr

IM Moon Whan, b. 7 April 1955, Seoul, Republic of Korea. Professor. Education: MD, 1980, School of Medicine, PhD, 1992, Postgraduate School, Seoul National University, Korea. Appointments: Army Physician, 1982-85; Rotating Internship, 1985-86, Residency, Department of Obstetrics & Gynecology, 1986-90, Seoul National University Hospital; Assistant Professor, 1990-96, Professor, 1996-, Obstetrics and Gynecology, School of Medicine, Inha University; Visiting Professor, Stanford University School of Medicine, 2001; Postdoctoral Fellow, Yale University School of Medicine, 2001-02; Visiting Professor, Harvard University School of Medicine, 2002; Member, Legislation and Judiciary Committee, Korean Society of Obstetrics and Gynaecology, 2010-. Publications: Numerous articles in professional journals; Reviewer, Journal of Perinatal Medicine, 2010-; Reviewer, Open Journal of Obstetrics and Gynaecology, 2011; Scoring Panel, Korean Health Industry Development Institute, 2011. Honours: Best Clinical Trainee, Seoul National University Hospital, 1986; Best Doctor, Korean Association of Obstetricians & Gynecologists, 1997; Director, Exam Board, Korean Society of Complementary & Integrative Medicine, 2004; Expert Advisor, Korean Medical Association, 2006; Vice President, World Congress of Arts, Sciences and Communications, 2010; Ambassador, World Congress of Arts, Sciences and Communications, 2010; IBC: International Hippocrates Award, 2010; Inner Circle of the IBC, 2010; 2000 Outstanding Intellectuals of the 21st Century, 2011; Lifetime Achievement Award, 2010; Top 100 Health Professionals, 2010-2012; Salute to Greatness Award, 2010; Order of International Fellowship Peace Prize, 2010; Medal of Wisdom, 2010; Da Vinci Diamond, 2011; Deputy Director General, 2011; Honorary Director General, 2011; ABI: Universal Award of Accomplishment, 2010; Deputy Governor, 2010; World Lifetime Accomplishment Award, 2011; Man of the Year, 2011; Order of International Ambassadors, 2011; Research Board of Advisers, 2011; Hippocrates Award, 2012; Who's Who in the World, 2010-13; Who's Who in Medicine and Healthcare, 2011-12; Who's Who in Science and Engineering, 2011-12; Who's Who in Asia, 2012. Memberships: Korean Medical Association; Korean Society of Obstetrics and Gynecology; Korean Society of Perinatology; Korean Association of Genetics; Korean Society of Complementary & Integrative Medicine; Korean Association of Gynaecologic Endoscopy; Korean Association of Voluntary Sterilization; International Gynaecologic Cancer Society; World Association of Perinatal Medicine; Life Fellow, IBA; Order of International Fellowship, IBC; Fellowship, ABI. Address: Unit 1-2106 1st World Apt, Songdo-dong, Yeonsu-gu, Incheon, 406-743, Republic of Korea. E-mail: mwim@inha.ac.kr

IMAISO Junko, b. Fukuoka prefecture, Japan. Nurse. Education: BA, Kobe University; BS, Oita University; MSN, Nagoya University, 2008. Appointments: Assistant, Mie Prefectural College of Nursing, 2002-04; Assistant, Japanese Red Cross Toyota College of Nursing, 2004-08; Lecturer, Ishikawa Prefectural Nursing University, 2008-10; Associate Professor, Ishikawa Prefectural Nursing University, 2010-. Publications: Collaboration between nurses and professional caregivers to provide medical care in Japan, 2009; Caregiver suctioning education for Japanese patients with an invasive home ventilator, 2009; Influential factors of long-term care in a Japanese rural community examined through interviews of family caregivers, 2010. Honours: Listed in international biographical dictionaries. Memberships: Sigma Theta Tau International Honour Society of Nursing; Japan Academy of Community Health Nursing; Japanese Society of Public Health. E-mail: junkoi@ishikawa-na.ac.jp

DICTIONARY OF INTERNATIONAL BIOGRAPHY 36th EDITION

IMAIZUMI Kiichi, b. 24 May 1948, Gumma, Japan. Linguist; Educator. m. Noriko. Education: BA, Tokyo University of Foreign Studies, 1973; MA, Graduate School of Tokyo University of Foreign Studies, 1975; PhD, Graduate School of Kyorin University, 2008. Appointments: Visiting Lecturer, Japanese Language, National University of Mongolia, 1979-80; Visiting Lecturer, Japanese Language, Karachi Consulate-General of Japan, 1981-85; Visiting Lecturer, Japanese Language, Autonomous University of Madrid, 1986-90; Professor, Kyorin University, Faculty of Foreign Studies & Graduate School, 1990-. Publications: Japanese Grammar for Conveying Deep Structure, 2000; Japanese Grammar for Conveying Deep Structure – Development A, 2003; A Study of the Japanese Structure of Verbal Voices – Development B, 2008. Honours: Listed in biographical dictionaries. Memberships: Society of Japanese Grammar; Society for Japanese Linguistics; Linguistic Society of Japan; Japanese Cognitive Association. Address: 17-4-805 Oiwake-cho, Hachioji-shi, Tokyo 192-0056, Japan. E-mail: imaizumi@ks.kyorin-u.ac.jp

IMAN (Iman Abdul Majid), b. 25 July 1955, Model. m. (1) Spencer Haywood, divorced 1987, 1 child, (2) David Bowie, 1992, 1 daughter. Education: Nairobi University. Appointments: Fashion Model, 1976-90; Has modelled for Claude Montana and Thierry Mugler; Signed Revlon Polish Ambers Contract (1st black model to be signed by an international cosmetics co), 1979; Numerous TV appearances; Appeared in Michael Jackson video. Creative Works: Films include: Star Trek VI: The Undiscovered Country; Houseparty II; Exit to Eden; The Deli, 1997; Omikron: The Nomad Soul, 1999. Publications: Naomi, 1996; I Am Iman, 2001; Beauty of Color: The Ultimate Beauty Guide for Skin of Color, 2006. Address: c/o Elite Model Management, 40-42 Parker Street, London WC2B 5PQ, England.

IMAPAN Aiyared, b. 8 July 1979, Thailand. Lecturer. m. Supalak Yooyod. Education: BS, 2002, MS, 2004, PhD, 2008, Mathematics, Naresuan University, Thailand. Appointments: Lecturer, Mathematics, Naresuan Phayao University, 2005-10; Lecturer, Mathematics, University of Phayao, 2011-. Honours: Listed in international biographical dictionaries. Address: Department of Mathematics, School of Science, University of Phayao, Phayao 56000, Thailand. E-mail: aiyared.ia@up.ac.th

IMMELMAN Niel, b. 13 August 1944, Bloemfontein, South Africa. Pianist. Education: Royal College of Music, 1964-69; Private studies with Ilona Kabos, 1969-70, Maria Curcio, 1970-76; LRAM; ARCM; LGSM; LTCL. Career: Debut with London Philharmonic Orchestra, 1969; Concert appearances, London's Royal Festival Hall, Royal Albert Hall and Amsterdam Concertgebouw; Concert tours of every continent; Compact disc recordings for Etcetera and Meridian labels; Professor of Piano, Royal College of Music, London, 1980-; Masterclasses at Berlin Hochschule, The Chopin Academy, Warsaw and Moscow Conservatoire. Publications: Commercial recordings of Beethoven, Schubert, Schumann, Dale, Suk, Novak and Bloch; First pianist in history to record complete piano works of Josef Suk; Articles on pianists Maria Curcio, Lamar Crowson and Annie Fischer, and on Czech Piano Music. Honours: Chappell Gold Medal, 1969; Fellow, Royal College of Music, 2000. Memberships: Royal Society of Musicians of Great Britain; EPTA. Address: 41 Ashen Grove, London, SW19 8BL, England. E-mail: niel@immelman.co.uk

IMYANITOV Naum Solomonovich, b. 31 December 1935, Novocherkassk, Russia. Scientist. m. Kira Rozinova, 1 son. Education: MS, 1958; PhD, 1964; DSc, 1980; Diplomas: Fine Chemical Engineering, 1958; Research Chemist, 1962; Senior Research Chemist, 1967. Appointments: Research Scientist, 1958-65; Senior Scientist, 1965-76; Department Leader, 1976-86; Chief Scientist, 1986-, VNII Neftekhim, Leningrad, St Petersburg; Project Leader, SciVision, St Petersburg, Academic Press, 1998-2000; Project Leader, MDL Information Systems, Inc, St Petersburg, 2000-; Chief Scientist, Eurochem-SPb-Trading, St Petersburg, 2003-. Publications: Author, 250 articles and patents; Editor, 2 monographs. Honours: Badge, Inventor of Czechoslovakia, 1979; Badge, Inventor of USSR, 1986; Medal, Veteran of Labour, 1988. Memberships: Mendeleev Chemical Society, 1959; World Wide Club Chemical Community, 1999. Address: ul Bryantseva 18, kv 155, 195269 St Petersburg, Russia. E-mail: naum@itcwin.com

IN Man-Jin, b. 11 October 1963, Dangjin, Chungnam, Korea. Professor. m. Ok-Joo Kim, 1 son, 1 daughter. Education: BS, 1985, MS, 1987, PhD, 1997, Seoul National University, Seoul. Appointments: Senior Researcher, Daesang Corp, Seoul, 1986-98; Research Professor, Korea Nutritional Research Institute, Korea University, 1998-99; Associate Professor, Chungwoon University, Hongseong, Korea, 1999-. Publications: Papers and articles in professional scientific journals. Honours: Young Scientist Award, Korean Society for Applied Biological Chemistry, 2006; Universal Award of Accomplishment, ABI, 2007; International Scientist of the Year, IBC, 2007. Memberships: Korean Academic Industrial Society; Korean Society of Food Science and Nutrition; Korean Food Professional Engineers; Korean Society of Microbiology and Biotechnology; Korean Society of Food Science and Technology; Korean Society of Applied Biological Chemistry. Address: Department of Human Nutrition and Food Science; Chungwoon University, San 29, Namjang-ri, Hongseong-eup, Hongseong-kun, Chungnam 350-701, Korea. E-mail: manjin@chungwoon.ac.kr

INAMDAR Jayshree Shashikant, b. 20 September 1974, Kalyan, India. Tabla Player. Education: SSC, Bombay, 1990; Higher Secondary Certificate, 1992; Commerce, University of Mumbai; Diploma in Music, Hindustani Vocal Light (HVL). Appointments: Artist, All India Radio; Casual Assistant, Churchgate, Mumbai; Artist, Doordarshan Kendra; Production Assistant, Resource Person, DD Mumbai (Sahyadri), Marathi and DD1 (National) in Hindi, 2006; Data input, Transport Section, Urdu Channel, 2006. Honours: Silver Medal Winner, NSMD, 1984; Bronze Medallion Winner, Running Competition, Dadoji Konddev Stadium, Thane; Kabbadi Winner; Rashtriya Saksharta Mission certificates, 1990 and 1991; Award, 8th Annual Essay Competition, National Society of Friends of the Trees, Kalyan Branch, 1991; Television channels winner: Apsara Film & Television; Radio Mirchi; Stardust; Star Screen, 2011; Filmfare, 2011; Listed in international biographical dictionaries. Address: Flat No 205, Second Floor, NAV SUNDER Co-operative Housing Society Ltd, near Dutta Mandir, Patharli, Kalyan Road, Dombivli (East), 421201, Taluka Kalyan, District Thane, India.

ING Bruce, b. 1 September 1937, London, England. Mycologist. m. Eleanor Scouller, 1 son, 1 daughter. Education: BA, 1960, MA, 1964, Cambridge University; MSc, St Andrews University, 1967; PhD, Liverpool University, 1979. Appointments: Assistant Organiser, Conservation Corps, 1960-64; Director, Kindrogan Field Study Centre, 1964-67; Conservation Officer, Hertfordshire and Middlesex Trust,

1967-71; Lecturer, Senior Lecturer in Biology, Chester College, 1971-94; Professor of Environmental Biology, University of Chester, 1999-. Publications: Over 200 papers on myxomycetes, fungi, ecology and conservation, 1959-; Publications in over 10 countries; The Phytosociology of Myxomycetes, 1994; The Myxomycetes of Britain and Ireland, 1999. Honours: Benefactors Medal, British Mycological Society, 1995. Memberships: Institute of Biology; Linnean Society; British Mycological Society; many other botanical, mycological and natural history societies worldwide. Address: 1 Rhue, Ullapool, Ross-shire, IV26 2TJ, Scotland. E-mail: myxoking@btinternet.com

INGEL Lev, b. 15 May 1946, Nizhny Tagil, USSR. Geophysicist. m. Irina Sklobovskaya, 1 daughter. Education: Graduate, Gorky State University, 1968; PhD, Institute of Experimental Meteorology, Obninsk, 1979; Dr in Physics and Mathematics, Hydrometeo Centre, Moscow, 1998. Appointments: Engineer, Institute 'Salute', Gorky, 1969-73; Engineer, Institute of Experimental Meteorology, Obninsk, 1973-75; Scientist, Senior Scientist, Head of Department, Institute of Experimental Meteorology, Obninsk, 1975-. Publications: More than 160 articles in scientific journals in meteorology, geophysics, hydrodynamics, astrophysics, quantum electronics. Honours: Alexander Chizhevsky Scientific Prize; Grantee, International Science Foundation; Russian Foundation of Basic Research, 1997, 1998, 2001, 2004; Listed in various international biographical dictionaries. Membership: Academic Board, Institute of Experimental Meteorology; Izvestia Newspaper Club, Moscow. Address: Mira St 4, Flat 45, 249038 Obninsk, Kaluga Reg, Russia. E-mail: ingeli@obninsk.ru

INGENITO Michele, b. 18 September 1945, Amalfi, Italy. University Professor. Education: MA (cum laude), English Language and Literature, Istituto Universitario Orientale, Naples, 1969. Appointments: Co-ordinator, Byron Society, southern Italy; Translator, English to Italian, main Italian publishers; Parliamentary Journalist and Freelance, Italian Parliament; Director, Institute of Foreign Languages, University of Salerno; Professor, Italian Language, University of Mogadiscio; Lector, Italian Language, University of Sheffield, England; Lecturer, English Language and Literature, Istituto Universitario Orientale, Naples; Associate Professor, English Language and Literature, University of Salerno, Italy. Publications: Main research and works in Victorian Age (Mary Barton, Il romanzo della denuncia, 1983; Carbone e diamanti, 1990); Shakespearian tragedy (Figlio di un dio minore. Otello, il moro di Venezia, 2000); English language and satire in the 1960s (I burloni del re, a trilogy, 2000); Lingua e traduzione-2, 2012; Other publications include essays and articles in professional journals and books; Novels: Il miracolo a rovescio, 1977, 2007 revised edition; Orizzonti di mezzanotte, 2005, special edition for first decade Twin Towers anniversary (11.9.2001 – 11.9.2011), 2011; Danza sul fiordo, 2007. Honours: International Prize on Political Satire, 2001; Listed in international biographical dictionaries. Memberships: Italian Association of English Studies; European Society for the Study of English. Address: University of Salerno, via Ponte don Melillo, Fisciano 84084, Italy. E-mail: m.ingenito@unisa.it

INGHAM John, b. 16 February 1958, Halifax, England. Journalist. m. Christine, 1 son, 1 daughter. Education: BA (Hons), 1980, PhD, 1990, History, Durham University; MA, American Studies, Bowling Green State University, Ohio, USA, 1981; Visiting Researcher, Georgetown University, Washington, 1982-83. Appointments: Freelance Sports Reporter, Sunday Express, 1986-89; Deputy Editor, BNFL News and Editor, Sellascene, 1984-87; Northern Correspondent, Building & Chartered Surveyor Weekly Magazines, 1987-89; News Reporter, Defence & Diplomatic Correspondent, Foreign Desk, Political Correspondent, Environment Correspondent, 1989-99, Environment, Transport & Defence Editor, 1999-2006, Daily Express. Address: Daily Express, 10 Lower Thames Street, London EC3, England. E-mail: john.ingham@express.co.uk

INGHAM Philip William, b. 19 March 1955, Liverpool, England. Deputy Director. m. Anita Taylor, 1 son, 2 daughters. Education: BA (Hons), Cambridge University, 1977; D Phil, University of Sussex, 1981; MA, Cambridge University, 1982; MA, Oxford University, 1987. Appointments: Research Scientist, MRC Laboratory of Molecular Biology, Cambridge, 1986; Research Scientist/Senior Scientist, ICRF Development Biology Unit, Oxford, 1986-94; Principal Scientist, Imperial Cancer Research Fund, London, 1994-96; Professor, Developmental Genetics and Director, MRC Centre for Developmental and Biomedical Genetics, University of Sheffield, 1996-2009; Deputy Director, A*STAR Institute of Molecular and Cell Biology, Singapore. Publications: Numerous articles in professional journals; 3 patents. Honours include most recently: Balfour Memorial Prize, 1990; Honorary Research Lectureship, Oxford University, 1990; Medal, 2005, Genetics Society of Great Britain; Visiting Professor, National University of Singapore, 2005; Honorary Fellow, Royal College of Physicians, London, 2007. Memberships: European Molecular Biology Organisation; Fellow, Institute of Biology, London; Fellow, Academy of Medical Sciences; Fellow, Royal Society, London; Life Member, Genetics Society of Great Britain.

INGLE Stephen James, b. 6 November 1940, Ripon, Yorkshire, England. Professor Emeritus. m. Margaret Anne Farmer, 1964, 2 sons, 1 daughter. Education: BA, 1962, DipEd, 1963, MA (Econ), 1965, University of Sheffield; PhD, Victoria University, New Zealand, 1967. Appointment: Professor, University of Stirling; Professor of Politics, 1991-2006, Emeritus Professor, 2006-, University of Stirling. Publications: Socialist Thought in Imaginative Literature, 1979; Parliament and Health Policy, 1981; British Party System, 1987, 1989, 2000; George Orwell: A Political Life, 1993; Narratives of British Socialism, 2002; Social and Political Thought of George Orwell: A Reassessment, 2006; British Party System, 2008; Many contributions to fields of Politics and Literature. Honours: Commonwealth Scholar, 1964-67; Erasmus Scholar, 1989; Visiting Research Fellow, Victoria University, New Zealand, 1993; Overseas Fellow, Open Society, 2005-08. Memberships: Political Studies Association; Society of Authors. Address: Department of Politics, University of Stirling, Stirling FK9 4LA, Scotland.

INGLIS-JONES Nigel John, b. 7 May 1935, London, England. Queen's Counsel. m. (1) Lenette Bromley-Davenport, deceased 1986, 2 sons, 2 daughters, (2) Ursula Jane Drury Culverwell, 1 son. Education: Trinity College, Oxford, 1955-58. Appointments: Subaltern, Grenadier Guards, National Service, 1953-55; Called to the Bar, 1959; Recorder of the Crown Court, 1978-93; Took Silk, 1982; Deputy Social Security Commissioner, 1993-2002; Bencher of the Inner Temple, 1981-. Publication: The Law of Occupational Pension Schemes, 1989. Honour: Queen's Counsel. Membership: MCC. Address: Outer Temple Chambers, 222 The Strand, London WC2R 1BA, England.

DICTIONARY OF INTERNATIONAL BIOGRAPHY 36th EDITION

INGRAM David Stanley, b. 10 October 1941, Birmingham, England. Botanist; Horticulturalist; Conservationist. m. Alison, 2 sons. Education: Yardley Grammar School, Birmingham; BSc, PhD, University of Hull; MA, ScD Cantab. Appointments: Research Fellow, University of Glasgow; Senior Scientific Officer, Agricultural Research Council Unit of Developmental Botany; Lecturer, then Reader in Plant Pathology, University of Cambridge; Regius Keeper, Royal Botanic Garden, Edinburgh; Master, St Catharine's College, Cambridge. Publications: 9 books; Newspaper and magazine articles; Research papers, reviews and articles in peer-reviewed scientific and specialist journals. Honours: OBE; FIBiol, 1986; FRSE, 1993; FIHort, 1995; FRCPEd, 1998; Hon FRSGS, 1998; Hon D University, Open University, 2000; Victoria Medal of Honour, Royal Horticultural Society, 2004; Honorary Member, British Society for Plant Pathology, 2008-. Memberships: Senior Visiting Fellow, Department of Plant Sciences, University of Cambridge; Honorary Professor and Special Adviser to University of Edinburgh on the Public Engagement with Science; Honorary Professor, Glasgow University; Honorary Fellow and Visiting Professor, Myerscough College, Lancashire; Honorary Fellow, Royal Botanic Garden, Edinburgh; Downing College and St Catharine's College, Cambridge, Worcester College, Oxford; Independent Member and Deputy Chair, Joint Nature Conservation Committee, 2002-08; Senior Visiting Fellow, ESRC Genomics Forum, Edinburgh; Programme Convenor and Chairman, Steering Group on Science and Society, Royal Society of Edinburgh; Formerly Chairman, Darwin Initiative for the Survival of Species; Visiting Professor, Napier University; Honorary Professor, Lancaster University. Address: c/o The Royal Society of Edinburgh, 22-26 George Street, Edinburgh, EH2 2PD, Scotland.

INKINEN Tommi Aleksanteri, b. 20 August 1974, Kuusankoski, Finland. Professor. m. Pirjo Venalainen. Education: MSc, 1998; MSoc Sc, 1999; PhD, University of Turku, 2001. Appointments: Docent, University of Turku, 2003-; Docent, 2006-, Professor, 2008-, University of Helsinki. Publications: European Planning Studies; Journal of Urban Technology; Industrial Management & Data Systems; Regional Studies; Springer; 101; Ashgate. Memberships: International Geographical Union; Regional Studies Association. Address: Niittaajankatu 2B30, 00810 Helsinki, Finland. E-mail: tommi.inkinen@helsinki.fi

INMAN Edward Oliver, b. 12 August 1948, Oslo, Norway. Chief Executive. 1 son, 2 daughters, 2 stepdaughters. Education: MA, Gonville and Caius College, 1969; School of Slavonic Studies, London, 1970. Appointments: Research Assistant, then Directing Staff, Imperial War Museum, London, 1972-78; Keeper, 1978-82, Director, 1982-2004, Imperial War Museum, Duxford, Cambridge; Chief Executive, South Bank Employers' Group, 2004-. Honours: Order of the British Empire, 1998; Fellow, Royal Aeronautical Society, 1999. Address: South Bank Employers' Group, 103 Waterloo Road, London SE1 8UL, England. E-mail: einman@iwm.org.uk

INNES Brian, b. 4 May 1928, Croydon, Surrey, England. Writer; Publisher. m. (1) Felicity McNair Wilson, 5 October 1956, (2) Eunice Lynch, 2 April 1971, 3 sons. Education: BSc, King's College, London, 1946-49. Appointments: Assistant Editor, Chemical Age, 1953-55; Associate Editor, The British Printer, 1955-60; Art Director, Hamlyn Group, 1960-62; Director, Temperance Seven Ltd, 1961-; Proprietor, Brian Innes Agency, 1964-66, Immediate Books, 1966-70, FOT Library, 1970-; Creative Director, Deputy Chairman, Orbis Publishing Ltd, 1970-86; Editorial Director, Mirror Publishing, 1986-88. Publications: Book of Pirates, 1966; Book of Spies, 1967; Book of Revolutions, 1967; Book of Outlaws, 1968; Flight, 1970; Saga of the Railways, 1972; Horoscopes, 1976; The Tarot, 1977; Book of Change, 1979; The Red Baron Lives, 1981; Red Red Baron, 1983; The Havana Cigar, 1983; Crooks and Conmen, 1993; Catalogue of Ghost Sightings, 1996; The History of Torture, 1998; Death and The Afterlife, 1999; Dreams, 1999; Bodies of Evidence, 2000; Profile of a Criminal Mind, 2003; The Body in Question, 2005; Fakes and Forgeries, 2005; Serial Killers, 2006; 'Til the Butcher Cut Him Down (ebook), 2011. Contributions to: Encyclopaedia Britannica; Grove Dictionary of Jazz; Man, Myth & Magic; Take Off; Real Life Crimes; Fire Power; The Story of Scotland; Discover Scotland; Marshall Cavendish Encyclopaedia of Science; Numerous recordings, films, radio and television broadcasts; Many photographs published. Honour: Royal Variety Command Performance, 1961. Memberships: Chartered Society of Designers; Royal Society of Literature; Royal Society of Chemistry; Royal Society of Arts; Institute of Paper, Printing and Publishing (IP3); Crime Writers Association; Society of Authors; British Actors' Equity; Chelsea Arts Club. Address: Les Forges de Montgaillard, 11330 Montgaillard, France.

INOUE Kazuko, b. 17 April 1919, Osaka Prefecture, Japan. Professor Emeritus. m. Iwao, 1 son, 1 daughter. Education: Tsuda College, 1936-39; MA, Teaching English as a Foreign Language, 1958, PhD, Linguistics, 1964, University of Michigan, USA. Appointments: Visiting Scientist, Massachusetts Institute of Technology, 1973-74; Visiting Scientist, Harvard University and MIT, 1976; Assistant Professor, 1965-67, Associate Professor, 1967-71, Professor, 1971-85, International Christian University; Professor, Tsuda College, 1985-88; Professor, 1988-2001, President, 1990-97, Academic Consultant, Center for Language Sciences, 2001-, Professor Emeritus, 2001-, Kanda University of International Studies. Publications: Books include: A study of Japanese Syntax, 1969; Transformational Grammar and Japanese: Part I: Syntax, Part II: Semantics, 1976; Grammatical Rules of Japanese, 1978; Introduction to Generative Linguistics, 1999; Numerous articles in professional journals. Honours include: Distinguished Service Medal, UNESCO, 1995; Third Order, Order of the Sacred Crown, 1996; Medal for Distinguished Academic Activities and Service in Linguistics, Japan Society of English Linguistics, 2007. Memberships: Honorary Member, Linguistics Society of America. Address: 1-chome, 7-21 Nishikata, Bunkyo-ku, Tokyo, 113-0024, Japan. E-mail: kinoue@tcn-catv.ne.jp

INSALL Sir Donald William, b. 7 February 1926, Clifton, Bristol, England. Architect. m. Amy Elizabeth (Libby) Moss, 2 sons, 1 daughter. Education: RWA School of Architecture, Bristol University, Bristol; Royal Academy School of Architecture, London; School of Planning and Research for Regional Development; Lethaby Scholar, The SPAB. Appointments: Founder (1958), Donald Insall Associates, Architects and Historic Building Consultants, London, Bath, Canterbury, Cambridge, Chester, Conwy, Shrewsbury; Member, Historic Buildings Council for England, 1971-84; Founder-Commissioner, English Heritage, 1984-89. Publications: The Care of Old Buildings Today; Historic Buildings: Action to Maintain the Expertise for their Care and Repair, Council of Europe; Chester: A Study in Conservation; Living Buildings: Architectural Conservation: Philosophy, Principles and Practice; Contributor: Encyclopaedia Britannica and numerous technical journals; Arts Council Film: Buildings: Who Cares? Honours: Queen's Silver Jubilee

Medal, 1977; OBE, 1981; CBE, 1995; Honorary LLD, 2004; Honorary Freeman of the City of Chester; Europa Nostra Medal of Honour; Harley J McKee Award, Association for Preservation Technology, International; Plowden Medal, Royal Warrant Holders' Association; Kt, 2011. Memberships include: Fellow, RIBA; Fellow (Rtd), RTPI; Fellow, Society of Antiquaries of London; Academician, Royal West of England Academy; Liveryman, Worshipful Company of Goldsmiths; Member, Europa Nostra; Member of Committees, European Union; Council Member, ICOMOS, UK; UK Committee, World Monuments Fund; Past and present Member of Fabric Committees, Westminster Abbey, Canterbury and Southwark Cathedrals; Vice-president, City of Winchester Trust; Honorary Life Member, Bath Preservation Trust; Patron; Kew Society, Environmental Trust for Richmond upon Thames, Bedford Park Society; Fellow, Royal Society of Arts; Rolls Royce Enthusiasts' Club; The Athenaeum. Address: Donald Insall Associates, 73 Kew Green, Richmond, Surrey, TW3 3AH, England. E-mail: donald.insall@insall-architects.co.uk

INSAROV Gregory E, b. 14 November 1948, Moscow, USSR. Ecologist. m. Irina D, 1 daughter. Education: MS, Mathematics, Moscow State University, USSR, 1970; PhD, Biology, Moscow State Forestry University, Moscow, USSR, 1975; Junior Research Scientist, 1976-77, Senior Research Scientist, 1978-79, Institute of Applied Geophysics, Moscow, USSR; Senior Research Scientist, Natural Environment and Climate Monitoring Laboratory, Moscow, USSR/Russia, 1979-91; Leading Research Scientist, Institute of Global Climate and Ecology, Moscow, Russia, 1991-. Publications: Over 100 publications as author or co-author; Books: Mathematical methods in forest protection, 1980; Effects of SO_2 on plants, 1984; Quantitative characteristics of the state of epiphytic lichenflora of biosphere reserves. The Zakatal reserve, 1987; Numerous book chapters, articles in scientific journals and conference proceedings include most recently: Assessment of lichen sensitivity to climate change, 1996; Computer-aided multi-access key IDENT for identification of the Negev lichens, 1997; A system to monitor climate change with epilithic lichens, 1999; Long term monitoring of lichen communities response to climate change and diversity of lichens in the Central Negev Highlands, Israel, 2001; Lichen Monitoring and Global Change, 2002; Towards an Early Warning System for Global Change, 2004; Assessment report on climate change and its consequences in the Russian Federation, 2008; Epiphytic montane lichens exposed to background air pollution and climate change: Monitoring and conservation aspects, 2010. Honours: Expedition leader, Russia, adjacent countries, and Sweden, co-ordinated and guided expeditions to remote protected areas with emphasis on lichen monitoring, 1978-2009; Editorial Board, Series Problems of Ecological Monitoring and Ecosystem Modelling, 1987-; Visiting Professor, University of Arkansas at Monticello, USA, 1990; Research Associate, Swedish Environmental Protection Agency, Sweden, 1991-92; Research Associate, Ben-Gurion University of the Negev, Israel 1993-97; Marie Curie Experienced Fellow, University of Evora, Portugal, 1997; Leading Research Scientist, Institute of Geography of the Russian Academy of Sciences, Moscow, Russia, 1998-; Director, NATO Advanced Research Workshop on Lichen Monitoring, Wales UK, 2000; Expert, Intergovernmental Panel on Climate Change, 2001-; Research Fellow, Acid Deposition and Oxidant Research Center, Japan, 2004; Network of Soil and Vegetation Monitoring Specialists of the Acid Deposition Monitoring Network in East Asia, 2004-; Project Leader, Air Quality Management in Moscow and London, 2006-07; Listed in national and international biographical directories. Memberships: Moscow Society of Naturalists, 1972-; British Lichen Society, 1993-; American Association for the Advancement of Science, 1997-98; American Bryological and Lichenological Society, 1998-; European Association for the Science of Air Pollution, 2001-; Russian National Committee on Human Dimensions on Global Environmental Change, 2004; Nordic Lichen Society, 2005-. Address: Institute of Global Climate and Ecology, Glebovskaya 20B, Moscow 107258, Russia. E-mail: insarov@lichenfield.com

INSOLL Christopher, b. 28 June 1956, London, England. Artist. m. Andrea, 1 son, 1 daughter. Education: Haileybury College, Hertfordshire, 1969-74; Chelsea School of Art, 1978; Camberwell School of Art, 1981; Falmouth School of Art, 1979-82. Appointments: Longcrofts Accountants, -1978; Founder, Portscatho Society of Artists, 1985; 1st exhibition, Royal Academy, 1985; Worked in France, exhibition at Paris Salon, 1992-93; Exhibition, Antwerp, 1994; Retrospective, Falmouth Art Gallery, 2001; Book published, 2006; Exhibition, Truro Museum, 2008. Publications: Portscatho, A Portrait of a Cornish Art Colony, 2006; Artists in Britain Since 1945, 2006; Paintings About Paintings, 2001; St Ives Art Colony in Transition, 2008; Numerous articles in professional journals. Honours: Prizewinner, La Federation Nationale de la Culture Française, 1992. Memberships: Chelsea Arts Club. Address: 5 The Square, Portscatho, TR2 5HW, England.

INTUWONGSE Chai-Sit, b. Nakornpranom, Thailand. Doctor of Medicine. m. Siriporn Intuwongse, 1 son, 2 daughters. Education: Doctor of Medicine, Siriraj Hospital, Mahidol University, Thonburi, Thailand, 1959; Thai Orthopaedics Board, Thailand, 1975; Thai Board of Family Medicine, Thailand, 2004. Appointments: Lieutenant, Royal Thai Navy, 1959; Head, Orthopaedic Department, Lerd-Sin General Hospital, Bangkok, Thailand, 1966-96; Medical Consultant, Tanksin General Hospital, Chareonkrung General Hospital, Bangkok Metropolitan Administration; Medical Consultant, Sports Authority of Thailand; Medical Consultant, Department of Medical Services, Ministry of Public Health, Thailand; Member, Sub-committee of Medical Board, Department of Labour, Thailand. Publications: Articles in medical publications including: Clinical Orthopaedics and Related Research, 1996; The Journal of Hand Surgery, 1998. Honours: Listed in Who's Who publications and biographical dictionaries. Memberships: Brain Bank, National Economic and Social Development Board; Royal College of Orthopaedic Surgeons of Thailand; International College of Surgeons. Address: 2 Soi 1 Saeree 1 Rankamhaeng 24, Haumark, Bangkapi, Bangkok, 10250 Thailand.

IOANNIDES Ouranios, b. 22 December 1944, Nicosia, Cyprus. Politician; Educator. m. Eleni Oratou-Ioannidou, 2 sons. Education: BSc, Natural Sciences, 1969; Graduate diploma, Educational Management, Educational Psychology, Educational Technology and Research Skills, 1990; Master, Education, 1993; Honorary Professor, Donetsk National University, 2002-; Doctorates: La Salle University, 1997; Middlesex University, 2004; Mariupol State University of Humanities, 2002; World Universities Association Plato, 2005; Professor and Academic Advisor, La Salle University, 1997-99; International Visiting Professor, World Academy Plato, 2005-. Appointments: Science schoolmaster, secondary schools, 1971-86; Lecturer, Biological Sciences, Pedagogical Academy of Cyprus, 1986-92; Assistant Headmaster, Secondary Education Schools, and Lecturer at Pedagogical Institute of Cyprus, 1992-95; Senior Education Officer, Ministry of Education and Culture, Republic of Cyprus, 1995-96; Member, House of Representatives, 1996-99;

Minister of Education and Culture, 1999-2003; President, Institute for the Eurodemocracy, 2003-04; Education, Culture and Science Consultant, 2003-; President, Interim Governing Board, 2005-07 and Chairman of the Council, 2008-12, Frederick University, Cyprus. Publications: Numerous articles in professional journals, books and manuals in the fields of science, sports, education, culture and politics; Books include most recently: Interviews to 20 reporters, 1999; Without Fear and Hatred, 2003; Anan Plan Before and After Referendum, 2004; Don't Expect Others to Do For You What You Must Do, 2005; The Last Turn, 2006; Stockholm Syndrome, 2007; Alchemies, 2010. Honours include most recently: The Decoration of National Cedar, of the Republic of Lebanon; Medal and Diploma of Honour, Republic of Cyprus, 2006; Honorary Citizen of Aspropirgos Municipality, 2009; Honorary Member, National Olympic of Cyprus, 2009; For Services to Education, 50th Anniversary Honour, Republic of Cyprus, 2010. Memberships: Scientist Council, UK; Institute of Biology, UK; Royal Society of Chemistry, UK; European Association for Sports Management; International Association for Sports Law; Union for Educational Management; Archbishop Macarios III Foundation. Address: PO Box 25163, 1307 Nicosia-Cyprus.

IOANNIDIS Orestis, b. 20 November 1980, Thessaloniki, Greece. Surgical Resident. Education: Medical Degree, Medical School, 2005, MSc, Medical Research Methodology, Medical School, 2008, PhD, Surgery, Medical School, 2009-, Aristotle University of Thessaloniki. Appointments: Surgical Resident, First Surgical Department, General Regional Hospital George Papanikolou, Thessaloniki, Greece, 2007-. Publications: Over 20 articles in professional journals. Honours: 1st place award, Asklipiada of Medical Knowledge, Medical School, Aristotle University of Thessaloniki, 2005; 2nd place award, Olympiada of Medical Knowledge, Scientific Society of Greek Medical Students, 2005. Address: Alexandrou Mihailidi 13, 54640, Thessaloniki, Greece.

IPATOV Sergei Ivanovich, b. 10 November 1952, Moscow, Russia. Applied Mathematician in Astronomy. m. Valentina Ipatova (Artioukhova), 14 June 1986, 1 son. Education: MS, Faculty of Mechanics and Mathematics, Moscow State University, 1970-75; PhD, Candidate of Physical and Mathematical Sciences, 1982; Doctor of Physical and Mathematical Sciences, 1997. Appointments: Probationer-Investigator, Keldysh Institute of Applied Mathematics of Russian Academy of Sciences, Moscow, 1975-77; Junior Scientist, 1977-87; Scientist, 1987-90; Senior Scientist, 1990-97; Leading Scientist, 1997-2003; Lecturer, Moscow State University, 1998; Visiting USA via NASA grants from July 2001; NRC Senior Research Associate in NASA Goddard Space Flight Centre, 2002-03; Visiting Senior Research Associate, George Mason University, USA, 2003-04; Research Associate, Catholic University of America, 2004. Publications: About 200 published scientific works; Book, Migration of celestial bodies in the solar system. Honours: Listed in numerous biographical directories. Memberships: European Astronomical Society; Euro-Asian Astronomical Society; American Astronomical Society; International Astronomical Union; Committee on Space Research; Russian Academy of Natural Sciences; Russian Academy of Sciences and Arts; New York Academy of Sciences. Address: Laboratory for Astronomy and Solar Physics, Building 21, NASA Goddard Space Flight Centre, Mail Code 685, Greenbelt, MD 20771, USA. E-mail: siipatov@hotmail.com

IRABOR-ESEZOBOR Helen Efese, b. 19 January 1963, Ujiogba Ishan, Nigeria. Accountant. m. Freddie Irabor-Esezobor, 2 sons, 2 daughters. Education: National Diploma, Accountancy, 1988; Higher National Diploma, Accountancy, 1991; Fellow Chartered Accountant, ICAN, 2009; Associate Chartered Tax Inspector, CITN, 2000; Loan Analysis School, Federal Deposit Insurance Corporation, Washington DC, USA, 2006; Bank Management Course, 2009, Asset and Liability Management Course, 2011, Board of Federal Reserve, Washington DC. Appointments: Management Assistant, Finance Department, 1992-95, Assistant Manager, Finance Department, 1996-2000, Deputy Manager, 2001-2004, Manager, 2005-09, Senior Manager, 2009-, Bank Examinations Department, Nigeria Deposit Insurance Corporation. Publications: Numerous articles in professional journals. Honours: Honourable Member, House of Representatives, Student Union Organisation, Auchi Polytechnic, 1989-90; Wife of the Year, Accountancy Department, Auchi Polytechnic, 1991. Memberships: Chairperson, Parent Teachers Association, Oak Crest Private School, Ijanikin, Lagos, 2001-2005; Financial Secretary, Parent Teachers Association, Regina Mundi Girls' High School, Iwo, Osun State; Treasurer, United Sisters Association (Charity Organisation), St Cecilia Catholic Church, Ijanikin, Lagos; Treasurer, Sacred Heart of Jesus and Immaculate Heart of Mary; Financial Secretary, Confraternity of Christian Mothers, 2000-03; Treasurer, Nigeria Deposit Insurance Co-operative Thrift Society, 2002-05; President, Catholic Women Organisation, St Cecilia Catholic Church, Ijanikin, Lagos, 2004-10; Patroness: Saint Anthony of Padua Society; Alter Servers; Catholic Youth Organisatin of Nigeria at Saint Cecilia Catholic Church. Address: Nigeria Deposit Insurance Corporation, 23A Marina Street, PMB 12881, Marina Lagos, Nigeria. E-mail: efese2001@yahoo.com

IRANZO Jose Alfredo, b. 27 April 1977, Zaragoza, Spain. Researcher. m. Paloma Pineda, 1 son. Education: Masters, Chemical Engineering, University of Zaragoza, 2000; MSc, Thermal Engineering Systems, 2010, PhD, 2011, University of Seville. Appointments: Undergraduate Reseracher, LITEC, Zaragoza, Spain, 1998-2000; Internship, Dow Chemical Company, Tarragona, Spain, 2000; Customer Support Engineer, ANSYS, Germany, 2001-05; Manager, R&D Analysis DSC, Madrid, 2005-08; Researcher, Energy Engineering Department, University of Seville, 2008-. Publications: Numerous articles in professional journals. Memberships: International Association for Hydrogen Energy. Address: Energy Engineering Department, School of Engineering, University of Seville, Camino de los Descubrimientos s/n, 41092 Sevilla, Spain.

IRONS Jeremy, b. 19 September 1948, Isle of Wight, England. Actor. m. (2) Sinead Cusack, 1978, 2 sons. Creative Works: TV appearances include: Notorious Woman; Love for Lydia; Langrishe Go Down; Voysey Inheritance; Brideshead Revisited; The Captain's Doll; Tales From Hollywood, 1991; Longtitude 2000; Films: Nijinsky, The French Lieutenant's Woman, 1980; Moonlighting, 1981; Betrayal, 1982; The Wild Duck, Swann in Love, 1983; The Mission, 1986; A Chorus of Disapproval, Dead Ringers, 1988; Australia, Danny, The Champion of the World, 1989; Reversal of Fortune, 1990; Kafka, Damage, 1991; Waterland, 1992; M. Butterfly, House of the Spirits, 1994; Die Hard with a Vengeance, 1995; Stealing Beauty, Lolita, 1996; The Man in the Iron Mask, 1997; Chinese Box, 1998; Dungeons and Dragons, 2000; The Time Machine, 2001; Callas Forever, 2002; The Merchant of Venice, Being Julia, 2004; Kingdom of Heaven, Casanova, 2005; Inland Empire, Eragon, 2006; The Pink Panther 2, 2009. Stage appearances: The Real Thing, Broadway, 1984; Rover, The Winter's Tale, Richard II, Stratford, 1986. Honours include: NY Critics Best Actor Award, 1988; Academy Award, 1991; Tony Award; European Film Academy Special Achievement Award, 1998. Address: c/o Hutton Management, 4 Old Manor Close, Askett, Buckinghamshire HP27 9NA, England.

IRONSIDE 2nd Baron, Edmund Oslac Ironside, b. 21 September 1924, Camberley, Surrey, England. Businessman. m. Audrey Marigold Morgan-Grenville, 1 son, 1 daughter. Education: Tonbridge School. Appointments: Lieutenant Royal Navy, 1943-52; Marconi Co, 1952-59; English Electric Leo Computers, 1959-64; International research and Development Co Ltd, 1968-84; NEI plc, 1984-89; Defence Consultant, Rolls Royce IPG, 1989-95. Publication: Book: Highroad to Command, 1972. Honours: Honorary FCGI, 1986; Member of Court of Assistants, Worshipful Company of Skinners, Master, 1981-82; Honorary Fellow, City and Guilds Institute (Hon FCGI). Memberships: Organising Committee, British Library, 1972-74, Select Committee European Communities, 1974-90; Chairman, Science Reference Library Advisory Committee, 1975-85; President: Electric Vehicle Association of Great Britain, 1975-83, European Electric Road Vehicle Association, 1980-82, Sea Cadet Corps, Chelmsford, 1959-88; Vice-President: Institute of Patentees and Inventors, 1976-90, Parliamentary and Scientific Committee, 1977-80, 1983-86; Treasurer, All Party Energy Studies Group, 1979-92; Honorary Secretary, 1992-94, Chairman 1994-2000, All-Party Defence Study Group; Privy Council Member of Court, City University, 1971-96 and Council, 1987-89; Court, University of Essex, 1982; Club: Royal Ocean Racing. Address: Priory House, Old House Lane, Boxted, Colchester, Essex CO4 5RB, England.

IRVIN Albert, b. 21 August 1922, London, England. Artist. m. Beatrice Nicolson, 2 daughters. Education: Northampton School of Art, 1940-41; Navigator, Royal Air Force, 1944-46; Goldsmiths College, University of London, 1946-50. Career: Teacher, Goldsmiths College, 1962-83; Solo exhibitions include: New Art Centre, London, regularly during 1960's and 70's; Gimpel Fils Gallery, London, regularly since 1982; Aberdeen Art Gallery, 1976, 1983; Third Eye Centre, Glasgow, 1983; Ikon Gallery, Birmingham, 1983; Talbot Rice Gallery, Edinburgh, 1989; Spacex Gallery, Exeter, 1990; Serpentine Gallery, London, 1990; Welsh Arts Council, Cardiff, 1990; Royal Hibernian Academy, Dublin, 1995; Centre d'Art Contemporain, Meymac, France, 1998; Royal West of England Academy, 1999; Storey Gallery, Lancaster and Scott Gallery, Lancaster University, 2003; Peppercanister Gallery, Dublin 2003, 2006, 2008; Gimpel Fils Gallery, London, 2004, 2007; Advanced Graphics Gallery, London, 2002, 2005; Tate Gallery, London, 2008; Kings Place, London, 2008; University of Northumbria Gallery, Newcastle, 2009; Gimpel & Müller Gallery, Paris, 2009; Churchill College, Cambridge, 2010; Advanced Graphics Gallery, London, 2010; Gimpel Fils Gallery, London, 2010; Kings Place Gallery, London, 2010; University of Northumbria, 2011; Peppercanister Gallery, Dublin, 2011; Galleries and museums in USA, Australia, Austria, Germany, France, Belgium, Spain, Dubai, Finland, Ireland, Italy, Saudi Arabia, Sweden, Switzerland; Works in public collections including Tate Gallery, Royal Academy, Victoria and Albert Museum, Arts Council, British Council and in public collections internationally; Commissions include: Painting for Homerton Hospital, Hackney, 1987; Design for Diversions Dance Company, 1994; Painting for Chelsea and Westminster Hospital, 1996. Publications: Albert Irvin: Life to Painting by Paul Moorhouse, 1998; Television: A Feeling for Paint, BBC2, 1983; Off the Wall: The Byker Show, BBC2 1994; Albert Irvin: Artist At Work, Artsworld, 2000; Albert Irvin: Portrait, Injam, Paris, 2001; Radio: Interview with Joan Bakewell, BBC Radio 3, 1990; Private Passions interview with Humphrey Berkeley, BBC Radio 3, 2001. Publications: Albert Irvin: The Complete Prints by Mary Rose Beaumont. Honours: Arts Council Awards, 1968, 1975, 1980; Prize Winner, John Moores Liverpool Exhibition, 1982; Gulbenkian Award for Printmaking, 1983; Giles Bequest Award, Victoria and Albert and British Museum, 1986; Korn/Ferry Award, Royal Academy, 1989; Honorary Fellow, Goldsmiths College, 2002; Listed in Who's Who publications and biographical dictionaries. Memberships: London Group, 1965-2006, re-elected as Honorary Member, 2009; Royal Academician, 1998, Honorary Member, Royal West of England Academy, 2000. Address: 19 Gorst Road, London SW11 6JB, England.

IRVINE Robin Francis, b. 10 February 1950, Wales. Professor of Molecular Pharmacology. m. Sandra Jane, 2 sons. Education: MA, BA (Hons), Biochemistry, St Catherine's College, Oxford, 1972; PhD, Agricultural Research Council Unit of Developmental Botany, Cambridge, 1976. Appointments: Beit Memorial Fellow, 1975-78, Higher Scientific Officer, 1978, Senior Scientific Officer, 1980, Principal Scientific Officer, 1983, Senior Principal Scientific Officer (UG6), 1987, Deputy Chief Scientific Officer (UG5) and Head of Development and Signalling, 1993-95, AFRC Institute of Animal Physiology, Babraham, Cambridge; Royal Society Research Professor of Molecular Pharmacology, Department of Pharmacology, University of Cambridge. Publications: Over 150 papers as author, co-author and first author published in refereed journals include: Back in the water: the return of the insitol phosphates, 2001; Inositol lipids are regulated during cell cycle progression in the nuclei of murine erythroleukaemia cells, 2001; Inositol 1,4,5-triphosphate 3-kinase A associates with F-actin and dendritic spines via its N terminus, 2001; Type IIα phosphatidylinositol phosphate kinase associates with the plasma membrane via interaction with type I isoforms, 2002. Honours: Pfizer Academic Award, 1988; Transoceanic Lecturer, The Endocrine Society, USA, 1989; FEBS Lecturer, 1993; FRS, 1993; Morton Lecturer, Biochemical Society, 1993; FIBiol, 1998; FMedSci (Founding Fellow), 1998. Memberships: Editorial Boards: Cellular Signalling, 1989-, Current Biology, 1994, Cell, 1996, Molecular Pharmacology, 2000-; Chairman, Molecular and Cellular Pharmacology Group 1999-, Council Member, 1999-, Biochemical Society; Royal Society Council, 1999-2001; Royal Society Research Fellowships Committee, 2000-. Address: Department of Pharmacology, University of Cambridge, Tennis Court Road, Cambridge CB2 1PD, England. E-mail: rfi20@cam.ac.uk

IRVING Amy, b. 10 September 1953, Palo Alto, California, USA. Actress. m. (1) Steven Spielberg, 1985, divorced, 1 son, (2) Bruno Barreto, 1996, divorced, 1 son, (3) Kenneth Bowser, 2007. Education: American Conservatory Theater and London Academy of Dramatic Art. Career: Plays: Romeo and Juliet, 1982-83; Amadeus, 1981-82; Heartbreak House, 1983-84; The Road to Mecca, 1988; Films: Carrie; The Fury; Voices; Honeysuckle Road; The Competition; Yentl; Mickey and Maude; Rumpelstiltskin; Crossing Delancey; A Show of Force; Benefit of the Doubt; Kleptomania; Acts of Love; I'm Not Rappaport; Carried Away; Deconstructing Harry; One Tough Cop, 1998; Blue Ridge Fall, 1999; The Confession; The Rage: Carrie 2, 1999; Traffic, 2000; Bossa Nova, 2000; Thirteen; Conversations About One Thing, 2002; Tuck Everlasting, 2002; Hide and Seek, 2005. Honours: SAG Award, 2001.

ISAACS Jeremy Israel, Sir, b. 28 September 1932. Arts Administrator. m. (1) Tamara Weinreich, 1958, 1 son, 1 daughter, (2) Gillian Widdicombe, 1988. Education: Glasgow Academy; Merton College, Oxford. Appointments: TV Producer, Granada TV, 1958, Associated Rediffusion, 1963, BBC TV, 1965; Controller of Features, Associated Rediffusion, 1967; Thames TV, 1968-78; Producer, The World at War, 1974, Cold War, 1998; Director of Programmes, 1974-78; Special Independent Consultant, TV Series, Hollywood ITV, A Sense of Freedom, ITV Ireland, TV Documentary, BBC, Battle for Crete, NZ TV, Cold War, Turner Broadcasting; CEO, Channel 4 TV Co, 1981-88; General Director, Royal Opera House, 1988-96 (director 1985-97); Chief Executive, Jeremy Isaacs Productions, 1998-. Publications: Storm Over Four: A Personal Account, 1989; Cold War, 1999; Never Mind the Moon, 1999; Look Me In The Eye: A Life In Television, 2006. Honours include: Desmond Davis Award, Outstanding Creative Contribution to TV, 1972; George Polk Memorial Award, 1973; Cyril Bennett Award, 1982; Lord Willis Award, Distinguished Service to TV, 1985. Memberships include: British Film Institute; Fellow, Royal TV Society, 1978.

ISAAK Robert Allen, b. 2 September 1945, Akron, Colorado, USA. Professor. m. Gudrun Kamm, 1 son, 1 daughter. Education: BA, Stanford University, 1966; MA, San Jose State University, 1967; PhD, New York University, 1971. Appointments: Associate Professor, Political Science, Fordham University, 1969-75; Fellow, Z Brzezinski's Research Institute of International Change and Institute on Western Europe, Columbia University, 1975-78; Associate Professor, Comparative Political Economy, Johns Hopkins School of Advanced International Studies, 1978-81; Henry George Professor of International Management, Pace University, 1981-2011; Guest Professor, Entrepreneurship, University of Mannheim, 2011-12. Publications: Politics for Human Beings, 1975; Individuals and World Politics, 1975; American Democracy & World Power, 1977; European Politics, 1980; Modern Inflation, 1983; The Real American Politics, 1986; American Political Thinking, 1994; The Making of the Ecopreneur (article), 1997; Green Logic, 1998; Managing World Economic Change, 2000; The Globalization Gap, 2005; From Collective Learning to Silicon Valley Replication (article), 2008; Brave New World Economy, 2011. Honours: Award for Innovation, 1992; Teacher of the Year, Pace University, 1993; Senior Fulbright Grant for research/teaching on environmental entrepreneurship, University of Heidelberg, 1996-97; Washington Irving Book Selection Award, 2007. Memberships: Eastern Economic Association, USA. Address: Untere Strasse 31, 69151 Neckargemund, Germany. E-mail: rasiaak@gmail.com

ISAEV Vyacheslav Konstantionovich, b. 3 June 1935, Volgograd, USSR. Research Scientist. m. E I Makarova, deceased, 3 daughters. Education: Diploma, 1958, Postgraduate School, 1961, Moscow Institute of Physics and Technology. Appointments: Research Scientist, TSAGI, 1958-; Candidate of Sciences in Technology, 1962; Doctor of Sciences, Physics and Mathematics, 1992; Professor, 1993; Assistant Professor, 1962-72, Associate Professor, 1972-93, Professor, 1993-, Moscow Institute of Physics and Technology. Publications: More than 200 articles in academician journals and proceedings of international and Russian congresses. Honours: Medal, Distinguished Service, 1974; Veteran of Labor Medal, 1985; Gold Jubilee Medal of Moscow Institute of Physics and Technology, 1985. Memberships: Academy of Non-Linear Sciences. Address: Chkalov str 31, Ap 3, Zhukovsky, Moscow Region, 140185, Russia.

ISAYEV Avraam Isayevich, b. 17 October 1942, Privolnoe, Azerbaijan. Professor. m. Lubov Dadasheva, 26 July 1969, 1 daughter. Education: MS, Chemical Engineering, Azerbaijan Institute of Oil and Chemistry, Baku, 1964; PhD, Polymer Engineering and Science, USSR Academy of Science, Moscow, 1970; MS, Applied Mathematics, Institute of Electronic Machine Building, Moscow, 1975. Appointments: Research Associate, State Research Institute of Nitrogen Industries, Severodonetsk, Ukraine, 1965-66; Predoctoral, Institute of Petrochemistry Synthesis, Russian Academy of Sciences, Moscow, 1967-69; Research Association, 1970-76, Senior Research Fellow, Israel Institute of Technology, Haifa, 1977-78; Senior Research Associate, Cornell University, Ithaca, New York, 1979-83; Associate Professor, Institute of Polymer Engineering, University of Akron, Ohio, 1983-87; Professor, 1987-2001; Director, Molding Technology, 1987-; Distinguished Professor, 2001-; Expert Witness, US House of Representatives, Washington DC, 1988; Guest Professor, University of Aachen, Germany, 1986, University of Linz, Austria, 1993, Kyoto Institute of Technology, Japan, 1996, Institute of Polymer Research, Dresden, Germany, 1997, University of Sao Carlos, Brazil, 1997; Treasurer, Polymer Processing Society, 1989-91; Expert on Plastics Processing Technologies, Malaysia, 1995; Editor in Chief, Advances in Polymer Technology, 2010. Publications: Injection and Compression Molding Fundamentals, 1987; Modeling of Polymer Processing, 1991; Liquid Crystalline Polymers Systems: Technological Advances, 1996; Recycling of Rubbers, 2005; Rheology: Concepts, Methods, Applications, 2006; Injection Molding: Technology and Fundamentals, 2009; Encyclopedia of Polymer Blends: Fundamentals, 2010; 260 articles in journals, books, encyclopaedias; 25 patents. Honours: Laureate of Young Scientist, USSR Academy of Sciences, 1970; NASA Faculty Fellow, 1985; Outstanding Achievement Awards, University of Akron Board of Trustees, 1988, 1993; Certificate of Recognition for Significant Contribution to Society and the Plastics Industry, SPE, 1994; Distinguished Corporate Inventor, American Society of Patent Holders, 1995; Outstanding Researcher Award, University of Akron Alumni Association, 1996; Silver Medal, Institute of Materials, London, 1997; Melvin Mooney Distinguished Technology Award, Rubber Division, American Chemical Society, 1999; Omnova Solutions Signature University Award, Akron, 2000; Vinogradov Prize, Society of Rheology, Moscow, 2000; Fellow, Society of Plastic Engineers, 2008; George Stafford Whitby Award for Distinguished Teaching and Research, Rubber Division, American Chemical Society, 2011; NorTech Award, 2011. Memberships: American Chemical Society; New York Academy of Sciences; Society of Plastic Engineers; Polymer Processing Society; Society of Rheology; American Association for Advancement of Science. Address: Institute of Polymer Engineering, University of Akron, Akron, OH 44325-0301, USA.

ISHIHARA Shintaro, b. 30 September 1932, Kobe, Japan. Politician; Author. m. Noriko, 4 sons. Education: Law Graduate, Hitotsubashi University, Tokyo, Japan. Appointments: Member, House of Councilors, 1968-72; Member, House of Representatives, 1972-95; Director-General, Environment Agency, 1976-77; Minister of Transport, 1987-88; Candidate, Liberal Democratic Party, Presidential Election, 1988; Governor of Tokyo, (currently serving fourth term), 1999-. Publications: The Season of the Sun, (Akutagawa Prize for Literature, 1956); The Forest of Fossils; The Japan that Can Say "No"; The State Becomes An Illusion; Undercurrents – Episodes from a Life on the Edge; Victorious Japan. Honours: Akutagawa prize, 1956. Memberships: Member, Selection Committee for Akutagawa

Prize, 1995. Address: Tokyo Metropolitan Government, 2-8-1, Nishi-Shinjuku, Shinjuku-ku, Tokyo 163-8001, Japan. E-mail: S0000573@section.metro.tokyo.jp

ISHII Shigemitsu, b. 15 April 1954, Fukuoka, Japan. University Teacher. m. Keiko Iwakami, 1 son. Education: BA, 1978, MA, 1980, Doshisha University, Japan. Appointments: Lecturer, Baika Junior College, Japan, 1982-99; Reader, 1999-, Professor, 2008-, Kinki University, Japan. Publications: Rorensu Sutahn: Sterne in Japan, The Shandean 8, 1996; Tokugawa Shogun's Tristram Shandy, The Shandean 12, 2001; Medical Realism and Fantasy in Tristram Shandy, The Shandean 18. Memberships: The Voltaire Foundation; The British Society for Eighteenth Century Studies. Address: 4-4-34 Kita Sakurazuka, Toyonaka, Osaka 560-0022, Japan.

ISHIMURA Ryuichi, b. 26 November 1953, Tokyo, Japan. Professor. m. Li-yuen Liu, 2 daughters. Education: MSc, Mathematics, 1978, DSc, 1985, Kyushu University. Appointments: Assistant, Kyushu University, 1979-87; Assistant Associé, University of Strasbourg, 1980-81; Associate Professor, 1987-99, Professor, 1999-, Chiba University; Maître de conférence Associé, University of Paris XIII, 1988-89, 1991. Publications: Existence locale de solutions holomorphes pour les equations differentielles d'ordre infini, 1985; The existence and the continuation of holomorphic solutions for convolution equations in tube domains, 1994. Memberships: Japan Mathematical Society. E-mail: ishimura@math.s.chiba-u.ac.jp Website: www.math.s.chiba-u.ac.jp/~ishimura

ISLAM Nazmul, b. 30 October 1983, Hariharpara, India. Assistant Professor. Education: PhD. Appointments: Assistant Professor, Department of Basic Science & HU, Techno Global-Balurghat, Dinajpur. Publications: 33 research papers in international journals; 14 book chapters; 6 books. Honours: Editorial boards of Journal of Chemical Engineering and International Journal of Physical Sciences and Material Science; Listed in biographical dictionaries. Memberships: International Journal of Physical Sciences; Journal of Chemical Engineering. Address: Vil PO PS Hariharpara Dist, Murshidabad, PIN 742166, West Bengal, India.

ISLAM Rafiqul, b. 31 March 1956, Bangladesh. University Professor. Education: MSc, Petro-Chemical Engineering & Technology, Azerbaijan Institute of Petroleum & Chemistry, 1980; PhD, Chemical Engineering, Azerbaijan Institute of Petro-Chemical Processes Academy of Sciences, 1985. Appointments: Process Engineer, Eastern Refinery Ltd, 1981; Scientist, Central Research Laboratory, Baku Petroleum Refinery, 1982-86; Engineer, Process Design, Bangladesh Chemical Industries Corporation (Chittagong Urea Fertilizer Ltd), 1986-87; Assistant Professor, 1987, Associate Professor, 1992, and Professor, 1997, Chairman, 2004-07, Department of Applied Chemistry & Chemical Technology, University of Dhaka. Publications: Around 50 articles in national and international journals. Honours: Winner, Moscow Olympiad of Young Scientists; Marie Curie Bursary, Commission of the European Communities; Great Wall Award, State Education Commission of China and UNESCO; Alexander von Humboldt Post-Doctoral Fellowship; Europe Research Fellowship; Commonwealth Academic Staff Fellowship; Ambassador Scientist, Alexander von Humboldt Foundation, Federal German Government, Bangladesh; Listed in international biographical dictionaries. Memberships: Environment Study Centre, Bangladesh; Bangladesh Chemical Society; Bangladesh Association for the Advancement of Science; Asiatic Society of Bangladesh; Institution of Engineers, Bangladesh; Association of Humboldt Fellows Bangladesh; Bangladesh Society of Pharmaceutical Chemists. Address: Department of Applied Chemistry & Chemical Engineering, Faculty of Engineering & Technology, University of Dhaka, Dhaka 1000, Bangladesh.

ISLAM Zafarul, b. 10 September 1950, Chhittey Pur, Azamgarh, India. Professor. m. Shamima Begum, 4 sons, 3 daughters. Education: BA, 1972; MA, 1974; M Phil, 1977; PhD, 1984; Diploma in West Asian Studies, 1983. Appointments: Research Associate, History, 1980-84; Lecturer, Islamic Studies, 1984-93; Reader, Islamic Studies, 1993-2001; Professor, Islamic Studies, 2001-. Publications: 16 books; 163 articles; 57 seminars attended. Honours: Listed in international biographical dictionaries, 2004-. Memberships: Idarah Ulumal-Quran; Madrasatul Islah; Darul Musannefin Shibli Academy. Address: Department of Islamic Studies, Aligarh Muslim University, Aligarh, 202002, India. E-mail: zafarul.islam@gmail.com

ISOBE Tetsuya, b. 7 December 1961, Osaka, Japan. Physician. m. Keiko Kodaira, 1 daughter. Education: MD, 1995, PhD, 2003, Osaka University; International Traditional Chinese Medicine Doctor, World Federation of Chinese Medicine Societies, Liaoning College of Traditional Chinese Medicine, 2011. Appointments: Physician, Western Medicine & Oriental Medicine, related hospitals with Medical Faculty of Mie University, 1995-2004; Chief, Reproductive Medical Center, Suzuka Kaisei Hospital, 2005-10; Chief, International Oriental Medical Center, Kishokai Bellnet, 2011-. Publications: The effect of RANTES on human sperm chemotaxis, 2002; Validity of trans-rectal ultrasound-guided embryo transfer against retroflexed uterus, 2003; Approach for estimating fetal body weight using two-dimensional ultrasound, 2004; Assessment of fertility by sperm mechanical energy using computer-assisted sperm analysis system, 2009; Discovery of natural law of sperm motion, and application to reproductive medicine. Honours: Listed in Who's Who in the World 2011. Memberships: Japan Society for Oriental Medicine; Japan Society for Ultrasonics in Medicine; Japan Society of Obstetrics and Gynecology; Japan Society for Reproductive Medicine. Address: 3-19-5 FLEZIO LA 8F, Marunouchi, Naka, Nagoya Kishokai Bellnet, Aichi 460-0002, Japan.

ITOH Chiaki, b. 4 February 1939, Akita, Japan. Professor. m. Katsuko, 1 son, 1 daughter. Education: PhD, Tokyo University of Education, 1966. Appointments: Lecturer, Meiji Gakuin University, Tokyo, 1968-71; Assistant Professor, 1971-78; Professor, 1978-2007; Professor Emeritus, 2007-. Publications: Unified Gauge Theory of Weak Electromagnetic and Strong Interactions, 1973. Honours: International Man of the Year, IBC, 1994-95; Most Admired Man of the Decade, ABI, 1995; The International Order of Merit, IBC, 1996. Memberships: The American Physical Society. Address: Department of Physics, Meiji Gakuin University, 1518 Kamikuratacho, Totsuka, Yokohama 244-8539, Japan. Website: http://www.meijigakuin.ac.jp/~citoh/eng.htm

ITZHAKI-WEINBERGER Paz, Computer Company Executive. Education: Degree, Computer Science, 2003, Degree, Japanese, 2005, The Open University, Tel-Aviv, Israel; Law degree, Tel Aviv University, 2005. Appointments: CEO, HobbitNet Israeli Communication Systems, Tel Aviv, 1995-96; CEO, PAZ Computer Corporation, Tel-Aviv, 1996-98; Captain, Intelligence IDF, 1998-2004; CEO and Chairman, Itzhaki-Weinberger Consultants Ltd, Netanya, Israel, 2004-; Information Security Expert, Gteko Ltd,

DICTIONARY OF INTERNATIONAL BIOGRAPHY 36th EDITION

Raanana, Israel, 2004-06; Security Expert, Microsoft Corp, Raanana, 2006-09; Law Practitioner, Eitan S Erez & Co, 2010-. Memberships: Israel-British Chamber of Commerce; IEEE. Address: Itzhaki-Weinberger Consultants Ltd, PO Box 102, Givataim 53100, Israel.

IVAKHIV Orest, b. 24 May 1945, Lviv, Ukraine. Professor. m. Oleksandra, 1 son, 1 daughter. Education: Engineer (Honorary), Lviv Polytechnic Institute, Lviv, 1963-68; PhD, Moscow Aviation Institute, Moscow, Russia, 1972-76; DSc, Lviv Polytechnic National University, Lviv, 2002. Appointments: Assistant, 1976-80, Senior Educator, 1980-81, Associated Professor, 1981-2002, Full Professor, 2002-, Head of Chair, 2002-, Lviv Polytechnic National University, Lviv. Publications: More than 200 papers; 14 patents; 3 textbooks. Honours: Prize, Ministry of Education, USSR, 1975; Honorary Educator, Ukraine, 2004. Memberships: IEEE; Ukrainian Professional Association; Scientific and organizing committees of international seminars and conferences. Address: 12 Bandera Str, Lviv 790073, Ukraine.

IVANCEVIC Tijana Tanya Tulasi, b. 8 July 1965, Leskovac, Yugoslavia. Research Scientist; Mathematician. m. Vladimir Ivancevic, 1 son, 2 daughters. Education: BS, 1991, MS, 1995, Biomechanics, University of Novi Sad, Yugoslavia; PhD, Mathematics, University of Adelaide, Australia, 2008. Appointments: Lecturer, University of Novi Sad, 1992-95; Researcher, 1999-2000, Senior Researcher, 2009-, University of South Australia; Researcher, University of Adelaide, 2000-08; Scientific Adviser of CEO, 2009-. Publications: Books: Natural Biodynamics, 2006; High Dimensional Chaotic & Attractor Systems, 2006; Humanlike Biomechanics, 2006; Complex Dynamics, 2006; Applied Differential Geometry, 2007; Computational Mind, 2007; Neuro Fuzzy Associate Machinery, 2007; Complex Nonlinearity, 2007; Quantum Leap, 2008; Complex Sports Biomechanics, 2008; Quantum Neural Computation, 2009; Handbook for Engineers, 2010; Paradigm Shift for Future Tennis, 2011; Gateway to Future Science with Nikola Teslak, 2011. Honours: Best Textbook Award, Novi Sad. Memberships: Nonlinear Human Factors. Address: 9 Pike Avenue, Mawson Lakes, Shoalhaven, 5095 South Australia, Australia. E-mail: tijana.ivancevic@alumni.adelaide.edu.au

IVANCEVIC Vladimir, b. 12 May 1955, Belgrade, Yugoslavia. Senior Defence Scientist. m. Tijana, 1 son, 2 daughters. Education: PhD, Biomechanics, University of Belgrade, 1986. Appointments: Associate Professor, Biomechanics, University of Novi Sad, Yugoslavia, 1990-95; Research Associate, Applied Mathematics, University of Adelaide, Australia, 1995-2000; Chief Scientist, Torson Gr Inc, 2000-02; Senior Research Scientist, Defence Science & Technology Organisation Australia, 2002-. Publications: Over 100 publications including 8 monographs. Honours: Excellence in Science & Technology, Defence Science & Technology Organisation Australia, 2005. Membership: IEEE.

IVANISEVIC Goran, b. 13 September 1971, Split, Croatia. Former Professional Tennis Player. Appointments: Winner, US Open Junior Doubles with Nargiso, 1987; Turned Professional, 1988; Joined Yugoslav Davis Cup Squad, 1988; Runner-up, Wimbledon Championship, 1992, 1994, 1998; Semi-Finalist, ATP World Championship, 1992; Winner, numerous ATP tournaments, include Kremlin Cup, Moscow, 1996; Winner, Wimbledon Championship, 2001; Winner, 22 tours singles and 9 doubles titles to date; Retired, 2004. Honours include: Bronze Medal, Men's Doubles, Barcelona Olympic Games, 1992; BBC Overseas Sports Personality of the Year Award, 2001. Membership: President, Children in Need Foundation, 1995. Website: www.goranivanisevic.com

IVANOV Viktor Petrovich, b. 12 May 1950, Novgorod, Russia. Deputy Head of Administration of the President of the Russian Federation. m. 1 son, 1 daughter. Education: Graduate, Leningrad Professor M. Bonch-Bruyevich Electrical Engineering Institute of Communications, 1974; Served in Soviet Army, 1974-75; Engineer, Leningrad Scientific-Production Association "Vector", 1975-77; Served in State Security Bodies, Specialisation - fight against organised crime, 1977-; Head, Directorate of Administrative Bodies, St Petersburg Mayor's Office, 1994-96; Director General, Teleplus Television Company, 1996-98; Head of Directorate, Federal Security Service of the Russian Federation, 1998-99; Deputy Director, Head of Department of Economic Security, Federal Security Service of the Russian Federation, 1999-2000; Deputy Head of Administration of the President of the Russian Federation, 2000-04; Adviser to the President, 2004-. Honours: Order "For Merits to the Motherland" 4th class; Order of Honour; Medal "For Merits in Combat". Address: Administration of President of Russian Federation, Staraya pl 4, 103132 Moscow, Russia.

IYENGAR Yogacharya B K S, b. 14 December 1918, Bellur, Kolar District, Karnataka, India. Yoga Expert. m. Shrimati Ramamani, 1943. Education: Yoga Teaching Assignment, Karnataka College, Dharward, 1936. Appointments: Yoga Instructor, Deccan Gymkhana, Pune, 1937-40; Private Yoga Teacher, pupils included Shri J Krishnamurthi, Shri Jayaprakash Narayan, Shri Achyutrao Patwardhan, G S Pathak, B D Jatti, General Shrinagesh, General B C Joshi and Yehudi Menuhin; Yoga class, Bombay, 1954-. Publications: Light on Yoga, 1966; Body the Shrine, Yoga thy Light, 1978; The Concise Light on Yoga 1980; Light on Prāṇāyāma, 1981; The Art of Yoga, 1985; The Tree of Yoga, 1988; Iyengar: His Life and Work, 1991; The Illustrated Light on Yoga, 1993; Light on Yoga Sūtras of Patañjali, 1993; Light on Astanga Yoga; Astadala Yogamala, Volumes 1-8, 2000-08; Yoga, the Path to Holistic Health, 2001; Light on Life, 2005; Yoga Wisdom and Practice, 2009; Yaugika Manas, 2010; books translated in to more than 25 languages. Honours: Subject of film, Guruji, 1985; Holds titles of: Yogi Ratna, Yoganga Shikshaka Chakravarti; Star named Yogacharya BKS Iyengar, 1988; Rajyotsava Award, 1988; Patañjali Award, 1990; Commemorative volume, 70 Glorious Years of Yogacharya BKS Iyengar, 1990; Vasistha Award, 1991; Gold Medal, All India Board of Alternative Medicine, 1991; Padma Shri Award, 1991; Scroll of Honours, Pune Municipal Corporation, 1991; Purna Swasthya Award, 1991; Doctor of Science degree, Open International University for Complementary Medicine, 1991; Shri Krishnanugraha Prashasti Patra, 1992; Pune Pride Gold Medal, 1992; Punya Bhushan Award, 1995; Gem of Alternative Medicine, 1995; Conducted Mega Classes in USA, Canada, Bombay, Bangalore and London, 1993; Health Care for 1996 Award; Doctorate of Science, University of Mysore, 1997; Vipra Ratna, Karnataka Brahman Mahasabha, 1997; Man of the Year, ABI, 1998; 20th Century Achievement Award, ABI; International Man of the Year, IBC, 1998; 20th Century Award for Achievement, IBC; 10 day Yoga Festival to celebrate 80th birthday and title of Arsa-Kula-Sresthah, 1998; Jeevan Sadhana Gaurav, Pune University, 1999; Gyan Kalyan Charitable Award, 1999; Abhinava Patanjali Maharsh, 1999; Rotary Excellence Award, 1999; Swami Vivekanand Puruskar Award, 1999; Best Citizen of India Award, 1999, 2000; Eminent Personalities of India, 1999; Yoga Dron Award, 1999; 2000 Millennium Medal of Achiever, 2001;

Hall of Fame Award, 2000; Priyadarshni Academy Award for Lifetime Achievement, 2000; Swasthya Seva Ratna, 2000; Rishi Award, 2001; Padmabhushan Award, 2002; Doctorate of Letters, 2002; Yoga Ratna Award, 2002; Yoga Panchajanya Pithamaha, 2002; Rising Personalities of India Award, 2002; Yoga Bhaskara Award, 2002; Fellow, Royal College of Physicians, 2003; Jewel of India, 2003; Lifetime Achievement Award, 2003; Vidya Vyas Award, 2003; Industrial Technology Foundation Award, 2004; Karnataka Legislature Council award, 2004; Ajit Kumar Memorial Yoga Research Centre Students of Yoga Center, 2004; Heroes and Icons, 2004; Indira Gandhi Excellence Award and Rajdhani Rattan Gold Medal Award, 2005; Suryadata Lifetime Achievement Award, 2005; Yoga Shikshana Puraskar Award, 2005; Bharati Jeevan Sadhana Gaurav Puraskar, 2005; Golden Lifetime Achievement Award, 2005; Kasba Ganapati Award, 2006; Yogiraj of the Millennium Award, 2007; Rising Personalities of India Award and Gold Medal, 2007; Certificate of Excellence, 2008; Economic Growth and National Unity certificate, 2008; Superior Achievement Award, 2008; Degree of Science, 2009; Readers Digest: India's Most Trusted 2009; Rajdhani Rattan Gold Medal Award, 2010; Rashtriya Gaurav Award, 2010; Jewel of India Gold Award, 2010; Maha Yoga Guru Puraskar; Participated in the First International Conference Yoga for Health and Social Transformation, 2011; Meeting with H H Dalai Lama; Listed in numerous national and international biographical directories. Memberships: Fellow, International Council of Ayurveda, 1991; President, India Yoga Association, 2008. Address: Ramamani Iyengar Memorial Yoga Institute, 1107 B/1 Hare Krishna Mandir Road, Model Colony, Shivaji Nagar, Pune – 411 016, Maharashtra, India.

IYER Saraswati Raju, b. 30 September 1968, Madras, India. Teacher. m. Raju, 1 son, 1 daughter. Education: Bachelor, 1990, Master, 1992, Social Work, College of Social Work, Hyderabad, Osmania University; Master of Arts, Sociology, Centre for Distance Education, Acharya Nagarjuna University, 2010; PhD, Stress, Anger and Myocardial Infarction – Its Relationship, Management and Counselling, Osmania University, 2002; Certificate Course in Guidance, IGNOU, New Delhi, 2003. Appointments: Lecturer, Social Work Department, SPMVV Tirupati; Lecturer, Department of Social Work, GRD College of Science, Coimbatore; Lecturer, Department of Social Work, Maris Stella College, Vijayawada; Lecturer, Assistant Professor, Department of Sociology & Social Work, Acharya Nagarjuna University. Publications: Over 60 articles in journals of repute; Editor, source book; Editor of books on Social Work for ANU Centre for Distance Education; Book chapters; Lesson writer. Honours: Award and Certificate of Appreciation, Best Youth at All India Youth Camp, Kerala, 1990; Gold Medal and Cash Award, Best Student of P G College of Social Work, 1991-92; Best Citizen of India Award, 2011. Memberships: Indian Society of Professional Social Workers; Andhra Pradesh Sociological Society; Indian Academy of Social Sciences; Child Rights Advocacy Foundation. Address: Department of Sociology and Social Work, Acharya Nagarjuna University, Nagarjuna Nagar, Guntur 522 510, Andhra Pradesh, India. E-mail: saras1_2rajuiyer2003@yahoo.com

IYER Vijayan Gurumurthy, b. 10 June 1964, Mayuram, India. University Professor. m. Shanthi. Education: Diploma, Mechanical Engineering, 1982; Diploma, Production Management, Annamalai University, 1988; Post Diploma, Automobile Engineering, Victoria Jubilee Technical Institute, Mumbai, 1992; AMIE, Mechanical Engineering, Institution of Engineers, India, 1990; Master's, 1997, PhD, 2003, Environmental Science and Engineering, Indian School of Mines University, Dhanbad; Post-doctoral Researcher, World Scientific and Engineering Academy and Society, Greece, 2006; Doctor of Science and Engineering, 2010; Doctor of Law, The Yorker International University, Italy, 2011. Appointments: Technical Officer, Indian Council of Agricultural Research Service, Central Institute of Agricultural Engineering, Bhopal, 1985-; Central Institute for Research on Cotton Technology, -1998; Professor, Hindustan College of Engineering, Rajalakshmi Engineering College, MNM Jain Engineering College; Professor, Environmental Engineering, Dr M G R University, Chennai, -2010; Principal, PDr KVCOET, Chennai, -2011. Publications: Over 150 research publications in the field of environmental science and mechanical engineering and education; Over 190 citations; Reviewer: WSEAS; ASABE; Environmental Monitor Journals. Honours: Kendriya Sachivalaya Hindi Parishad, 1988; Bharat Jyothi, 2000; Prominent citizens of India and Best Citizen of India, 2001; Rashtriya Ratna, 2001; NCERT Special Education Award, 2003; Rashtriya Gaurav, 2004, 2010; Tamil Nadu Government Best Environmental Research Essay Award, 2005; Postdoctoral Fellowship Award, 2006. Memberships: Indian Society for Technical Education; Loss Prevention Association of India; World Scientific and Engineering Academy and Society, Greece; Institution of Engineers, Bangladesh; Aeronautical Society of India; Bioinformatics Institute of India; Consultancy Development Center; Mining Engineers Association of India; Indian Society for Training and Development; American Society of Mechanical Engineers; Fellow: Institution of Engineers, India; Institution of Valuers, India; Textile Association, India; All India Management Association. Address A-2/31 III Floor, Kendriya Vihar 2, Poonamalee – Avadi Main Road, Paruthipattu, Avadi, Chennai 600 071, India. E-mail: vijayaniyergurumurthy@rediffmail.com

IZUMI Yasuo, b. 4 January 1965, Tokyo, Japan. Associate Professor. m. Emi, 2 sons, 1 daughter. Education: DSc, University of Tokyo, 1993. Appointments: Research Associate, 1992, Lecturer, 1998, Tokyo Institute of Technology; Monbu Sho Visiting Scientist, Stanford University, 1996-97; Associate Professor, Chiba University, 2007-. Publications: Numerous articles in professional journals. Honours: Young Scientist Prize, International Congress on Catalysis, 2000; Tejima Foundation Award, 2001; Special Lecture Prize, Chemical Society of Japan, 2001. Memberships: American Association for the Advancement of Science; Chemical Society of Japan; Catalysis Society of Japan; Japanese Society of Synchrotron Radiation Research. Address: Yayoi 1-33, Inage-ku, Chiba 263-8522, Japan. Website: http://www2.odn.ne.jp/yizumi/index_eng.html

J

JACK Kenneth Henderson, b. 12 October 1918, North Shields, Northumberland, England. University Professor. m. Alfreda Hughes, deceased 1974, 2 sons. Education: BSc, 1939, DThPT, 1940, MSc, 1944, King's College, University of Durham, Newcastle upon Tyne, England; PhD, 1950, ScD, 1978, Fitzwilliam College, University of Cambridge, England. Appointments: Experimental Officer, Ministry of Supply, London, England, 1940-41; Lecturer in Chemistry, King's College, University of Durham, 1941-45, 1949-52, 1953-57; Senior Scientific Officer, British Iron and Steel Research Association, 1945-49; Research, Crystallographic Laboratory, Cavendish Laboratory, Cambridge, 1947-49; Research Engineer, Westinghouse Electric Corporation, Pittsburgh, Pennsylvania, USA, 1952-53; Research Director, Thermal Syndicate Ltd, Wallsend, Tyne and Wear, 1957-64; Professor of Applied Crystal Chemistry, University of Newcastle Upon Tyne, 1964-84; Director, Wolfson Research Group for High-Strength Materials, England, 1970-84; Leverhulme Emeritus Fellow, 1985-87; Emeritus Professor, University of Newcastle Upon Tyne, 1984-; Consultant, Cookson Group plc, England, 1986-94; Honorary Professor of Materials Engineering, University of Wales, Swansea, 1996-2011. Publications: 200 papers in scientific journals and conference proceedings covering solid state chemistry, crystallography, metallurgy, ceramic science and glass technology. Honours: 18 major awards including: Saville-Shaw Medal, Society of Chemical Industry, 1944; Sir George Beilby Memorial Award, Institute of Metals et al, 1951; Kroll Medal & Prize, The Metals Society, 1979; Elected Fellow of The Royal Society (FRS), 1980; Prince of Wales Award for industrial Innovation and Production, 1984; Royal Society Armourers & Brasiers Company Award, 1988; World Materials Congress Award, ASM International, 1988; A A Griffith Silver Medal & Prize, The Metals Society, 1989; Centennial Award, Ceramic Society of Japan, 1991; Appointed Officer of the Most Excellent Order of the British Empire (OBE), 1997; Listed in international biographical dictionaries. Memberships: Fellow, The Royal Society (Elected); Elected Member, International Academy of Ceramics, 1989; Fellow, The Royal Society of Chemistry; Distinguished Life Member, The American Ceramic Society, 2007; Honorary Member, Société Française de Métallurgie et de Matériaux; Honorary Member, the Ceramic Society of Japan; Honorary Member, The Materials Research Society of India. Address: 147 Broadway, Cullercoats, Tyne and Wear, NE30 3TA, England.

JACK Ronald Dyce Sadler, b. 3 April 1941, Ayr, Scotland. University Professor. m. Kirsty Nicolson, 8 July 1967, 2 daughters. Education: MA, Glasgow, 1964; PhD, Edinburgh, 1968; DLitt, Glasgow. Appointments: Lecturer, Department of English Literature, Edinburgh University, 1965; Reader, 1978; Professor, 1987; Visiting Professor, University of Virginia, 1973-74; Director, Universities Central Council on Admissions, 1988-94; Visiting Professor, University of Strathclyde, 1993; Distinguished Visiting Professor, University of Connecticut, 1998-2004; Professor Emeritus, 2004-. Publications: Scottish Prose 1550-1700, 1972; The Italian Influence on Scottish Literature, 1972; A Choice of Scottish Verse 1560-1660, 1978; The Art of Robert Burns (co-author), 1982; Sir Thomas Urquhart (co-author), 1984; Alexander Montgomerie, 1985; Scottish Literature's Debt to Italy, 1986, 2nd revised edition, 2010; The History of Scottish Literature, Vol I, 1988; Patterns of Divine Comedy, 1989; The Road to the Never Land, 1991, 2nd edition, 2010; Of Lion and Unicorn, 1993; The Poems of William Dunbar, 1997; Mercat Anthology of Early Scottish Literature, 1997, 2nd revised edition, 2000; New Oxford Dictionary of National Biography (associate editor), 2004; Scotland in Europe (co-editor), 2006; Joyous Sweit Imaginahoun: Essays in honour of R D S Jack, 2007; Myths and the Mythmaker, 2010; Contributions to: Review of English Studies; Modern Language Review; Comparative Literature; Studies in Scottish Literature. Memberships: Medieval Academy of America; Scottish Text Society; Fellow, Royal Society of Edinburgh, 2001; Fellow, English Association, 2001. Address: David Hume Tower, George Square, Edinburgh EH8 9JX, Scotland.

JACKLIN Tony, b. 7 July 1944, Scunthorpe, England. Golfer. m. Vivien Jacklin, 1966, deceased 1988, 2 sons, 1 daughter, (2) Astrid May Waagen, 1988, 1 son, 1 stepson, 1 stepdaughter. Appointments: Lincolnshire Open Champion, 1961; Professional, 1962-85, 1988-; Won, British Assistant Professional's Title, 1965; Won, Dunlop Masters, 1967, 1973; First British player to win British Open since 1951, 1969; US Open Champion, 1970; First British player to win US Open since 1920 and first since 1900 to hold US and British Open titles simultaneously; Greater Greensboro Open Champion, USA, 1968, 1972; Won, Italian Open, 1973, German Open, 1979, Venezuelan Open, 1979, Jersey Open, 1981, British PGA Champion, 1982 and 15 major tournaments in various parts of the world; Played in 8 Ryder Cup matches and 4 times for England in World Cup; Captain of 1983 GB and European Ryder Cup Team; Captain of European Ryder Cup Team, 1985 (1st win for Europe since 1957), 1987; BBC TV Golf Commentator; Director of Golf, San Roque Club, 1988-; Golf course designer. Publications: Golf With Tony Jacklin, 1969; The Price of Success, 1979; Jacklin's Golfing Secrets, with Peter Dobereiner; The First Forty Years, with Renton Laidlaw, 1985; Your Game and Mine, with Bill Robertson, 1999. Honours include: Honorary Fellow, Birmingham Polytechnic, 1989. Memberships include: British Professional Golfers Association. Address: Tony Jacklin Golf Academy, Plaza del Rio Office Centre, 101 Riverfront Boulevard, Suite 610, Bradenton, FL 34205, USA.

JACKMAN Brian, b. 25 April 1935, Epsom, Surrey, England. Freelance Journalist; Writer. m. (1) 14 February 1964, divorced December 1992, 1 daughter, (2) January 1993. Education: Grammar School. Appointment: Staff, Sunday Times, 1970-90. Publications: We Learned to Ski, 1974; Dorset Coast Path, 1977; The Marsh Lions, 1982; The Countryside in Winter, 1986; My Serengeti Years, editor, 1987; Roaring at the Dawn, 1996; The Big Cat Diary, 1996; Touching the Wild, 2003. Contributions to: Sunday Times; The Times; Daily Telegraph; Daily Mail; Country Living; Condé Nast Traveller; BBC Wildlife; Harper's Bazaar. Honours: TTG Travel Writer of Year, 1982; Wildscreen Award, 1982. Memberships: Royal Geographical Society; Fauna and Flora Preservation Society; Patron, The Tusk Trust; Trustee, The George Adamson Wildlife Trust. Address: Spick Hatch, West Milton, Nr Bridport, Dorset DT6 3SH, England.

JACKMAN Hugh, b. 2 October 1968, Sydney, New South Wales, Australia. Actor; Singer; Producer. m. Deborra-Lee Furness, 1996, 1 son, 1 daughter. Education: BA, Communications, University of Technology, Sydney, 1991; Western Australian Academy of Performing Arts, Edith Cowan University, Perth, 1994. Career: Film: X-Men, 2000; Kate & Leopold, 2001; Swordfish, 2001; X2: X-Men United, 2003; Van Helsing, 2004; The Prestige, 2006; The Fountain, 2006; Scoop, 2006; Happy Feet, 2006; Flushed Away, 2006; Deception, 2008; Australia, 2008; X-Men Origins: Wolverine, 2009; X-Men: First Class, 2011; Snow Flower and the

Secret Fan, 2011; Real Steel, 2011; Butter, 2012; Rise of the Guardians, 2012; Les Miserables, 2012; Movie 43, 2013; The Wolverine, 2013; Theatre: Oklahoma!, 1998; Carousel, 2002; The Boy from Oz, 2003-04, 2006; A Steady Rain, 2009; One-man show, Curran Theatre, San Francisco, 2011. Honours include: Tony Award, 2004; Drama Desk Award, 2004; Emmy Award, 2005; Australian Dance Award, 2008; People's Choice Award, 2010; Scream Award, 2011; People's Choice Award, Favourite Action Movie Actor, 2012; Tony Award, 2012; Golden Globe for Best Actor, 2013.

JACKSON Betty, b. 24 June 1949, Lancashire, England. Couturier. m. David Cohen, 1985, 1 son, 1 daughter. Education: Birmingham College of Art and Design. Appointments: Chief Designer, Quorum, 1975-81; Founder, Betty Jackson Ltd, 1981, Director, 1981-; Opened, Betty Jackson Retail Shop, 1991; Part-time Tutor, RCA, 1982-; Visiting Professor, 1999; Established Award for Arts by Preston City Council, 2004. Memberships: Fellow, Birmingham Polytechnic, 1989; University of Central Lancashire, 1993. Honours: Designer of the Year, 1985; Royal Designer for Industry, Royal Society of Arts, 1988, 1989; Fil d'Or, International Linen, 1989; Honorary Fellow, 1989, part time tutor, 1982-, visiting professor, 1999, RCA; Contemporary Designer of the Year, 1999; CBE, 2007. Address: Betty Jackson Ltd, 1 Netherwood Place, Netherwood Road, London W14 0BW, England. Website: www.bettyjackson.com

JACKSON Caroline Frances, b. 5 November 1946, Penzance, Cornwall, England. Former Member of European Parliament. m. Robert Jackson, 1 son, deceased. Education: Classics and History, St Hugh's and Nuffield College, Oxford; Oxford Doctorate in Philosophy. Appointments: Research Fellow, St Hugh's College, Oxford; Member of Parliament, Wiltshire North and Bath; Member of European Parliament, South West Region, 1984-99, 1999-2009; Conservative Spokesman, Environment Committee, European Parliament, 1984-99; Deputy Chairman, Conservative Members of the European Parliament, 1997; First Member of the European Parliament to chair a session of the Conservative Party Conference, 1998; Chairman, European Parliament's Committee on the Environment, Public Health and Food Safety, 1999-2004; Chairman of Trustees, Institute for European Environment Policy, 2004-10; President, Environmental Protection UK, 2010-. E-mail: cf.jackson@homecall.co.uk Website: www.drcarolinejackson.com

JACKSON Colin Ray, b. 18 February 1967. Athlete. Career: Honours for 110m hurdles include: Silver Medal, European Junior Championships, 1985; Gold Medal, World Junior Championships, 1986; Silver Medal, Commonwealth Games, 1986; Silver Medal, European Cup, 1987; Bronze Medal, World Championships, 1987; Silver Medal, Olympic Games, 1988; Silver Medal, World Cup, 1989; Gold Medal, European Cup, 1989, 1993; Gold Medal, Commonwealth Games, 1990; Gold Medal, World Cup, 1992; Gold Medal (new world record), Silver Medal (relay), World Championships, 1993; Honours for 60 hurdles include: Silver Medal World Indoor Championships, 1989, 1993; Silver Medal, 1987, Gold Medal 1989, 1994, European Indoor Championships; Gold Medal, European and Commonwealth Championships, 1994; Gold Medal, European Championships, 1998, 2002; Gold Medal, World Championships, 1999; Numerous Welsh, UK, European and Commonwealth records; Most capped British athlete ever (70 vests), 2003; Total of 25 medals; Announced retirement in 2003. Honours: MBE, 1990; CBE, 1992; Hon BA, Aberystwyth, 1994; Hon BSc, University of Wales, 1999; Athlete of the Decade, French Sporting Council; Hurdler of the Century, German Athletic Association; Athlete of the Year, 1993-94; British Athletics Writers Sportsman of the Year, 1994; Sports Writers Association. Memberships: Brecon Athletics Club UK International, 1985-. Address: 4 Jackson Close, Rhoose, Vale of Glamorgan, CF62 3DQ, Wales. Website: www.mtc-uk.com

JACKSON Davina Gainor, b. 18 March 1956, Auckland, New Zealand. Writer. m. Chris Johnson. Education: Auckland University, 1972; Auckland Technical Institute, 1973; University of New South Wales, 1995-97; RMIT, 2003-07. Appointments: Auckland Star, 1974-77; Daily Mirror, 1977; Various decorating magazines, 1980-92; Editor, Architecture Australia, 1992-2000; Author, 1995-. Publications: D_City: Digital Earth, Virtual Nations, Data Cities, 2012; Australian Architecture Now, 2007; 40UP: Next Wave: Emerging Talents in Australian Architecture, 2007; Australian Architecture's Next Generation, 1999; Pink Fits: Australian Perspectives on Architecture, 1993-2006, 2006. Honours: National Association of Women in Construction, Vision Award, 2000. Memberships: International Society for Digital Earth; Australian Society of Authors; Fellow, Royal Society for Arts. E-mail: davina@davinajackson.com

JACKSON Glenda, b. 9 May 1936, Birkenhead, Cheshire, England. Member of Parliament; Actress. m. Roy Hodges, 1958, divorced 1976, 1 son. Education: Royal Academy of Dramatic Art. Appointments: Actress, Royal Shakespeare Company; Other Theatre includes: The Investigation, Hamlet, US, 1965; Three Sisters, 1967; The Maids, 1974; Hedda Gabler, 1975; The White Devil, 1976; Antony and Cleopatra, 1978; The House of Bernada Alba, 1986; Scenes from an Execution, 1990; Mermaid, 1990; Mother Courage, 1990; Mourning Becomes Electra, 1991; Films include: Women in Love, 1969; Sunday, Bloody Sunday, Mary, Queen of Scots and The Boyfriend, 1971; A Touch of Class, 1973; The Abbess of Crewe, 1976; House Calls, 1978; Salome's Last Dance, 1988; The Rainbow, 1989; The Secret Life of Sir Arnold Bax, 1992; TV includes: Elizabeth R, 1971; The Morecambe and Wise Show; Elected Labour MP Hampstead and Highgate, 1992-; Parliamentary Under Secretary of State, Department for the Environment and Transport, 1997-99; Adviser on Homelessness, GLA, 2000-. Honours: CBE, Honorary DLitt, Liverpool, 1978; Honorary LLM, Nottingham, 1992; Honorary Fellow, Liverpool Polytechnic, 1987; 2 Academy Awards, 1971, 1974. Memberships: President, Play Matters, 1976-; Director, United British Artists, 1986-. Address: c/o House of Commons, London SW1A 0AA, England.

JACKSON Janet, b. 16 May 1966, Gary, IN, USA. Singer; Actress. m. (1) El DeBarge, 1984, annulled 1986, (2) Rene Elizondo, 1991, divorced. Career: First appearance with family singing group The Jacksons, aged 7; Television actress, 1977-81; Appeared in US television series: Good Times, CBS-TV; Diff'rent Strokes; Fame; A New Kind Of Family; Solo recording artiste, 1982-; Concerts and tours include: Rhythm Nation World Tour (US, Europe, Far East), 1990; Film debut, Poetic Justice, 1993. Recordings: Albums: Janet Jackson, 1982; Dream Street, 1984; Control, 1986; Janet Jackson's Rhythm Nation, 1989; Janet, 1993; Design Of A Decade 1986-1996, 1995; The Velvet Rope, 1997; All For You, 2001; Damita Jo, 2004; 20 Y.O., 2006; Discipline, 2008. Hit singles include: What Have You Done For Me Lately, Nasty, When I Think Of You, 1986; Control, Let's Wait Awhile, The Pleasure Principle, 1987; Miss You So Much, 1989; Rhythm Nation, Escapade, Alright, Come Back To Me, Black Cat, 1990; Love Will Never Do (Without You), 1991; The Best Things In Life Are Free, duet with Luther

Vandross, from film Mo' Money, 1992; That's The Way Love Goes, If, Again, 1993; Whoops Now, Scream, Runaway, 1995; Twenty Foreplay, When I Think of You, 1996; Got Til It's Gone, Together Again, 1997; Go Deep, Every Time, I Get Lonely, 1998; Girlfriend, What's It Gonna Be, 1999; Doesn't Really Matter, 2000; All For You, Someone To Call My Lover, Got Til It's Gone, Son of a Gun, 2001; Just a Little While, All Nite Don't Stop, 2004; So Excited, 2006. Films: Poetic Justice, 1992; Nutty Professor II: The Klumps, 2000; Why Did I Get Married?, 2007. Numerous honours include: Billboard Awards, 1986-; American Music Awards, 1987-; Soul Train Awards, 1987-; MTV Video Music Awards, 1987-; Grammy, Best Music Video, Rhythm Nation 1814, 1990; Star on Hollywood Walk Of Fame, 1990; Janet Jackson Week, Los Angeles, 1990; Humanitarian Of The Year Award, Starlight Foundation of Southern California, 1990; Chairman's Award, NAACP Image Awards, 1992; First artist to have seven US Top 5 hits from one album, 1990-91; International Dance Award, Achievement In Dance, 1995. Address: RDWM Services (UK) Ltd, 37 Limerston Street, London, SW10 0BQ, England. Website: www.janet-jackson.com

JACKSON Jesse Louis, b. 8 October 1941, Greenville, South Carolina, USA. Clergyman; Civic Leader. m. Jacqueline Lavinia Brown, 1962, 3 sons, 2 daughters. Education: University of Illinois; Illinois Agricultural and Technical College; Chicago Theological Seminary. Appointments: Ordained to Ministry Baptist Church, 1968; Active, Black Coalition for United Community Action, 1969; Co-Founder, Operation Breadbasket, Southern Christian Leadership Conference; Coordinating Council, Community Organsations, Chicago, 1966, National Director, 1966-77; Founder, Executive Director, Operation PUSH (People United to Save Humanity), Chicago, 1971-; TV Host, Voices of America, 1990-. Honours include: President's Award, National Medical Association, 1969; Humanitarian Father of the Year Award, National Father's Day Committee, 1971; Medal of Freedom. Address: c/o Rainbow PUSH Coalition, 930 East 50th Street, Chicago, IL 60615, USA.

JACKSON Michael David (Gen Sir Mike), b. 21 March 1944, Sheffield, England. Soldier. m. Sarah Coombe, 1985, 2 sons, 1 daughter. Education: BSoc Sc, Birmingham University, 1967. Appointments: Chief of Staff Berlin Infantry Brigade, 1977-78; Co-Commander, 2nd Battalion, The Parachute Regiment, 1979-80; Directing Staff, Staff College, 1981-83; Commanding Officer, 1st Battalion, The Parachute Regiment, 1984-86; Directing Staff, Joint Services Defence College, 1987-88; Service Fellow, Wolfson College Cambridge 89; Commander, 39 Infantry Brigade, 1990-91; Director Personal Services, 1992-93; Commander 3 (UK) Division, 1994-96; Commander Multinational Division South West, Bosnia, 1996; Director, Development and Doctrine, MOD, 1996-97; Commander, Allied Command Europe Rapid Reaction Corps, 1997-1999; Commander, Kosovo Force, 1999; Commander in Chief, UK Land Force, 2000-03; Chief of the General Staff, 2003-. Honours: MBE, 1979; Freeman, City of London, 1988; CBE, 1992; CB, 1996; KCB, 1998; DS0, 1999; Kt Grand Cross, Order of the Bath, 2005. Membership: RUSI. Address: Office of the Chief of the General Staff, Ministry of Defence, Main Building, Whitehall, London, SW1A 2HB, England. E-mail: webmaster@dgics.mod.uk Website: www.mod.uki

JACKSON Peter, b. 31 October 1961, Pukerua Bay, North Island, New Zealand. Film Director. m. Frances Walsh, 1 son, 1 daughter. Films: Bad Taste, 1987; Meet the Feebles, 1989; Valley of the Stereos, 1992; Ship to Shore, 1993; Heavenly Creatures, 1994; Jack Brown Genius, 1994; Forgotten Silver, 1995; The Frighteners, 1996; The Lord of the Rings: The Fellowship of the Ring, 2001; The Lord of the Rings: The Two Towers, 2002; The Long and Short of It, 2003; The Lord of the Rings: The Return of the King, 2003; The Long and Short of it, 2003; King Kong, 2005; District 9, The Lovely Bones, 2009. Honours: Honorary Graduation, Massey University, 2001; BAFTA Award for Best Director, 2001; New Zealand Order of Merit, 2002; Voted Man of the Year 2002, Australian Empire Magazine, 2003; Golden Globe Award, Best Director, 2004; Critics' Choice Award, Best Director, 2004; Academy Award, Best Director, Best Picture, 2004; Oscar, Best Director, 2004. Address: c/o ICM, 8942 Wilshire Boulevard, Beverly Hills, CA 90211, USA.

JACKSON Samuel L, b. 21 December 1948, Washington, USA. Actor. m. LaTanya Richardson, 1 daughter. Education: Morehouse College. Appointments: Co-Founder, Member, Just Us Theatre Company, Atlanta. Creative Works: Stage appearances: Home; A Soldier's Story; Sally/Prince; Colored People's Time; Mother Courage; Spell No 7; The Mighty Gents; The Piano Lesson; Two Trains Running; Fences; TV appearances: Movin' On, 1972; Ghostwriter, 1992; The Trial of the Moke, 1978; Uncle Tom's Cabin, 1987; Common Ground, 1990; Dead and Alive: The Race for Gus Farace, 1991; Simple Justice, 1993; Assault at West Point, Against the Wall, 1994; Films include: Together for Days, 1972; Ragtime, 1981; Eddie Murphy Raw, 1987; Coming to America, School Daze, 1988; Do The Right Thing, Sea of Love, 1989; A Shock to the System, Def by Temptation, Betsy's Wedding, Mo' Better Blues, The Exorcist III, GoodFellas, Return of the Superfly, 1990; Jungle Fever, Strictly Business, 1991; Jumpin' at the Boneyard, Patriot Games, Johnny Suede, 1992; Jurassic Park, True Romance, 1993; Hail Caesar, Fresh, The New Age, Pulp Fiction, 1994; Losing Isaiah, Kiss of Death, Die Hard With a Vengeance, 1995; The Great White Hype, A Time to Kill, 1996; The Long Kiss Goodnight; Jackie Brown; Trees Lounge; Hard Eight; Out of Sight; The Negotiator; Deep Blue Sea; Sphere; Eve's Bayou; Star Wars Episode I: The Phantom Menace, Rules of Engagement, 1999; Shaft, Unbreakable, 2000; The Caveman's Valentine, The 51st State, 2001; Changing Lanes, Star Wars Episode II: Attack of the Clones, The House on Turk Street, XXX, 2002; Basic, S.W.A.T, 2003; Country of My Skull, Twisted, Kill Bill: Vol 2, The Incredibles (voice), 2004; Coach Carter, Mr Incredible and Pals, xXx: State of the Union, Star Wars: Episode III-Revenge of the Sith, The Man, 2005; Farce of the Penquins, Freedomland, Snakes on a Plane, Home of the Brave, 2006; Resurrecting the Champ, 1408, Cleaner, 2007; Jumper, Iron Man, Soul Men, 2008; Mother and Child, Astro Boy (voice), 2009; Unthinkable, Iron Man 2, 2010. Honours include: Best Actor Award, Cannes International Film Festival; New York Film Critics Award. Address: c/o ICM, 8942 Wilshire Boulevard, Beverly Hills, CA 90211, USA.

JACKSON Siti Mariah Mansor, b. 29 May 1953, Kedah, Malaysia. Artist. m. (1) Billy Morrow Jackson, deceased, (2) Brian John Sullivan, 2008. Education: Diploma in Art and Design (Textile Design) and Art Teacher's Diploma, Mara Institute of Technology, Malaysia, 1978-79; MA, Art Education, University of Illinois, 1988-2009. Appointments: Art Teacher, Lecturer, Malaysian Schools and Teachers Colleges, 1979-85; Ceramic Sculptor, 1988-; Vice President, Jackson Studios, Illinois; Invitational and Juried Local and National Group Art Exhibitions and Show Cases. Publication: Book, On This Island: An Artistic View of Martha's Vineyard, 2005; Founder, Champaign/Urbana International Artists Group, Champaign, Illinois, 2008-; International Art Juror, Penang State Museum and Art Gallery, Penang, 2010.

Publications: Full-colour art catalogue, Galeri Art Point, Penang, 2007; Full-colour art catalogue, International Women Artists, Beijing, China, 2008. Honours: First Award, Fabric Design on Paper for Stewardess Uniform, Malaysian Airline System, 1978; Federal Teaching Art Scholarship, Ministry of Education, Malaysia, 1985; Elected Member, Kappa Delta Pi, 1987; Award of Excellence, Manhattan Arts International Cover Art Competition, New York, 1995; 2nd Place, Watercolour, 10th International Juried Exhibition, Laredo Center for the Arts, 2002; Veenon B Christie Memorial Award of Recognition, 2009; 65th Annual Wabash Valley Juried Show, Swope Art Museum, Terre Haute, Indiana; Listed in international biographical dictionaries. Memberships: Smithsonian Institution, Washington, DC; National Museum of Women in the Arts, Washington, DC; International Women Artists Council, USA-Malaysia; Krannert Art Museum, University of Illinois, Champaign; Art Exhibition Advisory Committee, Springer Cultural Center, Champaign; Kedah Artist's Art Association, Malaysia; Penang State Museum & Art Gallery, Malaysia; Asian-American Culture Center, University of Illinois, USA. Address: 706 West White Street, Champaign, IL 61820, USA. E-mail: mrartist2@gmail.com Web site: http://www.soltec.net/jacksonstudios/

JACKSON William David, b. 15 July 1947, Liverpool, England. Freelance Journalist; Translator; Poet. m. Christine Range, 1972, 1 son, 1 daughter. Education: BA, Honours, English Language and Literature, St Catherine's College, Oxford, 1968. Publications: Then and Now, 2002; From Now to Then, 2005; Boccaccio in Florence, 2009. Contributions to: Acumen; Agenda; The Amsterdam Review; Babel; Blithe Spirit; The Dark Horse; Foolscap; Haiku Quarterly; The Interpreter's House; Iron; Leviathan Quarterly; The London Magazine; Metre; Modern Poetry in Translation; Oasis; Orbis; Outposts; Oxford Poetry; Pennine Platform; Poetry Nottingham; Poetry Review; Poetry Wales; The Rialto; The Shop; Stand; Staple. Address: Clemensstrasse 66, 80796 Munich, Germany.

JACOBI Derek George, Sir, b. 22 October 1938, London, England. Actor. Education: St Johns College, Cambridge. Appointments: Birmingham Repertory Theatre, 1960-63; National Theatre, 1963-71; Prospect Theatre Company, 1972, 1974, 1976-78; Artistic Association, 1976-; Old Vic Company, 1978-79; Joined Royal Shakespeare Company, 1982; Vice President, National Youth Theatre, 1982-; Artistic Director, Chichester Festival, 1995-. Creative Works: TV appearances include: She Stoops to Conquer; Man of Straw; The Pallisers; I Claudius; Philby; Burgess and Maclean; Tales of the Unexpected; A Stranger in Town; Mr Pye; Brother Cadfael, 1994-; Inquisition, 2002; Mr Ambassador, 2003; The Long Firm, 2004; Pinochet in Suburbia, 2007; Films: Odessa File; Day of the Jackal; The Medusa Touch; Othello; Three Sisters; Interlude; The Human Factor; Charlotte, The Man Who Went up in Smoke, The Hunchback of Notre Dame, 1981; Inside the Third Reich, 1982; Little Dorrit, 1986; The Tenth Man, 1988; Henry V, The Fool, 1990; Dead Again, Hamlet, 1996; Love is the Devil, 1997; Gladiator, 2000; Gosford Park, The Revengers Tragedy, Night's Noontime, Two Men Went to War, 2002; Cloud Cuckoo Land, Strings, 2004; Bye Bye Blackbird, Project Huxley, Nanny McPhee, 2005; Underworld: Evolution, 2006; Guantanamero, The Riddle, Anastezsi, 2007; Morris: A Life with Bells On, Adam Resurrected, 2008. Plays: The Lunatic; Lover and the Poet, The Suicide, 1980; Much Ado About Nothing; Peer Gynt; The Tempest, 1982; Cyrano de Bergerac, 1983; Breaking the Code, 1986; Richard II, 1988; Richard III, 1989; Kean, 1990; Becket, 1991; Mad, Bad and Dangerous to Know; Ambassadors, 1992; Macbeth, 1993; Hadrian VII, Playing the Wife, 1995; Uncle Vanya, 1996; God Only Knows, 2000; Director: Hamlet, 1988, 2000. Honours: Honorary Fellow, St Johns College, Cambridge; Variety Club Award, 1976; British Academy Award, 1976; Press Guild Award, 1976; Royal TV Society Award, 1976; CBE, 1985; KBE, 1994; Evening Standard Award Best Actor, 1998. Address: Chichester Festival Theatre, Oaklands Park, Chichester, West Sussex PO19 4AP, England.

JACOBS David Lewis, b. 19 May 1926, London, England. Broadcaster. m. (1) Patricia Bradlaw, 1949, divorced 1972, 1 son deceased, 3 daughters, (2) Caroline Munro, 1975, deceased 1975, (3) Lindsay Stuart Hutcheson, 1979, 1 stepson. Education: Belmont College, London. Career: Royal Navy; Impressionist, Navy Mixture, 1944; Chief Announcer, Radio SEAC, Ceylon; BBC announcer and newsreader; Freelance broadcaster; Radio includes: Housewives Choice; BBC Jazz Club; Pick Of The Pops; Saturday Show Band Show; Any Questions?; Any Answers?; Melodies For You; Founder member, Capital Radio; Own programme, BBC Radio 2, 6 years; Television includes: Juke Box Jury; Top Of The Pops; David Jacobs' Words And Music; Sunday Night With David Jacobs; Where Are They Now?; What's My Line?; Eurovision Song Contest; A Song For Europe; Miss World; Little Women; Come Dancing; Presents musical concerts and one-man show, An Evening with David Jacobs. Publications: Jacobs Ladder; Caroline; Any Questions? (with Michael Bowen). Honours: 6 Royal Command Performances; Top British DJ, BBC and Radio Luxembourg, 6 years; TV Personality of Year, Variety Club of Great Britain, 1960; BBC Radio Personality of Year, 1975; Sony Gold Award, 1984; Sony Hall of Fame; Richard Martin Award (animal welfare); Honorary Doctorate, Kingston University, 1994; CBE, 1996; Deputy Lieutenant of and for Greater London, 1983; Representative Deputy Lieutenant for the Royal Borough of Kingston-upon-Thames; Honorary Freeman of the Royal Borough of Kingston-upon-Thames, 1997; Chairman, Thames Radio. Memberships include: Vice-President, Society of Stars; Vice-President, Royal Star & Garter Home, Richmond; Vice-President, Kingston Arts Festival; Director, Chairman, Kingston Theatre Trust. Current Management: Billy Marsh Associates. Address: 174 North Gower Street, London, NW1 2NB, England.

JACOBS Peter, b. 21 March 1934, Pretoria, South Africa. m. Margaret Ann (Diane) Botbyl, 1961, 2 sons. Education: Matriculated, Prince Edward School, 1948; MB, BCh, 1959, MD, 1966, PhD, 1974, University of Witwatersrand; DSc, Medical Sciences, Stellenbosch University, 2010. Appointments: Chief Medical Technologist, Pasteur Institute and Public Health Laboratory, Salisbury; Chief Technologist, Dr George V Blaine Laboratory, Central Africa, 1951-54; Director, Division of Haematology, Department of Laboratory Medicine, University Hospital and King County Medical Centre, Seattle, USA; Therapeutic Trials Physician, Department of Medicine, University of the Witwatersrand and Johannesburg General Hospital; Foundation Professor of Haematology, University Cape Town, Chief Specialist, Groote Schuur Hospital, 1971; Director, University Cape Town Leukaemia Centre; Emeritus Professor of Haematology, University of Cape Town, 1995; Honorary Consultant Physician, Groote Schuur Hospital Teaching Group, 1995; Honorary Professor of Haematology, Stellenbosch University –Tygerberg Academic Hospital, 1996; Professor of Internal Medicine, College of Medicine – University of Nebraska Medical Centre; Foundation Professor and Head, Division of Clinical Haematology, Department of Internal Medicine, University of Stellenbosch and Tygerberg Academic Hospital, 2003; Extraordinary Professor, Haematological Pathology,

Stellenbosch University, 2010. Publications: Author of books, chapters and numerous professional articles in scientific journals. Honours include: Eli Lilly International Fellowship; Andries Blignault Memorial Medal; Ernest Oppenheimer Memorial Scholarship; Chalarick Solomon Memorial Scholarship; David Lurie Memorial Prize; Medical Graduate Prize in Medicine; University Washington Research Fellowship; S L Sive Memorial Travelling Fellowship; Ernest Oppenheimer Memorial Travelling Fellowship; Centenary Medal, Die Suid-Afrikaanse Akademie vir Wetenskap en Kuns, 2009; Fellowships: The Royal Society of Medicine; The Royal College of Physicians of Edinburgh; The Royal College of Pathologists in the UK; The American College of Physicians; American Society of Internal Medicine The Royal Society of South Africa; The Colleges of Medicine of South Africa. Memberships: Association of Cancer Research; The American Society of Clinical Haematology; The College of American Pathologists; Consultancies: Drug Monitoring for World Health Organization – Uppsala. Address: Haematology Research Group, Pathcare-Library Square, 20 Wilderness Road, Claremont, 7708, Cape Town, South Africa.

JACOBSON Dan, b. 7 March 1929, Johannesburg, South Africa. Professor Emeritus; Writer. m. Margaret Pye, 3 sons, 1 daughter. Education: BA, University of the Witwatersrand; Honorary Ph.D., University of Witwatersrand. Appointments: Visiting Fellow, Stanford University, California, 1956-57; Professor, Syracuse University, New York, 1965-66; Fellow, 1981, Australian National University; Lecturer, 1975-80, Reader, 1980-87, Professor, 1988-94, Professor Emeritus, 1994-, University College, London. Publications: The Trap, 1955; A Dance in the Sun, 1956; The Price of Diamonds, 1957; The Evidence of Love, 1960; The Beginners, 1965; The Rape of Tamar, 1970; The Confessions of Josef Baisz, 1979; The Story of the Stories, 1982; Time and Time Again, 1985; Adult Pleasures, 1988; Hidden in the Heart, 1991; The God Fearer, 1992; The Electronic Elephant, 1994; Heshel's Kingdom, 1998; A Mouthful of Glass, translation, 2000; Ian Hamilton in Conversation with Dan Jacobson, interview, 2002; All for Love, 2005. Contributions to: Periodicals and newspapers. Honours: John Llewelyn Rhys Memorial Award, 1958; W Somerset Maugham Award, 1964; H H Wingate Award, 1979; J R Ackerley Award, 1986; Honorary DLitt, University of the Witwatersrand, 1987; Mary Elinore Smith Prize, 1992; Honorary Fellow, University College, London, 2005. Address: c/o A M Heath & Co Ltd, 79 St Martins Lane, London WC2, England.

JACOBSON Howard, b. 25 August 1942, Manchester, England. Novelist. m. (1) Rosalin Sadler, 1978, divorced 2004, 1 son, (2) Jenny De Yong, 2005. Education: BA, Downing College, Cambridge. Appointments: Lecturer, University of Sydney, 1965-68; Supervisor, Selwyn College, Cambridge, 1969-72; Senior Lecturer, Wolverhampton Polytechnic, 1974-80; Television Critic, The Sunday Correspondent, 1989-90; Into the Land of Oz, (Channel 4), 1991; Writer/Presenter, Yo, Mrs Askew! (BBC2), 1991, Roots Schmoots (Channel 4 TV), 1993, Sorry, Judas (Channel 4 TV), 1993, Seriously Funny: An Argument for Comedy (Channel 4 TV), 1997; Columnist, The Independent, 1998-; Howard Jacobson Takes on the Turner (Channel 4 TV), 2000; Why The Novel Matters: A South Bank Show Special (ITV), 2002; Jesus the Jew (Channel 4 TV), 2009; Creation (Channel 4 TV), 2010; Flesh (Channel 4 TV), 2010. Publications: Shakespeare's Magnanimity: Four Tragic Heroes, Their Friends and Families, 1978; Coming From Behind, 1983; Peeping Tom, 1984; Redback, 1986; In the Land of Oz, 1987; The Very Model of a Man, 1992; Roots Schmoots, 1993; Seeing With the Eye: The Peter Fuller Memorial Lecture, 1993; Seriously Funny, 1997; No More Mister Nice Guy, 1998; The Mighty Walzer, 1999; Who's Sorry Now?, 2002; The Making of Henry, 2004; Kalooki Nights, 2006; The Act of Love, 2008; The Finkler Question, 2010. Honours: Winner Jewish Quarterly and Wingate Prize, 2000; Winner of the first Bollinger Everyman Wodehouse Prize, 2000; Winner, Man Booker Prize for Fiction, 2010; Winner, Sandford St Martin Trust Award, 2010. Address: Curtis Brown, Haymarket House, 28-29 Haymarket, London SW1Y 4SP, England.

JACOBSON Jerry I, b. 25 January 1946, New York, USA. Medical Researcher, Biophysicist; Theoretical Physicist. 1 son; 4 daughters. Education: BA, City University of New York, 1966; DMD, DDS, Temple University, Philadelphia, USA, 1970; PhD, Bundel Khand University, India, 2002. Appointments: Captain, Emergency Oral Surgeon; MEDDAC, 1970-72; Fort Rucker, Alabama/Lyster Army Hospital; President, Institute of Theoretical Physics and Advanced Studies for Biophysical Research; Chairman, President, The Perspectivism Foundation, Florida, USA; Chairman of the Board, President, CEO, Jacobson Resonance Enterprises Inc, Public Biotechnology Corporation; Chief Magnetic Therapist, Magnetic Resonance Therapy Inc, Nassau, Bahamas; Chief Science Officer, Applied Magnetics LLC, Denver, Colorado and Pico Tesla Magnetic Therapies LLC; Music Producer and Songwriter, Musicantu Productions LLC, Jupiter, Florida; Principal Investigator, Double Blind, Placebo Controlled, Randomized Clinical Studies in Fibromyalgia, Parkinsons, Alzheimers and Osteoarthritis. Publications: 17 US patents; 31 foreign patents; 87 scientific articles; 45 symposia presentations; 5 books; 4 book chapters; 80 full length science articles; 10 full length philosophy articles; 40 poems; 100 songs and clarinet concertos; 800 oil paintings; 2,000 drawings, inks, pastels and watercolours; 10 one-man art exhibitions; Composer and musician (clarinet and saxophone); Clinical Studies in Parkinson's Disease, Alzheimer's, Osteoarthritis, Fibromyalgia, Neuropathy, and Diabetes Mellitus Type II; Co-investigator, Director of Biophysics (20 basic science university-based studies utilising Jacobson Resonator); 20 books authored and held as Trade Secrets. Honours: International Order of Merit, IBC; Albert Einstein Genius Award; Champion of Freedom Award; Invited Lecturer, Karolinska Institute; Invited Lecturer, Weill Medical College of Cornell University; Invited Lecturer, City Conference Center, Stockholm; Invited Lecturer, Indian Medical Association, Calcutta; Special Achievement in Medical Research, Bundel Khand University; Certificate of Appreciation, President Richard Nixon, Meritorious Service in the Armed Forces of the USA during Vietnam War, 1973; Invited by Her Serene Highness Antoinette de Monaco to present a tutorial, Monaco, Les Entretiens Internationaux de Monaco, 2002; Chief Science Officer, Applied Magnetics LLC, Pico-Tesk Magnetic Therapies LLC, Denver, Colorado, Clearwater, Florida, Detroit, Michigan; Outstanding Achievement in Poetry, 2007; Listed in international biographical dictionaries. Memberships: Cardiology in Review; American Physical Society Medical Hypotheses; American Association for Advancement of Sciences; Bioelectromagnetics Society; Bundel Khand University; Advisory Board, Center for Frontier Sciences, Temple University, Philadelphia, USA; New York Academy of Sciences, USA; International Society for Biologically Closed Circuits and Electrochemical Treatment of Cancer; Editorial Consultant, Journal of Alternative Therapies in Health and Medicine; Editorial Consultant, Journal of the Italian Medical Association. Address: Institute of Theoretical

Physics & Advanced Studies for Biophysical Research, 2006 Mainsail Circle, Jupiter, FL 33477-1418, USA. E-mail: drjijacobson@yahoo.com

JAFFE Edward E, b. 22 September 1928, Vilna, Poland. Chemist. m. Ann Swirski, 1 son, 2 daughters. Education: BS, City College, City of New York, 1952; MS, 1954, PhD, 1957, New York University. Appointments: Research Chemist, 1957-63, Senior Research Chemist, 1963-65, Research Associate, 1965-73, Research Supervisor, 1973-75, Technical Superintendent, 1975-78, Research Manager, 1978-80, Research Fellow, 1980-84, DuPont Company; Distinguished Research Fellow, 1984-87, Director of Research, 1987-88, Vice President of R&D, 1988-95, CIBA-GEIGY Corporation; Retired, 1995-; Exclusive Consultant to CIBA Speciality Chemical Corp, 1995-2003; Independent consultant, 2003-. Publications: 67 US patents; Over 200 international patents; Many articles in professional journals and chapters in scientific books. Honours: Founders Day Award, New York University; Armin J Bruning Award, Outstanding Contribution to the Science of Colour; Recipient of the American Chemical Society Delaware Section Award, for Conspicuous Scientific Achievement in the Area of Chemistry, 2000. Memberships: American Chemical Society; Delaware Chemical Society Chapter; Organic Section of ACS; Sigma Xi Society. Address: 6 Penny Lane Court, Wilmington, Delaware 19803, USA. E-mail: eejaffe@comcast.net

JAGANNATH Mythili, b. 19 March 1958, Bangalore, India. Associate Professor. m. 2 sons. Education: BSc, Mount Carmel College, 1979; MSc, Central College, Bangalore University, 1981; PhD, St John's Medical College, Bangalore, 1990. Appointments: Junior Research Fellow, Research Assistant, Research Officer for Department of Science & Technology, Government of India and Indian Council of Medical Research, St John's Medical College, 10 years; Lecturer, Senior Lecturer, Associate Professor of Zoology, Mount Carmel College, 1993-. Honours: Young Scientist's Award, 1988; One of the Carmelites on Roll of Honour, Golden Jubilee Celebrations, 1948-98. Memberships: Indian Society of Human Genetics; Biotechnology Society of India; Bangalore University College Teachers Association. Address: Mount Carmel College, Palace Road, Vasanthnagar, Bangalore 560052, Karnataka, India.

JAGGER Bianca, b. 2 May 1945, Nicaragua. Actress; Film Maker; Human Rights Advocate. m. Mick Jagger, 1971, divorced, 1 daughter. Education: Political Science, Institute of Science Politics, Paris, France; Film School, New York University. Appointments: Lecturer, Colleges and Universities. Civic Activities: Executive Director, Leadership Council, Amnesty International, USA; Advisory Committee of Human Rights, Watch America; Coalition, International Justice; Board Director, People for The American Way; Special Advisor, Indigenous Development International, University of Cambridge, England. Publications: Several articles in professional journals, newspapers and magazines. Honours include: United Nations Earth Day International Award, 1994; Green Globe Award, Rainforest Alliance, 1997; Right Livelihood Award, 2004. Commissions and Creative Works: Produced and directed a documentary "Nicaragua in Transition"; Appeared in many feature films and television productions. Address: 530 Park Avenue, 18D New York, NY 10021, USA.

JAGGER Sir Michael (Mick) Philip, b. 26 July 1943, Dartford, Kent, England. Singer; Songwriter. m. (1) Bianca Pérez Morena de Macias, 1971, divorced, 1979, 1 daughter, (2) Jerry Hall, 2 sons, 2 daughters; 1 daughter by Marsha Hunt; 1 son Luciana Gimenez. Education: London School of Economics. Career: Member, Rolling Stones, 1962-; Numerous tours, concerts include: National Jazz & Blues Festival, Richmond, 1963; Debut UK tour, 1963; Debut US tour, 1964; Free concert, Hyde Park, 1969; Free concert, Altamont Speedway, 1969; Knebworth Festival, 1976; Live Aid, Philadelphia, 1985; Solo tour including Japan, 1988; Steel Wheels North American tour, 1989; National Music Day Celebration Of The Blues, with Gary Moore, 1992; Voodoo Lounge World Tour, 1994-95; Bridges to Babylon Tour, 1997-98; Films include: Ned Kelly, 1970; Performance, 1970; Freejack, 1992; Bent, 1996. Compositions: Co-writer for the Rolling Stones, with Keith Richards (under the pseudonym The Glimmer Twins). Recordings: Albums include: The Rolling Stones, 1964; The Rolling Stones No 2, 1965; Out Of Our Heads, 1965; Aftermath, 1966; Between The Buttons, 1967; Their Satanic Majesties Request, 1967; Beggar's Banquet, 1968; Let It Bleed, 1969; Get Yer Ya-Ya's Out, 1969; Sticky Fingers, 1971; Exile On Main Street, 1972; Goat's Head Soup, 1973; It's Only Rock And Roll, 1974; Black And Blue, 1976; Some Girls, 1978; Emotional Rescue, 1980; Still Life, 1982; Steel Wheels, 1989; Flashpoint, 1991; Stripped, 1995; Bridges to Babylon, 1997; Forty Licks, 2002; Live Licks, 2004; The Very Best of Mick Jagger, 2007. Solo albums: She's The Boss, 1985; Primitive Cool, 1987; Wandering Spirit, 1993; Goddess in the Doorway, 2001; Singles include: It's All Over Now; Little Red Rooster; (I Can't Get No) Satisfaction; Get Off Of My Cloud; Jumping Jack Flash; Let's Spend The Night Together; Brown Sugar; 19th Nervous Breakdown; Harlem Shuffle; Ruby Tuesday; Paint It Black; It's Only Rock'n'Roll; Start Me Up; Undercover Of The Night; Dancing In The Street (with David Bowie); Ruthless People, 1986; Let's Work, 1987; Sweet Thing, 1993; Don't Tear Me Up, 1993; God Gave Me Everything, 2001; Visions of Paradise, 2002; Old Habits Die Hard (with Dave Stewart), 2004. Honours: with Rolling Stones include: Grammy Lifetime Achievement Award, 1986; Inducted into Rock And Roll Hall Of Fame, 1989; Q Award, Best Live Act, 1990; Ivor Novello Award, Outstanding Contribution To British Music, 1991; Golden Globe Award for Best Original Song, 2005. Address: c/o Rupert Loewenstein, 2 King Street, London SW1Y 6QL, England.

JAGGI Satya Dev, b. 15 January 1937, Punjab, Pindigheb, India. Retired University Senior Lecturer (and Professor Designate); Poet; Writer. m. Santosh, 1974. Education: BA, Honours, English, 1958; MA, Philosophy, 1960; MA, English, 1963, PhD, English, 1977. Appointments: Lecturer, 1973-81, Reader, 1981-83, Hans Raj College, Delhi University; Senior Lecturer, 1981-97, Head, Department of English, Dean, Faculty of Arts, 1994-96, University of Maiduguri, Nigeria. Publications: Coleridge's and Yeats' Theory of Poetry, 1966; No More Words, 1966; Homewards and Other Poems, 1966; End of Hunger, 1968; The Point of Light, 1968; The Earthrise, 1969; The Moon Voyagers, 1970; One Looks Earthward Again, 1970; Our Awkward Earth, 1970; Readiness is All, 1970; Obscure Goodbyes, 1970; Lead No One by the Nose (play), 1983; Our Concern with Poetry, 1983; The Poet's Plenty, 1983; Far in Maiduguri, 1983; The Poet's Proposition, 1984; I A Richards on Poetic Truth, 1985; The Language of Poetry, 1990. Honour: 3rd Prize, BBC Poetry Competition, 1990. Address: 8258, B-XI, Vasant Kunj, New Delhi 110070, India.

JAGLAND Thorbjørn, b. 5 November 1950, Drammen, Norway. Secretary General of the Council of Europe. m. Hanne Grotjord, 2 sons. Education: Degree, Economics,

University of Oslo, 1975. Appointments: Member of Buskerud County Council, 1975-83; Many international political positions, 1987-, and European and transatlantic parliamentary positions, 1993-; Party Secretary, 1987-92, Chairman, 1992-2002, and various other positions within the Norwegian Labour Party; Member of Parliament, 1993-2009; Member, 1993-96, 1997-2000, Chairman, 2000, 2001-05, Standing Committee on Foreign Affairs and the Enlarged Foreign Affairs Committee; Member, 1994-96, 1997-2000, Chairman, 2000-05, EEA Consultative Committee; Prime Minister, Norway, 1996-97; Minister of Foreign Affairs, Norwegian Government, 2000-01; President, Norwegian Parliament, 2005-09; Member, Standing Committee on Defence and the Enlarged Foreign Affairs Committee, 2005-09. Publications: Numerous books and articles in professional journals, including Min Europeiske Drøm (My European Dream), 1990. Address: Council of Europe, 67075 Strasbourg Cedex, France. Website: www.coe.int

JAHR Ernst Håkon, b. 4 March 1948, Oslo, Norway. Professor. m. Inger Martinsen, 2 sons, 1 daughter. Education: Cand. Mag., 1973, Cand. Philol, Scandinavian Languages, 1976, University of Oslo; Dr Philos., University of Tromsø, 1984. Appointments: Research Assistant, University of Oslo, 1972-76; Assistant Professor, 1976-81, Associate Professor, 1981-86, Professor, 1986-98, University of Tromsø; Professor, 1999-, Rector, President, 2000-07, Agder University; Consultant Professor, Eötvös Loránd University, Budapest, 1994-; Visiting Scholar, University of Reading, UK, 1986; Visiting Professor, University of Hamburg, 1992-1993; Fulbright Researcher, University of California, Santa Barbara, California, 1997-98. Publications: About 40 books (authored and edited) within linguistics; About 170 articles; Fields of research: Language history, sociolinguistics, language contact, language planning, history of linguistics. Honours: The Norwegian Research Council's Prize for outstanding research in the humanities, 1990; Dr Honoris Causa, Linguistics, Adam Mickiewicz University, Poznań, Poland, 1995; Dr Phi Honoris Causa, Uppsala, Sweden, 2009. Memberships: President, Agder Academy of Sciences and Letters, 2002-; Fellow, Norwegian Academy of Science and Letters, 1994-; Fellow, Royal Norwegian Society of Sciences and Letters, 1994-; Fellow, Royal Gustav Adolf's Academy (Uppsala), 2007; Member, Academia Europaea, 2008; Fellow, Royal Society of Art and Sciences in Gothenburg, 2010; Fellow, Royal Skyttean Society (UMed), 2010-; The Swedish Academy's Nordic Prize, 2011. Address: Agder University, Box 422, N-4604 Kristiansand, Norway. E-mail: ernsthakon.jahr@uia.no

JAIN Parma Nand, b. 1 March 1943, India. Doctor; Professor. m. Sudha, 3 sons, 1 daughter. Education: BSc, 1962; MBBS, 1967; DTCD, 1968; MS, 1970. Appointments: House/Resident Doctor, 1967; Demonstrator, 1968-71; Lecturer, Assistant Professor, 1971-73; Associate Professor, 1973-86; Professor, 1986-. Publications: 35 papers in medical journals. Honours: Listed in international biographical dictionaries; Vijai Shree Award, 2005; Best Citizens of India, 2006. Memberships: Lions Club; Anatomical Society of India; Indian Medical Association; Indian Academy of Neurosciences. Address: Anand Hospital, Opposite Medical College, Jhansi (UP), 284128, India.

JAISWAL Shree Prakash, b. 14 November 1970, Bhopal, India. Consultant; Immunologist. 1 son. Education: HSC, 1986; BSc, Biology, 1989; MSc, Biochemistry, 1991; PhD, 1997; MBA, 2000; Professional Diploma in Clinical Research, 2010. Appointments: Lecturer, 1991-2000; Scientific Officer, 1997; Senior Scientific Officer, 1998-2000; Junior Consultant, 2000-10; Assistant Professor, 2000-10; Associate Professor, 2010-; Consultant, Immunology, 2010-. Publications: 22 articles in national and international journals on seroepidemiology of Hepatitis viruses, HIV, infection control, etc. Honours: Merit in MSc; Qualified NET & GATE; Best Paper Presentation Award for Hospital Infection Society of India Conferences, three consecutive years. Memberships: INASL; IAMM; IAPM; AIMLTA; ISBTJ; BTSI; Indian Immunological Society. Address: 46 Sector D, Slice 2, Scheme No 78, Vijaynagar, Indore (MP) 452010, India.

JAKAB Tibor, b. 5 September 1961, Tirgu-Mures, Romania. Photo Artist; Photo Journalist; Occupational Safety Inspector. Life partner, Edit Berecki. Education: Mechanical Engineer diploma, Technical University of Cluj Napoca, Romania, 1986; Graduate, New York Institute of Photography, 1995; Occupational Safety Inspector diploma, Ministry of Education and Work, Romania, 2007. Appointments: Freelance Photo Journalist, 1989-; Press Photographer: Romaniai Magyar Szo, 1989-91; Gazeta de Mures, 1991-94; Tabu Magazin, 1993-99; Kronika, 1999-2000; Casa de Vacanta, 2000-08; Casa Lux, 1998-2008; Saptamana turistica, 2006-; La Cucina, 2008-; Caminul, 2009-; Casa Mea, 2009-; National and international photo art exhibitions; Solo and group exhibitions around the world. Publications: Contributed over 1,500 illustrated articles to listed newspapers and magazines, 1989-; More than 100,000 photos published. Honours: AFIAP, 1992; EFIAP, 1995; Hon APSG, 1995; EFIAP (Bronze), 2000; KKL Friendship Prize, 2004; EFIAP (Silver), 2005; Associateship for Service to Photography, ASIIPC, 2005; Associateship, Photographic Society of America, 2006; Hon FPSG, 2008; Works found in museums, cultural centres and private collections around the world; Listed in international biographical dictionaries. Memberships: Romanian Photoartists Society; Photographic Society of America; Creative Monochrome, England; Kodak Professional Network; Fine Arts Union of Romania; IIWF, Germany; International Organization of Journalists; FIJET. Address: Str Slatina nr 3, 540431 Tirgu Mures, Romania. E-mail: jakabtibor@hotmail.com

JALAN Bimal, b. 3 July 1941, Calcutta, India. Economist. m. Divya, 1 son, 1 daughter. Education: MA, University of Cambridge, 1962; M Phil, University of Oxford, 1964; PhD, University of Bombay, 1974. Appointments: Governor, Reserve Bank of India; Finance Secretary, Chief Economic Adviser, Government of India; Executive Director, World Bank; Executive Director, IMF. Publications: Books: India's Economic Crisis: The Way Ahead, 1991; India's Economic Policy, 1996; The Future of India: Politics, Economics and Governance, 2005; India's Politics: A view from the Backbench, 2007. Honours: Presidential Nominee to Upper House of Parliament of India. E-mail: bjalan@nic.in

JAMES Alan Morien, b. 20 January 1933, Newport, Monmouthshire, Wales. Retired University Teacher. m. (1) Valerie Hancox, 4 sons, 2 daughters, (2) Lorna Lloyd. Education: BSc Economics, first class honours, London School of Economics and Political Science, 1954. Appointments: Civil service, 1955-57; Assistant Lecturer, Lecturer, Senior Lecturer, Reader in International Relations, London School of Economics, 1957-73; Professor of International Relations, Keele University, 1974-98. Publications: 8 books. Honours: Rockefeller Research Fellow, Columbia University, 1968; Visiting Professor, University of Ife, 1981; Visiting Professor, Jawaharlal Nehru University, 1983; Guest Professor, National Institute for Defense Studies, Japan, 1993. Memberships: Committees of Social Science Research Council; Council for National Academic Awards; University Grants Committee. Address: 23 Park Lane, Congleton, Cheshire CW12 3DG, England.

JAMES Anthony, (A R James), b. 17 March 1931, London, England. Literary Researcher; Author. m. (1) Jacqueline, 1952, deceased, (2) Anne, 1997, 1 son, 2 daughters. Appointments: General Manager, Wimbledon Stadium, 1956-91; Secretary, NGRC Racecourse Promoters, 1989-2005. Publications: W W Jacobs Companion, 1990; Wimbledon Stadium - The First Sixty Years, 1993, new enlarged edition, 2000; Informing the People, 1996; W W Jacobs (biography), 1999; WW Jacobs Book - Hunter's Field Guide, 2001. Contributions to: Book and Magazine Collector; Antiquarian Book Monthly; W W Jacobs Appreciation Society Newsletter; WWII HMSO Paperbacks Society Newsletter. Memberships: Secretary and Editor, W W Jacobs Appreciation Society, WWII HMSO Paperbacks Society. Address: 3 Roman Road, Southwick, W Sussex BN42 4TP, England.

JAMES Clive Vivian Leopold, b. 7 October 1939. m. Prue Shaw, 2 daughters. Writer; Broadcaster; Journalist. Education: Sydney University; Pembroke College, Cambridge. Appointments: President, Footlights, Cambridge; TV Critic, 1972-82, Feature Writer, 1972-, The Observer; Director, Watchmaker Productions, 1994-; Lyricist for Pete Atkin; TV series including: Cinema; Up Sunday; So It Goes; A Question of Sex; Saturday Night People; Clive James on Television; The Late Clive James; The Late Show with Clive James; Saturday Night Clive; Fame in the 20th Century; Sunday Night Clive; The Clive James Show; Numerous TV documentaries including: Clive James meets Katherine Hepburn, 1986; Clive James meets Jane Fonda; Clive James meets Mel Gibson, 1998; Clive James meets the Supermodels, 1998; Postcard series, 1989-; Publications: Non-Fiction: The Metropolitan Critic, 1974; The Fate of Felicity Fark in the Land of the Media, 1975; Peregrine Prykke's Pilgrimage Through the London Literary World, 1976; Britannia Bright's Bewilderment in the Wilderness of Westminster, 1976; Visions Before Midnight, 1977; At the Pillars of Hercules, 1979; First Reactions, 1980; The Crystal Bucket, 1981; Charles Charming's Challenges on the Pathway to the Throne, 1981; From the Land of Shadows, 1982; Glued to the Box, 1982; Flying Visits, 1984; Snakecharmers in Texas, 1988; The Dreaming Swimmer, 1992; Fame, 1993; The Speaker in Ground Zero, 1999; Novels: Brilliant Creatures, 1983; The Remake, 1987; Unreliable Memoirs (autobiography), 1980; Falling Towards England: Unreliable Memoirs Vol II, 1985; Unreliable Memoirs Vol III, 1990; May Week Was in June, 1990; Brrm! Brrm! or The Man From Japan or Perfume at Anchorage, 1991; Fame in the 20th Century, 1993; The Metropolitan Critic, 1993; Criticism: Clive James on Television, 1993; The Silver Castle, 1996; Evan as We Speak, 2005; North Face of Soho, 2006. 4 volumes of poetry. Address: c/o Watchmaker Productions, The Chrysalis Building, Bramley Road, London W10 6SP, England.

JAMES David Geraint, b. 2 January 1922, Treherbert, Wales. Doctor of Medicine. m. Sheila Sherlock, deceased, 2 daughters. Education: MA, MD, Jesus College, Cambridge; MRCS, LRCP, MRCP, Middlesex Hospital, University of London. Appointments: Surgeon-Lieutenant RNVR, 1946-48; Consultant Physician, Royal Navy, 1972-85; Dean of Studies, 1968-88, Consultant Physician, 1959-, Royal Northern Hospital, London; Professor of Medicine, University of London and Miami; Consultant Ophthalmic Physician, St Thomas' Hospital, London. Publications: Textbook of Infections, 1957; Colour Atlas of Respiratory Diseases, 1981; Sarcoidosis, 1985. Honours: Worshipful Society of Apothecaries, 1960-; Freeman, City of London; Honorary LLD University of Wales, 1982; FRCP, 1964; Honorary FACP, 1990. Memberships: President: Harvey Society, London; Osler Club, London; Medical Society, London; Member: London Medical Ophthalmology Society; World Congress History of Medicine; RCP; Hunterian Society; World Association of Sarcoidosis; International Journal of Sarcoidosis; Postgraduate Medical Federation; Thoracic Society of France, Italy and Portugal; French National Academy of Medicine; London Glamorganshire Society; White Robed Member, Bardic Circle of Wales. Address: 41 York Terrace East, London NW1 4PT, England.

JAMES Geraldine, b. 6 July 1950, Maidenhead, Berkshire, England. Actress. m. Joseph Blatchley, 1 daughter. Education: The Drama Centre, London. Career: Theatre includes: UN Inspector; The Cherry Orchard; Home; Faith Healer; Give Me your Answer Do; Death and the Maiden; Hedda Gabler; Lysistrata; The Merchant of Venice; Cymbeline; The White Devil; 4 years repertory including 18 months with the Northcott Theatre, Exeter; TV includes: Poirot; Jane Hall's Big Bad Bus Ride; Little Britain; White Teeth; The Sins; Kavanagh QC; Band of Gold; Blott on the Landscape; The Jewel in the Crown; The History Man; Dummy, Hearts of Gold; He Knew He Was Right; Hex; The Sins; White Teeth; Hearts of Gold; Little Britain; Jane Hall; The Battle of Rome; A Harlot's Progress, 2006; The Amazing Mrs Pritchard, 2006; The Time of Your Life, 2007; Medieval Heist, 2007; The Last Enemy, 2007. Films: Gandhi; The Tall Guy; Wolves of Willoughby Chase; She's Been Away; The Luzhin Defense; An Angel for May; Calendar Girls; Radio includes most recently: The Raj Quartet; Brought to Book; Turtle Diaries; King Lear; The Master and Marguerita; Alexander the Great; The Deptford Wives; The Hours; Whale Music; Richard III; Sherlock Holmes; Alice In Wonderland. Honours: TV Critics Award, Best Actress, 1978; Venice Film Festival Best Actress, 1989; Drama Desk Award, New York, 1990; OBE, 2003. Address: c/o Julian Belfrage Associates, Adam House, 14 New Burlington Street, London W15 3BQ, England.

JAMES Glen William, b. 22 August 1952, London, England. Solicitor. m. Amanda Claire Dorrell, 3 daughters. Education: New College, Oxford. Appointments: Articled Clerk, 1974-76, Assistant Solicitor, 1976-83, Partner, 1983-, Slaughter and May. Publications: Various professional articles contributed to books and other publications associated with corporate and commercial law. Memberships: Law Society; City of London Solicitors' Company; Securities Institute; Royal Automobile Club. Address: c/o 1 Bunhill Row, London EC1Y 8YY, England.

JAMES Michael Leonard, b. 7 February 1941, Cornwall, England. Government Official; Writer and Broadcaster. m. Jill Tarján, 2 daughters. Education: MA, Christ's College, Cambridge; FRSA. Appointments: Entered Government Service, GCHQ, 1963; Private Secretary to Rt Hon Jennie Lee, Minister for the Arts, 1966-68; DES, 1968-71; Planning Unit of Rt Hon Margaret Thatcher, Secretary of State for Education and Science, 1971-73; Assistant Secretary, 1973; Deputy Chief Scientific Officer, 1974; Adviser, OECD, Paris and UK Governor, International Institute for Management of Technology, Milan, 1973-75; International Negotiations on Non-Proliferation of Nuclear Weapons, 1975-78; Director, IAEA Vienna, 1978-83; Adviser, International Relations, 1983-85, Consultant, 1985-2001, Commission of the European Union, Brussels; Chair, Civil Service Selection Boards, 1983-93; Chair, The Hartland Press Ltd, 1985-2001,

Wade Hartland Films Ltd, 1991-2000; Feature Writer and Book Reviewer for The Times, (Resident Thriller Critic, 1990-91); Sunday Times, Guardian and Daily Telegraph, (Resident Thriller Critic, 1993-). Publications: Co-author, Internationalization to Prevent the Spread of Nuclear Weapons, 1980; Novels, as Michael Hartland: Down Among the Dead Men, 1983; Seven Steps to Treason, 1985 (South West Arts Literary Award, dramatised for BBC Radio 4, 1990); The Third Betrayal, 1986; Frontier of Fear, 1989; The Year of the Scorpion, 1991; As Ruth Carrington: Dead Fish, 1998; TV and radio include: Sonja's Report, ITV, 1990; Masterspy (interviews with KGB defector Oleg Gordievsky), BBC Radio 4, 1991. Honours: Honorary Fellow, University of Exeter, 1985-. Memberships: Governor, East Devon College of Further Education, Tiverton, 1985-91, Colyton Grammar School, 1985-90, Sidmouth Community College, 1988-; (Chair, Board of Governors, 1998-2002); Chair, Board of Governors, Axe Vale Further Education College, Seaton, 1987-91; Member, Immigration Appeal Tribunal, 1987-; Devon and Cornwall Rent Assessment Panel, 1990-; Chairman, General Medical Council, Professional Conduct Committee, 2000-. Address: Cotte Barton, Branscombe, Devon, EX12 3BH, England.

JAMES P(hyllis) D(orothy) (Baroness James of Holland Park), b. 3 August 1920, Oxford, England. Author. m. Ernest Connor Bantry White, 1941, deceased 1964, 2 daughters. Appointments: Member, BBC General Advisory Council, 1987-88, Arts Council, 1988-92, British Council, 1988-93; Chairman, Booker Prize Panel of Judges, 1987; Governor, BBC, 1988-93; President, Society of Authors, 1997-. Publications: Cover Her Face, 1962; A Mind to Murder, 1963; Unnatural Causes, 1967; Shroud for a Nightingale, 1971; The Maul and the Pear Tree (with T A Critchley), 1971; An Unsuitable Job for a Woman, 1972; Innocent Blood, 1980; The Skull Beneath the Skin, 1982; A Taste for Death, 1986; Devices and Desires, 1989; The Children of Men, 1992; Original Sin, 1994; A Certain Justice, 1997; Time to be in Earnest, 1999; Death in Holy Orders, 2001; The Murder Room, 2003; The Lighthouse, 2005; The Private Patient, 2008; Talking About Detective Fiction, 2011; Death Comes to Pemberley, 2013. Honours: Order of the British Empire; Honorary Fellow, St Hilda's College, Oxford, 1996, Downing College, Cambridge, 2000, Girton College, Cambridge, 2000; Honorary DLitt, University of Buckingham, 1992, University of Hertfordshire, 1994, University of Glasgow, 1995, University of Durham, 1988, University of Portsmouth, 1999; Honorary LittD, University of London, 1993; Dr hc, University of Essex, 1996; Grand Master Award, Mystery Writers of America, 1999. Memberships: Fellow, Royal Society of Literature; Fellow, Royal Society of Arts. Address: c/o Greene & Heaton Ltd, 37 Goldhawk Road, London W12 8QQ, England.

JAMESON Norma Marion, b. 18 January 1933, Stoke-on-Trent, England. Artist. m. Kenneth Jameson, deceased. Education: Thistley Hough Grammar School for Girls; Bath Academy of Art, Corsham; Liverpool University; Goldsmiths College, London. Appointments: Primary School Teacher; Senior Lecturer in Art; Freelance artist. Memberships: Royal Society of British Artists; Royal Institute of Oil Painters; Kent Potters Association. Address: 111 Hayes Way, Park Langley, Beckenham, Kent BR3 6RR, England.

JAMIL Tariq, b. 9 November 1965, Pakistan. Lecturer; Engineer. m. Saiqa, 1 son, 1 daughter. Education: BSc, Electrical Engineering, NWFP University of Engineering and Technology, Pakistan, 1989; MS, Computer Engineering, 1992; PhD, Computer Engineering, Florida Institute of Technology, USA, 1996. Appointments: Graduate Teaching Assistant, Florida Institute of Technology, USA, 1994-96; Assistant Professor, Faculty of Computer Science and Engineering, GIK Institute of Engineering Sciences and Technology, Pakistan, 1997; Lecturer, School of Computer Science and Engineering, University New South Wales, Sydney, Australia, 1997-98; Lecturer, School of Computing, University of Tasmania, Launceston, Australia, 1999-2000; Assistant Professor, Department of Electrical & Computer Engineering, Sultan Qaboos University, Muscat, Oman, 2000-. Publications: Numerous articles in professional journals; 1 patent; 1 book, Introduction to Associative Dataflow Processing, 2010. Honours include: National Talent Scholarship, 1981-89; President's Cash Award and Gold Medal, 1983, Best Graduate and Gold Medal, 1989; Quaid-e-Azam Scholarship, 1990-94; Award for Academic Excellence, IEEE Computer Society, 1996; Distinguished Speaker, IEEE Computer Society, 2005-07. Memberships: IEEE, USA; Institution of Engineering and Technology, UK; Institution of Electrical and Electronic Engineers, Pakistan; Chartered Engineer, UK; Professional Engineer, Pakistan; Member, International Association of Engineers, Hong Kong. Address: Electrical and Computer Engineering Department, Sultan Qaboos University, PO Box 33, Muscat 123, Sultanate of Oman.

JANA Asok Kumar, b. 25 December 1960, West Bengal, India. Chemistry Educator; Researcher. m. Papiya Sur, 1 son, 1 daughter. Education: BSc (Hons), 1982, MSc, 1984, Chemistry, Calcutta University; PhD, Jadavpur University, 1989; Graduate Aptitude Test Engineering, Ministry of Education, Government of India, 1985; National Educational Test, University Grants Commission, New Delhi, 1985. Appointments: Junior Research Fellow, 1985-88, Senior Research Fellow, 1988-90, Research Associate, 1990-91, Council of Science and Industrial Research, New Delhi; Assistant Professor, Head of Department, Chemistry Degree College, Directorate Higher Education, Khowai, Tripura, 1992-98; Guest Teacher, Tripura University, 1994-95; Senior Lecturer, Chemistry Degree College, Chief Secretariat (Edn), Mahe, Pondicherry, 1998-2000; Senior Lecturer, Reader, Chemistry Kanchi Mamuivar Centre for Postgraduate Studies, Chief Secretariat (Edn), Pondicherry, 2000-03, 2003-. Publications: Many papers and articles in professional scientific journals. Honours: National scholarships during Graduate & Post Graduate Studies; Junior Research Fellowship, Council for Scientific and Industrial Research, New Delhi, 1986; Research Associateship, Council of Scientific and Industrial Research, New Delhi, 1990; Research Associateship, University Grants Commission, New Delhi, 1990. Memberships: Life Member, Indian Association for the Cultivation of Science, 1986-; Member, Doctoral Committee, Pondicherry University, 2003-. E-mail: akjpgs@yahoo.com

JANES J(oseph) Robert, b. 23 May 1935, Toronto, Ontario, Canada. Writer. m. Gracia Joyce Lind, 16 May 1958, 2 sons, 2 daughters. Education: BSc, Mining Engineering, 1958, MEng, Geology, 1967, University of Toronto. Publications: Children's books: The Tree-Fort War, 1977; Theft of Gold, 1980; Danger on the River, 1982; Spies for Dinner, 1984; Murder in the Market, 1985. Adult books: The Toy Shop, 1981; The Watcher, 1982; The Third Story, 1983; The Hiding Place, 1984; The Alice Factor, 1991; St Cyr/Kohler series: Mayhem, 1992; Carousel, 1992; Kaleidoscope, 1993; Salamander, 1994; Mannequin, 1994; Dollmaker, 1995; Stonekiller, 1995; Sandman, 1996; Gypsy, 1997; Madrigal, 1999; Beekeeper, 2001; Flykiller, 2002. Non-Fiction: The Great Canadian Outback, 1978. Textbooks: Holt Geophoto Resource Kits, 1972; Rocks, Minerals and Fossils, 1973;

Earth Science, 1974; Geology and the New Global Tectonics, 1976; Searching for Structure (co-author), 1977. Teacher's Guide: Searching for Structure (co-author), 1977; Airphoto Interpretation and the Canadian Landscape (with J D Mollard), 1984. Contributions to: Toronto Star; Toronto Globe and Mail; The Canadian; Winnipeg Free Press; Canadian Children's Annual. Honours: Grants: Canada Council; Ontario Arts Council; J P Bickell Foundation; Thesis Award, Canadian Institute of Mining and Metallurgy; Works-in-progress Grant, Ontario Arts Council, 1991; Hammett Award Nominee, International Association of Crime Writers (North American Branch). Memberships: Crime Writers Association (UK); Historical Novel Society (UK); International Association of Crime Writers (North American Branch). Address: PO Box 1590, Niagara-on-the-Lake, Ontario L0S 1J0, Canada. Website: www.jrobertjanes.com

JANES Robert R, b. 23 April 1948, Canada. Editor-in-Chief; Museum/Heritage Consultant and Volunteer. m. Priscilla Bickel, 1 son, 1 daughter. Education: BA (cum laude), Anthropology, Lawrence University, USA, 1970; PhD, Archaeology, University of Calgary, Canada, 1976. Appointments: Founding Executive Director, Prince of Wales Northern Heritage Centre, Yellowknife, 1976-86; Postdoctoral Fellow, Arctic Institute of North America, University of Calgary, 1981-82; Founding Executive Director, Science Advisor, Science Institute of the NWT, Yellowknife, 1986-89; Adjunct Professor, Archaeology, University of Calgary, 1990-; President, Chief Executive Officer, Glenbow Museum, Calgary, 1989-2000; Museum/Heritage Consultant and Volunteer, 2000-; Editor-in-Chief, The Journal of Museum Management and Curatorship, 2003-. Publications: 6 books; Over 90 publications in professional journals; 55 principal public addresses. Honours: Received traditional Blackfoot name of Otahko Ohkiptopii (Yellow Horse Rider), 1995; Canadian Museums Association Outstanding Achievement Award for Museum Publications, 1996; Museums Alberta Award of Merit for Outstanding Achievement, 1996; Association of Cultural Executives Award for Outstanding Cultural Management, 1998; Commemorative Medal, Golden Jubilee of Her Majesty Queen Elizabeth II, 2003; Listed in various international biographical dictionaries. Memberships: Fellow, Glenbow-Alberta Institute, 1999; Fellow, Canadian Museums Association, 2002, Canadian Academy of Independent Scholars. Address: 104 Prendergast Place, Canmore, Alberta, Canada.

JANG Chang-Hyun, b. 22 April 1965, Seoul, Republic of Korea. Professor. m. Su-Youn Seo, 2 sons. Education: BS, 1988, MS, 1991, Chemistry, Hanyang University; PhD, Chemistry, Virginia Tech, 2004. Appointments: Sith Arty Rgt, Korea, 1991-92; Research Scientist, LG Chem, Daejeon, Korea, 1993-98; Secretary, Korean American Scientists & Engineers Association, Blacksburg, Virginia, 2000-01; Contributor, Choir Korean Baptist Church, Blacksburg, 2001-03; Research Associate, University of Wisconsin, Madison, USA, 2004-06; Senior Research Scientist, Korea Electrotechnical Research Institute, Ansan, Korea, 2006-07; Assistant Professor, 2007-11, Associate Professor, 2011-, Kyungwon University, Seongnam, Korea. Publications: Numerous articles in professional journals. Honours: Excellent Researcher Award, 1994, Best Project Award, 1997, LG Chem Ltd Research Pk. Memberships: American Chemical Society; Material Research Society; International Liquid Crystal Society; Korean American Scientists & Engineers Association. Address: Kyungwon University College College of BioNano Technology, San 65, Bokjeong-dong, Sujeong-gu, Seongnam, Gyeonggi-do 461-701, Republic of Korea. E-mail: chjang4u@kyungwon.ac.kr

JANG Ik-Gyu, b. 8 March 1978, Geojin-ri, Goseong-gun, Kangwon-do, Korea. Biomedical Researcher. Education: BS, Department of Control & Measurement, 2003, MS, Telecommunications & Multimedia, 2005, PhD, Electronic & Telecommunications, 2011, Kangwon National University. Appointments: Researcher, Biomedical Engineering branch division of Convergence Technology, National Cancer Center, 2009-. Publications: 3D gait analysis of limb salvage patients with osteoarticular knee allograft reconstruction, 2010. Honours: Listed in international biographical dictionaries. Memberships: Korean Society of Medical & Biological Engineering; Institute of Control, Robotics and Systems. Address: National Cancer Center, 323 Ilsan-ro, Gyeonggi-do, Goyang-si, ilsandong-gu, Madu 1-dong, 410-769, Republic of Korea. E-mail: eqjang@gmail.com

JANG Insoo, b. 21 November 1969, Seoul, Korea. m. Sanghee Kim, 2 sons. Education: Premedical course, Korean Medicine, 1990, College of Korean Medicine, 1994, Woosuk University; PhD, Korean Medicine, Kyunghee University, 2002. Appointments: Internship, 1994-95, Resident, 1995-96, 1999-2001, Woosuk University Hospital; Specialist for Internal Medicine of Korean Medicine, 2002; Instructor in Medicine, 2002-, Assistant Professor, 2004-, Associate Professor, 2008-, Woosuk University, College of Korean Medicine; Visiting Scholar, University of North Carolina at Chapel Hill, 2007-08. Publications: Laser therapy, clinical practice and scientific background, 2006; Laser needle acupuncture, 2007; Safety management guideline for acupuncture treatment, 2011. Honours: Medical Research Award, Korean Oriental Medicine Society, 2004; Annual Research Symposium, University of North Carolina at Chapel Hill, 2008; Knowledge Economy Minister's Award, 2010. Memberships: Association of Korean Oriental Medicine; Korean Oriental Medical Society; Korean Society of Toxicology; Korean Society for Oriental Internal Medicine; Korean Society of Joongpoong; World Association for Laser Therapy; Korean Medicine Association for Laser Therapy. Address: Woosuk University Hospital, 2-5 Junghwasan-dong, Jeonju, Jeonbuk, 560-833, Republic of Korea.

JANG Mi-Soon, b. 27 Janaury 1975, Yeogu, Republic of Korea. Researcher. m. Young Woo Kim. Education: PhD, Food Science & Technology, Tokyo University of Fisheries, 2003. Appointments: Researcher, Hansung Enterprise Co Ltd, 1997-99; Researcher, National Fisheries R&D Institute, 2004-. Publications: Eo-dim Chae, 2009; Seafood bibimbap, 2010; Food Science Biotechnology, 2009. Honours: Best Poster Presentation Award, International Commemorative Gymposium 70th Anniversary, Japanese Society of Fisheries Science; Appreciation Award, Korean Society of Food Science & Nutrition, 2009. Memberships: Korean Society of Food Science & Technology; Korean Society of Food Preservation. Address: National Fisheries R&D Institute, 152-1 Haeanro, Gijang-up, Gijang-Gun, Busan 619-705, Republic of Korea.

JANG PhilSik, b. 5 February 1967, Gangwon-do, Republic of Korea. Associate Professor. m. JooYang Lee, 2 sons. Education: BS, Seoul National University, 1990; MS, 1992, PhD, 1998, Korea Advanced Institute of Science and Technology. Appointments: Full time Lecturer, 1997-2000, Assistant Professor, 2000-04, Associate Professor, 2004-10, Professor, 2010-, Daebul University, Youngnam-gun, Jeollanam-do, Korea. Publications: 18 papers including:

Designing Acoustic and Non-Acoustic Parameters of Synthesized Speech Warnings to Control Perceived Urgency, 2007; 11 book including: Practical Programming with C++, 2002. Honours: Listed in international biographical dictionaries. Memberships: Ergonomics Society of Korea. Address: Department of Computer Education, Daebul University, Samho-eup, Yeongnam-gun, Jeollanam-do, 526-702, Republic of Korea. E-mail: philsjang@gmail.com

JANNER Greville Ewan, Baron Janner of Braunstone, b. 11 July 1928, Cardiff, South Wales. Working Peer; Barrister; Queen's Counsel; Author; Jewish Leader. m. Myra Louise Sheink, deceased, 1 son, 2 daughters. Education: MA, Trinity Hall, Cambridge, 1946-49; Harvard Law School, 1950-51; Hon PhD, Haifa, 1984; Hon LLD, De Montfort University, Leicester, 1998. Appointments: Member of Parliament, Leicester North West, 1970-74; Member of Parliament, Leicester West, 1974-97; Chairman, Select Committee on Employment, 1992-96; Vice Chairman, British Israel and British India Parliamentary Groups; Vice President, World Jewish Congress; Founder President, Commonwealth Jewish Council; Chairman, Holocaust Educational Trust; President, Maimonides Foundation; Former President, Board of Deputies of British Jews, 1978-84; Founder, President, JSB Ltd; Former Director, Labroke plc. Publications: Author, 65 books mainly on employment and industrial relations law, presentational skills and public speaking; One Hand Alone Cannot Clap. Memberships: Magic Circle; International Brotherhood of Magicians. Address: House of Lords, London SW1A 0PW, England.

JANSEN N Elly, b. 5 October 1929, Wisch, Holland. Retired Charity Director. m. Alan Brian Stewart (George Whitehouse), 3 daughters. Education: Paedologisch Institute, Free University, Amsterdam, Boerhave Kliniek (SRN), University of London. Appointments: Founder and CEO, Richmond Fellowship for Community Mental Health, 1959-91; Founder, Richmond Fellowship College, 1967; Founder and CEO, Richmond Fellowship International, 1981-2000; Founder and Executive Trustee, Fellowship Charitable Foundation (now Community Housing and Therapy), 1983-93; Founder, Richmond Fellowship Workshops, 1986; Founded: Richmond Fellowship of America (1968), Australia (1973), New Zealand (1977), Austria (1978), and subsequently of Barbados, Bangladesh, Bolivia, Canada, Costa Rica, France, Ghana, Grenada, Hong Kong, India, Israel, Jamaica, Malta, Mexico, Nigeria, Peru, Philippines, Trinidad & Tobago, Uruguay and Zimbabwe; Founder and CEO, Richmond Fellowships Foundation International, 2006; Organised international conferences on therapeutic communities and courses on mental illness and drug rehabilitation; Acted as adviser to many governments on issues of community care. Publications: Editor, The Therapeutic Community Outside the Hospital, 1980; Contributor: Mental Health and the Community, 1983; Towards a Whole Society, 1985; R D Laing, Creative Destroyer, 1997; Contributions to American Journal of Psychiatry, L'Information Psychiatrique and other journals. Honours: Fellowship, German Marshall Memorial Fund, 1977-78; OBE, 1980; Templeton Award, 1985. Address: Clyde House, 109 Strawberry Vale, Twickenham, TW1 4SJ, England.

JARPLID Bertil, b. 8 November 1930, Brooklyn, New York, USA. Veterinarian Pathologist. m. Ruth Edler. Education: Dr Vet Med, 1958, PhD, 1968, Royal Veterinary College. Appointments: Researcher, National Defence Institute, 1960-71; Assistant Professor, National Veterinary Institute, 1971-78; District Veterinarian, Ronneby, 1978-84; Director, SIDA International Courses on Veterinary Pathology, 1984-87; Professor, National Veterinary Institute, Uppsala, 1988-2000. Publications: Over 50 articles in professional journals including: Radiation induced asymmetry and lymphoma of thymus in mice, 1968; Pathological findings indicative of distemper in European seals, 1990; Pathogenesis of infective valvular endocarditis, 2010. Address: Cellovagen 85, 75654 Uppsala, Sweden. E-mail: jarplid@telia.com

JARRATT Sir Alexander Anthony, b. 19 January 1924, London, England. Retired Civil Servant; Company Executive. m. Mary Philomena Keogh, 1 son, 2 daughters. Education: BCom, 1st Class Honours, Birmingham University, 1946-49. Appointments: Petty Officer Fleet Air Arm; Civil Servant Ministry of Power, 1949-64; Seconded to the Treasury, 1953-54; Cabinet Office, 1964-65; Secretary, Prices and Incomes Board, 1964-68; Deputy Under Secretary, Department of Employment and Productivity, 1968-70; Deputy Secretary Ministry of Agriculture, 1970; Chief Executive IPC and IPC Newspapers, 1970-74; Chairman and Chief Executive, Reed International, 1974-85, Director, 1970-85; Chairman, Smiths Industries plc, 1985-91, Director, 1984-96; Director, Thyssen-Bornemisza Supervisory Board, 1972-89; Deputy Chairman: Midland Bank plc, 1980-91, Prudential Corporation, 1987-91 and 1992-94; Non-Executive Director, ICI plc, 1975-91; President Advertising Association, 1979-83; Former Member, NEDC; Former Chairman, CBI Economic Policy Committee; CBI Employment Policy Committee; Former Member, Presidents Committee, CBI; Chairman, Industrial Society, 1975-79; Henley Administrative Staff College, 1976-89; Centre for Dispute Resolution, 1990-2000, president, 2001-; Chancellor, University of Birmingham, 1983-2002. Honours: Companion of the Bath, 1968; Knight Bachelor, 1979; Honorary LLD, University of Birmingham; Honorary DSc, Cranfield; Honorary D Univ, Brunel and Essex; Honorary, CGIA; FRSA; Honorary FCGI. Address: Barn Mead, Fryerning, Essex CM4 0NP, England.

JARRE Jean-Michel, b. 24 August 1948, Lyons, France. Musician (synthesizers, keyboards); Composer; Record Producer. m. (1) Flore Guillard, 1975, divorced, 1 child, (2) Charlotte Rampling, 1977, divorced, 1 son, (3) Anne Parillaud, 2005-. Musical Education: Piano and guitar from age 5; Conservatoire de Paris, with Jeanine Reuff. Career: Solo debut, Paris Opera, 1971; Youngest composer to appear, Palais Garnier, 1971; Major concerts, often including lasers and fireworks, filmed for video releases include: Beijing, China, 1981; Bastille Day, Place De La Concorde, 1979; Houston, Texas (1.3 million audience), 1986; London Docklands, 1988; La Defense, Paris (2.5 million audience), 1990; Sun City, Johannesburg, South Africa, 1993; Member of jury, First International Visual Music Awards, Midem, France, 1992. Compositions include: Oxygène Part IV, used for several television themes; Ballet and film scores include: Des Garçons Et Des Filles, 1968; Deserted Palace, 1972; Les Granges Brûlées, 1973; La Maladie De Hambourg, 1978; Gallipoli, 1979. Recordings: Albums (all self-composed and produced): Deserted Palace, 1971; Oxygène, 1977; Magnetic Fields, 1981; The Concerts In China, 1982; The Essential Jean-Michel Jarre, 1983; Zoolook, 1984; Rendez-Vous, 1986; In Concert Lyons/Houston, 1987; Revelations (Number 2, UK), 1988; Jarre Live, 1989; Waiting For Cousteau, 1990; Images - The Best Of Jean-Michel Jarre, 1991; Chronologie, 1993; Jarre Hong Kong, 1994; Cities in Concert, 1997; Oxygène 7-13, 1997; China Concert, 1999; Odyssey Through 2, 1998; Metamorphoses, 2000; Aero, 2004; Teo & Tea, 2007. Honours: First Western artist to play in China, 1981; Grand Prix, Academie Du Disque, Zoolook, 1985; Best Instrumental

Album, Victoire de la Musique, 1986; Numerous Platinum and Gold discs worldwide. Address: c/o Dreyfus Records, 26 Avenue Kléber, 75116 Paris, France.

JARSKÝ Čeněk, b. 11 June 1953, Prague, Czech Republic. Civil Engineer; Professor of Technology of Structures. m. Václava Jarská, 1 son. Education: MSc, Civil Engineering, 1976, PhD, Technology of Structures, 1982, DSc, Technology of Structures, 2001, all at the Czech Technical University, Prague; Postgraduate Course in Theoretical Cybernetics, Charles University, Prague, 1983; Diploma of Chartered Engineer, Czech Chamber of Civil Engineers, Prague, 1991. Appointments: Lecturer, Czech Technical University, Prague, 1976-82; Scientific Officer, Building Research Establishment, Garston, UK, 1980-81; Scientific Officer, 1982-84, Division Head, 1984-90, Research Institute of Civil Engineering, Prague; General Manager, Owner, CONTEC Construction Technology Consulting, Kralupy n. Vlt, 1990-; Associate Professor, 1997-2005, Professor of Technology of Structures, 2005-, Czech Technical University, Prague. Publications: Automated Preparation and Management Realization of Structures (book, author), 2000; Planning and Realization of Structures (book, main author), 2003; Mathematical Modeling in Preparation and Management of Projects (monograph, author), 2005. Honours: Bronze Medal, Ministry of Civil Engineering, Prague, 1989; Award Certificate, Grand Prix For Arch (exhibition), 2000; Silver Plaque, Slovak Technical University, 2004. Memberships: Czech Society of Project Management, Prague; Czech Chamber of Chartered Civil Engineers, Prague; International Association for Bridge and Structure Engineering, Zurich; Fellow, ABI; International Association for Automation and Robotics in Construction. Address: Mánesova 819, 27801 Kralupy n. Vlt, Czech Republic. E-mail: jarsky@contec.cz Website: www.contec.cz

JART Aage, b. 5 May 1931, Nykobing on Falster, Denmark. Food Chemist. m. Una Kalmer Steensen, 1957, 2 sons, 2 daughters. Education: MSc, Chemical Engineering, Technical University of Denmark, 1955. Appointments: Research Engineer, Danish Soyacake Factory Ltd, 1955; Staff Member, Danish Fat Research Institute, 1956-61; Lecturer, Organic Chemical Department, Technical University of Denmark, 1961-74; Reader in Chemistry, Royal Danish Defence College, 1961-74; Senior Lecturer, Royal Veterinary and Agricultural University of Denmark, 1974-98. Publications: Fat Technology, university textbook, 4th edition, 1995; Articles in numerous journals on fat chemistry, biochemistry and organic chemistry. Membership: Associate Member, International Union Pure and Applied Chemistry, Analytical Chemistry Division, 1963-67. Address: Hojsgårds Allé 50, DK-2900 Hellerup, Denmark.

JARVIS Ruth, b. 5 September 1927, Belmont County, Ohio, USA. Teacher; Apartment Owner. 2 daughters. Education: BA, Asbury College; Master of Education, University of Florida; Unplanned program equivalent to 2 Master of Education degrees or a Doctors degree, Ohio State University. Appointments: Teacher, Florida and Ohio schools, 45 years; Apartment owner, Ohio and Florida. Honours: International Peace Prize, 2005; Woman of the Year 2005; Woman of Achievement, 2005; International Fellowship; President Bush's Advisory Staff, 2005; Listed in international and national biographical dictionaries. Address: 117 East Church St, Barnesville, OH 43713-1214, USA.

JASON Sir David, b. 2 February 1940, England. Actor. m. Gill Hinchcliffe, 2005, 1 daughter. Creative Works: Theatre includes: Under Milk Wood, 1971; The Rivals, No Sex Please...We're British!, 1972; Darling Mr London (tour), Charley's Aunt (tour), 1975; The Norman Conquests, 1976; The Relapse, 1978; Cinderella, 1979; The Unvarnished Truth (Middle/Far East tour), 1983; Look No Hands! (tour and West End), 1985; Films: Under Milk Wood, 1970; Royal Flash, 1974; The Odd Job, 1978; Only Fools and Horses, Wind in the Willows, 1983; TV includes: Do Not Adjust Your Set, 1967; The Top Secret Life of Edgar Briggs, 1973-74; Mr Stabbs, 1974; Ronnie Barker Shows, Open All Hours, Porridge, Lucky Feller, 1975; A Sharp Intake of Breath, 1978; Del Trotter in Only Fools and Horses, 1981-91; Porterhouse Blue, 1986; Jackanory, 1988; A Bit of A Do, 1988-89; Single Voices: The Chemist, Amongst Barbarians, 1989; Pa Larkin in The Darling Buds of May, 1990-92; A Touch of Frost, 1992-2010; The Bullion Boys, 1993; Micawber, 2001; The Second Quest, 2005; Diamond Geezer, 2005-2007; Ghostboat, Hogfather, 2006; The Colour of Magic, 2008; Albert's Memorial, 2009. Voice work: Dangermouse; Count Duckula; The Wind in the Willows. Honours include: Best Actor Award, BAFTA, 1988; BAFTA Fellowship, 2003; OBE, 2005. Address: c/o Richard Stone Partnership, 2 Henrietta Street, London WC2E 8PS, England.

JASON Gillian Brett, b. 30 June 1941, England. Art Gallery Director. m. Neville Jason, 1961, 1 son, 1 daughter. Education: Dominican Convent School, Brewood, Staffordshire; Royal Ballet School, London, 1958-60; London Opera Centre, London, 1965-67. Appointments: Director, Gillian Jason Gallery, London, 1981-94; Director, Jason and Rhodes, London, 1994-99; Gillian Jason, Modern and Contemporary Art, 1999-. Honours: BBO Award, Royal Ballet School, 1958; Countess of Munster Award, London Opera Centre, 1965. Membership: Society of London Art Dealers, 1994-. Address: 3 Ormonde Terrace, London, NW8 7LP, England. Email: art@gillianjason.com Website: www.gillianjason.com

JASPER David, b. 1 August 1951, Stockton on Tees, England. University Teacher; Clergyman. m. Alison Elizabeth Collins, 29 October 1976, 3 daughters. Education: Dulwich College, 1959-69; Jesus College, Cambridge, 1969-72; BA, MA, 1976, BD, 1980, Keble College, Oxford; PhD, Hatfield College, Durham, 1983; DD, Keble College, Oxford, 2002; Theol Dr hc, Uppsala University, 2007. Appointments: Director, Centre for the Study of Literature and Theology, Durham University, 1986-91, Glasgow University, 1991-; Editor, Literature and Theology; Professor of Literature and Theology, University of Glasgow, 1998-. Publications: Coleridge as Poet and Religious Thinker, 1985; The New Testament and the Literary Imagination, 1987; The Study of Literature and Religion, 1989; Rhetoric Power and Community, 1992; Reading in the Canon of Scripture, 1995; The Sacred and Secular Canon in Romanticism, 1999; The Sacred Desert, 2004; The Sacred Body, 2009; General Editor, Macmillan Series, Studies in Religion and Culture. Honours: Dana Fellow, Emory University, Atlanta, 1991; Honorary Fellow, Research Foundation, Durham University, 1991; Ida Cordelia Beam Distinguished Visiting Professor, University of Iowa, 2003; Doctorate of Theology – Honoris Causa, University of Uppsala, Sweden, 2007; Changyang Chair Professor, China, 2009-11. Memberships: International Society for Religion, Literature and Culture secretary; American Academy of Religion; Fellow, Society for Arts, Religion and Culture, 2000; Fellow, Royal Society of Edinburgh, 2006; Fellow, Royal Society of Arts, 2007. Address: Netherword, 124 Old Manse Road, Wishaw, Lanarkshire ML2 0EP, Scotland.

JAXYBEKOV Adilbek, b. 26 July 1954, Burli, Karabalykskii district, Kazakhstan. Economist. m. Lyazzat, 1 son. Education: Graduate, Faculty of Economics, All-Union State Institute of

Cinematography, Moscow, 1977; PhD, Moscow Institute of National Economy, 1987. Appointments: Worked in the system of State cinematography and State provision of Kazakh SSR; Head, multi-industry corporation Tsesna, 1988-95; Elected to Senate of the Parliament of the Republic of Kazakhstan, 1995; First Deputy and later Mayor, Akmolinskaya oblast, 1996; Mayor, Astana city (new capital city of Kazakhstan), 1997-2003; Minister of Industry and Trade, Republic of Kazakhstan, 2003-04; Chief of Administration of the President of the Republic of Kazakhstan, 2004-; First Deputy Chairman, People-Democratic Party, Nur Otan – adviser to the President of Republic of Kazakhstan, 2008; Extraordinary and Plenipotentiary Ambassador, Republic of Kazakhstan to the Russian Federation, 2008-09; Minister of Defence of the Republic of Kazakhstan, 2009-. Publications: Numerous books and articles in professional journals. Honours: Kazakhstand Respublikasynyn Toongush Presidenti Nursultan Nazarbayev; Barys of II and III degrees; Prince Yaroslav the Wise of III degree (Ukraine) and medals. Memberships: Football Federation of the Republic of Kazakhstan. E-mail: pressa@mod.gov.kz Website: www.mod.gov.kz

JAY Peter, b. 7 February 1937. Writer; Broadcaster. m. (1) Margaret Ann Callaghan, 1961, dissolved 1986, 1 son, 2 daughters, (2) Emma Thornton, 1986, 3 sons. Education: MA, 1st class honours, Politics, Philosophy and Economics, Christ Church Oxford, 1960. Appointments: Midshipman and Sub-Lieutenant, RNVR, 1956-57; Assistant Principal, 1961-64, Private Secretary to Joint Permanent Secretary, 1964, Principal, 1964-67, HM Treasury; Economics Editor, The Time, 1967-77; Associate Editor, Times Business News, 1969-77; Presenter, Weekend World, ITV series, 1972-77; The Jay Interview, ITV series, 1975-76; Ambassador to USA, 1977-79; Director, Economist Intelligence University, 1979-83; Consultant, Economist Group, 1979-81; Chairman and Chief Executive, TV-AM Ltd, 1980-83, and TV-AM News, 1982-83; President, TV-AM, 1983-; Presenter, A Week in Politics, Channel 4, 1983-86; COS to Robert Maxwell, Chairman of Mirror Group Newspapers Ltd, 1986-89; Visiting Scholar, Brookings Institution, Washington, 1979-80; Wincott Memorial Lecturer, 1975; Copland Memorial Lecturer, Australia, 1980; Shell Lecturer, Glasgow, 1985; Governor, Ditchley Foundation, 1982-; Author and Presenter, Road to Riches, BBC TV series, 2000. Publications: The Budget, 1972; Contributor, America and the World, 1979, 1980; The Crisis for Western Political Economy and other Essays, 1984; Apocalypse 2000, with Michael Stewart, 1987; Contributor, Foreign Affairs journal, Road to Riches, or The Wealth of Man, 2000. Honours: Political Broadcaster of the Year, 1973; Harold Wincott Financial and Economic Journalist of the Year, 1973; RTS Male Personality of the Year, Pye Award, 1974; SFTA Shell International TV Award, 1974; RTS Home News Award, 1992; Honorary DH, Ohio State University, 1978; Honorary DLitt, Wake Forest University, 1979; Berkeley Citation, University of California, 1979. Address: Hensington Farmhouse, Woodstock, Oxfordshire OX20 1LH, England.

JAY-Z, b. 4 December 1970, Brooklyn, New York, USA. Rapper; Songwriter; Businessman. m. Beyoncé Knowles, 2008. Career: Singer: Albums inclue: Reasonable Doubt, 1996; In My Lifetime, Vol 1, 1997; Vol 2, Hard Knock Life, 1998; Vol 3, Life and Times of S Carter, 1999; The Dynasty: Roc La Familia, 2000; The Blueprint, 2001; The Blueprint2: The Gift & The Curse, 2002; The Black Album, 2003; Kingdom Come, 2006; American Gangster, 2007; The Blueprint 3, 2009; Actor: Films: Streets Is Watching, 1998; Backstage, 2000; State Property, 2002; Paper Soliders, 2003; Fade to Black, 2004; Designer: Rocawear clothing brand.

JAYASURYA P K, b. 25 September 1971, Trivandrum, India. Environmental Scientist; Criminologist. M. L S Suja, 1 son, 1 daughter. Education: BSc, University of Kerala, 1992; MSc, 1995, M Phil, 2000, PhD, 2001, Manomaniam Sundarnar University; TTIM (Dip), Kerala Institute of Tourism & Travel Studies, 1996-97; Special Training, Annamalai University, 2003; PG, Criminology & Criminal Justice Administration, Kerala University, 2008; PG (Dip), Criminology & Police Administration, Madurai Kamaraj University, 2009. Appointments: Research Assistant, Indian Institute of Spices Research, Calicut, 1997-99; Junior Research Fellow, Kerala Forest Research Institute, Peechi, 1999-2000, 2001; Senior Research Fellow, Central Marine Fisheries Research Institute, Cochin, 2001, 2002, 2004; L D Clerk, Office of the Superintendent of Police, Malappuram, 2002, 2004; Junior Scientific Assistant, Kerala State Pollution Control Board, Trivandrum, 2004-09; UD Clerk, Office of the State Police Chief, Police Head Quarters, Trivandrum, 2009-10. Publications: Numerous articles in professional journals. Honours: Gold Medal, M Phil; First Rank, M Phil; Best Scientific Paper Award, 15th Swadeshi Science Congress, 2005; Listed in biographical dictionaries. Memberships: Krishnamoorthy Institute of Algology, Chennai; Orchid Society of India, Chandigarh. Address: Suryakanthi, TC16/1480, JPN-72, Behind DPI's Office, Jagathy PO, Trivandrum 695 014, Kerala, India. E-mail: pkjayashurya@yahoo.in

JAYAWARDENE Kirikankanange Albert Thistlethwayte Wilhelm Perera, b. 9 November 1928, Moratuwa, Sri Lanka. Consultant Anaesthetist. m. Amara, 1 son, 2 daughters. Education: MBBS, Ceylon, 1956; DA, London, 1962; FRCA, England, 1963; FACC, USA, 1985. Appointments: Retired Consultant Anaesthetist, Cardiothoracic Unit and Surgical Intensive Care Unit, National Hospital, Sri Lanka. Publications: Medical orations and presidential addresses, Sri Lanka, 1990-2009; Several articles in professional medical journals. Honours: Most Outstanding Citizen Award for Medicine, 1995; 20th Century Achievement Award; Vishva Prasadhini Award for Distinguished Service to the Nation, 1996; Honorary Senior Fellow, Postgraduate Institute of Medicine, University of Colombo,2009; Listed in national and international biographical dictionaries. Memberships: President, College of Anaesthesiologists of Sri Lanka, 1984, 1985, 1986; President, Sri Lanka Medical Association, 1991; Vice President, Sri Lanka Heart Association, 1994-2008; Vice President, Organisation of Professional Associations of Sri Lanka, 2001, 2006-07; Patron, Sri Lankan Critical Care and Emergency Medicine Society, 2002-; Director and Vice President, Critical Care, Ceylon Hospitals Ltd; Director, Durdans Medical and Surgical Hospital Ltd. Address: 14 Albert Place, Dehiwela, Sri Lanka.

JAYSTON Michael, b. 29 October 1935, Nottingham, England. Actor. m. (1) Lynn Farleigh, 1965, divorced 1970, (2) Heather Mary Sneddon, divorced 1977, (3) Elizabeth Ann Smithson, 1978, 3 sons, 1 daughter. Career: Actor, RSC, 1965-69, National Theatre, 1976-79; Films: Cromwell, 1970; Nicholas and Alexandra, 1971; Follow Me, 1972; Bequest to the Nation, 1972; Tales That Witness Madness, 1973; Craze, 1973; The Internecine Project, 1974; Dominique, 1978; Zulu Dawn, 1979; Element of Doubt, 1996. TV: Power Game; Charles Dickens; Beethoven; Solo-Wilfred Owen; Quiller, 1975; Tinker, Tailor, Soldier, Spy, 1979; Dr Who, 1986; A Bit of A Do, 1989; Kipling's Sussex, 1989; About Face, 1989; Darling Buds of May, 1992; Outside Edge, 1995-96; Only Fools and Horses, 1996; Flesh and Blood, 1980; Dust to Dust, 1985; Highlander III: The Sorcerer, 1994; The Bill, 2006;

The Royal, 2007; Emmerdale Farm, 2007-2008; Holby City, 2001-2010. Theatre: Private Lives, 1980; Sound of Music, 1981; Way of the World, 1984-85; Woman in Mind; Beethoven Readings with Medici String Quartet, 1989; Dancing at Lughnasa, 1992; Wind in the Willows, 1994; Racing Demon, 1998; Easy Virtue, 1999. Address: Michael Whitehall Ltd, 125 Gloucester Road, London SW7 4TE, England.

JEA Seung Youn, b. 8 November 1973, Seoul, South Korea. Ophthalmologist. Education: MD, 1998, PhD, 2007, Pusan National University. Appointments: Postdoctoral Research Fellow, Glaucoma Service, Harvard Medical School, Massachusetts Eye and Ear Infirmary, Boston, 2008-10. Publications: Numerous articles in professional journals. Honours: TaeJun-Santen Young Ophthalmologist fellowship grant, 2003. Memberships: Korean Glaucoma Society. Address: Goodmorning Saint Mary's Eye Centre, KB building 5th floor, 260-5, Bujeon-dong, Jin-gu, Busan 614-030, South Korea. E-mail: jeasy2@gmail.com

JEANNENEY Jean-Noël, b. 2 April 1942, Grenoble, France. Historian; Politician. m. Annie L Cot, 2 sons. Education: École Normale Supérieure; Agrégation in History, Doctorate in Letters, Paris Institute of Political Studies. Appointments: Teacher, University of Paris X, Nanterre, -1977; Maître de Conférences, Professeur des universités, 1979, Paris Institute of Political Studies; President, General Manager, Radio France International, 1982-86; Junior Minister, Foreign Trade, 1991-92; Junior Minister, Communication, 1992-93; Member, Conseil Régional, Franche-Comté région, 1992-98; Co-president (with Élisabeth Guigou), Europartenaires, 1998-; President, Bibliothèque nationale de France, 2002-07. Publications: Numerous books and articles in professional journals. Address: 44 rue de la Clef, 75005 Paris, France.

JEFFCOTT Leo B, b. England. Professor of Veterinary Science. m. Tisza Jacqueline Hubbard, 1969, 2 daughters. Education: Bachelor of Veterinary Medicine, Royal Veterinary College, University of London, 1961-66; PhD, 1972; FRCVS, 1978; DVr Pt 1, 1973; DVSc, 1989; Specialist in Equine Medicine, 1990; MA, 1994; VetMedDr hc (Uppsala), 2000. Appointments: Assistant Pathologist, 1967-71, Radiologist, 1972-77, Head of Clinical Department, 1977-82, Equine Research Station, Animal Health Trust, Newmarket, England; Accredited Equine Veterinarian, FEI, 1977-; Professor of Clinical Radiology, 1981-82, Visiting Professor, 1990-91, Swedish University of Agricultural Sciences, Uppsala, Sweden; Professor of Veterinary Clinical Sciences, 1982-91, Deputy Dean, Faculty of Veterinary Science, 1985, Head of Department, Veterinary Clinical Sciences, 1985-89, Director, Department of Veterinary Clinic & Hospital, 1986-91, University of Melbourne, Australia; Official Veterinarian at Olympic Games, 1988, 1992, 1996, 2000, 2004, 2008; Professor of Veterinary Clinical Studies, Department of Clinical Veterinary Medicine, 1991-2004, Dean, Veterinary School, 1991-2004, Professorial Fellow, Pembroke College, 1993-2004, University of Cambridge, England; Dean, Faculty of Veterinary Science, University of Sydney, 2004-09. Publications: Over 300 scientific publications related to equine science; Co-author of 10 textbooks. Honours include: Share Jones Lectureship in Veterinary Anatomy, 1993; Animal Health Trust Outstanding Scientific Achievement Award, 1994; Sefton Award 1997 for services to Equestrian Safety, 1997; Dalrymple Champneys Prize and Cup, 2001; J D Stewart Address, 2004; R R Pascoe Peroration, 2005; Honorary Member, Bureau of the Federation Equestre Internationale, 2006; Kentucky Colonel, 2011. Memberships: British Veterinary Association; British Equine Veterinary Association; Member, Bureau of Federation Equestre Internationale and Chairman, Veterinary Committee, 1998-2006; Royal College of Veterinary Surgeons; World Society for the Protection of Animals; International Committee on Equine Exercise Physiology. Address: Faculty of Veterinary Science, University of Sydney, University Veterinary Teaching Hospital, 410 Werombi Road, Camden, NSW 2570, Australia. E-mail: leo.jeffcott@sydney.edu.au

JEFFS Julian, b. 5 April 1931, Wolverhampton, England. Author; Editor. m. Deborah Bevan, 3 sons. Education: Downing College, Cambridge. Appointments: Sherry Shipper's Assistant, Spain, 1956; Barrister, Gray's Inn, 1958; QC, 1975; Recorder, 1975-96; Bencher of Hon Society of Gray's Inn, 1981; Deputy High Court Judge (Chancery Division), 1981-96; Retired from practice, 1991. Publications: Sherry, 1961, 5th edition, 2004; Clerk & Lindsell on Torts, 13th edition, 1969 to 16th edition, 1989 (an editor); The Wines of Europe, 1971; Little Dictionary of Drink, 1973; Encyclopaedia of UK and European Patent Law, 1977, co-editor; The Wines of Spain, 1999. Honours: Office International de la Vigne et du Vin, 1962, 2001; Gran Orden de Caballeros del Vino; Glenfiddich Wine Writers Award, 1974 and 1978. Memberships: Member of Committee, Wine and Food Society, 1965-67, 1971-82; Chairman, Patent Bar Association, 1980-89; President, Circle of Wine Writers, 1992-96. Address: Church Farm House, East Ilsley, Newbury, Berkshire RG20 7LP, England.

JEGART HOUSEWRIGHT Artemis Skevakis, b. 18 July 1927, Tampa, Florida, USA. Artist. m. (1) Rudolf A Jegart, 1952-67, 2 daughters, (2) Riley D Housewright, 1969-2003. Education: BA, 1949, MA, Painting, 1953, Florida State University, Tallahassee. Appointments: Artist, 1955-; Solo and group exhibitions across USA. Publications: Books: The Other Florida, 1967; The Grove, 1998; Coast to Coast, 1999; Voices, 2002. Honours: Numerous prizes and awards for work, 1955-; 50th Retrospective, Vero Beach Museum of Art, Florida, 2003; Formal Dedication of Oil Mural for Florida State University, 2003; Listed in international biographical dictionaries. Address: 9 Vista Estrella So, Lamy, Santa Fe, NM 87540, USA.

JEKABSONS Eriks, b. 14 January 1965, Riga, Latvia. Historian. m. Laima, 2 daughters. Education: Education course, University of Latvia, Riga, 1990; Dr hist diploma, 1995. Appointments: Assistant, 1990-95, Researcher, 1995-, Institute of History of Latvia; Head of Department, State Historical Archives of Latvia, 1996-2006; Assistant Professor, 2003-06, Professor, 2006-, University of Latvia. Publications: 14 books in Latvia and Poland; 180 scientific articles. Honours: Small Felix Prize of European Academy of Sciences and Arts; Gold Cross of Merits, Poland. Membership: Editorial board member of 15 scientific editions in Latvia, Poland, Lithuania, Romania and Belarus. Address: Raunas Str 45/3-107, Riga, LV-1084, Latvia. E-mail: eriksj@lu.lv

JENKINS Michael Nicholas Howard (Sir), b. 13 October 1932, Sevenoaks, Kent, England. Company Chairman. m. Jacqueline Frances, 3 sons. Education: Merton College, Oxford, 1953-56. Appointments: IBM, 1962-67; Management Consultant, Robson Morrow & Co, 1967-71; Technical Director, London Stock Exchange, 1971-77; Managing Director, European Options Exchange, 1977-80; Chief Executive, London International Futures and Options Exchange, 1981-92; Chairman, Futures and Options Association, 1992-2000; Chairman, London Commodity Exchange, 1992-96; London Clearing House, 1991-

DICTIONARY OF INTERNATIONAL BIOGRAPHY 36th EDITION

Chairman, 1996-; Deputy Chairman, Easyscreen plc, 1999-; Chairman, E. Crossnet Ltd, 1999-. Honours: OBE, 1991; Knighthood, 1997. Address: London Clearing House, Aldgate House, 33 Aldgate High Street, London EC3N 1EA, England.

JENKINS Michael R H (Sir), b. 9 January 1936. Former President, Boeing UK; Consultant. m. Maxine Louise Hodson, 1 son, 1 daughter. Education: BA Honours, King's College, Cambridge. Appointments: Entered HM Diplomatic Service, 1959; Foreign and Commonwealth Office and British Embassies, Paris and Moscow, 1959-68; Seconded, General Electric Company, London, 1968-70; British Embassy, Bonn, 1970-73; European Commission, Brussels, 1973-83; Assistant Under-Secretary of State, Foreign and Commonwealth Office, 1983-85; Minister and Deputy Head of Mission, British Embassy, Washington DC, 1985-87; British Ambassador, The Netherlands, 1988-93; Executive Director and Member of Group Board, Kleinwort Benson Group, 1993-96; Vice-Chairman, Dresdner Kleinwort Wasserstein, 1996-2003; President, 2003-2005, Part-time Consultant, 2005-, Boeing UK; President's Advisory Council, Atlantic Council, 1994; Non-Executive Director, Aegon NV, 1995; Chairman of Directors, Action Centre for Europe, 1995; Chairman, British Group, Member of the European Executive Committee, Trilateral Commission, 1996-98; Adviser, Sage International, 1997; Chairman, Dataroom Ltd, 1999-2002; Non-Executive Director, EO, 2000; Chairman, MCC, 2000-02, Trustee, 2002-; Council of Britain in Europe, 2000-; The Pilgrims, 2001-; Advisory Council Prince's Trust, 2002-; Companion, Royal Aeronautical Society, 2004. Publications: Arakcheev, Grand Vizier of the Russian Empire, 1969; A House in Flanders, 1992. Honour: KCMG, 1989. Address: The Boeing Company, 16 St James's Street, St James's, London SW1A 1ER, England.

JENNINGS Alex Michael, b. 10 May 1957, Upminster, Essex. Actor. Partner: Lesley Moors, 1 son, 1 daughter. Education: BA honours, Warwick University, 1978; Bristol Old Vic Theatre School, 1978-80. Career: Theatre includes: Richard II, 1990-91; The Importance of Being Earnest, 1993; Hamlet, 1997-98; Speer, 2000; The Winter's Tale, 2001; The Relapse, 2001; My Fair Lady, 2002 Films include: War Requiem, 1988; A Midsummer Night's Dream, 1996; The Wings of the Dove, 1997; The Hunley, 1998; Four Feathers, 2002; Five Children and It, 2004; Bridget Jones: The Edge of Reason, 2004; Riot at the Rite, 2005; Babel, 2006; The Queen, 2006; TV includes: Smiley's People; Inspector Morse; Ashenden; Inspector Alleyn Mysteries; Hard Times; Bad Blood; London; A Very Social Secretary; The State Within; Cranford Chronicles; Waking the Dead.. Honours: Best Actor for Too Clever By Half, London Theatre Critics Awards; Olivier Award, Best Comedy Performance for Too Clever By Half; Oliver Award, Best Actor for Peer Gynt; Helen Hayes Award, Best Actor for Hamlet, 1998; Hon D Litt, Warwick University, 2000; Best Actor, Evening Standard Drama Award, 2001. Address: c/o ICM, Oxford House, 76 Oxford Street, London W1N 0AX, England.

JENNINGS Marie Patricia, b. 25 December 1930, Quetta, India. Author; Consumer Affairs Consultant. m. Walter Hayman, 1 son. Education: Presentation Convent College, Strinagar, Kashmir. Appointments: Managing Director, The Roy Bernand Co Ltd, 1960-65; Special Adviser, Stanley Tools, 1961-89, The Unit Trust Association, 1976-90, The Midland Bank, now HSBC, 1978-2004; Director, Lexington Ltd, 1971-75, The PR Consultants Association, 1979-84, Cadogan Management Ltd, 1984-90; Patron and Former President, National Association of Womens Clubs, 1998-; Member, Council and Deputy Chairman, Insurance Ombudsman Bureau, 1986-2001; Member, Council of Financial International Managers and Brokers Regulatory Association, 1986-98; Executive Committee Member, Wider Share Ownership Council, 1987-91; Consumer Panel, Personal Investment Authority, PIA, Chairman, National Federation of Consumer Groups, 1998-2000; Chairman, President and Founder, Consumer Policy Institute, 2000-04; Consultant Editor, Finance, Good Housekeeping Magazine, 1992-2000; Founder and President, The Money Management Council, 1984-2004; Member, FSA Consumer Education Forum, 1998-2004. Publications: Many books including: Women and Money; Ten Steps to the Top; Guide to Good Corporate Citizenship; Perfect Insurance; National TV series: Moneyspinner, C4; Money Go Round, LWT; Translations; Articles for newspapers. Honours: MBE. Memberships: Institute of Directors; RAC Honorary Member, Public Relations Consultants Association; Institute of Public Relations; National Union of Journalists. Address: Cadogan Grange, Calfway Lane, Bisley, Stroud, Gloucestershire, GL6 7AT, England. E-mail: MLocke1162@aol.com

JENSEN Arthur S, b. 24 December 1917, Trenton, New Jersey, USA. Engineering Physicist. m. Lillian Elizabeth Reed, 2 sons, 1 daughter. Education: BS, Physics, 1938, MS, Physics, 1939, PhD, Physics, 1941, University of Pennsylvania; Diploma of Advanced Engineering, 1972, Computer Science, 1977, Westinghouse School of Applied Science, Baltimore. Appointments: Teacher of Physics and Physics of Aviation, Department of Electrical Engineering, US Naval Academy, 1941-46; Research Physicist, RCA Laboratories, Princeton, NJ, 1946-57; Consulting Physicist, Westinghouse Defence and Space Centre, 1957-94. Publications: Novel, Persian Gulf Jeopardy, 2007; 25 patents; 60 articles in physics and engineering journals and conferences. Honours: Captain, US Navy, retired; Westinghouse Special Corporate Patent Award; American Defence Service Medal; American Campaign Medal; World War II Victory Medal; Naval Reserve Medal; Armed Forces Reserve Medal; Biographical listing in several Who's Who books; Maryland Governor's Citation; Engineers' Council of Maryland's Outstanding Service Award. Memberships: American Association for Advancement of Science; Fellow, Institute of Electrical and Electronic Engineers; American Physical Society; SPIE; Fellow, Washington Academy of Science; Maryland Academy of Science; New York Academy of Science; Life Member, Retired Officers' Association; National Eagle Scout Association; Vigil Honor, Order of the Arrow; Sigma Xi; American Association of Physics Teachers. Address: Chapel Gate 1104, Oak Crest Village, 8820 Walther Boulevard, Parkville, MD 21234-9022, USA.

JEON Hyeong-Seop, b. 26 April 1972, Seoul, Republic of Korea. Engineer; Researcher. m. Suk-Gyeong Sin, 1 son, 1 daughter. Education: BS, Computer Engineering, 2001, MS, Computer & Information Communication, 2003, Youngsan University; PhD, Information Communications Engineering, Chungnam National University, 2011. Appointments: Post-Doctor, Korea Atomic Energy Research Institute, Daejeon, Republic of Korea. Publications: Multi-Point Measurement of Structure Vibration using Pattern Recognition from Camera Image, 2010. Memberships: Korea Nuclear Society; Korea Society for Noise and Vibration Engineering. Address: 704-705 Banseok Maeul 7 Danji Apt, Banseok-dong, Yuseong-gu, Daejeon 305-750, Korea. E-mail: jhs200@yahoo.co.kr

JEON Insu, b. 5 March 1968, Busan, Republic of Korea. Assistant Professor. m. Hyeonjeong Lee, 1 son, 1 daughter. Education: BS, Mechanical Design Engineering, Pusan National University, 1993; MS, 1995, PhD, 2000, Mechanical Engineering, KAIST. Appointments: Member of Technical Staff, PKG & Module R&D, HYNIX, Korea, 2000-03; Postdoctoral Researcher, Tokyo Institute of Technology, Japan, 2003-04; Research Scientist, AIST, Nagoya, Japan, 2004-06; Assistant Professor, 2006-10, Associate Professor, 2010-, School of Mechanical Systems Engineering, Chonnam National University. Publications: 20 articles in professional journals. Honours: Best Thesis Award, Department of Mechanical Engineering, KAIST, 2001; Yoo-Dam Award, KSME, 2005. Memberships: KSME, Reliability Engineering Division. Address: School of Mechanical Engineering, Chonnam National University, 300 Yongbong-dong, Buk-gu, Gwangju, 500-757, Republic of Korea. E-mail: i_jeon@chonnam.ac.kr Website: http://altair.chonnam.ac.kr/~i_jeon

JEON Joong-Kyun, b. 26 March 1955, Seoul, Republic of Korea. Professor. m. Jeehee, 2 son. Education: Bachelor, 1980, Master, 1982, Pukyong National University, Korea; PhD, University of Tokyo, Japan, 1986. Appointments: Principal Researcher, Korea Ocean Research & Development Institute, 1986-96; Professor, Gangneung-Wonju National University, 1996-. Publications: Studies on Paralytic Toxins in Several Marine Invertebrates, 1986; Changes in activity of hepatic xenobiotic-metalbolising enzymes in tiger puffer exposed to PSP toxins, 2008; Accumulation of tributyltin and triphenyltin compounds in laboratory exposure and their induction of imposex in rock shell, 2009; Plasma Protein Binding of Tetrodotoxin in the Marine Puffer Fish, 2010. Memberships: International Society of Toxinology; Society of Environmental Toxicology and Chemistry; Korean Society of Fisheries and Aquatic Science; Korean Society of Oceanography. Address: 301-803 Sindo-Branew, Songjeong, Gangneung, Gangwon 210-140, Republic of Korea. E-mail: jkjeon@gwnu.ac.kr

JEONG Chanyong, b. 3 December 1974, Seoul, Korea. Engineer. m. Rokkyung Hwang, 2 sons. Education: BS, Electrical Engineering, Dankook University, Seoul; MS, Electronics Engineering, Ajou University, Suwon; PhD, Electrical and Electronic Engineering, Korea University, Seoul. Appointments: Senior Engineer, Corporate R&D Institute, Samsung Electro-Mechanics Co Ltd, 1999-. Publications: Efficient discrete-time bandpass sigma-delta modulator and digital I/Q demodulator for multistandard wireless applications, 2008. Honours: Listed in international biographical dictionaries. Memberships: IEEE. Address: Corporate R&D Institute, Samsung Electro-Mechanics Co Ltd, 314 Maetan3-dong, Yeongtong-gu, Suwon, 443-743, Korea. E-mail: jeffjeong@samsung.com

JEONG Jin-Hwan, b. 3 March 1974, South Korea. Researcher. m. Eunah Kim. Education: PhD, Korea University, 2005. Appointments: Senior Research Staff, ETRI, 2005-. Publications: 15 international papers. Honours: Listed in international biographical dictionaries. Memberships: IEEE. Address: Jugong APT 203-1106, Daebang-dong, Dongjak-gu, Seoul, South Korea. E-mail: jhjeong.kr@gmail.com Website: http://jjhnote.blogspot.com

JEONG Myung Yung, b. 20 February 1920, Busan, South Korea. Engineer. m. Jin Hyung, 1 son, 2 daughters. Edcuation: BS, 1982, MS, 1984, Mechanical Engineering, Pusan National University; PhD, Mechanical Engineering, Korea Advanced Institute of Science & Technology, 2000. Appointments: Principal Researcher, Basic Research Laboratory, Electronics and Telecommunications Research Institute, 1983-2003; Associate Professor, Department of Cogno-Mechatronics Engineering, Pusan National University, 2003-. Publications: Over 100 papers in professional journals. Honours: Best Research Team Prize, ETRI, 2002; Best Researcher Prize, Nanoscience Technology College, Pusan national University, 2008 & 2010; Listed in biographical dictionaries. Address: Department of Cogno-Mechatronics Engineering, College of Nanoscience & Nanotechnology, Pusan National University, Busan, 627-706, South Korea. E-mail: myjeong@pusan.ac.kr

JEONG Seulki, b. 24 May 1968, Younggwang, South Korea. Hemorheology; Neurology. m. Jin, 3 sons. Education: PhD, Medical Science, Chonnam National University Medical School, Gwangju, 2004. Appointments: Associate Professor, Department of Neurology, Chonbuk National University Medical School & Hospital, 2009-. Publications: 28 scientific publications; 18 domestic articles. Honours: Young Researcher, Korean Stroke Society, 2006; Best Poster Award, Neurosonology and Stroke, 2006; Listed in international biographical dictionaries. Memberships: Korean Neurological Association; American Heart Association; American Stroke Association; World Stroke Organization. Address: Department of Neurology, Chonbuk National University Medical School & Hospital, 634-18 Geumam-dong, Deokjin-gu, Jeonju, Jeonbuk, 561-712, South Korea. E-mail: jeongsk@jbnu.ac.kr

JEONG Soon-Taek, b. 3 December 1960, Cheongju, Korea. Doctor; Professor. m. Hea-Ju Lee, 2 sons. Education: Premedical College, 1979-81, College of Medicine, 1981-85, Master's degree, Medicine, 1989, PhD, Medicine, Graduate School, 2000, Kyung-Pook National University; Intern, 1985-86, Resident, 1986-90, Kyung-Pook National University Hospital; Fellowship, Spine Surgery, Seoul National University Hospital, 1993-94. Appointments: Staff Surgeon, Department of Orthopaedic Surgery, Red Cross Hospital, Daegu, 1994-95; Staff Surgeon, 1995-97, 1997-2001, Chief Surgeon, 2001-07, 2007-, Spine Section, Gyeong-Sang National University Hospital; Senior Lecturer, 1995-97, Assistant Professor, 1997-2001, Associate Professor, 2001-07, Professor, 2007-, Department of Orthopaedic Surgery, School of Medicine, Gyeong-Sang National University; Research Fellow, Department of Orthopaedic Surgery, Okayama University Medical School, Japan, 1997; Research Fellow, Department of Orthopaedic Surgery, School of Medicine, Kanazawa University, Japan, 1997; Travelling Fellow, Korean Orthopaedic Association, Twin City Spine Center, Minnesota and Rush Medical Center, Chicago, USA, 1998; Visiting Professor and Research Fellow, Department of Orthopaedic Surgery, Rush Prebyterian St Luke's Medical Center and Rush University, Chicago, 2000-01. Publications: Numerous articles in professional journals. Memberships: Korean Orthopaedic Association; Korean Society of Spine Surgery; Korean Society of Fracture and Trauma; Korean Society of Orthopaedic Research; Korean Medical Association; Scoliosis Research Society; Pacific Asian Society of Minimally Invasive Spine Surgery. Address: Department of Orthopaedic Surgery, School of Medicine, Gyeong-Sang National University, 90 Chilam-dong, Jinju, 660-702, Republic of Korea. E-mail: ssurgeon@gsnu.ac.kr

JEREZ Magali R, b. Cuba. Administrator, Educator. Education: BA, Romance languages, University of Puerto Rico, Rio Piedras, Puerto Rico, USA, 1968; MA, Education/Counseling, Montclair State University, Upper Montclair, New Jersey, USA, 1977; ABD (Doctor of Education), Administration of Higher Education/Linguistics, Seton

Hall University, South Orange, New Jersey, USA, 2005; PhD summa cum laude, Educational Leadership, Belford University, Colbert, Georgia, USA, 2011. Appointments: Various clerical positions, 1964-75; Program Co-ordinator, Equal Opportunity Employment Officer, Bergen County Industry Council, Hackensack, New Jersey, 1975-83; Editor, Amanecer Publications, National Spanish Magazine, Union City, New Jersey, 1983-85; Research Co-ordinator, National Study in Language Assessment, Newark, New Jersey, US Department of Education, Pelavin Associates, Washington, DC, 1985-86; Reviewer, Evaluator, Videos on International Curricula, Rutgers, The State University, 1986; Adjunct Instructor of Spanish and English as a Second Language, Seton Hall University, South Orange, New Jersey, 1986-87; Full Professor of Spanish 1987-, Chair of the Department of World Languages and Cultures 2007-, Bergen Community College, Paramus, New Jersey, USA. Publications: Expertise and research in Spanish Language; Member of various committees, Bergen Community College; Local Committee Member, 1988-2010, Workshop Evaluator 1989-2009, Coordinator of Broadway Ticket Discount Program 2004-2006, Northeast Conference for the Teaching of Foreign Languages; Elementary Spanish I, 1990, 1991 and 1992; Español Primer Nivel, 1992 and 1994; Español Segundo Nivel, 1992, 1995 and 1997; Book review, Spanish for Spanish Speakers, 1993; Spanish Language Music Consultant, Roman Catholic Archdiocese of Newark, New Jersey, 1994-2005; Co-Author, Spanish Textbooks and Workbooks including Empecemos, first edition, 1995 and fifth edition, 2010; Reviewer, Civilización y Cultura, 2000; Coordinator, Broadway Ticket Discount Program, McGraw Hill Symposium on College Level Spanish Materials, New York, 2010; Numerous others. Honors: Doctoral Fellow, United States Department of Education, Office of Bilingual Educational and Minority Affairs, Seton Hall University, 1985-87; Latino Heritage Committee, 2008; President's Recognition Award, Bergen Community College, 2009; Woman of the Year in Education, American Biographical Institute, 2011; Award of Excellence in Educational Leadership, Belford University, 2011; Listed in numerous biographical reference books. Memberships: American Association of University Women; American Council on the Teaching of Foreign Languages; Foreign Language Educators of New Jersey; Foreign Language Educators of New Jersey; National Association of Cuban-American Educators; Jew Jersey Collegiate Consortium for International/ Intercultural education; Northeast Association of Two-Year Colleges; Cuban Cultural Center of New York; Garden State Immigration History Consortium; Instituto de Liturgia Hispana; Kappa Delta Pi Honor Society; National Association of Pastoral Musicians; Phi Delta Kappa Honor Society. Address: 316 Eighth Street, Union City, New Jersey 07087, USA. E-mail: magalirjerez@aol.com

JERVIS Simon Swynfen, b. 9 January 1943, Yoxford, Suffolk, England. Art Historian. m. Fionnuala MacMahon, 1 son, 1 daughter. Education: Corpus Christi College, Cambridge, 1961-64. Appointments: Student Assistant, Assistant Keeper of Art, Leicester Museum and Art Gallery, 1964-66; Assistant Keeper, 1966-75, Deputy Keeper, 1975-89, Acting Keeper, 1989, Curator, 1989-90, Department of Furniture, Victoria and Albert Museum; Director and Marlay Curator, Fitzwilliam Museum, Cambridge, 1990-95; Director of Historic Buildings, The National Trust, 1995-2002. Publications: 7 books on furniture and design; Many articles in learned journals. Memberships: Member, 1964-, Arts Panel, 1982-95, Chairman, 1987-95, Properties Committee, 1987-95, National Trust; Member, 1966-, Council, 1977-79, 1981-83, 1986-87, Editor, 1988-92, Chairman, 1999-, Furniture History Society; Member, 1968-, Stafford Terrace Committee, 1980-90, Victorian Society; Member, Southwark Diocesan Advisory Committee, 1978-87; Member, 1982-, Council, 1987-1991, Royal Archaeological Institute; Elected Fellow, 1983, Council, 1986-88, Executive Committee, 1987-92, House Working Party, 1988-, President, 1995-2001, Kelmscott Committee, 2001-, Society of Antiquaries of London; Director, 1993-, Trustee, 1996-, The Burlington Magazine; Member, 1988-, Council, 1990-95, Chair, 2004-, Walpole Society; Guest Scholar, The J Paul Getty Museum, 1988-89, 2003; Member, Museums and Galleries Commission, Acceptance in Lieu Panel, 1992-2000; Trustee, The Royal Collection Trust, 1993-2001; Trustee, 1998-2002, Life Trustee, 2002-, Sir John Soane's Museum; Member, Advisory Council, National Art Collections Fund, 2002-; Iris Foundation Award for Outstanding Contributions to the Decorative Arts, 2002. Address: 45 Bedford Gardens, London W8 7EF, England.

JESS Digby Charles, b. 14 November 1953, Plymouth, England. Barrister; Chartered Arbitrator. m. Bridie, 1 son, 1 daughter. Education: BSc Honours, Aston University, 1976; Called to the Bar, 1978; LLM, 1986, PhD, 1999, University of Manchester; FCIArb, 1992; Chartered Arbitrator, 1999. Appointments: Barrister, Private Practice specialising in insurance claims and building disputes, 1978-; Treasury Counsel (Northern Region), 1992-2003; Legal Assessor, General Medical Council, Fitness to Practice Panels, 2002-; Member, Association of Chartered Certified Accountants' Disciplinary and Licensing Committees, 2002-; Chairman CIArb North West Branch, 1992-93; Chairman, BIIBA Liability Society (NW), 1995-99; President, Manchester Liability Society, 2006-08; Sometime Part-time Lecturer in Law, University of Manchester; Legal Adviser, General Dental Council Fitness to Practise Committee, 2010-. Publications: The Insurance of Commercial Risks: Law and Practice, 1986, 3rd edition 2001; The Insurance of Professional Negligence Risks: Law and Practice, 1982, 2nd edition, 1989; Professional Indemnity Insurance Law (co-author with Enright), 2nd Edition, 2007; The Insurance of Commercial Risks: Law & Practice, 2011. Honours: Winner, British Insurance Law Association Book Prize, 2008. Memberships: Northern Circuit Commercial Bar Association; Technology and Construction Court Bar Association; Manchester Liability Society. Address: Exchange Chambers, 7 Ralli Courts, West Riverside, Manchester M3 5FT, England. E-mail: jess@exchangechambers.co.uk

JESTY Ronald Cyril Benjamin, b. 7 May 1926, Weymouth, Dorset, England. Graphic Designer; Artist. m. Margaret Ellen Johnson. Appointments: Apprentice Draughtsman, Vickers Armstrong, 1941-45; Freelance Graphic Designer, 1947-78; Artist (watercolours), 1978-; Part-time Art Teacher, 1978-2002. Publications: Learn To Paint Seascapes, 1996; Various articles in Leisure Painter Magazine and International Artist Magazine; Contributor to several books on art and painting. Membership: Royal Society of British Artists, 1982-92. Address: 11 Pegasus Court, South Street, Yeovil, Somerset, BA20 1ND, England.

JHAVER Bharat, b. 27 November 1977, Mumbai, India. Industrialist. 1 son. Education: B Tech, Chemical Engineering, Madras University; M Engineering, Chemical Engineering, Cornell University, Ithaca, New York, USA. Appointments: Executive Vice President, Strategic Alliances and Communication, Tablets India Ltd. Publications: Revolution of Probiotic Market in India through cross border collaboration in this field; Concept of 'Co-Marketing' established in India; Established high quality Probiotic Production facility. Honours: Award, Indian Pharma Association Convention, 2010. Memberships: Young President Organization (son); Young Indians; Round Table India; Indian Pharmaceutical Alliance. Address: Tablets India Ltd, Jhaver Centre, 72 Marshalls Road, Chennai 600 008, India. E-mail: bj@tabletsindia.com

JI Ho Seong, b. 20 April 1960, Busan, South Korea. Research Professor. Education: BA, 1986, PhD, 2001, Mechanical Engineering, Pusan National University; MA, Mechanical Engineering, Anjou University, 1993. Appointments: Postdoctoral Researcher, Tokyo University, 2004-05; Senior Researcher, POSTECH, 2005-08; Research Professor, Pusan National University, 2008-. Publications: 17 SCI-E Journal; 15 domestic journals; 22 international conferences; 32 domestic conferences; 4 patents. Honours: Outstanding Paper Award, CSC2, 2001; Best Paper Award, KSME Spring Conference, 2008. Memberships: European Society on Biomechanics; International Society on Biomechanics. Address: School of Mechanical Engineering, Pusan National University, Som 31, Jang Jeon 2-Dong, Geum Jeong Gu, Busan 609-735, South Korea. E-mail: hsji@pusan.ac.kr

JIMBOW Kowichi, b. 4 June 1941, Nagoya, Japan. Physician; Dermatologist; Professor. m. Mihoko Jimbow, 1 son, 4 daughters. Education: MD, Sapporo Medical College, Sapporo, Japan, 1966; PhD, Sapporo Medical College Graduate School, Sapporo, Japan, 1974. Appointments: Professor and Chair, Department of Dermatology, Sapporo Medical University, School of Medicine, 1995-; Chief, Division of Dermatology, Division of Plastic Surgery (Adjunct), Sapporo Medical University Hospital, 1995-; Adjunct Professor, Department of Medicine, Dermatology and Cutaneous Sciences, University of Alberta, Edmonton, Canada, 1996-; Dean, 2000, Professor Emeritus, Sapporo Medical University, Graduate School of Medicine; President, Institute of Dermatology & Cutaneous Sciences. Publications: Over 300 original articles; More than 60 miscellaneous publications; 76 books; 63 review articles. Honours include: Alfred Marchionini Prize, International Association of Dermatology, 1982; Seiji Memorial Award, Japanese Society of Dermatology, 1984; Alberta Heritage Medical Scientist Award, Canada, 1988, 1993; Henry Stanley Raper Award, European Society of Pigment Cell; Hokkaido Physician Award, Japan, 2001; Hokkaido Science and Technology Award, Japan, 2002; Myron Gordon Prize, 2008. Memberships: Alberta Medical Association; American Academy of Dermatology; American Association for Cancer Research; American Society for Cell Biology; American Society of Photobiology; Canadian Dermatological Association; Canadian Society for Clinical Investigation; Canadian Society for Investigative Dermatology; International Society of Pigment Cell Research; Society for Investigative Dermatology; Japanese Dermatological Association. Address: Sapporo Medical Care Bldg 4F, 1-27, Odori W17, Chuo-ku, Sapporo, Hokkaido, 060-0042, Japan. E-mail: jimbow@sapmed.ac.jp

JIMENEZ MOTTE Fernando, b. 7 May 1964, Lima, Peru. Director. Education: Electrical Engineer with PhD course work in Electrical Engineering and Master's Degree. Appointments: Telefonica SA, 2001-08; Director, Electrical Engineering and Telecommunications and Networks Career, Peruvian University of Applied Sciences UPC Laureate International Universities, 2008-11. Publications: Linear Quadratic Gaussian Design, 1993; Technology Writer, Business Technology Section IT/Users magazine, 2008; Book, Perú y America Latina en la Era Digital, 2008. Honours: Members, Department of Electronics Consulting Committee, 2006-08; Listed in biographical dictionaries. Memberships: Microsoft Research Faculty Summit, Brazil; Gerson Lehrman Group, Society of Industry Leaders Vista Research International Neural Network Society, USA. Address: Conde de la Monclova 378, Dpto 701, El Golf, San Isidro, Peru.

JIN Jae Won, b. 8 September 1973, Republic of Korea. Doctor. m. Jung Min Ahn, 1 daughter. Education: Medical Doctor, 2004. Appointments: Director, COBICO Otorhinolaryngologic Clinics. Publications: Tuberculous otitis media developing as a complication of typmanostomy tube insertion. Address: Cobico ENT Clinic, 2F 317-3 Byeongbang dong, Gyeyang gu, Incheon, Republic of Korea. E-mail: cafeer73@gmail.com

JIRA Reinhard, b. 11 April 1929, Cham, Germany. Chemist. m. Waltraut Riebl, 2 sons. Education: Chemistry, Technische Hochschule (now Technische Universitaet), Munich, 1948; Diploma, 1952; Dr rer nat (PhD), Walter Hieber and E O Fischer, 1955. Appointments: Research Chemist, Consortium fuer elektrochemische Industrie, Wacker-Chemie GmbH, 1955; Co-inventor of the Wacker process (oxidation of olefins to carbonyl compounds), 1956; Development of commercial process for the manufacture of acetaldehyde from ethylene, 1957-60; Research co-ordinator; Research Manager and Manager of Chemistry, Burghausen Factory, 1979; Abteilungsdirector, 1990; Retired, 1993. Publications: Numerous articles in professional journals. Honours: Prix de Cinquantenaire de la Société de Chemie Industrielle. Address: Kabastastrasse 9, DE 81243 Muenchen, Germany. E-mail: rw.jira@t-online.de

JIRAVA Emil, b. 26 April 1930, Praha, Czech Republic. Stomatologist; Maxillofacial Surgeon. 1 son, 1 daughter. Education: MUDr, Medical Faculty, Prague, 1953; DrSc, Charles University, Prague, 1981. Appointments: Assistant Professor, 1968-81, Professor, 1981-, Medical Faculty, Olomouc; Visiting Lecturer, Health Science University, Portland, Oregon, USA, 1996-; Maxillofacial Surgeon. Publications: Fractures of orbita and reconstruction of the orbital base; Fractures of the lower jar treatment; The phenomenon of latent pregnancy and cancer, 1989. Honours: National Award Czech Republic; Research Fellow, USA; Honorable Fellow J E Purkyne Medical Association, 1984; Plato Award, 2010; Listed in international biographical dictionaries. Memberships: Pierre Fauchard Academy, USA; ABI, USA; New York Academy of Sciences, 1994; Czech Medical Association. Address: Eranburga 42, 77900 Olomouc, Czech Republic. E-mail: jirava@seznam.cz

JO Baik-Hyeon, b. 17 February 1962, Andong city, Kyeongbuk, Republic of Korea. Breast Surgeon. m. Eun-Ah Yi, 1 son, 1 daughter. Education: College of Medicine, 1987, PhD, 2004, Resident, 1988-92, Department of General Surgery, Pil-Dong Hospital, Chung-Ang University, Seoul. Appointments: Chief of Staff, Department of General Surgery, Moon-Kyeong Hospital, Korea, 1992-95; Chief of Staff, Department of General Surgery, Je-Cheon Hyundai Hospital, Korea, 1995-97; Chairman, Je-Cheon Chung-Ang Anorectal Clinic, Korea, 1997-2001; Visiting Scientist, Department of Colorectal Surgery, Cleveland Clinic Florida, USA, 2001; Staff, 2003, Chief of Staff, 2007-, Department of General Surgery, Director, MizMedi Breast Center, 2005-07, MizMedi Hospital, Seoul; Visiting Scientist, Johns Hopkins Breast Center, Johns Hopkins Hospital, Baltimore, USA, 2004. Publications: Numerous articles in professional journals;

Book, Life Remodeling to Conquer Cancer, 2010. Honours: Dong-A Academic Award, Korean Breast Cancer Society, 2007; Listed in international biographical dictionaries. Memberships: The Korean Surgical Society; Korean Breast Cancer Society. Address: The Breast Center, MizMedi Hospital, 701-4 Naebalsan-dong, Kangseo-ku, Seoul, 157-280, Korea. E-mail: drjo514@yahoo.co.kr

JO Dae-Jean, b. 20 April 1971, Seoul, Republic of Korea. Neurosurgeon; Medical Educator. Education: MD, 1992-97, PhD, 2009, Kyung Hee University. Appointments: Assistant Professor, Spine Centre, Kyung Hee University Hospital at Gang-dong, 2010-. Publications: 18 articles in professional journals. Honours: Listed in international biographical dictionaries. Address: Kyung Hee University Hospital at Gang-dong, Department of Neurosurgery, Spine Centre, 149 Sangil-Dong, Gandong-Gu, Seoul 134-727, Republic of Korea. E-mail: apuzzo@hanmail.cnet

JO Jong Chull, b. 9 September 1955, Kyungnam-do, Republic of Korea. Research Scientist. m. Yeong-Kyeong Kim, 1 son, 1 daughter. Education: BS, 1979, MS, 1981, PhD, 1985, Mechanical Engineering, Hanyang University, Seoul. Appointments: Teaching and Research Assistant, 1979-81, Lecturer, 1985-86, Department of Mechanical Engineering, Hanyang University, Seoul; Assistant Professor of Mechanical Engineering, Induk Institute of Technology, Seoul, 1981-86; Senior Researcher, 1986-92, Principal Researcher, 1993-, Nuclear Safety Review and Inspection Department, Project Manager, Development of Integral-Type Reactor Regulatory Technology, 2002-, Chair, Safety Issue Research Department, 2005-, Korea Institute of Nuclear Safety; Visiting Scientist, Division of Nuclear Technology, TUEV Hannover eV, Germany, 1987-88; Visiting Scientist, Office of Nuclear Reactor Regulation, US Nuclear Regulatory Commission, 1995-96; Lecturer, Mechanical Engineering, Graduate School of Jeonju University, Jeonju, 2003-05; Member, National R&D Projects Evaluation Committee, 2007; Technical Consultant, OECD Nuclear Energy Agency, 2008-. Publications: Over 130 papers in professional scientific journals. Honours: Korean Prime Ministerial Citation, 1994; Korean Presidential Citation, 2004; Certificate of Recognition, 2005; Tenure Evaluation of an Associate Professor of Engineering Science and Mechanics, Penn State University, 2006; Outstanding Technical Paper Award, Korean Nuclear Society, 2006; Invited contributor, 3rd Edition of Companion Guide for ASME B&PV Codes, American Society of Mechanical Engineers, 2007; Invited author, Topic 'Fluid-Structure Interaction' for Pressure Vessels and Piping Systems, The Encyclopaedia of Life Support Systems, UNESCO, 2007-08; ASME Fellow, 2010; Listed in international biographical directories. Memberships: Korea Foundation of Science and Technology; American Society of Mechanical Engineers; Korean Society of Pressure Vessels and Piping; Korean Nuclear Society; Korean Society of Mechanical Engineers; and others. Address: Korea Institute of Nuclear Safety, 19 Kusung-dong, Yusung-gu, Taejeon (Daejeon) 305-338, Korea. E-mail: jcjo@kins.re.kr

JO Qtae, b. 12 December 1960, Busan, Korea. Research Scientist. m. Sung Hye Joo, 1 son, 1 daughter. Education: BA, 1986, MA, 1989, Marine Biology, National Fisheries University of Pusan; PhD, Molecular Biology, Pusan National University, Busan, 1998. Appointments: Research Scientist, National Fisheries Research and Development Institute, 1989-. Publications: 41 articles on shellfish physiology and aquaculture in domestic and international journals; Korean Aquaculture in General; Shellfish Aquaculture; Shellfish Aquaculture in the Ecosystem Integrity; Protocol for Hatchery Production of Shellfish. Honours: Outstanding Researcher Awards, Ministry for Food, Agriculture, Forest and Fisheries, 2004, 2009. Memberships: Korean Society of Fisheries Sciences; Journal of Environmental Biology. Address: National Fisheries Research and Development Institute, Haean-ro 216, Gijang, Busan 619-705, Korea. E-mail: qtjo@nfrdi.go.kr

JOEL Billy (William Martin Joel), b. 9 May 1949, Bronx, New York, USA. Musician (piano); Singer; Songwriter. m. (1) Elizabeth Small, 1973, divorced, 1982; (2) Christie Brinkley, 23 Mar 1989, divorced 1994, 1 daughter; (3) Katie Lee, 2004. Education: LHD (hon), Fairfield Univesity, 1991; HMD (hon), Berklee College Music, 1993. Career: Popular solo recording artist, 1972-. Compositions include: Just The Way You Are, 1978; Honesty, 1979; We Didn't Start The Fire, 1989; The River Of Dreams, 1994. Albums include: Turnstiles; Streetlife Serenade; The Stranger, 1978; 52nd Street, 1978; Glass Houses, 1980; Songs In The Attic, 1981; Nylon Curtain, 1982; An Innocent Man, 1983; Cold Spring Harbour, 1984; Piano Man, 1984; Greatest Hits, Volumes I & II, 1985; The Bridge, 1986; KOHUEPT-Live In Leningrad, 1987; Storm Front, 1989; River Of Dreams, 1994; Greatest Hits, 1997. Publications: Goodnight My Angel: A Lullabye, 2004. Honours: 6 Grammy Awards include: Record of Year, Song of Year, Best Male Vocal Performance, 1978; Best Album, 1979; 10 Grammy Nominations include: Best Song, Record, Producer, Male Vocal Performance of Year; American Music Award, Best Album, 1980; Grammy Legend Award, 1990; Inducted into Songwriters Hall of Fame, 1992; ASCAP Founders Award, 1997; Honorary DHL, Hofstra University, 1997. Address: c/o Maritime Music Inc., 200 West 57th Street, Suite 308, New York, NY 10019, USA.

JOFFE Joel Goodman (Lord Joffe), b. 12 May 1932. Human Rights Lawyer; Businessman; Chairman and Trustee of Charities; National Health Services Chairman. m. Vanetta Joffe, 3 daughters. Education: B Com LLB, Witwatersrand University, Johannesburg. Appointments: Solicitor, then Barrister, Johannesburg, 1952-65; Secretary and Administrative Director, Abbey Life Assurance, London, 1965-70; Founder Director, Joint Managing Director, Deputy Chairman, Allied Dunbar Assurance, 1971-91; Founding Trustee, Chairman, Allied Dunbar Charitable Trust, 1974-93; Chairman, Thamesdown Voluntary Services Council, 1974-1980; Trustee, Honorary Secretary, Chairman of the Executive Committee, Chair, Oxfam, 1979-2001; Chairman, Swindon Private Hospital plc, 1982-87; Council Member, IMPACT, 1984-; Chairman, Swindon Health Authority, 1988-93; Campaigner to protect consumers from the excesses of the Financial Services Industry, 1992-97; Chairman, Swindon and Marlborough National Health Trust, 1993-95; Special Adviser to South African Minister of Transport, 1997-98; Chair of The Giving Campaign, 2000-04; Trustee, J G and V L Joffe Charitable Trust. Memberships: Member, Royal Commission for the Care of the Elderly, 1997-99; Member, Home Officer Working Group on the Active Community, 1998-99. Address: Liddington Manor, Liddington, Swindon, Wiltshire SN4 0HD, England.

JOHANSSON Anita Christin, b. 12 November 1940, Kiruna, Sweden. Artist. m. B W Johansson, 1 daughter. Career: Paintings characterised by bold colours, billowing lines and variations in style and technique to create a feeling of freedom. Exhibitions in Sweden, Norway, Spain, Switzerland, Japan, USA: The Swedish Place, Half Moon Bay, California, 1990; Swedish American Museum, Chicago, 1991; Galleri Smedjan vid

Skabersjöslott, 1992, 1996; Galleri Valvet, Malmö, 1993, 1996, 1997, 2000; Galleri Salong Strandvägen, Stockholm, 1993; Tokyo Geijutsu Gekijyo 5F Gallery, Japan, 1994; Europ'Art, Geneva, 1997; Galleri Belsola, Rheinfelden, Switzerland, 1997; Nordic Art Fair, Sundsvall, 1997; Konsthallen Bryggeriet, Trelleborg, 1997; Delaware River Gallery, Yardley, Pennsylvania, 1998; Galleri Svarta Soffan, Stockholm, 1998; International Contemporary Art: Private Gallery, Möhlin-Riburg, Switzerland, 1998; Galleri Hamnen, Viken, 1999; Kullander & Kullander, Malmö, 1999; International Contemporary Art: Show-Room Belvedere, St Moritz, 1999; Galerie Rote Rose, Regensberg-Zurich, 1999; Kiruna Folkets Hus I samband med Kiruna Stads 100-årsjubileum, 2000; Galleri Belsola, Rheinfelden, Switzerland, 2000; LKAB: Kiruna-Narvik, Malmberget –Luleå, 2000; Kultur Huset, Kautokeino, Norway, 2001; Galleri Stand 4, Girona, Spain, 2002; Njut!, 2005; Chokladfabriken, Malmö, 2005. Address: Knutstorpsgatan 23, 216 22 Malmö, Sweden.

JOHANSSON Scarlett, b. 22 November 1984, New York City, USA. Actor; Singer. m. Ryan Reynolds, 2008, divorced 2011. Education: Professional Children's School, Manhattan, 2002. Career: Films: North, 1994; Just Cause, 1995; Manny & Lo, 1996; If Lucy Fell, 1996; Home Alone 3, 1997; The Horse Whisperer, 1998; My Brother the Pig, 1999; The Man Who Wasn't There, 2001; Ghost World, 2001; An American Rhapsody, 2001; Eight Legged Freaks, 2002; Lost in Translation, 2003; Girl with a Pearl Earring, 2003; A Love Song for Bobby Long, 2004; A Good Woman, 2004; The SpongeBob SquarePants Movie, 2004; The Perfect Score, 2004; In Good Company, 2004; The Island, 2005; Match Point, 2005; Scoop, 2006; The Black Dahlia, 2006; The Prestige, 2006; The Nanny Diaries, 2007; The Other Boleyn Girl, 2008; Vicky Cristina Barcelona, 2008; The Spirit, 2008; He's Just Not That Into You, 2009; Iron Man 2, 2010; We Bought a Zoo, 2011; The Avengers, 2012. Album: Anywhere I Lay My Head, 2008; Break Up, 2009. Honours: Best Actress in a Leading Role, BAFTA, 2003; Tony Award for Best Performance by a Featured Actress in a Play, 2010. Address: c/o United Talent Agency, 9560 Wilshire Boulevard, Floor 5, Beverly Hills, CA 90212-2400, USA.

JOHN Elton (Sir) (Reginald Kenneth Dwight), b. 25 March 1947, Pinner, Middlesex, England. Singer; Songwriter; Musician (piano). m. Renate Blauer, 1984, divorced 1988; partner, David Furnish, 2005, 2 sons. Musical Education: Piano lessons aged 4; Royal Academy of Music, 1958. Career: Member, Bluesology, 1961-67; Worked at Mills Music Publishers; Solo artiste, 1968-; Long-term writing partnership with Bernie Taupin, 1967-; Partnership wrote for Dick James Music; Founder, Rocket Records, 1973; Own publishing company, Big Pig Music, 1974; Performances include: Wembley Stadium, 1975; First Western star to perform in Israel and USSR, 1979; Live Aid, Wembley, 1985; Wham's farewell concert, Wembley, 1985; Prince's Trust concerts, London, 1986, 1988; Farm Aid IV, 1990; AIDS Project Los Angeles - Commitment To Life VI, 1992; Chair, The Old Vic Theatre Trust, 2002-; Concert for Diana, 2007. Film appearance, Tommy, 1975. Recordings: Hit singles include: Your Song, 1971; Rocket Man, 1972; Crocodile Rock (Number 1, US), Daniel, Saturday Night's Alright For Fighting, Goodbye Yellow Brick Road, 1973; Candle In The Wind, Don't Let The Sun Go Down On Me, 1974 (live version with George Michael, Number 1, UK and US, 1991); Philadelphia Freedom, Lucy In The Sky With Diamonds (Number 1, US), Island Girl (Number 1, US), 1975; Pinball Wizard, from film Tommy, Don't Go Breaking My Heart, duet with Kiki Dee (Number 1, UK and US), Sorry Seems To Be The Hardest Word, 1976; Song For Guy, 1979; Blue Eyes, 1982; I Guess That's Why They Call It The Blues, I'm Still Standing, Kiss The Bride, 1983; Sad Songs (Say So Much), 1984; Nikita, 1986; Sacrifice (Number 1, UK), 1989; True Love (with Kiki Dee), 1993; Made In England, Blessed, Believe, 1995; You Can Make History, 1996; If The River Can Bend, 1998; Written in the Stars, 1999; I Want Love, This Train Don't Stop There Anymore, 2001; Are You Ready for Love, 2003; All That I'm Allowed (I'm Thankful), 2004; Contributor, That's What Friends Are For, Dionne Warwick And Friends (charity record), 1986; Albums include: Elton John, 1970; Tumbleweed Connection, Friends, 17-11-70, 1971; Madman Across The Water, Honky Chateau, 1972; Don't Shoot Me, I'm Only The Piano Player, Goodbye Yellow Brick Road, 1973; Caribou, 1974; Captain Fantastic And The Brown Dirt Cowboy, Rock Of The Westies, 1975; Here And There, Blue Moves, 1976; A Single Man, 1978; Lady Samantha, 21 At 33, 1980; Jump Up!, 1982; Too Low For Zero, 1983; Breaking Hearts, 1984; Ice On Fire, 1985; Leather Jackets, 1986; Live In Australia, 1987; Reg Strikes Back, 1988; Sleeping With The Past, 1989; The One, 1992; Made In England, Love Songs, 1995; Big Picture, 1997; Aida, 1999; El Dorado, 2000; Songs From the West Coast, 2001; Elton John – Greatest Hits, 1970-2002, 2002; Peachtree Road, 2004; Wrote music for stage musicals, The Lion King, 1994 and Billy Elliot, 2004. Honours include: First album to go straight to Number 1 in US charts, Captain Fantastic..., 1975; Numerous Ivor Novello Awards for: Daniel, 1974; Don't Go Breaking My Heart, 1977; Song For Guy, 1979; Nikita, 1986; Sacrifice, 1991; Outstanding Contribution To British Music, 1986; Star on Hollywood Walk Of Fame, 1975; Madison Square Gardens Honours: Hall Of Fame, 1977; Walk Of Fame (first non-athlete), 1992; American Music Awards: Favourite Male Artist, Favourite Single, 1977; Silver Clef Award, Nordoff-Robbins Music Therapy, 1979; BRIT Awards: Outstanding Contribution To British Music, 1986; Best British Male Artist, 1991; Grammy, Best Vocal Performance By A Group, 1987; MTV Special Recognition Trophy, 1987; Hitmaker Award, National Academy of Popular Music, 1989; Honorary Life President, Watford Football Club, 1989; Inducted into Songwriters Hall Of Fame (with Bernie Taupin), 1992; Q Magazine Merit Award, 1993; Officer of Arts And Letters, Paris, 1993; KBE, 1998; Dr hc Royal Academy of Music, 2002; Grammy Lifetime, Achievement Award, 2000; Kennedy Center Honors, 2004. Address: c/o Simon Prytherch, Elton Management, 7 King Street Cloisters, Clifton Walk, London, W6 0GY, England.

JOHN Ricky, b. 2 May 1957, Trinidad, West Indies. Education: BSc, Electrical Engineering, New Jersey Institute of Technology (NJIT), 1981; MSc, Management, NJIT, 1992; PhD, Engineering Management, Kennedy-Western University, 2000. Appointments: Flight Test Engineer for experimental test flights of US Space Shuttle Columbia, member, NASA Space Shuttle Launch Team, Kennedy Space Center, 1981-82; Systems Engineer, Airway Facilities Modernization Program, US Federal Aviation Administration (FAA), 1983-85, Selected to test one of world's first Weather Radar Display Systems, 1983; Program Administrator, New Jersey Department of Energy, 1985; Conceptual designer and installer: first multi-campus integrated computerized energy management system, New Jersey University of Medicine and Dentistry; Largest geothermal energy system of its kind, Stockton State College, New Jersey; Visiting Lecturer, John Donaldson Technical Institute in Port-of-Spain, Trinidad, 1982; Member, New Jersey Martin Luther King Commission Education Committee, 1987-90; Technical Advisor, New Jersey Board of Public Utilities, 1996-; Judge and presenter,

NASA Awards for annual North New Jersey Regional Science Fair for secondary students, 1993-. Honours: US Department of Energy Certificate of Recognition, 1995; IEEE Regional Award, 2008; IEEE Power & Energy Society Outstanding Engineer Award, 2009. Memberships: New Jersey Institute of Technology Alumni Association, Board of Trustees, 1991-, Energy Manager of New Jersey Association of Energy Engineers, 1994, Vice President for Public Relations, 1996-98; Institute of Electrical and Electronic Engineers; New Jersey Aviation Hall of Fame; Notary Public, State of New Jersey, 1988-; Board of Directors, New Jersey Inventors Hall of Fame, 2003-, Listed in various international biographical dictionaries. Address: 1 Rieder Road, Edison, NJ 08817, USA.

JOHNS David John, b. 29 April 1931, Bristol, England. Chartered Engineer. Education: BSc (Eng), Aero Engineering, 1950-53, MSc (Eng), 1959, University of Bristol; PhD, 1967, DSc, 1985, Loughborough University. Appointments: Apprentice up to Section Leader, Bristol Aeroplane Co Ltd, 1949-57; Technical Officer, Sir W G Armstrong Whitworth Aircraft Ltd, 1957-58; Lecturer, Cranfield College of Aeronautics, 1958-64; Reader, Professor, 1964-83, Head of Department of Transport Technology, 1972-82; Senior Pro-Vice-Chancellor, 1982-83, Loughborough University; Foundation Director, City Polytechnic of Hong Kong, 1983-89; Vice-Chancellor and Principal, University of Bradford, 1989-98; Chairman, Prescription Pricing Authority, 1998-2001; Chairman, North and East Yorkshire and Northern Lincolnshire Strategic Health Authority; Chairman, Genetics and Insurance Committee. Publications: Monograph, Thermal Stress Analyses; 126 Technical articles; 40 papers on education, training et al. Honours: British Association for the Advancement of Science Brunel Lecturership in Engineering; Commander of the Order of the British Empire (CBE). Memberships: Chartered Engineer, Engineering Council, 1964; Fellow, Royal Aeronautical Society, 1969; Fellow, Institute of Acoustics, 1977-85; Fellow, Chartered Institute of Transport, 1977-85; Fellow, Hong Kong Institution of Engineers, 1984; Life Fellow, Aeronautical Society of India, 1986; Fellow, Royal Academy of Engineering, 1990. Address: 8 Swan Court, York Road, Harrogate, North Yorkshire HG1 2QH, England. E-mail: david@johnshg1.fsnet.co.uk

JOHNSON (Alexander) Boris, b. 19 June 1964, New York, USA. Mayor of London. m. Marina Wheeler, 2 sons, 2 daughters. Education: Brakenbury Scholar, BA, Balliol College, Oxford. Appointments: Trainee Reporter, The Times, 1987; Reporter, Wolverhampton Express and Star, 1988; Leader Writer, 1988, European Community Correspondent, Brussels, 1989-94, Assistant Editor, 1994, The Daily Telegraph; Editor, The Spectator, 1999-2005; Member of Parliament, Conservative, Henley-on-Thames, 2001-; Shadow Minister for the Arts, April-November 2004; Shadow Minister for Higher Education, 2005-07; MP for Henley-on-Thames, 2001-08; Mayor of London, 2008-; Appearances on Radio and TV. Publications: Books: Friends, Voters and Countrymen, 2001; Lend Me your Ears, 2003; Seventy Two Virgins, 2004; The New British Revolution, 2005; Dream of Rome; Weekly column for the Daily Telegraph. Honours: Political Commentator of the Year, What the Papers Say, 1997; National Journalist of the Year, Pagan Federation of Great Britain, 1998; Editors' Editor of the Year, 2003; Columnist of the Year, British Press Awards, 2004; Channel 4 News Award for the person who made the biggest impression on the politics of 2004, 2005; Columnist of the Year, What the Papers Say, 2005. Address: Greater London Authority City Hall, The Queen's Walk, More London, London SE1 2AA, England.

JOHNSON Benjamin Sinclair Jr, b. 30 December 1961, Falmouth, Jamaica. Professional Athlete; Coach. Honours: Phil Edwards Memorial Outstanding Track Athlete, 1984, 1985, 1986, 1987; Inducted into the Canadian Amateur Hall of Fame, 1985; Olympic Champion Award, 1985; Morton Crowe Award for Male Athlete of the Year, 1985, 1986, 1987; CTFA Track Jack W Davies Outstanding Athlete of the Year, 1985, 1986, 1987; Athlete of the Month, October 1985, January 1986, August 1987, January 1988, Sports Federation of Canada; Sports Excellence Award, 1986; IAAF/Mobil Grand Prix Standings (Indoor), 1986; Lionel Connacher Award for Male Athlete of the Year, 1986, 1987; Jesse Owens International Trophy for Athletic Excellence, 1987; World Champion Award, 1987; The Tribute to Champions; Outstanding Athlete of the Year, 1986, 1987; Order of Canada, 1987; Disqualified for doping lost 1987-88 records. E-mail: benjohnson979@mail.com

JOHNSON Betsey Lee, b. 10 August 1942, Hartford, Connecticut, USA. Fashion Designer. m. (1) John Cale, 1966, 1 daughter, (2) Jeffrey Olivier, 1981. Education: Pratt Institute, New York; Syracuse University. Appointments: Editorial Assistant, Mademoiselle Magazine, 1964-65; Partner, Co-Owner, Betsey, Bunky & Nini, New York, 1969-; Shops in New York, Los Angeles, San Francisco, Coconut Grove, Florida, Venice, California, Boston, Chicago, Seattle; Principal Designer for Paraphernalia, 1965-69; Designer, Alvin Duskin Co, San Francisco, 1970; Head Designer, Alley Cat by Betsey Johnson (division of LeDamor Inc), 1970-74; Freelance Designer for Junior Women's Division, Butterick Pattern Co, 1971, Betsey Johnson for Jeanette Maternities Inc, 1974-75; Designer for Gant Shirtmakers Inc (women's clothing), 1974-75, Tric-Trac by Betsey Johnson (women's knitwear), 1974-76, Butterick's Home Sewing Catalog (children's wear), 1975-; Head Designer, Junior Sportswear Co; Designed for Star Ferry by Betsey Johnson & Michael Miles (children's wear), 1975-77; Owner, Head Designer, B J Inc, Designer, Wholesale Co, New York, 1978; President, Treasurer, B J Vines, New York; Opened Betsey Johnson Store, New York, 1979. Honours include: Merit Award, Mademoiselle Magazine, 1970; Coty Award, 1971; 2 Tommy Print Awards; Fashion Walk of Fame, 2002. Memberships: Council of Fashion Designers; American Women's Forum. Address: 110 East 9th Street, Suite A889, Los Angeles, CA 90079, USA.

JOHNSON Charles (Richard), b. 23 April 1948, Evanston, Illinois, USA. Professor of English; Writer. m. Joan New, 1970, 1 son, 1 daughter. Education: BA, 1971, MA, 1973, Southern Illinois University; Postgraduate Studies, State University of New York at Stony Brook, 1973-76. Appointments: Assistant Professor, 1976-79, Associate Professor, 1979-82, Professor of English, 1982-, University of Washington, Seattle. Publications: Faith and the Good Thing, 1974; Oxherding Tale, 1982; The Sorcerer's Apprentice: Tales and Conjurations, 1986; Being and Race: Black Writing Since 1970, 1988; Middle Passage, 1990; All This and Moonlight, 1990; In Search of a Voice (with Ron Chernow), 1991; Dreamer, 1998; Turning the Wheel, 2003. Honours: Governor's Award for Literature, State of Washington, 1983; National Book Award, 1990. Address: c/o Department of English, University of Washington, Seattle, WA 98105, USA.

JOHNSON Christopher Louis McIntosh, b. 12 June 1931, Thornton Heath, England. Economic Adviser. m. Anne Robbins, 1958, 1 son, 3 daughters. Education: MA 1st class honours, Philosophy, Politics and Economics, Magdalen College, Oxford. Appointments: Journalist, 1954-76, Paris Correspondent, 1959-63, The Times and Financial Times;

Diplomatic Correspondent, Foreign Editor, Managing Editor, Director, Financial Times, 1963-76; Chief Economic Adviser, 1977-91, General Manager, 1985-91, Lloyds Bank; Visiting Professor of Economics, Surrey University, 1986-90; Visiting Scholar, IMF, 1993; Specialist Adviser to the Treasury Select Committee, House of Commons, 1981-97; Chairman, British Section of the Franco-British Council, 1993-97; UK Adviser, Association for the Monetary Union of Europe, 1991-2002. Publications: Editor, Lloyds Bank Review and Lloyds Bank Economic Bulletin, 1985-91; 4 books; Newspaper articles; Lectures on the euro and other economic and financial topics. Honours: Chevalier de la Legion d'Honneur, 1996. Memberships: Member, National Commission on Education, 1991-92; Member, Council of the Britain in Europe Campaign for the Euro; Member, Council of the Institute for Fiscal Studies; Chairman, New London Orchestra, 2001-04. Address: 39 Wood Lane, London N6 5UD, England. E-mail: johnson.c@blueyonder.co.uk

JOHNSON Daniel Benedict, b. 26 August 1957, London, England. Journalist; Writer. m. Sarah Johnson, 2 sons, 2 daughters. Education: BA 1st class, Modern History, Magdalen College, Oxford, 1978; Research Student, Cambridge, 1978-81; Shakespeare Scholar, Berlin, 1979-80. Appointments: Teaching Assistant, German History, Queen Mary College, London, 1982-84; Director of Publications, Centre for Policy Studies, 1983-84; The Daily Telegraph: Leader Writer, 1986-87; Bonn Correspondent, 1987-89; Eastern Europe Correspondent, 1989-90; The Times: Leader Writer, 1990-91; Literary Editor, 1992-96; Assistant Editor, Comment, 1996-98; The Daily Telegraph, Associate Editor, Culture, 1998-; Reported, New York Sun. Publications: Contributions to: The New Yorker; New York Times; Wall Street Journal; Washington Post; Commentary; The National Interest; Civilisation; The Spectator; Times Literary Supplement; Literary Review; Prospect; Encounter; many other journals; Books: Co-editor, German Neo-Liberals and the Social Market Economy, 1989; Introduction, Thomas Mann: Death in Venice and Other Stories; Introduction, Collected Stories, 2001. Address: c/o The Daily Telegraph, 1 Canada Square, Canary Wharf, London, E14 5DT, England. E-mail: daniel.johnson@telegraph.co.uk

JOHNSON Earvin (Magic Johnson), b. 14 August 1959, Lansing, Michigan, USA. Basketball Player. m. Cookie Kelly, 1 son. Education: Michigan University. Appointments: Professional Basketball Player, Los Angeles Lakers National Basketball Association (NBA), 1979-91, (retired), Returned to professional sport, 1992, later announced abandonment of plans to resume sporting career; Chairman, Johnson Development Corporation, 1993-; Magic Johnson Entertainment, 1997-; Vice-President, Co-Owner, Los Angeles Lakers, 1994-, Head Coach, 1994; Presenter, TV Show, The Magic Hour, 1998-. Publications: Magic, 1983; What You Can Do to Avoid AIDS, 1992; My Life (autobiography), 1992. Honours include: Named, Most Valuable Player, NBA Playoffs, 1980, 1982, 1987, NBA, 1987, 1989, 1990. Memberships include: NCAA Championship Team, 1979; National Basketball All-Star Team, 1980, 1982-89; National Basketball Association Championship Team, 1980, 1982, 1985, 1987, 1988; National AIDS Association. Address: Magic Johnson Foundation, Suite 1080, 1600 Corporate Pointe, Culver City, CA 90230, USA.

JOHNSON Gabriel Ampah, b. 13 October 1930, Aneho, Togo. Professor of Biology. m. Louise Chipan, 3 sons, 3 daughters. Education: Licence-es-Sciences, 1950-54, Doctorat-es- Sciences d'État, 1954-59, Universite de Poitiers, France. Appointments: Research Fellow, CNRS, France, 1958-60; Professor and Chair of Biology, 1966; Founding Rector, Universite du Benin, Lome, Togo, 1970-86; Chancellor of Togolese Universities, 1998-. Publications: Articles and papers in professional scientific journals. Honours: Chevalier de l'Ordre National de la Côte-d'Ivoire, 1966; Officier de la Légion d'Honneur, France, 1971; Commandeur de l'Ordre National du Gabon, 1977; Grand Officier de la Croix du Sud, Ordre du Cruzeiro do Sul, Brazil, 1977; Commandeur de l'Ordre du Mérite, France, 1983; Certificate of Merit, IBC, 1983; Commandeur de l'Ordre des Palmes Académiques, France, 1986; Commandeur de l'Ordre National de Mérite de la Tunisie, 1986; Commandeur de l'Ordre du Mono, Togo, 2000; Commandeur de l'Ordre des Palmes Académiques, Togo, 2006; Universal Award of Accomplishment, ABI, 2006; International Medal of Honor, IBC, 2006; American Medal of Honor, ABI, 2006. Memberships: The Africa Club; World Association of Social Prospective; UNESCO; Executive Board, UNESCO, 1997-2001; Administrative Council, International Fund for the Promotion of Culture, 2003; Chairman, Commission of the Extension of the Continental Shelf of Togo, 2008; National Academy of Pharmacy, Paris, France; International Committee of Bioethics; Academie Universale Umanesing Nuovo, Rome; New York Academy of Sciences; Zoology Society of France; Biology Society of France; Endocrinology Society of France; International Association of Universities, 1975-85; Panafican Institute for Development, 1978-84; Association of Partially or Fully French-Speaking Universities, 1975-85; President, Association of African Universities, 1977-80; Brazil-Togo Friendship Association. Address: Boîte Postale 7098, Lome, Togo, West Africa. E-mail: apa.g.johnson@ids.tg

JOHNSON Jenny, (Jennifer Hilary Harrower), b. 2 November 1945, Bristol, England. Choreographer; Comic Actor; Illustrator; Poet; Reiki Therapist. m. Noel David Harrower, 1990, 1 son. Education: The Red Maids' School, Bristol. Career: Choreographer; Illustrator; Reiki Practitioner; Writer. Publications: Poetry: The Wisdom Tree, 1993; Neptune's Daughters, 1999; Recent contributions to: Grapevine (The Circle Dance Network); The Green Door (International Arts Magazine); GreenSpirit Journal; Sarasvati. Honours: 4 Literature Awards, Southwest Arts (now Arts Council England, South West); BETW, 1978-1982. Memberships: The Reiki Association; GreenSpirit. Address: Ground Floor Flat, 6 Lyndhurst Road, Exmouth, Devon EX8 3DT, England. E-mail: jennyharrower@btinternet.com Website: www.jennyjohnsondancerpoet.co.uk

JOHNSON Michael, b. 13 September 1967, Dallas, USA. Athlete. Education: Baylor University. Appointments: World Champion 200m, 1991, 400m & 4 x 400m, 1993, 200m, 400m & 4 x 400m (world record), 1995, 400m, 1997; Olympic Champion 4 x 400m (world record), 1992, 200m, 400m, 1996, World Record Holder 400m (indoors) 44.63 seconds, 1995, 4 x 400m (outdoors) 2.55.74, 1992, 2.54.29, 1993; Undefeated at 400m, 1989-97; First man to be ranked World No 1 at 200m and 400m simultaneously, 1990, 1991, 1994, 1995; Olympic Champion, 200m (world record), 400m, Atlanta, 1996; Olympic Champion, 400m, Sydney 2000. Awards: Jesse Owens Award, 1994; Track and Field US Athlete of the Year (four times). Address: USA Track & Field, PO Box 120, Indianapolis, IN 46206, USA.

JOHNSON Rex Sutherland, b. 24 August 1928, Essex, England. Chartered Architect; Arbitrator; Expert Witness. m. Betty E Johnson, deceased, 2 sons. Education: Diploma of Architecture, London University. Appointments: Assistant

Architect, Senior Architect, T P Bennett and Son; Junior Partner, Oliver Law and Partners, 1961-63; T P Bennett and Son, 1963-65; Associate Partner, 1965-69, Senior Partner, 1969-90, Ronald Ward and Partners; Retired, 1990; Consultant, Design 5, London. Memberships: Fellow, Royal Institute of British Architects; Fellow, Chartered Institute of Arbitrators; Founder Member, Society of Expert Witnesses; Trustee, Royal Wanstead Childrens Foundation. Address: Whitepines, Longmill Lane, Crouch, Nr Sevenoaks, Kent TN15 8QB, England. Email: beejons@aol.com

JOHNSON Stanley P, b. 18 August 1940. Writer. m. (1) Charlotte Fawcett, 1963, dissolved 1979, 3 sons, 1 daughter, (2) Jennifer Arnell, 1981, 1 son, 1 daughter. Education: BA, MA, Exeter College, Oxford, 1959-63; Harkness or Commonwealth Fund Fellowship, State University of Iowa and Columbia University, New York, 1964; Diploma, Agricultural Economics, Oxford, 1964-65. Appointments: United Kingdom Foreign Office, 1964-65; World Bank, Washington DC, 1966-69; United Nations Association of the United States, UNA-USA, 1968-69; Ford Foundation Fellow, London School of Economics, 1969-70; Conservative Research Department, 1969-70; International Planned Parenthood Federation, 1970-73; Head of EC's Prevention of Pollution and Nuisances Division, Adviser to EC Director-General for Environment, European Commission, Brussels, 1973-79; MEP for East Hampshire and the Isle of Wight, Vice Chairman of Committee on the Environment, Public Health and Consumer Protection, European Parliament, 1979-84; Adviser to Director-General Environment, Director of Energy Policy (DG XVII), European Commission, Brussels, 1984-90; Food and Agriculture Organisation of the United Nations, 1990-92; Director, International and Policy Services, Environmental Resources Management, 1992-94; Special Adviser on the Environment to Coopers and Lybrand, 1994-96; Senior Adviser, International Fund for Animal Welfare, 1996-2003. Publications: Author, 20 books (11 non-fiction and 9 fiction); Articles in professor and popular journals; Speeches at national and international conferences. Honours: Newdigate Prize for English Verse, Oxford University, 1962; Greenpeace Prize for Outstanding Services to the Environment, 1984; Royal Society for the Prevention of Cruelty to Animals, Richard Martin Award for Outstanding Services to Animal Welfare, 1984; Cited by London Times as "environmentalist of the year" for work on EU habitats directive, 1989; Consultant, UNDP/UNFPA, 1969-97; Consultant, World Bank Operations Evaluation Unit, 1970; Member, UK Countryside Commission, 1971-73; General Editor, Kluwer Law International series of books on Environmental Law and Policy, 1987-97; Consultant (at Coopers and Lybrand) to UNEP, 1992-92; Consultant FAO for follow-up to Rio Forest Principles, 1994; Trustee, Earthwatch Institute Europe, 1995-2001; Trustee, Plantlife International, 2002-05; Trustee, Gorilla Organisation, 2004-10, Chairman, 2010-. Address: 34 Park Village East, London NW1 7PZ, England.

JOHNSTON Ronald John, b. 30 March 1941, Swindon, Wiltshire, England. Professor of Geography; Writer. m. Rita Brennan, 1 son, 1 daughter. Education: BA, 1962, MA, 1964, University of Manchester; PhD, Monash University, 1967. Appointments: Teaching Fellow, 1964, Senior Teaching Fellow, 1965, Lecturer, 1966, Monash University; Lecturer, 1967-68, Senior Lecturer, 1969-72, Reader, 1973-74, University of Canterbury, New Zealand; Professor of Geography, 1974-92, Pro-Vice Chancellor for Academic Affairs, 1989-92, University of Sheffield; Vice-Chancellor, Essex University, 1992-95; Professor of Geography, Bristol University, 1995-. Publications: The World Trade System: Some Enquiries Into Its Spatial Structure, 1976; Geography and Geographers: Anglo-American Human Geography Since 1945, 1979, 6th edition, 2004; Geography and the State, 1982; Philosophy and Human Geography: An Introduction to Contemporary Approaches, 1983, 2nd edition, 1986; On Human Geography, 1986; Bell-Ringing: The English Art of Change-Ringing, 1986; Money and Votes: Constituency Campaign Spending and Election Results, 1987; The United States: A Contemporary Human Geography (co-author), 1988; A Nation Dividing?: The Electoral Map of Great Britain, 1979-1987 (with C J Pattie and J G Allsopp), 1988; Environmental Problems: Nature, Economy and State, 1989, 2nd edition, 1996; The Dictionary of Human Geography (editor), 1989, 5th edition, 2009; An Atlas of Bells (co-author), 1990; A Question of Place: Exploring the Practice of Human Geography, 1991;The Boundary Commissions, 1999; From Votes to Seats, 2001; Putting Voters in their Place, 2006. Contributions to: Various books and professional journals. Honours: Murchison Award, 1985; Victoria Medal, Royal Geographical Society, 1990; Honors Award for Distinction in Research, Association of American Geographers, 1991; Lifetime Achievement Award, Association of American Geographers, 2010; Honorary doctorates, University of Essex, 1996, Monash University, 1999, University of Sheffield, 2002, University of Bath, 2005, Fellow, British Academy, 1999. Memberships: Institute of British Geographers, secretary, 1982-85, president, 1990. Address: School of Geographical Studies, Bristol University, Bristol BS8 1SS, England.

JOHNSTONE Alexander Henry, b. 17 October 1930, Edinburgh, Scotland. Retired University Professor. m. Martha Y Cuthbertson, 2 sons. Education: Leith Academy, 1942-49; BSc (1st Class), Chemistry, 1953, PGCE, 1954, University of Edinburgh; PhD, Chemical Education, University of Glasgow, 1972. Appointments: Chemistry Master, George Watson's College, Edinburgh; Principal Chemistry Master, Stirling High School; Senior Lecturer in Chemistry, Reader in Chemistry, Professor in Chemistry, Director of Teaching & Learning Service, Director of Centre for Science Education, Professor of Science Education, University of Glasgow. Publications: 8 chemistry textbooks; 226 academic research papers; Supervision of 80 higher degree students. Honours: Nyholm Medal, Royal Society of Chemistry; Illuminati Medal, Italian Chemical Society; Mellor Medal, Royal Australian Chemical Society; Brasted Medal, American Chemical Society; Verhagen Titular Chair, Limburg University; FECS Lecture, Federation of European Chemical Societies; Galen Lectureship, University of Dublin; American Chemical Society Award for Achievement in Research for the Teaching and Learning of Chemistry, 2009. Memberships: Fellow, Royal Society of Chemistry. E-mail: alexjo@btinternet.com

JOLIE Angelina, b. 4 June, 1975, USA. Actress. m. (1) Jonny Lee Miller, 1996, divorced 1999, (2) Billy Bob Thornton, 2000, divorced 2003, 2 adopted sons, 1 adopted daughter, 1 son and 2 daughters with Brad Pitt. Education: Lee Strasberg Institute, New York. Career: Goodwill Ambassador, UNHCR, 2001; Films: Lookin' To Get Out, 1982; Cyborg II: Glass Shadow, Hackers, 1995; Foxfire, Mojave Moon, Love Is All There Is, 1996; True Women, George Wallace, Playing God, 1997; Hell's Kitchen, Gia, 1998; Playing by Heart, Girl, Interrupted, 1999; Tomb Raider, Original Sin, 2001; Life or Something Like It, 2002; Lara Croft Tomb Raider: Cradle of Life, Beyond Borders, 2003; Taking Lives, Shark Tale (voice), Sky Captain and the World of Tomorrow, Alexander, 2004; Mr & Mrs Smith, 2005; The Good Shepherd, 2006; A Mighty Heart, Beowulf, 2007; Kung Fu Panda, Changeling, Wanted,

2008; Salt, The Tourist, 2010. Honours: Golden Globe, 1998, 1999; Screen Actors Guild Award, 1999; Academy Award for Best Supporting Actress, 1999. Address: c/o Richard Bauman & Associates, Suite 473, 5757# Wilshire Boulevard, Los Angeles, CA 90036, USA.

JONAS Peter (Sir), b. 14 October 1946, London, England. General and Artistic Director, Bavarian State Opera. m. Lucy Hull, 1989, divorced 2001. Education: BA honours, University of Sussex; LRAM, FRNCM, 2000, Royal Northern College of Music; CAMS, Fellow, FRCM 1989, Royal College of Music; Eastman School of Music, University of Rochester, USA. Appointments: Assistant to Music Director, 1974-76, Artistic Administrator, 1976-85, Chicago Symphony Orchestra; Director of Artistic Administration, Orchestral Association of Chicago, Chicago Symphony Orchestra, Chicago Civic Orchestra, Chicago Symphony Chorus, Allied Arts Association, Orchestra Hall, 1977-85; General Director, ENO, 1985-93; General and Artistic Director, Bavarian State Opera, 1993-; Chairman, Deutsche Opernkonferenz (Congress of German and European Opera House Directors), 1999-2005. Publications: with Mark Elder and David Pountney, Power House, 1992; Co-author, Eliten und Demokratie, 1999-2005; Lecturer, University of St Gallen (CH), 2001-; Lecturer, University of Zürich, 2003-. Honours: FRSA, 1989; CBE, 1993; Honorary DrMus, Sussex, 1994; Knighted 2000; Bayerische Verdienstorden (Distinguished Service Cross), 2001; Bavarian Constitutional Medal, 2001; Queen's Lecture, Berlin, 2001; Visiting Lecturer, St Gallen University, 2003-, University of Zurich, 2004-; Member, Bavarian Academy of Fine Arts, 2005-. Memberships: Advisory Board, Hypo-Vereinsbank, 1994-2004; Board of Governors, Bayerische Rundfunk, 1999-2006; Board of Management, National Opera Studio, 1985-93; Council, RCM, 1988-95; Council, London Lighthouse, 1990-94. Address: Bayerische Staätsoper, Nationaltheater, Max-Joseph-Platz 2, 80539 München, Germany.

JONCKHEERE Inge, b. 26 May 1977, Ghent, Belgium. Education: MSc, Bio-Engineering, Land and Forestry Management, 2000; PhD, BioScience Engineering, 2005. Appointments: Research Associate, Kuleuven, 2001-05; Postdoctoral Research Fellow, Kuleuven, 2005-06; European Collaborative Research Co-ordinator, European Science Foundation, 2006-09; Remote Sensing Scientific Expert, FAO-UN, 2009-. Publications: 25 peer-reviewed articles; 4 book chapters; More than 20 international conference proceedings. Honours: Postdoctoral Grant, Flemish Science Foundation, 2006-09; Laureate, Belgian Stichting Roeping, 2006; Listed in international biographical dictionaries. Memberships: IEEE; BES; EGU; AGU; EPWS; EuroScience. Address: Andre Devaerelaan 102, 8500 Kortrijk, Belgium. E-mail: inge-jonckheere@fao.org

JONES Catherine Zeta, b. 25 September 1969, Swansea, Wales. Actress. m. Michael Douglas, 1 son, 1 daughter. Creative Works: Stage appearances include: The Pyjama Game; Annie; Bugsy Malone; 42nd Street; Street Scene; TV appearances include: Darling Buds of May; Out of the Blue; Cinder Path, 1994; Return of the Native, 1995; Titanic, 1996; Film appearances include: Scheherazade; Coup de Foudre; Splitting Heirs, 1993; Blue Juice, 1995; The Phantom, 1996; The Mask of Zorro, 1997; Entrapment, 1998; The Haunting, 1999; Traffic, 2000; America's Sweethearts, 2001; Chicago, 2002; Monkeyface, 2003; Intolerable Cruelty, 2003; The Terminal, 2004; Ocean's Twelve, 2004; Legend of Zorro, 2005; No Reservations, 2007; Death Defying Acts, 2007. Honours: Best Supporting Actress, BAFTA Awards, 2003; Screen Actors Guild Awards, 2003; Academy Awards, 2003. Address: c/o ICM Ltd, Oxford House, 76 Oxford Street, London W1N 0AX, England.

JONES Douglas Gordon, b. 1 January 1929, Bancroft, Ontario, Canada. Retired Professor; Poet. Education: MA, Queen's University, Kingston, Ontario, 1954. Appointment: Professor, University of Sherbrooke, Quebec, 1963-94. Publications: Poetry: Frost on the Sun, 1957; The Sun Is Axeman, 1961; Phrases from Orpheus, 1967; Under the Thunder the Flowers Light Up the Earth, 1977; A Throw of Particles: Selected and New Poems, 1983; Balthazar and Other Poems, 1988; The Floating Garden, 1995; Wild Asterisks in Cloud, 1997; Grounding Sight (poetry), 1999; The Stream Exposed with All its Stones: Collected Poems, 2010; Other: Butterfly on Rock: A Study of Themes and Images in Canadian Literature, 1970. Honours: President's Medal, University of Western Ontario, 1976; Governor General's Award for Poetry, 1977, and for Translation, 1993; Honorary DLitt, Guelph University, 1982; OC, Officer of the Order of Canada, 2008. Address: 120 Hougton Street, North Hatley, Quebec J0B 2C0, Canada.

JONES George Glenn, b. 12 September 1931, Saratoga, Texas, USA. Country Singer; Musician (guitar). m. (1) Tammy Wynette, 1969-75; (2) Nancy Sepulveda, 1983. Career: Recording artist, 1953-; Worked under names of Johnny Williams, Hank Davis, Glen Patterson; Worked with The Big Bopper; Johnny Preston; Johnny Paycheck; Recorded duets with Gene Pitney; Melba Montgomery; Tammy Wynette; Elvis Costello; James Taylor; Willie Nelson. Compositions include: The Window Up Above, Mickey Gilley; Seasons Of My Heart, Johnny Cash, Jerry Lee Lewis. Recordings: 150 Country hits include: Why Baby Why; White Lightning; Tender Years; She Still Thinks I Care; You Comb Her Hair; Who Shot Sam?; The Grand Tour; He Stopped Loving Her Today; Recorded over 450 albums; Recent albums include: First Time Live, Who's Gonna Fill Their Shoes, 1985; Wine Coloured Roses, 1986; Super Hits, Too Wild Too Long, 1987; One Woman Man, 1989; Hallelujah Weekend, You Oughta Be Here With Me, 1990; And Along Came Jones, Friends In High Places, 1991; Salutes Bob Wills and Hank Williams, Live At Dancetown USA, Walls Can Fall, 1992; One, 1995; I Lived to Tell It All, 1996; In a Gospel Way, 1997; It Don't Get Any Better Than This, 1998; The Cold Hard Truth, Live with the Possum, 1999; with Tammy Wynette: We Can Go Together, 1971; Me And The First Lady, 1972; Golden Ring, 1976; Together Again, 1980. Address: Razor & Tie, 214 Sullivan Street, Suite 4A, New York, NY 10012, USA.

JONES George William, b. 4 February 1938, Wolverhampton, England. Retired University Professor. m. Diana Mary, 1 son, 1 daughter. Education: Jesus College, Oxford, 1957-60; Nuffield College, Oxford, 1960-63. Appointments: Assistant Lecturer in Government, 1963-65, Lecturer in Government, 1965-66, Leeds University; Lecturer in Political Science, 1966-71, Senior Lecturer in Political Science, 1971-74, Reader in Political Science, 1974-76, Professor of Government, 1976-2003, Professor Emeritus, 2003-, Honorary Fellow, 2009, London School of Economics; Honorary Professor, University of Birmingham, 2003-; Visiting Professor, Queen Mary College, London, 2004-; Visiting Research Fellow, De Montfort University, 2007-. Publications: Borough Politics, 1969; Herbert Morrison, 1973, 2nd edition 2001; Case for Local Government, 2nd edition 1985; West European Prime Ministers, 1991; At the Centre of Whitehall, 1998; Regulation Inside Government, 1999; Premiership, 2010. Honours: BA, 1960; MA, 1965; D Phil,

1965; FRHisS, 1980; OBE, 1999. Memberships: Honorary Fellow, University of Wolverhampton, 1986; Layfield Committee on Local Government Finance, 1974-76; Joint Working Party on Internal Management of Local Authorities, 1992-93; Beacon Councils Advisory Panel, 1999-2002; National Consumer Council, 1991-99; Honorary Member, Chartered Institute of Public Finance and Accountancy, 2003-; Honorary Member, Society of Local Authority Chief Executives, 2003-; Associate, Centre for Public Service Partnerships, 2010. Address: Department of Government, LSE, Houghton Street, London WC2A 2AE, England. E-mail: g.w.jones@lse.ac.uk

JONES Grace, b. 19 May 1948, Spanishtown, Jamaica. Singer; Model; Actress. m. (1) Chris Stanley, 1989, divorced; (2) Atila Altaunbay, 1996, divorced; 1 son with Jean-Paul Goude. Education: Syracuse University. Appointments: Fashion Model, New York, Paris; Made 1st Album, Portfolio, for Island Records, 1977; Debut as Disco Singer, New York, 1977; Founder, La Vie en Rose Restaurant, New York, 1987. Creative Works: Films include: Conan the Destroyer; A View to a Kill, 1985; Vamp; Straight to Hell; Siesta; Boomerang, 1991; Cyber Bandits, 1995; McCinsey's Island, 1998; Palmer's Pick Up, 1999; No Place Like Home, 2006. Albums include: Fame; Muse; Island Life; Slave to the Rhythm.

JONES (Dame) Gwyneth, b. 7 December 1936, Pontnewynydd, Wales. Soprano. 1 daughter. Education: Student, Royal College of Music, London; Accademia Chigiana, Siena, Italy; International Opera Centre, Zurich, Switzerland; Dr h c musica, University of Wales and Glamorgan. Appointments: Member, Royal Opera, Covent Garden, England, 1963-; Vienna State Opera, 1966-; Deutsche Opera, Berlin, 1966-; Munich Bavarian State Opera, 1967-; Guest performances in numerous opera houses including: Hamburg, Bayreuth, Dresden, Paris, Zurich, Rome, Chicago, San Francisco, Los Angeles, Tokyo, Buenos Aires, Munich, La Scala, Milan, Metropolitan Opera, New York City, Peking, Seoul, Bayreuth Festival, Hong Kong, Salzburg Festival, Verona; Appeared in 50 leading roles; Court Singer, Bavaria, Austria; Recording artist for Decca, Deutsche Grammophon, Philips, EMI, Chandos, Claves, Capriccio, Vai, CBS; Director, Producer: Der Fliegende Hollander, Weimar National Theatre, 2003; Films, TV and concert appearances. Honours: Dame Commander of the British Empire, 1986; Commandeur de l'Ordre des Arts et Lettres, France, 1992; Ehren-Krenz I Klasse, Austria Bundes Ver, 1998, others; Recipient, Shakespeare Prize, Hamburg, 1987; Verdienst Kreuz I Klasse, Federal Republic of Germany, 1988; Golden Medal of Honor, Vienna, 1991; Österreichische Ehren Kreuz Wissenschaft und Kunst Klasse, 1998; Premio Puccini Award, Toro Del Lago, 2003; Cymry for the World Honour, Wales Millennium Centre, 2004; Kammersängerin, Austria, Bavaria. Memberships: Royal Welsh College of Music and Drama; Royal College of Music; Honorary Member, Royal Academy of Music, London; Honorary Member, Rah; President, Wagner Society, London. Address: PO Box 2000, CH-8700 Küsnacht, Switzerland.

JONES Huw, b. 5 May 1948, Manchester, England. Broadcasting Executive. m. Siân Marylka Miarczynska, 1979, 1 son, 1 daughter. Education: BA, Modern Languages (French), MA, Oxon. Appointments: Pop Singer, Recording Artist, Television Presenter, 1968-76; Director, General Manager, Sain Recording Company, 1969-81; Chairman, Barcud Cyf (TV Facilities), 1981-93; Managing Director, Producer, Teledu'r Tir Glas Cyf (independent production company), 1982-93; First Chairman, Teledwyr Annibynnol Cymru (Welsh Independent Producers), 1984-86; Chief Executive, S4C (Welsh Fourth Channel), 1994-2005. Honours: Honorary Fellow, University of Wales, Aberystwyth; Member, Gorsedd of Bards National Eisteddfod of Wales; Fellow, Royal Television Society. Memberships: Chairman, Celtic Film and Television Co Ltd, 2001-2004; Director, Sgrin Cyf; Director, Skillset Ltd; Chairman, Skillset Cymru; Member, British Screen Advisory Council. Address: S4C, Parc Ty Glas, Llanishen, Cardiff, C14 5DU, Wales. E-mail: huw.jones@s4c.co.uk

JONES Jade, b. 21 March 1993, Bodelwyddan, Wales. Taekwondo Athlete. Career: Gold medal, Youth Olympic Games, Singapore, 2010; Bronze medal (bantamweight), European Championships, St Petersburg, 2010; Silver medal (featherweight), World Championships, Gyeongju, 2011; Bronze medal (featherweight), European Championships, Manchester, 2012; Gold medal, London Olympics, 2012.

JONES James Earl, b. 17 January 1931, Mississippi, USA. Actor. m. Cecilia Hurt, 1982, 1 child. Education: University of Michigan. Creative Works: Numerous stage appearances on Broadway and elsewhere including, Master Harold...And the Boys, Othello, King Lear, Hamlet, Paul Robeson, A Lesson From Aloes, Of Mice & Men, The Iceman Cometh, A Hand is on the Gate, The Cherry Orchard, Danton's Death, Fences; Frequent TV appearances; Voice of Darth Vader in films Star Wars, The Empire Strikes Back, The Return of the Jedi; Films include: Matewan; Gardens of Stone; Soul Man; My Little Girl; The Man; The End of the Road; Dr Strangelove; Conan the Barbarian; The Red Tide; A Piece of the Action; The Last Remake of Beau Geste; The Greatest; The Heretic; The River Niger; Deadly Hero; Claudine; The Great White Hope; The Comedians; Coming to America; Three Fugitives; Field of Dreams; Patriot Games; Sommersby; The Lion King (voice); Clear and Present Danger; Cry the Beloved Country; Lone Star; A Family Thing; Gang Related; Rebound; Summer's End; Undercover Angel, 1999; Quest for Atlantis, 1999; On the Q.T., 1999; Finder's Fee, 2001; Recess Christmas: A Miracle on Third Street (voice), 2001; Robots (voice), 2005; Star Wars: Episode III – Revenge of the Sith, 2005; The Benchwarmers (voice), 2006; The Better Man, 2008. Honours include: Tony Award; Golden Globe Award; Honorary DFA, Princeton, Yale, Michigan.

JONES John Henry, b. 29 April 1942, Lingfield, Surrey, England. Chemist; Historian. m. Patricia, 3 sons. Education: Balliol College, Oxford, 1961-67. Appointments: Fellow, 1966-2009, Dean, 1972-2002, Vicegerent, 2000-01, 2006, Vice-Master, 2002-2007, Emeritus Fellow, 2009, Balliol College, Oxford. Publications: Numerous papers and articles in professional scientific journals. Honours: MA; D Phil; C Chem; FRSC; FRHistS. Address: Balliol College, Oxford, OX1 3BJ, England. E-mail: john.jones@balliol.ox.ac.uk

JONES Lawrence William, b. 16 November 1925, Evanston, Illinois, USA. Professor Emeritus. 1 son, 2 daughters. Education: BSc, 1948, MSc, 1949, Northwestern University, Evanston, Illinois; PhD, University of California at Berkeley, 1952. Appointments: Professor of Physics, 1952-98, Chair, Department of Physics, 1982-87, Professor Emeritus, 1998, University of Michigan; Scientist, Midwestern Universities Research Association, 1956-57; Ford Foundation Fellow, CERN, Geneva, Switzerland, 1961-62; Guggenheim Foundation Fellow, CERN, 1965; Visiting Professor and Science Research Council Fellow, Westfield College, London, England, 1977; Visiting Professor, Tata Institute for Fundamental Research, Bombay, India, 1979; Distinguished Visiting Scholar, University of Adelaide, Australia, 1991;

Visiting Professor, University of Sydney, Australia, 1991; Visiting Scientist, University of Auckland, New Zealand, 1991. Publications: Over 400 journal publications; Over 200 publications in conference proceedings; Over 30 book chapters or sections. Honours: Phi Beta Kappa and Sigma Xi; Fellow, American Physical Society; Award, Quest for Technology, University of Michigan; Honoree, Symposium in Honor of LW Jones, CERN, Geneva. Memberships: American Physical Society; American Association for the Advancement of Science; Phi Beta Kappa. Address: Department of Physics, University of Michigan, 450 Church Street, Ann Arbor, MI 48109-1040, USA. E-mail: lwjones@umich.edu

JONES Martyn David, b. 1 March 1947, Crewe, Cheshire, England. Member of Parliament. Divorced, 1 son, 1 daughter. Education: Liverpool College of Commerce; CIBiol, Liverpool Polytechnic; MIBiol, Trent Polytechnic. Appointments: Microbiologist, Wrexham Lager Beer Company, 1969-87; Councillor, Clwyd County Council, 1981-89; MP for Clwyd South (formerly Clwyd South West), 1987-; Opposition Spokesperson on Food, Agriculture and Rural Affairs, 1994-95; Labour Whip; 1988-92; Speaker's Panel of Chairmen, 1993-94; Chairman, Welsh Affairs Select Committee, 1997. Memberships: Council Member, Royal College of Veterinary Surgeons; SERA, Fabian Society; Christian Socialist Movement; Federation of Economic Development Authorities; Institute of Biology. Address: House of Commons, London, SW1A 0AA, England. E-mail: jonesst@parliament.uk

JONES Norah, b. 30 March 1979, New York, USA. Singer; Pianist. Education: Booker T Washington High School for the Performing and Visual Arts, Dallas; North Texas University. Career: Member, Wax Poetic; Formed band with Jesse Harris, Lee Alexander and Dan Rieser; Solo artist, 2001-; Albums: Come Away With Me, 2002; Feels Like Home, 2004; Not Too Late, 2007; The Fall, 2009. Singles: First Sessions, 2001; Don't Know Why, 2002; Feelin' The Same Way, 2002; Come Away With Me, 2002; Turn Me On, 2003; Sunrise, 2004; What Am I To You? 2004; Here We Go Again, 2004. Honours: MOBO Award, Best Jazz Act, 2002; VH1 Best Young Female Singer Award, 2002; Grammy Awards: Best New Artist, 2003; Album of the Year, 2003, Best Pop Vocal Album, 2003, Record of the Year, 2003, Best Female Pop Vocal Performance, 2003, Best Female Pop Vocal Performance, 2005, Record of the Year, 2005; BRIT Award for International Breakthrough Artist, 2003; World Music Awards for Best Female Artist, 2004. Address: Macklam Feldman Management, Suite 200, 1505 W Second Avenue, Vancouver, BC V6H 3Y4, Canada. Website: www.norahjones.com

JONES Peter Ivan, b. 14 December 1942, Cosham, Hampshire, England. Chairman of the Tote. m. Elizabeth Gent, 2 sons, 2 daughters. Education: BSc Economics, London School of Economics, 1964; MIPA, 1967. Appointments: Chief Executive, Boase Massimi Pollitt, 1988-89; Chief Executive, 1989-93, Director, 1989-97, Omnicom UK plc; President, Racehorse Owners Association, 1990-93; Member, Horserace Betting Levy Board, 1993-95; Director, British Horseracing Board, 1993-97; President, Diversified Agency Services, 1993-97; Chairman, Dorset Police Authority, 1997-2003; Director, 1995-97, Chairman, 1997-, Horserace Totalisator Board. Publications: Trainers Record, annually, 1973-87; Editor, Ed Byrne's Racing Year, annually, 1980-83. Memberships: Bridport and West Dorset Golf Club. Address: Melplash Farmhouse, Melplash, Bridport, Dorset DT6 3UH, England. E-mail: pjones@tote.co.uk

JONES Quincy, b. 14 March 1933, Chicago, Illinois, USA. Record Producer; Composer; Arranger; Musician (trumpet); Conductor. 7 children. Education: Seattle University. Musical Education: Berklee College Of Music; Boston Conservatory. Career: Trumpeter, arranger, Lionel Hampton Orchestra, 1950-53; Arranger for various singers, orchestra leaders include: Count Basie; Frank Sinatra; Peggy Lee; Dinah Washington; Sarah Vaughn; Trumpeter, Dizzy Gillespie, 1956; Leader, own orchestra, concerts, television appearances, 1960-; Music Director, Mercury Records, 1961; Vice President, 1964. Recordings: Solo albums include: You've Got It Bad Girl, 1973; Walking In Space, 1974; Body Heat, 1974; Mellow Madness, 1975; I Heard That!, 1976; Quintessence, 1977; Sounds And Stuff Like That, 1978; The Dude, 1981; Bossa Nova, 1983; The Q, 1984; Back On The Block, 1989; QD III Soundlab, 1991; Producer, video Portrait Of An Album, 1986; Q's Jook Joint, 1995; Music, television series Fresh Prince Of Bel Air, 1990-; Guest musician, albums: with George Benson: Shape Of Things To Come, 1976; Give Me The Night, 1980; with James Ingram: It's Your Night, 1983; Never Felt So Good, 1986; with Michael Jackson: Thriller, 1982; Bad, 1987; Singles include: Blues in the Night, 1989; Listen Up, 1991; I'm Yours, 1999; Conductor, film music includes: In The Heat Of The Night, 1967; The Slender Thread, 1968; McKenna's Gold, 1968; For The Love Of Ivy, 1968; Banning, 1967; The Split, 1968; Bob And Carol And Ted And Alice, 1969; The Out-Of-Towners, 1970; The Anderson Tapes, 1971; The Hot Rock, 1972; The New Centurions, 1972; The Getaway, 1972; The Wiz, 1978; The Color Purple, 1985. Honours include: Golden Note, ASCAP, 1982; Hon degree, Berklee College, 1983; 27 Grammy Awards; Lifetime Achievement, National Academy of Songwriters, 1989; ASMAC Golden Score Award. Address: c/o Quincy Jones Productions, 3800 Barham Blvd #503, Los Angeles, CA 90067, USA.

JONES Richard Elfyn, b. 11 April 1944, Blaenau Ffestiniog, Wales. Composer; Academic. m. Gillian, 1 son, 2 daughters. Education: Friars School, Bangor; Colwyn High School; BA (1st class honours), Music, 1966; Fellow, Royal College of Organists, 1967; M Mus, 1968, PhD, 1978, University College, Bangor; King's College, Cambridge. Appointments: Lecturer, later Senior Lecturer, School of Music, Cardiff University, 1970-2011; Consultant, Classical Music, S4C (Welsh Fourth Channel), 1996-2004; Publications: Numerous orchestral, chamber and choral compositions; Film and television music including scores for 'Timeline' and 'After the Warming', 1988-93; Many academic papers and books on metaphysical aesthetics including 'Music and the Numinous', 2009. Honours: Limpus Prize, Royal College of Organists, 1967. Address: 10 Westbourne Crescent, Cardiff, CF14 2BL, Wales. E-mail: jonesre1@cf.ac.uk

JONES (Robert) Neil, b. 30 August 1939, Shrewsbury, England. University Professor. Divorced, 1 son, 1 daughter. Education: BSc (Hons), Agricultural Botany, PhD, 1967, Aberystwyth University, Wales; Fulbright Scholar, Genetics, Indiana University, 1963-64. Appointments: Teaching Assistant, Botany Department, Indiana University, 1963-64; Supernumerary Lecturer, 1967-68, Lecturer, 1968-69, Genetics, Queen's University, Belfast; Lecturer, Genetics, 1969-82, Senior Lecturer, 1982-88, Reader, 1988-91, Professor, 1991-2004, Leverhulme Emeritus Fellowship, 2004-06, Professor Emeritus, 2007, Part time Lecturer, 2009, Aberystwyth University; Visiting Professor, Kyoto University, Japan, 2004. Publications: Books and numerous articles in professional journals. Honours: Honorary Member, Spanish Genetical Society, 1981; Fellow, Institute of Biology, 2000; Professor Honoris Causa, Faculty of Biology, St

Petersburg State University 2000; Honorary Member, Vavilov Society of Geneticists and Breeders, 2000; Leverhulme Trust Emeritus Fellow, 2004-06; Member, Lithuanian Academy of Sciences; Honorary Member, St Petersburg Society of Naturalists. Memberships: Genetical Society of Great Britain; Spanish Genetical Society; Vavilov Society of Geneticists and Breeders, Russia; Federation European Genetical Societies. Address: Institute of Biological, Environmental and Rural Sciences, Aberystwyth University, Edward Llwyd Building, Penglais, Aberystwyth SY23 3DA, Wales. E-mail: rnj@aber.ac.uk

JONES Russell Alan, b. 26 May 1960. Director. Education: BA Honours, British Government and Politics and History (also studied with conductor and musicologist, Harry Newstone), University of Kent at Canterbury, 1978-81. Appointments: Orchestra Manager, Royal Liverpool Philharmonic, 1981-86; Concerts Manager, Scottish Chamber Orchestra, 1986; Chief Executive, National Federation of Music Societies, 1987-97; Chairman, National Music Council, 1995-2000; Numerous appointments (Director of Operations and Director of Policy & Public Affairs), ABSA/Arts and Business, 1997-2002; Co-creator, Arts & Business New Partners programme; Director, Association of British Orchestras, 2002-; Former Chairman, Young Musicians Symphony Orchestra; Former Vice Chairman, Academy of Live & Recorded Arts, -2005. Memberships: President, International Alliance of Orchestral Associations; Freeman, City of London; Liveryman, Worshipful Company of Musicians; Past Master, Billingsgate Ward Club; Fellow, Royal Society of Arts; Lords Taverner; Chevalier, Order of Champagne. Address: 12 Eastern Road, Bounds Green, London N22 4DD, England.

JONES Tom Sir (Thomas Jones Woodward), b. 7 June 1940, Pontypridd, Wales. Entertainer. m. Melinda Trenchard, 1956, 1 son. Career: Former bricklayer, factory worker, construction worker; Singing debut, aged 3, later sang in clubs, dance halls, with self-formed group The Playboys; Became Tom Jones, 1963; First hit record It's Not Unusual, 1964; Appeared on radio, television; Toured US, 1965; Television show, This Is Tom Jones, 1969-71; Many international hits, albums in Top 10 charts, Europe, USA; Over 30 million discs sold by 1970; Toured continuously, television appearances, 1970s-; Score, musical play Matador; Hit single: A Boy From Nowhere, 1987; Frequent Amnesty International; Simple Truth, 1991; Rainforest Foundation, 1993; Shelter, 1993; Television series: The Right Time, 1992; Glastonbury Festival of Contemporary Performing Arts, 1992; Live stage appearance, Under Milk Wood, Prince's Trust, 1992; Performed in Amnesty International 40th Anniversary Special, 2001. Recordings: Hits include: It's Not Unusual, 1964; What's New Pussycat, 1965; Thunderball, 1966; Green Green Grass Of Home, 1966; Delilah, 1968; Love Me Tonight, 1969; Can't Stop Loving You; She's A Lady; Letter To Lucille, 1973; Say You Stay Until Tomorrow, 1976; A Boy From Nowhere, 1987; It's Not Unusual (reissue), 1987; If I Only Knew, 1994; Burning Down The House, 1999; Baby It's Cold Outside, 1999; Mama Told Me Not To Come, 2000; Sex Bomb, 2000; You Need Love Like I Do, 2000; Tom Jones International, 2002. Albums include: Green Green Grass Of Home, 1967; Delilah, 1968; This Is Tom Jones, 1969; Tom, 1970; I Who Have Nothing, 1970; Close Up, 1972; The Body and Soul Of TJ, 1973; I'm Coming Home, 1978; At This Moment, 1989; After Dark, 1989; The Lead And How To Swing It, 1994; Reload, 1999; Mr Jones, 2002; Reload 2, 2002. Honours: OBE, 1999; BRIT Award for Best British Male Solo Artist, 2000; Nodnoff Robbins Music Therapy Silver Clef Award, 2001; Q Magazine Merit Prize, 2002; BRIT Award for Outstanding Contribution to Music, 2003; Knight Bachelor, 2006. Memberships: SAG; AFTRA: AGVA. Address: Tom Jones Enterprises, 10100 Santa Monica Blvd, Ste 205, Los Angeles, CA 90067, USA.

JONES Tommy Lee, b. 15 September 1946, San Saba, Texas, USA. Actor. m. (1) Kate Lardner, 1971, divorced; (2) Kimberlea Cloughley, 1981, divorced, 1 son, 1 daughter; (3) Dawn Laurel, 2001. Education: Harvard University. Creative Works: Broadway appearances include: A Patriot for Me; Four in a Garden; Ulysses in Night Town; Fortune and Men's Eyes; TV appearances include: The Amazing Howard Hughes; Lonesome Dove; The Rainmaker; Cat on a Hot Tin Roof; Yuri Nosenko; KGB; April Morning; Films include: Love Story, 1970; Eliza's Horoscope; Jackson County Jail; Rolling Thunder; The Betsy; Eyes of Laura Mars; Coal Miner's Daughter; Back Roads; Nate and Hayes; River Rat; Black Moon Rising; The Big Town; Stormy Monday; The Package; Firebirds; JFK; Under Siege; House of Cards; The Fugitive; Blue Sky; Heaven and Earth; Natural Born Killers; The Client; Blue Sky; Cobb; Batman Forever; Men in Black, 1997; Volcano, 1997; Marshals, 1997; Small Soldiers (voice), 1998; Rules of Engagement, 1999; Double Jeopardy, 1999; Space Cowboys, 2000; Men in Black II, 2002; The Hunted, 2003; The Missing, 2003; Man of the House, 2005; The Three Burials of Melquiades Estrada, 2005; A Prairie Home Companion, 2006; No Country for Old Men, 2007; In the Valley of Elah, 2007; In the Electric Mist, 2009; The Company Men, 2010. Honours include: Academy Award, Emmy Award, Cannes Film Festival Award, Golden Globe, MTV Movie Award, SAG Award.

JONES Trevor Mervyn, b. 19 August 1942, Wolverhampton, England. Director. m. Verity Ann Bates, 1 son, 1 daughter. Education: BPharm, Honours, PhD, Kings College, London. Appointments: Lecturer, University of Nottingham; Head of Development, The Boots Co Ltd; Director, Research and Development, Wellcome Foundation; Chairman, Reneuron Holdings plc; Director of Merlin Fund, Merlin Biosciences; Director General, Association of the British Pharmaceutical Industry; Director, Allergan Inc; Director, NextPharm Ltd. Publications: Numerous scientific papers in learned journals; Books: Drug Delivery to the Respiratory Tract; Advances in Pharmaceutical Science. Honours: Honorary degrees: PhD, University of Athens; DSc, University of Nottingham; DSc, University of Strathclyde; DSc, University of Bath; Honorary Fellowships: Royal College of Physicians, Faculty of Pharmaceutical Medicine; British Pharmacological Society; The School of Pharmacy; Charter Gold Medal, Pharmaceutical Society; Gold Medal, Comenius University. Memberships: Fellow, Kings College London; Fellow, Royal Society of Chemists; Fellow, Royal Pharmaceutical Society; Member, College of Pharmacy Practice; Member, WHO Commission on Intellectual Property Rights Innovation and Public Health; Liveryman, Worshipful Society of Apothecaries; Atheneum Club; Surrey County Cricket Club. Address: 18 Friths Drive, Reigate, Surrey, RH2 0DS, England. E-mail: trevor.m.jones@btinternet.com

JONG Erica (Mann), b. 26 March 1942, New York, New York, USA. Author; Poet. m. (4) Kenneth David Burrows, 5 August 1989, 1 daughter. Education: BA, Barnard College, 1963; MA, Columbia University, 1965. Appointments: Lecturer in English, City College of the City University of New York, 1964-66, 1969-70; University of Maryland Overseas Division, 1967-69; Faculty, Bread Loaf Writers Conference, Middlebury, Vermont, 1982, Salzburg Seminar, Austria, 1993. Publications: Fear of Flying, 1973; How to Save Your Own Life, 1977; Fanny, Being the True History of the Adventures of Fanny Hackabout-Jones, 1980; Parachutes and Kisses, 1984; Serenissima: A Novel of Venice, (reissued as Shylock), 1987; Any Woman's Blues, 1990; Fear of Fifty: A Midlife Memoir, 1994. Poetry: Fruits and Vegetables, 1971, 2nd edition, 1997; Half-Lives, 1973; Loveroot, 1975; The Poetry of Erica Jong, 1976; At the Edge of the Body, 1979; Ordinary Miracles, 1983; Becoming Light: Poems, New and Selected, 1992; Inventing Memory, 1997. Other: Four Visions of America (with others), 1977; Witches, 1981; Megan's Book of Divorce: A Kid's Book for Adults, (reissued Megan's Two Houses), 1984; Erica Jong on Henry Miller: The Devil at Large, memoir, 1994; Lyrics: Zipless: Songs of Abandon, from the Erotic Poetry of Erica Jong, 1995. Contributions to: Various publications. Honours: Academy of American Poets Award, 1963; Bess Hokin Prize, 1971; New York State Council on the Arts Grant, 1971; Alice Faye di Castagnola Award, 1972; National Endowment for the Arts Grant, 1973; Woodrow Wilson fellow; Mother of the Year, 1982; Memberships: PEN; Authors Guild USA, Council, 1975-, President, 1991-93; Phi Beta Kappa; Poetry Society of America; Poets and Writers; Writers Guild of America (West). Address: C/o Burrows, 451 Park Avenue South, New York, NY 10016, USA.

JORDAN Bill (Lord), b. 1936, Birmingham, England. m. Jean, 3 daughters. Appointments: Machine Tool Fitter, 1951; Joined engineering union, served as Shop Steward, Convenor at GKN and District President; Elected Divisional Organiser, West Midlands Division, 1977; Elected National President, Amalgamated Engineering Union, 1986; General Secretary, International Confederation of Free Trade Unions, 1994-2002. Honours: CBE; Honorary Doctorate, University of Central England, 1993; Honorary Doctorate, University of Cranfield, 1995. Memberships: General Council of the British TUC; National Economic Development Council; European Metalworkers' Federation; International Metalworkers' Federation; European Trade Union Confederation; Victim Support Advisory Committee; English Partnership; Winston Churchill Trust; Governor, London School of Economics; Governor, Ashridge Management College; RSA; Member, UN High Level Panel on Youth Employment; Member, UN Global Compact Advisory Council; Chairman, English Partnerships Pension Scheme, 2003-.

JORDAN Michael Jeffrey, b. 17 February 1963, Brooklyn, New York, USA. Basketball and Baseball Player. m. Juanita Vanoy, 1989, divorced, 2 sons, 1 daughter. Education: University of North Carolina. Appointments: Player, Chicago Bulls National Basketball Association (NBA), 1984-93, 1995-98, (NBA Champions, 1991, 1992, 1993, 1996, 1997, 1998), Birmingham Barons Baseball Team, 1993; Member, NCAA Championship Team, 1982, US Olympic Team, 1984, NBA All-Star Team, 1985-91; with Nashville Sounds, 1994-95; Holds record for most points in NBA Playoff Game with 63; Retired, 1998-; Came out of retirement to play for Washington Wizards, 2001-; Founder, Jordan Motorsports/ Suzuki, 2004. Publications: Rare Air: Michael on Michael (autobiography), 1993; I Can't Accept Not Trying: Michael Jordan on the Pursuit of Excellence. Honours include: Seagram's NBA Player of the Year, 1987; Most Valuable Player, NBA All-Star Game, 1988; NBA Most Valuable Player, 1988, 1991, 1992, 1996, 1998; Named, World's Highest Paid Athlete, Forbes Magazine, 1992. Memberships: President, Basketball Operations, Washington Wizards, 1999-. Address: Washington Wizards, 718 7th Street NW, Washington, DC 20004, USA.

JORDAN Neil Patrick, b. 25 February 1950, Sligo, Ireland. Author; Director. 3 sons, 2 daughters. Education: BA, 1st Class Honours, History/English Literature, University College, Dublin, 1972. Appointment: Co-Founder, Irish Writers Cooperative, Dublin, 1974. Publications: Night in Tunisia, 1976; The Past, 1979; The Dream of a Beast, 1983; Sunrise with Sea Monster, 1994; Nightlines, 1995. Films as a Director: Angel, 1982; The Company of Wolves, 1984; Mona Lisa, 1986; High Spirits, 1988; We're No Angels, 1989; The Miracle, 1990; The Crying Game, 1992; Interview With the Vampire, 1994; Michael Collins, 1996; The Butcher Boy, 1997; In Dreams, 1999; The End of the Affair, 1999; In Dreams, 1999; Double Dawn, 2001; The Good Thief, 2002; Shade, 2005; Breakfast on Pluto, 2005; The Brave One, 2007; Heart Shaped Box, 2007. Honours: Guardian Fiction Prize, 1979; The London Evening Standard's Most Promising Newcomer Award, 1982; London Film Critics Circle Awards, 1984; Oscar, 1992; Los Angeles Film Critics Award, 1992; New York Film Critics Circle Award, 1992; Writers Guild of America Award, 1992; BAFTA Award, 1992; Golden Lion, Venice Film Festival, 1996; Silver Bear, Berlin Film Festival, 1997; BAFTA Award, 2000. Address: c/o Jenne Casarotto Co Ltd, National House, 60-66 Wardour Street, London W1V 3HP, England.

JORIO Ado, b. 11 June 1972, Belo Horizonte, Brazil. Professor. m. Patricia Aguiar de Oliveira, 2 daughters. Education: Undergraduate, Physics, 1995, PhD, Physics, 1999, Universidade Federal de Minas Gerais; Technical specialisation: CNRS, Orleans, France, 1997, ILL, Grenoble, France, 1998; Postdoctoral Fellow, MIT, Cambridge, USA, 2000-01. Appointments: Associate Professor, 2002-10, Full Professor, 2010-, Department of Physics, Director of Technology Transfer Office, Universidade Federal de Minas Gerais (UFMG), Belo Horizonte, Brazil, 2002-10; Visiting Scientist: Tohoku University, Sendai, Japan, 2004; University of Tuebingen, Germany, 2005, 2006; Institute of Optics, Rochester University, 2006, 2007; and many others; General Coordinator of Strategic Studies, Brazilian National Institute of Metrology, 2006-09; Full Professor, Department of Physics, UFMG, 2010-; Director of Technology Transfer and Innovation, UFMG, 2010-. Publications: Carbon Nanotubes: Advanced Topics in the Synthesis, Structure, Properties and Applications, 2008; Applications of Group Theory to the Physics of Condensed Matter, 2008; Raman Spectroscopy on Graphene Related Systems, 2013; 16 book chapters; 147 scientific articles; Numerous citations. Honours: Profix, CNPq, Brazil, 2002; 26 founded grants; Productivity Fellowship, CNPq, Scopus Brasil, 2009, Elsevier/CAPES, 2009; Somiya, IUMRS, 2009. Memberships: Brazilian Physical Society; Brazilian Academy of Science. E-mail: adojorio@fisica.ufmg.br Website: http://www.fisica.ufmg.br/~adojorio

JOSEPH Jane Elizabeth, b. 7 June 1942, Dorking, Surrey. Painter; Printmaker. Education: Camberwell School of Arts & Crafts, 1961-65. Career: Solo shows include: Morley Gallery, London, 1973; The Minories, Colchester, 1982; Angela Flowers Gallery, London, 1987; Flowers East, London, 1989; Flowers East, London, 1992; Edinburgh Printmakers, 1994; Chelsea and Westminster Hospital, London, 1995; Morley Gallery, London, 1997; Scarborough Art Gallery, 1999; Twenty Etchings for Primo Levi, Morley Gallery, London, Hebrew Union College, New York, Italian Cultural Institute, London, 2000; The Stanley Picker Gallery, Kingston University, 2000; Worcester City Art Gallery, 2001; Etchings 1985-2001, Victoria Art Gallery, Bath, 2002; Commonplaces, School of Art Gallery, Aberystwyth, 2004; Group shows include: Royal Academy Summer Exhibition, London;

Flowers East, London; Rocket Gallery, London, 1996; Inaugural exhibition, Artsway, Lymington, 1997; The Hunting Art Prizes, London, 1997, 2003; Cheltenham Open Drawing Exhibition and tour, 1998, (prizewinner), 2000; Portrait of the Artist, touring exhibition, UK, 1999; Printworks, Eagle Gallery, London, 2002; The Art of Aging, Hebrew Union College, New York, 2003; International Biennieale of Graphic Arts, Ljubljana, 2005; Drawing Breath, Wimbledon College of Art and Touring, 2006-07; Eagle Gallery, London, 2007, 2008-09; Work in collections: School of Art Gallery, Aberystwyth; Ben Uri Art Gallery, London; Birmingham City Museum and Art Gallery; Brecknock Museum, Brecon; The British Museum; Chelsea and Westminster Hospital, London; Fitzwilliam Museum, Cambridge; New Hall College, Cambridge; Government Art Collection, London; Hebrew Union College, New York; Imperial College, London; Lindley Library, London; The Whitworth Art Gallery, Manchester; The National Art Library, Victoria and Albert Museum; Castle Museum, Norwich; Ashmolean Museum, Oxford; Unilever House, London; Royal Botanic Gardens, Kew; Morley College, London; Worcester City Art Gallery; Yale Center for British Art, New Haven, Connecticut, USA; The British Library, London; Commission: Chelsea and Westminster Hospital, 1994; Folio Society, etchings for "If This is a Man" by Primo Levi, 1999, and "The Truce" by Primo Levi, 2002. Publications: A Little Flora of Common Plants (with text by Mel Gooding), 2002; Kinderszenen (with text by Anthony Rudolf), 2007. Honours: Leverhulme Travelling Award, 1965-66; Invited Artist, Pécs Workshop for Graphic Art, Hungary, 1989, Abbey Award in Painting, British School at Rome, 1991, 1995; Elephant Trust Award, 1997; Wimbledon School of Art Research and Development Grant, 2000; Listed invarious international biographical dictionaries. Address: 6a Eynham Road, London W12 0HA, England. E-mail: janejoseph42@gmail.com Website: www.janejoseph.co.uk

JOSEPHSON Brian David, b. 4 January 1940, Cardiff, Wales. Physicist. Education: Cambridge University. Appointments: Fellow, Trinity College, Cambridge, 1962-; Research Assistant Professor, University of Illinois, 1965-66; Professor of Physics, Cambridge University, 1974-; Faculty Member, Maharishi European Research University, 1975; Helped discover the tunnelling effect in superconductivity, called the Josephson effect. Publications: Co-editor, Consciousness and the Physical World, 1980; The Paranormal and the Platonic Worlds, in Japanese, 1997; Research papers on superconductivity, critical phenomena, theory of intelligence, science and mysticism. Honours: Honorary Member, Institute of Electrical and Electronic Engineers; Foreign Honorary Member, American Academy of Arts and Sciences; New Scientist Award, 1969; Research Corporation Award, 1969; Fritz London Award, 1970; Hughes Medal, Royal Society, 1972; Joint Winner, Nobel Prize for Physics, 1973. Address: Cavendish Laboratory, Madingley Road, Cambridge, CB3 0HE, England. E-mail: bdj10@cam.ac.uk

JOSHI Rangnath Nathrao, b. 29 July 1940, Aite Tq Bhoom district Osmanabad, Maharashtra, India. Retired Superintendent in Law and Judiciary Department; Poet; Writer; Actor; Sweet Poetry Singer; Music Director Jagodguru. Education: HMDs; BTMD; DLit, Colombo; DLit, Nanded; PhD, Calcutta; 36 other literary degrees. Appointments: Composer of poems and lyrics in Marathi, Hindi, English and Sanskrit, Proze and Poetry; Singer of own compositions, 5000 performances in various states and cities in India; Singer, Actor, Director, Literary researcher, artist of radio and television; Many Performances; Approved Poet of AIR; Prominent personality in various posts in several sansthas and state institutions. Publications: 7,500 poems (gits). Honours: Nine First prizes, 1953, 1974, 1976, 1980, 1999, 2001, 2006, 2007, 2009, 2010; Special Merit Certificate Pune, 1976; Numerous medals, awards, cups, certificates, Sanman Patra for literary, musical, dramatic, poetic work, yoga; International Man of the Year 2001 & 2006; Presided at several literary, cultural, yoga conferences; Life member, Maharashtra Shahir Parishad Pune; Invited Chief Poet for Kavi Sammelen, arranged by Station Director of All India Radio Aurangabad, 1981, etc; Chief guest, invitee, president, inauguarator, examiner, many literary, musical, dramatic and social institutions; Chief and Judge in numerous competitions. Memberships include: All India Rajendra Samajik Kalyan Parishad Patna 1974-; Gita Ramayan Prachar Sangha Swargashram, 1975, etc; Chief Consultant, Editor, Dharma Prbha magazine, 1984-, and others; Master in Palmistry; Vishwaratna ShakatiPat [Kundlini] diksha Sadguru; Jyotish Maharshi; Pandit Samrat; Main Actor in 25 dramas; Composed samargits, war songs, national songs, performed programmes in national institutions and in public programmes; Has done social service, cultural service and national service; Posted on the greatest post of His Holiness as Kundlini Shakti Pat Dikshant Jagadguru Mahaswami. Address: 335 Kaviraj, Near Papnash Tirtha, At PO Tq, Tuljapur District, Osmanabad 413601, Maharashtra State, India.

JOSHI Sudhir, b. 11 April 1961, Delwada, India. Professor. m. Sadhana, 1 son. Education: PhD, Physics; M Phil, Physics; MSc, Physics; M Ed; DCS. Appointments: Associate Professor and Head, Physics Department. Publications: 3 papers in reputed international journals. Honours: MSc (University first); Minor Research Project; 3 Teacher Fellowships, by University and University Grants Commission. Memberships: Indian Association of Physics Teachers. Address: Vastushilp Society, Opp Shishu-Mangal, Near Darji Boarding, Junagadh 362001, India. E-mail: energyjoshi@rediffmail.com

JOSHUA Anthony Oluwafemi Olaseni, b. 15 October 1989, Watford, England. Amateur Boxer. Career: Winner, Haringey Box Cup, 2009 and 2010; Winner, Senior ABA Championships, 2010; Silver, World Amateur Championships, Baku, Azerbaijan, 2011; Gold (Super Heavyweight), London Olympics, 2012.

JOSIPOVICI Gabriel David, b. 8 October 1940, Nice, France. Professor of English; Writer; Dramatist. Education: BA, Honours, 1st Class, St Edmund Hall, Oxford, 1961. Appointments: Lecturer in English, 1963-76, Reader in English, 1976-84, Professor of English, 1984-99, Research Professor, Graduate School of Humanities, 1999-, University of Sussex. Publications: Novels: The Inventory, 1968; Words, 1971; Mobius the Stripper: Stories and Short Plays, 1974; The Present, 1975; Migrations, 1977; The Echo Chamber, 1979; The Air We Breathe, 1981; Conversations in Another Room, 1984; Contre-Jour, 1986; In the Fertile Land, Shorter Fiction, 1987; The Big Glass, 1990; In a Hotel Garden, 1993; Moo Pak, 1994; Now, 1998; Goldberg: Variations, 2002; Everything Passes, 2006; 2 Novels: After, and Making Mistakes, 2009; Non-Fiction: The World and the Book, 1971; The Lessons of Modernism, 1977; Writing and the Body, 1982 The Book of God: A Response to the Bible, 1988; Text and Voice, 1992; Touch, 1996; On Trust, 1999; A Life, 2001; The Singer on the Shore, 2006; Heart's Wings: New and Selected Stories, 2010; What Ever Happened to Modernism? 2010; Contributions to: Encounter; New York Review of Books; London Review of Books; Times Literary Supplement. Honours: Sunday Times Playwriting Award, 1969; BBC nominations for Italia Prize, 1977, 1989; South East Arts Literature Prize, 1978; Lord

Northcliffe Lecturer, University of London, 1981; Lord Weidenfeld Visiting Professor of Comparative Literature, University of Oxford, 1996-97; Fellow of the Royal Society of Literature, 1997; Fellow of the British Academy, 2001. Address: c/o John Johnson, Clerkenwell House, 45-47 Clerkenwell Green, London EC1R 0HT, England.

JOSS Timothy Hans, b. 27 June 1955, London, England. Artistic Director. Divorced, 1 daughter. Education: The Queen's College, Oxford, England, 1973-76; University of Grenoble, 1976; Royal Academy of Music, England, 1976-79. Appointments: Mathematics lecturer, Davies's College, London WC1; Community worker, Pitt Street Settlement, London SE15; Commissioned composer and record producer for 1980 World Energy Conference; Researcher for Richard Baker, 1979-81; Assistant Administrator, Live Music Now!, 1981-82; Music and Dance Officer, North West Arts, 1982-89; Concerts Director, Bournemouth Sinfonietta rising to Senior Manager, Bournemouth Orchestras, 1989-93; Director (Artistic Director and Chief Executive), Bath Festivals Trust, 1993-2004; Director, The Rayne Foundation, 2005-; Visiting Senior Fellow in Cultural Policy and Management, City University, 2010-. Publications: Editor: UK Directory of Black, Asian and Chinese Musics, 1989; UK Directory of Community Music, 1992; New Flow: A better future for artists, citizens and the state, 2008. Honours: Fellow, Royal Society of Arts; Honorary Associate, Royal Academy of Music; Chevalier Dans L'Ordre Des Arts Et Lettres. Memberships: Council Member, London Sinfonietta, Trustee, The Richard Feilden Foundation; Co-founder and Chairman, British Council for School Environments, 2006-08. Address: 15 Dukes Avenue, Muswell Hill, London, N10 2PS, England. E-mail: timjoss@timjoss.com

JOVANOVIC Bojan, b. 4 July 1966, Leskovac, Serbia. Senior Lecturer. m. Marija. Education: BSc, 1996, MSc, 2004, University of Novi Sad; PhD, Science, Biomechanics, University of Niš, 2010. Appointments: Senior Lecturer, Sports Academy, Belgrade, Serbia, 2010-11. Publications: Books: Complex Sports Biodynamics: With Practical Applications in Tennis, 2009; Paradigm Shift for Future Tennis, 2011; Gateway to Future Science with Nikola Tesla, 2011. Memberships: Society for NonLinear Dynamics in Human Factors. Address: Save Kovačevića 315, 21000 Novi Sad, Serbia. E-mail: jovanboj@yahoo.com

JOVANOVIC Sasha, b. 12 September 1972, Kula, Serbia. Scientist; Professional Artist. 1 son, 3 daughters. Education: Bachelor of Visual Art, 1997, Master of Visual Art, in progress, University of Novi Sad. Appointments: Lecturer, Academy of Art, Novi Sad, 2000-04; CEO, 2 plus 2 studio. Publications: 1 book chapter; 2 books. Honours: Member, Royal South Australian Society of Arts, 1996. Address: Fruskogorska 30/143, 21000 Novi Sad, Serbia. E-mail: 2plus2studio@gmail.com

JOWETT Jenny (Jennifer Ann), b. 15 March 1936, Bromley, Kent, England. Artist. 1 son, 1 daughter. Education: Bromley High School; NDD, Studley College, 1955-57; Lithography, Reading, 1979-82. Appointments: Watercolour workshops abroad; Teacher at home studio; Tutoring for British Field Studies Council, Flatford Mill; Freelance Botanical Artist. Publications: The White Garden; The Highgrove Florilegium; RHS Plantsman; Kew Curtis Magazine; Contemporary Botanical Artists; Fine Botanical Paintings; The Art of Botanical Painting; The Botanical Palette; The Treasures of the Royal Horticultural Society. Honours: National Diploma of Dairying; 4 Gold Medals, Royal Horticultural Society; Designed the Chelsea Plate. Memberships: Society of Botanical Artists; American Society of Botanical Artists; President, Society of Floral Painters. Address: West Silchester Hall, Silchester, Berkshire RG7 2LX, England.

JOYNER-KERSEE Jaqueline, b. 3 March 1962, East St Louis, Illinois, USA. Athlete. m. Bobby Kersee, 1986. Education: University of California, Los Angeles; Training: Husband as coach. Career: Athlete in the Heptathlon; Assistant Basketball Coach, UCLA; World Record Heptathlon Scores: 7,158 points, Houston, 1986; 7,215 points, US Olympic Trial, Indianapolis, 1988; 7,291 points, Seoul, 1988; 7,044 points, Olympic Games, Barcelona 1992; Honours: 3 Olympic Gold Medals; 4 World Championships; Record erased by IAAF, 1999; With Richmond Rage in American Basketball League; Winner, IAAF Mobil Grand Prix, 1994; Chair, St Louis Sports Commission, 1996-; Jim Thorpe Award, 1993; Jackie Robinson Robie Award, 1994; Jesse Owens Humanitarian Award, 1999; Hon DHL, Spellman College, 1998, Howard University, 1999, George Washington University, 1999. Publications: A Kind of Grace, autobiography, 1997. Address: Elite International Sports Marketing Inc, 1034 South Brentwood Boulevard, Suite 1530, St Louis, MO 63117, USA.

JOYO Ammer Ali, b. 25 October 1980, Jamshoro, Pakistan. Information Technologist. Education: Bachelor, Computer & Information Technology, 2003. Appointments: Executive Director, Institute of Imagine Technology, Hyderabad, 2008-. Honours: Student Secured Best Students; 2 times, Best Teacher; Best Administrator. Website: http://imaginetech.webs.com

JOZWIAK Ireneusz Jozef, b. 10 March 1951, Poddebice, Poland. Professor Dr Hab; Engineer. m. Elzbieta, 2 sons, 2 daughters. Education: School of Electronics Technology, Zdunska Wola, 1970; MSc, Department of Electronics, 1975, Dr, Institute of Engineering Cybernetics, 1979, Wroclaw University of Technology; Habilitation, Polish Academy of Sciences, 1994; Professor, Wroclaw University of Technology, 1998. Appointments: Secretary General, International Conference on Relcomex, Ksiaz Castle, 1979-89; Director, Catholic Secondary School, Wroclaw, 1996-; Councillor, City Council of Wroclaw, 1994-2002; Professor, Wroclaw University of Technology, Wroclaw, Poland, 1998-; Chancellor, High School of Teleinformatics Technologies, Swidnica, Poland, 2001-09. Publications: Co-editor, Performance Evaluation, Reliability and Exploitation of Computer Systems, 1989; Author, Application of the Weibull Proportional Hazards Model to the Engineering Systems Reliability Assessment, 1991; Co-author, O/S2 3.0 Warp Operating System Architecture and Function, 1998; Contributor of 150 articles to professional journals; Vice Chairman, National Conference on Strategy in Decision Making, 2005-. Honours: Gold Polish Medal for Work, 2008; National Education Committee Medal, 2009. Memberships: Member, Committee of Automatic Control and Robotics of Polish Academy of Sciences, 1994-; Society of Polish Informatics, President, 1995-; Association of Miraculous Medal, Member of Board, 1996-; Society of Education, President, 2005-; International Federation of Automatic Control; Member, TC3.3 and TC5.3, 2008-; Member, Polish Society for Measurement, Automatic Control and Robotics, 2008. Address: Wroclaw University of Technology, Institute of Informatics, Department of Computer Science and Management, Wybrzeze Wyspianskiego str 27, 50-370 Wroclaw, Poland. E-mail: ireneusz.jozwiak@pwr.wroc.pl

JU Heongkyu, b. 14 September 1970, Seoul, Korea. Assistant Professor. m. Hun I Choi, 2 sons, 1 daughter. Education: Bachelor, Physics, 1993, Master, Quantum Field Physics, 1998, Korea University; D Phil, Condensed Matter Physics, University of Oxford, 2003. Appointments: Postdoctoral Fellow, Department of Electrical Engineering, Findhoven University of Technology, The Netherlands, 2003-05; Research Associate, NTT Basic Research Laboratory, Japan, 2006-07; Assistant Professor, College of Bionano Technology, Kyungwon University, 2007-. Publications: More than 20 papers in peer-reviewed international journals. Honours: Overseas Korean Student Grant, Korean Government; Listed in international biographical dictionaries. Memberships: IEEE; Optical Society of America; Institute of Physics. Address: 109HO Mirae 2 Bldg, College of Bionano Technology, Kyungwon University, Seongnam-si, Gyeonggi-do, Korea.

JUAN CARLOS I (King of Spain), b. 5 January 1938, Rome, Italy. Education: Private, Fribourg, Switzerland, Madrid, San Sebastian; Institute of San Isidro, Madrid; Colegio del Carmen; General Military Academy, Zaragoza; University Madrid. Appointments: Inaugurated as King of Spain, 1975; Named as Captain-General of the Armed Forces, 1975. Honours include: Charlemagne Prize, 1982; Bolivar Prize, UNESCO, 1983; Gold Medal Order, 1985; Candenhove Kalergi Prize, Switzerland, 1986; Nansen Medal, 1987; Humanitarian Award, Elie Wiesel, USA, 1991; Houphouet Boigny Peace Prize, UNESCO, 1995; Franklin D Roosevelt Four Freedoms Award, 1995. Memberships include: Foreign Member, Académie des sciences morales et politiques. Address: Palacio de la Zarzuela, 28071 Madrid, Spain.

JUBERTHIE Christian, b. 12 March 1931, Brive, France. Director. m. Lysianne Jupeau, 1 son, 1 daughter. Education: Doctor-es-Sciences Naturelles, University of Toulouse, 1964. Appointments: Director of Research, CNRS, 1977-95; Director of the Underground Laboratory, CNRS, 1983-95; President de la Commission Aires Protégées, CNPN, 2005-09. Publications: Over 350 articles in professional journals including: La grotte Movilé, 1998; The diversity of the karstic and pseudokarstic hypogean habitats in the world, 2000; Interstitial habitat, 2003; Encyclopaedia Biospeologica, 1994-2001 and Europe, in print. Honours: Honorary Citizen of Lubbock, Texas, USA, 1973; Chevalier de l'ordre du Mérite, 1989; Chevalier dans l'ordre du Mérite Agricole, 1991; Membre d'honneur de l'Académie des Sciences de Roumanie, 1998-2011. Memberships: Comité National de Protection de la Nature; Comité de l'Environment Polaire; Société Internationale de Biospéologie; Société Européenne d'Arachnologie; European Evolutionary Society; Conseil d'Administration du Parc National des Pyrénées; Rotary Club de Saint-Girons Couserans. Address: La Basterne, 1 Impasse Saint-Jacques, 09190 Saint-Lizier, France. E-mail: christianjuberthie@wanadoo.fr

JUDD Frank Ashcroft, Baron Judd, b. 28 March 1935, Sutton, Surrey, England. Specialist in International Affairs. m. Christine Willington, 2 daughters. Education: City of London School, BScEcon, London School of Economics and Political Science, 1953-56. Appointments: F/O RAF, 1957-59; Secretary General, International Voluntary Service, 1960-66; Member of Parliament, Labour, Portsmouth West, 1966-74, Portsmouth North, 1974-79; Parliamentary Private Secretary to Leader of the Opposition, 1970-72; Member of the Parliamentary Delegation to the Council of Europe and Western European Union, 1970-73; Shadow Navy Minister, 1972-74; Parliamentary Under Secretary of State for Defence (Navy), 1974-76; Minister of State for Overseas Development, 1976-77; Minister of State, Foreign and Commonwealth Office, 1977-79; Associate Director, International Defence and Aid Fund for Southern Africa, 1979-80; Director, Voluntary Service Overseas, 1980-85; Director, Oxfam, 1985-91; Created Life Peer, 1991; Member, Sub-committee, (Environment, Agriculture, Public Health and Consumer Protection) of the European Community Committee in the House of Lords, 1997-2001; Member, Procedure Committee, 2001-04, and Ecclesiastical Committee in the House of Lords, 2001-; Joint Committee (Commons & Lords) on Human Rights, 2003-; Member, Parliamentary Assembly of the Council of Europe & Western European Union, 1997-2005; Joint Chair, Joint Working Group on Chechnya, Council of Europe, 2000-03; A Non-Executive Director, Portsmouth Harbour Renaissance Ltd; Trustee of Saferworld and of the Ruskin Foundation; Consultant Advisor to De Montfort University. Publications: Radical Future (jointly), 1967; Fabian International Essays (jointly), 1970; Purpose in Socialism (jointly), 1973; Imagining Tomorrow (jointly), 2000. Honours: Honorary DLitt, University of Bradford, University of Portsmouth; Honorary LLD, University of Greenwich; Honorary Fellow, University of Portsmouth and Selly Oak Colleges; Freeman of the City of Portsmouth; Member of Court, London School of Economics; Member of Court, University of Lancaster and University of Newcastle. Memberships include: Royal Institute of International Affairs; The Royal Society of Arts; The British Council; The Oxfam Association; The Labour Party; The Fabian Society; President, YMCA (England), 1996-2005; Vice-President Council for National Parks and United Nations Association; Convenor, Social Responsibility Forum of Churches Together in Cumbria, 1999-2005. Address: House of Lords, London SW1A 0PW, England.

JUERGENS Uwe, b. 29 January 1942, Frankfurt am Main, Germany. Zoologist. m. Christl, 1 daughter. Education: Abitur, Luitpold Gymnasium, Munich, 1961; Doctor Degree, 1969, Habilitation, 1976, University of Munich, Germany. Appointments: Research Associate, Max Planck Institute of Psychiatry, Munich, 1969-91; Professor, Zoological Institute, Head, Neurobiology Department, German Primate Centre, Goettingen, 1991-2007. Publications: Over 160 articles in international journals; Co-Editor, Nonverbal Vocal Communication, 1992; Co-Editor, Current Topics in Primate Vocal Communication, 1995; Associate Editor, Journal of Medical Primatology, 1996-2004. Retired in 2007. Address: 37075 Goettingen, Germany. E-mail: ujuerge@t-online.de

JUEZ VALDIVIELSO Eloy, b. 11 July 1944, Burgos, Spain. Civil Engineer. m. Graciela Beatriz Calle, 3 sons, 1 daughter. Education: Mercantil Skilful, 1961; Construction Engineer, Civil Engineer, La Plata National University, 1970-71; Professor, Teachers' College of Engineering Instruction; Professor, Center National University. Appointments: Project Engineer, Genaro Garcia SA, Dorrego Lopez y Noves SA, Cooperativa General Necochea Ltd; Structrual Engineer, Terminal Quequen SA, Puerto Quequen, Cooperativa General Necochea Ltd, Dorrego Lopez y Noves SA, Evasio Marmetto SA, Asociacion de Cooperativas Argentinas. Publications: Course on Reinforced Concrete Constructions, 1994, 2002; Numerous articles in professional journals. Honours: Professor of the Year, Domingo Lubrano Foundation, 1995; Laurel Award, Argentina Society of Writers, 1996; Honour and Merit Award, La Radio. Memberships: Necochea Engineer Association; Engineer Professional Center; Structural Engineer Association; Argentine Association of Concrete Technology; Argentine Association of Structural

Concrete; ASCE; Structural Engineering Institute. Address: 67-1305 Necochea, Drov Buenos Aires, Argentina. E-mail: ingejuez@satlink.com

JULA Nicolae, b. 14 December 1945, Hunedoara County, Romania. University Professor. m. Mioara Ana, 1 son. Education: Graduate, Faculty of Electrotechnics, Technical University Politehnica, Bucharest, 1969; PhD, Military Aircraft, 1986. Appointments: Scientific Researcher, Institute of Fluid Mechanics and Aerospace, 1969-78; Lecturer, 1978-90, Associate Professor, 1990-2000, Professor, 2000-, Military Technical Academy. Publications: 21 books; 120 articles and scientific communications published in Romania; 50 articles abroad; 850 standards from which 800 national standards for electrical and electronic equipment; 50 technical military standards. Memberships: Vice President, Stefan-Odobleja Academy of Cybernetics; Commission of Aero-Astronautics of Romanian Academy; Romanian Society of Ethical & Control Engineering; 6 technical committees of Romanian Standards Association. Address: Aleea Fetesti Nr 6-12, Bl I26, Sc A, Apt 13, Sector 3, Bucharest 032564, Romania. E-mail: nicolae.jula@gmail.com

JULIANO Bienvenido Ochoa, b. 15 August 1936, Los Baños, Laguna, Philippines. Cereal Chemist (Rice). m. Linda C Alvarez, 2 sons, 1 daughter. Education: BS (magna cum laude), Agriculture, University of the Philippines Los Baños, 1955; MSc, 1958, PhD, 1959, Organic Chemistry, Ohio State University, Columbus. Appointments: Assistant Instructor, 1955-56, Visiting Professor, 1962-93, Professorial Lecturer, 1993-2003, Institute of Chemistry, University of Philippines Los Baños; Project Chemist, Head, Laboratory & Development Sections, Philippine Refining Co, Manila, Philippines, 1959-61; Associate Chemist, 1961-67, Chemist, 1968-93, International Rice Research Institute, Los Baños; Research Fellow, MSU/AEC Plant Research Laboratory, Michigan State University, 1968; Visiting Professor, Department of Botany, University of Durham, England, 1975; Research Associate, Department of Nutritional Sciences, University of California-Berkeley, 1983; Senior Consultant, Philippine Rice Research Institute, Los Baños, 1993-. Publications: Author and co-author, over 350 articles/chapters on rice chemistry; Author, FAO/IRRI, Rice in Human Nutrition, 1993; Editor and Chapter Author, Rice Chemistry and Technology; 2nd Edition, 1985, American Association of Cereal Chemists; Co-author, IRRI Consumer Demand for Rice Grain Quality, 1992; IRRI Grain Quality Evaluation of World Rices, 1993; PhilRice; Rice Chemistry and Quality, 2003, 2007. Honours: Medal of Merit, Japanese Society of Starch Science, 1982; TB Osborne Medal, American Association of Cereal Chemists, 1988; 10 Outstanding Young Men, 1964; National Researcher Award, National Research Council, 1993; ASEAN Outstanding Scientist and Technologist Award, 1998; Conferred rank and title of National Scientist, President of the Philippines. Memberships: National Academy of Science and Technology, Philippines; Chemical Society of the Philippines; National Research Council of the Philippines; American Association of Cereal Chemists; World Innovation Foundation. Address: 9350 Lopez Avenue, Los Baños, Laguna, 4030, Philippines. E-mail: bienvenidojuliano@yahoo.com.ph

JUNCKER Jean-Claude, b. 9 December 1954, Redange-sur-Attert, Luxembourg. Prime Minister; Minister of State; Minister of the Treasury. m. Christiane Frising. Education: Master of Law, University of Strasbourg, 1979. Appointments: Member, 1974-, Parliamentary Secretary, 1979-, Christian Social Party; Secretary of State for Labour and Social Security, 1982-; Minister of Labour and Minister Delegate for the Budget, Luxembourg Parliament, 1984; Chair, Social Affairs, and Budget Councils, Council of European Communities, 1985; Minister of Finance and Minister of Labour, 1989; President, Ecofin Council, 1989-94; Governor of the World Bank, 1989-95; Governor, International Monetary Fund and Governor, European Bank for Reconstruction and Development; One of the signatories of the Maastricht Treaty, 1992; Leadership, Christian Social Party, 1990-95; Re-elected Minister of Finance and Minister of Labour, 1994-; Appointed Prime Minister and Minister of State by His Royal Highness Grand Duke Jean, 1995, re-elected 1999, 2004, and 2009; Minister of the Treasury, 2009-. Honours: Doctor honoris causa from numerous international universities; Several international decorations and many important political awards including: Grand Officer of the Legion of Honour 002; Honorary Citizen of the City of Trier, 2003; Charlemagne Prize, Aachen, 2006; Foreign Associate Member, Academy of Ethics and Political Science, Institute of France, 2007; Honorary Senator, European Academy of Sciences and Arts, 2009. Address: Ministere d'Etat, 4 rue de la Congregation, L-2910 Luxembourg.

JUNG Dong Hak, b. 12 January 1957, South Korea. Surgeon; Facial Plastic Surgeon. m. Hye Sun Jun, 1 daughter. Education: MD, Yonsei University, 1990; Master, Inha University, 2000. Appointments: Director, Shimmian Clinic, Seoul, South Korea; President, Asian Society of Asian Cosmetic Surgery; Clinical Professor, Yonsei University & Inha University; Vice Chairman, Korean Academy of Facial Plastic and Reconstructive Surgery. Publications: Subnasal flap for correction of columella base deviation in secondary unilateral cleft lip nasal deformity; Correction of severe alar retraction with use of a cutaneous alar rotation flap; The X-Graft for nasal tip surgery call; From Plastic and Reconstruction Surgery. Memberships: American Academy of Facial Plastic and Reconstruction Surgery; The International Academy of Cosmetic Surgery; Korean Board of Otolaryngology. Address: 137-070 6F, Seocho Hyundai Tower, 1319-13, Seocho-Dong, Seocho-Gu, Seoul, South Korea. E-mail: rhinojdh@hotmail.com

JUNG Hanmin, b. 5 April 1970, Seoul, Korea. Chief Researcher; Professor. m. Jiyoun Choi, 2 daughters. Education: BA, 1992, MA, 1994, Computer Science, PhD, Computer Science & Engineering, 2003, POSTECH. Appointments: Senior Researcher, ETRI, 1994-2000; CTO, DIQUEST Inc, 2000-04; Chief Researcher, KISTI, 2004-. Publications: On co-authorship for author disambiguation, 2009; Comparative evaluation of reliabilities on semantic search functions, 2009; Auto-complete for improving reliability on semantic web service framework, 2009. Honours: Listed in international biographical dictionaries. Memberships: British Computer Society; Korean Institute of Information Scientists & Engineers. Address: KISTI, 52-11 Eueon-Dong, Yuseong-Gu, Daejeon 305-806, Korea. E-mail: jhm@kisti.re.kr

JUNG In Su, b. 20 June 1972, Seoul, Korea. Researcher. m. Yo Hee Han, 1 son, 1 daughter. Education: Bachelor, 1995, Master, 1997, PhD, 2010, Electronics, Sungkyunkwan University. Appointments: Manager of Accelerator RF Team, Senior Researcher, Korea Institute of Radiological & Medical Sciences, 2001-. Publications: Design of a beam buncher for the KIRAMS-30 cyclotron, 2007; Development of a beam buncher for the KIRAMS-30 cyclotron, 2010. Honours: Listed in international biographical dictionaries. Address: 135-853 Kukje APT, 1-201, Daechi 1-dong, Gangnam-gu, Seoul, Korea.

JUNG Jae Hong, b. 4 February 1975, DaeGu, South Korea. Medical Doctor. m. Jee Young Park, 1 son, 1 daughter. Education: Bachelor, 1999, Master, 2004, Kungpook National University Medical School; Intern and Resident, Samsung Medical Center, 1999-2004. Appointments: Head, Internal Medicine in Population & Welfare Association Clinic, 2004-07; Gastrointestinal Fellowship, Samsung Medical Center, 2007-08; Head, Internal Medicine, Samsung Joen Clinic, 2008-09; Head, Internal Medicine, Median Hospital, 2009-. Publications: The Clinical Findings of Gastrointestinal Burkitt Lymphoma in Adults, 2008. Memberships: Korean Association of Internal Medicine; Korean Association of Gastrointestinal Endoscopy. Address: Kolong Apartment 103-1102, Bangi-dong, Songpa-Gu, Seoul, Korea. E-mail: redcomet20032@yahoo.co.kr

JUNG Tacksun, b. 3 December 1954, Seoul, Republic of Korea. Professor; Mathematician. m. Q-Heung Choi, 1 son, 1 daughter. Education: Bachelor, 1978, Master, 1980, PhD, 1988, Department of Mathematics, Seoul National University, Republic of Korea. Appointments: Lecturer, Department of Mathematics, Seoul National University, 1982-93; Visiting Scholar, Department of Mathematics, Connecticut University, USA, 1988-89; Professor, 1993-2011, Chairman, 1997-99, Department of Mathematics, Kunsan National University. Publications: Existence of Four Solutions of Some Nonlinear Hamiltonian System, 2008; Nonlinearities and Nontrivial Solutions for the nonlinear hyperbolic system, 2009; On the number of the periodic solutions of the nonlinear Hamiltonian system, 2009. Honours: Best Lecturer, Kunsan National University, 2009. Memberships: Korean Mathematical Society; Honam Mathematical Society. Address: Department of Mathematics, Kunsan National University, Kunsan 573-701, Republic of Korea. E-mail: tsjung@kunsan.ac.kr

JUNG Young Bok, b. 16 January 1946, Gyeongsangbukdo, Republic of Korea. m. 1 son, 2 daughters. Education: Graduate, College of Medicine, Kyung-buk National University, 1970; Postgraduate, Department of Orthopaedic Surgery, College of Medicine, Catholic University, Seoul, 1978; PhD, Orthpaedics, 1982. Appointments: Resident, 1974-78, Lecturer, 1978-79, Assistant Professor, 1979-84, Associate Professor, 1984-89, Professor, 1989-2011, Orthopaedic Surgery, College of Medicine, Catholic University, Seoul; Clinical Fellow, 1984-2001, Arthroscopic Surgery, Orthopaedic & Arthritic Hospital, Toronto University, 1986-87; Chairman, Orthopaedic Surgery Department, Yong-San Hospital, Chunag-Ang University, 1994-2001; Chairman, Department of Orthopaedic Surgery, College of Medicine, Chung-Ang University; Vice Director, Department of Orthopaedic Surgery, Hyundae General Hospital, 2011-. Publications: Numerous articles in professional journals. Honours: Best Paper Award, Korean Knee Society, 1998; Good Paper Award, 2004 and 2005, Best Poster Award, 2006, Korean Orthopaedic Association; Achievement Award, Chung-Ang University, 2009 and 2011. Memberships: Korean Orthpaedic Association; Korean Knee Society; Korean Arthroscopic Society; Korean Orthopaedic Sport Medicine Society. Address: Department of Orthopedic Surgery, 663 Janghyun-Ri, Jinjeop-Eup, Namyangju-City, Kyungki Do, 472-865, Republic of Korea.

JURADO-PALOMO Jesús, b. 30 July 1979, Córdoba, Spain. Medical Doctor; Allergist. Education: Medical Doctor, University of Córdoba, Spain, 2003; Clinical Research Degree, Autonomous University of Madrid, Spain, 2006; Allergy Specialist, University Hospital La Paz, Madrid, 2008; Graduate Expert in Clinical Genetics, University of Alcalá de Henares, Spain, 2010. Appointments: Department of Cellular Biology, Physiology and Immunology, School of Medicine, University of Córdoba, 1998-2003; Allergology Specialist, Department of Allergology, University Hospital La Paz, Madrid, 2004-08; Allergology Specialist, Department of Allergology, Complexo Hospitalario Universitario A Coruña, Spain, 2008-09; Allergology Specialist, Nuestra Señora del Prado General Hospital, Talavera de la Reina, Spain, 2009-. Publications: Numerous articles in professional journals, book chapters and clinical assays in areas of specialisation. Honours: Certificate of Excellence in Allergology and Clinical Immunology, European Academy of Allergology and Clinical Immunology, Barcelona, 2008 and London, 2010; Listed in international biographical dictionaries. Memberships: Madrid-Castille La Mancha Society of Allergology and Clinical Immunology; Spanish Society of Allergology and Clinical Immunology; European Academy of Allergology and Clinical Immunology; Spanish Study Group on Bradykinin-induced Angioedema; European Respiratory Society. Address: Department of Allergology, Planta Baja – Consultas Externas, Hospital General Nuestra Señora del Prado, Carretera de Madrid, KM 114, 45600 Talavera de la Reina (Toledo), Spain. E-mail: h72jupaj@yahoo.es

JUŠIĆ Anica, b. 26 July 1926, Zagreb, Croatia. Education: Medical Faculty, A von Humboldt Fellowship, Max-Planck Fellowship. Appointments: Foundation of Centre (later Institute for Neuromuscular Diseases), 1973; Full Professor, 1977; Retired, 1991; Started Hospice Movement in Croatia, Founded Croatian Society for Hospice/Palliative Care, 1994; Croatian Association of Hospice Friends, 1999; Regional Hospice Centre, 2002. Publications: Numerous articles in professional journals; Handbook, Neuromuskularne bolesti I klinicka Electromioneurografija, 1981; Key Ethical Discussions in Hospice/Palliative Care, 2008. Honours: Work Medal with Golden Wreath, 1975; Laureat of Academy of Medical Sciences; Medical Faculty, Zagreb Reward for Humanity and Ethics, 2008. Memberships: Honorary Member, Croatian Medical Association; Academy of Medical Sciences; Nominated for Royal Society of Medicine, UK. Address: Gunduliceva 49, 10000 Zagreb, Croatia.

JUSTO FILHO Joao Francisco, b. 21 December 1966, Sao Paulo, Brazil. Professor. m. Sonia Shiba, 1 son. Education: Bachelor, 1988, Master, 1991, Physics, University of Sao Paulo; PhD, Nuclear Engineering, Massachusetts Institute of Technology, 1997. Appointments: Professor, Escola Politecnica, University of Sao Paulo, 2001-; Visiting Associate Professor, University of Minnesota, 2007-08. Publications: More than 100 publications in international scientific journals. Honours: Member, Alpha Nu Sigma Honor Society; Member, Sigma Xi Honor Society. Memberships: Brazilian Physics Society. Address: Escola Politecnica, Universidade de Sao Paulo, CP 61548, CEP 05508-970, Sao Paulo – SP, Brazil. E-mail: jjusto@lme.usp.br

K

KAANG Shinyoung, b. 18 June 1949, Gwangju, Korea. Professor. m. Eunyoung Chun, 2 sons, 1 daughter. Education: B Eng (Chemical), College of Engineering, Chonnam National University, Korea, 1976; MSc, 1985, PhD, 1988, Polymer Science, University of Akron, Ohio, USA. Appointments: Professor, School of Applied Chemical Engineering, 1989-, Chairman, Department of Polymer & Fine Chemicals Engineering, 1995-97, Chairman, Admission Committee, 1998-99, Vice Chairman, Board of Trustees, 1999-2000, Dean, College of Engineering & Graduate School of Industry Technology, 2006-08, Chonnam National University, Korea; Visiting Professor, University of Washington, USA, 1993-94; Visiting Professor, University of Leeds, England, 1997, 1998; Editor in Chief of Elastomer journal, Korea, 1998-2001; President, The Rubber Society of Korea, 2008-09; Member, Editorial Board, Journal of Adhesion and Interface, Korea, 2000-; Member, Korean Industrial Standards Council & Head of Korean Delegates for ISO/TC45, Korean Agency for Technology and Standards, 2002-; Head, Korean Delegates, IRCO, London, England, 2003-; Trustee, Polymer Society of Korea, 2004-; Co-president, Citizens' Coalition for Scientific Society, Korea, 2005-09; President, Deans' Council for Graduate School of Industry Technology of National Universities, Korea, 2006-07; Vice President, Deans' Council for College of Engineering, Korea, 2006-08; Member, International Advisory Board and Scientific Committee, IRS, Czech Republic, 2007; Member, Presidential Advisory Council on Education, Science and Technology for President of Republic of Korea, 2008-09; Member, International Advisory Committee, 12th ISE, Thailand, 2010. Publications: Translator, An Introduction to Rubber Technology, 2005. Honours: Best Paper Awards, The Rubber Society of Korea, 2002, 2004; Best Book Award, Korean Government, 2005; Medal of Merit, Republic of Korea, 2009. Memberships: ACS, Rubber Division, USA; Editorial Board Member, Polymer Testing journal, Elsevier, UK, 2010-. Address: School of Applied Chemical Engineering, College of Engineering, Chonnam National University, Gwangju 500-757, Republic of Korea. E-mail: kaang@chonnam.ac.kr

KABASAKAL Osman Sermet, b. 16 June 1956, Ankara, Turkey. Chemical Engineer. m. Kadriye Aslan Kabasakal. Education: BS, Chemical Engineering Department, Faculty of Engineering, Hacettepe University, 1984; MS, 1989, PhD, 1995, Chemical Engineering Department, Institute of Science and Technology, Istanbul Technical University. Appointments: Assistant, Chemical Technologies Division, 1985-95, Doktor Associate, 1995-98, Associate Professor, 1998-99, Chemical Engineering Department, ITU Faculty of Chemistry-Metallurgy; Associate Professor, 1999-2005, Professor, 2005-, Chemical Engineering Department, Faculty of Engineering-Architecture, Eskisehir Osmangazi University. Publications: More than 20 articles authored or co-authored published in journals included in the Source Publications List of Science Citation Index (SCI) by Institute of Scientific Information (ISI). Memberships: Turkish Chamber of Chemical Engineers; Turkish Chemical Association; IUPAC Affiliate Member; American Chemical Society (ACS). Address: Eskisehir Osmangazi University, Faculty of Engineering & Architecture, Chemical Engineering Department, Bati Meselik, Eskisehir, 26480, Turkey. E-mail: osk@ogu.edu.tr

KABASAWA Uki, b. 21 January 1965, Namerikawa, Japan. Physicist. Education: Bachelor Degree, 1988, Master Degree, 1990, Osaka University. Appointments: Researcher, Central Research Laboratory, 1990-96, Engineer, Electronic Device Manufacturing Equipment and Engineering Division, 1996-99, Engineer, Instruments, Beam Technology Centre, 1999-2001, Hitachi Ltd; Engineer, Hitachi High-Technologies Corporation, Research and Development Division, 2001-. Publications: Translator: Quantum Theory of Many-Body Systems, 1999; Elements of Advanced Quantum Theory, 2000; Introduction to Mesoscopic Physics, 2000; The Physics of Quantum Fields, 2002; The Case of the Missing Neutrinos, 2002; The Physics of Low-Dimensional Semiconductor, 2004; An Introduction to the Standard Model of Particle Physics, 2005; Fundamentals of Semiconductor Devices, 2008; Quantum Mechanics – A Modern and Concise Introductory Course, 2009; Advanced Quantum Mechanics, 2010; Theory of Superconductivity, 2010; Quantum Field Theory, 2011. Memberships: American Association for the Advancement of Science; New York Academy of Sciences; Physical Society of Japan; Japan Society of Applied Physics. Address: Hitachi High-Technologies Corporation, Beam Technology Centre, 882 Ichige, Hitachinaka-shi, Ibaraki-ken 312-8504, Japan. E-mail: kabasawa-uki@naka.hitachi-hitec.com

KABBAH Alhaji Ahmad Tejan, b. 6 February 1932, Pendembu, Kailahun District, Sierra Leone. President of Sierra Leone. m.(1) Patricia Tucker (deceased), 4 children; (2) Isata Jabbie Kabbah, 2008 . Education: Bachelor's degree in Economics, University College, Aberystwyth, Wales, 1959; Law studies. Appointments: Barrister-at-Law, Honourable Society of Gray's Inn, London, 1969; National and international civil servant in Western Area and in all Provinces of Sierra Leone; District Commissioner, Bombali and Kambia (Northern Province), Kono (Eastern Province), and Moyamba and Bo (Southern Province); Permanent Secretary in various ministries (Trade and Industry, Social Welfare and Education); Deputy Chief, West Africa Division, UN Development Programme (UNDP), New York; Head and Resident Representative, UNDP's operation in Lesotho, 1973; Head of operations in Tanzania, Uganda and Zimbabwe, Head, Eastern and Southern Africa Division, Deputy Director and Director of Personnel, Director of Division of Administration and Management, UNDP; Leader, Sierra Leone Peoples Party; Elected President of Sierra Leone, 1996-1997, 1998-2007. Honours: Chancellor, University of Sierra Leone; Honorary Doctor of Laws degree, University of Sierra Leone; Honorary Doctor of Laws degree, Southern Connecticut State University, USA; Honorary Doctor of Laws, University of Bradford, England; Grand Commander, Order of the Republic of Sierra Leone; Grand Commander of the Republic of the Gambia, 2001. Address: Presidential Lodge, Hill Station, Freetown, Sierra Leone. E-mail: info@statehouse-sl.org Website: www.statehouse.sl

KABBARA Nijad, b. 1943, Fakhe, Lebanon. Scientific Researcher. Education: BS, Physics, Lebanese University, 1972; PostDoc, University of Delaware, Graduate College of Marine Studies, USA, 1999; PhD, Physical Oceanography, University of Perpignan, Department of Marine Geo-Environmental Studies, France, 2005. Appointments: Scientific Researcher. Honours: Fulbright Scholar grant, 1999; National Council for Scientific Research Award, 2007. Memberships: Lebanese Association; International Center for Scientific Culture, World Culture, Switzerland; National Committee, International Geosphere-Biosphere Programme; Ocean Color Community, NASA.

KAČERGIENĖ Nella (Vernickaitė), b. 19 October 1935, Minsk, Belarus. Physician; Paediatrician; Scientific Researcher. Education: Doctor's Assistant, Obstetrician,

Kaunas Paramedical and Obstetrical School, 1954; Physician, Kaunas Medical Institute, 1962; Clinical Physician diploma, 1970, Postgraduate, 1973, Diploma, Candidate of Medical Science, Institute of Paediatrics, USSR, Academy of Medical Sciences, Moscow, 1973; Senior Research Diploma, USSR, 1984; Diploma, Med Sci Doctor's degree, USSR Academy of Medical Sciences, 1987; Senior scientific researcher, Vilnius, 1984; Paediatrician of highest category, Vilnius, 1991; Diploma, Dr Sci habilitas, 1993. Appointments: Nurse, Surgery Department, Kaunas Town Hospital No 2, 1952-54; Doctor's Assistant-Obstetrician, Jieznas Hospital, 1954-56; Paediatrician, Prienai District Hospital, 1962-67, Republican Vilnius Children's Hospital, 1967-68; Clinical Physician of the Institute of Paediatrics, USSR, Academy of Medical Sciences, Moscow, 1968-70; Postgraduate of the Institute of Paediatrics, USSR Academy of Medical Sciences, Moscow, 1970-73; Junior Research Worker, 1973-79, Senior Research Worker, 1979-85, Department of Paediatrics of the Lithuanian Scientific Research Institute of Experimental and Clinical Medicine; Senior Research Worker, Lithuanian Scientific Research Institute of Mother and Child Care, 1985-91; Chief Scientific Researcher, Centre of Paediatrics of Vilnius University Children's Hospital, 1991-97, Centre of Paediatrics of Vilnius University, 1998-2001. Publications: (monograph) SOS to the Life on Earth: The Effect of Environmental Factors and Atmospheric Chemical Pollutants on the Human Organism at Certain Periods of Its Ontogenesis, 1999; Book, The Road to Happiness, 2006; 210 scientific works and 2 inventions. Honours include most recently: Albert Einstein, Genius Dedication, 2009; The International Hippocrates Award, 2009; Ultimate Achiver Award, 2009; Great Minds of the 21st Century, 2009; The International Hippocrates Award for Medical Achievement, 2009; Ultimate Achiever Award, 2009; Medal, Ambassador of Knowledge, 2010; Tesla Award, 2010; Listed in international biographical dictionaries. Memberships include: IBC, LIFBA, IBC Research Council Honorary Member, IBC, England; Honorary Member, Bulgarian Association of Clinical and Experimental Pathophysiology, Sofia; ABI Research Association; International Governors Club, ABI; United Cultural Convention; Order of American Ambassadors; International Women's Review Board; World Academy of Letters; World's Most Respected Expert; The Expert Elite; Committee for Defense of Doctoral Theses, Faculty of Medicine, Vilnius University. Address: Viršuliškių 89-22, LT-05117 Vilnius, Lithuania.

KADRY Seifedine, b. 20 November 1977, Rafid, Bekaa, Lebanon. Professor. m. Diana Fayyad. Education: PhD, Blaise Pascal University, France, 2007. Appointments: Associate Professor, American University of the Middle East. Publications: 42 articles in professional journals. Address: The American University of the Middle East, PO Box 220 Dasman, 15453 Kuwait. E-mail: skadry@gmail.com

KAFELNIKOV Yevgeny Aleksandrovich, b. 18 February 1974, Sochi, Russia. Tennis Player. m. 2 daughters. Education: Krasnodar Pedagogical Institute. Appointments: Started playing tennis in Sochi Children Sports School, 1982; Later with coach Anatoly Lepeshin; ATP Professional, 1992-; Won 17 ATP tournaments including Milan, St Petersburg, Gstaad, Long Island; Won French Open (singles and doubles), 1996; Won, Moscow Kremlin Cup, 1997; Won, Australian Open, 1999; Member, Russian Federation Davis Cup Championship Team, 1993; Runner-up, World Championship, Hanover, 1997; Highest ATP Rating 1st, 1999; Olympic singles champion, Sydney, 2000; Winner of 51 pro titles by 2002. Address: All-Russian Tennis Association, Luzhnetskaya nab 8, 119871 Moscow, Russia.

KAGAYA Hiroshi Kan, b. 8 August 1930, Tokyo, Japan. Professor Emeritus. m. Kazuko, 2 sons, 1 daughter. Education: MA, Humanities, Tokyo University, 1956. Appointments: Professor, Osaka University of Foreign Studies, 1960-95. Publications: History of Modern Iran, 1975; Urdu-Japanese Dictionary, 2005. Honours: Professor Emeritus, Osaka University of Foreign Studies; Sitara-i Quaid-i Aazam, Government of Pakistan, 2007; Zhuiho Chujusho Prize, Government of Japan, 2010. Memberships: Academic associations for Islamic, Iranian and South-Asian studies, Japan. Address: Nishiyamacho 4-59, Koyoen, Nishinomiya, Japan 662. E-mail: qq337h6@cure.ocn.ne.jp

KAHL Lesley Patricia, b. Newcastle, Australia. Research Scientist; Specialist in Clinical Drug Development. Divorced, 1 daughter. Education: BSc (Hons I), University of Newcastle, New South Wales, Australia, 1979; PhD, Medical Biology, University of Melbourne, Victoria, Australia, 1983. Appointments: Postdoctoral Research Fellow, Department of Medicine, Harvard Medical School, Boston, USA, 1983-86; Postdoctoral Research Fellow, Wellcome Laboratories, London, England, 1986-92; Principal/Senior Clinical Research Scientist, Wellcome/Glaxo Wellcome, London, 1992-2004; Senior Manager and Manager, Clinical Development, GlaxoSmithKline, London, 2005-. Publications: Numerous articles to professional journals including bench and clinical research mainly in the area of infectious disease. Honours: University Gold Medal for Excellence in the Science Faculty, University of Newcastle, New South Wales, 1979; NIH Fogarty International Post Doctoral Fellow, Harvard Medical School, Boston, 1983-86; Awarded Chartered Scientist status, The Science Council, UK, 2009; Listed in international biographical directories. Memberships: Assoc. Member, Royal Society of Medicine, London; Institute of Clinical Research. Address: Respiratory and Immuno-Inflammation CCSE, GlaxoSmithKline, Stockley Park West, Uxbridge, UB11 1BT, England. E-mail: lesley.p.kahl@gsk.com

KAHN Howard, Senior Lecturer. Education: MA (Hons), Political Economy and Modern History, University of Glasgow, 1967; MSc, Organisational Psychology, 1987, PhD, 1990, University of Manchester Institute of Science and Technology. Appointments: Analyst, British Steel Corporation, 1967-70; Senior Analyst, Corporation of Lloyd's of London, 1970-73; Principal Lecturer, Department of Business Information Technology, Faculty of Management and Business, Manchester Polytechnic, 1973-90; Director of Research, International University of East Africa, Kampala, Uganda; Management Consultant, Organisational Behaviour, School of Management, Heriot-Watt University, 1991-2009. Publications: Numerous articles in professional journals, consultancy reports and book contributions; 3 books. Honours: British Psychological Society Certificate in Competence in Occupational Testing; National Computing Centre Certificate in Systems Analysis; Chartered Information Systems Practitioner; Qualified Professional Reviewer and Licenced Membership Assessor of the British Computer Society; Outstanding Paper, 2007; Fellowship, 2008 Summer Institute, Israel. Memberships: British Academy of Management; Chartered Member, British Computer Society; British Psychological Society; Association for Coaching; Fellow, Higher Education Academy. Address: 27 Blinkbonny Road, Ravelston, Edinburgh, EH4 3HY, Scotland.

KAIDAR Abduali Tuganbai-uly, b. 13 December 1924, Enbekshi-Kazakh region, Kazakhstan. Professor. m. Altynbekova Sheker Isa-kysy, 3 daughters. Education: Philological Faculty, Kazakh State University, 1947-51;

Post-graduate Course, Uigur Linguistics, Kazakh Academy of Sciences, 1951-54; Candidate Dissertation, Alma-Ata, 1955; Doctor's degree, Baku, 1970. Appointments: Deputy Director, 1961-78, Director, 1978-94, Research Worker, 1994-, Institute of Linguistics, Academician, 1983, Kazakh Academy of Sciences; Honorable Academician, Bashkir Academy of Sciences, 1986. Publications: 450 publications including 54 books, textbooks, dictionaries and booklets. Memberships: Honorable Member, Turkey Linguistic Society Til-gurumy; President, International Society Kazakh Tili. Address: ap 8, 8-7272-91-00-61, Chokan Valikhanov street 128, Almaty, Kazakhstan.

KAKÁ (Ricardo Izecson dos Santos Leite), b. 22 April 1982, Brasilia, Brazil. Professional Footballer. m. Caroline Celico, 2005, 1 son. Career: Professional Football Player: Sao Paulo, 2001-03; Milan, 2003-09; Real Madrid, 2009-. Honours: Copa Sao Paulo de Juniores, 2000; FIFA World Cup, 2002; Torneio Rio-Sao Paulo, 2001; Serie A, 2003-04; Italian Super Cup, 2003-04; FIFA Confederations Cup, 2005, 2009; UEFA Champions League, 2006-07; UEFA Super Cup, 2003-04, 2007-08; FIFA Club World Cup, 2007; Ballon d'Or, 2007; FIFA World Player of the Year, 2007.

KAKATI Dinesh Chandra, b. 1 February 1941, Soalkuchi, Assam, India. Doctor of Medicine. m. Bhabani, 1 son, 1 daughter. Education: MBBS, Guwahati University, India, 1967; Diploma in Tropical Medicine, University of Liverpool, England, 1970; Diploma in Thoracic Medicine, Diploma in Cardiac Medicine, University of London, 1984; Diploma in Geriatric Medicine, Royal College of Physicians of London, 1985; Vocational Training Certificate, Royal College of General Practitioners, 1987; Intra-Uterine Device, Family Planning Certificate, Joint Committee on Contraception, 1987. Appointments: House Officer, Senior House Officer, Gauhati Medical College Hospital, Assam, India, 1967-68; General Medicine, Ingham Infirmary, South Shields, England, 1969; Senior House Officer, Registrar, Sunderland General Hospital, Sunderland, 1969-72; Registrar, Addenbrookes Hospital and Chesterton Hospital, Cambridge, 1972-74; Internal Medicine, University of Edinburgh, Scotland, 1973; Registrar, London Hospital and Bethnal Green Hospital, London, 1974-77; Specialist and Consultant, Oldchurch Hospital, Romford, 1977-83; Postgraduate Student, National Heart Hospital, Brompton Hospital, London Chest Hospital, London, 1983-84; Clinical Assistant, Romford Group of Hospitals based at St George's Hospital, Hornchurch, 1984-2002; General Practice Principal, Berwick Surgery, Rainham, 1997-. Publications: Numerous articles in professional journals. Honours: Class examination medals; 4th place, Guwahati University Order of Merit; Distinction, MBBS, Guwahati University; Glory of India Award, 2008; Listed in international biographical dictionaries. Memberships: Cultural Association of Assam in the UK; Chairman, Sankar Jayanty Celebration Committee, UK; Assamese Bihu Committee, UK; British Medical Association; Royal College of General Practitioners of London; Royal Society of Health; Chairman, Cultural Association of Asam; Cardiology Advsier to Havering Primary Care Trust. Address: Assam Manor, 99 Ardleigh Green Road, Hornchurch, Essex RM11 2LE, England. E-mail: dinesh.kakali@nhs.net

KALAL Milan, b. 24 March 1952, Jicin, Czech Republic. Physicist; University Educator. m. Vera Dudkova, 2 sons, 1 daughter. Education: MSc, 1976, PhD, 1984, Faculty of Nuclear Sciences and Physical Engineering, Associate Professor, 1999, Czech Technical University, Prague. Appointments: Long Term Research Visit, Australian National University, Canberra, Australia, 1984-87; Fellow, 1987-94, Senior Fellow, 1994-98, Deputy Head, Department of Physical Electronics, 1998-2000, Vice Dean, 2000-06, Faculty of Nuclear Sciences and Physical Engineering, Czech Technical University, Prague; Chair, School of Applied and Engineering Physics, 2006-. Publications: Over 80 papers in international scientific journals. Honours: Czech Technical University Medal, 2002; Ambassador of Peace, 2003; Leadership and Governance Medal. Memberships: Laser and Particle Beams Journal; European Conference on Laser Interaction with Matter; IAEA Fusion Energy Conference; Beam Plasma & Inertial Fusion Board, European Physical Society. Address: Bronzova 2011/3, 155 00 Prague 5, Czech Repbulic. E-mail: kalal@mymail.cz

KALBITZER Seigfried, b. 11 May 1934, Essen, Germany. Physicist. Education: Graduate, Nuclear Physics, 1961, Habilitation, 1995, University of Heidelberg. Appointments: Scientist, Brookhaven National Laboratory, New York, USA, 1962-65; Group Leader, Max Planck Institute for Nuclear Physics, Heidelberg, 1964-99; Professor, University of Pretoria, Republic of South Africa, 1994; Founder, Ion Beam Technology, 1999. Address: Bahofweg 2, 69121 Heidelberg, Germany. E-mail: skalbitzer@aol.com

KALEVO Ossi Mikael, b. 24 May 1968, Lohja Mlk, Finland. Technology Fellow. m. Mari Susanna Kacevo Ratto. Education: MSc, 1992, Licenciate of Technology, 1999, Tampere University of Technology. Appointments: Senior Researcher, Tampere University of Technology, 1991-96; Senior Researcher, Nokia Research Center, 1996-2003; Technology Fellow & Distinguished Specialist, Nokia Oyj, 2003-. Publications: 13 conference papers; 150 granted patents; 80 pending patent applications. Address: Ketunhanta 1, 37800 Toijala, Finland.

KALININ Vladimir, b. 24 May 1960, Novosibirsk, Russia. Physicist; Consultant. Divorced, 2 sons. Education: MSc, Physics, Novosibirsk State University, 1982; PhD, Physics & Numerical Methods, Institute of Theoretical and Applied Mechanics, Academy of Sciences of USSR, Novosibirsk, 1989; Docent, Applied Mathematics, Novosibirsk Construction University, Russia, 1999. Appointments: Engineer, Electro-Physicist, Institute of Power Generation, Novosibirsk, Russia, 1982-83; Junior Researcher, 1983-90; Research Scientist, 1990-92, Senior Research Scientist, 1995-96, Institute of Theoretical and Applied Mechanics, Russian Academy of Sciences, Novosibirsk; Business and Lecturing, 1992-94; Research Scientist, Halle-Wittenberg University, Germany, 1998-99; Senior Development Engineer, Engineering Solution International Ltd, Dublin, 1999-2003; Expert Engineer, Wavebob Ltd, Co Kildare, 2003-09; Director, Techno-Modelling Arts Ltd, Co Louth, Ireland. Publications: 37 articles in professional journals (before 1999, published under the name V Melesko, since 2000, surname changed to Kalinin). Honours: Listed in various international biographical dictionaries. Address: 8 Cul na Raithe, Omeath, Co Louth, Ireland.

KALKHOF Peter Heinz, b. 20 December 1933, Stassfurt, Germany. Painter; Lecturer in Fine Art. m. Jeanne The, deceased, 1 son. Education: Graduated, School of Arts and Crafts, Braunschweig, 1953-55; Academy of Fine Art, Stuttgart, 1956-60; Slade School of Fine Art, London, 1960-61; Ecole des Beaux Arts, Paris, 1962. Career: Exhibitions include Annely Juda Fine Art, London, 1970, 1974, 1977, 1979, 1997, 2002; Kulturgeschichtliches Museum, Osnabrück, 1977; Landesmuseum, Oldenburg,

1988; Camden Arts Centre, London, 1989; Ostpreussen Museum, Lueneburg, 1989; Prignitz Museum am Dom, Havelberg, 1994; Stadt Museum Schieder-Schwalenberg, 1996; Galerie Planie, Reutlingen, 1998; St Hugh's College, Oxford, 1998; Gallery Rösch, Houston, Texas, 2000; Gallery: t 1+2, London, 2004; Numerous group exhibitions; Mural painting commission, Treaty-Centre, Hounslow, London, 1987; Appointment: Lecturer in Fine Art, Fine Art Department, Reading University, 1966-99. Publications: Exhibition catalogues, including, Kulturgeschichtliches Museum, Osnabrück, 1977; Landesmuseum, Oldenburg, 1988; Annely Juda Fine Art, London, 1990, 1997, 2002; Gallery Rösch, Karlsruche, 1994; Galerie Planie, Reutlingen, 1998; Annely Juda Fine Art, London, 2002; Annely Juda Fine Art, London, 2007. Honours: First Prize, Portrait Competition, Academy of Fine Art, Stuttgart, 1959; Slade School travel grant, 1961; Artist-in-residence, Osnabrück, 1985; Künstlerhaus Schieder-Schwalenberg, Germany, 1995, 1996. Memberships: Member of the Friends of the British Museum Society; Member of the Friends of the Victoria and Albert Museum; Member of the Friends of the Royal Academy; Member, Tate Gallery, London. Address: 19 Lansdowne Crescent, London W11 2NS, England. E-mail: p.kalkhof@virgin.net

KALMBACH Gudrun, b. 27 May 1937, Grosserlach, Germany. Professor. Education: Dr rer. nat. University of Göttingen, Germany. Appointments: Assistant, University of Göttingen, Germany, 1963-66; Lecturer, University of Illinois, Urbana, USA, 1967-69; Assistant Professor, University of Massachusetts, Amherst, USA, 1970-71; Assistant Professor, Pennsylvania State University, University Park, USA, 1969-75; Professor, University of Ulm, Germany, 1975-2002; Director, MINT, 2003-. Publications: 12 books; Articles in professional journals on algebra, topology, quantum structures, education and women; Chief Editor, Journal MINT; Evolution of Physics, 2008; Macroscopic Proton Model, 2011. Honours: 4 medals; 2 titles; 3 books in honour of 60th Birthday; Albert Schweitzer Medal, 2008. Memberships: AMS; Emmy-Noether-Verein (Chair); FDP; LDA; OIA. Address: PF 1533, D-86818 Bad Woerishofen, Germany. E-mail: mint-01@maxi-dsl.de

KALRA G L, b. 1 July 1941, Londkhor, Pakistan. Teacher; Researcher. m. Raj Kalra, 2 daughters. Education: MSc, 1962, PhD, 1967, University of Delhi. Appointments: Senior Research Fellow, University of Delhi, 1966-69; Fellow, Flinders University of South Australia, 1969-70; RA, University of Delhi, 1970-74; Lecturer, 1974-84; Reader, 1984-86; Associate Professor, Al Fateh University, Tripoli, 1986-87; Reader, University of Delhi, 1984-94; Professor in Physics, University of Delhi, 1994-2006. Publications: 51 research papers mostly in international scientific journals. Honours: Hari Om Ashram Prerit Dr Vikram Sarabhai Research Award in Planetary and Space Sciences, 1985; Australia VC's Committee Visiting Fellowship, 1990; Offered New York Academy of Sciences Membership, also American Chemical Society Membership. Memberships: Founder Member, Astronomical Society of India; Founder Member of Plasma Science Society of India; Listed in Who's Who and biographical publications. Address: G-89 Ashok Vihar, Delhi 110052, India.

KALTENBACH Anneliese Elisabeth, b. Karlsruhe-Durlach, Germany. Retired Senior Civil Servant. Education: Diplomas, Commercial French and English, Germanic, General Linguistics, History Studies, Russian Language and Literature; Licenciée ès Lettres, 1957; PhD, Paris University, 1962; Appointments: Deputy Chief, Press and Information Office, Federal Government of Bonn; German Embassy, Paris, Ministry for Foreign Affairs, Bonn. Publications include: Ludwig Haeusser, Historien et patriote (1818-1867), 1965; Many contributions to scientific reviews and newspapers. Honours include: Gold Medal, Robert Schuman, Silver Gilt Medal, Municipality of Paris, Bronze Medal Académie Française, 1966; Officer Ordre de Leopold, Belgium, 1971; Commandeur, Ordre Oranje-Nassau, Netherlands, 1971; Commandeur Ordre du Mérite du Grand-Duché de Luxembourg, 1973; Commandeur de l'Ordre de Leopold II, Belgium, 1974; Silver Medal, French-German Youth Office, 1982; Officier, 1974, Commandeur de l'Ordre National du Mérite de la République Française, 1980; Order of Merit First Class, Federal Republic of Germany, 1982; Officer dans l'ordre des Palmes Académiques, 1995. Address: Duerenstrasse 29, D 53173 Bonn, Germany.

KALTENIS Petras, b. 12 November 1937, Berzyte, Kedainiai district, Lithuania. Retired. Education: Kaunas Medical University, 1955-61. Appointments: Senior Editor, Lithuanian Soviet Encylcopaedia, 1961-63; Assistant Professor, 1963-72, Associate Professor, Professor, 1974-90, Professor, 2002-09, Vilnius University; Head, Department of Medical Informatics, Institute of Experimental and Clinical Medicine, 1972-74; Head, Centre of Paediatrics, 1991-2002; Pensioner, 2009-. Publications: 3 monographs; Co-author of 3 textbooks. Honours: Lithuanian Science Award, 1994; Lithuanian Independence Medal, 2000; Award of 2nd degree for textbook, Children's Diseases, 2006. Memberships: Lithuanian Paediatric Society; Lithuanian Society of Paediatric Nephrology. Address: Antakalnio str 95-3, Vilnius, LT-10218, Lithuania.

KAMAL Ahmed, b. 5 April 1956, Hyderabad, India. Scientist. m. Kausar, 2 sons, 1 daughter. Education: BSc, Osmania, 1975; MSc, 1977, M Phil, 1979, PhD, 1982, Aligarh; Postdoctoral Research Work, Portsmouth, England, 1988-89. Appointments: Scientist B, 1983-89, Scientist C, 1989-92, Scientist, EI, 1992-97, Scientist EII, 1997-2002, Scientist F, 2002-07, Scientist G, 2007-10, Scientist H, 2010-, IICT, Hyderabad; Postdoctoral Trainee, University of Portsmouth, England, 1988-89; Visiting Scientist, University of Alberta, Canada, 1993-94; Project Director, NIPER, Hyderabad, 2009-; Visiting Professor, King Saud University, Saudi Arabia, 2011-. Publications: Over 270 scientific papers; 12 review articles; Around 60 patents. Honours: CSIR Young Scientist Award in Chemical Sciences, 1991; Fellow, National Academy of Sciences, India, 1999; Best Patent Award, Indian Drug Manufacturers Association, 2005; Medal, Chemical Research Society of India, 2005; Ranbaxy Research Award, 2005; UKIERI Standard Award for Biomedical Solutions, 2006; Andhra Pradesh Scientist Award, 2007; Organization of Pharmaceutical Producer of India (OPPI) Scientist Award, 2009. Memberships: Chemical Research Society of India; Indian Society of Bio-organic Chemists. Address: Chemical Biology Laboratory, Organic Chemistry, Indian Institute of Chemical Technology, Tarnaka, Hyderabad – 500 607 (AP), India. E-mail: ahmedkamal@iict.res.in

KAMALIAN Rafayel, b. 15 October 1962, Yerevan, Armenia. Scientist; Researcher; Lecturer. Education: Graduate, Physics-Mathematics School, 1979, Hon Dip, Department of Applied Mathematics, 1984, Yerevan State University; PhD, Graph Theory, Institute of Mathematics, Siberian Branch of the Academy of Sciences of USSR, Novosibirsk, 1990. Appointments: Lecturer, Ajevan Branch, Yerevan State University, 2004-; Postgraduate, 1985-88, Junior Researcher, 1987-91, Researcher, 1991-94, Adv Researcher, 1994-2006,

Senior Researcher, 2007-, IIAP of NASRA. Publications: More than 35 publications in professional journals. Honours: Gold Medal; Honours Diploma, Yerevan State University. Address: fl 50, build 22, 1st subst of Aygedzor street, Yerevan, 0019, Republic of Armenia. E-mail: rrkamalian@yahoo.com

KAMEDA Hisao, b. 15 April 1942, Gifu-City, Gifu, Japan. University Professor Emeritus. m. Mieko Kameda, 3 sons. Education: Bachelor of Science, 1965, Master of Science, 1967, Doctor of Science, 1970, University of Tokyo, Tokyo, Japan. Appointments: Research Associate, University of Tokyo, 1970-71; Assistant Professor, University of Electro-Communications, 1971-73; Visiting Scientist, IBM T J Watson Research Center, 1973-74; Visiting Researcher, University of Toronto, 1974-75; Associate Professor, 1973-85, Professor, 1985-92, University of Electro-Communications; Professor, 1992-96, Professor Emeritus, 2006-, University of Tsukuba. Publications: Articles in professional journals including: JACM, ACM Transactions on Computer Systems, IEEE Transactions on Computer, IEEE Transactions Software Engineering, IEEE Transactions on Automatic Control, IEEE Transactions on Parallel and Distributed Systems; IEEE Journal on Selected Areas in Communications. Honours: Fellow, IEEE; Fellow, IEICE; Fellow, IPSJ; Fellow, ORSJ; Best Paper Award, IEEE NACON '97; Listed in numerous Who's Who and biographical publications. Address: Department CS, Graduate School of SIE, University of Tsukuba, 1-1-1 Tennodai, Tsukuba Science City, Ibaraki 305-8573, Japan. Website: www.osdp.cs.tsukuba.ac.jp/kameda

KAMENAR Boris, b. 20 February 1929, Susak-Rijeka. University Professor. m. Maja Perusko, Vedrana. Education: Diploma in Chemical Technology, University of Zagreb, 1953; PhD, Chemistry, University of Zagreb, 1960; Postdoctoral Fellowship, University of Oxford, England, 1964. Appointments: Head, Testing Laboratory, Metal Factory, Rijeka, 1953-56; Research Scientist, Rudjer Boskovic Institute, Zagreb, 1956-62; Assistant and Associate Professor, 1962-72, Professor of Chemistry, 1972-99, Professor Emeritus, 1999-, University of Zagreb; Visiting Fellow, All Souls College, Oxford, 1971-72; Visiting Professor, University of Auckland, New Zealand, 1980; Visiting Professor, Massey University, Palmerston North, New Zealand, 1989-90, 1995. Publications: About 160 articles in scientific journals. Honours: Scientific Award, Republic of Croatia, 1970; Scientific Award, City of Zagreb, 1980; Scientific Award for Life Achievement, Republic of Croatia, 1999; Božo Težak Medal, Croatian Chemical Society, 2002. Memberships: Croatian Chemical Society; European Crystallographic Committee; Croatian Academy of Sciences and Arts; Fellow, World Academy of Art and Science; Croatian Crystallographic Association; Macedonian Academy of Sciences and Art. Address: Laboratory of General and Inorganic Chemistry, Faculty of Science, University of Zagreb, Horvatovac 102A, 10000 Zagreb, Croatia.

KAMERER Jocelyne Maria, b. 6 September 1950, Pont-a-Moussons, France. Poet. Education: Kaiserlautern American High School, Kaiserlautern, West Germany. Career: Secretary; Poet; Cocktail Waitress. Publications: Reflections, 1990; Contributions to many poetry journals including Poets of Now, Simply Words, Milo Rosebud, World of Poetry and others. Honours: 10 awards from Association for Advancement of Poetry including: Gold Quill Award, 1990, Silver Quill Award, 1990; Southern Poetry Association, 4 awards, 1991; Khepera, 3 awards, 1994; More than 15 1st Place, Robert Bennett's Viewpoint; Certificate for teaching Christian Doctrine in Kaiserslautern, West Germany and at St Thomas Aquinas Cathedral, Reno, Nevada, 1984-85; Listed in international biographical dictionaries; Nominee, International Peace Prize, 2006; Register of the World's Most Respected Experts, 2006; Woman of the Year, 2006. Memberships: Sponsor of veterans' groups such as Disabled American Veterans and Blind Veterans of America; Childrens' Burn Foundation, Burbank, California; Many animal charities. Address: 6256 Village Lane, Colorado Springs, CO 80918, USA.

KAMEYAMA Michitaka, b. 12 May 1950, Utsunomiya, Japan. Professor. m. Kimiko Owashi, 1 son, 2 daughters. Education: Bachelor Degree, Electronic Engineering, 1973, Master Degree, Electronic Engineering, 1975, Doctor Degree, Electronic Engineering, 1978, Tohoku University. Appointments: Research Associate, 1978-81, Associate Professor, 1981-91, Professor, 1991-, Tohoku University. Publications include: A Multiplier Chip with Multiple-Valved Bidirectional Current-Mode Logic Circuits, IEEE Computer, 1988. Membership: Fellow, IEEE. Address: 6-10-8 Minami-Yoshinari, Aoba-ku, Sendai, Japan.

KAMINSKI Wlodzimierz, b. 16 April 1924, Skierniewice, Poland. Scientist; Economist. m. Krystyna Tyszkowska, 1 son. Education: MS, 1947, LLD, 1948, University of Cracow; DAgricEcon, 1961, Professor, Economic Sciences, 1973-92, doctor honoris causa, 2000, Agricultural University, Warsaw. Appointments: Researcher, Economist, 1959-92, Extraordinary Professor, 1973-80, Ordinary Professor, 1980-92, Faculty of Food Technology, Agricultural University, Warsaw; Editorial Board, International Journal of Refrigeration, 1975-99; Ordinary Professor, 1997-2009, Prorector, 1998-2004, Warsaw College of Economics, Warsaw; Visiting Professor, various universities and institutions; Head, Division for Spatial Research, 1983-92, Director, 1990, Institute of Agricultural and Food Economics. Publications: 27 books, over 300 publications in 8 languages; Author, Regional Aspects of Food Economy, 1989; Booklet, Refrigeration and the Worldwide Food Industry on the Threshold of the 21st Century, 1995; Nobel Prize Winners in Economic Sciences (1969-2000) – my impressions and fascinations, 2004. Honours: Knight, Officer and Commander Cross of Polonia Restituta, 1964, 1979, 1987; 5 awards, Minister of Education, 1975-85; 1st scientific award, Minister of Agriculture, 1991; Cross of National Army, Polish Government, 1994; Croix d'Officier du Merite Agricole, French Government, 1995; Award, International Institute of Refrigeration, 1999; Man of the Year, 2004; Professor Pijanowski Award, Polish Scientific Society of Food Industry, 2006. Memberships: Polish Scientific Society of Food Industry; Polish Academy of Sciences; 2 committees, Association of Agricultural Economists; Hungarian Scientific Society of Food Industry; French Academy of Agriculture; International Institute of Refrigeration, Paris; New York Academy of Sciences, 1995-2004. Address: Smolna 15, Room 11, 00375 Warsaw, Poland.

KAMNEV Alexander Anatolievich, b. 17 December 1958, Saratov, Russian Federation (USSR). Chemist; Researcher. m. Angella B Mashkina, 1 son, 2 daughters. Education: MSc, Chemistry, 1980; Cand Sci (PhD), Physical Chemistry, 1992; DSc, Physical Chemistry, Saratov State University, 2002; Professor (in physical chemistry), Higher Attestation Committee of the Russian Federation (Moscow) 2010. Appointments: Junior Scientist to Scientist, Scientific Research Institute of Chemistry, Saratov State University, 1980-92; Senior Scientist to Leading Scientist, Institute of Biochemistry and Physiology of Plants and Microorganisms, Russian Academy of Sciences, Saratov, 1992-. Publications:

Over 100 papers in refereed specialised journals and edited volumes, book chapters. Honours: Several research grants and short-term fellowships. Memberships: Russian Microbiological Society; Russian Society of Biochemists and Molecular Biologists. Address: IBPPM RAS, 13 Prospekt Entuziastov, 410049 Saratov, Russia. E-mail: aakamnev@ibppm.sgu.ru Website: www.ibppm.saratov.ru

KAMU Okko, b. 7 Mar 1946, Helsinki, Finland. Conductor.Education: Violin studies with Väinö Arjava from 1949 and with Professor Onni Suhonen at the Sibelius Academy, Helsinki, 1952-67. Career: Leader of the Suhonen Quartet, 1964; Leader of the Finnish National Opera Orchestra, 1966-69; Conducted Britten's The Turn of the Screw in Helsinki, 1968; Guest Conductor, Swedish Royal Opera, 1969; Chief Conductor, Finnish Radio Symphony Orchestra, 1971-77; Music Director,Oslo Philharmonic, 1975-79; Music Director, Helsinki Philharmonic,1981-88; Principal Conductor, Dutch Radio Symphony, 1983-86; Principal Guest Conductor, City of Birmingham Symphony Orchestra, 1985-88;Principal Conductor, Sjaelland Symphony Orchestra (Copenhagen Philharmonic), 1988-89; Guest engagements with the Berlin Philharmonic,Suisse Romande Orchestra, Vienna Symphony Orchestra and orchestras in the USA, Far East, Australia, South America and Europe; Conducted the premieres of Sallinen's operas The Red Line and The King Goes Forth to France; Metropolitan Opera, 1983, US premiere of The Red Line; Covent Garden, 1987, in the British premiere of The King Goes Forth to France; Principal Conductor of the Helsingborg Symphony Orchestra, 1991-2000; Music Director of the Finnish National Opera, 1996-2000; Principal Guest Conductor, Singapore Symphony Orchestra, 1995-2001 and principal Guest Conductor of Lausanne Chamber Orchestra, 1999-2002. Recordings: About 70 recordings for various labels; Sallinen's Shadows, Cello Concerto and 5th Symphony. Honours: Winner, 1st Herbert von Karajan Conductors' Competition, Berlin, 1969; Member of the Royal Swedish Academy of Music. Address: Villa Arcadia, C/Mozart 7, Rancho Domingo, 29639 Benalmadena Pueblo, Spain.

KANAI Akifumi, b. 23 September 1967, Japan. Medical Doctor. m. 1 son. Education: MD, Kitasato University School of Medicine, Japan, 1994; PhD, 2001. Appointments: Medical Doctor. Publications: Numerous articles in professional journals. Honours: Listed in international biographical dictionaries. Address: 1-15-1 Kitasato, Minami-ku, Sagamihara 252-0374, Japan. E-mail: kanaiakifumi@aol.com

KANEMATSU Hideyuki, b. 21 November 1957, Sakai, Osaka, Japan. Researcher. m. Reiko Komori, 1 son, 1 daughter. Education: B Eng, 1981, M Eng, 1983, PhD, 1989, Materials Science and Engineering, Nagoya University. Appointments: Research Associate, Department of Materials Science and Engineering, Faculty of Engineering, Nagoya University, 1986; Research Associate, Department of Materials Science and Engineering, Faculty of Engineering, Osaka University, 1990; Research Associate, 1992, Assistant Professor, 1994, Associate Professor, 1997, Full Professor, 2007, Dean, 2010-, Department of Materials Science and Engineering, Director, Processing of Information Processing Center, 2009, Suzuka National College of Technology; Vice Director, Academic-Industrial Co-operation Centre, 2010-. Publications: 13 books; 290 scientific papers; 19 patent applications. Honours: Listed in international biographical dictionaries; Professional Member, 2001, Fellow, 2007, Institute of Metal Finishing in UK; Wood Badge, Scout Association of Japan, 2002; Outstanding Achievement Award, American Chemical Society, 2002; President Award, Association of National Colleges of Technology, Japan, 2003; Educational Incentive Award, Suzuka National College of Technology, 2003; Chem Luminary Award, American Chemical Society, 2004; Long Service Award for 20 Years, Institute of National Colleges of Technology, 2006; Visiting Professor, Clarkson University, USA, 2009; Creative Education Institute (Yonsei Complex), South Korea, 2009. Memberships: Institute of Metal Finishing in UK; National Association for Surface Finishing, USA The Minerals, Metals & Materials Society, USA; ASM International; American Society for Engineering Education, USA; Japan Institute of Metals; Iron and Steel Institute of Japan; Japanese Society for Engineering Education; Surface Finishing Society of Japan; Japan Society of Heat Treatment; Japan Industrial Archaeology Society; The Molten Salt Committee; The Japan Institute of Marine Engineering. Address: 2-4-31 Shinonome Nishi-machi, Sakai-ku, Sakai, Osaka 590-0013, Japan. E-mail: kanemats@mse.suzuka-ct.ac.jp

KANET Roger Edward, b. 1 September 1936, Cincinnati, Ohio, USA. University Professor. m. Joan Alice Edwards, 2 daughters. Education: PhB, Berchmanskolleg, Pullach-bei-München, Germany, 1960; AB, Xavier University, Cincinnati, Ohio, 1961; MA, Lehigh University, Bethlehem, Pennsylvania, 1963; AM, 1965, PhD, 1966, Princeton University, New Jersey. Appointments: Assistant Professor, 1966-69, Associate Professor, 1969-74, Associate Chairman, 1970-71, Department of Political Science, University of Kansas; Joint Senior Fellow, Research Institute on Communist Affairs and Russian Institute, 1972-73, Columbia University; Visiting Associate Professor of Political Science, 1973-74, Associate Professor, 1974-78, Professor, 1978-97, Professor Emeritus, 1997-, Department of Political Science, Member of Russian and East European Center, 1974-97, Member of Program in Arms Control, Disarmament and International Security, 1979-97, 2008-, Associate Vice Chancellor for Academic Affairs, Director of International Programs and Studies, 1989-97, University of Illinois at Urbana-Champaign; Professor, 1997-, Department of International Studies, Dean, 1997-2000, School of International Studies, University of Miami, Coral Gables. Publications: Author of 230 scholarly articles, primarily on Soviet/Russian and East European foreign and security policies and democratisation, and more than 400 other publications; Books include: Identities, Nations and Politics after Communism, 2008; The United States and Europe in a Changing World, 2009; A Resurgent Russia and the West: The European Union, NATO and Beyond, 2009; Russian Foreign Policy in the 21st Century, 2010; Key Players and Regional Dynamics in Eurasia: The Return of the Great Game, 2010. Honours include: NATO Faculty Fellow, 1977; College of Liberal Arts and Sciences and Campus Awards for Excellence in Undergraduate Teaching, University of Illinois at Urbana Champaign, 1981; Department of Political Science Pi Sigma Alpha/Clarence A Berdahl Award for Excellence in Undergraduate Teaching, University of Illinois at Urbana-Champaign, 1984. Memberships include: Council on Foreign Relations, New York; International Committee for Soviet and East European Studies; International Studies Association; American Association for the Advancement of Slavic Studies. Address: Department of International Studies, University of Miami, PO Box 248123, Coral Gables, FL 33124-2231, USA. E-mail: rkanet@miami.edu

KANEVSKAYA Regina Dmitrievna, b. 18 December 1960, Moscow, Russia. Petroleum Engineer; Educator; Researcher. m. Anatoly Vladimirovitsh Kanevsky, 1981, 1 son, 1 daughter. Education: M, 1983, DSc, 1999, Applied Mathematics, Russian State University of Oil and Gas,

Moscow; PhD, All-Union Research Institute of Oil and Gas, Moscow, 1988. Appointments: Researcher, 1983-89, Senior Researcher, 1989-91, All-Union Research Institute of Oil and Gas, Moscow; Head of Department, ENPETRO Research and Design Co, Moscow, 1991-2002; Head of Group, Sibneft Oil Co, Moscow, 2002-06; Head of Department, 2006-10, Deputy Director for Science of Research & Engineering Centre, 2010-, RUSSNEFT Oil Co, Moscow; Professor, Russian State University of Oil and Gas, Moscow, 2000-; Expert, State Commission of Resources, Moscow, 2003-. Publications: Books: Simulation of Oil and Gas Reservoir Engineering Using Hydraulic Fracturing, 1999; Simulation of Hydrodynamic Processes in Hydrocarbon Reservoirs, 2003; Subsurface Fluid Mechanics, 2005; Contributed to over 85 publications to professional journals. Memberships: Society of Petroleum Engineers; Russian Academy of Natural Sciences; Russian Society of Subsoil Use Experts. Address: RUSSNEFT Oil Co Research and Engineering Centre, 6A, Alexander Solgenizin St, Moscow 109004, Russia. E-mail: kanevskaya@ntc.russneft.ru

KANG Byung-Uk, b. 3 April 1969, Seoul, Korea. Doctor. m. NaRi Kim, 1 daughter. Education: MD, Kon-Kuk University, 1997; Neurosurgical Specialist, Catholic University, Korea, 2003; Fellowship, Wooridul Spine Hospital, Seoul, 2004; Fellowship, American Board of Minimally Invasive Spinal Surgery, 2005. Publications: Operative failure of PELD: an analysis of 55 cases, 2006; An evaluation of vascular anatomy for mini-laparotomic anterior L4-5 procedures, 2006; An analysis of general surgery-related complications, 2009; Surgical site infection in spinal surgery: detection and management, 2010. Honours: Award of Excellence, 2006 & 2007. Memberships: Korean Neurosurgical Society; Korean Spinal Neurosurgery Society. Address: Wooridul Spine Hospital 50-3, Dongin-dong, Jung-gu, Daegu, 700-732, Republic of Korea. E-mail: skulspine@hanmail.net

KANG Dae Kyung, b. 9 July 1966, Busan, Korea. Researcher. m. Myung Hee Lee, 3 daughters. Education: Master degree, Electrical Engineering, National Pukyung University, Busan, 1994. Appointments: Researcher, KT Central R&D Labs, 1995-. Address: 463-1 Jeonmin-dong, Yusung-gu, Daejeon 305 811, Korea. E-mail: kangdk@kt.com

KANG Dong-Gu, b. 9 March 1977, Busan, Republic of Korea. Nuclear Engineer. m. Yoon-Jung Choi, 1 daughter. Education: MS, Korea Advanced Institute of Science and Technology, 2006; BS, Pusan National University, 2003. Appointments: Senior Researcher, Korea Institute of Nuclear Safety, 2005-. Publications: Buoyant convection in an enclosure under time-periodic magnetizing force, 2007; CFD application to the Regulatory Assessment of FAC-caused CANDU Feeder Pipe Wall Thinning Issue, 2008; Numerical Calculation of Shear Stress Distribution on the Inner Wall Surface of CANDU Reactor Feeder Pipe Conveying Two-Phase Coolant, 2009; CFD analysis of thermally stratisfied flow and conjugated heat transfer in PWR pressurizer surgeline, 2010; Fluid-structure interaction analysis for pressurizer surgeline subjected to thermal stratification, 2011. Address: Korea Institute of Nuclear Safety, 62 Gwahak-ro, Yuseong-gu, Daejeon 305-338, Republic of Korea. E-mail: littlewing@kins.re.kr

KANG Doo-Kyoung, b. 15 March 1968, Incheon, Republic of Korea. Professor; Radiologist. m. Sun-Mi Lee, 1 son, 1 daughter. Education: MD, Yonsei University Wonju College of Medicine, 1994; Radiologist, Ajou University Hospital, 1999; Master's degree, Ajou University School of Medicine, 2004. Appointments: Fellow, 2000-, Assistant Professor, 2005-09, Associate Professor, 2009-, Ajou University School of Medicine. Publications: CT comparison of visual and computerised quantification of coronary stenosis according to plaque composition, 2010; DECT for integrative imaging of coronary artery disease, 2010; Reproductivty of CT signs of right ventricular dysfunction in acute pulmonary embolism, 2010. Honours: Cum laude, poster presentation, KCR, 2004; Cum laude, poster presentation, ESCR, 2010. Memberships: Korean Medical Association; Korean Society of Radiology. Address: Department of Radiology, Ajou University Hospital, San-5, Wonchon-dong, Yeongtong-gu, Suwon, Gyeonggi-do, 443-721, Republic of Korea. E-mail: kdklsm@ajou.ac.kr

KANG HyunKoo, b. 5 December 1970, m. Byungin Jung, 1 daughter. Education: MD, 1995, Master's degree, 2003, Hanyang University College of Medicine, Seoul. Appointments: Rotating Internship, 1995-96, Resident, Department of Radiology, 1999-2003, Hanyang University Medical Center, Seoul; Physician, ROK Army, 1996-99; Visiting Scholar, Department of Neuroradiology, Stanford University Medical Center, USA, 2009-10; Chief of Neuroradiology, Department of Radiology, Seoul Veterans Hospital, Seoul, 2003-. Publications: Sclerosing Stromal Tumour of the Ovary, 2002; Human Tail: A Case Report, 2002; Rapidly Aggravated Creutzfeldt-Jacob Disease: Autopsy-Proven Case, 2005; Association of Cholesterol Granuloma and Aspergillosis in the Sphenoid sinus, 2008; Pott's Putty Tumour Arising from Frontal Sinusitis, 2010. Memberships: Korea Medical Association; Korean Radiological Society; Korean Society of Neuroradiology and Head & Neck Radiology. Address: Department of Radiology, Seoul Veterans Hospital, 6-2 Dunchon-Dong, Gangdong-gu, 134-060, Seoul, Korea. E-mail: knroo@hanmail.net

KANG Jian, b. 2 August 1964, Shanxi, China. University Professor. m. Mei Zhang, 2 sons. Education: BEng, 1984, MSc, 1986, School of Architecture, Tsinghua University, Beijing; PhD, The Martin Centre, University of Cambridge, England, 1996. Appointments: Assistant Lecturer, 1987-89, Lecturer, 1989-92, Building Science Department, School of Architecture, Tsinghua University, Beijing; BFT Scholar, 1992-93, Humboldt Postdoctoral Fellow, 1997-98, Fraunhofer Institute of Building Physics, Stuttgart, Germany; Research Fellow, Wolfson College, University of Cambridge, England, 1996-99; Senior Research Associate, The Martin Centre, University of Cambridge, England, 1998-99; Lecturer, 1999-2001, Reader, 2001-03, Full Professor, 2003-, School of Architecture, University of Sheffield. Publications: 3 books; More than 150 refereed journals and book chapters; Over 300 refereed conferences. Honours: Newman Medal, Acoustical Society of America, 1996; Lloyd's of London Fellowship, 1998; A V Humboldt Fellowship, Germany, 1997-98; Fellow, Cambridge University Wolfson College, UK, 1996-99; Visiting Professor, Harbin Institute of Technology, and South China University of Technology, 2005-; Distinguished Overseas Experts, Chinese Academy of Sciences, 2005-; Chang-Jiang Visiting Chair Professorship, China Ministry of Education, 2007-; Tyndall Medal, Institute of Acoustics, 2008. Memberships: Fellow, Institute of Acoustics, UK; Fellow, Acoustical Society of America; German Society of Acoustics; Acoustical Society of China; European Acoustics Association; International Institute of Acoustics and Vibration; Chairman, UK Chinese Association of Resources and Environment. Address: School of Architecture, University of Sheffield, Western Bank, Sheffield S10 2TN, England. E-mail: j.kang@sheffield.ac.uk Website: www.shef.ac.uk/acoustics

KANG Leen-Seok, b. 2 December 1960, Seoul, Korea. Professor. m. Jin-Hee Jang, 1 son. Education: Postdoctoral studies, Stanford University, USA, 1996; Master's degree, 1986, PhD, 1990, Chungang University, Korea. Appointments: Professor, Gyeongsang National University, 1991-; Chief Researcher, Korea National Housing Institute, 1991; Invited Researcher, VTT, Finland, 1998; Head of Construction Committee, Korean Society of Civil Engineers, 2008-. Member, Advisory Board, Ministry of Construction and Maritime Affairs, 2000-; President of Local Chapter, Director, Korean Institute of Construction Engineering & Management, and Korean Institute of Procurement Management, 2000-; Member, Advisory Board, Korean Institute of Construction Technology, 2000-; Exchange Professor, Salford University, England, 2000-; Vice President, Research Institute of GSNU, 2004-; President, Regional Section, Korean Institute of Construction Engineering and Management, 2006-; Vice President, Korean Institute of Construction Engineering & Management, 2010-. Publications: Book, New Construction Engineering & Management, 2008; Book, New Construction Method for Civil Engineering Project, 2010; Papers and articles in professional scientific journals. Honours: Award for Best Paper, Korean Institute of Construction and Management, Korean Society of Civil Engineers, 2005; Official Commendation from Minister, Ministry of Construction, 2006; Listed in various international biographical dictionaries. Memberships: ASCE; KSCE; KICEM. Address: Department of Civil Engineering, Gyeongsang National University, Gajoa-dong 900, Jinju, Gyeongnam 660 701, South Korea. E-mail: Lskang@gnu.ac.kr

KANG Nam Yeo, b. 15 November 1965, Gwangju, Cheollanam-do, Korea. Ophthalmologist; Educator. m. Myungsang Kim, 2 daughters. Education: Diplomate, Korean Medical Association, 1990; MD, 1990, PhD, 1999, College of Medicine, Catholic University of Korea; Ophthalmology Board, Diplomate, Korean Ophthalmologist Association, 1995. Appointments: Instructor, 1995, Assistant Professor, 2000, Associate Professor, 2008, College of Medicine, Catholic University of Korea; Clinical Fellowship, Strabismus & Pediatric Ophthalmology, JSEI, UCLA, USA, 2004-05. Publications: Numerous articles in professional journals. Memberships: Korean Strabismologists Association; Korean Ophthalmologists Association. Address: Bucheon St Mary's Hospital, 2 Sosa-dong, Wonmi-gu, Bucheon, Kyunggi-do, 420-717, Korea. E-mail: nyeokang@catholic.ac.kr

KANG Sukwon, b. 26 February 1966, Seoul, Korea. Researcher. m. Eunjeong Yi. Education: BS, 1989, MS, 1991, Seoul National University; PhD, Cornell University, 1996. Appointments: Research Associate, US Department of Agriculture, Agricultural Research Service, 1996-98; Postdoctoral Associate, Bioresource Engineering Department, Rutgers the State University of New Jersey, 1998-2001; Research Associate, US Department of Agriculture, Agricultural Research Service, 2001-02; Researcher, Department of Agricultural Engineering, Rural Development Administration, 2002. Publications: Numerous articles in professional journals. Honours: Superior Paper Awards, 2000, IET Honorable Mention Paper Award, 2000, American Society of Agricultural & Biological Engineers; Listed in various international biographical dictionaries. Memberships: American Society of Agricultural & Biological Engineers; Korean Society for Agricultural Machinery; Korean Society of Food Science and Technology; Korean Society for Food Engineering. Address: Department of Agricultural Engineering, Rural Development Administration, Suinro 150, Seodun-dong, Suwon 441-707, Korea. E-mail: skang@rda.go.kr

KANLI Ali Ismet, b. 23 October 1968, Ankara, Turkey. Geophysical Engineer. m. Nurudil, 1 son. Education: BSc, 1989; MSc, 1994; PhD, 1998. Appointments: Associate Professor, Department of Geophysical Engineering, Istanbul University, 2010. Publications: More than 50 articles in professional journals. Memberships: SEG; EAGE; AGU; CGET. Address: Istanbul University, Engineering Faculty, Department of Geophysical Engineering, 34320, Avcilor Campus, Istanbul, Turkey. E-mail: kanli@istanbul.edu.tr

KANNAN Lakshmi (Kaaveri), b. 13 August 1947, Mysore, India. Writer. m. L V Kannan, 2 sons. Education: BA (Hons), MA, PhD, all in English. Appointment: Writer-in-Residence, University of Kent at Canterbury, 1993; Indian Participant, International Writing Program, Iowa, USA; British Council Visitor to Cambridge, England; Fellow, Indian Institute of Advanced Study, Shimla; Indian Participant, International Feminist Book Fairs, Montreal, Canada and Amsterdam, Holland. Publications: 20 books of poems, short stories, novel & translation; Titles include: Unquiet Waters: Poems; Going Home, 1999; Novel, India Gate, 1993; Short stories and other titles in Hindi and Tamil. Honours: Honorary Fellow in Writing, University of Iowa, USA; Ilakkiya Chintanai Award for Best Short-story; Charles Wallace Trust Fellowship for Writer-in-Residence, University of Canterbury, Kent, England; Sahitya Akademi Fellowship for Writer-in-Residence, Jama Millia Islamia University, Delhi; Kataa Award for Translation; Ilakkiya Chintanai Award for Best Short Story. Memberships: Founder-member and Treasurer, The Poetry Society, India; Indian Association for American Studies; Life Member, India International Centre, Delhi; American Studies Research Centre, Hyderabad; Bharat Soka Gakkai, The Indian Affiliate of Soka Gakkai International, a Global Organization for Lay Buddhists. Address: B-XI/8193, Vasant Kunj, New Delhi 110030, India.

KANTARIS Sylvia, b. 9 Jan 1936, Grindleford, Derbyshire, England. Poet; Writer; Teacher. m. Emmanuel Kantaris, 11 Jan 1958, 1 son, 1 daughter. Education: Diplome d'Etudes Civilisation Française, Sorbonne, University of Paris, 1955; BA, Honours, 1957, CertEd, 1958, Bristol University; MA, 1967, PhD, 1972, University of Queensland, Australia. Appointments: Tutor, University of Queensland, Australia, 1963-66, Open University, England, 1974-84; Extra-Mural Lecturer, Exeter University, 1974-. Publications: Time and Motion, 1975; Stocking Up, 1981; The Tenth Muse, 1983; News From the Front (with D M Thomas), 1983; The Sea at the Door, 1985; The Air Mines of Mistila (with Philip Gross), 1988; Dirty Washing: New and Selected Poems, 1989; Lad's Love, 1993. Contributions to: Many anthologies, newspapers, and magazines. Honours: National Poetry Competition Award, 1982; Honorary Doctor of Letters, Exeter University, 1989; Major Arts Council Literature Award, 1991; Society of Authors Award, 1992. Memberships: Poetry Society of Great Britain; South West Arts, literature panel, 1983-87, literary consultant, 1990-. Address: 14 Osborne Parc, Helston, Cornwall TR13 8PB, England.

KAO Po-Ching, b 22 July 1971, Tainan, Taiwan. Professor. m. Hsin-Hsuan Huang, 2 daughters. Education: PhD. Appointments: Assistant Professor. Publications: 3 articles in professional journals. Memberships: Photonics Program, Engineering Division, National Science Council, Taiwan. Address: Department of Electrophysics, National Chiayi University, Chiayi 600-83, Taiwan.

KAO Tsai-Sheng, b. 8 June 1975, Taiwan, ROC. Associate Professor. Education: PhD, Department of Electrical and Control Engineering, National Chiao-Tung University, Taiwan, 2004. Appointments: Associate Professor, Department of Electronic Engineering, Hwa-Hsia Institute of Technology, Taiwan. Memberships: IEEE: IACSIT; SERC. Address: No 111, Gongzhuan Road, Zhonge District, New Taipei City 235, Taiwan, ROC. E-mail: tsaishengkao@gmail.com

KAPLANOĞLU Hasan Semih, b. 22 February 1963, Izmir, Turkey. Director. m. Leyla. Education: BAs (Hons), Cinema & TV, 9 Eylul University, Izmir, 1984. Appointments: Writer for art journals (Gergedan, Gösteri, Cumhuriyet, Sanat Dunyamiz), 1987-2003; Columnist, Radikal daily paper, 1996-2000; Copywriter for ad agencies (Saatchi & Saatchi, Young & Rubicam, 1980-; Director & Writer, Sehnaz Tango tv series, 2000; Director, Away from Home, 2001; Director, Producer & Writer, Angel's Fall, 2005, Yumurta, 2007, Süt, 2008, Bal, 2010. Publications: Books and articles in professional journals. Honours: Numerous awards throughout the industry including: Honey International Awards; National Awards; Milk International Awards; Egg International Awards. Address: Av Sureyya Agaoglu Sok, 41/7 Hatay Ap, Tesvikiye, Istanbul, Turkey. E-mail: info@kaplanfilm.com Website: www.kaplanfilm.com

KAPUR Harish, b. 21 February 1929, India. Professor Emeritus. 1 daughter. Education: BA; MA; LLB; PhD. Appointments: Assistant Legal Adviser, Office of The United Nations High Commissioner For Refugees, Geneva, 1957-61; Research Associate, Harvard Russian Research Centre, Harvard University, 1961-62; Assistant Professor, Associate Professor, Professor, Graduate Institute of International and Development Studies, Geneva, 1962-96; Consultant, Office of the United Nations High Commissioner for Refugees, 1962-69; Special Adviser to the United Nations High Commissioner for Refugees, 1971-72; President, Scientific Council, Asian Documentation and Research Centre, Geneva, 1972-74; Director, Asian Centre, Geneva, 1977-82; Editor, World Affairs Quarterly, New Delhi, 1997-2000; Professor Emeritus, Graduate Institute of International Studies, Geneva, Switzerland, 1996-. Publications include: As China Sees The World: Perception of Chinese Scholars, 1987; Distant Neighbours: China and Europe, 1990; India's Foreign Policy 1947-1992: Shadows and Substance, 1994; Diplomacy of India: Then and Now, 2002; India's Prime Ministers and their Foreign Policies, 2008; India of Our Times: An Experiment in Democracy, 2011; Contributions to books. Address: Les Rapperins, 1928 Ravoire, Valais, Switzerland. E-mail: harkapur@yahoo.fr

KAPUSUZOGLU Ayhan, b. 1 January 1984, Ankara, Turkey. Research Assistant. Education: Graduate, Business Administration, Abant Izzet Baysal University, 2007; PhD, Business Administration, Hacettepe University, 2007-11; PhD Research, Bangor University, UK, 2010-11. Appointments: Research Assistant, Finance, Faculty of Economics and Administrative Sciences, Abant Izzet Baysal University, 2006-08; Research Assistant, Finance, Faculty of Economics and Administrative Sciences, Hacettepe University, 2008-11; Assistant Professor Dr, Faculty of Management, Department of Banking and Finance, Yildirim Beyazit University, 2011-. Publications: Numerous articles in professional journals. Honours: Undergraduate Success Scholarship, Izzet Baysal Foundation, 2001-05; 2nd Best Student of the University, Abant Izzet Baysal University, 2005; National Graduate Success Scholarship, TUBITAK, 2005-07; National Postgraduate Success Scholarship, TUBITAK, 2007-11; International Publication Exhortation Reward, TUBITAK, 2010; International Publication Exhortation Reward, Hacettepe University, 2010; Postgraduate Research Scholarship, The Council of Higher Education in Turkey, 2010-11. Memberships: International Journal of Management and Technology; Journal of Business Management and Economics; Advances in Management and Applied Economics; International Journal of Economics and Research; Journal of Basic and Applied Scientific Research; International Journal of Business Management and Economic Research; International Journal of Management Studies and Practices; International Review of Applied Financial Issues and Economics; Banking and Finance Letters; International Journals of Engineering and Sciences. Address: Sair Nedim Sokak, No 28/13, Asagiayranci, 06690, Ankara, Turkey. E-mail: ayhkap@gmail.com

KARAN Donna, b. 2 October 1948, Forest Hills, New York, USA. Fashion Designer. m. (1) Mark Karan, 1 daughter, (2) Stephen Weiss, 1983, deceased 2001. Education: Parsons School of Design, New York. Appointments: Designer, Anne Klein & Co, Addenda Co, 1968; Returned to Anne Klein, 1968, Associate Designer, 1971, Director of Design, 1974-84; Owner, Designer, Donna Karan Co, New York, DKNY, 1984-96; Designer, Donna Karan International, 1996-2001; Chief Designer, LVMH, 2001-. Honours: Coty Awards, 1977, 1981; Fashion Designers of America Women's Wear Award, 1996; FEMMY Designer of the Year Award, 1999; FIFI Best National Advertising Campaign of the Year Award, 2001; Fashion Group International Superstar Award, 2003. Membership: Fashion Designers of American. Address: Donna Karan International, 15th Floor, 5550 Seventh Avenue, New York, NY 10018, USA.

KARANDE Sunil, b. 29 July 1961, Mumbai, India. Paediatrician; Researcher. Education: MBBS, 1984; DCH, 1988; MD, 1989; Diploma in Information Technology, Advanced Computing Training School, Pune, 2000. Appointments: Medical Officer, Government of India, 1990-91; Surgeon Lieutenant, Indian Navy, 1991-92; Lecturer, Paediatrics, Seth GS Medical College and KEM Hospital, Mumbai, 1992-98; Associate Professor, Paediatrics, Lokmanya Tilak Municipal Medical College and Lokmanya Tilak Municipal General Hospital, Mumbai, 1998-2009; Associate Editor, Indian Journal of Pediatrics, 2008-; Professor, Paediatrics, Seth G S Medical College and KEM Hospital, 2009-. Publications: 99 indexed articles in peer reviewed journals; Reviewer for indexed journals; Written chapters in 2 books. Honours: Expert, Essential Drug List, Indian Pharmacological Society of Clinicians and Pharmacologists, 1994; First Prize, Free Paper, VII Maharashtra State Indian Academy of Paediatrics Conference, 1996; Fellow, Indian Academy of Pediatrics; Reviewer for Indian Paediatrics, Indian Journal of Paediatrics, Journal of Postgraduate Medicine and Neurology India, British Journal of Clinical Pharmacology, Paediatric Rehabilitation, Emerging Infectious Diseases, Indian Journal of Medical Sciences; Expert Review of Pharmacoeconomics and Outcomes Research; American Journal of Medical Genetics Part B, Neuropsychiatric Genetics, Journal of Pediatric Neurology indexed journals. Memberships: Member of Technical Committee: WHO/ Adverse Drug Reaction Monitoring Programme; Life Member, Indian Academy of Paediatrics; Life Member, Indian Medical Association; Member, New York Academy of Sciences; Fellow, International Academy for Research in Learning Disabilities, USA. Address: Flat 24, Joothica, 5th Floor, 22A Naushir Bharucha Road, Mumbai 400007, India. E-mail: karandesunil@yahoo.com

KARASIN Grigory B, b. 23 August, 1949, Moscow, Russia. Diplomat; Ambassador Extraordinary and Plenipotentiary. m. Olga V Karasina, 2 daughters. Education: Graduate, College of Oriental Languages, Moscow State University, 1971. Appointments: Embassy in Senegal, 1972-76; Embassy in Australia, 1979-85; Embassy in the United Kingdom, 1988-92; Director, Department of Africa, MFA, 1992-93; Director, Department of Information and Press, MFA, 1993-96; Deputy Minister of Foreign Affairs of the Russian Federation, 1996-2000; Ambassador to the Court of St James's, 2000-2005; Deputy Minister of Foreign Affairs of Russia, 2005-. Address: The Russian Embassy, 13 Kensington Palace Gardens, London W8 4QX, England.

KARAVANIĆ Ivor, b. 27 June 1965, Zagreb, Croatia. Archaeologist. m. Snježana, 1 daughter. Education: BA, Archaeology, 1990, MA, Archaeology, 1993, University of Zagreb; PhD, Archaeology, 1999, University of Zagreb. Appointments: Research Assistant, 1991-2001, Assistant, 1993-99, Senior Assistant, 1999-2001, Assistant Professor, 2001-05, Associate Professor, 2005-10, Head of Department, 2005-07, Full Professor, 2010-, Department of Archaeology, Faculty of Humanities and Social Sciences, University of Zagreb. Publications include: Néandertaliens et Paléolithique supérieur dans la grotte de Vindija, co-author, 1998; Gornjopaleolitičke kamene i koštane rukotvorine iz špilje Vindije, 1994; Upper Paleolithic occupation levels and late-occurring Neanderthal at Vindija Cave (Croatia) in the Context of Central Europe and the Balkans, 1995; The Middle/Upper Paleolithic Interface and the Relationship of Neanderthals and Early Modern Humans in the Hrvatsko Zagorje, co-author, 1998; The Early Upper Paleolithic of Croatia, 1998; Neanderthal Diet at Vindija and Neanderthal Predation: The Evidence from Stable Isotopes, co-author, 2000; Stones that Speak, Šandalja in the Light of Lithic Technology, co-author, 2000; Olschewian and Appearance of Bone Technology in Croatia and Slovenia, 2000; ESR and AMS-based ^{14}C dating of Mousterian Levels at Mujina Pećina, Dalmatia, Croatia, co-author, 2002; Osvit tehnologije, co-author, 2003; Život neandertalaca, 2004; Odiseja čovječanstva, co-author, 2005; Osvit čovječanstra, co-author, 2009. Honours: Fellowship, French Government, 1995, 2001; Constantin-Jireček Fellowship, 1995; Fulbright Fellowship, 1996-97; International Scientist of the Year, IBC, 2001; Plaquette of Zagreb City, 2006; Faculty of Humanities and Social Sciences Medal, 2006; Hall of Fame for Distinguished Accomplishments, 2009; Yearly Awards of Croatian Archaeological Society and Croatian Anthropological Society, 2010; Listed in several Who's Who and biographical publications. Memberships: Croatian Archaeological Society; Society for American Archaeology; INQUA National Committee, Croatia; Serra International, Zagreb; Croatian Fulbright Alumni Association; L'Association croate des boursiers du governement Français; HERA JRP Review Panel. Address: Department of Archaeology, Faculty of Humanities and Social Sciences, University of Zagreb, Ivana Lučića 3, 10000 Zagreb, Croatia. E-mail: ikaravan@ffzg.hr

KARDORFF Bernd, b. Mönchengladbach, Germany. Dermatologist; Laser Specialist; Author; Inventor; Allergologist. m. Maria, 1 son, 1daughter. Education: Doctor of Medicine, Heinrich-Heine University, Dusseldorf; Specialist in Dermatologic Radiotherapy, 1999; Specialist in Dermatologic Science Laboratory Tests, 2000; Specialist in Dermatology (Medical), Specialist in Allergology (Medical), Specialist in Environmental Medicine (Medical), Aerztekammer Nordrhein, 2000; Specialist in Acupuncture, 2006; Skin Cancer Specialist Trainer, 2008. Appointments: Head Physician, Laser Medicine, 1996-99, Registrar, 1998-99, St Barbara Hospital, Duisburg, Northrhine-Westphalia; Vice Head Physician, Rhein-Klinik St Joseph, Duisburg-Beeckerwerth, Northrhine-Westphalia 1996-99; Chief Dermatologist and Allergologist, Kardorff & Dorittke Out Patients Clinic, Mönchengladbach, 1999; President, Dachverband für Wohnortnahe Dermatologische Rehabilitation und Therapie chronischer Hautkrankheiten, 2000; Advisory Board Member, DERM Specialist periodical, Omnimed-Verlag, Hamburg, 2001; Head Physician, Skin, Allergy and Venous Clinic, Korschenbroich, 2007; Advisory Board Member, Cosmetic Medicine Specialist Periodical, Grosse-Verlag, Berlin, 2008. Publications: Papers and articles in professional scientific and medical journals; Author, several scientific books. Honours: Award for Paediatric Dermatology, 1999; Literary Awards, Georg Thieme Publishing Company, 1995, 1998, 2002; Cross of Merit on Ribbon, Knight's Cross, Bundesverdienstkreuz, 2009. Memberships: Deutsche Akademie für Akupunktur und Auriculomedizin; NVV Lions Mönchengladbach; Westgerman Basketball Mastership, 2000; Deutsche Dermatologische Gesellschaft; Arbeitsgemeinschaft Dermatologische Kosmetologie; Vereinigung für operative Dermatologie; Dachverband für Wohnortnahe Dermatologische Rehabilitation und Therapie chronischer Hautkrankheiten; Gesellschaft für Asthetische Chirurgie Deutschland GACD; PSV Mönchengladbach; Deutsche Gesellschaft für Dermatochirurgie DGDC. Address: Dermatology & Laser Out Patients Clinic, Marktstrasse 31, Mönchengladbach, Northrhine-Westphalia 41236, Germany. E-mail: info@dorittke-kardorff.de Website: www.dorittke-kardorff.de

KARGUL Józef, b. 18 June 1936, Zwiernik, Poland. Research Scholar. m. Alicja Kargulowa, 2 daughters. Education: PhD, Education, Adam Mickiewicz University, Poznan, 1971; Doctor habil, Wrocław University, 1978; Full Professor, 1992. Appointments: Director, Pedagogy Institute, Wrocław University, 1987-93; Head, Faculty of Culture Animation, University of Zielona Góra, 1999-2006; President, Regional Board, Association for the Advancement of Education, Wrocław, 2003-; Head, Faculty of Social Pedagogy and Counseling, University of Lower Silesia, 2006-. Publications: 7 books; 200 articles including: Cultural and Educational Worker, 1976; From Culture Dissemination to Culture Animation, 1978; Areas of Formal and Non-Formal Adult Education, 2005. Honours: 3 times winner, Ministry of Science and Higher Education Award for Scientific Achievements; Association of Polish Educators Award in Scientific Publication Competition. Memberships: Committee of Education of Polish Academy of Science; Wrocław Science Association; Honorary Member, Academic Association of Adult Education; Chair, Association of Counselling Science. Address: ul Pilnikarska 2, 53-206 Wrocław, Poland. E-mail: j.kargul@dswe.pl

KARIM Fawzi, b. 1 July 1945, Baghdad, Iraq. Poet; Writer; Editor; Publisher. m. 31 December 1980, 2 sons. Education: BA, Arabic Literature, College of Arts, Baghdad, 1967. Appointment: Editor-in-Chief and Publisher, Al-Lahda Al-Shiriya, quarterly, London. Publications: Where Things Begin, 1968; I Raise My Hand in Protest, 1973; Madness of Stone, 1977; Stumbling of a Bird, 1985; We Do Not Inherit the Earth, 1988; Schemes of Adam, 1991; Pestilential Continents, 1992; Collected Poems, 1968-1992, 1993. Other: Essays and short stories. Contributions to: Reviews and periodicals. Memberships: Poetry Society, England; Union of Iraqi Writers. Address: PO Box 2137, London W13 0TY, England.

KARIMOV Abdulaziz Vakhitovich, b. 11 January 1944, Tashkent, Uzbekistan. Physicist; Researcher. m. Gavkhar Khalilovna Khakimova, 4 daughters. Education: Diploma in Mathematics, State Pedagogical Institute, Tashkent, 1970; Candidate dissertation, 1980; PhD, 1995; DS, Physics and Mathematics, Institute of Physics and Technics, 1995. Appointments: Tashkent Cable Factory, 1962-64; Soviet Army, 1964-67; Senior Engineer, Tashkent University, 1967-68; Junior Researcher, 1968-71, Senior Researcher, 1971-86, Leading Scientist, 1986-96, Professor, 2006, Physical-Technical Institute, Academy of Sciences of Uzbekistan. Publications: More than 300 scientific articles; 2 monograph collections; 1 monograph; 1 academic textbook; 30 inventions. Address: Physical-Technical Institute, Academy of Sciences of Uzbekistan Bodomzor Str, 2b Tashkent, 100084, Uzbekistan. E-mail: karimov@uzsci.net

KARIMOV Kazimir, b. 10 March 1937, Chinkent town, Kazakhstan. m. Scientist. m. 2 sons. Education: Physicist, Kyrgyz State University, 1960; Scientific degree of candidate of Physical Mathematics Science in Radiophysics, Kazan State University, 1967; Doctor of Geophysics, Academy of Sciences of USSR, Moscow, 1986; Professor of Geophysics, High Attestation Committee under the Government of USSR, 1988. Appointments: Engineer, PB 53, Mountain-mining Enterprise, 1960-62; Scientific Researcher, Institute of Physics and Mathematics, Kyrgyz Academy of Sciences, Frunze City, 1963-68; Head of Scientific Group, Institute of Physics and Mathematics, Kyrgyz Academy of Science, 1968-77; Head, Laboratory of Atmospheric Processes of Institute of Physicotechnical Problems and Materials Science, National Academy of Kyrgyz Republic, 1978-. Publications: More than 300 papers; 11 books; More than 200 scientific reports. Honours: Honoured Worker of Science of Kyrgyz Republic; Honoured Scientist of National Academy of Sciences of Kyrgyz Republic; Gold Medal, International Ataturk Foundation; Listed in biographical dictionaries. Memberships: New York Academy of Sciences; National Geographic Society of USA; EUFAR. Address: Institute of Physicotechnical Problems and Materials Science, National Academy of Sciences, Chui Prosp 265-A, 720071 Bishkek, Kyrgyz Republic. E-mail: kazkarimov@yahoo.com

KARLSSON Gunnar, b. 26 September 1939, Iceland. Professor of History. m. Silja Adalsteinsdottir, 3 daughters. Education: MA, Icelandic Philology and History, 1970, PhD, 1978, University of Iceland. Appointments: Fellow, Scandinavian History, University College London, 1974-76; Lecturer, 1976-80, Professor, 1980-2009, History, University of Iceland. Publications: Iceland's 1100 Years, 2000; 20 books on Iceland; Numerous articles in Icelandic and English. Honours: Asa Wright Award, 2007. Address: Hristateigi 34, 105 Reykjavik, Iceland. E-mail: gunnark@hi.is

KARLUK Sadik Ridvan, b. 1948, Eskisehir, Turkey. Professor. Education: Political Sciences, Ankara University, 1970; PhD, 1975; Associate Professor's degree, 1979. Appointments: Ministry of Finance and Supreme Court of Public Accounts; Department of Economy, Eskisehir Administrative and Economic Sciences Academy, 1972; Scientific Researcher, Sussex University, 1975-76; The European Union Department of State Planning Organization (General Directorate), 1982; Elected Member, Board of Director of Economic Development Foundation, 1984-85; Adviser to Chairman, Board of Directors, Istanbul Chamber of Commerce; Lecturer, Military Academies, Istanbul, 1983-85; Member, Turkish Delegation, 6th UNCTAD Conference, Belgrade, 1983; Member, Turkish Delegation, UNIDO Conference, Vienna, 1984; Planning Undersecretary, OECD, Paris, 1985; Adviser to Undersecretary of DPT (State Planning Organization), 1990; Adviser to Prime Minister; Professor, Anatolia University, 1991; Lecturer, European Union-Turkey Relations, Ankara University ATAUM, 1991-2003, and T C Ziraat Bankasi AS Co Inc Banking School, 2004-05; Chairman, Scientific Board of Turkish Industrialists and Businessmen Foundation, 1996; Turkish Representative to International Chamber of Commerce, Commission on Trade and Investment Policy, Paris. Publications: 20 books; more than 300 articles; 5 co-authored and 3 translation works. Honours: 4 scientific research awards. Address: Dean of the Faculty of Economics, Anadolu University Eskisehir, Yunusemre Kampusu, Turkey. E-mail: rkarluk@anadolu.edu.tr

KARPOV Anatoliy Yevgenievich, b. 23 May 1951, Zlatoust, Russia. Chess Player. m. (1) Irina, 1 son, (2) Ntalia Bulanova, 1 daughter. Education: Leningrad University. Career: Member, CPSU, 1980-91; USSR Candidate Master, 1962, Master, 1966; European Junior Champion, 1967, 1968; World Junior Champion, 1969; International Master, 1969; International Grandmaster, 1970; USSR Champion, 1976, 1983, 1988; World Champion, 1975-85; Became world champion when holder, Bobby Fischer, refused to defend title; Retained title against Viktor Korchnoi, 1978 and 1981; Defended title against Garry Kasparov, Moscow, 1984 (match later adjourned due to illness of both players); Lost to Kasparov, 1985; Unsuccessfully challenged Kasparov, 1986, 1987, 1990; Won World Championship title under FIDE after split in chess organisations, 1993, 1996, 1998; Has won more tournaments than any other player (over 160); People's Deputy of USSR, 1989-91; President, Soviet Peace Fund (now International Association of Peace Funds), 1982-; President, Chernobyl-Aid organisation, 1989-; UNICEF Ambassador for Russia and Eastern Europe, 1998-; Chair, Council of Directors Federal Industrial Bank, Moscow. Publications: Chess is My Life, 1980; Karpov Teaches Chess, 1987; Karpov on Karpov, 1991; How to Play Chess; 47 other books. Honours: Winner, Oscar Chess Prize, 1973-77, 1979-81, 1984, 1994; Fontany di Roma Prize for Humanitarian Achievements, 1996; Honorary Texan; Honorary Citizen of Tula, Zlatoust, Orsk and other cities in Russia, Belarus and Ukraine. Memberships: Soviet (now Russian) UNESCO Affairs Commission; Board, International Chess Federation; Editor in Chief, Chess Review 64 magazine, 1980-91. Address: International Peace Fund, Prechistenka 10, Moscow, Russia.

KARPUSHKIN Evgeny, b. 13 November 1950, Murmansk, Russia. Engineer; Translator. Divorced. Education: MS, Mechanical Engineer, 1977-86, Foreign Languages Chair, Scientific and Technical Translator, 1978-81, Leningrad Technological Institute of Refrigeration Industry; Ship's refrigeration plant operator, training plant of Sevryba Association, Murmansk, 1982; IBM PC operator course, Sevrybsistemotekhnika Association, Murmansk, 1991; TOEFL certificate, Moscow Institute of Steel and Alloys, 1993; Ship's radio operator, I I Mesiatsev Marine Fish-Industrial College, Murmansk, 1994-99; Public Relations & State/ Municipal Management Manager, North-West Academy of State Service at the President of RF, Murmansk, 1997-2000; Exchange Student, Oulun University, Oulu, Finland, 2008. Appointments: Sailor, 1967-76; Ship's Refrigeration Plant Operator, Murmanrybprom Association, 1967-86; Design Engineer, Technical Translator, 1986-88, Scientific and Technical Translator, 1988-94, Sevrybsistemotekhnika Association; Foreign Trade Relations Manager, Trade Polaris Company, Murmansk, 1995; English Language Teacher,

Murmansk Middle School No 27, 1996; GMDSS English Language Teacher, Murmansk Training Centre, 1999-2000; Public Relations Manager, Union of Journalists, Murmansk, 2000; Fish Farmer, Ichthyologist, Translator, PanFish Norge AS & Murman SeaFood Co Ltd, Floro, Norway, 2001. Publications: The ABC of the Mathematical Infinitology, 2003; The paradoxial equilibrium, 2003; The aliens from the planetary system of the "α"-Taurus; The unusual graphics: the "sieve of Eratosphen" and "the spireal of Ulam" in Cartesian co-ordinates; Numerous articles in the internet. Honours: Veteran of Labour, medal in honour of 100 year anniversary of V I Lenin, 1970; Silver medal of V I Vernadsky, 2012; Adviser, Russian Academy of Human History. Memberships: President, Murmansk Regional Association of the Victims of Illegal Political Repressions; President, The Academy of Cartesian Infinitology & Euclidian fractals. Address: The Academy of Cartesian Infinitology and Euclidian Fractals, 105 Kolsky Avenue, Apt 36, Murmansk 14, 183014, Russia. E-mail: e.v.karpushkin@mail.ru

KARUNARATNE Vidanage Pemananda, b. 10 October 1942, Colombo, Sri Lanka, Professor and Management, Marketing and Training Consultant, Author and Novelist. m. Nanda Vijitha Karunaratne, 2 daughters. Education: BA, Economics (Ceylon), 1961-65; Expert's Certificate in Insurance Management (Japan), 1988; Postgraduate Diploma, Marketing Management (Sri Lanka), 1990-92; MBA (Sri Lanka), 1993-96; Associate of Ceylon Insurance College (Sri Lanka), 1993; Chartered Marketer, Chartered Institute of Marketing (UK), 1998. Appointments: Assistant Manager, Life Department, 1968-69, Assistant Manager and Manager, Housing Loans Department, 1970-79, Manager and Head, Publicity, Advertising, Training and Public Relations Department, 1980-91, Insurance Corporation of Sri Lanka; Manager, Training Department, Ceylinco Insurance Company, 1991-95; Academic and Administative Head, Ceylinco Insurance College, 1995-97; Visiting Senior Lecturer, University of Sri Jayewardenepura, Sri Lanka, 1991-; Management, Marketing and Training Consultant, 1997-; Professor, 2004. Publications: The Neglected But Essential Element of the Marketing Mix for Insurance - Personalised Service - The Case of Insurance in Sri Lanka; Transformation Through the People for the People – The Indian Experience: The Lessons Sri Lankans Can Learn From It; Sexual Truisms and Men and Women – A Guidance Manual; The Living Dead or the Vampire Legend; Manual for Co-operative Study Circle Leaders; Two Translation Volumes of Short Stories written by Anton Chekhov and Guy de Maupassant; Novels: The Enigmatic Sisters; When Loved Ones Are Far Away; The Case of the Pink Panties and Hankies; The Virgin Brides of the Undead; The Sublime Attachment; The Sublime Return; Sublime Love Never Withers, Book I and Book II. Honours: Honorary Member, Research Council, IBC, 2006; Consulting Editor, ABI, USA, 2002; Man of the Year 2005, ABI, USA, Listed in Who's Who publications and biographical dictionaries. Memberships: Chartered Institute of Marketing, UK, 1993; Chartered Management Institute, UK, 1994; Chartered Institute of Public Relations, 1995; Institute of Management of Sri Lanka, 1996; Research Board of Advisors, ABI, 2003; Research Council, IBC, 2006. Address: 3A Wimalawatta Road, Nugegoda, Sri Lanka.

KASAI Masataka, b. 12 March 1973, Mie Prefecture, Japan. Language Educator. m Tamami, 2 sons. Education: BA, English Language, Gifu University for Education and Languages, Japan, 1995; MA, 2001, PhD, 2007, Social Studies and Global Education, Ohio State University, USA. Appointments: Japanese Assistant Instructor, Gosford High School, Australia, 1996; English Instructor, 1997-2000, 2007, Global English School, Japan; English Instructor, Kwansei Gakuin University, Japan, 2007-09; Associate Professor, Kansai Gaidai University, Japan, 2008-. Publications: Numerous articles in professional journals. Honours: Antoinette Lowry Barr Scholarship, 2002; Listed in international biographical dictionaries. Memberships: Japanese Association for Language Teaching; Japan Association for International Education; Japan Association for Global Education. Address: 101 Doux Solaire II 4-49, Hirakatamotomachi, Hirakata-shi, Osaka 573-0052, Japan. E-mail: masatakasa@hotmail.com

KASCHNY Jorge Ricardo de Araujo, b. 11 October 1963, Porto Alegre, RS, Brazil. Physicist. m. Selma Rozane Vieira. Education: Bachelor, 1988, Master, 1991, PhD, 1995, Physics, Institute of Physics, UFRGS Brazil. Appointments: Postdoctoral Fellow, FZR Germany, 1996-97; Auxiliary Professor, Institute of Physics, UFRGS Brazil, 1998-99; Guest Scientist, FZR Germany, 2000; Professor, Department of Physics, UEFS, Brazil, 2001-06; Professor, Department of Electrical and Electronic Engineering, IFBA, Brazil, 2006-. Publications: Over 50 articles in scientific journals. Honours: Honoured Professor of Physics, UEFS, 2006. Memberships: Brazilian Physics Society; American Association of Physics Teachers, USA. Address: IFBA, Av Amazonas 3150, 45030-220 Vitoria da Conquista-BA, Brazil. E-mail: kaschny@cefetba.br

KASER Michael Charles, b. 2 May 1926, London, England. Economist. m. Elizabeth Piggford, 4 sons, 1 daughter. Education: BA, 1946, MA, 1950, Economics, King's College, Cambridge; MA, 1960, DLitt, 1993, Oxford University. Career: Chief Scientific Advisor's Department, Ministry of Works, 1946-47; HM Foreign Service, including HM Embassy, Moscow as Second Secretary, Commercial Secretariat, 1947-51; United Nations Economic Commission for Europe, Geneva, 1951-63; Fellow, 1960-93, Emeritus Fellow, 1993-, St Antony's College; Lecturer, 1963-72, Reader, 1972-93, Reader Emeritus, 1993-, University of Oxford; Honorary Chair, Institute for German Studies, University of Birmingham, 1993-. Publications: Author, Editor, 23 books and 390 articles in journals on the East European, Russian and Central Asian economies; Books include: Soviet Economics, 1970; Health Care in the Soviet Union and Eastern Europe, 1976; Privatisation in the CIS, 1995; The Economies of Kazakstan and Uzbekistan, 1997. Memberships: General Editor, International Economic Association, 1986-2007; Councillor, 1979-92, Chairman, 1980-92, Central Asia and Caucasus Advisory Board, 1993-2003, Royal Institute of International Affairs; Trustee, Council of the Keston Institute, 1994-2002 and Cumberland Lodge, Windsor, 1987-2006; Former President, British Association of Former UN Civil Servants; Former President, Albania Society of Britain; Member, Advisory Group on Former Soviet and East European Studies of the Higher Education Funding Council for England; Reform Club. Honours: Papal Knighthood, Order of St Gregory; Knight's Cross of the Order of Merit, Poland; Order of Naim Frasheri, Albania; Hon DSocSc, Birmingham; Honorary Member, European Association of Comparative Economics. Address: 31 Capel Close, Oxford, OX2 7LA, England.

KASIPATHI Chinta, b. 17 October 1955, Rajahmundry, India. Professor of Geology. m. Hemalatha, 2 sons. Education: BSc, 1973, M Sc (Tech), 1976, PhD, 1981, Andhra University. Appointments: Research Assistant, 1976-80; Research Associate, 1980-84, Officer Pool, 1984; Lecturer, Assistant

Professor, 1984-86; Reader, Associate Professor, 1986-94; Professor, 1998-; Supervised doctoral and masters theses; Supervised 36 PhD students; organised two national seminars and two national workshops; Consultant, several mining organisations; Adviser, national and international bodies. Publications: 254 research papers in field of Indian ore mineral studies; Editorial Board, 6 journals. Honour: Young Scientist Award, 1984; Recognised Qualified Person, Government of India; Man of the Year 2005; Vijay Rattan Award, IIFS, New Delhi; Glory of India Gold Medal, IISA; Bharata Jyothi Award, IISA; Gold Medal and Citation from Environmental Research Academy International, India. Memberships: New York Academy of Sciences; AGID; IGC; GSI; GMMSI; IMSA; IEA; IGC, India; IMA; IGI; IAGS; SGAT; MMR; JDW; FGW; INS; AEG; ISAG; Secretary, Andhra University Geology Alumni Association; FISCA; FAPA Sc; F GARC; FEnRA. Address: Head and Chairman, Board of Studies (PG), Department of Geology, Andhra University, Visakhapatnam 530 003, Andhra Pradesh, India.

KASMEL Tiiu, b. 9 April 1948, Polva, Estonian SSR. Teacher; Naturalist; Social Sciences Educator. Education: Nursing certificate, 1966; Diploma, Sport Pedagogy and Coaching, MA, Physical Education and Sport, Tartu State University, Tartu, 1978. Appointments: Various posts in the town and district of Valga, 1964-66; Teacher, Hargla Primary School, Estonia, 1966-70; Technician Chair, Track and Field, Tartu State University, Tartu, 1970-74; Teacher, Tartu Medical School, 1974-82; Teacher, Tartu Hiie School, Tartu, 1982-2001; Senior Teacher, Tartu Hiie School, Tartu, 2001-. Publications: More than 80 articles in scientific journals. Honours: Listed in biographical dictionaries. Memberships: European Anthropological Association; Estonian Naturalists Society. Address: 193-4 Jaama St, Tartu 50705, Estonia. E-mail: tiilem@hot.ee

KASPAR Suatopluk, b. 12 December 1952, Policka, Czech Republic. m. Libuse, 2 sons. Education: Faculty of Medicine, Charles University, Hradec Kralove. Appointments: Chief Surgeon, Felbocentrum, Hradec Kralove. Publications: More than 130 papers in Czech Republic and abroad. Honours: Honorary Member, Czech Society of Phlembology. Memberships: Czech societies of Surgery, Phlebology and Angiology; French societies of Phlebology, andVascular Pathology; European Society of Phlebectomy. Address: Liznerova 737, 50009 Hradec Kralove, Czech Republic.

KASPAROV Garri Kimovich, b. 13 April 1963, Baku, Azerbaijan. Chess Player. m. (1) Masha Kasparova, 1 daughter, (2) Yulia Kasparova, 1 son. Education: Azerbaijan Pedagogical Institute of Foreign Languages. Appointments: Azerbaijan Champion, 1975; USSR Junior Champion, 1975; International Master, 1979, International Grandmaster, 1980; World Junior Champion, 1980; Won USSR Championship, 1981, subsequently replacing Anatoliy Karpov at top of world ranking list; Won match against Viktor Korchnoi, challenged Karpov for World Title in Moscow, 1985, the match being adjourned due to the illness of both players; Won rescheduled match to become the youngest ever World Champion; Successfully defended his title against Karpov, 1986, 1987, 1990; Series of promotional matches in London, 1987; Won Times World Championship against Nigel Short, 1993; Stripped of title by World Chess Federation, 1993. Publication: Child of Change (with Donald Trelford), 1987; London-Leningrad Championship Games, 1987; Unlimited Challenge, 1990. Honours include: Oscar Chess Prize, 1982-83, 1985-89; World Chess Cup, 1989. Membership: Professional Chess Association. Address: Mezhdunarodnaya-2, Suite 1108, Krasnopresnenskaya nab 12, 123610 Moscow, Russia. E-mail: maiavia@dol.ru Website: www.kasparovchess.com

KASTEN Brigitte, b. 6 October 1955, Corrientes, Argentina. Historian. m. Dieter Kasten. Education: 1st German State Exam, 1979; PhD, 1984; Staatsexamen, 1985; Habilitation, 1996. Appointments: Assistant Lecturer, Heinrich Heine Universität Düsseldorf, 1979-83; Assistant Lecturer, 1994-99, Senior Assistant Lecturer, 1999-2002, University of Bremen; Professor, Medieval History, University of Saarland, 2002-. Publications: Numerous articles in professional journals. Honours: Deutsche Forschunsgemeinschaft, 1985-90. Address: Ölmühlweg 37d, 61462 Königstein im Taunus, Germany. E-mail: b.kasten@mx.uni-saarland.de

KASUYA Koichi, b. 1 February 1943, Osaka, Japan. University Professor. m. Keiko Nakamura, 2 sons. Education: BSME, 1965, MSME, 1967, PhD, Engineering, 1970, Osaka University, Japan. Appointments: Research Associate, Osaka University, 1970-78; Humbolt Fellow, University of Karlsruhe, Germany, 1976-77; Associate Professor, Tokyo Institute of Technology, 1978-; Member, Advisory Committee, International Symposium on Gas Flow and Chemical Lasers and High Power Laser Conference, 1982-; Research Collaborator, Nagoya University, 1978-91, Osaka University, 1992-. Publications: Several books and many research reports on plasma engineering, laser developments, plasma and laser applications, nuclear fusion (science and technology). Honours: Prize of Kudo Foundation in Japan; Travels Grants, 1967-; Grants-in-Aid for Research Work, Ministry of Education and Hattori Foundation. Memberships: Japan Society of Plasma Science and Nuclear Fusion; Laser Society of Japan. Address: Institute of Applied Flow & Institute of Laser Engineering, 3-24-4 Utsukushigaoka-Nishi, Aoba-ku, Yokohama, Kanagawa 225-0001, Japan.

KATAKAWA Jun'ichi, b. 9 July 1950, Osaka, Japan. Educator; Chemist. m. Chizuko Yoshimura, 1992. Education: ME, Osaka Institute of Technology, 1977; PhD, Pharmacology, Kyoto University, 1989. Appointments: Associate Professor, Setsunan University, Hirakata, Osaka, 2003-; Councilor, Japan Scientific Society of Biological Macromolecules, Kyoto, 2009-. E-mail: katakawa@pharm.setsunan.ac.jp

KATILIUS Ramunas, b. 15 October 1935, Kaunas, Lithuania. Physicist; Scientific Researcher. m. Elmira Sabirova, 2 sons. Education: Diploma (cum laude), Faculty of Physics and Mathematics, Vilnius University, 1959; Postgraduate Studies, Institute of Physics and Mathematics, Lithuanian Academy of Sciences, Vilnius, 1959-62; Candidate of Physics and Mathematics (PhD), Institute for Semiconductors of the Academy of Sciences of the USSR, Leningrad, 1969; Doctor of Science (Physics and Mathematics), Ioffe Physical-Technical Institute of the Academy of Sciences of the USSR, Leningrad, 1986; Senior Research Fellow, Academy of Sciences of the USSR, 1989; Doctor Habilitatus (Nat Sci), Republic of Lithuania, 1993; Professor (Nat Sci), Vytautas Magnus University, 1993. Appointments: Junior Research Fellow, Institute of Physics and Mathematics of the Lithuanian Academy of Sciences, Vilnius, 1962-66; Junior Research Fellow, Institute for Semiconductors of the Academy of Sciences of the USSR, Leningrad, 1966-72; Junior Research Fellow, Senior Research Fellow, Ioffe Physical-Technical Institute of the Academy of Sciences of the USSR, Leningrad, 1972-88; Extraordinary Professor, Faculty of Physics and Mathematics, 1992-93, Professor of Physics, Environment Research Faculty, 1993-2000, Vytautas

Magnus University, Kaunas; Principal Research Fellow, Semiconductor Physics Institute, Vilnius, 1988-. Publications: Over 130 papers in professional journals; 7 review articles and book chapters; 3 books. Honours: Lithuanian National Science Award, 1995; ISI Citation Index: 500+. Memberships: Lithuanian Physical Society; Associate Member, Institute of Physics, UK; Board Member, Lithuanian Association of Non-Linear Analysis; Editorial Board Member, Nonlinear Analysis – Modelling and Control; Board Member, Open Society Fund, Lithuania, 1990-2000. Address: Semiconductor Physics Institute, Gostauto 11, Vilnius, LT-01108, Lithuania. E-mail: katilius@pfi.lt

KATSANOS Nicholas, b. 14 January 1930, New Agathoupolis, Greece. University Professor. m. Hara Sideri, 3 sons. Education: Doctorate Degree, Chemistry, 1963; Post-graduate Diploma in Radiochemistry, 1961; Degree in Chemistry, 1954. Appointments: Teaching Assistant, University of Thessaloniki, Greece; Research Associate, Head of Research Group, Professor of Physical Chemistry, Director of Physical, Inorganic and Nuclear Chemistry Department, University of Patras, Greece. Publications: Articles in international journals and/or presented in scientific symposia; 180 original research papers; 10 books in Greek; 2 books in English. Honours: Empirikion Scientific Prize, 1972; Academy of Athens Prize, 1983; Desty Memorial Prize, Waters Ltd; Prize for Excellence in Physical Sciences, Academy of Athens, 2008. Memberships: Fellow and Chartered Chemist of Royal Society of Chemistry, England; Greek Chemist Association; Chromatography Society; New Academy of Sciences. Address: 5 Chilonos Patreos, 26224 Patras, Greece.

KATSIKI Niki, b. 7 November 1979, Thessaloniki, Greece. Doctor. 1 son. Education: MD, 2003; MSc, Medicine, 2006; PhD, in progress. Appointments: Research Fellow, AHEPA University Hospital, Thessaloniki; Trainee, Agios Dimitrios Hospital, Thessaloniki; General Practice, Health Centre, Lagador, Thessaloniki; Teacher of Medical Students, Medical School, Aristotle University of Thessaloniki. Publications: Numerous articles in professional journals; 60 abstracts in Greek and international scientific conferences; 3 chapters in Greek medical books. Honours: Honorary Clinical and Research Fellow, UCL, London; Scholarships from Greek State Scholarship Foundation for Best Under- and Post-Graduate Student, 1997-2006; Grants, Northern Greece Diabetes Association and the Hellenic Atherosclerosis Society. Memberships: Fellow, Royal Society of Public Health; SCOPE Member, EASO; Hellenic Diabetes Association; Hellenic Atherosclerosis Society; Hellenic Medical Association for Obesity-Northern Greece Diabetes Association. Address: Dionyssiou 12 St, Anopoli 54634, Thessaloniki, Greece. E-mail: nikikatsiki@hotmail.com

KATSURA Fumiko, b. 21 February 1944, Kyoto, Japan. Professor. Education: BA, 1966, MA, 1968, Kyoto University; Visiting Scholar, UCLA, 1977-78; Visiting Scholar, St Edmunds College, 1989-90; Visiting Scholar, Cambridge, 1997; Research Fellow, Kyoto University, 2001-02. Appointments: Assistant, Kyoto University, 1970-72; Instructor, 1972-76, Associate Professor, 1976-91, Professor, 1991-, Ryukoku University; Owner and manager, Kameoka Katsura Hall (a private hall for classical music and cultural activities). Publications: A History of English Poetry; Men and Literature; For Those Who Read English Poetry; George Meredith's The Ordeal of Richard Feveral; B T Gates' Victorian Suicide; E B Browning's Aurora Leigh; English Sonnets from Southey to Swinburne; English Sonnets from Carew to Coleridge; R Browning's Prince Hohenstiel-Schwangau, Saviour of Society 1871; A Study of Robert Browning, from Paracelsus to Inn Album. Memberships: The Browning Institute; The English Literary Society of Japan; The Victorian Studies Society of Japan. Address: 51 Hatago-Cho, Kameoka, Kyoto, Japan 621-0866.

KATZENBERG Jeffrey, b. 21 December, 1950, New York, USA. Film Executive. m. Marilyn Siegal, 1 son, 1 daughter. Appointments: Assistant to Chair, CEO, Paramount Pictures, NY, 1975-77; Executive Director, Marketing, Paramount TV, California, 1977, Vice President, Programming, 1977-78; Vice President, Feature Production, Paramount Pictures, 1978-80, Senior Vice President, Production, Motion Picture Division, 1980-82, President, Production, Motion Pictures & TV, 1982-94; Chairman, Walt Disney Studios, Burbank, California, 1994; Co-Founder, Dreamworks SKG, 1995-. Address: Dreamworks SKG, 100 Flower Street, Glendale, CA 91201, USA.

KAUFFMAN Teresa Jo, b. 24 August 1951, San Francisco, California. Professor; Creative Artist; Art Therapist; TV Writer; Producer; Director; Journalist. Education: Bachelor of Arts, University of California, Berkeley, 1974; Master Degree, Communications, University of Texas, Austin, 1980; PhD, Interdisciplinary Study of Psychology, Communication, and Creative Expression, The Union Institute, 1996. Appointments: Senior Writer, Producer, Director, World Headquarters, Ampex Corporation, California, 1981; Lecturer, Department of Communication, North Carolina State University, 1986-2001; Adjunct Faculty in Arts and Studies, NCSU; Adjunct Professor, Meredith College, Raleigh; Adjunct Faculty, Department of Radio, Television and Motion Pictures, University of North Carolina, Chapel Hill; Founder, Director, Creative Spaces. Honours: First Place National Award Winning Creative Artist; Over 15 first place national awards in writing, producing and directing for television and video; Outstanding Teacher, North Carolina State University; Dictionary of International Biography, International Biographical Centre; International Authors and Writers Who's Who; Memberships: American Psychological Association; California Scholastic Federation; Phi Kappa Phi; Former Member: National Association of Television Arts and Sciences, Wake Visual Arts Association, Texas Consumer Association, International Television Association. Address: 407 Furches Street, Raleigh, NC 27607, USA.

KAUP Mohamed, b. 27 May 1966, Bombay, India. Professor; Director. m. 2 sons. Education: PhD, 1995; FMRP, 1999; MCom, 2004; Doctorate in Business Administration, 2005. Appointments: Deputy Director, Head of Business Studies Department, Aff National American University, 1997-2002; Dean and Director, World of Knowledge Management DC, Dubai, United Arab Emirates, 2002-. Publications: Articles in management journals, newsletters, etc. Honours: Super Intellectual Award; Management Excellence Award; Fellow, All India Management Council. Memberships: Fellow, Management Studies and Promotion Institute; Fellow, All India Management Council, New Delhi. Address: PO 44548, Dubai, United Arab Emirates. E-mail: drkaup@emirates.net.ar

KAVATKAR Anita, b. 9 August 1969, Wai, Satara, India. Medical Doctor; Pathologist. m. Neelkanth C Kavatkar. Education: MBBS, 1990; MD, 1994. Appointments: Lecturer, 1995-2004, Associate Professor, 2004-, Department of Pathology, B J (Byramjee Jeejeebhoy) Medical College, Pune, Maharashtra, India. Publications: Articles in medical journals as co-author: Cytological study of neck masses with special emphasis on tuberculosis, 1996; Sclerosing mediastinitis with oesophageal involvement in miliary tuberculosis – A case report, 2000; Granulocytic sarcoma presenting as a mediastinal mass – a case report, 2002; Infantile Hepatic Hemangioendothelioma – A Case Report, 2003; Fatal Outcome of Colloid Cyst of Third Ventricle – A report of three cases, 2003; Histopathological patterns of tumor and tumor like lesions of ovary – a review of 191 cases, 2003; Fine needle aspiration cytology in lymphadenopathy of HIV positive patients, 2003; Autopsy study of maternal deaths, 2003; Benign linitis plastica – a case report, 2004; FNAC of Salivary Gland Lesions with Histopathological Correlation, 2006; Study of a manual method of liquid based cervical cytology, 2008. Honours: Smt Kuntidevi Mehrotra Award for research publication; International Fellowship, Indian Council of Medical Research, 2005; Listed in Who's Who publications and biographical dictionaries. Memberships: Life Member: Indian Association of Pathologists and Microbiologists, Research Society, BJ Medical College, Indian Academy of Cytologists. Address: BJ Medical College, Department of Pathology, Sassoon Road, Pune 411001, Maharashtra, India. E-mail: kavatkaranita@rediffmail.com

KAVOULAKOS Konstantinos, b. 4 October 1967, Athens, Greece. Assistant Professor. Education: Diploma, Sociology, 1989; PhD, Social and Political Philosophy, 1995. Appointments: Lecturer, Social and Political Philosophy, 1998-2002, Assistant Professor, Social and Political Philosophy, 2002-, Associate Professor, Social and Political Philosophy, Philosophy of Culture, 2011-, Department of Philosophy and Social Studies, University of Crete. Publications: 3 books; 8 book editions; Numerous articles in journals; Contributions in collective works. Memberships: Greek Philosophical Association. Address: Department of Philosophy and Social Studies, University of Crete, Panespitimioupoli Gallou, 74 100 Rethymno, Greece. E-mail: kavoulakos@phl.uoc.gr

KAWAGISHI Shigenori, b. 26 April 1950, Kushiro, Hokkaido, Japan. Neuroscientist; Educator. m. Akemi Tanaka, 1 son, 1 daughter. Education: BSc, 1974, MSc, 1976, PhD, 1980, Hokkaido University, Japan. Appointments: Research Associate, 1980-88, Assistant Professor, 1988-91, Associate Professor, 1991-, Department of Oral Neurosciences, Kyushu Dental College; Postdoctoral Fellow, Biochemistry Department, University of Toronto, 1985-87. Publications: Decrease in stereognostic ability of the tongue with age, 2009. Honours: Research grant, Japan Society for the Promotion of Science, Ministry of Education, Culture, Sports and Technology, 1982-84, 1991, 1995-97, 2008-13. Memberships: International Association of Dental Research; Physical Society of Japan; Japanese Association of Oral Biology; Japan Neuroscience Society; Japanese Society of Dysphagia Rehabilitation. Address: 2-18-13 Kurobaru, Kokurakita-ku, Kitakyushu, 802-0051, Japan. E-mail: kawagisi@kyu-dent.ac.jp

KAWAGUCHI Akihiko, b. 5 March 1942, Taipei, Taiwan. Professor. m. Ayako, 2 sons. Education: BS, Okayama University, 1964; PhD, Kyoto University, 1969. Appointments: Professor, Graduate School of Arts and Sciences, 1983-2002, Senator, 1991-95, Director of International Office, 1994-98, Director of University Museum, 1999-2001, University of Tokyo; Professor, 2000-06, Director of Department of Evaluation and Research, 2004-06, Vice President, 2006-10, Professor, 2010-, National Institution for Academic Degrees and University Evaluation. Publications: Biosynthesis and Degradation of Fatty Acids, 1999; Glossary of Quality Assurance in Japanese Higher Education, 2009; Quality Assurance for Higher Education in Japan, 2012. Honours: Vice President, Asian Pacific Quality Network, 2007-09; Chief Director, Institution for Beauty Business Evaluation, 2011-; Chida Prize, Japanese Conference on Biochemistry of Lipids; Young Investigator Award, Japanese Biochemical Society. Memberships: Japanese Biochemical Society; Japanese Society of Plant Physiologists; Botanical Society of Japan; Japan Association for Quality Assurance in Higher Education. Address: 1-29-1 Gakuen-Nishimachi, Kodaira, Tokyo 187-8587, Japan. E-mail: chombi@niad.ac.jp

KAY Chul-Seung, b. 19 August 1964, Seoul, South Korea. Professor. m. Seon Ra, 1 son, 1 daughter. Education: MD, The Catholic University of Korea, College of Medicine, 1990; MS, 1994, PhD, 2002, Medical Science, Graduate School, The Catholic University of Korea. Appointments: Board of Radiation Oncology, South Korea, 1995; Assistant Professor, 2002, Associate Professor, 2011-, Department of Radiation Oncology, The Catholic University of Korea, College of Medicine; Licence of Radioisotope Management, Ministry of Science and Technology, South Korea, 2005. Publications: Simultaneous multitarget irradiation using helical tomotherapy for advanced hepatocellular carcinoma with multiple extrahepatic metastasis, 2009; Helical tomotherapy for simultaneous multitarget radiotherapy for pulmonary metastasis, 2009. Honours: Listed in international biographical dictionaries. Memberships: Korean Liver Cancer Study Group; Korean Radiosurgery Society; Korean Cancer Association; Korean Society of Therapeutic Radiology and Oncology. Address: Department of Radiation Oncology, Incheon St Mary's Hospital, 665 Bupyeong-6-dong, Bupyeonggu, Incheon 403720, South Korea. E-mail: k41645@chol.com

KAY Steven Walton, b. 4 August 1954, Amman, Jordan. Lawyer; Barrister. m. Valerie, 1 son, 1 daughter. Education: Epsom College; LLB (Hons), Leeds University; Inns of Court School of Law, 1976-77. Appointments: Called to the Bar, Inner Temple, 1977; Bar Rights of Audience in the Crown Court, 1995; Bar Council Committee, Efficiency in the Criminal Justice System, 1994; Prime Minister's Special Committee on Victims in the Criminal Justice System, 1995; Secretary Criminal Bar Association, 1993-96; Queens Counsel, 1997; Recorder, 1997; Treasurer, European Criminal Bar Association, 1998-2000; Defence Counsel, Dusko Tadic, UN International Criminal Tribunal for the Former Yugoslavia , 1996; Defence Counsel, Alfred Musema, UN Criminal Tribunal for Rwanda, 1997-; Amicus Curiae, Trial of Slobodan Milosevic, UN International Tribunal for the Former Yugoslavia, 2001-04; Assigned Counsel, Slobodan Milosevic, 2004-2006; Advising Syria re: UN Resolutions 1595, 1636, 1644, 2005; Defence Counsel UNICTY, CERMAR - Trial of Croatia's Operation Storm, 2007-11; Defence Counsel ICC, Uhuru Kenyatta Deputy Prime Minister Kenya - Post Election Violence, 2008; Other notable trials include: R-v-Winzar (an allegation of murder by insulin injection); R-v-Lomas (a European agricultural regulations fraud); R-v-Hannon (an international time share fraud); R-v-Clemente (an international money laundering case). Publication: Role of Defence in International Criminal Court, Commentary on ICC (editors: Casese, Jones, Gaeta), 2003. Honour: QC, 1997. Memberships: Criminal Bar Association; Forensic Science Society; Association of Defence Council; Founder Member, International Criminal Law Bureau, 2008; Listed in national biographical dictionaries. Address: 9 Bedford Row, London WC1R 4HD, England. E-mail: goodnightvienna@gmail.com Website: www.internationallawbureau.com

KAY Vernon, b. 28 April 1974, Bolton, England. TV Presenter; DJ; Former Model. m. Tess Daly, 2003, 2 daughters. Career: Model; DJ, BBC Radio 1, 2004-; TV appearances: T4, Channel 4 TV; Boys and Girls, 2003; A Wife for William, 2004; HeadJam, 2004; Hit Me Baby One More Time, 2005; The Prince's Trust 30th Birthday: Live, 2006; All Star Family Fortunes, 2006-; Co-presenter, with Tess Daly, Just the Two of Us, 2006; Gameshow Marathan, 2006, 2007; Extras, 2007; Thank God You're Here, 2008; Happy Birthday Brucie! 2008.

KAZANTZIS Judith, b. 14 August 1940, Oxford, England. Poet; Fiction Writer. 1 son, 1 daughter. Education: Honours Degree, Modern History, Oxford, 1961. Appointments: General Council, Poetry Society, member, 1991-94; Royal Literary Fund fellow, University of Sussex, 2005-2006. Publications: Non Fiction: The Gordon Riots, 1966; Women in Revolt, 1968; The Florida Swamps pamphlet, 1990; The Great What of Who: By Mad King George Pertaining to Tom Paine Dec 1809 pamphlet, 2009; Poetry Collections: Minefield, 1977; The Wicked Queen, 1980; Touch Papers (co-author), 1982; Let's Pretend, 1984; Flame Tree, 1988; A Poem for Guatemala, pamphlet, 1988; The Rabbit Magician Plate, 1992; Selected Poems 1977-92, 1995; Swimming Through the Grand Hotel, 1997; The Odysseus Papers: Fictions on the Odyssey of Homer, 1999, reissued 2011; In Cyclops' Cave, Homeric translation, 2002; Just After Midnight, 2004; Fiction: Of Love And Terror, 2002; Short Fiction: London Magazine; Comparative Criticism; Critical Quarterly; Serpents Tail Anthologies; Contributions to: Stand; Agenda; London Magazine; Poetry London; Poetry Wales; New Statesman; Red Pepper; Poetry Review; Ambit; Verse; Honest Ulsterman; Anthologies: Poems on the Underground; Key West Reader; Faber Book of Blue Verse; Virago Book of Love Poetry; Second Light Anthologies; The Light Unlocked; Red Sky at Night; Criticism: Poetry in Poetry Review, London Magazine; Fiction, in Banipal, 2007-08. Honours: Judge, Sheffield Hallam Poetry Competition, 1995-96; Judge, Stand International Poetry Competition, 1998; Royal Literary Fund Fellow, University of Sussex, 2005-06; Cholmondeley Award, 2007. Memberships: CND; Palestine Solidarity Campaign. Address: 32 St Annes Crescent, Lewes, East Sussex, BN7 1SB, England. Website: www.judithkazantzis.com

KAZIM Pasha, b. 23 December 1946, Agra, India. TV Drama Director. m. Fehmida Nasreen, 1 son, 3 daughters. Education: Matriculation; FA (Intermediate), Economics, History & Geography; BA, Economics & Geography, 1968. Appointments: Banker, State Bank of Pakistan, 1965-74; Producer/Director, Pakistan Television, 1975-2011. Honours: PTV Award; Nigar Award; Luxstyle Award; Bhitai Award; Waheed Murad Memorial Award; Governor of Sind Award; Chief Minister Balochistan Award. Memberships: Arts Council of Pakistan, Karachi. Address: G-7/B-5 Block-17, Gulshan-E-Iqbal, Karachi, Pakistan. E-mail: kazimuddin.pasha@gmail.com

KEACH Stacy, b. 2 June 1941, Savannah, Georgia, USA. Actor; Director. m. Malgossia Tomassi, 1986, 2 daughters. Career: Plays: Hamlet, 1964; A Long Day's Journey into Night; Macbird; Indians; Deathtrap; Hughie; Barnum; Cyrano de Bergerac; Peer Gynt; Henry IV (Parts I & II); Idiot's Delight; The King and I, 1989; Love Letters, 1990-93; Richard III, 1991; Stieglitz Loves O'Keefe, 1995; Director: Incident at Vichy; Six Characters in Search of an Author; Films: The Heart is a Lonely Hunter; End of the Road; The Travelling Executioner; Brewster McCloud; Doc; Judge Roy Bean; The New Centurions; Fat City; The Killer Inside Me; Conduct Unbecoming; Luther; Street People; The Squeeze; Gray Lady Down; The Ninth Configuration; The Long Riders; Road Games; Butterfly; Up in Smoke; Nice Dreams; That Championship Season; The Lover; False Identity; The Forgotten Milena; John Carpenter's Escape from LA, Prey of the Jaguar, 1996; The Truth Configuration, American History X, 1998; Icebreaker, 1999; Unshackled, Militia, Mercy Streets, 2000; Sunstorm, 2001; When Eagles Strike, Jesus, Mary and Joey, 2003; Caught in the Headlights, Galaxy Hunter, El Padrino, The Hollow, 2004; Man with the Screaming Brain, Keep Your Distance, 2005; Come Early Morning, Jesus, Mary and Joey, Death Row, 2006; Honeydipper, 2007; The Portal, 2008; TV: Mike Hammer, Private Eye, 1997; The Courage to Love, Titus, 2000; Lightning: Fire From The Sky, 2001; Rods! The Santa Trap, 2002; Miracle Dogs, Frozen Impact, 2003; Prison Break, 2005-07; ER, 2007; Two and a Half Men, 2010. Publications: Keach, Go Home! 1996. Memberships: Artists Committee, Kennedy Center Honors, 1986-; Hon Chair, American Cleft Palate Foundation, 1995-. Honours: Vernon Rice Drama Desk Award; 3 Obie Awards; Pasadena Playhouse Alumni Man of the Year, 1995; Pacific Pioneers Broadcasters' Association Diamond Circle Award, 1996. Address: c/o Palmer & Associates, #950, 23852 Pacific Coast Highway, Malibu, CA 90265, USA.

KEANE Fergal Patrick, b. 6 January 1961, London, England. Journalist; Broadcaster. m. Anne Frances Flaherty, 1986, 1 son. Education: Terenure College, Dublin; Presentation College, Cork. Appointments: Trainee Reporter, Limerick Leader, 1979-82; Reporter, Irish Press Group, Dublin, 1982-84, Radio Telefis, Eireann, Belfast, 1986-89 (Dublin 1984-86); Northern Ireland Correspondent, BBC Radio, 1989-91, South Africa Correspondent, 1991-94, Asia Correspondent, 1994-97, Special Correspondent, 1997-; Presenter, Fergal Keane's Forgotten Britain, BBC, 2000. Publications: Irish Politics Now, 1987; The Bondage of Fear, 1994; Season of Blood: A Rwandan Journey, 1995; Letter to Daniel, 1996; Letters Home, 1999; A Stranger's Eye, 2000; There Will be Sunlight Later: A Memoir of War, 2004; All of These People, 2006. Honours: Reporter of the Year Sony Silver Award, 1992, Sony Gold Award, 1993; International Reporter of the Year, 1993; Amnesty International Press Awards; RTS Journalist of the Year, 1994; OBE, 1996; BAFTA Award, 1997; Hon DLitt, Strathclyde, 2001, Staffordshire, 2002. Address: c/o BBC Television, Wood Lane, London W12 7RJ, England.

KEATING Paul John, b. 18 January 1944. Australian Politician. m. Anna Johanna Maria Van Iersel, 1975, 1 son, 3 daughters. Education: De La Salle College, Bankstown, New South Wales. Appointments: Research Officer, Federal Municipal & Shire Council Employees Union of Australia, 1967; MP for Blaxland, 1969-96; Minister for Northern Australia, 1975; Shadow Minister for Agriculture, 1976, for Minerals & Energy, 1976-80, for Resources & Energy, 1980-83; Shadow Treasurer, 1983; Federal Treasurer of Australia, 1983-91; Deputy Prime Minister, 1990-91; Prime Minister of Australia, 1991-96. Publication: Engagement: Australia Faces the Asia Pacific, 2000. Memberships: Chairman, Australian Institute of Music, 1999-; Board of Architects of New South Wales, 2000-.

KEATING Ronan, b. 3 March 1977, Dublin, Ireland. Vocalist. m. Yvonne Connolly, 1 son, 2 daughters. Career: Lead Singer, Boyzone; Co-Host, Eurovision Song Contest, Ireland. Recordings: Singles: Working My Way Back To You, 1994; Key To My Life, Love Me For A Reason, So Good, Father and Son, Coming Home Now, 1995; Words, 1996; Isn't It A Wonder, Baby Can I Hold You Tonight, Mystical Experience, 1997; I Love The Way You Love Me, You Needed

Me, Solo: When You Say Nothing At All, Everyday I Love You, 1999; Life Is a Rollercoaster, The Way You Make Me Feel, 2000; Lovin' Each Day, 2001; If Tomorrow Never Comes, I Love The Way We Do, We've Got Tonight, 2002; Iris, 2006. Albums: Different Beat, 1996; Where We Belong, 1998; By Request – the Greatest Hits, 1999; Ronan, 2000; Destination, Turn It On, 2002; 10 Years of Hits, 2004; Bring You Home, 2006; Songs for My Mother, Winter Songs, 2009. Publications: No Matter What, 2000; Life is a Rollercoaster, 2000. Honours: BMI European song-writing Award, 2003; Fair Trade Ambassador for Christian Aid. Address: The Outside Organisation, 180-182 Tottenham Court Road, London, W1P 9LE, England.

KEATON Diane, b. 5 January 1946, California, USA. Adopted 2 children. Education: Student at Neighbourhood Playhouse, New York. Career: Theatre in New York includes: Hair, 1968; The Primary English Class, 1976; Films include: Lovers and Other Strangers, 1970; The Godfather, 1972; Sleeper, 1973; Annie Hall, 1977; Manhattan, 1979; Shoot the Moon, 1982; Crimes of the Heart, 1986; Baby Boom, 1988; The Godfather III, 1991; Manhattan Murder Mystery, 1993; Father of Bride II, 1995; Marvins's Room, The First Wives Club, 1996; The Only Thrill, 1997; Hanging Up (also director), The Other Sister, Town and Country, 1999; Sister Mary Explains It All, 2001; Wildflower, 2002; Something's Gotta Give, 2003; Terminal Impact, The Family Stone, 2005; Because I Said So, Smother, 2007; Mama's Boy, Mad Money, 2008. Publications: Reservations, Still Life, editor. Honours: Academy Award, Best Actress, 1977; Golden Globe Award, Best Actress in a Musical or Comedy, 2004. Address: c/o John Burnham, William Morris Agency, 151 El Camino, Beverly Hills, CA 90212, USA.

KEATON James, b. 29 October 1934, Manchester, England. Company Director. m. Angela Mary Gilbertson, 1 son, 1 daughter. Education: BSc, St Edward's College, Liverpool; FSDC, 1974; Advanced Management Certificate, Harvard University, 1978; FRSA, 1996; FCMI, 1998. Appointments: Director, ICI Organics Division, 1979-90; Chairman, ICI Dyestuffs Business Area, 1984-90; Board Member, ICI Espana, ICI Brasil, Deutche ICI, ICI France, ICI Italia, ICI China, Atic Industries (India), 1984-90; Chairman, Quarry Bank Mill Trustees, 1989-2004; Consultant to the Finance Department, 1991-, Deputy Chairman, Finance and Planning Board, 1992-, Diocesan Trustee, 1997-, Executive Chairman Shrewsbury Diocesan Commercial Company Ltd, 2000-, Shrewsbury Roman Catholic Diocese; Chairman, Dundee Textiles Ltd, 1992-97; Chairman, MGP Investment Management Ltd, 1994-2004; Chairman, Campus Ventures Ltd, 1995-2004; Member, Byers Committee on the Future of Daresbury Research Laboratories and Scientific Research in the NW; Chairman, Magna Colours Ltd, 1997-2004; Chairman, Roberts Bakeries Ltd, 2002-03; Vice President and Treasurer, University of Liverpool, 2005-09; Chairman, National Trust NW Regional Board, 2005-; Chairman, Management School Board, 2005-, Pro-Chancellor and Treasurer, University of Liverpool, 2010-, University of Liverpool; Trustee, Liverpool School of Tropical Medicine, 2011-; Chairman of Governors, Upton Hall Grammar School, 2005-; Director, Pro-Liverpool Ltd, 2007-. Publications: Numerous articles in professional journals. Honours: Honorary Professor, School of Management, University of Liverpool; LLD, University of Manchester, 1999; The Dyers Company, London; Freeman of the City of London; President, Society of Dyers and Colourists, 1986-87; Gold Medal, Silver Medal, Society of Dyers and Colourists; Pro Ecclesia et Pontifice, 2009. Memberships: The Athenaeum; The Sloane Club. Address: c/o University of Liverpool, Foundation Building, Liverpool, L69 7ZX, England. E-mail: jimkeaton@btinternet.com

KEATON Michael, b. 5 September 1951, Pittsburgh, USA. Actor. m. Caroline MacWilliams, divorced, 1 son. Education: Kent State University. Appointments: With Comedy Group, Second City, Los Angeles; TV appearances include: All in the Family; Maude; Mary Tyler Moore Show; Working Stiffs; Report to Murphy; Roosevelt and Truman (TV film); Body Shots (producer), 1999. Creative Works: Films: Night Shift, 1982; Mr Mom, 1983; Johnny Dangerously, 1984; Touch and Go, Gung Ho, 1987; Beetlejuice, Clean and Sober, 1988; The Dream Team, Batman, 1989; Much Ado About Nothing, 1992; My Life, The Paper, Speechless, 1994; Multiplicity, Jackie Brown, 1997; Desperate Measures, Jack Frost, 1998; A Shot at Glory, 2000; Quicksand, 2001; First Daughter, 2004; White Noise, Game 6, Herbie Fully Loaded, 2005; Cars (voice), The Last Time, 2006; The Merry Gentleman, 2008; Post Grad, 2009. Address: c/o ICM Management, 8942 Wilshire Boulevard, Beverly Hills, CA 90211, USA.

KEATS Reynold Gilbert, b. 15 February 1918, Pt Pirie, South Australia, Australia. Emeritus Professor of Mathematics. m. Verna Joy, 2 daughters. Education: Diploma in Accountancy, 1939; BSc, 1948, PhD, 1966, University of Adelaide. Appointments: Clerk, Savings Bank of South Australia, 1934-40; Private to Lieutenant, 2/48th Battalion, Australian Imperial Forces, 1940-45; Visiting Research Scientist, Royal Aircraft Establishment, Farnborough, England, 1948-51; Scientific Officer, Australian Government Department of Supply, Melbourne, Victoria, 1951, 1952; Senior Scientific Officer, 1952-57, Principal Scientific Officer, 1957-61, Australian Government Department of Supply, Weapons Research Establishment, Salisbury, South Australia; Senior Lecturer, University of Adelaide, South Australia, 1961-67; Professor of Mathematics, 1968-83, Dean, Faculty of Mathematics, 1971-76, 1980-83, Member of Council, 1977, 1978, Deputy Chairman of Senate, 1977, 1978, Emeritus Professor, 1983-, Honorary Professor, 1984-88, University of Newcastle, New South Wales. Honours: Fellow, Australian Society of Certified Practising Accountants, 1952; Fellow, Institute of Mathematics and its Applications, 1973; Honorary DMath, University of Waterloo, Ontario, Canada, 1979; Chartered Mathematician, Institute of Mathematics and its Applications, 1993; Fellow, Australian Mathematical Society, 1995; Fellow, Australian Computer Society, 1997. Address: Ridgecrest Retirement Village, Unit 105, 55 Burkitt Street, Page, ACT 2614, Australia.

KEEFE Denis Edward Peter Paul, b. 29 June 1958, Bury St Edmunds, Suffolk, England. Diplomat. m. Catherine Anne Mary, 3 sons, 3 daughters. Education: MA, Classics, Churchill College, Cambridge; Hertford College, Oxford; University of Malmo. Appointments: Greece Desk Officer, Southern European Department, FCO, 1982-84; Second Secretary, British Embassy, Prague, 1984-88; European Community Department (Internal), FCO, 1988-90; Germany Desk Officer, Western European Department, FCO, 1990-91; European Correspondent, CFSP Department, FCO, 1991-92; Head of Political Section, British High Commission, Nairobi, 1992-95; Deputy Head of South Asia Department, FCO, 1996-97; Head of ASEM Unit, FCO, 1997-98; Deputy Head of Mission, British Embassy, Prague, 1998-2002; CONTEST Team Leader, Cabinet Office, 2002-03; Head of Far Eastern Group, FCO, 2003-06; British Ambassador to Georgia, 2007-10; Minister and Deputy Head of Mission,

British Embassy, Moscow, 2010-. Address: c/o Foreign and Commonwealth Office, King Charles Street, London SW1A 2AH, England. Website: www.musicformass.co.uk

KEEFFE Barrie (Colin), b. 31 October 1945, London, England. Playwright. m. (1) Dee Truman, 1969, divorced 1979, (2) Verity Bargate, 1981, deceased 1981, 2 stepsons, (3) Julia Lindsay, 1983, divorced 1993, (4) Jacky Stoller, 2011. Appointments: Writer; Actor; Director; Journalist; Tutor; Dramatist-in-Residence, Shaw Theatre, London, 1977, Royal Shakespeare Company, 1978; Associate Writer, Theatre Royal Stratford East, London, 1986-91; Board of Directors, Soho Poly Theatre, 1976-81; Board of Directors, Theatre Royal, Stratford East, 1981-89; Ambassador, United Nations, 50th anniversary year, 1995; Tutor, City University, London, 2002-05; Judith E Wilson Fellow, Christ's College Cambridge, 2003-04; Honorary degree, Doctor of Letters, Warwick University, 2010; Tutor and Patron, Writing for Performance, Ruskin College, Oxford, 2010-. Plays: A Mad World, My Masters, 1977, Gimme Shelter, 1977; Barbarians, 1977; Frozen Assets, 1978, revised version, 1987; Sus, 1979; Heaven Scent, 1979; Bastard Angel, 1980; Black Lear, 1980; She's So Modern, 1980; Chorus Girls, 1981; A Gentle Spirit (with Jules Croiset), 1981; The Long Good Friday (screenplay), 1984; Better Times, 1985; King of England, 1986; My Girl, 1989; Not Fade Away, 1990; Wild Justice, 1990; I Only Want to Be With You, 1997; Shadows on the Sun, 2001; Still Killing Time, 2006; Sus (screenplay), 2010; Novels: Gadabout, 1969; No Excuses, 1983; Journalism: Numerous articles contributed to national newspapers, including Sunday Times; The Independent; The Guardian; Evening Standard. As Director: A Certain Vincent, 1974; A Gentle Spirit, 1980; The Gary Oldman Fan Club, 1998. Radio Plays: Good Old Uncle Jack, 1975; Pigeon Skyline, 1975; Self-Portrait, 1977; Paradise, 1990; On the Eve of the Millennium, 1999; Tales, 2000; Feng Shui and Me, 2000; The Five of Us, 2002. Television Plays: Gotcha, 1977; Champions, 1978; Hanging Around, 1978; Nipper, 1978; Waterloo Sunset, 1979; No Excuses Series, 1983; King, 1984; Honours: French Critics Prix Revelation, 1978; Giles Cooper Award, Best Radio Plays, 1978; Edgar Allan Poe Award, Mystery Writers of America, 1982. Membership: Société des Auteurs et Compositeurs Dramatiques. Address: 33 Brookfield Mansions, Highgate West Hill, London N6 6AT, England.

KEEGAN John (Desmond Patrick) (Sir), b. 15 May 1934, London, England. Editor; Writer; Defence Correspondent. m. Susanne Everett, 1960, 2 sons, 2 daughters. Education: BA, 1957, MA, 1962, Balliol College, Oxford. Appointments: Senior Lecturer in Military History, Royal Military Academy, Sandhurst, 1960-86; Fellow, Princeton University, 1984; Defence Editor, Daily Telegraph, 1986-; Delmas Distinguished Professor of History, Vassar College, 1997. Publications: The Face of Battle, 1976; Who's Who in Miltary History (co-author), 1976; World Armies (editor), 1979, new edition, 1982; Six Armies in Normandy, 1982; Zones of Conflict (co-author), 1986; The Mask of Command, 1987; The Price of Admiralty, 1988, reissued as Battle at Sea, 1993; The Times Atlas of the Second World War, 1989; Churchill's Generals (editor), 1991; A History of Warfare, 1993; Warpaths: Travels of a Military Historian in North America, 1995; War and Our World: The Reith Lectures, 1998; The Penguin Book of the War: great miltary writings (editor), 1999; Winston Chrucnill, 2002; Intelligence in War, 2003; The Iraq War, 2004; Atlas of World War II, 2006; The American Civil War, 2009. Honours: Officer of the Order of the British Empire, 1991; Duff Cooper Prize, 1994; Honorary Doctor of Law, University of New Brunswick, 1997; Honorary Doctor of Literature, Queen's University, Belfast, 2000; Knighted, 2000; Honorary Doctor of Letters, University of Bath, 2001. Address: The Manor House, Kilmington, near Warminster, Wilts BA12 6RD, England.

KEEGAN Kevin Joseph, b. 14 February 1951, Armthorpe, England. Professional football manager; Former professional football player. m. (1) Jean Woodhouse, 1974, 2 daughters. Career: Player: Scunthorpe United, Liverpool, 1971-77 (won League Championships three times, FA Cup 1974, European Cup, 1977, UEFA Cup, 1973, 1976), SV Hamburg, 1977-80, Southampton, 1980-82, Newcastle United, 1982-84; Retired, 1984; Scored 274 goals in approximately 800 appearances; Capped for England 63 times (31 as captain), scoring 21 goals; Manager: Newcastle United, 1992-97; Fulham, 1998-99, England national team, 1999-2000, Manchester City, 2001-05. Publications: Kevin Keegan, 1978; Against the World: Playing for England, 1979; Kevin Keegan: My Autobiography, 1997. Honours: Footballer of the Year, 1976; European Footballer of the Year, 1978, 1979. Address: c/o Manchester City Football Club, City of Manchester Stadium, Manchester, England.

KEEN Richard, b. 29 March 1954, Rustington, Sussex, England. Queen's Counsel. m. Jane Carolyn Anderson, 1 son, 1 daughter. Education: Beckman Scholar, University of Edinburgh. Appointments: Admitted to Faculty of Advocates (Scottish Bar), 1980; Counsel to DTI in Scotland, 1986-93; Queen's Counsel, 1993-; Chairman, Appeal Committee, Institute of Chartered Accountants Scotland (ICAS), 1996-. Treasure, Faculty of Advocates. Address: The Castle, Elie, Fife KY9 1DN, Scotland. E-mail: rskeenqc@compuserve.com

KEENE Raymond Dennis, b. 29 January 1948, London, England. Author; Publisher. m. Annette Sara Goodman, 1 son. Education: MA, Trinity College, Cambridge, 1967-72. Career: Co-owner, GM Racing (winner of 1984/85 UK historic Formula 3 Championship); Chess Correspondent, The Spectator, 1977-; The Times, 1985-; The Sunday Times, 1996-; International Herald Tribune, 2001-08; Organiser, World Chess Championships, London, 1986, 1993, 2000; Director, Hardinge Simpole Publishing; Organiser, World Memory Championship; Founding President, Commonwealth Chess Association; International Arbiter of Mental World Records & Director of The International Academy of Mental World Records. Publications: 161 books written and published on chess; Daily chess article in The Times; Weekly chess column in The Spectator and the Sunday Times; Weekly IQ column in The Times; Winner, 22 National Chess Championships. Honours: International Chess Grandmaster, 1976; OBE, 1985. Memberships: The Garrick; Director, The Brain Trust Charity; RAC; Pall Mall. Address: 86 Clapham Common, North Side, London SW4 9SE, UK. E-mail: rdkobe@aol.com

KEENER Craig S, b. 4 July 1960, Massillon, Ohio, USA. Professor. Education: BA, Central Bible College; MA, MDv, Assemblies of God Theological Seminary; PhD, Duke University Graduate School. Appointments: Associate Professor, Professor, Hood Theological Seminary, 1992-96; Visiting Professor of Biblical Studies, Eastern Seminary, 1996-99; Professor of New Testament, Palmer Seminary (previously Eastern Seminary), Eastern University, 1999-. Publications: 15 books; Numerous articles in professional journals. Memberships: Society for New Testament Studies; Institute for Biblical Research; Society of Biblical Literature. Address: Palmer Theological Seminary, 6 E Lancaster Ave, Wynnewood, PA 19096, USA.

KEESOM Pierre Henri Marie, b. 21 August 1943, Heerlen, The Netherlands. Trademark Attorney; Translator; Chartered Linguist. m. Xiaodu Liu, 3 sons. Education: Sworn Translator (English), Sworn Translator (French), 1981; JDrs, Catholic University, Nymegen, 1988; idem Interpreter (French), 2002; Diploma, Justice Department, Translator and Interpreter (English), 2004. Appointments: Trademark Attorney, Member of Management Team, Markgraaf, 1965-75; Principal, Keesom & Hendriks, 1975-. Publications: The New Benelux Trade Marks Act, 1986; Contributor of many articles to professional publications. Honours: Knight; Order of Orange – Nassau; Commander, Most Venerable Order of the Hospital of St John of Jerusalem; Knight jure sanguinis, Constantinian Order (Naples, Spain); Commander, Order Pro Merito Melitensi; Medal of Merit, Order of St John. Memberships: Fellow, Chartered Institute of Linguists; Fellow, Royal Society for the Encouragement of the Arts, Manufactures & Commerce; Member, Netherlands Association of Interpreters and Translators; Member, Royal Netherlands Society for Genealogy and Heraldry; BMM Attorney Member, Benelux Association of Trade Mark and Design Law; Member, Complaints Board Sworn Translators and Interpreters, Ministry of Security and Justice, The Netherlands. E-mail: phmkeesom@keesom.hl Website: www.keesom.nl

KEEY Roger Brian, b. 11 March 1934, Birmingham, England. Chemical Engineer. m. Daphne Pearl Griffiths, 1959, 1 son, 3 daughters. Education: BSc, 1954; PhD, University of Birmingham, 1957; DSc (Hon), Technical University of Łódź, 2002. Appointments: Chemical Engineer, DCL Ltd, Saltend, 1957-62; Lecturer, Senior Lecturer, Reader, University of Canterbury, New Zealand, 1962-78; Professor, 1978-97, Professor Emeritus, 1997-, Chemical Engineering; Director, Wood Technology Research Centre, 1997-2001; Forest Guardian, Hurunui District Council, 1999-; Hanmer Springs Community Board, 2001-07. Publications: Drying Principles and Practice; Introduction to Industrial Drying Operations; Reliability in the Process Industries; Drying of Loose and Particulate Materials; Wainui Incident; Kiln-Drying of Lumber; Management of Engineering Risk; Lambent Flames; Forest Affairs. Honours: Cadman Medal; NZIE Angus Award; NZIE Skellerup Award; IPENZ Rabone Award; IPENZ Skellerup Award; Proctor and Gamble Award, Excellence in Drying Research; Award for outstanding achievement and excellence in Drying R&D, 1st Nordic Drying Conference; Chemeca Medal, 2005; Distinguished Fellow IPENZ, 2006; Lifetime Achievement Award, 16th International Drying Symposium, Hyderabad, 2008; Community Services Award, Hurunui District Council, 2010; Listed in several Who's Who publications. Memberships: former Council Member IPENZ; former Council Member, Christchurch Polytechnic; former Council Member, New Zealand Dairy Research Institute; FRSNZ; FIChemE; Dist FIPENZ; FNZIC; Ceng; Address: PO Box 31080, Ilam, Christchurch, New Zealand 8444.

KEHAYOGLOU Aristides, b. 26 May 1931, Komotini, Greece. Emeritus Professor. m. Georgia Bechri, 1996. Education: Degree, Chemistry, Aristotle University, 1955; PhD, Organic Chemistry, 1968; DSc, Organic Chemical Technology, 1980. Appointments: Chemist Manager, Control Office Almopia Red Peper, Aridea, 1957-62; Assistant, Organic Chemistry, 1962-69, Senior Assistant, 1969-82, Assistant Professor, 1982-83, Associate Professor, 1983-87, Director, Organic Chemical Technology Laboratory, 1981-98, Professor, 1987-98, Aristotle University. Publications: Industrial Organic Chemistry, 1984; Several scientific papers in professional journals mainly on Polymers and Dye Chemistry. Honours: Fellow, Technical University, Delft, 1970-71; Honorary Staff Member, University of Manchester, Institute of Science and Technology, 1972. Memberships: Association of Greek Chemists; Hellenic Society of Polymers. Address: Them-Sofouli 3, GR 54646, Thessaloniki, Greece.

KEIGHTLEY Richard Charles, b. 2 July 1933, Aldershot, England. Army Major General. m. Caroline Rosemary Butler, 3 daughters. Education: Royal Military Academy Sandhurst, 1951-53; Army Staff College, 1963; National Defence College, 1971-72; Royal College of Defence Studies, 1980. Appointments: Various Regimental and Staff appointments, 1953-70; Commander, 5th Royal Inniskilling Dragoon Guards, 1972-75; Colonel GS, 1st Division, 1977; Commander 33 Armoured Brigade, 1978-79; Brigadier General Staff, UK Land Forces, 1981; GOC Western District, 1982-83; Commandant, Royal Military Academy Sandhurst, 1983-87; Chairman, Dorset Healthcare NHS Trust, 1995-97; Chairman, Dorset Health Authority, 1988-95, 1998-2001; Chairman, Southampton University Hospitals NHS Trust, 2002-. Honour: CB, 1987. Memberships: President, Dorset County Royal British Legion; President, Dorset Relate; Member, St John Council for Dorset. Address: Kennels Farmhouse, Tarrant Gunville, Dorset DT 11 8JQ, England.

KEILLOR Garrison, (born Gary Edward Keillor), b. 7 August 1942, Anoka, Minnesota, USA. Writer; Radio Host. Education: BA, University of Minnesota, 1966. Appointments: Creator-Host, national public radio programmes, A Prairie Home Companion and American Radio Company. Publications: Happy to Be Here, 1982; Lake Wobegon Days, 1985; Leaving Home, 1987; We Are Still Married: Stories and Letters, 1989; WLT: A Radio Romance, 1991; The Book of Guys, 1993; Wobegon Boy, 1997; Lake Wobegon Summer 1956, 2001; Love Me, 2004; Homegrown Democrat, 2004; Good Poems for Hard Times, 2005; Pontoon, 2007. Children's Books: Cat, You Better Come Home, 1995; The Old Man Who Loved Cheese, 1996; Sandy Bottom Orchestra, 1997; ME by Jimmy (Big Boy) Valente as Told to Garrison Keillor, 1999. Contributions to: Newspapers and magazines. Honours: George Foster Peabody Award, 1980; Grammy Award, 1987; Ace Award, 1988; Best Music and Entertainment Host Awards, 1988, 1989; American Academy and Institute of Arts and Letters Medal, 1990; Music Broadcast Communications Radio Hall of Fame, 1994; National Humanities Medal, 1999. Address: c/o Minnesota Public Radio, 45 East 7th Street, St Paul, MN 55101, USA.

KEINÄNEN Matti Tapio, b. 1 January 1953, Kuopio, Finland. Docent. m. Kristina, 2 sons, 1 daughter. Education: Licentiate of Medicine, 1977; Doctor of Medicine and Surgery, 1981; Specialist in Psychiatry, 1985; Psychoanalytic Psychotherapy Training, 1986; Specialist-level Psychotherapy Training, 1992; Advanced Specialist-level Individual Psychotherapy Training, 1997; Docent in Psychiatry, Turku University, 2002; Family Therapy Training, Finnish Mental Health Society, 1987; Licentiate Psychotherapist, 1995; Licentiate Advanced Specialist-level Individual Psychotherapist, 1998, National Authority for Medicolegal Affairs; Supervising Member, Finnish Balint-Group Organisation, 1999; Docent in Clinical Psychology, Jyväskylä University, 2000. Appointments: Psychiatrist, Finnish Student Health Service, Turku; Docent in Psychiatry, Turku University; Docent in Clinical Psychology, Jyväskylä University. Publications: Articles on biological basic study of psychiatry, family research and symbolic function research in individual psychoanalytic psychotherapy; Books: Psychosemiosis as a Key to Body-Mind Continuum. The Reinforcement of Symbolization – Reflectiveness in Psychotherapy, 2006; The Psychodynamic Psychotherapy of

Young Adults, 2007. Honours: International Peace Prize, 2005. Memberships: Finnish Medical Association; Finnish Psychiatric Association; International Semiotic Association; Finnish Psychodynamic Psychotherapy Association; Finnish Adolescent Psychiatry Association; Finnish Balint-Group Association; International Association of Relational Psychoanalysis and Psychotherapy, 2005. Address: Finnish Student Health Service, Kirkkotie 13, FIN-20540 Turku, Finland.

KEITEL Harvey, b. 13 May 1939, USA. Actor. m.(1) Lorraine Bracco, divorced, 1 daughter, (2) Daphna Kastner, 2001, 1 child. Education: Actors Studio. Appointments: US Marines. Creative Works: Stage appearances: Death of a Salesman, Hurlyburly; Films: Mean Streets; Alice Doesn't Live Here Anymore; That's the Way of the World; Taxi Driver; Mother Jugs and Speed Buffalo Bill and the Indians; Welcome to LA; The Duelists; Fingers; Blue Collar; Eagle's Wing; Deathwatch; Saturn 3; Bad Timing; The Border; Exposed; La Nuit de Varennes; Corrupt; Falling in Love; Knight of the Dragon Camorra; Off Beat; Wise Guys; The Men's Club; The Investigation; The Pick-up Artist; The January Man; The Last Temptation of Christ; The Two Jakes; Two Evil Eyes (The Black Cat); Thelma & Louise; Tipperary; Bugsy; Reservoir Dogs; Bad Lieutenant; Mean Streets; The Assassin; The Young Americans; The Piano; Snake Eyes; Rising Sun; Monkey Trouble; Clockers; Dangerous Game; Pulp Fiction; Smoke; Imaginary Crimes; Ulyssees' Gaze, Blue in the Face, 1995; City of Industry; Cop Land, Head Above Water; Somebody to Love, 1996; Simpatico, 1999; Little Nicky, U-571, Holy Smoke, 2000; Nailed, Taking Sides, Grey Zone, 2001; Nowhere, Ginostra, Red Dragon, Beeper, 2002; Crime Spree, Galindez File, Dreaming of Julia, Puerto Vallarta Squeeze, 2003; National Treasure, The Bridge of San Luis Rey, 2004; Shadows in the Sun, Be Cool, The Shadow Dancer, 2005; A Crime, The Stone Merchant, Arthur and the Invisibles (voice), 2006; My Sexiest Year, The Ministers, National Treasure: Book of Secrets, 2007; The Ministers, Inglorious Bastards (voice), Wrong Turn at Tahoe, 2009. Address: c/o William Morris Agency, 151 South El Camino Drive, Beverly Hills, CA 90212, USA.

KEITH Penelope Anne Constance, b. 2 April 1940, Sutton, Surrey, England. Actress. m. Rodney Timson, 1978. Education: Webber Douglas School, London. Creative Works: Stage appearances include: Suddenly at Home, 1971; The Norman Conquests, 1974; Donkey's Years, 1976; The Apple Cart, 1977; The Millionairess, 1978; Moving, 1980; Hobson's Choice, 1982; Captain Brassbound's Conversation, 1982; Hay Fever, 1983; The Dragon's Tail, 1985; Miranda, 1987; The Deep Blue Sea, 1988; Dear Charles, 1990; The Merry Wives of Windsor, 1990; The Importance of Being Ernest, 1991; On Approval, 1992; Relatively Speaking, 1992; Glyn and It, 1994; Monsieur Amilcar, 1995; Mrs Warren's Profession, 1997; Good Grief, 1998; Star Quality, 2001; Film appearances include: Rentadick; Take a Girl Like You; Every Home Should Have One; Sherlock Holmes; The Priest of Love; TV appearances include: The Good Life (Good Neighbors in USA), 1974-77; Private Lives, 1976; The Norman Conquests, 1977; To the Manor Born, 1979-81; On Approval, 1980; Spider's Web; Sweet Sixteen; Waters of the Moon; Hay Fever; Moving; Executive Stress; What's My Line?, 1988; Growing Places; No Job for a Lady, 1990; Law and Disorder, 1994; Teletubbies (voice) 1997; Next of Kin; Coming Home, 1999; Margery and Gladys, 2003. Honours include: Best Light Entertainment Performance, British Academy of Film & TV Arts, 1976; Best Actress, 1977; Show Business Personality, Variety Club of Great Britain, 1976; BBC TV Personality, 1979; Comedy Performance of the Year, Society of West End Theatre, 1976; Female TV Personality; TV Times Awards, 1976-78; BBC TV Personality of the Year, 1978-79; TV Female Personality, Daily Express, 1979-82; CBE, 2007. Address: London Management, 2-4 Noel Street, London W1V 3RB, England.

KELLEHER Graeme George, b. 2 May 1933, Sydney, Australia. Civil Engineer; National Resource Manager. m. Fleur Meachen, 1 son, 2 daughters. Education: BE (Civil), 1955. Appointments: Engineer Project Manager, 1955-75; Commissioner, Ranger Uranium Inquiry, 1976-77; Deputy Chair, Non-proliferation Task Force, 1977-78; Chair, CEO, Great Barrier Reef Marine Park Authority, 1979-94; Professor, Systems Engineering, James Cook University, 1991-94; Vice Chair, World Commission on Protected Areas, 1986-98; Leader, High Seas MPA Task Force, 1999-2007; Senior Advisor on High Seas Marine Protected Areas Task Force, World Commission on Protected Areas, 1999-; Chair, CSIRO Marine Advisory Committee, 1995-99; Co Chair, Life Sciences, Co-operative Research Centres Program, 1995-2002; Director, Graeme Kelleher and Associates, 1995-; Member, Religious and Scientific Committee, Religion, Science and the Environment, 1996-; Member, Independent Community Engagement Panel, Murray-Darling Ministerial Council, 2002-2004. Publications: Ranger Uranium Environmental Inquiry; Guidelines for Marine Protected Areas; A Global Representative System of Marine Protected Areas; Many papers and articles. Honours: Churchill Fellowship, 1972; Monash Medal, 1986; Member, Order of Australia, 1988; Officer of the Order of Australia, 1996; Packard International Parks Merit Award, 1998; Centenary Medal, 2003; Institution of Engineers, Canberra Hall of Fame, 2005; Lifetime Achievement Award, World Commission on Protected Areas, 2007; Top 100 Engineers of the World, 2007. Memberships: Institution of Engineers (Fellow); Australian Academy of Technological Sciences and Engineering (Fellow); Environmental Institute of Australia and New Zealand (Fellow); Peter Cullen Trust (Friend); Scientific Council for Marine Protected Areas in West Africa (RAMPAO) (Member); Energy Forum of Academy of Technological Sciences and Engineering (ATSE) of Australia, 2009-. Address: 12 Marulda Street, Aranda, Canberra ACT 2614, Australia.

KELLER Evelyn Fox, b. 20 March 1936, New York, New York, USA. Professor of History and Philosophy of Science; Writer. 1 son, 1 daughter. Education: BA, Brandeis University, 1957; MA, Radcliffe College, 1959; PhD, Harvard University, 1963. Appointments: Visiting Fellow, later Scholar, 1979-84, Visiting Professor, 1985-86, MIT; Professor of Mathematics and Humanities, Northeastern University, 1982-88; Senior Fellow, Cornell University, 1987; Member, Institute for Advanced Study, Princeton, New Jersey, 1987-88; Professor, University of California at Berkeley, 1988-92; President, West Coast History of Science Society, 1990-91; Professor of History and Philosophy of Science, Massachusetts Institute of Technology, 1992-; MacArthur Fellow, 1992-97; Guggenheim Fellowship, 2000-01; Moore Scholar, California Institute of Technology, 2002; Winton Chair, University of Minnesota, 2002-05; Dibner Fellow, 2003; Radcliffe Institute Fellow, 2005; Rothschild Lecturer, Harvard University, 2005; Plenary Speaker, International History of Science Congress, Beijing, 2005. Publications: A Feeling for the Organism: The Life and Work of Barbara McClintock, 1983, 2nd edition, 1993; Reflections on Gender and Science, 1985, new edition, 1995; Women, Science and the Body (editor with Mary Jacobus and Sally Shuttleworth), 1989; Conflicts in Feminism (editor with Marianne Hirsch), 1990; Keywords in Evolutionary Biology (editor with Elisabeth Lloyd), 1992; Secrets of Life, Secrets of Death: Essays on Language, Gender, and Science, 1992; Refiguring Life: Metaphors of Twentieth Century Biology, 1995; Feminism and Science (editor with Helen Longino), 1996; The Century of the Gene, 2000; Making Sense of Life, 2002. Contributions to: Scholarly journals. Honours: Distinguished Publication Award, Association for Women in Psychology, 1986; Alumni Achievement Award, Brandeis University, 1991; Honorary Doctorates, Holyoke College, 1991, University of Amsterdam, 1995, Simmons College, 1995, Rensselaer Polytechnic Institute, 1995, Technical University of Lulea, Sweden, 1996; John D and Catharine T MacArthur Foundation Fellowship, 1992-97; Medal of the Italian Senate, 2001; Numerous honorary degrees. Address: c/o Program in Science, Technology and Society, Massachusetts Institute of Technology, 77 Massachusetts Avenue, Cambridge, MA 02139, USA.

KELLEY Patricia Marie Hagelin, b. 8 December 1953, Cleveland, Ohio, USA. Geology Educator. m. Jonathan Robert Kelley, 1 son, 1 daughter. Education: BA, Geology, College of Wooster, 1975; AM, Geology, 1977; PhD, Geology, Harvard University, 1979. Appointments: Instructor, New England College, 1979; Assistant Professor, 1979-85, Associate Professor, 1985-89, Acting Associate Vice-Chancellor for Academic Affairs, 1988, Professor of Geology and Geological Engineering, 1989-90, University of Mississippi; Programme Director for Geology and Paleontology and Geological Record of Global Change Programmes, National Science Foundation, 1990-92; Professor and Chair of the Department of Geology and Geological Engineering, University of North Dakota, 1992-97; Professor and Chair, Department of Earth Sciences, 1997-2003, Professor of Geology, 2003-, University of North Carolina at Wilmington. Publications: Over 60 books, articles in scientific journals and book chapters as author and co-author include most recently: Role of Bioerosion in Taphonomy, in Current Developments in Bioerosion, 2008; From Evolution to Geobiology: Paleontology at the Start of a New Century, 2008; Stephen Jay Gould: Reflections on his view of life, 2009; Teaching Evolution in the Galapagos, 2009; Teaching Evolution During the Week and Bible Study on Sunday: Perspectives on Science, Religion and Intelligent Design, 2009; A College Honors Seminar on Evolution & Intelligent Design: Successes and Challenges, 2009; Shell repair as a reliable indicator of bivalve predation by shell-wedging gastropods in the fossil record, 2010. Honours include: Sigma Xi, 1975; National Science Foundation Graduate Fellowship, 1976-79; An Outstanding Young Woman of America, 1983; Outstanding Faculty Member, School of Engineering, University of Mississippi, 1989-90; Award Paper, 13th Annual Conference on College Teaching and Learning, 2002; Association for Women Geoscientists Outstanding Educator Award, 2003; Faculty Scholarship Award, University of North Carolina, Wilmington, 2005; Centennial Fellow of the Palentological Society, 2006. Memberships include: Fellow, Geological Society of America; Fellow, American Association for the Advancement of Science; President, Paleontological Society, 2000-2002; President, Board of Trustees, Paleontological Research Institution, 2004-2006; National Center for Science Education; Society for Sedimentary Geology; Association for Women Geoscientists; National Association of Geoscience Teachers. Address: Department of Geography and Geology, University of North Carolina Wilmington, 601 South College Road, Wilmington, NC 28403-5944, USA. E-mail: kellyp@uncw.edu

KELLY Anthony, b. 25 January 1929, Hillingdon, Middlesex, England. Consultant. Education: BSc, 1st class, Physics, University of Reading, 1949; PhD, Trinity College, Cambridge, 1953; ScD, University of Cambridge, 1968. Appointments: Research Associate, University of Illinois, 1953-55; ICI Fellow, University of Birmingham, 1955; Assistant Professor, Associate Professor, The Technological Institute, Northwestern University, Chicago, 1956-59; University Lecturer, University of Cambridge, 1959-67; Superintendent, 1967-69, Deputy Director, 1969-75, National Physical Laboratory, Middlesex; Seconded to ICI plc, 1973-75; Consultant to many international companies, 1973-; Vice Chancellor and Chief Executive, University of Surrey, 1975-94; Founder, Surrey Research Park, 1979; Director, Johnson Wax UK Ltd, 1981-96; Director, QUO-TEC Ltd, 1984-2000; Director, NPL Management Ltd, 1994-2001; Distinguished Research Fellow, Department of Materials Science and Metallurgy, University of Cambridge, 1994-. Publications: 200 papers in scientific and technical journals; Numerous books; Many lectures. Honours include: CBE, 1988; Gold Medal, American Society of Materials, 1991; Platinum Medal, Institute of Materials, 1992; Knight of St Gregory, 1992; Deputy Lieutenant for the County of Surrey, 1993; DUniv, University of Surrey, 1994; Honorary Fellow, Institution of Structural Engineers, 1996; Hon DSc, University of Birmingham, 1997; Honorary Fellow, Institution of Civil Engineers, 1997; Acta Metallurgica Gold Medal, 2000; Honorary DEng, Hanyang University, Korea, 2001; Honorary Doctor of Science, University of Reading, 2002. Memberships: Institute of Metals; British Non-Ferrous Metals Research Association; Engineering Materials Requirements Board, Department of Trade and Industry; European Association of Composite Materials; Royal National Institute for the Deaf; Institute of Materials. Address: Churchill College, Cambridge, CB3 0DS, England. E-mail: ak209@cam.ac.uk

KELLY Donald Francis, b. 20 July 1933, Manchester, England. Veterinary Pathologist. m. Patricia Ann Holt, 3 sons. Education: BVSc, Bristol, 1957; MRCVS, 1957; MA, PhD, Cantab, 1963; FRCPath, Dipl ECVP. Appointments: Demonstrator in Pathology, University of Cambridge, 1962-66; Assistant/Associate Professor, University of Pennsylvania, 1966-70; Senior Lecturer, University of Bristol, 1970-79; Professor of Veterinary Pathology, University of Liverpool, 1979-2000; Honorary Senior Fellow, Emeritus Professor, University of Liverpool, 2000-. Publications: 200 contributions to textbooks, scientific veterinary literature in medicine, surgery and pathology. Honours: C L Davis Foundation Award for Outstanding Service, 1988; British Small Animal Veterinary Association, Ameroso Award, 1993; University of Liverpool Teaching and Learning Excellence Award, 1994; Honorary Membership, European College of Veterinary Pathologists, 2010. Memberships: MRCVS; FRCPath; Diplomate, European College of Veterinary Pathologists. Address: Glenarch, 1 Wittering Lane, Heswall, Wirral, Merseyside, CH60 9JL, England. E-mail: donpatkel@gmail.com

KELLY John Philip, b. 25 June 1941, Tuam, Ireland. m. Jennifer, 1 son. Retired Diplomat and Historian. Education: Open University. Appointments: HM Diplomatic Service, 1959-2000; British Representative, Grenada, 1982-86; Deputy Governor, Bermuda, 1989-94; Governor, Turks and Caicos Islands, 1996-2000; President, Victoria League for Commonwealth Friendship, 2002-07. Honours: MBE, 1983;

LVO, 1994; CMG, 2000. Memberships: Rotary Club of Royston. Address: 56 Garden Lane, Royston, Hertfordshire, SG8 9EH, England. E-mail: john@johnphilipkelly.com

KELLY Matthias John, b. 21 April 1954, Dungannon, Ireland. Queen's Counsel; Senior Counsel. m. Helen Ann, 1 son, 1 daughter. Education: BA Hons, Legal Science, LLB, Trinity College, Dublin, 1977; Council of Legal Education, London, 1978. Appointments: Barrister, England and Wales, 1979-; Barrister, Inn of Court, Belfast, 1983; Barrister, King's Inn, Dublin, 1983; Attorney, New York Bar, 1986; Attorney, US Federal Bar, 1987; Member, Ogden Working Party (Actuarial tables), 1997-2002; Member, Bar Council, 1998-2003; Member, Blackwell Committee, 1999; Queen's Counsel, 1999; Chairman, Policy Committee Bar Council, 2000; Chairman, Public Affairs, Bar Council, 2001; Chairman, Personal Injuries, Bar Association, 2001-2002; Chairman, Bar Conference, London, 2002; Vice Chairman, Bar of England and Wales, 2002; Chairman of the Bar, 2003-. Publications: 5 books; Reviews and journals. Honours: Queen's Counsel, 1999; Senior Counsel, Ireland, 2005. Address: 39 Essex Street, London WC2R 3AT, England. E-mail: kelly@39essex.com

KELLY Michael Denis, b. 23 September 1964, Penrith, New South Wales, Australia. Surgeon. Education: Chevalier College, Bowral, NSW, 1977-82; MB BS (Hons), 1987, MS, 2001, University of NSW; Fellow, Royal Australasian College of Surgeons, 1994; Fellow, Royal College of Surgeons (England), 1998. Appointments: Training in Surgery, Colchester, Hammersmith, Dublin, Glasgow and Hong Kong, 1997-2003; Senior Lecturer, Surgery, St George Hospital, Sydney, 2001-02; Upper GI Surgeon, Frenchay Hospital, Bristol, 2004-. Publications: Over 40 articles/letters in professional journals. Honours: Grays Point Prize in Anatomy, University of NSW, 1983; The Prize in Practical Anatomy, University of NSW, 1984; Wellcome Prize for 1st Place in Medicine, 1985; Sam Cracknell Scholarship for Sports and Academic Achievement, University of NSW, 1986; Travelling Fellowship, RACS, 1999. Memberships: Research Editor, World Journal of Emergency Surgery; Catholic Medical Association, Bristol, UK. E-mail: mk@mdkelly.com

KELNER Simon, b. 9 December 1957, Manchester, England. Newspaper Editor. m. Sally Ann Lasson, 1 daughter. Education: Pre-entry Journalism course, Preston Polytechnic, 1975-76. Appointments: Trainee Reporter, Neath Guardian, 1976-79; Sports Reporter, Extel, 1979-80; Sports Editor, Kent Evening Post, 1980-83; Assistant Sports Editor, Observer, 1983-86; Deputy Sports Editor, The Independent, 1986-89; Sports Editor, Sunday Correspondent, 1989-90; Sports Editor, Observer, 1990-91; Editor, Observer magazine, 1991-93; Sports Editor, The Independent on Sunday (launched first national stand-alone sports section), 1993-95; Night Editor, The Independent, 1995; Features Editor, The Independent, 1995-96; Editor of Night & Day magazine (review section of Mail on Sunday), 1996-98; Editor-in-Chief, The Independent, 1998-. Honours: Winner, Magazine of the Year (Observer magazine), 1992; Honorary Fellowship, University of Central Lancashire; The Edgar Wallace Award, 2000; Editor of the Year, What the Papers Say Awards, 1999, 2003; Newspaper of the Year, What the Papers Say Awards, 2004; Newspaper of the Year, British Press Awards, 2004; Newspaper of the Year, London Press Club, 2004; GQ Editor of the Year, GQ Awards, 2004; Media Achiever of the Year, Campaign Media Awards, 2004; Marketeer of the Year, Marketing Week Effectiveness Awards, 2004. Publications: To Jerusalem and Back, 1996. Memberships: The Groucho Club; Kirtlington Golf Club. Address: The Independent, 191 Marsh Wall, London E14 9RS, England.

KELSALL Malcolm Miles, b. 27 February 1938, London, England. Professor Emeritus of English. m. Mary Emily Ives, 5 August 1961. Education: BA, Oxon, 1961; BLitt, Oxon, 1964; MA, Oxon, 1965. Appointments: Staff Reporter, The Guardian Newspaper, 1961; Assistant Lecturer, Exeter University, 1963-64; Lecturer, Reading University, 1964-75; Professor, 1975-2003, Professor Emeritus, 2005-, University of Wales, Cardiff; Visiting Professor: University of Paris VII, 1978, University of Hiroshima, 1979, Charles University, Prague, 1994, University of Madison, Wisconsin, 1996; Visiting Scholar in residence, International Centre for Jefferson Studies, 1997. Publications: Editor, Sarah Fielding, David Simple, 1969; Editor, Thomas Otway, Venice Preserved, 1969; Christopher Marlowe, 1981; Congreve: The Way of the World, 1981; Studying Drama, 1985; Byron's Politics, 1987; Editor, Encyclopaedia of Literature and Criticism, 1990; The Great Good Place: The Country House and English Literature, 1992; Editor, J M Synge, The Playboy of the Western World, 1997; Editor, William Congreve, Love For Love, 1999; Jefferson and the Iconography of Romanticism, 1999; Literary Representations of the Irish Country House, 2003. Contributions to: Byron e il segno plurale; Byron Journal; Cambridge Companions to Byron and Pope; DNB; Encyclopaedia of the Essay; Encyclopaedia of the Romantic Era; Essays in Criticism; Irish University Review; Theatre Research International; Review of English Studies; Studies in Romanticism; English Romanticism and the Celtic World; OHCREL. Honours: Elma Dangerfield Prize, 1991; British Academy Warton Lecturer, 1992; Marchand Lecturer, 2005; Honorary Fellow, Graduate School of European Romanticism, Glasgow University. Membership: Advisory Editorial Board, The Byron Journal, Litteraria Pragensia. E-mail: malcolm.kelsall@btinternet.com

KEMOKLIDZE Tariel, b. 1 October 1955, Kataisi, Georgia. Mathematician. m. Nino Kakhidze, 1 son. Education: Mathematics, Faculty of Physics and Mathematics, Kutaisi Alexandre Tsulukidze State Pedagogical Institute, 1972-76; High Educational, Department of Algebra, 1979-81, Postgraduate, 1981-84, Moscow V I Lenin State Pedagogical Institute. Appointments: Teacher, Mathematics, Kutaisi Secondary School N18, and Andrya Razmadze State Boarding School of Physics and Mathematics, 1976-77; Military Service, 1977-78; Reader (Teacher), 1984-93, Docent, 1994-2005, Associate Professor, 2006-, Department of Mathematics, Akaki Tsereteli Kutaisi State University. Publications: Numerous articles in professional journals. Honours: Candidate of Physical and Mathematical Sciences, Ivane Javakhishvili Tbilisi State University, 1994; Research grant, Ministry of Education and Science, 2004; Research grant, A Tsereteli Kutaisi State University, 2008; Travel grant, Georgia Science Foundation, 2009. Memberships: Georgian Mathematical Union. Address: 21 Jorjiashvili Str, Kutaisi 4600, Georgia.

KEMP Terence James, b. 26 June 1938, Watford, Hertfordshire, England. Professor. m. Sheila Therese, 1 son, 2 daughters. Education: BA, 1961, MA, DPhil, 1963, Jesus College, Oxford. Appointments: DSIR Research Fellow, Cookridge Laboratory, University of Leeds, 1962; Assistant Lecturer, 1966-66, Lecturer, 1966-70, Senior Lecturer in Chemistry, 1970-74, Reader in Chemistry, 1974-80, Professor of Chemistry, 1980-, Pro-Vice Chancellor, 1983-89, University of Warwick. Publications: Introductory Photochemistry, 1971; Dictionary of Physical Chemistry, 1992; 240 original scientific articles. Honours: Meldola Medal, Royal Institute of Chemistry, 1967; Order of Merit, Polish People's Republic, 1978; Nagroda, 2nd prize, Marie-Curie-Slodowska Society for

Radiation Research, 1992. Address: Department of Chemistry, University of Warwick, Coventry CV4 7AL, England. E-mail: t.j.kemp@warwick.ac.uk

KENDAL Felicity, b. 25 September 1946. Actress. m. (1) 1 son, (2) Michael Rudman, 1983, divorced 1991, 1 son. Career: Plays: Minor Murder; Henry V; The Promise; Back to Methuselah; A Midsummer Night's Dream; Much Ado About Nothing; Kean; Romeo and Juliet; 'Tis Pity She's a Whore; The Three Arrows; The Norman Conquests; Once Upon a Time; Arms and The Man; Clouds; Amadeus; Othello; On the Razzle; The Second Mrs Tanqueray; The Real Thing; Jumpers; Made in Bangkok; Hapgood; Ivanov; Hidden Laughter; Tartuffe; Heartbreak House; Arcadia; An Absolute Turkey; Indian Ink; Mind Millie for Me; The Seagul; Waste; Alarms and Excursions; Fallen Angels; Humble Boy; Happy Days; TV includes: The Good Life; Solo; The Mistress; The Woodlanders; Edward VII; Rosemary and Thyme, 2003-06. numerous other plays and serials; Films: Shakespeare Wallah, 1965; Valentino, 1976; Parting Shots. Publications: White Cargo, 1998. Honours: Variety Club Most Promising Newcomer, 1974; Best Actress, 1979; Clarence Derwent Award, 1980; Evening Standard Best Actress Award, 1989; Variety Club Best Actress Award, 2000. Address: c/o Chatto and Linnit, 123A Kings Road, London SW3 4PL, England.

KENDALL Bridget, b. 27 April 1956, Oxford, England. Journalist. Education: Lady Margaret Hall, Oxford, 1974-78; Harvard, USA, 1978-80; St Antony's College, Oxford, 1980-83; Voronegh State University, 1976-77; Moscow State University, 1981-82. Appointments: Trainee, BBC World Service, 1983; Presenter and Producer, Newsnight, BBC2, 1983-84; Producer, Reporter, Editor, BBC World Service Radio, 1984-89; BBC Moscow Correspondent, 1989-93; BBC Washington Correspondent, 1994-98; BBC Diplomatic Correspondent, 1998-. Publications: Co-author, David the Invincible, annotated translation (classical Armenian philosophy), 1980; Kosovo and After: The future of spin in the digital age (Jubilee Lecture for St Antony's College, Oxford), 2000; Co-author, The Day that Shook the World (BBC correspondents on September 11th 2001), 2001. Honours: British Council Scholar to USSR, 1976-77, 1981-82; Harkness Fellow, USA, 1978-80; Sony Award, Reporter of the Year (Bronze Award), 1992; James Cameron Award for distinguished journalism, 1992; Voice of the Listener and Viewer Award, 1993; MBE, 1994; Honorary Doctorate, University of Central England, Birmingham, 1999; Honorary Doctorate in Law, St Andrew's University, 2001; Honorary Doctorate in Law, Exeter University, 2002; Honorary Fellow, St Anthony's College, Oxford. Memberships: Advisory Board, Russian and Eurasian Programme at Chatham House, Royal Institute of International Affairs, 2000-; Member of Council, Royal United Services Institute, 2001-05; Member of Advisory Council, European Research Institute, University of Birmingham. Address: BBC Television Centre, Wood Lane, London W12, England.

KENNEDY Alexander, b. 20 April 1933, Manchester, England. Retired Consultant Histopathologist. Education: MB ChB, Liverpool, 1956; MD, Liverpool, 1964; MRCPath, 1967; FRCPath, 1985. Appointments: House Office, Stanley and Royal Liverpool Children's Hospitals, 1956-58; Short Service Commission, Royal Air Force Medical Branch, 1958-61; Pathologist, RAF Hospital, Wroughton, 1958-61; Lecturer, University of Liverpool, 1961-67; Visiting Assistant Professor, University of Chicago, 1968; Senior Lecturer, University of Sheffield, 1969-77; Consultant Histopathologist, 1977-97, Retired, 1997-, Northern General Hospital, Sheffield. Publications: 4 books; Over 50 articles in professional journals; Abstracts, letters and other publications. Memberships: Pathological Society of Great Britain and Ireland; British Thoracic Society; British Division of the International Academy of Pathology; Trent Regional Thoracic Society; Sheffield Medico-Chirurgical Society. Address: 16 Brincliffe Gardens, Sheffield, S11 9BG, England. E-mail: sandy.kennedy@care4free.net

KENNEDY Iain Manning, b. 15 September 1942, Northampton, England. Company Director. m. Ingrid Annette, 2 daughters. Education: Pembroke College, Cambridge, 1961-64. Appointments: Joined staff, 1969, Production Director, 1976, Chief Executive, 1998, Chairman, 2001, Church and Co plc; Chairman, SATRA, 1989; Governor, University College, Northampton, 1998; Retired, 2001. Honours: OBE, 2002. Address: 3 Townsend Close, Hanging Houghton, Northampton, NN6 9HP, England. E-mail: iain@hanghoughton.fsnet.co.uk

KENNEDY Jane Hope, b. 28 February 1953, Loughborough, England. Architect. m. John Maddison, 2 sons. Education: Dip Arch, Manchester Polytechnic; Registered Architect, RIBA. Appointments: British Waterways Board, 1978-80; Assistant, David Jeffcoate Architect, 1980-81; Self-employed, 1981-86; Norwich City Council Planning Department, 1986-88; Architect, 1988-, Partner, 1992-, Purcell Miller Tritton; Surveyor to the fabric of Ely Cathedral, 1994-. Memberships: Institute of Historic Building Conservation; Fellow, Royal Society of Arts; Architect Accredited in Building Conservation. Address: Purcell Miller Tritton, 46 St Mary's Street, Ely, Cambridgeshire CB7 4EY, England. E-mail: janekennedy@pmt.co.uk

KENNEDY Nigel, b. 28 December 1956, England. Violinist. Partner, Eve Westmore, 1 son. Education: Yehudi Menuhin School; Juilliard School of Performing Arts. Creative Works: Chosen by the BBC as the subject of a 5 year documentary on the development of a soloist following his debut with the Philharmonic Orchestra, 1977; Appeared with all the major British orchestras; Appearances at all the leading UK Festivals and in Europe at Stresa, Lucerne, Gstaad, Berlin & Lockenhaus; Debut at the Tanglewood Festival with the Boston Symphony under André Previn, 1985, at MN with Sir Neville Marriner, at Montreal with Charles Dutoit; Given concerts in the field of jazz with Stephane Grappelli at Carnegie Hall and Edinburgh, runs his own jazz group; Recordings include: Elgar Sonata with Peter Pettinger; Tchaikovsky; Sibelius; Vivaldi; Mendelssohn; Bruch; Walton Viola & Violin Concertos; Elgar Concerto with London Philharmonic Orchestra; Bach's Concerto with Berlin Philharmonic. Publication: Always Playing, 1991. Honours include: Best Classical Disc of the Year Award, London, 1985; Golden Rose of Montreux, 1990; Variety Club Showbusiness Personality of the Year, 1991; Hon DLitt, Bath, 1991; BRIT Award for Outstanding Contribution to British Music, 2000; Male Artist of the Year, 2001. Memberships include: Senior Vice President, Aston Villa FC, 1990-. Address: Askonas Holt Ltd, Lonsdale Chambers, 27 Chancery Lane, London WC2A 1PF, England. Website: www.askonasholt.co.uk

KENNEDY, Rt Hon Lord Justice, Rt Hon Sir Paul Joseph Morrow Kennedy, b.12 June 1935, Sheffield, England. m. Virginia Devlin, 2 sons, 2 daughters. Education: MA, LLM, Gonville and Caius College, Cambridge, 1955-59; Called to Bar at Gray's Inn, 1960, Bencher, 1982, Vice-Treasurer, 2001, Treasurer, 2002. Appointments: Recorder, 1972-83; Queen's Counsel, 1973; Presiding Judge, North East Circuit, 1985-89;

High Court Judge, Queen's Bench Division, 1983-92; Lord Justice of Appeal, 1992-; Member Judicial Studies Board and Chairman of Criminal Committee, 1993-96; Vice-President, Queen's Bench Division, 1997-2002; Member Sentencing Guidelines Council, 2004-. Honours: Kt, 1983; PC, 1992; Honorary Fellow, Gonville and Caius College, Cambridge, 1998; Honorary LLD, University of Sheffield, 2000. Address: Royal Courts of Justice, Strand, London WC2A 2LL, England.

KENNEDY Peter Graham Edward, b. 28 March 1951, London, England. Professor of Neurology. m. Catherine Ann Kennedy, 1 son, 1 daughter. Education: University College London and University College Hospital Medical School, 1969-74; MB BS, 1974; PhD, 1980; MD, 1983; FRCP (London), 1988; FRCP (Glasgow), 1989; DSc, 1991; FRSE, 1992; MPhil, 1993; MLitt, 1995; FRCPath, 1996; FMedSci, 1998. Appointments: Honorary Research Assistant, MRC Neuroimmunology Project, University College, London, 1978-80; Registrar, then Senior Registrar, National Hospital for Nervous Diseases, London, 1982-84; Visiting Assistant Professor of Neurology, Johns Hopkins University Hospital, USA, 1985; Senior Lecturer, Neurology and Virology, University of Glasgow, 1986-87; Burton Professor of Neurology, University of Glasgow and Consultant Neurologist, Institute of Neurological Sciences, Southern General Hospital, Glasgow, Scotland, 1987-. Publications: Numerous articles in learned journals on Neurology and Neurovirology; Books: Infections of the Nervous System (with R T Johnson), 1987; Infectious Diseases of the Nervous System (with L E Davis), 2000. Honours: BUPA Medical Foundation Doctor of the Year Research Award, 1990; Linacre Medal and Lectureship, Royal College of Physicians, London, 1991; TS Srinivasan Gold Medal and Endowment Lecturer, Madras, 1993; Fogarty International Scholar-in-Residence, National Institutes of Health, Bethesda, USA, 1993-94; James W Stephens Honored Visiting Professor, Department of Neurology, University of Colorado Health Sciences Center, Denver, USA, 1994; Livingstone Lecture, Royal College of Physicians and Surgeons of Glasgow, 2004. Memberships: Association of Physicians of Great Britain and Ireland; Corresponding Member, American Neurological Association; Association of British Neurologists; Fellow of the Royal Society of Edinburgh; Founder Fellow, Academy of Medical Sciences; Secretary, 2000-03, President, 2004-, International Society for Neurovirology; Chairman, EFNS Scientist Panel on Infections including AIDS; Member Editorial Boards several medical journals. Address: Glasgow University Department of Neurology, Institute of Neurological Sciences, Southern General Hospital, Glasgow G51 4TF, Scotland. E-mail: p.g.kennedy@clinmed.gla.ac.uk

KENNEFICK Christine Marie, b. 4 July 1962, Washington DC, USA. Materials Scientist. Education: BSc, 1984, MSc, 1986, Stanford University; PhD, Cornell University, 1991. Appointments: National Research Council Associate, NASA Lewis Research Center, Cleveland, Ohio, 1991-93; Guest Scientist, Max-Planck Institute, Stuttgart, Germany, 1994-96; ASEE Postdoctoral Fellow, US Army Research Laboratory, Aberdeen, Maryland, 1997-98; Senior Research Associate, Air Force Research Laboratory, Dayton, Ohio, 1998-2000; Visiting Assistant Professor, Shippensburg University, Pennsylvania, 2001-02; Lecturer and Principal Investigator, Howard University, Washington, DC, 2005-09; Senior Scientist, Alion Science & Technology Corporation, Alexandria, VA, 2010-. Honours: BSc with Distinction and in Departmental Honors Program; International Woman of Year, IBC, 1998-2001; Outstanding Woman of the Twentieth Century, ABI, 1999; Listed in biographical publications. Memberships: Life Fellow, International Biographical Association; Fellow, Deputy Governor, American Biographical Institute; International Order of Merit; Order of International Ambassadors.

KENNY Enda, b. 24 April 1951, Derrywash, County Mayo, Ireland. Irish Fine Gael Politician. m. Fionnuala O'Kelly, 1992, 2 sons, 1 daughter. Education: St Patrick's College of Education, Dublin; University College Galway. Appointments: Primary school teacher; Teachta Dala for Mayo, 1975-; Minister for Tourism and Trade, 1994-97; Leader, Fine Gael, 2002-; Taoiseach, 2011-.

KENNY Jason, b. 23 March 1988, Bolton, England. Track Cyclist. Education: Mount St Joseph Business & Enterprise College, Farnworth, Bolton. Career: 1st, British National Team Sprint Championships, 2005; 1st (team sprint), Track World Cup, Moscow, 2006-07; 1st (sprint and team sprint), Track World Cup, Manchester, 2008-09; 1st (team sprint), Track World Cup, Copenhagen, 2008-09; 1st, British National Team Sprint Championships, 2010; 1st (keirin), European Track Championships, 2010; 1st (sprint), UCI Track World Championships, 2010; 1st (sprint), UCI Track World Championships, 2011; Gold (team sprint and men's sprint), London Olympics, 2012. Honours: MBE, 2009.

KENSIT Patsy (Jude), b. 4 March 1968, London, England. Film Actress. m. (1) Dan Donovan, (2) Jim Kerr, divorced, 1 son, (3) Liam Gallagher, divorced, 1 son. Creative Works: Films include: The Great Gatsby; The Bluebird; Absolute Beginners; Chorus of Disapproval; The Skipper; Chicago Joe and The Showgirl; Lethal Weapon II; Twenty-One; Prince of Shadows; Does This Mean We're Married; Blame It On the Bellboy; The Turn of the Screw; Beltenebros; Bitter Harvest; Angels and Insects; Grace of My Heart; Human Bomb; Janice Beard; Pavillions, 1999; Best; Things Behind the Sun, 2000; Bad Karma; Who's Your Daddy, 2001; The One and Only, 2001; Darkness Falling, 2002; Quest for the Kingdom: A fairy tale; shelter Island, 2003; Played, 2006; TV appearances: Great Expectations; Silas Marner; Tycoon: The Story of a Woman; Adam Bede; The Corsican Brothers (US TV); Aladdin; Emmerdale; Holby City; Play: See You Next Tuesday, 2003; Played, 2006. Address: c/o Steve Dagger, 14 Lambton Place, London W11 2SH, England.

KENT Jeff (Jeffrey John William), b. 28 July 1951, Stoke-on-Trent, England. Writer; Musician; Lecturer; Campaigner. m. Rosalind Ann Downs, 1987. Education: BSc (Econ) (Hons), International Relations, University of London, 1973; Postgraduate Teaching Certificate, Crewe College of Higher Education, 1974. Career: Freelance Writer and Editor, 1972-; Lecturer in Humanities, various Staffordshire colleges, 1974-2010; Performing Musician and Songwriter, 1975-; Radical Campaigner, 1977-; Guest Speaker, 1986-; Lecturer in Writing and Publishing, Stoke on Trent College, 1994-2010. Publications: The Rise and Fall of Rock, 1983; Principles of Open Learning, 1987; Routes to Change, 1988; The Last Poet, 1989; Back to Where We Once Belonged!, 1989; The Valiants' Years, 1990; Port Vale Tales, 1991; 100 Walks in Staffordshire, 1992; The Port Vale Record 1879-1993, 1993; Port Vale Personalities, 1996; The Mercia Manifesto, 1997; Editor, Port Vale Grass Roots, 1997; The Potteries Derbies, 1998; A Draft Constitution for Mercia, 2001; The Mysterious Double Sunset, 2001; The Constitution of Mercia, 2003; Editor, A Potteries Past, 2010; Numerous articles. Recordings: Butcher's Tale (single), 1981; Tales from the Land of the Afterglow (album in two parts), 1984; Port Vale Forever (album), 1992; Only One World (CD album), 2000. Honours: Listed in international biographical dictionaries. Memberships: NATFHE/ICI, 1976-2010; The Green Party, 1980-89; Movement for Middle England, 1992-93; The Mercia Movement (co-ordinator), 1993-; The Mercian Constitutional Convention (convener), 2001-03; The Acting Witan of Mercia (convener), 2003-. Address: Cherry Tree House, 8 Nelson Crescent, Cotes Heath, via Stafford ST21 6ST, England. E-mail: witan@mail.com

KENT Paul Welberry, b. 19 April 1923, Doncaster, England. Biochemist. m. Rosemary Shepherd, 3 sons, 1 daughter. Education: BSc, PhD, Birmingham University; MA, DPhil, Jesus College, DSc, Christchurch, Oxford University. Appointments: Assistant Lecturer then ICI Fellow, Birmingham University; Visiting Fellow, Princeton University, New Jersey, 1948-49; Demonstrator in Biochemistry, Oxford University, 1950-72; Tutor and Dr Lees Reader, 1955-72, Emeritus Fellow (Student), 1973-, Censor of Degrees, 2000-10, Christ Church, Oxford; Master, Van Mildert College, Durham University, 1972-82. Publications: Biochemistry of Amino Sugars, 1955; Membrane-Mediated Information, 1973; Some Scientists in the Life of Christ Church, Oxford, 2001; Robert Hooke and the English Renaissance, 2005. Honours: JP; Honorary DSc, CNAA; Honorary LHD, Drury University, USA; Order of Merit, Germany. Memberships: Royal Society of Chemistry; Biochemical Society; Athenaeum. Address: 18 Arnolds Way, Cumnor Hill, Oxford OX2 9JB, England.

KENT Peter Edwin, b. 27 July 1925, Christchurch, Dorset, England. Maritime Radio Communications and Radio Navigation. m. Elsie Joan (deceased), 3 daughters. Education: Ordinary National Certificate, Electrical Engineering; Higher National Certificate, Electronic Engineering. Appointments: Royal Navy Radio Communications Branch, 1942-55; Government Service, 1955-71; Principal Adviser to the Marine Directorate, Department of Transport, 1971-88; IMD Sub-Committee on Radiocommunications Chairman, Technical Group, 1975-81, Chairman, Sub-Committee, 1981-88; Chairman, Technical Group, IMO Sub-Committee on Safety of Navigation, 1976-94; Chairman, Technical Committee, 1988 Conference of Contracting Governments to the International Convention for the Safety of Life at Sea, 1974 on the Global Maritime Distress and Safety System; Chairman, ITU-R Working Party 8C, 1978-97; Chair, International Radio Regulations Committee on maritime distress and safety matters, ITU World Radio Administrative Conference, 1987; Consultant, Maritime Radio Communications and Radionavigation, International Association of Marine Aids to Navigation and Lighthouse Authorities, 1988-2006. Honours: Diploma of Honour, International Telecommunications Union. Memberships: Fellow, Royal Institute of Navigation; Associate Academician, International Informatization Academy, Russia; Secretary, European Radionavigation Maritime Forum. Address: 38 Stanbury Road, Thruxton, Andover, Hampshire, SP11 8NS, England. E-mail: peter-kent@btconnect.com

KENTFIELD Graham Edward Alfred, b. 3 September 1940, Buckhurst Hill, Essex, England. Retired Bank of England Official. m. Ann Hewetson, 2 daughters. Education: BA (Lit Hum, 1st Class), St Edmund Hall, Oxford, 1963. Appointments: Head of Monetary Policy Forecasting, 1974-76, Governor's Speechwriter, 1976-77, Editor, Quarterly Bulletin, 1977-80, Senior Manager, Banking and Money Supply Statistics, 1980-84, Adviser, Banking Department, 1984-85; Deputy Chief Cashier, 1985-91, Chief Cashier and Chief of Banking Department, 1991-94, Chief Cashier and Deputy Director, 1994-98, Bank of England. Honour: Fellow of Chartered Institute of Bankers, 1991; Memberships: Bank of England Director BACS Ltd, 1988-95; Bank of England Director, Financial Law Panel, 1994-98; Bank of England Representative, Council of Chartered Institute of Bankers, 1991-98; Bank of England Representative, APACS Council, 1991-98; Member, Building Societies Investor Protection Board, 1991-2001; Member, Deposit Protection Board (Banks), 1991-98; Chairman, Insolvency Practices Council, 2000-04; Honorary Treasurer, Society for the Promotion of Roman Studies, 1991-; Trustee, 1994- Chairman, 2000-, Chartered Institute for Bankers Pension Fund; Trustee, 1999-, Chairman, 2005-, Overseas Bishoprics Fund; Member, Council of London University, 2000-. Address: 27 Elgood Avenue, Northwood, Middlesex, HA6 3QL, England.

KENWRIGHT Bill, b. 4 September 1945, England. Theatre Producer. Education: Liverpool Institute. Appointments: Actor, 1964-70; Theatre Producer, 1970-; Chairman, Everton Football Club, 2004; Launched, Everton Tigers basketball team, 2007. Creative Works: Plays directed include: Joseph and The Amazing Technicolor Dreamcoat, 1979; The Business of Murder, 1981; A Streetcare Named Desire, 1984; Stepping Out, 1984; Blood Brothers, 1988; Shirley Valentine, 1989; Travels With My Aunt, 1993; Piaf, 1994; Lysistrata, 1993; Medea, 1993; Pygmalion, 1997; A Doll's House; An Ideal Husband; The Chairs, 2000; Blood Brothers; Ghosts; The Female Odd Couple. Honours: CBE, 2000. Address: Bill Kenwright Ltd, 106 Harrow Road, London, W2 1RR, England.

KENYON Ronald James, b. 24 May 1951, Penrith, England. Chartered Accountant. m. Ann Christine Kenyon, 1 son, 1 daughter. Education: Trent Polytechnic, Nottingham; Foundation Course, Institute of Chartered Accountants. Appointments: Pricewaterhouse, Leeds, 1968-69; Chartered Accountant, 1974-, Partner, 1980-, F T Kenyon and Son, Kyle and Kenyon, Kyle Saint and Co, Saint and Co; Chairman, Cumberland Society of Chartered Accountants, 1991. Publications: Rock Climbing in the North of England, 1978; Rock Climbing Guide to Borrowdale, 1986, 1990. Honours: Fellow, Institute of Chartered Accountants; Vice President, Fell and Rock Climbing Club. Memberships: Fell and Rock Climbing Club; Eden Valley Mountaineering Club; Penrith Agriculture Society; Eden Sports Council; Penrith Partnership; Penrith Mountain Rescue Team, 1967-92; Penrith Lions Club, 1979-2004.

KENZO Takada, b. 27 February 1939, Kyoto, Japan. Fashion Designer. Education: Bunka Fashion College, Japan. Appointments: Designer of patterns, Tokyo magazine; Freelance Designer to Louis Feraud, Paris, 1964-70; Owner of own shop, Jungle Jap, 1970; Director and Writer of film, Yume, Yume no Ato, 1981; Head, Kenzo fashion house; Retired, 1999; Created Yume label, 2002.

KERC Janez, b. 22 May 1962, Podrecje. Pharmacist. Education: BSc, 1987, MSc, 1990, PhD, 1995. Appointments: Researcher, 1988-94, Senior Researcher, 1994-2002, Head of NDS Department, 2002-10, Head of Group NDS, 2009-, Lek Pharmaceuticals d.d. Ljubljana; Assistant Professor, 1997-2007, Associated Professor, 2007-, Faculty of Pharmacy, University of Ljubljana. Publications: Patents in pharmaceutical field; Articles in professional journals. Honours: KRKA Award, 1985; Minarik Award, 1999; Novartis VIVA Leading Scientists Award, 2007. Memberships: American Association of Pharmaceutical Scientists; Slovenian Pharmaceutical Society; Controlled Release Society. Address: Podrecje 6, 1230 Domzale, Slovenia.

KERCKHOVEN Guy Maria van, b. 25 January 1951, Louvain, Belgium. Professor. m. Fannes Anne-Marie, 2 sons, 1 daughter. Education: MA, University of Louvain, 1972; PhD, Institute of Philosophy, Husserl-Achives, 1985. Appointments: Sociale Hogeschool Heverlee, Louvain, 1989; Full Professor, Department of Architecture & Arts, Associated Faculty of Architecture & Arts, University of Louvain, 1998-. Publications: Numerous articles in professional journals; 4 books. Honours: A von Humboldt Fellowship, 1986-87, 1990, 2008. Memberships: President of the Board, St Lucas Archives; Architecture Archives, Brussels. Address: Platanen Laan-Oost 34, B-8420 De Haan, Belgium. E-mail: guy.van.kerckhoven@telenet.be

KERNER Boris, b. 22 December 1947, Moscow, Russia. Engineer; Physicist. m. Tatiana, 1 daughter. Education: Engineer, Electronics, Technical University MIREA, Moscow, 1972; PhD, Physics and Mathematics, 1976; Dr Sc degree, Physics and Mathematics, 1986. Appointments: Engineer, Semiconductor Research Institute Pulsar, Moscow, 1972-80; Senior Scientist, Head of Theoretical Department, Semiconductor Engineering, Research Institute Orion, Moscow, 1980-92; Professor, Technical University MIREA, Moscow, 1990-91; Senior Scientist, Daimler Research, Stuttgart, Germany, 1992-2000; Head, Resarch Field Traffic, Group Research and Advanced Engineering, DaimlerChrysler AG, 2000-. Publications: 4 books; Over 180 articles and review in professional journals; Over 100 patents. Honours: DaimlerChrysler Research Award, 1994. Memberships: Section Editor of Springer Encyclopaedia of Complexity and Systems Science. Address: Daimler AG, Head of Traffic, GR/ETF, HPC: G021, D-71059 Sindelfingen, Germany. E-mail: boris.kerner@daimler.com Website: http:/en.wikipedia.org/wiki/Boris_Kerner

KERNICK Robert Charles, b. 11 May 1927, Istanbul, Turkey. Wine Merchant. m. (1) Gillian Burne, 1 son, 1 daughter, (2) Adelaide Anne Elizabeth White. Education: Blundells and Sidney Sussex, Cambridge. Appointments: Director, Grandmetropolitan Ltd, 1972-75; Managing Director, International Distillers and Vintners, 1972-75; Clerk of the Royal Cellars, 1979-92; Chairman, Corney and Barrow Ltd, 1981-88; Clerk of the Prince of Wales's Cellar, 1992-99. Honours: Commander of the Royal Victorian Order; Chevalier de l'Ordre du Merite Agricole. Memberships: Merchant Taylors' Company; Leathersellers' Company; Cavalry and Guards Club; MCC; Swinley Forest Golf Club. Address: 79 Canfield Gardens, London NW6 3EA, England.

KERNS Christian R, b. 8 April 1953, Fredicksburg, Virginia, USA. Chemist. Education: BSc, Chemistry, West Virginia University, 1978. Appointments: Chemist, Florida Department of Agriculture, Tallahassee, Florida, 1986-96; Chemist, Harbor Branch, Oceanographic Institution, 1997; Chemist, Aerotek Scientific, Fort Lauderdale, Florida, 1999-2000; Engineer, Spectro Analytical Instruments, Fitchburg, Massachusetts, 2000-01; Chemist, Adecco, Leominister, Massachusetts, 2002-; President, United Methodist Men, Wesley United Methodist Church, Worcester, MA. Honours: Named 1st Team, All-State Colorado Men's Basketball Team, 1971; Captain Colorado State Championship Basketball Team, 1971; Man of the Year, 2011. Memberships: American Chemical Society; Lions Club; Phi Theta Kappa; Chairman, Missions Committee, St Paul's United Methodist Church, Tallahassee, Florida. Address: 14 Oread Street, #307 Worcester, MA 01608, USA.

KESBY John Douglas, b. 14 April 1938, London, England. Anthropologist; Educator. m. Sheila Anne Gregory. Education: BA, 1960, Diploma in Anthropology, 1961, BLitt, 1963, MA, 1967, DPhil, 1971, Oxford University, England. Appointments: Lecturer, Pitt Rivers Museum, Oxford, 1967-68; College Lecturer, King's and Newnham Colleges, Cambridge, 1968-71; Lecturer, University of Kent, Canterbury, 1971-98. Publications include: The Cultural Regions of East Africa, 1977; The Rangi of Tanzania, 1981; Progress and the Past among the Rangi of Tanzania, 1982; Rangi Natural History, 1986; Entry in Encyclopaedia Britannica: Eastern Africa: the Peoples: East Africa. Memberships include: Association of Social Anthropologists; University and College Union; Royal Society for the Protection of Birds; Kent Trust. Address: 32 St Michael's Place, Canterbury, Kent CT2 7HQ, England.

KESSELYÁK Péter, b. 7 February 1936, Budapest, Hungary. Research Engineer. m. Judit Bontó, 2 sons, 4 daughters. Education: MSc, Mathematics & Physics, University of Szeged, Hungary, 1958; Postgraduate: Environmental Testing, 1960, Reliability Engineering, 1962, Pulse Technique of Semiconductor Devices, 1963, Computer Engineering, 1977, Technical University of Budapest. Appointments: Research Engineer, BHG Telecommunication Works, Budapest, 1959-91; Senior Counsellor, Communications Authority, Hungary, 1991-2006; Board Member, European Telecom Standards Institute, 1996-2005 and Issue Manager of CEEC/EU Enlargement Affairs, 1996-2004; Committee Member, Hungarian Accreditation Body responsible for the field of Infocommunication, 2009-. Publications: Co-author of book, Hétpecsétes történetek, 2008; Over 50 articles in periodicals: Quality, Nachrichtentechnik, Hiradastechnika, many others. Honours: Annual Award of European Organisation for Quality, 1983; 2nd Prize, National Competition for Microelectronics, 1983; Baross Gábor Ministerial Award, 1994. Memberships: International Electrotechnical Commission (IEC TC56 WG4, System Aspects of Dependability); Hungarian National Committee for EOQ; EOQ Software Group; Hétpecsét Society for Information Security. Outstanding Achievements: field reliability data bank of telecom exchanges based on 100 billion component-hours; theoretical models: relativity principle of reliability in dependence of the fault criteria; fault capacity concept of large telecom systems (awarded by EOQ in 1983); SW dependability model based on multidimensional space of states; information content to be considered as the driving fuel of all intelligent systems. Address: Rátz László u 86, H-1116 Budapest, Hungary. E-mail: p.kesselyak@chello.hu

KETTLEY John Graham, b. 11 July 1952, Halifax, West Yorkshire, England. Presenter; Weather Consultant. m. Lynn, 2 sons. Education: BSc honours, Applied Physics, Coventry University. Appointments: Meteorological Office, 1970-2000; National BBC TV broadcast meteorologist, Domestic TV manager and lead presenter, 1985-2000; Founded, British Weather Services, 2000; Appearances on numerous TV series; Ambassador for Cricket World Cup, 1999; Presenter and host, Triangular NatWest One-day International cricket, 2001; Freelance presenter and weather consultant, John Kettley Enterprises; Contract weather presenter and sporting features for BBC Radio 5Live, 2001-. Publications: Several articles for cricket journals, travel and leisure brochures; Foreword, Rain Stops Play, book by Andrew Hignell, 2002. Memberships: Lord's Taverner, 1990-; Institute of Broadcast Meteorology, 1995-; Fellow, Royal Meteorological Society, 2001-. Address: c/o PVA Management, Hallow Park, Hallow, Worcester WR2 6PG, England. E-mail: johnkettley@bbc.co.uk

DICTIONARY OF INTERNATIONAL BIOGRAPHY 36th EDITION

KEYES Gregory James, b. 26 December 1952, Warrigul, Victoria, Australia. International Presenter. m. Evelyn Keyes, 1 son, 1 stepson, 1 daughter, 1 stepdaughter. Education: BA, 1997; MBA, 1999; PhD, Doctor of Business and Leadership Studies, 2001; Master of Science, Exercise Science, 2003. Appointments: Chief Executive Officer, Global Lifestyle Organisation Web; Chief Executive Officer, Global Aquatic Instructor Network; Chief Executive Officer, Absolute Concepts of Entertainment; Chief Executive Officer, Ready Steady Live Consulting; Professor, Vice President, Dean, Department of Education, Cyber LLB, USA, 2005-; FCEO, Mt Elephant Enterprises. Publications: Aquatics – The Umbilical into Lifestyle Wellness and Advancement, 2003; The Star of Communication Stratagem, 2003; Ready Steady Live – Adventurism into Lifestyle Development; The most unique Vehicle ever created – You!; Introduction to Human Physiology, 2004; Star to Leadership and Self Development, 2004; Hydrospinning and Aquatics, 2004; Concept creations: TAR – Total Audience Reality Concept; Keyes Core of Concept Creativity Method; Keyes Scopes of Excellence Appraisal System; Keyes "EGA" Scale of Exertion, Goal and Achievement System; Keyes Scale of Stress Rationality Method; Keyes Combat-A-Size System (A combination method course of Self Defence mixed with Education on Body Awareness/Fitness Exercise Prescription/Performance and Weight Loss Methodology). Honours: National Medal, Australia, 1988; Global Award Aquatics, USA, 2002; Emma Award, Aquatics Europe, 2003; Guinnes Book of Records, 2003, 2004. Address: 1184 Elephant Pass Road, St Marys, 7215, Tasmania, Australia. E-mail: gkeyes@intas.net.au

KEYS Alicia, b. 25 January 1981, New York, USA. Singer; Pianist; Songwriter. Education: Professional Performing Arts School, Manhattan; Classically trained pianist. Career: Signed to Clive Davis' new J Records label, 1999; Appeared in charity telethon in aid of World Trade Center victims, 2001; Prince's Trust Urban Music Festival, London, 2004; Collaborations with Angie Stone and Jimmy Cozier. Recordings: Albums: Songs In a Minor, 2001; The Diary of Alicia Keys, 2003; Unplugged, 2005; As I Am, 2007; The Element of Freedom, 2009. Singles: Girlfriend, 2001; Fallin', 2001; A Woman's Worth, 2001; How Come You Don't Call Me Any More, 2002; You Don't Know My Name, 2003; If I Ain't Got You, 2004. Honours: Grammy Award, Best New Artist, 2001; Grammy Award, Best R&B Album, 2001; Grammy Award, Song of the Year, Best Female R&B Vocal Performance, Best R&B Song, 2001; American Music Award Favorite New Artist, Pop/Rock, Favourite New Artist, Soul/R&B, 2002; MTV Award, Best R&B Act, 2002; MOBO Award for Best Album, 2002; American Music Award for Best Female Soul/R&B Artist, 2004; Source Hip Hop Music Award for Female Artist of the Year, 2004; Grammy Award, Best R&B Album, 2005; Grammy Award, Best R&B Song, 2005. Address: William Morris Agency, 1325 Avenue of the Americas, New York, NY 10019, USA. Website: www.aliciakeys.net

KEZIK Vitaly Yakov, b. 23 April 1951, Kiev, Ukraine. Senior Scientist. m. Helen, 1 son. Education: BS, MS, Electric Chemistry, State University of Chemical Engineering, Dnepropetrovsk, Ukraine, 1980; PhD, Physical Metallurgy, KPI, State Polytechnic University, Kiev, Ukraine, 1987. Appointments: More than 30 years professional experience; Senior Scientist, Academy of Science; Vice President of R&D, Specmask Corp; Scientific Consultant and Scientific Adviser; Co-founder and Co-owner, Start-up Water Treatment Technologies Co. Publications: More than 200 scientific papers including 16 individual editions and 30 patents. Memberships: American Chemistry Society. Address: 7 Ozka, Katszin 12900, Israel.

KHABAKHPASHEV Georgy Alekseevich, b. 1 April 1956, Moscow, USSR. Leading Researcher. 1 daughter. Education: Physics, Novosibirsk State University, 1979. Appointments: Special Student, Researcher, Junior Researcher, Research Fellow, Senior Researcher, Leading Researcher, Kutateladze Institute of Thermophysics SB RAS, Novosibirsk, 1979-. Publications: Numerous articles in professional journals. Memberships: European Mechanics Society; European Geosciences Union. Address: Kutateladze Institute of Thermophysics SB RAS, Academician Lavrentiev Avenue 1, Novosibirsk, 630090, Russia.

KHABAROVSKIY Nikolay, b. 27 May 1972, Moscow, USSR. System Engineer. Education: System Engineer, 1995, PhD, 1999, MAI. Appointments: Engineer/Designer, 1996-2000, Leader/Engineer, 2000-05, NPP Zvezda J-St Co; Head, Designed and Computed Research Sector, NIIchimmash J-St Co, 2006-. Publications: More than 60 articles and other publications. Honours: Ju A Gagarin Medals of FK Russia, 2001, 2002; S P Korolev Medal of FK Russia, 2003; V N Chelomey Medal of FK Russia, 2004; V M Komarov Medal of FK Russia, 2005. Address: 16 app, 63 Ryazanski avenu, 109428 Moscow, Russian Federation. E-mail: nik.khaba@gmail.com

KHALIFEH Ala' F, b. 27 March 1978, Amman, Egypt. Assistant Professor. Education: PhD, Electrical Engineering and Computer Science, University of California, Irvine, USA. Appointments: Assistant Professor, German University in Cairo. Publications: Numerous articles in professional journals, see website. Honours: Fulbright Scholarship, 2005-07; Listed in international biographical dictionaries. Memberships: IEEE. Address: German University in Cairo, New Cairo City, Egypt. E-mail: alafkh@gmail.com Website: http://newport.eecs.uci.edu/~akhalife

KHAN Imran Niaza, b. 25 November 1952, Lahore, Pakistan. Politician; Former Professional Cricketer. m. Jemima Goldsmith, 1995, divorced 2004, 2 sons. Education: Keble College, Oxford. Career: Right-arm fast bowler, middle-order right-hand batsman; Played for Lahore, 1969-71, Worcester, 1971-76, Oxford University, 1973-75 (Captain, 1974), Dawood, 1975-76, PIA, 1975-81, Sussex, 1974-88, NSW, 1984-85; 88 test matches for Pakistan, 1971-92, 48 as captain, scoring 3,807 runs and taking 362 wickets; Toured England 1971, 1974, 1975 (World Cup) 1979 (World Cup), 1982, 1983 (World Cup), 1987; Scored 17,771 first-class runs and took 1,287 first-class wickets; 175 limited-overs ints, 139 as captain (including 1992 World Cup victory); Special Representative for Sports, UNICEF, 1989; Editor in Chief, Cricket Life, 1989-90; Founder, Imran Khan Cancer Hospital Appeal, 1991-; Founder, 1996, Leader, 1996-, Tehrik-e-Insaf (Movement for Justice). Publications: Imran, 1983; All-Round View (autobiography), 1988; Indus Journey, 1990; Warrier Race, 1993; Syndicated newspaper column. Honours: Honorary Fellow, Keble College, Oxford, 1988; Wisden Cricketer of the Year, 1983; Hilal-e-Imtiaz, 1993. Address: c/o Shaukat Khanum Memorial Trust, 29 Shah Jamal, Lahore 54600, Pakistan.

KHAN Jemima, b. 30 January 1974, London, England. Charity fund-raiser. m. Imran Khan, 1995, divorced 2004, 2 sons. Education: Bristol University. Career: Developed own brand of tomato ketchup; Established Jemima Khan

Designs fashion label; Campaigned to improve literacy levels in Pakistan; UK Special Representative, UNICEF, 2001-; Founded Jemima Khan Appeal; Reporter and presenter, Channel 5, Bangladesh, 2002-; Fund-raiser, Shaukat Khanum Memorial Cancer Hospital. Honours: Rover People's Award for Best Dressed Female Celebrity, British Fashion Awards, 2001. Address: c/o UNICEF, 3 United Nations Plaza, New York, NY 10017, USA.

KHAN Kazim Ali, b. 12 November 1968, Hyderabad, India. General Dentist; Orthodontist. m. Sumaira, 2 sons. Education: BSc, Osmania University, 1989; Bachelor of Dental Surgeries, Gulbarga University, 1997; P G Diploma, Computer Applications, APTECH, 1998; Diploma in Tally, Focus, etc, 2000; Doctorate in Medicine, Kolkatta, 2005; P G Diploma, Forensic Sciences & Criminology, Annamalai University, Chennai, 2005; Residency in Orthodontics, International Association for Orthodontics (USA), 2006; Japanese Techniques in Orthodontics, Non-Extraction Techniques, 2006; Orthodontics for General Practitioners Session I to IV taken from Dr Brock Rondeau (IBO Diplomat), USA, 2007-08; PhD, Acupuncture, Italian University, 2007; Attended many post doctoral training programmes in India, USA, Canada in the field of Implants, Cosmetic dentistry, Orthodontics, Rhinoplasty, etc; International Instructor training in field of Orthodontics from pioneer Diplomats of IAO, International Association for Orthodontics Head Quarters, Milwaukee, USA, in progress. Appointments: Consultant to clinics in home town; Founder, BMS Dental Hospital, Hyderabad, 2000. Publications: Numerous articles in professional journals. Honours: BDS Gold Medalist; Gold Medal in Prosthodontia; Colgate-Palmolive Award in Periodontia; Rashtriya Ratna Award, New Delhi, 2001; Glory of India Award & Man of the Year Gold Medal, Bhopal, 2003; International Gold Star Award, Hyderabad, 2003; Prominent Citizen of India Award, 2004; Mother India International Gold Award, Hyderabad, 2005; Pride of India Award, 2007; Man of the Era Award, Hyderabad, 2009. Memberships: Indian Dental Association; Rural Health Society, Kolkatta; Council of Independent Medical Practitioners, Chennai; American Dental Association, Chicago; International Association for Orthodontics, Milwaukee, USA; Fellow, Academy of General Education, Manipal, India, 1998; Fellow, Rural Health Society, Kolkatta, 2001; Fellow, Pierre Fauchard Academy, USA, 2008; Fellow, International College of Dentistry, USA, 2010. Address: 23-2-53 to 56, First Floor, Mishal Estate, Moghulpura, Hyd, AP-2, India. E-mail: kk_bdh@yahoo.co.in

KHAN Mohammad Ibrahim, b. 19 August 1942, Kanpur, India. Educator. m. Zubaida Hamid, 2 sons, 5 daughters. Education: BS (Mech), 1963; ME (Prod), 1966; PhD (Prod), 1979. Appointments: Lecturer, University of Roorkee, India, 1966-70; Assistant Professor, MNNIT, Allahabad, India, 1970-80; Assistant Professor, Basrah University, Iraq, 1980-84; Professor (Mech), Garyousis University, Benghazi, Libya, 1984-2001; HOD (Mech), Dean, Engineering, Integral University, India, 2002-. Publications: 4 books; 47 research papers. Honours: Bharat Jyoti Award, 1976-77; Certificate of Merit, Institution of Engineers (India), 1978; Man of the Year for India, 2009; Jewel of India Award, Indian Solidarity Council; Eminent Educationist, International and Natl Compendium, New Delhi, India. Memberships: Fellow, Institution of Engineers; Senior Member, ASME, USA. Address: 94/6 Nai Sarak, Kanpur, Uttar Pradesh, 208001, India. E-mail: mikyh_20@yahoo.com

KHAN Shahjahan, b. 1 September 1953, Gopalgonj, Bangladesh. Professor. m. Anarkali Lutfun Nahar, 3 sons. Education: BSc (Hons), Statistics, 1977, MSc, 1979, Jahangirnagar University, Bangladesh; MSc, 1987, PhD, 1992, Statistics, University of Western Ontario, Canada. Appointments: University of Southern Queensland, Australia; University of Bahrain, Bahrain; Sultan Qaboos University, Oman; King Fahd University of Petroleum and Minerals, Saudi Arabia; University of Dhaka, Bangladesh; University of Western Ontario, Canada; Founding Chief Editor, Journal of Applied Probability and Statistics (JAPS), USA. Publications: Over 60 refereed journal articles; Over 40 book chapters, conference proceedings and other publications; 14 keynote addresses; 23 invited talks; Over 60 conference and seminar presentations. Honours: Queensland Multicultural Service Award, 20002; ISOSS Gold Medal, 2007. Memberships: President, Islamic Countries Society of Statistical Sciences; Elected Fellow, Royal Statistical Society, UK; Elected Member, International Statistical Institute, Netherlands; Member, Statistical Society of Australia; Member, Statistical Society of Canada. Address: Department of Mathematics & Computing, University of Southern Queensland, Toowoomba, QLD 4350, Australia. E-mail: drshahjahankhan@yahoo.com

KHAN Sujoy, b. 16 June 1976 (arrived in UK 2002). Consultant Immunologist. m. Sanchita Saha, 2004, 1 daughter. Education: MBBS, Christian Medical College & Hospital, Vellore, India, 1999; MRCP (UK), Royal College of Physicians of Edinburgh, 2004; FRCPath (London), 2010. Appointments: Resident, Christian Medical College & Hospital, Vellore, 2000-01; Senior House Officer Medicine, NHS Trust, Wales, 2002-05; Specialist Registrar, Immunology, Barts and the London NHS Trust, London, 2005; Specialist Registrar, Immunology, Scunthorpe & Hull, England, 2005-10; Consultant Immunologist, Surrey, 2010-. Publications: Numerous articles in peer-reviewed journals. Honours: Research Award, Christian Medical College & Hospital, Vellore, 1999; Myre Sim Research Grant, Royal College of Physicians of Edinburgh, 2007. Memberships: RCP (Edinburgh); RCPath (London); Association of Clinical Pathologists; European Academy of Allergy and Clinical Immunology; British Society for Immunology; European Society for Immunodeficiences. Address: Department of Immunology & Allergy, Frimley Park Hospital NHS Foundation Trust, Frimley, Surrey GU16 7UJ, England. E-mail: sujoy.khan@nhs.net

KHAN Taskeen Ahmad, b. 8 June 1955, Peshawar, Pakistan. Urologist/Genito-urinary Surgeon. m. Rubina Anwar (deceased), 1 daughter. Education: SSCE (Biology Group), Pakistan, 1969; IE (Pre-Medical Group), Pakistan, 1971; MBBS, Pakistan, 1976; DU, Austria, 1982; FU, Switzerland, 1983; FWMAAF, Austria, 1984; FA f Urol, West Germany, 1984; MDGU, Germany, 1990. Appointments: Assistant Professor, 1985-91, Associate Professor, 1991-96, Head of Department of Urology, 1996-, Professor, 1996-, Post-Graduate Medical Institute, Peshawar; Consultant Urologist, 1985-, In charge of Urology Unit, 1996-, Lady Reading Hospital, Peshawar; First ever Associate Dean, first ever Associate Faculty of Urology, Khyber Medical University, Peshawar, 2009-. Publications: Over 170 articles in scientific research journals. Honours include relatively recently: Contact Person (in Pakistan), European Urology Accredited Continuing Medical Education (EU-ACME) Programme, EU-ACME Committee/Office, European Board of Urology and European Association of Urology; Scientific Envoy (for Pakistan), six Members Asia and Australasia Section, International Relations Office, European Association of Urology; Secretary General, European Association of Urology, European Urology Support Fund – Award; Scientific Envoy (for Pakistan), Urological Academic/ Research, Professional Activities, etc, American Urological Association; Scientific Envoy (for Pakistan), 14 Members Asia and Australasia Section, International Relations Office, American Urological Association. Memberships: Advisory Panel, Integrated Mountain Research Centre, University of Punjab, Lahore; Deutsche Gesellschaft für Urologie EV; Osterreichisch-Pakistanischer Club; European Association of Urology; Pakistan Association of Urological Surgeons; European Society for Male Genital Surgery; Wakeup Club, Al-Borak International; European Society for Infections in Urology; American Urological Association; many others. Address: 52 - S J Afghani Road, University Town, PC 25120, Peshawar, Khyber Pakhtun Khwa, Pakistan. E-mail: prof.dr.taskeenamadkhan@gmail.com

KHANDELWAL Chiranjiva, b. 8 October 1952, Indian. Surgical Gastroenterologist and Oncologist. m. Dr Poonam, 2 sons. Education: MBBS, 1977; Master of Surgery, 1982; Diplomate National Board, 1985. Appointments: Professor, Head, Department G I Surgery, Indira Gandhi Institute of Medical Sciences. Publications: 31. Honours: International Fellow, Cleveland Clinic; International Cancer Technology Transfer Award Scholarship. Memberships: International Union Against Cancer; International College of Surgeons. Address: 6 Nehru, Nagar, Patna 800013, India. E-mail: drkhandelwal@hotmail.com

KHANNA Amit, b. 1 March 1951, Delhi, India. Entertainment Business. Education: BA (Hons), St Stephen's College, New Delhi, 1968-71. Appointments: Executive Producer: Feature Films: Shareef Budmaash, 1973; Heera Panna, 1974; Ishk Ishk Ishk, 1975; Jaaneman, 1976; Bullet, 1976; Des Pardes, 1977; Lootmaar, 1980; TV serials: Buniyaad, 1986; Chapte Chapte, 1985; Apne Aap, 1985; Producer: Feature Films: Man Pasand, 1981; Papa Kehta Hain, 1995; Aur Ek Prem Kahani, 1995; Is Raat Ki Subah Nahin, 1995; Gudgudee, 1996; Lalchee, 1996; Saaz, 1996; Bhairavi, 1996; Gudia, 1996; Sardari Begum, 1997; Do Rahein, 2000; Producer, Writer & Director: Feature Films: Sheeshay Ka Ghar, 1984; Shesh, 1988; Producer & Director: Namaskar, 1989; Business Plus, 1993-99; Mirch Masala, 1993-99; Mere Saath Chal, 1993; Sangeet Sitare, 1994-98; Jaldi Jaldi, 1994-99; Zameen Aasmaan, 1994; Rangoli, 1994; Swabhimaan, 1995-97; Badalte Rishte, 1995; A Mouthful of Sky, 1996-97; Star TV: Ajeeb Dastan, 1999-2000; Jubilee Plush, 1996-2000; Home TV: Bollywood Plus, 1997-98; Mumkin, 1997-98; Sony TV: Open House, 1999; Producer and director of several advertising shorts and documentaries; Producer and writer of several radio shows. Memberships: Indian Documentary Producers Association; Federation of Indian Chmabers of Commerce & Industry; Information, Communication & Entertainment Planning Commission, Government of India; Confederaton of Indian Industry; Ministry of Communications & IT; Workding Group for 11th Five Year & 12th Five Year Plan on Information & Broadcasting Sector; Advisory Board, Forum d'Avignon, Paris.

KHASANSHIN Rashid Khusainovitch, b. 5 August 1955, Russia. Lecturer. m. Marina Levdik, 1 son, 1 daughter. Education: Diploma, Engineer Physicist, Experimental and Theoretical Physics Department, Moscow Engineering Physics Institute; Diploma, Mathematician, Mechanico-Mathematics Department, Moscow M V Lomonosow State University. Appointments: Chief, Mathematical Modeling Laboratory, joint-stock company Kompozit; Senior Lecturer, Chair of Physics, Moscow Bauman State Technical University. Publications: 56 articles in professional journals. Address: 141080, Kosmonautov 41, Bld 2, Apt 43, Korolev, Moscow region, Russia.

KHASHARMEH Hussein Ali, b. 7 January 1949, Ajloun, Jordan. Associate Professor. m. Kierieh, 7 sons, 2 daughters. Education: BA, Yarmouk University, Jordan, 1982; MBA, Cardiff Business School, 1986; PhD, Middlesex, UK, 1995. Appointments: Teaching and Research Assistant, 1982-84, Instructor, 1987-93, Assistant Professor, 1995-99, Associate Professor, 1999-2002, Yarmouk University; Associate Professor, United Arab Emirates University, 2002-04; Associate Professor, Arab Academy of Financial Institutions, Amman, 2004-05; Associate Professor, Bahrain University, Kingdom of Bahrain, 2005-. Publications: Over 45 articles in national, regional and international refereed journals. Honours: Academic Excellence, Yarmouk University, 1982; Master and PhD Scholarship, Yarmouk University, 1985, 1993; Research Excellence, Yarmouk University, 1999; Research Excellence, Syria, 2000; Research Excellence, United Arab Emirates, 2004; Outstanding Research, GCBF Conference, USA, 2009. Memberships: Listed in international biographical dictionaries; GABER International Conference; Jordanian Certified Public Accountants. Address: PO Box 32038, Bahrain University, College of Business Administration, Accounting Department, Kingdom of Bahrain. E-mail: hkhasharmeh@hotmail.com

KHDARY Nezar, b. 28 February 1966, Taif, Saudi Arabia. Nano and Environmentalist. m. Rihab, 4 sons, 2 daughters. Education: PhD, Southampton University, England. Appointments: Researcher; Consultant. Publications: 110 articles in professional journals. Honours: Southampton Chemistry Nano Prize. Memberships: RSC. Address: PO Box 6086, King Abdulaziz City for Science & Technology, Riyadh-11442, Saudi Arabia. E-mail: nkhdary@kacst.edu.sa Website: www.nozor.info

KHINTIBIDZE Elguja, b. 7 June 1937, Georgia. Philologist. m. Mzia Menabde, 2 sons. Education: Student of Tbilisi State University, 1955-60; Postgrad Student, 1960-63; Cand Philol, 1963; DrPhilol, 1971; Professor, 1973; Corresponding Member, Georgian Academy Sciences, 1997. Appointments: Assistant Professor, 1966, Professor, 1973, Deputy Dean Philology Department, 1965-66, The Dean of Philology Department, 1976-85, Vice Rector, Tbilisi State University, 1985-93; Director, Centre of Georgian Studies, 1992-; Head, Laboratory of Georgian-Foreign Literature Contacts, 1993-2006; Head, Chair of Old Georgian Literature, 2000-06; Head, Institute for the History of Georgian Literature, 2007-. Publications: 200 scholarly works including 18 monographs; Georgian-Byzantine Literary Contacts, 1996; The Designations of Georgians and Their Etymology, 1998; Georgian Literature in European Scholarship, 2001; The Man in Panther-Skin in England in the Age of Shakespeare, 2008; Rustaveli's The Man in the Panther Skin and European Literature, 2011. Honours: Ivane Javakhishvili Prize, 1983; International Order of Merit, 1994; Georgia's Order of Merit, 2003. Memberships: Membre Titulaire de Société Internationale pour l'Etude de la Philosophie Médiévale (Belgique Louvan La Neuve). Address: Side Street Ateni 18A Apt 13, Tbilisi 0179, Georgia.

KHOLODOV Vladimir Nicolaevich, b. 21 August 1925, Moscow, USSR. Geologist; Lithologist; Ore-Geochemist. m. I A Kondratjeva-Mutso, 2 daughters. Education: Engineer, Institute of Oil and Gas, 1951; Candidate of Sciences, postgraduate course, 1955; Doctor of Geology-Mineral Sciences, 1970, Professor, 1987, Geological Institute of USSR. Publications: 400 scientific works and 9 monographs in professional journals. Honours: USSR State Prize for monograph, 1967; Academician of RANS, 1991; Honoured Scientist of Russian Federation, 2002. Memberships: International Association of Sedimentologists; Editorial Board of Geology of Ore Deposits Journal; Other scientific councils. E-mail: rostilann@jandex.ru

KHOO Boo-Chai, b. 24 April 1929, Singapore. Medical Doctor. m. Cheng Lui, 2 sons. Education: Anglo Chinese School, 1946; MBBS, University of Singapore, 1954. Appointments: Medical Officer, General Surgery Unit, Singapore General Hospital, 1954-58; Resident, Plastic Surgery Unit, Tokyo Metropolitan Police Hospital, Japan, 1959-61; Private Practice, Plastic Surgery, Singapore, 1962-; Deputy Editor, Chinese Journal of Plastic and Reconstructive Surgery. Publications: Clinics in Plastic Surgery: Plastic Surgery in non-Caucasian; Aesthetic Surgery for the Oriental; Oriental Eye Surgery; Concepts of Oriental Beauty; Surgery for the Oriental Eyelid; Sculpturing the Nasal Tip and Lobule Region; Many others. Honours: Man of the Year in Medicine and Healthcare, 2009. Memberships: American Society of Plastic and Reconstructive Surgeons; Israel Association of Plastic Surgeons; Association of Plastic Surgeons of India; International Society Aesthetic Plastic Surgery; Oriental Society Aesthetic Plastic Surgery; Singapore Medical Association. Address: 05-12 Parkway Parade Medical Centre, Singapore 449 269.

KHORANA Har Gobind, b. 9 January 1922, Raipur, Punjab Region, India (US Citizen). Chemist. m Esther Elizabeth Sibler, 1952, 1 son, 2 daughters. Education: Bachelor's Degree, 1943, Master's Degree, 1945, Chemistry, Punjab University; Doctorate, Liverpool University; Postdoctoral work in Zurich, Switzerland. Appointments: Organic Chemist, working with Sir Alexander Todd, Cambridge, 1950-52; Organic Chemist, National Research Institute, Canada, 1952-60; Professor and Co-Director, Institute of Enzyme Chemistry, University of Wisconsin, 1960-64; Conrad A Elvehjem Professor in Life Sciences, 1964-70; Andrew D White Professor at Large, Cornell University, Ithaca, 1974-80; Alfred P Sloan Professor, 1970-97, Professor Emeritus and Senior Lecturer, 1997-, Massachusetts Institute of Technology. Publications: Some Recent Developments in the Chemistry of Phosphate Esters of Biological Interest, 1961; Articles on Biochemistry in various journals. Honours: Joint Winner, Nobel Prize for Physiology or Medicine, 1968; Louisa Gross Horwitz for Biochemistry, 1968; American Chemical Society Award for creative work in Synthetic Chemistry, 1968; Lasker Foundation Award, 1968; American Academy of Achievement Award, 1971; Willard Gibbs Medal, 1974; Gairdner Foundation Annual Award, 1980; National Medal of Science, 1987; Paul Kayser International Award of Merit, 1987; Numerous honorary degrees and international awards. Memberships: NAS; Foreign Academician, USSR Academy of Sciences; Foreign Member, Royal Society, London; Pontifical Academy of Sciences. Address: Departments of Biology and Chemistry, Massachusetts Institute of Technology, 77 Massachusetts Avenue, Room 68-680, Cambridge, MA 02139, USA.

KHOVANOV Igor Aleksandrovich, b. 14 October 1971, Saratov, USSR. Assistant Professor. m. Natalia Aleksandrovna Sal'nikova, 2 sons. Education: MSc, 1993, PhD, 1997, Saratov State University. Appointments: Lecturer, 1996-99, Associate Professor (Docent), 1999-2003, Saratov State University; Humboldt Research Fellow, Humboldt University of Berlin, Germany, 2004-05; Research Associate, 2005, AR EPSRC Fellow, 2005-08, Lancaster University, UK; AR EPSRC Fellow (Assistant Professor), 2008-10, Assistant Professor, 2011-, University of Warwick. Publications: 49 publications in refereed scientific journals. Honours: Young Scientist Awards, 1994, 1995, Associate Docent Award, 2001, Soros Scientific Education Programme; Post-Doctoral Fellowship Award, CRDF (USA) and BRHE (Russian Federation), 2003; Alexander von Humboldt Research Fellowship, 2004-05; AR EPSRC Fellowship, 2005-10. Memberships: Institute of Physics. Address: School of Engineering, University of Warwick, Coventry, CV4 7AL, England. E-mail: i.khovanov@googlemail.com

KHREIS Khalid, b. 23 December 1955, Assammu, Jordan. Director General. m. Clara Amado, 2 daughters. Education: BA, Art Education, Hilwan University, Cairo, Egypt, 1978; MA, Drawing and Painting, Academy San Jordi of Fine Arts, Barcelona, Spain, 1982; PhD (cum laude), History of Art, Faculty of Fine Arts, University of Barcelona, Spain, 1993. Appointments: Director General, Jordan National Gallery of Fine Arts, 2002-. Publications: Numerous articles in professional journals around the world. Honours: First Prize, Joan Miro International Contest, Spanish Arab Institute, Madrid, Spain, 1985. Memberships: Art Reach Foundation; Noor Al Hussein Foundation; Jordanian-Spanish Friendship Association. Address: The Jordan National Gallery of Fine Arts, Jabal al Weibdeh, PO Box 9068, Amman 11191, Jordan. E-mail: k.khreis@nationalgallery.org Website: www.nationalgallery.org

KHURRAM SIDIKI Mohammad, b. 1 November 1976, Pakistan. Business Manager. m. Shagufta. Education: Intermediate, Engineering, PECHS Education Foundation College, 1994; BBA (Hons), American University in London, 1997; MBA, Finance, University of Sindh, Jamshoro, 1999. Appointments: Group Sales Manager, Hira Enterprises; Remittance Officer, Dubai Islamic Bank, 2007-08; Account Assistant, 1999-2007, Account Supervisor, 2008-10, Store Supervisor, Foreign Purchases (Technical), 2010-, Store Supervisor, Procurement Management, 2010-, Pakistan International Airlines Corporation. Address: A-216, W C H Society, Near K E S C Power House, Gulshan e Iqbal Bl-19, Karachi, Pakistan. E-mail: khurram11176@hotmail.com

KHURRAM SIDIKI Shagufta, b. 5 November 1978, Pakistan. Teacher. m. Muhammad Khurram Sidiki. Education: BSc, 1st Class, 1998, MA, 2nd class, English, 2003, M Ed, Shah Abdul Latif University, Khairpur; B Ed, University of Karachi. Appointments: English and Science Teacher, Iqra Public School, Gambat, 1998-2000; Language Instructor, Domino English Learning Centre, Gulshan-e-Iqbal Campus, 3 years; Lecturer, Department of English, Government Islamia Degree Science College, Karachi, 1 year; Senior English Teacher, BPS-17, SMI College. Address: A-216 WCH Society, BL-19 Gulshane Iqbal, Near KESC Power House, Karachi, Pakistan. E-mail: khurram11176@hotmail.com

KHURSHID Syed Javaid, b. 8 February 1951, Karachi, Pakistan. Scientist. m. Safoora, 1 son, 2 daughters. Education: BSc (Hons), 1972; MSc, 1973; MS, 1977; PhD, 1993. Appointments: Executive Secretary, INSC, PAEC; Director of Projects, Director of Biosciences, Chief Scientist, PAEC. Publications: 55 articles in professional journals. Honours: FPPS. Memberships: Pakistan Chemical Society; Pakistan Pharmacology Society; Pakistan Nuclear Society; Pakistan

Biosafety Association. Address: International Nathiagali Summer College, PO Box 1114, Islamabad, Pakistan. E-mail: syedjkhurshid@ballstate.bsu.edu

KHUTORYANSKIY Vitaliy, b. 1 May 1975, Almaty, Kazakhstan. Lecturer. m. Olga, 1 son. Education: BSc, 1996, MSc, 1998, Kazakh State National University; PhD, Kazakh National Technical University, 2000; PGCAP, University of Reading, England, 2008. Appointments: Senior Lecturer, Polymer Chemistry, Kazak National University, Kazakhstan, 2001-02; Postdoctoral Research Fellow, University of Strathclyde, Scotland, 2002-04; Postdoctoral Research Associate, University of Manchester, England, 2004-05; Lecturer, Pharmaceutics, 2005-10, Reader in Pharmaceutical Materials, 2010-, University of Reading, England. Publications: 1 edited book; 6 review articles; 77 original research papers in peer-reviewed journals. Honours: Research funding in excess of £1million. Memberships: Royal Society of Chemistry; Academy of Pharmaceutical Sciences; Higher Education Academy. Address: Reading School of Pharmacy, University of Reading, Whiteknights, PO Box 224, Reading, RG6 6AD, England.

KIDD Jodie, b. 25 September 1978, Canterbury, England. Fashion Model. Education: St Michael's School, W Sussex. Appointments: Modelled for numerous fashion magazines, also top international catwalk model for designers include: Gucci, Prada, Karl Lagerfeld, Yves Saint Laurent, Chanel, John Galliano, Calvin Klein, Yohji Yamamoto; Make-up Model for Chanel, 1999 season. Honours: Former National Junior Athletics Champion; Holder, Under 15s High Jump Record for Sussex; Many awards as junior show jumper. Address: c/o IMG Models, Bentinck House, 3-8 Bolsover Street, London, W1P 7HG, England.

KIDMAN Fiona (Judith) (Dame), b. 26 March 1940, Hawera, New Zealand. Writer; Poet. m. Ernest Ian Kidman, 1960, 1 son, 1 daughter. Appointments: Founding Secretary/Organiser, New Zealand Book Council, 1972-75; Secretary, 1972-76, President, 1981-83, New Zealand Centre, PEN; President, 1992-95, President of Honour, 1997-, New Zealand Book Council. Publications: Novels: A Breed of Women, 1979; Mandarin Summer, 1981; Paddy's Puzzle, 1983, US edition as In the Clear Light, 1985; The Book of Secrets, 1987; True Stars, 1990; Ricochet Baby, 1996; The House Within, 1997; Songs from the Violet Café, 2003; The Captive Wife, 2005. Short stories: Unsuitable Friends, 1988; The Foreign Woman, 1994; The Best of Fiona Kidman's Short Stories, 1998; A Needle in the Heart, 2002; Songs from the Violet Café, 2003; The Best New Zealand Fiction, 2004, 2005. Poetry: Honey and Bitters, 1975; On the Tightrope, 1978; Going to the Chathams, Poems: 1977-1984, 1985; Wakeful Nights: Poems Selected and New, 1991; Other: Search for Sister Blue (radio play), 1975; Gone North (with Jane Ussher), 1984; Wellington (with Grant Sheehan), 1989; Palm Prints (autobiographical essays), 1995; New Zealand Love Stories: An Oxford Anthology (editor), Best New Zealand Fiction, 1999. Contributions to: Periodicals. Honours: Scholarships in Letters, 1981, 1985, 1991, 1995; Mobil Short Story Award, 1987; Queen Elizabeth II Arts Council Award for Achievement, 1988; Officer of the Order of the British Empire, 1988; Victoria University Writing Fellowship, 1988; President of Honour, New Zealand Book Council, 1997; Dame Companion of the New Zealand Order of Merit, for services to literature, 1998. Memberships: International PEN; Media Women; New Zealand Book Council, president, 1992-95; Patron, Cambodia Trust Aotearoa. Address: 28 Rakau Road, Hataitai, Wellington 3, New Zealand.

KIDMAN Nicole, b. 20 June 1967, Hawaii, USA, Australian nationality. Actress. m. (1) Tom Cruise, 1990, divorced 2001, 1 adopted son, 1 adopted daughter, (2) Keith Urban, 2006, 2 daughters. Education: St Martin's Youth Theatre, Melbourne; Australian Theatre for Young People, Sydney. Appointments: Goodwill Ambassador, UNICEF. Acting début in Australian film aged 14; Actress, TV mini-series, Vietnam, 1987; Bangkok Hilton, 1989. Creative Works: Films: The Emerald City; The Year My Voice Broke; Flirting; Dead Calm, Days of Thunder, 1990; Billy Bathgate, 1991; Far and Away, 1992; Malice, My Life, 1993; Batman Forever, To Die For, 1995; Portrait of a Lady, 1996; The Peacemaker, Eyes Wide Shut, 1998; Practical Magic, 1999; The Others, 2000; Moulin Rouge, Birthday Girl, The Hours, 2001; Dogville, Cold Mountain, The Human Stain, Birth, 2003; The Interpreter, Alexander the Great, 2004; Bewitched, 2005; Fur: An Imaginary Portrait of Diane Arbus, Happy Feet, 2006; The Invasion, His Dark Materials: The Golden Compass, Margot at the Wedding, 2007; Australia, 2008; Nine, 2009; Rabbit Hole, 2010; Just Go With It, Monte Carlo, Trespass, 2011; Hemingway & Gellhorn, The Paperboy, 2012; Stoker, 2013; Play: The Blue Room, 1998-99. Honours: Best Actress Award, Australian Film Institute; Actress of the Year, Australia; Seattle International Film Festival Award, 1995; London Film Critics Award, 1996; Best Actress, Golden Globe Award, 1996; BAFTA Nominee, 1996; Best Actress in a Musical, Golden Globe Award, 2001; Best Dramatic Actress, Golden Globe Award, 2003; BAFTA Award for Best Actress in a Leading Role, 2003; Academy Award for Best Actress, 2003. Address: c/o Ann Churchill-Brown, Shanahan Management, PO Box 478, Kings Cross, NSW 2011, Australia.

KILMER Val, b. 31 December 1959, Los Angeles, USA. Actor. m. Joanne Whalley, divorced, 1 son, 1 daughter. Education: Hollywood's Professional's School; Juilliard. Creative Works: Stage appearances include: Electra and Orestes, Henry IV Part One, 1981; As You Like It, 1982; Slab Boys, 1983; Hamlet, 1988; Tis Pity She's A Whore, 1992; TV Films: Top Secret, 1984; Real Genius, 1985; Top Gun, 1986; Willow, 1988; Kill Me Again, 1989; The Doors, Thunderheart, 1991; True Romance, The Real McCoy, Tombstone, 1993; Wings of Courage, Batman Forever, Heat, 1995; The Saint, The Island of Dr Moreau, The Ghost and the Darkness, Dead Girl, 1996; Joe the King, 1999; Pollock, Red Planet, 2000; The Salton Sea, Run for the Money, 2002; Masked and Anonymous, Wonderland, The Missing, 2003; Spartan, Mind Hunters, Alexander, 2004; Kiss, Kiss, Bang, Bang, 2005; Moscow Zero, 10th & Wolf, Played, Summer Love, Déjà vu, The Ten Commandments: The Musical, 2006; Delgo, Have Dreams, Will Travel, 2007; Conspiracy, Columbus Day, Alpha Numeric, 2008; Streets of Blood, American Cowslip, The Thaw, 2009. Address: c/o CAA, 9830 Wilshire Boulevard, Beverly Hills, CA 90212, USA.

KIM Bong-Hyun, b. 17 May 1967, Seoul, Korea. Doctor. m. Young-Ah Oh, 2 sons. Education: MD, 1991, PhD, 2003, Chung-Ang University Medical School, Seoul, Korea; Fellowship, Harvard Medical School, Boston, USA, 2004-05. Appointments: Director, Department of Ophthalmology, St Columban's Hospital, Mokpo, Republic of Korea, 1996-99; President, HenAm Kim Eye Center, Haenam, Republic of Korea, 1997-2007; Fellow, Massachusetts Eye and Ear Infirmary, Boston, Massachusetts, USA, 2004-05; President, Seer & Partner Eye Institute, Seoul, Republic of Korea, 2007-. Publications: Lightless cataract surgery using a near-infrared operating microscope, 2006; Virtual training tool, 2006; Spontaneous cilia in the caractous lens, 2006. Honours: Winner, Film Festival, American Society of Cataract and Refractive Surgery, 2006 and 2007; Second Prize, European Society of Cataract and Refractive Surgery, 2006. Memberships: American Society of Cataract and Refractive Surgery; Korean Medical Association; American Academy of Ophthalmology; European Society of Cataract and Refractive Surgery. Address: 586-9 Sinsa-Dong, Kangnam-Gu, Seoul 135-892, South Korea. E-mail: nunsusul@yahoo.co.kr Website: www.seereye.org

KIM Byung Ki, b. 25 March 1962, Bonghwa Gun, Republic of Korea. Research Scientist. m. Myeong Ja Choi, 1 son, 1 daughter. Education: Bachelor, Agriculture, National Suncheon University, 1987; Master, Agriculture, National Suncheon University Graduate School, 1990; Doctor, Agriculture, National Gyeongsang University Graduate School, 1994; Master, Public Administration, National Andong University Graduate School, 2005; Doctor, Public Administration, Dongyang University Graduate School, 2011. Appointments: Dairy Farming Team Leader, Haetae Dairy Food Co, 1996-97; Contract Research Worker, National Institute of Animal Science, Rural Development Administration, 1990-95; Part-time Instructor, Sangju University, Department of Animal Husbandry, 2000-03; Expert Instructor, Agriculture CEO Course, Korean Native Cattle Class, Andong University, 2005-; Expert Instructor, Gyeongbuk Farmers Academy Course, Korean Native Cattle Class, Yeongnam University, 2005-. Publications: Numerous articles in professional journals. Honours: Up-to-date Knowledge Public Official, 2002, Outstanding Public Official, 2007, Secretary of Ministry of Public Administration and Security Award; Grand Prize Public Official, Gyeongsangbuk-do Governor, 2007; Over 70 TV appearances; Numerous articles in local/national newspapers. Memberships: Korean Society for Food Science of Animal Resources; Korean Society for Animal Science Technology. Address: Gyeongsangbukdo Livestock Research Institution, 275 Mookri Anjung-myeon, Yeongju, Gyeongsangbuk-do, 750-871, Republic of Korea. E-mail: bkkim017@korea.kr

KIM Byung Woon, b. 23 July 1967, Gohung, Jeonla-namdo, Republic of Korea. Research Scientist. m. Michelle, 1 son, 1 daughter. Education: PhD, Economics, Chosun University, 2000. Appointments: Principal Researcher/Head of Team, Electronics and Telecommunications Research Institute, 2000-. Publications: Economic analysis of the introduction of the MVNO system and its major implications for optimal policy decisions in Korea, 2007. Honours: Letter of Commendation, Korea Communications Commission, 2008. Memberships: Referee, Telecommunications Policy. Address: Electronics and Telecommunications Research Institute, Regulatory Policy Research Team, 138 Gajeongno, Yuseong-gu, Daejeon 305-700, Republic of Korea. E-mail: bukim@etri.re.kr

KIM Byung-Nam, b. 6 April 1962, Seoul, South Korea. Researcher. m. Eun-Kyung Lee, 1 son, 1 daughter. Education: Bachelor's degree, Yonsei University, Korea, 1986; Master's degree, 1989, Doctor's degree, 1992, University of Tokyo, Japan. Appointments: Researcher, 1992-93, Research Associate, 1995-98, University of Tokyo; Research Associate, Tokyo Metropolitan University, 1993-95; Senior Researcher, National Institute for Materials Science, 1998-; Visiting Scholar, University of Pennsylvania, USA, 2003-04. Publications: Articles and papers in professional scientific journals. Honours: Paper Award, 1994, Meritorious Honor Award, 2003, Japan Institute of Metals. Memberships: Japan Institute of Metals; Commendation for Science and Technology, Minister of Education, Culture, Sports, Science and Technology, Prizes for Science and Technology, 2007. Address: National Institute for Materials Science, 1-2-1 Sengen, Tsukuba, Ibaraki 305-0047, Japan. E-mail: kim.byung-nam@nims.go.jp

KIM Cherl-Jin, b. 10 May 1958, Jinju, Korea. Professor; Engineering Educator. m. Il-Sim Lee, 1983, 1 son, 1 daughter. Education: Bachelor's degree, 1980, Master's degree, 1983, PhD, 1991, Electrical Engineering, Hanyang University, Seoul. Appointments: Engineer, Korea Electrical Power Co, Seoul, 1979-82; Professional certifications, Electrical Engineers (1st class), Republic of Korea, 1981; Board Member, Director, Korean Institute of Electrical Engineering, Korea, 2002-11; Expert Adviser, Korea Government Gwacheon-si, Gyeonggi-do, Korea, 2003-11. Publications: Research, Design of Power LED Drive Circuit with Constant Current Control; Author, Scitechmedia, 2002; Author, Journal of Electrical Engineering & Technology, 2011. Honours: Appreciation Plaque, MOPAS, 2009; Academic Award, KIEE, 2010. E-mail: cjkim018@hotmail.com

KIM Choongsoo, b. 6 June 1947, Seoul, Republic of Korea. Central Banker. m. Ju Hea Hwang, 1 daughter. Education: BA, Economics, Seoul National University, 1973; PhD, Economics, University of Pennsylvania, USA, 1979. Appointments: Military Service, 1968-71; Senior Research Associate, Ohio State University, USA, 1979-83; Associate Research Fellow, 1983-84, Research Fellow, 1985-88, Director, Research Planning and Co-ordination, 1988, Senior Fellow, 1989, Director, Center for Economic Education, 1991-93, President, 2002-05, Korea Development Institute; Vice President, National Institute for Economic System and Information, 1989-91; Secretary to the President for Economic Affairs, Office of the President, 1993-95; Minister and Head, OECD Office, Korean Embassy in Paris, 1995-97; Assistant Minister and Special Adviser to the Deputy Prime Minister, Ministry of Finance and Economy, 1997; President, Korea Institute of Public Finance, 1997-98; Dean, 1998-2000, Professor, 1998-2002, Professor, 2005-07, GSP, Kyung Hee University; President, Hallym University, 2007-08; Senior Secretary to the President for Economic Affairs, Office of the President, 2008; Ambassdor and Permanent Representative of the Republic of Korea to the OECD, 2008-10; Governor of the Bank of Korea, 2010-. Publications: Numerous articles in professional journals. Honours: Civil Merit Medal, 1987; Order of Civil Merit, 1992. Address: The Bank of Korea, 39 Namdaemunno, Jung-Gu, Seoul 100-794, Korea.

KIM Dae-Soung, b. 22 December 1959, Seoul, Korea. Professor. m. Young-Sook Kwon, 1 son, 1 daughter. Education: BA, 1983, MA, 1985, Kwangwon National University, South Korea; PhD, Georgia State University, USA, 1995. Appointments: Research Assistant, Georgia State University, 1990-95; Postdoctoral, Pohang University, 1995-97; Postdoctoral, KAIST, 1995-97; Research Scholar, Clark Atlanta University, 1999-2000; Professor, Gyenggi College of Science and Technology, 2003-. Publications: Numerous articles in professional journals. Honours: Research Fund, Korea Research Foundation, 1997, 2000, 2006, 2007; Research Fund, Korea Science and Engineering Foundation, 2005. Memberships: American Physical Society; Korean Physical Society; Korea Academia-Industrial Co-operation Society. Address: Department of e-Business, Fyongai College of Science and Technology, Jungwong-Dong 2121-3, 429-450, Siheong, Gyonggi-PO, South Korea. E-mail: dskim@gtec.ac.kr

KIM Daesik, b. 14 June 1974, Seoul, Republic of Korea. Professor. Education: PhD, Mechanical Engineering, 2005. Appointments: Post-doctoral Researcher, Penn State University, USA; Senior Researcher, Samsung, Korea; Assistant Professor, Gangwon Provincial College, Korea. Publications: More than 50 research papers. Honours: Best Dissertation Award. Memberships: ASME; KSME; KOSCO. Address: 115, Kyohangro, Jumunjin, Gangneung, Gangwon 210-804, Republic of Korea. E-mail: dskim@gw.ac.kr Website: www.gw.ac.kr

KIM Dong Chung, b. 4 December 1967, Jeju, Republic of Korea. Professor. m. Yoon Jeong Hwang, 1 son. Education: Bachelor, 1990, Master, 1992, Yonsei University; PhD, Seoul National University, 2003. Appointments: Assistant Professor, Suncheong First College, 2000-07; Visiting Scholar, Cambridge University, 2006-07; Research Associate Professor, Sungkyunkwan University, 2007-09; Assistant Professor, Chungwoon University, 2009-. Publications: Journal of the American Oil Chemists' Society, 2009; Journal of Medicinal Food, 2010; Journal of Ginseng Research, 2010; Plant Foods for Human Nutrition, 2011. Honours: Small and Medium Business Administration Award, 2002; Chungwoon Distinguished Scholar Award, 2011. Memberships: Korean Society of Ginseng; Korean Society of Biotechnology and Bioengineering. Address: San 29, Namjang-ri, Hongseong-eup, Hongseong, Chungnam 350-701, Republic of Korea. E-mail: kimdc@chungwoon.ac.kr

KIM Dong Hyeon, b. 16 May 1962, Busan-city, Korea. Researcher; Engineering Educator. m. Hye-Jeong Kang, 2 sons. Education: Bachelor, 1986, Master, 1988, Mechanical Engineering, Chung-Ang University, Seoul; PhD, Mechanical Engineering, Seoul National University, 1993. Appointments: Senior Researcher, Vehicle Aerodynamics, Institute for Advanced Engineering, Seoul, 1994-95; Senior Researcher, Heat and Fluid Flow, Research Institute of Industrial Science and Technology, Pohang, 1995-96; Principal Researcher, Railroad Environment Research Department, Korea Railroad Research Institute, Uiwang, 1996-; Adjunct Professor, Mechanical Engineering Department, Chung-Ang University, Seoul, 2005-07; Visiting Professor, Mining Engineering Department, Colorado School of Mines, USA, 2007-08; Adjunct Professor, Department of Rolling Stock System, Graduate School of Railroad, Seoul National University of Technology, Seoul, 2009-. Publications: 43 papers; 16 reports; 22 patents. Honours: Three Minister's Prizes, Ministry of Construction & Transportation, 1999, 2003, 2005; President's Award, Industrial Property Right, 2003, President's Award, Contribution to Research Funds, 2003, Korea Railroad Research Institute; President's Award, Korea Institute of Contruction & Transportation, 2007; Listed in international biographical dictionaries. Memberships: Korean Society of Mechanical Engineers; Korean Society of Civil Engineers; Korean Society of Hazard Mitigation; Korean Society for Railway; Korean Tunnelling Association; Fire Investigation Society of Korea; Korea Disaster Prevention Association; Judging and Screening Committee, Railway Construction, Ministry of Land, Transport and Maritime Affairs, Korea; Public Enterprise Performance Evaluation Committee, Ministry of Strategy and Finance, Korea. Address: #503, Poonglim 2(I)-cha Apt, 104, Samseong-dong, Gangnam-gu, Seoul 135-090, Republic of Korea. E-mail: dhkim0516@gmail.com

KIM Dong Hyun, b. 17 January 1978, Seoul, Korea. Research Engineer. m. Hyun Joo Lee, 1 daughter. Education: PhD, Hanyang University, Seoul, 2007. Appointments: POSCO R&D, 2007-. Publications: 32 articles in professional journals; More than 20 patents. Honours: Best Graduation Essay, Hanyang University. Memberships: Korea Metal and Materials Society. Address: 1 Goedong-dong, Nam-gu, Pohang, Gyeongbuk 790-300, Korea. E-mail: dhk@posco.com

KIM Dong-Won, b. 13 January 1956, Seoul, Republic of Korea. Professor. m. Hwa-Yeong Lee, 1 son, 1 daughter. Education: Bachelor's degree, Department of Materials Engineering, Hanyang University, 1980; Unified Master's and Doctor's degree, Department of Materials Engineering, Korea Advanced Institute of Science and Technology, 1988. Appointments: Manager, Process Development Team, LG Semiconductor, 1988-91; Professor, Advanced Materials Engineering, 1991-, Head Professor, Renewable Energy & Fusion Technology Research Center, 2006-11, Associate Dean, Industrial University Co-operation Foundation, 2007-11, Kyonggi University; Consultant, Jusung Engineering Co Ltd, 1994-; Consultant, Samhan Electronics, 2004-; Consultant, DSLCD Co Ltd, 2008-; Consultant, Will Technology Co Ltd, 2010-; Consultant, Aegisco Co Ltd, 2010-. Publications: Numerous articles in professional journals, papers and patents. Honours: Prize for Patent Application, LG Semiconductor, 1989; 1st Sosung Academic Award, 1994; Outstanding Research Results Best 50, Ministry of Science and Technology, 2006; Prize for operational performance of business incubating center, Gyeonggi Provincial Government, 2010; Listed in international biographical dictionaries. Memberships: Materials Research Society of Korea; Korean Institute of Chemical Engineers; Bulgok Middle School Steering Committee; Bundang High School Steering Committee; National Industrial Security Center; Business Support Committee of Suwon-Si; Korea Venture Business Association. Address: 207-1501 Mujigaemaeul LG Apt Gumi-dong, Bundang-gu, Seongnam-si, Gyeonggi-do, 463-705, Republic of Korea. E-mail: dwkim@kgu.ac.kr

KIM Eung-ki (Monk Beob Hyeon), b. 20 June 1964, Seoul, Korea. Buddhist Monk. Education: Master's degree, Buddhist Historical Science, MA, Science of Religion, Dongguk University, 1995; PhD, Science of Religion, Wongwang University. Appointments: Entered Buddhist Priesthood, Bongwon temple, 1974; Professor, Korean Traditional Music Department, Dongguk University; No 50th Human Cultural Asset of Complete of Buddhist Chanting and Dance; UNESCO World Heritage Yeongsanjae Planning Republic Relations Executive; Special Assistant, Korean Taego Buddhist Order Cultural Art Department, Research Institute of Buddhist Music; Representative of the World Culture and Art Contents Exchange Federation; Special Secretary, Culture and Art Department,Korea Buddhism Taego Buddhist Order Affairs; Expert Advisor, Korean Music, Cultural Properties Protection Committee. Publications: 4 books on Buddhist Music and Dance; 43 theses; Founder of Gakpil Score; Numerous articles in professional journals. Website: www.pompae.or.kr

KIM Hae-Young, b. 15 November 1966, Korea. Dental Public Health. m. Jin-Young Choi, 1 son, 1 daughter. Education: BA, School of Dentistry, 1989, Master, 1998, PhD, 2002, Biostatistics, School of Public Health, Seoul National University; Post-doctoral Fellow, Department of Dental Ecology, School of Dentistry, University of North Carolina at Chapel Hill, USA, 2003-05. Appointments: Dentist, Gunpo Dental Clinic, Anyang, Korea, 1991-97; Adjunct Associate Professor, Department of Dental Ecology, School of Dentistry, University of North Carolina at Chapel Hill, 2005-08; Senior Researcher, Dental Research Institute, School of Dentistry, Seoul National University, 2006-08; Assistant Professor,

Department of Dental Hygiene, College of Health Science, Eulji University, 2009-10; Assistant Professor, Department of Dental Laboratory Science & Engineering, College of Health Science, Korea University, 2010-. Publications: Numerous articles in professional journals. Honours: Best Dissertation Award, 2002; Best Poster Award, 2006. Memberships: International Association of Dental Research; Korean Academy of Oral Health; Korean Association for Survey Research. Address: Department of Dental Laboratory Science & Engineering, College of Health Science, Korea University, San 1 Geongnung-3-dong, Seongbuk-gu, Seoul 136-703, Korea. E-mail: kimhaey@korea.ac.kr

KIM Hyung Hun, b. 31 January 1974, Kwang-Ju, South Korea. Gastroenterology. m. 1 son. Education: BSc, 1994, MD, 1998, Cheonnam National University; MSc, Medicine, Sungkyunkwan University Graduate School of Medicine, 2004; Graduate Degree in Law, Academic Credit Bank System, Ministry of Education, 2005; Medical MBA, Advanced Course for Pharmaceutical Medicine, Seoul National University, 2008. Appointments: Intern, Cheonnam National University, 1998-99; Resident, Samsung Seoul Hospital, 1998-2002; Epidemic Intelligence Service Officer Membership course, Korea Centers for Disease Control and Prevention, 2003-05; Internal Medicine Director, Young Clinic, Seoul, 2006-07; Medical Manager, Clinical Trial, Allergan, Seoul, 2007-09; Full time Instructor, Gastroenterology, 2010-, Board Member, Clinical Research Center, 2011-, Kosin University College of Medicine, Busan; Board Member, Education Department, Korean Society of Neurogastroenterology and Motility, Seoul, 2011-; Board Member, Korean Natural Orifice Trans-luminal Endoscopic Surgery, Seoul, 2011-; IRB Member, Kosin University, Busan, 2011-. Publications: Numerous articles in professional journals. Honours: 1st Prize, Korean University Student Academic Essay Contest, 1996; Excellent Resident Prize, Samsung Medical Center, 2001; Excellent Epidemic Intelligence Service Officer Prize, 2006; Best Clinical Research Performance Prize, BPH Phase III Clinical Trial, 2008; Japanese Society of Gastroenterology Research Fellowship Award, 2011; Gold Medal for Korea, 2011. Memberships include: Korean NOTES; Japanese Society of Gastroenterology; Korean Society of Gastroenterology; Helicobacter Research Society; Korean Board of Internal Medicine. Address: Shinbanpo Hanshin Apt 117-103, Jamwon-dong, Seocho-gu, Seoul, Korea. E-mail: drhhkim@gmail.com

KIM Jae Hee, b. 11 September 1956, Kangneung, Kangwondo, Korea. Mechanical Engineer; Researcher. m. Sun Mee Cho, 1 son, 2 daughters. Education: BS, 1980, MS, 1982, Seoul National University, Seoul, Korea; PhD, Korea Advanced Institute of Science and Technology, Taejon, Korea, 1992. Appointments: Project Manager, Korea Atomic Energy Research Institute, Taejon, Korea, 1983-2005; Visiting Scholar, Center of International Co-operation for Computerization, Tokyo, Japan, 1994; Associate Professor, Chungnam University, Taejon, Korea, 1995-2002; Guest Associate Professor, Korea University, Seoul, Korea, 1996-97; Visiting Scholar, University of California Irvine, USA, 2007-08. Publications: Laser-guided underwater wall climbing robot for reactor vessel inspection (patent); An improved dead-reckoning scheme for a mobile robot using neural networks (paper). Honour: Scientist of the Month Award, Korea Science and Engineering Foundation, 2003. Memberships: Fellow Institute of Control, Automation and Systems Engineers, Korea; The Korean Society of Systems Engineers. Address: 304-1301 Mockryun Apt., Dunsandong, Seogu, Taejon, Republic of Korea. E-mail: jaehkim@kaeri.re.kr

KIM Jae Hoon, b. 21 June 1963, Korea. Plastic & Reconstructive Surgeon. Education: Korean Medical Licence, 1988; Korean Plastic Surgeon Board Certification, 1993. Appointments: Full-time Research and Clinical Fellow, Department of Plastic Surgery, Soonchunhyang Medical College Hospital, Seoul, 1996-98; Full-time Instructor, Department of Plastic Surgery, College of Medicine, Soonchunhyang University, Seoul, 1998-2000; Director of Clinic, Kim Jae-Hoon Aesthetic Plastic Surgery Clinic, Seoul, 2000-06; Chief Director of Clinic, April 31 Aesthetic Plastic Surgery Clinic, Seoul, 2006-. Publications: Blessed Book (Parto f Physiognomic Plastic Surgery. Honours: Grand Prize, 68th Korean Society of Plastic Surgery. Memberships: Korean Society of Rhinoplasty Surgeons; Korean Medical Association; Korean Society of Plastic and Reconstructive Surgery; Korean Society of Aesthetic Plastic Surgery; Korean Association of Plastic Surgeon; International Society of Plastic and Reconstructive Surgery. Address: April 31 Aesthetic Plastic Surgery Clinic, Keon-Woo B/D, 120 Nonhyun-Dong, Kangnam-Ku, Seoul 135-010, Korea.

KIM Jae-Kwan, b. 1 July 1969, Chung-buk, South Korea. Researcher. m. Hye-Jeong Kim, 2 sons. Education: D Eng, Chemical Engineering, Korea University, 2000. Appointments: Researcher, R&D on Flue Gas Desulfurization Technology, KEPRI, KEPCO, 1994-2000; Assistant Manager, R&D for recycling of coal by-product, KEPRI, 2001-08; Assistant Director, R&D for combustion of renewable waste at coal power plant, KEPRI, 2009-. Publications: Numerous articles in professional journals. Honours: R&D Awards, KEPRI, 2000/05; Listed in international biographical dictionaries. Memberships: Korean Society of Industrial and Engineering Chemistry; Japan Society of Chemical Engineering; Korean Society of Waste Management. Address: Korea Electric Power Research Institute, Munji-Ro 65, Yusung-Gu, Daejon, 305-380, Republic of Korea. E-mail: jkkim@kepri.re.kr

KIM Jaemin, b. 7 July 1974, Seoul, Korea. m. Hyojung Yu, 2 sons. Professor. Educaiton: MD, 2001, Master, 2005, PhD, 2010, Rehabilitation Medicine, Medical College, Catholic University, Seoul. Appointments: Resident, Department of Rehabilitation Medicine, Catholic Medical Center, 2002-06; Clinical Fellowship, Korea University, Guro Hospital, Seoul, 2006-07; Assistant Professor, Department of Rehabilitation Medicine, 2007-. Publications: Scientific articles; Translation for text of ultrasound and musculoskeletal disease. Honours: Annual Meeting, Korean Association of EMH Electrodiagnostic Medicine, 2008; Annual Meeting, Korean Academy of Neuromusculoskeletal Sonography. Memberships: Korean Association of Rehabilitation Medicine; Korean Academy of Neuromusculoskeletal Sonography; Korean Association of Pain Medicine; Korean Society of Sports Medicine; Korean Academy of Medical Sciences. Address: Incheon St Mary's Hospital, #665 Bupyeong 6-Dong, Bupyeong Gu, Incheon 403-702, Republic of Korea.

KIM Jong-Un, b. 8 January 1984, North Korea. Military Leader. Education: Kim Il Sung Military University, Pyongyang. Appointments: Member, Central Committee, Workers' Party of Korea, 2010-; Vice Chairman, Central Military Commission, Workers' Party of Korea, 2010-; Four-Star General, Korean People's Army, 2010-; Supreme Commander, Korean People's Army, 2011-. Honours: Named one of the 10 Most Influential People in the World, Time magazine, 2010. Address: Workers' Party of Korea, Central Military Commission, Pyongyang, Democratic Peoples Republic of Korea.

KIM Jongwan, b. 9 October 1966, Republic of Korea. Research Professor. m. Education: BS, Business Administration, Sahmyook University, 1991; Engineer, Information Processing, Human Resources Development Service of Korea, 1996; Advanced Technical Expert and Advanced Auditor, Information and Communication, Korea Information & Communication Contractors Association, 2008; Technical Specialist on Software Development, Ministry of Knowledge Economy, 2009; MS, Software Engineering, Soongsil University, 2001; PhD, Distributed Systems, Korea University, 2007. Appointments: Freelancer, Project Manager, Information System Development, Josetongram Co, 1994-96; Lecturer & S/W Developer, Jeil Information and Communication Institute, 1996-2001; S/W Developer, JungPyung Mobile and Computer Co Ltd, 2002-03; Researcher, Research Institute of Computer Information and Communication Lab, 2003-07; Postdoctoral Researcher, 2007-08, Research Professor, 2008-09, Konkuk University; Research Professor, Sahmyook University, 2009-11; Researcher, University of New South Wales, Australia, 2011-. Publications: Numerous articles in professional journals on spatial data compression technology in location-based services; Numerous projects on Spatial data compression scheme, RFID middleware and Mobile games. Honours: Endeavour Awards, 2011; Listed in international biographical dictionaries. E-mail: wany@korea.ac.kr Website: www.phdkorea.com

KIM Kisun, b. 14 February 1962, Busan, Republic of Korea. Professor. m. Misun Lee, 1 son, 1 daughter. Education: Bachelor, Business Administration, Sogang University, 1985; Master, 1989, PhD, 1993, International Trade, Graduate School of Sogang University. Appointments: Professor, Department of International Trade, Kunsan National University; Director, Korean Research Institute of International Trade; President, Korean Association of Regional Development; Visiting Scholar, Southeast Missouri State University; Arbitrator, Korean Commercial Arbitration Board. Publications: Numerous articles in professional journals. Honours: Listed in biographical dictionaries. Address: 1170 Daihakro, Miryong-dong, Department of International Trade, Kunsan National University, Kunsan City, 573-701, Republic of Korea. E-mail: kks@kunsan.ac.kr

KIM Kwan-Sik, b. 30 July 1963, Namwon, Jeonbuk, Republic of Korea. Medical Doctor. m. Kyeong-Sik Kim, 2 sons. Education: MD, Chonbuk National University, 1987; PhD, Chonnam National University, 2000; Postdoctoral, Lerner Research Institute, Cleveland Clinic Foundation, USA, 2002-04. Appointments: Professor, Chonbuk National University Medical School, 1995-2008; Director, Department of Education and Research, Chonbuk National University Hospital, 2006-08; Director, GYN Women's Clinic, Jeonju. Publications: Numerous articles in professional journals. Memberships: Korean Medical Association; Korean Cancer Association; Korean Association of Obstetrics & Gynaecology. Address: GYN Women's Clinic, 700-1 Jungwhasandong, Wansangu, Jeonju, Jeonbuk, Republic of Korea. E-mail: ksjm@chonbuk.ac.kr

KIM Kyoung Soo, b. 15 March 1964, Seoul, Korea. Chief Executive Officer. m. Chun Kyun Park, 2 daughters. Education: BS, Chemistry, Kyung Hee University, Korea, 1986; MS, Chemistry, 1988, PhD, Chemistry, 1990, Korea Advanced Institute of Science and Technology (KAIST). Appointments: Senior Researcher, Korea Research Institute of Chemical Technology, 1990-95; Research Manager, Hanmi Pharmaceutical Co Ltd, 1995-98; Research Director, ChemTech Research Incorporation, 1998-2002; Chief Executive Officer, Chirogenix Co Ltd, 2002-; Advisor, HS Holdings Inc, 2005-. Publications: Numerous articles in professional journals; 59 patents. Honours: Award for Excellence, Kyung Hee University, Korea, 1986; Distinguished Service Award, Korea Research Institute of Chemical Technology, Korea, 1993; Distinguished Service Award, ChemTech Research Incorporation, Korea, 2001; International Order of Merit, IBC, England, 2005; The Order of International Fellowship, IBC, 2005; Lifetime Achievement Award, The World Congress of Arts, Sciences and Communications, England, 2005; The IBC Medal of Honour, IBC, 2005; Year 2005 Universal Award of Accomplishment, ABI, 2005; Top 100 Scientists Pinnacle of Achievement Award, IBC, 2005; 21st Century Award for Achievement, IBC, 2005; IBC Hall of Fame, 2005; IBC's Salute to Greatness Award, 2005; The IBC Meritorious Decoration, IBC, 2005; The Da Vinci Diamond, IBC, 2005; The Order of International Ambassadors, ABI, 2005; IBC Lifetime of Achievement Award, 2005; International Commendation of Success, ABI, 2005; The Key Award, ABI, 2005; American Medal of Honor, ABI, 2005; Decree of Excellence, IBC, 2005; Man of the Year, ABI, 2005; Award for Excellent Venture Entrepreneurs, Gyonggi Regional Service, Small and Medium Business Administration, 2005; International Medal of Vision, ABI, 2006; The Statesmen's Award of Ambassador of Grand Eminence, ABI, 2006; International Cultural Diploma of Honor, ABI, 2006; The Archimedes Award, IBC, 2006; World Lifetime Achievement Award, ABI, 2006; The World Medal of Freedom, ABI, 2006; International Peace Prize, UCC, 2006; Legion of Honor, UCC, 2006; Presidential Citation, The Korea Government, 2006; The Master Diploma, The World Academy of Letters, 2006; Scientist of the Year, IBC, 2006; Leading Scientists of the World, IBC, 2006; American Hall of Fame, ABI, 2006; Order of American Ambassadors, ABI, 2006; Presidential Award, The Korea Government, 2006; New Intelligent Korean of the Year, 2006; Small and Medium Business Administration, 2006; Letter of Commendation, Small and Medium Business Administration, 2006; Listed in numerous national and international biographical directories. Memberships: Life Fellow, Korean Chemical Society, Korea, 1990; Editorial Member, Korea Specialty Chemical Industry Association, 2001; Member, main committee of Clinical Trial Center for Functional Foods, 2004; Member, Venture Enterprises Special Committee, 2005; Regular Member, American Chemical Society, USA, 2005; Life Fellow, International Biographical Association, IBC, 2005; Life Patron, International Biographical Association, IBC, 2005; Member, International Order of Merit, IBC, 2005; Member, Order of International Fellowship, 2005; Member, The Research Board of Advisors, ABI, 2005; Lifetime Deputy Governor, ABI Research Association, USA, 2005; Founding Member, The American Order of Excellence, ABI, 2005; Honorary Director General, IBC, 2006; Deputy Director General, IBC, 2006; Governor, IBA, 2006; Adviser to Director General, IBC, 2006; Senator, World Nations Congress, 2006; Ambassador-General, United Cultural Convention, 2006; Vice-President, The World Congress of Arts, Sciences and Communications, 2006. Address: Celltrion Chemical Research Institute, 7th Floor, Daewoo Frontier Valley 2, 1028 Jung-dong, Giheung-gu, Yongin-si, Geyonggi-Do 446-016, Korea. E-mail: kskimpc@celltrionchem.com

DICTIONARY OF INTERNATIONAL BIOGRAPHY 36th EDITION

KIM Sang Ic, b. 4 July 1969, Seoul, Korea. Research Scientist. m. Eunmee Hong, 1 son. Education: PhD, Biological Sciences, Purdue University, 2006. Appointments: Postdoctoral Researcher, Department of Plant Sciences, University of California at Davis, 2006; Postdoctoral Research Affiliate, Crops Pathology and Genetics Research Unit, USDA-ARS, 2006-. Memberships: American Society of Plant Biologists; Crop Science Society of America. Address: 1305 PES Build, Department of Plant Sciences, University of California at Davis, CA 95616, USA. E-mail: sangkim@ucdavis.edu

KIM Sangeun, b. 16 May 1975, South Korea. Dermatologist. m. Ji-youn Choi, 1 son. Education: Medical Doctor, Dermatologist, 2000. Appointments: Medical Doctor, 2000-. Publications: Numerous articles in professional journals. Memberships: Association of Korean Dermatologists. Address: Yonsei-Zium Dermatologic Clinic, Nogosan-dong, Mapo-gu, Seoul 57-5, Korea. E-mail: expo9406@naver.com

KIM Seon Bong, b. 28 November 1955, Namhae, Gyeongsangnamdo, Republic of Korea. m. Jin Sook Cho, 1 son, 1 daughter. Education: PhD, University of Tokyo, 1985. Appointments: Invited Researcher, National Cancer Research Institute, Japan, 1990-91; Invited Professor, Kyoto University, Japan, 1993; Research Fellow, Institute of Pathology, Case Western Research University, USA, 1993-94; Professor, Department of Food Science & Technology, 1986-, Director, Food Analysis & Inspection Center, 2007-10, Director, Institute of Food Science, 2010-, Pukyong National University. Publications: Seafood Processing & Utilization, 1994; Introduction to Fisheries Processing, 1997; Fisheries Processing, 2003; many others. Honours: Korean Fisheries Society Award, 1988; Foundation for Promotion of Cancer Research Fellowship, 1990; Rotary Yoneyama Memorial Fellowship, 1993; Ochi Young Scholarship Award, 1995. Memberships: Fellow, Korean Academy of Science and Technology; Editor-in-chief, Korean Journal of Fisheries & Aquatic Science. Address: GS 305-403, Yongho-dong, Nam-gu, Busan 608-790, Republic of Korea. E-mail: owlkim@pknu.ac.kr

KIM Seong Hyun, b. 15 August 1965, Busan, Korea. Principal Researcher. m. Young Mi Kim, 1 son, 2 daughters. Education: BS, 1988, PhD, 1998, Physics, Pusan National University; MS, Physics, Oregon State University, USA, 1992. Appointments: Researcher, Dielectric Research Institute, Pusan, 1992-98; Post Doctorate, 1998-99, Principal Researcher, 1999-, Electronics & Telecommunications Research Institute, Daejeon. Publications: 3 articles in professional journals. Honours: Best Paper Award, Pusan National University, 1998; Patent Award (Sejong Daewang Award), Korean Intellectual Property Office, 2006. Memberships: Korean Physical Society; Korean Chemical Society; Polymer Society of Korea; Korean Vacuum Society. Address: 503-102, Jeonmin-Dong, Youseong-Gu, Daejeon, Korea.

KIM Tae Sung, b. 10 January 1967, Seoul, Korea. Associate Professor. m. Jee Yeoun Lee, 2 daughters. Education: Bachelor, Industrial Engineering, Dong Guk University, South Korea, 1991; Master, Industrial & Management Systems Engineering, New Jersey Institute of Technology, USA, 1993; PhD, Industrial Engineering, Louisiana State University, USA, 2000. Appointments: Master Consultant, Samsung SDS, 2001-03; Technical Consultative Professor, Samsung Electronics, Samsung Electro-Mechanics, 2003-08; Associate Professor, Kumoh National Institute of Technology, School of Industrial Engineering, 2003-; Associate Professor, University of Maryland, Baltimore, USA, 2009-10. Publications: Scheduling Optimization for Safety Decommissioning of Research Reactor, 2006; Intelligent Agent for Simultaneous Load Factors of Electric Power Reduction System in Korea, 2009; A Heuristic Approach for Workload Balancing Problems, 2010. Honours: Alpha Pi Mu, National Industrial Engineering Honor Society; Interactive Fuzzy Programming with Two-Phase Approach, Outstanding Research Award, Korean Society of Industrial and Systems Engineering, 2005; Scheduling Optimization for Safety Decommissioning of Research Reactor, Outstanding Research Award, Korea Safety Management & Science. Memberships: Korean Society for Supply Chain Management; Korean Society for Engineering Education; Korean Institute of Industrial Engineers; Korean Operations Research and Management; Science Society; Korea Safety Management & Science; Institute for Operations Research and the Management Sciences. Address: Kumoh National Institute of Technology, School of Industrial Engineering, Global #608, 1 Yangho-dong, Gumi City, Gyung-Buk, 730-710, Republic of Korea.

KIM Yong Jig, b. 26 January 1957, Choongju, Choongbuk, Korea. Professor of Naval Architecture. m. Sung Hee Yoon, 1 son, 1 daughter. Education: Bachelors, 1979; Masters, 1981; PhD, 1985, Seoul National University, Seoul, Korea. Appointments: Chairman of Department of Naval Architecture and Marine Systems Engineering, Pukyong National University, Busan, Korea, 1989-91, 1999-2001; Editorial Director, the Society of Naval Architects of Korea, Seoul, Korea, 2002-05; Full time Lecturer/Professor, Pukyong National University, Busan, Korea, 1984-. Publications: Over 70 technical papers including Numerical Calculation and Experiment of Green Water on the Bow-Deck in Regular Waves, Transactions of the Society of Naval Architects of Korea, 2005. Honours: Excellent Paper Award, the Society of Naval Architects of Korea, 1997; Excellent Paper Award, the Korean Federation of Science and Technology Societies, 2004. Memberships: The Society of Naval Architects and Marine Engineers; Life Member, the Society of Naval Architects of Korea; Life Member, the Korean Society of Ocean Engineers. Address: Department of Naval Architecture and Marine Systems Engineering, Pukyong National University, 599-1 Daeyeon 3-dong, Nam-gu, Busan, 608-737, Republic of Korea. E-mail: yjkim@pknu.ac.kr

KIM Yong-Ku, b. 4 March 1962, Seoul, Korea. Psychiatrist; Educator. m. So-Hyun Choi, 1 son. Education: MD, College of Medicine, 1987, MSc, 1994, PhD, 1998, Psychiatry, Graduate School, Korea University. Appointments: Army Surgeon, 1991-94; Associate Professor, 1996-2005, Professor, Psychiatry, 2005-, College of Medicine, Korea University. Publications: About 200 scientific papers; 8 book chapters. Honours: Dr Paul Janssen Schizophrenia Research Award, 1999; GSK Award, 2008; Astrageneca Award, 2009. Memberships: Collogicum Internationale Neuropsychopharmacology; International Society for Affective Disorder; World Federation Society of Biological Psychiatry. Address: Department of Psychiatry, Korea University, Ansan Hospital, Gojan-Dong, Danwon-gu, Ansan city, Kyunggido, Republic of Korea. E-mail: yongku@korea.ac.kr

KIMM Fiona, b. 24 May 1952, Ipswich, Suffolk, England. Singer (Mezzo Soprano). Education: Royal College of Music, National Opera Studio, London. Appointments: Mezzo Soprano with national and international operatic, oratorio and concert repertoire; Operatic roles include: Sextus (La Clemenza di Tito), Hansel, Orlofsky, Dido (Purcell), Hermia, Julie (Showboat), Olga, Fyodor, Nicklaus,

Baba the Turk, Wife/Sphinx/Doreen (Greek), Rosalind (The Mines of Sulphur), Clairon, Fricka, Mistress Quickly, Azucena, Ulrica, Kabanicha, Jezibaba, Marcellina and Orfeo; Companies include ROH, ENO, Opera North, Scottish Opera, Glyndebourne, COC, ETO, Nationale Reisopera; Major oratorio and concert performances in United Kingdom and abroad; Many contemporary performances including world premieres; Regular broadcaster; Appeared in several TV films; Soloist at prestigious state events. Recordings include: L'Enfance du Christ; Weill's Street Scene; Simon Holt's Canciones; Turnage's Greek; Goldschmidt's Beatrice Cenci; Turnage's Lament for a Hanging Man; Peter Maxwell Davies' Taverner. Address: James Black Management Ltd, The Old Grammar School, High Street, Rye, East Sussex TN31 7JF, England.

KIMURA Atsuo, b. 20 September 1956, Minamiuonuma City, Japan. Professor. m. Ikuko, 3 sons, 1 daughter. Education: Bachelor, 1979, Master, 1981, PhD, 1984, Agriculture, Hokkaido University, Japan. Appointments: Adjunct Lecturer, Hokkaido Prefectural School of Hygiene, 1984; Assistant Professor, 1985, Associate Professor, 1992, Professor, 2001-, Hokkaido University. Publications: More than 100 articles in professional journals. Honours: Excellent Young Scientist, Japanese Society of Applied Glycoscience, 1997. Memberships: Japan Bioscience, Biotechnology and Agrochemistry Society; Japanese Biochemical Society; Japanese Society of Applied Glycoscience; Japanese Society of Carbohydrate Research. E-mail: kimura@abs.agr.hokudai.ac.jp

KIMURA Shigeo, b. 20 May 1950, Ibaraki Prefecture, Japan. University Professor. m. Yukiko Satoh, 1 son. Education: BS, Mechanical Engineering, Waseda University, 1974; MS, 1980, PhD, 1983, Mechanical Engineering, University of Colorado. Appointments: Engineer, Mitsubishi Electric Corporation, 1974-77; Postdoctoral Fellow, University of California, Los Angeles, 1983-85; Researcher, Government Industrial Research Institute, Tohoku, 1985-95; Associate Professor, 1995-96, Professor, 1996-, Kanazawa University. Publications: More than 100 scientific journal papers on research interests including transport processes due to industrial and environmental fluid motions. Honours: Creative Work Award, University of Colorado, 1983; Best Paper Award, Geothermal Research Society of Japan, 1989; Best Paper Award, John Atanasoff Society of Automatic and Informatics, 2010. Memberships: Fellow, Japan Society of Mechanical Engineers; Member, Geothermal Research of Japan; Japan Society of Fluid Mechanics; American Society of Mechanical Engineers. Address: Nagasaka 1-3-18-207, Kanazawa, 921-8112, Japan. E-mail: skimura@t.kanazawa-u.ac.jp

KINDERSLEY Tania, b. 30 January 1967, London, England. Writer. Education: MA, Christ Church, Oxford. Publications: Goodbye, Johnny Thunders, 1997; Don't Ask Me Why, 1998; Elvis Has Left the Building, 2001; Nothing to Lose, 2002. Address: Home Farm, Aboyne, Aberdeenshire AB34 5JP, Scotland. E-mail: pulch66@totalscne.co.uk

KING B B (Riley), b. 16 September 1925, Itta Bena, Mississippi, USA. Singer; Musician (guitar). Musical Education: Self-taught guitar. Career: Performed with the Elkhorn Singers; Played with Sonny Boy Williamson, 1946; Regular broadcast slot, The Sepia Swing Show, Radio WDIA; Averaged 300 performances a year, 1950s-70s; Numerous worldwide tours with wide variety of R&B and pop artistes; Appearances include: Newport Jazz Festival, 1969, 1989; Atlantic City Pop Festival, 1969; Atlanta Pop Festival, 1970; Mar Y Sol Festival, Puerto Rico, 1972; Kool Jazz Festival, New York, 1983; Live Aid concert, Philadelphia, 1985; Benson & Hedges Blues Festival, Dallas, 1989; JVC Jazz Festival, Newport, 1990; Memphis In May Festival, 1991; Montreux Jazz Festival, 1991; San Francisco Blues Festival, 1991; Guitar Legends, Expo '92, Seville, Spain, 1991; Westbury Music Fair, New York, 1993; Pori Jazz, Finland, 1995; Opened B B King's Memphis Blues Club, Memphis, Tennessee, 1991. Recordings: Albums: Completely Well, 1970; The Incredible Soul Of B B King, 1970; Indianola Mississippi Seeds, 1970; Live In Cook County Jail, 1971; Live At The Regal, 1971; B B King In London, 1971; LA Midnight, 1972; Guess Who, 1972; The Best Of.., 1973; To Know You Is To Love You, 1973; Friends, 1974; Lucille Talks Back, 1975; King Size, 1977; Midnight Believer, 1978; Take It Home, 1979; Now Appearing At Ole Miss, 1980; There Must Be A Better World Somewhere, 1982; Love Me Tender, 1982; Blues'n'Jazz, 1984; Six Silver Strings, 1986; Live At San Quentin, 1991; Blues Summit, 1993; Lucille and Friends, 1995; Live in Japan, 1999; with Bobby Bland: Together For The First Time - Live, 1974; Together Again - Live, 1976; Hit singles include: Three O'Clock Blues; You Didn't Want Me; Please Love Me; You Upset Me Baby; Sweet Sixteen; Rock Me Baby; The B B Jones (used in film soundtrack For The Love Of Ivy); The Thrill Is Gone; Blues Come Over Me; Also featured on: Happy Anniversary, Charlie Brown!, 1989; When Love Comes To Town, U2, 1989; Heroes And Friends, Randy Travis, 1990; The Simpsons Sing The Blues, 1990. Honours include: Grammy Awards: Best Male R&B Vocal Performance, 1971; Best Ethnic or Traditional Recording, 1982; Best Traditional Blues Recording, 1984, 1986, 1991, 1992; Inducted into Rock And Roll Hall Of Fame, 1987; Lifetime Achievement Awards include: NARAS, 1988; Songwriters Hall Of Fame, 1990; Gibson Guitars, 1991; Star in Hollywood Walk Of Fame, 1990; MTV Video Award, with U2, 1989; Q Inspiration Award, 1992. Membership: Co-chairman, Foundation for the Advancement of Inmate Rehabilitation and Recreation. Current Management: Sidney A Seidenberg Inc, 1414 6th Avenue, New York, NY 10019, USA.

KING Billie Jean, b. 22 November 1943, California, USA. Tennis Player. m. Larry King, 1965, divorced. Education: Los Angeles State University. Career: Amateur status, 1958-67; Professional, 1967-; Championship Titles: Australia, 1968; South Africa, 1966, 1967, 1969; Wimbledon 20 Titles, 10 doubles, 4 mixed and 6 singles, 1966, 1967, 1968, 1972, 1973, 1975, Italy, 1970; Federal Republic of Germany, 1971; France, 1972; Winner, 1/046 singles tournaments, 1984; Other: Sports Commentator ABC-TV, 1975-78; Founded Women's Tennis Association, 1973; Publisher of Women's Sports, 1974-; US Tennis Team Commissioner, 1981-; CEO World Team Tennis, 1985-; US Federation Cup Team Captain, 1995-2004; Women's Olympic Tennis Coach, 1996, 2000; Virginia Simms Championship Series Consultant; Chair, US Tennis Association, Tennis High Performance Committee, 2005-. Publications: Tennis to Win, 1970; Billie Jean, w K Chapin, 1974; We Have Come a Long Way: The Story of Women's Tennis, 1988. Honour: Top Woman Athlete of the Year, 1973. Address: c/o World Team Tennis, 445 North Wells, Suite 404, Chicago, IL 60610, USA.

KING Don, b. 20 August 1931, Clevelend, USA. Boxing Promoter. m. Henrietta, 2 sons, 1 daughter. Career: Boxing promoter, 1972-; Owner, Don King Productions Inc, 1974-; Fighters promoted include: Mohammad Ali, Sugar Ray Leonard, Mike Tyson, Ken Norton, Joe Frazier, Larry Holmes, Roberto Duran, Tim Witherspoon, George Foreman, Evander Holyfield; Founder, The Don King Foundation; Actively supports other charities including: The Martin Luther King

Jr Foundation. Honours: International Boxing Hall of Fame, 1997. Address: Don King Productions Inc, 501 Fairway Drive, Deerfield Beach, FL 33441, USA.

KING Joy Rainey, b. 5 August 1939, Memphis, Tennessee, USA. Poet. m. Guy King, 1 son, 1 daughter. Education: Graduate, Whitehaven High School, 1957. Career: Retired Medical Secretary; Staff Writer, Majestic Records. Publications: 1 book in Mongolia; 3 books in India; 5 books in Italy; Writes personalised songs for sick children in hospitals in USA, England and Canada; Writer for the Songs of Love Foundation, New York City. Honours: International Poetry Hall of Fame; Millennium Hall of Fame; Woman of the Year, 1997; International Woman of the Year, 1998; Author of the Year, Edizioni Universum, Trento, Italy, 1999; Who's Who of American Women, 21st edition; International Peace Prize, 2002; Poem in Best Poems and Poets of the 20th Century, International Library of Poetry; Honorary Doctor of Literature, World Academy of Arts & Culture, 2007; Listed in many other international Who's Who publications; Numerous awards for poetry. Memberships: World Congress of Poets; Metverse Muse, India; World Poets Society, Greece; World Poets, China; International Society of Poets, USA. Address: 3029 Willow Branch, Herrin, IL 62948, USA. E-mail: guynjoy@shawneelink.net

KING Larry, b. 19 November 1933, Brooklyn, USA. Broadcaster. m. (1) Alene Akins, 1 daughter, (2) Sharon Lepore, 1976, (3) Julia Alexander, 1989, 1 son, (4) Shawn Southwick, 1997. Appointments: Disc Jockey, various radio stations, Miami, Florida, 1957-71; Freelance Writer, Broadcaster, 1972-75; Radio Personality, Station WIOD, Miami, 1975-78; Writer, Entertainment Sections, Miami Herald, 7 years; Host, The Larry King Show, 1978-, 1990 Goodwill Games, WLA-TV Let's Talk, Washington DC; Columnist, USA Today, Sporting News; Currently hosts Larry King Live, nightly on CNN. Appeared in films, Ghostbusters, 1984, Lost in America, 1985. Publications: Mr King, You're Having a Heart Attack (with B D Colen), 1989; Larry King: Tell Me More, When You're From Brooklyn, Everything Else is Tokyo, 1992; On the Line (jointly), 1993; Daddy Day, Daughter Day (jointly), 1997. Honours: Several broadcasting and journalism awards. Address: c/o CNN Larry King Live, 820 1st Street NE, Washington, DC 20002, USA.

KING Sir Mervyn Allister, b. 30 March 1948, Chesham Bois, England. Economist; Central Banker. Education: BA honours, King's College, Cambridge. Appointments: Junior Research Officer, 1969-73; Kennedy Scholarship, Harvard University, 1971-72; Research Officer, 1972-76; Lecturer, Faculty of Economics, Cambridge, 1976-77; Fellow, St John's College, Cambridge, 1972-77; Esmee Fairbairn Professor of Investment, University of Birmingham, 1977-84; Visiting Professor of Economics, Harvard University, 1982-83; Visiting Professor of Economics, Massachusetts Institute of Technology, 1983-84; Visiting Professor of Economics, Harvard University, and Senior Olin Fellow, National Bureau of Economic Research, 1990; Professor of Economics, London School of Economics, 1984-95; Chief Economist and Executive Director, Bank of England, 1991-98; Visiting Professor of Economics, London School of Economics, 1996-; Deputy Governor, Bank of England, 1998-2003; Governor, Bank of England, 2003-. Publications: Indexing for Inflation, 1975; Public Policy and the Corporation, 1977; The British Tax System, 1978, 5th edition, 1990; The Taxation of Income from Capital, a comparative study of the US, UK, Sweden & West Germany, 1984; Numerous articles in various journals. Honours include: Stevenson Prize, Cambridge University, 1970; Medal of the University of Helsinki, 1982; Honorary Fellow, St John's College, Cambridge, 1997; Honorary degrees from Birmingham and London Guildhall and City (London) and Wolverhampton Universities and London School of Economics; Honorary Fellow, King's College, Cambridge, 2004; Honorary Doctorate, University of Helsinki, 2006; Honorary Life Member of IFS, 2006; Honorary Degree, Doctor of Laws, University of Cambridge, 2006; Knighted, 2011; Other activities: Advisory Council, London Symphony Orchestra, 2001-; Chairman of OEDC's Working Party 3 Committee, 2001-03; Member, Group of Thirty, 1997-; President of Institute for Fiscal Studies, 1999-2003; Visiting Fellow, Nuffield College, Oxford, 2002-; Patron, Worcestershire County Cricket Club; Trustee, National Gallery; Committee Member, All England Lawn Tennis and Croquet Club. Address: Bank of England, Threadneedle Street, London EC2R 8AH, England.

KING Stephen Edwin, (Richard Bachman), b. 21 September 1947, Portland, Maine, USA. Author. m. Tabitha J Spruce, 1971, 2 sons, 1 daughter. Education: University Maine. Appointments: Teacher, English, Hampden Academy, Maine, 1971-73; Writer-in-Residence, University of Maine, Orono, 1978-79. Publications: Carrie, 1974; Salem's Lot, 1975; The Shining, 1977; The Stand, 1978; The Dead Zone, 1979; Firestarter, 1980; Danse Macabre, 1981; Cujo, 1981; Christine, 1983; Pet Sematary, 1983; The Talisman (w Peter Straub), 1984; Cycle of the Werewolf, 1985; It, 1986; The Eyes of the Dragon, 1987; Misery, 1987; The Tommyknockers, 1987; The Dark Half, 1989; Four Past Midnight, 1990; Needful Things, 1991; Gerald's Game, 1992; The Girl Who Loved Tom Jordan, 1999; Hearts in Atlantis, 1999; Storm of the Century (adapted to mini-series), 1999; Riding the Bullet, 2000; On Writing, 2000; Dreamcatcher, 2001; Everything's Eventual, 2002; From a Buick 8, 2002; The Dark Tower Stories: Vol I: The Gunslinger, 1982, Vol II: The Drawing of the Three, 1984, Vol III: The Waste Lands, 1991, Vol IV: Wizard and Glass, 1997, Vol: V: Wolves of the Cala, 2003, Vol VI: Song of Susannah, 2004, VII: The Dark Tower, 2004; The Girl Who Loved Tom Gordon, 2004; Faithful, 2005; The Colorado Kid, 2005; Cell, 2006; Lisey's Story, 2006; The Secretary of Dreams: Vol. 1, 2006; Blaze, 2007; Duma Key, 2008; Ur, 2009; Under The Dome, 2009. Short Story Collections: Night Shift, 1978; Different Seasons, 1982; Skeleton Crew, 1985; Gerald's Game, 1992; Dolores Claiborne, 1993; Nightmares & Dreamscapes, 1993; Insomnia, 1994; As Richard Bachman: Thinner, 1984; The Bachman Books: Rage, The Long Walk, Roadwork, The Running Man, 1985; Just After Sunset, 2008 Over 200 stories including 50 best selling horror and fantasy novels. Honours: Medal for Distinguished Contribution to American Letters, National Book Foundation, 2003. Memberships: Authors Guild of America; Screen Artists Guild; Screen Writers of America; Writers Guild. Address: 49 Florida Avenue, Bangor, ME 04401, USA. Website: www.stephenking.com

KING Victor Terence, b. 26 January 1949, Gorleston, Norfolk. Emeritus Professor. m. Judith Jane, 2 sons. Education: BA (Hons), Hull; MA (distinction), SOAS, London; PLD, Hull. Appointments: Lecturer, 1973-88, Senior Lecturer, 1988, South-East Asian Sociology; Professor, South-East Asian Studies, Hull, 1988-2005; Pro-Vice Chancellor, University of Hull, 1998-2000; Director, Graduate School, University of Hull, 2002-05; Professor, South-East Asian Studies, University of Leeds, 2005-10; Executive Director, White Rose East Asia Centre, University of Leeds, 2006-. Publications: The Peoples of Borneo, 1993; Images of Malay-Indonesian Identity, 1997; Environmental Challenges in South-East Asia,

1998; Anthropology and Development in South-East Asia, 1999; The Modern Anthropology of South-East Asia, 2006; The Sociology of Southeast Asia, 2008; Tourism in Southeast Asia: Challenges and New Directions, 2010; Heritage Tourism in Southeast Asia, 2011. Honours: Chair, RAE, Asian Studies Panel, 2008; Chair, Association of South-East Asian Studies in the United Kingdom; Listed in various international biographical dictionaries. Memberships: Fellow, Royal Society of Arts; Fellow, Borneo Research Council; Fellow, Royal Asiatic Society, Malaysia Branch. Address: 141 Newland Park, Hull, HU5 2DX, England.

KING OF BRIDGWATER, Baron of Bridgwater in the County of Somerset, Thomas Jeremy (Tom) King, b. 13 June 1933, Glasgow, Scotland. Politician. m. Elizabeth Jane Tilney, 1 son, 1 daughter. Education: Emmanuel College, Cambridge. Appointments: National Service, Somerset Light Infantry and Kings African Rifles, Tanganyika and Kenya; With E S & A Robinson Ltd Bristol, rising to Division General Manager; Director, 1965-79, Chairman, 1971-79, Sale Tilney & Co; Member of Parliament, Conservative, Bridgwater, 1970-2001; Parliamentary Private Secretary to Minister of Posts and Telecommunications, 1970-72, to Minister for Industrial Development, 1972-74; Vice-Chairman, Conservative Parliamentary Industry Committee, 1974; Shadow Secretary of State for Energy, 1976-79; Minister of State for Local Government, 1979-83; Secretary of State for Environment, 1983; Secretary of State for Transport, 1983; Secretary of State for Employment, 1983-85; Secretary of State for Northern Ireland, 1985-89, Secretary of State for Defence, 1989-92; Member of Nolan Committee on Standards in Public Life, 1994-97; Chairman of Intelligence and Security Committee which oversees MI5, MI6 and GCHQ, 1994-2001; Entered House of Lords as Lord King of Bridgwater, 2001; Chairman, London International Exhibition Centre Ltd; Director, Electra Investment Trust; Part Time Vice Chairman, Conservative National and International Security Policy Group, 2006-. Honours: PC, 1979; CH, 1992. Address: c/o The House of Lords, London SW1A 0PW, England.

KING-HELE Desmond George, b. 3 November 1927, Seaford, Sussex, England. Scientist; Author; Poet. m. Marie Therese Newman, 1954, separated 1992, 2 daughters. Education: BA, 1st Class Honours, Mathematics, 1948, MA, 1952, Trinity College, Cambridge. Appointments: Staff, 1948-68, Deputy Chief Scientific Officer, Space Department, 1968-88, Royal Aircraft Establishment; Editor, Notes and Records of the Royal Society, 1989-96; Various lectureships. Publications: Shelley: His Thought and Work, 1960, 3rd edition, 1984; Satellites and Scientific Research, 1960; Erasmus Darwin, 1963; Theory of Satellite Orbits in an Atmosphere, 1964; Space Research V (editor), 1965; Observing Earth Satellites, 1966, 2nd edition, 1983; Essential Writings of Erasmus Darwin (editor), 1968; The End of the Twentieth Century?, 1970; Poems and Trixies, 1972; Doctor of Revolution, 1977; Letters of Erasmus Darwin (editor), 1981; The RAE Table of Earth Satellites (editor), 1981, 4th edition, 1990; Animal Spirits, 1983; Erasmus Darwin and the Romantic Poets, 1986; Satellite Orbits in an Atmosphere: Theory and Applications, 1987; A Tapestry of Orbits, 1992; John Herschel (editor), 1992; A Concordance to the Botanic Garden (editor), 1994; Erasmus Darwin: A Life of Unequalled Achievement, 1999; Antic and Romantic (poems), 2000; Charles Darwin's Life of Erasmus Darwin (editor), 2002; The Collected Letters of Erasmus Darwin (editor), 2006. Contributions to: Numerous scientific and literary journals. Honours: Eddington Medal, Royal Astronomical Society, 1971; Charles Chree Medal, Institute of Physics, 1971; Lagrange Prize, Académie Royale de Belgique, 1972; Honorary Doctorates, Universities of Aston, 1979, and Surrey, 1986; Nordberg Medal, International Committee on Space Research, 1990; Society of Authors Medical History Prize, 1999. Listed in national and international biographical dictionaries. Memberships: British National Committee for the History of Science, Medicine and Technology, chairman, 1985-89; Fellow, Institute of Mathematics and Its Applications; Fellow, Royal Astronomical Society; Fellow, Royal Society; Bakerian Lecturer, Royal Society, 1974; Wilkins Lecturer, Royal Society, 1997. Address: 7 Hilltops Court, 65 North Lane, Buriton, Hampshire GU31 5RS, England.

KINGSLEY Sir Ben, b. 31 December 1943, England. Actor. m. (1) Angela Morant, 1966, divorced 1 son, 1 daughter; (2) Alison Sutcliff, 1978, divorced, 2 sons; (3) Alexandra Christmann, 2003, divorced; (4) Daniela Lavendar, 2007. Appointments: RSC, 1970-80, National Theatre, 1977-78; Associate Artist, RSC. Creative Works: Stage appearances include: A Midsummer Night's Dream; Occupations; The Tempest; Hamlet (title role); The Merry Wives of Windsor; Baal; Nicholas Nickleby; Volpone; The Cherry Orchard; The Country Wife; Judgement; Statements After An Arrest; Othello (title role); Caracol in Melons; Waiting for God; TV appearances include: The Love School, 1974; Kean; Silas Marner; The Train, 1987; Murderous Amongst Us, 1988; Anne Frank; Several plays; Films: Gandhi, Betrayal, 1982; Harem, Turtle Diary, 1985; Without A Clue, Testimony, Pascali's Island, 1988; Bugsy, 1991; Sneakers, Innocent Moves, Dave, 1992; Schindler's List, 1993; Death and the Maiden, 1994; Species, 1995; Twelfth Night, 1996; Photographing Fairies, 1997; The Assignment, Weapons of Mass Destruction, Sweeney Todd, 1998; The Confession, Sexy Beast, Rules of Engagement, What planet Are You From? Spooky House, 1999; A.I., Triumph of Love, Anne Frank, 2000; Tuck Everlasting, 2001; Sound of Thunder, Suspect Zero, House of Sand and Fog, 2002; Thunderbirds, Suspect Zero, 2004; A Sound of Thunder, Olive Twist, BloodRayne, 2005; Lucky Number Slevin, 2006; You Kill Me, The Last Legion, The Ten Commandments, Transsiberian, War, Inc, Elegy, 2007; War Inc., The Love Guru, 2008; Shutter Island, Prince of Persia: The Sands of Time, 2010; Hugo, 2011; The Dictator, A Therapy, 2012; Iron Man 3, Ender's Game, 2013. Honours include: 2 Hollywood Golden Globe Awards, 1982; NY Film Critics Award; 2 BAFTA Awards; Academy Award, Best Actor, 1983; Los Angeles Film Critics Award, 1983; CBE, 2000; Best Actor, British Industry Film Awards, 2001; Knighted, 2002; Screen Actors' Guild Award for Best Actor, 2002; Hollywood Walk of Fame, 2010; Padma Sri; Hon D Litt, Hull University, Sussex University; Hon MA, Salford University.

KINGSNORTH Jean, b. 9 April 1933, Hanwell, London, England. Artist. m. (1) Brian Brennan, 1 daughter, (2) Anthony Neville Kingsnorth. Education: Maidstone School of Art, 1951-55; Northwest London Polytechnic, 1957-58; BA (Hons), Courtauld Institute of Art, 1958-61; Postgraduate Diploma in Textiles, Goldsmiths College, 1979-81. Appointments: Theatrical Costume Design, Aubrey Samuels, 1955-57; Part time Lecturer, Chelsea School of Art and Regent Street Polytechnic, 1961-62; Writing for various art publications, including George Rainbird Ltd, 1962-64; Full time Lecturer, Design Department, Head of First Year Students, South East Essex College, 1964-74; Part time Lecturer, Education Department, North East London Polytechnic, 1975-76; Part time writing for Flax & Kingsnorth (book designers), 1975-81; Full time Artist, late 1970s-; Many solo and group exhibitions around London and the UK, also Japan and New Zealand; Work held in private collections in Britain, Australia, Malaysia, Singapore, South Africa, Egypt,

France and New Zealand. Publications: Contributions to books and encyclopaedias; Articles in professional journals. Memberships: Free Painters and Sculptors. Address: 45 Edenbridge Road, Bush Hill Park, Enfield, Middlesex, EN1 2LW, England. E-mail: jeankingsnorth@hotmail.com

KINGSOLVER Barbara, b. 8 April 1955, Annapolis, Maryland, USA. Author; Poet. m. (1) Joseph Hoffmann, 1985, divorced 1993, 1 daughter, (2) Steven Hopp, 1995, 1 daughter. Education: BA, DePauw University, 1977; MS, University of Arizona, 1981. Appointments: Research Assistant, Department of Physiology, 1977-79, Technical Writer, Office of Arid Land Studies, 1981-85, University of Arizona, Tucson; Journalist, 1985-87; Author, 1987-; Founder, Bellwether Prize to recognize a first novel of social significance, 1997. Publications: The Bean Trees (novel), 1988; Homeland and Other Stories, 1989; Holding the Line: Women in the Great Arizona Mine Strike of 1983 (non-fiction), 1989; Animal Dreams (novel), 1990; Pigs in Heaven (novel), 1993; Another America (poems), 1994, new edition, 1998; High Tide in Tucson: Essays from Now or Never, 1995; The Poisonwood Bible (novel), 1998; Prodigal Summer (stories), 2000; Small Wonder, 2002; Last Stand, 2002; Animal, Vegetable, Miracle, 2007; Notes to a Future Historian, 2007; The Lacuna, 2009. Contributions to: Many anthologies and periodicals. Honours: Feature-Writing Award, Arizona Press Club, 1986; American Library Association Awards, 1988, 1990; PEN Fiction Prize, 1991; Edward Abbey Ecofiction Award, 1991; Los Angeles Times Book Award for Fiction, 1993; PEN Faulkner, 1999; American Booksellers Book of the Year, 2000; National Humanities Medal, 2000; Governor's National Award in the Arts, Kentucky, 2002; John P McGovern Award for the Family, 2002; Physicians for Social Responsibility National Award, 2002; Academy of Achievement Golden Plate Award, 2003. Address: PO Box 31870, Tucson, AZ 85751, USA.

KINNEY Arthur F(rederick), b. 5 September 1933, Cortland, New York, USA. Author; Editor; Teacher; Director, Massachusetts Center for Interdisciplinary Renaissance Studies. Education: AB, magna cum laude, Syracuse University, 1955; MS, Columbia University, 1956; PhD, University of Michigan, Ann Arbor, 1963. Appointments: Instructor, Yale University, 1963-66; Assistant Professor, University of Massachusetts, Amherst, 1966-69; Associate Professor, 1969-75, Professor, 1975-84, Thomas W Copeland Professor of Literary History, University of Massachusetts, 1984-; Adjunct Professor of English, Clark University, 1971-; Adjunct Professor of English, New York University, 1991-. Publications: Over 30 books including: Humanist Poetics; Continental Humanist Poetics; John Skelton: Priest as Poet; Lies Like The Truth: Shakespeare Macbeth and the Cultural Moment; Shakespeare, Computers, and the Mystery of Authorship; Dorothy Parker Revisited; Faulkner's Narrative Poetics; Go Down, Moses: The Miscegenation of Time; Shakespeare by Stages; Shakespeare's Webs: Networks of Meaning; Shakespeare and Cognition; Backgrounds; Titled Elizabethans; Editor: Renaissance Historicism; Cambridge Companion to English Literature 1500-1600; Tudor England: An Encyclopedia; Elizabethan Backgrounds; Titled Elizabethans; Rogues, Vagabonds and Sturdy Beggars; Nicholas Hilliard's Art of Lymning; Women in the Renaissance; Renaissance Drama; New Critical Essays on Hamlet; A Companion to Renaissance Drama; Challenging Humanism; Elizabethan and Jacobean England; Oxford Handbook to Shakespeare; Founding Editor, English Literary Renaissance, journal; Massachusetts Studies in Early Modern Culture, book series; Twayne English Authors – Renaissance, book series. Honours: Phi Beta Kappa; Breadloaf Scholar in Fiction; Morse Fellow, Yale; Fulbright Scholar and Teacher, Oxford University, 1977-78; Chancellor's Medal; University Distinguished Teaching Award; Senior NEH Fellow, 1973-74, 1981-82, 2003-2004; Senior Folger Fellow, 1974, 1982, 1991, 1995; Senior Huntington Library Fellow, 1973, 1977, 1990; Paul Oskar Kristeller Lifetime Achievement Award; Jean Robertson Lifetime Achievement Award; Samuel F Conti Research Fellowship; Listed in several biographical publications. Memberships include: President, Renaissance English Text Society; President, MLA Council of Editors of Learned Journals; Trustee, Shakespeare Association of America; Executive Council, Renaissance Society of America; Executive Council, Folger Library Institute. Address: 25 Hunter Hill, Amherst, MA 01002, USA.

KINNOCK Glenys, b. 7 July 1944, Roade, Northamptonshire, England. Member of European Parliament, Wales. m. Neil Kinnock, 1 son, 1 daughter. Education: BA, Dip Ed, University College, Cardiff, 1962-66. Appointments: Primary and Secondary School Teacher, 1966-93; European Parliamentary Labour Party Spokesperson on Development, Co-President of the African, Caribbean and Pacific States ACP-EU Joint Parliamentary Assembly; Member of European Parliament, South Wales East, 1994-99; Member of European Parliament, Wales, 1999-. Publications: Books: Voices for One World, 1987; Eritrea – Images of War and Peace, 1989; Nambia - Birth of a Nation, 1991; Could Do Better – Where is British Education in the European League Tables?; By Faith and Daring, 1993; Zimbabwe: On the brink, 2003; The rape of Darfur, 2006. Honours: Honorary Fellow, University of Wales College, Newport and University of Wales, Bangor; Honorary Doctorates from: Thames Valley, Brunel and Kingston Universities; Fellow, Royal Society of Arts. Memberships: NUT; GMB; President, One World Action; Patron, Saferworld; Council Member, Voluntary Service Overseas; Patron, Drop the Debt Campaign; Vice President, Parliamentarians for Global Action; Board Member, World Parliamentarian Magazine; President, Coleg Harlech; Patron, Welsh Woman of the Year; Vice President, Wales Council for Voluntary Action, South East Wales Racial Equality Council; Vice President, St David's Foundation; Special Needs Advisory Project, Cymru; UK National Breast Cancer Coalition Wales; Community Enterprise Wales and Charter Housing; Patron, Burma Campaign UK; Crusaid; Elizabeth Hardie Ferguson Trust; Medical Foundation for Victims of Torture; National Deaf Children's Society; Council Member, Britain in Europe.

KINNOCK Neil Gordon (Lord Kinnock of Bedwellty), b. 28 March 1942, Wales, United Kingdom. Politician. m. Glenys Elizabeth Parry, 1967, 1 son, 1 daughter. Education: Lewis School, Pengam; University College, Cardiff. Appointments: Elected President, University College Cardiff Students Union, 1965-66; Tutor, Organiser, Industrial & Trade Union Studies, Workers' Educational Association, 1966-70; Labour MP for Bedwellty, 1970-83, for Islwyn, 1983-95; Member, Welsh Hospital Board, 1969-71; Parliamentary Private Secretary to Secretary of State for Employment, 1974-75; Member, National Executive Committee, Labour Party, 1978-94; Leader of Labour Party, 1983-92; Leader of the Opposition, 1983-92; EC Commissioner with Responsibility for Transport, 1995-99; President, Cardiff University, 1998-; Vice-President, European Commission, 1999-2004; Chairman, British Council, 2004-; Life Peer, 2005. Publications: Wales and the Common Market, 1971; Making Our Way, 1986; Thorns and Roses, 1992; Numerous contributions in periodicals, newspapers and books including The Future of Social

Democracy, 1999. Honours: Several honorary doctorates; Alex de Tocqueville Prize, 2003. Address: British Council, 10 Spring Gardens, London SW1A 2BN, England.

KINOSHITA Hiroyuki, b. 2 January 1972, Tokyo, Japan. Medical Doctor. m. Mayuko, 1 son, 1 daughter. Eduacation: MD, University of Yamanashi, 2001; PhD, Graduate School of Medicine and Faculty of Medicine, University of Tokyo, 2007. Appointments: October Massachusetts General Hospital, Harvard Medical School, USA, 2005; Tama North Medical Center, Tokyo, 2007; Tokyo Metropolitan Bokutoh Hospital, Tokyo, 2008. Publications: Numerous articles in professional journals. Honours: Listed in international biographical dictionaries. Memberships: Japanese Society of Internal Medicine. E-mail: hkinoshita-tky@umin.ac.jp

KINSKI Natassja, b. 24 January 1961, West Berlin, Germany. Actress. m. I Moussa, 1984, divorced, 1 son, 1 daughter; 1 daughter with Quincy Jones. Career: Debut in Falsche Bewegung, 1975; Films include: Stay as You Are, 1978; Cat People, 1982; Moon in the Gutter, 1983; Unfaithfully Yours; Paris; Texas and the Hotel New Hampshire, 1984; Magdalene, 1989; Terminal Velocity, 1994; One Night Stand, 1997; Sunshine, 1998; Town and Country, 1999; The Claim, 2000; The Day the World Ended, 2001; An American Rhapsody, 2001; Say Nothing, 2001; Beyond the City Limits, 2001; .com for Murder, 2002; Paradise Found, 2003; Á ton image, 2004; Inland Empire, 2006. Address: c/o Peter Levine, William Morris Agency, 151 South El Camino Drive, Beverly Hills, CA 90212, USA.

KINTHADA Prakash, b. India. Associate Professor. Education: BSc, Chemistry, 1979; MSc, Chemistry/ Inorganic Chemistry, 1981p; PhD, Analytical Chemistry/ Inorganic Chemistry, 1987; PDF, Organometallic Chemistry/Bioinorganic Chemistry, Bioorganic Chemistry, Pharmaceutical Chemistry, Cancer Research, Biotechnology, Medical Biotechnology, 1987, 1989, 1991, 1999, 2003, 2004. Appointments: CSIR Research Associate, Organometallic Laboratories, Indian Institute of Technology, New Delhi, India, 1988-90; Post doctoral Fellow, Organometallic Laboratories, Imperial College of Science, Technology and Medicine, London, England, 1990-91; CSIR Pool Officer, Department of Chemistry, University of Hyderabad, India, 1991-93; Leverhulme Visiting Fellow, Organometallic Laboratories, Department of Chemistry and Chemical Engineering, Aston University, Birmingham, England, 1999-2000; Royal Society Visiting Fellow, Inorganic Chemistry Laboratories, University of Oxford, England, 2004; NIH Visiting Fellow, Karmanos Cancer Research Institute, Department of Pathology, Wayne State University School of Medicine, Michigan, USA, 2005-06. Publications: 16 international papers; 5 national papers; 6 communicated. Honours: Junior Research Fellowship, 1982-84, Senior Research Fellowship, 1984-87, CSIR Pool Officership, 1993-95, Government of India; Nehru Centenary British Fellowship, British Council, 1991-92; Visiting Fellowship, Leverhulme Trust, 1999-2000; Royal Society Visiting Fellowship, Royal Society, London, 2004; NIH Visiting Fellowship, NIH Maryland, 2005-06; Cancer Prevention Fellowship, National Cancer Research Institute, 2011; Paper Presentation, 8th International Conference on Inorganic Chemistry, Heidelberg, Germany, 2011. Memberships: American Chemical Society; Royal Society of Chemistry, London; American Association of Cancer Research; American Association for the Advancement of Science; many others. Address: Department of Chemistry, GIT, GITAM University, Rushikonda, Vishakhapatnam, AP, India. E-mail: prakashkinthada@yahoo.com

KIRBY Michael Donald, b. 18 March 1939, Sydney, Australia. University Professor; Arbitrator; Mediator; Former Judge. Partner: Johan A van Vloten. Education: BA, 1959, LLB, 1962, LLM, first class honours, 1967, BEc, 1966, Sydney University. Career: Solicitor and Barrister; Deputy President, Australian Conciliation and Arbitration Commission, 1975-83; Foundation Chairman, Australian Law Reform Commission, 1975-84; Judge, Federal Court of Australia, 1983- 84; President, New South Wales Court of Appeal, 1984-96; President, Court of Appeal of Solomon Islands, 1995-96; Justice of the High Court of Australia (Australia's Federal Supreme Court), 1996-2009; Acting Chief Justice of Australia, 2007, 2008. Honours: Companion of the Order of St Michael and St George, 1983; Honorary Fellow, New Zealand Research Foundation, 1984; Honorary DLitt, University of Newcastle, New South Wales, 1987; Companion of the Order of Australia, 1991; Australian Human Rights Medal, 1991; Hon LLD, Macquarie University, 1994; Hon LLD, Sydney University, 1996; Hon LLD, National Law School, India, 1997; UNESCO Prize for Human Rights Education, 1998; Hon DLitt, University of Ulster, 1998; Hon LLD, Buckingham, 1999; Hon DUniv, Univerity of South Australia, 2002; Hon D Litt, James Cook University, 2003; Hon LLD, Australian National University, 2004; Lifetime Achievement Award, Australian Law Awards, 2005; Included in 100 Most Influential Australians, 2006; Honorary Bencher, Inner Temple, London, 2006; Hon D University, Southern Cross University, 2007; Hon LLD, University of South Wales, 2008; Hon D University, Griffith University, 2008; Hon LLD, Murdoch University, WA, 2009; Hon LLD, University of Melbourne, 2009; Hon LLD, Indiana University, 2009; Hon LLD, University of Technology, Sydney and Bond University, Queensland, 2009; Hon LLD, Colombo University, Sri Lanka, 2010; Gruber Justice Prize, Washington DC, 2010; Hon LLD, La Trobe University, 2011. Memberships include: Member, UNAIDS Global Reference Group on HIV/AIDS and Human Rights; Member, Judicial Integrity Group of UN Office on Drugs and Crime; Honorary Member, Australian National Commission for UNESCO, 1996-2007; Member, American Law Institute, 2000-; Honorary Counselor, American Society of International Law, 2009; Life Member, Australian Bar Association, 2009; Life Member, NSW Bar Association, 2009; Council Member, Human Rights Institute, International Bar Association, 2009-; Life Member, Law Council of Australia, 2009-10; Elected President, Institute of Arbitrators and Mediators Australia, 2009; Elected Board Member, Australian Centre for International Commercial Arbitration, 2009; International Privacy Champion Award, Electronic Privacy Information Center, Washington, DC, 2010; Member, UNDP Global Commission on HIV and the Law, 2010-; Member, Eminent Persons Group on Future of the Commonwealth of Nations, 2010-; Member, International Committee on Settlement of Investment Disputes (ICSID), World Bank (Arbitration Panel), 2010-. Address: LV7, 195 Macquarie Street, Sydney, NSW 2000, Australia. E-mail: mail@michaelkirby.com.au

KIRCI DENIZLI Betul, b. 28 April 1973, Izmir, Turkey. Engineer. m. Haluk. Education: BA, 1997, MSc, 2000, PhD, 2004, Department of Chemistry, Hacettepe University, Ankara. Appointments: Research Assistant, Department of Chemistry, Hacettepe University, 1998-2004; Visiting Scholar, 2001-02, Post-doctoral studies, 2006, Mellon Institute, Carnegie Mellon University, USA; R&D Project Leader, Standard Profil, Duzce, 2004-06; Invited Assistant Professor, Department of Chemistry, ITU, Istanbul, 2006; Assistant Professor, AIBU, Bolu, 2006; TPM & Environmental Project Management Engineer, ARCELIK AS, Bolu, 2006-.

Publications: Numerous articles in professional journals. Address: Argelik AS Cooking Appliances Plant, Yukari sokum Cele sok No 7, Bolu, Turkey.

KIRILLOVA Elena Nikolaevna, b. 18 September 1959, Khabarovsk, Russia. Physicist; Educator; Writer (Poet). m. Vladimir A Kirillov, 1 daughter. Education: MD, Physics, 1981, PhD, Theoretical Physics, 1990, MD, Psychology, 2000, Tomsk State University, Russia. Appointments: Associate Professor, Tomsk State Pedagogical University, Department of Theoretical Physics. Publications: Numerous articles in professional journals; Poems in Russian journals. Honours: Medal, Tomsk State Pedagogical University, 2009. Memberships: Journalists' Union, Russia; Russian Writers' Union. E-mail: kirillovaen@tspu.edu.ru

KIRK Nicholas Kenneth, b. 27 December 1945, Bradford, West Yorkshire, England. Musician (New Orleans Jazz Banjo); Electronics Engineer. Education: BSc, Honours, University of Wales; Postgraduate Diploma in Communications, Southampton University; Postgraduate Diploma in R F and Microwave Electronics, Bradford University. Career: Appearances on radio and television Wales with Clive Evan's River City Stompers, 1966-67; Appeared at the Keswick Jazz Festival, Bude Jazz Festival, Marsden Jazz Festival, and at jazz clubs and pubs in Yorkshire, Wales and South of England, with the Dennis Browne Creole Band; Appeared at the 100 Club in London with the New Era Jazzband; Currently proprietor, P&P Electronics and P&P Electrical; Toured Holland with Dennis Browne Creole Band. Publications: Author of British Patent for apparatus for Recording and Replaying Music (The Musical Arranger and Sequencer), subsequent sale of patent rights to Waddingtons House of Games. Composition: Clouds. Recording: Float Me Down The River, with the Dennis Browne Creole Band, cassette; City Of A Million Dreams, cassette; Live at the Ritz, CD, by the Dennis Armstrong Jazz Band; Alternative Theory of the Red Shift in the Universe; CD, Dennis Brown Creole Jazz Band, Live at Hawarden Club, Bude, Cornwall; CD, Clouds from Yorkshire; CD, Live at the Keswick Jazz Festival; CD with The New Orleans Wiggle Band, Over the Waves. Memberships: Fellow, Royal Microscopical Society; Musicians Union. Address: Harcadeia, 36 Kilpin Hill Lane, Staincliffe, Near Dewsbury, West Yorkshire WF13 4BH, England.

KIRK Raymond Maurice, b. 31 October 1923, Beeston, Nottinghamshire, England. Surgeon, retired. m. Margaret Schafran, 1 son, 2 daughters. Education: King's College, London; Charing Cross Hospital, London; University of London. Appointments: Ordinary Seaman to Lieutenant RNVR, 1942-46; House Surgeon and Casualty Officer, Charing Cross Hospital, 1952; Lecturer in Anatomy, King's College, London, 1952-53; House Surgeon and Resident Surgical Officer, Royal Postgraduate Medical School, Hammersmith Hospital, London, 1953-56; Registrar and Senior Registrar, Charing Cross Hospital, 1956-60; Senior Surgical Registrar, Royal Free Hospital, 1961; Consultant Surgeon, Willesden General Hospital, 1962-72; Consultant Surgeon and Honorary Senior Lecturer, Royal Free Hospital, 1964; Part-time Lecturer in Anatomy and Developmental Biology, University College, London; Honorary Professor of Surgery, Honorary Consulting Surgeon, Royal Free Hospital and Royal Free and University College, London School of Medicine, 1989-. Publications: Author and co-author, 8 books; Numerous articles and chapters in professional medical journals. Memberships: Royal College of Surgeons of England; Court of Examiners; Royal Society of Medicine; Hunterian Society; Medical Society of London; Association of Surgeons of Poland; Association of Surgeons of Sri Lanka. Address: 10 Southwood Lane, Highgate Village, London N6 5EE, England. E-mail: r.kirk@medsch.ucl.ac.uk

KIRK-GREENE Anthony (Hamilton Millard), b. 16 May 1925, Tunbridge Wells, England. m. Helen Sellar, 1967. University Lecturer; Fellow; Writer; Editor. Education: BA, 1949, MA, 1954, Clare College, Cambridge; Edinburgh University, 1965-66; MA, Oxford University, 1967. Appointments: Senior Lecturer in Government, Institute of Administration, Zaria, Nigeria, 1957-62; Professor of Government, Ahmadu Bello University, Nigeria, 1962-65; University Lecturer and Fellow, St Antony's College, Oxford, 1967-92, Emeritus Fellow, 1992-, Director, Oxford University Colonial Records Project, 1979-84; Director, Foreign Service Programme, Oxford University, 1986-90; Associate Professor, Stanford University (Oxford Campus), 1992-99; Co-editor/Academic Consultant: Methuen Studies in African History, 1969-75, Hoover Colonial Studies, 1975-85, Holmes and Meier, Africana, 1978-83, Gregg Press Modern Revivals in African Studies, 1990-95, Radcliffe Press Overseas Memoirs, 1992-; Reviews Editor: Corona Club Bulletin, 1984-2000, Britain-Nigeria Association Newsletter, 2001-07; Associate Editor, Oxford Dictionary of National Biography, 1996-2005. Publications: Adamawa Past and Present, 1958; Barth's Travels in Nigeria, 1962; The Emirates of Northern Nigeria (co-author), 1966; Crisis and Conflict in Nigeria, 1971; Teach Yourself Hausa (co-author), 1975; Nigeria Since 1970 (co-author), 1980; A Biographical Dictionary of British Colonial Service, 1939-66, 1991; On Crown Service, 1999; Britain's Imperial Administrators, 2000; The British Intellectual Engagement with Africa in the 20th Century (co-editor), 2000; Glimpses of Empire, 2001; Symbol of Authority, 2006. Contributions to numerous reference books and scholarly journals. Honours: Member of the Order of the British Empire, 1963; Hans Wolff Memorial Lecturer, 1973; Fellow, Royal Historical Society, 1985; Festschrift, 1993; Leverhulme Emeritus Fellowship, 1993; Companion of the Order of St Michael and St George, 2001; African Studies Association (UK) Distinguished Africanist Award, 2005. Memberships: Royal African Society; International African Institute; Britain – Nigeria Association, Council Member, 1985-2007; African Studies Association of UK, President, 1988-90; Vice President, Royal African Society, 1992-2006. Address: c/o St Antony's College, Oxford OX2 6JF, England.

KIRKHOPE Timothy John Robert, b. 29 April 1945, Newcastle upon Tyne, England. Solicitor. m. Caroline Maling, 4 sons. Education: Law Society College of Law, Guildford, Surrey. Appointments: Qualified as Solicitor, 1973; Partner, Wilkinson Maughan, now Eversheds, Newcastle upon Tyne, 1977-87; Conservative, Member of Parliament, Leeds North East, 1987-97; Government Whip, 1990-95; Vice Chamberlain to HM the Queen, 1995; Under Secretary of State, Home Office, 1995-97; Business Consultant, 1997-; Member of European Parliament, Yorkshire and the Humber, 1999-; Spokesman on Citizens Rights, Justice and Home Affairs, 1999-; Chief Whip, Conservative Delegation, 1999-2001; Member, Future of Europe Convention, 2002-. Memberships: Fountain Society; Northern Counties Club; Dunstanburgh Castle Golf Club; Newcastle Aero Club, private pilot. Address: c/o ASP 14E, 246 European Parliament, Rue Wiertz, B-1047 Brussels, Belgium. E-mail: tkirkhope@europarl.eu.int

KIROV Georgi, b. 16 December 1945, Malko Tarnovo, Bulgaria. Telecommunications Engineer. m. Tatiana Stefanova, 1 son, 1 daughter. Education: M Eng Sc, Electrical Engineering, 1968, PhD, Communications Sciences, 1980,

Associate Professor, 1988, Technical University of Varna. Appointments: Visiting Professor, University of Setif, Algeria, 1981-86; Vice Dean, Faculty of Electronics, 1990-92, Head, Department of Radioengineering, 1992-, Technical University of Varna; Visiting Professor and Researcher, University of Magdeburg, Germany, 2002-03; Specialization, University of Luxembourg, 2006. Publications: Impedance Matching Improvement for a Class of Wideband Antennas, 2004; Dual-band Assembly of Integrated Short Backfire Antennas, 2007; 70 articles; 4 patents; 10 books. Honours: Listed in international biographical dictionaries. Memberships: IEEE; Reseau Teledetection de l'Aupelf-Uref; Union of Scientists of Bulgaria; Federation of the Scientific and Technical Unions in Bulgaria. Address: Comlex Vladislavovo Bl 218, Bx 7, Ap 214, 9023 Varna, Bulgaria. E-mail: gkirov@abv.bg

KIRSZENSTEIN-SZEWINSKA Irena, b. 24 May 1946, Leningrad, Russia. Athlete. m. 2 sons. Education: Warsaw University. Appointments: Athlete, 1961-80 (100m, 200m, long jump, 4 x 100m relay, 4 x 400m relay); Took part in Olympic Games, Tokyo, 1964, Munich, 1972; 10 times world record holder for 100m, 200m, 400m; President, Polish Women's Sport Association, 1994-, Polish Athletic Association, 1997-; Vice President, Polish Olympic Committee, 1988, Polish Olympians Association, 1993, World Olympians Association, 1995-; Member, Council European Athletic Association, 1995-, Women's Committee, International Association of Athletics' Federation, International Olympic Committee, 1998-, President, Irena Szewinska Foundation-Vita-Aktiva, 1998, IOC Coordination Committee, Athens, 2004-; Head, Polish Federation of Athletics, 2004; Member, International Olympic Committee, 2004. Honours include: Gold Cross of Merit, 1964; Officer Cross, Order of Polonia Restituta, 1968; Commander's Cross, Order of Polonia Restituta, 1972, with Star, 1999; Order of Banner of Labour, 2nd class, 1976. Address: Polish Athletic Association, ul Ceglowska 68/70, 01-809 Warsaw, Poland.

KIS Károly István, b. 28 September 1944, Budapest, Hungary. Geophysicist. Education: MSc, Geophysics, 1969, Dr rer nat, 1972, PhD, Earth Sciences, 1995, Loránd Eötvös University, Budapest. Appointments: Postgraduate Fellowship, 1969-72, Assistant Professor, 1972-76, Scientific Adviser, 2006-, Loránd Eötvös University, Budapest; Research Associate, 1976-84, Senior Research Associate, 1984-2006, Honorary Associate Professor, 1984-, Research Group of Geophysics, Hungarian Academy of Sciences, Loránd Eötvös University, Budapest. Publications: Numerous articles in professional journals including: 3D reduction of satellite magnetic measurements to obtain magnetic anomaly coverage over Europe, 2002; Applicability of Poisson's relation to gravity and vertical magnetic anomalies, 2004; Bayesian inference in satellite gravity inversion, 2005; Effect of varying crustal thickness on CHAMP geopotential data, 2005; Application of magnetic field derivatives for locating Sarmatian graves, 2006; Magnetic Methods of Applied Geographics, 2009; 3 university text books; 6 university lecture notes; Contributions in 9 research reports; 66 papers in professional periodicals. Honours: Laszlo Egyed Prize, 2010. Memberships: Association of Hungarian Geophysicists; Society of Exploration Geophysicists, USA; Hungarian Astronautics Society. Address: Department of Geophysics and Space Sciences, Loránd Eötvös University, Pázmány Péter sétány 1/c, 1117 Budapest, Hungary. E-mail: kisk@ludens.elte.hu

KISBI Yahya Musa, b. 15 March 1949, Wadi Seer, Amman. Civil Engineer. m. Munira Ja'far, 2 sons, 2 daughters. Education: BSc, Civil Engineering, Ankara University, Turkey, 1974; Project Management, George Washington University, 1983; Project Management Using Computers, 1987, Higher Management Training Course, 1991, Jordan Management Institute. Appointments: General Manager, Buildings and World Bank Financed Projects, 1994-97; Assistant Secretary General, Ministry of Public Works and Housing, 1997-2001; General Manager, Government Tenders Directorate, 2001-09; Vice President, National Tourism Company, 2007-11; Minister, Publish Works and Housing, 2011-. Honours: Independence of the Second Degree. Memberships: Jordan Engineers Association; American Society of Civil Engineering; Turkish Society of Engineers. E-mail: y.kisbi@mpwh.gov.jo

KISSOON Anthony, b. 18 June 1952, Guyana. Economist. m. Maliba, 2 sons, 1 daughter. Education: Bachelor's degree, Economics, McGill University, 1974; Master's degree, Economics History, 1976. Appointments: Director, A H L Kissoon (family business). Publications: Book, Tales of the Spirits, 2002; Articles in professional journals. Honours: Listed in international biographical dictionaries. Memberships: Georgetown Cricket Club. Address: 73-74 Premnaranjan Place, Prashad Nagar, Georgetown, Guyana.

KITE Thomas O Jr, b. 9 December 1949, Austin, Texas, USA. Golfer. m. Christy Kite, 2 sons, 1 daughter. Appointments: Won Walker Cup, 1971; Turned Professional, 1972; Won Ryder Cup, 1979, 1981, 1983, 1985, 1987, 1989, 1993, European Open, 1980, US Open, Pebble Beach, CA, 1992; LA Open, 1993; 10 US PGA Wins; Appointed Captain, US Team for 1997 Ryder Cup, Valderrama, Spain; Joined Sr PGA Tour 2000; Numerous wins including The Countryside Tradition, 2000; MasterCard Championship, 2002; Spokesman for Chrysler Jr Golf Scholarship Programme. Address: c/o PGA Tour, 112 Tpc Boulevard, Ponte Vedra Beach, FL 32082, USA.

KITTL Pablo Alfredo, b. 18 November 1934, Buenos Aires, Argentina. Materials Scientist; Researcher. Education: Technical Constructor, National University de Cuyo, Argentina, 1953; Licence in Physics, University of San Luis, Argentina, 1964; Licence, University of Chile, Santiago, Chile, 1980. Appointments: Professor, Physics, University of San Luis, 1963-64; Researcher, IDIEM, 1965-80, Chief Electron Microscopy Laboratory, Materials Department, 1980-85, Professor, 1980-, University of Chile. Publications: Over 230 articles in scientific journals; Book: Scientific and Technical Development, particularly in the Case of Chile, 1995. Honours: Honorable mention in Latin American Journal of Metallurgy and Materials, 1987. Memberships: Fellow, American Academy of Mechanics; Chilean Academy of Sciences; Scientific Society of Argentina. E-mail: gediaz@ing.uchile.cl

KITTLEMAN Martha Adrienne, b. 31 December 1936, Houston, Texas, USA. Caterer; Decorator; Florist. m. Edmund Taylor Kittleman, 3 sons, 2 daughters. Education: BA, University of Mississippi; 2 years, University of Tulsa; UNC; Silver Jubilee, Oxford University, England, 1977; Correspondence degrees, Floristry, Interior Decorating, Antiques; Administrative Medical Assistant, Stratford Career Institute, 2005; Plainchant course in Latin, Liturgical Institute of Tulsa, 2007-09. Appointments: Owner, Chef, Adrienne's Tea Room, Bartlesville, Oklahoma, 1979; Head Cook, Bluestem Girl Scout Council, Bartlesville, 1993; Head Cook,

Washington/Nowata Counties Community Action Fund Inc (WNCCAF), Dewey, Oklahoma, 1993; Supervisor, Aftercare Program, St John School, Bartlesville, 1994-95; Gourmet Cook, International Mozart Festival, Bartlesville, 1998; Sampler, Auntie Anne's Pretzels, Bartlesville, 1998; Director Associate of RBC; Abundant Health Associates, Independent Member of RBC; Substitute Teacher, pre-kindergarten through 12; Hospital volunteer; Bakes European breads for Farmers' Market. Honours: Advisory Council, IBC; Nominee, Woman of the Year, IBC; Member, Society of Descendants of Knights of the Most Noble Order of the Garter; Listed in biographical dictionaries. Memberships: Bartlesville Choral Society; Eucharistic Minister; Magna Carta Dames; Plantagenet Society; Delta Delta Delta Sorority. Address: 110 Fleetwood Place, Bartlesville, OK 74006, USA. E-mail: kittlemanA@aol.com

KITTNAROVA Olga, b. 15 August 1937, Prague, Czechoslovakia (Czech Republic). Pedagogue; Journalist. Divorced, 1 daughter. Education: Musicology, Faculty of Philosophy and History, Charles University, Prague, 1955-60; PhD, 1971. Career: Editor, Supraphone, 1960-65; Teacher of Music, Music History and Theory, Prague Conservatoire, 1973-91; Pedagogue, Department of Musical Education, Pedagogical Faculty, Charles University, Prague, 1991-; Permanent Reviewer for newspapers and magazines including the musical journal Harmonie; Co-operation with 400 programmes for Prague Radio; Interested in musical ecology; Delivered the Women of Europe Award Lecture, The Excess of Sound in Contemporary Music, at Barcelona, 1994. Compositions include: Songs about Music with own texts, piano and Orff's instruments, published, 1995. Publications: Prague Quartet, 1974; Prague Quartet, Memorial Volume, UNESCO Symposium, 1978. Contributions to: Critical Miscellany, Musical Inventor A Hába, 1991; Jarmil Burghauser, 1992; Memorial Volume from Ecological Congress-Warning Memento of Sound Excess, 1995; Analysis of Musical Interpretation, University textbook, 1999; The Resounding Scores as a Guide of Performing Art, 2002; A History of Music in Outlines (in English), 2007. Memberships: Association of Musical Artists and Musicologists. Address: Benesovska 4, 10100 Prague 10, Czech Republic.

KIVELÄ Sirkka-Liisa, b. 14 January 1947, Temmes, Finland. Professor. m. Mauri Akkanen. Education: Medical Doctor, 1971; Doctor of Philosophy, 1983; Associate Professor in Family Medicine, 1984; Specialist in Family Medicine, 1976; Specialist in Geriatrics, 1985. Appointments: Chief Physician, Posio Health Centre, 1971-80; Senior Lecturer in Geriatrics, Tampere University, 1980-88; Professor in Public Health, Oulu University, 1988-90; Professor in Family Medicine, Oulu University, 1990-2000; Professor in Family Medicine, Turku University, 2000-. Publications: Over 300 scientific articles in national and international journals on depression, falls, abuse, coronary heart disease, chronic pulmonary diseases in old age; 40 publications for medical education; 6 books. Honours: Eeva Jalavisto Prize, 1996; Sv Aa og Magda Friederichens Prize, 1999. Membership: International Association of Psychogeriatrics. Address: University of Turku, Department of Family Medicine, Lemminkaisenkatu 1, 20014 University of Turku, Finland. Website: www.med.utu.fi/yleislaak/kivela.html

KIWERSKI Jerzy Edward, b. 24 June 1937, Warsaw, Poland. Physician. m. Szymczak Dorota, 1 son, 3 daughters. Education: Physician, 1963; Doctor of Medical Sciences, 1971; Habilitation, 1975; Professor of Medicine, 1984. Appointments: Head and Chairman, Rehabilitation Clinic, Warsaw Medical University, 1982-2007; Regional Consultant in Rehabilitation, 1981-2002; National Consultant in Rehabilitation, 2002-08; President, Public Health Foundation, 1990-; Vice President, 1990, President, 1999-2007, Committee of Rehabilitation, Polish Academy of Sciences; Director, Metropolitan Rehabilitation Center, 1991-98; President, Polish Society of Rehabilitation, 1992-99; Honorary Member, Polish Society of Rehabilitation, 2002-; New York Academy of Sciences, 1993; Vice-President, Polish Society of Biomechanics, 1994-2000; President (Rector), Warsaw Rehabilitation College, 2007-. Publications: 17 handbooks; Over 600 articles in national and international periodicals; Over 440 lecture and congress papers. Honours: Gold Cross, 1974, Knight's Cross, 1989, Order of the Rebirth of Poland; Ministry of Health Awards; President of Warsaw Award, National Orders; Outstanding Man of 21st Century, ABI; 2000 Outstanding Intellectuals of the 20th Century, IBC; Man of the Year 2001, 2004 ABI; One of the Genius Elite, ABI, 2004; Research Board of Advisors, ABI, 2005; Man of Science, ABI, 2006; Member, ABI, 2006; Charter Fellow, Advisory Directorate International, ABI, 2008; Gold Distinction of Polish Society of Physiotherapy, 2009; Man of the Year, ABI, 2009; National Education Medal, 2010; Listed in several biographical publications. Memberships: International Medical Society of Paraplegia; European Spine Society; International Rehabilitation Medical Association; European Board of Physical Medicine and Rehabilitation; The World Federation for Neurorehabilitation; International Society of Physical and Rehabilitation Medicine; Polish Society of Medical Engineering; Vice President, Polish Society of Biomedical Engineering. Address: Chyliczki, Orchidei 4, 05-500 Piaseczno, Poland.

KLANPRACHAR Amnart, b. 13 August 1954. Spiritual Painter; Meditation Teacher. Appointments: Individual Painting Artist, 1976-2003; Special Professor, Ratchasuda College, Mahidol University, 2001-03; Buddhist Monk, Wat Phra That Phakaew (Phasornkaew), 2003-11; Exhibitions include: The Oneness, Los Angeles and Denver, USA, 1996 and 1997; Bridge Linking the Mind, Thailand, 2000; Meditation, Thailand, 2001; Peace, Switzerland, 2002; Paticca Samuppada, Thailand, 2002; Prisna Phasomkaew, Thailand, 2006; The Art of Giving, Thailand, 2009; World Peace, Switzerland, 2010; and many others. Publications: Heaven Down to Earth, 1995; Flower Ring in Eyes, 1996; The Oneness, 1996; Bridge for Reaching to Heart, 2001; Tarot Roots of Asia, 2001; Gift, 2010. Honours: Award of Excellence, 8th Annual Art Exhibition, Petroleum Authority, Thailand, 1993; Honorary Award, Business and Administration Institute, 1992. Address: Wat Phra That Phakaew (Phasornkaew), 95 Moo 7, BaanTang Daeng, Campson, KhaoKoh, Petchaboon, 67280, Thailand.

KLAPKA Jindřich Ludvík, b. 19 March 1936, Zlín, Moravia, Czech Republic. Mathematician and Physicist. Education: Magister, 1959, Doctorate, 1967, Masaryk University, Brno, Czech Republic; PhD, Charles University, Prague, Czech Republic, 1968; Associate Professor, Technical University of Brno, Czech Republic, 1987; Professional Qualification: Mathematician, Theoretical Physicist, Applications of computers in automation. Appointments: Head of Research Group, Arms Works, Zbrojovka, Brno, 1959-66; Head of Creative Group, Institute of Theory and Methods of Engineering Production Management, and Institute of Theory and Methods of Industry Management, Technical University of Brno, 1966-89, Head of Pedagogical and Methodical Board, 1976-90; Visiting Professor, Università di Pisa, Italy, 1975; Head of Scientific Sector, 1989–91, Associate Professor, 1991-, Co-ordinator of PhD Studies in Technical

Cybernetics, 1996-2005, Faculty of Mechanical Engineering, Technical University of Brno; Head of scientific grand projects, 1986-97; Reviewer, Elsevier Science Publishing, World Scientific Publishing, IEEE Transactions in Systems, Man and Cybernetics, Springer Verlag, 2000-. Publications: More than 130 scientific publications in international journals, books and conference proceedings including: Theory of Propagation of the Transient Phenomena in Wave Guides, 1961; Assembler for Czechoslovak E1b Automatic Computer, 1964; Generalized Definition of Group Velocity of Signal in Dispersive Medium and its Application to Very Short Pulses in Waveguides, 1967; Dynamic Programming, 1970; Influence of Wall Losses on Energy Flow Center Velocity of Pulses in Waveguides, 1970; Optimization of Multistage Production System, 1975; Optimal lot size determination of multistage production-assembly system, 1986; Methods of operations research (with J Dvořák and P Popela), 1996; Decision support system for multicriterial R&D and information systems projects selection (with P Piňos), 2002; Optimal Distribution of Load between Cooperating Production Units with Combined Production of Heat and Electric Energy (with J Baláté, P Konečný, P Navrátil, B Chramcov), 2009. Honours include: Award of Honour of Merits for Development of the Faculty of Mechanical Engineering, Technical University of Brno, 1975; Lifetime Achievement Award, International Biographical Centre (IBC), 2004; World Lifetime Achievement Award, American Biographical Institute (ABI), 2004; American Medal of Honor, ABI, 2005; Legion of Honor, United Cultural Convention, 2005; Da Vinci Diamond Award, IBC, 2006; World Medal of Freedom, ABI, 2006; Man of the Year, ABI, 2006; Genius Laureate of Czech Republic, ABI, 2006; Gold Medal for the Czech Republic, ABI, 2007; International Peace Prize, United Cultural Convention, 2007; Honorary Director General, IBC, 2008; Legendary Leaders Hall of Fame, ABI, 2008; International Einstein Award, IBC, 2009; The Plato Award, IBC, 2009; Leading Intellectuals of the World (Charter Member), ABI, 2010; The Scientific Award of Excellence, ABI, 2011; Academician, ABI, 2011; International Order of Merit, IBC, 2012; Top 100 Scientists, IBC, 2012; Cambridge Certificate for Outstanding Scientific Achievement, IBC, 2012; Listed in national and international biographical dictionaries. Memberships include: Chairman, Moravian and Silesian Academy for Education, Science and Art; Promoting Fellow, Czech Operations Research Society; Honorary member, Project Management Society; Union of Czech Mathematicians and Physicists. Address: Brno University of Technology, Faculty of Mechanical Engineering, Institute of Automation and Computer Science, Technická 2, 61669, Brno, Czech Republic. E-mail: klapka@fme.vutbr.cz

KLÁRIK Béla William J Clark, b. 7 August 1931, Masontown, Pennsylvania, USA. Retired Education Administrator. Divorced, 3 sons, 1 daughter. Education: AB, cum laude, Education, majors in physical education and physical sciences, minor in mathematics, Fairmont State College, Fairmont, West Virginia, 1957; MEd, mathematics, University of Georgia, 1961; Postgraduate Work: West Virginia University, physics, secondary education, mathematics, summers of 1958, 1959, 1963; Antioch College, physics and mathematics, summer 1960; University of Maryland, mathematics education, curriculum and supervision, administration, summers and evenings, 1965-75. Appointments: Staff Sergeant, US Air Force, 1949-52; Professional Baseball Pitcher, Brooklyn Dodgers Minor Leagues, 1953-55; Math Teacher, Assistant Football Coach, Head Baseball Coach, Madison Memorial High School, Ohio, 1957-60; Math/Science Teacher, Euclid City Schools, Euclid, Ohio, 1961-62; Mathematics Department Head, Richard Montgomery High School, Rockville, Maryland, 1962-65; National Association of Secondary School Principals Administrative Intern, John F Kennedy High School, Silver Spring, Maryland, 1965-66; Vice-Principal, Colonel E Brooke Lee Junior High School, Silver Spring, Maryland, 1966-67; Supervisor of Mathematics, Montgomery County Public Schools, Maryland, 1967-75; Director, Department of Academic Skills, Montgomery County Public Schools, Maryland, 1975-91. Publications: Supervised and directed development and publication of numerous curriculum and instructional guides and documents in K-12 mathematics, reading, English language arts, foreign languages, social studies, science, early childhood learning. Honours: Awarded three National Science Foundation Summer Institute Fellowships; NSF Academic Year Institute Fellowship; Listed in numerous Who's Who publications and biographical dictionaries. Memberships: American Legion; Association for Advancement of Retired Persons; Maryland Retired School Employees Association; Montgomery County Retired Public School Employees Association; Burnt Store Isles Association; Burnt Store Isles Boat Club. Address: 5006 Ovideo Street, Punta Gorda, FL 33950, USA.

KLEIN Calvin Richard, b. 19 November 1942, New York, USA. Fashion Designer. m. (1) Jayne Centre, 1964, 1 daughter, (2) Kelly Rector, 1986, divorced 2006. Education: Fashion Institute of Technology, New York. Appointments: Own Fashion Business, 1968; President, Designer, Calvin Klein Ltd, 1969-; Consultant, Fashion Institute of Technology, 1975-. Honours: Coty Award, 1973, 1974, 1975; Coty Hall of Fame; FIT President's Award, Outstanding Design Council of Fashion Designers of America. Memberships: Council of Fashion Designers. Address: Calvin Klein Industries Inc, 205 West 39th Street, NY 10018, USA.

KLEIN George, b. 28 July 1925, Budapest, Hungary. Professor; Head of Department. Education: MD, Karolinska Institute, 1951; PhD (hc), Hebrew University, Jerusalem, 1989; DSc (hc), University of Nebraska, 1991; PhD (hc), Tel Aviv University, 1994; D Med Sc (Hon), Osaka University, 2001. Appointments: Instructor in Histology, 1945, Instructor in Pathology, 1946, Budapest University; Research Fellow, 1947-49, Assistant Professor of Cell Research, 1951-57, Professor of Tumour Biology and Head of Department of Tumour Biology, 1957-93, Research Group Leader, Microbiology and Tumour Biology Centre, 1993-, Karolinska Institute; Guest Investigator, Institute for Cancer Research, Philadelphia, USA, 1950; Visiting Professor, Stanford University, USA, 1961; Forgarty Scholar, NIH, USA, 1972; Visiting Professor, Hebrew University, Hadassah Medical School, 1973-93. Publications: Over 1,300 papers in professional scientific journals; 12 essay books. Honours include: DSc (hon), University of Chicago, 1966; MD (hon), University of Debrecen, Hungary, 1988; Institute of Human Virology Lifetime Achievement Award, 1998; Honorary Doctor of Medical Science, Osaka University, 2001; Paracelsus Medal, 2001; The Wick R Williams Memorial Lecture Award, 2001; Ingemar Hedenius Prize, 2002; Mendel Honorary Medal, 2005; IARC Medal of Honor, 2005; Karolinska Institute 200 Year Anniversary Medal, 2010; Royal Award, Swedish Academy, 2010; Distinguished Professorship Award, Karolinska Institute, 2010. Memberships: Royal Swedish Academy of Sciences; Foreign Member, Finnish Scientific Society; Foreign Associate, National Academy of Sciences of the United States; Honorary Member, Hungarian Academy of Sciences; Honorary Member, American Association of Immunologists; Foreign Member, American Philosophical Society; Honorary Member, French Society of Immunology;

Honorary Foreign Member, American Academy of Arts and Sciences; Honorary Member, American Association for Cancer Research; Member, Scientific Advisory Board, Ludwig Institute; Editor, Advances in Cancer Research; Member, Nobel Assembly of Karolinska Institutet; Titular Member, European Academy of Sciences, Arts and Humanities; Academy of Cancer Immunology; Honorary Fellow, European Association for Cancer Research. Address: Karolinska Institutet, Box 280, 171 77 Stockholm, Sweden. E-mail: georg.klein@ki.se

KLEIN Ladislau, b. 15 October 1942, Arad, Romania. Chemical Engineer; Assistant Professor. m. Katalin. Education includes: Engineer/Diploma, Chemical Engineering, Politechnical University of Timisoara, 1965; Certificates, Chemical Engineering, Center for Professional Development, Ministry for Chemical Industry, 1975 and 1976; Certificate, Water Resources Quality Protection, 2001; Doctoral Studies, Chemical Engineering, Polytechnic University of Timisoara, 2002; Master Diploma, Financial and Juridical Management of Enterprises, Vasile Goldis Western University, Arad, 2003. Appointments: Chemical Engineer, Dispatch Engineer, Milk Collecting and Processing Enterprise, Oradea, 1965-67; Engineer, Workshop Head, Railway Wagon Plant, Arad, 1967-71; Chemical Engineer, Office Head, Plant Head, Chemical Fertilizer Plant, Arad, 1971-83; Engineer, Office Head, Head of Department, Arad County Office for Water Management (later Arad Agency for Environment Protection, 1983-2001; Environmental Engineer, Quality Department, Arad Water Company, 2001-02; Chancellor, 2004-08, Assistant Professor, 2005-, Vice Dean, 2008-, Faculty for Economics, Vasile Goldis Western University, Arad. Publications: Numerous books, manuals and articles in professional journals; 2 patents. Honours: 24 university diplomas; Diploma, Arad Environment Agency for 10 Years Activity; Diploma, International Conference on Commerce, 2006; Diploma for Excellence, Association of Romanian Faculties for Economics, 2007. Memberships: American Chemical Society. E-mail: ladislauklein@yahoo.com

KLETZ Trevor Asher, b. 23 October 1922, Darlington, England. Chemical Engineer. m. Denise, deceased, 2 sons. Education: BSc, Chemistry, Liverpool University, 1941-44; DSc, Chemical Engineering, 1986, Hon D Tech, 2006, Loughborough University. Appointments: Various Research, Production and Safety appointments, ICI Ltd, 1944-82; Professor, Department of Chemical Engineering, 1978-86, Senior Visiting Research Fellow, 1986-2000, Visiting Professor, 2000-, Loughborough University; Adjunct Professor, Texas A&M University, 2003-10. Publications: 11 books; Over 100 peer-reviewed papers and many articles on process safety. Honours: OBE, 1997. Memberships: Fellow, Royal Academy of Engineering; Institution of Chemical Engineers; Royal Society of Chemistry; American Institute of Chemical Engineers; Honorary Fellow, Safety and Reliability Society and Institute of Safety and Health. Address: 64 Twining Brook Road, Cheadle Hulme, Cheadle, Cheshire SK8 5RJ, England. E-mail: t.kletz@lboro.ac.uk

KLIMES Jiri, b. 2 March 1956, Prerov, Czech Republic. Veterinary Surgeon. Education: Doctor of Veterinary Medicine, 1981; PhD, 1988; Associate Professor, 2005. Appointments: Veterinary Surgeon, University Teacher, Associate Professor, Zoology, Deputy Chief, Department of Biology and Wildlife Diseases, University of Veterinary and Pharmaceutical Sciences, Brno. Publications: Diseases of the Dog and Cat, Vol 1, 2, 1st and 2nd edition; Numerous articles in professional journals. Honours: Josef Hlavka Prize; Czech Literary Fund Prize; Listed in biographical dictionaries. Memberships: Czech Zoological Society; Czech Ornithological Society. Address: University of Veterinary and Pharmaceutical Sciences, Palackeho 1-3, 612 42 Brno, Czech Republic.

KLIMOVSKIY Konstantin, b. 14 January 1926, Kalinin, Russia. Assistant Professor. m. Lyubov Berger, deceased 2003, 1 daughter. Education: Moscow Aviation Institute. Appointments: Candidated Technical Sciences; Senior Research Fellow; Assistant Professor. Publications: 250 scientific works including monographs, one book and more than 100 articles in prestigious journals; 50 patents. Honours: USSR Inventor medal; Honorary Veteran of the Russian Space; Veteran of Labor of the USSR medal; Premium of Shnepp, 2003. Address: 2nd Sokolnicheskaya street, Haus 2, apt 123, 107014 Moscow, Russia.

KLINE Kevin Delaney, b. 24 October 1947, St Louis, USA. Actor. m. Phoebe Cates, 1989, 1 son, 1 daughter. Education: Indiana University; Julliard School of Drama. Appointments: Founding Member, The Acting Co, NY, 1972-76. Creative Works: Films include: Sophie's Choice; Pirates of Penzance; The Big Chill, 1983; Silverado, Violets Are Blue, 1985; Cry Freedom, 1987; A Fish Called Wanda, 1988; January Man, I Love You to Death, 1989; Soapdish, Grand Canyon, 1991; Consenting Adults, Chaplin, 1992; Dave, 1993; Princess Caraboo, 1994; Paris Match, French Kiss, 1995; Fierce Creatures, 1996; The Ice Storm, In and Out, 1997; A Midsummer Night's Dream, Wild Wild West, 1999; The Anniversary Party, Life as a House, 2001; Orange County, The Emperor's Club, The Hunchback of Notre Dame II (voice), 2002; De-Lovely, 2004; The Pink Panther, A Prairie Home Companion, As You Like It, 2006; Trade, 2007; Definitely, Maybe, 2008. Theatre includes: Numerous Broadway appearances in On the Twentieth Century, 1978; Pirates of Penzance, 1980; Arms and the Man, 1985; Several off-Broadway appearances including Richard III, 1983; Henry V, 1984; Hamlet (also director), 1986, 1990; Much Ado About Nothing, 1988; Measure for Measure, 1995; The Seagull, 2001. Honours include: Tony Award, 1978, 1980; Academy Award, Best Supporting Actor, 1989. Address: c/o William Morris Agency, 1325 Avenue of the Americas, New York, NY 10019, USA.

KLINGER Thomas Scott, b. 4 May 1955, Kalamazoo, Michigan, USA. Professor. 1 son, 1 daughter. Education: AA, Bradford College, 1974; BA, Macalester College, 1975; MA, 1979, PhD, 1984, University of South Florida. Appointments: Adjunct Assistant Professor, Saint Leo College, 1984-85; Assistant Professor, 1985-90, Associate Professor, 1990-96, Professor, 1996-, Bloomsburg University. Publications include: Numerous articles in scientific journals. Honours: Fellowship, University of South Florida, 1978-80; Honorable mention, Florida Academy of Sciences, 1980; Science Departmental Award, Bradford College; Midwest Newspapers Scholarship Prize; Mary C Barret Scholarship Prize; Mary C Barret Community Service Award; Antarctic Service Medal, 1999; Listed in numerous Who's Who and biographical publications. Memberships: Society for Integrative and Comparative Biology; American Microscopial Society; Sigma Xi; American Association for the Advancement of Science. Address: Department of Biology, Bloomsburg University, 400 East Second Street, Bloomsburg, PA 17815, USA. E-mail: tklinger@bloomu.edu

KLINSMANN Jurgen, b. 30 June 1964, Germany. Football Coach; Former Professional Football Player. m. Debbie, 1995, 1 son, 1 daughter. Appointments: Started career with

Stuttgarter Kickers, before moving to Stuttgart, 1984-89; Member, Winning Team, World Cup, 1990, UEFA Cup with Inter Milan, 1991 and Bayern Munich, 1996; With Inter Milan, 1989-92; AS Monaco, 1992-94; Tottenham Hotspur, 1994-95, 1997-98, played for Bayern Munich, 1995-97, Sampdoria, 1997; International Ambassador for SOS Children's Villages in partnership with FIFA; Founder, children's care charity AGAPEDIA; Vice President, Soccer Solutions; International Ambassador, FIFA World Cup Germany 2006; Head Coach, German National Football Team, 2004-. Honour: Footballer of the Year, 1988, 1994; English Footballer of the Year, 1995. Address: Soccer Solutions LLC, 744 SW Regency Place, Portland, OR 97225, USA. Website: www.soccersolutions.com

KLODT Claudia, b. 24 April 1960, Freiburg, Germany. Professor. Education: MA, Classics, Freiburg, 1986; Dr phil, Munich, 1991; Habilitation, Hamburg, 2001. Appointments: Lecturer, Classics, Rostock, Hamburg and Leipzig, 1991-2001; Professor, Classics, Bochum, 2002-. Publications: Ciceros Rede Pro Rabirio Postumo, 1992; Bescheidene Groesse, 2001; Numerous articles in professional journals. Memberships: Mommsen-Gesellschaft.

KLUM Heidi, b. 1 June 1973, Bergisch Gladbach, Germany. Model; Actress; TV host; Businesswoman; Fashion Designer; TV Producer; Artist. m. (1) Ric Pipino, 1997-2002, (2) Seal, 2005-12, 2 sons, 2 daughters. Career: Winner, Model 92, Germany, 1992; Designer of clothes, jewellery and fragrances; TV appearances: Malcolm in the Middle; I Get That a Lot; Spin City; Sex and the City; CSI: Miami; How I Met Your Mother; Yes, Dear; Project Runway, 2004; Germany's Next Top Model; Films: 54, 1998; Blow Dry, 2001; Ella Enchanted, The Life and Death of Peter Sellers, 2004; Blue Collar Comedy Tour, 2003; The Devil Wears Prada, 2006; Perfect Stranger, 2007; Hoodwinked Too! Hood vs Evil, 2011. Publications: Heidi Klum's Body of Knowledge, 2004; Contributions to German TV network RTL, and newspaper, Die Zeit. Honours: Peabody Award, 2008.

KNAPMAN Roger Maurice, b. 20 February 1944, Crediton, Devon, England. Chartered Surveyor. m. Carolyn Eastman, 1 son, 1 daughter. Education: Royal Agricultural College, Cirencester, England. Appointments: Conservative Member of Parliament for Stroud, 1987-97; Parliamentary Private Secretary to the Minister of State for the Armed Forces, 1991-93; Junior Government Whip, 1995-96; Senior Government Whip and Lord Commissioner of the Treasury, 1996-97; UKIP Political Advisor, 2000-01, Leader, 2001-2006, UK Independence Party; UKIP MEP for South West of England, 2004-. Address: Coryton House, Coryton, Okehampton, Devon, EX20 4PA, England.

KNECHT Robert Jean, b. 20 September 1926, London, England. Professor of French History Emeritus. m. (1) Sonia Hodge, deceased 1984 (2) Maureen White, 1986. Education: BA, 1948, MA, 1953, King's College, London; DLitt, Birmingham, 1984. Appointments: Assistant Lecturer, Modern History, 1956-59, Lecturer, Modern History, 1959-68, Senior Lecturer, Modern History, 1968-78, Reader in French History, 1978-85, Professor of French History, 1985-94, Emeritus Professor of French History and Honorary fellow of Institute for Advanced Research in the Humanities, 1998-, University of Birmingham. Publications: The Voyage of Sir Nicholas Carewe, 1959; Francis I and Absolute Monarchy, 1969; The Fronde, 1975; Francis I, 1982; French Renaissance Monarchy, 1984; The French Wars of Religion, 1989; Richelieu, 1991; Renaissance Warrior and Patron, 1994; The Rise and Fall of Renaissance France, 1996; Catherine de'Medici, 1998; Un Prince de la Renaissance: François Ier et son royaume, 1998; The French Civil Wars, 2000; The Valois, 2004; The French Renaissance Court, 2008. Honour: Chevalier dans l'Ordre des Palmes Académiques, 2001; Officier dans l'Ordre des Palmes Académiques, 2010. Memberships: Fellow, Royal Historical Society; Society of Renaissance Studies, chairman, 1989-92; Chairman, Society for the Study of French History, 1994-97. Address: 79 Reddings Road, Moseley, Birmingham B13 8LP, England.

KNEESE Carolyn C, b. 16 September 1941, Austin, Texas, USA. Retired Associate Professor. Education: BA, University of Texas, 1962; MA, Houston Baptist University, 1990; Ed D, University of Houston, 1994. Appointments: Teacher, Austin Independent School District, Texas, 1963-64; Teacher, Highland Park Independent School District, Texas, 1964-67; Research Assistant, University of Houston, 1993; Research Associate, Texas A&M University, 1994; Program Evaluator, Alameda Unified School District, California, 1995; Adjunct Professor, Center for Professional Teacher Education, University of Texas, 1998; Assistant Professor, 1998-2002, Associate Professor, 2003, Education Administration, Texas A&M Commerce. Publications: Co-author, School Calendar Reform: Learning in all Seasons, 2006; Co-editor with C Ballinger, Balancing the School Calendar: Perspectives from the Public and Stakeholders, 2009; Numerous journal articles, monographs, books and book chapters. Honours: Research Award, American Education Research Association, 2000; Committee for Review of Sex as Essential Knowledge and Skills for State Board of Education; Listed in international biographical dictionaries. Memberships: American Association of University Women; Texas Executive Women; Board Member, Baylor College of Medicine Partnership. Address: 1100 Uptown Park Blvd #121, Houston TX 77056, USA. E-mail: cckneese@aol.com

KNIGHT Edith Joan, b. 18 May 1932, Great Houghton, Barnsley, England. Retired Teacher; Singer; Poet. m. John Wyndham Knight, deceased. Education: Certificate in Education, Leeds University; RSA Diplomas in Shorthand, Typewriting Teaching, 1969; Qualifications in Music and Singing. Appointments: Secretarial Posts including Confidential Secretary, Barnsley British Co-operative Society, 1949-56; Head of Commercial Studies, 1969-87, Deputy Head of Middle School, 1973-76, Assistant to Head of Upper School, 1976-87, Wombwell High School; Solo singer for 63 years; Formerly, Oratorio Contralto Soloist, Joan Parkin. Publications: Anthologies: Voices on the Wind, 1996; A Lasting Calm, 1997; The Secret of Twilight, 1998; Way Back Then, 1999; Millennium Memories, 2000; A Word of Peace, 2000; The Triplet Times, 2001; The Prime of Life, 2002; Sweet Memories, 2002; Rondeau Challenge, 2003; A Story to Share, 2004; Love Hurts, 2004; Looking On, 2004; Labours of Love, 2005; The Way of God, 2005; Songs of Honour, 2006; Dodger & Friends, 2006; 15 Years of People's Poetry, 2006; Animal Antics, 2007; Sights to Behold, 2007; Count our Blessings, 2007; Memories are Made of This, 2007; Forever Spoken, 2007; 20 Years of Fwd Press, 2008; International Who's Who in Poetry, 2008; Collected Whispers, 2008; Forward Press Poets, 2008; Love's Many Mysteries, 2009; Poetry in magazines including: Poems of the World; Retford Writers; Triumph Herald (hymn); Poetry Now (The Great War Unvisited). Honour: Bronze Medallions, International Society of Poets' Conventions, 1997, 2005, 2006, 2007. Membership: Friend of Poetry-Next-The-Sea, Wells, Norfolk.

KNIGHT Gladys, b. 28 May 1944, Atlanta, Georgia, USA. Singer. Career: Singer, Gladys Knight and the Pips, 1957-89; Signed to Motown Records, 1966; Appearances include: Grand Gala Du Disque, Amsterdam, 1969; European tour, 1974; Kool Jazz Festival, San Diego, 1977; London Palladium, 1978; World Music Festival, 1982; Solo artiste, 1989-; Concerts include: Westbury Music Fair, New York, 1992; Recordings: Albums: Everybody Needs Love, 1967; Feelin' Bluesy, 1968; Silk'n'Soul, 1969; Gladys Knight And The Pips' Greatest Hits, 1970; If I Were Your Woman, 1971; Standing Ovation, 1972; Neither One Of Us, 1973; All I Need Is Time, 1973; Imagination, 1974; Anthology, 1974; Knight Time, 1974; Claudine, 1974; A Little Knight Music, 1975; I Feel A Song, 1975; 2nd Anniversary, 1975; The Best Of Gladys Knight And The Pips, 1976; Pipe Dreams, 1976; Still Together, 1977; 30 Greatest, 1977; The One And Only, 1978; About Love, 1980; A Touch Of Love, 1980; Visions, 1983; The Collection - 20 Greatest Hits, 1984; Solo: Good Woman, 1991; Just for You, 1994; Many Different Roads, 1998; At Last, 2000; Christmas Celebrations, 2002; Best Thing That Ever Happened To Me, 2003; One Voice, 2005; Before Me, 2006; A Christmas Celebration, 2006. Numerous honours include: Top Female Vocalist, Blues and Soul magazine, 1972; American Music Awards, 1975, 1976, 1984, 1989; Grammy Awards: Best Group Vocal Performance, Best R&B Vocal Performance, 1974; Heritage Award, Soul Train Music Awards, 1988; Honoured, Essence Awards, 1992; NAACP Image Award; Magazine awards from Cashbox, Billboard, Record World, Rolling Stone; Star on Hollywood Walk of Fame, 1995; Gladys Knight and the Pips inducted into Rock 'n' Roll Hall of Fame, 1996; Pinnacle Award, 1998. Current Management: Newman Management Inc, 2110 E Flamingo Road, Ste 300, Las Vegas, NV 89119, USA.

KNIGHT Gregory, b. 4 April 1949, Blaby, Leicestershire, England. Member of Parliament; Solicitor. Education: College of Law, London. Appointments: Member of Parliament for Derby North, 1983-97; Assistant Government Whip, 1989-90; Lord Commissioner of the Treasury, 1990-93; Government Deputy Chief Whip, 1993-96; Minister of State for Industry, Department of Trade and Industry, 1996-97; MP for East Yorkshire, 2001-; Shadow Deputy Leader, House of Commons, 2001-03; Shadow Minister for Culture, 2003; Shadow Minister for Railways and Aviation, 2003-05; Shadow Minister for Roads, 2005-. Publications: Westminster Words, 1988; Honourable Insults, 1990; Parliamentary Sauce, 1993; Right Honourable Insults, 1998; Naughty Graffiti, 2005. Honour: Privy Councillor, 1995. Memberships: Member of Conservative Party, 1966-; Member of Law Society, 1973; Member, Bridlington Conservative Club, 2001-. Address: House of Commons, Westminster, London SW1A 0AA, England. E-mail: secretary@gregknight.com

KNIGHT Michael James, b. 29 August 1939, London, England. Surgeon. m. Phyllis Mary, 1 son, 1 daughter. Education: MB BS (London), 1963; LRCP MRCS (Conjoint Board), 1963; FRCS (Royal College of Surgeons), 1967; MS, London, 1975. Appointments: Consultant Surgeon, St George's Hospital, London, St James Hospital, London, Royal Masonic Hospital, London; Honorary Senior Lecturer, St George's Hospital Medical School; Research Registrar, St George's Hospital; Research Registrar, Washington University, St Louis, USA. Publications: Chapters and articles on pancreatic and biliary diseases, and pancreatic islet transplantation. Honours: Hunterian Professor, Royal College of Surgeons, 1975; Member, Court of Examiners of the Royal College of Surgeons; Maingot Prize; External Examiner, Glasgow, Edinburgh, Sri Lanka and Abu Dhabi; Independent Adviser, Health Service Commissioner for England. Membership: Founder, Honorary Secretary and President, Pancreatic Society of Great Britain and Ireland. Address: 33 Sherwood Court, Chatfield Road, London SW11 3UY, England. E-mail: michaelknight119@btinternet.com

KNIGHT Sir Peter Leonard, b. 12 August 1947, Bedford, England. Educator. m. Christine, 2 sons, 1 daughter. Education: BSc, 1968, DPhil, 1972, University of Sussex. Appointments: Research Associate, University of Rochester, New York, USA, 1972-74; SRC Research Fellow, Sussex University, 1974-76; Jubilee Research Fellow, 1976-78, SERC Advanced Fellow, 1978, Royal Holloway College London; SERC Advanced Fellow, 1978-83, Lecturer, 1983-87, Reader, 1987-88, Professor, 1988-, Head of Physics Department, 2002-05, Principal, Faculty of Natural Sciences, 2005-08, Senior Principal, 2008-, Deputy Rector (Research) 2008-10, Imperial College London; Chief Scientific Advisor, National Physical Laboratory, 2002-05; Principal, Royal Society Kavli International Centre, Chicheley Hall. Publications: Principles of Quantum Optics, 1983; Introductory Quantum Optics, 2004; Author of over 400 articles in scientific literature. Honours: Honorary Doctorates: INAOE Mexico, Slovak Academy of Sciences, Sussex University, Heriot-Watt University; Alexander von Humboldt Research Award, 1993; Einstein Medal and Prize for Laser Science, Society of Optical and Quantum Electronics, 1996; Parsons Medal Institute of Physics and Royal Society, 1997; European Physical Society Lecturer, 1998-99; Thomas Young Medal and Prize, Institute of Physics, 1999; President, Optical Society of America, 2004; Knighthood, 2005; Ives Medal of the Optical Society of America, 2008; Glazebrook Medal of the Institute of Physics, 2009; Royal Medal of the Royal Society, 2010. Memberships: Fellow, Institute of Physics; Fellow, Optical Society of America; European Physical Society; The Royal Society; Mexican Academy of Sciences; Academia Europaea. Address: Kavli Royal Society International Centre, Chicheley Hall, Chicheley, Newport Pagnell, MK16 9JJ, England.

KNOBLER Robert, b. 6 December 1945, Bolivia. Professor of Dermatology. Education: BA, 1967, BS, 1969, Columbia University; MD, University of Vienna, 1977. Appointments: Lecturer, Department of Dermatology, Columbia University, 1983-; Professor, Dermatology, University of Vienna Medical School, 1996-; Head, Photoimmunotherapy Center, Dermatology, Vienna; Chairman, 2000-06, Past Chairman, 2006-, EORTC Cutaneous Lymphoma Task Force. Publications: Over 200 publications in professional medical journals. Honours: Unilever Award, 1981; Gold Medal, American Academy of Dermatology, 1992; Research Award, AESCA & Company, 1993. Memberships: New York Academy of Sciences; AAD; ILDS; SID; ESDR; EORTC; SIDLA; European Academy of Dermatology and Venerology (EADV). Address: Medical University of Vienna General Hospital, Department of Dermatology, Wahringerguertel 18-20, A-1090 Vienna, Austria.

KNOPFLER Mark, b. 12 August 1949, Glasgow, Scotland. Musician (guitar); Vocalist; Songwriter; Record Producer. m. Lourdes Salomone, Nov 1983, 2 sons. Education: English Graduate. Career: Former journalist, Yorkshire Evening Post; Member, Brewer's Droop; Café Racers; Founder member, Dire Straits, 1977-88, 1991-; Worldwide concerts and tours, 1978-; Major concerts include: San Remo Song Festival, Italy, 1981; Live Aid, Wembley, 1985; Princes Trust Rock Gala, Wembley, 1986; Nelson Mandela 70th Birthday Tribute, 1988; Guitarist and vocalist, Eric Clapton US tour, 1988; Nordoff-Robbins charity concert, Knebworth Park, 1990.

Numerous compositions include: Private Dancer, Tina Turner, 1985; Setting Me Up, Waylon Jennings, 1984; Co-writer, Money For Nothing, with Sting, 1985; Water Of Love, The Judds, 1989; Film music: Local Hero, 1983; Cal, 1984; The Princess Bride, 1987. Recordings: Albums: with Dire Straits: Dire Straits, 1978; Communique, 1979; Making Movies, 1980; Love Over Gold (Number 1, UK), 1982; Alchemy - Dire Straits Live, 1984; Brothers In Arms (Number 1, 20 countries), 1985; Money For Nothing (Number 1, UK), 1988; On Every Street (Number 1, UK), 1991; On The Night, 1993; with Chet Atkins: Neck And Neck, 1990; with Notting Hillbillies: Missing... Presumed Having, 1990; Solo: Local Hero (film soundtrack), 1983; Cal (film soundtrack), 1984; Golden Heart, 1996; Wag The Dog (film soundtrack), 1998; Metroland, 1999; Neck and Neck, 1999; Hit singles: with Dire Straits: Sultans Of Swing, 1979; Romeo And Juliet, 1981; Tunnel Of Love, 1981; Private Investigations, 1982; Twisting By The Pool, 1983; So Far Away, 1985; Money For Nothing (first video shown on MTV Europe), 1985; Brothers In Arms (first-ever CD single), 1985; Walk Of Life, 1986; Your Latest Trick, 1986; Calling Elvis, 1991; On Every Street, 1992; Solo singles: Going Home (theme from film Local Hero), 1983; Darling Pretty, 1996; Guest on albums including: Slow Train Coming, Bob Dylan, 1979; Solo In Soho, Phil Lynott, 1980; Gaucho, Steely Dan, 1980; Beautiful Vision, Van Morrison, 1982; The Phil Lynott Album, 1982; Boys And Girls, Bryan Ferry, 1985; Down In The Groove, Bob Dylan, 1988; The Shouting Stage, Joan Armatrading, 1988; Land Of Dreams, Randy Newman, 1988; As producer: Infidels, Bob Dylan, 1984; Knife, Aztec Camera, 1984. Honours include: Ivor Novello Awards: Outstanding British Lyric, 1983; Best Film Theme, 1984; Outstanding Contribution to British Music, 1989; Nordoff-Robbins Silver Clef Award, Outstanding Services To British Music, 1985; BRIT Awards: Best British Group, 1983, 1986; Best British Album, 1987; Grammy Awards: Best Rock Performance, Money For Nothing, 1986; Best Country Performance, with Chet Atkins, 1986, 1991; Honorary music doctorate, University of Newcastle Upon Tyne, 1993. Current Management: Ed Bicknell, Damage Management, 16 Lambton Place, London W11 2SH, England.

KNOWLES Colin George, Lord Knowles of Houghton and Burnett, b. 11 April 1939, Southport, England. Retired. 3 daughters. Education: CEDEP, Fontainebleau France; MA, PhD, Trinity College, Delaware, USA. Appointments: Company Secretary and Head of Public Affairs, Imperial Tobacco Ltd, 1960-80; Chairman, Griffin Associates, Ltd, UK, 1980-83; Director, TWS Public Relations (Pty) Ltd, Johannesburg, 1984; Chairman, Concept Communications (Pty) Ltd, Johannesburg, 1983-84; Director of Development and Public Affairs, University of Bophuthatswana, 1985-95; Chairman, Bophuthatswana Region Public Relations Institute of South Africa, 1988-91; Chairman, St John Ambulance Foundation, Bophutharswana, 1989-94; Member Chapter (Governing Body) Priory of St John for South Africa, 1992-99; Director, The Consumer Council of Bophuthatswana, 1991-94; Director, Association for Business Sponsorship of the Arts, 1975-84, Chairman, 1975-80; Director, The Bristol Hippodrome Trust Ltd, 1977-81; Director, The Bath Archaeological Trust Ltd, 1978-81; Director, The Palladian Trust Ltd, 1978-81. Honours: Freeman City of London, 1974; Liveryman, Worshipful Company of Tobacco Pipe Makers and Tobacco Blenders, London, 1973; OStJ, 1977, CStJ, 1991; KStJ, 1995; Lord Knowles of Houghton and Burnett, 2006; Listed in national and international biographical dictionaries. Memberships: Chancellor of the Duchy of Lancaster's Committee of Honour on Business and the Arts, 1980-81; MInstM; MIPR; FIMgt; FRSA; FPRI (SA); APR; Associate Member, Association of Arbitrators of South Africa (AAArb); Carlton Club; MCC. Address: 15 Standen Park House, Lancaster LA1 3FF, England. E-mail: lkhb@talktalk.net

KNOWLES Evelyn, b. 14 April 1931, London, England. Retired City Councillor. 1 son, 2 daughters. Education: BA Honours, Psychology, Ealing College of Higher Education. Appointments: President, Cambridge MS Society; Chair, Cambridge Citizens Advice Bureau; Cambridge City Councillor, 1986-2002; Director, St Lukes Community Centre, 1989-98; Mayor of Cambridge, 2000-01; Non-executive Director, Cambridge Primary Care Trust, 1998-2005; Member, Liberal Democrat Executive Committee, Isle of Wight, 2005-. Memberships: Fellow, Royal Society of Arts; Life Member, National Trust; Friend of University Botanic Garden; Friend of British Library; Member, Fawcett Society; Friends of the Earth. Address: Carisbrooke, 1b Madeira Road, Ventnor, PO38 1QP, England.

KNOX (Alexander John) Keith, b. 27 November 1933, Belper, Derbyshire, England. Electronic Engineer (retired); Record Producer. m. Ingrid Zakrisson Knox, 1 son, 2 stepchildren. Education: BSc, Physics and Maths, Southampton University, London; Brighton College of Advanced Technology; Course with Richard Goodman, Decision Mathematics for Management. Appointments: Electronic Engineer, with EMI, 1957-59, Brush Clevite Company, Hythe, Hampshire, UK, 1959-62; Redifon Ltd, Crawley, Sussex, UK, 1962-64; Amplivox Ltd, Wembley, Middlesex, UK, 1964-65, Transitron Electronic SA, Switzerland, 1965-67; Transitron Electronic Sweden AB, 1967-72; Freelance sound record producer, Caprice Records/ Sonet Records/WEA-Metronome Records (Stockholm), Storyville Records (Copenhagen), 1971-85; Manager for music group, "Sevda", 1971-74; Manager for music group "Music for Xaba", 1972-73; Marketing and liaison engineer, Sonab AB, Solna, Sweden, 1972-74; English language copywriter for advertising agency, Andersson and Lembke AB, Sundbyberg, Sweden, 1974-75; Support Engineer, Royal Institute of Technology (KTH), Stockholm, Sweden, 1975-98; Executive Producer, Silkheart Records, Stockholm, Sweden, 1986-. Publications: (biography, Lars Gullin) Jazz Amour Affair, 1986; Numerous articles for jazz publications and underground press. Address: c/o Silkheart Records, Sveavagen 17, 14tr, SE-11157 Stockholm, Sweden.

KNOX David Laidlaw (Sir), b. 30 May 1933, Lockerbie, Dumfriesshire, Scotland. Member of Parliament, retired. m. Margaret Eva Mackenzie, 2 stepsons, 1 deceased. Education: BSc Honours, Economics, London University. Appointments: Production Manager, printing industry, 1956-62; Internal Company Management Consultant, 1962-70; Parliamentary Adviser, Chartered Institute of Management Accountants, 1980-97; Member of European Legislation Select Committee, 1976-97; Member of Speakers Panel of Chairmen, 1983-97; Member of Parliament for Leek, 1970-83; Vice Chairman, Conservative Party, 1974-75; Member of Parliament for Staffordshire Moorlands, 1983-97; Chairman, London Union of Youth Clubs, 1998-99; Deputy Chairman, London Youth, 1999-. Publications: 4 pamphlets. Honours: Knighted, 1993. Memberships: Past member, Federation of Economic Development Authorities; Past member, Industry and Parliament Trust; Past Honorary Fellowship, Staffordshire University; Member, Conservative Party; Member, Conservative Group for Europe; Member, Tory Reform Group; Member, One World Trust. Address: The Mount, Alstonefield, Ashbourne, Derbyshire, DE6 2FS, England.

DICTIONARY OF INTERNATIONAL BIOGRAPHY 36th EDITION

KNOX Liz, b. 20 January 1945, Glasgow, Scotland. Painter. m. Peter Whittle, 2 sons. Education: Graduate, Edinburgh College of Art, 1971. Appointments: Lab Technician, James Anderson Colours Ltd (now Ciba), Paisley and J & P Coates Ltd, Paisley; Lecturer in Fine Art, Paisley, 1983-2003; Member, Advisory Panel, Gray's School of Art, Aberdeen 2001-03; President, Paisley Art Institute, 2007-; Painting full time, 2003-; Workshops and talks throughout Scotland; Work regularly exhibited throughout Britain and in 2003 in St Petersburg, Russia; Paintings in private collections in Europe, the Middle East and USA, and in corporate collections in London, Edinburgh and Glasgow; President, Paisley Art Institute, 2007-10; Council Member, Royal Glasgow Institute of Fine Arts, 2010-. Publications: Listed in international biographical dictionaries; 1 book cover, 2007. Honours: The Aspect Prize, 2003; The Bessie Scott Award, 2004; The Diploma of Paisley Art Institute (PAI), 2005; The University of the West of Scotland Award, 2006; The Blythswood Square Quaich, 2007; The Arnold Clark Award, 2010; Listed in international biographical dictionaries. Memberships: Paisley Art Institute; Visual Arts Scotland; Glasgow Art Club; Glasgow Society of Women Artists. Address: Jesmond, High Street, Neilston, Glasgow, G78 3HJ, Scotland. E-mail: lizknox1@ntlworld.com

KNOX-JOHNSTON Robin (Sir), b. 17 March 1939, London, England. Master Mariner m. Suzanne Singer, 1962, deceased 2003, 1 daughter. Education: Berkhamstead School; DOT Masters Certificate, 1965 Appointments: Merchant Navy, 1957-67; First Person to sail single-handed non-stop around the World, 1968-69; Managing Director, St Katharine's Yacht Haven Ltd, 1975-76; Director, Mercury Yacht Harbours Ltd, 1970-73; Rank Mariner International, 1973-75; Troon Marina Ltd, 1976-83; National Yacht Racing Centre Ltd, 1979-86; Knox-Johnston Insurance Brokers Ltd, 1983-; Managing Director, St Katharine's Dock, 1991-93; Chairman, Clipper Ventures plc; Set record for sailing circumnavigation, 1994; Completed 2nd solo circumnavigation of the World in Yacht, SAGA Insurance, finishing 4th in Velux 5 Oceans Race, 2007. Publications: A World of My Own, 1969; Sailing, 1975; Twilight of Sail, 1978; Last But Not Least, 1978; Bunkside Companion, 1982; Seamanship, 1986; The BOC Challenge 1986-1987, 1988; The Cape of Good Hope, 1989; History of Yachting, 1990; The Columbus Venture, 1991; Sea, Ice and Rock, 1992; Beyond Jules Verne, 1995. Honours: CBE, 1969; Sunday Times Golden Globe, 1969; Royal Institute of Navigation Gold Medal and fellowship, 1992; Jules Verne Trophy, 1994; Book of the Sea Award; Knighthood, 1995; Honorary DSc, Maine Maritime Academy; Honorary DSc, Nottingham Trent University. Memberships: Member, RNLI Council, 1972-; Younger Brother, Trinity House, 1972; Trustee, National Maritime Museum, Greenwich, 1993-2003; Trustee, National Maritime Museum, Cornwall, England; Sports Council Lottery Panel, 1995-99; Fellow, Royal Institute of Navigation; Member, English Sports Council, 1999-2003; President, Sail Training Association, 1992-2001; Honorary Member, Royal Yacht Squadron. Address: St Francis Cottage, Torbryan, Newton Abbot, Devon TQ12 5UR, England. Website: www.robinknox-johnston.co.uk

KNUDSEN Dagfinn Andreas, b. 11 April 1942, Drevja, Norway. Metallurgist. m. Karin Nilssen, 1 daughter. Education: Engineering Degree, Metallurgical Techniques, Trondheim Tekniske Skole, 1967. Appointments: Assistant Engineer, Årdal Verk, ÅSV, 1967-72; Project Engineer, Sunndal Verk, ÅSV, 1972-86; Process Engineer, Franzefoss Bruk, 1986; Service Engineer, Østlandsmeieriet, 1989; Service Engineer, Autodisplay AS, 1991. Publications: Microstructure of Commercial Silicon Material, 1983; Essay on Sensational Journalism, 1989; About Modern Industrial Culture; About Norwegian International Fish Industry; About Employees, Managers, Company & Loyalty. Honours: Vice President, World Congress of Arts, Sciences and Communications. Memberships: Order of International Fellowship, IBC. Address: Bergheim I Drevja, N-8664 Mosjøen, Norway.

KNUTSSON Henry Hoffding, b. 4 August 1930, Copenhagen, Denmark. Structural Engineer. 1 son, 1 daughter. Education: Structural Engineer, 1954. Appointments: Chairman or Secretary, Code of Practise for Lightweight Concrete, 1965-84; Masonry, 1978-97; Safety of Structures and Load for Design, 1974-99. Secretary for CEN/TC 124, Timber Structures, 1989-96. Publications: Wall ties for cramping veneer walls, 1976; Constructions for low rise houses until 2 floors, 1977, 1981; General control for building products, 1979, 1986; Foundation for low rise buildings, 1980 (editing only), 1985; Mortar, brickwork, plastering, 1981; Reinforced concrete floors, 1985; Constructions for low rise buildings, 1985; Veneer walls for external insulation, 1988; Wall ties for cramping veneer walls and cavity walls, 1989; Windloads on structures (editing only), 1989; Masonry: materials and properties, 1992; Low rise buildings: insulation, moisture, sound, fire, ventilation, carrying capacity (one of 8 editors), 1998; Author, chapter on brickwork, Handbook for Structures. Memberships: Board Member, 1947-57, Chairman, 1955-57, UNF (The Scientific Society for Youth); Editorial Committee Member, Eurocode 6 Masonry. Address: Askevaenget 39, 2830 Virum, Denmark.

KO Chien-Ho, b. 17 October 1974, Taipei, Taiwan. Professor. m. Li-Chen Tseng, 1 son, 1 daughter. Education: BS, 1997, MS, 1999, Construction Engineering, Certificate, High School Educational Programme, 1997, National Taiwan Institute of Technology; PhD, Construction Engineering, National Taiwan University of Science and Technology, 2002; Postdoctoral Researcher, University of California at Berkeley, 2004-05. Appointments: Construction Engineer Officer, Second Lieutenant, ROCA, Ministry of National Defense, 2002-04; Research Director, Co-founder, Lean Construction Institute, 2005-; Executive Director, Co-Founder, Asia Lean Construction Institute, 2005-; Assistant Professor, Department of Industrial Engineering & Technology Management, Da-Yeh University, 2005-08; Assistant Professor, Department of Civil Engineering, 2008-10, Associate Professor, 2010-, National Pingtung University of Science and Technology. Publications: 21 articles in professional journals. Honours: Lung-Shan Temple Scholarship, 1995; Lin Hsiung Scholarship, 1996; First Prize, Student Thesis Awards, 1999; Excellent Performance Award, 2000; Meritorious Award, Ministry of National Defense, 2004; Listed in international biographical dictionaries. Memberships: Taipei Association of Fire Protection Engineers; Editor in Chief, Journal of Engineering, Project and Production Management. Address: No 12, Alley 5, Lane 26, Sec 1, ZhongShun St, Taipei 116, Taiwan. E-mail: fpecount@yahoo.com.tw

KO Do-Young, b. 26 May 1973, Republic of Korea. Senior Researcher. Education: MSc, 2003, PhD, 2007, Electrical and Computer Engineering, University of Seoul. Appointments: Assistant Manager, Korea Electric Power Corporation, 1994-2001; Assistant Manager, Korea Hydro & Nuclear Power Company, 2001-03; Senior Researcher, Korea Hydro & Nuclear Power Company, Central Research Institute, 2003-. Publications: Nuclear Power Plants; Co-author, Development of Improved Installation Procedure & Schedule of RVI Modularization; Development of a remote measurement system for the gap between RV and CSB for RVI-modularization; and many others. Honours: Listed in biographical dictionaries. Memberships: Korea Nuclear Society; Korean Society for Noise and Vibration Engineering; Korean Institute of Electrical Engineering. Address: 70, 1312-gil, Yuseong-daero, Yuseong-gu, Daejeon, 305-343, Republic of Korea. E-mail: kodoyoung@khnp.co.kr

KO Eung Nam, b. 17 December 1955, Jeju, Korea. Professor. m. Chang-Mi Boo, 2 daughters. Education: BSc, Mathematics, Yonsei University, 1984; M Eng, Information & Communication, Soongsil University, 1991; D Eng, Computer, Sungkyunkwan University, 2000. Appointments: Seniority Researcher, Daewoo Communication, 1983-93; Professor, Dongwoo College, 1993-97; Professor, Shinsung College, 1997-2001; Professor, Baekseok University, 2001-. Publications: 70 international journal and proceedings lists; 18 domestic book publication lists; 200 domestic journal and proceedings; Most recent titles include: A Centralized-Abstraction and Replicated-View Architecture running on Ubiquitous Networks for Collaborative Multimedia Distance Education Services, 2007; An Intelligent Error Detection-Recovery System for Multimedia CSCW based on Situation-Awareness: AEDRS, 2007; An Application Program Sharing Model With Fault-Tolerance for Multimedia Distance Education System based on RCSM, 2007; An Adaptive Fault-Tolerance QoS for Whiteboard Errors based on RCSM for Ubiquitous Computing, 2007; An Adaptive Dynamic Window Binding Model for RCSM, 2007; An Error Sharing Agent for Multimedia Collaboration Environment Running on Pervasive Networks, 2007. Honours: Best Project Award, IITA, 2005; Best Teacher Award, Baekseok University, 2005; Best Paper Award, Korea Multimedia, 2006; Award of the Director of IITA, 2007; Award of the Ministry of Knowledge Economy, MKE, 2008; Best Paper Presentation Award, APIS, 2009; Best Academy Award of KIPS, 2009; Best Paper Award of DCS, 2009; Meritorious Award of KIPS, 2009; UCC Award of Backseok University, 2009; IBC Medal Award, 2009; Award of Prime Minister, 2010; Award of Minister of Public Administration and Security, 2010; Best Paper Award of SMT, 2010; Best Paper Award of ISS, 2011; Meritorious Award of ISS, 2011; Meritorious Award of KIPS, 201l. Memberships: IJSH; WSEAS; KIPS; KMMS; DCS; KI-IT; KONI; KIISE; IITA; Korea Multimedia Association; Public Procurement Service; NEMA. Address: Division of Information & Communication, Baekseok University, 115 Anseo-Dong, Cheonan, ChungNam, Korea 330-704, Korea. E-mail: ssken@bu.ac.kr Website: www.bu.ac.kr

KO Jih-Yang, b. 13 July 1955, Kaohsiung, Taiwan. Orthopaedic Surgeon. m. Lih-Ching Hsiu, 1 son, 1 daughter. Education: Department of Medicine, Taipei Medical University, Taiwan, 1980; Department of Orthopaedic Surgery, Jikei University School of Medicine, Tokyo, Japan, 1983-84; San Diego School of Medicine, University of California, 1993; Department of Orthopaedics, Mayo Clinic, Rochester, Minnesota, USA, 1993. Publications: Periacctabular osteotomy through a modified ollier transtrochanteric approach for treatment of painful dysplastic hips, 2002; Pathogenesis of partial tear of the rotator cuff: A clinical and pathologic study, 2006; Increased IL-1ß expression and myofibroblast recruitment in subacromial bursa is associated with rotator cuff lesion with shoulder stiffness, 2008; Increased Dickkopf-1 expression accelerates bone cell apoptosis in femoral head osteonecrosis, 2010. Honours: Award, President of Taiwan Shoulder & Elbow Society, 2006; Award, President of Taiwan Paediatric Orthopaedic Society, 2006-08; Award, President of Taiwan Orthopaedic Research Society, 2010-12. Memberships: Asia Shoulder Association; Orthopaedic Association, ROC; Western Pacific Orthopaedic Association. Address: 123, Ta Pei Road, Niao Sung Dist, Kaohsiung City, 83301, Taiwan. E-mail: kojy@adm.cgmh.org.tw

KO Kwang Sun, b. 4 October 1973, Korea. Director. m. Hyun Sun Ryu. Educaiton: BS, 1998, MS, 2004, PhD, 2007, Sungkyunkwan University. Appointments: Research Professor, Sungkyunkwan University, 2007-08; Director, Financial Security Agency, 2008-. Address: Financial Security Agency, 15F 36-1 Yoido-Dong, Youngdeungpo-Gu, Seoul, 150-886, Korea.

KO Sang-Hun, b. 1 August 1962, Seoul, South Korea. Professor. m. Hyun-Joo Lee, 2 daughters. Education: Harvard Shoulder Service, 2007. Appointments: Professor, University of Ulsan, College of Medicine, 2003; Chief Surgeon, Orthopaedics, Ulsan University Hospital, 2004; Harvard Shoulder Service, Harvard University, 2007. Publications: Single Row Supraspinatus Tendon Repair Using Modified Mattress Locking Stitches, 2008. Honours: Textbook Editing Award, Korean Shoulder Elbow Society, 2008. Memberships: Korean Shoulder Elbow Society; Korean Orthopaedic Association. Address: Orthopaedics, Ulsan University Hospital, 290-3, Jeon-Ha dong, Dong gu, Ulsan-Metropolitan City, Republic of Korea. E-mail: shkoshko@yahoo.co.kr

KO Woo Shin, b. 2 January 1963, Busan, Republic of Korea. Oriental Medicine Physician; Educator. m. Jung Soo Jung, 1992, 2 children. Education: MD, Oriental Medicine, WonKwang University, Iksan, 1995; PhD, Pusan National University, Busan, 2004; Licensed Oriental Medicine Physician, Ministry of Health & Welfare, 1988. Appointments: Korean Army, 1988-90; Chief, Clinical Research Centre for Oriental Medicine, Dongeui University, Busan, 2005-06; Director, Ulsan Dongeui Oriental Medicine Hospital, 2006-; Committee Member, Public Welfare of Srs, Korea, 2006-07. Publications: Author, Text of Traditional Korean Dermatology & Surgery. Honours: Grantee, Ministry of Health & Welfare, 2005; Grantee, KOSEF, 2005. Memberships: Korean Oriental Medicine; Ophthalmology, Otolaryngology & Dermatology. Address: Ulsan Dongeui Oriental Medicine Hospital, 479-7 Singung-Dong, Nam-Gu, Ulsan 680-824, Republic of Korea. E-mail: wsko@deu.ac.kr

KOBAYASHI Keiji, b. 15 May 1938, Yokkaichi-city, Mie, Japan. Researcher. m. Kazuko, 2 daughters. Education: Bachelor's degree, Nagoya Institute of Technology; Doctor, Tokyo Institute of Technology. Appointments: Central Research Laboratory, 1960, Chief Researcher, Research and Development Centre, 1977, Toshiba; Assembly man, Kuramae Association of Tokyo Institute of Technology. Publications: About 75 papers published; 200 patents held; Numerous articles in professional journals. Honours: Japan Ceramic Society Award, 1962; International Professional of the Year, 2007; 47 patent registration awards, Toshiba, 1960-2006. Memberships: Electrochemical Society of Japan; Ceramic Society of Japan; Chemical Society of Japan; Applied Physics Society of Japan. Address: 241-0814, 3-11-12, Nakazawa, Asahi, Yokohama, Japan.

KOGAN Pavel, b. 6 June 1952, Moscow, Russia. Conductor. 1 son. Education: Violin, 1969-74, Opera and Symphony Conductor, 1970-75, Master's degree, 1975-77, Moscow Conservatory. Appointments: Music Director, Zagreb Philharmonic Orchestra, 1987-90; Conductor, Bolshoi Opera Theatre, 1986-87; Music Director and Chief Conductor, Moscow State Symphony Orchestra, 1989-; Principal Guest

DICTIONARY OF INTERNATIONAL BIOGRAPHY 36th EDITION

Conductor, Utah Symphony Orchestra, USA, 1997-2005. Publications: Honours: 1st Prize, Sibelius Violin International Competition, Helsinki, 1970; People's Artist of Russia, 1994; The State Prize of the Russian Federation, 1997; Order of Friendship of RF, 2002; Order of Merit of Russia, 2007. Memberships: Russian Academy of Arts. Address: Brusov per 8-10/1, Apt 8, 1250-09 Moscow, Russia. E-mail: mssopr@mail.ru Website: www.msso-kogan.ru

KOH Bo Kyung, b. 30 November 1971, Kwangju, Republic of Korea. Medical Doctor. m. Sanghak Yoon, 1 son, 1 daughter. MD, 1997, PhD, 2003, Catholic University, Seoul; Dermatologist, Korean Dermatologic Association, 2003. Appointments: Instructor, Catholic University, Uijongbu St Mary's Hospital, Kyunggido, 2003-04; Doctor, CNP Skin & Laser Clinic, Seoul, 2004-10; Doctor, Department of Dermatology, Seoul Veterans Hospital, 2011-. Publications: A newly synthesized photostable retinol derivative (retinyl N-formyl aspartamate) for photodamaged skin: profilometric evaluation of 24-week study, 2006; Photorejuvenation with submillisecond neodymium-doped yttrium aluminum garnet (1064nm) laser: a 24-week follow-up, 2010. Honours: Hyundai Pharmacy Academy Awards, 2002; Korean Dermatologic American Association Scholarship, 2004; Listed in international biographical dictionaries. Memberships: Korean Medical Association; Korean Dermatologic Association.

KOH Young-Do, b. 13 April 1962, Seoul, Korea. Professor. m. Hyun-Soo An, 1 son, 1 daughter. Education: MD, Division of Welfare, 1987; Clinical Orthopaedic Board, Korean Medical Association, 1992; Philosophy Doctor, Seoul National University, Seoul, 1998. Appointments: Assistant Professor, Chungbuk National University, Chungju, 1992-96; Visiting Fellow, University of Utah, Saltlake City, USA, 1995; Visiting Fellow, Medical College of Wisconsin, Milwaukee, USA, 1996. Publications: Stress Fracture of the Pelvic Wing-Sacrum After Long-level Lumbosacral Fusion: A Case Report, 2005; Should an Ulnar Styloid Fracture be Fixed Following Volar Plate Fixation of a Distal Radial Fracture? 2010. Memberships: NASS; Korean Society of Spine Surgery. Address: Ewha Womans University, School of Medicine, 911-1, Mokdong, Yangcheongku, Seoul 158-710, Korea.

KOH Young-Sang, b. 12 November 1966, Jeju, Republic of Korea. Professor. m. Hwa-Jin Oh, 2 sons, 1 daughter. Education: BS (magna cum laude), 1989, MS, 1991, PhD, 1996, Seoul National University, Republic of Korea. Appointments: Postdoctoral Fellow, Harvard Medical School and Massachusetts General Hospital, Boston, 1996-97; Postdoctoral Fellow, Baylor College of Medicine, Houston, 1997-98; Full-time Lecturer, Assistant Professor, Associate Professor, Professor, Jeju National University, 1998-; Investigator, Microbial Genome Center for Skin Infection, Seoul National University College of Medicine, 2001-05; Chairman, Department of Microbiology, Jeju National University College of Medicine, 2001-06; Committee Member, Science Promotion Committee, Jeju National University, 2002-04; Assistant Dean for Basic Medicine, Jeju National University College of Medicine, 2003-05; Visiting Associate Professor, Dana-Farber Cancer Institute, Harvard Medical School, Boston, 2006-2008; Dean for Academic Affairs, Jeju National University, School of Medicine, 2010-12. Publications: Author, Medical Microbiology, 3rd edition, 2004, 4th edition, 2005, 5th edition, 2007; PNAS, 2007. Contribution of articles to professional journals including EMBO J, Journal of Bacteriology, Infection and Immunity. Honours: Excellent Dissertation Award, Seoul National University, 1996; Listed in national and international biographical dictionaries. Memberships: Fellow Member, Korean Society for Microbiology, 1998-; Fellow Member, Microbiological Society of Korea, 2000-. Address: Jeju National University School of Medicine, 102 Jejudaehakno, Jeju 690-756, Republic of Korea. E-mail: yskoh7@jejunu.ac.kr

KOIDE Samuel S, b. 6 October 1923, Honolulu, Hawaii, USA. Physician. m. Sumi M Mitsudo, 2 sons. Education: BS, University of Hawaii, 1945; MD, 1953, MS, 1954, PhD, 1960, Northwestern University. Appointments: Associate, Sloan Kettering Institute for Cancer Research, New York, USA, 1960-65; Senior Scientist, Population Council, New York, USA, 1965-2004. Publications: Over 300 paper in Biomedical Journals. Honours: Career Development Award, NIH, PHS, USA, 1963-65. Memberships: American Society of Molecular Biology and Biochemistry; The Biochemical Society; American Society of Cell Biology; Marine Biological Laboratory; USA Society for Experimental Biology and Medicine. Address: Koide Desk, 134 Lefurgy Ave, Dobbs Ferry, NY 10522, USA. E-mail: koide@optonline.net

KOKHANOVSKY Alexander, b. 4 June 1961, Minsk, Belarus. Physicist. m. Marina Bulash, 1 son, 1 daughter. Education: Diploma in Physics, 1983, PhD, Optics, 1991, Institute of Physics, Minsk, Belarus; Dr Sci (habil), Physics of Atmosphere and Hydrosphere, Main Geophysical Observatory, St Petersburg, 2011. Appointments: Institute of Physics, Minsk, Belarus, 1983-2004; Institute of Environmental Physics, Bremen, Germany, 2001-. Publications: Books: Light Scattering Media Optics, 1999, 2001, 2004; Polarization Optics of Random Media, 2003; Cloud Optics, 2006; Aerosol Optics, 2008; Satellite Aerosol Remote Sensing Over Land (editor), 2009; Light Scattering Reviews (editor), 2006-12. Honours: Science and Technology Agency of Japan, 1996. Memberships: American Geophysical Union; European Geophysical Union. Address: IUP, University of Bremen, O Hahn Allee 1, 28334 Bremen, Germany. E-mail: alexk@iup.physik.uni-bremen.de Website: www.iup.physik.uni-bremen.de/~alexk

KOLM Serge Christophe, b. 14 December 1932, Paris, France. Research. Education: Ecole Polytechnique, Paris, 1953; Corps et Ecole des Ponts et Chaussées. Appointments: Director, Senegal Development Mission, 1958-61; Professor and Vice Director, ENSAE, Paris, 1961-63; Professor, Harvard University, 1963-67; Professor, Stanford University, 1967-71; Professor, EHESS, ENPC, IEP, Paris, 1972-. Publications: Over 300 articles in scientific journals; 40 books including: Financial and Monetary Choices, 1966; Justice and Equity, 1971; Modern Theories of Justice, 1998; Macrojustice, 2004; The Good Economy, 1984; Reciprocity, 2006. Honours: Officier des Palmes Académiques. Memberships: Fellow, Econometric Society. Address: 20 rue Henrie-Heine, 75016 Paris, France. E-mail: serge.kolm@wanadoo.fr

KOLODIN Nikolay, b. 11 August 1941, Arzamas, Nizhniy Novgorod region, USSR. Journalist. Education: Graduate, Faculty of History and Philology, Ushinski Yaroslavl State Pedagogical Institute, 1964. Appointments: Editor, Medical Information and Analytical Centre, Department of Health and Pharmacy, Yaroslavl region. Publications: 10 books; 2 books of poetry. Honours: Medal, NI Pirogov Russian Red Cross Society; Diploma, Ministry of the Russian Federation for Press, Television and Radio and Mass Communications; Ministry of Health and Social Development; Winner of many regional art competitions. Memberships: Union of

Journalists of Russia. Address: House 16, Building 2, Apt 1, Suzdal Highway, Yaroslavl, Russian Federation. E-mail: miac@zdrav.yar.ru

KOMAN Alan J, Attorney; Educator. Education: BA, Cornell University; JD, Duke University School of Law; Certificate, Hague Academy of International Law; LLB, University of Munich School of Law. Appointments: Instructor, National Security Issues and Military History, Emory University, Atlanta, Georgia; Guest Lecturer, National Security Issues, Air University of the US Air Force, Montgomery, Alabama; Guest Lecturer in the Law Schools at Duke, Harvard, Munich, University of Pennsylvania, University of Virginia; Guest Lecturer at Johns Hopkins University and Swarthmore College. Publications: Princes of Darkness, 1996; The Last Surge to the South: The New Enemies of Russia in the Rhetoric of Zhirinovsky, 1996; The Legal Effects of War: When the Next Great War Comes, What Issues Will Face Attorneys in Private Practice? 1997; A Who's Who of Your Ancestral Saints, 2010; The Law of Trial by Combat in Medieval England. Honours: Most Venerable Order of St John, 2001, Officer Brother, 2004; Sovereign Military Order of the Temple of Jerusalem, 2004; Order of St Gregory the Great, 2005. Memberships: American Bar Association; International Society for Military Law and the Law of War; Saint Thomas More Society; State Bar of Georgia; Order of the Crown of Charlemagne; National Society of Americans of Royal Descent; Baronial Order of Magna Carta; Military Order of the Crusades; Order of Three Crusades 1096-1192; Descendants of the Knights of the Garter; St Andrew's Society; General Society of Colonial Wars; First Families of Georgia; Sons of the Revolution; Society of the War of 1812; Colonial and Antebellum Bench and Bar; Antebellum Planters; Military Order of the Stars and Bars; Order of Indian Wars; many other learned societies.

KOMAR Victor G, b. 29 September 1913, Sysran, Russia. Adviser. m. Lorena De Pascual, 2 sons. Education: Electrical Engineering diploma, All Union Industrial Institute, Moscow, 1937. Appointments: Engineer, Moscow Transformer Works, 1930-37; Researcher, Cinema Research Institute, 1937-42; Researcher, Deputy Director and Director, Head of 3-D Cinematography and Head of the Cine-holography Laboratory, Cinema and Photo Research Institute, 1942-95; Lecturer, Leningrad Cine and Television Institute, Samarkand; Professor, Moscow Energy Institute; Academician, International Informatization Academy, 1995-; Academician, Academy of Cinematography Arts, 2002-; Main Adviser, NIFKI on Science. Publications: More than 170 books and articles in professional journals. Honours: Order of Red Star, 1944; Honoured Science Worker, 1968; Order of Labour Red Star, 1971; NIKA, Russian Academy of Cinematographic Arts, 2003; Order of Merit for the Motherland, 2009; and others. Memberships: Cinematographer Society of Russia; Fellow, Motion Pictures and Television Engineer Society (USA); Honorary Member: British Kinematograph, Sound and TV Society; International Union of Technical Cinematography Associations. Address: Leningradsky Prospect 45-4-243, 125167 Moscow, Russia.

KOMATSU Toshiki, b. 16 November 1968, Japan. Chemical Scientist. Education: BS, 1991, MS, 1993, PhD, 2000, University of Tsukuba. Appointments: NEC Corp, Japan, 1998; AIST, MITI, Japan, 2000; IMS, University of Tsukuba, 2002; NIMS, Japan, 2004; Chisso Petrochemical Corp, 2005. Publications: Articles in professional scientific journals. Memberships: American Chemical Society; Chemical Society of Japan; Photochemical Society of Japan. Address: 56 Goi Research Center, Chisso Petrochemical Corp, Ichihara 290-8551, Japan. E-mail: komatsu@big.or.jp

KONDALARAO Tata, b. 25 December 1954, Balijipata, India. Professor. m. Rambhatla Padmavathi, 2 daughters. Education: MSc; M Phil; PhD. Appointments: Professor and Researcher, Nanochemistry. Publications: 5 international journals on nanomaterials. Honours: Convenor, Fujishima-Tata Foundation of Scholarships. Memberships: International Nanoscience Community; Council of Research Society of India; American Chemical Society; Board of Studies, Ambedkar University, Srikakulam. Address: AP4B Colony, Behind ZP, Srikakulam 532001, Andhra Pradesh, India.

KONDO Masayuki, b. 1 June 1950, Tokyo, Japan. Economics Professor. Education: BS, 1973, MS, 1976, Control Engineering, PhD, Management Engineering, Tokyo Institute of Technology; MS, Electrical Engineering, University of Washington, USA, 1975; MS, Engineering Economic Systems, Stanford University, USA, 1981. Appointments: Industrial Economist, World Bank, Washington, 1991-94; Director, Machinery Aerospace Research Development Ministry, International Trade and Industry, 1996-99; Director, Technology Evaluation Division, 1998-99; Professor, Kochi University of Technology; Associate, School Policy Science, Saitama University; Lecturer, French ENPC Graduate School of International Business, Tokyo; Visiting Scholar, FhG-ISI; Invited Professor, Beijing Aerospace University; Professor, Yokohama National University, 2001-. Publications: Strategy to Create University Spin-Offs, 2002; Co-editor and co-author, Innovation Networks and Knowledge Cluster, 2008; 21st Century Innovation Systems for Japan and the United States; Co-editor and co-author, 21st Century Innovation Systems for Japan and the United States, 2009; Numerous articles in professional journals. Honours: Erskine Fellow, University of Canterbury, New Zealand, 2004; Best Paper Award, 6th International Symposium on Management of Technology, 2009.

KONG Byeong Seon, b. 19 April 1968, Busan, Republic of Korea. Doctor. m. Kyung Ah Kim, 1 son, 1 daughter. Education: B Med, Busan National University Medical College, 1993; M Med, 2001, PhD, Medicine, 2004, Dong-A University Medicine Graduate School. Appointments: Guest Doctor, Orthopaedic Department, Wurzberg University, Germany, 1998-99; Doctor, Hand and Microsurgery Department, Seil Hospital, Busan, Korea, 1999-2001; Chief, Hand and Microsurgery Department, Choohae Hospital, Busan, 2001-06; Orthopaedic Specialist, Chief, Hand and Microsurgery Department, Chief, Orthopaedic Department, Good Moonwha Hospital, Busan, 2006-07; Hand and Microsurgery Department, Busan Centum Hospital, South Korea, 2007-08; Research Fellow, Hand Department, Massachusetts General Hospital, Boston, Massachusetts, USA, 2008; Doctor, Westbusan Centum Hospital, South Korea, 2009-. Publications: Numerous articles in professional journals. Honours: 2 Academic Prizes, Busan-Ulsan-Kyeongnam Orthopaedic Society, 2004 and 2010; Academic Prize, Korean Microsurgical Society, 2005. Memberships: Korean Orthopaedic Association; Korean Microsurgical Society; Korean Society for Surgery of the Hand; Korean Foot and Ankle Society. Address: Lucky APT 5-501, Ocheon 2 Dong, Dongrae Gu, Busan, South Korea. E-mail: gongja2000@yahoo.co.kr

KONG Surk-Key, b. 15 September 1955, Chonan City, Chung Namdo, Republic of Korea. University Professor. m. Sook Kim, 1 son, 1 daughter. Education: Department of Environmental Engineering, Soongsil University, 1987; PhD, Environmental Engineering, University of Seoul, 1997; Master, Department of Health, Chungnam National University, 2009. Appointments: Environmental Engineer, Lotte Construction Co, Jubail & Yombu Site, 1980-92; Full time Teacher, Joongbu University, 1992-. Publications: Wastewater Treatment, 2003; Environment & Health Hygiene, 2003; Human Health, 2009; Technological Control of Environmental Pollution, 2011. Honours: Listed in international biographical dictionaries; UCC International Peace Prize, 2011. Memberships: Korean Society for Urban Environment; Korean Society of Sanitation. Address: Hyundai Apt, 115-505, 2 dong, Joongbu University, Daijon City, Republic of Korea. E-mail: skkong@joongbu.ac.kr

KONUMA Michiji, b. 25 January 1931, Tokyo, Japan. Physicist. m. Masae Shinohara, 1 son, 1 daughter. Education: BSc, 1953, DSc, 1958, University of Tokyo. Appointments: Research Associate, University of Tokyo, 1958; Research Fellow, National Research Council, Italy, 1963-65; Visiting Professor, Scuola Normale Superiore, Italy, 1963-65; Visiting Professor, Catholic University of Louvain, Belgium, 1965-67; Associate Professor, Research Institute for Fundamental Physics, Kyoto University, 1967-83; Professor of Physics, 1983-96, Professor Emeritus, 1996-, Keio University, Japan; Professor and Dean, 1996-2001, Full-time Adviser, 2001-03, Professor Emeritus, 2005, Faculty of Environmental and Information Studies, Musashi Institute of Technology, Japan; Trustee, Kanagawa Dental College, Japan, 2009-. Publications: Numerous articles in professional journals. Honours: Honorary Member, Roland Eötvös Physical Society, Hungary, 1997; Honorary member, Hungarian Academy of Sciences, 1998; Soryushi Distinguished Service Medal, Committee for Research on Elementary Particle Theory, Physical Society of Japan, 2004. Memberships: Physical Society of Japan; Association of Asia Pacific Physical Societies; American Physical Society; History of Science Society of Japan; Pugwash Conferences of Science and World Affairs; many others. Address: 200-9 Kudencho, Sakaeku, Yokohama, 247-0014, Japan. E-mail: mkonuma@a8.keiv.jp

KOO Jae-Mean, b. 5 April 1956, Mokpo, Jeonnam, Korea. Educator. m. Sung-Hee Kim, 2 daughters. Education: BA, 1980, MA, 1982, PhD, 1991, Mechanical Engineering, Sung Kyun Kwan University, South Korea. Appointments: Adjunct Professor, 2001-06, Research Professor, 2006-, School of Mechanical Engineering, Sung Kyun Kwan University, South Korea. Publications: A new mixed Mode fracture Criterion: Maximum Tangential Strain Energy Dentistry Criterion, 1991. Honours: Best Paper Award, Energy Week, 2008; Ministry of Knowledge Economy, 2008. Memberships: ASME; Committee #7, ASME Nuclear Engineering Division. Address: School of Mechanical Engineering, Sung Kyun Kwan University, 300 Chunchun-dong, Jangan-gu, Suwon, Kyonggi-do 440-746, South Korea. E-mail: kjm9000@skku.edu

KOOK Youn-Gyou, b. 15 August 1972, Wanju, Korea. Researcher. Education: BA (Honours), 1999, MA, 2001, PhD, 2007, Computer Science, Kwangwoon University. Appointments: First Lieutenant, Infantry Corps, Republic of Korea Army, 1994-96; Lecturer, Computer Science, Kwangwoon University, Hongik University and Kyunghee University, 2001-06; Senior Researcher, Cellbig Inc, 2006-07; Principal Researcher, BISTel Inc, 2007-08; Lecturer, Information Technology Engineering, Korea University of Technology and Education, 2008-09; Senior Researcher, Department of National Science and Technology Information Service, Korea Institute of Science and Technology Information, 2009-11. Publications: 5 reports on information technology business; 40 articles in professional journal and proceedings. Honours: Listed in international biographical dictionaries. Memberships: Editorial Committee, International Journal of Advancements in Computing Technology. Address: 335, Gwahangno, Yuseong-gu, Daejeon, 305-806, Korea. E-mail: ykkook@kisti.re.kr

KOONTZ Dean R(ay), (David Axton, Brian Coffey, Deanna Dwyer, K R Dwyer, John Hill, Leigh Nichols, Anthony North, Richard Paige, Owen West), b. 9 July 1945, Everett, Pennsylvania, USA. Writer. m. Gerda Ann Cerra, 15 October 1966. Education: BS, Shippensburg University, 1966. Publications: Star Quest, 1968; The Fall of the Dream Machine, Fear That Man, 1969; Anti-Man, Beastchild, Dark of the Woods, The Dark Symphony, Hell's Gate, 1970; The Crimson Witch, 1971; A Darkness in My Soul, The Flesh in the Furnace, Starblood, Time Thieves, Warlock, 1972; A Werewolf Among Us, Hanging On, The Haunted Earth, Demon Seed, 1973; Strike Deep, After the Last Race, 1974; Nightmare Journey, The Long Sleep, 1975; Night Chills, Prison of Ice, 1976, revised edition as Icebound, 1995; The Vision, 1977; Whispers, 1980; Phantoms, 1983; Darkfall, 1984; Twilight Eyes, The Door to December, 1985; Strangers, 1986; Watchers, 1987; Lightning, 1988; Midnight, 1989; The Bad Place, 1990; Cold Fire, 1991; Hideaway, Dragon Tears, 1992; Mr Murder, Winter Moon, 1993; Dark Rivers of the Heart, 1994; Strange Hideways, Intensity, 1995; Tick-Tock, 1996; Fear Nothing, 1998; False Memory, 1999; From the Corner of the Eye, 2000; One Door Away from Heaven, 2001; By the Light of the Moon, 2002; The Face, Odd Thomas, 2003; Life Expectancy, 2004.; Forever Odd, 2005; The Husband, Brother Odd, 2006; The Good Guy, The Darkest Evening of the Year, 2007; Dead and Alive, 2008. Contributions to: Books, journals, and magazines. Honours: Daedalus Award, 1988; Honorary DLitt, Shippensburg University, 1989. Address: William Morris Agency, 1325 Avenue of the Americas, New York, NY 10019, USA.

KOPTAGEL-ILAL Günsel, b. 1 October 1933, Istanbul, Turkey. Psychiatrist; Psychoanalyst. m. Gürkan Ilal. Education: BA, American College for Girls, Istanbul, 1953; Dr med (MD), Istanbul University Medical Faculty, 1959; Neuro-psychiatrist, Free University of Berlin, 1964. Appointments: Assistant Doctor, Istanbul University Psychiatry Clinic, 1959-60; Resident Doctor, Free University Berlin, 1960-64; Chief Resident, 1964-68, Lecturer (Dozent), 1968-73, Professor, 1973-2000, Psychiatry, Istanbul University; Guest Professor, Giessen and Kassel Universities, Germany, 1985-88; Member, CPT Committee of the Human Rights Department at the Council of Europe, 2002-06. Publications: 71 books; 192 articles; 4 audio tapes; 4 book reviews. Honours: Foreign Publication Award, Turkish Mental Health Association, 1984; Successful Researcher Certificate, Istanbul University, 2001, 2002. Memberships: Turkish Society of Psychosomatics and Psychotherapy; German Psychoanalytic Association; German College of Psychosomatic Medicine; International College of Psychosomatic Medicine; International Society for the Psychopathology of Expression and Art Therapy; Turkish Society of Neuro-Psychiatry; Turkish Psychiatric Association; Turkish Academy of Medicine; Turkish Society of History of Medicine. Address: Ebekizi Sok No 14, D 9, Ebekizi Apt, Osmanbey, 34363 Istanbul, Turkey.

KORALEK Paul George, b. 7 April 1933, Vienna, Austria. Architect. m. Jennifer Koralek, 1 son, 2 daughters. Education: AA School of Architecture. Appointments include: Architect with Powell and Moya, London, 1956-57; Various work in France and Canada, 1957-59; Architect with Marcel Breuer, New York, USA, 1959-60; Founding Partner, Director and Consultant, Ahrends Burton and Koralek, 1961-; Member of Development Advisory Panel, Cardiff Bay Development Corporation, 1990-2000; Chair Works Committee, 1996, Member of Management Committee, 1997, Member of Architecture Committee, 2002-, Royal Academy of Arts; Chair, South East Regional Design Panel, 2002-; Assessor and Advisor for numerous design awards and competitions; Principal projects include most recently: North Tipperary County Council Offices, Nenagh, 2000; Trinity College Arts Faculty Building Extension, Dublin, 2000; Trinity College Dublin Innovation Centre, 2001; Trinity College Dublin Pearce Street Competition, 2002; Trinity College Dublin Enterprise Centre Bio Tech Units, 2003; Stockport Town Centre Design Competition, 2003; Collen House Extension, 2004; John Wheatley College, Glasgow, 2007. Publications: Ahrends Burton and Koralek (monograph), 1991; Collaborations: The Architecture of ABK, August/Birkhäuser; Numerous papers and lectures presented at national and international conferences and seminars. Honours: CBE, 1984; Associate, 1986, Member, 1993, Royal Academy of Arts. Memberships: RIBA; FRSA. Address: 3 Rochester Road, London NW1 9JH, England. E-mail: abk@abklondon.com Website: www.abk.co.uk

KORDA Petr, b. 23 January 1968, Prague, Czech Republic. Tennis Player. m. Regina Rajchrtova, 1992, 1 son, 2 daughters. Appointments: Coached by his father until 18 years old; Coached by Tomas Petera, 1991-; Winner, Wimbledon Junior Doubles, 1986; Turned Professional, 1987; Winner, Stuttgart Open, 1997, Australian Open, 1998, Qatar Open, 1998; Member, Czechoslovak Davis Cup Team, 1988, 1996; Retired, 1999, after winning 20 professional titles including 10 singles titles; Currently plays in Seniors Tour; Winner, Honda Challenge, 2002; Chairman, Board of Supervisors, Karlštejn golf resort.

KORDYUM Elizabeth L, b. 3 November 1932, Kyiv, Ukraine. m. Vitaly A Kordyum, 1 son, 1 daughter. Education: Graduate, Biology and Botany, Taras Shevchenko National Kyiv University, 1955; PhD, 1960; ScD, 1968; Professor, 1986. Appointments: Junior Scientist, O V Fomin Botanical Garden, Taras Shevchenko National Kyiv University, 1955-59; Junior Scientist, 1959-64, Senior Scientist, 1964-79, Head, Department of Cell Biology and Anatomy, 1976-, Deputy Director, Scientific Work, 1998-2003, Acting Director, 1998-99, Institute of Botany, National Academy of Sciences of Ukraine; Established Space and Gravitational Biology scientific school, Ukraine; Scientific Supervisor, Collaborative US/Ukrainian Experiment, 1995-98. Publications: Nearly 400 scientific articles in professional journals, including 11 monographs. Honours: Laureate, State Prize of Ukraine in Science and Technology, 1979; Honoured Scientist of Ukraine, 1984; Laureate, M G Kholodny Award, National Academy of Sciences of Ukraine, 1979; 1 Gold, 2 Silver and 3 Bronze medals, Exhibition of Achievements of National Economics of USSR, 1979-88; Order of Princess Olga, 3rd, 2nd and 1st degree, 1998, 2003, 2007; S G Navashin Medal, Russian Academy of Sciences; Yu V Kondratyuk Memorable Medal; Honorary medals and certificate, ABI and IBC, 1991-2007. Memberships: International Academy of Astronautics; National Academy of Sciences of Ukraine; Ukrainian Botanical Society; Ukrainian Society for Cell Biology; Co-ordinating Council on Botany and Mycology in Ukraine; COSPAR; International Society of Gravitational Physiology; ELGRA; American Society of Cell Biology; AAAS; American Society of Gravitational and Space Biology; Japanese Society of Plant Physiologists. Address: Institute of Botany, National Academy of Sciences of Ukraine, Tereschenkivska str 2, 01004 Kyiv, Ukraine.

KORNBERG Hans Leo, b. 14 January 1928, Herford, Germany (British Citizen). Professor of Biochemistry. Education: BSc, 1949, PhD, 1953, Sheffield University. Appointments: John Stokes Research Fellow, University of Sheffield, 1952-53; Member, Medical Research Council Cell Metabolism Research Unit, University of Oxford, 1955-61; Lecturer in Biochemistry, Worcester College, Oxford, 1958-61; Professor of Biochemistry, University of Leicester, 1961-75; Sir William Dunn Professor of Biochemistry, University of Cambridge, 1975-95; University Professor and Professor of Biology, Boston University, Massachusetts, USA, 1995-; Fellow, 1975-, Master, 1982-95, Christ's College, Cambridge. Publications: Numerous articles in scientific journals. Honours: Commonwealth Fund Fellow, Yale University and Public Health Research Institute, New York, 1953-55; Colworth Medal, Biochemical Society, 1963; Warburg Medal, Gesellschaft für biologische Chemie der Bundesrepublik, 1973; Honorary member of: Society of Biological Chemistry (USA), 1972; Japanese Biochemical Society, 1981; American Academy of Arts and Sciences, 1987; Honorary FRCP, 1989; Numerous honorary fellowships and degrees. Memberships: German Academy of Sciences, Leopoldina, 1982; Foreign associate, NAS, 1986; Academie Europaea, 1988; Fellow, American Academy of Microbiology, 1992; Foreign member, American Philosophical Society, 1993; Foreign member, Accademie Nazionale dei Lincei, Italy, 1997. Address: The University Professors, Boston University, 745 Commonwealth Avenue, Boston, MA 02215, USA.

KOROTCENKOV Ghenadii, b. 2 October 1949, Chita, Russia. Scientist. m. Irina, 2 daughters. Education: BA, Microelectronics, 1971, PhD, Physics and Technology of Semiconductor Materials and Devices, 1976, Technical University of Moldova; Dr Science (Habilitat), Physics and Mathematics, Academy of Science, Moldova, 1990. Appointments: Scientific Researcher, Technical University of Moldova, 1971-2007; Leader, gas sensor group; Manager of various national and international scientific and engineering projects, Laboratory of Micro- and Optoelectronics; Scientific Team Leader, nine international projects financed by EC, USA, and NATO, 1999-2007; Invited Scientist, Daejeon Institute of Energy Research, Daejeon, 2007-08; Research Professor, Department of Materials Science and Engineering, Gwangju Institute of Science & Technology, Korea, 2008-. Publications: Author and editor, 11 books; 18 patents; 10 review papers; 18 chapters; More than 190 scientific articles in refereed journals; More than 200 reports on international and national conferences and meetings. Honours: Best Student Scientific Work, 1970; Youth Award, Republic of Moldova, 1980; Best Young Scientific Researcher of Polytechnic Institute, 1980, 1984; Inventor of the USSR, 1984; Participant, International Millennium Celebration, Chicago, USA, 2000; Best Scientific Research, Technical University of Moldova, 2001, 2003; The Award of the Presidents of Ukrainian, Belarus and Moldovan Academies of Sciences, 2003; One of the Best Scientists in Moldova, 2004; Listed in biographical dictionaries. Memberships: Moldavian Society of Physics; International Society of Optical Engineering. Address: Bld Negruzzi 5, Chisinau, Republic of Moldova. E-mail: g.korotcenkov@yahoo.com

DICTIONARY OF INTERNATIONAL BIOGRAPHY 36th EDITION

KORYAGIN Sergey, b. 8 December 1973, Gorky, Russia. Astrophysicist. Education: BSc, 1995, MSc, 1997, Lobachevsky State University of Nizhni Novgorod; PhD, Institute of Applied Physics, Russian Academy of Sciences, 2001. Appointments: Junior Research Fellow, 1997, Research Fellow, 2002, Senior Researcher, 2006, Institute of Applied Physics, Russian Academy of Sciences; Associate Professor, Lobachevsky State University, Nizhni Novgorod, 2002-. Publications: Numerous articles in professional journals. Honours: State Premium of the Russian Federation for Young Scientists for Outstanding Works in Science and Technics, 2003; Associate Professor in Plasma Physics, 2010. Memberships: European Astronomical Society; Academic Council of Plasma Physics and High-Power Electronics Division at Institute of Applied Physics. Address: Institute of Applied Physics, 46 Uljanova Str, Nizhni Novgorod 603950, Russia. E-mail: koryagin@appl.science-nnov.ru

KORZENIK Diana, b. 15 March 1941, New York, New York, USA. Professor Emerita; Painter; Writer. Education: Oberlin College; BA, Vassar College; Master's Programme, Columbia University; EdD, Graduate School of Education, Harvard University. Appointments: Professor Emerita, Massachusetts College of Art, Boston. Publications: Chapter in Art and Cognition (editors, Leondar and Perkins), 1977; Drawn to Art, 1986; Art Making and Education (with Maurice Brown), 1993; The Cultivation of American Artists (co-editor with Sloat and Barnhill), 1997; The Objects of Art Education, 2004. Contributions to: Professional journals and to magazines. Honours: Boston Globe L L Winship Literary Award, 1986; National Art Education Association Lowenfeld Award, 1998; American Library Association LEAB Award for excellence in museum publications, 2005. Memberships: Friends of Longfellow House, founder, board member; American Antiquarian Society; Massachusetts Historical Society. Address: 7 Norman Road, Newton Highlands, MA 02461, USA.

KOSAREV Nikolai, b. 12 June 1962, Krasnoyarsk, Russia. Scientist. m. Larisa Vovnenko, 1 daughter. Education: Physicist, Teacher of Physics, Krasnoyarsk State University, 1980-85; Doctor of Physical and Mathematical Sciences, 2010. Appointments: Engineer, Junior Scientific Collaborator, Laboratory of Mathematical Problems of Laser Physics, Department of Computing Physics, Computer Centre of Siberian Branch of Academy of Sciences of USSR, 1987-92; Higher Teacher, Siberian Airspace Academy, 1992-97; Professor, Faculty of Information Technologies, Siberian Law Institute, 1997-. Publications: More than 50 scientific publications in professional journals. Honours: Listed in international biographical dictionaries. Address: Flat 52, 28 Ulianovski Street, Krasnoyarsk 660111, Russia. E-mail: rosarev_nikolai@mail.ru

KOSHINO Masanori, b. 13 July 1971, Yasugi-shi, Shimane, Japan. Scientist. m. Yukari, 1 daughter. Education: BSc, Tokyo University of Science, 1990-94; M Sci, 1994-96, Dr Sci course, 1999-2002, Dr Sci, 2005, Kyoto University; ELI, CUNY Queens College, 1996-97; ESF MS course, SUNY, 1997-98. Appointments: Researcher, a consortium among industry, government and academia, 2004-05; Lecturer, Institute for Chemical Research, 2002-04, Kyoto University. PD, JST-ERATO, 2005-07; Group Leader, Japan Science and Technology Agency (JST), ERATO project, 2008-10; Researcher, National Institute of Advanced Industrial Science and Technology, 2008-. Publications: Numerous articles in professional journals. Honours: Professional Technical Staff Award, 2005, 2007 Best Materials Paper Award, 2008, Microscopy Society of America. Memberships: American Chemical Society; Microscopy Society of America; Chemical Society of Japan; Japan Society of Microscopy; Fullerene-Nanotube Research Society; Society for DV-Xα. Address: AIST, Central 5, 1-1-1 Higashi, Tsukuba-city, Ibaraki 305-8565, Japan. E-mail: m-koshino@aist.go.jp

KOSSAKOVSKYI Anatolii, b. 8 October 1952, Rovensky reg, Ukraine. m. Nadia, 1 daughter. Education: MD, Chezneivetsky Medical Institute, Ukraine, 1975; Postgraduate, Kyiv State Institute of Advanced Medical Training of Physicians, Ukraine, 1982-85; PhD, 1985, DSc, 1994, Kyiv State Institute, Ukraine. Appointments: Postgraduate education, Head of Pediatric Otorhinolaryngology, Audiology and Phoniatrics Department, 2002-12, Vice Rector, 1998-2012, Shupyk National Medical Academy. Publications: Over 480 articles in professional journals including 70 inventions, 42 monographs and textbooks. Honours: Honored Rationaliser, Ukraine Supreme Soviet of Ukraine, 1990. Memberships: New York Academy of Sciences; International Pers Academy, USA. Address: 9 Dorogozhitska st, Kyiv 04112, Ukraine.

KOSSMANN Stefan A, b. 22 July 1933, Rybnik, Poland. Physician. m. Alina Piotrowska, 1 son. Education: Physicians Diploma, 1957, MD, 1964, PhD, 1976, Professor, 1985, Silesian Medical University School. Appointments: Assistant, 1957, Assistant Professor, 1976, Associate Professor, 1985, Full Professor, 1995-2003, Silesian Medical University School; Retired, 2003; Professor, Institute of Occupational Medicine and Environmental Health, Sosnowiec, 2005-06. Publications: 145 articles to professional journals and 105 congress abstracts, mainly on pulmonary medicine and industrial toxicology. Honours: Award granted by the Minister of Health for outstanding achievements in industrial toxicology; Polonia Restituta Cross. Memberships: New York Academy of Sciences (until 2003); Polish Society of Allergology. Address: ul. Żużlowa 55A, 44-200 Rybnik, Poland.

KOSTECKI Michel, b. 19 October 1946, Wroclaw, Poland. Economist. m. Anne Guimond, 1 son, 1 daughter. Education: Master, Economics, The Warsaw School of Economics (formerly SGPiS), 1969; Doctorate, The Graduate Institute of International Studies, University of Geneva, 1975. Appointments: Research Assistant, Institute of Operation Research and Applied Mathematics, University of Zurich, 1974-75; Associate Professor, The Graduate School of Business Administration, University of Montreal, 1975-81; Investment Manager, DELCON Financial Corporation, Geneva, 1981-82; Counsellor, GATT, Geneva, 1982-90; Professor, Founding Director, Enterprise Institute, University of Neuchatel, Switzerland, 1990-. Publications: Numerous articles in professional journals and 13 volumes including: The Political Economy of the World Trading System (with B Hockman), 2009. Honours: Outstanding Academic Book, 1995. Memberships: American Economic Association; Association Française du Marketing. Address: Villa Zadig, 1A Av Louis-Yung, 1290 Versoix, Switzerland.

KOSTER David, b. 5 November 1926, London, England. Artist. m. Katherine, 1 daughter. Education: Pinewood, Crowborough, Sussex; Clayesmore, Dorset; Slade School of Art. Appointments: Visiting Art Teacher, the Highlands, 1952-66; Teacher of Drawing & Printmaking, Folkestone School of Art, 1966-70; Medway College of Design, 1971-88; Assistant Art Director, Metropole Art Centre, Folkestone. Publications: Illustrations in various books and periodicals including: Down to Earth; Fellow Mortals; Artist, Printmaker & Naturalist. Memberships: Founder Member, Society of Wildlife Artists.

KOTELNIKOVA Elena, b. 15 March 1945, Saratov, Russia. Crystallographer. m. Arkady Glikin, 1 son. Education: Dipl Specialist, Geochemistry-Crystallography, 1968, PhD, Crystallography and Crystallophysics, 1982; Senior Scientist, 1991, Dr Sci, 1999, Mineralogy and Crystallography, Crystallography Department, Geological Faculty, St Petersburg State University. Appointments: Engineer, 1968-76, Scientific Researcher, 1976-85, Senior Scientist, 1985-99, Head of Laboratory, 1999-2001, Professor, 2001-, Crystallography Department, Geological Faculty, St Petersburg State University. Publications: 1 issued monograph; About 125 papers; More than 170 presentations at various conferences. Honours: Jubilee Medal, 275th Anniversary of St Petersburg University, 1999; Honorary Diploma, St Petersburg State University, 1999; Professor V A Frank-Kamenetsky Prize, St Petersburg University, 1999; Honorary Diploma, Russian Mineralogical Society, 2004; Diploma, University Prize for Scientific Labor, 2011; Honorary Diploma, International Centre for Diffraction Data, 1988, 2012; Research grants. Memberships: Russian Mineralogical Society; International Mineralogical Association; St Petersburg Society of Naturalists. Address: Liteiny prospect, 34, apt 44, 191028, St Petersburg, Russia. E-mail: kotelnikova.45@mail.ru

KOUBA Vaclav, b. 16 January 1929, Vrabi, Czech Republic. Epizootiologist. m. Anna Holcapkova, 1 son, 1 daughter. Education: Diploma, Veterinary Medicine, 1953, PhD, 1961, Habil Docent 1966, DrSc, 1978, Professor, Epizootiology, 1988, University of Veterinary Medicine, Brno, Czech Republic. Appointments: Lecturer, 1952-56, University of Veterinary Medicine, Brno, Czech Republic; National Chief Epizootiologist, Prague, 1956-78; Visiting Professor, University of Havana, 1967-71; Animal Health Officer (Research/Education), Animal Health Officer (Veterinary Intelligence), Senior Animal Health Officer, FAO-UN, Rome, Italy, 1978-85; Initiator and Founder, Veterinary Faculty, Lusaka University, Zambia, 1981; Professor, Founder of Faculty and Institute of Tropical Veterinary Medicine, Brno, 1985-88; Chief, Animal Health Service (responsible for United Nations animal health policy), Food and Agriculture Organisation of the United Nations, Rome, 1988-91; Visiting Professor, Mexico City University, 1993; Visiting Professor, University of Kosice, 1993-98; Visiting Professor, University of Prague, 1999-; Founder of modern epizootiology; Achievements as leading specialist: Eradication of bovine brucellosis, 1964, bovine tuberculosis, 1968, Teschen disease, 1973 and foot and mouth disease, 1975 in Czechoslovakia; Foot and mouth disease in Mongolia, 1964; African swine fever in Cuba, 1971; Myiasis Cochliomyia hominivorax in Northern Africa, 1991 regaining free status of the whole Eastern hemisphere; Co-responsible for global rinderpest eradication achieved in 2010 as the first animal infection in history; First isolation of Aujeszky disease virus in Czechoslovakia, 1954. Publications include: General Epizootiology textbooks in Czech, English and Spanish; World FAO-WHO-OIE Animal Health Yearbook, editor-in-chief; Over 800 articles on epizootiology and on infection long-distance spreading/globalization; Software: Epizoo, Epizmeth, Epiztext, electronic textbook. Honours: Polar Star Order, Mongolian Government; Outstanding Work Order, Czechoslovak Government; Veterinary Public Health Expert, World Health Organization, Geneva; Informatics Expert, International Office of Epizootics, Paris; Honourable President, Cuban Veterinary Scientific Society. Memberships: World Veterinary Association, Education Committee; International Society of Veterinary Epidemiology and Economics; World Association for the History of Veterinary Medicine. Address: Haskova 7, 170 00 Praha 7, Czech Republic. Website: http://vaclavkouba.byl.cz

KOUH Taejoon, b. 6 October 1970, Seoul, Korea. Professor. m. Imsoon Kim, 1 daughter. Education: BA, Boston University, USA, 1994; ScM, 1996, PhD, 2002, Physics, Brown University, USA. Appointments: Postdoctoral Research Associate, Boston University, 2002-05; Tenured Lecturer, 2005-07, Assistant Professor, 2007-, Kookmin University, Korea. Publications: Numerous articles in professional journals. Honours: Phi Beta Kappa; Sigma Xi. Memberships: American Physical Society; Korean Physical Society; Korean Magnetics Society. Address: Department of Physics, Kookmin University, 861-1 Jeongneung-dong, Seongbuk-gu, Seoul, 136-702, Korea. E-mail: tkouh@kookmin.ac.kr

KOURIS Stamatios Spyrou, b. 12 December 1933, Lefkimmi, Corfu, Greece. Professor. m. Amalia. Education: Dr Eng, 1960, Diploma, Radiocommunication, 1963, University of Rome, Italy; PhD, University of Edinburgh, Scotland, 1972; Diploma, Management and Administration, University of Pomona, California, USA, 1974. Appointments: Researcher, Founder, Ugo Bordoni, Rome, Italy, 1964-67; Researcher, University of Edinburgh, Scotland, 1967-71; Director, Electronics Department, Technological School of Thessaloniki, Greece, 1973-77; Full Professor, Chair of Telecommunications, Electrical and Computer Engineering Department, 1978-2002, Honorary Professor, 2002-, Aristotle University of Thessaloniki, Greece. Publications: More than 100 articles in professional journals. Honours: Honorary Member, Technical Chamber of Greece; Cavaliere (Knight) della Repubblica Italiana. Memberships: Technical Chamber of Greece; Union Radio Scientific International; International Reference Ionosphere. Address: Aigaiou 52, Kalamaria, GR-55133, Thessaloniki, Greece. E-mail: kouris@vergina.eng.auth.gr

KOVE Miriam, b. 17 February 1941, Chotin, Bassarabia. Psychoanalytic Psychotherapist. Divorced, 2 daughters. Education: BA, Sir George University, Montreal, Canada, 1962; MS, Education, Hunter College, 1976; Certificate in Psychoanalytic Psychotherapy, New Hope Guild Centres, New York, 1979; M of SW, Adelphi University, 1983; Diplomat, American Board of Examiners, NYC, 1991-. Appointments: Private practice, 25 years; Faculty Supervisor, New Hope Guild Centres Training Programme; Adjunct Lecturer, Early Childhood, Kingsborough: Intake Director, Marble Collegiate Church, Institute for Religion and Health. Publications: Articles to professional journals; Presentations; 2 books: Myths and Madness; Mid-Life Murders. Honours: Presenter, National Conference of the Society of Clinical Social Work, Chicago; Who's Who Among Human Service Professionals; Who's Who in American Women. Memberships: National Association of Social Work; American Board of Examiners in Clinical Social Work. Address: 320 E 25th St, #8EE, New York, NY 10010, USA.

KOWALSKA Maria T, b. 8 June 1932, Wielun, Poland. Research Scientist. m. W Kowalski, 1 son, 1 daughter. Education: BA, Lyceum of General Education, Lodz, Poland, 1950; MS in Pharmacy, 1954, PhD in Pharmacy, 1964, Dr Hab in Phytochemistry, 1978, Medical Academy, Poznan. Appointments: Assistant Professor, Pharmacy, Medical Academy, Poznan, 1955-67; Postdoctoral Fellowship, Department of Pharmacy, University of Paris, France,

DICTIONARY OF INTERNATIONAL BIOGRAPHY 36th EDITION

1969-70; Associate Professor of Agriculture, Department of Technology of Wood, Poznan, 1970-80; Professor of Pharmacognosy, National University of Kinshasa, Zaire, 1980-82; Research Associate, Research Center, Fairchild Tropical Garden, Miami, Florida, USA, 1985-90; Adjunct Assistant Professor, Department of Biochemistry and Molecular Biology, University of Miami, School of Medicine, 1990-2001. Publications: 53 scientific publications in the field of phytochemistry and pharmacognosy in international scientific periodicals. Honours: Dean's Award, Medical Academy in Poznan, 1962-64; PI grants, International Palm Society, 1986-87; PI grants, World Wildlife Fund, 1988. Memberships: Polish Pharmaceutical Society, 1960-72; American Society of Phytochemistry, 1990-92. Address: 6421 SW 106 Street, Miami, FL 33156, USA. E-mail: kellin242@aol.com

KOWALSKI Waldemar Zbigniew, b. 2 May 1957, Kielce, Poland. Historian. m. Mariola, 1 son. Education: MA, 1980; PhD, 1988; Habilitation, 1999; Professor, 2007. Appointments: Research Assistant, 1983-85, Kielce University Library, Lecturer, 1985-89, Senior Lecturer, 1989-99, Reader, 2000-07, Professor, 2007-, History Department, Jan Kochanowski University. Publications: Five books and numerous articles in professional journals. Honours: Elected Head, History Department, Kielce University, 2008-. Memberships: Polish Historical Association. Address: Department of History, Jan Kochanowski University, 25-369 Kielce, Poland. E-mail: kowalski@ujk.edu.pl

KOZÁK János, b. 20 December 1945, Kenderes, Hungary. Professor. m. Erzsébet Barna, 3 sons, 2 daughters. Education: Agricultural Engineer, 1968, Professional Agricultural Engineer, 1975, Agricultural Doctor of the University, 1979, University of Agricultural Sciences, Gödöllő, Hungary; Candidate of Economy (PhD), The Hungarian Committee of Scientific Qualifications, Budapest, Hungary, 1988; Habilitation, Szent István University, Gödöllő, Hungary 1998. Appointments: Assistant, Co-operative Farm, Aranykalász, Törökszentmiklós; Manager, Farm Machinery Institute, Gödöllő, 1970; Chief Animal Breeder, Co-operative Farm, Lenin, Kunság Népe, Kunhegyes, 1970-78; Director, Goose Breeding Research Station, 1978-99, 2001-05; Assistant Professor, Professor, University of Agricultural Sciences, Gödöllő, 1990-99; Professor, Szent István University, Gödöllő, 2000-. Publications: Books: Vertical relations and possibilities for the improvement of interest in goose production; Miscellaneous poultry breeding; Examination of environmental conditions in the light of European Union requirements; Poultry Industry in Hungary; Works on technologies, market regulation and animal welfare. Honour: Outstanding Worker of Agriculture Award, Ministry of Agriculture and Food Industry; Man of the Year, 2007. Memberships: World's Poultry Science Association Working Group No 8 Waterfowl, Hungarian Branch; Technical Commission of International Down and Feather Bureau, 1994-2005; Chairman, Hungarian Standard National Technical Committee MSZT/MB 626, Feather and Down; Poultry Breeding Department, Association of Hungarian Foodstuffs Industry Science; World Rabbit Science Association, Hungarian Branch; Hungarian Association of Agricultural Economists; World Council of Hungarian University Professors; Association of Hungarian Specialists; Public Body of the Hungarian Academy of Sciences. Address: Szent István University; Department of Animal Breeding, Pig, Poultry and Pet Husbandry, Páter Károly u 1, H-2103 Gödöllő, Hungary. E-mail: kozak.janos@mkk.szie.hu

KOZLOVSKIY Vladimir, b. 16 February 1928, Saint Petersburg, Russia. Physicist-Engineer. m. Irina Foox, 1 son. Education: Diploma, Polytechnic Institute of Saint Petersburg, 1944-50; Post Graduate Student, Institute of Silicate Chemistry, Saint Petersburg, 1952-56; Bachelor of Physical Mathematical Science, 1964; Doctor of Physical Mathematical Science, 1996. Appointments: Engineer, Works 211, Saint Petersburg, 1950-53; Scientific Collaborator, Institute of Semiconductors, Saint Petersburg, 1956-59; Scientific Collaborator, Raw Materials Synthesis Institute, Moscow, 1960-68; Lecturer and Scientific Collaborator, Technical University of Electronics and Mathematics, Moscow, 1968-91. Publications: 106 publications in Russian magazines and transactions of conferences and the Jewish Scientific Society, Berlin on the subject of solid corps physics, phase transitions, segnettelectricity. Honours: Medal for Defence of Leningrad; Man of the Year 2005; ABI Ambassador; ABI Fellow; Medal of Cambridge; Key of Success; Presidential Seal of Honor; Distinguished Service to Humankind Award; Academician ABI. Memberships: Jewish Scientific Society in Berlin; Moscow Mathematical Society. Address: Saarmunderstr 85, 14478 Potsdam, Germany. E-mail: v.kozlovskiy@gmx.de

KRAJICEK Richard, b. 6 December 1971, Rotterdam, Netherlands. Tennis Player. m. Daphne Dekkers, 1999, 1 son, 1 daughter. Appointments: Started playing tennis, 3 years; Reached semi-finals, Australian Open, 1992; Wimbledon Men's Singles Champion, 1996; Won 20 titles to date; Director, ABN AMRO World Tennis Tournament, 2004. Publications: Fast Balls, 2005. Address: ATP Tour, 201 ATP Tour Boulevard, Ponte Vedra Beach, FL 32082, USA.

KRAMER Herbert J, b. 24 December 1939, Bad Kreuznach, Germany. Professor Emeritus. m. Hella, 2 sons. Education: Medical School, Munich, 1958-60; Medical School, Sorbonne University, Paris, France, 1960-61; MD, 1963, PhD, 1967, Medical School, University of Saarland. Appointments: Resident, Research Fellow, UCLA, California, USA, 1968-70; Resident, 1964-68, Chief Resident, 1970-72, Medical Faculty, Assistant Professor of Medicine, 1972, University of Saarland; Associate Professor of Medicine, 1976, Professor of Medicine/Nephrology, 1980-2010, Professor Emeritus, University of Bonn. Publications: Approximately 400 publications in professional journals. Honours: Claude-Bernard Prize, University of Saarland, 1972; Theodor Frerichs Prize, German Society of Internal Medicine, 1973. Memberships: International Society of Nephrology; American Society of Nephrology; German Society of Nephrology; International Society of Hypertension; American Society of Hypertension; German Society of Hypertension; New York Academy of Sciences; American Society of Physiology; and others. Address: Augustastrasse 67, 53173, Bonn-Bad Godesberg, Germany. E-mail: hkramer@uni-bonn.de

KRAMER Stephen Ernest, b. 12 September 1947, Hampton Court, England. Circuit Judge. m. Miriam Leopold, 1 son, 1 daughter. Education: BA, 1969, MA, 1987, Keble College, Oxford; Université de Nancy, France. Appointments: Called to the Bar (Gray's Inn), 1970; Assistant Recorder, 1987-91, Recorder of the Crown Court, 1991-; Standing Counsel (Crime) to HM Customs and Excise South Eastern Circuit, 1989-95; Member, Bar Council, 1993-95, Committee, South Eastern Circuit, 1997-2000; Chairman Liaison Committee, Bar Council/Institute of Barristers' Clerks, 1996-99; Committee Member, 1993-98, Acting Vice Chairman, 1998-99, Vice Chairman, 1999-2000, Chairman, 2000-2001, Criminal Bar Association; Queen's Counsel, 1995; Bencher

Gray's Inn, 2001-; Head of Chambers, 2 Hare Court Temple, London, 1996-2003; Circuit Judge, 2003-05, Senior Circuit Judge sitting at Central Criminal Court, Old Bailey, 2005-.

KRASIN Yury Andreevich, b. 7 June 1929, Penza, Russia. Social Scientist. Widower, 1 daughter. Education: Graduate, Faculty of Philosophy, Leningrad University, 1952; PhD, Leningrad Pedagogical Institute, 1955; DSc, Philosophy, Institute of Philosophy, 1965; Professor, Moscow University, 1967; Full Member, Russian Academy of Natural Sciences, 1998; Board Member, Academy for Political Science, 1996; Honorary Doctor, Institute of Sociology, RAS, 2008. Appointments: Lecturer, Philosophy and Political Science, Leningrad Pedagogical Institute, 1952-60; Assistant Professor, Moscow University, 1960-75; Senior Fellow, Institute of Philosophy, USSR Academy of Sciences, 1963; Consultant, International Division, CPSU Central Committee, 1963-75; Professor, Head of Department, Prorector, Academy of Social Sciences, 1975-87; Rector, Institute of Social Sciences, 1987-91; General Director, Foundation for Social and Political Studies, 1991-92; Director, Center for Social Programs, Adviser of the Gorbachev Foundation, 1992-2011; Head, Department for Analysis of the Socio-Political Processes, Institute of Sociology, RAS, 1993-; Professor, Russian State Humanitarian University, 2009-. Publications: Over 500 articles in professional journals; 20 monographs. Honours: Medal for Labor of Valour, 1961; Lomonosov Prize, Moscow State University, 1968; Decoration of Esteem, 1971; Friendship of Peoples, 1979; USSR State Prize, 1980; Veteran of Labour, 1985; Pitirim Sorokin Silver Medal, 2008. Memberships: Russian Association of Political Science; Academy of Political Science; Russian Academy of Natural Sciences. Address: Malaya Philevskaya str, 44, fh 11, 121433, Moscow, Russia. E-mail: krasinyua@mtu-net.ru

KRASNOYAROVA Nadezhda, b. 14 November 1950, Almaty City, Kazakhstan. Doctor. m. Alexey Kraznoyarov, 1 son. Education: Medical Diploma (Distinction), 1975; Doctor of Medical Sciences, Russian Federation, 1997; Doctor of Medical Sciences, Kazakhstan, 2003; Professor of Medicine, 2005. Appointments: Medical Student, 1969-75; Neuropathologist, 1975-89; Junior Researcher, Neurology Department, 1989-93; Assistant, 1993-97, Associate Professor, 1997-2005, Professor, 2005-, Department of Traditional Medicine. Publications: 4 medical books; 141 articles. Honours: Woman of the Year, 2007; Woman of the Year in Medicine, 2008. Memberships: FIMM. Address: Gaydara Str, h87, f85, Almaty City, 050009, Kazakhstan.

KRAU Edgar, b. 9 April 1929, Stanislau, Poland. University Professor; Scientist; Educator. m. Mary Epure, 1 daughter. Education: MA, Psychology, Education, 1951, PhD, Psychology, 1964, University of Cluj, Romania. Appointments include: High School Teacher, Gherla, Romania, 1952-61; Chief Research Fellow, Institute of Pedagogical Sciences, Cluj, 1961-63; Consecutive positions, University of Cluj, 1963-77; Head, Psychological Department, Academy of the Romanian Republic, Cluj Branch, 1968-77; Member International Test Commission, 1971-73; Professor, University of Haifa, Israel, 1977-81; Professor, Tel-Aviv University, 1981-97; Chairman International Colloquium on Human Resources Development, Jerusalem, 1984; Member, Scientific Committee, XXI International Congress of Applied Psychology, 1986. Publications: Books: Co-author, Treatise of Industrial Psychology, 1967; Author, editor, Self-realization, Success and Adjustment, 1989; Author, The Contradictory Immigrant Problem, 1991; Co-author: Projet professionnel - projet de vie, 1992; Organizations and Management: Towards the Future, 1993; Author: The Realization of Life Aspirations through Vocational Careers, 1997; Social and Economic Management in the Competitive Society, 1998; A Meta-Psychological Perspective on the Individual Course of Life, 2003; Toward Globalization with a Human Face, 2009; Over 70 papers in leading scientific journals; Editor-in-Chief, Man and Work (journal of labour studies), 1987-. Honours include: Vasile Conta Prize, Romanian Academy, 1972; Award, High Centre for Logic and Comparative Sciences, Bologna, Italy, 1972; Honorary Mention, Journal of Vocational Behavior, 1986; Homagial Biography, Bibliography, Revue Européenne de Psychologie Appliquée, 1993; Dedication, Outstanding People of the 20th Century, IBC; 20th Century Achievement Award, ABI, 1999; Honours List, International Biographical Centre, 2000; Cavalier, World Order of Science, Education and Culture, 2002; American Order of Excellence, 2003; Legion of Honor, United Cultural Convention, 2005; Order of American Ambassadors, 2006; Honorary Director General, IBC, Cambridge, 2008; International Order of Merit, 2009; Listed in numerous international biographical publications. Memberships: International Association of Applied Psychology, Executive Committee, Division of Psychology and National Development; Member-Instructor, Israeli Psychological Association; Affiliate, American Psychological Association; Active Member, New York Academy of Sciences; Member of Academic Council, London Diplomatic Academy; Einsteinian Chair of Sciences, World Academy of Letters. Address: 2 Hess Str, 33398 Haifa, Israel.

KREBS John Richard (Lord Krebs of Wytham), b. 11 April 1945, Sheffield, England. Chairman; Professor; Principal. m. Katharine Anne Fullerton, 1968, 2 daughters. Education: BA, 1966, MA, 1970, D Phil, 1970, Pembroke College, Oxford. Appointments: Assistant Professor, Institute of Animal Resource Ecology, UBC, Canada, 1970-73; Lecturer in Zoology, University College of North Wales, Bangor, 1973-75; University Lecturer in Zoology, Edward Grey Institute of Field Ornithology, Oxford, 1976-88; Fellow, Wolfson College, Lecturer in Zoology, Oriel, St Anne's and Pembroke Colleges, 1976-81; E P Abraham Fellow in Zoology, Pembroke College, 1981-88; Storer Lecturer, University of California, 1985; Official Fellow, 1988-2005, Honorary Fellow, 2005-, Pembroke College; Royal Society Research Professor, Oxford University, 1988-2005; Director, AFRC Unit of Ecology and Behaviour, 1989-94; Director, NERC Unit of Behavioural Ecology, 1989-94; Chief Executive, Natural Environment Research Council, UK, 1994-99; Chairman, UK Food Standards Agency, 2000-05; Principal, Jesus College, Oxford University, 2005-. Publications: 2 books; 150 refereed publications; 45 book chapters; 50 other articles; 11 abstracts; 28 book reviews. Honours include: Association of the Study of Animal Behaviour Medal, 2000; Benjamin Ward Richardson Gold Medal, Royal Society for Promotion of Health, 2002; ISI Highly Cited Researcher, 2002; Wooldridge Medal, British Veterinary Association, 2003; Croonian Lecture, Royal Society, London, 2004; Lord Rayner Memorial Medal, 2005; Award for Outstanding Achievement, Society for Food Hygiene Technology, 2005; Harben Gold Medal, Royal Institute of Public Health, 2006; Life Peerage (cross bencher), 2007; Numerous DSc honoris causa. Memberships: Honorary Fellow, German Ornithologists' Society, 2003; Foreign Honorary Member, US National Academy of Sciences, 2004; Fellow, Academy of Medical Sciences, 2004. Address: Jesus College, Oxford OX1 3DW, England. E-mail: principal@jesus.ox.ac.uk

KRELLA Alicja Krystyna, b.16 September 1966, Gdynia, Poland. Scientist. m. Piotr, 1 son, 1 daughter. Education: MSc, 1990; PhD, 2003. Appointments: Scientist. Publications: Numerous articles in professional journals. Honours: Listed in international biographical dictionaries. Address: Cavitation Group, Institute of Fluid-Flow Machinery, Fiszera 14, 80-231 Gdansk, Poland. E-mail: akr@imp.gda.pl

KREMENYUK Victor, b. 13 December 1940, Odessa, Ukraine. Professor; Research Scholar. m. Liudmila. Education: Moscow Institute for International Relations of the Foreign Ministry (MGIMO), USSR, 1957-63; Courses at the Soviet Military Academy, 1963-64; PhD, MGIMO, 1965-67; Candidate, EconSci (World Economy), 1968; Doctor of History, Institute for USA and Canada Studies, 1980. Appointments: Military Service, 1963-68; Journalist, International Affairs, 1968-70; Research Scholar, Institute for USA and Canada Studies, 1970-; Lecturer and Professor: Salzburg seminar, Austria; NATO (SHAPE) School, Oberammergau, Germany; NATO Defense College, Rome, Italy; Marshall Center for European Security Studies, Garmisch-Partenkirschen, Germany; University of Paris, France; University La Sagesse, Beirut, Lebanon; Consultant and Advisor: USSR Supreme Soviet and Russian State Duma; Soviet and Russian Foreign Ministry; International Institute for Applied Systems Analysis, Laxenburg, Austria. Publications: Over 300 books, monographs, collective publications, articles in the press and academic journals worldwide. Honours: 2 medals for military service; Soviet National Prize for Science and Technology, 1980; CPR Institute for Dispute Resolution, New York, Book Award, 2002; Russian Ministry for Emergencies Prize for Strategic Risk Analysis, 2005. Memberships: US National Geographical Society, 1982-; Honorable Member, Association of Anciens, NATO Defense College, 2009-; Corresponding Member, Russian Academy of Sciences. Address: Institute for USA and Canada Studies, Russian Academy of Sciences, Khlebny per 2/3, Moscow 123995, Russian Federation. E-mail: vkremenyuk@gmail.com

KRIEGEL Hans-Peter, b. 1 October 1948, Borghost, Germany. Professor & Chair. m. Debra Lynn, 1 son, 1 daughter. Education: M Eng, 1973, PhD, Computer Science, 1976, University of Karlsruhe; Habilitation, Computer Science, University of Dortmund, Germany, 1982. Appointments: Postdoc and Visiting Assistant Professor, McMaster University, Canada, 1977-79; Assistant Professor, University of Dortmund, 1979-83; Associate Professor, University of Wuerzburg, 1983-87; Full Professor, University of Bremen, 1987-91; Full Professor, 1991-, Department Head alternating with Vice Head, 2003-, Ludwig-Maximilians-Universitaet Muenchen. Publications: Over 300 articles in professional journals and conferences. Honours: SIGMOD Best Paper Award, 1997; Ranked No 1 in Germany, Association for Computing Machinery, 2005; Best Paper Award, 11th International Conference on Database Systems for Advanced Applications, 2006; Nominated ACM Fellow, 2009; Most cited Computer Scientist in Germany, CiteSeer, 2010 and Microsoft Academic Search, 2010; Ranked among Top 10 Scientists in Data Mining, 2010. Memberships: Bavarian Academy of Science; Association for Computing Machinery; Institute of Electrical and Electronics Engineers; German Informatics Society. Address: Ludwig-Maximilians-Universitaet Muenchen, LFE Datenbanksysteme, Oettingenstr 67, 80538 Muenchen, Germany. E-mail: kriegel@dbs.ifi.lmu.de Website: www.dbs.ifi.lmu.de/cms/Haupsteite

KRISHNA Vinita, b. 3 February, Hazaribagh, Jharkhand, India. Educationist; Botanist; Scientist. Education: MSc, B Ed, Dip in Systems Management, Postgraduate Diploma, Intellectual Property Rights. Appointments: High School Science Teacher; Scientist, Government of India scheme, 2005; Researcher. Publications: National and international publications on climate change, intellectual property rights and science. Honours: 2nd prize, Indian Scientists Women's Conference, Mumbai; 2nd prize, National Conference for Lesson Plans; State Merit Scholarship from secondary classes to Masters level. Memberships: Indian National Science Congress, Kolkata; International Society for Environmental Botanists. Address: F-150, Sarita Vihar, New Delhi, 110076, India.

KRISHNAMURTHY Veeranki, b. 16 January 1950, Andhra Pradesh, India. Agricultural Scientist; Director. m. Jhansi Eswaramma, 1 son, 3 daughters. Education: BSc, 1972, MSc, 1975, AP Agri University, Hyderabad; PhD, Andhra University, Waltair, 1983. Appointments: Research Assistant, 1975, Scientist S, 1975-76, Scientist S-1, 1976, NDRI, Karnal, Haryana, Scientist S-1, 1976-77, Division of Soils & Agronomy, CSSRI, Karnal, Scientist S-1, 1977-82, Scientist S-2, 1983-85, Senior Scientist, 1986-88, Division of Soils & Agricultural Chemistry, CTRI, Rajahmundry, Senior Scientist & Officer in Charge, CTRI RS, Dihata, 1988-89, Senior Scientist, CTRI RS, Kandukur, 1989-91, Senior Scientist, 1991-98, Principal Scientist, 1998-2003, Head, 2003-06, Acting Director, 2006, Director, 2006-, CTRI, Rajahmundry, Indian Council of Agricultural Research, New Delhi. Publications: Over 250 articles in professional journals. Honours: Dr G S Murthy Award, 1987; First IPI-FAI Award, 1997; Sri K Devappa Award, 1998; Indian Tobacco Association Award, 2000; ISTS Award, 2005; Tobacco Board Award, 2009; Listed in international biographical dictionaries. Memberships: Institution of Chemists, Kolkata; Indian Society of Tobacco Science, Rajahmundry; NAARM Alumni Association, Hyderabad; Indian Society of Soil Science; Indian Science Congress Association. Address: Central Tobacco Research Institute, Bhaskar Nagar, Rajahmundry 533 105, East Godavari District, Andhra Pradesh, India. E-mail: krishnamurthy_ctri@yahoo.co.in Website: www.ctri.org.in

KRISHNARAJ Mannangatti, b. 19 February 1983, Puducherry, India. Research Associate. m. C Sathyavani, 1 son. Education: BSc, Botany, 2003, MSc, 2005, PhD, 2010, Industrial Microbiology, University of Madras, Chennai. Appointments: Junior Research Fellow, 2006-07, Senior Research Fellow, 2008-11, University of Madras, Chennai. Publications: 3 international journals; 4 national journals; 4 international conferences; 4 national level conferences. Honours: Student Project Scholarship, 2002-03; Medal, Anna Government College; Dr A S Laksmanachary Award, 2000-03; College Scholarship, Aringner Anna Government Arts College, Villupuram, 2000-03. Mem; Association of Microbiologists in India; Marine Biological Association of India; Asian Federation of Biotechnology; European Federation of Biotechnology; International Society of Ethnobiology; Madras Science Foundation; Madras Science Club. Address: No 37/43, Peeliyamman Koil Street, Kottur, Chennai 600 085, Tamil Nadu, India. E-mail: krishnoble@gmail.com

KRISTINSSON Magnús, b. 13 June 1943, Eyjafjörður, Iceland. Freelance Teacher; Teacher's Trainer; Translator; Interpreter; Tourist Guide; Editor; Lecturer. m. Brigitte Kristinsson, 1 son. Education: BA (Hons), English Language and Literature, German, Icelandic and Philosophy, University of Leeds, 1967; Study of German, University of Kiel, Germany, 1967-68; Study of Foreign Language Didactics, Computer Science and Data Processing, Giessen, Germany, 1987-88; Authorised Tourist Guide, Iceland (German, English, Icelandic), 1970-; Publicly appointed Translator and Interpreter for German, English and Icelandic in Iceland, Icelandic Ministry of Justice, 1975; Accredited Translator and Interpreter for German and Icelandic in Germany, Stuttgart Regional Court, 1998. Career: Junior Teacher, Secondary Boarding School Eiðar, Iceland, 1963-64; Director, Adult Education Department, Akureyri Junior College, 1975-81; Executive and Publicity Manager, Icelandic Social-Political Movement "Samtök um jafnrétti milli landshluta", 1985-86; Teacher of German and English, Junior College, Akureyri, Iceland, 1968-85, 1986-87, 1988-90; Part-time, 1970-90, Full-time, 1990-94, Tourist Guide and Translator, Iceland; Freelance Teacher (English, Icelandic, PC-Computing), Translator, Interpreter, Editor, Tourist Guide and Lecturer, Germany, 1994-. Publications: Several articles, books and book chapters in Icelandic include: Book: Úr torfbæjum inn í tækniöld (chief editor, translator, co-author), 2003; Fjallabálkurinn umhverfis Glerárdal (book chapter), 1991; Article: Glerárdalur, lýsing og örnefnatal, 1978; Translations of books from German and English into Icelandic. Honour: Best Non-Fiction Book of the Year in Iceland for "Úr torfbæjum inn í tækniöld", 2003. Memberships: BDÜ (Federal Association of Interpreters and Translators), Germany; FLDS (Association of Certified Court Interpreters and Document Translators), Iceland; VVU (Association of Accredited and Sworn Court Interpreters and Appointed and Sworn Document Translators) Baden-Württemberg, Germany; HAGÞENKIR (Union of Icelandic Non-Fiction Writers). Address: Schmidener Strasse 241, D-70374 Stuttgart, Germany. E-mail: kristinsson@gmx.net

KRITTAYAPHONG Rungroj, b. 12 October 1963, Bangkok, Thailand. Physician. Education: MD, Chulalongkorn University, Bangkok, Thailand, 1987; Internal Medicine, Prince of Songkhla, Songkhla, Thailand, 1991; Cardiology, Mahidol University, Bangkok, Thailand, 1993; Post Doctoral Research Associate, University of North Carolina at Chapel Hill, USA, 1996. Appointments: Instructor, 1997, Associate Professor, 2000, Professor, 2003, Division of Cardiology, Department of Medicine, Siriraj Hospital, Mahidol University; Fellowship of American College of Cardiology, 2005. Publications: Numerous articles in professional journals. Honours: Honor in Doctor of Medicine, Chulalongkorn University, 1987; Extern Award, Department of Pediatrics, Chulalongkorn University, 1987; Physician Award in Internal Medicine, 1989; Young Investigator Award Heart Association of Thailand, 1998. Memberships: Royal College of Physicians of Thailand; Heart Association of Thailand; American College of Cardiology; European Heart Rhythm Association. Address: Division of Cardiology, Department of Medicine, Siriraj Hospital, Bangkok 10700, Thailand. E-mail: sirkt@mahidol.ac.th

KROCKOVER Gerald Howard, b. 12 November 1942, Sioux City, Iowa, USA. Professor. m. Sharon Diane Shulkin, 2 sons. Education: BA, Chemistry, Secondary Education, 1964; MA, Science Education, Geology, 1966, PhD, Science Education, Geology, 1970, University of Iowa. Appointments: Science Teacher, Bettendorf and Iowa City, 1964-70; Assistant Professor, Associate Professor, Purdue University, West Lafayette, Indiana, 1970-80; Professor of Earth and Atmospheric Science Education, Purdue University, 1980-. Publications: 13 textbooks; 5 elementary science series; 121 journal publications. Honours include: Outstanding Science Educator, Association for the Education of Teachers of Science, 1973; Distinguished Teacher Educator Award, National Association of Teacher Educators, 1990. Memberships include: American Association for the Advancement of Science; International Organisation for Science and Technology Education. Address: Purdue University, 550 Stadium Mall Drive, West Lafayette, IN 47907-2051, USA.

KRONDAHL Hans, Professor Emeritus; Fibre Artist; Fabric Designer. Education: Graduate, University College of Arts Crafts and Design, Stockholm, Sweden; Further studies in Europe and the Far East. Appointments: Teacher, Fibre Art and Textile Design in art schools, 1960-; Working in own studio for Tapestry Weaving and Fabric Design, 1963-; Senior Lecturer, Head of Textile Department, University College of Arts Crafts and Design, Stockholm, Sweden, 1977-78; Head of Textile Design Department, National College of Art and Design, Oslo, Norway, 1978-79; Head of Textile Design Department, HDK College, 1981-88, Professor of Textile Art, Gothenburg University, Sweden, 1988-94; Worked as UNIDO Expert in Textile Design, Indonesia, 1979-80; Exhibits in Sweden and abroad most recently works included in "Katja of Sweden", Kulturen Museum, Lund, 2002-2003; "Heliga Kläder", Klostret Museum, Ystad, 2004-2005; Permanent representation in museum collections in Europe and USA; Tapestries, front curtains, rugs, carpets, ecclesiastical textiles and vestments commissioned for the public environment. Publications: Works included in: The Lunning Prize Exhibition Catalogue, 1986; Svenska Textilier 1890-1990, by Jan Brunius, etc, 1994; Contemporary Textile Art by Charles S Talley, 1982; Fiberarts Magazine, 1996; The Design Encyclopedia; Museum of Modern Art, New York, 2004. Honour: Prince Eugen Medal, 2002. Address: Smedjegatan 8, S 21421 Malmö, Sweden.

KROSNICK Mary Lou Wesley, b. 11 June 1934, Bayonne, New Jersey, USA. Musician; Pianist; Teacher. m. Aaron B Krosnick, 1 son. Education: BS, Juilliard School of Music, 1957; MA, University of Wisconsin, 1958; MM, Yale University School of Music, 1961. Appointments: Head of Piano Department, Sewanee Summer Music Center, 1976-85; Assistant Professor of Music, 1978, Associate Professor of Music, 1985, Professor of Music, 1992, Distinguished Performer-in-Residence, 2000-, Jacksonville University, Florida; Performances: Soloist with The Boston Pops Orchestra under Arthur Fiedler, 1961; Soloist with The Jacksonville Symphony Orchestra, Kennedy Center and Carnegie Hall under Willis Page, 1972; Soloist with The Jacksonville Symphony Orchestra under Morton Gould, 1981; Performances as a soloist and composer on Radio Stations: WaXR, WNYC, WOR-TV, Radio Free Europe, 1950-51; Composition: The Rain Comes (performed under Leopold Stokowsky in a version orchestrated by him by the New York Philharmonic-Symphony Orchestra, 1949). Publication: Book chapter in Isabella Vengerova: Beloved Tyranna by Joseph Rezits, 1995. Honours: 1st Place, New York Philharmonic Symphony's Young Composers' Contest, 1949; 1st Place, National Guild of Piano Teachers' International Recording Competition, Collegiate Division, 1957, Teachers' Division, 1972; 1st Place, University of Redlands, California, National American Music Competition, 1961; Excellence in Teaching Lifetime Award, Florida State Music Teachers' Association, 2010; Listed in national and international biographical dictionaries. Memberships include: Florida State Music Teachers; Music Teachers National Association; National Federation of Music Clubs; Address: 13734 Bermuda Cay Court, Jacksonville, FL 32225, USA. E-mail: abkmlk@hotmail.com

KRUG Arno, b. 16 February 1935, Schneidemuhl, Germany. Surgeon. m. Christine, 3 sons, 1 daughter. Education: MD, Berlin-Marburg, 1959; PhD, Surgery, 1972, Professor, 1978, Kiel. Appointments: Chief Surgeon, City Hospital, Hof/Saale, Germany, 1978-98; Retired, 1998-. Publications: Blood supply of the myocardium after temporary coronary occlusion; Alteration in myocardial hydrogen concentration: a sign of irreversible cell damage; The extent of ischemic damage in the myocardium of the cat after permanent and temporary coronary occlusion. Memberships: German Society of Surgery. Address: Theodor-Fontane-Str 20, D-95032 Hof/Saale, Germany. E-mail: arnokrug@yahoo.de

KRÜGER Eduardo L, b. 15 August 1965, Rio de Janeiro, Brazil. Associate Professor. m. Simone, 2 sons. Education: Civil Engineer, Civil Engineering, Universidade Católica de Petrópolis, 1983-89; MSc, Energy Planning, Universidade Federal do Rio de Janeiro, 1991-93; Dr Ing, Architecture, Universität Hannover, 1993-98. Appointments: Associate Professor, Universidade Tecnológica Federal do Paraná, 1999-. Publications: Over 30 peer-reviewed journal papers and numerous conference papers. Honours: Research Grants: Climatic Adequacy of Low-Cost Houses in 14 Brazilian Cities, 2003-04; Thermal Performance Analysis of Buildings and Passive Design Solutions, 2005-06; Preventive Conservation of Paper Collections and Utilization of Higrothermal Parameters for Three Climatic Regions in Brazil, 2008-10; International Research Project on Outdoor Thermal Comfort, 2008-10; Bioclimatic Considerations for Architecture and Urban Design, 2009-11; Visiting Researcher, Ben Gurion University of the Negev, 2005-06; Visiting Researcher, Glasgow Caledonian University, 2010-11; Listed in biographical dictionaries. Memberships: International Association for Urban Climate (IAUC). Address: Universidade Tecnológica Federal do Paraná, Campus Curitiba, Sede Ecoville, Rua Deputado Heitor Alencar Furtado, 4900, 81280-340 Curitiba – PR, Brazil. E-mail: ekruger@utfpr.edu.br

KRUKOWSKI Zygmunt Henderson, b. 11 December 1948, Crimond, Aberdeenshire, Scotland. Surgeon. m. Margaret Anne, 1 son, 2 daughters. Education: MB ChB, 1966-72, PhD, 1978, University of Aberdeen; FRCS (Edinburgh), 1976; FRCP (Edinburgh), 2001. Appointments: Basic and higher surgical training in Aberdeen, Inverness and London, Ontario; Lecturer in Surgery, 1977-86, Senior Lecturer, 1988-96, Reader, 1996-99, Professor of Clinical Surgery, 1999-, University of Aberdeen; Consultant Surgeon, 1986-; Surgeon to the Queen, 2004-. Publications: Publications on surgical audit, surgical infections, surgical technique, laparoscopic surgery, endocrine surgery and health services research. Honour: Honorary FRCS (Glasgow), 2000; A+ Merit Award, SACDA, 2008. Memberships: National Committees on Audit and Quality; President, British Association of Endocrine Surgeons, 2005-07; Member, Council Association, Laparoscopic Surgeons GB & Ireland, 2009-. Address: Aberdeen Royal Infirmary, Foresterhill, Aberdeen AB25 2ZN, Scotland.

KRUNKE Helle, b. 10 September 1970, Gentofte, Denmark. Professor in Constitutional Law. m. Mikkel Jarboel, 1 son, 1 daughter. Education: BA, 1996, MA, 1999, PhD, 2003, Law, Faculty of Law, University of Copenhagen. Appointments: Worked in Ministry of Economic Affairs, Denmark, 1999; Research Scholar, 1999-2003, Assistant Professor, 2003-07, Associate Professor, 2007-10, Professor, 2010-, Member of Management Team, Centre for European Constitutionalization and Security, 2010, Faculty of Law, University of Copenhagen; Visiting Academic, University of Bristol, England, 2000-01; Visiting Fellow, European University Institute, Florence, Italy, 2007. Publications: Numerous articles in professional journals and books including: From Maastricht to Edinburgh: The Danish Solution to the Maastricht Referendum, 2005; Developments in National Parliaments Involvement in Ordinary Foreign Policy and European Policy, 2007; Paradoxes of European Legal Integration, 2008. Honours: Danish Editor of Nordic Legal Journal, Retfaerd, 2003-05; Nordic Chief Editor, Retfaerd, 2006; Member, Academic Board, Faculty of Law, 2006-; Asked to give evidence to House of Lords, England, 2009; Listed in international biographical dictionaries. Address: Faculty of Law, University of Copenhagen, Studiestraede 6, 1455 Copenhagen K, Denmark. E-mail: helle.krunke@jur.ku.dk

KRUPATKIN Alexander Ilych, b. 17 February 1961, Moscow, Russia. Medical Doctor. Education: MD, Medical Institute, Tver, Russia, 1983; Dr Neurology, 1984; Consultant in Psychotherapy, 1987; PhD, 1989; DMSci, 1999; Professor of Pathophysiology, 2006. Appointments: Physician, Regional Hospital, Tver, Russia, 1983-84; Junior Researcher, Senior Researcher, Leading Researcher, Central Institute of Traumatology and Orthopaedics, Moscow, 1984-. Publications include: Polarographic Method in Traumatology and Orthopaedics, 1986; Laser Doppler Flowmetry in Traumatology and Orthopaedics, 1998; Clinical Neuroangiophysiology of the Limbs (perivascular innervation and nervous trophics), 2003. Honours: Man of the Year, 2000, IBC, England. Memberships: New York Academy of Sciences; Russian Association of Functional Diagnostics. Address: ul Priorova 10, CITO, 127299 Moscow, Russia.

KRUSZEWSKI Eugeniusz Stanislaw, b. 13 November 1929, Zbaszyn, Poland. Retired Professor; Historian. m. Marta Bialecka, 2 daughters. Education: MAEc, Poland, 1962; Post-graduate studies, Denmark, 1971-74; PhD, 1975, Dr hab, 1980, Polish University, London. Appointments: Drafted into Polish Army, 1950-57, 1962-64, Financial Officer, Warsaw, Gdynia; Teacher, Secondary School, Gdańsk, 1965-69; Civil Servant, Governmental Centre of Documentation and Information, Copenhagen, Denmark, 1976-97; Reader, 1980-85, Professor of the History of International Relations, 1985-2010, Polish University, London; Polish-Scandinavian Research Institute, Copenhagen, Denmark, 1985-2010; Retired, 2010. Publications: 10 books on Polish-Scandinavian history, immigration and emigrations history; Over 400 scientific articles, reviews, biographical articles. Honours: Army Medal, 1948; Home Army Cross, London, 1973; Knight Cross of the White Cross International, Sydney, Australia, 1990; Gold Medal of the Polish Cultural Congress, 1985, 1995; The Writers Award, Polish Combatants Association, London, 1992; Award of the Union of Polish Writers Abroad, London, UK, 2000; Honorary Member, Research Board of Advisors, ABI, 2007. Memberships: Danish Catholic Historians Society; Polish Historical Society in Great Britain; Polish Society of Arts and Sciences Abroad, London, UK; Union of Polish Writers Abroad, London; Albert Schweitzer Society, Cracow, Poland; President, Polish-Scandinavian Research Institute; Member, Polish PEN Club, Warsaw. Address: POB 2584, DK-2100 Copenhagen Ø – Denmark.

KRYUCHKOV Nickolay, b. 14 July 1982, Barnaul, Altay kray, USSR. Public Health; Biostatistics; Medicine. Education: MD, Stavropol State Medical Academy, 2005; PhD, National Research Centre, Institute of Immunology, Moscow, 2008; MPH, Hebrew University of Jerusalem, Israel, 2009; MBA, Moscow International Higher Business School, in progress. Appointments: Executive Director,

Russian Society of EBM Specialists, Moscow, 2006-10; Head, Clinical Trials Department, Valenta Pharm JSC, 2010-12; Associate Professor, Department of Public Health & Preventive Medicine, Sechenov First Moscow Medical University, 2010-; Deputy Head, Medical and Research Administration, Stata Pharm Development, Stada, CIS, 2012-. Publications: Auto-chronometric abnormalities, 2004; Course on Biostatistics, CD ROM, 2006; HIV infection and AIDS. EBM guidelines for health professionals and PLWH, 2009. Honours: Scholarships and travel grants from Hebrew University, American Association of Immunology, European Academy of Allergy and Clinical Immunology; Award at international and Russian conferences, 1998-99; Listed in biographical dictionaries. Memberships: Russian Society of Evidence-Based Medicine Specialists; Russian Anti-Tobacco Advocative Coalition; European Academy of Allergy and Clinical Immunology. E-mail: nkryuchkov@gmail.com Website: www.linkedin.com/in/nkryuchkov

KU Ja Hyon, b. 30 September 1966, Seoul, Republic of Korea. University Professor. m. Yoon Jung Choi, 1 son. Education: BS, 1989, MSc, 1995, PhD, 2002, Seoul National University. Appointments: Part time Instructor, Seoul National University, Konkuk University, Hongik University, Soongsil University, University of Seoul, Daejeon University. Publications: Rayleigh's Acoustical Research on the Fog Signal; Landmark Writings in Western Mathematics, 1640-1949, 2005; British Acoustics and its Transformation from the 1860s to the 1910s, 2006; Uses and Forms of Instruments: Resonator and Tuning Fork in Rayleigh's Acoustical Experiments, 2009. Honours: Korean History of Science Society Award, 2007; Plat Award; Top 100 Educators; International Educator of the Year, 2009; Listed in international biographical dictionaries. Memberships: History of Science Society; Korean History of Science Society. Address: 104-402 EG the One, Mojeon-ri, Jeonggwan-myeon, Gijang-gun, Busan, 619-962, Republic of Korea. E-mail: taramdge@hotmail.com

KUDRYAVTSEVA Anna, b. 14 November 1940, Moscow, Russia. Researcher. Widow, 1 son, 1 daughter. Education: Diploma, Moscow State University, 1966; PhD, Lebedev Physical Institute, 1975. Appointments: Researcher, 1966, Senior Researcher, Vice Head, Optical Department, 1995-, Leading Researcher, 2008-, Lebedev Physical Institute, Russian Academy of Sciences. Publications: 80 articles in professional journals. Honours: Diploma, Lebedev Physical Institute, Russian Academy of Sciences. Memberships: Optical Society of America. Address: Lebedev Physical Institute, Leninskii pr 53, 119991, Moscow, Russia. E-mail: akudr@sci.lebedev.ru

KUDZYS Antanas, b. 19 May 1925, Seirijai, Lithuania. Scientist. m. Birute Velickaite, 2 sons. Education: Faculty of Civil Engineers, Kaunas University, 1945-50; Postgraduate, 1955-58, DSc, 1959, Habil Doctor, 1967, Full Professor, 1967, Kaunas Polytechnical Institute. Appointments: Designer, Constructor, Kaunas Design Firms, 1950-60;, 1960-92; Professor, Vilnius Technical University, 1960-92; State Consultant, Lithuanian Government, 1992-95; Professor, Institute of Architecture and Construction, Kaunas Technological University, 1995-2011. Publications: 6 monographs; 5 textbooks in Lithuanian and Russian; More than 300 articles; Multilingual Dictionary, 2004; 4 collections of articles on engineer assessments and predictions in probabilistic structural reliability, 2011. Honours: Merited Engineer of Lithuania, 1965; Merited Scientist of Lithuania, 1975; State Science Prizes, 1974, 1982; Winner, Scientific Works of USSR Higher Schools, 1987; Honorary Doctor, Budapest University of Technology, Hungary, 1988; Full Member, Lithuanian Academy of Sciences, 1990. Memberships: Comité Euro-International du Béton, 1972; International Association for Bridge and Structural Engineering, 1991; European Mechanics Society, 1996; International Council for Research and Innovation in Building and Construction, 1997. Address: Jurates 15, Vilnius, LT 10311, Lithuania. E-mail: antanas.kudzys@gmail.com

KUHRT Gordon Wilfred, b. 15 February 1941, Madras, South India. Clergyman. m. Olive, 3 sons. Education: BD, Honours, London University, 1960-63; Oakhill Theological College, 1965-67; Doctor in Professional Studies, Middlesex University, 2001. Appointments: Religious Education Teacher, 1963-65; Curate, St Illogan, Truro, England, 1967-70; Curate, Holy Trinity, Wallington, England, 1970-73; Vicar of Shenstone, Lichfield, England, 1973-79; Vicar of Emmanuel, South Croydon, England, 1979-89; Rural Dean, Croydon Central, 1981-86; Honorary Canon of Southwark Cathedral, 1987-89; Archdeacon of Lewisham, 1989-96; Chief Secretary of the Advisory Board for Ministry, 1996-98; Director of Ministry, Ministry Division, Archbishop's Council, 1999-. Publications: Handbook for Council and Committee Members, 1985; Believing in Baptism, 1987; Doctrine Matters (editor), 1993; To Proclaim Afresh (editor), 1995; Issues in Theological Education and Training, 1998; Clergy Security, 1999; An Introduction to Christian Ministry, 2000; Ministry Issues for the Church of England – Mapping the Trends, 2001; Bridging the Gap: Reader Ministry Today, 2002. Membership: Fellow of the College of Preachers. Address: Ministry Division, Archbishops' Council, Church House, Great Smith Street, London SW1P 3NZ, England. E-mail: gordon.kuhrt@mindiv.c-of-e.org.uk

KUKLA Cynthia Mary, b. 23 June 1952, Chicago, Illinois, USA. Artist; Professor of Art. 2 sons. Education: BFA, School of the Art Institute of Chicago, Chicago, Illinois, 1973; MFA, University of Wisconsin-Madison, Madison, Wisconsin, 1983. Appointments: Assistant Professor of Art, 1983-1989, Associate Professor of Art, 1989-93, Northern Kentucky University, Highland Heights, Kentucky; Associate Professor of Art, 1993-2003, Professor of Art, 2004-, Illinois State University, Normal, Illinois; Visiting Professor, Aristotle Thessaloniki University, Thessaloniki, Greece, 2006; Visiting Professor/Masterclass, Art Academy of Tallinn, Estonia, 2009; Visiting Professor, Srinakharinwriot University, Bangkok, 2010, 2011; Exhibitions: Over 50 solo exhibitions include: Contemporary Art Center, Peoria, 2007; Tallinn Drawing Triennial, Tallinn, Estonia, 2009; Illinois Watercolour Society Member Exhibit, Chicago, Illinois, USA, 2009, 2010; Watercolor Honor Society, Japan Exhibition, 2010, Tokyo; Quincy University, 2011; Over 250 group exhibitions include: Springfield Art Museum, Springfield, Missouri, 1980, 1983, 2006; Laguna Beach Art Museum, Laguna Beach, California, 1983; American Embassy, Quito, Ecuador, 1989; Grand European National Centre, Arts e Lettres, Nice, France, 1990; Canton Art Institute, Canton, Ohio, 1992; Kharkov Art Museum, Ukraine, 1992; Arrowmount Center, Gatlinburg, Tennessee, 1993, 1995, 2004, 2006, 2008; Rockford Art Museum, Rockford, Illinois, 1995 and 2006; Ft. Sztuki Association, Krakow, Poland, 1998; Palace of Art, Budapest, Hungary, 1999; Lakeview Art Museum, Peoria, Illinois, 2002 and 2005; Vivarosi Gallery, Budapest, Hungary, 2004; Thailand Invitational, Hue, Viet Nam, 2011; No Greater Gods, University of Virginia, USA, 2011. Honours: University grants for sculpture, 1994, 1997, 2003; University technology grants to develop "Lost Art" website: www.cfa.ilstu.edu/cmkukla, 1997, 1998, 1999; Fellowships, Hungarian Multicultural

Council, Balatonfured, Hungary and Vermont Studio Center, Johnson, Vermont, 2003; Keynote Speaker, Cincinnati Art Museum, 2004; Fellowship, Virginia Center for Creative Arts, Amhurst, 2005; Travel grant for panel participation in Impact.Kontakt Art Conference, Berlin and Poznan, 2005; Impact 5, Tallinn, Estonia, 2007; SWU, Bangkok, 2010; Commission: 5 paintings for inauguration of Spurlock Museum of World Culture, University of Illinois, Champaign-Urbana, 2001. Memberships: American Association of University Women; Art Institute of Chicago; College Art Association; Contemporary Art Center, Cincinnati; McLean County Art Center, Bloomington; National Board Member, Watercolor Honor Society of America; National Museum of Women Artist, Washington, DC; Rotary International. Address: 1001 Broadmoor Drive, Bloomington, IL 61704-6109. E-mail: cmkukla@ilstu.edu

KULAGIN Victor V, b. 27 February 1960, Moscow, Russia. Scientist. m. Natalia B, 1 son, 1 daughter. Education: MS, Physics, 1983, Postgraduate course, 1983-86, PhD, Physics, 1987, Moscow State University. Appointments: Researcher, Institute of Radioengineering and Electronics, Russian Academy of Sciences, Moscow, 1986-92; Senior Researcher, 1992-2002, Senior Research Scientist, 2008-, Sternberg Astronomical Institute, Moscow State University; Research Scientist, Korea Electrotechnology Research Institute, Changwon, Republic of Korea, 2003-07; Visiting Scientist, Advanced Photonics Research Institute, Gwangju Institute of Science and Technology, Republic of Korea, 2007-08. Publications: More than 150 articles in professional journals. Memberships: Korean Physical Society. Address: Sternberg Astronomical Institute, Moscow State University, Universitetsky prosp 13, Moscow 119992, Russia. E-mail: victorvkulagin@yandex.ru

KULIKOV Leonid Igorevich, b. 4 July 1964, Moscow, Russia. Scholar. Education: MA, Theoretical Linguistics, Moscow State University, 1986; Candidate degree, Sanskrit, Institute of Oriental Studies, Moscow, 1989; PhD, Historical and Indo-European Linguistics, Sanskrit, Leiden University, 2001. Appointments: Research Fellow, Institute of Oriental Studies in Moscow, Department of Languages, 1989-93; Teacher of Sanskrit and Indology, Russian State University for Humanities, 1991-93; Research Assistant, Leiden University, Department of Comparative Linguistics, 1993-97; Post-doc Researcher, Leiden University, 2001; Post-doc Researcher, University of Nijmegen, 2002-04; Researcher, Teacher, Leiden University, Institute of Linguistics, 2004-; Humboldt Fellow, Göttingen University, 2005-07; Researcher, Institute of Linguistics, Moscow, 2009-; Lecturer, Uppsala University, 2010. Publications: Monograph: The Vedic-ya-presents: Passives and intransivity in Old Indo-Aryan, Amsterdam Rodopi, 2011; Numerous articles in professional journals. Honours: NWO/VENI Research Grant, 2004; Humboldt Fellowship, 2004. Memberships: Association of Linguistic Typology; Societas Linguistica Europaea; Editorial Board, Journal of Historical Linguistics, Lingua Posnaniensis Acta Orientalia Vilnensia. Address: Leiden University, Faculty of Humanities, Institute of Linguistics, PO Box 9515, 2300 RA, Leiden, The Netherlands. E-mail: l.kulikov@hum.leidenuniv.nl Website: www.hum.leiden.edu/lucl/organisation/kulikovli.jsp

KULKARNI Milind, b. 24 November 1972, Madha, India. Scientist. m. Manisha B Inamdar, 1 daughter. Education: MSc, Polymer Chemistry, 1996; PhD, Conducting Polymers, 2002. Appointments: Scientist B, 2001-06, Scientist C, 2006-, Centre for Materials for Electronic Technology (C-MET). Publications: Around 45 papers in international journals; Over 65 paper in international/national conferences; 2 Indian patents pending. Honours: First Rank, MSc, 1996; Junior Research Fellow, 1996; Senior Research Fellow, 1999; Young Associate of Maharashtra Academy of Science. Memberships: Materials Research Society of India. Address: Nanocomposite Laboratory, Centre for Materials for Electronic Technology, Panchawati, off Pashan Road, Pune – 8, India. E-mail: milindcmet@yahoo.com

KUMAMARU Takahiro, b. 28 March 1936, Kure, Japan. Professor. m. Taeko Shinagawa, 2 daughters. Education: BSc, Kyoto University, 1959; DSc, Hiroshima University, 1969. Appointments: Research Associate, Biophysics Research Laboratory, Harvard Medical School, Boston, USA, 1978-79; Professor, Department of Environmental Science, Faculty of Integrated Arts and Sciences, 1980-86, Professor, Department of Chemistry, Faculty of Science, 1986-99, Director, Instrument Center of Chemical Analysis, 1994-98, Professor Emeritus, 1999-, Hiroshima University; Professor, 1999-008, Vice President, 2001-06, Dean, Faculty of Human Ecology, 2006-08, Yasuda Women's University. Publications: Co-author, Environmental Science, 1983; Co-editor, co-author, Practice of Analytical Chemistry, 1992; Current Atomic Absorption Spectrometry, 1989; Analytical Chemistry, 2007; Contributions to analytical chemistr articles and professional journals. Honours: Japan Society for Analytical Chemistry Award, 1994. Memberships: Chemical Society of Japan; Japan Society for Analytical Chemistry. Address: 11-8-806 Tsurumi-cho, Naka-ku, Hiroshima 730-0045, Japan.

KUMAR Anil, b. 4 December 1974, Delhi, India. Associate Professor. m. Neelam, 1 son. Education: BS; M Pharm; PhD; MBA; DCRC; MNASc; CIC. Appointments: Associate Professor, Teaching and Research, UIPS. Publications: 119 research papers; 10 review articles; 5 reports; 4 book chapters. Honours: Raffelson Young Investigator Award; Lilly-Fellow Award; AICTE Career Award; INSA Visiting Fellowship; Boyscast Fellowship; IBRO Travel Award; Riken Brain Science Fellowship; several other travel awards. Memberships: IPS; IPA; APTI; IPGA; IRA; ANPA; ISN; APSN; MDS; ASN; ISBD; CIND; SFN; IBRO. Address: Panjab University, Chandigarh 160014, India.

KUMAR Chakresh, b. 10 July 1983, Sadabad, India. Teacher. Education: M Tech. Appointments: Teacher. Publications: Numerous articles in professional journals and international conferences. Honours: Scholarship, MHRD, New Delhi. Memberships: Indian Society of Technical Educaiton; Semiconductor of India; Materials Research Society of India; Materials Research Society of India; Institution of Electronics and Telecommunication Engineers; Indian Association of Physics Teachers; International Association of Engineers; Society of EMC Engineers, India. Address: s/o Prem Kuma, Mohalla Chawad Wala, Kaswa, Sadabad Hathras pin 281306, India. E-mail: chakreshk@gmail.com

KUMAR R Shashi, b. 8 May 1968, Tumkur, India. Reader in Economics. m. K L Rajeshwari, 1 son. Education: MA; M Phil; PhD. Appointments: Reader in Economics, Bangalore University, 1992-. Publications: Numerous articles in professional journals. Honours: 3 prestigious awards. Memberships: Many professional organisations. Address: Department of Economics, Bangalore University, Bangalore 560 056, Karnataka State, India. E-mail: drrshashi@yahoo.com

KUMAR Sandeep, b. 17 December 1983, Kurukshetra, India. m. Ankita Garg, 1 daughter. Education: B Tech, Kurukshetra University; PhD, Institute of Technology, Banaras Hindu University. Appointments: Assistant Professor, India Institute of Technology, Roorkee. Publications: 20 articles in international journals; 10 conferences; 4 books and book chapters. Honours: Best Research Paper Award, Hungary,2009; Gold Medal in B Tech. Address: Department of Electronics & Computer Engineering, Indian Institute of Technology, Roorkee 247667, Uttrarakhand, India.

KUNDT Wolfgang Helmut, b. 3 June 1931, Hamburg, Germany. Astrophysics Professor. m. Ulrike Schümann, 1 son, 1 daughter. Education: Dipl Phys, 1956, Promotion, 1959, Habilitation, 1965, Hamburg University, under Pascual Jordan. Career: Professor, Hamburg, Bielefeld, Bonn; Visiting Scientist: Pittsburgh, Pennsylvania; Edmonton; Cern; Kyoto; Boston; Bangalore; Linz; Maribor. Publications: Over 275 articles on fundamental physics, astrophysics, geophysics and biophysics; 6 books including: Astrophysics: a New Approach, 2004. Honours: NASA Group Achievement Award, 1975. Memberships: AG; EPS. Address: Institut für Astrophysik der Universität, Auf dem Hügel 71, D-53121, Bonn, Germany. E-mail: wkundt@astro.uni-bonn.de

KUNERT Günter, b. 6 March 1929, Berlin, Germany. Poet; Author; Dramatist. m. Marianne Todten. Education: Hochschule für angewandte Kunst, Berlin-Weissensee. Publications: Poetry: Wegschilder und Mauerinschriften, 1950; Erinnerung an einen Planeten: Gedichte aus Fünfzehn Jahren, 1963; Der ungebetene Gast, 1965; Verkündigung des Wetters, 1966; Warnung vor Spiegeln, 1970; Im weiteren Fortgang, 1974; Unterwegs nach Utopia, 1977; Abtötungsverfahren, 1980; Stilleben, 1983; Berlin beizeiten, 1987; Fremd daheim, 1990; Mein Golem, 1996; Erwachsenenspiele, autobiography, 1997; Nachtvorstellung, poems, 1999. Novel: Im Namen der Hüte, 1967. Other: Der ewige Detektiv und andere Geschichten, 1954; Kramen in Fächen: Geschichten, Parabeln, Merkmale, 1968; Die Beerdigung findet in aller Stille statt, 1968; Tagträume in Berlin und andernorts, 1972; Gast aus England, 1973; Der andere Planet: Ansichten von Amerika, 1974; Warum schreiben?: Notizen ins Paradies, 1978; Ziellose Umtriebe: Nachrichten von Reisen und Daheimsein, 1979; Verspätete Monologe, 1981; Leben und Schreiben, 1983; Vor der Sintflut: Das Gedicht als Arche Noah, 1985; Die letzten Indianer Europas, 1991. Honours: Heinrich Mann Prize, 1962; Heinrich Heine Prize, Düsseldorf, 1985; Hölderlin Prize, 1991; Georg-Trakl Prize, Austria, 1997. Memberships: Deutsche Akademie für Sprache und Dichtung e.v., Darmstadt. Address: Schulstrasse 7, D-25560 Kaisborstel, Germany.

KÜNG Hans, b. 19 March 1928, Lucerne, Switzerland. Professor of Ecumenical Theology Emeritus; Author. Education: Gregorian University, Rome; Institut Catholique, Paris; Sorbonne, University of Paris. Appointments: Ordained Roman Catholic Priest, 1954; Practical Ministry, Lucerne Cathedral, 1957-59; Scientific Assistant for Dogmatic Catholic Theology, University of Münster/Westfalen, 1959-60; Professor of Fundamental Theology, 1960-63, Professor of Dogmatic and Ecumenical Theology, 1963-80, Director, Institute of Ecumenical Research, 1963-96, Professor of Ecumenical Theology, 1980-96, Professor Emeritus, 1996- University of Tübingen; President, Foundation Global Ethic, Germany, 1995, Switzerland, 1997; Various guest professorships and lectureships throughout the world. Publications: The Council: Reform and Reunion, 1961; That the World May Believe, 1963; The Council in Action, 1963; Justification: The Doctrine of Karl Barth and a Catholic Reflection, 1964, new edition, 1981; Structures of the Church, 1964, new edition, 1982; Freedom Today, 1966; The Church, 1967; Truthfulness, 1968; Infallible?: An Inquiry, 1971; Why Priests?, 1972; On Being a Christian, 1976; Signposts for the Future, 1978; The Christian Challenge, 1979; Freud and the Problem of God, 1979; Does God Exist?, 1980; The Church: Maintained in Truth, 1980; Eternal Life?, 1984; Christianity and the World Religions: Paths to Dialogue with Islam, Hindus and Buddhism (with others), 1986; The Incarnation of God, 1986; Church and Change: The Irish Experience, 1986; Why I Am Still A Christian, 1987; Theology for a Third Millennium: An Ecumenical View, 1988; Christianity and Chinese Religions (with Julia Ching), 1989; Paradigm Change in Theology: A Symposium for the Future, 1989; Reforming the Church Today, 1990; Global Responsibility: In Search of a New World Ethic, 1991; Judaism, 1992; Mozart: Traces of Transcendence, 1992; Credo: The Apostles' Creed Explained for Today, 1993; Great Christian Thinkers, 1994; Christianity, 1995; Islam, 1995; A Global Ethic for Global Politics and Economics, 1997. Honours: Oskar Pfister Award, American Psychiatric Association, 1986; Many honorary doctorates. Address: Waldhäuserstrasse 23, 72076 Tübingen, Germany.

KUNGS Yan Aleksandrovich, b. 20 May 1932, Riga, Latvian Republic. Engineer. 1 son. Education: Siberian Technological Institute, 1957-61; Candidate of Science in Engineering, 1974; Professor, 1991. Appointments: Assistant, Krasnoyarsk Forestry Technical School, 1955-57; Assistant of the First Grade, 1957-60, Junior Research Scientist, 1960-62, Siberian Institute of Science and Research of Forestry and Forest Exploitation; Senior Engineer, 1962-64, Laboratory Chief, 1964-67, Regional Administration Krasnoyarskenergo; Laboratory Chief, Central Scientific and Research Economic Laboratory, 1967-70; Office Chief, 1970-74, Chief, Central Scientific and Research Laboratory of Electric Lighting, 1974-75, Chief of Laboratory of Electric Lighting, 1977-88, Sibenergotsvetmet; Head Teacher, Krasnoyarsk Polytechnic Institute, 1975-77; Chief of Laboratory of Electric Lighting, Sibtsvetmetenergo, 1988-91; Chief Engineer, 1991-92, Professor of Electrodrive Chair, 1992-95, Vice Department Chairman of the Chair of System Energetics, Professor, 1995-, Krasnoyarsk State Agrarian University. Publications: Numerous articles in professional journals. Honours: Merit Power Engineer of Russian Federation; Companion of Three Stars of Latvian Republic. Memberships: International Academy of Agrarian Education; Siberian Academy of Higher School; Russian Techological Academy. Address: Krasnoyarski Rabochy Avenue 155/58, Krasnoyarsk, ZIP 660093, Russia. E-mail: kungs@yandex.ru

KUNINAKA Akira, b. 16 January 1928, Tokyo, Japan. Professor. m. Sumiko Tanaka, 1 son, 2 daughters. Education: Bachelor of Agriculture, 1951, Doctor of Agriculture, 1959, University of Tokyo. Appointments: Researcher, 1953-2004, Director, 1978-86, Managing Director, 1986-95, Yamasa Corporation; Research Associate, Department of Biochemistry, MIT, 1963-66; President, Japan Immuno-Monitoring Centre, 1982-86; Chairman, Japan Sect Institute of Food Technologists, 1991-92; Guest Professor: Tokyo University of Agriculture, 1994-98, Chiba University, 1995-96, Chiba Institute of Science, 2005-11. Publications: Papers and articles in professional scientific journals. Honours: Agricultural Chemistry prize, 1960; Imperial Invention prize, 1964; Purple Ribbon medal, Prime Minister, Tokyo, 1983. Memberships: Japan Society for Bioscience, Biotechnology, and Agrochemistry; Japan Bioindustry Association; American

Chemical Society; Brewing Society of Japan. Address: 2-15-21 Araoi-cho, Choshi-shi, Chiba-ken 288-0056, Japan. E-mail: akuninakas@nexyzbb.ne.jp

KUO Ho-Chang, b. 1 March 1973, Taiwan. Pediatrician; Expert of Kawasaki disease. m. Mei-Fang Yao, 1 son, 1 daughter. Education: MD, National Yang-Ming University, Taiwan, 1999. Appointments: Attending Physician, Assistant Professor, Chang Gung Memorial Hospital, Kaohsiung Medical Center, Taiwan. Publications: More than 20 scientific papers in professional journals. Honours: Paediatric Research Travel Award, 2005; Physician Scientist Award, Institute of Biomedical Science, 2005-07; 2007 Annual Best Article Award; Best Research Article, Chinese Society of Pediatric Allergy, Asthma and Immunology, 2008; Professor Wen-Chang Liu's Research Award, Chinese Society of Immunology, 2009. Memberships: American Academy of Allergy Asthma and Immunology; European Academy of Allergy and Clinical Immunology; Asia Society for Pediatric Research; Marquis Who's Who in the World, 2011. Address: Department of Pediatrics, Chang Gung Memorial Hospital, Kaohsiung Medical Center, 123, Da-Pei Road, Niaosong Hsiang, Kaohsiung, Taiwan. E-mail: erickuo48@yahoo.com.tw Website (first for Kawasaki disease in Taiwan): http://tw.myblog.yahoo.com/erickuo48

KUO Yung-Chih, b. 1 March 1966, Taiwan. Professor. m. Yung-I Lou, 1 son, 1 daughter. Education: BSc, 1988; MSc, 1990; PhD, 1996. Appointments: Assistant Professor, 2001, Associate Professor, 2003, Professor, 2007-, Department of Chemical Engineering, National Chung Cheng University. Publications: Numerous articles in professional journals. Honours: Young Scholar Award, 2003; Excellent Research Award, 2011. Memberships: Phi-Tau-Phi Honor Society; American Association for the Advancement of Science; New York Academy of Sciences; Asian Federation of Biotechnology; American Nano Society; Asia-Pacific Chemical, Biological and Environmental Engineering Society.

KUPEK Emil, b. 16 October 1959, Zadar, Croatia. Epidemiologist. 1 daughter. Education: BSc, Clinical Psychology, 1984, MSc, Developmental Psychology, 1991, University of Belgrade, Yugoslavia; PhD, Public Health Medicine, Imperial College School of Medicine at St Mary's, University of London, England, 1997. Appointments: Assistant Professor, Department of Psychology, University of Belgrade, Yugoslavia, 1988-91; European Science Foundation Visiting Grant, Department of Experimental Psychology, University of Oxford, England, 1991-92; Research Posts in Statistics and Computing, St Mary's Hospital Medical School, Imperial College, London, 1992-95; Visiting Professor, Research Fellowship, 1997-99, Professor of Epidemiology, 1999-, Department of Public Health, Universidade Federal de Santa Catarina, Florianópolis, Brazil. Publications: Over 40 articles in international scientific journals as author and co-author on developmental psychology, anthropology, HIV/AIDS, methodology and statistics and other fields of medicine include most recently: Demographic and socio-economic determinants of community and hospital services costs for people with HIV/AIDS in London, 1999; Comparability of trends in condom use for different countries: Some methodological issues with secondary data analysis, 2000; The reduction of HIV transfusion risk in southern Brazil in the 1990's, 2001; Effectiveness of a mass immunisation campaign against serogroup C meningococci in children in the federal state of Santa Catarina, Brazil, 2001; Clinical, provider and sociodemographic predictors of late initiation of antenatal care in England and Wales, 2002. Honours: European Science Foundation Fellowship; Visiting Professor Fellowship, Brazilian Ministry of Education. Membership: American Association for the Advancement of Science. Address: Department of Public Health, Universidade Federal de Santa Catarina/CCS, 88040-900 Florianopolis-SC, Campus Universitario – Trindade, Brazil.

KURIĆ Lutvo, b. 22 August 1941, Sarajevo, Bosnia & Herzegovina. Independent Researcher. Education: BSc, Faculty of Economics. Appointments: Senior Expert Collaborant, Faculty of Economics, Sarajevo; Independent Researcher. Publications: 25 manuscripts on medicine and biochemistry; 100 manuscripts on economic science; 7 books. Honours: Great Minds of the 21st Century, 2010; Man of the Year in Medicine and Healthcare Designation for 2010; International Health Professional of the Year, 2010; The International Hippocrates Awards for Medical Achievement, 2010; Cambridge Certificate for Outstanding Medical Achievers, 2011, 2012; Gold Medal for Bosnia & Herzegovina, 2011; International Health Professional of the Year, 2012; Man of the Year, 2012. Address: Kalisnka 7/6, 72290 Novi Travnik, Bosnia & Herzegovina.

KURISU Kazutaka, b. 25 December 1971, Ube City, Yamaguchi, Japan. Linguist. m. Tamaki, 1 son, 1 daughter. Education: BA, English, 1994, MA, English Linguistics, 1996, Dokkyo University; PhD, Linguistics, University of California, Santa Cruz, 2001. Appointments: Assistant Professor, 2002-05, Associate Professor, 2005-, Department of English, Kobe College. Publications: Richness of the base and root fusion in Sino-Japanese, 2000; Gradient prosody in Japanese, 2005; Weak derived environment effects, 2007; Palatalisability via feature compatibility, 2009. Memberships: Phonological Society of Japan. Address: Department of English, Kobe College, 4-1 Okadayama, Nishinomiya, Hyogo 662-8505, Japan. E-mail: kurisu@mail.kobe-c.ac.jp

KURMAZENKO Eduard, b. 18 November 1942, Tokmak, USSR. Heating Engineer. m. 2 sons. Education: Heating Engineer, 1965; PhD, 1977; Assoicate Professor, Flight Maintenance and Safety Systems, 1988; Doctor of Engineering Science, 1994; Professor, Life-Support System, 1998. Appointments: NPO Nauka Engineer, Designer, 1965-75; Associate Professor, Professor, 1975-2002; Co-Head, Air Revitalization and Monitoring System Laboratory, 2002-. Publications: 250 articles and other publications; 32 patents. Honours: Ju A Gagarin Medals, 1980, 1983 and 1987; S P Korolev Medal, 1981; Ju V Kondratjuk Medal, 2004; Deserved Creator of Space Engineering, 2007. E-mail: e_kurmazenko@niichimmash.ru

KURODA Tatsuaki, b. 11 March 1955, Shirakawa, Japan. Professor of Economics. m. Junko Otani, 18 October 1980, 2 daughters. Education: BS, 1978, MS, 1980, Kyoto University; PhD, University of Pennsylvania, 1989. Appointments: Research Associate, Kyoto University, 1985; Assistant Professor, Toyahashi University of Technology, 1989; Associate Professor, 1991, Professor, 1998, Nagoya University; Visiting Scholar, LSE and University of Reading, England, 2003; Dean, Graduate School of Environmental Studies, 2004. Publications: City Planning for Promoting Amenity, 1984; Location of Public Facilities with Spillover Effects, 1989; A Power Index of Multistage and Multiagent Decision Systems, 1993; Advertising and City Formation with Local Public Goods, 1995. Honour: Graduate Prize, University of Pennsylvania, 1987. Membership: American Economic Association; Regional Science Association

International; Applied Regional Science Conference; Japan Economics Association. Address: 4-4-18 Takamoridai, Kasugai 487-0032, Japan.

KURTOVIC Sefko, b. 26 August 1937, Gacko, Bosnia and Herzegovina. Lawyer; University Professor. m. Nives, 1 son. Education: LB, 1962, LLM, 1968, University of Zagreb, Croatia; Postgraduate Diploma, Law, University of Strasbourg, France, 1965; Postgraduate Diploma, Law, King's College, London, 1970; LLD, University of Ljubljana, Slovenia, 1972. Appointments: Assistant, General History of State and Law, 1963-73, Associate Professor, General History of State and Law, Professor, History of Political Theories, 1973-84, Read Professor, General History of State and Law, Professor, History of Political Theories, 1984-2008, Law Faculty, University of Zagreb, Croatia. Publications: General History of the State and Law (from Antiquity to the Second World War) vols I-II, 1987-2007; Chrestomathy of General History of State and Law (from Hammurabian Law to the Second World War) vols I-II, 1999-; Studies and Articles in General History of State and Law, vols I-III, 2002; Articles include: Supreme executive power of French Third Republic, 1871-87; Historical premises of Paris Commune; Dissolution of parliament in French Third Republic; French Socialist Party, 1905-1914; Magna Carta 1215 and its constitutional analysis; Historical genesis of political representation; etc. Address: II Cvjetno naselje 26, 10000 Zagreb, Croatia.

KURUVILLA Bill (Kollanparampil), b. 20 July 1943, Kodukulanji, Kerala, India. Engineer. m. Santha, 1 son, 3 daughters. Education: BSc, Electrical Engineering, Kerala, India, 1965; MBA, Business Administration, USA; Student in Theology, USA (PhD on hold); PhD programme in Philosophy and Apologetics; PhD, Business Administration, USA, 1997; Diploma in Children's Writing, CT, USA, 2000. Appointments: Lecturer, MA College of Engineering, Kerala, India, 1965-66; Executive Engineer, Kerala State Electricity Board, India, 1966-88; Electrical Engineer, Zesco, Lusaka, Zambia, 1972-75; Chief of Power Station, Sher, Ministry of Power, Mozambique, 1979-81; Design Engineer, Septa, Philadelphia, PA, USA, 1989-. Publications: Numerous articles; Author, 5 books (4 unpublished); 1 US patent. Honours: Lifetime Royal Patronage and Citizen of the Year, 1994, 1996; Listed in national and international biographical directories; Honored Member, America's Registry of Outstanding Professionals for the Year, 2000-01, 2001-02, 2002-03, 2003-04, 2004-05, 2005-06; International Peace Prize, UCC, USA: Excellence Award and Gold Medal, 2006; Glory of India Award, Friendship Forum of India, 2006. Memberships: World Affairs Council of Philadelphia; Institute of Engineers (India); Associate, Library of Congress, USA; Handiham Club of USA. Address: 2407 Sentry Court, E Norriton, PA 19401, USA.

KUSHIRO Ikuo, b. 30 March 1934, Osaka, Japan. Professor Emeritus. m. Kazue Kushiro, 1 son. Education: BSc, 1957, PhD, 1962, University of Tokyo. Appointments: Postdoctoral Fellow, 1962-65, Staff Member, 1971-74 Geophysical Laboratory, Carnegie Institution of Washington; Associate Professor, 1970-71, Professor, 1974-94, Geological Institute, Dean, Faculty of Science, 1990-93, Vice-President, 1993-94, Professor Emeritus, 1995- University of Tokyo; Professor and Director, Institute for the Study of the Earth's Interior at Misasa, Okayama University, 1994-99; Director General, Institute for Frontier Research on Earth Evolution, Japan Marine Science and Technology Centre, 2001-2004. Publications: More than 200 papers in scientific journals include: Compositions of magmas formed by partial zone melting in the earth's upper mantle, 1968; Effect of water on the composition of magmas formed at high pressures, 1972; On the nature of silicate melt and its significance in magma genesis, 1975. Honours: Japan Academy Prize, 1982; Geological Society of Japan Award, 1988; Arthur Holmes Medal, European Union of Geosciences, 1999; Harry H Hess Medal, American Geophysical Union, 1999; Roebling Medal, Mineralogical Society of America, 1999; Goldschmidt Medal, Geochemical Society, 2001; Wollaston Medal, Geological Society of London, 2003; The Order of the Sacred Treasure, Gold and Silver Star, Japanese Government, 2009. Memberships: Japan Academy; Foreign Associate, National Academy of Sciences; Fellow, American Geophysical Union; Honorary Fellow, European Union of Geosciences; Honorary Fellow, Geological Society of London; Geochemistry Fellow, Geochemical Society; Life Fellow, Mineralogical Society of America. Address: 1-5-3-905 Takezono, Tsukuba, Ibaraki 305-0032, Japan. E-mail: ikushiro@r2.dion.ne.jp

KUSHNER Jack, b. 5 December 1939, Montgomery, Alabama, USA. Physician Executive. m. Annetta, 2 children. Education: University of Sheffield, England, 1959; BA (History), Tulane University, 1960; MD, University of Alabama, 1964; Surgical Intern, George Washington, 1965; Surgical Resident, Michigan, 1966; Neurosurgical Resident, Wake Forest, 1968-72; Master's (Finance) MGA, University of Maryland, 1990. Appointments: Chairman, American Opportunity Portal; Chief Executive Officer, Futuristic Instruments; Neurosurgeon, Annapolis. Publications: When Universities are Destroyed: How Tulane University and University of Alabama Rebuilt After Disaster; Courageous Judicial Decisions in Alabama. Honours: Bronze Star, Combat Surgeon, Viet-Nam, 1967; Board Certification, Neurological Surgery, 1975; Guest Speaker: British Neurological Surgeons, Cork, 1982; University of Chicago, USA, 1995; University of Alabama Medical, 1995-96; Pennsylvania State University Medical, 1996; Israeli Medical Society, Jerusalem, 1998; Wake Forest Medical, 1999; Galil Telemedicine, Technion University, Haifa, Israel, 2005, 2006; Man of the Year, ABI, 2004; Most Distinguished Alumnus, University of Maryland, 2004; Alpha Epsilon Delta Honor Society; Eta Sigma Phi Honor Society; Top 100 Health Care Professionals; America's Top Surgeons; Marie Curie Award, IBC, 2006; Lifetime Achievement Award, IBC; IBC Hall of Fame; Military Leadership Circle University of Maryland; Tulane University Alumni Board of Directors; Senior Tournament Director, United States Naval Academy Golf Association; Sovereign Ambassador of the Order of American Ambassadors, 2006; First Place, World Dance-o-Rama, Ball Room Dancing, Las Vegas, 2007; American Order of Merit, 2008; Listed in international biographical dictionaries. Memberships: American Association of Neurological Surgeons; Congress of Neurosurgeons; Southern Neurological Surgery; Pacific Neurosurgeons; Board of Managers, Anne Arundel Medical Center; Committee of Emerging Technology and Education, American College of Surgeons; National Security Forum @Air War College-Maxwell AFB; New York Academy of Sciences; Fellow, Tropical Medicine in Panama with Louisiana State University; White House Conference on Camp David Middle East Accords; Fellow, American College of Surgeons; Fellow, International College of Surgeons; 1902 Society for Anne Arundel Medical Center; Co-founder, Transcriptions International, 1989; Community Leaders of America, ABI; Men of Achievement, IBC, 1980; 2000 Outstanding People of the 20th Century, IBC, 1998. Address: 2030 Homewood Road, Ferry Farms, Annapolis, MD 21409, USA. E-mail: jkaoportal@comast.net Website: www.drjackkushner.com

KUTCHER Ashton (Christopher), b. 7 February 1978, Ceder Rapids, Iowa, USA. Actor. m. Demi Moore, 2005-12. Education: Biochemical Engineering Student, University of Iowa. Career: Sweeper, General Mills plant; Modeling. Film Appearances include: Coming Soon, 1999; Down To You, 2000; Reindeer Games, 2000; Dude Where's My Car?, 2000; Texas Ranger, 2001; Just Married, 2003; My Boss's Daughter, 2003; Cheaper by the Dozen, 2003; The Butterfly Effect, 2004; Guess Who, 2005; A Lot Like Love, 2005; Bobby, 2006; The Guardian, 2006; Open Season (voice), 2006; What Happens in Vegas, 2008; Spread, 2009; Personal Effects, 2009; Valentine's Day, Killers, 2010; No Strings Attached, New Year's Eve, 2011; Jobs, 2013. TV Appearances include: That 70's Show, 1998-2006; Just Shoot Me, 2001; Grounded for Life, 2002; Punk'd, 2003-07, 2012; Robot Chicken, 2005; Miss Guided, 2008; Two and a Half Men, 2011-. Honours: Young Artist Award, 1999; Sierra Award, 2000; MTV Movie Award, 2001; Teen Choice Award, 2003, 2004, 2005, 2006, 2012; Razzie Award, 2004, 2011; Hollywood Film Award, 2006; People's Choice Award, 2010.

KUTILEK Miroslav, b. 8 October 1927, Trutnov, Czech Republic. Professor of Soil Science and Soil Physics. m. Xena Radova, 1 son, 1 daughter. Education: Ing, CTU, Prague, 1946-51; CSc, 1952-55; DrSc, 1966. Appointments: Associate Professor, CTU Prague, 1968-73; Reader, University of Khartoum, Sudan, 1965-68; Professor, CTU, Prague, 1973-90, 1992-93; Deputy Dean, 1974-85; Visiting Professor, Institute de Mechanique, Grenoble, France, 1979-80, 1985, 1991; Visiting Professor, University of California, 1981-82; Visiting Professor, Technische Universitat, Braunschweig, 1989; Professor, Bayreuth University, Fachbereich Geookologie, Germany, 1990-92. Publications: Research papers in journals; Scientific Books in Czech; Four books on Soil Science, Soil Hydrology, Porous Materials; Scientific books and monograph chapters in English; Others; Seven fiction books in Czech; Facts about Global Warming, 2010. Honours: Felber's Award, Technical Sciences; Mendel's Award, Biological Sciences; Honorary Member, IUSS; Medal of Merit in Science, granted by the President of the Czech Republic. Memberships: International Soil Science Society; New York Academy of Sciences; International Commission on Irrigation and Drainage; International Council of Scientific Unions; European Cultural Club; Others. Address: Nad Patankou 34, 160 00 Prague 6, Czech Republic.

KUTTNER Paul, b. 20 September 1922, Berlin, Germany. Publicity Director; Author. m. (1) Myrtl Romegialli, 1956, divorced 1961, (2) Ursula Timmermann, 1963, divorced, 1970, 1 son. Education: Bismarck Gymnasium, Berlin, 1932-38; Bryanston College, Blandford, Dorset, 1939-40. Appointments: Child Actor, aged nine, in films including: Kameradschaft (directed by G W Pabst); Emil und die Detektive (based on Erich Kästner's international juvenile best-seller, opposite Fritz Rasp); M (directed by Fritz Lang, starring Peter Lorre), Germany, 1931; US Publicity Director for the Guinness Book of World Records, 1964-89; Publicity Director, Sterling Publishing Co Inc, 1989-98. Publications: Translator of nine American books from German into English, 1963-76; The Man Who Lost Everything, 1976 (Best Seller in Spanish Language Edition, 1982); Condemned, 1983; Absolute Proof, 1984; The Iron Virgin, 1985; History's Trickiest Questions, 1990; Arts & Entertainment's Trickiest Questions, 1993; Science's Trickiest Questions, 1994; The Holocaust: Hoax or History? - The Book of Answers to Those Who Would Deny the Holocaust, 1997; Autobiography, An Endless Struggle – Reminiscences and Reflections, 2010. Contributions to: Der Weg; London Week. Address: Apt 5C, 37-26 87th Street, Jackson Heights, NY 11372, USA.

KUZNETSOV Igor Vladimirovich, b. 11 December 1951, Khabarovsk, Russia. Writer. m. E Korsakova, 1 daughter. Education: Novosibirsk University, 1968-73. Appointments: Novosibirsk University, 1973-90; Russian Federation Ministry of Industry, 1990-97; Ministry of Foreign Economic Relations of the Russian Federation, 1997-2009. Publications: 6 books: Anthem for Doomed Youth; Vibres todo entero; Antes que la luna salga; Je te cherche par-delà l'attente; Selected Works; The Strength of Silent Minds. Honours: Dr Sc (Economics); Academician, Russian Academy of Sciences and Arts. Memberships: Union of Translators of Russia; Russian Literary Club; Authors and Publicists International Associations. Address: ul Ramenki 8-1-165, Moscow 119607, Russia. E-mail: natkk@mail.ru Website: www.igorkuznetsov.narod.ru

KVARATSKHELIA Elene, b. 27 August 1969, Tbilisi, Georgia. Chemist. Education: Engineer, Chemist, Researcher, Technical University of Georgia, 1986-92; English Course, Tbilisi Pedagogical Institute of Foreign Languages, 1988-90; Postgraduate Course, Institute of Inorganic Chemistry and Electrochemistry, 1992-95. Appointments: Junior Researcher, 1993-95, Researcher, 1995-2001, Senior Researcher, 2001-, Chief Technology Commercialization Officer, 2008-, R Agladze Institute of Inorganic Chemistry and Electrochemistry. Publications: 90 articles and papers in professional journals; 24 international conference abstracts. Honours: Candidate of Sciences, 1995; Doctor of Sciences, Chemistry, 2005; Certificate of Science and Technology Center of Ukraine, Technological Management: Commercialization of R&D Results, 2008. Honours: International Society of Electro-Chemistry; Bioelectrochemical Society. Address: 73 Javakhishvili st, 0112 Tbilisi, Georgia. E-mail: elicko@mail.ru

KVARATSKHELIA Ramaz, b. 15 November 1935, Tbilisi, Georgia. Chemist. m. Lyudmila Mladznovskaya, 1 son, 1 daughter. Education: Chemist-Engineer diploma, 1954-59, Candidate of Sciences, 1965, Georgian Polytechnical Institute; Institute of Inorganic Chemistry, 1959-; Doctor of Sciences, Kiev, Ukraine, 1987. Appointments: Junior, Senior and Chief Scientist, Institute of Inorganic Chemistry and Electrochemistry, 1959-; Professor, Georgian Technical University, 1989-95. Publications: 2 monographs; 1 invention; 160 articles in the fields of electrochemistry, physical chemistry and organic chemistry. Honours: American Medal of Honor. Memberships: New York Academy of Sciences. Address: I Javakhishvili str 73, 0112 Tbilisi, Georgia. E-mail: rkvaratskhelia@yahoo.com

KWATRA Saurabh, b. 12 April 1968, New Delhi, India. m. Archana Sagar, Education: Advanced Certificate, CAD/CAM, IIT, Delhi; Advanced Certificate Industrial Design, Hero Global Designs; PhD, Industrial Design. Appointments: Engineering Designer; Professor Triz User/Teacher Level 3, Institute of Innovative Design, Krasnoyarsk, Russia. Publications: Over 15 articles in professional journals. Honours: Leadership of Co-ordination Award, International Multidisciplinary Conference, Harvard University, USA, 2010. Address: B-6/42/1, Safdarjung Enclave, New Delhi, 110029, India.

KWEON Gichul, b. 23 January 1967, Korea. Professor. m. Youngyill Park, 1 son, 1 daughter. Education: BS, Civil Engineering, Yonsei University, 1989; MS, 1992, PhD,

1999, Civil Engineering, KAIST. Appointments: Researcher, Korean Highway Research Center, 1992-99; Professor, Department of Civil Engineering, Dongeui University, 1999-. Publications: Deterioration of Asphalt Concrete Complex Modulus with Impact Resonance test; Alternative Method of Determining Resilient Modulus of Subbase Soils Using Static Triaxial Test. Honours: Young and Promising Scholar Award, Society of Korean Geotechnical Engineers, 2004; Best Paper Award, Korena Society of Road Engineers, 2011. Memberships: Society of Korean Civil Engineers; Society of Korean Geotechnical Engineers; Korean Society of Road Engineers. Address: Department of Civil Engineering, Dongeui University, 995 Eomgwangno, Busanjin-gu, Busan 614-714, Korea. E-mail: gckweon@deu.ac.kr

KWON Jaehwan, b. 19 February 1970, Busan, Korea. Chairman. m. Jeonghyun Oh, 1 son, 1 daughter. Education: Pusan National Medical University, Busan, 1988-94; Postgraduate Course, Pusan National Medical University, 2004-06. Appointments: Intern, 1994-95, Resident, Otolaryngology Department, 1995-99, Clinical Fellowship, 2002-03, Chairman, ENT Department, 2003-, Maryknoll Medical Center, Busan; Military Service, Medical Officer, Korean Army, 1999-2002; Clinical Research Fellowship, Department of Facial Plastic Reconstructive Surgery, Stanford University, 2007-08. Publications: Numerous articles in professional journals. Honours: Listed in biographical dictionaries. Memberships: Korean Medical Association; Korean Otolaryngology, Head & Neck Surgery Society; Korean Rhinology Society; Korean Cosmetic Surgery Society; Korean Academy of Facial-Plastic Reconstructive Surgery; Korean Otology Society; Korean Skull Base Society; Busan-Ulsan-Kyongnam Branch, Korean Society of Otolaryngology. Address: Department of Otolaryngology, Head & Neck Surgery Society, Maryknoll Medical Center, 4-12 Daechung-dong, Jung-Gu, Busan, 600-730, Korea. E-mail: entkwon@hanmail.net

KWON Jongkwang, b. 16 June 1970, Republic of Korea. Researcher. m. Hyonjong Kim, 1 son, 2 daughters. Education: BS, 1991, MS, 1993, Department of Electronics Engineering, Kyungpook National University; PhD, Department of Electronics Engineering, Changnam National University, 2008. Appointments: Researcher, 1993-98, Senior Researcher, 1998-, Avionics Division, Agency for Defense Development; KT-1 Basic Trainer, KA-1, Flying Test Bed, Medium Unnamed Air Vehicle. Publications: Flight Tests of the KO-1 Aircraft at Night, 2007. Honours: Listed in international biographical dictionaries. Memberships: JSASS; KIMST; KSAS. Address: Yuseong PO Box 35-73, Daejeon 305-600, Korea. E-mail: aramy@chol.com

KWON Oh-Jin, b. 5 June 1968, Andong, Korea. Researcher. m. Seung-Nam Choo, 2 sons. Education: BA (Hons), 1990, MA, 1994, Computer Science, Kwangwoon University; PhD, Computer Science and Statistics, University of Seoul, 2009. Appointments: Platoon Leader, First Lieutenant, Wire Communication, Capital Corps, Republic of Korea Army, 1990-92; Senior Researcher, Department of Technology Information Analysis, KISTI, 1994-2010; Member, Organising Committee, University of Science and Technology, 2003; Assistant, Board of Audit of Inspection of Korea, 2003; Lecturer, Scientometrics, University of Science and Technology, 2009-10; Workshop Chair, CTIC, 2010. Publications: 6 books on information analysis and patent strategy; 10 reports on new technology business evaluation; 50 articles in professional journal and proceedings. Honours: Listed in international biographical dictionaries; Official Commendation of Republic of Korea Army, 1992; Letter of Approval, KISTI President, 1998, 2008-09. Memberships: Secretary General, Technical Committee, WF, ICT, Standardization & Technology; Secretary, Patent Information Research Association; Steering Committee, DQM Forum, DPC. E-mail: dbajin@kisti.re.kr

KWON Soon-Kyoung, b. 14 October 1940, Anjoo, Korea. Professor. m. Sin-Kang Park, 1 son, 1 daughter. Education: BS, Seoul, 1962; MS, Seoul, 1964; PhD, Munster, Germany, 1975. Appointments: Assistant Professor, Duksung Women's University, 1978-82; Associate Professor, 1982-87; Professor, 1987-2006; Honorary Professor 2006-. Vice President, 1992-93; Dean, College Pharmacy, 1998-2000; President, Duksung Women's University, 2001. Publications: Medicinal Chemistry, Textbook, 1985; The World of Drugs, 1988; Medicinal Chemistry, revised, 1996, 1999; The Advices of Drugs and Health, 2000. Honours: Prize for distinguished scientist, The Pharmaceutical Society of Korea, 1980; Golden Tower Prize for distinguished Pharmacists, Korea Pharmaceutical Association, 1992; Prize for commenter on pharmaceutical affairs, The Korean Medical News, 1997; Dong-Am Prize for the distinguished scientist in the field of pharmacy, Korean Pharmaceutical Industry News, 2001; A certificate of commendation from the President of Republic of Korea, Government, 2006; Prize for Distinguished Pharmaceutical Educator, 2006; Listed in various international biographical dictionaries. Memberships: American Chemical Society; Pharmaceutical Society of Korea; Korean Chemical Society; Korean Society of Applied Pharmacology. Address: Ui-dong 572-25, Kangbuk-ku, Seoul 142-880, Korea.

KWON Sun, b. 16 December 1977, Seoul, Korea. Neurosurgeon. Education: BA, Ulsan University College of Medicine, Seoul, 2002. Appointments: Intern, 2002-03, Resident, Neurosurgery, 2003-07, Asan Medical Center, Seoul; Director, Department of Neurosurgery, Armed Forces 3rd Military Academy Hospital, Young-Cheon, Kyong-Sang-Buk Do, 2007-08; Director, Department of Neurosurgery, Armed Forces Hong-Cheon Hospital, Hong-Cheon, Kang-Won Do, 2008-10; Fellow, Neurosurgeon, Wooridul Spine Hospital, Seoul, 2010-11; Neurosurgeon, Anyang Naun Spine Hospital, 2011-. Publications: Delayed in-situ fusion of thoracic fracture-dislocation in A case without neurologic deficits, 2005; Factors Associated with Cervical Myelopathy, 2006; Efficacy of tissue Plasminogen Activator in patients with Massive Subarachnoid hemorrhage by Aneurysmal Rupture, 2006; Facility of the Removal of Recurrent Disc Herniation due to use of Laser in Primary Operation, 2010. Memberships: Korean Neurosurgical Society; Korean Spine Neurosurgical Society; Fellow, American Board of Minimally Invasive Spinal Surgery; Fellow, Royal College of Surgeons. Address: Messe Building 5-6th floor, 676-91, Anyang 4-Dong, Anyang city, Kyeongki-Do, 430-832, Korea. Website: www.naeunhospital.com

KWONG Daniel W, b. 1 August 1958, Hong Kong. Business Owner; Investor; Global Strategist. Divorced, 1 daughter. Education: BA, Political Science, California State University at Los Angeles, USA, 1982; JD, Law, Thomas Jefferson College of Law, Florida, USA, 1993. Appointments: Chairman/CEO, Global Investment and Management Institute Inc; Chairman/CEO, Golden Harvest Holdings Ltd; Honorary Chairman and Non-Executive Director, KingHarvests.Com, Shanghai, China; Visiting Professor, World Eminent Chinese Business College, Beijing, China; Contributing Editor, Politics on Line. Publications: A Hidden Tool (an investment book), 1990; Cass' Story (song), 1991. Honours: Founding Sponsor, Flight

93 National Memorial Monument (invited by Governor Tom Ridge); Co-Founder, Ronald Reagan Republican Center, DC; Founder, National History Center, DC; Conference Chair/ Key Note Speaker, Real Estate Investments in China, San Francisco, 2007; Overseas Councillor, Nanjing Government, P R China, 2009; Co-chairman, Corporate Governance Summit in Asia, 2010; Pollie Award nominee, 2011; VIP Guest, Asian Financial Forum, Hong Kong, 2011. Memberships: Life Member, Republican National Committee; Life Member, Republican Presidential Task Force; Fellow, Hong Kong Institute of Directors; Vice Chairman, Board of Trustees, World Eminent Chinese Business Association, Beijing, China; Economic & Public Affairs Committee Member, Hong Kong Institute of Directors; National Committee on US-China Relations. Address: 1301 Bank of America Tower, Suite 500, 12 Harcourt Road, Central Hong Kong. E-mail: ghh_dwk@sbcglobal.net

KYRIAKOPOULOS Grigorios, b. 11 September 1972, Athens, Greece. Research Scientist. Education: Degree, Chemical Engineering, National Technical University of Athens, 1996; MS, Hellenic Open University, Patra, Greece, 2004; PhD, School of Chemical Engineering, National Technical University of Athens, Greece, 2005; MS, entitled Techno-economical Systems, National Technical University, Athens, Greece, 2007; PGCE, School of Pedagogical and Technological Education of Athens, 2010; BA (1st class Honours), Business and Management, London Metropolitan University, 2011; HND, Business Management, Bright School of Business and Management, 2012; CertHE, Psychology, University of Derby, 2012; CertHE, Human Resource Management, University of Leicester, 2013. Appointments: Research Fellow, Organic Chemical Technology, Laboratory of National Technical University of Athens, 1996-2006; Participant in the postgraduate programme "Protection of Monuments" organised by the Schools of Architectural Engineering, Chemical Engineering, Civil Engineering and Agronomist-Topographer Engineering, National Technical University of Athens with the experimental study: Removal of pesticides from aqueous solution by adsorption on polymeric resins, 1998-99 and 1999-2000; Academic Studies Auditor, Hellenic National Academic and Information Centre, Hellenic Ministry of Education, 2005-2006; Lecturer, Technical University of Pedagogical and Technical Education, Athens, Greece, 2004-2008; Lecturer, Hellenic Naval Academy of Greece, 2006-2008; Public Servant, Engineer, National Technical University of Athens, 2007-. Publications: Articles in scientific journals and papers in conference proceedings as co-author include: Treatment of contaminated water with pesticides via adsorption, 2006; Bio utilization for energy infrastructure and applications, 2009; European and international policy intervention of implementing the use of wood fuels in bioenergy sector, 2010; Power as resource – Power as discourse: An overview evaluation of the key-factors of "wind farms" and "riparian rights" as sources of power, 2011; The role of quality management for effective implementation of customer satisfaction, customer consultation and self-assessment, within service quality schemes: A review, 2011; A half a century of management by objectives (MBO): A review, 2011. Honours: Scholarships: National Technical University of Athens, 1998-2001; Hellenic Open University, 2001-2002, 2002-2003, 2003-2004; Postdoctoral Research, State Scholarship Foundation of Greece; Prix Afas, 2000, Société d'Encouragement au Progrès (French Institution) in the Municipality of Athens, 2000; Thomaidio Award, National Technical University of Athens, 2003, 2004 and 2005; Reviewer for 20 scientific journals of environmental orientation. Memberships: Technical Chamber of Greece; Panhellenic Society of Chemical Engineers; American Chemical Society; Global Alliance for International Advancement. Address: National Technical University of Athens, 9 Heroon Polytechniou Street, School of Electrical and Computer Engineering, Electric Power Division, Zografou Campus, GR 15780, Athens, Greece. E-mail: gregkyr@chemeng.ntua.gr

KYTE Peter Eric, b. 8 May 1945, Rawalpindi, Pakistan. Barrister. m. Virginia Cameron, 1 son, 1 daughter. Education: MA, Trinity Hall, Cambridge, 1968. Appointments: Teacher of Classics and French, 1964-65; Manager, Charter Consolidated Ltd, London, Mauritania and Congo, 1968-73; Account Executive, Merrill Lynch, London and New York, 1973-74; Joined Chambers of Daniel Hollis QC, now Hollis Whiteman Chambers, 1974-; Recorder, 1988; Queen's Counsel, 1996; Legal Assessor for the General Medical Council and General Dental Council. Honours: Recommended as Leading Silk in the field of Criminal Fraud in Chambers Guide to the Legal Profession, 2000-. Memberships: New York Stock Exchange; Chicago Board of Trade; Gray's Inn; Criminal Bar Association; Aula Club. Address: Forge House, Lower Heyford, Oxfordshire, OX25 5NS, England. E-mail: peter@kyte.u-net.com

L

LA PLANTE Lynda, b. 15 March 1946, Formby, England. Television Dramatist; Novelist. m. Richard La Plante, divorced. Education: Royal College of Dramatic Art. Appointments: Former Actress. Creative Works: Actress in The Gentle Touch, Out, Minder; Founder and Chair, La Plante Productions, 1994-; TV dramas include: Prime Suspect, 1991, 1993, 1995; Civvies; Framed; Seekers; Widows (series); Comics, 2 part drama, 1993; Cold Shoulder 2, 1996; Cold Blood; Bella Mafia, Trial and Retribution, 1997-; Killer Net, 1998; Mind Games, 2000; The Warden, 2001; Framed, Widows (mini-series), 2002; The Commander, 2003-. Publications include: The Widows, 1983; The Widows II, 1985; The Talisman, 1987; Bella Mafia, 1991; Framed, Civvies, Prime Suspect, 1992; Seekers, Entwined, Prime Suspect 2, 1993; Lifeboat, Cold Shoulder, Prime Suspect 3, 1994; She's Out, 1995; The Governor, Cold Blood, 1996; Trial and Retribution, 1997; Cold Heart, Trial and Retribution 2, 1998; Trial and Retribution 3, 1999; Trial and Retribution 4, Sleeping Cruelty, 2000; Trial and Retribution 5, Trial and Retribution 6, Royal Flush, 2002; Like a Charm (short stories), Above Suspicion (novel), 2004; The Red Dahlia, 2006; Clean Cut, 2007; Deadly Intent, 2008; Silent Scream, 2009; Blind Fury, 2010. Honours: CBE, 2008. Address: La Plante Productions Ltd, Paramount House, 162-170 Wardour Street, London, W1F 8ZX, England. Website: www.laplanteproductions.com

LAAR Mart, b. 22 April 1960, Tallinn, Estonia. Prime Minister. m. Katrin Laar, 1981, 1 son, 1 daughter. Education: MA, Philosophy, BA, History, Tartu University. Appointments: Member, Supreme Council, 1990-92; Member, Constitutional Assembly, 1992; Prime Minister of Estonia, 1992-94, 1999-2002; National Coalition Fatherland Party Chairman, 1992-95; Member of Parliament, Riikogu, VII Session, 1992-95; Member of Parliament, Riigikogu, VIII Session, 1995-98; Chairman, Pro Patria, 1998-; Prime Minister, Republic of Estonia, 1999. Publications: Variety of Estonian and English language books and publications on history. Honours: The Year's Best Young Politician in the World Award, 1993; European Tax Payer Association Year Prize, 2001; European Bull, Davastoeconomic Forum, Global Link Award, 2001; Adam Smith Award, 2002; Cato Institute's Milton Friedman Prize for Advancing Liberty, 2006. Memberships: Chairman, Jaan Tonisson Institute; Estonian Christian Democratic Union; Pen Club; Estonian University Students Society; Mont Pelerin Society, 2007. Address: State Chancellery, Lossi Plats 1a, Tallinn 15161, Estonia.

LABURTHE-TOLRA Philippe-Pierre, b. 9 July 1929, Paris, France. University Professor; Writer. m. Michéle Jouve, 1 son, 1 daughter. Education:, 1947-55, Agrégation de Philosophie, 1962, Doctorat d'Etat es lettres et Sciences Humaines, 1975, Sorbonne, Paris. Appointments: Founder, Benin University, 1962-64; Co-founder, Federal University of Cameroons, Yaounde, 1964-72; Headman, Social Sciences, Rennes University, 1972-77, University Paris V, Sorbonne, 1977-90, Dean, Social Science Faculty, Sorbonne, 1977-99. Publications: 12 books; Over 100 articles. Honours: Chevalier de la Legion d'Honneur et des Palmes Academiques Francaises; Chevalier du Merite et de la Valeur du Cameroun; President de la Societe des Africanistes. Memberships: Academie d'Education et de Sciences Sociales; Académie des Sciences d'Outre-Mer; Carrefour des Acteurs Sociaux; Academie des Sciences d'Outremer; Societe des Africanistes; Automobile Club de France. Address: 54 rue Saint Lazare, 75009 Paris, France. E-mail: philippe.laburthe@laposte.net

LACEY Nicholas Stephen, b. 20 December 1943, London, England. Architect. m. (1) Nicola, (2) Juliet, 2 sons, 3 daughters. Education: MA, Emmanuel College Cambridge; AADipl, Architectural Association, London. Appointments: Partner, Nicholas Lacey and Associates, 1971-83; Partner, Nicholas Lacey and Partners, 1983-. Honours: Winner, Wallingford Competition; Winner, Crown Reach (Millbank) Competition; Joint Winner, Arunbridge Competition; Prize Winner, Paris Opera House Competition; RIBA Regional Awards; Civic Trust Awards. Memberships: Royal Institute of British Architects (RIBA); Architecture Club; Athenaeum; Royal Dorset Yacht Club. Address: Reeds Wharf, 33 Mill Street, London SE1 2AX, England. E-mail: nicholaslacey@lineone.net

LACHELIN Gillian Claire Liborel, b. 5 February 1940, Reigate, Surrey, England. Emeritus Consultant in Obstetrics and Gynaecology. Education: MA, MB, BChir, 1964, MRCOG, 1969, MD (London), 1981, FRCOG, 1982, Cambridge University and St Thomas' Hospital Medical School. Appointments: Reader and Consultant in Obstetrics and Gynaecology, 1977-2000, Emeritus Reader and Consultant in Obstetrics and Gynaecology, 2000-, University College London and University College Hospitals Trust. Publications: Numerous articles on reproductive endocrinology; Books: Miscarriage: The Facts; Introduction to Clinical Reproductive Endocrinology. Memberships: Committee on Safety of Medicines, 1993-96; Society for Gynecologic Investigation (USA), 1982-. Address: Department of Obstetrics and Gynaecology, Royal Free and University College Medical School, 88-96 Chenies Mews, London WC1E 6HX, England.

LACHINOV Mikhail, b. 31 March 1957, Gorkovskaya Region, Russia. Engineer; Economist. 1 son, 1 daughter. Education: M Eng, Moscow Civil Engineering University, 1979; PhD, 1987; Master of Economics, State Financial Academy of the Russian Federation Government, 1991; Postgraduate Courses, London School of Business, Holborn College, London, England, 1994. Appointments: Professor of Economics, Moscow State Civil Engineering University, 1995-2002; Head, Director, Institution of Civil Engineers representation in Russia, 1996-2003; Deputy Director, Economics, "Mospromstroi" Construction Corporation, 2002-2006; International Construction and Industrial Association (Mossib), 2006; Department of Management Directors; Director General, JSC Zarubezhstroy Corporation for Construction in Foreign Countries, 2008-; Mountain Climatic Resort International Department Head, State Corporation on Construction of Olympic Venues and Development of Sochi, 2010-. Publications: Textbook: Foreign Economic Relations in Construction, 2001; More than 30 scientific articles. Honours: Medal, Krasnoyarsk Region Development Award; Medal, For International Links Development. Memberships: Fellow, Institution of Civil Engineers (UK); Fellow, Russian Society of Civil Engineering; Chartered Engineer. Address: Pokrovskyi boulvar 4/17, Build 10, Moscow 101000, Russia. E-mail: lachinov@rambler.ru

LACROIX Christian Marie Marc, b. 16 May 1951, Arles, France. Fashion Designer. m. Francoise Roesenstiehl, 1989. Education: Université Paul Valéry, Montpellier; Université Paris, Sorbonne; Ecole du Louvre. Appointments: Assistant, Hermès, 1978-79, Guy Paulin, 1980-81; Artistic Director, Jean Patou, 1981-87, Christian Lacroix, 1987-, Emilio Pucci, 2002-; Design for Carmen, Nîmes, France, 1988, for L'as-tu revue?, 1991, for Les Caprices de Marianne, 1994, for Phèdre a la Comèdie Francaise, 1995; Created costumes for Joyaux, Opera Garnier, 2000; Decorated the TGV Mediterranee, 2001;

DICTIONARY OF INTERNATIONAL BIOGRAPHY 36th EDITION

Creative Director, Emilio Gucci, 2002. Publications: Pieces of a Pattern, 1992; Illustrations for albums, Styles d'aujourd'hui, 1995; Journal d'une collection, 1996. Honours include: Dés d'or, 1986, 1988; Council of Fashion Designers of America, 1987; Prix Balzac, 1989; Goldene Spinnrad Award, Germany, 1990; Commander, Ordre des Arts es Lettres, 1991; Prix Molière, for costumes in Phèdre, 1996; Chevalier, Legion d'honneur, 2002. Address: 73 rue de Faubourg Saint Honoré, 75008 Paris, France.

LADY GAGA (Stefani Joanne Angelina Germanotta), b. 28 March 1986, New York City, USA. Singer; Songwriter. Education: New York University's Tisch School of the Arts, 2003. Career: Recording Artist, Streamline Records; Recording Artist, Kon Live Distribution: Albums: The Fame, 2008; The Fame Monster, 2009; Born This Way, 2011; Artpop, 2013; Singles: Just Dance; Poker Face; Bad Romance; Telephone; Alejandro; Born This Way; Judas; The Edge of Glory; You and I; Marry the Night; Tours: The Fame Ball Tour, 2009; The Monster Ball Tour, 2009-11. Honours: 5 Grammy Awards; Artist of the Year, Billboard, 2010; Listed in Time 100 and Forbes' annual lists.

LADYMAN Stephen John, b. 6 November 1952, Ormskirk, Lancashire, England. Member of Parliament. m. Janet Baker, 2 stepsons, 1 daughter, 1 stepdaughter. Education: BSc, Applied Biology, Liverpool Polytechnic; PhD, Strathclyde University. Appointments: Research Scientist, MRC Radiobiology Unit, 1979-85; Head of Computing, Kennedy Institute, 1985-91; Head, Computer Support, Pfizer Central Research, 1991-97; Member of Parliament, South Thanet, 1997-; Treasurer, All Party British Fruit Industry Group, 2000-; Chair, All Party Parliamentary Group on Autism, 2000-; Liaison MP for The Netherlands, 2001-; Chair, All Party British-Dutch Group, 2001-; Parliamentary Private Secretary to the Minister for the Armed Forces, 2001-. Address: House of Commons, London SW1A 0AA, England. E-mail: ladymans@parliament.uk

LAFAY Gérard Marie Rémi, b. 8 September 1940, Feurs, France. Emeritus Professor. m. Francoise Dumas, 2 sons, 2 daughters. Education: Master, Politics, Institut d'Etudes, 1963; Diploma, Institut d'Administration des Entreprises, 1965; PhD, Economics, University Paris I, 1973. Appointments: Head of Department, GEPI, 1967-77; Deputy Director, CEPII, 1978-93; Associate Professor, University Paris I, 1992-95; Professor, University Paris II, 1996-2008; Director, IRGEI. Publications: Articles in professional journals; 3 books. Address: 6 Rue du Général Lambert, 75007 Paris, France. E-mail: glafay@noos.fr

LAFON Jacqueline Lucienne, b. 4 October 1941, Paris, France. Law Educator. Education: Baccalaureat, Paris, France, 1960; Doctorate in Law, Paris University, 1972. Appointments: Associate Professor, Paris XI Law Faculty, 1973-2007; Associate Professor, Sorbonne University (Paris IV), 1973-80; Associate Dean, Paris XI Law Faculty, 1980-87; Lecturer, Florida State University Study Centre, Florence, Italy, 1983; Lecturer, Florida International University, Miami, USA, 1984; Lecturer, Harvard University, Massachusetts, USA, 1984; Lecturer, Boston University Overseas Programs, Paris, 1985; Lecturer, Missouri University, Kansas, USA, 1987; Associate Professor, University Pantheon-Sorbonne (Paris I), 1990-2008. Publications: 6 books; 8 articles in professional journals. Honours: Laureate in Private Roman Law, University of Paris, 1962; Award for thesis, University of Paris II, 1972; Award for thesis, Association of the Historians of Law, 1973; Grant, Centre National de la Recherche Scientifique, 1979. Memberships: Le cercle France-Amériques, Paris; Association Vieilles maisons Françaises, Paris.

LAGERFELD Karl-Otto, b. 1938, Hamburg, Germany. Fashion Designer. Education: Art School, Hamburg. Appointments: Fashion Apprentice, Balmain and Patou, 1959; Freelance Designer, associated with Fendi, Rome, 1963-, Chloe, Paris, 1964-83, Chanel, Paris, 1982-, Isetan, Japan; Designer, Karl Lagerfeld's Women's Wear, Karl Lagerfeld France Inc, 1983-; First collection under own name, 1984; Honorary Teacher, Vienna, 1983; Costume Designer for film, Comédie d'Amour, 1989; Designed tour outfits for Maddona; Kylie Minogue, Mariah Carey, 2004; New collection K Karl Lagerfeld, 2006. Publications: Lagerfeld's Sketchbook, 1990; Karl Lagerfeld Off the Record, 1995. Honours include: Golden Thimble, 1986. Address: Karl Lagerfeld France Inc, 75008 Paris, France.

LAGOS Ricardo, b. 2 March 1938, Santiago, Chile. Politician. m. Luisa Durán, 5 children. Education: University of Chile; Duke University, North Carolina, USA; PhD. Appointments: Professor, 1963-72, former Head, School of Political and Administrative Sciences, former Director, Institute of Economics, General Secretary, 1971, University of Chile; Chairman, Alianza Democrática, 1983-84; Chairman, Partido por la Democracia, 1987-90; Minister of Education, 1990-92; Minister of Public Works, 1994; President of Chile, 2000-06. Publications: Numerous books and articles on economics and politics. Address: Office of the President, Palacio de la Moneda, Santiago, Chile.

LAGOURI Theodota, b. 20 February 1970, Thessaloniki, Greece. Research Associate. Education: PhD, Physics, Aristotle University of Thessaloniki, Greece. Appointments: Research Associate, High Energy Physics, Universitad Autonoma de Madrid and CERN. Publications: Numerous articles in professional journals. Honours: Greek National Fellowships, 1987-91; Marie Curie Fellowships, 1998-2000, 2003-04, 2004-06. Memberships: Marie Curie Fellowship Association; High Energy Physics Greek Association. Address: Avenue de Mategnin 65, Meyrin, CH-1217, Switzerland.

LAGRAVENESE Richard, b. 30 October 1959, Brooklyn, New York, USA. Film Screenplay Writer, Director and Producer. m. Ann Weiss, 1986, 1 daughter. Education: Emerson College; BFA, New York University. Appointments: Producer, The Ref, film, 1994; Director, Living Out Loud, film, 1998. Creative Works: Screenplays: Rude Awakening, 1991; The Fisher King, 1991; The Ref, 1994; A Little Princess, 1995; The Bridges of Madison County, 1995; The Horse Whisperer, 1998; Living Out Loud (also Director), 1998; Unstrung Heroes; Defective Detective, 2002; Paris, je t'aime, 2006; The Secret Life of Walter Mitty, 2006; Freedom Writers, 2007; P.S. I Love You, 2008. Honours: Independent Film Project Writer of the Year. Address: c/o Kirsten Bonelli, 8383 Wilshire Boulevard, Suite 340, Beverly Hills, CA 90211, USA.

LAHOUD Emile (General), b. 1936, Baabdate, Lebanon. Politician; Naval Officer. m. Andrée Amadouni, 2 sons, 1 daughter. Education: Brumana High School; Cadet Officer, Military Academy, 1956; Naval Academy courses, UK, USA, 1958-80. Appointments: Ensign, 1959, Sub-Lieutenant, 1962, Lieutenant, 1968, Lieutenant-Commander, 1974, Commander, 1976, Captain, 1980, Rear-Admiral, 1985, General, 1989; Commander of Second Fleet, 1966-68, First Fleet, 1968-70; Staff of Army Fourth Bureau, 1970-72; Chief of Personal Staff of General and Commander of Armed Forces, 1973-79;

Director of Personnel, Army Headquarters, 1980-83; President of Military Office, Ministry of Defence, 1983-89; General and Commander of Armed Forces, 1989-1998; President of Lebanon, 1998-2007. Publications: Procedure and Modus Operandi, 1998. Honours: Medal of Merit and Honour, Haiti, 1974; Lebanese Medal of Merit, General Officer, 1989; War Medals, 1991, 1992; Dawn of the South Medal, 1993; National Unity Medal, 1993; Medal of Esteem, 1994; Grand Cordon, Order of the Cedar, Lebanon, 1993; Commandeur, Légion d' Honneur, France, 1993; Order of Merit, Senior Officer Level, Italy, 1997; Grand Cross of Argentina, 1998; Order of Hussein ibn Ali, Jordan, 1999; Necklace of Independence, Qatar, 1999. Address: Presidential Palace, Baabda, Lebanon. E-mail: opendoor@presidency.gov.lb

LAI Chin-Hung, b. 25 January 1974, Taipei, Taiwan, Republic of China. Professor. Education: Bachelor, Chemistry, Tunghai University, Taichung, 1997; Master, 1999, Doctor, 2003, Chemistry, National Tsing Hua University, Hsinchu. Appointments: Postdoctor, Institute of Bioinformatics and Structural Biology, National Tsing Hua University, Hsinchu, 2003-04; Postdoctor, 2004-10, Assistant Research Scientist, 2010, Department of Chemistry, National Taiwan University, Taipei; Assistant Professor, School of Applied Chemistry, Chung Shan Medical University, Taichung, 2010-. Publications: Numerous articles in professional journals. Honours: Listed in biographical dictionaries. Memberships: American Chemical Society. Address: No 110, Section 1, Jianguo North Road, Taichung 402, Taiwan. E-mail: chlai125@csmu.edu.tw

LAI Manhong, b. 15 July 1964, Macao, P R China. Assistant Professor. m. Leung Kin Sun. Education: BA, National Chung Hsing University of Taiwan,1986; Diploma in Education, Chinese University of Hong Kong (CUHK), 1987; MPhil, 1995, PhD, 2002, Chinese University of Hong Kong Graduate School. Appointments: Instructor, 2000-01, Senior Instructor, 2005-07, Assistant Professor, 2007-, Department of Education Administration & Policy, Chinese University of Hong Kong. Publications: Numerous articles in professional journals. Honours: Faculty Exemplary Teaching Award, Research Excellence Award, Chinese University of Hong Kong. Memberships: Comparative and International Education Society, USA. Address: Faculty of Education, The Chinese University of Hong Kong, Shatin, Hong Kong. E-mail: mhlai@cuhk.edu.hk

LAI Michael Ming-Chiao, b. 8 September 1942, Tainan, Taiwan. Professor; Educator; Medical Researcher. m. Wung Hwei-Ying Lai, 2 daughters. Education: MD, National Taiwan University College of Medicine, Taiwan, 1968; PhD, Molecular Biology, University of California, Berkeley, USA,1973. Appointments: Assistant Professor, 1973-78, Associate Professor, 1978-83, Professor, 1983-2002, Distinguished Professor, 2002-2007, University of Southern Carolina, USA; Investigator, Howard Hughes Medical Institute, 1990-2003; Distinguished Research Fellow and Vice President, Academia Sinica, 2003-06; Professor and President, National Cheng Kung University, 2007-11; Distinguished Research Fellow, Academia Sinica, 2011-. Publications: Over 300 articles in professional journals. Honours: Academician, National Academy of Sciences, Taiwan, 1992; Fellow, American Academy of Microbiology, 2002; Doctor Honoris Causa, The Central University, Taiwan, 2004; TWAS Fellow, 2006; Outstanding Scholar Awards, 2007; Lifetime Achievement Award, University of Southern California, 2008;

Lifetime Achievement Award, Society of Chinese Bioscientists in America, 2009. Memberships: American Society for Microbiology; American Society for Virology.

LAI Yukman, b. 25 February 1949, Canton, China. Artist. m. Ming-Yan Ng, 1997, 3 daughters. Education: Diploma, Hong Kong Sir Robert Black College of Education, 1974; BA, University of East Asia, Macau, 1986. Appointments: Board of Directors, Richmond Art Gallery Association, 1997-98; Curator, Chinese Canadian Arts Gallery; President, Chinese Canadian Artists Federation, Vancouver, Canada; Lecturer of Art, Simon Fraser University, Vancouver, Canada. Publications: Paintings, Calligraphy and Seals of Yukman Lai; My Rockies, Landscape Paintings by Yukman Lai; Yangtze River, A Sentimental Journey, The Landscape Paintings of Yukman Lai. Honours: 1st Class Prize, The Whole China Tabai Cup Competition of Chinese Painting, 1989. Memberships: Life Member, Chinese Canadian Artists Federation in Vancouver; Fellow, Huang Pu Art Academy, Shanghai, China. Address: 1280, Eastlawn Drive, Burnaby, BC, Canada.

LAIDLAW Christopher Charles Fraser (Sir), b. 9 August 1922. Business Executive. m. Nina Mary Prichard, 1952, 1 son, 3 daughters. Education: St John's College, Cambridge. Appointments: War Service, Europe, Far East, Major on General Staff, 1939-45; With British Petroleum Co Ltd, 1948-83: Representative, Hamburg, 1959-61, General Manager, Marketing Department, 1963-67, Director, BP Trading, 1967, President, BP Belgium, 1967-71, Director of Operations, 1971-72, Chairman, BP Germany, 1972-83, Managing Director, BP Co Ltd, 1972-81, Deputy Chairman, BP Co Ltd, 1980-81, Chairman, BP Oil Ltd, 1977-81, Chairman, BP Oil International 1981; Director, Commercial Union Assurance Co, 1978-83, Barclays Bank International Ltd, 1980-87, Barclays Bank, 1981-88; Chairman, ICL, 1981-84; President, ICL France, 1983; Director, Amerada Hess Corporation, 1983-94; Director, Barclays Merchant Bank, 1984-87; Chairman, Boving and Co, 1984-85; Chairman, UK Advisory Board, 1984-91, Director, 1987-94, INSEAD; Director, Amerada Ltd, 1985-98; Chairman, Bridon PLC, 1985-90; Director, Daimler-Benz UK Ltd, 1994-99. Honours: Honorary Fellow, St John's College, Cambridge. Memberships: President, German Chamber of Industry and Commerce, 1983-86; Master, Tallow Chandlers Company, 1988-89; Vice-President, British-German Society, 1996-. Address: 49 Chelsea Square, London SW3 6LH, England.

LAIDLAW (Henry) Renton, b. 6 July 1939, Edinburgh, Scotland. Journalist. Education: James Gillespie's School, Edinburgh, Scotland; Daniel Stewart's College, Edinburgh, Scotland. Appointments: Sports Reporter, Edinburgh Evening News, 1957-68; Newsreader, Interviewer, Grampian Television, 1968-70; BBC Reporting Scotland Anchorman, 1970-73; Golf Reporter, Evening Standard, London, 1973-98; BBC radio, ITV, TWI, Eurosport, Screensport, Sport on 2, BBC Radio Scotland, PGA European Tour Productions, 1985-; Golf Channel, USA, 1995-. Publications: Golfers Handbook (editor); Tony Jacklin – the First 40 Years; Play Better Golf; Play Golf (with Peter Alliss); Golfing Heroes; Ryder Cup 1985; Ryder Cup, 1987; Ryder Cup, 1989; Captain at Kiawah (with Bernard Gallacher); Wentworth – 70 Years; Sunningdale Centenary. Honours: Lifetime Achievement Award in Journalism, PGA of America, 2003; Memorial Journalism Award, USA, 2001. Memberships: R and A; Sunningdale; Royal Burgess; Ballybunion; Caledonian Club. Address: c/o Kay Clarkson, 10 Buckingham Place, London SW1E 6HX, England. E-mail: renton@rentonlaidlaw.com

LAIDMÄE Virve-Ines, b. 4 September 1941, Tallinn, Estonia. Sociologist. m. Valdur Randoja, 1 daughter. Education: BA, Tallinn Technical University, Estonia, 1966; MA, Sociology, Tallinn University, 2000. Appointments: Researcher, Institute of International and Social Studies, 1970-2007, Researcher, Institute of Social Work, 2007-10, Tallinn University. Publications: Author of articles and contributions to professional journals; Chapters to books, 2000-10. Honours: Grants: Elderly People – Coping with Life; Chronic Rheumatic Patients, 2000-08; Research, Population Surveys, 1973-2008. Memberships: European Sociological Association; Estonian Association of Sociologists, Tallinn; Estonian Rheumatic Association, Tallinn. E-mail: ines@tlu.ee

LAINE Cleo (Clementina Dinah Dankworth), b. 28 October 1927, Southall, Middlesex, England. Singer. m. (1) George Langridge, 1947, 1 son, (2) John Philip William Dankworth, 1958 (deceased), 1 son, 1 daughter. Appointments: Joined, Dankworth Orchestra, 1953; Lead, Seven Deadly Sins, Edinburgh Festival and Sadler's Wells, 1961; Acting roles in Edinburgh Festival, 1966, 1967; Founder, Wavendon Stables Performing Arts Centre, 1970; Many appearances with symphony orchestras; Frequent tours and TV appearances and productions including Last of the Blonde Bombshells, 2000. Publications: Cleo: An Autobiography, 1994; You Can Sing If You Want To, 1997. Honours include: Woman of the Year, 9th Annual Golden Feather Awards, 1973; Edison Award, 1974; Variety Club of GB Show Business Personality Award, 1977; TV Times Viewers' Award for Most Exciting Female Singer on TV, 1978; Grammy Award, Best Jazz Vocalist, Female, 1985; Best Actress in a Musical, 1986; Theatre World Award, 1986; Lifetime Achievement Award, 1990; Vocalist of the Year, British Jazz Awards, 1990; Lifetime Achievement Award, USA, 1991; ISPA Distinguished Artists Award, 1999. Memberships include: National Association of Recording Merchandisers. Address: The Old Rectory, Wavendon, Milton Keynes MK17 8LT, England.

LAING (John) Stuart, b. 22 July 1948, Limpsfield, England. Diplomat. 1 son, 2 daughters. Education: Rugby School; Corpus Christi College, Cambridge. Appointments: Served with the UK Diplomatic Service in Saudi Arabia, Brussels, Cairo, Prague and the Foreign and Commonwealth Office, London. British High Commissioner, Brunei, 1998–2002; British Ambassador to Oman, 2002-2005; British Ambassador to Kuwait, November 2005-08; Master of Corpus Christi College, Cambridge, 2008-; Trustee, CfBT Education Trust, 2008-. Memberships: Oxford & Cambridge. Address: Corpus Christi College, Cambridge, CB2 1RH, England. E-mail: master@corpus.cam.ac.uk

LAIRD Gavin Harry (Sir), b. 14 March 1933, Clydebank, Scotland. Trade Union Official. m. Catherine Gillies Campbell, 1956. Appointments: Shop Stewards Convener, Singer, Clydebank, 7 years; Regional Officer, 1972-75, Executive Councillor for Scotland and North-West England, 1975-82, General Secretary, Union Section, 1992-95, Amalgamated Engineering Union, formerly Amalgamated Union of Engineering Workers; Scottish Trades Union Congress General Council, 1973-75; Part-time Director, Highlands and Islands Development Board, 1974-75; Part-time Director, British National Oil Corporation, 1976-86; Trades Union Congress General Council, 1979-82; Industrial Development Advisory Board, 1979-86; Chairman, The Foundries Economic Development Committee, 1982-85; Arts Council, 1983-86; Director, Bank of England, 1986-94; Non-Executive Director, Scottish TV Media Group PLC, 1986-99; Non-Executive Director, Britannia Life, 1988-; Non-Executive Director, GEC Scotland, 1991-99; Non-Executive Director, Edinburgh Investment Trust, 1994-; Chairman, Greater Manchester Buses North, 1994-96; Armed Forces Pay Review Body, 1995-98; Employment Appeal Tribunal, 1996-; Non-Executive Director, Britannia Investment Managers Ltd and Britannia Fund Managers Ltd, now Britannia Asset Managers Ltd, 1996-; Chairman, Murray Johnstone Venture Capital Trust 4, 1999-; Murray Johnstone Private Acquisition Partnership Advisory Committee, 1999-. Honours: Commander, Order of the British Empire. Memberships: Trustee, John Smith Memorial Trust; Advisory Board, Know-How Fund for Poland, 1990-95; Trustee, Anglo-German Foundation, 1994-; President, Kent Active Retirement Association, 1999-; Vice-President, Pre-Retirement Association of Great Britain and Northern Ireland, 1999-; Editorial Board, European Business Journal. Address: 9 Cleavedon House, Holmbury Park, Bromley BR1 2WG, England.

LAKATANI Sani, Politician. Appointments: Leader, Niue People's Party; Prime Minister of Niue, 1999-2001; Minister for External Affairs, Finance, Customs and Revenue, Economic and Planning Development and Statistics, Business and Private Sector Development, Civil Aviation, Tourism, International Business Company and Offshore Banking, Niue Development Bank, 1999-2001; Chancellor, University of the South Pacific, Fiji, 2000-03; Deputy Premier and Minister for Planning, Economic Development and Statistics, the Niue Development Bank, Post, Telecommunication and Information Computer Technology Development, Philatelic Bureau and Numismatics, Shipping, Investment and Trade, Civil Aviation and Police, Immigration and Disaster Management, 2002-. Address: c/o Office of the Prime Minister, Alofi, Niue, South Pacific.

LAL Ganesh Prakash, b. 28 January 1929, Gaya, Bihar, India. Engineering. m. Brij Lata, 2 sons, 3 daughters. Education: BSc, Engineering, 1950; BL, 1969; FIE, India. Appointments: AE, EE, SE, CE, Engineer in Chief & Special Secretary, CMD BR DGE Const Corporation, Government of Bihar; President, Institute of Engineers, India; President, Federation of Engineering Organisations, South and Central Asia; Vice President, World Federatioin of Engineering Organisation. Publications: Engineering & Environment; Environment in Everyday Life. Honours: Abhiyanta Ratna; Excellence in Civil Engineering Award; National Research and Design Award; Gold Medal from WFEO for Service to Humanity. Memberships: Institute of Engineers (India); Indian Building Congress; Indian Roads Congress; Productivity Council; Concrete Institute; Lions Club; Vikas Parishad. Address: Ved-Shree Dujra, Patna 800001, Bihar, India. E-mail: er.gplal@gmail.com

LALLA AICHA (HRH Princess), b. 17 June 1930. Diplomatist. Appointments: Moroccan Ambassador to UK, 1965-69; Moroccan Ambassador to Italy and accredited to Greece, 1969-73. Honours: Grand Cordon, Order of the Throne of Morocco. Membership: President, Moroccan Red Crescent. Address: c/o Ministry of Foreign Affairs, ave Franklin Roosevelt, Rabat, Morocco.

LAMB Allan Joseph, b. 20 June 1954, Langebaanweg, Cape Province, South Africa. Cricketer. m. Lindsay Lamb, 1979, 1 son, 1 daughter. Education: Abbotts College. Appointments: Mid-Order Right-Hand Batsman; Teams: Western Province, 1972-82, 1992-93, OFS, 1987-88, Northamptonshire, 1978-95, Captain 1989-95; Qualified for England 1982 and played in 79 Tests, 1982-92, 3 as Captain, scoring 4,656 runs, average 36.0, including 14 hundreds; Toured Australia,

1982-83, 1986-87, 1990-91; Scored 32,502 1st Class Runs, 89 hundreds; 1,000 15 times; 122 limited-overs internationals; Director, Lamb Associates Event Management Company, Grenada Sports Ltd; Contributor, Sky Sports Cricket. Publication: Silence of the Lamb, autobiography, 1995. Address: Lamb Associates, First Floor, 4 St Giles Street, Northampton NN1 1JB, England.

LAMB Andrew (Martin), b. 23 September 1942, Oldham, Lancashire, England. Writer on Music. m. Wendy Ann Davies, 1970, 1 son, 2 daughters. Education: Corpus Christi College, Oxford, 1960-63; MA, Honours, 1967, D Litt, 2006. Publications: Jerome Kern in Edwardian London, 1985; Ganzl's Book of the Musical Theatre (with Kurt Ganzl), 1988; Skaters' Waltz: The Story of the Waldteufels, 1995; An Offenbach Family Album, 1997; Shirley House to Trinity School, 1999; 150 Years of Popular Musical Theatre, 2000; Leslie Stuart: Composer of Florodora, 2002; Fragson: The Triumphs and the Tragedy (with Julian Myerscough), 2004; The Merry Widow at 100, 2005; A Life on the Ocean Wave: The Story of Henry Russell, 2007. Editor: The Moulin Rouge, 1990; Light Music from Austria, 1992; Leslie Stuart: My Bohemian Life, 2003. Contributions to: Oxford Dictionary of National Biography; The New Grove Dictionary of Music and Musicians; The New Grove Dictionary of American Music; The New Grove Dictionary of Opera; Gramophone; Musical Times; Classic CD; BBC Music Magazine; American Music; Music and Letters; Wisden Cricket Monthly; Cricketer; Listener; Notes. Memberships: Fellow, Institute of Actuaries; Lancashire County Cricket Club. Address: 1 Squirrel Wood, West Byfleet, Surrey, KT14 6PE, England.

LAMBERT Nigel Robert Woolf, b. 5 August 1949, London, England. Barrister; Queens Counsel. m. Roamie Elisabeth Sado, 1 son, 1 daughter. Education: College of Law, London. Appointments: Called to the Bar, Gray's Inn, 1974; Ad eundem Member of Inner Temple, 1986; Chairman, South Eastern Circuit, Institute of Barristers Clerks Committee; Assistant Recorder, 1992-96; Recorder, 1996-; Queens Counsel, 1999; Chairman, North London Bar Mess, 2001-; Bencher, Gray's Inn, 2003. Memberships: Life Vice President, Cokethorpe Old Boys Association; North London Bar Mess Committee, 1991-; Criminal Bar Association, Committee, 1993-2000; Member, Bar Council, 1993-2000; Member, South Eastern Circuit, Executive Committee, 2001-; Inner Temple Bar Liaison Committee, 2002-04. Address: 2-4 Tudor Street, London EC4Y 0AA, England. E-mail: nigellambertqc@hotmail.com

LAMBERT Richard Peter, b. 23 September 1944. Journalist. m. Harriet Murray-Browne, 1973, 1 son, 1 daughter. Education: Balliol College, Oxford; BA Oxon. Appointments: Staff, 1966-2001, Lex Column, 1972, Financial Editor, 1978, New York Correspondent, 1982, Deputy Editor, 1983, Editor, 1991-2001, Financial Times; Lecturer and Contributor to The Times, 2001-; External Member, Bank of England Monetary Policy Committee, 2003-; Director, Confederation of British Industry, 2006-; Chancellor of University of Warwick, 2008-. Honours: Hon DLitt, City University, London, 2000; Princess of Wales Ambassador Award, 2001; World Leadership Forum Business Journalist Decade of Excellence Award, 2001. Memberships: Director, London International Financial Futures Exchange; AXA Investment Mans, International Rescue Committee, UK; Chair, Visiting Arts; Governor, Royal Shakespeare Co; UK Chair, Franco-British Colloque; Member, UK-India Round Table; Member, International Advisory Board, British-American Business Inc. Address: Bank of England, Threadneedle Street, London EC2R 8AH, England.

LAMINE LOUM Mamadou, b. Senegal. Politician. Appointments: Formerly Minister of Economics, Finance and Planning, Senegal; Prime Minister of Senegal, 1998-99. Memberships: Parti Socialiste. Address: Office of the Prime Minister, ave Leopold Sedar Senghor, Dakar, Senegal.

LAMONT Norman Stewart Hughson (Baron Lamont of Lerwick in the Shetland Islands), b. 8 May 1942, Lerwick, Shetland, Scotland. Politician; Writer; Businessman. m. Alice Rosemary White, 1971. Education: BA Economics, Fitzwilliam College, Cambridge. Appointments: Personal Assistant to Duncan Sandys MP, 1965; Staff, Conservative Research Department, 1966-68; Merchant Banker, N M Rothschild and Sons, 1968-79; Director, Rothschild Asset Management; Conservative Member of Parliament for Kingston-upon-Thames, 1972-97: Parliamentary Private Secretary to Norman St John Stevas, 1974, Opposition Spokesman on Prices and Consumer Affairs, 1975-76, Opposition Spokesman on Industry, 1976-79, Parliamentary Under-Secretary of State, Department of Energy, 1979-81, Minister of State, Department of Trade and Industry, 1981-85, Minister of State, Department of Defence Procurement, 1985-86, Financial Secretary to Treasury, 1986-89, Chief Secretary to Treasury, 1989-90, Chancellor of the Exchequer, 1990-93; Non-Executive Director, N M Rothschild and Sons Ltd, 1993-95; Chairman, Archipelago Fund, Food Fund and Indonesia Investment Trust, 1995-; Chairman, Conservatives Against a Federal Europe, 1998; Vice-Chairman, International Nuclear Safety Commission; Chair, Bruges Group, 2003-; House of Lords Select Committee on European Union, 2001-03; Director, Balli Group PLC. Publications: Sovereign Britain, 1995; In Office, 1999. Honour: Life Peeerage, 1998; Privy Councillor. Memberships: Chairman, Cambridge University Conservative Association, 1963; President, Cambridge Union, 1966. Address: c/o Balli Group plc, 5 Stanhope Gate, London, W1Y 5LA, England.

LAMPE Peter, b. 28 January 1954, Detmold, Germany. University Professor. m. Margaret Birdsong, 1 son, 1 daughter. Education: Dr habil; PhD; Cand theol (MTh); Studies of Theology, Philosophy, Archaeology, 1971-81. Appointments: Wissenschaftlicher Assistant, University of Bern, Switzerland, 1981-87; Associate Professor, 1987-89, Full Professor & Chair of Biblical Studies Department, 1989-92, Union Theol Sem Va, USA; Full Professor, Director of Institute of New Testament and Judaic Studies, University of Kiel, Germany, 1992-99; Dean, School of Theology, University of Kiel, 1996-98; Full Professor, University of Heidelberg, Germany, 1999-; Director, Phrygia Archaeological Surface Survey, University of Heidelberg, Co-discoverer, Discovery of Pepouza and Tymion, 2001-. Publications: More than 260 publications, books & scholarly articles. Honours: German Ecumenical Preaching Award, 2003; Honorary Professor, University of the Free State, South Africa, 2008. Memberships: Studiorum Novi Testamentum Societas; Society Bibl Lit; Societas Theologicum Ordinem Adiuvantium (founder, 1st chairman); K St J (Johanniter Order). Address: University of Heidelberg, WTS, Kisselgasse 1, 69117 Heidelberg, Germany. E-mail: p@uni-hd.de Website: www.rzuser.uni-heidelberg.de/~d04/wts/lampe/strt.htm

LAMPI Rauno Andrew, b. 12 August 1929, Gardner, Massachusetts, USA. Food Scientist; Engineer. m. Betty, 3 sons, 1 daughter. Education: BS, 1951, MS, 1955, PhD, 1957, Food Technology, University of Massachusetts. Appointments: Technical Director, New England Apple Products; Manager, Food Technology Section, Central Engineering, FMC Corporation; Research Physical Scientist,

US Army Natick R and D Centre; Physical Science Administrator, N Labs; Independent Food Scientist/Engineer. Publications: Over 80, including 5 book chapters: 3 patents. Honours: US Army Exceptional Civilian Service Medal; Institute of Food Technology's Industrial Achievement Award; Institute of Food Technology Riester-Davis Award. Memberships: Fellow, Institute of Food Technology. Address: 1110 North Henness Road, #212, Casa Grande, Arizona 85122, USA.

LAMY Pascal, b. 8 April 1947, Levallois-Perret, France. Director General of World Trade Organisation. m. Genevieve Luchaire, 3 sons. Education: Degree, Hautes Etudes Commerciales; Degree, Institut d'Etudes Politiques; Degree, Ecole Nationale d'Administration. Appointments: Chief of Staff for Jacques Delors, President of European Commission, 1985-94; Chief Executive Officer, Credit Lyonnais, 1994-99; Commissioner for Trade, European Commission, 1999-2004; Director General, World Trade Organisation, 2005-. Publications: Monde-Europe, 1993; Books: The Europe We Want with Jean Pisani-Ferry, 2002; L'Europe en premiere ligne, 2002; Towards World Democracy, 2004. Honours: Knight Commander's Cross (Badge and Star) of the Order of Merit of the Federal Republic of Germany, 1991; Commander, Order of Merit of Luxembourg, 1995; Officier de la Legion d'Honneur, 1999; Officer, Order of Merit of Gabon, 2000; Doctor Honoris Causa, University of Louvain, Belgium, 2002; Order of the Aztek Eagle, Mexico, 2003; Order of Merit of Chile, 2004; Doctor Honoris Causa, Geneva University, 2009; Doctor Honoris Causa, Warwick University, 2009; Doctor Honoris Causa, Montreal University, 2010; Chairman of the Board, Musiciens du Louvre-Grenoble, 2009. Address: World Trade Organisation, 154 rue de Lausanne, 1211 Geneva, Switzerland. Website: www.wto.org

LAND Ian Sherard, b. 15 February 1977, Boynton Beach, Florida, USA. Accounting Manager. m. Karla DaCosta, 1 son. Education: Bachelor's degree, Finance, Florida Atlanta University, 2000. Appointments: Lead Analyst, Franklin Templeton Investments, Fort Lauderdale, 2000-09; Accounting Manager, American Credit Counselors Inc, Boca Raton, 2009-. Address: 10675 Eland Street, Boca Raton, FL 33428, USA.

LANDERS Linda Anne, b. 27 December 1959, Borehamwood, England. Artist; Writer; Director. 2 sons. Education: Art Foundation Course, Watford School of Art, Ridge Street, Watford; BA, Fine Art Painting, Central-St-Martin's School of Art, 1987; Postgraduate Printmaking Studies, Morley College, Essendine School, Camden Arts Centre; Desmond Jones Physical Theatre & Mime Training, 2005-06; Laban Dance Centre, 2004-06. Appointments: Author, limited edition books under own imprints, 1993-; Author, Producer and Director: Outside The Cradle, 2006; Creator, short film: The Longing, 2007; Author and Producer, 2 plays: What's Left Behind, 2007, and Mamenschka, 2008. Publications: An Engraver's Globe, 2002; The Printmaker's Directory, 2006; Illustration Magazine, 2007; Live radio interview on plays and books, Life FM, 2008. Honours: Royal Society of Painter-Printmakers, 1995; John Purcell Paper Prize for Excellence in Printmaking, Mall Galleries, 2000. Memberships: Royal Society of Painter-Printmakers. E-mail: lindalanders87@hotmail.com

LANDSBERGIENE Grazina, b. 28 January 1930, Anyksciai, Lithuania. m. Vytautas Landsbergis, 1 son, 1 daughter. Education: Panevezys Gymnasium for Girls, 1948; Lithuanian Academy of Music, 1959. Appointments: Accompanist, National Theatre of Opera and Ballet, 1958-85; Associate Professor, Professor, Lithuanian Academy of Music, 1990-99; Numerous concerts and records with various singers. Honours: Vilnius Glory Award, 1998; Order of Grand Duke Gediminas, 1999; Barbora Radvilaite Award, Vilnius, 2005. Memberships: Lithuanian Society of Political Prisoners and Deportees; Chairperson, Vytautas Landsbergis Foundation. Address: Traidenio 34-15, LT 2004 Vilnius, Lithuania.

LANDSBERGIS Vytautas, b. 18 October 1932, Kaunas, Lithuania. Musicologist; Politician. m. Grazina Rucyte, 1 son, 2 daughters. Education: J Gruodis Music School, 1949, Ausra gymnasium, Kaunas, 1950; Lithuanian Music Academy, Vilnius, 1955. Appointments include: Chairman, 1988-90, Honorary Chairman, 1991-, Lithuanian Reform Movement, Sajudis; President of the Supreme Council of the Republic of Lithuania (Head of State), 1990-92; Member of Seimas (Parliament), Republic of Lithuania and Leader of Opposition, 1992-96, member, Lithuanian Delegation to Parliamentary Assembly of Council of Europe, 1992-96, 2000-02, and to the Baltic Assembly, 1992-96, 2000-04; Chairman, Lithuanian Conservative Party, 1993-2003; President, Seimas (Parliament) Republic of Lithuania, 1996-2000; Candidate, Presidential elections, 1997; Member of the Seimas (Parliament) of the Republic of Lithuania, 2000-04; Observer to the European Parliament, 2003-04, and MEP, 2004-. Publications include: Books (in Lithuanian, French, English, Japanese): The Act of 11 March. Facsimiles, 2000; The Heavy Freedom volumes I-III, 2000; The Cousin Mathew. The Book on Stasys Lozoraitis from His Letters and Messages, 2002, 2003; Koenigsberg and Lithuania, 2003; Unknown Documents on January 13, 2003, 2004; In the European Parliament I, II and III, 2004, 2005, 2006; Lithuania's Road to NATO, 2005; Forgotten Soviet war Crime, 2005, 2006, 2007; Soldier Seeks Justice, 2006; Correspondence and Conversations with François Mitterrand 1990-1992, 2007; Un peuple sort de prison, 2007; Vincas Kurdirka: Concern for Lithuanians, 2008; Crossroad of Europe, 2008; In the European Parliament IV, V and VI, 2007, 2008, 2009; That's Serious, Children (poems), 2007; Guilty of Negligence (essays and poems), 2007; All Ciurlionis (monograph), 2008; The Quality of Man, 2010; The 11th of March Twenty Years Agao and Friday, 2010; M K Ciurlionis, Time and Content, 1992. Honours include: Pleiade Ordre de la Frankophonie (France), 2000; Three Stars Order, 2nd Class, Latvia, 2001; Order of the Cross of St Mary's Land, 1st Class, Estonia, 2002; Order of Grand Duke Vytautas with Golden Collar, 2003; Constitutional Medallion of Saxonian Parliament, Germany, 2003; Award of Lithuanian Foundation, USA, 2004; Aschaffenburger Mutig-Preis, Germany, 2004; La Médaille Robert Schuman, EPP-ED, European Parliament, 2005; Mérite Européen Medal, Luxembourg, 2006; Honorary Citizen of the City of Turin, Italy, 2007; Knight Grand Cross of the Order of Orange-Nasau, Netherlands, 2008; Sixteen Honorary doctorates, including University of Sorbonne. Memberships include: Lithuanian Composers Union; European St Sebastian's Order of Knights; Honorary Doctor of St Lucas Academy, The Netherlands, 2004; Member of International Advisory Council of the Victims of Communism Memorial Foundation (USA), 1995-2007; Chairman: M K Ciurlionis Society; Knight of the Grand Order de Coeurs, 2004-. Address: Traidenio G 34-15, LT-08116 Vilnius, Lithuania.

LANE Nathan, b. 3 February 1956, Jersey City, New Jersey, USA. Actor. Education: St Peter's Preparatory High School. Career: Actor; Theatre: Broadway debut, Present Laughter, 1982; Merlin, 1983; The Wind in the Willows; Some Americans Abroad; Broadway Bound; On Borrowed Time; Guys and Dolls; Lips Together, Teeth Apart; The Lisbon Traviata; Bad Habits; Love! Valour! Compassion!;

Dedication; Laughter on the 23rd Floor; A Funny Thing Happened on the Way to the Forum; Wise Guys; TV includes: One of the Boys; The Days and Nights of Molly Dodd; The Man Who Came to Dinner; Teacher's Pet; Timon & Pumbaa; George and Martha; Miami Vice; Mad About You; Sex and the City; Frasier; Saturday Night Live; The Tony Awards; Great Performances – Alice in Wonderland; The Last Mile; Curb Your Enthusiasm; Absolutely Fabulous; 30 Rock; The Boys Next Door; Laughter on the 23rd Floor; Films: Valley of the Dolls, 1981; Miami Vice, 1985; Ironweed, 1987; The Lemon Sisters, 1990; Joe Versus the Volcano, 1990; He Said, She Said, 1991; Frankie and Johnny, 1991; Addams Family Values, 1993; Life with Mikey, 1993; Jeffrey, 1995; The Birdcage, 1996; Mousehunt, 1997; At First Sight, 1999; Love's Labours Lost, 2000; Isn't She Great, 2000; Trixie, 2000; Nicholas Nickleby, 2002; Austin Power in Goldmember, 2002; Win a Date with Tad Hamilton! 2004; The Producers, 2005; Trumbo, 2007; Swing Vote, 2008; Nutcracker: The Untold Story, 2009; Voice work: The Lion King, 1994; The Lion King II: Simba's Pride, 1998; Stuart Little, 1999; Titan AE, 2000; Stuart Little 2, 2002; The Lion King 1½, 2004; Teacher's Pet, 2004; Astro Boy, 2009. Honours: St Clair Bayfield Award, 1986; 5 Drama Desk Awards, 1990, 1992, 1995, 1996, 2001; 2 Obie Awards, 1992, 1996; 2 Tony Awards, 1996, 2001; 2 Daytime Emmy Awards, 1995, 2000; American Comedy Award, 1996; Screen Actors Guild Award, 1997; MTV Movie Award, 1997; 2 Golden Globe Awards, 1997, 2006; People's Choice Award, 1999; National Board of Review Award, 2002; GLAAD Media Award, Vito Russo Award, 2002; Olivier Award, 2005; American Theatre Wing, 2006; The Trevor Project Hero Award, 2007; Human Right Campaign Equality Award, 2007.

LANG Helmut, b. 10 March 1956, Vienna, Austria. Fashion Designer. Career: Established own studio, Vienna, 1977; Opened made-to-measure shop, Vienna, 1979; Developed ready-to-wear collections, 1984-86; Presented Helmut Lang's Women's Wear, 1986, Helmut Lang's Menswear, 1987-, Paris Fashion Week; Started licensed business, 1988; Professor, Masterclass of Fashion, University of Applied Arts, Vienna, 1993-; Helmut Lang Underwear, 1994; Helmut Lang Protective Eyewear, 1995; Helmut Land Jeans, 1996; Helmut Lang, Footwear and Accessories, 1990; Helmut Lang Fragrances, 1999. Honours: Council of American Fashion Designers of the Year Award, 1996; CFDA Designer of the Year, 2004; Fashion Group International "The Imagineers of Our Time" Award, 2004; LEAD Award, 2005. Address: c/o Michele Montagne, 184 rue St Maur, 75010 Paris, France.

LANG k d (Kathryn Dawn Lang), b. 2 November 1961, Consort, Alberta, Canada. Singer; Composer; Actress. Career: Played North American clubs with own band, 1982-87; Performed at closing ceremony, Winter Olympics, Calgary, 1988; Headlining US tour, 1992; Royal Albert Hall, 1992; Earth Day benefit concert, Hollywood Bowl, 1993; Sang with Andy Bell, BRIT Awards, 1993; Television includes: Late Night with David Letterman; Wogan; The Arsenio Hall Show; The Tonight Show; Top of the Pops; Subject, South Bank Show documentary, ITV, 1995; Film appearance, Salmonberries, 1991. Recordings: Albums: A Truly Western Experience, 1984; Angel with a Lariat, 1986; Shadowland, 1988; Absolute Torch and Twang, 1990; Ingénue, 1992; Even Cowgirls Get the Blues (soundtrack), 1993; All You Can Eat, 1995; Drag, 1997; Australian Tour, 1997; Invincible Summer, 2000; Live By Request, 2001; A Wonderful World (with Tony Bennett), 2003; Hymns of the 49th Parallel, 2004; Reintarnation, 2006; Features on soundtrack to Dick Tracy; Hit singles include: Crying (duet with Roy Orbison); Constant Craving; Mind of Love; Miss Chatelaine; Just Keep Me Moving; If I Were You. Honours: Canadian CMA Awards: Entertainer of Year, 1989; Album of Year, 1990; Grammy Awards: Best Female Country Vocal Performance, 1990; Best Pop Vocal, 1993; Album of the Year, Ingénue, 1993; Best Traditional Pop Vocal Album, 2004; American Music Award: Favourite New Artist, 1993; Songwriter of The Year, with Ben Mink, 1993; BRIT Award, Best International Female, 1995.

LANGDOWN Christopher, b. 15 June 1971. Pianist. Education: Bishop Walsh School, Sutton Coldfield, 1983-89; Royal College of Music, London, 1989-96. Appointments: Soloist and Chamber Musician; Recitals at major London concert halls including: Wigmore Hall, South Bank Centre, LSO St Luke's and St John's Smith Square; Appeared at music festivals through the UK and Europe; Teacher, The Godolphin & Latymer School, Hammersmith, 1993-97; Teacher, Ibstock Place, The Froebel School, Roehampton, 1996-97; Visiting Teacher, Birmingham Conservatoire Junior Department, 1998-99; Head of Piano, The Kingsley School, Leamington Spa, 1998-; Visiting Teacher, Royal Academy of Music in London, 2004. Honours: Numerous awards including: Finalist and Prize Winner, Brant UK Pianoforte Competition, 1997; RCM Wall Trust Scholar (twice); Listed in international biographical dictionaries. Memberships: Incorporated Society of Musicians. Address: 40 Mountford Drive, Sutton Coldfield, West Midlands B75 6TA, England. E-mail: info@christopherlangdown.com Website: www.christopherlangdown.com

LANGE Jessica, b. 20 April 1949, Cloquet, Minnesota, USA. Actress. m. Paco Grande, 1970, divorced, 1 daughter with Mikhail Baryshnikov; 1 son, 1 daughter with Sam Shepard. Education: University of Minnesota; Mime, Etienne DeCroux, Paris. Appointments: Dancer, Opera Comique, Paris; Model, Wilhelmina Agency, New York. Creative Works: Films include: King Kong, 1976; All That Jazz, 1979; How to Beat the High Cost of Living, 1980; The Postman Always Rings Twice, 1981; Frances, Tootsie, 1982; Country, 1984; Sweet Dreams, 1985; Crimes of the Heart, 1986; Everybody's All American, 1989; Far North, 1991; Night and the City, 1993; Losing Isaiah, Rob Roy, Blue Sky, 1994; A Thousand Acres, 1997; Hush, Cousin Bette, 1998; Titus, 1999; Prozac Nation, Normal, Masked and Anonymous, Great Performances, Big Fish, 2003; Don't Come Knockin', Neverwas, 2005; Bonneville, 2006; Play: Long Day's Journey Into Night, 2000; Star Showtime TV Production, Cat On A Hot Tin Roof, 1984. Honours include: 2 Academy Awards, 1983, 1995; Theatre World Award, Golden Globe, 1996. Address: c/o CAA, Ron Meyer, 9830 Wilshire Boulevard, Beverly Hills, CA 90212, USA.

LANGE Roderyk, b. 5 October 1930, Bydgoszcz, Poland. Choreologist; Anthropologist. Widower. 1 son. Education: Dance Studies prior to university; Movement and Notation studies, Folkwang Hochschule, Essen, Germany, 1959; MA, Cultural Anthropology, Universities of Toruń and Wrocław, Poland, 1965; PhD, Polish University, London, 1975; Habilitation, 1977; Professor nomination, 1979. Appointments: Lecturer, Laban Art of Movement Studio, Addlestone, Surrey, 1967-1972; Lecturer, Queen's University, Belfast, Northern Ireland, 1975-82; Director, Centre for Dance Studies, Jersey, Channel Islands, UK, 1971-2003; Lecturer, Laban Centre, Goldsmiths' College, London University, 1976-93; Professor, Polish University, London, 1979-92; Professor, A Mickiewicz University, Poznań, Poland, 1989-2003; Director, Institute of Choreology, Poznań, Poland, 1993-; Lecturer, Academy of Music, Warsaw, Poland, 1999-2006; Leader of the European Seminar for Kinetography, 1980-96. Publications: Numerous publications on the anthropology of dance, movement analysis and notation; Monographs include: The Nature of Dance: An Anthropological Perspective, 1975; Handbook of Kinetography according to the Laban-Knust method, 1975; Folklore of Cuiavia (co-author), 1979; Guidelines for Fieldwork on Traditional Dance: Methods and Checklist, 1984 . Honours: Honorary Citizen of Poznań, Poland, 1988; Oskar Kolberg Medal, Warsaw, 1990; Chevalier de L'Ordre des Arts et des Lettres, Paris, 2005. Memberships: Fellow, Royal Anthropological Institute, London; Co-chairperson, ICTM Study Group of Ethnochoreology, 1986-92; Fellow, International Council of Kinetography Laban; Member, Conseil International de la Danse, UNESCO, Paris and of other scholarly associations. Address: The Lodge – Hamptonne, La Rue de la Hague, St Peter, Jersey, JE3 7DB, Channel Islands.

LANGHAM John Michael, b. 12 January 1924, Stroxton, UK. Chartered Engineer. m. Irene Elizabeth Morley, 2 sons, 1 daughter. Education: MA (Cantab), Mechanical Sciences Tripos, Queen's College, Cambridge, England; Administrative Staff College. Appointments: Engineer Officer, Royal Navy, 1944-46; Various Appointments, 1947-67, Executive Director, 1967-80, Stone-Platt Industries, plc; Director, BPB Industries plc, 1976-92; Chairman: Vacu-Lug Traction Tyres Ltd, 1973-95; Chairman, Langham Industries, Ltd, 1980-; External Appointments: Member, CBI Council, 1967-79; Chairman, CBI Production Committee, 1970-79; Member, Executive Board, British Standards Institute, 1969-76; Deputy Chairman, Quality Assurance Council, 1971-79; Member, General Council, 1974-82, Member, Management Board, 1979-82, Vice-President, Executive Committee, 1978-82, E.E.F. Publications: Presented British Exchange Paper to 21st International Foundry Congress, Italy; Article: The Manufacture of Marine Propellers with Particular Reference to the Foundry. Honours: Commander of the Order of the British Empire (CBE); Diploma, Institute of British Foundrymen, 1954, 1963; British Foundry Medal and Prize, 1955; Award of American Foundrymen's Society, Detroit Congress, 1962, Dorset Business Man of the Year, 1996. Memberships: Fellow, Institution of Mechanical Engineers; Fellow, Institute of Marine Engineers; Fellow, Institute of British Foundrymen, Companion of the Institute of Management. Address: Bingham's Melcombe, Dorchester, Dorset DT2 7PZ, England.

LANKA Vaclav, b. 25 October 1941, Hredle, near Rakovník, Czech Republic. Teacher. 1 son. Education: Diploma, Faculty of Natural Science, Charles University, Prague, 1974; Diploma Biologist. Appointments: Teacher, to 1994; Vice-Mayor, Town of Rakovník, 1994-98; Currently Teacher. Publications: Co-author, books: Amphibians and Reptiles, 11 editions, 6 languages, 1985; Wolfgang Böhme, 1999; Handbuch der Reptilien und Amphibien Europas, Vol 3/IIA; Monographs: Dice Snake, Natrix tessellata, 1975; Variabilität und Biologie der Würfelnatter, Natrix tessellata LAURENTI, 1976; Several hundred popular articles on nature and ecology; Several hundred specialist and popular lectures. Membership: Entomological Society of the Czech Republic, 1956-; Species Survival Commission, International Union for the Conservation of Nature and Natural Resources. Address: Wintrovo nam 1787, 269 01 Rakovník, Czech Republic.

LANSBURY Angela Brigid, b. 16 October 1925, United Kingdom. Actress. m. (2) P Shaw, 1949, 1 son, 1 step-son, 1 daughter. Education: School of Singing and Dramatic Art, London; School of Drama and Radio, New York. Career: with MGM, 1943-50; Freelance, 1951-; Films include: Gas Light, National Velvet, 1944; The Picture of Dorian Gray, 1945; If Winter Comes, The Three Musketeers, 1948; Kind Lady, 1951; Please Murder Me, 1956; The Reluctant Debutante, 1958; Blue Hawaii, 1961; The Greatest Story Ever Told, The Amorous Adventures of Moll Flanders, 1965; Bedknobs and Broomsticks, 1971; Death on the Nile, 1978; The Mirror Crack'd, The Lady Vanishes, 1980; The Pirates of Penzance, 1982; The Company of Wolves, 1983; Voice of Mrs Potts in Beauty and the Beast, 1991; Nanny McPhee, 2005; Theatre includes: Broadway debut in Hotel Paradiso, 1957; Mame, New York Winter Garden, 1966-68; Gypsy, 1974; Anna, The King and I, 1978; Sweeny Todd, 1979; Mame, 1983; Deuce, 2007; TV includes: Madeira! Madeira!, The Ming Llama, Lace, Murder She Wrote, 1984-96; The Shell Seekers, 1989; Miss Arris Goes to Paris, 1992; Mrs Santa Claus, 1996; South by Southwest, 1997; A Story to Die For, 2000; The Blackwater Lightship, 2004; Law & Order: Special Victims Unit, 2005; Law & Order: Trial by Jury, 2005.; Kingdom Hearts II (voice), 2005. Publication: Positive Moves, co-author and video. Honours include: Academy Award Nomination, Best Supporting Actress, 1944; Nomination, Academy Award, The Manchurian Candidate; Pudding Theatre Woman of the Year, 1968; Antoinette Perry Awards for Mame, 1968; Dear World, 1969; Gypsy, 1975; Sweeney Todd, 1982; Sarah Siddons Awards, 1974, 1980; BAFTA Lifetime Achievement Award, 1992; CBE; National Medal of Arts, 1997; Nomination, 16 Emmy Awards; Winner, 6 Golden Globe Awards, nominated 8 Golden Globe Awards. Address: c/o MCA Universal, 100 Universal City Plaza, Universal City, CA 91608, USA.

LANSING Sherry, b. 31 July 1944, Chicago, Illinois, USA. Business Executive. m. (2) William Friedkin, 1991. Education: BS, Northwestern University, Evanston, Illinois. Appointments: Mathematics Teacher, Public High Schools, Los Angeles, California, 1966-69; Model, TV commercials, Max Factor Co and Alberto-Culver, 1969-70; Appeared in films Loving and Rio Lobo, 1970; Executive Story Editor, Wagner International, 1970-93; Vice-President for Production, Heyday Productions, 1973-75; Executive Story Editor, then Vice-President for Creative Affairs, MGM Studios, 1975-77; Vice-President, then Senior Vice-President for Production, Columbia Pictures, 1977-80; President, 20th Century Fox Productions, 1980-83; Founder, Jaffe-Lansing Productions, Los Angeles, 1982-; Produced films including Racing with the Moon, 1984, Firstborn, 1984; Fatal Attraction, 1987; The Accused, 1989; Black Rain, 1990; School Ties, 1992; Indecent Proposal, 1993; The Untouchables: Capone Rising, 2006; Chairperson, Paramount Pictures, 1992-. Honour: Jean Hersholt Humanitarian Award, 2007. Address: Paramount Pictures Corporation, 555 Melrose Avenue, Los Angeles, CA 90038, USA.

LAPRESTA-FERNANDEZ Alejandro, b. 10 September 1978, Granada, Spain. Researcher. Education: Bachelor degree, 2001, PhD, 2007, Analytical Chemistry, University of Granada. Appointments: Nanoparticles Researcher, Marie Curie Fellow, Friedrich-Schiller University, Jena, Germany, 2008-10; Researcher, Instituto de Ciencias de Materiales de Sevilla, Consejo Superior de Investigaciones Cientificas, Spain. Publications: 17 articles; 1 book chapter. Memberships: American Chemical Society; Spanish Chemistry Association. Address: Calle Estanco No 16, 18151 Ogijares, Granada, Spain. E-mail: lapresta@ugr.es

LAPTEV Vladimir, b. 28 April 1924, Moscow, Russia. Professor of Law. m. Maya Lapteva, 2 sons. Education: Graduate, Law Department, Moscow Institute for Foreign Trade, 1949. Appointments: Chief of Section of Economic Law, Institute of State and Law of Russian Academy of Sciences, Moscow, 1959; Chief, Centre of Entrepreneurial and Economic Law, 1992; Head of Chair of Entrepreneurial Law of Academic Law University, Moscow, 1997; Chief scientific researcher of the Institute, 1997. Publications: More than 360 scientific books and articles in fields of economic and entrepreneurial law. Honour: Professor, Doctor of Law, Honoured Scientist of Russian Federation. Membership: Russian Academy of Sciences. Address: Institute of State and Law, Znamenka 10, Moscow, Russia.

LARA Brian Charles, b. 2 May 1969, Santa Cruz. Cricketer. Appointments: Started playing cricket aged 6; Played football for Trinidad Under 14; Played cricket for West Indies Under-19; Captain, West Indies Youth XI against India, scoring 186; Left-Hand Batsman; Teams: Trinidad and Tobago, 1987-, Captain 1993-; Warwickshire, 1994, Captain 1988; Making world record 1st class score of 501 not out, including most runs in a day, 390, and most boundaries in an innings, 72, v Durham, Edgbaston, 1994; 112 Tests for West Indies 1990-, 18 as Captain, scoring 10,094 runs, average 52.84, including 26 hundreds, highest score 400, world record v England, St John's, Antigua, 2004; Has scored 19,835 1st class runs, 55 hundreds, to 2002, including 2,066 off 2,262 balls for Warwickshire, 1994, with 6 hundreds in his first 7 innings; Toured England, 1991, 1995; 246 One Day Internationals, scoring 9,031 runs (average 42.39); Retired, 2007. Honours: Wisden Cricketer of the Year, 1995; Federation of International Cricketers' Associations International Cricketer of the Year, 1999. Publication: Beating the Field, autobiography, 1995. Address: c/o West Indies Cricket Board, PO Box 616, St John's, Antigua.

LARGE Andrew McLeod Brooks (Sir), b. 7 August 1942, Goudhurst, Kent, England. Banker and Regulatory Official. m. Susan Melville, 1967, 2 sons, 1 daughter. Education: University of Cambridge; Euorpean Institute of Business Administration, Fontainebleau; MA, Economics; MBA. Appointments: British Petroleum, 1964-71; Orion Bank Ltd, 1971-79; With Swiss Bank Corporation, 1980-89, as Managing Director, 1980-83, Chief Executive, Deputy Chairman, 1983-87, Group Chief Executive, 1987-88, SBCI London; Board, Swiss Bank Corporation, 1988-90; Non-Executive Director, English China Clays, 1991-96; Chairman, Large, Smith and Walter, 1990-92; Chairman, Securities and Investments Board, 1992-97; Member, Board on Banking Supervision, 1996-97, Deputy Governor, 2002-, Bank of England; Deputy Chairman, 1997-2002, Director, 1998-2002, Barclays Bank; Chairman, Euroclear, 1998-2000. Address: Bank of England, Threadneedle Street, London EC2R 8AH, England. Website: www.bankofengland.co.uk

LARIKKA Martti Johannes, b. 27 July 1957, Helsinki, Finland. Physician. m. Marjatta Puustinen, 1 son, 1 daughter. Education: MD, 1983; PhD, 2004. Appointments: Researcher, University of Oulu, Finland; Chief Physician, Laboratory, Lansi-Pohja Central Hospital, Kemi, Finland. Publications: Articles in medical journals as co-author include: Extended combined 99mTc-white blood cell and bone imaging improves the diagnostic accuracy in the detection of hip replacement infections, 2001; Improved method for detecting knee replacement infections based on extended combined 99mTc-white blood cell/bone imaging, 2001; 99mTc-ciprofloxacin (Infecton) imaging in the diagnosis of knee prosthesis infections, 2002; Comparison of 99mTc-Ciprofloxacin, 99mTc white blood cell and three-phase bone imaging in the diagnosis of hip prosthesis infections: improved diagnostic accuracy with extended imaging time, 2002; Specificity of 99mTc-ciprofloxacin imaging, 2003. Membership: European Association of Nuclear Medicine. Address: Lansi-Pohja Central Hospital, Kauppakatu 25, FI-94100 Kemi, Finland. E-mail: martti.larikka@lpshp.fi

LARKIN William Vincent Jr, b. 19 July 1953, New York, USA. President of Industrial Businesses. m. Margaret Gunn, 2 sons. Education: AB (cum laude), Harvard University; MBA, Yale University. Appointments: President and CEO: Tuboscope Corporation; Travis International Inc; The Six Stars Club; Corrpro Companies Inc; Warren Alloy Inc; Shield Air Solutions Inc. Memberships: AD Club, Harvard; River Oaks Country Club; The Coronado Club. Address: 369 Piney Point Road, Houston, TX 77024, USA. E-mail: grottie12@gmail.com

LAROCA Sebastião, b. 15 April 1941, Castro, Brazil. Professor; Scientist. m. Aurora Gonçalves, 2 sons, 3 daughters. Education: Meteorology (Tech), IPE, Paraná, 1966; Natural History, UFPR, 1968; Geology and Geomorphology of Quaternary (Specialist), UFP, 1972; MSc, Biological Science, Entomology, UFPR, 1974; PhD, Biological Science, Entomology, The University of Kansas. Appointments: Senior Professor; Tech, Genetic Laboratory, Universidade Federal do Paraná, Brazil, 1959-2011; Editor, Acta Biológica Paranaense. Publications: 75 articles in scientific journals. Honours: Member, Sigma Xi, Kansas Chapter, 1978; Diploma of Honour and Merit, Brazilian Society of Zoology, 1988; Distinction, Nicolau, Journal de Cultura, 1988; Distinction, Rede Globo, Paraná, 1988; Prêmio Nacional de Ecologia, 1988; 90th anniversary medal and certificate, Universidade Federal do Paraná, 2003; Who's Who, 2011. Memberships: SBPC, Brazil; SBZ, Brazil; SBE, Brazil; Sigma Xi, USA. Address: Rua Coronel Alfredo Ferreira da Costa, 433, Curitiba, Paraná, CEP 81540-090, Brazil. E-mail: slaroca@netpar.com.br

LARSON Gary, b. 14 August 1950, Tacoma, Washington, USA. Cartoonist. m. Toni Carmichael, 1988. Education: Washington State University. Career: Performed in jazz duo, 1972-75; Worked in a music store; Sold first cartoons to Pacific Search magazine; Subsequently sold cartoons to Seattle Times, San Francisco Chronicle, Chronicle Features Syndicate; Founder, FarWorks Inc; Announded retirement, 1994. Exhibitions include: The Far Side of Science, Cálifornia Academy of Sciences, 1985; Smithsonian National Museum of Natural History; American Museum of Natural History, New York; Los Angeles County Museum of Natural History; Films: Gary Larson's Tales from The Far Side, 1994; Gary Larson's Tales from The Far Side II, 1997. Publications: The Far Side; Beyond The Far Side; In Search of The Far Side; Bride of The Far Side; Valley of The Far Side; It Came From The Far Side; Hound of The Far Side; The Far Side Observer: Night of the Crash-test Dummies; Wildlife Preserve; Wiener Dog Art; Unnatural Selections; Cows of Our Planet; The Chickens Are Restless; The Curse of Madame "C"; Last Chapter and Worse, 1996; Anthologies: The Far Side Gallery 1, 2, 3, 4 and 5; The PreHistory of The Far Side; There's A Hair in My Dirt! A Worm's Story, 1998. Honours: National Cartoonists Society Award for best syndicated panel of 1985; Outstanding Cartoonist of the Year Award, 1991, 1994; Max and Moritz Prize for Best International Cartoon, 1993; Insect named in his honour, Strigiphilus garylarsoni (biting louse), also butterfly, Serratoterga larsoni; Grand Prix, Annecy Film Festival, 1995. Address: c/o Andrews McMell Publishing, 4520 Main Street, Suite 700, Kansas City, MO 64111, USA. Website: www.thefarside.com

DICTIONARY OF INTERNATIONAL BIOGRAPHY 36th EDITION

LAŠAS Liudvikas, b. 4 June 1933, Kaunas, Lithuania. Biotechnologist. m. Danute Lašienė, 1 son, 1 daughter. Education: Biotechnologist diploma, 1956, PhD, 1962, Kaunas Technological University; Dr Sc, St Petersburg Technological Institute, 1989. Appointments: Assistant, Assistant Professor, Kaunas Technological University, 1959-78; Chief of Laboratory, Kaunas Branch Institute of Endocrinology of Medical Academy of former USSR, 1978-90; Director, Institute of Endocrinology, 1990-2004; Professor, Kaunas University of Medicine, 1993-; Director, Endocrinology Center of Lithuania, 1994-; Chairman of Council of Institute of Endocrinology, 2004-. Publications: Over 300 scientific articles and studies, including Human Growth Hormone, Deficiency and Treatment, 2003; Institute of Endokrinology, 2007; also author of 30 patents. Honours: Investigator USSR, 1986; Laureate of Vladas Lasas (Medicine), Premium of Academy of Sciences of Lithuania, 2002. Memberships: International Growth Hormone Research Society; New York Academy of Science ; Society of European Endocrinologists; International Osteoporosis Foundation; Society of Endocrinology of Lithuania. Address: Aukštaičių No 37, 44158 Kaunas ACP, Lithuania. E-mail: liudvikas.lasas@med.kmu.lt

LASZLO Pierre, b. France. Science Writer; Professor. m. Valerie Annette Jann. Appointments: Professor, Princeton University, USA; Professor, Université d'Orsay, France; Visiting professorships, universities of Connecticut, Kansas, California (Berkeley), Chicago, Colorado, Johns Hopkins, Lausanne, Hamburg, Toulouse and Cornell; Professor Emeritus, Chemistry, University of Liège, Belgium and École polytechnique, Palaiseau, France. Publications: 10 scientific monographs and textbooks; Popularizations include: Chemins et savoirs du sel, 1998; Le savoir des plantes, 1999; La découverte scientifique, 1999; Le savoir des plantes, 2000; Miroir de la chimie, 2000; Terre et eau, air & feu, 2000; Salt. Grain of Life, 2001, 2002; Peut-on boire l'eau du robinet? 2002; Pourquoi la mer est-elle bleue? 2002; L'architecture du vivant, 2002; Les odeurs nous parlent-elles? 2003; Qu'est-ce que l'alchimie? 2003; NO, 2003; Le Phénix et la salamandre, 2004; Communicating Science. A Practical Guide, 2006; Copal, et autres gemmes, 2007; Citrus: A History, 2007, 2008; Drôle de chimie, 2011. Honours: Maurice Pérouse Prize, Fondation de France, 1999; Paul Doistau-Emile Blutet Prize, French Academy of Sciences, 2004. Address: Cloud's Rest, Sénergues, 12320, France. Website: www.pierrelaszlo.net

LATHAM Anthony John Heaton, b. 30 October 1940, Wigan, England. University Lecturer. m. Dawn Catherine Farleigh, 1990, 1 son. Education: BA (Hons) Medieval and Modern History, Birmingham, 1964; PhD African Studies, Birmingham, 1970. Musical Education: Clarinet tuition, Johnny Roadhouse, Manchester. Career: Debut, Wigan Jazz Club, 1958; Penn-Latham Quintet, University of Birmingham, 1961-63; Harlech Television, 1967; Axiom Jazz Band, Swansea, 1967-68; J.J.'s Rhythm Aces, Swansea University, 1982-84; Speakeasy Jazz Band, Swansea, 1984-; John Latham's Jazztimers, 1995-; Brecon Jazz Festival, 1986-89, 1991, 1996-99; Cork Jazz Festival, 1987; Birmingham Jazz Festival, 1987, 1988; BBC Wales, 1989, 1990, 1992, 1994; Llangollen Jazz Festival, 1995-98; Bude Jazz Festival, 1998; Clubs: Fritzel's; Gazebo; Bonaparte's Retreat; In New Orleans, 1988; Blue Fox, Calcutta; Tower Records, Tokyo. Recordings: Blanche Finlay with The Speakeasy Jazzband, 1987; John Latham's Jazz Timers with Bill Nicholes, Sandy's Bar, Cardiff, 1997; John Latham's Jazz Timers, Sandy & Co, Bude Jazz Festival, 1998. Publications: Al Fairweather Discography, 1994; Eurojazz Discographies, No 34; Stan Greig Discography, 1995; Eurojazz Discography, No 42; Sandy Brown Discography, 1997; Eurojazz Discography, No 5; New Orleans Music; Jazz Journal; Just Jazz; Jazz Rag; International Association of Jazz Record Collectors Journal; Oxford Dictionary of National Biography, 2004; Contributions to professional journals. Honours: Listed in international biographical dictionaries. Membership: Musicians' Union; Secretary, Sandy Brown Society, 1997-. Address: 2 Church Meadow, Reynoldston, Swansea SA3 1AF, Wales.

LATHAM David Nicholas Ramsay, b. 18 September 1942, Blagdon, England. Lawyer. m. Margaret Elizabeth Forrest, 3 daughters. Education: Bryanston, 1956-60; Queens' College, Cambridge, 1960-63; Called to the Bar, 1964. Appointments: Barrister, 1964-92; Queens' Counsel, 1985-92; High Court Judge, 1992-2000; Presiding Judge, Midland – Oxford Circuit, 1994-99; Lord Justice of Appeal, 2000-09; Vice President of the Court of Appeal (Criminal Division), 2006-09; Chairman, Parole Board of England and Wales, 2009-. Honours: Master of the Bench, Middle Temple, 1987-; Knight Batchelor, 1992-; Privy Councillor, 2000-. Memberships: Travellers Club; Beefsteak Club; Leander Club; Fellow, Royal Society of Arts. Address: 3 Manor Farm Close, Pimperne, Blandford Forum, Dorset, DT11 8XL, England. E-mail: david@lathamonline.org

LAUDA Andreas-Nikolaus, b. 22 February 1949, Vienna, Austria. Racing Driver. m. Marlene Knaus, 1976, 2 sons. Appointments: Competed in hill climbs, 1968, later in Formula 3, Formula 2, Sports Car Racing; Winner, 1972 John Player Brit Formula 2 Championship; Started Formula 1 racing in 1971; World Champion, 1975, 1977, 1984, runner-up, 1976; Founder, Owner, Own Airline, Austria. Creative Works: Grand Prix Wins: 1974 Spanish, Ferrari, 1974 Dutch, Ferrari, 1975 Monaco, Ferrari, 1975 Belgian, Ferrari, 1975 Swedish, Ferrari, 1975 French, Ferrari, 1975 US, Ferrari, 1976 Brazilian, Ferrari, 1976 South African, Ferrari, 1976 Belgian, Ferrari, 1976 British, Ferrari, 1977 South African, Ferrari, 1977 German, Ferrari, 1977 Dutch, Ferrari, 1978 Swedish, Brabham-Alfa Romeo, 1978 Italian, Brabham-Alfa Romeo; Retired, 1979; Returned to racing, 1981; Won US Formula 1 Grand Prix, British Grand Prix, 1982, Dutch Grand Prix, 1985; Retired, 1985; Chair, Lauda Air, -2000; CEO Ford's Premier Performance Division, 2001-02; Head, Jaguar Racing Team, 2001-02. Honours include: Victoria Sporting Club International Award for Valour, 1977. Address: Sta Eulalia, Ibiza, Spain.

LAUDER Leonard Alan, b. 19 March 1933, New York City, New York, USA. Business Executive. m. Evelyn Hausner, 1959, 2 sons. Education: Wharton School, University of Pennsylvania. Appointments: Joined, 1958, Executive Vice-President, 1962-72, President, 1972-, Chief Executive Officer, 1982-, now also Chairman, Estee Lauder Inc, cosmetics and fragrance company, New York; Trustee, University of Pennsylvania, 1977-; President, Whitney Museum of American Art, 1977-; Trustee, Aspen Institute for Humanistic Studies, 1978-; Governor, Joseph H Lauder Institute of Management and International Studies, 1983-. Address: Estee Lauder Inc, 767 Fifth Avenue, New York, NY 10153, USA.

LAUGHTON Anthony Seymour (Sir), b. 29 April 1927. Oceanographic Scientist. m. (1) Juliet A Chapman, 1957, dissolved 1962, 1 son, (2) Barbara C Bosanquet, 1973, 2 daughters. Education: King's College, Cambridge; John Murray Student, Columbia University, New York, 1954-55; PhD. Appointments: Served Royal Naval Volunteer Reserve, 1945-48; Oceanographer, 1955-88, later Director, National Institute of Oceanography, later Institute of Oceanographic Sciences; Member, 1974-, Chairman, 1986-, Joint IOC-IHO

Guiding Committee, GEBCO, ocean charts; Member, 1981-, Chairman, 1995-, Governing Body, Charterhouse School; Council, University College, London, 1983-93; Co-ordinating Committee for Marine Science and Technology, 1987-91; Trustee, Natural History Museum, 1990-95. Publications: Papers on marine geophysics. Honours: Silver Medal, Royal Society of Arts, 1958; Prince Albert the 1st of Monaco Gold Medal, 1980; Founders Medal, Royal Geographical Society, 1987; Murchison, Geological Society, 1989. Memberships: Fellow, Royal Society; President, Challenger Society for Marine Science, 1988-80; President, Society for Underwater Technology, 1995-97; President, Hydrographic Society, 1997-99. Address: Okelands, Pickhurst Road, Chiddingfold, Surrey GU8 4TS, England.

LAUNDER Brian Edward, b. 20 July 1939, United Kingdom. Professor. m. Dagny Simonsen, 1 son, 1 daughter. Education: BScEng, Imperial College London; SM, ScD, Massachusetts Institute of Technology; DScEng, University of London; DSc, University of Manchester; DEng, UMIST. Appointments: Research Assistant, Massachusetts Institute of Technology, 1961-64; Lecturer in Mechanical Engineering, 1964-72, Reader in Fluid Mechanics, 1972-76, Imperial College London; Professor of Mechanical Engineering, University of California Davis, 1976-80; Professor of Mechanical Engineering, 1980-98, Head of Thermodynamics and Fluid Mechanics Division, 1980-90, Head of Mechanical Engineering Department, 1983-85, 1993-95, Research Professor, 1998-, Chairman Environmental Strategy Group, 1998-2004, UMIST (now University of Manchester since October 2004); Adjunct Professor, Pennsylvania State University, 1984-88; Associate Editor ASME Fluids Engineering Journal, 1978-81; Editor-in-Chief, International Journal of Heat and Fluid Flow, 1987-; Regional Director, Tyndall Centre for Climate Change Research, 2000-05. Publications: Mathematical Models of Turbulence (with D B Spalding), 1972; Turbulence Models and Their Application (with W C Reynolds and W Rodi), 1985; Closure Strategies for Turbulent and Transitional Flows (with N Sandham), 2002; Turbulence Modelling for Engineering and the Environment, 2011; Author of over 250 scientific articles. Honours: Honorary Professor, Nanjing University of Aeronautics and Astronautics, People's Republic of China, 1993; Hon DSc, INP, Toulouse, and Paul Cézanne University, Aix-en-Provence, France, and Aristotle University of Thessaloniki, Greece; FRS; FREng, 1994; James Clayton Lifetime Research Achievement Prize, 2004. Memberships: FIMechE, 1981; FASME, 1983; FRAeS, 1996. Address: Department of Mechanical, Aerospace and Civil Engineering, The University of Manchester, PO Box 88, Manchester M60 1QD, England. E-mail: brian.launder@manchester.ac.uk

LAUREN Ralph, b. 14 October 1939, Bronx, New York, USA. Couturier. m. Ricky L Beer, 1964, 2 sons, 1 daughter. Appointments: Salesman, Bloomingdale's, New York, Brooks Brothers, New York; Assistant Buyer, Allied Stores, New York; Representative, Rivetz Necktie Manufacturers, New York; Neckwear Designer, Polo Division, Beau Brummel, New York, 1967-69; Founder, Polo Menswear Company, New York, 1968-, Ralph Lauren Women's Wear, New York, 1971-, Polo Leathergoods, 1978-, Polo Ralph Lauren Luggage, 1982-, Ralph Lauren Home Collection, 1983-; Chair, Polo Ralph Lauren Corporation, 66 stores in USA, over 140 worldwide. Honours: Several fashion awards, including: American Fashion Award, 1975; Council of Fashion Designers of America Award, 1981. Address: Polo Ralph Lauren Corporation, 650 Madison Avenue, New York, NY 10022, USA.

LAURENTS Arthur, b. 14 July 1917, New York, New York, USA. Dramatist; Writer; Director. Education: BA, Cornell University, 1937. Publications: Plays: Home of the Brave, 1946; The Bird Cage, 1950; The Time of the Cuckoo, 1952; A Clearing in the Woods, 1956; Invitation to a March, 1960; The Enclave, 1973; Scream, Houston, 1978; The Hunting Season, The Radical Mystique, Jolson Sings Again, 1995; My Good Name, 1997; Big Potato, 2000; Venecia, Claude Lazlo, 2001; The Vibrator, Closing Bell, 2002; Attacks on the Heart, Two Lives, 2003; Collected Plays, 2004. Musical Plays: West Side Story, 1957; Gypsy, 1959; Anyone Can Whistle, Do I Hear a Waltz?, 1964; Hallelujah Baby, 1967; Nick and Nora, 1991. Screenplays: The Snake Pit, Rope, Caught, 1948; Anna Lucasta, 1949; Anastasia, 1956; Bonjour Tristesse, 1958; The Way We Were, 1973; The Turning Point, 1977. Novels: The Way We Were, 1972; The Turning Point, 1977; Original Story By (memoir), 2000. Honours: Tony Awards, 1967, 1984; Drama Desk Awards, 1974, 1978; Golden Glove Award, 1977; Writers Guild of America, 1977; Best Director Award, 1985; William Inge Festival Award, 2004. Memberships: Academy of Motion Picture Arts and Sciences; Authors League; Dramatists Guild; PEN; Screenwriters Guild; Theatre Hall of Fame. Address: c/o William Morris Agency, 1325 Avenue of the Americas, New York, NY 10019, USA.

LAURIE Hugh, b. 11 June 1959, Oxford, England. Actor; Comedian. m. Jo, 2 sons, 1 daughter. Education: Cambridge University. Appointments: President, Footlights, Cambridge University; TV Appearances include: Santa's Last Christmas; Alfresco, The Crystal Cube, 1983; Mrs Capper's Birthday, 1985; Saturday Live (writer), 1986; A Bit of Fry and Laurie, 1989-91; The Laughing Prisoner, Blackadder the Third, Up Line, 1987; Blackadder: The Cavalier Years, Les Girls, Blackadder's Christmas Carol, 1988; Blackadder Goes Forth, Hysteria 2! 1989; Jeeves and Wooster, 1990-92; Treasure Island, All or Nothing at All, 1993; Look at the State We're In! (also director), The Adventures of Mole, 1995; The Best of Tracey Takes On…, 1996; The Place of Lions, 1997; Blackadder Back & Forth, 1999; Little Grey Rabbit, Preston Pig, 2000; Life with Judy Garland: Me and My Shadows, Second Star to the Left, 2001; Spooks, 2002; Stuart Little, Fortysomething (also director), The Young Visiters, 2003; House, 2004-; Film Appearances include: Plenty, 1985; Strapless, 1989; Peter's Friends, 1992; A Pin for the Butterfly, 1994; Sense and Sensibility, 1995; 101 Dalmatians, The Snow Queen's Revenge, 1996; The Borrowers, Spice World, The Ugly Duckling, 1997; The Man in the Iron Mask, Cousin Bette, 1998; Stuart Little, 1999; Carnivale, Maybe Baby, Lounge Act, 2000; The Piano Tuner, Chica de Rio, 2001; Stuart Little 2, 2002; Flight of the Phoenix, 2004; Valiant (voice), Stuart Little 3: Call of the Wild, The Big Empty, 2005. Publications: Fry and Laurie 4, (with Stephen Fry), 1994; The Gun Seller, 1996. Honours: Golden Globe Award, Best Actor in a TV Series, 2006. Address: Hamilton Asper Ltd, Ground Floor, 24 Hanway Street, London W1P 9DD, England.

LAURIE Richard Thomas, b. 4 October 1935, Bagshot, Surrey, England. Writer; Musician; Gardener. m. Susan Dring, divorced, 2 sons; 1 daughter. Education: Bradfield College 1949-1954. Appointments: National Service, 2 Lieutenant, RASC; Creative Director, Brockie Haslam, 1970-81; Group Head, Ted Bates, 1982-84; Band Leader, Dick Laurie's Elastic Band, 1983-; Creative Director, Breen Bryan Laurie and Dempsey, 1985-89; Creative Director, The Medicine Men 1993-; Producer, Zephyr Records, 1995-2000; Woodville Records, 2008-; Director, The Jobbing Gardener, 2002-. Publications: Editor: Soho Clarion, 1977-99, Docklands Business News, 1994-96, Journal for European Private

Hospitals, 1995-96; Founder/Publisher/Editor, Allegedly Hot News International, 1987-; Numerous articles, reviews and interviews. Memberships: Soho Society Executive Committee, 1976-2000, Advertising Creative Circle Council Member 1980-90; Director, Creative Circle Radio Workshop, 1988-90; Listed in Who's Who publications and biographical dictionaries. Address: 27 Clarendon Drive, Putney, London SW15 1AW, England. E-mail: alasdick@waitrose.com

LAURISCH Soeren, b. 15 May 1981, Hannover, Germany. Physician. Education: Physician, 2008; MD (Dr Med), 2009. Appointments: Physician, Internal Medicine, Department of Cardiology, Hannover Medical School, 2009-10; Physician, Internal Medicine, Department of Oncology & Gastroenterology, Werner Forssmann Hospital, 2011-. Publications: Allopurinol-induced hypersensitivity syndrome resulting in death, 2010; Rolle des Murinen Poliovirusrezeptor-Orthologs (mCD155/TAGE4) bei Transendothelialen Migrationsprozessen von Lymphozyten, 2010. Honours: Book Prize, German Physical Society, 2000; Listed in international biographical dictionaries. E-mail: soelau@hotmail.de

LAURSEN (Kirsten Marie) Benedicte, b. 6 September 1933, Trustrup, Denmark. Doctor of Medical Science. Education: MD, Copenhagen University, Denmark, 1961; Authorised Specialist of Internal Medicine, 1969, Authorised Specialist of Haematology, 1983, National Health Service, Denmark. Appointments: Specialist Training, different departments in University Hospitals, Copenhagen, 1963-80; Extensive teaching and lecturing activity, 1963-2004; Consultant, Associate Head, Department of Haematology and Internal Medicine B, 1980-2004, Aalborg Hospital; Retired, 2004-. Publications: Over 50 papers and articles in professional medical journals. Honours: Research Fellowship, Department of Internal Medicine, Enzymology, Washington University School of Medicine, St Louis, Missouri, USA, 1970-71; Member, Regional Committee for Biomedical Research Ethics, 1990-98; Honorary Director General for Europe, IBC; Deputy Director General, IBC; Medical Adviser to the Director General, IBC; Inner Circle of the Director General; Life Fellow, IBA; Ambassador to the World Congress of Arts, Sciences and Communication; Order of the International Fellowship; The International Hippocrates Award for Medical Achievement; IBC Medal of Wisdom; Top 100 Health Professionals, 2011; Lifetime Deputy Governor, ABI; Ambassador of Knowledge Medallion, 2010. Memberships: Danish Medical Association; Danish Society of Haematology; International Society of Haematology; Danish National Committee for Biomedical Research Ethics, 1994-98. Address: Skolemestervej 10, 9000 Aalborg, Denmark.

LAVENDER Justin, b. 4 June 1951, Bedford, England. Opera Singer. m. Louise Crane, 1 son, 1 daughter. Education: Queen Mary College, University of London; Guildhall School of Music and Drama. Career: Operatic Tenor; Leading roles with most of the world's major opera houses, 1980-; Title role, Faust (Gounod) Royal Opera, Covent Garden, 2004; Concert engagements with major orchestras and conductors worldwide; Numerous recordings, most recently Schnittka's Faust Cantata. Publications: Regular contributions to The Irish Examiner, original articles and book reviews, 1996-; Contributions to various professional journals. Membership: Newlands Rowing Club. Address: c/o Athole Still International Management Ltd, 25-27 Westow Street, London SE19 3RY, England.

LAVER Rod(ney) George, b. 9 August 1938, Rockhampton, Queensland, Australia. Tennis Player. m. Mary Benson, 1966, 1 son. Education: Rockhampton High School. Career: Played Davis Cup for Australia, 1958, 1959, 1960, 1961, 1962, and first open Davis Cup, 1973; Australian Champion, 1960, 1962, 1969; Wimbledon Champion, 1961, 1962, 1968, 1969; USA Champion, 1962, 1969; French Champion, 1962, 1969; First player to win double Grand Slam, 1962, 1969; Professional from 1963; First Player to win over 1,000,000 US $ in prize money. Publications: How to Play Winning Tennis, 1964; Education of a Tennis Player, 1971. Honours: Member, Order of the British Empire; Melbourne Park centre court renamed Rod Laver Arena in his honour, 2000. Address: c/o Tennis Australia, Private Bag 6060, Richmond South, VIC 3121, Australia.

LAVERDANT Alain Michel, b. 2 February 1954, Thionville, France. Researcher. m. Patricia Simone Vandon, 1 son. Education: Aeronautics Engineer, ETACA, 1976; DEA Meca flu, Energ, 1978, Doctorat 3rd cycle, 1981, Orléans University; Doctor of Sciences, Rouen University, 1991. Appointments: Doctoral Candidate, 1978-81; Research Engineer, 1981-93; Master of Research, 1994. Publications: Papers and articles in professional scientific journals. Honours: Prix Estrade-Delcros; Houllevigue Saintour Jules Mahyer de l'Académie des Sciences, 1991. Address: 9 résidence de la Boële, 91700 Sainte-Geneviève-des-Bois, France. E-mail: laverdan@onera.fr

LAVIELLE Lisette, b. 14 April 1941, Mulhouse, France. Retired Researcher. m. Jean-Pierre Lavielle, 2 daughters. Education: Graduate, Chemical Engineering, École Nationale Supérieure de Chimie, Mulhouse, 1964; Doctor of Engineering, University of Strasbourg, France, 1968; DSc, University of Haute-Alsace, Mulhouse, 1971. Appointments: Research Associate, Thin Films Laboratory, CNRS, École Nationale Supérieure de Chimie, Mulhouse, 1964-70; Research Associate, Mineral Chemistry Laboratory, CNRS, Mulhouse, 1971-76; Engineer, European Society of Propulsion, Vernon, 1978-79; Research Associate, Macromolecular Chemistry Laboratory, CNRS, Rouen, 1980-81; Research Associate, Centre for Physical Chemistry Solid Surfaces, CNRS, Mulhouse, 1981-94; Research Associate, General Photochemistry Department, CNRS, 1995-2001. Publications: Polymer Surface Dynamics, chapter, 1987; Polymer Characterisation by Inverse Gas Chromatography, chapter, 1989; UV Phototreatment of Polymer Film Surface: Self-Organization and Thermodynamics of Irreversible Processes, chapter, 1999. Honour: Recipient, Emilio Noelting Prize, École Nationale Supérieure de Chimie de Mulhouse, 1964. Address: 6 rue la Fayette, 68100 Mulhouse, France.

LAVIGNE Avril, b. 27 September 1984, Belleville, Ontario, Canada. Singer; Musician; Songwriter; Actress; Model; Designer. m. Deryck Whibley, 2006, divorced 2009. Career: Singer; Singles: Complicated, Sk8er Boi, I'm With You, 2002; Losing Grip, 2003; Don't Tell Me, My Happy Ending, Nobody's Home, 2004; He Wasn't, 2005; Girlfriend, When You're Gone, Hot, 2007; The Best Damn Thing, 2008; Albums: Let Go, 2002; Under My Skin, 2004; The Best Damn Thing, 2007; DVDs: My World, 2003; Live at Budokan, 2005; Live in Toronto, 2008; Tours: Try to Shut Me Up Tour, 2003; Bonez Tour/Mall Tour, 2004/05; Promotional Tour, 2007; The Best Damn Tour, 2008; TV/Films: Sabrina, the Teenage Witch, 2002; Going the Distance, Saturday Live, MADtv, 2004; Fast Food Nation, Over the Hedge, 2006; The Flock, 2007. Honours: Best New Artist, MTV Video Music Awards,

2002; 4 Juno Awards, 2003; World's Best-Selling Canadian Singer, World Music Award, 2004; World's Best Pop/Rock Artist, World Music Award, 2004.

LAVIT Igor, b. 14 May 1951, Tula, Russia. m. Nadja, 1 daughter. Education: Tula Polytechnic Institute, 1974. Appointments: Research Engineer, KBP, Tula, 1974-88; Professor, Tula State University, 1988-; DPhil, 1989. Publications: Stable crack growth in an elastoplatic material, 1988; Crack growth in the process of quasibrittle fracture under an increasing or cyclic load, 2001. Honours: Listed in biographical dictionaries. Address: Tula State University, Mechanical & Mathematical Department, Lenin ave 92, Tula, Tula Region 300600, Russia. E-mail: igorlevit@yandex.ru

LAW Jude, b. 29 December 1972, London, England. Actor. m. Sadie Frost, 1997, divorced 2003, 2 sons, 1 daughter. Appointments: National Youth Music Theatre; Co-founder, Natural Nylon (production company), Director, 2000-03; Stage appearances include: Joseph and the Amazing Technicolour Dreamcoat; Les Parents Terribles, 1994; Ior, 1995; Tis Pity She's A Whore, 1999; Doctor Faustus, 2002; Film appearances include: Shopping, 1994; I Love You I Love You Not, 1996; Wilde, 1997; Gattaca, Midnight in the Garden of Good and Evil, 1997; Bent; Music From Another Room, Final Cut, The Wisdom of Crocodiles, 1998; eXistenZ, The Talented Mr Ripley, 1999; Final Cut; Enemy at the Gates, Love Honour and Obey, 2000; Artificial Intelligence: AI, 2001; Road to Perdition, 2002; Cold Mountain, 2003; Sky Captain and the World of Tomorrow, Alfie, I Heart Huckabees, The Aviator, Lemony Snicket's A Series of Unfortunate Events (voice), 2004; All the King's Men, Breaking and Entering, The Holiday, 2006; My Blueberry Nights, Sleuth, 2007; Sherlock Holmes, 2009; Repo Men, 2010. Honours: BAFTA Award, Best Supporting Actor, 1999. Address: c/o Julian Belfrage Associates, 46 Albemarle Street, London, W1S 4DF, England. Website: www.jude-law.net

LAWANDE Sandeep Anant, b. 11 February 1975, Mapusa, Goa, India. Peridontist; Oral Implantologist. m. Gayatri. Education: Bachelor of Dental Surgery, Goa University, 1996; Master of Dental Surgery, SDM College of Dental Sciences & Hospital, Dharwad, Karnataka, 2002; AAID Maxicourse on Implant Dentistry, 2004; The Osseointegrated Implant Course, 2006. Appointments: Private dental practice in general dentistry, 1998-2000; Lecturer, 2003-09, Assistant Professor, 2010-, Department of Periodontics, Goa Dental College & Hospital, Bambolim; Convenor, Council on Dental Health, 2005-06, President Elect, 2006-07, President, 2007-08, Indian Dental Association, Goa State Branch; Editorial Board Member, Journal of Dental Implants, 2005-; Editorial Board Member, Journal of Indian Dental Association; Chief Co-ordinator, Indian Dental Association, Colgate National Oral Health Program, 2006-; Key Resource Team member, Oral Healthcare Providers workshops, 2006-; National Co-ordinator, 11th Congress of International Congress of Oral Implantologists, Asia Pacific Section, 2007; Convenor, Continuing Dental Education, IDA Goa State Branch, 2009-10. Publications: Author, 2 books, Secrets of Dental Care, and Daataanchi Jatnaay – Kaain Samaj, Kaain Gairsamaj, 2011; Numerous articles in professional journals. Honours: Fellow, International Congress of Oral Implantologists, 2006; Associate Fellow, American Academy of Implant Dentistry, 2006; Best Scientific Paper Presentation Award, 2007; Gold Medal for Excellence in Dentistry, 2007; Certificate of Excellence for Outstanding Contribution in Dental Sciences, 2008; Certificate of Merit for Best Short Film on Dental Health Education, 2009; National Award for Excellence in Dentistry, 2009; AIDS Control Society Best Film Award, 2009; Health Achievement Award in Dentistry, 2010; National Award for Intellectual Development, 2010; Rajiv Gandhi Excellence Award, 2010; Indian Dental Association Appreciation Award, 2010; International Gold Star Award for Health Excellence, 2010; Appreciation Award for Publication, 2010; Nehru Youth National Award, 2010; Educational Development Council National Award for Excellence in Dentistry, 2010; Listed in international biographical dictionaries. Memberships: International Congress of Oral Implantologists; American Academy of Implant Dentistry; Implant Prosthodontic Section of the ICOI; Indian Society of Periodontology; Indian Society of Oral Implantologists; Indian Academy of Osseointegration; Indian Academy of Aesthetic and Cosmetic Dentistry; Academy of Implantology; Indian Dental Association; Global Achievers Foundation; Entertainment Society of Goa. Address: HNo 874/5 Saideep, New Pundalik Nagar, Porvorim, Goa, 403521, India. E-mail: drsanlaw@rediffmail.com

LAWRENCE Roderick John, b. 30 August 1949, Adelaide, Australia. m. Clarisse Christine Gonet, 3 sons. Education: BArch, University of Adelaide, 1972; MLitt, University of Cambridge, England, 1978; DSc, Ecole Polytechnique Fédérale de Lausanne, Switzerland, 1983. Appointments: Design-Research Architect, South Australian Housing Trust, Adelaide, 1974; Architect, Percy Thomas Partnership, Cardiff, Wales, 1978; Tutor, Department of Architecture, Ecole Polytechnique Fédérale de Lausanne, 1978-84; Consultant, Committee on Housing Building and Planning, Economic Commission for Europe, 1984-85; Visiting Lecturer, Faculty of Architecture and Town Planning, University of Adelaide, Visiting Research Fellow, School of Social Sciences, Flinders University, 1985; Master of Teaching and Research, Centre for Human Ecology and Environmental Sciences, University of Geneva, 1986; Professor, Faculty of Social and Economic Sciences, 1999-; Member of 4 Scientific Editorial Boards. Publications include: An Ecological Blueprint for Healthy Housing, 1993; Mythical and Ritual Constituents of the City, 1994; Type as Analytical Tool: Reinterpretation and Application, 1994; Sustaining Human Settlement: A Challenge for the New Millennium, 2000. Over 120 articles in scientific journals and 50 book reviews. Honours: Wormald Prize in Architecture, University of Adelaide, 1971; Milne Travelling Scholarship, 1974; Lawson Postgraduate Research Fellowship, 1974; Travel and Study Scholarship, National Science Foundation of Switzerland, 1984; Eurasmus Mundus Professor's Scholarship, 2007-08; Listed in national and international biographical dictionaries. Memberships: Associate Member, Royal British Institute of Architects, 1973-98; People and Physical Environment Research, Sydney; International Association for People – Environment Studies, Guildford, England; Co-ordinator, European Network for Housing Research, Working Group on Housing and Health; Member, Scientific Advisory Board of the World Health Organisation's European Centre for Environment and Health, 1994-98; Member, The New York Academy of Sciences, 1997-; Chairperson, Evaluation Advisory Committee of World Health Organisation's Healthy Cities Project, 1998-; Member, World Health Organization's European Taskforce on Housing and Health, 2001-. Address: Faculty of Social and Economic Sciences, Pole Environment, University of Geneva, Site Battelle, CH-12227 Carouge (ÇE), Switzerland. E-mail: roderick.lawrence@unige.ch

LAWSON Dominic Ralph Campbell (Hon), b. 17 December 1956, London, England. Journalist; Editor. m. (1) Jane Fiona Wastell Whytenead, 1982, divorced 1991, (2) Hon Rosamond

DICTIONARY OF INTERNATIONAL BIOGRAPHY 36th EDITION

Monckton, 1991, 2 daughters. Education: Christchurch, Oxford; BA Oxon. Appointments: World Tonight and The Financial World Tonight, BBC, 1979-81; Staff, Energy Correspondent, Lex Columnist, 1987-90, Columnist, 1991-94 The Financial Times; Deputy Editor, 1987-90, Editor, 1990-95, The Spectator; Editor, The Spectator Cartoon Book; Columnist, Sunday Correspondent, 1990; Columnist, Daily Telegraph, 1994-95; Editor, The Sunday Telegraph, 1995-2005; Columnist, The Independent, 2006-. Publications: Korchnoi, Kasparov, 1983; Britain in the Eighties, co-author, 1989; The Spectator Annual, editor, 1992, 1993, 1994; The Inner Game, editor, 1993. Honours: Editor of the Year, Society of Magazine Editors, 1990. Memberships: Fellow, Royal Society of Arts. Address: The Sunday Telegraph, 1 Canada Square, Canary Wharf, London E14 5AR, England.

LAWSON Lesley (Twiggy), b. 19 September 1949, London, England. Model; Singer; Actress. m. (1) Michael Whitney Armstrong, 1977, deceased, 1983, 1 daughter, (2) Leigh Lawson, 1988. Career: Model, 1966-70; Manager, Director, Twiggy Enterprises Ltd, 1966-; Own musical series, British TV, 1975-76; Founder, Twiggy and Co, 1998-; Made several LP records; Appearances in numerous TV dramas, UK and USA; Appeared in films including The Boy Friend, 1971, There Goes the Bride, 1979, Blues Brothers, 1981, The Doctor and the Devils, 1986, Club Paradise, 1986, Harem Hotel, Istanbul, 1988, Young Charlie Chaplin, TV film, 1989, Madame Sousatzka, 1989, Woundings, 1998; Appeared in plays: Cinderella, 1976; Captain Beaky, 1982; My One and Only, 1983-84; Blithe Spirit, Chichester, 1997; Noel and Gertie, USA, 1998; If Love Were All, New York, 1999; Blithe Spirit, New York, 2002; Play What I Wrote, 2002; Mrs Warren's Profession, 2003. Publications: Twiggy: An Autobiography, 1975; An Open Look,1985; Twiggy in Black and White, co-author, 1997. Honours: 2 Golden Globe Awards, 1970. Address: c/o Peters Fraser and Dunlop, Drury House, 34-43 Russell Street, London WC2B 5HA, England. E-mail: postmaster@pfd.co.uk

LAWSON of BLABY, Baron of Newnham in the County of Northamptonshire, Nigel Lawson, b. 11 March 1932, London, England. Politician. m. (1) Vanessa Salmon, divorced. 1980, deceased. 1985, (2) Thérèse Mary Maclear, 1980, 2 sons, 4 daughters, 1 deceased. Education: Christ Church, Oxford; MA Oxon. Appointments: Sub-Lieutenant, Royal Naval Volunteer Reserve, 1954-56; Editorial Staff, Financial Times, 2956-60; City Editor, Sunday Telegraph, 1961-63; Special Assistant to Prime Minister, 1963-64; Columnist, Financial Times and Broadcaster, BBC, 1965; Editor, The Spectator, 1966-70; Regular Contributor to Sunday Times and Evening Standard, 1970-71, The Times, 1971-72; Fellow, Nuffield College, Oxford, 1972-73; Special Political Adviser, Conservative Party Headquarters, 1973-74; Member of Parliament for Blaby, Leicestershire, 1974-92; Opposition Whip, 1976-77; Opposition Spokesman on Treasury and Economic Affairs, 1977-79; Financial Secretary to the Treasury, 1979-81; Secretary of State for Energy, 1981-83; Chancellor of the Exchequer, 1983-89; Non-Executive Director, Barclays Bank, 1990-98; Chairman, Central European Trust, 1990-; Adviser, BZW, 1990-91; Non-Executive Director, Consultant, Guinness Peat Aviation, 1990-93; Director, Institute for International Economics, Washington DC, 1991-; International Advisory Board, Creditanstalt Bankverein, 1991-; International Advisory Board, Total SA, 1994-; Advisory Council, Prince's Youth Business Trust, 1994-; President, British Institute of Energy Economics, 1995-; Chairman, CAIB Emerging Russia Fund, 1997-; Privy Councillor. Publications: The Power Game, co-author, 1976; The View from No 11: Memoirs from a Tory Radical, 1992; The Nigel Lawson Diet Book, co-author, 1996; Various pamphlets. Memberships: President, British Institute of Energy Economics, 1995-; Governing Body, Westminster School, 1999-2005; President, British Institute of Energy Economics, 1995-2004. Honours: Finance Minister of the Year, Euromoney Magazine, 1988; Honorary Student, Christ Church, Oxford, 1996. Address: House of Lords, London SW1A 0PW, England.

LAYARD, Baron of Highgate in the London Borough of Haringey, Peter Richard Grenville, b. 15 March 1934, Welwyn Garden City, England. Economist. m. Molly Meacher, 1991. Education: BA, Cambridge University; MSc, London School of Economics. Appointments: Schoolteacher, London County Council, 1959-61; Senior Research Officer, Robbins Committee on Higher Education, 1961-64; Deputy Director, Higher Education Research Unit, 1964-74, Lecturer, 1968-75, Head, Centre for Labour Economics, 1974-90, Reader, 1975-80, Professor of Economics, 1980-99, Director, Centre for Economic Performance, 1990-, London School of Economics; Consultant, Centre for European Policy Studies, Brussels, 1982-86; University Grants Committee, 1985-89; Chairman, Employment Institute, 1987-92; Ch-Chairman, World Economy Group, World Institute for Development Economics Research, 1989-; Economic Adviser to Russian Government, 1991-97. Publications: Cost Benefit Analysis, 1973; Causes of Poverty, co-author, 1978; Microeconomic Theory, co-author, 1978; More Jobs, Less Inflation, 1982; The Causes of Unemployment, co-editor, 1984; The Rise in Unemployment, co-author, 1986; How to Beat Unemployment, 1986; Handbook of Labour Economics, co-editor, 1987; The Performance of the British Economy, co-author, 1988; Unemployment: Macroeconomic Performance and the Labour Market, co-author, 1991; East-West Migration: the alternatives, co-author, 1992; Post-Communist Reform: pain and progress, co-author, 1993; Macroeconomics: a text for Russia, 1994; The Coming Russian Boom, co-author, 1996; What Labour Can Do, 1997; Tackling Unemployment, 1999; Tackling Inequality, 1999; What the Future Holds; Happiness: Lessons from a New Science, 2005. Honours: Created Life Peer, 2000. Memberships: Fellow, Econometric Society. Address: 45 Cholmeley Park, London N6 5EL, England.

LAYMAN Dale Pierre, b. 3 July 1948, Niles, Michigan, USA. Professor; Author. m. Kathleen Ann Jackowiak, 1 son, 3 daughters. Education: AS, Lake Michigan College, 1968; BSc with distinction, Anthropology and Zoology, University of Michigan, 1971; MSc, Physiology, University of Michigan Medical School, 1974; Educational Specialist in Physiology and Health Science, Ball State University, 1979; PhD, Health and Safety Studies, University of Illinois, 1986; Grand PhD, Medicine, World Info Distributed University, 2003. Appointments: Histological Technician in Neuropathology and a Teaching Fellow in Human Physiology, University of Michigan Medical School, Ann Arbor, 1971-74; Instructor in Human Anatomy, Physiology and Histology, Lake Superior State College, now Lake Superior State University, 1975; Professor of Medical Terminology, Human Anatomy and Physiology, Joliet Junior College, 1975-2007, Part-time, 2007-10. Publications: 2 textbooks: The Terminology of Anatomy and Physiology, 1983; The Medical Language: A Programmed Body-Systems Approach, 1995; 4 trade books: Biology Demystified, 2003; Anatomy Demystified, 2004; Physiology Demystified, 2004; Medical Terminology Demystified, 2006; Journal articles, Published interview, Unpopular Mechanics, Maxim magazine, 2005; Article on Transhumanism featured in Wikipedia, 2009. Honours:

Lifetime Achievement Award, IBC; International Man of the Millennium, Deputy Director General, Life Patron, Director General's Honours List, Order of International Fellowship, International Order of Merit, Outstanding Speaker of the 20th Century, International Intellectual for the Year 2001, International Scientist of the Year 2003, International Educator of the Year 2003, Medical Adviser to the Director General, Founding Member of the World Peace and Diplomacy Forum, Founding Member of the Scientific Faculty, The Inner Circle, 2010, The Cambridge Certificate for Outstanding Scientific Achievement, 2010, Top 100 Scientists, 2011, Top 100 Educators, 2011, International Biographical Centre; Outstanding Man of the 20th Century, World Lifetime Achievement Award, 20th Century Achievement Award, Continental Governor, Deputy Governor, Life Fellow, International Cultural Diploma of Honor; Who's Who of the Year, 1999; 2000 Millennium Medal of Honor, 2000 Platinum Record for Exceptional Performance, World Laureate, American Order of Excellence, The Presidential Seal of Honor, 2001, The Most 100 Intriguing People of 2002, The American Medal of Honor, International Peace Prize; Man of the Year 2003; Founding Cabinet, World Peace and Diplomacy Forum, 2003; International Writer of The Year 2004; The Seat of Wisdom, 2010; Ambassador of Grand Eminence, A Profile of Courage, 2010, The Order of International Ambassadors, 2010, American Biographical Institute; Kappa Delta Pi; Phi Kappa Phi. Memberships: Academic Counselor, London Diplomatic Academy; Human Anatomy and Physiology Society; Society of Leading Intellectuals of the World; World Order of Science-Education-Culture, Cavalier-Knight; Former, Council Member and Notable Author, Text and Academic Authors; Campus Co-ordinator, Illinois Community College Faculty Association; Secretary General, United Cultural Convention; Founder and President, Robowatch; VIP Member, Strathmore's Who's Who Registry; Life Member, International Association of Business Leaders. Address: 509 Westridge Road, Joliet, IL 60431, USA.

LE BLANC Matt, b. 25 July 1967, Newton, Massachusetts, USA. Actor. m. Melissa McKnight, 2003, 1 daughter. Education: Newton High School; Trained as carpenter. Career: Actor: Television includes: TV 101, 1988; Top of the Heap, 1991; Vinnie and Bobby, 1992; Red Shoes Diaries, 1993; Friends, 1994-2004; Reform School Girl, 1994; Red Shoes Diaries 7, 1997; Joey, 2004-2006; Commercials: Levi's 501 jeans, Coca Cola, Doritos, Heinz Ketchup; Producer, The Prince, 2006; Films include: Lookin' Italian, 1994; Ed, 1996; Lost in Space, 1998; Charlie's Angels, 2000; All the Queens Men, 2001; Charlie's Angels: Full Throttle, 2003; TV guest appearances include: Just the Ten of Us, 1989; Monsters, 1990; Married… with Children, 1991; The Rosie O'Donnald Show, 1996; The Tonight Show with Jay Leno, 1996; Entertainment Tonight, 2003; Opera Winfrey Show, 2003; Celebrities Uncensored, 2003; Tonight with Jay Leno, 2004. Honours: TV Guide Award, 2000; Teen Choice Award, 2002. Address: c/o United Talent Agency, 9560 Wilshire Boulevard, Suite 500, Beverly Hills, CA 90212, USA.

LE BRUN Christopher Mark, b. 20 December 1951, Portsmouth, England. Artist. m. Charlotte Verity, 2 sons, 1 daughter. Education: DFA, Slade School of Fine Art, 1970-74; MA, Chelsea School of Art, 1974-75. Career: Visiting Lecturer: Brighton Polytechnic, 1975-82, Slade School of Fine Art, 1978-83, Wimbledon School of Art, 1981-83; Professor of Drawing, RA, 2000-02, Chair, Education Committee RA, 2000-, Royal Academy; Trustee, Prince of Wales's Drawing School, 2004-; Trustee: Tate Gallery, 1990-95, National Gallery, 1996-2003, Dulwich Picture Gallery, 2000-05; Chair, Academic Advisory Board, Prince of Wales Drawing School, 2004-; Trustee, Princes' Drawing School, 2004-; Numerous one-man and group exhibitions internationally since 1979; Public Collections include: Tate Gallery, British Museum, Victoria and Albert, MOMA, New York; British Council; National Portrait Gallery; Scottish National Gallery of Modern Art; Walker Art Gallery. Publications: Works feature in: 50 Etchings, 1991; Christopher Le Brun, 2001. Honours: John Moores Liverpool Prizewinner, 1978, 1980; Gulbenkian Printmakers Commission, 1983; DAAD Fellowship, Berlin, 1987-88; Turner Watercolour Medal, 2005. Membership: Royal Academician (RA), 1996. Address: Royal Academy of Arts, Piccadilly, London W1J 0BD, England.

LE MARCHANT Francis Arthur (Sir), b. 6 October 1939, Hungerton, UK. Artist; Farmer. Education: Byam Shaw School of Drawing and Painting; Certificate, RAS, Royal Academy Schools. Career: One man exhibitions include: Museum of Art and Science, Evansville, USA; Agnews; Roy Miles Fine Art; Group exhibitions include: Royal Academy Summer Exhibitions; Leicester Galleries, Spink; Bilan de l'Art Contemporain, Paris; Spink; Collections include: Government Art Collections, 2 paintings; Financial Times; The Museum of Evansville, USA; University of Evansville, USA; Collection of the late Mrs Anne Kessler. Honour: Silver Medal, Bilan de l'Art Contemporain, Paris. Memberships: Savile Club; Reynolds Club (Alumni Association of Royal Academy Schools). Address: c/o HSBC, 88 Westgate, Grantham, Lincolnshire NG31 6LF, England.

LE ROUX Patricia, b. 16 May 1958, Lyon, France. Medical Doctor. m. Dominique, 2 sons, 2 daughters. Education: Medical Doctor, 1983; Specialist, Paediatrics, 1988; Homeopathic Training, 1995; Ethics Diploma, Medical Ethics, 1996. Appointments: Emergency Paediatrician; European Committee of Homeopathy, Brussels, 2000-. Publications: 6 books; Numerous articles in professional journals and at international conferences. Honours: Woman of the Year, 2010.

LEACH Henry (Conyers) (Admiral of the Fleet Sir), b. 18 November 1923. Naval Officer. m. Mary Jean McCall, 1958, deceased 1991, 2 daughters. Education: Royal Naval College, Dartmouth. Appointments: Served cruiser Mauritius, South Atlantic and Indian Ocean, 1941-42, battleship Duke of York, 1943-45, destroyers, Mediterranean, 1945-46; gunnery, 1947; Gunnery appointments, 1948-51; Gunnery Officer, cruiser Newcastle, Far East, 1953-55; Staff appointments, 1955-59; Commanded destroyer Dunkirk, 1959-61; Captain, 27th Squadron and Mediterranean, frigate Galatea, 1965-67; Director of Naval Plans, 1968-70; Commanded Commando Ship Albion, 1970; Assistant Chief of Naval Staff, Policy, 1971-73; Flag Officer, First Flotilla, 1974-75; Vice-Chief of Defence Staff, 1976-77; Commander-in-Chief and Allied Commander-in-Chief, Channel and Eastern Atlantic, 1977-79; Chief of Naval Staff, First Sea Lord, 1979-82; First and Principal ADC to the Queen, 1979-82; Deputy Lieutenant; Chairman, 1987-98, Honorary Vice-President, 1991-, Council, King Edward VII Hospital; Governor, Cranleigh School, 1983-93; Chairman, 1983-98, Honorary Vice-President, 1999-, St Dunstan's; Governor, St Catherine's, 1987-93. Publications: Endure No Makeshifts, autobiography. Honours: Knight Grand Cross, Order of the Bath; Honorary Freeman, Merchant Taylors, Shipwrights, City of London. Memberships: Royal Bath and West of England Society, President, 1993, Vice-President, 1994-; Royal Naval Benevolent Society, President, 1984-93; Sea Cadet Association, President, 1984-93; Patron, Meridian Trust

Association, 1994-; Patron, Hampshire Royal British Legion, 1994-. Address: Wonston Lea, Wonston, Winchester, Hants SO21 3LS, England.

LEACH Matthew John, b. Whyalla, South Australia. Academic. m. Pamela. Education: Bachelor of Nursing, 1995, Bachelor of Nursing (Honours), 2000, PhD, 2005, University of South Australia; Diploma of Applied Science (Naturopathy), South Australian College of Natural Medicine, 1999; Diploma, Clinical Nutrition, International Academy of Nutrition, 2008. Appointments: Registered Nurse, Adecco NSB, Adelaide, 1996-2000; Registered Nurse, Royal District Nursing Service, Adelaide, 2000; Lecturer, Nursing, 2001, Lecturer, Naturopathy, 2004, Programme Director, Bachelor of Health Science (Naturopathy), University of South Australia; Research Fellow, University of South Australia, 2008. Publications: Numerous articles in medical journals. Honours: RCNA High Achiever Award, 1995; ATMS Award for Excellence in Naturopathic Studies, 1999; Bachelor of Nursing (Honours) Scholarship, 2000; Australian Postgraduate Award, 2001-04; ATMS Simon Schot Education Grant, 2006; Division of Health Sciences Research Development Grant, 2006; NHMRC Project Development Grant, 2008. Memberships: Nurses Board of South Australia; Australian Traditional Medicine Society; International Society of Complementary Medicine Research; Australian Society of Medical Research; Canadian Interdisciplinary Network for Complementary and Alternative Medicine Research; Network of Researchers in the Public Health of Complementary and Alternative Medicine; Cochrane Metabolic and Endocrine Disorders Group. E-mail: matthew.leach@unisa.edu.au

LEAH Philip, b. 23 October 1948, Dulwich, London, England. Music Educator. Divorced, 2 sons. Education: Northern School of Music, Manchester, 1968-71; Awarded GNSM, 1971; Studies in flute, piano and composition; Padgate College of Education, Warrington, 1971-72; Postgraduate Certificate in Education. Appointments: Peripatetic Music Teacher, Glamorgan, 1972-73; Peripatetic Music Teacher, City of Birmingham, 1973-90; Lecturer, North Worcestershire College of Education, 1977-80; University of Wolverhampton, 1982-90; Founder and Musical Director, West Birmingham Schools Wind Band, 1985-90; Founder and Musical Director, Halesowen Symphony Orchestra, 1986-89; Examiner, Guildhall School of Music and Drama, 1988-; Flute Tutor, University of Wales, Aberystwyth, 2000-05; Resound workshops and Gong baths. Compositions: Concertino for bass tuba and orchestra; Sinfonia for flute and strings; Acme, a suite for chamber orchestra; Sinfonia for chamber orchestra; Elegy for string sextet; Prelude and Scherzo for string quartet; Three Penny Bit for wind; Wind quintet; Fanfare, 1969; Fanfare for a Golden Jubilee; Conversations for flute and piano; Chorale Prelude on 'Austria' for organ; Wedding Suite for organ; In Annum for tenor solo, SATB choir and string quartet; Winter for SATB choir and string quartet; Song: Meditation for soprano and piano; Psychological Songs for bass voice and piano; Various arrangements for woodwind instruments. Honours: First prize, Horatio Albert Lumb Composition Competition, 1992. Memberships: Royal Society of Musicians of Great Britain; Incorporated Society of Musicians; Musicians' Union. Address: 15 Oak Tree Crescent, Halesowen, West Midlands, B62 9DA, England. E-mail: philresound@aol.com

LEAPER David John, b. 23 July 1947, York, England. Professor of Surgery. m. Francesca Ann, 1 son, 1 daughter. Education: Leeds Modern Grammar School (Head Boy, 1965), 1957-65; MBChB with honours, University of Leeds Medical School, 1970; MD, 1979, ChM, 1982. Appointments: House Officer, Leeds General Infirmary, 1970-71; MRC Fellow, 1971-73; Registrar, Leeds General Infirmary and Scarborough, 1973-76; Senior Registrar in Surgery, CRC Fellow, Westminster and Kings College Hospitals, London, 1976-87; Professor of Surgery, University of Hong Kong, 1988-90; Senior Lecturer in Surgery, University of Bristol, 1981-95; Professor of Surgery, 1995-2004, Emeritus Professor, 2004-, University of Newcastle; Visiting Professor, Cardiff University, 2004-; Visiting Professor, Imperial College, London, 2006-. Publications: Books: International Surgical Practice; Oxford Handbook of Clinical Surgery; Oxford Handbook of Operative Surgery; Handbook of Postoperative Complications: Series: Your Operation, Preparation for the MRCS, 2006; Member, Editorial Board of Medical, Educational and Surgical Journals; Papers on wound healing, surgical infections, colorectal and breast cancer. Honours: Fellow, Royal College of Surgeons of England, 1975, of Edinburgh, 1974, of Glasgow, 1998; Hunterian Professor, 1981-82; Zachary Cope Lecturer, 1998; Fellow, American College of Surgeons, 1998; Past Member, Court of Examiners, Royal College of Surgeons of England; Intercollegiate Fellowship Examiner, 2000-04. Memberships: Founder Member, Past Recorder and Past President, European Wound Management Association; Surgical Infection Society of Europe; Past Vice President, Section of Surgery, Royal Society of Medicine; Past Committee Member, Surgical Research Society; Programme Director, Higher Surgical Training, Northern Deanery, 2000-04; Member, Specialist Advisory Committee, Higher Surgical Training, UK, 2000-05; Chair, Subcommittee Surgical Site Infection, Steering Group on Healthcare Associated Infection; Day Case Champion, Modernisation Agency, 2002-04; Member, 2015 Forum; Chair, NICE guideline development group, Surgical Site Infection; Expert Member Antimicrobial Resistance and Healthcare Associated Infection Advisory Group. Address: 33 Peverell Avenue East, Poundbury, Dorchester, Dorset DT1 3RH, England. E-mail: profdavidleaper@doctors.org.uk

LEAPMAN Michael Henry, b. 24 April 1938, London, England. Writer; Journalist. m. Olga Mason, 15 July 1965, 1 son. Appointment: Journalist, The Times, 1969-81. Publications: One Man and His Plot, 1976; Yankee Doodles, 1982; Companion Guide to New York, 1983; Barefaced Cheek, 1983; Treachery, 1984; The Last Days of the Beeb, 1986; Kinnock, 1987; The Book of London (editor), 1989; London's River, 1991; Treacherous Estate, 1992; Eyewitness Guide to London, 1993; Master Race (with Catrine Clay), 1995; Witnesses to War, 1998; The Ingenious Mr Fairchild, 2000; The World for a Shilling 2001; Inigo, 2003; The Biggest Beetroot in the World, 2008; Contributions to: Numerous magazines and journals. Honours: Campaigning Journalist of the Year, British Press Award, 1968; Thomas Cook Travel Book Award, Best Guide Book of 1983; Garden Writers Guild Award, 1995; Times Education Supplement Senior Book Award, 1999. Memberships: Society of Authors; Royal Society of Arts, National Union of Journalists. Address: 13 Aldebert Terrace, London SW8 1BH, England.

LEAVER Christopher (Sir), b. 3 November 1937, London, England. Business Executive. m. Helen Mireille Molyneux Benton, 1975, 1 son, 2 daughters. Appointments: Commissioned, Royal Army Ordnance Corps, 1956-58; Member, Retail Food Trades Wages Council, 1963-64; Justice of the Peace, Inner London, 1970-83; Council, Royal Borough of Kensington and Chelsea, 1970-73; Court of Common Council, Ward of Dowgate, 1973, Sheriff, 1979-80, Lord Mayor, 1981-82, City of London; Justice of the Peace, City,

1974-93; Board, Brixton Prison, 1975-78; Governor, Christ's Hospital School, 1975; Governor, City of London Girls School, 1975-78; Board of Governors, 1978-, Chancellor, 1981-82, City University; Chairman, Young Musicians Symphony Orchestra Trust, 1979-81; Trustee, Chichester Festival Theatre, 1982-97; Church Commissioner, 1982-83, 1996-; Chairman, London Tourist Board Ltd, 1983-89, Trustee, London Symphony Orchestra, 1983-91; Deputy Chairman, 1989-93, Chairman, 1993-94, Vice-Chairman, 1994-2000, Thames Water PLC; Adviser to Secretary of State on Royal Parks, 1993-96; Non-Executive Director, Unionamerica Holdings, 1994-97; Chairman, Eastbourne College. Honours: Knight Grand Cross, Order of the British Empire; Knight, Order of St John of Jerusalem; Honorary Colonel, 151 Regiment, Royal Corps of Transport (Volunteers), 1983-89; Honorary Colonel, Royal Corps of Transport, 1988-91; Honorary Liveryman, Farmers Company; Fellow, Chartered Institute of Transport; Honorary Freeman, Company of Water Conservators; Freeman, Company of Watermen and Lightermen; Order of Oman. Memberships: Vice-President, Playing Fields Association. Address: c/o Thames Water PLC, 14 Cavendish Place, London W1M 0NU, England.

LEAVER Peter Lawrence Oppenheim, b. 28 November 1944. Lawyer; Football Executive. m. Jane Rachel Pearl, 1969, 3 sons, 1 daughter. Education: Trinity College, Dublin; Called to Bar, Lincoln's Inn, 1967. Appointments: Member, Committee on Future of the Legal Profession, 1986-88, Council of Legal Education, 1986-91, General Council of the Bar, 1987-90; Chairman, Bar Committee, 1989, International Practice Committee, 1990; Director, Investment Management Regulatory Organisation, 1994-2000; Recorder, 1994-; Bencher, 1995; Queen's Counsel; Chief Executive, Football Association Premier League, 1997-99; Deputy High Court Judge. Memberships: Chartered Institute of Arbitrators; Member, Dispute Resolution Panel for Winter Olympics, Salt Lake City, 2002. Address: 5 Hamilton Terrace, London NW8 9RE, England.

LEBED Aleksey Ivanovich, b. 14 April 1955, Novocherkassk, Rostov Region, Russia. m. Yelizaveta Vladimirovna, 1 son, 1 daughter. Education: Ryazan Higher School of Airborne Troops; Military Academy; Saint Petersburg State University. Appointments: Served in the Soviet Army, 1979-88; Served in Afghanistan, 1982, Pskov, 1991; Military operations, various parts of USSR, 1980-92; Regimental Commander, 300th Paratroop Regiment, 1995-96; State Duma Deputy, 1996-; Head of Government, Republic of Khakassia, 1996-2001; Member, Council of Russian Federation, 1996-; Member, Congress of Russian Communities. Honours: Order of the Red Star; Medal for Courage; Honoris Causa Degree, Khakassia Kalanov State University; Peter the Great Prize, 2001. Address: House of Government, Prospect Lenina 67, R-665019 Abakan, Russia. E-mail: pressa@khakasnet.ru

LEBEDEV Vladimir Alekseyevich, b. 8 May 1940, Novosibirsk, Russia. Physicist-Researcher; Teacher-Psychologist. m. Valentine Aleksandrovna Rechling, 1965, 2 sons. Education: State Institute of Railway, Novosibirsk, 1957-59; MSc, State University of Novosibirsk, 1965; Patent Lawyer Diploma, Central Institute of Study of Patents, Moscow, 1971; History/Philosophy Educator Diploma, Regional University of History & Philosophy, Novosibirsk, 1979. Appointments: Probationer, State Institute of Railway, Novosibirsk, 1957-59; Probationer, Russian Academy of Sciences, Siberian Branch, Institute of Thermophysics, Novosibirsk, 1963-65; Probationer Researcher, 1965-67, Engineer, 1967-78, Research Assistant, 1978-2003, Senior Research Assistant, 2003-, one of the Organisers and First Ideologist, Teacher-Psychologist, The School for the Sick Child, The Centre for the Social Habilitation by Out-of-Medicine Methods, Novosibirsk, 1991-2004; Physics, Music, Art and History Lecturer, Home of Scientists, TV, Child Organisation, etc, Novosibirsk, 1970-; Consultant, Thermophysic in Russia, USA, Ukraine, Uzbekistan, 1986-; Consultant, Seminars on methods of child psychology correction, TV, various medical and educational organisations, Russia, 1992-2006; Teacher-Psychologist, Lecturer, State University, Novosibirsk, 2004-; Special Educator, Pedagogue, Clinic of Research Institute of Physiology, Medical Academy of Russia, 2005-. Publications: About 200 scientific books, papers, articles, and reports on gravitation, thermophysics and psychology. Honours: Medal, The Science in Siberia authors' competition, 1979; Honorary title and Medal, Honoured Veteran of Russian Academy of Science, 1997; Soros Foundation Grant, 1997; Grand Gold Medal of Siberian Market, Education XXI age, 1998; Honorary Insignia, Silver Sigma, 2007; 2000 Outstanding Intellectuals of the 21st Century medal, 2008; Man of the Year, Russia, 2008; Distinguished Service Order & Cross, 2011; Listed in international biographical dictionaries. Memberships: Emperor Peter I Academy of Sciences and Arts; Russian Physical Society International. Address: Institute of Thermophysics, Russian Academy of Sciences, Siberian Branch, Lavrent'ev Ave, 1, Novosibirsk, 630090, Russia. E-mail: leb_vlad@mail.ru

LECHEVALIER Hubert Arthur, b. 12 May 1926, Tours, France. Microbiologist. m. Mary Jean Pfeil, 2 sons. Education: Licence ès Sciences, 1947, MS, 1948, Laval University, Quebec, Canada; PhD, Rutgers University, New Brunswick, New Jersey, 1951. Appointments: Assistant Professor, Microbiology, College of Agriculture then Waksman Institute, Rutgers University, 1951-56; Associate Professor, Microbiology, 1956-66, Professor, Microbiology, 1966-91, Associate Director, 1980-88, Waksman Institute of Microbiology, Rutgers University; Professor Emeritus, Rutgers, The State University of New Jersey, 1991-. Publications: Author or co-author of over 140 scientific papers, co-author or co-editor of 10 books including: A Guide to the Actinomycetes and Their Antibiotics, 1953; Antibiotics of Actinomycetes, 1962; Three Centuries of Microbiology, 1965, reprint 1974; The Microbes, 1971; 4 US patents. Honours include: Honorary Member, the Société Française de Microbiologie 1972-; Charles Thom Award (jointly with Mary P Lechevalier), 1982; DSc, Laval University, 1983; Bergey Trust Award for contributions to bacterial taxonomy, 1989; New Jersey Inventors Hall of Fame, 1990; Honorary member of the Society for Actinomycetes, Japan, 1997. Address: 131 Goddard-Nisbet Rd, Morrisville, VT 05661-8041, USA. E-mail: mheques@comcast.net

LEDERER Helen, b. 24 September 1954, United Kingdom. Comedienne; Actress. m. Chris Browne, 1 daughter. Education: Hatfield Polytechnic (now Hatfield University); Central School of Speech and Drama. Career: Early work at the Comedy Store and similar venues; Theatre includes: Bunny in House of Blue Leaves, Lilian Bayliss Theatre; Rita in Educating Rita; Doreen in Having a Ball, Comedy Theatre; Vagina Monologues, West End, 2002; Full House and The Hairless Diva, Palace Theatre, Watford; Television appearances include: The Young Ones; Girls on Top; The French and Sauders Show; Flossie in Happy Families, BBC2; 4 series of Naked Video, writing and performing own material between sketches, BBC2; Wogan; Hysteria; The New Statesman; Bottom; 5 series of Absolutely Fabulous,

BBC; One Foot in the Grave, BBC; Heartbeat; Occasional presenter, The Heaven and Earth Show, BBC; Radio includes: In One Ear; Life With Lederer (writer and performer, 2 series), Radio 4; Short story readings, Radio3 and Radio 4; Comic Cuts, Radio 5; Regular writer and performer of comic monologues for Woman's Hour, Radio 4; Presenter of Home Truths (as stand in for the late John Peel), BBC Radio 4; Films: Solitaire for Two; Dance to Your Daddy; Speak Like a Child; Clark. Publications: Coping with Lederer; Single Minding; Contributing author: Girl's Night In/Big Night Out; Author of numerous articles for newspapers and magazines. Memberships: Groucho; Soho House; Princes Trust Ambassador; Fawcett Society. Address: Jessica Carney Associates, 4th Floor, 23 Golden Square, London, W1F 9JP, England. E-mail: info@jcarneyassociates.co.uk

LEE Ang, b. 1954, Pingtung, Taiwan (naturalized US citizen). Film maker. m. Jane Lin, 1983, 2 sons. Education: National Taiwan College of Arts, 1975; BFA Degree in Theatre/Theater Direction, University of Illinois Urbana-Champaign; Masters Degree in Film Production, New York University. Career: Films include: Joe's Bed-Stuy Barbershop: We Cut Heads, 1983; Pushing Hands, 1992; The Wedding Banquet, 1993; Eat Drink Man Woman, 1994; Sense and Sensibility, 1995; The Ice Storm, 1997; The Civil War drama Ride With The Devil, 1999; Crouching Tiger, Hidden Dragon, 2000; Hire, The Chosen (short film), 2001; Hulk, 2003; Brokeback Mountain, 2005; Lust, Caution, 2007; Taking Woodstock, 2009; Life of Pi, 2012. Honours: Berlin International Film Festival, 1993, 1996; Golden Globe Award, 1996, 2001, 2006; British Academy Film Awards, 1996, 2001, 2006; Directors Guild of America Award, 2001, 2006; Academy Awards, 2005; Venice Film Festival, 2005, 2007; Critics' Choice Award, 2006.

LEE Bruce, b. 3 December 1930, New York City, USA. Editor; Writer. m. (1) Nancy Faye Hatch, 1958, divorced 1980, 1 son, 1 daughter, (2) Janetta M Macpherson, 1981. Education: BA, Rollins College, Winter Park, Florida, 1954; MFA, Fordham University, 1959. Appointments: Reporter, Adirondack Daily Enterprise, Saranac Lake, New York, 1952-53; New York Daily News, 1954; Associate Editor, Newsweek, New York City, 1954-61; Washington Correspondent, Reader's Digest, Washington, 1961-65; Associate Editor, New York City, 1965-66; Senior Editor, 1966-72; Editor-in-chief, Reader's Digest Press, New York City, 1972-78; Senior Editor, McGraw Hill General Book Division, New York City, 1978-82; William Morrow & Co, New York City, 1982-90; Author, 1990-. Publications: The Boy's Life of John F Kennedy, 1962; Marching Orders: The Untold Story of World War II, 1995; Co-author, Pearl Harbor: Final Judgement, 1992; Editor, Bearing The Cross: The Biography of Martin Luther King Jr, 1997. Honours: Award for advancing the knowledge of cryptographic history, National Security Agency, 1995; Pulitzer Prize, 1997. Memberships: Royal Northern and Clyde Yacht Club; Royal Yacht Squadron; New York Yacht Club; Seawanhaka Corinthian Yacht Club; Life Member, Naval Order of the USA. Address: 115 E 67th St, New York, NY 10065, USA.

LEE Chan, b. 12 June 1963, Seoul, Korea. Professor; Food Scientist. Education: Bachelor, 1987, Master, 1989, Agriculture, Korea University; PhD, Engineering, Technical University of Berlin, Germany, 1992. Appointments: Postdoctoral Research Assistant, Sandoz Co Ltd, Switzerland, 1992-93; Postdoctoral Research Assistant, University of North Carolina at Chapel Hill, USA, 1993; Postdoctoral Research Assistant, POSTECH, Korea, 1994-95; Professor, Department of Food Science & Technology, Chung-Ang University, South Korea, 1995-; Editorial board, Mycotoxin Research, Germany, 2012-14. Publications: A new cytotoxic cyclic pentadepsipeptide, neo-N-methylsansalvamide produced by Fusarium Solani KCCM90040, isolated from potato, Food Chemistry, 2011. Honours: DAAD Scholarship, German Academic Exchange Program, 1989-92; Academic Award, Korean Society of Food Hygiene and Safety, 2010. Memberships: Korean Society of Food Science and Technology; Mycotoxin Research, Germany. Address: Department of Food Science & Technology, Chung-Ang University, South Korea. E-mail: chanlee@cau.ac.kr Website: www.chanlee.kr

LEE Cheng-Chi, b. 6 December 1975, Taiwan. Teacher. Education: PhD, 2006. Appointments: Assistant Professor, Fu Jen Catholic University, 2010-. Address: 510 Jhongjheng Road, Sinjhuang City, Taipei County 24205, Taiwan, ROC. E-mail: cclee@mail.fju.edu.tw

LEE Christopher Frank Carandini, b. 27 May 1922, London, England. Actor; Author; Singer. m. Birgit Kroenke, 1961, 1 daughter. Education: Wellington College. Appointments: Served RAF, 1941-46; Mentioned in Despatches, 1944; Film industry, 1947-; Appeared in over 200 motion pictures; Films include: Moulin Rouge, 1953; The Curse of Frankenstein, 1956; Tale of Two Cities, 1957; Dracula, 1958; The Hound of the Baskervilles, The Mummy, 1959; Rasputin the Mad Monk, 1965; The Wicker Man, The Three Musketeers, The Private Life of Sherlock Holmes, 1973; The Four Musketeers, The Man with the Golden Gun, 1975; To the Devil a Daughter, 1976; Airport 77, Return from Witch Mountain, How the West Was Won, Caravans, The Silent Flute, 1977; The Passage, 1941, Bear Island, 1978; The Serial, 1979; The Salamander, 1980; An Eye for an Eye; Goliath Awaits; Charles and Diana; The Return of Captain Invincible; The Howling Z; Behind the Mask; Roadstrip; Shaka Zulu; Mio my Mio; The Girl. Un Metier du Seigneur; Casanova; The Disputation (TV); Murder Story; Round the World in 80 Days (TV); Return of the Musketeers; Outlaws; Gremlins II, 1989; Sherlock Holmes; Rainbow Thief; L'Avaro; Wahre Wunder, 1990; Young Indy, Cybereden, 1991; Death Train, 1992; The Funny Man, Police Academy, Mission in Moscow, 1993; A Feast at Midnight, 1994; The Stupids, Moses, 1995; Jinnah, 1997; Sleepy Hollow, 1999; The Lord of the Rings, 2000, 2001, 2003; Star Wars Episode II, 2002 and Episode III, Charlie and the Chocolate Factory, The Corpse Bride, Greyfriars Bobby, 2005; The Heavy, 2008. Publications: Christopher Lee's Treasury of Terror, Christopher Lee's Archive of Evil, 1975; Christopher Lee's The Great Villains, 1977; Tall Dark and Gruesome, 1977, 2002; Christopher Lee: Lord of Misrule, 2004. Honours: Officier, Ordre des Arts et des Lettres, 1973; Commander, St John of Jerusalem, 1997; Commander of the Order of the British Empire, 2001. Address: c/o Diamond Management, 31 Percy Street, London, W1T 2DD, England.

LEE Dae-Woong, b. 20 January 1964, Jeonju, Jeonbuk, Korea. Professor. m. Jaeran, 1 son, 1 daughter. Education: BS, 1990, MS, 1992, PhD, 1996, Department of Mathematics, Chonbuk National University; Postdoctoral, Department of Mathematics, Wayne State University, Detroit, USA, 2000-01. Appointments: TA, 1991-94, Instructor, 1994-2000, Assistant Professor, 2003-07, Associate Professor, 2007-, Chonbuk National University; Instructor, Jeonju Technical College, 1996-2000; Instructor, Howon University, 1995-2000; Postdoctoral Fellow, Ministry of Education, Republic of Korea, 1997; Full Time Instructor, Myungsin University, 2000-03; Research Professor, Dartmouth College, 2008-09. Publications: Numerous articles in professional journals.

Address: Department of Mathematics, Chonbuk National University, Jeonju, Jeonbuk 561-756,Republic of Korea. E-mail: dwlee@jbnu.ac.kr

LEE Deog Ro, b. 6 January 1956, Uiseong-gun, Gyeongsangbuk-do. Professor. Education: Bachelor's degree, Business Administration, Youngnam University, 1982; Master's degree, 1984, PhD, 1989, Business Administration, Yonsei University. Appointments: Lecturer, Yonsei University, Chungang University, Korea University, 1984-2010; Professor, Seowon University, 1991-; Editorial Member, Journal of Human Resources Management, Review of Business History, 1997-; Head, Division of Management, Seowon University, 1999-2009; Visiting Scholar, Fuqua School of Business, Duke University, 2003-04; Vice President, Korean Association of Personnel Administration, 2004-; Public Interest Commissioner, Chungbuk Regional Labor Relations Commission, 2005-; Member, Local Administration Revolution, Ministry of Public Administration & Security, 2005-; Member, Inner Assessment Committee, Rural Development Administration, 2006-; Accreditation Member, Korean Academy of Business Education Accreditation, 2007-; Assessment Member, Multifunctional Administrative City Construction Agency, 2007-; Non-Standing Director, Korean Deposit Insurance Corporation, 2009-; Editor-in-chief, Korean Journal of Human Resources Development, 2010-. Publications: Numerous articles in professional journals. Honours: President Award, Yonsei University, 2004; President Awards, Seowon University, 2006, 2007, 2008, 2009; Research Director Award, Korea Research Institute of Bioscience & Biotechnology, 2006; Minister's Award, Ministry of Labor, 2007; Writing Award, Korean Academy of Personnel and Organization, 2009; Best Paper Award, Korean Academy of Human Resource Management, 2009. Memberships: Chungbuk Regional Labor Relations Commission; Chungbuk Economy Forum; Chungbuk Labor, Management, Government Forum, and others. Address: 241 Musimseoro, Heungdeok-gu, Cheongju, Chungcheongbuk-do, 361-742, Korea. E-mail: drlee@seowon.ac.kr

LEE Hong-Koo, b. 9 May 1934, Seoul, Korea. Politician; Political Scientist. m. 1 son, 2 daughters. Education: Seoul National University; Emory University; Yale University; PhD. Appointments: Assistant Professor, Emory University, USA, 1963-64; Assistant Professor, Case Western Reserve University, 1964-67; Assistant Professor, Associate Professor, Professor of Political Science,1968-88, Director, Institute of Social Sciences, 1979-82, Seoul National University, Korea; Fellow, Woodrow Wilson International Center for Scholars, Smithsonian Institution, Washington DC, 1973-74; Fellow, Harvard Law School, 1974-75; Minister of National Unification, Korea, 1988-90; Special Assistant to President, 1990-91; Ambassador to UK, 1991-93; Commission on Global Governance, 1991-95; Senior Vice-Chairman, Advisory Council for Unification, Chairman, Seoul 21st Century Committee, The World Cup 2002 Bidding Committee, 1993-94; Deputy Prime Minister, Minister of National Unification, 1994; Prime Minister, 1994-95; Chairman, New Korea Party, 1996; Ambassador to USA, 1998-. Publications: An Introduction to Political Science; One Hundred Years of Marxism; Modernization. Address: Embassy of the Republic of South Korea, 2450 Massachusetts Avenue NW, Washington, DC 20008, USA. E-mail:korinfo@koreaemb.org

LEE Hung, b. 21 November 1954, Taiwan. Professor. m. Colleen McCann, 1 son, 1 daughter. Education: BSc, honours, Biochemistry, University of British Columbia, 1977; PhD, Biochemistry, McGill University, 1982. Appointments: Research Associate, Division of Biological Sciences, National Research Council, Canada, 1983-86; Assistant Professor, Department of Environmental Biology, 1986-91, Adjunct Professor, School of Engineering, 1992-, Associate Professor, Department of Environmental Biology, 1991-99, University of Guelph; Visiting Professor, Biotechnology Laboratory, University of British Columbia, 1992-93; Affiliated Network Investigator, Protein Engineering Network Center of Excellence, 1998-2005; Professor, School of Environmental Sciences, University of Guelph, 1999-; Regional Associate Editor for the journal, Environmental Toxicology, 2000-; Network Investigator, Canadian Water Network Centre of Excellence, 2001-; Visiting Professor, Department of Wood Science, University of British Columbia, 2005-2006; Editorial Board Member of national and international journals; Co-Scientific Director, NSERC Bioconversion Network, 2008-. Publications: 162 original research papers, 28 original review papers, 16 refereed book chapters, 1 patent, 212 conference abstracts, 12 non-refereed technical reports, 4 disclosures. Honours include: Canadian MRC Studentship, McGill University, 1978-82; Research Excellence Citation, Imperial Oil Limited, 1990; President's Distinguished Professor Award, University of Guelph, 2002-04; Listed in national and international biographical dictionaries. Membership: American Society for Microbiology; Society for Industrial Microbiology. Address: School of Environmental Sciences, University of Guelph, Guelph, Ontario N1G 2W1, Canada.

LEE Jae-Man, b. 6 August 1930, Korea. Professor Emeritus. m. Eun-Hong Kim, 1 son, 1 daughter. Education: BS, 1956, MA, 1957, Jeon-Buk University; PhD, Tsukuba University, Japan, 1995. Appointments: Shin-Heung High School, Jeon-Ju, 1952-66; Korean Armed Forces, 1953-55; Professor, Kun-San National Junior Teachers College, 1966-78; Professor, Kun-San National Woman's College, 1978-79; Professor, 1979-95, Emeritus Professor, 1996, Kun-San National University; Professor, Ewha Woman's University, Seoul, 1979-80; Professor, Nagoya University, Japan, 1982; Professor, Tsukuba University, 1988-89; Seminar Speaker, Congress of International Commission for Optics, 1996. Publications: Author: Junior Science Education, 1968; Natural Science, 1970; University Physical Experiments, 1989. Honours: Education Merit Prize, Ministry of Education, Seoul, 1991; Kuhkmin-Huhnjang Dong-BaekJang, Merit Prize, Seoul, 1995. Memberships: Society of Korean Physics. Address: 185 Kosa-Dong, Jeon-Ju, Jeon-Buk, 560-802, Republic of Korea.

LEE John Arthur, b. 12 September 1937, Roodepoort, South Africa. Medical Doctor; Consultant in Public Health. m. Valerie Jill Jenkin. Education: MB BCh, University of the Witwatersrand, South Africa, 1960; DPH, London School of Hygiene and Tropical Medicine, England, 1966; MD, University of the Witwatersrand, 1973. Appointments: Epidemiologist, Public Health Laboratory Service, London, 1967-74; Member of Scientific Staff, Medical Research Council and Department of Health Epidemiology and Medical Care Unit, Northwick Park Hospital, London, 1974-76; Consultant in Public Health, Kingston and Esher Health Authority, Kingston-upon-Thames, London, 1976-82; Consultant in Public Health, Herefordshire Health Authority, Hereford, 1983-91. Publications: Numerous articles in professional journals including: Ischaemic Heart Disease and the Autonomic Nervous System, 1980; The Role of Animal Feeding Stuffs in the Causation of Human Salmonellosis in the United Kingdom, 1982; The Role of the Sympathetic Nervous System in Ischaemic Heart Disease: A review of epidemiological features and risk factors, integration with clinical and experimental evidence and hypothesis, 1983; Coronary Heart Disease Prevention, 1988. Honours: Elected Fellow, Faculty of Public Health, Royal College of Physicians, UK, 2006. Memberships: Life Fellow, Royal Society of Medicine; Member, British Medical Association; Member, Society for Social Medicine. Address: 1 Lugg View Close, Hereford, HR1 1JF, England. E-mail: drjohnalee@btinternet.com

LEE Jong Hun, b. 18 January 1974, Kyung Ju, South Korea. Scientist. m. You Mi Jang, 1 son, 1 daughter. Education: BS, 1996, MS, 1998, Electronics Engineering, PhD, Electrical and Electronics and Computer Science, 2002, SungKyunKwan University. Appointments: Senior Research Engineer, R&D Research Center, Division of Telecommunication Network, Samsung Electronics Company, 2002-05; Senior Research Engineer, Robotics Research Division, DGIST Daegu Gyeongbuk Institute of Science and Technology, Korea, 2005-. Publications: 36 papers in domestic and international journals; More than 90 papers in international and domestic conferences; 51 patents filed; 39 patents pending. Honours: 6 Best Paper awards: 5th Conference on Optoelectronics and Optical Communication, 1995; 1st, 4th & 5th International Symposium on Embedded Technology, 2006, 2009 & 2010; 4th & 6th, Conference on National Defense Technology, 2008 & 2010. Memberships: IEEE; IEE; IEICE; SPIE; KSAEC; IEEK; IEMEK; KSS; KICS. E-mail: jhlee@dgist.ac.kr

LEE Jong-Hyouk, b. 3 November 1978. Engineer. m. Eun-Sun Hwang, 1 son. Education: Master, PhD, Sungkyunkwan University, Korea. Appointments: Postdoctoral Researcher, 2010, Expert Engineer, 2011-, INRIA. Publications: Numerous articles in professional journals and conferences. Honours: Best Paper Award, International Conference on Systems Networks Comm, 2008; Excellent Research Awards, Sungkyunkwan University, 2009, 2010. Memberships: IEEE. Address: IMARA Team, Bt 7, INRIA, Domaine de Voluceau Rocquencourt, 78153, France.

LEE Jongjoo, b. 15 May 1971, Gyeongsan, Republic of Korea. Electrical Engineer. m. Juyeun Woo, 2000, 1 son, 2 daughters. Education: BS, Kyungpook National University, Daegu, 1994; MS, 1997, PhD, 2001, Korea Advanced Institute of Science & Technology, Daejeon. Appointments: Commission Researcher, Korea Research Institute of Standard Science, Daejeon, 1998-2002; Senior Engineer, IPT team, Memory Division, Samsung Electronics, Hwasung, Republic of Korea, 2002-09; DDR3-DRAM Samsung Member, Physical Working Group, 2003-04; Next-Generation DRAM's Samsung Member, 2006-09; DRAM Design team, 2009-10; Principal Engineer, 2010-; Solution Development team, Memory Division, 2010-. Publications: Numerous patents and articles in professional journals. Honours: Grant for Junior Researcher, Korean Research Foundation, 2000-01; Best Paper Award, Samsung Semiconductor Network, 2005; Bronze Prize, Samsung HumanTech, 2002; Bronze Award, Global Samsung Best Paper Award, 2009; Listed in international biographical dictionaries. Memberships: IEEE. E-mail: jongjoo.lee@samsung.com

LEE Jung Hwan, b. 26 January 1971, Seoul, Korea. Physician. m. Kyoung Sook, 1 daughter. Education: MD, Seoul National University, 1997; PhD, Ulsan University, 2010. Appointments: Chief Physician, Department of Physical Medicine & Rehabilitation, Wooridul Spine Hospital, 2007-. Publications: Numerous articles in professional journals. Honours: President's Citation Award, Annual Assembly of American Academy of Physical Medicine & Rehabilitation. Memberships: Korean Medical Association; Korean Society of Paediatric Rehabilitation Medicine; Korea Society of Sports Medicine; American Board of Electrodiagnostic Medicine; Korean Academy of Physical & Rehabilitation Medicine. Address: 47-4 Wooridul Spine Hospital, Chungdam-Dong, Gangnam-Gu, Seoul 135-100, Korea. E-mail: j986802@hanmail.net

LEE Kang Guk, b. 27 May 1971, Taegu, South Korea. Professor. m. 2010, 1 daughter. Education: Doctor of Engineering, 2007. Appointments: Professor, Research Centre of Urban Affairs, Kyungil University, 2007-. Publications: 19 articles in professional journals. Memberships: Asian Institute of Urban Environment. Address: No 425 18/33 Buho-ri Hayang-up, Gyeongbuk, Korea. E-mail: ggyi@naver.com

LEE Lung-Sheng, b. 15 May 1954, Nantou, Taiwan. Professor. m. Chun-Chin Lai, 1 son, 1 daughter. Education: Bachelor in Industrial Education, National Taiwan Normal University, 1978; Master in Industrial Education, National Taiwan Normal University, 1980; PhD, Technology Education, Ohio State University, 1991. Appointments: Instructor, National Taipei Institute of Technology, 1982-84; Instructor, National Taiwan Normal University, 1984-86; Associate Professor, National Taiwan Normal University, 1986-93; Professor, National Taiwan Normal University, 1993-; Dept Chair, National Taiwan Normal University, 1995-2001; College Dean, National Taiwan Normal University, 2001-2004; Adviser, Ministry of Education, Taiwan, Republic of China, 1997-2000; President, National United University, 2005-; President, Association for Curriculum and Instruction, Tawian, 2006-10; President, Ohio State University Alumni Club of Taiwan, 2007-. Publications: Over 100 articles; Issues in Technology Education and Vocational Education. Honours: Leader to Watch, International Technology Education Association, 1996; Alumni Award of Excellence, Technology Education, Ohio State University, 1999; Prakken Professional Co-operation Award, ITEA, 2002. Memberships: ITEEA; Industrial Technology Education Association, Taiwan. Address: National United University, 1 Lienda, Miaoli 36003, Taiwan. E-mail: lslee@nuu.edu.tw Website: www.nuu.edu.tw/

LEE Martin Chu Ming, b. 8 June 1938, Hong Kong. Politician; Barrister. m. Amelia Lee, 1969, 1 son. Education: BA, University of Hong Kong. Appointments: Queen's Counsel; Justice of the Peace; Hong Kong Legislative Council, 1985-; Basic Law Drafting Committee, 1985-90; Hong Kong Law Reform Commission, 1985-91; Chairman, Hong Kong Consumer Council, 1988-91; Founder, 1989, Leader, 1990-, United Democrats of Hong Kong; Chairman, Democratic Party, 1994-2002; Goodman Fellow, University of Toronto, 2000. Publications: The Basic Law: some basic flaws, co-author, 1988. Honours: International Human Rights Award, American Bar Association, 1995; Prize for Freedom, Liberal International, 1996; Democracy Award, National Endowment for Democracy, USA, 1997; Honorary LLD, Holy Cross College, 1997; Honorary LLD, Amherst College, USA, 1997; Statesmanship Award, Claremont Institute, USA, 1998; Schuman Medal, European Parliament, 2000. Memberships: Chairman, Hong Kong Bar Association, 1980-83. Address: Democratic Party of Hong Kong, 4th Floor, Hanley House, 776-778 Nathan Road, Kowloon, Hong Kong Special Administrative Region, China. E-mail: oml@martinlee.org.hk Website: www.martinlee.org.hk

LEE Min Ha, b. 2 October 1971, Seoul, Korea. Scientist. Education: BS, Materials Science & Engineering, Ajou University, 1996; MS, 1998, PhD, 2004, Metallurgical Engineering, Yonsei University. Appointments: Postdoctoral

Associate, Ames Laboratory, USA, 2004-06; Research Scientist, IFW Dresden, Germany, 2006-08; Senior Researcher, 2008-10, Principal Researcher, 2010-, KITECH, Korea. Publications: 47 scientific papers; 20 international conference presentations; 6 international patents. Honours: Korea Materials & Components Industry Agency President Award, 2009; R&D 100 Awards, 2007. Memberships: TMS; Korea Powder Metallurgy Institute; Korea Institute of Materials. Address: 7-42 Songdon-Dong, Yeonsu-Gu, 406-840 Incheon, Korea. E-mail: mhlee1@kitech.re.kr

LEE Pin-Chan, b. 11 December 1979, Taiwan. Construction Engineer. Education: PhD, Department of Construction Engineering, National Taiwan University of Science and Technology. Appointments: Department of Civil Engineering and Hazard Mitigation Design, China University of Technology. Honours: Listed in international biographical dictionaries. Memberships: Fellow, ABI. Address: No 56, Sec 3, Xinglong Road, Wunshan District, Taipei City 116, Taiwan (ROC). E-mail: pinchan.lee@gmail.com

LEE Sangsik, b. 18 April 1968, Sancheong-gun, Korea. Professor. m. Yunjeong Kim. Education: Bachelor, 1994, Master, 1996, PhD, 2000, Sungkyunkwan University. Appointments: Senior Researcher, LG Cable Co Ltd, R&D Centre, 1993-2000; Director, Monotech Co Ltd, Korea, 2001-04; Research Professor, Sankyunkwan University, Korea, 2004-10; Professor, Kwandong University, Korea, 2011-. Honours: Greating Award, Korea Institute of Information Electronic Communication Technology, 2009. Memberships: General Director, KIIECT. Address: 1202-ho, 101-dong, 796 KCCA, Dang-dong, 435-010, Gumpo-shi, Kyungki-do, Korea. E-mail: lsskyj@dreamwiz.com

LEE Shin-Da, b. 30 March 1970, Taichung, Taiwan. Cardiopulmonary Research Scientist. m. Shu-Ping. Education: BS, Physical Therapy, Kaohsiung Medical College, Taiwan, 1993; MS, 1999, PhD, 2001, State University of New York at Buffalo, USA. Appointments: Department Chair, Professor, Department of Physical Therapy, Graduate Institute of Rehabilitation Science, China Medical University, Taiwan. Publications: Over 86 journal articles. Honours: American Thoracic Society Grand Travel Award; Top Ten Outstanding Young Persons in Taiwan, 2010. Memberships: American Association of Cardiovascular and Pulmonary Rehabilitation; American College of Sports Medicine; American Heart Association. Address: 91 Hsueh-Shih Road, Taichung 40202, Taiwan. E-mail: shinda@mail.cmu.edu.tw Website: http://mail.cmu.edu.tw/~shinda/

LEE Spike (Shelton Jackson Lee), b. 20 March 1957, Atlanta, Georgia, USA. Film Maker; Actor. m. Tonya Lewis, 1993, 1 daughter. Education: Morehouse College; Atlanta University; New York University; Institute of Film and TV. Appointments: Wrote Scripts for Black College; The Talented Tenth; Last Hustle in Brooklyn; Produced, Wrote, Directed, Joe's Bed-Stuy Barbershop; We Cut Heads; Has directed music videos; TV Commercials; Films include: She's Gotta Have It, 1985; School Daze, 1988; Do the Right Thing, 1989; Love Supreme, Mo' Better Blues, 1990; Jungle Fever, 1991; Malcolm X, 1992; Crooklyn; Girl 6; Clockers, Tales from the Hood, 1995; Girl 6; Get on the Bus; 4 Little Girls; He Got Game, 1998; Summer of Sam, 1999; Bamboozled, The Original Kings of Comedy, 2000; Lisa Picard is Famous, A Huey P Newton Story, 2001; The 25th Hour, 2003; CSA: Confederate States of America, She Hate Me, 2004; Jesus Children of America, 2005; Inside Man, 2006; Lovers & Haters, 2007; TV includes: Sucker Free City, 2004; Miracle's Boys, 2005; When the Levees Broke: A Requiem in Four Acts, Shark, 2006; M.O.N.Y, 2007. Publications: Spike Lee's Gotta Have It: Inside Guerilla Filmmaking, 1987; Uplift the Race, 1988; The Trials and Tribulations of the Making of Malcolm X, 1992; Girl 6; Get on the Bus, 1996. Honours: Cannes Film Festival Prize for Best New Film, 1985; Cannes Film Festival, Best New Director, 1986; LA Film Critics' Association Awards, 1986, 1989; Chicago Film Festival Critics' Awards, 1990, 1992; Golden Satellite, Best Documentary, 1997; Dr h c, New York University, 1998; Inducted into National Association for the Advancement of Colored People Hall of Fame, 2003; Commander des Arts et des Lettres, 2003. Address: Forty Acres and a Mule Filmworks, 124 De Kalb Avenue, Brooklyn, New York, NY 11217, USA.

LEE Taewook, b. 28 May 1973, Ulsan City, Republic of Korea. Electronics Engineer; Educator. m. JungAe Moon, 2 sons. Education: BS, 1998, MS, 2000, PhD, 2004, University of Ulsan. Appointments: Part-time Lecturer, Ulsan Campus, Korea Polytechnic VII, 2000-03; Ulsan College, 2000-04; Sorabol College, 2002-03; Chief Research Engineer, LG Display, 2004-. Publications: Numerous articles in professional journals; Patents and patents pending in field of flat panel displays. Honours: Outstanding Poster Paper Award, IDW08; Best Presentation Award, Summer Conference, IEEK, 2003. Address: 404-602 Hanyang Sujain Apt, Garam-ro 70, Paju-si, Gyeonggi-do 413-190, Republic of Korea. E-mail: twlee00@lgdisplay.com

LEE Won Gu, b. 13 June 1973, Pusan, Republic of Korea. Research Scientist. m. Hyo Sill Yang. Education: BS, Control and Mechanical Engineering, 1996, MS, Mechanical and Precision Engineering, 2000, Pusan National University; PhD, Mechanical and Aerospace Engineering, Seoul National University, 2007. Appointments: Reserved Officer's Training Corps, Pusan National University, 1994-96; Intelligent Operation Officer, Republic of Korea Army, 1996-97; Full time Researcher, Research Institute of Mechanical Technology, Pusan, 2000-04; Senior Researcher, AUTOPOWER Co, 2001-02; Lecturer, Youngsan University, 2001-03; Researcher, NanoEnTek Inc, 2002-07; Teaching Assistant, College of Engineering, 2005-06, Graduate School, 2004-05, Research Assistant, School of Mechanical & Aerospace Engineering, 2003-07, Seoul National University; Researcher, Korea BIO-IT Foundry Centre, 2004-05; Senior Researcher, Advanced Micro Engineering Design Co, 2007; Research Associate, Harvard-MIT Health Sciences & Technology, Brigham & Women's Hospital, Harvard Medical School, 2007-. Publications: Numerous articles in professional journals. Honours: Full Scholarship, Pusan National University, 1992; Best Officer Award, 1998; New Young Researcher Award, KOSEF, 2001; Best Presentation Paper Award, Asan Medical Center, 2004; Next-Generation Scholar, KRF, 2007-08; Graduate Student Best Paper Award, Seoul National University, 2008. Memberships: Korea Nano Technology Research Association; Korean Society of Gene Therapy; Korean Physical Society; Korean Society of Mechanical Engineers; Korean Society for Precision Engineers; Institute of Control, Automation and System Engineers, Korea. Address: Department of Mechanical Engineering, College of Engineering, Kyung Hee University (Global Campus), 1 Seochon, Giheung, Yongin, Gyeonggi 446-701, Republic of Korea. E-mail: termylee@khu.ac.kr Website: http://ONE.khu.ac.kr

LEE Woo-Sun, b. 23 January 1952, Gwangju, Korea. Professor. m. Tom-Sook Ryoo, 2 sons. Education: PhD, Electrical Engineering, Jungang University, Seoul.

Appointments: Doctoral Fellow, Purdue University, West Lafayette, USA; Visiting Professor, University of California, Santa Barbara, USA; Professor, Chosun University, Gwangju, Korea. Publications: Research in Electrical and Electronics and their Processing; Photo Cells; Patents pending for chemical mechanical planarization technology. Honours: Award, Electric and Electronic Material Engineers; Academic Award, Korean Institute of Electric and Electronic Material Engineers. Memberships: American Vaccum Society; Korean Institute of Electrical Engineers; IEEE. Address: 375 Seosuk Dong, Donggu, Gwangju 501-759, Republic of Korea.

LEE Yeo Back, b. 6 September 1968, Republic of Korea. Theme Park Designer. m. Jin Won Jeong, 2 sons. Education: Bachelor, Landscape Architecture, Seoul National University, 1996; Master, Business Administration, Helsinki School of Business Administration and Economics, 1999. Appointments: Staff, Korea Racing Association, 1996-99; President, Jasper 123 Corp venture company, 1999-2001; Chairman, Artfamilia Inc Ltd, theme park design, 2002-. Publications: Numerous articles in professional journals, 2 patents for new materials for theme park construction. Honours: Seoul Economy Award, Innovation Company, 2004; Herold Economy Award, Competitive Company, 2004. Memberships: International Association of Amusement Parks and Attractions. Address: Suite 511, STX V-tower, 371-37 Ga-San dong, Keumcheun-gu, Seoul 153-803, Korea. E-mail: laspace7@hanmail.net

LEE Yoonjae, Researcher. Education: PhD, University of London. Appointments: Scientist/Engineer, Rutherford Appleton Laboratory, England.

LEE Young Woo, b. 9 March 1937, Ulsan City, Korea. Neuroscientist; Neurosurgeon; Biomedical Engineer. m. Kyung Ja Kim, 1 son, 1 daughter. Education: MD, School of Medicine, 1962, MSc, Medicine, 1965, PhD, 1973, Graduate School, Pusan National University, Pusan, Korea; Rotating Internship, 1962-63, Residency, General Surgery, 1963-65, Residency, Neurosurgery, 1965-67, Pusan National University Hospital, Pusan, Korea; Fellowship, Neurosurgery, Long Island College Hospital, Brooklyn, New York, USA, 1980-81. Appointments: Army Service, 1967-70; Instructor, Assistant Professor, Associate Professor, Professor, 1971-2002, Chairman, Department of Neurosurgery, 1975-2002, Pusan National University School of Medicine and Pusan National University Hospital, Pusan, Korea; Honorary Professor, Pusan National University, 2002-; Honorary Superintendent, Dong-Rae Bong Seng Hospital and Chairman of Department of Neurosurgery in Bong Seng Hospital, 2002-; Research Fellow, Department of Neurology, University of Alabama in Birmingham School of Medicine and Medical Center, USA, 1974-75; Fellowship, Department of Neurosurgery, Montreal Neurological Institute, McGill University, Montreal, Canada, 1998-99. Publications: Over 150 articles in scientific journals as author and co-author include most recently: Clinical Analysis Spondylolisthesis Treated with Pediatric Screw Instrumentation, 1998; Clinical Analysis of Thoracolumbar and Lumbar Spine Fracture Treated with Instrumentation; 1999; Prognosis of Surgically Treated Acute Subdural Hematoma, 2003; Chemical Hypoxia-Induced Cell Death in Human Glioma Cells: Role of Reactive Oxygen Species and Lipid Peroxidation; Role of Oxidative Stress in Amyloid-β Peptide-induced Death of Human Glioma Cells; H_2O_2-Induced Cell Death in Human Glioma Cells: Role of Lipid Peroxidation and PARP Activiation, 2001; Underlying Mechanism of Cisplatin-induced Apoptosis in PC-12 Cells, 1998; Modulation of Immune Responses by Capsaicin in Mice, 2000; Books in collaboration: Neurosurgery, 1989, 1996, 2001; The Great Medical Encyclopedia, 1991. Honours include: Military Medal in Vietnam War, President of the Republic of Korea, 1968; 2 Medals, Vietnam Government, 1969; Pfizer's Medical Company Prize, 1997; Madison Biomedical Prize, Korean Society of Biomedical Engineering, 1999; Educational Prizes, 2001, Korean Teacher Association, Pusan Teacher Association; Research Prize, Korean Neurosurgical Society, 2001. Numerous Memberships include: Korean Medical Association; Korean Neurosurgical Society; International College of Surgeons; Korean Society of Medical and Biological Engineering; New York Academy of Sciences; Korean Brain Tumour Study Group; Korean Society for Brain and Neural Science (Neuroscience); Korean Veterans Society.

LEE Yuan Tseh, b. 29 November 1936, Hsinchu, Taiwan. Professor of Chemistry. m. Bernice W Lee, 1963, 2 sons, 1 daughter. Education: National Taiwan University; National Tsinghua University, Taiwan; University of California, Berkeley; PhD. Appointments: Assistant Professor, 1968-71, Associate Professor, 1971-72, Professor of Chemistry, 1973-74, James Franck Institute and Department of Chemistry, University of Chicago, Illinois, USA; Professor of Chemistry, 1974-94, Professor Emeritus, 1994-, University of California, Berkeley; Head, Academia Sinica, 1994. Publications: Articles in professional journals. Honours: Sloan Fellow, 1969; Guggenheim Fellow, 1976; Miller Professorship, 1981; E O Lawrence Award, US Department of Environment, 1981; Co-recipient, Nobel Prize for Chemistry, 1986; Many other awards and prizes. Memberships: American Academy of Arts and Sciences. Address: Department of Chemistry, University of California, Berkeley, CA 94720, USA.

LEECH Geoffrey Neil, b. 16 January 1936, Gloucester, England. Emeritus Professor of English Linguistics; Writer. m. Frances Anne Berman, 29 July 1961, 1 son, 1 daughter. Education: BA, English Language and Literature, 1959, MA, 1963, PhD, 1968, University College London; DLitt, Lancaster University, 2002. Appointments: Assistant Lecturer, 1962-64, Lecturer, 1965-69, University College London; Reader, 1969-74, Professor of Linguistics and Modern English, 1974-2001, Emeritus professor of English Linguistics, 2002-, University of Lancaster; Visiting Professor, Brown University, 1972, Kobe University, 1984, Kyoto University, 1991, Meikai University, Japan, 1999, 2000. Publications include most recently: Longman Student Grammar of Spoken and Written English (with D Biber and S Conrad), 2002; Longman Student Grammar of Spoken and Written English Workbook (with S Conrad and D Biber), 2002; A Glossary of English Grammar, 2006; English – One Tongue, Many Voices (with J Svartvik), 2006; Language in Literature, 2008; Change in Contemporary English (with M Hundt, Ch Mair and N Smith), 2009. Contributions to: A Review of English Literature; Lingua; New Society; Linguistics; Dutch Quarterly Review of Anglo-American Letters; Times Literary Supplement; Prose Studies; The Rising Generation; Transactions of the Philological Society; Language Learning; International Journal of Corpus Linguistics; English Language and Linguistics. Honours: FilDr, University of Lund, 1987; British Academy, fellow, 1987; Hon DLitt, University of Wolverhampton, 2002; Honorary Fellowship, University of Lancaster, 2009; Listed in numerous Who's Who and biographical publications. Membership: Academia Europea; Member, Det Norske Videnskaps-Akademi, 1993. Address: Department of Linguistics and English Language, Lancaster University, Lancaster, LA1 4YL, England.

LEES Andrew John, b. 27 September 1947, Liverpool, England. Professor of Neurology. m. Juana Luisa Pulin Perez Lopez, 1 son, 1 daughter. Education: Royal London Hospital Medical College, University of London; Post Graduate Training, L'Hopital Salpetriere, Paris, University College London Hospitals, National Hospital for Neurology and Neurosurgery. Appointments: Consultant Neurologist, National Hospital for Neurology and Neurosurgery; Professor of Neurology, Institute of Neurology; Director, Reta Lila Weston Institute of Neurological Science; Appeal Steward to the British Boxing Board of Control. Publications: Ray of Hope, authorised biography of Ray Kennedy; Tic and Related Disorders; 820 articles in peer reviewed medical journals. Honours: Charles Smith Lecturer, Jerusalem, 1999; Cotzias Lecturer 2000, Spanish Neurological Association. Memberships: Member, Royal Society of Medicine; Fellow, Royal College of Physicians; President, of the Movement Disorders Society; Former Editor-in-Chief, Movement Disorders. Address: The Reta Lila Weston Institute for Neurological Studies, The Windeyer Building, 46 Cleveland Street, London, W1T 3AA, England. E-mail: a.lees@ion.ucl.ac.uk

LEGG Sir Thomas Stuart, b. 13 August 1935, London, England. Lawyer; Retired Civil Servant. m. 2 daughters, (3) Margaret Wakelin-Saint. Education: Horace-Mann Lincoln School, New York; Frensham Heights School, Surrey; MA, LLM, St John's College, Cambridge; 2nd Lieutenant, Royal Marines, 1953-55; Called to the Bar, Inner Temple, 1960 (Bencher, 1984). Appointments: Barrister in private practice, 1960-62; Served Lord Chancellor's Department (now Ministry of Justice), 1962, Permanent Secretary and Clerk of the Crown in Chancery, 1989-98, variety of posts connected with administration of justice and law reform, 1962-89, Chairman, Civil Service Benevolent Society, 1993-98; Consultant, Clifford Chance, 1998-2010; Conducted Sierra Leone Arms Investigation, 1998; Visitor, Brunel University, 2001-06; Chairman, London Library, 2004-09; Chairman, Hammersmith Hospitals NHS Trust, 2000-07; Director, Imperial College Healthcare NHS Trust, 2007-; Member, Audit Commission, 2005-11; External Member, House of Commons Audit Committee, 2000-09; Conducted ACA Review of MPs' Expenses, 2009-10. Honours: Companion of the Bath, 1985; Queen's Counsel, 1990; Knight Commander of the Bath, 1993; Hon LLD, Brunel University, 2006; Honorary Fellow, Royal College of Physicians, 2010. Memberships: Garrick Club. Address: The Blue House, Back Lane, Hampstead, London NW3 1EW, England. E-mail: tomlegg@talktalk.net

LEGGE-BOURKE Victoria Lindsay, b. 12 February 1950, Witchford, Cambridgeshire, England. Business Executive. Education: Benenden and St Hilda's College, Oxford. Appointments: Social Attaché, British Embassy, Washington, USA, 1971-73; Director, Junior Tourism LTD, 1974-81; Lady-in-Waiting, HRH The Princess Royal, 1974-86; Extra Lady-in-Waiting, HRH The Princess Royal, 1986-; Special Assistant, 1983-89, Head of Protocol, 1991-94, American Embassy, London; Council of the American Museum in Britain, 1995-; Executive Director, 1995-98, Executive Director of Cultural and Social Affairs, 1999-, Goldman Sachs International; Governor of the English Speaking Union, 1996-99; Director, Lehman Brothers, 1998-99. Honours: LVO, 1986; Meritorious Honor Award, US State Department, 1994. Membership: The Pilgrims. Address: 72 Albany Mansions, Albert Bridge Road, London SW11 4PQ, England. E-mail: victoria.legge-bourke@gs.com

LEGGIO Massimo, b. 7 August 1975, Rome, Italy. Cardiologist. 1 daughter. Education: BS, Medicine-Surgery, 1999, MS, Cardiology, 2003, La Sapienza University, Rome. Appointments: MD, Cardiovascular Department, San Filippo Neri Hospital, Rome. Publications: Reviewer for international peer-reviewed indexed journals. Honours: Reviewer, European Heart Journals, 2006-; Reviewer, international peer-reviewed indexed journals; Listed in various international biographical dictionaries. Address: San Filippo Neri Hospital (SI), Via Della Lucchina 14, Rome, 00135, Italy.

LEGH Davis Piers Carlis (The Hon), b. 21 November 1951, Compton, England. Chartered Surveyor. m. Jane Wynter Bee, 2 sons, 2 daughters. Education: Eton, Royal Agricultural College, Cirencester. Appointments: Senior Partner, John German, 1994-99; Senior Partner, Germans, 1999-2000; Chairman, Fisher, German Chartered Surveyors, 2000-. Honour: FRICS. Memberships: Chairman, Taxation Committee, CLA. 1993-97; Chairman, East Midlands Region Country Land and Business Association (CLA), 2002-. Address: Cubley Lodge, Ashbourne, Derbyshire DE6 2FB, England.

LEGKOSTUP Plamen, b. 4 April 1959, Veliko Turnovo, Bulgaria. m. Magdalena, 2 sons, 1 daughter. Education: MA, Fine Arts, 1983, Associate Professor, 1997, Professor, 2007, Methodology of Teaching Pictorial Art, Dr Habil, Doctor of Education Studies, 2006, St Cyril and St Methodius University, Veliko Turnovo; Specialisation, State Institute of Ornamental and Applied Art, Lvov, Ukraine, 1989-90. Appointments: Chairman of Trade Union of the Faculty of Education, 1991-95, Member of Academic Council, 1991-, Vice-Dean in Charge of Academic Affairs, 1995-99, Dean, 1999, 2003-07, Faculty of Education, Head, Department of Historical and Practical Theology, Faculty of Orthodox Theology, 2001-03, Rector, 2007-, St Cyril and St Methodius University. Honours: Gold Medal and Diploma, East-West Euro Intellect, 1998; Veliko Turnovo Municipality Award, 2005; Great Victory Decree Mdal, Presidium of the Academy of Safety, Defense and Legal Order, Moscow, 2006; Order of Lomonosov, Decree of the National Committee of Public Awrads, Moscow, 2007. Memberships:Young Artist's Studio, Sofia; Veliko Turnovo Artists' Group; Bulgarian Artists' Union. Address: St Cyril and St Methodius University, 2 T Turnovski Str, 5003 Veliko Turnovo, Bulgaria. E-mail: plamen_legkostup@abu.bg

LEGRIS Manuel Christopher, b. 19 October 1964, Paris, France. Ballet Dancer. Education: Paris Opera School of Dancing. Career: Member, Corps de Ballet, 1980, Danseur Etoile, 1986-, Paris Opéra; Major roles, Paris Opéra, include Arepo, Béjart, 1986, In the Middle Somewhat Elevated, Forsythe, 1987, Magnificat, Neumeier, 1987, Rules of the Game, Twyla Tharp, 1989, La Belle au Bois Dormant, Nureyev, 1989, Manon, MacMillan, 1990, Dances at the Gathering, Robbins, 1992; In Hamburg created Cinderella Story and Spring and Fall, Neumeier; Appearances, Bolshoi Ballet, Moscow, La Scala, Milan, Royal Ballet, London, New York City Ballet, Tokyo Ballet, Stuttgart Ballet, elsewhere. Honours: Gold Medal, Osaka Competition, 1984; Prix du Cercle Corpeaux, 1986; Nijinsky Prize, 1988; Benois de la Danse Prize, 1998; Chevalier des Arts et des Lettres, 1998; Nijinsky Award, 2000. Address: Théâtre National de l'Opéra de Paris, 8 rue Scribe, 75009 Paris, France.

LEHNERT Bo Peter, b. 30 March 1926, Stockholm, Sweden. Professor Emeritus. m. Ann-Marie, 1 stepdaughter. Education: MSc, 1950, Tekn Dr, 1955, Royal Institute of Technology, Stockholm. Appointments: Research Assistant, 1950-55,

Assistant Professor, 1955-63, Associate Professor, 1963-68, Royal Institute of Technology; Full Professor, Swedish Atomic Research Council and Swedish Natural Research Council, 1968-90; Full Professor, Royal Institute of Technology, 1990-; Emeritus, 1993-. Publications: Books: Electromagnetic Phenomena in Cosmical Physics, 1958; Dynamics of Charged Particles, 1964, Russian edition 1967; Extended Electromagnetic Theory (with S Roy), 1998; A Revised Electromagnetic Theory with Fundamental Applications, 2008; About 220 original publications. Honours: Edlund Prize of Royal Swedish Academy of Sciences, 1962; Celsius Gold Medal of Royal Society of Sciences, Uppsala, 1974; Medal of his Majesty the King of Sweden, 1996. Memberships: Royal Swedish Academy of Sciences; Royal Swedish Academy of Engineering Sciences; Fellow, Institute of Mathematics and its Applications, London; Fellow, Alpha Foundation, Institute of Advanced Study, Budapest; The Electromagnetics Academy, Cambridge, USA. Address: Alfvén Laboratory, Royal Institute of Technology, SE-10044 Stockholm, Sweden. E-mail: bol@ee.kth.se

LEIBOVITZ Annie, b. 2 October 1949, Connecticut, USA. Photographer. Education: San Francisco Art Institute. Career: Photographed rock'n'roll stars and other celebrities for Rolling Stone magazine, 1970s; Chief Photographer, Vanity Fair, 1983-; Proprietor, Annie Leibovitz Studio, New York; Celebrity portraits include studies of John Lennon, Mick Jagger, Bette Midler, Louis Armstrong, Ella Fitzgerald, Jessye Norman, Mikhail Baryshnikov, Arnold Schwarzenegger, Tom Wolfe; Retrospective exhibition, Smithsonian National Portrait Gallery, Washington DC, 1991. Publications: Photographs 1970-90, 1992; Women, with Susan Sontag, 2000. Honours: Innovation in Photography Award, American Society of Magazine Photographers, 1987. Address: Annie Leibovitz Studio, 55 Vandam Street, New York, NY 10013, USA.

LEIGH Jennifer Jason, b. 5 February 1962, Los Angeles, California, USA. Actress. Career: Appeared in Walt Disney TV movie The Young Runaways, age 15; Other TV films include The Killing of Randy Webster, 1981, The Best Little Girl in the World, 1981; Film appearances including Eyes of a Stranger, 1981, Fast Times at Ridgemont High, 1982, Grandview, USA, 1984, Flesh and Blood, 1985, The Hitcher, The Men's Club, 1986, Heart of Midnight, The Big Picture, 1989, Miami Blues, Last Exit to Brooklyn, 1990, Crooked Hearts, Backdraft, 1991, Rush, Single White Female, 1992, Short Cuts, 1993, The Hudsucker Proxy, Mrs Parker and the Vicious Circle, 1994, Georgia, 1995, Kansas City, 1996, Washington Square, 1997, eXistenZ, 1999; The King is Alive, 2000; The Anniversary Party, 2001; Crossed Over, Road to Perdition, 2002; In The Cut, 2003; The Machinist, Childstar, 2004; The Jacket, Palindromes, Easter Sunday, Rag Tale, 2005; Margot at the Wedding, Lymelife, 2007; Stage appearances including Sunshine, Off-Broadway, 1989. Address: c/o Elaine Rich, 2400 Whitman Place, Los Angeles, CA 90211, USA.

LEIGH Mike, b. 20 February 1943, Salford, Lancashire, England. Dramatist; Film and Theatre Director. m. Alison Steadman, 1973, divorced 2001, 2 sons. Education: Royal Academy of Dramatic Arts; Camberwell School of Arts and Crafts; Central School of Art and Design; London Film School. Publications: Plays: The Box Play, 1965; My Parents Have Gone to Carlisle, The Last Crusade of the Five Little Nuns, 1966; Nenaa, 1967; Individual Fruit Pies, Down Here and Up There, Big Basil, 1968; Epilogue, Glum Victoria and the Lad with Specs, 1969; Bleak Moments, 1970; A Rancid Pong, 1971; Wholesome Glory, The Jaws of Death, Dick Whittington and His Cat, 1973; Babies Grow Old, The Silent Majority, 1974; Abigail's Party, 1977, also TV play; Ecstasy, 1979; Goose-Pimples, 1981; Smelling a Rat, 1988; Greek Tragedy, 1989; It's a Great Big Shame!, 1993; Two Thousand Years, 2005. TV films: A Mug's Game, Hard Labour, 1973; The Permissive Society, The Bath of the 2001 F A Cup, Final Goalie, Old Chums, Probation, A Light Snack, Afternoon, 1975; Nuts in May, Knock for Knock, 1976; The Kiss of Death, 1977; Who's Who, 1978; Grown Ups, 1980; Home Sweet Home, 1981; Meantime, 1983; Four Days in July, 1984; Feature films: Bleak Moments, 1971; The Short and Curlies, 1987; High Hopes, 1988; Life is Sweet, 1990; Naked, 1993; Secrets and Lies, 1996; Career Girls, 1997; Topsy Turvy, 1999; All or Nothing, 2002; Vera Drake, 2004. Radio Play: Too Much of a Good Thing, 1979. Honours: Golden Leopard, Locarno Film Festival, 1972; Golden Hugo, Chicago Film Festival, 1972; George Devine Award, 1973; Evening Standard Award, 1981; Drama Critics Choice, London, 1981; Critics Prize, Venice Film Festival, 1988; Honorary MA, Salford University, 1991, Northampton, 2000; OBE, 1993; Best Director Award, Cannes Film Festival, 1993; Palme D'Or, Cannes Film Festival, 1996; Honorary DLitt, Stafford, 2000, Essex, 2002; Best British Independent Film, 2005; Best Director, British Independent Film Awards, 2005; Best Film, Evening Standard British Film Awards, 2005; David Lean Award for Achievement in Direction; BAFTA Awards, 2005. Address: The Peters, Fraser and Dunlop Group Ltd, 503/4 The Chambers, Chelsea Harbour, London SW10 0XF, England.

LEITH Prudence Margaret, b. 18 February 1940, Cape Town, South Africa. Caterer; Author. m. Rayne Kruger, 1 son, 1 daughter. Education: Haywards Heath, Sussex; St Mary's, Johannesburg; Cape Town University; Sorbonne, Paris; Cordon Bleu School, London. Appointments: Founder and Managing Director: Leith's Ltd (formerly Leith's Good Food Ltd), 1960-65; Leith's Restaurant, 1969-95; Leith's School of Food and Wine, 1975-95; Board Member: Whitbread plc, 1995-2005; Triven VCT, 1999-2003; Halifax plc, 1995-99; Safeway plc (formerly Argyll Group plc), 1989-96; Leeds Permanent Building Society, 1992-95; British Railways Board, 1980-85; British Transport Hotels, 1977-83; Cookery Correspondent: Daily Mail, 1969-73; Sunday Express, 1976-80; The Guardian, 1980-85; The Mirror, 1995-98; Non-Executive Director: Woolworths, 2001-; Omega International plc, 2004-; Consultant, Compass Group plc, 2001-. Publications include: 12 cookbooks including Leith's Cookery Bible with Caroline Waldegrave; 3 novels in print; TV series include: Best of British, BBC2; Take 6 Cooks, Channel 4; Tricks of the Trade, BBC1. Honours: Corning Award Food Journalist of the Year, 1979; Glenfiddich Trade Journalist of the Year, 1983; Honorary Fellow, Hotel, Catering and Institutional Management Association, 1986; Order of the British Empire, 1989; Veuve Clicquot Business Woman of the Year, 1990; Honorary Fellow, Salford University, 1992; Honorary Fellow, The City and Guilds of London Institute, 1992-97; Visiting Professor, University of North London, 1993; Freedom of the City of London, 1994; Honorary DSc, The University of Manchester, 1996; Honorary Doctor of Business Administration, Greenwich University, 1996; Honorary Doctor of Letters, Queen Margaret College, Edinburgh, 1997; Honorary Doctorate, The Open University, 1997; Master of the University of North London, 1997; Deputy Lieutenant of Greater London, 1998-; Doctor of the University, Oxford Brookes, 2000; Honorary Doctorate, City University, 2005. Memberships: Trustee/Director, Training for Life, 1999; Commissioner, Lord Griffiths Debt Commission, 2004-05; Chairman: The British Food Trust, 1997-; 3E's Enterprises Ltd, 1998; Kings College for Technology and the Arts, 2000-; Ashridge Management College, 2002-; 3C's Limited, 2002-. Address: Castleton Glebe, Moreton in Marsh, Gloucester, GL56 0SZ, England.

LELE Chitra, Management Consultant; Author; Motivational Speaker; Poet. Education: MS, Software Engineering; CompTIA Project +; Several certifications in project management. Appointments: Management consultant, motivational speaker, poet and multi-time record setting author. Publications: Books: The 6 Spheres of Life: Unlocking the Door to Success and Happiness; Organizational Democracy; More than 500 poems in various journals around the world. Honours: Peace Maker Certificate; Peace Writers Organization; Creative Giant Awards, Holi, 2009; Several appreciation letters from important personalities; The Editors Choice Awards, Enchanting Verses, Paris; Top Poem Awards, Asian American Poetry Journal; Letter of Commendation, Hon President of India; Editor's Choice Award for Creative Writing, HOLI, 2009; Highest Number of Commendation Letter for The 6 Spheres of Life; First Indian to receive Peace Maker Award, Peace Writer's Organization, USA; Versatile Writer with maximum number of books in 18 months; Distinguished Leadership Award, Home of Letters, India. Memberships: Writers Club International; Indian Writers Organization; United Minds for Peace Society; Eternity Journal; World Peace Organization, USA; several other literary, peace and professional bodies. Website: www.chitralele.com

LEMANN Thomas Berthelot, b. 3 January 1926, New Orleans, USA. Lawyer. m. (1) Barbara M London, 1951, deceased 1999, 1 son, 1 daughter, (2) Sheila Bosworth Bell, 2000. Education: AB summa cum laude, Harvard University, 1949; LLB, 1952; MCL, Tulane University, 1953; Bar, Louisiana, 1953. Appointments: Served with AUS, 1944-46; Associate, 1953-58, Partner, 1958-98, Munroe & Lemann, New Orleans; Trustee, 1956-71, President, 1967-70, Metairie Park Country Day School; New Orleans Philharmonic Symphony Society, 1956-78; Flint-Goodridge Hospital, 1960-70; Chairman, Mayor's Cultural Resources Committee, 1970-75; President, Louisiana Civil Service League, 1974-76; Board of Directors, Member of Visiting Committee of art museums, Harvard University, 1974-80; President, Arts Council, Greater New Orleans, 1975-80; New Orleans Museum of Art, 1986-92; Counsel, Liskow & Lewis, New Orleans, 1998-; Board of Directors, B Lemann & Bro, Mermentau Mineral and Land Co, Avrico Inc; Council Member, Secretary of Trust Advisory Committee, Louisiana State Law Institute; Board of Directors, Zemurray Foundation, Hever Foundation, Hawkins Foundation, Parkside Foundation, Azby Fund, Azby Art Fund, Greater New Orleans Foundation, 1996-2005; Arts Council, New Orleans, Musica da Camera. Publications: Numerous articles in professional journals. Memberships: ABA; Louisiana Bar Association; New Orleans Bar Association; Association Bar City New York; American Law Institute; Society Bartolus; New Orleans Country Club; Wyvern Club; Phi Beta Kappa.

LEMKE Dietrich, b. 31 January 1943, Stargard, Germany. University Professor. m. Wilma, 1 son, 2 daughters. Education: Staatsexamen, 1969; Dr phil, 1971; Assessor des Lehramts, 1971; Dipl paed, 1974; Habilitation, 1980. Appointments: Retired Professor of Education. Publications: Die Theologie Epikurs, 1973; Lernziel-orientierter Unterricht-revidiert, 1981; Many articles concerning teacher education and higher education; Two poetic works: Schüttelreime, 1992; Bruchsteinverse, 2010. Memberships: Deutscher Hochschulverband; Studienstiftung des Deutschen Volkes. Address: Vennkampweg 6, D-33659 Bielefeld, Germany. E-mail: dietrich.lemke@uni-bielefeld.de

LEMPER Ute, b. 4 July 1963, Munster, Germany. Singer; Dancer; Actress. Education: Max Reinhardt-Seminar, Vienna. Appointments: Leading Role, Viennese Production of Cats, 1983; Appeared in Peter Pan, Berlin, Cabaret, Düsseldorf and Paris; Chicago, 1997-99; Life's A Swindle tour, 1999; Punishing Kiss tour, 2000; Albums include: Ute Lemper Sings Kurt Weill, 1988; Vol 2, 1993; Threepenny Opera, 1988; Mahoganny Songspiel, 1989; Illusions, 1992; Espace Indécent, 1993; City of Strangers, 1995; Berlin Cabaret Songs, 1996; All that Jazz/The Best of Ute Lemper, 1998; Punishing Kiss, 2000; Film appearances include: L'Autrichienne, 1989; Moscou Parade, 1992; Coupable d'Innocence, 1993; Prêt à Porter, 1995; Bogus, 1996; Combat de Fauves, 1997; A River Made to Drown In, 1997; Appetite, 1998; Ute Lemper: Blood & Feathers, 2005. Honours: Moliere Award, 1987; Laurence Oliver Award; French Culture Prize, 1993. Address: c/o Oliver Gluzman, 40 rue de la Folie Regnault, 75011 Paris, France.

LENDL Ivan, b. 7 March 1960, Czechoslovakia (US citizen, 1992). Retired Professional Tennis Player. m. Samantha Frankel, 1989, 5 daughters. Appointments: Winner, Italian Junior Singles, 1978; French Junior Singles, 1978; Wimbledon Junior Singles, 1978; Spanish Open Singles, 1980, 1981; South American Open Singles, 1981; Canadian Open Singles, 1980, 1981; WCT Tournament of Champion Singles, 1982; WCT Masters Singles, 1982; WCT Finals Singles, 1982; Masters Champion, 1985. 1986; French Open Champion, 1984, 1986, 1987; US Open Champion, 1985, 1986, 1987; US Clay Court Champion, 1985; Italian Open Champion, 1986; Australian Open Champion, 1989, 1990; Finalist Wimbledon, 1986; Held, World No 1 Ranking for a Record 270 weeks; Named World Champion, 1985, 1986, 1990; Retired, 1994. Publication: Ivan Lendl's Power Tennis. Honours: Granted American Citizenship, 1992; ATP Player of the Year, 1985, 1986, 1987; Inducted, International Tennis Hall of Fame, 2001. Memberships: Laureus World Sports Academy. Address: c/o Laureus World Sports Academy, 15 Hill Street, London W1 5QT, England.

LENNARTSSON Olof Walter, b. 27 October 1943, Sweden. Physicist. m. Nancy Karllee, 1 son. Education: MEng, 1969, PhD, Plasma Physics, 1974, Royal Institute of Technology, Stockholm, Sweden. Appointments: NAS/NRC Research Associate, 1974-76; Docent, Royal Institute of Technology, Sweden, 1976-78; Staff Scientist, Lockheed Martin Missiles and Space, 1979-. Publications: Numerous articles in scientific journals and books. Memberships: American Geophysical Union; American Institute of Physics. Address: Lockheed Martin Space Systems Co, Advanced Technology Center, ADCS, B255, 3251 Hanover Street, Palo Alto, CA 94304, USA.

LENO Jay (James Douglas Muir Leno), b. 28 April 1950, New Rochelle, New York, USA. Comedian; TV host. m. Mavis Nicholson. Education: Emerson College, Boston, USA. Career: Standup comedian and comedy writer, 1970s; One of several guest hosts, 1986, Executive guest host, 1987-92, Host, 1992-, Tonight Show (NBC); Films include: American Hot Wax, 1978; Silver Bears, 1978; Americathon, 1979; What's Up; Hideous Sun Demon (voice), 1983; Collision Course, 1989; We're Back! A Dinosaur's Story (voice), 1993; The Flintstones, 1994; Providence (voice), 1999; The Fairly OddParents (voice), 2001-05; Robots (voice), 2005; Ice Age 2: The Meltdown (voice), 2006; The Jimmy Timmy Power Hour

3: The Jerkinators (voice), 2006; Payback, 2006; Christmas Is Here Again (narrator), 2007. Honours: Emmy Award, 1995. Address: The Tonight Show with Jay Leno, 3000 West Alameda Avenue, Burbank, CA 91523, USA. Website: www.nbc.com/The_Tonight_Show_with_Jay_Leno/index.shtml

LENTNER Csaba, b. 30 August 1962, Papa, Hungary. Vice Rector. m. Anita E Boros, 3 children. Education: BS, Economics, College of Finance and Accountancy, Zalaegerszeg, 1984; MSc, 1989, Doctorate, 1991, Economics, University of Economics, Budapest; Dr fin habil, West Hungarian University, Sopron, 2003; CPA, Hungarian Judicial Chamber, 1994; PhD, CSc, Economics, Hungarian Academy of Sciences, Budapest, 1995. Appointments: Analyst Economist, Hungarian National Bank, Budapest, 1990-91; Financing Section Head, Hungarian Foreign Trading Bank, Budapest, 1991-93; Director, Danube Bank Joint-Stock Co, Budapest, 1993-96; Board of Directors, Agricultural and Food Industrial Joint Stock Co, Fertod, 1994-98; President, Control Sub Commission, Budapest General Assembly, 1996-98; President, Control Commission, Funeral Joint-Stock Co, 1997-98; Associate Professor, Head of Department, West Hungarian University, Sopron, 1996-2007; Member, Hungarian Parliament, Budapest, 1998-2002; President, Hungarian-Slovanian Section, Interparliamentary Union, Brussels, 1998-2002; Vice-Dean, WHU for Faculty of Economics, 2003-05; Study of British monetary and fiscal policy, England, 2007-; Chairman, Advisory Board for Public Foundation of Gyor, 2007-; Professor, Head of Department, 2008-, Vice Rector, 2009-, Private Business College of Wekerle Alexander; Chief Editor, Econ and Soc Learned Journal, 2009-; Research Professor, Paris Sorbonne University, Paris, 2010; Chief in Editorial, Civic Review Learned Paper, 2011-. Publications: Books: Change-over and Financial Policy, 2005; Regulation of Money Markets in Hungary, 2006; Financial Policies Strategies at the Beginning of the XXI Century, The Health Care System as a New Competitive Factor in the Light of the Convergence Programme, 2007; Accounting and Audit in Hungary, 2009; Articles: The Competitiveness of Hungarian University-Based Knowledge Centres in European Economic and Higher Education Area, 2007. Honours: Honorary Professor, Kaposvar University, 2009. Memberships: Hungarian Academy of Sciences Committee for Future Research; Hungarian Accreditation Committee for Economics. Address: 51 Dozsa Gyorgy rkp, Gyor 9026, Hungary. E-mail: dr.lentnercsaba@gmail.com Website: www.lentnercsaba.hu

LEONARD Elmore (John, Jr), b. 11 October 1925, New Orleans, Louisiana, USA. Novelist. m. (1) Beverly Cline, 1949, 3 sons, 2 daughters, divorced 1977, (2) Joan Shepard, 1979, deceased 1993, (3) Christine Kent, 1993. Education: BA, University of Detroit, 1950. Publications: 33 novels including: Hombre, 1961; City Primeval, 1980; Split Images, 1981; Cat Chaser, 1982; Stick, 1983; Labrava, 1983; Glitz, 1985; Bandits, 1986; Touch, 1987; Freaky Deaky, 1988; Killshot, 1989; Get Shorty, 1990; Maximum Bob, 1991; Rum Punch, 1992; Pronto, 1993; Riding the Rap, 1995; Out of Sight, 1996; Pagan Babies, 2000; Fire in the Ole, 2001; When the Women Come Out to Dance, 2002; Tishomingo Blues, 2002; A Coyote's in the House, 2003; Mr Paradise, 2004; The Hot Kid, 2005; Up in Honey's Room, 2007. Other: The Tonto Woman and Other Western Stories, 1998; Screenplays: Cuba Libre, 1998; Be Cool, 1999. Honours: Edgar Allan Poe Award, 1984, and Grand Master Award, 1992, Mystery Writers of America; Michigan Foundation for the Arts Award for Literature, 1985; Honorary degrees in Letters from Florida Atlantic University, 1995, University of Detroit Mercy, 1997. Memberships: Writers Guild of America; PEN; Authors Guild; Western Writers of America; Mystery Writers of America. Address: c/o Michael Siegel, Brillstein-Grey Entertainment, 9150 Wilshire Boulevard, Beverly Hills, CA 90212, USA.

LEONARD Ray Charles (Sugar Ray), b. 17 May 1956, Wilmington, North Carolina, USA. Boxer. m. Juanita Wilkinson, 1980, divorced 1990, 2 sons. Appointments: Amateur Boxer, 1970-77; won 140 of 145 amateur fights; World amateur champion, 1974; US amateur athletic union champion, 1974; Pan-American Games Gold Medallist, 1975; Olympic Gold Medallist, 1976; Guaranteed Record Purse of $25,000 for first professional fight, 1977; Won, North American Welterweight title from Pete Ranzany, 1979; Won World Boxing Council Version of World Welterweight title from Wilfred Benitez, 1979; Retained title against Dave Green, 1980; Lost it to Roberto Duran, Montreal, 1980; Regained title from Duran, New Orleans, 1980; World Junior Middleweight title, World Boxing Association, 1981; Won, WBA World Welterweight title from Tommy Hearns to become undisputed World Champion, 1981; Drew rematch, 1989; 36 professional fights, 33 wins, lost 2, 1 draw; Retired from boxing, 1982; returned to ring, 1987; Won World Middleweight title; Lost to Terry Norris, 1991; retired, 1991, 1997; returned to ring, 1997; Lost International Boxing Council Middleweight title fight to Hector Camacho, 1992; Commentator, Home Box Office TV Co; Motivational speaker; Co-host, The Contender. Address: Suite 303, 4401 East West Highway, Bethesda, MD 20814, USA.

LEONG Lampo, b. 3 July 1961, Guangzhou, China. Artist; Educator. Education: BFA, Guangzhou Academy of Fine Arts, Guangdong, China, 1983; Graduate Studies, University of California at Berkeley, USA, 1988; MFA, California College of the Arts, San Francisco/Oakland, USA, 1988; PhD, Central Academy of Fine Arts, Beijing, China, 2009. Appointments: Assistant Professor, 2001-04, Associate Professor, 2005-11, Art Department Chair, 2007-09, Professor, 2011-, University of Missouri-Columbia, Missouri, USA. Publications: Works appear in more than 800 popular and professional journals; Over 61 solo and 320 group exhibitions worldwide. Honours: Over 47 awards including most recently: Mayoral Proclamation, Lampo Leong Day, 19 November 1999; Juror's Award, Ninth Great Plains National Art Exhibition, Fort Hays State University, USA, 2003; 3rd Place Award, Girardot National Juried Exhibition, Arts Council of Southeast Missouri, USA, 2003; Diploma of Excellence, Medial 1 Art Biennial, UK, 2005; Best of Show & Metro New York Award, 42nd Annual Juried Exhibition, USA, 2005; Faculty Award, University of Missouri-Columbia, 2007; Cover Award, New Art International, Woodstock, New York, 2009; Ten Best Entries, Exposicao Annual de Artes Visuais de Macau, Instituto Cultural, 2009, 2011; Gold Award, International Art Competition, Creative Quarterly: The Journal of Art & Design, No 18, New York, NY, USA. Address: Department of Art, A126 Fine Arts, University of Missouri-Columbia, MO 65211-6090, USA. E-mail: leongl@missouri.edu Website: http://www.lampoleong.com

LEONHARDT Joyce LaVon, b. 17 December 1927, Aurora, Nebraska, USA. Poet. Education: BS, Union College, Lincoln, 1952. Appointments: High School Teacher, 1952-76; Junior College Instructor, 1981-90. Contributions to: Several books of poems. Honours: Honourable Mention Certificates; Golden Poet; Silver Poet. Membership: World of Poetry. Address: 1824 Atwood Street, Longmont, CO 80501, USA.

LEONI Tea, b. 25 February 1966, New York, USA. Actress. m. David Duchovny, 1997, separated 2011, 1 son, 1 daughter. Career: Film appearances in Switch, 1991, A League of Their Own, 1992, Wyatt Earp, 1994, Bad Boys, 1995, Flirting with Disaster, 1996, Deep Impact, 1998, There's No Fish Food in Heaven, 1999; The Family Man, 2000; Jurassic Park III, 2001; Hollywood Ending, 2002; People I Know, 2002; House of D, 2004; Spanglish, 2004; Fun with Dick and Jane, 2005; You Kill Me, 2007; Ghost Town, 2008; The Smell of Success, 2009; Tower Heist, 2011; Appearances on TV: The Counterfeit Contessa, 1994; Flying Blind, 1995; Frasier, 1995; Naked Truth, 1995; The X-Files, 2000; Spring/Fall, 2011. Address: c/o ICM, 8942 Wilshire Boulevard, Beverly Hills, CA 90211, USA.

LEONIDOPOULOS Georgios, b. 19 April 1958, Kalamata, Messinia, Greece. Electrical, Computer and Electronics Engineer; Researcher; Educator. Education: Diploma, Electrical and Computer Engineering, Patra University, Greece, 1981; Postgraduate, Iowa State University, USA, 1982, Wayne State University, USA, 1983; MSc, 1984; PhD, Electronic and Electrical Engineering, Strathclyde University, Glasgow, Scotland, 1988. Appointments: Trainee Electrical Engineer, Public Electricity Co, Kalamata, Greece, 1979; Teaching Assistant, Strathclyde University, Scotland, 1984-87; Engineering Educator, Secondary School, Kalamata, Greece, 1991-94; Professor, Engineering, Institute of Technology, Kalamata, Greece, 1994-97; Professor, Engineering, Electrical Engineering Department, Institute of Technology, Lamia, Greece, 1997-. Publications include: A method for locating polymeric insulation failure of underground cables, 1998; On the convergence of three series, 1998; Root investigation of third degree algebraic equation, 1998; A mathematical method for solving a particular type of linear differential equations using complex symbolism, 2000; Trigonometric form of the quadratic algebraic equation solution, 2000; Greenhouse dimensions estimation and short time forecast of greenhouse temperature based on net heat losses through the polymeric cover, 2000; Greenhouse daily sun-radiation intensity variation, daily temperature variation and heat profits through the polymeric cover, 2000; Test methods of the four basic mathematical operations, 2001. Honours: Referee of research articles; Patentee in field; Examiner for Greek postgraduate scholarships; Selectee, Euratom research position, Joint European Torus, Culham, Oxford, England, 1990; Head of Electrical Engineering Department, 2000-03; Listee, expert evaluator of European Commission's scientific research and development programmes; European programme Socrates, Greece, 2000-; Grant, Schilizzi Foundation, 1987; Grant, Empeirikeion Foundation, 1994. Memberships: New York Academy of Sciences; IEEE; National Geographic Society; AMSE. Address: Kilkis 11, Kalamata 24100, Messinia, Greece. E-mail: georgiosleonidopoulos@yahoo.gr

LEONOV Aleksey Arkhipovich (Major-General), b. 30 May 1934, Listianka, Kamerovo Region, Russia. Cosmonaut. m. Svetlana Leonova, 2 daughters. Education: Chuguevsky Air Force School for Pilots; Zhukovsky Air Force Engineering Academy; Cosmonaut Training, 1960. Appointments: Pilot, 1956-59; Member, CPSU, 1957-91; Cosmonaut, space-ship Voskhod 2 flight, becoming first man to walk in space, 1965; Pilot Cosmonaut of USSR; Chairman, Council of Founders, Novosti Press Agency, 1969-90; Deputy Commander, Gagarin Cosmonauts Training Centre, 1971; Participant, Soyuz 19-Apollo joint flight, 1975; Major-General, 1975; Deputy Head, Centre of Cosmonaut Training, 1975-92; Director, Cheteck-Cosmos Co, 1992-; Vice-President, Investment Fund Alfa-Capital, 1997-; Vice President, Alpha Bank, 2000. Publications: Numerous books, papers and articles; Two Sides of the Moon (with David Scott), 2004. Honours: Honorary DrScEng; Hero of the Soviet Union, 1965, 1975; Hero of Bulgaria; Hero of Vietnam; Order of Lenin, twice; USSR State Prize, 1981. Memberships: Co-Chairman, Board, International Association of Cosmonauts. Address: Alfa-Capital, Academician Sakharov Prospect 12, 107078 Moscow, Russia.

LÉOTARD François Gérard Marie, b. 26 March 1942, Cannes, France. Politician. m. (1) France Reynier, 1976, (2) Isabelle Duret, 1992, 1 son, 1 daughter. Education: Faculté de Droit, Paris; Institut d'Etudes Politiques, Paris; Ecole Nationale d'Administration. Appointments: Secretary of Chancellery, Ministry of Foreign Affairs, 1968-71; Administration, Town Planning, 1973-76; Sous-Préfet, 1974-77; Mayor of Fréjus, 1977-92, 1993-97; Deputy to National Assembly, for Var, 1978-86, 1988-92, 1995-97, 1997-2002; Conseiller-Général, Var, 1980-88; Secretary, 1982-88, President, 1988-90, 1995-97, Honorary President, 1990-95, Général Parti Républicain; Vice-President, 1983-84, President, 1996-, Union pour la Démocratie Française; Minister of Culture and Communications, 1986-88; Member, Municipal Council, Fréjus, 1992; Minister of National Defence, 1993-95; With EU Special Envoy to Macedonia, 2001-; Inspector General de Finances pour l'extérieur, 2001-; Convicted of money-laundering and illegal party funding, received 10 month suspended sentence, 2004. Publications: A Mots Découverts, 1987; Culture: Les Chemins de Printemps, 1988; La Ville aimée: mes chemins de Fréjus, 1989; Pendant la Crise, le spectacle continue, 1989; Adresse au Président des Républiques françaises, 1991; Place de la République, 1992; Ma Liberté, 1995; Pour l'honneur, 1997; Je vous hais tous avec douceur, 2000; Paroles d'immortels, 2001. Honours: Chevalier, Order Nationale du Mérite. Address: Nouvelle UDF, 133 bis rue de l'Université, 75007 Paris, France.

LERKKANEN Marja-Kristiina, b. 13 October 1963, Oulu, Finland. Adjunct Professor. m. Jukka, 1 son, 1 daughter. Education: Teacher's Certificate, 1988, PhD, Education (with honours), 2004, University of Jyväskylä, Finland. Appointments: Associate Assistant of Didactics, Department of Teacher Education, 1987-92, Senior Lecturer, 1995-, Associate Professor, 1996-97, Researcher, Department of Psychology, 2000-01, Postdoctoral Researcher, 2005-08, Academic Research Fellow, Center of Excellence in Learning and Motivation, 2008-09, Senior Researcher, Department of Psychology, 2009-10, Adjunct Professor, 2010-, University of Jyväskylä. Publications: Over 120 articles in professional journals; 30 textbooks in Finnish. Honours: Excellent Pedagaogist Award, Student Union Pedago, 2004; Outstanding Publication Award, European Association for Research, Learning and Instruction, 2005; Reading/Literacy Research Fellowship Award, International Reading Association, 2007; Lagus Award, Finnish Academy of Sciences and Letters, 2008. Memberships: Society of Scientific Study of Reading; International Reading Association; European Educational Research Association; European Association of Research, Learning and Instruction. E-mail: marja-kristiina.lerkkanen@jyu.fi

LESIN Victor, b. 26 March 1950, Moscow, Russia. Divorced. 1 son, 1 daughter. Education: Faculty of Molecular and Chemical Physics, Dr Phy, Molecular Chemical Physics, 1977, Moscow Institute for Physics and Technology. Appointments: Junior Researcher, Institute of Chemical Physics, 1973-78; Senior Researcher, Institute for Biological Testing of Chemicals, 1978-85; Senior Researcher, Federal Institute of Oil & Gas, 1985-90; Leading Researcher, All Russian

Institute of Oil, 1990-2000; Leading Researcher, Oil & Gas Scientific Research Institute of RAS, 2000-. Publications: Magnetic field effects on reactions between organic radicals and triplet molecules; RYDUR effect theory and experiment, theory and experiment on magnetic field effects on oil industry processes, theory of non-Newtonian liquids. Honours: Silver medal for scientific achievements, USSR. Memberships: Oil & Gas Scientific Research Institute of RAS, Moscow; Institute of Crystallography of RAS, Moscow; Moscow Institute for Physics and Technology. Address: ul Zoi I Alex Kosmodemyanskikh, 4-140, 125171 Moscow, Russia.

LESSING Doris May, b. 22 October 1919, Kermanshah, Persia. Writer. m. (1) Frank Charles Wisdom, 1939, divorced 1943, 1 son, 1 daughter, (2) Gottfried Anton Nicholas Lessing, 1945, divorced 1949, 1 son. Publications: Novels: The Grass Is Singing 1950; Children of Violence, 1952; A Proper Marriage, 1954; Retreat to Innocence, 1956; The Golden Notebook, 1962; A Ripple from the Storm, 1965; The Four-Gated City, 1969; Briefing for a Descent into Hell, 1971; The Summer Before the Dark, 1973; The Memoirs of a Survivor, 1974; Canopus in Argos: Archives, 1979-1983; The Diary of a Good Neighbour, 1983; If the Old Could, 1984; The Diaries of Jane Somers, 1984; The Good Terrorist, 1985; The Fifth Child, 1988; Love, Again, 1996; Mara and Dann, 1999; Ben, in the World, 2000; The Old Age of El Magnifico, 2000; The Sweetest Dream, 2001; The Story of General Dann and Mara's Daughter, Griot and the Snow Dog, 2005; Short stories: Collected African Stories, 2 volumes, 1951, 1973; Five, 1953; The Habit of Loving, 1957; A Man and Two Women, 1963; African Stories, Winter in July, 1966; The Black Madonna, 1966; The Story of a Non-Marrying Man and Other Stories, 1972; A Sunrise on the Veld, 1975; A Mild Attack of Locusts, 1977; Collected Stories, 2 volumes, 1978; London Observed: Stories and Sketches, 1992; The Grandmothers, 2004; Non-fiction includes: Going Home, 1957, 1968; Particularly Cats, 1967; Particularly Cats and More Cats, 1989; African Laughter: Four Visits to Zimbabwe, 1992; Under My Skin, 1994; Walking in the Shade, 1997. Plays: Each to His Own Wilderness, 1958; Play with a Tiger, 1962; The Singing Door, 1973; Other publications include: Fourteen Poems, 1959; A Small Personal Voice, 1974; Doris Lessing Reader, 1990; Timebites, 2005. Honours: 5 Somerset Maugham Awards, Society of Authors, 1954-; Prix Médicis for French translation, Carnet d'or, 1976; Austrian State Prize for European Literature, 1981; Shakespeare Prize, Hamburg, 1982; W H Smith Literary Award, 1986; Palermo Prize and Premio Internazionale Mondello, 1987; Grinzane Cavour Award, Italy, 1989; Woman of the Year, Norway, 1995; Los Angeles Times Book Prize, 1995; James Tait Memorial Prize, 1995; Premi Internacional Catalunya, Spain, 1999; David Cohen Literary Prize, 2001; Principe de Asturias, Spain, 2001; PEN Award, 2002; Nobel Prize, 2007. Memberships: Associate Member, American Academy of Arts and Letters, 1974; National Institute of Arts and Letters, USA, 1974; Member, Institute for Cultural Research, 1974; President, Book Trust, 1996-. Address: c/o Jonathon Clowes Ltd, Iron Bridge House, Bridge Approach, London NW1 8BD, England.

LESTER Alexander Norman Charles Phillips, b. 11 May 1956, Walsall, England. Broadcaster. Education: Diploma, Communication Studies, Birmingham Polytechnic, 1978. Appointments: BBC Local and Independent Radio, 1977-86; BBC Radio 2, 1987-; Alex Lester Show, Radio 2, 1991-; Presenter, The Boat Show, BBC2 TV, Appearances on: Call My Bluff, BBC TV; Waterworld, Carlton TV; Lunchtime Live, Meridian TV; Announcer/Voice Over on numerous satellite and terrestrial TV and radio channels. Honours: Patron St Michael's Hospice, St Leonards-on-Sea; Ambassador, Hospital Radio Association. Memberships: Hastings Winkle Club; Equity. Address: c/o MPC Management, MPC House, 15-16 Maple Mews, Maida Vale, London NW6 6UZ, England. E-mail: alex.lester@bbc.co.uk

LESTER Richard, b. 19 January 1932, Philadelphia, USA. American Film Director. m. Deirdre V Smith, 1956, 1 son, 1 daughter. Education: William Penn Carter School; University of Pennsylvania. Appointments: TV Director, CBS, 1952-54; ITV, 1955-59; Composer, 1954-57; Film Director, 1959-; Films directed: The Running, Jumping and Standing Still Film, 1959; It's Trad ad, 1962; The Mouse on the Moon, 1963; A Hard Day's Night, 1963; The Knack, 1965; Help!, 1965; A Funny Thing Happened on the Way to the Forum, 1966; How I Won the War, 1967; Petulia, 1969; The Bed Sitting Room, 1969; The Three Musketeers, 1973; Juggernaut, 1974; The Four Musketeers, 1974; Royal Flash, 1975; Robin and Marian, 1976; The Ritz, 1976; Butch and Sundance: The Early Days, 1979; Cuba, 1979; Superman II, 1980; Superman III, 1983; Finders Keepers, 1984; The Return of the Musketeers, 1989; Get Back, 1990. Honours: Academy Award Nomination, 1960; Grand Prix, Cannes Film Festival, 1965; Best Director, Rio de Janeiro Festival, 1966; Gandhi Peace Prize, Berlin Festival, 1969; Best Director, Tehran Festival, 1974. Address: c/o Creative Artists Agency, 9830 Wilshire Boulevard, Beverley Hills, CA 90212, USA.

LESTER OF HERNE HILL, Baron of Herne Hill in the London Borough of Southwark, Anthony Paul Lester, b. 3 July 1936, London, England. Lawyer. m. Catherine Elizabeth Debora Wassey, 1971, 1 son, 1 daughter. Education: Trinity College, Cambridge; BA, Cantab; LLM, Harvard Law School; Called to Bar, Lincoln's Inn, 1963, Bencher, 1985. Appointments: Special Adviser to Home Secretary, 1974-76, to Northern Ireland Standing Advisory Commission on Human Rights, 1975-77; Appointed Queen's Counsel, 1975; Member, Board of Overseers, University of Pennsylvania Law School, Council of Justice, 1977-90; Member, Court of Governors, London School of Economics, 1980-94; Visiting Professor, University College London, 1983-; Board of Directors, Salzburg Seminar; President, Interights, 1996-2000; Recorder, South-Eastern Circuit, 1987-93; Co-Chair, Board, European Roma Rights Center; Governor, British Institute of Human Rights; Chair, Board of Governors, James Allen's Girls' School, 1987-93; Chair, Runnymede Trust, 1990-93; Governor, Westminster School, 1998-; Member, Advisory Committee, Centre for Public Law, University of Cambridge, 1999-; International Advisory Board, Open Society Institute, 2000-; Member, House of Lords Select Committee on European Communites Sub Committee E (Law and Insts), 2000-04, 2004-; Parliamentary Joint Human Rights Commission, 2001-04; Foreign Honorary Member, American Academy of Arts and Sciences, 2002; Foreign Member, American Philosophical Society, 2003; Adjunct Professor, Faculty of Law, University College, Cork, Ireland, 2005; Special Advisor on Constitutional Reform to the Secretary of State for Justice, 2007. Publications: Justice in the American South, 1964; Race and Law, co-author, 1972; Butterworth's Human Rights Cases, editor-in-chief; Halsbury's Laws of England Title Constitutional Law and Human Rights, 4th edition, consultant editor, contributor, 1996; Human Rights Law and Practice, co-editor, 1999; Articles on race relations, public affairs and international law. Honours: Honorary degrees and fellowships, Open University, University College, London University, Ulster University, South Bank

University; Liberty Human Rights Lawyer of the Year, 1997. Address: Blackstone Chambers, Blackstone House, Temple, London EC4Y 9BW, England.

LETSIE III, King of Lesotho, b. 17 July 1963, Morija, Lesotho. Monarch. m. Karabo Mots'oeneng, 1 son, 2 daughters. Education: National University of Lesotho; Universities of Bristol, Cambridge and London. Appointments: Principal Chief of Matsieng, 1989; Installed as King of Lesotho, 1990, abdicated, 1995, reinstated after father's death, 1996-; Patron, Prince Mohato Award. Address: Royal Palace, Masero, Lesotho.

LETTE Kathy, b. 11 November 1958, Sydney, Australia. Author. m. Geoffrey Robertson, 1990, 1 son, 1 daughter. Education: Sylvania High School, Sydney. Publications: Puberty Blues, 1980; HIT and MS, 1984; Girl's Night Out, 1988; The Llama Parlour, 1991; Foetal Attraction, 1993; Mad Cows, 1996; Altar Ego, 1998; Nip 'n Tuck, 2001; Dead Sexy, 2003; How to Kill Your Husband: And Other Handy Household Hints, 2006; Plays: Wet Dreams, 1985; Perfect Mismatch, 1985; Grommitts, 1988; I'm So Sorry For You, I Really Am, 1994; Radio: I'm So Happy For You, I Really Am; Essays: She Done Him Wrong, 1995; The Constant Sinner in Introduction to Mae West, 1995. Address: c/o Ed Victor, 6 Bayley Street, London, WC1B 3HB, England.

LETTERMAN David, b. 12 April 1947, Indianapolis, USA. Broadcaster. m. (1) Michelle Cook, 1969, divorced 1977; (2) Regina Lasko, 2009, 1 son . Education: Ball State University. Appointments: Radio and TV Announcer, Indianapolis; Performer, The Comedy Store, Los Angeles, 1975-; TV Appearances include: Rock Concert, Gong Show; Frequent guest host, The Twilight Show; Host, David Letterman Show, 1980; Late Night with David Letterman, 1982; The Late Show with David Letterman, CBS, 1993-; TV Scriptwriting includes, Bob Hope Special; Good Times; Paul Lynde Comedy Hour; John Denver Special. Publications: David Letterman's Book of Top Ten Lists, 1996. Honours: Recipient, Two Daytime Emmy Awards, Five Primetime Emmy Awards. Address: Late Show with David Letterman, Ed Sullivan Theater, 1697 Broadway, New York, NY 10019, USA.

LETTS Quentin Richard Stephen, b. 6 February 1963, Cirencester, Gloucestershire, England. Journalist. m. Lois Rathbone, 1 son, 2 daughters. Education: Trinity College, Dublin; Jesus College, Cambridge. Appointments: Daily Telegraph, 1988-95, 1997-2000; New York Bureau Chief, The Times, 1995-97; Parliamentary Sketchwriter, Daily Mail, 2000-. Publications: 50 People Who Buggered Up Britain; Bog-Standard Britain. Honours: British Press Award, Critic of the Year, 2010. Membership: The Savile Club. Address: Scrubs' Bottom, Bisley, Gloucestershire GL6 7BU, England.

LEUNG Ka Cheong, b. 4 October 1972, Hong Kong. Research Assistant Professor. Education: B Eng, Computer Science, HKUST, 1994; MSc, Electrical Engineering, Computer Networks, 1997; PhD, Computer Engineering, 2000, USC. Appointments: Senior Research Engineer, Nokia Research Center, Irving, 2001-02; Assistant Professor, Terre Tech University, 2002-05; Visiting Assistant Professor, 2005-09, Research Assistant Professor, 2009-, The University of Hong Kong. Publications: Around 38 international conference and journal articles; 1 US patent. Memberships: IEEE.

LEUNG Mei-Yung, Surveyor; Educator. Education: BSc, Quantity Surveying, University of Wolverhampton, England, 1994; Degree, Religious Science, Pontifical Urban University, Rome, 1996; PhD, University of Hong Kong, 2001. Appointments: Quantity Surveyor, Widnell QS Consultant Firm, Hong Kong, 1987-92; HA, Brechin QS Consultant Firm, Hong Kong, 1994-96; Lecturer, Assistant Professor, City University of Hong Kong, 1999-; Consultant, Learning Skills and Counselling, 2004; Facilitator, Ivan Ho Architects Ltd, Hong Kong, 2004; Ove Arup & Partners HK Ltd, Hong Kong, 2004; Highways Department, Hong Kong Special Administration Region, Hong Kong, 2004; Halcrow China Ltd, 2005; Tourism Commission, Hong Kong Special Administration Region, 2005; Consultant, Team Member, Planning Department, Hong Kong Special Administration Region, Hong Kong, 2005-06; with Kirk Associates LLC, NC, 2006; Massasell-Metcalf & Eddy Joint venture, 2006-08; Shai On Building Contractors Ltd, 2007; Region Water Supplies Department, Hong Kong Special Administration, 2007-09; Hong Kong Special Administration Housing Authority, 2007-08; Region Drainage Services Department, Hong Kong Special Administration, 2008; Archtectural Services Department and Shui On Building Construction Ltd, 2007; VM Modules I & II Training Workshops, 2009; Member, Editorial Board, AECOM, 2009; Caritas, 2009; Hong Kong Housing Authority, 2007-12. Publications: Numerous articles in professional journals. Honours: Barrie Tankel Partnership award, 1994; Education Prize, University of Wolverhampton, 1993, 1994; Tony Toy Memorial award, 2005; Thomas D Snodgrass Value Teaching award, 2005; Academic Best Paper award, Miles Value Foundation, 2008; Teaching Excellence award, 2008-09; Various research grants. Memberships: Hong Kong Institute of Value Management; SAVE International Value Society; Royal Institution of Chartered Surveyors; Hong Kong Institute of Surveyors; Australian Institute of Building; Chartered Institute of Building; Hong Kong Institute of Construction Managers. Address: City University of Hong Kong, Department of Building and Construction, Kowloon, Hong Kong. E-mail: bcmei@cityu.edu.hk

LEUNG Thomas Kim-Ping, b. 28 July 1955, Hong Kong. Associate Professor. m. May Mei-Lin Leung, 1 son. Education: BA, University of Saskatchewan, Canada; MComm, University of New South Wales, Australia; PhD, University of Western Sydney, Australia. Appointments: Various executive positions in multi-national companies, 1980-91; Lecturer, Assistant Professor, Associate Professor, Hong Kong Polytechnic University, 1991-. Publications: Over 90 articles in international referred journals, book chapters and referred conferences; 2 books: Guanxi: Relationship Marketing in a Chinese Context (co-author); Negotiate on a relationship in China. Address: Department of Management and Marketing, The Hong Kong Polytechnic University, Hung Hom, Kowloon, The Hong Kong SAR. E-mail: msthomas@polyu.edu.hk

LEUNG Wing Tai, b. 4 October 1949, Hong Kong. Educator; Youth Worker; Media Producer. m. Sharon Lo, 3 sons. Education: BSc, University of Hong Kong, 1972; MA, Gordon-Conwell Theological Seminary, 1976; MA, Bowling Green State University, 1977; MFA, University of Southern California, 1983; PhD, Regent University, 1994. Appointments: Director, Audio-Visual Centre, 1978-86, Associate General Secretary, 1986-2003, General Secretary, 2003-, Breakthrough, Hong Kong. Publications: The Making of a Communicator, 1983; The Glimpses of Tomorrow, 1990; The Age of Rapid Changes, 1998; Ideology in Multimedia World, 1998; Managing TV with Your Kids, 2000; The Thinkers' Eyes, 2003; Communication Exceed, 2003; New Leadership DNA, 2003; Second-Curve People, 2005; Decisions That Make Kids Outstanding, 2009. Honours:

Listed in international biographical dictionaries; Outstanding Graduate of the Year, University of Hong Kong, 1972; Distinguished Alumni, Faculty of Science, HKU, 2009; Honorary Fellow, City University of HK, 2010. Memberships: New Life Temple. Address: Breakthrough Youth Village, 33 A Kung Kok Shan Road, Shatin, NT, Hong Kong. E-mail: wingtai@breakthrough.org.hk

LEUTHOLD Dieter Georg, b. 18 March 1942, Berlin, Germany. Professor. m. Christine Lehmann, 1972, 2 daughters. Education: Studies at Universities of Bonn/Rhine and Free University of Berlin, 1961-66; Established Graduate Secondary School Teacher, 1970. Appointments: Lecturer, 1973, Professor, 1978, Vice-Rector and Vice Dean, 1977-91, 2002-06, Faculty of Economics, University of Applied Sciences of Bremen. Publications: More than 70 articles in professional journals. Honours: Knight, Royal Dutch Order of Orange-Nassau, 2007. Memberships: Wittheit Scientific Society, Bremen. Address: Werderst 72, 28199 Bremen, Germany. E-mail: dieter.leuthold@hs-bremen.de

LEVENE OF PORTSOKEN, Baron of Portsoken in the City of London, Peter Keith Levene, b. 8 December 1941, Pinner, Middlesex, England. Business Executive; Justice of the Peace. m. Wendy Ann Levene, 1 son, 1 daughter. Education: BA, University of Manchester. Appointments: Joined, 1963, Managing Director, 1968, Chair, 1982, United Scientific Holdings; Member, South-East Asia Trade Advisory Group, 1979-83; Personal Adviser to Secretary of State for Defence, 1984; Alderman, 1984, Sheriff, 1995-96, Lord Mayor, 1998-99, City of London; Chair, European NATO National Armaments Directors, 1990-91; Special Adviser to Secretary of State for the Environment, 1991-92; Chair, Docklands Light Railway Ltd, 1991-94; Chair, Public Competition and Purchasing Unit, H M Treasury, 1991-92; Deputy Chair, Wasserstein Perella and Co Ltd, 1991-94; Adviser to Prime Minister on Efficiency, 1992-97; Special Adviser to President of Board of Trade, 1992-95; Chair, Chief Executive Officer, Canary Wharf Ltd, 1993-96; Senior Adviser, Morgan Stanley and Co Ltd, 1996-98; Director, Haymarket Group Ltd, 1997-; Chair, Bankers Trust International, 1998-99; Chair, Investment Banking Europe, Deutsche Bank AG, 1999-2001; Director, 2001-04, Head, Chairman, nominations committee, 2004-, J Sainsbury plc; Vice Chair, Deutsche Bank, UK, 2001-02; Chair, Lloyds of London, 2002-; Member, Supervisory Bd Deutsche Boerse AG, 2004-. Honours: Honorary Colonel Commandant, Royal Corps of Transport, 1991-93; Master, Worshipful Company of Carmen, 1992-93; Honorary Colonel Commandant, Royal Logistics Corps, 1993-; Fellow, Queen Mary and Westfield College, London University, 1995; Knight Commander, Order of St John of Jerusalem; Commander, Ordre National du Mérite, 1996; Honorary DSc, City University, 1998; Knight Commandants Order of Merit, Germany, 1998; Middle Cross Order of Merit, Hungary, 1999; Knight Commander, Order of the British Empire. Memberships: Fellow, Chartered Institute of Transport; Companion, Institute of Management; Defence Manufacturers Association, Council, 1982-85, Vice-Chair, 1983-84, Chair, 1984-85. Address: 1 Great Winchester Street, London EC2N 2DB, England. E-mail: peter.k.levene@db.com

LEVENSON David, b. 8 October 1965, Bronx, New York, USA. Physician. m. Marissa, 4 sons. Education: BA cum laude, 1985, BS cum laude, 1985, University of Miami; MD, Honours in Physiology and Biophysics, New York University School of Medicine, 1989. Appointments: Residency Training Programme, Long Island Jewish Medical Centre, 1989-92; Endocrinology Fellowship, Cornell University Programme, 1992-94; Geriatric Fellowship, University of Miami, Florida, 1994-95; Private Practice, 1995-. Publications: Electrophysiologic Changes Accompanying Wallerian Degeneration in Frog Sciatic Nerve Brain Research; Candida Zeylenoides: Another opportunistic yeast; Peripheral facial nerve palsy after high dose radio iodine therapy in patients with papillery thyroid cancer; A review of calcium preparations; A multi-centre trail of Gallium Nitrate in patients with advanced Pagets disease of bone. Honour: AMA Physicians' Recognition Award. Memberships: Fellow, American College of Endocrinology; Fellow, American College of Physicians; American Association of Clinical Endocrinology; Endocrine Society. Address: 7301 West Palmetto Park Road, Suite 108B, Boca Raton, FL 33433, USA.

LEVER Tresham Christopher Arthur Lindsay (Sir) (3rd Baronet), b. 9 January 1932, London, England. Naturalist; Writer. m. Linda Weightman McDowell Goulden, 6 November 1975. Education: Eton College, 1945-49; BA, 1954, MA, 1957, Trinity College, Cambridge; PhD, 2011. Appointments: Commissioned 17th/21st Lancers, 1950; Peat Marwick Mitchell & Co, 1954-55; Kitkat & Aitken 1955-56; Director John Barran & Sons Ltd, 1956-64. Publications: Goldsmiths and Silversmiths of England, 1975; The Naturalized Animals of the British Isles, 1977; Naturalized Mammals of the World, 1985; Naturalized Birds of the World, 1987; The Mandarin Duck, 1990; They Dined on Eland: The Story of the Acclimatisation Societies, 1992; Naturalized Animals: The Ecology of Successfully Introduced Species, 1994; Naturalized Fishes of the World, 1996; The Cane Toad: The History and Ecology of a Successful Colonist, 200l; Naturalized Reptiles and Amphibians of the World, 2003; Naturalised Birds of the World, 2005; The Naturalised Animals of Britain and Ireland, 2009. Contributions to: Books, Art, Scientific and general publications. Honours: Honorary Life President, Tusk Trust, 2004; Fellow, WWF-UK, 2005; Editorial Board, Journal of Applied Herpetology, 2005-09; Vice-Patron, Conservation Foundation, 2005-2006. Memberships: Fellow, Linnean Society of London; Fellow, Royal Geographical Society; World Conservation Union Species' Survival Commission, 1988-; Council of Ambassadors, WWF (UK), 1999-2005; Honorary Life Member, Brontë Society, 1988. Address: Newell House, Winkfield, Berkshire SL4 4SE, England.

LEVICK William Russell, b. 5 December 1931, Sydney, Australia. Neuroscience Researcher. m. Patricia Lathwell, 1 son, 1 son deceased, 1 daughter. Education: BSc, honours, 1953, MSc, 1954, MBBS, honours, 1957, University of Sydney. Appointments: C J Martin Travelling Fellow, Cambridge University, University of California, Berkeley, 1963-64; Professorial Fellow, 1967-83, Professor, 1983-96, Emeritus Professor, 1997-, Australian National University, Canberra. Honours: Fellowship, Australian Academy of Sciences, 1973, Optical Society of America, 1977, Royal Society of London, 1982. Memberships: Society for Neuroscience; Australian Neuroscience Society; Australian Physiological Society. Address: 33 Quiros Street, Red Hill, ACT 2603, Australia.

LEVI-MONTALCINI Rita, b. 22 April 1909, Turin, Italy. Neuroscientist. Education: Graduated, Medicine, University of Turin, 1936. Appointments: Neurological research in Turin and Brussels, 1936-41, in Piemonte, 1941-43; In hiding in Florence during German occupation, 1943-44; Medical Doctor working among war refugees, Florence, 1944-45; Resumed academic positions at University of Turin, 1945; Worked with Professor Viktor Hamburger, 1947, Associate Professor, 1956, Professor, 1958-77, St Louis, USA; Director,

1969-78, Guest Professor, 1979-89, Guest Professor, Institute of Neurobiology, 1989-, Institute of Cell Biology of Italian National Council of Research, Rome. Publications: In Praise of Imperfection: My Life and Work, 1988. Honour: Joint Winner, Nobel Prize for Medicine, 1986. Address: Institute of Neurobiology, CNR Viale Marx 15, 00137, Rome, Italy.

LEVITAS Valery, b. 3 April 1956, Kiev, Ukraine. Researcher; Educator. m. Natasha Levitas, 20 January 1993, 2 sons. Education: MS honours, Mechanical Engineering, Kiev Polytechnic Institute, 1978; PhD, Materials Science, Institute of Superhard Materials, Kiev, 1981; DSc, Continuum Mechanics, Institute of Electronic Machine Building, Moscow, 1988; DEng habil, Continuum Mechanics, University of Hannover, Germany, 1995; Registered Professional Engineer, Texas, 2001. Appointments: Leader, Research Group, 1982-95, Associate Research Professor, 1984-88, Research Professor, 1989-95, Consultant, 1995-, Institute for Superhard Materials, Ukrainian Academy of Sciences, Kiev; Humboldt Research Fellow, 1993-95, Visiting and Research Professor, 1995-99, University of Hannover, Germany; Associate Professor, 1999-2002, Professor, 2002-08, Director, Center for Mechanochemistry and Synthesis of New Materials, 2002-2007, Texas Tech University, Lubbock; President, Firm "Material Modeling", Ames, 2002-; Consultant, Los Alamos National Laboratory, 2001-; Schafer 2050 Challenge Professor, Department of Mechanical Engineering, Department of Aerospace Engineering and Department of Material Science & Engineering, Iowa State University, Ames, Iowa, 2008-; Adjunct Professor, Department of Mechanical Engineering, Texas Tech University, Lubbock, 2008-. Publications include: Large Elastoplastic Deformations of Materials at High Pressure, 1987; Thermomechanics of Phase Transformations and Inelastic Deformations in Microinhomogeneous Materials, 1992; Large Deformation of Materials with Complex Rheological Properties at Normal and High Pressure, 1996; Continuum Mechanical Fundamentals of Mechanochemistry, 2004. Honours: Medal, Ukrainian Academy of Sciences, 1984; Alexander von Humboldt Foundation Fellowship, Germany, 1993-95; International Journal of Engineering Sciences Distinguished Paper Award, 1995; Richard von Mises Award, Society of Applied Mathematics and Mechanics, 1998; Best Professor Award, Pi Tau Sigma, Mechanical Engineering Department, Texas Tech University, 2001; American Medal of Honor, ABI, 2004; Barnie E Rushing Jr Faculty Distinguished Research Award, Texas Tech University, 2005. Memberships: International Association for the Advancement of High Pressure Science and Technology; American Society of Mechanical Engineers; American Physical Society; Society of Engineering Science; Society of Applied Mathematics and Mechanics; Minerals, Metals and Materials Society. Address: Iowa State University, Department of Mechanical Engineering, 2028 Black Engineering Bldg, Ames, IA 50011-2161, USA.

LEVITT Arthur, Jr, b. 3 February 1931, Brooklyn, New York, USA. Business Executive. m. Marylin Blauner, 1955, 1 son, 1 daughter. Education: Williams College. Appointments: Assistant Promotion Director, Time Inc, New York, 1954-59; Executive Vice-President, Director, Oppenheimer Industries Inc, Kansas City, 1959-62; Joined, 1962, President, 1969-78, Shearson Hayden Stone Inc, now Shearson Lehmann Bros Inc, New York; Chair, Chief Executive Officer, Director, American Stock Exchange, New York, 1978-89; Chair, Levitt Media Co, New York, 1989-93; Chair, New York City Economic Development Corporation, 1990-93; Chair, Securities and Exchange Commission, 1993-2001; Various directorships and other business and public appointments. Honours: Honorary LLD, Williams College, 1980, Pace, 1980, Hamilton College, 1981, Long Island, 1984, Hofstra, 1985. Address: Securities and Exchange Commission, 450 Fifth Street NW, Washington, DC 20001, USA.

LEVITT Stephan Hillyer, b. 9 February 1943, Brooklyn, New York, USA. Indologist. Education: Diploma, High School of Music and Art, New York City, 1956-60; BA, Columbia College, Anthropology, 1960-64; PhD, University of Pennsylvania, Department of Oriental Studies, 1964-73. Appointments: Cataloguer, Indic MSS, University of Pennsylvania Library for Institute for Advanced Studies of World Religions, Stony Brook, New York, 1971-72; Research Assistant, to Emeritus Professor, Dr W Norman Brown, University of Pennsylvania, 1972-74; Visiting Assistant Professor, Anthropology Department and Humanities Program, University of Denver, 1974-76; Tutor, English Department and Student/Faculty Co-ordinator, Humanities Program, Queensborough Community College, New York City, 1977-78; Private tutor, consulting work for University of Pennsylvania Library, Center for Advanced Judaic Studies, University of Pennsylvania (formerly Annenberg Research Institute), Burke Library, Union Theological Seminary, 1978-. Publications: Buddhist Tales for Young and Old, Vol 3: Stories of the Enlightenment Being, Jatakas 101-150, 2007; Explanations of Misfortune in the Buddha's Life: The Buddha's Misdeeds in his Former Human Lives and their Remnants, 2010; Buddhist Tales for Young and Old, Vol 4: Stories of the Enlightenment Being, 2009; Articles in professional journals. Honours: National Defense Foreign Language Fellowship (Tamil), 1964-67; American Council of Learned Societies Fellowship for Summer Study in Linguistics, 1967; American Institute of Indian Studies Travel-Study Award, 1974; University of Denver Faculty Research Grant, 1975. Memberships: American Oriental Society; Societas Linguistica Europaea; Bhandarkar Oriental Research Institute; Dravidian Linguistics Association. Address: 144-30 78th Road, Apt 1H, Flushing, New York 11367-3572, USA.

LEVY Alain M, b. 19 December 1946, France. Record Company Executive. Education: Ecole des Mines, France; MBA, University of Pennsylvania. Appointments: With CBS, Assistant to the President, CBS International, New York, 1972, Vice-President, Marketing for Europe, Paris, 1973, Vice-President, Creative Operations for Europe and Manager, CBS Italy, 1978; Managing Director, CBS Disques, France, 1979; Chief Executive Officer, PolyGram, 1984; Executive Vice-President, PolyGram Group, France and Federal Republic of Germany, 1988; Manager, US Operations PolyGram Group, 1990-; President, Chief Executive Officer, Member, Board of Management, PolyGram USA, 1991-; Member, Group Management Committee, Philips Electronics, 1991-; Majority Shareholder, PolyGram USA, 1991-98; Chair, Board EMI Group plc, 2001-, Chair and Chief Executive Officer, EMI Recorded Music, 2001-. Address: EMI Group plc, 4 Tenterden Street, Hanover Square, London W1A 2AY, England.

LEVY, His Honour Dennis Martyn, b. 20 February 1936, Liverpool, England. Queen's Counsel. m. Rachel Jonah, 1 son, 1 daughter. Education: BA, 1960, MA, 1963, Gonville and Caius College, Cambridge. Appointments: Called to the Bar, Gray's Inn, 1960, Hong Kong, 1985, Turks and Caicos Islands, 1987; Granada Group, 1960-63; Time Products Ltd, 1963-67; In practice at the Bar, 1967-91; Queen's Counsel, 1982; Recorder, 1989-91; Circuit Judge, 1991-2007; Accredited Mediator, 2007; Member: Employment Appeals Tribunal, 1994-2004, Lands Tribunal, 1998; Trustee of Fair Trials

International; Chairman, The United Kingdom Association of Jewish Lawyers and Jurists. Address: 25 Harley House, Marylebone Road, London, NW1 5HE, England.

LEVY John Court (Jack), b. 16 February 1926, London, England. Engineer; Consultant; Managing Director. m. Sheila F Krisman, 2 sons, 1 daughter. Education: BSc, Engineering, Imperial College of Science and Technology, London, England, 1943-46; MS, University of Illinois, USA, 1953-54; PhD, University of London, 1961. Appointments: Stress Analyst, Boulton Paul Aircraft, 1946-48; Assistant to Chief Engineer, Fullers Ltd, 1948-52; Lecturer, Senior Lecturer, Reader, 1952-66, Head (Professor) of Mechanical and Manufacturing Engineering, 1966-83, City University, London; Director, Engineering Profession at Engineering Council, 1983-90; Consulting Engineer, 1990-97; Consultant to Engineering Council, 1997-; Managing Director, Levytator Ltd, 2000-. Publications: Most recent publications include: UK Manufacturing – Facing International Challenge, 1994; Co-author, Sustaining Recovery, 1995; The University Education and Industrial Training of Manufacturing Engineers for the Global Market, 1996; UK Developments in Engineering Education, Including the Matching Section, 1998; Keynote address at international conference, The Impact of Globalization on Engineering Education and Practice, Balaton, Hungary, 1999. Honours: OBE, 1984; Member, Board of Governors, Middlesex University, 1990-2003; Freeman of City of London, 1991; Honorary Doctorates, City University, London, University of Portsmouth, Leeds Metropolitan University. Memberships: Fellow, Royal Academy of Engineering; Fellow, Institution of Mechanical Engineers; Fellow, Royal Aeronautical Society; Fellow, City and Guilds of London Institute; Fellow, Royal Society of Arts; Fellow, Institution of Engineers of Ireland. Address: 18 Woodberry Way, Finchley, London N12 0HG, England. E-mail: jack.levy1@btopenworld.com

LEVY, Baron of Mill Hill, Michael Abraham Levy, b. 11 July 1944, London, England. Consultant. m. Gilda Altbach, 1 son, 1 daughter. Education: Hackney Downs Grammar School (formerly the Grocers Company School); Qualified as Chartered Accountant. Appointments: Accountancy practice, 1967-73; Built up MAGNET, worldwide record and music publishing group of companies (sold to Warner Brothers) (now part of Time Warner), 1973-88; Built up and sold a second successful company in the music and entertainment business, 1992-97; Consultant to various international companies, 1998-; Chairman, International Standard Asset Management, 2008-. Publications: A Question of Honour, 2008. Honours: B'nai B'rith First Lodge Award, 1994; Elevated to the Peerage as Baron Levy of Mill Hill, 1997; Friends of the Hebrew University of Jerusalem Scopus Award, 1998; Honorary Doctorate, Middlesex University, 1999; Israel Policy Forum (USA) Special Recognition Award, 2003. Memberships: Vice Chairman, Central Council for Jewish Social Services, 1994-; Chairman, Chief Rabbinate Awards for Excellence, 1992-2007; Chairman, Foundation for Education, 1993-; Patron, British Music Industry Trust, 1995-; Member, World Commission on Israel-Diaspora Relations, 1995-; Chairman, Jewish Care Community Foundation, 1995-; Member, Advisory Council to the Foreign Policy Centre, 1997-; Patron, Prostate Cancer Charitable Trust, 1997-; Member, International Board of Governors, Peres Center for Peace, 1997-; Member, NCVO Advisory Committee, 1998-; Patron, Friends of Israel Educational Trust, 1998-; President, Community Service Volunteers, 1998-; Trustee, Holocaust Educational Trust, 1998-2007; President, Jewish Care, 1998-; Member, Community Legal Service Champions Panel, 1999-; Patron, Save A Child's Heart Foundation, 2000-; Member, Honorary Committee of the Israel Britain and the Commonwealth Association, 2000-; Honorary President, UJIA, 2000-; President, JFS School, 2001-; Patron, Simon Marks Jewish Primary School Trust, 2002-; Honorary Patron, Cambridge University Jewish Society, 2002-; President, Specialist Schools and Academies Trust, 2005-; Trustee and member of the Executive Committee of the Jewish Leadership Council JLC; President, Jewish Lads and Girls Brigade JLGB, 2006-; Member, Development Board, British Library, 2008-. Former positions: Founder, Former Chairman, British Music Industry Awards Committee (now Music Industry Trust); Vice-Chairman, British Phonographic Industry Ltd, 1984-87; Vice-Chairman, Phonographic Performance Ltd, 1979-84; Honorary Vice-president, UJIA, 1994-2000; Chairman, Jewish Care, 1992-97; National Campaign Chairman, JIA, 1982-85; Member, Keren Hayesod World Board of Governors, 1991-95; Member, World Board of Governors of the Jewish Agency, representing Great Britain, 1990-95; World Chairman, Youth Aliyah Committee, Jewish Agency Board of Governors, 1991-95; Governor, JFS School, 1990-95; Executive Committee Member, Chai-Lifeline, 2001-2002; Chairman, Academy Sponsors Trust; Chairman, Board of Trustees of New Policy Network Foundation, 2000-2007. Address: House of Lords, Westminster, London SW1, England.

LEVY Suzy Hug, b. 2 June 1944, Istanbul, Turkey. Plastic Arts; Sculptor; Installation, Performance, Video Artist. m. Henry Levy, 1 son, 1 daughter. Education: BA, Robert College, American College for Girls. Career: Artist and Sculptor; Numerous national and international exhibitions include most recently: Solo exhibitions: Newspapers, APEL Gallery, Istanbul and Emlak Bank Gallery, Ankara, Turkey, 1999; A Celebration, installation, video, performance, Milli Reasurans Art Gallery, Istanbul, Turkey, 2000; Fragile Images, installation, photography, performance, video, Iş Sanat Gallery, Istanbul, 2001; Arcadia, installation, performance, video, Milli Reasurans Art Gallery, Istanbul, 2001; INAX Gallery, Tokyo, Japan, 2001; To be a woman, G-art Gallery, Istanbul, 2005; Selected international group exhibitions: Finalists Show, London Jewish Museum of Art, Ben Uri Gallery and Tram Studios, London, England, 2004; Beijing Biennial, China, 2005; Ben Uri Art Gallery, London Jewish Museum of Art, 2005; Frankfurt Book Fair, Germany, 2007; Siena Book Fair, Italy, 2008; Buchdruckkunst, Frankfurt, 2009; Installed the Flying Carpets exhibit at Dolmabahçe Cultural Centre, Istanbul, 2000; Curator, Auschwitz exhibit, 2001, Anne Frank: A History for Today exhibit, 2002, Terezin Children's drawings exhibit, 2004, Schneidertempel Cultural Centre, Istanbul; Designed the Holocaust Menorah, 2002; Installed the Kuzgun Acar Retrospective exhibit, Kibele Art Gallery, Istanbul, 2004. Honours: Contemporary Artist of the Year Award, Painting and Sculpture Museum Association, Istanbul, 1991; Il Sharjah Biennial Award, United Arab Emirates, 1997; Artist of the Year on Sculpture, Ankara Arts Council, 1998, 1999, 2000; Tunis Biennial Award, 2002; International Jewish Artist of the Year Award in Sculpture, London Jewish Museum of Art, Ben Uri Gallery, 2004; Beijing Biennial, 2005; Listed in international biographical dictionaries. Memberships: Founder, Istanbul Modern Art Museum Foundation; Founder, Schneidertempel Cultural Centre; Istanbul Philharmonic Orchestra Association; PCD-UNESCO Plastic Arts Association; SANART Art and Cultural Organisation. Address: Karakütük Cad. 52, Sariyer, Istanbul, Turkey. E-mail: suzy@levi.com.tr

LEW Julian D M, b. 3 February 1948, South Africa. Lawyer; Queen's Counsel. m. Margot Gillian Perk, 2 daughters. Education: LLB honours, University of London, 1969; Doctorat special en droit international, Catholic University of Louvain, Belgium, 1977; Fellow, Chartered Institute of Arbitrators. Appointments: Called to Bar in England, 1970; Admitted Solicitor, 1981; New York State Bar, 1985; Barrister, Arbitrator, 20 Essex Street, London; Visiting Professor, Head of School of International Arbitration, Centre for Commercial Law Studies, Queen Mary, University of London; Partner, Herbert Smith, 1995-2005. Publications: Numerous books and articles on international commercial arbitration and international trade including: Applicable Law in International Commercial Arbitration, Oceana, 1978; Comparative International Commercial Arbitration, co-author, Kluwer, 2003. Memberships: General Council of the Bar of England and Wales; International Bar Association; American Bar Association; Swiss Arbitration Association; American Arbitration Association; French Committee for Arbitration; British Institute of International and Comparative Law; Chairman, Committee on arbitration practice guidelines of Chartered Institute of Arbitrators, 1996-2001; Chairman, Committee on Intellectual Property Disputes and Arbitration, International Chamber of Commerce, 1995-99; Member, Council of the ICC Institute of World Business Law; Director and Member of Court, London Court of International Arbitration. Address: 20 Essex Street, London WC2R 3AL, England. E-mail: jlew@20essexst.com

LEWIN Christopher George, b. 15 December 1940, Poole, Dorset, England. Actuary. m. Robin Lynn, 2 sons. Education: Cooper's Company School, London, 1951-55; Actuaries Tuition Course, Institute of Actuaries 1956-62. Appointments: Actuarial Assistant, Equity & Law Life, 1956-63; Actuarial Assistant, London Transport, 1963-67; Actuarial Assistant, 1967-70, Controller, Corporate Pensions, 1970-80, Co-ordinator, Private Capital, 1980-89, British Rail; Pensions Director, Associated Newspapers, 1989-92; Head of Group Pensions, Guinness PLC, 1992-98; Head of UK Pensions, Unilever PLC, 1998-2003; Pensions Manager, EDF Energy plc, 2005; Part-time appointments: Member of Investment Committee, The Pensions Trust, 2004-; Chairman of Training Standards Initiative, National Association of Pension Funds, 2004-2006; Chairman of Trustees, Marconi Pension Fund, 2004-05; Reviewer, Department of Work and Pensions Deregulatory Review of Private Pensions, 2007. Publications: Book: Pensions and Insurance Before 1800 - A Social History, 2003; Article: The Philosophers' Game (Games and Puzzles Magazine), 1973; Enterprise Risk Management and Civil Engineering, Civil Engineering, vol 159, Special Issue 2, 2006; Various papers in technical journals on investment appraisal, manpower planning, funding of pension schemes and capital projects. Honours: Sir Joseph Burn Prize, Institute of Actuaries, 1962; Finlaison Medal, Institute of Actuaries, 1999; Pensions Manager of the Year, Professional Pensions Magazine, 2003. Memberships: Fellow Institute of Actuaries, 1962; Fellow, Pensions Management Institute, 1976; Governor, Pensions Policy Institute; Governor, National Institute for Economic and Social Research; Chairman of joint working party with the Actuarial Profession and the Institution of Civil Engineers to develop a successful risk methodology for projects known as RAMP, 1992-; Member of Steering Group for the Stratrisk Initiative, 2002-. E-mail: thirlestane1903@aol.com

LEWINSKI Silke von, Academic in Law. Education: Law Studies, Johannes-Gutenberg University, Mainz; University of Geneva; Institut Universitaire des Hautes Internationales, Geneva; Ludwig-Maximilian University, Munich; Final Examination (Hons), Munich; Foreign Associate, Radon & Ishizumi, New York; Bar Exam (Hons), Munich; Doctor's degree, Public Lending Right, Free University, Berlin. Appointments: Legal Expert, European Commission, 1989-92; Chief Legal Expert, governments of Eastern and Central European and former Soviet countries on copyright legislation, 1995-; Delegate for European Communities, WIPO Diplomatic Conference, 1996; Delegate for Germany, WIPO Diplomatic Conference, 2000; Adjunct Professor, Franklin Pierce Center for iPat University of New Hampshire Law School, Concord, New Hampshire; Adjunct Professor, Munich Intellectual Property Law Center, Munich, 2003-; Visiting Professor at many universities worldwide; Head of Department, Max-Planck Institute for Intellectual Property and Competition Law, 1995-. Publications: Over 230 articles in professional journals; 12 books with focus on international and EC copyright law. Honours: Heinrich-Hubmann Award, 1991; First Distinguished Visitor, Intellectual Property Research Institute of Australia, 2002; Hosier Distinguished Visiting IP Scholar, DePaul University, Chicago, 2005. Memberships: Executive Committee, ALAI; Vice President, German ALAI; International Association for the Advancement of Teaching and Research in Intellectual Property; Advisory Council of Intellectual Property, Concord, New Hampshire. Address: Max Planck Institute for Intellectual Property, Marstallplatz 1, 80539 München, Germany. E-mail: svl@ip.mpg.de

LEWIS Adrian Mark, b. 25 June 1951, Swansea, Wales. University Lecturer. m. Valerie Josephine Barber. Publication: BA, Modern History, Oxford University, 1973; MA, History of Art, University of London, 1975; PhD, History of Art, University of Manchester, 1996. Appointments: Lecturer, Bristol Polytechnic, 1975-76; Education Officer, Walker Art Gallery, Liverpool, 1976-79; Lecturer, 1979-2011, MA Course Leader, 2000-2003, History of Art, De Montfort University Leicester; Visiting Associate Professor, Creighton University, Omaha, USA, 1999; External Assessor, Bristol Polytechnic, 1988-92. Publications: Books: The Last Days of Hilton, 1996; Roger Hilton, 2003; Exhibition catalogue: Roger Hilton: The Early Years, 1984; Numerous reviews and articles in Art History; Art Monthly; Art Book; Artscribe; Burlington Magazine; Connoisseur; Sculpture Journal. Address: 5 Impasse du Parc, Ruffec 16292, France.

LEWIS Bernard Walter, b. 24 July 1917, Lincoln, England. Flour Miller. m. Joyce Ilston Storey, 1943, 1 son, 1 daughter. Education: University of Manchester. Appointments: Joined King's Own Regiment, served in Middle East, 1940-46; RASC, 1941; Captain, 1942; Major, 1943; Chairman and Managing Director, Green's Flour Mills Ltd, 1955-90; General Tax Commissioner, 1957-93; Chairman, Dengie and Maldon Essex Bench, 1970-88; Chairman, Maldon Harbour Commissioners, 1978-2001; Chairman, Flour Advisory Bureau, 1979-88; President, National Association of British and Irish Millers, 1985-86; Chairman, Edward Baker Holdings Ltd, 1983-89; Retired, 1989. Honour: CBE, 1973. Memberships: Financial Board, Conservative Party, 1966-75; Chairman, Board of Governors, Plume School, 1968-83; Liveryman, Worshipful Company of Bakers, 1973. Address: Roughlees, 68 Highlands Drive, Maldon, Essex CM9 6HY, England.

LEWIS Carl, b. 1 July 1961, Birmingham, Alabama, USA. Athlete. Education: University of Houston. Appointments: Bronze Medal, Long Jump, Pan-American Games, 1979; Won World Cup Competition, 1981; First World Championships (with 8.55 metres); Achieved World Record 8.79 metre jump, 1983; Gold Medals, Olympic Games, 100 metres, 200 metres,

Long Jump, 4x100m, 1984; 65 Consecutive wins in Long Jump, 1985; Silver Medal, 200 metres; Gold Medal, 100 metres, Olympic Games, 1988; Jumped 8.64 metres, New York, 1991; World Record, 100 metres 9.86 seconds, 1991; Gold Medal, Long Jump, Olympic Games, 1992; Gold Medal for long jump (27ft. 10.75 in), Olympic Games, 1996; Retired, 1997; Attached to Trialtir, 1997. Honours: Track and Field News Athlete of the Decade, 1980-89; Athlete of the Century, IAAF, 1999. Address: c/o Carl Lewis International Fan Club, P O Box 57-1990, Houston, TX 77257-1990, USA.

LEWIS Denise, b. 27 August 1972, West Bromwich, England. Athlete. Career: Specialises in heptathlon; Commonwealth Heptathlon Record Holder (6,736 points), 1977; Fifth European Junior Championships, 1991; Gold Medal, Commonwealth Games, 1994; Gold Medal, European Cup, 1995; Bronze Medal, Olympic Games, 1996; Silver Medal, World Championships, 1997; Gold Medal, European Championships, 1998; Gold Medal, Commonwealth Championships, 1998; Silver Medal World Championship, 1999; New Commonwealth Record (6,831 points), 2000; Gold Medal, Olympic Games, 2000. Publications: Denise Lewis: Faster, Higher, Stronger, autobiography, 2001. Honours: British Athletics Writers Female Athlete of the Year, 1998, 2000; Sports Writers Association Sportswoman of the Year, 2000. Address: c/o MTC (UK) Ltd, 20 York Street, London, W1U 6PU, England. E-mail: info.mtc-uk.com

LEWIS Esyr ap Gwilym, b. 11 January 1926, Clydach Vale, Glamorgan, Wales. Retired Judge. m. Elizabeth Hoffmann, 4 daughters. Education: Exhibitioner and Foundation Scholar, Trinity Hall, Cambridge, 1947-50. Appointments: Army Intelligence Corps, 1944-47; Called to Bar at Gray's Inn, 1951; Law Supervisor, Trinity Hall, Cambridge, 1951-57; Queens Counsel, 1971; Recorder, Crown Court, 1972-84; Deputy High Court Judge, 1978-84; Official Referee, London Official Referees Courts, 1984-98, Senior Official Referee, 1994-98; Leader, Welsh Circuit, 1978-82; Member, Criminal Injuries Compensation Board, 1977-84. Publications: Articles in legal publications. Honour: Queen's Counsel. Memberships: Fellow, Chartered Institute of Arbitrators; Vice-President, Academy of Experts; Honorary Fellow, Society of Advanced Legal Studies; Bencher of Gray's Inn, 1978-, Treasurer, 1997. Address: 2 South Square, Gray's Inn, London WC1R 5HT, England.

LEWIS Geoffrey David, b. 13 April 1933, Brighton, East Sussex, England. Museum Consultant. m. Frances May Wilderspin, 3 daughters. Education: MA, University of Liverpool; Diploma of the Museums Association. Appointments include: Museum Assistant, 1950-58, Assistant Curator, 1958-60, Worthing Museum and Art Gallery; Deputy Director and Keeper of Antiquities, Sheffield City Museum, 1960-65; Honorary Lecturer in British Prehistory, University of Sheffield, 1965-72; Director, Sheffield City Museums, 1966-72; Director, Liverpool City Museums, 1972-74; Director, Merseyside County Museums, 1974-77; Director of Museum Studies, University of Leicester, 1977-89; Museum Consultant, 1989-; President, 1983-89, Chair, Ethics Committee, International Council of Museums, 1996-2004; Chair of Governors, Wolvey School, 1998-2003; President, Museums Association, 1980-81. Publications: The South Yorkshire Glass Industry, 1964; Prehistoric and Roman Times in the Sheffield Area (co-author), 1968; For instruction and recreation: a centenary history of the Museums Association, 1989; Manual of Curatorship: A guide to museum practice (co-editor), 1984, 2nd edition, 1992; Contributor to Encyclopaedia Britannica, 1984, 1998, 2006, Britannica On-line, 2011; Contributor to many books and articles relating to archaeology, ethics and museums. Honours: Honorary Fellow, Museums Association, 1989; Honorary Member, International Council of Museums, 2004; Listed in biographical dictionaries. Memberships: Diploma and Associate, 1958, Fellow, 1966, Museums Association; Fellow, Society of Antiquaries of London, 1969. Address: 4 Orchard Close, Wolvey, Hinckley LE10 3LR, England. E-mail: dib@geoffreylewis.co.uk

LEWIS, Baron of Newnham in the County of Cambridgeshire, Jack Lewis b. 13 February 1928, Barrow, England. Professor of Chemistry. m. Elfreida M Lamb, 1951, 1 son, 1 daughter. Education: Universities of London and Nottingham; PhD. Appointments: Lecturer, University of Sheffield, 1954-56; Lecturer, Imperial College, London, 1956-57; Lecturer-Reader, 1957-61, Professor of Chemistry, 1967-70, University College, London; Professor of Chemistry, University of Manchester, 1961-67; Professor of Chemistry, University of Cambridge, 1970-95; Fellow, Sidney Sussex College, Cambridge, 1970-77; Warden, Robinson College, Cambridge, 1975-. Publications: Papers in scientific journals. Honours include: Honorary Fellow, Sidney Sussex College, Cambridge; Honorary Fellow, Royal Society of Chemistry; 21 honorary degrees; Davy Medal, Royal Society, 1985; Chevalier, Ordre des Palmes Académiques; Commander Cross of the Order of Merit, Poland; Royal Medal, Royal Society, 2004. Memberships: Fellow, Royal Society; Foreign Associate, National Academy of Sciences, USA; Foreign Member, American Philosophical Society, 1994; Foreign Member, Accademia Nazionale dei Lincei, 1995; Numerous committees. Address: Robinson College, Grange Road, Cambridge CB3 9AN, England.

LEWIS Jerry (Joseph Levitch), b. 16 March 1926, Newark, New Jersey, USA. Comedian; Writer; Director; Producer; Actor. m. (1) Patti Palmer, 1944, divorced, 5 sons, (2) SanDee Pitnick, 1983, 1 daughter. Career: Comedian, night-clubs, then with Dean Martin, 500 Club, Atlantic City, New Jersey, 1946; Professor of Cinema, University of Southern California; Film debut with Dean Martin in My Friend Irma, 1949; Other films, many also as producer and director, include My Friend Irma Goes West, 1950, That's My Boy, 1951, The Caddy, Sailor Beware, 1952, Jumping Jacks, The Stooge, Scared Stiff, 1953, Living It Up, Three Ring Circus, 1954, You're Never Too Young, 1955, Partners, Hollywood or Bust, 1956, The Delicate Delinquent, 1957, The Sad Sack, Rock a Bye Baby, The Geisha Boy, 1958, Visit to a Small Planet, 1959, The Bellboy, Cinderfella, 1960, It's Only Money, 1961, The Errand Boy, 1962, The Patsy, The Disorderly Orderly, 1964, The Family Jewels, Boeing-Boeing, Three On a Couch, 1965, Way Way Out, 1966, The Big Mouth, 1967, Don't Raise the Bridge, Lower the River, 1968, One More Time, Hook, Line and Sinker, 1969, Which way to the Front?, 1970, The Day the Clown Cried, 1972, Hardly Working, 1979, King of Comedy, 1981, Slapstick of Another Kind, 1982, Smörgåsbord, 1983, How Did You Get In?, 1985, Mr Saturday Night, 1992, Funny Bones, Appeared in play, Damn Yankees, 1995, on tour, 1995-97; Television appearances including Startime, The Ed Sullivan Show and the Jazz Singer. Publications: The Total Film-Maker, 1971; Jerry Lewis in Person, 1982. Address: Jerry Lewis Films Inc, 3160 W Sahara Avenue, C-16, Las Vegas, NV 89102, USA. Website: www.jerrylewiscomedy.com

LEWIS Jerry Lee, b. 29 September 1935, Ferriday, Louisiana, USA. Singer; Musician (piano); Entertainer. m. 6 times. Career: Appeared on Louisiana Hayride, 1954; Film appearances: Jamboree, 1957; High School Confidential, 1958; Be My Guest, 1965; Concerts include: National Jazz

& Blues Festival, 1968; Rock'n'Revival Concert, Toronto, 1969; First appearance, Grand Ole Opry, 1973; Rock'n'Roll Festival, Wembley, 1974; Numerous appearances with own Greatest Show On Earth; Subject of biographical film, Great Balls Of Fire, 1989. Recordings: Hit singles include: Whole Lotta Shakin' Goin' On', 1957; Great Balls Of Fire, Breathless, High School Confidential, 1958; What I'd Say, 1961; Good Golly Miss Molly, 1963; To Make Love Sweeter For You, 1969; There Must Be More To Love Than This, 1970; Would You Take Another Chance On Me?, 1971; Me And Bobby Gee, Chantilly Lace, 1972. Albums include: Jerry Lee Lewis, 1957; Jerry Lee's Greatest, 1961; Live At The Star Club, The Greatest Live Show On Earth, The Return Of Rock, Whole Lotta Shakin' Goin' On, Country Songs For City Folks, 1965; By Request - More Greatest Live Show On Earth, Breathless, 1967; Together, with Linda Gail Lewis, 1970; Rockin' Rhythm And Blues, 1971; Sunday Down South, with Johnny Cash, 1972; The Session, with Peter Frampton, Rory Gallagher, 1973; Jerry Lee Lewis, 1979; When Two Worlds Collide, 1980; My Fingers Do The Talking, 1983; I Am What I Am, 1984; Keep Your Hands Off It, 1987; Don't Drop It, 1988; Great Balls Of Fire! (film soundtrack), 1989; Rocket, 1990; Young Blood, 1995; Many compilations; Contributor, film soundtracks: Roadie, 1980; Dick Tracy, 1990. Honours include: Inducted into Rock'n'Roll Hall Of Fame, 1986; Star on Hollywood Walk Of Fame, 1989. Address: Warner Bros Records, 75 Rockefeller Plaza, New York, NY 10019, USA.

LEWIS Leona, b. 3 April 1985, London, England. Singer; Songwriter. Education: Sylvia Young Theatre School; Italia Conti Academy; BRIT School. Singles: A Moment Like This, 2006; Bleeding Love, 2007; Footprints in the Sand, Better in Time, Forgive Me, Run, 2008; I Will Be, Happy, 2009; Albums: Spirit, 2007; Echo, 2009. Honours: Best Selling British Single, Ivor Novello Awards, 2007; Best Album, Best Video, MOBO Awards, 2008; Best UK & Ireland Act, MTV Europe Music Award, 2008; Breakthrough Artist, MTV Asia Award, 2008.

LEWIS Peter Tyndale, b. 1929, London, England. Retail Businessman. m. Deborah Anne Collins, 1 son, 1 daughter. Education: Christ Church, Oxford, 1949-52. Appointments: 2nd Lieutenant, Coldstream Guards, 1948-49; Pilot Officer, RAFVR, 1951-52; Barrister, Middle Temple, 1955-59; Joined John Lewis Partnership, 1959; Director, John Lewis Department Stores, 1967-71; Chairman, John Lewis Partnership plc and John Lewis plc, 1972-93. Honours: Companion, Institute of Management; Fellow, Royal Society of Arts. Memberships: Executive Committee, Industrial Society, 1968-79; Executive Committee, Design Council, 1971-74; Chairman, Retail Distributors Association, 1971-72; Governor, Windlesham House School, 1979-95; Governor, NIESR, 1983-2000; Trustee, Bell Educational Trust, 1987-97; Governor, Queen's College, Harley Street, 1994-2000; Trustee, Southampton University Development Trust, 1994-2004. Address: 34 Victoria Road, London W8 5RG, England.

LEWIS Roger Leslie, b. 2 September 1939, Strood, Kent, England. Artist. m. Elaine, 1 son, 1 daughter. Education: NDD course, Sutton and Cheam School of Art, 1954-58. Appointments: Commerical Airbrush Illustrator & Graphic Artist, 1962-; Manager, several prominent London art and design studios; Freelance artist, 1980-96; Fine Artist/Painter, 1997-; Numerous private commissions; Works appear in group and solo exhibitions around the UK; Exhibits in group exhibitions including: Dulwich Picture Gallery, Menier Gallery and Mall Gallery in London. Publications: Paintings feature in art technique books and magazines. Honours: Many honours and awards; Listed in international biographical dictionaries. Memberships: Silver Signature Member, United Kingdom Colour Pencil Society; Associate Member, Armed Forces Art Society; Croydon Art Society. Address: 27 Lorne Avenue, Croydon, Surrey CR0 7RQ, England.

LEWIS Sanchia, b. 31 March 1960, London, England. Artist. m. Jeremy Youngs. Education: Foundation Course, Medway College of Art & Design, Kent, 1978-79; Certificate in Printmaking (Distinction), City & Guilds of London Art School, London, 1982. Appointments: Printroom Tutor/Technician, City & Guilds of London School of Art, 1989-98; Gallery Manager, Honor Oak Gallery, London SE23, 1999-; Artist with group and solo exhibitions in UK, Holland, Malta, USA, Germany and France. Publications: Listed in international biographical dictionaries. Honours: First Prize, Portobello Open Exhibition, London W11, 1993; The Marlborough Gallery Prize, National Open Print Exhibition, London W2, 1994. E-mail: sanchia@sanchialewis.co.uk Website: www.sanchialewis.co.uk

LHO Young Hwan, b. 2 June 1954, Republic of Korea. Professor. m. Eun Sug Kim, 2 daughters. Education: BE, Kyungpook National University, 1982; MS, University of Mexico, USA, 1988; PhD, Texas A&M University, USA, 1993. Appointments: LG Information Communication, Korea, 1982-85; Korea Aerospace Research Institute, 1994-95; Professor, Woosong University, Korea, 1995-. Publications: More than 100 papers and articles in professional journals including: A study on the design of a pulse-width modulation DC/DC converter, 2010; Impact of Gamma Irradiation Effects on IGBT and Design Parameter Considerations, 2009. Honours: Korean Ambassador to USA, 1991; Award on Distinguished Paper, The Institute of Electronics Engineers of Korea, 2003; Minister of Education, Science and Technology. Memberships: IEEE: KSAS; IEEK; ICROS. Address: 602-1602 Songrim Apt, Hagi-Dong, Yusung-Gu, Daejeon, Korea. E-mail: yhlho@wsu.ac.kr

LI Andrew Kwok Nang, b. 12 December 1948, Hong Kong. Former Chief Justice. m. Judy Li Woo Mo Ying, 2 daughters. Education: Cambridge University, 1967-71. Appointments: Practice, Hong Kong Bar, 1973-97; Chief Justice, Hong Kong Special Administrative Region and President of Court of Final Appeal, 1997-2010. Honours: Honorary Degrees: Hong Kong University of Science and Technology, 1993; Hong Kong Baptist University, 1994; The Open University of Hong Kong, 1997; University of Hong Kong, 2001; Griffith University, 2001; University of New South Wales, 2002; University of Technology, Sydney, 2005; Chinese University of Hong Kong, 2006; Hong Kong Shue Yan University, 2009; City University of Hong Kong, 2010; Honorary Bencher, Middle Temple, 1997; Honorary Fellow, Fitzwilliam College, Cambridge University, 1999. Memberships: Honorary Steward, Hong Kong Jockey Club; Hong Kong Country Club; Hong Kong Club; Shek O Club; Athenaeum, London. Address: 2213 Bank of America Tower, 12 Harcourt Road, Hong Kong. E-mail: andrewknli@judiciary.gov.hk

LI Ching-Chung, b. 30 March 1932, Changshu, China. Professor of Electrical Engineering and Computer Science. m. Hanna Wu Li, 2 sons. Education: BSEE, National Taiwan University, 1954; MSEE, 1956, PhD, 1961, Northwestern University. Appointments: Professor, Electrical Engineering, University of Pittsburgh, 1967-; Professor, Computer Science, University of Pittsburgh, 1977-. Publications: Over 200 papers. Memberships: Fellow, IEEE; Fellow, IAPR; Fellow,

AAAS; Biomedical Engineering Society; Pattern Recognition Society. Address: 2130 Garrick Drive, Pittsburgh, PA 15235-5033, USA.

LI Hanna-Wu, b. 28 March 1934, Canton, China. Professor of Music. m. Ching-Chung Li, 2 sons. Education: BA, Piano, National Taiwan Normal University, Taipei; Master of Music, Piano, Northwestern University, Evanston, Illinois, USA. Appointments: Instructor of Piano, Department of Music, National Taiwan Normal University, Taipei, 1956-58; Instructor of Piano, Preparatory School, Department of Music, Carnegie-Mellon University, Pittsburgh, USA, 1969-84; Director, Preparatory School, 1984-; Instructor of Piano, Department of Music, 1974-79; Artist, Lecturer in Piano, 1979-88; Associate Professor of Music, 1988-2005, Professor of Music, 2005-. Publications: Can we learn good techniques by fixing mistakes?, 2006. Honours: Presidential Scholar's Distinguished Teacher Award, White House, 1997. Memberships: American Music Scholarship Association; Chairman, Eastern Region Piano Contest; Pittsburgh Concert Society; Music Teachers National Association; Pi Kappa Lambda. Address: School of Music, Carnegie-Mellon University, Pittsburgh, PA 15213, USA.

LI Lingwei, b. 1964. Badminton Player. Career: Participant in international championships; Won Women's Singles Title, 3rd World Badminton Championships, Copenhagen, 1982; Won Women's Singles and Women's Doubles, 5th ALBA World Cup, Jakarta, 1985; Won Women's Singles, World Badminton Grand Prix finals, Tokyo, 1985; Won Women's Singles at Dunhill China Open Badminton Championship, Nanjing, and Malaysian Badminton Open, Kuala Lumpur, 1987; Won Women's Singles at World Grand Prix, Hong Kong, China Badminton Open, and Danish Badminton Open, Odense, 1988; Won Women's Singles, All-England Badminton Championships, 1989; Winner, Women's Singles, 6th World Badminton Championships, Jakarta. Honours: Elected 7th in list of 10 Best Chinese Athletes. Address: China Sports Federation, Beijing, People's Republic of China.

LI Quan Sheng, b. 28 August 1940, Chongqing, China. Nuclear Medicine. m. Jun Xu, 1 daughter. Education: MD, 1966, MS, Graduate School, 1981, Shanghai First Medical College; Fellow, Nuclear Medicine, Johns Hopkins Medical Institute, Baltimore, 1986-91. Appointments: Physician, 1968-75, Physician in Nuclear Medicine, 1975-78, Nan-chong Hospital, Si-chuan, China; Physician in Nuclear Medicine, Zhong-shan Hospital, Shanghai, 1981-86; Senior Researcher, JNJ Pharmaceutical Institute, Spring House, Pennsylvania, USA, 1991-2010; Retired, 2010-. Publications: Improvement of the Technetium-99m Human Serum Albumin Kit, 1983; Radionuclide Exercise Test of Left Ventricular Ejection Fraction with a Nuclear Stethoscope, 1983; The Application of the Nuclear Stethoscope Before and After Cardiac Valve Replacement Operation, 1984; Tc-99m Methoxyisobutyl Isonitrile (RP-30) for Quantification of Myocardial Ischemia and Reperfusion in Dogs, 1988; Myocardial Redistribution of Technetium-99m-Methoxyisobutyl Isonitrile, 1990; Tomographic Myocardial Perfusion Imaging with Technetium-99m Teboroxime at Rest and After Dipyridamole, 1991. Address: 7420 Lintwhite Street, North Las Vegas, NV 89084, USA. E-mail: qli8282000@yahoo.com

LI Tzu-yin, b. 3 March 1931, Gulangyu District, Xiamen Municipality, Fujian Province, China. Professor; Research Scientist. m. Qing-Liang Huang, 3 daughters. Education: BS, Department of Biology, Beijing Normal University, China, 1954; MS, 1987; PhD, 1990; Postdoctor, 1990-93, Department of Entomology, Texas A and M University, USA. Appointments: Biology Teacher, Beijing 15th Middle School, 1954-56; Lecturer, Professor, Department of Biology, Beijing Normal University, 1956-85; Visiting Scientist, Department of Zoology, J W Gothe University, Frankfurt, Germany, 1981-82; Research Assistant, Postdoctoral, Research Scientist, Department of Entomology, Texas A and M University, USA, 1983-2001. Publications: 6 books (4 co-author); Numerous articles for scientific journals. Honours: Certified Outstanding Teacher in Beijing, 1956; Certificate of Honour for lifelong scientist, Department of Zoology, J W Gothe University, 1982; Board Certified Entomologist, 1993, Emeritus Membership, 1996, Entomology Society of America; Certified as one of 2000 Outstanding Scientists of the 20th Century by IBC, Cambridge England, 2000; Award for Scientific Achievement as one of 500 World Leaders of Influence, ABI, USA, 2001; Honourable Professor, Beijing Normal University, China, 2002; Certified Lifetime Achievement Award by IBC, 2007; Excellent Oversea Chinese Entrepreneur, Chinese Enterprises Association, 2007; Included in several most reputed international biographical dictionaries. Memberships: Entomological Society of America; Sigma Xi, Scientific Research Society; Honour Society of Agriculture, Gamma Sigma Delta. Address: 35-30 73rd Street, Apt 3H, Jackson Heights, NY 11372, USA. E-mail: litzuyin@yahoo.com

LIANG Xue-Zhang, b. 1 December 1939, Pingdu, Shandong, China. University Professor. m. Feng-Jie, 2 sons, 1 daughter. Education: Diploma, 1962; Postgraduate thesis and diploma, 1965. Appointments: Assistant, 1965; Lecturer, 1978; Associate Professor, 1983; Professor, 1990; PhD Supervisor, 1993. Publications: Articles in journals: Lagrange representation of multivariate interpolation, 1989; On the convergence of Hakopian interpolation and cubature, 1997; On the integral convergence of Kergin interpolation on the disk, 1998; Solving second kind integral equation by Galerkin methods with continuous orthogonal wavelets, 2001; The application of Cayley-Bacharach theorem to bivariate Lagrange interpolation, 2004; Some researches on trivariate Lagrange interpolation, 2006; Superposition interpolation in Cn, 2009; On a Hermite interpolation on the sphere, 2011. Honours: Natural Science Award, China, 1982; Scientific and Technical Progress Award, Education Committee of China, 1988. Membership: Jilin Province Expert Association of China. Address: Institute of Mathematics, Jilin University, Changchun, Jilin 130012, China.

LIDDLE Peter (Hammond), b. 26 December 1934, Sunderland, England. Historian; Author; Archive Director. Education: BA, University of Sheffield, 1956; Teacher's Certificate, University of Nottingham, 1957; Diploma in Physical Education, Loughborough University of Technology, 1957. Appointments: History Teacher, Havelock School, Sunderland, 1957; Head, History Department, Gateacre Comprehensive School, Liverpool, 1958-67; Lecturer, Notre Dame College of Education, 1967; Lecturer, 1967-70, Senior Lecturer in History, 1970-87, Sunderland Polytechnic; Keeper of the Liddle Collection, University of Leeds, 1988-99; Director, The Second World War Experience Centre, Leeds, 1999-2007; Founder and Editor, The Poppy and the Owl, 1990; Founder and Editor, Everyone's War, 1999. Publications: Men of Gallipoli, 1976; World War One: Personal Experience Material for Use in Schools, 1977; Testimony of War 1914-18, 1979; The Sailor's War 1914-18, 1985; Gallipoli: Pens, Pencils and Cameras at War, 1985; 1916: Aspects of Conflict, 1985; Home Fires and Foreign Fields (editor and contributor), 1985; The Airman's War 1914-18, 1987; The Soldier's War 1914-18, 1988; Voices of War, 1988; The Battle of the Somme, 1992;

The Worst Ordeal: Britons at Home and Abroad 1914-18, 1994; Facing Armageddon: The First World War Experienced (co-editor and contributor), 1996; Passchendaele in Perspective: The Third Battle of Ypres (editor and contributor), 1997; At the Eleventh Hour (co-editor and contributor), 1998; For Five Shillings a Day (co-author), 2000; The Great World War, 1914-45, volume I, 2000, volume II, 2001, (co-editor and contributor); D-Day: By Those Who Were There, 2004; Captured Memories 1900-1918, vol 1, 2010; Captured Memories 1930-45, vol 2, 2011. Contributions to: Journals and other books; Oral History Consultant. Honours: MLitt, University of Newcastle, 1975; PhD, University of Leeds, 1997; Life President, Second World War Experience Centre. Memberships: British Audio Visual Trust; Fellow, Royal Historical Society. Address: Woodlands Cottage, Mickley, Near Ripon, North Yorkshire, HG4 3JE, England.

LIEBERMAN Louis Stuart, b. 23 May 1938, Swan Hill, Victoria, Australia. Barrister; Solicitor; Director. m. Marjorie Cox, 2 sons, 1 daughter. Education: New South Wales Barristers and Solicitors Admission Board; Studied and worked as Articled Law Clerk; Qualified as a Solicitor, New South Wales and High Court and Barrister and Solicitor, Victoria; Diploma in Law (SAB). Appointments include: Senior Partner, Harris Lieberman & Co Barristers and Solicitors, 1974-76; Chair, House of Representatives Standing Committee on Aboriginal and Torres Strait Islander Affairs; Parliamentary Secretary to Leader of Opposition, Commonwealth Parliament; Shadow Minister for Health, Further Education, Water Resources, Property and Services; Minister for Planning, Assistant Health, Minerals and Energy, Mines; Member for Benambra, Legislative Assembly, Parliament of Victoria, 1976-92, retired; Member for Indi, House of Representatives, Commonwealth of Australia, 1993-2001, retired; Director, Hume Building Society Ltd, 1999. Memberships: Fellow, Australian Institute of Company Directors; Law Society of New South Wales; Law Institute, Victoria; Australian War Memorial Foundation; Patron Bandiana Military Museum; La Trobe University Council; Wodonga Technical College Council; Rotary. Address: PO Box 151, Wodonga, Victoria, Australia 3689.

LIEBESCHUETZ John Hugo Wolfgang Gideon, b. 22 June 1927, Hamburg, Germany. Retired Professor of Classical and Archaeological Studies; Writer. m. Margaret Rosa Taylor, 9 April 1955, 1 son, 3 daughters. Education: BA, 1951, PhD, 1957, University of London. Appointments: Professor and Head of Department of Classical and Archaeological Studies, University of Nottingham, 1979-92. Publications: Antioch, 1972; Continuity and Change in Roman Religion, 1979; Barbarians and Bishops, 1992; From Diocletian to the Arab Conquest, 1992; The Decline and Fall of the Roman City, 2000; Ambrose of Milan, Political Letters and Speeches, 2005; Decline and Change in Late Antiquity, 2006; Ambrose and John Chrysostom, 2011. Honours: Fellow, British Academy, 1992; Corresponding Fellow, German Archaeological Institute, 1994; Fellow, University College, London, 1997; Fellow, Society of Antiquaries. Address: 1 Clare Valley, The Park, Nottingham NG7 1BU, England.

LIEFTING Hendrik, b. 21 February 1952, Ede, Netherlands. Minister. m. Elizabeth van Middelkoop, 3 sons, 2 daughters. Education: Pedagogical Academy, Ede, 1973; Master, History, 1988, Master, Theology, 1992, Utrecht. Appointments: Teacher, elementary school, Wekerom, Netherlands, 1973-80; Teacher, History, secondary school, Nijkerk, Netherlands, 1980-87; Teacher, Social Science and Theology, School of Economics, Amersfoort, Netherlands, 1987-93; Minister, Dutch Reformed Church: Nieuwland and Oosterwijk, Netherlands, 1993-98; Schoonhoven, Netherlands, 1998-2005, Delft, 2005-; Teacher, Philosophy, Theology College, Ede, 1997-2008. Publications: Numerous articles in professional journals including Gereformeerd Weekblad; Oproer in het leger te Harskamp, Oktober 1918 in Bijdragen en Mededelingen. Deel LXXVIII, 1987. Address: Ruys de Beerenbrouckstraat 4, 2613 AT Delft, Netherlands.

LIENARD-YETERIAN Marie, b. 3 May 1966, Clermont-Ferrand, France. Associate Professor; Researcher. m. Frederic Yeterian. Education: Licence, Clermont-Ferrand II, 1986; Master's degree, Case Western Reserve University, 1991; PhD, Cornell University, 1996; Maitrise FLE, Paris VIII, 2001. Appointments: Lecturer, Case Western Reserve University, 1990-91; Lecturer, Cornell University, 1992-95; Assistant Professor, Bard College, 1995-97; Assistant Professor, American University, Aix-en-Provence, 1997-98; Associate Professor, Ecole Polytechnique, Paris, 1998-. Publications: Books: A Streetcar Named Desire: the play and the film, 2003; Nouvelles du Sud, 2006; Culture et Mémoire, 2008; Le Sud au Cinéma, 2009; Faulkner et le cinéma, 2010; Numerous articles in professional and academic journals. Honours: Sage Fellowship, 1992-94; IPS/PEO, 1992-94; Fulbright Grant, 2001. Memberships: MLA; Cornell University Club; Board Member: AFEA, France – Fulbright. E-mail: lienardmarie@yahoo.com

LI-LAN, b. 28 January 1943, New York, New York, USA. Artist. Appointments: Regional Council, Parrish Art Museum, Southampton, New York, 1984-87; Artists Advisory Board, East Hampton Center for Contemporary Art, East Hampton, New York, 1989-90. Publications: Canvas With an Unpainted Part: An Autobiography, Tokyo, Japan, 1976; Experiences of Passage: The Paintings of Yun Gee + Li-lan; Texts in exhibition catalogues and books, numerous articles. Commissions and Creative Works: Collections in numerous museums including: Virginia Museum of Fine Arts, Richmond, Virginia; The Parrish Art Museum, Southampton, New York; William Benton Museum of Art, Storrs, Connecticut; Arkansas Arts Center, Little Rock; The Baltimore Museum of Art, Baltimore, Maryland; San Diego Museum of Art, San Diego, California; The Sezon Museum of Modern Art, Karuizawa, Japan; Ohara Museum of Art, Kurashiki, Japan; Other collections include: Estee Lauder Inc, Mobil Oil Corporation, Lifetime TV, Chermayeff and Geismer Associates, New York; Gap Inc, Flagship Store, Oahu, Hawaii; Art For Peace Collection, Fischer Pharmaceuticals Ltd, Tel Aviv, Israel; Seattle First National Bank, Washington; Security Pacific National Bank, Los Angeles, California; Weatherspoon Art Gallery, Greensboro, North Carolina; Werner Kramarsky Collection, New York; Solo exhibitions in USA, Japan, Taiwan include: Robert Miller Gallery, New York, 1978; OK Harris Gallery, New York, 1983, 1985, 1987; The William Benton Museum of Art, Storrs, Connecticut, 1990; Nantenshi Gallery, Tokyo, Japan, 1971, 1974, 1977, 1980, 1985; Lin & Keng Gallery, Taipei, Taiwan, 1995, 1997, 2001, 2006 and 2008; Art Projects International, New York, New York, 1994, 1996; DoubleVision Gallery, Los Angeles, California, 2003; Nabi Gallery, New York, 2004; Jason McCoy Inc, New York, 2006, 2008 and 2009; Solo, 2010, A Decade of Reverie, 2010, Tina Keng Gallery, Taipei, Taiwan; Numerous group exhibitions in USA, Japan and Taiwan. Honours: Artists Grant, Artists Space, New York, 1988, 1990; Certificate of Merit: Chinese American Cultural Pioneer, New York City Council, 1993.

LILJE Christian, b. 24 November 1963, Freiburg, Germany. Pediatric Cardiologist. m. Miriam. Education: Graduate, Albert-Ludwigs University Medical School, Freiburg, Germany, 1992; Unrestricted License, German Medical Board, 1994; Certification, ECFMG, 1996; Certification, German Speciality Board, Pediatrics, 1999; Certification, German Subspeciality Board, Pediatric Cardiology, 2002; Unrestricted License, Louisiana, 2008; Certification, German Subspeciality Board, Adults with Congenital Heart Disease, 2009; Med. Ethics, Georgetown University. Appointments: Senior Faculty, 2000-02, Deputy Chief of Division, 2005-08, Department of Pediatric Cardiology, University Heart Center, Hamburg, Germany; Fellowship, Pediatric Cardiology, Tulane University Hospital for Children, New Orleans, Boston Children's Hospital, Children's Hospital of NY, USA, 2003-04; Faculty, Associate Professor, Clinical Pediatrics, Louisiana State University Health Sciences Center, New Orleans, 2008-. Publications: Numerous articles in peer reviewed journals, books and book chapters. Honours: Dissertation, Clinical Ethics Consultation (summa cum laude), 1994; Fulbright Scholar; Many travel, research and conference grants; Poster Prize, European Society of Cardiology XXIV Annual Congress, Germany, 2002; American College of Cardiology Travel Award, 2005; Listed in international biographical dictionaries. Memberships: Society of Pediatric Echocardiography; Association for European Pediatric Cardiology; German Society of Pediatric Cardiology; German Society of Pediatrics; Fellow, American College of Cardiology; German Academy of Ethics in Medicine; Fulbright Alumni Association; German National Scholarship Foundation Alumni; Fellow, German National Merit Foundation. Address: Pediatric Cardiology, Children's Hospital, Louisiana State University HSC, School of Medicine, 200 Henry Clay Ave, New Orleans, LA 70118, USA. E-mail: lilje@europe.com

LILLEY Right Honourable Peter Bruce, b. 23 August 1943, Kent, England. Politician. m. Gail Ansell, 1979. Education: Clare College, Cambridge; MA, Cantab. Appointments: Chairman, Bow Group, 1973; Member of Parliament for St Albans, 1983-97, for Hitchin and Harpenden, 1997-; Economic Secretary, 1987-89, Financial Secretary, 1989-90, to Treasury; Secretary of State for Trade and Industry, 1990-92, for Social Security, 1992-97; Opposition Front Bench Spokesman for Treasury, 1997-98; Deputy Leader of the Opposition, 1998-99; Former Director, Greenwell Montague, Oil Analyst; Chairman, Globalisation and Global Poverty policy group, 2007. Publications: The Delusion of Incomes Policy, co-author, 1977; The End of the Keynesian Era, 1980; Thatcherism: The Next Generation, 1990; Winning the Welfare Debate, 1996; Patient Power, 2000; Common Sense on Cannabis, 2001; Taking Liberties, 2002; Save on Pensions, 2003. Honour: Privy Councillor. Address: House of Commons, London SW1A 0AA, England.

LILLIE Betty Jane, b. 11 April 1926, Cincinnati, Ohio, USA. Professor of Biblical Studies. Education: BSEd, 1955, BA, 1961, College of Mt St Joseph; MA, 1967, MA, 1975, Providence College, Rhode Island; PhD, Hebrew Union College, Cincinnati, Ohio, 1982. Appointments: Teaching at graduate and undergraduate levels, Faculty, Athenaeum of Ohio, Cincinnati, Ohio, 1982-2011; Athenaeum Summer Program: Progoff Intensive Journal I, 1986, Progoff Intensive Journal II, 1987, Women in the Biblical Tradition, 1988; Athenaeum Israel Study Program in Israel, Summer 1989; Athenaeum Summer Lecture Series: Women in the Biblical Tradition, 1990; Participant in faculty development workshops, 1992-93, 1996-97, 1999, 2002-09; Faculty, Evening College of the University of Cincinnati, 1984-2003; Academic committees; Involvement in Church ministry and life. Publications: Book: A History of the Scholarship on the Wisdom of Solomon from the Nineteenth Century to our Time; Biblical Exegesis for Weekday Homily Helps; Weekly column on Sunday Scripture readings every third month, 1988-; Numerous articles and papers on religious topics. Honours include: International Peace Prize, 2003; World Medal of Freedom, 2006; Named Woman of the Year, 1993, 1994, 1995, 1996, 1997, 1999, 2000; International Woman of the Year, 1992-93, 1996-97, 1998-99, 1999-2000, 2001-02, 2007; Named for: Decree of International Letters for Cultural Achievement, 1996, 1997; Lifetime Achievement Award, ABI, 1997; International Cultural Diploma of Honour, 1997, 1999; Presidential Seal of Honor, 1997; Order of International Fellowship, 1997; Millennium Hall of Fame, 1998; Named Educator of the Year, IBC, 2006; Great Minds of the 21st Century, ABI, 2002, 2007-08; Listed in Cambridge Blue Book, IBC, 2007; International Peace Prize, United Cultural Convention, USA, 2003. Memberships: Catholic Biblical Association; Society for Biblical Literature; Biblical Archaeology Society; Eastern Great Lakes Biblical Society, Vice President, 1992; President, 1993; Council of Societies for the Study of Religion; Women's Center for Theological Studies; Ohio Humanities Council; Listed in Who's Who publications and biographical dictionaries. Address: 2704 Cypress Way Apt 3, Cincinnati, OH 45212-1773, USA.

LILLYWHITE Louis, b. 23 February 1948, Portsmouth, England. Surgeon General. m. Jean, 1 son, 2 daughters. Education: MB, BCh, University of Cardiff, 1966-71; Army Staff College, 1981-82; MSc, University of London, 1990. Appointments: Medical Officer, 3rd Battalion Parachute Field Ambulance; Section Officer, then Second in Command, 23 Parachute Field Ambulance; Second in Command, 2nd Armoured Division Field Ambulance; Staff Officer Medical Operations, Plans and Equipment Policy, 1983-84; Commanding Officer, 23 Parachute Field Ambulance, 1985-88; Staff Officer Preventive Medicine HQ 1st British Corps, 1989-90; Commander Medical 1st Armoured Division, 1991-93; Head, Army Medical Service Personnel Branch, 1993-95; Army Member, Defence Cost Study Implementation Team 15, 1995-97; Deputy Chief of Staff Medical HQ Land Forces, 1998-2000; Chief Medical Officer, Allied Forces North West Europe, 2000-01; Director, Medical Training Reserves & Clinical Policy MOD, 2001-03; Director (Chief Executive), British Forces Germany Health Service, 2003-05; Director General, Army Medical Services, 2005-06; Surgeon General, UK Armed Forces, 2007-10; Senior Research Consultant, Chatham House Centre for Global Health Security, 2010-; Chief Medical Officer, St John Ambulance England, 2010-; Fee Paid Medical Member of Tribunal Appeal Service, 2011-. Honours: MBE, 1984; Mentioned in Dispatches (Gulf War), 1991; QHS, 2001; CB, 2009. Memberships: Faculty Occupational Medicine; Fellow, Royal College of Physicians & Surgeons of Glasgow; Fellow, President, 2009-10, Medical Society of London; United States Defense Secretary Medal for Exceptional Public Service, 2009; Honorary Member, Society of Medical Consultants to the Armed Forces of the USA; Army & Navy Club; British Medical Association; Fell Running Association; British Army Orienteering Club. Address: 4 Cassways Orchard, Bratton, Westbury, Wiltshire, BA13 4TY, England.

LIM Bokman, b. 21 January 1978, Jangheung-Gun, Jeollanam-Do, Republic of Korea. Senior Engineer. Education: BS, Mechanical Engineering, Korea University, 2003; PhD, Mechanical & Aerospace Engineering, Seoul

National University, 2008. Appointments: Senior Engineer, Robot R&D Group, Samsung Electronics Mechatronics & Manufacturing Technology Center, 2008-. Publications: Some research articles in Robotics journals and proceedings. Honours: Bronze Award, Samsung Best Paper Award, 2010. Address: 416 Maetan-3 Dong, Yeongtang-Gu, Suwon, Gyeonggi-Do 443-742, Republic of Korea. E-mail: bokman.lim@samsung.com

LIM Chee Wah, b. 27 January 1965, Batu Pahat, Johor, Malaysia. Associate Professor. m. Moi Peng Choo, 1 son, 1 daughter. Education: BEng (honours), Mechanical Engineering (Aeronautics), University of Technology, Malaysia, 1989; MEng, Mechanical Engineering, National University of Singapore, 1992; PhD, Mechanical Engineering, Nanyang Technological University, Singapore, 1995. Appointments: Research Assistant, National University of Singapore, 1989-91; Research Assistant, Teaching Assistant, Nanyang Technological University, Singapore, 1992-94; Research Assistant, 1994-95, Postdoctoral Research Fellow, 1995-97, University of Queensland, Australia; Research Fellow, University of Hong Kong, 1998-2000; Assistant Professor, 2000-03, Associate Professor, 2003-, City University of Hong Kong; Professional Consultant, Green Technology Consultants Limited, Hong Kong, 2000-; Associate Editor (Asia-Pacific Region), Advances in Vibration Engineering, 2002-; Technical Reviewer for John Wiley & Sons, Kluwer Academic Publishers and more than 50 international journals. Publications: Contributed more than 180 technical papers to professional journals; 1 book; 1 book chapter; More than 80 international conference papers; miscellaneous research reports; Research papers cited more than 1,800 times by independent authors. Honours: Public Service Commission Scholarship, Malaysia, 1985-89; Best Academic Performance, Mechanical Engineering, (Aeronautics), 1989; University of Queensland Postdoctoral Research Fellowship, 1995-97; University of Hong Kong Research Fellowship, 1998-2000; Listed in several biographical dictionaries; Fellowship, International Biographical Association. Memberships: American Society of Mechanical Engineers; American Society of Civil Engineers; Acoustical Society of America; Structural Engineering Institute of ASCE. Address: Department of Building and Construction, City University of Hong Kong, Tat Chee Avenue, Kowloon, Hong Kong. E-mail: bccwlim@cityu.edu.hk

LIM Chwen Jeng, b. 1964, Malaysia. Architect. Education: AA Dipl, Architectural Association, School of Architecture, London, England, 1982-87. Appointments: Director, Studio 8 Architects, 1994-; Professor, Architecture and Cultural Design, University College, London; Visiting Professor, Glasgow School of Art, 2001-; Exhibitions include: RMIT, Melbourne, Australia, 1996; Stadelschule, Frankfurt, 1997; ARCHILAB Fonds Regional d'Art Contemporain du Centre, France, 1999; Mackintosh Museum, Glasgow, 2004; Venice Architecture Biennale 04, British Pavilion, 2004; Other group exhibitions include: Dulwich Picture Gallery, 1990; National Gallery Alexandros Soutzos Museum, Athens, 1990; Museo Nazionale Di Castel St Angelo, Rome, 1994; Nara World Architecture Triennale, Japan, 1996; Defence Corp Building, Jyvaskyla, Finland, 1997; CUBE Gallery, Manchester, 2000; Academie de France, Rome, 2000; RIBA, London, 2000; Architecture Foundation, London, 2001; Gallery 312, Chicago, USA, 2001; Rubelle + Norman Schafler Gallery, New York, 2001; Storefront Gallery, New York, 2001; Thread Waxing Gallery, New York, 2001; Chicago Architecture Foundation, USA, 2001; Mediatheque d'Orleans, France, 2002; Drawings in permanent collections include: The Victoria and Albert Museum, London; Fonds Regional d'Art Contemporain du Centre, France; RIBA British Architectural Library, London. Publications: Articles in international periodicals and newspapers; Monographs include: Sins and Other Spatial Relatives, 2001; How Green is Your Garden, 2003; Neo Architecture, 2005; 5 edited books. Honours: Award winning research-based architectural competitions include: Housing: A Demonstration Project, UK, 1987; Bridge of the Future, Japan, 1987; UCL Museum, UK, 1996; Ideal Home Concept House, UK, 1999; GlassHouse, Japan, 2001. RIBA Award for Academic Contribution in Architectural Education, 1997, 1998, 1999; Selected to represent the UK in the Venice Architecture Biennale 04, 2004; Chosen as one of the New British Talent in Architecture by the Guardian and Independent Newspapers, 2004. Address: Studio 8 Architects, 95 Greencroft Gardens, London NW6 3PG, England. E-mail: mail@cjlim-studio8.com Website: www.cjlim-studio8.com

LIM Hyeon-Kyo, b. 11 October 1959, Seoul, Republic of Korea. Professor. m. Hyeon-Joo Kim, 1 son, 1 daughter. Education: BS, Industrial Engineering, Seoul National University, 1982; MS, 1984, PhD, 1988, Industrial Engineering, Korea Advanced Institute of Science and Technology. Appointments: Professor, Chungbuk National University, 1988-; Research Fellow, University of Occupational & Environmental Health, Fukuoka, Japan, 1996-; Consulting Samsung Electronics Co Ltd, Suwon, Kyonggi, Republic of Korea, 1996-98; Safety Certification Committee Member, Korea Occupational Safety & Health Agency, Incheon, 1997-2011; Research Group Chairman, Korea Standards Association, Seoul, 2000-04; Consulting, Ssanyong Motor Co Ltd, Pyongtaek, Kyonggi, 2002-08. Publications: Numerous articles in professional journals including: Co-author, To QWL Enhancement in Digital Concept Era, 2005; Co-author, Work Improvement – Wisdom and Exquisite Skill of Occupational Ergonomics, 2008. Honours: Academic Award, Korean Society of Safety, 2010; Excellent Paper Award in Science and Technology, Korean Federation of Science and Technology Societies, 2010. Memberships: Korean Society of Safety; Ergonomic Society of Korea. Address: Department of Safety Engineering, Chungbuk National University, Cheongju, Chungbuk 361-763, Republic of Korea. E-mail: hklim@chungbuk.ac.kr

LIM Hyun-Sul, b. 15 July 1952, Iksan-si, Jeonbuk-do, Korea. Professor. m. Hae-Gyeong Kim, 1 son, 1 daughter. Education: MD, College of Medicine, 1978, MPH, School of Public Health, 1981, PhD, College of Medicine, 1986, Seoul National University. Appointments: Korean Medical License for Practice, Ministry of Health and Social Welfare, 1978; Korean Board of Preventive Medicine, 1983; Korean Board of Family Medicine, 1989; Korean Board of Occupational Medicine, 1997; Assistant Professor, 1990-94, Associate Professor, 1994-99, Full Professor & Chair, 1999-, Preventive Medicine, College of Medicine, Dongguk University; Visiting Scientist, Environmental Epidemiology Services, Department of Veterans Affairs, Washington DC, USA, 1999-2000; Head, Medical Institute of Dongguk University, 2001-03; President, Korean Society of Epidemiology, 2004-06; Committee Member, National Academy of Medicine of Korea, 2004-08; Reform Mass Screening, Korea Ministry of Health and Welfare, 2005-; Vice President, Korean Society for Zoonoses, 2006-08; President, Korean Association of Agricultural Medicine & Community Health, 2007-09; Dean of School of Medicine, Dongguk University, 2011-13. Publications: Books: Preventive Medicine, 2004; Environmental Epidemiology, 2005; From Glass Fiber Wastes to Avian Influenza, 2005; Preventive Medicine and Public Health, 2011; 5 articles in professional scientific journals. Honours: The Testimonial of the President in the Republic of Korea, 2003; Award of Academy for Veterans, 2006; Medal for Merit, 2010. Memberships: Korean Medical Association; Korean Society for Preventive Medicine; Korean Society of Epidemiology; Korean Academy of Independent Medical Examiners; Korean Academy of Family Medicine; Korean Society of Toxicology; Korean Association of Agricultural Medicine & Community Health; Korean Society of Occupational and Environmental Medicine; American Public Health Association; Korean Society for Indoor Environment; Korean Society for Zoonoses; Korean Society for Preventive Medicine (President, 2011-13). Address: Department of Preventive Medicine, Dongguk University, College of Medicine, 707 Seokjang-dong, Gyeongju-si, Gyeongsongbuk-do 780-714, Korea. E-mail: wisewine@dongguk.ac.kr

LIM Won Kyun, b. 4 July 1953, Incheon, South Korea. Professor. m. Chung-Hyo Lee, 2 sons. Education: BS, Mechanical Engineering, 1972-76, MS, Mechanical Engineering, 1979-81, PhD, Mechanical Engineering, 1981-88, Inha University, Incheon, South Korea. Appointments: Professor, 1981-, Mechanical Department Chairman, MyongJi University, Kyonggido, South Korea, 1986-88; Visiting Professor, Cornell University, Ithaca, New York, 1990-1991; Visiting Professor, University of Florida, Gainesville, Florida, USA, 1999-2000; Visiting Professor, Vienna University of Technology, Vienna, Austria, 2006-2007; Standard Development Committee Member, Korea Automotive Technology Institute, Cheonan, South Korea, 2001-2004; Editorial Board Member, Far East Journal of Applied Mathematics, 2004-; Director, Korean Society of Mechanical Engineers, Seoul, 2005-06; Central Construction Technical Committee Member, Ministry of Construction and Transportation, Seoul, South Korea, 2006-. Publications: Articles in scientific journals including: Engineering Fracture Mechanics, 1998, 2001; Journal of Composite Materials, 2002; International Journal of Fatigue, 2003; Transactions of the Korean Society of Mechanical Engineers, 2006; Composites B, 2009; International Journal of Fracture, 2011. Honours: Full Scholarship, Inha University, 1972-76; Grants, Korea Research Foundation, 1995-97. Memberships: Korean Society of Mechanical Engineers; Editor, Journal of Korean Society of Precision Engineering. Address: Department of Mechanical Engineering, MyongJi University, 38-2 Namdong, Yongin, Kyonggido 449-728, South Korea. E-mail: limwk@mju.ac.kr

LIMERICK, Sylvia Countess of; Sylvia Rosalind Pery, b. 7 December 1935, Cairo, Egypt. m. 6th Earl of Limerick, deceased 2003, 2 sons, 1 daughter. Education: MA, Lady Margaret Hall, Oxford. Appointments include: Research Assistant, Foreign Office, 1959-62; Volunteer, British Red Cross, 1962-66; President and Chairman, Kensington and Chelsea Division, British Red Cross, 1966-72; Member of Board of Governors, St Bartholomew's Hospital, 1970-74; Vice Chairman, Foundation for the Study of Infant Deaths, 1971-; Vice President, London Branch, British Red Cross, 1972-85; President, 1972-79, Vice President, 1979-99, UK Committee for UNICEF; Vice-Chairman, Community Health Council, 1974-77; Member, Committee of Management, Institute of Child Health, London, 1976-96; Member Area Health Authority, Kensington, Chelsea and Westminster, 1977-82; Member, St Mary's Hospital, W2 Medical School Council and District Ethics Committee, 1977-82; Council Member, King Edward's Hospital Fund for London, 1977-2008; Vice President, 1978-84, President, 1984-2002, Community Practitioners and Health Visitors' Association; Trustee, Child Accident Prevention Trust, 1979-87; President, 1973-84, Vice President, 1985-90, National Association for Maternal and Child Welfare; Member, DHSS Maternity Services Advisory Committee, 1981-84; Member, Working Group on Ethics of Clinical Research in Children, 1982-84; Reviewed National Association of Citizens' Advice Bureau for H M Government, 1983; Vice-Chairman, 1984-85, Chairman of Council, 1985-95, Chairman Emeritus, 1995-97, British Red Cross Society; Advisory Board, Civil Service Occupational Health Service, 1988-92; Board Member, Eastman Dental Hospital Special Health Authority, 1990-96; Trustee, Voluntary Hospital of St Bartholomew, 1991-2004; Vice President, International Federation of Red Cross and Red Crescent Societies, 1993-97; Vice Chairman, Institute of Neurology/Hospital for Neurology and Neurosurgery Joint Research Ethics Committee, 1993-2004; Non-Executive Director, University College London Hospitals NHS Trust, 1996-97; Chairman, CMO's Expert Group to Investigate Cot Death Theories, 1994-98; Trustee, Childhealth Research Appeal Trust, 1995-2006; Chairman, Committee of Management, Eastman Dental Institute, 1996-99; Chairman, Eastman Dental Research Foundation, 1996-2002; Chairman, CPHVA Charitable Trust, 1997-2002; Patron, Child Health Advocacy International, 1998-2009; Honorary Vice President, British Red Cross Society, 1999-; Patron, CRUSE, 1984; Member, Academy of Medical Sciences working group on Strengthening Clinical Research, 2002-3; Member, Queen Square Brain Bank Management Board, 2004-08; Patron, Lodge Hill Trust, West Sussex, 2006-; President, St Catherine's Hospice, Sussex, 2010-. Publications: Co-author, Sudden Infant Death: patterns, puzzles and problems, 1985; Over 65 articles in medical and other journals on cot death and on International Red Cross and Red Crescent Movement. Honours: CBE, 1991; Hugh Greenwood Lecturer, Exeter University, 1987; Hon D Litt, Council for National Academic Awards, 1990; Samuel Gee Lecturer, RCP, 1994; European Women of Achievement Humanitarian Award, 1995; Hon LLD, University of Bristol, 1998. Memberships: Fellow, Royal Society of Medicine, 1977-; Hon MRCP, 1990, Hon FRCP, 1994, Royal College of Physicians; Freeman Honoris Causa, Worshipful Company of Salters, 1992; Honorary Fellow, Institute of Child Health, London, 1996; Honorary Member, 1986, Honorary Fellow, 1996, Royal College of Paediatrics and Child Health; Freeman, Worshipful Company of World Traders, 2003; Order of the Croatian Star, 2003. Address: Chiddinglye, West Hoathly, East Grinstead, West Sussex, RH19 4QT. E-mail: srlimerick@aol.com

LIN Mei-Mei (Rose), b. 7 December 1958, Taipei, Taiwan. Historian. Education: BA, General History, 1981, MA, Modern China, 1984, National Cheng Chi University, Taiwan; MA, US History, 1987, PhD, US History, 1994, University of Texas at Austin, USA. Appointments: Associate Professor, Department of History, National Chung Cheng University, Chia-Yi, Taiwan, 1994-2000; Associate Professor, 2000-05, Full Professor, 2005-, Department of History, National Dong Hwa University, Hualien, Taiwan. Publications: Over 30 papers and articles in professional journals. Honours: Modern Chinese History Scholarship, Ministry of Education, Taiwan, 1982-84; US History Scholarship, National Society of the Colonial Dames of America in the State of Texas, 1990; Teaching Assistantship, 1986-91, Dora Boham Research Fund, 1991, History Department, UT-Austin; New Faculty Research Fund, National Chung Cheng University, 1994-95; National Science Council Research Grant, National Science Council Research Award, 1997-98, National Science Council, Taiwan; Scholarship, the USIA of State Department, USA, 1999; Special Book Grant, USIS Taipei and USIA of State

Department, USA, 2002; Taiwan Scholars and their Research on Christianity, 1945-2000; Project Grant, National Science Council, Taiwan, 2000-02, 2002-03; Research on Taiwan Episcopal Church, 1954-2000; First, Second and Third Year Project Grant, National Science Council, Taiwan, 2003-2006; Women in Missology: Taking the Four Churches of Taiwan Episcopal Church in Northern Taiwan as Case-in-point, Project Grant, 2006-07, 2007-08; National Science Council, Executive Yuan, Taiwan, ROC. Listed in national and international biographical dictionaries. Memberships: The Taiwan Association for Religious Studies; American Studies Association of the ROC; American Historical Association; Association for Asian Studies; Historical Society of American Episcopal Church; Organisation of American Historians; Chinese Society of the Modern History. Address: 2F, No1, Alley 11, Lane 208, Ray-An Street, Taipei (10661), Taiwan, ROC. E-mail: mmlin@mail2000.com.tw

LIN Tzu-Ping, b. 11 April 1974, Taiwan. Professor. m. Meng-Chi Chu, 2 sons. Education: PhD, Architecture, National Cheng Kung University, Taiwan, 2002. Appointments: Professor, Department of Leisure and Recreation, National Formosa University, Taiwan, 2010. Publications: More than 20 international journal papers. Honours: Best Oral Presentation Award for Young Scientists, 17th International Congress of Biometeorology, 2005; Listed in international biographical dictionaries. Memberships: Expert on Climate and Tourism; International Association for Urban Climate; International Society of Biometeorology. Address: No 206, Singjhong St, Chiayi City, 600, Taiwan. E-mail: tplin@nfu.edu.tw

LINDSAY Robert, b. 13 December, 1949, Ilkeston, Derbyshire, England. Actor. m. (1) Cheryl Hall, divorced 1980, 1 daughter with Diana Weston, (2) Rosemarie Ford, 2006, 3 sons. Education: Royal Academy of Dramatic Art. Career: Stage appearances: Me and My Girl, London, Broadway and Los Angeles, 1984-87; Henry II in Anouilh's Beckett, London, 1991; Cyrano de Bergerac, London, 1992; Becket, 1996; Oliver! 1997; The Entertainer, 2007; Onassis, 2010; The Lion in Winter, 2011; Film appearances: Bert Rigby, You're a Fool; Loser Takes All; Strike It Rich; Fierce Creatures, 1997; Divorcing Jack, 1998; Wimbledon; Television appearances: King Lear; Citizen Smith; Nightingales, 1990-93; GBH, 1991; Jake's Progress, 1995; Hornblower, 1998-2003; Oliver, 1999; My Family, 2000-11; Space Race (narrator), 2005; A Very Social Secretary, 2005; The Trial of Tony Blair; Jericho, 2005; Friends and Crocodiles, 2006; Gideon's Daughter, 2006; Falcon, 2012. Honours: Olivier, Tony and Fred Astaire Awards for performance in Me and My Girl; Olivier Award for Best Actor in a Musical, 1998. Address: Hamilton Asper Management, Ground Floor, 24 Hanway Street, London W1P 9DD, England.

LINEKER Gary Winston, b. 30 November 1960, Leicester, England. Former Footballer; Television Host. m. (1) Michelle Denise Cockayne, 1986-2006 (divorced) 4 sons; (2) Danielle Lineker, 2009. Career: Debut as professional footballer, Leicester City, 1978; Everton, 1985; Represented England, 1986 World Cup, Mexico, 1990 World Cup, Italy; Captain, England, 1991-92; FC Barcelona, Spain, 1986-89; Transferred to Tottenham Hotspur, 1989-92; 80 international caps; Scored 48 goals, June 1992; Grampus Eight Team, Japan, 1994; Presenter, Match of the Day, BBC TV, 1995-. Honour: MA, Leicester, 1992, Loughborough, 1992; OBE, 1992. Address: c/o SFX Sports Group, 35/36 Grosvenor Street, London W1K 4QX, England.

LING Maurice, b. 30 March 1979, Singapore. Senior Scientist. Education: BSc, 2003, BSc (Hons), 2004, PhD, Bioinformatics, 2009, University of Melbourne, Australia; BSc, Computing, University of Portsmouth, England, 2007; Certificate in Teaching, Singapore Polytechnic, 2009. Appointments: Resident Adviser and Tutor, University College, 2006-08; Honorary Fellow, Department of Zoology, 2010-, University of Melbourne; Lecturer, Singapore Polytechnic, 2008-11; Architect and Project Director, Cyber Laboratory Notebook, 2008-; Co-editor in Chief and Co-founder, The Python Papers Anthology, 2008-; Vice President, Python User group, 2009-; Publications and Conference Chair, PyCon Asia-Pacific, 2009-; Program Committee Member, Python for High Performance Computing and Scientific Computing, 2010-; Technical Reviewer, Packt Publishing, 2010-; Chief Editor, Computational and Mathematical Biology, 2010-; Editor-in-Chief, Methods and Cases in Computational, Mathematical and Statistical Biology, 2010-; Senior Scientist, Bioinformatics, Life Technologies, 2010-. Honours: Outstanding Mentor Award, Ministry of Education. Memberships: Association of Computing Machinery; Python User Group; Institute of Mathematical Statistics; Association of Medical and Bio-Informatics. Address: Apartment Block 627, #08-1600, Bedok Reservoir Road, Singapore 470627, Republic of Singapore.

LING Sergey Stepanovich, b. 7 May 1937. Politician and Agronomist. m. 3 children. Education: Belarus Agricultural Academy; Higher CPSU School, CPSU Central Committee. Appointments: Agronomist Sovkhoz, Lesnoye Kopylsk District; Chief Agronomist Sovkhoz, Chief Agronomist, Krynitsa Kopylsk District; Deputy Director, Lyuban Production Co; Chief, Soligorsk Production Agricultural Administration; Deputy Chairman, then Chairman, Slutsk District Executive Committee, Secretary, Smolevichi District CPSU Committee, 1960-72; Chief, Agricultural Division, Secretary, Minsk Regional Belarus Communist Party Committee, 1972-82; First Deputy Chairman, then Chairman, Executive Committee, Minsk Regional Soviet, 1982-86; Chairman, Belarus State Committee on Prices, Deputy Chairman, State Planning Committee, 1986-90; Head, Agricultural Division, Secretary, Central Committee, Belarus Communist Party, 1990-91; Deputy Chairman, Belarus Council of Ministers; Chairman, State Committee on Economics and Planning, 1991-; Deputy Prime Minister, 1994-96, Acting Prime Minister, 1996-97, Prime Minister, 1997-2000, Belarus. Address: c/o Council of Ministers, pl Nezavisimosti, 220010 Minsk, Belarus.

LINGARD Brian Hallwood, b. 2 November 1926, Melbourne, Australia. Architect. m. Dorothy, deceased 2006, 2 sons, 1 daughter. Education: DA, Manchester School of Architecture. Appointments: Royal Navy, 1944-46; Associate, Royal Institute of British Architects (ARIBA), 1949; Commenced private architectural practice, 1950; Fellow, Royal Institute of British Architects (FRIBA), 1957; Formed architectural partnership, Brian Lingard and Partners, 1972; Formed landscape architecture partnership, Ecoscape (now Lingard Styles Landscape), 1975; Formed architectural historians partnership, Gallery Lingard, 1982; Chairman, Architects Benevolent Society, 1988-92. Publications: The Opportunities for the Conservation and Enhancement of Our Historic Resorts; Special Houses for Special People; Thrifty Dwellings for Thrifty People, 2009. Honours: RIBA Regional Award (Wales); DOE/RIBA Housing Medals/Commendations (7 awards); Civic Trust Awards/Commendations (21 awards); TIMES/RICS Conservation Awards (2 awards); Prince of Wales Conservation Awards (3 awards); Life Vice-President, Architects Benevolent

Society, 2002. Memberships: Carlton Club; Royal Automobile Club; Sloane Club. Address: Le Bouillon House, St George's Esplanade, St Peter Port, Guernsey.

LINGEN-STALLARD Andrew Phillip, b. 10 August 1962, Worcester, England. Honorary Senior Midwife; Midwife Advisor. m. (1) Avril Clare Dove, 1985, divorced, 1996, 3 sons; Civil Partner, Lee Winter, 2005. Education: Registered General Nurse, 1985; Registered Midwife, 1988; BSc (Hons), Midwifery, 1996, MSc, Advancing Midwifery, 2006, Kings College, University of London; PhD, University of Manchester, in progress. Appointments include: Midwife, Grade E, Princess Margaret Hospital, Swindon, 1988-92; Midwife Grade F, Roehampton Hospital, Roehampton, 1992-93; Midwife Grade G, Kings College Hospital, NHS Trust, 1993-96; Supervisor of Midwives, Lambeth, Southwark and Lewisham SHA, 1997-; Clinical Midwifery Manager, Clerical and Administration Manager, Supervisor of Midwives, Grade H, 1996-99; Senior Nurse for Surgery Grade I, 2000-2001; Clinical Midwifery Manager (Acting Assistant and Head of Midwifery), Supervisor of Midwives, 2001, Lewisham University Hospital, Lewisham; Modern Matron, Senior Midwife Manager Grade I, Kings College Hospital, 2001-2005; Appointed by Secretary of State for Health to Midwifery Support Team, Department of Health, 2005; Honorary Senior Midwife, Kings College Hospital, 2005-; Midwife Advisor, London Ambulance Service, 2005-; Managing Director and Trustee, Royal College of Midwives, 2003-07; Managing Director, Lingen-Stallard & Winter Estates Ltd (Property portfolio), 2005-; Managing Director, Lingen-Stallard & MacDonald Entertainment Ltd, 2006-; Midwife Advisor, Nursing & Midwifery Council in UN, 2006-; Clinical Expert, Panel Member, Health Care London, 2008-09. Publications: Contributor of articles, letters and comment to professional journals. Honours: Grantee, Her Majesty's College of Arms, 2003; Fellow, Royal Society of Arts, 2005; Elected UK Council Member, Royal College of Midwives, 2003-07, Professional Policy Committee, 2003-07, Employment Relations Committee, 2003-2005. Memberships: Royal College of Midwives; Labour Party; Amnesty International; Genealogical Society; White Lion Society; Heraldic Society; National Trust; Royal Society for the Protection of Birds; Royal Horticultural Society. Address: 36 Romola Road, Tulse Hill, London SE24 9AZ, England. E-mail: aplingenstallard@aol.com

LINKLATER Richard, b. 30 July 1960, Houston, Texas, USA. Film Director. Appointments: Founder, Director, own film company, Detour Films, Austin, Texas; Founder, Artistic Director, Austin Film Society; Director, films, Slacker, 1991, Dazed and Confused, 1993, Before Sunrise, 1995, Suburbia, 1997, The Newton Boys, 1998; Waking Life, 2001; Tape, 2001; Live From Shiva's Dance Floor, 2003; The School of Rock, 2003; Before Sunset, 2004; $5.15/Hr, 2004; Bad News Bears, 2005; Fast Food Nation, 2006; A Scanner Darkly, 2006; Inning by Inning: A Coach's Progress, 2008; Me and Orson Welles, 2008. Honours: Silver Bear, Berlin Film Festival, 1995.

LINSCOTT Gillian, b. 27 September 1944, Windsor, England. Journalist; Writer. m. Tony Geraghty, 18 June 1988. Education: Honours Degree, English Language and Literature, Somerville College, Oxford University, 1966. Appointments: Journalist, Liverpool Post, 1967-70; Northern Ireland Correspondent, Birmingham Post, 1970-72; Reporter, The Guardian,1972-79; Sub Editor, BBC Radio News, Local Radio Parliamentary Reporter, 1979-90; Freelance Writer, 1990-. Publications: A Healthy Body, 1984; Murder Makes Tracks, 1985; Knightfall, 1986; A Whiff of Sulphur, 1987;

Unknown Hand, 1988; Murder, I Presume, 1990; Sister Beneath the Sheet, 1991; Hanging on the Wire, 1992; Stage Fright, 1993; Widow's Peak, 1994; Crown Witness, 1995; Dead Man's Music, 1996; Dance on Blood, 1998; Absent Friends, 1999; The Perfect Daughter, 2000; Dead Man Riding, 2002; The Garden, 2002; Blood on the Wood, 2003. Honours: Herodotus Award, The Historical Mystery Appreciation Society, 1999; Ellis Peters Historical Dagger, Crime Writers Association, 2000. Memberships: Society of Authors; Crime Writers Association. Address: Wood View, Hope Under Dinmore, Leominster, Herefordshire HR6 0PP, England.

LIOTTA Ray, b. 18 December 1954, Newark, New Jersey, USA. Actor. m. Michelle Grace, 1997-2004 (divorced), 1 daughter. Education: BFA, University of Miami. Career: Various television appearances: Another World, NBC, 1978-80; Hardhat & Legs, CBS movie, 1980; Crazy Times, ABC pilot, 1981; Casablanca, NBC, 1983; Our Family Honour, NBC, 1985-86; Women Men – In Love there Are No Rules, 1991; The Rat Pack, 1998; Point of Origin, 2002; Film appearances: The Lonely Lady, 1983; Something Wild, 1986; Arena Brains, 1987; Dominick and Eugene, 1988; Field of Dreams, 1989; Goodfellas, 1990; Article 99, Unlawful Entry, 1992; No Escape, Corrina, Corrina, 1994; Operation Dumbo Drop, 1995; Unforgettable, 1996; Turbulence, Phoenix, Copland, 1997; The Rat Pack, 1998; Forever Mine, Muppets From Space, 1999; Blow, Heartbreakers, Hannibal, 2001; John Q, A Rumor of Angels, Narc, 2002; Identity, 2003; Last Shot, Slow Burn, Control, 2004; Revolver, 2005; Even Money, Local Color, Comeback Season, Smokin' Aces, 2006; In the Name of the King: A Dungeon Siege Tale, Wild Hogs, Battle in Seattle, Crossing Over, Hero Wanted, 2007; Powder Blue, Observe and Report, Youth in Revolt, 2009; Crazy on the Outside, Snowmen, 2010. Address: c/o Endeavor Talent Agency, 9701 Wilshire Boulevard, 10th Floor, Beverly Hills, CA 90212, USA.

LIPMAN Maureen, b. 10 May 1946, Hull, England. Actor. m. Jack Rosenthal, deceased, 1 son, 1 daughter. Education: Newland High School for Girls, Hull; London Academy of Music and Dramatic Art. Appointments: TV: Cold Enough for Snow, 1997; Hampstead on the Couch, Coronation Street, George Eliot: A Scandalous Life, Jonathan Creek, 2002; Winter Solstice, 2003; Art Deco Designs, 2004; The Fugitives, 2005. Stage: The Rivals, 1996; Oklahoma! 1998, 1999, 2002; Peggy For You, 1999; Sitting Pretty, The Vagina Monologues, The Play What I Wrote, 2001; Thoroughly Modern Milly, 2004; Film: Captain Jack, 1997; Solomon & Gaenor, 1998; The Discovery of Heaven, The Pianist, 2001; Lighthouse Hill, Supertex, 2002; Standing Room Only, 2004; Stories of Lost Souls, 2006; Bridge of Lies, 2007. Radio: The Lipman Test, 1996-97; Choice Grenfell, 1998; Home Truths, 2002. Publications: How Was It For You? 1985; Something to Fall Back On, 1987; You Got an 'Ology?, with Richard Phillips, 1989; Thank You For Having Me, 1990; When's It Coming Out? 1992; You Can Read Me Like a Book, 1995; Lip Reading, 1999. Honours: CBE; Hon D Litt, Hull and Sheffield; Hon MA, Salford. Memberships: BAFTA; Equity. Address: c/o Conway van Gelder Ltd, 18-21 Jerryn Street, London SW1Y 6HP, England.

LIPWORTH Maurice Sydney (Sir), b. 13 May 1931, Johannesburg, South Africa. Barrister; Businessman. m. Rosa Liwarek, 1957, 2 sons. Education: BCom, LLB, University of Witwatersrand. Appointments: Practising Barrister, Johannesburg, 1956-64; Non-Executive Director, Liberty Life Association of Africa Ltd, 1956-64; Executive, Private Trading Companies, 1964-67; Executive Director, Abbey

Life Assurance PLC, 1968-70; Vice-President, Director, Abbey International Corporation Inc, 1968-70; Co-Founder, Director, 1970-88, Deputy Managing Director, 1977-79, Joint Managing Director, 1979-84, Deputy Chairman, 1984-88, Allied Dunbar Assurance PLC; Director, J Rothschild Holdings PLC, 1984-87; Director, BAT Industries PLC, 1985-88; Deputy Chairman of Trustees, 1986-93, Chairman, 1993-, Philharmonia Orchestra; Chairman, Monopolies and Mergers Commission, 1988-92; Non-Executive Director, Carlton Communications PLC, 1993-; Deputy Chairman, Non-Executive Director, National Westminster Bank, 1993-2000; Chairman, Financial Reporting Council, 1993-2001; Non-Executive Director, 1994-99, Chairman, 1995-99, Zeneca Group PLC; Member, Senior Salaries Review Body, 1994-; Trustee, South Bank Ltd, 1996-. Honours: Honorary Queen's Council, 1993. Memberships: Chairman, Bar Association for Commerce, Finance and Industry, 1991-91; European Policy Forum. Address: 41 Lothbury, London EC2P 2BP, England.

LISBERG Harvey Brian, b. 2 March 1940, Manchester, England. Impressario; Artist Manager. m. Carole Gottlieb, 5 November 1969, 2 sons. Education: Manchester University. Musical Education: Self-taught piano, guitar. Career: First in discovering: Graham Gouldman; Andrew Lloyd Webber; Tim Rice; Herman's Hermits; Tony Christie; Sad Café; Godley and Creme; 10cc; Currently representing: 10cc; Graham Gouldman; Eric Stewart; George Stiles; Anthony Drewe; Cleopatra. Address: Kennedy House, 31 Stamford Street, Altrincham, Cheshire WA14 1ES, England.

LISCHKE Gerhard, b. 10 May 1948, Apolda, Germany. Mathematician. m. Monika Berger, 1 son. Education: Diploma, Mathematics, 1971; Dr rer nat, 1976; Dr sc nat, 1989; Dr rer nat habil, 1991. Appointments: Scientific Assistant, 1971-90, Scientific Chief Assistant, 1990-94, Lecturer, 1994-, Friedrich-Schiller-University, Jena; Visiting Professor, Eötvös Loránd University, Budapest, 1997, 1999; Exchange Visitor, International Computer Science Institute, Berkeley, California, USA, 1992; Fellowship, Japan Society for the Promotion of Science, Kyoto Sangyo University, 2006 and 2011. Publications: Over 30 articles in professional journals including: Towards the actual relationship between NP and Exponential Time, 1999; Roots and powers of regular languages, 2003; Restorations of punctured languages and similarity of languages, 2006; Generalized periodicity and primitivity for words, 2007; The primitivity distance of words, 2010; Primitive words and roots of words, 2011. Honours: Listed in various international biographical dictionaries. Memberships: European Association for Theoretical Computer Science. Address: Institut fuer Informatik, Friedrich-Schiller-University, Ernst-Abbe-Platz 1-4, D-07743, Jena, Germany.

LISCIC Bozidar, b. 17 January 1929, Karlovac, Croatia. Professor of Mechanical Engineering. m. Biserka Liscic, 2 daughters. Education: BSc, Mechanical Engineering, Technical Faculty, 1954, PhD, Materials Science, 1975, University of Zagreb, Croatia. Appointments: Workshop Engineer, Technical Manager, Machine Tool Factory "Prvomajska", 1954-64; Counsellor for Metalworking Industry, Chamber of Commerce, 1964-68; Assistant Professor, Associate Professor, Professor, Faculty of Mechanical Engineering and Naval Architecture, University of Zagreb, 1968-99; Served as UNDP Expert for Heat Treatment on several assignments in Israel, Egypt, Turkey, India, Bangladesh and Pakistan, 1971-90; Retired, 1999. Publications: Books: Co-author, Eckstein, Technologie der Wärmebehandlung von Stahl, 1986; Editor and co-author, Theory and Technology of Quenching, 1992; Co-author, Steel Heat Treatment Handbook, 1999; Co-author, Fuels and Lubricants Handbook, 2003; First editor and co-author, Quenching Theory and Technology, 2nd edition, 2010; About 120 scientific papers published. Honours: Grand Medal of the Faculty for establishing heat treatment laboratory; State Award of the Republic of Croatia for achievements in scientific research, 1989; Adolf Martens Medaille, AWT, Germany, 2006. Memberships: American Society for Materials, 1980-, elected Fellow, 1998; Fellow, Croatian Academy of Sciences and Arts, 1997; President, International Federation for Heat Treatment and Surface Engineering, 2004-05; Adolf Martens-Medaille, 2006. Address: Svačićev trg 12, 10000 Zagreb, Croatia. E-mail: bliscic@fsb.hr Website: www.hazu.hr

LISTER David George, b. 19 September 1943, Tadcaster, Yorkshire, England. Physical Chemist. Education: BSc, University of Leeds, 1965; PhD, 1968, DSc, 1984, University of Glasgow. Appointments: Research Assistant, University College, London, 1968-70; Royal Society Fellowship, Istituto di Spettroscopia Molecolare, Bologna, Italy, 1970-71; Research Fellow, University of Wales, Bangor, Wales, 1971-73; Senior Lecturer, University of Dar Es Salaam, Tanzania, 1975-76; Professor of Physical Chemistry, University of Messina, Italy, 1987-. Publication: Book: Internal Rotation and Inversion, 1978 (co-author). Memberships: European Academy of Sciences; Royal Society of Chemistry; American Chemical Society. Address: Dipartimento di Chimica Industriale e Ingegneria dei Materiali, Salita Sperone 31, I98166 Sant'Agata di Messina, Italy. E-mail: listerd@unime.it

LITHERLAND Sheila Jacqueline, b. 18 September 1936, Birmingham, England. Poet; Creative Writing/Literature Tutor. Divorced, 1 son, 1 daughter. Education: Regent Street Polytechnic, 1955; Ruskin College, Oxford, 1986; BA, University College, London, 1989. Publications: The Long Interval; Fourpack; Half Light; Modern Poets of Northern England; New Women Poets; The Poetry of Perestroika; Flowers of Fever; The Apple Exchange; The Forward Book of Poetry, 2001; The Work of the Wind; The Homage; The Absolute Bonus of Rain. Contributions to: Iron Magazine; Writing Women Magazine; Oxford Magazine; Green Book. Honour: Annaghmakerrig Residence, 1994; Northern Writers Award, 2000. Memberships: The Cricket Society; Durham County Cricket Club; Poetry Society; Vane Women Writers' Collective. Address: 6 Waddington Street, Durham City DH1 4BG, England.

LITTEN Julian William Sebastian, b. 6 November 1947, Wolverhampton, England. Architectural Historian. Education: South West Essex Technical College and School of Art, Walthamstow, 1964-66; PhD, Department of History and Archaeology, Cardiff University, 1993-2002. Appointments: Museum Assistant, Department of Sculpture, 1966-74, Senior Museum Assistant, 1974-82, Research Assistant, 1982-84, Department of Prints and Drawings, Accommodation Officer, 1984-90, Front-of House Manager, 1990-99, Victoria and Albert Museum, London; Visiting Lecturer in Built Heritage Conservation, Canterbury Christ Church University College, Canterbury, 1999-2005. Publications: Books: St Mary's Church, Woodford, Essex, 1978; The English Way of Death: The Common Funeral Since 1450, 1991, 2nd edition, 1992, 3rd edition, 2002; Folklore Traditions of Our Lady, 1994; The Eucharistic Year, 2001; St Barnabas and St James the Greater, Walthamstow, 2003; Co-author: St Mary the Virgin, Radwinter, 1994; Guide to the Management of safety in Burial

Grounds, 2001; Numerous chapters and articles in academic journals. Honours: PhD; FSA; FSA (Scot). Memberships: Fellow, Society of Antiquaries of London; Fellow Society of Antiquaries of Scotland; International Institute of Risk and Safety Management. Address: Friarscot, Church Street, King's Lynn, Norfolk PE30 5EB, England. E-mail: julian.litten@btopenworld.com

LITTEN Nancy Magaret, b. 30 September 1951, Dartford, Kent, England. Musician. m. Clinton Davis, 2 sons, 1 daughter. Education: LRAM Violin (Teacher's), 1970, LRAM Piano (Teacher's), 1971, Royal Academy of Music; Cert Ed, Exeter, 1972; ATCL Voice (Performer's), 2001. Appointments: Teacher of Piano, Singing, Violin and Keyboard, Kent Music School, 1997-; ABRSM Examiner, 1998-; Founder, Director, Kent Keyboard Orchestra, 1999-, and Kent Music's Singing Days for Instrumentalists; Freelance Accompanist and Adjudicator. Publications: Contributor to the Federation of Music Services, A Common Approach, 2002, keyboard section; Consultant to ABRSM for Electronic Keyboard Music Medals, 2004-. Honours: Elizabeth Stokes Open Piano Scholarship, 1968; Janet Duff Greet Prize for most deserving British scholar, 1970, 1971. Membership: Incorporated Society of Musicians. Address: Springfield, 39 Ashford Road, Maidstone, Kent ME14 5DP, England.

LITTLE Tasmin, b. 13 May 1965, London, England. Violinist. m. Michael Hatch, 1 daughter. Education: Yehudi Menuhin School; Guildhall School of Music; Private studies with Lorand Fenyves, Canada. Career: Performed with New York Philharmonic, Leipzig Gewandhaus, Berlin Symphony, London Symphony, Philharmonia, Royal Philharmonic, Royal Liverpool Philharmonic, European Community Chamber, Royal Danish and Stavanger Symphony orchestras; Has played in orchestras conducted by Kurt Masur, Vladimir Ashkenazy, Leonard Slatkin, Tadaaki Otaka, Sir Charles Groves, Andrew Davis, Jerzy Maksymiuk, Vernon Handley, Yan Pascal Tortelier, Sir Edward Downes, Yehudi Menuhin and Sir Simon Rattle; Played at Proms since 1990; Concerto and recital performances in UK, Europe, Scandinavia, South America, Hong Kong, Oman, Zimbabwe, Australia, New Zealand, USA and Japan; Numerous TV appearances including BBC Last Night of the Proms, 1995, 1998. Recordings include: Concertos of Bruch, Dvořák, Brahms, Sibelius, Delius, Rubbra, Saxton, George Lloyd, Ravel, Debussy, Poulenc, Elgar, Bax, Finzi; Dohnanyi violin sonatas, Bruch Scottish Fantasy, Lalo Symphonie Espagnole, Part Spiegel im Spiegel and Fratres. Publication: paper on Delius' violin concerto. Honours: Hon DLitt (Bradford), 1996; Hon DMus (Leicester), 2002. Address: c/o Askonas Holt Ltd, 27 Chancery Lane, London WC2A 1PF, England.

LITTLE RICHARD (Richard Penniman), b. 5 December 1935, Macon, Georgia, USA. Singer; Musician (piano). Education: Theological college, 1957. Career: R&B singer, various bands; Tours and film work with own band, The Upsetters; Gospel singer, 1960-62; World-wide tours and concerts include: Star Club, Hamburg, Germany, with Beatles, 1962; European tour, with Beatles, Rolling Stones, 1963; UK tour with Everly Brothers, 1963; Rock'n'Revival Concert, Toronto, with Chuck Berry, Fats Domino, Jerry Lee Lewis, Gene Vincent, Bo Diddley, 1969; Toronto Pop Festival, 1970; Randall Island Rock Festival, with Jimi Hendrix, Jethro Tull, 1970; Rock'n'Roll Spectaculars, Madison Square Garden, 1972-; Muhammad Ali's 50th Birthday; Benefit For Lupus Foundation, Universal City, 1992; Westbury Music Fair, 1992; Giants Of Rock'n'Roll, Wembley Arena, 1992; Film appearances: Don't Knock The Rock, 1956; Mr Rock'n'Roll, 1957; The Girl Can't Help It, 1957; Keep On Rockin', 1970; Down And Out In Beverly Hills, 1986; Mother Goose Rock'n'Rhyme, Disney Channel, 1989. Recordings: Albums: Here's Little Richard, 1957; Little Richard Is Back, 1965; Greatest Hits, 1965; Freedom Blues, 1970; The King Of Rock'n'Roll, 1971; God's Beautiful City, 1979; Lifetime Friend, 1987; Featured on: Folkways - A Vision Shared (Woody Guthrie tribute), 1988; For Our Children, 1991; Shake It All About, 1992; Little Richard and Jimi Hendrix, 1993; Shag on Down by the Union Hall,1996; Hit singles include: Tutti Frutti, 1956; Long Tall Sally, 1956; The Girl Can't Help It, 1957; Lucille, 1957; She's Got It, 1957; Jenny Jenny, 1957; Keep A Knockin', 1957; Good Golly Miss Molly, 1958, Baby Face, 1959; Bama Lama Bama Loo, 1964. Honours include: Inducted, Rock'n'Roll Hall of Fame, 1986; Star, Hollywood Walk Of Fame, 1990; Little Richard Day, Los Angeles, 1990; Penniman Boulevard, Macon, named in his honour; Platinum Star, Lupus Foundation Of America, 1992; Grammy Lifetime Achievement Award, 1993.

LITTLEJOHN Joan Anne, b. 20 April 1937, London, England. Creative Artist. Education: Royal College of Music, 1955-59; Postgraduate Study, Howells and Others; LRAM, 1957; GRSM, 1958. Appointments: Freelance Composer, Musicologist, Photographer, 1959-; Administrative Staff, Royal College of Music, 1960-83; Piano Teacher, Harrow School, 1972-73. Publications: Poems and Music. Honours: RVW Trust and Patrons Fund Awards in the 1970's; Recipient Howells' Composing Piano, 1984; Award of Merit, Golden Poet Award, 1985 and Silver Poet Award, 1986; Millennium Medal of Honour, 1998; Archives destined for The Nation, to be housed at The Devon Record Office. Memberships: PRS; ABIRA. Address: Shepherds Delight, 49 Hamilton Lane, Exmouth, Devon EX8 2LW, England.

LITTLEMORE Christopher Paul, b. 8 March 1959, Warwickshire, England. Architect. m. Jane Evelyn Chalk, 1 son, 1 daughter. Education: BA (Hons), B.Arch, Manchester University, 1977-83; MSc, Conservation of Historic Buildings, Bath University, 1998-99. Appointments: Associate, 1986, Director, 1989, Managing Director, 2002, The Charter Partnership, Architects. Membership: Royal Institute of British Architects. Address: Meadow House, Broad Chalke, Nr Salisbury, Wilts, England. E-mail: cplittlemore@charter.eu.com

LITTON Andrew, b. 16 May 1959, New York City, New York, USA. Orchestral Conductor; Pianist. Education: Mozarteum, Salzburg; Juilliard School of Music; MM. Appointments: Assistant Conductor, La Scala, Milan, 1980-81; Exxon-Arts Endowment Assistant Conductor, then Associate Conductor, National Symphony Orchestra, Washington DC, 1982-86; Principal Guest Conductor, 1986-88, Principal Conductor, Artistic Adviser, 1988-94, Conductor Laureate, 1994-, Bournemouth Symphony Orchestra; Music Director, Dallas Symphony Orchestra, 1994-2006; Guest Conductor, many leading orchestras world-wide including Chicago Symphony, Philadelphia, Los Angeles Philharmonic, Pittsburgh Symphony, Toronto Symphony, Montreal Symphony, Vancouver Symphony, London Philharmonic, Royal Philharmonic, London Symphony, English Chamber, Leipzig Gewandhaus, Moscow State Symphony, Stockholm Philharmonic, RSO Berlin, RAI Milan, Orchestre National de France, Suisse Romande, Tokyo Philharmonic, Melbourne Symphony and Sydney Symphony orchestras; Opera debut with Eugene Onegin, Metropolitan Opera, New York, 1989; Conducted Leoncavallo, La Bohème and Falstaff, St Louis Opera, Hansel and Gretel, Los Angeles

Opera, 1992, Porgy and Bess, Royal Opera House, Covent Garden, 1992, Salome, English National Opera, 1996; Music Consultant to film The Chosen. Publications: Recordings including Mahler Symphony No 1 and Songs of a Wayfarer, Elgar Enigma Variations, complete Tchaikovsky symphony cycle, complete Rachmaninov symphony cycle, Shostakovich Symphony No 10, Gershwin Rhapsody in Blue, Concerto in F, Bernstein Symphony No 2, Brahms Symphony No 1; As piano soloist and conductor, Ravel Concerto in G. Honours: Winner, William Kapell Memorial US National Piano Competition, 1978; Winner, Bruno Walter Conducting Fellowship, 1981; Winner, BBC-Rupert Foundation International Conductors Competition, 1982; Honorary DMus, Bournemouth, 1992. Address: c/o IMG Artists Europe, Media House, 3 Burlington Lane, London W4 2TH, England.

LIU Angela Leitmannová, b. 14 January 1952, Slovakia (former Czechoslovakia). Professor in Biophysics. m. George Shih-jan Liu, 1 son, 1 daughter. Education: MSc, Humboldt University, Berlin, Germany, 1974; PhD, Biophysics, 1977; Associate Professor, 1989; DrSc, 1995, Professor, 2001. Appointments: Humboldt University, 1972-77; Slovak Academy of Sciences, 1977-81; Slovak Technical University, 1981-; Visiting Associate Professor, 1991-2001, Visiting Professor, Biophysics, Michigan State University, East Lansing, 2001-. Publications: Over 180 in professional journals. Honours: Several. Memberships: Union of Slovak Mathematicians and Physicists; Slovak Medical Society; Slovak Cybernetic Society at Slovak Academy of Sciences. Address: Learning Resources Center, Bessey Hall, Michigan State University, East Lansing MI 48824, USA.

LIU Hung-Huan, b. 12 December 1968, Penghu, Taiwan. Computer Communications. m. Chia-Tian Yu, 1 son, 1 daughter. Education: BS, 1994, MS, 1997, PhD, 2003, National Taiwan University of Science and Technology, Taipei, Taiwan. Appointments: Lecturer and Assistant Professor, National Penghu University of Science and Technology, Denghu, Taiwan, 2000-04; Assistant Professor, Chung Yuan Christian University, Chung Li, Taiwan, 2004-. Publications: Mobile Social Networks as Quality of Life Technology for People with Mental Illness, 2009. Memberships: IEEE; ACM Sigcomm. Address: Chung Yuan Christian University EL, 200, Chung-Pei Road, Chung-Li 32023, Taiwan. E-mail: hhliu@cycu.edu.tw

LIU Xiangming, b. 1 April 1951, Hunan, China. University Teacher. m. Miaozhen Ou, 1 son. Education: PhD, Biomedical Engineering, Huazhong University of Science and Technology, 2001. Appointments: Dean, Pharmacy College, South-Central University for Nationalities, 2000-. Publications: Effect of dragon's blood and its component loureirin B on tetrodotoxin-sensitive voltage-gated sodium currents in rat dorsal root ganglion neutrons, 2004; Modulation of dragon's blood on tetrodotoxin-resistant sodium currents in dorsal root ganglion neurons and identification of its material basis for efficacy, 2006; Material basis for inhibition of Dragon's Blood on evoked discharges of wide dynamic range neurons in spinal dorsal horn of rats, 2008; Inhibitory effect of cochinchmenin B on capsicin-activated responses in rat dorsal root ganglion neurons, 2008. Honours: 3rd Prize, Hubei Provincial Natural Science Award, 2004; World Congress of Arts, Sciences and Communications, Lifetime Achievement Award, 2011; IBC Lifetime Achievement Award, 2011. Address: College of Biomedical Engineering, South-Central University for Nationalities, Minyuan Road No 708, Wuhan, Hubei 430074, China. E-mail: liu.xiangming@263.net

LIU Yi-Xun, b. 5 May 1936, Shandong, China. Professor; Fellow of Chinese Academy of Sciences; Reproductive Biologist. m. Xue-Kun Zhao, 1967, 1 daughter. Education: Bachelor's degree, Fudan University, 1963; PhD, Academia Sinica, Beijing, 1966. Appointments: Research Associate, Reproductive Biology, 1967-72, Assistant Professor, Department of Endocrinology, 1976-84, Associate Professor, Reproductive Biology, 1987-89; Director, Department of Endocrinology, 1989-90; Professor, Vice Director and Academic Committee Director, State Key Laboratory of Reproductive Biology, Institute of Zoology, Chinese Academy of Sciences, Beijing, 1991; Visiting Scholar, Imperial Cancer Research Foundation, London, England, 1974-75; Visiting Scientist, University of California, San Diego, USA, 1984-86; Visiting Scientist, 1988-89, Visiting Professor, 1990-91, 1992, Umeå University, Sweden; Visiting Professor, Leicester University, England, 1995-97, 1999-; Fellow, Chinese Academy of Sciences; Chairman, Academic Committee of State Key Laboratory of Reproductive Biology, Institute of Zoology, Chinese Academy of Sciences; Chairman, 10 other academic committees of key laboratories in China; Director, WHO/Rockefeller Foundation & International Implantation Collaboration Research Center, China, 1999-2005; Chairman, Chinese Society for Reproductive Biology; Deputy Director, National Society for Endocrinology, Reproductive Biology and Metabolism; Member, National Science and Technology Committee, China Population and Family Planning Commission. Publications: More than 250 articles in professional journals. Honours: Natural Science Award of Academia Sinica, 1982, 1984, 1985, 1991, 1993, 1996, 1997; Beijing Award of Science and Technology, 1983; Postdoctoral Fellowship and Research Fund from Rockefeller Foundation, 1984-86, 1987-89; Science and Technology Awards of State Family Planning Commission, 1996; China Population Award, 2005; China Population and Family Planning Science and Technology Award, 2006; Listed in international biographical dictionaries. Memberships: Society for the Study of Reproduction, USA; USA Endocrine Society; American Association for the Advancement of Science; New York Academy of Sciences; Chinese Society for Reproductive Biology; Chinese Society for Physiology; Chinese Society for Cell Biology; Chinese Society for Comparative Endocrinology; Chinese Society for Physiology; Editorial board member of international journals: Human Reproduction; Archives of Andrology; Endocrine; Frontiers in Bioscience; Asian Journal of Andrology; Developmental and Reproductive Biology; Science in China. E-mail: liuyx@ioz.ac.cn

LIU Zhaorong, b. 1 June 1937, Zuoquan County, Shanxi Province, China. Educator. m. Shaohua Zhao, 1 son, 3 daughters. Education: Mathematical Department, Harbin Teachers' College. Appointment: Teacher, Yuci Railway Middle School, 1962-95. Publications: The Proof of Goldbach's Conjecture; Numerous other mathematical research papers. Honours: The Golden Medal of the First Special Contribution Experts awarded by the World ESCH Organisation; Listed in Who's Who publications and biographical dictionaries. Membership: Mathematical Association of America; World ESCH Group; American Mathematical Society. Address: #168 Anning Street, Yuci District, Jinzhong City, Shanxi Province 030600, People's Republic of China. E-mail: lzronga@163.com

LIUHTO Kari Tapani, b. 26 December 1967, Joutseno, Finland. Professor. m. Minna Kihlström. Education: MSc, 1991, DSc, 1999, Economics and Business Administration, Department of International Marketing, Turku School of Economics; PhD, Social Sciences, Institute of Russian and

DICTIONARY OF INTERNATIONAL BIOGRAPHY 36th EDITION

East European Studies, University of Glasgow, Scotland, 1997. Appointments: Assistant, 1991-92, Researcher, 1994-95, Research Fellow, 1995-97, Institute for East-West Trade, Project Researcher, 1994, Business Research and Development Center, Research Director, Pan-European Institute, 1998-99, Turku School of Economics; Associate Professor, 1997, Professor, 1997-98, Department of Industrial Engineering and Management, Professor, 2000-03, Lappeenranta University of Technology, Finland. Publications: Some 300 published articles/reports in over 20 countries. Honours: Knight, First Class, Order of the White Rose of Finland, 2007. Memberships: Finnish Centre for Russian and East European Studies, University of Helsinki; Editor in Chief, Baltic Rim Economies review. Address: Pan-European Institute, Rehtorinpellonkatu 3, 20500 Turku, Finland. E-mail: kari.liuhto@tse.fi

LIVELY Penelope Margaret, b. 17 March 1933, Cairo, Egypt. Writer. m. Jack Lively, 1957, 1 son, 1 daughter. Education: Honours Degree, Modern History, Oxford University, England. Publications: Fiction: The Road to Lichfield, 1977; Nothing Missing But the Samovar, and Other Stories, 1978; Treasures of Time, 1979; Judgement Day, 1980; Next to Nature, Art, 1982; Perfect Happiness, 1983; Corruption and Other Stories, 1984; According to Mark, 1984; Moon Tiger, 1986; Pack of Cards: Stories 1978-86, 1987; Passing On, 1989; City of the Mind, 1991; Cleopatra's Sister, 1993; Heat Wave, 1996; Beyond the Blue Mountains: Stories, 1997; Spider Web, 1998; The Photograph, 2003; Making It Up, 2005; Consequences, 2007; Family Album, 2009. Non-Fiction: The Presence of the Past: An Introduction to Landscape History, 1976; Oleander, Jacaranda, 1992; A House Unlocked, 2001. Children's Books: Astercote, 1970; The Whispering Knights, 1971; The Driftway, 1972; Going Back, 1973; The Ghost of Thomas Kempe, 1974; Boy Without a Name, 1975; Fanny's Sister, 1976; The Stained Glass Window, 1976; A Stitch in Time, 1976; Fanny and the Monsters, 1978; The Voyage of QV66, 1978; Fanny and the Battle of Potter's Piece, 1980; The Revenge of Samuel Stokes, 1981; Uninvited Ghosts and Other Stories, 1984; Dragon Trouble, Debbie and the Little Devil, 1984; A House Inside Out, 1987; In Search of A Homeland: The Story of the Aeneid, 2001; The House in Norham Gardens, 2004. Contributions to: Numerous journals and magazines. Honours: Officer of the Order of the British Empire, 1989; Hon DLitt (Tufts University), 1993, (Warwick), 1998; Hon Fellow, Swansea University, 2002; Commander of the British Empire, 2002; Several honorary degrees and literary awards. Memberships: Society of Authors; PEN. Address: c/o David Higham Associates, 5-8 Lower John Street, Golden Square, London W1R 4HA, England.

LIVESLEY Brian, b. 31 August 1936, Southport, Lancashire, England. Medical Practitioner. m. Valerie Anne Nuttall, 1 son, 2 daughters. Education: MB, ChB, Leeds University Medical School, 1960. Appointments: Clinical Training and Teaching posts, University and District Hospitals, Leeds, Manchester and Liverpool, 1961-69; Harvey Research Fellow, King's College Hospital Medical School, London, 1969-72; Consultant Physician, Geriatric Medicine, Southwark, London, 1973-88; University of London's Foundation Professor in the Care of the Elderly, Honorary Consultant Physician in General and Geriatric Medicine, Chelsea and Westminster Hospital NHS Trust, London, 1988-2001; North West Thames Regional Adviser, Postgraduate Education, British Postgraduate Medical Federation, 1990-96; Invited Expert on the care of adults for several Police Constabularies and HM Coroner's offices, 1999-2011; The University of London's Emeritus Professor in the Care of the Elderly, 2003-; John Keats Lecturer, 2009-. Publications: Over 150 professional publications. Honours: Officer Brother, 1992, Knight, 1994, Most Venerable Order of St John of Jerusalem. Memberships: Osler Lecturer, 1975, Gideon de Laune Lecturer, 2001, Master, 2005-2006, Past Master & Court of Assistants, Worshipful Society of Apothecaries of London; Royal Society of Medicine; Royal College of Physicians of London. Address: PO Box 295, Oxford OX2 9GD, England. E-mail: brian.livesley@doctors.org.uk

LIVINGSTON Dorothy Kirby, b. 6 January 1948, Gosforth, Northumberland. Solicitor. 2 daughters. Education: MA, Jurisprudence, Hugh's College, Oxford, 1966-69. Appointments: Trainee, 1970, Assistant Solicitor, 1972, Partner, 1980, Consultant, 2008, Herbert Smith; Member, City of London Law Society Competition Law Committee, 1998; Chairman, City of London Law Society Financial Law Committee, 1999; Solicitor Advocate (Civil), 2005; Member, Banking Liaison Panel established under Banking Act, 2009. Publications: Competition Law and Practice, 1995; The Competition Act 1998: A Practitioner's Guide, 2001; Competition Law chapters in Leasing and Asset Finance, 3rd edition 1997, 4th edition 2003. Address: Herbert Smith, Exchange House, Primrose Street, London EC2A 2HS, England. E-mail: dorothy.livingston@herbertsmith.com

LIYANAGE Sunil, b. 27 September 1941, Colombo, Sri Lanka. Consultant Rheumatologist. m. Isabella Nallamanickam, 2 sons. Education: MBBS (Ceylon), 1965; FRCP (UK); DCH (Eng); DipMedAc. Appointments: Consultant Rheumatologist in East Berkshire, 1975-2005; Medical Director, Heatherwood and Wexham Park NHS Trust, 1991-95. Publications: Chapters in: Recent Advances in Rheumatology; Textbook of Rheumatology; Handbook of Drug Interactions. Memberships: British Society for Rheumatology; American Society for Bone and Mineral Research; British Medical Acupuncture Society, former Chairman. Address: The Princess Margaret Hospital, Windsor, SL4 3SJ, England. E-mail: rheumatology@lineone.net Website: www.medicalacupuncture.co.uk

LLEWELLIN (John) Richard (Allan), b. 30 September 1938, Haverfordwest, South Wales. Bishop. m. Jennifer Sally House, 1 son, 2 daughters. Education: Clifton College, Bristol; Theological studies, Westcott House and Fitzwilliam College, Cambridge, 1961-64. Appointments: Articled to Messrs Farrer and Co of Lincoln's Inn Fields; Solicitor, Messrs Field Roscoe and Co, London; Assistant Curate, Radlett, Hertfordshire, 1964-68; Assistant Priest, Johannesburg Cathedral, South Africa, 1968-71; Vicar of Waltham Cross, 1971-79; Rector of Harpenden, 1979; Bishop of St Germans, 1985; Bishop of Dover and Bishop in Canterbury, 1992; Bishop at Lambeth and Head of Staff to the Archbishop of Canterbury, 1999-. Address: Lambeth Palace, London, SE1 7JU, England. Email: richard.llewellin@lampal.c-of-e.org.uk

LLEWELLYN SMITH Sir Christopher Hubert, b. 19 November 1942, Giggleswick, England. Physicist. m. Virginia Grey, 1 son, 1 daughter. Education: BA, Physics with First Class Honours, 1964, DPhil, Theoretical Physics, 1967, Oxford University. Appointments: Royal Society Exchange Fellow, Physical Institute, Academy of Sciences, Moscow, USSR, 1967-68; Fellow in the Theoretical Studies Division, European Laboratory for Particle Physics (CERN), Geneva, Switzerland, 1968-70; Research Associate, Stanford Linear Accelerator Center, Stanford, California, USA, 1970-72; Staff Member, Theoretical Studies Division, CERN, Geneva,

1972-74; Fellow, St John's College, Oxford, 1974-98; Lecturer, 1974-80, Reader, 1980-87, Professor of Theoretical Physics, 1987-98, Chairman of Physics, 1987-92; Science Research Council Senior Fellow, 1978-81; Director General of CERN (on secondment from Oxford), 1994-98; Provost and President, University College London, 1999-2002; Senior Research Fellow, Department of Physics, University of Oxford, 2002-2003; Director, UKAEA Culham Division and Head of the Euratom/UK Fusion Association, 2003-08; Chairman, Consultative Committee for Euratom on Fusion, 2004-09; Chairman, ITER (International Tokamak Experimental Reactor) Council, 2007-09; President, SESAME (Synchrotron-light for Experimental Science and its Applications in the Middle East), 2008-; Vice President, Council of the Royal Society, 2008-10; Director of Energy Research, Oxford University, 2011-. Publications: Numerous articles on high energy physics, fusion energy, science policy and international collaboration in science. Honours: Maxwell Prize and Medal, Institute of Physics, Fellow of the Royal Society, 1984; Academia Europaea, 1989; Fellow, American Physical Society, 1994; Honorary DSc, Bristol, UK, 1997; Honorary D.Cien., Granada, Spain, 1997; Honorary DSc, Shandong China, 1997; Medal, Japanese Association of Medical Sciences, 1997; Gold Medal, Slovak Academy of Science, 1997; Foreign Fellow, Indian National Science Academy; Honorary Fellow, University of Wales, Cardiff, 1998; Distinguished Associate Award, US Department of Energy, 1998; Distinguished Service Award, US National Science Foundation, 1998; Glazebrook Medal, Institute of Physics, 1999; Honorary Fellow, St John's College, Oxford, 2000; Knight Bachelor, 2001; Honorary Fellow, New College, Oxford, 2002; Honorary Fellow, Institute of Mathematics and its Applications, 2003. Address: Theoretical Physics, 1 Keble Road, Oxford OX1 3NP, England. E-mail: c.llewellyn-smith@physics.ox.ac.uk

LLEWELYN-EVANS Adrian, b. 5 August 1953, Wales. Mediator. m. Catherine, 3 sons. Education: University College, Durham. Appointments: Linklaters, London, 1977-82; Head of Commercial Litigation, Head of ADR Services, Burges Salmon, Bristol, 1982-2009; Independent Mediator. Memberships: International Bar Association. E-mail: adrianlle@btinternet.com

LLOYD Christopher, b. 22 October 1938, Stamford, Connecticut, USA. Actor. m. (1) Catherine Boyd, 1959-1971 (divorced), (2) Kay Tornborg, 1975-1987 (divorced), (3) Carol Vanek, 1988-1991 (divorced), (4) Jane Walker Wood, 1992-2005 (divorced). Education: Neighbourhood Playhouse, New York. Appointments: Film Debut, One Flew Over the Cuckoo's Nest, 1975; Films include: Butch and Sundance: The Early Days; The Onion Field; The Black Marble; The Legend of the Lone Ranger; Mr Mom; To Be or Not to Be; Star Trek III: The Search for Spock; Adventures of Buckaroo Banzai; Back to the Future; Clue; Who Framed Roger Rabbit?; Track 29; Walk Like a Man; Eight Men Out; The Dream Team; Why Me?; Back to the Future, Part II; Back to the Future, Part III; The Addams Family; Twenty Bucks; Dennis the Menace; Addams Family Values; The Pagemaster; Camp Nowhere; The Radioland Murders; Things To Do in Denver When You're Dead; Cadillac Ranch; Changing Habits; Dinner at Fred's; Baby Geniuses; My Favorite Martian; Man on the Moon; Chasing Destiny, 2000; When Good Ghouls Go Bad, 2001; Wit, 2001; Wish You Were Dead, 2003; Interstate 60, 2003; Haunted Lighthouse, 2003; Merry Christmas Space Case (voice), 2003; Admissions, 2004; Wallflowering, 2005; Enfants Terribles, 2005; Flakes, 2007; Fly Me to the Moon, 2007; Jack and the Beanstalk, 2008; Foodfight, 2008; The Tale of Despereaux, 2008. TV includes: Taxi; Best of the West; The Dictator; Tales from Hollywood Hills; Pat Hobby - Teamed with Genius; September Gun; Avonlea; Alice in Wonderland; Right to Remain Silent; The Edge; Quicksilver Highway; Spin City; Cyberchase; Tremors; Malcolm in the Middle; The Big Time; I Dream (series), 2004; Clubhouse (series), 2004; Stacked, 2005-2006; A Perfect Day, 2006. Honours: Winner, Drama Desk and Obie Awards, Kaspar, 1973; Three Primetime Emmys. Address: The Gersh Agency, 252 North Canon Drive, Beverly Hills, CA 90210, USA.

LLOYD Clive Hubert, b. 31 August 1944, British Guiana, now Guyana. Cricketer. m. Waveney Benjamin, 1 son, 2 daughters. Career: Left-Hard Batsman, Right-Arm Medium-Paced Bowler; Played for British Guiana and Guyana, 1963-83; Played, 1968-86, Captain, 1981-83, 1986, for Lancashire; 110 Tests for West Indies, 1966-85, with record 74 as Captain, scoring 7,515 runs, averaging 46.6, including 19 centuries; Toured England, 1969, 1973, 1975 in World Cup, 1976, 1979 in World Cup, 1980, 1983 in World Cup, 1984; Scored 31,232 first-class runs including 79 centuries; Director, Red Rose Radio PLC, 1981; Executive Promotions Officer, Project Fullemploy, 1987-; West Indies Team Man, 1988-89, 1996-; International Cricket Council Referee, 1992-95. Publications: Living for Cricket, co-author, 1980; Winning Captaincy, co-author, 1995. Honours: Commander, Order of the British Empire. Address: c/o Harefield, Harefield Drive, Wilmslow, Cheshire SK9 1NJ, England.

LLOYD (David) Huw (Owen), b. 14 April 1950, London, England. Family Doctor. m. Mary Eileen, 1 son, 3 daughters. Education: Gonville and Caius College, Cambridge, 1968-71; Guy's Hospital, London, 1971-74; Somerset Vocational Training Scheme, 1976-79. Appointments: Principal, Cadwgan Surgery, Old Colwyn; Clinical Governance Lead, Conwy Local Health Group. Memberships: Fellow, Royal College of General Practitioners; Chairman, Mental Health Task Group, RCGP; Deputy Chairman, North Wales Local Medical Committee; Member, Welsh Council, RCGP; General Practitioners Committee, Wales. Address: Maes yr Onnen, Abergele Road, Llanddulas; Abergele LL22 8EN, Wales. E-mail: huwlloyd@welshnet.co.uk

LLOYD Geoffrey (Ernest Richard) (Sir), b. 25 Jan 1933, Swansea, Wales. Emeritus Professor of Ancient Philosophy and Science; Writer. m. Janet Elizabeth Lloyd, 1956, 3 sons. Education: BA, 1954, MA, 1958, PhD, 1958, King's College, Cambridge. Appointments: Fellow, 1957, Senior Tutor, 1969-73, King's College, Cambridge; Assistant Lecturer in Classics, 1965-67, Lecturer in Classics, 1967-74, Reader in Ancient Philosophy and Science, 1974-83, Professor of Ancient Philosophy and Science, 1983-2000, Cambridge University; Bonsall Professor, Stanford University, 1981; Sather Professor, University of California at Berkeley, 1984; Visiting Professor, Beijing University and Academy of Sciences, 1987; Master, Darwin College, 1989-2000; Professor at Large, Cornell University, 1990-96. Publications: Polarity and Analogy, 1966; Early Greek Science: Thales to Aristotle, 1970; Greek Science After Aristotle, 1973; Magic, Reason and Experience, 1979; Science, Folklore and Ideology, 1983; Science and Morality in Greco-Roman Antiquity, 1985; The Revolution of Wisdom, 1987; Demystifying Mentalities, 1990; Methods and Problems in Greek Science, 1991; Adversaries and Authorities, 1996; Aristotelian Explorations, 1996; Editor: Hippocratic Writings, 1978; Aristotle on Mind and Senses (with G E L Owen), 1978; Le Savoir Grec (with Jacques Brunschwig), 1996. Contributions to: Books and journals. Honours: Sarton Medal, 1987; Honorary Fellow,

King's College, Cambridge, 1990; Honorary Foreign Member, American Academy of Arts and Sciences, 1995; Knighted, 1997. Memberships: British Academy, fellow; East Asian History of Science Trust, chairman, 1992-; International Academy of the History of Science, 1997. Address: 2 Prospect Row, Cambridge CB1 1DU, England.

LLOYD John Nicol Fortune, b. 15 April 1946. Journalist. m. (1) Judith Ferguson, 1974, divorced 1979, (2) Marcia Levy, 1983, divorced 1997, 1 son. Education: MA, University of Edinburgh. Appointments: Editor, Time Out, 1972-73; Reporter, London Programme, 1974-76; Producer, Weekend World, 1976-77; Industrial Reporter, Labour Correspondent, Industrial and Labour Editor, Financial Times; 1977-86; Editor, 1986-87, Associate Editor, 1996-, New Statesman; Other Financial Times assignments, 1987-, including Moscow Correspondent, 1991-95; Freelance journalist, 1996-. Publications: The Politics of Industrial Change, co-author, 1982; The Miners' Strike: Loss Without Limit, co-author, 1986; In Search of Work, co-author, 1987; Counterblasts, contributor, 1989; Rebirth of a Nation: an Anatomy of Russia, 1998; Re-engaging Russia, 2000; The Protest Ethic, 2001; What the Media are Doing to Our Politics, 2004. Honours: Journalist of the Year, Granada Awards, 1984; Specialist Writer of the Year, IPC Awards, 1985; Rio Tinto David Watt Memorial Prize, 1997. Address: New Statesman, Victoria Station House, 7th Floor, 191 Victoria Street, London SW1E 5NE, England. E-mail: info@newstatesman.co.uk

LLOYD Kathleen Annie, (Kathleen Conlon, Kate North), b. 4 January 1943, Southport, England. Writer. m. Frank Lloyd, 1962, divorced, 1 son. Education: BA, Honours, King's College, Durham University. Publications: Apollo's Summer Look, 1968; Tomorrow's Fortune, 1971; My Father's House, 1972; A Twisted Skein, 1975; A Move in the Game, 1979; A Forgotten Season, 1980; Consequences, 1981; The Best of Friends, 1984; Face Values, 1985; Distant Relations, 1989; Unfinished Business, 1990; As Kate North: Land of My Dreams, 1997; Gollancz, 1997. Contributions to: Atlantic Review; Cosmopolitan; Woman's Journal; Woman; Woman's Own. Membership: Society of Authors. Address: 26A Brighton Road, Birkdale, Southport PR8 4DD, England.

LLOYD Robert Andrew, b. 2 March 1940, Southend-on-Sea, England. Broadcaster; Opera Singer; Teacher; Writer. m. Lynda Anne Powell, 1 son, 3 daughters. Education: MA, Modern History, Keble College, Oxford, 1962; London Opera Centre Certificate, 1969. Appointments: Teacher, various secondary schools, 1962; Lieutenant, Royal Navy, 1962-65; Civilian Tutor, Bramshill Police College, 1966-68; Student, London Opera Centre, 1968-69; Principal Bass, Sadlers Wells Opera, 1969-72; Principal Resident Bass, Royal Opera, Covent Garden, 1972-83; Freelance Broadcaster, Opera Singer, Teacher and Writer, 1983-; Senior Artist, Royal Opera Covent Garden, 2004; Master Teacher, San Francisco Merola Program, 2004; Guest Artist: Vienna Slaatsops, Munich, Paris, Amsterdam, Salzburg, Metropolitan Opera (200 performances), La Scala Milan, Florence, Tokyo, Seoul, St Petersburg, Moscow, San Francisco, Dallas, Toronto, Buenos Aires. Publications: Over 80 recordings; Radio and TV performances. Honours: Charles Santley Award; Chaliapin Commemoration Medal, St Petersburg; Best Foreign Singer Award, Buenos Aires; Commander of the British Empire, 1990; Honorary Fellow, Keble College; Honorary Member, Royal Academy of Music, Fellow of Royal Welsh College of Music and Drama. Memberships: President, British Youth Opera; Member, Executive Committee, Musicians Benevolent Fund; President, Abertillery Orpheus Male Voice Choir; President, Southend Choral Society; President 2005-6, Incorporated Society of Musicians; Sponsor, Brecon Cathedral Endowment Appeal; Tooley Committee, HEFCE, Advisory Committee of Friends of Covent Garden. Address: 57 Cholmeley Crescent, London N6 5EX, England. E-mail: robert@robertandlynda.co.uk

LLOYD WEBBER Andrew, (Baron Lloyd Webber of Sydmonton) b. 22 March 1948, London, England. Composer. m. (1) Sarah Jane Hugill, 1971, divorced 1983, 1 son, 1 daughter, (2) Sarah Brightman, 1984, divorced 1990, (3) Madeleine Gurdon, 1991, 2 sons, 1 daughter. Education: Magdalen College, Oxford; Royal College of Music, FRCM, 1988. Career: Composer and producer, musicals; Composer, film scores; Deviser, board game, And They're Off; Owner, Really Useful Group. Compositions: Musicals: Joseph And The Amazing Technicolour Dreamcoat (lyrics by Tim Rice), 1968; Jesus Christ Superstar (lyrics by Tim Rice), 1970; Jeeves (lyrics by Alan Ayckbourn), 1975; Evita (lyrics by Tim Rice), 1976; Tell Me On A Sunday (lyrics by Don Black), 1980; Cats (based on poems by T S Eliot), 1981; Song And Dance, 1982; Starlight Express (lyrics by Richard Stilgoe), 1984; The Phantom Of The Opera (lyrics by Richard Stilgoe and Charles Hart), 1986; Aspects Of Love (lyrics by Don Black and Charles Hart), 1989; Sunset Boulevard (lyrics by Don Black and Christopher Hampton), 1993; By Jeeves (lyrics by Alan Ayckbourn), 1996; Whistle Down The Wind (lyrics by Jim Steinman), 1996; The Beautiful Game (book and lyrics by Ben Elton), 2000; The Woman in White (book by Charlotte Jones, lyrics by David Zippel), 2004; The Sound of Music, 2006 (lyrics by Oscar Hammerstein II); Love Never Dies, 2009 (book and lyrics by Glenn Slater). Film Scores: Gumshoe, 1971; The Odessa File, 1974; Jesus Christ Superstar, 1974; Others: Requiem, 1985; Variations On A Theme Of Paganini For Orchestra, 1986; Amigos Para Siempre (official theme for 1992 Olympic Games), 1992; When Children Rule The World (official theme for the opening ceremony 1998 Winter Olympics). Publications: Evita (with Tim Rice), 1978; Cats: The Book of the Musical, 1981; Joseph And The Amazing Technicolour Dreamcoat (with Tim Rice), 1982; The Complete Phantom of the Opera, 1987; The Complete Aspects of Love, 1989; Sunset Boulevard: From Movie to Musical, 1993; Restaurant Columnist, the Daily Telegraph, 1996-99; Film: The Phantom of the Opera, 2004-05. Honours include: 5 Laurence Olivier Awards; 6 Tony Awards; 4 Drama Desk Awards; 3 Grammy Awards; Triple Play Award, ASCAP, 1988; Knighthood, 1992; Praemium Imperiale Award, 1995; Richard Rogers Award, 1996; Oscar, Best Song, (with Tim Rice), 1997; Honorary Life Peer, 1997; Critics Circle Award Best Musical, 2000. Address: 22 Tower Street, London WC2H 9NS, England.

LLOYD WEBBER Julian, b. 14 April 1951, London, England. Cellist. m. (1) Celia M Ballantyne, 1974, divorced 1989, (2) Zohra Mahmoud Ghazi, 1989, divorced, 1999, son, (3) Kheira Bourahla, 2001. Education: Royal College of Music. Appointments: Debut, Queen Elizabeth Hall, 1972; Debut, Berlin Philharmonic Orchestra, 1984; Appears in major international concert halls; Undertaken concert tours throughout Europe, North and South America, Australasia, Singapore, Japan, Hong Kong and Korea; Numerous TV appearances and broadcasts in UK, Netherlands, Africa, Germany, Scandinavia, France, Belgium, Spain, Australasia, USA; Recordings include: World Premieres of Britten's 3rd Suite for Solo Cello; Bridge's Oration; Rodrigo's Cello Concerto; Holst's Invocation; Gavin Bryar's Cello Concerto; Philip Glass Cello Concerto; Tchaikovsky Rococo Variations; Sullivan's Cello Concerto; Vaughan Williams' Fantasia on Sussex Folk Tunes; Andrew Lloyd Webber's

Variations; Elgar's Cello Concerto; Dvorak Concerto; Saint Saens Concerto; Lalo Concerto; Walton Concerto; Britten Cello Symphony; Philip Glass Cello Concerto, Phantasia. Publications: Frank Bridge, Six Pieces, 1982; Young Cellist's Repertoire, 1984; Travels with my Cello, 1984; Song of the Birds, 1985; Recital Repertoire for Cellists, 1986; Short Sharp Shocks, 1990; The Great Cello Solos, 1992; The Essential Cello, 1997; Cello Moods, 1999; Classical Journeys, 2004; Elgar Cello Concerto, 2005. Honours: British Phonographic Industry Award for Best Classical Recording, 1986; Crystal Award World Economic Forum, 1998; FRCM; Honorary Doctorate, (University of Hull) 2003, (Thames Valley University) 2004. Address: c/o IMG Artists Europe, Lovell House, 616 Chiswick High Road, London, W4 5RX, England. Website: www.julianlloydwebber.com

LLOYD-HOWELLS David, b. 11 January 1942, Cardiff, Wales. Composer; Poet. Education: BMus Hon, University College, Cardiff, 1980; MMus Lond, Goldsmiths, University of London, 1983; Fellow: Trinity College of Music, 1979, London College of Music, 1980. Career: Composer of acoustic and electronic works; facilitator in educational and community health workshops, courses. Discography: Nightcity Pulses; Lethal Edge; Bleak Sleaze; Med; Fractosonic Graffiti; Thermal Vista; Holos; Freakspeak; Nok; Dark Clowns; Cosmic Liturgy; Wrath Conference; Triptych; Iconic States; Druidika; Chromosomes; Naked Performance; Passions; Vanquished; Digitalis; Threnody for Diana; Kwanta; Shadowself; Metro Canticles; Insects' Convention; Marginal Spaces; Kyros; Rainbows in the Weave; International performances of Sonic Art Music: Freakspeak; A Cosmic Liturgy; Insects' Convention; Druidika; Metro Canticles; The Screaming; Dark Clowns; Nightcity Pulses; Iconic States; Wrath Conference; Mec; Nok; Fractosonic Graffiti; Soundspaces; Shadowself; Lethal Edge; Chromosomes; Bleak Sleaze; Thermal Vista; Triptych; Kwanta; and others. Honours: Fellow: Trinity College of Music, 1979, London College of Music, 1980. Memberships: Sonic Arts Network.

LO Wen-Lin, b. 1 January 1958, Kaohsiung, Taiwan. Dermatologist. m. Yung-Jung Ho, 1 son, 1 daughter. Education: MD, National Yang-Ming Medical College, Taipei, 1982. Appointments: Resident, Dermatology, 1984-89, Attending Physician, 1989-91, Veterans General Hospital, Taipei; Lecturer, National Yang-Ming Medical College, 1989-91; Attending Physician, 1991-93, Section Chief, 1993-94, Chutong (Taiwan) Veterans Hospital; Private Practice, 1994-. Publications: Contributor of articles in professional journals. Memberships: Fellow, American Academy of Dermatology; Asian Dermatological Association; International Society of Dermatology; Chinese Dermatological Society; Laser Medicine Society. Address: 2/F #2 Lane 14, Chung Shan North Sec 7, Taipei 111, Taiwan.

LOACH Kenneth, b. 17 June 1936, Nuneaton, England. Film Director. m. Lesley Ashton, 1962, 3 sons (one deceased), 2 daughters. Education: St Peter's Hall, Oxford. Appointments: BBC Trainee, Drama Department, 1963; Freelance Film Director, 1963-; Films include: Poor Cow, 1967; Kes, 1969; In Black and White, 1970; Family Life, 1971; Black Jack, 1979; Looks and Smiles, 1981; Fatherland, 1986; Hidden Agenda, 1990; Riff Raff, 1991; Raining Stones, 1993; Ladybird Ladybird, 1994; Land and Freedom, 1995; Carla's Song, 1996; My Name is Joe, 1998; Bread and Roses, 2001; The Navigators, 2001; Sweet Sixteen, 2002; 11.09.01 UK Segment, 2002; Ae Fond Kiss, 2004; Tickets, 2007; McLibel, 2005; The Wind That Shakes the Barley, 2006; To Each His Cinema, 2007; It's a Free World, 2007. TV includes: Diary of a Young Man, 1964; Three Clear Sundays, 1965; The End of Arthur's Marriage, 1965; Up the Junction, 1965; Coming Out Party, 1965; Cathy Come Home, 1966; In Two Minds, 1966; The Golden Vision, 1969; The Big Flame, 1970; After a Lifetime, 1971; The Rank of File, 1972; Auditions, 1980; A Question of Leadership, 1980; The Red and the Blue, 1983; Questions of Leadership, 1983; Which Side are You On?, 1984; The View from the Woodpile, 1988; Time to Go, 1989; Dispatches: Arthur Scargill, 1991; The Flickering Flame, 1996; Another City, 1998. Honours: Hon DLitt, St Andrews; Staffordshire University, Bristol; Dr hc, Royal College of Art, 1988; Honorary Fellow, St Peter's College, Oxford; Léopard d'honneur for Lifetime Achievement, Locarno Film Festival, 2003; Praemium Imperiale, 2003; London Film Critics' Circle Award for Outstanding Contribution to Cinema, 2005. Address: c/o Parallax Pictures, 7 Denmark Street, London, WC2H 8LS, England.

LOADES David Michael, b. 19 January 1934, Cambridge, England. Retired Professor of History; Writer. m. Judith Anne Atkins, 1987. Education: Emmanuel College, Cambridge, 1955-61, BA, 1958, MA, PhD, 1961, LittD, 1981. Appointments: Lecturer in Political Science, University of St Andrews, 1961-63; Lecturer in History, University of Durham, 1963-70; Senior Lecturer, 1970-77, Reader, 1977-80, Professor of History, 1980-96, University College of North Wales, Bangor; Director, British Academy John Foxe Project, 1993-2004; Honorary Research Professor, University of Sheffield, 1996-. Publications: 22 books and collections include: Two Tudor Conspiracies, 1965; The Oxford Martyrs, 1970; The Reign of Mary Tudor, 1979; The Tudor Court, 1986; Mary Tudor: A Life, 1989; The Tudor Navy, 1992; John Dudley: Duke of Northumberland, 1996; Tudor Government, 1997; England's Maritime Empire, 2000; The Chronicles of the Tudor Queens, 2002; Elizabeth I, 2003; Intrigue and Treason: the Tudor Court 1547-1558, 2004; Mary Tudor: The Tragical History of the First Queen of England, 2006; Henry VIII: Court, Church and Conflict; 2006; The Cecils, 2007; The Princes of Wales, 2008; The Tudor Queens of England, 2009; Editor: The Papers of George Wyatt, 1968; The End of Strife, 1984; Faith and Identity, 1990; John Foxe and the English Reformation, 1997; John Foxe: an historical perspective, 1999; with C S Knighton, The Anthony Roll of Henry VIII, 2000; Letters from the Mary Rose, 2002; John Foxe: At Home and Abroad, 2004; Word and Worship, 2005; The Church of Mary Tudor (co-editor with E Duffy), 2006; The Religious Culture of Marian England, 2010; Henry VIII, 2011; Contributions to academic journals. Memberships: Royal Historical Society, Fellow; Society of Antiquaries of London, Member; Ecclesiastical History Society; Vice President, Navy Records Society. Address: The Cottage, Priory Lane, Burford, Oxon OX18 4SG, England.

LOBODA-CACKOVIC Jasna, b. Homec, Slovenia, resident in Berlin, Germany, 1970-. Scientist; Physicist; Artist; Author; Sculptor; Painter. m. Hinko Cackovic. Education: Art studied with father (Peter Loboda, artist and sculptor) and mother (Jelena Loboda Zrinski, artist and writer) at first then continued with self education; Diploma of Physics, 1960; MSc, Solid State Physics, University of Zagreb, Croatia, 1964; PhD, Fritz-Haber-Institut der Max-Planck-Gesellschaft, Berlin-Dahlem, Germany and University of Zagreb, Croatia, 1970. Appointments: Scientist, Atom Institute Ruder Boskovic, Zagreb, Croatia, 1960-71; Honorary Assistant, University of Zagreb, 1961-65; Scientist, Fritz-Haber-Institut der Max-Planck-Gesellschaft, Berlin-Dahlem, Germany, 1965-67, 1970-97; Freelance Artist and Scientist, 1997-; Author, 2010-; Innovative works, two-artists co-operation

JASHIN, with Hinko Cackovic, 1997-. Publications: Numerous articles in professional scientific journals. Honours (most recently): 20th and 21st Century Achievement Awards, 1999, 2003; New Century Award, Europe 500, 2000; Presidential Award, 500 Great Minds, 2001; Presidential Award, 500 Distinguished Professors & Scholars of the BWW Society, 2004; Gold Medal for Germany for: Success, Passion, Courage, Spirit, Commitment, Excellence, Virtue, 2006; Legion of Honour of the United Cultural Convention, USA, for Significance of Contribution to Worldwide Humanity, and Personal Excellence in Achievement, 2007; The Preeminent 500, 500 Exceptional Individuals of Achievement in Commerce, Science and Technology, Medicine and Arts and Letters, 2011; For Outstanding Contributions to the field of Physics: Distinguished Service to Science Award, for Various Aspects of Physical Science, 2007; Decree of Excellence in Science, 2007; Awards for Art, Science and their Creative Interaction: Da Vinci Diamond, 2004; Dedication, Dictionary of International Biography, 33rd Edition, 2007; Salute to Greatness Award, 2007; IBC Lifetime Achievement Award, 2007; The Roll of Honour, 2007-; The World Medal of Freedom, ABI, 2008; The International Einstein Award, for Scientific Achievement: Science, Art and Universal Harmony, ABI, 2008; Albert Einstein Genius Dedication, ABI, 2009. Memberships: New York Academy of Sciences; Deutsche Physikalische Gesellschaft; Virtual Gallery of Forschungs-Institut Bildende Künste (FIBK), Germany; Europäischer Kulturkreis Baden-Baden; Archaeology, Astronautics and Seti Research Association; Founding Member of the BWW Society (Bibliotheque: World Wide). Commissions and Creative Art Works: Over 300 sculptures and relief, and more than one thousand paintings presented in books, catalogues, art journals and at numerous exhibitions in Germany, Austria, France, Monaco, Switzerland, Croatia, Luxembourg and in Internet Galleries; Collection in Gallery for Sculpture (Bildhauergalerie Plinthe), Berlin, Germany, 1987-95, Gallery Kleiner Prinz, Baden-Baden, Germany; Permanent representations by the Cyber Museum at wwwARTchannel (www.art-channel.net) and in the Gallery of Forschungs-Institut Bildende Künste, Germany in Internet (www.fibk.de). Address: Im Dol 60, 14195 Berlin, Germany.

LOCKHART James, Conductor. Education: Edinburgh University, Scotland, 1947-1951; Royal College of Music, London, 1951-1954. Appointments: Assistant Conductor, Yorkshire Symphony Orchestra, Leeds, 1954-55; Repetiteur and Assistant Conductor, Städtische Bühnen, Münster, 1955-56; Repetiteur and Assistant Conductor, Bayerische Staatsoper, München 1956-57; Director of the Opera Workshop, University of Texas, Austin, Texas, 1957-59; Repetiteur and Assistant Conductor, Glyndebourne Festival Opera, 1957-59; Repetiteur and Assistant Conductor, The Royal Opera House, Covent Garden, 1959-60; Assistant Conductor, BBC Scottish Symphony Orchestra, Glasgow, 1960-61; Conductor, Sadlers Wells Opera, London, 1960-62; Repetiteur and Conductor, The Royal Opera House, Covent Garden, London, 1962-68; Professor, Royal College of Music, 1962-72; Music Director, Welsh National Opera, Cardiff, 1968-73; Generalmusikdirektor, Staatstheater, Kassel, 1972-80; Generalmusikdirektor, Koblenz Opera, 1981-88; Generalmusikdirektor, Rheinische Philharmonie, Koblenz, 1981-91; Principal Guest Conductor, BBC Concert Orchestra, 1982-87; Director of Opera, Royal College of Music, 1986-1992; Director of Opera, Royal College of Music and Royal Academy of Music, 1992-96; Opera Consultant, Royal College of Music and Royal Academy of Music, London, 1996-98; Guest Professor of Conducting, Tokyo National University of Fine Arts and Music, (Tokyo Geidai), 1998-2001; Professor of Conducting, Sydney Conservatorium of Music, 2005; Professor Emeritus, Tokyo National University of Fine Arts and Music, (Tokyo Geidai); Ehrendirigent, Rheinische Philharmonie, Koblenz; Freelance Conductor. Address: 5 The Coach House, Mill Street, Fontmell Magna, Shaftesbury, SP7 0NU, England. E-mail: lockgrog@zen.co.uk

LODER Robert Reginald (Robin), b. 12 November 1943, Titchfield, Hampshire, England. Landowner. m. Jane Royden, 2 sons, 2 daughters. Education: MA, Trinity College, Cambridge. Appointments: Owner, Leonardslee Gardens; High Sheriff of West Sussex, 2000-01. Address: Leonardslee Gardens, Lower Beeding, Horsham, West Sussex RH13 6PP, England. E-mail: gardens@leonardslee.com

LODGE David John, b. 28 January 1935. Honorary Professor of Modern English Literature. m. Mary Frances Jacob, 1959, 2 sons, 1 daughter. Education: BA, honours, MA (London); PhD, Birmingham; National Service, RAC, 1955-57. Appointments: British Council, London, 1959-60; Assistant Lecturer, 1960-62, Lecturer, 1963-71, Senior Lecturer, 1971-73, Reader of English, 1973-76, Professor of Modern English Literature, 1976-87, Honorary Professor, 1987-2000, Emeritus Professor, 2001-, University of Birmingham; Harkness Commonwealth Fellow, 1964-65; Visiting Associate Professor, University of California, Berkeley, 1969; Henfield Writing Fellow, University of East Anglia, 1977. Publications: Novels: The Picturegoers, 1960; Ginger, You're Barmy, 1962; The British Museum is Falling Down, 1965; Out of the Shelter, 1970, revised edition, 1985; Changing Places, 1975; How Far Can You Go?, 1980; Small World, 1984; Nice Work, 1988; Paradise News, 1991; Therapy, 1995; Home Truths, 1999; Thinks...., 2001; Author, Author, 2004; Deaf Sentence, 2009. Criticism: Language of Fiction, 1966; The Novelist at the Crossroads, 1971; The Modes of Modern Writing, 1977; Working with Structuralism, 1981; Write On, 1986; After Bakhtin (essays), 1990; The Art of Fiction, 1992; The Practice of Writing, 1996; Consciousness and the Novel, 2002; The Year of Henry James: The Story of a Novel, 2006. Honours: Yorkshire Post Fiction Prize, 1975; Hawthornden Prize, 1976; Whitbread Book of the Year Award, 1980; Sunday Express Book of the Year Award, 1988; Chevalier de L'Ordre des Arts et des Lettres, 1997; CBE, 1998. Address: Department of English, University of Birmingham, Birmingham B15 2TT, England.

LODGE Oliver Raymond William Wynlayne, b, 2 September 1922, Painswick, Goucestershire, England. Retired Barrister. m. Charlotte Young, deceased, 1990, 1 son, 2 daughters. Education: Officer Cadet, Royal Fusiliers, 1942; BA, 1943, MA, 1947, King's College, Cambridge. Appointments: Called to the Bar by Inner Temple, 1945; Practiced at Chancery Bar, 1945-74; Admitted ad eundam to Lincoln's Inn, 1949; Member of Bar Council, 1952-56, 1967-71; Member of Supreme Court Rules Committee, 1968-71; Bencher of Lincoln's Inn, 1973; Permanent Chairman of Industrial Tribunals, 1975-92, Part-time Chairman, 1992-94; Regional Chairman of London South Region of Industrial Tribunals, 1980-92; General Commissioner of Income Tax for Lincoln's Inn District, 1983-91; Treasurer of Lincoln's Inn, 1995. Publications: Editor, 3rd edition, Rivington's Epitome of Snedl's Equity, 1948; Editor, article on Fraudulent and Voidable Conveyances in 3rd edition of Halsbury's Laws of England, 1956. Memberships: Garrick Club; Bar Yacht Club. Address: Southridge House, Hindon, Salisbury, Wiltshire SP3 6ER, England.

LOENNING Per (Right Reverend), b. 24 February 1928, Bergen, Norway. Bishop; Professor. m. Ingunn Bartz-Johannessen, 1951, 3 sons, 1 daughter. Education: Candidate theology, 1949, Dr theology, 1955, Dr philosophy, 1959, University of Oslo. Appointments: Assistant Pastor, Oslo, 1951; Lecturer, Oslo Teachers Training College, 1954; Member, Norwegian Parliament, 1957-65; Dean, Bergen Cathedral, Church of Norway, 1964; Bishop of Borg, 1969; Professor, History of Christian Thought, University of Oslo, 1976; Research Professor, Institute of Ecumenical Studies, Strasbourg, France, 1981; Bishop of Bergen, 1987-94. Publications: The Dilemma of Contemporary Theology, 1962; Cet effrayant pari - Pascal, 1980; Der begreiflich Unergreifbare, 1986; Creation - An Ecumenical Challenge?, 1989; Is Christ a Christian, 2002; 40 books in Norwegian including studies on Kierkegaard and Pascal; Collections of 120 selfcomposed hymns, texts and melodies, 1999-2010. Honours: Pax Christi Award, St John's University, Collegeville, Minnesota, USA, 1975; DLitt hc, St Olaf College, Northfield, Minnesota, 1986; Commander of the Royal Order of St Olav, 2000. Memberships: Royal Norwegian Academy of Social Sciences and Letters; Norwegian Academy of Science. Address: Loevenskiolds gt 19A. N-0260 Oslo, Norway.

LÖFFLER di CASAGIOVE Harti Hanns, b. 21 March 1936, Munich, Bavaria. University Professor. Divorced, 1 son. Education: BA, Munich Interpreters' School, 1963; MA, Munich University, 1968; Teacher Training Exam, State of Bavaria, 1970; PhD, Harvard University, USA, 1978; Postgraduate Ethics Studies (Philosophy), Munich, State Exam, 1988. Appointments: Assistant Lecturer, German (English), Bocconi University, Milan, Italy, 1963-66; Assistant Researcher, Linguistics, Munich University, 1966-68; Faculty Member, Maryland University, European Division, 1968-71; Language Co-ordinator, German-English-Italian, Munich Olympics, 1971-72; Lecturer, Munich and Landshut Fachhochschulen, 1972-77; Civil Service High School Teacher, Languages, Munich, 1978-88; Co-ordinator, Munich Municipality Education Authority, 1988-91; Freelance Language and Ethics Teacher, Orbetello, Tuscany, Italy, 1991-95; Freelance Language Teacher and Interpreter, Munich, 1995-2001; Freelance Language Teacher and Interpreter, Pietrasanta, Tuscany, 2001-02, 2005-07; Faculty Member, European School of Economics, Italy, 2002-04; Associate Professor, German, Camerino University, Italy, 2004-05; Managing Member, CONI (National Olympic Committee of Italy), Lucca County, 2007; Probo viro, Member of the Disciplinary Court of Panathlon International, Lucca County, 2007. Publications: Grüß Gott, liebe Kinder, 1964; Corso di lingua tedesca, 1966; Dizionario base tedesco-italiano/italiano-tedesco, 1965; Ski Dictionary Italian-German, Italian-English, 1968. Honours: Viscount Casagiove; Fellow, Academy of Political Science; Judge of both German and Italian Sailing Federations; Lord of the Manor of the Italian Trinity Order of Knights, 1999; DDG, IBC, 2007. Address: cp 44, Marina di Pietrasanta, I-55044, Italy. E-mail: languages@harti-it.eu

LOFTHOUSE Geoffrey (Lord Lofthouse of Pontefract), b. 18 December 1925, Featherstone, England. Deputy Speaker, House of Lords. m. Sarah, deceased, 1 daughter. Education: Leeds University, 1954-57. Appointments: Member, Pontefract Borough Council, 1962; Mayor of Pontefract, 1967-68; Leader, Pontefract Borough Council, 1969-73; First Chairman, Wakefield MDC, 1973; Chairman, Housing Committee, 1973-79; Elected Member of Parliament for Pontefract and Castleford, 1978; Elected Deputy Speaker of the House of Commons, 1992-97; Elected Deputy Speaker of the House of Lords, 1997-; Chairman of Wakefield Health Authority, 1998. Publications: A Very Miner MP (autobiography), 1985; Coal Sack to Woolsack (autobiography), 1999. Honours: Knighthood, 1995; Peerage, 1997. Memberships: Member of the Imperial Society of Knights Bachelor; Appointed Magistrate, 1970; President, British Amateur Rugby League Association. Address: 67 Carleton Crest, Pontefract, West Yorkshire WF8 2QR, England.

LOGUE Christopher (John), b. 23 November 1926, Portsmouth, Hampshire, England. Poet; Writer; Dramatist. m. Rosemary Hill, 1985. Education: Prior College, Bath. Publications: Poetry: Wand and Quadrant, 1953; Devil, Maggot and Son, 1954; The Weakdream Sonnets, 1955; The Man Who Told His Love: 20 Poems Based on P Neruda's "Los Cantos d'amores", 1958, 2nd edition, 1959; Songs, 1960; Songs from "The Lily-White Boys", 1960; The Establishment Songs, 1966; The Girls, 1969; New Numbers, 1970; Abecedary, 1977; Ode to the Dodo, 1981; War Music: An Account of Books 16 to 19 of Homer's Iliad, 1981; Fluff, 1984; Kings: An Account of Books 1 and 2 of Homer's Iliad, 1991, revised edition, 1992; The Husbands: An Account of Books 3 and 4 of Homer's Iliad, 1994; Selected Poems (edited by Christopher Reid), 1996; All Day Permanent Red, 2003. Plays: The Lily-White Boys (with Harry Cookson), 1959; The Trial of Cob and Leach, 1959; Antigone, 1961; War Music, 1978; Kings, 1993. Screenplays: Savage Messiah, 1972; The End of Arthur's Marriage, 1965; Crusoe (with Walter Green), 1986. Other: Lust, by Count Plamiro Vicarion, 1955; The Arrival of the Poet in the City: A Treatment for a Film, 1964; True Stories, 1966; The Bumper Book of True Stories, 1980. Editor: Count Palmiro Vicarion's Book of Limericks, 1959; The Children's Book of Comic Verse, 1979; London in Verse, 1982; Sweet & Sour: An Anthology of Comic Verse, 1983; The Children's Book of Children's Rhymes, 1986. Honours: 1st Wilfred Owen Award, 1998; Whitbread Poetry Award, 2005. Address: 41 Camberwell Grove, London SE5 8JA, England.

LOHAN Lindsay, b. 2 July 1986, New York City, USA. Actress; Singer; Fashion Designer; Model. TV/Films: The Parent Trap, 1998; Life-Size, 2000; Get a Clue, 2002; Freaky Friday, 2003; Confessions of a Teenage Drama Queen, Mean Girls, 2004; Herbie: Fully Loaded, 2005; Just My Luck, A Prairie Home Companion, Bobby, 2006; Chapter 27, Georgia Rule, I Know Who Killed Me, 2007; Labor Pains, 2009; The Other Side, Machete, Dare to Love Me, 2010; TV: Another World, 1996; Bette, 2000; King of the Hill, 2004; That '70s Show, 2005; Ugly Betty, 2008; Project Runway, 2009; Singer: Speak, 2004; A Little More Personal (Raw), 2005.

LÖKER Altan, b. 6 November 1927, Kütahya, Turkey. Electrical Engineer, retired. Education: MS in Electrical Engineering, Technical University of Istanbul, 1951; MS in Physics, Stevens Institute of Technology, USA, 1957. Appointments: Electrical Engineer in Turkey, USA, Canada, and Saudi Arabia; Project Manager, Subcontractor, Contractor in Turkey; Graduate Assistant at the Technical University of Istanbul and Physics Department of Stevens Institute of Technology. Publications: Film and Suspense, 1976, 2nd edition, 2005; Dreams and Psychosynthesis, 1987; Cognitive-Cybernetic Theory and Therapy, 1993; Dreams, Migraine, Neuralgia, 1993; Theory in Psychology: The Journal of Mind and Behaviour, 1999; Cognitive Behavioural Cybernetics of Symptoms, Dreams, Lateralization, 2001, 2nd edition, 2002; Migraines and Dreams, 2003; Theory Construction and Testing in Physics and Psychology, 2007; New Facts about Dreams Deduced from Jung's Compensation Theory: The Journal of Jungian Theory and Therapy, 2007.

DICTIONARY OF INTERNATIONAL BIOGRAPHY 36th EDITION

Memberships: Turkish Chamber of Electrical Engineers, retired. Address: Lalasahin 23/5, Ferikoy, Istanbul 80260, Turkey. E-mail: alloker@superonline.com

LÖKK (Carl Thorild) Johan, b. 18 June 1951, Eskilstuna, Sweden. Senior Consultant. m. Karin Dellenvall, 2 sons. Education: MD, 1986; PhD, 1991; Assistant Professor, 1998; Professor, 2010. Appointments: Specialist, Internal Medicine and Geriatrics; Senior Consultant, Karolinska University Hospital, Stockholm, 25 years. Publications: 70 articles in professional journals on Parkinson's Disease, Alzeimer's Disease and stroke. Address: Department of Neurobiology, Caring Sciences & Society, Karolinska Institute, Stockholm, Sweden.

LOLLOBRIGIDA Gina, b. 4 July 1927, Sibiaco, Italy. Actress. m. Milko Skofic, 1949, divorced 1971, 1 son. Education: Liceo Artistico, Rome. Appointments: First Screen Role, Pagliacci, 1947; Appeared in numerous films including: Campane a Martello, 1948; Cuori Senza Frontiere, 1949; Achtung, bandit!, 1951; Enrico Caruso, 1951; Fanfan la Tulipe, 1951; Altri Tempi, 1952; The Wayward Wife, 1952; Les belles de la nuit, 1952; Pane, amour e fantasia, 1953; La Provinciale, 1953; Pane, amour e gelosia, La Romana, 1954; Il Grande Gioco, 1954; La Donna piu Bella del Mondo, 1955; Trapeze, 1956; Notre Dame de Paris, 1956; Solomon and Sheba, 1959; Never So Few, 1960; Go Naked in the World, 1961; She Got What She Asked For, 1963; Woman of Straw, 1964; Le Bambole, 1965; Hotel Paradiso, 1966; Buona Sera Mrs Campbell, 1968; King, Queen, Knave, 1972; The Bocce Showdown, 1990; Plucked, Bad Man's River; The Lonely Woman; Bambole; Donna in fuga, Una, 1996; XXL, 1997. Publications: Italia Mia, 1974; The Philippines. Address: Via Appia Antica 223, 00178 Rome, Italy.

LOMAS Herbert, b. 7 February 1924, Yorkshire, England. Poet; Critic; Translator. m. Mary Marshall Phelps, 1968, 1 son, 1 daughter. Education: BA, 1949, MA, 1952, University of Liverpool. Appointments: Teacher, Spetsai, Greece, 1950-51; Lecturer, Senior Lecturer, University of Helsinki, 1952-65; Senior Lecturer, 1966-72, Principal Lecturer, 1972-82, Borough Road College. Publications: Chimpanzees are Blameless Creatures, 1969; Who Needs Money?, 1972; Private and Confidential, 1974; Public Footpath, 1981; Fire in the Garden, 1984; Letters in the Dark, 1986; Trouble, 1992; Selected Poems, 1995; A Useless Passion, 1998; The Vale of Todmorden, 2003. Translations: Territorial Song, 1991; Contemporary Finnish Poetry, 1991; Fugue, 1992; Wings of Hope and Daring, 1992; The Eyes of the Fingertips are Opening, 1993; Black and Red, 1993; Narcissus in Winter, 1994; The Year of the Hare, 1994; Two Sequences for Kuhmo, 1994; In Wandering Hall, 1995; Selected Poems, Eeva-Lisa Manner, 1997; Three Finnish Poets, 1999; A Tenant Here, 1999; Not Before Sundown, 2003. Contributions to: London Magazine and other reviews, journals, and magazines. Honours: Prize, Guinness Poetry Competition; Runner Up, Arvon Foundation Poetry Competition; Cholmondeley Award; Poetry Book Society Biennial Translation Award; Knight First Class, Order of the White Rose of Finland, 1991: Finnish State Prize for Translation, 1991. Memberships: Society of Authors; Finnish Academy; Finnish Literary Society; President, Suffolk Poetry Society, 1999-. Address: North Gable, 30 Crag Path, Aldeburgh, Suffolk IP15 5BS, England.

LOMU Jonah, b. 12 May 1975, Auckland, New Zealand. Rugby Football Player; Athlete. m. (1) Tanya Rutter, divorced, (2) Fiona Taylor, 2003. Appointments: Bank Officer, ASB Bank of New Zealand; Youngest Ever Capped All Black; Wing; International Debut, New Zealand versus France, 1994; Semi Finalist at World Cup, South Africa, 1995; Affilliated to Rugby Union; Ran 100m in 10.7 Seconds; With All Blacks, 1999; Signed for Cardiff Blues, 2005. Website: www.jonahlomu.com

LONG Derek Albert, b. 11 August 1925, Gloucester, England. Scientist; Author; Antiquarian. m. Moira Hastings (Gilmore), 3 sons. Education: MA, D Phil, Jesus College, Oxford. Appointments: Fellow, University of Minnesota, USA, 1949-50; Research Fellow, Spectroscopy, University of Oxford, 1950-55; Lecturer, Senior Lecturer, Reader in Chemistry, University College, Swansea, 1956-66; Professor of Structural Chemistry, 1966-92, Professor Emeritus, 1992-, Chairman of the Board of Physical Sciences, 1976-79, Director, Molecular Spectroscopy Unit, 1982-88, University of Bradford; OECD Travelling Fellow, Canada and USA, 1964; Leverhulme Research Fellow, 1970-71; Visiting Professor: Reims, Lille, Bordeaux, Paris, Bologna, Florence, Keele; Chairman, Second International Conference on Raman Spectroscopy, Oxford, 1970; Co-Director, NATO Advanced Studies Institute, Bad Winsheim, 1982; Member, Italian-UK Mixed Commission for Implementation of Cultural Convention, 1985; Vice Chairman, Euro Laboratory for Non-Linear Spectroscopy, Florence, 1986-92. Publications: Founder, Journal of Raman Spectroscopy, Editor, Editor-in-Chief, 1973-99, Emeritus Editor, 2000-; Books (sole author): Raman Spectroscopy, 1977; The Raman Effect, 2002; Books (joint editor): Essays in Structural Chemistry, 1971; Specialist Periodical Reports in Molecular Spectroscopy (vols 1-6), 1973-79; Non-Linear Raman Spectroscopy and Its Chemical Applications, 1988; Proceedings Eleventh International Conference on Raman Spectroscopy, 1988; About 200 papers in scientific journals relating to Raman Spectroscopy; Other papers: Sevres Service des Arts Industriels, 1997; The Goodmanham Plane, 2002; More Early Planes, 2006; Fifteen Early Woodworking Planes Mostly dated to within the First Millennium, 2008. Honours: Fellow, Society of Antiquaries, London; Fellow, Royal Society of Chemistry, Chartered Chemist; Foreign Member, Lincei Academy, Rome, Italy; Honorary, Docteur es Sciences, Reims, France. Membership: Oxford and Cambridge Club. Address: 19 Hollingwood Rise, Ilkley, W Yorks, LS29 9PW, England. E-mail: dal@profdalong.demon.co.uk

LONG Eric Sydney, b. 16 April 1943, Manchester. England. Professor; Chartered Consulting Engineer. m. Pamela, 1 son. Education: BA (Honours), Business Management; MSc, Advanced Manufacturing Technology & Management; Doctor of Laws, Engineering Safety Law; Postgraduate diploma, Marketing; Postgraduate diploma, Safety, Health & Environmental Management; Associateship, Faculty of Risk Management. Appointments: Apprentice Mechanical Engineer, Metropolitan Vickers Electrical Company, Manchester; Research on Marine Power Plant, University of Manchester Institute of Science & Technology; Postgraduate training, Yarrow Admiralty Research Department on Marine Engineering; Senior & Principal Consultant Naval Engineer-Surveyor & Naval Architect (Nuclear); Director & Principal Consulting Engineer with a Consultancy Practice. Publications: Chapters on Engineering Safety Law and Statutory Engineering Inspections in text book, Safety at Work; Articles on Safety Management in a number of journals. Honours: Past President and Head of Mechanical Engineering Examinations, Society of Engineers; Visiting Professorship, Engineering Safety Law. Memberships: European Engineer; Chartered Engineer; Institution of Engineers of Ireland; Royal Institution of Naval Architects; Society of Consulting Marine

Engineers and Ship Surveyors; Federation of European Maritime Consultants & Surveyors. Address: Brookside Mews Cottage, 29 Mill Brow, Marple Bridge, Stockport, SK6 5LW, England. E-mail: eslonmarinesafety@talktalk.net

LONG John Cecil, b. 30 August 1964, Portadown, Northern Ireland. Painter; Lecturer. Education: Foundation Course in Art and Design, Belfast, 1983-84; BA, Painting, 1988, Higher Diploma, Painting, 1990, Slade School of Fine Art, London. Appointments: Artist in Residence, Byam Shaw School of Art, London, 1990-91; One Man Exhibition, European Modern Art, Dublin, 1993; Banquet Exhibition, Royal Hibernian Academy, 1992, Royal Hibernian Academy Annual Exhibition, 1993-2011, Gallagher Gallery, Dublin; Drawings of Distinction, 1995, One Man Exhibition, 1998, Theo Waddington Fine Art, London; Twentieth Century British Art Fair, Royal College of Art, London, 1996; One Man Exhibition, Jorgensen Fine Art, Dublin, 1999, 2003, 2010; Part-time Lecturer, 1999, Senior Lecturer, 2005, Painting, Canterbury Christchurch University; Visiting Lecturer, Taichung Academy of Fine Art, Taiwan, 2002. Publications: Royal Hibernian Academy Annual Exhibition Catalogue, 1993-2008; Exhibition Catalogues, Jorgensen Fine Art, 1999, 2003, 2010; British Art, Julian Freeman, 2006; Listed in international biographical dictionaries. Honours: Arts Council of Northern Ireland, 1993; Taylor de Vere, Dublin, 1993; Arts Council of Northern Ireland, 1994; Elizabeth Greenshields Foundation, Canada, 1998; Year of the Artist, South East Arts, 2001. Memberships: Elected Associate Member, 1995, Academician, 2010, Royal Hibernian Academy, Dublin. Address: c/o Jorgensen Fine Art, 16 Herbert Street, Dublin 2, Ireland. E-mail: jcl18@canterbury.ac.uk

LONGANI Vites, b. 1 January 1949, Chiang Mai, Thailand. Professor. m. Natdhapat, 2 daughters. Education: BSc, Chiuangmai University, 1972; MS, 1977, PhD, 1982, University of London, England. Appointments: Teacher, Researcher, Department of Mathematics and College of Arts, Media & Technology, Chiangmai University, Thailand. Publications: 13 research papers, 2005-10. Honours: Listed in international biographical dictionaries. Address: 222/16, MOO6, Mooban Emperor 2, Wongwan Robklang Road, Tambon Faham, Ampur Muang, Chiangmai 50000, Thailand. E-mail: vites@chiangmai.ac.th

LONGMORE, Rt Hon Lord Justice, Rt Hon Sir Andrew Centlivres, b. 25 August 1944, Liverpool, England. Judge. m. Margaret McNair, 1 son. Education: Lincoln College, Oxford. Appointments: Called to Bar, 1966; Queen's Counsel, 1983; Recorder of Crown Court, 1992; High Court Judge, 1993; Lord Justice of Appeal, 2001. Publications: Co-editor, 6th, 7th, 8th and 9th edition of MacGillirray's Law of Insurance. Honours: Knight, 1993; Privy Councillor, 2001. Memberships: Middle Temple, 1962-. Address: Royal Courts of Justice, London WC2A 2LL, England.

LONIGAN Paul R, b. 27 May 1935, New York City, USA. Professor Emeritus. m. Cynthia Hartley, 2 daughters. Education: BA, Romance Languages and Classics, Queens College, New York, 1960; PhD, Romance Languages, Johns Hopkins University, 1967. Appointments: Instructor, Russell Sage College, Troy, New York, 1963-65; Associate Professor, State University College, Oswego, New York, 1965-67; Queens College, CUNY, 1967-, Professor, 1983; Professor, CUNY Graduate Center, 1968-98; Deputy Executive Officer, PhD program in French, CUNY Graduate Center, 1969-72. Publications on subjects: Medieval epic, romance, hagiography, Early Irish church, the Druids, Chrétien de Troyes, Villon, Rabelais, Montaigne, Ruben Darío, Women in the Middle Ages, Shamanism in the Old Irish Tradition, The Romance Languages and the Celtic Monks, The Three Kings of the Nativity, Napoleon's Irish Legion; Editor, poetry of María Victoria Carreño Montás, Respuestas Del Corazón, 1999; 'Protest Through Fasting'; 'Seamus Heaney's translation of Beowulf'; The Song of Roland; General Richard Montgomery (of The American Revolution). Editor, Provincial prize winning poetry of María Victoria Carreño Montás, 'Fragmentos de una tarde', Dominican Republic, Cocolo Editorial, 2004. Honours: National Defence Fellow; Phi Beta Kappa; Delta Phi Alpha; Magna cum laude; Chevalier dans l'Ordre des Palmes Académiques; Medal of Distinction, Men of Achievement; Plaque of Distinction as Sponsor of Le Cercle Francais, Queens College; Presidential Certificate of Distinguished Service, Queens College, 1988; International Order of Merit, 1999; Commemorative Medal of Honour, 2001; Letter of Appreciation from the Trustees of Huguenot Heritage, 2003; Certificate of Recognition for Service during the Period of the Cold War, 2004; National Defence Service Medal, 2005; Korean Defence Service Medal, 2005; World Medal of Freedom, 2006; Research Board of Advisors, ABI, 2006; Charter Fellow, Advisory Directorate International, ABI, 2008; Paul Lonigan: A Rare Combination of Teaching Skills, 2009; Legion of Honor, UCC, 2010; Medal of Merit, Ajutant General, State of New York, Commander of all Military Naval Forces, 2010; Listed in national and international biographical dictionaries. Memberships: Founding Member, Círculo de Cultura Panamericano; Irish Texts Society; Contributing Editor of Oidhreacht, Newsletter of Celtic Heritage Books; Association of Literary Scholars and Critics; Archaeological Institute of America; American Society of the French Academic Palms; Hugenot Heritage, New York City, New York; The Biblical Archaeology Society. Address: PO Box 243, Montgomery, NY 12549, USA.

LOPATIN Pavel Konstantinovich, b. 29 May 1968, Kemerovo, Russia. Robotics Professor; Researcher. Education: Mechanical Engineering degree, Technical University of Budapest, Hungary, 1991; Candidate, Technical Sciences, Siberian State Aerospace University, Krasnoyarsk, Russia, 1998. Appointments: Programmer, Krasnoyarsk Polytechnical Institute, 1991-92; Krasnoyarsk Metallurgical Plant, 1992-93; Assistant, Siberian State Aerospace University, Krasnoyarsk, 1994-97; Senior Teacher, Siberian State Aerospace University, Krasnoyarsk, 1997-99; Docent, Siberian State Aerospace University, Krasnoyarsk, 1999-. Publications: Algorithm of a manipulator movement amidst unknown obstacles, 2001; Computer modeling of emotional reactions of members of a pair when a member of the pair gets material harm from beyond, 2003; Manipulating Robots: Kinematics Dynamics Control, 2005; Using the Forward Search and the Polynomial Approximation Algorithms for Manipulator's Control in an Unknown Environment, 2006; Using the Polynomial Approximation Algorithm in the Algorithm2 for Manipulator's Control in an Unknown Environment, 2007; Algorithm for Dynamic Systems' Control in an Unknown Static Environment, 2007; A7DOF Manipulator Control in an Unknown Environment based on an Exact Algorithm, 2008; A Manipulator Control in an Environment with Unknown Static Obstacles, 2009. Honours: Grantee, Russian Foundation for Basic Research, 2005; Scholar, President of Russia, 1996-97; Scholar, German Academic Exchange Service, 2003; Listed in international biographical dictionaries. Memberships: Krasnoyarsk Historical and Educational Society Memorial; IEEE; Krasnoyarsk Esperanto Club. E-mail: efa14@yandex.ru

LOPES Everaldo Antonio, b. 7 May 1979, Viçosa, Brazil. Professor; Researcher. m. Luciana, 1 son. Education: Degree, Agronomy 2002, MSc, 2004, DSc, 2007, Plant Pathology, Universidade Federal de Viçosa. Appointments: Professor, UNIPAM, 2009-10; Professor, Universidade Federal de Viçosa, 2010-. Publications: 34 articles; 1 book. Honours: Listed in international biographical dictionaries. Memberships: Brazilian Society of Nematology. Address: Universidade Federal de Viçosa, Campus Rio Paranaíba, Rodovia BR 354, Km 310, Caixa Postal 22, Rio Paranaíba, Minas Gerais 38810-000, Brazil. E-mail: everaldolopes@ufv.br

LOPEZ Jennifer, b. 24 July 1969, Bronx, New York, USA. Actress; Dancer; Singer. m. (1) Ojani Noa, 1997, (2) Cris Judd, 2001, (3) Marc Anthony, 2004, 1 son, 1 daughter. Appointments: Album: On the 6; J Lo, 2001; J To Tha L-O! This Is Me... Then, 2002; Rebirth, 2005; Como Ama una Mujer, Brave, 2007; Singles: If You Had My Love, Waiting for Tonight, 1999; Feelin' So Good, Let's Get Loud, 2000; Love Don't Cost a Thing, Amor se paga con amor, Play, Ain't It Funny, I'm Real, 2001; I'm Gonna Be Alright, Jenny From the Block, 2002; All I Have, I'm Glad, Reel Me, 2003; Baby I Love You, Shall We Dance? 2004. Film appearances include: My Little Girl, 1996; My Family – Mia Familia, Money Train, 1995; Jack, Blood and Wine, 1996; Anaconda, Selena, U-Turn, 1997; Out of Sight, 1998; Thieves, Pluto Nash, 1999; The Cell, The Wedding Planner, 2000; Angel Eyes, 2001; Enough, Maid in Manhattan, 2002; Gigli, 2003; Jersey Girl, Shall We Dance? 2004; Monster-in-Law, An Unfinished Life, 2005; Border Town, El Cantante, 2006; The Backup Plan, 2010; What to Expect When You're Expecting, Ice Age: Continental Drift, 2012; Parker, 2013; TV appearances include: Second Chances; Hotel Malibu; Nurses on the Line; The Crash of Flight 7; Will & Grace; How I Met Your Mother. Honours: Golden Globe, 1998; MTV Movie Award, 1999; Billboard Latin Award for Hot Latin Track of the Year, 2000; MTV Video Music Award for Best Dance Video, 2000; VH1/ Vogue Fashion Versace Award, 2000; MTV Europe Music Award for Best Female Act, 2001; MTV Award for Best Female, 2002. Address: International Creative Management, 8942 Wilshire Boulevard, Beverly Hills, CA 90211, USA. Website: www.jenniferlopez.com

LÓPEZ DE LACALLE Luis Norberto, b. 22 April 1964, Vitoria, Spain. Professor. m. Blanca E Gómez, 2 daughters. Education: PhD, Mechanical Engineering, 1995. Appointments: Professor, Mechanical Engineering, University of the Basque Country. Publications: Machine Tools for High Performance Machining, 2008. Memberships: Society of Manufacturing Engineering; DAAAM International; International Association of Engineers. Address: ETS Ingeniería, c/Alameda urquijo s/n, 48013 Bilbao, Spain. E-mail: norberto.lzlacalle@ehu.es Website: www.ehu.es/manufacturing

LOPEZ GARCIA Angel, b. Madrid, Spain. Telecommunication Engineer. m. Maria Del Mar, 2 daughters. Education: Telecommunication Engineer, ETSIT, Madrid, Spain, 1980-1986. Appointments: Systems Analyst, Siemens S A, 1986-1989; Project Leader, Sener S A, 1989-1991; Project Leader, Indra Sistemas S A, 1991-2005; Senior Consultant, IT Deusto SA, 2005-08; Executive Manager, OESIA SL, 2008. Honours: Graduate with honours, Telecommunication Engineering. Address: Caleruega, 73, 28033, Madrid, Spain. E-mail: alopezg@oesia.com

LOPEZ PALACIOS Iris Athamaica, b. 15 May 1971, Caracas, Venezuela. Mathematician. 1 son. Education: PhD, Sciences & Mathematics, University of Central Venezuela, 2006. Appointments: Mathematician. Publications: Numerous articles in professional journals; Chapters to books. Address: Apt 31025, Junquito, Caracas 1030, Venezuela. E-mail: iris.athamaica@gmail.com

LÓPEZ-COBOS Jesús, b. 25 February 1940, Toro, Spain. Orchestral Conductor. Education: DPhil, Madrid University; Composition, Madrid Conservatory; Conducting, Vienna Academy. Appointments: Worked with major orchestras including London Symphony, Royal Philharmonic, Philharmonia, Concertgebouw, Vienna Philharmonic, Vienna Symphony, Berlin Philharmonic, Hamburg NDR, Munich Philharmonic, Cleveland, Chicago Symphony, New York Philharmonic, Philadelphia, Pittsburgh; Conducted new opera productions at La Scala, Milan, Covent Garden, London, Metropolitan Opera, New York; General Musikdirektor, Deutsche Oper, Berlin, 1981-90; Principal Guest Conductor, London Philharmonic Orchestra, 1981-86; Principal Guest Conductor, Artistic Director, Spanish National Orchestra, 1984-89; Music Director, Cincinnati Symphony Orchestra, 1986-2000; Music Director, Lausanne Chamber Orchestra, 1990-2000; Orchestre Français des Jeunes, 1998-2001; Music Director, Tetro Real, Madrid, 2003-. Publications: Recordings including: Bruckner symphonies; Haydn symphonies; Donizetti's Lucia di Lammermoor; Rossini's Otello; Recital discs with José Carreras. Honours: 1st Prize, Besançon International Conductors Competition, 1969; Prince of Asturias Award, Spanish Government, 1981; Founders Award, American Society of Composers, Authors and Publishers, 1988; Cross of Merit, 1st Class, Federal Republic of Germany, 1989. Address: c/o Terry Harrison Artists, The Orchard, Market Street, Charlbury, Oxon OX7 3PJ, England.

LOPOT Frantisek, b. 30 September 1950, Cervena Voda, Czech Republic. Clinical Engineer. m. Olga Hladeckova, 1 son, 1 daughter. Education: Dipl Eng, Technical Cybernetics, 1973, PhD, Biocybernetics, 1978, Czech Technical University. Appointments: Biomedical Engineer, 1975-88, Clinical Engineer, 1988-, General University Hospital, Prague; Senior Lecturer, 1995-2000, Associate Professor, Biophysics, 2001-, 1st Medical Faculty, Charles University, Prague. Publications: Over 50 articles in professional journals; Editor, 2 monographs; Author, 2 book chapters. Honours: Golden Medal EDTNA-ERCA, 1996; Jan Brod Award, 1998; Best Poster Award, International Society for Blood Purification, 2005; Lifetime Membership, Czech Society for Biomedical Engineering, 2006. Memberships: Czech Nephrological Society; Czech Society of Biomedical Engineering; Czech Society for Vascular Access; European Renal Care Association (EDTNA-ERCA); International Society of Blood Purification (ISBP); International Society of Hemodialysis (ISH); International Society for Artificial Organs (ISAO); American Society for Artificial Internal Organs (ASAIO); Editorial Board Member of ASAIO Journal, Hemodialysis International, and Journal of Renal Care. E-mail: f.lopot@vfn.cz

LOREN Sophia, b. 20 September 1934, Rome, Italy. Actress. m. Carlo Ponti, 1957 (marriage annulled 1962) m. Carlo Ponti 1966-2007 (deceased), 2 sons. Education: Scuole Magistrali Superiori. Appointments: First Screen Appearance, as an extra in Quo Vadis; Appeared in many Italian and other Films including: E Arrivato l'Accordatore, 1951; Africa sotto i Mari (first leading role); La Tratta delle Bianche, La Favorita, 1952; Aida, Il Paesedei Campanelli, Miseria e Nobilta, Il Segno di Venere, Tempi Nostri, Carosello Napoletano, 1953; L'Oro di Napoli, Attila, 1954; Peccatoche sia una canaglia, la Bella Mugnaia, La Donna del Fiume, 1955; Boccaccio,

1970; Matromonio All; Italiana; American Films include: The Pride and the Passion, 1955; Boy on a Dolphin, Legend of the Lost, 1956; Desire Under the Elms, 1957; That Kind of Woman, Houseboat, The Key, 1958; The Black Orchid, 1959; The Millionairess, Two Women, El Cid, 1961; Yesterday, Today and Tomorrow, 1963; The Fall of the Roman Empire, 1964; Lady L, Judith, A Countess from Hong Kong, 1965; Arabesque, 1966; More than a Miracle, 1967; The Priest's Wife, Sunflower, 1970; Man of La Mancha, 1972; Brief Encounter, (TV), The Verdict, 1974; The Cassandra Crossing, A Special Day, 1977; Firepower, 1978; Brass Target, 1979; Blood Feud, 1981; Mother Courage, 1986; Two Women, 1989; Pret a Porter, Grumpier Old Men, 1995; Soliel, 1997; Francesca e Nunziata (TV), 2001; Between Strangers, 2002; Lives of the Saints (TV), Peperoni ripienie pesci in faccia, 2004; Nine, 2009. Memberships: Chair, National Alliance for Prevention and Treatment of Child Abuse and Maltreatment. Publications: Eat with Me, 1972; Sophia Loren on Women and Beauty, 1984. Honours: Venice Festival Award for the Black Orchid, 1958; Cannes Film Festival Award for Best Actress, 1961; Honorary Academy Award, 1991; Chevalier Legion d'Honneur; Goodwill Ambassador for Refugees, 1992. Address: Chalet Daniel, Burgenstock, Luzern, Switzerland.

LOSOWSKY Monty S, b. 1 August 1931, London, England. Physician; Medical Educator. m. Barbara, 1 son, 1 daughter. Education: Coopers' Company's School, London, 1945-49; MB ChB (Hons), 1955, MD, 1961, University of Leeds. Appointments: Assistant, Hôpital St Antoine, Paris, France, 1960-61; Research Fellow, Harvard University, 1961-62; Lecturer, Senior Lecturer, Reader in Medicine, 1962-69; Professor of Medicine, 1969-96, Dean of Medicine & Dentistry, 1989-94, University of Leeds; Retired, 1996; Executive Chairman, Thackray Museum, Leeds. Publications: Joint author/editor, 9 books on medical subjects; Author/joint author, over 20 chapters in books on medical topics; Author/ joint author, about 400 papers. Honours: Visiting Professor, Postgraduate Medical Institute, Chandigarh, India, 1975; Visiting Professor, Royal Postgraduate Medical School, London, 1994; Watson Smith Lecturer, 1995, Simms Lecturer, 1996, Royal College of Physician, London; Visiting Professor, University of Queensland, Australia, 1997. Memberships: British Society of Gastroenterology; British Nutrition Foundation; Royal Society of Medicine; FRCP, London. E-mail: mlosowsky@email.com

LOTOREV Alexander Nikolaevich, b. 10 September 1948, Alexandrovka Village, Zolotukhinsky District, Kursk Region, USSR. Public Servant. m. Liubov Lotoreva, 2 sons, 1 daughter. Education: Postgraduate Diplomas, Kursk State Pedagogical Institute and Russian Academy of Public Service; Valid State Adviser of the Russian Federation 1st class. Appointments: Served in the Red Army, 1967-69; Toolmaker and Secretary of the Comsomol Committee, State Steel Bearing Factory, Kursk, 1970-76; Assistant to the Commander of a Company and Commander of a Company, Armed Forces, 1976-78; Director, Technical Training College No 22, Kursk, 1978-82; Deputy Director, Technical Training College, Surgut, Director of the Technical Training College, Nefteyugansk, Autonomous Region of Khanty, 1982-90; Elected Chairman, Executive Committee of the City of Nefteyugansk, 1990-92, Vice-Head, Administration of Nefteyugansk, 1992-; Elected Deputy of the State Duma of Khanty-Mansyisk. 1995, re-elected. 1999; Vice-President of the Deputy Group "Regions of Russia"; State Duma Committee on Power Transport and Communication; State Duma Mandate Committee; Co-ordinator of the deputy group on relations with Turkmenia; Active participant in the Co-ordinations Council of the Centrist Deputy Association "Unity", "Fatherland-All Russia" "People's Deputy", "Regions of Russia"; Secretary General (Head of Staff), State Duma of the Federal Assembly, Russian Federation, 2002-. Honours: Honorary PhD, Economics; Medals: 60 Years of the USSR Armed Forces, 1978, In Memory of 850 Years of Moscow, 1997, 300 Years of Saint Petersburg, 2003; Honoured Certificate of the State Duma of the Federal Assembly of the Russian Federation, 2002; Order of Honour, 2003. Address: State Duma of the Federal Assembly of the Russian Federation, Okhotny ryad 1, 103265 Moscow, Russian Federation. E-mail: lotorev@duma.gov.ru

LOTT Pixie (Victoria Louise), b. 12 January 1991, Bromley, England. Singer. Education: Italia Conti Academy of Theatre Arts. Career: Appearances in West End productions; Recording Artist, Island Def Jam Music Group, Mercury Records, UK and Interscope Records, USA; Songwriter, Sony/ATV Music Publishing, 2007; Recordings: Albums: Turn It Up, 2009; Young Foolish Happy, 2011; Singles: Mama Do, 2009; Boys and Girls, 2009; Cry Me Out, 2009; Gravity, 2010; All About Tonight, 2011; What Do You Take Me For? 2011; Kiss the Stars, 2012. Honours: 2 MTV EMA Awards, 2009; Best UK & Ireland Act and Best Push Artist, 2009; Cosmopolitan 2009 Ultimate Women Award for Ultimate Newcomer, 2009; Caron Keating Breakthrough Talent Award, 2009; Virgin Media Awards, 2011.

LOUDEN Stephen Henry, b. 18 November 1941, Southport, England. Roman Catholic Clergyman. Education: St Joseph's College, Upholland; Ordained in Roman Catholic Priesthood, 1968; BA, Open University, 1975; MTh (Distinction), Oxford University, 1993; PhD, University of Wales, 1998. Appointments: All Saints, Anfield, 1968-72; St John's, Kirkdale, 1972-75; Our Lady's, Formby, 1975-78; Royal Army Chaplain's Department, Dortmund, 1978-79; Londonderry, 1979-80; Münster, 1980-82; Dhekelia, Cyprus, 1982-84; Royal Military Academy, Sandhurst, 1984-86; Berlin, 1986-88; Rheindahlen, 1988-90; Hong Kong, 1990-92; Lisburn, 1992-94; Principal Roman Catholic Chaplain and Vicar General (Army), 1994-97. Publications: Chaplains in Conflict, 1996; Co-author, The Naked Parish Priest, 2003; Numerous articles in professional journals. Honours: Prelate of Honour to his Holiness Pope John Paul II, 1994; Rt Rev Monsignor. Address: Chapel House, 57 Chapel Lane, Netherton, L30 7PF, England. E-mail: mgrshl@msn.com

LOUISY Calliopa Pearlette, b. 8 June 1946, St Lucia, West Indies. Governor General. Education: BA, University of the West Indies, 1969; MA, Laval University, 1975; PhD, University of Bristol, 1994. Appointments: Principal, St Lucia A Level College, 1981-86; Dean, 1986-94, Vice Principal, 1994-95, Principal, 1996-97, Sir Arthur Lewis Community College; Governor General, 1997. Publications: The Changing Role of the Small State in Higher Education; Globalisation and Comparative Education: A Caribbean Perspective; Whose Context for What Quality? Informing Eduation Strategies for the Caribbean; Nation Languages and National Development in the Caribbean: Reclaiming Our Own Voices. Honours: Student of the Year, 1968; Grand Cross of the Order of St Lucia, 1997; International Woman of the Year, 1998, 2001; Grand Cross of the Order of St Michael and St George, 1999; Honorary Degree of Doctor of Law (LLD) University of Bristol, 1999 and University of Sheffield, 2003; Dame of Grace of the Most Venerable Order of the Hospital of St John of Jerusalem, 2001; Listed in International Biographical

Dictionaries. Membership: Fellow, Royal Society of Arts, 2000. Address: Government House, Morne Fortune, Castries, St Lucia, West Indies. E-mail: govgenslu@candw.lc

LOVE Courtney, b. 9 July 1964, San Francisco, USA. Singer; Musician (guitar); Actress. m. Kurt Cobain, 1992, deceased 1994, 1 daughter. Career: Member, Faith No More, 1 year; Founder, singer/guitarist, Hole, 1991-2002; Solo artist, 2003-; Tours include: Support tour to Nine Inch Nails; Reading Festival, 1994, 1995; Film appearances: Straight To Hell; Sid And Nancy; Feeling Minnesota; The People vs Larry Flynt; Man on the Moon; Beat, 2000; Julie Johnson, 2001; Trapped, 2002; Trailer for a Remake of Gore Vidal's Caligula, 2005. Recordings: Albums: Pretty On The Inside, 1991; Live Through This, 1994; Celebrity Skin, 1998; Solo album: America's Sweetheart. Singles: Doll Parts, 1994; Ask for It, 1995; Celebrity Skin, 1998; Malibu, 1998; Awful, 1999; Solo single: Mono, 2004. Address: Q-Prime Inc, 729 Seventh Avenue, 14th Floor, New York, NY 10019, USA. Website: www.courtneylove.com

LOVELL (Alfred Charles) Bernard (Sir), b. 31 August 1913, Oldland Common, Gloucestershire, England. Professor of Radio Astronomy Emeritus; Writer. m. Mary Joyce Chesterman, 1937, deceased 1993, 2 sons, 3 daughters. Education: University of Bristol. Appointments: Professor of Radio Astronomy, 1951-80, Professor Emeritus, 1980-, University of Manchester; Director, Jodrell Bank Experimental Station, later Nuffield Radio Astronomy Laboratories, 1951-81; Various visiting lectureships. Publications: Science and Civilisation, 1939; World Power Resources and Social Development, 1945; Radio Astronomy, 1951; Meteor Astronomy, 1954; The Exploration of Space by Radio, 1957; The Individual and the Universe, 1958; The Exploration of Outer Space, 1961; Discovering the Universe, 1963; Our Present Knowledge of the Universe, 1967; The Explosion of Science: The Physical Universe (editor with T Margerison), 1967; The Story of Jodrell Bank, 1968; The Origins and International Economics of Space Exploration, 1973; Out of the Zenith, 1973; Man's Relation to the Universe, 1975; P M S Blackett: A Biographical Memoir, 1976; In the Centre of Immensities, 1978; Emerging Cosmology, 1981; The Jodrell Bank Telescopes, 1985; Voice of the Universe, 1987; Pathways to the Universe (with Sir Francis Graham Smith), 1988; Astronomer By Chance (autobiography), 1990; Echoes of War, 1991; The Effect of Science on the Second World War, 2000. Contributions to: Professional journals. Honours: Officer of the Order of the British Empire, 1946; Duddell Medal, 1954; Royal Medal, 1960; Knighted, 1961; Ordre du Mérite pour la Recherche et l'Invention, 1962; Churchill Gold Medal, 1964; Gold Medal, Royal Astronomical Society, 1981; Many honorary doctorates. Memberships: American Academy of Arts and Sciences, honorary foreign member; American Philosophical Society; International Astronomical Union, vice-president, 1970-76; New York Academy; Royal Astronomical Society, president, 1969-71; Royal Society, fellow; Royal Swedish Academy, honorary member. Address: The Quinta, Swettenham, Cheshire CW12 2LD, England.

LOVESEY Peter, (Peter Lear), b. 10 September 1936, Whitton, Middlesex, England. Writer. m. Jacqueline Ruth Lewis, 1959, 1 son, 1 daughter. Education: BA, Honours, English, University of Reading, 1958. Publications: The Kings of Distance, 1968; Wobble to Death, 1970; The Detective Wore Silk Drawers, 1971; Abracadaver, 1972; Mad Hatters Holiday, 1973; Invitation to a Dynamite Party, 1974; A Case of Spirits, 1975; Swing, Swing Together, 1976; Goldengirl, 1977; Waxwork, 1978; Official Centenary History of the Amateur Athletic Association, 1979; Spider Girl, 1980; The False Inspector Dew, 1982; Keystone, 1983; Butchers (short stories), 1985; The Secret of Spandau, 1986; Rough Cider, 1986; Bertie and the Tinman, 1987; On the Edge, 1989; Bertie and the Seven Bodies, 1990; The Last Detective, 1991; Diamond Solitaire, 1992; Bertie and the Crime of Passion, 1993; The Crime of Miss Oyster Brown (short stories), 1994; The Summons, 1995; Bloodhounds, 1996; Upon a Dark Night, 1997; Do Not Exceed the Stated Dose (short stories), 1998; The Vault, 1999; The Reaper, 2000; Diamond Dust, 2002; The Sedgemoor Strangler (short stories), 2002; The House Sitter, 2003; The Circle, 2005; The Secret Hangman, 2007; The Headhunters, 2008; Murder on the Short List (short stories), 2009; Skeleton Hill, 2009; Stagestruck, 2011. Honours: Macmillan/Panther 1st Crime Novel Award, 1970; Crime Writers Association Silver Dagger, 1978, 1995, 1996 and Gold Dagger, 1982 and Cartier Diamond Dagger, 2000; Grand Prix de Littérature Policière, 1985; Prix du Roman D'Aventures, 1987; Anthony Award, 1992; Macavity Award 1997, 2004. Memberships: Crime Writers Association, chairman, 1991-92; Detection Club; Society of Authors. Address: 59 Crescent Road, Leigh-on-Sea, Essex SS9 2PF, England.

LOWE Gordon, b. 31 May 1933, Halifax, England. University Professor. m. Gwynneth Hunter, 2 sons. Education: BSc, ARCS, 1954, PhD, DIC, 1957, Royal College of Science, Imperial College, London University; MA, Oxford University, 1960. Appointments: University Demonstrator, 1959-65, Weir Junior Research Fellow, University College, 1959-61, Official Fellow, Tutor in Organic Chemistry, Lincoln College, 1962-99, University Lecturer, 1965-88, Sub-Rector, Lincoln College, 1986-89, Aldrichian Praelector in Chemistry, 1988-89, Professor of Biological Chemistry, 1989-2000, Emeritus Professor of Biological Chemistry, Supernumerary Fellow, 2000-, Oxford University; Director, Founder, Scientific Consultant, Pharminox Ltd, 2002-. Publications: Around 240 articles in learned journals. Honours: CChem, FRSC, 1981; Charmian Medal for Enzyme Chemistry, Royal Society of Chemistry, 1983; FRS, 1984; DSc, Oxon, 1985; Royal Society of Chemistry Award for Stereochemistry, 1992. Memberships: Fellow, Royal Society, London; Fellow, Royal Society of Chemistry, London. Address: 17 Norman Avenue, Abingdon, Oxfordshire, OX14 2HQ, England. E-mail: gordon.lowe@chem.ox.ac.uk

LOWE Rob (Robert Hepler), b. 17 March 1964, Virginia, USA. Actor. m. Sheryl Berkoff, 1991, 2 sons. TV: A New Kind of Family, 1979; The West Wing, 1999-2006; Jane Doe, 2001; Framed, 2002; The Christmas Shoes, 2002; The Lyon's Den, 2003; Salem's Lot, 2004; Perfect Strangers, 2004; Beach Girls, 2005; The Christmas Blessing, 2005; Brothers and Sisters, 2006-08; Dr Vegas, 2004-06; A Perfect Day, 2006; Family Guy, 2007; Stir of Echoes: The Homecoming, 2007; Film: The Outsiders, 1983; St Elmo's Fire, 1985; About Last Night, 1986; Wayne's World, 1992; Austin Powers: The Spy Who Shagged Me, 1999; Under Presure, 2000; The Specials, 2000; Proximity, 2001; Austin Powers in Goldmember, 2002; View from the Top, 2003; Thank You for Smoking, 2005; The Invention of Lying, 2009.

LOWNIE Andrew (James Hamilton), b. 11 November 1961, Kenya. Literary Agent; Writer; Editor. m. Angela Doyle, 1998, 1 son, 1 daughter. Education: Magdalene College, Cambridge, 1981-84; BA, Cantab; MA, Cantab; MSc, University of Edinburgh, 1989. Appointments: Agent, 1985-86, Director, 1986-88, John Farquharson Literary Agents; Director, Andrew Lownie Associates, 1988-; Partner, Denniston and Lownie,

1991-93; Director, Thistle Publishing, 1996-. Publications: North American Spies, 1992; Edinburgh Literary Guide, 1992; John Buchan: The Presbyterian Cavalier, 1995; John Buchan's Collected Poems (editor), 1996; The Complete Short Stories of John Buchan, Vols 1 - 3 (editor), 1997-98; The Literary Companion to Edinburgh, 2000; The Edinburgh Literary Companion, 2005; Contributions to: Books and periodicals. Honour: English Speaking Union Scholarship, 1979-80. Memberships: Association of Authors' Agents; Society of Authors; Secretary, The Biographer's Club, 1998-; Executive Committee, PEN, 2000. Address: 36 Great Smith Street, London, SW18 3BU, England.

LOZANO BARRAGÁN Javier, b. 26 January 1933, Toluca, Mexico. Cardinal of the Catholic Church. Education: Humanities, Philosophy and Theology, Seminary of Zamora, Mexico, 1944-54; Master's and Doctor's degrees, Dogmatic Theology, Pontifical Gregorian University, Rome, Italy. Appointments: Professor, Dogmatic Theology, History of Philosophy and Pedagogy, Zamora's Seminary, 1958-78; President, Mexican Theological Society, 1973-75; Director, Theological-Pastoral Institute of Celam, 1977-79; Professor, Latin-American Theology, Universities of Comillas, Spain, and Louvain, Belgium, 1977-79; Auxiliary Bishop, Mexico's Archdiocese, 1979-85; Founder, Pontifical University of Mexico, 1982-85; Bishop of Zacatecas, 1984-97; President, Pontifical Council for Pastoral Assistance to Healthcare Workers, 1997-2009. Publications: Síntesis Dogmáticas Actuales, 1968; Puebla, Pueblo, Liberación, Educación, 1980; Cristo Alianza de la Familia, 1982; Hacia el Tercer Milenio, Teología y Cultura, 1988; Por qué soy Católico, 1991; Santo Domingo, Puerta Grande hacia el Tercer Milenio, 1994; Teología, Estado y Sociedad, 1997; Theology and Medicine, 2000; Metabioetics and Medicine, 2005; Life in Death, 2009; Balcón de Recuerdos alrededor del Mundo, 2010; 8 more books and many theological articles in several theological revues. Honours: Doctor "Honoris Causa": Catholic University of Taiwan, 2001, Pontifical University Madre y Maestra, Dominican Republic, 2002, and Pontifical University of Mexico, 2003; Member, various Vatican dicasteries. Memberships: Vatican Congregation for Bishops; Vatican Congregation for the Evangelization of Peoples; Pontifical Committee for International Eucharistic Congresses; Pontifical Congregation for the Cause of the Saints. Address: Piazza San Calisto 16, 00153 Vatican City. E-mail: jlozano@hlthwork.va

LU Frank Leigh, b. 2 May 1967, Bellefonte, Pennsylvania, USA. Medical Director. Education: MD, School of Medicine, College of Medicine, National Taiwan University, 1993. Appointments: Intern, 1992-93, Resident, 1994-97, National Taiwan University Hospital; Attending Physician, Pediatric Intensive Care Unit, 1999-, Director, Division of Pediatric Pulmonary and Critical Care Medicine, 2007-, Clinical Lecturer, 2010-, Department of Pediatrics, National Taiwan University Children's Hospital, Taipei; Trustee, Society of Pediatric Pulmonology, Taiwan, 2009-. Publications: Numerous articles in professional journals. Honours: Presidential Award, Department of Medicine, 1992; Best Interns of the Medical Department, 1993; Best Interns of the Surgical Department, 1993; Award for Excellence in Clinical Service, 1997, 2001, 2010; Teaching Award for Excellence in Medical Education, 2002, 2006. Memberships: Taiwan Pediatric Association; Society of Neonatology; Society of Pediatric Pulmonology; Society of Critical Care Medicine; Formosan Medical Association. Address: Department of Pediatrics, National Taiwan University Children's Hospital, 15F 8 Chung San South Road, Taipei 100, Taiwan. E-mail: frankllu@ntu.edu.tw

LUBBOCK John, b. 18 March 1945, Hertfordshire, England. Conductor. m. Christine, 4 sons. Education: Chorister, St Georges Chapel, Windsor; Radley College; Royal Academy of Music. Appointments: Founder & Artistic Director, Orchestra of St John's; Founder of charity, Music for Autism. Honours: GRSM; Fellow, Royal Academy of Music. Address: 7 Warborough Road, Shillingford, Oxfordshire OX10 7SA, England. E-mail: orchestra@osj.org.uk

LUCA TUDORACHE Rodica, b. 18 May 1962, Iasi, Romania. Professor. m. Mihai, 1 son. Education: Degree, 1984, PhD, 1996, Mathematics, Al I Cuza University, Iasi. Appointments: High School Professor, Pascani, Iasi district, 1984-86; Mathematician, ITC, Iasi, 1986-88; Assistant Professor, 1988-94, Lecturer, 1994-2001, Associate Professor, 2001-08, Professor, 2008-, Department of Mathematics, Gh Asachi Technical University, Iasi. Publications: Numerous articles in professional journals. Honours: Listed in international biographical dictionaries. Memberships: American Mathematical Society; European Mathematical Society; International Federation of Nonlinear Analysts; Research Group in Mathematical Inequalities and Applications; Societatea de Stiinte Matematice din Romania; Societatea Romana de Matematica Aplicata si Industriala. Address: Department of Mathematics, Gh Asachi Technical University, 11 Blvd Carol I, Iasi 700506, Romania. E-mail: rluca@math.tuiasi.ro

LUCAS Charles Clement, b. 1942, North Carolina, USA. Physician. m. Marcia Helen Clare (divorced), 1 son, 1 daughter. Education: BA, Chemistry, BA, American History, University of North Carolina at Chapel Hill, 1960-65. Appointments: Intern, Lexington, Kentucky, 1969-70; Military Service, US Public Health Service, 1970-72; Resident, Duke University Medical Center, Durham, North Carolina, 1972-74; Private practice, Chowan Hospital, Edenton, North Carolina, 1974-79; Group practice, Tuxedo Park, New York, 1980-83; Director of Clinic, Life Extension Institute, Madison Avenue, New York, 1984-88; Private family practice, Larchmont, New York, 1988-. Honours: Fellow, American Medical Association Physicians Recognition Award; Order of the Long Leaf Pine. Memberships: American Academy of Family Physicians; American Board of Family Medicine. Address: 76 Khakum Wood Road, Greenwich, CT 06831, USA. E-mail: cclmd@aol.com

LUCAS George, b. 14 May 1944, Modesto, California, USA. Film Director. m. Marcia Lou Griffin, 1969, divorced 1983, 1 adopted son, 2 adopted daughers. Education: University of South California. Appointments: Warner Brothers Studio; Assistant to Francis Ford Cappola, The Rain People; Director, Documentary on making The Rain People; Formed, Lucasfilm Ltd; Director; Author; Executive Producer; Actor; Films include: THX-1138, 1971; American Graffiti, 1973; Star Wars Episode IV: A New Hope, 1977; More American Graffiti, 1979; Star Wars Episode V: The Empire Strikes Back, 1980; Raiders of the Lost Ark, 1981; Star Wars Episode VI: Return of the Jedi, 1983; Indiana Jones and the Temple of Doom, 1984; Mishima: A Life in Four Chapters, 1985; Howard the Duck, 1986; Labyrinth, 1986; Willow, 1988; Tucker: The Man and His Dream, 1988; Indiana Jones and the Last Crusade, 1989; Hook, 1991; Beverly Hills Cop III, 1994; Star Wars Episode I: The Phantom Menace, 1999; Star Wars Episode II: Attack of the Clones, 2002; Star Wars Episode III: Revenge of the Sith, 2005; Indiana Jones and the Kingdom of the Crystal Skull, 2008; Star Wars: The Clone Wars, 2008; Red Tails, 2010. Honours: Dr hc, University of South California, 1994; Irving Thalberg Award, 1992. Address: Lucasfilm Ltd, P O Box 2009, San Rafael, CA 94912, USA.

LUCAS John (Randolph), b. 18 June 1929, England. Philosopher; Writer. m. Morar Portal, 1961, 2 sons, 2 daughters. Education: St Mary's College, Winchester; MA, Balliol College, Oxford, 1952. Appointments: Junior Research Fellow, 1953-56, Fellow and Tutor, 1960-96, Merton College, Oxford; Fellow and Assistant Tutor, Corpus Christi College, Cambridge, 1956-59; Jane Eliza Procter Visiting Fellow, Princeton University, 1957-58; Leverhulme Research Fellow, Leeds University, 1959-60; Gifford Lecturer, University of Edinburgh, 1971-73; Margaret Harris Lecturer, University of Dundee, 1981; Harry Jelema Lecturer, Calvin College, Grand Rapids, 1987; Reader in Philosophy, Oxford University, 1990-96. Publications: Principles of Politics, 1966, 2nd edition, 1985; The Concept of Probability, 1970; The Freedom of the Will, 1970; The Nature of Mind, 1972; The Development of Mind, 1973; A Treatise on Time and Space, 1973; Essays on Freedom and Grace, 1976; Democracy and Participation, 1976; On Justice, 1980; Space, Time and Causality, 1985; The Future, 1989; Spacetime and Electromagnetism, 1990; Responsibility, 1993; Ethical Economics, 1996; The Conceptual Roots of Mathematics, 1999; An Engagement with Plato's Republic, 2003; Reason and Reality, 2006; Contributions to scholarly journals. Memberships: British Academy, Fellow; British Society for the Philosophy of Science, president, 1991-93. Address: Lambrook House, East Lambrook, Somerset TA13 5HW, England. Website: http://users.ox.ac.uk/~jrlucas

LUCKE Bernhard, b. 24 April 1975, Bielefeld, Germany. Academic. Education: Dipl-Ing, BTU Cottbus, 2002; PhD, BTU Cottbus, 2007. Appointments: Research Assistant, 2002-04, Researcher, 2006-09, BTU Cottbus; Research Assistant, Pennsylvania State University, 2005; Assistant Professor, German Jordanian University, Amman, 2009-10; Academic Counsellor, FAU Erlangen-Nuremberg, 2010-. Publications: Numerous articles in professional journals. Honours: Fulbright Fellow, 2004-05; Honorary Research Fellow, Council for British Research, Levant, 2010. Memberships: Franconian Geographical Society; Council for British Research, Levant; German Water History Society; Society of Applied Excavation Methods; German Soil Science Society. Address: FAU Erlangen-Nuremberg, Institute of Geography, Kochstr 4/4, 91054 Erlangen, Germany. E-mail: bernhard.lucke@gmail.com

LUDOVICO Anna Maria, b. 16 July 1944, Vittorito, Italy. University Professor of Epistemology. Education: Degree, 1971; University Scholar, Ministry of Education, University of Chieti, Italy, 1972-74; University of Salerno, Italy, 1975-77; Researcher, Roma 1, 1978-80; Cons Rai, Rome, 1988-89. Appointments: Full Researcher, University of Roma 1 La Sapienza, 1980; Complementary (Aggregato) Professor, 2005; University Professor of Epistemology, Department of Philosophy, Roma-La Sapienza, Italy. Publications: The Dressed Ape, 1979; Brain and Computer, 1997; Heisenberg Effect, 2001; Body and Soul, 2006; To Heisenberg, 2006; Virtual Reality, 1994 and 2000; Natural Philosophy of Juan Huarte, 2007; Historicity of Perception, 2008; A Sign in the Space and History is Born, 2010; From Physics to Philosophy, 2011. Memberships: Honorary Member, A Study in Holmes. E-mail: anna.ludovico@uniroma1.it

LUGTON Charles Michael Arber, b. 5 April 1951, Johannesburg, South Africa. Government Civil Servant. m. Elizabeth Joyce Graham, 2 sons. Education: St John's College, Johannesburg; The Edinburgh Academy; University of Edinburgh. Appointments: Private Secretary to Permanent Under Secretary of State, Scottish Office, 1976-78; Head of Branch, Police Division, 1978-83; Head of Town and Country Planning Policy Branch, 1983-87; Head of Public Health Division, 1988-90; Head of Criminal Justice and Licensing Division, Scottish Home and Health Department, 1990-95; Principal Private Secretary to the Secretary of State for Scotland, 1995-97; Director of Corporate Development, 1998-99; Head of Constitution and Parliamentary Secretariat, Scottish Executive, 1999-2004; Head of Constitution and Legal Services Group, 2004-. Memberships: Governor, Merchiston Castle School, Edinburgh; Board Member, Civil Service Healthcare Society Limited. Address: Scottish Executive, Victoria Quay, Edinburgh EH6 6QQ, Scotland. E-mail: michael.lugton@scotland.gsi.gov.uk

LUK Keith Dip Kei, b. 6 November 1954, Hong Kong. Doctor. m. Katherine O'Hoy, 2 daughters. Education: MBBS (Hong Kong), 1977; FRCS (Edinburgh), 1981; FRCS (Glasgow), 1981; MCh (Orth) (Liverpool), 1984; FRACS (Orth) (Australia), 1985; FHKCOS, 1987; FHKAM (Orthopaedic Surgery), 1993. Appointments: Chair, Professor and Head, Department of Orthopaedics & Traumatology, The University of Hong Kong, 2003-; Chief of Service, Department of Orthopaedics & Traumatology, Queen Mary Hospital, Hong Kong, 2003-. Publications: Numerous articles in professional medical journals. Honours include: Commonwealth Medical Fellowship, 1984-85; A R Hodgson Award, 1986; Orthopaedic Basic Science Award, 1999; Best Paper Award, 21st Annual Congress of the Hong Kong Orthopaedic Association, 2001; Best Basic Science Paper Award, 23rd Annual Congress of the Hong Kong Orthopaedic Association, 2003; Research Output Prize/Faculty Outstanding Research Output Award, 2008. Memberships include: Hong Kong Medical Association; Hong Kong Orthopaedic Association; Hong Kong Academy of Medicine; Fellow, Biomedical Engineering Centre, University of Hong Kong; Fellow, Sau Po Centre on Aging, The University of Hong Kong. Address: Department of Orthopaedics & Traumatology, The University of Hong Kong, 5th Floor, Professorial Block, Queen Mary Hospital, Pokfulam Road, Hong Kong.

LUKE William Ross, b. 8 October 1943, Glasgow, Scotland. Chartered Accountant. m. Deborah Jacqueline Gordon Luke, 3 daughters, 1 deceased. Appointment: Senior Partner, Luke, Gordon & Co, Chartered Accountants, 1983-. Honours: Metropolitan Police Commendation, 1983; Life Vice-President, London Scottish Rugby Football Club, 1995-. Memberships: Fellow, Institute of Chartered Accountants in England and Wales; Member, London Scottish Rugby Football Club; Member, Caledonian Society of London; Qualified Sub-Aqua Advanced Open Water Diver (PADI). Address: 105 Palewell Park, London SW14 8JJ, England.

LUKOSEVICIUS Viktoras, b. 9 August 1939, Kaunas, Lithuania. University Teacher. m. Emilija Lukoseviciene, 2 sons. Education: Diploma Engineer of Geodesy, Kaunas Polytechnical Institute, Lithuania, 1962; PhD, Engineering, Institute of Surveying, Aerial Photography and Cartography, Moscow, 1966; Associate Professor, Kaunas Polytechnical Institute, 1970. Appointments: Head of Basic Science Department, 1967-70, Head of Civil Engineering Department, 1970-81, KPI; Vice Dean and Associate Professor, Panevezys Faculty, Kaunas University of Technology, 1981-87, Head of Civil Engineering Department, Associate Professor and Faculty Council Chair of Panevezys Campus, Kaunas University of Technology, 1988-2001; Head of Civil Engineering Department, Associate Professor of Panevezys Institute, KTU, 2002-04; Associate Professor of Panevezys Institute, KTU and Civil Engineering Department, Siauliai University, Lithuania, 2004-09; Associate Professor, Civil Engineering Department, Siauliai University, Lithuania, 2004-. Publications include: Books; Over 70 scientific articles; Participant in conferences in USA, Brazil, Sweden, Norway, Russia. Honours: Certificate, Governor of State of Ohio, USA for outstanding contribution of the continued success of the Columbus National Program, 1995; Fellowship Winner, NATO and Italy National Science Competition, 1996. Memberships: Senate Member, Kaunas University of Technology, 1992-2001; Council Member, KTU, Panevezys Institute, Faculty of Technology; International Association for Continuing Engineering Education; Association for the Advancement of Baltic Studies; Council Member, Lithuanian Liberal Society, 1992-2004; Candidate, Lithuanian Republic Parliament, 1992,1996; Board Member, Panevezys Department, Lithuanian Scientists Union; President, Panevezys Lithuanian and Swedes Society. Address: Statybininku 56-66, Lt 37348 Panevezys, Lithuania. E-mail: viktoras.lukosevicius@ktu.lt

LUMLEY Joanna, b. 1 May 1946, Kashmir, India. Actress. m. (1) Jeremy Lloyd, divorced, (2) Stephen Barlow, 1 son. Career: TV includes: Release; Comedy Playhouse; Satanic Rites of Dracula, 1973; Coronation Street; General Hospital, 1974-75; The New Avengers, 1976-77; Steptoe & Son; Are You Being Served?; Sapphire & Steel, 1978; Absolutely Fabulous, 1992-94, 1996, 2001; Class Act, 1994; Joanna Lumley in the Kingdom of the Thunder Dragon, 1997; Coming Home, 1998; A Rather English Marriage, 1998; Nancherrow; Dr Willoughby MD; Mirrorball, 1999; Giraffes on the Move, 2001; Up In Town, 2002; Absolutely Fabulous Special, 2002; Marple, 2004; Sensitive Skin, 2005, 2nd series, 2007; Jam and Jerusalem, 2006; The Friday Night Project, 2007; Films include: Some Girls Do; Tam Lin; The Breaking of Bumbo; Games That Lovers Play; Don't Just Lie There, Say Something; On Her Majesty's Secret Service; Trail of the Pink Panther; Curse of the Pink Panther; That Was Tory; Mistral's Daughter; A Ghost in Monte Carlo; Shirley Valentine; Forces Sweetheart; Innocent Lies; James and the Giant Peach; Cold Comfort Farm; Prince Valiant; Parting Shots; Mad Cows; Maybe Baby; The Cat's Meow; Ella Enchanted; Eurotrip, 2004; The Magic Roundabout (voice), 2005; The Corpse Bride (voice), 2005; Dolls, 2006; The Audition, 2006; Theatre includes: Blithe Spirit, 1986; Vanilla, 1990; The Letter, 1995; all in London. Publications: Stare Back and Smile, memoirs, 1989; Girl Friday, 1994; Joanna Lumley in the Kingdom of the Thunder Dragon, 1997; No Room for Secrets (autobiography), 2004. Honours: OBE; Hon DLitt, Kent, 1994; D University, Oxford Brookes, 2000; BAFTA Award, 1992, 1994; Special BAFTA, 2000. Address: c/o Caroline Renton, 23 Crescent Lane, London SW4, England.

LUMSDEN David (James) (Sir), b. 19 March 1928, Newcastle upon Tyne, England. Musician. m. Sheila Gladys Daniels, 28 July 1951, 2 sons, 2 daughters. Education: Selwyn College, Cambridge; MA, 1955; DPhil, 1957. Career: Fellow, Organist at New College Oxford; Rector, chori, Southwell Minster; Founder and Conductor of Nottingham Bach Society; Director of Music, Keele University; Visiting Professor at Yale University; Principal: Royal Scottish Academy of Music and Drama and Royal Academy of Music, London; Hugh Porter Lecturer at Union Theological Seminary, New York, 1967; Director, European Union Baroque Orchestra, 1985-. Publications: An Anthology of English Lute Music, 1954; Thomas Robinson's Schoole Musike 1603, 1971. Contributions to: The Listener; The Score; Music and Letters; Galpin Society Journal; La Luth et sa Musique; La musique de la Renaissance. Honours: Knight, 1985; Honorary Fellow, Selwyn College, Cambridge, 1986; Honorary DLitt, Reading, 1990; Honorary Fellow of Kings College, London, 1991; Honorary Fellow, New College, Oxford, 1996. Memberships: Incorporated Society of Musicians, President, 1984-85; Royal College of Organists, President, 1986-88; Incorporated Association of Organists, President, 1966-68; Honorary Editor, Church Music Society, 1970-73; Chairman, National Youth Orchestra of Great Britain, 1985-94; Chairman, Early Music Society, 1985-89; Board, Scottish Opera, 1977-83; Board, ENO, 1983-88. Address: Melton House, Soham, Cambridgeshire CB7 5DB, England.

LUNAN (Charles) Burnett, b. 28 September 1941, London, England. Medical Practitioner. m. Helen Russell Ferrie, 2 sons, 1 daughter. Education: MB ChB, 1965, MD, 1977, University of Glasgow. Appointments: Research Fellow, MRC Unit, Strathclyde University, UK, 1971-72; Lecturer, University of Aberdeen, UK, 1973-75; Senior Lecturer, University of Nairobi, Kenya, 1975-77; Consultant Obstetrician, Gynaecologist, North Glasgow University NHS Trust, 1977-; Consultant to WHO, Bangladesh, 1984-85; Short term Consultant to WHO, ODA, Bangladesh, 1988-94. Publications: Various chapters and articles on female sterilisation, infection in pregnancy, diabetes in pregnancy, Caesarean section, health care in the developing world. Honours: MRCOG, 1970, FRCOG, 1983, Royal College of Obstetricians and Gynaecologists, London; FRCS, 1985, Royal College of Physicians and Surgeons of Glasgow. Memberships: Secretary, 1978-82, Vice President, 1998-2002, President, 2002-, Glasgow Obstetrical and Gynaecological Society; Treasurer, 1982-90, Vice President, 1990-91, President, 1991-92, Royal Medico-Chirurgical Society of Glasgow. Address: Princess Royal Maternity, 16 Alexandra Parade, Glasgow G31 2ER, Scotland.

LUNDGREN Dolph, b. 3 November 1959, Stockholm, Sweden. Actor. Education: Washington State University; Massachusetts Institute of Technology; Royal Institute of Technology, Sweden. Career: Doorman, Limelight disco, New York; Films include: A View to a Kill; Rocky IV; Masters of the Universe; Red Scorpion; The Punisher; I Come in Peace; The Eleventh Station; Dark Angel; Showdown in Little Tokyo; Universal Soldier; The Joshua Tree; Meltdown; Army of One; Johnny Mnemonic; The Shooter; The Algonquin Goodbye; The Peacekeeper, 1997; The Minion; Sweepers, 1999; Storm Catcher, 1999; Bridge of Dragons, 1999; The Last Patrol, 2000; The Last Warrior, 2000; Agent Red, 2001; Hidden Agenda, 2001; Detention, 2003; Direct Action, 2004; Fat Slags, 2004; Retrograde, 2004; The Defender, 2004; The Mechanik, 2005; Diamond Dogs, 2007; Missionary Man, 2007; Direct Contact, 2009; Command Performance, 2009; Universal Soldier: Regeneration, 2009; Icarus, 2010.

LUNELLI Aldo, b. 30 May 1940, Udine, Italy. University Professor. m. Roberta Nordera, 1 daughter. Education: Degree, Classics, Faculty of Letters and Philosophy, University of Padova, 1964. Appointments: Lecturer, Languages and Literature, 1964, Chair, 1976, Chair, Philology, 1981-, University of Padova; Teacher, 1970, Professor, 1976, University of Ferrara. Publications: Some books and numerous articles in professional journals. Address: Università, Dip di Scienze del Mondo Antico, Piazza Capitaniato 7, I-35139 Padova, Italy. E-mail: aldo.lunelli@unipd.it

LUO Zhi-Shan, b. 20 August 1936, Da-pu, Guangdong, China. Teacher; Researcher of Mechanics. m. Wang Xiu-Yin, 2 sons. Education: Graduate, Tianjin University, China, 1958. Appointments: Assistant, 1958-79, Lecturer, 1979-85, Associate Professor, 1986-93, Director, Laboratory of Mechanics, 1984-85; Director, Teaching and Research Section, 1985-86, Professor of Mechanics, 1993-, Tianjin University; Visiting Professor, Mechanical Engineering, University of Hong Kong, 1992; Technical Consultant, Shanton Jingyi Machinery Co, Shanton, China, 1992-94, Hong Kong Press Publications, 1996-97; Chief Engineer, Director of Research, Tianjin Xingu Intelligent Optical Measuring Technique Company, 2000-02; Civil Engineering Inspect and Determine Institute Board of Tianjin University, 2002-; Member, ABI Research Board of Advisors, 2004-; Chief Expert, Enterprise Development Research Center Expert Committee, Chine Management Science Institute, 2006-. Publications: The Principle and Application of Sticking Film Moire Interferometry; Ultra-high Sensitivity Moiré Interferometry for Subdynamic Tests in Normal Light Environment; Research of Instrumentation and Intellectualization for Moiré Interferometry; Ultra-High Sensitivity Moiré Interferometry by the Aid of Electronic-liquid Phase Shifter and Computer; Moiré Interferometer of Intelligent Mode and Its Application; New Computer Adjusted-and-Processing Moiré Interferometer's Applied Research to Mechanical Property Measure of Concrete; Application of Moiré Interferometry in study for Destructive Mechanism of Concrete; The Advance Instrumentation and its Prospects of Engineering Application for Moiré Interferometry; Laser interferometer of computer controlled and processed, 2006; Experimental Study on Tubular Joints in Spatial Grids Structure by Microcomputer Controlling Instrument of Moiré Intervention, 2010; Application Development of Moiré Interferometry in Civil Engineering, 2010. Honours: Medal of Gold, 2nd Invention Exhibition of China, 1986; Advanced Award of Science and Technology, China Education, 1986, 1997; Medal of Gilding, 15th International Exhibition of Invention and New Technique, Geneva, 1987; National Award of Invention, China, 1987; Award of Invention, Tianjin, China, 1998; Gold Medal, WCC for Promotion of Patent, 2005; Award of Special Grade, 2006; Gold Medal of the Divine Land Personages, 2006; The Golden Title of Nobility Medal of 100 Excellent Personage, 2007; Honor Figure of Harmonius China, Gold Award, 2008; Highest Award of Gold, 2008; Special Gold Award of Advance Bravery Award, 60th Anniversary of State, 2009; Gold Award, All Trade Person of Outstanding Ability of Republic, 2009; Excellent Achievements Gold Award, 60th Anniversary of State, 2009; Literary Star of China's our time, 2009; Chinese medal for republic do protruding contribution, 2009; Republic's build great contributon, Five Star Gold Medal, 2009; Special Award, Republic's 60 Years of Great Theory Achievement, 2009; Great Learning Brings Forth New Ideas Award, 2010; Expert Theory Article in China's Theory of the State Gold Award, 2010. Listed in international biographical dictionaries. Memberships: China Mechanics Society; China Invention Society; Society for Experimental Mechanics Inc. Address: Department of Mechanics, Tianjin University, Tianjin 300072, China. E-mail: lzstju@sina com.cn

LUPU Radu, b. 30 November 1945, Galati, Romania (British citizen). Concert Pianist. Education: Piano lessons at age 6 with Lia Busuioceanu; Subsequent teachers: Florica Muzicescu and Cella Delavrancea; High School, Brasov;

Scholarship, Moscow Conservatoire, Russia, 1961-69; Studied with Heinrich Neuhaus and Stanislav Neuhaus. Appointments: Debut at age 12; Plays regularly with leading orchestras and conductors in all major capitals and centres throughout the world; London debut, 1969; Berlin debut, 1971; American debut, in New York with Cleveland Orchestra and Barenboim, and in Chicago with Chicago Symphony and Giulini, 1972; World Premiere of Andre Tchaikowsky Piano Concerto, London, 1975. Publications: Recording include: Beethoven Piano Concertos; Brahms 1; Schumann; Grieg; Mozart K467; Mozart Double with Murray Perahia; Solo repertoire by Brahms, Beethoven, Schubert and Schumann; Leider with Barbara Hendricks; Piano duets with Daniel Barenboim and Murray Perahia; Chamber Music with Kyung Wha Chung, and Szymon Goldberg. Honours: 1st Prize, Van Cliburn Competition, 1966; Enescu Competition, 1967; Leeds Competition, 1969; Abbiati Prize, 1989, 2006; Edison Award, 1995; Grammy Award, 1995; The Premio Internazionale Arturo Benedetti Michelangeli, 2006. Address: Terry Harrison Artists Management, The Orchard, Market Street, Charlbury, Oxfordshire OX7 3PJ, England. E-mail: artists@harrisonturner.co.uk Website: www.harrisonturner.co.uk

LURIE Alison, b. 3 September 1926, Chicago, Illinois, USA. Professor of English; Author. 3 sons. Education: AB, magna cum laude, Radcliffe College, 1947. Appointments: Lecturer, 1969-73, Adjunct Associate Professor, 1973-76, Associate Professor, 1976-79, Professor of English, 1979-, Cornell University. Publications: Love and Friendship, 1962; The Nowhere City, 1965; Imaginary Friends, 1967; Real People, 1969; The War Between the Tates, 1974; V R Lang: Poems and Plays, With a memoir by Alison Lurie, 1975; Only Children, 1979; Clever Gretchen and Other Forgotten Folktales (juvenile), 1980; The Heavenly Zoo (juvenile), 1980; The Language of Clothes (non-fiction), 1981; Fabulous Beasts (juvenile), 1981; Foreign Affairs, 1984; The Truth About Lorin Jones, 1988; Don't Tell the Grownups: Subversive Children's Literature, 1990; Women and Ghosts, 1994; The Last Resort, 1998. Contributions to: Many publications. Honours: Guggenheim Fellowship, 1966-67; Rockefeller Foundation Grant, 1968-69; New York State Cultural Council Foundation Grant, 1972-73; American Academy of Arts and Letters Award, 1984; Pulitzer Prize in Fiction, 1985; Radcliffe College Alumnae Recognition Award, 1987; Prix Femina Etranger, 1989; Parents' Choice Foundation Award, 1996. Literary Agent: Melanie Jackson Inc, 250 W 57th Street, New York 10107. Address: c/o Department of English, Cornell University, Ithaca, NY 14853, USA.

LUSCOMBE Lawrence Edward, b. 10 November 1924, Torquay, England. Anglican Bishop. m. Doris, deceased, 1 daughter. Education: Kings College, London, 1963-64; LLD, 1987, MPhil, 1991, PhD, 1993, University of Dundee. Appointments: Indian Army, 1942-47; Chartered Accountant, Partner, Galbraith, Dunlop and Co, later Watson and Galbraith, 1952-63; Rector, St Barnabas, Paisley, 1966-71; Provost of St Paul's Cathedral, Dundee, 1971-75; Bishop of Brechin, 1975-90; Primus of the Scottish Episcopal Church, 1985-90. Publications: The Scottish Episcopal Church in the Twentieth Century; A Seminary of Learning; Matthew Luscombe, Missionary Bishop; The Representative Man. Honours: Chaplain, Order of St John; Honorary Research Fellow, University of Dundee; Honorary Canon, Trinity Cathedral, Davenport, Iowa, USA. Memberships: Institute of Chartered Accountants of Scotland; Society of Antiquaries of Scotland; Royal Society of Arts. Address: Woodville, Kirkton of Tealing, By Dundee, DD4 0RD, Scotland.

LUSHNIKOR Alexey Alexeevich, b. 30 May 1939, Moscow, Russian Federation. Professor. Education: Yulia S Lyubovtseva, 1 daughter. Education: Engineering Physical Institute, Moscow, 1956-62. Appointments: Junior Researcher, Kurchatov Institute for Atomic Energy, 1962-71; Junior Researcher, 1971-74, Senior Researcher, 1974-76, Head of Laboratory, 1976-2010, Leading Researcher, 2010-, Karpov Institute for Physical Chemistry; Visiting Professor, University of Helsinki, 2003-08. Publications: More than 130 papers in peer reviewed journals. Honours: Fuchs Memorial Award, 2002; C Junge Award, 2007. Memberships: Geselschaft fuer Aerosol Research; Honorary Member, Finnish Association for Aerosol Research. Address: Department of Aerosols, Karpov Institute of Physical Chemistry, 10, Vorontsovo pole, 105064 Moscow, Russia.

LUTSENKO Yuriy Yurievich, b. 13 April 1962, Tomsk, Russia. Principal Engineer. Education: Diploma in Engineering, 1984, Postgraduate course, 1986-89, PhD, Plasma Physics and Chemistry, 1991, Tomsk Polytechnic Institute. Appointments: Engineer, 1984-86, Research Assistant, 1994-2001, Institute of Strength Physics and Materials Science; Research Assistant, 1989-92, Docent, 2003-, Tomsk Polytechnic Institute; Principal Engineer, Chemical Technology, 2001-03. Publications: 15 articles, 1 monograph. Honours: Honorary Doctor of the Yorker International University, 2009; Listed in various international biographical dictionaries. Address: 9 Sakko apt 32, Tomsk 634009, Russia. E-mail: luts@mail.ru

LUTTWAK Edward N(icholae), b. 4 November 1942, Arad, Romania (US citizen, 1981). Political Scientist; Author. m. Dalya Iaari, 14 December 1970, 1 son, 1 daughter. Education: Carmel College, England; BSc, London School of Economics and Political Science, 1964; PhD, Johns Hopkins University, 1975. Appointments: Associate Director, Washington Center of Foreign Policy Research, District of Columbia, 1972-75; Visiting Professor of Political Science, Johns Hopkins University, 1973-78; Senior Fellow, 1976-87, Research Professor in International Security Affairs, 1978-82, Arleigh Burke Chair in Strategy, 1987-, Director, Geo-Economics, 1991-, Senior Fellow, 2004, Center for Strategic and International Studies, Washington, DC; Nimitz Lecturer, University of California, Berkeley, 1987; Tanner Lecturer, Yale University, 1989. Publications: A Dictionary of Modern War, 1971, new edition with Stuart Koehl, 1991; The Grand Strategy of the Roman Empire: From the First Century A.D. to the Third, 1976; The Economic and Military Balance Between East and West 1951-1978 (editor with Herbert Block), 1978; Sea Power in the Mediterranean (with R G Weinland), 1979; Strategy and Politics: Collected Essays, 1980; The Grand Strategy of the Soviet Union, 1983; The Pentagon and the Art of War: The Question of Military Reform, 1985; Strategy and History, 1985; On the Meaning of Victory: Essays on Strategy, 1986; Global Security: A Review of Strategic and Economic Issues (editor with Barry M Blechman), 1987; Strategy: The Logic of War and Peace, 1987; The Endangered American Dream: How to Stop the United States from Becoming a Third World Country and How to Win the Geo-Economic Struggle for Industrial Supremacy, 1993; Turbo-Capitalism: Winners and Losers in the Global Economy, 1999; La renaissance de la puissance aerienne stategique, 1999; Che cos'é davvero la democrazia (with Susanna Creperio Verratti); Il Libro delle Liberta, 2000; Strategy Now (editor), 2000; Strategy: The Logic of War and Peace, 2002. Contributions to: Numerous books and periodicals. Address: c/o Center for Strategic and International Studies, Georgetown University, 1800 K Street North West, Washington, DC 20006, USA.

LUX Jonathan Sidney, b. 30 October 1951, London, England. Solicitor. m. Simone, 1 son, 2 daughters. LLB Honours, Nottingham University, 1973; Diplom d'Etudes Superieures, University of Aix-Marseilles, 1974; Solicitor: England and Wales, 1977, Hong Kong, 1986. Appointments: Trainee Solicitor, 1975-77, Solicitor, 1977-83, Partner, London Office, 1983-2001 and 2004-, Managing Partner, Hamburg, Germany, 2001-2003, Ince & Co LLP (international law firm); Director, London Shipping Law Centre. Publications: Co-author: The Law of Tug, Tow and Pilotage, 1994; The Law and Practice of Marine Insurance and Average, 1996; Alternative Dispute Resolution, 2002; Bunkers, 2004; Corporate Social Responsibility, 2005; Classification Societies, in preparation; Editor: Classification Societies, 1993; Getting the Deal Through Shipping, 2009, 2010, 2011; Maritime Law Handbook, ongoing. Contributor of articles to professional journals. Honours: University Exhibition, 1972; French Government Scholarship, 1973; Freeman of City of London; Fellow, Chartered Institute of Arbitrators; Honorary Consul to Cape Verde in London; Global Shipping and Maritime Lawyer of the Year, 2010. Memberships: Law Society; Fellow, Chartered Institute of Arbitrators; Accredited Mediator (CEDR, The Academy of Experts, ADR Net); London Maritime Arbitrators Association; German Maritime Arbitrators Association; China Maritime Arbitration Commission; Association of Average Adjusters; Steering Committee, London Shipping Law Centre; Former Chair and current Chair of various Committees, International Bar Association; Athenaeum Club; Arbitrator: CIETAC (China); Hong Kong Arbitration Commission (HKIAC); Sports Disputes Resolution Board (SDRP); International Bunker Industry Association (IBIA). Address: c/o Ince & Co LLP, International House, 1 St Katharine's Way, London E1W 1UN, England. E-mail: jonathan.lux@incelaw.com

LUXIMON Ameersing, b. 16 October 1970, Mauritius. General Manager. m. Yan Zhang, 1 daughter. Education: BTech, Electrical and Electronic Engineering, University of Mauritius, 1993; MSc, 1996, PhD, 2006, Industrial Engineering and Engineering Management, Hong Kong University of Science and Technology. Appointments: Engineer, Design 2 Ltd and Emtel Ltd, Mauritius, 1993-94; Research/Teaching Assistant Positions, Hong Kong University of Science and Technology, Hong Kong, 1996-2002; Assistant Professor, American University of Armenia, Armenia, 2002-03; Postdoctoral Research Fellow, Hong Kong Polytechnic University, Hong Kong, 2003-05; General Manager, Excel-last Ltd, Hong Kong, 2005-. Publications: Numerous articles in professional journals. Memberships: Hong Kong Ergonomics Society; Human Factors and Ergonomics Society; Associate Ergonomics Professional; International Society of Biomechanics. Address: 1st Floor, 188B, Clear Water Bay Road, Tai Po Tsai, Sai Kung, NT, Hong Kong. E-mail: ieshyam@yahoo.com

LYALL John Adrian, b. 12 December 1949, Thundersley, Essex, England. Architect. m. Sallie Davies, 1 son, 1 daughter. Education: Architectural Association, School of Architecture, London, 1968-74. Appointments: Partner, Alsop & Lyall, 1979-91; Managing Director, John Lyall Architects, 1991-; Chair and Deputy Chair, 2004-07, RIBA Vice President, RIBA Trust; Council Member, Architectural Association, 2005-09; CABE National Design Review Panel, 2007-; Chair, Peterborough Design Panel, 2009-; External Examiner, University of Greenwich, 2011-; Tutor, Bartlett School of Architecture (UCL). Publications: Books: A Guide to Recent Architecture: London, 1993; A Guide to Recent Architecture: England, 1995; Context: New Buildings in Historic Settings,

DICTIONARY OF INTERNATIONAL BIOGRAPHY 36th EDITION

1998; Architecture 99: The RIBA Awards, 1999; John Lyall: Contexts and Catalysts, 1999; Numerous articles and contributions to professional journals. Honours: RIBA National Awards, 1991, 1999; RIBA White Rose Award, 1991; Leeds Award for Architecture, 1990, 1992; Ironbridge Award, British Archaeological Society, 1990, 1992, 1998; Civic Trust Commendation, 1991; Europa Nostra Award, 1991; British Council of Shopping Centres Award, 1991; Design Week Award, 1991; Aluminium Imagination Award, 1993; RICS Urban Renewal Award, 1995; The Ironbridge Award of Awards, 1998; RIBA Regional Award, 1999; RIBA National Category Award, 1999; Civic Trust Commendation, 2000; Architectural Review/MIPIM Future Projects Award, 2005; Royal Institute of Chartered Surveyors Award, 2010; Royal Institute of Civil Engineers CEEQUAL Award, 2011. Memberships: Architectural Association; Royal Institute of British Architects; Fellow, Royal Society of Arts; Chelsea Arts Club; Committee Member, Stour Valley Arts and Music Society; Academy of Urbanism. Address: Newlands, Gandish Road, East Bergholt, Suffolk CO7 6TP, England. E-mail: john.lyall@johnlyallarchitects.com

LYKLEMA Johannes, b. 23 November 1930, Apeldoorn, The Netherlands. Professor. m. 2 children. Education: Studies in Chemistry and Physics, State University of Utrecht, 1948-55; PhD, Utrecht, 1956; Honorary Doctorate, Universite Catholic, Louvain-la-Neuve, Belgium, 1988, Royal Institute of Technology, Stockholm, Sweden, 1997; Universidad de Granada, Spain, 2007. Appointments: Military Service, 1956-58; Science Co-Worker, University of Utrecht, 1958-61; Visiting Associate Professor, University of South California, Los Angeles, USA, 1961-62; Professor, Physical and Colloid Chemistry, Wageningen University, 1962-; Visiting Professor, University of Bristol, England, 1971, Australian National University, Canberra, 1976, University of Tokyo, Japan, 1988; Visiting Professor, University of Florida, Gainesville, USA, 1997-. Publications: Over 350 articles in professional journals. Honours: Nightingale Award for Medical Electronics, 1963; Gold Medal, Centre for Marine Research, Ruder Boskovic, Zagreb, 1986; Knight in the Order of the Dutch Lion, 1991; Koninklijke Shell Prize, 1995; Thomas Graham Prize, 1995. Memberships: 90 national and local committees; 105 international. Address: Wageningen University, Department of Physical Chemistry and Colloid Science, De Dreijen 6, 6703 HB Wageningen, The Netherlands.

LYNCH David, b. 20 January 1946, Missoula, Montana, USA. Film Director. m. (1) Peggy Reavey, 1967, divorced, 1 daughter, (2) Mary Fisk, 1977, divorced, 1 son, (3) Mary Sweeney, 2006, divorced, 1 child, (4) Emily Stofle, 2009. Education: Hammond High School, Alexandria; Corcoran School of Art, Washington, DC; School of Museum of Fine Arts, Boston; Pennsylvania Academy of Fine Arts, Philadelphia. Appointments: Films include: The Grandmother, 1970; Eraserhead, 1977; The Elephant Man, 1980; Dune, 1984; Blue Velvet, 1986; Wild at Heart, 1990; Storyville, 1991; Twin Peaks; Fire Walk With Me, 1992; Lost Highway, 1997; Crumb, 1999; The Straight Story, 1999; Mullholland Drive, 2001; Darkened Room, 2002; Rabbits, 2002; Dumbland, 2002; Inland Empire, 2006; Boat, 2007; Surveillance, 2008; My Son, My Son, What Have Ye Done, 2009. TV includes: Twin Peaks, 1990; Mulholland Drive, 2000. Honours: Fellow, Centre for Advanced Film Study, American Film Institute, Los Angeles, 1970; Dr hc, Royal College of Art; Golden Palm, Cannes; Stockholm Institute Film Festival Lifetime Achievement Award, 2003; Best Director, Cannes Film Festival, 2001. Address: c/o CAA, 9830 Wilshire Boulevard, Beverly Hills, CA 90212, USA.

LYNCH John, b. 11 January 1927, Boldon, England. Professor Emeritus; Historian. Education: MA, University of Edinburgh, 1952; PhD, University of London, 1955. Appointments: Lecturer in History, University of Liverpool, 1954-61; Lecturer, Reader and Professor of Latin American History, University College, London, 1961-74; Professor of Latin American History and Director of Institute of Latin American Studies, University of London, 1974-87. Publications: Spanish Colonial Administration 1782-1810: The Intendant System in the Viceroyalty of the Río de la Plata, 1958; Spain Under the Habsburgs, 2 volumes, 1964, 1967, 2nd edition, revised, 1981; The Origins of the Latin American Revolutions 1808-1826 (with R A Humphreys), 1965; The Spanish American Revolutions 1808-1826, 1973, 2nd edition, revised, 1986; Argentine Dictator: Juan Manuel de Rosas 1829-1852, 1981; The Cambridge History of Latin America (with others), Vol 3, 1985, Vol 4, 1986; Bourbon Spain 1700-1808, 1989; Caudillos in Spanish America 1800-1850, 1992; Latin American Revolutions 1808-1826: Old and New World Origins, 1994; Massacre in the Pampas, 1872: Britain and Argentina in the Age of Migration, 1998; Latin America between Colony and Nation, 2001; Simón Bolívar, A Life, 2006; San Martín: Argentine Soldier, American Hero, 2009. Honours: Encomienda Isabel La Católica, Spain, 1988; Doctor, Honoris Causa, University of Seville, 1990; Order of Andres Bello, 1st Class, Venezuela, 1995. Membership: Fellow, Royal Historical Society. Address: 8 Templars Crescent, London N3 3QS, England.

LYNDEN-BELL Donald, b. 5 April 1935. Astronomer. m. Ruth Marion Truscott, 1 son, 1 daughter. Education: Marlborough College, Wiltshire, 1948-53; PhD, Theoretical Astrophysics, Clare College, University of Cambridge, 1960. Appointments: Harkness Fellow of the Commonwealth Fund New York, California Institute of Technology & Mt Wilson & Palomar Observatories, 1960-62; Research Fellow, Clare College, 1960-62; Assistant Lecturer in Mathematics, University of Cambridge, 1962-65; Director of Studies in Mathematics, Clare College, 1962-65; Official Fellow of Clare College, 1962-65; Principal Scientific Officer, later Senior Principal Scientific Officer, Royal Greenwich Observatory, Herstmonceux Castle, Sussex, 1965-72; Professor of Astrophysics, University of Cambridge, 1972-2001; Visiting Appointments: Oort Professor, Leiden University; Visiting Professor, University of Sussex, 1969-72; South African Astronomical Observatory, 1973-90; Fairchild Scholar, CALTECH, 1979; Mt Stromlo Observatory, Australia, 1987; Einstein Fellow, Israeli Academy, Jerusalem, 1990; Carnegie Observatories, Pasadena, California, 2002; Queen's University, Belfast, 1996-2003, David Bates Lecturer, 2003. Publications: Numerous papers in scientific journals; Monthly Notices of Royal Astronomical Society. Honours: Murgoci Prize for Physics, Clare College, 1956; Honorary Scholar of Clare College, 1957; Schwarzschild Lecturer and Medallist of the Astronomische Gesellschaft, 1983; Eddington Medal, 1984, Gold Medal, 1993, Royal Astronomical Society; Medal, Science Faculty, Charles University, Prague; Honorary DSc, Sussex, 1987; Brouwer Award in Dynamical Astronomy of the AAS, 1990; Bruce Medal of the Astronomical Society of the Pacific, 1998; J J Carty Award, NAS, 1999; Russell Lecturer, American Astronomical Society, 2000; CBE, 2000. Membership: Fellow, Clare College; Fellow, Royal Society; Fellow, Royal Astronomical Society; Fellow, Cambridge Philosophical Society; Honorary Fellow, Inter-University Centre for Astronomy and Astrophysics, Pune, India; Foreign Associate, US National Academy of Sciences; Honorary Foreign Member, American Academy of Arts and Sciences; Foreign Associate, Royal Society of South Africa;

Honorary Member, American Astronomical Society. Address: 9 Storey's Way, Cambridge CB3 0DP, England. E-mail: dlb@ast.cam.ac.uk

LYNDON SKEGGS Barbara Noel, b. 29 December 1924, London, England. Retired. m. Michael Lyndon Skeggs, 2 sons, 2 daughters. Appointments include: Served 6 months in Aircraft Factory and 2½ years in the WRNS during World War II; Joined Conservative Party, holding various constituency positions over the years, 1945-; Manager of Ford Primary School, 1963-88; Appointed Justice of the Peace, 1966-94; Conservative County Councillor for Crookham, 1968-81; Appointed Tax Commissioner, 1984-94; Appointed Deputy Lieutenant for Northumberland, 1988-; Appointed High Sheriff of Northumberland, 1994-95. Honours: Freeman of the City of London, 1973; Badge of Honour for Distinguished Service, BRCS, 1987; MBE, 1990. Memberships: Berwick Infirmary Management Committee, 1966-74; Area Health Authority, 1974-90; Northumberland Family Practitioner Committee, 1980-90; Northumberland Magistrates Committee, 1980-94; Ford and Etal PCC, 1961-96; Board of Northern Opera, 1971-81. Address: Dalgheal, Evanton, Ross-shire IV16 9XH, Scotland.

LYNN Vera (Margaret Lewis) (Dame), b. 20 March 1917. Singer. m. Harry Lewis, 1941, 1 daughter. Career: Debut performance, 1924; Appeared with Joe Loss, Charlie Kunz, 1935; Ambrose, 1937-40; Applesauce, Palladium, London, 1941; Became known as the Forces Sweetheart, 1939-45; Radio show Sincerely Yours, 1941-47; Tour of Burma, entertaining troops, 1944; 7 Command performances; Appearances, Europe; Australia; Canada; New Zealand; Performed at 50th Anniversary of VE Day Celebrations, London, 1995; Own television shows: ITV, 1955; BBC1, 1956; BBC2, 1970; First British artist to top Hit Parade. Numerous recordings include: Auf Wiederseh'n (over 12 million copies sold). Publication: Vocal Refrain (autobiography), 1975. Honours: Order of St John; LLD; MMus. Address: c/o Anglo-American Enterprises, 806 Keyes House, Dolphin Square, London SW1V 3NB, England.

LYON Martin, b. 10 February 1954, Romford, Essex, England. Librarian; Poet. Education: BA, 1976. Appointments: Principal Library Assistant, University of London. Publications: Sandcastles at Evening (pamphlet), 2010; Rome and Iona (book), 2011; Contributions to: Acumen; Agenda; Orbis; Outposts Poetry Quarterly; Pen International; Spokes. Honour: Lake Aske Memorial Award. Address: 63 Malford Court, The Drive, South Woodford, London E18 2HS, England.

LYON Patricia Anne, b. 31 July 1949, Richmond, Surrey, England. Fellow and Director of Development. m. Richard Lyon, 1972, 2 sons, 2 daughters. Education: Didcot Girls' School; Newnham College, Cambridge, 1967-73; BA (Muriel Edwards Prize), 1970; MA, 1974, PhD, 1974, Girton College, Cambridge. Appointments: Research Fellow, 1973-76, College Lecturer, 1973-78; Girton College; Appeal Director, The Perse Millennium Campaign, 1996-98; Fellow for Development, St Catharine's College, 1999-2001; Fellow and Director of Development, Gonville & Caius College, 2001-; Cambridge University Council and Colleges Joint Committee on Development, 2004-. Publications: The Structures of Di-N-Aroyl Derivatives of Adenosine and 2-Aminopyridine, 1974; Reaction between 2', 3', 5'-Tri-O-acetyladenosine and Aryl Chloroformates, 1978. Memberships: Governor, The Perse School, Cambridge, 1999-2009. Address: Gonville & Caius College, Cambridge, CB2 1TA, England. E-mail: AL265@cam.ac.uk Website: www.cai.cam.ac.uk/alumni

LYONS Roger Alan, b. 14 September 1942, London, England. Consultant. m. Kitty Horvath, 2 sons, 2 daughters. Education: BSc (Econ) Hons, University College London, 1966. Appointments: General Secretary, MSF Union, 1992-2002; Member, Merger and Monopolies Commission, 1996-2002; Member, Design Council, 1998-2004; Member, Central Arbitration Committee, 1998-; Judge, Employment Appeals Tribunal, 1999-; Joint General Secretary, Amicus Union, 2002-04; President, TUC, 2003-04; Adviser to business services companies, 2005-. Publications: Contributions to: Handbook on Industrial Relations; Handbook on Management Development; Free and Fair, 2004. Memberships: Fellow, University College London; Fellow, Royal Society of Arts. Address: 22 Park Crescent, London N3 2NJ, England. E-mail: rogerlyons22@hotmail.com

LYU Jae Jin, b. 18 April 1965, Seoul, Korea. Principal Engineer. Education: BSc, 1988, MSc, 1992, Chemistry, Konkuk University; PhD, Material Science and Engineering, Chonbuk University, 2010. Appointments: Anam Semiconductor, 1992-93; Samsung, 1993-; Visiting Researcher, Kent State, 1997-98; PVA Mode Mass Production, 1998-99, Project Leader, OCB Mode, 2000-02, Project Manager, TN & VA Technology, 2003-06, Project Manager, new LC Modes, 2007-09, Team Manager, LCD TV Technology; Visiting Scholar, Kyushu University, 2010-11; Group Manager, Next Generation Display, Samsung Electronics, 2011-. Publications: Numerous articles in professional journals include: Control of liquid crystal director near signal lines and reduction of load of signal lines by optimized pattern of common electrode in the patterned vertical alignment mode, 2008; Surface-modification on vertical alignment layer using UV-curable reactive mesagens, 2009; More than 60 US patents. Address: 692-1 Bunji, Yangbeol-ri Opo-eup, Gwangju Si, Gyeonggi-Do, Seoul 464-926, Korea.

M

MA Tsao-Tsung, b. 5 January 1963, Miaoli City, Taiwan, ROC. Education: m. Cheng-Ling Lee, 2 daughters. Education: BS, National Taiwan University of Science and Technology, Taiwan, 1989; MSc, University of Missouri, Columbia, USA, 1993; PhD, University of Strathclyde, Glasgow, Scotland, 1999. Appointments: Head, Applied Power Electronic Systems Research Group, NUU, Taiwan; Adviser of Postgraduate Students, Associate Professor, Department of E E, NUU, Taiwan. Publications: Articles and papers in professional scientific journals. Honours: Listed in international biographical directories. Memberships: IEEE member. Address: #1 Lien-Da, Kung-Ching Li, Miaoli City 360, Taiwan, ROC. E-mail: tonyma@nuu.edu.tw

MA Ying-Jeou, b. 13 July,1950, Hong Kong. President of the Republic of China. m. Christine Chow, 2 daughters. Education: LLB, National Taiwan University, 1972; LLM, New York University Law School, 1976; SJD, Harvard Law School, 1981. Appointments: Legal Consultant, First National Bank of Boston, 1980-1981; Research Consultant, University of Maryland School of Law, 1981; Associate Lawyer, Cole and Deits (New York), 1981; Deputy Director-General, First Bureau, Office of the President, 1981-1988; Minister of the Research, Development and Evaluation Commission, 1988-1991; Deputy Minister of Mainland Affairs Council, 1991-1993; Minister of Justice, 1993-1996; Minister without Portfolio,1996-1997; Associate Professor of Law, National Chengchi University, 1998; Mayor, Taipei City, 1998-2006; Chairman, Kuomintang, 2005-2007. Publications: Legal Problems of Boundary Delimitation in the East China Sea; Two Major Legal Issues Relating to the International Status of the ROC; Taipei & East Asian Stability: Implications for Europe; The ROC (Taiwan's) Entry into the WTO: Progress, Problem, etc. Address: Office of the President, No 122, Sect 1, Chongqing S Road, Taipei 10048.

MA Yue, b. 19 October 1963, Beijing, China. Professor of Economics. m. Hong Lin, 1 daughter. Education: BS, Optimal Control Theory, Xiamen (Amoy) University, China, 1985; Certificate of Graduate in Economics, Renmin University, China, 1986; PhD, Econometrics & Economics, Manchester University, England, 1991. Appointments: Senior Research Fellow (tenured), Strathclyde University, Scotland, 1990-95; Reader (tenured), 1995-99, Visiting Professor, 2004, Stirling University, Scotland; Associate Professor, 1999-2004, Professor, 2004-12, Head of Economics Department, 2008-12, Lingnan University, Hong Kong; Chair Professor of Finance, 2013-, City University of Hong Kong; Wang Yanan Visiting Chair Professor, Xiamen University, China, 2006-08. Publications: Textbook in English translated into Chinese and Russian, Natural Resource and Environmental Economics, 2011; More than 50 refereed research papers published in France, Germany, Hong Kong, Italy, Japan, Mainland China, Russia, Singapore, Taiwan, the Netherlands, the UK, and the US. Honours: The Best Paper Award of the Jensen Prize (the First Prize) by the Journal of Financial Economics in the area of corporate finance and organisations in 2011; First Prize of Best Research Papers, Chinese Academy of Social Sciences, Beijing, 2003; Second Prize of Best Papers, 12th An Zijie International Trade Award, China, 2004. Memberships: Hong Kong Economics Association; Chinese Economics Association (UK). Address: Department of Economics and Finance, City University of Hong Kong, Hong Kong. E-mail: yuema24@cityu.edu.hk

MAALOUF Aline Ibrahim, b. 4 February 1974, Hadath, Lebanon. Research Fellow. Education: BSc, Electrical Engineering, 1996, MSc, Electrical Engineering, 1998, Balamand University; M Phil, Control Engineering, Cambridge University, England, 2000; PhD, Control Engineering, University of New South Wales, Australia, 2011. Appointments: Design Engineer, S&AS Ltd, Lebanon, 2004-05; Project Engineer, Dargroub, Lebanon, 2005-08; Research Fellow, University of New South Wales at ADFA, 2010-11. Publications: 7 journal articles; 10 conference papers. Honours: Finalist, Best Student Paper Award, ACC, 2009; Fellow, Cambridge Overseas Trust; Listed in international biographical dictionaries. Memberships: IEEE; Order of Lebanese Engineers. Address: School of SEIT, University of New South Wales at ADFA, North Cott Drive, Canberra, ACT 2600, Australia. E-mail: alinemaalouf@hotmail.com

MAC KEY James Fredrik, b. 20 November 1919, Varberg, Sweden. Professor; Doctor. m. Kerstin Anne-Marie Madsen, 2 daughters. Education: MSc, Agronomy, 1945, DPh, Genetics, 1953, DSc, Genetics, 1954, Royal Agriculture College of Sweden, Uppsala. Appointments: Assistant Teacher, Chemistry, Royal Agriculture College of Sweden, 1942-44; Assistant Plant Breeder, (Uppsala substation) 1944-45, (Svalöf main station) 1945-57, Head Plant Breeder, 1958-62, Swedish Seed Association ; Professor of Plant Breeding, 1962-84, Active Professor Emeritus, 1985-, Royal Agricultural College and Swedish University of Agricultural Sciences, Uppsala. Publications: Over 200 scientific publications pertaining to applied and theoretical genetics with special reference to self-fertilising crops, spontaneous and induced mutations, race-specific disease resistance and yield structure including root patterns of cereals, evolution and revision of taxonomy of cultivated plants, evolution and genetics of polyploidy and origin of agriculture. Honours: Knight of the Royal Order of the Polar Star, Sweden 1967; The Nilsson-Ehle Gold Medal, Swedish Academy of Forest and Agriculture, 1994; Rockefeller Research Fellowship, USA, 1954-55; Foreign Senior Scientist Award, National Science Foundation, USA, 1970-71; Weseman Foreign Scientist Award, Iowa State University, Ames, USA, 1980. Memberships: Swedish Seed Association; Hungarian Academy of Sciences; Yugoslavian Society of Genetics; Mendelian Society; Royal Academy of Forest and Agriculture; Royal Society of Arts and Sciences, Uppsala; Royal Physiographic Society, Lund. Address: Department of Plant Biology and Forest Genetics, Swedish University of Agricultural Sciences, POB 7080, SE-750 07, Uppsala, Sweden.

MacCARTHY Fiona, b. 23 January 1940, London, England. Biographer; Cultural Historian. m. David Mellor, 1966, 1 son, 1 daughter. Education: MA, English Language and Literature, Oxford University, 1961. Appointments: Staff Writer, The Guardian, 1963-69; Women's Editor, Evening Standard, 1969-71; Reviewer, The Times, 1981-91, The Observer, 1991-98. Publications: The Simple Life: C R Ashbee in the Cotswolds, 1981; The Omega Workshops: Decorative Arts of Bloomsbury, 1984; Eric Gill, 1989; William Morris: A Life for our Time, 1994; Stanley Spencer, 1997; Byron Life and Legend, 2002; Last Curtsey: The End of the Debutantes, 2006; The Last Pre-Raphaelite: Edward Burne-Jones and the Victorian Imagination, 2011. Contributions to: Times Literary Supplement; New York Review of Books. Honours: Royal Society of Arts Bicentenary Medal, 1987; Honorary Fellowship, Royal College of Art, 1989; Wolfson History Prize, 1995; Honorary D Litt, University of Sheffield, 1996; Senior Fellowship, Royal College of Art, 1997; Fellow, Royal Society of Literature, 1997; Honorary Doctorate, Sheffield Hallam University, 2001; Honorary Fellowship, Lady

Margaret Hall, Oxford, 2007; OBE. Memberships: PEN Club; Royal Society of Literature. Address: The Round Building, Hathersage, Sheffield S32 1BA, England.

MacCORMACK Geoffrey Dennis, b. 15 April 1937, Canterbury, Kent, England. Retired Professor of Law. 1 daughter. Education: University of Sydney, Australia, 1954-60; University of Oxford, England, 1960-65. Appointment: Professor of Jurisprudence, University of Aberdeen, 1971-96. Publications: Traditional Chinese Law, 1990; The Spirit of Traditional Chinese Law, 1996. Address: School of Law, King's College, University of Aberdeen, Old Aberdeen AB24 3UB, Scotland. E-mail: g.maccormack@abdn.ac.uk

MacCRACKEN Michael, b. 20 May 1942, USA. Atmospheric Scientist. m. Sandra Svets, 2 sons. Education: BS, Engineering, Princeton University, 1964; PhD, University of California, Davis, 1968. Appointments: Physicist, Atmospheric Scientist, University of California, Lawrence Livermore National Laboratory, 1968-2002; Executive Director, National Assessment Co-ordination Office, 1997-2001; Senior Scientist, Office US Global Change Research Program, 2001-2002; Chief Scientist for Climate Change Programs, Climate Institute, Washington, DC, 2003-. Publications: Co-editor 5 books; Several dozen articles in professional journals. Memberships: Fellow, American Association for the Advancement of Science; American Geophysical Union; American Meteorological Society; International Association of Meteorology and Atmospheric Sciences, President 2003-2007; The Oceanography Society. Address: 6308 Berkshire Drive, Bethesda, MD 20814, USA.

MacDONALD Angus D, b. 9 October 1950, Edinburgh, Scotland. Headmaster. m. Isabelle M Ross, 2 daughters. Education: MA (Hons), Cambridge University, 1969-71; Dip Ed, Edinburgh University, 1971-72. Appointments: Assistant Teacher, Alloa Academy, 1972-73; Assistant Teacher, King's School, Paramatta, 1978-79; Assistant Teacher, Edinburgh Academy, 1973-82; Head of Geography, 1982, Deputy Principal, 1982-86, George Watson's College; Headmaster, Lomond School, 1986-. Honour: Exhibition to Cambridge University. Membership: Chairman, Clan Donald Lands Trust. Address: 8 Millig Street, Helensburgh, Argyll & Bute, Scotland.

MacDONALD Betty Ann Kipniss, b. Brooklyn, New York, USA. 4 children. Artist; Printmaker; Watercolourist. Education: Art School, Museum of Modern Art, Manhattan; Art Students League; Sumie Drawing, Chinese Institute night school; MA, Teachers College, Columbia University. Appointments: Teacher of Art, elementary school and junior high school, 5 years; Editorial Assistant of children's books; Teacher of Art, Montshire Museum; Board Member, New Hampshire Art Association; Teacher, Lebanon College; Printmaking; Teacher, Smithsonian Institution, 10 years; Artist, Central Intelligence Agency. Publications: Poetry published in the Potomac Quarterly; Commissions for music book covers; Washington Women's Investment Club funded murals for a shelter for the homeless; Press releases for Journal of the Print World. Honours: Purchase Award Prize, Delta National Small Prints Exhibition; Museum Award for Graphics, Washington County Museum of Fine Arts; Best in Show in "Small Prints, Big Impressions", Maryland Federation of Arts; 1st Place Award, 72nd Annual International Exhibition of Fine Art in Miniature; Artwork held in a dozen galleries across the USA and in many museums and permanent collections around the world. Address: PO Box 1202, McLean, VA 22101, USA.

MacDONALD Douglas Andrew, b. 2 June 1967, Barrie, Ontario, Canada. Psychologist; Associate Professor of Psychology. 2 daughters. Education: BA (Hons), Psychology, 1990, MA, Psychology, 1992, PhD, Clinical Psychology, 1998, University of Windsor, Windsor, Ontario. Appointments: Academic: Teaching/Graduate Assistant, 1989-92, Sessional Instructor, Department of Psychology, 1993-94, University of Windsor, Windsor, Ontario; Part-time Faculty, Saybrook Graduate School and Research Center, San Francisco, California, USA, 2001-; Associate Professor of Psychology, University of Detroit Mercy, Detroit, Michigan, USA, 2000-; Clinical/Applied: Practicum Student, Guelph Assessment and Treatment Unit, Guelph Correctional Centre, Guelph, Ontario, 1991; Intern (half-time), University of Windsor Psychological Services Centre, 1992-93, Intern (half-time), Windsor Regional Hospital, Western Campus, 1994-95; Behavioural Consultant (half-time), Essex County Board of Education, Essex, Ontario, 1995-97; Psychologist, Windsor Board of Education, 1997-98; Psychologist, Greater Essex County District School Board, 1998-2004. Publications: Book: Approaches to transpersonal measurement and assessment (co-editor), 2002; Peer-reviewed journal articles as co-author include most recently: Identity and spirituality – Conventional and Transpersonal Perspectives, 2009; Measures of spiritual and transpersonal constructs for use in yoga research, 2009; Examination of the Psychometric Properties of the Spiritual Fitness Assessment, 2010; Numerous papers presented at conferences and symposia. Honours: University of Windsor Tuition Scholarships, 1992-93, 1993-94; Ontario Graduate Scholarship, 1992-93; Research Development Grant, Floraglades Foundation; Recipient, 2006 Carmi Harari Early Career Contributions Award, American Psychological Association; Invited Reviewer for several psychological journals; Member of several editorial boards; Listed in Who's Who publications and biographical dictionaries. Memberships: American Psychological Association, 1998-, Division 32, Humanistic Psychology, 2005-; Canadian Psychological Association, 2000-. Address: University of Detroit Mercy, Department of Psychology, 4001 W McNichols Road, Detroit, MI 48221, USA. E-mail: macdonda@udmercy.edu

MacDONALD Simon Gavin George, b. 5 September 1923, Beauly, Inverness-shire, Scotland. University Professor of Physics, retired. m. Eva Leonie Austerlitz, 1 son, 1 daughter. Education: First Class Honours, Mathematics and Natural Philosophy, Edinburgh University, 1941-43, 1946-48; PhD, St Andrews University, 1953. Appointments: Junior Scientific Officer, Royal Aircraft Establishment, Farnborough, 1943-46; Lecturer in Physics, 1948-57, Senior Lecturer in Physics, 1962-67, University of St Andrews; Senior Lecturer in Physics, University College of the West Indies, Jamaica, 1957-62; Senior Lecturer in Physics, 1967-72, Dean, Faculty of Science, 1970-73, Professor of Physics, 1973-88, Vice-principal, 1974-79, University of Dundee. Publications: 3 books; Numerous articles in scientific journals on x-ray crystallography. Honours: Fellow, Institute of Physics, 1958; Fellow, Royal Society of Edinburgh, 1972; Chairman, Dundee Repertory Theatre; Chairman, Federation of Scottish Theatres. Address: 7a Windmill Road, St Andrews, Fife KY16 9JJ, Scotland.

MacDOWELL Andie, b. 21 April 1958, South Carolina, USA. Film Actress. m. (1) Paul Qualley, divorced, 1 son, 2 daughters, (2) Rhett DeCamp Hartzog, 2001-2004 (divorced). Appointments: TV appearances include: Women and Men 2, In Love There are No Rules, 1991; Sahara's Secret; Films include: Greystoke, 1984; St Elmo's Fire, 1985; Sex, Lies and Videotape, 1989; Green Card, 1990; Hudson Hawk,

1991; The Object of Beauty, 1991; The Player, 1992; Ruby, 1992; Groundhog Day, 1993; Short Cuts, 1993; Bad Girls, 1994; Four Weddings and a Funeral, 1994; Unstrung Heros, 1995; My Life and Me, 1996; Multiplicity, 1996; The End of Violence, 1997; Town and Country, 1998; Shadrack, 1998; The Scalper, 1998; Just the Ticket, 1998; Muppets From Space, 1999; The Music, 2000; Harrison's Flowers, 2000; Town and Country, 2001; Crush, 2001; Ginostra, 2002; The Last Sign, 2004; Beauty Shop, 2005; Tara Road, 2005; Barnyard (voice), 2006; Intervention, 2007; The Prince of Motor City, 2008; Inconceivable, 2008; The Six Wives of Henry Lefey, 2009; As Good As Dead, 2010. Address: c/o ICM 8942 Wilshire Boulevard, Beverly Hills, CA 90211, USA.

MacFARLANE Sheila Margaret, b. 2 May 1943, Aberdeen, Scotland. Artist. 1 daughter. Education: DA, Edinburgh College of Art, 1960-64, Dip Ed, Morray House College of Education, 1964-65; Atelier 17, Paris, 1967-68. Appointments: Lecturer in Charge of Printmaking, Duncan of Jordanstone College, Dundee, 1970-76; Founder, Director, Kirktower House Print Studio, Montrose, 1976-88; Art-Drama Specialist to children with special needs in Angus, Occasional Visiting Lecturer to Ruskin School, Oxford University, 1984-2004; Selector, Researcher for SAC Exhibition "Relief Printing", 1984-85. Publications: The Finella Prints, Printmaking Today, 1997; The Finella Prints, The Leopard Magazine, 2002. Membership: Dundee Contemporary Arts Print Studio. Address: 1 Tangleha, St Cyrus, Montrose, Angus, DD10 0DQ, Scotland.

MacGREGOR John Roddick Russell (Lord MacGregor of Pulham Market), b. 14 February 1937, Glasgow, Scotland. Politician; Businessman. m. Jean Mary Elizabeth Dungey, 1 son, 2 daughters. Education: MA, First Class Honours, St Andrew's University; LLB, King's College, London. Appointments: University Administrator, 1961-62; Editorial Staff, New Society, 1962-63; Hill Samuel & Co, 1968-79; Director, Hill Samuel and Co, 1973-79; Deputy Chairman, Hill Samuel Bank Ltd, 1994-96; Non-Executive Director: Slough Estates plc, 1995-, Associated British Foods plc, 1994, Unigate plc (now Uniq), 1996-, Friends Provident plc, 1998-; European Supervisory Board, DAFS Netherlands NV; Political Career: Special Assistant to Prime Minister, 1963-64; Head, Leader of Opposition's Office, 1965-68; Member of Parliament for South Norfolk, 1974-2001; Lord Commissioner of the Treasury, 1979-81; Parliamentary Under Secretary of State for Industry with particular responsibility for small businesses, 1981-83; Minister of State for Agriculture, Fisheries and Food, 1983-85; Chief Secretary to the Treasury, 1985-87; Minister for Agriculture, Fisheries and Food, 1987-89; Secretary of State for Education, 1989-90; Lord President of the Council and Leader of the Commons, 1990-92; Secretary of State for Transport, 1992-94; Member of the House of Lords, 1991-. Honours: OBE, 1971; PC, 1985; Honorary Fellow, King's College, London, 1990; Honorary LLD, University of Westminster, 1995. Address: House of Lords, London SW1A 0PW, England.

MACHIDA Curtis A, b. 1 April 1954, San Francisco, USA. Molecular Neurobiologist. Education: AB, University of California, Berkeley, 1976; PhD, Oregon Health Sciences University, 1982. Appointments: Postdoctoral Fellow, Biochemistry, Oregon Health Sciences University, 1982-85; Postdoctoral Fellow, Vollum Institute, 1985-88; Assistant Scientist, 1988-95, Assistant Professor, 1989-95; Associate Scientist, Associate Professor, 1995-2002 Neuroscience, Oregon National Primate Research Center, Oregon Health Sciences University; Research Associate Professor, Integrative Biosciences, Oregon Health Sciences University, 2002-05; Research Professor, Integrative Biosciences, 2005-07; Professor with Tenure, Integrative Biosciences, 2008-; Adjunct Faculty, Biochemistry and Biophysics, Oregon State University, 1997-2001; Editorial Board, Journal of Endodontics, Adjunct Faculty, Pediatric Dentistry, Oregon Health and Science University, 2010-. Publications: Over 100 articles and abstracts in professional journals; Patent holder; Editor, Adrenergic Receptor Protocols; Editor, Viral Vectors for Gene Therapy: Methods and Protocols; Member, Editorial Boards, Molecular Biotechnology, Frontiers in Bioscience and World Medicine/International Journal of Biomedical Sciences. Honours include: NIH First Award; AHA Established Investigator Award; NIH Grant Recipient; Finalist, OHSU Faculty Senate Award for Research; Finalist, OHSU Faculty Senate Award for Teaching. Memberships: AAAS; ASM; ASBMB; ASGT; AHA Scientific Council. Address: Department of Integrative Biosciences, School of Dentistry, Oregon Health Sciences University, 611 SW Campus Drive, Portland, OR 97239, USA.

MACHOCKI Andrzej Edward, b. 12 August 1947, Dabrowa Gornicza, Poland. Chemist; Researcher; Lecturer. Divorced, 1 daughter. Education: MS, 1971, PhD, 1979, DSc Habilitation, 1997, University of Marie Curie-Sklodowska, Lublin, Poland. Appointments: Assistant, 1972-77, Assistant Lecturer, 1977-79, Tutor, 1979-97, Assistant Professor, 1997-2001, Associate Professor, 2001-, University of Marie Curie-Sklodowska. Publications: Numerous articles in professional journals. Honours: President, University of Marie Curie-Sklodowska. Memberships: International Union of Pure and Applied Chemistry; Polish Chemical Society; Polish Catalysis Club; Yacht Club, University of Marie Curie-Sklodowska. Address: University of Marie Curie-Sklodowska, Faculty of Chemistry, 3 M Curie-Sklodowska Square, 20-031 Lublin, Poland. E-mail: machocki@umes.lublin.pl

MĂCIUCĂ Gina, b. 10 May 1961, Iasi, Romania. Professor. Divorced, 1 daughter. Education: BA, 1984, PhD, Comparative Philology, 2001, Al I Cuza University, Iasi; DAAD grant for PhD research, Ludwig-Maximillians University, Munich, 1994-95. Appointments: Senior Lecturer, 1993-2002, Associate Professor, 2002-11, Professor, 2011-, Stefan cel Mare University, Suceava; Director of Project, Word-Formation Characteristics of Romanian, 2005-07; Co-director, Research Centre, Inter Litteras, 2005-; Co-ordinator of ILET International Conference, 2007, 2012; Director of Project, Lexico-Morphological Idiosyncrasies of Romanian, 2009-11; Editor-in-Chief, Concordia Discors vs Discordia Concors, 2009-; Acquisitions Editor, Versita Editorial Board, 2011; Head, Department for Foreign Language and Literature Studies, 2011-. Publications: Author, 8 books on linguistics; 80 contributions to national and international journals; Co-author, 4 books. Honours: 1st Prize for Linguistics, Bukowina's International Foundation for Culture and Science, 2011; Listed in biographical dictionaries. Memberships: SKASE Journal of Theoretical Linguistics; Speech and Context; Language and Literature European Landmarks of Identity; ESSE; SLE; SRAA; DAAD; GGR.

MACKAY Donald Neil, b. 14 September 1936, Lima, Peru (d. 28 April 2012). Clinical Psychologist. m. Mary, 1 son, 1 daughter. Education: Royal High School, Edinburgh; MA, Edinburgh University; PhD, Queen's University of Belfast. Appointments: Consultant Clinical Psychologist, Muckamore Abby Hospital, Co Antrim. Publications: Numerous articles in professional journals. Honours: Honorary Lecturer, The

Queen's University of Belfast, 1972. Memberships: Associate Fellow, British Psychological Society. Address: 23 Bridge Park, Templepatrick, Co Antrim, BT39 0AE, Northern Ireland.

MACKAY William Morton, b. 26 March 1934, Dundee, Scotland. Educator. m. Catherine, 30 July 1959, 2 sons, 1 daughter. Education: MA (honours), St Andrews University; Dip Ed, St Andrews University, 1957; Diploma of Theological Studies, Free Church of Scotland College, Edinburgh, 1959. Appointments: Teacher, Buckhaven High School, 1959-61; Ordained, 1961; Teacher, Supervisor of Secondary Studies and Headmaster (1966-78), St Andrew's College, Lima, Peru, 1961-78; Teacher, Lothian Region, 1978-85; Principal, Presbyterian Ladies' College, Melbourne, Australia, 1986-97; Lecturer, Church History, Free Church of Scotland College, Edinburgh, 1998-2005; Clerk of Public Questions, Religion and Morals Committee, Free Church of Scotland, 1999-2002; Chairman, International Missions Board, 2002-07; Co-Vice-Chairman and Treasurer, Edinburgh Centre; Member of Council, 2003-06, 2008-, Royal Scottish Geographical Society; Member of Council, Clan Mackay Society. Publications: Thomas Chalmers: A Short Appreciation, 1980; Articles: Formative Aims in the Teaching of History, in "The Teaching of History", Catholic University of Peru, 1979; Church and School and the Care of Youth, in "Crown Him Lord of All", 1993; Andrew Melville and the Scottish Universities, and The Getting of Wisdom, in "A Witness for Christ", 1996. Honours: Diploma of Honour for services to Education in Peru, Peruvian Government, 1981; Moderator of Synod, Presbyterian Church of East Australia, 1993; Moderator of General Assembly, Free Church of Scotland, 2001. Memberships: Australian College of Educators; Association of Heads of Independent Schools of Australia; Associate Fellow, Australian Principals Centre; Fellow, Institute of Contemporary Scotland; Professional Associate, Royal Scottish Geographical Society; Fellow, Royal Geographical Society. Address: 53 Lauderdale Street, Edinburgh EH9 1DE, Scotland.

MacKENZIE Kenneth John, b. 1 May 1943, Glasgow, Scotland. Civil Servant. m. Irene Mary Hogarth, 1 son, 1 daughter. Education: Open Exhibitioner, BA, Modern History, 1964, MA, 1970, Pembroke College, University of Oxford; Dorothy Chandos Smyllie Scholarship in Department of History, Stanford University, California, 1964-65; Fulbright Travel Scholarship, 1964; Graduate AM in History, Stanford, 1965. Appointments: Principal Private Secretary to Secretaries of State for Scotland, 1977-79; 2 Assistant Secretary Posts in Scottish Office, 1979-85; 3 Under Secretary Posts in Scottish Office including Principal Finance Officer, 1985-92; Member, Biotechnology and Biological Sciences Research Council, 1992-95; Head of Scottish Office Agriculture and Fisheries Department, 1992-95; Head of Economic and Domestic Secretariat, 1995-97, Head of Constitution Secretariat, 1997-98, Cabinet Office; Head of Scottish Executive Development Department, 1998-2001; Quinquennial Reviewer, Lord Chancellor's Department, 2001-2002; Chairman, Historic Scotland Foundation, 2001-; Member, British Waterways Scotland Group, 2002-07; Honorary Professor, Department of Politics, University of Aberdeen, 2001-04; Lead Consultant with Public Administration International advising the Government of Kosovo on structure and organisation of a Prime Minister's Office, 2004-08; Board Member, Christian Aid, 2005-08; Chairman, Edinburgh City Centre Churches Together, 2010-. Publications: Articles: Planner Shortage in Strathclyde, 1976; Tears Before Bedtime: A Look Back at the Constitutional Reform Programme since 1999 in Public Policy and Administration, 2005 and in Reinventing Britain, 2007. Honour: Companion of the Bath (CB), 1996. Address: 23C/1 Ravelston Park, Edinburgh, EH4 3DX, Scotland. E-mail: kenneth@voltaire.plus.com

MACKESY Piers Gerald, b. 15 September 1924, Cults, Aberdeenshire, Scotland. Historian; Writer. Education: BA, Christ Church, Oxford, 1950; DPhil, Oriel College, Oxford, 1953; DLitt, Oxford, 1978. Appointments: War Service: Lieutenant, The Royal Scots Greys, N.W. Europe, 1943-7; Harkness Fellow, Harvard University, 1953-54; Fellow, 1954-87, Emeritus, 1988-, Pembroke College, Oxford; Visiting Fellow, Institute for Advanced Study, Princeton, New Jersey, 1961-62; Visiting Professor, California Institute of Technology, 1966. Publications: The War in the Mediterranean 1803-1810, 1957; The War for America 1775-1783, 1964, 1993; Statesmen at War: The Strategy of Overthrow 1798-1799, 1974; The Coward of Minden: The Affair of Lord George Sackville, 1979; War without Victory: The Downfall of Pitt 1799-1802, 1984; British Victory in Egypt, 1801: The End of Napoleon's Conquest (Templer Medal), 1995, 2010; FBA, 1988. Memberships: National Army Museum, council member, 1983-92; Society for Army Historical Research, council member, 1985-94, currently Vice President. Address: Westerton Farmhouse, Dess, by Aboyne, Aberdeenshire AB34 5AY, Scotland.

MACKEY James P, Appointments: Lecturer, Philosophy, Queen's University, Belfast, 1960-69; Professor, Religious Studies and Theology, University of San Francisco, 1969-79; Thomas Chalmers Professor of Theology, 1979-99, Dean, Faculty of Divinity, 1984-88, University of Edinburgh; Visiting Professor, University of California at Berkeley, 1974-75; Visiting Professor, Dartmouth College, USA, 1989; Curricular Consultant, University College, Cork, Ireland, 1999-2002; Visiting Professor, Trinity College, University of Dublin, 1999-. Publications: 18 books; Numerous articles in professional journals; Editor and associate editor; Presented television series for BBC and Channel 4; Participated in various other radio and television programmes. Memberships: Irish Philosophical Association; British-Irish Theological Society; Irish Theological Association; Catholical Theological Society of Great Britain; College Theology Society of America; International Study Group on the Foundations of Christian Morality, University of London; Centre for Hermeneutical Studies in Ancient and Modern Philosophy, University of California at Berkeley; Convivium of Philosophers from India and Great Britain. Address: 15 Glenville Park, Waterford, Eire.

MACKINTOSH Cameron Anthony (Sir), b. 17 October 1946, Enfield, England. Theatre Producer. Education: Prior Park College, Bath. Appointments: Stage Hand, Theatre Royal, Drury Lane; Assistant Stage Manager; Worked with Emile Littler, 1966; Robin Alexander, 1967; Producer, 1969-; Chair, Cameron Mackintosh, 1981-; Director, Delfont Mackintosh, 1991-; Productions: Little Women, 1967; Anything Goes, 1969; Trelawney, 1972; The Card, 1973; Winnie the Pooh, 1974; Owl and the Pussycat Went to Sea, 1975; Godspell, 1975; Side by Side by Sondheim, 1976; Oliver!, 1977; Diary of a Madam, 1977; After Shave, 1977; Gingerbread Man, 1978; Out on a Limb, 1978; My Fair Lady, 1979; Oklahoma!, 1990; Tomfoolery, 1980; Jeeves Takes Charge, 1981; Cats, 1981; Song and Dance, 1982; Blondel, 1983; Little Shop of Horrors, 1983; Abbacadabra, 1983; The Boyfriend, 1984; Les Miserables, 1985; Cafe Puccini, 1985; Phantom of the Opera, 1986; Follies, 1987; Miss Saigon, 1989; Just So, 1990; Five Guys Named Moe, 1990; Moby Dick, 1992; Putting it Together, 1992; The Card, 1992; Carousel, 1993; Oliver!, 1994; Martin Guerre, 1996; The Fix, 1997; Oklahoma!, 1999; The Witches of Eastwick, 2000; My Fair Lady, 2001. Honours:

Observer Award for Outstanding Achievement; Laurence Oliver Award, 1991; Knighted. Address: Cameron Mackintosh Ltd, 1 Bedford Square, London, WC1B 3RA, England.

MACKINTOSH Steven, b. 30 April 1967, Sawston, Cambridgeshire, England. Actor. m. Lisa Jacobs, 2 children. Education: Sawston Village College. Career: TV includes: Nanny; Doctor Who; The Secret Diary of Adrian Mole Aged 13¾; The Bill; Care; London Kills Me; The Buddha of Suburbia; Cadfael; Blue Juice; Prime Suspect; Undercover Heart; The Land Girls; Different for Girls; Criminal Justice; Our Mutual Friend; The Queen; Luther; Camelot; The Jury II; Inside Men; Theatre: Brighton Beach Memoirs; My Zinc Bed; Films: Lock, Stock and Two Smoking Barrels; The Other Boleyn Girl; Shining Shiny Bright New Hole in My Heart; Sugarhouse; The Beckoning Silence; The Escapist; Good; The Daisy Chain; Underworld: Rise of the Lycans; The Scouting Book for Boys; Mo. Honours: Best Actor, Brussels International Film Festival, 1997; Best Actor, BAFTA, 2001; Best Male Actor, RTS Television Award, 2001.

MACKLIN Elizabeth, b. 28 October 1952, Poughkeepsie, New York, USA. Poet. Education: BA in Spanish, State University of New York at Potsdam, 1973; Graduate School of Arts and Sciences, New York University, 1975-78. Appointment: Editorial Staff, 1974-99, Query Editor, 1981-99, The New Yorker Magazine; Poetry Editor, Wigwag Magazine, 1989-91; Freelance Editor and Writer, 2000-. Publications: A Woman Kneeling in the Big City, 1992; You've Just Been Told, Poems, 2000; Meanwhile Take My Hand, Poems by Kirmen Uribe (translation), 2007; Bar Puerto: Voices from the Edge (translation), 2010. Contributions to: Penguin Book of the Sonnet; 180 More: Extraordinary Poems for Every Day; Nation; New Republic; New York Times; New Yorker; Paris Review; Threepenny Review. Honours: Ingram Merrill Foundation Award in Poetry, 1990; Guggenheim Fellowship, 1994; Amy Lowell Poetry Travelling Scholarship, 1998-99; PEN Translation Fund grant, 2005; Listed in Who's Who publications. Memberships: Authors Guild; PEN American Center, executive board, 1995-96. Address: 207 West 14th Street, 5F, New York, NY 10011, USA. E-mail: email@elizabethmacklin.net

MacLACHLAN Kyle, b. 22 February 1959, Yakima, Washington, USA. Actor. m. Desiree Gruber, 2002-. Education: University of Washington, Seattle. Career: Stage: Regional Shakespeare productions and off-Broadway in Palace of Amateurs; Films: Dune, 1984; Blue Velvet, 1986; The Hidden, 1988; Don't Tell Her It's Me, 1990; The Doors, 1991; Where the Day Takes You, Twin Peaks: Fire Walk With Me, 1992; The Trial, Rich in Love, 1993; Against the Wall, The Flintstones, Roswell, 1994; Showgirls, 1995; Trigger Effect, Mad Dog Time, 1996; One Night Stand, 1997; X-Change, Hamlet, Timecode, 2000; Perfume, Me Without You, 2001; Miranda, 2002; Northfork, 2003; Touch of Pink, 2004; Free Jimmy (voice), 2006. Plays: Palace of Amateurs, Minetta Lane Theatre (off Broadway), New York; On An Average Day, Comedy Theatre, London, 2002; TV: Northwest Passage; The O'Conners; Twin Peaks, 1990-91; Sex and the City, 2000-02; Mysterious Island, 2005; In Justice, 2006; Desperate Housewives, 2006-2007. Address: UTA, 9560 Wilshire Boulevard, 5th Floor, Beverly Hills, CA 90212, USA.

MacLAINE Shirley, b. 24 April 1934, Richmond, Virginia, USA. Film Actress; Writer; Film Director. m. Steve Parker, 1954-1982 (divorced) 1 daughter. Education: Grammar School; Lee High School, Washington. Appointments: Chorus Girl and Dancer; Films include: The Trouble with Harry; Artists and Models; Around the World in 80 Days; Hot Spell; The Matchmaker; Can-Can; Career; The Apartment; Two for the Seesaw; The Children's Hour; Irma La Douce; What a Way to go; The Yellow Rolls-Royce; Gambit; Woman Times Seven; The Bliss of Mrs Blossom; Sweet Charity; Two Mules for Sister Sara; Desperate Characters; The Possessions of Joel Delaney; The Turning Point, 1977; Being There, 1979; Loving Couples, 1980; The Change of Seasons, Slapstick, 1981; Terms of Endearment, 1984; Out on a Limb, 1987; Madame Sousatzka, Steel Magnolias, 1989; Waiting for the Light, Postcards from the Edge, 1990; Used People, 1993; Wrestling Ernest Hemingway, Guarding Tess, 1994; Mrs Westbourne, The Evening Star, 1995; Mrs Winterbourne, The Celluloid Closet; The Evening Star, 1996; Looking for Lulu; Bet Bruce; Joan of Arc, 1999; The Dress Code, 2000; In Her Shoes, 2004; Bewitched, Rumor Has It, 2005; Closing the Ring, 2007; Valentine's Day, 2010. Revues: If My Friends Could See Me Now, 1974; To London with Love, 1976; London, 1982; Out There Tonight, 1990; TV Film: The West Side Waltz, 1994; Joan of Arc; These Old Broads, 2001; Video: Shirley MacLaines's Inner Workout, 1989; Producer and Co-director, The Other Half of the Sky - A China Memoir, 1973. Publications: Don't Fall From Here, 1975; Out on a Limb, 1983; Dancing in the Light, 1985; It's all in the playing, 1987; Going Within, 1989; Dance While You Can, 1991; My Lucky Stars, 1995; The Camino, 2000. Honours: Star of the Year Award, Theatre Owners of America, 1967; Best Actress Award, Desperate Characters, Berlin Film Festival, 1971; Academy Award, Best Actress, 1984; Golden Globe Award, Best Actress, 1989; Lifetime Achievement Award, Berlin Film Festival, 1999. Address: MacLaine Enterprises Inc, 25200 Malibu Road, Suit 101, Santa Monica, CA 90265, USA.

MACLAURIN Ian Charter (The Lord MacLaurin of Knebworth), b. 30 March 1937, Blackheath, Kent, England. Company Director. m. (1) Ann, 1 son, 2 daughters, (2) Paula Brooke, 2 stepdaughters. Education: Malvern College. Appointments: National Service, RAF Fighter Command, 1956-58; Management Trainee and subsequent numerous appointments, 1959, Board Member, 1970, Managing Director, 1973, Deputy Chairman, 1983, Chairman, 1985-97, Tesco; Chairman, Food Policy Group of the Retail Consortium, 1980-84; Non-Executive Director, Enterprise Oil plc, 1984-90; Non-Executive Director, Guinness, 1986-95; President, Institute of Grocery Distribution, 1989-92; Non-Executive Director, National Westminster Bank plc, 1990-96; Non-Executive Director, Gleneagles Hotels plc, 1992-97; Member, Stock Exchange Advisory Committee, 1988-91; Non-Executive Director, Whitbread plc, 1997-2002; Non-Executive Director, 1997-, Chairman, 2000-06, Vodafone; Chairman, Vodafone Group Foundation, 2006-09; Retired, 2009. Publications: Tiger by the Tail, 1999. Honours: Honorary Doctorate, Universities of Stirling, Bradford and Hertfordshire; Honorary Fellowship, University of Wales, Cardiff; Freedom of the City of London, 1981; Liveryman, Carmen Company, 1982; Knighted, 1989; Elevated to the peerage, 1996; Deputy Lord Lieutenant of Hertfordshire, 1992; Honorary Fellow, City and Guilds of London Institute, 1992; Deputy Lord Lieutenant of Wiltshire; Chancellor of the University of Hertfordshire, 1996-2005. Memberships: Fellow, Royal Society of Arts; Fellow, Institute of Marketing.

MACLAVERTY Bernard, b. 14 September 1942, Belfast, Northern Ireland. Novelist; Dramatist. m. Madeline McGuckin, 1967, 1 son, 3 daughters. Education: BA, Honours, Queen's University, Belfast, 1974. Publications: Bibliography: Secrets and Other Stories, 1977; Lamb (novel), 1980; A Time to Dance and Other Stories, 1982; Cal (novel),

1983; The Great Profundo and Other Stories, 1987; Walking the Dog and Other Stories, 1994; Grace Notes (novel), 1997; The Anatomy School (novel), 2001; Matters of Life & Death, 2006. For Young Children: A Man in Search of a Pet, 1978; Andrew McAndrew, 1988, US edition, 1993; Radio Plays: My Dear Palestrina, 1980; Secrets, 1981; No Joke, 1983; The Break, 1988; Some Surrender, 1988; Lamb, 1992; Grace Notes, 2003; The Woman from the North, 2007; Winter Storm, 2009; Television Plays: My Dear Palestrina, 1980; Phonefun Limited, 1982; The Daily Woman, 1986; Sometime in August, 1989. Screenplays: Cal, 1984; Lamb, 1985; Bye-Child, 2003; Drama Documentary: Hostages, 1992, US edition, 1993; Television Adaptation: The Real Charlotte by Somerville and Ross, 1989; Libretti: The King's Conjecture, 2008; The Letter, 2010. Honours: Northern Ireland and Scottish Arts Councils Awards; Irish Sunday Independent Award, 1983; London Evening Standard Award for Screenplay, 1984; Joint Winner, Scottish Writer of the Year, 1988; Society of Authors Travelling Scholarship, 1994; Shortlisted, Saltire Society Scottish Book of the Year, 1994, 2001; Grace Notes awarded The Saltire Scottish Book of the Year Award, 1997; A Scottish Arts Council Book Award; Shortlisted for: The Booker Prize; the Writers Guild Best Fiction Book; The Stakis Scottish Writer of the Year; The Whitbread Novel of the Year; Creative Scotland Award, the Scottish Arts Council, 2003; Nominated, BAFTA Best Short Film for Bye-Child, 2004; BAFTA Scotland, Best First Director for Bye-Child, 2004; The Lord Provost of Glasgow's Award for Literature, 2005.

MACLEAY John (Iain) Henry James, b. 7 December 1931, Inverness Scotland. Retired Clergyman. m. Jane Speirs Cuthbert, 1 son, 1 daughter. Education: BA, 1954, MA, 1960, St Edmund Hall, Oxford; College of the Resurrection, Mirfield, Yorkshire. Appointments: Deacon, 1957; Priest, 1958; Curate, St John's, East Dulwich, England, 1957-60; Curate, 1960-62, Rector, 1962-70, St Michael's, Inverness, Scotland; Priest-in-Charge, St Columba's, Grantown-on-Spey with St John the Baptist, Rothiemurchus, Scotland, 1970-78; Canon, St Andrew's Cathedral, Inverness, 1977-78; Rector of St Andrew's, Fort William, 1978-99; Synod Clerk of Argyll and the Isles, Canon of St John's Cathedral, Oban, 1980-87; Dean of Argyll and the Isles, 1987-99; Honorary Canon of Oban, 2001. Address: 47 Riverside Park, Lochyside, Fort William PH33 7RB, Scotland.

MacMAHON James Ardle, b. 25 November 1924, Curragh, Co Kildare, Ireland. Catholic Priest. Education: St Macartan's College, Monaghan; Holy Cross College, Clonliffe, Dublin; University College, Dublin; Gregorian University, Rome. Appointments: Ordained Priest, 1949; Doctorate in Canon Law, 1954; Secretary to the Archbishop of Dublin, 1954-72; Parish Priest, 1975-2000; Commission for Charitable Donations and Bequests for Ireland, 1975-2000; Director of Religious Education in Vocational Schools, 1976-79; Vicar Forane, 1977-80; Episcopal Vicar for Religious, 1980-86; Prelate of Honour of His Holiness, 1985; Chancellor, Dublin Metropolitan Chapter of Canons, 2003. Membership, Foxrock Golf Club, Dublin. Address: Sacred Heart Residence, Sybil Hill Road, Killester, Dublin 5, Ireland.

MacPHERSON Elle, b. 29 March 1963, Killara, Australia. Model; Actress; Business Executive. m. G Bensimon, divorced 1990, 2 sons with Arpad Busson. Career: Founder, Elle Macpherson Intimates, and Macpherson Men lingerie and underwear companies; Released fitness video, Stretch and Strengthen, The Body Workout, 1995; Chief Executive, Elle Macpherson Inc; Co-owner, Fashion Café, New York; Films: Sirens; Jane Eyre; If Lucy Fell; The Mirror Has Two Faces; Batman and Robin; The Edge; Beautopia; With Friends Like These; South Kensington. Address: c/o Artistmanagement Associates Inc, 414 East 52nd Street, Penthouse B, New York, NY 10022, USA.

MacQUEEN Hector Lewis, b. 13 June 1956, Ely, Cambridgeshire, England. Professor of Law. m. Frances Mary, 2 sons, 1 daughter. Education: LLB Honours, 1974-78, PhD, 1985, University of Edinburgh. Appointments: Lecturer, Senior Lecturer, Reader, 1979-94, Professor of Private Law, 1994-, Faculty of Law, Dean of the Faculty of Law, 1999-, University of Edinburgh; Visiting Professor, Cornell University, USA, 1991, Utrecht University, Netherlands, 1997; Director, The David Hume Institute, 1991-99. Publications: Copyright, Competition and Industrial Design, 1989, 2nd edition, 1995; Common Law and Feudal Society in Medieval Scotland, 1993; Studying Scots Law, 1993, 2nd edition, 1999; Contract Law in Scotland (with J M Thomson), 2000; Numerous articles in learned and professional journals and collections. Honour: Fellow of the Royal Society of Edinburgh. Memberships: Chair, Scottish Records Advisory Council, 2001-; Literary Director, Stair Society, 1999-; Heriots FP Cricket Club. Address: Faculty of Law, University of Edinburgh, Edinburgh EH8 9YL, Scotland. E-mail: hector.macqueen@ed.ac.uk

MacRAE (Alastair) Christopher (Donald) (Summerhayes) (Sir), b. 3 May 1937, Burleigh, Gloucestershire, England. Retired Diplomat. m. Mette Willert, 2 daughters. Education: BA Hons, Lincoln College, Oxford; Henry Fellow, Harvard University, USA. Appointments: Royal Navy, 1956-58; Second Secretary, Dar es Salaam, Tanzania, 1963-65; Middle East Centre for Arab Studies, 1965-67; Second Secretary, Beirut, Lebanon, 1967-68; Principal, Near East Department, Foreign and Commonwealth Office, 1968-70; 1st Secretary and Head of Chancery, Baghdad, Iraq, 1970-71; 1st Secretary and Head of Chancery, Brussels, Belgium, 1972-76; On loan to European Commission, 1976-78; Ambassador to Gabon, 1978-80, concurrently to Sao Tome and Principe; Head of West Africa Department, Foreign and Commonwealth Office, and Non-resident Ambassador to Chad, 1980-83; Political Counsellor, Paris, France, 1983-87; Head of Mission, Tehran, Iran, 1987; Assistant Under Secretary, Cabinet Office, 1988-91; British High Commissioner to Nigeria, 1991-94 and concurrently Ambassador to Benin; British High Commissioner to Pakistan, 1994-97; Secretary General Order of St John, 1997-2000. Honours: CMG, 1987; KCMG, 1993; KStJ, 1997. Memberships: Royal Commonwealth Society; Board Member, Aga Khan Foundation (UK); Chairman, Pakistan Society; President St John Ambulance, Ashford District. Address: 4 Church Street, Wye, Kent TN25 5BJ, England. E-mail: christophermacrae@btinternet.com

MACVEAGH Colin Lincoln, b. 28 March 1948, Mt Kisco, New York, USA. Investment Banker. Education: BA, History, Harvard College, 1970; MBA, Finance & Accounting, Columbia University School of Business, 1978. Appointments: International Lending Officer, First National Bank, Boston, 1972-76; Vice President, Dillon, Read & Co Inc, New York, 1978-82; Managing Director, Morgan Grenfell Inc, New York, 1982-88; Director, Mergers & Acquisitions, Merrill Lynch, New York, 1989-90; Director and Head, Mergers & Acquisitions Group, Citicorp, Milan, 1991-92; Managing Director and Group Head, Mergers & Acquisitions Group (US & Europe), London and New York, 1993-96; Managing Director, ISSI (International Strategy Services Inc), New York and Sao Paulo, 1996-. Memberships: Spee Club, Harvard Lampoon; Harvard College; Harvard

Club; President, American-Portuguese Society; Downtown Association. Address: 444 East 75th St 19D, New York, NY 10021, USA. E-mail: cmacveagh@aol.com

MACY William H, b. 13 March 1950, Miami, Florida, USA. Actor. m. Felicity Huffman, 2 daughters. Education: Goddard College, Vermont. Appointments: Co-founder, St Nicholas Theatre Company; Atlantic Theatre Company; Stage appearances include: The Man in 605, 1980; Twelfth Night; Beaurecrat; A Call from the East; The Dining Room; Speakeasy; Wild Life; Flirtations; Baby With the Bathwater; The Nice and the Nasty; Bodies Rest and Motion; Oh Hell!; Prairie du Chien; The Shawl; An Evening With Dorothy Parker; The Dining Room; A Call From the Sea; The Beaver Coat; Life During Wartime; Mr Gogol and Mr Preen; Oleanna; Our Town; Play director: Boy's Life; Film appearances include: Without a Trace; The Last Dragon; Radio Days; Somewhere in Time; Hello Again; House of Games; Things Change; Homicide; Shadows and Fog; Benny and Joon; Searching for Bobby Fischer; The Client; Oleanna; The Silence of the Lambs; Murder in the First; Mr Holland's Opus; Down Periscope; Fargo; Ghosts of Mississippi; Air Force One; Wag the Dog; Pleasantville; A Civil Action; Psycho; Magnolia; State and Maine; Panic; Focus; Boogie Nights; Jurassic Park III; Welcome to Collinwood; The Cooler; Stealing Sinatra; Out of Order; Seabiscuit; Spartan; Cellular; Sahara; Bobby, 2006; Inland Empire, 2006; Wild Hogs, 2007; He Was a Quiet Man, 2007; The Deal, 2008; The Tale of Despereaux (voice), 2008; Film director: Lip Service; TV appearances include: Chicago Hope; The Murder of Mary Phagan; Texan; A Murderous Affair; The Water Engine; Heart of Justice; A Private Matter; The Con; A Slight Case of Murder; ER. Address: 8383 Wilshire Blvd, #550, Beverly Hills, CA 90211, USA.

MADAN Man Mohan, b. 28 August 1954, Badwasi, Rajashthan. Engineer. m. Rachna, 1 son, 1 daughter. Education: B Tech, Civil Engineering, GB Pant University of Agriculture & Technology, Pantnagar, 1976; DIM, 1997, PGDIM, 1999, PGDHRM, 1999, MBA, 2000, Indira Gandhi National Open University; Fellow, 1995, Chartered Engineer (India), 1996, Institution of Engineers, Calcutta; Fellow, Institution of Valuers, Delhi, 1997. Appointments: M/s M N Dastur & Co, Bombay, 1976; Various positions, leading to Executive Director, Public Sector Hydro Power Company NHPC Ltd, 1977-2008; Chief Executive Officer, Malana Power Company Ltd and AD Hydro Power Ltd; Director, Business Development, GVK Group. Publications: Over 110 technical papers in professional journals, seminars, symposiums and conferences; Book, Brief History of Tunnel Construction at Loktak. Honours: Professor V K Kulkarni Award for best paper, Indian Concrete Journal, 1987; Best Citizen of India Award, 1998; 2nd Prize, Indira Gandhi award scheme for writing Original Technical Books in Hindi Language, 1999; Certificate of Excellence and Gold Medal, Friend Forum of India, 2000; CBIP-I N Sinha Award 2001-02, 2003; 1st Prize for original book in Hindi Language, Power Minister. Memberships: Fellow, Institution of Engineers (India); Fellow, Institution of Valuers; Member, Indian Society for Rock Mechanics and Tunnelling Technology; Member, Indian National Hydropower Association, Faridabad. Address: MPCL, LNJ Bhilwara Group, Bhilwara Towers, A-12, Sector-1, NOIDA-201301, India. E-mail: mmmadan2007@gmail.com

MADAN Sanjeev, b. 1 September 1966. Consultant Orthopaedic Surgeon. m. Education: D'Orth, College of Physicians and Surgeons, Bombay, India, 1992; MBBS, Bombay University, 1992, MS (Orth), 1994, Bombay University; DNB (Orth), National Board, New Delhi, 1994; MSc (Orth), University of Wales, Cardiff, 2002. Appointments: Senior House Officer, Paediatric Orthopaedics, AlderHey Children's Hospital, Liverpool, 1996; Visiting Specialist Orthpaedic Registrar: Salisbury District Hospital, UK, 1996-97, 2000-01; Poole and Royal Bournemouth Hospital, 1997-98; Southampton University Hospital, 1998-99; Royal Bournemouth and Poole Hospital, 1999-2000; Travelling Orthopaedic Fellow, Campbell Clinic, Memphis, USA, 2001; Paediatric Orthopaedic Fellow, Hospital for Joint Diseases Orthopedic Institute, New York, 2001-02; Specialist Registrar, St Richards Hospital, Chichester, UK, 2002; Specialist Registrar, Southport and Formby Hospital, Southport, 2002; National Paediatric Orthopaedic Fellow, Sheffield Children's Hospital, Sheffield, 2003; Fellow, Hip and Pelvis Surgery, Inselspital, Bern, Switzerland, 2004; Consultant Orthopaedic Surgeon, Doncaster and Bassetlaw NHS Trust, UK, 2004-06; Consultant Orthopaedic Surgeon, Sheffield Children's Hospital Foundation Trust, Doncaster and Bassetlaw Foundation Trust, 2006-. Publications: Numerous articles in professional journals. Honours: Listed in international biographical dictionaries; Clinical Excellence Award, Department of Health. Memberships: British Orthopaedic Organisation; British Society for Children's Orthopaedic Surgery; British Orthopaedic Food and Ankle Society; British Limb Reconstruction Society; Skeletal Dysplasia Society, UK; Fellow of Institute of Leadership and Management, 2009-; and others. Address: Whim Cottage, Sheffield Road, Hathersage, Hope Valley, S32 1DA, England. E-mail: eashrish@aol.com

MADAU Fabio A, b. 21 October 1973, Sassari, Italy. Education: Graduate, Agricultural Sciences, University of Sassari; PhD, Agricultural Economics and Policy, University of Bologne. Appointments: Researcher and Teacher, Agricultural Economics and Policy, University of Sassari and National Institute of Agricultural Economics. Publications: More than 70 published works including peer-reviewed journals, books, book chapters, etc. Memberships: European Association of Agricultural Economics; International Association of Agricultural Economics. Address: via Cottoni 9, 07100 Sassari, Italy.

MADDEN John, b. 8 April 1949, Portsmouth, England. Film Director. Appointments: TV includes: Inspector Morse; Prime Suspect IV; Ethan Frome; Films: Mrs Brown, 1997; Shakespeare in Love, 1998; Captain Corelli's Mandolin, 2001; Proof, 2005; Killshot, 2008. Honours: Academy Award for Best Film; BAFTA Award for Best Film, 1998.

MADDY Penelope Jo, b. 4 July 1950, Tulsa, Oklahoma, USA. Professor. Education: BA, Mathematics, University of California, Berkeley, 1972; PhD, Philosophy, Princeton University, 1979. Appointments: Assistant Professor, University of Notre Dame, 1978-83; Associate Professor, University of Illinois, Chicago, 1983-87; Associate Professor 1987-89, Full Professor, 1989-, Distinguished Professor, 2007-, University of California, Irvine. Publications: Believing the Axioms, 1988; Realism in Mathematics, 1990; Naturalism in Mathematics, 1997; Second Philosophy, 2007; Defending the Axioms, 2011. Honours: Westinghouse Scholarship, 1968; Marshall Scholarship, 1972; American Academy of Arts & Science, 1998; Lakatos Prize, 2002. Memberships: Association for Symbolic Logic; American Philosophical Association; Philosophical Science Association. Address: Department of Logic & Philosophy of Science, University of California Irvine, Irvine, CA 92697-5100, USA.

MADJIROVA Nadejda Petrova, b. 7 November 1945, Plovdiv, Bulgaria. Psychiatrist. m. Petko Tanev Valkov, 27 May 1973, 1 daughter. Education: English Language Scholar, 1959-64; Higher Medical Institute, 1971; PhD, Medical Academy, Sofia, Bulgaria, 1985; Psychiatrist, Psychiatric Hospital, Radnevo. Appointments: Assistant Professor, Higher Medical Institute, Plovdiv, 1976-85; Chief Assistant Professor, 1985-89, Associate Professor, 1989. Publications include: Chronobiological Aspects in Psychiatry, 1995; Child Complexes, 1996; 2 textbooks: Course of Clinical Psychology, 2001; Medical Psychology, 2001; 1 monograph: Chronobiology and Chronobiometeorology in Bulgarian Medicine (editor), 2001; Textbook: Psychopathology of Childhood, 2002. Memberships: New York Academy of Sciences; International Society of Chronobiology; Psychiatric Society of Bulgaria; Association for Child Psychiatry, Bulgaria; President, Bulgarian Chronobiology and Biometeorology Society. Address: Peter Stoeve 123, 4004 Plovdiv, Bulgaria.

MADONNA (Madonna Louise Veronica Ciccone), b. 16 August 1958, Bay City, Michigan, USA. Singer; Songwriter; Actress. m. (1) Sean Penn, 1985, divorced 1989; 1 daughter with Carlos Leon, (2) Guy Ritchie, 2000, divorced 2008, 1 son, 1 adopted son, 1 adopted daughter. Education: University Of Michigan, 1976-78. Career: Dancer, New York, 1979; Actress, 1980-; Solo singer, 1983-; Film appearances include: Vision Quest, Desperately Seeking Susan, 1985; Shanghai Surprise, 1986; Who's That Girl, 1987; Bloodhounds On Broadway, Dick Tracy, 1990; A League Of Their Own, 1992; Evita, 1996; The Next Best Thing, 2000; Swept Away, Die Another Day, 2002; Numerous worldwide concerts, 1983-; Major appearances include: Live Aid, Philadelphia, 1985; Don't Bungle The Jungle, ecological awareness benefit, 1989; Television includes: In Bed With Madonna, documentary, 1991; Stage performance, Speed The Plow, Broadway, 1988; Up For Grabs, Wyndhams Theatre, 2002; Owner, Maverick record label. Compositions include: Co-writer, own hits: Live To Tell; Open Your Heart; Justify My Love; Co-writer, Each Time You Break My Heart, Nick Kamen, 1986. Recordings: Hit singles include: Holiday, 1983; Lucky Star, Borderline, Like A Virgin, 1984; Material Girl, Crazy For You, Angel, Into The Groove, Dress You Up, Gambler, 1985; Live To Tell, Papa Don't Preach, True Blue, Open Your Heart, 1986; La Isla Bonita, Who's That Girl, Causin' A Commotion, The Look Of Love, 1987; Like A Prayer, Express Yourself, Cherish, Dear Jessie, 1989; Oh Father, 1990; Keep It Together, Vogue, I'm Breathless, Hanky Panky, Justify My Love, Rescue Me, 1991; This Used To Be My Playground, Erotica, Deeper And Deeper, 1992; Bad Girl, Fever, Rain, 1993; Frozen, Ray of Light, Power of Goodbye, 1998; Nothing Really Matters, Beautiful Stranger: theme song from Austin Powers: The Spy Who Shagged Me, 1999; American Pie, Music, Don't Tell Me, 2000; What It Feels Like For A Girl, 2001; Die Another Day, 2002; American Life, Hollywood, 2003; Hung Up, 2005; Sorry, Get Together, Jump, 2006; 4 Minutes, Give It 2 Me, Miles Away, 2008; Celebration, Revolver, 2009; Give Me All Your Luvin', Girl Gone Wild, Turn Up the Radio, 2012; Albums: Madonna, 1983; Like A Virgin, 1985; True Blue, 1986; Who's That Girl?, film soundtrack, 1987; You Can Dance, 1988; Like A Prayer, 1989; I'm Breathless, The Immaculate Collection, Dick Tracy, film soundtrack, 1990; Erotica, 1992; Bedtime Stories, 1994; Something To Remember, 1995; Evita, film soundtrack, 1996; Ray of Light, 1997; Music, 2000; American Life, 2003; Remixed and Revisted, 2004; Confessions on a Dance Floor, 2005; Hard Candy, 2008; MDNA, 2012. Publications: Sex, 1992; The English Roses, 2003; Mr Peabody's Apples, 2003; Yaokov and the Seven Thieves, 2004; The Adventures of Abdi, 2004. Honours include: Numerous MTV Video Awards, including Vanguard Award, 1986; American Music Awards: Favourite Female Video Artist, 1987; Favourite Dance Single, 1991; Oscar, Best Song, 1991; Juno Award, International Song Of The Year, 1991; Grammy Award, Best Longform Music Video, 1992; Grammy Award, Best Electronic/Dance Album, 2007; Numerous awards from Billboard, Vogue and Rolling Stone magazines. Address: c/o Norman West Management, 9348 Civic Centre Drive, Beverly Hills, CA 90210, USA.

MADSEN Michael, b. 25 September 1958, Chicago, USA. Actor. m. (1) Jeannine Bisignano, divorced, 1 son, (2) Georganne La Piere (divorced), (3) De Anna Morgan 1996-, 4 sons. Appointments: Began acting career, Steppenwolf Theatre, Chicago; Appeared in plays including: Of Mice and Men; A Streetcar Named Desire; Appeared in Broadway Production of A Streetcar Named Desire, 1992; Films: Wargames; The Natural; Racing with the Moon; The Killing Time; Shadows in the Storm; Iguana; Blood Red; Kill Me Again; The Doors; The End of Innocence; Thelma and Louise; Fatal Instinct; Inside Edge; Reservoir Dogs; Straight Talk; Almost Blue; Free Willy; A House in the Hills; Money for Nothing; Trouble Bound; Wyatt Earp; The Getaway; Dead Connection; Species; Free Willy II: The Adventure Home; The Winner; Red Line; Mulholland Falls; Man with a Gun; The Last Days of Frankie the Fly; Rough Draft; The Marker; Donnie Brasco; Catherine's Grove; Papertrail; The Girl Gets Moe; Executive Target; The Thief and the Stripper; Supreme Sanction; The Florentine; Species II; Detour; Code of the Dragon, 2000; The Ghost, 2000; High Noon, 2000; LAPD Conspiracy, 2001; LAPD To Protect and Serve, 2001; Welcome to America, 2002; Die Another Day, 2002; My Boss's Daughter, 2003; Kill Bill 1,2, 2003-04; Smatyvay udochki, 2004; Hoboken Hollow, 2005; Sin City, 2005; The Last Drop, 2005; Last Hour, 2006; Scary Movie 4, 2006; House, 2007; Vice, 2007; Deep Winter, 2007; Hell Ride, 2008; The Portal, 2008; Corruption.Gov, 2010. TV: Our Family House, 1985-86; Special Bulletin, 1983; War and Remembrance, 1988; Montana, 1990; Baby Snatcher, 1992; Beyond the Law, 1994; 24, 2010. Address: Grant and Tane, 9100 Wilshire Boulevard, Beverly Hills, CA 90212, USA.

MAEL-AININ Mohamed, b. 1952, Tantan, Morocco. Ambassador. m. 3 children. Education: Bachelor degree, Economic Sciences, Mohamed V University, Rabat. Appointments: Journalist, 1974-77; Adviser to Foreign Affairs Minister, 1977-80, Bureau Manager of Foreign Affairs, 1980-83, Bureau of the Minister of Foreign Affairs and Co-operation; Bureau Manager, Minister of State, Mr M'hamed Boucetta, 1983-85; Ambassador of His Majesty the King of Morocco to the Republic of Uruguay, 2000-05; Ambassador of His Majesty the King of Morocco to the Republic of Argentina, 2000-05; Ambassador of His Majesty the King of Morocco to the Hashemite Kingdom of Jordan, 2006-08; Ambassador of His Majesty the King of Morocco to Australia, 2009-. Publications: Many essays, studies and files on Moroccan Sahara Cause. Address: PO Box 3531, Manuka, ACT 2603, Australia. E-mail: sifmacan@moroccoembassy.org.au Website: www.moroccoembassy.org.au

MAENDLE Markus, b. 17 November 1967, Geislingen/Steige, Germany. Economics Professor. m. Nicole Simone, 2 daughters. Education: Diploma, PhD, Economics, University of Hohenheim. Appointments: Professor, Economics, 2002-, Director, Institute for Co-operative Studies, 2005-, Nürtingen-Geislingen University. Publications: Numerous articles in professional journals; 2 book series and real estate dictionary. Memberships: Verein für Socialpolitik; European Real Estate Society; American Real Estate and Urban Economics Association. Address: Nürtingen-Geislingen University, Institute for Co-operative Studies, Parkstr 4, 73312 Geislingen/Steige, Germany. E-mail: markus.maendle@hfwu.de Website: www.ifk-office.de

MAGEE Bryan, b. 12 April 1930, London, England. Writer. m. Ingrid Söderlund, 1 daughter. Education: MA, Keble College, Oxford University, 1956; Yale University, 1955-56. Appointments: Theatre Critic, The Listener, 1966-67; Lecturer in Philosophy, Balliol College, Oxford, 1970-71; Visiting Fellow, All Souls College, Oxford, 1973-74; Regular Columnist, The Times, 1974-76; Member of Parliament for Leyton, 1974-83; President, Critics Circle of Great Britain, 1983-84; Honorary Senior Research Fellow, 1984-94, Visiting Professor, 1994-2000, King's College, London; Honorary Fellow, Queen Mary College, London, 1988-; Fellow, Queen Mary and Westfield College, London, 1989-; Visiting Fellow: Wolfson College, Oxford, 1991-94, New College, Oxford, 1995, Merton College, Oxford, 1998, St Catherine's College, Oxford, 2000, Peterhouse College, Cambridge, 2001. Publications: Go West Young Man, 1958; To Live in Danger, 1960; The New Radicalism, 1962; The Democratic Revolution, 1964; Towards 2000, 1965; One in Twenty, 1966; The Television Interviewer, 1966; Aspects of Wagner, 1968; Modern British Philosophy, 1971; Popper, 1973; Facing Death, 1977; Men of Ideas, 1978, reissued as Talking Philosophy, 2001; The Philosophy of Schopenhauer, 1983; The Great Philosophers, 1987; On Blindness, 1995, reissued as Sight Unseen, 1998; Confessions of a Philosopher, 1997; The Story of Philosophy, 1998; Wagner and Philosophy, 2000; Clouds of Glory, 2003; A Hoxton Childhood, 2003. Contributions to: Numerous journals. Honours: Silver Medal, Royal Television Society, 1978; J R Ackerley Prize for Autobiography, 2004. Memberships: Critics Circle; Society of Authors; Arts Council of Great Britain and Chair, Music Panel, 1993-94; Honorary Fellow, Keble College, Oxford, 1994-; Silver Medal, Royal TV Society; Life Member, Clare Hall, Cambridge, 2004. Address: Wolfson College, Oxford OX 2 6UD, England.

MAGER Peter Paul, b. 18 June 1946, Klostergeringswalde, Saxony, Germany. m. Christine, 2 daughters. Education: Approbation in Medicine, Leipzig, 1973; MD, 1974; Mathematics in Chemistry, 1975, Degree in Pharmacology and Toxicology, 1978, Halle; DSc, 1982; Degree in Educational and Didactic Methodology in University Teaching, 1983; Facultas docendi, 1990; Dr med habil, 1991. Appointments: Assistant, Pharmacology and Toxicology, University of Greifswald, 1973-75; Assistant in Internal Medicine, Doesen/Saxony, 1975-76; Senior Researcher, Institute of Pharmacy, University of Halle, 1976-80; Head of Research Group of Pharmacochemistry, University of Leipzig, 1980-; Co-ordinator, Research Programme, FMC Co, Princeton, New Jersey, USA, 1984-90; Consultant, Clinical Pharmacology, Leipzig, 1985-90; Consultant, Biostructure SA, France, 1991-94; Managing Director, Institute of Pharmacology and Toxicology, University of Leipzig, 1993-95; Professor, 1996. Publications: Co-editor and Referee of scientific periodicals; Around 230 papers in scientific periodicals and handbooks; 3 monographs. Honour: Leibniz Award. Memberships include: New York Academy of Sciences; American Association for the Advancement of Science; Affiliate, International Union of Pure and Applied Chemistry; German Society of Pharmacology and Toxicology; Medicinal Chemistry Division, Computer Chemistry Division, German Chemical Society; Deutsche Hochschulverband. Address: Am Wohnpark 3, Neuweißenborn b. Bennewitz, 04828, Germany. E-mail: magp@server3.medizin.uni-leipzig.de

MAGIEIRA-COELHO Alvaro, b. 26 May 1932. Research Director. m. Ana Maria, 3 sons, 1 daughter. Education: School of Medicine, Lisbon, Portugal. Appointments: Inter, Santa Maria Hospital, Lisbon; Research Associate, Wistar Institute, Philadelphia, USA; Research Associate, Department of Pathology, Uppsala University, Sweden; Research Director, French National Institute of Health. Publications: 160 papers in scientific journals; 9 books. Honours: Doctor Honoris Causa, Linköping University, Sweden; Fritz Verzär Prize, University of Vienna, Austria; Johananof Visiting Professor, Marionegri University, Milan, Italy; Seeds of Science Career Award, Lisbon, Portugal. Memberships: American Society of Cell Biology; American Association for Cancer Research. Address: 73 Bis Rue Marchal Foch, 78000 Versailles, France.

MAGNUSSON Tomas Herbert, b. 1 April 1949, Linköping, Sweden. Dentist. m. Annica Birgitta Hedmo, 3 daughters. Education: L D S, 1974; Odont Dr, PhD, 1981; Docent, Reader, 1986; Professor, 2006; Certified Specialist in Stomatognathic Physiology, 1993. Appointments: General Practitioner, Jokkmokk, Sweden, 1974-1979; Assistant Professor, University of Göteborg, Sweden, 1979-1980; Head, Senior Consultant, Lulea, Sweden, 1980-1988; Senior Consultant, 1988-2000, Head, Senior Consultant, 2000-10, Jonkoping, Sweden; Professor, School of Health Sciences, Jonkoping University, 2010-. Publications: Published more than 100 scientific papers in peer review national and international journals mainly in the field of temporomandibular disorders; One out of two authors of four textbooks and author of seven separate book chapters, all in the field of temporomandibular disorders. Honours: The Forsberg Dental Foundation Award for extraordinary clinical achievements, 1990; The Henry Beyron Award for unique research, 2000; Corresponding member, Finnish Dental Society, 2002. Memberships: Swedish Dental Association; Swedish Dental Society; Swedish Academy of Temporo Mandibular Disorders; Board member and past president of the Society of Oral Physiology. Address: School of Health Sciences, PO Box 1026, SE-55111 Jonkoping, Sweden. E-mail: tomas.magnusson@lj.se

MAGNY Michel Marie René, b. 7 April 1952, Héricourt, France. Research Scientist. m. Beatrice Jacquinot, 1 son, 1 daughter. Education: PhD, Prehistory, 1978, PhD, Live Sciences, 1994, University of Franche-Comté, Besançon, France. Appointments: Teacher, Ministry of Education Nationale, France, 1978-83; Research Scientist, CNRS, France, 1983. Publications: Book, Une Histoire de Climat, 1995; Numerous articles in professional journals. Honours: Silver Medal, CNRS, 2006. Address: UMR 6249 du CNRS, Laboratoire de Chrono-Environnement, University of Franche-Comté, Besançon, 16 route de Gray, 25030 Besançon, France. Address: michel.magny@univ-fcomte.fr

MAGUIRE Adrian Edward, b. 29 April 1971, Ireland. Jockey. m. Sabrina, 1995, 1 daughter. Education: Kilmessan National School; Trim Vocational School. Appointments: Champion Pony Race Rider, 1986; Champion Point to Point Rider, 1990-91; Champion Conditional Jockey, 1991-92; Winner of the Following Races: Cheltenham Gold Cup; Irish Grand National; Galway Plate; Imperial Cup; Greenalls Gold Cup; Queen Mother Champion Chase; King George VI Chase; Triumph Hurdle and Cathcort Chase; Holds record for most Point to Point winners in a season; Most winners in a season for a conditional jockey (71), 1991-92; Retired due to neck injury having won over 1,000 races, 2002. Address: The Jockey Club (Jockey Section), 42 Portman Square, London, W1H 0EM, England.

MAGUIRE Janet, b. Chicago, USA. Composer. Education: BA, Colorado College; Studied composition with René Liebowitz, Paris; Student, Darmstadt Ferienkurse. Appointments: President, Venezia Nuova Musica, Venice, Italy, 1992-2003, Musica in Divenire, Venice, Italy, 2004-; Composer. Compositions: Per Acqua, 1990; Shuffle, 1991; Ebb & Flow, 1992; Trieze à Table, 1993; Così, 1993; Inno a Dio, 1994; Hark, 1995; La mia serra, 1995; Canzone d'Amore, 1996; Invenzione, 1996; Il Fiume Tchirek, 1996; Glass, 1997; Discussion, 1997; Etude Osmotique, 1998; Fumées d'Ivresse, 1998; Lace Knots, 1998; Danza, 1999; L'altro Quartetto, 1999; Le Jardin de Versailles, 2000; L'intervista, 2000; Quest, 2000; Cummings Lieder, 2000; Five Chinese Poems, 2001; Hier bin Ich, Wo bist Du?, 2002; Un Momento, 2002; Moondust, 2002; A Trois, 2002; Southern Trees, 2002; Frills, 2002; Rain, 2003; Fingers, 2003; Vagheggiando, 2003; Gone, 2004; Sonata-Suonata, 2005; Variations, 2005; Tragedy, 2006; Please, 2007; Wisp, 2007; Lightly, 2002; Operas: Envoys, 1996; Hèrèsie, 2008; Ballets: Taigà. 2001; Orchestrations: Les Nuits Parisiennes; Die drei Pintos; Arrangements: Operas Finale Turandot by Giacomo Puccini. Honours: Fellow, John Simon Guggenheim Memorial Foundation, 2008; Copland House resident, Aaron Copland Foundation, 2006. Memberships: European Society for Culture. Address: Via Fogazzaro 18, 30172 Mestre, Venice, Italy. E-mail: janetdmaguire@yahoo.com

MAGUIRE Robert Alfred, b. 6 June 1931, London, England. Retired Architect; Sculptor. m. (1) Robina, 4 daughters, (2) Alison Margaret. Education: Leverhulme Scholar, AA Diploma with Honours, Architectural Association School of Architecture, London, 1948-53. Appointments: Buildings Editor, Architects' Journal, 1954-59; Sole Principal in architectural practice, 1956-59; Partner, Robert Maguire & Keith Murray, 1959-88; Chairman, Maguire & Co, 1988-2003, Maguire & Co International, 1989-2002; Consultant, Maguire & Co, 2003-2004; Surveyor of the Fabric to The Queen's Free Chapel of St George at Windsor Castle, 1975-87; Head, Oxford School of Architecture, 1976-85; Trustee, Stowe House Preservation Trust, 1998-2007. Publications: Book: Modern Churches of the World (co-author with Keith Murray); Numerous articles on architectural theory, conservation, and architectural critiques; Major paper: Continuity and Modernity in the Holy Place (Annual Lecture to the Society of Architectural Historians of Great Britain), 1995. Honours: OBE, 1983; 4 buildings of his own design listed as Buildings of Historic Interest: St Paul's Church, Bow Common, London; St Matthew's Church, Perry Beeches, Birmingham; St Mary's Abbey Church, West Malling; Residences at St Mary's Abbey, West Malling. Memberships: Royal Society of Arts; Oxford University Club. Address: Hopewater House, Ettrickbridge, Selkirk TD7 5JN, Scotland.

MAGUIRE Tobey Vincent, b. 27 June 1975, Santa Monica, California, USA. Actor. m. Jennifer Meyer, 2007, 1 son, 1 daughter. Career: Various Commercials as child; Films include: Pleasantville, 1998; Ride with the Devil, 1999; Tales from the Whoop: Hot Rod Brown Class Clown, 1990; Empire Records, 1995; Fear and Loathing in Las Vegas, 1998; The Cider House Rules, 1999; Wonder Boys, 2000; Cats and Dogs, voice, 2001; Dons Plum, 2001; Spider-Man, 2002; Seabiscuit, 2003; Spider-Man 2, 2004; The Good German, 2006; Spider-Man 3, 2007; Brothers, 2009. TV appearances include: Celebrities Uncensored; The Tonight show with Jay Leno; Rove Live; Tracey Takes On…; Roseanne; The Wild and Crazy Kids; Great Scott!. Honours include: Academy of Science Fiction, Fantasy & Horror Films, USA, Best Performance by a Young Actor, Pleasantville, 1999; Best Actor, Spider Man 2, 2005.

MAH Boon Yih, b. 4 February 1979, Georgetown, Penang, Malaysia. Lecturer. m. Hui Mee Wong, 2 daughters. Education: BA, Education in ELS (Hons), 2003, PhD, in progress, Universiti Sains Malaysia, Penang; MA, Applied Linguistics, Universiti Utara Malasia, Sintok, Kedah, 2007. Appointments: Lecturer, Kedah Matriculation College, 2003-07; Lecturer, Universiti Teknologi MARA (UiTM), 2007. Publications: Mah Boon Yih's Blog (http://mahboonyih.blogspot.com); Mobile Curriculum Vitae (http://m-curriculumvitae.blogspot.com); Ubiquitous Academic (http://ubiquitousacademic.blogspot.com); Can Adults Acquire a Second Language Successfully?, 2006; Group Autonomy and Peer Assessment in Conducting Reading Comprehension Activity Using Newspapers, 2008; Bringing Blogs into ESL Writing Classroom, 2008; GAT-a Teaching Module of Restructuring Basic Mandarin Sentences to UiTM Malay Students, 2009; An Investigation on Students' Acceptance of Writing Web Logs: A Test of Technology Acceptance Model, 2009; Expanding ESL Classroom Horizons with Weblogs: Educators' Perspective, 2009; Measuring Students' Preception of Writing Web Logs in ESL Classroom Employing the Technology Acceptance Model, 2009; The Manifestation of Native Language Transfer in ESL Learning, 2009; Writing Web Logs in the ESL Classroom: A Study of Student Perceptions and the Technology Acceptance Model, 2009; Learning Style Preferences of English Language Learners among UiTM Penang Diploma Students, 2010; Preference of Learning Style among the Diploma Students of UiTM Penang: An Overview, 2010; The Process of Designing and Developing a Romanised Mandarin Web-based Instruction on ISD Methodology for Non-native Learners in Malaysia, 2010; The Impact of Chinese ESL Learner Interlanguage on Writing: A Syntactical Analysis, 2010; Part Time Students, Part Time Assessors. How Reliable Are Students to Fit Two Roles in Reading Comprehension Activity? 2011; A Cross-discipline Survey on University Students' Acceptance of Mobile Curriculum Vitae Developed Using Weblog, 2011; Developing a Mobile Curriculum Vitae Using Weblog: A Cross-disciplinary Survey on University Students' Perception Based on Technology Acceptance Model, 2011; Enhancing Student-centred Learning through Usage of Television Commercials via Wiki, 2011; Are You Ready to Blog? 2011; Publishing Curriculum Vitae Using Weblog: An Investigation on its Usefulness, Ease of Use, and Behavioural Intention to Use, 2012. Honours: Silver Certificate Publication Award, 2008; Platinum Certificate Publication Award, 2009; Gold Medal, 7th IID, 2010; ITEX Silver Medal, 2010; Silver Award, IID Kedah, 2010; Gold Medal, IID 2010 SE, 2010; Silver Certificate Publication Award, 2010; Listed in biographical dictionaries. Memberships: International Association of Computer Science and Information Technology; Asia Association of Computer Assisted Language Learning; Asian Association of TEFL; Malaysian English Language Teaching Association.

MAHESHWARI Monika, b. 9 February 1977, Barielly, India. Doctor; Physician. Education: MBBS, 1998, MD, 2004, DNB, 2006, PhD, 2011, J L N Medical College; DM (Cardiology), 2010. Appointments: Registrar, 2002-04, Assistant Professor, 2005-, J L N Medical College. Publications: 6 book chapters; Numerous articles in professional journals. Honours: Gangadhar Verma Memorial Award, 2004, 2006; Jaipur Apicon Award, 2007, 2008, 2009, 2010; Dr D P Basu Award, 2009, 2010, 2011; Dr D S Mungekar Award, 2010. Memberships: Association of Physicians of India; Indian Medical Association; National Academy of Medical Science; Cardiology Society of India; Indian Society of Electrocardiology; Indian Academy of Electrocardiology. Address: Navin Niwas 434/10, Bapu Nagar, Ajmer (Raj), India. E-mail: opm11@rediffmail.com

MAHMOUD Dina, b. 14 April 1968, Cairo, Egypt. Assistant Professor. Education: BSc, Pharmaceutical Sciences, 1990; MSc, 1995, PhD, 2000, Pharmaceutics, Faculty of Pharmacy, Cairo University. Appointments: Research Assistant, -1996, Assistant Researcher, 1996-2000, Researcher, 2000-08, Assistant Professor, 2008-, Pharmaceutical Technology Department, National Research Centre, Egypt. Publications: 12 publications; Numerous articles in professional journals. Honours: Listed in biographical dictionaries. Memberships: Pharmaceutical Society of Egypt; Egyptian Society of NanoTechnology & Materials Science. E-mail: dnamm2005@yahoo.com

MAIDEN Colin James, b. 5 May 1933, Auckland, New Zealand. Engineer. m. Jenefor Mary, 1 son, 3 daughters. Education: BE, 1955, ME, 1956, University of New Zealand; D Phil, University of Oxford, 1957; Hon LLD, University of Auckland, 1994. Appointments: Defence Research Board, Canada, 1958-60; Manager, General Motors Corporation, USA, 1961-70; Vice Chancellor, University of Auckland, 1971-94; Director and Chairman of numerous public companies in New Zealand and Australia, 1972-2011; Member, Director and Chairman of various NZ government bodies and enterprises, 1973-2004. Publications: An Energetic Life, 2008; Numerous articles in professional journals. Honours: Queen Elizabeth Silver Jubilee Medal, 1977; Medal of University of Bonn, 1983; Thomson Medal, Royal Society of New Zealand, 1986; Knight Bachelor, 1991; Symons Award, Association of Commonwealth Universities, 1999. Memberships: Northern Club; Remuera Rackets Club; Royal Auckland Golf Club. Address: Apt 503, 10 Middleton Road, Remuera, Auckland 1050, New Zealand.

MAINWARING Scott Patterson, b. 18 July 1954, Pittsburgh, Pennsylvania, USA. Political Scientist; Educator. m. Susan M Elfin, 1 son, 1 daughter. Education: BA, Political Science, 1972-76, MA, Political Science, 1975-76, Yale University; PhD, Political Science, Stanford University, 1978-83. Appointments: Assistant Professor, Government, 1983-88, Associate Professor, Government, 1988-93, Professor of Government, 1993-96, Chair, Government Department 1996-97, Eugene Conley Professor of Political Science, 1996-, Director, Kellogg Institute for International Studies, 1997-2002, 2003-, University of Notre Dame, Indiana, USA. Publications: Author, The Catholic Church and Politics in Brazil 1916-1985, 1986; Author, Rethinking Party Systems in the Third Wave of Democratization: The Case of Brazil, 1999; Edited books: The progressive Church in Latin America, 1989; Issues in Democratic Consolidation, 1992; Building Democratic Institutions: Party Systems in Latin America, 1995; Presidentialism and Democracy in Latin America, 1997; Christian Democracy in Latin America, 2003; The Third Wave of Democratization in Latin America, 2005; Democratic Accountability in Latin America, 2003; The Crisis of Democratic Representation in the Andes, 2006; Democratic Governance in Latin America, 2010. Honours: Phi Beta Kappa, Yale University; Magna Cum Laude, Yale University, 1976; Washburn Clark Prize, Yale University, 1976; Hubert Herring Prize for the best dissertation on a Latin American subject, 1983-84; 7 Research Grants and Fellowships include: Fulbright Hays, 1980-81; Social Science Research Council, 1980-81; Fulbright-Hays, 1987-88; Hoover Institute, Stanford, 1990-91; Woodrow Wilson Centre, 1995-96; Guggenheim Fellow, 2000; American Academy of Arts and Sciences, 2010; Listed in national and international biographical dictionaries. Memberships: Council on Foreign Relations, 1986-91; Research Council, International Forum for Democratic Studies, National Endowment for Democracy, Washington DC, 1994-. Address: Kellogg Institute for International Studies, 231 Hesburgh Center, Notre Dame, IN 46556, USA. E-mail: mainwaring.1@nd.edu

MAIONE Guido, b. 10 August 1967, Naples, Italy. Engineer. Education: Laurea, Electronic Engineering, 1992, PhD, Electrical Engineering, 1997, Technical University of Bari, Italy. Appointments: Lecturer, 1996-99, Senior Lecturer, 1999-2002, School of Engineering, University of Lecce; Senior Lecturer, 2nd School of Engineering, Technical University of Bari, 2002-. Publications: 60 articles in professional journals, book chapters, conferences and workshops. Memberships: IEEE; IEEE Control Systems Society; IFAC; SIDRA, Italy.

MAIORANO Domenico, b. 10 November 1966, Vibo Valentia, Italy. Professor. m. Helen Guillon, 1 son, 1 daughter. Education: Institute of Human Genetics, CNRS UPR 1142, 141, rue de la Cardonille 34396, Montpellier, Cedex 5, France. Education: Laurea (Masters), Biology, University of Milan, 1990; D Phil, Molecular Genetics and Cell Biology, University of Oxford; Clearance to Direct Research, University of Montpellier II. Appointments: Research Assistant, University of Oxford, 1996; Postdoctoral Researcher, Institute Jacques Monod, Paris, France, 1997-98; Postdoctoral Researcher, Institute of Human Genetics, Montpellier, 1998-2001; Assistant Professor, University of Insubria, Italy, 2000; Staff Researcher, Institute of Health and Medical Research, 2001-. Publications: Numerous articles in professional journals; 3 patents. Memberships: French Society of Cell Biology; Faculty of 1000 Biology; American Association for the Advancement of Science; Trinity College, Oxford. Address: Institute of Human Genetics, CNRS-UPR 1142, 141 rue de la Cardonille, 34396, Montpellier, Cedex 5, France.

MAJ Barnaba, b. 3 October 1949, Balsorano, Italy. Professor. 2 sons. Education: Secondary School Diploma, 1967; University Law Degree, 1972. Appointments: Research Fellow, 1980-; Professor, 2005-. Publications: Heimat: la cultura tedesca contemporanea, 2001; Idea dei tragico e consienza storica, 2003; Il volto e l'allegoria della storia, 2007; Franz Kafka davanti alia legge, 2008. Memberships: Internationales Graduiertes Kolleg. Address: Vicolo Viazzolo 1, I-40124 Bologna, Italy. E-mail: barnaba.maj@jui.it

MAJAGI Suneel Ishwar, b. 28 July 1972, Belagavi, Karnataka, India. Associate Professor. m. Girija, 1 daughter. Education: MBBS; MD; MSc (HPE), in progress. Appointments: Associate Professor, Department of Pharmacology, J N Medical College, Nehrunagar, Belagavi. Publications: Book, Pharmaovigilance & Safety Monitoring, 2007; 13 international indexed journals; 1 national and a 1 regional journal. Honours: Best Branch Award, APPF, Belgaum Branch, 2009-10. Memberships: Indian Pharmacological Society; Association of Physiologists and Pharmacologists of India; J N Medical College Scientific Society. Address: Department of Pharmacology, J N Medical College, Belagavi 590010, Karnataka, India.

MAJERUS Steve, b. 3 May 1975, Luxembourg. Senior Scientist. 2 sons. Education: Master, Psychological Sciences, 1999; Advanced Master, 2001, PhD, 2002, Psychological Sciences, University of Liege. Appointment: Research Professor, FRS-FNRS, University of Liege. Publications: Over 80 international publications; 2 books. Honours: Max Wajskop International Scientific Prize. Memberships: Academy of Aphasia; ESCOP; BAPS. Address: Department of Psychology, University of Liege, Boulevard du Rectorat, B33 4000 Liege, Belgium.

MAJOOR Frank A M, b. 1 April 1949, Tilburg, Netherlands. Diplomat. m. Danielle F Krakauer, 2 daughters. Education: Civil Law, University of Leiden, Netherlands, 1976. Appointments: Joined Ministry of Foreign Affairs, 1976, Third Secretary, Netherlands Embassy, Dar es Salaam, Tanzania, 1977-79; Second Secretary, Netherlands Embassy, Bonn, Germany, 1979-82; Head, Environmental Affairs Division, Economic Co-operation Department, MFA, 1982-85; Assistant to Director General for Political Affairs, 1985-86, First Secretary, 1986-88, Minister Plenipotentiary, 1988-92, Netherlands Mission to the United Nations, New York; Special Advisor, Political Security Matters, Deputy Director, Atlantic Co-operation and Security Affairs Department, 1992-93; Director, Security Policy Department, 1993-97, Ministry of Foreign Affairs; Ambassador; Permanent Representative of the Netherlands, Conference on Disarmament, Geneva, Switzerland, 1997-99; Ambassador at Large, Ministry of Foreign Affairs, 1999-2000; Secretary General, Netherlands Ministry of Foreign Affairs, The Hague, 2000-05; Permanent Representative of the Netherlands, United Nations, New York, 2005-09; Permanent Representative of the Netherlands, North Atlantic Council, 2009-. Address: NATO HQ, Boulevard Leopold III 39, 1110 Brussels, Belgium.

MAJOR Clarence, b. 31 December 1936, Atlanta, Georgia, USA. Poet; Writer; Artist; Professor. m. (1) Joyce Sparrow, 1958, divorced 1964, (2) Pamela Ritter. Education: BS, State University of New York at Albany, 1976; PhD, Union Graduate School, 1978. Appointments: Editor, Coercion Review, 1958-66, Writer-in-Residence, Center for Urban Education, New York, 1967-68, Teachers and Writers Collaborative-Teachers College, Columbia University, 1967-71, Aurora College, Illinois, 1974, Albany State College, Georgia, 1984, Clayton College, Denver, 1986, 1987; Associate Editor, Caw, 1967-70, Journal of Black Poetry, 1967-70; Lecturer, Brooklyn College of the City University of New York, 1968-69, 1973, 1974-75, Cazenovia Collge, New York, 1969, Wisconsin State University, 1969, Queens College of the City University of New York, 1972, 1973, 1975, Sarah Lawrence College, 1972-75, School of Continuing Education, New York University, 1975; Columnist, 1973-76, Contributing Editor, 1976-86, American Poetry Review; Assistant Professor, Howard University, 1974-76, University of Washington, 1976-77; Visiting Assistant Professor, University of Maryland at College Park, 1976, State University of New York at Buffalo, 1976; Associate Professor, 1977-81, Professor, 1981-89, University of Colorado at Boulder; Editor, 1977-78, Associate Editor, 1978-, American Book Review; Professor, 1989-, Director, Creative Writing, 1991-, University of California at Davis. Publications: Poetry: The Fires That Burn in Heaven, 1954; Love Poems of a Black Man, 1965; Human Juices, 1965; Swallow the Lake, 1970; Symptoms and Madness, 1971; Private Line, 1971; The Cotton Club: New Poems, 1972; The Syncopated Cakewalk, 1974; Inside Diameter: The France Poems, 1985; Surfaces and Masks, 1988; Some Observations of a Stranger at Zuni in the Latter Part of the Century, 1989; Parking Lots, 1992; Configurations: New and Selected Poems 1958-1998, 1998; Waiting for Sweet Baby, 2002. Fiction: All-Night Visitors, 1969; new version, 1998; NO, 1973; Reflex and Bone Structure, 1975; Emergency Exit, 1979; My Amputations, 1986; Such Was the Season, 1987; Painted Turtle: Woman with Guitar, 1988; Fun and Games, 1990; Dirty Bird Blues, 1996. Other: Dictionary of Afro-American Slang, 1970; The Dark and Feeling: Black American Writers and Their Work, 1974; Juba to Jive: A Dictionary of African-American Slang, 1994; Necessary Distance: Essays and Criticism, 2001; Come by Here: My Mother's Life, 2002. Editor: Writers Workshop Anthology, 1967; Man is Like a Child: An Anthology of Creative Writing by Students, 1968; The New Black Poetry, 1969; Calling the Wind: Twentieth Century African-American Short Stories, 1993; The Garden Thrives: Twentieth Century African-American Poetry, 1995. Honours: Fulbright-Hays Exchange Award, 1981-83; Western States Book Award, 1986; Pushcart Prize, 1989; National Book Award Bronze Medal Finalist, 1998. Address: c/o Department of English, 1 Shields Avenue, University of California at Davis, Davis, CA 95616, USA.

MAJOR John (Sir), b. 29 March 1943. Politician; Former Member of Parliament. m. Norma Major, 1970, 1 son, 1 daughter. Education: Associate, Institute of Bankers. Appointments: Various executive positions, Stand Chartered Bank, UK and overseas, 1965-80; Served, Lambeth Borough Council, 1968-71, including Housing and Finance Committees, also Chairman, Accounts Committee and Housing Committee, 1969; Contested Camden, St Pancras North, February and October 1974; Member, Board, Warden Housing Association, 1975-93; Member of Parliament for Huntingdonshire, 1979-83, for Huntingdon, 1983-2001; Parliamentary Private Secretary to Ministers of State, Home Office, 1981-83; Assistant Government Whip, 1983-84; Lord Commissioner of Treasury, Senior Government Whip, 1984-85; Parliamentary Under-Secretary of State, Department of Health and Social Security, 1985-86; Minister of State, Social Security and the Disabled, 1986-87; Chief Secretary to the Treasury, 1987-89; Secretary of State for Foreign and Commonwealth Affairs, 1989; Chancellor of the Exchequer, 1989-90; Elected Leader, Conservative Party, 1990; Prime Minister, 1st Lord of the Treasury, Minister for the Civil Service, 1990-97. Publication: The Autobiography, 1999. Honours: Member, Order of the Companions of Honour, 1999; Knight Companion of the Most Noble Order of the Garter, 2005. Memberships: Parliamentary Consultant to Guild of Glass Engravers, 1979-83; President, Eastern Area Young Conservatives, 1983-85; National Asthma Campaign, 1998-; Chair, Carlyle Group, 2001-; Non-Executive Director, Mayflower Corporation, 2000-; Member, Main Committee, MCC, 2001-; Honorary Master of the Bench of the Middle Temple, 1992.. Address: House of Commons, London, SW1A 0AA, England.

MAJOR Malvina (Lorraine) (Dame), b. 28 January 1943, Hamilton, New Zealand. Opera Singer (Soprano). m. Winston William Richard Fleming, 1965, deceased 1990, 1 son, 2 daughters. Education: Grade VIII, Piano, Singing, Theory, Convent at Ngaruawahia, Waikato; Singing continued under Dame Sister Mary Leo, St Mary's Music School, Auckland, 1960-65 and Ruth Packer, Royal College of Music, London, London Opera Centre, UK, 1965-67. Debut: Camden Town Festival, 1968 in Rossini's La Donna del Lago. Career includes: Performances as: Belle, Belle of New York, New Zealand, 1963; Pamina, Magic Flute, London Opera Centre, 1967; 1st non Mormon Soloist to sing with Mormon Tabernacle Choir, 1987; Matilda in Elisabetta Regina d'Inghilterra, Camden Town, 1968; Rosina, Barber of Seville, Salzburg (conductor, Claudio Abbado), 1968-69; Gala

Concert, King and Queen of Belgium, Centenary Antwerp Zoological Society, 1969; Marguerite, Gounod's Faust, Neath and London, 1969; Bruckner's Te Deum, conductor Daniel Barenboim, 1968; Cio Cio San, Madam Butterfly; Widow, The Merry Widow; Gilda in Rigoletto; Tosca; Constanze in Die Entführung; Arminda in La Finta Giardiniera, Brussels, 1986; Donna Elvira, Don Giovanni, Brighton Festival, 1987; Donna Anna in Don Giovanni at Sydney, Australia, 1987; Operas include recent productions of Rosalinda (Die Fledermaus) and Lucia di Lammermoor, Mimi in La Bohème and Constanze in New York and Australia; Sang Arminda at Lausanne, 1989, Constanze with the Lyric Opera of Queensland; Season 1992-93 with Lucia at Adelaide, Arminda at Salzburg, Violetta and Gilda at Wellington; Sang in Eugene Onegin and Don Giovanni with Wellington City Opera, 1997. Recordings: To The Glory of God, 1964; L'amico Fritz, opera (Caterina), 1969; Songs for All Seasons, Mahler Symphony No 4, 1970; Scottish Soldiers Abroad, 1975; Alleluia, 1974; Operatic Arias, conductor John Matheson, 1987; La Finta Giardiniera, Brussels. Contributions to: London Sunday Times (article by Desmond Shawe-Taylor). Honours: New Zealand Mobil Song Quest, 1963; Melbourne Sun Aria, Australia, 1964; Kathleen Ferrier Scholarship, London, 1966; OBE, 1985; DBE, 1991; Honorary D Litt, 1993; Honorary D Waik, 1993. Address: P O Box 4184, New Plymouth, New Zealand.

MAKAM Roshan, b. 12 December 1963, Bangalore, India. Research Scientist. Education: BE, Chemical Engineering, Bangalore University, 1987; MS, Chemical/Biochemical Engineering, 1993, PhD, Environmental Engineering, 2005, Arizona State University, USA. Appointments: Research Fellow, Tribiology, Indian Institute of Science, Bangalore, India, 1987-88; Research/Graduate Assistant, Biotechnology Processing, Tufts University, USA, 1988-89; Research Associate, Process Development, Arizona State University, 1989-92; Process Engineer, Genzyme Corporation, Massachusetts, 1992-97; Application Engineer, ProSoft Systems, Massachusetts, 1997-99; Research Scientist, Environmental Engineering Laboratory, Arizona State University, 1999-2006; Assistant Professor, Engineering Research Laboratory, Chemical Engineering Department, SIT, Tumkur, India, 2007-09; Assistant Professor, Biotechnology Processing Laboratory, Biotechnology Department, PESIT, Bangalore, 2009-. Publications: Numerous articles in professional journals. Honours: National Merit Scholarship, 1988-89; Regents Scholarship, 1989-92; Rashtreeya Gaurav Award, 2011. Memberships: Board of Examiners of Autonomous Courses, Biotechnology Department, MSRIT, 2010. Address: 82 East End 'B' Main Road, Jayanagar 9th Block, Bangalore, Karnataka, 560069, India.

MAKAROV Anatoly Nikolaevich, b. 8 June 1949, Tvyerskaya obl, Russia. m. Natalia Victorovna Ivanova, 1 son. Education: Graduate, Tver State Technical University, Russia, 1978; Postgraduate, Moscow Power Institute, 1979-82; Dr Sci Tech, St Petersburg State Electro-Technical University, Russia, 1995. Appointments: Technical Engineer, 1973-78, Person with Higher Degree, 1979-82, Senior Lecturer, Assistant Senior Educator, 1983-94, Professor, 1995-, Dr Sci Tech, 1996-, St Petersburg State Electro-Technical University, Russia. Publications: 245 scientific works; 5 monographs; 5 text books; 62 articles in main journals of power field. Honours: Patented inventions; Honour Certificate, Administration Tver Area, 1997; Ministry of Education, Russia, 2000; Honorary Worker of Higher Education award, Ministry of Education and Science, Russia, 2007; Grantee for Researches in the Field of Electronic Engineers, Power Metallurgy. Memberships: ACS; AAAS; Academy of Electrotechnician Scientific Russian Federation. Address: RF, Tver, Pashi Savelyevoy Street, 170039, Russia.

MÄKELÄINEN Pentti Keijo, b. 17 June 1944, Hiitola, Finland. Professor. Education: MSc (Tech), 1970, DSc (Tech), 1976, Helsinki University of Technology. Appointments: Research Assistant, 1969-77, Acting Professor, 1978-80, 1987-89, Professor of Steel Structures, 1989-, Helsinki University of Technology; Senior Research Fellow, Academy of Finland, 1980-84; Post-doctoral Researcher, RWTH Aachen, Germany, 1977; Visiting Professor, TNO Delft, The Netherlands, 1986-87; Visiting Professor, EPFL Lausanne, Switzerland, 1992-93; Visiting Professor, Queensland University of Technology, Brisbane, Australia, 2000-01. Publications: 180. Honours: Doctor honoris causa, Tallinn Technical University, 2003. Memberships: European Convention for Construction Steelwork; International Association for Bridge and Structural Engineering; Association for Steel-Concrete Composite Structures. Address: Jukolanahde 6E18, FI-02180 Espoo, Finland.

MAKEPEACE John, b. 6 July 1939, Solihull, Warwickshire, England. Designer; Furniture Maker. Education: Denstone College, Staffordshire, 1952-57; Pupil to Keith Cooper, Furniture Maker, 1957-59; City and Guilds Teaching Certificate (Crafts), 1957-59; Study tours in: Scandinavia, 1957; USA, 1961, 1974; Italy, 1968; West Africa, 1972. Career: Established own furniture-making business Director, John Makepeace Furniture Ltd, 1963-; Founder Member, Crafts Council, 1972-77; Furniture commissioned by corporate and private clients in UK, Europe and USA; Consultancy Tours: India, 1974, 1977; Australia, 1980; Japan, 1978, 1994; Korea, 2001; Trustee, Victoria and Albert Museum, 1987-91; Founder and Director, The Parnham Trust, 1976-2001. Publications: Publisher, Conran Octopus, 1995; Makepeace: A Spirit of Adventure in Craft and Design by Professor Jeremy Myerson; Numerous articles in professional and popular journals. Honours: Observer Design Award, 1972; OBE for services to furniture design, 1988; Master's Award, Worshipful Company of Furniture Makers, 1999; Award of Distinction, The Furniture Society, USA, 2002; Sponsor, Furniture Futures, Victoria and Albert Museum, 2009; Nominated for the Prince Philip Designers Prize, Special Commendation, 2011; Arts Council Touring Exhibition, 2010-11. Memberships: Chartered Society of Designers; Royal Society for the Arts; Member, Contemporary Art Society; Member, Contemporary Applied Arts. Address: Farrs, Whitcombe Road, Beaminster, Dorset DT8 3NB, England.

MAKHZOUMI Fouad, b. 30 August 1952, Beirut, Lebanon. Executive Chairman & CEO. m. May, 2 daughters. Education: MSc, Chemical Engineering, Michigan Technological University, USA, 1975. Appointments: Executive Chairman and CEO of Future Group Holding SA, 1984; President, 1995-97, President, International Desalination Association, Vice Chairman, Institute for Social and Economic Policy in the Middle East, John F Kennedy School of Government, Harvard University, USA, 1995-98; Founder, Makhzoumi Foundation, 1997, Makhzoumi Foundation (USA) Inc, 1998. Memberships: International Board of the Council on Foreign Relations: US/Middle East Project; Board of Arab Reform Initiative; Center for Strategic and International Studies; Board of the International Council for Middle East Studies; Board of the US Middle East Project; International Institute for Strategic Studies; Middle East Board of the S Olayan Business School, American University of Beirut.

DICTIONARY OF INTERNATIONAL BIOGRAPHY 36th EDITION

Address: 10th Floor, Liberty House Tower, Office 1007, Dubai International Financial Centre, PO Box 506835, Dubai. Website: www.futuregroup.com

MAKOWER Peter, b. 12 September 1932, Greenwich, London, England. Architect; Town Planner. m. Katharine Chadburn, 2 sons, 1 daughter. Education: The Royal Engineers, 1951-52; Territorial Army, 1952-56; Master of Arts, Trinity College, University of Cambridge, 1959; Diploma in Architecture, The Polytechnic, London, 1959; Diploma in Town Planning, University of London, 1969. Appointments: Architect, 1959-62, Associate, 1962-82, Frederick Gibberd Partners, London; Executive Architect, Chapman Taylor Partners, 1982-85; Solo Principal, Peter Makower Architects and Planners, 1985-99. Publications: The World is Not Enough – an account of the filming of part of the river chase in the Bond film of that name; The Boater, The Quarterly Magazine of the Thames Vintage Boat Club, 2000. Honours: Conservation and Design Award, London Borough of Richmond upon Thames and the Mortlake with East Sheen Society; Lay Reader, Church of England. Memberships: Associate, 1961-70, Fellow, 1970-, Royal Institute of British Architects; Royal Town Planning Institute, 1972-. Address: 89 Hartington Road, Chiswick, London W4 3TU, England.

MAKRIS Nikolaos, b. 11 July 1964, Athens, Greece. University Professor. m. Maria Louisa, 1 son, 1 daughter. Education: Civil Engineering, National Technical University, Athens, 1988; MSc, 1990, Doctorate, 1992, Civil Engineering, State University of New York at Buffalo. Appointments: Research Assistant, 1988-92, Instructor, summer, 1991, Senior Research Scientist, 1992, State University of New York at Buffalo; Assistant Professor, University of Notre Dame, 1992-96; Assistant Professor, 1996-98, Associate Professor, 1998-2002, Professor, 2002-05, University of California at Berkeley; Professor, University of Patras, 2003-. Publications: More than 85 papers in archival journals; More than 85 papers in conference proceedings; More than 25 technical reports. Honours: Member, Academia Europaea; Walter L Huber Civil Engineering Research Prize, American Society of Civil Engineers; Shah Family Innovation Prize, Earthquake Engineering Research Institute; T K Hsieh Award, Institution of Civil Engineers London, UK; Henry Pusey Award, Program Committee, 67th Shock and Vibration Symposium; NSF Career Award, National Science Foundation; Director of Reconstruction, Temple of Zeus at Nemea, 2004-09. Memberships: Technical Chamber of Greece; American Society of Civil Engineers; Society of Earthquake and Civil Engineering Dynamics; Society of Rheology; Society of Industrial and Applied Mathematics; Earthquake Engineering Research Institute; Metal Structures Research Society of Greece; Greek Society of Earthquake Engineering; Greek Society of Theoretical and Applied Mechanics. Address: Division of Structures, Department of Civil Engineering, University of Patras, Patras GR-26500 Greece. E-mail: nmakris@upatras.gr

MAKSIMOV Maksim, b. 9 June 1964, Odessa, Ukraine. Educator; Scientist. m. Oksana, 3 sons. Education: Nuclear Engineer; Doctor of Philosophy, 1990; Doctor of Science, 2000. Appointments: Engineer, postgraduate student, 1986-90; Researcher, Associate Professor, Odessa National Polytechnic University, 1990-2000; Scientific Director, Professor, Atomspetsavtolmatika R&D Lab, 1998-2011; Head of Heat and Power Engineering Processes Automation Chair, 2010-11. Publications: Model of cladding failure estimation for a cycling nuclear unit, 2009; Method for evaluating the service life of VVER-1000fuel-element cladding in different loading regimes, 2010; Theory of fuel life control methods at Nuclear Power Plants with Water-Water Energetic Reactor, 2012. Address: Odessa National Polytechnic University, Shevchenko av 1, Odessa 65044, Ukraine. E-mail: prof.maksimov@gmail.com

MALAJ Maksim, b. 13 December 1958, Vlora, Albania. Military Professional; Officer. m. Luljeta, 1 son, 1 daughter. Education: Military Academy Skanderbeg Infantry, Tirana, 1978-81; Defense Academy, Tirana, 1990-92; Staff Officer Course, Netherlands, 1999; Armed Control Course, Croatia, 2001; Coure for Disaster Influence in Security Environment, Croatia, 2002; Training Course on Vienna Document 1999, England, 2004; Seminar, General Inspection of USA AF, Germany, 2005; Staff of Joint Operation Forces' Course, Netherlands, 2006. Appointments: Fire-Drill Instruction, Instruction School, Zall-Herr, Tirana, 1981-82; Training Instructor, Military Garrison, Tirana, 1982-87; Instructor, Instructor Branch 8th Infantry Division, Tirana, 1987-88; Battalion Commander, Military Battalion, Tirana, 1988-89; Territorial Battalion Commander, Tirana, 1989-90; Instructor, Operational Branch, 8th Infantry Division, 1992-93; Operational Chief in Military Unit, Tirana, 1993-94; Instructor, Operational Branch in Infantry Division, Tirana, 1994-97; Inspector, General Audition Directory in MOD, 1997-2005; Military Representative, Arm Contro Centre, Croatia, 2001; Chief of Staff, 2005-07, Commander, 2000-08, Rapid Reaction Brigade; Chief, General Staff, Albanian Armed Forces (CHOD), 2008-; Albanian Armed Forces General, 2011-. Publications: Numerous articles in various military journals. Honours: 25 Years Medal of Career; Medal for Distinguished Services; Medal for Distinguished Service in MOD. Address: Ministria e Mbrojtjes, Bulevardi Deshmoret e Kombit, Tirana, Albania. E-mail: maksim.malaj@aaf.mil.al

MALAMATENIOU Flora, b. 27 September 1970, Athens, Greece. Assistant Professor. Education: BS, Statistics, University of Piraeus, Greece, 1992; MA, 1996, PhD, 2002, Health Informatics, University of Athens, Greece. Appointments: R&D Project Manager, Health Informatics Lab, Department of Informatics, University of Piraeus, Greece, 1997-2000; Informatics Consultant, Public Sector, Research & Academic Computer Technology Institute, Greece, 2002-05; Senior Researcher, Informatics & Telematics Institute, Greece, 2005-07; Assistant Professor, Department of Digital Systems, University of Piraeus, Greece, 2008-; Adjunct Lecturer, Department of Digital Systems, University of Piraeus, Greece, 2000-03, 2006-08. Memberships: IEEE. Address: 80 Karaoli & Dimitriou Street, 18534 Piraeus, Greece. E-mail: flora@unipi.gr

MALETA Yulia, b. 31 March 1976. Academic. Education: Office and Administration Q's; Certificate of Advertising and Marketing; Diploma of Business; Diploma of Marketing; Diploma of Advertising; B Arts, Social and Cultural Analysis; B Arts (Honours); PhD, Sociology, in progress. Appointments: McNair Ingenuity Researcher, ACA Research, Social and Market Research, 2001-11; Research Assistant, Social Policy Research Centre, UNSW, 2008; Reviewer, International Journal of Diversity in Organisations, Communities & Nations, 2010; Associate Editor, International Journal of Interdisciplinary Social Sciences, 2010-11; Casual Academic Marker, School of Nursing, 2010-, Casual Academic Marker, School of Social Science, 2011, Guest Lecturer, School of Social Sciences, 2011, University of Western Sydney, 2011; Research Assistant, School of Education, University of Western Sydney; Research Assistant, Commonwealth Scientific & Industrial Research Organisation, 2011-;

Reviewer, Journal of Sociology, 2011. Publications: Playing with Fire: Gender at Work and the Australian Female Cultural Experience within Rural Fire Fighting, 2009; Social Dimensions of Gender and Hegemony within Environmental Organisations and Communities, 2011; International Journal of Diversity in Organisations, Communities and Nations, 2011; The Politics of the Environment: Australian Womens Activism (International Journal of Interdisciplinary Social Science). Honours: Australian Postgraduate Award; Dean's Merit List, University of Western Sydney, 2005 and 2007. Memberships: ANZTSR; EIANZ; ESA; CANA; GKIHS. E-mail: y.maleta@uws.edu.au Website: www.uws.edu.au

MALFITANO Catherine, b. 18 April 1948, New York City, New York, USA. Singer (Soprano). Education: High School of Music and Art; Manhattan School of Music; With violinist father and dancer/actress mother; Voice with Henry Lewis. Debut: Nannetta in Falstaff, Central City Opera, 1972. Career: With Minnesota Opera, 1973, New York City Opera, 1973-79, debut as Mimi/La Bohème; Netherlands Opera: Susanna in Figaro, 1974, Eurydice, 1975, Mimi, 1977; Tosca 1998; Salzburg Festival: Servilia in Tito, 1976, 1977, 1979, 3 Hoffmann roles, 1981, 1982, Salome, 1992, 1993, Elvira in Giovanni, 1994, 1995, 1996; Jenny in Mahagonny, 1998; Met debut as Gretel, 1979, returning for many other roles; Vienna Staatsoper: Violetta, 1982, Manon, 1984, Grete in Schreker's Der Ferne Klang, 1991, Salome and Butterfly, 1993; Wozzeck, 1997; Maggio Musicale Florence: Suor Angelica, 1983, Jenny in Weill's Mahagonny, 1990, Salome, 1994; Teatro Comunale, Florence: Antonia in Hoffmann, 1980-81, Mimi, 1983, Faust, 1985, Butterfly, 1988, Poppea, 1992; Munich: Berg's Lulu, 1985, Mimi, 1986, Daphne, 1988; Covent Garden: Susanna, Zerlina, 1976, Butterfly, 1988, Lina (Stiffelio), Tosca, Tatyana, 1993, Salome, 1995, 1997; Berlin Deutsche Oper: Butterfly, 1987, Amelia in Boccanegra, Mimi, Susanna, 1989, Salome, 1990; Berlin Staatsoper, Marie (Wozzeck), 1994, Leonore (Fidelio), 1995; Geneva: Fiorilla (Turco), 1985, Poppea, Manon, 1989, Leonore, 1994; La Scala: Daphne, 1988, Butterfly, 1990; Wozzeck, 1997; Lyric Opera, Chicago: Susanna, 1975, Violetta, 1985, Lulu, 1987, Barber's Cleopatra, 1991, Butterfly, 1991-92, Liu, 1992; McTeague/Bolcom, 1992; Makropulos Case, 1995-96; 3 Roles/Il Trittico, 1996; Salome, 1996; Butterfly 1997, 1998; Mahagonny, 1998; View from Bridge/Bolcom, 1999; Macbeth, 1999; World premiere roles created: Conrad Susa's Transformations, 1973, Bilby's Doll (Carlisle Floyd), 1976, Thomas Pasatieri's Washington Square, 1976, William Bolcom's McTeague, 1992. Recordings: Rossini Stabat Mater, conductor Muti; Gounod Roméo et Juliette, conductor Plasson; Strauss's Salome, conductor Dohnányi; Music for Voice and Violin with Joseph Malfitano; Tosca - Zubin Mehta; Others; Videos include Tosca with Domingo; Stiffelio with Carreras and Salome. Honours: Emmy, Best Performance in Tosca film; Honorary Doctorate De Paul University, Chicago.

MALHERBE Johannes A G, b. 15 March 1940, Cape Town, South Africa. Retired Vice Principal. m. Margaret, 1 daughter. Education: PhD, 1974; D Eng, 1987. Appointments: Professor, -1988, Dean, Engineering, 1989-99, Executive Director, 2000-01, Vice Principal, 2001-03, Institute Professor, 2003-05, University of Pretoria. Publications: Approximately 70 articles in professional journals. Honours: Havenga Prize for Engineering, 1995; IEEE Third Millennium Medal, 2000. Memberships: Life Fellow, IEEE; Fellow, SA Academy for Engineering; Fellow, SA Institute for Electrical Engineers; SA Academy of Science. Address: 94 Copse Lane, Lynnwood Glen, Pretoria 0081, South Africa. E-mail: jagm@up.ac.za

MALICK Terrence, b. 30 November 1943, Ottawa, Illinois, USA. Film Director. Education: Center for Advanced Film Study; American Film Institute. Appointments: Films: Bedlands; Days of Heaven, 1978; The Thin Red Line, 1998; The Moviegoer; The New World, 2005. Honours: NewYork Film Critics Award, National Society of Film Critics Award, 1978; Cannes Film Festival Award, 1978; Golden Bear Award, 1999; Chicago Film Critics Association Award, 1999; Golden Satellite Award, 1999. Address: c/o DGA, 7920 Sunset Boulevard, Los Angeles, CA 90046, USA.

MALIK Art. b. 13 November, 1952. Actor. m. Gina Rowe, 1980, 2 daughters. Career: TV: The Jewel in the Crown; Chessgame; The Far Pavilions; The Black Tower; Death is Part of the Process; After the War; Shadow of the Cobra; Stolen; Cleopatra; In the Beginning, 2000; The Seventh Scroll, 2001; Holby City, 2003-05; The English Harem, 2005; Mayo, 2006; Dalziel and Pascoe, 2006; The Path to 9/11, 2006; Jackanory Junior, 2007. Films: Richard's Things; A Passage to India; Underworld; Living Daylights; Side Streets; City of Joy, 1992; Wimbledon Poisoner, 1994; True Lies, 1994; A Kid in King Arthur's Court, 1995; Path to Paradise, 1997; Booty Call, 1997; Side Streets, 1998; Tabloid, 2001; Out Done, 2002; Tempo, 2003; Fakers, 2004; Nina's Heavenly Delights, 2007; Dean Spanley, 2008; Franklyn, 2008; Hotel, 2009; The Wolfman, 2010. Theatre: Othello; Cymbeline; Great Expectations.

MALIK Zubeida, Journalist. Appointments: Correspondent, Today programme, Radio 4, Reporter, Newsnight, BBC2; Interviewed key figures including: Kofi Anan, President Musharraf, Tony Blair, Prince Saud Al Faisal, Archbishop Tutu, Hamas Sheikh Yassin. Honours: BT Press Award for Radio News Broadcaster of the Year, 1997; Young Journalist of the Year, Foreign Press Association, 2000; Best Radio News Journalist, EMMA, 2001, 2002; Media Personality of the Year, Asian Women of Achievement Awards, 2002; Winner, Carlton TV Multicultural Achievement Award for Television and Radio, 2003; Voted as one of the Good Housekeeping Role Models, 2004. Publications: Contributions to September 11 2001, Feminist Perceptives. Address: Today Programme, BBC Radio 4, Room G630, Stage 6, Television Centre, Wood Lane, London W12 7RJ, England.

MALINEN Mikko Ilari, b. 23 July 1969, Helsinki, Finland. Researcher. Education: BSc (Tech), 2006, MSc (Tech), 2009, Helsinki University of Technology, Espoo. Appointments: Manager, 1989-2002, Board Member, 1989-2002, Entry-Valmennus Oy, Espoo; Research Assistant, Helsinki University of Technology, 2001; Instructor, 2009, Researcher, 2009-, University of Eastern Finland. Publications: Contributor of chapters to books; Inventor of several inventions in science and engineering. Memberships: IEEE; Society for Industrial and Applied Mathematics; Mensa Finland. Address: Kartanontie 6, 82200 Hammaslahti, Finland. E-mail: mikko.i.malinen@gmail.com Website: http://koti.kapsi.fi/~mmalinen

MALKAWI Bashar Hikmet, b. 20 November 1976, Irbid, Jordan. Professor of Law. m. Sana A Jaradat, 1 daughter. Education: Doctorate of Juridical Science, American University, Washington College of Law, 2005. Appointments: Associate Professor of Law, University of Sharjah. Publications: More than 35 articles. Honours: One year seniority in rank and salary of Assistant Professor, for distinction and excellence in research work and teaching, Hashemite University, Zarqa, Jordan, 2009. Address:

Department of Private Law, College of Law, University of Sharjah, PO Box 27272, Sharjah, United Arab Emirates. E-mail: bmalkawi@gmail.com Website: www.sharjah.ac.ae

MALKOVICH John, b. 9 December 1953, Christopher, Illinois, USA. m. (1) Glenne Headley, 1982, divorced, (2) Nicoletta Peyran, 1989, 2 children. Education: Eastern Illinois and Illinois State University. Appointments: Co-Founder, Steppenwolf Theatre, Chicago, 1976; Theatre appearances include: True West, 1982; Death of a Salesman, 1984; Burn This, 1987; Director, Balm in Gilead, 1984-85; Arms and the Man, Coyote Ugly, 1985; The Caretaker, 1986; Burn This, 1990; A Slip of the Tongue, 1992; Libra, Steppenwolfe, 1994; Film appearances include: Places in the Heart, The Killing Fields, 1984; Eleni, 1985; Making Mr Right, The Glass Menagerie, Empire of the Sun, 1987; Miles from Home, 1988; Dangerous Liaisons, Jane, La Putaine du roi, Queen's Logic, The Sheltering Sky, 1989; The Object of Beauty, 1991; Shadows and Fog, Of Mice and Men, 1992; Jennifer Eight; Alive; In the Line of Fire; Mary Reilly, 1994; The Ogre, 1995; Mulholland Falls, Portrait of a Lady, 1996; Con Air; The Man in the Iron Mask, 1997; Rounders, Tune Regained, 1998; Being John Malkovich, The Libertine, Ladies Room, Joan of Arc, 1999; Shadow of the Vampire, 2000; Je Rentre à la Maison, Hotel, Knockaround Guys, 2001; The Dancer Upstairs, director and producer, 2002; Ripley's Game, Johnny English, Um Filme Falado, 2003; The Libertine, 2004; The Hitchiker's Guide to the Galaxy, Colour Me Kubrick; 2005; Art School Confidential, Klimt, The Call, Eragon, 2006; In Transit, Drunkboat, Gardens of the Night, Beowulf, Disgrace, 2007; The Mutant Chronicles, The Great Buck Howard, Afterwards, 2008. Executive Producer, The Accidental Tourist. Address: c/o Artists Independent Network, 32 Tavistock Street, London, WC2E 7PB, England.

MALLARD John Rowland, b. 14 January 1927, Northampton, England. Professor of Medical Physics and Medical Engineering. m. Fiona Lawrance, 1 son, 1 daughter. Education: BSc honours, Physics, University College, Nottingham, 1947; PhD, Magnetism, 1952, DSc, Medical Physics, 1972, University of Nottingham. Appointments: Assistant Physicist, Radium Institute, Liverpool, 1951-53; Senior then Principal Physicist, 1953-56, Head, Department of Physics, 1956-62, Hammersmith Hospital, London; Reader, Medical Physics, Postgraduate Medical School, University of London, 1962-64; Reader, Biophysics, St Thomas's Hospital Medical School, London, 1964-65; Professor of Medical Physics, Head of Department of Bio-Medical Physics and Bio-Engineering, University of Aberdeen and Grampian Health Board, 1965-92. Publications: Over 240 papers, review articles and lectures in medical and scientific journals. Honours include: OBE, 1992; Royal Society Wellcome Gold Medal, 1984; Royal Society Mullard Gold Medal, 1990; Honorary DSc, University of Hull, 1994; Norman Veall Prize Medal, British Nuclear Medicine Society, 1995; Honorary DSc, University of Nottingham, 1996; Keith of Dunottar Silver Medal, Royal Scottish Society of Arts, 1996; Honorary DSc, University of Aberdeen, 1997; Royal Gold Medal, Royal Society of Edinburgh, 2002; Gold Medal, Royal College of Radiologists, 2004; Medal of European Federation of Organisations of Medical Physics, 2004; Freedom of the City of Aberdeen as a Pioneer of Medical Imaging, 2004. Memberships include: Fellow: Royal Society of Edinburgh; Royal Academy of Engineering; Institution of Electrical Engineers; Institute of Physics; Royal College of Pathologists; Honorary Fellow: Institute of Physics and Engineering in Medicine; British Institute of Radiology; British Nuclear Medicine Society; Founder Fellow, International Society of Magnetic Resonance and Medicine; Founder President, International Union of Physics and Engineering in Medicine. Address: 121 Anderson Drive, Aberdeen, AB15 6BG, Scotland. E-mail: h.parry@biomed.abdn.ac.uk

MALLET Philip Louis Victor, b. 3 February 1926, London, England. Member of HM Diplomatic Service (Retired). m. Mary Moyle Grenfell Borlase, 3 sons. Education: Balliol College, Oxford, England. Appointments: Army, 1944-47; HM Foreign Diplomatic Service, 1949-82; Served in Iraq, Cyprus, Aden, Germany, Tunisia, Sudan and Sweden; British High Commissioner in Guyana and non-resident Ambassador to Suriname, 1978-82. Honour: CMG. Address: Wittersham House, Wittersham, Kent TN30 7ED, England.

MALLON Maurus Edward, b. 10 July 1932, Greenock, Scotland. Teacher. Education: MA, Honours, University of Glasgow, 1956; BEd, University of Manitoba, Winnipeg, 1966. Appointments: Retired after 30 year teaching career. Publications: Basileus, 1971; The Opal, 1973; Pegaso, 1975; Way of the Magus, 1978; Anogia, 1980; Bammer McPhie, 1984; Treasure Mountain, 1986; Postcards to a Certain Michel (essays), 1991; Ex Novo Mundo (short stories), 1992; Poems, Satire, Philosophy Compendium, 1993; A Matter of Conscience (play), 1994. Honours: Gold Records of Excellence, 1994, 1995, Lifetime Achievement Award, 1996, Platinum Records for Exceptional Performance, 1997, 1998, ABI; Gold Medal of Honor, 2000. Memberships: Living Authors' Society; National Writers' Association, USA; PEN, Canada. Address: Box 331, Deep River, Ontario K0J 1P0, Canada.

MALOIY Geoffrey Moriaso, b. 10 August 1939, Nairobi, Kenya. Professor. m. Josephine, 2 sons, 1 daughter. Education: BSc, University of British Columbia, Canada, 1964; PhD, 1968, DSc, 1985, University of Aberdeen; DSc, University of Nairobi, 2012. Appointments: Visiting Scientist, Institute of Animal Physiology, Cambridge, 1971; Professor, Animal Physiology, University of Nairobi, 1975; Dean, Faculty of Veterinary Medicine, 1976-80; Visiting Professor, Zoology, University of Tel Aviv, Israel, 1978; Principal, College of Agricultural & Veterinary Science, 1983-88; Senior Fulbright Fellow, Harvard University, 1975; Visiting Alexander Agassiz Professor of Biology, Harvard University, 1979; Research Associate, Museum of Comparative Zoology, Harvard University, 1990-91; Visiting Professor of Zoology, Duke University, 1990-91. Publications: Over 190 articles in professional journals; 5 books and chapters in books. Honours: Hon DSc, Duke University, NC, USA; American Order of Merit; Elder of the Burning Spear, Kenya. Memberships: Fellow, African Academy of Science; Fellow, Norwegian Academy of Science & Letters; American Chemical Society; American Association for Advancement of Science. Address: Comparative and Integrative Physiology Laboratory, University of Nairobi, PO Box 34206-00100, Nairobi, Kenya.

MALONE Vincent, b. 11 September 1931, Liverpool, England. Bishop. Education: BSc, Liverpool University, 1959; Cert Ed, 1960, Dip Ed, 1962, Cambridge University. Appointments: Chaplain to Notre Dame Training College, Liverpool, 1955-59; Assistant Priest, St Anne's, Liverpool, 1960-61; Assistant Master, Cardinal Allen Grammar School, Liverpool, 1961-71; Chaplain to Liverpool University, 1971-79; Administrator (Dean), Liverpool Metropolitan Cathedral, 1979-89; Auxiliary Bishop of Liverpool, 1989-2006; Vicar General, 2006-. Membership: Fellow, College of Preceptors. Address: 17 West Oakhill Park, Liverpool L13 4BN, England. E-mail: vmalone@onetel.com

MALOUF (George Joseph) David, b. 20 March 1934, Brisbane, Queensland, Australia. Poet; Novelist. Education: BA, University of Queensland, 1954. Appointments: Assistant Lecturer in English, University of Queensland, 1955-57; Supply Teacher, London, 1959-61; Teacher of Latin and English, Holland Park Comprehensive, 1962; Teacher, St Anselm's Grammar School, 1962-68; Senior Tutor and Lecturer in English, University of Sydney, 1968-77. Publications: Poetry: Bicycle and Other Poems, 1970; Neighbours in a Thicket: Poems, 1974; Poems, 1975-1976, 1976; Wild Lemons, 1980; First Things Last, 1981; Selected Poems, 1981; Selected Poems, 1959-1989, 1994. Fiction: Johnno (novel), 1975; An Imaginary Life (novel), 1978; Child's Play (novella), 1981; The Bread of Time to Come (novella), 1981, republished as Fly Away Peter, 1982; Eustace (short story), 1982; The Prowler (short story), 1982; Harland's Half Acre (novel), 1984; Antipodes (short stories), 1985; The Great World (novel), 1990; Remembering Babylon (novel), 1993; The Conversations at Curlow Creek (novel), 1996; Dream Stuff (stories), 2000; Made in Britain, 2003; Every Move You Make, 2006; Typewriter Music, 2007. Play: Blood Relations, 1988. Opera Libretti: Voss, 1986; Mer de Glace; Baa Baa Black Sheep, 1993. Memoir: Twelve Edmondstone Street, 1985. Editor: We Took Their Orders and Are Dead: An Anti-War Anthology, 1971; Gesture of a Hand (anthology), 1975. Contributions to: Four Poets: David Malouf, Don Maynard, Judith Green, Rodney Hall, 1962; Australian; New York Review of Books; Poetry Australia; Southerly; Sydney Morning Herald. Honours: Grace Leven Prize for Poetry, 1974; Gold Medals, Australian Literature Society, 1975, 1982; Australian Council Fellowship, 1978; New South Wales Premier's Award for Fiction, 1979; Victorian Premier's Award for Fiction, 1985; New South Wales Premier's Award for Drama, 1987; Commonwealth Writer's Prize, 1991; Miles Franklin Award, 1991; Prix Femina Etranger, 1991; Inaugural International IMPAC Dublin Literary Award, 1996; Neustadt Laureat, 2000. Address: 53 Myrtle Street, Chippendale, New South Wales 2008, Australia.

MALPAS John Peter Ramsden, b. 14 December 1927, Colombo, Ceylon. Stockbroker. m. Rosamond Margaret Burn, 3 sons. Education: MA (Oxon), P.P.E., New College Oxford. Appointments: Imperial Chemical Industries, 1951-56; Chase, Henderson and Tennant, 1956-58; Deputy Chairman, Quilter Goodison, 1959-87; London Stock Exchange, 1961-88; Non Executive Director, Penny & Giles International, 1988-92; Management Board, 1988-2002, Honorary Treasurer, 1988-98, Royal Hospital for Neuro Disability; Non Executive Director, West Wittering Estate, 1998. Honour: MA (Oxon). Memberships: Itchenor Sailing Club; Ski Club Great Britain. Address: 48 Berwyn Road, Richmond, Surrey TW10 5BS, England. E-mail: peter.malpas@ukgateway.net

MAMET David Alan, b. 30 November 1947, Chicago, USA. Playwright; Director. m. (1) Lindsay Crouse, 1977, divorced, 2 children (2) Rebecca Pidgeon, 1991, 2 children. Education: Goddard College, Plainfield, Vermont. Appointments: Artist in Residence, Goddard College, 1971-73; Artistic Director, St Nicholas Theatre Company, Chicago, 1973-75; Guest Lecturer, University of Chicago, 1975, 1979; New York University, 1981; Associate Artistic Director, Goodman Theatre, Chicago, 1978; Associate Professor of Film, Columbia University, 1988; Director, House of Games, 1986; Things Change, 1987; Homicide, 1991; Play, A Life in the Theatre, 1989. Publications: The Duck Variations, 1971; Sexual Perversity in Chicago, 1973; The Reunion, 1973; Squirrels, 1974; American Buffalo, 1976; A Life in the Theatre, 1976; The Water Engine, 1976; The Woods, 1977; Lone Canoe, 1978; Prairie du Chien, 1978; Lakeboat, 1980; Donny March, 1981; Edmond, 1982; The Disappearance of the Jews, 1983; The Shawl, 1985; Glengarry Glen Ross, 1984; Speed-the-Plow, 1987; Bobby, Guild in Hell, 1989; The Old Neighborhood, 1991; Oleanna, 1992; Ricky Jay and his 52 Assistants, 1994; Death Defying Acts, 1996; Boston Marriage, 1999; Screenplays: The Postman Always Rings Twice, 1979; The Verdict, 1980; The Untouchables, 1986; House of Games, 1986; Things Change, 1987; We're No Angels, 1987; Oh Hell!, 1991; Homicide, 1991; Hoffa, 1991; Glengarry Glen Ross, 1992; The Rising Sun, 1992; Oleanna, 1994; The Edge, 1996; The Spanish Prisoner, 1996; Wag the Dog, 1997; Boston Marriage, 2001; Childrens' books: Mr Warm and Cold, 1985; The Owl, 1987; The Winslow Boy, 1999; Lakeboat, 2000; State and Main, 2000; Hannibal, 2001; Heist, 2001; Spartan, 2004; Edmond, 2005; Redbelt, 2008. Essays: Writing in Restaurants, 1986; Some Freaks, 1989; On Directing Film, 1990; The Hero Pony, 1990; The Cabin, 1992; A Whore's Profession, 1993; The Cryptogram, 1994; The Village (novel), 1994; Passover, 1995; Make-Believe Town: Essays and Remembrances, 1996; Plays, 1996; Plays 2, 1996; The Duck and the Goat, 1996; The Old Religion, 1996; True and False, 1996; The Old Neighbourhood, 1998; Jafsie and John Henry, 2000; State and Maine, (writer, director), 2000. Honours: Outer Critics Circle Award, for contributions to American Theatre, 1978; Honorary DLitt (Dartmouth College), 1996; Pulitzer Prize for Drama, New York Drama Critics Award. Address: c/o Howard Rosenstone, Rosenstone/Wender Agency, 38 East 29th Street, 10th Floor, New York, NY 10016, USA.

MANA Samira Al, b. 25 December 1935, Basra, Iraq. Writer. m. Salah Niazi, 1959, 2 daughters. Education: BA, Honours, University of Baghdad, 1958; Postgraduate Diploma in Librarianship, Ealing Technical College, 1976; Chartered Librarian, British Library Association, 1980. Appointments: Arabic Language and Literature Teacher, Secondary School, Baghdad, 1958-65; Chief Librarian, Iraqi Cultural Centre, London, 1976-81; Assistant Editor, Alightrab Al-Adabi (Literature of the Exiled), 1985-2002. Publications: The Forerunners and the Newcomers (novel), 1972; The Song (short stories), 1976; A London Sequel (novel), 1979; Only a Half (play in two acts), 1979; The Umbilical Cord (novel), 1990; The Oppressers (novel), 1997; The Soul and Other Stories, 1999; Just Look at Me, Look at Me (novel), 2002; Knowing Not What They Want (novel), 2010. Contributions to: Alightrab Al-Adabi; Many short stories in Arabic magazines; Translations in Dutch and English periodicals; Translation into English, The Umbilical Cord, 2005. Address: 46 Tudor Drive, Kingston-Upon-Thames, Surrey KT2 5PZ, England.

MANAF Pengiran DiRaja Mohammed Zaini, b. 24 February 1941, Muar, Johore, Malaysia. Certified Management Consultant; Consulting Engineer & Arbitrator; University Professor. m. Noor Aini Md Zin, 3 children. Education: Maur HS & English College, Johore, Bahru, 1952-59; Cornwall Technical College, Redruth, Cornwall, Chiswick Polytechnic (now London Brunel University), Isleworth Polytechnic (now Middlesex University), City of London College (now London Metropolitan University), London School of Economics and Political Science University, London, UK, 1960-67; MSc (distinction), Transportation Engineering, Pacific Western University, 1978; PhD, Kensington University, Glendale, California, 1979; DBA, Industrial Engineering, Pacific Western University, 1982; DSc, Aero Engineering, Pepperdine University, 1983; LL D, 1983, DSc, Bedford University, 1983; DLitt, 1984, D Phil, Transporation, 1983, Clayton University; Dr in Engineering Sciences, Pacific Western University, 1987;

D Tech, 1988, Litt D, 1994, American Coastline University; D Litt, 1993, DCL, 1994, Summit University of Louisiana; Dr, Faculty, Commonwealth Open University, British Virgin Islands, 1999; Litt D, Colegio de Sto Nino de Jasaan, 1999; Certified Manufacturing Engineer, USA; P Mgr, Canada. Appointments: Administrative Assistant, Borneo Company (London) Ltd, & Inchcape Export Ltd (London), 1963-67; Bank Officer, Chase Manhattan Bank, Kuala Lumpur, 1967-68; Marketing Manager, Sarawak Motor Industries and Sales Manager, Wearne Group of Companies, 1968-75; Director, Sing Kwang Kee Shipping Pte Ltd, Singapore, 1972-75; Director, Far East Baggage & Transport Sdn Bhd, 1973-83; General Manager, Pernas Jardine Aviation, 1975-77; Chairman & Principal Consultant, Manaf & Company, 1977-88; Manaf Sutter Inc, Los Angeles, 1984-88; Visiting Lecturer, Air Transport Studies, Mara Institute of Technology, 1970-73; Associate Professor, 1984-87, Professor, 1988-98, Engineering & Business Management, Pacific Western University, Los Angeles; Associate, Pepperdine University, Malibu, California, 1984-; Professor, Engineering, Clayton University, 1986; Honorary Visiting Fellow, Faculty of Business and Visiting Professor, Transportation Engineering, Department of Civil Engineering, North East London Polytechnic, 1986-96; Professor & Fellow, Faculties of Engineering & Management, American Coastline University, 1988-2002. Publications: Numerous articles in professional journals; Author, Professional Organizations of Malaysia, 1979; The Malaysian Universities, 1981. Honours: Frank Haskell Silver Medal; Diploma, Pi Epsilon Tau, 1981; Honorary Fellow, Institute of Engineers, London, 1982; Distinguished Service Award, US Air Force, 1983; President's Distinguished Award, 1983; Honorary Citizen Award, Ambassador at Large Award, 18 Governors, commissioners and mayors, Philippines; 8 royal titles, various Sultanates; Honorary Admiral Gt State Ala Navy Gov George C Wallace, Governor and Commander-in-Chief state Ala Sec State the Hon Mr D Diegelman, 1983; Diploma of Honor, Phi Kappa Phi, 1984; Knight Commander of Merit, Sovreign Order of St John of Jerusalem, 1986; Honorary Consultant, Imperial College of Science, Technology & Medicine, University of London, 1986-96; Knight Grand Commander, 1987; High Commissioner for Order of St John in Moslem countries (with rank of Brigadier in emergency medical corps), 1987; Baron of Hampstead and Petaling Jaya, 1993; Honorary Member, Louisiana Sheriff, 1996; Phi Delta Kappa, Moslem; Life Member, Oxford University Society; Titled of The Right Honourable Pengiran Raja Dato Mahkota of Mindanao, Professor Dr M Z Manaf, University of Oxford; Many awards and recognition from organisations worldwide; Listed in 29 international biographical dictionaries. Memberships: 98 professional bodies and learned institutions including: American Association of University Professors; F Coll P; FRGS; FRSA; FSA Scot; IEEE; FIEC; F Inst Pet; FMS; FCIM; FICS; MCIT; MCIArb; FIEScot; 18 Academies of Science in the US. Address: Hampstead Lodge, PO Box 1052 J Semangat, 46860 Petaling Jaya, Malaysia.

MANANDRA Wadamany, b. 8 December 1971, Nawalapitiya, Sri Lanka. Associate Professor. m. Inbaverni. Education: BSc, Zoology, St John's College, Tirunelveli, 1995; MSc, Zoology, V O Chidambaram College, Tuticorin, 1997; Post Graduate Diploma in Coastal Aquaculture, Manonmaniam Sundaranar University, Tamil Nadu, 1998. Appointments: Senior Technician, Trisea Shrimp Hatchery, Chettikulam, 1998-99; Junior Research Fellow, Centre for Marine Science and Technology, Manonmaniam Sundaranar University, Rajakkamangalam, 2002-04; Research Consultant & Overseas Representative, Greenlines International, Sri Lanka, 2004-07; Associate Professor, Biotechnology, ARJ College of Engineering and Technology, Mannargudi, 2007-. Publications: Numerous articles in professional journals, research papers and contributions to books. Honours: PhD, Zoology, Open International University for Complimentary Medicine, Colombo, 2004; Review Member, African Journal of Microbial Research, Nairobi. Memberships: European Federation of Biotechnology; Australian and New Zealand Society for Comparative Physiology and Biochemistry; International Carotenoid Society; Environment and Eco-planning Association of India. Address: No 21 Elango Street, Ayyappa Nagar, Trichirappalli, Tamil Nadu – 620 021, India. E-mail: wmanandra@gmail.com

MANDAL Mrinal Kanti, b. 22 September 1978, Birbhum, West Bengal, India. Assistant Professor. m. Sonali, 1 son. Education: BSc (Hons), 1998, MSc, 2000, Physics, PhD, Science (Physics), 2008, Burdwan University. Appointments: Assistant Professor, Department of Physics, National Institute of Technology, Dwigapur, 2003-. Publications: More than 15 research papers in national and international journals; Published and attended more than 10 national and international conferences. Honours: National scholarship in MSc level; CSIR Research Fellowship during PhD degree. Memberships: Life Member, Indian Physical Society; Life Member, Indian Association of Physics Teachers; Life Member, Institute of Electronics and Telecommunication Engineering. Address: Department of Physics, National Institute of Technology, M G Avenue, Dwigapur, 713209, West Bengal, India. E-mail: nitmkm@yahoo.co.in

MANDELA Nelson Rolihlahla, b. 1918, Umtata, Transkei. President (retired); Lawyer. m. (1) Evelyn Mandela, divorced 1957, 4 children, 2 deceased, (2) Winnie Mandela, 1958, divorced 1996, 2 daughters, (3) Graca Machel, 1998. Education: University College, Fort Hare; University of Witwatersrand. Appointments: Legal Practice, Johannesburg, 1952; On trial for treason, 1956-61 (acquitted); Sentenced to 5 years imprisonment, 1962; Tried for further charges, 1963-64, sentenced to life imprisonment; Released, 1990; President, African National Congress, 1991-97; President of South Africa, 1994-99; Chancellor, University of the North, 1992-; Joint President, United World Colleges, 1995-. Publications: No Easy Walk to Freedom, 1965; How Far We Slaves Have Come: South Africa and Cuba in Today's World, co-author, 1991; Nelson Mandela Speaks: Forging a non-racial democratic South Africa, 1993; Long Walk to Freedom, 1994. Honours: Jawaharlal Nehru Award, India, 1979; Simon Bolivar Prize, UNESCO, 1983; Sakharov Prize, 1988; Liberty Medal, USA, 1993; Nobel Peace Prize (Joint Winner), 1993; Mandela-Fulbright Prize, 1993; Honorary Bencher, Lincoln's Inn, 1994; Tun Abdul Razak Award, 1994; Anne Frank Medal, 1994; International Freedom Award, 2000; Honorary QC, 2000; Honorary Freeman of London; Johannesburg Freedom of the City Award, 2004; Numerous honorary doctorates.

MANDELBROT Benoit B, b. 20 November 1924, Warsaw, Poland (French Citizen). Mathematician. Education: Graduated, Ecole Polytechnique, Paris, 1947; MS, California Institute of Technology, 1948; PhD, Sorbonne, Paris, 1952. Appointments: Staff Member, Centre National de la Recherche Scientifique, Paris, 1949-57; Institute of Advance Study, New Jersey, 1953-54; Assistant Professor of Mathematics, University of Geneva, 1955-57; Junior Professor of Applied Mathematics, Lille University; Professor of Mathematical Analysis, Ecole Polytechnique, Paris; Research Staff Member, IBM Thomas J Watson Research Centre, New York, 1958; IBM Fellow, 1974; Abraham Robinson Professor of

Mathematical Science, 1987-99, Sterling Professor, 1999-, Professor Emeritus, 2005-, Yale University, New Haven, Connecticut; Visiting Professor, Harvard University, 1962-64, 1979-80, 1984-87; Devised the term Fractal to describe a curve or surface. Publications: Logique, Langage et Théorie de l'Information, co-author, 1957; Fractals: Form, Chance and Dimension, 1977; Fractal Geometry of Nature, 1982; Fractals and Scaling in Finance: Discontinuity, Concentration, Risk, 1997; Fractales, hasard et finance, 1997; Multifractals and Low-Frequency Noise: Wild Self-Affinity in Physics, 1998; Gaussian Self-Similarity and Fractals, 2000; Nel mondo dei frattali, 2001; Globality, The Earth, Low-frequency Noise and R/S, 2002; Fractals, Graphics and Mathematical Education, with M L Frame, 2002; Fractals in Chaos and Statistical Physics, 2003; The (Mis) Behaviour of Markets: A Fractal View of Risk, Ruin and Reward, 2004; Numerous scientific papers; Editorial Boards, several journals. Honours: Several honorary degrees; Numerous awards and medals including Chevalier, L'Ordre de la Légion d'Honneur, 1989; L F Richardson Medal for Geophysics, 2000; Procter Prize of Sigma Xi, 2002; Japan Prize for Science and Tech, 2002. Address: Mathematics Department, Yale University, New Haven, CT 06520, USA.

MANDELL Gordon Keith, S, b. 6 March 1947, New York City, New York, USA. Aerospace Engineer. Education: BS, Aeronautics, Astronautics, 1969, MS, Aeronautics, Astronautics, 1970, Massachusetts Institute of Technology. Appointments: Staff Member, Fluid Dynamics Research Laboratory, Massachusetts Institute of Technology, 1970-72; Consulting Aerospace Engineer, 1973-76; Federal Aviation Administration Designated Engineering Representative, 1976-82; Federal Aviation Administration Aerospace Engineer, determining compliance of aircraft designs with safety standards, 1982-2007; Independent Researcher, 2007-. Publications: Missile Recovery by Extensible Flexwing, 1966; Numerous articles in Model Rocketry magazine, 1968-72; Co-author, Lenticular Re-entry Vehicle, 1970; Co-author, editor, book, Topics in Advanced Model Rocketry, 1973. Honours: Louis de Florez Award; James Means Memorial Prize; Grumman Scholar, Massachusetts Institute of Technology, 1965-69; National Science Foundation Fellow, Massachusetts Institute of Technology, 1969-70; Admitted to: Tau Beta Pi; Sigma Gamma Tau; Sigma Xi; Listed in International Biographical Dictionaries. Memberships: National Association of Rocketry; National Space Society; Planetary Society; Team SETI. Address: Post Office Box 671388, Chugiak, AK 99567-1388, USA.

MANDL Anita Maria, b. 17 May 1926, Prague, Czechoslovakia. Sculptor. m. Denys Jennings, deceased. Education: BSc honours, Zoology, Birkbeck College, University of London, 1947; Part-time, Birmingham College of Art. Appointments: Research Assistant, London Hospital, 1946-47; Lecturer and Senior Lecturer, Reader in Reproductive Physiology, Department of Anatomy, University of Birmingham, 1948-65; Freelance Sculptor, 1965-. Publications: Numerous scientific papers in professional journals; Exhibitions of artwork in London, across the UK and Channel Islands. Honours: PhD, 1951, DSc, 1960, University of Birmingham; RWA, 1978; FRBS, 1980. Memberships (past and present): Society of Endocrinology; Devon Guild of Craftsmen; Royal West of England Academy; Royal Society of Marine Artists; Royal British Society of Sculptors; National Trust; Campaign for the Protection of Rural England; Zoological Society of London.

MANDRULEANU Constantin, b. 17 March 1952, Craiova, Romania. IT Specialist. m. Nirvana, 3 daughters. Education: Carol 1st High School; Mathematics-Informatics Faculty. Appointments: University Teacher, Automation Faculty; County Councilor; Vice President, Chamber of Commerce and Industry, Israel; Vice President, National Union of the Romanian Employers; President, Oltenia Regional Employers' Association. Publications: Cobol Language, 1985. Honours: 2nd Prize, The Companies' Top, 2002; 2nd Prize, The Companies' Top, 2003; 3rd Prize, The Companies' Top, 2004; 1st Prize, The Companies' Top, 2005. Memberships: Substitute Member of Parliament; Democratic Liberal Party Member, Vice President of Dolj Branch. Address: Parului St, 8A-8C, Craiova, Dolj County, 260346, Romania. E-mail: micro@microcomputer.ro

MANFREDI Roberto, b. 22 June 1964, Bologna, Italy. Professor of Infectious Diseases. Education: MD, 1988; Infectious Disease Specialist, University of Bologna, 1992. Appointments: Researcher, Grantee, 1986-91, Medical Assistant, Infectious Diseases, 1991-93, Associate, 1993-2005, Contract Professor of Infectious Diseases, Postgraduate School of Infectious Diseases, 1996-2005, Associate Professor of Infectious Diseases, 2005-, University of Bologna; Board of Associate Professors of Infectious Diseases, 2003. Publications: Over 2,000 scientific publications in textbooks, congress proceedings and professional journals; 16 monographs. Honours: L Concato Award, University of Bologna, 1988; F Schiassi Award, 1989; G Salvioli Award, University of Bologna, 1991; FESCI Young Investigator Award, 2000; Heracles Award, 2006-08. Memberships: International Society of Infectious Diseases; Italian Society for Infectious and Tropical Diseases; European AIDS Clinical Society; Editorial Board and Reviewer of many scientific journals. Address: Via di Corticella 45, I-40128, Bologna, Italy.

MANGLA Pramod B, b. 5 July 1936, Chhachhrauli, India. University Professor. m. Raj Mangla, 1 son, 1 daughter. Education: MA, History (Pb); MLibSC, Delhi; MSLS, Columbia, New York; DLSc, MI Inf Sc, London; FILA. Appointments: Professor and Head, Department of Library & Information Science, 1967-69, 1972-79, 1985-88 and 1994-96; Dean, Faculty of Arts, University of Delhi, 1976-78, 1984-88; Professor and Head/Visiting Professor, Department of Library Science, Tabriz University, Iran, 1970-72, 1974-75; UNESCO Expert, Guyana, West Indies, 1978-79; Associated with numerous organisations including Government of India, State governments, universities and other academic institutions in India and abroad, 1970-; Visited around 45 countries on professional assignments. Publications: Author of numerous research articles, books, and technical reports, etc. Honours: Rockefeller Foundation Grant for Higher Studies, 1961; Travel/exchange fellowship grants from organisations such as: UGC (India) National Lecturer, 1984-86; British Council, IDRC and UNESCO; Honorary Fellowship, ILA, 1983; Shiromani Award for Human Excellence, 1990; IFLA Gold Medal, 1991; 2-volume Festschrift, India, 1997; Certificate of Honour, IASLIC, 2006; Indian Library Association Life Time Achievement Award, 2009; Tagore National Fellowship, 2010. Memberships: President, 1981-84, Indian Library Association; IASLIC; Executive Board, 1985-91, Vice President, 1987-91, IFLA; Board of Management, National Library of india, Kolkata, 2003-; Working Group, National Knowledge Commission, Government of India, 2006-; Member, Delhi Library Board, Government of India, Ministry of Culture. Address: EB-210 Maya Enclave, New Delhi –110064, India. E-mail: manglapb@rediffmail.com

MANILOW Barry (Pinkus), b. 17 June 1943, Brooklyn, New York, USA. Singer; Musician (piano); Songwriter. Education: Advertising, New York City College; Musical Education: NY College Of Music; Juilliard School Of Music. Career: Film Editor, CBS-TV; Writer, numerous radio and television commercials; Member, cabaret duo Jeanne and Barry, 1970-72; MD, arranger, producer for Bette Midler; Solo entertainer, 1974-; Numerous world-wide tours; Major concerts include: Gala charity concert for Prince and Princess of Wales, Royal Albert Hall, 1983; Arista Records 15th Anniversary concert, Radio City Music Hall, 1990; Royal Variety performance, London, 1992; Television film Copacabana, 1985; Numerous television specials and television appearances; Broadway show, Barry Manilow At The Gershwin, 1989; West End musical, Copacabana, 1994. Recordings: Albums include: Barry Manilow, 1973; Barry Manilow II, 1975; Tryin' To Get The Feelin', 1976; This One's For You, 1977; Barry Manilow Live (Number 1, US), 1977; Even Now, 1978; Manilow Magic, 1979; Greatest Hits, 1979; One Voice, 1979; Barry, 1981; If I Should Love Again, 1981; Barry Live In Britain, 1982; I Wanna Do It With You, 1982; Here Comes The Night, 1983; A Touch More Magic, 1983; Greatest Hits Volume II, 1984; 2.00 AM Paradise Café, 1984; Barry Manilow, Grandes Exitos En Espanol, 1986; Swing Street, 1988; Songs To Make The Whole World Sing, 1989; Live On Broadway, 1990; The Songs 1975-1990, 1990; Because It's Christmas, 1990; Showstoppers, 1991; The Complete Collection And Then Some, 1992; Hidden Treasures, 1993; The Platinum Collection, 1993; Singin' with the Big Bands, 1994; Another Life, 1995; Summer of '78, 1996; Manilow Sings Sinatra, 1998; Here at the Mayflower, 2001; A Christmas Gift of Love, 2002; Two Nights Live, 2004; The Greatest Songs of the Seventies, 2007. Scores: Songs from Copacabana and Harmony, 2004; Hit singles include: Mandy (Number 1, US), 1975; Could It Be Magic, 1975; I Write The Songs (Number 1, US), 1976; Tryin' To Get The Feelin', 1976; Weekend In New England, 1977; Looks Like We Made It (Number 1, US), 1977; Can't Smile Without You, 1978; Copacabana (At The Copa), from film Foul Play, 1978; Somewhere In The Night, 1979; Ships, 1979; I Made It Through The Rain, 1981; Let's Hang On, 1981; Bermuda Triangle, 1981; I Wanna Do It With You, 1982. Honours: Grammy Awards: Song Of The Year, I Write The Songs, 1977; Best Male Pop Vocal Performance, Copacabana (At The Copa), 1979; Emmy Award, The Barry Manilow Special, 1977; American Music Awards, Favourite Male Artist, 1978-80; Star on Hollywood Walk Of Fame, 1980; Tony Award, Barry Manilow On Broadway show, 1976; Academy Award Nomination, Ready To Take A Chance Again, 1978; Hitmaker Award, Songwriters Hall Of Fame, 1991; Named, Humanitarian of the Year, Starlight Foundation, 1991; Society of Singers Ella Award, 2003; Platinum and Gold records. Address: Arista Records, 6 W 57th Street, NY 10019, USA.

MANIRUZZAMAN A F M, Professor; Research Director. Education: LLB (Hons), 1977 (first class first), LLM, 1978 (first class first), University of Dhaka; M Int'l Law (Distinction), The Australian National University, 1984; PhD, International Law, University of Cambridge, 1993. Appointments: Professor, International and Business Law, 2004-, Director of Research, 2004-, Director, Postgraduate Research Degrees in Law, 2004-, School of Law, University of Portsmouth; Honorary Professorial Fellow, Centre for Energy, Petroleum, Mineral Law and Policy, University of Dundee, 2005-. Publications: Numerous books and articles in professional and academic journals. Honours: Visiting Fellow, Lauterpacht Centre for International Law, University of Cambridge, 1998; Visiting Scholar, St John's College, University of Oxford, 1999; many other honours and awards. Memberships: Fellow, Royal Geographical Society; Fellow, Society for Advanced Legal Studies, London; Fellow, Royal Society of Arts, London; many other prestigious organisations. Address: School of Law, University of Portsmouth, Richmond Building, Portland Street, Portsmouth, PO1 3DE, England. E-mail: munir.maniruzzaman@port.ac.uk

MANN (Colin) Nicholas Jocelyn, b. 24 October 1942, Salisbury, Wiltshire, England. Emeritus Professor. m. (1) Joëlle Bourcart, 1 son, 1 daughter, divorced, (2) Helen Stevenson, 2 daughters. Education: BA 1st class, Modern and Medieval Languages, 1964, MA, PhD, 1968, King's College, Cambridge. Appointments: Research Fellow, Clare College, Cambridge, 1965-67; Lecturer in French, University of Warwick, 1967-72; Visiting Fellow, All Souls College, Oxford, 1972; Fellow and Tutor in Modern Languages, 1973-90, Dean of Graduates, 1976-80, Senior Tutor, 1982-86, Emeritus Fellow, 1991-2007, Honorary Fellow, 2007, Pembroke College, Oxford; Member of Council, Museum of Modern Art, 1984-92; Director of the Warburg Institute and Professor of the History of the Classical Tradition, 1990-2001, Senior Research Fellow of the Warburg Institute, 2002-08, University of London; Member of Council of Contemporary Applied Arts, 1994-2006; Distinguished Visiting Scholar, Center for Reformation and Renaissance Studies, Victoria University, Toronto, Canada, 1996; Professeur au Collège de France, 1998; Visiting Professor, University of Calabria, Cosenza, 1999-2000; Fellow, 1992-; Foreign Secretary and Vice President of the British Academy, 1999-2006; Dean of the School of Advanced Study and Professor of Renaissance Studies, 2002-07, Pro-Vice Chancellor, 2003-07, Emeritus Professor, 2007-, University of London; Vice President, ALLEA (Federation of European Academies), 2007-. Publications: Books and articles on Petrarch and other topics in professional journals. Honours: CBE, 1999; Hon DLitt, University of Warwick, 2006; Member of many advisory and editorial boards. Address: Rue du Tourneur, 46160 Cajarc, France. E-mail: nicholas.mann@free.fr

MANN Jessica, b. England. Writer. Publications: A Charitable End, 1971; Mrs Knox's Profession, 1972; The Only Security, 1973; The Sticking Place, 1974; Captive Audience, 1975; The Eighth Deadly Sin, 1976; The Sting of Death, 1978; Funeral Sites, 1981; Deadlier Than the Male, 1981; No Man's Island, 1983; Grave Goods, 1984; A Kind of Healthy Grave, 1986; Death Beyond the Nile, 1988; Faith, Hope and Homicide, 1991; Telling Only Lies, 1992; A Private Inquiry, 1996; Hanging Fire, 1997; The Survivor's Revenge, 1998; Under a Dark Sun, 2000; The Voice From the Grave, 2002; Out of Harm's Way (non-fiction), 2005; The Mystery Writer, 2006; Godrevy Light, 2009. Contributions to: Daily Telegraph; Sunday Telegraph; Various magazines and journals. Memberships: Detection Club; Society of Authors: PEN; Crime Writers Association. Address: Lambessow, St Clement, Cornwall, England.

MANN Michael K, b. 5 February 1943, Chicago, USA. Producer; Director; Writer. m. Summer Mann, 1974, 4 children. Education: University of Wisconsin; London Film School. Appointments: Executive Producer, (TV) Miami Vice, Crime Story, Drug Wars: Camarena Story, Drug Wars: Cocaine Cartel, Police Story, Starsky & Hutch. Creative Works: Films directed include: The Jericho Mile, 1981; The Keep, 1983; Manhunter, 1986; Last of the Mohicans, 1992; Heat, 1995; The Insider, 1999; Ali, 2001; Collateral, 2004; The Aviator, 2005; Miami Vice, 2006; The Kingdom, 2007; Nobody Loves Alice, 2008; Hancock, 2008; Public Enemies,

2009. Honours include: 2 Emmy Awards; Best Director, National Board of Review, 2004; BAFTA Awards, Best Film, 2005. Memberships: Writers Guild; Directors Guild. Address: c/o Creative Artists Agency, 9830 Wilshire Boulevard, Beverly Hills, CA 90212, USA.

MANNEPALLI Venkata Aditya Nag, b. 27 June 1988, Nellore, India. Academic. Education: B Tech, Mechanical Engineering; M Tech in progress; PGDip, Patent Law, in progress. Appointments: Assistant Professor, Gokaraju RangaRaju Institute of Engineering & Technology, Hyderabad, 2009-. Publications: Numerous articles in professional journals. Honours: South India Regional Finalist, International Climate Champions, 2009; British Council, Chennai, 2009; Reviewer Board, International Conference of Mechanical Engineering & International Conference of Manufacturing Engineering and Engineering Management, International Association of Engineers, 2011; Editorial Board, Technical and Non-Technical Journal; Reviewer, Journal of Mechanical Science and Technology; Best Paper Award, ICSCI 2009; Organiser, ICSCI 2008 & ICSCI 2009. Memberships: International Society of Condensed Matter and Nuclear Sciences; AMIMechE, AMINANO, MIAEngg; MIACSIT; Indian Red Cross Society. Address: H No 2-2-647/22, Central Excise Colony, Bagh Amberpet, Andhra Pradesh 500013, India. E-mail: nagaditya88@yahoo.com

MANNING Jane Marian, b. 20 September 1938, Norwich, Norfolk, England. Singer (Soprano); Lecturer. m. Anthony Payne. Education: Royal Academy of Music, London; Scuola di Canto, Cureglia, Switzerland. Career: Freelance solo singer specialising in contemporary music; More than 350 world premiers including operas; Regular appearances in London, Europe, USA, Australia, with leading orchestras, conductors, ensembles and at major festivals; Lectures and master classes at major universities in USA including Harvard, Princeton, Cornell, Stanford; UK universities and leading conservatories in Europe and Australia; Visiting Professor, Mills College, Oakland, USA, 1981, 1984, 1986; Artistic Director, Jane's Minstrels, 1988-; Artist-in-Residence, universities in USA, Canada, Australia and New Zealand; Currently AHRC Creative Arts Research Fellow, Kingston University, UK, 2004-07; Visiting Professor, Royal College of Music, London; Honorary Professor, Keele University, 1996-2002; Many CDs, radio broadcasts worldwide. Publications: Books, New Vocal Repertory – An Introduction; New Vocal Repertory 2; Chapter on the vocal cycles in A Messiaen Companion; Numerous articles and reviews in newspapers and professional journals. Honours: Special Award, Composers Guild of Great Britain; FRAM, 1980; Honorary Doctorate, University of York, 1988, OBE, 1990; FRCM, 1998; Hon Doctorate, University of Keele, 2004. Memberships: Vice-President, Society for the Promotion of New Music; Chairman, Nettlefold Trust (Colourscape Festival); Executive Committee, Musicians Benevolent Fund; Royal Philharmonic Society; Incorporated Society of Musicians. Address: 2 Wilton Square, London N1 3DL, England. E-mail: janetone@gmail.com

MANNING Peter, b. 11 June 1947, Bethnal Green, London, England. Fire Officer (retired). m. Christine A Pynn, 1 son. Education: Territorial Army, 1965-69; Kent Fire Brigade Training Centre, 1969; Fire Service College, Moreton in Marsh, 1996. Appointments: Postman, General Post Office, South London, 1965-66; Kent Fire Brigade (Kent Fire & Rescue Service), 1969-2000; Industrial Fire Safety Officer, Henry Schein UK Holdings Ltd, Gillingham, Kent, 2000-08. Publications: Numerous articles in genealogical research journals. Honours: RSA (English), Senior Woodwork Award, and Knight Prize, Bush Elms School; Member, 1981, Fellow, 1987, Chairman, 2001-10, General Secretary, 2010-, Irish Genealogical Research Society; Long Service & Good Conduct Medal, Kent Fire Brigade. Memberships: East of London Family History Society; Irish Genealogical Research Society. Address: 18 Stratford Avenue, Rainham, Gillingham, Kent ME8 0EP, England. E-mail: peter@manningpeter.demon.co.uk

MANOCHA Anshu, b. 10 October 1971, India. Pharmacologist. Education: B Pharm, 1993, M Pharm, 1995, Faculty of Pharmacy, Jamia Hamdard (Hamdard University), India; PhD, Pharmacology, University College of Medical Sciences and Guru Teg Bahadur Hospital, Delhi University, India, 2000. Appointments: Junior Research Fellow, Department of Pharmacology, Faculty of Pharmacy, Jamia Hamdard, India, 1993-95; Senior Research Fellow, Department of Pharmacology, University College of Medical Sciences and Guru Teg Bahadur Hospital, Shahdara, India, 1996-2000; Lecturer, 2000-04, Senior Lecturer, 2004-, Department of Pharmacology, Faculty of Pharmacy, Jamia Hamdard, New Delhi, India. Publications: 14 published articles in national and international journals; 8 published abstracts. Honours include: University Gold Medal for B Pharm and M Pharm, Jamia Hamdard; National Merit Scholarship, 1987; Hakim Abdul Majeed Scholarship, 1992-93; Junior Research Fellowship, Indian Institute of Technology, 1993-95; Senior Research Fellowship, Council of Scientific and Industrial Research 1996-2000; Servier Young Investigators' Award, Institutet de Recherches Internationales Servier, France, 1999. Memberships: Life Member, Indian Pharmaceutical Association; Life Member, Indian Pharmacological Society; Listed in international biographical dictionaries. Address: Department of Pharmacology, Faculty of Pharmacy, Jamia Hamdard, New Delhi 110062, India. E-mail: anshumanocha@hotmail.com

MANSEL Robert Edward, b. 1 February 1948, Carmarthen, Wales. Surgeon. m. Elizabeth Skone, 2 sons, 4 daughters. Education: Llandovery College, 1959-66; Charing Cross Medical School, 1966-71. Appointments: Professor of Surgery, University of Manchester, 1989-92; Professor of Surgery, 1992-, Head, Department of Surgery, Gynaecology and Obstetrics, Anaesthetics, Pain Medicine and Intensive Care, 2008-, University of Cardiff. Publications: Over 200 papers in refereed medical journals; Senior Editor, Benign Diseases of the Breast, 2009. Honours: CBE, 2006. Memberships: British Breast Group; Welsh Surgical Society; British Association of Surgical Oncology; Lead Cancer Clinician, Wales. Address: The University Department of Surgery, Cardiff University, Heath Park, Cardiff CF14 4XN, Wales; American Society of Oncology. E-mail: manselre@cf.ac.uk

MANSELL Nigel, b. 8 August 1953, Upton-on-Severn, England. Racing Driver. m. Rosanne Perry, 2 sons, 1 daughter. Appointments: Began in Kart-racing, then Formula Ford, Formula 2, 1978-79, first Grand Prix, Austria, 1980; Winner, South African Grand Prix, 1992; Member, Lotus Grand Prix Team, 1980-84, Williams Team, 1985-88, 1991-92, Ferrari Team, 1989-90, Newman-Haas IndyCar Team, 1992-95, McLaren Team, 1995; Winner of 31 Grand Prix; Surpassed Jackie Stewart's British Record of 27 wins; World Champion, 1992; PPG IndyCar World Series Champion, 1993; Editor-in-Chief, Formula One Magazine, 2001. Publications: Mansell and Williams (with Derick Allsop), 1992; Nigel Mansell's IndyCar Racing (with Jeremy Shaw), 1993; My Autobiography (with James Allen), 1995. Honours include: Honorary DEng, Birmingham, 1993; OBE, 1990; BBC

Sports Personality of the Year, 1986, 1992; Special Constable for 12 years; Awarded Honorary Fellowship of Centre for Management of Industrial Reliability, Cost and Effectiveness (MIRCE), 1997; Awarded Grand Fellowship of the MIRCE Akademy, 2000; Appointed President, UK Youth Charity, 2002; President, Institute of Advanced Motorists. Address: c/o Nicki Dance, Woodbury Park Golf & Country Club, Woodbury Castle, Woodbury, Exeter, Devon EX5 1JJ, England.

MANSER Martin Hugh, b. 11 January 1952, Bromley, England. Reference Book Editor; Language Trainer; Consultant. m. Yusandra Tun, 1979, 1 son, 1 daughter. Education: BA, Honours, University of York, 1974; MPhil, C.N.A.A., 1977. Publications: Concise Book of Bible Quotations, 1982; A Dictionary of Everyday Idioms, 1983, 2nd edition, 1997; Listening to God, Pocket Thesaurus of English Words, Children's Dictionary, 1984; Macmillan Student's Dictionary, 1985, 2nd edition, 1996; Penguin Wordmaster Dictionary, 1987; Guinness Book of Words, Dictionary of Eponyms, Visual Dictionary, Bloomsbury Good Word Guide, Printing and Publishing Terms, Marketing Terms, Guinness Book of Words, 1988, 2nd edition, 1991; Bible Promises: Outlines for Christian Living, 1989; Oxford Learner's Pocket Dictionary, 2nd edition, 1991; Get To the Roots: A Dictionary of Words and Phrase Origins, The Lion Book of Bible Quotations, Oxford Learner's Pocket Dictionary with Illustrations, 1992; Guide to Better English, Chambers Compact Thesaurus, Bloomsbury Key to English Usage, 1994; Collins Gem Daily Guidance, 1995; NIV Thematic Study Bible, 1996; Chambers English Thesaurus, Dictionary of Bible Themes, NIV Shorter Concordance, 1997; Guide to English Grammar, Crash Course in Christian Teaching, Dictionary of the Bible, Christian Prayer (large print), 1998; Bible Stories, Editor: Millennium Quiz Book, I Never Knew That Was in the Bible, Pub Quiz Book, Trivia Quiz Book, Children's Dictionary, Compiler, Lion Bible Quotation Collection, Common Worship Lectionary, 1999; The Eagle Handbook of Bible Promises, 2000; The Westminster Collection of Christian Quotation, Wordsworth Crossword Companion, Biblical Quotations: A Reference Guide, NIV Comprehensive Concordance, 365 Inspirational Quotations, Writer's Manual, The Facts On File Dictionary of Proverbs, 2001; Dictionary of Foreign Words and Phrases, 2002; Getting to Grips with Grammar, A Treasury of Psalms, Dictionary of Classical and Biblical Allusions, The Joy of Christmas, 2003; Editor, Synonyms and Antonyms, Editor, The Chambers Thesaurus, Compiler, Best Loved Hymns, Poems and Readings, Editor, The Really Useful Concise English Dictionary, Editor, Dictionary of Saints, 2004; Editor, World's Best Mother, A Treasury of Quotations, 2005; Editor, Wordsworth Thesaurus, Editor, Wordsworth Dictionary of Proverbs, Editor Pocket Writer's Handbook, Editor, Collins Dictionary for Writers and Editors, Editor, Thematic Dictionary 1, Thematic Dictionary 2, 2006; Editor, Facts on File Dictionary of Proverbs 2nd edition, Editor, Good Word Guide, 6th Edition, 2007; Compiler, Wordworth Book of Hymns, 2006; Co-author, Facts on File Guide to Style, 2006. Address: 102 Northern Road, Aylesbury, Bucks HP19 9QY, England.

MANSFIELD Eric Arthur, b. 14 April 1932, Southend, Essex, England. RAF Officer; Consulting Engineer. m. Marion Byrne, 1 son, 1 daughter. Education: RAF Apprenticeship, 1949-52; MA, St John's College, Cambridge, England, 1953-56; RAF Flying and Training to Wings Standard, 1957-58; MSc, Southampton University, 1962-63; RAF Staff College, 1968-69. Appointments: Tours with RAF Chief Scientist, Exchange with USAF, 1963-68; Nimrod Aircraft Engineering Authority and OC Engineering Wing, RAF Cottesmore, 1969-74; Chief Electrical Engineer, HQ RAF Germany, 1974-78; Staff, HQ 18 Group, 1978-82; Staff, Ministry of Defence, 1983-86; Staff, NATO HQ AFSOUTH, 1986-88; Staff, RAF Support Command, 1986-89; Association of Consulting Engineers, 1989-94; Independent Consultant, 1994-95; Retired, 1995. Memberships: Royal Aeronautical Society; Chartered Engineer. Address: 33 Chalgrove End, Stoke Mandeville, Bucks HP22 5UH. E-mail: ericandmarion@eamansfield.freeserve.co.uk

MANSFIELD Michael, b. 12 October 1941, London, England. Barrister. m. (1) Melian, 1967, divorced 1992, 3 sons, 2 daughters, (2) Yvette, 1992, 1 son. Education: Keele University. Appointments: Began Practising, 1967; Founder, Tooks Court Chambers, 1984; Speciality, Civil Liberties Work; Professor of Law, Westminster University, 1996. Creative Works: Films for BBC TV: Inside Story, 1991; Presumed Guilty. Publication: Presumed Guilty. Honours: Honorary Fellow, Kent University; Several Honorary Degrees. Membership: Patron Acre Lane Neighbourhood Chambers, Brixton, 1997-. Address: Tooks Court Chambers, 14 Tooks Court, Cursitor Street, London EC4Y 1JY, England.

MANTHE Cora, b. 10 October 1928, Alton, Iowa, USA. President & Treasurer, "C" Manthe Realty Ltd. m. Carl Manthe (deceased), 2 sons. Education: BA, Economics, University of Iowa, 1950; Postgraduate studies, University of Wisconsin, Madison & Oshkosh, 1972-75; Graduate Realtors Institute, 1983. Appointments: Research Analyst, Department of Defense, Washington DC; Social Work Investigator, Dane County Welfare Department, Madison; Civic Hostess Welcome Wagon, International Beaver Dam, Wisconsin; Real Estate Broker, "C" Manthe Realty Ltd, Property Manager, President & Treasurer, Investor, 1979-. Honours: Salutatorian, Alton Public High School, 1946; One of 470 people invited to the Hour of Power, Crystal Cathedral, Garden Grove, California, 2005 to help the church plan for their next 50 years; Listed in international biographical dictionaries. Memberships: Graduate of the Realtors Institute, 1983; Elder and Deacon, Grace Presbyterian Church; Life Member, American Association of University Women; Life Member, Optimists International, Alumnus Life Member, University of Iowa; International Platform Association. Address: 404 De Clark Street, Beaver Dam, WI 53916-1714, USA.

MANTHIRAM Arumugam, b. 15 March 1951, Amarapuram, India. Teacher; Researcher. m. Rajeswari, 1 son, 1 daughter. Education: BS, 1974; MS, 1976; PhD, 1980. Appointments: Lecturer, Madurai Kamaraj University, 1981-85; Postdoctoral Fellow, University of Oxford, 1985-86; Postdoctoral Researcher, University of Texas, Austin, 1986-91, Assistant Professor, 1991-96, Associate Professor, 1996-2000, Professor, 2000-; Director, Texas Materials Institute, 2011-. Publications: 420 research papers. Honours: Faculty Excellence Award, 1994; Faculty Leadership Award, 1996; Charlotte Maer Patton Centennial Fellowship in Engineering, 1998; Ashley H Priddy Centennial Professorship in Engineering, 2002; Fellow, American Ceramic Society, 2004; Fellow, World Academy of Materials and Manufacturing Engineering, 2006; BFGoodrich Endowed Professorship in Engineering, 2006; Jack S Josey Professorship in Energy Studies, 2008; Joe C Walter Chair in Engineering, 2009; Outstanding Teaching Award, 2011; Fellow, Electrochemical Society, 2011. Memberships: American Ceramic Society; American Chemical Society; Materials Research Society; Electrochemical Society; National Institute of Ceramic Engineers; American Association for the

Advancement of Science. Address: Department of Mechanical Engineering, 1 University Station C2200, University of Texas, Austin, TX 78712, USA.

MANTLE Anthony Dod, b. 14 April 1955, Witney, Oxfordshire, England. Director of Photography. m. Susanne, 1 son. Education: BA (Hons), Visual Communication, London College of Printing, 1984; Cinematography, National Film School of Denmark, 1989. Appointments: Director of Photography: Julien Donkey Boy, 1999; 28 Days Later, 2002; Dogville, 2003; Millions, 2004; Dear Wendy, 2005; The Last King of Scotland, 2006; Slumdog Millionaire, 2008; Antichrist, 2009. Publications: Diverse articles in professional journals. Honours: European Cinematographer of the Year, 2004; Evening Standard Award, 2007; Golden Frog/Camera Image, 2008, 2009; Oscar, 2009; ASL Award, 2009; BAFTA (twice), 2009; 4 Danish Academy Awards; New York Critics Award, 2009. Memberships: BSC, Great Britain; DFF, Denmark; ACS, Australia; American Academy; European Academy; Danish Academy.

MANVILLE Stewart Roebling, b. 15 January 1927, White Plains, New York, USA. Archivist; Curator. m. Ella Viola Brandelius-Ström Grainger, 17 January 1972. Education: Hunter College Opera Workshop, 1950-52; Akademie für Musik und Darstellende Kunst, Vienna, 1952-53; BS, Columbia University, 1962. Appointments: Assistant Stage Director, European Opera Houses, 1952-57; Editor, 1959-63; Archivist of Percy Grainger's music, curator of the Percy Grainger Home and Studio in White Plains New York, 1963-. Publications: Manville-Manvel Genealogy, 1948-; Seeing Opera in Italy, 1955; Seeing Opera in Central Europe, 1956. Memberships include: Soc des Antiquaires de Picardie; National Trust for Historic Preservation; Westchester County Historical Society; St Nicholas Society of New York. Address: 46 Ogden Ave, White Plains, NY 10605-2323, USA.

MANZONI Giacomo, b. 26 September 1932, Milan, Italy. Composer; Teacher. m. Eugenia Tretti, 1960, 1 son. Education: Liceo Musica Laudamo, Messina and Conservatorio Verdi, Milan (Composition); Foreign Languages, Università Bocconi, Milan; Piano Diploma, Milan; -. Career: Teacher of Composition, Conservatorio Verdi, Milan, 1962-64, 1968-69, 1974-91, Conservatorio Martini, Bologna, 1965-68, 1969-74, Masterclass, Composition, Scuola di Musica, Fiesole, 1988-, and Accademia Pescarese, 1992-97; Composer, international festivals, Amsterdam, Berlin, Osaka, Prague, Warsaw, Venice, Vienna, Salzburg; Master courses for composition held in San Marino, Santiago, Paris, Granada, Osaka, Buenos Aires, Vancouver, Tokyo, Beijing, etc. Compositions: Operas: La Sentenza (Bergamo), 1960; Atomtod (Piccola Scala, Milan), 1965; Per Massimiliano Robespierre (Bologna), 1975; Doktor Faustus, by Thomas Mann (La Scala, Milan), 1989; Orchestral includes: "Insiemi", 1967; Masse: omaggio a E Varèse, piano, orchestra, 1977; Modulor, 1979; Ode, 1982; Scene Sinfoniche per il Dr Faustus, 1984; Dedica, texts by B Maderna, bass, flute, orchestra, choir ad lib, 1985; Chorus, orchestra: 5 Vicariote, 1958; Ombre, to memory of Che Guevara, 1968; Parole da Beckett, 1971; Hölderlin (frammento), 1972; Il deserto cresce (Nietzsche), 1992; Trame D'Ombre for tenor, soprano, choir, and ensemble, 1998; KOKIN b, for 2 voices and orchestra, 2009; Chamber includes: Musica notturna, 7 instruments, 1966; Quadruplum, 4 brass instruments, 1968; Spiel, 11 strings, 1969; String quartet, 1971; Percorso GG, clarinet, tape, 1979; D'improvviso, percussion, 1981; Klavieralbum 1956; Incontro, violin, string quartet, 1983; Opus 50 (Daunium), 11 instruments, 1984; 10 versi di E Dickinson, soprano, harp, strings, 1988; Quanto Oscura Selva Trovai (Dante) for trombone, chorus and live electronics, 1995; Moi, Antonin A, texts by A Artaud, for soprano, narrator and orchestra, 1997; Quarto Rivolto for string sextet, 2011. Recordings: Masse: omaggio a E Varèse; Parole da Beckett; Ode; Dedica; Quadruplum; Musica notturna; 10 Versi di E Dickinson; Scene Sinfoniche per il Dr Faustus, etc; Other chamber music. Publications: Guida all'ascolto della musica sinfonica, 1967; A Schoenberg - L'uomo, l'opera, i testi musicati, 1975, 1997; Per M Robespierre - Testo e materiali per le scene musicali (with L Pestalozza and V Puecher), 1975; Scritti, 1991; Tradizione e Utopia, 1994; Écrits, 2006; Parole per Musica, 2007; Musica e Progetto Civile, 2009; Translations: many works by T W Adorno and A Schoenberg. Contributions to: Music critic, L'Unità, 1958-66; Many Italian and foreign periodicals. Membership: Accademia Santa Cecilia, Rome. Address: Viale Papiniano 31, 20123 Milan, Italy.

MAO Zai-Sha, b. 3 July 1943, Chengdu, China. Research Chemical Engineer. m. Junxian Zhou, 2 daughters. Education: BEng, Department of Chemical Engineering, Tsinghua University, Beijing, China, 1966; MS, Institute of Chemical Metallurgy, Chinese Academy of Sciences, Beijing, China, 1981; PhD, Department of Chemical Engineering, University of Houston, Texas, USA, 1988. Appointments: Research Professor, Institute of Process Engineering, Chinese Academy of Sciences; Associate Editor in Chief, Chinese Journal of Chemical Engineering, Beijing; Associate Editor in Chief, Chinese Journal of Process Engineering, Beijing. Publications: 130 papers in peer-reviewed journals; 10 patents on multiphase chemical reactor design. Honours: Best Fundamental Paper, South Texas Section, AIChE, USA, 1992; Excellent Postgraduate Adviser, Graduate School, Chinese Academy of Sciences, Beijing, 2001; 2nd prize of State Natural Science Award, China, 2009. Memberships: Chemical Industry and Engineering Society of China. Address: Institute of Process Engineering, CAS, PO Box 353, Beijing 100190, China.

MAOGOTO Jackson Nyamuya, b. 12 October 1975, Nairobi, Kenya. Senior Lecturer in Law. Education: Bachelor of Laws (1st class honours), Moi University, 1999; LLM (honours), University of Cambridge, England, 2001; PhD, University of Melbourne, Australia, 2002; LLM, University of Technology Sydney, Australia; G Cert PTT, University of Newcastle, Australia. Appointments: Graduate Assistant, Moi University; Research Assistant, Sessional Lecturer, University of Melbourne; Senior Lecturer, University of Newcastle, Australia; Member, International Criminal Law Committee, International Law Association; Senior Lecturer, University of Manchester, England. Publications: Prolific publications in leading international specialist journals: Over 40 refereed journal articles; 6 books: International Criminal Law & State Sovereignty, 2003; War Crimes & Realpolitik, 2004; Battling Terrorism, 2005; Legal Control of the Private Military Corporation, 2008; International Law in a Nutshell, 2008; The Militarization of Outer Space and International Law, 2009. Honours: Fellow, Cambridge Commonwealth Society; Melbourne International Scholarship; Shell Centenary Award; Chancellor's Medal. Memberships: Royal Institute of International Affairs; Australian Institute of International Affairs; Australian Lawyers for Human Rights; American Society of International Law; Newcastle Law Society; Australian & New Zealand Society of International Law; Nuclear Age Foundation; European Society of International Law; International Institute of Space Law; International Society for Military Law and the Law of War. E-mail: jacksonmaogoto@aol.com

MAOUTSOS Vassilis A, b. 3 September 1948, Athens, Greece. Psychoanalyst. m. Galyna Semenyuk, 1 son, 1 daughter. Education: MD, Athens, 1973; Psychiatry, Cambridge/Athens, 1979; Psychoanalysis, London, 1983; Psychotherapist, 2008. Appointments: Senior Registrar, Psychiatry, Fulbourn Hospital; Consultant Psychotherapist, St George's Hospital; Consultant Psychotherapist/Psychiatrist, Alexandroupoli University; Chairman, Education Committee, Hellenic Institute of Classic Psychoanalysis. Publications: Book, The Invisible Human Brain; Numerous papers in Greek psychoanalytic journals. Honours: Lady Bullogh Award in Psychotherapy. Memberships: British Association of Psychotherapists; Hellenic Institute of Classic Psychoanalysis; International Psychanalytic Association. Address: 43 Karaiskaki Street, Kefalari, Athens 14562, Greece. E-mail: vam@otenet.gr

MAPUNDA Emmanuel, b. 10 December 1935, Peramiho. Education: Philosophical Studies, Peramiho Senior Seminary, 1957-59; Systematic Theology, 1959-65; MS, Moral Theology, Gregorian University, Rome, 1970-72; Doctorate, Alfonsiana University of Rome, 1984. Appointments: Ordained to Priesthood, 1965; Teaching Mission, Hanga Junior Seminary, 1966-67; Curate, Matogoro Parish, 1966; Curate, Songea Parish 1968-69; Lecturer, Moral Theology, Alma Mater - Peramiho Senior Seminary, 1973-80; Professor, 1984-86; Bishop, Diocese of Mbinga, 1986. Honours: Consecrated in Rome by His Holiness Pope John Paul II, 1987. Address: Bishop's House Mbinga, PO Box 94, Peramiho, Tanzania, E Africa.

MAQSOOD Sajid, b. 26 February 1982, Srinagar, India. Research Scientist. Education: Bachelor, Fisheries Science; Master, Fisheries Science; PhD, Food Science and Technology. Appointments: Research Assistant, Seafood Technology Project, 2008-10. Publications: Numerous articles in professional journals. Honours: Gold Medal, Bachelor and Master degree; Alltech Young Scientist Award, 2010; Listed in international biographical dictionaries. Memberships: European Association for Integrating Food Science and Engineering Knowledge into the Food Chain; International Association for Computer Science and Information Technology; Institute for Research on Environment and Sustainability; Fisheries Society of Nigeria; African Network for Fish Technology and Safety; Professional Fisheries Graduate Forum. Address: Maqsood House, Shivpora, BB Cantt, Srinagar, Jammu and Kashmir, 190004, India.

MAR AND KELLIE, Earl of, James Thomas Erskine (Jamie), b. 10 March 1949, Edinburgh, Scotland. Peer. m. Mary. Education: Diploma in Social Work, Moray House College of Education, 1968-71; Certificate in Building, Inverness College, 1987-88. Career: Social Work, 20 years; Building Work, 4 years; Hereditary Peer, 1994-99; Life Peer, 2000-; Liberal Democrt Assistant Whip; Liberal Democrat Assistant Transport Spokesman. Honours: Life Peerage: Lord Erskine of Alloa Tower, 2000. Memberships: Chairman, Clackmannanshire Heritage Trust; Non-Executive Director, Clackmannanshire Enterprise; Select Committee on the Constitution, 2001-04. Address: Hilton Farm, Alloa FK10 3PS, Scotland.

MARABLE Darwin William, b. 15 January 1937, Los Angeles, California, USA. Historian; Lecturer; Critic; Curator. m. Joan Ynez Frazell. 1 daughter. Education: BA, University of California at Berkeley, 1960; MA, San Francisco State University, 1972; PhD, History of Photography, University of New Mexico, 1980. Appointments: Lecturer, San Francisco State University, 1977-78, 1982, California College of the Arts, Oakland, 1977-79; San Francisco Art Institute, 1977, 2001; St Mary's College, Moraga, 1990-91, 1992; Academy of Art University, 2001, 2006; Instructor, University of California at Berkeley Extension, 1995-2004, 2008; Mentor, University of California at Berkeley Student-Alumni Mentor Program; Volunteer, University of New Mexico Outreach; Board Member, Diablo Symphony Orchestra, Walnut Creek, 1979-81, Lafayette Arts and Science Foundation, 1980-81, Contra Costa Alliance for the Arts, 1981-82; Docent, Friends of Photography, San Francisco, 1995-2001; Arts Commissioner, Contra Costa County Arts Commission, 2003-. Publications: Numerous articles in popular and professional journals. Honours: Listed in Who's Who publications and biographical dictionaries. Memberships: History of Photography Group; Friends of Photography; San Francisco Museum of Modern Art; Society for Photographic Education; Photo Alliance, San Francisco. Commissions and Creative Works: Guest Curator: Hearst Art Gallery, St Mary's College, Moraga, The Crucifixion in Modern Art, 1992; California College of Arts and Crafts, Oakland, Vilem Kriz Memorial Exhibition, 1996; JJ Brookings Gallery, San Francisco, Visual Dialogue Foundation, Revisited, 2000. Address: 166 Valley Hill Drive, Moraga, CA 94556, USA.

MARADONA Diego Armando, b. 1960, Lanus, Argentina. Footballer. m. Claudia Villafane, 1989-2004 (divorced) 2 daughters. Appointments: Boca Juniors, Argentina, 1982; Barcelona Football Club; Naples Football Club, 1984-91, Sevilla (Spain), 1992, Boca Juniors, 1997, Badajoz, 1998-; Founder, Maradona Producciones; Former Ambassador for UNICEF; Banned from football for 15 months after drugs test; Convicted by Naples Court on charges of possession of cocaine, 14 month suspended sentence and fine of 4 million lira, 1991; Federal Court in Buenos Aires ruled he had complied with the treatment; Suspended for 15 months for taking performance-enhancing drugs in World Cup Finals, 1994; Indicted for shooting an air rifle at journalists, 1994; Resigned as coach of Deporto Mandiyu, 1994; Captain of Argentina, 1993. Sports Vice President, Boca Juniors, 2005-2006; Television Host, 2005-. Publication: Yo Soy El Diego, 2000. Honour: Footballer of the Century Award, Féderation Internationale de Football Association (France), 2000. Membership: President, International Association of Professional Footballers, 1995-.

MARBER Patrick, b. 19 September 1964, London, England. Playwright; Director. 1 son. Education: BA, English Language and Literature, Wadham College, Oxford University, 1983-86. Publications: Plays: Dealer's Choice, 1995; After Miss Julie, 1996; Closer, 1997; Howard Katz, 2001; Old Street, 2004; Closer, 2004; Asylum, 2005; Notes on a Scandal, 2006; The Tourist, 2007; Saturday, 2008. Honours: Writer's Guild Award for Best West End Play, 1995; Evening Standard Award for Best Comedy, 1995; Evening Standard Award for Best Comedy, 1997; Critic's Circle Award for Best Play, 1997; Olivier Award for Best Play, 1997; New York Critics' Award for Best Foreign Play, 1999. Address: c/o Judy Daish Associates, Ltd, 2 St Charles Place, London W10 6EG, England.

MARCEAU Sophie (Sophie Danièle, Sylvie Maupu), b. 17 November 1966, Paris, France. Actress. 1 son, 1 daughter. Creative Works: Stage appearances include: Eurydice, 1991; Pygmalion, 1993; Films: La Boum, 1981; La Boum 2, 1982; Fort Saganne, 1984; Joyeuses Pâques, 1985; L'Amour Braque, 1985; Police, 1985; Descente aux Enfers, 1986; Chouans!, 1987; L'Etudiante, 1988; Mes Nuits Sont Plus Belles Que Vos Jours, 1989; Pacific Palisades, 1989; Pour Sacha, 1991; La Note Bleue, 1991; Fanfan, 1993; La Fille de D'Artagnan, 1994; Braveheart, 1995; Beyond the Clouds, 1995; Firelight, 1988; Anna Karenina, 1996; Marquise, 1997; The World is

Not Enough, 1998; La Fidelité, 1999; Belphégor, 2001; Alex and Emma, 2003; Je reste! 2003; Les Clefs de bagnole, 2003; Nelly, 2004; Anthony Zimmer, 2005; Disparue de Deauville, La, 2007; Cendrillon, 2008; Femmes be l'ombre, Les, 2008. Publication: Menteuse, 1996. Address: c/o Artmedia, 10 avenue George V, 75008 Paris, France.

MARCH Andrew, b. 14 November 1973, Nuneaton, Warwickshire, England. Composer. Education: Composition, Royal College of Music, 1992-96; Studies with Jeremy Dale Roberts. Appointments: Composer. Publications: Compositions include: Two Songs of Laurie Lee, 1993; Poem I from Chamber Music by James Joyce, 1996; Easdale, 1996; Marine - à travers les arbres, 1997; Irish Reel, 2000; A Stirring in the Heavenlies, 2000; Alto Flute and Harp Book, 2000; Be Still and Know, 2001; Nymphéas for 2 Pianos, 2001; Boy in Ice, 2002; In Memoriam, 2002; Spiritus, 2004; Sanguis Venenatus, 2009. Honours: Royal Philharmonic Composition Prize, 1996; English Song Prize; Cobbett & Hurlstone Prize; United Music Publishers Prize; Constant & Kit Lambert Award. Address: c/o Chester Novello, Head Office, 14-15 Berners Street, London W1T 3LJ, England. Website: www.andrewmarch.com/57448/index.html

MARC'HADOUR Germain, b. 16 April 1921, Langonnet, Brittany. Priest; Professor. Education: Licence ès Lettres, 1945; Doctorat ès Lettres, 1969; Honorary Doctorate of Theology, 1999. Appointments: High School Teacher, 1945-52; Assistant Professor, 1952, Professor, 1969, Catholic University; Founding Secretary, Amici Thomae Mori, 1963. Publications: 6-volume work on Thomas More and the Bible; 200 articles in professional journals; 12 books on St Thomas More & Erasmus, including: The Bible in the Works of Thomas More; Praying with St Thomas More. Honours: 4 medals; Dedicatee of a Festschrift, 1989; Dr honoris causa, Maynooth, 1999; Palmers Academiques, 2000; Honorary President, 2005. Memberships: Renaissance Society of America; Modern Language Association; Third Order of St Francis; Editorial Board of Tyndale Project; Charter member of Erasmus of Rotterdam Society. Address: 126, rue Chèvre, 49044 Angers, France.

MARCINIAK Jan Józef, b. 10 March 1943, Tarnowskie Góry, Poland. Mechanical Engineer. m. Marianna Joanna Melcer, 3 daughters. Education: MA, 1968, PhD, 1972, DSc, 1982, Professor, 1990, Silesian University of Technology, Gliwice, Poland. Appointments: Master of Metal Physics Team, Institute of Metal Science, Silesian University of Technology, 1975-80; Director of Science, 1982-85; Head, Metal Science Department, 1984-88; Director of Institute, 1985-93; Head, Special Materials and Techniques, 1991; President, Association of Faculty Mechanics, Gliwice, 1983-88; Chairman of Board, Silesian University of Technology, 1985; Director of Centre of Bioengineering, 1999-. Publications: Biomaterials in Surgery, 1992; Biomaterials, 2002; Menace of Electromagnetic Environment, 1995, 2000; Co-author: Metal Science and Head Treatment of Tool Materials, 1990; Intramedullary Nailing in Osteosynthessis, 2006; Stents for Minimal Invasive Surgery, 2006; Biomaterials in Stomatology, 2008; Problems of Bone Union Electrostimulation, 2010; 28 books; 31 patents; 360 publications. Honours: Award in Gold, Chief Technical Organization, Katowice, 1980; Order of Merits for Development, Voivode of Katowice, 1986; Order of Merits, Leszno, 1988; Gold Medal, INPEX XIII, Pittsburgh, 1997; Golden Key Award, London International Inventions Fair, 1997. Memberships: Rehabilitations Engineering and Social Adaption Committee, Committee of Materials Engineering; Applied Mechanics Committee, Polish Academy of Science; Scientific Committee of journals; Acta of Bioengineering and Biomechanics, Engineering of Biomaterials; Member, scientific committees of Internationale Conference on Materials, Mechanical and Manufacturing Engineering; Polish Society of Biomechanics; Polish Society of Biomaterials; Polish Society of Applied Electromagnetics; Polish Club of Ecology. Address: Silesian University of Technology, Institute of Engineering and Biomedical Materials, Konarskiego 18a, 44-100 Gliwice, Poland.

MARCOS Imelda Romualdez, b. 1930, Philippines. Politician; Social Leader. m. Ferdinand E Marcos deceased, 1 son, 2 daughters. Appointments: Governor, Metro Manila, 1975-86; Roving Ambassador; Visited Beijing, 1976; Took part in negotiations in Libya over self-government for southern province, 1977; Leader, Kilusan Bagong Lipunan (New Socialist Movement), 1978-81; Member, Batasang Pambansa (Interim Legislative Assembly), 1978-83; Minister of Human Settlements, 1978-79, 1984-86, of Human Settlements and Ecology, 1979-83; Meber, Cabinet Executive Committee, 1982-84; Chair, Southern Philippines Development Authority, 1980-86; Indicated for embezzlement, 1988, acquitted, 1990; Returned to Philippines, 1991; Sentenced to 18 to 24 years imprisonment for criminal graft, 1993; Convicted of two charges of corruption, sentenced to 9-12 years on each, 1993; Sentenced on appeal to Supreme Court; Facing 4 charges of graft, 1995; Presidential Candidate, 1992; Senate, 1995-; 10 pending graft cases, 2007. Creative Works: Records include: Imelda Papin, featuring songs with Mrs Imelda Romualdez Marcos, 1989.

MARDON Austin Albert, b. 1962, Edmonton, Alberta, Canada. Geographer; Writer; Researcher. m. (2) Catherine Mardon, 2006. Education: BA, Geography, University of Lethbridge, Alberta, 1985; MSc, Geography, South Dakota State University, 1988; MEd, Educational Curriculum and Instruction, Texas A&M University, 1990; Graduate work in Space Science, University of North Dakota, 1990; PhD, Geography, Greenwich University, Australia, 2000; Graduate work Newman Theological College, 2001-03 and Kharkiv National University, 2002-04; Study, University of South Africa, postgraduate, 2008-09. Appointments include: Private, Primary Reserves, Artillery Lethbridge, 1981, 1985; Teaching Assistant, Department of Geography, South Dakota State University, 1986; Teaching Assistant, Department of Geography, Texas A&M University, 1986; Expedition Field Member, NASA/NSF Antarctic meteorite field expedition, 1986-87; Chair, Antarctic Institute of Canada, 1986-; Research Assistant, Alberta Culture and Multiculturalism, 1989; Freelance Writer, 1991-; Adjunct Faculty, Akamai University, 2004-; Adjunct Faculty, Greenwich University, 2000-04; Honorary Professor, Penza State University, 2005-07; Co-ordinator, Alberta Mental Health Self Help Network/Canadian Mental Health Association, 1999-2006; Trustee, Edmonton Library Board, 2000-06; Vice Chair, Alberta Disabilities Forum Steering Committee, 2004-07; Chair, Alberta Disabilities Forum Low-Income Working Group, 2005-06; Board Member, Premier's Council on Status of Persons with Disabilities, 2005-12; Board Member, The Champion's Centre national Board, 2005-07; Chair, The Champion's Centre, Edmonton Advisory Committee, 2006-; Committee Member, Service Integration Working Group, AHS, 2007-08; Board of Alberta College of Social Workers, 2009-13; Deputy Ministers Strategic Planning Committee for Addiction and Mental Health. Publications: Author, co-author, translator and editor, over 50 books and over 206 articles. Honours include most recently: Queen Elizabeth II Golden

Jubilee Medal, 2002; Alberta Centennial Medal, 2005; Ron LaJeunnesse Leadership Award, Canadian Mental Health Association, 2005; Order of Canada, 2006; Bill Jefferies Family Award, Schizophrenia Society of Canada, 2007; CM Hincks Award, National Canadian Mental Health Association, 2007; Alberta Medical Association, Medal of Honour, 2010; Listed in various international biographical dictionaries. Memberships: The Explorers Club; Schizophrenia Society of Alberta; International Academy of Astronautics; American Polar Society; International Noble Academy; Sigma Pi Sigma; Gamma Theta Upsilon; International Committee on Space Research; Antarctice Institute of Canada. Address: PO Box 1223, Station Main, Edmonton, Alberta T5J 2M4, Canada. E-mail: aamardon@yahoo.ca Website: www.austinmardon.org

MARGOLYES Miriam, b. 18 May 1941, Oxford, England. Actor. Education: BA (Hons) English Literature, Cambridge University. Career: Films: Stand Up Virgin Soldiers; The Awakening; The Apple; Reds; Coming Out Of The Ice; Scrubbers; Yentl; Electric Dreams; Handel - Honour, Profit And Pleasure; The Good Father; Little Shop Of Horrors; Little Dorrit; Wiesenthal - The Murderers Among Us; I Love You To Death; Pacific Heights; The Fool; Dead Again; The Butcher's Wife; As You Like It; The Age Of Innocence; Ed And His Dead Mother; The White Horse; Immortal Beloved; Babe (Voice); James And The Giant Peach; Crossing The Border; Romeo and Juliet; Sunshine; End Of Days; Alone; Harry Potter and the Chamber of Secrets; Cold Comfort Farm; Different For Girls; Dreaming Of Josephe Lees; Cats & Dogs; The First Snow Of Winter; The Life And Death Of Peter Sellers; Modigliani; Being Julia; Ladies In Lavender; Sir Billi the Vet (voice); Flushed Away; Happy Feet (voice); The Dukes. Television: Fall Of Eagles; Girls Of Slender Means; Kizzy; The Widowing Of Mrs Holroyd; Glittering Prizes; Stanley Baxter Christmas Show; Tales Of The Unexpected: Fat Chance; The History Man; The Lost Tribe; Take A Letter Mr Jones; A Kick Up The 80s (Various); Scotch And Wry; The First Schlemiel; Freud; Strange But True: Flight Of Fancy; A Rough State: The Mexican Rebels; The Young Ones; Alternative Society; Oliver Twist; Blackadder; Blackadder II; Blackadder III; Life And Loves Of A She Devil; The Little Princess; Poor Little Rich Girl; Body Contact; Mr Majeika; The Finding; Doss; City Lights; Old Flames; Orpheus Decending; Hands Across The Sea; Ways And Means; The Comic Strip - Secret Ingredient; Frannie's Turn; Just William; Phoenix And The Carpet; Fall Of The House Of Windsor; The Lost Tribe; Tuscany To Go; Miss Marple; Wallis And Edward; Theatre: The Cherry Orchard; The Killing Of Sister George; She Stoops To Conquer; Dickens' Women; Orpheus Descending; Man Equals Man; Gertrude Stein And A Companion; 84 Charing Cross Rd; Flaming Bodies; Cloud Nine; The White Devil; Threepenny Opera; Kennedy's Children; Canterbury Tales; Fiddler On The Roof; Romeo And Juliet; The Vagina Monologues; The Way Of The World; Blithe Spirit. Honours: Joint winner (with Genevieve Bujold), Best Supporting Actress, LA Critics Circle, 1989; Talkies Performer of the Year, 1991; BAFTA Best Supporting Actor, 1993; Sony Radio Best Actress on Radio, 1993; Best Children's Entertainment, The Royal Television Society, 1999; Best Animation for Children, BAFTA, 1999; Best Independent Production, The Prix Danube, 1999; 2nd Prize, Children's Jury for Best Animation, Chicago International Children's Film Festival, 1999; Grand Prize, Best Short Film, Kinderfilmfest, Tokyo, 1999; Best Film Audience Award Jury Award, Washington DC International Film Festival, 1999 Prix Jeunesse, Best Children's Programme (0-6 fiction), 2000; OBE, 2001. Memberships: BAFTA: Equity; AFTRA; Academy of Motion Pictures. Address: c/o PFD, Drury House, 34-43 Russell Street, London WC2B 5HA, England. Website: www.miriammargolyes.com

MARGRETHE II H.M. (Queen of Denmark), b. 16 April 1940, Denmark. m. Count Henri de Laborde de Monpezat (now Prince Henrik of Denmark), 1967, 2 sons. Education: University of Copenhagen; University of Aarhus; University of Cambridge; University of Sorbonne, Paris; London School of Economics. Appointments: Illustrator, The Lord of the Rings, 1977, Norse Legends as Told by Jorgen Stegelmann, 1979, Bjarkemaal, 1982; Poul Oerum's Comedy in Florens, 1990; Cantabile poems by HRH the Prince Consort, 2000. Publications: (trans) All Men are Mortal (with Prince Henrik), 1981; The Valley, 1988; The Fields, 1989; The Forest (trans), 1989. Honours include: Honorary LLD, Cambridge, 1975, London, 1980; Honorary Bencher, Middle Temple, 1992; Honorary Fellow, Girton College, Cambridge, 1992; Medal of the Headmastership, University of Paris, 1987; Hon KG, 1979. Address: Amalienborg Palace, 1257 Copenhagen K, Denmark.

MARÍN CARRIÓN Ismael, b. 23 October 1979, Albacete, Spain. Computer Engineer; Researcher. Education: ME, 2003, BE, 2001, Computer Science,M Res, 2006, PhD, 2010, Advanced Computer Science, University of Castilla-La Mancha. Appointments: Pre-doctoral Fellow, 2005, Research Assistant, 2005-08, University of Castilla-La Mancha; Visiting Researcher, HPC-Europa Transnational Access Program, University of Amsterdam, 2006; Visiting Researcher, ICTS Mobility Program, Barcelona Supercomputing Center, 2007; Visiting Researcher, HPC-Europa Transnational Access Program, University of Stuttgart, 2007; Visiting Researcher, Hong Kong Polytechnic University, 2008; IT Systems Engineer, maat GKnowledge, 2008-09; Research Project Associate, Complutense University of Madrid, 2010-. Publications: Numerous articles in professional journals. Honours: PhD awarded with the European Doctorate Mention, 2010; Best Paper Award, ICPDC, 2010. Memberships: International Association of Engineers. E-mail: i.marin@fdi.ucm.es

MARINELLI Carlo, b. 13 December 1926, Rome, Italy. Musicologist; Discologist; Discographer. 1 son, 1 daughter. Education: Degree in Letters, La Sapienza University of Rome, 1948. Career: Founder and Editor, Microsolco magazine, 1952-59; Professor, History of Music, 1970-98, Associate, 1985-98, Associate, History of Modern and Contemporary Music, 1992-98, Department of Comparative Cultures, Faculty of Letters, University of L'Aquila; Professor, Discography and Musical Videography, 1998-2002, DAMS, Faculty of Letters, University of Bologna; President, Institute for Research on Musical Theatre, Rome. Publications: Discographies of Mozart, Rossini, Monteverdi, Donizetti, Bellini, Verdi, Puccini; Editor, catalogues of Italian audiovisual and sound sources of Mozart and Rossini; Editor: Notizie Videoarchivio Opera e Balletto, Notizie Archivio Sonoro Musica Contemporanea, IRTEM "Quaderni"; Le cantate profane di J S Bach, 1966; La musica strumentale da camera di Goffredo Petrassi, 1967; Lettura di Messiaen, 1972; Cronache di musica contemporanea, 1974; L'opera ceca, l'opera russa, l'opera in Polonia e Ungheria, 1977; Opere in disco. Da Monteverdi a Berg, 1982; Di Goffredo Petrassi, un'antologia, 1983; Prolegomeni ad una nuova disciplina scientifica: Discografia e videografia musicale, 1998; Prolegomena to a new scientific discipline: musical discography and videography, 2000; I documenti musicali sonori e visivi quali fonti di conoscenza, informazione e transmissione, 2002; Sound and Visual Musical Documents as Sources of Knowledge, Information and Transmission, 2002; Rilettura digitale come alterazione di documenti sonori originali, 2004; Analogue-to-Digital Conversion Viewed as an Alteration of Original Sounds Documents, 2004; Discological Critical Edition: Giovanni Paisiello, Il re Teodoro in Venezia, 1994. Discographies: Faust e Mefistofele nelle opere sinfonico-vocali, 1986; Le opere di Mozart su libretti di Da Ponte, 1988; Mozart Singspiele, 1993; Mozart, Opere serie italiane, 1995; Monteverdi, Balli e Madrigali in genere rappresentativo, 1996; De Falla, Atalantida, 1996; Rossini, Il barbiere di Siviglia, 1998; Verdi, Rigoletto, Il trovatore, La traviata, 1999; Monteverdi, Opere teatrali, 2000; Rossini, Opere teatrali 1820-1829, 2001; Verdi, Don Carlo, Otello, Falstaff, 2002; Verdi, Oberto, Giorno di regno, Nabucco, Lombardi, Ernani, Due Foscari, 2003; Verdi, Don Carlos, La forza del destino, 2003, Verdi, Aida, 2004; Mozart, Opere buffe italiane, Serenate, azioni teatrali, balletti, Drammi sacri e oratori, 2006; Un itinerario donizettiano, 2006; Verdi 1844-1850, Giovanna d'Arco, Alzira, Atilla, Macbeth, I masnadieri, Jerusalem ll corsaro, La battaglia di Legnano, Luisa Miller, Stiffelio, 2007; Opera Discography Encyclopaedia, 2004-09 onwards. Honours: Honorary Member, International Association of Sound and Audiovisual Archives; Academician, Accademia Santa Cecilia, Rome: Memberships: President, Associazione Italiana Archivi Sonori Audiovisivi; Board Member, Internationales Musik Zentrum, 1993-95; Chairman, Discography Committee, IASA, 1996-99; International, American, Australian, French, Spanish and Italian Musicological Societies; International Association of Music Libraries; Association of Recorded Sound Collectors; Australasian Sound Recording Association; Association Française Archives Sonores; Associazione Italiana Studi Nord Americani; Associazione Docenti Universitari Italiani Musica. Address: Via Francesco Tamagno 65-67, I-00168 Rome, Italy. E-mail: carlomarinelli@mclink.it Website: www.carlomarinelli.it

MARINO Marialuisa, b. 4 January 1945, Milan, Italy. Artist; Writer; Poet. 3 sons. Education: Ballet Diploma, La Scala Opera House, Italy, 1962; Teachers Diploma, Advanced Diploma, Chechetti, Italy, 1963; Principal Soloist, Performing Arts Council of Transvaal, South Africa; Studies in art, Witwatersrand Technical College of Art, South Africa; Imperial Society of Teachers of Dance (Advanced Teachers). Appointments: 6 appointments for voluntary community and honorary officer, 1976-85; First solo art exhibition, 1990; Joined family business founded by father in 1967, became Managing Director, 1978, Marmernova and Building Products Pty Ltd; Only woman member, Master Mason Association and the Building Industries Federation; Trustee and Director of Events, City Ballet of London; Chair of Fine Art Committee, Fine Art Trade Guild. Publications: Illustrations, Diana: An English Rose, 1998; Beyond Fantasy, painting and poetry book, 2000; Annuario d'Arte Moderna Artisti Contemporanei, 2000; Merry Mischief – A Childhood Celebration of Queen Elizabeth, The Queen Mother, 2001; Royalty; Savonarola; Childrens books: The Fantastical Journey of George Green I, 2007, II, 2007, III, 2008; A Leap Through Time at the Speed of Light, 2010; Portraits: Alexander Thynn, Marquis of Bath; Homage to the Queen, 2006; George Green, Miller Mathematician of Nottingham, 1793-1843; Dame Alicia Marcova; HRH Prince William of Wales; Queen Elizabeth, The Queen Mother; Sir Malcolm Arnold CBE; Paloma Picasso. Honours: La Scala Opera House, 1962; 10 gold medals, South Africa Premiere Exhibition, Witwatersrand Easter Show, 1976-85; Annuario d'Arte Moderna, 1999, 2000; Paul Harris Fellow, Rotary Foundation; Citta di Firenze: Professore HC, for painting "Diana, Princess of Wales", 2000; Cavaliere dell'Etruria: Grosetto, Italy, 2000; Coppa Libertas, for Symphony No 9, 2001; New Art Promotion "Sirena del Mare", Cervia, Italy, 2001; Statua della Liberta, Accademia del Fiorano, New York, USA, 2001; Award for "Merry Mischief", Accademia Italiana Etruschi, Cita di Milano, 2001; Cavaliere della Pace, Firenze, Italy, for painting of President Nelson Mandela, 2001; N D Marialuisa Marino, Accademica Gentilizia (Classe) Belle Arti, 2001; N D Professor Marialuisa Marino, Il Marzocco dalla Firenze dei Signori l'Illustrissimo Corpo Accademico, (Classe) Belle Arti, 2001; Arte in Italia l'Elite, 2002, 2003; Associazione Culturale: Amici del Quadro Gold Medal, Milan, 2003; Gold Medal, Artist of the Year, S Ambrogio d'Oro, 2003; Accademia il Marzocco, Gran Premio Internazionale, Genova la Superba citta della Cultura, 2004; Promotore della Pace, for Celebration: A Portrait of Julian Lloyd Webber, 2004; Accademia Internazionale Città Di Roma Award for Venus Through a Mirror of Time, 2004; Athena Gold Medal, Rassegna Nazionale Artisti d'Avanguardia, 2005; Salento Porta d'Oriente, 2006, Premio Rembrandt, 2006, Regione Publica Università di Studi di Lecce; Grand Prix Mediceo Cosimo I Granduca della Toscana città di Livorno, 2007; International Prize, Unversita del Salento, Dipartimento di Scienza dei Materiali, 2007; Rassegna "Folgore" Dr Livorno (Caserma Vannucci) "Premio Italia 2008" for painting and poetry, 2008; International Gallery Exhibitor, Ambassador for England and Italy, Forum Speaker, World Forum, Washington DC, 2009; Woman of the Year Representing England, 2009; USA World Academy of Letters, Masters Diploma for Literature, 2009; Lifetime Achievement Award, 2010. Memberships: Life Member, British/Italian Society; International Society of Poets, 2000; Accademia Il Marzocco ND for Belle Arte, 2001; Rotary International Rotary Club of Kensington; The Fine Art Trade Guild, 2000; Academical Commander Ordine Accademico del Verbano, 2004; Avanguardie Artistiche, 2004, 2005; Universitá di Salento, Premio Speciale 'Human Rights' 60th Anniversary, New York, 10 December 1948; Premio Internazionale 'Michelangelo Buonarotti', 2008; Maestro: Honorary Member, Ministero per i Beni Culturali, Departmento di Scienza dei Materiali, 2009; United Cultural Convention. Address: The Mill House, 12 Belvoir Hill, Sneinton, Nottingham NG2 4LF, Nottinghamshire, England.

MARIOTTINI Gian Luigi, b. 19 December 1954, Genova, Italy. Biologist; Physician. m. Maria Carla Casarino, 3 sons. Education: MSc, Biological Sciences, 1984; MD, Medicine and Surgery, 2009; Qualified Biologist, 1985; Physician, 2009. Appointments: Apprentice Biologist, San Martino Hospital, Genova; Teacher in middle and secondary schools; Bursary Biologist, Research Laboratory of Pediatric Oncology, G Gaslini Children's Hospital, Genova; High Professional Scientific Technician, University of Genova, 1987-. Publications: 126 articles in professional journals including 9 teaching books. Honours: Scholarship for Research on Neuroblastoma; ABEO Giannina Gaslini Children's Institute, Genova. Memberships: Italian Society for Experimental Biology; Spera Commission, Friendship Project and Resources for Africa. Address: Dipteris, University of Genova, Viale Benedetto XV 5, I-16132 Genova, Italy. E-mail: gian.luigi.mariottini@unige.it

MARK Thomas, b. 24 March 1973, Viborg, Denmark. Associate Professor. m. Alicja Budek, 1 son. Education: MSc, University of Copenhagen, 1999; PhD, Swedish University of Agricultureal Sciences, 2005. Appointments: Project Manager, Danish Cattle Federation, 1999-2000; Research Genetisist, Interbull Centre, 2000-05; Assistant Professor, 2005-07,

Associate Professor, 2007-, Quantitative and Systems Genetics. Address: Genetics & Bioinformatics, Faculty of Life Sciences, University of Copenhagen, Denmark.

MARKHAM Richard, b. 23 June 1952, Grimsby, England. Concert Pianist. Education: Wintringham Grammar School, piano privately with Shirley Kemp and Max Pirani; National Youth Orchestra of Great Britain; Royal Academy of Music, London, 1969-73. Career: Concert Pianist; Tours in over 40 countries as David Nettle/Richard Markham Piano Duo, 1977-; Examiner for Associated Board of the Royal Schools of Music, 1984-. Recordings include: Nettle and Markham in America; Nettle and Markham in England; Nettle and Markham in France; Complete Two-Piano Works of Brahms; Holst's The Planets (two pianos); Stravinsky's Petrushka & The Rite of Spring (piano duet). Honours: ARCM, 1967; LRAM, 1968; Nora Naismith Scholarship, 1969; Bronze Medal, Geneva International Competition, 1972; Countess of Munster Musical Trust Awards, 1973, 1974; Frederick Shinn Fellowship, 1975; Gulbenkian Foundation Fellowship, 1976-78; ARAM 1983; MRA Award for Excellence, 1985. Memberships: Incorporated Society of Musicians; RAM Club; Friend of Stonewall. Address: The Old Power House, Atherton Street, London SW11 2JE, England. E-mail: richardpianouk@gmail.com

MARMEFELT Thomas Dan-Olof, b. 4 July 1962, Gothenburg, Sweden. Economist. m. Jurgita, 1 son, 2 daughters. Education: Augsburg College, 1982-83; Fil Kand, Social Sciences, University of Gothenburg, 1985; Diploma, International Studies, 1986, MA, History, 1987, Johns Hopkins University; University of Lund, 1987-89; EHESS, 1989-93; Ekon Dr (Economics), Jönköping University, 1998. Appointments: Lecturer, Economics, Jönköping International Business School, Jönköping University, 1996-98; Assistant Professor, Economics, Gävle University, 1999; Assistant Professor, 2000-08, Associate Professor, 2008-, Economics, University of Södertörn; Adjunct Professor, Economics, Åbo Akademi University, 2008-. Publications: Monograph, Bank-Industry Networks and Economic Evolution: An Institutional-Evolutionary Approach; Articles in professional journals and book chapters including: Culture, Social Interactions and Natural Resources: Some Reflections on Culture as Social Capital and Julian Simon's Ultimate Resource in Lithuania and Sweden; Human Knowledge, Rules, and the Spontaneous Evolution of Society in the Social Thought of Darwin, Hayek, and Boulding; Civil Society Formation and Global Exchange: Lithuania, Sweden, the Baltic Sea Area and the World. Memberships: European Association for Evolutionary Political Economy; Society for the Development of Austrian Economics; Association for Social Economics; World Economics Association. Address: University of Södertörn, Department of Social Sciences, SE-14189 Huddinge, Sweden. E-mail: thomas.marmefelt@sh.se

MAROCHKIN Sergei Y, b. 16 November 1956, Zaozerny city, Russia. Lawyer. m. Galina, 1 son, 1 daughter. Education: Lawyer, Law Faculty, Irkutsk State University, 1979; Candidate of Juridical Sciences, 1984; Docent (Associate Professor), 1987; Doctor of Juridical Sciences, 1998; Professor, 1999. Appointments: Assistant Professor, 1979; PhD Candidate, 1981; Lecturer, 1984; Senior Lecturer, Docent, 1987; Head of Department (Chair), Law Faculty, 1991; Dean, Law Faculty, 1998, Director, Institute of Continuing Education, 2000-, Tyumen State University. Publications: More than 130 publications including: Monograph, Action and Realization of International Law norms in the Legal System of the Russian Federation, 2011; Textbook, International Law – a Russian Introduction, 2009. Honours: Honoured Jurist, Russian Federation, 2007; Gold Medal, Tyumen State University; G Tunkin Medal, Russian Association of International Law. Memberships: 20 Semakov St, Tyumen State University, 625003 Tyumen, Russia. E-mail: mar@utmn.ru Website: www.tumidpo.ru

MAROVIC Pavao, b. 26 January 1954, Split, Croatia. University Professor; Civil Engineer. m. Vladica Herak, 1 son. Education: Faculty of Civil Engineering, University of Zagreb, 1972-77; Graduate, Civil Engineer, 1977; PhD, Faculty of Civil Engineering, University of Zagreb, 1987. Appointments: Teaching Assistant, 1978-88, Assistant Professor, 1988-92, Head of Department, Testing and Technology of Materials, 1988-91, Vice Dean of the Faculty, 1991-94, President, University Assembly, 1991-93, Associated Professor, 1992-96, Vice Rector, 1994-98, Professor, 1996-, Head of the Chair for Strength of Materials, Testing of Structures, 1998-, Dean of the Faculty, 2000-2006, University of Split; Associated Member, Croatian Academy of Technical Sciences, 2000. Publications: International Conference on Nonlinear Engineering Computations, 1991; Nonlinear Calculations of R/C Structures, 1993; International Congress of Croatian Society of Mechanics, 1997, 2000; Symposium on The Use of Computers in Civil Engineering; Co-editor of 25 Croatian Conference proceedings; Approximately 160 scientific and professional papers in journals and conference proceedings; Many others. Honours: Rector's Student Award; Plaque of the CAD/CAM Congress; Decorated by the President of the Republic of Croatia; County Splitsko-dalmatinska Yearly Award for Science; 2000 Outstanding Scientists of the 20th Century Silver Medal, International Biographical Centre; World Lifetime Achievement Award, American Biographical Institute; Acknowledgement, Faculty of Civil Engineering, University of Mostar, 2003; Plaque, University of Split, 2008. Memberships: International Association for Computer Methods in Geomechanics; International Association for Bridge and Structural Engineering; Central European Association for Computational Mechanics; European Scientific Association for Material Forming; National Geographic Society; Croatian Society of Mechanics; Croatian Society of Structural Engineers; Many others. Address: Faculty of Civil Engineering and Architecture, University of Split, Matice hrvatske 15, HR-21000 Split, Croatia.

MARQUES Eduardo Jorge de Sousa Ferreira, b. 2 February 1964, Tondela, Portugal. Medical Doctor; Eye Surgeon. Education: Medical Degree, 1987, Clinical Oncology Fellowship, 1989, University of Coimbra, Portugal; Assistant in Ophthalmology, Ministry of Health, Portugal, 1995; Ophthalmology Specialty, Portuguese Medical Association, 1995. Appointments: Member, National Executive Board, Portuguese Medical Association, 1992-98; Ophthalmology Assistant, Coimbra University Hospital, Portugal, 1995-96; Ophthalmology Assistant, Clipóvoa Hospital, Portugal, 1996-99; President, Permanent Working Group of European Junior Doctors, 1998-2001; Ophthalmology Consultant, Centro Oftalmológico de Lisboa, Lisbon, Portugal, 1999-; Member, European Board of Ophthalmology, 2000-03; Member, Consulting Board, Portuguese Medical Association, 2001-; Member, Continuing Medical Education Committee, European Board of Ophthalmology; Head, Ophthalmology Department, Hospital da Cruz Vermelha, Lisbon, Portugal, 2008-. Publications: Over 100 presentations; 33 publications including 25 articles and 8 books. Honours: Portuguese Society of Ophthalmology Award, 1995. Memberships: Portuguese Medical Association; Portuguese Society of Ophthalmology; Portuguese Group of Implant and Refractive

Surgeons; European Society of Cataract and Refractive Surgeons; American Society of Cataract and Refractive Surgeons; Portuguese Board of Ophthalmology; American Academy of Ophthalmology; International Society of Refractive Surgeons; European Society of Retina Specialists. E-mail: em.lx@netcabo.pt

MARQUES-PEREIRA Bérengère, b. 17 May 1951, Uccle, Belgium. Professor. m. Marc Rayet. Education: Licence, 1976, Doctorat, 1986, en Sciences Politiques et Relations Internationales de l'Université Libre de Bruxelles. Appointments: Assistant, 1979, Professor, -2011, Professor Emeritus, Faculty of Political and Economic Social Sciences, l'Université Libre de Bruxelles; Visiting Professor to many universities in Europe, Canada, and Latin America; Visiting Professor, Institut d'Etudes Politiques, Paris. Publications: 3 books; About 100 articles in international or Belgian publications. Memberships: Association Francaise de Sciences Politiques; European Sociological Association; International Political Science Association; ECPR; and others. Address: 54 rue Dautzenberg, Bt 2, 1050 Brussels, Belgium. E-mail: bmarques@ulb.ac.be

MARR Leslie Lynn, b. 14 August 1922, Durham, England. Artist; Painter; Draftsman. m. Maureen, 2 daughters. Education: BA, 1942, MA, 1947, Pembroke College, Cambridge; Borough Polytechnic, 1947-49. Appointments: Teacher, Oil Painting, Barnstaple Polytechnic, University of East Anglia; Painter and Draftsman in oil, watercolour, etc; Group, solo and retrospective exhibitions held around the UK; Work held in public and private collections. Publications: Book, From My Point of View, 1979; 2 albums of piano solos. Memberships: The Borough Group; The London Group; The National Society. Address: c/o Piano Nobile Fine Paintings, 129, Portland Road, London W11 4LW, England. Website: www.piano-nobile.com

MARSDEN Simon Neville Llewelyn (Sir), b. 1 December 1948, Lincoln, Lincolnshire, England. Photographer; Author. m. Caroline Stanton, 1 son, 1 daughter. Education: Ampleforth College, Yorkshire, England; Sorbonne, Paris, France. Career: Professional photographer and author; Photographs in the following collections: J Paul Getty Museum, California, USA; Victoria and Albert Museum, London; Bibliothéque Nationale, Paris, France; The Cleveland Museum of Art, USA; The Maryland Historical Society, Baltimore, USA; The University of Arizona, USA; Flanders Field Museum, Ypres, Belgium. Publications: In Ruins: The Once Great Houses of Ireland, 1980; The Haunted Realm – Ghosts, Witches and Other Strange Tales, 1986; Visions of Poe- A Personal Selection of E A Poe's Stories and Poems, 1988; Phantoms of the Isles – Further Tales from the Haunted Realm, 1990; The Journal of a Ghosthunter – In search of the Undead from Ireland to Transylvania, 1994; Beyond the Wall – The Lost World of East Germany, 1999; Venice - City of Haunting Dreams, 2002; The Twilight Hour – Celtic Visions from the Past, 2003; This Spectred Isle – A Journey Through Haunted England, 2005. Memberships: Chelsea Arts Club; The Arthur Machen Society. Address: The Presbytery, Hainton, Market Rasen, Lincolnshire LN8 6LR, England. E-mail: info@marsdenarchive.com Website: www.simonmarsden.co.uk

MARSDEN-SMEDLEY Christopher, b. 9 February 1931, London, England. Retired Architect. m. Susan Penelope King, 2 sons 1 daughter. Education: BA, (Arch), University College, London, 1956. Appointments: Partner, 1961-96, Senior Partner, 1990-96, Nealon Tanner Partnership; High Sheriff, Avon, 1994-95; Deputy Lieutenant, Somerset, 2000. Publications: Burrington, Church and Village; Articles in various architectural papers. Honours: ARIBA, 1959; FRIBA, 1969. Memberships: Honorary Secretary, Bristol Civic Society, 1966-71; Governor, 1969-75, Chairman, 1972-75, Fairfield School; Committee Member, 1974-97, Chairman, 1988-97, Vice President, 1997-, Bristol Age Care; President, Bristol Commercial Rooms, 1988; Trustee, Wells Cathedral, 1997-; Committee Member, 1997-, President 2000-2001, Canynges Society. Address: Church Farm, Burrington, Near Bristol BS40 7AD, England.

MARSH Eric M, b. 25 July 1943, Preston, England. Hotelier. m. Elizabeth Margaret, 2 sons, 2 daughters. Education: National Diploma in Hotelkeeping and Catering, Courtfield Catering College, Blackpool, Lancashire, England, 1960-63. Appointments: Dorchester Hotel, London, 1963-68; Rank Hotels, London, 1968-73; Director and General Manager, Newling Ward Hotels, St Albans, Hertfordshire, England, 1973-1975; Tenant of Cavendish Hotel from Chatsworth Estate, 1975-; Managing Director, Paludis Ltd (Trading as Cavendish Hotel), 1975-; Managing Director of Eudaemonic Leisure Ltd (Trading as George Hotel), 1996-; Managing Director, Cavendish Aviation Ltd (Operating at Gamston Airfield), 1975-. Publications: Several articles in Caterer and Hotelkeeper magazine and Pilot magazine. Memberships: Institute of Marketing; Institute of Advanced Motorists; Director, Committee Member, British Aerobatic Association. Address: Cavendish Hotel, Baslow, Derbyshire DE45 1SP, England. E-mail: info@cavendish-hotel.net

MARSH Francis Patrick, b. 15 April 1936, Birmingham, England. Consultant Physician. m. Pamela Anne Campbell, 1 son, 2 daughters. Education: BA, Natural Science Tripos, Gonville and Caius College, 1957; London Hospital Medical College, 1957-60; MB BChir, Cambridge, 1960; MA, Cambridge, 1961; MRCP, London, 1963; FRCP, London, 1976. Appointments: House Physician, 1960-61, House Surgeon, 1961, The London Hospital; Senior House Officer in Medicine, Kent and Canterbury Hospital, 1961-62; Registrar in Medicine, Royal Free Hospital, 1962-63; Registrar in Medicine, The London Hospital, 1963-65; Research Fellow, 1965-67, Lecturer, Senior Registrar, 1967-70, The London Hospital and London Hospital Medical College; Honorary Consultant Physician, Bethnal Green Hospital, 1970-71; Senior Lecturer in Medicine, The London Hospital Medical College, now St Bartholomew's and the Royal London School of Medicine and Dentistry, 1970-2001; Consultant Nephrologist, Barts and the London NHS Trust, 1971-2001; Dean of Medical Studies and Governor, The London Hospital Medical College, 1990-95; Board of Directors, American University of the Caribbean, 2000-; Honorary Senior Lecturer in Medicine, Bartholomew's and the Royal London School of Medicine and Dentistry, 2001-; Emeritus Consultant Nephrologist, Barts and the London NHS Trust, 2001-. Publications: Around 80 original research papers; Author, 26 book chapters; Editor, Postgraduate Nephrology; Refereed many medical journals and for regional and national prizes. Memberships include: Joint Formulary Committee, British National Formulary; Renal Association; Specialist Advisory Committee on Renal Disease; North East Thames Regional Medical Advisory Committee; North East Thames Regional Committee for Hospital Medical Services; Council of the Section of Medicine, Experimental Medicine and Therapeutics (Royal Society of Medicine); Central Committee for Hospital Medical Services. Address: Butchers End, 20 Butchers Lane, East Dean, West Sussex, PO18 0JF, England. E-mail: frank.marsh@virgin.net

MARSH Michael John, b. 19 November 1935, Sydney, Australia. Surgeon. m. Carol Jopson, 2 sons, 1 daughter. Education: Knox Grammar School, Sydney; Sydney University; Royal College of Surgeons, England. Appointments: Consultant Surgeon, WACHS; Consultant General Surgeon, KEMH; Relieving Surgeon, RPH; Surgeon, Bentley Hospital; Surgeon, St John of God Hospital; Surgeon, The Mount Hospital; Surgeon, South Perth Community Hospital. Publications: Universal Spirituality; Gnosticism The Essenes and Christianity; The God Experience and Evolving Spirituality; Steps in Academic Achievement and Career Success. Memberships: Royal Australian College of Surgeons; Royal College of Surgeons, England; Royal College of Surgeons, Edinburgh; Australian Medical Association. Address: 6 Linden Gardens, Floreat, WA 6014, Australia. E-mail: marshmjr@iinet.net.au Website: http://marshm.com.au/

MARSHALL Albert Selwyn, b. 26 September 1934, Tatsfield, Surrey, England. Retired Diplomat. m. Joan Margaret Lashwood, deceased, 1985, 1 son, 1 daughter. Education: Kent Horticultural College, Kent, England. Appointments: Royal Corps of Signals, Korea, Suez Canal, Cyprus, 1952-57; Foreign Office, 1957-61; Communications Officer, UK Mission to UN, New York, 1961-64; Archivist, British Embassy, Prague, 1954-65; ECO, British High Commission, Kingston, Jamaica, 1965-68; Foreign and Commonwealth Office, London, England, 1968-72; Management Officer, British Embassy, Addis Ababa, Ethiopia, 1972-75; British Vice-Consul, Belgrade, Yugoslavia, 1975-77; HM Vice-Consul, Tokyo, Japan, 1977-81; Foreign and Commonwealth Office, London, England, 1981-86; Management Officer, British Embassy, Washington DC, USA, 1986-90; HM Consul, Tel Aviv, Israel, 1990-94; Retired, 1994. Honour: MBE, 1968. Memberships: Treasurer, Merrow Horticultural Society; Volunteer, National Trust, Polesden Lacey. Address: 4 Tansy Close, Guildford, Surrrey GU4 7XN, England. E-mail: albert@asmarshall.freeserve.co.uk

MARSHALL Hugh Phillips, b. 13 July 1934, London, England. Anglican Priest (Retired). m. Diana Elizabeth Gosling, 1 son, 3 daughters. Education: BA, MA, Sidney Sussex College, Cambridge; Bishops Hostel, Lincoln. Appointments: Royal Navy, 1952-54; Ordained Deacon, 1959, Priest, 1960, Diocese of London; Curate, St Stephen and St John, Westminster, 1959-65; Vicar of St Paul, Tupsey, Hereford, 1965-74; Vicar and Team Rector of Wimbledon, 1974-87; Rural Dean of Merton, 1979-85; Vicar of Mitcham, Surrey, 1987-90; Chief Secretary, ABM, 1990-96; Vicar of Wendover, 1996-2001. Honours: Honorary Canon, Southwark Cathedral, 1989; Honorary Canon Emeritus, 1990; Canon St John's Cathedral Bulawayo, 1996; Commissary to Bishop of Matabeleland, 1989-. Memberships: Chairman, Betty Rhodes Fund, 1966-2007, Member, 1989-2007; South East Regional Committee, National Lottery Charities Board, 1998-2002; Honorary Secretary, Oxford Diocesan Board of Patronage, 2001-08; Foundation Governor, Deddington Voluntary Aided School, 2002. Address: 7 The Daedings, Deddington, Oxon OX15 0RT, England.

MARSHALL-ANDREWS Robert, b. 10 April 1944, London, England. Member of Parliament; Queen's Counsel; Writer. m. Gillian Diana, 1 son, 1 daughter. Education: University of Bristol; Gray's Inn. Appointments: Member of Bar, 1967; Recorder, Crown Court, 1982; Queen's Counsel, 1987; Deputy High Court Judge, 1996; Bencher, Gray's Inn, 1996; Member of Parliament, 1997-. Publications: Numerous political articles in national (UK) newspapers and publications: Novels: Palace of Wisdom, 1989; A Man Without Guilt, 2002. Honours: Winner Observer Mace, 1967; Spectator Parliamentary Award, 1997. Address: House of Commons, London SW1A 0AA, England.

MARTIN Bill, b. 9 November 1938, Govan, Glasgow, Scotland. Songwriter; Music Publisher. m. Jan, 1 son, 3 daughters. Education: Govan High School; Royal Scottish Academy of Music Certificate. Career: Songwriter; First song, Kiss Me Now, released 1963; Writing partnership with Tommy Scott, 1964-65; Writing partnership with Phil Coulter, 1965-83; Martin-Coulter publishing company, 1970-; Producer of musical, Jukebox, 1983; Producer, publisher and writer, Angus Publications; Acquisitions and Back Catalogue Consultant, SONY/ATV Music, 2000-. Honours: 20 Gold albums; 4 Platinum albums; 3 Ivor Novello Awards; 3 ASCAP Awards; First British Winner, Eurovision Song Contest with Puppet on a String, 1967; Rio de Janeiro Award of Excellence, 1967, 1969; Antibes Song Festival Award for the Best Song, 1971; Japanese Yamaha Best Song Award, 1978; Variety Club Silver Heart, 1979; Scotland's Songwriter of the Decade, 1980; Four No 1s in the UK and three in USA. Memberships: BASCA; PRS; Society of Distinguished Songwriters; Freeman of the City of London; Freeman of the City of Glasgow; Member, Worshipful Company of Distillers; Member, MCC; Past Golf Captain, Royal Automobile Club; Member, St George's Hill Golf Club. Address: 14 Graham Terrace, Belgravia, London SW1W 8JH, England. E-mail: bill.puppetmartin@virgin.net Website: www.billmartinsngwriter.com

MARTIN David (Alfred), b. 30 June 1929, London, England. Professor of Sociology Emeritus; Priest; International Fellow; Writer. m. (1) Daphne Sylvia Treherne, 1953, 1 son, (2) Bernice Thompson, 30 June 1962, 2 sons, 1 daughter. Education: DipEd, Westminster College, 1952; External BSc, 1st Class Honours, 1959, PhD, 1964, University of London; Postgraduate Scholar, London School of Economics and Political Science, 1959-61. Appointments: Assistant Lecturer, Sheffield University, 1961-62; Lecturer, 1962-67, Reader, 1967-71, Professor of Sociology, 1971-89, Professor Emeritus, 1989-, London School of Economics and Political Science; Ordained Deacon, 1983, Priest, 1984; Scurlock Professor of Human Values, Southern Methodist University, Dallas, 1986-90; International Fellow, Institute for the Study of Economic Culture, Boston University, 1990-; Various visiting lectureships. Publications: Pacifism, 1965; A Sociology of English Religion, 1967; The Religious and the Secular, 1969; Tracts Against the Times, 1973; A General Theory of Secularisation, 1978; Dilemmas of Contemporary Religion, 1978; Crisis for Cranmer and King James (editor), 1978; The Breaking of the Image, 1980; Theology and Sociology (co-editor), 1980; No Alternative (co-editor), 1981; Unholy Warfare (co-editor), 1983; Divinity in a Grain of Bread, 1989; Tongues of Fire, 1990; The Forbidden Revolution, 1996; Reflections on Sociology and Theology, 1997; Does Christianity Cause War?, 1997; Pentecostalism: The World Their Parish, 2000; Christian Language and the Secular City, 2002; Christian Language and its Mutations; On Secularization, 2005. Honours: Honorary Assistant Priest, Guildford Cathedral, 1983-; Honorary Professor, Lancaster University, 1993-2002; Sarum Lecturer, Oxford University, 1994-95; Honorary Doctor of Theology, Helsinki, 2000. Membership: International Conference of the Sociology of Religion, president, 1975-83. Address: Cripplegate Cottage, 174 St John's Road, Woking, Surrey GU21 7PQ, England.

DICTIONARY OF INTERNATIONAL BIOGRAPHY 36th EDITION

MARTIN David McLeod, b. 30 December 1922, Glasgow, Scotland. Artist; Teacher. m. Isobel A F Smith, deceased, 2000, 4 sons. Education: Glasgow School of Art, 1940-42; RAF War Service, 1942-46; Completed training at Glasgow School of Art, 1948; Diploma in Art, 1948; Jordanhill Teachers' Training College, 1948-49. Career: Commenced a teaching career in Glasgow schools in 1949 ending as a Principal Teacher of Art, Hamilton Grammar School; Retired early in 1983 to paint full-time. Publications: Works appear in books including: Paintings from the Clydesdale Bank Collection by Patrick Bourne; Scottish Watercolour Painting by Jack Firth; Articles in the Artist Magazine. Honours: Elected Professional Member: Society of Scottish Artists, 1949, Royal Society of Painters in Watercolour, 1961, Royal Glasgow Institute of the Fine Arts, 1982; Honorary membership, Society of Scottish Artists, 1993; Retrospective Exhibition, Perth Museum & Art Gallery, 1999; Listed in biographical dictionaries. Address: The Old Schoolhouse, 53 Gilmour St, Eaglesham, Glasgow G76 0LG, Scotland.

MARTIN George (Henry), b. 3 January 1926, England. Music Industry Executive; Producer; Composer. m. (1) Sheena Rose Chisholm, 1948, 1 son, 1 daughter, (2) Judy Lockhart Smith, 1966, 1 son, 1 daughter. Education: Guildhall School of Music and Drama. Appointments: Sub-Lieutenant, RNVR, 1944-47; Worker, BBC, 1950, EMI Records Ltd, 1950-65, Chair, 1965-; Built AIR Studios, 1969; Built AIR Studios, Montserrat, 1979; Completed new AIR Studios, Lyndhurst Hall, Hampstead, 1992; Co-merged with Chrysalis Group, 1974, Director, 1978-; Chair, Heart of London Radio, 1994-; Scored the music of 15 films; Produced by George Martin, 2001; The Family Way, 2003. Publications: All You Need is Ears, 1979; Making Music, 1983; Summer of Love, 1994; Playback (autobiography), 2002. Honours include: Ivor Novello Awards, 1963, 1979; Grammy Awards, 1964, 1967 (two), 1973, 1993, 1996; CBE, 1996. Address: c/o AIR Studios, Lyndhurst Hall, Hampstead, London, NW3 5NG, England.

MARTIN George Whitney, b. 25 January 1926, New York City, USA. Writer. Education: BA, Harvard College, 1948; Fiske Scholar, Trinity College, Cambridge, England, 1949-50; LLB, Law School, University of Virginia, 1953. Appointments: Practising law in New York City, 1955-59; Writing books, lecturing full-time, 1959-. Publications: The Opera Companion, a Guide for the Casual Operagoer, 1961, 1999; The Battle of the Frogs and the Mice, An Homeric Fable, 1962, 1987; Verdi, His Music, Life and Times, 1963, 1965, 1982, 1984, 2001; The Red Shirt and the Cross of Savoy, the Story of Italy's Risorgimento 1748-1871, 1970; Causes and Conflicts, the Centennial History of the Association of the Bar of the City of New York 1870-1970, 1970, 1997; Madam Secretary, Frances Perkins, 1976; The Companion to Twentieth Century Opera, 1979, 1989; The Damrosch Dynasty, America's First Family of Music, 1983; Aspects of Verdi, 1988, 1994; Verdi at the Golden Gate, Opera and San Francisco in the Gold Rush Years, 1993; Twentieth Century Opera, A Guide, 1999; Verdi in America, Oberto through Rigoletto, 2011. Address: 53 Crosslands Drive, Kennett Square, PA 19348-2010, USA.

MARTIN Michael John, b. 3 July 1945. Politician. m. Mary McLay, 1 son, 1 daughter. Education: St Patrick's Boys' School, Glasgow, Scotland. Appointments: Glasgow City Councillor, 1973-79; Member of Parliament, Glasgow, Springburn (now Glasgow North East), 1979-2009; Deputy Speaker and Deputy Chairman of Ways and Means, 1997-2000; Speaker of the House of Commons, 2000-2009. Address: Speaker's House, House of Commons, London SW1A 0AA, England.

MARTIN Ricky, (Enrique Martin Morales), b. 24 December 1971, Puerto Rico. Singer; Actor. Career: Joined group Menudo, aged 13; Numerous tours and recordings; Left Menudo, 1989; Acted in Mexican soap opera Alcanzur una Estrella II; Began releasing Spanish language albums; Role as bartender in General Hospital; Won the role of Marius in Broadway production of Les Miserables; Dubbed voice in Spanish version of Disney film Hercules; Released first English Language album including a duet with Madonna; Numerous television appearances and tour dates. Recordings: Singles: Maria, 1996; 1 2 3 Maria, 1997; Cup of Life, 1998; La Bomba, 1999; Livin' La Vida Loca, 1999; She's All I Have Had, 1999; Shake Your Bon-Bon; Story, with Christine Aguilera; Albums: Ricky Martin, 1991; Me Amarás, 1993; A Medio Vivir, 1995; Vuelve, 1998; Ricky Martin, 1999; Sound Loaded, 2000; La Historia, 2001; Almas del Silencio, 2003; Life, 2005; MTV Unplugged, 2006. Honour: Grammy Award, Best Latin Pop Album, 1999; Hollywood Walk of Fame, 2007. Address: c/o Sony Music Latin, 550 Madison Avenue, New York, NY 10022, USA.

MARTIN Steve, b. 14 August 1945, Waco, Texas, USA. Actor; Comedian. m. Victoria Tennant, 1986-1994 divorced, (2) Anne Stringfield, 2007, 1 child. Education: Long Beach State College; University of California, Los Angeles. Appointments: TV Writer, several shows; Nightclub Comedian; TV Special, Steve Martin: A Wild and Crazy Guy, 1978. Creative Works: Recordings: Let's Get Small, 1977; A Wild and Crazy Guy, 1978; Comedy is Not Pretty, 1979; The Steve Martin Bros; Film appearances include: The Absent Minded Waiter; Sgt Pepper's Lonely Hearts Club Band, 1978; The Muppet Movie, 1979; The Jerk, 1979; Pennies From Heaven, 1981; Dead Men Don't Wear Plaid, 1982; The Man With Two Brains, 1983; The Lonely Guy, 1984; All of Me, 1984; Three Amigos, 1986; Little Shop of Horrors, 1986; Roxanne, 1987; Planes, Trains and Automobiles, 1987; Parenthood, 1989; My Blue Heaven; L.A. Story; Grand Canyon; Father of the Bride; Housesitter, 1992; Leap of Faith, 1992; Twist of Fate, 1994; Mixed Nuts, 1994; Father of the Bride 2; Sgt Bilko, 1995; The Spanish Prisoner; The Out of Towners; Bowfinger, 1999; Joe Gould's Secret, 2000; Novocaine, 2002; Bringing Down the House, 2003; Cheaper By The Dozen, 2003; Jiminy Glick in La La Wood, 2004; Shopgirl, 2005; Cheaper By The Dozen 2, 2005; The Pink Panther, 2006; Baby Mama, 2008; The Pink Panther 2, 2009; It's Complicated, 2009; The Big Year, 2011. Honours: Emmy Award, 1969; Grammy Award, 1977, 1978; National Society of Film Critics Actor's Award. Address: ICM, 8942 Wilshire Boulevard, Beverly Hills, CA 90211, USA.

MARTIN Todd, b. 8 July 1970, Hinsdale, Illinois, USA. Tennis Player. Education: Northwestern College. Appointments: Winner, New Haven Challenger, 1989; Turned professional, 1990; Semi-Finalist, Stella Artois Grass Court Championships, London, 1993, Champion, 1994, Champion (doubles with Pete Sampras), 1995; Finalist, Australian Open, 1994, Grand Slam Cup, Munich, 1995; Semi-Finalist, US Open, 1994, Wimbledon, 1994, 1996, Paris Open, 1998; Champion, Scania Stockholm Open, 1998; Winner of 13 pro titles by end of 2002; Special Adviser, US Tennis High Performance Program, 2003-; Retired, 2004-. Honours include: Adidas/ATP Tour Sportsmanship Award, 1993, 1994; ATP Tour Most Improved Player, 1993. Memberships: US

Davis Cup Team, 1994-99; President, ATP Players' Council, 1996-97. Address: c/o Advantage International, 1751 Pinnacle Drive, Suite 1500, McLean, VA 22102, USA.

MARTIN Vivian, b. Detroit, Michigan, USA. Opera and Concert Singer. m. Education: Graduate, Wayne State University, Detroit; Conservatoire de Fountainebleau, France; Detroit Conservatory of Music; France; New York; Munich; Berlin; Detroit. Debut: Operatic debut, Leonardo, Verdi's La Forza Del Destino, 1971. Career: Major opera roles including Leonora, Verdi's Il Trovatore; Rezia, Weber's Oberon; Selika, Meyerbeer's L'Africane; Bess, Gershwin's Porgy and Bess, more than 500 times; Major opera houses and concert halls in Europe, Asia, USA, South America; TV and radio appearances; Toured and soloist with numerous orchestras; Symphonies in Sweden, Berlin, Munich, Nurenberg; Philharmonic orchestras in Germany, Slovenska Philharmonia, Detroit Symphony Orchestra; Sang in Tivoli Garden, Copenhagen, Denmark; Grosser Konzert Saal, Vienna, Austria; Théâtre des Champs Elysees, Paris, France, Kongress Saal, Munich, Germany; Participated in World of Gershwin; Festival with concerts with St Petersburg National Symphony Orchestra in Shostakovich Philharmonic Hall, St Petersburg; Moscow Symphony Orchestra in Tschaikovsky, Moscow, Russia; Concerts and performances in USA and abroad during 1994-2004. Honours: First prize and Jean Paul award, Conservatoire de Fountainbleau, 1953; Eighteen singing scholarships and awards. Memberships: AFTRA; American Guild of Music Artists; Actors Equity Association; Wayne State University Alumni Association; Alpha Kappa Alpha. Address: c/o Dr Gösta Schwark International APS, Opera-Concert-Theatre, 18 Groennegade, 1 Floor, DK-1107 Copenhagen, Denmark.

MARTINAC Vanja, b. 28 January 1959, Split, Croatia. Full Professor. 1 son. Education: BSc, 1982, MSc, Chemical Engineering, 1987, PhD, Chemical Engineering, 1994, Faculty of Technology, University of Split. Appointments: Trainee, Graduate Student, 1984-87, Scientific Assistant, 1987-94, Assistant PhD, 1994-96, Faculty of Technology, Assistant Professor, 1996-2001, Associate Professor, 2001-06, Full Professor, 2006-, Faculty of Chemistry and Technology, University of Split. Publications: 37 scientific articles in field of chemical engineering; Co-author, The Book of Technical Thermodynamics, 2nd edition, 2007; Author, The Book of Magnesium Oxide from Seawater, 2010. Honours: Dean Award, 1982. Memberships: Croatian Chemical Society; Croatian Society of Chemical Engineering & Technologists; Association of Chemical Engineering & Technology, Split. Address: Faculty of Chemistry and Technology, Teslina 10/V, 2100 Split, Croatia. E-mail: martinac@ktf-split.hr

MARTINEZ Conchita, b. 16 April 1972, Monzon, Spain. Tennis Player. Appointments: Turned Professional, 1988; Reached last 16, French Open, 1988, quarter-finals, French Open, 1989, 1990, 1991, 1992, 1993, semi-finals, Italian Open, 1991, French Open, 1994, Australian, French and US Opens and Wimbledon, 1995, French and US Opens, 1996, quarter-finals, Olympic Games, 1992; With Arantxa Sanchez-Vicario, won Olympic Doubles Silver Medal, 1992; Won, Italian Open, 1993, Hilton Head (SC), Italian Open, Stratton (Vt), 1994; Wimbledon Singles Champion, 1994; by end of 2002 had won 42 WTA tour titles; Retired 2006. Honours: WTA Tour Most Impressive Newcomer, 1989; Most Improved Player, Tennis Magazine, 1994; ITF Award of Excellence, 2001; International Tennis Hall of Fame, 2001.

MARTINEZ Elizabeth Cruz, b. 19 December 1968, Bayamo, Gramma, Cuba. Microbiologist. m. Ramiro E Almaguel Gonzalez, 2 daughters. Education: Microbiologist, 1991; Master's degree, Water Sciences, 1998. Appointments: Researcher. Publications: Numerous articles in professional journals. Honours: National Award for Research-Development, Ministry of Agriculture of Cuba. Memberships: Cuban Swine Society; Cuban Animal Production Society; Cuban Forest & Agricultural Technicians Society. Address: calle46 No 4310 entre 43 y 45, Caimito, La Habana, CP 32 300, Cuba. E-mail: ecruz@iip.co.cu

MARTINS Grasiele de Lourdes, b. 11 February 1979, Umuarama, Parana, Brazil. Paediatric Endocrinologist; Researcher of Metabolic Syndrome and Physical Activity. Education: Master's degree, Fundação Universidade Federal do Rio Grande, 2002. Appointments: Medical Residency in Paediatrics, 2005, Medical Residency in Paediatric Endocrinology, 2007, Clinical Hospital of Federal University of Parana; Sport Medicine, 2008, Researcher in Metabolic Syndrome and Effects of Physical Activity, 2010, Federal University of Parana. Honours: Highest Scores, Federal University Foundation of Rio Grande, 2002; Best Monograph Presentations, Paediatrics Department, Federal University of Parana, 2006; Outstanding Achievement in Endocrinology, International Endocrine Scholars Program, Endocrine Society, 2007; Award, Endocrine Trainee Day, ENDO 2008, San Francisco, USA, 2008. Memberships: Endocrine Society; Professional Association, International Endocrine Scholars Program Award; American Association of Clinical Endocrinologists; Brazilian Society of Paediatrics. Address: CEDIBE – Diabesity and Well-Being Center, 825 Conselheiro Laurindo St, Room 901, Downtown, Curitiba, Parana, Brazil. E-mail: grasiendo@hotmail.com

MARTINS Herbert Ernst, b. 27 January 1950, St Veit an der Glan, Austria. Economist. m. Doris Martins, 2 daughters. Education: Master of Economics, University of Vienna, Austria, 1972; Doctor of Economics, Vienna School of Economics and Business Administration, Austria, 1975; Fulbright Scholar Postgraduate, University of Oregon, USA, 1975, University of Chicago, USA, 1976. Appointments: Research Associate, University of Chicago, USA, 1976-77; Secretary to Minister of State for Economic Affairs, Austria, 1978; Deputy Director for Foreign Economic Policy Co-ordination, 1987-91, Director for Multilateral Economic Affairs, 1991-2009, Senior Economic Adviser, 2009-10, Federal Chancellery, Department for Co-ordination, Vienna, Austria; Lecturer in Economics, Vienna School of Economics and Business Administration, 1987-96; Member of the Bureau of the Senior Economic Advisors of the UNO Economic Commission for Europe, 1989-90; Minister Counsellor, Permanent Delegation of Austria to the Organisation for Economic Co-operation and Development (OECD), Paris, France, 1990; Member, OECD Committee for International Investment and Multinational Enterprises, 1990-94. Publications: Books: The Dangerous Force – Unemployment, Inflation and Social Justice, 2001; Poverty and Wealth – Problems of the World of Today, 2004. Honours: Recipient of various scholarships and grants, 1969-75; Fulbright Scholarship, 1975. Memberships: Austrian Economic Association; Austrian Association for Foreign Policy and the United Nations; Austrian Association for Public Finance; Center for Peace Research at the University of Vienna; Austrian Society for Political and Strategic Studies. Address: Arsenal 7/2/14, A-1014 Vienna, Austria. E-mail: herbert.martins@gmx.at

DICTIONARY OF INTERNATIONAL BIOGRAPHY 36th EDITION

MARTUCCELLI Silvio, b. 19 April 1968, Rome, Italy. Professor; Lawyer. m. Maria Chiara Romano, 2 sons, 2 daughters. Education: Law degree, La Sapienza University of Rome, 1991; LLM, Columbia University Law School, USA, 1993; PhD, Civil Law, University of Turin, Italy, 1997; Associate Professor of Law, 2000; Full Professor of Law, 2001. Appointments: Director, Private Law Department, 2001-05, Vice-Dean, Law School, 2001-05, University of Teramo, Italy; Partner, Studio Legale Martuccelli, 1994-2008; Partner, Chiomenti Studio Legale, 2010-. Publications: Numerous articles in professional journals. Honours: Admitted to Bar Association, Rome, 1994; Admitted to Italian Supreme Court of Cassation, 2001. Memberships: Italian Bar Association; Directive Council, Society Italian Studiosi Dir Civile, 2007; Circolo Canottieri Amene. Address: Chiomenti Studio Legale, Via G Verdi, 2-20121 Milan, Italy. E-mail: silvio.martuccelli@chiomenti.net

MARZEC Anna Maria, b. 10 March 1933, Kopyczynce, Poland. Chemist. Education: MSc, Technology University, Gliwice, 1956; PhD, 1962; Habilitation, 1969; Professor, Polish Academy of Sciences, 1976. Appointments: Assistant Professor, Associate Professor, Technology University, Gliwice, 1954-70; Associate Professor, 1970, Professor, 1976, Chemistry and Technology of Fuels, Institute of Coal Chemistry, Polish Academy of Sciences, 1974-84; Vice Director, Institute of Coal Chemistry, Polish Academy of Sciences; Professor Emeritus, 2007-. Publications: Numerous articles in professional journals; 55 articles in popular scientific magazines. Honours: Special Guest, International Coal Science Conference, USA, 1984; Peter H Given Memorial Lecturer, Pennsylvania State University, College Earth and Mineral Sciences, University Park, 1990; Research Awards, Ministry Higher Education and Polish Academy of Sciences, 1969, 1973, 1980, 1984; Listed in international biographical dictionaries. E-mail: marzeca@neostrada.pl Website: www.amarzec.republika.pl

MÁŠA Jaromír Amadeus, b. 16 July 1937, Prague, Czech state. Linguist; Translator; Indologist. m. Darie Savelaková, 3 sons, 3 daughters. Education: Philosophical Faculty, Charles University, Prague, 1966; High School of Astronomy, Observatory V Mezirici, 1979; Faculty of Electrotechnics, Czech Technical University, Prague, 1983; United Nations' University, International Leadership Academy, Amman, 1991. Appointments: Book Reviewer, 1966-68; Delegation Interpreter, Czech Ministry of Education and Culture, 1968-73; Technical Interpreter and Translator, 1973-93; Manager and Author, European Association of Children and Youth Leisure Time, 1993-97; Professor of Languages at Orthodox Academy, High School of Arts, Second Age University; Freelance Translator of belles lettres and poetry; Professor of Sanskrit Studies and General Linguistics. Publications: Numerous articles in professional journals. Honours: St Cyrilus and Methodius Medal in Silver, 1997. Memberships: Australian Institute of NDT; Czech Astronomic Society; Czech Society of Music; Czech Society for Nanotechnology; Czech Union of Translators; Huygens-Fokker Stichting; International Academy of Philosophy; International Academy of Yoga; Internationale Ekmelische Gesellschaft. E-mail: jaromir.masa@gmail.com

MASADA Hiromitsu, b. 3 February 1938, Nishinomiya, Hyogo, Japan. Chemistry Researcher. m. Yoko Danno, 1 daughter. Education: Bachelor of Engineering, Osaka University, 1962; Master of Engineering, 1964, Doctor of Engineering, 1967, Kyoto University. Appointments: Assistant Professor, 1967-72, Associate Professor, 1972-96, Professor, 1996-2003, Kanazawa University. Honour: Seikyo Newspaper Culture Award, Tokyo, 1986; Who's Who in the World, 1998; Nominator, Nobel Prize in Chemistry, 2001. Address: 7-6 Hongo 3 Chome, Kashiwara City, Osaka Prefecture 582-0001, Japan.

MASO Giuseppe, b. 20 October 1952, Mirano, Venezia, Italy. Family Doctor; Teacher. m. Antonella Livieri, 1 son. Education: Maturitá Scientifica, 1971; MD, 1977; Certificate in Nephrology, 1980; Certificate in Internal Medicine, 1986. Appointments: Family Physician, Local Health Unit, Mirano, 1999; Teacher, Family Medicine, Udine University, Research CHE Facilitator, Veneto Region, 1985; President, Society Italiana Medician Generale, Venezia, 1987-91; Leader, Cancer Registry, 1988-93; President, Italian Academy of Family Physicians, Milan, 2000-03; Editor-in-Chief, Italian Journal of Primary Care, 2009. Publications: Books: Author: Registro Tumori per la Medicina Generale; La Disciplina Invisible; La Ricerca in Medicina di Famiglia; Le Eta' Della Vita; Il Progetto RTMG SIMG Venezia; RTHG Venezia FASE Operativea; La Giornata del Medico Di Famiglia Italiano; Infermiera e Medico Di Famiglia; Editor: The European Textbook of Family Medicine. Memberships: American Academy of Family Physicians. Address: Via Sabbiona, 68, 30034, Mira, Venezia, Italy. E-mail: giuseppe.maso@gmail.com

MASON Dean Towle, b. 20 September 1932, Berkeley, California, USA. Physician; Cardiologist. m. Maureen O'Brien, 2 daughters. Education: BA, 1954, MD, 1958, Duke University; Resident, Johns Hopkins Hospital, Baltimore, 1958-61; Cardiology Fellow, National Heart Institute, National Institutes of Health, Bethesda, 1961-63. Appointments: Co-Director, Cardiac Catheterization Laboratory, National Institues of Health, 1963-68; Professor of Medicine and Physiology, Chief of Cardiology Division, University of California at Davis, 1968-82; Editor-in-Chief, American Heart Journal, 1980-96; Physician-in-Chief, Western Heart Institute, Chairman, Department of Cardiovascular Medicine, St Mary's Medical Centre, San Francisco, California, 1983-2000; Honorary Staff, 2000-. Publications: Over 1000 scientific publications; 35 books on cardiovascular medicine. Honours: American Therapeutic Society Research Award, 1965; Outstanding Professor, 1972; Faculty Research Award, 1978; Wisdom Society Award Honour, 1997; Winston Chrchill Society Medal, 1998; Dean T Mason, Eminent Physician of Wisdom Award, 2000. Memberships: American Society for Clinical Investigation, 1965; American College of Cardiology, President, 1977-78, Master, 1998. Address: 44725 Country Club Drive, El Macero, CA 95618, USA.

MASON OF BARNSLEY, Baron of Barnsley in the County of South Yorkshire, Roy Mason, b. 18 April 1924, England. Member of the House of Lords. m. Marjorie Sowden, 2 daughters. Education: TUC Scholarship, London School of Economics; D University, Hallam University, Sheffield. Appointments: Coal Miner, 1938-53; Labour Candidate for Bridlington, 1951-53; Member of Parliament for Barnsley, 1953-83, Barnsley Central, 1983-87; Opposition Spokesman on Defence and Post Office Affairs, 1960-64; Minister of State for Shipping, Board of Trade, 1964-67; Minister of Defence Equipment, 1967-68; Postmaster General, 1968; Minister of Power, 1968-69; President, Board of Trade, 1969-70; Principal Spokesman on Board of Trade Affairs, 1970-74; Member, Council of Europe and Western European Union, 1973; Secretary of State for Defence, 1974-76; Secretary of State for Northern Ireland, 1976-79; Principal Opposition Spokesman on Agriculture, Fisheries and Food, 1979-81. Publication: Paying the Price, autobiography. Honours: PC, 1968; Peerage,

1987. Memberships: Yorkshire Miners' Council, 1949-53; Council of Europe, 1970-71; Yorkshire Group of Labour MPs, 1970-74, 1981-84; Miners' Group of MPs, 1973-74, 1980-81; Railway and Steel Union MPs, 1979-80; National Rivers Authority, 1989-92. Address: 12 Victoria Avenue, Barnsley, South Yorkshire, S70 2BH, England.

MASSEY Roy Cyril, b. 9 May 1934, Birmingham, England. Cathedral Organist. m. Ruth Carol Craddock. Education: University of Birmingham, 1953-56; Private tuition under Sir David Willcocks, Worcester Cathedral. Appointments: Accompanist, City of Birmingham Choir, 1953-60; Church and School appointments, 1956-65; Warden, Royal School of Church Music, 1965-68; Organist and Master of the Choristers, Birmingham Cathedral, 1968-74; Organist and Master of the Choristers, Hereford Cathedral, 1974-2001. Publication: The Organs of Hereford Cathedral (in Hereford Cathedral, a history), 2000. Honours: Honorary Fellowship, Royal School of Church Music, 1971; Lambeth Degree, Doctor of Music, 1991; MBE for Services to Music, 1997; Honorary Fellowship, Guild of Church Musicians, 2000; President, Royal College of Organists, 2003-05. Address: 2 King John's Court, Tewkesbury, Gloucestershire GL20 6EG, England. E-mail: drroymassey@ukonline.co.uk

MASTERSON Kleber Sanlin Jr, b. 26 September 1932, San Diego, California, USA. Physicist; Military Operations Researcher. m. Sara Cooper Masterson, 2 sons. Education: BS (Engineering), US Naval Academy, 1954; MS (Physics), US Naval Postgraduate School, 1961; PhD (Physics), University of California at San Diego, 1963; Graduate, Advanced Management Programme, Harvard Business School, 1980. Appointments: Commanding Officer, USS Preble; Antiship Missile Defence Project Manager; Assistant Deputy Commander, Naval Sea Systems Command for Anti-Air and Surface Warfare Systems; Chief, Studies Analysis and Gaming Agency; Office of the Joint Chiefs of Staff; Retired as Rear Admiral, US Navy, 1950-82; Principal, 1982-87, Vice President, Partner, 1987-92 Booz, Allen and Hamilton; Senior Vice President, Science Applications International Corporation, 1992-96; President, The Riverside Group Ltd, 1994-2007; President, Military Operations Research Society, 1988-89; President, Massachusetts Society of the Cincinnati, 2001-04; Assistant Secretary-General, The Society of the Cincinnati, 2001-04; Treasurer General, The Society of the Cincinnati, 2004-2007; Vice President General, The Society of the Cincinnati, 2007-10: President General, The Society of the Cincinnati, 2010-. Publications: Numerous articles and invited presentations; Editor, The Book of Navy Songs, 1954; Created NELIAC ALGOL compiler, 1958-59. Honours: Defence Superior Service Medal; Legion of Merit with 2 gold stars for subsequent awards; Navy Commendation Medal with Combat 'V' and 2 gold stars; Listed in various international biographical dictionaries. Memberships: American Physical Society; Society of Sigma Xi; Society of the Cincinnati; Trustee Emeritus, US Naval Academy Foundation. Address: 101 Pommander Walk, Alexandria, VA 22314-3844, USA. E-mail: skidmasterson@cs.com

MASUCH Jürgen Bruno Wilhelm, b. 25 October 1940, Berlin, Germany. Scientist. m. Monika Schmieder, 1 son, 1 daughter. Education: Bachelor's degree, 1959, Dipl Ing (Mechanical Engineer), 1965, Dr Ing (HVAC), 1971, Technical University, Berlin; Researcher, Comité Scientifique et technique du Chauffage, de la Ventilation et du Conditionnement d'Air (COSTIC), Paris, France, 1971-72. Appointments: Head, Development Department, LTG Lufttechn GmbH, Stuttgart, 1972-88; Head, Consultancy Group, HL Technik AG, Stuttgart, 1989-91; Chief Manager, M&E for building developer Technoteam Wiesbaden, 1991-94; Chief Manager, Consulting Firm RP+K Sozietät GmbH, Berlin and Maidenhead, England, 1994-; Head, Innovation Center, Scholze Ing GmbH, Stuttgart, 2001-. Publications: 68 papers and articles in professional scientific journals. Honours: VDI Honour Ring, 1975; VDI Honour Medal, 2000. Memberships: VDI, ASHRAE. Address: Alemannenstr 16, D-71726, Benningen, Germany. E-mail: masuch@scholze.de

MASUMI Taizo, b. 31 March 1932, Kyushu, Japan. Professor Emeritus; Research Scientist. m. Mifune Taeko, 1 daughter. Education: BS, 1954, MEng, 1956, DEng, 1959, University of Tokyo, Japan. Appointments: Research Scientist, Institute of Physical and Chemical Research, 1959-64; Research Associate, University of Illinois, USA, 1959-62; Associate Professor, 1964-77, Professor, 1977-92, Professor Emeritus, 1992-, University of Tokyo; Professor, Gunma University, 1992-97; COE Special Research Scientist, National Research Institute for Metals, 1997-2001; COE Special Scientist, 2001-03, Visiting Research Scientist, 2003-05, Professor, 2006-, National Institute for Materials Science, Tsukuba. Publications: Over 120 scientific papers and reviews on polarons and excitons, and space-time aspects of superconductivity; Book, Quasi-Particle Physics in Condensed Matters, 1996; 30 patents on superconductive optoelectronics. Honour: Grant for Specially Distinguished Research, Ministry of Education, Science and Culture, Japan, 1989-92; Listed in several international scientific biographical directories, including 2000 Outstanding Scientists of the 20th Century; 2000 Outstanding Scientists of the 21st Century. Memberships: Physical Society of Japan; Japan Society of Applied Physics; American Physical Society; LFIBA; IBC. Address: 4-55-10, Utsukushigaoka, Aoba-ku, Yokohama City, Kanagawa Prefecture 225-0002, Japan. E-mail: MASUMI.Taizo@nims.go.jp

MAT ARSHAD Adzemi, b. 26 May 1955, Bachok, Kelantan, Malaysia. Senior Lecturer. m. An'am Fauzi, 5 sons, 6 daughters. Education: Bachelor, 1986, Master, 1990, Agricultural Science; PhD, 1999. Appointments: Head, Department of Agrotechnology, 2005-. Publications: Journal of Environmental Science & Engineering; Journal of Agriculture, Science and Technology. Honours: Excellent Service Award, 2006, 2007, 2008, 2009, 2010 & 2011. Memberships: Malaysia Society of Soil Science; Internal Peat Society. Address: Faculty of Agrotechnology and Food Science, Universiti Malaysia Terengganu, 21030 Kuala Terengganu, Terengganu, Malaysia. E-mail: adzemi@umt.edu.my

MATEOS Oscar Ignacio, b. 16 June 1963, Madrid, Spain. Researcher; Educator; Professor. Education: Graduate, Political Sciences and Sociology, 1990, Graduate in Law, 1999, Doctor in Political Sciences, 1996, University of Complutense, Madrid; Doctor in Right, 2005, Master Degree, Advanced Studies in Public Law, 2003, University of King Juan Carlos. Appointments: Regular Professor, Constitutional Law, University of King Juan Carlos, Madrid; Scientific Adviser, Foundation Joaquin Costa, Institute of Studies Altoaragoneses of the Excellent Deputation of Huesca, 2002-. Publications: Numerous articles in professional journals on legal, political and historical matters. Honours: Extraordinary Reward for Best Doctoral Thesis, University of King Juan Carlos, 2010. Memberships: Lawyer in Madrid; Association of Constitutionalists from Spain. Address: University of King Juan Carlos, Paseo de los Artilleros S/N, 28032 Madrid, Spain. E-mail: oscar.mateos@urjc.es

MATHESON Michael, b. 8 September 1970, Glasgow, Scotland. Member of the Scottish Parliament. Education: BSc, Occupational Therapy, Queen Margaret College, Edinburgh, 1988-92; BA, Diploma in Applied Social Sciences, Open University, 1992-96. Appointments: Community Occupational Therapist, Stirling Council, Central Regional Council and Highland Regional Council, 1992-99; Member of the Scottish Parliament, 1999-; Shadow Minister for Culture and Sport, 2004-2006; Falkirk West, 2007; Member, Health & Sport Committee, 2007-11; Minister for Public Health, 2011. Memberships: State Registered Occupational Therapist, Health Professions Council; Member, Ochils Mountain Rescue Team; Former Member, Scottish Parliament Justice Committee; Member, Enterprise and Culture Committee. Address: The Scottish Parliament, Edinburgh, EH99 1SP, Scotland. E-mail: michael.matheson.msp@scottish.parliament.uk

MATHIAS Peter, b. 10 January 1928. Historian. m. Elizabeth Ann Blackmore, 2 sons, 1 daughter. Education: BA, 1951, MA, 1954, Jesus College, Cambridge; LittD (Oxon), 1985; DLitt (Cantab), 1987. Appointments include: Research Fellow, Jesus College, Cambridge, 1952-55; Assistant Lecturer, Lecturer, Faculty of History, University of Cambridge, 1955-68; Director of Studies in History, Fellow, Queens' College, Cambridge, 1955-68; Tutor, 1957-68, Senior Proctor, 1965-66, University of Cambridge; Chichele Professor of Economic History, University of Oxford, Fellow All Souls College, 1969-87; Curator Bodleian Library, 1972-87; Master, Downing College, Cambridge, 1987-95; Visiting Professor: Toronto University, 1961; Delhi University, 1967; California University, Berkeley, 1967; Pennsylvania University, 1972; Virginia Gildersleeve Professor, Columbia University, 1972; Johns Hopkins University, 1979; Natal University, 1980; Australian National University, 1981; Geneva University, 1986; Leuven University, 1990; San Marino University, 1990; Waseda University, 1996; Osaka Gakuin University, 1998; Bolzano Free University, 1999; Kansai University, 2006; Chairman, Business Archives Council, 1967-72, President, 1984-95, Vice-President, 1995-;Chairman, International Advisory Committee, University of Buckingham, 1979-84; National Advisory Council, British Library, 1994-2000; Chairman, 1997-2005, President, 2005-, Great Britain Sasakawa Foundation; Member Syndicate Fitzwilliam Museum, Cambridge, 1987-98; Chairman, Fitzwilliam Museum Enterprises, 1990-99; Member, Board of Patrons, European Association for Banking History; Honorary Treasurer, British Academy, 1980-89. Publications: The Brewing Industry in England 1700-1830, 1959, reprinted 1993; English Trade Tokens, 1962; Retailing Revolution, 1967; The First Industrial Nation, 1969, revised edition, 1983; The Transformation of England, 1979; Editor and contributor, Science and Society, 1972; Co-editor and contributor, The First Industrial Revolutions, 1989; Co-editor and contributor, Innovation and technology in Europe, 1991; L'Economia Britannica dal 1815-1914, 1994; Cinque lezioni de teoria e storia, Naples, 2003; L'Idea di Europa, Naples, 2009; General editor, Cambridge Economic History of Europe, 1968-93. Honours: Fellow, Royal Historical Society, 1972; Fellow, British Academy, 1977; CBE, 1984; Honorary Fellow, Jesus College, 1987, Queens' College, 1987, Downing College, 1995; Honorary LittD, University of Buckingham, 1985, University of Hull, 1992, University of Warwick, 1995, De Montfort University, 1995; Honorary DLitt, University of Birmingham, 1988, UEA, 1999; Honorary Doctorate, Russian Academy of Sciences, 2002; Grand Cordon, Order of the Rising Sun, 2003; Honorary Doctorate, Kansai University, Japan, 2006; Honorary Doctorate, Keio University, Japan, 2008. Memberships include: President, 1974-78, Honorary President, 1978- International Economic History Society; Vice President, 1975-80, Honorary Vice-President, 2001-, Royal Historical Society; President, 1989-92, Vice President, 1992-, Economic History Society; Academia Europaea; Foreign Member: Royal Danish Academy, Royal Belgian Academy. Address: 33 Church Street, Chesterton, Cambridge, CB4 1DT, England.

MATHUR Anand Behari Lal, b. 8 November 1939, Jaipur, Rajasthan, India. Retired Education Educator. m. Kanti, 4 children. Education: M Com, First Division, 1960, PhD in Commerce, 1971, University of Rajasthan, Jaipur. Appointments: Teacher of B Com, M Com, M Phil, BSc Management Studies, MBA and PG Diploma students, University of Rajasthan, University of Calabar (Nigeria) on foreign assignment by the Government of India to the Government of Nigeria for 4 years, and J N Vyas University (Jodhpur, India), 39 years; Guest Faculty, Indira Gandhi National Open University, the Bhartiya Vidya Bhawan, the Indian Institute of Rural Management, the Aravali Institute of Management, and the Pacific Institute of Management; Founder Editor, Editor and Chairman of Editorial Board, The Indian Journal of Business Administration, 1996-97, 1997-98, 1998-99, and Head of Department of Business Administration, J N Vyas University, Jodhpur, India, 1996-99, Retired, 1999. Publications: Author of over 50 research papers published nationally and internationally including World Bank Publication, widely recognised by experts and authorities like the International Trade Centre, UNCTAD/GATT, Geneva, Switzerland and the Indian institute of Management, Ahemadabad; Indo-US Trade Relations, 2001 (doctoral thesis updated); Readings in Marketing, 2002; Readings in Management, 2002. Supervisor of over 30 research projects in India and Nigeria in the fields of Marketing and General Management; Participated in numerous national and international seminars, conferences, workshops and symposia. Honours: Secretary, Appointments and Promotion Committee, Department of Management Studies, University of Calabar, Nigeria, 1981-85; Invited by the Irish Export Board, Dublin (Ireland) to co-operate in Trade Development Training Programme, 1989; Served as expert at several prominent organisations in India including the University Grants Commission, Banking Service Recruitment Board, and Public Service Commissions; Founded Research Cell, Department of Business Administration, J N Vyas University, 1997; International Educator of the Year, IBC, 2005; Man of the Year, 2009; Listed in prestigious biographical directories. Memberships: Life Member, The Indian Commerce Association; The Indian Marketing Association; The Pitman Fellowship, London, 1964; A scout; Participated in National Service Scheme. Address: Nrasingh Krapa, B14/1, Kesar Marg, JLN Marg, Jaipur 302017, India. E-mail: mathur1alok@rediffmail.com

MATIN Abdul, b. 1 March 1932, Sawabi, Mardan, Pakistan. Economist. m. Azra, 3 sons. Education: MA, PhD, Economics, Bonn, Germany. Appointments: Minister, Foreign Service, Pakistan Embassy, Ankara, 1973-76; Secretary, Senior Executive Director, Agricultural Development, Bank of Pakistan, 1977-85; Vice Chancellor, Peshawar University, 1987-89; Chairman, Thinkus Forum, NWFP, Hamdard Foundation, Karachi. Publications: Industrialization of NWFP, 1970; 95 articles in professional journals, 1957-; Numerous official reports, 1992-. Honours:

Award for Excellence of Services, Hamdard Foundation, Karachi, 1992; Award for outstanding services, Khawaja Farid Sang, Lahore, 2004. Membership: Several finanical, economic, educational and cultural commissions, 1992-2007. Address: House No 27, Street No 9, D3, Phase – I, Hayatabad Peshawar Pakhturhwa KPP, Pakistan.

MATOUŠEK Jiří, b. 4 April 1930, Příbram, Czech Republic. Chemical Engineer. m. Dagmar Matoušková, 1 son, 1 daughter. Education: Dipl Eng (Chem), Czech Technical University, Prague and Military Technical Academy, Brno, 1954; PhD (CSc), Military Technical Academy, Brno, 1958; DSc, Military Academy of Chemical Protection, Moscow, 1967; Associate Professor, Special Technology, Military Academy, Brno, 1966; Professor, Organic Chemistry, Palacký University, Olomouc, 1983. Appointments: Assistant Professor, Military Technical Academy, Brno, 1954-59, Head of Department, 1959-63; Director, NBC Defence R & D Establishment, Brno, 1963-71; Deputy Head, Department of Toxicology, Purkyne Medical Research Institute, Hradec Králové, 1971-81; Director for Research, NBC Defence R & D Establishment, Brno, 1981-89; Senior Research Fellow, Academy of Science, Prague, 1989-90; Professor of Toxicology, Masaryk University, Brno, 1990-; Visiting Professor International Institute for Peace, Vienna, 1990-; Director Institute of Environmental Chemistry and Technology, Brno University of Technology, 1992-2000. Publications: Over 520 articles in professional and scientific journals; About 135 research reports, 90 patents and improvement suggestions, mostly realised in production and use; More than 570 conference papers, mostly international; 27 books and 43 chapters in monographs dealing with chemistry and analysis of toxic agents, chemical and biological disarmament, verification, conversion, ecological, environmental and other global problems, mostly in English but also in German, French, Russian, Czech and Slovak. Honours: 12 state and military orders and medals; Memorial Medal of Masaryk University, 1991; Memorial Medal of Brno University of Technology, 1999; American Medal of Honor, 2002; International Peace Prize, 2005; Czech Golden Rescue Cross, 2007. Memberships: International Network of Engineers and Scientists; World Federation of Scientific Workers; Pugwash Conferences; Accredited Representative of World Federation of Scientific Workers at UNO and conference of NGOs; Foreign Member, Bologna Academy of Sciences; Honorary Member, NBC Defence Forum, Vienna; Many other professional organisations. Address: Krásného 26, CZ-636 00 Brno, Czech Republic. E-mail: matousek@recetox.muni.cz

MATSUDA Wakoto, b. 6 April 1968, Onomichi, Hiroshima, Japan. Neurosurgeon, Researcher. m. Kiyoe Nakazawa, 2 sons, 1 daughter. Education: MD, Faculty of Medicine, University of Tsukuba, Tsukuba, Ibaraki, Japan, 1990-96; Diplomate in Neurosurgery, Japan Neurosurgical Society, 2002; PhD, Kyoto University, Japan, 2009. Appointments: Residency, Department of Neurosurgery, Tsukuba University Hospital, 1996-2002; Clinical fellow, Department of Neurosurgery, Tsukuba Medical Centre Hospital, 2002-2003; Postgraduate, 2003-06, Research Assistant, 2004-06, Department of Morphological Brain Science, Graduate School of Medicine, Kyoto University, Kyoto, Japan; Assistant Professor, Division of Anatomy and Cell Biology, Department of Anatomy, Shiga University of Medical Science, 2006-. Publications: Articles in Journal of Neurology, Neurosurgery and Psychiatry, 2003, 2004; Neuropsychological Rehabilitation, 2005; Paediatric Neurosurgery, 2006; Neuroscience Research, 2008; Journal of Trauma, 2008; Journal of Neuroscience, 2009; Neurologia medico-chirurgical, Tokyo, 2010; European Journal of Neuroscience, 2011. Honours: The Best Resident Award of the Year, Department of Neurosurgery, Institute of Clinical Medicine, University of Tsukuba, 2002; Iwadare Scholarship, Iwadare Scholarship Foundation, 2003; Grantee: General Insurance Association of Japan, 2009; Zenkyoren, 2010; Shiga Prefectural Rehabilitation Centre, 2010, 2011; Mitsui Sumitomo Insurance Welfare Foundation, 2010; Grant-in-Aid for Scientific Research, 2010-12; Listed in international biographical dictionaries. Memberships: Society for Neuroscience, USA; Japan Neurosurgical Society; Japanese Congress of Neurological Surgery; Japan Neuroscience Society, Tokyo; Japanese Association of Anatomists, Tokyo. Address: Division of Anatomy and Cell Biology, Department of Anatomy, Shiga University of Medical Science, Tsukinowa-cho, Seta, Otsu, Shiga, 520-2192, Japan. E-mail: matsuda2@belle.shiga-med.ac.jp

MATSUHASHI Nobuyuki, b. 7 November 1956, Tokyo. Physician. 3 daughters. Education: BM, 1982, MD, 1991, University of Tokyo. Appointments: Resident, University of Tokyo, 1982-84; Assistant Professor, Tokyo Women's Medical College, 1984-85; Resident, Jichi Medical School, 1985-86; Research Fellow, National Institute of Radiological Sciences, 1988-89; Assistant Professor, University of Tokyo, 1989-2003; Chairman, Department of Endoscopy and Department of Gastroenterology, 2006-, Kanto Medical Center, NTT East. Publications: Articles in professional medical journals including: Journal of Immunology, Gut, Lancet, Gastroenterology, Gastrointestinal Endoscopy, Journal of Experimental Medicine, Cancer Research. Honours: Academic Prize of the Japanese Gastroenterological Endoscopy Society, 1999. Memberships: Japanese Society for Gastroenterology; Japanese Society for Gastroenterological Endoscopy; Japanese Society for Immunology; Japanese Society for Internal Medicine; American Gastroenterological Association; Society for Mucosal Immunology; American Society for Gastrointestinal Endoscopy. Address: Department of Gastroenterology, Kanto Medical Center, NTT East, 5-9-22 Higashi-gotanda, Shinagawa-ku, Tokyo 141-8625 Japan. E-mail: nmatuha-tky@umin.ac.jp

MATSUI Masayuki, b. 15 November 1945, Japan. Professor. m. Kazuko Oguni, 1 son, 1 daughter. Education: BS, 1968, MS, 1970, Engineering, Hiroshima University; Doctor of Engineering, Tokyo Institute of Technology, 1981. Appointments: Visiting Scholar, UC Berkeley, Purdue University, 1996-97; Editor, Journal of Japan Industrial Management Association, 2000-03; President, JIMA, Japan, 2007-09; Board Member, International Foundation for Production Research, 2007-. Publications: Numerous articles in professional journals. Honours: JIMA Prize and Award, Japan, 2005; 5 Year Anniversary, 2010; Emeritus, Professor, University of Electro-Communications, 2011. Memberships: Institute of Industrial Engineers; Japan Industrial Management Association. Address: 1-8-73 Fujimi-cho, Chofu-shi, Tokyo 182-0033, Japan. E-mail: mmatsui55@nifty.com

MATSUMOTO Ken'ichi, b. 13 March 1982, Hyogo, Japan. Academic. Education: School of Policy Studies, 2000-03, PhD, Graduate School of Policy Studies, 2004-07, Kwansei Gakuin University; MSc, Graduate School of Information Production and Systems, Waseda University, 2003-04. Appointments: JSPS Research Fellow (DC2), 2006-07, JSPS Research Fellow (PD), 2007-08, Researcher, 2007-08, Kwansei Gakuin University; Post-doctoral Fellow, National Institute for Environmental Studies, 2008-11; Assistant Professor, The University of Shiga Prefecture, 2011-. Publications:

Economic Analysis of CO2 Emission Abatement Applying a Dynamic CGE Model with Endogenous Technological Change: Impacts of Time Horizon, 2011; Many other papers in environmental economics and policies. Memberships: Society for Environmental Economics and Policy Studies; Society of Environmental Science, Japan.

MATSUMURA Sowjun, b. 22 February 1947, Fukui, Japan. Researcher. m. Nahomi, 1 son, 1 daughter. Education: Master, Kohnan University, Japan, 1972; Doctor, Tsinghua University, China, 2004. Appointments: Researcher, C Uyemura Co Ltd, Japan; General Manager, Okuna Chemical Co Ltd, Japan; Representative, Matton Laboratory Solution, Japan. Publications: Composite Plating, 1986; New Composite Plating, 1998; Absolutely Easy Functional Plating, 2008. Honours: Technical Prize, Surface Finishing Society, Japan, 1981; Technical Award, Kinki Chemical Society, Japan, 1983. Memberships: Electrochemical Society, Japan; Surface Finishing Society, Japan. Address: 1-4-26 Tachibana-cho, Toyonaka, Osaka 560-0025, Japan.

MATSUURA Koichiro, b. 29 September 1937, Tokyo, Japan. Director-General of UNESCO. m. Takako Kirikae, 2 sons. Education: Faculty of Law, University of Tokyo, 1956-59; Faculty of Economics, Haverfod College, USA, 1959-61. Appointments: Third Secretary, Embassy of Japan, Ghana, 1961-63; Second Secretary, then First Secretary, Japanese Delegation to the OECD, Paris, 1968-72; Various posts in central administration, 1963-68, 1972-74, Director, First North American Division (Political Affairs), 1974-75, Director, Development Co-operation Division, 1975-77, Director, Aid Policy Division, 1980-82, Director-General, Economics Co-operation Bureau, 1988-90, Director-General, North American Affairs Bureau, 1990-92, Ministry of Foreign Affairs; Counsellor, Embassy of Japan, USA, 1977-80; Director, General Affairs Division, Deputy Director-General, Foreign Minister's Office, 1982-85; Consul General of Japan in Hong Kong, 1985-88; Deputy Minister for Foreign Affairs (Sherpa for Japan at the G-7 Summit), 1992-94; Ambassador of Japan to France and concurrently to Andorra and Djibouti, 1994-99; Chairperson, World Heritage Committee of UNESCO, 1998-99; UNESCO Director-General (elected for a 6-year term on 15 November 1999), 1999-2005; Re-elected UNESCO Director-General for a 4-year term on 15 November 2005), 2005-. Publications: In the Forefront of Economic Co-operation Diplomacy, 1990; History of Japan-United State Relations, 1992; The G-7 Summit: Its History and Perspectives, 1994; Development & Perspectives of the Relations between Japan and France, 1995; Japanese Diplomacy at the Dawn of the 21st Century, 1998. Address: Office of the Director-General, UNESCO, 7, place de Fontenoy, 75352 Paris 07 SP, France. Website: www.unesco.org

MATTESSICH Richard, b. 9 August 1922, Trieste, Italy. Professor Emeritus. m. Hermine. Education: Mech Engineer Diploma, 1940; Dipl Kaufmann, 1944; Dr rer pol, 1945; Dr honoris causa, Madrid, 1998; Bordeaux, 2006; Malaga, 2006; Graz, 2008. Appointments: Research Fellow, Austrian Institute of Economic Research, 1945-47; Lecturer, Rosenberg College, Switzerland, 1947-52; Department Head, Mount Allison University, Canada, 1953-58; Associate Professor, University of California, Berkeley, 1959-67; Professor, Ruhr University, Bochum, 1965-66; Professor, University of British Columbia, 1967-88; Professor, University of Technology, Vienna, 1976-78; Professor Emeritus, University of British Columbia, 1988-. Publications: Books: Accounting and Analytic Methods, 1964; Simulation of the Firm, 1964; Instrumental Reasoning and Systems Methods, 1978; Modern Accounting Research, 1984; Accounting Research in the 1980's, 1991; Critique of Accounting, 1995; Foundational Research in Accounting, 1995; The Beginnings of Accounting, 2000; La Representacion Contable y el modelo de Capas-Cebolla de la Realidad, 2003; Two Hundred Years of Accounting Research, 2008. Honours: Ford Founding Fellow, USA, 1961, 62; Erskine Fellow, New Zealand, 1970; Killam Senior Fellow, Canada, 1971; Literary Awards, AICPA, 1972, CAAA, 1991; Drhc, University of Montesquieu, Bordeaux, 2006; Drhc, University of Málaga, 2006; Dr hc, Graz, 2008; Listed in Who's Who publications. Memberships: Accademia Italiana di Econ Aziendale, 1980-; Austrian Academy of Science, 1984-; Life member, American Accounting Association; Life member, Academy of Accounting Historians; Officially Nominated for the Nobel Prize in Economics, 2002; Drhc. (Univ. of Madrid, 1998). Address: 1807 Knox Road, Vancouver, British Columbia, Canada V6T 1S4. E-mail: richard.mattessich@sauder.ubc.ca

MATTHEW Christopher Charles Forrest, b. 8 May 1939, London, England. Writer and Broadcaster. m. Wendy Mary Matthew, 1979, 2 sons, 1 daughter. Education: King's School, Canterbury; MA (Hons), St Peter's College, Oxford. Appointments: Editor, Times Travel Guide, 1972-73; Radio: Freedom Pass (Radio 4), with Alan Coren, 2003-06; Touchline Tales (Radio 4), with Des Lynam, 2010-. Publications: A Different World; Stories of Great Hotels, 1976; Diary of a Somebody, 1978; Loosely Engaged, 1980; The Long-Haired Boy, 1980; The Crisp Report, 1981; Three Men in a Boat, annotated edition, with Benny Green, 1982; The Junket Man, 1983; How to Survive Middle Age, 1983; Family Matters, 1987; The Amber Room, 1995; A Nightingale Sang in Fernhurst Road, 1998; Now We Are Sixty, 1999; Knocking On, 2000; Now We Are Sixty (And a Bit), 2003; Summoned by Balls, 2005; When We Were Fifty, 2007; Contributions to: Many leading newspapers; Columnist for Punch, 1983-88; Restaurant Critic for English Vogue, 1983-86; Book reviewer for Daily Mail. Membership: Society of Authors; Chelsea Arts Club. Address: 4 Fleming House, 20 Danvers Street, London SW3 5AT, England.

MATTHEWS Donald John, b. 21 December 1933, New Jersey, USA. Financial Consultant. m. Ann Lind Bowers. Education: Georgetown Preparatory School; BS, University of Notre Dame, 1955. Appointments: President, Midland Insurance Co; Managing Director, Johnson & Higgins; President, American Capital Access Inc; Director, Syncora Capital Assurance Inc. Honours: America's Cup Defence, 1958-62. Memberships: Trustee, University of Notre Dame; Director, Mercy College; Retired Chairman, Guiding Eyes for the Blind; Knight of Malta.

MATTISON Keith, b. 27 November 1921, Dewittville, New York, USA. Military Fighter Pilot; Engineer. m. (1) Virginia Keller Gettmann (deceased), (2) Florence Larson (deceased), (3) Carol Ann Parker, 2 sons (1 deceased), 2 daughters. Education: BSME, Lehigh University; MBA, Auburn University; PhD, California Western. Appointments: Serendipity Songsters and Presbyterian Church Choir; Three Singing Groups Silver Saints, Volusia County Chorus; Kiwanis Club serving the Children of the World; Retired and serving in volunteer organizations. Publications: A Pacific Fighter; The Dive; Friendly Fire; Effective Communication. Honours: Fighter Pilot WWII; Air Medal with Clusters; Distinguished Flying Cross; Purple Heart. Memberships: Kiwanis Club of Deltona South West Volusia; Toastmasters International; Volusia County Chorus; Serendipity Songsters;

Singing Silver Saints; Deltona Presbyterian Church and Choir. Address: 1345 N Shadow Ridge Drive, Deltona, FL 32725, USA. E-mail: kwmatt1127@aol.com

MATUSSEK Thomas, b. 18 September 1947, Lauda, Germany. Ambassador. m. Ursula Matussek, 1 son, 2 daughters. Education: Studied Law and History at the Universities of Paris (Sorbonne) and Bonn, 1979-72; First State Examination in Law, 1973. Appointments: Judge's Assistant/Assistant Lecturer, University of Bonn, 1973-76; German Foreign Office, Bonn, 1975-77; German Embassy, London, 1977-80; Federal Chancellery, European Affairs, 1980-83; German Embassy, New Delhi, 1983-86; German Embassy, Lisbon, 1986-88; German Foreign Office, Bonn, 1988-92; Head of the Minister's Office, 1992-93, Chief of the Cabinet of the Minister, 1993-94, Foreign Office, Bonn; Deputy Chief of Mission, German Embassy, Washington, 1994-99; Director-General, Political Department, Foreign Office, Berlin, 1999; Ambassador of the Federal Republic of Germany to the Court of St James's, 2002-; German ambassador to the United Nations, 2006. Memberships: Athenaeum; Royal Automobile; Naval and Military Club; Travellers Club; Beefsteak Club; Capital Club. Address: German Embassy, 23 Belgrave Square, London SW1X 8PZ, England. E-mail: amboffice@german-embassy.org.uk

MATZKA Christian, b. 31 October 1959, Vienna, Austria. Teacher; Lecturer. m. Ulrike, 2 daughters. Education: Teacher's Diploma, Geography, 1985; PhD, History, 2004. Appointments: Teacher, College of Tourism, 1985-2007; Lecturer, Faculty of History, Geography & Education, Vienna University, 1989-; Headmaster, College of Tourism, Vienna, 1999-2001; Vice Rector, 2007-11, Professor, 2008-, University of Education, Vienna; Vice Mayor, Purkersdorf, 2010-. Publications: Numerous articles in professional journals. Honours: Thanks of Board of Education in Vienna; Head, City Museum of Purkersdorf. Memberships: Austrian Geographical Society; Herodot Network; Austrian Society of Didactics of History. Address: Wienerstrasse 10, A-3002 Purkersdorf, Austria. E-mail: christian.matzka@univie.ac.at

MAUNDER Leonard, b. 10 May 1927, Swansea, Wales. Engineer. m. Moira Anne Hudson (deceased), 1 son, 1 daughter. Education: BSc, University College of Swansea, 1947; PhD, Edinburgh University, 1950; ScD, MIT, 1954. Appointments: Instructor and Assistant Professor, Mechanical Engineering, MIT, 1950-54; Section Leader, Aeronautical Research Lab, Wright Air Development Center, US Air Force, 1954-56; Lecturer, University of Edinburgh, 1956-61; Professor, Applied Mechanics, King's College, Professor, Mechanical Engineering and Dean of Engineering, University of Newcastle upon Tyne, 1961-92. Publications: Numerous articles in professional journals; Books: Gyrodynamics and its Engineering Applications with R N Arnold, 1961; Machines in Motion, 1986. Honours: OBE, 1977; I Mech E Leonardo da Vinci Lecturer, 1978; Royal Institution Christmas Lecturer, 1983. Memberships: Fellow, Royal Academy of Engineering; Fellow, Institution of Mechanical Engineers; Fellow, University of Swansea, Wales; Honorary Foreign Member, Polish Society of Applied Mechanics. Address: 46 Moorside South, Newcastle upon Tyne, NE4 9BB, England. E-mail: leonard.maunder@ncl.ac.uk

MAURICE-WILLIAMS Robert Stephen, b. 14 June 1942, Southampton, England. Consultant Neurosurgeon. m. Elizabeth Anne Meadows, 1 son, 3 daughters. Education: Winchester College; Pembroke College, Cambridge, St Thomas' Hospital Medical School, London; MA, MB, BChir, Cambridge; FRCS (England); FRCP(London). Appointments: Chief Assistant in Neurosurgery, St Bartholomew's Hospital, 1973-77; Consultant Neurosurgeon, Brook Hospital, 1977-80; Consultant Neurosurgeon, 1980-2007, Senior Neurosurgeon, 1982-2007, The Royal Free Hospital; Editor, British Journal of Neurosurgery, 1992-99; Member, Court of Examiners, Royal College of Surgeons, 1992-98. Publications: Books: Spinal Degenerative Disease, 1981; Subarachnoid Haemorrhage, 1988; Over 80 papers in peer-reviewed scientific journals and 8 chapters in medical textbooks. Honours: Open Scholarship in Natural Sciences, Pembroke College, Cambridge, 1960; First Class Honours, Natural Sciences Tripos, Cambridge, 1964; Cheselden Medal, St Thomas' Hospital, 1967; Hallett Prize, Royal College of Surgeons, 1971; President, Clinical Neurosciences Section, Royal Society of Medicine, 2009-10. Memberships: Athenaeum Club, London; Pitt Club, Cambridge; Society of British Neurological Surgeons, Officer, 1996-2006, Member of the Council, 1992-2006. Address: Neurosurgical Unit, Wellington Hospital, London NW8 9LE, England.

MAVRIKAKIS Ioannis, b. 5 November 1973, Athens, Greece. Ophthalmologist. Education: MUDr, 3rd Faculty of Medicine, Charles University, Prague, Czech Republic, 1997; Specialist qualification, Ophthalmology, 2004, PhD, 2005, University of Athens, Greece. Appointments: Clinical Research Fellow, Ophthalmology, Queen Victoria Hospital, East Grinstead, England, 1999-2000; Ophthalmology Resident: Eastbourne District General Hospital, England, 2000-01; Brighton & Sussex University Hospital, England, 2001-03; Royal Berkshire Hospital, Reading, England, 2003-04; Oculoplastic and Lacrimal Fellow: Brighton & Sussex University Hospital, 2003-04; Queen Victoria Hospital, East Grinstead, 2004-05; Orbital Fellow, UBC, Vancouver, Canada, 2005-06; Oculoplastic, Lacrimal Orbital Surgeon, University of Athens, 2006-. Publications: 45 high quality peer-reviewed scientific papers in most prestigious international ophthalmic journals. Memberships: American Society of Ophthalmic Plastic and Reconstructive Surgery; European Society of Ophthalmic Plastic and Reconstructive Surgery; British Oculoplastic Surgery Society; American Academy of Ophthalmology. Address: Solonos 18, Kolonaki, 10673, Athens, Greece. E-mail: jmavrikakis@yahoo.com

MAVROPOULOS Georgios, b. 30 July 1964, Moschato, Attiki, Greece. Mechanical Engineer; Researcher. Education: Dipl Ing, Mechanical Engineering, 1989, Dr Ing, 2001, National Technical University of Athens; Certificate of Proficiency in English, University of Michigan, USA, 2004. Appointments: Research Assistant, National Technical University of Athens, 1993-97; Product Design Engineer, Ceremetal se SA, 1998-2000; Product Development Engineer, 2000-05, Responsible for Cooling Systems Development, 2006-, Bosch-Siemens Oikiakes Syskeves; Senior Research Associate, National Technical University of Athens, 2000-. Publications: Author, more than 30 papers in international journals and conferences; Scientific consultant on university textbook, Internal Combustion Engines – Exercises in Dynamics. Honours: Two-year Scholarship for Postgraduate Studies, National Technical University of Athens, 1993-95; Annual Scholarship, Toyota Hellas, 1995-96; Excellence in Research and Development, Bosch-Siemens Oikiakes Syskeves, 2002, 2003, 2005; Society of Automotive Engineers, Best Presentation Award, 2004; Society of Automotive Engineers, Longtime Member Service Award, 2006. Memberships: Technical Chamber of Greece; Hellenic Association of Mechanical and Electrical Engineers; Society of Automotive Engineers; American Chemical Society, ACS-USA, 2010. Address: 7 Pallikaridi Street, 18345 Moschato, Greece. E-mail: mavrop@otenet.gr

MAWBY Colin, b. 9 May 1936, Portsmouth, England. Musician. m. Beverley Courtney, 2 sons. Education: Westminster Cathedral Choir School, 1946-51; Royal College of Music, 1951-54. Appointments: Master of Music, Westminster Cathedral, 1961-77; Professor, Trinity College of Music, 1977-81; Choral Director, Radio Telefís, Eireann, 1981-95; Freelance Composer, Artistic Director, National Chamber Choir of Ireland, 1995-2002. Publications: Over 50 masses; 2 children's operas; 2 cantatas; Over 200 motets; Anthems, psalms, hymns and a large amount of organ music, including 1 sonata; Articles published in popular and professional journals. Honours: Officer of Merit, Knights of Malta, 1975; Honorary Fellow, Guild of Church Musicians; Knighthood of St Gregory, 2006. Address: 29b Lawrence Road, East Ham, London E6 1JN, England. E-mail: colinmawby@btinternet.com

MAXWELL DAVIES Peter (Sir), b. 8 September 1934, Manchester, England. Composer. Education: Royal Manchester College of Music; Mus B (Hons), Manchester University, 1956. Musical Education: Studies with Goffredo Petrassi in Rome, 1957; Harkness Fellowship, Graduate School, Princeton University, studied with Roger Sessions, Milton Babbitt, Earl Kim. Career: Director of Music, Cirencester Grammar School, 1959-62; Founder and co-director (with Harrison Birtwistle) of the Pierrot Players, 1967-71; Founder, Artistic Director, Fires of London, 1971-87; Founder, Artistic Director, St. Magnus Festival, Orkney Islands, Scotland, 1977-86; Artistic Director, Dartington Summer School of Music, 1979-84; President, Schools Music Association, 1983-; President, North of England Education Conference, 1985; Visiting Fromm Professor of Composition, Harvard University, 1985; Associate Composer/Conductor, Scottish Chamber Orchestra, 1985-94; President, Composer's Guild of Great Britain, 1986-; President, St Magnus Festival, Orkney Islands, 1986-; President, National Federation of Music Societies, 1989-; Major retrospective festival as South Bank Centre, London, 1990; Conductor/Composer, BBC Philharmonic, 1992-; Associate Conductor/Composer, Royal Philharmonic Orchestra, 1992-; President, Cheltenham Arts Festival, 1994-; Composer Laureate of Scottish Chamber Orchestra, 1994-; President, Society for the Promotion of New Music, 1995-. Compositions: Stage: Operas Taverner 1962-70; The Martydom of St Magnus 1976-77; The Two Fiddlers 1978; The Lighthouse, 1979; Theatre Pieces: Notre Dame des Fleurs 1966; Vesalii Icones 1969; Eight Songs for a Mad King 1969; Nocturnal Dances, ballet 1969; Blind Man's Buff 1972; Miss Donnithorne's Maggot 1974; Salome, ballet 1978; Le Jongleur de Notre Dame 1978; Cinderella 1980; The Medium 1981; The No 11 Bus 1983-84; Caroline Mathilde, ballet, 1990; Operas: Resurrection 1987 and The Doctor of Myddfai 1996. Orchestra and Ensemble: Alma Redemptoris Mater for 6 wind instruments 1957; St Michael, sonata for 17 wind instruments 1957; Prolation 1958; Ricercar and Doubles for 8 instruments 1959; 5 Klee Pictures 1959, rev 1976; Sinfonia 1962; 2 Fantasias on an In Nomine of John Taverner 1962-64; 7 In Nomine 1963-65; Shakespeare Music 1965; Antechrist 1967; Stedman Caters 1968; St Thomas Wake 1969; Worldes Blis 1969; Renaissance Scottish Dances 1973; Ave Maris Stela 1975; 4 Symphonies 1973-76, 1980, 1984, 1988; Runes from a Holy Island 1977; A mirror of Whitening Light 1977; Dances from Salome, 1979; The Bairns of Brugh 1981; Image Reflection, Shadow 1982; Sinfonia Concertante 1982; Sinfonietta Accademica 1983; Unbroken Circle 1984; An Orkney Wedding, with Sunrise 1985; Jimmack the Postie, overture 1986; 10 Strathclyde Concertos for Violin 1985, Trumpet 1987, Oboe 1988, Clarinet 1990, Violin and Viola, 1991, Flute 1991, Doublebass 1992, Bassoon, 1993, Chamber Ensemble 1994, Orchestra 1995; Vocal: 5 Motets 1959; O Magnum Mysterium 1960; Te Lucis ante Terminum 1961; Frammenti di Leopardi, cantata 1962; Veni Sancte Spiritus 1963; Revelation and Fall; The Shepherds' Calendar 1965; Missa super L'Homme Arme 1968, rev 1971; From Stone to Thorn 1971; Hymn to St Magnus 1972; Tenebrae super Gesualdo 1972; Stone Litany 1973; Fiddlers at the Wedding 1974; Anakreontika 1976; Kirkwall Shopping Songs 1979; Black Pentecost 1979; Solstice of Light 1979; The Yellow Cake Review, 6 cabaret songs 1980; Songs of Hoy 1981; Into The Labyrinth for tenor and orchestra 1983; First Ferry to Hoy 1985; The Peat Cutters 1985; House of Winter 1986; Excuse Me 1986; Sea Runes, vocal sextet 1986; Hymn to the Word of God, for tenor and chorus, 1990; The Turn of the Tide for orchestra and children's choir, 1992; Chamber music includes: String Quartet 1961; The Kestrel Paced Round the Sun 1975; Sonatina 1981; The Pole Star 1982; Sea Eagle 1982; Sonata for violin and cimbalon 1984; Piano Sonata 1981; Organ Sonata, 1982; Latest works: Sails in St Magnus I-III, 1997-98; Job, oratorio for chorus, orchestra and soloists, 1998; A Reel of Seven Fishermen for orchestra, 1998; Sea Elegy, for chorus, orchestra and soloists, 1998; Roma Amor Labyrinths, 1998; Maxwell's Reel with Northern Lights, 1998; Swinton Jig, 1998; Temenos with Mermaids and Angels, for flute and orchestra, 1998; Spinning Jenny, 1999; Sails in Orkney Saga III: An Orkney Wintering, for alto saxophone and orchestra, 1999; Trumpet Quintet, for string quartet and trumpet, 1999; Mr Emmet Takes a Walk, 1999; Horn Concerto, 1999; Orkney Saga IV: Westerly Gale in Biscay, Salt in the Bread Broken, 2000, Symphony No 7, 2000; Antarctic Symphony, Symphony No 8, 2000; Canticum Canticorum, 2001; De Assumtione Beatae Mariae Virginis, 2001; Crossing Kings Reach, 2001; Mass, 2002; Naxos Quartet No 1, 2002; Piano Trip, 2002; Naxos Quartet No 2, 2003. Honours: Many honours including: Fellow, Royal Northern College of Music, 1978; Honorary Member, Royal Academy of Music, 1979; Honorary Member, Guildhall School of Music and Drama, 1981; CBE, 1981; Knight Bachelor, for services to music, 1987; L'officier dans L'Ordre des Arts et des Lettres, France, 1988; First Award, Association of British Orchestras, outstanding contribution and promotion of orchestral life in UK; Gulliver Award for Performing Arts in Scotland, 1991; Fellowship, Royal Scottish Academy of Music and Drama, 1994; Charles Grove Award, outstanding contribution to British Music, 1995; Master of the Queen's Music, 2007. Member of the Bayerische Akademie der Schönen Künste, 1998. Address: c/o 50 Hogarth Road, London SW5 0PU, England.

MAY Derwent James, b. 29 April 1930, Eastbourne, Sussex, England. Author; Journalist. m. Yolanta Izabella Sypniewska, 1 son, 1 daughter. Education: MA, Lincoln College, Oxford, 1952. Appointments: Theatre and Film Critic, Continental Daily Mail, Paris, 1952-53; Lecturer in English, University of Indonesia, 1955-58; Senior Lecturer in English, Universities of Lodz and Warsaw, 1959-63; Chief Leader Writer, Times Literary Supplement, 1963-65; Literary Editor, The Listener, 1965-86; Literary and Arts Editor, Sunday Telegraph, 1986-90, The European, 1990-91; European Arts Editor, The Times, 1992-. Publications: Novels: The Professionals, 1964; Dear Parson, 1969; The Laughter in Djakarta, 1973; A Revenger's Comedy, 1979. Non-Fiction: Proust, 1983; The Times Nature Diary, 1983; Hannah Arendt, 1986; The New Times Nature Diary, 1993; Feather Reports, 1996; Critical Times: The History of the Times Literary Supplement, 2001;

The Times: A Year in Nature Notes, 2004. Contributions to: Encounter; Hudson Review. Honours: Member, Booker Prize Jury, 1978; Hawthornden Prize Committee, 1987-; FRSL. Membership: Beefsteak Club; Garrick Club. Address: 45 Burghley Road, London, NW5 1UH, England.

MAY Geoffrey John, b. 7 May 1948, London, England. Chartered Engineer. m. Sarah, 2 sons. Education: MA, Double First Class Honours, Natural Sciences Tripos, Materials Science, Fitzwilliam College, University of Cambridge; PhD, Department of Metallurgy and Materials Science; Fellow of the Institute of Metals; Chartered Engineer. Appointments: Research Officer, Central Electricity Generating Board, 1973-74; Technical Manager, Chloride Silent Power Ltd, 1974-78; Design and Development Manager, Chloride Technical Ltd, 1978-82; Technical Director, 1982-86, Operations Director, 1986-88, Tungstone Batteries Ltd; General Manager, Brush Fusegear Ltd, 1988-90; Managing Director, Barton Abrasives Ltd, 1990-91; Group Director of Technology, Hawker Batteries, 1991-97; Group Director of Technology, BTR Power Systems, 1997-2000; Chief Technology Officer, Fiamm SpA, 2000-03; Principal, The Focus Partnership, 2003-. Publications: Numerous publications in technical and trade journals and conference proceedings. Address: Troutbeck House, Main Street, Swithland, Loughborough, Leicestershire LE12 8TJ, England. E-mail: geoffrey.may@tiscali.co.uk

MAY John F, b. 10 March 1950, Elisabethville, Belgian Congo. Demographer. m. Anne Legrand, 1 son, 1 daughter. Education: BA, Modern History, 1973; MA, Demography, 1985, University of Louvain, Leuven; PhD, Demography, University of Paris, Sorbonne, 1996. Appointments: Associate Expert in Demography, United Nations, Haiti, 1976-79; Expert in Demography, United Nations South Pacific Commission, 1980-83; Training Co-ordinator, International Union for the Scientific Study of Population, 1985-86; Senior Scientist, The Futures Group International, 1987-97; Lead Population Specialist, Africa Region, World Bank, 1997-. Publications: Numerous papers in peer-reviewed journals. Honours: Andrew W Mellon Foundation Visiting Scholarship at the Population Reference Bureau. Memberships: International Union for the Scientific Study of Population; Population Association of America. Address: The World Bank, 1818 H Street NW, MSN # J10-1004, Washington, DC 20433, USA. E-mail: jmay@worldbank.org

MAY Naomi Young, b. 27 March 1934, Glasgow, Scotland. Novelist; Journalist; Painter. m. Nigel May, 3 October 1964, 2 sons, 1 daughter. Education: Slade School of Fine Art, London, 1953-56; Diploma, Fine Art, University of London. Publications: At Home, 1969, radio adaptation, 1987; The Adventurer, 1970; Troubles, 1976. Contributions to: Anthologies, newspapers, and magazines. Honour: History of Art Prize, Slade School of Fine Art. Membership: Writers in Prison Committee; English PEN. Address: 6 Lion Gate Gardens, Richmond, Surrey TW9 2DF, England.

MAY OF OXFORD, Baron of Oxford in the County of Oxfordshire, Sir Robert McCredie May, b. 1 August 1936, Professor. Education: BSc, PhD, Theoretical Physics, Sydney University. Appointments: Gordon MacKay Lecturer, Applied Mathematics, Harvard University; Senior Lecturer in Theoretical Physics, Personal Chair in Physics, Sydney University; Class of 1877 Professor of Zoology, 1973, Chairman of the Research Board, 1977-88, Princeton University, USA; Royal Society Research Professor, 1988; Chief Scientific Adviser, UK Government, 1995-2000; Head, UK Officer of Science and Technology, 1995-2000; Joint Professorship, Department of Zoology, Oxford University and Imperial College, London; Fellow, Merton College, Oxford University; President, The Royal Society, 2000-05. Publications: Numerous books; Several hundred papers in major scientific journals; Broader contributions to scientific journalism in newspapers, radio and TV. Honours: Knighthood, 1996; Companion of the Order of Australia, 1998; Crafoord Prize, Royal Swedish Academy; Swiss-Italian Balzan Prize; Japanese Blue Planet Prize; Order of Merit (OM), 2002. Memberships: Foreign Member, US National Academy of Sciences; Overseas Fellow, Australian Academy of Sciences. Address: Department of Zoology, University of Oxford, South Parks Road, Oxford, OX1 3PS, England. E-mail: robert.may@zoo.ox.ac.uk

MAY Theresa Mary, b. 1 October 1956. Politician. m. Philip John May, 1980. Education: St Hugh's College, Oxford. Career: Bank of England, 1977-83; Inter-Bank Research Org, 1983-85; Association for Payment Clearing Services, 1985-97 (Head of European Affairs Unit, 1989-96); Member, (Conservative Party) Merton, London Borough Council, 1986-94; Contested (Conservative Party), Durham NW, 1992, Barking, 1994; MP (Conservative), Maidenhead, 1997-; Opposition Frontbench Spokeswoman on Education and Employment, 1998-99; Shadow Secretary of State for Education and Employment, 1999-2001; Shadow Secretary of State for Transport, Local Government and the Regions, 2001-02; Chair, Conservative Party, 2002-03; Shadow Secretary of State for Environment and Transport, 2003-04, for Families, 2004-05; Shadow Leader of the House, 2005. Address: House of Commons, Westminster, London SW1A 0AA, England.

MAYALL Richard Michael (Rik), b. 7 March 1958, England. Comedian; Actor; Writer. m. Barbara Robin, 1 son, 2 daughters. Education: University of Manchester. Creative Works: Theatre includes: The Common Pursuit, 1988; Waiting for God, 1991-92; Bottom Live, 1993; Bottom Live: the Big Number Two Tour, The Government Inspector, Cell Mates, 1995; Bottom Live 3: Hooligan's Island, 1997; Bottom Live 2001: An Arse Oddity, 2001; Bottom Live 2003: Weapons Grade Y-Fronts Tour, 2003; The New Statesman, 2006; TV includes: The Young Ones (also creator and co-writer), 1982, 1984; The Comic Strip Presents, 1983-2005; George's Marvellous Medicine, 1985; The New Statesman, 1987-88, 1990, 1994; Bottom, 1990, 1992, 1994; Rik Mayall Presents, 1992-94; Wham Bham Strawberry Jam!, The Alan B'Stard Interview with Brian Walden, 1995; In the Red, 1998; The Bill, Jonathan Creek, 1999; The Knock, Murder Rooms, Tales of Uplift and Moral Improvement, 2000; All About George, 2005; SpongeBob SquarePants, 2006; Agatha Christie's Marple, Midsomer Murders, 2009; Who Let the Dogs Out? 2012; Hooligan's Island, 2013; Films include: Whoops Apocalypse, 1982; Drop Dead Fred, 1990; Horse Opera, 1992; Remember Me, Bring Me the Head of Mavis Davis, 1996; Guest House Paradiso, Merlin – The Return, 1999; Kevin of the North, Jesus Christ, Super Star, 2000; Churchill: The Hollywood Years, 2004; Valiant, 2005; Blanche-Neige, la suite, 2007; Eldorado, 2012; Several voices for animations; Live Stand Up includes: Comic Strip, 1982; Kevin Turvey and Bastard Squad, 1983; Rik Mayall, Ben Elton, Andy De La Tour, UK tour and Edinburgh Fringe 1983; Rik Mayall and Ben Elton, 1984-85, Australian tour 1986, 1992; Rik Mayall and Andy De La Tour, 1989-90; Rik Mayall and Adrian Edmondson, UK tours, 1993, 1995, 1997, 2001. Honours include: BAFTA, Best New Comedy, 1990; British Comedy

Awards, Best New Comedy, 1992; Primetime Emmy Award, 1997. Address: c/o The Brunskill Management Ltd, Suite 8A, 169 Queen's Gate, London SW7 5HE, England.

MAYER Sydney L, b. 2 August 1937, Chicago, USA. Publisher. m. Charlotte W M Bouter. Education: BA, MA, University of Michigan; MPhil, Yale University. Appointments: Lecturer, University of Maryland, USA, 1966-77; Visiting Assistant Professor, University of Southern California, 1969-74; UK Director, University of Maryland, 1972-73; Managing Director, Bison Books Ltd, 1973-95; President, CEO, Brompton Books Corporation, 1982-98; President, Twin Books Corporation, 1985-98; Chairman, Twin Films Ltd, 1997-. Publications: 22 books including: The World of Southeast Asia (with Harry J Benda), 1971; The Two World Wars (with William J Koenig), 1976; Signal, 1975; World War Two, 1981; hundreds of articles. Honours: Angell Society, University of Michigan, 1989; Honorary Fellow, Oriel College, Oxford, 1993; Fulbright Advisory Board, London, 1993-. Address: 2 Shrewsbury House, 42 Cheyne Walk, London, SW3 5LN, England.

MAYERHOFF David Isak, b. 3 September 1958, Brooklyn, New York, USA. Psychiatry. Education: BA, Yeshiva University, 1979; MD, Sony Downstate College of Medicine, 1983; Adult Psychiatry Residency, 1983-87; Biological Psychiatry & Schizophrenia Research Fellowship, 1987-89, Hillside Hospital, LIJMC. Appointments: Staff Psychiatrist, Greystone Park Psychiatric Hospital, 2003-; Medical Director, Essex County Hospital Center, 1999-2003; Clinical Director, Director, Ambulatory Mental Health, Nassau County Medical Center, 1994-99; Assistant Director, Research & Staff Psychiatrist, Hillside Hospital, 1989-94; Clinical Professor of Psychiatry, UMDNJ-NJ Medical School, Newark, 2008-. Publications: Articles in professional journals. Honours: Board of Chosen Freeholders; Essex County Proclamation on Health Care Professional Day; Essex County Executive Certificate of Appreciation. Memberships: American Medical Association; Distinguished Fellow, American Psychiatric Association, 2008-. E-mail: drsyke@aol.com

MAYER-KOENIG Wolfgang, b. 28 March 1946, Vienna, Austria. University Professor; Writer. 1 son. Education: DFA, DLitt; University Professor, Austrian Government, 1987. Appointments: Founder, Literarische Situation, Austrian University Cultural Centre, 1968; Head of Division, Corporation of Public Law, Austrian universities, 1968-70; Member, Cabinet of Chancellor Kreisky, Austria, 1971-78; Coordinator, International Governmental Meeting on Future of Science and Technology, 1972; Chairman, Austrian Meetings of Executives, 1972-77; Lecturer, universities in France, Italy, Germany, USA, 1973-86; Coordinator, negotiations between Austria and Arab States, 1975; Member, Board of Austrian Research Conflict, 1975-82; Industrial Director, Board member, Porr Cy, 1978-90; Chairman, Munich-Brenner-Verona infrastructure consortium, 1986-90; Permanent Representative UN, 1991-92; Founder of high quality wine production in Vienna, Poetenfass Vineyards, 1994-; President, Mozart Company; Member of Board, Karl Renner Institute; Vice President, Pro Austria Nostra; Executive Director, Transportbeton KG; Member, Advisory Board, Porr International AG; Chairman, Humanitarian Aid and Recovery Programme, Indochina and earthquake victims, Italy; Editor of LOG, international journal and magazine. Publications: Visible Pavilions, 1968; Stichmarken, 1968; Psychology and Language, 1975; Language-Politics-Aggression, 1977; Goethes Journey to Italy, 1978; Possibilities of Robert Musil; Chagrin non dechiffre, 1986; Colloqui nella Stanza, 1986;

The Corselet of the Mighty, 1986; Modern Grammar, 1986; Fire and Ice, 1986; Mirror Wading, 1986; A hatalom bonyolult angyala, 1989; Behind Desires Deficits, 1997; Confessions of an angry loving European, 1998; Grammatik der Seele, 2004; Verzögertes Vertrauen, 2004; The Three Dolphins, 2005; The Adoption, 2005; The Own Antagonist, 2006; Undefended – unprotected child, 2007; Runkelsteiner Elegien, 2007; The Language of Adele Kurzweil, 2007; The Divorced Child, 2009; Alpha One, 2010. Honours include: Cross of Honour for Science and Arts, Austria, 1976; Ordre des Arts et des Lettres, France, 1987; Officer, Order of Merit, Egypt; Grand Cross of Merit, Austrian Province of Carinthia; Commendatore, Republic of San Marino; Order of the Eagle in Gold of the Province of Tyrol; Cross of Honour, Lower Austria; Papal Lateran Cross; Papal Cross of Leo XIII; American Medal of Honor; Gold Cross in Honour of Greek Orthodox Patriarch of Alexandria; Golden Medal, Chamber of Agriculture and Poetenfass Wines granted as "Best Viennese Wines"; International Peace Prize, 2005; Plato Award; Austrian Cross of Honour for Science and Arts First Class, 2006; Grand Cross of Honour of Styrias Government, 2006; Medal of Honour for Culture, Government of Upper Austria; Honorary Medal of City of Vienna. Memberships include: International PEN Club; Accademia Tiberina Roma; Accademia Cosentina; Grand Master of the Order "Pour le Merite"; Grand Master of the Order Merito Navali; Honorary President of Literary Society (St. Pölten). Address: Hernalser Guertal 41, A-1170 Vienna, Austria. E-mail: univprofmayerkoenig@a1.net

MAYO Edward John, b. 24 May 1931, Lyme Regis, England. Army Officer. m. (1) Jacqueline Margaret Anne Armstrong, deceased, 1 son, (2) Pamela Joyce Shimwell. Education: King's College, Taunton, 1943-49. Appointments: Commissioned, Royal Artillery, 1951; ADC to Governor of Malta, 1953-54, 2 RHA, 1955-57; ADC to Commander in Chief, BAOR, 1958-60; Adjutant 20 FD Regiment, Malaya, 1961-63; Instructor, RMAS, 1964-66; Instructor, Staff College, 1970-72; Commanded 17 Training Regiment, 1972-75; Colonel General Staff, 1979-93; Director General, Help the Aged, 1983-97; Trustee, Helpage, India, 1984-2001; Trustee, Helpage, Sri Lanka, 1986-; Trustee, Helpage, Kenya, 1984-; Trustee, Ex-Services Mental Welfare, 1996-2005; Trustee, Global Cancer, 1996-2004; Patron, Global Cancer, 2005-; Patron, The Homeless Fund, 1998-2000; Patron, Employers' Retirement Association, 2004-; Chairman of Commissioners, Jurby, Isle of Man, 2002-04, 2008-09; Director, Executive Communication Consultants, 1999-2008. Publications: Miscellaneous articles on military matters; Articles on ageing. Honour: OBE, 1976. Memberships: Army and Navy Club; Special Forces Club; MCC; Royal Society of Arts, 1985-97; Woodroffes. Address: Ballamoar Castle, Sandygate, Jurby, Isle of Man, IM7 3AJ, United Kingdom. E-mail: mayo@manx.net

MAYS Sally, b. Melbourne, Australia. Pianist; Composer; Teacher. m. John Elsom, 2 sons. Education: AMusA, aged 13 years; LRSM, aged 15 years; ARCM, aged 19 years; Studied at University Conservatorium; Clarke Scholarship, Royal College of Music, London; Further studies with Marcel Ciampi in Paris and Irene Kohler in London. Appointments: Recital pianist in Australia, aged 12 years; First UK recital, Wigmore Hall, 1956; Numerous tours of Australia, New Zealand and South Africa; Appearances in Europe, San Diego, Singapore and Abu Dhabi; Piano tuition and music appreciation, Goldsmiths College, University of London, the City Literary Institute, Marylebone Institute and Roehampton Institute in London; Examiner for the Associated Board of the Royal Schools of Music, in UK and all over the world,

1984-2005; Played with Alexandra Ensemble and leading orchestras around the world; Featured solo performer with London Ballet Orchestra on Margot Fonteyn's Farewell Tour; Premiered: Ann Carr-Boyd's Piano Concerto in Hobart, 1991; Eric Gross's Piano Concerto in Melbourne and Perth, 1983-84; and Edwin Carr's Second Piano Concerto in Wellington and Perth, 1987 and 1992; Broadcasts for Australian Broadcasting Corporation and other broadcasting stations annually; Currently, member of Trio LaVolta and Sounds Positive. Publications: Compiler and editor, four volume series of contemporary Australian Piano Music; Choices contemporary piano works by Australian composers, publisher, Wirripang; Composed for Sounds Positive and for the stage; Featured on Jade series of CS of Australian music; Appears in Anthology of Australian Music on Disc; From the Dark Side, John Carmichael (Orientis); in Piano Music by Edwin Roxburgh; with Paul Goodey (oboe) in Oboe Classics; with Linda Berwick (clarinet) in Dynamics of Matter; in Undercurrents by Sounds Positive; in Music of Barry Anderson by Continuum. Honours: Sounds Australia Award for services to music; Chappell Gold Medal, Royal College of Music. Memberships: Founder Member, The Mouth of Hermes, 1968-72; Member, Sounds Positive, 1988-; Fellow, Trinity College, London. Address: 30 Landseer Road, New Malden, Kingston-upon-Thames, Surrey KT3 5NH, England.

MAZZOLI Dino (Leopoldo), b. 10 May 1935, Terni, Italy. Artist; Illustrator. m. Visnja, 1 son, 1 daughter. Education: Oriani College, Rome; Studies under Renato Guttuso, Villa Massimo, Rome, 1953; Villa Medici, Rome, 1954-56; Studies with Dorothy Swain, Royal College of Art. Career: Artist in oil and watercolours; Illustrator; Group and solo exhibitions: Don Orione, Farnesina, Rome; Heathfield AG; East Grinstead Autumn Show; Towner Museum and AG Eastbourne; Brighton Museum and AG; Star Gallery, Lewes; Blackheath Gallery, London; Dusseldorf, Germany; St Laurent en Grandvaux, France; Birmingham, Alabama, USA; Works held in public and private collections in France; Copied out complete text of the Bible and illustrated it with approximately 5,000 colour illustration in 23 volumes. Honours: Listed in international biographical dictionaries including Who's Who in Art.

McALEESE Mary Patricia, b. 27 June 1951, Belfast, Northern Ireland. President of Ireland. m. Martin, 1976, 1 son, 2 daughters. Education: LLB, The Queen's University, Belfast, 1969-73; BL, Inn of Court of Northern Ireland, 1973-74; MA, Trinity College, Dublin, 1986; Diploma in Spanish, The Chartered Institute of Linguistics, 1991-94. Appointments: Reid Professor, Criminal Law, Criminology and Penology, Trinity College, Dublin, 1975-79, 1981-87; Current Affairs Journalist, Presenter, Irish National TV, 1979-81; Part-time Presenter, -1975; Director, Institute of Professional Legal Study, Queen's University of Belfast, 1987-97; Pro-Vice Chancellor, 1994-97; President, Ireland, 1997-. Publications: The Irish Martyrs, 1995; Reconciled Being, 1997. Honours: Several honorary degrees; Silver Jubilee Commemoration Medal, Charles University, Prague. Memberships: European Bar Association; International Bar Association; Inns of Court, North Ireland; King's Inn, Dublin; Former Member: Institute of Advanced Study; Irish Association of Law Teachers; Society of Public Teachers of Law; British and Irish Legal Technology Association. Address: Áras an Uachtaráin, Phoenix Park, Dublin 8, Ireland. E-mail: webmaster@president.ie

MCARTHUR Liam, b. 8 August 1967, Edinburgh, Scotland. Member of the Scottish Parliament for Orkney. m. Tamsin, 2 sons. Education: Sanday Junior High School, Orkney; Kirkwall Grammar School, Orkney; MA (Hons), Politics, Edinburgh University. Appointments: Researcher, Jim Wallace MP, House of Commons, 1990-92; Trainee, European Commission (External Affairs Directorate), 1992-93; Account Executive, various EU public affairs consultancies, 1993-96; Associate Director, APCO and APCO Europe, 1996-2002; Special Adviser to Deputy First Minister, Jim Wallace MSP, 2002-05; Director, Greenhaus Communications, 2005-06; Self-employed Political Consultant, 2006-07; Member of the Scottish Parliament for Orkney, 2007-. Memberships: Member, Rural Affairs and Environment Committee; Substitute Member, Finance Committee. Address: 31 Broad Street, Kirkwall, KW15 1DH, Scotland. E-mail: liam.mcarthur.msp@scottish.parliament.uk

McCALL Carolyn Julia, b. 13 September 1961, Bangalore, India. Chief Executive. m. Peter Framley, 2 sons, 1 daughter. Education: BA, PGCE (Distinction), MA (Distinction); Advanced Management Programme, Wharton, 2000. Appointments: Analyst, Costain Group plc, 1984-86; Planner/ Sales Executive/Group Head, 1986-92; Advertisement Manager/Deputy Advertisement Director, 1992-95, Commercial Director, 1995-2000, Guardian Newspapers Limited; Non-Executive, New Look plc, 1999-2005; CEO, Guardian News & Media Ltd, 2000-06; Chair, Opportunity Now, 2005-; Non-Executive, Tesco plc, 2005-08; Group CEO, Guardian Media Group, 2006-. Address: Guardian Media Group, 60 Farringdon Road, London EC1R 3GA, England.

McCALL Davina, b. 16 October 1967, London, England. TV Presenter. m. (1) Andrew Leggett, 1997, divorced; (2) Mathew Robertson, 2000, 1 son, 2 daughters. Education: St Catherine's, Bramley; Godolphin & Latymer, London. Appointments: God's Gift, MTV; Don't Try This At Home, 4 series; The Brits, 2000, 2003; Big Brother, 7 series, 2000-06; Sam's Game, 2001; Popstars – The Rivals, 2002; Reborn in the USA, 2003; Love on a Saturday Night, 2004; Comic Relief, 2004, 2007; The BAFTA Television Awards, ITV, 2004, 2006; He's Having a Baby, 2005; Davina, BBC, 2006; Sport Relief, 2006; Let's Talk Sex, 2007. Address: c/o John Noel Management, 2nd Floor, 10A Belmont Street, London NW1 8HH, England.

McCARTER Keith Ian, b. 15 March 1936, Scotland. Sculptor. m. Brenda, 1 son, 1 daughter. Education: The Royal High School of Edinburgh, 1948-54; Edinburgh College of Art, 1956-60. Appointments: Designer, Steuben Glass, New York, USA, 1961-63; Self-employed Sculptor, 1964-; Over 40 public-sited works worldwide. Publications: Many articles published relative to work. Honours: Otto Beit Medal, Royal Society of British Sculptors; Fellow, Royal Society of Arts; DA (Edin). Memberships: The Farmers Club; Melrose RFC. Address: 10 Coopersknowe Crescent, Galashiels, TD1 2DS, Scotland. E-mail: keith@keith-mccarter.com Website: www.keith-mccarter.com

McCARTHY Cormac, (Charles McCarthy Jr), b. 20 July 1933, Providence, Rhode Island, USA. Author; Dramatist. m. Lee Holleman, 1961, divorced 1 child, (2) Anne deLisle, 1967, divorced, (3) Jennifer Winkley, 2006, 1 son. Publications: Novels: The Orchard Keeper, 1965; Outer Dark, 1968; Child of God, 1974; Suttree, 1979; Blood Meridian, or The Evening Redness in the West, 1985; All the Pretty Horses, 1992; The Crossing, 1994; Cities of the Plain, 1998; No Country for Old Men, 2005; The Road, 2006; The Sunset Limited, 2006. Plays: The Gardner's Son, 1977; The Stonemason, 1994. Honours: Ingram Merrill Foundation Grant, 1960; William Faulkner Foundation Award, 1965; American Academy of

DICTIONARY OF INTERNATIONAL BIOGRAPHY 36th EDITION

Arts and Letters Travelling Fellowship, 1965-66; Rockefeller Foundation Grant, 1966; Guggenheim Fellowship, 1976; John D and Catharine T MacArthur Foundation Fellowship, 1981; National Book Award, 1992; National Book Critics Circle Award, 1993; Pulitzer Prize, 2007; James Tait Black Memorial Prize, 2007. Address: 1011 N Mesa Street, El Paso, TX 79902, USA.

McCARTNEY (James) Paul (Sir), b. 18 June 1942, Liverpool, England. Singer; Songwriter; Musician. m. (1) Linda Eastman, 1969, deceased 1998, 1 son, 2 daughters, 1 stepdaughter, (2) Heather Mills, 2002, divorced 2006, 1 daughter, (3) Nancy Shevell, 2011. Education: Self-taught in music. Appointments: Member, The Quarrymen, 1957-59, The Beatles, 1960-70; Founder, Apple Corporation Ltd; Founder, MPL Group of Companies; Founder, Wings, 1970-81; Solo Artiste, 1970-; International tours, concerts, TV, radio, films; Founder, Liverpool Institute of Performing Arts, 1995. Creative Works: Numerous albums with The Beatles. Solo Albums: McCartney, 1970; Ram, 1971; McCartney II, 1980; Tug of War, 1982; Pipes of Peace, 1983; Give My Regards to Broad Street, 1984; Press to Play, 1986; All the Best, 1987; Flowers in the Dirt, 1989; Tripping the Light Fantastic, 1990; Unplugged, 1991; Choba b CCCP, 1991; Paul McCartney's Liverpool Oratorio, 1991; Off the Ground, 1993; Paul is Live, 1993; Flaming Pie, 1997; Standing Stone, symphonic work, 1997; A Garland for Linda, composition with 8 other composers for a capella choir, 2000; Paul McCartney: The Music and Animation Collection, DVD, 2004; The McCartney Years, DVD, 2007. Publications: Paintings, 2000; The Beatles Anthology (with George Harrison and Ringo Starr), 2000; Sun Prints (with Linda McCartney), 2001; Many Years From Now, autobiography, 2001; Blackbird Singing: Poems and Lyrics 1965-1999, 2001. Honours: MBE, 1965; Numerous Grammy Awards; 3 Ivor Novello Awards; Freeman, City of Liverpool, 1984; Doctorate, University of Sussex, 1988; Guinness Book of Records Award, 1979; Q Merit Award, 1990; Knighted, 1997; Fellowship, British Academy of Composers and Songwriters, 2000. Address: c/o MPL Communications, 1 Soho Square, London W1V 6BQ, England.

McCARTNEY Stella, b. 13 September 1971. Fashion Designer. m. Alasdhair Willis, 2 sons, 2 daughters. Education: Central St Martins College of Art and Design. Appointments: Work with Christian Lacroix at age 15 and later with Betty Jackson; Work experience in Fashion Department, Vogue magazine; After graduation, set up own design company in London; Chief Designer for Chloe, Paris; Designed collection for Gucci, 2001; Established own fashion house, in partnership with Gucci Group, 2001-; Launched clothes line with Adidas, 2004-10; Designed range of clothing for H&M, 2005; Launched skincare line CARE, 2007; Lingerie collection with Bendon, 2008; Designed luggage and accessory line for LeSportsac, 2008; Jewellry design for Disney, 2010; Launched Stella McCartney Kids, 2010. Honours: VH/1Vogue Fashion and Music Designer of the Year, 2000; Woman of Courage Award, 2003; Designed costumes for film, Sky Captain and the World of Tomorrow, 2004. Address: Stella McCartney London, 30 Bruton Street, London, W1J 6LG, England. Website: www.stellamccartney.com

MCCAUGHREAN Geraldine Margaret, b. 6 June 1951, Enfield, Middlesex, England. Author. m. John, 1 daughter. Education: B Ed (Hons), Christ Church College of Education, Kent, 1977. Appointments: Secretary, Thames Television, London, 1970-73; Secretary, 1977, Sub-Editor, 1978-79 and 1983-88, Marshall Cavendish publishers, London; Editorial Assistant, Rothmans International, Ware, 1980-82; Editor, Banbury Focus, Oxfordshire, 1982; Freelance Author, 1988-. Publications include: For young adults: A Little Lower than the Angels, 1987; A Pack of Lies, 1988; Gold Dust, 1993; Plundering Paradise, 1996; Forever X, 1997; The Stones are Hatching, 1999; The Kite Rider, 2001; Stop The Train! 2001; Showstopper! 2003; Not the End of the World, 2004; The White Darkness, 2005; Cyrano, 2006; Tamburlaine's Elephants, 2007; The Death Defying Pepper Roux, 2009; Pull Out All the Stops! 2010; For younger children: Doctor Quack, 2003; Dancing the Night Away, 2003; Oxford Treasury of Fairy Tales, 2003; Dog Days, 2003; Jalopy, 2003; Smile! 2004; Sky Ship, 2004; Fig's Giant, 2006; Think Again! 2005; MO, 2006; Father and Son, 2006; The Nativity Story, 2007; Peter Pan in Scarlet (adapted edition), 2008; For adults: The Maypole, 1989; Fires' Astonishment, 1990; Vainglory, 1991; Lovesong, 1996; The Ideal Wife, 1997; Cyrano, 2006; many other books published in 62 countries and 43 languages. Honours include: All London Literary Competition, 1978; Whitbread Children's Novel Award, 1987, 1994, 2004; Carnegie Medal, 1988, 2001; Guardian Award, 1988; Smarties Book Prize, Bronze Award, 1996, 2001, 2002, 2004; United Kingdoim Reading Association Book Award, 1998; Blue Peter Book of the Year Award, 2000; Michael L Printz Award, 2008; many others. Memberships: FRSL; Fellow, English association; Honorary Fellow, Christ Church University, Canterbury; Society of Authors; Association of Storytellers. E-mail: mccaughrean@btinterest.com

McCAUSLAND Christine, b. 17 February 1944, Scotland. Painter. Career: Painter, specialising in city panoramas and urban landscapes in oil; Exhibitions in Grafton Gallery; Royal Academy; Saltire Gallery; Pall-Mall Galleries; Festival Hall; Bear Lane Gallery; South London Art Gallery. Listed in Who's Who in Art. Address: 88 Clarendon Road, London W11 2HR, England.

McCOLGAN Elizabeth, b. 24 May 1964, Dundee, Scotland. Athlete. m. Peter McColgan, 3 sons, 1 daughter. Education: Coached by Grete Waitz. Appointments: Gold Medal Commonwealth Games 10,000 m, 1986, 1990; Silver Medal, Olympic Games 10,000m, 1988; Silver Medal, World Indoor Championships 3,000m, 1989; Bronze Medal, Commonwealth Games, 3,000m, 1990; Gold Medal, World Championships 10,000m, 1991; Gold Medal, World Half Marathon Championships, 1992; First in New York City Marathon, 1991; First in Tokyo Marathon, 1992; Third in London Marathon, 1993; Fifth in 1995; First in 1996; Second in 1997, 1998; Retired, 2001; Returned to competitive athletics with victory in Scottish Cross Country Championships, 2004; Runs own fitness centre and coaches young athletes in Dundee. Honours: MBE. Address: c/o Marquee UK, 6 George Street, Nottingham NG1 3BE, England.

McCONAUGHEY Matthew, b. 4 November 1969, Ulvade, Texas, USA. Actor. m. Camila Alves, 2012, 2 sons, 1 daughter. Education: University of Texas, Austin. Appointments: Film appearances include: Dazed and Confused; The Return of the Texas Chainsaw Massacre; Boys on the Side; My Boyfriend's Back, 1993; Angels in the Outfield, 1994; Scorpion Spring; Submission, 1995; Glory Daze; Lone Star; A Time to Kill, 1996; Larger Than Life, 1997; Amistad; Contact; Making Sandwiches; Last Flight of the Raven; Newton Boys; South Beach; EdTV, 1999; U-571, 2000; The Wedding Planner, 2001; Reign of Fire, 2001; Frailty, 2001; 13 Conversations About One Thing, 2001; Tiptoes, 2003; How to Lose a Guy in Ten Days, 2003; Sahara, 2005; Two for the Money, 2005; Failure to Launch, 2006; We Are Marshall, 2006; Surfer Dude, 2008; Fool's Gold, 2008; Tropic Thunder, 2008;

Ghosts of Girlfriends Past, 2009; Eastbound & Down, 2010; The Lincoln Lawyer, Bernie, Killer Joe, 2011; The Paperboy, Mud, Magic Mike, 2012; The Dallas Buyer's Club, Thunder Run, The Wolf of Wall Street, 2013. Address: c/o J K Livin, POB 596, Zachary, LA 70791, USA.

McCRYSTAL Cahal, (Cal McCrystal), b. 20 December 1935, Belfast, Northern Ireland. Journalist; Broadcaster; Author. m. Stella Doyle, 15 October 1958, 3 sons. Education: St Mary's College, Dundalk; St Malachy's College, Belfast. Appointments: Reporter, Northern Herald; Labour Correspondent, Belfast Telegraph; Crime Reporter, Chief Reporter, Foreign Correspondent, New York Bureau Chief, News Editor, Foreign Features Editor, Sunday Times, London; Senior Writer, Independent-on-Sunday; Senior Writer, The Observer. Publications: Watergate: The Full Inside Story (co-author), 1973; Reflections on A Quiet Rebel, 1997. Contributions to: Vanity Fair, British Magazines, British Journalism Review and London Evening Standard; Independent-on-Sunday and Financial Times (book reviews); Poetry, Ireland Review; Melbourne Sunday Age; London Evening Standard; The Daily Telegraph. Honours: Various journalism awards; Belfast Arts Council Literary Award, 1998; Broadcasts for BBC, Radio Eireann, ABC TV and CBC. Membership: Editorial Board, British Journalism Review. Address: c/o 37 Goldhawk Road, London W12 8QQ, England.

McCULLOCH Nigel Simeon (The Right Reverend Bishop of Manchester), b. 17 January 1942, Anglican Bishop. m. Celia Hume, 2 daughters. Education: Selwyn College, Cambridge; Cuddesdon College, Oxford. Appointments: Assistant Curate, Ellesmere Port, 1966-70; Chaplain and Director of Studies in Theology, Christ's College, Cambridge, 1970-73; Diocesan Missioner, Norwich, 1973-78; Rector of St Thomas's, Salisbury, 1978-86; Archdeacon of Sarum, 1979-86; Bishop of Taunton, 1986-92; Bishop of Wakefield, 1992-2003; Bishop of Manchester, 2003-. Member of the House of Lords, 1997-; Lord High Almoner to H.M. The Queen, 1997-. Publications: A Gospel to Proclaim; Barriers to Belief; Credo Columnist for the Times, 1996-2000. Honour: MA. Memberships: Chairman, Sandford St Martin Religious Broadcasters Awards; National Chaplain, The Royal British Legion; National Chaplain, The Royal School of Church Music. Address: Bishop's Lodge, Wakefield WF2 6JL, England. E-mail: bishop@wakefield.anglican.org

MCCULLOUGH Colleen, b. 1 June 1937, Wellington, Australia. Author. m. Ric Robinson, 1984. Education: Holy Cross College, Woollahra; Sydney University Institute of Child Health, London University. Appointments: Neurophysiologist, Sydney, London, Yale University Medical School, USA. Publications: Novels: Tim, 1974; The Thorn Birds, 1977; An Indecent Obsession, 1981; A Creed for the Third Millennium, 1985; The Ladies of Missalonghi, 1987; The First Man in Rome, 1990; The Grass Crown, 1991; Fortune's Favorites, 1993; Caesar's Women, 1996; Caesar, 1997; The Song of Troy, 1998; The Courage and the Will, 1999; Morgan's Run, 2000; Cooking with Colleen McCullough and Jean Easthope, 1982; Roden Cutler, VC The Biography, 1998; Morgan's Run, 2000; The October Horse, 2002; The Touch, 2003; Angel Puss, 2004; On, Off, 2006; Antony and Cleopatra, 2007; The Independence of Miss Mary Bennet, 2008; Too Many Murders, 2009. Honour: DLitt, Macquaire University. Address: "Out Yenna", Norfolk Island, Oceania, Via Australia.

McDAID Perry, (Phoenix Martin, Pam Louis, Blythe Stitt, Naomi de Plume), b. 10 October 1959, Derry City, Ireland. Writer; Poet. Education: BTEC, Business Studies, 1984; BA (Hons), Social Sciences; Certificate in Creative Writing, 2005; BSc (Hons) Open (Open). Appointments: Branch Secretary, NICSA, 1980; Civil Servant; Regional Administrative Officer, Industrial Development Board; Manager, Foyle Chess Club; Accounting Officer, Author Operations Manual for Civil Service Pensions; Quizmaster; Retired due to ill health; Managing Editor, Narwhal Publishing. Publications: Over 700 different poems in 900 listings worldwide; Short Stories: Earlyworks, Banksnotes, Professional Anthologies; The Milesian. Honours: Honorary Appointment, The Research Board of Advisors, ABI, 2006; Numerous editor's choice awards; Distinguished Member, International Society of Poets. Memberships: Lifetime member, Metverse, ISP; PCOF; Salopean Society. Address: 6 Rathmore Road, Rathmore Estate, Derry, BT48 9BS, Northern Ireland.

McDERMOTT Patrick Anthony, b. 8 September 1941, Ripley, Surrey, England. Her Majesty's Diplomatic Service, Retired. m. (1) 2 sons, (2) Christa Herminghaus, 2 sons. Education: Clapham College, London. Appointments: Foreign and Commonwealth Office, London, 1961-63; Mexico City, 1963-66; New York, 1966-71; Belgrade, 1971-73; Foreign and Commonwealth Office, London, 1973; Bonn, 1973-76; Paris, 1976-79; Foreign and Commonwealth Office, London, 1979-83; HM Consul-General and Economic and Financial Adviser to the British Military Government, West Berlin, 1984-88; Foreign and Commonwealth Office, London, 1988-89; Counsellor, Paris, 1990-95; Foreign and Commonwealth Office, London, 1996-97; HM Consul General, Moscow and to the Republic of Moldovia, 1998-2001; Retired, 2001-; Management Consultant, Diplomatic Consulting, 2001-02; Deputy Burser, Ampleforth College, 2002-; Board of Trustees, Helmsley Walled Garden, 2005-. Honours: Member, Royal Victorian Order, 1972; Freeman of the City of London, 1986. Address: Linkfoot House, 10 Acres Close, Helmsley, York YO62 5DS, England.

McDONALD Catherine Donna, b. 20 December 1942, Vancouver, British Columbia, Canada. Writer; Arts Administrator; Project Manager. m. Robert Francis McDonald, 1965. Education: BA, 1964. Publications: Illustrated News: Juliana Horatia Ewing's Canadian Pictures 1867-1869; The Odyssey of the Philip Jones Brass Ensemble; Lord Strathcona; A Biography of Donald Alexander Smith; Milkmaids and Maharajas: A History of 1 Palace Street. Contributions to: Periodicals and journals. Address: 10 Chelwood Gardens, Richmond, Surrey TW9 4JQ, England.

McDONALD Forrest, b. 7 January 1927, Orange, Texas, USA. Distinguished University Research Professor; Historian; Writer. m. (1) 3 sons, 2 daughters, (2) Ellen Shapiro, 1 August 1963. Education: BA, MA, 1949, PhD, 1955, University of Texas. Appointments: Executive Secretary, American History Research Centre, Madison, Wisconsin, 1953-58; Associate Professor, 1959-63, Professor of History, 1963-67, Brown University; Professor, Wayne State University, 1967-76; Professor, 1976-87, Distinguished University Research Professor, 1987-, University of Alabama, Tuscaloosa; Presidential Appointee, Board of Foreign Scholarships, Washington, DC, 1985-87; Advisor, Centre of Judicial Studies, Cumberland, Virginia, 1985-92; James Pinckney Harrison Professor, College of William and Mary, 1986-87; Jefferson Lecturer, National Endowment for the Humanities, 1987. Publications: We the People: The Economic Origins of the Constitution, 1958; Insull, 1962; E

DICTIONARY OF INTERNATIONAL BIOGRAPHY 36th EDITION

Pluribus Unum: The Formation of the American Republic, 1965; The Presidency of George Washington, 1974; The Phaeton Ride, 1974; The Presidency of Thomas Jefferson, 1976; Alexander Hamilton: A Biography, 1979; Novus Ordo Seclorum, 1985; Requiem, 1988; The American Presidency: An Intellectual History, 1994; States' Rights and the Union 1776-1876, 2000; Recovering the Past: A Historian's Memoir, 2004. Contributions to: Professional journals. Honours: Guggenheim Fellowship, 1962-63; George Washington Medal, Freedom's Foundation, 1980; Frances Tavern Book Award, 1980; Best Book Award, American Revolution Round Table, 1986; Richard M Weaver Award, Ingersoll Foundation, 1990; First Salvatori Award, Intercollegiate Studies Institute, 1992; Salvatori Book Award, Intercollegiate Studies Institute, 1994; Mount Vernon Society Choice, One of the Ten Great Books on George Washington, 1998. Memberships: American Antiquarian Society; Philadelphia Society; The Historical Society. Address: PO Box 155, Coker, AL 35452, USA.

McDONALD Paul Ian, b. 20 December 1946, Stockport, England. Managing Director. Education: BA (Hons), Geography, University College London, 1965-68; PhD, Civil Engineering, University of Leeds, 1968-71; Cert Ed, New College Oxford, 1971-72. Appointments: Research Fellow, University of Aston, 1975-78; Head of Information Services, National Oil Company of Saudi Arabia, 1978-83; Senior Oil Analyst, Shearson Lehman Brothers, 1983-86; Managing Director, Pearl Oil Ltd, Hong Kong, 1986-2003; Managing Director, Pearl Oil, Great Britain. Publications: Various articles in Nature; New Scientist; Times Literary Supplement; Economist Foreign Report; International Affairs; Japanese Institute of Middle Eastern Economies Review; Zeitschrift für Internationale Politik; Books on Middle East and North Africa; Oil Trading in Asia; Deregulation in Japan; Chinese Oil Industry; Oil and Gas in Iraq; The Oil Industry in the USSR; Agriculture in Thailand. Honour: University research exhibited at the Science Museum, London. Memberships: Institute of Petroleum; Oxford Union; Sri Lanka Club, Hong Kong; Devon & Exeter Institution. Address: Springfields, Hawker's Lane, Hambridge, Langport, Somerset TA10 0AU, England.

MCDONALD Tracey Therese Anne, b. 10 April 1949, Bathurst, New South Wales, Australia. Nurse; Researcher. Divorced, 2 sons. Education: General Nursing Certificate, 1969; Diploma in Nursing Education, 1976; Midwifery Certificate, 1983; Bachelor of Health Administration, 1988; MSc (Hons), Community Health, 1994; Doctor of Philosophy, 2003. Appointments: Student Nurse, St Vincent's Hospital, Bathurst, 1965-66; Student Nurse, 1966-69, Educator and Senior Educator, Nurse Education Centre, 1978-80, Continuing Education Co-ordinator, 1980-82, Registered Nurse, 1983, Community Liaison & Discharge Planner, 1983-84, Assistant Director of Nursing, Executive Projects Co-ordinator, 1984-85, Prince Henry Hospital, Little Bay; Registered Nurse, various hospital and community services, 1969-74; Nurse Educator, St Vincent's Hospital, Darlinghurst, 1974-78; Lecturer, Faculty of Health & Behavioural Sciences, 1985-90, Senior Lecturer, Nursing, 1990-95, 1997-99, University of Wollongong; Head, School of Nursing, Monash University, Frankston Campus, 1995-97; Manager, Professional Services NSW Nurses' Association, 1999-2003; Management Consultant, Australian Nursing Homes and Extended Care Association, NSW 2003-04; Manager, Resarch, Policy & Professional Services, Aged Care Association, Australia, 2004-05; Professor, Ageing RSL LifeCare Chair, Australian Catholic University, 2005-. Publications: Numerous articles in professional journals, books, reports and chapters. Honours: Lions Nurse of the Year, NSW and ACT, 1977; Certificate of Notable Achievement, 1990; Vice-Chancellor's Award for Excellence in Teaching, 1991; Ethyl Hayton Trophy for Outstanding Contribution to the Community, 1994. Memberships: World Alliance for Patient Safety; United Nations Network on Ageing. Address: Australian Catholic University, North Sydney Campus, 40 Edward Street North, Sydney, NSW 2060, Australia. E-mail: tracey.mcdonald@acu.edu.au

McDONALD Sir Trevor, b. 16 August 1939, Trinidad. Broadcasting Journalist. m. 2 sons, 1 daughter. Appointments: Worked on newspapers, radio and TV, Trinidad, 1960-69; Producer, BBC Caribbean Service and World Service, London, 1969-73; Reporter, Independent TV News, 1973-78; Sports Correspondent, 1978-80; Diplomatic Correspondent, 1980-87; Newscaster, 1982-87; Diplomatic Editor, Channel 4 News, 1987-89; Newscaster, News at 5.40, 1989-90; News at Ten, 1990-99; ITV Evening News, 1999-2000; ITV News at Ten, 2001-04, News at 10.30, 2004-2005; Chairman, Better English Campaign, 1995-97; Nuffield Language Inquiry, 1998-2000; Governor, English-Speaking Union of the Commonwealth, 2000; President, European Year of Languages, 2000. Publications: Clive Lloyd: a biography, 1985; Vivian Richard's biography, 1987; Queen and Commonwealth, 1989; Fortunate Circumstances, 1993; Favourite Poems, 1997; World of Poems, 1999. Honours: Hon DLitt, Nottingham, 1997; Dr hc, Open University, 1997; Honorary Fellow, Liverpool John Moores University, 1998; Newscaster of the Year, TV and Radio Industries Club, 1993, 1997, 1999; Gold Medal, Royal Television Society, 1998; Richard Dimbleby Award for Outstanding Contribution to Television, BAFTA, 1999; OBE; Knighted, 1999. Royal Television Society Lifetime Achievement Award, 2005. Address: c/o ITN, 200 Gray's Inn Road, London, WC1 8XZ, England.

McDORMAND Frances, b. 23 June 1957, Illinois, USA. Actress. m. Joel Coen 1984, 1 adopted son. Education: Yale University, School of Drama. Appointments: Stage Appearances include: Awake and Sing, 1984; Painting Churches, 1984; The Three Sisters, 1985; All My Sons, 1986; A Streetcar Named Desire, 1988; Moon for the Misbegotten, 1992; Sisters Rosenzweig, 1993; The Swan, 1993; Films include: Blood Simple, 1984; Raising Arizona, 1987; Mississippi Burning, 1988; Chattaboochee, 1990; Darkman, 1990; Miller's Crossing, 1990; Hidden Agenda, 1990; The Butcher's Wife, 1991; Passed Away, 1992; Short Cuts, 1993; Beyond Rangoon, 1995; Fargo, 1996; Paradise Road, 1997; Johnny Skidmarks, 1997; Madeline, 1998; Talk of Angels, 1998; Wonder Boys, 1999; Almost Famous, 2000; The Man Who Wasn't There, 2001; Upheaval, 2001; Laurel Canyon, 2002; City By the Sea, 2003; Something's Gotta Give, 2003; Last Night, 2004; North Country, 2005; Æon Flux, 2005; Friends with Money, 2006; Miss Pettigrew Lives for a Day, 2008; Burn After Reading, 2008; Transformers: Dark of the Moon, This Must Be the Place, 2011; Moonrise Kingdom, Madagascar 3: Europe's Most Wanted, Promised Land, 2012. Has appeared in several TV series. Honours: Screen Actors' Guild Award, 1996; London Film Critics' Circle Award, 1996; Independent Spirit Award, 1996; American Comedy Award, 1997; Academy Award, Best Actress, 1997; LA Film Critics Award, 2000. Address: c/o William Morris Agency, 1325 Avenue of the Americas, New York, NY 10019, USA.

McDOUGALL Bonnie Suzanne, b. 12 March 1941, Sydney, Australia. Professor of Chinese. m. H Anders Hansson, 1 son. Education: BA honours, 1965, MA honours, University Medal, 1967, PhD, 1970, University of Sydney. Appointments: Lecturer in Oriental Studies, University of Sydney, 1972-76;

Research Fellow, East Asian Research Center, Harvard University, 1976-79; Associate in East Asian Studies, John King Fairbank Center, Harvard University, 1979-80; Visiting Lecturer on Chinese, Harvard University, 1977-78; Editor and Translator, Foreign Languages Press, Peking, 1980-83; Teacher of English, College of Foreign Affairs, Peking, 1984-86; Senior Lecturer in Chinese, University of Oslo, 1986-87; Professor of Modern Chinese, University of Oslo, 1987-90; Professor of Chinese, University of Edinburgh, 1990-. Publications: Numerous books and articles on Chinese Literature. Memberships: Association for Asian Studies; European Association of Chinese Studies; British Association of Chinese Studies; Universities' China Committee in London; Scots Australian Council. Address: Scottish Centre for Chinese Studies, School of Asian Studies, University of Edinburgh, 8 Buccleuch Place, Edinburgh EH8 9LW, Scotland.

McDOWALL David Buchanan, b. 14 April 1945, London, England. Writer. m. Elizabeth Mary Risk Laird, 1975, 2 sons. Education: MA, 1966-69, MLitt, 1970-72, St John's College, Oxford. Appointments: Subaltern, Royal Artillery, UK and Hong Kong, 1963-70; British Council, Bombay, Baghdad and London Headquarters, 1972-77; Contributions Officer, United Nations Relief and Works Agency for Palestine Refugees in the Near East, 1977-79; Consultant to voluntary agencies re development in Middle East, 1979-84; Full-time Writer, 1984-. Publications: Lebanon: A Conflict of Minorities, 1984 Palestine and Israel: The Uprising and Beyond, 1989; An Illustrated History of Britain, 1989; Europe and the Arabs: Discord or Symbiosis?, 1992; Britain in Close Up, 1993, 1998; The Palestinians: The Road to Nationhood, 1994; A Modern History of the Kurds, 1996; Richmond Park: The Walker's Historical Guide, 1996; Hampstead Heath: The Walker's Guide (co-author Deborah Wolton), 1998; The Kurds of Syria, 1998; The Thames from Hampton to Richmond Bridge: The Walkers Guide, 2002; The Thames From Richmond to Putney Bridge: The Walker's Guide, 2005. Contributions to: World Directory of Minorities, Middle East section, 1997. Honour: The Other Award. Address: 31 Cambrian Road, Richmond, Surrey TW10 6JQ, England.

McDOWELL Malcolm, b. 13 June 1943, Leeds, England. Actor. m. (1) Mary Steenburgen, 1980, 1 son, 1 daughter, (2) Kelley Kuhr, 1991, 3 sons. Appointments: Began career with Royal Shakespeare Company, Stratford, 1965-66; Early TV appearances in such series as Dixon of Dock Green; Z Cars; Stage Appearances: RSC, Stratford, 1965-66; Entertaining Mr Sloane, Royal Court, 1975; Look Back in Anger, New York, 1980; In Celebration, New York, 1984; Holiday Old Vic, 1987; Another Time, Old Vic, 1993; Films Include: If..., 1969; Figures in a Landscape, 1970; The Raging Moon, A Clockwork Orange, 1971; O Lucky Man, 1973; Royal Flash, 1975; Aces High, 1976; Voyage of the Damned, Caligula, 1977; The Passage, 1978; Time After Time, 1979; Cat People, 1981; Blue Thunder, Get Crazy, 1983; Britannia Hospital, 1984; Gulag, 1985; The Caller, Sunset, 1987; Sunrise, 1988; Class of 1999, Il Maestro, 1989; Moon 44; Double Game; Class of 1999; Snake Eyes, Schweitzer; Assassin of the Tsar, 1991; The Player; Chain of Desire; East Wind; Night Train to Venice; Star Trek: Generations, Tank Girl, 1995; Kids of the Round Table; Where Truth Lies; Mr Magoo, 1998; Gangster No 1, Island of the Dead, 2000; Just Visiting, The Void, Dorian, 2001; The Barber, Between Strangers, Superman: Shadow of Apokolips, I Spy, 2002; I'll Sleep When I'm Dead, Tempo, Inhabited, Red Roses and Petrol, The Company, 2003; Hidalgo, Evilenko, Bobby Jones, Stroke of Genius, Tempesta, Pinocchio 3000, 2004 (voice); Rag Tale, 2005; Cut Off, Bye Bye Benjamin, 2006; The List, Exitz, Halloween, Doomsday, 2007; Delgo, 2008; Bolt (voice), 2008; Halloween II, 2009; The Book of Eli, 2010. Numerous TV appearances including: Our Friends in the North; War and Peace; Phineas and Ferb. Address: c/o Markham and Froggatt, 4 Windmill Street, London, W1P 1HF, England.

McENROE John Patrick, b. 16 February 1959, Wiesbaden, Federal Republic of Germany. Lawn Tennis Player. m. (1) Tatum O'Neil, 1986, 2 sons, 1 daughter, (2) Patty Smyth, 2 daughters, 1 step-daughter. Education: Trinity High School, New Jersey; Stanford University, California. Appointments: Amateur Player, 1976-78; Professional, 1978-93; USA Singles Champion, 1979, 1980, 1981, 1984; USA Doubles Champion, 1979, 1981, 1989; Wimbledon Champion (doubles), 1979, 1981, 1983, 1984, 1992 (singles) 1981, 1983, 1984; WCT Champion, 1979, 1981, 1983, 1984, 1989; Grand Prix Champion, 1979, 1983, 1984; Played Davis Cup for USA, 1978, 1979, 1980, 1982, 1983, 1984, 1985; Only Player to have reached Wimbledon semi-finals (1977) as pre-tournament qualifier; Semi Finalist, 1989; Tennis Sportscaster, USA Network, 1993; Member, Men's Senior's Tours Circuits, 1994; Winner, Quality Challenge, Worldwide Senior Tennis Circuit, 1999; ATP Tour, 2006 (doubles); Owner, John McEnroe Gallery; Coach, British Lawn Tennis Association, 2003-; TV: Presenter, The Chair (game show), 2002; McEnroe (talk show), CNBC, 2004. Publication: You Cannot Be Serious, autobiography, 2002. Honour: National Father of the Year Award, 1996; International Tennis Hall of Fame, 1999. Address: The John McEnroe Gallery, 41 Greene Street, New York, NY 10013, USA.

McEWAN Geraldine, b. 9 May 1932, Old Windsor, Berkshire, England. Actress. Education: Windsor County Girls' School. Career: TV: The Prime of Miss Jean Brodie, 1978; L'Elégance, The Barchester Chronicles, Come Into the Garden, Maude, 1982; Mapp and Lucia, 1985-86; Oranges are Not the Only Fruit, 1990; Mulberry, 1992-93; Red Dwarf, 1999; Thin Ice, Victoria Wood's Christmas Special, 2000; Carrie's War, 2003; Marple, 2004-2007; Films: The Adventures of Tom Jones, 1975; Escape from the Dark, 1978; Foreign Body, 1986; Henry V, 1989; Robin Hood: Prince of Thieves, 1991; Moses, 1995; The Love Letter, 1999; Titus, Love's Labours Lost, The Contaminated Man, 2000; The Magdalene Sisters, Food for Love, Pure, 2002; The Lazarus Child, Vanity Fair, 2004; Stage: Debut, Theatre Royal, Windsor, 1949; London stage: Who Goes There? 1951; Sweet Madness; For Better, For Worse; Summertime; Shakespeare Memorial Theatre, Straford on Avon, 1956, 1958, 1961; USA stage: School for Scandal, 1962; The Private Eat and The Public Eye, 1963; Member, National Theatre, 1965-71; Numerous other theatre appearances; Radio: Arrived, 2002; Director: As You Like It, 1988; Treats, 1989; Waiting for Sir Larry, 1990; Four Door Saloon, 1991; Keyboard Skills, 1993. Honours: TV Critics Best Actress Award, 1978; BAFTA Best Actress Award, 1990; Evening Standard Drama Award for Best Actress, 1983 and 1995. Address: c/o ICM Oxford House, 76 Oxford Street, London W1D 1BS, England.

McEWAN Ian, b. 21 June 1948, Aldershot, Hampshire, England. Author. m. (1) Penny Allen, 1982, divorced, 1995, 2 sons, 2 step daughters, (2) Annalena McAfee, 1997. Education: Woolverstone Hall; University of Sussex; University of East Anglia; Hon D Phil, Sussex, 1989; East Anglia, 1993. Publications: First Love, Last Rites, 1975; In Between the Sheets, 1978; The Cement Gardens, 1978; The Imitation Game, 1980; The Comfort of Strangers, 1981; Or Shall we Die?, 1983; The Ploughman's Lunch, 1983; The Child in Time, 1987; Soursweet (screenplay), 1987; A Move

Abroad, 1989; The Innocent, 1990; Black Dogs, 1992; The Daydreamer, 1994; The Short Stories, 1995; Enduring Love, 1997; Amsterdam (novel), 1998; Atonement, 2001; Saturday, 2005; On Chesil Beach, 2007; For You (Opera), 2008; Solar, 2010. Honours: Somerset Maugham Prize, 1975; Primo Letterario, Prato, 1982; Whitbread Fiction Prize, 1987; Prix Femina, 1993; Booker Prize, 1998; Shakespeare Prize, 1999; CBE, 2000; National Book Critics Circle Award, 2003; James Tait Black Memorial Prize, 2005. Address: c/o Jonathan Cape, Random Century House, 20 Vauxhall Bridge Road, London SW1V 2SA, England. Website: www.ianmcewan.com

McFADYEN Jock, b. 18 September 1950, Paisley, Scotland. Artist. m. (1) Carol Hambleton, divorced, 1 son, (2) Susie Honeyman, 1 daughter, 1 son. Education: BA, MA, Chelsea School of Art, London, 1973-77. Career: Over 40 solo exhibitions including: Artist-in-Residence, National Gallery, 1982; Camden Arts Centre, 1988; Imperial War Museum, 1991; Talbot Rice Gallery, Edinburgh, 1998; Pier Arts Centre, Orkney, 1999; Agnew's Gallery, London, 2001; Rude Wercs, London, 2005; Grey Gallery, Edinburgh Festival, 2007; Grey Gallery, London, 2009; Works in over 30 public collections, including the Tate Gallery, the National Gallery, the Victoria and Albert Museum, the British Museum; Works in many private and corporate collections in Britain, Europe and America. Publication: Jock McFayden – A Book About a Painter, by David Cohen, 2001. Honours: Arts Council Major Award, 1979; Prizewinner John Moores Liverpool, 1991; Designed sets and costumes for Sir Kenneth MacMillan's ballet, The Judas Tree, Royal Opera House, 1992. Membership: Vintage Japanese Motorcycle Club. Address: 15 Victoria Park Square, Bethnal Green, London E2 9PB, England.

McFALL John, b. 4 October, 1944, Member of Parliament. m. Joan McFall, 3 sons, 1 daughter. Education: BSc honours, Chemistry; BA honours, Education; MBA. Appointments: School Teacher, Assistant Head Teacher, -1987; Member of Parliament for Dumbarton, 1987-; Opposition Whip with responsibility for Foreign Affairs, Defence and Trade and Industry, 1990; Deputy Shadow Secretary of State for Scotland with responsibility for Industry and Economic Affairs; Employment and Training; Home Affairs, Transport and Roads; Highland and Islands, 1992-97; Lord Commissioner, 1997-98; Parliamentary Under Secretary of State, Northern Ireland Office, 1998-99; Chairman of the Treasury Select Committee, 2001-05. Memberships: British/Hong Kong Group; British/Italian Group; British/Peru Group; Retail Industry Group; Roads Study Group; Scotch Whisky Group; Parliamentary and Scientific Committee; Select Committee on Defence; Select Committee on Sittings of the House; Executive Committee Parliamentary Group for Energy Studies; Information Committee; Executive Committee Parliamentary Group for Energy Studies. Address: House of Commons, London SW1A 0AA, England. E-mail: mcfallj@parliament.uk

McGAVIN David Douglas Murray, b. 9 August 1938, Shanghai, China. Doctor of Medicine. m. Ruth, 2 sons, 1 deceased, 1 daughter. Education: Kelvinside Academy, Glasgow, 1945-46; Shanghai British School, 1947-48; Kelvinside Academy, Glasgow, 1949-56; University of Glasgow, 1956-62. Appointments: Project & Medical Director, Noor Eye Institute, Kabul, Afghanistan, 1976-81; Founder Editor, Journal of Community Eye Health, London, 1988-2003; Medical Director, International Resource Centre for the Prevention of Blindness, 1990-2003; Executive Director, 1999-2008, President, 2008-09, International Community Trust for Health & Educational Services. Publications: Editorial Consultant (Founder): Journal of Developing Mental Health, Journal of Community Ear & Hearing Health and Journal of Community Dermatology; Chapters in international medical textbooks; Editor, online text book on Prevention of World Blindness, 2003. Honours: Listed in international biographical dictionaries; Honorary Fellowship, Royal College of Physicians of Edinburgh; MBE, Queen's New Year Honours, 2010. Memberships: Royal College of Surgeons, Edinburgh; Royal College of Ophthalmologists; Royal College of Physicians, Edinburgh; Royal Geographical Society; Afghan Ophthalmological Society. Address: West Hurlet House, Glasgow Road, Hurlet, Glasgow G53 7TH, Scotland.

McGEACHIE Daniel, b. 10 June 1935, Barrhead, Glasgow, Scotland. Journalist; Company Director. m. Sylvia Andrew, 1 daughter. Appointments: Journalist, Scotland and Fleet Street, 1955-60; Foreign Correspondent, Daily Express, 1960-65; Parliamentary Correspondent, Diplomatic and Political Correspondent, Daily Express, 1965-75; Political Advisor, Conoco UK Ltd, 1975-77; Director, General Manager, Government and Public Affairs, Conoco UK Ltd, 1977-2000. Honours: OBE for services to Industry and Government relations, 1992. Memberships: Member, Royal Institute of International Affairs; Member, Reform Club. Address: 27 Hitherwood Drive, London SE19 1XA, England. E-mail: danmcgeachie@ukgateway.net

McGEOUGH Joseph Anthony, b. 29 May 1940, Kilwinning, Ayrshire, Scotland. University Professor. m. Brenda Nicholson, 2 sons, 1 daughter. Education: BSc, 1963, PhD, 1967, Glasgow University; DSc, Aberdeen University, 1982. Appointments: Senior Research Fellow, Queensland University, 1967; Research Metallurgist, International Research and Development Co Ltd, Newcastle, 1968-69; Senior Research Fellow, Strathclyde University, 1969-72; Lecturer, 1972-77, Senior Lecturer, 1977-80, Reader, 1980-83, University of Aberdeen; Regius Professor of Engineering, 1983-2005, Emeritus Professor, 2005-, Senior Honorary Professorial Fellow, 2007-11, University of Edinburgh; Vice-President, Institution of Mechanical Engineers, 2006-10. Publications: Books include: Principles of Electrochemical Machining, 1974; Advanced Methods of Machining, 1988; Micromachining of Engineering Materials (editor), 2001. Honour: FRSE, 1990; FREng, 2008. Memberships: FIMechE; MRi; FCIRP; Vice President, Institution of Mechanical Engineers, 2006-10; President, Colinton Parish Church Literary Society, 2009-12; Listed in national and international biographical dictionaries. Address: 39 Dreghorn Loan, Edinburgh EH13 0DF, Scotland. E-mail: j.a.mcgeough@ed.ac.uk

MCGOUGH Roger, b. 9 November 1937, Liverpool, England. Poet. m. 1986, 3 sons, 1 daughter. Education: St Mary's College, Crosby; BA and Graduate Certificate of Education, Hull University. Appointments: Fellow of Poetry, University of Loughborough, 1973-75; Writer-in-Residence, West Australian College of Advanced Education, Perth, 1986; Honorary Fellow, John Moores University, Honorary Professor, Thames Valley University, 1993. Publications: The Mersey Sound (with Brian Patten and Adrian Henri), 1967; Strictly Private (editor), 1982; An Imaginary Menagerie, 1989; Blazing Fruit (selected poems 1967-87), 1990; Pillow Talk, 1990; The Lighthouse That Ran Away, 1991; You at the Back (selected poems 1967-87, Vol 2), 1991; My Dad's a Fire Eater, 1992; Defying Gravity, 1992; The Elements, 1993; Lucky, 1993; Stinkers Ahoy!, 1994; The Magic Fountain, 1995; The Kite and Caitlin, 1996; Sporting Relations, 1996;

Bad, Bad Cats, 1997; Until I Met Dudley, 1997; The Spotted Unicorn, 1998; The Ring of Words (editor), 1998; The Way Things Are, 1999; Dotty Inventions, 2002; Everyday Eclipses, 2002; Good Enough to Eat, 2002; Moonthief, 2002; What On Earth? 2002; Collected Poems, 2003; Said and Done (autobiography), 2005; Slapstick, 2008; That Awkward Age, 2009; As Far As I Know, 2012. Honours: Honorary Professor, Thames Valley University, 1993; Officer of the Order of the British Empire, 1997; Honorary MA, Nene College of Further Education, 1998; Fellow, John Moores University, Liverpool, 1999; CBE, 2004; Honorary D Litt, University of Hull, 2004, Roehampton University, 2006, University of Liverpool, 2006; Fellows of the Royal Society of Literature, 2004. Address: c/o The Peters, Fraser and Dunlop Group Ltd, Drury House, 34 – 43 Russell Street, London WC2B 5HA, England.

McGREGOR Ewan, b. 31 March 1971, Perth, Scotland. Actor. m. Eve Mavrakis, 1995, 3 daughters. Education: Guildhall School of Music and Drama. Appointments: Formerly with Perth Repertory Theatre; Theatre includes: What the Butler Saw; Little Malcolm and his Struggle against the Eunuchs, Hampstead Theatre Club, 1989; TV includes: Lipstick on Your Collar; Scarlet and Black; Kavanagh QC; Doggin Around; Tales from the Crypt; ER; Films include: Being Human; Family Style; Shallow Grave; Blue Juice; The Pillow Book; Trainspotting; Emma; Brassed Off; Nightwatch; The Serpent's Kiss; A Life Less Ordinary; Velvet Goldmine; Star Wars Episode I: The Phantom Menace; Little Voice; Rogue Trader; Eye of the Beholder; Nora; Moulin Rouge, 2001; Black Hawk Down, Stars Wars Episode II: Attack of the Clones, 2002; Down with Love, Young Adam, Faster, Big Fish, 2003; Robots (voice), Stay, Valiant (voice), Star Wars Episode III: Revenge of the Sith, The Island, 2005; Stormbreaker, Scenes of a Sexual Nature, Miss Potter, 2006; Cassandra's Dream, The Tourist, 2007; Incendiary, Jackboots on Whitehall, 2008; I Love You Phillip Morris, Angels & Demons, The Men Who Stare at Goats, Amelia, 2009; The Ghost Writer, Nanny McPhee and the Big Bang, Jackboots in Whitehall, Beginners, 2010; Perfect Sense, Fastest, Haywire, 2011; Salmon Fishing in the Yemen, The Impossible, 2012; Jack the Giant Slayer, August: Osage County, 2013. Documentary and book: The Long Way Round, motorcycle trip around the world for UNICEF with Charley Boorman, 2004; Long Way Down, 2007. Honours: Best Actor Dinard Film Festival, 1994; Best Actor, Berlin Film Festival; Empire Award; Variety Club Awards; Film Critics' Awards.

McGREGOR Richard Ewan, b. 22 March 1953, Glasgow, Scotland. Professor of Music. m. Helen Frances Card (divorced), 1 son, 1 daughter. Education: B Mus (Hons), University of Glasgow, 1971-75; PhD, University of Liverpool; PGCE, Westminster College, Oxford. Appointments: Director of Music, Luton Sixth Form College, 1981-92; Head of Performing Arts, 1992-99, Principal Lecturer in Music, 1999-2006, Professor of Music, 2006-, Director of Research and Graduate Studies, St Martin's College, Lancaster (now University of Cumbria). Publications: The Early Music of Peter Maxwell Davies, 1986; The Maxwell Davies Manuscripts in the British Library, 1996; Perspectives on Peter Maxwell Davies, 2000; Reading the Runes, 2000; Laus Deo: Composers' Views of Their Spirituality, 2005; The Persistence of Parody in Peter Maxwell Davies's Music, 2007; Stepping Out: Salome as Transitional Work, 2006; Transubstantiated into the Musical: a critical study of Veni Veni Emmanuel by James Macmillan, 2007; Hunting and Forms: an interview with Wolfgang Rihm, 2009; Interpreting Compositional Process in Wolfgang Rihm's Chiffre Cycle, 2007; Janet MacMillan's OP Bone Jesus; A Metaphor for the Deeper Wintriness: Exploring James MacMillan's Musical Identity; James MacMillan: A Conversation and a Commentary; Hunting and Forms: An Interview with Wolfgang Rihm; Because the Drummed Rhythm was Seven; Maxwell Davies sources: reflections on origins, meanings and significance, 2009; Numerous compositions. Honours: Glasgow University Class Prize, 1973; Goudie Prize for Harmony, 1974; Martha Vidor Scholarship, University of Liverpool, 1976-79; Italian Government Scholarship, 1982; Paul Sacher Stiftung Stipendium, 2002. Memberships: Fellow, Higher Education Academy; Scottish Music Centre (Composer); Fellow, Society of Antiquaries (Scotland). Address: University of Cumbria, Lancaster Campus, Bowerham Road, Lancaster LA1 3JD, England. E-mail: richard.mcgregor@cumbria.ac.uk

MCGRIGOR James Angus Rhoderick (Sir), b. 19 October 1949, London, England. Conservative MSP. m. Emma, 1 son, 5 daughters. Education: Cladich primary school, Argyll; Sunningdale school, Berkshire; Eton College; Commercial French, Neuchatel University, Switzerland. Appointments: Shipping Agent, J & A Gardner Shipping, 1969-71; Stockbroker, Laurence Prust & Co, 1972-74; Owner and manager of hill farm (sheep and cattle), 1976-; Scottish Conservative List MSP for Highlands and Islands, 1999-, re-elected, 2003, 2007. Publications: Numerous articles in local journals; Gut Feelings, MSP recipe book. Honours: Created Kentucky Colonel, 2010. Memberships: Patron, Marie Curie (Cancer Care); Governor, RNLI; Chelsea Arts Club Member; New Club, Edinburgh; Whites; Honorary President, Highland Disabled Ramblers Association; Member, Royal Company of Archers; Council Member, Atlantic Salmon Trust; Chairman, Loch Awe Improvement Association.

McGUINNESS Martin, b. 23 May 1950, Derry, Northern Ireland. Politican. m. Bernadette Canning, 1974, 2 sons, 2 daughters. Appointments: Took part in secret London Talks between Secretary of State for Northern Ireland and Irish Republicans Army (IRA), 1972; Imprisoned for six months during 1973, Irish Republic, after conviction for IRA membership; Elected to North Ireland Association, Refused Seat; Stood against John Hume in General Elections of 1982, 1987, 1992; MP for Mid-Ulster, House of Commons, 1997-; Member, Ulster-Mid, Northern Ireland Association, 1998-2000, Association suspended 11 February 2000; Minister of Education, 1999-2007; Deputy First Minister of Northern Ireland, 2007- ; Spokesperson for Sinn Féin; Member of National Executive; Involved in Peace Negotiations with British Government.

McINTYRE Ian (James), b. 9 December 1931, Banchory, Kincardineshire, Scotland. Writer; Broadcaster. m. Leik Sommerfelt Vogt, 1954, 2 sons, 2 daughters. Education: BA, 1953, MA, 1960, St John's College, Cambridge; College of Europe, Bruges, Belgium, 1953-54. Appointments include: National Service, Commissioned in the Intelligence Corps, 1955-57; BBC Current Affairs Talks Producer, 1957; Editor, At Home and Abroad, 1959; Programme Services Officer, Independent Television Authority, 1961-62; Director of Information and Research, Scottish Conservative Central Office, 1962-70; Writer, Broadcaster, 1970-76, Controller, Radio 4, 1976-78, Controller, Radio 3, 1978-87, British Broadcasting Corporation; Associate Editor, The Times, London, 1989-90. Publications: The Proud Doers: Israel After Twenty Years, 1968; Words: Reflections on the Uses of Language, editor, contributor, 1975; Dogfight: The Transatlantic Battle over Airbus, 1992; The Expense of Glory: A Life of John Reith, 1993; Dirt and Deity: A Life of Robert Burns, 1996; Garrick, 1999; Joshua Reynolds: The Life and

Times of the First President of the Royal Academy, 2003. Honour: Winner, Theatre Book Prize, 1999. Memberships: Union Society, Cambridge; Beefsteak Club. Address: Spylaw House, Newlands Avenue, Radlett, Hertfordshire WD7 8EL, England.

McINTYRE James Archibald, b. 2 September 1926, Stranraer, Scotland. Retired Farmer. m. Hilma Wilson Brown, 1 son, 2 daughters. Education: Oxford University, 1944, 6 months short army course. Commissioned 12 H Royal Lancers, 1945-47; West of Scotland Horticultural College, 1948-49. Appointments: Council Member, 1962-72, President, 1969, National Farmers Union, Scotland; Member, 1973-, Chairman, 1985-95, Dumfries and Galloway Health Board; Board Member, NFU Mutual Insurance, 1983-93. Honours: JP, 1989; OBE, 1989; CBE, 1995; O St J, 1979; C St J, 2000. Memberships: National Farmers Union, Scotland, 1950-; Member, Order of St John, 1972-. Address: Glenorchy, Broadstone Road, Stranraer, Scotland.

McISAAC Ian, b. 13 July 1945. Chartered Accountant. m. (1) Joanna Copland, dissolved, 1 son, 1 daughter, (2) Debrah Ball, 1 son, 1 daughter. Education: Charterhouse scholar. Appointments: Partner, Touche Ross (UK), 1979-88; Touche Ross (Canada), 1983-85; Chief Executive, Richard Ellis Finanacial Services, 1988-91; Partner, Deloitte and Touche (formerly Touche Ross), 1991-2005; Global Head, Reorganisation Service, 1999-, UK Chairman, Emerging Markets, 2000-; Chairman, Society of Turaround Professionals, Director, Care International (UK). Honours: Freeman of the City of London; Member of the Worshipful Company of Chartered Accountants; ACA, 1969; FCA, 1979. Memberships: City of London Club; Hurlingham Club; Royal Mid-Surrey Golf Club; High Post Golf Club; OCYC. Address: 28 Hereford Square, London SW7, England. E-mail: imcisaac@deloitte.co.uk

McKAY Brenda Doris, b. 26 January 1947, Johannesburg, South Africa. Writer; Academic Researcher. Education: BA, Classical Culture, History of Art, English and Biblical Studies, 1979, Honours in Ancient History and Latin, 1981, 3rd year course in English III (equivalent to BA major in English), 1981, University of Witwatersrand, Johannesburg; Diploma, Abnormal Psychology, London University, 1986; MA (cum laude) Victorian Studies, 1990, PhD, English Research, 1996, Birkbeck College, London University. Appointments: Antiques dealer, -1988, South Africa and London; Lecturer, English, Birkbeck College, -1996; Teacher, Gender Studies, English and American Literature, University of Hertfordshire, 1997; Independent Scholar and Writer, 1997-; Research interests: George Eliot, Elizabeth Gaskell, Charlotte Brontë, Charles Darwin, A R Wallace, Robert Knox, and Harriet Beecher Stowe. Publications: Helped to edit and wrote Preface to Nabil Hamad, Broken Poems, 2009; Contributed to Adapting Gaskell: Screen and Stage Versions of Elizabeth Gaskell's Fiction, 2013. Honours: Monograph, George Eliot & Victorian Attitudes to Racial Diversity, Darwinism, Colonialism, Class, Gender and Jewish Culture & Prophecy, honoured by CHOICE as one of 2003's outstanding academic books. Memberships: George Eliot Society; Gaskell Society; Brontë Society; The Society of Authors. Address: 11 Pinehurst Court, London W11 2BH, England.

MCKEEVER Ed (Edward Daniel), b. Bath, Somerset, England. Kayak Athlete. Education: BA (Hons), Accountancy and Finance, Kingston University; ACCA, in progress. Career: Gold (K-1 200m) and Silver (K-1 4x200m), ICF Canoe Sprint World Championships, Poznan, 2010; Winner (K-1 200m), European Championships, Trasona, Spain, 2010; Silver (K-1 200m), ICF Canoe Sprint World Championships, Szeged, Hungary, 2011; Winner (K-1 200m), World Cup, Poznan, 2012; Gold (K-1 200m), Canoe Sprint World Cup, 2012; Gold (K-1 200m) Canoe Sprint, London Olympics, 2012.

McKELLEN Ian Murray (Sir), b. 25 May 1939, Burnley, Lancashire, England. Actor. Education: Bolton School; St Catherines College, Cambridge. Appointments: First stage appearance, Roper (A Man for All Seasons), Belgrade Theatre, Coventry, 1961; Numerous other parts including: Royal National Theatre: Bent, Max; King Lear, Kent; Richard III, world tour then US tour, 1990-92; Napoli Milionaria, 1991; Uncle Vanya, 1992; An Enemy of the People, Peter Pan, 1997; The Seagull, Present Laughter, The Tempest, West Yorkshire Playhouse, 1998-99; Dance of Death, Broadhurst Theatre, New York, 2001, London, 2003, Australia, 2004; Aladdin, Old Vic, London, 2004-05; Films include: Alfred the Great, The Promise, A Touch of Love, 1969; Priest of Love, 1981; The Keep, 1982; Plenty, Zina, 1985; Scandal, 1988; The Ballad of Little Jo, I'll do Anything, 1992; Last Action Hero, Six Degrees of Seperation, 1993; The Shadow, Jack and Sarah, Restoration, 1994; Richard III, 1995; Bent, Swept From Sea, 1996; Apt Pupil, 1997; Gods and Monsters, 1998; X-Men, 1999; Lord of the Rings: The Fellowship of the Ring, 2001; Lord of the Rings: The Two Towers, 2002; X-Men 2, Emile, Lord of the Rings: The Return of the King, 2003; Neverwas, 2005; The Da Vinci Code, X-Men: The Last Stand, Flushed Away (voice), 2006; For the Love of God, Stardust (voice), The Golden Compass (voice), 2007; TV appearances include: David Copperfield, 1965; Ross, 1969; Richard II; Edward II; Hamlet, 1970; Hedda Gabler, 1974; Macbeth; Every Good Boy Deserves Favour, Dying Day, 1979; Acting Shakespeare, 1981; Walter; The Scarlet Pimpernel, 1982; Walter and June, 1983; Countdown to War, 1989; Othello, 1990; Tales of the City, 1993; Cold Comfort Farm, 1995; Rasputin, 1996; Coronation Street, 2005. Publications: William Shakespeare's Richard III, 1996. Honours: Clarence Derwent Award, 1964; Hon D Litt, 1989; Variety and Plays and Players Awards, 1966; Actor of the Year, Plays and Players, 1976; Society of West End Theatres Award for Best Actor in a Revival, 1977, for Best Comedy Performance, 1978, for Best Actor in a New Play, 1979; Tony Award, 1981; Drama Desk, 1981; Outer Critics Circle Award, 1981; Royal TV Society Performer of the Year, 1983; Laurence Olivier Award, 1984, 1991; Evening Standard Best Actor Award, 1984, 1989; Cameron Mackintosh Professor of Contemporary Theatre Oxford University, 1991; Screen Actor's Guild Award for besting supporting Actor, 2000; British Industry Film Awards, Variety UK Personality Award, 2003. Address: c/o ICM 76 Oxford Street, London, W1N 0AX, England.

McKENDRICK Melveena Christine, b. 23 March 1941, Crynant, Neath, Wales. Hispanist. m. Neil McKendrick, 2 daughters. Education: BA 1st class honours, Spanish, King's College, London; PhD, Girton College, Cambridge, 1967. Appointments: Jex-Blake Research Fellow, 1967-70, Tutor, 1970-83, Senior Tutor, 1974-81, Director of Studies in Modern Languages, 1984-95, Girton College, Cambridge; Lecturer in Spanish, 1980-92, Reader in Spanish Literature and Society, 1992-99, Professor of Spanish, Golden-Age Literature, Culture and Society, 1999-, University of Cambridge; British Academy Reader, 1992-94, Visiting Professor, University of Victoria, 1997; Fellow of the British Academy, 1999-; Pro-Vice-Chancellor (Education), University of Cambridge, 2004-. Publications: Author and co-author, numerous books; Articles on Early Modern Spanish theatre in many journals. Memberships: General Board, Cambridge University, 1993-97;

Humanities Research Board, British Academy, 1996-98; Arts and Humanities Research Board, 1998-99; Consultant Hispanic Editor, Everyman, 1993-99; Editorial board, Donaire, 1994-; Revista Canadiense de Estudios Hispanicos, 1995-; Bulletin of Hispanic Studies, Glasgow, 1998-. Address: Department of Spanish & Portuguese, Faculty of Modern and Medieval Languages, University of Cambridge, Sidgwick Avenue, Cambridge, CB3 9DA, England.

McKENDRICK Neil, b. 28 July 1935, Formby, Lancashire, England. Historian. m. Melveena Jones, 2 daughters. Education: BA 1st class honours with Distinction, History, 1956, MA, 1960, Christ's College, Cambridge; FRHistS, 1971. Appointments: Research Fellow, 1958, Christ's College Cambridge; Assistant Lecturer in History, 1961-64, Lecturer, 1964-95, Secretary to Faculty Board of History, 1975-77, Chairman, History Faculty, 1985-87, Cambridge University; Fellow, 1958-96, Lecturer in History, 1958-96, Reader in Social and Economic History, 1995-2002, Director of Studies in History, 1959-96, Tutor, 1961-69, Master, 1996-2005, Gonville and Caius College; Lectures: Earl, University of Keele, 1963; Inaugural, Wallace Gallery, Colonial Williamsburg, 1985; Chettyar Memorial, University of Madras, 1990; Master, Gonville and Caius College, 2006-. Publications: Author and Editor of numerous publications; Author of articles in learned journals. Memberships: Tancred's Charities, 1996; Sir John Plumb Charitable Trust, 1999-; Properties Committee, National Trust, 1999-; Vice President, Caius Foundation in America, 1998-; Glenfield Trust, 2001-. Address: The Master's Lodge, Gonville and Caius College, Cambridge, CB2 1TA, England.

McKENNA Virginia Anne, b. 7 June 1931, London, England. Actress; Conservationist. m. Bill Travers, deceased 1994, 3 sons, 1 daughter. Education: Central School of Speech and Drama, London. Career: TV includes: The Whistle Blower; Pucini; The Camomile Lawn; The Deep Blue Sea; A Passage to India; Waters of the Moon; September; Films include: Born Free; Ring of Bright Water; Carve Her Name with Pride; The Cruel Sea; The Smallest Show on Earth; Waterloo; The Barretts of Wimpole Street; Staggered; An Elephant Called Slowly; Sliding Doors. Theatre includes: Season, Old Vic; The Devils; A Winters Tale; Penny for a Song; The River Line; A Little Night Music; The Beggars Opera; Winnie; I Capture the Castle; Hamlet; The King and I. TV includes: The Whistle-Blower; The Scold's Bridle; Marple: A Murder Is Announced,. Publications: Books: On Playing with Lions (with Bill Travers); Some of My Friends Have Tails; Into the Blue; Back to the Blue; Journey to Freedom; Co-editor and contributor to: Beyond the Bars; Contributor to: Women at Work. Honours: Best Actress Award for Born Free, Variety Club; Belgian Prix Femina for Carve Her Name with Pride; SWET Award for The King and I (theatre); Best Actress Award, Romeo and Juliet (TV); Best Actress Award for A Town Like Alice, BAFTA; OBE, 2004. Memberships: Special Forces Club; Patron of: Plan International UK, Children of the Andes, Elizabeth Fitzroy Support; Wildlife Aid, Swallows and Amazons; Founder, Trustee, The Born Free Foundation. Address: The Born Free Foundation, 3 Grove House, Foundry Lane, Horsham, West Sussex RH13 5PL, England. E-mail: wildlife@bornfree.org.uk

McKENZIE Dan Peter, b. 21 February 1942, Cheltenham, England. Earth Scientist. m. Indira Margaret, 1 son. Education: BA, MA, PhD, King's College, University of Cambridge. Appointments: Senior Assistant in Research, 1969-75, Assistant Director of Research, 1975-79, Reader in Tectonics, 1979-84, Royal Society Professor of Earth Sciences, Department of Earth Sciences, University of Cambridge. Publications: Author of various papers in learned journals. Honours: Honorary MA, University of Cambridge, 1966; Fellow, Royal Society, 1976; Foreign Associate, US National Academy of Sciences, 1989; Balzan Prize (with F J Vine and D H Matthews), International Balzan Foundation, 1981; Japan Prize (with W J Morgan and X Le Pichon), Technological Foundation of Japan, 1990; Royal Medal of the Royal Society, 1991; Crafoord Prize, 2002; Companion of Honour, 2003. Address: Bullard Laboratories, Madingley Road, Cambridge CB3 0EZ, England.

MCKEOWN Donal, b. 12 April 1950, Belfast, Northern Ireland. Auxiliary Bishop of Down and Connor. Education: Mount St Michael's Primary School, Randalstown, 1954-61; St MacNissi's College, Garron Tower, 1961-68; BA (Hons), German and Italian, Queen's University, Belfast, 1973; Licence in Sacred Theology, Pontifical Gregorian University, Rome, 1978; Masters in Business Administration, University of Leicester, 2000. Appointments: Ordained as a Priest, Diocese of Down and Connor, 1977; Teacher, St Patrick's College, Belfast; Teacher, St MacNissi's College, Garron Tower; Teacher, President, 1995-2001, St Malachy's College, Belfast; Ordained Titular Bishop of Killossy and Auxiliary to the Bishop of Down and Connor, 2001. Publications: Numerous articles in professional journals; Appearances on radio and television. Memberships: NI Government's Post-Primary Review Working Group; Chair, NI Commission for Catholic Education. Address: 96 Downview Park West, Belfast, BT15 5HZ, Northern Ireland. E-mail: dmck@downandconnor.org

McLAIN John Anthony (Lain), b. 5 June 1933, Chingford, London, England. Composer; Songwriter; Retired Statistician. Education: BSc Mathematics, London University, 1955. Appointments: National Service (REME), 1955-57; Statistical Officer, Royal Society for the Prevention of Accidents, 1959-70; Manpower Planner, ICI Plastics, 1970-85; Television performances: Our Father, Who Art in Heaven, performed by the Gibside Singers, Tyne Tees TV. Recordings: Now You Have Gone, by Tony Jacobs with Jim Barry (piano); Why Don't They Write the Songs?, by Tony Jacobs with Jim Barry Sextet; Adlestrop (poem by Edward Thomas); I Came to Oxford (Gerald Gould); The Old Railway Line (Anne Allinson); The Demise of Harpenden Junction Box (Sue Woodward), by Gordon Pullin (tenor) with John Gough (piano); Winter's Spring, Clock-a-Clay, November, The Cuckoo (settings of John Clare poems), by Gordon Pullin with Andrew Plant (piano). Other compositions (published): Psalm (The Lord is my Shepherd); Mamble (John Drinkwater); Faintheart in a Railway Train; Yellow-hammer, Day-close in November, And So Do I (Thomas Hardy); Dream Awhile; The Poop Scoop Song. Listed in national and international biographical dictionaries. Memberships: Performing Right Society Ltd; British Academy of Songwriters, Composers and Authors; Light Music Society; Robert Farnon Society; Mensa. Address: 42 Osidge Lane, Southgate, London N14 5JG, England.

McLEAN Don, b. 2 October 1945, New Rochelle, New York, USA. Singer; Instrumentalist; Composer. m. Patrisha Shnier, 1987, 1 son, 1 daughter. Education: Villanova University; Iona College. Appointments: President, Benny Bird Corporation Inc; Member, Hudson River Slope Singers, 1969; Solo concert tours throughout USA, Canada, Australia, Europe, Far East; Numerous TV appearances; Composer of film scores for Fraternity Row; Flight of Dragons; Composer of over 200 songs including Prime Time; American Pie; Tapestry; Vincent; And I Love You So; Castles in the Air; Recordings include: Tapestry, 1970; American Pie, 1971; Don McLean, 1972;

Playin' Favourites, 1973; Homeless Brother, 1974; Solo, 1976; PrimeTime, 1977; Chain Lightning, 1979; Believers, 1982; For the Memories, Vol I, Vol II, 1986; Love Tracks, 1988; Headroom, 1991; Don McLean Christmas, 1992; Favourites and Rarities, 1993; The River of Love, 1995; Christmas Dreams, 1997; Sings Marty Robbins, 2001; Starry Starry Night (Live), 2001; You've Got to Share: Songs for Children, 2003; The Western Album, 2003; Christmas Time, 2004; Rearview Mirror: An American Musical Journey, 2005. Numerous compilation packages. Publications: Songs of Don McLean, 1972; The Songs of Don McLean, Vol II, 1974. Honours: Recipient of many gold discs in USA, Australia, UK and Ireland; Israel Cultural Award, 1981. Address: Benny Bird Co, 1838 Black Rock Turnpike, Fairfield, Connecticut 06432, USA.

McLEAN Donald Millis, b. 26 July 1926, Melbourne, Australia. Professor Emeritus of Pathology. m. Joyce. Education: MBBS, 1950; MD, University of Melbourne, 1954; MRCPath, 1963; FRCPC, 1967; FRCPath, 1970. Appointments: Harrison Watson Research Fellow, Clare College, Cambridge, 1955-56; Virologist, The Hospital for Sick Children, Toronto, 1958-67; Professor, Medical Microbiology, University of British Columbia, 1967-91; Professor Emeritus, Pathology, 1991-. Publications: 6 books, 120 original scientific papers. Memberships include: British Medical Association; American Society of Virology. Address: 2720 Yukon Street, Vancouver, British Columbia V5Y 3R1, Canada.

McLELLAN David Thorburn, b. 10 February 1940, Hertford, England. Professor of Political Theory; Writer. m. Annie Brassart, 1 July 1967, 2 daughters. Education: MA, 1962, DPhil, 1968, St John's College, Oxford. Appointment: Professor of Political Theory, Goldsmiths College, University of London. Publications: The Young Hegelians and Karl Marx, 1969; Karl Marx: His Life and Thought, 1974; Engels, 1977; Marxism After Marx, 1980; Ideology, 1986; Marxism and Religion, 1987; Simone Weil: Utopian Pessimist, 1989; Unto Caesar: The Political Importance of Christianity, 1993; Political Christianity, 1997; Karl Marx: A Biography, 2006; Marxism after Marx, 2007. Contributions to: Professional journals. Address: 13 Ivy Lane, Canterbury, Kent, CT1 1TU, England. E-mail: david@mclellankent.com

MCLELLAND Richard J, b. 9 December 1953, Indianapolis, Indiana, USA. Club Executive. m. Ana Ledesma, 2 daughters. Education: AB, Psychology, 1978, MLS, Library Science, 1985, Indiana University. Appointments: Assorted Manager positions, Chicago Public Library, 1985-2009; Vice President, Private Clubs, International Club Network, Toronto. Honours: Listed in biographical dictionaries. Memberships: Georgian Club, Atlanta; Royal Canadian Military Institute, Toronto; Adventurers Club, Chicago; Universities & Colleges Club, Chicago; Public Schools Club, Adelaide, Australia; Eccentric Club, London, UK; City University Club, London, UK. Address: 310 South Union Street, Bloomington, Indiana 47408, USA. E-mail: richjmcl2003@yahoo.com

McLEOD James Graham, b. 18 January 1932, Sydney, Australia. Neurologist. m. Robyn Edith Rule, 13 January 1962, 2 sons, 2 daughters. Education: BSc, 1953, MB BS, 1959, DSc, 1997, University of Sydney; DPhil, Oxon, 1956; Institute of Neurology, London University, 1963-65; Harvard University, Department of Neurology, 1965-66; MD, University of Sydney, 2008. Appointments: Pro-Dean, Faculty of Medicine, University of Sydney, 1974-94; Chairman, Department of Neurology, Royal Prince Alfred Hospital, 1978-95; Bosch Professor of Medicine, 1972-97, Bushell Professor of Neurology, 1978-97, Professor Emeritus, 1997-, University of Sydney; Consultant Neurologist, Royal Prince Alfred Hospital, Sydney, 1997-. Publications: A Physiological Approach to Clinical Neurology (co-author), 1981; Introductory Neurology (co-author), 1995; Peripheral Neuropathy in Childhood (co-author), 1991, 1999; More than 200 principal scientific publications. Honours: Rhodes Scholarship, 1953; Nuffield Travelling Fellowship, 1964-65; Sir Arthur Sims Commonwealth Travelling Professorship, 1983; AO, 1986; Commonwealth Medical Senior Fellowship; Honorary Doctorate, University of Aix-Marseille; Centenary Medal, 2003. Memberships: Fellow, Royal Australian College of Physicians, 1971; Fellow, Royal College of Physicians, 1977; Fellow, Australian Academy of Science, 1981; Fellow, Australian Academy of Technological Sciences and Engineering, 1987; Australian Science and Technology Council, 1987-93. Address: 2 James Street, Woollahra, NSW 2025, Australia. E-mail: james.mcleod@sydney.edu.au

McMANUS Jonathan Richard, b. 15 September 1958, Heywood, England. Barrister. Education: First Class Honours in Law, Downing College, Cambridge, 1978-81; Called to the Bar, 1982; Appointments: Commenced practice at the bar, 1983; Government A panel of Counsel, 1992-1999; QC, 1999. Publication: Education and the Courts, 1998. Honour: Maxwell Law Prize, Cambridge, 1981. Memberships: Administrative Law, Bar Association; National Trust; English Heritage; Friend of the Royal Opera House. Address: 4 and 5, Gray's Inn Square, Gray's Inn. London WC1R 5AH, England.

McMICKLE Robert Hawley, b. 30 July 1924, Paterson, New Jersey, USA. Physicist. m. Gwendolyn Gill, 3 sons, 2 daughters. Education: BA, Physics, Oberlin College, 1947; MS, Physics, University of Illinois, 1948; PhD, Physics, Pennsylvania State University, 1952. Appointments: Research Physicist, BF Goodrich Company, Brecksville, Ohio, 1952-59; Professor, Physics, Robert College, Istanbul, Turkey, 1959-71, University of the Bosphorus, Istanbul, Turkey, 1971-79, Schreiner College, Kerrville, Texas, 1979-80, Luther College, Decorah, Iowa, 1980-81; Adjunct Professor, Physics, Memphis State University, Tennessee, 1981-83; Accreditation Co-ordinator, Northeast Utilities, Seabrook, New Hampshire, 1983-94, Retired, 1994. Publications include: Diffusion Controlled Stress Relaxation, 1955; The Compressions of Several High Molecular Weight Hydrocarbons, 1958; Introduction to Modern Physics, 1979. Honours include: Fellowship, American Petroleum Institute, 1950-52; Research grant, Optics, Innovative Systems Research Inc, Pennsauken, New Jersey, 1976; Distinguished Service Award, University of the Bosphorus, Istanbul, Turkey, 1989. Memberships: American Association of Physics Teachers; Physical Society of Turkey; Sigma Xi. Address: 3032 Fernor Street, Allentown, PA 18103, USA.

MCNAIR Clarissa, b. 26 January 1947, Jackson, Mississippi, USA. Private Detective; Writer. Education: BA, American History, Briarcliff College; New York School of Interior Design; Advanced Degree, Cordon Bleu di Roma. Appointments: Publisher and Founder, Fedora Press; President, Green Star Investigations; Published Novelist; True Crime Writer; International cases; Undercover work with the FBI, the Organized Crime Intelligence Division of the New York Police Department and the Joint Terrorist Task Force; Collaborated with Charles Hill on chapter called The Art of Crime (The Art Business) used for the Master's degree programme at Sotheby's (London) Institute of Art. Publications: Garden of Tigers; A Flash of Diamonds; Dancing with Thieves; Detectives Don't Wear Seatbelts; Never Flirt with a Femme Fatale. Memberships: Overseas

Press Club; Mystery Writers of America; Pen & Pencil Club, Philadelphia; PA Association of Licensed Investigators; PEN America; World Investigators Network. E-mail: clarissamcnair@gmail.com Website: www.mcnairwrites.com, www.greenstarinvestigations.com and www.fedorapress.com

McNEAL Jane Erskine, b. 29 October 1958, Somers Point, New Jersey, USA. Musician; Music Teacher. Education: Music Studies, Wheaton College, Illinois; BA, Psychology, Stockton State College, Pomona, New Jersey; Crescendo Music Training, Academy of Community Music, Philadelphia area, Pennsylvania; Kindermusik Certification, Westminster Choir College, Princeton, New Jersey. Appointments: Piano and Vocal Instructor, 1975-; Recitalist and Professional Accompanist, 1980-; Church and Synagogue Organist and Music Director, Organist, 1982-; Advocate for the mentally ill. Honours: Music Scholarship, Wheaton College; National Merit Corporate Scholarship; Psi Chi Honor Society; Graduated College cum laude; Marquis Who's Who; ABI; Biltmore Who's Who; Da Vinci Diamond, 2009; International Profiles of Accomplished Leaders, ABI; 500 Great Leaders, ABI; IBC; Life Member, Order of Merit, Republican National Committee, 2010; Republican National Committee Order of Merit, 2010 & 2011. Memberships: Life Member, Republican National Committee; American Federation of Musicians; American Guild of Organists; Fellow, IBA; National Association of Professional Women. Address: 2112 Newcombtown Road, Millville, NJ 08332, USA.

MCPARTLIN Anthony David, b.18 November 1975, Newcastle, England. m. Lisa Armstrong, 2006. TV Presenter. Career: Presenter: SMTV Live; Friends like These; Pop Idol; I'm a Celebrity...Get Me Out of Here!; Ant & Dec's Saturday Night Takeaway; Britain's Got Talent; PokerFace; Push the Button; Red or Black?; Actor: Byker Grove; A Tribute to The Likely Lads, 2002; Alien Autopsy, 2006; Singer (as PJ and Duncan): Let's Get Ready to Rumble; Stepping Stone; Shout; and others. Honours: 16 National Television Awards; 6 British Comedy Award; BAFTA; many others.

MCPHILLIPS Julian Lenwood Jr, b. 13 November 1946, Birmingham, Alabama, USA. Attorney. M. J Leslie, 1 son, 2 daughters. Education: AB, Princeton University, 1968; JD, Columbia University Law School, 1971. Appointments: Admitted New York Bar, 1972, Alabama Bar, 1975, Supreme Court of Alabama, 1975, Supreme Court of United States, 1976, and many federal court bars; Associate Attorney, Davis, Polk & Wardwell, New York, 1971-73; Associate Counsel, American Express Company, 1973-75; Assistant Attorney General, State of Alabama, 1975-77; Senior Partner, President & Founding Attorney, McPhillips Shinbaum, LLP, and predecessor firms, 1977-2009. Publications: From Vacillation to Resolve: The Role of French Communist Party in the Resistance Movement Against the Nazis 1939-45, 1968; The People's Lawyer, the Colorful Life and Time of Julian L McPhillips Jr, 2nd edition, 2005; History of Christ the Redeemer Episcopal Church, 2005. Honours: Communication & Leadership Award, Toastmaster's International, 1985; Leadership Award, 2000, Legacy of the Dreamer Award, 2001, Martin Luther King Jr Social Consciousness Award, 2003, and Humanitarian Award, 2005, Southern Christian Leadership Conference; Humanitarian Award, Alabama State Association of Elks, 2008; Alabama Citizens for Life Individual Community Leader Award, 2008. Address: 831 Felder Ave, Montgomery, AB 36106, USA.

MCQUILLAN Robert, b. 13 February 1942, Belfast, Northern Ireland. Counsellor; Minister; Wordsmith; Exhortationist. m. Maureen, 1 son, 1 daughter. Education: Dip Th, Crusade Bible College, Adelaide, Australia, 1978; Cert Th, 1978, Dip Th, 1982, Vision College, Sydney, Australia; DLitt, MM, BBTh, Jubilee International, Brisbane, Australia, 1989; LHD, 1999, PhD, 2005, ThD, 2009, Scholae Theologicae Regentiae, LA, California, USA. Appointments: Service & Warehouse Manager, Singer Australia, Melbourne, 1974; Marketing Manager, Charlicks International, Adelaide, 1976-80; Senior Minister, Christian Life Centre, Adelaide, 1978-85; State Secretary, Christian Revival Crusade, Adelaide, 1983-84; National Publications Director, AOG in Australia, 1986-89, 1991-98; State Secretary, AOG South Australia, 1988-89; Founder/Director, Life Focus Inc, 1998-; Senior Minister, Life Focus Centre, 1999-2008. Publications: Editorials, features, general reporting, news and conference reporting, articles, biographies, 'ghost writing', specials and numerous articles in professional journals. Honours: Dip Creative Writing, CCE, Penrith, NSW, Australia; Guest speaker at conferences, AGMs, men's sessions, churches, business people's 'breakthrough' sessions and leadership sessions, locally and internationally. Memberships: Live Focus Inc; Australia Counselling Association. Address: PO Box 405, Leopold, VIC 3224, Australia. E-mail: lifefocus1@bigpond.com Website: http://lifefocus.blogspot.com

MCRAE Steven James, b. 19 December 1985, Sydney, Australia. Dancer. Education: St Paul's Grammar School, Sydney; Royal Ballet School, London, England. Appointments: Principal Dancer, Royal Ballet, London; Guest performer with companies around the world including: Japan, Hong Kong, Europe, Australia, USA, Cuba; Roles include: Romeo, Oberon (The Dream), Prince (Nutcracker, Cinderella, Sleeping Beauty, Swan Lake), Basilio (Don Quixote), Colas (La Fille mal Gardee), Bronze Idol (La Bayadere), Bluebird, Blueboy, Bratfish, Fire (Homage to the Queen), Chroma, DGV, Polyphonia, Sinfonietta, Pas de Trois (Swan Lake), Symphonic Variations, Napoli, La Sylphide, Les Lutins, Concerto (MacMillan), Theme and Variations, Stars and Stripes, Symphony in C. Honours: RAD Solo Seal Award; Adeline Genee Gold Medal; 1st Prize, Prix de Lausanne; Emerging Male Artist, Critics Circle; International Rising Star Award; Olivier Award Nominee; Evening Standards 1000 Most Influential Londoners, 2009 & 2010. E-mail: tappuppy@hotmail.com

MCTEER Janet, b. 8 May 1961, Newcastle upon Tyne, England. Actress. Education: Royal Academy of Dramatic Art. Career: TV, theatre and film actress; TV: The Black Velvet Gown, 1991; The Amazing Mrs Pritchard; Hunter; Agatha Christie's Marple; Damages; Parade's End, 2012; Theatre: A Doll's House, 1996; Mary Stuart; God of Carnage, 2008, 2010; Film: Half Moon Street, 1986; Wuthering Heights, 1992; Carrington, 1995; Tumbleweeds, 1999; Songcatcher; Waking the Dead; The King is Alive; The Intended; Tideland; Into the Storm, 2009; Albert Nobbs, 2011; The Woman in Black, 2012 . Honours: Laurence Oliver Theatre Award, 1996; Critics' Circle Theatre Award, 1996; Tony Award, 1997; Theatre World Award, 1997; 2 Drama Desk Awards; Golden Globe, 1999; OBE, 2008.

McVIE J Gordon, b. 13 January 1945, Glasgow, Scotland. Director Cancer Intelligence; Professor. Education: BSc (Hons), Pathology, 1967, MB, ChB, 1969, University of Edinburgh, Scotland; ECFMG, USA, 1971; Accreditation in Internal Medicine and Medical oncology, Joint Committee on Higher Medical Training, 1977; MD, Edinburgh, 1978;

FRCPE, Edinburgh, 1981; FRCPS, Glasgow, 1987; DSc (Hon), University of Abertay, Dundee, Scotland, 1996; DSc (Hon), University of Nottingham, England, 1997; FRCP, 1997; FMedSci, 1998; DSc (Hon), University of Portsmouth, England; FRCSE, Edinburgh, 2001. Appointments: House Officer, Royal Infirmary, Edinburgh and Royal Hospital for Sick Children, Edinburgh, 1969-1970; Medical Research Council Research Fellow, Department of Pathology and Therapeutics, Edinburgh University; 1970-1971; Temporary Lecturer in Therapeutics, 1971-73, Lecturer in Therapeutics, 1973-76, Edinburgh University; Honorary Registrar, 1971-73, Honorary Senior Registrar, 1973-76, Lothian Health Board, Scotland; Senior Lecturer, The Cancer Research Campaign Department of Clinical Oncology, University of Glasgow, 1976-1980; Honorary Consultant in Medical Oncology, Greater Glasgow Health Board, 1976-1980; Head, Clinical Research Unit, Consultant Physician, and Chairman, Division of Experimental Therapy, The National Cancer Institute, Amsterdam, The Netherlands, 1980-84; Clinical Research Director, The National Cancer Institute of the Netherlands, 1984-1989; Scientific Director, 1989-1996, Director General, 1996-2002, The Cancer Research Campaign; Director General, Cancer Research UK, 2002-; Director, Cancer Intelligence, 2003-. Publications: Extensive within this field; Membership of numerous medical editorial boards. Honours: Gunning Victoria Jubilee Prize in Pathology, 1967; Honeyman Gillespie Lecturer in Oncology 1977; Visiting Fellow, Department of Medical Oncology, University of Paris, 1978; Visiting Fellow, Netherlands Cancer Institute, Amsterdam; Consultant, Carcinogenesis of Cytostatic Drugs, International Agency, Research in Cancer, WHO, Lyon, 1980; Visiting Professor, University of Sydney, NSW, Australia; Visiting Professor, British Postgraduate Medical Federation, London University; 1990-96; Chairman, UICC Fellowships Program, 1990-98; President, European Organisation for Research and Treatment of Cancer, 1994-97; First European Editor of Journal of the National Cancer Institute, 1994-; Visiting Professor, University of Glasgow, 1996-; Semmelweis Medal for Excellence in Science. Memberships: European Organisation for Research on Treatment of Cancer (EORTC), 1979-; Numerous advisory committees and examination boards including: Member, Steering Committee, Alliance of World Cancer Research Organisations, 1999; Cancer Research Funders Forum, 1999-2001; Member, AACR Membership Committee, 2000-01; Member, AACR Clinical Cancer Research Committee, 2001-. Address: Cancer Intelligence, 4 Stanley Rd, Cotham, Bristol BS6 6NW, England. E-mail: gordonmcvie@doctors.org.uk

MEACHER Michael Hugh (Rt Hon), b. 4 November 1939, Hemel Hempstead, Hertfordshire, England. Member of Parliament. m. Lucianne Sawyer, 2 sons, 2 daughters. Education: Greats, Class 1, New College, Oxford; Diploma in Social Administration, London School of Economics. Appointments: Lecturer, Social Administration, York and London School of Economics, 1966-70; Member of Parliament for Oldham West, 1970-; Minister for Industry, 1974-75; Minister for the Department of Health and Social Security, 1975-76; Minister for Trade, 1976-79; Member of the Shadow Cabinet, 1983-97; Minister for the Environment, 1997-2003. Publications: Taken for a Ride (about the care of the elderly), 1972; Socialism with a Human Face, 1982; Diffusing Power, 1992. Memberships: Labour Party; Fabian Society; Child Poverty Action Group. Address: House of Commons, Westminster, London, SW1A 0AA, England.

MEDEIROS José Augusto da Silva, b. 22 September 1947, Maia, São Miguel Azores, Portugal. Professor; Medical Doctor. m. Maria Paula Gonçalves da Silva Marques, 1 daughter. Education: Graduate, Medicine, 1976, PhD, Medicine and Physiology, 1992, Assistant of Physiology, 1985-92, Auxiliary Professor of Physiology, 1992-2000, Associate Professor, 2000-06, Associate Professor with Aggregation to Full Professor, 2006-11, Faculty of Medicine, Coimbra University. Appointments: Intern, Gastroenterology, Queen's University Hospitals, Kingston, Ontario, Canada, 1981-84; Director, Medical University Clinic, Coimbra University, 1998-2011; Gastroenterologist, Hospital Cova da Beira-Covilhã, 2007-10; Professor, Gastroenterology, Faculty of Health Sciences, Covilhã, 2007-10. Publications: Over 50 articles in national and international medical journals. Honours: 3 times winner, Award of Best Teacher of the Year, Faculty of Medicine, Coimbra University; Golden Medal, City Hall of Ponta Delgada, São Miguel, Azores. Memberships: Portuguese Society of Gastroenterology; Portuguese Society of Coloproctology; European Society of Neurogastroenterology and Motility. Address: Quinta do Vale de Figueiras, Estrada do Vale de Figueiras, 3020-403, Coimbra, Portugal. E-mail: jmedeiros@fmed.uc.pt

MEDEL Jose de Jesus, b. 6 April 1970, Mexico. m. Gabriela Benitez, 2 sons, 1 daughter. Education: Aeronautics Engineer, 1991; MSc, Automatic Control, 1995; Dr Sc, Automatic Control, 1998. Appointments: Professor, Simon Bolivar University, 1998-2000; Full-time Professor, Computer Research Centre, 1999-; Professor, Americas University, 2002; Professor, Monterrey Technology, 2004; Invited Professor, Advanced Technology and Applied Sciences Centre, 2004-; Professor, Pan-American University, 2006. Publications: More than 35 original indexed papers; 20 considered in International Science Index; 70 international proceedings; 4 international books; 4 national books; 2 patents. Honours: Great American Educator, 2004; PhD, Management Education, 2006; Master on Management Education, 2006; Best Doctoral Direction, 2006. Memberships: Mexican Academic of Sciences; Titular Professor, National Polytechnic Institute; Listed in international biographical dictionaries. Address: Gral FCO, Molinos del Campo #34, Col San Miguel Chapultepec, Zip 11850, Mexico. E-mail: jjmedelj@yahoo.com.mx

MEDVEDEV Dmitry Anatolyevich, b. 14 September 1965, Leningrad, Russia SFSR, Soviet Union. President of Russia. m. Svetlana Linnik, 1 son. Education: Graduate, Law Department, 1987, PhD, Private Law, 1990, Leningrad State University. Appointments: Docent, Saint Petersburg State University (previously Leningrad State University), 1991-99; Legal Expert, International Relations Committee, St Petersburg Mayor's Office, 1991-96; Legal Affairs Director, Ilim Pulp Enterprise, St Petersburg, 1993; Elected Member, Board of Directors, Bratskiy LPK Paper Mill, 1998-99; Deputy Head, Presidential Staff, Russian Government, 1999-; Chair, 2000-01, 2002, Deputy Chair, 2001-02, Gazprom's Board of Directors; Presidential Chief of Staff, 2003; First Deputy Prime Minister, Russian Government, 2005-; President of Russia, 2008-. Publications: Numerous articles in professional journals. Honours: Person of the Year, Expert magazine, 2005. Address: The Kremlin, Moscow, Russia.

MEDVEDKIN Gennady, b. 30 October 1954, St Petersburg, Russia. Physicist; Researcher. m. Liza Shvets, 2 sons, 1 daughter. Education: MS, Electrical Engineering University, St Petersburg, 1977; PhD, 1981, DSc, 1993, Ioffe Physical Technical Institute, St Petersburg; Vocational Certificate in X-Ray Diffraction, Stanford University, 2006. Appointments:

Laboratory Assistant, 1972-77, Probationer-Researcher, 1977-79, Junior Researcher, 1979-86, Researcher, 1986-99, Senior Scientist, 1999-2005, Ioffe Physical Techn Institute, St Petersburg; Director General, Joint-St Co Standard, St Petersburg, 1997-98; Vice Director, Profit Ltd, St Petersburg, 1999-2000; Visiting Professor, Tokyo University of Agriculture and Technology, 1999-2001; Director General, FERROBIT Ltd, St Petersburg, 2004-2006; Visiting Scholar, Stanford University, 2005-2006; Program Manager & Research Scientist, Physical Optics Corporation, 2007-10; Principal Scientist, Advanced Science & Novel Technology Co, 2010-. Publications: Monograph, Semiconductor Crystals for Optical Sensors of Linearly Polarized Radiation, 1992; Patentee in field; Over 90 publications in professional refereed journals; More than 70 presentations at international conferences including 5 invited talks. Honours: Honour Plaque for Outstanding Inventors of Russian Federation, 1984; Outstanding Poster Award, Boston, 2000; Best Publication Award, Japan, 2001; American Medal of Honor, ABI, USA, 2007; Listed in Who's Who publications and biographical dictionaries. Memberships: OSA; SPIE. Address: 21305 Payne Ave, Torrance CA 90502, USA. E-mail: g.a.medvedkin@hotmail.com

MEDVIDOVIĆ-KOSANOVIĆ Martina, b. 10 January 1975, Vinkovci, Croatia. Doctor of Chemistry. m. Aleksej Kosanović, 1 daughter. Education: Bachelor, Chemical Engineering, 1998, MSc, 2003, 2011, Field Chemistry, Faculty of Science, Zagreb. Appointments: Assistant, Faculty of Food Technology, 1999-2008; Expert Assistant, 2008-11, Senior Assistant, 2011-, Department of Chemistry, Josip Juraj Strossmayer University of Osijek. Publications: 12 articles in professional journals including most recently: Electrochemical and Antioxidant Properties of (+)-Catechin, Quercetin and Rutin, 2010; Electrochemical and Antioxidant Properties of Rutin, 2010; Electroanalytical Characterization of a Copper (II)-Rutin Complex, 2011. Memberships: Croatian Chemical Society; International Society of Electrochemistry. Address: Department of Chemistry, Josip Juraj Strossmayer University of Osijek, Kuhačeva 20, Osijek, HR 31 000, Croatia. E-mail: mmkosano@kemija.unios.hr

MEFED Anatoly Egorovich, b. 7 December 1938, Gorodische, Bryansk, Russia. Physicist; Researcher of NMR in solids and of NQR in explosives; Consultant. m. Lyudmila Ivanovna Putilova, 1 daughter. Education: Graduate, Moscow University, 1962; PhD, Russian Academy of Sciences, 1972. Appointments: Professor, Physics and Maths, Institute Radioengineering and Electronics Russian Academy of Sciences, Fryazino, 1989; Professor, Kazan State University, 1989. Publications: Author and co-author: Discovery, A New Physical Law in Spin Thermodynamics in Solids, 1968; Contribution to more than 95 research papers to professional journals. Honours: Recipient USSR diploma for discovery of a new physics law in spin thermodynamics in solids, 1987; USSR inventor medal Russian Academy of Sciences; Listed in various international biographical publications. Membership: New York Academy of Sciences, Russian Academy of Natural Sciences. Address: Russian Academy of Sciences Institute of Radioengineering & Electronics, Vvedenskogo Sq, 141190 Fryazino, Moscow, Russia. E-mail: aem228@ire216.msk.su

MEGALI Giuseppe, b. 17 October 1981, Reggio Calabria, Italy. System Engineer. Education: Bachelor's degree, 2000, Master's degree, 2007, Electronic Engineering; Engineer of Information, 2007; Preliminary English Test, 2009; PhD, Computer, Biomedical and Telecommunication Engineering, 2011. Appointments: Associate, Academic Spin-Off Neuratek srl, 2007-; Researcher, Electromagnetic measure in the Provice of Reggio Calabria programme, 2009; Business Control Agent, ControlTEST, Reggio Calabria, 2009; Associate, Cooperativa TEC, Reggio Calabria, 2009-10; Scientific Collaborator for Research Works, University Mediterranea, Reggio Calabria, 2011; System Engineer, ANSALDO STS, a Finmeccanica Company, 2011-. Publications: 7 books, book chapters and book series; 14 international journals; 1 patent; 11 international conferences; 3 technical reports; 2 Italian journals; 7 Italian conferences; Scientific reviewer of professional journals. Honours: Best ENNS Poster Award, 2008; Anassilaos Youth Award, 2010; Listed in biographical dictionaries. Memberships: Italian Society of Neural Networks. Address: 41 Via Fontana Piria, 89018, Ferrito di Cannitello, Villa San Giovanni (RC), Italy. E-mail: giuseppe.megali@unirc.it

MEHROTRA Hunny, b. 4 September 1982, Kanpur, India. Research Scholar. Education: B Level (MCA), Computer Science & Engineering, DOEACC, New Delhi, 2005; M Technology (Research), 2010, PhD, in progress, Computer Science & Engineering, National Institute of Technology, Rourkela. Appointments: Project Associate, 2005, Senior Project Associate, 2005-08, Indian Institute of Technology, Kanpur; Teaching Assistant, National Institute of Technology, Rourkela, 2008-10. Publications: Numerous articles in professional journals. Honours: First Prize, SKOCH Summit, 2009; Scholarship Grant, Grace Hopper Celebration of Women in Computing, 2009; Innovative Student Project Award, 2010; Google India Women in Engineering Award, 2010. Address: Department of Computer Science & Engineering, National Institute of Technology Rourkela, Rourkela 769 008, India. E-mail: hunny04@gmail.com

MEHTA Jigar, b. 31 May 1983, Baroda, India. Research Scientist. Education: MSc, Organic Chemistry, Bhavnagar University, 2005; MBA, Supply Chain Management, NIM, 2010. Appointments: Executive, Quality Control Department, Torrent Pharma Ltd, 2005-08; Research Scientist 1, Analytical Research Laboratory, Cadila Pharma Ltd, 2008-. Publications: 5 research papers in professional journals. Honours: Reviewer in reputed journals such as Eurasian Journal of Analytical Chemistry and Journal of AOAC International. Address: Analytical Research Laboratory, Cadila Pharma Ltd, 1389 Trasad road, Dholka 387810, Gujarat, India. E-mail: jigarmehta@gmail.com

MEHULIC Ketij, b. 23 July 1963, Split, Croatia. Professor. m. Muharem, 1 son, 1 daughter. Education: Graduate, 1988, Master, 1992, School of Dental Medicine, University of Zagreb; PhD, 1996; Specialist, Prosthodontics, Dental University Clinic, 1997. Appointments: Assistant, 1993, Assistant Professor, 1999, Professor, 2004, Department of Prosthodontics, School of Dental Medicine, University of Zagreb; Main investigator in scientific projects supported by Ministry of Science, 2007-; Main investigator in Bilateral Project, 2010-. Publications: Numerous articles in professional journals. Honours: Valedictorian in High School; Award for Student Scientific Research. Memberships: Croatian Medical Association; Croatian Society for Prosthodontics; European Prosthodontic Association; Croatian Dental Chamber. Address: Department of Prosthodontics, School of Dental Medicine, University of Zagreb, Guduliceva 5, 10 000 Zagreb, Croatia. E-mail: mehulic@sfzg.hr

MEIĆ Zlatko, b. 4 September 1938, Šid, Serbia. Professor. m. Paulina, 2 daughters. Education: BSc, Chemical Engineering, 1962, MSc, Chemistry, 1967, PhD, Chemistry, 1969,

DICTIONARY OF INTERNATIONAL BIOGRAPHY 36th EDITION

University of Zagreb, Croatia. Appointments: Head, 1977-99, NMR Service, Head, Laboratory of Molecular Spectroscopy, 1991-2000, Rudjer Boskovic Institute; Head, Laboratory of Analytical Chemistry, Department of Chemistry, University of Zagreb, 2000-08; Visiting Professor at University of Ulm,Technical, University of Munich, University of Mainz, Technical University of Vienna and other. Publications: Over 100 publications including: 82 scientific papers; 3 book chapters; Two book translations for students. Honours: Chairman XXth Congress on Molecular Spectroscopy, Zagreb, 1991; President, Croatian Chemical Society, 1996-98; Award of the City of Zagreb, 2001; State Award for Scientific Achievements, 2006; many others. Memberships: Croatian Chemical Society; Croatian Society of Chemical Engineers; American Chemical Society. Address: Dept of Chemistry, Faculty of Science, 10000 Zagreb, Croatia. E-mail: zmeic@chem.pmf.hr

MEIGHAN Roland, b. 29 May 1937, Sutton Coldfield, England. Writer; Publisher; Consultant. m. (1) Shirley, deceased, (2) Janet, 1 son, 2 stepsons. Education: DSocSc; PhD; BSc; LCP. Appointments: Various school teacher positions; Lecturer, Senior Lecturer in Education, University of Birmingham; Special Professor of Education, University of Nottingham; Independent Writer and Consultant; Director and owner, Educational Heretics Press, Nottingham; Director and Trustee, Centre for Personalised Education Trust. Publications: A Sociology of Educating, 1981, 2nd edition, 1986, 3rd edition, 1999, 4th edition, 2003, 5th edition, 2006; Flexischooling, 1988; Theory and Practice of Regressive Education, 1993; The Freethinkers' Guide to the Educational Universe, 1994; John Holt: Personalised Education and the Reconstruction of Schooling, 1995; The Next Learning System, 1997; The Next Learning System: Pieces of the Jigsaw, 2000; Natural Learning and the Natural Curriculum, 2001; Learning Unlimited, 2001; John Holt: personalised learning instead of 'uninvited teaching', 2002; Comparing Learning Systems, 2005. Contributions to: Natural Parent Magazine; Observer; Yorkshire Post; Times Educational Supplement. Membership: Fellow of the Royal Society of Arts. Address: 113 Arundel Drive, Bramcote Hills, Nottingham NG9 3FQ, England. Website: www.rolandmeighan.co.uk

MELEZINEK Adolf, b. 3 October 1932, Vienna, Austria. Emeritus University Professor. m. Vera Melezinek, 1 son, 1 daughter. Education: Dipl Ing, Electronics, 1957; Dr phil, Pedagogy, 1969. Appointments: Chief Engineer; Assistant Professor; University Professor, Chair of Engineering Pedagogy. Publications: More than 200 publications including 20 specialist books such as: Ingenieurpädagogik, in German, Czech, Hungarian, Slovenian, Ukrainian, Polish and Russian editions. Honours: Gold Ring, International Society for Engineering Education; Golden Felber Medal, Czech Technical University, Prague; Honorary Senator, Technical University, Budapest; Grand Gold Medal, Carinthia; Austrian Honorary Cross 1st Class for Science and Art; Grand Decoration of Honour in Silver for Services to the Republic of Austria, 2007, 2008; Dr honoris causa, 1997, 2000, 2001, 2005, 2007, 2008; Listed in several Who's Who and biographical publications. Membership: Founder and Honorary Life President, International Society for Engineering Education (IGIP). Address: Akazienhofstrasse 79, A-9020 Klagenfurt, Austria. E-mail: adolf.melezinek@uni-klu.ac.at

MELLANO Paolo, b. 24 August 1963, Cuneo, Italy. Architect; Professor. m. Raffaella Brondino, 1 son, 1 daughter. Education: Master, Architecture, Politecnico di Torino, 1988; Architectural Restoration, Palazzina di Stupinigi Foundation, 1991. Appointments: Researcher, Architectural Composition, Politecnico di Torino, 1994; Associate Professor, 2003; Confirmed Associate Professor, 2006; Assistant President of course of studies in Architecture, 2007. Publications: Architecture nel Paesaggio, 2006. Honours: International Prize of Architecture, A Palladio, 1993; Finalist and Honourable Mention, Prize of Architecture L Cosenza, 1992, 1994, 1996, 1998, 2000, 2002; Selection and Honourable Mention of Jury, 1st Prize of Accademia di San Luca, Rome, 2003; 1st Prize, Regione Piemonte, 2004. Memberships: Siat-Societa degu Ingegneri e degli Architetti di Torino. Address: Via Senator Toselli, 1, 12100 Cuneo, Italy. E-mail: mellano@bruna-mellano.it Website: www.burna-mellano.it

MELLING John Kennedy, b. 11 January 1927, Westcliff-on-Sea, Essex, England. Drama Critic; Editor; Writer; Lecturer; Broadcaster; Chartered Accountant. Appointments: Drama Critic, The Stage, 1957-90; Drama Critic, Fur Weekly News, 1968-73; Editor, The Liveryman Magazine, 1970-75, Chivers Black Dagger Series of Crime Classics, 1986-91; Radio Crime Book Critic, BBC London, 1984-85, BBC Essex, 1987; Conducting Master Classes for Arts Council, 2004-. Publications: Discovering Lost Theatres, 1969; Southend Playhouses from 1793, 1969; Discovering London's Guilds and Liveries, 6 editions, 1973-03; Discovering Theatre Ephemera, 1974; The Poulters of London Booklet, 1977; She Shall Have Murder, 1987; Murder in the Library, 1987; Crime Writers' Handbook of Practical Information (editor), 1989; Gwendoline Butler: Inventor of the Women's Police Procedural, 1993; Alchemy of Murder, 1993; Murder Done to Death, 1996; Scaling the High C's (with John L Brecknock), 1996; A Little Manual of Etiquette for Gentlemen, 2004; The Constructors: Genesis and Growth, 2004; Plays include: George....From Caroline, 1971; Diarists' Pleasures, 1982; Murder at St Dunstan's, 1983; The Toast Is ... (series); The Gilbertian Consequences of Mr Sullivan; Regular columnist, Crime Time magazine, 1996-2002. Honours: Knight Grand Cross; Order of St Michael; Master of the Worshipful Company of Poulters, 1980-81; Police Medal of Honour, USA, 1984; Knight, Order of St Basil, 1984; Crime Writers Association Award for Outstanding Services, 1989; Listed in national and international biographical dictionaries. Memberships: British Academy of Film and Television Arts; Institute of Taxation, fellow; Faculty of Building, Royal Society of Arts, fellow; Crime Writers' Association, committee member, 1985-88; Governor of the Corporation of the Sons of the Clergy, 1981-; Member, Drugs Task Force, National Association of Chiefs of Police, USA; Honorary International Life Vice-President, American Federation of Police; Founder-President, First Honorary Life Member, Westcliff Film and Video Club; Member, Cookery and Food Association; Member, City Livery Club; Liveryman, Worshipful Companies of Bakers, Farriers, and Constructors; Marylebone Rifle and Pistol Club; Edinburgh Press Club; Friend, Clowns International. Addresses: 44 A Tranquil Vale, Blackheath, London SE3 0BD, England; 85 Chalkwell Avenue, Westcliff-on-Sea, Essex, SS0 8NL, England.

MELLOR D(avid) H(ugh), b. 10 July 1938, England. Professor of Philosophy; Writer. Education: BA, Natural Sciences and Chemical Engineering, 1960, PhD, 1968, ScD, 1990, M in English, 1992, Pembroke College, Cambridge; MSc, Chemical Engineering, University of Minnesota, 1962. Appointments: Research Student in Philosophy, Pembroke College, 1963-68, Fellow, Pembroke College, 1965-70, University Assistant Lecturer in Philosophy, 1965-70, University Lecturer in Philosophy, 1970-83, Fellow, 1971-, and Vice-Master, 1983-87, Darwin College, University Reader in Metaphysics, 1983-85, Professor of Philosophy, 1986-99,

Professor Emeritus, 1999-, Pro-Vice-Chancellor, 2000-01, Cambridge University; Visiting Fellow in Philosophy, Australian National University, Canberra, 1975; Honorary Professor of Philosophy, University of Keele, 1989-92. Publications: The Matter of Chance, 1971; Real Time, 1981; Cambridge Studies in Philosophy, (editor), 1978-82; Matters of Metaphysics, 1991; The Facts of Causation, 1995; Real Time II, 1998; numerous articles on philosophy of science, metaphysics and philosophy of mind. Contributions to: Scholarly journals. Memberships: Aristotelian Society, president, 1992-93; British Academy, fellow; British Society for the Philosophy of Science, president, 1985-87; British Humanist Association. Address: 25 Orchard Street, Cambridge CB1 1JS, England.

MELNIKOVA Tamara Mikhailovna, b. 15 November 1940, Ukraine. Teacher. m. Gennadiy Valentinovich Salkov, 1 son, 1 daughter. Education: Penzian State Pedagogical University, 1963. Appointments: Kindergarten Teacher, Teacher of Russian, 1962-68; Head Scientific Worker, 1969, Head Guardian, 1969-75, Tarkhany Museum Reserve; Deputy Director, Scientific Work, 1975-77, Director, 1977-, Federal State Establishment, State Lermontov Tarhany Museum Reserve. Publications: Numerous articles in professional journals; 1 book; 1 photoalbum; 1 guidebook. Honours: Order of the Nations Friendship, 1981; Just Culture Worker, Russian Federation, 1986; M U Lermontov Laureate, 2000; Honoured Sign of Social Acknowledgement, 2001; Russian Orthodox Church Order, 2007; Government of the Russian Federation Award, 2008; The Golden Order Chest Sign; Best People of Russia medal; Honour Order, Russian Literature, 2008. Memberships: Russian Committee, International Museum House. Address: 7 Ovsianka street, Lermontovo, Belinsky raion, Penza oblast, 442280, Russia. E-mail: muslerm@sura.ru

MELTON Gary Bentley, b. 4 June 1952, Salisbury, North Carolina, USA. Professor. m. Robin J Kimbrough-Melton, 2 daughters. Education: BA (High Distinction), Psychology, University of Virginia, 1973; MA, 1975, PhD, 1978, Boston University Clinical Community Psychology Program. Appointments include: Director of Research, Institute of Law, Psychiatry and Public Policy, and Assistant Professor of the General Faculty and Psychology, University of Virginia, 1978-81; Assistant Professor, Psychology, 1981-82, Associate Professor, Law, 1983-85, Associate Professor, Psychology, 1982-85, Director, Law/Psychology Program, Department of Psychology and College of Law, 1982-94, Professor of Psychology and Law, 1985-87, Director, Center on Children, Families and the Law, 1987-94, Carl Adolph Happold Professor of Psychology and Law, 1987-94, University of Nebraska-Lincoln; Consultant, Institute for Families in Society, 1993-94, Affiliated Faculty, Women's Studies Program, 1998-99, Adjunct Professor of Paediatrics, 1995-99, Adjunct Professor of Law and Psychology, 1994-99, Professor of Neuropsychiatry and Behavioural Science, 1994-99, Director, Institute for Families in Society, 1994-99, University of South Carolina; Professor of Psychology and Director, Institute on Family and Neighbourhood Life, Clemson University, 1999-; Extraordinary Professor, Centre for Psychology & Law, University of the Free State, 2010-; Consultant and Psychologist in public and private sectors. Publications: Numerous articles in professional scientific journals; Co-editor, American Journal of Orthopsychiatry. Honours include: Karl Heiser Award, APA, 1998; Award for Distinguished Contributions to Public Service, American Psychological Association, 1999; Lynn Stuart Weiss Lectureship, American Psychological Foundation, 2000; Media Award, South Carolina Professional Society on Abuse of Children, 2003; Award for Distinguished Contributions to the International Advancement of Psychology, APA, 2005; Award for Career Achievement in Research, American Professional Society on Abuse of Children, 2005; Distinguished Presidential Award, American Orthopsychiatric Association, 2006; Blanche L Ittleson Award, American Orthopsychiatric Association, 2009; Listed in national and international biographical dictionaries. Memberships: American Psychological Association; American Orthopsychiatric Association; South Carolina Psychological Association; International Society for Prevention of Child Abuse and Neglect; American Professional Society on Abuse of Children; International Society for Child Indicators. Address: Institute on Family and Neighborhood Life, Clemson University, 225 South Pleasantbury Drive, Ste B11, Greenville, SC 29607, USA. E-mail: gmelton@clemson.edu Website: www.clemson.edu/ifnl

MEMOS Constantine Demetrius, b. 26 November 1946, Patras, Greece. Civil Engineer. m. Maria Antonopoulou, 2 sons. Education: MEng, Civil Engineering, National Technical University of Athens, Greece, 1969; Diploma, Mathematics, University of Patras, Greece, 1972; DIC, PhD, University of London, Imperial College, 1977. Appointments: Educator, School of Civil Engineering, National Technical University of Athens, 1978-; Professor, Maritime Hydraulics and Port Engineering, 2004-; Engineer, Consultant, Port Planning and Design, 1978-. Publications: Over 150 articles in journals and conference proceedings, including Journal of Fluid Mechanics, Coastal Engineering, ASCE Journal of Ports and Waterways, Coastal Engineering Conference, Journal of Hydraulic Research. Honours: Unwin Prize, Imperial College, 1977; Embeirikeio Prize of Technological Science, with Award, Greece, 1988; David Hislop Award, Institution of Civil Engineers, London, 2004; President, ASCE Hellenic Group; Engineers of the Earth. Memberships: Technical Chamber of Greece; Fellow, ASCE; Member, PIANC; Chair, Committee on Coastal and Maritime Hydraulics, IAHR; New York Academy of Sciences; Member, Higher Education Quality Assurance Agency, Greece. Address: National Technical University of Athens, 5 Heroon Polytechneiou, 15780 Zografos, Greece. E-mail: memos@hydro.ntua.gr

MENCINGER Jože, b. 5 March 1941, Slovenia. Lawyer; Economist; Politician. Education: Law, University of Ljubljana, 1964; MA, University of Belgrade, 1966; PhD, University of Pennsylvania, USA, 1975. Appointments: Minister of Economy, 1990; Vice President, Government for Economic Co-ordination, 1990-91; Member, Democratic Party, 1992-96; Rector, 2001-05, Chair of Legal and Economic Science, University of Ljubljana. Publications: Numerous articles in professional journals. Membership: Slovenian National Council. Address: University of Ljubljana, Poljanski nasip 2, 1000 Ljubljana, Slovenia.

MENDELSON Paul Anthony, b. 6 April 1951, Newcastle upon Tyne. Scriptwriter. m. Michal Mendelson, 2 daughters. Education: MA Law, Emmanuel College, Cambridge. Appointments: Group Head, Ogilvy & Mather, 1973-80; Deputy Creative Director, Wasey Campbell-Ewald, 1980-82; Creative Group Head Dorland Advertising, 1982-88; Creative Director, Capper Granger, 1988-90; Scriptwiter, 1990-; Creator and writer: Losing It, ITV; My Hero, BBC1; So Haunt Me, BBC1; May to December, BBC1; The Dover Series, Radio 4; Snap, Radio 4; A Meeting in Seville, Radio 4; Neighbours from Hell, Dreamworks Animation/Fox. Honours: TV and Best Radio Commercial and Best Radio Campaign for Don't Drink and Drive, 1980; Best Media Commercial Clio, 1982;

Best Radio Commercial (food) Clio, 1986 BAFTA Nomination for From May to December, 1990; Nomination, Best Writing (Losing It) Televisual Awards, 2007. Memberships: Writers Guild of Great Britain; Groucho Club. Address: c/o Alan Brodie Representation, Paddock Suite, The Courtyard, 55 Charterhouse Street, London EC1M 6HA, England.

MENDES Alexandre Schalch, b. 27 August 1973, Sao Paulo, Brazil. Mechanical Engineer. Divorced, 1 daughter. Education: Mechanical Engineering, FEI, 1997; MSc, Mechanical Engineering, UNICAMP, 2005. Appointments: Research Engineer, Structural Analysis in Internal Combustion Engines, MWM International Motores, 1998-. Publications: Experimental validation of a methodology for torsional vibration analysis in internal combustion engines, 2007; Analysis of torsional vibration in internal combustion engines: Modelling and experimental validation, 2008. Honours: Society of Automotive Engineers Congress, 2003. E-mail: alexandre.schalch@navistar.com.br

MENDES Sam, b. 1 August 1965, England. Theatre Director. m. Kate Winslet, 2001, divorced 2011, 1 son. Education: Magdalen College School; Oxford University; Peterhouse, Cambridge University. Appointments: Artistic Director, Minerva Studio Theatre, Chichester; Artistic Director, Donmar Warehouse, 1992-2002. Creative Works: Plays directed include: London Assurance, Chichester; The Cherry Orchard, London; Kean, Old Vic, London; The Plough and the Stars, Young Vic, London; Troilus and Cressida, RSC, The Alchemist, RSC, 1991; Richard III, RSC, 1992; The Tempest, RSC, 1993; National Theatre debut with The Sea, 1991; The Rise and Fall of Little Voice, National and Aldwych, 1992; The Birthday Party, 1994; Othello (also world tour); Assassins, Translations, Cabaret, Glengarry Glen Ross, The Glass Menagerie, Company, Habeas Corpus, The Front Page, The Blue Room, To the Green Fields Beyond, (all at Donmar Warehouse) 1992-2000; Uncle Vanya and Twelfth Night, Donmar Warehouse, 2002; Oliver!, London Palladium; Cabaret, The Blue Room, Broadway, New York; Gypsy, Broadway; The Vertical Hour, Broadway, 2006; The Winter's Tale, The Cherry Orchard, BAM, Old Vic, 2009; As You Like It, The Tempest, BAM, Old Vic, 2010; Richard III, Old Vic, 2011, BAM, 2012; Films: American Beauty, 1999; The Road to Perdition, 2002; Jarhead, 2005; Starter for Ten, 2006; The Kite Runner, 2007; Things We Lost in the Fire, 2007; Revolutionary Road, 2008; Away We Go, 2009; Richard II, Henry IV, Part I, Henry IV, Part II, 2012; Skyfall, 2012. Honours include: Commander of the British Empire, 2000; Critics' Circle Award, 1989, 1993, 1996; Olivier Award for Best Director, 1996; Tony Award, 1998; LA Critics' Award, Broadcast Critics' Award, Toronto People's Choice Award, Golden Globe Award, 1999; Shakespeare Prize, Academy Award for Best Director (also Best Film) for American Beauty, 2000; The Hamburg Shakespeare Prize; Oliver Award for Best Director (also Special Award), 2003. Address: 26-28 Neal Street, London, WC2H 9QQ, England. E-mail: mleigh@scampltd.com

MÉNDEZ RODRÍGUEZ José Manuel, b. 19 March 1955, Reinosa, Spain. Professor of Logic. 2 sons. Education: BA, History, 1978; BA, Philosophy, 1979; PhD, 1983. Appointments: Assistant Lecturer, 1980, Associate Professor, 1981, Professor, 1988-. Publications: Several articles in professional journals. Honours: 1st Class Distinction 1979; Special Distinction, 1983. Member of the Association for Symbolic Logic. Address: Departmento de Filosofia, Universidad de Salamanca, Edificio FES, Campus Unamuno, 37007 Salamanca, Spain. E-mail: sefus@usal.es Website: http//web.usal.es/n.sefus

MENEM Carlos Saul, b. 2 July 1930, Anillaco, La Rioja, Argentina. Politician. m. (1) Zulema Fatima Yoma, 1966, divorced, 1 son, deceased, 1 daughter, (2) Cecilia Bolocco, 2001, 1 child. Education: Cordoba University. Appointments: Founder, Juventud Peronista, Peron Youth Group, La Rioja Province, 1955; Defended political prisoners following 1955 Coup; Legal Advisor, Confederacion General del Trabajo, La Rioja Province, 1955-70; Candidate, Provincial Deputy, 1958; President, Partido Justicialista, La Rioja Province, 1963-; Elected Govenor, La Rioja, 1973, re-elected, 1983, 1987; Imprisoned following military coup, 1976-81; Candidate for President, Argentine Republic for Partido Justicialista, 1989; President of Argentina, 1989-2001; Vice President, Conference of Latin-American Popular Parties, 1990-; Arrested for alleged involvement in illegal arms sales during his presidency, June 2001, charged, July 2001, placed under house arrest for five months; Presidential Candidate, 2003; National Senator, 2005- . Publications: Argentine, Now or Never; Argentina Year 2000; The Productive Revolution, with Eduardo Duhalde. Address: Casa de Gobierno, Balcarce 50, 1064 Buenos Aires, Argentina.

MENG Ru Ling, b. 16 March 1937, China. Research Professor. m. D Huang, 1 son, 1 daughter. Education: BS, Central South University of Technology, Mining and Metallurgy College, Hunan, PR China, 1958. Appointments: Instructor, Central South University of Technology, Mining and Metallurgy College, Hunan, PR China, 1958-59; Research Assistant, Metallurgy and Materials Science Division, Institute of Mining and Metallurgy, PR China, 1959-73; Research Associate, Institute of Physics, Chinese Academy of Science, Beijing, PR China, 1973-79; Research Associate, Department of Physics, University of Houston, Texas, USA, 1979-81; Visiting Scholar, Department of Physics, University of Konstanz, Germany, 1981; Research Associate, Institute of Physics, Academy of Science, Beijing, PR China, 1982-84; Research Associate, Department of Physics, 1984-86, Senior Research Scientist, Research Professor, Department of Physics, Texas Center of Superconductivity, 1987-, University of Houston, Texas, USA; Editorial Board, Central European Journal of Physics, 2002-. Publications: More than 300 publications include most recently as co-author: Formation and Morphology of Superconducting Hg-1223 thick film on Ni substrate, 2000; High pressure study on MgB_2, 2002; Field dependence of intragrain superconductive transition in $RuSr_2EuCu_2O_8$, 2002; Study of binary and preudo-binary internetallic compounds with AIB_2 structure, 2002. Honours: Ranked 25th out of 100 most cited physicists, 1981-97, Institute for Scientific Information; Honorary Professorships: Zhong-Shan University (Sun Yat-Sen University), 1992; Central South University of Technology, 1992; Beijing Polytechnic University, 1998; Hainan University, 2003; Hainan Normal University, 2003; Senior Consultant, Chan-Sha Research Institute of Mining and Metallurgy, 1992. Memberships: Materials Research Society; Phi Beta Delta International Association; Chinese Association of Professionals in Science and Technology. Address: Texas Center for Superconductivity, University of Houston, 202 Houston Science Center, Houston TX 77204-5002, USA. E-mail: rmeng@uh.edu

MENKEN Alan, b. 22 July 1949, New York, USA. m. Janis, 1972, 2 children. Composer. Education: New York University. Creative Works: Theatre music including: God Bless You

Mr Rosewater, 1979; Little Shop of Horrors, with Howard Ashman; Kicks; The Apprenticeship of Duddy Kravitz; Diamonds; Personals; Let Freedom Sing; Weird Romance; Beauty and the Beast; A Christmas Carol; Film music includes: Little Shop of Horrors, 1986; The Little Mermaid, 1988; Beauty and the Beast, 1990; Lincoln, 1992; Newsies, 1992; Aladdin, 1992; Life with Mikey, 1993; Pocahontas, with Stephen Schwartz, 1995; The Hunchback of Notre Dame, 1996; Hercules, 1997; Home on the Range, 2004; Noel, 2004; The Shaggy Dog, 2006; Enchanted, 2007. Honours include: Several Academy Awards, 1989, 1993, 1996; Golden Globe Award, 1996. Address: The Shukat Company, 340 West 55th Street, Apt 1A, New York, NY 10019, USA.

MENNEN Ulrich, b. 1 July 1947, Barberton, Mpumalanga, South Africa. m. Johanna Margaretha Louw, 2 sons, 1 daughter. Education: MBChB, University of Pretoria, 1970; FRCS, Glasgow, 1978, Edinburgh, 1978; FCS (SA) Ortho, 1979; MMed, Orthopaedics, University of Pretoria, 1979; FHMVS (DUMC) 1983; MD, Orthopaedics, 1983; DSc (Med), 2007. Appointments include: Professor and Head, Department of Hand- and Microsurgery, Medical University of Southern Africa, 1985-; Honorary Head, Hand Surgery Unit, Pretoria Academic Hospital; Head, Department of Orthopaedic Surgery, Medical University of Southern Africa, 1990-91; Visiting Professor, Hong Kong, Australia, USA, Vietnam, Iran, South Korea, Botswana, Ethiopia, Uganda, Tanzania, Egypt; Private Hand Surgery Practice, 1992-; Founder and Member, Pretoria Hand Institute, Jakaranda Hospital, 1997-. Publications: Chirurgiese Sinopsis, 1978; Co-author, Surgical Synopsis, 1983; Editor, The Hand Book, 1988, second edition, 1994, third edition, 2007; Co-editor, Principles of Surgical Patient Care, vols 1 and 2, 1990, second edition, 2003; The History of South African Society for Surgery of the Hand 1969-1994, 1994; 202 articles in professional journals and book chapters. Honours include: 15 times winner, SASSH Annual Isidore Kaplan Literary Prize; Numerous other literary prizes; Originator and developer of the Mennen Clamp-on Bone Fixation System, the Mennen Interposition Replacement Arthroplasty for Digital Joints (MIRA prostheses) the Radial Swivel Head Arthroscopy Prothesis; The Functional Wrist Fusion Plate; Pioneer in End-to-side Nerve Suture Technique; Developer, EPL opponensplasty, Distal-Dorstal-Scaphoid approach, Internalisation of splints for Tetraplegic patients (tendon transfers); The South African Orthopaedic Association Presidents Essay Medal, 2005. Memberships include: South African Medical Association; SA Orthopaedic Association; SA Association for Arthritis and Rheumatic Diseases; Cripples Research Association of South Africa; International Member, American Society for Surgery of the Hand; Executive Member and Past President, Historian, South African Society for Surgery of the Hand; Founding and Honorary Member, South African Society for Hand Therapy; Executive Member, Past-Secretary-General and President, International Federation of Societies for Surgery of the Hand (IFSSH) Editor of IFSSHezine electronic magazine. Address: 374 Lawley Street, Waterkloof, 0181, Pretoria, South Africa.

MENON Parakkat Ramakrishnan, b. 22 July 1938, Trichur, India. Professor. m. Annalaxmi, 1 son. Education: BSc, 1958; MSc, 1960; PhD, 1964. Appointments: Lecturer, Assistant Professor, 1968; Professor, 1976; Professor and Head of the Department, 1978; Professor and Chief Co-ordinator, 1981; Professor Emeritus, IIT, Bombay. Publications: 15 books; More than 450 technical papers in international and national journals. Memberships: ASM International (USA); APMI International (USA); Indian Institute of Metals and Powder Metallurgy Association of India. Honours: National Metallurgist Award, The Government of India; Binani Gold Medal; Bilateral Awards of Grants, Indo-USA, Indo-UK, Indo-Israel, etc. Address: 402, Opal, Powai-Vihar Complex, Powai, Mumbai 400076, India.

MENUGE Angus John Louis, b. 23 June 1964, Woking, Surrey, England. Philosophy Professor. m. Vicki Hubert, 2 sons. Education: BA, First Class Honours, Philosophy, University of Warwick, England; MA, Philosophy, 1987, PhD, Philosophy, 1989, University of Wisconsin-Madison, USA. Appointments: Teaching Assistant, Philosophy, 1985-88, Fellow in Philosophy, 1988-89, University of Wisconsin-Madison, USA; Computer Programmer, British Rail, Crewe, England, 1989-91; Assistant Professor of Philosophy, 1991-97, Associate Professor of Philosophy, 1997-2004, Professor of Philosophy, 2004-, Concordia University, Wisconsin, USA. Publications: Books: C S Lewis Lightbearer in the Shadowlands: The Evangelistic Vision of C S Lewis (editor and author of a chapter and introduction), 1997; Christ and Culture in Dialogue: Constructive Themes and Practical Applications (general editor and author of a chapter and introduction), 1999; Debating Design: From Darwin to DNA (assistant to the editors), 2004; Reading God's World: The Scientific Vocation (editor and author of a chapter and the introduction), 2004; Agents Under Fire: Materialism and the Rationality of Science (author), 2004; Over 20 articles in academic journals. Honours: International Personality of the Year for promoting dialogue between faith and science, 2001; Fellow of the Discovery Institute for 2002; Who's Who Among American Teachers, 2003-05; Faculty Laureate, Concordia University, Wisconsin, 2008-09; Listed in international biographical directories. Memberships: Philosophy of Science Association; American Scientific Affiliation; Evangelical Philosophical Society; Board of Directors of the Cranach Institute; Wisconsin Philosophical Society. Address: Department of Philosophy, Concordia University Wisconsin, 12800 N Lake Drive, Mequon WI 53097, USA. E-mail: angus.menuge@cuw.edu Website: www.cranach.org

MERKEL Angela, b. 17 July 1954, Hamburg, Germany. Chancellor of Germany. Education: Physics doctorate, 1978. Appointments: Chemist, scientific academy, East Berlin; Joined the Christian Democratic Union (CDU), 1990; Minister for Women and Youth, 1991-94; Minister for Environment, Nature Protection and Reactor Safety, 1994-98; General Secretary, 1993-2000, Chairman, 1998-2000, CDU Deutschlands; Chairman, CDU/CSU-Bundestagsfraktion, 2002-; Chancellor of Germany, 2005-. Publications: The Price of Survival: Ideas and Conversations about Future Tasks for Environmental Policy, 1997. Member: Council of Women World Leaders, 2007. Address: Office of the Federal Chancellor, Willy-Brandt-Strasse 1, D-10557, Berlin, Germany. Website: www.cdu.de

MERKURYEV Yuri, b. 30 April 1954, Riga, Latvia. Educator. m. Galina Merkuryeva, 1 daughter. Education: Electrical Engineer, Automation and Remote Control, 1976, Candidate of Technical Sciences, 1982, Doctor of Engineering, 1992, Habilitated Doctor of Engineering, 1997, Riga Technical University; Sabbatical year in Finland: Abo Akademi, Turku and Helsinki University of Technology, Helsinki, 1987-88. Appointments: Research Assistant, Department of Automatic Control Systems, 1976-78, Doctoral Student, 1978-81, Teaching Assistant, Senior Lecturer, Associate Professor, Acting Head of the Department of Automatic Control Systems, 1982-93; Associate Professor, Head of the Department of Modelling and Simulation, 1993-97, Full Professor, Head of the Department of

Modelling and Simulation, 1997-, Riga Technical University; Part-time Professor, University of Rezekne, 1998-2002. Publications: Over 300 publications including 6 books and a textbook: Logistics Information Systems; About 250 scientific papers including chapters in the books: Bounding Approaches to System Identification, 1996, Supply Chain Optimisation: Product/process design, facility location and flow control, 2005; Supply Chain Configuration: Concepts, Solutions, and Applications, 2007; Simulation-based Case Studies in Logistics: Education and Applied Research, 2009; Managing Risk in Virtual Enterprise Networks: Implementing Supply Chain Principals, 2010; Papers in scientific journals and conference proceedings; 23 teaching publications and 31 edited books. Honours: Best Paper Award, European Simulation Symposium, Dresden, Germany, 1992; Annual Award of the Latvian National Organisation on Automation, 1997; Corresponding Member, Latvian Academy of Sciences, 2004. Memberships include: Senior Member, Board Member, European Council, 1991-2006; Director, Latvian MISS Centre; Society for Modelling and Simulation International; Board Member, Federation of European Simulation Societies; EUROSIM; Chartered Fellow, British Computer Society; President, Latvian Simulation Society; Baltic Operations Research Society; National Geographic Society; Latvian Scientists Union; Latvian Association of University Professors; Latvian Transport Development and Education Association; Editorial Boards: Simulation & Gaming: An Interdisciplinary Journal of Theory, Practice and Research; International Journal of Simulation and Process Modelling; Simulations: Transactions of the Society for Modeling and Simulation International; SCS Publishing House. Address: Riga Technical University, Kalku Street 1, LV-1658 Riga, Latvia. E-mail: merkur@itl.rtu.lv

MEURGEY Francois, b. 22 December 1971, Paris, France. Curator. 1 daughter. Education: Degree, Biology, 1991; Degree, Medieval Archaeology, 1993. Appointments: Curator of Insects and Birds, Museum d'Histoire Naturelle de Naules; Insect Biosystematist, Parc National de Guadeloupe. Publications: Book, Les Libellules des Antilles Francaises, in press; 75 papers on dragonflies; Description of new species, Protoneura Romanae, 2006, Argia telesfordi, 2010; Revision of the Genus Dythemis in the less Antilles. Honours: Listed in international biographical dictionaries. Memberships: Worldwide Dragonfly Association; Société des Sciences Naturelles de l'Ouest de la France. Address: 21 rue Villebois-Dareuil, 44000 Nantes, France. E-mail: francois.meurgey@mairie_nantes.fr

MEUSBURGER Peter, b. 14 March 1942, Lustenau, Germany. University Professor. m. Annemarie Oehner, 3 daughters. Education: PhD, 1968, Habilitation, 1980, Innsbruck University. Appointments: Distinguished Senior Professor, Department of Geography, Heidelberg University. Publications: Over 250 articles in professional journals; 20 edited books. Honours: Honorary ring of Austrian President; Presidential Achievement Award, Association of American Geographers; Honorary Doctorate, Eotvos Lorant University, Budapest. Memberships: Association of American Geographers. Address: Department of Geography, Heidelberg University, Berlinerstrasse 48; D-69120 Heidelberg, Germany.

MEYER Conrad John Eustace, b. 2 July 1922, Bristol, England. Retired Roman Catholic Priest. m. Mary Wiltshire. Education: Pembroke College, Cambridge; Westcott House, Cambridge; Ordained Priest in the Roman Catholic Church, 1995. Appointments: War Service, 1942-46; Lieutenant (S), Chaplain, RNVR, retired 1954; As Anglican: Diocesan Secretary for Education, 1960-69; Archdeacon of Bodmin, Truro Diocese, 1969-79 Honorary Canon, Truro Cathedral, 1960-79; Provost, Western Division of Woodard Schools, 1970-92; Examining Chaplain to the Bishop of Truro, 1973-79; Area Bishop of Dorchester, Oxford Diocese, 1979-87; Honorary Assistant Bishop, Truro Diocese, 1990-94; As Roman Catholic: Honorary Canon, Plymouth Roman Catholic Cathedral, 2001. Memberships: Formerly Chairman of Appeal Committee, Vice-Chairman of Society, 1989-90, Vice-President, 1990-, Society for Promoting Christian Knowledge (SPCK); Chairman, Cornwall Civil Aid and County Commissioner, 1993-96; Honorary Fellow, Institute for Civil Defence and Disaster Studies. Address: Hawk's Cliff, 38 Praze Road, Newquay, Cornwall TR7 3AF, England.

MEYER Jens Eduard, b. 23 December 1970. Professor. m. Eva Varhegyi, 1993, 3 sons. Education: MD (Hons), Christian-Albrechts-University, Kiel, Germany, 1997; PhD, Luebeck University, Germany, 2006; Full Professor of ENT, 2009. Appointments: Research Fellow, Yale University, Veterans Affairs Hospital, West Haven, Connecticut, 1997; Subintern, Yale University, 1998; Resident, 1998-2003, Fellow, 2003-05, Department of Otorhinolaryngology, Head and Neck Surgery, Kiel, Schleswig-Holstein, Germany; Lecturer, Sch Speech Therapy, Kiel, 1999-2005; Visiting Assistant Professor, Surgery, Yale University, 2003-; Attending, Department of Otorhinolaryngology, Head and Neck Surgery, 2005-, Department of Otorhinolaryngology, Facial Plastic Surgery, 2006-, Luebeck; Consultant in field. Publications: Editor, Journal of Otolaryngology, 2000-; Head, Department of Otorhinolaryngology, Head, Neck and Plastic Surgery, AK St Georg, Hamburg, 2011-. Contributed articles to professional journals. Honours: Hensel Prize, 2003, Grantee, Medical Faculty, 2004, Christian-Albrecht University. Memberships: European Academy of Allergy and Clinical Immunology; North German Association for Facial Surgery; German Otorhinolaryngology, Head and Neck Society; American Head and Neck Surgery. Address: Department of Otorhinolaryngology, Head and Neck Surgery, Lohmuehlenstr 5, Hamburg 20099, Germany. E-mail: jens.meyer@asklepics.com

MIANIYE Mikhail, b. 2 January 1964, Lugansk region, Ukraine. Scientist. Widower, 1 son. Education: Graduate, Kharkov Institute of Radio Electronics, 1988; Post-graduate course, 1989-92; Academy of Yoga, 1988-92. Appointments: Teacher, 1988-92, Pro-rector, 1992, Academy of Yoga; Development of the Personality Centre, 1993-; President, Founder, Scientific Supervisor, other organization of the Development of the Personality System, 2006-. Publications: More than 30 articles in professional journals; 4 monographs. Honours include: Order of St Alexander Nevsky, 1st degree; Silver George Medal, 4th degree; International Award of the Millennium, 2007; J W Goethe Medal, 2010; Award of Italy, 2010. Memberships: Russian Academy of Natural Sciences; European Academy of Natural Sciences; New York Academy of Sciences; International Diplomatic Academy; Academy of Security, Defense, Law and Order; Italian Academy of Economics and Social Sciences; International Personnel Academy; Senator of the International Knight's Union; Knight of the Sovereign Military Teutonic Order of the Levant; Sovereign Military Order of St John of Jerusalem; Order of Malta; St George Order. Address: Ground Floor, 38 Kirov Street, Kharkov, 61002, Ukraine. E-mail: info@mianie-system.org

MICHAEL George (Georgios Kyriacos Panayiotou), b. 25 June 1963, Finchley, London, England. Singer; Songwriter; Producer. Career: Singer, The Executive, 1979; Singer, pop duo Wham! with Andrew Ridgeley, 1982-86; Solo artiste, 1986-; Worldwide appearances include: Live Aid, with Elton John, Wembley, 1985; Prince's Trust Rock Gala, 1986; Wham's 'The Final' concert, Wembley, 1986; Nelson Mandela's 70th Birthday Tribute, 1988; Rock In Rio II Festival, Brazil, 1991; A Concert For Life, tribute to Freddie Mercury, Wembley Stadium, 1992; Elizabeth Taylor AIDS Foundation Benefit, Madison Square Garden, New York, 1992; Dispute with Epic record label, and parent company Sony Entertainment, 1992-95; Television special, Aretha Franklin: Duets, 1993. Recordings: Albums: with Wham!: Fantastic (Number 1, UK), 1983; Make It Big (Number 1, UK and US), 1984; The Final, 1986; Solo albums: Faith (Number 1, US), 1987; Listen Without Prejudice, Vol 1, 1990; Older, 1996; Older and Upper, 1998; Ladies and Gentlemen: The Best of George Michael, 1998; Songs from the Last Century, 1999; Contributor, Duets, Elton John, 1991; Two Rooms, 1992; Hit singles include: with Wham!: Wham Rap, 1982; Young Guns (Go For It), 1982; Bad Boys, 1983; Club Tropicana, 1983; Wake Me Up Before You Go Go (Number 1, UK), 1984; Last Christmas, 1984; Careless Whisper (Number 1, US and UK), 1984; Everything She Wants (Number 1, US), 1984; Freedom, 1985; I'm Your Man (Number 1, UK), 1985; The Edge Of Heaven (Number 1, UK), 1986; Solo: A Different Corner (Number 1, UK), 1986; I Knew You Were Waiting For Me, duet with Aretha Franklin, (Number 1, UK), 1987; I Want Your Sex, 1987; Faith (Number 1, US), 1987; Father Figure (Number 1, US), 1988; One More Try (Number 1, US), 1988; Monkey (Number 1, US), 1988; Kissing A Fool, 1988; Praying For Time (Number 1, US), 1990; Freedom 90, 1990; Don't Let The Sun Go Down On Me, duet with Elton John (Number 1, UK and US); Too Funky, 1992; Five Live EP (Number 1, UK), 1993; Somebody To Love, with Queen, 1993; Jesus To A Child (Number 1, UK), 1995; Fast Love, 1996; Star People, 1997; You Have Been, 1997; Outside, 1998; Contributor, Do They Know It's Christmas?, Band Aid, 1985; Nikita, Elton John, 1985. Publication: Bare, with Tony Parsons (autobiography). Honours include: BRIT Awards: Best British Group, 1985; Outstanding Contribution to British Music, 1986; Best British Male Artist, 1988; Best British Album, 1991; Ivor Novello Awards: Songwriter Of The Year, 1985, 1989; Most Performed Work (Careless Whisper), 1985; Hit Of The Year (Faith), 1989; Grammy, with Aretha Franklin, 1988; Nordoff-Robbins Silver Clef Award, 1989; American Music Awards: Favourite Pop/Rock Male Artist, Soul R&B Male Artist, Favourite Album, 1989; ASCAP Golden Note Award, 1992. Address: c/o Connie Filipello Publicity, 17 Gosfield Street, London W1P 7HE, England.

MICHAEL (H M King), b. 25 October 1921, Romania. King of Romania. m. Princess Anne of Bourbon-Parma, 1948, 5 daughters. Appointments: Declared heir apparent, ratified by Parliament 1926; Proclaimed King, 1927, deposed by his father, 1930; Succeeded to the throne of Romania following his father's abdication, 1940; Led coup d'etat against pro Nazi dictator Ion Antonescu, 1944; Forced to abdicate following communist takeover of Romania, 1947; Subsequently ran chicken farm in Hertfordshire, England; Went to Switzerland as a Test Pilot, 1956; Worked for Lear Incorporated; Founder, Electronics Company; Stockbroker; Deported from Romania on first visit since exile, 1990; Returned to Romania, 1992; Romanian citizenship and passport restored, 1997; Undertook official mission for Romania's integration into NATO and EU 1997. Honours: Order of Victoria, USSR, 1945; Chief Commander, Legion of Merit, USA, 1946; Honorary KCVO. Address: 17 La Croix-de-Luisant, 1170 Aubonne, Vaud, Switzerland.

MICHALEK Pavel, b. 27 April 1968, Pardubice, Czech Republic. Consultant Anaesthetist. m. Michaela Vesela, 2 sons, 1 daughter. Education: MD, Medical Faculty, Charles University, Prague, Czech Republic, 1992; Board Certification of 2nd Degree, Anaesthesia and Intensive Care, Prague, 2000; PhD, Medical Faculty, Masaryk University, Brno, 2002; Diplomate, European Society of Anesthesiologists, 2008. Appointments: Registrar, SHO, District Hospital, Louny, Czech Republic, 1992-98; Consultant, Specialist Registrar, IKEM, Prague, 1998-2001; Chief, Department of Cardiovascular Anaesthesiology and Intensive Care, NaHomolce Hospital, Prague, 2001-05; Senior Lecturer, Medical Faculty, Charles University, Prague, 2001-; Consultant Anaesthetist, Antrim General Hospital, 2005-; Associate Professor, Anaesthesia and Intensive Medicine, Charles University, Prague, Czech Republic, 2009; Consultant Anaesthetist, Antrim Area Hospital, 2005-11; Consultant Anaesthetist, General University Hospital, Prague, 2011-. Publications: Articles in professional medical journals including: Interventional pain management, 2002; Techniques of regional anaesthesia and analgesia, 2002; Sedation in dental office, 2007. Honours: Reviewer, Journal of Clinical Anaesthesia, USA; Reviewer, BMJ Learning, UK; Reviewer, Journal of Paramedic Practice, UK; Associate Editor, Journal of Medical Case Reports. Memberships: European Society of Regional Anaesthesia; Difficult Airway Society; International Association for Study of Pain; Czech Pain Society; Board Member, Czech Society of Anaesthesia and Intensive Care. AddressNad Panenskou 1, Prague 6, 169 0-0, Czech Republic. E-mail: pafkamich@yahoo.co.uk

MICHEL Louis, b. 2 September 1947, Tienen, Belgium. Member of European Parliament. m. Martine Pierre, 2 sons. Education: Teaching qualification, English, Dutch and German Literature, 1968. Appointments: Teacher, Professor of Germanic Languages, Dutch, English and German Literature; Professor, Ecole Normale provinciale de Jodoigne, 1968-78; Invited Professor, University of Liège, Belgium; Elected Member, Belgian Parliament, 1978-; Representative of Belgian Government, European Convention on the Future of Europe and in the Intergovernmental Convention; Deputy Prime Minister and Minister for Foreign Affairs, Belgian Government, 1999-2004; European Commissioner for Science and Research, 2004; European Commissioner for Development and Humanitarian Aid, 2004-09; Member, European Parliament, 2009-. Publications: Numerous articles in professional journals. Honours: Minister of State; Honorary mayor of Jodoigne; Knight in the Order of Leopold; Officer in the Order of Leopold; Commander in the Order of Leopold; Grand Cross in the Royal Swedish Order of the Polar Star; Grand Cross in the Order of the Infante Dom Henrique; Grand Cross in the Order of Orange Nassau; Grand Cross of Isabella the Catholic; Grand Cross in the Order of Danneborg; Grand Croix de l'Ordre de l'Honneur; Grand Cross in the Order of the Star of Romania; Grand Officier de l'Ordre de la Pléiade; Grand Officier de l'Ordre de la Légion d'honneur; Grand Cordon de l'Ordre du Mérite; Ordre Stara Planina de 1ère Classe; Ordre Duarte Sanchez et Mella, Dominican Republic; Doctor Honoris causa of the University of Antananarivo, Madagascar; Doctor Honoris causa of the University of Gembloux, Belgium. Memberships: Committee on Civil Liberties, Justice and Home Affairs; Committee on Development; Joint Parliamentary Assembly. Address: European Parliament, Rue Wiertz, 60, 1047 Brussels, Belgium.

DICTIONARY OF INTERNATIONAL BIOGRAPHY 36th EDITION

MICHELL Alastair Robert, b. 28 December 1940, London, England. Veterinarian; Academic. m. Pauline Selley, 1 daughter. Education: Dulwich College, London; State Scholarship, 1958, First class honours, Physiology, 1962, B Vet Med, 1964, PhD, 1969, DSc, 1996, University of London, Royal Veterinary College. Appointments: Harkness Fellowship, Commonwealth Fund of New York, 1969-71; Beit Memorial Fellowship for Medical Research, 1971-73; MRC Research Fellow, Pritzker School of Medicine, Nephrology Section, University of Chicago, 1974-76; Personal Chair, Applied Physiology and Comparative Medicine, University of London, 1993; Elected Member, University of London Senate; Member, Academic Advisory Board in Medicine; Chair, Board of Studies in Veterinary Medicine; Chair, Examiners in Veterinary Medicine; Various external examinerships; Former Member, Technology Foresight Health Sciences Panel; Head, Companion Animal Referral Hospital, Animal Health Trust, 1997-99; Visiting Professor, University of Sydney, Department of Veterinary Clinical Science, 2000. Publications: Over 300 scientific publications in professional journals; Reviews, articles and textbook chapters; 6 textbooks including: Veterinary Fluid Therapy, The Advancement of Veterinary Medicine and The Clinical Biology of Sodium. Honours: Blaine Award for outstanding contributions to the advancement of companion animal medicine and surgery, 1990; George Fleming Prize, 1992, 2005; Dalrymple-Champneys Cup & Medal for outstanding contributions to veterinary science and comparative medicine, 2007; Honorary Member, Royal Pharmaceutical Society, 2010; BVA Chiron Award, 2012. Memberships: Royal College of Veterinary Surgeons (President, 1999-2000); Veterinary Research Club; Association of Veterinary Teachers & Research Workers; Central Veterinary Society; RPS; Patient Governor, Addenbrookes Hospital Foundation Hospital Trust; St Nicholas Hospice Users Forum; Professional Leadership Body for Pharmacists; Health Professionals for Assisted Dying; many others. Address: Pinecroft, Upper Cleveley, Oxon, OX7 4DX, England.

MICLE Valer, b. 6 November 1958, Ceaca, Salaj County, Romania. Professor; Engineer. m. Michaela, 1 son, 1 daughter. Education: Mechanical Engineer, Technological Equipment, Technical University of Cluj-Napoca, 1983; PhD, Foundry, 1995. Appointments: IMUAS Baia-Mare, 1983-85; Assistant, 1985-91, Lecturer, 1991-96, Reader, 1996-2000, Professor, 2000-, Deputy Dean, Faculty of Materials Science & Engineering, 2004-, Doctorship Supervisor, 2005-, Technical University of Cluj-Napoca. Publications: 7 books; 105 published scientific papers in professional journals. Memberships: Romanian Foundry Technical Association; General Association of Engineers in Romania. Address: Technical University of Cluj-Napoca, Faculty of Materials Science & Engineering, Str Memorandumului 28, RO 400114, Cluj-Napoca, Romania. E-mail: valer.micle@sim.utcluj.ro

MIDLER Bette, b. 1 December 1945, Honolulu, Hawaii, USA. Singer; Actress; Comedienne. m. Martin von Haselberg, 1984, 1 daughter. Education: Theatre studies, University of Hawaii. Career: As actress: Cast member, Fiddler On The Roof, Broadway, 1966-69; Salvation, New York, 1970; Rock opera Tommy, Seattle Opera Company, 1971; Nightclub concert performer and solo artiste, 1972-; Numerous television appearances include: Ol' Red Hair Is Back, NBC, 1978; Bette Midler's Mondo Beyondo, HBO, 1988; Earth Day Special, ABC, 1990; The Tonight Show, NBC, 1991; Now, NBC, 1993; Films include: Hawaii, 1965; The Rose, 1979; Jinxed!, 1982; Down And Out In Beverly Hills, 1985; Ruthless People, 1986; Outrageous Fortune, 1987; Big Business, 1988; Beaches, 1988; Stella, 1990; Scenes From A Mall, 1990; For The Boys (also co-producer), 1991; Hocus Pocus, 1993; Gypsy, 1993; The First Wives Club, 1996; That Old Feeling, 1997; Drowning Mona, 2000; Isn't She Great, 2000; The Stepford Wives, 2004; Then She Found Me, 2007. Own company, All Girls Productions, 1989-. Recordings: Albums include: The Divine Miss M, 1972; Bette Midler, 1973; Songs For The New Depression, 1976; Broken Blossom, 1977; Live At Last, 1977; Thighs And Whispers, 1979; The Rose, film soundtrack, 1979; Divine Madness, film soundtrack, 1980; No Frills, 1984; Beaches, film soundtrack, 1989; Some People's Lives, 1991; Best Of, 1993; Bette Of Roses, 1995; Experience the Divine, 1997; Bathhouse Betty, 1998; From a Distance, 1998. Singles include: The Rose; Wind Beneath My Wings (Number 1, US), from Beaches soundtrack, 1989; From A Distance, 1991. Publications: A View From A Broad; The Saga Of Baby Divine. Honours: After Dark Award, Performer Of The Year, 1973; Grammy Awards: Best New Artist, 1973; Best Female Pop Vocal Performance, The Rose, 1981; Record Of The Year, Song Of The Year, Wind Beneath My Wings, 1990; Special Tony Award, 1973; Emmy, Ol' Red Hair Is Back, 1978; Golden Globe Awards: The Rose, 1979; For The Boys, 1991; Oscar Nomination, Best Actress, The Rose, 1980; Contributor, We Are The World, USA For Africa, 1985; Oliver And Company, 1988. Address: c/o All Girls Productions, Animation Bldg #3B-10, 500 South Buena Vista, Burbank, CA 91521, USA.

MIKIC Pavao, b. 19 September 1945, Orasje, Bosnia-Herzegovina. Philosopher; Linguist; Educator. m. Anna Margarete Schneider, 1979. Education: Graduate, Theology, University of Sarajevo, Bosnia-Herzegovina, 1969, University of Bonn, Germany, 1973; Graduate in Philosophy and Germanistics, 1975, PhD, 1980, University of Bonn. Appointments: Developer of Language Department, Academy Klausenhof Adult Education Institute, Hamminkeln, Germany; Assistant Professor, 1982-86, Professor, 1986-90, Full Professor, 1990-, Dean, 1997-2000, Head, Department of German Language, 2005-07, University of Zadar, Croatia. Publications: German for Advanced Tourism and Hotel Business Students, 1991; Comparative Dictionary of Proverbs, 1992; Proverbs of the Bible in Croatian Language, 1994; Swearwords in Croatian and German Language, 1999; German for German Language Students, 1999, 1997, 2000; Translation Studies in the Context of Culture Specifics, 2004; Croatian Touristic Advertising in German Translation, 2008; Religious Dictionary, Croatian-German, 2009-10. Address: University of Zadar, Department of German, M Pavlinovica 2, 23000 Zadar, Croatia. E-mail: pmikic@unizd.hr

MIKOLAJEWSKA Barbara, b. 3 December 1947, Poland. Sociologist; Author; Publisher. m. FEJ Linton. Education: Master's degree, Sociology. 1970, PhD, Sociology, 1979, Warsaw University, Poland. Appointments: Assistant, Warsaw Polytechnic University, 1970-72; Senior Assistant, 1972-79, Adjunct Professor, 1979-2002, Warsaw University; Co-proprietor, The Lintons' Video Press, New Haven, Connecticut, 1997-. Publications: Sociology of Small Groups, 1985; Ethnic Names as a Factor in Ethnic Distance, 1987; Community, 1989, second edition, revised, 1999; Who are Jews, 1989; Polish Translation of René Girard's A Theater of Envy: William Shakespeare, 1996; Desire Came Upon That One in the Beginning, 1997, 1999; This Is Us – Doing Math, 1999, Symposium, 1999, Facing Off, 1999; Child's Play, 2000; The Adventures of Marysia, 14 volumes, 2000-04; Good Violence Versus Bad, 2004; The Mahabharata Retold (in Polish): Books I & II, 2007, Book III, 2007, Books IV & V, 2009, Books VI & VII, 2010, Books VIII-XI, 2011; Numerous web publications in English and Polish. Honours: Rector's Achievement Awards, Warsaw University, 1980, 1987, 1988, 1989, 1990. Memberships: Colloquium on Violence and Religion; Society for Indian Philosophy and Religion; Inner Circle, GCT. Address: 36 Everit Street, New Haven, CT, 06511-2208, USA. E-mail: bmikolajewska@gmail.com

MIKROYANNIDIS Alexander J, b. 29 October 1980, Patras, Greece. Electrical & Computer Engineer. Education: B Eng, University of Patras, Greece, 2003; M Phil, 2004, PhD, 2007, University of Manchester, England. Appointments: Laboratory Demonstrator, 2003-06, Teaching Assistant, 2003-07, Research Assistant, 2004-05, School of Informatics, Teaching Assistant, School of Education, 2006-07, University of Manchester; Research Assistant, 2007-08, Research Fellow, Institute of Communication Studies, 2008-09, University of Leeds; Research Fellow, Knowledge Media Institute, The Open University, 2009-. Publications: Numerous articles in professional journals, book chapters, conferences and workshops. Honours: Honorary Distinction Award, Technical Chamber of Greece, 1998-2003. Memberships: IEEE; IEEE Computer Society; Technical Chamber of Greece. Address: Knowledge Media Institute, The Open University, Milton Keynes, MK7 6AA, England. E-mail: a.mikroyannidis@computer.org

MIKRUT Leszek Andrzej, b. 13 January 1958, Lublin, Poland. Lecturer; Sworn Translator. m. Elzbieta Leja, 1 son, 1 daughter. Education: MA, 1979, PhD, 1988, Russian Philology, Maria Sklodowska-Curie University; Certificate of Pedagogical Training Teacher, 1979; Certificate of Tourist Guide, 1984; Russian Language Sworn Translator & Interpretor Certificate, 1991; Ukrainian Language Sworn Translator & Interpretor Certificate, 1998. Appointments: Junior Member of teaching staff, Senior Lecturer, Institute of Slavonic Philology, Maria Sklodowska-Curie University; Tourist Guide Trainer/Coach, Sworn Translator & Interpreter (Russian and Ukrainian language); Consultant, Polish Society of Sworn & Specialised Translators (TEPIS); Speaker, Cracow Tertium Society for the Promotion of Language Studies; Russian Language Interpreter, J Osterwy Theatre, Lublin; Chairman, Statutory Committee, Scholarly Training in Moscow, Petersburg, Warsaw and Cracow. Publications: Numerous articles in professional journals. Honours: Medal of Commission of National Education, 2006; Gold Medal of Long Service, 2009; Numerous awards granted by rector of Maria Sklodowska-Curie University. Memberships: Lublin Scholarly Association. Address: Przy Stawie 4/38, 20-067 Lublin, Poland. E-mail: leszek.mikrut@wp.pl Website: www.tlumacz-przysiegly.biz

MILENKOVIC Zoran, b. 19 February 1940, Skopie, Yugoslavia. Medical Doctor. m. Jelena, 2 sons. Education: Bachelor, Medical School, University of Belgrade, 1965; PhD, University of Niš, Yugoslavia, 1980. Appointments: Teaching Fellow, 1965-, Institute of Anatomy, Instructor of Neurosurgery, Assistant Professor, Associate Professor and Full Professor of Neurosurgery, Department of Surgery, Faculty of Medicine, Rector, 2000-04, University of Niš. Publications: Over 150 papers in international and national journals; 2 books; 4 manuals. Memberships: World and European Member, Neurosurgeons. Address: Tolstoieva 10, D Vrezina, Niš, Serbia.

MILES June Sylvia, b. 4 July 1924, London, England. Painter. m. (1) Paul Feiler, 1 son, 2 daughters, (2) Paul Mount. Education: Slade School of Fine Art; West of England College of Art. Appointments: Teacher, Bristol Polytechnic, 1967-78. Honours: Medallist (as June Feiler), Womens' International, Paris, 1968. Memberships: Royal West of England Academy; Penwith Society of Art, St Ives. Address: Nancherrow Studio, 34 Nancherrow Terrace, St Just, Penzance, TR19 7LA, England.

MILES Sarah, b. 31 December 1941, England. Actress. m. Robert Bolt, 1967, divorced 1976, re-married 1988, deceased 1995. Education: Royal Academy of Dramatic Art, London. Creative Works: Films include: Those Magnificent Men in Their Flying Machines, 1964; I Was Happy Here, 1966; The Blow-Up, 1966; Ryan's Daughter, 1970; Lady Caroline Lamb, 1972; The Hireling, 1973; The Man Who Loved Cat Dancing, 1973; Great Expectations, 1975; Pepita Jiminez, 1975; The Sailor Who Fell From Grace With the Sea, 1976; The Big Sleep, 1978; Venom, 1981; Hope and Glory, 1987; White Mischief, 1988; The Silent Touch, 1992; Jurij, 2001; Days of Rage, 2001; The Accidental Detective, 2003. Theatre appearances include: Vivat! Regina!; Asylum, 1988; TV appearances: James Michener's Dynasty; Great Expectations; Harem; Queenie; A Ghost in Monte Carlo; Dandelion Dead; Ring Around the Moon; The Rehearsal. Publications: Charlemagne, play, 1992; A Right Royal Bastard, memoirs, 1993; Serves Me Right, memoirs, 1994; Bolt From the Blue, memoirs, 1996.

MILICHOVSKY Miloslav, b. 13 February 1945, Babice, near Havlickuv Brod, Czech Republic. Senior Lecturer. m. Svatava Dostalova, 2 sons. Education: MS, Physical Chemistry, Institute of Chemical Technology, Pardubice, 1968; Organic Chemistry, ICT, Prague, 1975; CSc, Macromolecular Chemistry, ICT Pardubice, 1977; DrSc, Wood Chemistry and Technology, 1989. Appointments: Graduate Technologist, South Bohemian Papermill Vetrni, 1968; Assistant Professor, ICT Pardubice, 1976; Full Professor, Chemistry and Technology of Wood, Pulp and Paper, ICT Pardubice,2003; Head of Department, Wood, Pulp, Paper, University of Pardubice. Publications: More than 100 scientific articles in more than 8 scientific and professional journals. Memberships: Technical Association of Pulp and Paper Industry TAPPI; Association of Pulp and Paper Industry SPPaC; Czech and Slovak Papermaking Association SPPC. Address: University of Pardubice, Department of Wood, Pulp and Paper, Studentska 95, CZ 53210 Pardubice, Czech Republic.

MILLER (James) David Frederick, b. 5 January 1935, Wolverhampton, England. Retired Company Director. m. Saffrey Blackett, 3 sons, 1 deceased, 1 daughter. Education: MA, Emmanuel College, Cambridge, Diploma, IPM, London School of Economics. Appointments: Director, J & P Coats Ltd, 1972-79, Coats Patons plc, 1977-92, Royal Scottish National Orchestra, 1985-93, Outward Bound Trust, Ltd, 1985-95, Coats Viyella plc, 1986-92, The Wolverhampton & Dudley Breweries plc, 1984-2001, (chairman 1992-2001), Scottish Life Assurance Co, 1995-2001, J&J Denholm Ltd, 1997-2005, Scottish Enterprise Forth Valley, 1994-2003 (vice-chairman, 1996-2003). Honours: Freeman City of London, 1983; Freeman, Worshipful Company of Needlemakers, 1983; Honorary DUniv: University of Stirling, 1984, University of Paisley, 1997; CBE, 1997. Memberships: Chairman: Scottish Vocational Education Council, 1992-97, Court, University of Stirling, 1992-99, Scottish Examination Board, 1995-97, Scottish Qualifications Authority, 1996-2000, Fairbridge in Scotland, 1998-2006, Clackmannon College of Further Education, 1992-99, 2004-05; Director, Edinburgh Military Tattoo, 1990-2000., 2003-05. Address: Blairuskin Lodge, Kinlochard, Aberfoyle, by Stirling FK8 3TP, Scotland.

DICTIONARY OF INTERNATIONAL BIOGRAPHY 36th EDITION

MILLER Jacques Francis Albert, b. 2 April 1931, Nice, France. Medical Research. M. Margaret Houen. Education: University of Sydney, Medical School, Australia, 1949-1955; BSc (Med), 1953, MB, BS, 1955, University of Sydney; PhD Experimental Pathology, 1960, DSc Experimental Pathology and Immunology, 1965, University of London; BA, University of Melbourne, 1985. Appointments: Junior Resident Medical Officer, Royal Prince Alfred Hospital, Sydney, Australia, 1956; Pathological Research, University of Sydney, 1957; Cancer research, 1958, Assistant Professor, 1960, Chester Beatty Research Institute, London, England; Eleanor Roosevelt Fellowship, NIH, Bethesda, Maryland, USA, 1963; Associate Professor in Experimental Pathology, University of London, 1965; Head, Department of Experimental Pathology, Walter and Eliza Hall Institute of Medical Research, Melbourne, Australia, 1966; Visiting Fellow, Basel Institute for Immunology, Switzerland, 1972; Visiting Fellow, Centre d'Immunologie, Luminy, France, 1979; Visiting Fellow, Deutches Krebsforschungszentrum, Heidelberg, Germany, 1986; Professor, Chair of Experimental Immunology, 1990, Professor Emeritus, 1997, University of Melbourne and The Walter and Eliza Hall Institute of Medical Research, Australia. Publications: Excluding abstracts, over 400 mostly on immunology. Honours: Numerous including: Inaugural Sandoz Prize for Immunology, 1990; Inaugural Peter Medawar Prize of the Transplantation Society, 1990; Honorary Life Membership, Australian Society of Immunology, 1991; Elected Corresponding Member, Belgium Royal Academy of Science, 1991; Croonian Lecture of the Royal Society, London, 1992; Honorary Life Membership, Transplantation Society of Australia and New Zealand, 1992; J Alwyn Taylor International Prize for Medicine, London, Ontario, Canada, 1995; Elected Emeritus Member of the International Transplantation Society, 1999; Elected Honorary Member of the German Society for Immunology, 1999; Faulding-Florey Medal and Prize, Australian Institute of Political Science, 2000; Copley Medal and Prize, Royal Society, London, 2001. Memberships: Include: American Association of Immunologist; Australian Academy; Australian and New Zealand Association for the Advancement of Science; Australian Society of Immunology; Royal Society (London); Royal Society of Arts (London); Transplantation Society; WHO Expert Advisory Panel on Immunology, 1984-2000. Address: The Walter and Eliza Hall Institute of Medical Research, Post Office, Royal Melbourne Hospital, Victoria, 1050, Australia.

MILLER Jonathan (Wolfe), b. 21 July 1934, London, England. Theatre, Film, and Television Director; Writer. m. Helen Rachel Collet, 1956, 2 sons, 1 daughter. Education: MB, BCh, St John's College, Cambridge, 1959. Appointments: Theatre, film, and television director; Resident Fellow in the History of Medicine, 1970-73, Fellow, 1981-, University College, London; Associate Director, National Theatre, 1973-75; Visiting Professor in Drama, Westfield College, London, 1977-; Artistic Director, Old Vic, 1988-90; Research Fellow in Neuropsychology, University of Sussex; Actor in TV/Films: Beyond the Fringe, 1964; One Way Pendulum, 1964; Sensitive Skin, 2005; Director: Alice in Wonderland, 1966; Whistle and I'll Come to You, 1968; BBC Television Shakespeare, 1978-85; Presenter and writer for numerous TV programmes. Publications: Harvey and the Circulation of Blood: A Collection of Contemporary Documents (editor), 1968; McLuhan, 1971; Censorship and the Limits of Personal Freedom, 1971; Freud: The Man, His World, His Influence, 1972; The Uses of Pain, 1974; The Body in Question, 1978; Darwin for Beginners, 1982; The Human Body, 1983; States of Mind, 1983; The Facts of Life, 1984; Subsequent Performances, 1986; Laughing Matters: A Serious Look at Humour, 1989; Acting in Opera, 1990; The Don Giovanni Book: Myths of Seduction and Betrayal (editor), 1990; The Afterlife of Plays, 1992; Dimensional man, 1998; On Reflection, 1998; Nowhere in Particular, 1999. Honours: Special Tony Award, 1963; Distinguished Supporter, British Humanist Association; Honorary Associate, National Secular Society; Honorary Fellow, University College London; Honorary Fellow, Royal College of Art; Associate Member, Royal Academy of Dramatic Art; Honorary Fellow, St John's College, Cambridge, 1982; Honorary Fellow, Royal College of Physicians; Honorary D Phil, University of Cambridge; CBE, 1983; Knight Bachelor, 2002; Foreign Member, American Academy of Arts and Sciences; President, Rationalist Association, 2006-. Memberships: Royal Academy, Fellow; American Academy of Arts and Sciences. Address: c/o IMG Artists, Media House, 3 Burlington Lane, London W4 2TH, England.

MILLER Leigh Martin, b. 22 May 1927, Olympia, WN, USA. International Finance Consultant. m. Lynden R Breed, 4 sons. Education: BA, Yale University, 1948; JD, Yale Law School, 1952. Appointments: US Navy, 1945-46; US Army, 1953-54; Attorney, Pillsbury, Madison & Sutro, San Francisco, California; Associate Assistant Administrator, Agency for International Development, Department of State, Washington, DC; VP & Special Assistant of President, J Henry Schroder Banking Corp, New York City; Deputy Superintendent of Banks, Secretary, New York State Banking Board, New York City; SVP, American Express Bank, New York City; Managing Director, AMEX Bank Ltd, London, England; Vice Chairman, Realty Factors Ltd; President, American Express Export Credit Corp, New York City. Memberships: Appointed Trustee, New York Public Library, New York City, USA; Chairman, International Science and Technology Institute, Washington DC, USA; Director Emeritus, Americans for UNFPA. Address: 1170 Fifth Avenue, New York, NY 10029, USA.

MILLER Michael Dawson, b. 12 March 1928, London, England. Solicitor; Insurance Manager. m. Gillian Margaret Gordon, 3 daughters. Appointments: Regular, Parachute Regiment, 1946-49; Parachute Regiment TA, 1949-55; 1st Regiment Hon. Artillery Company TA, 1957-63; Articled Clerk to Solicitor, 1949-53; Practice as a Solicitor, 1953-55; Executive, 1955-61, Partner, 1962-90, Thos R Miller & Son, Mutual Insurance Managers; Partner, Thos R Miller & Son (Bermuda), 1969-90; Directorships: Shipowners Assurance Management, Montreal, 1973-84, A/B Indemnitas, Stockholm, 1980-90, Thomas R Miller War Risks Services Ltd, 1985-90; Technical Adviser, Planning Board for Ocean Shipping, 1970-; National Shipping Advisory Committee, 1970-90; Arbitrator, London Maritime Arbitrators Association, 1963-. Publications: Marine War Risks, 1990, 2nd edition, 1994, supplement, 1999, 3rd edition, 2005; Uncommon Lawyer, 2001; Wars of the Roses, forthcoming; Numerous articles in journals and conference proceedings include: Shipowners Liabilities, Singapore Seminar, 1980; Shipping, 4th Arm of Defence, Hong Kong, 1982; Shipping Under Fire, Athens, 1987. Honour: Silver Medal, Hellenic Merchant Marine. Memberships: Liveryman, Worshipful Company of Solicitors of the City of London, 1974-; Liveryman, Worshipful Company of Shipwrights, 1977-; Royal Bermuda Yacht Club, 1970-; Royal Ocean Racing Club, 1983-; Royal Thames Yacht Club, 1992-; Hurlingham Club, 1964-; City of London Club, 1974-. Address: 52 Scarsdale Villas, London W8 6PP. E-mail: somersisle@btinternet.com

MILLIKEN Peter, b. 12 November 1946, Kingston, Ontario, Canada. Lawyer. Member of Parliament. Education: Queen's University; Oxford University; Dalhousie University. Appointments: Lawyer and Partner, Cunningham, Swan, Carty, Little and Bonham, 1973-89; President, Kingston and the Islands Liberal Association, 1985-87; Elected to House of Commons, 1988; Re-elected, 1993; Parliamentary Secretary to the Government House Leader, 1993-96; Councillor, Canadian NATO Parliamentary Association, 1996; Elected Deputy Chairman of Committees of the Whole House, 1996-97; Re-elected, 1997; Deputy Speaker and Chairman of the Committees of the Whole House, 1997; Member, Board of Internal Economy; Re-elected, 2000; Speaker, 2001, Chair of the Board of Internal Economy; Re-elected, 2004; Speaker of the House of Commons, 2004; Re-elected, 2006, 2008; Speaker of the House of Commons, 2006, 2008. Address: Room 316-N, House of Commons, Ottawa, Ontario K1A 0A6, Canada.

MILLINGTON Barry (John), b. 1 November 1951, Essex, England. Music Journalist; Writer. Education: BA, Cambridge University, 1974. Appointments: Music Critic, Times, 1977-2001; Reviews Editor, BBC Music Magazine; Artistic Director, Hampstead and Highgate Festival. Publications: Wagner, 1984, revised edition, 1998; Selected Letters of Richard Wagner (translator and editor with S Spencer), 1987; The Wagner Compendium: A Guide to Wagner's Life and Music (editor), 1992; Wagner in Performance (editor with S Spencer), 1992; Wagner's Ring of the Nibelung: A Companion (editor with S Spencer), 1993. Contributions to: Articles on Wagner to New Grove Dictionary of Opera, 1992, New Grove Dictionary of Music and Musicians, 2nd edition, 2001; Newspapers and magazines. Membership: Critics' Circle. Address: 50 Denman Drive South, London NW11 6RH, England.

MILLOT Jean-Louis, b. 21 August 1947, Noisy-le-Sec, France. Medical Advisor. Widower. Education: MD, Faculty of Medicine, Lyon, 1975; Maitrise Biomathematics and Statistics, Faculty of Medicine, Kremlin-Bicêtre, France, 1985-. Appointments: Private Practitioner, France, 1976-80; Medical Advisor, EDF Gaz de France, Annecy, France, 1980-. Publications: La place du lithium dans le traitement de l'hyperthyroïdie, 1977; Les accidents de sport chez les salariés d'EDF Gaz de France des régions Rhône-Alpes et Bourgogne-Fréquence et Gravité, 2000; Reduced efficiency of influenza vaccine in prevention of influenza-like illness in working adults: a 7-month perspective survey in EDF Gaz de France employees in Rhône-Alpes 1996-97, 2002. Address: EDF Gaz de France Distribution, 5 bd Decouz, BP 2334, 74011 Annecy Cedex, France. E-mail: jean-louis.millot@erdf-grdf.fr

MILLS Hayley Catherine Rose Vivien, b. 18 April 1946, London, England. Actress. m. Roy Boulting, 1971, divorced 1977, 2 sons. Education: Elmhurst Ballet School; Ist Alpine Vidamanette. Creative Works: Films include: Tiger Bay, 1959; Pollyanna, 1960; The Parent Trap, 1961; Whistle Down the Wind, 1961; Summer Magic, 1962; In Search of the Castaways, 1963; The Chalk Garden, 1964; The Moonspinners, 1965; The Truth About Spring, 1965; Sky West & Crooked, 1966; The Trouble with Angels, 1966; The Family Way, 1966; Pretty Polly, 1967; Twisted Nerve, 1968; Take a Girl Like You, 1970; Forbush and the Penguins, 1971; Endless Night, 1972; Deadly Strangers, 1975; The Diamond Hunters, 1975; What Changed Charley Farthing?, 1975; The Kingfisher Caper, 1975; Appointment with Death, 1987; After Midnight, 1990; A Troll in Central Park (voice), 1994; 2BPerfectlyHonest, 2004; Stricken, 2005. TV appearances include: The Flame Trees of Thika, 1981; Parent Trap II, 1986; Good Morning Miss Bliss; Murder She Wrote; Back Home; Tales of the Unexpected; Walk of Life, 1990; Parent Trap III, IV, Amazing Stories; Back Home; Wild At Heart; Numerous stage appearances. Publication: My God, 1988. Honours include: Silver Bear Award, Berlin Film Festival, 1958; British Academy Award; Special Oscar, USA; Golden Globe Award. Address: c/o Chatto & Linnit, Prince of Wales Theatre, Coventry Street, London W1V 7FE, England.

MILLS Ian (Sir), b. 19 November 1935, Hampshire, England. Chartered Accountant. m. Elizabeth Dunstan, 1 son, 1 daughter. Education: Taunton's Grammar School, Southampton, 1946-54; Beal, Young & Booth, Chartered Accountants, Southampton, 1954-60. Appointments: Financial Consultant, World Bank team, Pakistan, 1962; Chief Accountant, University of Ibadan, Nigeria, 1965-68; Manager, Price Waterhouse, London, 1960-65, 1968-70; Partner, then Senior Partner, Price Waterhouse, London, 1973-92, (i/c Management Consultancy Services (MCS), Newcastle-upon-Tyne & Scotland, 1970-73; MCS, Africa, 1973-83; Central Government Services, 1983-85; Business Development, Europe, 1988-92); Director of Finance, NHS Executive, 1985-88; Chair, Lambeth, Southwark & Lewisham Health Authority, 1991-96; Chair, North Thames Region of NHS, 1996-98; Chair, London Region of NHS, 1998-2001; Appointments Commissioner, London Region of NHS, 2001-03. Publications: Articles on management, information systems and financial planning and control in professional journals, 1965-88; Pamphlets and brochures on heritage issues, 1984-; Rebirth of a Building: the story in pictures of a 16-year programme of renovation, 2000; Craftsmen of St Margaret: illustrations of the work of 12 Victorian architects and craftsmen, 2007; Boone's Chapel: History in the Making – with Madeleine Adams and Charlie MacKeith, 2010. Honours: Knighted, 2001; Fellow, Royal Society of Arts, 1994-; Fellow, Institute of Health Service Management, 1985-; Fellow, Chartered Institute of Management Consultants, 1963-; Fellow, Institute of Chartered Accountants, 1960-. Memberships: Chair, Independent Remuneration Panel, London Borough of Lewisham, 2001-10; Chair, Blackheath Historic Buildings Trust, 2003-11; Chair, Age Exchange Theatre Trust, 2008-. Address: 60 Belmont Hill, London SE13 5DN, England. E-mail: ianmills@googlemail.com

MILNER Arthur David, b. 16 July 1943, Leeds, England. Professor of Cognitive Neuroscience. Education: BA, 1965, MA, 1970, University of Oxford, England; Dip Psych, London, 1966; PhD, Experimental Psychology, University of London, 1971. Appointments: Research Worker, Institute of Psychology, London, 1966-70; Lecturer and Senior Lecturer in Psychology, 1970-85, Reader in Neuropsychology, 1985-90, Head Department of Psychology, 1983-88, 1994-97, Professor of Neuropsychology, 1990-2000, Dean, Faculty of Science, 1992-94, Honorary Professor of Neuropsychology, 2000-, University of St Andrews, Scotland; Professor of Cognitive Neuroscience, University of Durham, 2000-; Professor Emeritus, 2008-. Publications: Co-author and/or editor or co-editor of 6 books; Author and co-author of over 160 chapters in books and articles in refereed journals; Numerous invited lectures and workshops. Honours: Fellow, Royal Society of Edinburgh, 1992; Leverhulme Trust Research Fellow, 1998-2000; FC Donders Lecturer, Max-Planck-Institut, Nijmegen, 1999; Member, Scientific Council, Helmholtz Instituut, Netherlands, 2002-; Chichele Lecturer and Visiting Fellow, All Souls College, Oxford, Trinity Term, 2006; Fellow, Royal Society of London, 2011. Memberships: Honorary Member, Experimental Psychology Society; International Neuropsychological Symposium; International Association of Attention and Performance;

Royal Society of Edinburgh; European Brain and Behaviour Society. Address: Wolfson Research Institute, University of Durham, Queen's Campus, Stockton-on-Tees TS17 6BH, England. E-mail: a.d.milner@durham.ac.uk

MIN Byung-Chan, b. 7 June 1962, Daejeon, Korea. Professor. m. Sang-Shim Choi, 1 son, 1 daughter. Education: B Eng, Department of Industrial and Management Engineering, Hanbat National University, Republic of Korea, 1991; M Eng, Department of System Engineering, Chuo University, Tokyo, 1994; PhD, Department of Industrial and Systems Engineering, The University of Electro-Communications, Tokyo, 1998; BA, Department of North Koreanology, Korea University, 2008. Appointments: Writing Committee Member, National Technology and Research Map; Selection Committee Member of the Public Service, Daejeon Metropolitan City; Edit Director, Society of Kroea Industrial and Systems Engineering Corporate Juridical Person, Seoul, Korea; Director of General Affairs, Korean Society for Emotion and Sensibility, Corporate Juridical Person, Seoul; International Director, Ergonomics Society of Korea, Corporate Juridical Person, Seoul; President, Consultative Committee Member, Advisory Council on Democratic and Peaceful Unification, Korea. Publications: 7 books; Numerous articles in professional journals; Over 30 articles. Honours: Hanbaek Academic Award, Society of Korea Industrial and Systems Engineering, 2001; Service Prize, Japan Society of Kansei Engineering, 2001; Service Prize, Korean Society for Emotion & Sensibility, 2001; Best Posters Award, 2002; President's Commendation Award, Korea, 2005; Excellent Studies Award, 2005, Excellent Studies Award, 2008, 3 Excellent Studies Awards, 2009, Korean Industrial & Systems Engineering, Seoul; Alumni Association Award, UEC, Tokyo, 2006; Celebrated Scholar, 2007, Research and Co-operation Performance Excellence, 2008, Hanbat National University; Science and Technology Medal, 2010. Memberships: Consultative Committee Member, Patent Review Committee of Korean Intellectual Property Office; Director, Alumni Association of Seoul National University; Director, Alumni Association of UEC, Tokyo. Address: San 16-1, Duckmyung-dong, Yuseong-Ku, Daejeon, Republic of Korea. E-mail: bcmin@hanbat.ac.kr

MIN Jae Hyung, b. 18 June 1959, Seoul, Korea. Professor. m. Mihyun Kim, 1 son, 1 daughter. Education: PhD, Indiana University, USA, 1989. Appointments: Professor of Management Science, Graduate School of Business, Sogang University, Seoul; Dean, Sogang Business School, 2010-. Honours: British Chevening Scholar; Best Paper Award, Korea Customer Satisfaction Management Association; Teaching Excellence Award, Sogang Business School; Teaching Excellence Award, Sogang Graduate School of Business, MBA Program; Listed in international biographical dictionaries. Memberships: Life Member, Clare Hall, University of Cambridge, England; Beta Gamma Sigma, USA. Address: Graduate School of Business, Sogang University, #1 Shinsu-dong, Mapo-gu, Seoul 121-742, Korea.

MIN Kyung Hoon, b. 17 July 1974, Gunpo, Republic of Korea. Pulmonologist; Allergist; Medical Educator. Education: MD, 2000, MA, 2004, PhD, 2006, Medicine, Chonbuk National University Medical School, Jeonju. Appointments: Intern, 2000-01, Resident, Internal Medicine, 2001-05, Clinical and Research Fellowship, Pulmonology and Allergology, 2005-07, Clinical Professor, Pulmonology and Allergology, 2010, Chonbuk National University Medical School, Jeonju; Military Service, Captain, Pulmonology and Allergology, Armed Forces Capital Hospital, Seongnam, 2007-10. Publications: 30 articles in professional journals. Memberships: Korean Medical Association; Korean Association of Internal Medicine; Korean Academy of Tuberculosis and Respiratory Diseases; Korean Academy of Asthma, Allergy and Clinical Immunology; Korean Association for the Study of Lung Cancer; American Thoracic Society. Address: Division of Pulmonology and Allergology, Department of Internal Medicine, Chonbuk National University Hospital, Geumam 2-dong, Deokjin-gu, Jeonju, Jeonbuk 561-712, Republic of Korea. E-mail: mkhmd@jbnu.ac.kr

MIN Kyung Hwan, b. 2 May 1981, Hae-nam Gum, Cheon-nam, Republic of Korea. Education: BA, Civil and Environmental Engineering, 2005, MS, Structural Engineering, 2007, PhD, Structural Engineering, in progress, Korea University. Appointments: Researcher, High Performance Concrete Laboratory, 2005-07, Senior Researcher, FCP Composites and Structural Laboratory, 2007-, Korea University. Memberships: Korea Concrete Institute; Korea Institute for Structural Maintenance Inspection; Korean Society of Civil Engineers; Korean Tunnelling and Underground Space Association. Address: School of Civil, Environmental and Architectural Engineering, Korea University, 5ka-1, Anam-dong, Seongbuk-gu, Seoul 136-701, Republic of Korea.

MINA Fayez Mourad, b. 29 July 1940, Sohag, Egypt. University Professor. m. Theresa Nabih Abdo, 1 son, 1 daughter. Education: BSc, Mathematics and Education, 1964, Special Diploma in Education, 1969, MA, Education, 1973, Faculty of Education, Ain Shams University, Egypt; PhD, University of London, Institute of Education, 1978. Appointments: Mathematics Teacher, 1964-72, Demonstrator and Assistant Lecturer, 1972-78, Lecturer, 1978-83, Associate Professor, 1988-89, Professor, 1989-2000, Emeritus Professor, 2000-, Faculty of Education, Ain Shams University, Egypt; Assistant Professor, 1983-84, Associate Professor, 1984-88, University of Bahrain. Publications: More than 150 publications including books, articles, studies, conference papers and researches (individually and jointly) in the areas of curriculum, mathematics education, comparative education, teacher education, sociology of education, adult education, research methodology and futurology. Honours: The State Prize in Education, Egypt, 1983; Medal of Science and Arts of the First Degree, Egypt, 1985; The Recognition Award Fellowship, Project Milestones, Columbia University, 1992. Memberships: Fellow Institute of Mathematics and its Applications; Elected Member, International Statistical Institute; Board Member, WCCI, 1984-98; Vice-President, ECCI. Address: Faculty of Education, Ain Shams University, Roxy, Heliopolis, Cairo, Egypt. E-mail: fmmina@link.com.eg

MINDE Jan, b. 27 February 1954, Gällivare, Sweden. Senior Orthopedic Consultant. m. Anita Stöckel, 2 sons, 1 daughter. Education: Med kand, Practice Medicine, Uppsala University, 1973-76; Medicine licentiate, Karolinska Institute, 1976-79; MD, PhD, Medicine, Orthopedic Surgery, University of Umea, 2000-06; MD, Medicine, Mayo Medical School, 2007. Appointments: General Junior Doctor, Boden Hospital, 1983-89; Resident Doctor, Orthopedic Surgeon, Orthopedic Surgery, Gallivare Hospital, 1983-89; Senior Orthopedic Consultant, Gallivare Hospital, 1982-; Visiting Clinician, Mayo Clinic, Rochester, USA, 2007; Senior Orthopedic Consultant, Harstads Hospital, Norway, 2000-06; Senior Orthopedic Consultant, Torshavn, Faero Islands, 2005. Publications: Numerous articles in professional journals; 1 patent. Honours: Listed in biographical dictionaries;

Neuroscience Award, J Tempelton Foundation, Pennsylvania University, USA, 2011. Address: Skogssnavav 7, SE-98235 Gällivare, Sweden. E-mail: janminde@gmail.com

MINH Hoang-Ngoc, b. 29 July 1929, Vietnam. Doctor of Medicine. m. Nguyen Thi Long, 2 sons, 2 daughters. Education: MD, 1958, Postgraduate Training Residency, Johns Hopkins, MD, USA, 1958-60. Appointments: Chief, Department Gynaeco-Surgical Tu Du Hospital, Saigon, Vietnam, 1965; Assistant Professor, Saigon Faculty of Medicine, 1968; Associated Professor, CHU Amiens, France, 1971. Publications: 280 publications. Memberships: President, French Society of Gynaecology, 1996-98; General Secretary of French Society of Gynaeco-Pathology; Vice President, European Society of Gynaecology, 2001-2003; Life Member, American Society for Reproductive Medicine, Senior Member: ICGS, ISGYP, New York Academy of Sciences. Address: 4 Rue Eugene Delacroix, 94410 Saint Maurice, France.

MINNELLI Liza May, b. 12 Mar 1946, Los Angeles, California, USA. Singer; Actress; Dancer. m. Peter Allen, 1967 (divorced), (2) Jack Haley Jr, 1974 (divorced), (3) Mark Gero, 1979 (divorced), (4) David Gest, 2002 (divorced). Career: Singer and entertainer, stage, film and television; Major appearances include: Best Foot Forward (off-Broadway), 1963; Touring productions: Carnival; The Pajama Game; The Fantasticks; Performed with mother (Judy Garland), London Palladium, 1964; Broadway debut, Flora And The Red Menace, 1965; The Act, 1977; The Rink, 1984; The Ultimate Event, international tour with Frank Sinatra, Sammy Davis Jr, 1988; Film appearances: Charlie Bubbles, 1967; The Sterile Cuckoo, 1969; Cabaret, 1972; Tell Me That You Love Me Junie Moon, 1974; Lucky Lady, 1975; A Matter Of Time, 1976; Silent Movie, 1976; New York, New York, 1977; Arthur, 1981; Arthur 2 - On The Rocks, 1988; Stepping Out, 1991; Television appearances include: Liza With A 'Z', 1972; Goldie And Liza Together, 1980; Baryshnikov On Broadway, 1980; The Princess And The Pea; Showtime, 1983; A Time To Live, 1985; Sam Found Out, 1988. Recordings: Albums include: Liza! Liza!, 1964; It Amazes Me, 1965; There Is A Time, 1966; New Feelin', 1970; Liza With A 'Z', 1972; Liza Minnelli The Singer, 1973; Live At The Winter Garden, 1974; Lucky Lady, 1976; Tropical Nights, 1977; Live At Carnegie Hall, 1987; Live From Radio City Music Hall, 1992; Film and stage soundtracks: Best Foot Forward, 1963; Dangerous Christmas Of Red Riding Hood, 1965; Flora And The Red Menace, 1965; Cabaret, 1972; with Judy Garland: Live At The London Palladium, 1964; with Pet Shop Boys: Results, 1989; Liza, 1994; Gently, 1996; Rink (oringinal Broadway cast), 1999. Single: Losing My Mind, with Pet Shop Boys, (first UK chart entry), 1989. Honours: Promising Personality Award, 1963; 2 Tony Awards, Best Foot Forward, 1965, The Act, 1977; Academy Award Nomination, 1969; Oscar, Best Actress, Cabaret, 1972; Emmy Award, Lisa With A 'Z', 1972; Golden Globe Award, Best Actress, A Time To Live, 1985. Current Management: Krost/Chapin Management, Penthouse 1, 9911 West Pico Blvd, Los Angeles, CA 90035, USA.

MINOGUE Kylie (Ann), b. 28 May 1968, Melbourne, Victoria, Australia. Singer; Actress. Career: Actress, Australian television dramas: Skyways, 1980; The Sullivans, 1981; The Henderson Kids, 1984-85; Neighbours, 1986-88; Film appearances: The Delinquents, 1989; Streetfighter, 1994; BioDome, 1995; Cut, 2000; Sample People, 2000; As singer, biggest selling single of decade in Australia, Locomotion, 1987; Highest UK chart entry for female artist, Locomotion, 1988; Highest debut album chart entry, Australia, UK, Kylie, 1988; First ever artist with 4 Top 3 singles from an album; First female artist with first 5 singles to recieve Silver discs; Performances include: Australian Royal Bicentennial Concert, 1988; John Lennon tribute, Liverpool, 1990; Cesne Music Festival, Turkey, 1992; Sydney Gay Mardi Gras, 1994, 1998; Prince's Trust Concert, 1994; T In The Park Festival, Glasgow, 1995; Tours of UK, Europe, Asia, and Australia. Recordings: Albums: Kylie, 1988; Enjoy Yourself, 1989; Rhythm Of Love, 1990; Let's Get To It, 1991; Kylie - Greatest Hits, 1992; Kylie Minogue, 1994; Impossible Princess, 1997; Light Years, 2000; Fever, 2001; Body Language, 2003; X, 2007; Aphrodite, 2010. Singles include: Locomotion, 1987; I Should Be So Lucky, 1988; Je Ne Sais Pas Pourquoi, 1988; Especially For You, with Jason Donovan, 1988; Never Too Late, 1989; Confide In Me, 1994; Put Yourself In My Place, 1995; Where Is The Feeling, 1995; Where The Wild Roses Grow (duet with Nick Cave), 1995; Some Kind Of Bliss, 1997; Did It Again, 1997; Breathe, Cowboy Style, 1998; Spinning Around, On a Night Like This, Please Stay, 2000; Your Disco Needs You, Can't Get You Out of My Head, 2001; In Your Eyes, Love at First Sight, Come into My World, 2002; Slow, 2003; Red Blooded Woman, Chocolate, I Believe in You, 2004; Giving You Up, 2005; 2 Hearts, 2007; Wow, In My Arms, All I See, The One, 2008; All the Lovers, Get Outta My Way, Better Than Today, 2010; Put Your Hands Up, 2011; Timebomb, Flower, On a Night Like This, 2012. Honours: Numerous Platinum, Gold and Silver discs; 6 Logies (Australia); 6 Music Week Awards (UK); 3 Smash Hits Awards (UK); 3 Australian Record Industry Association Awards; 3 Japanese Music Awards; Irish Record Industry Award; Canadian Record Industry Award; World Music Award; Australian Variety Club Award; MO Award (Australian Showbusiness); Amplex Golden Reel Award; Diamond Award, (Belgium); Woman of the Decade (UK); MTV Video of the Year, Did It Again, 1998; 25 Top Ten singles worldwide. Address: c/o Terry Blamey Management, PO Box 13196, London SW64WF, England.

MINOGUE Valerie Pearson, b. 26 April 1931, Llanelli, South Wales. Professor Emeritus. m. Kenneth Robert Minogue, 16 June 1954, separated 1978, divorced 2001, 1 son, 1 daughter. Education: BA, 1952, MLitt, 1956, Girton College, Cambridge. Appointments: Assistant Lecturer, University College, Cardiff, Wales, 1952-53; Contributor, Cambridge Italian Dictionary, 1956-61; Lecturer, 1963-74, Senior Lecturer, 1975-81, French Department, Queen Mary, London University, England; Professor, 1981-88, Research Professor, 1988-96, Professor Emeritus, 1996-, Swansea University. Publications: Proust: Du Côté de chez Swann, 1973; Nathalie Sarraute: The War of the Words, 1981; Zola: L'Assommoir, 1991; Eight texts, Pléiade Oeuvres complètes of Nathalie Sarraute (co-editor, with notes and critical essays), 1996. Contributions to: Romance Studies, Editor, 1982-98, General Editor, 1998-2004; Quadrant; Literary Review; Modern Language Review; French Studies; Romance Studies; Forum for Modern Language Studies; New Novel Review; Revue des Sciences Humaines; The Times; Times Literary Supplement; Esprit Créateur; Theatre Research International, Roman 20-50; Numerous chapters in books. Honours: Listed in international biographical dictionaries. Memberships: Modern Humanities Research Association; Society for French Studies; Institute of Germanic and Romance Studies; Emile Zola Society (President, 2005-); Société des Dix-Neuviémistes; The Art Fund; Friends of the Royal Academy; Friends of Wigmore Hall; Friends of the Victoria and Albert Museum. Address: 23 Richford Street, London, W6 7HJ, England.

DICTIONARY OF INTERNATIONAL BIOGRAPHY 36th EDITION

MIR Mohammad Afzal, b. 6 May 1936, Kashmir. Physician. m. Lynda, 1 son, 2 daughters. Education: MBBS, 1962; DCH, 1965; MRCP, 1972; FRCP, 1985. Appointments: Senior House Officer, Alder Hey Children's Hospital, Liverpool; Medical Registrar, North Ormesby Hospital, Middlesborough; Resident Medical Officer, Queen Mary's Hospital, Sidcup; Medical Registrar, Manchester Royal Infirmary; Senior Medical Registrar, Manchester Royal Infirmary; Senior Lecturer and Consultant Physician, University of Wales, College of Medicine. Publications: Numerous papers in acute leukaemia, metabolic disorders, sodium transport and obesity; 10 books on basic clinical skills, PLAB and MRCP; 38 video tapes on basic clinical skills. Honours: Young Research Investigator's Award, British Cardiac Society, 1976; British Heart Foundation, European Travelling Fellowship, 1977. Memberships: British Cardiac Society; British Diabetic Association; British Hypertension Society; Medical Research Society; British Hyperlipidaemia Association. E-mail: afzal.mir@virgin.net

MIRCI Liviu-Eduard, b. 19 March 1942, Timisoara, Romania. Divorced, 1 daughter. Education: MSc, Chemical Engineer, Politehnica Timisoara, 1964. Appointments: Assistant Professor, Lecturer, Associate Professor, Full Professor, Faculty of Chemical Engineering, Politehnica Timisoara, 1964-. Publications: Books in the field of rubber technology, lacquers and varnishes; Numerous articles in professional journals. Memberships: American Chemical Society; Romanian Chemical Society. Address: Pta Rusel No 4, Sc B, Ap 7, 300056 Timisoara, Romania.

MIRONENKO Vladimir Ivanovich, b. 9 February 1942, Bych, Belarus. Mathematician. m. Svetlana Tarasevich, 1 son, 1 daughter. Education: Candidate of Science, Belorussian University, Minsk, USSR, 1970; Professor, Gomel State University, Gomel, 1992. Appointments: Postgraduate, 1965-67, Researcher, 1968-70, Assistant Professor, 1970-75, Belgos University, Minsk; Head, Sub-Faculty, 1975-2010, Professor, 2010-, Gomel State University. Publications: Books: Linear dependence of functions along solutions of DE, 1981; Reflecting Function and Periodic Solutions of DE, 1986; Reflecting Function and Investigation of Multidimensional DE Systems, 2004. Memberships: Mathematics Society of Belarus. Address: Gomel State University, Sovetskaya 104, Gomel 246699, Belarus. E-mail: vmironenko@tut.by

MIRREN Dame Helen, b. 26 July 1945, London, England. Actress. m. Taylor Hackford, 1997. Creative Works: Theatre include: The Faith Healer, Royal Court, 1981; Antony & Cleopatra, 1983, 1998; The Roaring Girl, RSC, Barbican, 1983; Extremities, 1984; Madame Bovary, 1987; Two Way Mirror, 1989; Sex Please, We're Italian, Young Vic, 1991; The Writing Game, New Haven, Connecticut, 1993; The Gift of the Gorgon, NY, 1994; A Month in the Country, 1994; Orpheus Descending, 2001; Dance of Death, New York, 2001; Mourning Becomes Electra, 2003; Phedre, 2009; Films include: Age of Consent, 1969; Savage Messiah, O Lucky Man!, 1973; Caligula, 1977; The Long Good Friday, Excalibur, 1981; Cal, 1984; 2010, 1985; Heavenly Pursuits, 1986; The Mosquito Coast, 1987; Pascali's Island, 1988; When the Whales Came, 1988; Bethune: The Making of a Hero, 1989; The Cook, the Thief, his Wife and her Lover, 1989; The Comfort of Strangers, 1989; Where Angels Fear to Tread, 1990; The Hawk, The Prince of Jutland, 1991; The Madness of King George, 1995; Some Mother's Son, 1996; Killing Mrs Tingle, 1998; The Pledge, 2000; No Such Thing, 2001; Greenfingery, 2001; Gosford Park, 2001; Calendar Girls, 2003; The Clearing, 2004; Raising Helen, 2004; The Hitchiker's Guide to the Galaxy (voice), 2005; Shadowboxer, 2005; The Queen, 2006; National Treasure: Book of Secrets, 2007; Inkheart, 2008; State of Play, 2009; The Last Station, 2009; Love Ranch, The Tempest, Brighton Rock, RED, Legend of the Guardians: The Owls of Ga'Hoole, 2010; Arthur, The Debt, 2011; The Door, Hitchcock, 2012; Monsters University, RED 2, 2013; TV include: Miss Julie; The Apple Cart; The Little Minister; As You Like It; Mrs Reinhardt; Soft Targets, 1982; Blue Remembered Hills; Coming Through; Cause Celebre; Red King, White Knight; Prime Suspect, 1991; Prime Suspect II, 1992; Prime Suspect III, 1993; Prime Suspect IV: Scent of Darkness, 1996; Prime Suspect V: Errors of Judgement, 1996; Painted Lady, 1997; The Passion of Ayn Rand, 1998; Prime Suspect VI: The Last Witness, 2003; Elizabeth I, 2005; Prime Suspect: The Final Act, 2006; Glee, 2012. Honours include: BAFTA Award, 1991; Emmy Award, 1996; Screen Actor's Guild Award for Best Supporting Actress, 2001; Screen Actor's Guild Award for Best Supporting Actress, 2002; DBE, 2003; BAFTA, The Queen, 2007; Broadcast Film Critics Association Awards, Best Actress, The Queen, 2007; Oscar, Best Performance by an Actress in a Leading Role for The Queen, 2007; Star on the Hollywood Walk of Fame, 2013. Address: c/o Ken McReddie Ltd, 91 Regent Street, London W1R 7TB, England.

MIRZA Qamar, b. 19 March 1927, Ferozepur, India. Librarian. Education: BA, 1947; Certificate in LSc, 1951; Registration Exam Library Association, London, 1953-54; Masters degree in LSc, 1968-69. Appointments: Assistant Librarian, Northumberland County Library, 1954-62; Deputy Librarian, University of Peshawar, Pakistan, Teacher at Department of LSc, 1962-68, 1971-74; Graduate Librarian, Western Institute of Technology, Australia, 1975-76; Librarian, Umm Al-Qura University, Makkah, Saudi Arabia, 1977-98. Publications: Perspective of Past, Present and Future of L-Services in the University of Peshawar, in Pakistan Librarianship, 1963-64; Islamic Subject Headings in LC Subject Headings, 1992. Honours: Beta Phi Mu. Memberships: Life Member, Pakistan Library Association; Former Associate Library and Information Association of Australia. Address: 17/46 Wahdat Colony, Disposal Road, Gujranwala, Pakistan.

MIRZOEFF Edward, b. 11 April 1936, London, England. Television Producer. m. Judith Topper, 3 sons. Education: MA (Oxon), Open Scholarship in Modern History, The Queen's College, Oxford. Appointments: Market Researcher, Social Surveys (Gallup Poll) Ltd, 1959-58; Public Relations Executive, Duncan McLeish and Associates, 1960-61; Assistant Editor, Shoppers' Guide, 1961-63; BBC Television, 1963-2000; Executive Producer, Documentaries, 1983-2000; Freelance TV Producer, Director, 2000-; Director and Producer of many film documentaries including: Metro-land, 1973; A Passion for Churches, 1974; The Queen's Realm: A Prospect of England, 1977; The Front Garden, 1977; The Ritz, 1981; The Englishwoman and the Horse, 1981; Elizabeth R, 1992; Torvill and Dean: Facing the Music, 1994; Treasures in Trust, 1995; John Betjeman - The Last Laugh, 2001; Series Editor: Bird's-Eye View, 1969-71; Year of the French, 1982-83; In at the Deep End, 1983-84; Just Another Day, 1983-85; Editor, 40 Minutes, 1985-89; Executive Producer of many documentary series including: The House, 1992, Full Circle with Michael Palin, 1997; The 50 Years War: Israel and the Arabs, 1998; Children's Hospital, 1998-99; Queen Elizabeth The Queen Mother, 2002; The Lords'Tale, 2003; A Very English Village, 2005. Honours: CVO, 1993; CBE, 1997; BAFTA Award for Best Documentary, 1981; BAFTA Awards for Best Factual Series, 1985, 1989; BFI TV Award, 1988; Samuelson Award, Birmingham Festival, 1988; British Video

Award, 1993; BAFTA Alan Clarke Award for Outstanding Creative Contribution to Television, 1995; International EMMY, 1996; Royal Philharmonic Society Music Award, 1996; British Press Guild Award for Best Documentary Series, 1996. Memberships: Vice-Chairman TV, 1991-95, Chairman, 1995-97, Trustee, 1999-, British Academy of Film and Television Arts (BAFTA); Trustee, 1999-, Vice Chair, 2000-02, Chair, 2002-06, Grierson Trust; Board Member, Director's and Producer's Rights Society, 1999-; Salisbury Cathedral Council, 2002-. Address: 9 Westmoreland Road, London, SW13 9RZ, England.

MISHRA Ajay Kumar, b. 8 January 1976, Varanasi UP, India. Associate Professor. m. Shivani, 2 daughters. Education: BSc, MSc, UP College, Varanasi; M Phil, PhD, University of Delhi. Appointments: Postdoctoral Fellow, University of Free State, South Africa, 2006-08; Postdoctoral Fellow, 2008-09, Senior Lecturer, 2009-11, Associate Professor, 2011-, University of Johannesburg, South Africa. Publications: 52 international research papers; 25 book chapters; 7 books; many keynote invited lectures and conference attendance. Honours: AVI Award, 2009; IAAM Scientist Award, 2011; AML Medal, 2011. Memberships: ACS Nano Society; SACI; ACS; CoESM; IAAM; ICS. Address: R No 3208, Department of Chemical Technology, University of Johannesburg, PO Box 17011, Doornfontein 2028, South Africa. E-mail: qmishra@uj.ac.za

MISHRA Subhash, b. 31 December 1958, Manendragarh, CG, India. Eye Specialist. m. Sarita, 1 daughter. Education: MBBS, 1980, DOMS, 1983, Jabalpur University; MS, 1990, LLB, 1994, Ravishankar University. Appointments: Programme Officer, National Programme for Control of Blindness at Kanker, Bastar, 1983-88; Resident Surgeon, Medical College, Raipur, 1988-91; Medical Officer, Deeken, 1991-92; Eye Specialist and Chief Eye Surgeon, Central Eye Mobile Unit, Medical College, Raipur, 1993-. Publications: Various articles, booklets and materials for educating people about common eye diseases, eye donation, and ocular rhinosporodiosis. Honours: Bharat Jyoti Award; Dr J L Arya Award; Highest operation in Motia Mukt Raipur; Honour for maximum lens implants; Honoured for highest eye operation in State. Memberships: All India Ophthalmological Society; Chhattisgarh State Ophthalmological Society; Raipur Divisional Ophthalmological Society; Lions Club of Kanker. Address: Aminpara, Purani Basti, opposite Police Station, Raipur, Chhattisgarh, India. E-mail: drsubhashm@yahoo.com

MITCHELL David John, b. 24 January 1924, London, England. Writer. m. 1955, 1 son. Education: Bradfield College, Berkshire; MA, Honours, Modern History, Trinity College, Oxford, 1947. Appointment: Staff Writer, Picture Post, 1947-52. Publications: Women on the Warpath, 1966; The Fighting Pankhursts, 1967; 1919 Red Mirage, 1970; Pirates, 1976; Queen Christabel, 1977; The Jesuits: A History, 1980; The Spanish Civil War, 1982; Travellers in Spain, 1990; The Spanish Attraction, editor, 2001. Contributions to: Newspapers and magazines. Honours: Civil List Pension for services to Literature. Membership: Society of Authors. Address: 20 Mountacre Close, Sydenham Hill, London SE26 6SX, England.

MITCHELL Enid G D, b. London, England. Sculptor; Ceramist. 1 son, 2 daughters. Education: The Lady Eleanor Holles School; Intermediate Arts and Crafts, Ealing School of Art, 1947-50; Study of Sculpture with Robert Thomas FRBS, ARCA, Ealing School of Art, 1964-68; Visual Arts Diploma, London University (Extra Mural), 1967-71; Diploma in Art and Design with Merit, Ceramics, Chelsea School of Art, 1976-79. Career: Independent Sculptor and Ceramist; Exhibitions: Regular exhibitor, Society of Portrait Sculptors, 1967-78; Exhibitor, Royal Society of British Sculptors, 1974-; RBS Exhibitions include: Scone Palace, Scotland; Taliesin Centre, Swansea University; Work in permanent collection, Leamington Spa Museum and various schools; Work in private collections in England, Eire, Israel, Holland, Australia, Brunei (ceramics), USA and Wales. Honour: Gilchrist Prize, London University, 1971. Memberships: Society of Portrait Sculptors, 1967-78; Associate, 1974, Fellow, 1983, Royal Society of British Sculptors. Address: Medmenham 2, 32 Stanier Street, Swindon, Wiltshire SN1 5QX, England.

MITCHELL George John, b. 20 August 1933, Waterville, USA. Politician; Lawyer. 1 daughter. Appointments: Called to Bar, 1960; Trial Attorney, US Department of Justice, Washington, 1960-62; Executive Assistant to Senator Edmund Muskie, 1962-65; Partner, Jensen & Baird, Portland, 1965-77; US Attorney for Maine, 1977-79; US District Judge, 1979-80; US Senator from Maine, 1980-85; Majority Leader, US Senate, 1988-95; Special Advisor to President Clinton for Economic Initiatives in Ireland, 1995; Chancellor designate, Queen's University, Belfast, 1999; Adviser, Thames Water, 1999; Chairman, The Walt Disney Company, 2004-2007; United States Special Envoy for the Middle East, 2009- . Publications: Great American Lighthouses, 1989; World on Fire, 1991; Not For America Alone, 1997; Making Peace, 2000. Memberships: Chair, Maine Democratic Committee, 1966-68; Member, National Committee, Maine, 1968-77; Chair, Committee on Northern Ireland, 1995. Honours: Hon LLD, Queens University, Belfast, 1997; Honorary KBE, 1999; Shared, Honphouet-Boigny Peace Prize, 1999; Presidential Medal of Freedom, 1999; Tipperary International Peace Award, 2000. Address: c/o Verner, Liipfert, Bernhard, 901 15th Street, NW, #700, Washington, DC 20005, USA.

MITCHELL Julian, b. 1 May 1935, Epping, Essex, England. Author; Dramatist. Education: BA, Wadham College, Oxford, 1958. Appointment: Midshipman, Royal Naval Volunteer Reserve, 1953-55. Publications: Imaginary Toys, 1961; A Disturbing Influence, 1962; As Far as You Can Go, 1963; The White Father, 1964; A Heritage and Its History (play), 1965; A Family and a Fortune (play), 1966; A Circle of Friends, 1966; The Undiscovered Country, 1968; Jennie Lady Randolph Churchill: A Portrait with Letters (with Peregrine Churchill), 1974; Half-Life (play), 1977; Another Country (play), 1982, (film), 1984; Francis (play), 1983; After Aida (play), 1985; Falling Over England (play), 1994; August (adaptation of Uncle Vanya) (play), 1994, (film), 1995; Wilde (film script), 1997; Consenting Adults (TV play), 2007; The Good Soldier (play), 2010; The Wye Tour and its Artists, 2010; Family Business (play), 2011. Contributions to: Welsh History Review; Monmouthshire Antiquary; Gwent County History, 2009. Honours: Scottish BAFTA Award, 2007; FRSL; FSA; Listed in various international biographical dictionaries. Address: 11 St Tysoi Close, Llansoy, Usk, NP15 1EF, Wales.

MITCHINER John Edward, b. 12 September 1951. HM Diplomatic Service (retired). m. Elizabeth Mary Ford, 1983. Education: John Fisher School, Purley; Beaumont College, Old Windsor; BA, Bristol University, 1972; MA, 1973, PhD, 1977, School of Oriental and African Studies, London University. Appointments: ACU Research Fellow, Visva Bharati University, Santiniketan, 1977-78; Bipradas Palchaudhuri Fellow, Calcutta University, 1978-79; Joined FCO, 1980; Third, later Second Secretary (Information), Istanbul, 1982-85; FCO, 1985-87; Second Secretary (Develt), New Delhi, 1987-91; Second, later First Secretary (Political), Berne, 1991-95; Head, Japan Section, FCO,

1995-96; Ambassador to Armenia, 1997-99; Deputy High Commissioner, Kolkata, India, 2000-03; High Commissioner to Sierra Leone and Ambassador (non-resident) to Liberia, 2003-06. Publications: Studies in the Indus Valley Inscriptions, 1978; Traditions of the Seven Rsis, 1982, 2nd edition 2000; The Yuga Purana, 1986, 2nd edition 2002; Guru: the search for enlightenment, 1992; Contributions to learned journals. Memberships: Royal Commonwealth Society. Address: Bower Farm, Whitland, SA34 0QX, Wales.

MITCHINER Michael Bernard, b. 8 February 1938, Croydon, England. Medical Practitioner. m. Rosaleen Mary, 2 sons, 2 daughters. Education: St George's College, Weybridge, Surrey; Guy's Hospital Medical School, London, 1957-64; BSc, Physiology, 1961, MBBS, 1964, PhD, Pathology, 1969, London University; LRCP, MRCS, 1964. Appointments: House Physician and House Surgeon, Royal Surrey County Hospital, Guildford, 1964-65; University Lecturer in Pathology, Guy's Hospital Medical School, London University, 1965-71; General Medical Practitioner, Sanderstead, 1971-92; Medical and numismatic work, India, 1992, 1993; General Practice, England and abroad, 1993-2009. Publications: A car journey across Asia, 1964; Articles in professional medical journals; Numerous books and articles on coinage and history. Honours: Harris Prize for Anatomy, 1960; Wooldridge Prize for Physiology, 1960; First Prize for Proficiency, 1960; Lubbock Prize Certificate of Honour for Clinical Pathology, 1962; Nuffield Foundation Travelling Scholarship to Hong Kong University, 1963. Memberships: British Medical Association; Royal Society of Medicine; Royal Numismatic Society; Royal Asiatic Society; British Numismatic Society.

MITKOVIC Milorad, b. 7 June 1950, Lebane, Serbia. Orthopaedic Surgeon. m. Gordana, 1 son, 1 daughter. Education: MD, Medical Faculty, 1976, Master of Multidisciplinary Science, 1984, University of Belgrade; PhD, Medical Faculty, University of Nis, 1987; Orthopaedic Surgery Researcher; Hammersmith Hospital, London, England, 1983, 1984, 1988; General Hospital, Cambridge, 1984; Erasme l'hopital, Brussels, Belgium, 1985; Uni-Clinic, Ulm, Germany, 1986; John Radcliff Hospital, Oxford, England, 1987; Institute of Traumatology and Orthopaedics, Moscow, Russia, 1988; Institute of Traumatology, Riga, 1989; AO Institute, Davos, Switzerland, 1997, 1998, 2000, 2002, 2004; University Trauma and Orthopaedic Clinic, Tuebingen, Germany, 2001; University Trauma and Orthopaedic Clinic, Hannover, Germany, 2001; Department of Orthopaedic, School of Medicine, Kyungpook National University, 2002, 2009. Appointments: GP, Leskovac, 1974-78; Orthopaedic clinic, Clinical Centre, 1978-82, Associate Professor, 1990-96, Professor of Surgery, 1996-, Medical Faculty, University of Nis; Director, University Orthopaedic and Traumatology Clinic, Nis, 1994-; Founder and Chief, Orthopaedic Clinic, Al-Salam Hospital, Kuwait, 1995-2008; Chief, Orthopaedic Department, Institute of Niska Banja, 1996-2001; Visiting Professor, AO Orthopaedic Institute, Davos, Switzerland, 1998, 2004. Publications: Over 390 articles in professional journals; Inventor, 44 inventions, including Mitkovic exernal in internal fixation systems. Honours: 20 national and international rewards for inventions and introducing new concept in orthopaedic surgery including: 1st Prize, World Inventions Exhibition, Brussels, 1990; 1st Prize, Nikola Tesla, 1996; 1st Prize, Mihajlo Pupun, 1994; 1st Prize for invention, Yugoslavia, 1989; Gold Medal, Riga's Traumatology Institute, 1988; Gold Plaque, Clinical Centre, Nis; Man of the Year in Medicine and Healthcare, 2010. Address: Bulevar Nemanjica 67/18, 18000 Nis, Serbia. E-mail: mikovic@gmail.com Website: www.mitkovic.net

MITROVIĆ R Ljubiša, b. 16 February 1943, Mokra, Bela Palanka, Serbia. Sociologist; Professor. m. Svetlana, 2 daughters. Education: Graduate, Sociology, Faculty of Philosophy, University of Belgrade, 1970; Master's Degree, Political Sciences, University of Belgrade, 1975; PhD, Sociological Sciences (General Sociology), University of Niš, 1977. Appointments include: Assistant Teacher, Faculty of Philosophy, 1971, Dean of the Faculty of Philosophy, 1983-87, Full-time Professor, Faculty of Philosophy, 1987, Vice-Rector, 1987-89, University of Niš; Director, several microproject dealing with regional and cultural co-operation in the Balkans, identity of the Balkan nations, interethnic relationships and the culture of peace, 1996-; Professor, by invitation, World University Association "Plato", Greece, 2001; Director, Centre for Balkan Studies, 2002-; Writer of poetry. Publications: 40 books; Over 400 papers and articles; Most recent books: Balkan Crossroads and Alternatives, 2006; The Balkans in the Maelstrom of Transition, 2006; Geoculture of Development, Identities and the Culture of Peace, 2007; The Contemporary Balkans and Geopolitics, 2008; The Makers of New Paradigms in Sociology, 2008; Homoturisticus and the Culture of Peace, 2009; Transition into Peripheral Capitalism, 2009; Hono Religiosus and the Culture of Peace, 2009; The Development Geoculture of the Balkans and Contemporary Sociology, 2011; 17 volumes of poetry: New Barbarians, 2000; Orpheus under the Suva Mountain, 2001; Fires of Disquiet, 2002; From the Garden of Niketas of Remesiana, 2003; Archipelago of Memories, 2004; Home Country Garland, 2004; Under the Sokolica – Lyric Recollections on the Despot and Manasija, 2004; Flight over the Suva Mountain, 2005; Terror of a Big Beast, 2005; Space Nomads, 2005; Dance of the White Horses, 2005; Far Away, Deep Down, 2007; Charm of Unknown Coasts, 2007; Poems Choose Poets, 2008; The Gifst of Hypnos, 2009; The Midnight Weaver, 2010; Between Self and Everything, 2011; Through Prayer to Stars, 2011; Some scientific and literary works translated into English, French, Bulgarian and Macedonian. Honours: October Prize of the City of Niš, 1987; University Rewards, 1985, 1987; Medal for Deserving Citizens of the Socialist Federative Republic of Yugoslavia, 1988; Listed in international biographical dictionaries. Memberships: Sociological Association of Serbia; Association for Political Sciences of Serbia; Centre for Balkan Studies; Writers' Association of Serbia. Address: Oblačića Rada 24/4, 18000 Niš, Serbia.

MITTAL Vinod A, b. 8 August 1950, Mumbai, India. Orthopaedic Surgeon. m. Bharati, 2 sons. Education: Bachelor of Medicine, Bachelor of Surgery, 1975, Master of Surgery (Orthopaedics), 1979, Bombay University; Diploma, Psychological Counselling, Institute of Health Care Administration, Madras, 1993. Appointments: Resident, Assistant Medical Officer, King Edward Memorial Hospital, Bombay, 1975-81; Orthopaedic Registrar, All India Institute of Physical Medicine and Rehabilitation, Bombay, 1981-83; Orthopaedic Specialist, General Hospital, Kuala Lumpur, Malaysia, 1983-84; Orthopaedic Specialist and Unit Head, ESIS Hospitals, Bombay, 1985-98; Self employed, 1998-2001; Medical Interpreter, Cambridge Health Alliance, Cambridge, Massachusetts, USA, 2001-. Publications: Book, Low Back Pain and Low Back Care; Numerous articles in professional journals. Honours: Bombay Orthopaedic Society Travelling Fellowship, 1982; Indian Orthopaedic Association Travelling Fellowship, 1991; Distinguished Scientist, 1991. Memberships: Bombay Orthopaedic Society; Indian Orthopaedic Association; International Medical Interpreters Association. Address: 5 Sunrise, 3rd Pasta Lane, Colaba, Mumbai 400005, India. E-mail: drvinodmittal@yahoo.com

MIURA Kimihisa, b. 23 January 1948, Japan. Engineering Educator; Researcher. m. Masako, 1 son, 1 daughter. Education: PhD, Engineering, Akita University, 1997. Appointments: Technician, 1972-92, Associate Research, 1992-98, Lecturer, 1998-2002, Associate Professor, 2002-, Akita University. Honours: Yamazaki Award, 2001. Memberships: Japan Society of Mechanical Engineers; Japanese Society for Non-Destructive Inspection; Society of Materials Engineering for Resources of Japan. Address: Department of Mechanical Engineering, Faculty of Engineering and Resource Science, Akita University, 1-1, Tegata-Gakuen-Cho, Akita, 010-8502, Japan. E-mail: kmiura@ipc.akita-u.ac.jp

MIYACHI Iwao, b. 27 September 1916, Kochi, Japan. Professor of Engineering. m. Kazuko Nagano, 2 daughters. Education: Bachelor in Engineering, 1940, Doctor in Engineering, 1953, University of Tokyo. Appointments: Lecturer, 1940, Professor, 1957, Nagoya University; Professor, 1980, Guest Professor, 1989, Aichi Institute of Technology. Publications: Articles for Institute of Electrical Engineers, Japan, on Power Transmission and Distribution, Electrical Power Engineering, Electrical Power Generation. Honours: Meritorious Contribution Award and four others, Institute of Electrical Engineers, Japan, 1968-90; Officier des Palmes Académiques, France, 1975; Second Order of National Merits, Japan, 1990. Memberships: SEE, France, 1960-; Honorary Member, Institute of Electrical Engineers of Japan, 1986; Distinguished Member, Conférence Internationale des Grands Réseaux Electriques, 1996. Address: 3-6-5 Nishizaki-cho, Chikusa, Nagoya 464-0825, Japan.

MIYAKE Issey, b. 22 April 1939, Tokyo, Japan. Fashion Designer. Education: Tama Art University; Tokyo and La Chambre Syndicale de la Couture Parisienne, Paris. Appointments: Assistant Designer to Guy Laroche, Paris, 1966-68, to Hubert de Givenchy, Paris, 1968-69; Designer, Geoffrey Beene (ready-to-wear firm), New York, 1969-70; Founder, Miyake Design Studio, Tokyo, 1970; Director, Issey Miyake International, Issey Miyake and Associates, Issey Miyake Europe, Issey Miyake USA, Issey Miyake On Limits, Tokyo; Executive Advisor, Planner, First Japan Culture Conference, Yokohama, 1980. Creative Works: Works exhibited in Paris, Tokyo and MIT, appears in collections of Metro Museum of Art, New York and Victoria and Albert Museum, London. Honours: Japan Fashion Editors Club Awards, 1974, 1976; Mainichi Design Prize, 1977; Pratt Institute Award, New York, 1979; Dr.h.c. Royal College of Art, 1993.

MIYAN M Alimullah, b. 15 February 1942, Comilla, Bangladesh. Vice-Chancellor. m. Selina Nargis, 1 son. Education: B Com (Hons), 1962, M Com, 1963, Dhaka University, Bangladesh; MBA, Indiana University, USA, 1968; PhD, Victoria University of Manchester, England, 1976. Appointments: Lecturer, Saadat College, Tangail, 1963; Research Associate, Social Science Research Committee, 1963-64, Senior Lecturer, Department of Commerce, 1964-68, Assistant Professor, 1968-73, Director & Professor, 1986-93, Founder Chairman, Centre for Population Management and Research, 1979-84, Associate Professor, 1973-90, Director and Professor, 1986-93, Institute of Business Administration, Dhaka University; Visiting Professor, Department of Vocational and Technical Education, Nigeria, 1981; Founder & President, 1991-94, Vice Chancellor & Professor, 1994-, International University of Business Agriculture & Technology. Publications: 16 books; 51 articles; 14 research reports; 20 case researches; 45 applied researches & consultancies. Honours: Rotary International Award, 75th Anniversary for saving lives; Institute of Business Administration Alumni Day Award; Listed in various international biographical dictionaries. Memberships: Association of Private Universities of Bangladesh; Association of Management Development Institutions in South Asia; UN Global Assessment Report on Disaster Risk Reduction; Quality Assurance and Improvement Council; Committee on Quality Assurance; International Society for Labor and Social Security Law; International Labor and Employment Relations Association; National Geographic Society; Bangla Academy; AMDISA; Uttara Sector 10 Welfare Association; Bangladesh Economic Association; Comilla Peoples Welfare Association; Association for Total Social Advancement; Rural and Urban Poverty Eradication Association; Chandina Thana Advisory Council; Dhaka Club; Uttara Club; Life Member: BETA; BAMA; SIGMA; IBA Alumni Association; American Alumni Association of Bangladesh; International Association of University Presidents. Address: 4 Embankment Drive Road, Sector 10, Uttara Model Town, Dhaka 1230, Bangladesh. E-mail: miyan@iubat.edu Website: www.iubat.edu

MIYOSHI Isao, b. 15 July 1932, Tokushima, Japan. Physician; Educator. m. Shigeko Kagawa, 3 sons. Education: MD, 1957, PhD, 1965, Okayama University, Japan. Appointments: Intern US Army Hospital, Tokyo, 1957-58; Resident Ohio State University, Columbus, 1958-59; Fellow, University of Texas, Houston, 1959-60; Member, Okayama University Hospital, Japan, 1966-81; Associate Professor, Kochi Medical School, Japan, 1981-82; Professor of Medicine, 1982-98; Professor Emeritus, 1998-. Publications: Numerous articles published in Medical Journals, 1961-2006. Honours: Recipient Hideyo Noguchi Prize, 1983; Princess Takamatsu Cancer Prize, 1984; Hammer Prize, 1985; Asahi Prize, 1987; Medal with Purple Ribbon, 1996. Memberships: Japanese Cancer Association; American Association of Cancer Research. Address: Kochi Medical School, Kochi 783-8505, Japan.

MIZRAHI Isaac, b. 14 October 1961, Brooklyn, New York, USA. Fashion Designer. Education: Parsons School of Design. Appointments: Apprenticed to Perry Ellis, 1982, full-time post, 1982-84; Worked with Jeffrey Banks, 1984-85, Calvin Klein, 1985-87; Founder, own design firm in partnership with Sarah Hadad Cheney, 1987; First formal show, 1988, First spring collection, 1988; First menswear line launched, 1990, Announced closure of firm, 1998; Designer for Isaac Mizrahi for Target line, 2002-2008; Head designer for Liz Claiborne, 2009.

MIZUNO Reiko, b. 13 January 1953, Tokyo, Japan. Science Writer. m. Kichi, 2 sons, 1 daughter. Education: BA, 1975, MA, 1978, Sociology, Sophia University, Tokyo, Japan. Appointments: Director, Japan Children's Environmental Health Circles, 1998-; Director, Japan Endocrine-disruptor Prevention Action, 2005-. Publications: The male/female ratio of fetal deaths and births in Japan, 2000; Increase in male fetal death in japan and congenital abnormalities of the kidney and urinary tract, 2010. Memberships: Japan Society of Endocrine Disruptors Research; Yusho Support Center, Tokyo. Address: 3-6-13 Shoan, Suginami-ku, Tokyo 167-0054, Japan.

MLADENOV Georgiev, b. 29 June 1937, Sofia, Bulgaria. Physicist. m. Maria, 1 son, 1 daughter. Education: Dipl, Physicist, 1960; Junior Researcher, 1964; Senior Researcher, 1985; Research Professor, 1994. Appointments: Institute of Physical Chemistry; Institute of Solid State Physics; Bulgarian Academy of Sciences. Publications: 130 articles in professional journals; 60 preprints, 1960-2010. Honours: JSPS

1 year grant, 1990; Fulbright Research Fellow, UCSD, 1999. Memberships: European Physical Society. Address: Veslets 18, Sofia 1000, Bulgaria. E-mail: mladenlz@gmail.com

MO Timothy (Peter), b. 30 December 1950, Hong Kong. Writer. Education: Convent of the Precious Blood, Hong Kong; Mill Hill School, London; BA, St John's College, Oxford. Publications: The Monkey King, 1978; Sour Sweet, 1982; An Insular Possession, 1986; The Redundancy of Courage, 1991; Brownout on Breadfruit Boulevard, 1995; Renegade or Halo2, 2000. Contributions to: Periodicals. Honours: Gibbs Prize, 1971; Geoffrey Faber Memorial Prize, 1979; Hawthornden Prize, 1983; E M Forster Award, American Academy of Arts and Letters, 1992; James Tait Black Memorial Prize, 1999. Address: c/o Chatto & Windus, 20 Vauxhall Bridge Road, London SW1V 2SA, England.

MOAT John, b. 11 September 1936, India. Author; Poet. m. 1962, 1 son, 1 daughter. Education: MA, Oxford University, 1960. Publications: 6d per Annum, 1966; Heorot (novel), 1968; A Standard of Verse, 1969; Thunder of Grass, 1970; The Tugen and the Toot (novel), 1973; The Ballad of the Leat, 1974; Bartonwood (juvenile), 1978; Fiesta and the Fox Reviews and His Prophecy, 1979; The Way to Write (with John Fairfax), 1981; Skeleton Key, 1982, complete edition, 1997; Mai's Wedding (novel), 1983; Welcome Overtunes, 1987; The Missing Moon, 1988; Firewater and the Miraculous Mandarin, 1990; Practice, 1994; The Valley (poems and drawings), 1998; 100 Poems, 1998; Rain (short stories), 2000; Hermes & Magdalen (poems and etchings), 2004; The Founding of Arvon (belles lettres), 2006; The Best of Dydimus (selected comment), 2007; Blanche (novel), 2011; SM & The Fabrication of Gold (novel), 2011. Address: Crenham Mill, Hartland, North Devon EX39 6HN, England.

MOBBERLEY David Winstone, b. 12 July 1948, Birmingham, England. Poet; Didgeridoo Player. Divorced, 1 son. Appointments: Pharmaceutical Process Technician, 1964-71; Postman, 1971-2005. Publications: Equilibrium of Forces, 1992; Beneath the Darkness A Light is Shining, 1993; Sacred Journey, 1995; Revelations, 2007; First and Last, 2007; Contributions to Iota; San Fernando Poetry Journal, USA; Envoi; The Plowman Journal; Poetry Now. Honours: 1st Prize, The Plowman Poetry Contest, 1997, 1999, 2001; World Record, Greatest Draw of a Flatbow, Commandery Civil War, Centre, Worcester, 1999. Memberships: Reivers Archery Club, Gordon, Scotland; A Friend of the Classic Malts, Glasgow, Scotland. Address: 87 Woodthorpe Road, Kings Heath, Birmingham B14 6EG, England.

MOBERLEY Gary Mark, b. Sydney, New South Wales, Australia. Musician (keyboards); Composer; Writer; Programmer. Musical Education: Grade 6, Australian Conservatory of Music, New South Wales. Career: Left Australia for London, 1971; Musical Director for soul acts with American Promotions Bureau, 1973; Recorded and toured with Tina Charles, 1974-76; Joined John Miles touring GB, Europe, USA and Canada, supporting Elton John, 1976; Joined The Sweet, 1978; Session work in Florida, USA recording with many Spanish artists, 1981; Returned to London and become involved with major recording studios and recording labels as a session musician, 1982; Live work/recorded with: The Sweet; John Miles Band; Terence Trent D'Arby; Prefab Sprout; Wet Wet Wet; The Damned; The Alarm; Hipsway; The The (Infected Album); Jodie Watley; Girlschool; Drum Theatre; Sigue Sigue Sputnik; Little Richard; Haywoode; Nicole; Big Country (remix); Loose Ends; The Associates; Talk Talk; Kiki Dee; Band Of Holy Joy; Dangerous Grounds; Funkadelia; Steel Pulse; Trevor Horn; The JBs; Red Beans and Rice; ABC; Fine Young Cannibals; The Foundations; Jean Jacques Perrey; Live work with: Bee Gees; Paul Rodgers; Bonnie Tyler; Wilson Pickett; Eddie Floyd; Rufus Thomas; Ben E King; Arthur Conley; Andrew 'Junior Boy' Jones; Cookie McGhee; Texas Blues Summit; Memphis Blues Summit; 34 European tours; 9 American tours; 3 world tours; 5 albums of radio and TV themes used world-wide, including Eastenders theme. Address: 43 High Street, Haddenham, Bucks, HP17 8ET, England. E-mail: garymoberley@btinternet.com

MOBINI Sirous, b. 23 July 1964, Sarab, Iran. Psychologist. m. Zohreh Laieghi, 2 daughters. Education: BSc, Clinical Psychology, University of Tabriz, Iran, 1987; MS, Clinical Psychology, Tehran Institute of Psychiatry, Iran University of Medical Sciences, Iran, 1989; PhD, Neuropsychology, University of Nottingham, England, 2001; MSc, Cognitive Psychotherapy, University of Brighton, 2005; PGCertHE, University of Sussex, 2007; Doctorate in Clinical Psychology, School of Medicine, Health Policy & Practice, University of East Anglia, 2010. Appointments: Lecturer, Clinical Psychology, Tabriz University of Medical Sciences, 1992-97; Research Associate/Fellow, School of Psychology, University of Birmingham, 2001-02; Research Fellow, Department of Psychology, School of Life Sciences, University of Sussex, 2002-07; Clinical Psychologist, Cambridgeshire & Peterborough Mental Health Foundation Trust, 2007-10. Publications: Numerous articles in professional journals. Honours: Honorary Research Fellow, School of Psychology, University of Birmingham, 2002-10. Memberships: British Psychological Society; British Association for Behavioural and Cognitive Psychotherapies; Higher Education Academy. Address: School of Medicine, Health Policy and Practice, University of East Anglia, Norwich, NR4 7TJ, England. E-mail: s.mobini@uea.ac.uk

MOBY, b. 11 September 1965, New York, New York, USA. Musician (Guitar, Drums, Keyboards); Producer; Composer; Remixer. Education: University Philosophy Student, University of Connecticut; Private Classical Education, 1976-83. Career: Production & remixes for: Metallica; Smashing Pumpkins; Michael Jackson; Depeche Mode; Soundgarden; Blur; David Bowie; Orbital; Prodigy; Freddie Mercury; Brian Eno; B-52's; Ozzy Osbourne; John Lydon; Butthole Surfers; Erasure; Aerosmith; OMD; Pet Shop Boys; Jon Spencer Blues Explosion; Tours: Lollapalooza, 1995; Red Hot Chili Peppers, 1995; Soundgarden, 1996; Big Top, 1997; Prodigy, 1993, 1995; many solo tours. Recordings: Albums: Moby, 1992; Underground, 1993; Move, 1994; Ambient, 1994; Everything is Wrong, 1995; Underwater, 1995; Animal Rights, 1996; Collected B-Sides, 1996; I Like to Score, 1997; The End of Everything, 1997; Play, 1999; Mobysongs, 2000; 18, 2002; Play: The B Sides, 2004; Hotel, 2005; Last Night, 2008; Wait for Me, 2009; Destroyed, 2011; Singles: That's When I Reach for My Revolver; Come on Baby; Dog Heaven; Why Can't It Stop?; Fucked Up; Higher/Desperate; Into the Blue; Everytime You Touch Me; Feeling So Real; Hymn; Move; UHF; Rock the House; James Bond Theme; Go; Drug Fits the Face; Honey; Run On; Bodyrock; Next Is The E; Why Does My Heart Feel So Bad?; Natural Blues; Full movie score: Double Tap, 1997; Movie soundtrack contributions: Cool World, 1993; Heat, Scream, Joe's Apartment, 1996; Tomorrow Never Dies, the Saint, The Jackal, Spawn, 1997; Gattaca, Senseless, Rounders, Species II, Ever After, Blade, The Bumblebee Flies Anyway, Dangerous Beauty, Permanent Midnight, Playing By Heart, 1998; Any Given Sunday, The Next Best Thing, The Beach, Big Daddy. Honours include:

MTV Video Music Award, 2001; NRJ Music Award, 2001; NME Award, 2001; Q Award, 2002; MTV Video Music Award, 2002; Billboard Music Awards, 2002; BMI Pop Songs Award, 2002; IFPI Platinum Europe Awards, 2001, 2002, 2003. Memberships: BMI; PMRS; AF of M; SAG; AFTRA. Address: c/o Mr Eric Härle, Deutsch-Englische Freundschaft Ltd, PO Box 2477, London NW6 6NQ, England.

MOCUMBI Pascoal Manuel, b. 10 April 1941, Maputo, Mozambique. Medical Doctor. m. Adelina Isabel Bernadino Paindane, 3 January 1966, 2 sons, 2 daughters. Education: MD, University of Lausanne, 1973; Diploma, Health Planning, Institut Planification Sanitaire, University of Dakar, 1975. Appointments: Chief Medical Officer, Sofala Province, 1976-80; Minister of Health, 1980-87; Foreign Minister, 1987-94; Prime Minister, 1994-2004; High Commissioner, European-Developing Countries Clinical Trials Programme, 2004-. Publications: Co-author, Manual de Obstetricia Pratica, Intervencoes Obstétricas; Health for All by the Year 2000?, 1996. Honours: National decorations; International decorations, Brazil, Chile. Memberships: Mozambique Medical Association; Mozambique Public Health Association; Mozambique Family Development Association. Address: Praça da Marinha, Maputo, Mozambique. E-mail: dgpm.gov@teledata.mz

MOELIONO Anton Moedardo, b. 21 February 1929, Bandung, Indonesia. Emeritus Professor. m. Cecile Soeparni Josowidagdo, 2 daughters. Education: MA, Indonesian Studies, 1958, LHD, Sociolinguistics, 1981, University of Indonesia, Jakarta; MA, General Linguistics, Cornell University, USA, 1965. Appointments: Lecturer, 1962, Professor, Indonesian and Linguistics, 1982-94, Chair, Linguistics Graduate Program, 1987-2000, University of Indonesia, Jakarta; Director, 1984-89, Terminology Consultant, 1990-, National Language Centre, RI Department of National Education; Chair, Applied English Linguistics Graduate Program, Atma Jaya University, 2000-04. Publications: Language Development and Cultivation: Alternative approaches, 1984; Pacific Linguistics, 1986; A Grammar of Standard Indonesian, 1988; Manual of Terminography, 2005. Honours: Knight, Order of St Gregory the Great, Vatican, 1993; Honorary Doctor of Letters, University of Melbourne, Australia, 1995; Knight Officer, Order of Orange-Nassau, Netherlands, 1996; RI Medal for Outstanding Service, 2006. Memberships: Royal Netherlands Institute of Southeast Asian and Caribbean Studies Language, Netherlands; Linguistic Society of America; Atma Jaya Foundation. Address: Jalan Kertanegara 51, Jakarta 12110, Indonesia.

MOELLER Christoph, b. 27 December 1969, Muensingen, Germany. Child and Adolescent Psychiatrist; Psychotherapist. 2 daughters. Education: Medical Doctor, University of Witten/Herdecke, 1997. Appointments: Paediatric Physician, Herdecke, 1997-98; Child and Adolescent Psychiatrist, Osnabrueck, Hannover, 1998-2001; Consultant and Head of Department, Child and Adolescent Psychiatrist/ Psychotherapist and Family Therapist, Group Therapist, Hannover, 2002-10; Head, Department of Child Adolescent Psychiatry, 2010-; Teaching: Balintgroups and Group Therapy. Publications: Author, Seeking Adolescence, 2009; Author and editor, Drug Abuse in Adolescence, 2009; Author and Editor, The Positive Sight of Addiction in Adolescent, 2007; Computer and Internet Addiction, 2011; Several articles in journals, newspapers and on TV. Honours: Listed in international biographical dictionaries. Address: Kinderkrankenhaus auf der Bult, Janusz-Korczak-Allee 12, 30173 Hannover, Germany.

MOFFATT Henry Keith, b. 12 April 1935, Edinburgh, Scotland. Emeritus Professor. m. Katharine (Linty) Stiven, 2 sons, 1 deceased, 2 daughters. Education: George Watson's College, Edinburgh, 1943-53; Lycee Henri IV, Paris, France, 1953; BSc (1st class honours), Mathematical Science, Edinburgh University, 1953-57; Wrangler, 1958, BA (1st class), 1959, Smith's Prize, 1960, PhD, Magnetohydrodynamic Turbulence, 1962, ScD, 1987, Cambridge University. Appointments: Assistant Editor, 1962-65, Editor, 1966-83, Journal of Fluid Mechanics; Professor of Applied Mathematics, Bristol University, 1977-80; Fellow, 1962-76, 1980-, Tutor, 1970-74, Senior Tutor, 1975-76, Trinity College, Cambridge; Assistant Lecturer, 1962-64, Lecturer, 1964-76, Head of Department of Applied Mathematics and Theoretical Physics, 1983-91, Professor of Mathematical Physics, 1980-2002, Cambridge University; Director, Isaac Newton Institute for Mathematical Sciences, Cambridge, 1996-2001; Blaise Pascal Professorship, ENS, Paris, 2001-03; Leverhulme Emeritus Fellowship, 2003-05. Publications: Numerous papers and articles in professional scientific journals; Books: Magnetic Field Generation in Electrically Conducting Fluids, 1978; Topological Aspects of the Dynamics of Fluids and Plasmas (editor), 1992; Tubes, Sheets and Singularities in Fluid Dynamics (editor), 2002. Honours: FRS, 1986; FRS (Edin), 1988; Doctor hc: Institut National Polytechnique de Grenoble, 1987; State University of New York (Utica), 1990; Edinburgh University, 2001; Technical University of Eindhoven, 2006; Glasgow University, 2007; Foreign Member: Royal Netherlands Academy of Arts and Sciences, 1991; Academia Europaea, 1994; Académie des Sciences, Paris, 1998; Accademia Nazionale dei Lincei, Rome, 2001; Lisbon Academy of Sciences, 2010; US National Academy of Science, 2008; Officier des Palmes Académiques, 1998; Panetti-Ferrari International Prize and Gold Medal, 2001; Euromech Prize in Fluid Mechanics, 2003; Caribbean Award for Fluid Dynamics, 2004; London Mathematical Society Senior Whitehead Prize, 2005; Royal Society Hughes Medal, 2005; David Crighton Medal, 2009. Memberships: Member of Bureau, 1992-, President, 2000-04, Vice President, 2004-, International Union of Theoretical and Applied Mechanics; Trustee and Member of Council, African Institute for Mathematical Sciences, 2003-; Fellow, American Physical Society, 2003-. Website: www.damtp.cam.ac.uk/user/hkm2

MOGILENKO Alexander, b. 23 March 1976, Leninsk, Kazakhstan. Power Engineer. m. Maya, 1 son. Education: MR, 1999, Ph Dr (Hon), 2003, Novosibirsk State Technical University. Appointments: Teacher, Novosibirsk State Technical University, 2003-05; Head, Power Loss Department, 2003-06, Head, Power Losses and QA Audit Division, 2006, Main expert of technical audit department, 2007-09, Main expert of power engineering department, 2009-, Open Joint Stock Company, Novosibirskenergo. Publications: More than 100 publications. Honours: Honorary Medal for contribution to Power Engineering, 2006; Listed in various international biographical dictionaries. Memberships: VDE, Germany; SEV Electrosuisse, Switzerland; ÖVE, Austria. Address: Trolleynaya 3/1-50, Novosibirsk 630108, Russia. E-mail: a.mogilenko@mail.ru

MOHAMMED Eshrat Halim, b. 11 November 1964, Shiraz, Iran. Medical Researcher. 1 son. Education: BSc, Chemistry, Biochemistry, Analytical Chemistry, 1986; MSc, Biochemistry, 1993; PhD, Chemistry, 2003. Appointments: Post-doctoral Research, 2004-08; Volunteer Peer Reviewer for Medical Journals; Volunteer in Indian Hospitals; Fellowships and Research Associate positions. Publications: Journal of Clinical Biology; Indian Journal of Clinical Biochemistry;

Indian Journal of Experimental Biology; Journal of Medicinal Plants Research. Honours: Junior and Senior Research Fellow; Listed in international biographical dictionaries. Memberships: Canadian Diabetes Association; Canadian Obesity Network. Address: 6-154 Osgoode St, Ottawa, ON K1N 6S6, Canada. E-mail: halim222003@yahoo.co.in

MOHANTY Kailash Chandra, b. 4 April 1948, Gandibed, India. Doctor. m. Suravi, 1 son, 1 daughter. Education: MBBS, 1970; MD (Doctor of Medicine), 1977; Dip Ven, 1977; DipHCE (Ethics), 1992; LLB, Leeds Metropolitan University, 1996; LLM, Sheffield Hallam University, 2003; DFFP, 2004; FRCP, 2009. Appointments: Consultant Physician, Bradford Teaching Hospital NHS Trust, England, 1982-2003; Consultant Physician, North East Lincolnshire & Goole NHS Hospitals Trust, 2003-07; Permanent Member, Employment Appeal Tribunal (High Court), London, 2003-; Consultant Physician, County Durham & Darlington Foundation Hospitals NHS Trust, 2007-. Publications: 95 scientific papers; 2 books; Chapters in textbooks. Honours: Merit Award 'C', 1995; Clinical Excellence Awards, 2006, 2007, 2008, 2009 (9 points, Bronze Award). Memberships: Fellow, Royal Society of Medicine; Fellow, British Association for Sexual Health & HIV; Fellow, Royal College of Physicians, London; Member, British HIV Association. Address: Darlington Memorial Hospital, Hollyhurst Road, Darlington DL3 6HX, England. E-mail: kailash.mohanty@cddft.nhs.uk

MOHANTY Rakesh, b. 16 June 1976, Balangir, Orissa, India. Lecturer. m. Suchismita Pattanaik, 1 daughter. Education: BE, Computer Science & Engineering, Veer Surendra Sai University of Technology, 1998; M Technology, Computer Science & Technology, Jawaharalal Nehru University, 2002; PhD, Computer Science & Engineering, Indian Institute of Technology, Madras, 2012. Appointments: Teaching Faculty, 1998-2000, Teaching Assistant, 2005-08, Department of Computer Science & Engineering, University College of Engineering, Burla; Lecturer, Department of Computer Science & Engineering, Veer Surendra Sai University of Technology, 2001-. Publications: 23 research publications. Honours: Rashtriya Gaurav Award, 2011; Asia Pacific Excellence Award, 2011; Best Citizens of India, 2011; Global Achievers Award, 2011; AICTE-QIP Merit Scholarship, 2005-08; Merit Scholarship Holder. Memberships: International Association of Engineers. Address: c/o Rabinarayan Mohanty, Umabhawn, Radharanipara, Balangir, Orissa 767001, India. E-mail: rakesh.iitmphd@gmail.com Website: http://sites.google.com/site/rakbgr3/personal

MOIR (Alexander) (Thomas) Boyd, b. 1 August 1939, Bolton, Lancashire, England. Medical Practitioner; Scientist. m. Isobel May Shechan, deceased, 1 son, 2 daughters. Education: MBChB, BSc, PhD, Edinburgh University. Appointments: Rotating Intern, New York City, USA; 1964-65; Scientific Staff, 1965-67, Clinical Scientific Staff, 1968-73, Medical Research Council; Senior Medical Officer, 1972-77, Principal Medical Officer, 1977-85, Director of Chief Scientist Organisation, 1986-96, Scottish Health Department; Currently, Honorary Appointments, Edinburgh and Glasgow Universities; Consultancy and Clinical Services. Publications: Publications on Neuroscience, Pharmacology, Biochemistry, Toxicology, Research Management, Public Health. Honours: FRCP (Edin); FRCP (Glasgow); FRCPath; FFPHM; FIBiol; FIFST; MFOM; MFPM; FRSS. Memberships: UK Royal Colleges of Physicians and their Faculties; Royal College of Pathologists; Institute of Biology; Association of Chemists and Biochemists; Pharmacology Society. Address: 23 Murrayfield Gardens, Edinburgh EG 12 6DG, Scotland. E-mail: boyd_moir@msn.com

MOKRICKY Vadim, b. 9 June 1937, Zhitomir, Ukraine. Lecturer; Professor. m. Zhanna, 1 son, 1 daughter. Education: Electronics Engineer, Odessa State Polytechnic Institute, 1961; Doctor of Technical Science. Appointments: Head, Microelectronics Chair, 1972-2000; Dean, Computer Engineering Faculty, 1985-87; Pro-Rector, Odessa State Polytechnic Institute, 1975; Professor, Information Technology Chair, 2001-. Publications: Numerous articles in professional journals and 15 monographs of science. Honours: High Achiever of Higher Education of Ukraine. Memberships: International Informatization Academy; International Higher Technical Education Academy; Ukrainian Telecommunication Academy. Address: Phontanskaya Road str 16/3, ap 48, Odessa 65049, Ukraine. E-mail: mokrickiy@mail.ru

MOKRUSHIN Anatoly, b. 16 October 1948, Votkinsk, Russia. Researcher. Education: Leningrad National University, USSR, 1974; PhD, Postgraduate Student, Pavlov Institute of Physiology, Academy of USSR, 1974-77; DSc, 1997. Appointments: Junior Researcher, Laboratory of Physiology, 1977-82; Research Associate, 1982-86, Researcher, 1986-, Laboratory of Experimental Endocrinology; Senior Researcher, 1990-, Lead Researcher, 1997-, Laboratory of Regulation of Brain Neurons Functions, Pavlov Institute of Physiology, Russian Academy of Sciences. Publications: 120 research papers in scientific journals; 3 monographs; 15 patents for invention. Honours: Grant, pharmacological company ASGL, 1998; Grant, President of Russia, 2001; Grant, RFFI, 2003-05. Address: Pavlov Institute of Physiology, Russian Academy of Sciences, Nab Makarova 6, 199034 St Petersburg, Russia. E-mail: mok@inbox.ru

MOLDEN Nigel Charles, b. 17 August 1948, Oxford, England. Company Director. m. Julia, 3 sons. Education: BSc (Hons), London University, 1970; MSc, Brunel University, 1986; PhD, Fairfax University, 1996. Appointments: General Manager, Warner Bros. Records, 1976-78; International General Manager, WEA Records, 1978-80; Head of International Marketing, Thorn EMI Screen Entertainment, 1980-84; Chairman, Magnum Music Group, 1984-97; Chairman, Magnum America Inc, 1995-97; Chief Executive, Synergie Logistics, 1997-; Thames Valley Magistrates Courts Service, 2002-2005; HM Courts Service for the Thames Valley, 2005-, Chairman, 2007-10; HM Courst Service for Bucks, Herts & the Thames Valley, 2010-11; Governor, 2000-11, Chairman, 2006-09, Claremont High School; Member of Court, Brunel University, 2008-; Governor, Claremont High School Academy, 2011-; Governor, Oxford Spires Academy, 2011-. Publications: Enemies Within, 1993; Research Provides No Scapegoat, 1993; Thinking Positive, 1994; Adrift On The Waves, 1995. Honours: Fellow, Chartered Institute of Marketing, 1988; Freeman of the City of London, 1990; Fellow, Institute of Directors, 1994; Fellow, Royal Society of Arts, 1995; Fellow, Chartered British Management Institute, 1995. Address: Ashcombe House, Deanwood Road, Jordans, Buckinghamshire HP9 2UU, England. E-mail: synergielogistics@btconnect.com

MÖLDER Leevi, b. 4 July 1933, Tudulinna, Estonia. Professor of Chemical Engineering. m. Maila Vägi, 1961, 2 sons, 1 daughter. Education: MSc, Chemical Engineering, 1957, PhD, 1963, Tallinn Technical University. Appointments: Researcher, 1957-62, Associate Professor, 1962-73, Professor, 1973-85, 1992- 2000, Emeritus Professor, 2000-, Tallinn

Technical University; Head of Department, Institute of Chemistry, Estonian Academy of Sciences, 1983-97; Vice Chairman, Council Oil Shale, Estonian Academy of Sciences, 1989-99; Chairman, Commission on Liquid Fuels Quality Specification, Ministry of Economics, Tallinn, 1994-97; Consultant, RAS Kiviter Chemical Co, Kohtla-Jarve, Estonia, 1995-98. Publications: Technology of Heavy Chemicals, co-author, 1970; English-Estonian-Russian Dictionary of Chemistry, co-author, 1998; Chemical Nomenclature, co-author, 2000; 203 articles in professional journals; 11 inventions. Honours: Mente et manu Medal, Tallinn Technical University, 1983, 1993; Paul Kogerman Medal, Estonian Academy of Sciences, 1987; White Star Order of Merit, 2004; Listed in various international biographical dictionaries. Memberships: American Society for Testing and Materials; Estonian Chemical Society; Union of Estonian Scientists; Estonian Society for Nature Conservation. Address: Tallinn Technical University, 5 Ehitajate tee, Tallinn 19086, Estonia. E-mail: leevi.molder@ttu.ee

MOLDOVEANU Anca Maria, b. 18 June 1956, Orastie, Romania. Medical Educator. m. Constantin Moldoveanu, 1 son. Education: Medical Doctor degree, University of Medicine & Pharmacy, Timisoara, 1981; PhD, Medicine, University of Medicine and Pharmacy, Bucharest, 1997; Certificates, World Health Organization, 1995 and 1996, London School of Hygiene and Tropical Medicine, 1996 and 1997, and Michigan State University, 2005 and 2006. Appointments: Medical Doctor, Clinical Hospital Coltea Bucharest, Romania, 1981-84; Specialist, Hygiene and Environmental Medicine, 1985-91, part time, 1991-, Institute of Hygiene and Public Health, Bucharest; Chair, 1991-, Assistant Professor, 1991-97, Lecturer, 1997-2005, Associate Professor, 2005-, Hygiene and Medical Ecology, University of Medicine and Pharmacy Carol Davila, Bucharest. Publications: Author, 4 books; 3 book chapters; 66 articles; 37 communications in scientific events in Romania and abroad. Memberships: Society of Hygiene and Public Health, Romania; Balkan Medical Union; Romanian Society of Microbiology; Romanian Society of Laboratory Medicine; Balkan environmental Association; College of Physicians of Romania; Romanian Society of History of Medicine. Address: Dionisie Lupu, nr 37, Bucharest, 020021, Romania. E-mail: anca.moldoveanu@gmail.com

MOLIN Yury, b. 3 February 1934, Romodanovo Village, USSR. Chemist. m. Galina Jakovleva, 2 daughters. Education: MA, Moscow Institute of Physics and Technology, 1957; Candidate (PhD), 1962, Doctor, 1971, Institute of Chemical Kinetics and Combustion, Novosibirsk. Appointments: Researcher Institute of Chemical Physics, Moscow, 1957-59; Researcher, 1959, Head of Laboratory, 1967, Director, 1971, Head of Laboratory, 1993, Advisor of Russian Academy of Sciences, 2004-, Institute of Chemical Kinetics and Combustion, Novosibirsk; Lecturer, 1966, Professor, 1974-, Novosibirsk State University. Publications: Spin Exchange, 1980; Spin Polarization and Magnetic Effects in Radical Reactions, 1984; Infrared Photochemistry, 1985; 300 articles in scientific journals. Honours: National (Lenin) Prize, 1986; Mendeleev Lecturer, 1992; Fellow of EPR/ESR Society, 1998; N N Semenov Golden Medal, Russian Academy of Sciences, 2006. Memberships: Corresponding Member, 1974, Full Member, 1981, USSR (Now Russian) Academy of Sciences; Editorial boards of journals. Address: Institute of Chemical Kinetics and Combustion, 3 Institutskaya Str, Novosibirsk 630090, Russia. E-mail: molin@ns.kinetics.nsc.ru

MOLINA Alfred, b. 24 May 1953, London, England. Actor. m. Jill Gascoigne, 2 stepsons, 1 daughter from previous relationship. Education: Guildhall School of Music and Drama. Career: Theatre: RSC and National Theatre, Royal Court Theatre, Donmar Warehouse, Minskoff Theater and Broadway; Films: Indiana Jones and the Raiders of the Lost Ark, 1981; Anyone for Denis, 1982; Number One, 1984; Eleni, Ladyhawke, A Letter to Brezhnev, 1985; Prick Up Your Ears, 1987; Manifesto, 1988; Not Without My Daughter, American Friends, Enchanted April, 1991; When Pigs Fly, The Trial, American Friends, 1993; White Fang 2: Myth of the White Wolf, Maverick, 1994; Hideaway, The Perez Family, A Night of Love, The Steal; Species, 1995; Before and After, Dead Man, Scorpion Spring, Mojave Moon, 1996; Anna Karenina, The Odd Couple II, Boogie Nights, The Man Who Knew Too Little, 1997; The Imposters, 1998; Magnolia, Dudley Do-Right, 1999; The Trial, Chocolat, 2000; Texas Rangers, Agatha Christie's Murder on the Orient Express, 2001; Pete's Meteor, Road to Perdition, 2002; Frida, My Life Without Me, Coffee and Cigarettes, 2003; Spider-Man 2, Steamboy (voice), 2004; Sian Ka'an, 2005; The Da Vinci Code, As You Like It, The Hoax; Orchids, 2006; The Moon and the Stars, Silk, The Little Traitor, The Ten Commandments (voice), 2007; The Lodger, An Education, The Pink Panther 2, Wonder Woman (voice), Lessons in Self Defense, Yes, Virginia, 2009; Prince of Persia: The Sands of Time, The Sorcerer's Apprentice, 2010; Abduction, Rango (voice), 2011; TV: El Cid; Year in Provence; Nervous Energy; Ladies Man; Murder on the Orient Express; Bram and Alice; Justice League; Joan of Arc; The Company; Law & Order: LA; Roger and Val Have Just Got In; Harry's Law; Gravity Falls; Monday Mornings. Honours: Royal Television Society Award, 1989; Florida Film Critics Circle Award, 1997, 1999; Imagen Award, 2002; Spider-Man 2, 2004. Website: www.alfred-molina.com

MOLINERO Carme, b. 8 January 1955, Barcelona, Spain. Professor. Education: PhD, History, 1983. Appointments: Universitat de Barcelona, 1987-91; Universitat Autònoma de Barcelona, 1991-; Director, Studies Center on Francoism and Democracy, 2001-06. Publications: La captacion de las masas. Politica social y propaganda en el regimen franquista, 2005; Anatomía del franquismo. De la supervivencia a la agonia 1945-77, 2008. Memberships: Board of the Contemporary History Association, Spain. Address: Autònoma de Barcelona, Dept Historia Contemporanea, Edifici B, 08193 Cerdanyola del Vallès (Barcelona), Spain. E-mail: carme.molinero@uab.es

MØLLER Jesper Vuust, b. 24 January 1938, Ebeltoft, Denmark. Professor. m. Birgit Irene. Education: MD, 1963, Gold Medal thesis, 1965, DSc, 1968, University of Aarhus. Appointments: Assistant Professor, 1963-66, Associate Professor, 1966-89, Chairman, 1980-88, Associate Professor (docent), 1989-90, Department of Medical Biochemistry, University of Aarhus; Senior Research Fellow, Medical Faculty, University of Aarhus, 1973-76, Professor, 1990-2008, Chairman, 1999-2004, Department of Biophysics, University of Aarhus; Research Assistant, Department of Biochemistry, Manchester University, England, 1968-69; Visiting Professor, Department of Biochemistry, Duke University, North Carolina, USA, 1973-74; Senior Research Fellow, Aarhus University Research Foundation, 1988-89; Chairman, Danish Biomembrane Research Centre, 1992-99; Board of Pumpkin (Centre for Membrane Pumps in Cells and Disease), Danish National Research Foundation, 2007-. Publications: Around 130 papers and monographs. Honours: Aa Th B Jacobsen Prize, 1967; Hanstedgaard-Foundation Prize, 2005. Memberships:

Danish Academy of National Sciences; Sigma-Chi; American Biographical Institute. Address: Karetmagervej23, 8920 Randers NV, Denmark. E-mail: jvm@biophys.au.dk

MOLNÁR Gábor, b. 17 July 1951, Debrecen, Hungary. Psychiatrist; Neurologist; Researcher. m. Jelena Aseva, 2 sons, 1 daughter. Education: Medical Diploma, Sechenow Medical School, Moscow, Russia, 1975; Specialist in Psychiatry, Debrecen Medical School, 1979; Specialist in Neurology, National Institute of Neurology and Psychiatry, 1982; Psychotherapeutical Education, Debrecen and Budapest, 1980-83. Appointments: Senior Assistant Professor, Debrecen Medical School, 1975-90; Senior Registrar, County Hospital, Debrecen, 1990-94; Consultant for numerous organizations, Debrecen, 1994-98; Psychiatrist-Neurologist, Researcher, 1998-, Chief Psychiatrist, 2005-, Budapest Social Centre. Publications: 110 papers and summaries; 8 expert reports. Honours: Award, Hungarian Medical Association, 1995; Award, National Institute of Psychiatry and Neurology, 1996; 2000 Achievement Diploma, 1998; International Man of the Millennium, 1999; Millennium Medal of Honour, 1999; Study Award, Hungarian Academy of Sciences, 2002; Listed in international biographical dictionaries. Memberships: International Society of Psychoneuroendocrinology, 1998; Collegium Internationale Neuro-Psychopharmacologicum, 1990; New York Academy of Sciences, 1994; WPA Section on Women's Mental Health, 1997-2002; International Society of Neuro-Psycho-Endocrinology, 1998-2001. Address: Solymárvölgyi ut 78, Budapest H-1037, Hungary.

MONGKHONVANIT Jomphong, b. 28 March 1977, Bangkok, Thailand. Academic. Education: BA, University of Wisconsin, 1999; MPA, Columbia University, 2003; EdM, Harvard University, 2004; DBA, University of Bath, 2008. Appointments: President, Sian Institute of Technology; Trustee and Assistant President, Siam University. Publications: Model of Technological University; Development of Knowledge Standard for Teacher's Profession. Honours: Outstanding Lecturer of Education; Deans' Council of Thailand; Golden Key Honour; Royal Decoration of Direkunaporn. Address: 235 Petkasem Road (Siam University), Pasichareon, Bangkok 10160, Thailand. E-mail: jomphong1@gmail.com

MONSAN Pierre Frédéric, b. 25 June 1948, Prades, France. Professor. m. Dominique Picard, 1 son, 1 daughter. Education: Biochemical Engineering, 1969, Doctor-Engineer, 1971, INSA, Toulouse; Doctor of Sciences, University of Toulouse, 1977. Publications: 200 scientific papers; 2 books; 57 patents. Honours: Chaptal Award for Chemical Art, 1999; Knight Academic Palms, 2002; Officer Academic Palms, 2007; Founding Member, French Academy of Technology. Memberships: French Society of Microbiology; French Society of Biochemistry and Molecular Biology. Address: LISBP-INSA, 135 Avenue de Rangueil, 31077 Toulouse, Cedex 4, France. E-mail: pierre.monsan@insa-toulouse.fr Website: www.lisbp.insa-toulouse.fr

MONTAGU OF BEAULIEU Edward John Barrington Douglas-Scott-Montagu, 3rd Baron, b. 20 October 1926, London, England. Museum Administrator; Author; Elected Peer. m. (1) Elizabeth Belinda, 1959, divorced, 1974, 1 son, 1 daughter, (2) Fiona Herbert, 1974, 1 son. Education: St Peter's Court, Broadstairs; Ridley College, St Catharines, Ontario; New College, Oxford. Appointments: Founder, Montagu Motor Car Museum, 1952, world's first Motor Cycle Museum, 1956, National Motor Museum, Beaulieu, 1972; Founder-Editor, Veteran and Vintage magazine, 1956-79; Chairman, Historic Buildings and Monuments Commission, 1983-92; Free-lance motoring journalist; Hereditary Peer, 1947-99, Elected Peer, 1999-, House of Lords. Publications: The Motoring Montagus, 1959; Lost Causes of Motoring, 1960; Jaguar: A Biography, 1961, revised edition, 1986; The Gordon Bennett Races, 1963; Rolls of Rolls-Royce, 1966; The Gilt and the Gingerbread, 1967; Lost Causes of Motoring: Europe, 2 volumes, 1969, 1971; More Equal Than Others, 1970; History of the Steam Car, 1971; The Horseless Carriage, 1975; Early Days on the Road, 1976; Behind the Wheel, 1977; Royalty on the Road, 1980; Home James, 1982; The British Motorist, 1987; English Heritage, 1987; The Daimler Century, 1995; Wheels within Wheels, 2000. Memberships: Federation of British Historic Vehicle Clubs, president, 1989-; Federation Internationale des Voitures Anciennces, president, 1980-83; Historic Houses Association, president, 1973-78; Museums Association, president, 1982-84; Union of European Historic Houses, president, 1978-81; Guild of Motoring Writers. Address: Palace House, Beaulieu, Brockenhurst, Hants SO42 7ZN, England.

MONTAGU-POLLOCK Sir Giles Hampden (5th Baronet of the Khyber Pass), b. 19 October 1928, Oslo, Norway. Management Consultant. m. Caroline Veronica Russell, 1 son, 1 daughter. Education: Eton College; de Havilland Aeronautical Technical School. Appointments: Airspeed Ltd, 1949-51; G P Eliot at Lloyd's, 1951-52; de Havilland Engine Co Ltd, 1952-56; Advertising Manager, Bristol Aeroplane Co Ltd, 1956-59; Advertising Manager, Bristol Siddeley Engines Ltd, 1959-61; Associate Director, J Walter Thompson Co Ltd, 1961-69; Director: C Vernon & Sons Ltd, 1969-71, Acumen Marketing Group, 1971-74, 119 Pall Mall Ltd, 1972-78; Management Consultant in Marketing, 1974-; Associate: John Stork & Partners, Ltd, 1980-88, Korn/Ferry International, 1988-2002. Address: The White House, 7 Washington Road, London SW13 9BG, England.

MONTGOMERIE Colin, b. 23 June 1963, Glasgow, Scotland. Golfer. m. Eimear Wilson, 1990-2006 divorced) 1 son, 2 daughters. Education: Baptist University, Texas, USA. Career: Professional Golfer, 1987-; Member, Walker Cup team, 1985, 1987, Ryder Cup team, 1991, 1993, 1995, 1997, 1999, 2002, 2004, Dunhill Cup Team, 1988, 1991-2000, World Cup Team, 1988, 1991, 1992, 1993, 1997, 1998, 1999; Leader, European Tour Order of Merit, 1993-99; 28 European Tour wins as at end December 2002; Signed contract to play Yonex Clubs from 2004. Honours: Winner: Scottish Stroke Play, 1985; Scottish Amateur Championship, 1987; European Tour Rookie of the Year, 1988; Portuguese Open, 1989; Scandinavian Masters, 1991, 1999, 2001; Heineken Dutch Open, 1993; Volvo Masters, 1993; Spanish Open, 1994; English Open, 1994; German Open, 1994; Volvo German Open, 1995; Trophee Lancome, 1995; Alfred Dunhill Cup, 1995; Dubai Desert Classic, 1996; Murphy's Irish Open, 1996, 1997, 2001; Canon European Masters, Million Dollar Challenge, 1996; World Cup Individual, 1997; Andersen Consulting World Champion, 1997; Compaq European Grand Prix, 1997; King Hassan II Trophy, 1997; PGA Championship, 1998, 1999, 2000; German Masters, 1998; British Masters, 1998; Benson and Hedges International Open, 1999; BMW International Open, 1999; Standard Life Loch Lomond Invitational, 1999; Cisco World Matchplay, 1999; Skins Game, US, 2000; Novotel Perrier Open de France, 2000; Ericsson Australian Masters, 2001; Volvo Masters Andalucia, 2002; TCL Classic, 2002; Macan Open, 2003; Caltex Masters Singapore, 2004; Dunhill Links Championships, 2005; Hong Kong Open, 2006; Smurfit Kappa European Open, 2007. Member: winning European Ryder Cup team, 1995, 1997, 2002, 2004. Address: c/o IMG, McCormack House, Burlington Lane, London W4 2TH, England.

MONTGOMERY John Warwick, Baron of Kiltartan, Lord of Morris, Comte de St Germain de Montgommery, b. 18 October 1931, Warsaw, New York, USA. m. Lanalee de Kant, 26 August 1988, 1 adopted son. Education: AB, Philosophy with distinction, Cornell University, 1952; BLS, 1954, MA, 1958, University of California at Berkeley; BD, 1958, MST, 1960, Wittenberg University, USA; PhD, University of Chicago, USA, 1962; Docteur de l'Universite, mention Theologie Protestante, University of Strasbourg, France, 1964; LLB, La Salle Extension University, 1977; Diplome cum laude, International Institute of Human Rights, Strasbourg, 1978; MPhil in Law, University of Essex, England, 1983; Dr (hon), Institute of Religion and Law, Moscow, 1999; LLM, 2000, LLD, 2003, Cardiff University, Wales; Bar: Virginia, 1978; California, 1979; DC, 1985; Washington State, 1990; US Supreme Court, 1981; England & Wales, 1984; Paris, 2003; Certified Fraud Examiner, 2008; Licenced Real Estate Broker, California; Certificate, Law Librarian; Diplomate, Medical Library Association; Ordained to ministry, Lutheran Church, 1958; Librarian, general reference service, University of California Library, Berkeley, 1954-55; Instructor, Biblical Hebrew, Hellenistic Greek, Medieval Latin, Wittenberg University, Springfield, Ohio, 1956-59; Head Librarian, Swift Library of Divinity and Philosophy, member Federated Theological Faculty, University of Chicago, 1959-60; Associate Professor, Chairman, Department of History, Wilfred Laurier University, Ontario, Canada, 1960-64; Professor, Chairman, Division of Church History, History of Christian Thought, Director, European Seminar Programme, Trinity Evangelical Divinity School, Deerfield, Illinois, 1964-74; Professor, Law and Theology, International School of Law, Washington DC, 1974-75; Theology consultant, Christian Legal Society, 1975-76; Director of Studies, International Institute of Human Rights, Strasbourg, France, 1979-81; Founding Dean, Professor Jurisprudence, Director of European Programme, Simon Greenleaf University School of Law, Anaheim, California, 1980-88; Distinguished Professor of Theology and Law, Faith Evangelical Lutheran Seminary, Tacoma, Washington, 1989-91; Principal Lecturer, Reader in Law, 1991-93, Professor of Law and Humanities, Director, Centre of Human Rights, 1993-97, Emeritus Professor, 1997-, Bedfordshire University, England; Distinguished Professor of Apologetics, Law, and History of Christian Thought, Vice President, Academic Affairs, UK and Europe, 1997-2007, Trinity College and Theological Seminary, Newburgh, Indiana; Director, International Academy of Apologetics, Evangelism and Human Rights, Strasbourg, France, 1997-; Distinguished Research Professor of Philosophy and Christian Thought, Patrick Henry College, Purcellville, Virginia, 2007-; Honorary Professor, Lavengamalie College, Tonga, 2010-; Distinguished Professor of Law, Regent University, Virginia, 1997-99; Senior Counsel, European Centre for Law and Justice, 1997-2001; Visiting Professor, Concordia Theological Seminary, Springfield, Illinois, 1964-67, DePaul University, Chicago, 1967-70, Concordia University, Irvine, California, 2006; Honorary Fellow, Revelle College, University of California, San Diego, 1970; Lecturer, Research Scientists Christian Fellowship Conference, St Catherine's College, Oxford University, 1985; International Anti-Corruption Conference, Beijing, China, 1995; Pascal Lecturer on Christianity and the University, University of Waterloo, Ontario, Canada, 1987; A Kurt Weiss Lecturer, Biomedical Ethics, University of Oklahoma, 1997; Adjunct Professor, Puget Sound University School of Law, Tacoma, Washington, 1990-91; Worldwide Advocacy Conference lecturer, Inns of Court School of Law London, 1998; Law and Religion Colloquium lecturer, University College, London, 2000; IVR World Congress of the Philosophy of Law, Crackow, Poland, 2007 and Shanghai, China, 2009; numerous other functions. Publications: Author, 60 books, most recently: The Transcendental Holmes, 2000; The Repression of Evangelism in Greece, 2000; Christ Our Advocate, 2002; Tractatus Logico-Theologicus, 2002; Consultant Editor (Religion & Law), Amicus Curiae, 2010-; Editor, Contributing Editor, Film and TV series; Contributor of articles to academic, theological, legal encyclopaedias and journals, and chapters to books. Honours: Ordre des chevaliers du Saint-Sepulcre Byzantin; Patriarch's Medal, Romanian Orthodox Church; Phi Beta Kappa; Phi Kappa Phi; Beta Phi Mu; Awards: National Lutheran Educational Conference Fellow, 1959-60; Canada Council Postdoctoral Senior Research Fellow, 1963-64; American Association of Theological Schools Faculty Fellow, 1967-68; Recipient Angel Award, National Religious Broadcasters, 1989, 1990, 1992; Honorary Chairman, Academic Board, International Institute for Religious Freedom, 2007-; Fellow: Trinity College, Newburgh, Indiana; Royal Society of Arts, England; Victoria Institute, London (Honorary Vice-President); Academie Internationale des Gourmets et des Traditions Gastronomiques, Paris; American Scientific Affiliation; Society for Advanced Legal Studies, UK. Memberships: European Academy of Arts, Sciences and Humanities; Heraldry Society, UK (Advanced Certificate); Lawyers' Christian Fellowship (Honorary Vice-President, 1993-2010); National Conference of University Professors; International Bar Association; World Association of Law Professors; Middle Temple and Lincoln's Inn; American Society for International Law; Union Internationale de Avocats; National Association of Realtors; ALA; Tolkien Society of America; New York C S Lewis Society; American Historical Society; Society for Reformation Research; Creation Research Society; Tyndale Fellowship, England; Stair Society, Scotland; Presbyterian Historical Society, Northern Ireland; American Theological Library Association; Bibliographical Society, University of Virginia; Evangelical Theological Society; International Wine and Food Society; Societe des Amis des Arts; Chaine des Rotisseurs; Athenaeum Club; Freeman of the City of London and Liveryman of the Scriveners' Company; Players' Theatre Club; Sherlock Holmes Society of London; Honorary Member, Societe Sherlock Holmes de France; Club des Casseroles Lasserre, Paris. Address: 2, rue de Rome, 67000 Strasbourg, France. E-mail: 106612.1066@CompuServe.com

MONTGOMERY Jonathan Robert, b. 29 July 1962, Epsom, Surrey, England. Law Professor. m. Elsa Montgomery, 2 daughters. Education: BA (Hons), Cantab, 1983; LLM, Cantab, 1984. Appointments: Chair, Southampton Community Health Services NHS Trust, 1998-2001; Professor, Health Care Law, University of Southampton, 2001-; Chair, Hampshire Partnership NHS Trust, 2001-04; Chair, Hampshire & Isle of Wight SHA, 2004-06; Chair, Advisory Committee on Clinical Excellence Awards, 2005-14; Chair, NHS Hampshire, 2006-13; Chair, Human Genetics Commission, 2009-12; Chair, Nuffield Council on Bioethics, 2012-17; Chair, Health Research Authority, 2012-. Publications: Health Care Law, 2003; Health Care Choices: Making decisions with children, 1996; Law and the Demoralisation of Medicine, 2006; 26 Legal Studies 1-26; Time for a paradigm shift? Medical law in transition, 2000. Honours: Hon FRCPCH, 2005. Address: Southampton Law School, University of Southampton, Highgield, Southampton SO17 1BJ, England. E-mail: jrm@soton.ac.uk

MONTOYA Jaime, b. 16 July 1961, Manila, Philippines. Physician. m. Rosalyn Bermudez, 1 son. Education: BS, Biology, University of the Philippines, 1981; MD, UP College of Medicine, 1985; MSc, 1989, Diplomate, 1999, Clinical Tropical Medicine, London School of Hygiene and Tropical Medicine, University of London, England; Residency Training, UP-PGH Medical Centre, 1987-92; Specialty Training, University of California, USA, 1997, Cornell University, USA, 1998. Appointments: Professor V, Section of Infectious Diseases, UP College of Medicine, 1993-; Training Officer, Department of Medicine, UP College of Medicine, 1994-2005; Assistant Professor III, Faculty of Medicine and Surgery, University of Santo Tomas, 1997-2002; Chairman, Department of Internal Medicine, St Dominic Medical Centre, Bacoor, Cavite, 1998-2001; Head, Department of Medicine, Medical Research Laboratories, UP-PGH, 2001-05; Executive Officer, Chief, Section of Infectious and Tropical Diseases, 2000-01, 2001-02; Dr Elpidio Gamboa Oriented Medical Education Unit, UP College of Medicine, 2003-05; Medical Director, Bristol Myers Squibb, Philippines and Hong Kong, 1998-2004; Member, Advisory Committee, National Institutes of Health, UP Manila, 2005-; Executive Director, Philippines Council for Health Research and Development, Department of Science and Technology, 2005-; Focal Person and Head, Philippine Science Heritage Center, Department of Science and Technology, 2008-. Publications: Numerous articles in professional journals, books, articles and newsletters. Honours include most recently: UP Alumni Association Distinguished Alumnus Award, 2010; One of the Outstanding Graduate of the Institute of Biology, 2011; Outstanding Service Award, UP Medical Alumni Society, 2011; Achievement Award, National Research Council of the Philippines, 2011; Fellow, American College of Physicians, 2011; Honorary Fellow, Royal College of Physicians of Thailand, 2011. Memberships: American College of Physicians; Royal Institute of Doctors, Singapore; Royal College of Physicians of Thailand; Royal Society for Tropical Medicine and Hygiene, London; Institute of Biology, UK; and others. Address: 36 Rubueno St Philamlife Village, Pamplona, Las Pinas City, Philippines. E-mail: mnty_jm@yahoo.com

MOODALIYAR Kasturi, b. 2 March 1977, Durban, South Africa. Law Lecturer. m. Keith Weeks. Education: B Proc, 1999; LLB, 2000; LLM, 2001; M Phil, Criminology Research, 2002. Appointments: Junior Investigator, 2002-03, Merger Analyst, 2003-05, Competition Commission, South Africa; Senior Lecturer, Competition Law, University of Witwatersrand, 2005-. Honours: Mandela Magdalene Scholarship, Cambridge University; Carnegie Sandwich Fellowship; World Trade Institute Fellowship. Memberships: Academic Society for Competition Law; American Bar Association; International Antitrust Committee; Non-Government Adviser, International Competition Network. E-mail: kasturi.moodaliyar@wits.ac.za

MOODY A David, b. 21 January 1932, New Zealand. University Teacher; Writer. m. Joanna S Moody. Education: BA, 1951, MA, 1952, Canterbury College, University of New Zealand; BA, 1st Class Honours, Oxford University, 1955. Appointments: Assistant Information Officer, UNHCR, Geneva; Lecturer, Senior Lecturer in English, University of Melbourne, 1958-65; Member, Department of English and Related Literature, 1966-99, Emeritus Professor of English and American Literature, 1999-, University of York. Publications: Virginia Woolf, 1963; Shakespeare: The Merchant of Venice, 1964; The Waste Land in Different Voices (editor), 1974; Thomas Stearns Eliot: Poet, 1979, 1994; At the Antipodes: Homage to Paul Valéry, 1982; News Odes: The El Salvador Sequence, 1984; Cambridge Companion to T S Eliot (editor), 1994; Tracing T S Eliot's Spirit: essays on his poetry and thought, 1996; Ezra Pound: Poet, A Portrait of the Man and His Work, vol 1, The Young Genius 1885-1920, 2007; Ezra Pound to his Parents: Letter 1895-1929, 2010. Honours: Shirtcliffe Fellow, University of New Zealand, 1953-55; Nuffield Foundation Travelling Fellow, 1965; British Academy/Leverhulme Visiting Professor, 1988; Honorary Member, T S Eliot Society, USA; Fellow, English Association. Memberships: Association of University Teachers; Member of the Editorial Board: Paideuma: A Journal of Scholarship on British and American Modernist Poetry, 2002-; Society of Authors. Address: Church Green House, Old Church Lane, Pateley Bridge, North Yorkshire HG3 5LZ, England.

MOOK Sarah, b. 29 October 1929, Brooklyn, New York, USA. Chemist. Education: BA, Hunter College, 1952; Graduate Coursework, Columbia University, 1954-57; Coursework, University of Hartford, 1958-59; Language Course, Columbia University, 1962-65; New York City Citizens Police Academy, 2001. Appointments: Cartographic Aide, US Geological Survey, 1952-54; Research Assistant, Columbia University, 1954-57; Analytical Chemist, Combustion Engineering, 1957-59; Research Scientist, Radiation Applications Inc, 1959-62; Chemist, Marks Polarised Corp, 1962-64; Senior Chemist, NRA Inc, 1964-74; Clinical Technologist, Coney Island Hospital, 1974-84; Supervisor, 1984-89, Principal Chemist, 1989-95, Bellevue Hospital; Retired, 1995-. Publications: Several professional articles. Honours: Woman of the Year, New York City Council, 2004; Margaret M McCord Woman of Year Memorial Award, Sheepshead Bay Historical Society, 2004; Woman of the Year Humanitarian Award, New York State Senate, 2004; Distinguished Leadership in Community Award, New York City Office of Comptroller, 2004; Marjorie Matthews Community Advocate Recognition Award, 2008. Memberships: American Chemical Society; American Association for the Advancement of Science; American Association for Clinical Chemistry; New York Academy of Science; Van Slyke Society; Citizens Police Academy Alumni Association. Address: 2042 East 14th Street, Brooklyn, NY 11229, USA.

MOON Chan-Seok, b. 13 July 1965, Busan, Korea. Professor. m. Jin-Hee Kim, 2 daughters. Education: BSc, Department of Biology, Inje University, Kimhae, Korea, 1988; Master of Public Health, Department of Environmental Health, Inje University, Korea, 1990; Doctor of Medical Science, Department of Public Health, Kyoto University Faculty of Medicine, Kyoto, Japan, 1997. Appointments: Full-time Lecturer, Inje University, Institute of Industrial Medicine, Busan, 1997-2000; Associated Researcher, Yangsan College, Institute of Industrial Technology, Yangsan, 2000-01; Research Professor, Pohang University of Science and Technology, School of Environmental Science & Engineering, Pohang, 2002-04; Assistant Professor, Department of Public Health, Catholic University of Pusan, Busan, 2007-. Publications: Dietary intake, blood, urinary cadmium and lead among general population in Korea, 1995-2005; Pollutant levels in ambient air and human blood, 1996; Nutritional evaluation, 1997; Urinary cadmium and lead as markers of background exposure, 1999; Use of solvents in industries, 2001; Evaluation of serum PCDD/Fs congeners among the residents near the continuously burning municipal solid waste incinerators, 2005. Honours: Listed in international biographical dictionaries. Memberships: Editorial Board, Journal of Environmental Health Services; Korean Society of Environmental Health; Director, Korean Society of Occupational and Environmental Hygiene. Address: Department of Industrial Health, Catholic University of Pusan, #9, Bugok3-dong, Kumjeong-ku, Busan 609-757, Korea. E-mail: csmoon@cup.ac.kr

MOON Doo-Gyung, b. 16 January 1966, Jeju Island, Korea. Agricultural Researcher. m. Sun-Bog Lee, 2 sons, 1 daughter. Education: BS, Jeju City, 1991, MS, 1993, Jeju National University; PhD, Ehime University, Matsuyama City, Japan, 2001. Appointments: Cheju Citrus Research Institute, Rural Development Administration, 1993-96; Mie Agricultural Station, Tsu City, Mie Prefecture, Japan, 1996-97; Cheju Agricultural Station, Jeju City, 1997-98; National Institute of Subtropical Agriculture, Jeju City, 2001-05; Research and Development Bureau, Suwon City, Gyeonggi Prefecture, 2005-07; NISA, RDA, Jeju City, 2007-08; Agricultural Research Center for Climate Change, National Institute of Horticultural and Herbal Science, RDA, 2009-. Publications: Soluble solids and titratable acid in different portions in maturing satsuma mandarin fruit as affected by water stress; Seasonal fluctuations in myconhizal spore populations and infection rates of vineyards soils planted with five legume cover crops; Gradient in sugar and acid content among different portions of pulp in the axial direction of several citrus fruit at harvest season; Nitrogen fixation and N-balance studies of candidate legume cover crops for use in orchards; The relationship between fruit shapes and acid content in different part of citrus fruits; Partitioning pattern of 13C-assimilate in different portions of maturing satsuma mandarin fruit; Sugar and acid contents in different portions of 'Shiranuhi' mandarin fruit as affected by water stress; Sugars and organic acid contents in different parts of juice sacs in 'Shiranuhi' mandarin fruit at harvest, 2009. Honours: Listed in international biographical dictionaries. Memberships: International Society for Horticultural Science; Korean Society for Horticultural Science; International Society of Citriculture. Address: Agricultural Research Center for Climate Change, National Institute of Horticultural & Herbal Science, Rural Development Administration, 316 Ayeonno (1696 O-Deung Dong), Jeju, 690-150, Republic of Korea. E-mail: dgmoon@korea.kr

MOON Gi-Seong, b. 8 August 1972, Jinju, South Korea. Professor. m. Hye-Jean Lee, 2 sons. Education: BSc, 1998, MSc, 2000, Gyeongsang National University; Jinju, PhD, Yonsei University, Seoul, 2005. Appointments: Research Scientist, Korea Food Research Institute, Seongnam, 2000-05; Visiting Scientist, Institute of Food Research, Norwich, England, 2005-06; Professor, Chungju National University, Jeungpyeong, 2006-. Publications: 22 research papers in professional journals. Honours: Listed in international biographical dictionaries. Memberships: Korean Society for Lactic Acid Bacteria; Korean Society of Food Science and Nutrition; Society of General Microbiology; Korean Society of Food Science and Technology; Korean Society of Microbiology and Biotechnology. Address: Department of Biotechnology, Chungju National University, 61 Daehak-ro, Jeungpyeong, Chungbuk 368-701, South Korea. E-mail: gsmoon@cjnu.ac.kr

MOON Yang Ho, b. 10 January 1969, Jeon-joo, Korea. Engineer. m. Young Mee Kim, 1 daughter. Education: BS, Hanyang University, 1991; MS, Korean Advanced Science and Technology, 1993. Appointments: KIA Motors, 1993-97; Samsung Electromechanics, 1998-. Publications: Fatigue analysis of rigid-flexible PCB for cellular phone and bending endurance reliability tester; Thermal cycle analysis of MLCC using finite element method; Tolerance analysis of injection mould for plastic lens; Vibration analysis of smooth picture module for projection TV. Honours: Silver Award, 1998, Gold Award, 2001, Samsung Group CAE Conference; Best Paper Award, MSC User Conference, 2004. Memberships: Society for Information Display; American Ceramic Society; American Society of Mechanical Engineers. Address: 1-201 Sun-kyung-APT, Sung-Po-Dung, Ansan, Kyung-gi-do, 425-767, Republic of Korea. E-mail: yanghomoon@gmail.com

MOORE Brian C J, b. 10 February 1946. Professor of Auditory Perception. Education: BA, 1968, MA, 1971, Natural Sciences, PhD, Experimental Psychology, 1971, University of Cambridge, England. Appointments: Lecturer, Psychology, University of Reading, England, 1971-73; Fulbright-Hayes Senior Scholar and Visiting Professor, Department of Psychology, Brooklyn College of CUNY, 1973-74; Lecturer, Psychology, University of Reading, 1974-77; Lecturer, Experimental Psychology, University of Cambridge, 1977-89; Fellow, Wolfson College, Cambridge, 1983-; Visiting Researcher, University of California at Berkeley, USA, 1985; Reader in Auditory Perception, 1989-95, Professor of Auditory Perception, 1995-, University of Cambridge. Publications: 14 books; Over 90 book chapters and papers in conference proceedings; 388 publications in refereed journals; 3 CDs. Honours include: Silver Medal, Acoustical Society of America in Psychological and Physiological Acoustics, 2003; Carhart Memorial Lecturer, American Auditory Society, 2003; International Award in Hearing, American Academy of Audiology, 2004; TS Littler Prize, British Society of Audiology, 2006; Award of Merit, Association for Research in Otolaryngology, 2008; Hugh Knowles Prize for Distinguished Achievement, Northwestern University, 2008. Memberships: Experimental Psychology Society; Fellow, Acoustical Society of America; Cambridge Philosophical Society; British Society of Audiology; American Speech-Language-Hearing Association; Audio Engineering Society; Acoustical Society of Japan; American Auditory Society; Association for Research in Otolaryngology; American Academy of Audiology; Fellow, Academy of Medical Sciences; Fellow, Royal Society. Address: Department of Experimental Psychology, University of Cambridge, Downing Street, Cambridge CB2 3EB, England. Website: http://hearing.psychol.cam.ac.uk

MOORE David Moresby, b. 26 July 1933, Barnard Castle, County Durham, England. Professor Emeritus of Botany. m. Ida Elizabeth Shaw, 2 sons. Education: BSc, Honours, Botany, 1954, PhD, 1957, DSc, 1984, University College and Botany Department, University of Durham. Appointments: Research Officer, Genetics Section, Division of Plant Industry, CSIRO, Canberra, ACT, Australia, 1957-59; Research Fellow, Department of Botany, University of California at Los Angeles, 1959-61; Lecturer, Genetics, Department of Botany, University of Leicester, England, 1961-68; Reader, Plant Taxonomy, 1968-76, Professor of Botany, 1976-94, Reading University, England. Publications: About 100 articles on taxonomy, geography, cytogenetics of plants; 19 books include: Vascular Flora of the Falkland Islands, 1968; Plant Cytogenetics, 1976, Flora Europaea Check-List and Chromosome-Number Index, 1982; Green Planet, 1982; Flora of Tierra del Fuego, 1983; Garden Earth, 1991. Honours: Botany Field Prize, University of Durham, 1954; British Association Studentship, University of Durham; Plaque for services to Magellanic Botany, Instituto de la Patagonia, Punta Arenas, Chile, 1976; Premio Perito Francisco P Moreno, Sociedad Argentina de Estudios Geográficos, 1985; Enrique Molina Gold Medal, University of Concepción, Chile. Memberships: Botanical Society of the British Isles; Editorial Committees: Webbia, Italy, Polish Botanical Journal, Anales del Instituto de la Patagonia, Flora de Chile. Address: 26 Eric Avenue, Emmer Green, Reading, Berks, RG4 8QX, England.

MOORE Demi, b. 11 November 1962, Roswell, New Mexico, USA. Actress. m. (1) Freddy Moore, 1980, divorced 1984, (2) Bruce Willis, 1987, divorced 2000, 3 daughters; (3) Ashton Kutcher, 2005, divorced 2012. Career: Started in TV, also Model; Films include: Blame it on Rio; St Elmo's Fire; One Crazy Summer; About Last Night…; Wisdom; The Seventh Sign; Ghost; Mortal Thoughts, also co-producer; The Butcher's Wife; A Few Good Men; Indecent Proposal; Disclosure; The Scarlet Letter; Striptease, 1995; The Juror, 1996; GI Jane, 1996; The Hunchback of Notre Dame, 1996; Now and Then, produced & acted, 1996; Deconstructing Harry, 1997; Passion of Mind, 2000; Airframe; Charlie's Angels: Full Throttle, 2003; Half Light, 2006; Bobby, 2006; Flawless, 2007; Mr Brooks, 2007; Flawless, 2008; Happy Tears, The Joneses, Bunraku, 2010; Margin Call, Another Happy Day, 2011; LOL, 2012; Very Good Girls, 2013; Producer, Austin Powers: International Man of Mystery, 1997; Austin Powers: The Spy Who Shagged Me, 1999; Austin Powers in Goldmember, 2002; Theatre: The Early Girl; TV: General Hospital, Bedroom. Honour: Theatre World Award for The Early Girl. Address: c/o Creative Artists Agency, 9830 Wilshire Boulevard, Beverly Hills, CA 90212, USA.

MOORE John Richard, b. 20 May 1929, Newbury, Berkshire, England. Master Grocer; Geneaology Lecturer. m. (1) Muriel Young, 1 son, 2 daughters, (2) Marjorie Thompson. Education: St Bartholomew's, Newbury. Appointments: Master Grocer; Wholesale trade; Lecturer. Memberships: Fellow, Society of Genealogists; Founder, Vice President, Wiltshire FHS; Vice President, Guild of One Name Studies. Address: 1 Cambridge Close, Swindon, Wiltshire SN3 1JQ, England.

MOORE Julianne, b. 3 December 1960, USA. Actress. Education: Boston University School for Arts. m. (1) Sundar Chakravarthy 1983-85 (divorced); (2) John Gould Rubin 1986-1995 (divorced); (3) Bart Freundlich 2003-, 2 children. Creative Works: Stage appearances include: Serious Money, 1987; Ice Cream with Hot Fudge, 1990; Uncle Vanya; The Road to Nirvana; Hamlet; The Father; Film appearances include: Tales From the Darkside, 1990; The Hand That Rocks the Cradle, The Gun in Betty Lou's Handbag, 1992; Body of Evidence, Benny & Joon, The Fugitive, Short Cuts, 1993; Vanya on 42nd Street, 1994; Roommates, Safe, Nine Months, Assassins, 1995; Surviving Picasso, 1996; Jurassic Park: The Lost World, The Myth of Fingerprints, Hellcab, Boogie Nights, 1997; The Big Lebowski, 1998; Eyes Wide Shut, The End of The Affair, Map of the World, Magnolia, Cookie's Fortune, An Ideal Husband, 1999; Hannibal, The Shipping News, 2000; Far From Heaven, The Hours, 2002; Marie and Bruce, Laws of Attraction, The Forgotten, 2004; Trust the Man, The Prize Winner of Defiance, Ohio, 2005; Freedomland, Children of Men, 2006; Next, Savage Grace, I'm Not There, 2007; Blindness, 2008. TV appearances include: As the World Turns, series; The Edge of Night, series; Money, Power Murder, 1989; Lovecraft, 1991; I'll Take Manhattan; The Last to Go; Cast a Deadly Spell. Honours: Best Actress, Venice Film Festival, 2002. Address: c/o Creative Artists Agency, 9830 Wilshire Boulevard, Beverly Hills, CA 90212, USA.

MOORE Sir Roger, b. 14 October 1927, London, England. Actor. m. (1) Doorn van Steyn, divorced, (2) Dorothy Squires, 1953, divorced, (3) Luisa Mattioli, 2 sons, 1 daughter, divorced; (4) Christina 'Kiki' Tholstrup, 2002. Education: Royal Academy of Dramatic Arts. Appointment: Special Ambassador for UNICEF, 1991-. Creative Works: Films include: Crossplot, 1969; The Man With the Golden Gun, 1974; That Lucky Touch, Save Us From Our Friends, Shout At The Devil, 1975; Sherlock Holmes in New York, The Spy Who Loved Me, 1976; The Wild Geese, 1977; Escape to Athens, Moonraker, 1978; Esther, Ruth and Jennifer, 1979; The Sea Wolves, Sunday Lovers, For Your Eyes Only, 1980; Octopussy, The Naked Face, 1983; A View to a Kill, 1985; Key to Freedom, Bed and Breakfast, Bullseye!, 1989; Fire, Ice and Dynamite, 1990; The Quest, 1997; Boat Trip, 2002; The Fly Who Loved Me (voice), 2004; Here Comes Peter Cottontail: The Movie (voice), Foley & McColl: This Way Up, 2005; Agent Crush (voice), 2008. TV appearances include: The Alaskans; The Saint, 1962-69; The Persuaders, 1972-73; The Man Who Wouldn't Die, 1992; The Quest, 1995. Publication: James Bond Diary, 1973.

MOORE Terence, b. 24 December, 1931, London, England. Retired Businessman. m. Tessa Catherine, 2 sons, 1 daughter. Education: BSc, Economics, London; AMP, Harvard, USA. Appointments: Various positions, Shell International, 1948-64; Economics Analyst, Investment Banking, 1964-65; Various positions, 1965-87, Managing Director, Supply and Trading, 1979-87, Chief Executive Officer, Conoco Ltd, 1987-95; Currently, Trustee Energy Institute Pension Fund. Publications: Various technical and business articles. Honour: CBE. Memberships: Fellow, Energy Institute; Associate, Chartered Insurance Institute; Associate, Institute of Chartered Shipbrokers; Friend: Royal Academy of Art, Tate Gallery, Imperial War Museum, National Trust. Address: 67 Merchant Court, 61 Wapping Wall, London EW1 3SJ, England. E-mail: terrymoore@terrymoore.demon.co.uk

MOORHOUSE (Cecil) James (Olaf), b. 1 January 1924, Copenhagen, Denmark. European Politician. m. (1) 1 son, 1 daughter, (2) Catherine Hamilton Peterson. Education: King's College, 1942-44 and Imperial College, 1945-46, University of London: BSc (Eng); DIC Advanced Aeronautics; C Eng. Appointments: Designer with De Havilland Aircraft Co, 1946-48; Project Engineer, BOAC, 1949-53; Technical Adviser, 1953-68, Environmental Conservation Adviser, 1968-72, Shell International Petroleum; Environmental Adviser, Shell Group of Companies in UK, 1972-73; Group Environmental Affairs Adviser, Rio-Tinto Zinc Corporation, 1973-80; Consultant, 1980-84; MEP for London South, 1979-84; MEP, London South and Surrey East, 1984-99. Publications: Righting the Balance: A New Agenda for Euro-Japanese Trade (with Anthony Teasdale), 1987; Numerous articles and papers on aviation. Memberships: Club: Sloane; University (Washington, DC); The English Speaking Union; President, Help Tibet Trust (UK). Address: 180 Piccadilly, London W1J 9HF, England. E-mail: jamesmoorhouse@aol.com

MORA Renzo, b. 6 July 1970, Savona, Italy. Medical Doctor. m. Barbara Crippa, 1 son, 1 daughter. Education: Graduate, Medicine and Surgery, 1994, Otorhinolaryngology, ENT Department, 1998, Genoa University. Appointments: First Level Medical Manager, San Giovanni Bosco Hospital, Turin, 1999; First Level Medical Manager, ENT Department, 2000-, Professor, Audiometry Techniques, Speciality School in Audiology, 2002-, Research Doctor, 2002-, Associate Professor, Otorhinolaryngology, 2005-, University of Genoa. Publications: Regular reviewer for several scientific journals; Author, Over 80 articles in national and international journals; 26 book chapters; 155 other publications. Honours: Professor on the new diagnostic and rehabilitation techniques in otorhinolaryngology, Speciality School in Otorhinolaryngology of the University of Genoa, 1999; Polito Prize, 1999; AUORL Prize, 2000; Calearo AUORL Prize, 2002. Memberships: Italian Society of Otorhinolaryngology

Head and Neck Surgery; University Otorhinolaryngology Italian Association; American Academy of Otolaryngology – Head and Neck Surgery. E-mail: renzomora@libero.it

MORAŃSKA Danuta Izabela, b. 5 April 1963, Czeladź, Poland. Academic; Researcher. 1 daughter. Education: MA, 1988, PhD, Pedagogical Sciences, 1999, University of Silesia. Appointments: University Teacher, Faculty of Computer Science and Material Science, Division of Didactics of Technical Subjects, 1988-98, 1998-99, Supervisor of Scientific Club of Alternative Education, Faculty of Pedagogy and Psychology, Institute of Pedagogy, Department of Early School Pedagogy and Media Pedagogy, Division of Media Pedagogy, 2000-, University of Silesia, Katowice, Poland; Teacher, Electronics, Electronics Secondary School Complex, Sosnowiec, Poland, 1988-89; Teacher, Information Technology, Technical and Trade Secondary School Complex, Bedzin, Poland, 1993-99. Publications: Numerous articles in professional journals; Co-author, 1 book. Honours: 12 awards, University of Silesia, 1995-2010. Memberships: Polish Cognitive Society; Polish Society of Technology and Educational Media. Address: University of Silesia Katowice, Grazynskiego 53, Katowice, Slaskia 40-126, Poland.

MORARU Alexandru, b. 16 August 1948. Professor. Education: High School Graduate, 1968; University degree, 1972; Doctor's degree, Orthodox Theology, 1986. Appointments: Rev Teacher, World Church History and Romanian Orthodox Church History, 1972-90; Headmaster, Orthodox Theological Seminary, Cluj-Napoca, 1990; Rev Lecturer Dr, 1990; Rev University Professor, Romanian Orthodox Church History, 1990-; Rector, Orthodox Theological Institute, Cluj-Napoca, 1990-92; Rev University Professor, 1990-, Dean, 1992-96, Orthodox Theological Faculty, Babes-Bolyai University, Cluj-Napoca. Publications: 11 books; 265 studies and articles; Editor, 6 books. Memberships: WCC, Unit IV; Anglican-Orthodox Dialogue, 1990; National Ecclesiastical History Commission; Ioan Lupas Foundation, Cluj-Napoca. Address: Orthodox Theological Faculty, Babes-Bolyai University, No 18 Avram Iancu Street, RO-400090 Cluj-Napoca, Romania.

MORAWIEC Henryk Zygmunt, b. 14 September 1933, Katowice, Poland. Professor Emeritus retired 2009. m. Jadwiga Grabowska. Education: MSc, Technical University, Gliwice, Poland, 1958; PhD, 1967; DSc, Technical University Silesia, Katowice, Poland, 1976. Appointments: Head of Workshop, Institute of Non-ferrous Metals, Gliwice, 1961-72; Head of Department, 1972-78, Dean of Faculty, 1982-90, Director of Institute, 1990, University of Silesia, Katowice. Publications: Several articles in professional journals. Honours: Award of the Polish Academy of Sciences, 1961, 1990; Diploma, Technical University, Brno, 1986; Award, Foundation for Electron Microscope, Polish Science Foundation, 1994; Honorary Doctorate, Aristotle University of Thessalonika, Greece, 2009; Listed in various international biographical dictionaries. Memberships: Committee, Materials Science and Committee of Crystallography, Polish Academy of Sciences, 1980. Address: Kormoranów 16, 40-521 Katowice, Poland.

MOREHEN John Manley, b. 3 September 1941, Gloucester, England. Emeritus Professor. m. Marie Catherine Jacobus. 1 son, 1 daughter. Education: Royal School of Church Music, 1960-61; FRCO (Chm); BA (MA), Organ Scholar, New College, Oxford, 1961-64; PhD, King's College, Cambridge, 1964-67; Ralph H Lane Memorial Scholar, College of Church Musicians, Washington DC, 1966. Appointments: Assistant Director of Music, St Clement Danes Church, Strand, Hampstead Parish Church, London, 1964-67; Keyboard Player, Hampstead Choral Society, Martindale Sidwell Choir, London Bach Orchestra; Lecturer, College of Church Musicians, Washington Cathedral, and American University, Washington, DC, 1967-68; Sub-Organist, St George's Chapel, Windsor Castle, 1968-72; Lecturer, 1973-82, Senior Lecturer, 1982-89, Professor, 1989-2002, Head, School of Humanities, 1998-2001, Emeritus Professor of Music, 2002-, University of Nottingham. Publications: Editor, English Choral Practice, 1996; Chapters in: Byrd Studies, 1992; The Blackwell History of Music in Britain: The Sixteenth Century, 1995; Many critical editions of music by English and Italian composers of the 16th and 17th centuries; Contributions to professional publications; Numerous broadcasts as organist, speaker and conductor; Recital and lecture visits to Europe, North America and Australia; Many presentations on computer applications in music at conferences in the UK, USA, Canada, France and the Netherlands. Honours: Hon FGCM, 2004; D Litt, University of Nottingham, 2005. Memberships: Justice of the Peace, Nottingham; Freeman, City of London, and Junior Warden of the Worshipful Company of Musicians; Examiner, Associated Board of the Royal Schools of Music; Member, Academic Board and Council of the Guild of Church Musicians; Trustee, Member of Editorial Committee, Musica Britannica; Governor, Chetham's School of Music. Address: Chestnut Barn, Syerston Hall Park, Newark, Nottinghamshire, NG23 5NL, England. E-mail: j.morehen@athenaeumclub.co.uk Website: www.morehen.com

MOREL Pierre Jean Louis, b. 27 June 1944, Romans, France. Diplomat. m. Olga Bazanoff, 2 sons, 1 daughter. Education: Ecole Nationale d'Administration; Licence en Droit; Institut d'Etudes Politiques de Paris. Appointments: Political Director, Ministry of Foreign Affairs, 1985-86; Ambassador to the Conference on Disarmament, 1986-90; Diplomatic Adviser to the President, 1991-92; Ambassador in Russia, 1992-96; Ambassador in China, 1996-2002; Ambassador in the Holy See, 2002-05; European Union Special Representative for Central Asia, 2006; EU Special Representative for the Crisis in Georgia, 2008. Honours: Officier de la Legion d'Honneur; Commandeur de l'Ordre National du Merite. Memberships: International Institute for Strategic Studies, London, England. Address: 42 rue du Bac, 75007 Paris, France. E-mail: pierre.morel@consilium.europa.eu

MOREY DE MORAND C, b. Paris, France. Artist. m. James Corcoran, 1 son, 1 daughter. Education: Fine Art Certificate, Queens University (Dept Fine Arts), Kingston, Canada, 1965-1968; Manawatu (Massey) University Wellington, New Zealand, 1969-1972; Diploma (Hons) General Design, Painting, Photography, Lithography, Etching It Digital Printing And Design, Acava & Wornington College, London, 2001-2002. Appointments: Teaching: School of Fine Art, University of Canterbury, Christchurch, 1975, 1976, 1977; Art & Education workshops, AIR Gallery 1980, 1985, 1987; Morley College, London, Life Drawing 1981, 1982, 1983; Taught Drawing private pupils, 1983, 1984, 1985; Hertfordshire College of Art & Design, St. Albans, 1988, 1987; Sphere Centre, Moscow, Russia, 1990; Gallery Talk, Camden Art Centre, 1993; Michigan State University Art School, 1993, 1991, 1989; American University in London, studio practice experience, 2004, 2005; Artist In Residence: Triangle Artists Workshop, New York State withAnthony Caro, Clement Greenberg, Larry Poons, Helen Frankenthaler, Sheila Girling, 1983; House of Creativity, Chelyuskinskaya, USSR, 1989; Sphere Centre, Moscow, USSR, 1990; Society of Artists, Burgas, Bulgaria, 1990; Leighton Foundation, Alberta,

Canada, 1991; Sarabhai Residency, Ahmedabad, India, with John Baldessari, 1992; Symposium residency, Burgas Bulgaria, 1996; Denizli International Art Colony, Turkey, 1998; Milchhof Berlin Residency, Germany, 2006-2007; Short Listed British School at Rome, 2008; Cill Rialaig, Residency, Ireland, 2009; Artist, group and solo exhibitions in UK and abroad; Work held in public and private collections in 18 countries worldwide. Publications: Numerous articles in professional journals. Honours: QEII Arts Council of New Zealand Grant, 1973; Greater London Arts Grant, 1979; Arts Council of Great Britain, Artists Payment, 1980; Elephant Trust Grant,1983; Europe Prize for Painting, - Bronze Medal, 1986; British Council Grant, 1988; Leighton Foundation Grant, Alberta, Canada, 1991; Arts Council England Award, 2006; Irish Cill Rialaig Award, 2009. Memberships: Fellow, Royal Geographical Society; The London Group; Riverside Artists Group. Address: 61D Oxford Gardens, London W10 4UJ, England. E-mail: colettemoreydemorand@yahoo.co.uk Website: www.cmoreydemorand.co.uk

MORGAN David Gwyn, b. 24 July 1944, Llandeilo, South Wales. Veterinary Pathologist. m. Patricia, 1 son, 2 daughters. Education: BVSc (Hons), University of Liverpool, 1967; PhD, Viral Oncology, University of Bristol, 1975; Member of the Royal College of Veterinary Surgeons. Appointments: Adjunct Associate Professor, Department of Pathology, School of Veterinary Medicine, University of Pennsylvania, 1982-2001; Assistant Lecturer, Lecturer, Veterinary Comparative Pathology, University of Bristol, 1968-78; Assistant Director, Associate Director and Group Director of Pathology, Group Director, Pathology and Toxicology, Vice-President of Safety Assessment, SmithKline and French laboratories, Philadelphia, USA, 1978-90; Vice-President and Director, Worldwide Safety Assessment, SmithKline Beecham Pharmaceuticals, 1990-2001; Member, Board of Trustees, Health and Environmental Sciences Institute (International Life Sciences Institute, Washington, DC), 1997-2001; Chair, Drug Safety Sub-Section Steering Committee, Pharmaceutical Research and Manufacturers Association, USA, 1994-97; Chair, International Safety Evaluation Advisory Board, Centre for Medicines Research, London, England, 1998-2001; Scientific Advisor to the Academy of Medical Sciences Forum, London, 2002-05. Publications: More than 70 publications: Articles in peer reviewed journals, book chapters, and abstracts on topics related to veterinary pathology, immunotoxicology, arterial toxicity, nephrotoxicity, molecular toxicology and drug safety assessment; 52 invited presentations to international scientific societies and academic departments. Honours: World Health Organisation (IARC) Post-doctoral Research Training Fellowship, Yale University School of Medicine, New Haven Connecticut, USA, 1976; SmithKline Beecham Vice-President's Award for significant scientific contribution, 1993; SmithKline Beecham President's Award for significant scientific contribution, 1994; Safety Pharmacology Society Award for Meritorious Service to the Discipline of Safety Pharmacology, 2004. Memberships: Pathological Society of Great Britain and Ireland; Society of Toxicologic Pathologists, USA; Elected Regional Fellow, Royal Society of Medicine, 2004. Address: Trefri Hall, Aberdovey, Gwynedd LL35 0RD, Wales. E-mail: drgwynmorgan@aol.com

MORGAN David Vernon, b. 13 July 1941, Llanelli, Wales. Distinguished Research Professor. m. Jean, 1 son, 1 daughter. Education: BSc (Wales), 1963; MSc (Wales), 1964; PhD (Cambridge), 1967; DSc (Leeds). Appointments: University of Wales Fellow, Cavendish Laboratory Cambridge, 1966-68; Fellow, Harwell, 1968-70; Lecturer, 1970-77, Senior Lecturer, 1977-80, Reader, 1980-85, University of Leeds; Professor, 1985-, Head of School, 1992-2002, Distinguished Research Professor, Microelectronics, 2002-, Cardiff University. Publications: 230 papers published in scientific journals and international conferences; Authored and Edited 14 books including: An Introduction to Semiconductor Microtechnology, 1983, 2nd edition, 1990. Honours: FREng, 1996; FCGI for Services to Higher Education, 1998; Papal Cross (Pro Ecclesia et Pontifice) Services to Academe, 2004; Hon Fellowship, University of Wales, 2005. Memberships: FInstP; FIEE; Welsh Livery Guild. Address: School of Engineering, Cardiff University, Cardiff CF24 0YF, Wales. E-mail: morgandv@cf.ac.uk

MORGAN Edward Patrick William, b. 17 September 1927, Shorncliff, Kent, England. Retired; Lay Theologian. m. Nora Jane, 1 son, 1 daughter. Education: English, Honours, University of Birmingham, Teaching Diplomas, St Mary's College, University of London, 1950-53; B Theol, Honours, University of South Africa, 1982-87; Diploma, Credit Management Institute of South Africa; Diploma, Public Relations Institute of South Africa and of Market Research Institute, South Africa. Appointments: Secondary School Teacher, Hertfordshire County Council, Barnet then at St Dominic's, Haverstock Hill, (LCC), 1953-57; Rhodesia Government High School Teacher, Chaplin High School, Gwelo, Southern Rhodesia, 1957-63; St George's Jesuit College, Salisbury, Rhodesia, 1963-67; National Fund Raising Manager, Marist, South Africa, 1967-70; South African Government High School Teacher, Johannesburg, 1970-72; National Marketing Manager, then National Credit Manager in Johannesburg and Director of companies in Harare and Johannesburg, 1965-93; Retired 1993. Publications: Life of St Paul (series for Jesuit Magazine, Salisbury, Rhodesia), 1961; Regional Correspondent for weekly "Southern Cross", South Africa. Memberships: Executive Member for Wexford, Irish Senior Citizens' Parliament, 2005-; Public Relations Institute and Marketing Management Institute, South Africa; Founder-Treasurer, Catenian Association of South Africa; Catholic Theological Society of South Africa and Theology Associations of Great Britain and Ireland; European Society of Theologians. Address: 21 St Brendan's, Rosslare Harbour, County Wexford, Ireland. E-mail: patemorgan@eircom.net

MORGAN Kenneth, b. 9 June 1945, Llanelli, Wales. Professor. m. Elizabeth Margaret Harrison, 2 sons. Education: BSc, 1966, PhD, 1970, DSc (Eng), 1987, University of Bristol; CMath; CEng; FIMA, 1978; FICE, 1993; FREng, 1997; FLSW, 2011. Appointments: Scientific Officer, Mathematical Physics Division, UKAEA, AWRE Aldermaston, 1969-72; Lecturer, Department of Mathematics, University of Exeter, 1972-75; Lecturer, 1975-84, Senior Lecturer, 1984-86, Reader, 1986-88, Professor, 1988-89, Department of Civil Engineering, University of Wales, Swansea; Zaharoff Professor of Aviation, Department of Aeronautics, Imperial College, London 1989-91; Professor, Department of Civil Engineering, 1991-2002, Head of Department, 1991-96, Dean of Engineering, 1997-2000, Head, Civil and Computational Engineering Centre, 2002-08, University of Wales, Swansea; Professor, Computational Modelling, Wales Institute of Mathematical and Computational Sciences, School of Engineering, Swansea University, 2008-; Visiting Scientist, Joint Research Centre of the EC, Ispra, Italy, 1980; Visiting Research Scientist, Institute for Computer Applications in Science and Engineering, NASA, Langley Research Center, Virginia, USA, 1985; Visiting Research Professor, Old Dominion University, Norfolk, Virginia, 1986-87; Visiting Research Professor, University of Virginia, 1988-92; Council,

DICTIONARY OF INTERNATIONAL BIOGRAPHY 36th EDITION

International Association for Computational Mechanics, 1993-; Management Board, European Committee for Computational Methods in the Applied Sciences, 1993-2008; Inter Research Council High Performance Computing Management Committee, 1995-98; Ludwig Prandtl Medal, European Community on Computational Methods in Applied Sciences, 2008. Publications: Finite Elements and Approximations (co-author), 1983; The Finite Element Method in Heat Transfer Analysis (co-author), 1996. Honours: Special Achievement Award, NASA, Langley Research Center, 1989; Computational Mechanics Award, International Association for Computational Mechanics, 1998; Honorary Fellow, International Association for Computational Fluid Dynamics, 2003; Fellow, International Association for Computational Mechanics, 2004. Address: 137 Pennard Drive, Southgate, Swansea SA3 2DW, Wales. E-mail: k.morgan@swansea.ac.uk

MORGAN Piers Stefan, b. 30 March 1965, Guildford, England. Journalist. m. Marion E Shalloe, 1991 (divorced) 3 sons. Education: Harlow Journalism College. Career: Reporter, Surrey and South London newspapers, 1987-89; Showbusiness Editor, The Sun, 1989-94; Editor, The News of the World, 1994-95, Daily Mirror (later The Mirror) 1995-2004; First News, 2006.TV: Presenter, The Importance of Being Famous, Channel 4, 2004; Morgan & Platell, Channel 4, 2005-; America's Got Talent, 2006; Comic Relief Does The Apprentice, 2007; Britains Got Talent, 2007; You Can't Fire Me, I'm Famous, 2007; Piers Morgan on Sandbanks, 2008. Publications: Private Lives of the Stars, 1990; Secret Lives of the Stars, 1991; Phillip Schofield, To Dream A Dream, 1992; Take That, Our Story, 1993; Take That: On the Road, 1994; Va Va Voom!: A Year with Arsenal, 2003-04; The Insider (memoir), 2005; Don't You Know Who I Am?, 2007; God Bless America: Misadventures of a Big Mouth Brit, 2009. Honours: Atex Award for National Newspaper Editor of the Year, 1994; What the Papers Say Newspaper of the Year Award, 2001; GQ Editor of the Year, 2002; British Press Awards Newspaper of the Year, 2002; Magazine Design & Journalism Awards, Columnist of the Year Live, 2007.

MORGAN Ronald, b. 28 February 1936, Landywood, Staffordshire, England. Artist. Education: Walsall School of Art. Appointments: Local Government Graphic Designer, London Borough's of Haringey, Hammersmith and Tower Hamlets; Senior Local Government Officer, 1988-91; Full time Self Employed Artist, 1991-; Governor, Federation of British Artists, 2004-. Publications: Articles on painting for the Leisure Painter magazine. Honours: 1st Prize, Lord Mayor of London Art Award, 1974; Crane Gallery Award, 1989; Usiskin Contemporary Art Award, 1990; Gourley Memorial Award, 1996; Dover Federation for the Arts Award, Royal Society of British Artists, 2008; Le Clerc Fowle Gold Medal, Royal Institute of Oil Painters, 2009; many others. Memberships: Royal Society of British Artists; Royal Institute of Oil Painters; Chelsea Art Society; Small Paintings Group. Address: 8 Marina Court, Alfred Street, Bow, London E5 2BH, England.

MORGAN Trefor Owen, b. 11 March 1936, New South Wales, Australia. Medical Researcher; Vigneron. m. Olive Lawson, 1 son, 1 daughter. Education: University of Sydney, 1953-59; BScMed, 1958; MBBS, 1960; MD, 1972; Fellow, Royal Australian College of Physicians, 1972; Charles Stuart University, 1987-91; BApplSci, Wine, 1992. Appointments: Intern, Resident, Registrar, Clinical Supervisor, Royal Prince Alfred Hospital, 1960-66; Visiting Scientist, National Institutes of Health, USA, 1966-69; Renal Physician, Princess Alexandra Hospital, Australia, 1969-71; Assistant in Medicine, 1971-77, Professor of Physiology, 1984-2004, University of Melbourne, Victoria; Distinguished Professor of Medicine, Universiti Tecknologica Mara, Shah Alam, Malaysia, 2004-07; Visiting Professor, University of Munich, Germany, 1975; Foundation Professor of Medicine, University of Newcastle, Australia, 1977-81; Specialist in Charge of Medicine, Repatriation Hospital, 1981-84; Visiting Professor, University Lausanne, 1996. Publications: 350 scientific papers; 3 books. Honour: Honorary Professor, Shandong Academy of Medical Sciences, China. Memberships: International Society of Hypertension; High Blood Pressure Research Council of Australia; Secretary, Asian Pacific Society of Hypertension. Address: Department of Physiology, University of Melbourne, Parkville 3052, Victoria, Australia.

MORGAN William Richard, b. 27 March 1922, Cambridge, Ohio, USA. Mechanical Engineer. m. Marjorie Eleanor Stevens, 17 February 1946, 1 son, 1 daughter. Education: BSME, Ohio State University, 1944; MSME, Purdue University, 1950; PhD, Mechanical Engineering, 1951. Appointments: Power Plant Design Engineer, Curtiss Wright Corp, Columbus, Ohio, 1946-47; Instructor and Westinghouse Research Fellow, Purdue University; West Lafayette Indiana, 1947-51; Supervisor, Experimental Mechanical Engineering, GE, Cincinnati, 1951-55; Manager, Controls Analysis Development, Aircraft Gas Turbine Division, GE, 1955-59; Manager, XV5A vertical take-off and landing aircraft programme, GE, 1959-65; Manager, Acoustic Engineering, Flight Propulsion Division, GE, 1965-69; Manager, quiet engine programme 1969-71; President, Cincinnati Research Corporation, 1971-73; Vice President, SDRC International, Cincinnati, 1973-79; Engineering and Management Consultant, Cincinnati, 1979-. Publications: Geometric Configuration Factors in Radiant Heat Transmission (PhD Dissertation), 1951; Numerous papers presented in seminars and symposia and articles in professional journals. Memberships: ASME; Sigma Xi; Pi Tau Sigma; Pi Mu Epsilon. Address: 312 Ardon Ln, Cincinnati, OH 45215, USA.

MORISSETTE Alanis, b. 1 June 1974, Ottawa, Canada. Singer. m. Mario "MC Souleye" Treadway, 2010, 1 child. Career: Solo recording artiste; Appeared on Canadian cable TV, aged 10; Signed contract as songwriter with MCA Publishing aged 14; Tours: Vanilla Ice Tour, 1991; Jagged Little Pill, 1995; Can't Not Tour, 1996; Club Tour, 1998; Junkie Tour, 1999; 5 ½ Weeks Tour, 1999; One Tour, 2000; Under Rug Swept Tour, 2001; Toward Our Union Mended Tour, 2002; All I Really Want/Feast on Scraps Tour, 2003; So-Called Chaos/Au Naturale Tour, 2004; Diamond Wink Tour, 2005; Exile in America, 2008; Flavors of Entanglement Tour, 2008; The Guardian Angel Tour, 2012; 16 million albums sold. Recordings: Albums: Alanis, 1991; Now Is The Time, 1992; Jagged Little Pill, 1995; Space Cakes (live), Supposed Former Infatuation Junkie, 1998; Alanis Unplugged (live), 1999; Under Rug Swept, 2002; So-called Chaos, 2004; Jagged Little Pill Acoustic, Alanis Morissette: The Collection, 2005; Flavors of Entanglement, 2008; Havoc and Bright Lights, 2012. Singles: Fate Stay With Me; You Oughta Know, One Hand In My Pocket, 1995; Ironic, You Learn, Head Over Feet, 1996; All I Really Want, Thank U, You Oughta Know, 1998; Joining You, Unsent, So Pure, So Real, That I Would Be Good, 1999; Hands Clean, Precious Illusions, 2002; So-called Chaos, 2004; Flavors of Entanglement, 2008; TV: You Can't Do That on Television, 1986; Malhacao, 1996; Sex and the City, 2000; Curb Your Enthusiasm, 2002; Celebridade, 2003; American Dreams, 2004; Degrassi: The Next Generation, 2005; Lovespring International, Nip/Tuck, 2006; Weeds,

2009-10; Up All Night, 2012; Stage: The Vagina Monologues, 1999; The Exonerated, 2004; An Oak Tree, 2010; Film: Dogma, 1999; De-Lovely, 2004; Fuck, Just Friends, 2005; Radio Free Albemuth, 2010; As Cool As I Am, 2012. Honour: BRIT Award, Best International Newcomer, 1996; Four Grammy Awards, including Album of the Year and Best Rock Album; Best Female Award, MTV European Music Awards, 1996. Address: Maverick Recording Company, 9348 Civic Center Drive, Suite 100, Beverley Hills, CA 90210, USA. Website: www.alanismorissette.com

MORITZ Ralf, b. 2 May 1941, Leipzig, Germany. University Professor. m. Marlies Ludwig, 1 son. Education: Diploma, Philosophy and Sinology, Leipzig University, 1963, Peking, 1966; Doctor's Degree, Leipzig, 1969; Habilitation, 1980. Appointments: Assistant Professor, Leipzig University, 1966-69; Fellow, Academy of Social Sciences, Berlin, 1969-80; Lecturer, 1981-84, Professor, 1984-, Vice-Director for African and Middle East Studies, 1983-86, Director, Asian Department, 1988-93, Director of East Asia Institute, 1994-98, 2001-06, Leipzig University; Director, Confucius Institute, Leipzig, 2007-. Publications: Confucius. Analects (editor, translator), 1982; Classes and class-structure in PRC (in Russian) (co-editor, co-author), 1982; How and why did philosophy arise in different regions of the world ? (co-editor, co-author), 1988; Philosophers. A Reader (co-editor, co-author), 1988; The Philosophy of Ancient China (author), 1990; Sinological Traditions in the Mirror of New Researches (editor, co-author), 1993; Middle German Studies of East Asia (book series, co-editor), 1998; The Confucianism (co-editor, co-author), 1998; The Great Learning (editor, translator), 2003. Honours: University Medal, Leipzig University, 2006. Memberships: German Society for Chinese Studies; European Association for Chinese Studies. Address: Kurt-Weill-Str 7, D-04347 Leipzig, Germany. E-mail: moritz-ralf@t-online.de

MORPURGO Michael Andrew Bridge, b. 5 October 1943, St Albans, England. Author; Poet; Playwright; Librettist. m. Claire. Education: The King's School, Canterbury; Royal Military Academy, Sandhurst; King's College London. Appointments: Primary School Teacher, Kent; Author. Publications include: War Horse, 1982; Little Foxes, 1984; Why the Whales Came, 1985; Waiting for Anya, 1990; Colly's Barn, 1991; The Sandman and the Turtles, 1991; Martians at Mudpuddle Farm, 1992; The War of Jenkins' Ear, 1993; The Wreck of the Zanzibar, 1995; The Butterfly Lion, 1996; Kensuke's Kingdom, 1999; Cool! 2002; Private Peaceful, 2003; Alone on a Wide, Wide Sea, 2006; Beowulf, 2006. Honours: Prix Socières, 1993, 1999, 2001; Whitbread Children's Book Award, 1995; Nestlé Smarties Book Prize, 1996, 2002; MBE, 1999; Children's Laureate, 2003-05; Red House Children's Book Award, 2000, 2004; Blue Peter Book of the Year Award, 2005; Hampshire Book Award, 2005; OBE, 2006; California Young Reader Medal, 2007. Website: www.michaelmorpurgo.org

MORRELL David William James, b. 26 July 1933, Glasgow, Scotland. University Administrator; Ombudsman. m. Margaret Rosemary, 2 sons, 1 daughter. Education: MA (Hons), 1954, LLB, 1957, University of Edinburgh. Appointments: Apprentice Solicitor, Shepherd & Wedderburn WS, 1954-57; Administrative Assistant, King's College, University of Durham, 1957-60; Assistant Registrar, University of Exeter, 1960-64; Senior Assistant Registrar, University of Essex, 1964-66; Academic Registrar, 1966-73; Registrar and Secretary, 1973-89, University of Strathclyde; Consultant to Institutional Management in Higher Education Programme of OECD, Paris, 1989-90; Lay Observer for Scotland, 1989-91; Scottish Legal Services Ombudsman, 1991-94; Chairman, 1995-96, Vice-Chairman, 1996-99, Lomond Healthcare NHS Trust; Member, Argyll and Clyde Health Board, 1999-2001; Chairman of University of Paisley, 1997-2002. Publications: Various on management in higher education and on lawyer/client relationships. Honours: Honorary Degree, Doctor of the University, University of Paisley, 2005. Memberships: National Trust for Scotland; Historic Scotland; Church of Scotland; Fellow, Institute of Contemporary Scotland.

MORRELL Peter Richard, b. 25 May 1944, Ruislip, Middlesex, England. Clerk in Holy Orders; Retired Circuit Judge. m. Helen Mary Vint Collins, 2 daughters. Education: Orley Farm Preparatory School, 1952-57; Westminster School, 1957-62; University College, Oxford, 1963-66; College of Law, 1967-70; Eastern Region Ministry Course, Anglia Ruskin University, 2006-08. Appointments: Admitted as Solicitor, 1970; Called to the Bar, Gray's Inn, 1974; Recorder, 1990; Circuit Judge, 1992; Reader, 2005; Deacon, 2008; Assistant Curate, Benefice of Uppingham with Ayston, and Wardley with Belton, Diocese of Peterborough, 2008; Priest, 2009; Assistant Curate, Benefice of Nassington with Yarwell, and Woodnewton with Apethorpe, Diocese of Peterborough, 2010. Memberships: Countryside Alliance; Game Conservancy; Council of Circuit Judges; Company of St Peter, Peterborough. Address: New Sulehay Lodge, Nassington, Peterborough PE8 6QT, England. E-mail: pmorrell@btinternet.com

MORRIS Desmond John, b. 24 January 1928, Purton, Wiltshire, England. Zoologist; Author; Broadcaster; Artist. m. Ramona Baulch, 1 son. Education: BSc, Birmingham University, 1951; DPhil, Oxford University, 1954. Appointments: Zoological Research Worker, University of Oxford, 1954-56; Head of Granada TV and Film Unit, Zoological Society of London, 1956-59; Curator of Mammals, Zoological Society of London, 1959-67; Director, Institute of Contemporary Arts, London, 1967-68; Privately engaged writing books, 1968-73; Research Fellow, Wolfson College, Oxford, 1973-81; Privately engaged writing books and making television programmes, 1981-2005. TV series: Zootime, 1956-67; Life, 1965-67; The Human Race, 1982; The Animals Roadshow, 1987-89; The Animal Contract, 1989; Animal Country, 1991-96; The Human Animal, 1994; The Human Sexes, 1997; Solo exhibitions (paintings): Art galleries across England and in Holland, Belgium, France, USA and Ireland. Publications include: The Biology of Art, 1962; The Big Cats, 1965; Zootime, 1966; The Naked Ape, 1967; The Human Zoo, 1969; Patterns of Reproductive Behaviour, 1970; Intimate Behaviour, 1971; Manwatching, 1977; Animal Days, 1979; The Soccer Tribe, 1981; Bodywatching: A Field Guide to the Human Species, 1985; Catwatching, 1986; Dogwatching, 1986; Catlore, 1987; The Human Nestbuilders, 1988; The Animal Contract, 1990; Animal-Watching, 1990; Babywatching, 1991; Christmas Watching, 1992; The World of Animals, 1993; The Naked Ape Trilogy, 1994; The Human Animal, 1994; Bodytalk: A World Guide to Gestures, 1994; Catworld: A Feline Encyclopaedia, 1996; The Human Sexes: A Natural History of Man and Woman, 1997; Illustrated Horsewatching, 1998; Cool Cats: The 100 Cat Breeds of the World, 1999; Body Guards: Protective Amulets and Charms, 1999; The Naked Ape and Cosmetic Behaviour (with Kaori Ishida), 1999; The Naked Eye, Travels in Search of the Human Species, 2000; Dogs: a Dictionary of Dog Breeds, 2001; Peoplewatching, 2002; The Silent Language (in Italian), 2004; The Nature of Happiness, 2004; The Naked Woman, 2004; Linguaggio muto, 2004;

Watching, 2006; The Naked Man, 2008; Baby: A Portrait of the First Two Years of Life, 2008; Planet Ape, 2009; Owl, 2009; Child: How Children Think, Learn and Grow in the Early Years, 2010. Contributions to: Many journals and magazines. Honour: Honorary DSc, Reading University, 1998. Membership: Scientific Fellow, Zoological Society of London; Honorary Fellow, Linnenan Society, London. Address: c/o Jonathan Cape, Random Century House, 20 Vauxhall Bridge Road, London SW1V 2SA, England.

MORRIS Richard Francis Maxwell, b. 11 September 1944, Sussex, England. Chief Executive. m. Marian Sperling, 9 April 1983, 2 daughters. Education: New College, Oxford, 1963-66; College of Law, London, 1967. Appointments: Solicitor, Farrer & Co, 1967-71; Banker, Grindlay Brandts, 1971-75; Director, Invicta Radio plc, 1984-92; General Manager, Corporate Finance, SG Warburg & Co, 1975-79; Managing Director, Edward Arnold Ltd. 1987-91; Finance Director, Joint Managing Director, Hodder & Stoughton, 1979-91; Founder, Almaviva Opera, 1989-; Trustee, Governor, Kent Opera, 1985-90; Director, Southern Radio plc, 1990-92; Chief Executive, Associated Board of the Royal Schools of Music, 1993-; Trustee, Director, Kent Music School, 2001-; Member, Executive Committee, Chairman, Music Education Council, 1995-; Trustee, Council for Dance Education and Training, 1999-2005; Governor, The Yehudi Menuhin School, 2004-. Honours: Honorary RCM; Honorary RNCM; MA (Oxon). Memberships: Incorporated Society of Musicians. Address: 24 Portland Place, London W1B 1LU, England. E-mail: rmorris@abrsm.ac.uk

MORRIS Richard Graham Michael, b. 27 June 1948, Worthing, Sussex, England. Neuroscientist. m. Hilary Ann Lewis, 2 daughters. Education: MA, Trinity Hall, University of Cambridge, 1966-69; DPhil, Sussex University, 1969-73. Appointments: Senior Scientific Officer, British Museum, Natural History, Researcher, BBC Television, Science and Features Department, 1973-75; Lecturer, Psychology, 1977-86, MRC Research Fellow, 1983-86, University of St Andrews; Reader in Neuroscience, 1986-93, Professor of Neuroscience, 1993-, Director, Centre for Neuroscience, 1993-97, Chairman, Department of Neuroscience, University of Edinburgh, 1998-2002; Co-Director, Edinburgh Neuroscience, 2005-; Editorial roles in various scientific journals, 1990-. Publications: Over 150 papers in academic journals; Neuroscience: The Science of the Brain (booklet for secondary school children); Parallel Distributed Processing: Implications for Psychology and Neurobiology (editor), 1989; Neuroscience: Science of the Brain, 1994, 2003; Long Term Potentiation, 2004. Honours: Fellow, Academy of Medical Sciences, 1998-; Decade of the Brain Lecturer, 1998; Zotterman Lecturer, 1999; Forum Fellow, World Economics Forum, 2000; Life Sciences Co-ordinate OST Foresight Project on Cognitive Systems, 2002-04; Yngve Zotterman Prize, Karolinska Institute, 1999; Henry Dryerre Prize, Royal Society of Edinburgh, 2000. Memberships: Experimental Psychology Society, Honorary Secretary, 1984-88; British Neuroscience Association, Chairman, 1991-95; Society for Neuroscience, USA; European Brain and Behaviour Society; American Academy of Arts and Sciences, 2004-. Address: Neuroscience, University of Edinburgh, 1 George Square, Edinburgh EH8 9JZ, Scotland.

MORRIS William (Bill), Baron Morris of Handsworth, b. 1938, Jamaica. Trade Union General Secretary. m. Minetta, deceased 1990, 2 sons. Appointments include: Joined engineering company, Hardy Spicers, Birmingham; Joined T&G, 1958; Elected Shop Steward, Hardy Spicers, 1962; Involved in first industrial dispute, 1964; Elected Member, T&G's General Executive Council, 1972; District Officer, T&G, Nottingham/Derby District, 1973; Northampton District Secretary, T&G, 1976; National Secretary of the Passenger Service Trade Group, T&G, 1979; Deputy General Secretary, T&G, 1986-92; Elected General Secretary, 1991, re-elected, 1995-2003; Member, TUC General Council, 1988-2003; Member, TUC Executive Committee, 1988-; Member, Commission for Racial Equality, 1980-87; Member, Executive Board of the International Transport Worker's Federation, 1986; Member, New Deal Task Force, 1997-2000; Member, Court of the Bank of England, 1998-; Member of Committee for Integrated Transport, 1999-; Member, Governing Councils, Luton University and Northampton University; Chancellor, University of Technology, Jamaica, 1999-, Staffordshire University, 2004-; Chair, Morris Enquiry, 2003-04; Non-executive Director, England and Wales Cricket Board, 2007-. Honours: Numerous Honorary Degrees; Honorary Professorship, Thames Valley University, 1997; Honorary Fellowship, Royal Society of Arts, 1992; Honorary Fellowship City & Guilds London Institute, 1992; Order of Jamaica, 2002; Public Figure of the Year, Ethnic Multicultural Media Awards, 2002; Knighted, 2003. Memberships: Board of Fullemploy, 1985-88; Trustee, 1987-90, Advisory Committee, 1997- Prince's Youth Business Trust. Address: 156 St Agnells Lane, Grove Hill, Hemel Hempstead, Hertfordshire, HP2 6EG, England.

MORRISON Madison, b. 28 June 1940, USA. Writer. Education: BA, Yale University, 1961; AM, 1962, PhD, 1969, Harvard University. Appointments: Assistant, Humanities courses, 1963-1965, Tutor, 1967-1969, Harvard University; Instructor, University of Maryland on military bases in Germany, France and Greece, 1965-1967; Professor, University of Oklahoma, 1969-92. Publications: 23 of the 26 volumes in Sentence of the Gods; 7 other books; Academic monograph: Frank W Stevenson, Chaos and Cosmos in Morrison's Sentence of the Gods, Collection of essays about: MM: The Sentence Commuted. Honours: National Endowment for the Arts; National Endowment for the Humanities; Ingram Merrill Foundation; Fulbright Lecturer, India; Visiting Professor, University of Rome, Italy; Visiting Professor, Thammasat University, Thailand, etc. Address: PO Box 22-106, Taipei 10699, Taiwan. Website: www.madisonmorrison.com

MORRISON Samuel James, b. 18 February 1917, Glasgow, Scotland. Engineer. m. Mary, 2 daughters. Education: Shawlands Academy, Glasgow, 1922-29; Allan Glen's School, Glasgow, 1929-34; BSc, Electrical Engineering, University of Glasgow, 1935-40. Appointments: Apprentice, 1940-42, Research Engineer, 1945-56, British Thomson Houston; Shrinkage Engineer, Cosmos Manufacturing, 1942-45; Statistician, Standard Telephones & Cables, 1956-60; Statistician, British Ropes, 1960-63; Lecturer, 1963-78, Head of Department of OR, 1978-82, Honorary Research Associate, 1982-86, Retired, Senior Fellow, 1986, University of Hull. Publications: Over 30 articles in various professional journals; Numerous conference presentations; Author, Statistics for Engineers: an Introduction, 2009. Honours: National Academic Prize, Undiscovered Authors Competition, 2006; Greenfield Industrial Medal, Royal Statistical Society, 2007; IET Achievement Medal, Institution of Engineering and Technology, 2007. Memberships: Fellow, Institution of Mechanical Engineers; Fellow, Chartered Management Institute; Fellow, Royal Statistical Society; Senior Member, American Society for Quality. Address: Rm 51, St Mary's Care Centre, Beverley Road, Anlaby, HU10 7BQ, England.

MORRISON Toni (Chloe Anthony), b. 18 February 1931, Lorain, Ohio, USA. Novelist. m. Harold Morrison, 1958, divorced 1964, 2 children. Education: Howard University; Cornell University. Appointments: Teacher, English and Humanities, Texas Southern University, 1955-57, Howard University, 1957-64; Editor, Random House, New York, 1965-; Associate Professor of English, State University of New York, 1971-72; Schweitzer Professor of the Humanities, 1984-89; Robert F Goheen Professor of the Humanities, Princeton University, 1989-. Publications: The Bluest Eye, 1970; Sula, 1974; Song of Solomon, 1977; Tar Baby, 1983; Beloved, 1987; Jazz, 1992; Playing in the Dark: Whiteness and the Literary Imagination, 1992; Nobel Prize Speech, 1994; Birth of a Nation'hood: Gaze, Script and Spectacle in the O J Simpson Trial, 1997; The Big Box (poems), 1999; The Book of Mean People, 2002; Love, 2003; Remember: The Journey to School Integration, 2004. Who's Got Game?: The Ant or the Grasshopper, The Lion or the Mouse, 2003; Poppy or the Snake, 2004; The Mirror or the Glass, 2007. Honours include: Pulitzer Prize and Robert F Kennedy Book Award, for Beloved, 1988; Nobel Prize for Literature, 1993; Commander, Ordre des Arts et des Lettres; National Medal of Arts, 2000. Membership: Council, Authors' Guild. Address: c/o Suzanne Gluck, International Creative Management, 40 57th Street West, NY 10019, USA.

MORRISON Van (George Ivan Morrison), b. 31 August 1945, Belfast, Northern Ireland. Singer; Songwriter; Composer; Musician. 1 daughter; Partner, Michelle Rocca, 1 son, 1 daughter. Career: Founder, lead singer, Them, 1964-67; Solo artiste, 1967-; Appearances include: Knebworth Festival, 1974; The Last Waltz, The Band's farewell concert, 1976; Played with Bob Dylan, Wembley Stadium, 1984; Self Aid, with U2, Dublin, 1986; Glastonbury Festival, 1987; Prince's Rock Trust Gala, 1989; Performance, The Wall, by Roger Waters, Berlin, 1990; Concert in Dublin, with Bono, Bob Dylan, 1993; Phoenix Festival, 1995. Recordings: Singles include: Gloria; Brown-Eyed Girl; Moondance; Domino; Wild Night; Albums include: Blowin' Your Mind, 1967; Astral Weeks, 1968; Moondance, 1970; His Band And Street Choir, 1973; Tupelo Honey, 1971; St Dominic's Preview, 1972; Hard Nose The Highway, 1973; It's Too Late To Stop Now, 1974; TB Sheets, 1974; Veedon Fleece, 1974; This Is Where I Came In, 1977; A Period Of Transition, 1977; Wavelength, 1978; Into The Music, 1983; Bang Masters, 1990; Common One, 1980; Beautiful Vision, 1982; Inarticulate Speech Of The Heart, 1983; Live At The Opera House Belfast, 1984; A Sense Of Wonder, 1984; No Guru, No Method, No Teacher, 1986; Poetic Champions Compose, 1987; Irish Heartbeat, 1988; Best Of..., 1990; Avalon Sunset, 1989; Enlightenment, 1990; Hymns To The Silence, 1991; Too Long In Exile, 1993; Best Of..., Vol 2, 1993; A Night in San Francisco, 1994; Days Like This, 1995; Songs of the Mose Allison: Tell Me Something, 1996; The Healing Game, 1997; The Skiffle Sessions: Live in Belfast, 1998, 2000; Brown Eyed Girl, 1998; The Masters, 1999; Super Hits, 1999; Back on Top, 1999; You Win Again, 2000; Down The Road, 2002; What's Wrong With This Picture? 2003; Magic Time, 2005; Pay the Devil, 2006; Live at the Austin City Limits Festival, 2006; Keep it Simple, 2008; Astral Weeks Live at the Hollywood Bowl, 2009; Born to Sing: No Plan B, 2012; Also recorded on albums: with The Band: Cahoots, 1971; The Last Waltz, 1978; with John Lee Hooker: Folk Blues, 1963; Mr Lucky, 1991; with Bill Wyman: Stone Alone, 1976; with Jim Capaldi: Fierce Heart, 1983; with Georgie Fame: How Long Has This Been Going On, 1996. Honours include: Inducted into Rock And Roll Hall Of Fame, 1993; BRIT Award, Outstanding Contribution to British Music, 1994; Q Award, Best Songwriter, 1995; OBE, 1996; Officuer de l'Ordre des Arts et des Lettres, 1996; BMI Icon Award, 2004; Best International Male Singer, 2007; Hollywood Walk of Fame, 2010. Website: www.vanmorrison.co.uk

MORRISS Peter, b. 7 January 1940, Chesterfield, England. Retired. m. Joan Margaret, 1963, 1 son, 1 daughter. Publications: Published in over 100 anthologies of poetry by: Poets England; Forward Press; Poetry Now; Arrival Press; Anchor Books; Poetic Hours; Dogma Publications; United Press; Aural Images; Poetry Today; United Reformed Church Sounds of Fury Anthology; Through My Eyes (poetry collection), 1999; Painting the Town Red (epic Poem), 2002; Tape, Just Poetry (for the Leicestershire Royal Society for the Blind), 1994; Poetry also published in various magazines. Honours: Commendation Poetry Club, 1996, Triumph House, 1997; Editors Choice Award, International Society of Poets, 1996; Editors Choice Award International Library of Poetry, 1998. Membership: Society of Authors; Lapidus (Literary Arts In Personal Development); Poetry Society; British Haiku Society. Address: Pitnamoon Farmhouse, Laurencekirk AB30 1ES, Scotland. E-mail: petermorriss@btinternet.com Website: www.scribesnook.co.uk

MORT Graham Robert, b. 11 August 1955, Middleton, England. Poet. m. Maggie Mort, 12 February 1979, 3 sons. Education: BA, University of Liverpool, 1977; PGCE, St Martin's College, Lancaster, 1980; PhD, University of Glamorgan, 2000. Appointment: Creative Writing Course Leader, Open College of the Arts, 1989-2000; Senior Lecturer in Creative Writing, Lancaster University, 2002. Publications: A Country on Fire; Into the Ashes; A Halifax Cider Jar; Sky Burial; Snow from the North; Starting to Write; The Experience of Poetry, Storylines; Circular Breathing; A Night on the Lash; Visibility: New and Selected Poems; Touch, 2010. Contributions to: Numerous literary magazines and journals. Honours: 1st Prizes, Cheltenham Poetry Competition, 1979, 1982; Duncan Lawrie Prizes, Arvon Poetry Competition, 1982, 1992, 1994; Major Eric Gregory Award, 1985; Authors Foundation Award, 1994; Bridport Prize for Short Fiction, 2007. Memberships: Society of Authors; National Association of Writers in Education. Address: Hollins House, Duke Street, Burton-in-Lonsdale, Carnforth, Lancashire LA6 3LG, England.

MORTENSEN Finn Hauberg, b. 26 July 1946, Copenhagen, Denmark. Professor. m. Ella Bredsdorff, 3 sons, 2 daughters. Education: Cand Phil, 1972, Mag Art, 1975, Lic Phil, 1979, Copenhagen University, Denmark. Appointments: Research Fellow, 1972-74, Assistant Professor, 1974-76, Associate Professor, 1976-89, Docent, 1989-91, Professor, 1991-2007, University of Southern Denmark; Research Professor, 1994-91, Professor, 2007-, Copenhagen University; Guest Professor, Kwansei Gakuin University, 1997, 2002; Research Fellow, University of California, Berkeley, 2003, 2004, 2005, 2006, 2007, 2008, 2009, 2011; Chair, Institute of Philosophy, Education and the Study of Religions; University of Southern Denmark, 2005-06; Chair, Institute of Scandinavian Studies and Linguistics, University of Copenhagen, 2007-. Publications: Litteraturfunktion og symbolnorm 1-2, 1973; Danskfagets didaktik 1-2, 1979; Kierkegaards Either/Or, 1989; A Tale of Tales – H C Andersen, 1989; Funderinger over faget dansk, 1993; Kierkegaard Made in Japan, 1996; Villy Sørensen: Talt, 2002; Abe and Søko, Uddannelsesdebat 1969-2001, 2002; Bibliografi over Villy Sørensens Forfatterskab, 2003; Laeselist, Litteraturpaedagogiske essays 1-2, 2003; Litteratur & Symbol, 2009; H C Andersen, Skeve Skrifter, 2011. Honours: Gold Medal, Copenhagen University, 1969; Knighted by the Queen of Denmark. Memberships: Royal Danish Academy of Sciences and Letters; Council of Arts, Ministry of Culture; Chairman, Society for Danish Language and Literature; Chairman, Council of Literature, Ministry of Culture. Address: Thorsvej 33, 3140 DK-Ålsgårde, Denmark.

MORTON Newton Ennis, b. 21 December 1929, Camden, New Jersey, USA. Professor. 3 sons, 2 daughters. Education: BA, Zoology, University of Hawaii, 1951; MS, 1952, PhD, 1955, Genetics, University of Wisconsin. Appointments: Geneticist, Atomic Bomb Casualty Commission, NRC-NAS, 1952-53; Postdoctoral Fellow, National Cancer Institute, 1955-56, Assistant Professor, 1956-60, Associate Professor, 1960-62, University of Wisconsin; Professor, Genetics and Public Health, 1962-85, Director, Population Genetics Laboratory, 1968-85, University of Hawaii; Head, Department of Epidemiology and Biostatistics, Memorial Sloan-Kettering Cancer Center, 1985-87; Adjunct Professor, Rockefeller University, 1985-87; Professor and Director, CRC Research Group in Genetic Epidemiology, 1988-95, Professor and Senior Professorial Fellow in Human Genetics, 1995-, University of Southampton. Publications: More than 500 articles; 8 books. Honours: Phi Beta Kappa, 1951; Lederle Medical Faculty Award, 1958; Allan Award, American Society of Human Genetics, 1961; Foreign Member, Academia Brasiliera de Ciências, 1963; MD (Hon), University of Umea, Sweden, 1976; Regents' Excellence in Research Award, University of Hawaii, 1982; Fellow, American Association for the Advancement of Science, 1983; Fellow, Japan Society of Human Genetics, 1983; Member, National Academy of Sciences, USA, 1990; President, 9th International Congress of Human Genetics, 1996; Honorary Fellow, Royal College of Physicians, 1997; Honorary Symposium, American Society of Human Genetics, 2009. Memberships: American Society of Human Genetics; International Genetic Epidemiology Society; European Society of Human Genetics; British Society for Human Genetics; Genetics Society. Address: School of Medicine, University of Southampton, Human Genetics Division, Duthie Building (Mailpoint 808), Tremona Road, Southampton, SO16 6YD, England.

MOSES Daniel, b. 4 December 1954, Hartsville, South Carolina, USA. Human Resources Consultant; Author. m. Burlean Smith, 1 son. Education: BS, Business Management, Coker College; Masters Degree, Human Resources, Kennedy Western; PhD, Business Administration. Appointments: Manager, Jewel Companies, Jacksonville, Florida, 1981-85; Manager, Pharmor Drug Store, Columbia, South Carolina, 1985-88; Agent, Lincoln Benefit Life, Columbia and Lincoln, Nebraska, 1989-97; Consultant, Bridge Counseling Centre, Benedict College, Columbia, 1989-92; Recruiter, Edward Waters College, Jacksonville, Florida, 1995-96; Publisher, Researcher, Genealogist, Daniel Moses Inc, Delaware, South Carolina, 1994-; Co-founder, Project Heritage Quest Inc; Former Professor, Jones College, Jacksonville; Professor, Phoenix University, Jacksonville; Board of Directors, Theatre Works. Honours: Recipient, Towney Award, Town Theater, Columbia, South Carolina, 1987; Merit Award, International Music Festival, 1993; Junior Achievement, Carolina Music Academy, 1992-94; Ramses Hilton Award; Listed in various international biographical dictionaries. Memberships: SHRM; American Parliamentary Association; International Platform Association; American Institute of Parliamentarians; South Carolina Philharmonic Orchestra; WWII Tank Destroyer Society; Southside Businessmen's Club; Fort Mose Historical Society; African-American Community of Freedom Inc; Congress World Poets; World Academy of Arts and Sciences;

Honorable Order of Kentucky Colonels; Columbia C of C; Jacksonville C of C; Southside Business Mens Club. Address: PO Box 2403, Jacksonville, FL 32203, USA.

MOSIENKO Boris Alexandrovich, b. 31 December 1928, Omsk region, Russia. Retired Geophysicist; Researcher. m. Olga Nicolaevna Rybalova, 1975, 1 son, 1 daughter. Education: Astronomy, Gorki University, 1953; MSc, Council of Phys-Math and Techn Sciences, Siberian Branch of Academy of Sciences, USSR, 1974. Appointments: Teacher, secondary school, Vladivostock, Russia, 1953-56; Engineer, Measure Lab, Ust-Kamenogorsk, Russia, 1956-60; Research Scientist, Siberian Research Institute of Geology, Geophysics and Mineral Resources, Novosibirsk, Russia, 1960-90. Publications: Articles in professional journals. Address: Saltykova Schedrina 1/43, Novosibirsk 630004, Russia. E-mail: b.mosienko@ngs.ru

MOSIMANN Anton, b. 23 February 1947, Switzerland. Chef; Restaurateur. m. Kathrin Roth, 1973, 2 sons. Appointments: Apprentice, Hotel Baeren, Twann; Worked in Canada, France, Italy, Sweden, Japan, Belgium, Switzerland, 1962-; Cuisinier, Villa Lorraine, Brussels, Les Prés d'Eugénie, Eugénie-les-Bains, Les Frères Troisgros, Roanne, Paul Bocuse, Collonges au Mont d'Or, Moulin de Mougins; Joined Dorchester Hotel, London, 1975, Maitre Chef des Cuisines, 1975-88; Owner, Mosimann's, 1988-, Mosimann's Party Service, 1990-, The Mosimann Academy, 1995-, Creative Chefs, 1996-; Numerous TV appearances. Publications: Cuisine a la Carte, 1981; A New Style of Cooking: The Art of Anton Mosimann, 1983; Cuisine Naturelle, 1985; Anton Mosimann's Fish Cuisine, 1988; The Art of Mosimann, 1989; Cooking with Mosimann, 1989; Anton Mosimann – Naturally, 1991; The Essential Mosimann, 1993; Mosimann's World, 1996. Honours: Freedom of the City of London, 1999; Royal Warrant from HRH the Prince of Wales for Caterers, 2000; OBE, 2004; Lifetime Achievement Award (Hotel & Caterer), 2004; Numerous others. Address: c/o Mosimann's, 11B West Halkin Street, London SW1X 8JL, England.

MOSS Kate, b. 16 January 1974, Addiscombe, England. Model. 1 daughter. Career: Modelled for Harpers and Queen; Vogue; The Face; Dolce & Gabana; Katherine Hamnett; Versace, Yves St Laurent; Exclusive world-wide with Calvin Klein, 1992-99. Publication: Kate, 1994. Film: Unzipped, 1996. TV: Inferno, 1992; Blackadder Back & Forth, 1999. Honour: Female Model of the Year, VH-1 Awards, 1996. Address: Storm Model Management, 1st Floor, 5 Jubilee Place, London SW3 3TD, England.

MOSS Sir Stirling, b. 17 September 1929, London, England. Racing Driver. m. (1) Katherine Stuart Moson, 1957, dissolved 1960, (2) Elaine Barbarino, 1964, 1 daughter, dissolved 1968, (3) Susie Paine, 1980, 1 son. Education: Haileybury and Imperial Service College. Appointments: British Champion, 1951; Built Own Car, The Cooper-Alta, 1953; Drove in HWM Formula II Grand Prix Team, 1950, 1951, Jaguar Team, 1955; Leader, Maserati Sports & Grand Prix Teams, 1956, Aston Martin Team, 1956; Member, Vanwall, Aston Martin, Maserati Teams, 1958; Events include New Zealand, Monaco Grand Prix, Nurburgring 1,000km, Argentine 1,000km. UK, Pescara, Italy, Moroccan Grand Prix; Managing Director, Stirling Moss Ltd; Director, 28 companies; Journalist; Lecturer; President, Patron, 28 Car Clubs. Publications: Stirling Moss, 1953; In the Track of Speed, 1957; Le Mans 59, 1959; Design and Behaviour of the Racing Car, 1963; All But My Life, 1963; How to Watch Motor Racing, 1975; Motor Racing and All That, 1980;

My Cars, My Career, 1987; Stirling Moss: Great Drives in the Lakes and Dales, 1993; Motor Racing Masterpieces, 1995; Stirling Moss, autobiography, 2001. Honours include: Honorary FIE, 1959; Gold Star, British Racing Drivers Club, 10 times, 1950-61; Driver of the Year, Guild of Motoring Writers, 1954; Sir Malcolm Campbell Memorial Award, 1957; International Motorsports Hall of Fame, 1990; Segrave Trophy, 2005; FIA gold medal, 2006. Address: c/o Stirling Moss Ltd, 46 Shepherd Street, Mayfair, London W1Y 8JN, England. E-mail: stirlingmossltd@aol.com

MÖSSBAUER Rudolf Ludwig, b. 31 January 1929, Munich, Germany. Physicist. Education: Graduated, Munich Institute of Technology, 1952; PhD, 1958; Postgraduate Research, Max Planck Institute for Medical Research, Heidelberg, 1958. Appointments: Professor of Physics, California Institute of Technology, Pasadena; Concurrent Professorship, Munich Institute of Technology; Discovered the Mössbauer Effect. Publications: Papers on Recoilless Nuclear Resonance Absorption and on Neutrino Physics. Honour: Nobel Prize for Physics, 1961. Address: Fachbereich Physik, Physik Department E 15, Technische Universität Menchen, D-85747 Garching, Germany. E-mail: beatrice.vbellen@ph.tum.de

MOSSELMANS Carel Maurits, b. 9 March 1929, East Knoyle, Wiltshire, England. Investment Banker. m. Prudence Fiona McCorquodale, 2 sons. Education: Stowe; MA, Trinity College, Cambridge. Appointments: Joined Sedgwick Collins & Co, 1952, Director, 1963; Director, Sedgwick Forbes Holdings, 1978; Sedgwick Forbes Bland Payne, 1979; Chairman, Sedgwick Ltd, 1981-84; Deputy Chairman, 1982-84, Chairman, 1984-89, Sedgwick Group plc; Chairman, Sedgwick Lloyd's Underwriting Agents (formerly Sedgwick Forbes (Lloyds Underwriting Agents), 1974-89; Chairman, The Sumitomo Marine & Fire Insurance Co (Europe), 1981-90 (Director, 1975-81); Chairman, Rothschild Asset Management, 1990-93 (Director, 1989-99); Director, Coutts & Co, 1981-95; Director, Rothschild Continuation Ltd, 1990-97; Director, Tweedhill Fisheries, 1990-; Chairman, Committee of Management, Lionbrook Property Fund 'B' (formerly Five Arrows Property Unit Trust Manager Ltd), 1993-2003; Member, Investors' Committee Lionbrook Property Partnership, 1997-2003; Chairman, Indoor Golf Clubs plc, 1998-2004; Vice President, BIIBA, 1987-89. Honours: Regular Army, 1947-49, commissioned to Second Lieutenant Queen's Bay 2nd Dragoon Guards; Joined Territorial Army, The City of London Yeomanry (Rough Riders) TA (later Inns of Court and City Yeomanry TA); Territorial Decoration, 1961; Lieutenant Colonel, Inns of Court and City Yeomanry Regiment, 1962. Memberships: Clubs: White's; Cavalry and Guards; Royal St George's Golf; Sunningdale Golf; Swinley Forest Golf; Royal & Ancient Golf, St Andrews. Address: 15 Chelsea Square, London SW3 6LF, England.

MOSZCZYNSKI Paulin, b. 3 January 1936, Janów, Lubelski, Poland. Haematologist. m. Maria Otto, 1 son, 1 daughter. Education: University Medical School, Cracow, Poland, 1960; MD, 1968; Full Professor of Medicine, 1991. Appointments: Head, Department of Medicine, L Rydygier Hospital, Brzesko, Poland, 1975-2007; Head, Provincial Immunology Laboratory, Brzesko, 1978-2007; Consultant Haematologist, 1975-; President, International Institute of University Medicine, Tarnow, Poland, 1996-2003; Lecturer, Moloposka University, Brzesko, 2008-. Publications: Over 435 publications to professional journals; Epidemiology, The Analyst, Arch, Medicine, Research; Industrial Hematology; Drugs in Poland; Co-author, Industrial Hematology. Honours: Individual Prize Ministry of Health and Social Welfare, 1989; Gloria Med Medal, 1994; Health, 1995; A Schweitzer Golden Medal, 1996, 1999; Chivalry and Officer Cross of Order of Rebirth of Poland, 1992, 1999. Memberships: Polish Academy of Medicine; New York Academy of Sciences; Albert Schweitzer World Academy of Medicine; Polish Medical Society. Address: Wyzwolenia 7, 32-800 Brzesko, Poland.

MOTION Andrew, b. 26 October 1952, England. Biographer; Poet; Poet Laureate of the United Kingdom, 1999-. m. (1) Joanna J Powell, 1973, dissolved 1983, (2) Janet Elisabeth Dalley, 1985, 2 sons, 1 daughter. Education: Radley College and University College, Oxford. Appointments: Lecturer in English, University of Hull, 1977-81; Editor, Poetry Review, 1981-83; Poetry Editor, Chatto & Windus, 1983-89, Editorial Director, 1985-87; Professor of Creative Writing, University of East Anglia, Norwich, 1995-2004; Professor of Creative Writing, Royal Holloway, University of London, 2004-; Chair, Literary Advisory Panel Arts Council of England, 1996-98; Poet Laureate of the United Kingdom, 1999-2009. Publications: Poetry: The Pleasure Steamers, 1978; Independence, 1981; The Penguin Book of Contemporary British Poetry (anthology), 1982; Secret Narratives, 1983; Dangerous Play, 1984; Natural Causes, 1987; Love in a Life, 1991; The Price of Everything, 1994; Selected Poems, 1996-97, 1998; Salt Water, 1997; Here to Eternity, anthology, 2000; Public Property, 2001; Here to Eternity: An Anthology of Poetry, 2001; As Poet Laureate: Remember This: An Elegy on the Death of HM Queen Elizabeth The Queen Mother, 2002; A Hymn for the Golden Jubilee, 2002; On the Record (for Prince William's 21st birthday), 2003; Spring Wedding (for the wedding of Prince Charles and Camilla Parker Bowles), 2005; In the Blood, 2006; The Five Acts of Harry Patch, 2007; The Cinder Path, 2009. Criticism: The Poetry of Edward Thomas, 1981; Philip Larkin, 1982; William Barnes Selected Poems (ed), 1994; Biography: The Lamberts, 1986; Philip Larkin: A Writer's Life, 1993; Keats, 1997; Wainewright the Poisoner, novel, 2000; The Invention of Dr Cake, novel, 2003. Honours include: Rhys Memorial Prize, 1984; Somerset Maugham Award, 1987; Whitbread Biography Award, 1993; Honorary DLitt, Hull, 1996, Exeter, 1999, Brunel, 2000, APU, 2001, Open University, 2002; Sheffield Hallam, 2003; Sheffield, 2005. Address: c/o Faber & Faber, 3 Queen Square, London WC1, England.

MOUILLET Alain Charles Maurice Yves, b. 11 September 1944, Saint Germain Sur Meuse, France. Retired Professor. m. Viviane Albert, 1 son, 2 daughters. Education: Agregation de Sciences Physiques, Paris, 1968; PhD, University of Technology, Compiegne, 1975. Appointments: Assistant Professor, University of Paris XI, Cachan, Val de Marne, 1968-73; Assistant Professor, University of Technology, Compiegne-OISE, 1973-88; Professor, University of Burgundy, IVT Le Creusot, 1988-93; Professor, University Paul Cezanne, 1993-2006. Publications: 35 papers on electrical engineering and electromagnetism. Memberships: Societe des Electriciens et Electroniciens. Address: 140 Avenue Anselme Mathieu, F-84810 Aubignan, France. E-mail: amouil@club-internet.fr

MOUTSOPOULOS Nicolas, b. 27 December 1927, Athens, Greece. Architect; Professor. m. Euthymia Thanopoulos, 2 sons. Education: Architect, 1953, PhD, 1956, Technical University, Athens; Theological Diploma, Aristot University, Thessaloniki, 1963; Postdoctoral studies, Institute d'Art et d'Archeologie, Sorbonne, Paris, France. Appointments: Past President, Greek Institute of Castles; Past President, Greek Institute of CIAV/ICOMOS/UNESCO; Member, Academy of Athens; Member, Sciences Academy of Sofia,

Bulgaria; Member, Academia Pontaniana, Naples, Italy; Doc Honoris Causa, Clemens Ohridski University of Sofia and Paisii Hilandarski University of Plovdiv; Professor, Aristotle University, Thessaloniki. Publications: Churches & Monasteries of Gortynia, Arcadia, Greece; Gothic Churches in Greece; The Mansion of Casa Bianca, Thessaloniki; Excavation of Basilica S Achillios at Prespa; Excavations of Redina, Greece; Grevena (Castles & Churches); and others. Honours: Brig of Kts of Holy Grave of Jerusalem; Gold Medal of Lions; Conf Brig Phoenix, 1978. Address: 23 Ave Megalou Alexandrou, Thessaloniki, 54640, Greece.

MOWAT David, b. 16 March 1943, Cairo, Egypt (British citizen). Playwright. Education: BA, New College, Oxford, 1964. Publications: Jens, 1965; Pearl, 1966; Anna Luse, 1968; Dracula, Purity, 1969; The Normal Woman, and Tyypi, Adrift, The Others, Most Recent Least Recent, Inuit, 1970; The Diabolist, John, 1971; Amalfi (after Webster), Phoenix-and-Turtle, Morituri, 1972; My Relationship with Jayne, Come, 1973; Main Sequence, The Collected Works, The Memory Man, The Love Maker, 1974; X to C, 1975; Kim, 1977; Winter, 1978; The Guise, 1979; Hiroshima Nights, 1981; The Midnight Sun, 1983; Carmen, 1984; The Almas, 1989; Jane, or The End of the World, 1992. Radio Plays. Honour: Arts Council Bursaries. Address: 7 Mount Street, Oxford OX2 6DH, England.

MOWLE Arthur Frank, b. 21 November 1946, Perth, Western Australia. Psychotherapist; Educationalist; Biomedical Scientist. Education: LTh, Melbourne College of Divinity, 1971; Hospital Based Diploma in Nursing, Royal Perth Hospital, WA, 1972; BA, Immanuel College, 1974; WA Teachers Certificate & Diploma, College of Preceptors, England, 1978; PG Dip in Clinical Nutrition, Sydney & DSc (Health Science), CPU, 1982; EdD, California Coast University, 1988; B Hum, Pastoral Studies, CSR, 1992; Dip Specific Learning Difficulties, Royal Society of Arts, 1995; MA, CSR, 1997; Dip Psynth Cnslg, South Australia, 2000; ThSoc, CSR, 2004; Cert Clin Hypnotherapy, NSW School of Hypnotic Sciences, 2005; Cert Clin Hypnotherapy, American Institute of Hypnotherapy, 2006; D Litt, European-American University, 2008. Appointments: Commissioned Officer RAAMC (Reserve), 1972-78; Registered Nurse, Royal Perth Hospital, 1972-73; Teacher and Registered Nurse, Salvado College, New Norcia, 1973-74; Teacher and Registered Nurse, St Mark's Christian Brothers College, Bedford, 1975-80; Teacher and Registered Nurse, Christian Brothers Agricultural School, Tardun, 1981-82; Senior Nurse Educator, Gippsland Base Hospital, Victoria, and in Western Australia, 1983-85; Senior Teacher, Health Officer & Counsellor, Servite College, Tuart Hill, 1986-99; Senior Teacher & Counselling Therapist, Kolbe Catholic College, Rockingham, 2000-10; Ordained Priest, (Liberal Catholic Rite), 2002; Director, Liberal Catholic Institute of Studies, 2003-10; Vicar, Cathedral Church of St John the Divine, Perth, 2005-10. Publications: Numerous articles in professional medical and religious journals; Research into role of Vitamin C in health and disease conditions as well as in HIV/AIDS. Honours: The Plato Award, 2006. Memberships: Fellow, College of Nursing, 1980; Fellow, Australasian College of Biomedical Scientists, 1980; Fellow, Central School of Religion, 1995; Full Member, Psychotherapists & Counsellors Association of Western Australia, 1993; Psychotherapy & Counselling Federation of Australia, 2004; Western Australian College of Teaching, 2005; Australian Society of Clinical Hypnotherapists, 2006; Order of Corporate Reunion, 2011. Address: 13 Yulgering Road, Calingiri WA 6569, Australia. E-mail: psychehealth@westnet.com.au

MOXLEY Raymond James (Ray), b. 28 June 1923, Sheffield, England. Chartered Architect. m. Ann March, 1 son, 2 daughters. Education: Oxford School of Architecture, 1939-42; War service, 1942-46; Demobilised as Captain Royal Engineers; Dipl Arch, Oxford School of Architecture, 1946-49. Appointments: Assistant Architect, Bristol City Architects Department, 1949-51; Own Practice, 1953; Senior Partner, Moxley, Jenner and Partners, 1970-95; Commissions: Chelsea Harbour & Excel Exhibition Centre, London, et al; Founder, Chairman of the Society of Alternative Methods of Management; Co-Founder, Association of Consultant Architects; Commodore, Cargreen Yacht Club, Cornwall, 2002-2004; Designer of MOX12 Lateral Schooner Catamaran. Publications: Architects Eye; Building Management by Professionals; An Architects Guide to Fee Negotiation. Honours: Honorary Fellow, University of the West of England; First Honorary Librarian of the Royal Institute of British Architects. Memberships: Fellow, Past Vice President, Royal Institute of British Architects; Past President, Association of Consultant Architects; Fellow, Royal Society of Arts; The Worshipful Company of Chartered Architects; Academician, Royal West of England Academy; The Royal West of England Yacht Club; Cargreen Yacht Club, Cornwall. Address: March House, Cargreen, Cornwall PL12 6PA, England.

MOYLE Robert, b. 31 January 1952, Leamington Spa, England. Civil Engineer. m. Alexandra, 2 daughters. Education: Uppingham School; Birmingham University. Appointments: Various roles, later Chairman and Chief Executive, North Midland Construction plc, 1973-. Honours: BSc (Hons); C Eng. Memberships: FICE. Address: North Midland Construction plc, Nunn Close, The County Estate, Huthwaite, Sutton-in-Ashfield, Nottinghamshire, NG17 2HW, England. E-mail: robert.moyle@northmid.co.uk

MOYLES Chris (Christopher David), b. 22 February 1974, Leeds, England. Radio DJ; Presenter. Career: Presenter, Radio Aire; The Pulse of West Yorkshire; Chiltern Radio; Horizon Radio; Capital FM; Radio Luxembourg; Presenter Radio 1, 1997; Afternoon Show Radio 1, 1998; The Breakfast Show, 2004. TV Appearances: Live With Chris Moyles, The Chris Moyles Show, Look North, 1999; Later With Jools Holland, 2001; Fame Academy, 2002; Liquid News, 2003; Top Of The Pops, 2004; The Great Big Bid, Destination Three, Chris Moyles' Red Nose Rally, Comic Relief In Da Bungalow, Dick And Dom In The Bungalow, Mercury Music Prize, Newsround – Newsround Showbiz, Live 8, Comic Relief Does Fame Academy, 2005; Midlands Today, 2004; Powerhouse, 2004; Jools' 11th Annual Hootenanny, 2003; Ou – Steel/03; Sigmund Freud, 2003; Celebdaq, 2003; Dale's Wedding, 2003; This Is Your Life – David Dickinson, 2003; Patrick Kielty Almost Live, 2002; The Saturday Show, 2002; Radio 1 TV, 2001; Urban Icons – Instant Food, 2001; East Midlands Today, 2001; A Question Of Pop, 2000; Children In Need, 1999; Radio 1 Live From Heaton Park, Manchester, 1999; Real Lives – Radio 1 Goes Mad In Ibiza, 1999; Clubbing Night, 1999; Never Mind The Buzzcocks, 1998; The O Zone, 1998; Fully Booked, 1998; News, 1998; Stupid Punts, 2001; I Love The Nineties, 1992; Look East, 1998; BBC Breakfast News, 1999; Monster Wars, 1998; Viz, 2006; The X Factor: Battle Of The Stars, 2006. Singles Released: Dogz Don't Kill People (Wabbitz Do), 2004. Publications: The Gospel According to Chris Moyles, 2006; The Difficult Second Book, 2007. Honours: Faces For '97, Sky Magazine, 1997; DJ Of The Year, Sony Silver Awards, 1998; DJ Of The Year, The Sun Readers, Best Entertainment Show, Sony Gold Radio Award, 2006; Fastest-Ever Selling Download, Guinness Book Of Records.

DICTIONARY OF INTERNATIONAL BIOGRAPHY 36th EDITION

MOZHEIKO Zinaida, b. 6 December 1933, Orsha, Belarus. Ethnomusicologist. m. Kovban Evgeny. Education: Belarusian State University; Belarusian Academy of Music. Appointments: Doctor of Art Criticism, 1992; Chief Research Worker, Institute of Art Criticism, Ethnography and Folklore, Academy of Sciences of Belarus. Publications: Songs of Belarusian Poozerje, 1981; Songs of the Belarusian Polesye, release 1-2, 1983-84; Calendar Songs in the Culture of Belarus, 1985; Co-author, Belarusian Ethomusicology, Essays of History (XIX-XX centuries), 1997; Co-author, Songs of Belarusian Podneprovje, 1999; Compiler-editor, Gippius E V Selected Works in Belarusian Ethnomusicology Context, 2004; Co-author, Belarusians, T11 Music, 2008; Ecology of Traditional Folk Music Culture, 2011. Honours: State Prize of Belarus, 1994; Honoured Artist of Belarus, 1987; Grand Prize, French Musical Academy, Paris, France, 1984. Memberships: Belarusian Composers' Union; Belarusian Cinema Union; European Seminar in Ethnomusicology; International Organisation of Folk Art; International Commission of Slavic Folklore. Address: Zaslavskaia, 25-277, Minsk 220004, Belarus.

MOZSIK Gyula, b. 7 June 1938, Dancshaza, Hungary. Professor. m. Ilona Vizi, 1 son. Education: MD, 1962, PhD, Medicine, 1970, University of Debrecen; Specialist, International Medicine, University Medical School of Debrecen, 1967; DSc, Medicine, University of Pécs, 1977; Specialist, Gastroenterology, University Medical School, Pécs, 1980. Appointments: Assistant, Second Department of Medicine, 1962, Visiting Scientist, Department of Pharmacology, 1968-69, University of Medical School of Debrecen; Associate Professor, First Department of Medicine, University College of Medicine, Pécs, 1975; Visiting Scientist, Chemical Pathology Laboratory, Harvard Medical University, Boston, Massachusetts, 1985; Full Professor, 1989; Head of Department, 1993; Professor of Internal Medicine, Head, First Department of Medicine, University Medical School of Pécs. Publications: 18 textbooks for college students; Author, 3 monographs; Numerous book chapters; Regular papers and medical abstracts; Editor, 17 books. Honours: Excellent Worker in Education by the Hungarian Ministry of Education, 1983; Hungarian Society of Gastroenterology; Hungarian Society of Nutrition; Géza Hetényi Medal, 1983; Pro Optimo Merito Medal in Gastroenterologia, 1989; József Sós Medal, 1984; Medal of the International Brain-Gut Society, 1994; Excellent Health Worker Award, Hungarian Ministry of Health, 1997; Széchenyi Scholarship for Professors, 1999-2002. Memberships: New York Academy of Sciences; IUPHAR Gastro-Intestinal Section; International Brain-Gut Society; International Society of Internal Medicine; International Society of Metabolic Therapy; European Society for Clinical Investigation; American Gastrenterological Association; Hungarian Society of Physiology; Hungarian Society of Pharmacology. Address: First Department of Medicine, University Medical School of Pécs, H-7643 Pécs, Hungary.

MTHOKO November Ananias, b. 22 November 1943, Onyaanya, Namibia. Teacher; Administrator. m. Ndahambelela, 1 son, 2 daughters. Education: Secondary School Teacher's Diploma, Nkrumah Teacher's College, in Association with the University of Zambia, 1972; BA, Hons, Adult Education, University of Lagos, Nigeria, 1980; Certificate, Biblical Studies and the Christian Ministry, Namibia Evangelical Theological Seminary, Windhoek, Namibia, 2004. Appointments: School Teacher, Zambia, 1971-73; Teacher, Namibia Health and Education Centres, 1976-77, 1980-81; Executive Director, UNIN-Namibian Extension Unit 1981-90; Director, Lifelong Learning Programmes, Ministry of Basic Education, Sport and Culture, Namibia, 1990-2003. Publications: Co-author of several course textbooks, including Basic Agriculture Course; English Course; Primary Health Care Course for the Namibian Extension Unit Students, 1980-85; Junior Secondary Geography of Namibia, 1990; Graded Reader for the National Literacy Programme of Namibia, 1998; Co-author, Unity in Diversity: A Culture Booklet for Adult Basic Education in Namibia, 2000; Co-author: Unity in Diversity: A Culture Booklet for Adult Basic Education in Namibia, 2000; Farming with Animals and Fish in Namibia, 2001; Co-author, Supplementary Reader for Adult Literary Programme, 2002; Author: The Life and Selected Passages from the Works of N A Mthoko, 1943-2003, 2003. Memberships: International Diabetic Federation, Belgium, 1992-; New York Academy of Sciences, 1998-; National Geographic Society, Washington DC, 1984-. Address: PO Box 776, 89 Bach Strasse Windhoek West, Windhoek 9000, Namibia.

MUELLER Rudhard Klaus, b. 20 August 1936, Glauchau, Saxony. Forensic Toxicologist; University Professor. m. Ursula Hanni, 3 daughters. Education: Study of Chemistry, College of Chemistry, Merseburg, 1954-55 and Leipzig University, Diploma (MSc equivalent), 1955-60; Study of Medicine, Leipzig University, 1956-61. Appointments: Member, Institute of Forensic Medicine, Leipzig University, 1960-2003; Dr rer nat in Chemistry, Leipzig University, 1965; Expert in Toxicology, Academy of Advanced Medical Studies, Berlin, 1981; Head, Postgraduate Study Programme Toxicology, Leipzig University, 1987-2003; Professor of Forensic Toxicology, Leipzig University, 1989; Expert in Forensic Toxicology, Society for Toxicological and Forensic Chemistry, 1991; Director, Institute of Doping Analysis and Sports Biochemistry, Dresden, 1992-2006; Member, Thuringian Academy of Sciences, 1993; Federal Commissioner for Doping Analysis, Federal Institute of Sports Sciences, Cologne, 1996-2006; EUROTOX Registered Toxicologist, 1998, 2003. Publications: Over 400 publications including numerous books; Over 600 presentations at scientific meetings. Honours: Virchow Award, Ministry of Health, Berlin, 1977; Leibniz Award, University of Leipzig, 1979; Kockel Medal, Society of Forensic Medicine, Leipzig, 1982; Honorary Member, Society of Medical Sciences, Czech Federal Republic, Prague, 1983; Order of Merit, Federal Republic of Germany, 2003; Alan Curry Award, International Association of Forensic Toxicologists, 2004. Memberships: International Association of Forensic Toxicologists; National Antidoping Agency, Germany; Working Group on Science, Antidoping Convention of the European Council; World Antidoping Agency, 2000-06. Address: Pirolweg 1, D-04821 Brandis, Germany. E-mail: rkmueller.leipzig@t-online.de

MUKHERJEE Tara Kumar, b. 20 December 1923, Calcutta, India. Retired. Education: Scottish Church College; Calcutta University, India. Appointments: Shop Manager, Bata Shoe Company, India, 1941-44; Buyer, Brevitt Schoes, 1951-56; Sundries Buyer, British Shoe Corporation, 1956-66; Production Administrator, Priestly Footwear Ltd, 1966-68; Head Store Manager, British Shoe Corporation, 1968-70; District Manager, 1970-78, Branch Manager, 1978-84, Save and Prosper Group; Area Manager, Guardian Royal Exchange, 1985-88; Managing Director, OWL Financial Services, 1988. Honours: Honorary Doctor of Philosophy, Middlesex University; FLIA; FRSA. Memberships: First Class Cricketer, Ranjy Trophy, Bihar, India; Leicestershire County Cricket Club; Indian National Club; Chairman, European Multicultural Foundation; President, Confederation of Indian Organisations (UK); President, European Union

Migrants Forum; Royal Commonwealth Society; European Movement; President, India Film Society. Address: 51 Viking Way, Brentwood, Essex CM15 9HY, England. E-mail: emf@mbebrentwood.co.uk

MULDOON Paul, b. 20 June 1951, Portadown, County Armagh, Northern Ireland. Poet; Writer; Dramatist; Professor in the Humanities. Education: BA, English Language and Literature, Queen's University, Belfast, 1973. Appointments: Producer, 1973-78, Senior Producer, 1978-85, Radio Arts Programmes, Television Producer, 1985-86, BBC Northern Ireland; Judith E Wilson Visiting Fellow, University of Cambridge, 1986-87; Creative Writing Fellow, University of East Anglia, 1987; Lecturer, Columbia University, 1987-88; Lecturer, 1987-88, 1990-95, Director, Creative Writing Programme, 1993-, Howard G B Clark Professor in the Humanities, 1998-, Princeton University; Professor of Poetry, Univerity of Oxford, 1999-04; Writer-in-Residence, 92nd Street Y, New York City, 1988; Roberta Holloway Lecturer, University of California at Berkeley, 1989; Visiting Professor, University of Massachusetts, Amberst, 1989-90, Bread Loaf School of English, 1997-; Elected Honorary Professor of Poetry, Oxford University, 1999-2004. Publications: Poetry: Knowing My Place, 1971; New Weather, 1973; Spirit of Dawn, 1975; Mules, 1977; Names and Addresses, 1978; Immram, 1980; Why Brownlee Left, 1980; Out of Siberia, 1982; Quoof, 1983; The Wishbone, 1984; Meeting the British, 1987; Madoc: A Mystery, 1990; Incantata, 1994; The Prince of the Quotidian, 1994; The Annals of Chile, 1994; Kerry Slides, 1996; New Selected Poems, 1968-94, 1996; Hopewell Haiku, 1997; The Bangle (Slight Return), 1998; Hay, 1998; Moy Sand and Gravel, 2002; Horse Latitudes, 2006; General Admission, 2006; When the Pie was Opened, 2008; Plan B, 2009; Maggot, 2010. Theatre: Monkeys (television play), 1989; Shining Brow (opera libretto), 1993; Six Honest Serving Men (play), 1995; Bandanna (opera libretto), 1999. Essays: To Ireland, I, 2000. Translator: The Astrakhan Cloak, by Nuala Ni Dhomhnaill, 1993; The Birds, by Aristophanes (with Richard Martin), 1999. Editor: The Scrake of Dawn, 1979; The Faber Book of Contemporary Irish Poetry, 1986; The Essential Byron, 1989; The Faber Book of Beasts, 1997. Children's Books: The O-O's Party, 1981; The Last Thesaurus, 1995; The Noctuary of Narcissus Batt, 1997. Contributions to: Anthologies and other publications. Honours: Eric Gregory Award, 1972; Sir Geoffrey Faber Memorial Awards, 1980, 1991; Guggenheim Fellowship, 1990; T S Eliot Prize for Poetry, 1994; American Academy of Arts and Letters Award, 1996; Irish Times Poetry Prize, 1997; Pulitzer Prize for Poetry, 2003; Griffin Prize, 2003; Shakespeare Prize, 2004; John William Corrington Award for Literary Excellence, 2009. Memberships: Aosdana; Poetry Society of Great Britain, president, 1996-; Royal Society of Literature, fellow; American Academy of Arts and Sciences, 2000. Address: c/o Faber and Faber, 3 Queen Square, London WC1N, England.

MULHOLLAND John Henry, b. 23 May 1933, Stockton-on-Tees, England. Retired. m. Maureen O'Brien, 2 sons, 1 daughter. Education: St Mary's College, Middlesbrough; BA, MSc, University of Manchester. Appointments: Commissioned Officer, Royal Signals, 1954-56; Production Manager, Procter and Gamble, 1957-61; Personnel Manager, ICI and Ilford Limited, 1961-68; Head, St Helens School of Management Studies and Dean of Faculty, 1968-87; ACAS Arbitrator, 1975-; Chairman, Final Appeals Board, GIST Ltd-Unite National Agreement, 1984-2008; Chairman, Courts of Inquiry, Isle of Man, various dates 1985-95; Chairman, Industrial Disputes Tribunal, Guernsey, various dates 1993-2005; Chairman, NHS Independent Review Panels and Central Adjudication Panels, 1994-2003; Arbitrator under GCHQ-GCG National Agreement, 1998-2010; Nominated Arbitrator under the National Probation Service Agreement for Disciplinary Cases, 1998-2010; Mediator under OECD Guidelines, International Employment Disputes, 2008-. Publications: Occasional articles in professional employment relations journals and Catholic publications. Honours: Fellow, Chartered Institute of Personnel and Development. Memberships: Trustee, Catholic Diocese of Shrewsbury; Chairman of Governors, Blessed Thomas Holford Catholic College, Altrincham; Member, Liberal Democrats and Former Westminster and European Parliamentary Candidate; Chairman and Trustee, Altrincham Choral Society; Member, Royal British Legion; Durham Country Cricket Club; World Development Movement; Ramblers' Association; Campaign for Real Ale; Pax Christi; Friend of Westminister Cathedral; Bar Convent; Opera North; Welsh National Opera; Clonter Opera; Buxton Festival. Address: 12 Arthog Drive, Hale, Altrincham, Cheshire, WA15 0NB, England.

MULLANY Kevin Fergus, b. 7 June 1968, New York, USA. Music Teacher. 1 daughter. Education: BA, English, 1997, MFA English (Creative Writing), 2010, Queens College, New York; MA, Music Education, Hunter College, New York, 2004. Appointments: English Tutor, Queensborough Community College, CUNY, 1991-94; Music Teacher, Forest Hills Montessori School, New York, 1992-97; Music Teacher, Harbor Conservatory, New York City, 1994-96; Organist/Choir Director, St Lucy-St Patrick R C Church, Brooklyn, New York, 1995-2002; Childrens Choir Director, St John Evangelist R C Church, Brooklyn, New York, 1996-98; Music Director, Garden School, New York, 1997-98; Chorus Director, Flushing High School, New York City, 1999-. Honours: Fredric Kurzwell Memorial Award in Music, 1991; NYS Permanently Certified English Teacher; Dean's Honor List, 1991, 1992, 1994; English Club Award for Writing, 1994; Silverstein-Peiser Award in Writing, 1996; NYS School Music Association Annual Choral Festival, 2000; NYS Assembly Certificate of Merit for Community Service, 2001; Honorable Mention, Composers Guild International Music Composition Competition, 2005; Silver Award Level IV, 2006; NYS School Music Association Annual Choral Festival; NYS Permanently Certified Music Teacher Tenured; First Place Winner, 2008, Honorable Mention, 2008, Composers Guild's Annual Choral Writing Contest; Listed in international biographical dictionaries. Memberships: National Association of Composers, USA; American Choral Directors Association; Composers Guild; Tri-M Music Honor Society; TRI-M Music Honor Society Faculty Lifetime Membership; Music Educators Association of NYC; Music Educators National Conference; Chorus America. Address: 40-10 73 St, 2nd Floor,, NY 11377, USA. E-mail: mullanykevin@aol.com

MÜLLER Kurt Bernd, b. 3 September 1943, Blens/Eifel, Germany. Professor (retired). m. Rosa Gomez Cagigal, 1 son, 1 daughter. Education: State Exam, English and German Philology, University of Cologne, Germany, 1970; PhD, 1976, Habilitation, 1988, University of Freiburg, Germany. Appointments: Academic Councillor, University of Freiburg, Germany, 1979-90; Deputy Professor, University of Trier, Germany, 1990-92; Professor and Chair of American Studies, University of Jena, Germany, 1992-2008. Publications: Books: Konventionen und Tendenzen der Gesellschaftskritik im expressionistischen amerikanischen Drama der zwanziger Jahre, 1977; Identität und Rolle bei Theodore Dreiser: Eine Untersuchung des Romanwerks unter rollentheoretischem Aspekt, 1991; Inszenierte Wirklichkeiten: Die Erfahrung der Moderne im Leben und Werk Eugene O'Neills, 1993;

Ernest Hemingway: Der Mensch, der Schriftsteller, das Werk, 1999; Das amerikanische Drama, 2006. Co-editor, Literaturwissenschaftliches Jahrbuch; Numerous articles as author and co-author in professional journals. Memberships: Deutscher Anglistenverband; Deutsche Gesellschaft für Amerikastudien; Gesellschaft für Kanadastudien; Görres-Gesellschaft zur Pflege der Wissenschaften. Address: Ernst-Abbe-Platz 8, D-07743 Jena, Germany. E-mail: kurt.mueller@uni-jena.de

MÜLLER Margit Gabriele, b. 9 October 1968, Weissenhorn, Germany. Director; Veterinary Surgeon. Education: Doctor of Veterinary Medicine, University Giessen, 1996; MBA, University of Strathclyde, Scotland, 2007; PhD, Veterinary Medicne, University of Munich, 1999; Diploma, Veterinary Homeopathy, British Institute of Homeopathy, 2001; Board certification in veterinary dentistry, Bavarian Chamber of Veterinary Surgeons, 2000. Appointments: Scientist, 2001-02, Manager, 2002-07, Director, 2007-, Abu Dhabi Falcon Hospital, Abu Dhabi, United Arab Emirates. Publications: 2 books: Practical Handbook of Falcon Husbandry and Medicine, 2009; Modern Veterinary Practice Management, 2011/2012; Numerous articles in professional journals. Honours: Erasmus Grant for students, 1993, 1994; Abu Dhabi Award, Abu Dhabi Government, 2008; Diamond Eye Award for Quality Commitment & Excellence, Management Association, Rome, Italy, 2009; World Leader Businessperson Award, Certificate of Excellence in Business Leadership, 2010, 2011, Certificate for Excellence in Business Management, 2010, 2011, Certificate for Excellence in Quality Management, 2010, Certificate for Excellence in Marketing Management, 2011, World Leader Businessperson Award, 2011, World Confederation of Business, Houston, Texas, USA; Honorary Falconer, King Juan Carlos I of Spain, 2010. Memberships: World Journal of Gastrointestinal Endoscopy; Royal College of Veterinary Surgeons, UK; Bavarian Chamber of Veterinarians, Germany; Association of Veterinary Practitioners, Germany; Association of Avian Veterinarians, USA. Address: PO Box 131588, Abu Dhabi, United Arab Emirates. E-mail: vet_uae@hotmail.com

MÜLLER Thomas, b. 13 December 1960, Clausthal-Zellerfeld, Germany. Professor. Education: Universities of Bochum, Essen and Munich, 1980-87; Licence to practice, 1987. Appointments: Department of Psychiatry, University of Würtzburg, 1987-90; Department of Neurology, University of Marburg, 1990-91; Department of Neurology, University of Bochum, 1992-2007; University Lecturer, Senior Physician, Specialist and Consultant in Neurology, Psychiatry and Psychotherapy, 1996; Faculty for Neuroscience, University of Bochum, 2001; Professor, 2002; Head, Department of Neurology, Berlin Weissensee, St Joseph Hospital, Berlin, 2007-; Consultant, Neurology/Psychiatry, St Joseph Berlin Tempelhof, 2008; Outpatient Unit for Multiple Sclerosis, 2009; MFSZ, 2010. Publications: Over 300 peer-reviewed papers; 51 book chapters; 16 book and edited journal supplements. Memberships: MFSZ; IGSN. Address: Department of Neurology, St Joseph Hospital Berlin-Weissensee, Gartenstr 1, 13088 Berlin, Germany. E-mail: th.mueller@alexius.de

MUN Ji-Hun, b. 24 December 1973, Pusan, Republic of Korea. Researcher. m. 1 son. Education: Master's degree, Material Science and Engineering, 2001; PhD, Material Science and Engineering, Tohoku University, Japan, 2006. Appointments: Silicon Crystal Growth, R&D Center, L G Siltron, 2006-09; Strategic Planning Team, Gyeongbuk Hybrid Technology Institute, 2009-. Publications: Tm^{3+} doped Y_2D_3 Investigated for quantum light storage application, 2008; Effects of Strontium gallate additions on Sintering behaviour and electrical Conductivity of Samaria doped ceria, 2009. Honours: Listed in international biographical dictionaries. Memberships: Editor, Journal of the Korean Crystal Growth and Crystal Technology; Committee Member, Ministry of Knowledge Economy, Korea. Address: 104dong 1502ho, Seoboo Buyoung 1-Cha, Okgok-dong, Gyeongsan-Si, Gyeongsangbuk-do, 712-781, Seoul, Republic of Korea. E-mail: m1004y@hanmail.net

MUNI PRABAHARAN Muniappan, b. 28 March 1989. Design Engineer. Education: BE, Mechanical Engineering, Sri Ramakrishna Engineering College, Anna University, 2010. Appointments: Design Engineer, Mahindra Satyam, 2010-. Publications: 63 research papers in professional scientific journals. Honours: Rajya Puraskar, 2004; Sri P Ramaswamy Naidu Memorial Prize, 2008-09; Vellay Chidambaram, 2008-09; Smt M S P Nagarathinam Ammal Memorial Gold Medal; Pat on the Back, 2011; Associate of the Month (April), 2011. Memberships: International Association of Engineers; Mechanical Engineering; Artificial Engineering; Industrial Engineering; International Association of Computer Science and Information Technology. Address: 99, Govindaswamy Layout, Chetty Street, Coimbatore, Tamil Nadu, India. E-mail: mp.me89@gmail.com

MUNITIC Ante, b. 26 August 1941, Omis, Croatia. Scientist. m. 1970, 1 son. Education: Master, Electronics. Publications: Books: Computer Simulation; Computer Application in Marin; System Dynamics. Honours: Doctor of Science; Award for Lifework; Man of the Year 2011. Memberships: System Dynamics Society; many others. Address: Marina Getaldica 31, 21000 Split, Croatia.

MUÑOZ-ROJAS David, b. 31 July 1976, Barcelona, Spain. Researcher. 2 sons. Education: Degree, Organic Chemistry, 1999, Chemical Engineer, 2000, Institut Quimic de Sarria; MBA, 2002, Universitat Ramon Llull, 2002; Diploma, 2002, Master, 2003, Materials Science, Diploma, Advanced Studies in Physical Chemistry, 2003, DSc, Materials Science, 2004, ICMAB-CSIC/UAB. Appointments: Trainee, Pinturas HEMPEL SA, 1999; Degree project, Polymer Institute, University of Detroit, USA, 1999-2000; PhD thesis, 2000-04, Postdoctoral Contract, 2004, Instituto de Ciencias de Materiales de Barcelona, Spain; Postdoctoral Contract, Université de Picardie Jules Verne, France, 2005; Postdoctoral Grant I3P, Nanoscience and Nanotechnology Research Centre, Barcelona, 2006-08; Marie Curie Intra-European and Beatriu de Pinós Fellow, Department of Materials Science & Metallurgy, University of Cambridge, England, 2008-12. Publications: 26 articles in peer-reviewed journals; 2 books; 2 patents; 2 proceedings and others. Honours: P Salvador Gil, SI, 2000; 2nd Prize, Scientific Photography Contest, 2003; European Doctor Mention, 2004; Best Poster Award, 2008; Finalist, Science as Art, 2009, 2010; Best Poster Award, University of Cambridge, 2010; Platinum 1st Poster Prize, Nanotechnology for Sustainable Energy, 2010; Winner, Materials Today cover competition, 2011; 2nd Prize, Science as Art Scientific Photography Contest, 2011. Memberships: Materials Research Society; Institute of Physics; Societat Catalana de Quimica. Address: Flat 7, 96 Lexham Gardens, London W8 6JQ, England. E-mail: davidmunozrojas@gmail.com Website: http://sites.google.com/site/workdmr/

MUNRO Alice, b. 10 July 1931, Wingham, Ontario, Canada. Author. m. (1) James Armstrong Munro, 29 December 1951, divorced 1976, 3 daughters, (2) Gerald Fremlin, 1976. Education: BA, University of Western Ontario, 1952. Publications: Dance of the Happy Shades, 1968; A Place for Everything, 1970; Lives of Girls and Women, 1971; Something I've Been Meaning to Tell You, 1974; Who Do You Think You Are?, 1978, US and British editions as The Beggar Maid: Stories of Flo and Rose, 1984; The Moons of Jupiter, 1982; The Progress of Love, 1986; Friend of My Youth, 1990; Open Secrets, 1994; Selected Stories, 1996; The Love of a Good Woman, 1998; Hateship, Friendship, Courtship, Loveship, Marriage, 2001; Runaway (short stories), 2004; The View from Castle Rock, 2006; Too Much Happiness, 2009. Honours: Governor-General's Awards for Fiction, 1968, 1978, 1986; Guardian Booksellers Award, 1971; Honorary DLitt, University of Western Ontario, 1976; Marian Engel Award, 1986; Canada-Australia Literary Prize, 1994; Lannan Literary Award, 1995; W H Smith Literary Award, 1996; National Book Critics Circle Award, 1998; Giller Prize, 1999; O Henry Award, 2001; Man Booker International Prize, 2009. Address: The Writers Shop, 101 5th Avenue, New York, NY 10003, USA.

MUNTEANU COLÁN Dan, b. 22 May 1944, Şoşdea, Romania. Professor. m. Eugenia Alexe Munteanu. Education: Degree, Spanish and Romanian Philology, Faculty of Foreign Languages, 1967, PhD, Romance Philology, 1981, University of Bucharest, Romania. Appointments: Researcher, Hispanic Linguistics, Institute of Linguistics of the Romanian Academy, Bucharest, 1971-90; Visiting Professor, University of Oviedo, Spain, 1990-91; Professor, Romance Philology, University of Las Palmas de Gran Canaria, Spain, 1991-. Publications: El léxico indigena del español americano, 1977; El español de América, 1982; El papiamento, origen, evolución y estructura, 1991; El papiamento, lengua criolla hispánica, 1996; Breve historia de la lingüística románica, 2005; La posición del catalán en la Romania, 2008. Honours: Centenary of the Mexican Academy Award, 1975; Bucharest Writers' Association Award, 1981; National Prize for Translation, Spanish Ministry of Culture, 1984; Union of Romania Writers' Award, 1984; Listed in international biographical dictionaries. Memberships: Societé de Linguistique Romane; Asociación de Lingüística y Filología de la América Latina; Society for Pidgin and Creole Linguistics; Sociedad Española de Lingüística; and others. Address: Av de José Mesa y López 58, es 2, 5°A, 35010 Las Palmas de Gran Canaria, Spain.

MURADOVA Aliki, b. 26 November 1968, Tbilisi, Georgia. Mathematician. m. Emmanuel Contadakis, 1 son, 1 daughter. Education: Honours Diploma, 1990, PhD, 1998, Applied Mathematics, Tbilisi State University, Georgia. Appointments: Postdoctoral Research, Department of Projective Methods, Institute of Applied Mathematics, 1999-2003, Research Fellow, Department of Mineral Resources and Engineering, and Department of Manufacturing Engineering and Management, 2005-, Technical University of Crete; Visiting Fellow, Center for Mathematics and its Applications, Mathematical Sciences Institute, Australian National University, 2003-05. Publications: Numerous articles in professional journals. Honours: State Scholarship, Foundation of Greece; Certificate with Merit of Completion, Graduate Teaching Programme, Australian National University. Address: Department of Manufacturing Engineering and Management, Technical University of Crete, Kounoupidiana, Chania 73100, Crete, Greece. E-mail: aliki@mred.tuc.gr

MURARIU Dumitru, b. 21 September 1940, Ungureni-Botosani, Romania. Biologist. m. Angela, 1 son, 1 daughter. Education: University Diploma, 1966; PhD, Biology, 1981. Appointments: Biologist, Bacteriologist, 1966-69; Museologist, 1969-76; Head of Department, 1976-88; Director, 1988-; Senior Researcher, 1991-. Publications: 195 scientific papers and articles; 16 books; 65 reviews and forewords. Honours: Order Cultural Merit; Degree Officer, Category E, 2004; Four awards for scientific research and management of patrimony, Ministry of Culture; Corresponding Member, Romanian Academy, 2006. Memberships: Life Member, American Society of Mammalogists; Seven other professional associations. Address: Str Amman Nr 20, 011614 Sectorul 1, Bucharest, PO 63, Romania. E-mail: dmurariu@antipa.ro

MURDOCH Keith Rupert, b. 11 March 1931, Melbourne, Australia (American citizen, 1985-). Publishing and Broadcasting Executive. m. (1) Patricia Booker, divorced, 1 daughter, (2) Anna Maria Torv, 1967, divorced, 2 sons, 1 daughter, (3) Wendy Deng, 1999, 2 daughters. Education: MA, Oxon, Worcester College, Oxford, England, 1953. Appointments: Chief Executive Officer, 1979-, Chairman, 1991-, News Corporation; Owner, numerous newspapers, magazines and TV operations in UK, US, Italy, Asia and Australia. Honours: AC, 1984; Commander of the White Rose, First Class, 1986; Knight of St Gregory the Great, 1998. Address: News Corporation, 1211 Avenue of the Americas, New York, NY 10036, USA.

MURDOCH Lachlan Keith, b. 8 September 1971, London, England (American citizen). Business Executive. m. Sarah O'Hare, 1999, 2 sons, 1 daughter. Education: Princeton University. Appointments: Reporter, San Antonio Express News, The Times (UK); Sub-Editor, The Sun (UK); General Manager, Queensland Newspapers Pty Ltd, 1994-95; Executive Director, News Ltd, 1995; Director, Beijing PDN Xinren Information Technology Co Ltd, 1995-; Deputy Chair, Star Television, 1995-; Deputy Chief Executive, News Ltd, 1995-96; Director, The Herald & Weekly Times Ltd, 1996-, News Corporation, 1996-, Deputy COO, 2000-, Independent Newspapers Ltd (NZ), 1997-; Executive Chair, Chief Executive Officer, News Ltd, 1997; Senior Executive Vice-President, US Print Operations News Corporation, 1999-2005; Publisher, NY Post newspaper, 2002-2005; President, Illyria Pty Ltd, 2005- . Address: New York Post, 1211 Avenue of the Americas, New York, NY 10036-8790, USA. Website: www.nypost.com

MURÍN Gustáv, b. 9 April 1959, Bratislava, Slovakia. Author. m. Jana, 2 daughters. Education: BSc, 1983, MSc, 1984, PhD, 1991, Comenius University, Bratislava. Publications: 27 books (including 6 in Czech, 1 in French and 1 in Hindi, 1 in Croatian translations): Novel, novella, 2 collections of stories, collection of sci-fi stories, 8 collections of essays, collection of articles about culture and media, extensive essay study about biology, 2 popular studies (about marriage, about longevity), 4 retrospective studies about organised crime in capitol city and in Slovakia (with more than 90,000 copies sold), 2 popular encyclopaedias, 3 collections of travel stories; Author of more than 2,000 articles in more than 50 major Slovak, Czech and international newspapers and magazines; More than 200 texts translated into 43 other languages and published around the world. Honours: Best Slovak story, 1979; Best Czech and Slovak story, 1981; Best Czech and Slovak novella, 1986; Special prize in Slovak radio drama, 1988; Honorary Fellow in Writing, University of Iowa, 1995; Best Essay of the Year, 1996; E E Kisch Award, 2003; Fifik's Children

Jury Award, 2005; 3rd place at journalist CEE Award, 2006; Panta Rhei Award, 2009; Active participation at international literary conferences. Memberships: Slovak Centre of the PEN International; Slovak Syndicate of Journalists; World Innovation Foundation. Address: Hagaru 17, 831 51 Bratislava, Slovak Republic. E-mail: gmurin@fns.uniba.sk Website: http://gustavmurin.webgarden.cz/biography

MURPHY Eddie (Edward Regan), b. 3 April 1961, Brooklyn, New York, USA. Film Actor. m. (2) Nicole Mitchell, divorced, 5 children. Creative Works: Films include: 48 Hours, 1982; Trading Places, Delirious, 1983; Best Defence, Beverly Hills Cop, 1984; The Golden Child, 1986; Beverly Hills Cop II, Eddie Murphy Raw, 1987; Coming to America, 1988; Harlem Nights, 1989; 48 Hours 2, 1990; Boomerang, Distinguished Gentleman, 1992; Beverly Hills Cop III, 1994; The Nutty Professor, 1996; Dr Dolittle, Holy Man, Life, 1998; Bowfinger, Toddlers, Pluto Nash, 1999; Nutty Professor II: The Klumps; Dr Dolittle 2, 2001; Showtime, 2002; I-Spy, Daddy Day Care, The Haunted Mansion, Shrek 4-D (voice), 2003; Shrek 2 (voice), Far Far Away Idol (voice), 2004; Dreamgirls, 2006; Norbit, Shrek 3 (voice), 2007; Starship Dave, 2008; Imagine That, 2009; Shrek Forever After (voice), 2010. Tours with own comedy show; Comedy Albums: Eddie Murphy, 1982; Eddie Murphy: Comedian, 1983; How Could It Be, 1984; So Happy, 1989; Recorded 7 albums of comedy and songs. Honours include: Numerous awards and nominations. Address: c/o Jim Wiatt, ICM, 8942 Wilshire Boulevard, Beverly Hills, CA 90211, USA.

MURRAY Andrew (Andy), b. 15 May 1987, Dunblane, Scotland. Tennis Player. Education: Schiller International School, Spain. Career: Started playing tennis aged 3 years; Won Orange Bowl, Florida aged 12 years; Won U S Open Tennis Boys' Title, 2004; Turned professional aged 18 years; Won doubles with David Sherwood for Great Britain's Davis Cup team against Israel, 2005; Reached semi-finals of the Boys' tournament at the French Open, 2005; Reached the third round of the Stella Artois tournament, 2005; Reached the third round of Wimbledon, 2005; Beat Tim Henman at the Swiss Indoors in Basel, 2005; Won the SAP Open tournament, 2006; Took over from Tim Henman as British number one, 2006; World Ranking 11, 2007; Winner, Qatar ExxonMobil Open, 2008, 2009; Winner, exhibition tournament, Abu Dhabi, 2009; Winner, Queen's, 2009; Winner, Thailand Open, 2011; Gold (men's singles) and Silver (mixed doubles), London Olympics, 2012. Honours: BBC Young Sports Personality of the Year, 2005. Website: www.murraysworld.com

MURRAY Bill, b. 21 September 1950, Evanston, Illinois, USA. Actor; Writer. m. (1) Margaret Kelly, 1980, divorced, 2 son; (2) Jennifer Butler, 1997, 4 children. Education: Loyola Academy; Regis College, Denver; Second City Workshop, Chicago. Appointments: Performer, Off-Broadway National Lampoon Radio Hour; Regular Appearances TV Series Saturday Night Live; Appeared in Radio Series Marvel Comics' Fantastic Four; Co-Producer, Director, Actor, Quick Change, 1990; Writer, NBC-TV Series Saturday Night Live, 1977-80; Films: Meatballs, 1977; Mr Mike's Mondo Video, 1979; Where the Buffalo Roam, Caddyshack, 1980; Stripes, 1981; Tootsie, 1982; Ghostbusters, The Razor's Edge, Nothing Lasts Forever, 1984; Little Shop of Horrors, 1986; Scrooged, 1988; Ghostbusters II, 1989; Quick Change, 1990; What About Bob?, 1991; Mad Dog and Glory, Groundhog Day, 1993; Ed Wood, 1994; Kingpin, Larger Than Life, Space Jam, 1996; The Man Who Knew Too Little, 1997; With Friends Like These, Veeck as in Wreck, Rushmore, 1998; Wild Things, 1998; The Cradle Will Rock, Hamlet, Company Man, 1999; Charlie's Angels, 2000; The Royal Tenenbaums, Osmosis Jones, 2001; Lost in Translation, Coffee and Cigarettes, 2003; Garfield: The Movie (voice), The Life Aquatic with Steve Zissou, 2004; Broken Flowers, The Lost City, 2005; Garfield: A Tail of Two Kitties, (voice), 2006; The Darjeeling Limited, 2007; Get Smart, City of Ember, 2008; The Limits of Control, Get Low, Fantastic Mr. Fox (voice), 2009. Honours include: Emmy Award, Best Writing for Comedy Series, 1977; BAFTA Award for Best Actor, 2004. Address: c/o William Carroll Agency, 139 N San Fernando Road, Suite A, Burbank, CA 91502, USA.

MURRAY Noreen Elizabeth, b. 26 February 1935, Read, Nr Burnley, Lancashire, England. Scientist; University Teacher. m. Kenneth Murray. Education: BSc, Botany, King's College, London, 1953-56; PhD, Microbial Genetics, University of Birmingham, 1956-59; Honorary Degree, University of Sheffield, 2010. Appointments: Research Associate, Department of Biological Sciences, Stanford University, 1960-64; Research Fellow, Botany School, Cambridge, 1964-67; Member, MRC Molecular Genetics Unit, 1968-74, Lecturer, 1974-80, Department of Molecular Biology, University of Edinburgh; Group Leader, European Molecular Biology Laboratory, Heidelberg, Germany, 1980-82; Reader, Department of Molecular Biology, 1982-88, Professor of Molecular Genetics (Personal Chair), 1988-2001, Professor Emeritus 2002-, University of Edinburgh. Publications: Numerous publications in scientific journals, including early papers in the field of genetic engineering. Honours: Member, European Molecular Biology Organisation, 1980; Fellow Royal Society, 1982; Fellow Royal Society of Edinburgh, 1989; Member, Academica Europaea, 1989; Royal Society Gabor Medal, 1989; Society of General Microbiology Fred Griffiths Lecturer, 2001; CBE for services to science, 2002; AstraZeneca Award, The Biochemical Society, 2005; Honorary DSc, UMIST, Birmingham, Warwick and Lancaster; Fellow, King's College London. Memberships: Genetics Societies of UK and USA; UK Societies of Biochemistry and General Microbiology; President, Genetics Society of UK, 1987-90; Trustee, The Darwin Trust of Edinburgh, 1990-; Member of Board, International Genetics Federation, 1998-2002; Council Member of BBSRC, 1994-98; Council Member, The Royal Society, 1992-93, 2002-2004; Royal Commission of the Exhibition of 1851, Science Fellowship Committee, 2002-07; Honours Committee for Science and Technology, 2005-; Member of the Athenaeum Club, 2001. Address: Institute of Cell Biology, University of Edinburgh, Darwin Building, King's Buildings, Mayfield Road, Edinburgh, EH9 3RJ, Scotland. E-mail: noreen.murray@ed.ac.uk

MURRAY-LYON Iain Malcolm, b. 28 August 1940, Edinburgh, Scotland. Consultant Physician. m. Teresa, 1 son, 1 daughter. Education: University of Edinburgh, 1958-64. Appointments: Consultant Physician and Gastroenterologist, Charing Cross Hospital and Chelsea and Westminster Hospital, London, 1974-2002; Honorary Consultant Physician and Gastroenterologist, Chelsea and Westminster Hospital, 2002-; Honorary Senior Lecturer in Medicine, Imperial College School of Medicine, 1993-. Publications: More than 200 articles on topics in gastroenterology and liver disease and the medical effects of chewing Khat (Qat) leaves. Honours: BSc (Hons), 1962; MB ChB, 1964; MD, 1973; FRCP, 1980; FRCPE, 1980; International Fellowship, National Institute of Health (NIH), USA, 1971-72. Memberships: British Society of Gastroenterology; British Association for the Study of the Liver; European Association

DICTIONARY OF INTERNATIONAL BIOGRAPHY 36th EDITION

for the Study of the Liver; International Association for the Study of the Liver; Brooks's; Hurlingham Club. Address: 116 Harley Street, London W1G 7JL, England.

MURS Olly (Oliver Stanley), b. 14 May 1984, Witham, England. Singer; Songwriter; Musician; TV Presenter. Education: Notley High School, Braintree. Career: Recruitment Consultant, Prime Appointments; Appeared on The X Factor, BBC Television, 2009; Singer, Epic Records and Syco Music, 2010-; Songwriter; Musician; TV Presenter, The Xtra Factor, 2011. Publications: Singles: Please Don't Let Me Go, 2010; Thinking of Me, 2010; Heart Skips a Beat, 2011; Albums: Olly Murs, 2010; In Case You Didn't Know, 2011. Honours: Best Male Artist, BT Digital Music Awards; Best Album, BBC Radio 1 Teen Awards.

MURSELL (Alfred) Gordon, b. 4 May 1949, Guildford, England. Priest in Church of England. m. Anne. Education: Pontifical Institute of Sacred Music, Rome, 1966-67; Brasenose College, Oxford, 1967-71; Cuddesdon College, Oxford, 1971-73; BA, History; BA, Theology; ARCM, Organ Performance; BD, Theology. Appointments: Curate, Walton, Liverpool, 1973-77; Vicar, St John's East Dulwich, London, 1977-86; Tutor, Salisbury-Wells Theological College, Salisbury, 1986-91; Team Rector, Stafford, 1991-99; Provost, 1999-2002, Dean, 2002-2005, Birmingham Cathedral. Publications: The Theology of Carthusian Life, 1989; Out of the Deep: Prayer as Protest, 1989; The Wisdom of the Anglo-Saxons, 1997; The Story of Christian Spirituality (editor), 2001; English Spirituality (2 volumes), 2001. Address: 103a Selly Park Road, Birmingham, B29 7LH, England. E-mail: gordonmursell@beeb.net

MURUGANADAM M, b. 21 September 1976, Salem, India. Assistant Professor. m. Indumathi, 1 son. Education: Diploma, Electrical and Electronics Engineering, Salem Polytechnic, 1996; BE, Periyar University, Salem, 2003; ME, 2005, PhD, in progress, Anna University, Chennai. Appointments: Electrical Supervisor, Tambbi Modern Spinning Mills Pvt Ltd, Salem, 3 years; Trainee, Tamilnadu Electricity Board, Salem, 1 year; Lecturer, 2005, Assistant Professor and Head, 2009, Electronics and Instrumentation Engineering, Muthayammal Engineering College, Namakkal-Dt. Publications: 4 national conferences; 1 international journal; 3 international conference; 4 books. Honours: Listed in biographical dictionaries. Memberships: IEEE; ISTE. Address: 55 Adhiselva Ganapathi Street, Ammapet, Salem 636003, Tamil Nadu, India.

MURUGAVEL Thanikachalam, Language Educator. Education: BSc, Botany, Pachaiyappa's College, University of Madras, 1985; MA, English Literature, 1987; M Phil, English Literature, 1989; PhD, English Language Teaching, 2005. Appointments: Lecturer, 1991-99, Senior Lecturer, 1999-2001, Assistant Professor, 2003-09, Professor, 2009-, Sri Venkateswara College of Engineering. Publications: Contributor of scientific papers to professional journals, articles, chapters to books. Honours: Exceptional Service Award, SVCE; Best Faculty Award by CTS; Listed in international biographical dictionaries; Committed environmentalist. Memberships: Trust Restoration Ecology and Environment. Address: 101, 4th St, AI Block, Shanthi Colony, Chennai, Tamil Nadu 600 040, India. E-mail: mcwhale@svce.ac.in

MUSHA Takaaki, b. 17 September 1951, Toumi-shi, Nagano-ken, Japan. Government Official. m. Yumiko Suzuki, 1 son, 1 daughter. Education: BE, 1974, ME, 1977, Shunshu University; PhD, Mechanical Engineering, 1994. Appointments: Technical Officer, Japan Maritime Self Defense Force, 1977-89; Researcher, Acoustics Laboratory, ONO SOKKI Co Ltd, 1989-94; Research Member, Advanced Space Propulsion Investigation Committee, 1994-96; Research Engineer, 5th Research Center, Technical Research & Development Institute, Defense Agency of Japan, 1995-2006; Deputy Director, Department of Naval Systems Development, TRDI, Ministry of Defense, Japan, 2006-08; Program Manager, Naval Research Center, TRDI, Ministry of Defense, Japan, 2008-09; Director, Kawasaki Branch, Naval Research Center, TRDI, 2009-10; Director, (NPO) Advanced Science Technology Research Organization, 2010-. Publications: Speculations in Science and Technology, 1998; Journal of Theoretics, 2000, 2001, 2002, 2004; Infinite Energy, 2004, 2006, 2008; International Journal of Simulation and Process Modeling, 2006; Physics Essays, 1994, 2005; Applied Acoustics, 1993, 1999, 2004, 2005, 2008; Journal of Sound and Vibration, 2007; Journal of the British Interplanetary Society, 2008; Online Journal of Biological Sciences, 2008; BioSystems, 2009; Far East Journal of Applied Mathematics, 2009, 2010; Advances and Applications and Mathematical Sciences, 2010; Far East Journal of Mathematical Sciences, 2010; JP Journal of Algebra, Number Theory and Applications, 2010; Natural Science, 2011; Books: Computer Science Research and Technology (Chap 4, Possiblity of High Performance Computation in Biological Brains), 2011; Field Propulsion System for Space Travel, 2011. Honours: Best Paper Award, Marine Acoustics Society of Japan, 2000 and 2003. Memberships: Advanced Space Propulsion Investigation Committee, Japan Society for Aeronautical and Space Sciences; IEEE Aerospace and Electronic Systems Society; Japan Society of Mechanical Engineers; Marine Acoustics Society of Japan; Listed in international biographical dictionaries. Address: 3-11-7-601, Namiki, Kanazawa-ku, Yokohama 236-0005, Japan. E-mail: takaaki.musha@gmail.com

MUSIL Robert Kirkland, b. 27 October 1943, New York, USA. Professor. m. Caryn McTighe, 2 daughters. Education: BA, Yale University, 1964; MA, 1966, PhD, 1970, Northwestern University; MPH, Johns Hopkins University, 2001; LHD, Mitchell College, 2009; ScD, Lincoln Memorial University, 2011. Appointments: Executive Director, The Professionals' Coalition for Nuclear Arms Control, 1988-92; Executive Director and CEO, Physician for Social Responsibility, 1992-2006; Senior Fellow, Center for Congressional and Presidential Studies, American University, School of Public Affairs, 2010-; Adjunct Professor, American University, 1997-; Visiting Scholar, Churches' Center for Theology and Public Policy, Wesley Theological Seminary, 2007-09. Publications: Hope for a Heated Planet: How Americans are Fighting Global Warming and Building a Better Future, 2009. Memberships: Board of Trustees, Mitchell College; Treasurer, Board of Directors, Population Connection; Board of Directors, The Council for a Livable World; President, The Scoville Peace Fellowships. Honours: The Armstrong Award for Excellence in Radio Broadcasting, 1985, 1986; Visiting Fellow, The London School of Hygiene & Tropical Medicine, 2001; Visiting Fellow, Pembroke College, Cambridge University, 2001. Address: 8600 Irvington Avenue, Bethesda, MD 20817, USA. E-mail: bmusil1@yahoo.com

MUSIL Rudolf, b. 5 May 1926, Brno, Czech Republic. Emeritus University Professor. m. Ing Liba Kochová, 26 July 1952, 2 sons. Education: RNDr, 1952, CSc, 1960, Habil, 1966, DSc, 1968, Full Professor, 1980, Education, Masaryk

University, Charles University. Appointments: Full Professor, Institute of Geological Sciences, Faculty of Science, Masaryk University, Brno. Publications include: Domestication of wolves in Central European Magdalenien sites, 2005; Animal prey in Pavlov I Southeast. A window into the Gravettian Lifestyles; Die Bärenpopulation von Bilzingsleben – eine neue mittelpleistozäne Arot, 2005-2006; Environmental changes spanning the Early-Middle Pleistocene transition, 2005; The Moravian Karst – the cradle of karst research in Central Europe, 2007; Die Pferde von Schöningen: Skelettreste einer ganzen Wildpferdeherde, 2007; The Paleoclimatic and Paleoenvironmental Conditions at Předmostí, 2008; Überlebensstrategien von Elephanten, Survival strategies of elephants) 2010; Das Austerben der Megafauna am Ende des Pleistozäns, The extinction of megafauna at the end of the Pleistocene, 2010; The environment of the middle Palaeolithic sites in Central and Eastern Europe, 2010; Palaeoenvironment at Gravettian Sites in Central Europe with emphasis on Moravia, Czech Republic, 2010. Honours: Silver Medal, National Museum, 1968; Silver Medal, Humboldt Universität, Berlin; Medal, Moravian Museum, 1968; Medal, Slaskie University, Poland, 1983; Medal, Velkopolskie Towarzystwo, 1983; Silver Medal, Czech Academy, 1986; Gold Medal, Masaryk University, 1997; Medal, Faculty of Science, Komensky University, Slovakia, 2006. Memberships: Czech Society of Geology and Mineralogy; Czech Society of Speleology; National Committee INQUA; International Commission on History of Geological Sciences. Address: Kotlárska Str 2, 61137 Brno, Czech Republic. E-mail: rudolf@sci.muni.cz

MUSK Arthur William (Bill), b. 12 August 1943, Kalgoorlie, Western Australia. m. Criena Fitzgerald, 1 son, 1 daughter. Education: MBBS, University of Western Australia, 1967; MSc, Occupational Health, Harvard University, USA, 1977; MD, University of New South Wales, 1987. Appointments: Physician, Respiratory Medicine, Sir Charles Gairdner Hospital, Western Australia; Clinical Professor of Medicine and Population Health, University of West Australia. Publications: Over 280 scientific articles; Numerous reviews, editorials, reports, etc. Honours: Order of Australia, 1982; Wunderly Medal, 1991, Research Medal, 2010, Thoracic Society, ANZ. Memberships: Australasian College of Physicians; Australian Faculty of Occupational Medicine; American College of Chest Physicians; Royal College of Physicians, Faculty of Occpational Medicine. Address: 19 Kinninmont Avenue, Nedlands, Western Australia.

MUSKER Alison Awdry Chalmers, b. 9 September 1938, Southampton, England. Watercolour Painter. m. Roger, 1 son, 2 daughters. Education: Sherborne School for Girls; SRN, The Middlesex Hospital, London; Studied under Jacqueline Groag and Edward Wesson, Ecole des Arts, Paris, 1956, and under Leslie Orriss, Reading College of Art, 1968. Career: Solo exhibitions: Brotherton Gallery, Walton Street, London, 1981; King Street Gallery, St James's, London, 1983, 1985; The Royal Geographical Society, London, 1986, Richmond Gallery, Cork Street, London, Italy and Albania, 1990; Ebury Galleries, London, 2008; Watercolour auctioned for Red Cross Appeal for the Gulf War, 1991; Pennant Melangell Church, Wales for CADW, 1990; Richmond Gallery, Cork St WI, Save Britain's Heritage, 1992; Numerous group exhibitions include: Royal Institute of Painters in Watercolours, 1958, 1977-91; Singer and Friedlander Exhibition, Mall Galleries, 1998, 1999, 2000; Royal Academy, 1999, 2002, 2003, 2005, 2006; New English Art Club, Mall Galleries, 1993-98, 2003, 2004, 2005; The Small Paintings Group, Century Gallery, 2003; W H Patterson and Select Seven Exhibition, 1995-2009; Watercolours and Drawings Fair, London W1 and WC2, 2006-09; Royal Society of British Artists, Mall Galleries, 2009; W H Patterson, 1995-2009; Work in collections including: John Julius Norwich, Lady Dashwood, Barry Munn, Martin Vandersteen, HRH The Prince of Wales, 1995; Peter Boizot Collection, 1998, The late Queen Mother, 2000; Charity work includes: The Landmark Trust, 1994; Guest Lecturer for National Trust, 1993; Wardour Chapel Appeal, Christies, London, 1994; British Red Cross Society, 1994, 1995; Friends of the City Churches, London, 1995; APA, Mall Galleries, London, 1995; Music in country churches succeeding Sir Hugh Casson PPRA, 1996-2009; Painswick House, Rococco Garden Exhibition, 1998; Watercolour donated to North Hampshire Hospital, 2001; Paintings given to Koestler Award Trust, 2002 and 2003. Publications: Works mentioned reference works; The Artist's Manual, 1995; Light and Colour Techniques in Watercolour, 1997; Travellers' Survival Kit – Indian drawings, 1997; Creative Watercolour Techniques, 1997; The Enchanted River, 200 Years of the RWS by Simon Fenwick, 2004; The Watercolour Expert by Royal Watercolour Society, Cassell, 2004; Watercolour Masters – Then and Now, by Royal Watercolour Society, 2006; The Dictionary of Artists in Britain since 1945 – David Buckman, 2005; Who's Who in Art, 30th edition, 2002, 30th and 32nd edition, 2006; Whitehall Palace painted for Music in Country Churches, 2005; Watercolour Masters: Then & Now, 2006; Cassell. Honours: Agnes Reeve Memorial Prize, 1989, 1991; Award, Presentation Prize, International Watercolour Biennale, Mexico, 2000; The William-Powlett Prize, 2001; Rotary Club Prize, 2008; Freeman of the Worshipful Company of Painter-Stainers, 2008; Listed in international biographical dictionaries. Memberships: Chelsea Art Society, 1980; The Small Paintings Group, 2000; Reading Guild of Artists, 2002; Associate Member of RWS, 2000, Full member, Royal Watercolour Society, 2003. Address: Rose Cottage, Beech Hill, Reading, Berkshire RG7 2AZ, England.

MUSTAFA Saleem, Professor. m. Rashedah Ayob, 1 son. Education: BSc; MSc; PhD; Postdoctorate Research, Centre de Recherche en Ecologie Marine et Aquaculture de L'Houmeau, France. Appointments: Associate Professor, 1993-2004; Professor, 2004-. Publications: 5 books; Numerous articles in professional journals; 7 book chapters. Honours: Ten Year Service Award, 1994-2004; Honorary Associate, Centres of Excellence in the South, 2000; Excellent Services Award, 2002, 2003; Quality Award, 2003; Australia-Asia Award, 2003-04; Silver Medal, 32nd International Exhibition of Inventions, Switzerland, 2004; Silver Medal, 33rd International Exhibition of Inventions, Switzerland, 2005; Saintis Cemerlang, 2005; Bronze Medal, Biotechnology Asia, 2006; Silver Medal, BioInno Awards, 2008; Silver Medal, Research and Innovation Competition, Kota Kinabalu, 2008; Gold Medal, Seoul International Invention Fair, 2009; Silver Medal, 20th International Invention, Innovation and Technology Exhibition, Kuala Lumpur, 2009; 2 Bronze Medals, International Exhibition of Inventions, Switzerland, 2009; Special Award for Excellent Service, 2009; 2 Bronze Medals, Research and Innovation Competition, Kota Kinabalu, 2010; Leading Scientist of the World, 2010. Memberships: Malaysian Fisheries Society; International Maritime Club Newsletter; Malaysian Network for Holothurian Conservation and Sustainable Management; Technical Committee, Environmental Management, Department of Standards Malaysia; Editorial Board Member, Journal of Environmental Biotechnology and Journal of Applied Aquaculture; Chair, Centre for Collaborative Research in Aquaculture, Japan.

Address: Borneo Marine Research Institute, Universiti Malaysia Sabah, Jalan UMS, 88400 Kota Kinabalu, Sabah, Malaysia. E-mail: saleem@ums.edu.my

MUTAFOVA-ZABERSKA Yulia, b. 27 February 1942, Bulgaria. Psychologist. m. Petio Zaberski, 1 son, 1 daughter. Education: National Sports Academy, 1960-65; Doctor of Sport Psychology, St Petersburg University, 1971; Professor, Psychology, National Sports Academy, Sofia, 1971. Appointments: Lecturer, Psychology; Sport Psychologist to national teams; Member, National Science Council, 1990-2003; Head & Reviewer of Doctorates, Editor of scientific publications; Head, Dean's Office, 1986-91; Head, Department of Psychology, Pedagogy & Sociology, 2003-08. Publications: 10 monographs on sport and social psychology; More than 200 journal publications; Participation in more than 150 conferences. Honours: Award, Artistic Gymnastics Federation, 1978; Award, Wrestling Federation, 1982; Award, Weight Lifting Federation, 1984; Award, Basketball Federation; Special honours from the Rector/President of National Sports Academy, 2007. Memberships: Bulgarian Society of Psychology; FEPSAK. Address: Bul Tsarigradsko shose No 35, 1127 Sofia, Bulgaria. E-mail: yulia@gbg.bg

MUTH Richard Ferris, b. 14 May 1927, Chicago Illinois, USA. Economist. m. Helene Louise Martin, 2 daughters. Education: US Coast Guard Academy, 1945-47; AB, 1949, MA, 1950, Washington University, St Louis; PhD, University of Chicago, 1958; Master of Theology Studies, Emory University, 1995. Appointments: Associate Professor, University of Chicago, 1959-64; Professor of Economics, Washington University St Louis, 1966-70; Professor, Stanford University, 1970-83; Professor, 1983-2001, Chair, 1983-90, Professor Emeritus, 2001-, Emory University. Publications: With others: Regions, Resources & Economic Growth, 1960; Cities & Housing, 1969; Public Housing, 1974; Urban Economic Problems, 1975; The Economics of Housing Markets (with Allen C Goodman), 1989. Honour: Phi Beta Kappa. Address: Department of Economics, Emory University, Atlanta, GA 30322-2240, USA. E-mail: rmuth@emory.edu

MUTTER Raoul Josua, b. 12 October 1970, Zurich, Switzerland. Palaeontologist. m. Yolanda Martina. Education: BSc, 1994, MSc, 1997, PhD, Palaeontology, 2002, University of Zurich, Switzerland. Appointments: Research Assistant & Instructor, Palaeontological Institute and Museum, University of Zurich, Switzerland, 1997-2002; Postdoctoral Fellow and Sessional Lecturer, University of Alberta, Edmonton, Canada, 2002-05; Researcher, Natural History Museum, London, 2005-08; Postdoctoral Fellow, University of the Witwatersrand, Johannesburg, South Africa, 2008-09. Publications: Over 50 articles in professional journals. Honours: Grants and fellowships: Borso Premio Postuniversitatie (Balerna), Switzerland, 2001; Awards: Swiss National Science Foundation, 2002-05; Theodore Roosevelt Memorial Foundation, New York, 2003; Foundation Dr Robert & Lina Thyll-Durr, Arlesheim, Switzerland, 2003; SANW Foundation, Dr Joachim de Giacomi, Chur, Switzerland, 2003-05; Zurcher Universitatsverein Zurich, Switzerland, 2003-05; Swiss National Science Foundation, 2005-06; Marie Curie Fellowship, 2006-08; Swiss Academy of Sciences, 2007-08; BPI, University of the Witwatersrand; Honorary Research Fellow, 2010-12. Memberships: Geological Society of America; Schweizerische Palaeontologische Gesellschaft; Zurcher Naturforschende Gesellschaft; Palaeontological Association; Palaeontologische Gesellschaft; Society of Vertebrate Paleontology. E-mail: r.mutter@permotriassicfishes.org

MUMINA John M Kasyoka, b. 4 October 1965, Mbooni, Makueni, Kenya. Catholic Priest. Education: Diploma, Theology & Philosophy, St Thomas Aquinas Seminary, Nairobi, 1991; Bachelor, Theology, 1991, Bachelor, MA, PhD, Philosophy, 1997-2002, Urbaniana University, Rome; MA, Praxi Administrative Canonica, Rome, Vatican, 2002; many other certificates. Appointments: Parish Priest; Lecturer, Dean of Studies, National Philosophicum; Chairman, Philosophy Department; Administrator, MIDS; Scripture course, Broken Bay Institute of Education (with Newcastle University, Australia), in progress. Publications: 2 books: Human Suffering and Existence; Philosophy of Religion, An Introduction; Many articles in local magazines. Address: PO Box 1419, Machakos 90100, Kenya. E-mail: jkmufuku@yahoo.com

MUZUR Amir, b. 12 January 1969, Rijeka, Croatia. Professor; Head of Department. Education: MD, University of Rijeka, 1993; MA, Medieval Studies, Central European University, Budapest, Hungary, 1996; PhD, Cognitive Neuroscience, International School for Advanced Studies, Trieste, Italy, 2000. Appointments: Postdoctoral Researcher, Harvard Medical School, Boston, USA, 2001-02; University of Rijeka, School of Medicine and School of Philosophy, 2003-, Associate Professor and Head of Department for Social Sciences and Medical Humanities, 2008-; Mayor of Opatija, Croatia, 2005-09. Publications: Around 20 books; About 120 papers in scientific journals; More than 300 articles in non-scientific periodicals. Honour: Mayor of the Year in Croatia, 2006; Commendatore della Stella della Solidarieta Italiana, 2008; Honorary Consul of the Republic of Poland, 2011; Listed in international biographical dictionaries.

MYERS Mike, b. 25 May 1963, Toronto, Ontario, Canada. Actor; Writer. m. Robin Ruzan, 1993 (divorced). Creative Works: Stage appearances: The Second City, Toronto, 1986-88, Chicago, 1988-89; Actor and Writer, Mullarkey & Myers, 1984-86; TV show, Saturday Night Live, 1989-94; Films: Wayne's World, 1992; So I Married an Axe Murderer, 1992; Wayne's World II, 1993; Austin Powers: International Man of Mystery, 1997; Meteor, 1998; McClintock's Peach, 1998; Just Like Me, 1998; It's A Dog's Life, 1998; 54, 1998; Austin Powers: The Spy Who Shagged Me, 1998; Pete's Meteor, 1999; Austin Powers: Goldmember, 2002; Shrek (Voice), 2003; Cat in the Hat, 2003; Shrek 2 (Voice), 2004; Far Far Away Idol, (voice), 2004; Shrek 3, (voice), 2007; The Love Guru, 2008; Inglorious Bastards, 2009; Shrek Forever After (voice), 2010. Honours: Emmy Award for outstanding writing in a comedy or variety series, 1989; MTV Music Award, 1998; Canadian Comedy Award, 2000; American Comedy Award, 2000; Blockbuster Entertainment Award, 2000; Teen Choice Award, 2000; MTV Music Award, 2003; AFI Star Award, 2003. Address: c/o Creative Artists Agency, 9830 Wilshire Boulevard, Beverly Hills, CA 90212, USA.

MYONG Seung Yeop, b. 28 September 1992, Seoul, Korea. CTO/R&D Director. Education: BS, 1995, MS, 1997, Department of Electronic Engineering, PhD, Department of Electronic Engineering & CS, 2002, KAIST. Appointments: Visiting Professor, Institute of Microtechnology, EPFL, Switzerland, 2005-06; Researcher (Professor), Department of Physical Electronics, Tokyo Institute of Technology, 2006-07; Production Team Leader, 2007-09, CTO/R&D Director, 2009-, KISCO Energy Division. Publications: 245

on thin-film Si Solar Cells and ZnO TCO; 40 international journal papers; 44 international conference papers; 3 domestic journal papers; 12 domestic conference papers; 100 external patents; 47 domestic patents. Honours: Minister of Knowledge Economy Prize, NEWTECH, Korea, 2008; PVSEC Scientist Award, PVSEC-19, 2009. Memberships: Advisory Council, Photovoltaics in Korea; Editorial Advisory Member, Recent Patents on Nanotechnology. E-mail: myongsy@kaist.ac.kr

N

NA Hyung-Gi, b. 18 May 1969, Kyungsan, Kyungbuk, Korea. Research Engineer. m. Kyung-Hee Choi, 2 sons. Education: BS, 1991, MS, 1993, PhD, 1996, Electronic and Electrical Engineering, POSTECH, Korea. Appointments: Antenna Engineer, Lignex1, 1996-. Publications: Numerous articles in professional journals. Memberships: IEEE; Korean Institute of Electromagnetic Engineering Science. Address: ISR Center, Lignex1, 148-1 Mabuk-Dong, Giheung-Gu, Yongin-City, Gyeonggi-Do, 446-912, Korea. E-mail: hyunggi.na@lignex1.com

NA Sang Ho, b. 3 July 1952, Incheon, South Korea. Researcher. m. Yeon Soon Kim, 1 son, 1 daughter. Education: Bachelor, Metallurgical Engineering, Inha University, 1979; Master, 1987, PhD, 1995, Material Engineering, KAIST; Professional Engineer, Nuclear Fuel, HRD Korea, 1988. Appointments: R&D (fabrication, process design, equipment design, characteristics analysis, etc), Nuclear Fuel, 1979-. Publications: Introduction to Nuclear Fuel Cycle; Plutonium Fuel Engineering. Address: 305-755 Hanbit Apt 110-103, Yuseong-Gu, Eoeun-Dong, Daejeon, South Korea. E-mail: shna@kaeri.re.kr

NACHAZEL Karel, b. 11 November 1934, Ceske Budejovice, Czech Republic. Hydrology and Water Management. Education: Engineering degree, Faculty of Civil Engineering, 1958, DrSc, 1977, Professor, 1990, Czech Technical University. Appointments: Chief Engineer, Water Management, Development and Construction, Prague, Czech Republic, 1959-68; Research Worker, Faculty of Civil Engineering, 1968-90, Professor, Engineering Educator, 1990-, Czech Technical University, Prague. Publications: More than 100 articles in professional journals. Honours: Honour of Czech Com Hydrology, 1985; International President's Award for Iconic Achievement, IBC, 2010. Memberships: Czech Comm Science-Tech Cooperation; Czech Com Hydrology; Czech Com Tech Liter. Address: Karel Nachazel, Czech Tech University, Thakurova 7, Prague 16629, Czech Republic. E-mail: milecova@fsv.cvut.cz

NADAL Rafael, b. 3 June 1986, Manacor, Majorca, Spain. Professional Tennis Player. Career: Winner, French Open, 2005, 2006, 2007, 2008; Winner, Wimbledon Championships, 2008; Winner, London Queen's Club, 2008; Semi-finalist, US Open, 2008; World No 1 ranking, 2008; Winner, Australia Open, 2009. Honours: Gold Medal (Men's Singles), Beijing Olympics, 2008; Prince of Astruias Award, 2008.

NADYROV Ramil, b. 24 July 1967, Kurgan-Tyube, Tajikistan. Chief of General Staff, Armed Forces of Tajikistan; First Deputy of the Minister of Defense. m. Alina, 3 daughters. Education: Chernigovsky High Military Aviation School of Pilots, 1988; Graduated with Gold Medal, Y A Gagarin Air Military Academy, 1998. Appointments: Flight Control Officer Assistant, 105 Aviation Regiment, 1989; Officer of Combat Department, 1992, then Senior Officer of the Unit, Air Force, 105 A R Check Point; Deputy Chief of Main Staff, 1998, Chief of Main Staff, 2001, Chief of General Staff, 2006-, Armed Forces; First Deputy of the Minister of Defense. Honours: Government Awards; Sharaf Order; 21 medals. Address: 59 Bokhtar Street, 734025, Dushambe, Tajikistan. E-mail: rknadirov@mail.ru

NAESS Orvar Almar, b. 25 October 1922, Horten, Norway. Lector (Lecturer). m. Margit, deceased 2006, 1 son, 2 daughters. Education: Examen Artium, 1942; Teachers' College, 1942-44; Cand phil, Oslo University, 1945-51; Master's degree, American Literature, Fulbright stipend, University of Illinois, USA, 1951-52. Appointments: Teacher, elementary school, Oslo, 1944-51; Teacher, state school, Tingvoll, 1952-53; Lector (Lecturer), Molde secondary school, 1953-59; Lector (Lecturer), Sofienberg secondary school, 1959-70; Secretary, Ministry of Education, 1962-65; Vice Principal, Hovin secondary school (gymnasium for adult education), Oslo, 1973-75; Lecturer, Main Teacher, Persbraaten secondary school, 1975-92; Lecturer, Teacher, People's University (Oslo gymnasium), Oslo, 1992-2007; Lecturer, Aftenskolen, Oslo, 2008-. Publications: John Ruskin – The Personality of a Great Artist, 1951; Series of articles on literary themes in Norwegian newspapers. Honours: Stipend from Norway-America Association, 1966; 7th Degree Order of Druids, Norway; Vice President, IGLD, 1970-80. Memberships: Norway-America Association; Norway Conservative Party. Address: Vestliveien 20A, 0750 Oslo, Norway. E-mail: orvnae@frisurf.no

NAG Debabrata, b. 3 February 1943, Sylhet, India (now Bangladesh). Teacher; Researcher. m. Lakshmi, 1 son, 1 daughter. Education: BSc (Hons), Chemistry, 1965, MSc, 1967, PhD, 1974, Biochemistry, Calcutta University. Appointments: Teacher, Chemistry and Biochemistry, different colleges under Calcutta University, 1968-2003; Professor & Head, Department of Biochemistry, Government Medical College, 1977-2003; Retired, 2003; Professor and Head, Department of Biochemistry, Gurunanak Institute of Dental Sciences & Research, Kolkata, 2003-. Research: Neurotropic drug action on membrane bound enzymes of brain; Viral hepatitis; Eclampsia; Gallstone; Tuberculosis; Arecoline and endocrine functions. Memberships: Indian Society of Cell Biology; The Zoological Society, Kolkata. Address: F6, Panchasayar, PO Panchasayar, Kolkata 700094, West Bengal, India. E-mail: debabrata43@hotmail.com

NAGASAWA Shin'ya, b. 21 September 1955, Niigata City, Japan. Professor. m. Sachiko Kato, 2 daughters. Education: B Eng, 1978, M Eng, 1980, Dr Eng, 1986, Waseda University, Tokyo. Appointments: Research Associate, Meiji University, Tokyo, 1981-88; Assistant Professor, Sanno College, Tokyo, 1988-90; Associate Professor, Asia University, Tokyo, 1990-95; Professor, Ritsuneikan University, Kyoto, 1995-2003; Professor, Waseda Business School, Tokyo, 2003-; Visiting Professor, ESSEC Business School, France, 2008-09. Publications: Creating Customer Experience on Long-Standing Companies, 2006; Marketability of Environment-Conscious Products, 2007; The Principles of Louis Vuitton: The Strongest Brand Strategy, 2007; Secrets of Louis Vitton, 2009; Chanel Strategy: Ultimate Luxury Brand, 2010; Translator, The Luxury Strategy, 2011. Honours: Nikkei Publishing Award in Quality Control, 2001, 2010; Best Paper Award, EcoDesign, 2003; Publishing Award in Waste Technology, 2006; Publishing Awards, Japan Society of Kansei Engineering, 2002, 2005, 2006, 2007, 2009. Memberships: Japan Society of Kansei Engineering (former Vice President); Association of Product Development and Management (Executive Director); International Society of Management Engineering (Life Fellow). Address: 1-6-1 Nish-Waseda, Shinjuku-ku, Tokyo 1698050, Japan. E-mail: nagasawa@waseda.jp Website: www.waseda.jp/wbs

NAGASHIMA Kazunori, b. 20 May 1965, Japan. Physician. Education: MD, Akita University, 1992; PhD, Tokyo Medical University, 2003. Appointments: Research fellow, Tokyo Medical University, Tokyo, Japan; Research Scholar, Postdoctoral fellow, Columbia University, New York, USA;

Health Care Physician, Isesaki-Sawa Medical Association Hospital, Gunma, Japan; Isesaki Municipal Hospital, Gunma, Japan; Chief of Clinical Medicine; The Minister of Ministry of Health, Labor and Welfare Accredited East-Japan Labor-Health Center, Gunma, Japan. Publications: Articles in medical journals: Clarification of changes of serum lipids according to age in males and females who requested a medical health check up, 2000; Changes regarding age and correlations between serum lipids and body mass index in humankind, 2002; Effects of the PPARγ agonist pioglitazone on lipoprotein metabolism in patients with type 2 diabetes mellitus, 2005. Honours: Symposiast, 40th Annual Congress of Japanese College of Angiology, Hiroshima, Japan, 1999; Man of the Year 2005, ABI, 2005; Great Minds of the 21st Century, ABI, 2005; Noble Order of International Ambassadors, ABI, 2005; 2000 Outstanding Intellectuals of the 21st Century, IBC, 2005, 2006; Deputy Director General, IBC, 2006; 500 Greatest Geniuses of the 21st Century, ABI, 2006; Deputy Governor, ABI, 2006; Great Lives of the 21st Century, IBC, 2006; American Medal of Honor, ABI, 2006; International Order of Merit, IBC, 2006; Gold Medal for Japan, ABI, 2006; Top 100 Health Professionals, IBC, 2006; Director Generals Roll of Honour, IBC, 2007; Greatest Minds of the 21st Century, ABI, 2007; The Establishment of the Kazunori Nagashima, MD, PhD Award Foundation, ABI, 2007; Man of Achievement, ABI, 2007; Dictionary of International Biography, 2007; 500 Great Leaders, 2008; Top Two Hundred of the IBC, 2008; Cambridge Blue Book, 2009. Memberships: International Health Evaluation and Promotion Association; Japanese Society of Internal Medicine; Japanese Circulation Society; Japan Atherosclerosis Society; Japanese College of Angiology; Japan Society of Health Evaluation and Promotion; Japan Society of Ningen Dock; American Heart Association; Council on Arteriosclerosis, Thrombosis and Vascular Biology; International Atherosclerotic Society; Council on Epidemiology and Prevention; Interdisciplinary Working Group of Atherosclerotic Peripheral Vascular Disease; American Diabetes Association; New York Academy of Sciences; Japan Society for Occupational Mental Health. Address: 23-13 Chuo-cho, Prime Square ISESAKI Rm 901, Isesaki-shi, Gunma-ken, 372-0042, Japan. E-mail: kanagashima-circ@umin.ac.jp

NAGY Endre László, b. 25 December 1942, Terehegy, Baranya, Hungary. Electrical Engineer; Researcher; Educator. m. Ritsuko Mine. Education: Budapest Technical University, 1961-66; PhD, Computing and Automation Research Institute of Hungarian Academy of Sciences, and Budapest Technical University, 1970-73. Appointments: Scientific Associate, Research Institute for Electric Energy Industry, Budapest, 1966-70, 1973-74; Associate Professor, Kandó Kálmán College for Electrical Engineering, Budapest, 1974-84; Chief Researcher, Birds Information Research Institute, Tokyo, 1987-89; Head of Department, Sanrura Inc, Tokyo/Yokohama, 1990-93; Basic research on control systems, 1994-. Publications: Several articles, studies and presentations at conferences: International Federation of Automatic Control; World Multi-Conference on Systematics, Cybernetics and Informatics; International Conference on Nonlinear Problems in Aviation & Aerospace; American Control Conference, etc. Honours: Diploma Prize, Electrotechnical Society, Budapest, 1966; Member of the Year, Madison Who's Who, 2007-08; Deputy Governor, ABI Research Association, 2008; Proclamation Plaque of Recognition, ABI, 2008; Universal Award of Accomplishment, ABI, 2008; Listed in Dedication section of Great Minds of the 21st Century, 2008; Man of the Year, 2008, ABI, 2009; International Peace Prize, United Cultural Convention, 2009; American Hall of Fame, ABI, 2009; International Ambassador, ABI, 2009; Honorary Freeman of Harkány, Hungary, 2009; ABI World Laureate, 2009; Listed in international biographical dictionaries. Memberships: International Federation of Automatic Control; International Institute of Informatics & Systematics; Society of Instrument and Control Engineers of Japan. E-mail: nagy@mtd.biglobe.ne.jp

NAGY István, b. 12 August 1931, Budapest, Hungary. Research Professor. m. Georgia Tassy, 1 daughter. Education: MSc, Technical University, Budapest, 1953; University Dr, 1960; MS, Intech, Hungarian Academy of Sciences, Budapest, 1959; Dr, Technical Science, 1975. Appointments: Researcher, 1957-65, Head of Department, 1976-96, Head of Group, 1996-, Technical University; Part time Project Engineer, Ganz Electric Work, Budapest, 1960-74; Chief Researcher, 1967-70, Head of Department, 1970-90, Computation and Automation Institute, Budapest. Publications: 8 textbooks; 7 handbooks; 100 journal papers; 200 conference proceeding papers; 34 reports; 13 patents. Honours: Eugene Mittellmann Achievement Award, 2009; William E Newell Power Electronics Award, 2008; Szechenyi Prize; Csaki Award, Zipernowskey Prize. Memberships: Fellow, IEEE; Hungarian Cigre Committee; EPE-PEMC Council, Budapest; European Power Electronics Society; EPE Executive Council; Full Member, Academy of Sciences (HAS). Address: Budapest University of Technology and Economics, Magyar Tudosok Korutja 2, Building Q, H-1117 Budapest, Hungary.

NAH Hwan-Seon, b. 11 January 1962, Mogpo, South Korea. Research Scientist. m. Sun-Jin Lim, 1 son, 1 daughter. Education: Doctoral degree, Kongju national University. Appointments: Research Scientist. Honours: Awards of Ministry of Knowledge and Economy, Korea. Memberships: Korea Society of Steel Construction; Architectural Institute of Korea; Korea Green Building Council. Address: Korean Electric Power Research Institute 65, Munji-Ro, Yusung-Gu, Daejon, 305-760, Korea. E-mail: hsnah@kepri.re.kr

NAIK Vihang, b. 2 September 1969, Surat, India. Lecturer. Education: BA, 1993, MA, 1995, Maharaja Sayajirao University of Baroda. Appointments: Lecturer, English, Smt MC Desai Arts and Commerce College, 1996-97; Lecturer in English, Shree Ambaji Arts College, 1997-. Publications: City Times & Other Poems, Writer's Workshop, Calcutta, 1993; Jeevangeet, 2001; Making a Poem, 2004; Poetry Manifesto, 2010; Poems published in leading journals and various anthologies including: Poems 96; Poems 97; Wanderlust; Dayspring; World Poetry 1996, 1997, 1998, 1999; Translations include: (from Gujarati into English) A Sahitya Akedemi's Journal. Honours: International Man of the Year 1997-98, IBC; Honorary appointment, Research Board of Advisers, ABI; Michele Madhusudhan Prize for City Times & Other Poems. Memberships: Various prominent literary organisations including Poetry Society (India); Poetry Circle (Mumbai); World Poetry Society International; The Poetry Society, India. Address: Shree Ambaji Arts College, Kumbhariya, Danta Highway, Ambaji 385110, Dist BK, North Gujarat, India.

NAIR Vipin Devi Prasad Purushothaman, b. 10 May 1978, Neyoor, India. Research Assistant Professor. m. Lekshmi. Education: Bachelor, Pharmacy, 1999; Master, Pharmacy, 2001; PhD, Pharmaceutical Sciences, Rhodes University, 2006. Appointments: Scientist 2, TRC, Research Fellow, BIT, 2001; Postdoctoral Fellow, Rhodes University, 2006; Postdoctoral Fellow, University of Kentucky, 2006-08; Research Associate, 2008-09, Assistant Professor, 2009-,

Arkansas Bioscience Institute. Publications: Numerous articles in professional journals. Honours: Scientist II, Sun Pharmaceutical Advanced Research Center, Mumbai; Senior Lecturer, Faculty of Pharmacy, University of KwaZulu-Natal, South Africa; Fee waiver (LMM in Intellectual Property), Turin University. Memberships: Sigma Xi, Scientific Research Society; American Chemical Society; American Association of Pharmaceutical Scientists; American Association for the Advancement of Science; South African Pharmacy Council; Indian Pharmaceutical Association. Address: 264/C, 1389, Devi Priya, Behind RB Office, Vanamaleeswaram, South Road, Parvathipuram, Nagercoil, KK Dist, Tamil Nadu, 629003, India. E-mail: vipindeviprasad@rediffmail.com Website: www.astate.edu

NAKAGAWA Masahiko, b. 4 September 1968, Tokyo, Japan. Forestry Researcher. Education: Bachelor of Science, Humboldt State University, 1992; Master of Agriculture, University of Tokyo, 1995.; Doctor of Agriculture, University of Tokyo, 2006. Appointments: Bureaucrat, Forestry Agency, Ministry of Agriculture, Forestry and Fisheries, 1995-96; Forester, Shibiutan Forester Office, Japan National Forest, 1996-98; Forester, Tokyo Metropolitan Government, Tokyo Metropolitan Forest, 1998-99; Forester, Abasiri-seibu Forest Centre, Hokkaido Prefectural Forest, 1999-2003; Forestry Researcher, Hokkaido Forestry Research Institute, 2003-. Publications: Numerous articles in professional journals. Honours: Phi Kappa Phi; magna cum laude, 1992; Listed in national and international biographical dictionaries. Memberships: Japan Forest Society; Forest Management and Research Network. Address: RC-97-1-101, Minami3 jo, Nishi 2 chome, Shimizu-cho, Hokkaido, 089-0104, Japan.

NAKAMURA Yukio, b. 15 January 1955, Kanazawa city, Japan. Medical Doctor. m. Sanae Arai, 2 sons, 1 daughter. Education: MD, School of Medicine, 1979; PhD, Doctor of Medical Science, 1987, Kanazawa University. Appointments: Resident, 1979, Medical Staff, 1981-82, 1983-84, Kanazawa University Hospital; Postdoctoral Fellow, Montreal Heart Institute, Quebec, Canada, 1987-89; Instructor, 1990-93, Associate Professor, 1994-95, Kanazawa University; Director, Clinical Research Institute, Kanazawa Medical Center, 1996-. Publications: Effects of endoscopic transthoracic sympathicotomy on hemodynamic..., 2002; Relation between hemodynamic changes after endoscopic transthoracic..., 2003; Effects of endoscopic transthoracic sympathicotomy on plasma natriuretic..., 2005. Honours: Listed in international biographical dictionaries. Memberships: Fellow, Japanese College of Cardiology; Japan Society of electrocardiology; Japan Society of Internal Medicine; Japan Clinical Society; Japan Heart Failure Society; Japan College of Angiology; Japan Heart Rhythm Society; Japan Society of Phlebology. Address: Kanazawa Medical Center, 1-1 Shimoishibiki-machi, Kanazawa, Ishikawa 920-8650, Japan. E-mail: nakay@kinbyou.hosp.go.jp

NAKANISHI Tohru, b. 24 September 1964, Shiga, Japan. m. 3 daughters. Education: PhD, Engineering, Kyoto University, 2006. Appointments: Component Engineering, Design Methodology, IBM, 1987; Design Optimization with Numerical Analysis, Lenovo, Japan, 2011-. Publications: Advanced Engineering of Mobile Phone; Advanced Electronics Packaging; Thermal Engineering of Electronics Products. Memberships: IEEE; Japan Society of Mechanical Engineers. Address: 6-10-10 Moriyama, Moriyama-shi, Shiga-ken, 524-0022, Japan.

NAKASHIMA Kazuya, b. 18 September 1945, Japan. Dentist. 2 sons. Education: Los Alamos High School, New Mexico; BA, University of New Mexico; DDS, Tohoku Dental University, Japan. Appointments: Horiuchi Dental Office, Japan; Ogura Dental Office, Japan; Head, Dental Department, Asaka Hoyoen Hospital, Japan. Memberships: International Member, American Academy of Periodontology; Associate Member, American Association of Endodontist; ADA; AGD; AACD; ALD; Japan Dental Association. Address: Nakashima Medical Coporation, Nakashima Dental Office, Roppongi U Bldg 4F, 4-5-2 Roppongi, Minato-ku, Tokyo 106, Japan. E-mail: hahaha@dentist_nakashima.jp Website: www.dentist-nakashima.jp

NAM Charles Benjamin, b. 25 March 1926, Lynbrook, New York, USA. Demographer; Sociologist. m. Marjorie Tallant, deceased, 1 son, 1 daughter. Education: BA, Applied Statistics, New York University, 1950; MA, Sociology, 1957, PhD, Sociology, 1959, University of North Carolina. Appointments: Staff, 1950-53, Branch Chief, 1957-63, US Bureau of the Census; Professor, Florida State University, 1964-95; Professor Emeritus and Author, Research Associate, Centre for Demography and Population Health, Florida State University, 1995-; Distinguished Research Professor Emeritus. Publications: 13 books, including The Golden Door, 2006; Over 100 articles and chapters. Honours: Fellow, American Association for the Advancement of Science; Fellow, American Statistical Association; Listed in international biographical dictionaries. Memberships: American Association for the Advancement of Science; Population Association of America, Past President; American Statistical Association; Society for the Study of Social Biology; American Sociological Association; International Union for the Scientific Study of Population. Address: 820 Live Oak Plantation Road, Tallahassee, FL 32312-2413, USA. E-mail: charlesnam2@embarqmail.com

NAM Ho-Yun, b. 7 April 1951, Gyeongju, Korea. Researcher. m. En-Sook Yoon, 1 son, 2 daughters. Education: BS, Physics, Seoul National University, 1978; MS, 1986, PhD, 1994, Nuclear Engineering, KAIST. Appointments: Experimental Researcher, Thermal-Hydraulic for Nuclear Reactor, 1978-, Project Manager, 1993-98, Korea Atomic Energy Research Institute (KAERI); Deputy Director General, IBC, 2011. Publications: Experimental and theoretical investigation of waterhammer induced by steam-water countercurrent flow in a long horizontal pipe, 1994; A criterion for the onset of slugging in horizontal stratified air-water counter-current flow, 1995; Experimental study on the amplitude of a free surface fluctuation, 2008; Thermal hydraulic design of a double wall tube steam generator with an online leak detection system, 2009; Steam generator for sodium cooled fast reactor, heat transfer tubes thereof, and leak detection unit, patent application. Honours: Awards of the Minister of Education and Technology of Korea, 2009; Man of the Year, ABI, 2011; Top 100 Scientists, IBC, 2011. Memberships: Korea Nuclear Society; Fellowship of IBA. Address: Korea Atomic Energy Research Institute, 1045, Daedeok-daero, Yuseong-gu, Daejeon 305-353, Republic of Korea. E-mail: hynam@kaeri.re.kr

NAM Hye Jeong, b. 17 November, Seoul, Korea. Assistant Professor. Education: BBA, Inha University, 1999; MS, 2004, PhD, 2008, Seoul National University. Appointments: Assistant Professor, 2008-, Admission Officer, 2009-10, Dongguk University. Publications: The effect of Regulation

Fair disclosure on conference calls: The case of earnings surprise, 2009; Firm location and Earnings Management: Korean Evidence, 2011.

NAM Ki Chang, b. 10 August 1972, Seoul, Korea. Research Professor. m. Hyejin Yang, 2 daughters. Education: BS, 1997, MS, 1999, PhD, 2004, Biomedical Engineering, Yonsei University. Appointments: Research Fellow, 2004-05, Research Professor, 2010-, Yonsei University College of Medicine; Principal Engineer, Siemens, Korea, 2005-06; Postdoctoral Researcher, AIST, Japan, 2006-07; Senior Researcher, Korea Electrotechnology Research Institute, 2007-10. Publications: 20 SCI(E) papers, 2000-; Biomedical Engineering, 2009. Honours: Best Employee, Siemens, 2006; Distinguished Service Award, IEEK, 2010. Memberships: Institute of Electronics Engineers of Korea; Institute of Electronics, Information and Communication Engineers; Korean Society of Medical & Biological Engineering. E-mail: kichang.nam@gmail.com

NAM Ki-Bong, b. 26 February 1955, Masan, South Korea. Professor. m. Young Hee Esther, 1 son, 1 daughter. Education: BS, 1981, MS, 1983, Mathematics, Hanyang University, Korea; MA, 1996, PhD, 1998, Mathematics, University of Wisconsin-Madison, USA. Appointments: Teaching Assistant, Hanyang Graduate, 1981-83; Teaching Assistant, Iowa State University, 1983-84; Lecturer, 1999-2002, Assistant Professor, 2003-06, Associate Professor, 2006-, University of Wisconsin-Whitewater. Publications: Generalised S-type Lie Algebras, 2007; Weyl type non-associative algebra using additive groups I, 2007; Presented a paper, ICM, 2002, 2006, 2010; Presented a paper, ICA, 2010, Indonesia, 2010; Editor and reviewer for professional journals. Honours: Research Award, College of Letters & Sciences, 2006-07; University Research Award, University of Wisconsin-Whitewater, 2006-07. Memberships: American Mathematics Society; Southeast Asian Math Society; Editorship of professional scientific journals. Address: Department of Mathematics & Computer Science, University of Wisconsin-Whitewater, 800 West Main Street, Whitewater, WI 53190, USA. E-mail: namk@uww.edu

NAMBA Kanji, b. 12 April 1939, Sojya, Okayama Prefecture, Japan. Professor. m. Toshiko Hosaya, 2 sons. Education: Graduate, Department of Mathematics, Okayama University, 1962; Master of Mathematics, 1964, Dr Sci, 1968, Graduate School of Science, Tokyo University of Education. Appointments: Assistant, 1964-67, Lecturer, 1967-70, Department of Applied Mathematics, Tokyo University of Education; Associate Professor, College of General Education, Nagoya University 1970-79; Associate Professor, 1979-86, Professor, 1986-92, Faculty of General Education, University of Tokyo; Professor, Graduate School of Mathematical Science, University of Tokyo, 1992-2000; Retired, 2000; Professor Emeritus, University of Tokyo, 2001; Professor, 2002-05, Professor Emeritus, 2006-, Hirosaki University. Publications: Several papers in professional scientific journals. Memberships: Director, Association of the Philosophy of Sciences; Mathematics Society of Japan; American Mathematical Society; Association of Applied Mathematics of Japan; Association of Symbolic Logic. Address: 463-3 Kitamizote, Sojya, Okayama 719-1117, Japan.

NAMMAS Wail Mostafa, b. 1972, Damietta, Egypt. Assistant Professor. m. Education: MBBCh (Hon), 1989, Master Degree, Cardiology, 1999, Doctor Degree, Cardiovascular Medicine, 2003, Ain Shams University, Faculty of Medicine. Appointments: Medical House Officer Service, 1996-97, Medical Resident Service, Cardiology, 1997-2000, Ain Shams University Hospitals; Assistant Lecturer, 2000-04, Lecturer, 2004-09, Assistant Professor, 2009-, Cardiology, Ain Shams University; International Reviewer, Echocardiography journal, 2009-; Member of the Advisory Board, Anatolian Journal of Cardiology, 2009-; International Reviewer, Expert Opinion on Pharmacotherapy journal, 2010-. Publications: Numerous articles in professional journals. Honours: Listed in international biographical dictionaries. Memberships: Egyptian Society of Cardiology; European Society of Cardiology. Address: 3 Wageb Street, 1st Province, Nasr City, Cairo, Egypt. E-mail: wnammas@hotmail.com

NANDANWAR Tukaram Upasrao, b. 1 April 1940, Nagpur, India. Journalist; Professor; Advocate; Anthropologist. m. Shrimati Sindhutai, 2 sons, 3 daughters. Education: BA; BJ; LLB; DBM; DIRPM; DPR; PDDA & TD; DRTM; MCJ; MIRPM; MMS/MBA; PhD; Worker Teacher CBWE, Government of India. Appointments: Journalist Advocate, Faculty Member, Mass Communication & Journalism; Faculty Member of Social Science and Management; National Secretary General, National Federation of Human Rights Council, Mumbai, India; Director, Nagpur International Human Rights Association. Publications: Numerous articles in professional journals; Monograph on Halba, Halbi Tribes of Madhya Pradesh, Maharashtra State, Amendment to the Constitution of India, 1950; The Constitution (Scheduled Castes and Scheduled Tribes, Other Backward Classes and Scheduled Area). Honours include most recently: Netaji Rashtriya Award, 2009; Babu Jagjivam Rao International Award, 2010; Babu Jagjivam Rao National Sanman Award, 2010; Shree Jagnnath Rashtriya Shreekhetra Sanman Award, 2010; Mahatma Phuie Talen National Sanman, 2010; WF Manya Tilak Srimaj Bhushan Puraskar, 2010; Maharashtra Deep Puraskar, 2010; Samajshtra Acharya Puraskar, 2010. Memberships: Secretary Tribal Research Centre, Nagpur; Secretary Tribal Research and Development Centre, Nagpur; Founder, Nandanwar Tribal Research, Welfare Development, Documentation Council, Nagpur; Editor in Chief, Weekly Tribal Welfare newspaper, Nagpur. Address: Plot No 30, Rajaram Nagar, Housing Society, Behind Pandey Nursery Garden, Near Rout Sabha Gruha, Police Line Takli, Nagpur 440 013 Maharashtra, India. E-mail: nandanwar_tribal@yahoo.co.in

NAPINEN Leo, b. 17 April 1948, County of Paide, Estonia. Philosopher; Educator. Education: MSc, Chemistry, University of Tartu, Estonia, 1975; PhD, Philosophy, Latvian Academy of Sciences, Riga, Latvia, 1984. Appointments: Researcher and Teacher, 1978-80, Postgraduate Student and Teacher, 1980-83, Lecturer, 1983-85, Senior Lecturer, Department of Philosophy, 1985-87, University of Tartu; Research Fellow, Department of Philosophy, Institute of History, Tallinn, Estonia, 1987-88; Senior Research Fellow, 1989-96, and Project Leader, 1995-96, Department of Philosophy, Institute of Philosophy, Sociology and Law, Tallinn; Lecturer, 1996-99, and Acting Head of the Chair, 1999, Associate Professor, 1999-, Chair of Philosophy, Tallinn University of Technology. Publications: Author, numerous articles in professional journals; Co-author, Boston Studies in the Philosophy of Science, vol. 219, Synergetic Paradigm. Cognitive and Communicative Strategies of Modern Scientific Reason, 2004. Honours: Letter of Thanks Award, Tallinn University of Technology, 2008. Memberships: Estonian Society for the History and Philosophy of Science; Organising Committee, 24th International Baltic Conference on the History of Science, Tallinn. Address: Tallinn University of Technology, Faculty of Social Sciences, The Chair of Philosophy, Akadeemia tee 3, Tallinn 12618, Estonia. E-mail: leo.napinen@ttu.ee

NARAGHI Akhtar, Writer. m. Javad Ebadi, deceased, 1 son, 1 daughter. Education: PhD, English Literature, McGill University, Canada, 1991. Appointments: Teacher at Teachers Training College, Tehran; Teacher, McGill University. Publications: Legacy: Selected Poems, 1992; The Big Green House: A Novel in Twelve Short Stories (translated into German, French and Persian), 1994, 5th edition, 2001; Solitude: Selected Poems, 1996; Blue Curtains: A Novel in Six Stories, 1999; With Mara That Summer: A Novel in Four Stories, 2004; Ghazal: The Poems of Safai Naraghi (editor), 1972; Contributor of forewords, articles, short stories and poems to numerous journals. Honours: The Big Green House shortlisted for the 1995 QSPELL Hugh MacLennan Prize for Fiction; Several interviews for newspapers, radio and television Listed in Who's Who publications and biographical dictionaries. Memberships: Founding President, International Organisation of the Helen Prize for Women, 1987; Member, Quebec Writers' Association. Address: PO Box 781, Place du Parc, Montreal, QC H2X 4A6, Canada. E-mail: persica@sympatico.ca

NARAYANAN Geetha, b. 20 May 1959, Kerala, India. Medical Oncologist. Education: MBBS; MD; DNB; DM, Oncology. Appointments: Lecturer, Assistant Professor, Associate Professor, Additional Professor of Medical Oncology, Regional Cancer Centre, Trivandrum. Publications: 40 articles in professional journals. Memberships: American Society of Haematology; American Society of Clinical Oncology; European Society of Medical Oncology; Indian Association of Pediatrics; Indian Medical Association.

NAROTZKY Norman David, b. 14 March 1928, Brooklyn, New York, USA. Artist. m. Mercedes Molleda, 10 March 1957, 2 daughters. Education: High School of Music and Art, New York City, New York, 1941-45; Art Students League, New York City, 1945-49; BA, Brooklyn College, 1949; Cooper Union Art School, New York City, 1949-52; Atelier 17, Paris, 1954-56; Kunstakademie, Munich, 1956-57; New York University Institute of Fine Arts, 1957-58; BFA, Cooper Union Art School, 1979. Appointments: 56 solo exhibitions in Europe and USA. Creative Works: Group shows at Brooklyn Museum; National Gallery, Oslo; Salon de Mai and Salon des Réalités Nouvelles, Paris; VI Bienal Sao Paulo, Brazil; Museum of Modern Art, New York; Baltimore Museum of Art; San Francisco Museum of Art; Whitney Museum of Art, New York; Palazzo Strozzi, Florence; Haus Der Kunst, Munich; Fundació Miro, Barcelona; Work in the collection of museums in Europe and USA. Publications: 9 original colour etchings for limited edition artist's book, The Raven, by Edgar Allan Poe; Several articles in professional journals and magazines. Honours: Cooper Union Award for Excellence in Graphic Arts, 1952; Award, Texas Watercolor Society, San Antonio, Texas, 1954; Wooley Foundation Fellowship, 1954; French Government Fellowship, 1955; Fulbright Fellowship, 1956; Philadelphia Museum Purchase Prize, 1956; 1st Prize, Hebrew Educational Society, Brooklyn, 1959; Award, 2nd Mini Print International Cadaques, 1982; Painting Grant, Generalitat de Catalunya, 1983; Grand Prize, II Bienal D'Art Fc Barcelona, 1987; Listed in national and international biographical dictionaries. Memberships: Art Students League, New York; Cercle D'Art Sant Lluc, Barcelona; Catalan Association of Visual Artists. Address: Diputación 294, 1-2, 08009 Barcelona, Spain. E-mail: ndnarotzky@gmail.com

NASHEED Mohamed, b. 17 May 1967, Male', Republic of Maldives. President of Maldives. Eduation: BA, Maritime Studies, Liverpool John Moores University, 1989. Appointments: Established political magazine, Sangu, 1990; Elected MP for Male', 1999; Co-founder, Maldivian Democratic Party (in exile in Sri Lanka), 2004; Granted refugee status, UK government, 2004; Returned to Maldives to establish MDP, 2005; Elected Chair, MDP, 2005; Initiated campaign of non-violent civil disobedience in Maldives, 2005-08; Elected President of the Maldives, 2008. Honours: Anna Lindh Prize, 2009; Hero of the Environment, 2009. Address: Office of the President, Bodhuthakurufaanu Magu, Male', Republic of Maldives. E-mail: info@presidencymaldives.gov.mv

NASKOU-PERRAKI Paroula, b. 19 January 1947, Thessaloniki, Greece. Professor of International Law. 1 son, 1 daughter. Education: Law degree, Master, International Law, Aristotle University; PhD, International Law, Demokritus University. Appointments: Professor, International Law and International Organisations, University of Macedonia, Department of International and European Studies, Thessaloniki, Greece. Publications: 64 books; 35 articles on human rights, international law and international organisations. Honours: Professor of Honor, Blagoevgrad University, Bulgaria; Friend of the United Nations; Deputy Director, Center of International and European Economic Law; Visiting Professor, Capital Law School, Columbus, Ohio; UNESCO Chair Holder, Intercultural Policy. Memberships: International Law Association; Hellenic Society of International Law and International Relations. Address: K Karamauli 173, Thessaloniki 54249, Greece. E-mail: perraki@uom.gr

NASR Seyyed Hossein, b. 7 April 1933, Tehran, Iran. University Professor. m. Soussan Daneshvary, November 1958, 1 son, 1 daughter. Education: BS, MIT, 1954; MSc, 1956, PhD, History of Science and Philosophy, 1958, Harvard University. Appointments: Professor of Philosophy and History of Science, 1958-79, Dean of Faculty of Letters, 1968-72, Vice Chancellor, 1970-71, Tehran University; Visiting Professor, Harvard University, 1962, 1965; Aga Khan Professor of Islamic Studies, American University of Beirut, 1964-65; President, Aryamehr University, 1972-75; Founder, 1st President, Iranian Academy of Philosophy, 1974-79; Distinguished Visiting Professor, University of Utah, 1979; Professor of Religion, Temple University, 1979-84; University Professor, The George Washington University, 1984-; A D White Professor-at-Large, Cornell University, 1991-97. Publications: Over 50 books and 500 articles in magazines and journals throughout the world. Honours: Royal Book Award of Iran, 1963; Honorary Doctorate, University of Uppsala, 1977; Gifford Lecturer, 1981; Honorary Doctorate, Lehigh University, 1996. 2001 volume of the Library of Living Philosophers; International Gittler Prize, Brandeis University, 2010; Keynote Speaker, Beijing Forum, 2009; Listed in various international biographical dictionaries. Address: The George Washington University, Gelman Library, 709-R, 2130 H Street, NW Washington, DC 20052, USA.

NASTASE Ilie, b. 19 July 1946, Bucharest, Romania. Tennis Player. m. (1) 1 daughter, (2) Alexandra King, 1984. Appointments: National Champion (13-14 age group), 1959, (15-16 age group) 1961, (17-18 age group) 1963, 1964; Won, Masters Singles Event, Paris, 1971, Barcelona, 1972; Boston, 1973, Stockholm, 1975; Winner, Singles, Cannes, 1967, Travemunde, 1967, 1969, Gauhati, Madras, 1968, 1969, New Delhi, 1968, 1969, Viareggio, 1968, Barranquilla,

DICTIONARY OF INTERNATIONAL BIOGRAPHY 36th EDITION

Coruna, Budapest, Denver, 1969, Salisbury, Rome, 1970, Omaha, Nice, Monte Carlo, 1971, 1972, Baastad, Wembley, Stockholm, Richmond, Hampton, Istanbul, 1971, Forest Hills, Baltimore, Madrid, Toronto, S Orange, Seattle, 1972, Roland Garros, US Open, 1973; Winner, Doubles, Roland Garros (with Ion Tiriac), 1970; Played 130 matches for the Romanian team in the Davis Cup; Retired, 1985. Publication: Breakpoint, 1986. Honours: ILTF Grand Prix, 1972, 1973; Best Romanian Sportsman of the Year, 1969, 1970, 1971, 1973. Address: Clubul Sportiv Steaua, Calea Plevnei 114, Bucharest, Romania.

NATH Indranil, b. 11 September 1969, Kolkata, India. Managing Director. m. Sumitra, 2 sons. Education: BA (Hons), Japanese and Linguistics, 1991; MBA, 1995; Graduate Diploma in Training & Development, 1995; PhD, Engineering Management, 2006; Certified IT Project Manager, 2002; Chartered IT Professional, 2007. Publications: Several articles in professional journals. Honours: Fellow, Chartered Management Institute, England. Memberships: IEEE; Project Management Institute; Indian Society of Training & Development; Institute of Corporate Directors; British Computer Society. Address: 3-80-4 Chiyozaki-cho, Naka-ku, Yokohama 231-0864, Japan. E-mail: indranil@nathonline.com

NATH Kamal, b. 18 November 1946, Kampur, India. Minister. m. Alka, 2 sons. Education: B Com, St Xavier's College, Calcutta. Appointments: Youth Worker, Indian National Congress Party, 1968; First elected to Parliament, Chhindwara constituency, 1980; Indian Representative, United Nations General Assembly, 1982, 1983; Board of Directors, Housing and Urban Development Corporation; First inducted into Union Council of Ministers, 1991; Minister of Environment & Forests, 4 years; Textiles Minister, 1995-96; Commerce & Industry Minister, 2004-09; Minister for Road Transport and Highways, 2009-. Publications: Book, India's Century; Minister of Urban Development, 2011-. Honours: Honorary Doctorate, Rani Durgavati University, 2006.

NATHAN Ramaswamy Jeya Gandhi, b. 18 February 1948, Mandaitivu, Ceylon. Mechanical Engineer. 1 son, 1 daughter. Education: BSc, Mechanical Engineering, University of Hertfordshire, England, 1978; Diploma (Postgraduate), Management Studies, University of Coventry, England, 1982; PhD, Mechanical Engineering, Curtin University of Technology, Australia, 1994. Appointments: Test Engineer, Jaguar Rover Triumph Ltd, 1978-80; Senior Engineer, British Leyland Technology Ltd, UK, 1980-83; Research Engineer, National Materials Handling Bureau, Sydney, 1984-85; Plant Performance Engineer, 1985-87, Mechanical Design Engineer, 1987-94, System Engineer, 1994-95, Mechanical Engineer Generation, 1995-98, Western Power Corporation; Engineering Consultant/Lecturer, Contract & Consulting Employment with Various Organisations, 1999-2002; Reliability Engineer, Alcoa World Alumina Australia, 2002-07; Principal Maintenance Engineer, Transfield Worley, Woodside Energy Ltd, 2007-. Publications: Numerous articles in professional journals. Memberships: Institution of Engineers, Australia; Institution of Mechanical Engineers, UK; Chartered Management Institute, UK; Registered Professional Engineer. Address: PO Box 197, Bull Creek, Western Australia 6149, Australia. E-mail: rjnathan@iinet.net.au

NAUGHTIE (Alexander) James, b. 9 August 1951, Aberdeen, Scotland. Journalist. m. Eleanor Updale, 1986, 1 son, 2 daughters. Education: University of Aberdeen; Syracuse University. Appointments: Journalist, The Scotsman (newspaper), 1977-84; The Guardian, 1984-88; Chief Political Correspondent; Presenter, The World at One, BBC Radio, 1988-94; The Proms, BBC Radio and TV, 1991-; Today, BBC Radio 4, 1994-; Book Club, BBC Radio 4, 1998-. Publication: The Rivals, 2001; The Accidental American, 2004. Honour: LLD, Aberdeen. Membership: Council, Gresham College, 1997-. Radio Personality of the Year, 1991; Voice of the Listener and Viewer Award, 2001. Address: BBC News Centre, London W12 7RJ, England.

NAUMOV (Panche) Panče, b. 30 March 1975, Štip, Macedonia. Associate Professor. Education: BSc, Chemistry, SS Cyril and Methodius University, 1997; PhD, Chemistry, Tokyo Institute of Technology, 2004. Appointments: Undergraduate Research Associate, 1996-97, Graduate Research Fellow, 1997-2000, Associate Professor, 2005-09, SS Cyril and Methodius University; Research Fellow, 2000-01, Graduate Research Fellow, 2001-04, Tokyo Institute of Technology; Research Fellow, National Institute for Materials Science, Tsukuba, Japan, 2004-07; Associate Professor, Osaka University, Japan, 2007-. Publications: Over 110 research articles in scientific journals; More than 950 citations; Over 100 participations in scientific meetings; Referee in more than 100 papers; 2 book chapters: 1 patent. Honours: Best Student Award, 1997; Japanese Ministry of Science and Education Fellowship, 2000-04; Best Presentation Award, CRSJ, 2005; Best Presentation Award ASCA, 2006; Finalist, European Young Chemist Award, 2008; Global Center of Excellence Fellowship, 2011; Human Frontier Research Project, 2011; Listed in various international biographical dictionaries. Memberships: American Chemical Society; Crystallographic Society of Japan; Society of Chemists and Technologists of Macedonia; Councilor, European Crystallographic Association; Japan Society of Co-ordination Chemistry; Member, The Japanese Photochemistry Association; Member, The Materials Research Society of Japan; Councillor, European Crystallographic Association; Co-editor, Macedonian Journal of Chemistry and Chemical Engineering. Address: Graduate School of Engineering, Osaka University, 2-1 Yamadaoka, Suita 565-0871, Osaka, Japan. E-mail: npance@wakate.frc.eng.osaka-u.ac.jp

NAVARRETE Juan Manuel, b. 25 February 1933, Mexico City, Mexico. Chemical Engineer. m. Celia Luna, 3 sons. Education: Chemical Engineer, 1958, BSc, Human Philosophy, 1968, National University of Mexico; Postgraduate Diploma, Radiochemistry, Leicester College of Technology, England, 1965; Docteur en Chimie, l'Université Pierre et Marie Curie (Paris 6), France, 1992. Appointments: Director, Nuclear Studies Centre, 1971-76, Titular Professor C, Faculty of Chemistry, 1981-2010, National University of Mexico; Scientific Counselor, Embassy of Mexico, Paris, France, 1976-77. Publications: 72 scientific articles in international journals; 2 books: Mathematics and Reality, 1976, 1982; Introduction to the Study of Radioisotopes, 1979, 1993. Honours: Invited Speaker, Winter Meeting of American Nuclear Society, Washington DC, USA, 2005; Session Chairperson, Asia Pacific Symposium on Radiochemistry, Beijing, China, 2005; Vice President, International Nuclear Chemistry Society, Turkey, 2005-10; Session Chairperson, Modern Trends in Activation Analysis, Tokyo, Japan, 2007; Head, Second International Nuclear Chemistry Congress, Cancun, Mexico, 2008; Invited Speaker, Nuclear and Radiochemistry Symposium, Bombay, India, 2009; National Researcher, Level I (1982-88, 1992-2001), Level II, (2001-09), Level III (2010-14). Memberships: National System of Researchers; International Nuclear Chemistry Society; Mexican Academy of Engineering; Chemical Society of Mexico.

NAVARRO David Michael, b. 7 June 1967, Santa Monica, California, USA. Songwriter, Writer, Musician (piano, guitar, drums and bass guitar). m. (1) Tania Goddard, 1990 (divorce); (2) Rhian Gittins, 1994 (divorced); (3) Carmen Electra, 2003 (divorced). Musical Education: Piano lessons aged 6; Guitar lessons. Career: Various TV and radio show appearances; Co-hosting Tv show Rock Star:INXS; Bands: South Dakota Railroad, Dizastre, 1983; Jane's Addiction, 1986; Red Hot Chilli Peppers, 1993; Nancy Raygun (Swallow), 1999; Spread, 1997; Camp Freddy, 2002; The Panic Channel, 2004. Recordings: Singles released include: Rexall; Hungry; Sunny Day; Mourning Son; Everything; Not for Nothing; Avoiding the Angel; Very Little Daylight; Venus in Furs; Slow Motion Sickness; The Bed; Somebody Else; Easy Girl; Why Cry; Teahouse of the Spirits. Albums include: Nothing's Shocking, 1988; Trust No One, 2001; One, 2006. Publications: Don't Try This at Home, 2004. Website: www.6767.com.

NAVRATILOVA Martina, b. 18 October 1956, Prague, Czech Republic (now American Citizen). Tennis Player. Career: Defected to the US in 1975, professional Player since; Titles: Wimbledon Singles, 1978, 1979, 1982, 1983, 1984, 1985, 1986, 1987, 1990; Doubles: 1976, 1979, 1982, 1983, 1984, 1985; Avon, 1978, 1979, 1981; Aust, 1981, 1983, 1985; France, 1982, 1984; US Open, 1983, 1984, 1986, 1987; Finalist at Wimbledon, 1988, 1989; Federation Cup for Czechoslovakia, 1973, 1974, 1975; 54 Grand Slam Titles (18 Singles, 37 Doubles); World Champion, 1980; Ranked No 1, 1982-85; 8 Wimbledon Titles, 1993; Women's Record for Consecutive wins, 1984; 100th Tournament win, 1985; only player to win 100 Matches at Wimbledon, 1991; Record 158 singles victories, 1992; 1,400 Victories, 1994; 167 Singles Titles, 1994; Made comeback in 2000 (in doubles only); Winner, Mixed Doubles, Australian Open, 2003 (oldest winner of a grandslam title); 177 doubles titles; Retired doubles, 2006. Appointments: President, Women's Tennis Association, 1979-80; Designs own fashionwear; Representative of USA in Federation Cup, 2003. Publications: Being Myself, 1985; The Total Zone (with Liz Nickles, novel, 1994); The Breaking Point (with Liz Nickles), 1996; Killer Instinct, (with Liz Nickles), 1998. Address: IMG, 1360 E 9th Street, Cleveland, OH 44114, USA.

NAYLOR Andrew Ross, b. 22 March 1958, Chester, England. Professor. m. May, 1 son, 1 daughter. Education: MBChB, 1981, MD, 1990, Aberdeen University. Appointments: Consultant Vascular Surgeon, Aberdeen Royal Infirmary, 1993-95; Consultant Vascular Surgeon, 1995-2003, Professor of Vascular Surgery, 2003-10, Leicester Royal Infirmary. Publications: Over 300 papers in peer reviewed journals; 49 book chapters on vascular disease management; Editor, textbook. Honours: Royal College of Surgeons Hunterian Professor of Surgery, 2002; Associate Editor, European Journal of Vascular and Endovascular Surgery; Senior Editor, European Journal of Vascular & Endovascular Surgery, 2011; Elected President, Vascular Society of Great Britain & Ireland, 2012. Memberships: Vascular Society of Great Britain & Ireland; European Society of Vascular Surgery; FRCS, Edinburgh; FRCS, London.

NAYLOR Peter Russell, b. 5 October 1933, London, England. Composer. Education: MA, University of Cambridge, 1958; B Mus, London University, 1961; Fellow, Royal College of Organists, London, 1961. Appointments: Lecturer, City Literary Institute, London, 1963-65; Lecturer, Harmony, Counterpoint & History, Royal Scottish Academy of Music and Drama, 1965-71; Organist, Ashwell Festival, Hertfordshire, 1964-69; Associate Organist, Glasgow Cathedral, 1972-85; Music Associate, Opera for Youth (Scottish Opera), 1975-80; Repetiteur, Shepway Youth Opera, Kent, 1982-85; Organist, Lyminge Methodist Church, Kent, 1982-; Organist, Postling Church, Kent, 1985-. Publications: The Oak Tree and the Cypress, 1998; Movement and Stillness, 1998; Tides of Summer, 2001; Echoes and Reflections, 2002; Variations for Organ, 2007. Compositions: Tides and Islands (orchestra); Organ Concerto, Beowulf for symphonic wind band; Odysseus Returning (three-act opera); Pied Piper (one-act opera); The Mountain People (workshop opera); Earth was Waiting (cantata); Wassail Sing We for chorus, piano and percussion; A Hero Dies (22 voices and clarsach); Movement for Organ, Air and Variations (2 pianos); Clarinet Quintet; Trio (violin, clarinet and piano); Variations (violin and organ); Four Minatures (double bass and piano); Kilda Kaleidoscope (double bass and piano); Spring Fantasia (violin, clarinet, chorus and piano); Carols and Anthems. Recordings: The Voice of My Beloved; Eastern Monarchs, Elizabethan Singers, Louis Halsey; and the Choir of St John's College, Cambridge, George Guest; Now the Green Blade Riseth, Choir of Glasgow Cathedral, John R Turner; Clarinet Quintet, Colin Bradbury and the Georgian Quartet; Movement and Stillness, Stephen Pusey. Honours: London University Convocation Trust Prize, 1959; Aschenberg Composition Prize, 1959. Memberships: British Academy of Songwriters, Composers and Authors; Scottish Music Centre. Address: Greenacres, Brady Road, Lyminge, Folkestone, Kent CT18 8HA, England.

NAYRAL DE PUYBUSQUE Jean, b. 25 August 1923, Toulouse, France. Magistrate. m . Clarisse Delval. Appointments: Magistrat, Premier President de la Cour d'Office de Toulouse; Actuallment Secretaire Perpetuel de l'Academie de Jeux Floraux de Toulouse. Honours: Officer de la Legion d'Honeur; Commandeur de l'Ordre National du Merite. Address: Fabie, Chemin des Combes, 31140 Launaguet, France.

NAZARETYAN Akop P, b. 5 May 1948, Baku, Azerbaijan. Psychologist. 1 son, 1 daughter. Education: Moscow State Linguistic University, 1971; PhD, Psychology,1978; Big History, 1990; Full Professor, M Lomonosov Moscow State University, 1982. Appointments: Psychologist; Anthropologist; Historian; Editor-in-Chief, Historical Psychology & Sociology academic journal; Senior Researcher, Institute for Oriental Studies; Director, Euroasian Center for Big History & System Forecasting. Publications: About 300 academic publications; 7 books; Evolution of Non-Violence: Studies in Big History, Self Organization and Historical Psychology. Memberships: Russian Academy of Natural Sciences; Russian Academy of Cosmonautics; Society for Cross-Cultural Research; World History Association. Address: Rossoshanskaya 1-1-688, Moscow 117535, Russia.

N'DOUR Youssou, b. 1 October 1959, Dakar, Senegal. Musician; Singer; Songwriter. Career: Member, Sine Dramatic, 1972; Orchestre Diamono, 1975; The Star Band (houseband, Dakar nightclub, the Miami Club), 1976-79; Founder, Etoile De Dakar, 1979; Re-formed as Super Etoile De Dakar, 1982-; International tours include support to Peter Gabriel, US tour, 1987. Recordings: Albums: A Abijan, 1980; Xalis, 1980; Tabaski, 1981; Thiapathioly, 1983; Absa Gueye, 1983; Immigres, 1984; Nelson Mandela, 1985; The Lion, 1989; African Editions Volumes 5-14, 1990; Africa Deebeub, 1990; Jamm La Prix, 1990; Kocc Barma, 1990; Set, 1990; Eyes Open, 1992; The Best Of Youssou N'Dour, 1994; The Guide, 1995; Gainde - Voices From The Heart Of Africa (with Yande Codou Sene), 1996; Immigrés/Bitim Rew, 1997; Inedits 84-85, 1997; Hey You : The Essential Collection,

DICTIONARY OF INTERNATIONAL BIOGRAPHY 36th EDITION

1988-1990; Best of the 80's, 1998; Special Fin D'annee Plus Djamil, 1999; Joko: From Village to Town, 2000; Batay, 2001; Le Grand Bal, Bercy, 2000; Le Grand Bal 1 & 2, 2001; Birth of a Star, 2001; Nothing's in Vain, 2002; Et Ses Amis, 2002; Sant Allah (Homage to God), 2003; Egypt, 2004; The Best of Youssou N'Dour, 2004; Rokku Mi Rokka, 2007; Instant Karma, 2007; Special Fin D'annee: Salegne-Salenge, 2009; Dakar – Kingston, 2010. Hit Single: Seven Seconds, duet with Neneh Cherry, 1995; How Come Shakin' the Tree, 1998; Recorded with: Paul Simon, Graceland, 1986; Lou Reed, Between Thought and Expression, 1992; Otis Reading, Otis! The Definitive Otis Reading, 1993; Manu Dibango, Wafrika, 1994; Cheikh Lo, Ne La Thiass, 1996; Alan Stivell, I Dour, 1998. Honours: Best African Artist, 1996; African Artist of the Century, 1999; BBC Radio 3 World Music Award for Album of the Year, 2005. Address: Youssou N'Dour Head Office, 8 Route des Almadies Parcelle, BP 1310, Dakar, Senegal. E-mail: yncontact@yahoo.fr Website: www.youssou.com

NEAGU Stefan Ilie, b. 13 September 1949, Bucharest, Romania. Education: MD, Faculty of Medicine, Bucharest, 1974; Diploma, Cancer Surgery, Cancer Institute, Bucharest, 1982; PhD, 1984; Diploma, Transplantation Surgery, Strasbourg University, 1992; Diploma, Visceral Surgery (AFSA), Strasbourg, 1994. Appointments: Assistant Professor of Surgery, 1976-79, Assistant Professor Titular, 1980-93, Associate Professor of Surgery, 1993-, Professor of Surgery, 2009-, Faculty of Medicine, Bucharest; Head, 2nd Department of Surgery, University Hospital, Bucharest, 1998-; President, Alexis Carrel Foundation for Medical Research, 2000; Professor of Surgery, 2009. Publications: Author, Renal Preservation by Cold Storage, 1990; Surgery, 1992, 1994; Surgical Pathology, 2002; Inventor in field: Enterovasculoplasty; Epiploonoplasty for treatment of infection complication of orthopaedic prosthesis; Rectal Cancer, Clinic and Epidemiology, 2007. Honours: Vice President, Romanian Society of Emergency Surgery and Trauma; University Member, IASGO, 2007; Listed in international biographical dictionaries. Memberships: French Association of Surgery; International Association of Pancreatology; IASG; European Hernia Society; European Digestive Surgery; New York Academy of Sciences; Honorary Member, Surgical Society of Serbia, 2005; Honorary Doctorate, Yorker University, 2010; Academician, IBC, 2010. Address: Str Viitorului Nr 22, Ap 2, Bucharest 020502, Romania. E-mail: stephanneagu@gmail.com

NEELY William Robert Nicholas (Bill), b. 21 May 1959, Belfast, Northern Ireland. TV Journalist. m. Marion Kerr, 2 daughters. Education: BA Honours, Queens University, Belfast. Appointments: Reporter, BBC, Northern Ireland, 1981-87; Reporter, BBC Network, 1987-88; Reporter, Presenter, Sky TV, 1989 (January to June); ITN Reporter, 1989-90, ITN Washington Correspondent and US Bureau Chief, 1990-97, Europe Correspondent, 1997-2002, International Editor and Newscaster, 2002-, ITN. Honours: Royal Television Society News Award, 1999, 2001, 2006; Golden Nymph Trophy, Monte Carlo TV Festival, 2000; BAFTA (for Television News), 2009, 2010, 2011; Broadcasting Journalist of the Year, London Press Club, 2011. Listed in biographical dictionaries. Address: 200 Gray's Inn Road, London WC1X 8XZ, England. E-mail: bill.neely@itn.co.uk

NEESON Liam, b. 5 June 1952, Ballymena, Northern Ireland. Actor. m. Natasha Richardson, 1994 (deceased), 2 children. Education: St Mary's Teachers College, London. Appointments: Forklift Operator; Architect's Assistant. Creative Works: Theatre includes: Of Mice and Men, Abbey Theatre Co, Dublin; The Informer, Dublin Theatre Festival; Translations, National Theatre, London; The Plough and the Stars, Royal Exchange, Manchester; The Judas Kiss; Films include: Excalibur; Krull; The Bounty; The Innocent; Lamb; The Mission; Duet for One; A Prayer for the Dying; Suspect Satisfaction; High Spirits; The Dead Pool; The Good Mother; Darkman; The Big Man; Under Suspicion; Husbands and Wives; Leap of Faith; Ethan Frome; Ruby Cairo; Schindler's List; Rob Roy; Nell; Before and After; Michael Collins; Les Misérables, 1998; The Haunting; Star Wars: Episode 1 – The Phantom Menace; Gun Shy, 1999; Gangs of New York, 2000; K19: The Widowmaker, 2002; Love Actually, 2003; Kinsey, 2004; Kingdom of Heaven, 2005; Batman Begins, 2005; The Proposition, 2005; Breakfast on Pluto, 2005; The Chronicles of Narnia: The Lion, the Witch and the Wardrobe, 2005; Seraphim Falls, 2006; Taken, 2008; The Other Man, 2008; Five Minutes of Heaven, 2009; Chloe, 2009; Clash of the Titans, The A-Team, The Chronicles of Narnia: The Voyage of the Dawn Treader, The Next Three Days, The Wildest Dream, 2010; Unknown, 2011; The Grey, Wrath of the Titans, Battleship, The Dark Knight Rises, Taken 2, 2012; Non-Stop, Khumba, 2013; TV includes: Arthur the King; Ellis Island; If Tomorrow Comes; A Woman of Substance; Hold the Dream; Kiss Me Goodnight; Next of Kin; Sweet As You Are; The Great War and the Shaping of the 20th Century; Comic Relief VIII; Empires: The Greeks – Crucible of Civilization; The Endurance: Shackleton's Legendary Antarctic Expedition; Inside the Space Station; The Man Who Came to Dinner; The Greeks; Revenge of the Whale; Nobel Peace Prize Concert; Uncovering the Real Gangs of New York; The Maze; Inside the Playboy Mansion; Martin Luther; Evolution; Liberty's Kids: Est 1776; Happy Birthday Oscar Wilde; Star Wars: The Clone Wars; Life's Too Short. Honours include: Best Actor, Evening Standard Award, 1997; OBE, 1999; Best Actor, Los Angeles Film Critics' Association, 2004; Honorary Doctorate, Queen's University, Belfast, 2009. Address: c/o ICM, 8942 Wilshire Boulevard, Beverly Hills, CA 90211, USA.

NEGISHI Ei-ichi, b. 14 July 1935, Changchun, China. Professor; Researcher. m. Sumire Suzuki, 2 daughters. Education: B Eng, Applied Chemistry, University of Tokyo, 1958; PhD, Organic Chemistry, University of Pennsylvania, 1963. Appointments: Postdoctorate, 1966-68, Assistant, 1968-72, H C Brown, Purdue University; Assistant Professor, Syracuse University, 1972; Professor, Purdue University, 1979-; Inaugural Herbert C Brown Distinguished Professor of Chemistry, 1999. Publications: 450 publications including 45 miscellaneous papers and several patents. Honours: Japan Chemical Society Award, 1996; ACS Award in Organometallic Chemistry, 1998; ACS Award for Creative Research in Synthetic Organic Chemistry, 2010; Nobel Prize in Chemistry (joint), 2010; Order of Culture and Man of Cultural Distinction Award, Japan, 2010. Memberships: ACS; Chemical Society of Japan; AAAS. Address: Purdue University, H C Brown Laboratory of Chemistry, 560 Oval Drive, West Lafayette, IN 47907, USA. E-mail: negishi@purdue.edu

NEGM Abdelazim, b. 15 April 1962, Egypt. Educator; Researcher. 1 son, 3 daughters. Education: BSc, MSc, and PhD, Civil Engineering. Appointments: Vice Dean, Academic and Students Affairs, Faculty of Engineering, Zagazig University, Egypt. Publications: More than 170 scientific papers; 5 books. Honours: 3 international awards. Memberships: IAHR. Address: Faculty of Engineering, Zagazig University, Zagazig 44519, Egypt. E-mail: amnegm@zu.edu.eg Website: www.name.eg/negm

NEGRIN Lukas Leopold, b. 30 May 1984, Vienna, Austria. Trauma Surgeon. Education: MD, Human Medicine, 2009. Appointments: President, Department of Trauma Surgery, Medical University, Vienna, 2009-. Publications: Articles on microfracture, polytrauma, intramedullary nailing, acetabular fractures, pelvic fractures and outcome measures. Honours: Sportehrenzeichen des Landes Niederosterreich. Memberships: Oesterrichische Gesellschaft fuer Unfallchirurgie; Gesellschaft fuer Orthopaedisch-Traumatologische Sportmedicin; European Society for Trauma and Emergency Surgery; Gerhard Kuentscher Society; Alumni Club of the Medical University of Vienna; Young Scientist Association of the Medical University of Vienna. E-mail: lukas.negrin@meduniwein.ac.at

NEHORAI Arye, b. Haifa, Israel. Professor. m. Shlomit, 1 son, 1 daughter. Education: BSc, Technion, Israel, 1976; MSc, Technion, Israel, 1979; PhD, Stanford University, 1983. Appointments: Research Engineer, Systems Control Technology Inc, 1983-85; Assistant Professor, Yale University, 1985-89; Associate Professor, Yale University, 1989-95; Professor, University of Illinois, Chicago, 1995-2005; The Eugene and Martha Lohman Professor and Chair, Electrical and Systems Engineering, Washington University in St Louis, St Louis, 2006-. Publications: More than 160 journal papers; 250 conference papers. Honours: University Scholar, University of Illinois; IEEE Signal Processing Society Senior Award for Best Paper, 1989; Magazine Paper Award, 2003; Fellow, IEEE; Fellow, Royal Statistical Society; Editor in Chief, IEEE Transactions on Signal Processing, 2000-2002; Vice President, Publications, IEEE Signal Processing Society, 2003-05; Technical Achievement Award, Meritorious Service Award, IEEE Signal Processing Society, 2006. Memberships: IEEE; Royal Statistical Society; IEEE Signal Processing Society Distinguished Lecturer, 2003-05. Address: ESE Department, Washington University in St Louis, One Brookings Drive, St Louis, MO 63130, USA. E-mail: nehorai@ese.wustl.edu

NEIL Andrew, b. 21 May 1949, Paisley, Scotland. Publisher; Broadcaster; Editor; Columnist; Media Consultant. Education: MA, University of Glasgow. Appointments: Conservative Party Research Department, 1971-73; Correspondent, The Economist, 1973-83; UK Editor, 1982-83, Editor, Sunday Times, 1983-94; Executive Chairman, Sky Television, 1988-90; Executive Editor and Chief Correspondent, Fox News Network, 1994; Contributing Editor, Vanity Fair, New York, 1994-; Freelance Writer and Broadcaster, 1994-97; Publisher, (Chief Executive and Editor-in-Chief), The Scotsman, Edinburgh, The Business, London, 1996-; Chief Executive, The Spectator and Apollo magazines, handbag.com, London, 2004-; Anchorman, BBC TV's Despatch Box, ITV's Thursday Night Live; BBC Radio's Sunday Breakfast, 1998-2000; BBC TV's This Week with Andrew Neil; BBC TV's Daily Politics, 2003-; Lord Rector, University of St Andrews, 1999-2002; Fellow, Royal Society for Arts, Manufacture and Commerce. Publications: The Cable Revolution, 1982; Britain's Free Press: Does It Have One?, 1988; Full Disclosure (autobiography), 1996: British Excellence, 1999, 2000, 2001. Address: Glenburn Enterprises Ltd, PO Box 584, London SW7 3QY, England.

NEILL John Robert Winder, b. 17 December 1945, Dublin, Ireland. Archbishop. m. Betty Anne Cox, 3 sons. Education: Foundation Scholar, 1965, First Class Moderatorship, 1966, Trinity College, Dublin, 1962-66; Theological Tripos, 1968, Jesus College, Cambridge, 1966-69; General Ordination Examination, 1969, Ridley Hall, Cambridge, 1968-69. Appointments: Ordained Deacon, 1969, Priest, 1970, Bishop, 1986; Curate of Glenageary, Dublin, 1969-71; Bishop's Vicar, St Canice's Cathedral, Ossory, 1971-74; Rector of Abbeystrewry, Cork, 1974-78; Vicar of Saint Bartholomew's, Dublin, 1978-84; Dean of Waterford, 1984-86; Bishop of Tuam, 1986-97; Bishop of Cashel and Ossory, 1997-2002; Archbishop of Dublin and Primate of Ireland, 2002-. Honours: BA, University of Dublin, 1966; BA, University of Cambridge, 1968; MA, University of Dublin, 1969; MA, University of Cambridge, 1972; LLD (Honoris Causa), National University of Ireland, 2003. Address: The See House, 17 Temple Road, Dublin 6, Ireland. E-mail: archbishop@dublin.anglican.org

NEILL Norma Christine, b. 30 August 1933, Liverpool, England. Teacher. m. Eric Neill, 2 daughters. Education: Broad Square County Primary School, Liverpool; Childwall Valley High School, Liverpool; City of Leeds Training College, Leeds, 1951-53. Appointments: Teacher, Liverpool and Yorkshire, 1953; Adult Lecturer, Family History, 1985-91, Remedial Specialist, 1961-65, 1977-91, Lecturer, Los Angeles and Kentucky, USA; Primary School Teacher, various schools in Lincolnshire, 1967-77; Lecturer, Family History, UK, 1980-; Retired, 1991. Publications: The Elam Family, Quaker Merchants of England and America, 1996; Editor, The Islonian Magazine, 21 years; Editor, Quaker FHS magazine, 4 years; Articles in various FH magazines and Family Tree; Book, Historic Haxey Parish, 1988; Book, More About History Haxey Parish, 1989; Editor of book, 900 Years of Haxey Parish Church; Book, Haxey Parish, Day by Day, 1991, 2008. Honours: Teaching Fellowship, Kingston-Upon-Hull; Teacher Training College, Hull, 1976. Memberships: President, Chairman & Secretary, Haxey & Westwoodside Heritage Society; Chairman and Secretary, Isle of Axholme FHS. Address: Colywell, 43 Commonside, Westwoodside, Doncaster, DN9 2AR, England.

NEILL Sam, b. 14 September 1947, Northern Ireland. Actor. m. Noriko Watanabe, 1989, 1 daughter, 1 stepdaughter. 1 son by Lisa Harrow. Education: University of Canterbury. Creative Works: Toured for 1 year with Players Drama Quintet; Appeared with Amamus Theatre in roles including Macbeth and Pentheus in The Bacchae; Joined New Zealand National Film Unit, playing leading part in 3 films, 1974-78; Moved to Australia, 1978, England, 1980; TV appearances include: From a Far Country; Ivanhoe; The Country Girls; Reilly: Ace of Spies; Kane and Abel (mini-series); Submerged (film), 2001; Framed (film), 2002; Dr Zhivago (mini-series), 2002; Stiff, 2004; Jessica, 2004; To The Ends of the Earth, 2005; Mary Bryant, 2005; The Triangle, 2005; Merlin's Apprentice, 2006; The Tudors, 2007; Crusoe, 2008-10; Happy Town, 2009; Rake, 2010; Alcatraz, 2012; Films: Sleeping Dogs, 1977; The Journalist; My Brilliant Career; Just Out of Reach; Attack Force Z; The Final Conflict (Omen III); Possession; Enigma; Le Sand des Autres; Robbery Under Arms; Plenty; For Love Alone; The Good Wife; A Cry in the Dark; Dead Calm; The French Revolution; The Hunt for Red October; Until the End of the World; Hostage; Memoirs of an Invisible Man; Death in Brunswick; Jurassic Park; The Piano; Sirens; Country Life; Restoration; Victory; In the Month of Madness; Event Horizon; The Horse Whisperer; My Mother Frank; Molokai; The Story of Father Damien; Bicentennial Man; The Dish, 2000; Monticello; The Zookeeper, 2001; Jurassic Park III, 2001; Dirty Deeds, 2002; Perfect Strangers, 2002; Yes, 2004; Wimbledon, 2004; Little Fish, 2005; Irresistible, 2006; Angel, 2007; Dean Spanley, 2008; I Am You, Iron Road, Under the Mountain, Daybreakers, 2009; Legend of the Guardians: The Owls of Ga'Hoole, 2010; The Dragon Pearl, The Hunter,

2011; The Vow, 2012. Honours: Distinguished Companion of the New Zealand Order of Merit. Address: c/o ICM, 8942 Wilshire Boulevard, Beverly Hills, CA 90211, USA.

NĚMEC Ivan, b. 22 November 1945, Žarošice, Czech Republic. University Teacher. m. Jana, 1 son, 2 daughters. Education: Ing (MSc), 1969; CSc (PhD), 1991; Associate Professor, 2002. Appointments: University Lecturer, 1969; Head, Computing Centre, Dopravodpkojekt, Brno, 1975; Director, The Software Company, FEM Consulting, 1991; Associate Professor, University of Technology, Brno, 2002. Publications: 6 books, including: Modelling the Soil-Structure Interaction, 1989; Finite Element Analysis of Structures, 2010; More than 100 articles. Memberships: Society for Mechanics. Address: Dillingerova 16, 62100 Brno, Czech Republic. E-mail: nemec@fem.cz

NEMOV Viktor Vadimovich, b. 13 December 1930, Krasnodar, Russia. Physicist. m. Zoya Vladimirovna, 1 son. Education: Degree, Electrical Engineering, Odessa Polytechnic Institute, 1954; Degree, Physics, Kharkov State University, 1966; PhD, Physics and Mathematics, Donetsk State University, 1972; Senior Research Scientist, 1977; Doctor of Sciences, Physics and Mathematics, Kharkov State University, 1994. Appointments: Electrical Engineer, Industry, Kotel'nich, Kirov, Russia, 1954-56; Engineer Investigator, Kharkov Electromechanical Plant, 1956-59; Senior Researcher, All-Union Electrodevice Research Institute, Kharkov, Ukraine, 1959-66; Research Associate, Kharkov Institute of Physics and Technology, 1966-77; Senior Researcher in Staff, 1977-96, Leading Research in Staff, 1996-, KhIPT. Publications: Numerous articles in professional journals. Memberships: Ukrainian Physics Society. Address: National Science Centre, Kharkov Institute of Physics and Technology, Akademicheskaya str 1, 61108, Kharkov, Ukraine. E-mail: nemov@ipp.kharkov.ua

NENE Bhagwan, b. 27 September 1940, Maharashatra, India. Consulting Physician. m. Anjali, 3 daughters. Education: MD, FRCP (London). Appointments: Director, Nargis Dutt Memorial Cancer Hospital, Barshi; Chairman, Ashwini Rural Cancer Research & Relief Society, Barshi; Physician, Hiremath Co-op Hospital, Barshi. Publications: More than 25 articles in professional journals. Honours: Outstanding Rural Cancer Effort Plaque of Merit; Fellow, Royal College of Physicians, London, 2000; National Award, Women's Development through Application of Science and Technology, 2003. Address: Ashwmedh Subhash Nagar, Barshi 413 401, Solapur, Maharashtra State, India.

NESHIGE Ryuji, b. 10 December 1954, Takeo City, Saga Prefecture, Japan. Medical Doctor. m. 1 son, 1 daughter. Education: Faculty of Medicine, 1974-80, PhD, 1984, Yamaguchi University. Appointments: Clinical Associate, Department of Internal Medicine, Saga Medical School, 1984-90; Special Fellow, The Cleveland Clinic Foundation, USA, 1985-86; Assistant Director, Yanagawa Rehabilitation Hospital, 1991-99; Director, Neshige Neurological Clinic, 1999-. Publications: Event-related brain potentials as indicators of visual recognition and detection of criminals by their use, 1991; Communications aid device utilizing event-related potentials for patients with severe motor impairment, 2007. Honours: Best Doctor in Japan, 2006-08; Board Certified Neurology Specialist, 1984-; Board Certified EEG Specialist, 2006-; Listed in international biographical dictionaries. Address: 38-17 Tyuou-machi, Kurume city, Fukuoka, Japan. E-mail: neshiryu@yahoo.co.jp

NETANYAHU Benjamin, b. 21 October 1949. Politician; Businessman. m. 3 children. Education: BSc, 1974, MSc, 1976, MIT. Appointments: Managing Consultant, Boston Consulting Group, 1976-78; Executive Director, Jonathan Institute, Jerusalem, 1978-80; Senior Manager, Rim Inds, Jerusalem, 1980-82; Deputy Chief of Mission, Israeli Embassy, Washington DC, 1982-84; Permanent Representative to UN, 1984-88, Deputy Minister of Foreign Affairs, 1988-91, Deputy Minister, PM's Office, 1991-92; Leader, Likud, 1993-99; 2006-; Minister of Foreign Affairs, 2002-03, of Finance, 2003-2005; Leader of the Opposition, 2006-2009; Prime Minister of Israel, 2009-. Publication: A Place Among the Nations: Israel and the World, 1993; Fighting Terrorism, 1995; A Durable Peace, 2000. Address: Ministry of Finance, POB 13191, 1 Rehov Kaplan, Kiryat Ben-Gurion, Jerusalem 91008, Israel.

NETTLETON Michael Arthur, b. 30 August 1932, Leeds, Yorkshire, England. Retired Academic. Widower, 2 daughters. Education: BSc, Applied Chemistry, Glasgow University & ARTC, Royal Technical College, 1953; PhD, Applied Physical Chemistry, Imperial College, London University, 1960; DSc, Strathclyde University, 1979. Appointments: REME, Malaysia, 1953-55; Electrochemical Engineering, 1955-58; Imperial College, 1958-60; Vickers Research, 1960-62; Central Electricity Research Laboratories, 1962-85; Mechanical Engineering and later Chemical Engineering, University of Queensland, 1985-97; Campaigner for the Restoration of Civil Liberties to the UK. Publications: Over 80 articles in reputable scientific journals. Honours: Research Fellow, Physics Department, University College of Wales; Research Fellow, Mechanical Engineering Department, Leeds University; Hunterhill Bursary, Glasgow, General Service Medal; Honorary Professor, University of Queensland. Memberships: Returned Servicemen Club, Australia. Address: Acorns, 11 Grendon Close, Horley, Surrey RH6 8JW, England. E-mail: MNettl5993@aol.com

NEVO Eviatar, b. 2 February 1929, Tel Aviv, Israel. Professor of Evolutionary Biology. Divorced, 1 son, deceased, 1 daughter. Education: MSc, 1958 (with Special Distinction), Biology, PhD (summa cum laude), Biology, 1964, Hebrew University, Jerusalem. Appointments: Lecturer, Oranim Teachers State College, 1956-63; Visiting Professor in Zoology, University of Texas, 1964-65; Fellow in Biology, Harvard University, 1965-66; Research Associate, 1967-68, Lecturer, 1968-70, Senior Lecturer, 1970-71, Genetics, Hebrew University, Jerusalem; Research Associate, Museum of Vertebrate Zoology, University of California, Senior Postdoctoral Research Fellow, Department of Biology, University of Chicago, 1972-73; Associate Professor, 1973-75, Professor, Biology, 1975-, Director, Institute of Evolution, 1977-2008, Incumbent Chair of Evolutionary Biology, 1984-2008, Director, International Graduate Center of Evolution, 2004-, University of Haifa. Publications: Over 1,200 papers in various fields of Evolutionary Biology (genetics, ecology, physiology, morphology and behaviour of bacteria, plants, fungi, animals and humans); 26 Books (author, co-author or editor) include: Mosaic Evolution of Subterranean Mammals: Regression, Progression and Global Convergence, 1999; Coleoptera of "Evolution Canyon", 1999; Evolution of Wild emmer and wheat improvement, 2002; Population Genetics, Genetic Resources and Genome Organisation of Wheat's Progenitor, *Triticum dicoccoides*, 2002; Fungal Life in the Dead Sea (co-editor), 2003. Honours: Numerous from American Biographical Institute and International Biographical Centre; Fulbright and Guggenheim Fellowships. Memberships include: Fellow, Explorers Club,

1980; Fellow, 1989-, Foreign Member, 1990, Linnean Society of London; Honoured Member, Ukrainian Botanical Society, 1995; Foreign Member, National Academy of Sciences of Ukraine, 1997; First Foreign Member, Advisory Board, Ankara University Center for International Agricultural Research and Scientific Cooperation, 1999; Foreign Member, National Academy of Sciences, USA, 2000. Address: Institute of Evolution, Haifa University, Haifa 31905, Israel.

NEVZOROV Anatoly, b. 31 October 1934, Nizhny Novgorod, Russia. Scientist. m. N P Grishina, 1 son. Education: Diploma, Moscow Physico-Technology Institute, 1958; PhD, Institute of Applied Geophysics, 1965. Appointments: Engineer; Junior Scientist; Senior Scientist; Leading Scientist. Publications: More than 120 articles in Russian and foreign journals. E-mail: an-nevzorov@yandex.ru

NEWBY Richard Mark (Baron of Rothwell in the County of West Yorkshire), b. 14 February 1953, UK. Member of the House of Lords. m. Ailsa Ballantyne Thomson, 2 sons. Education: BA, Philosophy, Politics and Economics, 1971, MA, St Catherine's College, Oxford. Appointments: Private Secretary to Permanent Secretary, 1977-79, Principal Planning Unit, 1979-81, HM Customs and Excise; Secretary, SDP Parliamentary Committee, 1981; National Secretary, SDP, 1983-88; Executive, 1988-90, Director, 1991, Corporate Affairs, Rosehaugh plc; Director, Matrix Communications Consultancy Ltd, 1992-99; Chairman, Reform Publications, 1993-; Liberal Democrat, Treasury Spokesman, House of Lords, 1997-2010; Member, Centre Forum Advisory Board; Director, Flagship Group, 1999-2001; Chief of Staff to Charles Kennedy MP, 1999-2006; Chairman, Live Consulting, 2001-; Director, Elmwood Design Ltd, 2004-; Co-Chair, Lib Dem Parliamentary Treasury Committee, 2010-; Chair, Live Sport, CIC, 2010-. Honour: OBE, 1990. Memberships: Trustee, Coltstaple Trust; MCC; IDS UK; NW University UK; FRSA. Address: House of Lords, London SW1A 0PW, England. E-mail: newbyr@parliament.uk

NEWCOME James William Scobie, b. 24 July 1953, Aldershot, England. Minister of Religion. m. Alison Clarke, 2 sons, 2 daughters. Education: Marlborough College; Trinity College, Oxford; Selwyn College, Cambridge. Appointments: Curate, All Saints, Leavesden, 1978-82; Minister, Bar Hill LEP, 1982-94; Tutor, Ridley Hall, 1983-88; Rural Dean, North Stowe, 1993-94; Canon Residentiary, Chester Cathedral, 1994-2002; Director of Ordinands, 1994-2000; Director of Ministry, Chester Diocese, 1996-2002; Bishop of Penrith, 2002-09; Bishop of Carlisle, 2009-; Lead Bishop for Healthcare; Chairman, National Stewardship Committee. Honours: Listed in international biographical dictionaries. Address: Bishop's House, Ambleside Road, Keswick, Cumbria, LA12 4DD, England.

NEWELL Mike, b. 28 March 1942, St Albans, England. Film Director. m. Bernice Stegers, 1979, 3 children. Education: University of Cambridge. Appointments: Trainee Director, Granada TV, 1963. Creative Works: TV work includes: Big Breadwinner Hog (series), 1968; Budgie (series); Thirty Minute Theatre and other TV plays; Director, European Premiere of Tennessee Williams' The Kingdom of the Earth, Bristol Old Vic; Films: The Man in the Iron Mask, 1976; The Awakening, 1979; Bad Blood, 1980; Dance with a Stranger, 1984; The Good Father, 1985; Amazing Grace and Chuck, 1986; Soursweet, 1987; Common Ground, 1990; Enchanted April, 1991; Into the West; Four Weddings and a Funeral, 1994; An Awfully Big Adventure, 1994; Donnie Brasco, 1997; Pushing Tin, 1998; Photographing Fairies (executive producer), 1997; 200 Cigarettes, 1999; Best Laid Plans, 1999; High Fidelity, 2000; Traffic, 2000; I Capture the Castle, 2003; Mona Lisa Smile, 2003; Harry Potter and the Goblet of Fire, 2005; Love in the Time of Cholera, 2007; Prince of Persia: The Sands of Time, 2010. Honours include: BAFTA Award, Best Director, 1995. Address: c/o ICM, Oxford House, 76 Oxford Street, London W1N 0AX, England.

NEWEY Jon Wilton, b. 12 January 1951, London, England. Editor; Publisher. m. Jill Newey, 1 son, 1 daughter. Education: Bec Grammar School; Graphic Art Diploma Course, Kennington College. Appointments: Professional Musician, 1970-74; Department Head, Dalton's Weekly, 1974-77; Advertisement Manager, Sounds Magazine, 1977-91; Publisher, Top Magazine, 1991-99; Editor and Publisher, Jazzwise Magazine, 2000-. Publications: Books: The Tower Jazz Guide (editor); Tapestry of Delights (consultant editor); Music Mart Drum Guide (author); Jazz-Rock – A History (discographer); Articles in magazines including: Sounds, Music Mart, Mojo, Record Collector, Jazzwise, Jazz on CD, Jazz at Ronnie Scotts, Music Business, MI PRO. Honour: Journalist of the Year, Parlimentary Jazz Awards, 2006; Publication of the Year, Parliamentary Jazz Awards, 2007; Publication of the Year, Ronnie Scott's Jazz Awards, 2007; Publication of the Year, Parliamentary Jazz Awards, 2010. E-mail: jonnewey@jnal.com

NEWING Peter, b. 10 May 1933, Littlebourne, Canterbury, England. Clerk in Holy Orders. m. Angela Newing. Education: Cert Ed, Birmingham, Worcester College of Education, 1953-55; BA and Long Prize (Proxime Accesit), St John's College, Durham, 1960-65; B Ed, Bristol University, 1976; BSc, State University of New York, USA, 1985; Ed D, Pacific Western University, USA, 1988; Diploma, Religious Studies, Cambridge University, 1991. Appointments: National Service, RAF, London, 1951-53; Science Teacher, Bedfordshire County Council, 1955-60; Curate of Blockley with Aston Magna, 1965-69; Deacon, 1965, Priest, 1966, Gloucester; Priest in Charge of Taynton and Tibberton, 1969-75; Lecturer, Gloucestershire College of Arts and Technology, now University of Gloucestershire, 1972-82; Tutor, Open University, 1975-76; Rector of Brimpsfield, Elkstone and Syde, 1975-95; Rector of Brimpsfield, Daglingworth, The Duntisbournes, etc, 1995-2001; Curate of Redmarley, Bromesberrow, Dymock, etc, 2001-03, Honorary Curate, 2003-10; Chaplain to the High Sheriff of Herefordshire and Worcestershire, 2009-10; Retired, 2010. Publications: Pamphlet, The Literate's Hood and Hoods of the Theological Colleges of the Church of England, 1959; Various articles on church bells. Honours: Fellow Society of Antiquaries, Scotland, 1959; Fellow Royal Society of Arts, London, 1960; Fellow The College of Preceptors, London (F.Coll.P), 1995; Honorary Fellow, Victoria College of Music, London; B Th, Trinity College, 2007; BA (honoris causa), University of Worcester, 2012. Memberships: Bishop of Gloucester's Visitor to Church Schools, 1976-94; Member of Court, University of Bristol, 1977-2004; Member, Gloucester Diocesan Synod, 1982-2001, re-elected 2003-2009; Member, Gloucester Diocesan Board of Finance, 1982-2004; Member, Gloucester Diocesan Board of Patronage, 1985-93, 2001-09; Member, Panel of Advisers Incumbents (Vacation of Benefices) Measure 1977, 1985-2009; Member, Central Council of Church Bellringers, 1985-2004. Address: 42 Born Court, New Street, Ledbury, HR8 2DX, England.

NEWKIRK Herbert William, b. 23 November 1928, Jersey City, New Jersey, USA. Materials Scientist. m. Madeleine Dorothy, 2 sons, 1 daughter. Education: AA, Pre-Engineering,

DICTIONARY OF INTERNATIONAL BIOGRAPHY 36th EDITION

Jersey City Junior College, 1948; BSc, Polytechnic Institute of Brooklyn, 1951; PhD, Ohio State University, 1956. Appointments: Research Associate, Phosphor Laboratory, Department of Chemistry, Polytechnic Institute of Brooklyn, 1950-51; Research Chemist, Allied Chemical and Dye Corporation Research Center, 1951-52; Research Associate, Engineering Experiment Station, 1952-54, Teaching Assistant, 1954-55, Research Fellow, 1955-56, Department of Chemistry, Ohio State University; Chemist, General Electric, Hanford Research Laboratories, 1956-59; Chemist, Consultant, RCA, David Sarnoff Research Center, 1959-60; Group Leader, Materials Scientist, Lawrence Livermore National Laboratory, 1960-92; Consultant and Participating Guest, Environmental Restoration Division, Lawrence Livermore National Laboratory; Visiting Research Professor, Consultant, Aachen Technical Institute and Philips Laboratories, Aachen, Germany, Philips Laboratories, Eindhoven, Netherlands, 1969-71. Publications: Over 50 publications and articles on various topics of materials science; 2 inventions. Honours: First Prize and Best of Show – Ceramographic Exhibit, American Ceramic Society, 1965; Research and Development 100 Magazine Award for Technologically Most Significant Invention, 1991; William L Dickinson High School Scholastic Hall of Fame, 2001. Memberships: American Association of Crystal Growth, Treasurer, Northern California Section; Phi Lambda Upsilon; Sigma Xi Fraternity. Address: 1141 Madison Avenue, Livermore, CA 94550, USA. E-mail: newkirk01@sbcglobal.net

NEWMAN Nanette, b. 29 May 1934 Northampton, England. Actress. m. Bryan Forbes, 1955, 2 daughters. Education: Italia Conti School; Royal Academy of Dramatic Art. Appointments: Varied Career in Films, Stage and TV. Creative Works: Appearances in Films including: The Wrong Box; The Stepford Wives; The Raging Moon; International Velvet; The Endless Game; The Mystery of Edwin Drood; Talk Show, The Fun Food Factory; TV Series, Stay With Me Till Morning; Comedy Series, Let There Be Love, Late Expectations. Publications: God Bless Love, That Dog, The Pig Who Never Was, Amy Rainbow, The Root Children; The Fun Food Factory; Fun Food Feasts; My Granny Was a Frightful Bore; The Cat Lovers Coffee-Table Book; The Dog Lovers Coffee-Table Book; The Cat and Mouse Love Story; The Christmas Cookbook; Pigalev; The Best of Love; Archie; The Summer Cookbook; Small Beginnings; Bad Baby; Entertaining with Nanette Newman and Her Two Daughters Sarah and Emma; Charlie The Noisy Caterpillar; Sharing; Cooking for Friends; Spider the Horrible Cat; There's A Bear in the Bath; A Bear in the Classroom; Take 3 Cooks; To You With Love, 1999; Up to the Skies and Down Again, 1999; Bad Baby Good Baby, 2002; Small Talk, 2004; Ben's Book, 2005; Eating In, 2005. Honours include: Best Actress Award, Variety Club; Best Actress, Evening News. Address: Chatto & Linnit Ltd, 123 King's Road, London SW3 4PL, England.

NEWTON Keith, b. 10 April 1952, Liverpool, England. Priest. m. Gillian, 2 sons, 1 daughter. Education: BD Hons, AKC, PGCE, Kings College, University of London, 1970-73; Christchurch College, Canterbury, 1973-74; St Augustine's College, Canterbury, 1974-75. Appointments: Anglican Deacon, 1975, Anglican Priest, 1976, Chelmsford Cathedral; Curate, St Mary's Great, Ilford, 1975-78; Team Vicar, St Matthew's Wimbledon, Wimbledon Team Ministry, 1978-85; Malawai, Central Africa, 1985-91; Dean of Blantyre, Malawi, 1986-91; Honorary Canon, St Paul's Cathedral, Blantyre, 1986-; Vicar, Holy Nativity, Knowle, 1991-2002; Rural Dean, Brislington, 1995-99; Priest in Charge, All Hallows, Easton, 1997-2002; Area of Dean of Bristol South, 1999-2001; Honorary Canon, Bristol Cathedral, 2000-02; Consecrated Anglican Bishop, 2002; Bishops of Richborough and Provincial Episcopal Visitor, 2002-10; Ordained Catholic Priest, 2011; Ordinary of the Personal Ordinariate of Our Lady of Walsingham, 2012-; Protonary Apostolic, 2011. Address: 6 Mellish Gardens, Woodford Green, Essex IG8 0BH, England. E-mail: mgr.newton@gmail.com

NEWTON Thandie, b. 6 November 1972, Zambia. Actress. m. Oliver Parker, 1998, 2 daughters. Education: Downing College, Cambridge. Career: Films: Flirting, 1991; The Young Americans, 1993; Interview with a Vampire, 1994; Loaded, 1994; Jefferson in Paris, 1995; The Journey of August King, 1995; The Leading Man, 1996; Gridlock'd, 1997; Besieged, 1998; Beloved, 1998; Mission Impossible II, 2000; It Was An Accident, 2000; The Truth About Charlie, 2002; Shade, 2003; The Chronicles of Riddick, 2004; Crash, 2004; The Pursuit of Happyness, 2006; Norbit, 2007; Run, Fat Boy, Run, 2007; W., 2008; 2012, 2009. TV: Pirate Prince, 1991; In Your Dreams, 1997; ER, 2003-09.

NEWTON-JOHN Olivia, b. 26 September 1948, Cambridge, England. Singer; Actress. m. (1) Matt Lattanzi, 1984-1995 (divorced) 1 daughter; (2) John Esterling, 2008. Career: Moved to Australia, aged 5; Singer in folk group as teenager; Local television performer with Pat Carroll; Winner, National Talent Contest, 1964; Singer, actress, 1965-; Represented UK in Eurovision Song Contest, 1974; Music For UNICEF Concert, New York, 1979; Film appearances include: Grease, 1978; Xanadu, 1980; Two Of A Kind, 1983; It's My Party, 1995; Sordid Lives, 2001; Own clothing business, Koala Blue, 1984-. Recordings: Albums: If Not For You, 1971; Let Me Be There, 1974; Music Makes My Day, 1974; Long Live Love, 1974; If You Love Me Let Me Know (Number 1, US), 1974; Have You Ever Never Been Mellow, 1975; Clearly Love, 1975; Come On Over, 1976; Don't Stop Believin', 1976; Making A Good Thing Better, 1977; Greatest Hits, 1978; Grease (film soundtrack), 1978; Totally Hot, 1979; Xanadu (film soundtrack), 1980; Physical, 1981; 20 Greatest Hits, 1982; Olivia's Greatest Hits Vol 2, 1983; Two Of A Kind, 1984; Soul Kiss, 1986; The Rumour, 1988; Warm And Tender, 1990; Back To Basics: The Essential Collection 1971-92, 1992; Gaia - One Woman's Journey, 1995; More than Physical, 1995; Greatest Hits, 1996; Olivia, 1998; Back with a Heart, 1998; Highlights from the Main Event, 1999; Greatest Hits: First Impressions, 1999; Country Girl, 1999; Best of Olivia Newton John, 1999; Love Songs: A Collection: Hit singles include: If Not For You, 1971; What Is Life, 1972; Take Me Home Country Roads, 1973; Let Me Be There, 1974; Long Live Love, 1974; If You Love Me (Let Me Know), 1974; I Honestly Love You (Number 1, UK), 1974; Have You Never Been Mellow (Number 1, US), 1975; Please Mr Please, 1975; Something Better To Do, 1975; Fly Away, duet with John Denver, 1976; Sam, 1977; You're The One That I Want, duet with John Travolta (Number 1, US and UK, third-best selling single in UK), 1978; Summer Nights, duet with John Travolta (UK Number 1, 9 weeks), 1978; Hopelessly Devoted To You (Number 2, UK), 1978; A Little More Love, 1979; Deeper Than The Night, 1979; I Cant Help It, duet with Andy Gibb, 1980; Xanadu, with ELO (Number 1, UK), 1980; Magic (Number 1, US), 1980; Physical (US Number 1, 10 weeks), 1981; Make A Move On Me, 1982; Heart Attack, 1982; Twist Of Fate, from film soundtrack Two Of A Kind, 1983; Back with a Heart, 1998; Grease (Remix), 1998; I Honestly Love You, 1998; Physical Remix 1999, 1999. Honours include: OBE; Grammy Awards: Record of the Year, 1974; Best Country Vocal Performance, 1974; Best Pop Vocal Performance, 1975; Numerous American Music Awards,

1975-77, 1983; CMA Award, Female Vocalist Of Year (first UK recipient), 1975; Star on Hollywood Walk Of Fame, 1981; Numerous other awards from Record World; Billboard; People's Choice; AGVA; NARM; Goodwill Ambassador, UN Environment Programme, 1989. Address: MCA, 70 Universal City Plaza, North Hollywood, CA 91608, USA.

NICHOLLS Paul Edward, b. 1 April 1948, Colchester, Essex, England. Artist. m. Jennifer Valerie, 6 sons, 3 stepsons, 1 stepdaughter. Education: Epsom College of Art and Design, 1965-66; Portsmouth College of Art and Design, 1966-69; Department of Educational Studies, Brighton College of Art, 1969-70. Appointments: Graphic Artist, Roebuck Theatre Club, 1971; Scenic Artist, Richmond Theatre, Surrey, 1971; Teacher of Art, Greenway School, Uxbridge, and Harlington School, London, 1970-71, 1972; Teacher, St Paul's Junior School, Penzance, 1973-76; Teacher, Acting Head, St Michael Penkivel VA CP School, 1979-70; Teacher, Deputy Head, Acting Head, Treleigh CP School, Redruth, 1976-84; Visiting Lecturer, 1980-81, Host Tutor, 1998, External Moderator, University of Exeter, College of St Mark and St John; Headteacher, Leedstown CP School, 1985-95; External Marker, Key Stage 2, SATs, 1995-2002; Headteacher, Stithians CP School, 1996-2006; Primary Curriculum Advisor for Art, 1998; Part-time Tutor, University of Plymouth, St Mark and St John, 2006-. Full time Artist, 2006-; Work held in public and private collections around the world. Publications: Numerous articles in professional journals; Totally Eclipsed, Cornwall series of cards, 1999. Illustrator of numerous books. Honours: Cornwall County Council Long Service Medal, 1998; Prize Winner, Finding Fan Gogh, 2007; Listed in various biographical dictionaries. Memberships: Newlyn Society of Artists; Design Artists Copyright Society. Address: South Barn, Mithian, St Agnes, Cornwall, TR5 0QH, England. E-mail: south_barn@yahoo.co.uk

NICHOLS Mike (Michael Igor Peschowsky), b. 6 November 1931, Berlin, Germany. Stage and Film Director. m. (1) Patricia Scott, 1957-60, (2) Margot Callas, 1963-74, 1 daughter, (3) Annabel Davis-Goff, 1 son, 1 daughter, (4) Diane Sawyer, 1988. Education: University of Chicago. Creative Works: Shows directed: Barefoot in the Park, New York, 1963; The Knack, 1964; Luv, 1964; The Odd Couple, 1965; The Apple Tree, 1966; The Little Foxes, 1967; Plaza Suite, 1968; Films (director/producer): Who's Afraid of Virginia Woolf?, 1966; The Graduate, 1967; Catch-22, 1969; Carnal Knowledge, 1971; Day of the Dolphin, 1973; The Fortune, 1975; Annie, 1977; Gilda Live, 1980; Silkwood, 1983; Heartburn, 1985; Biloxi Blues, 1987; Working Girl, 1988; Postcards From the Edge, 1990; Regarding Henry, Wolf, 1994; Mike Nicholas, 1995; The Birdcage, 1998; Primary Colors, 1998; What Planet Are You From?, 2000; All the Pretty Horses, 2000; Closer, 2004; Charlie Wilson's War, 2007. Plays directed: Streamers, 1976; Comedians, 1976; The Gin Game, 1978; Lunch Hour, 1980; The Real Thing, 1984; Hurlyburly, 1984; Waiting for Godot, 1988; Death and the Maiden, 1992; Blue Murder, 1995; The Seagull, 2001; Spamalot, 2005; Country Girl, 2008. Honours include: Numerous Tony Awards, Emmy Awards and Drama Desk Awards; National Association of Theatre Owners' Achievement Award. Address: c/o Mike Ovitz, CAA, 9830 Wilshire Boulevard, Beverly Hills, CA 90212, USA.

NICHOLSON Bryan Hubert (Sir), b. 6 June 1932, Rainham, Essex, England. Chairman. m. Mary, 1 son, 1 daughter. Education: Politics, Philosophy and Economics, Honours, Oriel College, Oxford, 1952-55. Appointments include: Unilever Management Trainee then District Manager, 1955-60; Sales Manager, Jeyes Group, 1960-64; Sales Director, UK, General Manager, Australia, Managing Director, UK and France, Remington, 1964-72; Director, Operations, 1972-76, Executive Main Board Director, 1976-79, Chairman, UK, Chairman, Germany, Supervising Director, France and Italy, Executive Main Board Director, 1979-84, Rank Xerox Ltd; Chairman, Manpower Services Commission, 1984-87; Chairman, The Post Office, 1987-92; Chairman, Council for National Academic Awards, 1988-91; Chairman, National Council for Vocational Qualifications, 1990-93; Chancellor, Sheffield Hallam University, 1992-2001; Chairman, Varity Europe Ltd, 1993-96; President, Confederation of British Industry, 1994-96; Non-Executive Director, Equitas Holdings plc, 1996-2005; Chairman, Cookson Group plc, 1998-2003; Pro-Chancellor and Chair of the Council of the Open University, 1996-2004; Chairman, 2001-2003, Deputy Chairman, 2003-2004, Chairman, 2004-2005, Goal plc (renamed Educational Development International plc); Chairman, 1992-2001, Vice-president, 2001-05, President, 2005-, BUPA; Chairman, Financial Reporting Council, 2001-05; Non-Executive Director, Education Development International plc, 2005-10; President, Wakefield Trinity Wildcats, 2000-; President, 2005-11, Life Vice President, 2011, National Centre For Young People with Epilepsy (NCYPE); Trustee, International Accounting Standards Committee Foundation (IASCF); Member, Public Interest Oversight Board (PIOB) of the International Federation of Accountants (IFAC); Senior Advisor, Penfida, 2006-. Honours: KB, 1987; GBE, 2005; Companion of the Institute of Management, 1985-; FRSA, 1986-; Honorary FGCI, 1989; Honorary Fellow: Oriel College, Oxford, Manchester Metropolitan University, 1990, Scottish National Vocational Council, 1994-, Scottish Qualifications Authority, 1997; Elected Fellow, Chartered Institute of Marketing, 1991; Hon D Ed, Council for National Academic Awards, 1992; Honorary Doctor, Open University, 1994; Honorary Companion, Chartered Institute for Personnel and Development, 1994; Honorary Doctor of Letters, Glasgow Caledonian University, 2000; Honorary Doctor, Sheffield Hallam University; Honorary Fellow, Open University, 2006; Honorary Fellow, Institute of Chartered Accountants in England and Wales, 2011; Listed in national and international biographical dictionaries. Membership: Oxford and Cambridge Club. Address: Flat 21, 192 Emery Hill Street, London SW1P 1PN, England. E-mail: bryanhnicholson@aol.com

NICHOLSON Jack, b. 22 April 1937, Neptune, New Jersey, USA. Actor; Film Maker. m. Sandra Knight, 1962, divorced 1968, 1 daughter, 1 daughter by Winnie Hollman, 1 son and 1 daughter by Rebecca Broussard. Career: Films include: Cry-Baby Killer, 1958; Studs Lonigan, 1960; The Shooting; Ride the Whirlwind; Hell's Angels of Wheels, 1967; The Trip, 1967; Head, 1968; Psych-Out, 1968; Easy Rider, 1969; On a Clear Day You Can See Forever, 1970; Five Easy Pieces, 1971; Drive, He Said, 1971; Carnal Knowledge, 1971; The King of Marvin Gardens, 1972; The Last Detail, 1973; Chinatown, 1974; The Passenger, 1974; Tommy, 1974; The Fortune, 1975; The Missouri Breaks, 1975; One Flew Over the Cuckoo's Nest, 1975; The Last Tycoon, 1976; Goin' South, 1978; The Shining, 1980; The Postman Always Rings Twice, 1981; Reds, 1981; The Border, 1982; Terms of Endearment, 1984; Prizzi's Honor, 1984; Heartburn, 1985; The Witches of Eastwick, 1986; Ironweed, 1987; Batman, 1989; The Two Jakes, 1989; Man Trouble, 1992; A Few Good Men, 1992; Hoffa, 1993; Wolf, 1994; The Crossing Guard, 1995; Mars Attacks! The Evening Star, Blood and Wine, 1996; As Good As It Gets, 1997; The Pledge, 2000; About Schmidt, 2002; Anger Management, 2003; Something's Gotta Give, 2003; The Departed, 2006; The Bucket List, 2007; How Do You

Know, 2010. Honours: Academy Award, Best Supporting Actor, 1970, 1984; Academy Award, Best Actor, 1976; Cecil B De Mille Award, 1999; Kennedy Center Honor, 2001; Commander des Arts et des Lettres; Golden Globe for Best Dramatic Actor, 2003. Address: 12850 Mulholland Drive, Beverly Hills, CA 90210, USA.

NICHOLSON John William, b. 9 February 1955, Hampton Court, Middlesex, England. University Lecturer. m. Suzette, 2 sons, 2 daughters. Education: BSc, Kingston University, 1977; PhD, South Bank University, 1981. Appointments: Research Fellow, South Bank University, 1981-83; Higher Scientific Officer, Senior Scientific Officer, Principal Scientific Officer, Laboratory of the Government Chemist, 1983-94; Senior Lecturer in Biomaterials Science, King's College, London, 1995-97; Reader in Biomaterials Science, King's College, London, 1997-2002; Professor of Biomaterials Chemistry, University of Greenwich, 2002-. Publications: Approximately 150 scientific articles; 4 books: The Chemistry of Polymers, 1991, 2nd edition, 1996, 3rd edition, 2006; Acid Base Cements (with A D Wilson), 1993; Polymers in Dentistry (with M Braden, R Clarke and S Parker), 1996; The Chemistry of Medical and Dental Materials, 2002. Honours: EurChem; CChem; FRSC; Jordan Award, Oil and Colour Chemists Association, 1987; President, 2001, Treasurer, 2003-, UK Society for Biomaterials. Memberships: Fellow, Royal Society of Chemistry; UK Society for Biomaterials; European Society for Biomaterials; International Association for Dental Research. Address: School of Science, University of Greenwich, Chatham, Kent ME4 4TB, England. E-mail: j.w.nicholson@gre.ac.uk

NICKLAUS Jack William, b. 21 January 1940, Columbus, Ohio, USA. Professional Golfer. m. Barbara Jean Bash, 1960, 4 sons, 1 daughter. Education: Ohio State University. Career: Professional, 1961-; Winner: US Amateur Golf Championship, 1959, 1961; US Open Championship, 1962, 1967, 1972, 1980; US Masters, 1963, 1965, 1966, 1972, 1986; US Professional Golfers' Association, 1963, 1971, 1973, 1975, 1980; British Open Championship, 1966, 1970, 1978; 6 times, Australian Open Champion; 5 times, World Series winner; 3 times individual winner, 6 times on winning team, World Cup; 6 times, US representative in Ryder Cup matches; 97 tournament victories; 76 official tour victories; 58 times second, 36 times third; Won US Senior Open, USA; 136 tournament appearances, 1996; Played in 154 consecutive majors, 1999; Designer of golf courses in USA, Europe, Far East; Chairman, Golden Bear International Inc; Captain, US team which won 25th Ryder Cup, 1983 Co-chair, The First Tee's Capital Campaign, More Than A Game, 2000; Retired at the Open Championship at St. Andrews, 2005. Publications: My 55 Ways to Lower Your Golf Score, 1962; Take a Tip From Me, 1964; The Greatest Game of All, autobiography, 1969; Lesson Tee, 1972; Golf My Way, 1974; The Best Way to Better Your Golf, vols 1-3, 1974; Jack Nicklaus' Playing Lessons, 1976; Total Golf Techniques, 1977; On and Off the Fairway, autobiography, 1979; The Full Swing, 1982; My Most Memorable Shots in the Majors; My Story, 1997. Honours: Athlete of the Decade Award, 1970s; Hon LLD, St Andrew's, 1984; 5 times US PGA Player of the Year; Golfer of the Century, 1988. Address: 11780 US Highway #1, North Palm Beach, FL 33408, USA.

NICKS Stevie (Stephanie Nicks), b. 26 May 1948, California, USA. Singer; Songwriter. Appointments: Songwriter with Lindsey Buckingham; Recorded album, Buckingham Nicks, 1973; Joined Group, Fleetwood Mac, 1973. Creative Works: Albums with Fleetwood Mac: Fleetwood Mac, 1975; Rumours, 1977; Tusk, 1979; Fleetwood Mac Live, 1980; Mirage, 1982; Tango in the Night, 1987; Behind the Mask, 1990; 25 Years - The Chain, 1992; Solo albums include: Bella Donna, 1981; The Wild Heart, 1983; Rock a Little, 1985; Time Space, 1991; Street Angel, 1994; Composer of Songs Rhiannon, Landslide, Leather and Lace, Dreams, Sara, Edge of Seventeen, If Anyone Falls (with Sandy Stewart), Stand Back (with Prince Rogers Nelson), I Can't Wait (with others), The Other Side of the Mirror, Time Space, Street Angel, Seven Wonders (with Sandy Stewart). Address: WEA Corporation, 79 Madison Avenue, Floor 7, New York, NY 10016, USA.

NICOROVICI Nicolae-Alexandru, b. 26 August 1944, Buftea, Romania. Physicist. Divorced. Education: Diploma, Nuclear Physics, University of Bucharest, Romania, 1967; PhD, Physics, Institute of Atomic Physics, Romanian Academy, 1972. Appointments: ARC Research Associate, 1991-94, 1995-98, Research Associate, 1998, Department of Theoretical Physics, Research Associate, Theoretical Physics Group, 1998-2003, Research Fellow, 2006-, School of Physics, University of Sydney; Senior Research Assistant, School of Mathematical Sciences, 1995, Instructional Designer & Programmer, Faculty of Mathematical and Computing Sciences, 1998-99, Research Associate, 2003-05, Senior Research Consultant, 2005-06, Casual Academic, 2005-, Department of Mathematical Sciences, University of Technology, Sydney. Publications: 4 books; 10 book chapters; Numerous articles in professional journals. Memberships: Australian Optical Society; Senior Member, Optical Society of America; American Institute of Physics; European Physical Society. E-mail: nicoalex@ozemail.com.au

NIDDRIE Robert Charles, b. 29 January 1935, Southampton, England. Chartered Accountant. m. Maureen Joy, 1 son, 2 daughters. Education: Brockenhurst Grammar School. Appointments: National Service 1959-61; Whittaker, Bailey & Co, 1952-59, 1962-75, Partner, 1963-75; Senior Partner in Charge, Southampton Office, Price Waterhouse, 1975-92; Trustee, Duphar Pension Scheme, 1992-2003; Local Director, Coutts & Co, 1992-2002; Non-Executive Director: Bournemouth Orchestras, 1986-96, Meridian Broadcasting Charitable Trust, 1993-2000, Sovereign Employee Benefits Ltd, 1993-95, Chairman, Southampton Cargo Handling plc, 1993-98, Hotel du Vin Ltd, 1994-2004; Founder Chairman, Hampshire Branch of Institute of Directors, 1980-86, Member, Institute of Directors Council, 1980-86; Trustee, Mayflower Theatre Trust, 1988-99; Governor King Edward VI School, Southampton, 1989-2003; Winchester Cathedral Guild of Voluntary Guides, 1995-2010; Trustee, Deputy Chairman, Royal Marines Museum, 1996-2006. Memberships: Fellow, Institute of Chartered Accountants; Associate, Chartered Institute of Taxation; Associate, Institute of Directors. Address: Morestead House, Morestead, Winchester, Hampshire SO21 1LZ, England.

NIEMINEN-VON WENDT Taina Solveig, b. 21 November 1960, Lappajärvi, Finland. Chief Executive Officer; Medical Doctor. m. Lennart von Wendt, 1 daughter. Education: Undergraduate, Kokkola, 1979; MD, 1988, Specialist in Children's Diseases, 1994, University of Oulu; Specialist in Child Neurology, 1997, PhD, Medical Faculty, 2005, University of Helsinki. Appointments: Locum Medical Doctor, Department of Paediatrics, 1988-90, Department of Child Neurology, 1991, Vaasa Central Hospital; Locum Assistant Medical Doctor, 1991-92, Assistant Medical Doctor, 1991-92, Department of Paediatrics, Locum Assistant Medical Doctor, Department of Child Neurology, 1994, Oulu University Hospital; Assistant Medical Doctor, Department of

Child Neurology, 1995-97, Locum Assistant Medical Doctor, Department of Paediatrics, 1997-99, Helsinki University Hospital; On-duty Medical Doctor (weekends), Health Centre, Kannus, Lappajärvi, 1985-94; On-duty Paediatrician (weekends), Pietarsaari, Malmi Hospital, 1993-99; Private clinic, Vaasa, 1989-91, Oulu, 1993-95, and Helsinki, 1995-; CEO, Leading MD and PhD, Neuropsychiatric private clinic, Helsinki Asperger Centre, 1999-2007; Research MD, Neurology, 1999-2004, Senior Research MD, PhD, 2005-, Helsinki University; Locum Medical Doctor, Department of Adolescent Psychiatric Hospital District of Helsinki and Uusimaa, Jorvi Hospital, 2005-10; Leading MD, PhD, CEO, Neuropsychiatric private clinic, Helsinki, 2007-. Publications: Numerous articles in professional journals. Memberships: Finnish Autism and Asperger Society. Address: Rakuunanpiha 14 b, 02620 Espoo, Finland. E-mail: taina.nieminen@kolumbus.fi

NIGAM Pranesh, b. 18 June 1943, Banda UP, India. Physician. m. Laxmi K, 3 daughters. Education: BSc, 1959, MBBS, 1965, MD (Med), 1969, Lucknow University; MNAMS, N Acad Med Sc, 1988; FCCP; FICP; FICA; FFCH; FIAMS; FAIMS. Appointments: Medical Officer, Physician, District Hospital, Hamirpur & Jhansi; Lecturer in Medicine, MLB Medical College, Jhansi, UP; Associate Professor of Medicine, BRD Medical College, Gorakhpur; Professor and Head, Department of Medicine, Medical College, Gorakhpur; Professor & Head, Department of Medicine, UFHT Medical College, Haldwani. Publications: 240 papers in professional medical journals; Editorial Board Member, JAPI. Honours: Diabetes Research Award, API; Bronchitis & Asthma Award, API. Memberships: Indian Medical Association; Association of Physicians of India; Indian Association of Ch Physicians; Indian Association of Gastroenterologists; Diab-Association, India. Address: Lakshmi Grah, C-14 Rapti Nagar Phase II, Medical College Road, Chargawa, Gorakhpur 273009, UP, India.

NIGHY William (Bill) Francis, b. 12 December 1949, Caterham, Surrey, England. Actor. m. Diana Quick, 1 daughter. Education: St John Fischer School, Purley, Surrey, England. Career: National Theatre: A Map of the World and Skylight by David Hare; Pravda by David Hare and Howard Brenton; The Seagull by Chekov; Arcadia by Tom Stoppard; Mean Tears by Peter Gill; Blue Orange by Joe Benhall; A Kind of Alaska and Betrayal by Harold Pinter; Blue/Orange by Joe Penhall; The Vertical Hour by David Hare; Valkyrie by Christopher McQuarrie; Films: Still Crazy; Lawless Heart; Lucky Break; Underworld, I Capture the Castle, Love Actually, 2003; Shaun of the Dead, Enduring Love, 2004; The Magic Roundabout, The Hitchhiker's Guide to the Galaxy, The Constant Gardener, 2005; Underworld Evolution, Pirates of the Caribbean: Dead Man's Chest, Stormbreaker, Flushed Away, Notes on a Scandal, 2006; Hot Fuzz, Pirates of the Caribbean: At World's End, 2007; Valkyrie, 2008; Underworld: Rise of the Lycans, The Boat That Rocked, G-Force, Astro Boy, Statuesque, Glorious 39, 2009; Wild Target, Harry Potter and the Deathly Hallows – Part I, 2010; Rango, Chalet Girl, Arthur Christmas, 2011; The Best Exotic Marigold Hotel, Wrath of the Titans, Total Recall, 2012; TV: Absolute Hell; The Maitlands; The Men's Room; A Masculine Ending; Eye of the Storm; Unnatural Causes; Don't Leave Me This Way; The Maitlands; Kiss Me Kate; Longitude, 2000; The Inspector Lynley Mysteries: Well Schooled in Murder, 2002; Ready When You Are Mr McGill, The Lost Prince, State of Play, The Canterbury Tales (The Wife of Bath's Tale), The Young Visiters, Life Beyond the Box: Norman Stanley Fletcher, 2003; He Knew He Was Right, Poliakoff Films 2004 – 2, The Girl in the Café, Gideons Daughter, 2005; Doctor Who, 2010; Page Eight, 2011; Numerous radio performances. Honours: Theatre Managers Best Actor, 1996; Best Actor, Barclays Theatre Award, 1996; Best Comedy Performance, Evening Standard Peter Sellars Award, 1998; Best Actor, Broadcasting Press Guild Award, 2003; Barclays Best Actor Award, 2004; BAFTA Award for Best Actor in a TV Drama, 2004; Best Supporting Actor, LA Critics' Circle Award, 2004; London Film Critic's Award, 2004; Best Supporting Actor, LA Critics' Circle Award, 2004; BAFTA Award for Best Supporting Actor, 2004. Address: c/o Markham & Froggatt Ltd, Julian House, 4 Windmill Street, London W1P 1HF, England. Website: www.markhamfroggatt.com

NIJNIK Maria, b. 7 April 1956, Lviv, Ukraine. Senior Research Scientist. m. Albert Nijnik, 1 daughter. Education: Dipl Engineer/MSc with Distinction, Ukrainian University of Forestry and Wood Technology, 1978; PhD, Economics, National Academy of Sciences of the USSR, 1984; MSc, Environmental Policy and Management, Netherlands, 1995; Diploma, General and Quantitative Economics, Netherlands Network of Economics, 1999; Diploma, Mansholt Graduate School of Social Sciences, Netherlands, 2002; PhD, Social Sciences, Wageningen University, 2002. Appointments: Researcher, Senior Scientific Fellow, National Academy of Sciences of the USSR, Institute of Economics, 1980-91; Associate Professor, Ukrainian National University, 1991-94; Researcher, Institute for Environmental Studies, Vrije Universiteit, Amsterdam, 1995-2000; Post-Doc Research Fellow, Agricultural Economics and Rural Policy, Wageningen University, 2002; Research Scientist, 2002-08, Senior Research Scientist, 2008-, Socio-Economic Research Programme, Macaulay Institute and Fellow of the University of Aberdeen, UK; James Hutton Institute, UK, 2011-. Publications: Over 225 articles and papers in professional scientific journals, books and proceedings of societies. Honours: Honorary Fellow, University of Aberdeen; Associate, Institute for Rural Research, Scotland; Canadian Institute of Forestry; International Union of Forest Research Organizations; European Association for Environmental and Resource Economists; International Association of Agricultural Economists; many others. Memberships: Scottish Economic Society; UK Women Experts in Science, Engineering and Technology; Advisory Group, Agriculture and Rural Development, USA; Royal Netherlands Society for Agricultural Sciences; Academician, Ukrainian Ecological Academy; Ukrainian Scientific Society; European and International Societies for Ecological Economics; International Union of Forest Research Organisations; International Association of Agricultural Economists; International Association for Society and Natural Resources; European Association of Environmental & Resource Economics. Address: The James Hutton Institute, Craigiebuckler, Aberdeen, AB15 8QH, Scotland. E-mail: m.nijnik@macaulay.ac.uk Website: www.hutton.ac.uk

NIKBERG Illya, b. 19 November 1929, Kiev, Ukraine, USSR. Professor of Preventive Medicine. m. Lana Tsodicova, 1 son, 1 daughter. Education: Diplom (Hon), Kiev Medical Institute, 1952. Appointments: Doctor –Specialist, San Epid Sta, Makeevka, Ukraine, 1952-56; Scientific Staffer, Head of Department of Hygiene of Institute of Epidemiology, Microbology, Hygiena, Kishinev, Moldova, 1956-64; Lecturer (Docent), National Medical University, Kiev, Ukraine, 1964-96; Professor, Head of Department of Preventive Medicine, Medical Institute, Kiev, Ukraine, 1996-2000; Medical Columnist, Russian and Ukrainian Mass Media, Sydney, Australia, 2000-. Publications: Author or co-author of over 470 scientific publications including 18 monographs and textbooks. Honours: Professor, Laureat of Ukrainian State Prize, 1997; Advanced Specialist of Public Education of Ukraine, 1999; Honorary Member, Australian and Ukrainian Diabetes Association, 1997, 2003. Memberships: New York Academy of Science; Ukrainian and International Federation of Journalists; Ukrainian Doctors Society in Australia. Address: 2/2 A Edmund Str, Waverley, Sydney, NSW 2024, Australia. E-mail: inikberg@hotmail.com

NIKS Inessa, b. 6 November 1938, St Petersburg, Russia. Piano Teacher; Musicology Teacher. m. Mikhail Niks, deceased, 1 son, 1 daughter. Education: Studied Piano, Special Music School for Gifted Children, St Petersburg, 1948-56; Master in Musicology, Diploma with Distinction, St Petersburg Conservatory, 1956-61. Career: Teacher of Musicology and Piano, Music College, Novgorod, Russia, 1961-64; Teacher of Musicology and Piano, Music School, St Petersburg, 1966-76; Head of Musicology Department, Pskov Music College, 1976-79; Owner, piano and musicology studio, Redlands, California, 1983-; Co-Founder, Niks Hand Retraining Center, 1991-; Special course for composers based on new research of sound. Publications: Numerous articles in specialist music journals concerning newly developed piano technique; Co-Inventor of Hand Guide, piano training device, 1991; Manual, Play Without Tension, supplement to piano training device, 1998; Cassette, Mystery of Singing Tone – acoustical breakthrough in piano sound, 1998; Manual, Type Without Tension, 2000; CD of own compositions, Dedications, 2011. Honours: Silver Medal, 1983, Bronze Medal, 1984, International Piano Recording Competition; Finalist, Audio-Visual Piano, 1995; The piano device "Hand Guide" was exhibited in Germany and will stay permanently in R Schumann Museum. Memberships: Music Teachers' Association of California, 1983-; European Piano Teachers' Association, 1983-2009; The National League of American Pen Women, 2002-10. Address: 405 Northcliff Road, Pasadena, CA 91107, USA. Website: www.nikstechnique.com

NIMMO Ian Alister, b. 14 October 1934, Lahore, Pakistan. Journalist. m. Grace, 1959, 2 sons, 1 daughter. Education: Royal School of Dunkeld; Breadalbane Academy. Appointments: Lieutenant, Royal Scots Fusiliers, 1956; Editor, Weekly Scotsman, 1962; Editor, Evening Gazette, Teesside, 1970; Editor, Evening News, Edinburgh, 1976-89; Publishing Consultant, 1989-. Publications: Robert Burns, 1968; Portrait of Edinburgh, 1969; The Bold Adventure, 1969; Scotland at War, 1989; The Commonwealth Games, 1989; Edinburgh The New Town, 1991; Edinburgh's Green Heritage, 1996; Walking With Murder, 2005; Rhythms of the Celts, stage musical, 1997; Numerous articles and radio programmes. Membership: Scottish Arts Club; Robert Louis Stevenson Club; Edinburgh Sir Walter Scott Club; Vice-President, Newspaper Press Fund. Address: The Yett, Whim Farm, Lamancha, By West Linton, Peeblesshire EH46 7BD, Scotland. E-mail: i.nimmol@skg.com

NIMOY Leonard, b. 26 March 1931, Boston, Massachusetts, USA. Actor; Director. m. (1) Sandi Zober, 1954, divorced, 1 son, 1 daughter. (2) Susan Bay, 1988, 1 child. Education: Boston College; Antioch University. Appointments: US Army, 1954-56; TV appearances include: Star Trek, 1966-69; Eleventh Hour; The Virginian; Rawhide; Dr Kildare; Films include: Old Overland Trail, 1953; Satan's Satellites, 1958; Valley of Mystery, 1967; Catlow, 1971; Invasion of the Bodysnatchers, 1978; Star Trek - The Motion Picture, 1979; Star Trek: The Wrath of Khan, 1982; Star Trek III: The Search for Spock, 1984; Star Trek IV: The Voyage Home, 1986; Three Men and a Baby, 1987; The Good Mother, 1988; Star Trek V: The Final Frontier, 1989; Funny About Love, 1990; Star Trek VI: The Undiscovered Country, 1991; Holy Matrimony, 1994; The Pagemaster, 1994; Carpati: 50 Miles, 50 Years, 1996; A Life Apart: Hasidism in America, 1997; David, 1997; Brave New World, 1998; Sinbad, 2000; Atlantis: The Lost Empire, 2001; Civilization IV, 2005; Star Trek, Land of the Lost, 2009; Fringe, 2009-12; Star Trek Online, Kingdom Hearts Birth by Sleep, 2010; Transformers: Dark of the Moon, 2011; The Big Bang Theory, Kingdom Hearts 3D, Zambezia, 2012. Publications: I Am Not Spock, autobiography, 1975; We Are All Children, 1977; Come Be With Me, 1979; I am Spock, 1995; Shekhina, 2005: The Full Body Project, 2008. Address: c/o Gersh Agency Inc, 222 North Cannon Drive, Beverly Hills, CA 90210, USA.

NISH Ian Hill, b. 3 June 1926, Edinburgh, Scotland. Retired Professor. m. Rona Margaret Speirs, 1965, 2 daughters. Education: University of Edinburgh, 1943-51; University of London, 1951-56. Appointments: University of Sydney, New South Wales, Australia, 1957-62; London School of Economics and Political Science, England, 1962-91. Publications: Anglo-Japanese Alliance, 1966; The Story of Japan, 1968; Alliance in Decline, 1972; Japanese Foreign Policy, 1978; Anglo-Japanese Alienation 1919-52, 1982; Origins of the Russo-Japanese War, 1986; Contemporary European Writing on Japan, 1988; Japan's Struggle with Internationalism, 1931-33, 1993; The Iwakura Mission in America and Europe, 1998; Japanese Foreign Policy in the Inter-War Period, 2002; The Japanese in War and Peace 1942-48, 2011. Honours: Commander of the Order of the British Empire, 1990; Order of the Rising Sun, Japan, 1991; Japan Foundation Award, 1991; Honorary Member, Japan Academy, 2007. Memberships: European Association of Japanese Studies, president, 1985-88; British Association of Japanese Studies, president, 1978. Address: Oakdene, 33 Charlwood Drive, Oxshott, Surrey KT22 0HB, England.

NISHIGAKI Ikuo, b. 2 January 1926, Nagoya, Japan. Medical Doctor; Biochemist. m. Yuko, 1 son, 1 daughter. Education: MD, 1962, PhD, 1967, Nagoya University, School of Medicine; Study under Professor Kunio Yagi, Graduate School of Nagoya University, 1963-67. Appointments: Assistant Professor, then Associate Professor under Professor Kunio Yagi, Laboratory of Biochemistry, Nagoya University, 1967-88; Study under Professor Lowell E Hokin, University of Wisconsin, USA, 1972-75; Vice Director, then Director, Institute of Applied Biochemistry, Gifu, Japan, 1988-2004; Director, NPO Inuyama Scientific and Cultural Exchange Center, 2004-; Director, NPO International Laboratory of Biochemistry, Nagoya, 2004-; Visiting Professor, University of Madras, India, 2007-. Honours: Silver medal, Polish Academy. Publications: A method for determining 2 thiobarbituric acid (TBA) reactive substances in fractionated blood serum, 1967; Studies on the characterization of the sodium-potassium transport adenosine triphosphatase XV. Direct chemical characterization of the asyl phosphate in the enzyme as an aspartyl-phosphate residue, 1974; Purification of aromatic L-amino acid decarboxylase from bovine brain with a monoclonal antibody, 1988; Glycated protein-iron chelate increases lipid peroxide level in cultured aortic endothelial and smooth muscle cells, 1998; Cytoprotective Role of Astaxanthin against Glycated Protein/Iron Chelate- induced Toxicity in Human Umbilical Vein Endothelial Cells, 2010; Stimulatory role of glycated fetal bovine serum along with iron on in vitro production of insulin by differentiated mouse embryonic stem cell, 2011. Memberships: Amateur Painter, Churchill Club. Address: 1-166 Uchide, Nakagawa-ku, Nagoya, 454-0926, Japan. E-mail: nishigaki@se.starcat.ne.jp

NISHIMATSU Yuichi, b. 16 January 1932, Japan. Consultant Engineer; Professor Emeritus, University of Tokyo. m. Teiko Kawaguchi, 2 daughters. Education: Graduate, Department of Mining, University of Tokyo, 1954; DEng, University of Tokyo, 1969. Appointments: Research Engineer, Coal Research Institute, Tokyo, 1957; Professor, Department of Mining, University of Tokyo, 1976; Professor Emeritus, 1992-. Publications: Several articles in professional journals. Honours: 4 Prizes, Excellent Research Papers. Membership: Engineering Academy of Japan. Address: 31-9-1003 Honcho, Wako City, Saitama 351-0114, Japan.

NISHIMURA Toshihiko, b. 7 February 1958, Mie, Japan. Engineer. m. Chieko, 3 sons. Education: Bachelor, 1980, Master, 1982, Nagoya Institute of Technology; Doctor, Tokyo Institute of Technology, 1992. Appointments: Manager, Mitsubishi Heavy Industries Ltd, Nagoya Aerospace Systems. Memberships: Japan Society of Mechanical Engineers, ASTM International, 1012-1, Tottori, Toin-cho, Inabe-gun, Mie 511-0241, Japan. E-mail: toshihiko_nishimura@mhi.co.jp

NISHIMURA Yukio, b. 4 September 1951, Kagoshima, Japan. Researcher; Cell Biologist; Associate Professor. Education: BSc, 1974, MSc, 1976, PhD, 1979, Kyushu University, Fukuoka, Japan. Appointments: Research Associate, New York University School of Medicine, New York, 1981-84; Research Associate, 1979-81, 1984-92, Associate Professor, 1992-, Kyushu University, Fukuoka; Trustee, Japanese Association for Metastasis Research, Osaka, Japan, 2005-. Publications: Numerous articles in professional journals. Honours: Grants, Ministry of Education, Culture, Sports, Science and Technology, Japan, 1989, 1990, 1993, 1996; Grants, Kyushu University, 2007; Prize, Outstanding Presentation Award, Japanese Society for Metastasis Research, 2004. Memberships: Japanese Association for Metastasis Research; Professional Association; Japanese Cancer Association; Professional Association. Address: 6-15-3-406, Yoshizuka, Hakata-ku, Fukuoka, 812-0041, Japan. E-mail: ynkio443@yahoo.co.jp

NISHIURA Hiroyuki, b. 15 February 1953, Itami, Hyogo Prefecture, Japan. Scientist; Professor. Education: BS, 1976, MS, 1978, DS, 1981, Osaka University, Japan. Appointments: Postdoctoral Fellow, Soryushi Shogakukai Foundation, 1981-82; Postdoctoral Fellow, Japan Society for the Promotion of Science, Kyoto University, 1982-83; Postdoctoral Fellow, Johns Hopkins University, 1983-85; Associate Professor, 1991-2000, Professor, 2000-2005, Osaka Institute of Technology, Junior College; Professor, Faculty of Information Science and Technology, Osaka Institute of Technology, 2005-. Memberships: Physical Society of Japan; American Physical Society. Address: Faculty of Information Science and Technology, Osaka Institute of Technology, 1-79-1 Kitayama, Hirakata-city, Osaka 573-0196, Japan. E-mail: nishiura@is.oit.ac.jp

NISHIYAMA Misuzu, b. 15 December 1951, Sapporo, Japan. Anaesthesiologist. m. Hiroaki Nishiyama, 1 daughter. Education: Graduated, 1976, Hokkaido University, Sapporo, Japan. Appointments: Resident, Hokkaido University, 1975-76; Staff Anaesthesiologist, St Luke's International Hospital, Tokyo, 1986-96; Staff Anaesthesiologist, Jikei University School of Medicine, 1996-2000; Staff Anaesthesiologist, Asahi Central Hospital, 2001-04; Staff Anaesthesiologist, Ito Municipal Hospital, 2007-09; Chief Anaesthesiologist, Shizuoka Kosei Hospital, 2010-. Publication: Anaesthesiology Resident Manual, 1994, 2nd edition, 2000, 3rd edition, 2008. Address: 4982-1317 Futo Ito, Shizuoka-ken, Japan.

NISKANEN Toivo Kalle Antero, b. 16 October 1949, Kuhmo, Finland. Senior Adviser. m. Helena Raitomaa, 2 sons, 2 daughters. Education: MSc, Construction Engineering, University of Oulu, 1975; Doctor, Technology, Technical University of Helsinki, 1993. Appointments: Safety Inspector, Finnish Board of Labour Protection, 1975-77; Senior Researcher, Finnish Institute of Occupational Health, 1978-90; Senior Adviser, Legislation University, Department for Occupational Safety and Health, Ministry of Social Affairs and Health, 1990-. Publications: Numerous articles in professional journals. Address: Ministry of Social Affairs and Health, PO Box 33, 00023 Government, Helsinki, Finland. E-mail: toivo.niskanen@stm.fi

NISSAN Ephraim, b. 9 May 1955. Academic Scholar. Education: Dottore, Ingegneria Elettronica, 1982; Engineering Certification Exam, 1983; PhD, Computer Science, 1989. Appointments: Various posts, 1983-94; Visiting Professor, University of Urbino, Italy, 1993; Researcher, University of Greenwich, London, 1994-2003; Researcher (later Visiting Scientist), Computing Department, Goldsmiths College, University of London, 2004. Publications: About 325 publications of which 115 articles in professional journals; 20 times guest editor for scholarly journals. Honours: Listed in international biographical dictionaries; Honorary posts at University of Manchester, University of Urbino, and Universidad del Salvador in Buenos Aires; Award for PhD project, 1988; Award for second Laurea thesis, nationwide contest, Italy, 1982; Guest Editor, Annals of Mathematics and Artificial Intelligence; Applied Artificial Intelligence; Artificial Intelligence and Law; Artificial Intelligence for Engineering Design, Analysis and Manufacturing; Computational Intelligence; Computers and Artificial Intelligence; Computing and Informatics; Cybernetics and Systems; Information and Communications Technology Law; International Journal on Artificial Intelligence Tools; Journal of Educational Computing Research; Journal of Intelligent and Fuzzy Systems; Journal of Intelligent and Robotic Systems; New Review of Applied Expert Systems; Founding Joint Editor, Melilah, Manchester; Founding Associate Editor, IJHR. E-mail: ephraimnissan@hotmail.com

NOEL Carol Adele, b. Chicago, Illinois, USA. Teacher; Former Opera Singer. Education: Bachelor of Music, Boston Conservatory of Music; Master, Music, Northwestern University. Appointments: State Opera Houses, Rendsburg and Hagen, Germany; Lyric Opera of Chicago; Teacher, Music and Elementary Education, Chicago Public Schools; Substitute Teaching, Suburban and Catholic Schools, Chicago area; Vocal Soloist, St Stephen's Evangelical Church, Chicago; Vocal Recording in Process of Gospel Music. Publications: Numerous articles in Music Kg-8 (professional journal). Honours: Frederik A Chramer Opera Award, Northwestern University; Voice Scholarship, Boston Conservatory of Music and on and Dean's List; Rosary College Scholarship; Alderman, Pacini, First Place in Vocal Contest; Certificate of Commendation, Metropolitan Opera National Council; Outstanding Service Plaque, Grant Community Academy. Memberships: Music Educators National Conference. Address: 6629 S Whipple St, Chicago, Illinois 60629-2915, USA. E-mail: Cancatlady11@aol.com

DICTIONARY OF INTERNATIONAL BIOGRAPHY 36ᵗʰ EDITION

NOLTE Nick, b. 8 February 1941, Omaha, USA. Film Actor. m. (1) Sheila Page, 1966 (divorced); (2) Sharyn Haddad, 1978 (divorced); (3) Rebecca Linger, 1984, divorced 1995, 1 son. Education: Pasadena City College; Phoenix City College. Creative Works: Films: Return to Macon County, 1975; The Deep, 1977; Who'll Stop the Rain, 1978; North Dallas Forty, 1979; Heartbeat, 1980; Cannery Row, 48 Hours, 1982; Under Fire, 1983; The Ultimate Solution of Grace Quigley, Teachers, 1984; Down and Out in Beverly Hills, 1986; Weeds, Extreme Prejudice, 1987; Farewell to the King, New York Stories, 1989; Three Fugitives; Everybody Wins; Q & A, Prince of Tides, 1990; Cape Fear, 1991; Lorenzo's Oil, 1992; Blue Chips, I'll Do Anything, Love Trouble, Jefferson in Paris, 1994; Mulholland Falls, Mother Night, 1996; Afterglow, 1997; Affliction, U-Turn; Breakfast of Champions, The Thin Red Line, 1998; The Golden Bowl, 2000; Investigating Sex, Double Down, 2001; The Good Thief, Northfork, Hulk, 2003; Hotel Rwanda, 2004; Neverwas, 2005; Over the Hedge (voice), Paris, I Love You, Peaceful Warrior, A Few Days in September, Off the Black, 2006; The Mysteries of Pittsburgh, 2007; The Spiderwick Chronicles, Tropic Thunder, 2008; My Horizon, 2009; My Own Love Song, 2010; Arcadia Lost, 2010; Arthur, 2011; Warrior, 2011. Numerous TV and theatre appearances. Address: 6153 Bonsall Drive, Malibu, CA 90265, USA.

NORBECK Jack C, b. 8 December 1940, Greensburg, Pennsylvania, USA Education: University of Connecticut, Ratcliffe Hicks School of Agriculture, 1964; Dale Carnegie, 1967; Opticians Institute, 1971. Appointment: President, Norbeck Research (educational library exhibits on steam and draft animals), 1978-; Lectured on North American steam traction engines and work horses; Owner one of largest private collections of photographs of operational steam traction engines and draft horses still working farmlands; Gymnast for the University of Connecticut. Publication: Author, the Encyclopedia of American Steam Traction Engines; 93 magazine covers; over 101 magazine articles; Over 365 photo educational exhibits world-wide. Honours: International Man of the Year, International Biographical Centre, Cambridge; Order of International Ambassadors Medal, ABI, 2000; Winner, numerous medals for proficiency on side horse; One Thousand Great Americans Medal, 2000; Gold Record of Achievement, American Biographical Institute, 2001; American Medal of Honor, American Biographical Institute 2001; Noble Prize, American Biographical Institute, 2001; Vice Chancellor, World Academy of Letters, ABI, 2011; Listed in biographical publications including Who's Who in Gymnastics. Memberships: Historical Steam Associations; American Society of Agricultural and Biological Engineers; The Author's Guild; Union Historical Fire Society; YMCA; American Legion; USA Gymnastics. Address: 117N Ruch Street, 8 Coplay, PA 18037 1712, USA.

NORDGREN Mats Olav, b. 9 May 1959, Malmö, Sweden. Head & Neck Surgeon; Consultant. m. Margareta Petersson, 2 sons. Education: Medical Licenciate, 1989; Specialist in Otorhino-laryngology, Head & Neck Surgery, 1997; Specialist, Phoniatrics, 2005; PhD, Lund University, 2005. Appointments: Resident, Thoracic Surgery, 1990-91; Resident, Urologic Surgery, 1993-94; Resident, Head and Neck Surgery, 1994-97; Consultant, Head and Neck Surgery and Phoniatrics, 1997-2009; Head of Surgery, 2007-09; Private practice in Otorhinolaryngology & Phoniatrics, 2009-. Publications: Thesis, Health-Related Quality of Life in Head and Neck Cancer – a Five Year Prospective Multicenter Study. Honours: Listed in international biographical dictionaries. Memberships: International Member, American Academy of Otorhinolaryngology – Head and Neck Surgery; Corresponding member, American Head and Neck Society; Fellow, Swedish Association of Otorhinolaryngology; Member, European Laryngological Society, 2008. Address: Ehrensvardsgatan 15A, 21213 Malmö, Sweden. E-mail: mats.nordgren@med.lu.se

NORMAN Barry Leslie, b. 21 August 1933, London, England. Writer; Broadcaster. m. Diana Narracott, 1957, 2 daughters. Appointments: Entertainments Editor, Daily Mail, London, 1969-71; Weekly Columnist, The Guardian, 1971-80; Writer and Presenter, BBC 1 Film, 1973-81, 1983-88, The Hollywood Greats, 1977-79, 1984, The British Greats 1980, Omnibus, 1982, Film Greats, 1985, Talking Pictures, 1988; Barry Norman's Film Night, BSkyB, 1998-2001; Radio 4 Today, 1974-76, Going Places, 1977-81, Breakaway, 1979-80. Publications: Novels: The Matter of Mandrake, 1967; The Hounds of Sparta, 1968; End Product, 1975; A Series of Defeats, 1977; To Nick a Good Body, 1978; Have a Nice Day, 1981; Sticky Wicket, 1984. Non-Fiction: Tales of the Redundance Kid, 1975; The Hollywood Greats, 1979; The Movie Greats, 1981; Talking Pictures, 1987; 100 Best Films of the Century, 1992, 1998; And Why Not? 2002. Thriller: The Birddog Tape, 1992; The Mickey Mouse Affair, 1995; Death on Sunset, 1998. Honours: British Association of Film and Television Arts Richard Dimbleby Award, 1981; Magazine Columnist of the Year, 1991; Honorary DLitt, University of East Anglia, 1991, University of Hertfordshire, 1996; Magazine Columnist of the Year, 1991; Commander of the Order of the British Empire, 1998.

NORMAN Geraldine (Lucia), (Geraldine Keen, Florence Place), b. 13 May 1940, Wales. Chief Executive. m. Frank Norman, 1971. Education: MA, Honours, Mathematics, St Anne's College, Oxford, 1961; University of California at Los Angeles, USA, 1961-62. Appointments: Chief Executive, Hermitage Foundation UK, St Petersburg. Publications: The Sale of Works of Art (as Geraldine Keen), 1971; 19th Century Painters and Paintings: A Dictionary, 1977; The Fake's Progress (co-author), 1977; The Tom Keating Catalogue (editor), 1977; Mrs Harper's Niece (as Florence Place), 1982; Biedermeier Painting, 1987; Top Collectors of the World (co-author), 1993; The Hermitage: The Biography of a Great Museum, 1997. Contributions to: The Times, The Independent, The Daily Telegraph and other Newspapers. Honour: News Reporter of the Year, 1976; Russian Federation Medal in memory of 300 years of St Petersburg, 2005; Order of the British Empire, 2011. Address: 5 Seaford Court, 220 Great Portland Street, London W1, England.

NORMAN Gregory John, b. 10 February 1955, Queensland, Australia. Professional Golfer. m. (1) Laura, 1981, divorced, 1 son, 1 daughter, (2) Chris Evert, 2008, divorced. Career: Professional, 1976-; Numerous major victories including: Doral Ryder Open, 1990, 1993, 1996; South African Open, 1996; Players Championship, 1994; PGA Grand Slam of Golf, 1993, 1994; British Open, 1986, 1993; Canadian Open, 1984, 1992; Australian Masters, 1981, 1983, 1984, 1989, 1990; New South Wales Open, 1978, 1983, 1986, 1988; Australian Open, 1980, 1985, 1987; European Open, 1986; World Match-Play, 1980, 1983, 1986; Australian Team, Dunhill Cup, 1985, 1986. Publications: My Story, 1982-83; Shark Attack, 1987-88; Greg Norman's Instant Lessons, 1993; Greg Norman's Better Golf, 1994. Honours: Inducted into World Golf Hall of Fame, 2001. Address: Great White Shark Enterprises Inc, PO Box 1189, Hobe Sound, FL 33475-1189, USA.

NORODOM RANARIDDH Prince, b. 2 January 1944, Cambodia. m. 1968, 2 sons, 1 daughter. Appointments: President, United National Front for an Independent, Neutral, Peaceful & Co-operative Cambodia; Co-Chair, Provisional National Government of Cambodia; Minister of National Defence, Interior and National Security, 1993; Member, National Assembly, 1993-; Co-Prime Minister, Member, Throne Council, 1993; 1st Prime Minister of Royal Government of Cambodia, 1993-97; Chair, National Development Council, 1993-97; Found guilty of conspiracy with Khmer Rouges to overthrow the government, sentenced to 30 years imprisonment; In Exile; Returned from exile 1998; Professor of Public Law.

NORODOM SIHANOUK Samdech Preah, b. 31 October 1922, Cambodia. King of Cambodia. m. Princess Monique, 14 children (6 deceased). Education: Saigon; Vietnam; Paris; Military Training, Saumur, France. Appointments: Elected King, 1941, Abdicated, 1955; Prime Minister, Minister of Foreign Affairs, 1955, 1956, 1957; Permanent Representative to UN, 1956; Elected Head of State, 1960; Took Oath of Fidelity to Vacant Throne, 1960; Deposed by Forces of Lon Nol, 1970; Resided, Peking; Established, Royal Government of National Union of Cambodia, (GRUNC) 1970; Restored as Head of State when GRUNC forces overthrew Khmer Republic, 1975, Resigned, 1976; Special Envoy of Khmer Rouge to UN, 1979; Founder, National United Front for an Independent Neutral, Peaceful and Co-operative Kampuchea, 1981-89; President, Tripartite National Cambodian Resistance, in exile 13 years, returned to Cambodia, 1991-93; Crowned King of Cambodia, 1993-2004; Colonel in Chief, Armed Forces, 1993-; Abdicated, 2004. Publications: L'Indochine vue de Pékin (with Jean Lacouture), 1972; My War With the CIA (with Wilfred Burchett), 1973; War and Hope: The Case for Cambodia, 1980; Souvenirs doux et amers, 1981; Prisonnier des Khmers Rouges, 1986; Charisme et Leadership, 1989. Address: Khemarindra Palace, Phnom Penh, Cambodia.

NORTH Anthony Charles Thomas, b. 7 February 1931, Derby, England. University Professor. m. Margaret, 3 daughters. Education: BSc (Hons), Physics, 1951, PhD, Biophysics, 1955, University of London King's College. Appointments: Professor, Molecular Biophysics, 1972, Professor of Biophysics, Head, 1973, Astbury Department of Biophysics; Astbury Professor of Biophysics, Department of Biochemistry and Molecular Biology, 1990; Professor Emeritus, University of Leeds; Secretary-General, International Union for Pure & Applied Biophysics, 1993-2002. Publications: Numerous articles in professional journals. Honours: Honorary Member, British Biophysical Society; Honorary Member, Hungarian Biophysical Society. Memberships: Fellow, Institute of Physics; Chartered Physicist; Member, British Biophysical Society; Member, Biochemical Society; Member, British Crystallographic Association; Member, Molecular Graphics and Modelling Society; President, Leeds Philosophical and Literary Society. Address: 27 Breary Lane, Bramhope, Leeds LS16 9AD, England. E-mail: actnorth@talktalk.net

NORTON Hugh Edward, b. 23 June 1936, London, England. Business Executive. m. (1) Janet M Johnson, 1965, deceased, 1 son, (2) Joy Harcup, 1998. Education: Winchester College; Trinity College, Oxford. Appointments: Joined British Petroleum Company, 1959, Exploration Department, 1960, in Abu Dhabi, Lebanon & Libya, 1962-70, subsequently held appointments in Supply, Central Planning; Policy Planning, Regional Directorate Mid E & International & Government Affairs departments; Managing Director, BP's Associate Companies, Singapore, Malaysia, Hong Kong, 1978-81, Director of Planning, 1981-83, Regional Director for Near East, Middle East & Indian Sub-Continent, 1981-86, Director of Administration, 1983-86, Managing Director, CEO, BP Exploration Co, 1986-89, Chair, 1989-95, Managing Director, British Petroleum Co PLC, 1989-95; Chair, BP Asia Pacific Private Co Ltd, 1991-95; Director, Inchcape PLC, 1995-, Standard Chart PLC, 1995-, Lasmo PLC, 1997-. Memberships: Council, Royal Institute of Economic Affairs, 1991-. Address: c/o BP Asia Pacific Pte Ltd, BP Tower, 25th Storey, 396 Alexandra Road, 0511 Singapore.

NORWICH John Julius (The Viscount Norwich), b. 15 September 1929, London, England. Writer; Broadcaster. m. (1) Anne Clifford, 1952, 1 son, 1 daughter, (2) Mollie Philipps, 1989. Education: University of Strasbourg, 1947; New College, Oxford, 1949-52. Appointments: Writer, Royal Navy, 1947-49; Foreign Office, 1952-64; Third Secretary, British Embassy, Belgrade, 1955-57; Second Secretary, British Embassy, Beirut, 1957-60; First Secretary, Foreign Office, London, 1961; British delegation to Disarmament Conference, Geneva, 1960-64; Writer, Broadcaster, 1964-; Chairman: British Theatre Museum, 1966-71; Venice in Peril Fund, 1970-; Executive Committee, National Trust, 1969-95; Franco-British Council, 1972-79; Board, English National Opera, 1977-81. Publications: Mount Athos, 1966; Sahara, 1968; The Normans in the South, 1967; The Kingdom in the Sun, 1970; A History of Venice, 1977; Christmas Crackers 1970-79, 1980; Glyndebourne, 1985; The Architecture of Southern England, 1985; A Taste for Travel, 1985; Byzantium: The Early Centuries, 1988; More Christmas Crackers 1980-89, 1990; Venice: A Traveller's Companion (editor), 1990; The Oxford Illustrated Encyclopaedia of the Arts (editor), 1990; Byzantium, the Apogee, 1991; Byzantium: The Decline and Fall, 1995; A Short History of Byzantium, 1997; Shakespeare's Kings, 1999; Still More Christmas Crackers 1990-99, 2000; Paradise of Cities, 2003; The Middle Sea: A History of the Mediterranean, 2006. Honours: Commander, Royal Victorian Order; Commendatore, Ordine al Merito della Repubblica Italiana; Award, American Institute of Architects. Memberships: Fellow, Royal Society of Literature; Fellow, Royal Geographical Society; Fellow, Royal Society of Arts. Address: 24 Blomfield Road, London W9 1AD, England.

NOVAK Pavel, b. 7 September 1918, Stribro, Czech Republic. Civil Engineer; University Teacher. m. R Elizabeth Maurer, 1 son, 1 daughter. Education: BSc (Hon), University of London (external), 1941; Ing Dr, 1949, CSc (PhD), 1958, Czech Technical University, Prague; Dr Sc, Technical University, Brno, 1965. Appointments: Assistant Engineer, Trent Navigation Co, Nottingham, 1941-42; Assistant Lecturer, University College, Nottingham, 1942-45; Scientific Officer to Principal Scientific Officer, Hydraulic Research Institute, Prague, 1945-67; Director, Institute of Hydrodynamics, Academy of Sciences, Prague, 1967-68; Senior Lecturer, Department of Civil Engineering, 1968-70, Professor of Civil and Hydraulic Engineering, 1970-83, Head of Department of Civil Engineering, 1981-83, Head of School of Civil & Mining Engineering, 1982-83, University of Newcastle. Publications: Over 100 papers in refereed journals and at international conferences; Author, Co-author and editor of 23 books. Honours: Corresponding Member, Academy of Science, Toulouse, 1967; James Hardie Speaker, Institution of Engineers, Australia, 1987; Honorary Member, International Association for Hydraulic Engineering and Research, 1989; Hlavka Medal, 1992, Bechyne Gold Medal, 1994, Czechoslovak Academy of Sciences; Hydraulic Structures Medal, American Society of Civil Engineers, 2003;

Medal, De Scientia et Humanitate Optime Meritis, Czech Academy of Sciences, 2008; Honorary Citizenship of Stribro. Memberships: Fellow, Institution of Civil Engineers, UK; Fellow, Chartered Institution of Water and Environmental Management; Honorary Member, International Association for Hydraulic Engineering and Research. Address: 5 Glendale Avenue, Whickham, Newcastle upon Tyne, NE16 5JA, England. E-mail: pavel.novak@ncl.ac.uk

NOVIKOV Alexander F, b. 6 September 1941, Yaroslavl, Russian Federation. Engineering. m. Rimma V, 1 daughter. Education: Mechanical Engineering, Leningrad Polytechnic Institute, 1964; PhD, Sciences, Leningrad State Optical Research Institute (Vavilov GOI), 1974; Doctor Sci Techn, St Petersburg State University, ITMO, 1995. Appointments: Senior Engineer, Research Institute of Radiocomponents, 1964-74; Senior Researcher, Mendeleev State Institute of Metrology, 1974-77; Tutor, Assistant Professor, Professor, Physical Engineering Department, St Petersburg State University ITMO, 1977-; Invited Researcher, Harbin Institute of Technology, China, 1989-92; Invited Researcher, Siegen University, Germany, 2000-05. Publications: About 100 scientific papers in professional journals; Monograph, Colour of Molecules, Time, Light, 2011; Contribution, Book of Translations of the Nobel Bio & Lectures in Physics and Economics; 7 books of novels. Honours: Honoured Worker of Higher Education in Russia; Numerous government awards; Several literary awards; Named as one of The Best Men & Women in Russia III; Listed in international biographical dictionaries. Memberships: International Optoelectronics Society; American Chemical Society; Awarding University councils; Writers Union of Russia. E-mail: afnovikov@mail.ru

NOVOSAD Pavel, b. 13 June 1945, Zlin, Czech Republic. Doctor of Medicine. m. Pavla Novosadova, 2 sons. Education: Medical Faculty, UJEP BRNO, 1969; Postgraduate diploma, Internal Medicine, 1974; Postgraduate diploma, Clinical Chemistry, 1979; Postgraduate diploma, Clinical Osteology, 2010. Appointments: Chief, Special Science Laboratory specialized in Metabolic Diseases, Internal Teaching Clinic, Zlin, 1979-92; Chief, Mediekos Labor Ltd, 1992-; Chief, Osteology Academy, 2007-. Publications: Numerous articles in professional journals. Honours: Chief of Workgroup for Problematic Metabolic Diseases of Bones, Czech Medicine Society, 2007. Memberships: International Osteoporosis Foundation; Society of J E Purkyne; Osteology and Clinical Chemistry. Address: Strane 506, Zlin 76001, Czech Republic. E-mail: pnovosad@mediekoslabor.cz

NOVOTNA Bronislava, b. 19 January 1954, Brno, Czech Republic. m. Jan, 1 son, 1 daughter. Education: Faculty of Medicine, 1979; Certification in Paediatrics, 1988; Certification in Allergology and Clinical Immunology, 1991; PhD, 2006. Appointments: Secondary Physician, Department of Microbiology and Pediatrics, Head, Allergology Unit, Department of Internal Medicine and Gastroenterology, 1993-, University Hospital, Brno. Publications: About 120 articles in Czech literature; About 15 original papers in the form of abstracts. Honours: Team of Authors; Internal Medicine monographs and textbooks; Professor Vladimir Zerazol Prize, 2004. Memberships: Czech Society of Allergology and Clinical Immunology; EAACI; ERS; WAO. Address: Straznicka 3, 62700, Brno, Czech Republic.

NOVOTNA Jana, b. 2 October 1968, Brno, Czech Republic. Tennis Player. Appointments: Won US Open Junior Doubles, 1986; Turned Professional, 1987; Won 1st Title, Adelaide, 1988; Olympic Silver Medal, Doubles wih Helena Sukova, 1988; Won Australian and US Open Mixed Doubles with Pugh, 1988; Won 6 Women's Doubles Titles, 1989;With Sukova, won Australian Open, French Open, Wimbledon Doubles, 1990; Reached Quarter Finals, French Open, 1991; Won 7 Doubles Titles with Savchenko Neiland, 1992; Won Singles Titles, Osaka and Brighton, 1993; Singles Titles, Leipzig, Brighton, Essen, 1994; Won Wimbledon Singles and Doubles, 1998; Announced retirement, 1999. Honours: Olympic Bronze Medal in Singles, Silver Medal in Doubles, Atlanta, 1996.

NTIBA Micheni Japhet, b. 7 August 1958, Chuka, Kenya. m. Catherine Karimi Micheni, 3 sons. Education: MSc, Hydrobiology, 1987, BSc (Hons), Botany and Zoology, 1984, University of Nairobi; PhD, Fisheries Biology, University of East Anglia, 1990. Appointments: Tutorial Fellow, 1988-89, Lecturer, 1989-93, Senior Lecturer, 1993-97, Associate Professor, 1997-, Chairman, Department of Zoology, 2004-06, Director, School of Biological Sciences, 2006-08, University of Nairobi; First Executive Secretary, Lake Victoria Fisheries Organization, Uganda, 1997-2002; Permanent Secretary, Ministry of Fisheries Development of the Government of Kenya, 2008-; Chairman of Council, Presbyterian University of East Africa, 2010. Publications: 30 articles in professional journals. Honours: DAAD Scholarship, 1984; Rutherford Scholarship, 1986; Presidential Award for First Class Service, 2009. Memberships: International Society for Mangrove Ecosystems; Hydrobiological Society of Africa; East African Wildlife Society; Editorial Board of Endangered Species International Journal; Scientific Advisory Committee, Western Indian Ocean Marine Science Association. Address: School of Biological Sciences, College of Biological and Physical Sciences, University of Nairobi, PO Box 30197-00100, Nairobi, Kenya. E-mail: mjntiba@uonbi.ac.ke Website: ww.uonbi.ac.ke

NUGEE Edward George, 9 August 1928, Godalming, Surrey, England. Barrister-at-Law. m. Rachel Elizabeth Makower, 4 sons. Education: Law Moderations (Distinction), 1950, BA, Jurisprudence (1st Class), 1952, Eldon Law Scholarship, 1955, MA, 1956, Worcester College, Oxford; Barrister-at-Law, 1955. Appointments: Royal Artillery (Office of Chief of Staff FARELF), 1947-49; Captain, Intelligence Corps (100APIU(TA)), 1950-64; Barrister-at-Law, 1955; Inner Temple: Bencher, 1976, Treasurer, 1996 (read as a pupil with Lord Templeman and Lord Brightman, 1954-55); Queen's Counsel, 1977; Deputy High Court Judge (Chancery Division), 1982-97; Chairman, Committee of Inquiry into the Management of Privately Owned Blocks of Flats, 1984-85. Publications: Joint editor, Halsbury's Laws of England: Landlord and Tenant (3rd edition 1958); Real Property (3rd edition 1960, 4th edition, 1982, re-issue, 1998); Nathan on the Charities Act, 1962; Various articles in legal journals. Honour: TD, 1964. Memberships: The Institute of Conveyancers; Legal Advisory Commission of General Synod; Association of Pension Lawyers; Chancery Bar Association; Property Bar Association; Temple Music Trust; Nugee Foundation; Bhopal Hospital Trust. Address: Wilberforce Chambers, 8 New Square, Lincoln's Inn, London WC2A 3QP, England. Website: www.wilberforce.co.uk

NUNN Trevor Robert, Sir, b. 14 January 1940, Ipswich, England. Theatre Director. m. (1) Janet Suzman, 1969, 1 son, (2) Sharon Lee Hill, 1986, 2 daughters, (3) Imogen Stubbs, 1994, separated 2011, 1 son, 1 daughter. Education: Downing College, Cambridge. Appointments: Trainee Director, Belgrade Theatre, Coventry; Associate Director, Royal Shakespeare Company, 1964-86, Director Emeritus, 1986-; Founder, Homevale Ltd, Awayvale Ltd; Artistic

Director, Royal National Theatre, 1996-2001. Creative Works: Productions include: The Merry Wives of Windsor, 1979; Once in a Lifetime, 1979; Juno and the Paycock, 1980; The Life and Adventures of Nicholas Nickleby, 1980; Cats, 1981; All's Well That Ends Well, 1981; Henry IV (pts I and II), 1981, 1982; Peter Pan, 1982; Starlight Express, 1984; Les Misérables, 1985; Chess, 1986; The Fair Maid of the West, 1986; Aspects of Love, 1989; Othello, 1989; The Baker's Wife, 1989; Timon of Athens, 1991; The Blue Angel, 1991; Measure for Measure, 1991; Heartbreak House, 1992; Arcadia, 1993; Sunset Boulevard, 1993; Enemy of the People, 1997; Mutabilitie, 1997; Not About Nightingales, 1998; Oklahoma, 1998; Betrayal, 1998; Troilus and Cressida, 1999; The Merchant of Venice, 1999; Summerfolk, 1999; Love's Labour's Lost, 2002; We Happy Few, 2004; The Woman in White, 2004; Acorn Antiques, 2005; Hamlet, 2004; King Lear, 2007; The Seagull, 2007; Rock n Roll, 2007-08; Gone With the Wind, 2008; Inherit the Wind, 2009; A Little Night Music, 2009-10; Aspects of Love, Birdsong, 2010; Flare Path, The Lion in Winter, 2011; A Chorus of Disapproval, 2012; TV: Antony and Cleopatra, 1975; Comedy of Errors, 1976; Every Good Boy Deserves Favour, 1978; Macbeth, 1978; Shakespeare Workshops Word of Mouth, 1979; The Three Sisters, Othello, 1989; Porgy and Bess, 1992; Oklahoma!, 1999; Merchant of Venice, 2001; King Lear, 2008; Films: Hedda, Lady Jane, 1985; Lady Jane, 1986; Twelfth Night, 1996; Operas: Idomeneo, 1982; Porgy and Bess, 1986; Cosi Fan Tutte, 1991; Peter Grimes, 1992; Katya Kabanova, 1994; Sophie's Choice, 2002. Publications: British Theatre Design, 1989. Honours: Tony Award, 1982, 1983, 1987; Drama Desk Award, 1975, 1983, 1999; Laurence Olivier Awards, 1995, 2000, 2002; CBE; Knighted, 2002. Address: Royal National Theatre, Upper Ground, South Bank, London SE1 9PX, England.

NUSEIBEH Taj-Ul-Deen, b. 15 September 1933, Jersualem, Palestine. Engineer. m. Amal Hasan, 2 sons, 2 daughters. Education: Bachelor, Mathematics and Physics, East Texas State College, USA, 1958; BSc, Mechanical Engineering, Oklahoma State University, USA, 1960. Appointments: Mechanical Engineer, Industrial Section, Ministry of National Economy, Amman, 1961-62; Safety Engineer, Ministry of Social Affairs and Labour Department, 1962-71; Consultant Engineer, Grand Amman Hospital & Basheer Hospital, Amman Ministry of Health, 1971-72; Consultant Maintenance Engineer, Ministry of Public Works, Amman, 1972-73; Occupational Safety & Health Adviser, Ministry of Labour, 1973-83; Mechanical Engineer, Tender Department, Ministry of Water, Amman, 1985-86. Publications: Numerous articles in professional journals. Honours: Model of Respect, Risk Assessment Symposium, Cairo, 1975; Diploma for Outstanding Contributions in the field of Safety & Health Works, Ministry of Labour, 2004. Association of Jordan Engineer and General Safety Commission; American Society of Mechanical Engineers, USA; Institution of Occupational Safety & Health, UK; American Confederation of Government Industrial Hygiene, USA; Jordanian Society for Prevention of Road Accidents; Jordanian Society for Control of Environment Pollution. Address: Dahyet Al-Rabyeh, PO Box 950280, Amman 11195, The Hashemite Kingdom of Jordan. E-mail: hn14@hotmail.com

NUSS Joanne Ruth, b. 2 May 1951, Great Bend, Kansas, USA. Sculptor. Education: Valparaiso University, Indiana, 1969-71; University of Kansas, Kansas, 1972-73; University of Copenhagen, Denmark, 1974; BA, Fort Hays State University, Kansas, 1975; Master's program with Beverly Pepper, 1st Prize in Class Presentation, New Mexico Institute of Fine Arts, Santa Fe, New Mexico, 1991. Career: Bronze casting producing sculptures, 1975-; Exhibited worldwide for over 30 years; Work held in private collections of: King Hassan II of Morocco, Prince of Brunei and Bandarseri Begawan, Brunei; First foreign female artist commissioned for architectural project in Tangiers, Morocco, 1988-90; Exhibits in juried shows throughout USA. Publications: Kansas City's Single Professionals: Women and Men, 1981; Dictionary of American Sculptors, 18th Century to the Present. Honours: Award of Excellence, Period Gallery, Omaha; First Place Award, University of Northern Iowa Gallery, Cedar Falls, Iowa; Artist in Residence Grants, Taos, New Mexico, 1984, 1990; Best 3-D Award, Kansas Artist Craftsman Award, Wichita, Kansas; Dictionary of American Sculptors 18th Century to the Present, New York, 1984; First Kansas Artist Purchase Award, Kansas Professional Artists Collection, Fort Hays State University, Kansas, 1985; Artist featured working in Morocco, BBC Radio Network, London, 1986; Award of Excellence, Upstream People Gallery, Omaha, Nebraska, 2001-02; Woman of Achievement Award, 2005; America's Registry of Outstanding Professionals, 2005-06; Who's Who in American Art, 2010. Memberships: National Association of Women Artists; New York National Museum of Women in the Arts; National Sculpture Society, New York; International Sculpture Center, Hamilton, New York. Address: Unique Bronze Sculptures, 4843 Camelot West, Great Bend, KS 67530, USA.

NYE Robert, b. 15 March 1939, London, England. Author; Poet; Dramatist; Editor. m. (1) Judith Pratt, 1959, divorced 1967, 3 sons, (2) Aileen Campbell, 1968, 1 daughter. Publications: Fiction: Doubtfire, 1967; Tales I Told My Mother, 1969; Falstaff, 1976; Merlin, 1978; Faust, 1980; The Voyage of the Destiny, 1982; The Facts of Life and Other Fictions, 1983; The Memoirs of Lord Byron, 1989; The Life and Death of My Lord Gilles de Rais, 1990; Mrs Shakespeare: The Complete Works, 1993; The Late Mr Shakespeare, 1998. Children's Fiction: Taliesin, 1966; March Has Horse's Ears, 1966; Wishing Gold, 1970; Poor Pumpkin, 1971; Out of the World and Back Again, 1977; Once Upon Three Times, 1978; The Bird of the Golden Land, 1980; Harry Pay the Pirate, 1981; Three Tales, 1983; Lord Fox and Other Spine-Chilling Tales, 1997. Poetry: Juvenilia 1, 1961; Juvenilia 2, 1963; Darker Ends, 1969; Agnus Dei, 1973; Two Prayers, 1974; Five Dreams, 1974; Divisions on a Ground, 1976; A Collection of Poems, 1955-1988, 1989; 14 Poems, 1994; Henry James and Other Poems, 1995; Collected Poems, 1995, 1998; The Rain and the Glass: 99 Poems: 99 Poems, New and Selected, 2004; Plays: Sawney Bean (with Bill Watson), 1970; The Seven Deadly Sins: A Mask, 1974; Penthesilea, Fugue and Sisters, 1976. Translator: Beowulf, 1968. Editor: A Choice of Sir Walter Raleigh's Verse, 1973; The English Sermon, 1750-1850, 1976; The Faber Book of Sonnets, 1976; PEN New Poetry 1, 1986; First Awakenings: The Early Poems of Laura Riding (co-editor), 1992; A Selection of the Poems of Laura Riding, 1994. Contributions to: Magazines and journals. Honours: Eric Gregory Award, 1963; Guardian Fiction Prize, 1976; Hawthornden Prize, 1977. Membership: Royal Society of Literature, fellow.

NYIRI Ferenc (Baron), b. 25 August 1964, Hódmezövásárhely, Hungary. Basstrombone Player. Education: Academy of Music, Franz Liszt, Szeged, 1985. Appointments: Symphony Orchestra of Pécs, 1985-89; Nationaltheater of Szeged, 1989-93; Symphony Orchestra of Szeged, 1993-. Publications: Journal of Hungarian Trombone-Tuba Association. Honours: Competition of Trombone, III Prize, 1984, II Prize, 1985; Prize of Artisjus,

2001; Listed in biographical dictionaries. Memberships: Hungarian Trombone-Tuba Association. Address: Ipoly sor 11/B, H-6724 Szeged, Hungary.

NYONG Christopher Etim, b. 17 March 1960, Ikotene, Nigeria. Accountant. m. Cecilia, 2 daughter. Education: BSc (Hon), Accounting, 1985; MBA, 1992; ACA, 1992; ACTI, 1995; FCA, 2006; CFA, 2011. Appointments: Company Secretary/Accountant, Johnell Agro Ind Ltd, 1986-88; Auditor, Office of the Auditor-General CRS; Officer, MIS; Manager, Accounts Control; Head, Finance & Planning; Head, Energy Sector; Branch Manager, Chartered Bank plc; Auditor-General of CRS. Publications: Numerous articles in professional journals. Honours: Distinguished Member Award, CALCHP, 2001; Distinguished Member Award, Unical Alumni, Rivers State; Distinguished Member Award, Institute of Chartered Accountants of Nigeria, Calabar District Society; Listed in biographical dictionaries. Memberships: Fellow, Institute of Chartered Accountants of Nigeria; Chartered Institute of Taxation of Nigeria. Address: Office of the Auditor-General, 11/13 Adazi Street, Calabar, Nigeria. E-mail: chris_nyong@yahoo.com

O

Ó LAOIRE Muiris, b. 13 June 1958, Ireland. Lecturer. Education: BA, 1977, MA, 1981, PhD, 1995, National University of Ireland. Appointments: Lecturer, MA in Language Pedagogy, National University of Ireland, Galway; Senior Lecturer, Institute of Technology, Tralee, 1997-; Chief Examiner and External Examiner, Irish Language at European Schools, 2005-; Professor, Language Revitalization Studies, AUT, New Zealand, 2011. Publications: Numerous articles in professional journals; 6 books, 2 in progress; Invited lectures, plenary lectures and keynote addresses. Memberships: International Association for Multilingualism; Educational Studies Association of Ireland; Association of Language Awareness; North American Celtic Language Teachers Association; European Second Language Association; Royal Irish Academy Committee for Modern Language, Literary and Cultural Studies.

OAKLEY Ann (Rosamund), b. 17 January 1944, London, England. Professor of Sociology and Social Policy; Writer. 1 son, 2 daughters. Education: MA, Somerville College, Oxford, 1965; PhD, Bedford College, London, 1974. Appointments: Research Officer, Social Research Unit, Bedford College, London, 1974-79; Wellcome Research Fellow, Radcliffe Infirmary, National Perinatal Epidemiology Unit, Oxford, 1980-83; Deputy Director, Thomas Coram Research Unit, 1985-90, Director, Social Science Research Unit, 1990-, Professor of Sociology and Social Policy, 1991-, University of London. Publications: Sex, Gender and Society, 1972; The Sociology of Housework, 1974; Housewife, 1974, US edition as Women's Work: A History of the Housewife, 1975; The Rights and Wrongs of Women, 1976; Becoming a Mother, 1980; Women Confined, 1980; Subject Women, 1981; Miscarriage, 1984; Taking It Like a Woman, 1984; The Captured Womb: A History of the Medical Care of Pregnant Women, 1984; Telling the Truth about Jerusalem, 1986; What Is Feminism, 1986; The Men's Room, 1988; Only Angels Forget, 1990; Matilda's Mistake, 1990; Helpers in Childbirth: Midwifery Today, 1990; The Secret Lives of Eleanor Jenkinson, 1992; Social Support and Motherhood: The Natural History of a Research Project, 1992; Essays on Women, Medicine and Health, 1993; Scenes Originating in the Garden of Eden, 1993; Young People, Health and Family Life, 1994; The Politics of the Welfare State, 1994; Man and Wife, 1996; The Gift Relationship by Richard Titmuss, 1997; Who's Afraid of Feminism? 1997; Welfare Research: A critical review, 1998; Experiments in Knowing: Gender and Method in the Social Sciences, 2000; Welfare and Wellbeing: Richard Titmuss's contribution to social policy, 2001; Overheads, 2000; Gender on Planet Earth, 2002; Private Complaints and Public Health: Richard Titmus on the National Health Service, 2004; The Ann Oakly Reader: Gender, women and social science, 2005; Fracture: Adventures of a broken body, 2007. Contributions to: Professional journals; Many chapters in academic books. Honours: Hon DLitt, Salford, 1995; Honorary Professor, University College, London, 1996-; Honorary Fellow, Somerville College, Oxford, 2001-. Address: c/o The Sayle Agency, 8B Kings Parade, Cambridge, CB2 1SJ, England.

OAKLEY Robin Francis Leigh, b. 20 August 1941, Kidderminster, Worcestershire, England. Journalist. m. Carolyn, 1 son, 1 daughter. Education: MA, Brasenose College, Oxford. Appointments: Liverpool Daily Post, 1964-70; Crossbencher Columnist and then Assistant Editor, Sunday Express, 1970-79; Assistant Editor, Now! Magazine, 1979-81; Assistant Editor, Daily Mail, 1981-86; Political Editor, The Times, 1986-92; Political Editor, BBC, 1992-2000; European Political Editor, CNN, 2000-08; CNN Contributer, 2008-; Turf Columnist, The Spectator, 1996-; Contributor, Financial Times, 2003-; Trustee, Thompson Foundation, 2001-. Publications: Valley of the Racehorse – a portrait of the racing community of Lambourn, 2000; Inside Track – thirty years of political reporting, 2001; Frankincense and More – The Barry Hills Biography, 2010; The Cheltenham Festival: A Centenary History, 2011. Honour: OBE, 2001. Membership: RAC. Address: 24 Bridge End, Dorchester-on-Thames, Wallingford, Oxfordshire OX10 7JP, England. E-mail: robin.oakley278@gmail.com

OBAMA Barack Hussein, b. 4 August 1961, Honolulu, Hawaii, USA. 44th president of the United States of America. m. Michelle, 1992, 2 daughters. Education: Occidental College, Los Angeles, California, 2 years; BA, Political Science, Columbia University, New York, 1983; JD (magna cum laude), Harvard Law School, 1991. Appointments: Board Member, Woods Fund of Chicago; Member, Trinity United Church of Christ; Leadership for Quality Education; Lawyer's Committee for Civil Rights under the Law; Board Member, Joyce Foundation; Cook County Bar Association Community Law Project; Cook County Bar; Chicago Annebery Challenge; Center for Neighborhood and Technology; Senator, Illinois State Senate, 1997-2004; Senator, United States Senate, 2005-; President of the United States, 2009-12, re-elected 2013. Publications: Dreams From My Father: A Story of Race and Inheritance, autobiography, 1995; The Audacity of Hope: Thoughts on Reclaiming the American Dream, 2006. Honours: Nobel Peace Prize Laureate, 2009.

OBAMA Michelle LaVaughn Robinson, b. 17 January 1964, Chicago, USA. First Lady of the United States. m. Barack Obama, 1992, 2 daughters. Education: BA, Princeton University, 1985; JD, Harvard Law School, 1988. Appointments: Associate, Sidley Austin, Chicago; Assistant to the Mayor, Chicago; Assistant Commissioner of Planning and Development; Executive Diretor, Chicago Office of Public Allies, 1993-96; Associate Dean of Student Services, University of Chicago, 1996; Executive Director for Community Affairs, 2002, Vice President for Community and External Affairs, 2005, University of Chicago Hospitals. Honours: Honorary Member, Alpha Kappa Alpha.

OBERNDORFER Ulrich, b. 6 March 1981, Weiden, Germany. Energy Expert. Education: Diplom-Volkswift (MSc, Economics), Free University, Berlin, 2006; Dr rer pol, Oldenburg University, 2009. Appointments: Research Assistant, Institute for Ecological Economy Research, Berlin, 2003-06; Research Fellow, Centre for European Economic Research, Mannheim, 2006-08; Energy Expert, Federal Ministry of Economics & Technology, Berlin, 2008-. Publications: Monograph, Environment, Energy and Economic Performance; Articles in professional scientific journals. Honours: Erasmus Grant, EU, 2002-03; Young Scholar Best Paper Award, IEWT, Vienna, Austria, 2007; Young Economist International Presentation Award, Dt Bundesbank, 2007. Memberships: Verein für Socialpolitik; British-German Forum Alumni; Economics for Sustainability Project Advisory Board; many others. Address: BMUi, Scharnhorststr 34-37, 10115 Berlin, Germany. E-mail: ulrich.oberndorfer@bmwi.bund.de Website: www.bmwi.de

O'BRIEN Denis Patrick, b. 24 May 1939, Knebworth, Hertfordshire, England. Economist. m. (1) Eileen Patricia O'Brien, deceased, 1985, 1 son, 2 daughters (2) Julia Stapleton, 1 daughter. Education: BSc, Economics, 1960,

University College, London; PhD, Queen's University, Belfast, 1969. Appointments: Assistant Lecturer, 1963-65, Lecturer, 1965-70, Reader, 1970-72, Queen's University, Belfast; Professor of Economics, 1972-97, Emeritus Professor, 1998-, Durham University. Publications: J R McCulloch, 1970; The Correspondence of Lord Overstone (3 volumes), 1971; Competition in British Industry (jointly), 1974; The Classical Economists, 1975; Competition Policy, Profitability and Growth (jointly), 1979; Pioneers of Modern Economics in Britain (jointly), 1981; Authorship Puzzles in the History of Economics (jointly), 1982; Lionel Robbins, 1988; Thomas Joplin and Classical Macroeconomics, 1993; Methodology, Money and the Firm (2 volumes), 1994; The Classical Economists Revisited, 2003; History of Economic Thought as an Intellectual Discipline, 2007, The Development of Monetary Economics, 2007; Taxation and the Promotion of Human Happiness. An Essay by George Warde Norman (editor, with J Creedy), 2009; Darwin's Clever Neighbour. George Warde Norman and his Circle (editor, with J Creedy), 2010. Honours: FBA, 1988; Distinguished Fellow, History of Economics Society, 2003. Address: c/o Dr Julia Stapleton, Department of Politics, South End House, South Road, Durham DH1 3TG, England.

O'BRIEN Edna, b. 15 December 1930, Tuamgraney, County Clare, Ireland. Author; Dramatist. m. 1954, divorced 1964, 2 sons. Education: Convents; Pharmaceutical College of Ireland. Publications: The Country Girls, 1960; The Lonely Girl, 1962; Girls in Their Married Bliss, 1963; August is a Wicked Month, 1964; Casualties of Peace, 1966; The Love Object, 1968; A Pagan Place, 1970; Night, 1972; A Scandalous Woman, 1974; Mother Ireland, 1976; Johnnie I Hardly Knew You, 1977; Mrs Reinhardt and Other Stories, 1978; Virginia (play), 1979; The Dazzle, 1981; Returning, 1982; A Christmas Treat, 1982; A Fanatic Heart, 1985; Tales for Telling, 1986; Flesh and Blood (play), 1987; Madame Bovary (play), 1987; The High Road, 1988; Lantern Slides, 1990; Time and Tide, 1992; House of Splendid Isolation, 1994; Down by the River, 1997; James Joyce: A Biography, 1999; Wild Decembers, 1999; In the Forest, 2002; Iphigenia (play), 2003; Triptych, 2004; The Light of Evening, 2006; Haunted (play), 2009; Byron in Love, 2009. Honours: Yorkshire Post Novel Award, 1971; Los Angeles Times Award, 1990; Writers' Guild Award, 1993; European Prize for Literature, 1995; American National Arts Gold Medal. Address: David Godwin Associates, 14 Goodwin Court, Covent Garden, London WC2N 4LL, England.

O'BRIEN Keith Patrick, b. 17 March 1938, Ballycastle, County Antrim, Northern Ireland. Cardinal in Catholic Church. Education: BSc, University of Edinburgh, 1955-59; St Andrew's College, Drygrange, Melrose, 1959-65; Dip Ed, Moray House College of Education, 1965-66. Appointments: Teacher and Chaplain, St Columba's Secondary School, Fife, 1966-71; Priest, St Patrick's Kilsyth, 1972-75; Priest, St Mary's, Bathgate, 1975-78; Spiritual Director, St Andrew's College, Drygrange, Melrose, 1978-80; Rector, Blairs College, Aberdeen, 1980-85; Archbishop of St Andrew's and Edinburgh, 1985-; Cardinal, 2003. Honours: Equestrian Order of the Holy Sepulchre of Jerusalem, Grand Prior of the Scottish Liertenancy of the Order, 2001; Cardinal in Catholic Church, 2003; Knight Grand Cross, 2003; Honorary LLD, University of St Francis Xavier, Antigonish, Nova Scotia, 2004; Honorary DD, University of St Andrew's, 2004; Honorary DD, University of Edinburgh, 2004; Sovereign Military Order of Malta; Bailiff Grand Cross of Honour and Devotion, 2005. Address: The Archbishop's House, 42 Greenhill Gardens, Edinburgh EH10 4BJ, Scotland. E-mail: cardinal@staned.org.uk

O'BRIEN Stephen, b. 1 April 1957, East Africa. Member of Parliament. m. Gemma, 2 sons, 1 daughter. Education: MA (Hons) Law, Emmanuel College, Cambridge, 1976-79; Final Professional Examination, College of Law, Chester, 1979-80. Appointments: Solicitor, Senior Managing Solicitor, Freshfields Solicitors, City of London, 1981-88; Executive Assistant to the Board, 1988-89, Director of Corporate Planning, 1989-94, Director, International Operating Group, 1994-98, Deputy Chairman, Director, Redland Tile & Brick Ltd (Northern Ireland), 1995-98, Group Committee Member, 1990-98, Group Secretary and Director, Corporate Affairs, 1991-98, Redland PLC; International Business Consultant, 1998-; Member of Parliament for Eddisbury, South West Cheshire, 1999-; Parliamentary Private Secretary to the Chairman of the Conservative Party, 2000-2001; Opposition Whip (Front Bench), 2001-2002; Shadow Paymaster General, 2002-03; Shadow Secretary of State for Industry, 2003-05; Shadow Minister for Skills and Higher Education, 2005; Shadow Minister for Health, 2006. Memberships: CBI, Elected Member, South East Regional Council, 1995-98; Scottish Business in the Community, Council of Members, 1995-98; BMP Construction Products Association, 1995-99. Address: House of Commons, London SW1A 0AA, England. E-mail: obriens@parliament.uk

OBROUCHEVA Natalie, b. 4 January 1931, St Petersburg, Russia. Biologist; Plant Physiologist. m. A G Kovalev, 1 son. Education: Lomonosov Moscow University, 1953; PhD, Institute of Plant Physiology, 1961; DSc (Biol), Institute of Plant Physiology, 1991. Appointments: Assistant, Department of Plant Physiology, Faculty of Biology, Moscow University, 1953-61; Junior Researcher, Institute of General and Inorganic Chemistry, 1961-70; Senior, then Leading Researcher, Institute of Plant Physiology, 1970-. Publications: Books: Physiology of Growing Root Cells, 1965; How to Translate Biochemical Texts from Russian to English, 1972; English-Russian Dictionary on Physiology of Higher Plants, 1979; Seed Germination: a guide to the early stages, 1999; 4 book chapters. Honours: Full Member, Russian Academy of Natural Sciences, 1998; Winner, Timiryazev Prize, Russian Academy of Sciences, 2000. Memberships: International Society of Root Research; International Society of Seed Research; Editorial Board, Russian Journal of Plant Physiology. Address: Botanicheskaya str 35, Institute of Plant Physiology, Russian Academy of Sciences, Moscow 127276, Russia. E-mail: obroucheva@ippras.ru

O'CONNOR Raymond Francis, b. 23 January 1959, Cork City, Ireland. Medical Educator. m. Margaret, 3 children. Education: MBBCh, BAO, Medicine, University College Cork, 1982; Family Planning diploma, 1984; Child Health diploma, 1984; Obstetrics diploma, 1985; Medical Education certificate, 2005; Medical Education diploma, 2008; MSc, 2009. Appointments: GP principal in the GMS, 1990-, Chairman, Mid-West Regional Diabetes Steering Committee, 2006-, HSE West, Limerick; Clinical Tutor with UCC, UCD, UL and TCD Medical School, 1996-; Assistant Programme Director, Mid-West Specialist Training Programme in General Practice, University of Limerick, 2000-; Projects Assessor, ICGP Distance Learning Unit, 2002-04, Member, ICGP Quality Committee, 2005-, ICGP, Dublin. Publications: Numerous articles in professional journals. Honours: Charles Gold Medal, Physiology, 1979; Fellow, RCGP, 2006; Finalist, Irish Journal of Medical Science, 2007. Memberships: Royal College of General Practitioners, 1988; Irish College of General Practitioners, 1990. Address: 19 Cregan Avenue, Kileely, Limerick, Ireland. E-mail: rocthedoc@eircom.net

O'CONNOR Sinead, b. 8 December 1966, Dublin, Ireland. Singer. m. (1) John Reynolds, divorced, 1 child, (2) Nicholas Sommerlad, 2002, 1 child with Frank Bonadio, (3) Steve Cooney, 2010, divorced 2011, (4) Barry Herridge, 2011. Education: Dublin College of Music. Appointments: Band Member, Ton Ton Macoute, 1985-87. Creative Works: Singles include: Heroin, 1986; Mandinka, 1987; Jump in the River, 1988; Nothing Compares 2 U, 1990; Three Babies, 1990; You Do Something to Me, 1990; Silent Night, 1991; My Special Child, 1991; Visions of You (with Jan Wobble's Invaders of the Heart), 1992; Emperor's New Clothes, 1992; Secret Love, 1992; Success Has Made a Failure of Our Home, 1992; No Man's Woman, 2000; Jealous, 2000; Guide Me God, 2003; I Don't Know How To Love Him, 2007.Albums include: The Lion and the Cobra, 1987; I Do Not Want What I Haven't Got, 1990; Am I Not Your Girl?, 1992; Universal Mother, 1994; Gospeloak, 1997; Sean-Nós Nua, 2002; She Who Dwells in the Secret Place of the Most High Shall Abide Under the Shadow of the Almighty, 2003; Collaborations, 2005; Throw Down Your Arms, 2005; Theology, 2007; How About I Be Me (And You Be You)? 2012. Video films: Value of Ignorance, 1989; The Year of the Horse, 1991; TV film: Hush-a-Bye-Baby. Honours include: MTV Best Video, Best Single Awards, 1990; Grammy Award, Best Alternative Album, 1991; World Soundtrack Award, 2012. Address: c/o Principle Management, 30-32 Sir John Rogerson Quay, Dublin 2, Ireland.

ODELL Robin Ian, b. 19 December 1935, Totton, Hampshire, England. Writer. m. Joan Bartholomew, 1959. Publications: Jack the Ripper in Fact and Fiction, 1965; Exhumation of a Murder, 1975; Jack the Ripper: Summing-up and Verdict (with Colin Wilson), 1977; The Murderers' Who's Who (with J H H Gaute), 1979; Lady Killers, 1980; Murder Whatdunit, 1982; Murder Whereabouts, 1986; Dad Help Me Please (with Christopher Berry-Dee), 1990; A Question of Evidence, 1992; Lady Killer, 1992; The Long Drop, 1993; Landmarks in Twentieth Century Murder, 1995; The International Murderer's Who's Who, 1996; Ripperology, 2006; Murderers' Row (with Wilfred Gregg), 2006; Written & Red, 2009; Bizarre Crimes, 2010. Contributions to: Crimes and Punishment; The Criminologist. Honours: FCC Watts Memorial Prize, 1957; International Humanist and Ethical Union, 1960; Edgar Award, Mystery Writers of America, 1980 and 2007; Gold Medal, IP Book Awards, 2007. Memberships: Our Society; Police History Society. Address: 11 Red House Drive, Sonning Common, Reading RG4 9NT, England.

O'DONNELL Augustine Thomas (Gus), b. 1 October 1952, London, England. Economist. m. Melanie, 1 daughter. Education: BA, First Class, Economics, University of Warwick, 1973; M Phil, Nuffield College Oxford, 1975. Appointments: Lecturer, Department of Political Economy, University of Glasgow, 1975-79; Economist, H M Treasury, 1979-85; First Secretary, British Embassy, Washington DC, USA, 1985-88; Senior Economic Advisor, H M Treasury, 1988-89; Press Secretary to the Chancellor of the Exchequer (Nigel Lawson then John Major), 1989-90; Press Secretary to the Prime Minister, 1990-94; Deputy Director, H M Treasury, UK Representative to the EU Monetary Committee, 1994-97; UK Executive Director to the International Monetary Fund and the World Bank, Minister (Economic), British Embassy, Washington DC, 1997-98; Head of the Government Economic Service with professional responsibility for 730 economists, 1998-2003; Director, 1998-99, Managing Director, 1999-2002, H M Treasury, Macroeconomic Policy and Prospects; Permanent Secretary to H M Treasury, 2002-2005; Cabinet Secretary Head of the Home Civil Service, 2005-. Publications: Adding It Up (PIU report), 2000; Reforming Britain's Economic and Financial Policy (co-editor), 2002; UK Policy Coordination: The Importance of Institutional Design, 2002; Microeconomic Reform in Britain (co-editor), 2004. Honours: Honorary Fellow, Nuffield College, Oxford; Honorary Degrees: Warwick University, Glasgow University. Memberships: Chairman, Treasury Gym Club; Member of World Economics International Advisory Board. Address: H M Treasury, 1 Horse Guards Road, London SW1A 2HQ, England.

O'DONNELL Chris, b. 26 June 1970, Winnetka, Illinois, USA. Actor. m. Caroline Fentress, 1997, 3 sons, 2 daughters. Creative Works: Films include: Men Don't Leave, 1990; Fried Green Tomatoes, 1991; Scent of a Woman, 1992; School Ties, 1992; The Three Musketeers, 1993; Blue Sky, 1994; Circle of Friends, 1995; Mad Love, 1995; Batman Forever, 1995; The Chamber, In Love and War, Batman and Robin, Cookie's Fortune, 1998; The Bachelor, 1998; Vertical Limit, 2000; 29 Palms, 2002; Kinsey, 2004; The Sisters, 2005; Kit Kittredge: An American Girl, 2008; Max Payne, 2008. TV includes: Head Cases, 2005; Grey's Anatomy, 2006; The Company, 2007; Navy NCIS, 2009; NCIS: Los Angeles, 2009-2010. Address: c/o Kevin Huvane, CAA, 9830 Wilshire Boulevard, Beverly Hills, CA 90212, USA.

O'DONOGHUE (James) Bernard, b. 14 December 1945, Cullen, County Cork, Ireland. University Teacher of English; Poet. m. Heather MacKinnon, 1977, 1 son, 2 daughters. Education: MA in English, 1968, BPhil in Medieval English, 1971, Lincoln College, Oxford. Appointments: Lecturer and Tutor in English, Magdalen College, Oxford, 1971-95; Fellow and University Lecturer in English Wadham College, Oxford, 1995-. Publications: The Courtly Love Tradition, 1982; Razorblades and Pencils, 1984; Poaching Rights, 1987; The Weakness, 1991; Seamus Heaney & the Language of Poetry, 1994; Gunpowder, 1995; Here Nor There, 1999; Outliving, 2003; A Stay in a Sanatorium and Other Poetry, 2005; Sir Gawain and the Green Knight, 2006; Selected Poems, 2008. Contributions to: Norton Anthology of Poetry; Poetry Ireland Review; Poetry Review; Times Literary Supplement. Honours: Southern Arts Literature Prize, 1991; Whitbread Poetry Award, 1995. Memberships: Poetry Society, London, 1984-; Fellow, Royal Society of Literature, 1999; Fellow, English Society, 1999; Association of University Teachers. Address: Wadham College, Oxford OX1 3PN, England.

O'DONOGHUE Rodney (Rod) Charles, b. 10 June 1938, Woodford, Essex, England. Retired Director; Historian; Writer. m. Kay Patricia Lewis, 2 sons, 1 daughter. Education: Merchant Taylor's School, 1951-56; Fellow of the Institute of Chartered Accountants. Appointments: Accounting Profession, 1956-63; To Finance and Administration Director, Kimberly-Clark Ltd, 1963-72; To Group Controller, Rank Xerox Group, 1972-83; Group Finance Director (Finance and IT), Pritchard Services Group plc, 1983-86; Main Board and Group Finance Director (Finance and IT), 1986-97, Main Board Director, 1997-1998, Inchcape plc; Retired 1998; Historian, Genealogist and Writer, Founder of The O'Donoghue Society, 1998-; Founder, The O'Donoghue Society and The Irish Folklore Centre. Publications: The O'Donoghue Trail, 1990-95; O'Donoghue People and Places, 1999; Quarterly Journal for the O'Donoghue Society, 2000-; Heroic Landscapes: Irish Myth & Legend, 2011; 1 book in progress. Memberships: Society of Genealogists; Irish Genealogical Research Society; Guild of One Name Studies; Highgate Golf Club; The National Trust; English Heritage; RSPB; The Arts Club; Blacks Club. Address: 30 Canonbury Park South, London N1 2FN, England. E-mail: rod@odonoghue.co.uk Website: www.odonoghue.co.uk

OEIJORD Nils Kornelius, b. 10 May 1947, Mo I Rana, Norway. Researcher; Science Writer. m. Hanne Nystad, 1 son, 2 daughters. Education: Cand agric, Agricultural University of Norway, 1973; Mathematics, University of Trondheim; Mathematics, University of Tromso. Appointments: Researcher, Plant Production, 1973-76; High School Teacher, 1978-2009; Assistant College Professor, 1998-2000; Researcher, General Genetic Castastrophe, Science Writer, 1999-. Publications: Agricultural Science papers; Books on Waldsterben, general genetic castastrophe, derailed evolution, evolutionary psychology and mathematics. Honours: Discoverer of general genetic castastrophe due to manmade local and global mutagenic pollution; Listed in international biographical dictionaries. Memberships: Founder of several groups on the internet; Founder, International Association for DNA Protection. Address: Styrmannsveien 62, 9014 Tromso, Norway. E-mail: n-oeij@online.no

OESER Hans-Christian, b. 12 June 1950, Wiesbaden, Germany. Literary Translator; Travel Book Author; Editor. m. Barbara Proctor, 1 son, 1 daughter. Education: German, Politics, Philosophy and Pedagogy, Marburg and Berlin (West), Germany, 1971-77; First State Examination, 1978; Second State Examination, 1980; MA, 1980; ITI Diploma in Translation, 1989. Appointments: Lecturer in German, University College, Dublin, 1980-83; Lecturer in German, National Institute for Higher Education (now Dublin City University), 1983-84; Teacher, Goethe Institute, Dublin, 1984-2000. Publications: Irland (with M Schmidt), 1989; Dublin, Stadt und Kultur (with J Schneider and R Sotscheck), 1992; Treffpunkt Irland. Ein literarischer Reiseführer, 1996; Irland (with E Wrba and R Sotscheck), 1998; Oscar-Wilde-ABC, 2004; Dublin. Ein Reisebegleiter, 2005; James Joyce (with J Schneider), 2007. Editor of anthologies, almanacs and foreign language editions; Translator of non-fiction, fiction and poetry titles by numerous authors; Author of many essays, articles, reviews and translations in newspapers, journals, anthologies, encyclopaedias and websites. Honours: European Translation Prize Aristeion, 1997; Honorary Membership for Life of the Irish Translators' and Interpreters' Association, 2003; Rowohlt Prize, 2010. Memberships: Society for Exile Studies; Founder Member, Treasurer, 1986-89, Honorary Secretary, 1989-98, Editor of Translation Ireland, 1995-99, Irish Translators' and Interpreters' Association; Secretary, 2009-, PEN Centre of German Speaking Writers Abroad; PEN Centre Germany; Irish Writers' Union; Member, Board of Directors, Ireland Literature Exchange, 1995-99. Address: 114 Ballinclea Heights, Killiney, Co Dublin, Ireland. E-mail: hcoeser@eircom.net Website: www.hanschristianoeser.com

O'FERRALL Patrick Charles Kenneth, b. 27 May 1934, Wrecclesham, Surrey, England. Clerk in Holy Orders (Non-Stipendiary). m. (1) Mary Dorothea Lugard, deceased, 1 son, 2 daughters, (2) Wendy Elizabeth Barnett. Education: MA, New College, Oxford, 1954-58; Advanced Management Program, Harvard Business School, USA, 1983. Appointments: Various positions, Iraq Petroleum Group, 1958-70; BP Area Co-ordinator for Abu Dhabi Marine Areas Ltd and BP Eastern Agencies, 1971-73; Total CFP, Paris, 1974-77; Commercial Manager, 1977-82, Alwyn North Co-ordination Manager, 1983-85, Projects Co-ordination Manager, 1985-90, Total Oil Marine, London; Director, Total Oil Marine (Engineering Construction) Ltd, 1983-89; Deputy Chairman, 1991-93, Chairman, 1993-99, Lloyd's Register of Shipping; Member, Offshore Industry Advisory Board, 1991-94; Lay Reader, Church of England, 1961-2000; Ordained, Deacon, 2000, Priest, 2001; Curate, Saints Peter and Paul, Godalming, 2000-01. Honours: Longstaff Exhibition, New College, Oxford; Fellow, Royal Society of Arts; Honorary Fellow, Royal Academy of Engineering; Companion, Chartered Management Institute. memberships: Past master, Worshipful Company of Coachmakers and Coach Harness Makers, 1993-94; Liveryman, Worshipful Company of Shipwrights; Member of Court of Common Council, City of London, 1996-2001; Chairman, City Branch Outward Bound Association, 1993-97; President Aldgate Ward Club, 1998, currently Honorary Chaplain; Retired Member of Baltic Exchange, currently Honorary Chaplain. Address: Catteshall Grange, Catteshall Road, Godalming, Surrey GU7 1LZ, England. E-mail: patrick@oferrall.co.uk

OFFER Clifford Jocelyn, b. 10 August 1943, Ightham, Kent, England. Retired. m. Catherine, 2 daughters. Education: St Peter's College, Oxford (sent down); BA, Exeter University; Westcott House, Cambridge. Appointments: Curate, Bromley Parish Church, 1969-74; Team Vicar, Southampton (City Centre), 1974-83; Team Rector of Hitchin, 1983-94; Archdeacon of Norwich and Canon, Librarian, Norwich Cathedral, 1994-2008; Bishops Adviser, 1994-. Publications: King Offa in Hitchin, 1992; In Search of Clofesho, 2002. Membership: FRSA.

OGATA Shijuro, b. 16 November 1927, Tokyo, Japan. Retired Central Banker. m. Sadako Nakamura, 1 son, 1 daughter. Education: BA, University of Tokyo, 1950; MA, Fletcher School of Law and Diplomacy, 1955. Appointments: Deputy Governor for International Relations, Bank of Jordan, 1984-86; Deputy Governor, Japan Development Bank, 1986-91; Non-Executive Director, Barclays Bank plc, 1991-95; Non-Executive Director, Fuji Xerox Co Ltd, 1991-2001 (among others). Publications: Co-author, International Financial Integration – The Policy Challenges, 1989; Yen and Bank of Japan, 1996; Showa Years in Distant Past, 2005. Honours: Japan Society Award, 1992; CBE, 2002; Fletcher Class of 1947 Distinguished Leadership Award, 2005. Memberships: Group of Thirty. Address: 3-29-18 Denenchofu, Ota-ku, Tokyo 145-0071, Japan. E-mail: ogata40@nifty.com

OGAWA Tomoya, b. 19 March 1939, Tokyo, Japan. Director. m. Sachiko Ogita, 1 son, 1 daughter. Education: BS, Agricultural Chemistry, 1962, PhD, Organic Chemistry, 1967, University of Tokyo; Postdoctoral, Carbohydrate Chemistry, University of Montreal, USA, 1972-74. Appointments: Assistant, University of Tokyo, 1967-68, Councilor, 1997-98, Professor, Cellular Biochemistry, Graduate School of Applied Animal Resource Science and Veterinary Medical Science, 1990-98, Professor Emeritus, 1999-, University of Tokyo; Research Associate, University of Montreal, 1972-74; Scientist, Laboratory of Pesticide Synthesis II, 1968-79, Head, Synthetic Cellular Chemistry, 1979-98, RIKEN Institute; Executive Director, 1998-2001, Vice President, 2001-04, Executive Director, 2004-05, RIKEN; Director, RIKEN Yokohama Institute, 2001-10; Director, RIKEN Wako Institute, 2010-. Honours: Society of Agricultural and Biological Chemistry Award, Japan, 1978; Fellow, Royal Society of Chemistry, 1981; Japanese Minister of Science and Technology Agency Award, 1982; Okochi Prize, Japan, 1984; International Carbohydrate Award, Whistlers Award, 1984; Upjohn Fellowship Award for Scientific Research, 1988; Senior Alexander von Humboldt Research Award, Germany, 1991; Haworth Memorial Medal, Royal Society of Chemistry, 1993; Japan Society for Bioscience, Biotechnology and Agrochemistry Award, Japan, 1995; C S Hudson Award, American Chemical Society, 1995; Japan Academy Award,

Japan, 1995; Science Spot Light Award, American Chemical Society, 2003. Address: 5-16-13 Mejiro, Toshima-ku, Tokyo 171-0031, Japan.

OGIHARA Shigeki, b. 23 January 1955, Tokyo, Japan. Dentist. m. Naoyo. Education: DDS degree, Nihon University School of Dentistry, 1979; Phd, Physiology, Nihon University School of Medicine, 1989. Appointments: Private Practice, Ogihara Dental Clinic, 1981-. Publications: Numerous articles in professional journals. Memberships: American Academy of Peridontology; Academy of Osseointegration; Global Academy for Biologic Dentistry. Address: 7-16 Adachi 3 Chome, Adachi-ku, Tokyo 1200015, Japan.

O'GRADY Barbara Ann Vinson, b. 6 July 1928, Alhambra, California, USA. Public Health Nurse. m. Joseph Putnam O'Grady, 3 sons, 2 daughters. Education: Diploma in Nursing, Los Angeles County General Hospital, 1945-48; Baccalaureate in Science (major in Public Health Nursing), UCLA, 1948-51; Masters in Science (major in Public Health Nursing), University of Minnesota, 1970-72. Appointments: Staff Nurse, Los Angeles County General Hospital; Private Duty Nurse, Scripps Hospital; Staff Nurse, University of Minnesota Hospital, periodically between 1951-70; Assistant Professor in Nursing, Gustavus Adolphus College, St Peter, Minnesota, 1972-77; Appointed Director of Ramsey County Public Health Nursing Service, St Paul, Minnesota, 1977-88. Publications: The Collection of Baseline Data for Evaluating Patient Care, 1982. Honours: Innovative State and Local Government Initiatives, Ford Foundation, 1981; Outstanding Achievement Award, Board of Ramsey County Commissioners, 1987; Community Service Award, Minnesota Public Health Association, 1988. Memberships: American Academy of Nursing; American Nurses Association; Women's Environmental Watch; Valley Community Mentoring. Address: 3955 Edgehill Lane, PO Box 624, Santa Ynez, CA 93460, USA. E-mail: barbandjohn624@gmail.com

OGRAM Geoffrey Reginald, b. 14 October 1937, Ealing, England. Retired College Principal Lecturer. m. Margaret Mary, 3 daughters. Education: BSc (Hons) Industrial Metallurgy, 1958, PhD, 1961, University of Birmingham. Appointments: Research Fellow, University of Birmingham, 1960-62; Research Metallurgist, GKN Group Research Centre, Wolverhampton, 1962-65; Lecturer, Senior Lecturer, Principal Lecturer in Metallurgy, Sandwell College, West Midlands, 1965-95. Publications: Articles in scientific journals: Effect of Alloying Additions in Steel, 1965; Directionality of Yield Point in Strain-aged Steel, 1967; Magical Images – A Handbook of Stereo Photography (author's publication); The Music of Gordon Jacob (in preparation). Memberships: British Magical Society; Catenian Association (Stafford Circle); Stereoscopic Society; Governor St Anne's Roman Catholic Primary School, Stafford; Organist, St Anne's Roman Catholic Church, Stafford; Stafford Recorded Music Society. Listed in Catholic Directory. Address: 6 Silverthorn Way, Wildwood, Stafford ST17 4PZ, England. E-mail: geoff.ogram@talktalk.net

OH Jong-Taek, b. 28 December 1957, Pusan, South Korea. Professor. m. Ok-Nam Kim, 1 son, 1 daughter. Education: BS, 1985, MD, 1987, PhD, 1992, Pukyong National University. Appointments: Professor, Chonnam National University, 1989-; Postdoctoral, University of Tokyo, Japan, 1994-95; Editorial Director, KAR, 1995-2006; Visiting Professor, University of Tokyo, Japan, 1998; Member, National Technical Roadmap Committee, 2002-; Visiting Research, University of Illinois at Urbana-Champaign, USA, 2004-06; DI (Refrigerated Storage) Commission of IIR, 2006-; General Director, SAREK, 2007-08; President of Low Temperature Facilities Engineering Division, SAREK, 2009-. Publications: 210 articles in professional journals; Pressure drop and heat transfer during two-phase flow vaporization of propane in horizontal smooth minichannels, 2009. Honours: Best of Award in R&D, Ministry of Maritime Affairs and Fisheries, Korea, 1999; Service Certificate of Commendation, Korean Committee of International Vocational Training Competition, 2008; Person of Merit in Research and Development of Heating, Air-Conditioning, Refrigeration and Fluid Industry in Korea, 2011; Listed in international biographical dictionaries, Who's Who in the World, 2010-11; Top 100 Engineers, IBC, 2010; ABI, 2010. Memberships: International Institute of Refrigeration; KSME; SAREK; JSRAE; JSME; KAR; KACCR. Address: Department of Refrigeration and Air-Conditioning Engineering, Chonnam National University, San 96-1, Dunduk-dong, Yeosu, Chonnam 550-749, South Korea. E-mail: ohjt@chonnam.ac.kr

OH Jutaek, b. 4 September 1969, Seoul, Korea. Professor. m. Sang Young Jang, 1 son, 1 daughter. Education: BS, Hanyang University, 1995; MCRP, Rutgers, The State University of New Jersey, 1998; PhD, Georgia Institute of Technology, 2002. Appointments: Research Associate, University of Arizona, 2002-03; Research Fellow, Korea Transport Institute, 2003-11; Professor, Chungju National University, 2011-. Publications: Numerous articles in professional journals. Honours: Award, Korean Minister of Construction and Transportation, 2006. Memberships: Korean Society of Civil Engineers; Korean Society of Transportation Engineers; Korean ITS; American Society of Civil Engineers. Address: Department of Urban Engineering, Chungju National University, 50 Daehakro, Chungju, 380-702, Korea. E-mail: jutaek@cjnu.ac.kr

OH Kye-Heon, b. 4 September 1956, Seoul, Republic of Korea. Professor. m. Jungwon Hahn, 1 son. Education: BS, Biology, 1980, MS, Microbiology, 1986, Korea University; PhD, Microbiology, Ohio State University, 1991. Appointments: GRA/GTA, Ohio State University, 1986-91; Postdoctorate, Purdue University, 1991; Postdoctorate, University of Wales, Bangor, 1996-97; Research Fellow, University of California, Riverside, 2006-07; Professor, Soonchunhyong University, 2009-; Editor in Chief, Korean Journal of Microbiology, 2010-11. Publications: 48 papers including: Antimicrobial activity and biofilm formation inhibition of green tea polyphenols on human teeth, 2010; Synergistic anti-bacterial proteomic effects of epigallocatechin gallate on clinical isolates of imipenem-resistant Klebsiella pneumoniae, 2011. Honours: British Chevening Scholarship, 1996-97; Excellent Researcher, Soonchunhyong University, 2009. Memberships: American Society for Microbiology; Microbiological Society of Korea. Address: Department of Biotechnology, Soonchunhyong University, 646 Eupnae-ri, Shinchang-myon, Asan-si, Chung-Nam, 336-745, Republic of Korea. E-mail: homecoming.oh@gmail.com

OHLSSON Bertil Gullith, b. 24 July 1954, Malmö, Sweden. Scientist. Education: BS, Biology and Chemistry, 1979, PhD 1987, University of Lund, Sweden; Postdoctoral Fellow, Rockefeller University, New York, New York, 1987-90. Appointments: Assistant Professor, Department of Molecular Biology, University of Gothenburg, Sweden, 1991-92; Associate Professor, 1993-96, Research Associate, 1997-2004, Associate Professor, 2004-, Wallenberg Laboratory, Sahlgren's University Hospital, Göteborg, Sweden; Research Co-ordinator, University of Gothenburg,

Göteborg, Sweden, 2005-; Research Adviser, University of Gothenburg, Göteborg, Sweden, 2010-. Publication: Article in Journal of Clinical Investigation, 1996. Address: Research and Innovation Services, External Relations, University of Gothenburg, Box 100, SE 405 30 Göteborg, Sweden. E-mail: bertil.ohlsson@gu.se

OHNISHI Shun-ichi, b. 9 January 1930, Osaka, Japan. Professor Emeritus. m. Yoko Kajiki, 2 sons, 1 daughter. Education: Bachelor of Science, 1956, Dr of Science, 1961, Osaka University. Appointments: Research Scientist, Japanese Association for Radiation Research on Polymers, Osaka, 1957-63; Associate Professor, 1963-68, Professor, 1968-93, Professor Emeritus, 1993-, Kyoto University; Visiting Researcher, Stanford University, USA, 1964-66; President, Biophysical Society of Japan, 1988-89; Professor, Ryukoku University, 1993-98. Publication: The Dynamic Structure of Biological Membranes, 1993. Honours: Award for Young Chemist, The Chemical Society of Japan, 1964; Award for Promotion of Science, The Naito Foundation of Science, 1966. Memberships: The Biophysical Society of Japan, Emeritus. Address: 2-6-123 Myojyo-cho, Uji, Kyoto 611-0014, Japan.

OISO Naoki, b. 31 May 1968, Hyogo, Japan. Dermatology. m. Hisako, 1 son, 1 daughter. Education: Student, Osaka City University School of Medicine, Osaka, Japan, 1988; Graduate Student, Osaka City University Graduate School of Medicine, 1997; Postdoctoral Fellow, Human Medical Genetics Program, University of Colorado Health Sciences Center, USA, 2001. Appointments: Resident, Department of Dermatology, Osaka City University School of Medicine, Osaka, 1994; Assistant Chief Doctor, Department of Dermatology, Saiseikai Tondabayashi Hospital, Osaka, 2003; Assistant Professor, Department of Dermatology, Kinki University Faculty of Medicine, 2005. Publications: Numerous articles in professional journals. Honours: Kinki University Prize, 2006, 2007, 2010, 2011; Encouragement Prize, Japanese Society for Pigment Cell Research, 2010. Memberships: American Society of Human Genetics; Japanese Dermatological Association. Address: Department of Dermatology, Kinki University Faculty of Medicine, 377-2 Ohno-Higashi, Osaka-Sayama, Osaka 589-8511, Japan. E-mail: naoiso@med.kindai.ac.jp

OJHA Ek Raj, b. 23 September 1957, Mauwa, Dotee, Nepal. Education: BSc, Agriculture, University of Agricultural Sciences, 1984; BA, English, Tribhuvan University, Kathmandu, 1985; MSc, 1990, PhD, 1995, Rural and Regional Development Planning, Asian Institute of Technology. Appointments: Assistant Agriculture Officer, Department of Agriculture, Kathmandu, 1985-86; Agriculture Officer, Central Bank of Nepal, Kathmandu, 1986-90; Research Associate, 1991-95, Resource Person (Socio-economic Research), 1993, Asian Institute of Technology (AIT), Bangkok; United Nations Researcher, United Nations Centre for Regional Development (UNCRD), Japan, 1995-97; Senior Instructor, Banker's Training Centre, 1998-2000, Research Officer, Research Department, 2000, Central Bank of Nepal; Development Economist, United States Agency for International Development (USAID), Kathmandu, 2000; Visiting Scholar, Indiana University, USA, 2001; Associate Professor (and Associate Director, Human and Natural Resources Studies Centre), Environmental Economics and Entrepreneurship courses, Kathmandu University, 2000-02; Faculty Member, Sustainable Rural Development, 2003-07, Agriculture and Rural Development, 2007, Tribhuvan University; Contract Faculty, Human Dimensions of Development course, Kathmandu University, 2004; Visiting Faculty, Economic Development, 2004-09; Nepalese Economy, Kathmandu College of Management (KCM), 2007-09; Rural Development, and Rural Development and Conservation courses, 2006-08, Institute of Forestry, Pokhara; Sustainable Rural Development, Padma Kanya Campus, 2005-06; Natural and Human Resources Management, and Rural Resources, Environment and Management courses, Classic College International (CCI), 2006-07; Founder Chairman and Director, Centre for Rural Research and Development (CERRED), 2006-; Sustainable Rural Development, K & K College, 2007-; Economics Faculty Head and Extended Essay Co-ordinator, International Baccalaureate Diploma Programme (IBDP), Ullens School, Lalitpur, Nepal, 2009-. Publications: Co-author: 1 monograph; 1 working paper; 3 institutional reports; Author: 4 books; Numerous articles in professional journals. Memberships: World Futures Studies Federation; Aaroyga Aashram; Kirateshwar Sangeetashram. Address: GPO Box 13313, Kathmandu, Nepal. E-mail: erojha@hotmail.com

O'KANE Stephen Granville, b. 26 April 1951, Harrow, Middlesex, England. Writer; Researcher. Education: BA, Politics, History (subsidiary), University of Nottingham, England, 1970-73; MA, Political Thought, University of Keele, England, 1973-75; PhD, Christianity and Socialism in British thought, University of London, London School of Economics, 1975-79; Numerous computer courses, 1978-98; Business Enterprise Programme and Extended Business Training, 1989-91. Career: Owing to difficult health (asthma and ME/CFS) became researcher and writer rather than pursue an institutional career; Writings and research on the confluence between ethical and political issues and the implications of that for ethics itself, 1979-; Research into political affairs in individual members of the European Union, 1988-; Part-time Adult Education Teacher, Clerical and Market Research work, 1980-81, 1984-86, 1993; Set up own website (http://www.o-kane.f2s.com); Member of Assert, charity working for people with Aspergers Syndrome, 2003-. Publications: Books: Politics and Morality under Conflict, 1994; Ethics and Radical Freedom, 2006; Essays on website: Freedom and Thematic Decentralisation; The Spider and the Fly; Moral Judgement: True or Wise?; The Independence of Consciousness; The Fantasy of Western Liberal Assumptions; Freedom, Free Will, and Technology; Authority and Truth; "Speakers Corner" on website includes a philosophical dialogue entitled "Rachel: A Dialogue"; Several articles for The Radical Quarterly, 1987-90; 2 articles in FSI News/ Business News (Sussex), 1989, 1990; Article, What Right to Private Property? In Economy and Society, 1997; Paper: Ethical Systems and Expansion in Information Circulation, 2003. Memberships: British Society for Ethical Theory. Address: Flat 25, Homedrive House, 95-97 The Drive, Hove, East Sussex, BN3 6GE, England. E-mail: gs@o-kane.f2s.com Website: www.o-kane.f2s.com

OKAWARA Yoshio, b. 5 February 1919, Japan. Former Diplomat. m. Mitsuko Terashima, 1 son. Education: BA, Law Faculty, Tokyo Imperial University, 1942; Honorary Doctor of Law, Williams College, USA. Appointments: Director, American Affairs Bureau, 1972, Deputy Vice Minister for Administration, 1974, Ministry of Foreign Affairs; Ambassador to Australia, 1976; Ambassador to the US, 1980. Publications: To Avoid Isolation, 1985; Oral History: Japan/ US Diplomacy, 2006. Honours: First Class Order of Sacred Heart. Memberships: Tokyo Club; IISS, London. Address: 1-22-20 Seito, Setagaya-ku, Tokyo.

OKOH Anthony Ekle Joseph, b. 25 August 1945, Okpoga, Benue State, Nigeria. Veterinarian. m. Mary Lovina, 4 sons, 3 daughters. Education: DVM, 1971, Doctor of Philosophy, Veterinary Pathology & Microbiology, 1986, Ahmadu Bello University, Zaria; Master, Preventive Veterinary Medicine, University of California, Davis, 1977. Publications: Over 40 articles in professional journals; 3 books and monographs; Numerous conference, seminar and workshop papers. Honours: Listed in international biographical dictionaries; Member, National Advisory Committee on Control and Prevention of Rabies; Oyalobu of Aiatta of Okpoga, 2005; Gold Medal for Nigeria, 2007; World Medal of Freedom, 2007; Man of the Year, 2007; Outstanding African Achievers Gold Award, 2007. Memberships: Nigeria Veterinary Medical Association; Fellow, College of Veterinary Surgeons, Nigeria; Member, Nigerian Society of Animal Production. Address: PO Box 579, Makurdi, Benue State, Nigeria. E-mail: profokohanton@yahoo.co.uk

OKPARA Godwin Chigozie, b. 18 May 1958, Obinaulo Ngodo Isuochi, Nigeria. Senior Lecturer. m. Ugomma Flicia, 2 sons, 3 daughters. Education: NCE, Economics/Maths,. 1983; BSc, Economics, 1987; MSc, Economics, 1988; MSc, Financial Management, 2006; PhD, Finance and Banking, 2011. Appointments: Lecturing & Research, 1989-; Member, University Consultancy Committee, 1993-94; Co-ordinator, School of Economics, Banking and Finance, 1999-2001; Head, Department of Economics, 2005-07. Publications: 6 books in Finance and Economics; 35 international journal articles; 12 local journal articles; 8 book chapters; Many monographs. Honours: Listed in biographical dictionaries; Professional Excellence International Award, Institute of Global Resource Management; Fellow, Strategic Institute for Natural Resources and Human Development, INRHD. Memberships: University Senate, 1999-2007; University Consultant Committee, 1993-94; Academic Staff Union, 1989-; Editorial Board, Journal of Dist; NJEFR. Address: Department of Banking and Finance, Abia State University, PMB 2000 Uturu, Nigeria. E-mail: chigoziegodwin@yahoo.com

OKRI Ben, b. 15 March 1959, Minna, Nigeria. British Author; Poet. Education: Urhobo College, Warri, Nigeria; University of Essex, Colchester. Appointments: Broadcaster and Presenter, BBC, 1983-85; Poetry Editor, West Africa, 1983-86; Fellow Commoner in Creative Arts, Trinity College, Cambridge, 1991-93. Publications: Flowers and Shadows, 1980; The Landscapes Within, 1982; Incidents at the Shrine, 1986; Stars of the New Curfew, 1988; The Famished Road, 1991; An African Elegy, 1992; Songs of Enchantment, 1993; Astonishing the Gods, 1995; Birds of Heaven, 1995; Dangerous Love, 1996; A Way of Being Free, 1997; Infinite Riches, 1998; Mental Fight, 1999; In Exilus (play), 2001; In Arcadia, 2002; Starbook Rider, 2007. Contributions to: Many newspapers and journals. Honours: Commonwealth Prize for Africa, 1987; Paris Review/Aga Khan Prize for Fiction, 1987; Booker Prize, 1991; Premio Letterario Internazionale Chianti-Ruffino-Antico-Fattore, 1993; Premio Grinzane Cavour, 1994; Crystal Award, 1995; FRSL, 1997; Honorary DLitt: Westminster, 1997, Essex, 2002, Exeter, 2004; OBE, 2000; Premio Palmi, 2000; FRSA, 2004. Memberships: Society of Authors; Council, Royal Society of Literature, 1999-2004; Vice-president, English Centre, International PEN, 1997-; Board, Royal National Theatre of Great Britain, 1999-. Address: c/o Vintage, Random House, 20 Vauxhall Bridge Road, London SW1 2SA, England.

OLAZABAL Jose Maria, b. 5 February 1966, Spain. Professional Golfer. Career: Member, European Ryder Cup team, 1987, 1989, 1991, 1993, 1997, Kirin Cup Team, 1987, Four Tours World Championship Team, 1989, 1990, World Cup Team, 1989, Dunhill Cup Team, 1986, 1987, 1988, 1989, 1992; Winner, Italian Amateur Award, 1983, Spanish Amateur Award, 1983, European Masters-Swiss Open, 1986, Belgian Open, 1988, German Masters, 1988, Tenerife Open, 1989, Dutch Open, 1989, Benson & Hedges International, 1990, Irish Open, 1990, Lancome Trophy, 1990, Visa Talhoyo Club Masters, 1990, California Open, 1991, Turespana Open de Tenerife, 1992, Open Mediterrania, 1992, US Masters, 1994, 1999, Dubai Desert Classic, 1998; Benson & Hedges International Open 2000, French Open, 2001, Buick Invitational, 2002; Omega Hong Kong Open, 2002; Mallorca Classic, 2005. Tour victories include: NEC World Series of Golf, 1990; The International, 1991; US Masters, 1994, 1999; Dubai Desert Classic, 1998; Golf course designer. Address: PGA Avenue of Champions, Palm Beach Gdns, FL 33418, USA. Website: www.aboutgolf.com/jmo

OLDFIELD Bruce, b. 14 July 1950, England. Fashion Designer. Education: Sheffield City Polytechnic; Ravensbourne College of Art; St Martin's College of Art. Appointments: Founder, Fashion House, Producing Designer Collections, 1975; Couture Clothes for Individual Clients, 1981; Opened Retail Shop, Couture & Ready-to-Wear, 1984; Managing Board, British Knitting & Clothing Export Council, 1989; Designed for films, Jackpot, 1974; The Sentinel, 1976; Vice-President, Barnardo's, 1998; Govenor, London Institute, 1999-; Trustee, Royal Academy, 2000-. Publication: Seasons, 1987. Exhibition: Retrospective, Laing Galleries, Newcastle-upon-Tyne, 2000. Honours: Fellow, Sheffield Polytechnic, 1987; Royal College of Art, 1990; OBE, 1990; Durham University, 1991; Hon DCL (Northumbria), 2001; Hon DUniv (University of Central England), 2005. Publications: Seasons, 1987; Rootless (autobiography), 2004. Address: 27 Beauchamp Place, London SW3, England.

OLDFIELD Richard John, b. 11 October 1955, London, England. Investment Manager. m. (1) Alexandra Davidson, 1982, deceased 1991, 2 sons, 1 daughter, (2) Amicia de Moubray, 1997, 1 son. Education: Eton College; New College Oxford. Appointments: SG Warburg and Mercury Asset Management, 1977-96; Chief Executive, Alta Advisers Ltd, 1996-2005; Chief Executive, Oldfield Partners LLP, 2005-. Publications: Simple But Not Easy, 2007. Memberships: Trustee, Leeds Castle Foundation, 2000-; Chairman, Keystone Investment Trust plc, 2001-; Chairman, Oxford University Endowment Management Ltd and investment committee of Oxford University, 2007-; Trustee, Canterbury Cathedral Trust, 2008-; President, Demelza House Children's Hospice. Address: Oldfield Partners LLP, 130 Buckingham Palace Road, London SW1W 9SA, England. E-mail: rjo@oldfieldpartners.com

OLDMAN Gary, b. 21 March 1958, New Cross, South London, England. Actor. m. (1) Lesley Manville, 1 son, (2) Uma Thurman, 1991, divorced 1992, (3) Donya Fiorentino, divorced, 2 children. Education: Rose Bruford Drama College; Greenwich Young People's Theatre. Career: Theatre: Massacre in Paris; Chincilla; Desparado Corner; A Waste of Time; Minnesota Moon; Summit Conference; Real Dreams; The Desert Air; War Play I, II, III; Serious Money; Women Beware Women; The Pope's Wedding; The Country Wife; Films: Sid and Nancy; Prick Up Your Ears; Track 29; Criminal Law; We Think The World of You; Chattachoochee; State of Grace; Exile; Before and After Death; Rosencrantz and Guildenstern are Dead; JFK; Dracula; True Romance; Romeo is Bleeding; Immortal Beloved; Murder in the First; Dead Presidents; The Scarlet Letter; Basquiat; Nil by Mouth, The Fifth Element, Air Force One, 1997; Lost in Space, 1998; Anasazie Moon, 1999; Hannibal, The Contender, 2000; Nobody's Baby, Hannibal, 2001; Interstate 60, The Hire: Beat the Devil, 2002; Medal of Honor: Allied Assault – Spearhead (voice), Tiptoes, True Crime: Streets of LA (voice), Sin, 2003; Harry Potter and the Prisoner of Azkaban, Dead Fish, 2004; Batman Begins, Harry Potter and the Goblet of Fire, 2005; Bosque de sombras, 2006; Harry Potter and the Order of the Phoenix, 2007; The Dark Knight, 2008; The Unborn, Rain Fall, A Christmas Carol, 2009; The Book of Eli, 2010; Tinker Tailor Soldier Spy, Guns, Girls and Gambling, 2011; The Dark Knight Rises, Lawless, 2012; Paranoia, 2013; TV: Remembrance; Meantime; Honest, Decent and True; Rat in the Skull; The Firm; Heading Home; Fallen Angels. Honours: BAFTA Award, 1997; USA Film Festival, 2001; Scream Awards, 2008; People's Choice Awards, 2009; Empire Awards, 2011; San Francisco Film Critics Circle Award, 2011; Richard Attenborough Regional Film Awards, 2012. Address: c/o Douglas Urbanski, Douglas Management Inc, 515 N Robertson Boulevard, Los Angeles, CA 90048, USA.

OLIVEIRA Carlos A, b. 1 December 1942, Barras-Piauí, Brazil. Medical Doctor. Widowed, 3 daughters. Education: MD, Faculdade Nacional de Medicina, Rio de Janeiro, 1966; Specialist in Otolanyngology, American Board of Otolaryngology, Chicago Illinois, 1979; Doctor of Philosophy, Otolaryngology, University of Minnesota Graduate School, Minneapolis, Minnesota, USA, 1977; Postdoctoral Fellowship, Harvard Medical School, Boston, Massachusetts, USA, 1989. Appointments: Associate Professor, 1977-97, Professor and Chairman, Department of Otolanryngology, 1997-, Brasilia University Medical School, Brasilia, Brazil. Publications: 82 scientific articles published in Brazil; Over 40 international publications. Honours: Physician Recognition Award, American Medical Association, 1977; International Scientist of the Year, IBC. Memberships: Prosper Menière Society; Schuknecht Society, Boston, Massachusetts, USA; Neuroquilibriumetric Society, Bad Kinssingen, Germany; Brazilian Otolaryngology Society; American Otological Society. Address: Avda W-3 Sul Quadra 716, Bloco E, Sala 202, Brasilia DF, Brazil. E-mail: oliv@abordo.com.br

OLIVEIRA João Richardo Mendes de, b. 22 October 1974, Recife, Brazil. Professor; Psychiatrist. m. Mariana de Lacerda Oliveira, 1 daughter. Education: Biological Sciences, University of São Paulo, 1992; Medical School, State University of Pernambuco, 1993 and 1994; Medical Doctor degree, 2000, PhD, 2004, Biological Sciences, Federal University of Pernambuco. Appointments: Post-doctoral Fellow and Teaching Assistant, Psychiatry Department, 2001-02, Post-doctoral Fellow and Teaching Assistant, Department of Neurology, 2002-04, University of California, Los Angeles; Professor, Neuropsychiatry, Federal University of Pernambuco, 2005-; Member, Editorial Board, Journal of Molecular Neuroscience, 2009-; Adviser, National Organization of Rare Disorders, USA, 2009-. Publications: Numerous articles in professional journals. Honours: John Simon Guggenheim Fellowship, 2010. Memberships: Brazilian Genetics Society. Address: Department of Neuropsychiatry, Av Professor Moraes Rego, 1235 – Cidade Universitaria, Recife – PE – CEP 50670-901, Pernambuco, Brazil. E-mail: joao.ricardo@ufpe.br

OLIVER Jamie Trevor, b. 27 May 1975, Essex, England. Chef. m. Juliette Norton, 1 son, 3 daughters. Education: Westminster Catering College. Career: Head Pastry Chef, The Neal Street Restaurant; Chef, River Café, 3 years; Established Fifteen, chain of charity restaurants; TV: The Naked Chef, 1999; Comic Relief: Red Nose Ground Force in Practice, 2001; Pukka Tukka, 2001; Jamie's Kitchen, 2002; The Rise of the Celebrity Class, 2004; Jimmy's Farm, 2004; Jamie's School Dinners, 2005; Comic Relief: Red Nose Night Live 05, 2005; Jamie's Kitchen Australia, 2006. Publications: The Naked Chef; Something for the Weekend; The Return of the Naked Chef; Happy Days with the Naked Chef; The Naked Chef Takes Off; Jamie's Kitchen; Jamie's Dinners; Jamie's Italy; Cook With Jamie; Jamie at Home; Jamie's Ministry of Food; Jamie's Red Nose Recipes; Jamie's America; Jamie does … Spain, Italy, Sweden, Morocco, Greece, France; Jamie's 30-Minute Meals; Jamie's Great Britain; Jamie's 15 Minute Meals. Honours: MBE, 2003; Beacon Fellowship Prize, 2005; 2010 TED Prize.

OLIVER-JONES Stephen, b. 6 July 1947, Birmingham, England. Circuit Judge. m. Anne, 1 son, 1 daughter. Education: Marling School, 1958-65; University College, Durham University, 1965-68. Appointments: Lecturer, 1968-70; Barrister, 1970-96; Queen's Counsel, 1996-2000; President, Mental Health Review Tribunal, 1997-; Designated Civil Judge, West Midlands & Warwickshire, 2001-09; Circuit Judge, 2000-. Honours: Queen's Counsel, 1996. Memberships: Civil Procedure Rules Committee, 2002-08; Bencher, Inner Temple, 2010-.

OLLERENSHAW Kathleen Mary (Dame), b. 1 October 1912, Manchester, England. Mathematician. m. Robert G W Ollerenshaw, deceased, 1 son, 1 daughter both deceased. Education: Open Scholarship, Mathematics, Somerville College, Oxford, 1931-34; Oxford D Phil, Mathematics, 1945. Appointments: Chairman: Association of Governing Bodies of Girls' Public Schools, 1963-69, Manchester Education Committee, 1967-70, Manchester Polytechnic, 1968-72; Elected to Manchester City Council, 1956-81: Alderman, 1970-74, Lord Mayor, 1975-76, Deputy Lord Mayor, 1976-77, Leader of the Conservative Opposition, 1977-79, Honorary Alderman, 1981; Honorary Freeman of the City of Manchester, 1984-; Vice-President, British Association for Commercial and Industrial Education; Member: Central Advisory on Education in England, 1960-63, CNAA, 1964-74, SSCR, 1971-75, Layfield Committee of Enquiry into Local Government Finance, 1974-76; President, St Leonards School, St Andrews, 1976-2003; Deputy Pro Chancellor, University of Lancaster, 1978-91; Pro Chancellor, University of Salford, 1983-89; Director, Manchester Independent Radio Ltd, 1972-83; Deputy Lieutenant, Greater Manchester, 1987-; Honorary Colonel, Manchester and Salford Universities' Officer Training Corps, 1977-81. Publications: Books: Education of Girls, 1958; The Girls Schools, 1967; Returning to Teaching, 1974; The Lord Mayor's Party, 1976; First Citizen, 1977; Most-Perfect Pandiagonal Magic Squares, their Construction and Enumeration (with David Brée), 1998; To Talk of Many Things (autobiography), 2004; Constructing pandiagonal magic squares of arbitrarily large size, 2006; Numerous research papers in mathematical journals, 1940-2004. Honours: Mancunian of the Year, Junior Chamber of Commerce, 1977; DStJ, 1983; Honorary Fellow: Somerville College, Oxford, 1978; Honorary Fellow, City and Guilds, London, 1980; Honorary Fellow, Institute of Mathematics and Its Applications, 1990, Fellow, 1964, Member, Council, 1972-, President, 1979-80; Honorary Fellow, UMIST, 1987; Freeman City of Manchester, 1984-;

Honorary DSc Salford, 1975; Honorary LLD, Manchester, 1976; Honorary DSc, CNAA; Honorary DSc, Lancaster, 1992; Honorary LLD, Liverpool, 1994; Honorary FIMA, 1988; Catherine Richards Prize, Institute of Mathematics and Its Applications, 2006. Memberships: President: Manchester Technological Association, 1981, Manchester Statistical Society, 1983-85; Patron, Museum of Science and Technology, Manchester, 2003-; Vice President, Manchester Astronomical Society, 1998-; Chairman, Council Order of St John, Greater Manchester, 1974-89; Member, Chapter General Order of St John, 1978-96; Chartered Mathematician. Address: 2 Pine Road (side door), Manchester M20 6UY, England.

OLLONGREN Alexander, b. 9 November 1928, Kepamiang, Sumatra. Professor. m. Gunvor, 1 son, 1 daughter. Education: PhD, Dynamical Astronomy, Leiden University, 1962; Postdoctoral Research in Celestial Mechanics, Lecturer in Mathematics, Research Center of Celestial Mechanics, Yale University, USA, 1965-67. Appointments: Associate Director, Computer Centre, 1967-69; Lecturer, Numerical Mathematics and Computer Science, Associate Professor, Theoretical Computer Science, 1969-80, Department of Applied Mathematics, Emeritus Professor, 1993-, Leiden University; Visiting Research Member, IBM Laboratory, Vienna, Austria, 1970; Full Professor, Theoretical Computer Science, Leiden Institute of Advanced Computer Science, 1980-93; Visiting Professor, Department of Computer Science and Artificial Intelligence, Linköping University, Sweden, 1980; Member and Professor, Leiden University Council, University Level Courses for Elderly Citizens, 1995-2005. Publications: Numerous articles in professional journals. Honours: Fulbright Travel Grant, 1965. Memberships: International Astronomical Union; European Astronomical Society; Dutch Astronomical Society; International Astronautical Academy. Address: Cartesiuslaan 31, 2341 AM Oegstgeest, The Netherlands. E-mail: gunvor.ollongren@ziggo.nl

OLSEN Ashley, b. 13 June 1986, Sherman Oaks, California, USA. Actress; Producer; Fashion Model; Fashion Designer. Career: Actress: TV: Full House, 1987-95; The Adventures of Mary-Kate & Ashley; Two of a Kind; Switching Goals, 1999; 7th Heaven, 2000; Film: Our Lips Are Sealed, 2000; New York Minute, 2004; Fashion designer (with Ashley Olsen), pre-teen range for Wal-Mart, The Row, and Elizabeth and James; Chief Executive Office, Dualstar, 2004-. Publications: Influence, 2008. Honours: Best Young Actor/Actress Under 5 Years of Age (with Mary-Kate Olsen), 1989; Outstanding Performance by an Actress Under Nine Years of Age (with Mary-Kate Olsen), 1990; Exceptional Performance by a Young Actress Under Ten (with Mary-Kate Olsen), 1992; Best Youth Actress in a TV Mini-Series (with Mary-Kate Olsen), 1994; Favorite Movie Actress (with Mary-Kate Olsen), 1996; Favorite TV Actress (with Mary-Kate Olsen), 1999; Franchise Performers Award (with Mary-Kate Olsen), 2003; Choice Movie Blush (with Mary-Kate Olsen), 2004; Star on Walk of Fame (with Mary-Kate Olsen), 2004.

OLSEN Mary-Kate, b. 13 June 1986, Sherman Oaks, California, USA. Actress; Producer; Fashion Model; Fashion Designer. Career: Actress: TV: Full House, 1987-95; The Adventures of Mary-Kate & Ashley; Two of a Kind; So Little Time; Weeds; Samantha Who? 2008; Film: New York Minute, 2004; Factory Girl, 2006; The Wackness, 2008; Fashion designer (with Ashley Olsen), pre-teen range for Wal-Mart, The Row, and Elizabeth and James; Chief Executive Office, Dualstar, 2004-. Publications: Influence, 2008. Honours: Best Young Actor/Actress Under 5 Years of Age (with Ashley Olsen), 1989; Outstanding Performance by an Actress Under Nine Years of Age (with Ashley Olsen), 1990; Exceptional Performance by a Young Actress Under Ten (with Ashley Olsen), 1992; Best Youth Actress in a TV Mini-Series (with Ashley Olsen), 1994; Favorite Movie Actress (with Ashley Olsen), 1996; Favorite TV Actress (with Ashley Olsen), 1999; Franchise Performers Award (with Ashley Olsen), 2003; Choice Movie Blush (with Ashley Olsen), 2004; Star on Walk of Fame (with Ashley Olsen), 2004.

OLSZEWSKA Joanna Isabelle, b. 19 October 1978. Electrical Engineer; PhD; Researcher. Education: MSc, Electrical Engineering, Swiss Federal Institute of Technology, Lausanne, 2003; DEA, Computer Vision, Signal and Image Processing, 2007, PhD, 2009, UC Louvain, Belgium. Appointments: Research Engineer, ETH Zurich, Switzerland, 2003-04; Research Engineer, UC Louvain, Belgium, 2005-07; NSF Researcher, UC Louvain, Belgium, 2007-09; Research Fellow, University of Huddersfield, UK, 2010-. Publications: A New Hybrid-Ring Geometry well suited for CAD Implementation, 2004; Speeded-Up Gradient Vector Flow B-Spline Active Contours for Robust and Real-Time Tracking, 2007; Non-Rigid Object Tracker Based on a Robust Combination of Parametric Active Contour and Point Distribution Model, 2007; Multi-Feature Vector Flow for Active Contour Tracking, 2008; Unified Framework for Multi-Feature Active Contours, 2009; Ontology-Coupled Active Contours for Dynamic Video Scene Understanding, 2011; Spatio-Temporal Visual Ontology, 2011. Honours: FRIA Grant, Belgian National Science Foundation, 2007-09; Fellow, Higher Education Academy, UK; Listed in international biographical dictionaries including Who's Who in the World, 2009-12; Great Minds of the 21st Century. Memberships: IEEE Signal Processing Society; IEEE Computer Society; SPIE Imaging Society; CNRS Groupement de Recherche en Information, Signal, Images et Vision; IEEE Computational Intelligence Society; British Machine Vision Association and Pattern Recognition Society. Address: Rue de la Boisette, 31, B-1340 Ottignies, Belgium.

OLSZEWSKI Stanislaw Marian, b. 8 December 1932, Warsaw, Poland. Physicist. m. Anna Kalinowska, deceased 1996, 1 son (from a previous marriage). Education: MSc, Theoretical Physics, Warsaw, 1954; Chemical Engineer, Warsaw, 1954; Doctor degree, Solid State Physics, Paris-Orsay, 1962; Habilitation, Chemical Physics, Warsaw, 1964; Professor, 1971. Appointments: Research Worker, Institute of Physical Chemistry, Polish Academy of Sciences, 1955-; Visiting Professor, University of Grenoble, 1982, 1989; Visiting Professor, University of Paris-Sud, 1988; Head of Division, Institute of Physical Chemistry, Polish Academy of Sciences, 1985-2002. Publications: Over 100 research papers. Honours: Golden Cross of Merit, 1980. Memberships: European Academy of Sciences and Arts, Austria; Polish Physical Society; Polish Chemical Society; Friends of Cardinal S Wyszynski Circle. Listed in various international biographical dictionaries. Address: Institute of Physical Chemistry, Polish Academy of Sciences, Kasprzaka 44/52, 01-224 Warsaw, Poland. E-mail: olsz@ichf.edu.pl

OLURINOLA Philip Folaranmi, b. 4 October 1939, Iwo, Isin Local Government Area, Kwara State, Nigeria. Professor of Pharmaceutical Microbiology. m. Dorcas Omowumi Taiwo, 2 sons, 3 daughters. Education: Pharmaceutical Chemist Diploma, Chemists and Druggists Diploma, ABUZ, Nigeria, 1966; Bachelor of Science, Pharmacy, ABUZ, Nigeria, 1974; Doctor of Philosophy, Pharmacy, Bradford, UK, 1979; Several continuing education workshops in Pharmacy and Pharmaceutical Microbiology, 1981-; Diploma in Ministerial

Studies, GRBTI, Zaria, 2000. Appointments: Staff, Superintendent Pharmacist, Northern Nigeria Civil Service, Kaduna, 1966-68, Kano, 1968-74; Lecturer in Pharmacy to Reader, 1975-92, Head, Pharmaceutics Department, 1985-91, Dean, Faculty of Pharmaceutical Sciences, 1988-92, Professor of Pharmaceutical Microbiology, 1992-, Ahmadu Bello University, Zaria, (ABUZ), Nigeria; Voluntary retirement of tenure appointment, 2004; On yearly contract appointment, 2004-08; Professor, Pharmaceutical Microbiology, Niger Delta University, 2008-10; Pioneer Professor, Pharmaceutical Microbiology, Faculty of Pharmaceutical Sciences, University of Ilorin, 2010-; Ag Dean, Faculty of Pharmaceutical Sciences, 2010-. Publications: Over 90 academic, research and professional articles in journals and conference proceedings, mostly on antimicrobial agents and chemotherapy; Latest book: The Pharmacy Profession: A Focus on Nigeria. Honours: Fellow, West African Postgraduate College of Pharmacists, 1994; Kaduna State PSN Merit Award, 1994; Fellow, Pharmaceutical Society of Nigeria, 1997; Iwo Community Highest Merit Award (Certified Compatriot of Iwo), 2003; Merit Award, Nigerian Association of Academic Pharmacists, 2004; Faculty Merit Award, 2004; International Order of Merit, 2007; Merit Award, 2008. Memberships: Pharmaceutical Society of Nigeria, 1966-; Nigerian Association of Academic Pharmacists, 1980-; Gideons International, 1982-; Society for Applied Bacteriology, UK, 1988-94; American Society for Microbiology, 1991-94; Member, Institute of Public Analysts of Nigeria (MIPAN), 2005-. Address: Faculty of Pharmaceutical Sciences, University of Ilorin, Ilorin, Nigeria. E-mail: pfolurinola@yahoo.com

OMAE Iwao, b. 7 August 1939, Takao, Japan. Chemist; Researcher. m. Junko Hasegawa, 1 son, 2 daughters. Education: BA, Japan National College, 1962; MA, 1965, PhD, Organotin Chemistry, 1968, Osaka University. Appointments: Assistant Professor, Osaka University, 1968-70; Researcher, Teijin Central Research Institute, 1970-77; Adviser, Teijin Technical Information Ltd, 1977-97; Lecturer, Osaka City University, 1997; Professor, Tsuzuki Integrated Education Institute, 1997-2006; Founder and Head, Omae Research Laboratories, 1998-; Lecturer, Nihon Pharmaceutical University, 2006-09. Publications: Books as author: Organometallic Intramolecular-coordination Compounds, 1986; Organotin Chemistry, 1989; Applications of Organometallic Compounds, 1998; Global Warming and Carbon Dioxide, 1999; Plastic Recycles, 2000; Associate Editors, Research Journal of Chemistry and Environment, Indore, India, 2003-. Honour: Prize for Outstanding Paper on Organotin Antifouling Paints, 6th International Conference for Maritime Safety and the Environment, NEVA 2001, Russia; Prize for Outstanding Paper on Tin-free Antifouling Paints, 8th International Conference for Maritime Industries and Shipping, NEVA, Russia, 2005. Memberships: Chemical Society of Japan; Society of Synthetic Organic Chemistry, Japan; American Chemical Society. Address: 335-23, Mizuno, Sayama, Saitama 350-1317, Japan. E-mail: um5i-oome@asahi-net.or.jp

O'MEARA Bernard Raymund, b. 2 October 1955, Melbourne, Australia. Senior Academic. m. Cheryl Anne Crosbie, 2 sons. Education: BA, La Trobe, 1977; MBA, RMIT, 1987; Graduate Diploma of Educaiton, University of South Australia, 1996; PhD, Deakin, 2003; Diploma of Editing, 2010, Diploma of Publishing, 2010, Australian College. Appointments: Corporate Personnel Manager, Containers Packaging, 1979-89; Principal Consultant, CBO Consulting, 1989-94; Lecturer, 1993, MGT/HR Discipline Co-ordinator, 1996-98, Deputy Head of School, 1997-99, Head of School, 1998-99, Senior Lecturer (Human Resource Manager) and Acting Discipline Co-ordinator, University of Ballarat. Publications: Education and Training for Emergency Services, 2009; Author and co-author of monographs and texts; Contributing author to several international academic peer-reviewed journals. Memberships: University of Ballarat; Australian Human Resource Institute. Address: School of Business, University of Ballarat, University Drive, Mt Helen, Victoria 3350, Australia. E-mail: b.omeara@ballarat.edu.au

O'MEARA Mark, b. 13 January 1957, Goldsboro, North Carolina, USA. Golfer. Education: Long Beach State University. Career: Professional Golfer, 1980-; Ryder Cup Team, 1985, 1989, 1991, 1997; Won US Amateur Championship, 1979, Greater Milwaukee Open, 1984, Bing Crosby Pro-American, 1985, Hawaii Open, 1985, Fuji Sankei Classic, 1985, Australian Masters, 1986, Lawrence Batley International, 1987, AT&T Pebble Beach National Pro-American, 1989, 1990, 1992, 1997, H-E-B TX Open, 1990, Walt Disney World/Oldsmobile Classic, 1991, Tokia Classic, 1992, Argentine Open, 1994, Honda Classic, 1995, Bell Canada Open, 1995, Mercedes Championships, 1996, Greater Greensboro Open, 1996, Brick Invitational, 1997, US Masters, 1998, British Open, 1998, World Matchplay 1998; Best Finish 2002, 2nd in Buick Invitational and 2nd in Buick Open; Champions Tour, 2007. Honour: All-American Rookie of the Year, Long Beach State University, 1981; PGA Tour Player of the Year, 1998. Address: c/o PGA, Box 109601, Avenue of Champions, Palm Beach Gardens, FL 33410, USA.

OMIDVAR Hedayat, b. 3 January 1966, Abadan, Iran. Senior Expert. Education: BSc, 1995, MSc, 2001, Industrial Engineering. Appointments: Project Management, 1995-2001, Senior Expert, 2001-, Responsible for Strategic Studies, Research and Technology Department, National Iranian Gas Company; Head, Communication Affairs with Science & Research Centers, Research & Technology Department, NIGC. Publications: Articles in international journals and international conferences. Honours: Letter of Commendation as the Exemplary Research Expert, received from the Deputy Petroleum Minister & Managing Director of NIGC, 2008; Letter of Commendation, Deputy Minister & Managing Director, NIGC, 2011. Memberships: Institute of Industrial Engineers, 1992; American Industrial Hygiene Association, 1994; Iran Institute of Industrial Engineering, 2001; International Gas Union, 2003. Address: No 6 Arghavan Alley, Sabory St, Kashanak, Tehran 1978975981, Iran. E-mail: omidvar@nigc.ir

OMOMIA Robinson, b. 24 December 1948, Oyo Town, Oyo State, Nigeria. Businessman. Education: Diploma, Business Management, University of Wisconsin, USA, 1979; Postgraduate diploma, International Business, MBA, International Marketing, London School of International Business, 1983; Diploma, Property Law & Secured Credit Transaction, 1993, Diploma, Business & Industrial Law, 1995, Advanced Diploma, Commercial Law & Practice, 1996, Master in Legal Study, International Law & Diplomacy, 1997, Faculty of Law, Diploma, Banking & Finance, Faculty of Business Administration, 1994, University of Lagos; Postgraduate diploma, Maritime Management & Technology, Federal University of Technology, Owerri, 1998; Postgraduate diploma, Maritime Law, Institute of Maritime Law, 1999, MSc, Environmental Resources Management, Centre for Environment & Science Education, 2002, Lagos State University; MSc, Transport Management, Ladoke Akintola University of Technology, Ogbomosho, 2000; Diploma, Marine Surveying, Lloyd's Martime Academy, London, 2004;

Management and development courses. Appointments: Sales, Market Development, Project Co-ordination, Oasis Inc, West African Region; Sales, Distribution, Marketing, Training, Johnson & Johnson, Slough, England, 1971-78; General, Sales, Product Development, Marketing, Management, GlaxoSmithKline, Welwyn Garden City, England, 1981; Technical Consultant, National Automotive Council, Abuja, 1993-95; Member, OAU/AEC All Africa Trade Fair, Addis Ababa, Ethiopia, 1996-97; Team Leader, International Chamber of Commerce, 2001-02; Steering Committee Member, GEF/UNEP/FAO Shrimp Project, Environmental & Natural Resources Management, 2003-07; Member, The Codex Alimentarius Commission, 2003-07; Member, National Martime Joint Security Council, 2003-07; Deputy Co-ordinator, Nigerian Fisheries Laboratories, 2003-07. Memberships: Market Research Society, London; Institute of Commercial Management, UK; Chartered Institute of Taxation of Nigeria; Nigerian Institute of Management; Institute of Construction Industry Arbitrators; Chartered Institute of Marketing, UK; The Institute of Export, UK; American Marketing Association, USA; International Trade Association, USA; British Institute of Management; American Arbitration Association; National Institute of Marketing of Nigeria; Chemical Society of Nigeria; American Chemical Society; American Association of Cereal Chemists. Address: House One, B Close, 112 Road, 1st Avenue, PO Box 3302, Festac Town, Lagos, Nigeria. E-mail: robomomia@hotmail.com

O'MOORE Mona, b. 2 March 1945, Oslo, Norway. Child & Educational Psychologist. m. Rory O'Moore, 3 sons. Education: BA, Trinity College, Dublin University, 1966; MA, University of Nottingham, 1968; PhD, University of Edinburgh, 1977. Appointments: Assistant Lecturer, Developmental & Educational Psychology, University College, Cork, 1968-69; Child Psychologist, Institute of Child Psychology, London, 1973-75; Founder & Director, Anti-Bullying Research and Resource Centre, 1996-, Lecturer, 1975-90, Senior Lecturer, 1991-99, Child & Educational Psychology, Head of School of Education, 2000-07, Associate Professor of Education, 2003-, Trinity College, Dublin. Publications: Numerous articles in professional journals and books, including: Inclusion or Illusion? Educational Provision for Primary School Children with Mild General Learning Difficulties, 2009; The Relationship Between Workplace Bullying and Suicide in Ireland, 2010; Understanding School Bullying: A Guide for Parents and Teachers, 2010. Honours: Fellowship, Trinity College Dublin, 1995-; Fellowship, Royal Society of Arts, Manufacturers & Commerce, 2007-; Fellow, St Columba's College, Dublin, 2001-; Governor, National Children's Hospital, Dublin, 1992-97. Memberships: British Psychological Association; Psychological Association of Ireland; International Society for Research on Aggression; Irish Association of Teachers in Special Education; British-Irish Anti-Bullying Forum. Address: School of Education, Trinity College, Dublin 2, Ireland. E-mail: momoore@tcd.ie

ONDAATJE Michael, b. 12 September 1943, Colombo, Sri Lanka. Author. m. Linda Spalding; 2 sons. Education: Dulwich College, London; Queen's University; University of Toronto. Publications include: Poetry: The Dainty Monsters, 1967; The Man With Seven Toes, 1968; There's a Trick with a Knife I'm Learning to Do, 1979; Secular Love, 1984; Handwriting, 1998; The Story, 2006. Fiction: The Collected Works of Billy the Kid; Coming Through Slaughter; Running in the Family; In the Skin of a Lion; The English Patient; Handwriting; Anil's Ghost, 2000; The Conversations: Walter Murch and the Art of Editing Film, 2002; The Story, 2005; Divisadero, 2007. Honour: Booker Prize for Fiction, 1992; Prix Medicis, 2000; American Cinema Editors Awards, 2003; Kraszna-Krausz Book Award, 2003. Address: 2275 Bayview Road, Toronto, Ontario N4N 3MG, Canada.

O'NEAL Ryan, b. 20 April 1941, Los Angeles, USA. Actor. m. (1) Joanna Moore, divorced, 1 son, 1 daughter, (2) Leigh Taylor-Young, divorced, 1 son, 1 son with Farrah Fawcett. Career: Numerous TV appearances; Films include: The Big Bounce, 1969; Love Story, 1970; The Wild Rovers, 1971; What's Up, Doc? 1972; The Thief Who Came To Dinner, 1973; Paper Moon, 1973; Oliver's Story, 1978; The Main Event, 1979; So Fine, 1981; Partners, 1982; Irreconcilable Differences, 1983; Fever Pitch, 1985; Tough Guys Don't Dance, 1986; Chances Are, 1989; Faithful, 1996; Hacks, 1997; Burn Hollywood Burn, 1997; Zero Effect, 1998; Coming Soon, 1999; Epoch, 2000; People I Know, 2002; Malibu's Most Wanted, 2003; Waste Land, 2007.

ONEGA JAÉN Susana, b. 17 November 1948, Madrid, Spain. Professor of English Literature. m. Francisco Curiel Lorente, 2 sons. Education: Degree, 1975, PhD, 1979, English Philology, University of Zaragoza; Numerous certificates for aptitude in English, French, Italian and German, Madrid, Cambridge, Heidelberg, 1967-77. Appointments: Teacher of English, Official School of Languages, Madrid, 1968-69; Untenured Lecturer, 1975-77, Untenured Associate Professor, 1977-83; Tenured Associate Professor, 1983-86, Full Professor, 1986, Vice-Head of Department, 1989-90, 1995-97, 2000-03; Head of Department, 1987-89, 1991-93, 1993-95, 1997-99, Department of English, University of Zaragoza; Head of Competitive Research Team, 2003-05, 2005-07, Head of Excellence Research Team, 2008-, Government of Aragon; Research Manager for The Philologies and Philosophy, Ministry of Science and Technology, 2001-03; Member of Committee for recognition of foreign degrees in the Philologies, Ministry of Education and Science, 2005-; Member of Committee for Quality Assessment of Staff in the Humanities, National Agency for Quality Assessment and Validation, 2005-, President, 2008-. Publications: Books include: Análisis estructural, método narrativo y "sentido" de The Sound and the Fury de William Faulkner, 1980; Estudios literarios ingleses II: Renacimiento y barroco (editor and author of introduction), 1986; Form and Meaning in the Novels of John Fowles, 1989; Telling Histories: Narrativizing History/Historicizing Literature (editor and author of introduction), 1995; Narratology: An Introduction (co-editor and co-author of introduction), 1996; Peter Ackroyd. The Writer and his Work, 1998; Metafiction and Myth in the Novels of Peter Ackroyd, 1999; London in Literature: Visionary Mappings of the Metropolis (co-editor and co-author of introduction), 2002; Refracting the Canon in Contemporary British Literature and Film (co-editor and co-author of introduction), 2004; George Orwell: A Centenary Celebration, 2005; (Co-editor and co-author of introduction), Jeanette Winterson, 2006; The Ethical Component in Experimental British Fiction since the 1960s (co-editor and co-author of introduction), 2007; Ethics and Trauma in Contemporary British Fiction (co-editor and co-author of introduction), 2010; Numerous articles in professional journals, book chapters, conference papers and translations. Honours: Extraordinary Prize for Degree in Philosophy and Letters, University of Zaragoza, 1976; Extraordinary Prize for Doctorate in Philosophy and Letters, University of Zaragoza, 1980; Enrique García Díez Award, 1990; Honorary Research Fellowship, Birkbeck College, University of London, 1995-96. Memberships: Spanish Association for Anglo-American Studies, 1977-; European Association for American Studies, 1977-; European Society for the Study of English, 1990-; International Association of

University Professors of English, 1995-; National Federation of Associations of Spanish University Professors, 1997-2002; Corresponding Fellow, The English Association, 2003-08; Association of Women Researchers and Technologists, 2003-; Member, Academia Europaea, 2008-. Address: Dpto de Filología Inglesa y Alemana, Facultad de Filosofía y Letras, 50009 Universidad de Zaragoza, Spain. E-mail: sonega@unizar.es

ONG Hean-Choon, b. 10 November 1945, Malaysia. Doctor. m. It-Tean Lim, 2 sons. Education: MBBS, University of Malaya, 1970; MRCOG, 1975; MMEd, University of Singapore, 1982; FICS, USA, International College of Surgeons, 1983; FRCOG, UK, 1989; FAMM, Academy of Medicine of Malaysia, 1997; FRCPI, 2000. Appointments: Consultant, Obstetrician and Gynaecologist, Panta Medical Centre; Chairman, Malaysian Representative Committee, RCOK, UK; Member, Executive Council, Malaysian Menopause Society; Member, National Estrogen Deficiency Awareness Faculty of Malaysia. Publications: Over 75 Scientific Papers in local, regional and international journals. Honours: Many honours. Memberships: Royal College of Ob-Gyn, UK; International College of Surgeons; O and G Society of Malaysia; Malaysian Medical Association. Address: 14 Jalan Desa Ria Satu, Taman Desa, Jalan Klang-Lama, 58100 Kuala Lumpur, Malaysia.

ONG Marcus Eng Hock, b. 7 November 1969, Singapore. Senior Consultant. m. Frances Lim Hsiu Yih, 2 sons, 1 daughter. Education: MBBS, 1993; FRCS, Accident & Emergency, Edinburgh, 2000; USLME Part I, 2001; USLME Part II, 2002; Exit certified in Emergency Medicine, Academy of Medicine, Singapore, 2002; ECFMG Certification, USA, 2003; Specialist Accreditation, Singapore Medical Council, 2003; Fellow, Academy of Medicine, Singapore, 2005; Masters of Public Health, Virginia Commonwealth University, 2005. Appointments: Houseman, TTSH General Surgery, AH Paediatrics, NUH Medicine, 1993; Medical Officer, NUH ENT, Family Health Services, 1994; Captain, SAF, 1995; MSO III, TTSH Eye, NUH Cardiology, TTSH A&E, 1997, AH Medicine, NUH General Surgery, 1998, AH Orthopaedics, SGH A&E, 1999; MO (Specialist), NUH A&E, 1999; Registrar, SGH Department of Emergency Medicine, 1999; Clinical Tutor, 2000, Clinical Teacher, 2004, Faculty of Medicine, NUS; Registrar, Attached to NUH Emergency Medicine Department, 2002; Associate Consultant, SGH Department of Emergency Medicine, 2003; Clinical Fellow, Department of Emergency Medicine, University of Ottawa, Canada, 2003; Research Fellow, Ottawa Health Research Institute, Canada, 2003; NMRC Research Fellow, Virginia Commonwealth University, 2004; Consultant, SGH Department of Emergency Medicine, 2005; Senior Medical Scientist, SingHealth and SGH, 2006; Senior Fellow, Reanimation Engineering Shock Centre, Virginia Commonwealth University, 2007; Adjunct Associate Professor, 2007, Associate Professor, 2010, Duke-National University of Singapore; Clinical Lecturer, 2007, Senior Clinical Lecturer, 2008, Yong Loo Lin School of Medicine, National University of Singapore; Consultant, Ministry of Health, Hospital Services Division, 2008; Clinical Scientist, NMRC and SGH, 2010; Senior Consultant, SGH Department of Emergency Medicine, 2010. Publications: Numerous articles in professional journals. Honours include most recently: Best Abstract Award, Singapore Cardiac Society Annual Scientific Meeting, 2011; Young Investigator Award, Best Oral Paper, 19th SGH Annual Scientific Meeting, 2011; Listed in biographical dictionaries. Address: Singapore General Hospital, Department of Emergency Medicine, Outram Road, 169608, Singapore.

ONIFADE Ademola, b. 26 May 1956, Osogbo, Nigeria. University Teacher. m. Toyin Oluyede, 1 son, 3 daughters. Education: B Ed (Hons), University of Ibadan, 1978; MPE, University of New Brunswick, Fredricton, Canada, 1980; PhD, University of Maryland, College Park, USA, 1983. Appointments: Head, Department of Physical and Health Education, Adeyemi College, Ondo State, Nigeria, 1985-86; Head, Department of Physical and Health Education, 1988-90, 1999-2000, Professor, 2000-, Dean, Faculty of Education, 2000-2004, Lagos State University. Publications: Psycho-Social Perspective of Sports, 1993; History of Physical Education in Nigeria, 2001; Emergent Issues in Sociology of Sports, 2001; Britain, Sport and Nation Building in Nigeria, 2004. Honours: Listed in Who's Who publications and biographical dictionaries. Memberships: Nigeria Academy of Education; Nigerian Association for Physical and Health Education and Recreation; International Council for Health, Physical Education Recreation, Sports and Dance; Member and Vice Chair for Africa, UNESCO Intergovernmental Committee for Physical Education and Sports. Address: Department of Physical and Health Education, Lagos State University, PMB 1087, Apapa, Lagos, Nigeria. E-mail: ademolaonifade@yahoo.com

ONOZAWA Masaki, b. 1 January 1945, Shibukawa, Gumma, Japan. Professor. m. Nitaya, 1 daughter. Education: BA, University of Tokyo, 1968; MA, Graduate School of University of Tokyo, 1972; PhD, University of Tsukuba, 1995; Honorary PhD, Tashkent State Institute of Oriental Studies, Uzbekistan, 2006. Appointments: Instructor, 1972-77, Associate Professor, 1977-83, University of Kyushu; Associate Professor, 1983-95, Professor, 1995-2008, University of Tsukuba; Secretary General, International Academic Society for Asian Community, 2006-; Professor, 2008-, Vice President, 2012-, Ikuei College; Chair, Board of Directors, Shibusawa Fund for Promotion of Ethnological Sciences, 2008-. Publications: Continuity and Change in Oversears Chinese Communities in the Pan-Pacific Area, 1993; Thailand, 1994; Studies in Cultural Anthropology, 2002. Honours: Honorable Professor, Kyrgyz National University of Isup Barasagyn, Kyrgyztan, 2005. Memberships: Japanese Society of Cultural Anthropology; Japanese Society of Thai Studies; International Academic Society for Asian Community; Siam Society, Thailand. Address: 702-65 Shimohirooka, Tsukuba, Ibaraki, 305-0042, Japan. E-mail: onozawa.masaki@snow.plala.or.jp

ONYECHE Theodore, b. 8 October 1960, Nigeria. Engineer. m. Renate, 4 sons. Education: B Eng, Chemical/Petroleum Engineering, 1987; Dipl Ing (MSc), Petroleum Engineering, 1995; PhD, Environmental Engineering. Appointments: Research Engineer; Project Engineer; Project Co-ordinator; Assistant Head of Department; Manager, International Operations. Publications: Numerous articles in professional journals. Honours: Best Graduate in Chemical/Petroleum Engineering; Distinguished Fellow, Federal University of Technology, Nigeria. Memberships: International Water Association; Fellow, Nigeria Society of Engineers; Fellow, Environmental Association of Nigeria. Address: Cutec-Institut GmbH, Leibnizstr 21 & 23, 38678 Clausthal Zellerfeld, Germany. E-mail: theodore.onyeche@cutec.de Website: www.cutec.de

ONYSZKIEWICZ Janusz, b. 18 December 1937, Lwów, Poland. m. Joanna Jaraczewska, 2 sons, 3 daughters. Education: PhD, Pure Mathematics, Warsaw University; Dr Hon Causa, Leeds University. Appointments: Member, National Executive, Solidarity Trade Union, 1980-89; Member of Parliament, 1989-2001; Member of European Parliament, and Vice President, 2004-09; Minister of Defence, 1992-93, 1997-2001; President of Polish Mountaineering Association. Publications: Book, From Summits to NATO, 1999; Biography, Onyszkiewicz's Family, 2005. Honours: Polonia Restituta Cross; Great Cross of Gedyminas Order, Lithuania; Great Cross of Leopold, Belgium. Address: Narbutta 17, Warsaw 02 536, Poland.

OPALSKY Chester D, b. 31 August 1926, Braddock, Pennsylvania, USA. Retired Toxicologist. Education: University of Pittsburgh, Pennsylvania; The American University, Washington, DC; University of Florida, Gainesville, Florida; Clayton School of Natural Healing, Birmingham, Alabama. Appointments: Undergraduate and Graduate, University of Pittsburgh, and the American University, Washington, DC; Founder, Dynamic Health Services, Arlington, Virginia; Researcher, Nosocomial Infections, Bronx Veterans Administration Hospital, New York; Researcher, Department of Agriculture and the Environment Protection Agency, Beltsville, Maryland and Washington, DC; Toxicologist, Federal Civil Service, 30 years; Senior Scientist, American Association for the Advancement of Science. Publications: Reviewer of manuscripts and manuals in conjunction with American Association for the Advancement of Science. Honours: Republican Senatorial Medal, 2003. Memberships: Pittsburgh Alumni Association; University of Florida National Alumni Association; The American University Alumni Association; American Bar Association; American Association for Justice; National Health Lawyers Association; American Medal Association; American Naturopathic Association; American Holistic Medical Association; American Board of Hydrotherapy; American Society for Microbiology; Senior Scientists and Engineers; American Audiological Society.

OPIE Iona, b. 13 October 1923, Colchester, England. Writer. m. Peter Opie, 2 September 1943, deceased, 2 sons, 1 daughter. Publications: A Dictionary of Superstitions (with Moira Tatem), 1989; The People in the Playground, 1993; With Peter Opie: The Oxford Dictionary of Nursery Rhymes, 1951, new edition, 1997; The Oxford Nursery Rhyme Book, 1955; The Lore and Language of Schoolchildren, 1959; Puffin Book of Nursery Rhymes, 1963; A Family Book of Nursery Rhymes, 1964; Children's Games in Street and Playground, 1969; The Oxford Book of Children's Verse, 1973; Three Centuries of Nursery Rhymes and Poetry for Children, 1973; The Classic Fairy Tales, 1974; A Nursery Companion, 1980; The Oxford Book of Narrative Verse, 1983; The Singing Game, 1985; Babies: an unsentimental anthology, 1990; Children's Games with Things, 1997. Honours: Honorary MA, Oxon, 1962, Open University, 1987, DLitt, University of Southampton, 1987, University of Nottingham, 1991, Doctorate, University of Surrey, 1997; CBE, 1998; FBA, 1998. Address: Mells House, Liss, Hampshire GU33 6JQ, England.

OPIK Lembit, b. 2 March 1965, Bangor, County Down, Northern Ireland. Member of Parliament. Education: BA, Philosophy, Bristol University. Appointments: President, Bristol Students Union, 1985-86; Member, National Union of Students National Executive, 1987-88; Brand Assistant, 1988-91; Corporate Training and Organisation Development Manager, 1991-96; Global Human Resources Training Manager, 1997, Proctor and Gamble; Elected to Newcastle City Council, 1992; Elected as MP for Montgomeryshire, 1997-2010; Party Spokesperson on Northern Ireland and Young People, 1997; Spokesperson for Wales, Leader of the Welsh Liberal Democrats, Member of Shadow Cabinet, 2001-2007; Liberal Democrat spokesman for Business, Enterprise and Regulatory Reform, 2007. Publications: Articles on politics in newspapers and magazines; Weekly column in Shropshire Star, The Week in Politics. Honours: Nominated for Channel 4 House Magazine New MP of the Year, 1998; Nominated for Country Life Rural MP of the Year, 1999. Memberships: Agriculture Select Committee, 1998-2001; Co-Chair, All Parliamentary Middle Way Group; Member, Spinal Injuries Association; Speaks on behalf of British Gliding Association; Chair, All Party Parliamentary Motorcycle Group; President, Shropshire, Astronomical Society. Address: House of Commons, London, SW1A 0AA, England. E-mail: opikl@parliament.uk

ORBAN Radu Liviu, b. 26 January 1941, Abrud city, District Alba, Romania. Professor. m. Magdalena, 1 son, 1 daughter. Education: Diploma, Machine Building, 1962, PhD, Materials Technology and Metallography, 1973, Technical University, Cluj-Napoca; Diploma, Fulbright Program, USA, 1995; Diploma, Management of Change & Innovation Program, University College, Dublin, 1998. Appointments: Assistant, Lecturer, Associate Professor, 1962-92, Senior Researcher, 1973-78, Director of Research Centre for Powder Metallurgy, 1992-98, Full Professor, Doctorate Director, Materials Science and Engineering, 1992-2006, Head, Materials Science and Technology Department, Member, Faculty Board and University Senate, Director, Materials Science Research Centre, 2001-06, Consulting Professor, Doctorate Director, 2007-, Technical University, Cluj-Napoca; Associate Senior Researcher, Department of Materials Engineering, Drexel University, Philadelphia, USA, 1994-95; Associate Senior Researcher, Department of Advanced Materials, National R&D Institute for Electronic Engineering, Bucharest, 2004-10. Publications: 5 books, 1 in progress; More than 200 articles in professional journals; Over 70 reports; 9 patents. Honours: Co-chairman, 1996, Chairman, 2000, 2005, International Powder Metallurgy Conferences; Member, Liaison Committee, International Journal of Powder Metallurgy, USA, 1995-; Member, International Advisory Board, Powder Metallurgy Progress, 2001-; Member, Scientific or Technical Committees of 5 European Powder Metallurgy Congresses, 1998-2009; Powder Metallurgy World Congresses, 2004, 2010; Alexandru Domsa Award of Excellence in Scientific Research, 2005. Memberships: Powder Metallurgy Society of Romania; Expert Panel for Material Science & Engineering of the European Commission; Commission for Engineering Science; National Council of Science Research in Higher Education of Romania; American Ceramic Society. Address: 84 General Eremia Grigorescu Street, 400304 Cluj-Napoca, Romania.

ORING Stuart August, b. 28 August 1932, Bronx, New York, USA. Publisher; Writer; Photographer; Researcher. m. Mary Carolyn Barth Oring, 2 daughters. Education: Associate Degree, Applied Sciences, 1957, BFA, 1959, Rochester Institute of Technology; MA, American University, 1970. Appointments: Visual Info Specialist, ARS of US Department of Agriculture, 1964-67; AV Specialist, National AV Center, 1967-69; Photojournalist, Office of Economic Opportunity, 1971-74; Visual Information Specialist (Photography), ASCS of US Department of Agriculture, 1974-94; Founded ISIS Visual Communications (researcher, writer, photographer), 1992-. Publications: Books: Understanding Pictures;

Theories, Exercises and Procedures; A Beginners Guide to Pictures; Understanding Pictures: A Teacher's Planning Guide; Numerous articles and photographs published. Honour: Certificate of Appreciation, Eastman Kodak Co; Research and development of new approaches for analysing and interpreting art and photographs. Memberships: International Visual Literary Association; American Society for Psychopathology of Expression; Member of Board, ASPE; Listed in national and international biographical dictionaries. Address: 2570 Redbud Lane, Owings, MD 20736, USA.

ORLACCHIO Antonio, b. 24 February 1972, Perugia, Italy. Assistant Professor. m. Marialuisa Miele, 1 daughter. Education: MD, 1996, Board Certification, Neurology, 2000, University of Perugia; PhD, Neurosciences, University of Rome Torvergata, 2004; Postdoctoral Fellow, Centre for Research in Neurogenerative Diseases, University of Toronto, Canada, 1997-2002. Appointments: Head, Laboratory of Neurogenetics, CERC-IRCCS Santa Lucia, Rome; Attending Neurologist, Head, Outpatient Clinic and Clinical Programme of Neurogenetics, Division of Neurology, Clinical Department of Neurosciences, PTV; Assistant Professor, Neurology, Academic Department of Neurosciences, University of Rome Torvergata. Publications: 61 peer reviewed papers; 6 book chapters; 130 abstracts; 7 other publications. Honours: European Neurological Society Award, 2003; San Valentino d'Oro International Award, 2010. Memberships: Italian Neurological Society; European Neurological Society. Address: CERC IRCCS, Santa Lucia, Neurogenetica 64, Via del Fosso di Fiorano, Rome 00143, Italy.

ORLOV Alexei M, b. 28 May 1960, Orekhovo-Zuevo, USSR. Fisheries Biologist. m. Inessa Kasatkina, 1 daughter. Education: Diploma in Pisciculture and Ichthyology, Faculty of Fisheries, Astrakhan Technical University, Astrakhan, Russia, 1977-82. Appointments: Doctor of Biological Sciences, Principal Research Fellow, Chief of Section of International Fisheries Problems, Russian Federal Research Institute of Fisheries and Oceanography. Publications: Over 70 articles, more than 20 in English. Honours: R E Foerster Award as co-author of outstanding scientific publication of 1999; Membership of the American Association for the Advancement of Science, 2003. Memberships: Moscow Naturalists Society, 1999-; European Society of Ichthyologists, 2001-; Russian Hydrobiological Society, 2003-; American Fisheries Society, 2004-. Address: VNIRO, V Krasnoselskaya, Moscow 107140, Russia. E-mail: orlov@vniro.ru Website: www.vniro.ru

ORLOV Valery Alexandrovich, b. 16 April 1949, Novosibirsk, Russia. Physicist. m. Nina V Platonova, 1971, 2 daughters. Education: MSc, Quantum Radiophysics, State University Novosibirsk, 1972; Doctor of Philosophy, 2000, Doctor, Physics and Mathematics Sciences, 2004, Institute of Laser Physics, Novosibirsk. Appointments: Research Scientist, Institute of Semiconductor Physics, Novosibirsk, 1972-78; Research Scientist, Institute of Thermophysics, Novosibirsk, 1979-87; Senior Researcher, 1987-89, Head of Laboratory, 1989-91, Head, Laboratory of Applied Laser Interferometry, 1991-. Publications: More than 120 scientific publications. Honours: Gold Medal, Leipzig Exhibition, 1986; Medal, Nikolas Roerich for achievements in the field of Ecology, 2010; Listed in international biographical dictionaries. Memberships: Laser Assn; Science Council of Geophysical Service; Siberian Branch, Russian Academy of Sciences; IEEE. Address: Lesosechnaya 5 - 264, Novosibirsk 630060, Russia. E-mail: lss@lasser.nsc.ru

ORMAN Stanley, b. 6 February 1935, London, England. Consultant. m. Helen Hourman, 1 son, 2 daughters. Education: BSc, 1st Class Honours, Chemistry and Physics, 1957, PhD, Chemistry, 1960, Kings College, London; Fulbright Fellow, Brandeis University Massachusetts, USA, 1960-91. Appointments: Scientist Ministry of Defence, 1961-82, positions held include: Chief Weapons Systems Engineer Chevaline, 1980-82, Minister, British Embassy, Washington, USA, 1982-84, Deputy Director Atomic Weapons research Establishment, 1984-86, Founding Director General, SDI Participation Office, 1986-90; Under Secretary of State, UK Ministry of Defence, 1982-90; Chief Executive Officer, General Technology Systems, USA, 1990-96; Chief Executive Officer, Orman Associates, 1996-. Publications: Author book: Faith in G.O.D.S – Stability in Nuclear Age, 1991; 150 published papers and articles on chemistry, corrosion science, adhesion and defence issues including over 90 articles on missile defence; Participation in workshops and presentations at over 70 international conferences on defence issues. Honours: Captained London University Track Team, 1956-57; Represented Britain in World Student Games, 3rd in 100m and 7th in Long Jump, 1956; Jelf Medalist, King's College, London, 1957. Address: 17825 Stoneridge Drive, North Potomac, MD 20878, USA. E-mail: or2withdog@comcast.net

ORME Michael Christopher L'Estrange, b. 13 June 1940, Derby, England. University Professor; Medical Practitioner. m. (Joan) Patricia Orme, 1 son. Education: MA, MB, BChir (Cantab), 1964-65; MD, 1975; MRCP, 1967; FRCP, 1980. Appointments: Senior Lecturer, Clinical Pharmacology, 1975, Professor, 1984, Dean, Faculty of Medicine, 1991-96, University of Liverpool; Director of Education and Training, North West Regional Office, NHS Executive, 1996-2001; Retired 2001; Currently Professor Emeritus, University of Liverpool; Consultant Physician Emeritus, Royal Liverpool Hospital. Publications: 275 peer reviewed publications in journals; Books and book chapters on drug interactions, clinical pharmacology of oral contraceptives, drugs in tropical disease, anticoagulants and anti-rheumatic drugs. Honours: FRCGP (Hon), 1996; F Med Sci, 1998; DSc (Hon), Salford, 2000; FFPHM, 2000; Honorary Fellow, University of Central Lancashire, 2001; Honorary MD, International Medical University, Kuala Lumpur, Malaysia, 2004. Memberships: Association of Physicians; British Pharmacological Society. Address: Lark House, Clapton-on-the-Hill, Cheltenham, Gloucestershire GL54 2LG, England. E-mail: michaelorme@larkhouse.co.uk

ORMOND Julia, b.4 January 1965, England. Actress. m.(1) Rory Edwards, divorced; (2) Jon Rubin, 1999, 1 child. Education: Farnham Art School; Webber Douglas Academy. Appointments: Worked in Repertory, Crucible Theatre, Sheffield, Everyman Theatre, Cheltenham; On tour with Royal Exchange Theatre, Manchester; Appeared in Faith, Hope and Charity, Lyric, Hammersmith; Treats, Hampstead Theatre; West End Debut in Anouilh's The Rehearsal; My Zinc Bed, 2000. Creative Works: TV appearances: Traffik (Channel 4 series); Ruth Rendell Mysteries; Young Catherine, 1990; Stalin, 1992; Animal Farm (voice), 1999; Varian's War, 2001; Iron Jawed Angels, 2004; The Way, 2006. Films: The Baby of Macon; Legends of the Fall; First Knight; Sabrina; Smilla's Sense of Snow, 1997; The Barber of Siberia, 1998; The Prime Gig, 2000; Resistance, 2003; The Nazi Officer's Wife, 2003; Inland Empire, 2006; I Know Who Killed Me, 2007; Surveillance, 2008; Kit Kittredge; An American Girl, 2008; The Curious Case of Benjamin Button, 2008. Address: c/o CAA, 9830 Wilshire Boulevard, Beverly Hills, CA 90212, USA.

ORMOS Jenö, b. 21 December 1922, Hódmezővásárhely, Hungary. Physician. m. Judit Lantos, 1960, 2 sons, 1 daughter. Education: MD, Halle/Saale, 1945; MD, Szeged, 1946; PhD, Budapest, 1963; DSc, Budapest, 1980. Appointments: Professor and Chairman,1963-93, Professor Emeritus, 1993-, Department of Pathology, Albert Szent-Györgyi University of Medicine, Szeged; Deputy Rector, Albert Szent-Györgyi University of Medicine, Szeged, 1967-73. Honours: Baló Medal, Genersich M, Romhányi M, Hungarian Society of Pathology, 1984, 1992, 1995; Purkyne A Czechoslovak Medical Society, 1987; Thomasius A, Martin Luther University, Halle, 1987; Jancsó Miklós A, Albert Szent-Györgyi University of Medicine, 1989; Medal University, Poznan, 1989; Korányi A, Hungarian Society of Nephrology, 1998; Pro Urbe Hódmezővásárhely, 2003. Memberships: Hungarian Society of Pathology, 1947-, President, 1964-66; Polish Society of Pathology, Honorary Member, 1976; Cuban Society of Pathology, Honorary Member, 1982-; International Academy of Pathology; German Society of Pathology. Address: H-6720, Szeged Tömörkény u 2/C, Hungary.

ORMSBY Frank, b. 30 October 1947, Enniskillen, County Fermanagh, Northern Ireland. Poet; Writer; Editor. Education: BA, English, 1970, MA, 1971, Queen's University, Belfast. Appointment: Editor, The Honest Ulsterman, 1969-89. Publications: A Store of Candles, 1977; Poets from the North of Ireland (editor), 1979, new edition, 1990; A Northern Spring, 1986; Northern Windows: An Anthology of Ulster Autobiography (editor), 1987; The Long Embrace: Twentieth Century Irish Love Poems (editor), 1987; Thine in Storm and Calm: An Amanda McKittrick Ros Reader (editor), 1988; The Collected Poems of John Hewitt (editor), 1991; A Rage for Order: Poetry of the Northern Ireland Troubles (editor), 1992; The Ghost Train, 1995; The Hip Flask: Short Poems from Ireland (editor), 2000; The Blackbird's Nest: Anthology of Poetry from Queen's University Belfast (editor), 2006; Selected Poems of John Hewitt (editor with Michael Longley), 2007; Fireflies, 2009. Address: 33 North Circular Road, Belfast BT15 5HD, Northern Ireland

ORTIZ George, b. 10 May 1927, Paris, France (Bolivian Embassy). Companies Administrator. m. Catherine Haus, 3 sons, 1 daughter. Education: Studied under Professor Wolfson and read Aristotle's Exegesis of Metaphysics in original Greek, Harvard University, USA. Appointments: Founder of company to create a new tri-leaflet aortic heart valve; Fought for free circulation of art as being the patrimony of humanity; Collector, advocate for connoisseurship; Patron of the arts. Publications: The George Ortiz Collection; Numerous articles in professional and popular journals.

ÖRVELL Claes Gunnar, b. 22 April 1945, Stockholm, Sweden. Physician; Virologist. m. Eva Reimert, 2 sons, 3 daughters. Education: MD, 1973, PhD, 1977, Karolinska Institutet. Appointments: Researcher, Department of Virology, Karolinska Institutet, 1978-79; Researcher, Virology, National Bacteriological Laboratory, 1980-92; Associate Professor, Karolinska Institutet, 1988-; Senior Physician, Stockholm City Council, 1992-. Publications: Numerous scientific articles on the subjects structural, clinical and epidemiological studies on viruses. Honours: International Order of Merit, IBC, 2000; Order of International Fellowship, IBC, 2001; Fellow, International Biographical Association, 2001; Founding Member American Order of Excellence, 2001; Presidential Seal of Honor, 2001; Lifetime Achievement Award, IBC, 2001; World Biographee Day, ABI, 2001; Deputy Governor, ABI, 2001; Noble Prize for Outstanding Achievements and Contribution to Humanity, UCC, 2001; Continental Governor, ABI, 2001; Deputy Director General, IBC, 2001; Adviser to the Director General, IBC, 2001; Ambassador of Grand Eminence, ABI, 2002; ABI Hall of Fame, 2002; Minister of Culture, ABI, 2003; International Peace Prize, UCC, 2004; Order of Distinction, IBC, 2004; Life Fellow, ABI, 2005; Order of American Ambassadors, ABI, 2006; Hall of Fame, IBC, 2006. Memberships: FABI. Address: Department of Clinical Virology, Huddinge University Hospital, F68, S-14186 Huddinge, Sweden. E-mail: claes.orvell@karolinska.se

OSBORN John Holbrook (Sir), b. 14 December 1922, Sheffield, England. Semi-retired: Politician; Industrialist; Scientist; Soldier. m. (1) Molly Suzanne Marten, divorced 2 daughters, (2) Joan Mary Wilkinson, deceased, (3) Patricia Felicity Read. Education: MA Cantab, Part II Tripos Metallurgy, Trinity Hall, Cambridge University, England, 1943; Diploma in Foundry Technology, National Foundry College, Wolverhampton Technical College, 1949. Appointments: Royal Corps Signals, 1943-47; Battery Commander, Royal Artillery TA, 1948-55; Assistant Works Manager, Production Controller, Cost Controller, 1947-51, Company Director, 1951-79, Samuel Osborn and Company Limited, Sheffield, England; Conservative Candidate and Member of Parliament, Sheffield Hallam, 1959-87; Parliamentary Private Secretary to Minister for Commonwealth Relations, 1962-64; Joint Honorary Secretary, Conservative 1922 Committee, 1968-87; Former Chairman, Conservative Transport Committee, All-Party Road Study Group, Parliamentary Group Energy Studies; All-Party Channel Tunnel Group; Member of the European Parliament, 1975-79; Former Member of the Interim Licensing Authority; Friends of Progress. Publications: Co-author: Conservative publications: Export of Capital; Trade not Aid; Change or Decay; A Value Added Tax; European Parliamentary publications: Help for the Regions; Energy for Europe; Also Chairman of a Parliamentary and Scientific Committee report on Information Storage and Retrieval. Honours: Knight Bachelor, Birthday Honours 1983, for Public and Political Services; Chairman, Business in Development Committee, UK Chapter of Society of International Development, 1990-1995, attached to Worldaware; Member Executive, 1968-75, 1979-82, Life Member, 1987, IPU, UK branch; Life Member, CPA, UK branch, 1987-; Officer, 1960-87, Life Member, 1987, Parliamentary and Scientific Committee; European Atlantic Group Committee, 1990-; Member, Royal Institute of International Affairs, 1985-; Member, Conservative Group for Europe, European Movement, 1975-; Council Member, 1963-79, Life Member, Industrial Society; Junior Warden-Searcher, Assistant Searcher, Freeman, 1987-, Company of Cutlers in Hallamshire. Memberships: Fellow, Royal Society for Encouragement of the Arts, Manufacture and Commerce, 1966-; Trustee of many Sheffield Charitable Trusts; President, 1960-96, Honorary Patron, Sheffield Institute of Advanced Motorists; Fellow, Institute of Directors, 1955-; Fellow, Institute of Materials (now IM3), 1947-. Address: Newlands, 147 Hawton Road, Newark, Nottinghamshire, NG24 4QG, England. E-mail: j.p.osborn147@ntlworld.com

OSBORNE Margaret Elizabeth Brenda, b. 21 December 1931, Clifton, Bristol, England. Artist; Painter; Poet. m. Stuart John Osborne (deceased), 1 daughter. Education: Intermediate Certificate in Arts and Crafts, West of England College of Art, 1950; National Diploma in Design, 1952; Art Teacher's Diploma, Painting, 1953; Ministry of Education Certificate in Education, 1953. Career: Art Teacher in Schools and Art College for 26 years; Currently, Professional Freelance Painter in oils, gouache painting figurative portraits to commission and domestic pets; Worked for Galleries, Tarmac, Cadbury's and Glynweb for retiring directors and for private collectors; Over 100 commissions; Exhibitions: The Young Contemporaries Exhibition, London, 1952; Works sent to the Pastel Society in the Mall Gallery in London, selected to tour in the provinces in the 1960's; Showed work via one-woman exhibition, Lichfield Art Centre, mid 1970s; Still available for commissions. Honours: Intermediate Art Scholarship, 1948; City Senior Scholarship, Bristol Education Committee, 1950; Senior Drawing Prize, West of England College of Art, 1952; Listed in Who's Who publications and biographical dictionaries. Membership: The Fawcett Society, 2003-. Address: 64 Burton Manor Road, Stafford ST17 9PR, England.

OSBOURNE Ozzy (John), b. 3 December 1948, Aston, Warwickshire, England. Vocalist. m. Sharon Arden, 1982, 3 children. Career: Vocalist, Black Sabbath (formerly Earth), 1967-79; Numerous concerts worldwide include: Madison Square Garden, New York, 1975; Reunion concerts include: Live Aid, Philadelphia, 1985; Solo artiste, with own backing band Blizzard Of Ozz, 1979-; US Festival, 1983; Rock In Rio festival, 1984; Monsters of Rock Festival, Castle Donington, 1986; Moscow Music Peace Festival, 1989; No More Tears world tour, 1992; Created highly successful yearly touring festival, Ozz Fest, 1996; Has recorded with artists including: Alice Cooper, Motorhead, Ringo Starr, Rick Wakeman. Recordings: Hit singles: with Black Sabbath include: Paranoid; Iron Man; War Pigs; Never Say Die; Solo/with Blizzard Of Ozz: Mr Crowley, 1980; Crazy Train, 1980; Bark At The Moon, 1983; So Tired, 1984; Shot In The Dark, 1986; The Ultimate Sin, 1986; Close My Eyes Forever, duet with Lita Ford, 1989; No More Tears, 1991; Perry Mason, 1995; I Just Want You, 1996; Get Me Through, 2001; Dreamer, 2002; Changes (with Kelly Osbourne), 2003; Listen and Learn, 2003; Albums: with Black Sabbath: Black Sabbath, 1969; Paranoid, 1970; Sabbath Bloody Sabbath, 1973; Sabotage, 1975; Technical Ecstasy, 1976; Never Say Die, 1978; Reunion, 1998; Numerous compilations; with Blizzard of Ozz/solo: Blizzards Of Ozz, 1980; Diary Of A Madman, 1981; Talk Of The Devil, 1982; Bark At The Moon, 1983; The Ultimate Sin, 1986; Tribute, 1987; No Rest For The Wicked, 1988; Just Say Ozzy, 1990; No More Tears, 1991; Live & Loud, 1993; Ozzmosis, 1995; The Ozzman Cometh, 1997; OzzFest Vol 1: Live, 1997; Diary of a Madman/Bark at the Moon/Ultimate, 1998; Down to Earth, 2001; Live at Budokan, 2002; X-Posed, 2002; Under Cover, 2005; Black Rain, 2007; Scream, 2010. Publications: I Am Ozzy, 2009. Honour: Grammy Award, 1994; NME, 2004. Address: Sharon Osbourne Management, PO Box 15397, Beverly Hills, CA 90209, USA. Website: www.ozzy.com

OSHIKOYA Kazeem Adeola, b. 2 March 1968, Lagos, Nigeria. Medical Practitioner; Lecturer; Researcher. m. Mariam Oluremi, 1 son, 1 daughter. Education: MBBS, 1996, MSc, Pharmacology, 2000, University of Lagos, Nigeria; PhD, University of Nottingham, England, in progress. Appointments: Medical Officer, Federal Staff Clinic, Kano, Kaduna State, Nigeria, 1998-99; Medical Officer, Ajayi Medical Centre, Ikorodu, Lagos, Nigeria, 1999-2000; Medical Officer, Lagos State Health Service Commission, 2000-01; Lecturer (currently on study leave), Lagos State University College of Medicine, 2001-. Publications: Numerous articles in professional journals. Honours: Lagos State Scholarship Award to Study in the United Kingdom for PhD in Clinical Paediatric Pharmacology, 2008-12; Listed in international biographical dictionaries. Memberships: American Society for Clinical Pharmacology & Therapeutics; International Society for Pharmaco-Epidemiology; European Society for Developmental, Perinatal & Paediatric Pharmacology; West African Society for Pharmacology; Nigerian Medical Association. Address: 101A Normanton Road, Derby DE1 2GG, England. E-mail: med_modhospital@yahoo.com

OSTEN Carlota Suzanne, b. 20 June 1944, Stockholm, Sweden. Director; Professor. 1 daughter. Education: Literature and Art Studies, 1965, Honorary Doctor, 2000, Lund University; Professor, Dramatical Institute, 1996. Appointments: Independent Pocket Theatre, 1967-71; Leader, Ungaklara, City Theatre of Stockholm, 1971-. Publications: 9 feature films. Honours: Film awards from Sweden and France; Steffan Preis, Germany, 1998; Assitey B16 P, Korea, 2002. E-mail: suzanne.osten@ungaklara.se

OSTERMANN Marlies, b. 25 March 1964. Consultant; Honorary Senior Lecturer. Education: PhD, MD; Training in General Medicine, Nephrology and Critical Care, different hospitals in UK and Canada, 1991-2004; ECFMG Certificate, USA, 1993; European Diploma in Intensive Care, 2000; Postgraduate Degree, Medical Education, 2005; MD, University of London, 2009. Appointments: Fellowship, Critical Care, University of Western Ontario, Canada, 1996-98; Consultant, Critical Care & Nephrology, Guy's & St Thomas' Foundation Hospital, London, UK, 2003-; Honorary Senior Lecturer, King's College London, 2009. Publications: Numerous articles in professional journals. Honours: Ballantyne Award, London Health Sciences Centre, Canada, 1998; Travel Bursary, Renal Association UK, 2000; Honorary Prize, Royal Society of Medicine, London, 2003. Memberships: Fellow, Royal College of Physicians, London; European Society of Intensive Care Medicine; Intensive Care Society, UK; Renal Association, UK; British Transplantation Society; Renal Disaster Relief Task Force; Medicine Sans Frontieres. Address: Guy's & St Thomas' Foundation Hospital, Academic Health Sciences Center, Department of Critical Care, Westminster Bridge Road, London SE1 7EH, England. E-mail: marlies.ostermann@gstt.nhs.uk

O'SULLEVAN Peter John (Sir), b. 3 March 1918. Racing Correspondent; Commentator. m. Patricia Duckworth, 1951. Education: Hawtreys, Charterhouse, College Alpin, Switzerland. Appointments: Chelsea Rescue Service, 1939-45; Editorial work and manuscript reading with Bodley Head Publisher; Racing Correspondent, Press Association, 1945-50, Daily Express, 1950-86, Today, 1986-87; Race Broadcaster, 1946-98; Chair, Osborne Studio Gallery, 1999-. Publication: Calling the Horses: A Racing Autobiography, 1989. Honours include: CBE; Derby Award, Racing Journalist of the Year, 1971, 1986; Racehorse Owner of the Year Award, Horserace Writers Association, 1974; Sport on TV Award, Daily Telegraph, 1994; Services to Racing Award, Daily Star, 1995; Media Awards Variety Club of Great Britain, 1995; Lester's Award, Jockeys' Association, 1996; Special Award, TV and Radio Industries Club, 1998. Address: 37 Cranmer Court, London SW3 3HW, England.

O'SULLIVAN Sonia, b. 28 November 1969, Cobh, Ireland. Athlete. Education: Accounting Studies, Villanova, USA. Career: Gold Medal 1500m, Silver Medal 3000m, World Student Games, 1991; Holds 7 national (Irish) records; Set new world record (her first) in 2000m, TSB Challenge, Edinburgh, 1994, new European record in 3000m, TSB Games London, 1994; Gold Medal in 3000m European Athletic Championships, Helsinki, 1994; Winner, Grand Prix 3000m, 2nd overall, 1993; Silver Medal, 1500m World Championships, Stuttgart, 1993; Gold Medal, 5000m World Championships, Gothenburg, 1995; Gold Medal, World Cross Country Championships 4km, 8km, 1998; Gold Medal,

European Championships 5000m, 10,000m, 1998; Silver Medal, 5,000m 2000 Olympic Games; Silver Medal, 5,000m, 10,000m European Championships, 2002; Retired, 2007. Publications: Running to Stand Still. Honours: Female Athlete of the Year, 1995; Texaco Sports Star of the Year (Athletics), 2002. Address: c/o Kim McDonald, 201 High Street, Hampton Hill, Middlesex TW12 1NL, England.

OSWALD Angela Mary Rose (Lady), b. 21 May 1938, London, England. Lady-in-Waiting. m. Sir Michael Oswald, 1 son, 1 daughter. Appointments: Extra Woman of the Bedchamber to H M Queen Elizabeth the Queen Mother, 1981-83; Woman of the Bedchamber to H M Queen Elizabeth the Queen Mother, 1983-2002. Honours: LVO, 1993; Freeman of the City of London, 1995; CVO, 2000. Address: The Old Rectory, Weasenham St Peter, King's Lynn, Norfolk, PE32 2TB, England.

OSWALD (William Richard) Michael (Sir), b. 21 April 1934, Walton-on-Thames, Surrey. Racehorse Stud Manager. m. Lady Angela Oswald, 1 son, 1 daughter. Education: MA, King's College Cambridge. Appointments: 2nd Lieutenant, King's Own Regiment, BAOR, Korea, 1953-54; Captain, Royal Fusiliers (TA), 1955-60; Manager, Lordship and Egerton Studs, Newmarket, 1962-69; Director, Royal Studs, 1970-98; Racing Manager for H M Queen Elizabeth, The Queen Mother, 1970-2002; National Hunt Advisor to H M The Queen, 2002-; Member, Council of Thoroughbred Breeder's Association, 1964-2001, President, 1997-2001; Chairman, Bloodstock Industry Committee, Animal Health Trust, 1986-2002; Liveryman, Worshipful Company of Shipwrights. Honours: LVO, 1979; CVO, 1988; KCVO, 1998; Honorary DSc, De Montfort University, 1997; Honorary Air Commodore, 2620 Sqdn Royal Auxiliary Air Force, 2001-. Memberships: Jockey Club; Army and Navy Club; Royal Air Force Club. Address: The Old Rectory, Weasenham St Peter, King's Lynn, Norfolk PE32 2TB, England.

OTAKI Masayuki, b. 18 November 1957, Iwaki city, Fukushima province, Japan. Professor. m. Midori, 2 sons. Education: BA, Department of Economics, University of Tokyo, 1981; PhD, Graduate School of Economics, University of Tokyo. Appointments: Lecturer, 1986-88, Associate Professor, 1988-91, Department of Economics, Kanagawa University; Associate Professor, Department of Economics, Aoyama Gakuin University, 1991-96; Associate Professor, 1996-2001, Professor, 2001-, Institute of Social Science, University of Tokyo. Publications: Numerous articles in professional journals. Honours: 37th Nikkei Tosho Bunka Sho Award. Memberships: Japanese Economic Association; Europe Economic Association; American Economic Association; Econometric Society. Address: Institute of Social Science, University of Tokyo, 7-3-1 Hongo, Bunkyo, Tokyo 113-0033, Japan.

OTLACAN Eufrosina, b. 23 February 1936, Bucharest, Romania. University Professor Emeritus. m. Romulus-Petru Otlacan, 2 daughters. Education: Graduate, Faculty of Mathematics, 1958, PhD, Mathematics, 1976, University of Bucharest. Appointments: Assistant Professor, 1959-73, Lecturer Professor, 1973-75, Institute of Petroleum, Gas and Geology; Lecturer Professor, 1975-80, Associate Professor, 1980-95, University Professor, 1995-99, Military Technical Academy; University Professor, 1999-2007, Emeritus Professor, 2007-, Gheorghe Cristea Romanian University for Sciences and Arts. Publications: 13 university mathematical books; Over 130 papers including: About the mathematical expression of the observation operators, 2000; The Synergy and the Chaos Identified in the Constitutive Equation of a Dynamic System, 2004; Information Topology and Globalisation Process, 2006; Systems in a Retardation on Anticipation Relation, 2008; Symmetry of Conjugate Systems with Anticipation and Retardation, 2009. Honours: Highly Commended Award, Literati Club Excellence, 2001; Best Paper Award, Belgium, 2003; IIAS Excellence in Research Award, University of Windsor, Canada; Kybernetics Research Award, Highly Commended Paper, 2005; Best Paper Award, Belgium Crystal, 2007. Memberships: Romanian Committee for History and Philosophy of Science and Technology; International Honorary Committee of World Organisation of Cybernetic and Systems; International Scientific Committee of Centre for Hyperinclusion and Anticipation in Orderer Systems; Romanian Society of Mathematics; Emerald Literati Network, UK. Address: Aleea Haiducului 1, bl A3, apt 9, sect 6, 061581 Bucharest, Romania. E-mail: eufrosinaotl@gmail.com

O'TOOLE Peter Seamus, b. 2 August 1932, Eire, Ireland. Actor. 1 son, 2 daughters. Education: RADA (Diploma), Associate, RADA. Career: Joined Bristol's Old Vic Theatre, played 73 parts, 1955-58; West End debut in Oh My Papa, 1957; Stratford Season, 1960; Stage appearances in, Pictures in the Hallway, 1962; Baal, 1963; Ride a Cock Horse, Waiting for Godot, 1971; Dead Eye Dicks, 1976; Present Laughter, 1978; Bristol Old Vic Theatre Season, 1973; Macbeth Old Vic, 1980; Man and Superman, 1982-83; Pygmalion, 1984, 1987; The Applecart, 1986; Jeffrey Barnard is Unwell, 1989, 1991, 1999; Films include: Kidnapped, The Day They Robbed the Bank of England, 1959; Lawrence of Arabia, 1960; Becket, 1963; Lord Jim, 1964; What's New Pussycat?, 1965; The Bible, 1966; Night of the Generals, Great Catherine, 1967; The Lion in Winter, 1968; Goodbye Mr Chips, 1969; Brotherly Love, Country Dance, 1970; Murphy's War, 1971; Under Milk Wood, The Ruling Class, Man of La Mancha, 1972; Rosebud, 1974; Man Friday, Foxtrot, 1975; Caligula, 1977; Power Play, Stuntman, Zulu Dawn, 1978; The Antagonists, My Favourite Year, 1981; Supergirl, 1984; Club Paradise, The Last Emperor, 1986; High Spirits, 1988; On a Moonlit Night, 1989; Creator, King Ralph, 1990; Wings of Fame, 1991; Rebecca's Daughters, Our Song, Civies, 1992; Fairytale: the True Story, 1997; Coming Home, The Manor, 1998; Molokai: The Story of Father Damien, 1999; Global Heresy, The Final Curtain, 2002; Bright Young Things, 2003; Troy, 2004; Lassie, 2005; Venus, One Night with the King, 2006; Ratatouille (voice), Stardust, Thomas Kinkade's Home for Christmas, 2007; Eldorado, Cristiada, 2012. Publications: The Child, 1992; The Apprentice, 1996. Honours: Commander of the Order of Arts and Letters, France; Outstanding Achievement Award, 1999. Address: c/o William Morris Agency, Stratton House, Stratton Street, London, W1X 5FE, England.

OU Wen-Sheng, b. 15 January 1962, Tainan, Taiwan. Architect. m. Xue-Ying Ke, 2 daughters. Education: Bachelor, 1998; Master, 2000; PhD, 2005. Appointments: Interior Designer, 1997; Architect, 2000; Lecturer, 2004-05; Assistant Professor, 2005-09; Associate Professor, 2009-. Publications: More than 50 international referred papers. Honours: Golden Rudder Award, 2011; Best Paper Award, ICFMD, 2011. Memberships: Fellow, International Congress of Disaster Management. Address: No 57, Chung Shan Road, Sect 2, Taiping, Taichung, Taiwan. E-mail: wsou@ncut.edu.tw

OUGHTON Douglas Robert, b. 22 April 1942, Hendon, London, England. Building Services Engineer. 1 son. Education: MSc (Arch), Bristol University, 1979. Appointments: London-based contractor, 6 years; Engineer,

1967, Director, 1981, Divisional Director, 2001, Oscar Faber (now AECOM), St Albans and Northern Ireland; Building Services Research Information Association Council, 1975-87; Chairman, European Intelligent Building Group, 1992-95; CIBSE Professional Practices Committee, 1992-94; External Examiner, University of Ulster, 1994-99; Professional Advisory Panel, University of Hertfordshire, 1998-99; Engineering Council respresentative on UNESCO Science Committee, 2000-03; Chairman, CIBSE Patrons, 1999-2001; CIBSE Education, Training & Membership Committee, 2000-, Chairman, 2003-06; Executive Board, 1999-2006, Council, 1995-2006, President, 2002-03, CIBSE; Chairman, CIBSE Careers Panel, 2003-; Chairman, Education for Engineering Operational Group, 2009-. Publications: Heating and Air Conditioning of Buildings, 1989, 1995, 2001, 2008; Numerous technical papers on topics including energy, controls and intelligent buildings, relating to building services. Memberships: Honorary Member, CIBSE; Fellow, Royal Academy of Engineering. E-mail: doug.oughton@btinternet.com

OUZTS Eugene Thomas, b. 7 June 1930, Thomasville, Georgia, USA. Minister; Secondary educator. m. Mary Olive Vineyard. Education: MA, Harding University, 1957; Postgraduate: Murray State University, University of Arkansas, Arizona State University, University of Arizona; Northern Arizona University. Appointments: Certificated Secondary Teacher, Arkansas, Missouri, Arizona; Ordained Minister Church of Christ, 1956; Minister in various Churches in Arkansas, Missouri, Texas, -1965; Teacher, various public schools, Arkansas, Missouri, 1959-65; Teacher, Arizona, 1965-92; Minister in Arizona Church of Christ, Clifton, Morenci, Safford and Duncan, 1965-. Honours: Civil Air Patrol, Arizona Wing Chaplain of Year, 1984; Thomas C Casaday Unit Chaplain, 1985; Arizona, Wing Safety Officer, 1989; Arizona Wing Senior Member, 1994; Meritorious Service Award, 1994; Southwestern Region Senior Member, 1995; Exceptional Service Award, 1997; Life Fellowship, IBA, Cambridge, England. Memberships: Military Chaplains Association; Disabled American Veterans; Air Force Association; American Legion; Elks; Board, Arizona Church of Christ Bible Camp; Airport Advisory Board, Greenlee County, Arizona; Civil Air Patrol/Air Force Auxiliary (Chaplain, 1982, 1st Lieutenant advanced through grades to Lieutenant Colonel, 1989, Retired, 2008); Assistant Wing Chaplain. Address: 739E, Cottonwood, Duncan, Arizona 85534-8108, USA.

OVENDEN John Anthony, b. 26 May 1945, Epping, Essex, England. Clergyman. m. Christine, 2 sons, 1 daughter. Education: BA, Open University; MA, Kings College, London. Appointments: Precentor and Sacrist, Ely Cathedral; Vicar of St Mary's, Primrose Hill, London; Canon of St George's Chapel, Windsor; Chaplain in the Royal Chapel, Windsor Great Park; Chaplain to H M The Queen; Canon Chaplain, 1998-; Precentor, 2007-. Honours: Lieutenant, Victorian Order, 2007. Address: Little Croft, Great Rissington, Glos, GL54 2LN, England.

OVERILL Richard Edward, b. 29 January 1950, Halstead, Essex, England. Computer Scientist. m. Geraldine, 2 sons. Education: St Christopher School, Letchworth, England, 1960-68; BSc, 1971; PhD, 1976, University of Leicester, England. Appointments: Senior Analyst/Advisor, 1975-1986; Lecturer in Computer Science, 1987-1994; Senior Lecturer in Computer Science, 1994-, King's College London. Publications: 85 papers and articles in academic journals, professional journals and conference proceedings, covering computational science, parallel computing and information security. Memberships: Fellow, British Computer Society; Fellow, Institute of Mathematics; Fellow, Higher Education Academy; Member, Institute of Engineering and Technology; Member, Royal Society of Chemistry. Address: Department of Informatics, King's College London, Strand, London WC2R 2LS, England. E-mail: richard.overill@kcl.ac.uk

OVODOV Yury S, b. 28 August 1937, Kharkov, Ukraine, USSR. Chemist; Immunochemist. m. Raisa G Ovodova, 1 son. Education: Lomonosov State University, Moscow, 1959; Candidate of Chemical Sciences, 1963; Doctor of Chemical Sciences, 1972; Professor in Bioorganic Chemistry, 1973. Appointments: Senior Laboratory Worker, Novosibirsk Institute of Organic Chemistry, Siberian Branch of the USSR Academy of Sciences, 1959-62; Intern, Institute of Chemistry of Natural Compounds, the USSR Academy of Sciences, Moscow, 1960-62; Junior Scientist, Laboratory of Chemistry of Natural Substances, Vladivostok, 1962-64; Deputy Director, 1967-87, and concurrently Head of Department, 1975-94, Head of Laboratory, 1964-75 and 1979-94, Pacific Institute of Bioorganic Chemistry, Far Eastern Branch, Academy of Sciences, Vladivostok; Elected Corresponding Member of the USSR Academy of Sciences, 1990; Full Member, Russian Academy of Sciences, 1992; Head, Department of Molecular Immunology, 1994-2004, Director, 2004-, Institute of Physiology, Komi Science Centre, the Urals Branch of the Russian Academy of Sciences, Syktyvkar; Concurrently, Director, Educational Scientific Centre, Syktyvkar State University, 2000-; Chief Scientist, Institute of Chemistry, Komi Science Centre, The Urals Branch of the Russian Academy of Sciences, Syktyvkar, 2002-06; Head of Syktyvkar and Vyatsky State University Magistracies, Syktyvkar and Kirov, 2010-. Publications: Triterpenic Glycosides of Gypsophila spp; Bioglycans-immunomnodulators; Bacterial Lipopolysaccharides; Oncofetal Antigens and Oncoprecipitins; The Chemical Foundations of Immunity; Selected Chapters of Bioorganic Chemistry; Structural Features and Physiological Activities of Plant Polysaccharides; Pectic Substances of Plants of the European North of Russia. Honours: Lenin Komsomol Prize, 1972; I I Mechnikov Award, 1993; Y A Ovchinnikov Award, 2003; Laureate Medal, Russian Academy of Sciences and Arts, 2007; Laureate of Competition, 100 Best Russian Institutions, Science, Innovations, Scientific Elaboration, Nomination: The Scientist of the Year, 2010; Some Soviet and Russian Orders and Medals; Listed in Who's Who publications and international biographical dictionaries. Memberships: The Slav Academy of Science; New York Academy of Sciences; International Endotoxin Society; American Chemical Society; American Association for the Advancement of Science; Russian Biochemical Society; The Urals Immunology Society; Russian Physiological Society; Society of Biotechnologists of Russia. Address: Institute of Physiology, Komi Science Centre, The Urals Branch of the Russian Academy of Sciences, 50 Pervomaiskaya str, 167982 Syktyvkar, Russia.

OWEN, Baron of the City of Plymouth, David Anthony Llewellyn Owen, b. 2 July 1938, Plymouth, Devon, England. Physician; Politician; Businessman. m. Deborah Schabert, 2 sons, 1 daughter. Education: MA, MB BChir, Cantab, 1962. Appointments: Neurological Registrar, St Thomas' Hospital, London, 1964-65; Research Fellow, Medical Unit, St Thomas, 1966-68; Member of Parliament for Plymouth, 1966-92; Minister for Navy, 1968-70; Minister of Health, 1974-76; Minister of State for Foreign and Commonwealth Affairs, 1976-77; Foreign Secretary, 1977-79; Leader of the SDP Parliamentary Party, 1981-82; Deputy Leader of

SDP, 1982-83; Leader of SDP, 1983-87 and 1988-92; EU Negotiator in Former Yugoslavia, 1992-95. Publications: Papers and articles in medical journals; The Politics of Defense; In Sickness and in Health; Face the Future; The United Kingdom; Our NHS; Autobiography, Time to Declare, 1991; Anthology of poetry, Seven Ages, 1992 and Balkan Odyssey, 1995. Honours: Companion of Honour, 1994; Baron Owen of the City of Plymouth, 1992; Chancellor of Liverpool University, 1996; FRCP, 2005. Address: House of Lords, Westminster, London SW1A 0PW, England.

OWEN Nicholas David Arundel, b. 10 February 1947, United Kingdom. Journalist; Television Presenter. m. Brenda, 2 sons, 2 daughters. Appointments: Journalist: Surrey Mirror, 1964, London Evening Standard, 1968-70, Daily Telegraph, 1970-71, Financial Times, 1972-79, Now! Magazine, 1979-81; Reporter and Presenter, BBC Television News, 1981-84; Presenter, ITN, 1984-; Royal Correspondent, ITV News, 1994-2000; Channel 4 News Business and Economics Correspondent; Presented ITV1's live hour and a half Budget Programme, 2004; Anchor, Parliament Programme, Channel 4's first daytime political series; Presenter of ITV Lunchtime News, 2002-2007; Presenter, BBC New 24, 2007-. Publications: History of the British Trolleybus, 1972; Diana – The People's Princess. Address: c/o Independent Television News, 200 Gray's Inn Road, London WC1X 8XZ, England. E-mail: nicholas.owen@itn.co.uk

OWENS Jonathan David, b. 1 June 1973, Wales. Associate Professor. Education: B Eng (Hons), Manufacturing Management; M Eng (Hons), Advanced Manufacturing Engineering and Management; M Phil; Eng D; Post Graduate Certificate in Higher and Further Education. Appointments: Mechanical Apprentice, 1989-93, Shift Mechanical Craftsman, 1993-94, Shift Engineer, 1994, Engineering Placement, 1995, 1996, British Steel plc, Shotton Works, Deeside; Project Engineer, School of Electrical Engineering, University of Salford, Greater Manchester, 1997; Research Fellow, School of Management, University of Salford, 1998-2000; Lecturer, Operations and Logistics Management, Buckinghamshire Business School, Buckinghamshire Chilterns University College, 2000-03; Associate Professor, Operations and Logistics Management, Lincoln Business School, University of Lincoln, 2003-. Publications: Numerous articles in professional journals. Honours: Buck and Hickman Apprentice of the Year Award, 1989; Deans Medal and Commendation for Bachelor's dissertation, 1997; Best Paper in Conference Track, 2005; Best Conference Paper, 2007; Listed in international biographical dictionaries. Memberships: Fellow, Higher Education Academy; Chartered Fellow, Institute of Logistics and Transport; Fellow, Institute of Operations Management; Member, Institute of Engineering and Technology; Chartered Engineer; European Engineer. Address: Lincoln Business School, University of Lincoln, Brayford Pool, Lincoln, Lincolnshire LN6 7TS, England. E-mail: jowens@lincoln.ac.uk

OXLEY William, b. 29 April 1939, Manchester, England. Poet; Writer; Translator. m. Patricia Holmes, 1963, 2 daughters. Education: Manchester College of Commerce, 1953-55. Appointments: Dubbed Britain's First Europoet after publication of works on European continent during 1980s and 1990s; Only British poet to have read in Shangri-la, Nepal; Consultant Editor, Acumen magazine; Editor, Completing the Picture anthology, 1995; Co-editor (with Patricia Oxley), Modern Poets of Europe, 2004. Publications: The Dark Structures, 1967; New Workings, 1969; Passages from Time: Poems from a Life, 1971; The Icon Poems, 1972; Sixteen Days in Autumn (travel), 1972; Opera Vetera, 1973; Mirrors of the Sea, 1973; Eve Free, 1974; Mundane Shell, 1975; Superficies, 1976; The Exile, 1979; The Notebook of Hephaestus and Other Poems, 1981; Poems of a Black Orpheus, 1981; The Synopthegms of a Prophet, 1981; The Idea and Its Imminence (philosophy), 1982; Of Human Consciousness (philosophy), 1982; The Vitalist Reader, 1982; The Cauldron of Inspiration, 1983; A Map of Time, 1984; The Triviad and Other Satires, 1984; The Inner Tapestry, 1985; The Mansands Trilogy, 1988; Mad Tom on Tower Hill, 1988; The Patient Reconstruction of Paradise, 1991; Forest Sequence, 1991; In the Drift of Words, 1992; The Playboy, 1992; Cardboard Troy, 1993; The Hallsands Tragedy, 1993; Collected Longer Poems, 1994; Completing the Picture (editor), 1995; The Green Crayon Man, 1997; No Accounting for Paradise (autobiography), 1999; Firework Planet (for children), 2000; Reclaiming the Lyre: New and Selected Poems, 2001; Namaste: Nepal Poems, 2004; London Visions, 2005; Poems Antibes, 2006; Sunlight in a Champagne Glass, 2009. Honours: Millennium Year Poet-in-Residence, Torbay; Torbay Arts Base Award for Literature, 2008; First prize for Hills of Hampstead, by online long poem magazine, Echoes of Gilgamesh; Many other contributions to anthologies and periodicals. Memberships: Founder Member, Long Poem Group. Address: 6 The Mount, Furzeham, Brixham, South Devon TQ5 8QY, England. E-mail: PWoxley@aol.com Website: www.poetrypf.co.uk

OYAT Christopher, b. 31 July 1966, Gulu, Uganda. Teacher. m. Doris Laker, 2 sons, 3 daughters. Education: BA, Social Sciences, Makerere University, Uganda, 1991; Certificate in Human Rights and Humanitarian Law, University of Lund, Sweden, 1995; MA, Development Studies, Uganda Martyrs University, Uganda, 1997; Certificate in Law, Law Development Center, Kampala, Uganda, 1998; Diploma, Public and Local Government Administration, Institute of Management, Science & Technology, Uganda, 2000; Doctor of Letters, Business Organization, St Clements University, Turks and Caicos Islands, 2005; PhD, Management, California University FCE, USA, 2011; Postdoctoral Degree, Management, Isles Internationale Universite, Belgium; many others. Appointments: Licensed Primary School Teacher, 1986-88; Licensed Secondary School Teacher, 1989-90; Lecturer, Department of Business Management and Marketing, Kiima College of Commerce, 1990; Town Clerk, Kalongo Town Board, 1992-95; Assistant Town Clerk, Kitgum Town Council, 1995-2000; Deputy Town Clerk, 2000, Ag Town Clerk, 2001, Gulu Municipal Council; Lecturer, Gulu University, 2003-. Publications: 21 papers and articles in professional journals. Honours: Gold Medal from India; Doctor of Excellence, EQAC. Memberships: International Association of Distance Learning; International Council for Open and Distance Education; United States Distance Learning Association; British Learning Association; Oxford Association of Management; Cambridge Academy of Management; Intergovernmental Higher Academic Council; Institute of Management Specialists; Design, Technology and Management Society International; Institute of Professional Financial Managers; Academy of Multi-Skills. Address: PO Box 166, Gulu University, Gulu, Uganda.

OYLER Edmund John Wilfrid, b. 8 February 1934, London, England. Chartered Accountant. m. Elizabeth Kathleen Larkins, 1961, 2 sons, 1 daughter. Education: Trinity College, Cambridge, 1953-56; BA, 1956; MA 1960; University College, London, 1970-72; LLM, 1972; Heythrop College, London, 1997-2000; MTh, 2000. Appointments: National Service, 2nd Lieutenant, Royal Signals, 1951-53; Chartered accountant in public practice, ACA, 1961, FCA,

DICTIONARY OF INTERNATIONAL BIOGRAPHY 36th EDITION

1972; Articled – Pannell Crewdson and Hardy, 1956-60; Whinney Smith and Whinney, 1961; Partner, Whinney Murray and Co, 1967-79; Partner, Ernst and Whinney, 1979-89; Partner, Ernst and Young, 1989-97; Partner specialising in taxation of insurance companies, 1967-92; National tax partner, 1978-81; Partner with national responsibility for trusts, 1985-89; National compliance partner, 1988-97; Sole Practitioner, 1997-99. Memberships: Athenaeum; Madrigal Society; Georgian Group; Royal Geographical Society; Activities for ICAEW include: Co-opted Member of Council, 1996-99, Chairman, Financial Services Authorisation Committee, 1995-2001, Chairman, Joint Investment Business Committee, 1995-2001, Chairman, London Society of Chartered Accountants, 1996-97, Chairman, Joint Monitoring Unit Limited, 1997-2001; Chairman, Chartered Accountants Compensation Scheme Limited, 2010-. Address: 20 Bedford Gardens, London, W8 7EH, England.

OZ Amos, b. 4 May 1939, Jerusalem, Israel. Author; Professor of Hebrew Literature. m. Nily Zuckerman, 5 Apr 1960, 1 son, 2 daughters. Education: BA cum laude, Hebrew Literature, Philosophy, Hebrew University, Jerusalem, 1965. Appointments: Teacher, Literature, Philosophy, Hulda High School and Givat Brenner Regional High School, 1963-86; Visiting Fellow, St Cross College, Oxford, England, 1969-70; Writer-in-Residence, Hebrew University, Jerusalem, 1975, 1990; Visiting Professor, University of California, Berkeley, USA, 1980; Writer-in-Residence, Professor of Literature, The Colorado College, Colorado Springs, 1984-85; Writer in Residence, Visiting Professor of Literature, Boston University, Massachusetts, 1987; Full Professor of Hebrew Literature, Ben Gurion University, Beer Sheva, Israel, 1987-; Writer-in-Residence, Tel Aviv University, 1996; Writer in Residence, Visiting Professor of Literature, Princeton University, (Old Dominion Fellowship), 1997; Weidenfeld Visiting Professor of European Comparative Literature, St Anne's College, Oxford, 1998. Publications: Novels: Elsewhere; Perhaps, 1966; My Michael, 1968; Touch the Water, Touch the Wind, 1973; A Perfect Peace, 1982; Black Box, 1987; The Know a Woman, 1989; The Third Condition, 1991; The Same Sea, 1991; Don't Call It Night, 1994; Panther in the Basement, 1995; Novellas and short stories: Where the Jackals Howl, 1965; Unto Death, 1971; Different People (anthology), 1974; The Hill of Evil Counsel, 1976; Soumchi (children's story), 1978; Telling Tales (charity anthology), 2004; Essays: Under This Blazing Light, 1979; In the Land of Israel, 1983; The Slopes of Lebanon, 1987; Report of the Situation, 1992; Israel, Palestine and Peace, 1994; A Story Begins, 1996; All Our Hopes, 1998; But These Are Two Different Wars, 2002; Other: A Tale of Love and Darkness (memoir), 2002. Honours include: Holon Prize, 1965; Wingate Prize, London, 1988; Honorary Doctorate, Tel Aviv University, 1992; Cross of the Knight of the Legion D'Honneur, 1997; Honorary Doctorate, Brandeis University, USA, 1998; Israel Prize for Literature, 1998; Freedom of Speech Prize, Writers' Union of Norway, 2002; International Medal of Tolerance, Polish Ecumenical Council, 2002; Goethe Cultural Prize, Frankfurt, Germany, 2005. Address: Ben Gurion University of the Negev, PO Box 653, Beersheva 84105, Israel. Website: www.bgu.ac.il

OZAKI Miwako, b. 25 July 1961, Nagoyo, Japan. Researcher; Professor. m. Manabu Nakayama, 1 son. Education: BS, 1987, MS, 1989, Pharmacology, Tokyo University of Science; PhD, Molecular Genetics, National Institute of Genetics, 1992. Appointments: Postdoctoral Fellow, Kyoto University, 1992-93; Research Associate, Osaka Bioscience Research Institute, 1993-94; Postdoctoral Research Fellow, National Institutes of Health, USA, 1994-96; Senior Researcher, 1996-2001, Staff Scientist, 2001-05, Brain Science Institute, RIKEN; Professor, Institute for Biomedical Engineering, 2005-, Visiting Professor, Comprehensive Research Organization, 2006-, Waseda University; Principal Investigator, 2005-09, Vice Director, Research Director, 2006-09, Waseda-Olympus Bioscience Research Institute. Publications: Numerous articles in professional journals. Honours: Fellowship, Japan Society for the Promotion of Science for Japan Junior Scientist, 1991-93; Fellowship, National Institutes of Health, USA, 1994-96; 7th Award, Japan Academy of Women Scientists, 2002; NeuroSignals/ Award for Excellent Selected Paper, Hong Kong, 2002; International Hippocrates Award for Medical Achievement, 2010. Memberships: Society for Neuroscience, USA; Asian Pacific Society for Neurochemistry; European Society of Neuroscience; New York Academy of Science; The Molecular Biology Society of Japan; Japanese Neuroscience Society; The Society of Japanese Women Scientists.

OZEKHOME Mike Agbedor Abu, b. 15 October 1957, Iviukwe, Agenebode. Law. m. Josephine, 1991, 4 sons, 3 daughters. Education: Baptist Academy, Lagos, 1975; University of IFE, ILE-IFE, 1975-80; LLB honours, Nigeria Law School, Lagos, 1980-81; LLM, University of IFE, ILE-IFE, 1982-83. Appointments: State Counsel, Federal Ministry of Justice, Lagos; Graduate Assistant at Law, University of IFE, 1982-83; Counselor, Deputy Head of Chambers, Gani Fawehinmij Chambers, Lagos, 1984-85; Chief Counsel, Head of Chamber, Mike Ozekhome's Chambers, 1986-; Graduate Assistant, University of Ife; Lecturer, Benson Idahusa University, Benin City; Senior Advocate of Nigeria. Publications: Over 200 learned articles published in journals and magazines, and as chapters in books. Honours: Distinguished Alumnus, University of IFE; Most Outstanding Alumnus; Most Outstanding Youth of Nigeria; Senior Advocate of Nigeria (Senior Advocate of the Masses, SAM), Macres Ecowas and Royal Achievers Gold Awards; Bendel State Merit Scholarship; 10 Chieftaincy titles in different parts of Nigeria; Patron, Trustee, Over 30 students, Youth Organisations, Nigeria; Notary Public of Nigeria. Memberships: International Bar Association; Nigerian Bar Association; Commonwealth Lawyers Association; American Bar Association; African Bar Association; Amnesty International; Universal Defenders of Democracy; Democratic Rights Initiative; Mike Ozekhome Foundation, Peace Initiative; Civil Liberties Organization; Joint Action Committee of Nigeria; Vision 2020 National Political Reform Conference; many others. Address: Ukwe House, Plot 226, Census Close, off Babs Animashaun Street, P O Box 6811, Surulere, Lagos, Nigeria.

ÖZSOYLU N Şinasi, b. 29 August 1927, Erzurum, Turkey. Physician. m. F Selma, 2 sons, 1 daughter. Education: Istanbul University, 1951; Ankara University, 1959; Washington University, 1960, 1961; Harvard University, 1963; Johns Hopkins University, 1971. Appointments: Associate Professor, Paediatrics, Hacettepe University, 1964; Professor of Paediatrics and Haematology, 1969; Visiting Professor, Department of Paediatrics, Maryland University, 1972; Head, Paediatrics Department, 1976; Head, Haematology and Hepatology Departments, 1973-94; Professor of Paediatrics and Haematology, Fatih University, 1994-2005. Publications: Around 990 in professional journals. Honours include: İhsan Dogramaci Award, 1979; Mustafa N Parlar Award, 1989; Hacettepe University Excellence in Science Achievement Award, 1991; TUSAV Honorary Award, 2002; Help to Health Honorary Award, 2003; Fatih

University Award, 2004; SAMEDER Award, 2005; Physician of the Year, 2007; Interdisciplinary Hematology Expert for International Pediatric Association (IPA); Listed in Who's Who publications and international biographical dictionaries. Memberships: American Academy of Paediatrics, Honorary Fellow; American Paediatrics Society, Honorary Member; Islamic Academy of Sciences; Turkish Paediatric Society; International Paediatric Association; Turkish Hematology Society; Turkish Paediatric Hematology Society; Turkish Hegatology Society; 10 national and 8 international societies. Address: Fatih University Medical Faculty, Alparslan Türkeş Cad No 57 Emek, Ankara 06510, Turkey.

P

PACINO Al (Alfredo James), b. 25 April 1940, New York, USA. Actor. 1 son, 2 daughters. Education: The Actors Studio. Appointments: Messenger, Cinema Usher; Co-Artistic Director, The Actors Studio Inc, New York, 1982-83; Member, Artistic Directorate Globe Theatre, 1997-. Creative Works: Films include: Me, Natalie, 1969; Panic in Needle Park, 1971; The Godfather, 1972; Scarecrow, 1973; Serpico, 1974; The Godfather Part II, 1974; Dog Day Afternoon, 1975; Bobby Deerfield, 1977; And Justice For All, 1979; Cruising, 1980; Author! Author!, 1982; Scarface, 1983; Revolution, 1985; Sea of Love, 1990; Dick Tracy, 1991; The Godfather Part III, 1990; Frankie and Johnny, 1991; Glengarry Glen Ross, 1992; Scent of A Woman, 1992; Carlito's Way, 1994; City Hall, 1995; Heat, 1995; Donny Brasco, 1996; Looking For Richard, 1996; Devil's Advocate, 1997; The Insider, 1999; Chinese Coffee, 1999; Man of the People, 1999; Any Given Sunday, 1999; Insomnia, 2002; Simone, 2002; People I Know, 2002; The Recruit, 2003; Gigli, 2003; The Merchant of Venice, 2004; Two for the Money, 2005; 88 Minutes, 2007; Ocean's Thirteen, 2007; Righteous Kill, 2008; You Don't Know Jack, 2010; Jack and Jill, The Son of No One, Wilde Salome, 2011; Stand Up Guys, 2012. Honours include: 1 Oscar; 2 BAFTAs; 2 Primetime Emmy Awards; 2 Tony Awards; Lifetime Achievement Award, American Film Institute, 2007; 4 Golden Globe Awards. Address: c/o Rick Nicita, CAA, 9830 Wilshire Boulevard, Beverly Hills, CA 90212, USA.

PADFIELD Peter Lawrence Notton, b. 3 April 1932, Calcutta, India. Author. m. Dorothy Jean Yarwood, 23 April 1960, 1 son, 2 daughters. Publications: The Sea is a Magic Carpet, 1960; The Titanic and the Californian, 1965; An Agony of Collisions, 1966; Aim Straight: A Biography of Admiral Sir Percy Scott, 1966; Broke and the Shannon: A Biography of Admiral Sir Philip Broke, 1968; The Battleship Era, 1972; Guns at Sea: A History of Naval Gunnery, 1973; The Great Naval Race: Anglo-German Naval Rivalry 1900-1914, 1974; Nelson's War, 1978; Tide of Empires: Decisive Naval Campaigns in the Rise of the West, Vol I 1481-1654, 1979, Vol II 1654-1763, 1982; Rule Britannia: The Victorian and Edwardian Navy, 1981; Beneath the Houseflag of the P & O, 1982; Dönitz, The Last Führer, 1984; Armada, 1988; Himmler, Reichsführer - SS, 1990; Hess: Flight for the Führer, 1991, revised, updated edition; Hess: The Führer's Disciple, 1993; War Beneath the Sea: Submarine Conflict 1939-1945, 1995; Maritime Supremacy and the Opening of the Western Mind: Naval Campaigns that Shaped the Modern World 1588-1782, 1999; Maritime Power and the Struggle for Freedom: Naval Campaigns that Shaped the Modern World 1788-1851, 2003; Maritime Dominion and the Triumph of the Free World: Naval Campaigns that Shaped the Modern World 1852-2001, 2009; Novels: The Lion's Claw, 1978; The Unquiet Gods, 1980; Gold Chains of Empire, 1982; Salt and Steel, 1986. Honour: Winner Mountbatten Maritime Prize, 2003.

PAE Tae-Il, b. 16 May 1966, Pusan, South Korea. Professor. m. Gye-Hee Lee, 1 son. Education: BA, 1989, MA, 1991, Language & Literature, Seoul National University; PhD, Education, Purdue University, USA, 2002. Appointments: Associate Professor, Yeungnam University; Consultant, Korea Institute of Curriculum & Evaluation; Authors of English Textbooks for Secondary Students; Executive Officer, The Korea Association of Teachers of English. Publications: Many articles in prestigious journals such as Language Testing, Learning & Individual Differences; Journal of Language & Solid Psychology, American Biology Teacher, etc. Honours: Best Paper Award, Korea National Research Foundation, 2007, 2009; Best Paper Award, Korea Association of Teachers of English; Listed in international biographical dictionaries. Memberships: Fellow, Pan-Korea English Teachers' Association; Fellow, The Korea Association of Secondary English Education. E-mail: paet@ynu.ac.kr

PAGE Annette (Annette Hynd), b. 18 December 1932, Manchester, England. Retired Ballerina. m. Ronald Hynd, 1957, 1 daughter. Education: Royal Ballet School, 1944. Appointments: Ballerina, Sadler's Wells Theatre Ballet (Royal Ballet touring company), 1950-55; Ballerina, Sadler's Wells Ballet, (major Royal Ballet company), 1955-67; Ballet Mistress, Bayerischestaatsoper, Munich, 1984-86; Roles include: The Firebird; Princess Aurora in Sleeping Beauty; Odette-Odile in Swan Lake; Giselle; Lise in La Fille Mal Gardée; Juliet in Romeo and Juliet; Cinderella; Swanhilda in Coppelia; Nikiya in La Bayadère; Les Sylphides; Miller's Wife in Three Cornered Hat; Terpsichore in Apollo; Blue Girl in Les Biches; Mamzelle Angot; Ballerina in Petrouchka; Symphonic Variations; Les Rendezvous; Beauty and the Beast; La Capricciosa in Lady and the Fool; Queen of Hearts in Card Game; Agon; Polka in Solitaire; Ballerina in Scènes de Ballet; Queens of Fire and Air in Homage to the Queen; Blue Girl in Les Pâtineurs; Tango and Polka in Façade; Julia and Pèpe in A Wedding Bouquet; Moon and Pas de Six in Prince of the Pagodas; Danses Concertantes; Faded Beauty and Young Lover in Noctambules; Flower Festival Pas de Deux; Ballerina in Ballet Imperial; Assists husband, Ronald Hynd, with many of his productions, including The Merry Widow, Sleeping Beauty, etc. Memberships: Arts Council of Great Britain, 1976-79.

PAGET Julian Tolver (Lt. Col. Sir), b. 11 July 1921, London, England. Army Officer. m. Diana Farmer, 1 son, 1 daughter. Education: MA, Modern Languages, Christ Church Oxford, 1939-40. Appointments: Commission in Coldstream Guards, 1940-68; Served Northwest Europe, 1944-45; Retired as Lieutenant Colonel, 1968; Author, 1967-; Gentleman Usher to H M The Queen, 1971-91. Publications: Counter Insurgency Campaigning, 1967; Last Post, Aden 1964-67, 1969; The Story of the Guards, 1976; The Pageantry of Britain, 1979; The Yeoman of the Guard, 1984; Wellington's Peninsular War, 1990; Hougoumont, 1992; The Coldstream Guards 1650-2000, 2000; The Crusading General, 2008. Honours: Succeeded as 4th Baronet, 1972; CVO, 1984. Memberships: Cavalry and Guards Club; Flyfishers Club.

PAGLIA Camille (Anna), b. 2 April 1947, Endicott, New York, USA. Professor of Humanities; Writer. Education: BA, State University of New York at Binghamton, 1968; MPhil, 1971, PhD, 1974, Yale University. Appointments: Faculty, Bennington College, Vermont, 1972-80; Visiting Lecturer, Wesleyan University, 1980; Visiting Lecturer, Yale University, 1980-84; Assistant Professor, 1984-87, Associate Professor, 1987-91, Professor of Humanities, 1991-2000, Philadelphia College of the Performing Arts, later the University of the Arts, Philadelphia; Columnist, Salon.com, 1995-2001; University Professor and Professor of Humanities and Media Studies, University of the Arts, 2000-; Contributing Editor, Interview magazine, 2001-. Publications: Sexual Personae: Art and Decadence from Nefertiti to Emily Dickinson, 1990; Sex, Art, and American Culture: Essays, 1992; Vamps and Tramps: New Essays, 1994; Alfred Hitchcock's "The Birds", 1998; Break, Blow, Burn: Camille Paglia Reads Forty-Three of the World's Best Poems, 2005. Contributions to: Journals and periodicals and Internet communications. Address: University of the Arts, 320 South Broad Street, Philadelphia, PA 19102, USA.

DICTIONARY OF INTERNATIONAL BIOGRAPHY 36th EDITION

PAHANG H.R.H. Sultan of, b. 24 October 1930, Istana Mangga Tunggal, Pekan, Malaysia. m. (1) Tengku Hajjah Afzan binti Tengku Muhammad, 1954, deceased 1988, 2 sons, 5 daughters, (2) Sultanah Hajah Kalsom, 1991, 1 son. Education: Malay College, Kuala Kangsar; Worcester College, Oxford; University College, Exeter. Appointments: Tengku Mahkota (Crown Prince), 1944; Captain, 4th Battalion, Royal Malay Regiment, 1954; Commander, 12th Infantry Battalion of Territorial Army, 1963-65, Lieutenant-Colonel; Member, State Council, 1955; Regent, 1956, 1959, 1965; Succeeded as Sultan, 1974; Timbalan Yang di Pertuan Agong (Deputy Supreme Head of State), Malaysia, 1975-79, Yang di Pertuan Agong (Supreme Head of State), 1979-84, 1985; Constitutional Head, International Islamic University, 1988. Honours include: DLitt, Malaya, 1988, LLD, Northrop, USA, 1993. Address: Istana Abu Bakar, Pekan, Pahang, Malaysia.

PAHOS Spiro J, b. 22 November 1980, Athens, Greece. Naval Engineer. Education: BSc, Shipbuilding Technology, Technological Education Institution of Athens, 2003; M Eng, Naval Architecture & Ocean Engineering, Universities of Glasgow and Strathclyde, 2006; PhD, Reliability-based Vulnerability Requirements for Asymmetric Threats in the Ship Design Process, 2009. Appointments: Intern, Groenendijk & Soetermeer, Rotterdam, 2002; Intern, Vuyk Engineering, Rotterdam, 2003; Research Staff, Helsinki University of Technology, 2004; Research Staff, Universities of Glasgow and Strathclyde, 2005, 2006; Research Staff, Universities of Glasgow and Strathclyde, 2006-09; Sergeant Ranger, Systems Engineering, Hellenic Army Amphibious Assault Unit, 2009-10; Naval Engineer, Marine & Offshore Technical Services, Ansys UK Ltd, 2010-. Publications: Numerous articles in professional journals. Honours: Tertiary Education Scholarship, TEI, Athens, 1999; 3-year Marstruct Post-graduate Scholarship, 2006-09; Listed in various international biographical dictionaries. Memberships: RINA; SNAME; ASNE. Address: Ansys UK Ltd, 3 Horsham Gates, North Street, Horsham, W. Sussex, RH13 5PJ, England. E-mail: spiro.pahos@ansys.com

PAHYS Nick Jr, b. 18 May 1933, Cleveland, Ohio, USA. Author; Museum Curator; Restauranteur. m. Joanne Pahys, 2 sons, 1 daughter. Education: American College, Brigham Young University Extension; Life Underwriters Training Council; Limbre-Dale Carnegie. Appointments: Buckaroo Kid in Cleveland Theatre District; Master of Ceremonies working with Jack Paar, Bob Hope and Hugh O'Brian, 1950's; Insurance Business, Western & Southern, 1960's; Restaurant and Hotel Business, 1980's; Curator, author, founder, The One and Only Presidential Museum in the World, Williamsfield, Ohio, USA, 1990's. Publication: Book: The Books of the Centuries. What Every American Should Know! John Hanson. The first president of the United States of America. Fact or Fiction. You be the Judge, 2001. Honours include: 2000 Outstanding Intellectuals of the 21st Century, 500 Founders of the 21st Century, Great Minds of the 21st Century, Deputy Director General, 100 Great Americans, Lifetime Achievement Award, International Register of Profiles, Vice Consul, Adviser to the Director General, International Biographical Association, Cambridge, England; American Medal of Honor, Man of the Year 2001, Dedication Section, Great Minds of the 21st Century, Ambassador of Grand Eminence, American Biographical Institute, Raleigh, North Carolina, USA; Delegate, 29th International Congress on Arts and Communications, Vancouver, British Columbia, Canada, 2002; National Honour's List of National Register's Who's Who in Executive and Professionals; Charter Member, London Diplomatic Academy; Nominated twice for the Noble Peace Prize; The only Presidential Museum in the World Honoring all 54 US Presidents Honorary Peace Prize Medal; The new Museum is now handicap accessible and equipped to take care of bus tours. Membership: American Biographical Institute; International Biographical Association. Address: 6585 Howard Road, Williamsfield, OH 44093, USA. E-mail: nickpahysjr@embargmail.com Website: www.oneandonly presidentialmuseum.com

PAIGE Elaine, b. 5 March 1948, Barnet, England. Singer; Actress. Education: Ada Foster Stage School. Career: Stage appearances include: Hair, West End, London, 1968; Jesus Christ Superstar, 1973; Grease, 1973; Billy, 1974; Lead role of Eva Peron, Evita, 1978; Cats, 1981; Abbacadabra, London, 1983; Chess, 1986; Anything Goes, 1989; Piaf, 1993-94; Sunset Boulevard, 1995. Recordings: Solo albums include: Elaine Paige, 1982; Stages, 1983; Cinema, 1984; Love Hurts, 1985; Christmas, 1986; Memories - The Best Of Elaine Paige, 1987; The Queen Album, 1988; Romance and the Stage, 1994; Encore, 1996; From a Distance, 1998; Stages, 1998; Sings the Music of Edith Piaf, 1998; Appears on Tim Rice Collection: Stage and Screen Classics, 1996; Christmas with the Stars Vol 2, 1999. Honours: Platinum and Gold albums; Society of West End Theatre Award, Best Actress In A Musical, Evita, 1978; Variety Club Awards: Showbusiness Personality of the Year, Recording Artist Of Year, 1986; BASCA Award, 1993. Address: c/o D&J Arlon Enterprises Ltd, Pinewood Studios, Pinewood Road, Iver, Bucks SL10 0NH, England.

PAIK Chang-Nyol, b. 13 September 1969, Seoul, Korea. Assistant Professor. m. Jin Lee, 1 son, 1 daughter. Education: BS, 1996, Master of Medicine, 2009, Catholic University College of Medicine, Seoul, Korea. Appointments: Clinical & Research Fellow, Gastroenterology, Kangnam St Mary's Hospital, 2005-06; Clinical Assistant Professor, 2007-09; Assistant Professor, Gastroenterology, Catholic University College of Medicine, St Vincent's Hospital. Memberships: Korean Association of Internal Medicine; Korean Society of Gastrointestinal Endoscopy; Pancreatobiliary Disease; Neurogastroenterology & Motility. E-mail: cmcu@catholic.ac.kr

PAINTING Suzanne Jane, b. 12 March 1960, Welkom, South Africa. Scientist. m. Walter Shave, 2 sons. Education: BSc (Hons), PhD, University of Cape Town, South Africa. Appointments: Postgraduate Researcher, University of Cape Town, 1982-84; Biological Oceanographer, Sea Fisheries Research Institute/Marine and Coastal Management, South Africa, 1984-2002; Scientific Co-ordinator and Project Leader, Sardine and Anchovy Recruitment Project, Benguela Ecology Programme, 1992-96; Specialist Scientist, Fisheries Oceanography, 1999; Head, Pelagic Section, 2000; Convenor of Pelagic Working Group, 2001, Ecosystem Scientist, Centre for Environment, Fisheries and Aquaculture Research (CEFAS), Lowestoft, England, 2002-. Publications: Numerous articles in professional journals, conference presentations and project reports. Honours: Listed in international biographical dictionaries. Memberships: Institute of Ecology and Environmental Management. Address: CEFAS, Pakefield Road, Lowestoft, NR33 0HT, England. E-mail: suzanne.painting@cefas.co.uk

PAISLEY Ian Richard Kyle, b. 6 April 1926, Ireland. Politician. m. Eileen E Cassells, 1956, 2 sons, 3 daughters. Education: South Wales Bible College; Reformed Presbyterian Theological College, Belfast. Appointments: Ordained, 1946; Minister, Martyrs Memorial Free Presbyterian Church, 1946-; Moderator, Free Presbyterian Church of

DICTIONARY OF INTERNATIONAL BIOGRAPHY 36th EDITION

Ulster, 1951; Founder, The Protestant Telegraph, 1966; Leader (co-founder), Democratic Unionist Party, 1972; MP (Democratic Unionist), 1974-, (Protestant Unionist 1970-74), resigned seat, 1985 in protest against the Anglo-Irish Agreement; Re-elected, 1986; MP (Protestant Unionist) for Bannside, Co Antrim, Parliament of Northern Ireland (Stormont), 1970-72, Leader of the Opposition, 1972, Chair, Public Accounts Committee, 1972; Member, Northern Ireland Assembly, 1973-74, elected to Second Northern Ireland Assembly, 1982; Member, European Parliament, 1979-2008 for Antrim North, Northern.Ireland Assembly, 1998-2000; Member, Political Committee European Parliament Northern Ireland Assembly, 1998-2008; First Minister of Northern Ireland, 2007-2008 Publications include: Jonathan Edwards, The Theologian of Revival, 1987; Union with Rome, 1989; The Soul of the Question, 1990; The Revised English Bible: An Exposure, 1990; What a Friend We Have in Jesus, 1994; Understanding Events in Northern Ireland: An Introduction for Americans, 1995; My Plea for the Old Sword, 1997; The Rent Veils at Calvary, 1997; A Text a Day Keeps the Devil Away, 1997. Address: The Parsonage, 17 Cyprus Avenue, Belfast BT5 5NT, Northern Ireland.

PAJE Ramon Jesus Palmiano, b. 27 November 1960, Guinobatan, Albay, Philippines. Professional Environmental Planner; Professional Forester. m. Joseliza Santos, 1 son, 1 daughter. Education: BS, Forestry, 1982, MA, Urban and Regional Planning, 1988, Doctor of Public Administration, 1999, University of the Philippines; Certificate, Human Resources Development & Management, Australian National University, 1992; Certificate, Environmental Economics & Policy Analysis, Harvard University, USA, 1994. Appointments: Secretary, Department of Environment and Natural Resources, 2010-. Honours: Outstanding Professional of the Philippines, 1996; Ten Outstanding Young Men, 1996; Dr Jose Rizal Huwarang Pilipino Award for Public Service, 1999; Distinguished Alumnus, Harvard Club of the Philippines, 2010; Outstanding Alumnus in Government Service, University of the Philippines Los Banos, Laguna, 2011. Memberships: Eastern Regional Organization for Public Administration; Ten Outstanding Young Men Foundation; Rotary Club of Sta Mesa, Quezon City; University of the Philippines Los Banos College of Forestry Alumni Association; Philippine Institute of Environmental Planners; Society of Filipino Foresters; Association of Outstanding Professionals of the Philippines; Philippines Constitution Association. Address: Department of Environment and Natural Resources, Visayas Ave, Diliman, Quezon City 1101, Philippines. E-mail: osec@denr.gov.ph Website: www.denr.gov.ph

PAJIC Bojan, b. 25 October 1966, Luzern, Switzerland. Ophthalmologist; Ophthalmic Surgeon; Researcher & Scientist. m. Brigitte Pajic-Eggspuehler, 1 son, 1 daughter. Education: Doctor Diploma, 1992, Medical Thesis, 1995, Inselspital Bern, The Medical Faculty, University of Bern; Swiss Board of Certification, Ophthalmology and Ophthalmic Surgery, 1998; Diploma, Fellow of European Board of Ophthalmology, 2005; PhD, University of Novi Sad, 2010. Appointments: Medical Director, ORASIS Eye Clinic, Reinach, 2009-; President, Swiss Eye Research Foundation, Reinach, 2009-; Belegarzt, Spital Menziken, 2009-; Consultant, University Eye Clinic, Geneva, 2010-; Scientific Consultant, University of Novi Sad, 2010-; Surgeon, Vidar ORASIS Swiss, Novi Sad, 2010-. Publications: 12 original peer-reviewed publications; 63 book chapters in 24 books; 17 book editions; 121 conference proceedings. Honours: 9 honours and awards in ophthalmology, ophthalmic surgery, research and science from India, USA and Great Britain. Memberships: Foederatio Medicorum Helveticorum; Société Suisse d'Ophthalmologie; Société Français d'Ophthalmologie; American Advancing Science Serving Society; American Academy of Ophthalmology; European Society for Cataract and Refractive Surgery. Address: Titlistrasse 44, 5734 Reinach AG, Switzerland.

PAKARINEN Eeva Terttu, b. 22 July 1946, Mäntyharju, Finland. Professor Emerita. Education: M Arch, 1974; Dr Technology, 1985. Appointments: Research Assistant, 1974-76; Planner, 1976; University Lecturer, 1977-78; University Lecturer, Senior Lecturer, Assistant Professor, 1978-97; Full Professor, 1998-2011; Member of the Board, Academy of Finland, 1992-94, 1996-97, 1998-99. Publications: Over 100, including most recently: Metaphors in Planning, 2010. Honours: 1st Class Decoration, Finland's White Rose Order. Address: Teekkannkatu 13 D66, FIN 33720, Tampere, Finland. E-mail: pakarinen.terttu@gmail.com

PAL Satyabrata, b. 5 April 1945, Calcutta, West Bengal, India. University Professor. m. Sm Swastika Pal, 1 son, 1 daughter. Education: BSc, Honours, 1964, MSc, 1966, PhD, Statistics, 1979, Calcutta University. Appointments: Lecturer, Ashutosh College, Calcutta, 1967-69; Assistant Professor, Kalyani University, 1969-74, Bidhan Chandra Krishi Viswavidyalaya (BCKV), 1974-75; Associate Professor, 1975-82, Professor, 1983-2007, Head, 1979-82, 1985-88, 1995-98, Dean, Post-Graduate Studies, 2003-05, BCKV; Principal, NSHM College of Management and Technology, Durgapur, West Bengal, 2007-08; Principal, Swami Vivekananda Institute of Management and Technology, 2008-. Publications: 115 papers in international and national journals; 2 books on statistics. Honours: Elected Member, International Statistical Institute, Permanent Officer: Netherlands; Fellow: Academy of Science and Technology, West Bengal, Calcutta, India; Inland Fisheries Society of India, Barrackpore, West Bengal, India; Indian Association of Hydrologists, Roorkee, India; Senior Post Doctoral Fellow, International Rice Research Institute, Manila, Philippines; Former Chairman, Finance Committee, International Biometric Society, USA; Bharat Excellence Award and Gold Medal, Friendship Forum of India, New Delhi, India; Rajib Gandhi Shrimoni Award, India International Friendship Society, New Delhi, India; Shiksha Rattan Puroskar and Certificate of Excellence, 2007 by India International Friendship Society, New Delhi, India. Memberships: Governing Body Member, Life Member of 12 societies and associations. Address: 101/B, Bakul Bagan Road, Kolkata 700025, West Bengal, India. E-mail: satyabrata.pal@hotmail.com

PALANISWAMI Rajendran, b. 17 May 1960, Thondamuthur, India. Associate Professor. Education: BSc, Vivekananda, Madurai Kamaraj, 1980; MSc, Pachaiappas, Chennai, 1982; M Phil, Bharathiar, Coimbatore, 1983; PhD, Madurai Kamaraj, Madurai, 2004. Appointments: Associate Professor, Research Head, Department of Applied Zoology and Biotechnology, Vivekananda College; Visiting Foreign Researcher, Ryukyus University, Okinawa, Japan, 2006-07. Publications: 4 books/proceedings; Numerous articles in professional journals. Honours: Tamil Nadu State Government Award for Environment Management. Memberships: International Society for Zoology; Biotech Research Society. Address: PG & Research Department of Advanced Zoology & Biotechnology, Tiruvedakam West, Sholavandan, Maudurai – 625 214, India. E-mail: sinsir_1960@yahoo.com

PALGRAVE Derek Aubrey, b. 16 September 1932, Norwich, England. Chartered Chemist. m. Pamela Pearl Spilling, 2 sons, 1 daughter. Education: City of Norwich School, 1944-52; MA, Selwyn College, Cambridge, 1957; M Phil, Anglia Ruskin University, 2003. Appointments: Pilot Officer, RAF National Service, 1952-54; Research Chemist, Albright & Wilson Ltd, 1957-64; Chief Chemist and Technical Director, J W Chafer Ltd, 1964-91; Consultant & Freelance Lecturer, Science & History, 1991-. Publications: Editor and major contributor, 3 textbooks; 8 British & US patents, 1966-84; Numerous articles in professional journals. Honours: Patron Suffolk Family History Society; President, Guild of One-Name Studies; President, Doncaster & District FHS; Vice President, Federation of Family History Societies; Vice President, Cambridge University H&GS. Memberships: Fellow, Royal Society of Chemistry; Fellow, Institute of Risk Management; Fellow, Society of Genealogists; Fellow, College of Teachers; East of England Regional Archive Council; Heraldry Society; British Agricultural History Society; Society of Chemical Industry; International Fertiliser Society; Norfolk Record Society; Suffolk Record Society; Suffolk Local History Council; Ecclesiological Society; Halsted Trust; many others. Address: Crossfield House, Dale Road, Stanton, Suffolk IP31 2DY, England. E-mail: palgrave@one-name.org

PALIN Michael Edward, b. 5 May 1943, Sheffield, Yorkshire, England. Freelance Writer and Actor. m. Helen M Gibbins, 1966, 2 sons, 1 daughter. Education: BA, Brasenose College, Oxford, 1965. Appointments: Actor, Writer: Monty Python's Flying Circus, BBC TV, 1969-74; Ripping Yarns, BBC TV 1976-80; Writer, East of Ipswich, BBC TV, 1986; Films: Actor and Joint Author: And Now for Something Completely Different, 1970; Monty Python and the Holy Grail, 1974; Monty Python's Life of Brian, 1978; Time Bandits, 1980; Monty Python's The Meaning of Life, 1982; Actor, Writer, Co-Producer, The Missionary, 1982; Around the World in 80 Days, BBC, 1989; Actor: Jabberwocky, 1976; A Private Function, 1984; Brazil, 1984; A Fish Called Wanda, 1988; Contributor, Great Railway Journeys of the World, BBC TV, 1980; Actor, Co-Writer, American Friends, film, 1991; Actor, GBH, TV Channel 4, 1991; Actor, Fierce Creatures, 1997; Michael Palin's Hemingway Adventure, BBC TV, 1999; Sahara, 2002; Himalaya with Michael Palin, 2004; Michael Palin's New Europe, 2007. Publications: Monty Python's Big Red Book, 1970; Monty Python's Brand New Book, 1973; Dr Fegg's Encyclopaedia of All World Knowledge, 1984; Limericks, 1985; Around the World in 80 Days, 1989; Pole to Pole, 1992; Pole to Pole - The Photographs, 1994; Hemingway's Chair, 1995; Full Circle, 1997; Full Circle - The Photographs, 1997; Michael Palin's Hemingway Adventure, 1999; Sahara, 2002; Himalaya, 2004; For Children: Small Harry and the Toothache Pills, 1981; The Mirrorstone, 1986; The Cyril Stories, 1986. Honours: Writers Guild, Best Screenplay Award, 1991; Dr hc (Sheffield), 1992, (Queen's, Belfast), 2000; Lifetime Achievement Award, British Comedy Awards, 2002; BCA Illustrated Book of the Year Award, 2002; British Book Award, TV & Film Book of the Year, 2005; BAFTA Special Award for Outstanding Contribution to TV, 2005. Address: 34 Tavistock Street, London WC2E 7PB, England.

PALM Franz Christian, b. 15 May 1948, Rocherath, Belgium. Professor. Education: MS, 1971, PhD, 1975, Economics, University of Louvain. Appointments: Research Associate, CORE, University of Louvain; Research Assistant, Graduate School of Business, University of Chicago; Professor of Econometrics, Free University, Amsterdam; Professor of Econometrics, Maastricht University; Visiting Professor, University of Louvain; Visiting Professor, University of Chicago; Dean, Economics & Business Administration, Maastricht University; Professor, Royal Netherlands Academy of Sciences. Publications: The Structural Econometric Time Series Analysis Approach, 2004. Honours: Fellow, American Statistical Association; Fellow, European Economic Association; Fellow, CESIFO; Member, Royal Netherlands Academy of Sciences; Doctorate Honoris Causa, University of Fribourg, Switzerland, 2009. Memberships: European Economic Association; Econometric Society; American Statistical Association. Address: Maastricht University, School of Business and Economics, PO Box 616, 6200 MD Maastricht, The Netherlands. E-mail: f.palm@maastrichtuniversity.nl

PALMER Arnold Daniel, b. 10 September 1929, Latrobe, USA. Golfer; Business Executive. m. Winifred Walzer, 1954, 2 daughters. Education: Wake Forest University, North Carolina. Appointments: US Coast Guard, 1950-53; US Amateur Golf Champion, 1954; Professioanl Golfer, 1954-;Winner, 92 professional titles, including British Open 1961, 1962, US Open 1960, US Masters 1958, 1960, 1962, 1964, Candadian PGA 1980, US Seniors Championship 1981; Member, US Ryder Cup Team, 1961, 1963, 1965, 1967, 1971, 1973, Captain 1963, 1975; President, Arnold Palmer Enterprises; Board of Directors, Latrobe Area Hospital. Publications: My Game and Yours, 1965; Situation Golf, 1970; Go for Broke, 1973; Arnold Palmer's Best 54 Golf Holes, 1977; Arnold Palmer's Complete Book of Putting, 1986; Playing Great Golf, 1987; A Golfer's Life (with James Dodson), 1999; Playing by the Rules, 2002; Memories, Stories and Memorabilia, 2004. Honours: LLD, Wake Forest National College of Education; DHL, Florida Southern College; Athlete of the Decade, Associated Press, 1970; Sportsman of the Year, Sports Illustrated, 1960; Hickok Belt, Athlete of the Year, 1960. Address: PO Box 52, Youngstown, PA 15696, USA.

PALMER Frank Robert, b. 9 April 1922, Westerleigh, Gloucestershire, England. Retired Professor; Linguist; Writer. m. Jean Elisabeth Moore, 1948, 3 sons, 2 daughters. Education: MA, New College, Oxford, 1948; Graduate Studies, Merton College, Oxford, 1948-49. Appointments: Lecturer in Linguistics, School of Oriental and African Studies, University of London, 1950-52, 1953-60; Professor of Linguistics, University College of North Wales, Bangor, 1960-65; Professor and Head, Department of Linguistic Science, 1965-87, Dean, Faculty of Letters and Social Sciences, 1969-72, University of Reading. Publications: The Morphology of the Tigre Noun, 1962; A Linguistic Study of the English Verb, 1965; Selected Papers of J R Firth, 1951-1958 (editor), 1968; Prosodic Analysis (editor), 1970; Grammar, 1971, 2nd edition, 1984; The English Verb, 1974, 2nd edition, 1987; Studies in the History of Western Linguistics (joint editor) 1986; Semantics, 1976, 2nd edition, 1981; Modality and the English Modals, 1979, 2nd edition, 1990; Mood and Modality, 1986, 2001; Grammatical Roles and Relations, 1994; Grammar and Meaning, 1995 (editor) 1995; Modality in Contemporary English (joint editor), 2003; English Modality in Perspective (co-editor), 2004. Contributions to: Professional journals. Memberships: Academia Europaea; British Academy, fellow; Linguistic Society of America; Philological Society. Address: Whitethorns, Roundabout Lane, Winnersh, Wokingham, Berkshire RG41 5AD, England.

PALTROW Gwyneth, b. 27 September 1972, Los Angeles, USA. Actress. m. Chris Martin, 2003, 1 son, 1 daughter. Education: University of California, Santa Barbara. Creative

Works: Films include: Flesh and Bone, 1993; Hook; Moonlight and Valentino; The Pallbearer; Seven; Emma, 1996; Sydney; Kilronan; Great Expectations, 1998; Sliding Doors, 1998; A Perfect Murder, 1998; Shakespeare in Love, 1998; The Talented Mr Ripley, 1999; Duets, 1999; Bounce, 2000; The Intern, 2000; The Anniversary Party, 2001; The Royal Tenenbaums, 2001; Shallow Hal, 2001; Possession, 2002; View From the Top, 2003; Sylvia, 2003; Sky Captain and the World of Tomorrow, 2004; Proof, 2004; Infamous, 2006; Love and Other Disasters, 2006; Running with Scissors, 2006; The Good Night, 2007; Iron Man, 2008; Two Lovers, 2008; Iron Man 2, Country Strong, 2010; Glee: The 3D Concert Movie, Contagion, 2011; The Avengers, 2012; Iron Man 3, 2013. Honours include: Academy Award, Best Actress, 1998. Address: c/o Rick Kurtzman, CAA, 9830 Wilshire Boulevard, Beverly Hills, CA 90212, USA.

PALUMBO Peter Garth, Baron Palumbo of Walbrook in the City of London, b. 20 July 1935. m. (1) Denia, 1959, deceased 1986, 1 son, 2 daughters; (2) Hayat, 1986, 1 son, 2 daughters. Education: Eton College; MA (Hons), Law, Worcester College, Oxford. Appointments: Governor, London School of Economics and Political Science, 1976-94; Chairman: Tate Gallery Foundation, 1986-87; Painshill Park Trust Appeal, 1986-96; Serpentine Gallery, 1994-; Board Member and Director, Andy Warhol Foundation for the Visual Arts, 1994-97; Trustee: Mies van der Rohe Archive, 1977-; Tate Gallery, 1978-85; Whitechapel Art Gallery Foundation, 1981-87; Natural History Museum, 1994-2004; Design Museum, 1995-2005; Trustee and Honorary Treasurer, Writers and Scholars Educational Trust, 1984-99; Chairman, Arts Council of Great Britain, 1989-94; Member of Council, Royal Albert Hall, 1995-99; Chairman of Jury, Pritzker Architecture Prize, 2004-; Chancellor, Portsmouth University, 1992-2007; Governor, Whitgift School, 2002-10; Adviser Emeritus to the Board of Governors, Whitgift School, 2010-. Honours: Liveryman, Salters' Co, 1965-; Honorary FRIBA, 1986; Created Life Peer, 1991; Honorary FFB, 1994; Honorary FIStructE, 1994; Honorary DLitt Portsmouth, 1993; National Order of Southern Cross, Brazil, 1993; Patronage of the Arts Award, Cranbrook Academy of Arts, Detroit, 2002.

PALVA Ilmari Pellervo, b. 5 May 1932, South Pirkkala, Finland. Physician; Haematologist. m. Seija Kaivola, 9 June 1956, 1 son, 3 daughters. Education: MD, 1956, PhD, 1962, University of Helsinki. Appointments: Registrar, 1959-63, Consultant, 1964-65, Department of Medicine, University Hospital, Helsinki; Instructor, University of Helsinki, 1963-64; Associate Professor, Internal Medicine, University of Oulu, 1965-74; Professor, Internal Medicine, University of Kuopio, 1974; Acting Professor, Medical Education, University of Tampere, 1975-76; Consultant, City Hospitals, Tampere, 1977-92, Retired, 1992. Publications: Over 250 scientific papers in professional journals. Honours: Knight of 1st Rank Order of Finnish White Rose, 1986; Honorary Member, Finnish Society of Haematology, 1992. Memberships: Finnish Medical Association; Finnish Society of Internal Medicine; Finnish Society of Haematology; International Society of Haematology; American Society of Hematology. Address: Oikotie 8, FIN 33950 Pirkkala, Finland.

PAN Chai-fu, b, 8 September 1936, Loshon, Szechwan, China. Emeritus Professor. m. Maria C Shih, 1 son, 1 daughter. Education: BS, Chemical Engineering, National Taiwan University, 1956; PhD, Physical Chemistry, University of Kansas, USA, 1966. Appointments: Associate Professor, 1966-71, Professor, 1971-91, Emeritus Professor of Chemistry, 1991-, Alabama State University, USA. Publications: Contributions to Journal of Physical Chemistry, Journal of Chemical and Engineering Data, Canadian Journal of Chemistry, Journal of Chemical Society, Faraday Transaction 1, other professional journals. Honours: Phi Lambda Upsilon, 1963; Fellowship, American Institute of Chemists, 1971; Alabama State University Research Award, 1985; More than 30 listings. Memberships: American Chemical Society; Fellow, American Institute of Chemists. Address: 2420 Wentworth Drive, Montgomery, AL 36106, USA. E-mail: ppan@charter.net

PANAGOS Lisa Marie, b. 4 December, Potomac, Maryland, USA. Actor; Singer; Songwriter; Dancer; Producer. Education: Connelly School of the Holy Child; BFA, Syracuse University. Appointments: Owner, Panagos Global Entertainment LLC; Owner, Bijoux Music Publishing; Owner, Bijoux Music Productions; Actor: Film: Mansion Directive; The Bookcase; Where's Tuesday Monday; Kinescoping Dr Travis; Red Red Rope; Dinner with a Guest; Donnie Brasco; Coco; Everlong; TV: Yes, Dear; 90210 Spoof; Wonderland; Hercules Strikes Manhattan; Sophisticated Ladies; Theatre: (Broadway) Annie Get Your Gun; (US/Europe) Annie Get Your Gun; It's Not Funny; Sophisticated Ladies; Jesus Christ Superstar; Phantom of the Opera; Camelot. Publications: Greek Hollywood Reporter; Radio Indie; Girl Indie; Washington Post; Gaithersburg Gazette. Honours: Honorable Mention, Dance National Endowment for the Arts; Girl Indie Award for Music/Songwriting. Memberships: SAG; AFTRA; AEA; BMI; Women in Film. Address: 8491 W Sunset Blvd #671, West Hollywood, CA 90069, USA. Website: www.lisapanagos.com

PANCHENKO Yurii Nikolayevich, b. 6 April 1934, Kharkov, Ukraine. Chemist. m. Larisa Grigoriyevna Tashkinova, 1 son. Education: Department of Chemistry, MV Lomonosov Moscow State University, 1959; PhD, Chemistry (Molecular Spectroscopy), 1970. Appointments: Junior Researcher, Karpov Physico-Chemical Institute, 1959-61; Junior Researcher, 1961-77, Senior Researcher, 1977-, Department of Chemistry, Moscow State University. Publications: More than 200 scientific works in numerous scientific journals. Honours: Silver Medal (secondary school), Medal of Eötvös Lorand Budapest University. Membership: Fellow, World Association of Theoretically Oriented Chemists. Address: Laboratory of Molecular Spectroscopy, Division of Physical Chemistry, Department of Chemistry, MV Lomonosov Moscow State University, Moscow 119992, Russia. E-mail: panchenk@phys.chem.msu.ru

PANDEY Satrugna Prasad, b. 22 July 1941, Chaita, Bihar, India. Teacher. m. Rubina Thakur, 1 February 1976, 1 son, 1 daughter. Education: MA, English, Patna University, Patna, 1966; PhD, English, 1992; Postgraduate Diploma in Teaching of English, CIEFL, 1993; Numerous courses in Theology including: Church History, Christology, Cults, Christian Counseling, Apologetics. Appointments: Teacher of English, Notre Dame Academy, Patna, 1964-68; Lecturer/Assistant Professor, in English, BSK College, Maithon, Ranchi University, 1968-85; Reader/Associate Professor, in English, BSK College, Maithon, 1985-; Professor-in-Charge, , 1993-2000, Head, Department of English, 2001-, BSK College, Maithon. Publications: Hindi Translations of William Branham's Sermons: Women Preachers, 1980; Presenting Islam, 1980; The Mystery of the Father and the Son, 1992; Was it an Apple?, 1993; The Festival of Easter, 1993; The Siege of Jerusalem, 1993; The Beginning of Sorrows, 1994; The Influence of William Branham in India, 1995; What IS the Messiah's Actual Name?, 1995; What You can Do for the Environment: Greening the

Curriculum Through Language Teaching, 1996; A General Service List of English Words; National Consultation on Reconciliation, Religious Liberty and Social Justice: A New Perspective, 1998; Translations of Sermons into Hindi: I Indict This Generation, 1989; Recognising Your Day and Its Message, 1989; The Anointed Ones at the End Time, 1989; Choosing a Bride, 1990; Deceived Church, 1990; Marriage and Divorce, 1990; The Laodicean Church Age, 1991. Honours: The Twentieth Century Award for Achievement, 1998; International Man of the Year, 1996-2010; The 2000 Millennium Medal of Honour, ABI, 1998; Decree of Merit, IBC, 1999. Memberships: Indian Institute of Alternative Medicine, Calcutta, 1991-; American Studies Research Centre, Hyderabad; Indian Association for English Studies; Postgraduate Research Council, Vinoba Bhave University, Hazaribag; Indian Society for Commonwealth Studies; Life Member, Adviser, Tutor of Homoeopathy, Grace Medical Mission, Kerala, 2000-. Address: Bible Way, Maithon (Dhanbad), India 828 207.

PANG Chee Khiang, b. 20 March 1976, Singapore. Assistant Professor. Education: BEng (Hons), MEng, PhD, Electrical & Computer Engineering, National University of Singapore. Appointments: Several visiting appointments; Researcher (Tenure), Central Research Lab, Hitachi Ltd, Japan, 2006-08; Assistant Professor, Department of Electrical & Computer Engineering, National University of Singapore, 2009-. Publications: Numerous articles in professional journals. Honours: NUS Overseas Postdoctoral Fellowship, 2008/2009; Hitachi Global Storage Technologies Graduate Assistantship. Memberships: Institute of Electrical & Electronics Engineers. Address: Department of Electrical & Computer Engineering, National University of Singapore, 4 Engineering Drive 3, 117586, Singapore. E-mail: justingpang@nus.edu.sg Website: www.ece.nus.edu.sg

PANKOV Yuri, b. 10 February 1930, Leningrad, USSR. Biochemist; Molecular Biologist. m. Svetlana Chumachenko, 1 son, 1 daughter. Education: Biochemist, Leningrad State University, 1953; PhD, 1963; DSc, 1968; Biophysicist, Moscow State University, 1972; Academician of the USSR Academy of Medical Sciences, 1986; Professor, 1987, MOIF, 2000. Appointments: Senior Scientist, Institute of Experimental Endocrinology and Hormone Chemistry (IEEHC), 1965-70; Deputy Director, IEEHC, 1970-83; Director of IEEHC, 1983-90; Director of Moscow WHO Collaborating Center on Human Reproduction, 1984-97; Director, Moscow WHO Collaborating Center on Diabetes, 1984-90; Head of Laboratory Molecular Endocrinology Endocrine Research Centre, 1990-. Publications: Biochemistry of hormones and hormonal regulation, 1976; Several articles in Nature; Biochemistry; Molecular Biology; Bioorganic chemistry, Vestnick of Russian Academy of Medical Sciences; Problem Endocrinology. Honours: Honorary member, Cuban Society of Endocrinology Metabolism, 1984; Honorary Citizen of Lexington, Kentucky, USA, 1987; Listed in numerous international biographical publications. Memberships: Endocrine Society; Planetary Society; European Association for the Study of Diabetes; American Diabetes Association; Adjunct Professor, Special Educational Programme on Biochemistry, Immunology, Molecular and Cellular Biology, A N Belozersky Institute, Moscow State University, 1999. Address: Endocrine Research Centre, Moscvorechye Str 1, 115478, Moscow, Russia. E-mail: yuri-pankov@mtu-net.ru

PAPADEMOS Lucas, b. 11 October 1947, Athens, Greece. Bank Executive. Education: BSc, Physics, 1970, MSc, Electrical Engineering, 1972, PhD, Economics, 1977, Massachusetts Institute of Technology. Appointments: Research Assistant, Teaching Fellow, Massachusetts Institute of Technology, 1973-75; Lecturer, Economics, 1975-77, Assistant and Associate Professor of Economics, 1977-84, Columbia University, New York; Senior Economist, Federal Reserve Bank of Boston, 1980; Visiting Professor of Economics, Athens School of Economics and Business, 1984-85; Professor of Economics, University of Athens, 1988-; Economic Counsellor (Chief Economist), 1985-93, Head, Economic Research Department, 1988-93, Deputy Governor, 1993-94, Governor, 1994-2002, Bank of Greece; Vice-President, European Central Bank, 2002-; Member, Greece's Council of Economic Experts. Publications: Numerous articles in professional journals and books chapters as author and co-author. Honour: Grand Commander of the Order of Honour, Greece, 1999-. Memberships include: Governor, International Monetary Fund for Greece, 1994-; General Council, 1999-, Governing Council, 2001-, European Central Bank; Chairman, Governor's Club, 2001-. Address: European Central Bank, Kaiserstr 29, D-60211 Frankfurt am Main, Germany.

PÁPAI Éva, b. 20 November 1951, Szombathely, Hungary. Painter; Sculptor. m. Endre Nagy. Education: Graduate, School of Art, Cluj-Napoca, Romania, 1985; Scholarship, Nürenberg, Germany, 1985-86. Career: Painter; Sculptor; Represented in permanent collections: Calvary Church of Szombathely, 1985; Church of St Ludwig, Nürenberg, 1986; Bronze Coat of Arms, Güssing, Austria; Candlestick and Corpus to the altar on the visit of Pope John Paul II, Trausdorf, Austria, 1988; Basilika, alter and ambo, Nagyvarad, Romania, 2000; Built chapel and associated works of art, Torony, 1992; Works include: Lief of St Francis, 1985; Brick clayrelief on alter, Church of St Paul, 1985; Lief of St Michael, 1986; Bronze Coat of Arms, Church of St Francis, 1986; 3 candlesticks and corpus of brickclay, 1988; Chapel of St Francis and art works, 1991-92; Bronze reliefs, Oradea cathedral, 2000; Bronze reliefs, St Ladislas, Oradea, 2005. Publications: Snow-Prince and Snow-Princess, 1995; Funny Girl, 1995; Christmas of Birds, 2000; Carpet of Colours, 2000; On the Wings of Birds, 2003; I Put a Seed on the Curb, 2005; Star-Enchanting, 2005; Travel-Pictures – Peking and its Environs, 2006; Haiku, 2007. Honours: Prize, Competition of St Ludwig, Nürenberg, 1985; Scholarship, Nuremburg, 1985-86; Prize, Competition of Osterkirche Oberwart, 1988; Torony plaque, 2004; World Exhibition and Bookfair, 2006; Women of the Year, USA, 2009; Knight, Hungary, 2010; Listed in international biographical dictionaries. Address: Harsta St 23, H-8200, Veszprem, Hungary. E-mail: papai50@freemail.hu Website: papaieva.fw.hu

PAPP Laszlo, b. 6 December 1963, Dorog, Hungary. Consultant Vascular Surgeon. m. Eva Helga Biczo, 1 son. Education: MD, University of Debrecen, 1987; PhD, University of Edinburgh & University of Debrecen, 2002; EBSQ-Vasc, European Board of Vascular Surgery, 2003. Appointments: Consultant Vascular Surgeon, Royal Infirmary of Edinburgh, 2001-02; Consultant Vascular Surgeon, Addenbrooke's Hospital, Cambridge, 2002-03; Head of Department, Associate Professor, University Department of Vascular Surgery, University of Debrecen, 2005-06; Consultant Vascular Surgeon, University Hospital of North Staffordshire, 2007-. Publications: Honours: Founder and Chief Operating Officer, Eastern Hungarian Breast Cancer Foundation, 1992-96; International Expert in Vascular Surgery; Visiting Professor, Yale University, 2004; Member, European Board of Vascular Surgery Examinations; Won rights to stage 27th Annual Meeting of European Society for Vascular Surgery, 2013. Memberships: Hungarian Society of Surgery; Hungarian Society of Angiology and Vascular Surgery; European Society for Vascular Surgery; European Board of Vascular Surgery. E-mail: pl1963@hotmail.com

PARAMEI Galina V, b. 25 May 1956, Ivano-Frankovsk, USSR. Professor of Psychology. m. Martin Rainer Blaszcyk. Education: BSc and MSc, Psychology, 1979, PhD, 1983, General Psychology, Moscow Lomonosov State University, Moscow, USSR; Dr habil, Cognitive Psychology, Institute of Psychology, Ruhr-University Bochum, Germany, 2003; Privat-Dozent, Cognitive Neuroscience, Otto-von-Guericke University of Magdeburg, Germany, 2003. Appointments: Research Assistant, 1977-79, Research Associate, 1980-82, Research Scientist, 1989-91, Senior Lecturer, 1994-95, Faculty of Psychology, Moscow State University, Russia; Lecturer, 1983-85, Senior Lecturer, 1986-88, Department of Psychology, Grodno State University, USSR; Research Scientist, Institute for Occupational Physiology, University of Dortmund, Germany, 1995-2001; Associate Professor, Institute of Medical Psychology, Otto-von-Guericke University of Magdeburg, 2003-04; Interim Professor of General Psychology, Institute of Psychology, Darmstadt University of Technology, Germany, 2005-07; Senior Lecturer, 2007-08, Professor of Psychology, 2008-, Department of Psychology, Liverpool Hope University, UK. Honours: Fellow, A von Humboldt Foundation, Institute of Psychology, Ruhr-University Bochum, Germany, 1992-94, 1999; Grantee, Invited Oversea Visitor, University of Tokushima, Japan, 1996; McDonnell Foundation Grantee, Invited Visiting Professor, Department of Experimental Psychology, University of Sao Paulo, Brazil, 2002; Fellow, Hanse Institute for Advanced Study, Delmenhorst & Institute of Psychology, University of Oldenburg, Germany, 2004-05. Memberships: International Colour Vision Society; International Society for Psychophysics; Applied Vision Association (UK); The Colour Group (Great Britain). Address: Department of Psychology, Liverpool Hope University, Hope Park, Liverpool, L16 9JD, UK. E-mail: parameg@hope.ac.uk

PARASKEVAS Spyridon, b. 1 February 1937, Athens, Greece. University Professor. m. Mary Keskos, 1 son, 1 daughter. Education: Dipl Chemical Engineer, 1965, Doctor of Physical Sciences, 1968, Techische Hochschule Stuttgart, Germany; Docent of Organic Chemistry, University of Athens, 1977. Appointments: Assistant, Laboratory of Organic Chemistry, 1970, Assistant Professor, 1983, Associate Professor, 1990, Professor of Chemical Organic Chemistry, 1995, Emeritus Professor, 2001, University of Athens. Publications: Numerous articles in professional journals. Honours: Medal, Graduate Society of 1st Gymnasium, Athens. Memberships: Association of Greek Chemistry; Greek Technical Chamber; Philological Society, Parnassos; Dechema. Address: odos Trivonianou 77, 11636, Athens, Greece. E-mail: msparaskevas@gmail.com

PARAVICINI Nicolas Vincent Somerset, b. 19 October 1937, London, England. Private Banker. m. Susan Rose Phipps. 2 sons, 1 daughter. Education: Royal Military Academy, Sandhurst. Appointments: British Army, The Life Guards, 1957-69, retired as Major; Director, Joseph Sebag & Co, 1972-79; Chairman and Chief Executive, Sarasin Investment Management Ltd, 1980-89; Consultant, Bank Sarasin & Co, 1990-; Chief Executive, Ely Place Investments Ltd, 1992-98. Honours: Freeman City of London, 1984, Deputy Lieutenant for Powys, 2006, Listed in biographical dictionary. Memberships: London Stock Exchange, 1972-80; President, Becknockshire Agricultural Society, 1998-99; SSAFA Powys, 2002-; Clubs: White's; Pratt's; Corviglia Ski; Cardiff & County. Address: Glyn Celyn House, Brecon, Powys LD3 0TY, Wales.

PARIS Richard Bruce, b. 23 January 1946, Bradford, England. University Academic. m. Jocelyne Marie-Louise Neidinger, 1 son, 1 daughter. Education: BSc, 1967, PhD, 1971, DSc, Mathematics, 1999, University of Manchester. Appointments: Postdoctoral Fellow, Royal Society of London, 1972-73, Foreign Collaborator, 1973-74, Research Scientist, Euratom, Theory Division, Controlled Thermonuclear Fusion, 1974-87, Commissariat à l'Energie Atomique, France; Senior Lecturer, University of Abertay Dundee, 1987-99; Honorary Readership, University of St Andrews, 1998-2007; Reader in Mathematics, 1999-2010, Emeritus Reader, 2011-, University of Abertay Dundee. Publications: Books: Asymptotics of High Order Differential Equations (with A D Wood), 1986; Asymptotics and Mellin-Barnes Integrals (with D Kaminski), 2001; Hadamard Expansions and Hyperasymptotic Evaluation, 2011; Author of 150 papers and technical reports; Publications in Proceedings A Royal Society, Journal of Computational and Applied Mathematics, Physics of Fluids; Author of 2 chapters in Handbook of Mathematical Functions. Honours: Fellow of the Institute of Mathematics and Applications, 1986; CMath, 1992, DSc, 1999. Memberships: Institute of Mathematics and its Applications; Edinburgh Mathematical Society; Mathematical Association. Address: University of Abertay Dundee, Dundee DD1 1HG, Scotland. E-mail: r.paris@abertay.ac.uk

PARK Chung Hae, b. 30 June 1973, Jinhae, South Korea. Associate Professor. m. Eun Young Lee, 1 son. Education: BSc, 1996, MSc, 1998, Mechanical Engineering, PhD, Mechanical & Aerospace Engineering, 2003,Seoul National University; Dr, Mechanical & Material Engineering, Ecole des Mines de Saint-Etienne, France, 2003; Habilitation, Mechanics, University of Le Harve, France, 2011. Appointments: Senior Research Engineer, LG Chem, Korea, 2003-05; Lecturer, 2005-06, Assistant Professor, Maitre de Conferences, 2006-11, Associate Professor, 2011-, University of Le Havre, France. Publications: 20 papers in international journals; 5 papers in domestic journals; 1 international patent; 2 domestic patents; 3 articles for book chapters. Honours: Prime d'Excellence Scientifique, 2010-14; Editorial Board Member, American Journal of Materials Science; Scholarship for PhD thesis, Ministry of Foreign Affairs. Memberships: American Chemical Society; Association Française de Mécanique; Association pour les Matériaux Composites; European Scientific Association for Material Forming; Korean Society of Composite Materials. Address: 2 rue Bellot, 76600 Le Havre, France.

PARK Dong-Suk, b. 24 August 1949, Busan, South Korea. Oriental Medical Doctor; Professor. m. Eun-Ok Lee, 1 son, 2 daughters. Education: Bachelor, 1974, Master, 1976, Doctor of Medicine, 1983, Kyunghee University; Oriental Medical Doctor, Korean Ministry of Health and Welfare,1974. Appointments: Professor, Kyunghee University, 1979-; Chief of Research, Kyunghee Oriental Medical Center, 1996-98; Chairman, Korean Acupuncture and Moxibustion Society, 1997-99; Medical Advisory Committee Member, Ministry of National Defense, 2002-07; Chairman, Korean Oriental Medical Society, 2003-06; President, East-West Medical Graduate School, 2005-06; Private Sector Commissioner, Presidential Committee on Healthcare Innovation, 2006-07; Director, Oriental Medical Hospital, East-West Neo Medical Center, 2006-08; Chairman, Korean Oriental Medicine Education and Evaluation Institute, 2011-. Publications: 159

domestic and 28 international articles including: Biphasic positive effect of formononetin on metabolic activity of human normal and osteoarthritic subchondral osteoblasts, 2010; Bee venom inhibits tumor angiogenesis and metastasis by inhibiting tyrosine phosphorylation of VEGER-2 in LLC-tumor-bearing mice, 2010; The analgesic and anti-inflammatory effect of WIN-34B, a new herbal formula of osteoarthritis composed of Lonicera japonica Thunb and Anemarrhena asphodeloides BUNGE in vivo, 2010; Effect of Phellodendron amurense in protecting human osteoarthritic cartilage and chondrocytes, 2010. Honours: Kyunghee University Medical Award, 2006; Master (Honorary), Korean Oriental Medical Society. Memberships: Korean Oriental Medical Society; Korean Acupuncture and Moxibustion Society. E-mail: dspark49@yahoo.co.kr

PARK Haeryong, b. 4 February 1974, Gwangju, Republic of Korea. Researcher. m. Myunghee Song, 2 sons. Education: Bachelor, Mathematics, 1999, PhD, Information Security, 2006, Chonnam National University; Master, Mathematical Sciences, Seoul National University, 2001. Appointments: Sergeant, Army, 1994-96; Principal Researcher, General Manager, Korea Internet & Security Agency, Seoul, 2000-; Part-time Professor, Chonnam National University, 2009-. Publications: Numerous articles in professional journals. Honours: Special Award, Korean Mathematical Competition, 1997-98; Best Paper Award, Korean Society for Internet Information, 2008. Address: KISA, IT Venture Tower, Jundaero 135, Songpa-gu, Seoul 138-950, Republic of Korea. E-mail: snupark@dreamwiz.com

PARK Han Woo, b. 20 June 1971, Yeung-ju, Korea. Professor. m. Ju-Yeon Woo. Education: BA, Department of Communication & Information, Hankuk University of Foreign Studies, Seoul, 1995; MA, Department of Communication & Information, Seoul National University, Seoul, 1997; PhD, Department of Communication, State University of New York at Buffalo, USA, 2002. Appointments: Researcher, Korean Agency for Digital Opportunity, 1997-98; Research Associate, Royal Netherlands Academy of Arts & Sciences, 2002-03. Publications: Numerous articles in professional journals. Memberships: International Communication Association; International Networks for Social Network Analysis; Association of Internet Researchers; Korean Society for Journalism & Mass Communication Studies. Address: YeungNam University, 214-1 Dae-dong, KyeongSanBuk-do, KyeongSan-si, 712-749 South Korea. E-mail: parkhanwoo@hotmail.com Website: http://www.hanpark.net

PARK Heung Sik, b. 5 December 1963, Seoul, Korea. Plastic Surgeon. m. Eun Hee Kim, 1 son, 2 daughters. Education: MD, Medical School, 1988, MS, 1996, PhD, 2001, Department of Plastic, Reconstructive and Aesthetic Surgery, Seoul National University. Appointments: Intern, Seoul National University Hospital, 1998-89; Military Service, 1988-92; Resident, 1992-96, Fellowship, 1996-97, Department of Plastic, Reconstructive and Aesthetic Surgery, Seoul National University Hospital; Full time Instructor, 1997-2000, Assistant Professor, 2000-04, Associate Professor, 2004-05, Chief Professor, 2004-05, Attending Professor, 2005-, Department of Plastic, Reconstructive and Aesthetic Surgery, Ewha Woman's University Hospital; Attending Professor, Department of Plastic, Reconstructive and Aesthetic Surgery, Seoul National University Hospital, 2000-; Visiting Professor, Hwangsi Aesthetic Plastic Surgery Hospital, Beijing, China, 2005; Principal, AT Aesthetic Plastic Clinic, 2005-. Publications: Numerous articles in professional journals; 1 patent. Honours: Scholarship, Medical School, Seoul National University, 1994 and 1997; Letter of Appreciation, 2002 and 2006; Superior Presentation Winner, 60th Annual Meeting, Korean Society of Plastic and Reconstructive Surgeons, 2006; Certificate of Appreciation, 2007; Listed in biographical dictionaries. Memberships: Korean Society of Plastic, Reconstructive and Aesthetic Surgery; Korean Society of Aesthetic Plastic Surgery; Korean Society of Cleft Palate; Craniofacial Association; Korean Society of Medical Informatics; Korean Society for Biomaterials; International Confederation of Plastic, Reconstructive and Aesthetic Surgery Society; International Society of Aesthetic Plastic Surgery; COAPT Endocrine Systems Medical Advisory Board. Address: AT Aesthetic Plastic Clinic, 5th F Daesung Bld 1318, Seocho 4-dong, Seocho-gu, Seoul, Korea. E-mail: pseyes@dreamwiz.com Website: www.atro.co.kr

PARK Hwagyoo, b. 12 April 1964, Seoul, Korea. Professor. m. Mi Kyung Jung, 1 son, 1 daughter. Education: PhD, Healthcare Management. Appointments: Professor. Publications: 100 articles in professional journals. Honours: Listed in international biographical dictionaries. Memberships: CSCWD. Address: Department of Healthcare Management, Soonchunhyung University, 66 Shinchang Eupnali Asan, Korea. Website: www.sch.ac.kr/u-healthcare

PARK Jae-Gwan, b. 25 July 1958, Jeon-nam, Korea. Research Scientist. m. Hee-Jung Cha, 2 daughters. BA, 1982, MA, 1984, Seoul National University, Seoul; PhD, Alfred University, New York, USA, 1995. Appointments: Researcher, 1985-95, Senior Researcher, Principal Researcher, 1995-, Head of Multifunctional Ceramics Research Center, 2002-07, Head of Nano-Materials Research Center, 2007-09, Korea Institute of Science and Technology; Research Assistant, Alfred University, New York, USA, 1991-95. Publications: More than 150 articles in professional journals. Memberships: Materials Research Society; American Ceramic Society; American Chemical Society. Address: Nano-Materials Center, Korea Institute of Science and Technology, 39-1 Hawolgok-dong, Seongbuk-gu, Seoul 136-791, Republic of Korea. E-mail: jgpark@kist.re.kr

PARK Jong Woong, b. 30 January 1965, Seoul, Korea. Professor. m. You Jung Lee, 1 son, 1 daughter. Education: BA, College of Medicine, MA and PhD, Graduate School Medicine, Korea University. Appointments: Intern and Resident, Department of Orthopaedic Surgery, Korea University Hospital, Seoul; Fellow, Department of Orthopaedic Surgery, Korea University and Duke University, Durham, North Carolina, USA; Professor, College of Medicine, Korea University. Publications: Numerous articles in professional journals. Honours: Outstanding Clinical Paper Award, 1998, 2009; Outstanding Scientific Paper Award, 2000, 2002, 2006; Outstanding Basic Research Award, 2006; Listed in international biographical dictionaries. Memberships: Korean Association of Orthopaedic Surgery; Korean Society for Surgery of the Hand; Korean Society for Microsurgery; Korean Society for Foot & Ankle Surgery; Korean Society for Sports Medicine; Korean Society for Traumatology; The Korean Fracture Society. Address: Department of Orthopaedic Surgery, Korea University, Ansan Hospital, 516 Grojan, Danwon, Ansan City, Gyeonggi, 425-707, Korea. E-mail: ospark@korea.ac.kr

PARK Nae-Man, b. 22 December 1972, Korea. Research Engineer. m. Mi-Sook Chin, 4 daughters. Education: BS, MS, Physics, Hanyang University, Seoul; PhD, Material Science, Gwangju Institute of Science and Technology, Gwangju. Appointments: Research Engineer, Senior Engineer, Project

Manager, Electronics and Telecommunications Research Institute, 2002-. Publications: 44 scientific papers including: 72 presentations in conference; 39 patents. Honours: Silver Prize, Samsung Human Technology, 2001; Best Patent Prize, ETRI, 2004. Memberships: MRS; E-MRS; ECS; KPS; SPIE. Address: 161 Gajeong-dong, Yuseong-gu, Daejeon 305-700, Korea. E-mail: nmpark@etri.re.kr

PARK Namje, Information Scientist. Education: BS, Dongguk University, Republic of Korea, 2000; MS, 2003, PhD, Computer Engineering, 2008, Sungkyunkwan University, Republic of Korea. Appointments: Researcher, Newreka Co Ltd, Daejeon, 2000-03; Officer, Korean Association of Local Informatization, Seoul, 2003; Senior Researcher, Electronics and Telecom Research Institute, Daejeon, 2003-08; Associate Development Engineer, University of California, Los Angeles, USA, 2009; Research Scientist, Arizona State University, USA, 2010; Professor, Department of Computer Education, Teachers College, Jeju National University, Korea, 2010-; On-line Customs Officer, Korea Customs Service, 2004; Committee Member, Korea Institute of Industrial Technology Evaluation and Planning, Seoul, 2004; Independent Consultant, IT Consulting, Korea IT Information Center, 2004; Session Chairman, Personal Wireless Commission Conference, Spain, 2006; Researcher, Dongguk University, Republic of Korea, 2006; Lecturer, 2007; Vice President, IBC, 2008. Publications: Author, Ubiquitous Knowledge Test, 2008; Author, RFID (GL) Technical Qualification Test, 2008; Author and Translator, Applications Technology, Security and Privacy, 2007; Author, Techniques, Protocols and System-On-Chip Design; Numerous articles in professional journals. Honours: Early Graduation, Dongguk University, 2000; Recipient, Research Excellence Award, Electronics and Telecom Research Institute, 2005; Best Paper Award, Guest Journal, 2006; Recognition Award, Mobile RFID Forum, 2007. Memberships: Open Mobile Alliance; IEEE; Organisation for Advancement of Structured Information Standards; Korean Information Processing Society; Korea Institute of Information Security & Cryptology; Mobile RFID Forum. Address: Department of Computer Education, Teachers College, Jeju National University, 61 Iljudong-ro, Jeju-si, Jeju-do, 690-781, Republic of Korea. E-mail: namjepark@gmail.com

PARK Nick (Nicholas W), b. 6 December 1958, Preston, Lancashire, England. Film Animator. Education: Sheffield Art School; National Film & TV School, Beaconsfield. Appointments: Aardman Animations, 1985, partner, 1995-. Creative Works: Films include: A Grand Day Out, 1989; Creature Comforts, 1990; The Wrong Trousers, 1993; A Close Shave, 1995; Chicken Run (co-director), 2000; Wallace & Gromit: Curse of the Were-Rabbit, 2005.; Shaun the Sheep, (TV), 2007; Creature Comforts, (TV), 2007; A Matter of Loaf and Death, 2008. Honours: BAFTA Award, Best Short Animated Film, 1990; Academy Award, 1991, 1994; Oscar, Best Animated Feature Film, 2006. Address: Aardman Animations Ltd, Gas Ferry Road, Bristol BS1 6UN, England.

PARK Noh-Hyuck, b. 4 September 1969, Chungdo, Korea. Professor. m. Tae Yeon Rho, 1 son, 1 daughter. Education: MD, 1993, Master degree, 1996, Kyungpook National University, College of Medicine; PhD, Chungnam National University, 2009. Appointments: Intern, 1993-94, Resident, 1994-98, Kyungpook National University Hospital; Associate Professor, Myongji Hospital, 2003-. Publications: Numerous articles in professional journals. Honours: Listed in biographical dictionaries. Memberships: Asian-Society of Cardiac Imaging; Asian and Oceanian Society of Pediatric Radiology. Address: Department of Radiology, Myongji Hospital, Kwandong University College of Medicine, 694-24 Hawjeong-dong, Duckyang-gu, Goyang-shi, Gwonggi, Korea.

PARK Sangjo, b. 24 March 1961, Republic of Korea. Professor. m. Munsuk Lim, 1 son, 1 daughter. Education: M, Seoul National University, Republic of Korea, 1985; PhD, Osaka University, Japan, 1999. Appointments: Senior Researcher, Samsung Electronics Ltd, Suwon, 1984-91; ETRI, Daejeon, Republic of Korea, 1992-2000; Professor, Seowon University, Cheongju, Republic of Korea, 2000-. Publications: Numerous articles in professional journals. Honours: Listed in biographical dictionaries. Memberships: IEICE, Japan. Address: 102-1004 Hyundai Apt, Gaesin-dong, Cheongju-city, Chungbuk 361-751, Korea. E-mail: parks@seowon.ac.kr

PARK Seung Young, b. 28 September 1974, Kwang-ju, Republic of Korea. Professor. m. Heekyung Cho, 1 son. Education: BS, 1997, MS, 1999, PhD, 2002, Korea University. Appointments: Post Doctoral Research Fellow, Korea University, 2002; Senior Engineer, Samsung Advanced Institute of Technology, Republic of Korea, 2003-05; Post Doctoral Research Fellow, Purdue University, USA, 2006; Associate Professor, Kangwon National University, Republic of Korea, 2007-. Publications: Over 20 technical papers on digital communications in international refereed journals. Memberships: IEEE; IEICE; KICS. Address: School of Information Technology, Kangwon National University, 192-1 Hyoja-dong, Chuncheon, Kangwon 200-701, Republic of Korea. E-mail: young@ieee.org Website: http://cc.kangwon.ac.kr/~parksy

PARK Tong Choon, b. 23 August 1945, Gyungnam Province, Korea. Medicine; Urology. m. Hee Ok Shin, 1 son, 3 daughters. Education: Bachelor's degree, 1970, Master's degree, 1974, Medicine, Doctor of Medical Science, 1980, Kyungpook National University School of Medicine. Appointments: Internship, 1970-71, Resident, Urology, 1971-75, KNU Hospital; Instructor, 1978-80, Assistant Professor, 1980-83, KNU School of Medicine; Associate Professor, College of Medicine, Yeungnam University, Head, Department of Urology, Yeungnam University Hospital, 1983; Director, Medical Library, 1988-89, Professor, College of Medicine, 1988-2010, Emeritus Professor, 2010, Yeungnam University; Head, Research and Education Department, Yeungnam University Medical Centre (YUMC), 1991-93; Vice Director, Yeungnam University Hospital, 1993-95; Medical Advisor, Military Medicine, Ministry of Defense, 1995-97; Head, Planning and Co-ordination Department, YUMC, 1995-97; Director, Yeungnam University Hospital, 1997-99; Director, Yeongcheon Hospital, YUMC, 1999-2001; Advisory Committee, Korean Urological Oncology Society, 2002-04; Vice President, 2004-05, President, 2006-07, Korean Urological Association; Vice President, Medical Affairs, Yeungnam University, Director, YUMC, 2005-07; Head, Department of Urology, Uljin-Gun Medical Center, 2010; Member, Board of Directors, Chunma Medical Research Institute, 2007-11. Publications: Numerous articles in professional journals. Honours: Certificate of Commendation, KNU Hospital, 1971; Citation for Outstanding Service, Yeungnam University, 2003; Letter of Appreciation, Korean Urological Association, 2009; Medal of Okjo Geunjeong, 2010. Memberships: Korean Medical Association; Korean Urological Association; Korean Urological Oncology Society; Endourological Society; Society of International

Urology. Address: #116-502 Suseong-Dongil Highvil Lake City, Sang-dong, Suseong-gu, Daegu 706-950, Korea. E-mail: tcparkuro@naver.com

PARK Yong-Il, b. 5 January 1962, Chuncheon, Kangwon-do, Korea. Professor. m. Young Nan Kim, 1 daughter. Education: Bachelor of Engineering, 1987, MS, 1989, Kon-Kuk University, Seoul; PhD, University of Florida, Gainesville, USA, 1996. Appointments: Research/Teaching Assistant, University of Florida, 1992-96; Postdoctoral & Associate Research Scientist, Johns Hopkins University, Baltimore, USA, 1997-99; Research Scientist, Korea Research Institute of Bioscience and Biotechnology, 1999-2001; Professor, Department of Biotechnology, The Catholic University of Korea, 2002-; Director, Biomaterials Engineering Center of Catholic University of Korea, 2002-. Publications: Articles in professional scientific journals. Honours: Listed in international biographical directories. Memberships: Korean Society for Glycoscience; Korean Society for Microbiology and Biotechnology. Address: Department of Biotechnology, The Catholic University of Korea, 43-1, Yokkok 2-dong, Wonmi-gu, Bucheon, Gyeonggi-do 420-743, Korea. E-mail: yongil382@catholic.ac.kr

PARK Yonmook, b. 1 December 1972, Seoul, Republic of Korea. Senior Engineer. m. Younkyung Moon. Education: BS, 1995, MS, 1999, Control and Instrumentation Engineering, Korea University; PhD, Mechanical Engineering, Korea Advanced Institute of Science and Technology, 2004. Appointments: First Lieutenant, 3-Artillery Brigade, Republic of Korea, 1995-97; Education Assistant, Department of Control and Instrumentation Engineering, Korea University, 1997-99; Invited Speaker, 1st Matlab User Conference, Republic of Korea, 1999; Research Assistant, Division of Aerospace Engineering, Department of Mechanical Engineering, KAIST, 2000-03; Session Chair, 4th Asian Control Conference, Singapore, 2002; Senior Engineer, Satellite Technology Research Center, KAIST, 2003-04; Satellite Attitude Control Team Leader, Satellite Technology Research Center, KAIST, 2004; Invited Speaker, Sensor and Intelligent Control Laboratory, Department of Aerospace Engineering, Sejong University, Republic of Korea, 2004; Senior Engineer, 2004-, Project Leader, 2005, Project Leader, 2006-12, Mechatronics and Manufacturing Technology Center, Samsung Electronics Co Ltd; Invited Speaker, Micro Thermal System Research Center, Seoul National University, 2005; Session Chair, 2007 IEEE International Conference on Mechatronics and Automation, China, 2007; Visiting Scientist, Laboratory for Manufacturing and Productivity, MIT, 2008-09; Chief Technology Officer, Synapse Imaging Co Ltd, 2012-. Publications: Numerous articles in professional journals including: Optimal stabilization of Takagi-Sugeno fuzzy systems with application to spacecraft control, 2001; Robust and optimal attitude control law design for spacecraft with inertia uncertainties, 2002; Least squares based PID control of an electromagnetic suspension system, 2003; LMI-based design of optimal controllers for Takagi-Sugeno fuzzy systems, 2004; Design and analysis of optimal controller for fuzzy systems with input constraint, 2004; Robust and optimal attitude stabilization of spacecraft with external disturbances, 2005. Honours include: Korea University Staff Scholarship, 1991, 1992, 1993; Work-Study Scholarship, Korea University, 1992, 1993; Special Scholarship, Korea University, 1994; Welfare Scholarship, Korea University, 1994; 3-Artillery Brigade Commander Award, 1997; Education Assistant Scholarship, Korea University, 1997, 1998, 1999; Silver Prize, 9th Annual Humantech Thesis Prize, Samsung Electronics Co Ltd, 2003; Best Conference Paper Award, 2007 IEEE International Conference on Mechatronics and Automation, China, 2007; Meritorious Service Award, Samsung Electronics Co Ltd, 2008. Memberships: Korean Institute of Electrical Engineers; Institute of Electrical and Electronics Engineers, USA; Institute of Control, Robotics and Systems, Republic of Korea; Korean Society for Aeronautical and Space Sciences. Address: Synapse Imaging Co Ltd, #102-505, SK Ventium, 522, Dangjeong-dong, Gunpo, Gyeonggi-do 435-776, Republic of Korea. E-mail: ym-park@kaist.ac.kr

PARKER Alan William (Sir), b. 14 February 1944, London, England. Film Director; Writer. m. Annie Inglis, 1966, divorced 1992, 3 sons, 1 daughter. Education: Owen's School, Islington, London. Appointments: Advertising Copywriter, 1965-67; TV Commercial Director, 1968-78; Writer, Screenplay, Melody, 1969; Chair, Director's Guild of Great Britain, 1982-, British Film Institute, 1998-; Member, British Screen Advisory Council, 1985-. Creative Works: Writer, Director: No Hard Feelings, 1972; Our Cissy, 1973; Footsteps, 1973; Bugsy Malone, 1975; Angel Heart, 1987; A Turnip Head's Guide to the British Cinema, 1989; Come See the Paradise, 1989; The Road to Wellville, 1994; Director: The Evacuees, 1974; Midnight Express, 1977; Fame, 1979; Shoot the Moon, 1981; The Wall, 1982; Birdy, 1984; Mississippi Burning, 1988; The Commitments, 1991; Evita, 1996; Angela's Ashes, 1998; The Life of David Gale, 2003. Publications: Bugsy Malone, 1976; Puddles in the Lane, 1977; Hares in the Gate, 1983; Making Movies, 1998. Honours include: BAFTA Michael Balcon Award for Outstanding Contribution to British Film; National Review Board, Best Director Award, 1988; Lifetime Achievement Award, Director's Guild of Great Britain Lifetime Achievement Award; BAFTA Award, Best Director, 1991; CBE; Officier, Ordre des Arts et des Lettres, 2005. Address: c/o Creative Artists Agency, 9830 Wilshire Boulevard, Beverly Hills, CA 90212, USA.

PARKER James Mavin (Jim), b. 18 December 1934, Hartlepool, England. Composer. m. Pauline Ann, 3 daughters. Education: Guildhall School of Music. Career: Composer. Compositions include: A Londoner in New York, 10 brass; Light Fantastic, 10 brass and percussion; Mississippi Five, woodwind quintet; The Golden Section, 5 brass; Clarinet Concerto; Mexican Wildlife, 5 brass and percussion; Boulevard, woodwind quintet; Follow the Star, musical with Wally K Daly; Film and TV music includes: Mapp and Lucia; Wynne and Penkovsky; Good Behaviour; The Making of Modern London; Girl Shy (Harold Lloyd); The Blot; Wish Me Luck; Anything More Would be Greedy; House of Cards; Parnell and the Englishwoman; Soldier Soldier; The House of Elliott; Body and Soul; Goggle Eyes; The Play the King; The Final Cut; Moll Flanders; Tom Jones; A Rather English Marriage; Lost for Words; Foyle's War; The Midsomer Murders. Honours: BAFTA Awards for Best TV Music for: To Play the King, 1993, Moll Flanders, 1997, Tom Jones, 1997, A Rather English Marriage, 1998; GSM Silver Medal, 1959; LRAM, 1959; Honorary GSM, 1985. Membership: BAFTA. Address: 16 Laurel Road, London SW13 0EE, England. E-mail: jimparker@fairads.co.uk

PARKER John Richard, b. Great Britain. Chartered Architect; Chartered Town Planner; Urban Designer. Education: Polytechnic of Central London and University College London; PhD, DipArch, DipTP; ARIBA; FRTPI; FRSA. Appointments: Job Architect, Department of Architecture and Civic Design, Schools Division, London County Council, 1961-64; Group Leader, Directorate of Development Services, London Borough of Lambeth,

1964-70; Head of Central Area Team, Department of Transportation and Development, Greater London Council, 1970-86; Consultant Planning Inspector, Department of the Environment, 1986-88; Founding Partner and Managing Director, Greater London Consultants Limited (and Partnership), 1986-96; Principal, John Parker Associates, 1996-; Director, Greater London Consultants, 1996-; Voluntary Advisor, BESO, 1997-2004; Consultant, Council of Europe and Editor of Revised European Urban Charter, 2003-08; Adviser, British Consultancy Ltd, 2004-08; Chairman, International Development Forum, 2000-04; Leader, RTPI International Development Network, 2004-; Trustee, Jubilee Walkway Trust, 2002-. Publications: Over 50 publications and public lectures, most recently: Character of Cities, 2002; Built Environment of Towns: Towards a Revised Urban Charter, 2002. Honours: 3 prize-winning entries in architectural competitions; Winston Churchill Fellow, 1967; RIBA Pearce Edwards Research Award, 1969; BALI Landscape Award, 1980; Edwin Williams Memorial Award, 1980; RICS/Times Conservation Award, 1985; British Council Anglo/ Soviet Exchange Award, 1989. Memberships: Associate, Royal Institute of British Architects; Fellow, Royal Town Planning Institute; Fellow, Royal Society of Arts. Address: 4, The Heights, Foxgrove Road, Beckenham, Kent BR3 5BY, England. E-mail: glc@btinternet.com

PARKER Sarah Jessica, b. 25 March 1965, Nelsonville, Ohio, USA. Actress. m. Matthew Broderick, 1997, 1 son, 2 daughters. Creative Works: Stage appearances include: The Innocents, 1976; The Sound of Music, 1977; Annie, 1978; The War Brides, 1981; The Death of a Miner, 1982; To Gillian on Her 37th Birthday, 1983-84; Terry Neal's Future, 1986; The Heidi Chronicles, 1989; How to Succeed in Business Without Really Trying, 1996; Once Upon a Mattress, 1996; Film appearances include: Rich Kids, 1979; Somewhere Tomorrow, 1983; Firstborn, 1984; Footloose, 1984; Girls Just Want to Have Fun, 1985; Flight of the Navigator, 1986; LA Story, 1991; Honeymoon in Vegas, 1992; Hocus Pocus, 1993; Striking Distance, 1993; Ed Wood, 1994; Miami Rhapsody, 1995; If Lucy Fell, 1996; Mars Attacks!, 1996; The First Wives Club, 1996; Extreme Measures, 1996; Til There Was You, 1997; A Life Apart: Hasidism in America, 1997; Isn't She Great, 1999; Dudley Do-Right, 1999; State and Main, 2000; Life Without Dick, 2002; Strangers with Candy, 2005; The Family Stone, 2005; Failure to Launch, 2006; Spinning Into Butter, 2007; Smart People, 2008; Sex and the City, 2008; Did You Hear About the Morgans?, 2009; Sex and the City 2, 2010; New Year's Eve, I Don't Know How She Does It, 2011; Escape from Planet Earth, Lovelace, 2013. Numerous TV appearances include: Equal Justice, 1990-91; Sex and the City, 1998-2004; Glee, 2012-. Honours: Golden Globe for Best Actress in a TV Series, 2000, 2001, 2002, 2004; Emmy, 2001, 2004. Address: Creative Artists Agency, 9830 Wilshire Boulevard, Beverly Hills, CA 90212, USA.

PARKINSON, Baron of Carnforth in the County of Lancashire (Cecil Edward Parkinson), b. 1 September 1931. Politician. m. Ann Mary Jarvis, 1957, 3 daughters, 1 daughter by Sarah Keays. Education: Emmanuel College, Cambridge. Career: Manual trainee, Metal Box Co; Articled Clerk, 1956, Partner, 1961-71, West, Wake, Price & Co; Founder, 1967-, Chair, 1967-79, Director, 1967-79, 1984-, Parkinson Hart Securities Ltd; Director of several other companies, 1967-79; Branch Treasurer, Hemel Hempstead Conservative Association, 1961-64, Constituency Chair, 1965-66, Chair and ex-officio member all committees, 1966-69; Chair, Herts 100 Club, 1968-69; President, Hemel Hempstead Young Conservatives, 1968-71, Northampton Young Conservatives, 1969-71; Contested Northampton, General Election, 1970; MP for Enfield West, 1970-74, for Hertfordshire South, 1974-83, for Hertsmere, 1983-92; Secretary, Conservative Backbench Finance Committee, 1971-72; Parliamentary Private Secretary to Minister for Aerospace and Shipping, 1972-74; Assistant Government Whip, 1974; Opposition Whip, 1974-76; Opposition Spokesman on Trade, 1976-79; Minister of State for Trade, 1979-81; Paymaster General, 1981-83; Chair, Conservative Party, 1981-83, 1997-98; Secretary of State for Trade and Industry, 1983, for Energy, 1987-89, for Transport, 1989-90; Chair, Conservative Way Forward Group, 1991-; Chancellor of the Duchy of Lancaster, 1982-83; Leader, Institute of Directors, Parliamentary Panel, 1972-79; Secretary, Anglo-Swiss Parliamentary Group, 1972-79, Chair, 1979-82; Chair, Anglo-Polish Conservative Society, 1986-98; Chemical Dependency Centre Ltd, 1986-, Jarvis (Harpenden) Holdings, Usborne, 1991-, Midland Expressway Ltd, 1993-, Dartford River Crossing Ltd, 1993-; Director, Babcock International, 1984-87, Sports Aid Foundation, Save and Prosper, 1984-87, Tarmac, 1984-87; Sears PLC, 1984-87. Publication: An Autobiography: Right at the Centre, 1992. Address: House of Lords, London SW1A 0PW, England.

PARKINSON Michael, b. 28 March 1935, Yorkshire, England. TV Presenter; Writer. m. Mary Heneghan, 3 sons. Appointments: The Guardian, Daily Express, Sunday Times, Punch, Listener; Joined Granada TV Producer, Reporter, 1965; Executive Producer and Presenter, London Weekend TV, 1968; Presenter, Cinema, 1969-70, Tea Break, Where in the World, 1971; Hosted own chat show "Parkinson", BBC, 1972-82, 1998-2004, ITV, 2004-2007, "Parkinson One to One", Yorkshire TV, 1987-90; Presenter, Give Us a Clue, 1984-, All Star Secrets, 1985, Desert Island Discs, 1986-88, Parky, 1989, LBC Radio, 1990; Help Squad, 1991, Parkinson's Sunday Supplement, Radio 2, 1994, Daily Telegraph, 1991-; Going for a Song, 1997-; Parkinson's Choice, Radio 2, 1999-2004. Publications: Football Daft, 1968; Cricket Mad, 1969; Sporting Fever, 1974; George Best: An Intimate Biography, 1975; A-Z of Soccer, co-author, 1975; Bats in the Pavilion, 1977; The Woofits, 1980; Parkinson's Lore, 1981; The Best of Parkinson, 1982; Sporting Lives, 1992; Sporting Profiles, 1995; Michael Parkinson on Golf, 1999; Michael Parkinson on Football, 2001. Honours: Sports Feature Writer of the Year, British Sports Jounalism Awards, 1995, 1998; Yorkshire Man of the Year, 1998; BAFTA Award for Best Light Entertainment, 1999; Media Society Award for Distinguished Contribution to Media, 2000; CBE, 2000. Address: CSS Stellar Management Ltd, 1st Floor, Drury House, 34-43 Russell Street, London WC2B 5HA, England.

PARLIER Greg H, b. 10 May 1952, San Luis Obispo, California, USA. Retired Colonel, US Army; Operations Research/Systems Analyst; Engineer; Independent Consultant; Defense Analyst; Educator; Author; Advisor to Foreign Governments. Education: BS, USMA, West Point, 1974; MS, Naval Postgraduate School, 1983; MA, Walsh School of Foreign Service, Georgetown, 1988; US Marine Corps Command and Staff College, 1989; National Defense Fellow, MIT, 1995; US Army War College, 1996; MIT Sloan Executive Series on Management, Innovation and Technology, 1997-2008; PhD, Wesleyan, 2004. Appointments: Assistant Professor, Operations Research, Department of Engineering, 1984-86, Associate Professor, Department of Systems Engineering, 1990-94, USMA, West Point; Battalion Commander, 5th Battalion (Avenger), 2nd Air Defense Artillery Regiment, 69th ADA Brigade, V Corps, USAREUR, 1992-94; Chief, Resource Plans and Analysis Division, Directorate of Program Analysis and Evaluation,

Office of the Chief of Staff, Army, 1996-98; Director, Program Analysis and Evaluation, US Army Recruiting Command, 1998-2002; Director for Transformation and Principal Assistant Deputy Commander, US Army Aviation and Missile Command, 2002-03; Senior Research Scientist, University of Alabama, Huntsville, 2003-05; Adjunct Research Staff, Institute for Defense Analyses, 2003-; Independent Consultant, 2003-; Senior Systems Analyst, SAIC, 2005-09; Vice President, Strategic Planning, RSAE Inc, 2005-07. Publications: One text; One book chapter; One professional monograph; Numerous technical reports, research project summaries, conference papers, professional journal articles and the Congressional Record. Honours: Legion of Merit (3); Bronze Star; Meritorious Service Medal (7); Army Commendation Medal (3); Plaque of Appreciation: Korean National Assembly; German Efficiency Badge in Gold (2nd Award); Honorary Commander, Flugabwehrkanonregiment 8, 1st German Mountain Division; Canadian Parachutist Badge; MORS Graduate Research Award, 1983; Finalist, ORSA Koopman Prize, 1985, 1987; DA Operations Research Analyst of the Year, 1987; US Navy League Cates Award for Superior Research, 1989; Finalist, DA Payne Memorial Award for Excellence in Analysis, 1997, 2001; Finalist, MORS Rist Prize, 1998, 2002; Finalist, INFORMS Edelman Award, 2001; Edelman Laureate, INFORMS, 2006; Military Delegate, Eisenhower People-to-People Ambassador Program to South Africa, 2007. Memberships: California Scholarship Federation; 82nd Airborne Division Association; Air Defense Artillery Association; Association of the US Army; INFORMS Military Applications Society, Vice President, 2008-10, President, 2010-12, American Red Cross; Research Affiliate, Center for Technology, Policy & Industrial Development, MIT, 2010-. Address: 255 Avian Ln, Madison, AL 35758, USA. E-mail: gparlier@knology.net

PARPAL LLADO Pedro, b. 19 September 1936, Palma de Mallorca, Spain. Teacher. m. Aurora. Education: Baccalaureate; Teacher; Philosophy Graduate; Psychology degree; Master's degree in Human Relations. Appointments: Ensign, Lieutenant, Captain, Spanish Army; Lawyer; Teacher; Professor of Therapeutic Pedagogy; Chair, Literary Group; Military Judge; Director, Stella College; Director, Terman Academy; President, Research Institute, Mallorca; Co-ordinator of Fine Arts Circle. Publications: Numerous articles in professional journals. Honours: Caballero de la Real y Militar de San Hermene Gildo; Insignia de Honor del Colegio Oficial de Doctores y Licenciados en Filosofia y Letras y Ciencias de Baleares; Academio de la Academia Internacional de Napoles; and others. Memberships: Circle of Arts, Palma de Mallorca; Board of the Hispanic Group of Writers; Board of Directors, Friends of the Mallorca Mills; and others. Address: Ricardo Ankerman 38, 07006 Palma de Mallorca, Spain.

PARR John Brian, b. 18 March 1941, Epsom, England. University Researcher. m. Pamela Harkins, 2 daughters. Education: BSc (Econ), University College London, University of London, 1959-62; PhD, University of Washington, Seattle, USA, 1962-67. Appointments: Assistant Professor of Regional Science, 1967-72, Associate Professor of Regional Science, 1972-75, University of Pennsylvania, USA; Lecturer, Senior Lecturer in Urban Economics, 1975-80, Reader in Applied Economics, 1980-89, Professor of Regional and Urban Economics, 1989-, University of Glasgow. Publications include: Regional Policy: Past Experience and New Directions (co-edited book), 1979; Market Centers and Retail Location: Theory and Applications (co-authored book), 1988; Refereed papers in professional journals include: Outmigration and the depressed area problem, 1966; Models of city size in the urban system, 1970; Models of the central place system: a more general approach, 1978; A note on the size distributions of cities over time, 1985; The economic law of market areas: a further discussion, 1995; Regional economic development: an export-stages framework, 1999; Missing elements in the analysis of agglomeration economies, 2002; Spatial-structure differences between urban and regional systems, 2012. Honours: Guest, Polish Academy of Sciences, Warsaw, Poland, 1977; Speaker, August Lösch Commemoration, Heidenheim an der Brenz, Germany, 1978; Speaker at the Ehrenpromotion (award of honorary doctorate) of Professor Dr Martin Beckmann, University of Karlsruhe, Germany, 1981; Participant in Distinguished Visitors Program, University of Pennsylvania, Philadelphia, 1983; Academician, Academy of Social Sciences, 2000; Moss Madden Memorial Medal, 2003; Elected Fellow, Regional Science Association International, 2006; Listed in various international biographical dictionaries. Memberships: Royal Economic Society; Regional Science Association International and British and Irish Section; Regional Studies Association; Member of various editorial boards of scientific journals. Address: School of Social and Political Sciences, University of Glasgow, Glasgow G12 8QQ, United Kingdom.

PARRINDER (John) Patrick, b. 11 October 1944, Wadebridge, Cornwall, England. Professor of English; Literary Critic. 2 daughters. Education: Christ's College, 1962-65, Darwin College, 1965-67, Cambridge; MA, PhD, Cambridge University. Appointments: Fellow, King's College, Cambridge, 1967-74; Lecturer, 1974-80, Reader, 1980-86, Professor of English, 1986-2008, Emeritus Professor, 2008-, University of Reading. Publications: H G Wells, 1970; Authors and Authority, 1977, 2nd edition, enlarged, 1991; Science Fiction: Its Criticism and Teaching, 1980; James Joyce, 1984; The Failure of Theory, 1987; Shadows of the Future, 1995. Editor: H G Wells: The Critical Heritage, 1972; Science Fiction: A Critical Guide, 1979; Learning from Other Worlds, 2000; Nation and Novel, 2006. Contributions to: London Review of Books; Many academic journals. Honour: President's Award, World Science Fiction, 1987; Fellow, English Association, 2001. Memberships: H G Wells Society; Science Fiction Foundation; Society of Authors. Address: 82 Hillfield Avenue, London N8 7DN, England.

PARRIS Matthew, b. 7 August 1949, Johannesburg, South Africa. Writer; Broadcaster. Civil partner, Julian Glover. Education: Clare College, Cambridge; Yale University. Career: FOC, 1974-76; With Conservative Research Department, 1976-79; MP (Conservative) for West Derbyshire, 1979-86; Presenter, Weekend World, LWT, 1986-88; Parliamentary Sketchwriter for The Times, 1988-2002; Columnist, for The Times, 1988-, for The Spectator, 1992-; Member, Broadcasting Standards Council, 1992-97. Publications: IncaKola, 1990; Scorn, 1994; Great Parliamentary Scandals, 1995; Chance Witness (memoir), 2001; A Castle in Spain, 2005; Various books about travel, politics, insult, abuse and scandal. Honours: Columnist of the Year, British Press Awards, 1991, 1993, 1995; Columnist of the Year, What The Papers Say, 1992, 2004, 2006; Politico's Book of the Year Award, 2002; Winner, George Orwell Prize, 2004; Comment Award (Chairman's Prize), 2009; Commentator of the Year, The Press Gazette, 2010; Various awards for writing and journalism. Address: c/o The Times, Pennington Street, London E1 9XN, England.

PARSONS David Robert, b. 14 August 1950, Bristol, England. Council Leader. m. Elizabeth Dolby, 2 sons, 1 daughter. Education: BSc (Hons), University of Salford; MA, St John's

College, Oxford; DEM, Bristol Polytechnic. Appointments: Leader, Blaby District Council, 2001-03; Chairman, East Midlands Regional Assembly, 2002-10; Chairman, East Midlands Councils, 2010-; Leader, Leicestershire County Council, 2003-; Member, Committee of the Regions, EU, 2005-; Chairman, Improvement Board (LGA), 2008-; Deputy Chairman, Local Government Association, 2008-; Member, Regional Economic Cabinet, 2008-10; Member, Regional Economic Council, 2008-10. Publications: Outlook opinion on the European Single Market, 2007. Honours: CBE, 2009. Address: County Hall, Glenfield, Leicestershire LE3 8RA, England. E-mail: david.parsons@leics.gov.uk

PARTHASARATHY Panamalai Ramarao, b. 16 September 1948, Cuddalore, India. Mathematics Educator. m. Narasimhan Manorama, 2 children. Education: BS, Madras University, 1968; MS, 1970, PhD, 1976, Annamalai University. Appointments: Lecturer, Annamalai University, 1974-75; National Council of Education Research & Training, New Delhi, 1975-76; Lecturer, Mathematics, 1977-80, Assistant Professor, 1980-88, Associate Professor, 1988-90, Professor, 1990-, Chairman of Department, 1996-, Indian Institute of Technology, Madras; Visiting Scientist, McMaster University, Hamilton, Canada, 1988; International Centre for Theoretical Physics, Trieste, 1982, 1986; Member, Board of Governors, Indian Institute of Technology, 2010-11; Researcher in field. Publications: Author, Applied Birth and Death Models, 2004; Numerous articles in professional journals. Honours: Alexander von Humboldt Fellow, 1984-85; Jacob Wolfowitz Award for Best Paper, 2005; Distinguished Professor, DAAD, Karlsruhe Institute of Technology, 2007-09. Memberships: Fellow, Institute of Mathematical Statistics; International Statistics Institute; International Center for Theoretical Physics. Address: Indian Institute of Technology, Department of Mathematics, Madras 600 036, India. E-mail: prp@iitm.ac.in

PARTON Dolly Rebecca, b. 19 January 1946, Sevier County, Tennessee, USA. Singer; Composer. m. Carl Dean, 1966. Creative Works: Films include: Nine to Five, 1980; The Best Little Whorehouse in Texas, 1982; Rhinestone, 1984; Steel Magnolias, 1989; Straight Talk, 1991; The Beverly Hillbillies; Frank McKlusky, C.I., 2002; Miss Congeniality 2: Armed and Fabulous, 2005; Albums include: Here You Come Again, 1978; Real Love, 1985; Just the Way I Am, 1986; Heartbreaker, 1988; Great Balls of Fire, 1988; Rainbow, 1988; White Limozeen, 1989; Home for Christmas, 1990; Eagle When She Flies, 1991; Slow Dancing with the Moon, 1993; Honky Tonk Angels, 1994; The Essential Dolly Parton, 1995; Just the Way I Am, 1996; Super Hits, 1996; I Will Always Love You and Other Greatest Hits, 1996; Hungary Again, 1998; Grass is Blue, 1999; Best of the Best –Porter 2 Doll, 1999; Halos and Horns, 2002; Just Because I'm a Woman: Songs of Dolly Parton, 2003; For God and Country, 2003; Live and Well, 2004; Those Were The Days, 2005; Backwoods Barbie, 2008. Composed numerous songs including: Nine to Five. Publication: Dolly: My Life and Other Unfinished Business, 1994. Honours include: Vocal Group of the Year Award (with Porter Wagoner), 1968; Vocal Duo of the Year, All Music Association, 1970, 1971; Nashville Metronome Award, 1979; Female Vocalist of the Year, 1975, 1976; Country Star of the Year, 1978; Peoples Choice, 1980; Female Vocalist of the Year, Academy of Country Music, 1980; East Tennessee Hall of Fame, 1988. Address: RCA, 6 West 57th Street, New York, NY 10019, USA.

PARTRIDGE Derek William, b. 15 May 1931. London, England. Retired Diplomat. Appointments: HM Diplomatic Service: Foreign Office, London, England, 1951-54, Oslo, 1954-56, Jedda, 1956, Khartoum, 1957-60, Sofia, 1960-62, Manila, 1962-65, Djakarta, 1965-67, FCO, 1967-72, Brisbane, 1972-74, Colombo, 1974-77; Head, Migration and Visa Department, FCO, 1981-83; Head, Nationality and Treaty Department, FCO, 1983-86; British High Commissioner, Freetown, Sierra Leone, 1986-91; Liberal Democrat Councillor, London Borough of Southwark, 1994-2002. Honours: CMG, 1987. Memberships: National Liberal Club; Royal African Society. Address: 16 Wolfe Crescent, Rotherhithe, London SE16 6SF, England.

PASCOE Jane, b. 9 May 1955, Bristol, England. Artist. 1 son. Education: Foundation Course, Art and Design, 1973-74, BA Hons, Fine Art, 1st Class, 1977, Bristol Polytechnic Faculty of Art and Design; Art Teacher's Certificate, Brighton Polytechnic School of Art Education, 1977-78. Appointments: Art Teacher, Highbury School, Salisbury, 1979-84; Art Teacher, Blandford Upper School, 1984-86; Head of Art, Bournemouth School for Girls, 1986-88; Head of Art, Kingdown School, Warminster, 1988-89; Head of Art, The Atherley School, Southampton, 1989-2006; Head of Art, Hampshire Collegiate School, Romsey, 2006-. Work exhibited in: Royal West of England Academy of Art; The Festival Gallery; The Victoria Gallery; Beaux Arts Gallery, Bath; Wessex Artists Exhibition, Salisbury; The Eye Gallery, Bristol; The Manor House Gallery, Cheltenham; Parkin Fine Art, London; The Mall Gallery, London; Work also included in numerous private collections including The Cheltenham and Gloucester Building Society and the Public Collection of the RWA, Bristol. Honour: Listed in several Who's Who and biographical publications. Memberships: Associate Member, 1983, Full Member, 1987, Royal West of England Academy of Art. Address: Honeysuckle Cottage, Charmus Road, Old Calmore, Southampton, Hampshire SO40 2RG, England.

PASQUIER-VERDIN Laurent, b. 22 March 1974, Versailles, France. Program Manager. m. Muriel, 1 son, 1 daughter. Education: EFREI Engineering School, 1998; MSc, University Pierre et Marie Curie, Paris VI, 1998. Appointments: Research Engineer, 1998-2002, Senior Engineer, R&D, 2002-06, Philips; Principal Engineer, NXP Semiconductor; Program Manager, ST-ERICSSON. Publications: Numerous articles in professional journals. Honours: Best Presentation Award, 2000; Design of the Year Bronze Award, 2005.

PASTINE Maureen Diane Hillman, b. 21 November 1944, Hays, Kansas, USA. Teacher. m. Jerry Pastine. Education: AB, Bachelor of Arts, English, Fort Hays State University, Kansas, 1967; Master's degree, Library Science, Emporia State University, Kansas, 1970. Appointments: Reference Librarian, Head of Reference Department, University of Nebraska at Omaha, Nebraska, 1971-77; Head of Undergraduate Library, 1977-79, Reference Librarian and Head of Reference Department, 1979-80, University of Illinois at Urbana-Champaign, Urbana, Illinois; University Librarian, San Jose State University, California, 1980-85; Director of Libraries, Washington State University, Pullman, 1985-89; Central University Librarian, Southern Methodist University, Dallas, Texas, 1989-97; University Librarian, Temple University, Philadelphia, Pennsylvania, 1997-2004; General oversight for Temple University Press, 1999-2002; Grants and Contacts Officer, Yavapai-Apache Nation, Campverde, Arizona, 2004-08. Publications: Numerous articles in professional journals including most recently: A Case Study of Libraries and University Presses Working Together, 2001. Honours include: Miriam B Dudly Bibliographic Instruction Librarian of the Year Award, 1989; Service Award, Information Resources Committee, EDUCAUSE, 1996-2001; National Conference on Cultural Property Protection Museum Security Certificate, 1999; Fundraising Achievement Award, Emporia State University, 2002; Alumni Achievement Award, Fort Hays State University, 2002. Memberships: Online Computer Library Center; American Library Association; Association of Research Libraries; Research Libraries Group; Washington Library Network; Coalition for Networked Information; EDUCAUSE; Center for Library and Information Resources; National Museum of Women in the Arts; National Museum of Women in History. Address: PO Box 237, 901 South Madison, Plainville, KS62663, USA. E-mail: mdpastine@yahoo.com

PATEL Mohan, b. 19 July 1963, Thasra, Gujarat, India. Principal. m. Jaya Patel, 1 son, 2 daughters. Education: BA, Economics; MA, Economics; PhD, Economics. Appointments: Research Ast; Lecturer; Reader; Principal. Publications: 26 research papers; 15 books; Editor, 5 volumes; Presented 36 papers at conference. Honours: Man of the Year, ABI, 2003; Rastriya Gaurav Award, 2004; Jewel of India Award, 2007; National Environmental Awareness Award, 2007; Eminent Educationalist Award, 2007; Kutch Shakti: Best Educationalist, National Award, 2008. Memberships: Gujarat Economic Association; Sardar Patel University; All India Kutch Kadva Chhabhaiya Parivar; Indian Economic Association, Bombay. Address: NS Patel Arts College, Bhalej Road, Anan (Gujarat), India. E-mail: mohannsp@yahoo.co.in

PATIL Rajesh Ramesh, b. 26 March 1978, Dombivli, India. Resesarcher. m. Manisha, 1 son. Education: B Pharm, 2000, M Pharm, 2003, Bombay College of Pharmacy, University of Mumbai, Maharashtra, 2000; Post Graduate Diploma, Patent Law, NALSAR University of Law, Hyderabad, 2006; PhD, Institute of Chemical Technology, University of Mumbai, 2008. Appointments: Research Officer, Sun Pharmaceutical Advanced Research Center, Mumbai, 2002-04; Postdoctoral Fellow, Department of Materials Science & Engineering, Johns Hopkins University, Baltimore, USA, 2008-10. Publications: Numerous articles in professional journals. Honours: Best Research Poster Presentation Award, NANO NIPER, 2006; Best Research Poster Presentation Award, Indo-US symposium on Nanotechnology in Advanced Drug Delivery, 2006; One of 25 Top Indian Scientists, 1st Summer School on Nanotechnology in Advanced Drug Delivery, 2007; Travel Grant, 2008; Invited editor, Journal of Drug Delivery, 2010. Memberships: International Controlled Release Society; American Society of Cell and Gene Therapy. Address: 14 Ramdarshan Co Hsc Society, Chitranjandas Path, Ram Nagar, Dombivli (East) Maharashtra, PIN 421201, India. E-mail: rajeshrpatil@gmail.com

PATTEN Brian, b. 7 February 1946, Liverpool, England. Poet; Writer. Appointment: Regents Lecturer, University of California at San Diego. Publications: Poetry: The Mersey Sound: Penguin Modern Poets 10, 1967; Little Johnny's Confession, 1967; The Home Coming, 1969; Notes to the Hurrying Man: Poems, Winter '66-Summer '68, 1969; The Irrelevant Song, 1970; At Four O'Clock in the Morning, 1971; Walking Out: The Early Poems of Brian Patten, 1971; The Eminent Professors and the Nature of Poetry as Enacted Out by Members of the Poetry Seminar One Rainy Evening, 1972; The Unreliable Nightingale, 1973; Vanishing Trick, 1976; Grave Gossip, 1979; Love Poems, 1981; New Volume, 1983; Storm Damage, 1988; Grinning Jack: Selected Poems, 1990; Armada, 1996; The Utterly Brilliant Book of Poetry (editor), 1998. Editor: Clare's Countryside: A Book of John Clare, 1981; The Puffin Book of 20th Century Children's Verse, 1996; The Story Giant, 2001. Children's Books: Prose: The Jumping Mouse, 1972; Mr Moon's Last Case, 1975; Emma's Doll, 1976; Jimmy Tag-along, 1988; Grizzelda Frizzle, 1992; Impossible Parents, 1994; Beowulf, a version, 1999. Poetry: Gargling With Jelly, 1985; Thawing Frozen Frogs, 1990; The Magic Bicycle, 1993; The Utter Nutters, 1994; The Blue and Green Ark, 1999; Juggling with Gerbils, 2000; Little Hotchpotch, 2000; Impossible Parents Go Green; The Monsters Guide to Choosing a Pet (with Roger McGough), 2004. Contributions to: Journals and newspapers. Honour: Special Award, Mystery Writers of America, 1977; Arts Council of England, Writers Award, 1998; Freedom of the City of Liverpool, 2000; The Cholmondeley Award for Poetry, 2001; Honorary Fellow, John Moores University, 2002; Fellow, RSL. Membership: Chelsea Arts Club. Address: c/o Rogers, Coleridge and White, 20 Powis Mews, London W11 1JN, England.

PATTERSON Most Hon Percival Noel James, b. 10 April 1935, Dias Hanover, Jamaica. Politician; Lawyer. 1 son, 1 daughter. Education: BA, English, University of West Indies, 1958; BLL, London School of Economics, 1963. Appointments: Joined People's National Party, 1958; Party Organiser, People's National Party, 1958; Vice President, People's National Party, 1969; Minister of Industry, Trade and Tourism, 1972; Deputy Prime Minister and Minister of Foreign Affairs and Foreign Trade, 1978-80; Chairman, People's National Party, 1983; Deputy Prime Minister and Minister of Development, Planning and Production, 1989-90; Deputy Prime Minister and Minister of Finance and Planning, 1990-99; President and Party Leader, People's National Party, 1992; Prime Minister, 1992-96. Honours: Sir Hughes Parry Prize for excellence in the Law of Contract; Leverhulme Scholarship, London School of Economics; Appointed to Privy Council of the United Kingdom, 1992; Honorary Doctor of Letters, Northeastern University, 1994; Honorary Degree of Doctor of Laws, Brown University, 1998; Numerous foreign awards include: Order of Jose Marti, Cuba, 1997; Order of the Volta, Ghana, 1999; Food and Agriculture Organisation Agricola Medal, Jamaica, 2001; Juan Mora Fernandez Great Silver Cross, Costa Rica, 2001. Address: Office of the Prime Minister, 1 Devon Road, Kingston 6, Jamaica. E-mail: jamhouse@cwjamaica.com

PAUL Vattapparumbil Issac, b. 31 May 1966, Vengola, Kerala, India. Associate Professor. m. V M Rincy, 1 daughter. Education: MSc, Zoology (Gold Medal), Christ College, Irinjalakuda, B Ed (First Rank), Natural Science, Department of Education, University of Calicut; M Phil, Zoology, Department of Zoology, University of Calicut; PhD, Zoology, Banaras Hindu University. Appointments: Lecturer, Zoology, Nagaland University, 1997-99; Lecturer, Senior Scale, 2001-07, Reader, 2007-10, Associate Professor, Zoology, 2010-, Annamalai University. Publications: 32 research articles; 2 edited books. Honours: Inspiring Pillar of India Award; Bharat Excellence Award; Leading Scientists of the World, 2012; Famous India: Nation's Who's Who, 2012; Asian Admirable Achievers Vol VI. Memberships: Indian Science Congress Association; National Environmental Science Association; Academic Council, Annamalai University. Address: Department of Zoology, Annamalai University, Annamalai Nagar 608002, Tamil Nadu, India. E-mail: drissacpaul@gmail.com

PAVLICHENKOV Igor Mikhailovitch, b. 4 December 1934, Reutov City, Moscow Region, Russia. Physicist; Theoretician. m. Olga Yavorskaya, 1972, 1 son. Education:

Physics, Moscow University, 1958; Candidate of Physics, JINR, Dubna, 1964; DPhys, Kurchatov Institute, 1982. Appointments: Junior Researcher, 1958-83, Senior Researcher, 1983-87, Leading Researcher, 1987-93, Principal Researcher, 1993-, Kurchatov Institute. Publications: Several research papers in professional journals. Honours: I V Kurchatov Annual Prize, 1988, 1994. Memberships: Russian Nuclear Research Programme Committee, Moscow, 1986-90; Several scientific boards. Address: National Research Centre, Kurchatov Institute, 123182 Moscow, Russia.

PAVLOVIC Dragan, b. 4 August 1949, Vranje, Serbia. Physician. m. Snezana Divac. Education: MD, Belgrade, Yugoslavia, 1976; DSM, London, 1984; Dr Med, Germany, 2002; Habilitation, Germany, 2007. Appointments: General Practice, 1977-78; Anaesthesiologist, 1978-79, 1981-83; Sports Medicine, 1979-81, 1983-84; Research Fellow, Paris, 1985-2000; Research Director, Germany, 2000-. Publications: Over 150 articles in professional journals. Memberships: Societe de Pneumology; Mind Association, Oxford.

PAVLOVSKA Larisa, b. 6 August 1952, Zlatoust, Chelyabinsk region, Russia. Professor. Divorced, 1 son, 1 daughter. Education: Philology Faculty, Kishinev University, 1969-74; Candidate of Pedagogical Sciences, Scientific Research Institute of the USSR, Academy of Pedagogical Sciences for Teaching Russian in National Schools, Moscow, 1979-82; Doctor of Pedagogical Sciences, Russian Language Institute, Moscow, 1997-2000. Appointments: Lecturer, 1976-85, Senior Lecturer, 1986-88, Docent, 1988-2007, Associate Professor, 2008-, Liepaja University, Latvia; Professor, Rzeszow University, Poland. Publications: Numerous articles in professional journals. Memberships: International Association of Teacher of the Russian Language and Literature. E-mail: larisa.pavlovska@liepu.lv

PAXMAN Jeremy Dickson, b. 11 May 1950, Leeds, England. Journalist; Author. Education: St Catherine's College, Cambridge. Appointments: Journalist, Northern Ireland, 1973-77; Reporter, BBC TV Tonight and Panorama Programmes, 1977-85; Presenter, BBC TV Breakfast Time, 1986-89, Newsnight, 1989-, University Challenge, 1994-, Start the Week, Radio 4, 1998-2002. Publications: A Higher Form of Killing (co-author), 1982; Through the Volcanoes, 1985; Friends in High Places, 1990; Fish, Fishing and the Meaning of Life, 1994; The Compleat Angler, 1996; The English, 1998; The Political Animal, 2002; On Royalty, 2006; The Victorians, 2010; Numerous articles in newspapers and magazines. Honours include: Royal TV Society Award, International Reporting; Richard Dimbley Award, BAFTA, 1996, 2000; Interview of the Year, Royal TV Society, 1997, 1998; Voice of the Viewer and Listener Presenter of the Year, 1994, 1997; Dr h c, Leeds, Bradford, 1999; Variety Club Media Personality of the Year, 1999; Fellow, St Edmund Hall, Oxford, St Catharine's College, Cambridge, 2001. Address: c/o BBC TV, London W12 7RJ, England.

PAYNE Margaret Allison, b. 14 April 1937, Southampton, England. Artist; Educationalist. Education: NDD, Painting, Etching, Relief Printmaking, Harrow School of Art, 1955-59; ATC, Goldsmith's College, London University, 1959-60; BA (Hons), History of Art, Birkbeck College, London University, 1977-81; MA, Institute of Education, London University, 1981-83. Appointments: Art Teacher: Haggerston School, London, 1960-61, Harrow Art School, 1961-62, St Hilda's School, Bushey, 1965-68, Sarum Hall School, 1995-97; Senior Lecturer, University of Surrey, Roehampton, 1968-94; Exhibitions include: Annually with the Royal Society of Painter-Printmakers, 1962-90; Royal Academy Summer Exhibition: 1958, 1959, 1960, 1961, 1973, 1977; Young Contemporaries, 1960-61; Paris Salon, 1962-63; Norwich Art Gallery, 1964; Harrogate Art Gallery, 1977; Cardiff Art Gallery, 1978, 1979; Arts Club, London, 1987; Dickens Gallery, Bloxham, 1990; Many Educational Displays include: Art and Appreciation in a Multicultural Nursery School, 1989; Eastwood Nursery School at the Tate, 1989; Works in Sheffield City Art Gallery; Nottinghamshire and Sheffield Pictures for Schools. Publications: Articles in journals include: Under Fives at the Tate, 1989; Teaching Art Appreciation, 1990; Games Children Play, 1993; Froebelian Principles and the Art National Curriculum, 1993; What's in a Picture, 1994; Take Another Look, 1995. Membership: Fellow, Royal Society of Painter Etchers. Address: 11A Wallorton Gardens, East Sheen, London SW14 8DX, England.

PAYRET (Astem Bé) Alice Marie Thérèse, b. 17 November 1918, Pollestres, P-O, France. Ex-Professor of Mathematics; Painter; Writer. 2 daughters. Education: École Normale (teacher training school), Perpignan, 1935-38; École Normale, Toulouse, 1938-39; École Superieure (higher teacher training school), Paris, 1939-42; Certificate of Aptitude for Professorship, Mathematical section, 1942; École des Beaux Arts, Perpignan, 1980-85. Appointments: Professor of Mathematics: École Normale d'Institutrices, Chaumont, 1946-49; College, Ceret, France, 1942-46; École Normale d'Institutrices, Albi, France, 1949-52; Lycée, Rabat, Maroc, 1952-53; Lycée, Casablanca, Maroc, 1953-56; Lycée, Lille, 1957-59; Lycée, Jean Lurcat, Perpignan, 1959-65; Lycée, Berthelot, Toulouse, 1965-72; Painter, 1980-; Literary activity, 2004-. Publications: Numerous articles in professional journals; Letters and Stories, 2005; Am I the Soil or the Fruit? 2006; Seasons and Heat-Wave, 2006; Adolescence, 2007; Solitude, 2007; Moscou-Pekin, 2008; En Pologne, 2008; Voyage en Hongrie, 2009; Maroc: 1953-1956, 2008; Images du Roussillon, 2008; Vagabondage, 2009; Au gré des jours, 2010; Philosophie et Poésie, 2011; Avant tout, le coeur, 2011. Memberships: Ordre des Palmes Académiques; Anciens élèves d'École Normale Supérieure; Association of Painting in Roussillon; Association of Art and Culture Astembé, France; Universala Esperanto Asocio. Address: Chemin des Arcades, Perpignan, 66100 France.

PAZ Regina Celia Rodrigues da, b. 6 March 1972, Sorocaba ISP, Brazil. Veterinarian; Researcher. Education: Degree, University Estadual de Londrina, 1995; Master's degree, 2000, PhD, 2004, São Paulo University. Appointments: Clinvet, Sorocaba, Brazil, 1996-98; Universidad Federal de Mato Grosso, Cuiabá, Brazil, 2005. Publications: Papers and articles in professional scientific journals. Honours: Best Student Report Award, 5th International Symposium, Canine and Feline Reproduction, 2004; Listed in international biographical dictionaries. Address: Avenida Fernando Correa da Costa, Mato Grosso, Cuiabá 78060-600, Brazil. E-mail: repaz@usp.br

PEARCE Leslie Dennis, b. 20 April 1945, Bow, East London, England. Factory Worker; Road Worker; Security Officer; Local Government Officer; Retired. m. Anne Black, 21 December 1990. Appointments: J Compton Sons & Webb, Uniform Clothing, Cap Cutter; R M Turner and Hunter, Timber Merchants, Trainee Sales; Poplar Borough Council, Road Labourer; United Dairies, Milk Roundsman; Securicor, Brinks Mat, Security Express, Cash In Transit Security Guard; London Borough of Hackney, Cashier, 1975-95, early retired. Publications include: Making Matters Verse; Pre-Conception, poem, 1997; Travellers Moon, 1997; Mirrors of the Soul,

1996; Voices in the Heart, 1997; Expressions, 1997; Tibby, 1998; Winter Warmer, 1998; What Love, 1998; Science, 1998; A Moving Sonnet, 1998, 1999; Three Cheers (poem), 1999; The Love Verses, 2004; This Endless Joy, 2006; The Poet's Dream; A Seasonal Sonnet, 2008. Honour: Editors Choice Award, 1996; National Poetry Champion (Death and Dreams), Bexhill-on-Sea, 2010. Membership: International Society of Poets, Distinguished Member. Address: 29 Eastwood Road, Bexhill-on-Sea, East Sussex, TN39 3PR, England.

PEARSALL Derek Albert, b. 28 August 1931, Birmingham, England. Emeritus Professor of English. m. Rosemary Elvidge, 30 August 1952, 2 sons, 3 daughters. Education: BA, 1951, MA, 1952, University of Birmingham. Appointments: Assistant Lecturer, Lecturer, King's College, University of London, 1959-65; Lecturer, Senior Lecturer, Reader, 1965-76, Professor, 1976-87, University of York; Visiting Professor, 1985-87, Gurney Professor of English, 1987-2000, (Emeritus), Harvard University, Cambridge, Massachusetts, USA. Publications: John Lydgate, 1970; Landscapes and Seasons of the Medieval World (with Elizabeth Salter), 1973; Old English and Middle English Poetry, 1977; Langland's Piers Plowman: An Edition of the C-Text, 1978; The Canterbury Tales: A Critical Study, 1985; The Life of Geoffrey Chaucer: A Critical Biography, 1992; John Lydgate (1371-1449): A Bio-bibliography, 1997; Chaucer to Spenser: An Anthology of Writings in English 1375-1575, 1999; Gothic Europe 1200-1450, 2001; Arthurian Romance: A Short Introduction, 2003; Langland's Piers Plowman: A New Annotated Edition of the C-Text, 2008. Memberships: Early English Text Society, council member; Medieval Academy of America, fellow; New Chaucer Society, president, 1988-90; American Academy of Arts and Sciences, fellow. Address: 4 Clifton Dale, York YO30 6LJ, England.

PECHÁČEK Tomáš, b. 5 May 1981, Opočno, Czech Republic. Astrophysicist. Education: Master, Charles University, Prague, 2004; PhD, Theoretical Astrophysics, Astronomical Institute, Academy of Sciences of the Czech Republic, 2008. Appointments: Lecturer, M R Stefanik Observatory, Petrin, 1998-2005; Research Scientist, Astronomical Institute, Ondrejov, 2008-; Visiting Scientist, CAMK, Warsaw, Poland, Observatoire Astronomique de Strasbourg, France, and Silesian University, Opava, Czech Republic. Publications: The relativistic shifts, 2005; Power-spectra from spotted accretion discs, 2006; Hot-spot model of accretion disc variability, 2008; many others. Honours: High Schoolers' Scholarly Activity Award for Work on SYROP Compositions; Sprostak Honour of J Klokocnik. Memberships: IAU; Czech Astronomical Society. Address: Astronomical Institute Academy of Sciences, Boĉhi II/1401a, Prague 14131, Czech Republic. E-mail: pechacek_t@seznam.cz

PEDERSEN K George, b. 13 June 1931, Alberta, Canada. Educator. m. Penny, 1 son, 1 daughter. Education: Diploma, BC Provincial Normal School, 1952; BA, University of British Columbia, 1959; MA, University of Washington, 1964; PhD, University of Chicago, 1969. Appointments: Teacher, Vice President and Principal, various public schools, 1952-65; Academic appointments at University of Toronto, 1968-70, University of Chicago, 1970-72; Dean and Academic Vice President, University of Victoria, 1972-79; President, Simon Fraser University, 1979-83; President, University of British Columbia, 1983-85; President, University of Western Ontario, 1985-94; Interim President, University of Northern British Columbia, 1995; Founding President, Royal Roads University, 1995-96. Publications: The Itinerant Schoolmaster; Several book chapters; Innumerable articles. Honours: 10 major scholarships; Fellow, Canadian College of Teachers, Commonwealth Medal, 1992; Officer, Order of Canada, 1993; Order of Ontario, 1994; Order of British Columbia, 2002; Queens Jubilee Medal, 2002; LLD, McMaster University, 1996; DLitt, Emily Carr University of Art and Design, 2003; LLD, Simon Fraser University, 2003; LLD, University of Northern British Columbia; Fellow, Royal Society for the Advancement of the Arts; many others. Address: 2232 Spruce St, Vancouver, BC V6H 2P3, Canada.

PEDERSEN Mette Katharina, b. 24 August 1939, Copenhagen, Denmark. Medical Doctor; Ear-Nose-Throat Specialist. 1 son, 1 daughter. Education: MD; PhD. Appointments: Ear-Nose-Throat Specialist and Voice Disorders, The Medical Centre, Copenhagen. Publications: Numerous papers and articles in professional scientific and medical journals latest including: Acid Reflux Treatment for Hoarseness, 2006; High speed films evaluation of the larynx with running objective voice management at the same time gives more secure results than videos alone, 2006; A discussion of the evidence based approach in research of the singing voice, 2006. Honours: The Danish School System; The Finnish Phoniatic Society; many others. Address: The Medical Centre, Voice Unit, Ostergade 18, 3, DK-1100 Kbh, K, Denmark. E-mail: m.f.pedersen@dadlnet.dk Website: www.mpedersen.org

PEHCEVSKI Jovan, b. 14 June 1972, Skopje, Republic of Macedonia. Academic. m. Irena, 2 sons. Education: PhD, Computer Science, RMIT University, Melbourne, Australia, 2006. Appointments: PhD candidate, Part-time Tutor and Lecturer, RMIT University, Melbourne, 2002-06; Post-doctoral Research Scientist, INRIA Rocquencourt, France, 2006-07; Assistant Professor and Dean, Faculty of Computer Science and Technology, MIT University, Republic of Macedonia, 2007-09; Assistant Professor, Faculty of Informatics and Head of Research, European University, Republic of Macedonia, 2009-. Publications: Over 25 scientific publications; Book, XML Information Retrieval: Approaches, Relevance and Evaluation, 2010; Numerous articles in professional journals. Honours: Scholarship, Ministry of Education and Science, Republic of Macedonia, 1991-96; Best Undergraduate Student Award, University of St Cyril and Methodius, Republic of Macedonia, 1993-96; Australian International Postgraduate Research Scholarship, RMIT University, 2002-06; Google Industry Award for Academic Excellence in PhD program, RMIT University, 2005. Memberships: ACM; IEEE; MASIT Experts Council. Address: Gjorgji Sugare 2/2-14, 1000 Skopje, Republic of Macedonia. E-mail: jovan.pehcevski@acm.org Website: www.cs.rmit.edu.au/~jovanp

PELÉ (Edison Arantes do Nascimento), b. 23 October 1940, Tres Coracoes, Minas Gerais State, Brazil. Football Player; Author. m. Rosemeri Cholbi, 1966, divorced 1978, 1 son, 2 daughters. Education: Santos University. Appointments: Football Player at Bauru, Sao Paulo, Bauru Athletic Club; Joined Santos FC, 1955; 1st International Game v Argentina; Played in World Cup, 1958, 1962, 1966, 1970; Retired with New York Cosmos; Chair, Pelé Soccer Camps, 1978-; Director, Santos FC, 1993-; Special Minister for Sports, Government of Brazil, 1994-; Director, Soccer Clinics. Publications: Eu Sou Pelé, 1962; Jogando com Pelé, 1974; My Life and the Beautiful Game, 1977; Pelé Soccer Training Program, 1982; The World Cup Murders (novel), 1988. Honours: 3 World Cup Winner medals; 2 World Club Championship medals; 110 international caps; 97 goals for

Brazil; 1,114 appearances for Santos, 1,088 goals; 9 league championship medals; 4 Brazil Cup medals; Goodwill Ambassador for 1992; UN Conference on Environment and Development, Rio De Janeiro; International Peace Award, 1978; WHO Medal, 1989; Honorary KBE, 1997; FIFA World Footballer of the Century, 2000; Hans Christian Andersen Ambassador, 2003-. Address: 75 Rockefeller Plaza, New York, NY 10019, USA.

PELLANDA Anna Angela Maria, b. 15 February 1939, Venice, Italy. University Professor. Divorced. Education: Degree in Philosophy, Padua University, 1962; Diploma in Advanced International Studies, Johns Hopkins University, Bologna Center attended with a Fulbright Scholarship, 1963; MSc (Econ), LSE (scholarship from Italian Ministry of Foreign Affairs), 1966. Appointments: Voluntary, 1963, Appointed Assistant of Political Economy, 1969, University of Padua; Associate Professor, Political Economy, Universities of Parma, Venice and Verona, 1972; Full Professor, Naples and Padua Universities, 1986; President of the Diploma of the Faculty of Law, Rovigo, 1995-98; President, Council of the Degree in Law, 1969-99, Vice Dean, 2004-07, Padua University. Publications: 3 monograhs; Translation, notes and introduction of 3 books; Around 40 articles and 30 book reviews in Italian and international economic magazines. Honours: Listed in international biographical dictionaries. Memberships: Johns Hopkins Alumni Association; LSE; Life Member, Italian Society of Economists. Address: Via dei Livello, 56-35139 Padua, Italy. E-mail: anna.pelland@unipd.it

PELLI Moshe, b. 1936, Israel (US citizen). Professor. m. 2 children. Education: BS, Journalism and Liberal Studies, New York University, 1957-60; PhD, The Dropsie College for Hebrew and Cognate Learning, Philadelphia, 1961-67. Appointments: Editor, NIV, Hebrew Literary Quarterly, New York, USA, 1957-66; Executive Director, Hebrew Month, 1962-66; Executive Director, Hanoar Haivri (Hebrew Youth Organization), 1962-66; Founding Editor, 1964-66, Editor, 1983-85, Lamishpaha, Hebrew Illustrated Monthly, New York; Assistant Professor Co-ordinator of Hebrew Language Program, University of Texas, 1967-71; Abstractor, Religious and Theological Abstracts, 1968-71; Senior Lecturer, Staff Representative on University Instructors National Board, Ben-Gurion University, Israel, 1971-74; Associate Professor, Modern Hebrew Language and Literature, Cornell University, New York, USA, 1974-78; Associate Professor, Yeshiva University, Erna Michael College, New York, 1978-84; Judaic Studies Program, 1985-, Associate Professor, Department of Foreign Languages, 1985-88, Director, Interdisciplinary Program in Judaic Studies, Office of the Dean of Arts & Sciences, 1988-, Professor and Director, 1989-, The Abe and Tess Wise Endowed Professor in Judaic Studies, 2004-, College of Arts and Humanities, University of Central Florida. Publications: 13 scholarly books; 2 novels; 8 children's books; Numerous papers presented in scholarly conferences and articles published in professional journals. Honours include: Abraham Friedman Prize for Hebrew Culture in America, 1991; College of Arts and Sciences Excellence Award in Research, 1996; University of Central Florida Distinguished Researcher of the Year, 1996; Lucian N Littauer Foundation grant, 2005; Elected Fellow, Moses Mendelssohn Center, University of Potsdam, Germany, 2000; I Edward Kiev Library Foundation Grant, 2005; Member, Editorial Board, Kesher, 2005; Member, Editorial Board, Hebrew Higher Education, 2005; Elected Vice President, National Association of Professors of Hebrew in USA, 2005-07; Elected President NAPH, 2007-09; University of Central Florida Research Incentive Award, 2006; Distinguished Researcher of the Year, College of Arts and Humanities, University of Central Florida, 2006. Memberships: Association for Jewish Studies; American Academy of Religion; American Society of 18th Century Studies; National Association of Professors of Hebrew; World Union of Jewish Studies. Address: University of Central Florida, Judaic Studies Program, PO Box 161992, Orlando, FL 32816-1992, USA. E-mail: pelli@mail.ucf.edu

PELLOW Andrew Charles Henry (Newman), b. 29 September 1944, Nettlestone, Isle of Wight, England. Musician; Writer. Education: Diploma, History of Church Music, Williams School, 1986; Testamur, The Canterbury Award, 2010. Appointments: Organist, Nettlestone Methodist Chapel, 1956-93; Clerk, Legal Cashier, John Robinson & Jarvis, 1961-66, Robinson, Jarvis & Rolf, 1967-90; Freelance Piano Teacher, Accompanist, Calligrapher, 1990-; Musician and Calligrapher, Taylorian Fine Arts, 1990-; Organist, Choir Master, St Helen's (IW) Parish Church, 1993; Organist, Choir Master, Sandown Parish Church, Christ Church, Broadway, 1994-97; Director of Music, Organist, Choir Master, Parish and Priory Church of St Mary-the-Virgin, Carisbrooke, 1997-99; Freelance Organist, 1999-; Sub-Deacon with Traditional Anglican Church in Britain, St Barnabas Mission, Isle of Wight, 2004, Licensed to Office 2005; Pupil & Friends Soirée, St Alban-the-Martyr Church, Ventnor, 2009, also various other concerts there 2010/11; Narrator & Performer, Garlands for a Lady concert, St Thomas's Heritage Centre, Ryde, 2009; Lunchtime Organ Recitalist, Wesley's Chapel, City Road, London, 2009. Publications: Robella Ruby (poems), 1985; Numerous poems in anthologies; Many articles in professional & church magazines and newsletters; Periodic letters and concert critiques in local press. Honours: Associate of the Institute of Legal Cashiers and Administrators, 1984; Winner, Piano, Organ, Composition, Speech, Drama, Poetry and Prose, Isle of Wight and Portsmouth Musical Competition Festivals, 1989-2003, 2005, 2006, 2007, 2009, 2010, 2011 (IW) three awards for composition, six for performance (piano); Twice winner, four times runner-up, Isle of Wight County Press/ Tritone Singers Annual Carol Competition, 1996, 1998, 2000, 2001, 2002 and 2004; LGMS, 1996; Admitted Fellow, Guild of Musicians and Singers (FGMS), 2006; 1st Prize, Poetry, Poetry Today, 1998; Elected a Fellow of the Academy of St Cecilia, 2001; Granted Life Membership of the Central Institute, London (MCIL), 2002; Life Fellow (FCIL), 2006; Piano-Oxford Music Festival, 2003, 2004, 2006, 2007, 2008, 2009, 2010; Ceremonially admitted to CIL, 2003; Honorary Fellowship (Hon NCM), National College of Music, London, 2007; Juror, HMCS, 2011. Memberships include: Parochial Church Council & Concert Series' Co-ordinator, St Michael and All Angels, Swanmore, IW, 2000-03; The Folio Society, 2001, 2003-2007; Ryde Arts Festival (Planning Group), 2002-05; Amateur Actor, Bembridge (IW) Little Theatre Club, 2005; Centenary Pageant Carisbrooke Castle (Sir George Carey AD1588), 2007; The Guild of Church Musicians, 2004-; Cornwall Family History Society, 2005-; Trinity College, London – Local Teachers' Forum; Ryde (IW) Social Heritage Group, 2006; Friend of St Michael's Church, Brighton, 2006-; Associate, European Piano Teachers Association (UK) Ltd, 2007; Regular Contributor to CFHS Journal; Poem 'In Memoriam' in Forward Press 'Poets 2008', 'The Betjemanian' Journal, 2009, 'Pilgramage', 2009 & 'Call of the Infinite', 2010; Appointed First Custodian & Clerk of the Catalogue of Dispersed Objects to the Willis Fleming Historical Trust, 2007; Accompanist for 'Evenings with James Pellow' (brother) at the Manor Pavilion Theatre, Sidmouth, Devon, 2007, 2008 & 2009; Honorary Founder Fellow & Scriptum British Academy of Music, 2009; Friends of Northwood Cemetery, IW, 2009, Life Member, 2011;

Campaign for the Traditiona Cathedral Choir, 2010-; Trustee, Langbridge Chapel, IW, 2001; Honorary Director of Music, St Alban the Martyr Church, Upper Ventnor, IW (Parish of Godshill), 2010-. Address: 2 Radley Cottages, Nettlestone Hill, Nettlestone, Isle of Wight, PO34 5DW, England.

PELYKH Sergey Nikolayevich, b. 8 November 1968, Anadyr, Russia. Nuclear Scientist. Education: Engineer, Nuclear Power Stations and Plants, 1989; Doctor of Philosophy, Heat and Nuclear Power Plants, 1999. Appointments: Engineer-Researcher, Senior Scientist, 1999-2010, Leading Scientist, 2010-11, Odessa National Polytechnical University. Publications: Neutron-thermoacoustic instability in nuclear reactor channels; Model of cladding failure estimation for a cycling nuclear unit, 2009; Translation of monograph, Modelling of a light water reactor fuel element behaviour of different loading conditions, 2010; Theory of fuel life control methods at Nuclear Power Plants with Water-Water Energetic Reactor, 2012. Honours: Listed in international biographical dictionaries. Address: Odessa National Polytechnic University, Shevchenko av 1, Odessa 65044, Ukraine. E-mail: kingfisher@renome-i.net

PELYUKH Grigorij, b. 1 February 1944, Hmelnicky region, vil Bubnovka, Ukraine. Professor. m. Taisa Gorb, 1 son, 1 daughter. Education: Specialist, Kamenec-Podolsk, Pedagogical Institute, 1961-66; Aspirant, Institute of Mathematics, 1967-70; Candidate, Physics and Mathematics, 1970; Doctor, Physics and Mathematics, 1991. Appointments: Junior Staff Member, 1967-75, Senior Staff member, 1975-92, Leading Staff Member, 1992-, Institute of Mathematics, Professor, Mathematics, Polytechnic Institute. Publications: Introduction to the theory of functional equations; More than 150 scientific papers; Research in functional, difference and differential-functional equations. Honours: Grantee, Ukraine Government and International George Soros Fund, 1995. Address: Institute of Mathematics, Tereshchenkivska str 3, Kiev, Ukraine.

PENA Lorenzo, b. 29 August 1944, Alicante, Spain. University Professor. m. Teresa Alonso, 1969. Education: American Studies Diploma, Liège University, Belgium, 1978; PhD, Philosophy, Liège University, 1979; Master of Law, Spanish Open University, Madrid, Spain, 2004; Master of Jurisprudence, Madrid Autonomous University, 2007. Appointments: Professor of Philosophy, Pontifical University of Ecuador, 1973-75, 1979-83; Professor, University of Léon, Spain, 1983-87; Senior Scientific Researcher, 1987-2006, Science Professor, 2006-, CSIC; Visiting Position, Australian National University, Research School of Social Sciences, 1992-93; Leader, Logic-and-Law Research Group (JuriLog), CSIC. Publications: Rudiments of Mathematical Logic (Madrid), 1991; Philosophical Findings, 1992; Republican Studies (Madrid), 2009; Ethics and Public Service, co-authored, 2010. Honours: National Prize for Literary Creation in the Humanities, Madrid, 1988. Memberships: Australian Association of Philosophy; Mind Association; Aristotelian Society; European Society of Analytical Philosophy; Spanish Society of Legal and Political Philosophy. Address: Spanish Institute for Advanced Study, Department of Philosophy, Albasanz 26, E28037 Madrid, Spain.

PENCHEVA Tania, b. 20 June 1971, Kazanlak, Bulgaria. Scientist. m. Iasen Hristozov. Education: MSc, Engineering Pedagogics, University of Chemical Technology and Metallurgy, Sofia, 1993; MSc, Bioengineering, Technical University, Sofia, 1994; MSc, Applied Mathematics and Informatics, 1998, PhD, 2003, Technical University, Sofia. Appointments: Research Fellow, 1998-2005, Associate Professor, 2005-10, Centre of Biomedical Engineering Professor Ivan Daskalov, Bulgarian Academy of Sciences, Sofia; Chairman, Organising Committee, International Symposium of Bioprocess Systems, Sofia, 2005-; Deputy Chief Editor, International Electronic Journal of Bioautomation, 2006-; Member, Editorial Board, Notes on Generalised Nets, 2006-; Associate Professor, Institute of Biophysics & Biomedical Engineering, Bulgarian Academy of Sciences, 2010-. Publications: Author, 6 books; 60 articles in international and national journals; 46 presentation at international and national conferences. Honours: Young Scientist's Achievement Award, Union of the Scientists in Bulgaria, 2006; Best Poster Award, 21st International Symposium, Bioprocess Systems-BIOPS'08, Bulgaria, 2008; Diploma and Second Prize for Presentation, 7th National Young Scientific – Practical Session, Bulgaria, 2009; Diploma & 2nd Prize, 9th National Young Scientific-Practical Session, Bulgaria, 2011. Memberships: Union for Automation and Informatics; Union of the Scientists of Bulgaria; Union of Bulgarian Mathematicians; Scientific Monitoring and Advisory Committee, Australian Institute of High Energy Materials. Address: Institute of Biophysics and Biomedical Engineering, Bulgarian Academy of Sciences, 105 Acad Georgi Bonchev Str, 1113 Sofia, Bulgaria. E-mail: tania.pencheva@clbme.bas.bg Website: www.clbme.bas.bg/pwp/tania_pencheva/cv.htm

PENDLETON Victoria Louise, b. 24 September 1980, Stotfold, England. Retired Track Cyclist. Education: Fearnhill School, Letchworth Garden City; Sport and Exercise Science, Northumbria University, Newcastle upon Tyne. Career: 3 silver and 1 bronze, British National Track Championships, 2001; Gold medal (women's sprint), World Championships, 2005; Silver medal (500m time trial) Gold medal (sprint), Commonwealth Games, Melbourne, 2006; Winner (team sprint), Gold (women's sprint) and Gold (women's keirin), UCI Track World Championships, 2007; 2 Gold medals (women's sprint and women's team sprint), UCI Track World Championships, 2008; Gold medal (women's individual sprint event), Beijing Olympics, 2008; Winner (sprint), UCI Track World Championships, Pruszkow, 2009; Silver and Bronze (team sprint and sprint), World Championships, 2011; Winner (sprint), World Championships, Melbourne, 2012; Gold (keirin), London Olympics, 2012; Retired from professional cycling, 2012. Honours: Sportswoman of the Year, 2007; Sports Journalists' Association of Great Britain's Sportswoman of the Year, 2007; MBE, 2009.

PENEV Borislav Georgiev, b. 16 August 1962, Karlovo, Bulgaria. Engineer. m. Elena Lyubenova Gyuzeleva, 1 daughter. Education: MSc, Tula State University, Russia, 1987; PhD, Technical University – Sofia, Bulgaria, 1999. Appointments: Leading Designer, Vazov Machinery Plants, Sopot, Bulgaria, 1987-88; Assistant Professor, 1988-2007, Vice Head, Department of Opto-Electronics and Laser Engineering, 2000-2007, Associate Professor, Control Theory, 2007; Vice Dean of Faculty Electronics and Automatics, Technical University – Sofia, 2007; Head, Department of Optoelectronics and Laser Engineering, 2011. Publications: Numerous articles in professional journals. Honours: Gold Medal, International Plovdiv Fair, 1994; Listed in international biographical dictionaries. Memberships: Bulgarian Union of Automatics and Informatics. Address: Technical University – Sofia, Branch Plovdiv, 61 Sanct Petersburg Blvd, Plovdiv 4000, Bulgaria. E-mail: bpenev@tu-plovdiv.bg

PENIWATI Kirti, b. 28 June 1946, Jogyakarta, Indonesia. Decision Making Facilitator. Education: Electro Engineering, Bandung Institute of Technology, 1972; MBA, 1986, PhD, Decision Science, 1996, Katz Graduate School of Business, University of Pittsburgh. Appointments: Managerial positions in product design, quality, production and engineering, Tranka Kabel, Jakarta; Head, Department of Operations in Management & Decision Science, PPM Institute of Management; Dean, PPM Graduate School of Management. Publications: Group Decision Making: Drawing Out and Reconciling Differences; Numerous articles in professional journals. Honours: Beta Gamma Sigma, Pittsburgh Chapter, 1996; 2000 Outstanding Intellectuals of the 21st Century; Universal Award, 2011; American Hall of Fame, 2011; Great Minds of the 21st Century Hall of Fame, 2012; Dedication Honoree, Inaugural Edition of International Profiles of Accomplished Leaders; Listed in international biographical dictionaries. Memberships: International Committee, International Symposium on the Analytic Hierarchy Process; Indonesian Institute for Corporate Directorship; Soroptimist International of Jakarta; Orsin Club, Jakarta. Address: Jl Andara Dalam Kav 7, Pondok Labu, Jakarta 12450, Indonesia. E-mail: kirti@indo.net.id

PENN Sean, b. 17 August 1960, Burbank, California, USA. Actor. m. (1) Madonna, 1985, (2) Robin Wright, 1996, 2 children. Creative Works: Theatre appearances include: Heartland; Slab Boys; Hurlyburly, 1988; Film appearances: Taps, 1981; Fast Times at Ridgemont High, 1982; Bad Boys, 1983; Crackers, 1984; Racing with the Moon, 1984; The Falcon and the Snowman, 1985; At Close Range, 1986; Shanghai Surprise, 1986; Colors, 1988; Judgement in Berlin, 1988; Casualties of War, 1989; We're No Angels, 1989; State of Grace, 1990; Carlito's Way, 1993; Dead Man Walking, 1996; U Turn, 1997; She's So Lovely, 1997; Hurlyburly, 1998; As I Lay Dying, 1998; Up at the Villa, 1998; The Thin Red Line, 1998; Sweet and Lowdown; Being John Malkovich; The Weight of Water; The Pledge, 2000; Up at the Villa, 2000; I am Sam, 2001; Mystic River, 2003; 21 Grams, 2003; The Assassination of Richard Nixon, 2005; The Interpreter, 2005; All the King's Men, 2006; Persepolis, 2007; Crossing Over, 2007; Milk, 2008; Fair Game, 2010. Director, Writer: The Indian Runner, 1991, The Crossing Guard, 1995; The Pledge, 2000. Honours include: Best Actor Award, Berlin Film Festival, 1996; Oscar for Best Actor, Mystic River, 2004; Golden Globe, Best Dramatic Actor, 2004; Critics' Choice Award, Best Actor, 2004; Academy Award, Best Actor, 2004. Address: Suite 2500, 2049 Century Park East, Los Angeles, CA 90067, USA.

PENROSE Roger, b. 8 August 1931, Colchester, Essex, England. Mathematician. Education: University College, London; Doctorate, Cambridge University, 1957. Appointments: Worked with father in the devising of seemingly impossible geometric figures; Lecturing and Research posts in Britain and the USA; Professor of Applied Mathematics, Birkbeck College, London, 1966-73; Rouse Ball Professor of Mathematics, Oxford University, 1973-98; Professor Emeritus, 1998- Important contributions to the understanding of astrophysical phenomena, especially Black Holes. Publications: Techniques of Differential Topology in Relativity, 1973; Spinors and Space-time, with W Rindler, volume I, 1984, volume II, 1986; The Emperor's New Mind, 1989; The Nature of Space and Time, with S Hawking, 1996; The Large, the Small and the Human Mind, 1997; White Mars, with B Aldiss, 1999; The Road to Reality: A Complete Guide to the Laws of the Universe, 2004; articles in scientific journals. Honours: Adams Prize, 1966-67; Dannie Heinemann Prize, 1971; Eddington Medal, 1975; Royal Medal, 1985; Wolf Foundation Prize for Physics, 1988; Dirac Medal and Prize, Institute of Physics, 1989; Einstein Medal, 1990; Science Book Prize, 1990; Naylor Prize, London Mathematics Society, 1991; 8 Dr h c; Hon D University, 1998. Memberships: London Mathematical Society; Cambridge Philosophical Society; Institute for Mathematics and its Applications; International Society for General Relativity and Gravitation; Fellow, Birkbeck College, 1998; Institute of Physics, 1999; Foreign Associate, National Academy of Sciences, USA, 1998. Address: Mathematical Institute, 24-29 St Giles, Oxford, OX1 3LB, England.

PEPE Frank A, b. 22 May 1931, Schenectady, New York, USA. Emeritus Professor. Education: BS, Chemistry, Union College, 1953; PhD, Physical Chemistry, Yale University, 1957. Appointments: Instructor, 1957-60, Associate, 1960-63, Assistant Professor, 1963-65, Associate Professor, 1965-70, Professor, 1970-92, Department of Anatomy, School of Medicine, University of Pennsylvania, Chairman, Department of Anatomy, 1977-90, Professor, Department of Cell and Development Biology, 1992-96, Emeritus Professor, 1996-. Publications: Numerous articles in professional journals; Editor, Motility in Cell Function, 1979. Honours: Fellow, AAAS, 1987; Raymond C Truex Distinguished Lecture Award, Hahneman University, 1988; Listed in various international biographical dictionaries. Memberships: American Association of Anatomists; American Chemical Society; AAAS; Sigma Xi; Micro Society of America. Address: 4614 Pine Street, Philadelphia, PA 19143-1808, USA. E-mail: fpepe@mail.med.upenn.edu

PEPPÉ Rodney Darrell, b. 24 June 1934, Eastbourne, East Sussex, England. Author; Artist. m. Tatjana Tekkel, 1960, 2 sons. Education: Eastbourne School of Art, 1951-53, 1955-57; London County Council Central School of Art, 1957-59; NDD, Illustration (special subject) and Central School Diploma. Appointments: Art Director, S H Benson Ltd, 1960-64; J Walter Thompson & Co Ltd, 1965-65; Consultant Designer to Ross Foods Ltd, 1965-72; Freelance Graphic Designer, Illustrator, 1965-98; Children's Author and Illustrator, 1968; Toymaker and Automatist. Publications: The Alphabet Book, 1968; Circus Numbers, 1969; The House That Jack Built, 1970; Hey Riddle Diddle!, 1971; Simple Simon, 1972; Cat and Mouse, 1973; Odd One Out, 1974; Henry series, 1975-78; Picture Stories, 1976; Rodney Peppe's Puzzle book, 1977; Ten Little Bad Boys, 1978; Three Little Pigs, 1979; Indoors Word Book, Outdoors Word Book, 1980; Rodney Peppé's Moving Toys, 1980; The Mice Who Lived in a Shoe, 1981; Run Rabbit, Run!, 1982; The Kettleship Pirates, 1983; Little Toy Board Book series, 1983; Make Your Own Paper Toys, 1984; Block Books, 1985; The Mice and the Flying Basket, 1985; Press-Out Circus, Press-Out Train, 1986; Tell the Time with Mortimer, 1986; The Mice and the Clockwork Bus, 1986; Open House, 1987; First Nursery Rhymes, 1988; Thumbprint Circus, 1988; Noah's Ark Frieze, 1989; Huxley Pig series, 1989-90; The Animal Directory, 1989; ABC Index. ABC Frieze, 1990; The Shapes Finder, 1991; The Colour Catalogue, 1992; The Mice on the Moon, 1992; The Mice and the Travel Machine, 1993; The Magic Toybox, 1996; Gus and Nipper, 1996; Hippo Plays Hide and Seek, 1997; Angelmouse Series, 2000; Automata and Mechanical Toys, 2002; Toys and Models, 2003; Making Mechanical Toys, 2005; TV Series: Huxley Pig, ITV, 1990; Angelmouse, BBC, 2000. Contributions to: Periodicals. Membership: Society of Authors. Address: Stoneleigh House, 6 Stoneleigh Drive, Livermead, Torquay, Devon TQ2 6TR, England.

PERA Marcello, b. 28 January 1943, Lucca, Tuscany, Italy. President of the Italian Senate. Education: Accountancy degree, F Carrara High School, Lucca, 1962; Degree (summa cum laude), Philosophy, University of Pisa, 1972. Appointments: Employee, Banca Toscana, Lucca, 1962-63, Agliana, Pistoia, 1963-64; Employee, Lucca Chamber of Commerce, 1964-73; Assistant Professor, 1976-80, Associate Professor, 1980-89, Full Professor, 1992, Philosophy of Science, University of Pisa; Visiting Fellow, Center for Philosophy of Science, University of Pittsburgh, USA, 1984; Visiting Fellow, The Van Leer Foundation, Jerusalem, Israel, 1987; Full Professor, Theoretic Philosophy, University of Catania, 1989-92; Visiting Fellow, Department of Linguistics and Philosophy, MIT, Cambridge, Massachusetts, USA, 1990; Co-ordinator, Convention for Liberal Reform, 1995; Visiting Fellow, Centre for the Philosophy of Natural and Social Sciences, London School of Economics, England, 1995-96; Senator, Lucca constituency, Freedom Alliance, 13th Parliament, 1996-2001; Deputy Leader, Forza Italia parliamentary group, 1996-2001; Member, Standing Committee on Education and Cultural Properties, 1996-97; Member, Standing Committee on the Judiciary, 1997-; Member, Joint Committee on Constitutional Reform, 1997-; Member, Forza Italia Steering Committee; Head, Forza Italia Judiciary Department; Re-elected to Senate, Lucca constituency, House of Freedoms, 2001; Elected President of the Senate, 2001-2006. Publications: Contributions to scientific magazines and editorial activity; Member of advisory panels of and contributor to several journals; Contributions to Italian daily and weekly papers; Co-author (with Cardinal Joseph Ratzinger) of book entitled, Senza radici (Without Roots). Address: Gabinetto del Presidente, Senato della Repubblica, Palazzo Madama, 00186 Rome, Italy. E-mail: d.citi@senato.it

PERAK H.H. Sultan of, Sultan Azlan Muhibbuddin Shah ibni Al-Marhum Sultan Yussuf Ghafarullahu-Lahu Shah, b. 19 April 1928, Batu Gajah, Malaysia. Ruler. m. Tuanku Bainun Mohamed Ali, 1954, 2 sons, 3 daughters. Education: Malay College; University of Nottingham. Appointments: Called to Bar, Lincoln's Inn; Magistrate, Kuala Lumpur; Assistant State Secretary, Perak; Deputy Public Prosecutor; President, Sessions Court, Seremban and Taiping; State Legal Advisor, Pahang and Johre; Federal Court Judge, 1973; Chief Justice of Malaysia, 1979; Lord President, 1982-83; Raja Kechil Bongsu (6th in line), 1962, Raja Muda (2nd in line), 1983; Sultan of Perak, 1984-; Yang di-Pertuan Agong (Supreme Head of State), 1989-94; Pro-Chancellor, University of Saina Malaysia, 1971, Chancellor, University of Malaya, 1986; Honorary Colonel-in-Chief, Malaysian Armed Forces Engineers Corps; Manager, Malaysian Hockey Team, 1972; President, Malaysian Hockey Federation, Asian Hockey Federation; Vice-President, International Hockey Federation, Olympic Council of Malaysia.

PEREDELSKIY Gennadiy Ivanovich, b. 16 September 1937, Prokopyevsk, Russia. University Professor. Divorced, 1 son. Education: Graduated, Tomsk Polytechnical Institute, 1960; Postgraduate Candidate of Technical Science, 1969; Docent, 1971; Doctor of Technical Science, 1989; Professor, 1993. Appointments: Assistant Lecturer, Industrial Electronics Chair of Tomsk Polytechnical Institute, 1960-64; Docent, Industrial Electronics Chair of Tomsk Institute of Radioelectrics and Electronics Engineering, 1964-74; Head, Chair, Industrial Electronics of Tomsk Institute, Automatised Controlling Systems and Radioelectronics, 1974-91; Head, Chair, Industrial Electronics and Automatics of Kursk Polytechnical Institute, 1991-95; Professor, Orel State Technical University, 1995-2004; Professor, Kursk State Technical University, 2004-. Main research interests: use of test-signals in the form of consecutive pulses with voltage change during their duration, according to extent functions law. Publications: Over 300 articles and papers and 2 monographs; Titles include: A property of potentially frequency independent two-terminal networks, 2000; About the Equivalency of Frequency Independent Two-Pole Networks, 2002; Mating of pulsed power supply bridge circuits with electron assembly, 2002; Use of potentially frequency-independent, two-terminal networks for solutions of problems for measuring equipment, 2003; Improvement of electric bridges with electronic units coupling based on analogue adder, 2004; Zero biopolar measuring circuit, 2004; About the Frequency-Independent Two-Pole Network of Two Structures, 2006; Multiarm bridge circuits to determine the parameters of multielement two-port network with heterogeneous reactive element, 2006; Puise power supply bridge-type circuits with expanded functional capabilities, 2009; Electric Bridge with Expanded Functional Capabilities, 2010; Electric Bridge Chains with the Expanded Functional Possibilities and Uniform Reactive Balancing Elements, 2010; Bridge Electric Circuits with Expanded Functional Abilities Constructed on the Basis of Potentially Frequency-Independent Dipoles, 2010. Honours: Academician of the Electroengineering Sciences Academy of the Russian Federation; Academician of the Metrological Academy of the Russian Federation. Memberships: Scientific-Methodological Council in Industrial Electronics, 1975-80. Address: ul Pyatdesyat Lyet Oktyabrya, 96B-54, 305040 Kursk, Russia. E-mail: rector@kstu.kursk.ru

PERELOMOV Askold, b. 10 January 1935, Vologda Region, Russia. Mathematical Physics. m. Liudmila Muzeus, 1 son, 1 daughter. Education: Physical Faculty, Moscow State University, 1959; PhD, Physics and Mathematical Sciences, 1963, Doctorate, Mathematical Physics, 1973, Institute of Theoretical and Experimental Physics, Moscow. Appointments: Leading Scientific Researcher, Institute of Theoretical and Experimental Physics, Moscow, 1973-2010. Publications: 250 articles in professional journals; 3 books: Author, Generalized Coherent States and Their Applications, 1986; Author, Integrable Systems of Classical Mechanics and Lie Algebras, 1990; Co-author, Quantum Mechanics – Selected Topics, 1998. Memberships: International Association of Mathematical Physics; Moscow Mathematical Society.

PERERA Vimal Marcelline, b. 2 June 1939, Colombo, Sri Lanka. Chartered Accountant. m. Irma Marie Frances, 1 daughter. Education: BSc (Hons), University of Sri Lanka, 1962. Appointments: Assistant Teacher, Royal College, Sri Lanka; Trainee, Ford Rhodes Thornton, Chartered Accountants, 1963-65; Assistant/Director, Associate Management Services Ltd, 1966-77; Financial Controller, Galle Face Hotel, Sri Lanka, 1978-80; Group Organisation and Systems Manager, Mercantile Credit Ltd, Sri Lanka, 1981-82; Financial Controller, Hotel Sofitel Doha Palace, Qatar, 1983-84; Assistant, Mervyn Smith, Chartered Accountant, UK, 1985-86; Chief Accountant/Financial Controller, Hotel Lanka Oberoi, Sri Lanka, 1987-90; Deputy General Manager, Ceylon Glass Company Ltd, Sri Lanka, 1990-94; Administrative Accountant/Financial Manager, SANE UK, 1996-. Publications: Numerous articles in professional journals. Honours: Grand Knight, Knights of Columba. Memberships: Fellow, Institute of Chartered Accountants of Sri Lanka; Fellow, Chartered Institute of Management Accountants, UK; Member, Chartered Institute of Management. Address: 44 Sigrist Square, Canbury Park Road, Kingston Upon Thames, Surrey KT2 6JT, England.

DICTIONARY OF INTERNATIONAL BIOGRAPHY 36th EDITION

PERETZ Arna, b. 10 December 1941, New York, USA. Senior Lecturer. m. Josef Babai, 1 son, 3 daughters. Education: BA, Brandeis University, Waltham, Massachusetts, 1962; MA, Columbia University, New York City, 1964; PhD, University of New Mexico, Albuquerque, 1982; Life Certificate, Teacher English as a Second Language – Adults, California. Appointments: Chair, Department of EFL, Ben-Gurion University of the Negev, Israel, 1972-77, 1985-86, 1997-2001; Director, Service Teacher Education Course, EFL Teachers and Co-Director Internship Project, Department of Education, 1982-84, 1991, Senior Lecturer, 1971-2008, Ben-Gurion University; Director, Academic Writing Program and Program for Students with Special Needs, 2001-07. Publications: Numerous articles in professional journals and book chapters. Honours: Study and travel grants: British Council; Ford Foundation; BGU; University of NM; Outstanding Teacher: International School Desert Studies, Ben-Gurion University, 2001-02; Department EFL, Ben-Gurion University, 1994; Excellence in Teaching, Ben-Gurion University, 2002-07. Memberships: Asia TEFL; Organizing Committees, ECEL and ICEL; Reader, The Journal of Aisa TEFL. Address: 10/68 Hativat Harel, Modiin 71721, Israel. E-mail: aperetz@bgu.ac.il

PÉREZ-LIZAUR Marisol, b. 17 December 1944, Mexico City, Mexico. Social Anthropologist. m. Manuel Burgos, 1 son, 1 daughter. Education: Bachelor, Anthropology, 1970, Master, Social Anthropology, 1970, PhD, Social Sciences with Anthropology, 1994, Universidad Iberoamericana, Mexico City. Appointments: Consultant on University Planning to Vice Minister of Education, 1973-76; Consultant to Vice Minister of Technological Education and Research, 1980-83; Researcher, Centro para la Innovación Tecnológica, Universidad Nacional Autonóma de México, 1983-87; Professor, Social Sciences Department, Universidad Iberoamericana, Mexico City, 1997-. Publications: Numerous articles in professional journals. Honours: 2nd prize, Best PhD Dissertation in Social Anthropology, Fray Bernardinon de Sahagun Award, 1995; Member, National Research System II, 1998. Memberships: American Anthropological Association; LASA; UNICAES; Colegio de Etnólogos y Antropólogos Sociales; CALACS; The Society for Applied Anthropology; Asociacion Mexicana de Historia Economica. Address: Departamento de Ciencias Sociales y Políticas, Universidad Iberoamericana, Prol Paseo de la Reforma 880, México DF 01210, México.

PERHAM Michael Francis, b. 8 November 1947, Dorchester, Dorset, England. Bishop of Gloucester. m. Alison Jane Grove, 4 daughters. Education: Hardye's School, Dorchester, 1959-65; BA, 1974, MA, 1978, Keble College, Oxford; Cuddesdon Theological College, Oxford, 1974-76; Honorary Doctor of Philosophy, University of Gloucestershire, 2007. Appointments: Ordained Deacon in Canterbury Cathedral, 1976; Assistant Curate, St Mary's Addington, Croydon, 1976-81; Ordained Priest in Canterbury Cathedral, 1977; Domestic Chaplain to Bishop of Winchester (Bishop John Taylor), 1981-84; Rector, Oakdale Team Ministry, Poole, 1984-92; Canon Residentiary and Precentor, Norwich Cathedral, 1992-98; Vice Dean of Norwich, 1995-98; (Last) Provost of Derby, 1998-2000; (First) Dean of Derby, 2000-04; Ordained Bishop in St Paul's Cathedral, 2004; (40th) Bishop of Gloucester, 2004-. Publications include: A New Handbook of Pastoral Liturgy, 2000; Signs of Your Kingdom, 2003; Glory in our Midst, 2005; To Tell Afresh, 2010; The Hospitality of God, 2011. Honours: Honorary Fellow, Royal School of Church Music, 2003-. Memberships: Member, Governing Body of SPCK, 2002-, Chairman, 2006-; President, Alcuin Club, 2005-; Bishop Protector of the Society of St Francis, 2005-; Council Member, Pro-Chancellor, University of Gloucestershire, 2007-; President, Retired Clergy Association, 2007-; Chair, Hospital Chaplaincies Council, 2007-10; Chair of Governors, Ripon College, Cuddesdon, 2009-; House of Lords, 2009-; President of Affirming Catholicism, 2010-. Address: 2 College Green, Gloucester, GL1 2LR, England. E-mail: bshpglos@glosdioc.org.uk

PERIČIĆ Helena, b. 13 September 1961, Zadar, Croatia. University Professor. 1 daughter. Education: Graduate, Comparative Literature/English Language and Literature, 1985, Master's degree, 1989, University of Zagreb; Doctor's degree, Faculty of Philosophy, University of Split, 1997. Appointments: Lecturer, 2002, Guest Professor, 2004, Institute for Slavic and East European Studies, Charles University, Prague, Czech Republic; Head, Postgraduate Studies in Literature, 2005-, Head, Croatian Department, 2007-08, University of Zadar; Visiting Researcher, Department of Comparative Literature, NYU, 2009; Guest Professor, Institute for Slavistics, University of Klagenfurt, Austria, 2006, 2008; Lecturer, Institute for Slavic Languages, University of Amsterdam, Netherlands, 2007; Teacher, Doctoral Studies, Department of Comparative Literature, University of Zagreb, 2007. Publications: Poetry, prose and drama. Honours: Zadar County Annual Award, 2010. Memberships: Croatian Centre of PEN; Croatian Writers' Association; UNIMA; Croatian Association of Theatrologists and Theatre Critics; Croatian Centre of ITI; UNESCO. Address: Lojenov prilaz 6, 10 020 Zagreb, Croatia. E-mail: hpericic@gmail.com Website: www.helena-pericic.com

PERINA Jan, b. 11 November 1936, Mestec Kralove, Czech Republic. Professor of Physics. m. Vlasta Perinova, 1 son, 1 daughter. Education: Palacky University, 1964; PhD, Palacky University, 1966; RNDr, Palacky University, 1967; DSc, Charles University, 1984; Professor, 1990. Appointments: Laboratory of Optics and Joint Laboratory of Optics, Palacky University Olomouc, 1964-; Department of Optics, Palacky University Olomouc, Czech Republic, 1990-. Publications: About 300 publications on coherence and statistics of light; Books: Van Nostrand, 1972; Mir, 1974, 1987; Kluwer, 1984, 1985, 1991, 1994; World Scientific, 1998; J. Wiley, 2001. Honours: Awards of: Columbia University, 1983; Ministry of Education, 1991; Slovakia Academy of Sciences, 1996; Town of Olomouc, 2001; State Award of the Czech Republic, 2002; European Academy of Sciences and Arts, 2006. Memberships: Fellow of American Optical Society, 1984; Learned Society Bohemica, 1995. Address: Kmochova 3, 77900 Olomouc, Czech Republic.

PEROT (Henry) Ross, b. 27 June 1930, Texarkana, Texas, USA. Industrialist. m. Margot Birmingham, 1956, 4 children. Education: US Naval Academy. Appointments: US Navy, 1953-57; IBM Corporation, 1957-62; Founder, Electron Data Systems Corporation, 1962, Chair of Board, CEO, 1982-86; Director, Perot Group, Dallas, 1986-; Founder, Perot Systems Corporation, WA, 1988-, Chair, 1988-92, 1992-, Board Member, 1988-; Chair, Board of Visitors, US Naval Academy, 1970-; Candidate for President of USA, 1992, 1996; Founder, Reform Party, 1995. Publications: Not For Sale at Any Price, 1993; Intensive Care, 1995. Address: The Perot Group, PO Box 269014, Plano, TX 75026, USA.

PERRETT Bryan, b. 9 July 1934, Liverpool, England. Author; Military Historian. m. Anne Catherine Trench, 13 August 1966. Education: Liverpool College. Appointment: Defence Correspondent to Liverpool Echo, during Falklands War and Gulf War. Publications: The Czar's British Squadron (with A Lord), 1981; A History of Blitzkrieg, 1983; Knights of the Black Cross: Hitler's Panzerwaffe and its Leaders, 1986; Desert Warfare, 1988; Encyclopaedia of the Second World War (with Ian Hogg), 1989; Canopy of War, 1990; Liverpool: A City at War, 1990; Last Stand: Famous Battles Against the Odds, 1991; The Battle Book: Crucial Conflicts in History from 1469 BC to the Present, 1992; At All Costs: Stories of Impossible Victories, 1993; Seize and Hold: Master Strokes of the Battlefield, 1994; Iron Fist: Crucial Armoured Engagements, 1995; Against All Odds! More Dramatic Last Stand Actions, 1995; Impossible Victories: Ten Unlikely Battlefield Successes, 1996; The Real Hornblower: The Life and Times of Admiral Sir James Gordon, GCB, 1998; The Taste of Battle, 2000; The Changing Face of Battle, 2000; Gunboat!, 2000; Last Convoy, 2000; Beach Assault, 2000; Heroes of the Hour, 2001; Trafalgar, 2002; Crimea, 2002; Waterloo, 2003; For Valour – Victoria Cross and Medal of Honor Battles, 2003; D Day, 2005; U-Boat Hunter, 2005; British Military History for Dummies, 2007; North Sea Battleground, 2011; The Hunted and the Hunters, 2012. Contributions to: War Monthly; Military History; World War Investigator; War in Peace (partwork); The Elite (partwork). Memberships: Rotary Club of Ormskirk. Address: 7 Maple Avenue, Burscough, Nr Ormskirk, Lancashire L40 5SL, England.

PERRIE Walter, b. 5 June 1949, Lanarkshire, Scotland. Poet; Author; Critic. Education: MA, Honours, Mental Philosophy, University of Edinburgh, 1975; MPhil, English Studies, University of Stirling, 1989. Appointments: Editor, Chapman, 1970-75; Scottish-Canadian Exchange Fellow, University of British Columbia, Canada, 1984-85; Managing Editor, Margin: International Arts Quarterly, 1985-90; Stirling Writing Fellow, University of Stirling, 1991; Part-Time Lecturer, Philosophy and Creative Writing, Perth College, 2000-08. Publications: Metaphysics and Poetry (with Hugh MacDiarmid), 1974; Poem on a Winter Night, 1976; A Lamentation for the Children, 1977; By Moon and Sun, 1980; Out of Conflict, 1982; Concerning the Dragon, 1984; Roads that Move: A Journey Through Eastern Europe, 1991; Thirteen Lucky Poems, 1991; From Milady's Wood and Other Poems, 1997; The Light in Strathearn (poems), 2000; Decagon – Selected Poems 1995-2005, 2004; Caravanserai (Poems), 2005; Rhapsody of The Red Cliff (Poems), 2006; As Far As Thales – Beginning Philosophy, 2006; The King of France is Bald: Philosophy and Meaning, 2007; Editor (with John Herdman), FRAS magazine, 2004-; Lyrics & Tales in TWA Tongues, 2011; Contributions to: Journals and periodicals. Honours: Scottish Arts Council Bursaries, 1976, 1983, 1994, and Book Awards, 1976, 1983; Eric Gregory Award, 1978; Ingram Merrill Foundation Award, 1987 Scottish Arts Council Writers Bursary, 1999; Society of Authors, Travelling Scholarship, 2000; Scottish Arts Council Writer's Bursary, 2009. Address: 10 Croft Place, Dunning, Perthshire PH2 0SB, Scotland.

PERRONI Carol, b. 28 July 1952, Boston, Massachusetts, USA. Artist. m. John Richard Mugford, 1 son. Education: Boston Museum School, 1970-71; BA, Bennington College, Vermont, 1976; Skowhegan School of Painting and Sculpture, Maine, 1978; MFA, Hunter College, New York City, 1983; M Ed, The College of Santa Fe, New Mexico, 2003. Appointments: Studio Assistant, for artist Isaac Witkin, Bennington, Vermont, 1973-74; Library Assistant, Simmons College Library, Boston, 1977-78; Studio Assistant for artist Mel Bochner, New York City, 1979; Bookeeper, International House, New York City, 1979-80; Studio Assistant for Lee Krasner, East Hampton, New York, 1980; Research Assistant, Art News Magazine, 1981; Intern, Greenespace Gallery, New York City, 1982-83; Technical Assistant, Avery Architectural and Fine Arts Library, Columbia University, 1981-83; Library Researcher, Kennedy Galleries Inc, 1984-86; Program Specialist, Art Teacher, Swinging Sixties Senior Citizen Center, Brooklyn, 1986-87; Arts in Education Program, Rhode Island, 1993-96; Teacher, Santa Fe Public Schools, 2007-09; Teacher, Private School, 2004-06; Works included in Rhode Island Hospital Art Collection and private collections. Publications: Work published in The Art of Layering: Making Connections, 2004; Work published in Visual Journeys: Art of the 21st Century, 2010; Author of 35 biographies of American artists in Aspects of America: The Land and the People, 1810-1930, 1985. Honour: Flintridge Foundation Grant, 1993; Residencies: Vermont Studio Center, Johnson, Vermont, 1990, Dorland Mountain Arts Colony, California, 1993; Anderson Ranch Arts Center, Colorado, 2004. Membership: Hera Educational Foundation, Rhode Island, 1993-99; The Society of Layerists in Multi-Media; Associate Member: American Academy of Women Artists, National Collage Society. Address: 2089 Plaza Thomas, Santa Fe, NM 87505-5438, USA. E-mail carolpi56@msn.com

PERRY Matthew, b. 19 August 1969, Williamstown, Massachusetts, USA. Actor. Education: Ashbury College, Ottawa, Canada. Career: Films: A Night in the Life of Jimmy Reardon, 1988; She's Out of Control, 1989; Getting In, 1994; Fools Rush In, 1997; Almost Heroes, 1998; Three to Tango, 1999; Imagining Emily, 1999; The Whole Nine Yards, 2000; Serving Sara, 2002; The Whole Ten Yards, 2004; Hoosiers 11: Senior Year, 2005; Numb, 2007; The Laws of Motion. 2008;The Beginning of Wisdom, 2008; Birds of America, 2008; 17 Again, 2009; TV: Boys Will be Boys; Home Free; Sydney; Who's The Boss?; The Tracey Ullman Show; Empty; The John Laroquette Show; Beverly Hills 90210; Growing Pains; 240 Roberts; Friends, 1994-2004; Studio 60 on the Sunset Strip, 2006-07; TV films: Second Chance, 1987; Dance 'Til Dawn, 1988; Sydney, 1990; Call Me Anna, 1990; Home Free, 1993; Deadly Relations, 1993; Parallel Lives, 1994; Scrubs, 2001; Play: Sexual Perversity in Chicago, London, 2003; Writing includes: Maxwell House; Imagining Emily. Address: William Morris Agency, 151 El Camino Drive, Beverly Hills, CA 90212, USA.

PESALA Nageswara Rao, b. 10 August 1954, Kavali, India. Nuclear Medicine. m. Sampath Kumari, 1 son, 1 daughter. Education: BSc Sri Venkateswara University, Tirupathi, India, 1976; DMRIT, Radiation Medicine Centre, Mumbai, 1981; MSc, LTM Medical College, Mumbai, 1988; PhD, Sri Krishnadevaraya University, Ananthapur, 1997. Appointments: Technical Officer, Bombay Hospital, Mumbai, 1981-83; Faculty, Department of Nuclear Medicine, Kidwai Memorial Institute of Oncology, Bangalore, 1984-2000; Associate Professor, Department of Nuclear Medicine, Kasturba Medical College, 2000-06; Lead Medical Physics Technician, City Hospital, Nottingham, England, 2006-. Publications: Numerous articles in professional journals. Memberships: Society of Nuclear Medicine of India; AMPI; British Nuclear Medicine Society; Institute of Physics and Engineering in Medicine, UK. Address: 223 Edwards Lane, Nottingham, NG5 6EQ, England. E-mail: drpesala@yahoo.com

PESCI Joe, b. 9 February 1943, USA. Film Actor. Creative Works. m. Claudia Haro (divorced), 1 child. Films include: Death Collector, 1976; Raging Bull, 1980; I'm Dancing as Far as I Can, 1982; Easy Money, 1983; Dear Mr Wonderful, 1983; Eureka, 1983; Once Upon a Time in America, 1984; Tutti Dentro, 1984; Man On Fire, 1987; Moonwalker, 1988; Backtrack, 1988; Lethal Weapon II, 1989; Betsy's Wedding,

1990; Goodfellas, 1999; Home Alone, 1990; The Super, 1991; JFK, 1991; Lethal Weapon III, 1992; Home Alone II, 1992; The Public Eye, 1992; My Cousin Vinny, 1992; A Bronx Tale, 1993; With Honours, 1994; Jimmy Hollywood, 1994; Casino, 1995; 8 Heads in a Duffel Bag, 1997; Gone Fishing, 1997; Lethal Weapon 4, 1998; The Good Shepherd, 2006. Honours include: Academy Award, Best Supporting Actor, 1991.

PESCOD Mainwaring Bainbridge, b. 6 January 1933, Leadgate, Co Durham, England. Academic; Consultant. m. Mary Lorenza Coyle, 2 sons. Education: BSc, Civil Engineering, King's College University of Durham, 1954; SM, Sanitary Engineering, Massachusetts Institute of Technology, Cambridge, USA, 1956. Appointments: Research Associate, Department of Civil Engineering, University of Newcastle upon Tyne, 1956-57; Lecturer, Engineering, Acting Head, Department of Engineering, University College of Sierra Leone, West Africa, 1957-61; Assistant Engineer, Babtie Shaw & Morton, Consulting Civil Engineers, Glasgow, Scotland, 1961-64; Chairman, Division of Environmental Engineering, Asian Institute of Technology, Bangkok, Thailand, 1964-76; Professor, Environmental Control Engineering, 1976-98, Head, School of Civil & Mining Engineering, 1985-88, Head, Department of Civil Engineering, 1985-98, Emeritus Professor, 1998-, University of Newcastle; Member, Northumbrian Water Authority, 1986-89; Partner, Environmental Technology Consultants, 1986-88; Non-Executive Director, Motherwell Bridge Envirotec Ltd, 1991-95; Non-Executive Director, Northumbrian Water Group plc, 1989-97; Chairman and Managing Director, Environmental Technology Consultants, Motherwell Bridge Group, 1988-2003; Corporate Fellow, Safety & Ecology Corporation Ltd, Newcastle upon Tyne, 2003-08; Senior Environmental Consultant, Cundall Johnston & Partners LLP, Newcastle upon Tyne, 2008-09. Publications: Over 140 articles in professional journals. Honours: Premium Award, Council of the Institution of Water Engineers, 1965; Officer of the Order of the British Empire, 1977; President's Prize, Institute of Water Engineers and Scientists, 1982; Diploma, New England Water Works Association, 1982; Honorary Fellow, Pakistan Society of Public Health Engineers, 1988. Memberships: Chartered Engineer, Engineering Council, UK; Chartered Water and Environmental Manager, UK; Fellow, Institution of Civil Engineers, UK; Fellow, Chartered Institution of Water and Environmental Management, UK; Fellow, Chartered Institution of Wastes Management, UK. Address: Tall Trees, High Horse Close, Rowlands Gill, Tyne & Wear, NE39 1AN, England. E-mail: mpescod1@gmail.com

PESEK Jiri R V, b. 19 April 1936, Prague, Czech Republic. Geologist. m. Jarmila Dobiasova, 2 daughters. Education: Graduate, Faculty of Science, Charles University, 1959; Postgraduate Study, 1962-66; PhD, 1967; DSc, 1988. Appointments: Assistant Professor, 1967-88, Associate Professor, 1988-91, Professor of Economic Geology, 1991-, Faculty of Science, Charles University. Publications: 16 books and textbooks; About 309 papers in professional journals. Honours: Gold Medal, Faculty of Science; Commemorative Medal, Charles University. Memberships include: Czech Geological Society, Sub-Commission on Carboniferous Stratigraphy. Address: Charles University Prague, Faculty of Science, 12843 Prague 2, Albertov 6, Czech Republic.

PETER Gernot, b. 26 April 1942, Linz, Donau, Austria. Chemist. m. Agnes, 1 son, 1 daughter. Education: Diploma in Organic, Inorganic and Physical Chemistry, Dr phil nat in Biochemistry, Physical Chemistry and Clinical Chemistry, Faculty of Biochemistry and Pharmacy, Johann-Wolfgang-von-Goethe-University, Frankfurt, Germany. Appointments: Scientific Assistant, Centre of Biological Chemistry, Johann-Wolfgang-von-Goethe-University, 1973-81; Part-time Scientific Assistant, Institute of Laboratory Diagnostics and Haematological Paternity Testing, Giessen, 1973-78; Head, Laboratory of Pharmacokinetics, ASTA Medica AG, Frankfurt, 1981-90; Head, Group of Nonclinical Pharmacokinetics, ASTA Medica, 1990-2000; Manager, Senior Scientist, Preclinical Sciences, ADME (since 2002: VIATRIS GmbH & Co KG), 2001-03; Retired. Publications: 30 scientific articles and meeting abstracts; Patents in field of cytostatics; Contribution of pharmacokinetic parts to more than 10 expert opinions in connection with the international approval of drugs; International study reports. Memberships: Society of German Chemists; German Cancer Society; Society of Laboratory Animal Science; European Society for Autoradiography; German Society of Natural Scientists and Physicians; ADME panel in IPACT I and II. Address: Dr-Carl-Henss-Str 28, D-61130 Nidderau, Germany.

PETERSEN Sergio, b. 9 September 1943, Porto Alegre, RS, Brazil. Dentist. 1 son, 1 daughter. Education: DDS, MSc, PhD, Federal University of Rio de Janeiro; Post-graduate studies, Pediatric Dentistry, Visiting Scientist, Indiana University School of Dentistry, USA. Appointments: Head, Hospital Dentistry, Head, Handicapped Patients' Unit, Research Division, Federal University of Rio de Janeiro, Assistant Guest Professor, Pediatric Dentistry, Postdoctoral Programme, Dentistry School, New York University, USA; More than 100 lectures given in Brazil and abroad. Publications: A case of neonatal tooth causing ulceration of the tongue; The history of conscious sedation in Brazil; The beautiful smile conquest; The computer in dentistry; The importance to consult the dentist; the Bruxism origin may be stress; The benefits of aesthetic dentistry; Harmony and aesthetic in dentistry; Bleaching the teeth; Oral examination, how and why?; Bottle-mouth syndrome; Mucicutaneous lesions simulating allergic reactions to local anesthetics. Honours: 1st place student in class rank, Federal University of Rio de Janeiro; Winning article, Oral Manifestation in Children Carrying HIV, Brazilian Magazine of Dentistry, 1993. Memberships: Brazilian Society of Dentistry; American Academy of Cosmetic Dentistry; Fellow, International College of Dentists; Emeritus Councillor, Federal University of Rio de Janeiro. Address: Rua Carlos Gois 375 sls, 301/302, Leblon, Rio de Janeiro, RJ, Brazil.

PETIT Jean-Yves, b. 19 January 1945, St Jean de Beugne, France. Retired Professor. m. Annick Le Cadre, 1 son, 1 daughter. Education: Pharmaceutical Degree, 1969; PhD, Pharmacology, University of Nantes, 1975. Appointments: Professor, Faculty of Pharmacy, University of Nantes, 1972-2009; Referee, Conseil National des Universités Françaises, 1987-88; Charge of laboratory animals care in experimental research, 1989-2002; Pharmacologist Referee on doping drugs, Comité National Olympique et Sportif Français, Paris; Main Organiser, Joint Congress of French Pharmacological and Italian Pharmacologicals Societies, Nantes, 1999. Publications: 2 subjects for experimental research; 3 book chapters; Co-author, Doping: How to Jeopardize One's Health, CD-ROM, 2010. Honours: Academic Palms Officer; Marine Officer (Health Service); Referee, AFSSAPS (Rheumatology); Listed in international biographical dictionaries. Memberships: French Pharmacological Society; Societé de Chimie Thérapeutique; French Inflammation Society/GREMI. Address: 34 Rue Felibien, 44000 Nantes, France. E-mail: jean-yves.petit@univ-nantes.fr

PETRICA Ligia, b. 20 March 1958, Zalau, Romania. Physician. m. Maxim Petrica, 1 son, 1 daughter. Education: Graduate, University of Medicine & Pharmacy, Timisoara, Romania, 1983; PhD, 1998. Appointments: Assistant Professor, 1991, Senior Consultant Internist, 1998, Senior Consultant Nephrologist, 2000, Lecturer, 2003, Associate Professor, 2008, Victor Babes University of Medicine and Pharmacy, County Emergency Hospital, Department of Nephrology, Timisoara, Romania. Publications: Books, Cerebrovascular Disease within the Frames of Chronic Kidney Disease; Update in Nephrology; Numerous articles in professional journals. Honours: Listed in international biographical dictionaries. Memberships: International Society of Nephrology; European Renal Association; European Dialysis and Transplant Association; World Federation of the Societies of Ultrasound in Medicine and Biology; Romanian Society of Nephrology; Romanian Society of Immunology. Address: Str Telegrafului C11, Et 3, Ap 7, 300125 Timisoara, Timis, Romania. E-mail: ligiapetrica@rdslink.ro

PETROSYAN Aram, b. 4 November 1949, Kirovabad, USSR. Professor. m. Sofya Yesayan, 2 sons, 1 daughter. Education: Diploma, Physics, Armedian State Pedagogical Institute, 1970; Postgraduate studies, Karpov Physico-Chemical Institute, Moscow, 1975-78; PhD, Physical Chemistry, 1980. Appointments: Chief of Laboratory, Institute of Condensed Media Physics, 1979-91; Assistant Professor, Leading Researcher, Yerevan State University, 1991-2004; Leading Researcher, Head of Research Group, Molecule Structure Research Centre, 2004-09; Head of Research Group, Institute of Applied Problems of Physics, 2009-. Publications: More than 140 publications; More than 40 abstracts at conferences; More than 90 articles; 6 inventions. Honours: Research Grants, CRDF, 1996, 1998, 2004, and ANSEF, 2001, 2003, 2010; Prize of the President of Armenia in the Field of Natural Sciences, 2008. Memberships: USA Materials Research Society; Editorial board member, Journal of Crystallization Physics and Chemistry. Address: 2-83 Bakunts str, Yerevan, 0033, Armenia.

PETROSYAN Gevorg, b. 2 September 1940, Solak, Yerevan, Republic of Armenia. Professor. m. Marieta, 1 son, 1 daughter. Education: State Engineering University of Armenia (SEUA); Mechanical Engineer, 1962; PhD, Bauman Technical University (BTU), Moscow, 1968; Doctor of Technical Sciences, Institute of Problem of Materials Sciences (Ukranian National Academy of Sciences) in Kiev, Ukraine, 1983. Appointments: Assistant Professor, BTU Moscow; Head, Materials Treatment by Pressure Division, Head of Strength of Materials Division, Leader of the Cycle of the New Specialty Dynamics and Strength of Machines, and Head of the Mechanics Division, SEUA. Publications: Author of 150 articles including 25 Materials of Conference Reports; 1 book; 14 inventions. Honours: Armenian-American Professional Union Award, 1993; Best Scientific Leader of master's dissertation (1997), best scientific SEUA publication (2000) and Best Scientific Leader of Post-Graduate Student (2000-01); Best Invention (2004-05), and Best Scientific Publications in the area of "Technological Problems of Plasticity Theory" (2006), SEUA. Memberships: Scientific Technical Council of SEUA; Committee of Scientific Technical Councils of SEUA "Mechanics and Machine Science" and "Materials Science"; Academician, Armenian Scientific Technological National Academy; Corresponding member, Armenian Engineering Academy; Armenian National Committee of Theoretical and Applied Mechanics. Address: Teryan 105, Yerevan 0009, Armenia.

PETROV Vadim, b. 24 May 1932, Prague, Czech Republic. Composer; Professor of Composition. m. Marta Votápková, 1954, 1 son, 2 daughters. Education: Graduate, Department of Composition, Academy of Fine Arts, Prague, Czech Republic, 1956. Career: The Giant Mountains Fairy Tales; There Are Some Limits; The Romance of Water Spirit; The Good Old Band; Sonets Chi Seled in Stone; Pax Rerum Optima; The Swans' Lament; The Nightingale and Rose; The Twelve; Johan Doctor Faust Nocturno in G; Burlesque; The Valessian Intermezzo; Song of the Night; The Ditty. Compositions: Melancholical Waltz; Tango Habanero; Scherzo Poetico; Riva Dei Pini; Romans; The Silver Serenade; Russian Evangelium; Song for Jane Eyre; The Autumn Memory; Nigh Tango; Song of Hoping and Belief. Recordings: The Maple Violin; Lucy and Miracles; Anna Snegina; Don Quigxot; Don Jean and others. Publications: Czech and Slovak Composer, 1980; Film and Time, 1983; The Little Czechoslovak Encyclopedia, 1986. Honours: Award Of The Association of Czechoslovak Composers; Czech Television, 1997; Svobodné Slovo, Prague, 1997. Address: Hlubocinka 844, 25168 Kamenice, Czech Republic. E-mail: prof.petrov@seznam.cz Website: www.prof-vadim-petrov.cz

PETU-IBIKUNLE Abiona Michael, b. 13 May 1966, Nigeria. Lecturer. m. Grace Folashade, 2 sons, 1 daughter. Education: PhD, Agronomy, 2010. Appointments: Assistant Lecturer, Department of Agricultural Science & Technology. Publications: Numerous articles in professional journals. Honours: Commissioned Evangelist of Church of Nigeria Anglican Communion. Memberships: Bio-Technology Society of Nigeria; Nigeria Society for Experimental Biology. Address: No A 10 Mission Road, Oke Ero Ilofa, Kwara State, Nigeria. Website: www.nou.edu.ng

PEXIDR Karel (Charles), b. 4 November 1929, Praha, Czech Republic. Lawyer; Philosopher; Composer; Writer. m. Ludmila, 1 son. Education: JUDr, Charles University, Praha, 1955; Philosophy and composition, private study. Appointments: Lawyer, 1955-89; Teacher, Westczeche University, 1994-2000. Publications: Relativistic Philosophy, Psychology and Gnoseology; Kosmology out of a View of a Philosopher; Causality (with Dr Nikola Demjancuk); Philosophy for Everybody; Many other novels, poetry and fiction; More than 100 compositions (orchestra, chamber music, songs). Honours: First Prize in Literature, Plzeň, 2008. Memberships: Association of Writers and Composers, Praha and Plzeň. Address: Libusina 5, 323 00 Plzeň, Czech Republic.

PEYTON Kathleen Wendy, (Kathleen Herald, K M Peyton), b. 2 August 1929, Birmingham, England. Writer. m. Michael Peyton, 1950, 2 daughters. Education: ATD, Manchester School of Art. Publications: As Kathleen Herald: Sabre, the Horse from the Sea, 1947; The Mandrake, 1949; Crab the Roan, 1953. As K M Peyton: North to Adventure, 1959; Stormcock Meets Trouble, 1961; The Hard Way Home, 1962; Windfall, 1963; Brownsea Silver, 1964; The Maplin Bird, 1964; The Plan for Birdsmarsh, 1965; Thunder in the Sky, 1966; Flambards Trilogy, 1969-71; The Beethoven Medal, 1971; The Pattern of Roses, 1972; Pennington's Heir, 1973; The Team, 1975; The Right-Hand Man, 1977; Prove Yourself a Hero, 1977; A Midsummer Night's Death, 1978; Marion's Angels, 1979; Flambards Divided, 1981; Dear Fred, 1981; Going Home, 1983; The Last Ditch, 1984; Froggett's Revenge, 1985; The Sound of Distant Cheering, 1986; Downhill All the Way, 1988; Darkling, 1989; Skylark, 1989; No Roses Round the Door, 1990; Poor Badger, 1991; Late to Smile, 1992; The Boy Who Wasn't There, 1992; The Wild Boy and Queen Moon, 1993; Snowfall, 1994; The Swallow

DICTIONARY OF INTERNATIONAL BIOGRAPHY 36th EDITION

Tale, 1995; Swallow Summer, 1995; Unquiet Spirits, 1997; Firehead, 1998; Swallow the Star, 1998; Blind Beauty, 1999; Small Gains, 2003; Greater Gains, 2005; Blue Skies and Gunfire, 2006; Minna's Quest, 2007; No Turning Back, 2008; Far From Home, 2009; Paradise House, 2011. Honours: New York Herald Tribune Award, 1965; Carnegie Medal, 1969; Guardian Award, 1970. Address: Rookery Cottage, North Fambridge, Chelmsford, Essex CM3 6LP, England.

PFEFFER Philip E, b. 8 April 1941, New York, NY, USA. Biophysicist. m. Judith Stadlen, 2 sons, 1 daughter. Education: BS Chemistry, Hunter College of the City University of New York, 1962; MS, Chemistry, 1964, PhD, Chemistry, 1966, Rutgers University, New Brunswick, NJ. Appointments: Teaching Assistant, 1962-64, Research Assistant, 1964-66, Department of Chemistry, Rutgers University, New Brunswick, NJ; NIH Postdoctoral Research Fellow with Gerhardt Closs, University of Chicago, 1966-68; Research Chemist, Lipid Research Lab, Eastern Regional Research Center, 1968-76; Physical Leader, Physical Chemistry Lab, 1976-80; Lead Scientist, 1980-2006, Emeritus, 2006-, Microbial Biophysics and Biochemistry Lab; Visiting Scientist, Department of Plant Physiology, Centre d'Etudes Nucleaires de Grenoble, 1986; Oxford Research Fellow, Department of Plant Science, Oxford University, 1989; Visiting Professor, Insititut de Biologie Vegetale Moleculaire, Universite Bordeaux, 1998; Adjunct Full Professor, Department of Bioscience and Biotechnology, Drexel University, Philadelphia, 1996-. Publications: Author and Co-author of 156 publications. Honours include: Bond Award, American Oil Chemists Society, 1976; Philadelphia Federal Service Award for Scientific Achievement, 1979; Philadelphia American Chemical Society Award, 1982; USDA Science and Education Award, 1982; Agricultural Research Service North Atlantic Area Scientist of the Year, 1986; Competitive ARS Postdoctoral Research Associate Grants, 1986-1989; New Orleans ACS Award, 1987; Oxford University Visiting Scientist Stipend, 1989; OECD Fellowship, 1995, 1996; National Research Initiative Grant, Awardee, 1997-2000, 2002-2004. Memberships: American Society of Plant Biologists; American Chemical Society; International Society for Plant Microbial Interactions; AAAS. Address: USDA/ARS/Eastern Regional Research Center, Microbial Biophysics and Residue Chemistry, 600 E Mermaid Lane, Wyndmoor, PA 19038, USA.

PFEIFFER Michelle, b. 29 April 1958, Santa Ana, California, USA. Actress. m. (1) Peter Horton, divorced 1988, (2) David E Kelly, 1993, 2 children. Career: Films include: Grease 2; The Witches of Eastwick; Scarface; Married to the Mob; The Fabulous Baker Boys; Tequila Sunrise; Dangerous Liaisons, 1989; Frankie and Johnnie, 1990; Batman Returns, 1992; The Age of Innocence, 1993; Wolf, 1994; Dangerous Minds, 1997; Up Close and Personal, 1997; To Gillian on Her 37th Birthday, 1997; One Fine Day, 1997; A Thousand Acres, 1997; Privacy, 1997; The Story of US, 1999; The Deep End of the Ocean, 1999; A Midsummer Night's Dream, 1999; Being John Malkovitch, 1999; What Lies Beneath, 2000; I am Sam, 2001; White Oleander, 2002; Sinbad: Legend of the Seven Seas (voice), 2003; I Could Never Be Your Woman, 2007; Hairspray, 2007; Stardust, 2007; Cheri, 2009; Personal Effects, 2009. TV includes: Delta House; Splendour in the Grass. Address: c/o ICM, 8942 Wilshire Boulevard, Beverly Hills, CA 90211, USA.

PHELPS Michael Fred II, b. 30 June 1985, Maryland, USA. Retired Swimmer. Career: 3 gold, 2 silver, Yokohama, 2002; 4 gold, 2 silver, World Championships, 2003; 6 gold, 2 bronze, Athens Olympics, 2004; 5 gold, 1 silver, World Championships, 2005; 5 gold, 1 silver, Victoria, 2006; 7 gold, World Championships, 2007; 8 gold, Beijing Olympics, 2008; Founder, Michael Phelps Foundation, 2008; 5 gold, 1 silver, World Championships, 2009; 5 gold, Irvine, 2010; 4 gold, 2 silver, 1 bronze, World Championships, 2011; 4 gold, 2 silver, London Olympics, 2012. Honours: Swimmer of the Year, Swimming World Magazine, 2003, 2004, 2006, 2007, 2008, 2009; American Swimmer of the Year Award, 2001, 2002, 2003, 2004, 2006, 2007, 2008, 2009; Male Performance of the Year, 2004, 2006, 2007, 2008, 2009, Relay Performance of the Year, 2006, 2007, 2008, 2009, Male Athlete of the Year, 2004, 2007, 2008, Golden Google; USCO Sportsman of the Year Award, 2004, 2008; James E Sullivan Award, 2003; Laureus World Sportsman of the Year Award, 2004, 2005, 2008, 2009; Sports Illustrated Sportsman of the Year, 2008.

PHILIPSON Nittala Lloyd George, b. 24 January 1936, Bhimavaram, AP, India. Government Service. m. Blandeena, deceased 2004. Education: BA, Andhra University, 1956; Doctor of Divinity, Doctor of Philosophy, All Truth Bible Theological University International. Appointments: Progress Assistant, Community Development Blocks, 1962-64; Taluk Statistical Assistant, Tahsil Offices, 1965-81; Statistical Officer, Chief Planning Officer's Office, Eluru, 1982-86; Divisional Deputy Statistical Officer, Sub-Collectors Office, Nardsapur, Andhra Pradesh Economic and Statistical Service, Government of AP, India; Established Blandeena Bhavan Christian, Cultural and Spiritual Revival Centre, 2006. Publications: The Spiritual Stream; The Bond of Love; The Spiritual Bond; Numerous articles in professional journals. Honours: President's Silver Medal, 1971. Memberships: The State Employees Co-operative Building Society; The Lutheran Welfare and Service Centre. Address: Sudeepa Soudha, H No 19-10-22, 23rd Ward, Bhimavaram, WGDt, AP, India. E-mail: nlgphilipson@gmail.com

PHILLIPS Anthony Charles Julian, b, 2 June 1936, Falmouth, Cornwall, England. Headmaster. m. Victoria Ann Stainton, 2 sons, 1 daughter. Education: Solicitors Articled Clerk, 1953-58; Qualified as a Solicitor, 1958; Law Society's Honours Examination, 1958; BD First Class, AKC First Class, King's College, London, 1963; PhD, Gonville & Caius College, Cambridge, 1967; Pre-ordination, The College of the Resurrection, Mirfield, 1966. Appointments include: Solicitor, London, 1958-60; Curate, The Good Shepherd, Arbury, Cambridge, 1966-69; Dean, Chaplain and Fellow, Trinity Hall, Cambridge, 1969-74; Honorary Chaplain to the Bishop of Norwich, 1970-71; Chaplain and Fellow, St John's College, Oxford, 1975-86; Lecturer, Theology, Jesus College, Oxford, 1975-86; Examining Chaplain to the Bishop of Oxford, 1979-86; Examining Chaplain to the Bishop of Manchester, 1980-86; Domestic Bursar, St John's College, Oxford, 1982-84; Chairman, Faculty of Theology, 1983-85; S A Cook Bye Fellowship, Gonville and Caius College, Cambridge, 1984; Lecturer, Theology, Hertford College, Oxford, 1984-86; Archbishops of Canterbury and York Interfaith Consultant for Judaism, 1984-85; Examining Chaplain to the Bishop of Wakefield, 1984-86; Canon Theologian of the Diocese of Truro, 1985-2002; Headmaster, The King's School, Canterbury, 1986-96; Honorary Canon of Canterbury Cathedral, 1987-96; County Chaplain to St John Ambulance, 1996-2002; Chapter Canon of Truro Cathedral, 2001-2002, Emeritus Canon, 2002-; The Royal Cornwall Polytechnic Society, Board Member, 2003-08, Chairman, 2004-08, President, 2008-11, Honorary Vice-President, 2011-; Governor, SPCK, 1998-2006, Chair of Publishing, 2000-05. Publications: Books: Ancient Israel's Criminal Law, 1970; Deuteronomy, 1973, 2008; God BC, 1977; Lower than Angels:

Questions raised by Genesis 1-11, 1983, 1996; Preaching from the Psalter, 1988; The Passion of God, 1995; Entering into the Mind of God, 2002; Essays on Biblical Law, 2002, paperback, 2004; Standing Up to God, 2005; David: A Life of Passion and Tragedy, 2008; Numerous articles in academic journals and newspapers. Honours: Archibald Robertson Prize, 1962, Junior McCaul Hebrew Prize, 1963, King's College, London; Serving Brother to the Order of St John, 2003. Memberships: Society of Old Testament Study; Worshipful Company of Broderers. Address: The Old Vicarage, 10 St Peter's Road, Flushing, Nr Falmouth, Cornwall TR11 5TP, England.

PHILLIPS Francis Douglas, b. 19 December 1926, Dundee, Scotland. Artist; Painter. m. Margaret Parkinson, 1 daughter. Education: DA, Dundee College of Art, 1951. Career: Military service with Army; Illustrator, D C Thomson & Co Ltd; Full time painter, 1966-; Illustrator, over 100 books; Taught water colour painting, Dundee Art Centre; Taught illustration, Dundee College of Commerce; Several paintings reproduced as Limited Edition Prints; Over 1200 covers for magazine, Peoples Friend; Cover work for British and French Readers Digest and Scottish Field; Article in Artists and Illustrators Magazine, 2007; TV interviews, 1991, 1992, 1993, 1996; Radio Tay interview, 1995; Exhibited widely in commercial galleries including: Group Exhibitions: The Royal Scottish Academy; The Royal Glasgow Institute of Fine Art; The Royal Scottish Society of Painters in Watercolour; The Royal Institute of Painters in Watercolour, London; One Person Exhibitions: Stables Gallery, Bathgate, 1986; Dundee Art Galleries, 1987; Step Gallery, Edinburgh, 1998; Cornerstone Gallery, Stirling, 1998; Two Person Exhibitions: Victoria Art Galleries-Albert Institute, Dundee, 1955; Cornerstone Gallery, Dunblane, 1992; Cornerstone Gallery, Stirling, 1995, 1998; Queens Gallery, Dundee, 2002; Leith Gallery, Edinburgh, 2002; Numerous Four Person Exhibitions, Collections, Private Collections and Group Exhibitions. Publications: Contributions to several magazines including: The Artist Magazine; The International Artists Magazine; The Scots Magazine. Listed in Who's Who in Art. Membership: Life Member, Royal Glasgow Institute of Fine Art. Address: 278 Strathmore Avenue, Dundee, DD3 6SJ, Scotland.

PHILLIPS Leslie Samuel, b. 20 April 1924, London, England. Actor; Producer; Director. m. four children. Career: Child actor; Vice President, Royal Theatrical Fund, Disabled Living Foundation; Films include: A Lassie From Lancashire, 1935; The Citadel; Train of Events; The Galloping Major; Sound Barrier; The Fake; The Limping Man; Value for Money; The Gamma People; As Long As They're Happy; The Big Money; Brothers in Law; The Barretts of Wimpole Street; Just My Luck; Les Girls; The Smallest Show on Earth; I Was Monty's Double; The Man Who Liked Funerals; Carry on Nurse; This Other Eden; Carry on Teacher; Please Turn Over; Doctor in Love; Watch Your Stern; Carry on Constable; In The Doghouse; Crooks Anonymous; The Fast Lady; Father Came Too; Doctor in Clover; The Magnificent 7 Deadly Sins; Not Now Darling; Don't Just Lie There; Out of Africa; Empire of the Sun; Scandal; King Ralph; Carry on Columbus; Caught in the Act; Day of the Jackal; Cinderella; Saving Grace; August; Lara Croft – Tomb Raider; Harry Potter and the Philosopher's Stone; Thunderpants; Collusion; Doctor in Trouble; Pool of London; Churchill – The Hollywood Years; Maroc 7; Colour Me Kubrick; With Shadows; Venue. Radio: numerous plays including Navy Lark; Les Miserables; Tales from the Backbench; Round the World in 80 Days; Wind in the Willows; TV: Our Man at St Mark's; Time and Motion Man; Reluctant Debutante; A Very Fine Line; Casanova 74; You'll Never See Me Again; Rumpole; Summer's Lease; Chancer; Lovejoy; Boon; House of Windsor; Love on the Branch Line; Canteville Ghost; The Pale Horse; Dalziel & Pascoe; The Sword of Honour; Into the Void; The Oz Trial; Take a Girl Like You; Tales of the Crypt, Who Bombed Birmingham? Holby City; Midsomer Murders; Where the Heart Is; Theatre: The Merry Wives of Windsor; On the Whole Life's Been Jolly Good; Love for Love; Naked Justice; For Better or Worse; Ghosts of Albion; Charley's Aunt; Camino Real; Deadly Game; Diary of a Nobody; Man Most Likely to…; Passion Play; Walking with Shadows; Heartbeat; Marple: By the Pricking of My Thumbs, The Last Detective. Honours: Evening Standard Lifetime Achievement in Films Award, 1997; OBE, 1998; CBE, 2008. Address: c/o Diamond Management, 31 Percy Street, London W1T 2DD, England.

PHILLIPS Sian, b. 14 May 1933, Bettws, Carmarthenshire, Wales. Actress. m. (1) D H Roy, 1954, (2) Peter O'Toole, 1960, divorced 1979, 2 daughters, (3) Robin Sachs, 1979, divorced 1992. Education: University of Wales; RADA. Career: Child actress, BBC Radio Wales and BBC TV Wales; Newsreader, Announcer, Member of BBC repertory company, 1953-55; Toured for Welsh Arts Council with National Theatre Company, 1953-55; Arts Council Bursary, 1955; Royal TV Society annual televised lecture, 1992; Theatre includes: Lettice and Loveage, 2001; Divas at The Donmar Season, 2001; My Old Lady, Doolittle Theatre, Los Angeles, 2002, Promenade Theatre, New York, 2002-03; National Tour with The Old Ladies, 2003; The Dark, Donmar, London, 2004; Falling in Love Again, Cabaret, London, Europe, Israel, New York, UK tour; Films include: Becket, 1963; Goodbye Mr Chips, 1969; Laughter in the Dark, 1968; Murphy's War, 1970; Under Milk Wood, 1971; The Clash of the Titans, 1979; Dune, 1983; Ewok II; The Two Mrs Grenvilles; Sian, 1988; Dark River, 1990; The Age of Innocence, 1993; House of America, 1997; Coming and Going, 2001; Gigolo, 2004; TV: Shoulder to Shoulder, 1974; How Green Was My Valley, 1975; I, Claudius, 1976; Boudicca; Off to Philadelphia in the Morning, 1977; The Oresteia of Aeschylus, 1978; Crime and Punishment, 1979; Tinker, Tailor, Soldier, Spy, 1979; Sean O'Casey, 1980; Churchill: The Wilderness Years, 1981; How Many Miles to Babylon, 1982; Smiley's People, 1982; George Borrow, 1983; A Painful Case; Beyond All Reason; Murder on the Exchange; The Shadow of the Noose, 1988; Snow Spider, 1988; Freddie & Max; Emlyn's Moon; Perfect Scoundrels, 1990; Heidi, 1992; The Borrowers, 1992; The Chestnut Soldier, 1992; Huw Weldon TV Lecture, 1993; Summer Silence; The Vacillations of Poppy Carew; Mind to Kill; Ivanhoe, 1997; The Scold's Bridle, 1998; The Aristocrats, 1998; Alice Through the Looking Glass, 1998; Aristocrats, 1999; Nikita, 1999; The Magician's House, 1999, 2000; Cinderella, 2000; Attila, 2001; The Last Detective: The Murder Room; Numerous recordings and radio work. Honours: Honorary Fellow: University of Cardiff, 1981, Polytechnic of Wales, 1988, University of Wales, Swansea, 1998, Trinity College, Carmarthen; Honorary DLitt (Wales), 1984; CBE, 2000; Many awards for work in cinema, theatre and on TV including BAFTA Wales Lifetime Achievement Award, 2001. Memberships: Vice President, Welsh College of Music and Drama; Member, Gorsedd of Bards for services to drama in Wales, 1960; Member, Arts Council Drama Committee for 5 years; Governor, St David's Trust; Former Governor, Welsh College of Music and Drama; Fellow, Royal Society of Arts; Vice President, Actors Benevolent Fund. Address: L King, PDF, Drury House, 34-43 Russell Street, London, WC2B 5HA, England.

PHYSICK John Frederick, b. 31 December 1923, London, England. Museum Curator. m. Eileen Mary Walsh, 1954, 2 sons, 1 daughter. Education: Battersea Grammar School; Dr of the Royal College of Art; D Litt, Lambeth. Appointments: Home Guard, 1940-42; Royal Navy, 1942-46; Victoria and Albert Museum, 1948-84, retired as Deputy Director; Vice-Chairman (retired 2011), Rochester Cathedral Fabric Advisory Committee. Publications: The Engravings of Eric Gill, 1965; Designs for English Sculpture 1680-1860, 1969; The Wellington Monument, 1970; Marble Halls, 1975; The Victoria and Albert Museum: the history of its building, 1982; Sculpture in Britain 1540-1840 (editor 2nd edition), 1988; The Albert Memorial (contributor), 2000; Westminster Abbey, Henry VII's Chapel (contributor), 2003; A Biographical Dictionary of British Sculptors 1660-1851, (contributor) 2009. Honours: CBE; Fellow, Society of Antiquaries. Memberships: Kent Archaeological Society; Ancient Monument Society; Victorian Society; Society of Architectural Historians; Vice-President, Public Monuments and Sculpture Association; Vice-President, Church Monuments Society. Address: 49 New Road, Meopham, Kent DA13 0LS, England.

PICARD Robert George, b. 15 July 1951, Pasadena, California, USA. Professor; Author. m. Elizabeth Carpelan, 1979, 2 daughters, 1 son. Education: BA, Loma Linda University, 1974; MA, California State University, Fullerton, 1980; PhD, University of Missouri, 1983. Appointments: Editor, Riverside Community News, 1977-79; Copy Editor, Wire Editor, Ontario Daily Report, 1979-80; Publications Editor, Freedom of Information Center, Columbia, 1980-83; Assistant to Associate Professor, Louisiana State University, Baton Rouge, 1983-87; Associate Professor, Director of Communications Industries Management, Emerson College, Boston, 1987-90; Professor, California State University, Fullerton, 1990-98; Turku School Economics, 1998-2003; Hamrin Professor, Media Economics, Jonkoping International Business School, Sweden, 2003-; Chair, Committee for Media Diversity, Boston, 1987-2003; Visiting Professor, Turku School of Economics, Finland, 1993-94. Publications: The Press and the Decline of Democracy, 1985; The Ravens of Odin: The Press in the Nordic Nations, 1988; Media Economics: Concepts and Issues, 1989; In the Camera's Eye: News Coverage of Terrorist Events, 1991; Media Portrayals of Terrorism, 1993; Editor, Press Concentration and Monopoly, 1988; The Cable Network's Handbook, 1993; Media Firms: Structures, Operations and Performance, 2002; The Economics and Financing of Media Companies, 2004; Strategic Responses to Media Market Changes, 2004; Digital Terrestrial Televisin in Europe, 2005; Media Product Portfolios: Issues Management Multiple Products and Services, 2005; Internet and Mass Media, 2008; Editor, Journal of Media Economics, 1988-96; Journal of Media Business Studies, 2004-; Associate Editor, Political Communication and Persuasion, 1988-91; Chapter President, ACLU, Baton Rouge, 1985-87; Board of Directors, New England Institute for Peace, Boston, 1988-90; Co-ordinator of Publicity, Habitat for Humanity, Riverside, 1991-92. Honours: International Research Award, Association for the Advancement of Policy, Research and Development, 1984; Outstanding Research Award, Phi Kappa Phi, 1986; Joan Shorenstein Centre on Press, Politics, Public Policy Fellowship, Harvard University, 2006. Memberships: Association for Education in Journalism and Mass Communication. Address: Reuters Institute, Department of Politics and International Relations, University of Oxford, 13 Norham Gardens, Oxford OX2 6PS, England. E-mail: robert.picard@robertpicard.net Website: www.robertpicard.net

PICASSO Paloma, b. 19 April 1949, Paris, France. Designer. m. Rafael Lopez-Cambil (Lopez-Sanchez) 1978, divorced 1998, (2) Eric Thevennet, 1999. Education: University of Paris; Sorbonne; Studied jewellery design and manufacture. Career: Designer, fashion jewellery for Yves St Laurent, 1969; Designer, jewellery for Zolotas, 1971; Designer, costumes and sets, Parisian theatre productions: L'Interpretation, 1975, Succès, 1978; Created Paloma Picasso brand and creations designed for: Tiffany & Co, 1980; L'Oreal; Metzler Optik Partner AG; Villeroy & Boch; KBC; Motif; Pieces in permanent collections of Smithsonian Institute, Musée des Arts Décoratifs and Die Neue Zamlang; Council of Fashion Design of America Accessory Award, 1989. Address: Paloma Picasso Parfums, 1 rue Pasquier, 92698 Levallois-Perret Cédex, France.

PICHAY Regta, b. 12 March 1953, Alcala, Pangasinan, Philippines. Obstetrician-Gynecologist. Education: BSc, Preparatory Medicine, D Med, University of Santo Tomas, Manila; Medical Internship, Veterans Memorial and Medical Center, Quezon City; Pre-Licensure Rural Health Practice, Mt Province Provincial Hospital. Appointments: Assistant Professor I, 1986, Gynecology Co-ordinator, 1992-96, Section Head, Gynecologic Endoscopy, 1993-2001, Training Officer, 1997-2000, Department of Obstetrics and Gynecology, Editor in Chief, Philippine Scientific Journal, 2000-07, Chair, 2001-07, Chair, Promotional Board, 2003-04, Associate Professor II, 2004-06, Associate Professor III, 2007-09, Professor I, 2010-, College of Medicine, Manila Central University – Filemon D Tanchoco Medical Foundation. Publications: Numerous articles in professional journals. Honours include most recently: Leadership Awardee, St Luke's Medical Center, 2006 and 2010; Plaque of Recognition, Bulacan Medical Mission Group Health Services Cooperative Inc, 2008; Most Outstanding Alcalenean in field of Meidcine, 2008; Top Faculty Students' Choice, 2009, Certificate of Recognition, 2009, Top Faculty Awardee, 2010, College of Medicine, MCU-FDT Medical Foundation; Distinction Award, 2010, Meritorious Achievement Award, 2010, Philippine Obstetrical & Gynecological Society. Memberships: Philippine Obstetrical and Gynecological Society; Philippine Society for Gynecologic Endoscopy; Philippine Society of Climacteric Medicine Inc; Philippine Society of Reproductive Endocrinology and Infertility; Philippine Medical Society; Philippine Medical Women's Society; Philippine Association of Pernatologists; American Association of Gynecologic Laparoscopists; International Society for Gynecologic Endoscopy; Asia Pacific Association for Gynecologic Endoscopy. Address: College of Medicine, Manila Central University – Filemon D Tanchoco Medical Foundation, Epifanio delos Santos Avenue(EDSA), Caloocan City, Philippines 1400.

PICK Stepan, b. 26 December 1949, Prague, Czech Republic. Physicist. Education: Graduate, 1973, RNDr, 1976, Charles University; CSc, Czechoslovak Academy of Sciences, 1981. Appointments: J Heyrovsky Institute of Physical Chemistry, 1974, Researcher, 1986-; Visiting Professor, University of Nancy, France, 1992, 1993; Visiting Professor, University of Louis Pasteur, Strasbourg, France, 2006. Publications: Over 100 articles in professional journals. Memberships: Union of Czech Mathematicians and Physicists; Czech Union of Nature Conservation. Address: J Heyrovsky Institute of Physical Chemistry, Academy of Sciences of the Czech Republic, Dolejskova 3, CZ 182 23 Prague 8, Czech Republic.

PICKERING Alan Michael, b. 4 December 1948, York, England. Company Chairman. m. Christine. Education: BA (Hons), Politics and Social Administration, University of Newcastle, 1969-72. Appointments: British Rail Clerical Officer, 1967-69; Head of Membership Services, Electrical, Electronics, Telecommunications and Plumbing Union, 1972-92; Partner, Watson Wyatt, 1992-2009; Member Occupational Pensions Board, 1992-97; Chairman, National Association of Pension Funds, 1999-2001; Chairman, European Federation for Retirement Provision, 2001-04; Chairman, Plumbing Industry Pension Scheme, 2001-; Non-Executive Director, The Pension Regulator, 2005-; Chairman, Life Academy, 2005-; Chairman, Bestrustees, 2009-. Publication: A Simpler Way to Better Pensions, HMSO, 2002. Honour: CBE; Memberships: Blackheath and Bromley Harriers, President, 1992; Pensions Management Institute. Address: BESTrustees plc, Five Kings House, 1 Queen Street Place, London EC4R 1QS, England.

PICKETT John Anthony, b. 21 April 1945, Leicester, England. Michael Elliott Distinguished Research Fellow; Honorary Professor. m. 2 children. Education: BSc (Hons), 1967, PhD, Organic Chemistry, 1971, University of Surrey; Chartered Chemist, 1975; DSc, University of Nottingham, 1993; Chartered Scientist, 2004; Honorary DSc, University of Aberdeen, 2008. Appointments: Postdoctoral Fellowship, University of Manchester Institute of Science and Technology, 1970-72; Senior Scientist, Brewing Research Foundation, Redhill, Surrey, 1972-76; Principal Scientific Officer, Rothamsted Experimental Station, 1976-83; Head, Band 2, Individual Merit, Biological Chemistry Division, Rothamsted, 1984-2010; External Examiner, Imperial College, Silwood Park, 1992-95; Chairman, Advisory Committee, School of Applied Chemistry, University of North London, 1993-95; Honorary Member, Academic Staff, University of Reading, 1995-; External Examiner, Environmental Science, University of Sussex, 1997-2000; Michael Elliott Distinguished Research Fellow, 2010-. Publications: Over 400 publications and patents. Honours: Honorary Professor, University of Nottingham, 1991; Rank Prize, 1995; Fellow, Royal Society, 1996; Member, Deutsche Akademie der Naturforscher Leopoldina, 2001; International Society of Chemical Ecology medal, 2002; CBE, 2004; Honorary Life Membership, Association of Applied Biologists, 2004; Foreign Member, Royal Swedish Academy of Agriculture and Forestry, 2005; Wolf Foundation Prize in Agriculture, 2008; Royal Society Croonian Prize Lecture, 2008; Honorary Fellowship, Royal Entomological Society, 2010; Honorary Member, Chemical Society of Ethiopia, 2010; Honorary BSc, University of Surrey, 2011; Millennium Award, Assocham's 9th Knowledge Millennium Summit, New Delhi, India and presenter of Millennium Address, 2011. Address: Department of Biological Chemistry, Rothamsted Research, Harpenden, Hertfordshire AL5 2JQ, England. E-mail: john.pickett@rothamsted.ac.uk

PICKWOAD Michael Mervyn, b. 11 July 1945, Windsor, Berkshire, England. Film Designer. m. Vanessa Orriss, 3 daughters. Education: BSc, Honours, Civil Engineering, Southampton University. Career: Exhibitor, Director's Eye, MOMA, Oxford, 1992; Exhibition Design of Treasures of the Mind, Trinity College, Dublin Quatercentury (400 years), 1992; Design of Eastern Art Gallery, Ashmolean Museum, Oxford, 1996; Films: Comrades, 1985; Withnail & I, 1986; The Lonely Passion of Judith Hearne, 1987; How to Get Ahead in Advertising, 1988; The Krays, 1989; Let Him Have It, 1990; Century, 1992; Food of Love, 1996; Honest, 1999; High Heels, 2000; Television: Running Late, 1992; The Dying of the Light, 1994; Cruel Train, 1994; Cider With Rosie, 1998; A Rather English Marriage, 1998; David Copperfield, 1999; Last of the Blonde Bombshells, 1999; Hans Christian Andersen, 2001; Death in Holy Orders, 2002; The Deal, 2003; Death on the Nile, 2003; Archangel, 2004; The Queen's Sister, 2005; Sweeney Todd, 2005; Longford, 2006; Miss Marple, 2006-07; Old Curiosity Shop, 2007; Lost in Austen, 2007; The Prisoner, 2008; Kidnap and Ransom, 2010; Dr Who, 2010/11. Publications: Architectural paper models for the National Trust, 1972; Landmark Trust, 1973; St Georges Chapel, 1974; Architectural drawings for Hugh Evelyn Prints, 1973. Memberships: BAFTA; GBFD. Address: 3 Warnborough Road, Oxford OX2 6HZ, England.

PIERCE Mary, b. 15 January 1975, Montreal, Canada. Tennis Player. Career: Turned Professional, 1989; Moved to France, 1990; Represented France in Federation Cup, 1991; 1st Career Title, Palermo, 1991; Runner-up, French Open, 1994; Winner, Australian Open, 1995, Tokyo Nichirei, 1995; Semi-Finalist, Italian Open, Candian Open, 1996; Finalist, Australian Open singles, 1997, doubles with Martina Hingis, 2000; Winner of singles and doubles, with M Hingis, French Open, 2000; Highest singles ranking No 3; Winner of doubles, with M Hingis, Pan Pacific; French Federation Cup team, 1990-92, 1994-97; French Olympic team, 1992, 1996; 24 WTA Tour singles and doubles titles (by end 2002); France's (rising star) Burgeon Award, 1992; WTA Tour Comeback Player of the Year, 1997. Address: c/o WTA, 133 First Street North East, St Petersburg, FL 33701, USA.

PIGOTT-SMITH Tim (Timothy Peter), b. 13 May 1946, Rugby, England. Actor; Director. m. Pamela Miles, 1 son. Education: BA (Hons), Bristol University, 1964-67; Bristol Old Vic Theatre School, 1967-69. Career: Extensive theatre work includes most recently: Mourning Becomes Electra at the Royal National Theatre; Hecuba at the Donmar; Broadway: Sherlock Holmes and the Iceman Cometh; Television includes: The Lost Boys; Angelo and Hotspur for BBC Shakespeare series; Francis Crick in Life Story; Ronald Merrick in Jewel in the Crown; The Chief; The Vice; Richard Hale in North and South; The Last Flight to Kuwait, 2007; Holby City, 2007. Films include: Clash of the Titans; Escape to Victory; Remains of the Day; Bloody Sunday; Alexander; V for Vendetta, 2005; Entente Cordiale, 2005; Flyboys, 2005; Quantum of Solace, 2008; Alice in Wonderland, 2010; Director: The Real Thing, National Tour, 2005; Royal Hunt of the Sun for a National Tour, 1989; Hamlet in Regent's Park, 1994; Samuel Beckett's Company, Edinburgh Fringe and the Donmar; Regular broadcaster. Publications: Out of India, 1986, 1990, 1997; Numerous audio-books. Honours: BAFTA, TV Times and Broadcasting Press Guild Best Actor Awards for the Jewel in the Crown, 1984; Fringe First, Edinburgh Festival for Samuel Beckett's Company; Honorary Dlitt, Leicester University, 2002. Memberships: Special Lecturer, Bristol University Drama Department. Address: Actual Management, 7 Gt Russell Street, London WC1B 3NH, England. Website: www.timpigott.smith.co.uk

PIKE David Alan Wingeate, b. 2 October 1930, Kent, England. Distinguished Professor Emeritus. m. Carol Lynn Tjernell, 2 daughters. Education: BA, McGill University, 1960; MA, Universidad Interamericana Mexico, 1961; Docteur de l'Université de Toulouse, 1966; PhD, Stanford University, 1968. Appointments: Allied Intelligence G2/GSI Trieste, 1950-52; Lloyds Broker, London, 1952-55; Assistant Director, Institute of Hispanic American and Luso-Brazilian Studies, Stanford, 1962-64; Professor of Contemporary History and Politics, 1968-, Distinguished Professor, 1993-, Emeritus, 2001-, The American University of Paris; Vice-Chairman, California Institute of International Studies, Stanford, 1996-; Director of Research, American Graduate School of International Relations and Diplomacy, 2003-; Board, World Association of International Studies, Stanford, 2006. Publications: Les Français et la Guerre d'Espagne, 1975; In the Service of Stalin, 1993; Españoles en el Holocausto, 2003; Betrifft: KZ Mauthausen, 2005; Franco and the Axis Stigma, 2008; Crimes Against Women, 2010. Honours: Sociétaire des Gens de Lettres de France; Fellow of the Royal Historical Society; Medalla de la Universidad Autónoma de Madrid. Listed in Who's Who publications and biographical dictionaries. Memberships: Association de la Presse anglo-américaine de Paris. Address: 62 rue Jean-Baptiste Pigalle, 75009 Paris, France. E-mail: david.pike@aup.fr Website: www.ac.aup.fr

PIKE Edward Roy, b. 4 December 1929, Perth, Western Australia. Physicist. Education: BSc, Mathematics, 1953, BSc, Physics, 1954, PhD, Physics, 1957, University College, Cardiff, Wales. Appointments: Fellow, American Society for Testing Materials, University College, Cardiff, 1954-58; Research Assistant, University of Wales, Cardiff, 1957-58; Instructor, Massachusetts Institute of Technology, USA, 1958-60; Senior Scientific Officer to Chief Scientific Officer, Royal Signals and Radar Establishment, Malvern, England, 1960-86; Visiting Professor of Mathematics, Imperial College of Science and Technology, London, 1984-85; Non-Executive Director, Richard Clay plc (Printers), 1984-86; Clerk Maxwell Professor of Theoretical Physics, King's College, London, 1986-; Head of School of Physical Sciences and Engineering, King's College, London, 1991-94; Chairman, Stilo Technology Ltd (Publishing and World Wide Web software), 1995-2002; Chairman, 2000-02, Non-Executive Director, 2002-04, Stilo International plc; Director, Phonologica Ltd, 2004-. Publications: 300 papers and 10 books in the fields of theoretical physics, X-Ray diffraction, statistics, imaging and optics, inverse problems, compact disc technology. Honours: Charles Parsons Prize, Royal Society, 1975; McRobert Award, Confederation of Engineering Institutions, 1977; Annual Achievement Award, Worshipful Company of Scientific Instrument Makers, 1978; Civil Service Award to Inventors, 1980; Guthrie Medal and Prize, Institute of Physics, 1995; Fellow, University College Cardiff; Fellow King's College London; Fellow of the Institute of Mathematics and Applications; Fellow of the Institute of Physics; Fellow of the Optical Society of America; Fellow of the Royal Society. Address: Physics Department, King's College London, Strand, London WC2R 2LS, England.

PIKE Lionel John, b. 7 November 1939, Bristol, England. University Professor; Organist. m. Jennifer Marguerite Parkes, 2 daughters. Education: BA, Class I, Music, B Mus, MA, D Phil, Pembroke College, Oxford; FRCO; ARCM. Appointments: Organist, 1969-2005, Lecturer in Music, 1965-80, Senior Lecturer in Music and College Organist, 1980-2004, Professor of Music, 2004-05, Royal Holloway College (University of London), UK; Retired, 2005. Publications: Beethoven, Sibelius and "The Profound Logic", 1978; Hexachords in Late Renaissance Music, 1998; Vaughan Williams and the Symphony, 2003; Pills to Purge Melancholy: The Evolution of the English Ballet, 2004; Tudor Anthems, 2010. Honours: Book: Beethoven, Sibelius and "The Profound Logic", named by Choice Magazine as one of the three best academic books in any subject for the year 1978-79; Limpus Prize for FRCO; Honorary Fellowship, Royal Holloway College, 2007. Memberships: Royal College of Organists; Havergal Brian Society; Robert Simpson Society; Herbert Howells Society; Ralph Vaughan Williams Society. Address: 34 Alderside Walk, Englefield Green, Egham, Surrey, TW20 0LY, England. E-mail: lionel.pike@hotmail.co.uk

PILIPAVICIUS Vytautas, b. 10 July 1973, Vilnius, Lithuania. Professor; Agronomist; Educator. m. Vilma, 2 daughters. Education: Degree (cum laude), Agronomy, Lithuanian University of Agriculture, 1996; Dr, Biomedical Sciences, 2000; Habilitation procedure, Biomedical Sciences, 2007. Appointments: Inspector for organic farming, Gaja and Ekoagros, Kaunas, Lithuania, 1996-99; Researcher, 1999-2002, 2004-05, Associate Professor, 2000-07, Vice-dean, Agronomy Faculty, 2005-08, President of Professors Union, 2008-11, Lithuanian University of Agriculture; Expert, Lithuanian State Science and Studies Foundation, Vilnius, 2003-09; Professor, Weed Science and Agroecology of Soil Management Department, 2007-; Eureka Technical Expert, 2008-, Court Expert, 2010-, Brussels; Bulgaria National Foundation Expert, 2008-; EWRS National Representative for Lithuania, 2008-; Editor in Charge, Journal of Agronomy Research, 2009-; Editorial Board Member, Lithuanian University of Agriculture Journal, Vagos, 2009-10, and Agricultural Sciences, 2011-. Publications: General Agronomy, 2000, 2001, 2004, 2006, 2009; Organic Crop Production and Horticulture, 2006; Crop Communities and Their Investigations, 2008; Renewable Resources and Waste Treatment, 2008; Agroecology, 2008; Organic Agriculture, 2008; Basics of Organic Agriculture, 2009; Plant growing technologies in Organic Agriculture, 2009; Feedstuffs: Conventional and Organic, 2010; Weed Control System in Organic Agriculture, 2010; Over 100 articles in professional journals. Honours: Lithuanian Academy of Science, 2002; Lithuanian University of Agriculture, 2001, 2003, 2005, 2010; Research Fellowship, Ministry of Science & Education, 2003; Acknowledgement Awards, Lithuanian University of Agriculture, 2004, 2008; Diploma for best articles, Zemes ukis journal, 2006; Education Mobility Foundation Award, Erasmus Exchange Programme, 2007; Diploma, Lithuanian Ministry of Agriculture, 2008; Chamber of Agriculture, Republic of Lithuania, 2009; Centre of Programme Leader and Farmers' Training Methodology, 2009; State of Lithuania Medal of January 13. Memberships: European Weed Research Society; International Soil Tillage Research Organisation; International Weed Science Society; Japan Weed Science Society; Nordic Association of Agricultural Scientists; European Network of Organic Agriculture University Teachers; Lithuanian Weed Science Society; Lithuanian Soil Tillage Research Organisation; Lithuanian Society of Agronomy; Lithuanian Association of Researchers; Union of Professors of Lithuanian University of Agriculture; Lithuanian Society of Soil Science. Address: Lithuanian University of Agriculture, Department of Soil Management, Studentu street 11, LT-53361 Kaunas-Akademia, Lithuania.

PILIPOSYAN Vahagn, b. 4 January 1970, Yerevan, Armenia. Lawyer. m. Ruzanna, 1 son, 1 daughter. Education: Diploma of Higher Education, Law Department, Yerevan State University. Appointments: Advocate and Professor. Publications: Numerous articles in professional journals; 3 brochures of translated UN conventions. Honours: Doctor of Law, Honorary Professor. Memberships: APSA; Chamber of Armenian Advocates. Address: Home 24, Noy District, Yerevan, 0065, Armenia. E-mail: vpiliposyan@mail.ru

PILLAY Gerald John, b. 21 December 1953, Natal, South Africa. Vice Chancellor; Rector. m. Nirmala, 2 sons. Education: Bachelor of Arts, 1975, Bachelor of Divinity (with distinction), 1979, DTheol, University of Durban-Westville,

1985; Doctor of Philosophy, Rhodes University, 1983; BA, BD, D Theol, Philosophical Theology, Durban; PhD, Ecclesiastical History, Rhodes University. Appointments: Lecturer, Senior Lecturer, Church History, University of Durban-Westville, 1979-87; Professor, Modern Church History, University of South Africa, 1988-96; Foundation Professor of Theology, 1997-2003, Dean of Liberal Arts, 1998-2003, Otago University, New Zealand; Rector & Chief Executive, 2003-05, Vice Chancellor & Rector, 2005-, Liverpool Hope University. Publications: Voices of Liberation, vol 1, 1993; Religion at the Limits?: Pentecostalism among Indian South Africans, 1994; Editor, A History of Christianity in South Africa, vol 1, 1994; Contributions to books and learned journals. Honours: DL, Merseyside, 2009; FRSA. E-mail: pillayg@hope.ac.uk

PILLINGER Colin Trevor, b. 9 May 1943, Bristol, England. Professor of Planetary Sciences. m. Judith Mary, 1 son, 1 daughter. Education: BSc, PhD, University of Wales; DSc, University of Bristol. Appointments: Research Assistant, Research Associate, University of Bristol, 1968-76; Research Associate, Senior Research Associate, University of Cambridge, 1976-84; Open University Senior Research Fellow, 1984-90; PI of NASA Apollo Programme; Personal Chair in Planetary Services, Department of Earth Sciences, Open University, 1990-97; Principal Investigator, ESA Inc, Rosetta Cometary Mission, 1994-2000; Gresham Professor of Astronomy, 1996-2000; Lead Scientist, Beagle 2 Project for ESA Mars Express Mission, 1997-; Head, Planetary & Space Sciences Research Institute, 1997-2005; Professor, Planetary Sciences, 1997-; Emeritus Gresham Professor of Astronomy. Publications: Over 1,000 refereed papers, conference proceedings, abstracts, reports and scientific journalism; 4 books. Honours: Aston Medal, 2003; CBE, 2004; A C Clarke Award, 2004; BIS Space Achievement Medal, 2005; Reginald Mitchell Memorial Medal, 2006; Asteroid 15614 named Pillinger. Memberships: FRAS, 1981; Fellow, Meteoritical Society, 1986; FRS, 1993; FRGS, 1993; Fellow, IAU, 1993; Fellow, University College, Swansea, 2003. Address: Planetary & Space Sciences Research Institute, The Open University, Walton Hall, Milton Keynes, Buckinghamshire MK7 6AA, England. E-mail: c.t.pillinger@open.ac.uk

PINCHER (Henry) Chapman, b. 29 March 1914, Ambala, India. Author. m. (1), 1 daughter, 1 son, (2) Constance Wolstenholme, 1965. Education: BSc Honours, Botany, Zoology, 1935. Appointments: Staff, Liverpool Institute, 1936-40; Royal Armoured Corps, 1940; Defence, Science and Medical Editor, Daily Express, 1946-73; Assistant Editor, Daily Express, Chief Defence Correspondent, Beaverbrook Newspapers, 1972-79; Academician, Russian Academy for Defence, Security and Internal Affairs, 2005-. Publications: Breeding of Farm Animals, 1946; A Study of Fishes, 1947; Into the Atomic Age, 1947; Spotlight on Animals, 1950; Evolution, 1950; It's Fun Finding Out (with Bernard Wicksteed), 1950; Sleep and How to Get More of It, 1954; Sex in Our Time, 1973; Inside Story, 1978; Their Trade is Treachery, 1981; Too Secret Too Long, 1984; The Secret Offensive, 1985; Traitors - the Labyrinth of Treason, 1987; A Web of Deception, 1987; The Truth about Dirty Tricks, 1991; One Dog and Her Man, 1991; Pastoral Symphony, 1993; A Box of Chocolates, 1993; Life's a Bitch!, 1996; Tight Lines!, 1997; Treachery, 2009. Novels: Not with a Bang, 1965; The Giantkiller, 1967; The Penthouse Conspirators, 1970; The Skeleton at the Villa Wolkonsky, 1975; The Eye of the Tornado, 1976; The Four Horses, 1978; Dirty Tricks, 1980; The Private World of St John Terrapin, 1982; Contamination, 1989. Honours: Granada Award, Journalist of the Year, 1964; Reporter of the Decade, 1966; Honorary DLitt, University of Newcastle upon Tyne, 1979; King's College, London, fellow, 1979; Elected, Moscow Academy for Defence, Security & Law & Order, 2005; Russian Order of the Great Victory, 2006. Address: The Church House, 16 Church Street, Kintbury, Near Hungerford, Berkshire RG17 9TR, England.

PINCHUK Leonid, b. 14 May 1938, Gomel, Belarus. Engineer. m. L Kasatkina, 1966, 1 son, 2 daughters. Education: Graduated Engineer-Mechanic, Belarus Institute of Railway Engineers 1960; PhD, Engineering, 1972; DrSci, Engineering, 1983; Full Professor, Materials Science, Moscow,1990. Appointments: Technologist, Engineer-Designer, Locomotive Plant, Yaroslavl, 1960-68; Engineer, Researcher, Laboratory Chief, Department Head, Metal-Polymer Research Institute, Academy of Sciences of Belarus, Gomel, 1968-. Publications: 25 books; More than 409 articles in magazines and journals; 323 inventions. Honour: Honoured Inventor of Belarus, 2004. Memberships: Academician, Belarus Engineering Academy; Active Member, New York Academy of Sciences; National Geographical Society; Correspondent Member, International Eurasian Academy of Science. Address: MPPI Belarus NAS, Kirov Str, 32A Gomel, 246050, Belarus. E-mail: mpri@mail.ru

PINE Courtney, b. 18 March 1964, London, England. Jazz Musician (saxophone). 1 son, 3 daughters. Career: International tours, with own reggae and acoustic jazz bands; Trio (with Cameron Pierre, Talvin Singh) opened for Elton John and Ray Cooper, The Zenith, Paris and Royal Albert Hall, London, European Tour, 1994; Teacher's Jazz European tour, 1996; Support to Cassandra Wilson, US and Canada, 1996; Tours, Japan, South Africa and UK, 1996; Festivals in Europe, Japan, Thailand, 1996; Television appearances; Regular guest, Later With Jools Holland; Black Christmas, Channel 4; The White Room, 1996; Featured Artist on BBC's Perfect Day recording. Recordings include: Albums: Journey To The Urge Within, 1987; Destiny's Song, 1988; The Vision's Tale, 1989; Closer To Home, 1990; Within The Realms Of Our Dreams; To The Eyes Of Creation; Modern Day Jazz Stories', 1996; Underground, 1997; Another Story, 1998; History is Made at Night (soundtrack), 1999; Back in the Day (soundtrack), 2000; Devotion, 2003; Resistance, 2005; Transition in Tradition, 2009; Featured guest on: Wandering Spirit (with Mick Jagger); Jazzmatazz, Guru; Jazzmatazz II - The New Reality, Guru; Summertime, track on The Glory of Gershwin (Larry Adler tribute album); Evita (with Madonna); Devotion, 2003; Radio: Presenter, BBC Radio 2 series, Millennium Jazz, 1999; 5 series of BBC Radio 2 Jazz Crusade, 1999-2004; UK Black 2003, Jazz Makers. Honours: Mercury Music Prize, one of Albums of the Year, 1996; Best Jazz Act, MOBO, 1996, 1997; Best Jazz Act, BBC Jazz Awards, 2001; Gold Badge, Academy Composers and Songwriters, 2002. Address: c/o 33 Montpelier Street, Brighton, BN1 3DI, England. Website: www.courtney-pine.com

PINHEIRO Marcia Ricci, b. 6 January 1971, Porto Alegre, Brazil. Researcher. Education: PG Dip, Translation/Interpretation, 1991; PG Dip, Systems Analysis, 1992; PG Dip, Logic, 2000; PhD, Inequalities, 2001; PhD, Networks, 2002; PhD, ODES, 2003; others. Appointments: Postgraduate Student & Tutor, University of Queensland, 2000; Postgraduate Student & Tutor, VUT, 2001; Postgraduate Student, Tutor & Relief Lecturer, RMIT, 2002-03; Cancer Research Educator, Cancer & Bowel Research Trust, 2010-12; others. Publications: A solution to the Sorites Paradox-Semiotica, 2006; Starants – Applied Mathematics and Computation, 2007; First Note on S_2-convexity, Advances in Pure Mathematics, 2011; others. Honours: Listed in biographical dictionaries; International

Postgraduate Research Scholarship, VUT, 2001, and RMIT, 2002; Chancellor's Scholarship, RMIT, 2002; others. Memberships: Research Group on Mathematical Inequalities in Pure and Applied Mathematics. Address: PO Box 12396, A'Beckett St, Melbourne, VIC 8006, Australia.

PINSENT Sir Matthew Clive, b. 10 October 1970, Norfolk, England. Former Oarsman. m. Dee, 2 sons, 1 daughter. Education: University of Oxford. Career: First represented UK at Junior World Championships, 1987, 1988; Gold Medal, coxless pairs (with Tim Foster), 1988; Competed 3 times in University Boat Race for Oxford, 1990, 1991, 1993, winning twice; Gold Medal, coxless pairs (with Steve Redgrave), World Championships, 1991, 1993, 1994, 1995; Olympic Games, Barcelona, 1992, Atlanta, 1996; Gold Medal, coxless fours (with Steve Redgrave, Tim Foster and James Cracknell), World Championships, 1997, 1998, 1999, Olympic Games, Sydney, 2000; Gold Medal, coxless pairs (with James Cracknell), World Championships, 2001, 2002 (new world record); Gold Medal, coxless fours (with Cracknell, Coode and Williams) Olympic Games, Athens, 2004; Member, International Olympic Committee, 2002-04; Retired, 2004. Publication: A Lifetime in a Race, 2004. Honours: International Rowing Federation Male Rower of the Year; Member, BBC Sports Team of the Year, 2004; Knighted, 2004. Address: c/o Professional Sports Partnerships Ltd, The Town House, 63 The High Street, Chobham, GU24 8AF, England. Website: www.matthewpinsent.com

PIOMBINO-MASCALI Dario, b. 16 September 1977, Messina, Italy. Anthropologist. Education: MA, Archaeology, 2002; PhD, Palaeoanthropology and Pathocoenosis, 2007. Appointments: Senior Researcher, European Academy of Bolzano, 2008-; Consultant, Vatican Museums, 2009-; Research Associate, Reiss-Engelhorn Museen, Mannheim, 2010-; Curator, The Capuchin Catacombs, Palermo, 2010-. Honours: Grantee, National Geographic Society, 2008; Honorary Member, American Society of Embalmers, 2008. Memberships: Paleopathology Association. Address: EURAC, Viale Druso 1, 39100, Bolzano, South Tyrol, Italy. E-mail: dario.piombino@eurac.edu

PIPERAKI Stavroula Ina, b. 14 September 1965, Athens, Greece. Pharmacist. m. George Theodossopoulos, 2 sons. Education: French Literature Course, Sorbonne IV, 1984; Computer Sciences Course, Hellenic Center of Productivity, 1985; PhD, Pharmaceutical Sciences, University of Athens, 1993. Appointments: Special Postgraduate Scholar, Division of Pharmaceutical Chemistry, Laboratory of Pharmaceutical Analysis, 1990-93; Scientific Training Manager, Pancosmetics Hellas, 1991-92; Researcher Program, National Drug Organisation, 1991-93; Regulatory Affairs Manager, Aventis SA, 1993-96; Researcher, Department of Chemistry, University of York, 1993; Teacher, Postgraduate Program, Division of the Pharmaceutical Technology, University of Athens, 1995; Teacher, Postgraduate Program, Division of the Pharmaceutical Chemistry, University of Athens, 1996-97; Manager, Department of Regulatory Affairs, Pharmacovigilance Department, Aventis SA, 1996-98; Manager and Owner, pharmacy, Athens, 1997-. Publications: Co-author, 17 articles in scientific journals; 20 conference papers; Participant in several congresses, meetings, seminars and workshops. Honours: National School Awards for Excellency, 1979-83; Listed in international biographical dictionaries. Memberships: Pharmaceutical Association of Pharmacists of Attica; Panhellenic Association of Pharmacists; American Association for the Advancement of Science; AMICAL; European Society of Regulatory Affairs.

PIQUET Nelson, b. 17 August 1952, Rio de Janeiro, Brazil. Racing Driver. m. (1) Maria Clara, (2) Vivianne Leao, 1 son. Appointments: 1st Grand Prix, Germany, 1978; Member, Ensign Grand Prix Team, 1978, BS McLaren Team, 1978, Brabham Team, 1978-85, Williams Team, 1986-87, Lotus Team, 1988-89, Benetton Team, 1990; Winner of 23 Grand Prix; Formula One World Champion, 1981, 1983, 1987.

PISARCHIK Alexander N, b. 3 June 1954, Minsk, Belarus. Physicist. m. Liudmila Kotashova, 1 son, 4 daughters. Education: MS, Belorussian State University, 1976; PhD, Institute of Physics, Minsk, 1990. Appointments: Visiting Professor, University Libre, Brussels, 1992; Visiting Professor, Universitat Autonoma de Barcelona, 1993-94; 1997-99; Visiting Professor, University of Iceland, Reykjavik, 1995; Senior Researcher, Institute of Physics, Minsk, 1996-99; Research Professor, Centro de Investigaciones en Optica, Leon, Gto, Mexico, 1999-. Publications: Contributor, articles to professional journals including Physics review A and E; Physics review Letters; Physica D; Physics Letters A; Optical Communications; Editor, Recent Advances in Laser Dynamics: Control and Synchronization, 2008. Honours: First Prize, National Academy of Science, Minsk, 1999. Memberships: European Physical Society; Academia Mexicana de Optica; Society for Industrial and Applied Mathematics; Mexican National System of Researchers (SNI, level 3); Mexican National System of Evaluators on Science and Technology (SINECYT); Institute of Electrical and Electronics Engineers. Address: Centro de Investigaciones en Optica AC, Loma del Bosque # 115, Col Lomas del Campestre, 37150 Leon, Guanajuato, Mexico. E-mail: apisarch@foton.cio.mx

PITCHER Harvey John, b. 26 August 1936, London, England. Writer. Education: BA, 1st Class Honours, Russian, University of Oxford. Publications: Understanding the Russians, 1964; The Chekhov Play: A New Interpretation, 1973; When Miss Emmie was in Russia, 1977; Chekhov's Leading Lady, 1979; Chekhov: The Early Stories, 1883-1888 (with Patrick Miles), 1982; The Smiths of Moscow, 1984; Lily: An Anglo-Russian Romance, 1987; Muir and Mirrielees: The Scottish Partnership that became a Household Name in Russia, 1994; Witnesses of the Russian Revolution, 1994; Chekhov: The Comic Stories, 1998; Responding to Chekov: The Journey of a Lifetime, 2010. Contributions to: Times Literary Supplement. Address: 37 Bernard Road, Cromer, Norfolk NR27 9AW, England.

PITKEATHLEY Jill Elizabeth, b. 4 January 1940, Guernsey, Channel Islands. Peer of the Realm. 1 son, 1 daughter. Education: Ladies College, Guernsey. Appointments President, Community Council, Berkshire; Chair, CHRE (Council for Healthcare Regulatory Excellence); Labour Peer. Publications: Only Child, 1994; Cassandra and Jane, 2005; Dearest Cousin Jane, 2009. Honours: Honorary Degrees from Bristol and Metropolitan Universities; OBE, 1993; Peerage, 1997. Address: House of Lords, London, SWIA 0PW, England.

PITMAN Jennifer Susan, b. 11 June 1946, England. Racehorse Trainer. m. (1) Richard Pitman, 1965, 2 sons, (2) David Stait, 1997. Career: National Hunt Trainer, 1975-99; Director, Jenny Pitman Racing Ltd, 1975-99; Racing and Media Consultant, 1999-; Winners include: Corbiere, Welsh National, 1982, Grand National, 1983; Burrough Hill Lad, Welsh National, 1984, Cheltenham Gold Cup, 1984, King George VI Gold Cup, 1984, Hennessy Gold Cup, 1984; Smith's Man, Whitbread Trophy, 1985; Gainsay, Ritz Club National Hunt Handicap, 1987, Sporting Life

Weekend Chase, 1987; Garrison Savannah, Cheltenham Gold Cup, 1991; Wonderman, Welsh Champion Hurdle, 1991; Don Valentino, Welsh Champion Hurdle, 1992; Royal Athlete, Grand National, 1995; Willsford, Scottish National, 1995; Last Winner, Scarlet Emperor, Huntingdon, 1999. Publications: Glorious Uncertainty (autobiography), 1984; Jenny Pitman: The Autobiography, 1999; On the Edge, 2002; Double Deal, 2002; The Dilemma, 2003; The Vendetta, 2004. Honours include: Racing Personality of the Year, Golden Spurs, 1983; Commonwealth Sports Award, 1983, 1984; Piper Heidsieck Trainer of the Year, 1983-84, 1989-90; Variety Club of Great Britain Sportswoman of the Year, 1984; OBE, 1998. Address: Owls Barn, Kintbury, Hungerford, Berkshire, RG17 9XS, England.

PITT Brad, b. 18 December 1963, Shawnee, Oklahoma, USA. Film Actor. m. Jennifer Anniston, 2000, divorced, 2005, 1 daughter, twins (son and daughter) with Angelina Jolie. Creative Works: TV appearances include: Dallas (series); Glory Days (series); Too Young to Die? (film); The Image (film); Films include: Cutting Glass, Happy Together, 1989; Across the Tracks, 1990; Contact, Thelma and Louise, 1991; The Favor, Johnny Suede, Cool World, A River Runs Through It, 1992; Kalifornia, 1993; Legend of the Fall, 1994; 12 Monkeys, 1995; Sleepers, Mad Monkeys, Tomorrow Never Dies, 1996; Seven Years in Tibet, The Devil's Own, 1997; Meet Joe Black, 1998; Fight Club, Snatch, 2000; The Mexican, Spy Game, Ocean's Eleven, 2001; Confessions of a Dangerous Mind, 2002; Sinbad: Legend of the Seven Seas (voice), 2003; Troy, Ocean's Twelve, 2004; Mr & Mrs Smith, 2005; Babel, 2006; Ocean's Thirteen, The Assassination of Jesse James by the Coward Robert Ford, 2007; Burn after Reading, The Curious Case of Benjamin Button, 2008; Inglourious Bastards, 2009; Moneyball, 2011; Killing Them Softly, 2012; 12 Years a Slave, World War Z, The Counselor, 2013. Address: Creative Artists Agency, 9830 Wilshire Boulevard, Beverly Hills, CA 90212, USA.

PIUNOVSKIY Alexei, b. 16 March 1954, Moscow, Russia. Mathematician. m. Galina Piunovskaya, 2 daughters. Education: MSc, Electrical Engineering, 1971-76, MSc, Applied Mathematics, 1980, PhD, Applied Mathematics, 1981, Moscow Institute of Electronic Technology. Appointments: Engineer, Researcher, Moscow Institute of Electronic Technology, 1976-84; Head of Group, Moscow Institute of Physics and Technology, 1984-2000; Senior Lecturer, Reader, University of Liverpool, 2000-. Publications: 90 publications in total; Editor, Modern Trends in Controlled Stochastic Processes, 2010. Honours: Multiple grants from Russian Fund of Basic Research, EPSRC, Royal Society, LMS, British Council. Membership: The OR Society; American Mathematical Society. Address: Department of Mathematical Sciences, Peach Street, The University of Liverpool, Liverpool L69 7ZL, England.

PLATT Jan Kaminis, b. 27 September 1936, St Petersburg, Florida, USA. County Official. m. William R Platt, 1 son. Education: BA, Florida State University, 1958; Postgraduate, University of Florida Law School, 1958-59, University of Virginia, 1962, Vanderbilt University, 1964. Appointments include: Public School Teacher, Hillsborough County, Tampa, Florida, 1959-60; Field Director, Girl Scouts Suncoast Council, Tampa, 1960-62; City Councilman, Tampa City Council, 1974-78; County Commissioner, Hillsborough County, 1978-94, 1996-2004; Chairman, Hillsborough County Board County Commissioners, 1980-81, 1998-99; Chairman, Tampa Bay Regional Planning Council, 1982; Chairman, Hillsborough Area Regional Transit Authority, 2002-03; Co-Chairman, National Association of Counties Energy and Land Use Steering Committee; Board, Florida Aquarium, 2003-; Board Member, 1984-94, 2001-03, Hillsborough County Hospital Authority, Tampa; Chairman of numerous other local government and community committees. Honours: Numerous awards and honours include most recently: Freedom to Read Roll of Honor, American Library Association, 1999; Community Service Award, Tampa Bay Muslim Alliance, 2000; Liberty Bell Award, Hillsborough County Bar Association, 2000; Black Bear Award, Tampa Bay Sierra Club, 2001; Jan Kaminis Platt Regional Library Dedicated, 2000; League of Women Voters Lifetime Achievement Award; Hermann A Goldner Regional Leadership Award, 2010; Listed in Who's Who publications and biographical dictionaries. Memberships include: President, Suncoast Girl Scout Council; President, Tampa Bay Area Phi Beta Kappa Alumni; President, Hillsborough County Head Start Foundation; Vice-President, Hillsborough County Bar Auxiliary; Chair, Friends of the Library Development Committee; Board, Sierra Club of Tampa Bay; Board, Tampa Audubon Society; Board, Tampa Historical Society; Member, American Association of University Women; President, Tampa/Hillsborough County Literary Council.

PLESKO Ivan, b. 13 June 1930, Selpice, Slovakia. Physician. m. Anna, 2 daughters. Education: MD, Comenius University, Bratislava, 1955; PhD, 1964; DSc, Slovak Academy of Sciences, Bratislava, 1987; Associate Professor, 1968. Appointments: Research Assistant, 1955-68; Assistant Professor, Epidemiology, Comenius University, Bratislava, 1968-76; Host Researcher, Institute Pasteur, Paris, 1968-; Assistant Professor, University of Constantine, Algery, 1971-73; Head, Department of Epidemiology, Cancer Research Institute, Slovak Academy of Sciences, 1976-; Head, National Cancer Registry of Slovakia, 1980-2005. Publications: Atlas of Cancer Occurrence in Slovakia; Epidemiology of Lung Cancer; Atlas of Cancer Mortality in Central Europe; More than 190 papers in professional journals. Honours: Jesenius Medal, Research in medical sciences; Golden Medal, Research and Art; Gold medal of Health Promotion Foundation, Warsaw, Poland; Gold medal of the Slovak Medical Society; Award Panacea for lifelong research activities, 2004; Important individuality of Slovak Academy of Sciences, 2005; others; Listed in national and international dictionaries. Memberships: League Against Cancer, Slovakia; International Association of Cancer Registries; Science Council; Czech National Cancer Registry; European Institute of Oncology. Address: Pri Suchom mlyne 62, 811 04 Bratislava, Slovakia.

PLEVA Jaroslav, b. 27 May 1941, Prag, Czech Republic. Chemist; Corrosion Engineer. m. Zita, 2 daughters. Education: MSc, Analytical Chemistry, 1972; PhD, Corrosion Engineering, 1976. Appointments: Swedish Corrosion Institute, 1976-79; Uddeholm Steel Works, 1979-2001; Retired, 2001-. Memberships: International Academy of Oral Medicine & Toxicology; Swedish ABS of Dental Mercury Patients. Address: Lakheden 20, SE-68392 Hagfors, Sweden.

PLOWRIGHT Dame Joan Anne, b. 28 October 1929, Brigg, Lancashire, England. Actress. m. (1) Roger Gage, 1953, (2) Sir Laurence (later Lord) Olivier, 1961-89 (his death)1 son, 2 daughters. Education: Old Vic Theatre School. Appointments: Member, Old Vic Company, toured South Africa, 1952-53. Creative Works: Plays and films include: Britannia Hospital, 1981; Richard Wagner, Cavell, Brimstone and Treacle, 1982; The Cherry Orchard, 1983; The Way of the World, 1984; Mrs Warren's Profession, Revolution, 1985;

DICTIONARY OF INTERNATIONAL BIOGRAPHY 36th EDITION

The House of Bernardo Alba, 1986; Drowning by Numbers, 1987; Uncle Vanya, The Dressmaker, The Importance of Being Earnest, 1988; Conquest of the South Pole, And a Nightingale Sang, I Love You to Death, 1989; Avalon, 1990; Time and the Conways, Enchanted April, Stalin, 1991; Denis the Menace, A Place for Annie, 1992; A Pin for the Butterfly, Last Action Hero, 1993; Widow's Peak, On Promised Land, Return of the Natives, Hotel Sorrento, A Pyromaniac's Love Story, The Scarlet Letter, Jane Eyre, 1994; If We Are Women, Surviving Picasso, Mr Wrong, 1995; 101 Dalmatians, The Assistant, 1996; Shut Up and Dance, Tom's Midnight Garden, It May Be the Last Time, 1997; America Betrayed, Tea with Mussolini, 1998; Return to the Secret Garden, Frankie and Hazel, 1999; Bailey's Mistake, Global Heresy, 2000; George and the Dragon, Bringing Down the House, 2002; The Great Goose Caper, Absolutely Perhaps, I Am David, 2003; George and the Dragon, 2004; Mrs Palfrey at the Claremont, 2005; Goose on the Loose, Curious George (voice);2006; The Spiderwick Chronicles, Knife Edge, 2008. Publications: And That's Not All, autobiography, 2001. Honours include: Best Actress, Tony Award, 1960; Best Actress, Evening Standard Award, 1964; Variety Club Award, 1976; Variety Club Film Actress of the Year Award, 1987; Golden Globe Award, 1993; 18th Crystal Award for Women in Film, USA, 1994. Address: c/o The Malthouse, Horsham Road, Ashurst, Steying, West Sussex BN44 3AR, England.

PLUMMER Christopher, b. 13 December 1929, Toronto, Canada. Actor. m. (1) Tammy Lee Grimes, 1956, 1 daughter, (2) Patricia Audrey Lewis, 1962 (divorced 1966), (3) Elaine Regina Taylor, 1970. Career: Theatre includes: Professional debut, Ottawa Repertory Theatre; Broadway debut, 1951-52; Numerous appearances in USA: Julius Caesar; The Tempest; The Lark; L'Histoire du Soldat; JB, 1951-61; The Resistable Rise of Arturo Ui; The Royal Hunt of the Sun, 1965-66; The Good Doctor, 1973; Othello, 1981; Macbeth, 1988; No Man's Lane, 1994; Barrymore, 1996; Many leading Shakespearean roles, Stratford Canadian Festival Co; British debut, Richard III, 1961; Leading actor, National Theatre Co of Great Britain, 1971-72; Many TV roles; Films include: The Fall of the Roman Empire; The Sound of Music; Inside Daisy Clover; Triple Cross; Oedipus the King; Nobody Runs Forever; Lock Up Your Daughters; The Royal Hunt of the Sun; Battle of Britain; Waterloo; The Pyx; The Spiral Staircase; Conduct Unbecoming; The Return of the Pink Panther; The Man Who Would Be King; Aces High, 1976; The Disappearance, 1977; International Velvet, The Silent Partner, 1978; Hanover Street, 1979; Murder by Decree, The Shadow Box, 1980; The Disappearance, The Janitor, 1981; The Amateur, 1982; Dreamscape, 1984; Playing for Keeps, Lily in Love, 1985; Dragnet, 1987; Souvenir, 1988; Shadow Dancing; Mindfield, Where the Heart Is, 1989; Star Trek VI: The Undiscovered Country, 1991; Malcolm X, 1992; Wolf, Dolores Claiborne, 1994; Twelve Monkeys, 1995; Skeletons, 1996; The Arrow, 1997; The Insider, All the Fine, 1999; The Dinosaur Hunter, Dracula, 2000; Lucky Break, Blackheart, A Beautiful Mind, Full Disclosure, 2001; Ararat, Nicholas Nickleby, 2002; Blizzard, Cold Creek Manor, 2003; National Treasure, Alexander, 2004; Tma, Our Fathers, Must Love Dog, Syriana, The New World, 2005; Inside Man, The Lake House, 2006; Man in the Chair, Closing the Ring, Emotional Arithmetic, Already Dead, 2007; My DogTulip, 2008; The Last Station, 2009; The Tempest, 2010; Priest, 2011 Barrymore, 2011; The Girl with the Dragon Tattoo, 2011. Honours: Companion of the Order of Canada, 1968; 2 Emmy Awards; Genie Award; 2 Tony Awards, 1974, 1997; Edwin Booth Lifetime Achievement Award, 1997; Jason Robards Award for Excellence in Theatre, 2002; Honorary Doctor of Laws, University of Western Ontario, 2004; Screen Actors Guild Award, 2012; Academy Award, 2012. Address: c/o Lou Pitt, The Pitt Group, 9465 Wilshire Boulevard, Suite 480, Beverly Hills, CA 90212, USA.

PODBERSCEK Anthony Louis, b. 27 October 1963, Cairns, Queensland, Australia. Research Associate. Education: BVSc, 1985, BVSc (First Class Post-graduate Honours), 1986, PhD, 1992, University of Queensland, Australia; Commonwealth Post-graduate Scholarship, 1987. Appointments: Tutor, Emmanuel College, 1988, Tutor, Department of Farm Animal Medicine and Production, 1989, 1991, Invited Lecturer, Tutor, Animal Behaviour and Animal Husbandry, 1990, University of Queensland; Veterinary Consultant, Brisbane City Council, Australia, Member of Companion Animal Task Force, 1991-92; Post-doctoral Research Associate, Centre for Animal Welfare & Anthrozoology, Department of Veterinary Medicine, University of Cambridge, 1992-; Editor, International Society for Anthrozoology newsletter, 1993-99; Editor-in-Chief, Anthrozoös, 1997-; Senior Member, Wolfson College, Cambridge, 2001-; Tutor, online course on animal welfare, Cambridge e-Learning Institute, 2004-06; Course Organiser, course on Animal Welfare Science, Ethics and Law, St Catherine's College, Cambridge, 2010-. Memberships: International Society for Anthrozoology; Society for Editors and Proofreaders; International Association of Veterinary Editors; International Society for Applied Ethology; Universities Federation for Animal Welfare; Society for Companion Animal Studies; Companion Animal Behaviour Therapy Study Group; Cambridge Philosophical Society; Association of Pet Behaviour Counsellors. Address: University of Cambridge, Centre for Animal Welfare & Anthrozoology, Department of Veterinary Medicine, Madingley Road, Cambridge, CB3 0ES, England. E-mail: alp18@cam.ac.uk

PODSIADLO Elzbieta, b. 9 August 1938, Doly Opacie, Kielce voivodship, Poland. Lecturer. Education: MS, Natural Sciences, University of Wroclaw, 1962; PhD, Agricultural Sciences, 1972, Assistant Professor in Agricultural Sciences, 1987, The Agricultural University of Warsaw; Professor, Biological Sciences, Silesian University, 2009. Appointments: Teacher, secondary school, 1962-63; Laboratory Assistant, Senior Research Assistant, Assistant Professor, Professor, Department of Zoology, Agricultural University of Warsaw, 1963-2008; Retired, 2008-. Publications include: Concept of the species of Asterodiaspis variolosa, 1990; Morphological adaptations for respiration in Coccidae, 2005; Study on Larval Diapause Development of Kermes quercus in Warsaw, Poland, 2011. Memberships: The Polish Entomological Society. Address: Department of Zoology, Agricultural University of Warsaw, Ciszewskiego 8, 02-786 Warsaw, Poland. E-mail: elzbieta_podsiadlo@sggw.pl

POITIER Sidney, b. 20 February 1927, Miami, Florida, USA. Actor. m. (1) Juanita Hardy, 4 daughters, (2) Joanna Shimkus, 2 daughters. Appointments: Army service, 1941-45; Actor with American Negro Theatre, 1946; Member, 1994-2003, President, 1994-2003, Board of Directors, Walt Disney Company; Ambassador to Japan from the Commonwealth of the Bahamas; Actor, films including: Cry the Beloved Country; Red Ball Express; Go, Man, Go; Blackboard Jungle, 1955; Goodbye My Lady, 1956; Edge of the City, Something of Value, 1957; The Mark of the Hawk, The Defiant Ones, 1958; Porgy and Bess, 1959; A Raisin in the Sun, Paris Blues, 1960; Lilies of the Field, 1963; The Long Ships, 1964; The Bedford Incident, 1965; The Slender Thread, A Patch of Blue, Duel at Diablo, 1966; To Sir With Love, In the Heat of the Night, 1967; Guess Who's Coming to Dinner, 1968; For the Love of

Ivy, 1968; The Lost Man, 1970; They Call Me Mister Tibbs, 1970; The Organization, 1971; The Wilby Conspiracy, 1975; Shoot to Kill, 1988; Deadly Pursuit, 1988; Separate But Equal, TV, 1992; Sneakers, Children of the Dust, TV, 1995; To Sir With Love II, TV, 1996; Actor, director, Buck and Preacher, 1972; Warm December, 1973; Uptown Saturday Night, 1974; Let's Do It Again, 1975; A Piece of the Action, 1977; One Man, One Vote, 1996; Mandela and de Klerk, (TV), 1997; Director, Stir Crazy, 1980; Hanky Panky, 1982; Got For It, 1984; Little Nikita, 1987; Ghost Dad, 1990; Sneakers, 1992; The Jackal, 1997; David and Lisa (TV), 1998; Free of Eden (TV), 1999; The Simple Life of Noah Dearborn (TV), 1999; The Last Brickmaker in America (TV), 2001. Publication: This Life, 1980. Honours: Silver Bear Award, Berlin, 1958; NT Film Critics Award, 1958; Academy Award, Oscar, Best Actor of 1963; Cecil B De Mille Award, 1982; Life Achievement Award, American Film Institute, 1992; Kennedy Centre Honours, 1995; Honorary KBE; Honorary Academy Award for Lifetime Achievement, 2002. Address: c/o CAA, 9830 Wilshire Boulevard, Beverly Hills, CA 90210, USA.

POLAŃSKI Roman, b. 18 August 1933, Paris, France. Film Director; Writer; Actor. m. (1) Barbara Kwiatkowska-Lass, divorced, (2) Sharon Tate, 1968, deceased 1969, (3) Emmannuelle Seigner, 1989, 2 children. Education: Polish Film School, Łódź. Career: Actor: A Generation; The End of the Night; See You Tomorrow; The Innocent Sorcerers; Two Men and a Wardrobe; The Vampire Killers; What? 1972; Blood for Dracula, 1974; Chinatown, 1974; The Tenant, 1976; Chassé-croisé, 1982; Back in the USSR, 1992; A Pure Formality, 1994; Dead Tired, 1994; Tribute to Alfred Lepetit, 2000; The Revenge, 2002; Director: Two Men and a Wardrobe, 1958; When Angels Fall; Le Gros et Le Maigre; Knife in the Water; The Mammals; Repulsion; Cul de Sac; The Vampire Killers, 1967; Rosemary's Baby, 1968; Macbeth, 1971; What? 1972; Lulu (opera), Spoleto Festival, 1974; Chinatown, 1974; The Tenant, 1976; Rigoletto (opera), 1976; Tess, 1980; Vampires Ball, 1980; Amadeus (play), 1981; Pirates, 1986; Frantic, 1988; Tales of Hoffman (opera), 1992; Bitter Moon, 1992; Death and the Maiden, 1984; Dance of the Vampire (play), 1997; The Ninth Gate, 1999; Icons; A Pure Formality; In Stuttgart, 2000; The Pianist, 2002; Zemsta, 2002; Oliver Twist, (Director), 2005; Rush Hour 3, 2007. Publications: Roman (autobiography), 1984. Honours: Prize, Venice Film Festival, 1962; Prize, Tours Film Festival, 1963; Prize, Berlin Film Festival, 1965, 1966; Best Director Award, Society of Film and TV Arts, 1974; Le Prix Raoul-Levy, 1975; Golden Globe Award, 1980; Pris René Clair for Lifetime Achievement, Academy Française, 1999; Best Film, Cannes Film Festival, 2002; Academy Award for Best Director, 2003; BAFTA Award for Best Film and Best Director, 2003. Address: c/o ICM, 8942 Wilshire Boulevard, Beverly Hills, CA 90211-1934, USA. Website: www.icmtalent.com

POLIAKOFF Stephen, b. 1952, London, England. Dramatist; Director. m. Sandy Welch, 1983, 1 son, 1 daughter. Education: Westminster School; University of Cambridge. Theatre: Clever Soldiers, 1974; The Carnation Gang, 1974; Hitting Town, 1975; City Sugar, 1976; Strawberry Fields, 1978; Shout Across the River, 1978; The Summer Party, 1980; Favourite Nights, 1981; Breaking the Silence, 1984; Coming into Land, 1987; Playing with Trains, 1989; Sienna Red, 1992; Sweet Panic, 1996; Blinded by the Sun, 1996; Talk of the City, 1998; Remember This, 1999; Sweet Panic, 2003; My City, 2011; Films: Hidden City, 1992; Close My Eyes, 1992; Century, 1995; The Tribe, 1998; Food of Love, 1998; Glorious 39, 2009; Astonish Me, 2011; TV plays include: Caught on a Train; She's Been Away; Shooting the Past, 1999; Perfect Strangers, 2001; The Lost Prince, 2003; Friends and Crocodiles, 2005; Gideon's Daughter, 2005; Joe's Palace, 2007; A Real Summer, 2007; Capturing Mary, 2007; Dancing on the Edge, 2013. Publications: Plays One, 1989; Plays Two, 1994; Plays Three; Sweet Panic; Blinded by the Sun; Talk of the City; Shooting the Past; Remember This. Honours include: Best British Film Award, 1992; Critic's Circle Best Play Award; Prix Italia; BAFTA Award; Venice Film Festival Prize; CBE, 2007. Address: 33 Donia Devonia Road, London N1 8JQ, England.

POLIDORI Paolo, b. 30 September 1963, Ripatransone, Italy. Professor. Degree, Science of Agriculture, 1990, PhD, Animal Husbandry, 1995, University of Milan. Appointments: Senior Researcher, 1993-2000, Associate Professor, Animal Husbandry, 2000-06, Full Professor, Animal Nutrition, 2006-, University of Camerino. Publications: Over 30 peer-reviewed articles in professional journals. Honours: Invited Lecturer, XVIII Congress of the Italian Scientific Association of Animal Production, Palermo, 2009. Memberships: Scientific Association of Animal Production, Italy; Italian Society of Veterinary Sciences, Italy. Address: University of Camerino, School of Pharmacy, via Circonvallazione 93, 62024 Matelica (MC), Italy. E-mail: paolo.polidori@unicam.it

POLLMANN Olaf Axel, b. 4 October 1972, Hannover, Germany. Doctor; Civil Engineer. m. Nelli, 2 daughters. Education: Dipl Ing, Civil Engineer, 2000; Dr Ing, Doctoral Degree in Environmental Engineering, 2006; Cand Dr rer nat, Faculty of Natural Sciences, 2011. Appointments: Research Scientist, Lemphana University of Luneberg, Germany, 2001-06; Self-employed Consulting Engineer, Water, Waste, Environment, 2001-; Postdoctoral Researcher, North-West University, South Africa, 2007-10; Senior Scientist, Project Management Agency, Federal Ministry of Education and Research, 2010-. Publications: Sustainable Agricultural Development (chapter 3), Optimising Anthopogenic Material Streams; Mine Tailings: Waste or Valuable Resource?; Optimising the Rehabilitation of polluted mine tailings; Using Evolutionary Algorithm; Numerous articles in professional journals. Honours: Certified International Lecturer for Higher Education; Certified Mining-Engineer; Listed in international biographical dictionaries. Memberships: DWA; IWMSA; WISA; ASK-Network; ResearchGATA. E-mail: info@ibp-pollman.de

POLYAKOV Petr Vasiljevich, b. 5 June 1935, Pyatigorsk, Stavropol region, Russia. m. Galina Vasiljevna Stepanova, 1 son, 1 daughter. Education: Engineer, Politechnical Institute, Leningrad, USSR, 1951-57; Candidate of Science, Politechnical Institute, Leningrad, USSR, 1961-64; Doctor of Science, Sverdlovsk Institute of Electrochemistry, Sverdlovsk, 1980. Appointments: Shift Supervisor, Magnesium Smelter, Berezniky, Perm, 1957-59; Scientific Fellow, Alumnium-Magnesium Institute of Affiliation, Berezniky, 1959-61; Postgraduate, Politechnical Institute, Leningrad, 1961-64; Associate Professor, Siberian Federal University, Krasnoyarsk, 1964; Director, Light Metals Ltd, Krasnoyarsk, 1993-. Publications: 300 articles in professional journals; 130 patents. Honours: Honoured Metallurgist. Memberships: TMS, USA; ACS, USA; Corresponding Member, Russian Academy of Technological Sciences; 2 Doctoral Academic Councils; Academic Council of Institute of Chemistry and Chemical Technology; SB RAS. Address: Room 16, Bld 19, 160 Krasnoyarskiy Rabochiy St, Krasnoyarsk, 660010, Russia.

DICTIONARY OF INTERNATIONAL BIOGRAPHY 36th EDITION

PONCELET Christian, b. 24 March 1928, Blaise, Ardennes, France. Chairman of the Senate. m. Yvette Miclot, 1 son, 1 daughter. Education: Saint-Sulpice College, Paris; Post and Telecommunication National School. Appointments include: Auditor, French Post and Telecommunication, 1950-53; Member, National Confederation Committee of French Christian Workers, 1953-62; MP, Gaullist Party, 1962; Member, Union Democratic Group of the National Assembly, 1962; Elected General Councillor, Remiremont, 1963, re-elected 1964, 1970, 1982, 1988, 1994; Elected Municipal Councillor, Remiremont, 1965; Re-elected MP, Republic Defense Union group, 1967, 1968, 1973; Social Affairs State Secretary, 1972, State Secretary to the Work, Employment and Population Minister, 1973, Civil Service State Secretary to Prime Minister, 1974, Messmer government; Budget State Secretary to the Economy and Finances Minister, Chirac government, 1974; Chairman, General Council of Vosges Department, 1976, re-elected 1979, 1982, 1985, 1988, 1992, 1994; Budget State Secretary to the Economy and Finance Minister, 1976, Parliamentary Relations State Secretary to the Prime Minister, 1977, Barre government; Elected Senator, Vosges Department, 1982, re-elected 1986, 1995, 2004; Elected Mayor of Remiremont (Vosges), 1983, re-elected 1989, 1995; Elected Chairman, Finance, Budgetary Control and National Economic Audit Standing Committee of the Senate, 1986, re-elected 1989, 1992, 1995; Elected Chairman of the Senate, 1998, re-elected 2001, 2004. Address: 17 rue des Etats-Unis, 88200 Remiremont, France.

PONTIER Jean-Marie, b. 23 May 1946, Manosque, France. University Professor. m. Dominique, 1 son, 2 daughters. Education: Graduate, Institute for Political Science, 1966, Graduate in Law, Faculty of Law, 1967, PhD, Law, 1975, Professor, 1980, Aix-en-Provence, France. Appointments: Assistant, Faculty of Law, Aix-en-Provence, 1969; Maitre Assistant, 1977; Professor, 1980; Head, Unit of Legal, Political and Social Research, 1995-2004; Head, Doctoral School of Legal and Political Sciences, 2000-07; Head, Administrative Research Center, 2002-08; Member, National Council of the Universities, 2003-07; Professor, Sorbonne Law School, Paris I, 2007; Member, Scientific Council, GRALE-CARS, 2008-; Member, Orientation Council of Nimes University, 2008-. Publications: 55 publications and 400 articles in professional journals. Memberships: International Scientific Committees of Review and Centres at Taipei (Taiwan), Braga (Portugal), Madrid (Spain) and Seoul (South Korea).

PONTIUS Anneliese Alma, b. 19 May 1921, Chemnitz, Saxony, Germany (US Citizen, 1962). Associate Clinical Professor. m. Dieter Johann Jakob Pontius (deceased). Education: Dr med, Johann Wolfgang Goethe University, Frankfurt, Germany, 1950; Graduate, Munich Analytical Institute, 1953; Resident Trainee, Psychiatry, McGill University, Montreal and Massachusetts Training Faculty; Certified by USA Specialty Board of Psychiatry and Neurology, 1963;Research Fellow, Child Psychiatry, Lennox Hill Hospital, New York. Appointments: Medical Advisor/Expert, USA Department of Health & Human Services, 1968-99; Assistant Professor, New York University; Associate Clinical Professor of Psychiatry, Harvard Medical School, retired 2001. Publications: 93 in reviewed professional journals including: Proposing new syndrome of limbic nonconvulsive behavior epilepsy; Evolution of visual-spatial representation using 2 neurological tests in remote areas on 4 continents. Honours: Visiting Professor (4 summers), Department of Neurology, University of Heidelberg, Germany, 1975-80; Visiting Scientist, National Institute of Mental Health, 1971-72. Memberships: American Psychiatric Association; Association for the Advancement of Science; American Academy of Law & Psychiatry; New York Academy of Medicine; New York Academy of Science; New York Travellers' Club. Address: Waldschmidt Str 6, 60316 Frankfurt, Germany. E-mail: anneliese_pontius@hms.harvard.edu

POOCHAROEN Ora-Orn, b. 29 October 1973, Bangkok, Thailand. Professor. m. Qamaruzzaman Amir. Education: LLB, International Relations, Hitotsubashi University, 1998; LLM, Political Science, University of Tokyo, 2000; PhD, Public Administration, Syracuse University, 2005. Publications: Bureaucratic Politics and Administrative Reform: Why Politics Matter, 2010; The Bureaucracy: Problem or Solution to Thailand's Far South Flames?, 2010. Honours: United World College Scholarship, 1990-92; Japanese Government Scholarship, 1993-2000; Royal Thai Government Scholarship, 1999-2003. Address: 30 Bukit Batok St 21, #07-05, Singapore 659636.

POOL Adam de Sola, b. 5 November 1957, Palo Alto, California, USA. Venture Capitalist. m. Kristina Gjerde, 1 son. Education: BA, University of Chicago, 1981; MA, University of California, 1982; MBA, Massachusetts Institute of Technology. Economist, First National Bank of Chicago, 1980; Research Officer, 1982-83, International Officer, 1983-86, Assistant Vice President, 1986, Industrial Bank of Japan, New York; Associate, Corporate Finance, Salomon Brothers Inc, New York, 1987, 1988-92; Principal Banker, 1992-94, Senior Banker, 1994-95, European Bank for Reconstruction and Development; Chief Investment Officer, Yamaichi Regent ABC Polska, 1995-97; Owner, PP Investments, 1998-. Publications: Published photographer. Memberships: Board member: Relpol Centrum SA; Finesco SA; Korte-Organica RT; Honorary Member, Yale Club. Address: ul Piaskowa 12c, 05-510 Konstanin, Poland. E-mail: pool@eip.com.pl

POP Iggy (James Jewel Osterburg), b. 21 April 1947, Ypsilanti, Michigan, USA. Singer; Musician (guitar); Actor. Education: University of Michigan. Career: Formed Iguanas, High School band, 1962; Prime Movers, 1966; Concerts in Michigan, Detroit and Chicago; Formed The Stooges (originally the Pyschedelic Stooges), 1967; 3 albums, 1969-73; Solo artiste, 1976-; Collaborations with David Bowie, 1972-; Numerous tours and television appearances; Actor, films including: Sid And Nancy; The Color Of Money; Hardware; Cry-Baby; Atolladero; Tank Girl; Dead Man; The Crow – City of Angels; The Brace; The Rugrats Movie (voice); Snow Day; Coffee and Cigarettes; Actor, television series: Miami Vice; The Adventures of Pete & Pete; Compositions include: Co-writer, China Girl, David Bowie; Many film songtracks. Recordings: Albums: with The Stooges: The Stooges, 1969; Jesus Loves The Stooges, 1977; I'm Sick Of You, 1977; Solo albums: Fun House, 1970; Raw Power, 1973; Metallic KO, 1976; The Idiot, 1977; Lust For Life, 1977; TV Eye Live, 1978; Kill City, 1978; New Values, 1979; Soldier, 1980; Party, 1981; I'm Sick Of You, 1981; Zombie Birdhouse, 1982; I Got The Right, 1983; Blah Blah Blah, 1986; Rubber Legs, 1987; Live At The Whiskey A Go Go, 1988; Death Trip, 1988; Raw Stooges, 1988; Raw Stooges 2, 1988; The Stooges Box Set, 1988; Instinct, 1988; Brick By Brick, 1990; American Caesar, 1994; Naughty Little Doggie, 1996; Heroin Hates You, 1997; King Biscuit Flower Hour, 1997; Your Pretty Face is Going to Hell, 1998; Sister Midnight, 1999; Avenue B, 1999; Iggy Pop, 1999; Hippodrome Paris '77 (live), 1999; Beat 'Em Up, 2001; Skull Ring, 2003; Singles: Beside You, 1993; Wild America, 1993; Corruption, 1999; Appears on: Rock at the Edge, 1977; Low, David Bowie, 1977; Trainspotting, 1996;

Death in Vegas, Contino Sessions, 1999; Contributor, Red Hot And Blue AIDs charity record. Publications: Autobiographies: I Need More; Iggy Pop's A-Z, 2005. Address: Art Collins Management, PO Box 561, Pine Bush, NY 12566, USA.

POP Nadia-Cella, b. 13 March 1948, Ariuşd, Romania. Professor; Poet. Education: Master of Arts in Philosophy, Babeş-Bolyai University, 1973. Appointments: High School Teacher; Newspaper Reporter; Poet. Publications: Poems published in popular journals and poetry anthologies around the world; 5 poetry books including: The Lordship of the Word, 2007; Shipwrecks Delayed, 2010; Works translated into 21 languages; Many poems published in literary anthologies around the world; Contributor, 5 plays, Braso, Vienna and Bucharest. Honours: 157 awards for poetry: Medaille d'Or, Halaf; Grand Prix de l'Europe, Guerande; Medaille d'Argent, Paris; Premio internazionale Goccia di luna, La Spezia; 3 Premio Internazional di Poesia e Prosa, Pomezia Roma; Diplome, La plume ardente, Liege; Medaille de bronze, Luxemburg; Die Goldmedaille und Grosen intern Preis Friedrich Holderlin, Gildekamer; The Best Poet of the Year 2004, Chongqing; Professor Honoris causa, St Lucas Academy, Bamberg, Germany; Academical Knight, Greci-Marino Academy, Vinzaglio, Italy; Honorary Citizen of Saint Etienne, France; Several honours and nominations from ABI and IBC. Memberships: 23 literary societies and academies in France, Italy, Germany and USA; Accademia Letteraria Italo-Australiana Scrittori, Melbourne, Australia; Asociation Mundial de Escritores, Spain. Address: Apt 9, 6 Soarelui Street, 500427 Brasov, Romania.

POPOVSKA Cvetanka, b. 26 August 1951, Skopje, Macedonia. Professor. m. Mirko Popovski, 1 son. Education: BSc, Civil Engineering, 1976, MSc, Technical Sciences, 1983, PhD, Technical Sciences, 1988, University of Ss Cyril & Methodius, Skopje; MSc, Hydraulic Engineering, Delft, The Netherlands, 1981. Appointments: Researcher, 1975, Assistant, 1976, Assistant Professor, 1989, Associate Professor, 1992, Full Professor, 1996, Civil Engineering Faculty, Skopje. Publications: 15 books; Numerous articles in professional journals. Honours: Best Student, Hydraulic Engineering Course, 1972, Best Graduated Student, Faculty of Civil Engineering, 1975, University of Ss Cyril & Methodius; Best Achieved MSc Results, 1983, Best Achieved PhD Results, 1990, Yugoslav Fund Yaroslav Černy, Belgrade; Listed in international biographical dictionaries. Memberships:International Association for Hydraulic Research; International Network of Water Environment Centres for the Balkans; Macedonian Association for Theoretical and Applied Mechanics; Macedonian Hydrological Association; Water Management and Hydraulic Engineering Symposiums; International Association for Danube Research; Modern Management of Mine Producing, Geology and Environmental Protection. Address: Blvd Partizanski odredi 24, 1000 Skopje, Macedonia. E-mail: popovska@gf.ukim.edu.mk

POPPER Frank Geoffrey, b. 17 April 1918, Prague, Czech Republic. University Professor. m. Aline Dallier. Education: Licence-es-Lettres, 1960, Docteur-es-Lettres, 1970, Sorbonne, Paris, France. Appointments: Director, 1969-85, Full Professor, 1976, Emeritus Professor, 1985-, Arts Department, University of Paris 8. Publications: Origins of Kinetic Art, 1968; Art, Action and Participation, 1975; Art of the Electronic Age, 1993; From Technological to Virtual Art, 2007. Honours: Commandeur dans l'Ordre des Arts et des Lettres, 2004; Chevalier de la Légion d'Honneur, France, 2010. Memberships: Honorary Editor, Leonardo Journal. Address: 6 rue du Marché Saint-Honoré, 75001 Paris, France. E-mail: fpopper@club-internet.fr

PORIEL Cyril, b. 31 August 1976, Dovarnenez, France. CNRS Researcher. m. Flo Vigouroux, 1 son. Education: DEA, Chimie, Rennes, 2000; PhD, Chemistry, Rennes, 2003. Appointments: Postdoctoral Researcher for Professor Chris Moody, Exeter, England, 2003-05; Senior CNRS Researcher, Rennes, 2005-. Publications: 42 articles in professional journals. Honours: Young Chemist Award, 2009. Address: UMR CNRS 6226, 1-263 ave du gen Leclerc, 35042 Rennes, France. E-mail: cyril.poriel@univ-rennes1.fr

PORNPITAKPAN Chanthika, b. 19 October 1962, Bangkok, Thailand. Professor. Education: BA (first class honours), 1983, MBA (distinction), 1987, Sasin Graduate Institute of Business Administration, Chulalongkorn University, Thailand; PhD, University of British Columbia, Vancouver, Canada, 1995. Appointments: Assistant Professor, National University of Singapore; Associate Professor, Monash University, Malaysia; Dean, Associate Professor, University of the Thai Chamber of Commerce, Thailand; Program Co-ordinator, BBA in Marketing, Associate Professor, University of Macau, China. Publications: :Numerous articles in professional journals; Various international conference proceedings. Honours: Outstanding Academic of University of Macau; Listed in biographical dictionaries. Memberships: American Marketing Association; Academy of International Business; Association of Consumer Research. Address: Faculty of Business Administration, University of Macau, Avenida Padre Tomás Pereira, Taipa, Macau, China. Website: www.chanthika.110mb.com

POROSHKIN Alexander Grigorjevich, b. 8 September 1930, Zelenets, Russia. m. Diana Vasiljevna Koktomova, 1 son, 1 daughter. Education: Diploma, Komi Pedagogical Institute, Syktyvkar, 1951; PhD, Mathematics, Leningrad Pedagogical Institute, 1970. Appointments: Mathematics Teacher, Secondary School, Lozym, 1951-52; Assistant, Department of Mathematics, Komi Pedagogical Institute, Syktyvkar, 1952-69; Dozent, 1969-76, Professor, 1992-2012, Department of Mathematics, Syktyvkar State University. Publications: Ordered Sets: Author: Boolean Algebras, 1987; Vector Measures, 1990; Measure and Integral Theory, 1996, 2006; Functional Analysis, 2004; Editor: Ordered Spaces and Operator Equations, 1989; Problems of Functional Analysis, 1991; Author: Differential Mappings, 1999; Series Theory, 2008; Elements of Set Theory, 2009. Memberships: American Mathematical Society. Address: Comuniticheskaya St 39-112, 167001, Syktyvkar, Russia.

PORTMAN Natalie, b. 9 June 1981, Jerusalem, Israel. Actress. m. Benjamin Millepied, 2012, 1 son. Education: Harvard University. Career: Model, aged 11; Films: Léon, 1994; Developing, 1995; Heat, 1995; Beautiful Girls, 1996; Everyone Says I Love You, 1996; Mars Attacks! 1996; The Diary of Anne Frank, 1997; Star Wars: Episode I – The Phantom Menace, 1999; Anywhere But Here; Where the Heart Is, 2000; The Seagull, 2001; Zoolander, 2001; Star Wars: Episode II – Attack of the Clones, 2002; Cold Mountain, 2003; Garden State, 2004; True, 2004; Closer, 2004; Star Wars: Episode III – Revenge of the Sith, 2005; V for Vendetta, 2006; Paris, Je t'aime, 2006; Goya's Ghosts, 2006; My Blueberry Nights, 2007; Hotel Chevalier, 2007; The Darjeeling Limited, 2007; Mr Magorium's Wonder Emporium, 2007; The Other Boleyn Girl, 2008; New York, I Love You, 2009; Love and Other Impossible Pursuits, 2009; Brothers, 2009; Hesher,

2010; Black Swan, 2010; No Strings Attached, 2011; Your Highness, 2011; Thor, 2011; Thor: The Dark World, 2013. Theatre: A Midsummer Night's Dream; Cabaret; Anne of Green Gables; Tapestry. Honours: Teen Choice Award, 2002, 2011; Golden Globe Awards, 2005, 2011; Academy Award, 2005, 2011; Screen Actors Guild Award, 2011; BAFTA, 2011. Address: c/o ICM, 8942 Wilshire Boulevard, Beverly Hills, CA 90211, USA.

POSPÍŠIL Jaroslav, b. 19 February 1935, Charváty, Czech Republic. Professor. Education: MSc, 1957; MEng, 1964; RNDr, 1968; PhD, 1968; DSc, 1992; Graduated in Physics and Mathematics, Palacký University, Olomouc, Electrical Engineering, University of Technology, Brno. Appointments: Researcher, Optics, Institute of Industrial Sciences, Tokyo University; Professor, Optics and Quantum 275 research papers in professional journals mainly in the field of transfer, statistical, digital and informational properties of optical, electrooptical, photographical, optoelectrical and human vision systems. Honours: Gold Medal, Palacký University, 1995; Merit Member and Honorary Member, Union of Czech Mathematicians and Physicists, 1996 and 2002. Memberships: International Society for Optical Engineering; Union of Czech Mathematicians and Physicists; Czech Committee, International Commission for Optics; Optics and Electronics Division of European Physical Society; Czech and Slovak Society for Photonics; Czech Society for Metrology. Address: Ovesná 10, 77900 Olomouc, Czech Republic.

POSTGATE John Raymond, b. 24 June 1922, London, England. Microbiologist. m. Mary Stewart, 3 daughters. Education: First Class Honours, Chemistry, D Phil, Chemical Microbiology, Balliol College, Oxford; DSc, Oxford. Appointments: Senior Research Investigator to Principal Scientific Officer, Microbiology Group, Chemical Research Laboratory, 1948-59; Principal to Senior Principal Scientific Officer, Microbiological Research Establishment, 1959-63; Assistant Director, 1963-80, Director, 1980-87, AFRC Unit of Nitrogen Fixation, Professor now Emeritus of Microbiology, 1965-, University of Sussex; Visiting Professor, University of Illinois, Champaign-Urbana, USA, 1962-63; Visiting Professor, Oregon State University, Corvallis, USA, 1977-78. Publications include: Scientific books: The Sulphate-Reducing Bacteria, 1979, 1984; The Fundamentals of Nitrogen Fixation, 1982; Nitrogen Fixation, 1978, 1987, 1998; Microbes and Man, 1969, 1986, 1992, 2000; The Outer Reaches of Life, 1994, 1995; Other books: A Plain Man's Guide to Jazz, 1973; A Stomach for Dissent (with Mary Postgate), 1994; Lethal Lozenges and Tainted Tea, 2001; Looking for Frankie (with Bob Weir), 2003; Over 200 research papers; 30 articles on popular science; Numerous record reviews and writings on jazz music. Honours: Williams Exhibition to Balliol College, Oxford; Honorary DSc, University of Bath, 1990; Honorary LLD, University of Dundee, 1997. Memberships: Fellow, Institute of Biology, 1965, President, 1982-84; Elected Fellow, Royal Society, 1977; President, Society for General Microbiology, 1984-87, Honorary Member, 1988; Honorary Member, Society for Applied Microbiology, 1988; Honorary Associate, Rationalist Press Association, 1995. Address: 1 Houndean Rise, Lewes, East Sussex BN7 1EG, England. E-mail: johnp@sussex.ac.uk

POTOTSKIY Grigory Victorovich, b. 13 February 1954, Malyshevo, Kurgankiy region, Russia. Sculptor; Artist. m. Olga Andreevna Bare, 1 daughter. Education: PhD, Sculpture, State University of Kishinyov. Appointments: Sculptor; Artist. Publications: Numerous articles in professional journals. Honours: Best Sculptor of Russia, 2007; Golden Order of Peacemaker, 2009. Memberships: Member, USSR Union of Artists, 1985-; Member, International Academy of Arts; Member, International Informatization Academy, 1998-; Member, International Academy of Culture and Art, 2007-. Address: Art Gallery of Gregory Pototsky, Office 1, 27 Gogolevsky Boulevard, Moscow, 119019, Russia. E-mail: grpototsky@mail.ru Website: www.gpototsky.com

POTYOMKINA Anna, b. 31 July 1965, Yelizova, Kamchatka region, Ukraine. Scientist; Writer; Bibliographer. 1 son. Education: Faculty of Library Science and Bibliography, Kharkov State Academy of Culture, 1981-86. Appointments: Deputy Chairman, Person and Absolute, non-governmental organization, 1995-98; Co-ordinator, Center for Development of Personality, 1998-. Publications: Co-author, Happiness; Other titles include: Esoterics in Practice; The History of the Centre for Development of Personality 1993-2000;Esoterics. Society. Person. Honours: Academician, EANS, Germany; IAELPS, Russia; Honorary Academician, IPA, Ukraine; Honorable Professor, European University, Hannover; Senator, International Knight Union; Knight IKU; Star of Senator Award, EANS and IKU; The Honour Award, EANS; Award for Development of Science and Education, IPA; M V Lomonosov Award, IAELPS. Memberships: EANS, Germany; IAELPS, Russia; IPA, Ukraine; European University, Hannover; International Knight Union. Address: Flat 43, 26 Smolnaya street, Kharkov, Ukraine. E-mail: leoncrch@mail.ru

POUND Keith Salisbury, b, 3 April 1933, London, England. Clergyman. Education: BA, MA, St Catharine's College, Cambridge, 1951-54; Cuddesdon College, Oxford, 1955-57. Appointments: Curate, St Peter, St Helier, Morden, 1957-61; Training Officer, 1961-64, Warden, 1964-67, Hollowford Training Centre, Sheffield; Rector, Holy Trinity, Southwark, 1968-78; Rector, Thamesmead, 1978-86; Chaplain General and Archdeacon to H M Prison Service, 1986-93; Chaplain, Grendon and Springhill Prisons, 1993-98; Chaplain to H M The Queen, 1990-2003. Publication: Creeds and Controversies, 1965. Membership: Civil Service Club. Address: Adeleine, Pett Road, Pett, East Sussex TN35 4HE, England.

POWELL Robert, b. 1 June 1944, Salford, Lancashire, England. Actor. m. Barbara Lord, 1975, 1 son, 1 daughter. Career: TV roles include: Doomwatch, 1970; Jude the Obscure, 1971; Jesus of Nazareth, 1977; Pygmalion, 1981; Frankenstein, 1984; Hannay (series), 1988; The Sign of Command, 1989; The First Circle, 1990; The Golden Years, 1992; The Detectives, 1992-97; Escape, 1998; Dalziel and Pascoe, 2005; Marple: The Murder at the Vicarage, 2004; Holby City, 2005-. Theatre roles include: Hamlet, 1971; Travesties (RSC), 1975; Terra Nova, 1982; Private Dick, 1982; Tovarich, 1991; Sherlock Holmes, 1992; Kind Hearts and Coronets, 1998; Film include: Mahler, 1974; Beyond Good and Evil, 1976; Thirty Nine Steps, 1978; Imperative, 1981; Jigsaw Man, 1982; Shaka Zulu, 1985; D'Annunzio, 1987; Chunuk Bair, 1992; The Mystery of Edwin Drood, 1993; Colour Me Kubrick: A True…ish Story, 2005; Hey Mr DJ, 2005. Honours: Best Actor, Paris Film Festival, 1980; Venice Film Festival, 1982; Hon MA, 1990, Hon DLitt (Salford), 2000. Address: c/o Jonathan Altans Associates Ltd, 13 Shorts Gardens, London, WC2H 9AT, England.

POWELL Sandy, b. 7 April 1960. Costume and Set Designer. Education: St Martin's College of Art and Design, Central School of Art, London. Career: Costume designer for Mick Jagger on Rolling Stones European Urban Jungle tour, 1990, all shows by The Cholmondeleys and the Featherstonehaughs; Stage sets include: Edward II (RSC); Rigoletto (Netherlands

Opera); Dr Ox's Experiment (ENO); Costumes for films include: Cobachan; The Last Of England; Stormy Monday; The Pope Must Die; Edward II; Caraveggio; Venus Peter; The Miracle; The Crying Game; Orlando; Being Human; Interview with a Vampire; Rob Roy; Michael Collins; The Butcher Boy; The Wings of the Dove; Felicia's Journey; Shakespeare in Love; Velvet Goldmine; Hilary and Jackie; The End of the Affair; Miss Julie; Gangs of New York; Far From Heaven; Sylvia; The Aviator; The Departed; The Other Boleyn Girl; The Young Victoria; Shutter Island. Honours: Best Technical Achievement Award, Evening Standard Awards, 1994; Academy Award, 1998, 2005, 2010; BAFTA Award, 1998. Address: c/o PFD, Drury House, 34-43 Russell Street, London, WC2B 5HA. E-mail: lmamy@pfd.co.uk

POZDEEV Valery Aleksandrovich, b. 14 May 1940, Arhangelsk, Russia. Professor. m. Olga Ivanovna, 1 son, 1 daughter. Education: Diploma of Engineer-Mechanic, 1963, Candidate of Technical Science, 1975, Mykolayiv Shipbuilding Admiral Makarov Institute; Doctor of Physical and Mathematical Sciences, 2001, Professor, 2007, National Academy of Sciences of Ukraine, Kiev Institute of Hydromechanics. Appointments: Posts in various organisations; Head, Scientific Department of Theoretical Hydrodynamics, Institute of Pulse Processes and Technologies, National Academy of Ukraine; Associate Director, Scientific Work Department, European University; Head, Applied Mathematics Department, Mykolayiv National V O Sukhomlynsky University, 2009-. Publications: 5 monographs; 14 scientific articles in professional journals. Memberships: New York Academy of Sciences. Address: 142 Kosmonavtov street, Flat 29, Mykolayiv, 54056, Ukraine. E-mail: valer.al.pozdeev@mail.ru

PRASAD Braj Kishore, b. 24 January 1956, Bekobar, Jharkhand, India. Research and Development. m. Meera, 1 daughter. Education: BSc Engg, Metallurgical Engineering, BIT, Sindri, 1981; MTech, Metallurgical Engineering, IIT, Kanpur, 1983; PhD, Metallurgical Engineering, University of Roorkee, 1994. Appointments: Research Officer, RRL, Bhopal, 1983-84; Lecturer, Metallurgical Engineering Department, REC Durgapur, 1984-85; Scientist B, 1985-90, Scientist C, 1990-95, Scientist EI, 1995-2000, Scientist EII, 2000-05, Scientist F, 2005-, RRL, Bhopal. Publications: 134 papers in international journals; 50 papers in conference proceedings. Honours: Best Paper Award, 1995; Khosla Research Award, 1997; Maximum Publications Impact Award, RRL Bhopal, 2002-03; Bronze Medal, The Mining, Geological and Metallurgical Institute of India, 2004-05; Listed in national and international biographical dictionaries. Memberships: IIM; SAEST; MSI; MRSI; IE(I); ISE; ISNT; IIME. Address: Advanced Materials & Processes Research Institute, Habibganj Naka, Bhopal 462 026, India. E-mail: braj_kprasad@yahoo.co.in

PRASAD Kodali Siva Rama Krishna, b. 7 June 1950, Thurumella, India. Doctor; Orthopaedic Surgeon. Education: Graduate, Guntur Medical College, Andhra University, 1972; ECFMG, 1974, VQE, 1983, Philadelphia. Appointments: Resident, Surgery and Trauma & Orthopaedic Surgery, India and United Kingdom; Staff Grade Orthopaedic Surgeon, Prince Charles Hospital, Merthyr Tydfil, 1994-. Publications: Several articles in peer-reviewed journals; International Associate Editor/International Reviewer, Food and Ankle International; Consultant Reviewer, Journal of Bone and Joint Surgery, USA; Reviewer, Journal of Bone and Joint Surgery, UK; Reviewer, Clinical Orthopaedics and Related Research; Reviewer, Journal of Foot and Ankle Surgery; Regular presentations in regional, national and international conferences. Honours: Special Merit Scholarship for top-ranking scholars, Government of Andhra Pradesh, 1966-72; De Puy Summer University Award, Sheffield, UK, 2007; Making a Difference Award, and Team Award, Prince Charles Hospital, 2007; Glory of India Award, 2012; Listed in international biographical dictionaries. Memberships: British Orthopaedic Association, London; EFORT, Zurich; SICOT, Brussels; British Trauma Society; British Orthopaedics Specialists Association; Indian Orthopaedic Society, London; Footeuroclub, Italy; Orthopaedic Research UK, London; British Medical Association; Science Advisory Board, Arlington, USA. Address: Prince Charles Hospital, Merthyr Tydfil, Mid Glamorgan, CF47 9DT, Wales. E-mail: ambakrishna1950@yahoo.co.uk

PRASHAR Usha Kumari (Baroness of Runnymede), b. 29 June 1948, Nairobi, Kenya. Member of the House of Lords. m. Vijay Sharma, July 1973. Education: BA, Honours, University of Leeds, 1967-70; Dip Soc, University of Glasgow, 1970-71. Appointments include: Conciliation Officer, Race Relations Board, 1971-76; Director, Runnymede Trust, 1976-84; Fellow, Policy Studies Institute, 1984-86; Director, National Council for Voluntary Organisations, 1986-91; Numerous activities from 1992-96 include: Membership of the Royal Commission on Criminal Justice, Lord Chancellors Advisory Committee on Legal Education and Conduct; The Arts Council; Chairman Parole Board of England and Wales, 1997-2000; First Civil Service Commissioner, 2000-; Chairman, National Literacy Trust, 2001-04; Chancellor, De Montfort University, 2000-; Chairman, Royal Commonwealth Society, 2001-; Board Member, Salzburg Seminar, 2000-04; BBC World Service Trust, 2002; Judicial Appointments Commission, 2005. Publications include: Contributed to: Britain's Black Population, 1980; The System: a study of Lambeth Borough Council's race relations unit, 1981; Scarman and After, 1984; Sickle Cell Anaemia, Who Cares? A survey of screening, counselling, training and educational facilities in England, 1985; Acheson and After: primary health care in the innercity, 1986. Honours: CBE 1994; Peerage, 1999; Honorary LLD: De Montfort, 1994; South Bank University, 1994; Greenwich, 1999; Leeds Metropolitan, 1999; Ulster, 2000; Oxford Brookes, 2000; Asian Women of Achievement Award, 2002. Address: House of Lords, London SW1A 0PW, England. E-mail: prasharu@parliament.uk

PRATCHETT Sir Terry, b. 28 April 1948, Beaconsfield, Buckinghamshire, England. Author. m. Lyn Marian Purves, 1 daughter. Appointments: Journalist; Writer. Publications: The Carpet People, 1971, revised 1992; The Dark Side of the Sun, 1976; Strata, 1981; The Colour of Magic, 1983; The Light Fantastic, 1986; Equal Rites, Mort, 1987; Sourcery, Wyrd Sisters, 1988; Pyramids, Eric, The Unadulterated Cat, Co-author, Good Omens: The Nice and Accurate Predictions of Agnes Nutter, Truckers, Guards! Guards!, 1989; Moving Pictures, Diggers, Wings, 1990; Reaper Man, Witches Abroad, 1991; Small Gods, Only You Can Save Mankind, 1992; Johnny and the Dead, Lords and Ladies, Men at Arms, Co-author, The Streets of Ankh-Morpork, 1993; Soul Music, Co-author, Interesting Times, The Discworld Companion, 1994; Maskerade, Co-author, The Discworld Map, 1995; Johnny and the Bomb, Feet of Clay, Hogfather, The Pratchett Portfolio, 1996; Jingo, 1997; The Last Continent, Co-author, A Tourist Guide to Loncre, Carpe Jugulum, 1998; Co-author, Death's Domain, Co-author, The Science of Discworld, The Fifth Elephant, Co-author, Nanny Ogg's Cookbook, 1999; The Truth, 2000; Thief of Time, 2001; The Amazing Maurice and His Educated Parents, Night Watch, The Science of the

Discworld I, II, III, 2002; Monstrous Regiment, The Wee Free Men, 2003; A Hat Full of Sky, Going Postal, 2004; Nation, 2008; Dodger, 2012. Honours: OBE, 1998; Hon DLitt, (Warwick), 1999; Carnegie Medal, 2001; World Fantasy Award for Lifetime Achievement, 2010; Margaret A Edwards Award, 2011. Address: c/o Colin Smythe, PO Box 6, Gerrards Cross, Buckinghamshire SL9 8XA, England.

PREBBLE Richard, b. 7 February 1948, Kent, England. Leader and List Member of Parliament, ACT New Zealand Party. m. (1) Nancy Prebble, 1970, (2) Doreen Prebble, 1991. Education: BA, LLB honours, Legal-economic problems, Auckland University; Lizzie Rathbone Scholar, 1967-70. Appointments: Admitted to Supreme Court as Barrister and Solicitor, 1971; Admitted to the Fiji Supreme Court Bar, 1973; Chair, Cabinet Committee, 1983-84; Headed privatisation programme; Key Minister, Labour Government, 1984-87; Elected Member of Parliament, Auckland Central, 1975-90; Professional Company Director, Works and Development Corporation, 1994-96; Elected Member of Parliament, Wellington Central, 1996-99; Leader and List Member of Parliament for ACT New Zealand Party, 1996-2004; Speaker and Advisor on regulatory, public sector, labour market, communications and transport reform; Speaking engagements in Europe, UK, USA, Indonesia, Australia and South America. Publications: I've Been Thinking, 1996; What Happens Next, 1997; I've Been Writing, 1999; Out of the Red, 2006. Address: Parliament Buildings, Wellington 1, New Zealand. E-mail: richard.prebble@parliament.govt.nz

PREDA Dumitru, b. 17 June 1951, Bucharest, Romania. Diplomat; Minister-Counselor; Director for Romanians Abroad, Ministry of Foreign Affairs. m. Maria Preda, 1 son, 2 daughters. Education: Chief of 1974 series, Faculty of History, Bucharest; Doctorate, History of International Relations, University of Bucharest; Fulbright Alumnus. Appointments: Principal Archivist, Scientific Researcher, Senior Scientific Researcher, Center of Studies and Researches of History and Military Theory, Institute of History and Military Theory (1991-), Bucharest, 1974-97; Diplomat, Chief, Historical Office, Romanian Diplomatic Archives, 1997-98; Counselor, Director, Direction of Diplomatic Archives, Ministry of Foreign Affairs, Bucharest, 1999-2002; Minister-Counselor, Deputy Permanent Delegate to UNESCO, 2002-07; Chargé d'Affaires ai, 2004, 2006; Member, Bureau of the Romanian Commission of Military History, 1991-2003; Vice President, Romanian Committee of Military Archives, 1997-2003; Founder and Vice President of European Committee of History and Strategy of the Balkans, 2000-; Member, Committee of Bibliography, 1990-, and the Committee of Military Archives, 1991-, of the International Commission of Military History (ICMH); Member of the Board, Commission of the History of International Relations (CHIR), Milan, 2006-; Treasurer, 2011; Former Invited Professor, The Military Academy, Bucharest; Professor and Honorary Dean, University of Banat, Timisoara; Associate Professor, University Ovidius, Constanta, 2006-; Conferences in various European countries and USA; Congresses and international conferences on history in over 20 countries. Publications: Over 50 books and manuals of history; Over 150 studies and articles in Romania and abroad. Honours: Romanian Academy Prize, 1994; 3 times winner of the Grand Prix of the Romanian Review of Military History, 1994, 1996, 1998; Magazin istoric Review and Foundation Prize, 1999, 2002, 2009; MFA Diploma of Merit for Outstanding Activity, 2002. Address: Ministry of Foreign Affairs, Direction for Romanian Abroad (DOR), No 14, Aleea Modrogan, Sector 1, Bucharest, Romania.

PREMERU Donata, b. 4 June 1939, Petrovgrad, Yugoslavia. Musicologist; Journalist; Broadcaster; Music Writer; Lecturer. Education: State Music School/Diploma: Musicology, Academy of Music, Zagreb; History of Arts, University of Zagreb; Post Diploma, Early and Contemporary Music, University of London; Language Diplomas: English, Italian, French, German and Hungarian. Career: Lecturer, broadcaster, Radio Zagreb; Music Editor, Radio Belgrade – as first musicologist started its III Programme and in 1983, its first stereo weekend music programme, STEREORAMA with special edition, MUSIC MATTERS/MUZIKAS POVODOM; Jury member, International Competition, Rome; Initiator of the first overall opera by Isidora Zebeljan, Zora D, which won one of the Genesis Foundation Prizes, 2003; Vasilije Mokranjac Piano Competition, Novi Sad, 2006; Appearances on Radio and Television, Zagreb, BBC London, Novi Sad and Belgrade. Publications: On Childrens Operas, 1997; Conversations with contemporary Composers and Musicians, 2000/2012; Il Mondo della Musica; CEJ/European Journalists Newsletter; OKO; III Programme Magazine, Radio Belgrade; Pro Musica; Pro Femina; Novi Zvuk/New Sound; REČ; Continuo; TEATRON; Knjizevnost/Prosveta; Projekat, Pozoriste; Knjizevni magazin; Muzika Klasika; Koraci; Articles in daily newspapers; Articles on 13 mainly contemporary operas in the first Opera Encyclopedie in Belgrade, 2008. Honours: 1st Prize, Radio Belgrade, 1965; The Golden Microphone, Radio Belgrade, 1990; Listed in biographical dictionaries; Nominated for many other awards around the world. Memberships: Union of Yugoslav Composers & Musicologists; Union of European Journalists.

PREMKUMAR Thathan, b. 19 March 1976, Ooty, Nilgris, Tamilnadu, India. Researcher. Education: BSc, 1996, MSc, 1998, Chemistry, Sri Ramakrishna Mission, Vidyalaya College of Arts and Science, Coimbatore; PhD, Chemistry, Bharathiar University, Coimbatore, 2003. Appointments: Senior Research Fellow, CSIR, 2002-04, Research Fellow, 1999-2002, Department of Chemistry, Bharathiar University; Postdoctoral Fellow, 2004-08, Research Professor, 2008-, Applied Macromolecular Chemistry Laboratory, Department of Materials Science and Engineering, Gwangju Institute of Science and Technology, South Korea. Publications: Numerous articles in professional journals. Honours: Best Out-going Post Graduation Student Award, Sri Ramakrishna Mission, Vidyalaya College of Arts and Science 1997-98; University Research Fellowship, Bharathiar University, 1999-2002; Young Scientist Award, Indian Council of Chemists, 2001; Senior Research Fellowship, Council of Scientific and Industrial Research, 2002-04; IUCr Young Scientist Support, Asian Crystallographic Association, 2004; Cover picture, Macromolecular Rapid Communications, 2006; Listed in international biographical dictionaries. Memberships: Polymer Society of Korea; Korean Chemical Society. Address: 1/76-A, Balacola Village, Mudugula PO Lovedale via, The Nilgiris 643 003, Tamil Nadu, India. E-mail: thathanpremkumar@gmail.com

PRENDERGAST Francis Joseph (Frank), b. 13 July 1933, Ireland. Retired. m. Mary Sydenham, 3 sons, 1 deceased, 3 daughters, 1 deceased. Education: Christian Brothers School, Limerick; Diploma, Social and Economic Science, University College, Cork, Ireland; MA, Industrial Relations, Keele University, England. Appointments: Baker, Keane's Bakery, Limerick, 1950-73; General President, Irish Bakers and Confectioners and Allied Workers Union, 1967-70; Branch Secretary, ITGWU, Shannon, Clare County Branches, 1973-77; Regional Secretary, ITGWU, Limerick, Clare, 1977-82; Head Office Representative,

ITGWU, Clare County, Limerick No 2 Branches, 1987-88; District Secretary, SIPTU, Limerick, 1990-93; Member, Board of Management, Crescent College Comprehensive SJ, 1973-91; Member, Governing Body, University of Limerick, 1974-79; President, Christian Brothers School Past Pupils Union, Limerick, 1995-99; Member, Limerick City Council, 1974-99; Mayor of Limerick, 1977-78, 1984-85; Dáil Eireann (Irish Parliament), Labour Party TD (Member of Parliament), Limerick East Constituency, 1982-87; Vice-President, Bureau of Consultative Council for Regional and Local Authorities Europe, 1990-94; Alternate Member, Committee of Regions, European Union, 1994-98; Chairman, Assembly of Regional Authorities, Ireland, 1995-96; Chairman, General Council of County Councils, Ireland, 1996-97; Chairman, Mid-West Regional Authority, Ireland, 1995-96; Member, Irish Language Steering Group, Department of Local Government and Environment, Ireland, 1984-99; Member, Irish Language Television Council, 1994-2000; Member, Governing Body, School of Celtic Studies, Dublin Institute of Advanced Studies, Dublin, 1996-2000; Member, Irish Place Names Commission, 1997-; Member, Executive Trust, Hunt Museum, Limerick, 2000-; Member, Irish Parliament Trust, 1985-; Chairman, Board of Management, Árd Scoil Ris Christian Brothers School, Limerick, 2003-2006; Cathaoirleach, Gaelcholaiste Luimnigh, 2006-. Publications: History of St Michael's Parish, Limerick, 2000; Limerick's Glory: From Viking Settlement to the New Millennium (co-author), 2002; Articles in: Remembering Limerick – Historical Essays, 1997, North Munster Antiquarian Journal, Old Limerick Journal, AMDG Publications, Ireland, Made in Limerick – Historical Essays, 2003; Dála an Scéil, a book of published newspaper articles in Irish, 2003; Weekly column in Irish for the Anois and Limerick Leader newspapers. Memberships: Garryowen Football Club; Voices of Limerick Choir; Thomond Archaeological Society; Limerick Thomond Probus Club. Address: "Avondonn", Cratloe Road, Mayorstone Park, Limerick, Ireland.

PRENGLER Mara, b. 1963, Buenos Aires, Argentina. Medical Doctor; Paediatrician. Education: MD, School of Medicine, University of Buenos Aires, 1988; Certificate of Specialist in Paediatrics, Ministry of Health and Social Services, 1993; PhD, Child Health, University College, University of London, England, 2005. Appointments: Complete Residence in Clinical Paediatrics, Hospital de Ninos Dr Ricardo Gutierrez Children's Hospital, Buenos Aires, 1989-93; Practitioner, Neurology Unit, Hospital Dr Ramos Mejia, Buenos Aires, 1993-94; Practitioner, Child Neurology Unit, Hospital de Ninos Dr Ricardo Gutierrez Children's Hospital, Buenos Aires, 1994-96; Fellowship, Center for Developmental Medicine and Child Neurology, Beth Israel Medical Center, University Hospital and Manhattan Campus for the Albert Einstein College of Medicine, New York, USA, 2001; Research Fellow, Specialist Clinical Fellowship in Paediatric Neurology, Institute of Child Health and Great Ormond Street Hospital for Sick Children, London, England, 1996-2000; PhD Student and Research Fellow in Paediatric Neurology, Institute of Child Health, University College, London, 2000-04; Honorary Research Fellow in Paediatric Neurology, Registrar to Professor Robert Surtees, Professor of Child Neurology, Neurosciences Unit, Great Ormond Street Hospital for Children NHS Trust, 2004-2006; UK Co-ordinator, Silent Infarct Transfusion Trial in Sickle Cell Disease, 2005. Publications: 15 refereed articles in professional medical journals; 2 book chapters; Book, Stroke and Cerebrovascular Disease in Childhood, 2011. Honours: K Horemis Prize, Greek Pediatric Society Meeting, 2003; Listed in various international biographical dictionaries. Memberships: Fellow, Royal Society of Medicine; Member, British Medical Association; Member, British Paediatric Neurology Association. E-mail: mprengler@hotmail.com

PRENTICE David, b. 4 July 1936, Birmingham, England. Artist. m. Dinah White, 4 daughters. Education: Moseley School of Arts & Crafts, 1949-52; Birmingham College of Art & Crafts, 1952-57. Appointments: National Service, Royal Artillery, 1957-59; Part time Teacher, Birmingham College of Art & Crafts, and Mid-Warwickshire School of Art, 1959-; Lecturer, Basic Studies, Birmingham College of Art & Crafts, 1968-71; Founder and Co-Director, Ikon Gallery, Birmingham, 1964-72; Senior Lecturer in Charge, Experimental Workshop, City of Birmingham Polytechnic, 1971-82; Member, East Midlands Arts, Visual Arts Panel, 1978-81; Course Director, BA Fine Art, City of Birmingham Polytechnic, 1982-86; Retired, 1986; Artist in Residence, Nottingham University, 1986-87; Visiting Artist, BA Fine Art, Trent Polytechnic, 1986-89; Visiting Artist, Ruskin School of Fine Art, Oxford University, 1987-88; Visiting Artist, BA Fine Art, University of Central England, 1988-92; Patron, Autumn in Malvern Festival, 1997-2008; Landscape Painter; Exhibits with John Davies Gallery, Moreton in Marsh, Gloucestershire; Work held in public and private collections in UK and USA. Publications: Some of the Best Things in Life Happen Accidentally, 2004; England's Landscape: The West Midlands, 2006; Paul Martin's Britain, 2007; British Art – A Walk Round the Rusty Pier, 2007; The Public Catalogue Foundation – Oil Paintings in Public Ownership, 2008; Landscapes of the Wye Tour, 2008. Honours: Singer & Friedlander/Sunday Times Watercolour Prizes: First Prize, 1990; Second Prize, 1999; Third Prize, 1996 & 2007. Memberships: Veteran Cycling Club; Tricycle Association.

PRESCOTT John Leslie (Baron Prescott), b. 31 May 1938, Prestatyn, Wales. Politician; Trade Unionist. m. Pauline Tilston, 1961, 2 sons. Education: Ruskin College, Oxford; Hull University. Appointments: Trainee Chef, 1953-55; Steward, Merchant Navy, 1955-63; Recruitment Officer, General and Municipal Workers Union, 1965; Contested Southport for Labour, 1966; Full-time officer, National Union of Seamen, 1968-70; Member of Parliament, Kingston upon Hull East, 1970-83, Hull East, 1983-97, Kingston upon Hull East, 1997-; Member Select Committee, Nationalised Industries, 1973-79, Council of Europe, 1972-75, European Parliament, 1975-79; Personal Private Secretary to Secretary of State for Trade, 1974-76; Opposition Spokesman on Transport, 1979-81, Regional Affairs and Devolution, 1981-83, on Transport, 1988-89, on Employment, 1993-94; Member, Shadow Cabinet, 1983-97; Member, National Executive Deputy Council, 1989-; Deputy Leader, Labour Party, 1994-2007; Deputy Prime Minister and Secretary of State for the Environment, Transport and the Regions, May 1997-2001; Deputy Prime Minister and First Secretary of State, 2001-2007. Publications: Not Wanted on Voyage: report of 1966 seamen's strike, 1966; Alternative Regional Strategy: A framework for discussion, 1982; Planning for Full Employment, 1985; Real Needs - Local Jobs, 1987; Moving Britain into the 1990s, 1989; Moving Britain into Europe, 1991; Full Steam Ahead, 1993; Financing Infrastructure Investment, 1994; Jobs and Social Justice, 1994; Fighting Talk, 1997; Punchlines: A Crash Course in English with John Prescott, 2003. Honours: North of England Zoological Society Gold Medal, 1999; Priyadarshni Award, 2002. Address: House of Commons, London, SW1A 0AA, England.

PRESCOTT Laurence Francis, b. 13 May 1934, London, England. m. (1) 1 son, 3 daughters, (2) Jennifer Ann. Education: BA, 1957, MBBChir, 1960, MA, 1960, MD, 1968, Cantab; Diploma in Clinical Pharmacology (honoris causa), 1998. Appointments: Junior hospital appointments in London and Scotland, UK, and Boston, Massachusetts, USA; Research Fellow, Clinical Pharmacology, Johns Hopkins Hospital, Baltimore, Maryland, USA; Lecturer, Department of Therapeutics and Pharmacology, University of Aberdeen; Senior Lecturer and Reader, Clinical Pharmacology, Department of Therapeutics, University of Edinburgh and Honorary Consultant Physician, Professor of Clinical Pharmacology, Department of Clinical Pharmacology and Honorary Consultant Physician, The Royal Infirmary of Edinburgh. Publications: Nearly 350 articles in professional journals, articles, editorials, book chapters and books. Honours: Lilly Prize in Clinical Pharmacology, British Pharmacological Society; Cullen Prize, Royal College of Physicians, Edinburgh; Fellow, Royal Society, Edinburgh; Honorary Fellowship, British Pharmacological Society; Honorary Member, Swedish Association for Clinical Pharmacology. Memberships: MRCP Edinburgh; FRCP Edinburgh; FRS Edinburgh; FFPM; FRCP London. Address: Redfern, 24 Colinton Road, Edinburgh EH10 5EQ, Scotland. E-mail: laurie.prescott@ed.ac.uk

PRESCOTT Mark (Sir), b. 3 March 1948, London, England. Racehorse Trainer. Education: Harrow. Appointment: Trainer at Newmarket, 1970-; Training over 1,800 winners including: Pivotal, Alborada, Albanova, Hooray. Publications: The Waterloo Cup – The First 150 Years (co-author); Occasional contributor to publications including: The Racing Post and Horse and Hound. Address: Heath House, Newmarket, Suffolk CB8 8DU, England

PRESCOTT Richard Chambers, b. 1 Apr 1952, Houston, Texas, USA. Poet; Writer. m. Sarah Elisabeth Grace, 13 Oct 1981. Education: Self-taught. Publications: The Sage, 1975; Moonstar, 1975; Neuf Songes (Nine Dreams), 1976, 2nd edition, 1991; The Carouse of Soma, 1977; Lions and Kings, 1977; Allah Wake Up, 1978, 2nd edition, 1994; Night Reaper, 1979; Dragon Tales, 1983; Dragon Dreams, 1986, 2nd edition, 1990; Dragon Prayers, 1988; Dragon Songs, 1988, 2nd edition, 1990; Dragon Maker, 1989, 2nd edition, 1990; Dragon Thoughts, 1990; Tales of Recognition, 1991; Kings and Sages, 1991; Dragon Sight: A Cremation Poem, 1992; Three Waves, 1992; Disturbing Delights: Waves of the Great Goddess, 1993; Kalee Bhava: The Goddess and Her Moods, 1995; Because of Atma, 1995; The Skills of Kalee, 1995; Measuring Sky without Ground, 1996; Kalee: The Allayer of Sorrows, 1996; The Goddess and the God Man, 1996; Living Sakti: Attempting Quick Knowing in Perpetual Perception and Continuous Becoming, 1997; The Mirage and the Mirror, 1998; Inherent Solutions to Spiritual Obscurations, 1999; The Ancient Method, 1999; Quantum Kamakala, 2000. Contributions to: Articles and essays to professional publications. Address: 8617 188th Street South West, Edmonds, WA 98026, USA.

ROY Michael Presley-, b. 20 April 1928, London, England. Artist (Drawing and Painting). Education: Oxford School Certificate, 1944; Newland Park College, Bucks, 1967-70; Teacher's Certificate, Art Advanced Level, Distinction, Reading University; Hornsey College of Art, Postgraduate Department, Diploma in Art Education, London University, 1973-76. Appointments: From 1950, various teaching and commercial positions including: Head of Art Department, Orchard School, Slough; Art Lecturer, Langley College, Berkshire; Semi-retirement, 1984-; The State Apartments, Windsor Castle, 1985-88; A professional artist in multi-media (landscapes, religious themes, figurations, flower-pieces and abstract/fantasy idiomatic motifs); Originator of "Art Lark" monoprint series from original works by Michael Roy; Group exhibitions of Wessex Biennial and exhibitions curated by/ at Southampton Civic AG (viz: Aquarium, Le Coq dans la Boîte, The Artist's Chair, Art From Words – Self Portrait, 2001, Pattern, 2006). Publications: Author: The Rôle of the Art Teacher, 1976; The Art Lark, 1992; Featured in: British Contemporary Art, 1993; International Panorama of Contemporary Art, 1998; Ahoy Clausentum, 1994; Outstanding Artists and Designers of the 20th Century, 2001; Who's Who in Art, 2010; Cambridge Blue Book, 2005/06; Sotheby's charity auction catalogues. Commissions and Creative Works: In various private and public collections in UK and abroad including: Flight of the Holy Family, Allington Castle, Kent, 1958; Mary Magdalene, Crowmarsh Church, Oxon, 1959; Carisbrooke Halt, Trustees, Carisbrooke Castle Museum, Isle of Wight, 1957; Calvary, Windsor Parish Church, Berks, 1967; Flamingo Dancers, Red Swans, Reading AG, Berks, 1980; Quarr Abbey from the South, Quarr Abbey, Isle of Wight 1970; Oil painting, Sailing into the Millennium 2000, presented by Gosport Borough Council, Hants, 2005 to Holy Trinity Church, Gosport, Hants (www.holytrinitygosport.co.uk); Holy Trinity Church, Crucifixion, 1970, Madonna and Child Jesus, 1970. Honours: Los Peroquitos (Diploma Award, international section, visual poetry Biennial) Mexico City, 1996; Bronze Medal, Best Poetry of 1996, International Society of Poetry, Maryland, USA, 1996; Ambassador of England and Speaker, World Forum held at St John's College, Cambridge University, 17th-22nd August 2010; Lifetime Achievement Award for excellence in created Artworks, UCC, USA, 2010. Address: Flat 73, Homefort House, 82 Stoke Road, Gosport, Hants, PO12 1QQ, England.

PRESS Vello, b. 13 October 1934, Tallinn, Estonia. Scientific Worker. m. Lubomira Maria Broniarz. Education: Graduate Engineer, Technical University of Tallinn, 1957; PhD, Academy of Sciences of Estonia 1970; Diploma of Senior Researcher, 1974. Appointments: Heat Power Engineer, The Shipyard and the Factory Building Materials, Tallinn, 1957-60; Junior Researcher, Institute of Thermal Physics and Electrophysics, 1960-70; Senior Researcher, 1970-93; Senior Lecturer, Poznan University of Technology, 1994-2004; Retired, 2004. Publications: Over 50 papers and reports, field of combustion of fuels and the mass transport in multicomponent media. Honours: Millennium Medal of Honour, ABI, 2000; American Medal of Honor, ABI, 2005; World Medal of Freedom, ABI, 2006. Address: Brzoskwiniowa Str 4, PL 62-031, Lubon, Poland.

PRESSER Cary, b. 20 June 1952, Brooklyn, New York, USA. Research Engineer. m. Karen Leslie, 2 daughters. Education: BSc, Aerospace Engineering, Polytechnic Institute of Brooklyn, New York, 1974; MSc, Aeronautical Engineering, Polytechnic Institute of Brooklyn, Farmingdale, New York, 1976; DSc, Aeronautical Engineering, Technion, Israel Institute of Technology, Haifa, Israel, 1980. Appointments: Engineering Assistant, Student Internship Program, Hypersonic Vehicles Division, Langley Research Center, Langley, Virginia, 1973; Teaching Fellow, Department of Aeronautical Engineering, Polytechnic Institute of Brooklyn, Farmingdale, 1975-75; Teaching Instructor, Department of Aeronautical Engineering, Technion, Israel Institute of Technology, Haifa, Israel, 1975-80; Research Engineer, 1980-94, Group Leader, High Temperature Processes Group,

1994-99, Group Leader, Thermal and Reactive Processes Group, 1999-2004, Research Engineer, 2004-, Process Measurement Division, Chemical Science and Technology Laboratory, National Institute of Standards and Technology, Gaithersburg, Maryland. Publications: Numerous articles as author and co-author include most recently: Application of a Benchmark Experimental Database for Multiphase Combustion Modeling, 2006; Transport of High Boiling-Point Fire Suppressants in a Droplet-Laden Homogeneous Turbulent Flow Past a Heated Cylinder, 2006; PIV Measurements of Water Mist Transport in a Homogeneous Turbulent Flow Past an Obstacle, 2006; Droplet Size and Velocity Measurements from Commercial 'Fogger' Type Pepper Spray Products, 2008; Thermal and Chemical Kinetic Characterization of Multiphase and Multicomponent Substance by Laser Heating, 2008; A Simple Method to Access the Thermal Effectiveness of a Fire Suppressant, 2011; Fire Suppression (chapter in Handbook of Atomization and Spays: Theory and Applications, 2011. Honours include: Silver Medal Award for Meritorious Federal Service, 1991, SMART Bonus Award, 1992, US Department of Commerce; AIAA Terrestrial Energy Systems Technical Committee Best Paper Award, 1994; Listed in Who's Who publications and biographical dictionaries. Memberships include: Associate Fellow, American Institute of Aeronautics and Astronautics; Fellow, American Society of Mechanical Engineers; Institute for Liquid Atomization and Spray Systems: The Combustion Institute; Air Quality Research Subcommittee, Committee for Environmental and Natural Resources; Atmospheric Composition Interagency Working Group, Climate Change Science Program; New York Academy of Science; Sigma Xi; Sigma Gamma Tau. Address: Nanoscale and Optical Metrology Group, Process Measurements Division, Chemical Science and Technology Laboratory, National Institute of Standards and Technology, 100 Bureau Drive, Stop 8360, Gaithersburg, MD 20899-8360, USA. E-mail: cpresser@nist.gov

PRESSINGER Selwyn Philip Hodson, b. 9 December 1954, Guildford, Surrey, England. Writer; Company Director. Education: Graduate, Aix-en-Provence University France; Graduate, Oxford Brookes University; Postgraduate, The College of Law, Chancery Lane, London, 1973-78. Appointments: Management Consultancy (Company Law, Marketing and Trade Finance), 1981-2011:- SCF (UK), SCT Lille (France), Tennant FM International Ltd, Maygrove Consulting Ltd, Wilton & Partners; Legal Training and Practice, 1977-80:- Solicitors Professional Course and Thicknesse Hull Solicitors, Westminster. Publications: Books: Rupert Pressinger OSB 1688-1741, Benedictine Prior, 1998; Major W.S.R. Hodson 1821-1858 – In Memoriam, 2001; Military & Equine Works of Captain Adrian Jones, 2005; Torphichen & The Knights of St John (Knights of Malta) 1100s-200 Scotland, 2011; Contributions to national newspapers and literary magazines including: The Times, The Financial Times, The Universe, The Literary Review, 1990-2010; Articles in historical journals including: Army Quarterly and Defence Journal, Catholic Ancestor Journal, Journal of the Victorian Military Society, Journal of the Society for Army Historical Research, 1998-2010. Honours: Fellow, Royal Geographical Society, 1993; Fellow, Royal Society of Arts, 1999; Fellow, Society of Antiquaries of Scotland, 2007. Memberships: Associate, Law Society, 1978; British Institute of Management, 1985; Institute for the Management of Information Systems, 1990; Chartered Institute of Marketing, 1994; Catholic Writers' Guild, 1996; Society of Authors, 2006. Address: c/o 28 Old Brompton Road, South Kensington, London SW7 3SS, England.

PRESTON-GODDARD John, b. 5 May 1928, Liverpool, England. Painter. Partner, Kathleen Preston-Goddard. Education: Croydon School of Art. Career: Own studios since 1948; Freelance painter in oils and watercolour; Works sold in UK, USA, Europe, South Africa, Canada and South America. Publications: Numerous international publications. Address: The Studio House, 46 Selborne Road, Park Hill Village, Croydon, Surrey CR0 5JQ, England.

PRETSCH Thorsten, b. 5 January 1976, Berlin, Germany. Chemist. m. Sandra Birgit, 1 son. Education: Diploma, 2001, PhD, 2004, Chemistry, FU, Berlin. Appointments: Postdoctoral Research Fellow, Molecular Materials Group, School of Chemistry, University of Sydney, Australia, 2005; Postdoctoral Research Fellow, 2006-09, 2010-, BAM Federal Institute for Materials Research and Testing. Publications: Numerous articles in professional journals. Honours: Deutsche Akademie der Naturforscher Leopoldina Fellowship, University of Sydney, Australia, 2005; Best Paper Award, World Materials Research Institute Forum, Tsukuba, Japan, 2008. Memberships: CEN/TC 248 WG31 Smart Textiles; DIN NA 106-01-19 AA Arbeitsauschuss Intelligente Textilien. Address: BAM Federal Institute for Materials Research and Testing, Division 6.3, Unter den Eichen 87, 12205 Berlin, Germany. E-mail: thorsten.pretsch@bam.de Website: http://profile.bam.de/802

PREVIN André George, b. 6 April 1929, Berlin, Germany. Conductor; Pianist; Composer. m. (1) Betty Bennett, divorced, 2 daughters, (2) Dory Langan, 1959, divorced 1970, (3) Mia Farrow, 1970, divorced 1979, 3 sons, 3 daughters, (4) Heather Hales, 1982, 1 son; (5) Anne-Sophie Mutter, 2003, divorced 2006. Education: Berlin and Paris Conservatories. Appointments: Music Director, Houston Symphony, USA, 1967-69; Music Director, Principal Conductor, London Symphony Orchestra, 1968-79, Conductor Emeritus, 1979-; Composer, conductor, approximately 50 film scores; Guest Conductor, Guest Conductor most major world orchestras also, Royal Opera House, Covent Garden, Salzburg, Edinburgh, Osaka, Flanders Festival; Music Director, London South Bank Music Festival, 1972-74, Pittsburgh Symphony Orchestra, 1976-84, Los Angeles Philharmonic Orchestra, 1984-89; Music Director, Royal Philharmonic Orchestra, 1985-86, Principal Conductor, 1987-92; Chief Conductor and Music Director, 2004-06, Conductor Laureate, 2006-, Oslo Philharmonic Orchestra; Series of TV specials for BBC and American Public Broadcasting Service. Publications: Compositions, major works include: Every Good Boy Deserves a Favour (text by Tom Stoppard), 1977; Pages from the Calendar, 1977; Peaches, 1978; Principals, 1980; Outings, 1980; Reflections, 1981; Piano Concerto, 1984; Triolet for Brass, 1987; Variations for Solo Piano, 1991; Six Songs for Soprano and Orchestra, 1991; Sonata for Cello and Piano, 1992; The Magic Number, 1995; Trio for Bassoon, Oboe and Piano, 1994; Sonata for Violin, 1996; Sonata for Bassoon and Piano, 1997; Streetcar Named Desire (opera), 1998; Books: Music Face to Face, 1971; Orchestra (editor), 1977; Guide to Music, 1983; No Minor Chords: My Days in Hollywood, 1991. Honours include: TV Critics Award, 1972; Academy Awards for Best Film Score, 1959, 1960, 1964, 1965; Honorary KBE, 1995; Glenn Gould Prize, 2005. Address: c/o Columbia Artists, 165 W 57th Street, New York, NY 10019, USA.

PRICE Barrie, b. 13 August 1937, Bradford, England. Chartered Accountant. m. Elizabeth, 4 sons, 1 daughter. Education: St Bede's Grammar School, Bradford, 1948-53; ACA, 1959; FCA, 1968; ACCA, 1974; FCCA, 1980; MCMI, 1979; FCMI, 1980. Appointments: Trainee Accountant,

DICTIONARY OF INTERNATIONAL BIOGRAPHY 36th EDITION

1953-58; Partner, 1962, Senior Partner 1974-, Lishman Sidwell Campbell and Price; Chairman and Managing Director, Lishman Sidwell Campbell & Price Ltd (formerly Slouand Ltd), 1968-; Director, Eura Audit International, 1999-; Senior Partner, LSCP LLP, 2003-10; Senior Partner, ABS LLP, 2004-; Senior Partner, Eura Audit UK, 2005-; Director: Lishman Sidwell Campbell & Price Trustees Ltd, Lishman Sidwell Campbell and Price Financial Services Ltd, Tywest Investments Ltd, Slouand Ltd, Ripon Accountants Ltd, Ripon Improvement Trust Ltd, Lyons St John Ltd, LSCP Ltd, Yorks Image Ltd, LSCP Properties Ltd, LSCP Nominees Ltd, Accountant UK On Line Ltd, A2Z Financial Services Ltd; Director, Eura Audit International, 1999-; Senior Partner, Eura Audit, UK, 2005-; Vice President Eura Audit International 2006; Various appointments: AUKOL Ltd, Development Sharing (High Skellgate) Ltd, Gibsons Hotel (Harrogate) Ltd, Online Administrator Ltd; Board Member, Eura Audit International Paris, 2001-; Councillor, 1968-91, Mayor, 1980-81, Deputy Mayor, 1974-75, 1982-83, 1987-88, Ripon City Council; Councillor, 1974-91, Deputy Leader, 1987-88, 1990-91, Chairman, Economic Development Committee, Harrogate Borough District Council; Chairman: Ripon Life Care and Housing Trust, Ripon City and District Development Association, 1969-90, Harrogate Theatre Appeal, 2001-06, Harrogate Theatre Forward Appeal, 2002-06; President, Ripon City Conservative Association; Trustee: City of Ripon Festival, Chairman, 1981-, York Film Archive, Chairman, 1981-91, Ripon Cathedral Appeal, 1994-97, Ripon Museum Trust Appeal, Chairman, 1998-2000. Honours: Foundation Degree, Theology and Ministry, 2008. Memberships: Ripon Chamber of Trade and Commerce, 1962-83, President, 1975-77, Life Member, 1983-; Roman Catholic Diocese of Leeds Finance Committee and Board, 1989-94; Ripon Tennis Centre; RSC; Ripon Civic Society; Life Member, Yorkshire Agricultural Society; Life Member, National Trust; Skipton and Ripon Conservative Association; ACA, 1959; FCA, 1968; FCCA; FCMI. Address: Prospect House, 54 Palace Road, Ripon, North Yorkshire HG4 1HA, England. E-mail: b.price@euraudituk.com

PRICE Janet, b. 5 February 1938, Abersychan, Pontypool, Gwent, South Wales. Singer (Soprano). m. Adrian Beaumont. Education: BMus (1st class honours) and MMus, University of Wales, Cardiff, 1956-62; LRAM (Singing Performer); ARCM (Piano Performer); LRAM (Piano Accompanist); Studied singing with Olive Groves, 1962-64; Special Study of French Vocal Music with Nadia Boulanger, France, 1966. Appointments: Singing career encompassing opera, concerts and recitals throughout the UK and Western Europe, parts of Canada and USA; Worked with leading orchestras and conductors including Haitink, Rozhdestvensky, etc; Sang opera with Glyndebourne Festival Opera, Welsh National Opera, Opera Rara, Kent Opera Co, Handel Opera Society, Northern Ireland Opera Trust, San Antonio Grand Opera Texas, BBC TV, etc; Specialty of resurrecting neglected heroines of the Bel Canto period in operas by Mercadante, Donizetti, Bellini, etc; Numerous important premieres including Belgian premiere of Tippett's 3rd Symphony, Festival of Flanders, 1975; Adjudicator at competitions including Arts Council's Young Welsh Singers' Competition, RTE's Musician of the Future Competition, Dublin, Grimsby International Singers' Competition, Llangollen International Eisteddfod; Singing Professor at Royal Welsh College of Music & Drama, 1984-2004, 2006- and at Royal Academy of Music, London, 1997-2007. Publications: Commercial recordings for EMI, Argo, Philips, Decca, Opera Rara, etc; Role of Hecuba in video of Tippett's opera, King Priam, 1985; Article entitled Haydn's Songs from a Singer's Viewpoint, Haydn Yearbook, 1983. Honours: Winner, Arts Council's first Young Welsh Singers' Competition, 1964; Honorary ARAM, 2000; FRWCMD, 2004. Memberships: Royal Society of Musicians of Great Britain. Address: 73 Kings Drive, Bishopston, Bristol BS7 8JQ, England.

PRICE Nick, b. 28 January 1957, Durban, South Africa. Professional Golfer. m. Sue, 1 son, 1 daughter. Career: Professional Golfer, 1977-; Winner, PGA Championship, 1992, 1994, British Open, 1994, 3rd PGA Tour Money Leader, 1992; PGA Tour Money Leader, 1993; Zimbabwe Open, 1995; MCI Classic, 1997; Suntory Open, 1999; CVS Charity Classic, 2001; Mastercard Colonial, 2002; Founder, Nick Price golf course design, 2001; 10 US PGA victories, 25 world-wide victories. Honours: Vardon Trophy, 1993; Named Player of the Year, 1993; Bob Jones Award, United States Golf Association, 2005. Address: c/o PGA Tour, 100 Avenue of the Champions, Palm Beach, FL 33410, USA.

PRICE Roger (David), b. 7 January 1944, Port Talbot, Wales. Professor of Modern History; Writer. Education: BA, University of Wales, University College of Swansea, 1965. Appointments: Lecturer, 1968-82, Senior Lecturer, 1982-83, Reader in Social History, 1984-91, Professor, European History, 1991-94, University of East Anglia; Professor of Modern History, University of Wales, Aberystwyth, 1994-. Publications: The French Second Republic: A Social History, 1972; The Economic Modernization of France, 1975; Revolution and Reaction: 1848 and The Second French Republic (editor and contributor), 1975; 1848 in France, 1975; An Economic History of Modern France, 1981; The Modernization of Rural France: Communications Networks and Agricultural Market Structures in 19th Century France, 1983; A Social History of 19th Century France, 1987; The Revolutions of 1848, 1989; A Concise History of France, 1993, second edition, 2005; Documents on the French Revolution of 1848, 1996; Napoleon III and the French Second Empire, 1997; The French Second Empire: an Anatomy of Political Power, 2001; People and Politics in France, 1848-1870, 2004. Contributions to: Numerous Magazines and journals. Honour: DLitt, University of East Anglia, 1985. Membership: Fellow, Royal Historical Society, 1983. Address: Department of History and Welsh History, University of Wales, Aberystwyth, Ceredigion SY23 3DY, Wales.

PRIDEAUX Humphrey Povah Treverbian, b. 13 December 1915, London, England. Soldier; Businessman. m. Cynthia Birch Reynardson, 4 sons. Education: BA, Hons, 1936, MA, 1945, Trinity College Oxford, 1933-36. Appointments: Regimental and Staff appointments, Regular Army, 1936-53; Director, 1956-73, Chairman, 1963-73, NAAFI; Director, 1964-88, Chairman, 1973-88, London Life; Director, 1968-81, Chairman, 1972-81, Brooke Bond Liebig; Director, 1969-81, Vice-Chairman, 1977-81, W H Smith; Director, 1981-93, Chairman, 1983-93, Morland & Co. Honours: Kt, 1971; OBE; DL. Memberships Cavalry and Guards Club. Address: Kings Cottage, Buryfields, Odiham, Hook, Hampshire RG29 1NE, England. E-mail: hptprideaux@aol.com

PRIEST Jean Hirsch, b. 5 April 1928, Chicago, Illinois, USA. Professor Emeritus. m. Robert Eugene, deceased, 1 son, 2 daughters. Education includes: PhB Hons, 1947, BS, 1950, MD Hons, 1953, University of Chicago; MD, Illinois, 1957-1970; MD, Washington, 1959-1965; MD, Georgia, 1971-; MD, Montana, 1991-97. Appointments include: Clinical Instructor, Department of Pediatrics, Epidemiologist, Laboratory Bacteriologist, 1957-58, University of Illinois, Chicago, Illinois; Staff Physician, Respiratory

Center, Columbus Hospital, Chicago Illinois, 1957-58; Clinical Instructor, Department of Pediatrics, University of Washington, Seattle, 1960-62; Instructor, Department of Pediatrics, 1963-65, Director, Birth Defects Clinic, 1964-67, Assistant Professor, Department of Pediatrics and Pathology, 1965-71, University of Colorado Medical Center, Denver, Colorado; Visiting Member of staff, Department of Zoology, University of St Andrews, Scotland, 1969-70; Visiting Professor, Department of Community Health, Research Cytogeneticist, University of Auckland, New Zealand, 1980-81; Director, Prenatal Diagnosis Program, 1973-90, Professor Emeritus, 1990-, Emory University, Atlanta, Georgia; Director, Genetics Laboratory, Physician, Shodair Hospital, Helena, MT, 1990-95; Professor Emeritus, Faculdade de Medicina de Marilla, SP, Brasil, 2000-; American Cytogenetics Conference, Distinguished Cytogeneticist Award, 2006. Publications: 3 books; 8 book chapters; 7 book reviews; 27 abstracts; 86 refereed. Memberships: American Society for Cell Biology; American Society of Human Genetics; American Board of Medical Genetics; Tissue Culture Association; American Dermatoglyphics Society; International Dermatoglyphics Society; Association of Cytogenetic Technologists; Sigma Xi; American Medical Association; American Society for Experimental Pathology; American Society for Human Genetics; American College of Medical Genetics; American Academy of Pediatrics. Address: 4350 E Lincolnway # 410, Cheyenne, WY 82001-2191, USA. E-mail: jpriest517@aol.com

PRIMOST Norman Basil, b. 25 June 1933, London, England. Barrister. m. Debbie Doris Ferster, 3 sons, 1 daughter. Education: LLB (Hons), London School of Economics, University of London, 1950-53; Research on Comparative Law of Agency, Trinity Hall, Cambridge, 1953-54. Appointments: National Service, Censoring Mail RASC, Military Corrective Establishment, Colchester, 1954-56; Called to the Bar, Middle Temple, 1954; Pupillage with Montague Waters QC, 1956-57; General Common Law Practice specialising in property law with particular emphasis on landlord and tenant law, 1957-2011; Head of Chambers, Temple Gardens Temple, 1986-94. Publications: Legal Correspondent, Stock Exchange Journal, 1967-69; Editor, Restrictive Practices Reports, 1969-71; President, B'nai B'rith First Lodge of England, 2005-07. Listed in various international biographical dictionaries. Memberships: King's Head Theatre; Hampstead Theatre. Address: Grande Vue, 98 West Heath Road, London NW3 7TU, England. E-mail: sprimost@hotmail.com

PRINCE (Prince Rogers Nelson), b. 7 June 1958, Minneapolis, Minnesota, USA. Singer; Songwriter; Producer. m. (1) Mayté Garcia, 1996 (divorced), 1 son (deceased), (2) Manuela Testolini, 2001 (divorced). Appointments: Leader, Prince and The Revolution; Singer, New Power Generation, 1991-; Numerous tours and concerts. Creative Works: Singles: 1999; Alphabet Street; Controversy; I Could Never Take The Place; If I Was Your Girlfriend; Let's Go Crazy; Little Red Corvette; Purple Rain; Raspberry Beret; Sign O' The Times; U Got The Look; When Doves Cry; Cream; Gold. Albums: For You, 1978; Dirty Mind, 1979; Controversy, 1979; Prince, 1979; 1999, 1983; Purple Rain, 1984; Around the World in a Day, 1985; Parade, 1986; Sign of the Times, 1987; Lovesexy, 1988; Batman, 1989; Graffiti Bridge, 1990; Diamond and Pearls, 1991; Come, 1995; The Gold Experience, 1995; The Rainbow Children, 2002; One Nite Alone – Live! 2002; Musicology, 2004; 3121, 2006; Ultimate, 2006; Planet Earth, 2007; LOtUSFLOW3R, 2009. Honours: Academy Award, Best Original Score, 1984; 3 Grammy Awards, 1985; Brit Awards, 1992, 1993, 1995; Q Award, Best Songwriter, 1990; Special Award, World Soundtrack Awards, 2004; Golden Globe, Best Original Song – Motion Picture, Happy Feet, 2007. Address: Paisley Park Enterprises, 7801 Audoban Road, Chanhassen, MN 55317, USA. Website: www.npgmusicclub.com

PRINGLE Charles Norman Seton (Air Marshal Sir), b. 6 June 1919, Dublin, Ireland. Retired Engineer. m. Margaret Sharp, 1 son (deceased). Education: BA, MA, St John's College, Cambridge. Appointments: Royal Air Force, 1941-76, final appointment, Controller of Engineering and Supply and Chief Engineer; Senior Executive, Rolls-Royce (1971) Ltd, 1976-78; Non-Executive Director, Hunting Engineering, 1976-78; Chairman, Council of Engineering Institutions, 1977-78; The Director, Chief Executive, Society of British Aerospace Companies Ltd, 1978-84; Non-Executive Director, Cobham plc, 1985-89. Publications: Technical papers, Royal Aircraft Establishment, 1949. Honours: CBE 1967; KBE, 1973; Honorary Fellow (President, 1975-76), Royal Aeronautical Society; Fellow, Royal Academy of Engineering; Life Fellow, Wildfowl & Wetland Trust; Life Fellow, RSPB. Memberships: President, Smeatonian Society of Civil Engineers, 2006; Freeman City of London; Liveryman, Worshipful Company of Coachmakers. Address: Appleyards, Fordingbridge, Hampshire SP6 3BP, England

PRINGLE Jack Brown, b. 13 March 1952, Cambuslang, Glasgow, Scotland. Architect. 2 daughters. Education: BA Honours, Bristol University, 1970-73; DipArch, 1974-75; RIBA Pt II, 1977. Appointments: Powell and Moya, 1973-81; Jack Pringle Architects, 1981-86; Pringle Brandon, 1986-; Royal Institute of British Architects, Council, 1980-86, 2003-, Vice-President, 2003-2005, President, 2005-07; Vice Chair, Construction Industry Council, 2010-. Honours: RIBA; FRSA; FICPD; Commandeur des Arts et Lettres. Memberships: PPRIBA; Hon AIA; FRSA; Chelsea Arts Club; Royal Ocean Racing Club; Royal Southern Yacht Club. Address: 10 Bonhill Street, London EC2A 4QJ, England.

PRITZKER Andreas E M, b. 4 December 1945, Baden, Switzerland. Physicist. m. (1) Marthi Ehrlich, 1970, deceased 1998, (2) Ursula Reist, 2003. Education: PhD, Physics, Swiss Federal Institute of Technology (ETH), Zurich, Switzerland. Appointments: Scientist, Alusuisse, 1975-77; Consulting Engineer, Motor Columbus, 1977-80; Scientist, Swiss Institute for Nuclear Research, 1980-83; Assistant to President Board of Swiss Federal Institutes of Technology, 1983-87; Head Administration, Paul Scherrer Institute, 1988-98; Head, Logistics and Marketing, Paul Scherrer Institute, 1998-2002; Founder and Chairman, Munda Publishing Company, 2003-. Publications: Filberts Verhangnis, 1990; Das Ende der Tauschung, 1993; Eingeholte Zeit, 2001; Die Anfechtungen des Juan Zinniker, 2008; Allenthalben Lug und Trug, 2010; Several short stories. Memberships: Swiss Writers Association; PEN Swiss-German Centre. Address: Rebmoosweg 55, CH 5200 Brugg, Switzerland. E-mail: apritzker@bluewin.ch

PROCTER (Mary) Norma, b. 15 February 1928, Cleethorpes, Lincolnshire, England. Opera and Concert Singer. Education: Wintringham Secondary School, Grimsby; Vocal and Music studies in London with Roy Henderson, Alec Redshaw, Hans Oppenheim and Paul Hamburger. Career: London debut, Southwark Cathedral, 1948; Operatic debut, Aldeburgh Festival in Britten's Rape of Lucrecia, 1959, 1960; Royal Opera House, Covent Garden in Gluck's Orpheus, 1961; Specialist in concert works, oratorios and recitals;

Performed at festivals and with major orchestras in France, Germany, Netherlands, Belgium, Spain, Italy, Portugal, Norway, Denmark, Sweden, Finland, Austria, Luxembourg, Israel, South America; Performances with conductors including: Bruno Walter, Leonard Bernstein, Jascha Horenstein, Bernard Haitink, Raphael Kubelik, Karl Richter, Pablo Casals, Malcolm Sargent, Charles Groves, David Willcocks, Alexander Gibson, Charles Mackerras, Norman del Mar. Recordings include: The Messiah; Elijah; Samson; Second, Third and Eighth Symphonies and Das Klagende Lied by Mahler; First Symphony by Hartmann; Scenes and Arias by Nicholas Maw; Le Laudi by Hermann Suter; Brahms and Mahler Ballads with Paul Hamburger; Songs of England with Jennifer Vyvyan, 1999; The Rarities by Britten including world premier release of 1957 recording of Canticle II – Abraham and Isaac with Peter Pears and Benjamin Britten, 2001. Honour: Honorary RAM, 1974. Membership: President, Grimsby Philharmonic Society. Address: Nor-Dree, 194 Clee Road, Grimsby, Lincolnshire DN32 8NG, England.

PROKOPIUK Jerzy Stefan, b. 5 June 1931, Warsaw, Poland. Translator; Essayist. Education: Oriental Philology, 1949-54, English Philology, 1961-62, Philsophy, 1962-63, University of Warsaw. Appointments: Translator; Essayist. Publications: 17 books; 524 papers, essays and articles; 134 books of translations. Honours: Prize of Deutsches Polen Institut Darmstadt, 1987; Prize, Society of Polish Translator, 1989; Prize, Nieznany Swiat, 2005. Memberships: Allgemeine Anthroposophische Gesellschaft; Honorary President, Gnosis. Address: Nowolipie 20A/23, 01-115 Warsaw, Poland. E-mail: intermediarius@go2.pl

PROST Alain Marie Pascal, b. 24 February 1955, Lorette, France. Motor Racing Team Owner; Former Racing Driver. 2 sons. Education: College Sainte-Marie, Saint-Chamond. Career: French and European Champion, Go-Kart racing, 1973; French Champion, 1974-75; French and European Champion, Formula Three Racing, 1979; Joined Marlboro MacLaren Group, 1980; Winner, French, Netherlands and Italian Grand prix, 1981; World Champion, 1985, 1986, 1989, 1993; Winner, Brazilian, French, Mexican, Spanish and British Grand Prix, 1990; South African, San Marino, Spanish, European, Canadian, French, British, German Grand Prix, 1993; Silverstone Grand Prix, 1993; Estoril Grand Prix; 51 Grand Prix wins; Retired from Grand Prix racing in 1993.Technical consultant to McLaren Mercedes, 1995; Founder and President, Prost Grand Prix team, -. Publication: Vive ma vie, 1993. Honours: Officer, Legion d'honneur; Honorary OBE, 1994. Address: Prost Grand Prix, 7 avenue Eugène Freyssinet, 78286 Guyancourt Cedex, France.

PROUDFOOT (Vincent) Bruce, b. 24 September 1930, Belfast, Northern Ireland. Geographer. m. Edwina V W Field, 2 sons. Education: BA, 1951, PhD, 1957, Queen's University, Belfast. Appointments: Research Officer, Nuffield Quaternary Research Unit, 1954-58; Lecturer, 1958-59, Queen's University, Belfast; Lecturer, 1959-67, Tutor, 1960-63, Librarian, 1963-65, Hatfield College, University of Durham; Associate Professor, 1967-70, Professor, 1970-74, University of Alberta, Canada; Professor of Geography, 1974-93, Emeritus Professor of Geography, 1993-, University of St Andrews; Member of Council, 1975-78, 1992-93, Honorary Editor, 1978-92, Chairman of Council, 1993-99, Vice-President, 1993-, Royal Scottish Geographical Society; Council, 1982-85, 1990-91, Vice President, 1985-88, General Secretary, 1991-96, Royal Society of Edinburgh. Publications: Books: Frontier Settlement Studies (joint editor with R G Ironside et al), 1974; Site, Environment and Economy (editor), 1983; The Downpatrick Gold Find, 1955; Author and co-author of numerous papers in geographical, archaeological and soils journals and book chapters. Honours: Lister Lecturer, British Association for the Advancement of Science, 1964; Estyn Evans Lecture, Queens University Belfast, 1985; Bicentenary Medal, Royal Society of Edinburgh, 1997; FSA, 1963; FRSE, 1979; FRSGS, 1991; OBE, 1997. Memberships: Fellow Royal Society of Arts; Fellow Royal Anthropological Institute; Fellow Royal Geographical Society with Institute of British Geographers; Fellow Society of Antiquaries Scotland. Address: Westgate, 12 Wardlaw Gardens, St Andrews, Fife KY16 9DW, Scotland.

PROULX E(dna) Annie, b. 22 August 1935, Norwich, Connecticut, USA. Writer. m. (1) H Ridgeley Bullock, 1955, divorced, 1 daughter, (2) James Hamilton Lang, 1969, divorced 1990, 3 sons. Education: BA, University of Vermont, 1969; MA, Sir George Williams University, Montreal, 1973. Publications: Heart Songs and Other Stories, 1988; Postcards, 1992; The Shipping News, 1993; Accordion Crimes, 1996; Brokeback Mountain, 1998; Close Range: Wyoming Stories, 1999; That Old Ace in the Hole, 2002; Bad Dirt: Wyoming Stories 2, 2004; Fine Just the Way It Is: Wyoming Stories 3, 2008; Contributions to: Periodicals. Honours: Guggenheim Fellowship, 1992; PEN/Faulkner Award, 1993; National Book Award for Fiction, 1993; Chicago Tribune Heartland Award, 1993; Irish Times International Fiction Award, 1993; Pulitzer Prize in Fiction, 1994; Alumni Achievement Award, University of Vermont, 1994; New York Public Library Literary Lion, 1994; Dos Passos Prize for Literature, 1996; American Academy of Achievement Award, 1998; The New Yorker Book Award for Best Fiction, 2000; English Speaking Union Ambassador Book Award, 2000; Aga Khan Prize for Fiction, 2004. Memberships: Phi Alpha Theta; Phi Beta Kappa; PEN American Centre. Address: c/o Simon and Schuster Inc, 1230 Avenue of the Americas, New York, NY 10020, USA.

PRYCE John Derwent, b. 29 January 1941, Bowness on Windermere, England. University Lecturer. m. (1) Christine, 1967, divorced 1988, 2 sons, 1 daughter, (2) Kate, 1990, 1 daughter. Education: Dragon School, Oxford; Eton College; BA, Mathematics, Trinity College, Cambridge, 1962; PhD, Mathematics, University of Newcastle Upon Tyne, 1965; Cert Ed, University of Bristol, 1966. Appointments: Mathematics Teacher, 1966-68; Lecturer, University of Aberdeen, 1968-75; Lecturer, University of Bristol, 1975-88; Sabbatical Professor, University of Toronto, Canada, 1982-83; Lecturer, Senior Lecturer, Royal Military College of Science, Cranfield University, 1988-2006; Leverhulme Emeritus Fellow, 2006-08; Senior Technical Editor, Institute of Electrical and Electronic Engineers Working Group P1788 on Standardisation of Interval Arithmetic, 2008-. Publications: Books: Basic Methods of Linear Functional Analysis, 1973, reprinted 2011; Numerical Solution of Sturm-Liouville Problems, 1993; 55 articles in refereed journals/conference proceedings. Honours: Co-director, Uniben International Conferences on Scientific Computing, Benin City, Nigeria, 1992, 1994; Guest Editor, Volume on Differential Equations, Special Millennium Edition of Journal Computational and Applied Mathematics, 2000; Steering Committee Member, International Interval Subroutine Library project, 2005-; Senior Technical Editor, IEEE Working Group P1788 for standardisation of interval arithmetic, 2008-. Memberships: Fellow, Institute of Mathematics and Applications; Chartered Mathematician; Chartered Scientist. Address: 46 Ponting Street, Swindon, Wiltshire, SN1 2BW, England.

PRYCE Jonathan, b. 1 June 1947, North Wales. Actor. Partner, Kate Fahy, 2 sons, 1 daughter. Education: Royal Academy of Dramatic Art. Career: Stage appearances include: The Comedians, 1975, 1976; Hamlet, Royal Court, London, 1980; The Caretaker, National Theatre, 1981; Accidental Death of an Anarchist, Broadway, 1984; The Seagull, Queen's Theatre, 1985; Macbeth, RSC, 1986; Uncle Vanya, 1988; Miss Saigon, Drury Lane, 1989; Oliver!, London Palladium, 1994; My Fair Lady, 2001; A Reckoning, 2003; The Goat, 2004; TV appearances include: Roger Doesn't Live Here Anymore (series), Timon of Athens, 1981; Martin Luther, Praying Mantis, 1983; Whose Line is it Anyway?, 1988; The Man from the Pru, 1990; Selling Hitler, 1991; Mr Wroe's Virgins, Thicker Than Water, Great Moments in Aviation, 1993; David, 1997; Hey, Mr Producer! The Musical World of Cameron Mackintosh, 1998; The Union Came: A Rugby History, 1999; Victoria & Albert, 2001; Confessions of an Ugly Stepsister, 2002; HR, Baker Street Irregulars, 2007. Films include: Something Wicked This Way Comes, 1982; The Ploughman's Lunch, 1983; Brazil, 1985; The Doctor and the Devils, Haunted Honeymoon, 1986; Jumpin' Jack Flash, 1987; Consuming Passions, The Adventures of Baron Munchausen, 1988; The Rachel Papers, 1989; Glen Garry Glen Ross, 1992; The Age of Innocence, A Business Affair, 1993; Deadly Advice, 1994; Carrington, 1995; Evita, 1996; Tomorrow Never Dies, 1997; Regeneration, 1997; Ronin, 1998; Stigmata, 1999; Very Annie Mary, Unconditional Love, The Affair of the Necklace, Bride of the Wind, 2001; Unconditional Love, Mad Dogs, 2002; What a Girl Wants, Pirates of the Caribbean: The Curse of the Black Pearl, 2003; De-Lovely, 2004; The Brothers Grimm, Living Neon Dreams, Brothers of the Head, The New World, 2005; Ranaissance (voice), Pirates of the Caribbean: Dead Man's Chest, 2006; The Moon and the Stars, Pirates of the Caribbean: At World's End, 2007; My Zinc Bed, Leatherheads, Bedtime Stories, 2008; Echelon Conspiracy, GI Joe: The Rise of Cobra, 2009. Recordings: Miss Saigon, 1989; Nine-The Concert, Under Milkwood, 1992; Cabaret, 1994; Oliver!, 1995; Hey! Mr Producer, 1998; My Fair Lady, 2001. Honours: Tony Award, 1976; Oliver and Variety Club Awards, 1991; Tony and Drama Desk Awards, 1994; Best Actor, Cannes Film Festival, 1995; Best Actor, Evening Standard Film Awards, 1996; CBE, 2009. Address: c/o Julian Belfrage Associates, 46 Albemarle Street, London W1X 4PP, England.

PRYLUTSKYY Valery Pavlovich, b. 30 December 1939, Kyiv, Ukraine. 1 son. Education: Graduate, National Technical University, Kyiv Polytechnic Institute, 1966. Appointments: E O Paton Electric Welding Institute, 1958-; Candidate of Technical Science, 1982-; Senior Staff Scientist of Department, 1984; Deputy Chief of Department, 2006. Publications: Numerous articles in professional journals. Honours: Laureate, State Prize of Ukraine, 1988; Listed in biographical dictionaries. Address: 41 Solomenska St, Bldg 1, Apt 70, 03141 Kyiv, Ukraine.

PULATOV Valentine Borisovitsh, b. 13 August 1935, Odessa, Ukraine. Electromechanical Engineer. m. (1) Nadejda Prysyajnaya, 1958, deceased 1992, 1 son, 1 daughter, (2) Yaremchook Evgenya, 2000. Education: Graduate, Electromechanical Faculty, Polytechnic University, Odessa, Ukraine. Appointments: Work in industry, 1958-61; Lecturer, 1961-67; Engineer of Auxiliary Teaching Personnel, Odessa National Academy of Food Technologies, 1967-; Collaborated as optician with scientific group doing auxiliary works for aviation and space technology, 1970-90. Publications: Monograph: Electric Stations with Asynchronous Generator, 1967; 3 articles on this subject, 1965-67; 4 Author's Certificates and articles in scientific journals including: Magnetic Propulsion Systems, 2001; Physics of Magnetic Propulsion, 2005. Address: Apartment 58, 11-A Seminarskaya Street, Odessa 65039, Ukraine. E-mail: valentin.pulatov@gmail.com

PULLMAN Bill, b. 17 December, 1953, Hornell, New York, USA. Actor. Education: University of Massachusetts. m. Tamara, 3 children. Appointments: Former drama teacher, building contractor, director of theatre group; Started acting in fringe theatres, New York; Moved to Los Angeles; Films include: Ruthless People; A League of Their Own; Sommersby; Sleepless in Seattle; While You Were Sleeping; Caspar; Independence Day; Lost Highway, 1997; The End of Violence, 1997; The Thin Red Line, 1998; Brokedown Palace, 1998; Zero Effect, 1998; A Man is Mostly Water, 1999; History is Made at Night, 1999; The Guilt, 1999; Lake Placid, 1999; Coming to Light: Edward S Curtis and the North American Indians (voice), 2000; Titan AE, 2000; Numbers, 2000; Ignition, 2001; Igby Goes Down, 2002; 29 Palms, 2002; Rick, 2003; The Grudge, 2004; The Orphan King, 2005; Dear Wendy, 2005; Alien Autospy, 2006; Scary Movie 4, 2006; You Kill Me, 2007; Nobel Son, 2007; Your Name Here, 2008; Surveillance, 2008; Bottle Shock, 2008; Phoebe in Wonderland, 2008; The Killer Inside Me, 2010; Peacock, 2010. Address: c/o J J Harris, 9560 Wilshire Boulevard, Suite 50, Beverly Hills, CA 90212, USA.

PULLMAN Philip, b. 19 October 1946, Norwich, England. Author. m. Jude Speller, 1970, 2 sons. Education: BA, Oxford University, 1968. Appointments: Teacher, Middle School, 1972-86; Lecturer, Westminster College, Oxford, England, 1986-96. Publications: The Ruby in the Smoke, 1986; The Shadow in the North, 1987; The Tiger in the Well, 1990; The Broken Bride, 1992; The White Mercedes, 1992; The Tin Princess, 1994; Northern Lights, 1995; The Golden Compass, 1996; Spring-Heeled Jack, 1997; Puss in Boots, 1997; The Subtle Knife, 1997; Count Karlstein, 1998; Clockwork, 1998; I Was a Rat! 2000; The Amber Spyglass, 2000; Lyra's Oxford, 2003; The Scarecrow and his Servant, 2004; Once Upon A Time in the North, 2008; The Good Man Jesus and the Scoundrel Christ, 2010; Fairy Tales from the Brothers Grimm, 2012. Contributions to: Reviews in Times Educational Supplement; The Guardian. Honours: Carnegie Medal, 1996; Guardian Children's Fiction Award, 1996; British Book Awards Children's' Book of the Year, 1996; British Book Awards WH Smith Children's Book of the Year, 2000; Whitbread Children's Book of the Year Prize, 2001; Whitbread Book of the Year Award, 2001; BA/Book Data Author of the Year Award, 2001; Booksellers' Association Author of the Year, 2001, 2002; British Book Awards Author of the Year Award, 2002; Whitbread Book of the Year Award, 2002; CBE, 2004. Address: c/o Caradoc King, AP Watt Ltd, 20 John Street, London WC1N 2DR, England. Website: www.philip-pullman.com

PUNCOCHAR Pavel, b. 20 March 1944, Pelhrimov, Czech Republic. Biologist; Ecologist. 1 daughter. Education: MSc, Faculty of Life Sciences, Charles University, Prague, 1966; RNDr, Hydrobiology, 1969; PhD, Hydromicrobiology, 1972, Appointments: Czech Academy of Sciences, Hydrobiological Laboratory, 1967; Institute of Landscape Ecology, Prague, 1985-86; Water Research Institute, Prague, 1986-97; Director, 1990-97; Director, Department of Watermanagement Policy, 1998, General Director, Section of Watermanagement, 2003, 2008-, Deputy Minister, 2006-07, Ministry of Agriculture. Publications: More than 350 papers, contributions in Czech and or international journals. Memberships: International Commission for Elber River Protection, President, 2011-;

International Commission for Danube River Protection; International Commission for Oder River Protection, President, 2011-; Member, Research Board, Institute of Hydrobiology and Fishery of South Bohemia University; Institute of Soil Protection and Drainage, Prague; Faculty of Biological Sciences, Agricultural University, Prague; Others. Address: Zitkova 225, 15300 Prague 5, Czech Republic.

PUNTER David Godfrey, b. 19 November 1949, London, England. Professor of English; Writer; Poet. m. Caroline Case, 1988, 1 son, 2 daughters. Education: BA, 1970, MA, 1974, PhD, 1984, University of Cambridge. Appointments: Lecturer in English, University of East Anglia, 1973-86; Professor and Head of Department, Chinese University of Hong Kong, 1986-88; Professor of English, University of Stirling, 1988-2000; Professor of English, University of Bristol, 2000-. Publications: The Literature of Terror, 1980; Blake Hagel and Dialectic, 1981; Romanticism and Ideology, 1982; China and Class, 1985; The Hidden Script, 1985; Introduction to Contemporary Cultural Studies (editor), 1986; Lost in the Supermarket, 1987; Blake: Selected Poetry and Prose (editor), 1988; The Romantic Unconscious, 1989; Selected Poems of Philip Larkin (editor), 1991; Asleep at the Wheel, 1997; Gothic Pathologies, 1998; Spectral Readings (editor), 1999; Selected Short Stories, 1999; Companion to the Gothic (editor), 2000; Writing the Passions, 2000; Postcolonial Imaginings, 2000; The Influence of Postmodernism on Contemporary Writing, 2005; Methaphor, 2007; Modernity, 2007. Contributions to: Hundreds of articles, essays, and poems in various publications. Honours: Fellow, Royal Society of Arts; Fellow, Society of Antiquaries (Scotland); Scottish Arts Council Award; Founding Fellow, Institute of Contemporary Scotland; DLitt, University of Stirling. Address: Department of English, University of Bristol, Bristol BS8 1TB, England.

PUPPE Ingeborg, b. 1 January 1941, Lodz, Poland. Professor of Law. Education: Arbitur, Bremen girls' school, 1961; Law, first state bar exam, 1965, second state bar exam, 1970, Doctorate, 1970, University of Heidelberg; Trainee Lawyer, higher regional court, Bremen, 1966-70; Postdoctoral lecture qualification, 1977. Appointments: Assistant to Professor Dr Karl Leckner, Chair for Criminal Law and Proceedings, 1971-77; Chair for Criminal Law and Proceedings, Rheinischen Friedrich-Wilhelms-Universitaet, Bonn, 1977-. Publications: Numerous articles in professional journals. Honours: Venia Legendi for Criminal Law Proceedings and Legal Theory, 1977. Memberships: Active Member, Hildegartis-Verein for Disabled Women. Address: Rechts und Staatswissenschaftliche Fakultat, Adenauerallee 24-42, 53113 Bonn, Germany. Website: www.jura.uni-bonn.de/puppe

PURI Sanjay, b. 23 November 1961, Rampur, India. Physicist. m. Bindu Puri, 2 sons. Education: MS Physics, IIT Delhi, India, 1982; PhD, Physics, University of Illinois at Urbana-Champaign, USA, 1987. Appointments: Assistant Professor, 1987-93, Associate Professor, 1993-2001, Professor, 2001-, Jawaharlal Nehru University (JNU), New Delhi. Publications: Approximately 150 papers and books on statistical physics and nonlinear dynamics. Honours: Young Scientist Medal, Indian National Science Academy, 1993; Satyamurthy Medal, Indian Physics Association, 1995; Birla Science Award, Birla Science Centre, 2001; Homi Bhabha Fellowship, Bhabha Fellowships Council, 2003; Elected Fellow, Indian Academy of Sciences, Bangalore, 2006; S S Bhatnagar Prize, Council of Scientific and Industrial Research, 2006. Address: School of Physical Sciences, Jawaharlal Nehru University, New Delhi 110067, India. E-mail: puri@mail.jnu.ac.in

PURKIS Andrew James, b. 24 January 1949, London, England. Charity Director. m. Jennifer Harwood Smith, 1 son, 1 daughter. Education: 1st Class Honours Modern History, Corpus Christi College, Oxford, 1967-70; St Antony's College, Oxford, 1971-74; Doctor of Philosophy, 1978. Appointments: Administrative Trainee, 1973-76, Private Secretary, 1976-77, Principal, 1977-80, Northern Ireland Office; Head of Policy Analysis, 1980-84, Head of Policy Planning, 1984-86, Assistant Director, 1986-87, National Council for Voluntary Organisations; Director, Council for the Protection of Rural England, 1987-91; Public Affairs Secretary to the Archbishop of Canterbury, 1992-98; Chief Executive, Diana, Princess of Wales Memorial Fund, 1998-2005; Chief Executive, Tropical Health and Education Trust (THET), 2005-09; Board Member, Charity Commission, 2007-10; Member, Parole Board, 2010-; Board Member, Office of the Adjudicator for Higher Education, 2010-; Chair, Action Aid, 2010-. Publications: Housing and Community Care (with Paul Hodson), 1982; Health in the Round (with Rosemary Allen), 1983; Housing Associations and the Future of Voluntary Organizations in England, 2010. Honours: OBE; DPhil; MA. Membership: FRSA, 1989. Address: 38 Endlesham Road, Balham, London SW12 8JL, England.

PURNELL John, b. 8 January 1954, England. Lecturer. Education: Foundation Certificate, Bournville College of Art and Design, 1990; City and Guilds, Hall Green Technical College, 1991; BA (Hons), Cardiff Institute of Higher Education, School of Fine Art, 1994; MA, 1996, PhD, 2000, University of Wales Institute, Cardiff. Appointments: Photographic Tutor, 1994-97, Senior Department Tutor and Internal Verifier, 1997-2001, Howardian Community Education Centre; Art Tutor, United World College of the Atlantic, 1994-2002; Technician, Cardiff Institute of Higher Education, School of Fine Art, 1991-1996; Technician, 1996-98, Lecturer, 1996-2005, School of Fine Art, Tutor, Student Services, 2001-, University of Wales Institute, Cardiff. Honours: Vice Chancellor's Staff Award for Excellence, University of Wales Institute, Cardiff, 2007, 2009. Memberships: Mensa; Fellow, Royal Geographical Society; Fellow, Royal Society of Arts; Fellow, Higher Education Academy; Fellow, British Professional Photographers Association; Associate, Royal Photographic Society; Associate, British Institute of Professional Photographers; Associate, British Amateur Photography Associates; Licentiate, City and Guilds Institute; Member, International Society of Philosophical Enquiry. Address: Flat 13, 132 Newport Road, Roath, Cardiff CF24 1DJ, Wales.

PURVES Libby, (Elizabeth Mary Purves), b. 2 February 1950, London, England. Journalist; Broadcaster; Writer. m. Paul Heiney, 2 February 1980, 1 son (deceased), 1 daughter. Education: BA, 1st Class Honours, University of Oxford, 1971. Appointments: Presenter-Writer, BBC, 1975-; Editor, Tatler, 1983; Chief Theatre Critic, The Times, 2010-. Publications: Adventures Under Sail (editor), 1982; Britain at Play, 1982; The Sailing Weekend Book, 1984; How Not to Be a Perfect Mother, 1987; One Summer's Grace, 1989; How Not to Raise a Perfect Child, 1991; Casting Off, 1995; A Long Walk in Wintertime, 1996; Home Leave, 1997; More Lives Than One, 1998; Holy Smoke, 1998; Regatta, 1999; Passing Go, 2000; A Free Woman, 2001; Acting Up, 2004; Love Songs and Lies, 2007; Shadow Child, 2009; Contributions to: Newspapers and magazines. Honours: Best Book of the Sea, 1984; OBE, Services to Journalism, 1999; Columnist of the Year, 1999; Desmond Wettern Award, 1999. Membership: RSA. Address: c/o Rogers Coleridge White, 20 Powis Mews, London W11 1JN, England.

PUTIN Vladimir Vladimirovich, b. 7 October 1952, Leningrad, USSR. President, Prime Minister of the Russian Federation. m. Ludmila Alexandrovna Putina, 2 daughters. Education: Graduate, Faculty of Law, Leningrad State University, 1975. Appointments: National Security Service, 1975-90; Assistant Rector, International Affairs, Leningrad State University, Adviser to Chairman, Leningrad City Council, 1990; Head, International Committee, St Petersburg Mayor's Office, 1991-96, concurrently, First Deputy Chairman of the Government of St Petersburg, 1994-96; Deputy Property Manager, under President Yeltsin, Moscow, 1996; Deputy Chief of Staff, Main Control Department of the Administration of the Russian Federation, 1997; First Deputy Chief of Staff in Charge of Russian Regions and Territories, 1998; Director, Russian Federal Security Service, 1998; Secretary, Russian Security Council, 1999; Prime Minister of the Russian Federation, 1999; Acting President, 1999, President of the Russian Federation, 2000-04, 2004-08; Prime Minister of the Russian Federation, 2008-1012, President of Russia, 2012-. Honours: Master of Sports in sambo wrestling, 1973; Master of Sports in judo, 1975; Won sambo championships in St Petersburg many times; Candidate of Economic Sciences. Address: The Kremlin, Moscow, Russia. E-mail: president@kremlin.ru

PUTTNAM David Terence (Baron), b. 25 February 1941, London, England. Film Producer. m. Patricia Mary Jones, 1 son, 1 daughter. Appointments: Advertising, 1958-66; Photography, 1966-68; Film production, 1968-; Chairman, Enigma Productions Ltd, 1978-, Spectrum Strategy Ltd, 1999-; Director, National Film Finance Corporation, 1980-85, Anglia TV Group, 1982-99, Village Roadshow Corporation, 1989-99, Survival Anglia, 1989-, Chrysalis Group, 1993-96; Chairman, CEO, Columbia Pictures, USA, 1986-88; President, Council for Protection of Rural England, 1985-92; Visiting Lecturer, Bristol University, 1984-86; Visiting Industrial Professor, 1986-96; Governor, Lecturer, LSE, 1997-; Governor, 1974-, Chair, 1988-96, National Film and TV School; Chair, Teaching Council, 2000-02; Productions include: That'll Be the Day; Mahler; Bugsy Malone; The Duellists; Midnight Express; Chariots of Fire; Local Hero; The Killing Fields; Cal; Defence of the Realm; Forever Young, 1984; The Mission, 1985; Mr Love, 1986; Memphis Belle, 1989; Meeting Venus, 1990; Being Human, 1993; War of the Buttons, 1993; Le Confessional, 1995; My Life So Far, 2000. Publications: Rural England: Our Countryside at the Crossroads, 1988; Undeclared War: The Struggle to Control the World's Film Industry, 1997; My Life So Far, 1999. Honours: Honorary FCSD; Honorary degrees (Bristol, Leicester, Manchester, Leeds, Bradford, Westminster, Humberside, Sunderland, Cheltenham and Gloucester, Kent, London Guildhall Universities, Royal Scottish Academy, Imperial College London; Special Jury prize for the Duellist, Cannes, 1977; 2 Academy Awards, 4 BAFTA Awards for Midnight Express, 1978; 4 Academy Awards, 3 BAFTA Awards for Chariots of Fire, 1981; 3 Academy Awards and 9 BAFTA Awards for The Killing Fields, 1985; Michael Balcon Award, BAFTA, 1982; Palme d'Or, Cannes, 1 Academy Award, 3 BAFTA Awards for The Mission, 1987; Officier, Ordre des Arts et des Lettres, 1986. Memberships include: Vice President, BAFTA; Chancellor, University of Sunderland; Chairman, National Endowment for Science, Technology and the Arts, National Museum of Photography, Film and TV; Education Standards Task Force, 1997-2000. Address: Enigma Productions, 29A Tufton Street, London, SW1P 3QL, England.

PYNE Kenneth John (Ken), b. 30 April 1951, London, England. Cartoonist. Partner: Pamela Todd. Education: Holloway County School, London. Appointments: First cartoon published in Punch, 1968; Numerous jobs including layout artist on Scrap & Waste Reclamation & Disposal Weekly; Full-time freelance cartoonist, 1970; Work has appeared in Punch, Private Eye (since 1976, notably the 'Corporation Street' strip from October 1986), Today, The Times, Independent, Guardian, Evening Standard, Hampstead & Highgate Express, Oldie, New Statesman, People, Observer, Which?, The Spectator, Sunday Express, Sunday Times and Stern; Considerable amount of advertising work; Illustrated three guidebooks for English Heritage; Illustrated six editions of the Good Beer Guide, 1985-9, and 1992. Publications: The Relationship, 1981; Martin Minton, 1982; Silly Mid-Off, 1985; This Sporting Life, 1986; In the Bleak Mid-Winter, 1987; Illustrations reproduced in numerous books. Honours: CCGB Joke Cartoonist of the Year, 1981; Strip Cartoonist of the Year, Cartoon Art Trust, 2001; Caricaturist of the Year, Cartoon Art Trust, 2006; Exhibitions of Work: Cartoonist Gallery, 1991 and 1996; Barbican Centre, 1992; Burgh House, Hampstead, 2001; Work exhibited in V&A, British Museum and Cartoon Museum; Hampstead Cartoonist of the Year, 2010. Memberships: British Cartoonist Association. Address: 15 Well Walk, Hampstead, London NW3 1BY, England. E-mail: pyneken@yahoo.co.uk

Q

QIU Jinquan, b. 15 July 1939, Shanghai, China. Atomic Chemistry. 2 sons. Education: Graduate, Atomic Energy Chemistry, University of Science & Technology of China, 1963. Appointments: Deputy Director, Shanghai Institute of the Science of Sciences, 1980-84; Professor, Shanghai University, 1982-84; Deputy Secretary-General, Shanghai Municipal Committee of Science & Technology, 1984-86; Standing Deputy Director, Shanghai Municipal Research Centre of Development, 1986-91; Visiting Professor, Columbia University, 1991-94; General Director, Shanghai International Enterprise Co-operative Corporation, 1994-2001; Retired, Shanghai Municipal Committee of Commerce, 2001-. Publications: On the Yangtse Delta Regional Economy Planning Study, 1982; On Industry Instrument Research of Shanghai, 1988; A Selected Writing on Co-ordinating Development, 2003. Honours: Shanghai Philosophy Social Science Award, 1982; Shanghai High Education Best Achievement Prize of Philosophy & Science, 1982. Memberships: Shanghai Overseas Returned Scholars Association. E-mail: jinquanqiu@sina.com

QUADRIO CURZIO Alberto, b. 25 December 1937, Tirano, Italy. Professor. Education: Degree, Political Science, Catholic University of Milan, 1961. Appointments: Professor, University of Cagliari, 1965-67; Professor, 1968-75, Dean of Faculty, Political Sciences, 1974-75, University of Bologna; Founder, Institute of Economic Sciences, University of Bergamo, 1975-76; Director, 1977-2010, President of Scientific Committee, Research Centre in Economic Analysis; Professor of Political Economy, 1976-2010, Professor Emeritus, Dean of the Faculty of Political Sciences, 1989-2010, Catholic University of Milan; Lecturer, various universities world-wide; Speaker, conferences and seminars world-wide; Columnist, Corriere della Sera Journal. Publications: about 450, concerning economic theory, history of economic thought; stylized facts of economics, applied and institutional economics relating to economic development. Honours: Prizes for Economics include S Vincent, Walter Tobagi, Cortina Ulisse; Gerolamo Cardano, Rotary Club Pavia International Prize; Targa Premio Nuova Spoleto, Associazione Premio Nuova Spoleto, XXIV Premio Canova; Gold Medal for cultural merit, from President of Italian Republic, Benemeriti della Scienza e della Cultura, 2000. Memberships include: Many review and research institutions, scientific councils; Representative Economists, Council National Research, CNR, 1977-87; President, Italian Economists Society, 1995-98; Co-founder then Director, Economia Politica, Journal of Analytical and Institutional Economics (Il Mulino), 1984-; Member, Past President, Istituto Lombardo Accademia di Scienze e Lettere; President, Scientific Committee Edison Foundation, 2000-; Member, International Balzan Prize Foundation's Board, 2006-; Vice President, National Academy Lincei, 2009-; President, Class of Moral Sciences, National Academy Lincei, 2009-. Address: Universita Cattolica del Sacro Cuore, Largo Gemelli 1, 20923 Milano, Italy. E-mail: alberto.quadriocurzio@unicatt.it

QUAID Dennis, b. 9 April 1954, Houston, Texas, USA. Actor. m. (2) Meg Ryan, 1991, divorced, 1 son, (3) Kimberley Buffington, 2004, 2 children. Education: University of Houston. Career: Stage appearances in Houston and New York; Performances with rock band The Electrics; Songwriter for films: The Night the Lights Went Out in Georgia; Tough Enough; The Big Easy; TV appearances: Bill: On His Own; Johnny Belinda; Amateur Night at the Dixie Bar and Grill; Everything That Rises; Films: September 30 1955, 1978; Crazy Mama; Our Winning Season; Seniors; Breaking Away; I Never Promised You a Rose Garden; Gorp; The Long Riders; All Night Long; Caveman; The Night the Lights Went Out in Georgia; Tough Enough; Jaws 3-D; The Right Stuff; Dreamscape; Enemy Mine; The Big Easy; Innerspace; Suspect; DOA; Everyone's All-American; Great Balls of Fire; Lie Down With Lions; Postcards from the Edge; Come and See the Paradise; A 22 Cent Romance; Wilder Napalu; Flesh and Bone; Wyatt Earp; Something To Talk About, 1995; Dragonheart, 1996; Criminal Element, 1997; Going West, 1997; Gang Related, 1997; Savior, 1997; Switchback, 1997; The Parent Trap, 1998; On Any Given Sunday, 1999; Frequency, 2000; Traffic, 2000; The Rookie, 2002; Far From Heaven, 2002; Cold Creek Manor, 2003; The Alamo, 2004; The Day After Tomorrow, 2004; Flight of the Phoenix, 2004; Synergy, 2004; In Good Company, 2004; Yours, Mine and Ours, 2005; American Dreamz, 2006; Terra (voice), 2006; Smart People, 2008; Vantage Point, 2008; The Express, 2008; The Horseman, 2008; GI Joe: The Rise of Cobra, 2009; Pandorum, 2009; Legion, 2010. Address: POB 742625, Houston, TX 77274, USA.

QUANT Mary, b. 11 February 1934, London, England. Fashion, Cosmetic and Textile Designer. m. Alexander Plunket Greene, 1957, deceased 1990, 1 son. Education: Goldsmith's College of Art, London, England. Career: Started in Chelsea, London, 1954; Director, Mary Quant Group of Companies, 1955-; Joint Chair, Mary Quant Ltd; Design Council, 1971-74; UK-USA Bicentennial Liaison Committee, 1973; Retrospective exhibition of 1960s fashion, London Museum, 1974; Victoria and Albert Museum Advisory Council, 1976-78; Senior Fellow, Royal College of Art, 1991; Director (non-executive), House of Fraser, 1997-. Publications: Quant by Quant, 1966; Colour by Quant, 1984; Quant on Make-up, 1986; Mary Quant Classic Make-up and Beauty Book, 1996. Honours: OBE, 1966; Honorary Fellow, Goldsmiths College, University of London, 1993; Honorary FRSA, 1995; Sunday Times International Fashion Award, Rex Award, USA, Annual Design Medal, Society of Industrial Artists and Designers, Piavolo d'Oro, Italy, Royal Designer for Industry, Hall of Fame Award, British Fashion Council (for outstanding contribution to British fashion), 1990; Fellow, Chartered Society of Designers, winner of the Minerva Medal, the Society's highest award; Dr hc, Winchester College of Art, 2000. Address: Mary Quant Ltd, 3 Ives Street, London SW3 2NE, England.

QUEEN LATIFAH, (Dana Owens), b. 18 March 1970, East Orange, New Jersey, USA. Rap Artist; Actress. Career: Worked for Burger King; Worked with female rap act Ladies Fresh; Recorded with producers Dady-O, KRS-1, DJ Mark the 45 King and members of De La Soul; Moved to Motown Records; Established own label and management company, Flavor Unit; Guest appearance on Shabba Ranks's single Watcha Gonna Do; Other recording collaborations with De La Soul and Monie Love; Films include: Living Single; Jungle Fever, 1991; House Party 2, 1991; Juice, 1992; My Life, 1993; Set It Off, 1996; Hoodlum, 1997; Sphere, 1998; Living Out Loud, 1998; The Bone Collector, 1999; Bringing Out the Dead, 1999; The Country Bears, 2002; Brown Sugar, 2002; Chicago, 2002; Bringing Down the House, 2003; Scary Movie 3, 2003; Barbershop 2: Back in Business, 2004; The Cookout, 2004; Beauty Shop, 2005; Last Holiday, 2006; Ice Age: The Meltdown (voice), 2006; Stranger Than Fiction, 2006; Lost Historical Films on the Ice Age Period (voice), 2006; Life Support, 2007; Hairspray, 2007; The Perfect Holiday, 2007; Mad Money, 2008; What Happens in Vegas, 2008; The Secret Life of Bees, 2008; Ice Age: Dawn of the Dinosaurs (voice), 2009; Valentine's Day, 2010; Just Wright, 2010. Many TV appearances. Recordings: Singles: Wrath of My Madness, 1990; How Do I Love Thee, 1990; Ladies First, 1990; Mama Gave Birth to the Soul Children, 1990; Come Into My House, 1993; U.N.I.T.Y., EP, 1994; Just Another Day, EP, 1994; Mr Big Stuff, 1997; It's Alright, 1997; Paper, 1998; Albums: All Hail the Queen, 1989; Latifah's Had It Up 2 Here, 1989; Nature of a Sista, 1991; Black Reign, 1993; Queen Latifah and Original Flava Unit, 1996; Order in the Court, 1998. Address: c/o Universal Records, 2220 Colorado Avenue, Santa Monica, CA 90404, USA. Website: www.queenlatifahmusic.com

QUEIROZ Fernando Diniz, b. 21 October 1977, Belo Horizonte, Brazil. Civil Engineer. m. Joelma C Lima. Education: B, Civil Engineering, 2000, MSc, Structural Engineering, 2003, Federal University of Minas Gerais, Brazil; Diploma, Structural Engineering, Imperial College London, 2007; PhD, Structural Engineering, University of London, UK, 2007. Publications: 3 papers in international journals; 9 papers in international conferences. Honours: Arthur Guimarães Award, Gold Medal, 2000; Professor Jayme Ferreira da Silva Junior Award, 2000; PhD scholarship, Brazilian Foundation CAPES, 2003; Science Director Top 25 Hottest Articles, 2007-10; Listed in international biographical dictionaries. Memberships: American Association for the Advancement of Science; American Chemical Society. E-mail: fernando.dq@terra.com.br

QUEIROZ Joelma Costa de Lima, b. 22 March 1976, Ipatinga/MG, Brazil. Civil Engineer. m. Fernando Diniz Queiroz. Education: Bachelor, Civil Engineering, 2000, MSc, Hydrology, 2003, Federal University of Minas Gerais; Diploma, Hydrology, Imperial College London, 2009; PhD, Hydrogeology, University of London, 2009. Appointments: Independent Consultant, Water Resources Planning, Hydrology and Hydrogeology Engineering. Publications: 3 published papers in international journals; 5 papers at international conferences. Honours: PhD Scholarship, Brazilian Foundation Capes, 2003; Michigan Examination for the Certificate of Proficiency in English; Listed in international biographical dictionaries. E-mail: joelma.clq@terra.com.br

QUEL Eduardo Jaime, b. 12 January 1940, Mar del Plata, Argentina. Professor. m. Maria Silvia, 2 sons, 1 daughter. Education: Graduate, Physics, University of La Plata, Argentina, 1962; Doctor, Physical Sciences, University of Louvain, Belgium, 1970; Doctor, Physics, University of La Plata, Argentina, 1973. Appointments: Professor, National Technical University, 1964; Head, Laser Group, Citefa, Argentina, 1972-1980; Director, Ceilap Investigation Centre for Lasers and Applications, 1980-; Professor, National University of San Martin, 1995. Publications include: Laser scientific works presented at international and national Congresses; Papers and articles published in important international and national magazines; Co-Author of 2 books; Co-Editor of 1 book. Honour: Recorrido Dorado Award, 1992. Memberships: Sociedad Cientifica Argentina; Asociacion Fisica Argentina; Optical Society of America; American Geophysical Union. Address: Ceilap (Citefa-Conicet), Juan B. De La Salle 4397, 1603 Villa Martelli, Argentina. Email: quel@citefa.gov.ar

QUIGLEY Stephen Howard, b. 29 May 1951, Boston, Massachusetts, USA. Associate Publisher. m Suzanne Elizabeth Daley, 2 sons, 1 daughter. Education: BA, French and International Relations, Dartmouth College, Hanover, New Hampshire, 1973. Appointments: College Sales Representative, Acquisitions Editor, Regional Sales Manager, Addison-Wesley Publishing Co Inc, Boston, Chicago and DC, 1973-84; Acquisitions Editor, Scott, Foresman and Company, Chicago, 1985-88; Senior Mathematics Editor, PWS Publishing Company, Boston, 1988-95; Executive Editor, Associate Publisher, John Wiley & Sons Inc, Hoboken, New Jersey and Marblehead, 1995-. Honours: Editor of the Year, 1990; Man of Achievement Award, 2002; Listed in Who's Who publications and biographical dictionaries; Dartmouth Club of the Year, 1990; Association of American Publishers Professional/Scholarly Publications Book of the Year, 2001, 2002, 2006, 2007 and 2010. Memberships include: American Mathematical Society; MAA; National Council of Teachers of Mathematics; American Statistical Association; Association for Supervision and Curriculum Development; Geological Society of America; Massachusetts Bar Association; Boston Rotary International; American Red Cross; Boy Scouts of America; Corinthian Yacht Club, Goldthwaite Reservation; YMCA. Address: John Wiley & Sons Inc, Two Hooper Street, Marblehead, MA 01945, USA. E-mail: squigley@wiley.com

QUIN Louis DuBose, b. 5 March 1928, Charleston, South Carolina, USA. Professor of Chemistry. m. Gyöngyi Szakal Quin, 2 sons, 1 daughter (by previous marriage). Education: BS, The Citadel, 1947; MA, 1949, PhD, 1952, University of North Carolina. Appointments: Chemical Industry and US Army, 1952-56; Department of Chemistry, Duke University, 1956-86, Assistant Professor to J B Duke Professor, Chair, 1970-76; Department Chemistry, University of Massachusetts, 1986-96, Head, 1986-94; Distinguished Visiting Professor, 1997-99, Adjunct Professor, 1999-2009, Chemistry Department, University of North Carolina at Wilmington. Publications: 250 research publications, 9 authored or edited books. Honours: AE and BA Arbusov Award in Phosphorus Chemistry, 1997; North Carolina Distinguished Lecturer, 1999; Fellow, American Association for the Advancement of Science. Membership: American Chemical Society, Sigma Xi. Address: 15 Aldersgate Court, Durham, NC 27705, USA.

QUINN Aiden, b. 8 March 1959, Chicago, USA. Actor. m. Elizabeth Bracco, 1987, 2 daughters. Career: Worked with various theatre groups, Chicago; Off-Broadway appearances in Sam Shepard plays: Fool for Love; A Lie of the Mind; Hamlet, Chicago; TV: An Early Frost; Empire Falls, 2004; Films: Reckless, 1984; The Mission; All My Sons; Stakeout; Desperately Seeking Susan; Crusoe; The Handmaid's Tale; At Play in the Fields of the Lord; Avalon; Legends of the Fall; Mary Shelley's Frankenstein, 1994; The Stars Fell on Henrietta, 1994; Haunted, 1994; Michael Collins, 1996; Looking for Richard, 1996; Commandants, 1996; The Assignment, 1997; Wings Against the Wind, 1998; This is My Father, 1998; Practical Magic, 1998; Blue Vision, 1998; The Imposters, 1998; 50 Violins, 1999; In Dreams, 1999; Two of Us, 2000; See You In My Dreams, 2000; Evelyn, 2002; A Song for a Raggy Boy, 2003; Bobby Jones: Stroke of Genius, 2004; Plainsong, 2004; Return to Sender, 2005; Nine Lives, 2005; The Exonerated, 2005; Empire Falls, 2005; Dark Matter, 2007; 32A, 2007; Wild Child, 2008; A Shine of Rainbows, 2009; The Eclipse, 2009; Handsome Harry, 2009. Address: CAA, 930 Wilshire Boulevard, Beverly Hills, CA 90212, USA.

QUINTANA HIDALGO Alfredo, b. 14 February 1958, Palma Soriano City, Santiago del Cuba's Province, Cuba. University Teacher; Theatre Director. Education: Lic. in Philology, Universidad de Oriente, 1987; Diplomate in Socio-Theatre Studies, 2001. Appointment: Master in Cuban and Caribbean Studies; Director of "Actors' Workshop", Culture House, Palma Soriano; Currently, Master in Communitary Cultural Development. Publications: Articles in many magazines and newspapers; Memorie de Trompo (poetry book), 1992.

Membership: Literary Group "ARCA"; Cultural Society José Marti. Address: Apartado Postal 305, 90100 Santiago de Cuba 1, SCU, Cuba. E-mail: alfredo@mupalma.uo.edu.cu

QUIRK Sir Randolph (Baron Quirk of Bloomsbury), b. 12 July 1920, Isle of Man, England. Emeritus Professor of English Language and Literature; Writer. m. (1) Jean Williams, 1946, divorced 1979, 2 sons, (2) Gabriele Stein, 1984. Education: BA, 1947, MA, 1949, PhD, 1951, DLitt, 1961, University College, London. Appointments: Lecturer in English, 1947-54, Professor of English Language, 1960-68, Quain Professor of English Language and Literature, 1968-81, University College, London; Commonwealth Fund Fellow, Yale University and University of Michigan, 1951-52; Reader in English Language and Literature, 1954-58, Professor of English Language, 1958-60, University of Durham; Vice Chancellor, 1981-85, University of London. Publications: The Concessive Relation in Old English Poetry, 1954; Studies in Communication (with A J Ayer and others), 1955; An Old English Grammar (with C L Wrenn), 1955, enlarged edition (with S E Deskis), 1994; Charles Dickens and Appropriate Language, 1959; The Teaching of English (with A H Smith), 1959, revised edition, 1964; The Study of the Mother-Tongue, 1961; The Use of English, 1962, enlarged edition, 1968; Prosodic and Paralinguistic Features in English (with D Crystal), 1964; A Common Language (with A H Marckwardt), 1964; Investigating Linguistic Acceptability (with J Svartvik), 1966; Essays on the English Language: Mediaeval and Modern, 1968; Elicitation Experiments in English (with S Greenbaum), 1970; A Grammar of Contemporary English (with S Greenbaum, G Leech, and J Svartvik), 1972; The English Language and Images of Matter, 1972; A University Grammar in English (with S Greenbaum), 1973; The Linguist and the English Language, 1974; Old English Literature: A Practical Introduction (with V Adams and D Davy), 1975; A Corpus of English Conversation (with J Svartvik), 1980; Style and Communication in the English Language, 1982, revised edition, 1984; A Comprehensive Grammar of the English Language (with S Greenbaum, G Leech and J Svartvik), 1985; English in the World (with H Widdowson), 1985; Words at Work: Lectures on Textual Structure, 1986; English in Use (with G Stein), 1990; A Student's Grammar of the English Language (with S Greenbaum), 1990, revised edition 1997; An Introduction to Standard English (with G Stein), 1993; Grammatical and Lexical Variance in English, 1995. Contributions to: Scholarly books and journals. Honours: Commander of the Order of the British Empire, 1976; Knighted, 1985; Life Peerage, 1994; Numerous honorary doctorates; Various fellowships. Memberships: Academia Europaea; British Academy, president, 1985-89. Address: University College London, Gower Street, London WC1E 6BT, England.

R

RAAFAT Safanah Mudheher, b. 13 April 1963, Baghdad, Iraq. Lecturer. Education: BSc, Control & System Engineering, 1985, MSc, Control & Instrumentation Engineering, 1991, UOT, Baghdad; PhD, Mechatronics Engineering, IIUM, Malaysia, 2011. Appointments: Lecturer. Publications: Numerous articles in professional journals; 3 book chapters. Honours: Bronze Medal, Intelligent Robust Control of High Precision Positioning Systems Using ANFIS, IIUM Research Invention and Innovation Exhibition, 2010; IEEE Control System Travel Award, IEEE Multi-Conference on Systems & Control, Japan, 2010; Listed in biographical dictionaries. Memberships: IEEE. Address: Blk 7-2-8, Bukit OUG, Condo Jln 3A/155, Kuala Lumpur Klang Lama 58200, Malaysia.

RABBANI Dildar, b. 10 February 1953, Lahore, Pakistan. Director General. m. Blanche, 1 son, 1 daughter. Education: MBA; MSc Eco; JD, International Law. Appointments: Director General, IBMS Geneva, Switzerland. Publications: Human Development in Business Organization. Memberships: Diplomatic Club de Geneve-Swiss. Address: 36 Rue du 31 Décembre, Case Postale 6067, 1207 Geneva, Switzerland. E-mail: ibmsgeneva@gmail.com

RABINOWITZ Harry, b. 26 March 1916, Johannesburg, South Africa. Conductor; Composer; Musical Director. m. (1) Lorna Thurlow Anderson, 1944, 1 son, 2 daughters, divorced 2000, (2) Mary Cooper Scott, 2001. Education: University of the Witwatersrand; Guildhall School of Music, London. Career: Corporal, SA Forces, 1942-43; Conductor, BBC Radio, 1953-60; Head of Music, BBC Television Light Entertainment, 1960-68; LWT, 1968-77; Freelance Conductor, Composer, Hollywood Bowl, 1983-84, Boston Pops, 1985-92, London Symphony Orchestra, Royal Philharmonic Orchestra; Conductor for Films including: Chariots of Fire, Manhattan Project, Heat and Dust, The Bostonians, Time Bandits, Camille Claudel, Howard's End, The Remains Of The Day, Shirley Valentine, Business Affair, Le Petit Garçon, La Fille de d'Artagnan, Death And The Maiden, Nelly and Mr Arnold, Secret Agent, La Belle Verte, Surviving Picasso, The English Patient, Amour Sorcier, City of Angels, A Soldier's Daughter Never Cries; Message In A Bottle; Cotton Mary; The Talented Mr Ripley; The Golden Bowl; Cold Mountain; Possession; Television, New Faces, 1987-88, Paul Nicholas Special, 1987-88, Julia MacKenzie Special, 1986, Nicholas Nickleby, Drummonds, the Insurance Man, Absent Friends, Simon Wiesenthal Story, Marti Caine Special, Alien Empire, Battle of the Sexes; Theatre Conductor, World Premieres of Cats and Song & Dance. Compositions: Film: Sign Of Four; TV: Reilly Ace of Spies; The Agatha Christie Hour; Thomas and Sarah; Crocodile Bird. Honours: MBE, 1978; Basca Gold Award, 1986; Radio and Television Industries Award, 1984; Freeman City of London, 1996. Memberships: British Academy of Composers And Songwriters. Address: Yellow Cottage, Walking Bottom, Peaslake, Surrey GU5 9RR, England. E-mail: mitziscott@aol.com

RACZKA Tony Michael, b. 16 January 1957, Pottsville, Pennsylvania, USA. Artist; Educator. m. Patricia G Martinez, 1 daughter, 1 step-daughter. Education: BFA, Northern Arizona University, Flagstaff, USA, 1978; MFA, Northern Illinois University DeKalb, USA, 1980; Postgraduate Studies, University of California, San Diego, USA, 1991-92. Appointments: Gallery Co-ordinator (and Part-time Instructor of Art), Southwestern College, Chula Vista, California, 1981-84; Instructor of Art, Northern Arizona University, Flagstaff, Arizona, 1983; Registrar, Mingei International Museum of Folk Art, San Diego California, 1985-86; Instructor of Art, San Diego State University, 1987; Senior Museum Preparator, University Art Gallery, University of California, San Diego, 1989-95. Publications: To Consociate and Foster the Self, 2000; Words of Wonder, Wit, and Well?....Well Being, 2000; The Blending of Natures and the Perception of the Real, 2000. Honours: Exhibitions at commercial galleries: Quint Gallery, La Jolla, San Diego, 1982, 1983; Printworks, Chicago, 1982, 1984; Paris Green Gallery, La Jolla, California, 1987; Queens College Art Center, CUNY, Flushing, New York, 1999-; Recipient, Pollock-Krasner Foundation Award, 2001. Memberships: International Society of Phenomenology and the Sciences of Life; San Diego Museum of Art. Address: 4430 42nd Street #2, San Diego, CA 92116, USA. E-mail: raczkatony@aol.com

RADCLIFFE Daniel, b. 23 July 1989, London, England. Actor. Education: Sussex House School; City of London School. Career: Films: David Copperfield, 1999; Harry Potter and the Philosopher's Stone, The Tailor of Panama, 2001; Harry Potter and the Chamber of Secrets, 2002; Harry Potter and the Prisoner of Azkaban, 2004; Harry Potter and the Goblet of Fire, 2005; Harry Potter and the Order of the Phoenix, Ballet Shoes, 2007; The Tale of Despereaux (voice), 2008; Harry Potter and the Half-Blood Prince, 2009; Harry Potter and the Deathly Hallows: Part 1, 2010; Harry Potter and the Deathly Hallows: Part 2, 2011; The Woman in Black, 2012; Kill Your Darlings, Horns, 2013; Theatre: The Play What I Wrote, 2002; Equus, 2007; How to Succeed in Business Without Really Trying, 2011-12; TV: Extras, 2006; December Boys, 2006; My Boy Jack, 2007; The Simpsons, QI, 2010; Saturday Night Live, Robot Chicken, A Young Doctor's Notebook, Have I Got News For You, 2012. Honours: Male Youth Discovery of the Year, 2001; Outstanding New Talent, Targa d'Oro, Person of the Year, 2002; Best Young Actor, Best Actor, 2003; Best Film Star/Actor, Best Movie Actor, Young Talent of the Year, Best Junior Achiever, Best Breakthrough Male Actor, Top 10 Child Stars, 2004; Best Young Actor, 2005; Best Actor/Movie, Best Male Film Star, Best Actor, 2006; Best Male Performance, 2007; Dewynters London Newcomer of the Year, 2008; Favorite Breakthrough Performance, Favorite Leading Actor in a Broadway Play, 2009.

RADCLIFFE Paula Jane, b. 17 December 1973, Northwich, England. Athlete. m. Gary Lough, 1 daughter. Education: University of Loughborough. Career: Distance Runner; World Junior Cross Country Champion, 1992; Started senior career, 1993; 5th, 5,000m, Olympic Games, 1996; Winner, Fifth Avenue Mile, New York, 1996, 1997; 3rd, International Association of Athletics Federations World Cross Challenge series, 1997; 4th, 5,000m, World Championships, 1997; European Cross Country Champion, 1998; 2nd, 10,000m European Challenge, 1998; Silver Medal, 10,000m World Championships, 1999; 4th, 10,000m, Olympic Games, 2000; World Half Marathon Champion, 2000, 2001; World Cross Country Champion, 2002; Gold Medal, 5,000m, Commonwealth Games, 2002; Gold Medal, 10,000m, European Championships, 2002; Winner, London Marathon, 2002, 2003, 2005; Chicago Marathon, 2002, New York Marathon, 2004, 2007; Set world best time for 5,000m in Flora Light 5km, 2003; Winner, Great North Run Half Marathon in world best time, 2003; World record holder for 10,000m, 20,000m and marathon; Captain, GB's Women's Athletic Team, 1998-; Helsinki World Championships, Gold Medal, 2005; Winner San Silvestre Vallecana, 10 Km race, New Years Eve, 2005. Athlete Representative, International Association of Athletics Federations. Publication: Paula: My Story So Far, 2004. Honours: Hon DLitt (De Montfort,

Loughborough); British Female Athlete of the Year, 1999, 2001 and 2002; IAAF World Female Athlete of the Year, 2002; BBC Sports Personality of the Year, 2002; Sunday Times Sportswoman of the Year, 2002; MBE, 2002. Address: c/o Bedford and County Athletics Club, 3 Regent Close, Bedford MK41 7XG, England.

RADEBE Jeffrey Thamsanqa, b. 18 February 1953, Kwazulu Natal, South Africa. Cabinet Minister. m. Brigdette, 1 son, 2 daughters. Education: B Jur degree, University of Zululand, 1976; LLM, International Law, Leipzig University, 1981; Lenin International School, Moscow, 1985. Appointments: Minister of Public Works, 1994-99; Minister of Public Enterprises, 1999-2004; Minister of Transport, 2004-09; Minister of Justice and Constitutional Development, 2009-. Publications: Journalist, Radio Freedom, Dar Es Salaam, Tanzania. Honours: Honorary Doctorate, Human Letters, Chicago State University, 1996; Leucospermum flower named Radebe Sunrise, 2005; Honorary Colonel, SA Air Force, Mobile Deployment Wing, 2006. Memberships: African National Congress; South African Communist Party. Address: 329 Pretorius Street, Pretoria, South Africa. E-mail: jradebe@justice.gov.za

RADEV Lachezar Nikolaev, b. 1 November 1963, Kardjali, Bulgaria. Chemist; Researcher. 1 son. Education: Assen Zlatarov University, Burgas, 1984; PhD, Institute of Organic Chemistry, Bulgarian Academy of Sciences, Sofia, 1997. Appointments: Senior Assistant, 1999-2001, Chief Assistant, 2001-09, Associate Professor, 2010, Head, Department of Fundamental Chemical Technologies, 2010, University of Chemical Technology and Metallurgy, Sofia. Publications: Numerous articles in professional journals. Honours: Listed in biographical dictionaries; Albert Einstein Award of Excellence, 2011. Memberships: Union of Chemists of Bulgaria; American Chemical Society. Address: Botunetz-2, bl 17, vh B, app 17, Sofia 1870, Bulgaria.

RADHAKRISHNAN Nerukav V, b. 17 March 1949, Ernakulam, Kerala, India. Doctor of Medicine. m. Shoba, 1 son, 1 daughter. Education: MBBS, Calicut Medical College, Kerala, India, 1973; MRCP (UK), 1982; Certificate of Independent Practitioner in Gastro-Intestinal Physiological Measurements, Association of GI Physiologists, UK, 2004; FRCP (London), 2006; Specialist, Gastroenterology and General Internal Medicine, Postgraduate Medical Education Board, UK, 2007. Appointments: Pre-registration House Officer, 1972-73, Senior House Officer, Medicine, 1973-75, Calicut Medical College, Kerala, India; Resident, General Duty Medical Officer, Ministry of Health, Tabriz, Iran, 1975-76; General Duty Medical Officer, Government Health Services, Kerala, India, 1976-79; Senior House Officer, General Medicine & Gastroenterology, NHS hospitals in Greater Manchester, England, 1979-82; Registrar, Gastroenterology & General Medicine, District General Hospital, Bury, England, 1983-84; Medical Specialist, General Medicine & Gastroenterology, Dammam, Saudi Arabia, 1984-87; Staff Physician, General Medicine & Gastroenterology, Birch Hill Hospital, Rochdale, 1990-94; Associate Specialist, General Medicine & Gastroenterology, The Penning Acute Hospitals, NHS Trust, Rochdale, UK, 1994-. Publications: Addition of local antiseptic spray to parenteral antibiotic regime reduces the incidence of stomal infection following percutaneous endoscopic gastrostomy – a randomised controlled trial, 2006; The Quill Technique – another method for managing buried bumper syndrome, 2006; A case of intractable nausea & vomiting following posterior fossa crainiotomy – a unique case report with discussion of possible hypothetical pathogenesis.

Memberships: British Society of Gastroenterology; Association of Gastrointestinal Physiologists. Address: 7 Woodcock Close, Bamford, Rochdale, OL11 5QA, Lancashire, England. E-mail: nerukavr@gmail.com

RADOIU Marilena, b. 24 November 1967, Bucharest, Romania. R&D Manager. Education: BSc, 1993, MSc, 1993, Techological Organic Chemistry; Radiochemistry, Nuclear Chemistry, 1998. Appointments: Principal Scientific Researcher, Institute of Atomic Physics, Romania, 1993-2000; Senior Development Chemist, BOC Edwards, UK, 2001-03; Section Leader, Chemistry, Edwards Ltd, UK, 2003-08; R&D Manager, 2008, Director/ Marketing Director, 2009-, Sairem SAS, France. Publications: 2 chapters in thematic books; 7 international patents; 30 articles in scientific journals; 75 papers at international conferences. Honours: Chartered Chemist, Royal Society of Chemistry; Chartered Scientist, RSC; CFIA Rennes, France, 2011; Trophees de l'Innovation, 2011; Listed in international biographical dictionaries. Memberships: Royal Society of Chemistry; American Chemical Society; Association for Microwave Power in Europe for Research & Education. Address: Sairem SAS, 12 Porte du Grand Lyon, 01702 Neyron, France.

RADONS Jürgen, b. 21 February 1960, Lünen, Germany. Biologist. m. Vera Beatrix Langhammer, 1999. Education: Diploma, Biology, 1985; PhD, Biochemistry, 1991; Habilitation, Experimental Medicine, 2004. Appointments: Postgraduate Fellow, Cellular and Molecular Immunology, Biochemistry, 1986-91; Postdoctoral Fellow, Immunology and Biochemistry, 1991-92, Diabetology, 1992-96; Research Fellow, Rheumatology, 1996-98, Molecular Immunology, 1998-2006; Lecturer, Senior Scientist, Experimental Medicine, 2004-06; Group Leader in Tumour Biology and Molecular Oncology, Lecturer in Biochemistry/Pathobiochemistry, University of Greifswald, Germany, 2006-; Professor, Medical Biochemistry, 2010-. Publications: Several articles in professional journals. Honours: International Scientist of the Year 2001; Leader of Science, Technology and Engineering, 2001; Great Minds of the 21st Century; One of 500 Leaders of Influence; 2000 Outstanding Scientists of the 20th Century; 2000 Outstanding Scientists of the 21st Century; 2000 Outstanding Intellectuals of the 21st Century; 2000 Eminent Scientists of Today. Membership: The American Biographical Institute, Research Fellow; International Society of Exercise and Immunology. Address: Obere Bachstrasse 6a, D-17509 Hanshagen, Germany.

RADULESCU Elena, b. 14 May 1927, Rosiorii-de-Vede, Romania. Professor; Senior Specialist in Haematology; Immunocytochemist; Researcher. m. Alexandru A Matusah, divorced 1969, 1 child. Education: Faculty of General Medicine, Cluj, 1953; MD, PhD, Medical Sciences, University of Medicine and Pharmacy "Iuliu Hateganu", 1977; Postgraduate studies in London, 1983, 1987, 1990, and York University, 2000, England; Certificate as a University Professor, Romanian Medical Sciences Academy, 1999. Appointments: Laboratory Physician, Oradea Hospital, -1957; Laboratory Specialist, CFR Hospital; Researcher, Department of Haematology, Oncologic Institute "Ion Chiricuta", Cluj, 1966-91; Senior Researcher, Cluj-Napoca branch of Biotehnos SA, Bucharest, 1991-93; Senior Researcher, 2nd Paediatric Clinic, Cluj, 1993-2002; Senior Specialist, Clinical Laboratory, Pvt Polyclinic, 2002-. Publications: Co-author, Cancer Malignant Haemopathies; Chairman, International Congress of Histochemistry and Cytochemistry, Helsinki, 1984, Washington, 1988, Paris, 1991; Numerous papers and articles; Contributions to the study of leukaemia, lymphomas and myelodysplastic syndromes. Honours: Honorary Member, Professor's Council of University Medicine and Pharmacy, 1992; First degree Diplomas of Excellence; Listed in national and international biographical dictionaries. Memberships: International Federation of Researchers for Science and Technology, Gt Britain; World Society of Cellular and Molecular Biology, NY; International Society of Haematology. Address: Henri Coandă Nr 1, Ap 16, Cluj-Napoca, 400417, Romania.

RAGULSKY Valeri Valerianovich, b. 18 January 1943, Michurinsk, Russia. Physicist. Education: MS, Moscow State University, 1966; PhD, Lebedev Physics Institute, Moscow, 1973; DSc, State Optical Institute, Leningrad, Russia, 1982. Appointments: Researcher, Lebedev Physics Institute, 1967-77; Professor, Institute for Problems in Mechanics, Moscow, 1977-. Publications: Numerous articles in professional journals. Honours: State Diploma for Discovery of Optical Phase Conjugation, 1972; State Prize of USSR for Discovery, Investigation and Use of Optical Phase Conjugation, Moscow, 1983. Memberships: Russian Academy of Sciences. Address: Institute for Problems in Mechanics, Verkadskogo 101, Moscow 119526, Russia. E-mail: ragulsky@mail.ru

RAHMAN Md Mizanur, b. 19 July 1978, Dhaka, Bangladesh. Civil Engineer. m. Tamanna Zaman, 1 daughter. Education: BSc, Civil Engineering, Rajshahi University of Engineering & Technology, Bangladesh; PhD, Civil Engineering, University of New South Wales, Australia. Appointments: Lecturer, UniSA, Australia; Postdoctoral Fellow, University of Canterbury, New Zealand; Assistant Professor, Lecturer, RUET, Bangladesh. Publications: Numerous articles in professional journals and conferences. Honours: UNSW Global & EIPRS Scholarship, Australia; Institution Gold Medal and Jaynal Memorial Award, RUET, Bangladesh. Memberships: International Society of Soil Mechanics & Geotechnical Engineering; IAEG; ASCE, USA; IEB, Bangladesh. Address: School of Natural & Built Environment, Mawson Lakes, UniSA, South Australia 5095, Australia. E-mail: md.rahman@canterbury.ac.nz

RAI K B, b. 20 June 1935, Sarai Sidhu, West Pakistan. Retired Administration Officer. m. Umesh Wig, 1970, 1 son. Education: MA, English Literature, Delhi University, 1968. Appointments: Administration Officer, International Commission on Irrigation and Drainage, New Delhi, 32 years; Retired, 1995. Publications: Men and Gods and Other Poems, 1985; Miscellany (poems), 1994; The Will (play), 1998; Emotions (poems), 1998; Soul 'n Fire (poems), 2001; The Destiny (play), 2002 (approved as text book); Soul Tears (poems), 2005; Pearls of Wisdom (poems), 2005; Soul Smiles (poems), 2006; The Money Lender (play), 2008; Soul Dances (poems), 2009; Soul Speaks (poems), 2011; Words Speak (poems), 2011; Included in various anthologies published in India; Included in World Poetry from 1990 to 2009, Chennai. Honours: Michael Madhusuddan Award for Poetry, 1997; Poet of the Year, Poets International, 2003; Honorary Litt D, World Academy of Arts and Culture, 2007; Marian Love Trust Award, 2008; Lifetime Achievement Award, International Poets Academy, 2009; Editor's Choice Award, 2009; Poetic-works figure in several of M Phil dissertations in Jharkhand University, Dhanbad; Included in various reference publications of IBC, England and American Biographical reference publications. Memberships: International Writers and Artists Association, USA; Fellow, United Writers Association, Chennai; Writers Forum, Ranchi; Chetna Literary Group, Mangalore; World Academy of Arts and Culture, USA. Address: BB/18C First Floor, Janakpuri, New Delhi 110058, India.

RAIJADA Rajendrasinh, b. 1 July 1943, Sondarda, India. Headmaster. m. Gulab Kumari, 1969, 1 son, 1 daughter. Education: BA, Gujarat University, Ahmedabad, 1966; BEd, 1973, MA, 1975, Saurashtra University, Rajkot; PhD, Sardar Patel University, Vallabhvidyanaga, 1979. Appointments: Language Expert, 1975-82, Central Committee Member, 1997-2000, Gujarat State Textbook Board, Gandhinagar; Author. Publications: Radha Madhav, 1970; Farva avyo chhun, 1976; Gulmahor ni niche, 1977; Rahasyavad, 1980; Hun, Kali chhokari ane Suraj, 1982; Darsdhan ane Itishas, 1983; Sant Parampara Vimarsh, 1989; Tantra Sadhana, Mahapanth Ane Anya Lekho, 1993; Pat Upasana ane Pratiko num Rahasya, 2002; Radhasoami Mat Par Pravachan, 2004; Prarthana Na Shabdo, 2007; Bhajan Maram no Marag, 2009; Numerous articles in professional journals. Honours: 2nd prize in painting, Gujarat State Youth Festival, 1964; 1st prize, Pathik, 1976; 1st prize, Kumar, 1980; National Award for Best Teacher, 1990; State Award, Best Teacher, 1993; Sister Nivedita, Best Teacher Award, 2002. Memberships: Puratatva Mandal; Gujarati Sahitya Parishad. Address: Sondarda, via Kevadra 362227, Gujarat, India.

RAINE Craig (Anthony), b. 3 December 1944, Shildon, County Durham, England. Poet; Writer. m. Ann Pasternak Slater, 1972, 3 sons, 1 daughter. Education: Honours Degree in English Language and Literature, 1966, BPhil, 1968, Exeter College, Oxford. Appointments: Lecturer, Exeter College, Oxford, 1971-72, Lincoln College, Oxford, 1974-75, Christ Church, Oxford, 1976-79; Books Editor, New Review, London, 1977-78; Editor, Quarto, London, 1979-80; Poetry Editor, New Statesman, London, 1981, Faber & Faber, London, 1981-91; Fellow, New College, Oxford, 1991-; Editor, Arete magazine, 1999-. Publications: Poetry: The Onion, Memory, 1978; A Journey to Greece, 1979; A Martian Sends a Postcard Home, 1979; A Free Translation, 1981; Rich, 1984, 1953: A Version of Racine's Andromaque, 1990; History: The Home Movie, 1994; Clay. Whereabouts Unknown, 1996; A la recherche du temps perdu, 2000; Collected Poems 1978-99, 2000. Other: The Electrification of the Soviet Union (libretto), 1986; A Choice of Kipling's Prose (editor), 1987; Haydn and the Valve Trumpet (essays), 1990; In Defence of T S Eliot (essays), 2000; Collected Poems 1978-1999, 2000; Rudyard Kipling: The Wish House and Other Stories (editor), 2002; T.S. Eliot: Image, Text and Context, 2007. Contributions to: Periodicals. Honours: 1st Prizes, Cheltenham Festival Poetry Competition, 1977, 1978; 2nd Prize, National Poetry Competition, 1978; Prudence Farmer Awards, New Statesman, 1979, 1980; Cholmondeley Poetry Award, 1983; Sunday Times Award for Literary Excellence, 1998. Memberships: PEN; Royal Society of Literature. Address: c/o New College, Oxford OX1 3BN, England.

RAITT Bonnie, b. 8 November 1949, Burbank, California, USA. Musician (guitar, piano). m. Michael O'Keefe, 1991-1999 (divorced). Education: Radcliffe College. Career: Performer, blues clubs, US East Coast; Concerts include: MUSE concert, Madison Square Garden with Bruce Springsteen, Jackson Browne, Carly Simon, The Doobie Brothers, 1979; Roy Orbison Tribute Concert with artists including: Whoopi Goldberg; kd lang; Bob Dylan; B B King, 1990; Performances with artists including: Stevie Wonder, Bruce Springsteen, Aretha Franklin, Willie Nelson, Elton John. Recordings: Albums include: Bonnie Raitt, 1971; Give It Up, 1972; Takin' My Time, 1973; Streetlights, 1974; Home Plate, 1975; Sweet Forgiveness, 1977; The Glow, 1979; Green

Light, 1982; Nine Lives, 1986; Nick Of Time, 1989; The Bonnie Raitt Collection, 1990; Luck Of The Draw, 1991; Road Tested, 1995; Fundamental, 1998; Silver Lining, 2002; Souls Alike, 2005; The Best of Bonnie Raitt on Capital, 1989-2003, 2003; Bonnie Raitt and Friends, 2006. Singles include: Something to Talk About, 1991; Not the Only One, 1992; You Got It, 1995; Lover's Will, 1999; I Will Not Be Broken, 2005; I Don't Want Anything to Change, 2006.. Honours include: 4 Grammy Awards: Album of Year; Best Rock Vocal Performance; Best Female Pop Vocal Performance; Best Traditional Blues Performance (with John Lee Hooker), and numerous nominations; Rock and Roll Hall of Fame, 2000. Address: PO Box 626, Los Angeles, CA 90078, USA.

RAJAMOHAN Guindy Durairajan, b. 14 February 1939, Madurai, India. Engineer. m. R Thaovamani, 1 son, 3 daughters. Education: B Eng, University of Madras, India, 1960. Appointments: Lecturer, Senior Scale, Mechanical Engineering, Delhi College of Engineering, Delhi, 1967; Principal, various polytechnics, Tamilnadu, India, -1989. Publications: Hyperstatic Method of Photoelasticity; German University Racism. Honours: Listed in international biographical dictionaries. Memberships: CEG Alumni Association. Address: W9 New W 17 Fifth Main Road, Anna Nagar, Chennai, Tamilnadu 600 040, India. E-mail: rajamohan.du@gmail.com

RAJAN K T, Medical Adviser. Education: BSc, 1953; MBBS, 1958; DT, CD (Wales), Welsh National School of Medicine, 1962; PhD (Cantab), Kings College Cambridge, 1970. Appointments: NHS Consultant Physician, 1974-97; Locum, 1997-2000; Advisory role on behalf of Mid Glamorgan Health Authority, Manpower Services Commission for disabled persons, 1983-91; Medicine Lead Co-ordinator, Cardiff Community Health Council (Health Watchdog), Minister of Health & Social Services, Welsh Assembly Government Appointment, 2004-10; Member representative, Health Council to Equality and Diversity Committee of Health Trust in Cardiff, 2008-; Expert Panel Member, Welsh Audit Commission on MRSA and Hospital Acquired Infection; Panel Member, Public Reference Group, Butetown, 2005-; Chairman, Local Arthritis & Rheumatism Council, and Arthritis Care; Chair, Area Rehabilitation Division; Established first osteoporosis centre and bone scanner in Wales; Scientific staff member, Medical Research Council, Pnumoconiosis Unit, Cardiff; Chaired numerous committees at national and international meetings; Pioneered growing human fingers in organ culture and human pleura; Medical Adviser, Red Sock Campaign, Prostate Cancer Awareness, 2010-. Publications: Over 60 papers in peer reviewed journals; 2 papers published in Nature; Chapters in scientific publications. Memberships: Emeritus Member, British Society of Rheumatology, 1997-2009; Emeritus Member, American College of Rheumatology & American Bone Mineral Society, 1997. Address: Naples House, 158 Judkin Court, Heol Tredwen, Cardiff Bay, Cardiff, CF10 5AX, Wales.

RAJENDRAN Sulochana, b. 25 October 1934, Rangoon, Burma. Cultural Columnist; Critic in Music & Dance. m. S Rajendran, 2 daughters. Education: SSLC, Madras Board, 1950; BA (Hons), 1955, MA (Hist), 1956, Madras University; PhD (Hist), Bombay University, 1962; Karnatic Music Vocalist, private studies with Sangeetha Bhushanam K A Venkateswaran, Alathur School, 15 years. Appointments: Assistant Lecturer, Ismail Yusuf College, Bombay 1955-56; Assistant Editor, Thought (weekly), New Delhi, 1959-64; Freelance Art Critic, Music & Dance, 1959-; Lecturer, Sri Venkateswara College, New Delhi, 1964-66; Editor, Shanmukha Journal, 1989-2002; Director, Shanmukhanand Sangeeta Vidyalaya, Bombay, 1991-2002; Visiting Faculty, Music, Mumbai University, 1991-2002; Performing Artiste, 3 decades. Publications: Numerous articles in professional journals. Honours: Sri Rajarajeshwari Bharata Natya Kala Mandir, 1996; Kalasevaka Sudhakara Award, Music Triangle, 1998; Sri Shannukhananda Fine Arts & Sangeetha Sabha, 2000; Nadalaya, Mumbai, 2000; Sangeetha Choodamani, Padam, Mumbai, 2003; Geeta Dhvani, Mohiniatta Nritya Kalakshetra, Mumbai, 2010. Memberships: Managing Committee, Sri Shanmukhananda Fine Arts & Sangeetha Sabha, Bombay; Editorial Advisory Board, Shanmukha; Ad hoc Committee (Music), Mumbai University, 2009; Music Forum, Western Region. Address: 502 Sunshine CHS Ltd, N P Marg, Matunga, Mumbai 400019, Maharashtra, India.

RAKOTOMAHANINA Andrianiaina Franklin James, b. 11 September 1975, Antananarjvo, Madagascar. Education: Bachelor of Law and Communication; Master of Political Science, Master of Public Law, University Antananarivo, 2000; Master of Private Law (Business), 2001; Diploma of Magistrate, National High School for Judge, Antananarivo; Magistere CNTEMAD. Appointments: Journalist, Correspondent in Chief, 1993-2002; Training Career, Mairie d'Antsirabe, Training Career, 2004; Training Career, Regional Chamber of Account of Rhone Alpes, France, 2005; Auditor, Supreme Audit Institution, 2005; Counselor, Finanacial Court of Toliary, 2005; Counselor, Account Court of Fianarantsoa, 2007; Counselor, Financial Account Court of Antananarivo, 2009. Publications: Flambeau, school newspaper of LJJR; Zo, The Student Express Journa; Gazetinao, APEC; Le Fonio, Business Plan; The Privatisation, Global Phenomena; Travelling Around Madagascar on a Camel's Back; La Lutte Contre le Blanchiment d'Argent; La Lutte Contre la Criminalite Axee Sur le Profit. Honours: 1st Prize, Dissertation Competition, Embassy of India; First Award, Malagasy Academies of Science and Art; 3rd Award, Embassy of the People's Republic of China; Hong Kong Great Award, Embassy of the People's Republic of China. Memberships: Reseau des Anciens Stagiaires de France, 2006; Fikambanan'ny Mpikabary eto Madaga, 2007; Friends of English Language in Toliara, 2007; Zaref Translation and Production, 2008; President, Syndicat du Travailleur de Madagascar Mutuelle Syndicale des Auditeurs & Consultants. Address: Lot IPA 37, Anosimasina Bemasoandro, Antananarivo 102, Madagascar. E-mail: jamesdigne@yahoo.fr

RAKOWSKI Andrzej, b. 16 June 1931, Warsaw, Poland. Musicologist; Acoustician. m. Magdalena Jakobczyk, 1 son, 2 daughters. General Education: MSc (electronic engineer), 1957, DSc, 1963, Warsaw University of Technology; Upper PhD (habilitation in musicology), 1977, Warsaw University. Musical Education: MA, State College of Music in Warsaw, 1958. Appointments: Music Producer, Polish Disc Recording Company, 1956-58; Acoustic Consultant, Opera National Theatre, 1966-70; Assistant, Associate, Professor of Musical Acoustics, 1955-2001-, Deputy Rector, 1972-75, Rector (President), 1981-87, Head of the Chair of Music Acoustics, 1968-2001, Chopin Academy of Music, Warsaw; Part-time Professor, Institute of Musicology, Warsaw University, 1987-2003, A Mickiewicz University, Poznan, 1997-; Visiting Professor: Central Institute for the Deaf and Washington University St Louis, USA, 1977-78, McGill University, Montreal, 1985, Hebrew University, Jerusalem, 1991, New University of Lisbon, 2004. Publications: Books: Selected Topics on Acoustics, 1959; Categorical Perception of Pitch in Music, 1978; The Access of Youth to Musical Culture, 1984; Studies on Pitch and Timbre of Sound in Music (editor), 1999; Creation and Perception of Sound Sequences in

Music (editor), 2002; Over 120 articles to scientific journals. Honours: Union of Polish Composers, 1956-; Awards of the Minister of Culture in Poland, 1966, 1968, 1982, 1987; Polish State Awards, Silver Cross of Merit, 1971, Golden Cross of Merit, 1973; Order of the Revival of Poland, Bachelor's Cross, 1982, Officers Cross, 2002. Memberships: Polish Music Council; Polish Academy of Sciences, Acoustical Committee President, 1996-2007; European Society for Cognitive Sciences of Music, President, 2000-03; Honorary Member, Polish Acoustical Society; Honorary Member, Polish Phonetic Association; Fellow, Acoustical Society of America; Listed in Who's Who publications and biographical dictionaries. Address: Pogonowskiego 20, Warsaw 01564, Poland. E-mail: rakowski@chopin.edu.pl

RALHA-SIMOES Helena, b. 18 November 1953, Lisbon, Portugal. Professor. m. Carlos Alberto, 1 daughter. Education: Degree, Clinical Psychology, Higher Institute of Applied Psychology, Lisbon, Portugal; Post-graduate degree, Developmental Psychology, Catholic University of Leuven, Belgium, 1983; PhD, Educational Psychology, University of Aveiro, Portugal, 1993. Appointments: Assistant Professor, Polytechnic Institute of Faro, 1985-90; Adjunct Professor, 1991-2003, Co-ordinator Professor, 2003-, University of Algarve; Director, Department of Social and Educational Sciences, 2009-11. Publications: Personal and Professional Development of Teachers, 1995; Developmental Contexts and Psychological Theories, 1999; Resilience and Personal Development, 2000. Honours: Academic Scholarship of the Ministry of Culture, Catholic University of Leuven, Belgium, 1981-83; Research Fellowship, National Institute of Scientific Research, University of Montreal, Canada, 1989. Memberships: Giordano Bruno Institute; Interdisciplinary Center for the Study of Sciences and Arts; Portuguese Society of Eduational Sciences; CiDinE, Center for Research, Dissemination and Educational Intervention. Address: URB, Quinta da Palmeira, Rua Vergilio Ferreira, 41, 8005-546 Faro, Algarve, Portugal.

RALPH Richard Peter, b. 27 April 1946, London, England. Diplomat. (1) Margaret Elizabeth Coulthurst, 1970, divorced 2001, 1 son, 1 daughter, (2) Jemma Victoria Elizabeth Marlor, 2002. Education: Honours Degree, Politics, Edinburgh University, Scotland. Appointments: Joined, HM Diplomatic Service, 1969; Third Secretary, Foreign and Commonwealth Office (FCO), 1969-70; Third, then Second, Secretary, Laos, 1970-74; Second, then First, Secretary, Portugal, 1974-77; First Secretary, FCO, 1977-81; First Secretary and Head of Chancery, Zimbabwe, 1981-85; First Secretary, then Counsellor, FCO, 1985-89; Counsellor, Washington, USA, 1989-93; Ambassador, Latvia, 1993-95, Governor, Falkland Islands, Commissioner for South Georgia and the South Sandwich Islands, 1996-99; Ambassador, Romania (also accredited to Moldova), 1999-2002; Ambassador to Peru, 2003-2006. Honours: Companion of the Order of St Michael and St George (CMG); Commander of the Royal Victorian Order(CVO). E-mail: richard.ralph@fco.gov.uk

RAMAKRISHNAN Srinivasan, b. 23 March 1977, India. Professor. Education: BE, Electronics and Communicaton Engineering, Bharathidasan University, Trichy, 1998; ME, Communication Systems, Madurai Kamaraj University, 2000; PhD, Information and Communication Engineering, Anna University, Chennai, 2007. Appointments: Engineer, R&D Department, Venus Electronics, Thiruthuraipundi, 1998-99; Teaching Assistant, Department of ECE, Thiagarajar College of Engineering, Madurai, 1999-2000; Lecturer, Department of ECE, Priyadarshini Engineering College, Vaniyambadi, 2000-01; Lecturer, 2001-05, Senior Lecturer, 2005-08, Department of Information Technology, PSG College of Technology, Coimbatore; Associate Professor and Head, 2008-10, Professor and Head, 2010-, Department of Information Technology, Dr Mahalingam College of Engineering & Technology, Pollachi. Publications: 45 articles in professional journals. Honours: Certificate of Appreciation, EMC Corp, Bangalore; Outstanding Reviewer Award, International Journal of Computer Theory and Engineering; Best Paper Award, 3rd National Level Workshop on Intelligent Data Analytics and Image Processing, 2010; Certificate of Appreciation, BE 5th Semester University Examinations. Address: Department of Information Technology, Dr Mahalingam College of Engineering & Technology, Pollachi 642003, India. E-mail: ram_f77@yahoo.com

RAMASAMY Rajesh Kumar, b. 9 February 1983, Puthiyamputtur, India. Research Scholar. Education: BSc, Microbiology; MSc, Biotechnology; M Phil, Biotechnology; Post Graduate Diploma, Bioinformatics. Appointments: Technical Assistant; Research Trainee; Lecturer; Junior Research Fellow. Publications: 15. Honours: Junior Research Fellowship, DRDO; Rajiv Gandhi National Research Fellowship, UGC. Memberships: Indian Society for Technical Education. Address: Department of Environmental Biotechnology, Bharathidasan University, Tiruchirapalli 620 024, Tamilnadu, India. Website: www.rajeshkumar.tk

RAMELLI Ilaria, b. 26 September 1973, Piacenza, Italy. Academic Research Professor. Education: Master in Classics, Master in Philosophy, Catholic University of the Sacred Heart, Milan; PhD, Classical Philology and Culture of the Ancient World, State University of Milan, 1998-2000; Postdoctoral research, Late Antique Religion and Culture, Catholic University of Milan, 2000-02. Appointments: Young Researcher, Catholic University of the Sacred Heart, 2000-02; Assistant, Roman History, Assistant, History of Historiography, Assistant, History of Ancient Philosophy, 2003-, Catholic University of the Sacred Heart, Milan; Professor, History of the Roman Near East, G D Annunzio University, Chieti, 2001-02; Chair, Examination Commission; Full Professor, Roman History, Geneva University offered, 2002-; Director, international research project, Bardaisan of Edessa and the Liber Legum Regionum, 2009-; Church History Visiting Professor, 2012; Senior Visiting Professor of Greek Thought, 2012-13; Co-Director, international research project, Ancient Jewish Thinkers in Dialogue with Others; Director, international Oxford Workshop, The Soul in the Origenian Tradition; Director, international research project, Early Christian and Jewish Novels. Honours: Awards for Excellence, Liceo Classico, 1988-92; Italian Mathematics Olympiad Medal, 1991; Award for Excellence in Classics Licence, Fondazione Cassa di Risparmio di Parma e Piacenza, 1992; Yearly bursary awards, Catholic University, 1992-96; Agostino Gemelli Prize, 1997; Bursary awards, 1997-98, 1998-99, 1999-2000; Bursary awards, 2000-01; Marcello Gigante Classics International Prize, 2006; Formal Mention in Appreciation for Distinguished Scholarly Service, 2010, 2011, 2012; Calliope Cultural Prize, 2012; Listed in international biographical dictionaries. Memberships: Society of Biblical Literature; Studiorum Novi Testamenti Societas; American Philological Association; Classical Association; International Association for Patristic Studies; North American Patristics Society; International Society for Neoplatonic Studies; Italian Society for the History of Religions; European Association for the Study of Religion; International Association for the History of Religion; Patristic Society; Honorary Member, Fraternitas Aurigarum in Urbe; Society of ISSCAS; Directive

Board, many scholarly series and journals. Address: Catholic University of the Sacred Heart, Largo Gemelli 1, 20123 Milan, Italy. E-mail: ilaria.ramelli@unicatt.it

RAMOS Theodore Sanchez de Piña, b. 30 October 1928, Oporto, Portugal (Spanish) (British citizen). Portrait Painter. m. Julia Nan Rushbury, separated, 4 sons, 1 deceased. Education: Colégio Araújo Lima, Oporto; The Northern Polytechnic, London; Hornsey School of Art; RAS Dip, Royal Academy Schools, 1949-54. Appointments: Portrait painter; Former Visiting Lecturer, Harrow School of Art; Brighton College of Art; Royal Academy Schools; Represented in permanent collections: National Portrait Gallery; Royal Academy of Arts; Guards Museum; Windsor Guildhall; Chatsworth House; Government House, Perth, Western Australia; Louisiana University; Portraits include: Her Majesty The Queen; Her Majesty Queen Elizabeth the Queen Mother; HRH Prince Philip, Duke of Edinburgh; HRH Prince Charles; The Grand Duke of Luxembourg; Andrew, 11th Duke of Devonshire. Publications: Numerous illustrations for Penguin books and other publishers. Honours: RAS Silver Medal, 1953. Memberships: East India Club; Marylebone Cricket Club; Reynolds Club; Liveryman, The Worshipful Company of Painter-Stainers; The Worshipful Company of Founders. Address: Studio 3, Chelsea Farm House, Milmans Street, London SW10 0DA, England.

RAMPLING Charlotte, b. 5 February 1946, London, England. Actress. m. (2) Jean Michel Jarre, 1978 (divorced), 2 sons, 1 stepdaughter (1 son from previous marriage). Career: Films include: The Knack, 1963; Rotten to the Core, Georgy Girl, The Long Duel, Kidnapping, Three, The Damned, 1969; Skibum, Corky, 1970; 'Tis Pity She's a Whore, Henry VIII and His Six Wives, 1971; Asylum, 1972; The Night Porter; Giordano Bruno, Zardoz, Caravan to Vaccares, 1973; The Flesh of the Orchid, Yuppi Du, 1974-75; Farewell My Lovely, Foxtrot, 1975; Sherlock Holmes in New York, Orca – The Killer Whale, The Purple Taxi, 1976; Stardust Memories, 1980; The Verdict, 1983; Viva la Vie, 1983; Beauty and Sadness, 1984; He Died with His Eyes Open, 1985, Max mon Amour, Max My Love, 1985; Angel Heart, 1987; Paris by Night, 1988; Dead on Arrival, 1989; Helmut Newton, Frames from the Edge, Hammers Over the Anvil, 1991; Time is Money, 1992; La marche de Radetsky, TV Film, 1994; Asphalt Tango, 1995; Wings of a Dove, 1996; The Cherry Orchard, 1998; Signs and Wonders, 1999; Aberdeen, 1999; Fourth Angel, Under the Sand, Superstition, 2000; See How They Run, 2002; Summer Things, 2003; I'll Sleep When I'm Dead, 2003; Swimming Pool, 2003; The Statement, 2003; Jerusalem, 2003; Vers le sud, 2004; Basic Instinct 2, 2006; Désaccord parfait, 2006; Angel, 2007; Caótica Ana, 2007; Boogie Woogie, 2008; Babylon A.D., 2008; The Duchess, 2008; Life During Wartime, 2009; StreetDance 3D, 2010; TV: numerous appearances. Honours: Chevalier Ordre des Arts et des Lettres, 1986; OBE, 2000; Cesar d'honneur, 2001; Chevalier, Legion d'honneur, 2002. Address: c/o Artmédia, 20 avenue Rapp, 75007 Paris, France.

RAMRAKHIANI Meera, b. 5 June 1951, Mhow, India. Teaching & Research. Education: BSc, Physics, Pure Mathematics & Applied Mathematics, M H College of Home Science, Jabulpur, 1971; MSc, 1973, PhD, 1978, Physics, Jabalpur University. Appointments: Lecturer, Physics, Hawabagh Women's College, Jabalpur, 1977-89; Senior Lecturer, 1989-90, Reader, 1990-2005, Professor, 2005-, Physics, Rani Durgavati University, Jabalpur. Publications: Co-author, Bhoutiki Part II; Numerous articles in professional journals. Honours: Vijaya Shree Award, 1997; Women of the Year, 1997; 20th Century Award, 1998; Woman of the Year Jewel, 2005; Bharat Jyoto Award, 2006; Plato Award, 2006. Memberships: Indian Science Congress Association; Association of Physics Teachers; Luminescence Society of India; Third World Organization of Women in Science; Biophysical Society of India. Address: HIG-5, Govind Bhawan Colony, South Civil Lines, Jabalpur 482001, India. E-mail: mramrakhiani@hotmail.com

RAMSDEN Jeremy Joachim, b. 13 August 1955, Amersham, England. Biophysics and Nanotechnology Scientist. Education: MA, Cambridge University, 1981; Dr ès Sciences, Ecole Polytechnique Fédérale, Lausanne, Switzerland, 1985. Appointments: Research Scientist, Ilford Ltd, Warley, Essex, England, 1977-81; Research Associate, Princeton University, New Jersey, 1986; Visiting Scientist, Hungarian Academy of Sciences, Bioctr, Szeged, 1987; Scientist, 1988-2002, Privat-docent, 1994-, Basel University, Switzerland; Visiting Scientist, USSR Academy of Sciences, Moscow, 1990; President, Institute of Advanced Study, Basel, 1999-; Chair of Nanotechnology, Cranfield University, 2002-; Research Director, Bionanotechnology, Cranfield University, Kitakyushu, 2003-09; Academician Secretary of the Section of Natural Sciences and Engineering, Euro Mediterranean Academy of Arts and Sciences, 2010-. Publications: The New World Order, 1991; Bioinformatics, 2004, 2009; Nanotechnology in Paper Production, 2005; Spiritual Motivation: New Thinking for Business and Management, 2007; Biomedical Surfaces, 2008; Complexity and Security, 2008; Applied Nanotechnology: the Conversion of Research Results to Products, 2009; Nanotechnology: an Introduction, 2011; Contributor of articles to professional journals. Memberships: Oxford & Cambridge Club; Swiss Biochemical Society; Mathematical Association of America; Institute of Materials, Minerals and Mining. Address: Department of Materials, Cranfield University, Bedfordshire, MK43 0AL, England. E-mail: j.ramsden@cranfield.ac.uk

RANADE Ashok Da, b. 25 October 1937, India. m. Hamida Ebrahim. Education: LLB, MA, English Literature, MA, Marathi Literature, University of Bombay; Hindustani Vocal Classical Training with Pt Gajanauruo Joshi and others. Career: All India Radio, Bombay; Lecturer, English and Marathi, Siddharth College of Commerce and Economics; First Director of University Music Centre, Bombay, 1968-83; Associate Director, Archives and Research Centre, Ethnomusicology, American Institute of Indian Studies, 1983-84; Deputy Director, Theatre Research and Ethnomusicology, National Centre for Performing Arts, Bombay, 1984-94; Conducts many workshops and courses in voire culture singing, music appreciation and ethnomusicology; Numerous seminars. Compositions: Composed music for Akar, International Exhibition of Calligraphy, New Delhi, 1988; Discovery of India, Nehru Centre, Bombay, 1989; Composed music for plays and films; Composed and compered many thematical music presentations. Recordings: Cassettes: Baithakchi Lavani, 1989; Devgani, 1991. Publications include: Lok Sangget Shastra, 1975; On Music and Musicians of Hindustan, 1984; Marathi Stage Music, 1986; Keywords and Concepts: Hindustani Classical Music, 1990; Music and Drama in India, 1991; Essays in Indian Ethnomusicology, 1998. Honours: Appointed National Lecturer in Music, University Grants Commission, New Delhi, 1990-91; Appointed, Tagore Chair, M S University of Baroda, 1994-95; Awarded Master Krishnarao Phulambrikar Puraskar, Maharashtra Sahitya Parishad, 1998; Award for Music Research, Music Forum, Mumbai, 1998. Address: 7 Dnyanadevi, Sahitya Sahawas, Kalanagar, Kalelkar Marg, Mumbai 400051, India.

RANSFORD Tessa, b. 8 July 1938, Bombay, India. Poet; Writer; Editor. m. (1) Iain Kay Stiven, 1959, divorced 1986, 1 son, 3 daughters, (2) Callum Macdonald, 1989, deceased. Education: MA, University of Edinburgh, 1958; Teacher Training, Craiglockhart College of Education, 1980. Appointments: Founder, School of Poets, Edinburgh, 1981-; Founder, 1982, Director, 1984-99, Scottish Poetry Library; Editor, Lines Review, 1988-98; Retired, 1999; Freelance Poetry Practitioner and Adviser, 1999-; Royal Literary Fund Writing Fellow, 2001-04, 2006-08. Publications: Light of the Mind, 1980; Fools and Angels, 1984; Shadows from the Greater Hill, 1987; A Dancing Innocence, 1988; Seven Valleys, 1991; Medusa Dozen and Other Poems, 1994; Scottish Selection, 1998; When it Works it Feels Like Play, 1998; Indian Selection, 2000; Natural Selection, 2001; Noteworthy Selection, 2002; The Nightingale Question: five poets from Saxony, 2004; Shades of Green, 2005; Sonnet Selection, 2007; Not Just Moonshine, New and Selected Poems, 2008. Contributions to: Anthologies, reviews, and journals. Honours: Scottish Arts Council Book Award, 1980; Howard Sergeant Award for Services to Poetry, 1989; Heritage Society of Scotland Annual Award, 1996; OBE, New Years Honours, 2000; Society of Authors Travelling Scholarship, 2001; Honorary Fellow, Association for Scottish Literary Studies, 2010. Memberships: Saltire Society, honorary member 1993; Scottish Library Association, honorary member, 1999; Scottish Poetry Library, ex-officio honorary member, 1999; Fellow, Centre for Human Ecology, 2002; Honorary Doctorate, Paisley University (DUniv), 2003; Scottish International PEN, President, 2003-6; Institute of Contemporary Scotland, Honorary Fellow, 2005. Address: 31 Royal Park Terrace, Edinburgh EH8 8JA, Scotland. Website: http://www.wisdomfield.com www.scottish-pamphlet-poetry.com

RANTANEN Jussi-Pekka, b. 18 December 1975, Pori, Finland. Presenter; Editor. m. Saga Kaisa Inkeri Wiklund, 1 son, 1 daughter. Education: Undergraduate and Graduate Studies, University of Austin, Texas, USA, 1998-99; Master of Social Sciences, University of Tampere, Finland, 2000. Appointments: Journalist, Satakunnan Kansa, Pori, 1996; Reporter and News Presenter, 1997, Freelancer, 1998, YLE Radio News; Reporter and News Presenter, YLE Morning TV, 1998, 1999, 2000; Director and Presenter, Book Adventure Series, YLE Morning TV, 2001, Host and Reporter of YLE Morning TV, 2002-05, Presenter, Kult-TV, 2005, Presenter and Editor, Culture Corner, YLE Morning TV, 2006-, Channel YLE TV1; TV News Presenter, Finnish Broadcasting Company, Helsinki, 2007-; Talk Show Host, Mansikkapaikka, Channel YLE TV2, 2011. Publications: Pure Illusion – Puhtaan illusion puolesta, 2000; Newsreports, broadcasts, newspaper articles and various interview programmes. Honours: Stipend, Finnish Broadcasting Company (YLE) and the Union of Journalists in Finland (UJF), 2005. Memberships: Union of Journalists in Finland; Finnish Reserve Officers' Federation. E-mail: jussi-pekka.rantanen@yle.fi

RANTZEN Esther, b. 22 June 1940. Television Presenter. m. Desmond Wilcox, 1977, deceased 2000, 1 son, 2 daughters. Education: MA, Somerville College, Oxford. Appointments: Studio manager, making dramatic sound effects, BBC Radio, 1963; Presenter, That's Life, BBC TV 1973-94; Scriptwriter, 1976-94; Producer, The Big Time (documentary series), 1976; Presenter: Esther Interviews..., 1988; Hearts of Gold, 1988, 1996; Drugwatch; Childwatch; The Lost Babies (also producer); Esther (talk show), 1994-; The Rantzen Report, 1996-; Excuse my French, 2006; Old Dogs New Tricks, 2006. Publications: Kill the Chocolate Biscuit (with D Wilcox), 1981; Baby Love, 1985; The Story of Ben Hardwick (with S Woodward), 1985; Once Upon a Christmas, 1996; Esther: The Autobiography, 2000; A Secret Life, 2003. Honours include: BBC TV Personality of 1975, Variety Club of Great Britain; Richard Dimbleby Award, BAFTA, 1988; OBE, 1991; Snowdon Award for Services to Disabled People, 1996; Royal TV Society Hall of Fame Award, 1998; Champion, Community Legal Service, 2000; Hon DLitt, South Bank University, 2000. Memberships: National Consumer Council, 1981-90; Health Education Authority, 1989-95; Chairman, Childline. Address: BBC TV, White City, 201 Wood Lane, London, W12 7RJ, England.

RAO Erranguntla Venkata, b. 1 July 1931, Priyagraharam, India. Teacher; Researcher. m. Kameswari, 1 son, 1 daughter. Education: BSc, 1950, MSc, 1952, DSc, 1959, Andhra University; PhD, Newcastle University, 1964. Appointments: CSIR Research Assistant, 1953-58, Lecturer, Pharmacy, 1958-65, Reader, Pharmacy, 1965-75, Professor, Pharmaceutical Sciences, 1975-91, Head of Department, 1985-88, Andhra University; Professor & Principal, Benhampur University Pharmacy College, 1992-93; PI Investigator, UGC Project, 1993-96; Adviser, NatcoPharma Ltd, Hyderabad, 1996-2001; Visiting Professor, Kathmandu, 2004. Publications: 175 publications in Indian and international scientific journals including 15 review articles and 5 Indian patents. Honours: K N Welch Memorial Prize, UK, 1964; A P State Government Best Teacher Award, 1989; Professor G P Srivastava Memorial Award, 1990; Professor M L Khohana Memorial Lecture Award, 1991; IPA Fellowship Award, 1997; APTI Lifetime Achievement Award, 2003. Memberships: Royal Society of Chemistry; Indian Pharmaceutical Association; Association of Pharmaceutical Teachers of India; A P Akademi of Sciences; Current Science Association. Address: Flat GB, Geethika Residency, #50-121-49/1/2, B S Layout, Seethammadhara, Visakhapatnam – 530013, India. E-mail: profevrao@hotmail.com

RAO Nagaraja B K, b. 23 March 1934, Bangalore, India. Professor; Editor; Publisher. m. 2 daughters. Education: BSc, University of Mysore, India, 1955; MSc, University of Southampton, England, 1971; DIISc, The Indian Institute of Science, India, 1963; PhD, 1978, University of Birmingham, England; DTech, University of Sunderland, England, 2004. Appointments: Head of Packaging, LRDE, Bangalore, India, 1956-64; Head of Packaging, Hairlok Co, Bedford, England, 1965-67; Research Fellow, University College London, 1969-70; Post Doctoral Research Fellow, University of Birmingham, England, 1971-79; Senior Lecturer, Birmingham Polytechnic, 1980-89; Reader/Professor, Southampton Institute, 1990-96; Past Visiting Professor, University of Exeter, University of Sunderland and Glasgow Caledonian University; Past External Examiner for numerous universities throughout UK, also universities in India, Republic of South Africa, Sweden and Canada; Organised international congresses and exhibitions in UK, France, India, Canada, Finland, Australia, USA, Sweden, Portugal, Czech Republic; Published and edited COMADEM congress proceedings distributed worldwide. Publications: Over 120 technical papers in well-known journals; Editor and author, Handbook of Condition Monitoring; Contributed chapters in The Handbook of Condition Monitoring, and Infrasound & Low Frequency Vibration; Editor in chief and publisher, International Journal of Condition Monitoring and Diagnostic Engineering Management. Honours: Visiting Professor, University of Glamorgan, Wales; External Examiner, University of Wales Institute of Cardiff, Wales; Visiting Lecturer: Vaxjo University, Sweden; Lulea University of

Technology, Sweden; Vellore Institute of Technology, India. Address: 307 Tiverton Road, Selly Oak, Birmingham, B29 6DA, England. E-mail: rajbknrao@btinternet.com

RAOOF Mohammed, b. 1955, Tehran, Iran. University Professor. Education: BSc (Eng), Civil Engineering (1st class honours), 1975-78, MSc, Concrete Structures and Technology. 1978-79, PhD, Structural Analysis, 1979-83, DSc (Eng), Structural Engineering and Mechanics, 2002, Imperial College, London University. Appointments: Research Assistant, Imperial College, 1981-85; Structural Engineer, Wimpey Offshore Engineers and Constructors Ltd, 1985-86; Lecturer II, 1986, Senior Lecturer, 1988, Bridon Reader, 1991, Bridon Professor of Structural Mechanics, 1992, South Bank University, London, 1986-94; Professor of Structural Engineering, Structures and Materials Group Leader, Civil and Building Engineering Department, Loughborough University, 1994-; Visiting Professor, The Steel Structures Department, Civil Engineering Faculty, Czech Technical University, Prague, 1996; Visiting Professor, The Hydraulic Structures Department, Georgian Technical University, Tbilisi, 1999-; External examiner/assessor for 14 universities/ institutions in the UK, Canada, Malta, Georgia, Saudi Arabia and Malaysia; Consultancy for several international construction companies on a number of major structures including the Millennium Footbridge, London, The Severn Suspension Bridge, Bristol and The Queen Elizabeth II Cable Stayed Bridge, Dartford. Publications: Sole author of 21 international journal and 19 refereed international conference papers; Co-author of 56 international and 17 refereed national journal and 54 refereed international conference papers; Papers presented in 59 international conferences with 46 of them having been held outside the UK in 23 different countries across 4 continents; Reviewed papers for 34 different international journals. Honours: T K Hsieh Award, Institution of Civil Engineers in Conjunction with the Society of Earthquake and Civil Engineering Dynamics, 1985; James Watt Gold Medal, Institution of Civil Engineers, 1991; CEGB (Central Electricity Generating Board) Prize, Institution of Mechanical Engineers, 1991; Trevithick Premium, Institution of Civil Engineers, 1993; Henry Adams Award (Diploma), Institution of Structural Engineers, 1993; First winner of the 14th Khwarizmi International Award 2000-2001, Endorsed by UNESCO and presented personally by the President of Iran (Mr Seyed Mohammad Khatami), 2001; Honorary Doctorate (Honoris Doctor), Technical University of Georgia, 2008. Memberships: Diploma of Membership of Imperial College, 1979; Member, 1995-2000, Fellow, 2000-, Institution of Structural Engineers; Fellow, Institution of Civil Engineers, 2002-. Address: Civil and Building Engineering Department, Loughborough University, Loughborough, Leicestershire LE11 3TU, England. E-mail: m.raoof@lboro.ac.uk

RASHBA Emmanuel Iosif, b. 30 October 1927, Kiev, Ukraine. Physicist. m. Erna Kelman, 1 son, deceased, 1 daughter. Education: Diploma with Honour, Kiev, 1949; PhD, Kiev, 1956; Doctor of Sciences, Ioffe Institute for Physics and Technology, St Petersburg, 1963; Professor of Theoretical and Mathematical Physics, Landau Institute for Theoretical Physics, Moscow, 1967. Appointments: Junior and Senior Scientist, Institute of Physics, Kiev, 1954-60; Head of Theoretical Department, Institute for Semiconductors, Kiev, 1960-66; Head of Department and Principal Scientist, Landau Institute for Theoretical Physics, Moscow, 1966-97; Research Professor, University of Utah, Salt Lake City, 1992-2000; Research Professor, SUNY at Buffalo, 2001-2003; Research Associate, Harvard University, Cambridge, 2004-; Rutherford Professorship in Spintronics, England, 2007-10. Publications: Collection of Problems in Physics, in Russian, 1978, 1987, in English 1986, in Japanese, 1989; Spectroscopy of Molecular Excitons, in Russian, 1981, in English, 1985; Over 240 contributed and review papers in professional journals. Honours: National Prize in Science, USSR, 1966; Ioffe Prize of the Academy of Sciences of the USSR, 1987; ICL Prize, Conference on Lumin. and Optical Spectroscopy, 1999; Arkady Aronov Memorial Lecture, Israel, 2005; Sir Nevill Mott Lecture, England, 2005; Solomon Pekar Prize, National Academy of Sciences, Ukraine, 2007. Membership: Fellow American Physical Society. Address: Department of Physics, Harvard University, Cambridge, MA 02138, USA. E-mail: erashba@physics.harvard.edu

RASHED Mohamed Buajela, b. 14 June 1951, Sabrata, Libya. Orthopaedic Surgeon. m. Halima, 4 sons, 1 daughter. Education: Mb Bch; FRCSI. Appointments: Chairman, Libyan Orthopaedic Association; Head of Orthopaedic Department, Khadra Hospital; President, Libyan Sports Medicine Federation. Publications: 4th Floor Principles of Orthopaedics & Fractures; Sports Injuries Early Managements. Honours: Supreme Libya, 2003. Memberships: LOA; SICOT; SAFO; PANARAB; MARENSTRUM. Address: Khadra Hospital, Tripoli, Libya. E-mail: mohbrashed@yahoo.com

RASI-ZADEH Arthur Tahir, b. 26 February 1935, Ganja city, Azerbaijan. Mechanical Oil Engineer. m. Zeynalova Aida Ibrahim, 1 daughter. Education: Mechanical Engineer, Azerbaijan Industrial Institute, 1957. Appointments: Engineer, Head of Department, Deputy Director, Scientific Affairs of Oil Machinery, Azerbaijan SSR, 1957-73; First Deputy, Chief Engineer, Oil Machinery Corporation, Azerbaijan SSR, 1973-77; Director, Oil Machinery Institute, Azerbaijan SSR, 1977-78; Deputy Chairman, State Plan Committee, Azerbaijan SSR, 1978-81; Head, Machinery Department, Central Committee of Communist Party, Azerbaijan SSR, 1981-86; First Deputy Prime Minister, Republic of Azerbaijan, 1986-92, 1996, 2003; Adviser, Economic Reforms Foundation, 1992-96; Assistant to President of the Republic of Azerbaijan, 1996; Prime Minister, Republic of Azerbaijan, 1996-2003, 2003-present. Publications: Author of 7 inventions; 33 articles. Honours: Laureate, USSR State Prize, 1971; Badge of Honour Order, USSR Supreme Soviet Presidium, 1980; Order of the Red Banner of Labour, USSR Supreme Soviet Presidium, 1986; Certificates of Honour, Supreme Soviet Presidium; Order of Istiglal (Independence), late President of the Republic of Azerbaijan, Heydar Aliyev, 2005; Order of Sharaf (Honour), President of the Republic of Azerbaijan, Ilham Aliyev, 2010. Address: Cabinet of Ministers, 68 St Lermontov, Baku, AZ1066, Republic of Azerbaijan. E-mail: nk@cabmin.gov.az Website: www.cabmin.gov.az

RATH Banamali, b. 1 April 1938, BD Pur Sāsan, Ganjām, India. Professor. m. Sushilā, 1 son, 2 daughters. Education: Sāhityāchārya, 1955; BA, 1957; Hindi Sāhitya Ratna, 1957; MA, Sanskrit, 1959; MA, Oriya, 1960; PhD, Arts, 1974; Certificates, General Linguistics, Applied and Advanced Linguistics, 1974, 1975, 1976. Appointments: Lecturer, Oriyā, Orissa Education Service, Government of Orissā, & Visvabhārati University, Sānti Niketan, 1960-82; Reader/ Professor, Principal; Senior Administrative Grade, OES (1); Retired, 1996. Publications include: History of Sanskrit Literature, Orissa Sāhitya Academy, 1962; Glimpses of Vaisnavisim in Orissa, 1983; A Study in the Immitations of Gitagovinda, 1984; A Study on the Sri Krishna Iliamritam, 1984; Sāhitya Darpan of Viswanāth Kavirāj – A Critical Study, A Critique on Gitagovinda, A New Light on Indian Poetics, Orissa Text Book Bureau, 1981; 39 papers published in national and international research journals of repute. Honours: Best Meritorious Student Award, Government of Orissa, 1955; Best Orator Award, Rāmakrishna Mission, 1955; Nātyapravina, 1958; Best Researcher Award, Mithila Research Institute, Darbhangā, 1959; UGC Award for University Level Books by Indian Author, 1978; Bhārati Bhānam, 1978; Jnanasri, 1981; Bhanja Bhārati Honour Kalinga Sāhitya Samāj, Berhampur, 2003; Honorary Member, ABI Research Board of Advisors, Carolina, USA, 2003; PRATIBHĀ Honour, Berhampur University, 2011; Listed in international biographical dictionaries. Memberships: World Congress of Orientalists, Vienna; Indian Council of Cultural Relations, New Delhi; All India Linguistic Conference, Poona; All India Oriental Conference, Poona; Bhārat Vikash Parisad, New Delhi. Address: Medical Bank Colony, Front Line, Berhampur 760004, Dist Ganjam (Orissa), India.

RATHER Dan, b. 31 October 1931, Wharton, Texas, USA. Broadcaster; Journalist. m. Jean Goebel, 1 son, 1 daughter. Education: BA, Journalism, Sam Houston State College, Huntsville, Texas, 1953; University of Houston; South Texas School of Law. Appointments: Staff, United Press International, Houston Chronicle, KTRH Radio, Houston, KHOU-TV, Houston; White House Correspondent, 1964-65, 1966-74, Chief, London Bureau, 1965-66, CBS-TV; Anchorman-Correspondent, CBS Reports, 1974-75; Co-Editor, 60 Minutes, CBS-TV, 1975-81; Anchorman, Dan Rather Reporting, CBS Radio, 1977-; Anchorman and Managing Editor, 1981-2005, co-anchorman, 1993-2005, CBS Evening News with Dan Rather; CBS News special programmes; Dan Rather Reports, 2006. Publications: The Palace Guard (with Gary Gates), 1974; The Camera Never Blinks Twice (with Mickey Herskowitz), 1977; Memoirs: I Remember (with Peter Wyden), 1991; The Camera Never Blinks Twice: The Further Adventures of a Television Journalist, 1994; Deadlines and Datelines: Essays at the Turn of the Century, 1999. Honours: Many Emmy Awards; Dan Rather Communications Building named in his honour, Sam Houston State University, Huntsville, Texas; Honorary Doctor of Humane Letters, Siena College, New York, 2007. Address: c/o CBS News, 524 West 57th Street, New York, NY 10019, USA.

RATNAYAKE Ratnayake Mudiyanselage Jayaratna Bandara, b. 1 October 1950. Retired; Visiting Lecturer. m. 1 daughter. Education: BSc (Eng), University of Peradeniya, 1981; Postgraduate diploma, Industrial Engineering, National Institute of Business Management, 1986; LLB, Open University of Sri Lanka, 2000; Postgraduate diploma, Transportation, University of Moratuwa, Sri Lanka, 2002; Postgraduate diploma, Management, University of Rajarata, Mihintale, Sri Lanka, 2004; MBA, University of Northwest, USA, 2007; PhD, University of Honolulu, USA, 2009; Advanced Diploma, Psychology, 2009; Advanced diploma, Psychological Counselling & Psychotherapy, 2009; LLM (University of Wales), Institute of Advanced Legal Studies, Sri Lanka Law College, Colombo, 2009-11. Appointments: Visiting Lecturer, Faculty of Engineering, Assistant Lecturer, Industrial Training Division, University of Peradeniya, Sri Lanka; Visiting Lecturer, Construction Industry Training Project; Visiting Lecturer, Higher National Diploma in Engineering, Polytechnical College, Kandy; Visiting Lecturer, Diploma in Management Programme, OUSL; Visiting Lecturer, Postgraduate Institute of Business Management. Memberships: Institution of Engineers' Sri Lanka; Chartered Management Institute, UK; Institute of Management, Sri Lanka; Institute of Psychology, Counseling, Psychotherapy and Allied Professions of Sri Lanka; Project Management Institute, USA; Chartered Institute of Marketing, UK. Address: No 88, Turuviyana, Bulugolla, Potuhera, Sri Lanka. E-mail: ramujbr@yahoo.com

RATTLE Sir Simon, b. 19 January 1955, Liverpool, England. Conductor. m. (1) Elise Ross, 2 sons, (2) Candace Allen, 1996. Education: Royal Academy of Music. Career: Has conducted orchestras including: Bournemouth Symphony, Northern Sinfonia, London Philharmonic, London Sinfonietta, Berlin Philharmonic, Los Angeles Philharmonic, Stockholm Philharmonic, Vienna Philharmonic, Philadelphia Orchestra, Boston Symphony; Début: Queen Elizabeth Hall, 1974, Royal Festival Hall, 1976, Royal Albert Hall, 1976, Assistant Conductor, BBC Symphony Orchestra, 1977; Associate Conductor, Royal Liverpool Philharmonic Society, 1977-80; Glyndebourne début, 1977, Royal Opera, Covent Garden, 1990; Artistic Director London Choral Society, 1979-84; Principal Conductor and Artistic Advisor, City of Birmingham Symphony Orchestra (CBSO), 1980-90, Music Director, 1990-98; Artistic Director, South Bank Summer Music, 1981-83; Joint Artistic Director, Aldeburgh Festival, 1982-93; Principal Guest Conductor, Los Angeles Philharmonic, 1981-94, Rotterdam Philharmonic, 1981-84; Principal Guest Conductor, Orchestra of the Age of Enlightenment, 1992-; Chief Conductor and Artistic Director, Berlin Philharmonic Orchestra, 2002-. Publications: Over 30 recordings with CBSO. Honours: Edison Award, 1987; Grand Prix du Disque, 1988; Grand Prix Caecilia, 1988; Gramophone Record of the Year Award, 1988; Gramophone Opera Award, 1989; International Record Critics' Award, 1990; Grand Prix de l'Academy Charles Cros, 1990; Gramophone Artist of Year, 1993; Montblanc de la Culture Award, 1993; Officier des Arts et des Lettres, 1995; Toepfer Foundation Shakespeare Prize, 1996; Gramophone Award for Best Concerto recording, Albert Medal (RSA), 1997; Choc de l'Année Award, 1998; Gramophone Award for Best Opera Recording, 2000; Gramophone Awards for Best Orchestral Recording and Record of the Year, 2000; Comenius Prize, Germany, 2004; Classical BRIT Award, 2004. Address: c/o Askonas Holt Ltd, Lonsdale Chambers, 27 Chancery Lane, London, WC2A 1PF, England.

RATUSHNYAK Anna, b. 14 December, Chirchik, Uzbekistan. Chemist; Ecologist; Hydrobiologist. m. Jury Ratushnyak, 2 sons. Education: Degree, Chemistry, Kazan State University, Tatarstan, Russia, 1970; Postgraduate, Institute of Biology, Kazan branch, Russian Academy of Sciences, 1971-76; PhD, Hydrobiology, Moscow State University, 1993; DSc, Ecology, Nizhny Novgorod State University, Russia, 2002. Appointments: Senior Scientific Employee, Institute of Chemical Products, Tatarstan, Kazan, 1976-83; Senior Scientific Employee, Institute for Ecology of Natural Systems, Tatarstan Academy of Sciences, 1993-2003; Laboratory Manager, Institute for Ecology of Natural Systems, Tatarstan Academy of Sciences, 2003-08; Laboratory Manager, State Budgetary Establishment Research Institute for Problems of Ecology and Mineral Wealth Use of Tatarstan Academy of Sciences, 2008-. Publications: Numerous articles in professional journals. Address: State Budgetary Establishment Research Institute for Problems of Ecology and Mineral Wealth Use, Tatarstan Academy of Sciences, Daurskaya 28, Kazan 420087, Russia. E-mail: allelop@rambler.ru

RAUDKIVI Arbed Jaan, b. 14 March 1920, Estonia. Professor. m. Aino Jalg, 2 sons, 1 daughter. Education: Dipl Eng, Braunschweig, 1949; PhD, Auckland, 1966; Fellow, Institute of Professor Engineers of New Zealand, 1970; Fellow, Institute of Civil Engineers, London, 1971.

DICTIONARY OF INTERNATIONAL BIOGRAPHY 36th EDITION

Appointments: Civil Engineering, Ministry of Works, New Zealand, 1950-55; Lecturer, 1956, Assistant Professor, 1965, Professor, Civil Engineering, 1969-86, University of Auckland; Visiting Professor, Germany and Singapore, 1986-87; Co-ordinator, Coastal Engineering Research, Germany, 1988-94; Scientific Advisor, European Marine Science and Technology Program, 1995-99. Publications: Approximately 100 papers; 7 books. Honours: Carnegie Fellowship, 1966; German Academy Exchange, 1966; British Council, 1973; Minna-James-Heineman Fellowship, 1977, 1981; Dr Ing hc, Braunschweig, 1982. Memberships: Institute of Professional Engineers, New Zealand. Address: 7 Coates Road, Howick, Auckland 2014, New Zealand. E-mail: a.raudkivi@auckland.ac.nz

RAULINE Jean-Yves, b. 24 December 1958, Caen, France. Master of Conferences. Education: Agregation of Music, 1992; Doctorate of Musicology, University of Paris Sorbonne, 2000. Appointments: Music Teacher, 2nd degree general teaching establishment, 1980-2004; Master of Conferences, 2004-, Director, 2005-10, Department of Musicology, University of Rouen. Publications: Numerous articles in professional journals. Memberships: Galpin Society; Societe Française de Musicologie. Address: 38 rue des Bruyeres, St Julien, 76300 Sotteville-lès-Rouen, France. E-mail: jean-yvesrauline@university.rouen.fr

RAVERTY Aaron (Thomas), b. 13 March 1950, Stillwater, Minnesota, USA. Benedictine Monk; Anthropologist; Editor. Education: BA, Anthropology, 1972; MA, Theology, 1977; MA, Anthropology, 1979; PhD, Sociocultural Anthropology, 1990; Certificate, Graphoanalysis, 1996; Basic Manuscript Editing, University of Chicago, 2009. Appointments: Editor, The Liturgical Press, Collegeville; General Editor, Worship magazine; College Teacher, St John's University, Collegeville; Teacher, St John's Preparatory School, Collegeville; Teaching Assistant, University of Minnesota; Judge, St Cloud (Minnesota) Area High School Bowl; Book review editor, Bulletin of Monastic Interreligious Dialogue; Co-ordinator of Communications and Development, St John's Abbey. Publications: Articles and reviews in professional and religious journals and magazines. Honours: Fellowship Status Award, American Anthropological Association; Certificate of Merit, Academic Affairs Committee of the Student Activities Board, St John's University; Paul Lawson Administrative Development Award, St John's University, Collegeville, 2000, 2002, 2006, 2008; Entries in Who's Who and international biographies. Memberships: American Benedictine Academy; International Graphoanalysis Society; Secretary of the Board, Monastic Interreligious Dialogue; American Anthropological Association; Communications Committee Member, St John's University Alumni Board of Directors; St John's University Board of Regents; American Men's Studies Association, 2003-. Address: St Johns Abbey, PO Box 2015, Collegeville, MN 56321-2015, USA.

RAVN Helle Weber, b. 28 April 1957, Haderslev, Denmark. Senior Scientist. m. Kari Henny Hansen, 1 daughter. Education: Cand pharm; Lic pharm (PhD); Diploma in Leadership. Appointments: Senior Scientist, Aarhus University. Publications: 3 patents; 35 scientific publications; 100 posters. Honours: Incuba Science Park Price, 2011; Knight of the French Academic Palms. Memberships: Pharmaceutical Association. Address: Institute of Biosciences, Aarhus University, Vejlsoevej 25, 8600 Silkebong, Denmark.

RAWAT Tarun Kumar, b. 15 July 1979, Bijnore, UP, India. m. Deepti, 2 sons. Education: Master of Technology; Doctor of Philosophy. Appointments: Assistant Professor. Publications: Numerous articles in professional journals; Textbook, Signals & Systems, 2010. Honours: VP Pradhan Memorial Award, 2000; 2nd Prize, M V Chauhan All India Students' Paper Contest, 2007; Dr S Radhakrishnan Memorial National Teacher Award, 2007; Dr Rajendra Prasad Award, 2007; Listed in biographical dictionaries. Memberships: Institution of Electronics & Telecommunication Engineers; Life Member, Indian Society of Technical Education. Address: Room No 135/IV, ECE division, Netaji Subhas Institute of Technology, Sector 3, Dwarka, New Delhi 110078, India.

RAWNSLEY Andrew Nicholas James, FRSA (Fellow of the Royal Society of Arts) b. 5 January 1962, Leeds, England. Journalist; Broadcaster; Author. m. Jane Hall, 1990, 3 daughters. Education: Sidney Sussex College, Cambridge; MA, History, Cambridge. Appointments: BBC, 1983-85; Reporter, Feature Writer, 1985-87, Political Columnist, 1987-93, The Guardian; Writer, Presenter, A Week in Politics, 1989-97, Bye Bye Blues, 1997, Blair's Year, 1998, Channel 4 series; Associate Editor, Chief Political Commentator, The Observer, 1993-; Writer, Presenter, The Agenda, ITV series, 1996, The Westminster Hour, Radio 4 series, 1998-2006; The Unauthorised Biography of the United Kingdom, 1999; The Sunday Edition (with Andrea Catherwood), 2006. Publication: Servants of the People: The Inside Story of New Labour, 2000. Honours: Student Journalist of the Year, 1983; Young Journalist of the Year, 1987; Columnist of the Year, What the Papers Say Awards, 2000; Book of the Year, Channel 4/House Magazine Political Awards, 2001; Journalist of the year, Channel 4 Awards, 2003. Address: The Observer, 119 Farringdon Road, London EC1R 3ER, England. E-mail: andrew.rawnsley@observer.co.uk

RAY Asim Kumar, b. 6 October 1937. Teacher; Researcher. m. Parul Basu, 1 daughter. Education: BSc (honours), Physics, University of Calcutta, 1956; MSc, Physics, University of Calcutta, 1958; PhD, Particle Physics, Carnegie Mellon University, 1969. Appointments: Trainee, Atomic Energy Establishment, Trombay, Bombay, 1959-60; Research Associate, Tata Institute of Fundamental Research, Bombay, 1960-63; Lecturer, 1969-76, Reader, 1976-84, Professor, 1984-, Head of Department of Physics, 1981-87, Dean of Faculty of Science, 1990-92, Professor in Charge, Computer Centre, 1991-97, Registrar, 1992-93, Retired, 2002, Visva-Bharati University, India; Visiting Scientist, USA, Japan and Italy, 1980-95; Senior Associate, IUCAA, Pune, India, 1994-97; Currently Visiting Faculty, S N Bose National Centre for Basic Sciences, Salt Lake Sector III, Kolkata, India, 2004-10. Publications: Editor and co-editor, Dirac and Feynman, Pioneers in Quantum Mechanics; Editor and co-editor, Proceedings of XI DAE Symposium on High Energy Physics; Over 40 professional research papers. Honours: Fulbright Scholar. Memberships: Indian Physics Association; Indian Physical Society; Indian Association of Cultivation Science; Indian Association of General Relativity and Gravitation. Address: Flat No E5, Cluster IX, Purbachal Housing Estate, Salt Lake Sector III, Kolkata 700097, India. E-mail: asimkray@yahoo.co.in

RAYNER Desmond, b. 31 October 1928, London, England. Artist; Writer; Actor. m. Claire Rayner, 2 sons, 1 daughter. Education: Certificate in Acting, LGSM, Guildhall School of Music and Drama, 1950-51. Career: RAF, 1946-49; Professional Actor, 1952-57; Numerous advertising and public relations posts, 1957-; Agent and manager to wife, Claire

- 865 -

Rayner. Creative works: Designed productions: Heaven and Charing Cross Road; A Murder Has Been Arranged; The Boy With A Cart; Lady Windermere's Fan; Numerous art exhibitions, 1975-2008, including Art Deco in Egypt, New York – Another Perspective, London – Another Perspective; and many others; Private collections in Australia, Canada, USA and UK. Publications: Novels: The Dawlish Season, 1984; The Husband, 1992. Memberships: Royal Academy of Fine Art; Actors Centre. Address: Holly Wood House, Roxborough Avenue, Harrow-on-the-Hill, Middlesex, HA1 3BU, England.

RAZAFINDRALAMBO Hary Lanto, b. 3 December 1967, Antananarivo, Madagascar. Research Scientist. m. Rabetafika Holy, 1 son, 1 daughter. Education: MSc, Chemical Engineering and Bioindustries, 1990; PhD, Agronomic Sciences and Biological Engineering, 1996. Appointments: Research Assistant, 1996-97; Research Associate, postdoctoral research, 1998-. Publications: Author and co-author of book chapters, letters, patent, and regular articles in physics, chemistry, biotechnology and biochemistry areas. Honours: Academy of Science of New York; Listed in international biographical dictionaries. Memberships: American Chemical Society; Belgian Particle and Interface Science; Belgian Family League; Consumer Protection Association. Address: Gembloux Agro-Bio Tech University of Liege, Passage des Deportes 2, B-5030 Gembloux, Belgium. E-mail: h.razafindralambo@ulg.ac.be

RÉ Paul Bartlett, b. 18 April 1950, Albuquerque, New Mexico, USA. Artist; Writer; Poet; Peace Worker. Education: BSc, Physics (with High Honours), California Institute of Technology, Pasadena, California, 1972. Career: Artist, Writer, Poet, 1972-; Artist Advisory Board (Access to Art), Museum of American Folk Art, 1987-94; Director, the Paul Ré Collection and Archives, 1994-; Advisor, Paul Bartlett Ré Peace Prize Committee, University of New Mexico, 2007-; Exhibit "Touchable Art: An Exhibit for the Blind and Sighted" shown 18 times in USA and Canada, 1981-; 22 solo exhibitions in 13 states including Jonson Gallery of the University of New Mexico Art Museum, Albuquerque Museum, Triangle Gallery, Wichita Museum, Sumter Gallery, JB Speed Museum, Colorado Springs Museum, Karpeles Museum. Publications: Books: Touchable Art: A Book for the Blind and Sighted (embossings with text), 1983; The Dance of the Pencil. Serene Art by Paul Ré (drawings, essays, poetry), 1993; Articles in: La Mamelle, 1975; Journal of Visual Impairment and Blindness, 1983; Leonardo Art Journal, 1980-82; New America, 1984; Design Journal, 1992; SCETV TV documentary, Touchable Art, 1990; Chapter in Spirit of Enterprise: The 1990 Rolex Awards; 7 covers and poems, Spirit Magazine, 1985; Journal of the Print World, 2009; 4 books in progress (Réograms (hybrid hand-digital prints), humour, essays and poetry). Honours: First Place in Physics and NASA Awards, International Science Fair, 1967 and 1968; Wurlitzer Foundation Residencies, 1982, 1984; The Dance of the Pencil cited as one of the outstanding art books of the year, Journal of the Print World; The Torchbearers of Caltech, 2002; World Lifetime Achievement Award, American Biographical Institute, 2004; Great Minds Dedicatee, ABI, 2004; Legion of Honor, United Cultural Convention, 2005; 21st Century Award for Achievement, IBC, 2005; Who's Who in the World, 2005; Genius Laureate of the United States, ABI, 2005; 500 Greatest Geniuses of the 21st Century, ABI, 2006; Listed in many Who's Who publications and biographical encyclopaedias; The Paul Bartlett Ré Peace Prize and the Paul Ré Gallery and Sculpture Garden, University of New Mexico, Albuquerque; IBC Hall of Fame, 2006; Sovereign Ambassador, Order of American Ambassadors, 2006; Da Vinci Diamond, IBC, 2006; World's Most Respected Expert, ABI, 2006; IBC Roll of Honour, 2007; Cited for Serene Art that Elevates and Unites; Albert Einstein Genius Dedication Award, ABI, 2008; Decree of Excellence in Art, IBC, 2008; The Popejoy Society, University of New Mexico, 2008; Greatest Minds Honoree, ABI, 2009; International Peace Prize, United Cultural Convention, 2009; Great Minds Hall of Fame, cited for Serene, Universal Art, ABI, 2009; Dedicatee, 2000 Outstanding Intellectuals of the 21st Century, IBC, 2010; Legendary Leader Honoree, Hall of Fame and extensive essay, 500 Great Leaders, 2011; Greatest Minds Honoree and essay, Great Minds, 5th edition, 2011; Dedication essay, Dictionary of International Biography, 36th edition, 2011; named to The Global 100, 2011; Works highly regarded by Raymond Jonson, Georgia O'Keeffe, Nobel Laureates Richard Feynman and Subrahmanyan Chandrasekhar, College Presidents and other notables; Acclaimed by art critics as "a virtuoso of the pencil" and for his art of "quiet greatness and noble simplicity", its aim is to harmonise the world. Memberships: Life Member, CALTECH Alumni Association; Life Member, The Nature Conservancy. Address: 10533 Sierra Bonita Avenue NE, Albuquerque, NM 87111, USA. E-mail: paulre@centurylink.net Website: www.paulre.org

READ Anthony, b. 21 April 1935, Staffordshire, England. Writer; Dramatist. m. Rosemary E Kirby, 29 March 1958, 2 daughters. Education: Queen Mary's Grammar School, Walsall, 1945-52, Central School of Speech and Drama, London, 1952-54. Publications: The Theatre, 1964; Operation Lucy (with David Fisher), 1980; Colonel Z (with David Fisher), 1984; The Deadly Embrace (with David Fisher), 1988; Kristallnacht (with David Fisher), 1989; Conspirator (with Ray Bearse), 1991; The Fall of Berlin (with David Fisher), 1992; Berlin: The Biography of a City (with David Fisher), 1994; The Proudest Day: India's Long Road to Independence (with David Fisher), 1997; The Devil's Disciples, 2003; The Baker Street Boys: The Case of the Disappearing Detective, 2005; The Baker Street Boys: The Case of the Captive Clairvoyant, 2006; The Baker Street Boys: The Case of the Ranjipur Ruby, 2006; Baker Street Boys: The Case of the Limehouse Laundry, 2007; The World on Fire, 2008; The Baker Street Boys: The Case of the Stolen Sparklers, 2008; The Baker Street Boys: The Case of the Haunted Horrors, 2009; Other: Over 200 television films, plays, series and serials. Honours: Best Drama Series, BAFTA, 1966; Pye Colour TV Award, 1983; Wingate Literary Prize, 1989. Membership: Trustee, Past Chairman, Writers Guild of Great Britain. Address: 7 Cedar Chase, Taplow, Buckinghamshire, England.

READE John Brian, b. 4 July 1938, Wolverhampton, England. University Lecturer. m. (1) Alison Mary, 1 son, 1 daughter, (2) Suzanne Mary, 2 sons, 1 daughter. Education: LRAM (Piano), 1956; MA, 1962, PhD, 1965, Trinity College, Cambridge. Appointments: Lecturer in Mathematics, Birmingham University, 1965-67; Lecturer in Mathematics, University of Manchester, 1967-2003. Publications: Books: Introduction to Mathematical Analysis, 1986; Calculus with Complex Numbers, 2003; Various research papers on mathematics. Memberships: London Mathematical Society; Cambridge Philosophical Society. Address: 123 Andover Avenue, Middleton, Manchester M24 1JQ, England. E-mail: sue.reade@uwclub.net

READER Alec Harold, b. 1957, Dartford, Kent, England (arrived in Netherlands, 1983). Physicist; Researcher; Business Leader. Education: BS (honours), Physics, 1979, PhD, Materials Science, 1983, Birmingham University; Postgraduate studies: Cranfield University of Technology and Engineering, 1990-96; Ashridge Management College, London, 1999; Management Centre Europe, Brussels, 1999; Certified Physicist. Appointments: Postdoctoral Research Fellow, Materials Department, Delft University, Holland, The Netherlands, 1983-85; Research Scientist, 1985-90, Research Project Leader, 1990-, Philips Research Laboratories, Eindhoven, The Netherlands; Head, Failure Analysis and Characterization Department, SGS Thomson, Crolles, France, 1993-; Semiconductor Marketing Director and Vice President, Philips Analytical, Almelo, The Netherlands, 1999-; Chief Marketing Officer, Business Development Director, Sales, Marketing and Technology Director, Member of Supervisory Board, INNOS Ltd, Southampton, England, 2004-; Director and CEO, Nanotechnology KTN, 2008-; Reviewer in international journals and project applications; Presenter at international conferences, including NATO; Examiner for European PhDs; Project Leader, European Union R&D Projects. Publications: Book: Microstructural Defects in IC-Materials, 1990; Transmission Electron Microscopy, 1991; Silicides in Future IC's, Transition Metal Silicides in SI Technology, 1992; Silicides Data Review IEE (UK), 1995; In Encyclopedia of Analytical Science, 1995; Contributor to articles to professional journals; Reviewer of technical and science journals; 14 patents in field of microelectronics. Memberships: IEEE; Materials Research Society; London Institute of Metals and Materials; London Institute of Physics. Address: NANOKTN Office, Viewpoint, Basing View, Basingstoke, RG21 4RG, England.

REARDON Raymond (Ray), b. 8 October 1932, Tredegar, Wales. Snooker Player. m. (1) Susan Carter, divorced, 1 son, 1 daughter. (2) Carol Lovington, 1987. Career: Welsh Amateur Champion, 1950-55; English Amateur Champion, 1965; Turned professional, 1967; Six times World Snooker Champion, 1970-78; Benson & Hedges Masters Champion, 1976; Welsh Champion, 1977, 1981, 1983; Professional Players Champion, 1982; Retired, 1992; Active in running World Professional Billiards and Snooker Association; Occasional TV appearances. Publications: Classic Snooker, 1974; Ray Reardon (autobiography), 1982. Honour: MBE.

REDFORD Robert, b. 18 August 1936, Santa Monica, California, USA. Actor. m. Lola Van Wegenen, divorced, 4 children. Education: University of Colorado. Creative Works: Films include, War Hunt, 1961; Situation Hopeless But Not Serious, 1965; Inside Daisy Clover, 1965; The Chase, 1965; This Property is Condemned, 1966; Barefoot in the Park, 1967; Tell Them Willie Boy is Here, 1969; Butch Cassidy and the Sundance Kid, 1969; Downhill Racer, 1969; Little Fauss and Big Halsy, 1970; Jeremiah Johnson, 1972; The Candidate, 1972; How to Steal a Diamond in Four Uneasy Lessons, 1972; The Way We Were, 1973; The Sting, 1973; The Great Gatsby, 1974; The Great Waldo Pepper, 1974; Three Days of the Condor, 1975; All the President's Men, 1976; A Bridge Too Far, 1977; The Electric Horseman, 1980; Brubaker, 1980; The Natural, 1984; Out of Africa, 1985; Legal Eagles, 1986; Havana, 1991; Indecent Proposal, 1993; The Clearing, Sacred Planet, 2004, Director, Ordinary People, 1980; Milagro Beanfield War (also producer), 1988; Promised Land (executive producer), 1988; Sneakers, 1992; A River Runs Through it (also director), 1992; Quiz Show (director), 1994; The River Wild, 1995; Up Close and Personal, 1996; The Horse Whisperer, 1997; The Legend of Bagger Vance, (also director, producer), How to Kill Your Neighbour's Dog (executive producer), 2000; The Last Castle, 2001; Spy Game, 2001; The Motorcycle Diaries, 2004; The Clearing, 2004; An Unfinished Life, 2005; Charlotte's Web (voice), 2006; Lions for Lambs, 2007. Honours: Academy Award, Golden Globe Award, Best Director, 1981; Audubon Medal, 1989; Dartmouth Film Society Award, 1990; Screen Actors' Guild Award for Lifetime Achievement, 1996; Honorary Academy Award, 2002. Address: c/o Creative Artists Agency, 9830 Wilshire Boulevard, Beverly Hills, CA 90212, USA.

REDGRAVE Sir Steve (Steven Geoffrey), b. 23 March 1962, Marlow, England. Former Oarsman. m. Ann, 1 son, 2 daughters. Education: Doctor Civil Law, honoris causa. Appointments: Represented, UK at Junior World Championships, 1979; Silver medal, 1980; Stroke, British Coxed 4, Gold Medal Winners, Los Angeles Olympic Games, 1984; Gold Medals, Single Scull, Coxless Pair (with Andy Holmes) and Coxed 4, Commonwealth Games, 1986; Coxed Pair (with Holmes), World Championships, 1986; Coxless Pair Gold Medal and Coxed Pair Silver Medal (with Holmes), World Championships, 1987; Gold Medal (with Holmes), Coxless Pair and Bronze Medal, Coxed Pair, Olympic Games, Seoul, 1988; Silver Medal (with Simon Berrisford), Coxless Pairs, World Championships, 1989; Bronze Medal, Coxless Pair (with Matthew Pinsent), World Championships, Tasmania, 1990; Gold Medal, Coxless Pair (with Pinsent), World Championships, Vienna, 1991; Gold Medal, Olympic Games, Barcelona, 1992; Gold Medals at World Championships, Czech Republic, 1993, USA, 1994, Finland, 1995; Gold Medal, Olympic Games, Atlanta, 1996; Winners of World Cup, Gold Medal, Coxless 4, France, (with Pinsent, Foster, Cracknell), 1997; Gold Medal Winners, Coxless 4, World Championships, Cologne, 1998; Gold Medal Winners, Coxless 4, St Catherines (with Pinsent, Coode, Cracknell), 1999; Gold Medal, Olympic Games, Sydney, 2000. Publications: Steven Redgrave's Complete Book of Rowing, 1992; A Golden Age (autobiography), 2000; You Can Win At Life, 2005. Honours: MBE, 1987; CBE, 1997; Sports Personality of the Year, 2000; British Sports Writers; Association Sportsman of the Year, 2000; Laurens Lifetime Achievement Award, 2001; Honorary DSc (Buckingham, Hull), 2001; Knighted, 2001; BBC Golden Sports Personality, 2003. Address: c/o British International Rowing Office, 6 Lower Mall, London W6 9DJ, England.

REDGRAVE Vanessa, b. 30 January 1937, England. Actress. m. (1) Tony Richardson, 1962, divorced 1967, deceased 1991, 2 daughters, (2) Franco Nero, 2006, 1 son. Education: Central School of Speech and Drama. Career: Films include: Morgan – A Suitable Case for Treatment; Sailor from Gibraltar, 1965; Charge of the Light Brigade; The Seagull; Isadora Duncan, 1968; The Devils, 1970; Mary Queen of Scots, 1971; Murder on the Orient Express, 1974; Julia, 1977; Playing for Time, 1980; Wetherby, 1984; Howard's End, 1992; Breath of Life, The Wall, Sparrow, They, The House of the Spirits, Crime and Punishment, Mother's Boys, Little Odessa, A Month by the Lake, 1996; Mission Impossible, 1996; Looking for Richard, 1997; Wilde, 1997; Mrs Dalloway, 1997; Bella Mafia (TV), 1997; Deep Impact, 1998; Girl, Interrupted, 1999; Cradle Will Rock, 2000; The House of the Spirits; Crime and Punishment; Little Odessa; The 3 Kings, 2000; A Rumor of Angels, 2000; The Pledge, 2001; Crime and Punishment, 2002; Good Boy (voice), 2003; The Fever; 2004; Short Order, 2005; The White Countess, 2005; The Thief Lord, 2006; The Riddle, 2007; How About You, 2007; Evening, 2007; Atonement, 2007; Eva, 2009; Letters to Juliet, The Whistleblower, Miral, Animals United, 2010; Coriolanus, Cars 2, Anonymous, 2011; Song for Marion, 2012. Produced and narrated documentary film The Palestinians, 1977; Theatre includes: A Midsummer Night's Dream, 1959; The Prime of Miss Jean Brodie, 1966; Cato Street, 1971; Threepenny Opera, 1972; Macbeth, 1975; Ghosts, 1986; A Madhouse in Goa, 1989; Heartbreak House, 1992; Antony and Cleopatra, Houston, Texas (also directed), 1996; John Gabriel Borkman, 1996; Song at Twilight, 1999; The Cherry Orchard, 2000; The Tempest, 2000; Lady Windermere's Fan, 2002. Publications include: An Autobiography, 1991. Honours: Variety Club Award; Evening Standard Award for Best Actress, 1961; Cannes Film Festival Best Actress (Morgan-A Suitable Case for Treatment, 1966); CBE, 1967; UK Film Critic's Guild and National Society of Film Critics Leading Actress Award (Isadora Duncan,) 1969; Academy Award Best Supporting Actress (Julia, 1978); TV Award for Best Actress (Playing for Time, 1981); Laurence Olivier Award, 1984; Dr hc, Massachusetts, 1990. Memberships: Co-Founder Moving Theatre, 1974; Workers' Revolutionary Party (Candidate for Moss Side, 1979); Fellow, BFI, 1988.

REDINA Nataliia Ivanivna, b. 5 June 1947, Przhevalsk, Kirgizia. Rector. 1 daughter. Education: Graduate, Moscow State Historical and Archival Institute, 1970; Candidate, Economic Science, The Supreme Certifying Committee of Ukraine, 1997; Professor; Academician, Academy of Economic Science of Ukraine. Appointments: Rector, Dnipropetrovsk State Financial Academy, 1977-. Publications:The Formation of Shares market, 1997; Finances of Ukraine, 1997; Money, Finances and Financial Markets, 1998; External Economic Activities of Enterprises, 2002; Budget System, 2003; Management, 2005; Knowledge About Taxes to Each Family, 2006; The Control Over Groups, 2nd edition, 2007; Management, 2nd edition, 2007; Taxation in Ukraine, 2009; Control Over State Budget of Ukraine, 2010; Budget System Reforming on Innovative Principles, 2010; Theoretical and Practical Commentary on The Budget Code of Ukraine, 2010. Honours: Commendations from the Cabinet Council of Ukraine, the Ministry of Education, Youth and Sport of Ukraine, the Ministry of Finance of Ukraine, the State Administration of Dnipropetrovsk Region, and the Mayor of Dnipropetrovsk; Gold Medal, Presidium of International Academy of Human Resources; Decoration for Development of the Region, Head of State Administration of Dnipropetrovsk Region; Commemorative Medal for Great Services to the City; Medal of Grand Prince St Vladimir, Equal-to-the-Apostles, for Great Services to the Ukrainian Orthodox Church; Order of the Second Degree of the Ukrainian Orthodox Church of St Barbara; Distinguished Educationalist of Ukraine by Decree of the President of Ukraine, 2007; International Quality Certificate of International Organization for Standardization, ISO 9001:2009. Address: Dnipropetrovsk State Financial Academy, 12 Arzhanov street, 49083, Dnipropetrovsk, Ukraine. E-mail: id@dsfa.dp.ua

REDMAN Christopher Willard George, b. 30 November 1941, Pretoria, South Africa. Emeritus Professor of Obstetric Medicine. m. Corinna Susan Page, 4 sons, 1 daughter. Education: MB BChir, Cambridge University, 1967; MRCP, London, 1972; FRCP, London, 1981. Appointments: Training in Baltimore, USA, Oxford and Sheffield UK, 1967-70; Lecturer in Medicine, Oxford University, 1970-76; University Lecturer, 1976-89, Clinical Reader, 1989-92, Clinical Professor, 1992-, Obstetric Medicine, University of Oxford. Publications: More than 200 research and review articles on pre-eclampsia and medical disorders of pregnancy, 1973-. Honours: Chesley Award, International Society for the Study of Hypertension in Pregnancy; Barnes Award, International Society of Obstetric Medicine. Memberships: Fellow of the Royal College of Physicians, London; Fellow of Lady Margaret Hall, Oxford. Address: Nuffield Department of Obstetrics and Gynaecology, John Radcliffe Hospital, Oxford OX3 9DU, England.

REDTENBACHER Andreas Gottlieb, b. 8 May 1953, Vienna, Austria. Roman Catholic Priest. Education: Mag Theol, University of Vienna, Austria, 1977; Lic Theol, 1979, Dr Theol, 1983, Gregorian University, Rome; Postgraduate Student for Habilitation, University of Trier, Germany; Dr habil, Vallendar, 2007. Appointments: Ordained Priest, 1978; Religions Professor and Rector for Students, 1979; University Assistant in Liturgy and Lecturer in Liturgy, University of Vienna, Austria, 1981; Parish Priest in St Vitus, 1990; Nominated President, Committee for Liturgy in the Episcopal-Vikariat of the City of Vienna, Austria, 1981; Nominated President of the Conference of Liturgists in the Austrian Roman Catholic Church, 1995; Professor in Liturgy, University of Klosterneuburg and of Vallendar (BRD), Germany, 2008. Publications: Presbyter und Presbyterium, 1980; Zukunft aus den Erbe, 1984, second edition, 2007: Wo Sich Wege Kreuzen, 1985; Liturgie und Leben, 2002; Reihe: Pius – Parsch-Studien, bisher Bd I-IX; Die Zukunft der Liturgie, 2004; Kultur der Liturgie, 2006; Protokolle zue Liturgie, bisher Bd I-IV; Many published articles. Honour: Archiepiscopal Konsistorialrat. Memberships: International Societas Liturgica; European Academy of Finances and Arts; Editorial Board, Heiliger Dienst; Corresponding Member, Editorial Board, Bibel und Liturgie. Address: Stiftplatz 1, A-3400 Klosterneuburg, Austria. E-mail: a.redtenbacher@stift-klosterneuburg.at

REDVALDSEN David Aly, b. 22 May 1975, Oslo, Norway. Historian. Education: BA, Durham University, 1998; MA, University College, London, 1999; PhD, 2007, Certificate of Learning and Teaching in Higher Education, 2007, University College, London. Appointments: Teaching Assistant, University College, London, 2005; Lecturer, Social Science, 2008-09 and 2010-11, Lecturer, Social Science and History, 2009-10, Finnmark University College; Guest Lecturer, History, Azerbaijan University of Languages, 2009. Publications: The Representational Base of the Norwegian Labour Party in the 1930's, 2008; Today is the Dawn: The Labour Party and the 1929 General Election, 2010. Honours: Dame Gillian Brown Postgraduate Scholarship, 2003. Memberships: Fellow, Higher Education Academy. Address: Finnmark University College, PHF, Follums Vei 31, 9509 Alta, Norway. E-mail: davidredvaldsen@hotmail.com

REDWOOD John Alan (Rt Hon), b. 15 June 1951, Dover, England. Member of Parliament. Divorced, 1 son, 1 daughter. Education: BA, Honours 1971, MA, DPhil, 1975, Oxford University. Appointments: Fellow, All Souls College, Oxford, 1972-86, 2003-2005; Manager, then Director, NM Rothschild & Sons, 1977-89; Chairman Norcros Plc, 1987-89; MP for Wokingham, 1987-; Minister, UK Government, 1989-95; Shadow President, Board of Trade, 1997-99; Shadow Front Bench Spokesman on the Environment, 1999-2000; Head, Parliamentary Campaigns Unit, 2000; Shadow Secretary of State for Deregulation, 2004-; Chair, Murray Financial Corporation, 2002-04; Chairman Concentric plc, 2003-. Publications: Reason, Ridicule and Religion, 1976; Public Enterprise in Crisis, 1980; Co-author, Value for Money Audits, 1981; Co-author, Controlling Public Industries, 1982; Going for Broke, 1984; Equity for Everyman, 1986; Popular Capitalism, 1989; Global Marketplace, 1994; The Single European Currency, with others, 1996; Our Currency, Our Country, 1997; The Death of Britain? 1999; Stars and Strife, 2001; Just Say No, 2001; Third Way – Which Way, 2002; Singing the Blues, 2004; Superpower Struggles, 2005. Honours: Parliamentarian of the Year Awards, 1987, 1995, 1997. Address: House of Commons, London, SW1A 0AA, England.

REED Lou (Louis Firbank), b. 2 March 1943, Freeport, Long Island, New York, USA. Singer; Songwriter; Musician (guitar); Poet; Journalist. m. Sylvia Morales, 14 Feb 1980. Career: Founder member, lead singer, songwriter, Velvet Underground, 1964-1970, 1993-; Tours as part of Andy Warhol's Exploding Plastic Inevitable show; Solo artiste, 1971-93; Appearances include: Montreal World Fair, 1967; Crystal Palace Garden Party, 1973; Reading Festival, 1975; Nelson Mandela - A International Tribute, Wembley Stadium, 1990; John Lennon Tribute Concert, Liverpool, 1990; Glastonbury Festival, 1992; Bob Dylan 30th Anniversary Concert, New York, 1992. Recordings: Albums: with the Velvet Underground: The Velvet Underground And Nico, 1967; White Light, White Heat, 1968; The Velvet Underground, 1969; Loaded, 1970; Solo albums: Lou Reed, 1972; Transformer, 1973; Berlin, 1973; Rock'n'Roll Animal, 1974; Sally Can't Dance, 1974; Lou Reed Live, 1975; Metal Machine Music, 1975; Coney Island Baby, 1976; Rock And Roll Heart, 1976; Walk On The Wild Side - The Best Of Lou Reed, 1977; Street Hassle, 1978; Take No Prisoners, 1979; The Bells, 1979; Vicious, 1979; Growing Up In Public, 1980; Rock And Roll Diary, 1980; The Blue Mask, 1982; Transformer, 1982; Legendary Hearts, 1983; Rock Galaxy, 1983; New Sensations, 1984; Mistrial, 1986; Retro, 1989; New York, 1989; Songs For Drella - A Fiction (with John Cale), 1990; Magic And Loss, 1992; Set The Twilight Reeling, 1996; Also appears on: Sun City single, Artists Against Apartheid, 1985; Soul Man (with Sam Moore), theme for film Soul Man, 1987; Duets album, Rob Wasserman, 1988; Victoria Williams benefit album, 1993; Set the Twilight Reeling, 1996; Live, in Concert, 1997.. Publications include: Between Thought And Expression (poetry), 1992. Honours: Q Magazine Merit Award, 1991; Knight of the Order of Arts and Letters, France, 1992; Inducted into Rock'n'Roll Hall Of Fame (with Velvet Underground), 1996. Memberships: AFofM; Screen Actors Guild. Current Management: Sister Ray Enterprises, 584 Broadway, Suite 609, New York, NY 10012, USA.

REES David Benjamin, b. 1 August 1937, Wales. Minister of Religion; Lecturer; Author. m. 31 July 1963, 2 sons. Education: BA, BD, MSc, University of Wales; MA, University of Liverpool; PhD, University of Salford; FRHisS. Appointments: Minister, Presbyterian Church of Wales, Cynon Valley, 1962-68, Bethel, Heathfield Road, Liverpool, 1968-2008; Part-time Lecturer, Open University, 1969-90; Part-time Lecturer, University of Liverpool, 1970-99; Editor, Angor, Liverpool, 1979-; Professor, Ecclesiastical History, North West University, South Africa, 1999-; Editor, Peace and Reconciliation Magazine, 2000-02; Emeritus Minister, 2008-.. Publications: Chapels in the Valley: Sociology of Welsh Non-Conformity, 1975; Wales: A Cultural History, 1980; Preparation for a Crisis: Adult Education in England and Wales 1945-1980, 1981; Liverpool, Welsh and Their Religion, 1984; Owen Thomas: A Welsh Preacher in Liverpool, 1991; The Welsh of Merseyside, 1997; Local and Parliamentary Politics in Liverpool from 1800 to 1911, 1999; Mr Evan Roberts: The Revivalist in Anglesey 1905, 2005; Labour of Love in Liverpool, 2008; John Calvin and his Welsh Disciples, 2009; The Saga of a Revival: Early Welsh Pentecostal Methodism, 2010. Contributions to: Magazines and newspapers such as Independent and Guardian. Honour: Ellis Griffith Prize, 1979; Paul Harris Fellow, Rotary International, 2005; Vice President, Liverpool Welsh Choral Union; Listed in Who's Who publications and biographical dictionaries. Memberships: Cymmrodorion Society; Welsh Academy; Wales and the World; Assistant District Governor, 1995-98, Editor of Rotary District 1180 magazine, 1995-2011, Rotary Club of Liverpool; Chairman and Founder Member of Merseyside Welsh Heritage Society, 1999-2009; University of Wales, Aberystwyth Court of Governors, 2003-08. Address: 32 Garth Drive, Liverpool L18 6HW, England. E-mail: ben@garthdrive.fsnet.co.uk

REES David William Alan, b. 12 March 1947, Ruislip, Middlesex, England. Engineering Educator; Author; Researcher. Education: Student Apprentice, Black & Decker Ltd, Harmondsworth and Maidenhead, England; National Diploma and Engineering Institutions examinations, Southall Technical College, Middlesex, 1963-68; Postgraduate Student, Applied Mechanics, Imperial College, London, 1969-70; PhD, Research, Kingston University, 1973-76. Appointments: Engineering Apprentice, 1963-68, Engineering Designer, 1968-69, Black & Decker Ltd; Postgraduate Student, 1969-70, Experimental Officer, 1970-71, Imperial College, London; Research Assistant, 1971-72, Lecturer, 1972-77, Kingston University; Lecturer, Trinity College, Dublin, 1977-84; Lecturer, Surrey University, 1984-85, Lecturer, 1985-95, Senior Lecturer, 1995-2006, Brunel University; Visiting Fellow, Joint Research Centre, Petten, 1982; National Physical Laboratory, 1983, 1985; Regional Fellow, Royal Society of Medicine, London, 2007. Publications: Books: The Mechanics of Solids and Structures, 1990; Basic Solid Mechanics, 1997, Mechanics of Solids & Structures, 2000; Basic Engineering Plasticity, 2006; Mechanics of Optimal Structural Design: Minimum Weight Structures, 2009; Mechanics of Deformable Solids, 2011. Recent articles: Deformation and rupture of stainless steel under cyclic torsional creep, 2008; Descriptions of reversed bending of a solid circular bar in torsion, 2008; A theory for swaging of discs and lugs, 2011; The telescopic cantilever beam: Part I, Deflection analysis, Part II, Stress analysis, 2011. Honours: National Diploma Prize, 1968; MSc/ DIC, Imperial College, 1970; PhD, Kingston University, 1976; Honorary MA, Trinity College, Dublin, 1981; DSc, Brunel University, 2004; Best Paper, Fylde Prize, Strain, 1993; Best Paper, CEGB Prize, Journal of Strain Analysis, 1998; Listed in international biographical dictionaries. Memberships: Institution of Mechanical Engineers; Council of Engineering Institutions; Royal Society of Medicine. Address: Brunel University, School of Engineering and Design, Kingston Lane, Uxbridge, Middlesex UB8 3PH, England. E-mail: david.rees@brunel.ac.uk

REEVES Colin L, b. 4 April 1949, Orrell, Greater Manchester, England. Accountant. m. Christine, 2 daughters. Education: MA, Economics, Clare College, Cambridge, 1970; MSc, Finance, 1971, PhD, Monetary Economics, 1973, University College of North Wales, Bangor; CPFA, John Moores University, 1976; Diploma in Business Administration, Cornell University, New York, USA, 1991. Appointments: Director of Finance, Paddington & Kensington District Health Authority, 1985-86; Regional Director of Finance, North West Thames Regional Health Authority, 1986-94; National Director, Finance and Performance of the NHS, 1994-2001; Director, Review Board, Accountancy Foundation, 2001-03; Self-employed Management Consultant, 2003-. Publications: The Applicability of the Monetary Base Hypothesis to the UK, the USA, France and West Germany; Feasibility Study into the Implementation of a Capital Charges System in Chile; Regular contributions to various professional journals. Honours: Examiner for CIPFA, 1980-85; Chair, National Steering Group on Costing, 1992-94; Member, Culyer Task Force, 1993-94; Member, Department of Health/Home Office Advisory Committee on Mentally Disordered Offenders, 1993-94; Member, Chancellor of the Exchequer's Private Finance Panel, 1994-96; Member, Butler Review on Audit Commission, 1995; Member, National Screening Committee,

1996-2001; Member, Liddell Review, Office of National Statistics, 1999; Head, UK team to develop controls assurance in Australia, 1999; Head, UK trade delegation to promulgate PFI in South Africa, 1999; CBE, 1999; Honorary Treasurer, The Florence Nightingale Foundation. Memberships: Vice Chair and Chair of Audit Committee, Oxford Radcliffe Hospitals NHS Trust, 2005-09; Honorary Treasury of Headway; Audit Committee, Oxfam International; MCC; Goring and Streatley Golf Club; Flying Ferrets Golf Society; Henley Hawks RFC; Royal Automobile Club. Address: Battle Hill, Elvendon Road, Goring on Thames, Oxon RG8 0DT, England. E-mail: colinlreeves@aol.com

REEVES Keanu, b. 2 September 1964, Beirut, Lebanon. Actor. Education: Toronto High School for Performing Arts; Training at Second City Workshop. Career: Stage appearances include: Wolf Boy; For Adults Only; Romeo and Juliet; with rock band Dogstar, 1996-; TV films: Letting Go, 1985; Act of Vengeance, 1986; Babes in Toyland, 1986; Under the Influence, 1986; Brotherhood of Justice, 1986; Save the Planet (TV special), 1990; Films: Prodigal, Flying, 1986; Youngblood, 1986; River's Edge, 1987; Permanent Record, 1988; The Night Before, 1988; The Prince of Pennsylvania, 1988; Dangerous Liaisons, 1988; I Love You to Death, 1990; Tune in Tomorrow, 1990; Bill and Ted's Bogus Journey, 1991; Point Break, 1991; My Own Private Idaho, 1991; Bram Stoker's Dracula, 1992; Much Ado About Nothing, 1993; Even Cowgirls Get the Blues, Little Buddha, 1993; Speed, 1994; Johnny Mnemonic, 1995; A Walk in the Clouds, 1995; Chain Reaction, Feeling Minnesota, The Devil's Advocate, 1996; The Last Time I Committed Suicide, 1997; The Matrix, 1998; The Replacements, 2000; The Watcher, 2000; The Gift, 2000; Sweet November, 2001; The Matrix: Reloaded, 2003; The Matrix: Revolutions, 2003; Something's Gotta Give, 2003; Constantine, 2005; A Scanner Darkly, 2006; The Lake House, 2006; The Night Watchman, 2008; Street Kings, 2008; The Day the Earth Stood Still, 2008; The Private Lives of Pippa Lee, 2009; Henry's Crime, 2010; Side by Side, 2012; Man of Tai Chi, 47 Ronin, 2013. Honour: Star on Hollywood Walk of Fame, 2005. Address: c/o Kevin Houvane, 9830 Wilshire Boulevard, Beverly Hills, CA 90212, USA.

REEVES Saskia, b. 1962, London, England. Actress. Education: Guildhall School of Music and Drama, London. Career: Toured South America, India and Europe, Cheek By Jowl Theatre Company; Stage appearances include: Metamorphosis; Who's Afraid of Virginia Woolf?; Measure for Measure; Separation; Smelling A Rat; Ice Cream; The Darker Face of the Earth; TV includes: In My Defence; A Woman of Substance, 1983; Children Crossing, 1990; Cruel Train, 1995; Plotlands, 1997; A Christmas Carol, 1999; Dune, 2000; Suspicion, 2003; Waking the Dead, 2003; Island at War, 2004; A Line in the Sand, 2004; The Commander: Virus, 2005; Afterlife, 2005; The Inspector Lynley Mysteries, 2006; Spooks, 2006; Bodies, 2006; The Fixer, 2008; Midsomer Murders, 2009; Canoe Man, 2010; Luther, 2010; Wallander, 2010; Women in Love, 2011; Lewis, 2011; Page Eight, 2011; Films: December Bride, 1990; Antonia and Jane, 1991; Close My Eyes, 1991; In the Border Country, 1991; The Bridge, 1992; Traps, 1994; ID, 1995; The Butterfly Kiss, 1995; Different for Girls, 1996; Much Ado About Nothing, 1998; LA Without a Map, 1998; Heart, 1999; Ticks, 1999; Bubbles, 2001; The Tesseract, 2003; The Knickerman, 2004; Fast Learners, 2006. Address: Markham & Froggat Ltd, 4 Windmill Street, London W1P 1HF, England.

REGIS John, b. 13 October 1966, Lewisham, London, England. Athlete. Career: Winner, UK 200m (tie), 1985; 100m, 1988, Amateur Athletics Association 200m, 1986-87; UK record for 200m, Silver Medal, Olympic Games Seoul, 1988; 300m indoor record holder Commonwealth Games, 1990; Silver Medal 200m, 1991; Gold medal 4 x 100m relay, 1991; Gold Medal 200m 4 x 400m relay, 4 x 400m relay, 1993; Gold Medal World Cup, 1994; Member, British team Olympic Games, Atlanta, 1996; Retired, 2000; Member, Great Britain bobsleigh training team, 2000-; Founder, Stellar Athletes Ltd, 2001; Coach, UK Athletics sprint relay team, 2001-. Address: c/o Belgrave Harriers Athletic Club, Batley Croft, 58 Harvest Road, Englefield Green, Surrey, England.

REHMAN Atiq-ur, b. 4 February 1942, Agra, India. Consultant Neurosurgeon. m. Shamima Azhar, 1 son, 1 daughter. Education: MBBS (MD), Dow Medical College, Karachi, Pakistan, 1965; Fellow, Royal College of Surgeons of Edinburgh, 1974; Educational Commission for Foreign Medical Graduates, 1974; Fellow, International College of Surgeons, USA, 1985. Appointments: House Surgeon, General Surgery, 1965-66, Plastic Surgeon, 1966-67, Senior House Officer, General Medicine, 1967, Civil Hospital, Karachi; Casualty Officer, 1967-68, Senior House Officer, 1969, Royal Infirmary, Sunderland, UK; Senior House Officer, Orthopaedics, Accident Hospital, Sunderland, 1968; Senior House Officer, Neurology & Mental Subnormality, Prudhoe Hospital, UK, 1970-71; Senior House Officer, Casualty Department, 1971, General Surgery, 1972, General Hospital, Middlesborough, UK; Senior House Officer, Orthopaedics, Hemlington Hospital, Middlesborough, 1972; Senior House Officer, General Surgery, Southport, UK, 1973; Resident Surgical Officer, General Surgery, General Hospital, Hartlepool, UK, 1973-74; Registrar General Surgery, Ancoats Hospital, Manchester, UK, 1974-77; Consultant General Surgeon, Baqai Hospital & Al-Rehman General Hospital, Karachi, 1977-80; Assistant Professor, Neurosurgery, Jinnah Postgraduate Medical Centre, Karachi, 1980-82; Assistant Professor, Neurosurgery, Civil Hospital & Dow Medical College, Karachi, 1982-85; Assistant Professor, Neurosurgery, Liaquat Medical College, Hyderabad, 1985-87; Consultant Neurosurgeon, King Fahd Hospital, Medina, Saudi Arabia, 1988-89; Locum Registrar, Neurosurgery, Royal Free Hospital, London, 1990, 1992; Consultant Neurosurgeon, Social Insurance Hospital, Riyadh, Saudi Arabia, 1996-98; Consultant Neurosurgeon, Fakhri Azam Clinic, Rigga Road, Dubai, UAE, 2002-04; Consultant (Attending) Neurosurgeon & Chief, Department of Neurosurgery and Spinal Surgery Units, King Fahd Specialist Hospital, Buraidah, Saudi Arabia, 1991-96, 1998-2002, 2004-. Publications: Numerous articles in professional journals. Honours: Merit Scholarship Award, Medical College, 1960; Top Neurosurgeon Award, Ministry of Health, Saudi Arabia, 2005-08; Research Award for Stereotactic Device patent, Research Award for Aneurysm Clipping System patent, New Mexico Neurosurgical Society. Memberships: American Association of Neurological Surgeons; Pakistan Medical and Dental Council; Saudi Medical Council; General Medical Council. Address: King Fahd Specialist Hospital, PO Box 2290, Buraidah, Al-Gassim, Saudi Arabia. E-mail: atiq_ur@yahoo.com

REHMAN MALIK Abdul, Pakistan Minister of Interior. Appointments: Bureau of Emigration, Government of Pakistan, 1973-; In charge, FIA/Interpol; Deputy Director, Federal Investigation Agency (FIA), 1987; Deputy Secretary, Ministry of Interior, 1989; Chairman/Secretary, security installations of Pakistan, 1 year; Director, FIA Headquarters and Principal Staff Officer to DG/FIA, 1989; Chief

Co-ordinator, FIA; Pakistan representative, SAARC Meeting of Experts, Sri Lanka, 1990; Director/Head, FIA Frontier province/FATA and Northern Areas, 1992-93; Director, FIA Immigration and Anti-Smuggling, FIA Headquarters, 1993; Additional Director General, FIA, 1995; Appearances on TV as expert on war on terror; President, DM Digital World TV Ltd; Ran numerous companies in the fields of security, telecommunication, food and oil, UK, 1998-2007; Adviser/Minister to the Prime Minister for Interior, 2008; Senator, Sindh Province and Minister of Interior, 2008-; Chairman, SAARC Interior/Home Minister's Summit, 2010; Visiting Speaker, NDU Pakistan. Honours: Fellowship, International Migration, University of Philippines, 1984-85; Sitara-e-Shujaat (Gallantry), Government of Pakistan, 1995. Memberships: Central Executive Committee, PPP.

REID John, b. 8 May 1947, Bellshill, Lanarkshire, Scotland. Politician. m. (1) Cathie, deceased 1998, 2 sons, (2) Carine Adler 2002. Education: PhD, History, Stirling University; PC, 1998. Appointments include: Research Officer, Labour Party in Scotland, 1979-83; Political Adviser to Labour Leader, Neil Kinnock, 1983-85; Scottish Organiser, Trade Unionists for Labour, 1986-87; Member of Parliament representing Motherwell North and then Hamilton North and Bellshill for the past 17 years; Parliamentary Posts: Opposition Spokesman on Children, 1989-90; Opposition Spokesman in Defence, 1990-97; Minister of Defence, 1997-98; Minister for Transport, 1989-99; Secretary of State for Scotland, 1999-2001; Secretary of State for Northern Ireland, 2001-2002; Party Chair and Minister without Portfolio, 2002-2003; Leader of the House of Commons, 2003; Secretary of State for Health, 2003-05, for Defence, 2005-2006; Home Sectretary, 2006-2007; Chairman, Celtic F.C., 2007-. Address: House of Commons, London, SW1A 0AA, England.

REIF Stefan Clive, b. 21 January 1944, Edinburgh, Scotland. Professor; Writer. m. Shulamit Stekel, 19 September 1967, d. 19 February 2010, 1 son, 1 daughter. Education: BA, Honours, 1964, PhD, 1969, University of London; MA, 1976, LittD, 2002, University of Cambridge, England. Appointments: Emeritus Professor of Medieval Hebrew Studies and Founder Director of Genizah Research Unit, University of Cambridge; Editor, Cambridge University Library's Genizah Series, 1978-2006. Publications: Shabbethai Sofer and his Prayer-book, 1979; Interpreting the Hebrew Bible, 1982; Published Material from the Cambridge Genizah Collections, 1988; Genizah Research after Ninety Years, 1992; Judaism and Hebrew Prayer, 1993; Hebrew Manuscripts at Cambridge University Library, 1997; A Jewish Archive from Old Cairo, 2000; Why Medieval Hebrew Studies, 2001; The Cambridge Genizah Collections, 2002; Problems with Prayers, 2006; Charles Taylor and the Genizah Collection, 2009. Contributions to: Over 300 articles in Hebrew and Jewish studies. Memberships: Fellow, St John's College, Cambridge; Fellow, Royal Asiatic Society; Jewish Historical Society of England, ex-president, 1991-92; Honorary Fellow, Mekize Nirdamim Society, Jerusalem; British Association for Jewish Studies, ex-president, 1992; Society for Old Testament Study; Theological Society, Cambridge, ex-president, 2002-04. Address: Cambridge University Library, West Road, Cambridge CB3 9DR, England.

REINER Rob, b. 6 March 1947, New York, USA. Actor; Writer; Director. (1) Penny Marshall, 1971, divorced, (2) Michele Singer, 1989, 3 children. Education: University of California at Los Angeles. Career: Appeared with comic improvisation groups: The Session; The Committee; Scriptwriter for Enter Laughing, 1967; Halls of Anger, 1970; Where's Poppa, 1970; Summertree, 1971; Fire Sale, 1977; How Come Nobody's on Our Side, 1977; TV appearances: All in the Family, 1971-78; Free Country, 1978; Thursday's Game, 1974; More Than Friends, 1978; Million Dollar Infield, 1972; Director, This is Spinal Tap, 1984; The Sure Thing, 1985; Stand By Me, 1986; The Princess Bride, 1987; Misery, 1990; Co-producer, director, When Harry Met Sally, 1989; A Few Good Men, 1992; North, The American President, 1995; Ghosts of the Mississippi, 1996; The Story of Us, 1999; Alex and Emma, 2003; Rumor Has It ..., 2005; Everyone's Hero (voice), 2006; The Bucket List, 2007. Address: c/o Castle Rock Entertainment, 335 North Maple Drive, Suite 135, Beverly Hills, CA 90212, USA.

REITMAN Ivan, b. 27 October 1946, Komarno, Czechoslovakia. Film Director and Producer. m. Genevieve Robert, 1 son, 2 daughter. Education: MusB, McMaster University. Career: Producer, stage shows: The Magic Show, 1974; The National Lampoon Show, 1975; Merlin (also director), 1983; Director and Executive Producer, films: Cannibal Girls, 1973; They Came From Within, 1975; Death Weekend, 1977; Blackout, 1978; National Lampoon's Animal House, 1978; Heavy Metal, 1981; Stop! Or My Mom Will Shoot, 1992; Space Jam, 1996; Private Parts, 1996; Producer and Director: Foxy Lady, 1971; Meatballs, 1979; Stripes, 1981; Ghostbusters, 1984; Legal Eagles, 1986; Twins, 1988; Ghostbusters II, 1989; Kindergarten Cop, 1990; Dave, 1993; Junior, 1994; Executive Producer: Rabid, 1976; Spacehunter: Adventures in the Forbidden Zone, 1983; Big Shots, 1987; Casual Sex?, 1988; Feds, 1988; Beethoven, 1992; Beethoven's 2nd, 1993; Commandments, 1996; Road Trip, 2000; Evolution, 2001; Killing Me Softly, 2002; Old School, 2003; Eurotrip, 2004; Trailer Park Boys: The Movie, 2006; Disturbia, 2007; Hotel for Dogs, 2009; Up in the Air, 2009. Producer and director, TV series: The Late Shift, 1996; Father's Day, 1997. Membership: Director's Guild of America. Address: c/o CAA, 9830 Wilshire Boulevard, Beverly Hills, CA 90212, USA.

REMNICK David J, b. 29 October 1958, Hackensack, New Jersey, USA. Journalist; Writer. m. Esther B Fein, 2 sons, 1 daughter. Education: AB, Princeton University, 1981. Appointments: Reporter, Washington Post, 1982-91; Staff writer, 1992-, Editor-in-Chief, 1998-, The New Yorker. Publications: Lenin's Tomb: The Last Days of the Soviet Empire, 1993; The Devil Problem (and Other True Stories), 1996; Resurrection: The Struggle for a New Russia, 1997; King of the World: Muhammad Ali and the Rise of an American Hero, 1998; Life Stories: Profiles from The New Yorker (editor), 1999; Wonderful Town: Stories from The New Yorker (editor), 1999; Reporting: Writings from the New Yorker, 2006; Contributions to: Newspapers and periodicals. Honours: Livingston Award, 1991; Pulitzer Prize for General Non-Fiction, 1993; Helen Bernstein Award, New York Public Library, 1994; George Polk Award, 1994; Editor of the Year, 1999. Address: The New Yorker, Four Times Square, New York, NY 10036, USA.

RENA Ravinder, b. 5 June 1969, India. Senior Lecturer. Education: BA, Economics, Kakatiya Government Degree College, 1990; BEd, Annamalai University, 1994; LLB, University College of Law, Kakatiya University, 1996; National Eligibility Test, 1996; MA, 1992, M Phil, 1995, PhD, 2001, Economics, Osmania University. Appointments: Lecturer, Economics, Osmania University, 1992-97; Senior Lecturer, Head of Department of Economics, Banking and Finance, Asmara Commercial College, Eritrea, 1997-2004; Associate Professor of Economics, 2004-06, Associate

Professor of Economics, 2006-08, Department of Business and Economics, Eritrea Institute of Technology; Senior Lecturer, Head of Economics, Department of Business Studies, The Papua New Guinea University of Technology, 2008-09; Senior Lecturer, Economics, Harold Pupkewitz Graduate School of Business, Polytechnic of Namibia, 2010-. Publications: 8 books; Numerous articles in professional journals. Honours: Vemuri Seshayya Sastry University Gold Medal, 2001; Invited speaker, European Patent Forum, 2008. Address: Harold Pupkewitz Graduate School of Business, Polytechnic of Namibia, Post Box 26896, Windhoek, Namibia. E-mail: ravinder.rena2006@gmail.com

RENDELL Ruth Barbara (Baroness Rendell of Babergh), (Barbara Vine), b. 17 February 1930, England. Writer. m. Donald Rendell, 1950, divorced 1975, 1 son, remarried Donald Rendell, 1977, deceased 1999. Publications: From Doon with Death, 1964; To Fear a Painted Devil, 1965; Vanity Dies Hard, 1966; A New Lease of Death, 1967; Wolf to the Slaughter, 1967 (televised 1987); The Secret House of Death, 1968; The Best Man to Die, 1969; A Guilty Thing Surprised, 1970; One Across Two Down, 1971; No More Dying Then, 1971; Murder Being Once Done, 1972; Some Lie and Some Die, 1973; The Face of Trespass, 1974 (televised as An Affair in Mind, 1988); Shake Hands for Ever, 1975; A Demon in My View, 1976 (film 1991); A Judgement in Stone, 1977; A Sleeping Life, 1978; Make Death Love Me, 1979; The Lake of Darkness, 1980 (televised as Dead Lucky, 1988); Put on by Cunning, 1981; Master of the Moor, 1982 (televised 1994); The Speaker of Mandarin, 1983; The Killing Doll, 1984; The Tree of Hands, 1984 (film 1989); An Unkindness of Ravens, 1985; Live Flesh, 1986; Heartstones, 1987; Talking to Strange Men, 1987; A Warning to the Curious: The Ghost Stories of M R James (editor), 1987; The Veiled One, 1988 (televised 1989); The Bridesmaid, 1989; Ruth Rendell's Suffolk, 1989; Going Wrong, 1990; Kissing the Gunner's Daughter, 1992; The Crocodile Bird, 1993; Simisola, 1994; The Reason Why (editor), 1995; Road Rage, 1997; A Sight for Sore Eyes, 1999; Harm Done, 1999; The Babes in the Wood, 2002; The Rottweiler, 2003; Thirteen Steps Down, 2004; End in Tears, 2005; The Water's Lovely, 2006; Not in the Flesh, 2007. As Barbara Vine: A Dark-Adapted Eye, 1986 (televised 1994); A Fatal Inversion, 1987 (televised 1992); The House of Stairs, 1988; Gallowglass, 1990; King Solomon's Carpet, 1981; Asta's Book, 1993; The Children of Men, 1994; No Night is Too Long, 1994; The Keys to the Street, 1997; The Brimstone Wedding, 1996; The Chimney Sweeper's Boy, 1998; Grasshopper, 2000; The Blood Doctor, 2002; The Minotaur, 2005; The Thief, 2006; The Birthday Present, 2008; Short Stories: The Fallen Curtain, 1976; Means of Evil, 1979; The Fever Tree, 1982; The New Girl Friend, 1985; Collected Short Stories, 1987; Undermining the Central Line (with Colin Ward), 1989; The Copper Peacock, 1991; Blood Lines, 1995; Piranha to Scurfy and Other Stories, 2000. Honours: Arts Council National Book Award for Genre Fiction, 1981; Royal Society of Literature, Fellow, 1988; Sunday Times Award for Literary Excellence, 1990; Cartier Diamond Dagger Award, Crime Writers Association, 1991; Commander of the Order of the British Empire, 1996; Life Peerage, 1997. Memberships: Royal Society of Literature, Fellow. Address: 26 Cornwall Terrace Mews, London, NW1 5LL, England.

RENFREW (Andrew) Colin (Baron Renfrew of Kaimsthorn), b. 25 July 1937, Stockton-on-Tees, England. Educator; Archaeologist; Author. m. Jane M Ewbank, 1965, 2 sons, 1 daughter. Education: St John's College, Cambridge; BA Honours, 1962, MA, 1964, PhD, 1965, ScD, 1976, Cambridge University; British School of Archaeology, Athens. Appointments: Lecturer, 1965-70, Senior Lecturer in Prehistory and Archaeology, 1970-72, Reader, 1972, University of Sheffield; Head of Department, Professor of Archaeology, University of Southampton, 1972-81; Head of Department, Disney Professor of Archaeology, University of Cambridge, 1981-2004; Master, 1986-97, Professor Fellow, 1997-2004, Emeritus Fellow, 2004-, Jesus College, Cambridge; Director, 1990-2004, Fellow, 2004-, McDonald Institute for Archaeological Research; Guest Lecturer, universities, colleges; Narrator, television films, radio programmes, British Broadcasting Corporation. Publications include: The Emergence of Civilisation: The Cyclades and the Aegean in the Third Millennium BC, 1972; Before Civilisation: The Radiocarbon Revolution and Prehistoric Europe, 1973; Problems in European Prehistory, 1979; Approaches to Social Archaeology, 1984; The Archaeology of Cult: The Sanctuary at Phylakopi, 1985; Archaeology and Language: The Puzzle of Indo-European Origins, 1988; The Idea of Prehistory, co-author, 1988; Archaeology: Theories, Methods, and Practice, co-author, 1991, 2nd edition, 1996; The Cycladic Spirit: Masterpieces from the Nicholas P Goulandris Collection, 1991; The Ancient Mind: Elements of Cognitive Archaeology, co-editor, 1994; Loot, Legitimacy and Ownership, 2000; Archaeogenetics (editor), 2000; Contributor to: Journals including Archaeology; Scientific American. Honours: Rivers Memorial Medal, Royal Anthropological Institute, 1979; Fellow, St John's College, Cambridge, 1981-86; Sir Joseph Larmor Award, 1981; DLitt, Sheffield University, 1987; Huxley Memorial Medal and Life Peerage, 1991; Honorary Degree, University of Athens, 1991; DLitt, University of Southampton, 1995; Foreign Associate, National Academy of Sciences, USA, 1997; Fyssen Prize, 1997; Language and Culture Prize, University of Umeå, Sweden, 1998; Rivers Memorial Medal, European Science Foundation Latsis Prize, 2003; Bolzan Prize, 2004. Memberships include: Fellow, British Academy; Ancient Monuments Board for England, 1974-84; Royal Commission on Historical Monuments, 1977-87; Historic Buildings and Monuments Commission for England, 1984-86; Ancient Monuments Advisory Committee, 1984-; British National Commission for UNESCO, 1984-86; Trustee, British Museum, 1991-. Address: McDonald Institute for Archaeological Research, Downing Street, Cambridge, CB2 3ER, England.

RENO Janet, b. 21 July 1938, Miami, Florida, USA. Lawyer. Education: BA, Cornell University; LLB, Harvard University. Appointments: Florida Bar, 1963; Associate, Brigham & Brigham, 1963-67; Partner, Lewis & Reno, 1971-72; Administrative Assistant State Attorney, 11th Judicial Circuit Florida, Miami, 1973-76, State Attorney, 1978-93; Partner, Steel, Hector & Davis, Miami, 1976-78; US Attorney-General, 1993-2001. Memberships: American Bar Association; American Law Institute; American Judicature Society. Honours: Women First Award, YWCA, 1993; National Women's Hall of Fame, 2000. Address: Department of Justice, 10th Street and Constitution Avenue, NW Washington, DC 20530, USA.

RENO Jean, b. 30 July 1948, Casablanca, Morocco. Actor. m. (1) Geneviève, 1977, (divorced) 1 son, 1 daughter, (2) Nathalie Dyszkiewicz, 1996-2000, (divorced) 1 son, 1 daughter; (3) Zofia Borucka, 2006, 2 sons. Career: Films: Clair de Femme, 1979; Le Dernier Combat, 1983; Signes Extérieurs de Richesse, 1983; Notre Histoire, 1984; Subway, 1985; I Love You, 1986; The Big Blue, 1988; L'Homme au Masque d'Or, 1990; La Femme Nikita, 1991; L'Operation Corned Beef, 1991; Loulou Graffitti, 1991; The Visitors (also wrote screenplay), 1993; Leon, 1994; French Kiss, 1995;

Roseanna's Grave, 1997; Les Couloirs du Temps, 1998; Godzilla, 1998; Les Rivieres pourpres, 2000; Just Visiting, 2001; Wasabi, 2001; Decalage horaire, 2002; Rollerball, 2002; Tais-toi, 2003; Les Rivieres pourpres 2 – Les anges de l'apocalypse, 2004; Onimusha 3, 2004; L'Enquête corse, 2004; Hotel Rwanda, 2004; L'Empire des loups, 2005; The Pink Panther, 2005; The Tiger and the Snow, 2005; The Da Vinci Code, 2006; Flyboys, 2006; Flushed Away (voice), 2006; Margaret, 2007; Cash, 2008; The Pink Panther 2, 2009; Armored, Couples Retreat, 2009; The Round Up, L'immortel, 2010; Margaret, The Late Late Show with Craig Ferguson, 2011; Alex Cross, Comme un chef, 2012. Honours: National Order of Merit (France), 2003. Address: Chez Les Films du Dauphin, 25 rue Yves-Toudic, 75010 Paris, France.

RESENDE Marcelo, b. 26 August 1963, Rio de Janeiro, Brazil. Researcher; Lecturer. Education: BA, Economics, 1985, BS, Psychology, 1990, State University of Rio de Janeiro; MSc, Pontifical Catholic University of Rio de Janeiro, 1989; MA, Economics, University of Pennsylvania, 1993; DPhil, Economics, University of Oxford, 1997. Appointments: Lecturer, Pontifical Catholic University, 1987-89; Assistant Professor, State University of Rio de Janeiro, 1990; Assistant Professor, 1990-98, Associate Professor, 1998-, Federal University of Rio de Janeiro; Visiting Fellow, European University Institute, Italy, 2005-06. Publications: Several articles in professional journals. Honours include: Listed in Who's Who and biographical publications; Scholarships, Ministry of Science and Technology and Ministry of Education, Brazil. Membership: Econometric Society. Address: Av Pasteur 250, URCA, 22290-240 Rio de Janeiro, Brazil. Email: mresende@ie.ufrj.br

REYNDERS Didier, b. 4 August 1958, Liège, France. Deputy Prime Minister; Minister of Finance. m. Bernadette Prignon, 2 sons, 2 daughters. Education: Degree in Law, University of Liège, 1981. Appointments: Director General, Local Authorities Department of the Ministry of the Walloon Region, 1985-88; Chief of Staff of the Deputy Prime Minister, Minister of Justice and of Institutional reforms, Mr Jean Gol, 1987-88; Chairman, Societe Nationale des Chemin de fer belges (SNCB-NMBS), 1986-91; Member, Liège Town Council, 1988; Leader, PRL group, Provincial Council of Liège, 1991; Chairman, National Society of Airways, 1991-93; Chairman, Board of Directors of the SEFB Record Bank, 1992-99; Deputy Chairman, PRL, 1992; Member of Parliament, 1992; Chairman of the group PRL-FDF group, 1995; Leader, PRL group, Liège, 1995-; Chairman, Provincial and District PRL Federation (later the MR), 1995; Minister of Finance, 1999-; Chair, Euro group and Ecofin, 2001; Chair, G10, 2002-; Deputy Prime Minister, 2004-; President, Mouvement Réformateur, 2004-.

REYNOLDS Albert, b. 3 November 1935, Rooskey, County Roscommon, Ireland. Politician; Company Director. m. Kathleen Coén, 2 sons, 5 daughters. Education: Notre Dame University; Stoney Hill College, Boston; National University of Ireland; University of Philadelphia, Jesuits; University of Melbourne; University of Aberdeen. Appointments include: Company Director, own family business: C&D Foods, Edgeworthstown, Co Longford, Ireland; Director, many Irish and international companies; Political Career: Entered national politics, 1977, Elected to Dáil; Minister for Posts and Telegraphs and Transport, 1979-81; Minister for Industry and Energy, 1982; Minister for Industry and Commerce, 1987-88; Minister for Finance and Public Service, 1988-89; Minister of Finance, 1989-91; Vice-President, 1983-92, President, 1992-94, Fianna Fáil Party; Elected Taoiseach (PM), 1992-94; Chair, Bula Resources, 1999-2002, Longford Recreational Devt Centre. Memberships: Board of Governors: European Investment Bank; World Bank International Monetary Fund. Honour: Hon LLD (University College, Dublin), 1995. Address: Leinster House, Dáil Éirann, Kildare Street, Dublin 2, Ireland.

REYNOLDS Graham, b. 10 January 1914, Highgate, London, England. Writer; Art Historian. Education: BA, Honours, Queens' College, Cambridge. Publications: Nicholas Hilliard and Isaac Oliver, 1947, 2nd edition, 1971; English Portrait Miniatures, 1952, revised edition, 1988; Painters of the Victorian Scene, 1953; Catalogue of the Constable Collection, Victoria and Albert Museum, 1960, revised edition, 1973; Constable, The Natural Painter, 1965; Victorian Painting, 1966, revised edition, 1987; Turner, 1969; Concise History of Watercolour Painting, 1972; Catalogue of Portrait Miniatures, Wallace Collection, 1980; The Later Paintings and Drawings of John Constable, 2 volumes, 1984; English Watercolours, 1988; The Earlier Paintings of John Constable, 2 volumes, 1996; Catalogue of European Portrait Miniatures, Metropolitan Museum of Art, New York, 1996; The Miniatures in the Collection of H.M. the Queen, The Sixteenth and Seventeenth Centuries, 1999; Daphne Reynolds, A Memoir, 2007. Contributions to: Times Literary Supplement; Burlington Magazine; Apollo; New Departures. Honours: Mitchell Prize, 1984; Officer of the Order of the British Empire, 1984; Commander of the Victorian Order, 2000; British Academy, Fellow, 1993; Honorary Keeper of Miniatures, Fitzwilliam Museum, Cambridge, 1994-. Address: The Old Manse, Bradfield St George, Bury St Edmunds, Suffolk IP30 0AZ, England.

RHODES Richard (Lee), b. 4 July 1937, Kansas City, Kansas, USA. Writer. m. Ginger Untrif, 1993, 2 children by previous marriage. Education: BA, cum laude, Yale University, 1959. Publications: Non-Fiction: The Inland Ground, 1970; The Ozarks, 1974; Looking for America, 1979; The Making of the Atomic Bomb, 1988; A Hole in the World, 1990; Making Love, 1992; Dark Sun, 1995; How to Write, 1995; Deadly Feasts, 1997; Trying to get some Dignity (with Ginger Rhodes), 1996; Visions of Technology, 1999; Why They Kill, 1999; Masters of Death, 2001; John James Audobon, 2004; Arsenals of Folly: The making of the nuclear arms race, 2007; Fiction: The Ungodly, 1973; Holy Secrets, 1978; The Last Safari, 1980; Sons of Earth, 1981. Contributions to: Numerous journals and magazines. Honours: National Book Award in Non-Fiction, 1987; National Book Critics Circle Award in Non-Fiction, 1987; Pulitzer Prize in Non-Fiction, 1988. Membership: Authors Guild. Address: c/o Janklow and Nesbit Associates, 455 Park Avenue, New York, NY10021, USA.

RHODES Zandra Lindsey, b. 19 September 1940. Fashion Designer. Education: Royal College of Art. Career: Designer (textile, 1964-); Print Factory/Studio with A McIntyre, 1965; Fashion Industry, 1966-; Produced dresses from own prints in partnership with S Ayton, shop on Fulham Rd, 1967-68; US solo collection, 1969; annual fantasy shows in US, founded Zandra Rhodes (UK) Ltd; with A Knight & R Stirling, 1975-86; now world-wide, currently works in: interior furnishings, fine art with various collections in US and England, Speaker; Chancellor, University for the Creative Arts, 2009; Collection designed for Marks & Spencers, 2009; Several jewellery collections; Handbag range by Bluprint, 2010. Publications: The Art of Zandra Rhodes, 1984; The Zandra Rhodes Collection by Brother, 1988. Honours include: English Designer of the Year, 1972; Emmy for Best Costume

(Romeo and Juliet, US, 1984); Lifetime Achievement at the British Fashion Awards, 1995; CBE, 1997. Address: 79-85 Bermondsey Street, London, SE1 3XF, England.

RHYS David Garel, b. 28 February 1940, Swansea, Wales. Economist. m. Charlotte Mavis, 1 son, 2 daughters. Education: University of Wales, Swansea; University of Birmingham. Appointments: Lecturer and Assistant Lecturer, University of Hull; Lecturer and Senior Lecturer, University College, Cardiff; Professor of Motor Industry Economics and Director of the Centre for Automotive Research, Cardiff University Business School; Emeritus Professor, Cardiff University, 2005; Chairman, Welsh Automotive Forum; Chairman, Economic Research Advisory Panel of the Welsh Assembly Government. Publications: The Motor Industry: An Economic Survey, 1972; The Motor Industry in the European Community, 1989; Contributions to: Journal of Industrial Economics; Journal of Transport History; Journal of Transport Economics; Bulletin of Economic Research; Scottish Journal of Political Economy; Journal of Economic Studies; Journal of Accounting and Business Research; World Economics. Honours: OBE, 1989; Castrol – IMI Gold Medal, 1989; Welsh Communicator of the Year, 1993; Neath Port Talbot Business Award, 1999; Motortrader Outstanding Achievement in the Motor Trade, 2001; Honorary Fellow, University of Wales Swansea Institute, 2003. Memberships: Royal Automobile Club, Pall Mall; Fellow, Royal Society for Arts Commerce and Manufacture; Fellow, Institute of Transport Administration; President until 2009 now Vice President, Institute of the Motor Industry; Freeman of the City of London and Liveryman, Carmen's Company, C.B.E. 2007, Listed in biographical dictionaries. Address: 14 Maes-yr-Awel, Radya, Cardiff CF15 8AN, Wales. E-mail: rhysg@cardiff.ac.uk

RHYS-JAMES Shani, b. 2 May 1953, Melbourne, Australia. Artist. m. Stephen Alexander West, 2 sons. Education: St Martins College of Art, London. Appointments: Artist; Solo exhibitions include: Layers, Martin Tinney, Cardiff, 2005; New Paintings, Martin Tinney, 2008; Brussels Exhibition, 2009; Connaught Brown, London, 2009; Hillsboro Fine Art, Dublin, 2010. Publications: The Blackcot Monograph; Imaging the Imagination, 2005; Cassandra's Rant, 2007; CASW Print Collection, 2008; New Paintings/Martin Tinney Essay, 2008. Honours: Gold Medal for Fine Art, National Eisteddfod, 1992; First Prize, Hunting/Observer Prize, 1993; Winner, Jerwood Painting Prize, 2003; Wales Woman of Culture, 2004; MBE, Arts Council of Wales Creative Award, 2006; Honorary Fellowship, UWIC, Owain Glyndwr Award, 2007; Honorary Fellowship, Hereford College of Art, 2008. Memberships: Royal Cambrian Academy; Artist Advisor, Dereck Williams Trust/National Museum Purchasing Panel, 2006; Appointed to DACS Creator's Council, 2006. E-mail: shanirhysjames@btinternet.com

RIAUD Xavier, b. 28 March 1972, Nantes, France. Dental Surgeon. m. Education: Doctor, Dental Surgery, 1997; PhD, History of Sciences, 2007. Appointments: Dental Surgeon. Publications: 134 articles in French, English, Spanish and German; 14 books; 70 internet articles. Honours: Officer of the Academic Corps as delegate in the Scientific and Research Committee of Instituto Napoleonico Mexico-Francia; Life Member, American Academy of Dentistry; Elected Member, Academy of People of Letters in France; Member, Pierre Fauchard Academy; Winner, French Dental Academy; Associate Member, French Dental Academy. Memberships: Researcher, François Viete Centre in History of Sciences and Technics; Major, French Army Dental Corps. Address: 145 route de Vannes, 44800, Saint Herblain, France.

RIBBANS William John, b. 28 November 1954, Northampton, England. Orthopaedic Surgeon. m. Sian Williams, 3 daughters. Education: BSc, 1977, MB BS, 1980, Royal Free Hospital School of Medicine; MChOrth, University of Liverpool, 1990; FRCSEd, 1985; FRCSOrth, 1990; PhD, 2003; FFSEM (UK), 2006. Appointments: Orthopaedic Consultant, Royal Free Hospital, London, 1991-96, Northampton General Hospital, 1996-. Honour: Professor of School of Health, The University of Northampton. Address: Department of Orthopaedic Surgery, Northampton General Hospital, Northampton NN1 5BD, England. E-mail: wjribbans@uk-consultants.co.uk

RICCI Christina, b. 12 February 1980, Santa Monica, California, USA. Film Actress. Career: Actor in commercials then in films: Mermaids, 1990; The Hard Way, 1991; The Addams Family, 1991; The Cemetery Club, 1993; Addams Family Values, 1993; Casper, 1995; Now and Then, 1995; Gold Diggers: The Secret of Bear Mountain, 1995; That Darn Cat, 1996; Last of the High Kings, 1996; Bastard Out of Carolina, 1996; Ice Storm, 1997; Little Red Riding Hood, 1997; Fear and Loathing in Las Vegas, 1998; Desert Blue, 1998; Buffalo 66, 1998; The Opposite Sex, 1998; Small Soldiers, 1998; Pecker, 1999; 200 Cigarettes, 1999; Sleepy Hollow, 1999; The Man Who Cried, 2000; Monster, 2003; Cursed, 2005; Penelope, 2006; Black Snake Moan, 2006; Home of the Brave, 2006; Speed Racer, 2008; New York, I Love You, 2009; All's Fair in Love, 2009; After Life, 2009; Alpha and Omega, 2010; Bucky Larson: Born to be a Star, 2011; Bel Ami, 2012; Around the Block, 2013; TV: HELP, 1990; The Simpsons, 1996; The Laramie Project, Malcolm in the Middle, Ally McBeal, 2002; Joey, 2005; Grey's Anatomy, 2006; Saving Grace, 2009; Pan Am, 2011-12; The Good Wife, 2012. Honours: Young Artist Award, 1991; Special Award, 1995; Saturn Award, 1996, 2000; Golden Space Needle Award, 1998; NBR Award, 1998; Young Star Award, 1998; Golden Satellite Award, 1999; FFCC Award, 1999; Blockbuster Entertainment Award, 2000, 2001; Young Hollywood Award, 2001; Half-Life Award, 2006; Giffoni Award, 2009. Address: c/o ICM, 8942 Wilshire Boulevard, Beverly Hills, CA 90211, USA.

RICE Condoleezza, b. 14 November 1954, Birmingham, Alabama, USA. Government Official; Academic. Education: University of Denver; University of Notre Dame. Appointments: Teacher, 1981-2001, Provost, 1993-99; Currently Hoover Senior Fellow and Professor of Political Science, Stanford University, California; Special Assistant to Director of Joint Chiefs of Staff, 1986; Director, then Senior Director, Soviet and East European Affairs, National Security Council, 1989-91; Special Assistant to President for National Security Affairs, 1989-91; Primary Foreign Policy Adviser to Presidential Candidate, George W Bush, 1999-2000; Assistant to President for National Security Affairs and National Security Advisor, 2001-04; Secretary of State, 2004-09. Publications: Uncertain Allegiance: The Soviet Union and the Czechoslovak Army, 1984; The Gorbachev Era (co-author), 1986; Germany Unified and Europe Transformed (co-author), 1995; numerous articles on Soviet and East European foreign and defence policy. Honours: Dr hc (Morehouse College) 1991, (University of Alabama) 1994, (University of Notre Dame) 1995, (Mississippi College School of Law) 2003, (University of Louisville) 2004. Memberships: Board of Directors: Chevron Corporation; Charles Schwab Corporation; William and Flora Hewlett Foundation; numerous other boards; Senior Fellow, Institute for International Studies, Stanford; Fellow, American

RICE Susan Ilene, b. 7 March 1946, Providence, Rhode Island, USA. Banker. m. C Duncan Rice, 2 sons, 1 daughter. Education: BA, Wellesley College; M Litt, Aberdeen University. Appointments: Medical Researcher, Yale University Medical School, 1970-73; Dean of Saybrook College, Yale University, 1973-79; Staff Aide to the President, Hamilton College, 1980-81; Dean of Students, Colgate University, 1981-86; Senior Vice President, NatWest Bancorp, 1986-96; Head of Branch Banking, then Managing Director, Personal Banking, Bank of Scotland, 1997-2000; Chief Executive, 2000-09, Chairman, 2008-09, Lloyds TSB Scotland; Member, HM Treasury Policy Action Team on Access to Financial Services, 1997-2000; Member, Aberdeen Common Purpose Advisory Board, 1999-2006; Member, Foresight Sub-Committee on Retail Financial Services, 2000; Trustee, David Hume Institute, 2000-05; Member, Scottish Advisory Task Force on the New Deal, 2000-05; Chair, Edinburgh International Book Festival, 2001-; Treasurer, The March Dialogue, 2001-04; Director, Scottish Business in the Community, 2001-10; Director, UK Charity Bank, 2001-08; Chair, Advisory Committee of the Scottish Centre for Research on Social Justice, 2002-07; Member, BP Scottish Advisory Board, 2002-2003; Director, Scottish and Southern Energy plc, 2003-; Member, HMT Financial Inclusion Taskforce, 2005-11; Director, Scotland's Futures Forum, 2005-; Big Soc Capital, 2011-; 2020 Climate Change Leadership Group, 2008-; Director, Bank of England, 2007-; Chair, Edinburgh Festivals Forum, 2008-; Trustee, Lloyds TSB Foundation for Scotland, 2009-10; Chair, Governor's Patrons of the National Galleries of Scotland, 2011-; Regent, Royal College of Surgeons, Edinburgh, 2010-; Managing Director, Lloyds Banking Group Scotland, 2009-; President, Scottish Council for Development and Industry, 2012-. Publications: Articles on banking, insurance, business, marketing, diversity, corporate responsibility and financial exclusion published in The Scotsman, The Herald, Scotland on Sunday, Insurance Day, New Statesman, Finance Ethics Quarterly, Scottish Banker, Scottish Homes, Business AM, Holyrood Magazine, Business Insider Magazine, Being Scottish and in the proceedings of several conferences; Co-author of several articles published in medical journals, early 1970's. Honours: CBE; Chartered Banker; FCIBS; CCMI; FRSA; FRSE; Spirit of Scotland Annual Business Award, 2002; Corporate Elite Business Award, 2002, 2008; Logica Business Leadership Award, Scotland, 2007; HRH Ambassador for Corporate Responsibility in Scotland, 2005-2006; President, cdfa, 2007-; DBA (Hon), The Robert Gordon University; Dr honoris causa, Edinburgh University; DLitt (Hon), Heriot-Watt University; DUniv (Hon), Queen Margaret University; LLD (Hon), Aberdeen University; DUniv (Hon), Paisley University; DUniv (Hon), Glasgow University. Address: Lloyds Banking Group, N Bank Street, The Mound, Edinburgh EH1 1YZ, Scotland. E-mail: susan.rice@lloydsbanking.com

RICE Tim (Sir) (Miles Bindon), b. 10 November 1944, Amersham, Buckinghamshire, England. Songwriter; Broadcaster. m. Jane Artereta McIntosh, 1974, 1 son, 1 daughter. Education: Lancing College. Career: EMI Records, 1966-68; Norrie Paramor Organisation, 1968-69; Founder, Director, GRRR Books Ltd, 1978-, Pavilion Books Ltd, 1981-97. Appearances on TV and radio including Just A Minute, Radio 4; Creative Works: Lyrics for stage musicals (with Andrew Lloyd Webber): Joseph and the Amazing Technicolor Dreamcoat, 1968; Jesus Christ Superstar, 1970; Evita, 1976; Cricket, 1986; Other musicals: Blondel, with Stephen Oliver, 1983; Chess, with Benny Andersson and Bjorn Ulvaeus, 1984; Tycoon, with Michel Berger, 1992; Selection of songs, Beauty and the Beast, with Alan Menken, 1994; Heathcliff, with John Farrar, 1996; King David, with Alan Menken, 1997; Aida, with Elton John, 1998; Lyrics for musical films: Aladdin, with Alan Menken, 1992; The Lion King, with Elton John, 1994, theatre version, 1997; Aida, with Elton John, 1998; El Dorado, with Elton John, 1999; Lyrics for songs with other composers including Paul McCartney, Mike Batt, Freddie Mercury, Graham Gouldman, Marvin Hamlisch, Rick Wakeman, John Barry. Publications: Songbooks from musicals; Co-author of over 20 books in the series Guinness Book of British Hit Singles, Albums, etc; Fill Your Soul, 1994; Cricket Writer, National Newspapers and Cricket Magazines; Treasures of Lords, 1989; Oh, What a Circus, autobiography, 1995. Honours: Oscar, Golden Globe, Best New Song, A Whole New World, 1992, for Can You Feel The Love Tonight, with Elton John, 1994, and for You Must Love Me with Andrew Lloyd Webber, 1996; Gold and platinum records in numerous countries; 11 Ivor Novello Awards; 2 Tony Awards; 5 Grammy Awards, 3 Academy Awards; Kt, 1994. Memberships: Chairman, Stars Organisation for Spastics, 1983-85; Shaftesbury Avenue Centenary Committee, 1984-86; President, Lords Taverners, 1988-90; Dramatists' Saints and Sinners, Chairman, 1990; Cricket Writers; Foundation for Sport and the Arts, 1991-; Garrick Club; Groucho Club; Main Committee, 1992-94, 1995-, President, 2002-03, MCC. Address: c/o Lewis & Golden, 40 Queen Anne Street, London, W1M 0EL, England.

RICH Adrienne (Cecile), b. 16 May 1929, Baltimore, Maryland, USA. Poet; Writer. m. Alfred H Conrad, 1953, deceased 1970, 3 sons. Education: AB, Radcliffe College, 1951. Appointments: Visiting Poet, Swarthmore College, 1966-68; Adjunct Professor, Columbia University, 1967-69; Lecturer, 1968-70, Instructor, 1970-71, Assistant Professor, 1971-72, Professor, 1974-75, City College of New York; Fannie Hurst Visiting Professor, Brandeis University, 1972-73; Professor of English, Douglass College, New Brunswick, New Jersey, 1976-78; A D White Professor-at-Large, Cornell University, 1981-85; Clark Lecturer and Distinguished Visiting Professor, Scripps College, Claremont, California, 1983; Visiting Professor, San Jose State University, California, 1985-86; Burgess Lecturer, Pacific Oaks College, Pasadena, California, 1986; Professor of English and Feminist Studies, Stanford University, 1986-94; Board of Chancellors, Academy of American Poets, 1989-91; Clark Lecturer, Trinity College, Cambridge, 2002. Publications: Poetry: A Change of World, 1951; (Poems), 1952; The Diamond Cutters and Other Poems, 1955; Snapshots of a Daughter-in-Law: Poems 1954-1962, 1963; Necessities of Life: Poems 1962-1965, 1966; Selected Poems, 1967; Leaflets: Poems 1965-1968, 1969; The Will to Change: Poems 1968-1970, 1971; Diving into the Wreck: Poems 1971-1972, 1973; Poems Selected and New, 1975; Twenty-One Love Poems, 1976; The Dream of a Common Language: Poems 1974-1977, 1978; A Wild Patience Has Taken Me This Far: Poems 1978-1981, 1981; Sources, 1983; The Fact of a Doorframe: Poems Selected and New 1950-1984, 1984; Your Native Land, Your Life, 1986; Time's Power: Poems 1985-1988, 1989; An Atlas of the Difficult World: Poems 1988-1991, 1991; Collected Early Poems 1950-1970, 1993; Dark Fields of the Republic: Poems 1991-95, 1995; Midnight Salvage: Poems 1995-1998, 1999; Arts of the Possible: Essays and Conversations, 2001; Fox: Poems 1998-2000, 2001; The Fact of a Doorframe: Poems 1950-2000, 2002; The School Among the Ruins: Poems, 2000-04, 2004; Poetry and Commitment, 2007; Telephone

Ringing in the Labyrinth, 2007. Other: Of Woman Born: Motherhood as Experience and Institution, 1976; On Lies, Secrets and Silence: Selected Prose 1966-1978, 1979; Blood, Bread and Poetry: Selected Prose 1979-1985, 1986; What Is Found There: Notebooks on Poetry and Politics, 1993, revised 2003; Arts of the Possible: Essays and Conversations, 2001. Honours: Yale Series of Younger Poets Award, 1951; Guggenheim Fellowships, 1952, 1961; American Academy of Arts and Letters Award, 1961; Bess Hokin Prize, 1963; Eunice Tietjens Memorial Prize, 1968; National Endowment for the Arts Grant, 1970; Shelley Memorial Award, 1971; Ingram Merrill Foundation Grant, 1973; National Book Award, 1974; Fund for Human Dignity Award, 1981; Ruth Lilly Prize, 1986; Brandeis University Creative Arts Award, 1987; Elmer Holmes Bobst Award, 1989; Commonwealth Award in Literature, 1991; Frost Silver Medal, Poetry Society of America, 1992; Los Angeles Times Book Award, 1992; Lenore Marshall/Nation Award, 1992; William Whitehead Award, 1992; Lambda Book Award, 1992; Harriet Monroe Prize, 1994; John D and Catharine T MacArthur Foundation Fellowship, 1994; Academy of American Poets Dorothea Tanning Award, 1996; Lannan Foundation Lifetime Achievement Award, 1999; Bollingen Prize for Poetry, 2003; Editor, Muriel Rukeyser, Selected Poems, 2004; National Book Critics Circle Award, 2005; Honorary doctorates. Address: c/o W W Norton & Co, 500 Fifth Avenue, New York, NY 10110, USA.

RICH Frank Hart, b. 2 June 1949, Washington, District of Columbia, USA. Journalist. m. (1) Gail Winston, 1976, 2 sons, (2) Alexandra Rachelle Witchel, 1991. Education: BA, Harvard University, 1971. Appointments: Co-Editor, Richmond Mercury, Virginia, 1972-73; Senior Editor and Film Critic, New York Times Magazine, 1973-75; Film Critic, New York Post, 1975-77; Film and Television Critic, Time Magazine, 1977-80; Chief Drama Critic, 1980-93, Op-Ed Columnist, 1994-, New York Times; Columnist, New York Times Sunday Magazine, 1993. Publications: The Theatre Art of Boris Aronson (with others), 1987; Hot Seat: Theater Criticism for the New York Times 1980-93, 1998; Ghost Light, 2000. Contributions to: Newspapers and periodicals. Address: c/o The New York Times, 229 West 43rd Street, New York, NY 10036, USA.

RICHARD Cliff (Harry Webb) (Sir), b. 14 October 1940, Lucknow, India. Singer. Appointments: Leader, Cliff Richard and The Shadows; Solo Artist; International Concert Tours, 1958-; Own TV Show; Numerous TV and radio appearances. Creative Works: Films: The Young Ones; Expresso Bongo; Summer Holiday; Wonderful Life; Musicals: Time, 1986-87; Heathcliff, 1996-97; Albums include: 21 Today, 1961; The Young Ones, 1961; Summer Holiday, 1963; 40 Golden Greats, 1977; Love Songs, 1981; Private Collection, 1988; The Album, 1993; Real as I Wanna Be; Something's Goin' On, 1994; Over 120 singles. Publications: Questions, 1970; The Way I See It, 1972; The Way I See It Now, 1975; Which One's Cliff, 1977; Happy Christmas from Cliff, 1980; You, Me and Jesus, 1983; Mine to Share, 1984; Jesus, Me and You, 1985; Single-Minded, 1988; Mine Forever, 1989; My Story: A Celebration of 40 Years in Showbusiness, 1998. Honours: OBE, 1980; Knighted, 1995; Numerous music awards. Membership: Equity. Address: c/o PO Box 46C, Esher, Surrey KT10 0RB, England.

RICHARDS Isaac Vivian Alexander (Sir) (Viv), b. 7 March 1952, St John's, Antigua. Cricketer. m. Miriam Lewis, 1 son, 1 daughter. Career: Right-hand batsman, off-break bowler; Played for Leeward Islands, 1971-91 (Captain 1981-91); Somerset, 1974-86, Queensland, 1976-77, Glamorgan, 1990-93; 121 tests for West Indies, 1974-91, 50 as Captain, scoring 8,540 runs (average 50.2) including 24 hundreds and holding 122 catches; Scored 36, 212 first-class runs (114 hundreds, only West Indian to score 100 hundreds); Toured England, 1976, 1979 (World Cup), 1980, 1983 (World Cup), 1984, 1988 (as Captain), 1991 (as Captain); 187 limited-overs internationals scoring 6, 721 runs (11 hundreds including then record 189 not out v England at Old Trafford, 1984; Chair, Selectors, West Indies Cricket Board, 2002-. Publication: Co-author, Viv Richards (autobiography); Hitting Across the Line (autobiography), 1991; Sir Vivian, 2000. Honour: Wisden Cricketer of the Year, 1977; One of Wisden's Five Cricketers of the Century, 2000; Cricket Hall of Fame, 2001; Dr hc (Exeter), 1986. Address: West Indies Cricket Board, PO Box 616, St John's, Antigua.

RICHARDS Keith, (Keith Richard), b. 18 December 1943, Dartford, Kent, England. Musician; Vocalist; Songwriter. m. (1) Anita Pallenberg, 1 son, 1 daughter, (2) Patti Hansen, 1983, 2 daughters. Education: Sidcup Art School. Career: Member, The Rolling Stones, 1962-; Co-Writer (with Mick Jagger) numerous songs and albums, 1964-. Creative Works: Albums: The Rolling Stones, 1964; The Rolling Stones No 2, 1965; Out of Our Heads, 1965; Aftermath, 1966; Between the Buttons, 1967; Their Satanic Majesties Request, 1967; Beggar's Banquet, 1968; Let it Bleed, 1969; Get Yer Ya-Ya's Out, 1969; Sticky Fingers, 1971; Exile on Main Street, 1972; Goat's Head Soup, 1973; It's Only Rock'n'Roll, 1974; Black and Blue, 1976; Some Girls, 1978; Emotional Rescue, 1980; Still Life, 1982; Steel Wheels, 1989; Flashpoint, 1991; Voodoo Lounge, 1994; Stripped, 1995; Bridges to Babylon, 1997; No Security, 1999; Forty Licks, 2002; Live Licks, 2004; Singles: It's All Over Now; Little Red Rooster; (I Can't Get No) Satisfaction; Jumping Jack Flash; Honky Tonk Women; Harlem Shuffle; Start Me Up; Paint It Black; Angie; Going to a Go-Go; It's Only Rock'n'Roll; Let's Spend the Night Together; Brown Sugar; Miss You; Emotional Rescue; She's So Cold; Undercover of the Night; Highwire, 1991; Love Is Strong, 1994; Out of Tears, 1994; I Go Wild, 1995; Like A Rolling Stone, 1995; Wild Horses, 1996; Anybody Seen My Baby, 1997; Saint of Me, 1998; Out of Control, 1998; Don't Stop, 2002; Films: Sympathy for the Devil, 1970; Gimme Shelter, 1970; Ladies and Gentlemen, the Rolling Stones, 1974; Let's Spend the Night Together, 1983; Hail Hail Rock'n'Roll, 1987; Flashpoint, 1991: Pirates of the Caribbean: At World's End, 2007; Pirates of the Caribbean: On Stranger Tides, 2011. Honours: Grammy, Lifetime Achievement Award, 1986; Rock'n'Roll Hall of Fame, 1989; Q Award, Best Live Act, 1990; Ivor Novello Award, Outstanding Contribution to British Music, 1991; Songwriters Hall of Fame, 1993. Address: c/o Jane Rose, Raindrop Services, 1776 Broadway, Suite 507, New York, NY 10019, USA.

RICHARDS Rex Edward (Sir), b. 28 October 1922, Colyton, Devon, England. Academic. m. Eva Vago, 2 daughters. Education: BA (Oxon), 1945; FRS, 1959, DSc (Oxon), 1970; FRIC, 1970; FRSC, FBA (Hon), 1990; Hon FRCP, 1987; Hon FRAM 1991. Appointments: Fellow of Lincoln College, Oxford, 1947-1964; Dr Lee's Professor of Chemistry, Oxford, 1964-70; Warden of Merton College, Oxford, 1969-84; Vice-Chancellor, Oxford University, 1977-81; Chairman, Oxford Enzyme Group, 1969-1983; Chancellor, University of Exeter, 1982-98; Commissioner, Royal Commission for Exhibition of 1851, 1984-1997; Director, The Leverhulme Trust, 1984-94; Chairman, British Postgraduate Medical Federation, 1986-93; President, Royal Society of Chemistry, 1990-92; Retired, 1994. Publications: Numerous in scientific journals. Honours: Corday-Morgan, Chemical Society, 1954;

Fellow of the Royal Society, 1959; Tilden Lecturer, Chemical Society, 1962; Davy Medal, The Royal Society, 1976; Theoretical Chemistry and Spectroscopy, Chemical Society, 1977; Knight Bachelor, 1977; EPIC, 1982; Medal of Honour, University of Bonn, 1983; Royal Medal, The Royal Society, 1986; President's Medal, Society of Chemical Industry, 1991; Associé étranger, Académie des Sciences, Institut de France, 1995; Honorary degrees: East Anglia, 1971; Exeter, 1975; Dundee, 1977; Leicester, 1978; Salford, 1979; Edinburgh, 1981; Leeds, 1984; Kent, 1987; Cambridge, 1987; Thames Polytechnic (University of Greenwich) Centenary Fellow, 1990; Birmingham, 1993; London, 1994; Oxford Brookes, 1998; Warwick, 1999. Memberships: Trustee: National Heritage Memorial Fund, 1980-84, Tate Gallery, 1982-88, 1991-93, National Gallery, 1982-88, 1989-93; National Gallery Trust, 1996-, Chairman, 1996-99; National Gallery Trust Foundation, 1997-, (Chairman, 1997-1999); Henry Moore Foundation 1989-, (Chairman, 1994-2001). Address: 13 Woodstock Close, Oxford, OX2 8DB, England. E-mail: rex.richards@merton.oxford.ac.uk

RICHARDSON Joely, b. 9 January 1965, Lancashire, England. Actress. m. Tim Bevan, divorced, 1 daughter. Education: The Thacher School, Ojai, California; Royal Academy of Dramatic Art. Career: London stage debut in Steel Magnolias, 1989; TV appearances include: Body Contact, Behaving Badly, 1989; Heading Home, Lady Chatterly's Lover, 1993; The Tribe, 1998; Echo, 1998; Nip/Tuck, 2003-2007; Fallen Angel, 2003; Lies My Mother Told Me, 2005; Wallis & Edward, 2005; Fatal Contact: Bird Flu in America, 2006; Films: Wetherby, 1985; Drowning by Numbers, 1988; Shining Through, 1991; Rebecca's Daughters, 1992; Lochness, 1994; Sister, My Sister, 1995; 101 Dalmatians, 1995; Believe Me, 1995; Hollow Reed, 1996; Event Horizon, 1996; Wrestling with Alligators, Under Heaven, The Patriot, Maybe Baby, Return to Me, 2000; The Affair of the Necklace, 2001; Shoreditch, 2003; The Fever, 2004; The Last Mimzy, The Christmas Miracle of Jonathan Toomey, Freezing, 2007; The Day of the Triffids, 2009; The Tudors, 2010; Anonymous, The Girl with the Dragon Tattoo, 2011; Red Lights, Titanic: Blood and Steel, 2012. Address: c/o ICM, Oxford House, 76 Oxford Street, London, W1N 0AX, England.

RICHARDSON Miranda, b. 3 March 1958, Southport, England. Actress. Education: Old Vic Theatre School, Bristol. Career: Theatre appearances include: Moving, 1980-81; All My Sons; Who's Afraid of Virginia Woolf?; The Life of Einstein; A Lie of the Mind, 1987; The Changeling; Mountain Language, 1988; Etta Jenks; The Designated Mourner, 1996; Aunt Dan and Lemon, 1999; The Play What I Wrote, 2002-03; One Knight Only, 2005; Grasses of a Thousand Colours, 2009; Film appearances: Dance With a Stranger, 1985; The Innocent; Empire of the Sun; The Mad Monkey; Eat the Rich; Twisted Obsession; The Bachelor, Enchanted April, The Crying Game, 1992; Damage, 1993; Tom and Viv, La Nuit et Le Moment, 1994; Kansas City; Swann, 1995; Evening Star, The Designated Mourner, Apostle, 1996; All for Love; Jacob Two Two and the Hooded Fang; The Big Brass Ring, 1998; Sleepy Hollow, 1998-99; Get Carter, 1999; Snow White, The Hours, Spider, Rage on Placid Lake, 2001; The Actors, Falling Angels, 2002; The Prince and Me, Phantom of the Opera, 2003; Wah-Wah, Harry Potter and the Goblet of Fire, 2004; Provoked, 2005; Paris I Love You, Southland Tales, 2006; Puffball, Spinning Into Butter, Fred Claus, 2007; The Young Victoria, 2009; Made in Dagenham, Harry Potter and the Deathly Hallows: Part I, 2010; Maleficent, 2014; TV appearances include: The Hard Word; Sorrel and Son; A Woman of Substance; After Pilkington; Underworld; Death of the Heart; Blackadder II and III; Die Kinder (mini series), 1990; Sweet as You Are; Fatherland; Saint X, 1995; Magic Animals; Dance to the Music of Time, 1997; The Scold's Bridle; Merlin, 1997; Alice, 1998; Ted and Ralph, 1998; The Miracle Maker (voice), 2000; Snow White, 2001; The Lost Prince, 2003; Gideon's Daughter, 2005; Merlin's Apprentice, 2006; The Life and Times of Vivienne Vyle, 2007; Rubicon, 2010; Parade's End, World Without End, Dead Boss, 2012. Honours: Golden Globe Award for Best Comedy Actress, 1993; BAFTA Award for Best Supporting Actress, 1993; Golden Globe Award, 1995; Royal TV Society's Best Actress. Address: c/o ICM, 76 Oxford Street, London, W1N 0AX, England.

RICHARDSON Nigel Peter Vincent, b. 29 June 1948. Educational Consultant; Author. m. Joy James, 1979, 2 sons. Education: MA, Trinity Hall, Cambridge, 1970; PGCE, Bristol University, 1971; PhD, University College London, 2007. Appointments: Second Master, Uppingham School, 1983-89; Headmaster, Dragon School, Oxford, 1989-92; Deputy Head and Director of Studies, The King's School, Macclesfield, 1992-94; Headmaster, The Perse School, Cambridge, 1994-2008; Chairman, HMC, 2007. Publications: Numerous articles in professional journals; School books: Edith Cavell; Martin Luther King; John F Kennedy; Everyday Life in Britain in the 1960s; The July Plot; Monograph, Typhoid in Uppingham: Analysis of a Victorian Town and School in Crisis 1875-7, 2008; Training booklets; Book of School Anecdotes, 2009. Memberships: Friends of Choir of St John's College, Cambridge; East India Club; Governor, King's School, Ely, Norwich School, Magdalen College School, Oxford; Education Committee Member, Haileybury. Address: 6 High Meadow, Harston, Cambridge, CB22 7TR, England. E-mail: npvrichardson@btinternet.com

RICHES Naomi Joy, b. 15 June 1983, Hammersmith, London, England. Athlete (Rower). Education: BA (Hons), Metalwork and Jewellery Design, Buckinghamshire Chilterns University, 2006. Appointments: Volunteer Member of Staff, RNIB New College, Worcester, 2001; Volunteer Coach, London Regatta Centre, London, 2004-05; Full Time Performance Athlete, Great Britain Paralympic Rowing Squad, 2004-. Honours: World Champion, Mixed Cox Fours, 2004-06; Bronze Medal, Mixed Coxed Fours, Beijing Paralympics, 2008; World Champion and holder of World's Best Time in Mixed Coxed Fours, Poznan World Championships, 2009; Honorary Masters degree, Bucks New University, 2010. Memberships: Leander Rowing Club, Henley; Honorary Member, Marlow Rowing Club, Marlow. E-mail: naomijriches@googlemail.com

RICHIE Lionel, b. 20 June 1949, Tuskegee, Alabama, USA. Singer; Songwriter; Musician (piano); Actor; Record Producer. m. Diane Alexander, 1996. Education: BS, Econs, Tuskegee University, 1971. Career: Member, the Commodores, 1968-82; Support tours with The Jackson 5, 1973; The Rolling Stones, 1975; The O'Jays, 1976; Numerous other concerts; Solo artiste, 1982-; Concerts include: Closing ceremony, Olympic Games, Los Angeles, 1984; Live Aid, Philadelphia, 1985. Compositions: Hits songs with the Commodores: Sweet Love, 1975; Just To Be Close To You, 1976; Easy, 1977; Three Times A Lady (Number 1, US and UK), 1979; Sail On, 1980; Still (Number 1, US), 1980; Oh No, 1981; for Kenny Rogers: Lady (Number 1, US), 1981; for Diana Ross: Missing You, 1984; Solo hits: Endless Love, film theme duet with Diana Ross (Number 1, US), 1981; Truly (Number 1, US), 1982; All Night Long (Number 1, US), 1983; Running With The Night, 1984; Hello (Number 1, US and UK), 1984; Stuck On You, 1984; Penny Lover (co-writer with Brenda Harvey), 1984; Say You Say Me (Number 1, US), 1986; Dancing On The Ceiling,

1987; Love Will Conquer All, 1987; Ballerina Girl, 1987; My Destiny, 1992; Don't Wanna Lose You, 1996; Contributor, We Are The World (co-writer with Michael Jackson), USA For Africa (Number 1 worldwide), 1985; Recordings: Albums with the Commodores: Machine Gun, 1974; Caught In The Act, 1975; Movin' On, 1975; Hot On The Tracks, 1976; Commodores, 1977; Commodores Live!, 1977; Natural High 1978; Greatest Hits, 1978; Midnight Magic, 1979; Heroes, 1980; In The Pocket, 1981; Solo albums: Lionel Richie, 1982; Can't Slow Down, 1983; Dancing On The Ceiling, 1986; Back To Front, 1992; Louder Than Words, 1996; Time, 1998; Renaissance, 2000; Encore, 2002; Just For You, 2004; Coming Home, 2006. Solo singles: All Night Long, 1985; Do It To Me, 1992; My Destiny, 1992; Ordinary Girl, 1996; Don't Wanna Lose You, 1996. Honours include: ASCAP Songwriter Awards, 1979, 1984-96; Numerous American Music Awards, 1979-; Grammy Awards: Best Pop Vocal Performance, 1982; Album Of The Year, 1985; Producer Of The Year (shared), 1986; Lionel Richie Day, Los Angeles, 1983; 2 NAACP Image Awards, 1983; NAACP Entertainer of the Year, 1987; Oscar, Best Song, 1986; Golden Globe, Best Song, 1986. Current Management: John Reid. Address: 505 S Beverly Drive, Ste 1192, Beverly Hills, CA 90212, USA.

RICHMOND Douglas, b. 21 February 1946, Walla Walla, Washington, USA. History Professor. m. Belinda González, 1 daughter. Education: BA, 1968, MA, 1971, PhD, 1976, University of Washington. Appointments: Assistant Professor, 1976-82, Associate Professor, 1982-92, Professor of History, 1992-, Department of History, University of Texas, Arlington. Publications: Venustiano Carranza's Nationalist Struggle, 1983; Carlos Pellegrini and the Crisis of the Argentine Elites, 1880-1916, 1989; The Mexican Nation: Historical Continuity and Modern Change, 2001. Honour: Harvey P Johnson Award, 1985, 2004 and 2006; Capitán Alonso de Léon Medalla, 2004. Memberships: Southwest Council on Latin American Studies; Conference on Latin American History. Address: Department of History, Box 19529, University of Texas, Arlington, TX 76019-0529, USA.

RICHMOND, LENNOX AND GORDON, Duke of, Charles Henry Gordon Lennox, b. 19 September 1929. London, England. Chartered Accountant. m. Susan Monica Grenville-Grey, 1 son, 4 daughters. Education: Eton, 1944-48; William Temple College, Rugby, 1956-58; Chartered Accountant, 1956. Appointments: 2nd Lieutenant, KRRC (60th Rifles), 1949-50; Lieutenant, Queen's Westminsters (KRRC) TA, 1951-54; Financial Controllers Department, Courtaulds Ltd, Coventry, 1959-64; Director of Industrial Studies, William Temple College, 1964-68; Member, West Midlands Regional Economic Planning Council, 1965-68; Member, West Sussex Economic Forum Steering Group, 1996-2002; Chairman, Rugby Council of Social Service, 1961-68; Chairman, Goodwood Group of Companies, 1969-, Dexam International (Holdings) Ltd, 1965-, Trustees of Sussex Heritage Trust, 1978-2001; Sussex Rural Housing Partnership, Action in rural Sussex, 1993-2005, Wiley Europe Limited, 1993-98; Boxgrove Priory Trust, 1994-2008, and Member, Boxgrove Almshouses Trust, 1955-; Chairman, Chichester Cathedral Development Trust, 1985-1991; Chairman, West Sussex Coastal Strip Enterprise Gateway, 2000-05; Member, 1960-80, Chairman, Board for Mission and Unity of the General Synod, 1969-78, Church of England General Synod/Church Assembly; Church Commissioner, 1963-76; Member, Central and Executive Committees, World Council of Churches, 1968-75; Chairman, Christian Organisations Research and Advisory Trust, 1965-87; Lay Chairman, Chichester Diocesan Synod, 1976-79;

Vice-Chairman, Archbishops' Commission on Church and State, 1966-70; Treasurer, 1979-82, Chancellor, 1985-98, University of Sussex; Deputy Lieutenant, 1975-1990, Lord Lieutenant, 1990-94, West Sussex. Honours: Honorary LLD Sussex University, 1986; Medal of Honour, British Equestrian Federation, 1983; Winner, FT Arts and Business Award for Individuals, 2000. Memberships: Institute of Chartered Accountants, 1956-; Companion, Institute of Management, 1982-; Honorary Treasurer, 1975-82, Deputy President, 1982-86, Chairman South East Region, 1975-78, Historic Houses Association; Chairman, Bognor Regis Regeneration and Vision Group, 2002-07; Member, Joint Steering Group on Bognor Regis Regeneration, 2002-07; President: Sussex Rural Community Council (Action in rural Sussex), 1973-2005; Chichester Festivities, 1975-; South East England Tourist Board, 1990-2004; Sussex County Cricket Club, 1994-2000, Patron, 2000-; President, British Horse Society, 1976-78; African Medical and Research Foundation UK, 1996-; Chairman, Sussex Community Foundation, 2006-08; Freedom of the City of Chichester, 2008; Lifetime Achievement Award, Chichester Observer Business Awards, 2008. Address: Molecomb, Goodwood, Chichester, West Sussex PO18 0PZ, England. E-mail: richmond@goodwood.com

RICKETT John Francis, b. 7 September 1939, Laugharne, South Wales. Retired Army Officer; Military Historian. m. Frances Seton, 1 son, 1 daughter. Education: Eton College; Royal Military College of Science; Defence Services Staff College, India; Royal College of Defence Studies. Appointments: Served Fed Regular Army, South Arabian Emirates, 1963-65; Served Aden, India, Hong Kong, Kenya, Germany, USA, Northern Ireland, Falkland Islands; Commanding Officer, 1st Battlion Welsh Guards, 1980-82 (Falklands War, 1982); Commander, 19 Infantry Brigade and Colchester Garrison, 1984-86; Regimental Colonel, Welsh Guards, 1988-94; Deputy Commander/Chief of Staff, S E District, Aldershot, 1987-90; Military Attache, Paris, 1991-94; Comptroller, Union Jack Club, London, 1995-2009; Battlefield tour organizer, 2009-. Publications: Articles in war magazines/papers; Former articles in Royal United Service Institute; Lecturer on Civil War; Lecturer on WWI and WW2 battles. Honours: Queen's Commendation for Brave Conduct, 1964; MBE, 1967; Mentioned in Despatches, 1974; Knight of Magistral Grace, Order of Malta; Chevalier of Order of Danneburg (Denmark), 1975; OBE, 1982; CBE, 1990; Commander, Order of Merit, France, 1992; Liveryman, Worshipful Company of Gunmakers, 2008; Freeman, City of London, 2008. Memberships: Fellow, Institute of Directors; President, Colonie Franco-Britannique, Paris; President, Veterans Aid, London; Deputy Chairman of Governors, Penhurst School, Chipping Norton; Chairman, Barton Parish Council; Trustee, Airborne Assault, Normandy Trust. E-mail: reddragon.barton@yahoo.co.uk Website: www.battlefieldsdirect.com

RICKMAN Alan, b. 21 February 1946, Actor. Education: Chelsea College of Art; Royal College of Art; Royal Academy of Dramatic Art (RADA). Career: 2 seasons with Royal Shakespeare Company, Stratford; Stage Appearances include: Bush Theatre, Hampstead and Royal Court Theatre; Les Liaisons Dangereuses; The Lucky Chance; The Seagull; Tango at the End of Winter, 1991; Hamlet, 1992; Director, The Winter Guest, 1997; Antony and Cleopatra, 1998; Private Lives, 2001-02; John Gabriel Borkman, 2010; Seminar, 2011; TV appearances include: Obadiah Slope, The Barchester Chronicles, 1982; Pity in History, 1984; Revolutionary Witness, Spirit of Man, 1989; Rasputin (USA), 1995; Victoria Wood with All The Trimmings, 2000; Films include: The

January Man; Close My Eyes; Truly Madly Deeply; Die Hard; Robin Hood: Prince of Thieves; Bob Roberts, 1992; Mesmer, 1993; An Awfully Big Adventure, 1994; Sense and Sensibility, 1995; Michael Collins, 1996; Rasputin, 1996; Mesmer; Dark Harbour, 1997; The Judas Kiss, 1997; Dogma, 1998; Galaxy Quest, 1999; Blow Dry, 1999; Play, 2000; The Search for John Gissing, 2000; Harry Potter and the Philosopher's Stone, 2001; Harry Potter and the Chamber of Secrets, 2002; Love Actually, 2003; Harry Potter and the Prisoner of Azkaban, 2004; Something the Lord Made, 2004; Harry Potter and the Goblet of Fire, 2005; Snow Cake, 2006; Perfume: The Story of a Murderer, 2006; Nobel Son, 2007; Harry Potter and the Order of the Phoenix, 2007; Sweeney Todd: The Demon Barber of Fleet Street, 2007; Bottle Shock, 2008; Harry Potter and the Half Blood Prince, 2009; Alice In Wonderland (voice), Harry Potter and the Deathly Hallows – Part I, Wildest Dream, The Song of Lunch, 2010; Harry Potter and the Deathly Hallows – Part II, 2011; Gambit, 2012. Honours: Time Out Award, 1991; Evening Standard Film Actor of the Year, 1991; BAFTA Award, 1991; Golden Globe Award, 1996; Emmy Award, 1996; Variety Club Award, 2002; James Joyce Award, 2009. Address: c/o ICM, Oxford House, 76 Oxford Street, London, W1N 0AX, England.

RICKS Sir Christopher (Bruce), b. 18 September 1933, London, England. Professor of the Humanities; Writer; Editor. m. (1) Kirsten Jensen, 1956, divorced 1975, 2 sons, 2 daughters, (2) Judith Aronson, 1977, 1 son, 2 daughters. Education: BA, 1956, BLitt, 1958, MA, 1960, Balliol College, Oxford. Appointments: Lecturer, University of Oxford, 1958-68; Visiting Professor, Stanford University, 1965, University of California at Berkeley, 1965, Smith College, 1967, Harvard University, 1971, Wesleyan University, 1974, Brandeis University, 1977, 1981, 1984; Professor of English, University of Bristol, 1968-75, University of Cambridge, 1975-86; Professor of the Humanities, Boston University, 1986-; Co-Director, Editorial Institute, 1999-; Andrew W Mellon Distinguished Achievement Award, 2004-07. Publications: Milton's Grand Style, 1963; Tennyson, 1972, revised edition, 1987; Keats and Embarrassment, 1974; The Force of Poetry, 1984; Eliot and Prejudice, 1988; Beckett's Dying Words, 1993; Essays in Appreciation, 1996; Reviewery, 2002; Allusion to the Poets, 2002; Decisions and Revisions in T S Eliot, 2003; Dylan's Visions of Sin, 2003. Editor: Poems and Critics: An Anthology of Poetry and Criticism from Shakespeare to Hardy, 1966; A E Housman: A Collection of Critical Essays, 1968; Alfred Tennyson: Poems, 1842, 1968; John Milton: Paradise Lost and Paradise Regained, 1968; The Poems of Tennyson, 1969, revised edition, 1987; The Brownings: Letters and Poetry, 1970; English Poetry and Prose, 1540-1674, 1970; English Drama to 1710, 1971; Selected Criticism of Matthew Arnold, 1972; The State of the Language (with Leonard Michaels), 1980, new edition, 1990; The New Oxford Book of Victorian Verse, 1987; Inventions of the March Hare: Poems 1909-1917 by T S Eliot, 1996; Oxford Book of English Verse, 1999; Selected Poems of James Henry (editor), 2002; Reviewery, 2003; Dylan's Visions of Sin, 2003; Decisions and Revisions In, T S Eliot, 2003; Samuel Menashe: Selected Poems, 2005. Contributions to: Professional journals. Honour: Honorary DLitt, Oxford, 1998; Honorary D Litt, Bristol, 2002. Memberships: American Academy of Arts and Sciences, fellow; British Academy, fellow; Tennyson Society, vice-president; Housman Society, vice-president. Address: 39 Martin Street, Cambridge, MA 02138, USA.

RIDLEY Brian Kidd, b. 2 March 1931, Newcastle upon Tyne, England. Physicist. m. Sylvia Jean Nicholls, 1 son, 1 daughter. Education: BSc 1st Class Honours, Physics, 1953, PhD, 1957, University of Durham. Appointments: The Mullard Research Laboratory, Redhill, 196-64; Lecturer, 1964-67, Senior Lecturer, 1967-71, Reader, 1971-84, Professor, 1984-90, Research Professor, 1990-2008, Professor Emeritus, Department of Physics, University of Essex, Colchester; Visiting appointments: Distinguished Visiting Professor, 1967, Research Fellow, 1976, 1990-, Cornell University; Visiting Professorships: Stanford, 1967, Danish Technical University, 1969, Princeton, 1973, Lund, 1977, Santa Barbara, 1981, Eindhoven Technical University, 1983, Hong Kong University of Science and Technology, 1997, 1999, Cornell, 3 months annually, 1990-2004; Consultancies: UK Ministry of Defence, Great Malvern; British Telecom (now Corning), Office of Naval Research. Member: Programme Committee International Conference on Hot Carriers, 1986-89; Honorary Editorial Board, Solid State Electronics, 1990-95; Advisory Editorial Board of Journal of Physics Condensed Matter, 1996-2000; Executive Board, Journal of Physics, 2000-2003; Physics College of Engineering and Physical Sciences Research Council of the UK. Publications: Over 200 research papers; Books include: Time, Space and Things, 1976, 3rd edition, 1995, reprinted 2000; The Physical Environment, 1979; Quantum processes in Semiconductors, 1982, 4th edition, 1999; Electrons and Phonons in Semiconductor Multilayers, 1997, 2nd edition, 2009; On Science, 2002; Reforming Science: Beyond Belief, 2010; 7 book chapters. Honours: Fellow of the Royal Society; Paul Dirac Medal and Prize; Fellow of the Institute of Physics. Membership: American Physical Society. Address: Department of Electronic Systems Engineering, University of Essex, Colchester, Essex CO4 3SQ, England.

RIDPATH Ian (William), b. 1 May 1947, Ilford, Essex, England. Writer; Broadcaster. Publications: Over 40 books, including: Worlds Beyond, 1975; Encyclopedia of Astronomy and Space (editor), 1976; Messages From the Stars, 1978; Stars and Planets, 1978; Young Astronomer's Handbook, 1981; Hamlyn Encyclopedia of Space, 1981; Life Off Earth, 1983; Collins Guide to Stars and Planets, 1984-2011; Gem Guide to the Night Sky, 1985; Secrets of the Sky, 1985; A Comet Called Halley, 1985; Longman Illustrated Dictionary of Astronomy and Astronautics, 1987; Monthly Sky Guide, 1987-2009; Star Tales, 1989; Norton's Star Atlas (editor), 1989-2003; Book of the Universe, 1991; Atlas of Stars and Planets, 1992-2004; Oxford Dictionary of Astronomy (editor), 1997-2011; Eyewitness Handbook of Stars and Planets, 1998-2010; Gem Stars, 1999; Times Space, 2002; Times Universe, 2004. Membership: Fellow, Royal Astronomical Society; Member, Society of Authors, Association of British Science Writers. Address: 48 Otho Court, Brentford Dock, Brentford, Middlesex TW8 8PY, England. Website: www.ianridpath.com

RIEB William John Jr, b. 22 April 1937, USA. Mathematician; Physicist; Jurist. Education: PhD; PhD; JD. Career: First and only mathematician to unlock the secrets and mysteries of prime numbers; Currrently working with prime numbers in factoring infinitely-many integers. Publications: Book, Epiphany: How I Solved the Greatest and Oldest Mystery in Mathematics. First-Time-Ever Discovered Secrets of Prime Numbers, their Frequencies and How They are Perfectly and Endlessly Distributed Towards Infinity, 2009; Numerous articles in professional journals. Honours: Listed in international biographical dictionaries. Memberships: Many professional organisations. Address: Suzhou, Jiangsu Province, People's Republic of China. E-mail: WJRmath@gmail.com

RIEGER Gebhard, b. 10 March 1940, Vienna, Austria. Researcher; Medical Educator. m. Irmgard Strasser, 3 sons, 1 daughter. Education: Degree, Secondary School in Linz, 1959; Med Dr, Medical School University, Vienna, 1966; Assistant, I U Eye Clinic, Vienna, 1966-72; Eye Specialist, 1972. Appointments: Emeritus Head, Department of Ophthalmology, Paracelsus Institute, Bad Hall, Austria, 1972; Lecturer, 1998, Professor, 2003, University Eye Clinic, Innsbruck, Austria. Publications: Over 80 papers on dry eye syndrome and balneological themes. Honours: Grantee, Dr Heinz and Helen Adam, Frankfurt, 1990; Gold Medal, Upper Austrian country, 2007; Austrian Cross of Honour for Science and Art I Class, 2009. Memberships: Austrian Ophthalmology Society; Vienna Ophthalmology Society; German Ophthalmology Society; New York Academy of Sciences; Society of Free Radical Research; Austrian Society of Balneology and Medical Climatology; Association of Austria Cure Physicians; Paracelsus Society of Balneology and Iodine Research; Medical Society of Upper Austria; Van Swieten Society, Vienna. Address: Paracelsus Society, Kurpromenade 1, A-4540 Bad Hall, Upper Austria.

RIESENHUBER Klaus, b. 29 July 1938, Frankfurt am Main, Germany. Professor of Philosophy; Jesuit Priest. Education: Study of Philosophy, St Georgen, Frankfurt, 1957-58; Study of Philosophy, Berchmanskolleg Pullach, 1960-62; Lic Phil, 1962; Study of Philosophy, Universität München, 1962-67; Dr Phil, 1967; Study of Japanese Culture, Kamakura, Japan, 1967-69; Study of Theology, Sophia University, 1969-72; Master of Theology, 1972; Dr of Theology, 1989. Appointments: Lecturer, Philosophy, Sophia University, 1969; Assistant Professor, 1974; Director, Institute of Medieval Thought, Sophia University, 1974-2004; Professor, 1981-2009; Professor Emeritus, 2009-; Director, Zen-Hall Shinmeikutsu, Tokyo, 1990-; Part time Guest Professor: Tokyo University; Kyushu University; Tohoku University; Japanese Broadcast University; Keio University; Waseda University; Tokyo Metropolitan University. Publications: Die Transzendenz der Freiheit zum Guten, 1971; Existenzerfahrung und Religion, 1968 (Portuguese translation, 1972); Freedom and Transcendence in the Middle Ages (in Japanese), 1988; History of Ancient and Medieval Philosophy (in Japanese), 1991; Fundamental Streams of Medieval Philosophy (in Japanese), 1995; Internal Life (in Japanese), 1995; History of Medieval Thought, in Japanese 2002, Korean translation 2007; Man and Transcendence (in Japanese), 2004; Faith Searching for Understanding (in Japanese), 2004; Rationality and Spirituality in the Middle Ages (in Japanese), 2008; Editor and co-editor of 72 books in Japanese; Co-editor of Nishida Kitaro Collected Works (24 volumes, in Japanese). Memberships: Japanese Society of Medieval Philosophy; Japanese Society of Philosophy; Japanese Fichte Society; 5 other philosophical associations. Address: S J House, Sophia University, 7-1 Kioicho, Chiyoda-ku, Tokyo 102-8571, Japan.

RIFFARD Jean-Francois, b. 6 October 1968, Chamalieres, France. Professor of Law. m. Anne Raulin, 1 daughter. Education: Diplome d'Etudes juridiques Anglo-Americaines, 1994; PhD in Law, Université d'Auvergne, 1995; Habilitation à Diringer les Recherches, 2008. Appointments: Professor of Law, Auvergne University School of Law, 1996-; Arbitrator, ICC; Visiting Professor, Drake University School of Law, USA; Visiting Professor, McGill University School of Law, Montreal, Canada, 2010. Publications: Le security interest ou l'approche unitaire et fonctionnelle des sûretes, 1999; Droit des Sûretes, 2010. Honours: 1er prix de thése, Centre Français de Droit comparé. Memberships: United Nations Commission for International Trade Law; Societé de Legislation Companée, Paris. Address: Faculté de Droit, Université d'Auvergne, 41 bd François Mitterrand, 63000 Clermont Ferrand, France. E-mail: jfriffard@aol.com

RIGG (Enid) Diana (Elizabeth) (Dame), b. 20 July 1938, Doncaster, England. Actress. m. (1) Manahem Gueffen, 1973, divorced 1976, (2) Archibald Hugh Stirling, 1982, divorced 1993, 1 daughter. Education: RADA. Career: Professional début as Natella Abashwilli, The Caucasian Chalk Circle, York Festival, 1957; Repertory Chesterfield and Scarborough 1958; Films include: A Midsummer Night's Dream, 1969; On Her Majesty's Secret Service, 1969; Julius Caesar, 1970; The Hospital, 1971; Theatre of Blood, 1973; A Little Night Music, 1977; The Great Muppet Caper, 1981; Evil Under the Sun, 1982; A Good Man in Africa, 1993; Parting Shots, 1999; Heidi, 2005; The Painted Veil, 2006. TV appearances include: Emma Peel in the Avengers, 1965-67; Women Beware Women, 1965; Married Alive, 1970; Diana (USA), 1973; In This House of Brede, 1975; Three Piece Suite, 1977; The Serpent Son, 1979; The Marquise, 1980; Hedda Gabler, 1981; Rita Allmers in Little Eyolf, 1982; Reagan in King Lear, 1983; Witness for the Prosecution, 1983; Bleak House, 1984; Host Held in Trust, A Hazard of Hearts, 1987; Worst Witch, 1987; Unexplained Laughter, 1989; Mother Love, 1989; Host Mystery! (USA), 1989; Running Delilah, 1994; Zoya, 1995; The Haunting of Helen Walker, 1995; The Fortunes and Misfortunes of Moll Flanders, 1996; Samson and Delilah, 1996; Rebecca, 1997; The Mrs Bradley Mysteries, 1998-99; In the Beginning, 2000; The American, 2001; The 100 Greatest TV Characters (Mrs Peel), 2001; Victoria & Albert, 2001; Charles II: The Power and the Passion, 2003; Many leading roles with RSC and with theatres in UK and USA. Publications: No Turn Unstoned, 1982; So To The Land, 1994; Honours include: Plays and Players Award for Best Actress, 1975, 1978; Honorary doctorates, Stirling University, 1988; Leeds, 1991, South Bank, 1996; BAFTA Award, Best Actress, 1990; Evening Stand Award, 1993, 1996, 1996; Tony Award, Best Actress, 1994; Emmy, Best Supporting Actress, 1997; BAFTA, 2000; Theatregoers' Award for Best Actress, 2005. Memberships include: Vice-President, Baby Life Support Systems (BLISS), 1984-; Chancellor, University of Stirling, 1997-.

RIHANNA (Robyn Rihanna Fenty), b. 20 February 1988, Saint Michael, Barbados. Singer; Songwriter; Model. Career: Singer; Albums: Music of the Sun, 2005; A Girl Like Me, 2006; Good Girl Gone Bad, 2007; Rated R, 2009; Loud, 2010; Talk That Talk, 2011; Unapologetic, 2012; Singles: Pon de Replay, If It's Lovin' That You Want, 2005; SOS, Unfaithful, We Ride, Break It Off, 2006; Umbrella, Shut Up and Drive, Don't Stop the Music, Hate That I Love You, Don't Stop the Music, 2007; Take a Bow, Disturbia, Rehab, 2008; Russian Roulette, Hard, Wait Your Turn, 2009; Rude Boy, Rockstar 101, Te Amo, Only Girl, What's My Name? Raining Men, 2010; S&M, California King Bed, Man Down, Cheers, We Found Love, You da One, 2011; Talk That Talk, Princess of China, Birthday Cake, Where Have You Been, Cockiness Remix, Diamonds, 2012; Stay, Pour It Up, 2013. Films: Bring It On: All or Nothing, 2006; Battleship, 2012; This Is the End, 2013. Honours: 7 Grammy Awards; 5 American Music Awards; 18 Billboard Music Awards; 2 BRIT Awards.

RIIHENTAUS Leo Juhani, b. 4 March 1942, Helsinki, Finland. Docent. m. Leena Anneli Laurio, 1965, deceased 2011, 1 son, 1 daughter. Education: PhD, Mathematics, University of Helsinki, Finland, 1975. Appointments: Assistant, University of Jyvaskyla, 1966-68; Assistant, Helsinki Technical University, 1968-70; Temporary Associate Professor, 1970-71; Temporary Associate

Professor, Lapeenranta Technical University, 1971-72; Lecturer, University of Joensuu, 1972-77; Senior Lecturer, Oulu College of Technology, 1977-94, South Carelia Polytechnic, 1994-2005; Docent, University of Eastern Finland, 1980-; Docent, University of Oulu, 1983-; Retired, 2005. Publications: Numerous articles in professional journals. Memberships: Finnish Mathematical Society; European Mathematical Society; American Mathematical Society; Mathematical Association of America; Société Mathematique de France. Address: Lahettilaantie 5 c37, 01520 Vantaa, Finland.

RILEY Patrick Anthony, b. 22 March 1935, Neuilly-Sur-Seine, France. Pathologist. m. Christine E Morris, 1 son, 2 daughters. Education: MB, BS (Lond), 1960; PhD (Lond), 1965; DSc (Lond), 1990; FRCPath, 1985; FIBiol, 1976. Appointments: Rockefeller Scholar, 1962-63; MRC Junior Clinical Research Fellow, 1963-66; Beit Memorial Research Fellow, 1966-68; Wellcome Research Fellow, 1968-70; Lecturer in Clinical Pathology, University College Hospital Medical School, London, 1970-73, Senior Lecturer in Biochemical Pathology, 1974-76, Reader in Cell Pathology, 1976-84, Professor of Cell Pathology, 1984-2000, Emeritus Professor, 2000-, University College, London; Currently, Director, Totteridge Institute for Advanced Studies and Honorary Research Associate, Gray Cancer Institute. Publications: Reviews and chapters in books; Dictionary of Medicine; More than 250 substantive research contributions to learned journals. Honours: Myron Gordon Award, 1993; Centenary Medal, Charles University, Prague, Czech Republic, 1996. Memberships include: Linnean Club; Athenaeum Club; Royal Society of Medicine; NCUP. Address: 2 The Grange, Grange Avenue, London N20 8AB, England.

RIMAN Joseph Vavrinec Prokop, b. 30 January 1925, Horni Sucha, Czech Republic. Biochemist; Scientist. m. Vera Tomek. Education: MD, Charles University, Prague, 1950; PhD, Chemistry, CS Academy of Sciences, 1955; DSc, Chemistry, 1966; Associate Professor, Habil Doc, Medical Faculty, Charles University, 1967; Full Professor, Biochemistry, Science Faculty, 1984; DSc, Biology h c, Purkynje University, 1987. Appointments: Research Physician, 1st Clinic Paediatrics, Medical Faculty, Charles University, Prague, 1950-51; Scientist, Senior Scientist, Organic Chemistry and Biochemistry, CS Academy of Sciences, Prague, 1951-74; Founder, Director, Institute of Molecular Genetics, 1975-91; Science Secretary, 1977-81; Vice President, 1981-85; President, CS Academy of Sciences, 1986-90; Vice President, Central European Academy of Science, Art and Letters, 2010-. Publications: Published in various international journals; 128 original experimental papers, Biochemistry of retroviruses and growing vertebrate cells. Honours include: Gold Plaque of J G Mendel, Czechoslovak Academy of Sciences, 1980; Silver Medal, Charles University, 1985; Gold Einstein-Russel Pugwash Medal, 1987; Skrjabin's Medal, 1987; J E Fogarty NIH Medal, 1987; Hippocrates Medal, Kyoto University Medical School, 1988; Gold Lomonosov Medal, 1986; Gold Medal, Slovak Academy of Sciences for Merits, 1989; Gold Medal, Meidji University, Nagoya, 1990; K Yagis Gold Memorial Medal, 1990; Gold Plaque for Merits for Science and Mankind. Memberships include: Full Member, CS Academy of Sciences, 1976; Honorary Member, Hungarian Academy of Science; Foreign Member, Bulgarian Academy; Foreign Member, Russian Academy of Science; Foreign Fellow, Indian National Science Academy; Foreign Member, G W Leibniz Society, Germany; Foreign Member German Society of Biological Chemistry; Full Member, Central European Academy of Science and Art, 1997-. Address: Institute of Molecular Genetics, Academy of Science, Fleming n 2, Prague 6 16637, Czech Republic.

RIMINGTON Dame Stella, b. 1935. Civil Servant. m. John Rimington, 1963, 2 daughters. Education: Edinburgh University. Career: Director-General, Security Service, 1992-96; Non Executive Director, Marks and Spencer, 1997-2004, BG PLC, 1997-2000, BG Group, 2000-, GKR Group (now Whitehead Mann), 1997-2001; Chair, Institute of Cancer Research, 1997-2001. Publications: Open Secret (autobiography), 2001; At Risk, 2004; Secret Asset, 2006; Illegal Action, 2007; Dead Line, 2008; Present Danger, 2009. Honours: Honorary Air Commodore 7006 (VR) Squadron Royal Auxiliary Air Force, 1997-2001; Hon LLB (Nottingham) 1995, (Exeter) 1996, (London Metropolitan University) 2004; DCB, 1996. Address: PO Box 1604, London SW1P 1XB, England.

RINALDI Giacomo, b. 25 July 1954, Bergamo, Italy. University Professor. Education: Classical studies, Lovere, Bergamo; Graduated with honours, Philosophy, State University of Milan, 1978; Fellowship, Istituto Italiano di Studi Storici. Appointments: Researcher, Methodology of the Human Sciences, 1991-, Professor, Moral Philosophy, 2001-, Theoretical Philosophy, 2002-, University of Urbino. Publications: Critica della gnoseologia fenomenologica, 1979; Dalla dialettica della materia alla dialettica dell'Idea. Critica del materialismo storico, 1981; A History and Interpretation of the Logic of Hegel, 1992; Essenza e dialettica della percezione sensibile, 1993-94; Dialettica, arte e società. Saggio su Theodor W. Adorno, 1994; Fondamenti di filosofia del linguaggio, 1997-98; L'idealismo attuale tra filosofia speculativa e concezione del mondo, 1998; Prolegomeni ad una teoria generale della conoscenza, 1999; Idea e realtà della Logica, Part I, 2001-02, Part II, 2003-04; Teoria etica, 2004; Ragione e Verità. Filosofia della religione e metafisica dell'essere, 2010; Absoluter Idealismus und zeitgenössische Philosophie. Bedeutung und Aktualität von Hegels Denken, 2012. Honours: Listed in biographical dictionaries. Memberships: Hegel Society of America; Internationale Hegel-Gesellschaft; Internationaler Arbeitskreis zu Hegels Naturphilosophie; Johann-Gottlieb-Fichte Gesellschaft; Internationale Gesellschaft System der Philosophie. Address: Department DESP, University of Urbino, Via Saffi, 15, I-61029 Urbino (PU), Italy. E-mail: giacomo.rinaldi@uniurb.it

RIOS-DALENZ Jaime L, b. 13 November 1932, Cochabamba, Bolivia. Physician; Pathologist. m. Maria Haydee Ismael, 1 son, 1 daughter. Education: Bachelor of Humanities, La Salle College, La Paz, 1952; San Simon University Medical School, Chochamaba, 1952-60; MD and National License in Medicine, Bolivia, 1960; Resident in Pathology: University El Valle, Cali, Colombia, 1961; Balt Memorial Hospital, Muncie, USA, 1961-64; Temple University Hospital, 1965-66; Neuropathology, National Hospital, University of London, UK, 1969; Certificate of Specialist in Anatomical Pathology, 1965, and Clinical Pathology, 1966, American Board of Pathology, USA. Appointments: Pathologist, 1968-93, Chief of Pathology Department, 1993-96, Hospital Obrero No 1, NCS, La Paz; Director, La Paz Cancer Registry, 1987-; Professor, Pathology, 1968-86, Chief of Pathology Department, 1986-96, Emeritus Professor, 1996-, Medical School, San Andres University, La Paz; President, National Commission Against Tobacco, 1983-96; Vice President, Latin American Co-ordinating Committee of Smoking Control, 1964-86; National Conference of Bolivian Network of Health Sciences

Information. Publications: Numerous articles in professional journals. Honours: Diploma and Medal for tobacco control in Bolivia, 1992; Physician of the Year Certificate and Medal, Bolivian Medical Association, 1995; Jaime Rios-Dalenz Award Certificate and Medal for best undergraduate research study, San Andres University Medical School, 1996. Memberships: Bolivian Medical Academy; Bolivian Division, International Academy of Pathology; Bolivian Society of Pathology; Bolivian Academy of Medical History. Address: PO Box 490, La Paz, Bolivia. E-mail: jriosdal@gmail.com

RIPA Rinaldo, b. 25 May 1935, Mercatino Conca, Italy. Physician; Endocrinologist; Educator. m. Anne Mary Balardinelli, 1 son, 3 daughters. Education: MD, Bologna University, Italy, 1959; Degree, State Abilitation Medical Activity, 1960; Medical Semeiology degree, 1968, Medical Pathology degree, 1969, Endocrinology degree, 1971, Italian Ministry of University, Rome. Appointments: Sport Medicine Specialist, Chieti University, Italy, 1974; Specialist in Cardiology, University of Turin, 1961; Specialist in Endocrinology, University of Florence, Italy, 1963; Specialist in Geriatry & Gerontology, 1964, Specialist in Infectious Diseases, 1965, University of Modena, Italy; Specialist in Isotopic Techniques, University of Bologna, 1967; Specialist in Internal Medicine, 1973, Specialist in Medical Nephrology, 1971, University of Parma, Italy; Head, Internal Medicine, Civil Hospital of G Marconi, Cesenatico, Forli-Cesena, Italy, 1970-80; Head, Internal Medicine, Hospital Santa Maria delle Croci, Ravenna, Italy, 1980-82; Head, Internal Medicine, Casa di Cura Villa Maria, Rimini, Italy, 1982-; Professor, General Physiology, 1968-69, Professor of Endocrinology, 1969-76, University of Ferrara, Italy; Medical Consultant, Casa di Cura St Lorenzino, Cesena, 1982-94. Publications: Editor, Renin-Angiotensin System; Numerous articles in professional journals. Honours: 1st Award, A Azzi Ferrara, Italy, 1968. Memberships: Carim Financial Bank, Rimini; Economic-Finance Expert, Cassa Risparmio Rimini; European Institute of Oncology, Milan; AAAS; Rotary Club International. Address: v Sirio 4, 47923 Rimini (RN), Italy. E-mail: rinaldoripa@libero.it

RIPPON Angela, b. 12 October 1944, Plymouth, Devon, England. Television and Radio Presenter; Writer. m. Christopher Dare, 1967, divorced. Education: Grammar School, Plymouth, England. Appointments: Presenter, Reporter, BBC TV Plymouth, 1966-69; Editor, Presenter, Producer, Westward Television, 1967-73; Reporter, BBC TV National News, 1973-75, Newsreader, 1975-81; Founder, Presenter, TV-am, 1983; Arts Correspondent, WNETV (CBS), Boston, 1983; Reporter, Presenter, BBC and ITV, 1984; TV appearances: Angela Rippon Meets...; Antiques Roadshow; In the Country; Compere, Eurovision Song Contest, 1976; The Morecombe and Wise Christmas Show, 1976, 1977; Royal Wedding, 1981; Masterteam, 1985, 1986, 1987; Come Dancing, 1988-; What's My Line? 1988-; Healthcheck; Holiday Programme; Simply Money, 2001-; Channel 5 News, 2003-; Cash in the Attic, 2007; Radio: Angela Rippon's Morning Report for LBC, 1992; Angela Rippon's Drive Time Show, LBC, 1993; The Health Show, BBC Radio 4; Friday Night with Angela Rippon, BBC Radio 2; LBC Arts Programme, 2003-. Publications: Riding, 1980; In the Country, 1980; Mark Phillips: The Man and His Horses, 1982; Angela Rippon's West Country, 1982; Victoria Plum, 1983; Badminton: A Celebration, 1987; Many recordings. Honours: Dr hc, American International University, 1994; New York Film Festival Silver Medal, 1973; Newsreader of the Year, Radio and Television Industries Awards, 1976, 1977, 1978; Television Personality of the Year, 1977; Emmy Award, 1984; Sony Radio Award, 1990; New York Radio Silver Medal, 1992; Royal TV Society Hall of Fame, 1996; European Woman of Achievement, 2002; OBE, 2004. Memberships: Vice-President, International Club for Women in Television; British Red Cross; NCH Action for Children; Riding for the Disabled Association; Director, Nirex, 1986-; Chair, English National Ballet, 2000-. Address: Knight Ayton, 114 St Martin's Lane, London, WC2N 4AZ, England.

RISS Ilan, b. 7 August 1950, Bishkek, Kyrgyzstan. Sociologist. m. Belina, 1 son, 2 daughters. Education: PhD, Moscow University of Econometrics, Statistics and Informatics, 2004. Appointments: Head of Sector, IT Department, Central Bureau of Statistics, Jerusalem, 2003. Publications: Books: Mudy and Jesus; By the Broken Hot Stone. Address: Hel HaAviv str 41/6, Pisgat Zeev, Jerusalem, 97535, Israel. E-mail: ilanriss@hotmail.com

RISTIC Renata, b. 22 March 1964, Varazdin, Croatia. Viticulturalist. m. Radomir, 1 son, 1 daughter. Education: Bachelor, Agricultural Science, 1988; PhD, Viticulture, 2004. Appointments: Scientist, 1996-2004, Research Scientist, 2009-, University of Adelaide; Scientist/Technical Officer, Lalemand, Australia, 2004-06; Scientist, CSIRO, 2006; Scientist, AMDEL, 2007-08. Publications: Book, From Grapes Into Wines, 2009; Numerous articles in professional journals. Memberships: Australian Society of Viticulture & Oenology; American Chemical Society. Address: University of Adelaide, School of Agriculture, Food & Wine, Wine Innovation Central Building, Level 4, Urbrrae, South Australia 5064, Australia. E-mail: renata.ristic@adelaide.edu.au

RITCHIE Guy, b. 10 September 1968, Hatfield, Hertfordshire, England. Film Director. m. Madonna Ciccone, 2000 (divorced), 1 son, 1 adopted son, 1 step-daughter, 1 son with Jacqui Ainsley. Education: Standbridge Earls. Career: Directed numerous 1980s pop videos; Films: The Hard Case, 1995; Lock, Stock and Two Smoking Barrels, 1998; Snatch, 2000; What it Feels Like for a Girl (video), 2001; The Hire: Star, 2001; Swept Away, 2002; Mean Machine (supervising producer), 2002; Revolver, 2005; Suspect, 2007; RocknRolla, 2008; Sherlock Holmes, 2009; Sherlock Holmes: A Game of Shadows, 2011; TV: The Hard Case, 1995; Lock, Stock and Two Smoking Barrels (series executive producer), 2000. Honours: British Industry Film Award, 1998; London Film Critics' Circle Award, 1999.

RITCHIE Ian Russell, b. 27 November 1953, Leeds, England. Chief Executive. m. Jill Evelyn, 2 sons. Education: Leeds Grammar School; MA, Jurisprudence, Trinity College, Oxford; Barrister at Law, Middle Temple, Council of Legal Education. Appointments: Barrister, called to Middle Temple, 1976-78; Worked with television and media organisations including: Granada Television, Yorkshire Tyne Tees, London News Network, Channel 5 (CEO), Middle East Broadcasting Ltd (CEO); Managing Director, Russell Reynolds Associates; Former Chairman, Click4e.com; Director, West Ham United plc; Chairman, Newcastle Common Purpose; Governor of the University of Northumbria at Newcastle; Chairman, ITV Programme Rights Committee. Memberships: Fellow, Royal Society of Arts. E-mail: ian.ritchie@aeltc.com

RITCHIE Sir Lewis Duthie, b. 26 June 1952, Fraserburgh, Scotland. Academic General Practitioner. m. Heather Skelton. Education: BSc, Chemistry, 1978, MBChB, Commendation, 1978, University of Aberdeen; MSc, Community Medicine, University of Edinburgh, 1982; MD, University of Aberdeen, 1993; Vocational Training in General Practice, 1979-82; Specialist Training in Public Health Medicine, 1982-87. Appointments: General Practice Principal, Peterhead Health Centre, 1984-; Consultant in Public Health Medicine, Grampian Health Board, 1987-92; Honorary Consultant in Public Health Medicine, Grampian Health Board, 1993-; Sir James Mackenzie Professor of General Practice, University of Aberdeen, 1993-; Membership of a number of national medical advisory committees on behalf of the Scottish Executive Health Department and the Department of Health England, 1989-. Publications: Book: Computers in Primary Care, 1986; Over 150 publications on computing, cardiovascular prevention, lipids, hypertension, immunisation, oncology, intermediate care, community hospitals, and fishermen's health. Honours: Munday and Venn Prize, University of Aberdeen, 1977; John Watt Prize, University of Aberdeen, 1977; Kincardine Prize, North East Faculty, Royal College of General Practitioners, 1978; John Perry Prize, British Computer Society, 1991; Ian Stokoe Memorial Award, Royal College of General Practitioners, 1992; Blackwell Prize, University of Aberdeen, 1995; OBE, 2001; Eric Elder Medal, Royal New Zealand College of General Practitioners, 2007; James Mackenzie Lecture and Medal, Royal College of General Practitioners, UK, 2010; Knight Bachelor, 2011. Memberships: Diploma of the Royal College of Obstetricians and Gynaecologists, 1980; British Computer Society, 1985; Fellow, Royal Society of Medicine, 1987; Member Royal Environmental Health Institute for Scotland, 1991; Fellow, Faculty of Public Health Medicine, 1993; Fellow Royal College of General Practitioners, 1994; Fellow, Royal College of Physicians of Edinburgh, 1995; Fellow, British Computer Society, 2004; Chartered Computer Engineer, 1993; Fellow, Royal Society of the Arts, 2001; Founding Fellow of the Institute of Contemporary Scotland, 2001; Chartered Information Technology Professional, 2004. Address: Centre for Academic Primary Care, University of Aberdeen, Forstelhill, Aberdeen AB25 2ZD, Scotland. E-mail: l.d.ritchie@abdn.ac.uk

RIVERS Ann, b. 26 January 1939, Texas, USA. Poet. Education: BA, 1959. Appointments: Editor-Publisher, SHY, 1974-79; Guest Editor, As-Sharq, 1979; Contributing Editor, Ocarina, 1979-82. Publications: Samos Wine, 1987; A World of Difference, 1995; Pilgrimage and Early Poems, 2000; Pluto Probe, 2003; Good Timing, 2009. Contributions to: Ore; Iotà; Orbis; Poetry Nottingham; Pennine Platform. Address: Hydra, GR 180 40 Greece.

RO Kideok, b. 16 June 1953, Gyeongnam, Korea. Fluid Engineer. m. 1980, 1 son, 1 daughter. Education: Master, PhD, Kobe University. Appointments: Marine Engineer, Mobil Oil Company, 1977-79; Professor, Gyeongsang National University, 1979-2011. Publications: Performance Improvement of Weis-Hogh Type Ship's Propulsion Mechanism Using a Wing Restrained by an Elastic Spring. Honours: 2 theses, Korean Society of Marine Engineering, 2003 and 2008. Memberships: KSME. Address: 38 Cheondaegukchi-gil, Tongyeong, Gyeongnam 650-160, Korea. E-mail: rokid@gnu.ac.kr Website: http://gshp.gsnu.ac.kr/~rokid

ROBBINS Tim, b. 16 October 1958, New York, USA. Actor; Director; Screen Writer. 2 sons with Susan Sarandon. Education: University College of Los Angeles. Career: Member, Theatre for the New City; Founder, Artistic Director, The Actor's Gang, 1981-; Theatre includes: As actor: Ubu Roi, 1981; As director, A Midsummer Night's Dream, 1984; The Good Woman of Setzuan, 1990; As writer: (with Adam Simon): Alagazam; After the Dog Wars; Violence; The Misadventures of Spike Spangle; Farmer; Carnage – A Comedy (Represented USA at Edinburgh International Festival, Scotland); As writer: Embedded, 2004; Films: As actor: No Small Affair, Toy Soldiers, 1984; The Sure Thing, Fraternity Vacation, 1985; Top Gun, Howard the Duck, 1986; Five Corners, 1987; Bull Durham, Tapeheads, 1988; Miss Firecracker, Eric the Viking, 1989; Cadillac Man, Twister, Jacob's Ladder, 1990; Jungle Fever, 1991; The Player, Bob Roberts, Amazing Stories: Book Four, 1992; Short Cuts, 1993; The Hudsucker Proxy, The Shawshank Redemption, Prêt-à-Porter, IQ, 1994; Nothing to Lose, 1997; Arlington Road, The Cradle Will Rock, Austin Powers: The Spy Who Shagged Me, 1999; Mission to Mars, High Fidelity, 2000; Antitrust, Human Nature, 2001; The Truth About Charlie, 2002; The Day My God Died, Mystic River, Code 46, 2003; The Secret Life of Words, Zathura: A Space Adventure, 2005; Catch a Fire, Tenacious D in The Pick of Destiny, 2006; Noise, The Lucky Ones, City of Embers, 2008; Green Lantern, Cinema Verite, 2011; Back to 1942; As writer/director: Bob Roberts, 1992; Dead Man Walking, 1995; Cradle Will Rock, 1999. Honours: Golden Globe, Best Supporting Actor, 2004; Critics' Choice Award, Best Supporting Actor, 2004; Screen Actors Guild, Best Supporting Actor Award, 2004; Academy Award, Best Supporting Actor, 2004. Address: c/o Elaine Goldsmith Thomas, ICM, 40 West 57th Street, New York, NY 10019, USA.

ROBERT Leslie (Ladislas), b. 24 October 1924, Budapest, Hungary. Biochemist. m. Jacqueline Labat, 3 daughters. Education: MD, Paris, 1953; PhD, Lille, 1977; Postdoctoral Training, Department of Biochemistry, University of Illinois, Chicago; Columbia University, New York; Honorary Research Director, French National Research Center (CNRS), 1994-. Appointment: Research Director, Department of Ophthalmic Research, Hotel Dieu Hospital, Paris, France. Publications: 7 books on ageing biology; 1 book on time-regulations in biology; 12 books on connective tissues; 1000 publications in international journals. Honours: Honorary doctorate, Semmelweis Medical University, Budapest, 1972; Verzar Medal for Gerontology Research, University of Vienna, 1994; Novartis Prize, International Gerontological Association, 1997. Memberships: Academy of Sciences of Hungary and Germany (Nordrhein-Westfalen); Scientist of the Year, French Society for Antioxydents, 2008; French and International Biochemical Societies; Past president, French Society for Connective Tissue Research; Past president, French Society of Atherosclerosis. Address: 7 Rue J B Lully, 94440 Santeny, France. E-mail: lrobert5@wanadoo.fr

ROBERTS Brian, b. 19 March 1930, London, England. Writer. Education: Teacher's Certificate, St Mary's College, Twickenham, 1955; Diploma in Sociology, University of London, 1958. Appointments: Teacher of English and History, 1955-65. Publications: Ladies in the Veld, 1965; Cecil Rhodes and the Princess, 1969; Churchills in Africa, 1970; The Diamond Magnates, 1972; The Zulu Kings, 1974; Kimberley: Turbulent City, 1976; The Mad Bad Line: The Family of Lord Alfred Douglas, 1981; Randolph: A Study of Churchill's Son, 1984; Cecil Rhodes: Flawed Colossus, 1987; Those Bloody Women: Three Heroines of the Boer War, 1991. Address: 7 The Blue House, Market Place, Frome, Somerset, BA11 1AP, England.

ROBERTS Denys Tudor Emil, b. 19 January 1923, London, England. Judge. m. (1) Brenda Marsh, 1949, dissolved 1973, 1 son, 1 daughter, (2) Fiona Alexander, 1985, 1 son. Education: MA, Wadham College, Oxford 1948; BCL, 1949; Bar, London, 1950. Appointments: Crown Counsel, Nyasaland,

1953-59; Attorney General, Gibraltar, 1960-62; Solicitor General, Hong Kong, 1962-66; Attorney General, Hong Kong, 1966-73; Chief Secretary, Hong Kong, 1973-78; Chief Justice, Hong Kong, 1979-88; Chief Justice, Brunei Darussalam, 1979-2001; President, Court of Appeal, Bermuda, 1988-94; Member, Hong Kong Court of Final Appeal, 1997-2003; President, Court of Appeal, Brunei Darussalam, 2002-03. Publications: Books: Smuggler's Circuit, 1954; Beds and Roses, 1956; The Elwood Wager, 1958; The Bones of the Wajingas, 1960; How to Dispense with Lawyers, 1964; I'll Do Better Next Time, 1995; Yes Sir, But, 2000; Another Disaster, 2006. Honours: OBE, 1960; CBE, 1970; KBE, 1975; SPMB, Brunei, 1984. Memberships: Honorary Fellow, Wadham College, Oxford; Honorary Bencher, Lincoln's Inn; President, MCC, 1989-90. Address: The Grange, North Green Road, Pulham St Mary, Norfolk IP21 4QZ, England.

ROBERTS John Hughes, b. 6 July 1932, Gravesend, Kent, England. Theoretician. m. Diana, 1 son, 1 daughter, deceased. Education: Gravesend County Grammar School, 1940-51; BSc, Mathematics, Reading University, 1954. Appointments: 40 years in Maths Departments of GEC, Plessey, Siemens; Retired 1993. Publications: Numerous authored and co-authored papers in Electronics Literature; Author, Angle Modulation, No 5 in the IEE Telecommunications series, 1977. Honours: Awarded Premiums by the IEE for published papers 3 times. Membership: Fellow, Institute of Mathematics and Its Applications. Address: 61 Pine Crescent, Chandler's Ford, Hampshire, SO53 1LN, England.

ROBERTS Julia, b. 28 October 1967, Georgia, USA. Actress. m. (1) L Lovett, 1993, divorced 1995, (2) Daniel Moder, 2002, 2 sons, 1 daughter. Career: Actor; Films include: Blood Red; Mystic Pizza; Steel Magnolias; Flatliners; Sleeping with the Enemy; Pretty Woman; Hook; Batman; The Pelican Brief, 1993; Pret á Porter; I Love Trouble, 1994; Something to Talk About, 1996; Michael Collins, 1996; Everyone Says I Love You, 1996; My Best Friend's Wedding, 1997; Conspiracy Theory, 1997; Notting Hill, 1998; Stepmom, 1998; Runaway Bride, 1999; Erin Brockovich, 2000; The Mexican, 2001; America's Sweethearts, 2001; Ocean's Eleven, 2001; Full Frontal, 2002; Confessions of a Dangerous Mind, 2003; Mona Lisa Smile, 2003; Closer, 2004; Ocean's Twelve, 2004; Charlie Wilson's War, 2007; Fireflies in the Garden, 2008; Duplicity, 2009; Valentine's Day, 2010; Eat Pray Love, 2010; Love, Wedding, Marriage, Larry Crowne, 2011; Mirror, Mirror, 2012; UNICEF Goodwill Ambassador, 1995. Honour: Academy Award (Best Actress), BAFTA Award (Best Actress), Screen Actors Guild Award, and many others for Erin Brockovich, 2000. Address: ICM, 8942 Wilshire Boulevard, Beverly Hills, CA 90211, USA.

ROBERTS Mary Belle, b. 27 September 1923, Akron, Ohio, USA. Social Worker. Education: Bachelor of Psychology, University of Michigan, 1948; MSW, 1950; New York School of Social Work, Third Year Social Work, 1953-54. Appointments: Instructor of Alabama Medical School, Department of Psychiatry, 1951-53; ALA, Department of Public Health, Division of Mental Hygiene, 1950-53; Bur MH, Div Com Serv, Pennsylvania Department of Public Welfare, 1954-55; DHEW, PHS, NIMH, Com Services, 1955-64; Private practice, 1964-68; Family Counseling Service of Miami and prior organisations, 1968-90; Private practice, 1990-; Apogee, 1994-96. Publications: JPSW Effective Mental Health by Activation of Community's Potential; Edit the Vocational Rehabilitation of the Mentally Ill; Leadership Training for Mental Health Promotion; Editorials, Alabama Mental Health Bulletin. Honours: Phi Kappa Phi; Licensed Fl; Life Fellow, Royal Society for the Promotion of Health; Diplomate, NASW; AAUW named gifts, 1978 and 1981. Memberships: NASW; ACSW; Royal Society for the Promotion of Health; ABECSW; DAR; USD of 1812; AAUW; YWCA; IBC; ABI; University of Michigan Alumni Association; Smithsonian; AARP. Address: 8126 SW, 105th Place, Ocala, FL 34481-9132, USA.

ROBERTS Michael Victor, b. 23 September 1941, High Wycombe, England. Librarian. m. Jane Margaret, deceased, 1 son, 1 daughter. Education: Bachelor of Arts, Clare College, Cambridge, 1960-63; Loughborough Technical College, 1963-64; Master of Arts, 1966. Appointments: Various junior professional posts in Loughborough, Leeds and City of London, 1964-70; Principal Cataloguer, 1970-73, Keeper of Enquiry Services, 1973-82, Guildhall Library, City of London; Deputy Director, City of London Libraries and Art Galleries, 1982-95. Publications: Numerous articles in professional and academic journals; Editor, Guildhall Studies in London History, 1973-82; Editor, Branch Journal of the Library Association Local Studies Group, 1996-98; Editor, Archives and the Metropolis, 1998; Editor, Framlingham Historical Society, 1997-. Honours: Associate of the Library Association, 1967; Chartered Librarian, 1967; Member, Chartered Institute of Library and Information Professionals, 2002; Silver Badge, Royal National Lifeboat Institution, 2009. Memberships: Chairman, Council of British Records Association; East of England Regional Archives Council; Housing the Homeless Central Fund; Framlingham Town Council; Officer/Trustee of various local societies and charities. Address: 43 College Road, Framlingham, Suffolk IP13 9ER, England.

ROBERTSON David, b. 19 July 1958, Santa Monica, California, USA. Conductor; m. Orli Shaham. Education: Royal Academy of Music, London, England. Career: Conductor, Jerusalem Symphony Orchestra, 1985-87; Musical Director, Ensemble Intercontemporain, Paris, 1992-2000; Musical Director, Orchestre National de Lyon and Artistic Director, Lyon Auditorium, 2000-2004; Music Director, St Louis Symphony Orchestra, 2005-; Principal Guest Conductor, BBC Symphony Orchestra, 2005-. Has conducted orchestras including: Berlin Philharmonic, Royal Concertgebouw, Orchestre de Paris, Hamburg NDR Symphony, Bayerischer Rundfunk Symphonieorchester, Staatskapelle Dresden, Filharmonica della Scala (Milan), Tonhalle (Zürich), the New York and Los Angeles Philharmonics, and the symphony orchestras of Atlanta, Boston, Dallas, Detroit, Chicago, Cleveland, and San Francisco; Conducted US premieres of: Saariaho's Mirage, Turnage's A Prayer Out of Stillness, and Mackey's Violin Concerto and Time Release (2009), as well as Adams's "Doctor Atomic" Symphony (2008), with Saint Louis Symphony Orchestra; Saariahols Adriana Songs, New York Philharmonic, 2006, and Berio's Stanze, Pittsburgh Symphony Orchestra, 2005; world premiers of Rouse's Symphony No 3 with Saint Louis Symphony Orchestra, Roukens's Out of Control with the Royal Concertgebouw Orchestra and Dorman's Uriah with San Francisco Symphony, 2011; Monk's Weave with the Saint Louis Symphony Orchestra and Stephen McNeff's ConcertO-Duo with the BBC Symphony Orchestra, 2010; Fedele's Les 33 noms with Filarmonica della Scala and Hayden's complete Substratum with the BBC Symphony Orchestra, 2009; Danielpour's Songs of Solitude with Philadelphia Orchestra and Thomas Hampson, 2005; French premiere of Birtwistle's Theseus Games with the Ensemble Intercontemporain, 2005; Danielpour's Songs of Solitude with Philadelphia Orchestra and Thomas Hampson, 2005; Opera engagements have included the Metropolitan Opera, Opera de Lyon, La

Scala, Bayerische Staatsoper, Paris Châtelet, Hamburg State Opera, San Francisco Opera; Has given master classes at Paris Conservatory, The Juilliard School, Tanglewood, Aspen Music Festival. Recordings include: Edouard Lalo, Namouna, Musique de Ballet, 1994; Silvestrov, Symphony No 5, 1996; Jessye Norman, In the Spirit, 1996; Manoury, 60th Parallel, 1999; Milhaud, Works for Piano and Orchestra, 1999; Dusapin, Extenso, 2000; Ginastera, Estancia, 2001; Bartók, The Miraculous Mandarin, 2002; Boulez, Rituel in Memoriam Bruno Maderna, 2003; Steve Reich, Different Trains, 2004; Dvořák, Secrets of Dvořák's Cello Concerto, 2005; Bolcom, Satie and Schoenberg, Surprise, 2007; Adams, Doctor Atomic Symphony, 2009. Download releases include: Adams, Harmonielehre, 2007; Szymanowski, Violin Concerto No 1, 2008; Scriabin Poem of Ecstasy, 2008. Honours: Musical America Conductor of the Year, 2000; Ditson Conductor's Award, 2006; ASCAP Morton Gould Award for Innovative Programming, 2006; ASCAP Award for Programming of Contemporary Music, 2009; Excellence in the Arts award, St Louis Arts and Education Council, 2010; American Academy of Arts and Sciences, Fellow, 2010; Honorary Doctorates: Maryville University, 2007, Webster University, 2009, Westminster Choir College, 2010. Address: c/o FALCONE, Public Relations, 155 West 68th Street, Ste 1114, New York, NY 10023, USA.

ROBERTSON George Islay McNeill (Lord Robertson of Port Ellen), b. 12 April 1946. Politician. m. Sandra Wallace, 1970, 2 sons, 1 daughter. Education: MA honours, Economics, University of Dundee, 1968. Appointments: Research Assistant Tayside Study, 1968-69; Scottish Organiser, General and Municipal Workers Union, 1969-78; MP for Hamilton, 1978-97, for Hamilton South, 1997-99; Parliamentary Private Secretary to Secretary of State for Social Services, 1979; Opposition Spokesman on Scottish Affairs, 1979-80, on Defence, 1980-81, On Foreign and Commonwealth Affairs, 1981; Principal Spokesman for Scotland, 1994-97; Secretary of State for Defence, 1997-99; Secretary General, NATO, 1999-2003; Executive Deputy Chair, Cable & Wireless, 2003-; Non-Executive Director, Smiths Group, 2004-, Weir, 2004-. Honours: Grand Cross, Order of Merit (Germany, Hungary, Italy, Luxembourg, etc); Joint Parliamentarian of the Year, 1993; Received life peerage, 1999; Grand Cross of the Order of the Star of Romania, 2000; Knight, Order of the Thistle, UK, 2004; Knight Grand Cross, Order of St Michael and St George, UK, 2004; Honorary Regimental Colonel of the London Scottish Volunteers; Honorary Doctorates: University of Dundee, St Andrews; University of Bradford; Cranfield University-Royal Military College of Science; Baku State University, Azerbaijan; The French University, Yerevan, Armenia; Academy of Sciences, Azerbaijan and Kirgyz Republic; National School of Politics and Administration Studies, Bucharest. Memberships: Vice-Chairman, Board British Council, 1985-94; Governor, Ditchley Foundation, 1989-; Member, Her Majesty's Privy Council, 1997; President, Royal Institute of International Affairs, 2001-; Elder Brother, Trinity House, 2002-; President, Hamilton Burns Club, 2002-. Address: House of Lords, London SW1A 0PW, England. Website: www.cwplc.com

ROBERTSON George Wilber, b. 20 December 1914, Alberta, Canada. Agrometeorologist. m. Lucille Eileen Davis, 1 son, 1 daughter. Education: BSc, Mathematics and Physics, University of Alberta, 1939; MA, Physics and Meteorology, University of Toronto, 1948. Appointments: Meteorological Assistant, Meteorological Service of Canada, 1938; Officer in Charge, Meteorological Section, No 2 Air Observer School, British Commonwealth Air Training Plan, Edmonton, 1940; Meteorologist, MSC Meteorological Office, Edmonton Airport, 1945; Meteorologist, Central Meteorological Analysis Office of MSC, Ottawa, 1950; Agrometeorologist, Field Husbandry, Soils and Agricultural Engineering Division of Experimental Farms Service, Canada Department of Agriculture, Ottawa, 1951; Expert in Agrometeorology and Climatology, World Meteorological Organization, Philippines, 1969; Senior Scientist, Head of Environment Section, Research Station, Swift Current, Saskatchewan, 1971; Consultant, Food and Agriculture Organisation, Rome, Italy, 1972; Retired from Government Service, 1973; Consultant, Canadian Wheat Board, Winnipeg, 1973; Consultant, WMO, Geneva, 1974; Project Manager, FAO/UNDP Technical Assistance Project with Malaysia Federal Land Development Authority, 1975; Private Consultant in Agrometeorology, several short term projects in developing countries with various international agencies, 1977-98. Publications: Numerous scientific papers, technical reports, feasibility studies and press articles. Honours: Literary A Pin, University of Alberta, 1938; President's Award, 1951, Darton's Prize, 1953, Canadian Branch, Royal Meteorological Society; Accredited as Consulting Meteorologist, Canadian Meteorological and Oceanographic Society, 1987; Elected Fellow, Canadian Society of Agrometeorology, 1987; John Patterson Medal, Atmospheric Environmental Service, Canada, 1992; Honouree, Baier & Robertson Symposium on Modeling and Measurement of Soil Water Content, 1995. Memberships: American Meteorological Society; Fellow, Royal Meteorological Society, London; Agricultural Institute of Canada; Canadian Society of Agronomy; Ontario Institute of Professional Agrologists; Canadian Meteorological and Oceanographic Society; American Association for the Advancement of Science; The New York Academy of Sciences; Canadian Society of Agricultural and Forestry Meteorology. Address: AMICA at Westboro Park, 619-491 Richmond Road, Ottawa, ON K2A 1G4, Canada. E-mail: georger400@aol.com

ROBINSON (Alfred) Christopher, b. 18 November 1930, York, England. Soldier; Charity Worker. m. Amanda Boggis-Rolfe, dissolved, 2 sons, 2 daughters. Education: Royal Military Academy, Sandhurst. Appointments: Major, 16th/5th The Queen's Royal Lancers, 1951-65; Trade Indemnity Company Ltd. 1066-70; Glanvill Enthoren Ltd, 1970-73; The Spastic's Society, now Scope, 1973-91; Ferriers Barn Centre for Young Disabled People, 1973-, President, 1987; The Little Foundation, 199-, Chairman, 1996; The Mother & Child Foundation, 1994-, Chairman, 2001. Memberships: Institute of Fundraising, Welfare Committee Chairman, Royal British Legion, Bures Branch; Executive Committee, Dedham Vale Society; Vice-Chairman, Colne Stow Countryside Association; Fundraising Committee Chairman, British Red Cross, Suffolk Branch; Lay Chairman, Sudbury Deanery Synod; Member, St Edmundsbury and Ipswich Diocesan Synod. Address: Water Lane Cottage, Bures, Suffolk CO8 4DE, England.

ROBINSON Anne Josephine, b. 26 September 1944, Crosby, Liverpool, England. Journalist; Broadcaster. m. John Penrose, 1 daughter. Education: Farnborough Hill Convent, Hampshire; Les Ambassadrices, Paris. Appointments: Reporter, Daily Mail 1967-68; Reporter, Sunday Times, 1968-77; Women's Editor, 1979-80, Assistant Editor, 1980-93, Columnist, 1983-93, Daily Mirror; Columnist, Today, 1993-95; Columnist, The Sun, 1995-97; Columnist, The Express 1997-98; Columnist, The Times, 1998-2001; Columnist, Daily Telegraph, 2003-; Television: Afternoon Plus, Thames TV, 1986; Breakfast Time, BBC TV, 1987;

Presenter and Writer, Points of View, BBC TV, 1988-98; Presenter and Editor, The Write Stuff, Thames TV, 1990; Presenter, Questions, TVS, 1991; Presenter, Watchdog, BBC TV, 1993-2001; Presenter, Going for a Song, BBC TV, 2000; Presenter, The Weakest Link, BBC TV, 2000-; Presenter, The Weakest Link, NBC Television, 2001-2002; Presenter, Test the Nation, BBC TV, 2002- Presenter, Guess Who's Coming to Dinner, BBC TV, 2003; Presenter, Out Take TV, BBC TV, 2003-; Travels with My Unfit Mother, 2004; Radio: Presenter, The Anne Robinson Show, BBC Radio 2, 1988-93. Honour: Honorary Fellow, Liverpool John Moores University, 1996. Membership: Vice-President Alzheimer's Society. Address: c/o Drury House, 34-43 Russell Street, London WC2B 5HA, London. E-mail: tracey.chapman@css-stellar.com

ROBINSON Derek, (Dirk Robson), b. 12 April 1932, Bristol, England. Writer. m. Sheila Collins, 29 April 1968. Education: MA, Downing College, Cambridge, England. Publications: Goshawk Squadron, 1971; Rotten With Honour, 1973; Kramer's War, 1977; The Eldorado Network, 1979; Piece of Cake, 1983; War Story, 1987; Artillery of Lies, 1991; A Good Clean Fight, 1993; Hornet's Sting, 1999; Kentucky Blues, 2002; Damned Good Show, 2002; Invasion, 1940, 2005; Red Rag Blues, 2006; Better Rugby Refereeing, 2007; Hullo Russia, Goodbye England, 2008; Operation Bamboozle, 2010. Honour: Shortlisted for Booker Prize, 1971; Listed in biographical dictionaries. Address: Shapland House, Somerset Street, Kingsdown, Bristol BS2 8LZ, England.

ROBINSON Ivor, b. 28 October 1924, Bournemouth, England. Artist-Bookbinder. m. Olive Trask, 14 April 1952, 1 son, 1 daughter. Education: Southern College of Art, Bournemouth 1939-42. Appointments: Royal Navy, 1942-45; Lecturer, Bookbinding, Salisbury School of Art, 1946-53; Lecturer, Bookbinding, London School of Printing and Graphic Arts, 1953-58; Lecturer, Bookbinding, Bookworks and Visual Studies, Oxford Polytechnic, 1959-89; External Examiner, Ecole National Superieur D'Architecture et des Arts Visuels, Brussels, 1979; Adviser, Banbury School of Art, 1995-96. Publications: Introducing Bookbinding, 1st edition, 1969, 2nd edition, 1984; Contributor to the annual publication The New Bookbinder, 1981-. Creative Works: One-Man Exhibitions: Hantverket, Stockholm, Sweden, 1963; Galleria Del Bel Libro, Ascona, Switzerland, 1969; The Prescote Gallery, Cropredy, Oxfordshire, 1981; Contributor to 107 group exhibitions, 1951-2009; Work represented in collections of: The British Library; The Victoria & Albert Museum; The Bodleian Library, Oxford; Crafts Council Collection; The Keatley Trust, UK; The Rhösska Museum, Gothenburg, Sweden; The Royal Library, Copenhagen, Denmark; The Royal Library, Stockholm, Sweden; The Royal Library, The Hague, Netherlands; British Royal Collections and major public and private collections in Great Britain and overseas. Honours: MBE; Honorary Fellow, Oxford Brookes University; Honorary Fellow, Designer Bookbinders; Honorary Fellow, Meister Der Einbandkunst, Germany; Triple Medaillist, Priz Paul Bonet, Ascona, Switzerland, 1971. Membership: Fellow, Designer Bookbinders, 1955-2003, President, 1968-73. Address: Trindles, Holton, Oxford, OX33 1PZ, England.

ROBINSON Karen, b. 15 August 1958, New Brunswick, New Jersey, USA. Dietician. m. Richard A Robinson. Education: BS, Home Economics, Montclair State College, New Jersey, 1980; Certified Food Services Sanitation Manager, New Jersey, 1984; Dietetic Internship, Veterans Affairs Medical Center, Virginia, 1991; Masters Degree, Health Sciences, Dietetics, James Madison University, Virginia, 1992. Appointments: Temporary Sales Secretary, Banquet preparation Staff, Boar's Head Inn, Charlottesville, Virginia, 1986-88; Head Diet Counsellor, Diet Center, Charlottesville, Virginia, 1986-90; Public Health Nutritionist, Central Shenandoah Health District, Waynesboro, Virginia, Health Department, 1993-97; Dietetic Intern Mentor, 1993-97; Consulting Dietician, Hebrew Hospital Home, Bronx, New York, 1998; Food Service Manager, Sodexho Marriot Services, Morningside House Nursing Home, Bronx, New York, 1998-99; Clinical Dietician, Yonkers General Hospital, Yonkers New York, 1999-2001; Community Services Instructor, Westchester Community College, Valhalla, New York, 2001; Inpatient/Outpatient Dietician, Park Care Pavilion (formerly Yonkers General Hospital, 2001-); Clinical Dietician, St John's Riverside Hospital, Yonkers, New York, 2002-; Outpatient Dietician, St John's Riverside, Valentine Lane Family Practice, Yonkers, 2005, 2007-08; Outpatients Dietician, Park Care Pavilion, 2001-10; Inpatient Dietician, Park Care Pavilion, 2001-; Pulmonary Rehabilitation Dietician, St John's Riverside Hospital, Yonkers, New York, 2010-. Publications: Abstract as co-author: The psychological predictors of successful weight loss, 1992; Contributed articles to local newspapers and journals. Honours: Recipient, New York State Dietetic Association Grant. Listed in Who's Who publications and biographical dictionaries. Memberships: American Dietetics Association; Healthy Aging; Consultant Dieticians in Health Care Facilities; Westchester Rockland Dietetic Association; Virginia Dietetics Association, 1993-97; Virginia Public Health Association, 1995-97. Address: 102 Hunter Lane, Ossining, NY 10562, USA.

ROBINSON Sir Kenneth (Ken), b. 4 March 1950, Liverpool, England. Educator. m. Marie Thérése, 1 son, 1 daughter. Education: B Ed (with Honours), English and Drama, University of Leeds, 1972; Certificate of Education (with Distinction); Doctor of Philosophy, University of London, 1980. Appointments: Co-ordinator, Drama 10-16, National Development Project , Schools Council of England and Wales, 1974-77; Freelance lecturer, writer, 1977-79; Director, Calouste Gulbenkian Foundation National Committee of Inquiry on The Arts in Schools, 1979-81; Director, Gulbenkian Foundation/Leverhulme Inquiry: The Arts and Higher Education, 1981-82; Director, Calouste Gulbenkian Foundation, Arts Education Development Programme, 1981-83; Publisher, Managing Editor, Arts Express, national monthly magazine, 1983-85; Director, National Curriculum Council's, Arts in Schools Project, 1985-89; Professor of Arts Education, 1989-2001, Professor Emeritus, 2001-, University of Warwick; Currently, Senior Adviser, J Paul Getty Trust, Los Angeles, California, USA. Publications: 18 books and monographs; 17 book chapters and journal papers; Numerous newspaper features and interviews and appearances on radio and television. Honours: Knighted for services to the arts, June 2003. Memberships include: Member of Board and Chairman, Education Committee, Birmingham Royal Ballet; Education Adviser, Chairman Education Policy Group, Arts Council of Great Britain; Education Advisory Council, Independent Television Commission; Director, British Theatre Institute; Adviser to Outreach Programme, The Royal Academy. Address: J Paul Getty Trust, 1200 Getty Center Drive, Los Angeles, 90049, USA.

ROBINSON Mary, b. 21 May 1944, Ballina, County Mayo, Ireland. International Civil Servant; Former Head of State. m. Nicholas Robinson, 1970, 2 sons, 1 daughter. Education: Trinity College, Dublin; King's Inns, Dublin; Harvard University, USA. Appointments: Barrister, 1967, Senior Counsel, 1980; Called to English Bar (Middle Temple), 1973; Reid Professor of Constitutional and Criminal Law,

Trinity College, Dublin, 1969-75, Lecturer, European Community Law, 1975-90; Founder, Director, Irish Centre for European Law, 1988-90; Senator, 1969-89; President, Ireland, 1990-97; UN High Commissioner for Human Rights, 1997-2002; Chancellor, Dublin University, 1998-; Professor of Practice, Columbia University School of International and Public Affairs, New York, 2004-; The Elders, 2007. Honours include: LLD honoris causa (National University of Ireland; Cambridge; Brown; Liverpool; Dublin; Montpellier; St Andrews; Melbourne; Columbia; National University of Wales; Poznan; Toronto; Fordham; Queens University, Belfast); Dr honoris causa Public Services (Northeastern University); Honorary Docteur en Sciences Humaines (Rennes), 1996; Honorary LLD (Coventry), 1996; Berkeley Medal, University of California; Medal of Honour, University of Coimbra; Medal of Honour, Ordem dos Advogados, Portugal; Gold Medal of Honour, University of Salamanca; Andrés Bello Medal, University of Chile; New Zealand Suffrage Centennial Medal; Freedom Prize, Max Schmidheiny Foundation (Switzerland); UNIFEM Award, Noel Foundation, Los Angeles; Marisa Bellisario Prize, Italy, 1991; European Media Prize, The Netherlands, 1991; Special Humanitarian Award, CARE, Washington DC, 1993; International Human Rights Award, International League of Human Rights, New York, 1993; Liberal International Prize for Freedom, 1993; Stephen P Duggan Award (USA), 1994; Freedom of the City of Cork; Honorary AO; Council of Europe North South Prize, Portugal, 1997; Collar of Hussein Bin Ali, Jordan, 1997; F D Roosevelt Four Freedoms Medal, 1998; Erasmus Prize, Netherlands, 1999; Fulbright Prize, USA, 1999; Garrigues Walker Prize, Spain, 2000; William Butler Prize, USA, 2000; Indira Gandhi Peace Prize, India, 2000; Sydney Peace Prize, 2002. Memberships include: Royal Irish Academy; Honorary Bencher Kings Inns, Dublin, Middle Temple, London. Address: Columbia University School of International and Public Affairs, 420 West 118th Street, New York, NY 10027, USA. Website: www.sipa.columbia.edu

ROBINSON Tony, b. 15 August 1946, London, England. Actor; Writer; TV Presenter. 1 son, 1 daughter. Education: Central School of Speech and Drama. Career: Theatre: Numerous appearances as a child actor including the original stage version of the musical Oliver!; Several years in repertory theatre; Theatre director, 2 years, then Chichester Festival Theatre, Royal Shakespeare Company and National Theatre; Touring in 1 man show, Tony Robinson's Cunning Night Out, 2005; Television: Ernie Roberts in Horizon's Joey; Baldrick in Black Adder (4 series, BBC); Sheriff of Nottingham in Maid Marian and Her Merry Men (also writer, 4 series); Alan in My Wonderful Life (3 series, Granada); Leading role in Channel 4 series, Who Dares Wins; As presenter: Points of View; Stay Tooned; Time Team (Channel 4,); Social history series: The Worst Jobs in History, 2004; Historical Documentaries for Channel 4 on: The Peasants Revolt, the Roman Emperors, Macbeth, Robin Hood, the Holy Grail. Publications: Children's television programmes include: 30 episodes of Central TV's Fat Tulips Garden; 13 part BBC series based on Homer's Iliad and Odyssey: Odysseus – The Greatest Hero of Them All; 26 episodes of the Old Testament series Blood and Honey; Mrs Caldicot's Cabbage War, 2000; Tales from the Madhouse, 2000; Spider Plant Man, 2005; Hogfather, 2006; 17 children's books include: Tony Robinson's Kings and Queens; Adult books include most recently: The Worst Jobs in History; Archaeology is Rubbish – A Beginners Guide (with Professor Mick Aston); In Search of British Heroes; Currently putting the entire works of Terry Pratchett onto audio tape. Honours: 2 Royal Television Society Awards; BAFTA Award; International Prix Jeunesse; Honorary MA: Bristol University, 1999, University of East London, 2002; Honorary Doctorate: University of Exeter, 2005; Open University, 2005. Memberships: British Actors Equity, Vice-President, 1996-2000; President, Young Archaeology Club; National Executive Committee, Labour Party, 2000-2004. Address: c/o Jeremy Hicks Associates, 114-115 Tottenham Court Road, London W1T 5AH, England.

ROBINSON William Peter, Professor Emeritus; Social Psychology. Education: MA, D Phil (Oxon); Fellow, Australian and British Psychological Societies; Chartered Psychologist; CSCE Qualified Interpreter in Russian. Appointments: Academic positions at Universities of Hull, London, Southampton; Chairs of Education at Macquarie and Bristol Universities; Chair of Social Psychology, Bristol University; Currently, University and Leverhulme Senior Research Fellow and Professor Emeritus, Bristol University; Trustee: College of St Paul and St Mary, Cheltenham; Chair, Deaf Studies Trust; Chair and Vice-Chair, The Red Maid's School, Bristol; Bristol Municipal Charities. Publications: 6 authored books; 2 technical reports; 6 edited books; 4 edited series; More than 100 journal articles and chapters; Including most recently: Books: The New Handbook of Language and Social Psychology (co-editor), 2001; Language in Social Worlds, 2003; Arguing To Better Conclusions, 2006. Honours include: DSIR (ESRC) Postgraduate Award; Honorary Professor, Instituto Superior de Psicologia Aplicada, Lisbon; Visiting Professor, Monash University, Cheltenham CHE; Fellow, Japanese Society for the Promotion of Science; Visiting Scholar, Wolfson College, Oxford; JV Smyth Memorial Lecturer, Melbourne; Centenary Lecturer, University of Hanover; 13 funded research projects; listed in national and international biographies. Memberships: Various committees, SSRC/ESRC; Chair and Committee Member Social Psychology Section, Member of Council, British Psychological Society; Co-founder and Foundation President, International Association of Language and Social Psychology; Research Committee, International Communication Association; Co-founder triennial international conferences on language and social psychology, 1979-. Address: Holmbury, Thorncliffe Drive, Cheltenham, GL51 6PY, England.

ROBSON Bryan, b. 11 January 1957, Chester-le-Street, England. Professor Football Manager; Former Professional Football Player. m. Denise, 1979, 1 son, 2 daughters. Education: Birtley Lord Lawson Comprehensive. Career: Player with: West Bromwich Albion, 1974-81; Manchester United (FA Cup winners) 1983, 1985, 1990; Euro Cup Winners' Cup, 1991; Winner, League Championship, 1992-93, 1993-94; 90 caps (65 as captain), scoring 26 international goals; Player, Manager, Middlesborough FC, 1994-2001, Bradford City, 2003-04, West Bromwich Albion, 2004-2006; Sheffield United, 2007-2008; Formed Robson Lloyd Consultancy Ltd, 2007. Assistant Coach, national team, 1994. Publications: Autobiography: Robbo, 2006. Honours: OBE; Hon MA (Salford), 1992, (Manchester), 1992; English Football Hall of Fame, 2002. Address: West Bromwich Albion, The Hawthorns, West Bromwich, West Midlands B71 4LF, England. Website: www.wba.co.uk

ROBSON Stephen, b. 1 April 1951, Carlisle, England. Priest. Education: BSc, 1974, MTh, 1986, University of Edinburgh; STL, 2000, STD, 2003, JCL, 2006, Pontifical Gregorian University, Rome. Appointments: Ordained, 1979; Assistant Priest, St Mary's Cathedral, Edinburgh, 1979; Assistant Priest, Our Lady of Perpetual Succour (St Marie's), Kirkcaldy, 1979-81; Chaplain, St Andrew's High School, 1979-81; Teacher Training in-service, 1981; Professor,

St Mary's College, Blairs (National Junior Seminary), 1981-86; Secretary to Archbishop O'Brien, 1986-88; Postgraduate, Edinburgh University, 1986-88; Assistant, Holy Cross Edinburgh, 1986-88; Parish Priest, Duns, 1988-89; Ampleforth Abbey, 1989-90; Parish Priest Dunbar, 1990-93; Assistant, Episcopal Vicar for Education, 1990-93; Vicar, Episcopal for Education, 1993-98; Parish Priest, St John Vianney, Edinburgh, 1993-97; Parish Priest, St Theresa's East Calder, 1997-98; Spiritual Director, Pontifical Scots College, Rome, 1998-2006; Professor, BEDA College, Rome, 1999-2001; Postgraduate, Pontifical Gregorian University, Rome, 1998-2006; Vice-Postulator, Cause for Canonisation of Ven Margaret Sinclair, 2000-; Parish Priest, North Berwick & Dunbar, 2006-; Judge, Scottish National Tribunal, 2006-; Chancellor, Archdiocese of St Andrew's and Edinburgh, 2007-; Chaplain of His Holiness, 2008-; President, Archdiocesan Arts & Heritage Commission, 2009-. Publications: With the Spirit and Power of Elijah, 2004. Memberships: Institute of Biology; Chartered Biologist, Institute of Biology; Canon Law Society of Great Britain and Ireland. Address: Our Lady, Star of the Sea, 9 Law Road, North Berwick EH39 4PN, Scotland. E-mail: stephen.robson@staned.org.uk Website: www.archdiocese-edinburgh.org.uk

ROCCA Costantino, b. 4 December 1956, Bergamo, Italy. Golfer. m. 1 son, 1 daughter. Career: Former factory worker and caddie; Turned professional, 1981; Qualified for PGA European Tour through 1989 Challenge Tour; Won Open V33 Da Grand Lyon and Peugeot Open de France; First Italian Golfer to be member European Ryder Cup team, 1993; Member, winning European Ryder Cup team, 1995; AIB Irish Seniors Open, 2007.

ROCHA John, b. 23 August 1953, Hong Kong. Fashion Designer. Education: London College of Fashion. Career: Founder, own fashion design company, 1980, menswear line, 1993, jeans line, 1997; Regular collections at all major international fashion shows; Designed interiors for hotels and office blocks including: The Morrison Hotel, Dublin; Designed glassware for Waterford Crystal; Runs own brand labels for Debenhams. Honours: British Designer of the Year, 1993. Address: John Rocha, 12-13 Temple Lane, Dublin 2, Ireland.

ROCHA-PEREIRA Maria Helena, b. 3 September 1925, Oporto, Portugal. Professor Emeritus. Education: MA, Classics, University of Coimbra, Portugal, 1947; Student, University of Oxford, England, 1950-51, 1954, 1959; DLitt, University of Coimbra, 1956. Appointments: Lecturer, Latin and Greek, Centre for Humanistic Studies attached to the University of Oporto, 1948-57; Lecturer, 1951-56, Senior Lecturer, 1956-62, Reader, 1962-64, Professor, 1964-95, Professor Emeritus, 1995-, University of Coimbra; Visiting Professor, Federal University of Minas Gerais, Brazil, 1980; Lectures and Seminars, Federal University of Minas Gerais and Federal University of Rio de Janeiro, 1987, 96; Vice-Chancellor, University of Coimbra, 1970-71; Dean, Coimbra Faculty of Arts, 1976-77; President, Scientific Council, Coimbra Faculty of Arts, 1977-89. Publications: Numerous articles in professional journals. Honours: Essay Prize, Portuguese Ministry of Education, 1966; Essay prize, PEN Club, 1988; Woman of the Year, American Biographical Institute, 1994; Great Cross of the Order of St Jacob-of-the-Sword, Portugal, 2004; Essay Prize, Center for Iberian Studies, 2004; International Educator of the Year, IBC, 2004; Essay Prize, International Association of Literary Critics, 2006; University of Coimbra Prize, 2006; The Plato Award, IBC, 2006; Latinity Prize, Union Latine, 2006; Essay Prize, Jacinto do Prado Coelho, 2006; Golden Medal of the City of Oporto, 2007; Essay Prize Manuel Antunes, 2008; Honorary Member, Circulo José de Figueiredo, Oporto, 2008; Doctor honoris causa, University of Lisbon, Portugal, 2009; Golden Medal of the City of Coimbra, 2009; Prize Literary Life, Lisbon, 2010. Memberships: National Council for University Education; Scientific Council for the Humanities of the National Institute for Scientific Research; President, National Committee for the Evaluation of Portuguese State Universities, Classical and Modern Languages and Literatures; Representative of the Lisbon Academy of Sciences in the Standing Committee for the Humanities of the European Science Foundation, 1988-98; Representative of Portugal in the Scientific Council of the Lexicon Iconographicum Mythologiae Classicae; Honorary member of the Foundation for Hellenic Culture, Athens. Address: 1 Praceta Dias da Silva, 3000 Coimbra, Portugal. E-mail: classic@ci.uc.pt

ROCHE DE COPPENS Peter G, b. 24 May 1938, Vevey, Switzerland. Professor, Author. m. Maria Teresa Crivelli. Education: BS, Columbia University, New York, 1965; MA, 1966, PhD, 1972, Fordham University, New York. Appointments: Professor of Sociology/Anthropology, East Stroudsburg University of Pennsylvania, 1970-; Created TV program: Soul Sculpture, East Stroudsburg University, 1991-; Consultant, United Nations, PNUCID, 1997; Adjunct Professor, Department of Culture and Values in Education, McGill University, Montreal, 1998. Publications: Divine Light and Fire and Divine Light and Love, 1992, 1994; L'Alternance Instinctive and La Voie Initiatique de l'An 2000 (Louise Courteau); Prayer: the Royal Path of the Spiritual Tradition, 2003; True and Great Love Stories, 2005; The Spiritual family in the 21st Century, 2005. Medicine and Spirituality with 13 vols. Of which 9 are published: Medicina e Spiritualita 2003; La Preghiera, Strumento di Guarigione. La Thea Flora 2004; Il Perdono, Il Destino 2005; Religion, Spirituality and Healthcare, 2007; Religion et Spiritualite, 2008; Incontro con Santi e Saggi, 2006; Il Pellegrinaggio, 2006; La Natura Umana, 2007; La Medicina Differenziale e Qualitativa, 2007; La Reincarnazione ed il Karma, 2008; La Motivazione, 2008; The Great Theory of Human and Spiritual Evolution, 2010; L'Illuminazione nella Practica Medica, 2009; Medicina e Spiritualita': Manuale Sintetico, 2009; La Grande Opera, 2010; Il Potero Psiconoetico, 2010. Honours: Phi Beta Kappa; Woodrow Wilson Fellow; Knight Commander of Malta; American Biographical Institute's Commemorative Medal of Honor; Listed in national and international biographical dictionaries. Memberships: American Sociological Association; American Orthopsychiatric Association; New York Academy of Sciences; American Association for the Advancement of Science. Address: 124 S Kistler Street, East Stroudsburg, PA 18301 2604, USA.

ROCK David Annison, b. 27 May 1929, Sunderland, England. Architect. m. (1) Daphne Elizabeth Richards, 3 sons, 2 daughters, (2) Lesley Patricia Murray. Education: B Arch Hons (Dunelm), School of Architecture, Kings College, University of Durham, 1947-52; Cert TP (Dunelm), Department of Town Planning, Kings College, University of Durham, 1950-52; School of Town Planning, University of London, 1952-53. Appointments: 2nd Lieutenant, Royal Engineers, 1953-55; Basil Spence & Partners, 1952-53, 1955-59; David Rock Architect, 1958-59; Partner, Building Design Partnership, 1959-71; Chairman, Managing Director, Rock Townsend, 1971-92; Head, Lottery Architecture Unit, Arts Council of England, 1995-99; Partner, Camp 5, 1992-; Chairman, 5 Dryden Street Collective, 1971-80; Chairman, Barley Mow Workspace, 1973-92; Chairman, Society of Architect Artists, 1985-93; Lottery Awards Panel, Sports

Council of England, 1995-97; Vice-President, 1987-88, 1995-97, President, 1997-99, Royal Institute of British Architects; Vice-President, 2000-02, 2007-, President, 1997-99, 2002-07, Architects Benevolent Society; Trustee, Montgomery Sculpture Trust, 2000-2004; Trustee, South Norfolk Building Preservation Trust, 2002-2005; Finance Director, Huguenot Court Limited, 2003-05, 2006-; Honorary Treasurer, Harleston & Waveney Art Trail Collective, 2008-. Publications: Books: Vivat Ware! 1974; The Grassroots Developers, 1980; Numerous articles in building press, 1960-. Honours: Department of the Environment Housing Medals, RIBA Architecture Awards, Civic Trust Awards, 1965-92; Glover Medal, 1949; HB Saint Award, 1950; Crown Prize, 1951; Soane Medallion, 1954; Owen Jones Studentship, 1960; RIBA/Building Industry Trust Fellow, 1979; President's Medal, AIA, 1998; Honorary Fellow, American Institute of Architects, 1998. Memberships: Past President, RIBA; Fellow, Chartered Society of Designers. Address: The Beeches, 13 London Road, Harleston, Norfolk IP20 9BH, England. E-mail: david.rock1@keme.co.uk

RODMAN Dennis Keith, b. 13 May 1961, Trenton, New Jersey, USA. Basketball Player. Education: Cooke County Junior College; Southeastern Oklahoma State University. Career: West Detroit Pistons, 1986-93; Forward San Antonio Spurs, 1993-95, Chicago Bulls, 1995-99; L A Lakers, 1999; Dallas Mavericks, 2000; Retired, 2000; Resumed career with Long Beach Jam (American Basketball Association), 2003; Orange County Crush, 2004-. Honours: NBA Defensive Player of Year, 1990, 1991; NBA Championship Team, 1989-90, 1996; All-Defensive First Team, 1989-93, All-Defense Second Team, 1994; All Star Team, 1990, 1992. Film appearances: Cutaway; Simon Sez; Double Team. Publications: Bad as I Wanna Be, 1997; Walk on the Wild Side, 1997; Words from the Worm: An Unauthorized Trip Through the Mind of Dennis Rodman, 1997; I Should Be Dead By Now, 2005. Address: L A Lakers, 3900 West Manchester Boulevard, Inglewood, CA 90306, USA.

RODRIGUES DA PAZ Regina Celia, b. 3 June 1972, Sorocaba, Sao Paulo, Brazil. Professor. Education: Veterinary Medicine, University Estadual de Londina, 1995; Master, 2000, PhD, 2004, Animal Reproduction, University of Sao Paulo. Appointments: Professor, Universidade Federal de Mato Grosso, 2006-; Postdoctorate, Conservation & Research Centre, Smithsonian, USA, 2009-10. Publications: Numerous articles in professional journals. Honours: Best Student Report, 5th International Symposium on Canine and Feline Reproduction, 2004; Listed in biographical dictionaries. Memberships: AMC; ABRAVAS. Address: Avenida Fernando Correa da Costa, 2367, Boa Esperanca, Zip Code 78060-900, Cuiaba, MT, Brazil.

RODRIGUEZ VELASQUEZ Javier Oswaldo, b. 8 August 1969, Bogota, DC, Colombia. Physician. 3 sons, 2 daughters. Education: Physician and Surgeon, Universidad Nacional de Colombia, 1996. Appointments: Researcher, Ctr Investigaciones sobre Dinámica Social, Bogota, 1997-98; Director, Insight Group, 2001-; Researcher, Fundacion Cardio Infantil, Bogota, 2002-; Researcher, Clinica del Country, Bogota, 2006-; Researcher, Hospital Militar Central, Bogota, 2003-04; Teacher and Researcher, Universidad Nacional de Colombia, 2008-10; Teacher and Researcher, Universidad Militar Nueva Granada, 2008-; Referee, Journal of Medical System; Referee, Panamerican Journal of Public Health. Publications: Entropia proporcional de los sistemas dinámicos cardiacos: Predicciones fisicas y matematicas de la dinamica cardiaca de aplicacion clinica, 2010; Metodo para la prediccion de la dinamica temporal de la malaria en los municipios de Colombia, 2010; Theoretical generalization of normal and sick coronary arteries with fractals dimensions and the arterial intrinsic mathematical harmony, 2010. Honours: Honorary Mention on Clinical Sciences, Academica Nacional de Medicina of Colombia and Abbott Laboratories, 2010. Memberships: Director, Insight Group; Researcher, Clinica del Country, Bogota; Professor and Researcher, Universidad Militar Nueva Granada, Bogota. Address: Cra 79 B No 51-16 Sur, Int 1, apto 102, Bogota, DC, Colombia. E-mail: grupoinsight2025@yahoo.es

RÖHLING Horst Rudolf, b. 28 October 1929, Zwickau/Sa, Germany. Retired Librarian. Education: University final examination, 1953; Doctor's Degree, 1956; Librarian Examination, 1963. ᒪAppointments: University Assistant, 1955-58; Collaborator in University and Library, 1958-61; Librarian, 1963-94; Lecturer in Eastern Churches History, 1979-2008. Publications: Studien zur Geschichte der balkanslavischen Volkspoesie, 1975; Slavica-Bibliotheca-Ecclesia Orientalis, 1981; Drei Bulgaro-Germanica, 1983; Publikationsformen als verbindendes Element, 1992; Numerous publications on slavistics, eastern churches and library science. Honours: Fellow, American Biographical Institute; Bundesverdienstkreuz am Band; Marin-Drinov-Medaille am Band (Bulgarian Academy of Sciences); IBC Medal of Honor, International Peace Prize, 2004; Final Honours List, IBC; Man of the Year, IBC, 2011; Man of the Year, ABI, 2011; Roll of Honour, IBC. Memberships: Wolfenbütteler Arbeitskreis für Bibliotheks-, Buch- und Mediengeschichte; Deutsche Gesellschaft für die Erforschung des 18 Jahrhunderts; Study Group on 18th Century Russia; Südosteuropa-Gesellschaft; Honorary Member ABDOS; 4C's Club; Honorary Member Deutsch-Bulgarische Gesellschaft; Verein der Freunde der Ratsschulbibliothek Zwickau; Gesellschaft der Freunde und Förderer der Sächsischen Landesbibliothek Dresden; Gesellschaft Anna Amalia Bibliothek Weimar; Dombauförderverein Zwicken; Internationale Buchwissenschaftliche Gesellschaft. Address: Unterkrone 37, D-58455 Witten, Germany. L H o₂ DL

ROESKY Herbert, b. 6 November 1935, Laukischken, Germany. Chemist. m. Christel, 2 sons. Education: Diplom thesis, 1961; PhD thesis, 1963; Habilitation, 1967. Appointments: Professor, University of Frankfurt/Main, 1971; Director, 1980, Professor Emeritus, 2003, Institute of Inorganic Chemistry, Goettingen. Publications: More than 1,000 articles in professional journals. Honours: Leibniz Award, 1987; Grand Prix de la Fondation de la Maison de Chimie, Paris, 1998; ACS Award, Fluor Chem, 1999; ACS Award, Inorganic Chemistry, 2004; Moisson Prize, 2009. Memberships: German Chemical Society; American Chemical Society; Royal Society of Chemistry; Akademie d Wissenschaften, Goettingen. Address: University of Goettingen, Institute of Inorganic Chemistry, Tammann str 4, 37077 Goettingen, Germany.

ROGANTE Massimo, b. 2 October 1958, Macerata, Italy. Nuclear Scientist; Researcher. m. Natalija Miltakytė, 2 sons. Education: Diploma di Pianoforte, Conservatoire G Rossini, Pesaro, 1983; Mechanical Engineering Graduate, University of Ancona, Italy, 1984; PhD, Nuclear Engineering, University of Bologna, Italy, 1999. Appointments: General Manager, Rogante D&C Shipowners, Civitanova Marche, Italy, 1978-; Researcher in Materials Science, University of Ancona, 1994-98; Director, Rogante Engineering Office, Civitanova Marche, 1996-; Researcher in Nuclear Engineering, University of Bologna, 1999-. Publications:

Contributed articles to professional and scientific journals. Honours: Italian member, International Scientific Advisory Board, Budapest Research Reactor; Academia de Catenati Academia Georgia. Memberships: Neutron Scattering Society of America; Swiss Society for Neutron Scattering; Nuclear Energy Institute; World Directory of Crystallographers; many others. Address: Rogante Engineering Office, Contrada San Michele, 61-62012, Civitanova Marche, Italy. E-mail: main@roganteengineering.it Website: www.roganteengineering.it/

ROHATGI Pradip Krishna (Roy), b. 10 November 1939, Calcutta, India. Professor; Consultant. m. Pauline Mary Rohatgi. Education: Bachelor of Commerce, Calcutta University, 1960; Bachelor of Science, Economics, University of London, 1964; Associate Examinations of the Institute of Taxation (UK), 1967; Associate Member, 1969, Fellow, 1974, Institute of Chartered Accountants of England and Wales; Fellow, Institute of Chartered Accountants of India, 1980. Appointments: Senior Economist and Statistician in industrial market research, London, 1963-66; Articled and qualified as a Chartered Accountant, Mann Judd & Co, London, 1966-70; Arthur Andersen Worldwide Organisation, 1970-94, London Office Manager, 1974, Partner 1980, Head of Accounting and Audit Division for Gulf Countries, Dubai Office, 1980-84, Managing Partner for South Asia, Mumbai, India, 1980-89; Senior Partner and Consultant, London, 1990-94, retired as Partner, 1994; International Taxation and Strategy Advisor, 1994-2004; Conference Director, Annual International Taxation Conference, Mumbai, India, 1995-; Visiting Professor in International Taxation, RAU University, South Africa, 1996; Advisor to the Mauritius Offshore Business Activities Authority (subsequently Financial Services Promotion Agency) and Ministry of Economic Affairs, Financial Service and Corporate Affairs, 2000-05; Professor of International Tax Planning, St Thomas University School of Law, Miami, USA, 2002-06; Visiting Professor, Vienna University of Economics and Business Administration, Austria, 2007-. Publications: Book: Basic International Taxation, 2001, 2nd edition, 2005; More than 300 articles and over 1,000 presentations. Memberships: International Fiscal Association; International Tax Planning Association. Address: Olympus Apartments 512, Altamount Road, Mumbai 400026, India. E-mail: royrohatgi@gmail.com

ROHEN Edward, (Bruton Connors), b. 10 February 1931, Dowlais, South Wales. Poet; Writer; Artist. m. Elizabeth Jarrett, 4 April 1961, 1 daughter. Education: ATD, Cardiff College of Art, 1952. Appointments: Art Teacher, Ladysmith High, British Columbia, Canada, 1956-57; Head of Art, St Bonaventures, London, 1958-73; Ilford County High for Boys, Essex, 1973-82. Publications: Nightpriest, 1965; Bruised Concourse, 1973; Old Drunk Eyes Haiku, 1974; Scorpio Broadside 15, 1975; Poems/Poemas, 1976; A 109 Haiku and One Seppuku for Maria, 1987; Sonnets for Maria Marriage, 1988; Sonnets: Second Sequence for Maria, 1989. Contributions to: Poetry Wales; Anglo-Welsh Review; Irish Press; Mabon; Tribune; Argot; Edge; Little Word Machine; Second Aeon; Planet; Carcanet; Poetry Nippon; Riverside Quarterly; Littack; Wormwood Review; Twentieth Century Magazine. Honours: U.N. Medal (Korea); Listed in various international biographical dictionaries. Memberships: Korean War Veterans Writers and Arts Society; Academician, Centro Cultural Literario e Artistico de o Jornal de Felgeiras, Portugal; Welsh Academy; Poet's Society of Japan. Address: 57 Kinfauns Road, Goodmayes, Ilford, Essex IG3 9QH, England.

RÖHSER Günter, b. 27 July 1956, Rothenburg ob der Tauber, Germany. m. Hedwig Röhser, 3 sons. University Professor. Education: Studies in Protestant Theology in Erlangen, Heidelberg and Neuendettelsau, 1975-81; Doctor of Theology, 1986; Habilitation in New Testament Theology, 1993. Appointments: Director of Studies, Ecumenical Institute, University of Heidelberg, 1982; Pastor, Lutheran Church, Bavaria, 1987; Associate Professor, University/ GHS Siegen, 1994; Professor for Bible Studies, RWTH Aachen, 1997; Professor for the New Testament, University of Bonn, 2003. Publications: Metaphorik und Personifikation der Sünde, 1987; Prädestination und Verstockung, 1994; Stellvertretung im Neuen Testament, 2002. Memberships: Studiorum Novi Testamenti Societas; Academic Society for Theology; Society for Protestant Theology; Society of Biblical Literature; International Society for the Study of Deuterocanonical and Cognate Literature; Centre for Religion and Society, University of Bonn. Address: Faculty of Protestant Theology, Section for the New Testament, University of Bonn, Am Hof 1, D-53113 Bonn, Germany. E-mail: g.roehser@ev-theol.uni-bonn.de

ROMANO Sergio, b. 7 July 1929, Vicenza, Italy. Diplomat; Writer. m. Mary Anne Heinze, 2 sons, 1 daughter. Education: Doctor of Law, University of Milan, 1952. Appointments: Vice Consul, Innsbruck, 1955; IRST Secretary, Italian Embassy, London, 1958-64; IRST Counsellor, later Minister, Italian Embassy, Paris, 1968-77; Director General, Cultural Affairs, Italian Ministry of Foreign Affairs, 1977-83; Ambassador to NATO, 1983-85; Ambassador to USSR, 1986-89. Publications: Latest books: Avanti! Chroniques Italinnes, 2007; Briefan einen Judischen Freund, 2007; Con Gli Occhi Dell'Islam, 2008. Honours: Grand Cross; Order of Merit, Italian Republic; Commande Legion d'Honneur; and others. Address: via P Verri 6, 20121 Milan, Italy. E-mail: sergio.romano@fastwebnet.it

ROMANSKII Igor, b. 29 September 1937, Moscow, Russia. Retired. m. Galina Baronchesco. Education: Chemist, Basic Organic Synthesis, M V Lomonosov Moscow Institute of Fine Chemical Technology, 1961; PhD, L Ya Karpov Physiochemical Research Institute, 1981. Appointments: Junior Research Fellow, Research Institute of Chlorine Industry, 1961-65; L Ya Karpov Physicochemical Research Institute, 1965-73; Scientific Associate and Senior Scientific Associate, Research Institute for Organic Semi-Product and Dye Stuffs, 1974-2000; Retired, 2000. Publications: Numerous articles in professional journals. Honours: Listed in international biographical dictionaries. Memberships: American Chemical Society; Physical Chemistry Division. E-mail: ceng37@yandex.ru

RON Gad, b. 17 September 1927, Tel Aviv, Israel (arrived Holland, 1975). Civil Engineer. m. Noemi Deutsch, 1951, 2 daughters. Education: Diploma, Civil Engineering (Dipl Ing), Haifa Institute of Technology, Israel, 1950; Chartered CE, MICE, The Institute of Civil Engineers, UK, 1960, awarded Fellow, FICE, 2000; Certificates in Heavy Civil Engineering, Harbour Works, Airfields, Offshore Technology and Housing Development Projects. Appointments: Royal Netherlands Harbour Works Co, 1951-75; PE, Harbour Construction Zonguldak, Turkey, 1951-54; PR Manager, NATO airfields construction, Batman & Malatya, Turkey, 1955-60; International Projects Tenders, HO Holland, 1960-62; Project Manager, Oil Jetty Construction, Mombasa, Kenya, 1962-64; Project Manager, Construction of Harbour, Airfields Hangars, US Naval Base, Rota, Spain, 1964-70; Project Manager, Harbour extension, Dar es Salam, Jetty Construction, Tanga,

DICTIONARY OF INTERNATIONAL BIOGRAPHY 36ᵗʰ EDITION

Tanzania, 1970-72; Board Director, Joint Venture, SKANSA Hydroelectric power project, Kidatu, Tanzania, 1970-72; Managing Director, CPTP Aff Company of RNHW Group, Portugal Marine & Harbour works, 1972-75; Managing Director, Overseas projects, KNB – RNHW Group HO Gouda, Holland, Ogem Group, LA, 1975-81; Managing Director, Dutch Offshore Consortium, HO Mexico City, 1981-84; Vice President, Latin America & Caribbeans, Reynolds Construction Co, HO, New York, 1984-86; Managing Director, Resort Developments, J V Persimmon (UK), R Bachmann (Portugal), Balaia Golf Village and others, Algarve, Portugal, 1987-2007. Memberships: Institute of Civil Engineers, England; Rotary International; UK-Portugal Chamber of Commerce. Address: Balaia Golf Village, 8200 Albufeira, Portugal. E-mail: gadron@live.com.pt

RONALDINHO GAÚCHO (Ronaldo de Assis Moreira), b. 21 March 1980, Pôrto Alegre, Brazil. Footballer. 1 son. Career: Player: Gremio de Pôrto Alegre, 1998-2001, Paris St Germain, France, 2001-03, FC Barcelona, Spain, 2003-; 42 caps for Brazil, won Copa America, 1999 (scoring 6 goals), won World Cup, 2002. Honours: Won World Youth Cup with Brazil Under 17 team; EFE Trophy, 2004; FIFA World Footballer of the Year, 2004. Address: c/o Futbol Club Barcelona, Avenida Arístides Maillol, 08028 Barcelona, Spain. Website: www.fcbarcelona.com

RONALDO, b. 22 September 1976, Bento Ribero, Rio de Janeiro, Brazil. Retired Football Player. Career: Player: Social Ramos, Rio (12 games, 8 goals), Sao Cristovao, Rio Second Division (54 games, 36 goals), Cruzeiro, Brazil (60 games, 58 goals), PSV Eindhoven, Netherlands (58 games, 54 goals), Barcelona, Spain (49 games, 47 goals), Inter Milan, 1997-2002 (90 games, 53 goals); Real Madrid, 2002-2007; Brazilian National Team, 1994-2011 (67 international caps, 47 goals); A C Milan, 2007-08; Corinthians, 2009-11. Honours: Winning team, World Cup, 1994, 2002 and Copa America, 1997; Spanish Cup and European Cup Winners' Cup, 1997; World Soccer Magazine World Player of the Year, 1996; FIFA World Footballer of the Year, 1996, 1997, 2002; European Footballer of the Year, 1997, 2002.

RONAY Egon, b. Pozony, Hungary (UK citizen). Publisher; Journalist. m. (1) 2 daughters, (2) Barbara Greenslade, 1967, 1 son. Education: LLD, University of Budapest; Academy of Commerce, Budapest; Trained in kitchens of five family restaurants and abroad. Appointments: Manager, 5 restaurants within family firm; Emigrated from Hungary, 1946; General Manager, 2 restaurant complexes in London before opening his Marquee Restaurant, 1952-55; Founder, The Egon Ronay Guides, 1957, Publisher, 1957-85; Gastronomic and good living weekly columnist, Sunday Times, 1986-91, Sunday Express, 1991. Publications: The Unforgettable Dishes of My Life, 1989; Weekly columnist on eating out, food, wine and tourism, Daily Telegraph and later Sunday Telegraph, 1954-60; Weekly column, the Evening News, 1968-74; Editor-in-Chief, Egon Ronay Recommends (Heathrow Airport Magazine), 1992-94. Honours: Médaille de la Ville de Paris, 1983; Chevalier de l'Ordre du Mérite Agricole, 1987. Memberships: Academie des Gastronomes (France), 1979 Founding Vice-President, International Academy of Gastronomy; Founder, President, British Academy of Gastronomes. Address: 37 Walton Street, London SW3 2HT, England.

ROONEY Coleen, b. 3 April 1986, Liverpool, England. TV presenter; Columnist. m. Wayne Rooney, 2008, 1 son. Education: St John Bosco School. Career: Columnist, Closer magazine, -2008; Columnist, OK! Magazine, 2008-; Co-presenter, Tonight with Trevor McDonald, 2006; Presenter, Coleen's Real Women; Own fragrance, Coleen X; Celebrity endorsement of: L G Electronics; Nike Women Sportswear; George at Asda. Publications: Autobiography, Welcome to My World, 2007; DVD, Coleen McLoughlin's Brand New Body Workout. Honours: Ariel High Street Fashion Award.

ROONEY Mickey (Joe Yule Jr), b. 23 September 1920, Brooklyn, USA. Actor. m. (1) Ava Gardner, (2) Betty J Rase, 2 sons, (3) Martha Vickers, (4) Elaine Mahnken, (5) Barbara Thomason, 4 children, (6) Margie Lang, (7) Carolyn Hockett, 2 sons, (8) Jan Chamberlin, 2 stepsons. Education: Pacific Military Academy. Career: Served AUS, World War II; TV programmes including series: The Mickey Rooney Show; Films include: Judge Hardy's Children; Hold That Kiss; Lord Jeff; Love Finds Andy Hardy; Boys Town; Stablemates; Out West With the Hardys; Huckleberry Finn; Andy Hardy Gets Spring Fever; Babes in Arms; Young Tom Edison; Judge Hardy and Son; Andy Hardy Meets Debutante; Strike up the Band; Andy Hardy's Private Secretary; Men of Boystown; Life Begins for Andy Hardy; Babes on Broadway; A Yank at Eton; The Human Comedy; Andy Hardy's Blonde Trouble; Girl Crazy; Thousands Cheer; National Velvet; Ziegfeld Follies; The Strip; Sound Off; Off Limits; All Ashore; Light Case of Larceny; Drive a Crooked Road; Bridges at Toko-Ri; The Bold and the Brave; Eddie; Private Lives of Adam and Eve; Comedian; The Grabbers; St Joseph Plays the Horses; Breakfast at Tiffany's; Somebody's Waiting; Requiem for a Heavyweight; Richard; Pulp; It's a Mad Mad Mad Mad World; Everything's Ducky; The Secret Invasion; The Extraordinary Invasion; The Comic; The Cockeyed Cowboys of Calico County; Skidoo; BJ Presents; That's Entertainment; The Domino Principle; Pete's Dragon; The Magic of Lassie; Black Stallion; Arabian Adventure; Erik the Viking; My Heroes Have Always Been Cowboys, 1991; Little Nemo: Adventures in Slumberland (Voice), 1992; Silent Deadly Night 5; The Toymaker; The Milky Life; Revenge of the Baron; That's Entertainment II; The Legend of OB Taggart, 1995; Kings of the Court, 1997; Killing Midnight, 1997; Boys Will Be Boys, 1997; Animals, 1997; Sinbad: The Battle of the Dark Knights, 1998; Babe: Pig in the City, 1998; The Face on the Barroom Floor, 1998; The First of May, 1998; Holy Hollywood, 1999; Internet Love, 2000; Lady and the Tramp II: Scamp's Adventure, 2001; Topa Topa Bluffs, 2002; Paradise, 2003; Strike the Tent, 2004; The Happy Elf (voice), 2005; Night at the Museum, 2006; The Yesterday Pool, 2007; A Christmas Too Many, 2007; Bamboo Shark, 2007; Lost Stallions: The Journey Home, 2007; Wreck the Halls, 2008. Address: PO Box 3186, Thousand Oaks, CA 91359, USA.

ROONEY Wayne, b. 24 October 1985, Croxteth, Liverpool, England. Footballer. m. Colleen McLoughlin, 1 son. Teams: Everton, 2002-04; England, 2003-; Manchester United, 2004-. Sponsers: Coca-Cola; Nike. Shirt Numbers: 8; 9; 18; 21; 23. Awards: October Goal Of The Month, ITV, 2002; Young Sports Personality of the Year, 2002; PFA Fans Player of the Month, 2004; Golden Boy, Best Young Player in Europe, 2004; Match of the Day's Goal of the Season, 2004-05, 2006-07; FIFPro Young Player Award, 2005; PFA Fans' Player of the Year (Premiership), 2006.

ROSARIO Nelson Augusto, b. 7 February 1949, Londrina, Brazil. Professor. m. Teresa, 1 son, 3 daughters. Education: MD; PhD. Appointments: Professor of Pediatrics, University of Parana. Publications: Numerous articles in professional journals. Memberships: WAO; ACAAI; AAAAI; SBP; ASDAI. Address: Rua Gen Carneiro 181, Curitiba, Parana 80060 900, Brazil.

ROSE Sir Clive Martin, b. 15 September 1921, Banstead, Surrey, England. British Diplomatist (retired). m. Elisabeth MacKenzie Lewis, 1946, deceased 2006, 2 sons, 3 daughters. Education: Marlborough College; Christ Church, Oxford. Appointments: Rifle Brigade (rank of Major, mentioned in despatches), Europe, India, Iraq, 1941-46; Commonwealth Relations Office, 1948; High Commission, Madras, 1948-49; Foreign Office, 1950; Served in Bonn, Montevideo, Paris, Washington and London, 1950-73; Imperial Defence College, 1968; Ambassador and Head of UK Delegation to Mutual and Balanced Force Reduction talks, Vienna, 1973-76; Deputy Secretary to Cabinet Office, 1976-79; UK Permanent Representative on North Atlantic Council, 1979-82; Consultant to Control Risks Group Ltd, 1983-95; Director, 1986-93, Chair, 1991-93, Control Risks Information Services Ltd. Publications: Campaigns Against Western Defence: NATO's Adversaries and Critics, 1985; The Soviet Propaganda Network: a Directory of Organisations Serving Soviet Foreign Policy, 1988; The Unending Quest: A Search for Ancestors, 1996; Alice Owen: the life, marriages and times of a Tudor Lady, 2006; Contributor, Détente, Diplomacy and MBFR, 2002. Memberships: President, Emergency Planning Association, 1987-93; Member, Advisory Board, Royal College for Defence Studies, 1985-92; Chair, 1983-86, Vice President, 1986-93, Vice Patron, 1993-2001, Council, Royal United Services Institute; Chair, 1985-88, Vice President, 1988-, Suffolk Preservation Society. Address: Chimney House, Lavenham, Suffolk CO10 9QT, England.

ROSEANNE (Roseanne Barr), b. 3 November 1952, Salt Lake City, USA. Actress. m. (1) Bill Pentland, 3 children, (2) Tom Arnold, divorced 1994, (3) Ben Thomas, 1994-2002 (divorced) 1 son. Appointments: Former window dresser, cocktail waitress; Comic in bars and church coffee-house, Denver; Producer, forum for women performers Take Back the Mike, University of Boulder, Colorado; Performer, The Comedy Store, Los Angeles; Featured, TV special Funny and The Tonight Show; TV special, On Location: The Roseanne Barr Show, 1987; Star, TV series, Roseanne ABC, 1988-97; Host, Roseanne Show, 1998-; Actress in films: She Devil, 1989; Freddy's Dead, 1991; Even Cowgirls Get the Blues, 1994; Blue in the Face, 1995; Unzipped, 1995; Meet Wally Sparks, 1997; Home on the Range (voice), 2004. Publications: My Life as a Woman, 1989; Roseanne: My Lives, 1994. Honours: Emmy Award, Outstanding Actress in a Comedy Series, 1993. Address: c/o Full Moon and High Tide Productions, 4024 Radford Avenue, Dressing Room 916, Studio City, CA 91604, USA.

ROSEN Michael, b. 17 October 1927, Dundee, Scotland. Medical Practitioner. m. Sally Cohen, 2 sons, 1 daughter. Education: MB ChB, St Andrew's University, 1949; FFARCS, 1957. Appointments: House appointments, Bolton, Portsmouth, Bradford, 1949-53; RAMC, 1953-55; Registrar, Anaesthesia, Royal Victoria Infirmary, Newcastle upon Tyne, 1954-57; Senior Registrar, Cardiff, 1957-60; Fellow, Case Western University, Ohio, USA, 1960-61; Consultant Anaesthetist, Cardiff Hospitals, 1961-94; Honorary Professor in Anaesthetics, 1986; Member, GMC, 1989-92. Publications: Percutaneous Cannulation of Great Veins, 1981, 2nd edition, 1991; Obstetric Anaesthesia Safe Practice, 1982; Patient-Controlled Analgesia, 1984; Tracheal Intubation, 1985; Awareness and Pain in General Anaesthesia, 1987; Ambulatory Anaesthesia, 1991; Quality Measures Emergency, 2001. Honours: CBE, 1990; Honorary Member, French and Australian Societies of Anaesthesia; Honorary FFARCSI, 1990; Honorary Fellow, Academy of Medicine, Malaysia; Honorary LLD, Dundee, 1996; FRCOG, 1989; FRCS, 1994. Memberships: President, Association of Anaesthetists, 1986-88; President, Royal College of Anaesthetists, 1988-91. Address: 45 Hollybush Road, Cardiff CF 23 6TZ, Wales. E-mail: rosen@mrosen.plus.com

ROSEN Norma, b. 11 August 1925, New York, New York, USA. Writer; Teacher. m. Robert S Rosen, 1960, 1 son, 1 daughter. Education: BA, Mt Holyoke College, 1946; MA, Columbia University, 1953. Appointments: Teacher, Creative Writing, New School for Social Research, New York City, 1965-69, University of Pennsylvania, 1969, Harvard University, 1971, Yale University, 1984, New York University, 1987-95. Publications: Joy to Levine! 1962; Green, 1967; Touching Evil, 1969; At the Center, 1982; John and Anzia: An American Romance, 1989; Accidents of Influence: Writing as a Woman and a Jew in America (essays), 1992; Biblical Women Unbound: Counter-Tales (narratives), 1996; The Lovemaking of I B Singer, 1996; Elixir, 1998; My Son, the Novelist, 1999; Desperately Seeking Siblings, 1999; Orphan Lovers, 2000; Writers' Gift, Writers' Grudge, 2001; The Greatest Challenge Ever Told, 2002; What Goes Down Must Go Up, 2003; Of Need and Guilt, 2004; Deconstructing Jacques, 2005; The Writers Among Us, 2006; Betrayal: A Name Change, 2007; The Lord is One, with Facets, 2008; Unfinished Lives, 2010; Saul Bellow's Enigmatic Love, 2010; Contributions to: Anthologies and other publications; Commentary, New York Times Book Review & Magazine, MS, Raritan, etc. Honours: Saxton; CAPS; Bunting Institute; Listed in national biographies. Memberships: PEN; Authors Guild; Phi Beta Kappa.

ROSENBERG Marilyn R, b. 11 October 1934, Philadelphia, USA. m. 1955, 2 daughters. Education: Bachelor of Professional Studies in Studio Arts, Empire State College, State University of New York, 1978; MA, Liberal Studies, Graduate School of Arts and Science, New York, 1993. Career: Author; Artist. Publications: Over 1000 titles that include visual poems, artists books, mail art, drawings, small press/chap books, unique sculptural bookworks and more. Address: 67 Lakeview Avenue, West, Cortlandt Manor, NY 10567, USA. E-mail: bmrosenberg2@netscape.net

ROSS Diana, b. 26 March 1944, Detroit, Michigan, USA. Singer; Entertainer; Actress; Fashion Designer. m. (1) Robert Ellis Silberstein, 1971, 3 daughters; (2) Arne Ness, 1985, divorced 2002, 1 son. Career: Backing singer, the Temptations, Marvin Gaye, Mary Wells; Lead singer, Diana Ross and The Supremes; Solo artiste, 1969-; Appearances include: Opening ceremonies, Football World Cup, USA, 1994; Rugby World Cup, South Africa, 1995; Film appearances: Lady Sings The Blues, 1972; Mahogany, 1975; The Wiz, 1978; Television specials: An Evening With Diana Ross, 1977; Diana, 1980; Christmas In Vienna, 1992; Business ventures: Diana Ross Enterprises Inc; Anaid Film Productions; RTM Management Corp; Chondee Inc. Recordings: Albums include: Diana Ross, 1970; Lady Sings The Blues, 1972; Touch Me In The Morning, 1973; The Boss, 1979; Why Do Fools Fall In Love?, 1981; Eaten Alive, 1984; Silk Electric, 1982; Chain Reaction, 1986; Ain't No Mountain High Enough, 1989; The Force Behind The Power, 1991; Motown's Greatest Hits, 1992; Live...Stolen Moments, 1993; One Woman - The Ultimate Collection, 1993; The Remixes, 1994; Take Me Higher, 1995; Very Special Christmas, 1998; Every Day is a New Day, 1999; Voice of Love, 2000; Gift of Love, 2000. Publication: Secrets Of A Sparrow (autobiography), 1993. Honours include: Citations: Vice-President Humphrey; Mrs Martin Luther King, Rev Abernathy; Billboard award: Record World award, World's Outstanding Singer; Grammy Award, 1970; Female

Entertainer Of The Year, NAACP, 1970; Golden Globe, 1972; Antoinette Perry Award, 1977; Nominated Rock and Roll Hall Of Fame, 1988; BET Lifetime Achievement Award, 2007; Kennedy Center Honors Award, 2007. Address: RTC Management, PO Box 1683, New York, NY 10185, USA.

ROSS James Magnus, b. 3 March 1972, United Kingdom. Orchestra Conductor. Education: MA, History, 1993, MST, Music, 1994, D Phil, Music, 1998, Christ Church, Oxford University. Appointments: Music Director: Christ Church Festival Orchestra, 1993-, Chorus and Orchestra, Royal College of Paediatricians, 1994-, Northampton University Orchestra, 2001-, Welwyn Garden City Music Society, 2000-, St Albans Symphony Orchestra, 2001-; Oxford Unib Sinfonietta, 2005-; Guest Conductor: Sarajevo Philharmonic Orchestra, Bosnia, 1998, 1999, Oxford University Philharmonia, UK, 1999, Camden Chamber Orchestra, UK, 1999, Oxford Opera Society, UK, 1999; Bologna University Chamber Choir, Italy, 2002, Harbin Symphony Orchestra, China, 2002; Nis Symphony Orchestra, Serbia, 2002, Symphony Orchestra of Sri Lanka, Sri Lanka, 2001, 2003, 2005. Publications: Book chapters: Music in the French Salon in French Music since Berlioz (eds. C Potter and R Langham Smith), 2005; Republican Patriotism in the Third Republic Opera in Nationalism and Identity in Third Republic France (ed. B Kelly), 2005; Vincent d'Indy l'interpreté in Vincent d'Indy et son temps, 2005; Articles and reviews in professional journals include: D'Indy's Fervaal: Reconstructing French Identity at the Fin de Siècle, 2003. Honours include: British Academy Studentship, 1993-97; Osgood Award, 1996; Sir Donald Tovey Memorial Prize, 1998. Memberships: Performers and Composers Section, Incorporated Society of Musicians, UK; Conductors Guild, USA. E-mail: conductor@saso.org.uk Website: www.james-ross.com

ROSS Nicholas David (Nick), b. 7 August 1947, London, England. Broadcaster. m. Sarah Patricia Ann Caplin, 3 sons. Education: BA (Hons), Psychology, Queen's University Belfast. Appointments: Broadcaster and Moderator; Freelance 1971-; Television: Northern Ireland's main news, 1971-72; Man Alive, BBC2, 1976-83; Out of Court, BBC2, 1981-84; Breakfast Time & Sixty Minutes, BBC1, 1983-85; Crimewatch UK, BBC1 1984-2007; A Week in Politics, Channel 4, 1985-87; Star Memories, BBC1, 1985; Crimewatch File, BBC1, 1986-2007; Watchdog, BBC1, 1985-86; Crime Limited, BBC1, 1992-95; Westminster with Nick Ross, BBC2, 1994-97; Party Conferences live coverage, BBC2, 1997; Election Campaign, BBC2, 1997; Trail of Guilt, BBC1, 1999; Nick Ross, BBC2, 1999; Destination Nightmares, BBC1, 1999-2000; Storm Alert, BBC1, 1999; The Syndicate, BBC1, 2000; The Search, BBC1, 1999-2000; British Bravery Awards, BBC1, 2000; So You Think You're a Good Driver, BBC1, 1999-2002; Nick Ross Debates, 2000; The Truth About Crime with Nick Ross, 2009; Radio: Call Nick Ross, 1986-97; The Commission, 1998-. Publications: Various newspaper and magazine articles. Honours: Honorary Fellow, Visiting Professor, University College, London; Doctor of the University, Queen's University, Belfast; Honorary Fellow, Academy of Experimental Criminologists. Memberships: Fellow, Royal Society of Arts, Fellow Royal Society of Medicine. Address: PO Box 999, London W2 4XT, England. E-mail: nickross@lineone.net

ROSSE 7th Earl of, Sir Brendan Parsons, 10th Bart, also: Baron Ballybritt and Oxmantown. Lord of the Manors of Womersley and Woodhall in England and Parsonstown, Newtown and Roscomroe in Ireland, b. 21 October 1936 (Irish National). Director. m. Alison Cooke-Hurle, 2 sons, 1 daughter. Education: Grenoble University; MA, Christ Church, Oxford University. Appointments: United Nations Official, 1963-80; Successively, UNDP and UNESCO Representative, UN Volunteer Field Director, Iran; UN Disaster Relief Co-Ordinator, Bangladesh; Director, Historic Irish Houses and Gardens Association, 1980-91; Director, Agency for Personal Service Overseas, 1981-89; Appointed to Irish Government's Advisory Council in Development Co-Operation, 1983-88; Founding Director, Birr Scientific and Heritage Foundation, responsible for Ireland's Historic Science Centre. Honours: LLD, Honoris causa, Dublin; Honorary FIEI; Honorary Life Member, RDS. Memberships: RAS; RNS; Royal Society for Asian Affairs. Address: Birr Castle, Co. Offaly, Ireland.

ROSSELLINI Isabella, b. 18 June 1952, Rome, Italy (US citizen). Actress; Model. m. (1) Martin Scorsese, 1979, divorced 1982, (2) J Wiedemann, 1983, divorced 1986, 1 daughter, also 1 son. Education: Rome Academy of Fashion and Costume; New York School for Social Research. Career: Costume Designer for Roberto Rossellini (father), New York, 1972; Journalist for Italian TV; Vogue Cover Girl, 1980; Contracted to Lancome Cosmetics, 1982-95; Vice President, Marketing Department, Lancaster Cosmetics GPs, 1995-; As Actress: Films include: A Matter of Time, 1976; Blue Velvet, 1986; Cousins, 1989; Wild at Heart, 1990; Death Becomes Her, 1994; Immortal Beloved, 1994; Wyatt Earp, 1994; The Innocent, 1995; The Funeral, 1996; Big Night, 1996; Crime of the Century, 1996; Left Luggage, 1998; The Imposters, 1998; The Real Blonde, 1998; Don Quixote, 2000; Il Cielo cade, 2000; Empire, 2002; Roger Dodger, 2002; The Tulse Luper Suitcases, Part 1: The Moab Story, 2003; The Saddest Music in the World, 2003; The Tulse Luper Suitcases, Part 2: Vaux to the Sea, 2004; King of the Corner, 2004; Heights, 2005; La Fiesta del Chivo, 2005; The Architect, Infamous, Infected, Oh La La, 2006; The Accidental Husband, 2008; Two Lovers, My Dog Tulip, 2009; The Solitude of Prime Numbers, 2010; Keyhole, Chicken with Plums, Late Bloomers, 2011; TV: Ivory Hunters, 1990; Lies of the Twins, 1991; The Gift, 1994; Crime of the Century, 1996; The Odyssey, 1997; Don Quixote, 2000; Napoleon, 2002; Monte Walsh, 2003; Earthsea, 2004; Alias, 2004-05; Discovery Atlas: Italy Revealed, Iconoclasts, 2006; 30 Rock, 2007; Green Porno, 2008-09; The Phantom, 2009; Treme, 2012. Address: c/o United Talent Agency, 9560 Wilshire Boulevard, Floor 5, Beverly Hill, CA 90212, USA.

ROSSI Graziano, b. 14 December 1978, Vicenza, Italy. Astrophysicist. Education: Laureate, Astronomy, Università degli Studi di Padova, Padua, Italy, 2003; MS, Physics, University of Pittsburgh, USA, 2004; PhD, Astrophysics, University of Pennsylvania, USA, 2008. Appointments: Research Fellow Instructor, University of Pennsylvania, 2007-08; Postdoctoral Research Scientist, Korea Institute for Advanced Study, Seoul, South Korea, 2008-. Publications: Numerous articles in professional journals. Honours: Numerous visiting grants and invitations to international conferences; Prize for Excellence in Research, KIAS 15th Anniversary, 2011. Memberships: SDSS-III (BOSS) Collaboration; AAS International Affiliate Membership. Address: KIAS Hoegiro 87, Dongdaemun-gu, Seoul 130-722, South Korea. E-mail: graziano@kias.re.kr Website: www.grazianorossi.com

ROSSWICK Robert Paul, b. 1 June 1932. Consultant, General and Endocrine Surgery. Education: MB BS (Lond), The London Hospital Medical College, 1955; D Obst, RCOG, 1957; FRCS (Eng), 1961; MS (Surgery), Illinois, 1963; MAE, 1997. Appointments: House Surgeon, Poplar

Hospital, London, England, 1955-1956; House Physician, Swindon Hospital, Wiltshire, 1956; Obstetric SHO, Greenwich Hospital, London, 1957; Lecturer in Anatomy, Kings College, London, 1957-59; Surgical SHO, 1959-1960, Locum SHO, 1963, The London Hospital; Surgical Registrar, St Andrew's, Bow, London, 1961-62; Surgical Registrar, Harold Wood Hospital, Essex, 1963-64; Surgical Registrar, 1964-66, Senior Registrar, 1966-70, St George's Hospital, London; Senior Registrar, Winchester and Royal Marsden Hospital, 1966-1970; Consultant-in-Charge, Accident and Emergency Department, 1970-74, Consultant Surgeon, 1970-93, Honorary Senior Lecturer in Surgery, St George's Hospital Medical School, 1970-93, St George's Hospital, London; Surgeon, The Royal Masonic Hospital, 1975-1993; Examiner in Surgery: The University of London; The Society of Apothecaries; PLAB. Publications: Numerous papers on abdominal surgery, thyroid surgery; Letters in medical journals; Addresses to medical societies; Presidential address, The Medical Society of London, a review of 1000 thyroidectomies, 1990. Honours: Robertson-Exchange Fellow in Surgery, Rush-Presbyterian-St Luke's Hospital, Chicago, USA, 1962-63; Past member of Council, Section of Surgery, Royal Society of Medicine; Chairman, Wandsworth Division, 1984-87, Delgate, ARM, etc, British Medical Association; Councillor, Hunterian Society, 1987-1995; Editor, 1984-1989, President, 1990-1991, Treasurer and Trustee, 1994-, The Medical Society of London. Memberships: Fellow: The Association of Surgeons; The British Association of Endocrine Surgeons; The CRC Multiple Endocrine Neoplasia Group; The British Society of Gastroenterology; The Collegium Internationale of Chirurgicae Digestiva; The Chelsea Clinical Society; Liveryman: The Worshipful Society of Apothecaries, Treasurer, Livery Committee, 1992-96; Member: Independent Doctors Forum; Medical Appeals Tribunals, Independent Tribunal Service; The Academy of Experts; UK Register of Expert Witnesses. Address: 5 Staffordshire House, 50 Broughton Avenue, London N3 3EG, England.

ROTA Eugenia, b. 31 July 1965, Torino, Italy. Education: Graduate (summa cum laude), Medicine and Surgery, 1997, Specialization in Neurology, 2003, Master, Clinical Neurophysiology, 2004, Master, Clinical Methodology of Headaches and Cranial Neuralgias, 2005, University of Turin. Appointments: Research Fellow, Neuro-Immunology Laboratory, Department of Neuroscience, Research Fellow, Unit of Headache-Facial Pain, Department of Clinical Pathophysiology; Contract Professor, Neurological Aspects of the Headaches, Gnatologic Clinic, 2003-04, University of Turin; Neurologist, Neurology Unit, Alba and Bra Hospitals, CN, Italy. Publications: Numerous articles in professional journals. Honours: Listed in international biographical dictionaries. Memberships: Italian Neurological Society; Società Italiana per lo Studio delle Cefalee. Address: Str Gariglio 14, 12042 Bra (CN), Italy. E-mail: eugenia_rota@yahoo.it

ROTARU Florin, b. 11 November 1952, Romania. Historian. m. Julieta, 1 daughter. Education: BA, History, University of Bucharest, 1978; Cultural Management training, Denmark, 1992; PhD, History, 2002; Certificate, Archaeology, Ministry of Culture, 2003; CertiDoc Expert, European Council of Information Associations, 2007. Appointments: Expert in old Romanian/foreign books, National Heritage Department, History Museum, Bucharest, 1979-87; Collaborations with Romanian television, 1980-2002; Organizing book exhibitions, 1980-2011; President, Commission of Old Rare Book Survey and Assessment, 1987-90; Academic lectures in Bucharest, 1987-92; Area Adviser, Ministry of Culture, 1990-96; State Ministry of Culture, 2000-02; Senator, Romanian Parliament, 2003-04; President, National Committee of Libraries of Romania, 2002-04; Vice-President, Romanian Libraries Federation, 2000-09; President, Association of Librarians and Documentarists of Romania, 1996-; General Manager, Metropolitan Library, Bucharest, 1996-. Publications: Scientific Research Studies Regarding the Beginning of Printing in Romania, 1979-2006; Notes, Forwards and Supervised Books, 1990-2001; Bibliography of Bucharest Book, from its origins up to present (4 volumes), 2006-07; Publishers and Print Houses in Bucharest, from origins up to present, 2007; History of Books in Bucharest, from origins up to present, 2007; Founder, National Virtual Library of Romania DACOROMANICA (www.dacoromanica.ro), 2008; Chief Editor, Biblioteca Bucurestilor, 1998-; Chief Editor, BBF, Romanian version, 2008-; Chief Editor, Literatorul magazine, 2010. Honours: National Award for Book Rennaisance, Ministry of Culture, 2002; National Cultural Award, President of Romania, 2002; Romanian Cultural Radio Award for Science Department, 2004; Excellence Diploma, Brazilian Ambassador in Romania, 2005. Memberships: Romanian Librarians Association; Executive Committee, Metropolitan Libraries Section, IFLA (formerly INTAMEL), 1998-2002; EBLIDA; Romanian Libraries Federation; NAPLE. Address: Str Tache Ionescu nr 4, Sector 1, 010354, Bucharest, Romania. E-mail: florinrotaru@bmms.ro Website: www.bibliotecametropolitana.ro

ROTENBERG Vadim, b. 5 August 1941, Kirov, USSR. Physician; Scientist. m. Samarovich Nataly, 2 daughters. Education: MD, 1st Moscow Medical Institute, 1964; Postgraduate Student, Academy of Sciences, USSR, 1966-69; PhD, 1970; DSc, 1979. Appointments: Junior Doctor, City Hospital, Moscow, 1964-66; Junior Scientist, 1st Moscow Medical Institute, 1969-78, Senior Scientist, 1978-88, Head of Laboratory, 1988-90; Emigration to Israel, 1990; Head Laboratory Abarbanel Mental Health Centre Bat-Iam, Israel, 1992-2001; Senior Lecturer, Tel Aviv University, 1995-; Head Psychologic Project Zionist Forum, 1996-2002. Publications: Over 150 scientific articles in professional journals; Books: The Adaptive Function of Sleep, 1982; Search Activity and Adaption, 1984; Self Image and Behaviour, 2001; Dreams, Hypnosis and Brain Activity, 2001. Honours: Best Annual Science Publication, Moscow Medical Institute, 1982, 1984; Wolfsson Grant for Outstanding Scientists, Tel-Aviv, 1992; Listed in Who's Who publications. Memberships: European Society Sleep Research; International Psychophysiological Society; New York Academy of Sciences. Address: Abarbanel Mental Health Centre, Keren Kayemet 15, Bat-Yam, Israel.

ROTH Tim, b. 14 May 1961, Dulwich, England. Actor. 1 son with Lori Baker, m. Nikki Butler, 1993, 2 sons. Education: Brixton and Camberwell College of Art. m. Nikki Butler, 1993, 2 sons (1 son from previous relationship). Career: Fringe groups including: Glasgow Citizens Theatre, The Oval House and the Royal Court; Appeared on London stage in Metamorphis; Numerous TV appearances; Films: The Hit; A World Apart; The Cook, The Thief, His Wife and Her Lover; Vincent and Theo; Rosencrantz and Guildenstern are Dead; Jumpin at the Boneyard; Resevoir Dogs; Bodies Rest and Motion; Pulp Fiction; Little Odessa; Rob Roy; Captives; Four Rooms; Hoodlums; Everyone Says I Love You; Liar; The War Zone (director); The Legend of 1900, Vatel; Lucky Numbers; Planet of the Apes; Invincible; The Musketeer; Emmett's Mark; Whatever We Do; To Kill A King; With It, 2004; The Beautiful Country, 2004; Silver City, 2004; New France, 2004; The Last Sign, 2004; Don't Come Knockin', 2005; Dark Water, 2005; Jump Shot, 2005; Even Money, 2006; Youth Without Youth, 2007; Funny Game US, 2007; Virgin

Territory, 2007; The Incredible Hulk, 2008; King Conqueror, Skellig, 2009; Arbitrage, The Absinthe Drinkers, Broken, 2012. Address: Ilene Feldman Agency, 8730 West Sunset Boulevard, Suite 490, Los Angeles, CA 90069, USA.

ROTHSCHILD Evelyn de (Sir), b. 29 August 1931. Banker. m. (1) Victoria Schott, 1972, dissolved 2000, 2 sons, 1 daughter, (2) Lynn Forester, 2000. Education: Trinity College, Cambridge. Appointments: Chairman, Economist Newspaper, 1972-89, United Racecourses Ltd, 1977-94, British Merchant Banking and Securities Houses Association (formerly Accepting Houses Committee), 1985-89; Chairman, N M Rothschild and Sons Ltd, 1976-. Address: N M Rothschild & Sons Ltd, New Court, St Swithin's Lane, London, EC 4, England.

ROTTE Karl Heinz, b. 18 October 1933, Pasewalk, Germany. Retired Radiologist. m. Ursula Kambach, 1 son. Education: Studies at Humboldt University, Berlin, Germany, 1953-58; MD, 1958; Resident, General Hospital Prenzlau, Germany, 1959-62. Appointments: Specialisation in Diagnostic Radiology, Robert-Rössle Cancer Research Institute, Berlin-Buch, 1962-77; Habilitation, 1974; Chairman, Department Diagnostic Radiology, Lung Research Institute Berlin-Buch, 1977-80; Chairman, Department of Computed Tomography and Department of Diagnostic Radiology, Cancer Research Institute, Berlin-Buch, 1980-96; Interim Chairman, Department of Diagnostic Radiology, Kuwait Cancer Control Centre, 1984-86; Professor of Diagnostic Radiology, Academy of Sciences, Berlin, 1987. Publications: 2 monographs: Computer aided diagnosis of peripheral bronchial cancer, 1977; Computed tomography in oncology, 1989; 200 publications in scientific journals and book contributions. Honours: Leibnitz Medal, Academy of Sciences, Berlin, 1974; W-Friedrich Award, Society of Radiology of Germany, 1976. Memberships: German Roentgen Society; Roentgen Society of Berlin. Address: Grabbe-Allee 14, D-13156 Berlin, Germany. E-mail: krotte@t-online.de

ROURKE Mickey Philip Andre, b. 16 September 1952, New York, USA, Actor; Boxer. m. (1) Debra Fuer, 1981, divorced 1989, (2) Carre Otis, 1992, divorced 1998. Education: Actor's Studio, New York, USA. Career: Film appearances include: Fade to Black, 1941, 1979; Heaven's Gate, 1980; Body Heat, 1981; Diner, 1982; Eureka, 1983; Rumblefish, 1983; Rusty James, 1983; The Pope of Greenwich Village, 1984; 9½ Weeks, 1984; Year of the Dragon, 1985; Angel Heart, 1986; A Prayer for the Dying, 1986; Barfly, 1987; Johnny Handsome, 1989; Homeboy, 1989; Francesco, 1989; The Crew, 1989; The Desperate Hours, 1990; Wild Orchid, 1990; On the Sport, 1990; Harley Davidson and the Marlboro Man, 1991; White Sands, 1992; FTW; Fall Time; Double Time; Another 9½ Weeks; The Rainmaker, 1997; Love in Paris, 1997; Double Team, 1997; Buffalo '66, 1997; Thursday, 1998; Shergar, 1999; Shades, 1999; Out in Fifty, 1999; The Animal Factory, 2000; Get Carter, 2000; The Pledge, 2001; The Hire: Follow, 2001; Picture Claire, 2001; They Crawl, 2001; Spun, 2002; Masked and Anonymous, 2003; Once Upon A Time in Mexico, 2003; Driv3r (voice), 2004; Man on Fire, 2004; Domino, 2005; Stormbreaker, 2006; The Wrestler, 2008; Killshot, 2008; 13, 2010; Iron Man 2, The Expendables, Passion Play, 2010; Black Gold, Immortals, 2011. Honours: BAFTA Award, Best Actor, 2009; Golden Globe Award, Best Actor, 2009.

ROUX Albert Henri, b. 8 October 1935, Smur-en-Broinnais, France. Chef; Restaurateur. m. Monique Merle, 1959, 1 son, 1 daughter. Appointments: Military service, Algeria; Founder (with brother Michel Roux), Le Gavroche Restaurant, London (now co-owner with son Michel J), 1967-; The Waterside Inn, Bray (now sole owner), 1972-; Opened 47 Park Street Hotel, 1981; Opened Le Poulbot, le gamin, Gavvers, Les Trois Plats and Rouxl Britannia (all as part of Roux Restaurants Ltd), 1969-87; Began consultant practice, 1989. Publications: (with Michel Roux) New Classic Cuisine, 1983; The Roux Brothers on Pâtisserie, 1986; The Roux Brothers on French Country Cooking, 1989; Cooking for Two, 1991. Honours: Maître Cuisinier de France, 1968; Honorary Professor, Bournemouth University, 1995-; Chevalier du Mérite Agricole; Honorary DSc (Council for National Academic Awards), 1987. Memberships: Founder Member, Academy Culinaire de Grande Bretagne. Address: Le Gavroche, 43 Upper Brook Street, London, W1Y 1PF, England.

ROUX Michel André, b. 19 April 1941. Chef; Restaurateur. m. (1) Francoise Marcelle Becquet, divorced 1979, 1 son, 2 daughters. (2) Robyn Margaret Joyce, 1984. Appointments: Commis Patissier and Cuisinier, British Embassy, Paris, 1955-57; Commis Cook to Cécile de Rothschild, 1957-59, Chef, 1962-67; Military Service, 1960-62; Proprietor: Le Gavroche, 1967, The Waterside Inn, 1972, Le Gavroche, Mayfair, 1981. Publications: New Classic Cuisine, 1983; Roux Brothers on Patisserie, 1986; At Home With the Roux Brothers, 1987; French Country Cooking, 1989; Cooking for Two, 1991; Desserts, A Lifelong Passion, 1994; Sauces, 1996; Life is a Menu, autobiography, 2000; Only the Best, 2002; Eggs, 2005. Honours: Numerous Culinary Awards including: Gold Medal, Cuisiniers Français, Paris, 1972; Laureate Restaurateur of the Year, 1985; Chevalier, Ordre National du Mérite, 1987; Ordre des Arts et des Lettres, 1990; Honorary OBE, 2002; Chevalier de la légion d'Honneur, 2004; Numerous other awards and decorations. Memberships: Academician, Culinaire de France, English Branch; Association Relais et Desserts; Association Relais et Chateaux. Address: The Waterside Inn, Ferry Road, Berkshire SL6 2AT, England.

ROWE John Richard, b. 1 August 1942, Woodford, Essex, England. Film and Television Producer and Director. m. Rosa Mary Balls. Education: Royal Society of the Arts Education Certificate in English Literature. Appointments: Cutting Rooms and Film Library, 20th Century Fox, 1958-61; Film Researcher, Associated Redifusion, 1962-65; Film Researcher first major ITV documentary series, The Life and Times of Lord Mountbatten, 1965-69; Film Researcher, Thames Television, 1965-69; Principal Film Researcher, The World at War, 1971-74; Head of Production Research, Thames Television, 1972-82; Head of Programming, Sky Television, 1982-84; Head of Production, British Sky Broadcasting, 1984-93; Executive Producer and set up television side of QVC, The Shopping Channel, 1993-95; Producer and Director TV commercials for various clients, 1995-96; Producer, Director for Screeners, 13 half hour shows on the cinema, 1997; Producer, Director, children's series, Blue's Clues, 1997-2002; Producer, Director, children's comedy show, Havakazoo, 65 half hour shows, 2001; Director, Documentary on Anthony Quinn, Reflections in the Eye, 2001; Director, Monkey Makes, 2003; Director, Big Cook Little Cook, 2004, 2005; Writer/Director, Nickelodeon Jump Up Event, 2005, 2006, 2007-08; Currently, Chief Executive John Rowe Productions. Publications: In depth interview, Televisual, 1983; Contributor to: Satellite Wars, Channel 4, 1993. Honour: Part of the Emmy Award winning team for The World at War. Member, Research Board of Advisors, ABI. Address: 24 Long Hill, Mere, Warminster, Wiltshire, BA12 6LR, England.

ROWLANDS Robert Trevor, b. 15 September 1949, London, England. Scientific Consultant. Education: BSc (Honours), Biological Science, University of Leicester,

England, 1971; PhD, Microbial Genetics, University of Bristol, England, 1974. Appointments: Beit Memorial Medical Research Fellow, University of London, England, post held at Department of Bacteriology, University of Bristol Medical School, 1974-77; Section Head, Genetics and Screening Sections, Glaxo Operations, Ulverston, Cumbria, England, 1977-81; Senior Section Head, Strain Improvement Section, Beecham Pharmaceuticals, Worthing, England, 1981-84; Director, Biotechnology Services, Panlabs Inc, Cardiff, Wales, 1984-98; Self-employed Consultant under the name of Dragon Associates, 1998-. Publications: Over 30 publications in scientific journals and presented at conferences as author and co-author include most recently: The future of the fermentation industry. The shift to developing economic areas of the world, 1999; Rapid and sensitive quantitation of antibiotics in fermentations by electrospray mass spectrometry, 2001; Fermentation yield improvement – Part I. Strain improvement by traditional methods, Part II. Strain improvement by rational screening, Part III. Scale up for selected mutant strains, 2003. Honour; Honorary Lecturer in Applied Microbiology, University of Wales, Cardiff, 1996-2009. Address: 22 Adventurers Quay, Cardiff, CF10 4NP. E-mail: dragonassociates@aol.com

ROWLEY Rosemarie (Rose Mary, Rosemary) Teresa, b. 7 October 1942, Dublin, Ireland. 1 son. Writer; Poet; Essayist. Education: BA, 1969, MLitt, 1984, Trinity College, Dublin, Ireland; Dip Psych, National University of Ireland, 1996. Career: Green Activist, 1983-87; Poet and Essayist. Publications: The Broken Pledge, 1985; The Sea of Affliction (a work of ecofeminism), 1987 reprinted 2010; Betrayal into Origin, 1987, revised 1996; The Wake of Wonder, 1987, revised 1996; Freedom & Censorship – why not have both?, 1987, reprinted 1996; Flight into Reality, 1989, reprinted 2010, issued on CD, 2011; Hot Cinquefoil Star (including The Puzzle Factory, Letter to Kathleen Raine, A Ruby Garland), 2002; Seeing the Wood and the Trees, co-editor, 2003; In Memory of Her, 2008. Honours: Image/Maxwell House Award, 1988; Scottish International Open Poetry Competition, Long Poem Award, 1996, 1997, 2001, 2004. Memberships: MENSA, UK and Ireland; President, Irish Byron Society at United Arts Club; Trinity College Dublin Alumni; Long Poem Group, UK. Address: Booterstown, Co Dublin, Ireland. E-mail: rowleyrosie@yahoo.ie Website: www.rosemarierowley.ie

ROWLING J(oanne) K(athleen), b. 1965, Bristol, England. Writer. (1) divorced, 1 daughter, (2) Neil Murray, 2001, 1 son, 1 daughter. Education: Graduated, University of Exeter, 1986. Publications: Harry Potter and the Philosopher's Stone, 1997; Harry Potter and the Chamber of Secrets, 1998; Harry Potter and the Prisoner of Azkaban, 1999; Harry Potter and the Goblet of Fire, 2000; Quidditch Through the Ages, 2001; Fantastic Beasts and Where to Find Them, 2001; Harry Potter and the Order of the Phoenix, 2003; Harry Potter and the Half-Blood Prince, 2005; Harry Potter and the Dealthy Hallows, 2007; The Tales of Beedle the Bard, 2008; The Casual Vacancy, 2012. Honours: British Book Award Children's Book of the Year, 1997; Rowntree Nestle Smarties Prizes, 1997, 1998; Officer of the Order of the British Empire, 2000; Premio Príncipe de Asturias, 2003; WHSmith People's Choice fiction prize, 2004; Variety UK Entertainment Personality Award, British Industry Film Awards, 2004; LLD, University of Aberdeen, 2006; Pride of Britain Award, 2007; Order of the Forest, Markets Initiative, 2007; Hans Christian Andersen Literature Award, 2010; British Academy Film Awards, 2011; Freedom of the City of London, 2012. Address: c/o Christopher Little Literary Agency, Ten Eel Brook Studios, 125 Moore Park Road, London SW6 4PS, England. Website: www.jkrowling.com

ROWSELL Joyce (Joyce Gwyther), b. 20 November 1928, Mardy, Glamorgan, South Wales. Artist. m. Geoffrey Norman Rowsell, 2 sons. Education: BA, University of London, History of Art, 1988. Career: Draughtswoman, British Telecom, 1947-60; Freelance Illustrator; Self Employed artist exhibiting in UK and abroad; Miniaturist, USA and UK; Permanent Collections: Miniature Artists of America; The Dutch Foundation of Miniature Art; The Hilliard Collection; Miniature Art Society of Florida. Publications: Somerset Magazine, 2001; The Artist (UK), 2001; West Country Life, 2001; Countryman, 2005. Honours: Over 70 awards for miniature painting including 6 at the Royal Miniature Society; Chosen to participate in 300th anniversary exhibition at St Paul's Cathedral, London; Title, Miniature Artist of America. Memberships: Founder Member, Hilliard Society; Miniature Art Society, Florida; Miniature Painters, Sculptors and Gravers Society of Washington DC; Royal Society of Miniature Painters, Sculptors and Gravers; Cider Painters of America; Roswell Fine Art Society, NM. Address: Spring Grove Farm, Milverton, Somerset, TA4 1NW, England. E-mail: joycerowsell@btinternet.com Website: www.joycerowsell.com

ROY Arundhati, b. 24 November 1961, Bengal, India. Writer. m. (1) Gerard da Cunha, divorced, (2) Pradeep Krishen. Education: Delhi School of Architecture. Appointments: Artist; Actress; Film and Television Writer. Publications: The God of Small Things, 1997; The End of Imagination, essay, 1998; The Great Common Good, essay, 1999; The Cost of Living, collected essays, 2002; The Algebra of Infinite Justice, collected essays, 2002; Power Politics, 2002; The Ordinary Person's Guide to Empire, 2004; Public Power in the Age of Empire, 2004; The Checkbook and the Cruise Missile: Conversations with Arundhati Roy, 2004; The Shape of the Beast, 2008; Listening to Grasshoppers: Field Notes on Democracy, 2009. Screenplays: In Which Annie Gives It Those Ones, 1988; Electric Moon, 1992; DAM/AGE, 2002. Contributions to: Periodicals. Honour: Booker Prize, 1997; Lannan Prize for Cultural Freedom, 2002. Address: c/o India Ink Publishing Co Pvt Ltd, C-1, Soami Nagar, New Delhi 110 017, India.

ROY Dinesh, b. 31 May 1974, Thiruvananthapuram, India. Cytogeneticist. m. Indu, 1 son, 1 daughter. Education: M Phil; PhD. Appointments: Cytogeneticist. Publications: More than 50 articles in various national and international journals. Memberships: Indian Society of Human Genetics; Indian Association for the Study of Population; Society of Clinical Chemists of Kerala. Address: Genetika, Centre for Advanced Genetic Studies, Pettah Trivandram, 695024, Kerala, India.

ROY-DELGADO Juan Francisco, b. 25 September 1972, Zaragoza, Spain. Professor. Education: MS, Psychology, University of Valencia, 1998; PhD magna cum laude, University of Zaragoza, 2006. Appointments: Research Fellow, Faculty of Medicine, 2002-06, Professor of Psychology, 2010-, University of Zaragoza; Associate Professor, Department of Psychology, 2006-09; Research Associate, National Centre for Biomedical Network Research into Mental Health, 2007-09. Publications: More than 50 articles in professional journals. Honours: Recipient, International Award, European Association for Consultation Liasion Psychiatry and Psychosomatics & European Conference on Psychosomatic Research, 2003, 2005, 2008; National Award, Geriatric Depression Research Spanish Society Psychogeriatrics, 2002,

2008. Memberships: Spanish Society for Behavioural Medicine & Health Psychology; Spanish Society for Experimental Psychology; American Association for the Advancement of Science; American Psychosomatic Society.

ROZGONYI Ferenc, b. 21 September 1938, Tarcal, Hungary. MD; Professor for Medical Microbiology. m. (1) Gertrúd Mária Szécsi (deceased), (2) Katalin Szitha. Education: Medical Doctor, summa cum laude, Medical University of Debrecen, 1963; Diploma, Specialist for Laboratory Medicine, 1967; Diploma, Specialist for Medical Microbiology, 1979; Medical Microbiology Expert in Forensic Medicine, 1999-. Appointments: USA Scholarship, Department of Pharmacology, Faculty of Medicine, University of Kentucky, Lexington, USA, 1969-70; 1978; Dr Med Sciences, 1988; Visiting Professor, Department of Bacteriology and Epizootology, Swedish University of Agricultural Sciences and Department of Biochemistry, University of Uppsala, 1984-85; Department of Bacteriology, Royal Infirmary, University of Glasgow, 1994; Dr Med/Habil, Debrecen, 1995; University Professor in Debrecen, 1995; Chief, Central Bacterial Diagnostic Laboratory, Medical University, Debrecen, 1993-96; Director, Chairman, Institute of Medical Microbiology, 1996-2003 (retired), PhD Programme Leader (10 PhD student qualifications), Doctoral School, 1997-2008, University Professor, Medical and Dental Microbiology, 2003-08, University Professor, Scientific and Microbiology Diagnostic Advisor, Department of Dermatology, Venerology and Dermatooncology, National STD Diagnostic Center, 2008-, Semmelweis University, Budapest. Publications: 140 peer-reviewed articles; 16 conference proceedings; Around 480 lectures and posters presented in national and international conferences; 3 notebooks; 52 book chapters; 3 books on medical microbiology; Author: (manual) Rapid Microbiology Diagnostic Methods for General Practitioners, 1994; Clinical Microbiology Fast Diagnostics, 2006; Oral Microbiology, Immunity, Diagnostics and Infection-Control, 2007. Honours: Eminent Student Medal, Ministry of Education, 1957; Doubly awarded by Hungarian Academy of Sciences, 1972, 1985; Honoured twice for excellent teaching, Ministry of Public Health, 1980, Ministry of Welfare, 1991; L Batthyány – Strattmann Award, Minister of Public Health, Welfare and Family Affairs of Hungary, 2003, in recognition of his outstanding professional activity and achievement of several decades; Recipient, Doctoral School Medal, Semmelweis University, 2000; Honourable Certification, Hungarian Association for Innovation, 2003; Gold Seal-Ring, Ignác Semmelweis plaquette, Semmelweis University, 2003; Rezső Manninger plaquette, Hungarian Society for Microbiology, 2003; Pro Universitate, Semmelweis University, 2008. Memberships: Chairman, Curators Board for the Foundation of Struggle for Health, Hungary, 1990-; Executive Board, 1991-2007, Secretary, 1997-2007, Hungarian Society of Chemotherapy; Hungaria Helvetia Association, Debrecen, 1991-2004; Editorial Boards: J Chemotherapy, 1993-96; Zbl Bakt, Ab I, 1994-97; Acta Microbiologica et Immunologica Hungarica, 1996-; Hungarian Venerology Archive, 1998-; Board of Advisors, Focus Medicinae, 1999-; Member, Hungarian Medical Chamber, 1992-; European Society for Clinical Microbiology and Infectious Diseases, 1992-, Hungarian Representative at its European Council, 2001-05; New York Academy of Science, 1997-; World-wide Hungarian Medical Academy, 1999-; American Association for the Advancement of Science, 2002-; ECDC Roster of Scientists, 2005-; Chairman, Curators Board for the Foundation of the Hungarian Society of Microbiology, 2008-. Address: Department of Dermatology, Venerology and Dermatooncology, Semmelweis University, Maria utca 41, Budapest, H-1085, Hungary. E-mail: ferenc.rozgonyi@bor.sote.hu

ROZSÍVAL Pavel, b. 27 September 1950, Cheb, Czech Republic. Ophthalmologist; Surgeon; Educator. m. Iva Fišerová, 1 son, 1 daughter. Education: MD, Charles University, Prague, 1974; Diploma in Nuclear Chemistry, Czech Technical University, 1977; PhD, 1979; Board Certified, 1981; Associate Professor, 1991; Professor, 1996. Appointments: Scientific Worker, Charles University, Hradec Králové, 1979-84; Head, District Department, Ophthalmology, Teplice, 1984-86; Head of Regional Department, Ophthalmology, Ústí nad Labem, 1986-93; Head of Department, Ophthalmology, Charles University, 1993-; Consultant, National Medical Library, Prague, 1978-92. Publications: Over 350 articles in professional journals; Over 740 lectures; Ophthalmology for Family Physicians; Modern Cataract Surgery; Diabetic Macro and Microangiopathy; Eye Infections; Modern Trends in Ophthalmology II, 2005; Modern Trends in Ophthalmology III, 2006; Textbook of Ophthalmology, 2006; Modern Trends in Ophthalmology IV, 2007; Modern Trends in Ophthalmology V, 2008; Modern Trends in Ophthalmology VI, 2009; Modern Trends in Ophthalmology, 2011. Honour: Medal, 650th Anniversary of Charles University. Memberships: Czech Ophthalmological Society, President, 1997-2006; Scientific Advisory Board, Czech Ministry of Health, 1998-2004; Czech Glaucoma Society; Czech Society for Cataract and Refractive Surgery; American Academy of Ophthalmology; American Society of Cataract and Refractive Surgery; International Society for Cataract Surgery (Binkhorst Society); Deutschesprachigen Gesellschaft für Intraokularlinsenimplantationen; New York Academy of Sciences. Honours: Listed in Who's Who and other national and international biographical dictionaries. Address: Department of Ophthalmology, Charles University, 500 05 Hradec Králové, Czech Republic.

RUBANOV Lev Izrailevich, b. 20 June 1954, Moscow, Russia. Scientific Researcher. m. Galina, 3 sons. Education: MS, Applied Mathematics, Moscow Institute of Electronics and Mathematics, 1976; PhD, Technical Systems Control, Institute for Information Transmission Problems of the Russian Academy of Sciences, 1988. Appointments: Software Engineer to Head of Software Development Group, Computer Center of Oil Products Supply State Committee of Russia, 1976-86; Leading Scientist, Institute for Information Transmission Problems of the Russian Academy of Sciences, Moscow, 1986-. Publications: More than 50 scientific papers in scientific journals worldwide; Books: Computer Understanding of Texts with Errors, 1991; Activity and Understanding – Structure of Action and Orientated Linguistics, 1995. Honours: Honorary Diploma Russian Academy of Sciences, 1999; Gratifying Charter of the President of Russian Academy of Sciences, 1999; Listed in international biographical dictionaries. Memberships: Scientific Council, IITP RAS. Address: IITP RAS, 19 Bolshov Karetnyj Per, Moscow 127994, Russia. E-mail: rubanov@iitp.ru

RUCKMAN Robert Julian Stanley, b. 11 May 1939, Uxbridge, Middlesex, England. Chartered Engineer; Civil Servant. m. Josephine Margaret Trentham, 1 son, deceased 31 January 2005, 1 daughter. Education: ONC, Electrical Engineering, 1957-60, HNC, Electrical and Electronic Engineering, 1960-62; IERE Endorsements, 1963, Harrow Technical College; MSc Transport Studies, Cranfield University, 1974-75. Appointments: Computer Testing and Commissioning, Elliott Bros Ltd, Borehamwood, Hertfordshire, 1961-64; Logic and Systems Designer, Serck Controls, Leamington Spa, Warwickshire, 1964-66; Research into satellite digital communication systems, Technical Staff, System Sciences Corporation, Falls Church, USA, 1966-67; Transitron Electronic Corporation, Boston, USA, 1967-68; J Langham Thompson Ltd, Luton, Bedfordshire, 1968-70; Ministry of Transport, 1970-74; Birmingham Regional Office, Department of Transport, 1975-78; Cost Benefit Analyst, Computer Analyst, Department of Transport Road construction Unit, 1978-87; Computer Manager (Senior Professional Technical Officer), Department of Transport, West Midlands Region, Birmingham, 1987-95; Assessor, British Computer Society Professional Review Panel. Publications: Articles in scientific journals include: A Data Logger Scaler and Alarm Limit Comparator, 1967; Alarm Detection Using Delay Line Storage, 1966; Integral Alarms for Data Loggers, 1967; The Effects of Trip Characteristics on Interurban Model Choice, 1975; Guide for WMRO Geographical Information System, 1991. Honours: Department of Transport Award in recognition of work for development of Accident Analysis Geographical Information System, 1991; UCC International Peace Prize, ABI, 2005; Man of the Year, 2004-2007; World Lifetime Achievement Award, 2005; Fellow, ABI; Lifetime Deputy Governor, ABI; Hall of Fame, ABI, 2005-06; Research Fellow, ABI; Ambassador of Knowledge: Cambridge University 2010 (ABI); Listed in various biographical dictionaries. Memberships: Member of the Institution of Electrical Engineers; Member of The British Computer Society; Fellow, Institution of Analysts and Programmers; Member, Institute of Logistics and Transport; Chartered Engineer (C.Eng); European Engineer (Eur-Ing); Supporter of the Cranfield Trust. Address: 13 Alexander Avenue, Droitwich Spa, Worcestershire WR9 8NH, England. E-mail: robert_ruckman@tinyworld.co.uk

RUDKIN (James) David, b. 29 June 1936, London, England. Dramatist. m. Alexandra Margaret Thompson, 3 May 1967, 2 sons, 1 deceased, 2 daughters. Education: MA, St Catherine's College, Oxford, 1957-61. Appointment: Judith E Wilson Fellow, University of Cambridge, 1984; Visiting Professor, University of Middlesex, 2004-; Honorary Professor, University of Wales, 2006-. Publications: Afore Night Come (stage play), 1964; Schoenberg's Moses und Aron (translation for Royal Opera), 1965; Ashes (stage play), 1974; Cries From Casement as His Bones are Brought to Dublin (radio play), 1974; Penda's Fen (TV film), 1975; Hippolytus (translation from Euripides), 1980; The Sons of Light (stage play), 1981; The Triumph of Death (stage play), 1981; Peer Gynt (translation from Ibsen), 1983; The Saxon Shore (stage play), 1986; Rosmersholm (translation from Ibsen), 1990; When We Dead Waken (translation from Ibsen), 1990; Red Sun (stage play), 2011; Merlin Unchained (stage play), 2011; Opera Libretti: The Grace of Todd, music by Gordon Crosse, 1969; Inquest of Love, music by Jonathan Harvey, 1993; Broken Strings, music by Param Vir, 1994; Black Feather Rising, music by Param Vir, 2008. Book: Dreyer's Vampyr (monograph), 2005. Contributions to: Drama; Tempo; Encounter; Theatre Research Journal. Honours: Evening Standard Most Promising Dramatist Award, 1962; John Whiting Drama Award, 1974; Obie Award, New York, 1977; New York Film Festival Gold Medal for Screenplay, 1987; European Film Festival Special Award, 1989; Sony Silver Radio Drama Award, 1994. Memberships: Hellenic Society. Address: c/o Casarotto Ramsay and Associates Ltd, Waverley House, 7-12 Noel Street, London W1F 8GQ, England.

RUDOLF (Ian) Anthony, b. 6 September 1942, London, England. Literary Critic; Poet; Translator; Publisher. Divorced, 1 son, 1 daughter. Education: BA (Modern Languages Tripos, Part One; Social Anthropology Part Two) Trinity College, Cambridge, 1964; Diploma, British Institute, Paris, 1961. Appointments: Co-Founder and Editor, Menard Press, London, 1969; Adam Lecturer, Kings' College, London, 1990; Pierre Rouve Memorial Lecturer, University of Sofia, 2001; Visiting Lecturer, Arts and Humanities, London Metropolitan University, 2001-2003; Royal Literary Fund Fellow, University of Hertfordshire, 2003-2004, 2004-2005; Royal Literary Fund Fellow, University of Westminster, 2005-2008. Publications: The Same River Twice, 1976; After the Dream: Poems 1964-79, 1980; Primo Levi's War Against Oblivion (literary criticism), 1990; Mandorla (poetry), 1999 and 2007; The Arithmetic of Memory (autobiography), 1999; Kafka's Doll, 2007; Engraved in Flesh, 2007; Zigzag (poetry), 2010; Silent Conversations: A Reader's Life, 2013; A Vanished Hand, 2013; Translations include: Yesterday's Wilderness Kingdom (poetry) by Yves Bonnefoy, 2001; Blood from the Sky (novel) by Piotr Rawicz, 2004; Contributions to periodicals. Honours: Chevalier de l'Ordre des Arts et des Lettres, 2004; Fellow, Royal Society of Literature, 2005; Fellow, English Association, 2010. Address: 8 The Oaks, Woodside Avenue, London N12 8AR, England. E-mail: anthony.rudolf@virgin.net

RUENGSAKULRACH Permyos, b. 4 October 1966, Bangkok, Thailand. m. Kanokrat Limnitda. Education: MD, 1990, Diploma, Thai Board of General Surgery, 1994, School of Medicine, Prince of Songkla University, Thailand; Diploma, Thai Board of Thoracic Surgery, Mahidol University, 1996; PhD, Faculty of Medicine, Dentistry and Health Sciences, University of Melbourne, Australia, 2001; PhD, Faculty of Science, Department of Mathematics, Mahidol University, Thailand, 2007. Appointments: Lecturer, Department of Surgery, Prince of Songkla University, 1990-96; Fellow in Cardiac Surgery, Townsville General Hospital, Queensland, Australia, 1997; Fellow in Cardiac Surgery, 1996-2001, Honorary Fellow, Department of Surgery, 2000-01, The University of Melbourne; Cardiac Surgeon, Heart Institute, 2001-03, Vice Chairman, Research Ethics Committee, 2002-03, St Louis Hospital and Foundation, Bangkok; Honorary Cardiac Surgeon, Ramathibodi Hospital, Mahidol University, 2002-03; Fellow in Cardiovascular Surgery, University of Toronto, Canada, 2003-04; Cardiac Surgeon, Bangkok Heart Hospital, 2004-. Publications: Numerous articles in professional journals; 2 books. Honours: TAG Young Achievers Award, 1998; Finalist, Ralph Reader Prize Presentation, 1998; Finalist, Vivien Thomas Young Investigator Award, 1998; Investigators Award in Clinical Research, 1999; Travel Award, 2000; Finalist, TAG Young Achievers Award, 2000; Royal Golden Jubilee PhD Program, 2001; Governor's Community Service Awards, 2003; Semifinalist, Young Investigator Award, 2007; Listed in international biographical dictionaries. Memberships: Medical Council of Thailand; Medical Association of Thailand; Royal College of Surgeons of Thailand; Australia Thailand Association; Society of Thoracic Surgeons of Thailand; American College of Chest Physicians; International Society for Minimally Invasive Cardiothoracic Surgery; European Association for Cardio-Thoracic Surgery; Society of Thoracic Surgeons. Address: Division of Cardiac Surgery, Bangkok Heart Hospital, 2 Soi Soonvijai 7, New Petchburi Road, Bangkok 10320, Thailand. E-mail: lpermyos@hotmail.com

DICTIONARY OF INTERNATIONAL BIOGRAPHY 36th EDITION

RUIN Olof Kristian, b. 8 November 1927, Helsinki, Finland. Lars Hierta Professor of Political Science (Retired). m. Inger Björck, 3 sons. Education: BA, 1948, MA, 1954, PhD, 1960, Lund University. Appointments: Associate Professor, Lund University, 1966; Associate Professor, 1969-73, Professor, 1973-93, Stockholm University; Visiting Professor, University of Michigan, 1971-72, University of California, 1981, 1991; Member of the Board, International Political Science Association, 1982-88; Member of the Board, European Consortium of Political Research, 1976-82; Dean, Stockholm University, 1974-84; Deputy Chancellor of Swedish Universities and Colleges, 1978-79; Chairman, The Swedish Institute for Future Studies, 1987-95; Chairman, Swedish Research Council on Humanities and Social Sciences, 1995-98; Member of the Board, European University Institute, 1997-2001; Chairman, The Swedish Foundation for International Co-operation in Resaerch and Higher Educaiton, 1998-99; President, The Swedish School of Advanced Asian Pacific Studies, 2001-05; Chairman, several Royal Commissions on constitutional matters. Publications: Books about Swedish Politics; Tage Erlander Serving the Welfare State, 1946-1969; Articles in international and Swedish academic journals; Articles on current political issues in daily papers; Memoir, Trilogy on Finland, the US and Sweden respectively. Memberships: The Royal Academy of Letters, History and Antiquities; Finnish Academy of Sciences; Finnish Society of Sciences and Letters. Address: Department of Political Science, Stockholm University, 106 91 Stockholm, Sweden. E-mail: olof.ruin@statsvet.su.se

RUMANE Abdul Razzak, b. 8 June 1948, Chandve, India. Electrical Engineer; Consultant. m. Noor Jehan, 1 son, 1 daughter. Education: BE, (Electrical), Government College of Engineering, Marathwada University, Aurangabad, India, 1972; Diploma in Modern Management, British Career Training College, 1982; Diploma in International Trade, British Management Association, 1983; MS, General Engineering, Kennedy-Western University, USA, 2002; PhD, Kennedy Western University, USA, 2005; Honorary Doctorate in Engineering, The Yorker International University, Italy, 2007. Appointments: Trainee Engineer, Electro Sales Corporation, 1972-73; Assistant Officer, Ruttonsha Electronics, 1973-76; Assistant Engineer, Mandovi Pellets Ltd, 1976-79; Staff Engineer, Crompton Greaves Ltd, 1979-80; Officer, Dynacraft Machine Co, Ltd, 1981-83; Officer/Engineer, Toyo Engineering, India, Ltd, 1981-83; Electrical Engineer, Mansour Al Subaie Est, Kuwait, 1983-84; Electrical Engineer, Abdullah Al Otaibi Est. Kuwait, 1984-86; Electrical Engineer, Jassim Shaban and Sons Co. Kuwait, 1986-90; Electrical Engineer, Al Othman Centre for Architectural and Engineering Design, Al Khobar, Saudi Arabia, 1991; Senior Electrical Engineer, Pan Arab Consulting Engineers, Bahrain and Kuwait, 1991-99; Senior Electrical Engineer, Dar Al Handasah (Shair and Partners), Kuwait, 1999-2004; Senior Electrical Engineer, Pan Arab Consulting Engineers, Kuwait, 2004-08; Senior Electrical Engineer, SSH International, Kuwait, 2008-. Publications: Numerous papers and articles in technical journals and newsletters; Author, Quality Management in Construction Projects; Author, Quality Management in Construction Projects. Honours: Listed in numerous international biographical publications, Deputy Director-General, International Order of Merit, Lifetime Achievement Award, IBC; Top 100 Engineers of IBC; Continental Governor, American Order of Excellence, Magna Cum Laude, ABI; Global Award of Accomplishment, Who's Who Institute, USA; The World Order of Science-Education-Culture with title of "Cavalier", European Academy of Informatisation; Medal of Science and Peace, Albert Schweitzer International University Foundation; Bharat Gaurav Award, Gem of India Award, Lifetime Achievement, India International Friendship Society; ASIF Gold Medal, Albert Schweitzer International Foundation; Meritorious Service Bronze Medal, The Sovereign Order of the Knights of Justice. Memberships: Associate Member, American Society of Civil Engineers; Fellow, ABI; Patron, IBA; Fellow, The Institution of Engineers, India; Senior Member, Institute of Electrical and Electronics Engineers (USA); American Society for Quality; Member, Save International (The Value Society); Kuwait Society of Engineers; Project Management Institute; Chartered Engineer, IEI; Honorary Fellowship, Chartered Management Association, Hong Kong; MEW Kuwait Registration (Supervisor First Class); Member, National Geographic Society; Member, London Diplomatic Academy; Member, Board of Governors; Honorary Vice Governor, International Benevolent Research Forum; Honorary Fellow, Chartered Management Association (HK); Associate, Value Specialist (SAVE); President, Frontliners, Kuwait. Address: PO Chandve, Talk – Mahad District, Raigad, Maharashtra, India, 402301. E-mail: rarazak@yahoo.com

RUMELT Shimon, b. Jaffa, Israel. Ophthalmologist. Education: BSc, 1983, MD, 1990, Diploma in Ophthalmology, 1994, Tel Aviv University. Appointments: Intern, Assaf Harofeh Medical Centre, Zerifin, 1988-89; Fellow, Tribhuvan University Teaching Hospital, Nepal, 1989; Resident, 1989-94, Senior Ophthalmologist, 1994-95, Department of Ophthalmology, Western Galilee Regional Hospital, Nahariya; Clinical Fellow, Oculoplastics, Massachusetts Eye & Ear Infirmary, Boston, USA, 1995-96; Clinical Fellow, Retina, Boston University Medical Center, 1996-97; Senior Ophthalmologist, Hadassah University Hospital, Jerusalem, 1997-2002; Research Ophthalmologist, 1997-, Senior Ophthalmologist, 2002-, Western Galilee Medical Centre, Nahariya; Senior Ophthalmologist, Leumit Health Care Provider, 1997-. Publications: Numerous articles in professional journals; 2 books. Honours: Outstanding Student Awards, Tel Aviv University, 1981-84; Dr Dov Ehrlich Prize for Outstanding Presentation of a Family, 1988; World Fellowship Award, Israel Medical Association, 1995; Retina Foundation Travel Award, Association for Research in Vision & Ophthalmology, 1997; Best Lecture Award, Israel Ophthalmology Society, 2000; Achievement Award, American Academy of Ophthalmology, 2004. Memberships: Israel Medical Association; Israel Ophthalmological Society; Israel Society for Eye & Vision Research; American Academy of Ophthalmology; Association for Research in Vision & Ophthalmology; American Society for Microbiology. Address: Western Galilee Nahariya Medical Center, Nahariya 22100, Israel. Website: www.health-tip.info

RUMSEY Patricia Margaret (Sister Francisca), b. 1 January 1944, Rugby, England. Nun; Lecturer. Education: Rugby Girls' High School, 1955-60; Wolsey Hall, Oxford, 1966-70; MA, 2001, PhD, 2006, Post doctoral Licence, 2009, University of Wales, Lampeter, 1998-2009. Appointments: Part time Lecturer, University of Wales, Lampeter; Part time Lecturer, Sarum College, Salisbury. Publications: Book, Sacred Time in Early Christian Ireland, 2007; Women of the Church: The Religious Experience of Monastic Women, 2011; Numerous articles in professional journals. Honours: Visiting Scholar, Sarum College, Salisbury. Memberships: Society for Liturgical Society; Catholic Theological Association of Great Britain. E-mail: p.rumsey@hotmail.co.uk

RUSH Geoffrey, b. 6 July 1951, Toowoomba, Queensland, Australia. Actor. m. Jane Menelaus, 1988, 1 son, 1 daughter. Education: Jacques Lecoq of Mime, Paris. Career: Began with Queensland Theatre Company; Films include: The Wedding, 1980; Starstruck, 1982; Twelfth Night, 1986; Midday Crisis, 1994; Dad and Dave on our Selection, 1995; Shine; Children of the Revolution, 1996; Elizabeth, 1998; Shakespeare in Love, 1998; The Magic Pudding, 1999; Mystery Men, 1999; House on Haunted Hill, 1999; Quills, 1999; The Tailor of Panama, 2000; Lantana, 2001; Frida, 2002; The Banger Sisters, 2002; Swimming Upstream, 2003; Ned Kelly, 2003; Finding Nemo (voice), 2003; Pirates of the Caribbean: The Curse of the Black Pearl, 2003; Intolerable Cruelty, 2003; Harvie Krumpet (voice), 2003; Munich, 2005; Candy, 2006; Pirates of the Caribbean: At World's End, Elizabeth: The Golden Age, 2007; $9.99, 2008; Bran Nue Dae, 2009; Legend of the Guardians: The Owls of Ga'Hoole, The King's Speech, Lowdown, The Warrior's Way, 2010; Pirates of the Caribbean: On Stranger Tides, Green Lantern, The Eye of the Storm, 2011; Theatre includes; Hamlet; The Alchemist; The Marriage of Figaro; The Small Poppies; TV includes: Menotti, 1980-81; The Burning Piano, 1992; Mercury, 1995; Bonus Mileage, 1996; The Life and Death of Peter Sellers (TV), 2004. Honours: Academy and BAFTA Awards, Australian Film Institute Award, Golden Globe Award for Shine; BAFTA Award for Best Supporting Actor, 1998; Golden Globe, Best Actor in a Miniseries or TV Movie, 2005; Screen Actors Guild Awards, 2005; Australian Film Institute Longford Life Achievement Award, 2009; Santa Barbara International Film Festival Montecito Award, 2011; Australian of the Year, 2012. Address: C/o Shanahan Management, PO Box 478, Kings Cross, NSW 2011, Australia.

RUSHDIE (Ahmed) Salman, Sir, b. 19 June 1947, Bombay, India. Writer. m. (1) Clarissa Luard, 1976, dissolved 1987, died 1999, 1 son, (2) Marianne Wiggins, 1988, divorced 1993, 1 stepdaughter, (3) Elizabeth West, 1997, divorced, 1 son, (4) Padma Lakshmi, 2004, separated. Education: MA, King's College, Cambridge. Appointments: Actor, Fringe Theatre, London, 1968-69; Advertising Copywriter, 1969-73; Part-time Copywriter, 1976-80. Publications: Grimus, 1975; Midnight's Children, 1981; Shame, 1983; The Jaguar Smile: A Nicaraguan Journey, 1987; The Satanic Verses, 1988; Haroun and The Sea of Stories, 1990; Imaginary Homelands (essays), 1991; The Wizard of Oz, 1992; The Ground Beneath Her Feet, 1999; Fury, 2001; Step Across the Line: Collected Non-Fiction 1992-2002, 2002; Telling Tales (anthology), 2004; Shalimar the Clown, 2005; The Enchantress of Florence, 2008. TV Films: The Painter and The Pest, 1985; The Riddle of Midnight, 1988; Contributions to professional journals. Honours: Booker McConnell Prize for Fiction, 1981; Arts Council Literary Bursary, 1981; English Speaking Union Literary Award, 1981; James Tait Black Memorial Book Prize, 1981; Prix du Meilleur Livre Etranger, 1984; Nominated for Whitbread Prize, 1988; Booker Prize, 1993; Commander of the Order of Arts and Letters of France, 1999, Knighted, 2007. Memberships: PEN; Production Board, British Film Institute; Advisory Board, Institute of Contemporary Arts; FRSL; Executive, Camden Committee for Community Relations, 1975-82. Address: c/o Aitken & Stone Ltd, 29 Fernshaw Road, London SW10 0TG, England.

RUSHIN Linda Jordan, b. 13 May 1959, Sandersville, Georgia, USA. Writer. Divorced, 2 sons, 3 daughters. Education: Data Processing & Clerical Certificate, IBM Atlanta, Georgia, 1979; Business Management Word Processing VII, Vocational/Technical School, Atlanta Urban League, 1984; Associate Degree, Georgia Military College, Milledgeville, 1984; Licensed Insurance Agent, 1991; Bachelor of Arts degree, Organizational Management, Ashton University, 2009. Appointments: Executive Producer, Haywood's Studio, 1977-84; Co-owner, Rushins Income Tax Service, 1985-95;Teacher, Washington County High School Board of Education, 1994-2009; Marketing Representative, Glamour Magic, 1995-98; Independent Contractor, Pinkerton/Choice, 1999. Publications: Song, Believe in Yourself; Poems published in professional journals. Honours: Listed in international biographical dictionaries. Memberships: Building for Equal Equality, Atlanta Urban League; Elizabeth Baptist Church, Atlanta; NAFE; ASCAP; Atlanta Songwriters' Association; Tennille Grove Baptist; Springfield Baptist Church. Address: 512 Reeve Street, Sandersville, GA 31082, USA. E-mail: rushin9995@bellsouth.net

RUSHMAN Geoffrey Boswall, b. 20 August 1939, Northampton, England. Medical Practitioner. m. Gillian Mary, 3 daughters. Education: MB BS, St Bartholomew's Hospital, 1957-62; Conjoint Diploma (MRCS LRCP), 1962; Royal College of Anaesthetists (FFARCS), 1970. Appointments: Trainee Anaesthetist, St Bartholomew's Hospital, 1968-73; Consultant Anaesthetist, Southend Hospital, 1974-99; Examiner Royal College of Anaesthetists, 1991-99; Council Member, 1985-88, Secretary, 1991-92, President, 1999-2000, Section of Anaesthetics, Royal Society of Medicine; Council Member, Royal Society of Medicine, 2001-2005; Licensed Lay Minister, Diocese of Oxford. Publications: Parenteral Nutrition for the Surgical Patient (jointly), 1971; Synopsis of Anaesthesia (jointly), 8th, 9th, 10th, 11th and 12th editions, 1977, 1982, 1987,1993, 1999 (with Greek, Polish, Spanish, Italian and German Editions); Short History of Anaesthesia (jointly), 1996; Short Answer Questions in Anaesthesia, 1997. Honours: Hichens Prize (jointly), 1962; Police Award for Bravery, 1969; Association of Anaesthetists Prize for contributions to anaesthesia (jointly), 1971. Address: Aylesbury Road, Thame, Oxon, England.

RUSPOLI Francesco, b. 11 December 1958, Paris, France. Artist; Painter. Education: MA, Set and Costume design, Central St Martin, England, 1995. Career: Abstract figurative painter and colourist; Theatre designer of set and costumes; Exhibitions: Numerous exhibitions in UK and abroad 1983- include most recently: Group shows: Galiere d'Art, Nice, 2000; Agora Gallery, New York, 2000, 2001; Llewellyn Alexander Gallery, London, 2000, 2001; Hay's Gallery, London, 2001; Royal Free Hampstead Hospital, London, 2001; Nobleart Gallery, Cambridge, 2001; Salon des Arts, London, 2002; Plus One Plus Two Galleries, London, 2002; Artlands, Norfolk, 2002; DACS, London, 2002; Colouris, London, 2003; One man shows: Sylvia White Gallery, New York, 2000; Ministere des Finances, Paris, 2000; Mayfair Festival, London, 2000, 2003; Hay's Gallery, London, 2001; Artlands, London, 2003, 2004; Set and Costume Design: Shakespeare's Universe, Barbican, 1994; Loves Labours Lost, Cochrane Theatre, 1994; Triangle, Cochrane Theatre, 1995; Commercial, CTVC Studios, 1995; Snuff, London Film Festival, 1995; The May, Barons Court Theatre, 1997; Mind the Gap, Canal Café Theatre, 1999; Commissions: Painting, The Rating and Evaluation Association, London; Painting, Temple, Barristers, London; Mural, Le Cigale Restaurant, London; Mural, Insurance MGA, Nice, France; Painting, Hotel Grau Roig, Andorra; Private collections and museums: Robert Hardy; Dame Felicity Lott; Decia De Pauw; Gauguin Museum, Tahiti; Works in private collections in London, Paris, Tel-Aviv, Barcelona, Rome, Milan, Glasgow, Deauville, Cannes, Nice, Lille, Lyon, New York. Publications: Works featured in Exhibit A Magazine; Observer Magazine.

Honours: Silver Medal, Grand Prix of Rome, 1985; Bronze Medal, Biennial, Villeneuve-Loubet, 1985; Golden Painting, 1986, Silver Medal, 1986, Gold Medal, 1988, Institute of French Culture; Eugene Frometin, Federation Latin, France, 1987; Bronze Medal, Mairie 17e Arrond Paris, France, 1991; Academician, 1994, Knight of the Art, 1998, Academy Geci-Marino, Italy; Gold Medal, Beijing Olympics, China, 2008. Address: 54 Chestnut Grove, Balham, London SW12 8JJ, England. E-mail: info@francesco-ruspoli.com Website: www.francesco-ruspoli.com

RUSSELL Kurt von Vogel, b. 17 March 1951, Springfield, Massachusetts, USA. Actor. m. Season Hubley, 1979, divorced, 1 son, 1 son with Goldie Hawn. Career: Child actor, Disney shows and films; Professional baseball player, 1971-73; Films include: It Happened at the World's Fair, 1963; Unlawful Entry, 1992; Captain Ron, 1992; Tombstone, 1993; Stargate, 1994; Executive Decision, 1996; Escape from LA, 1996; Breakdown, 1997; Soldier, 1998; Vanilla Sky, 2001; Interstate 60, 2002; Dark Blue, 2002; Miracle, 2004; Sky High, 2005; Dreamer: Inspired by a True Story, 2005; Poseidon, 2006; Grindhouse, 2007; Death Proof, 2007; Cutlass, 2007. TV series include: lead role in Travels With Jamie McPheeters, 1963-64; The New Land, 1974; The Quest, 1976; TV films include: Search For the Gods, 1975; The Deadly Tower, 1975; Christmas Miracle in Caulfield USA, 1977; Elvis, 1979; Amber Waves, 1988; Numerous guest appearances. Honours: 5 acting awards; 10 baseball awards; 1 golf championship. Memberships: Professional Baseball Players' Association; Stuntman's Association. Address: Creative Artists' Agency, 9830 Wilshire Boulevard, Beverly Hills, CA 90212-1825, USA.

RUSSELL Martin James, b. 25 September 1934, Bromley, Kent, England. Writer. Publications: No Through Road, 1965; The Client, 1975; Mr T, 1977; Death Fuse, 1980; Backlash, 1981; The Search for Sara, 1983; A Domestic Affair, 1984; The Darker Side of Death, 1985; Prime Target, 1985; Dead Heat, 1986; The Second Time is Easy, 1987; House Arrest, 1988; Dummy Run, 1989; Mystery Lady, 1992; Leisure Pursuit, 1993. Memberships: Crime Writers' Association; Detection Club. Address: 15 Breckonmead, Wanstead Road, Bromley, Kent BR1 3BW, England.

RUSSELL Norman Atkinson, b. 7 August 1943, Belfast, Northern Ireland. Anglican Priest. m. Victoria Christine Jasinska, 2 sons. Education: MA, Churchill College, Cambridge; BD, London. Appointments: Articled Clerk, Cooper Brothers & Company, London, 1966-67; Curate, Christ Church with Emmanuel, Clifton, Bristol, 1970-74; Curate, Christ Church, Cockfosters, London and Anglican Chaplain, Middlesex Polytechnic, 1974-77; Rector of Harwell with Chilton, 1977-84; Priest in Charge of Gerrrards Cross, 1984-88 and Fulmer, 1985-88; Rector of Gerrards Cross and Fulmer, 1988-98; Archdeacon of Berkshire, 1998-. Honour: Honorary Canon, Christ Church, Oxford, 1995-98. Address: Foxglove House, Love Lane, Donnington, Newbury, Berkshire RG14 2JG, England. E-mail: archdber@oxford.anglican.org

RUSSELL Willy, (William Martin Russell), b. 23 August 1947, Liverpool, England. Dramatist; Writer. m. Ann Seagroatt, 1969, 1 son, 2 daughters. Education: Certificate of Education, St Katherine's College of Education, Liverpool. Appointments: Teacher, 1973-74; Fellow, Creative Writing, Manchester Polytechnic, 1977-78. Publications: Theatre: Blind Scouse, 1971-72; When the Reds (adaptation), 1972; John, Paul, George, Ringo and Bert (musical), 1974; Breezeblock Park, 1975; One for the Road, 1976; Stags and Hens, 1978; Educating Rita, 1979; Blood Brothers (musical), 1983; Our Day Out (musical), 1983; Shirley Valentine, 1986; The Wrong Boy (novel), 2000; Films: Dancin' Tru the Dark, 1990; Terraces, 1993. Songs and poetry; Hoovering The Moon (Album), 2003. Television Plays: King of the Castle, 1972; Death of a Young Young Man, 1972; Break In (for schools), 1974; Our Day Out, 1976; Lies (for schools), 1977; Daughter of Albion, 1978; Boy With Transistor Radio (for schools), 1979; One Summer (series), 1980. Radio Play: I Read the News Today (for schools), 1979. Screenplays: Band on the Run, 1979; Educating Rita, 1981. Honours: Honorary MA, Open University; Honorary Director, Liverpool Playhouse. Address: c/o Margaret Ramsay Ltd, 14A Goodwin's Court, St Martin's Lane, London WC2, England.

RUSSELL BEALE Simon, b. 12 January 1961, Penang, Malaya. Actor. Education: Gonville & Caius College, Cambridge; Associate Artist, RSC, 1986; Theatre: Traverse Theatre, Edinburgh; Lyceum, Edinburgh; Royal Court, London; Royal National Theatre; Donmar Warehouse, London; Almeida, London; RSC Productions: The Winter's Tale; The Art of Success; Everyman in his Humour; The Fair Maid of the West; The Storm; Speculators; The Constant Couple; The Man of Mode; Restoration; Mary and Lizzie; Some Americans Abroad; Playing with Trains; Troilus and Cressida; Edward II; Love's Labours Lost; The Seagull; Richard III; The Tempest; King Lear; Ghosts; Othello; Films: Orlando, 1992; Persuasion, 1995; Hamlet, 1996; The Temptation of Franz Shubert, 1997; An Ideal Husband, 1999; Blackadder Back & Forth, 1999; The Gathering, 2002; TV: A Very Peculiar Practice; Downtown Lagos, 1992; The Mushroom Picker, 1993; A Dance to the Music of Time, 1997; The Temptation of Franz Schubert, 1997; Alice in Wonderland, 1999; The Young Visiters, 2003; Dunkirk, 2004. Honours: Royal TV Society Award for Best Actor, 1997; BAFTA Award for Best Actor, 1998; Olivier Award, Best Actor, 2003.

RUSSO René, b. 17 February 1954, California, USA. Actress. m. Dan Gilroy, 1992, 1 daughter. Career: Formerly model Eileen Ford Agency; Film appearances include: Major League, 1989; Mr Destiny; One Good Cop; Freejack; Lethal Weapon 3; In the Line of Fire; Outbreak; Get Shorty; Tin Cup; Ransom; Buddy; Lethal Weapon 4, 1998; The Adventures of Rocky and Bullwinkle, 1999; The Thomas Crown Affair, 1999; Showtime, 2002; Big Trouble, 2002; 2 for the Money, 2005; Yours, Mine and Ours, 2005; Thor, 2011; Thor: the Dark World, 2013; TV appearance: Sable (series). Address: c/o Progressive Artists Agency, 400 South Beverly Drive, Suite 216, Beverly Hills, CA 90212, USA.

RUSTAN Peter Agne, b. 21 February 1941, Köping, Västmanland, Sweden. Mining Engineer. m. Brita Järvhammar, divorced 2002, 1 son, 3 daughters. Education: Mining Engineer, 1965; Technical Licentiate, 1973; Technical Dr, Mining, 1995; Associate Professor, Mining, 1995. Appointments: Stockholm Assistant in Mining, Royal Institute of Technology, 1965-70; Mine Planning Engineer, Luossavaara-Kirunavaara, Malmberget, Sweden, 1971-74; Researcher and Teacher, Lulea University of Technology, Lulea, Sweden, 1974-98; Consultant, 1998-. Secretary-General, International Society of Explosives Engineers – Flagblast Section and the International Organizing Committee for Rock Fragmentation by Blasling Symposia. Publications: Co-author, Underground Ventilation, Stiftelsen Bergteknisk Forskning, Sweden, 1984; Editor-in-Chief, Rock Blasting Terms and Symbols; A A Balkenna, Rotterdam, 1998; Mining and Rock Construction Technology, 2010.

Memberships: International Society of Explosives Engineers, USA. Address: Lagmansvagen 20, SE-954 32 Gammelstad, Sweden. E-mail: agne.rustan@spray.se

RUTHERFORD Greg, b. 17 November 1986, Milton Keynes, England. Athlete. Education: Denbigh School, Bletchley. Career: Long Jump, personal best 8.32m; Sprinter, personal best of 100m in 10.26 seconds; Youngest ever winner (long jump), European Junior Championships, 2005; 8th, Commonwealth Games, 2006; Silver medal (long jump), European Athletics Championships. Gothenburg, Sweden, 2006; Winner (long jump), London Grand Prix, Crystal Palace, 2008; 10th (long jump), Beijing Olympics, 2008; 5th, World Athletics Championships, Berlin, 2009; Silver medal (long jump), Commonwealth Games, 2010; Gold medal (long jump), London Olympics, 2012.

RUTSKAYA Yulia, b. 14 May 1981, Vitebsk, Belarus. Pop Music Singer. Education: Graduate, International Comparative Politics Department, American University of Central Asia, 2002. Appointments: Host, Good Evening with Yulia Rutskaya television programme; Goodwill Ambassador, MIV Kyrgyzstan, 2006. Honours: Miss Kyrgyzstan, 2000; 1st place, Spring of Bishkek, 2002; 1st place, Brdaily kongyuz urlaryn, 2002; Diplomat, Slavonic Bazaar, Vitebsk, 2004; Diplomat, Edir, 2004; 1st place, Kosh Iyldyz, 2009; Diplomat, Golden Voices, 2010; Audience Prize, Canzoni dal mondo, 2010; 4th place, Golden Melody, 2011; Special prize, Reconocimiento artistico, Universong, 2011; 2nd place, Nova Latinitas, 2011; Grand-prix, Evrofest, 2011; Listed in biographical dictionaries. Memberships: American University of Central Asia Alumni Association; World Association of Festivals and Artists. E-mail: yulia.rutskaya@gmail.com Website: www.rutskaya.com

RÜTTGERS Jürgen, b. 26 June 1951, Cologne, West Germany. Minister-President, State of Northrhine-Westphalia. m. 3 children. Education: Law and History studies at university. Appointments: State Chairman, Christian Democratic Union's youth wing, Junge Union, 1980-86; Erftkreis County Chairman, CDU, 1985-99; Chairman, Parliamentary Technology Assessment Commission, 1987-89; Member, Bundestag, 1987-2000; CDU/CSU Party Whip, Bundestag, 1989-90; Chief Whip, CDU/CSU Parliamentary Party, 1990-94; Deputy Chairman, 1993-99, Chairman, 1999-, CDU's North Rhine-Westphalia state branch; Federal Minister for Education, Research and Technology, 1994-98; Deputy Leader, CDU/CSU Parliamentary Party, Bundestag, 1998-2000; Deputy Chairman, Federal CDU, 2000-; Member, Landtag, 2000-; Leader, CDU/CSU Parliamentary Party, Landtag, 2000-05; State Premier, North Rhine-Westphalia, 2005-. Address: Staatskanzlei Nordrhein-Westfalen, 40190 Düsseldorf, Germany. E-mail: juergen.ruettgers@stk.nrw.de

RUZICKA Marek Captain, b. 29 August 1960, Sobeslav, Czech Republic. Naturalist. m. Magdalena Zhofova, 2 sons. Education: MSc, Environmental Engineering, 1984; Postgraduate course, Enzyme Engineering, 1988; Postgraduate studies, Applied Mathematics, 1987; PhD, Chemical Engineering, 1990; Partial study of Physics, Charles University, Prague, 1990-94; Ing-Paed IGIP, 2009. Appointments: Scientist, Institute of Chemical Process Fundamentals, Academy of Sciences, Prague, Czech Republic, 1990-; Associate Professor of Chemical Engineering, Prague Institute of Chemical Technology, Prague, Czech Republic, 2005-; Head of Department of Multiphase Reactors, Institute of Chemical Process Fundamentals, Prague, Czech Republic, 2009-. Publications: Over 30 articles in professional scientific journals; 5 chapters in scientific books. Honours: British Chevening Scholarship, University of Birmingham, 1994-95; Honorary Research Fellow, University of Birmingham. Memberships: Union of Czech Mathematicians and Physicists; Euromech; Golden Jubilee visiting Fellow, University of Mumbai, India, 2007-8. Address: Institute of Chemical Process Fundamentals, Rozvojova 135, 16502 Prague, Czech Republic. E-mail: ruzicka@icpf.cas.cz

RYABINKINA Yelena, b. 21 August 1941, Sverdlovsk, Russia. Ballet Artist; Teacher. Education: Ballet School, Bolshoi Theatre, 1951-59; Moscow School of Choreography, 1959; MB, Russian Academy of Theatre Arts, 1984. Appointments: Debut, Odette & Odille, Swan Lake, State Academic Bolshoi Theatre, 1959; Soloist Principal, Bolshoi Ballet, 1959-81; Classic Choreography Teacher, Moscow Academic School of Choreography, 1983-92; Ballet Mistress, Grigorovich Ballet Company, 1992-93; Senior Choreography Teacher, Moscow State Academy of Choreography, 1999-2004; Head, Department of Classic Choreography, Moscow State University of Culture and Art, 1999-2009. Honours: Winner, International Ballet Competition, Vienna, 1959; Honoured Artists of the Russian Federation, 1967; Order of the Red Banner of Labour, 1976; Best Performance of Contemporary Dance, All-Union Talent Show, 1971; Associate Professor, 2005. Address: c/o Academic Bolshoi State Theatre, Moscow Teatralnaya 1, Russia.

RYAN Meg, b. 19 November 1961, Fairfield, Connecticut, USA. Actress. m. Dennis Quaid, 1991, divorced, 1 son, 1 adopted daughter. Education: New York University. Career: Formerly in TV commercials; TV appearances: As The World Turns; One of the Boys; Amy and the Angel; The Wild Side; Charles in Charge; Owner, Prufrock Pictures; Films: Rich and Famous, 1981; Amytyville III-D; Top Gun; Armed and Dangerous; Innerspace; DOA; Promised Land; The Presidio; When Harry Met Sally; Joe Versus the Volcano; The Doors; Prelude to a Kiss; Sleepless in Seattle; Flesh and Bone; Significant Other; When a Man Loves a Woman; IQ; Paris Match; Restoration; French Kiss, 1995; Two for the Road, 1996; Courage Under Fire, 1996; Addicted to Love, 1997; City of Angels, 1998; You've Got Mail, 1998; Hanging Up, 1999; Lost Souls, 1999; Proof of Life, 2000; Kate & Leopold, 2001; In the Cut, 2003; Against the Ropes, 2004; In the Land of Women, 2007; My Mom's New Boyfriend, 2008; The Deal, 2008; The Women, 2008; Serious Moonlight, 2009; New Year's Eve, 2011. Address: c/o ICM, 8942 Wilshire Boulevard, Beverly Hills, CA 90211, USA.

RYAN Terence J, b. 24 July 1932. Professor. m. Anne, 1968, 1 son, 1 daughter. Education: Doctor of Medicine, Worcester College, Oxford, 1950. Appointments: Green (now Green Templeton) College, Oxford; Adjunct Professor, Jefferson Medical School, Philadelphia, USA; Honorary Professor, Institute of Microcirculation, Beijing, China; Consultant Dermatologist, NHS, Oxford, -1996; Clinical Professor of Dermatology, Emeritus Professor of Dermatology, 1997-, Oxford University; Emeritus Professor, Oxford Brookes University, 1997-; Honorary Professor, Peking University, Nanjing; Adjunct Professor, Department of Physics, Limerick University, Ireland, 2007-; Medical Adviser, St Francis Leprosy Guild; Advisor, Institute of Applied Dermatology, Kasaragod, Kerala, India; Consultant, Wound Healing Unit, Department of Dermatology, Churchill Hospital, Oxford; Consultant, Oxford International Wound Foundation. Publications: Over 570 articles in professional journals on dermatology, international public health, and lymphology. Honours: Awardee and member, Brazilian and Venezuelan

Academies of Medicine; Archibald Gray Medal, British Association of Dermatology; Distinguished Services Award, International League of Dermatological Societies, 2007; Honorary member of numerous National Dermatology Societies; Gold medals, British Association of Dermatology and European Tissue Repair Society; Lifetime Achievement Award, World Union of Wound Healing Societies, 2008. Memberships: International Society of Dermatology; International League of Dermatological Societies; Consultant, LEPRA; Global Initiative for Traditional Systems of Health; Oxford International Biomedical Centre; British Lymphology Interest Group; Hon Life Member, Indian Association of Dermatology, 2011; Adjunct Professor, School of Nursing, University of Missouri, 2011. Address: Brook House, Brook Street, Great Bedwyn, Wiltshire SN8 3LZ, England. E-mail: userry282@aol.com

RYCHNOVSKÁ Milena Jana, b. 17 October 1928, Brno, Czech Republic. Professor. m. Otomar Rychnovský, 2 sons. Education: RNDr, Masaryk University, Brno, 1951; CSc (PhD), 1959, Dr Sc, 1969, Czech Academy of Sciences, Prague. Appointments: Scientist, Czech Academy of Sciences, 1955-90; Assistant Professor, 1990-93, Professor, 1994-2008, Professor Emeritus, 2008-, Palacký University, Olomouc. Publications: Chapter in Grassland Ecosystems, 1979; Chapter in Ecosystems of the World, 1993; Structure and Functioning of Seminatural Meadows, 1993; 2 books on Grasslands; 106 papers. Honours: J G Mendel Award, 2008; M Paulova Award, 2009. Memberships: CZ-IALE; Czech Botanical Society; Slovak Botanical Society; Slovak Ecological Society. Address: Drobneho 44, Brno, CZ-60200, Czech Republic. E-mail: milena.rychnovska@upol.cz

RYDER Winona, b. 29 October 1971, Minnesota, USA. Actress. Education: American Conservatory Theatre, San Francisco. Career: Films include: Lucas, 1986; Beetlejuice, 1988; Great Balls of Fire; Heathers, 1989; Edward Scissorhands, 1990; Bram Stoker's Dracula, 1992; Age of Innocence, 1993; Little Women; How to Make an American Quilt; The Crucible; Looking for Richard; Boys; Alien Resurrection; Girl Interrupted, 1999; Lost Souls, 1999; Autumn in New York, 1999; Mr Deeds, 2002; S1m0ne, 2002; The Day My God Died, voice, 2003; The Heart is Deceitful Above All Things, 2004; The Darwin Awards, 2006; A Scanner Darkly, 2006; The Ten, 2007; Sex and Death 101, 2007; Welcome, 2007; The Last Word, 2008; The Informers, 2008; Water Pills, 2009; The Private Lives of Pippa Lee, 2009; Star Trek, 2009; When Love is Not Enough: The Lois Wilson Story, Black Swan, 2010; The Dilemma, 2011; Frankenweenie, The Letter, The Iceman, 2012. Honours: Golden Globe Best Supporting Actress, 1994. Address: 10345 W Olympic Boulevard, Los Angeles, CA 90064, USA.

RYN Zdzislaw Jan, b. 21 October 1938, Szczyrk, Poland. Professor. m. Halina Grażyna, 2 daughters. Education: University School of Medicine, 1956-62; Doctoral thesis, 1970; Habilitation thesis, 1979; Professor of Psychiatry, 1994. Appointments: Assistant, General Hospital, Bielsko-Biala, 1963-65; Assistant, Chair of Psychiatry, 1965-74, Assistant Professor, 1974-83, Associate Professor, 1984-94, University School of Medicine, Kraków; Head of Department, Clinical Psychology, 1984-89, Head of Department, Social Pathology, 1984-2007, Professor, Chair of Psychiatry, 1994-2007, Jagiellonian University; Ambassador of Poland to Chile and Bolivia, 1991-96, to Argentina, 2007-08; Honorary Consol of Chile to Cracow, Poland, 1997-2000; Professor, Institute of Rehabilitation, Academy of Physical Education, Kraków, 1997-; University School of Physical Education, 1997-; Department of Psychology, Katowice School of Economics, 2009-. Publications: Over 400 articles in professional journals; 30 books. Honours include: Bene Meritus, Polish Medical Association; Cruz Grande Orden Merito de Chile, 1996; Medicina Cracoviensis, 2000; Kolosy 2000 Prize, Chile, 2004; Honourable Caballero Cruz del III Milenio, Chile, 2004; Doctor Honoris Causa Universidad Cientifica del Sur, Lima, Peru, 2006; Castello Roca Award in Mountain Medicine, Spain, 2006; Man of the Year, USA, 2008; International Order of Merit, IBC, 2009. Memberships: Polish Medical Association; Polish Psychiatry Association; Polish Psychological Association; Polish Academy of Sciences; Polish Academy of Medicine; The Explorers' Club; Many international and honorary memberships. Address: ul Norwida 10/1, 31-521 Kraków, Poland. E-mail: mzryn@cyf-kr.edu.pl

RYOO Cheon Seoung, b. 12 June 1966, Korea. Professor. Education: BA, 1987, MA, 1989, DSc, 1995, Mathematics, Kyungpook National University, Taegu; PhD, Mathematics, Graduate School of Mathematics, Kyushu University, Japan, 1998. Appointments: Researcher, Kyungpook National University, Taegu, 1998-2000; Researcher, POSTECH, Pohang, 2000; Contact Professor, Department of Mathematics, Kyungpook National University, Taegu, 2000-02; Assistant Professor, 2002-05, Associate Professor, 2006-11, Professor 2011-, Department of Mathematics, Hannam University, Daejeon. Publications: Over 100 articles in professional journals. Address: Department of Mathematics, Hannam University, Daejeon 306-791, Korea. E-mail: ryoocs@hnu.kr

RYU Byoung Yoon, b. 30 April 1955, Daejeon, Republic of Korea. Doctor; Professor. m. Hee Soon Woo, 2 daughters. Education: MD, College of Medicine, Chungnam National University, 1981; Master's degree, Graduate School, Department of Medicine, Hallym University, 1993; PhD, Graduate School, Department of Medicine, Kyung Hee University, 2003. Appointments: Internship and Resident, Kangnam Sacred Heart Hospital, Hallym University, 1981-86; Medical Officer, army conscription, 1986-88; Clinical Fellow, Department of Surgery, 1989-90, Full time Instructor, 1990-92, Professor, 2001-, Chief & Surgery, 2007-11, Chunchon Sacred Heart Hospital, Hallym University. Memberships: Korean Surgical Society; Korean Society of Endoscopic & Laparoscopic Surgeons; Korean Gastric Cancer Association. Address: Chunchon Sacred Heart Hospital, Department of Surgery, 153 Kyo-Dong, Chunchon-Si, Kangwon-Do, 200-704, Korea. E-mail: byryu@hallym.or.kr

RYU Chan-Su, b. 3 December 1952, Jeonju, Korea. Professor. m. 1977, 2 daughters. Education: BSc, Department of Earth Science, Chosun University, 1975; MSc, Department of Earth Science, Korea University, 1981; DSc, Department of Atmospheric Science, Pusan Nat University, 1997. Appointments: Military Service, ROTC Officer of Korea, 1975-77; Professor, Chosun University, 1978-. Publications: Books: Living Environments and Weather, 1999; The Atmosphere, 2008; Environmental Science, 2008; Radar Meteorology, 2009; Aeronautical Meteorology, 2011; Life and Weather, 2011; Climate Change Report of Gwangju and Jeonnam in Korea, 2011; Climate Change Report of Jeonbuk in Korea, 2011; Numerous articles in professional journals. Honours: Minister Prize, Korea Meteorological Administration, 1998; Minister Prize, Science and Technology Administration, 1999; National Prize, 2001; University Prize, Chosun University, 2001; Science Prize, Korean Data Analysis Society, 2003; National Medal, 2004; Science Prize, Korean Federation of Water Science & Engineering

Society, 2010; Head Librarian, 2011-. Memberships: Korean Meteorological Society; Korean Earth Science Society; Korean Environmental Science Society; Japan Meteorological Society; Academic Society. Address: Department of Science Education, Chosun University, Gwangju, 501-759, Korea. E-mail: csryu@chosun.ac.kr

RYU Hojeong, b. 3 February 1983, Daegu, Republic of Korea. Scientist. Education: BA, Electronic Engineering & Physics, 2009, MA, Electronic Engineering, 2011, Yonsei University. Appointments: Research Scientist, National Core Research Centre, Yonsei University, 2011-. Publications: Influence of surface roughness on the polarimetric characteristics of a wire-grid polarizer, 2008; Probe-based Charge Injection Study of DNA Charge Transfer for Applications to Molecualr Electro-optic Switching, 2011. Honours: Bronze Medal, 4th Yonsei Idea Competition, 2007; LG-Yonam Honor Scholarship, 2009. Memberships: LG Yonam Foundation (Scholarship Member). Address: 3rd Engineering Building C731, Yonsei University, Sinchondong, Seodaemungu, Seoul 120-749, Republic of Korea. E-mail: nemorhj02@hanmail.net

RYU Kwang-Sun, b. 1 September 1963, Geochang County, Korea. Professor. m. Jik-Kyung Yoon, 2 daughters. Education: Bachelor, 1986, MSc, 1990, PhD, 1996, Yonsei University, Seoul. Appointments: Postdoctoral studies, Electronics & Telecommunication Research Institute, 1996-97; UBL Researcher, Tokyo University of Agriculture & Technology, 1997; Senior Researcher, Electronics & Telecommunication Research Institute, 1998-2007. Publications: 119 international papers; 12 domestic papers. Memberships: Korea Chemical Society; Korea Battery Society; Korean Electrochemical Society; Korean Society of Industrial & Engineering Chemistry; Polymer Society of Korea. Address: Department of Chemistry, Mugerdong, Ulsan 680-749, Korea.

RYU Yeon-Taek, b. 9 July 1970, Gwangju, South Korea. Professor. m. Hyunjoo Jung, 1 son, 1 daughter. Education: BA, 1995, ME, 1997, Seoul National University; PhD, University of Minnesota, USA, 2002. Appointments: Lecturer, 2003, Postdoctoral Fellow, 2003-04, University of Minnesota; Visiting Assistant Professor, University of Arizona, Tucson, USA, 2004-05; Visiting Research Fellow, Seoul National University, 2005-06; Assistant Professor, Chungbuk National University, Cheongju, South Korea, 2006-. Publications: Book, Cities and Architecture in the World, 2007, 2nd edition, 2008; Article, The Politics of Scale: the Social and Political Construction of Geographical Scale in Korean Housing Politics, 2007. Honours: AAG Urban Geography Specialty Group Doctoral Dissertation Award, 2002; Listed in international biographical dictionaries. Memberships: United Nations Conference on the Standardization of Geographical Names; United Nations Group of Experts on Geographical Names. Address: Department of Geography Education, Chungbuk National University, 410 Seongbong-ro, Heungduk-gu, Cheongju, Chungbuk 361-763, South Korea. E-mail: ytryu@chungbuk.ac.kr

RYZHIKOV Vladimir, b. 8 January 1940, Ukraine. Physicist. m. Lisetskaya Helen, 1 daughter. Education: Radiophysicist, Kharkov State University, 1967; Candidate of Physics, Maths Science, 1973; Doctor Ph M Science, 1990; Professor, 1993. Appointments: Engineer, Kharkov State University, 1967-70; Assistant, Post-graduate, Institute of Single Crystals, 1970-73; Researcher, Head of Laboratory, Head of Department Radiation Instrument, 1973-2012. Publications: More than 510 articles; 12 monographs. Memberships: IEEE Society; MRS Society; SPIE Society; Council for Nondestructive Control. Address: 61024 Kharkov, AB 7097, Pushkinskaya 8/7, Ukraine.

RZEDOWSKI Jerzy, b. 27 December 1926, Lwów, Poland. Botanist. m. Graciela Calderón, 3 daughters. Education: Biology, National School of Biological Sciences, National Polytechnic Institute, Mexico, 1954; Doctor of Biology, Faculty of Science, National University of Mexico, 1961. Appointments: Professor, San Luis Potosí University, 1954; Professor, Researcher, Postgraduate College, 1959; Professor, National School of Biological Sciences, National Polytechnic Institute, 1961; Researcher, Institute of Ecology, 1984-. Publications: 120 articles in scientific journals; 26 fascicles; 45 book chapters; 6 books. Honours: Diploma al mérito botánico; Ordre des palmes académiques; Doctorado honoris causa, Universidad Autónoma Chapingo; Doctorado honoris causa, Universidad Michoacana de San Nicolás de Hidalgo; Premio al mérito ecologico; Asa Gray Award; Botany Millennium Award; José Cuatrecasas Medal for Excellence in Tropical Botany. Memberships: Botanical Society of America; American Society of Plant Taxonomists; Sociedad Argentina de Botánica; International Association of Plant Taxonomy; Sociedad Botánica de México. Address: Apartado postal 386, 61600 Pátzcuaro, Michoacán, Mexico. E-mail: jerzy.rzedowski@inecol.edu.mx

RZHAVSKAYA Faina, b. 22 September 1916, Kiev, Russia. Researcher. Widow. Education: MSc, Astrachan Technical Fisheries Institute, 1939; PhD, Moscow Technical Fisheries Institute, 1948; Dr Sc, 1982; Professor, 1991. Appointments: Senior Research Worker, Allunion Scientific Research Institute for Oils, Leningrad, Moscow Branch, 1948-60; Senior Research Worker, 1960-86, Principal Research Worker, 1986-95, Allunion Scientific Research Institute for Marine Fisheries and Oceanography, Moscow (VNIRO). Publications include: Fish and Marine Mammal's Oils (monograph), 1976; 6 Brochures; Sections in collections: Chemical composition of food products, 1979; Application of World Ocean biological resources, 1980; Numerous articles in scientific journals and proceedings including: Colloidal Journal, 1958; News of Higher Educational Establishments, Food Technology, 1970, 1982; Questions of Nutrition, 1975, 1977, 1978; News of Latvian SSR Academic Science, 1980; Fishery Economy, 1966, 1969, 1970, 1971, 1973, 1975, 1976, 1978, 1980, 1981, 1984, 1985, 1986, 1988, 1990; Storage and Processing of Agricultural Crops, 1995; Moscow Technical Fisheries Institute, Proceedings, 1953; Allunion Scientific Research Institute for Oils, Proceedings, 1965; Allunion Scientific Research Institute for Marine Fisheries and Oceanography, Proceedings, 1967, 1971, 1972, 1974, 1977, 1979, 1981, 1983, 1985, 1986, 1990, 1997; International Conference on processing sea products, 1993; 11 patents. Honours: Medals: For Success in the Economy of the USSR, 1972; Veteran of Labour, 1985; For Distinguished Labour in WW2 1941-45, 1991; 50 Year and 60 Year of Victory in WW2 1941-1945, 1995, 2005. Memberships: Editorial Board, VNIRO's Proceedings, 1967-95; Scientific Supervisor of Postgraduates, 1972-95; VNIRO's Academic Council of Conferment of Academic Degrees, 1974-95. Address: 22/5 Haorgim Street, Bat Yam, 59674 Israel.

S

SAAGE Richard, b. 3 April 1941, Tülau, Germany. Political Science Professor. m. Ingrid Thienel, 1 daughter. Education: PhD, University of Frankfurt/Main, 1972; Dr disc pol habil, University of Göttingen, 1981. Appointments: Assistant Professor, 1972-76, Lecturer, 1976-92, University of Göttingen; Professor of Politics, 1992-2006, Dean, Section of History and Social Sciences, 1998-2000, Dean, Faculty of Philosophy, 1998-2000, University of Halle/Saale, Germany. Publications: Numerous articles in professional journals. Honours: Visiting Scholar, Harvard University, Cambridge, Massachusetts, USA, 1972-73; Two Festschriften, 2001, 2006. Membership: Member, Saxonian Academy of Sciences, Leipzig. Address: Dohnenstieg 6, 14195 Berlin, Germany. E-mail: saage@gmx.net

SAAIMAN Nolan, b. 21 December 1960, Pretoria, South Africa. Internal Auditor. m. Anita, 2 sons. Education: B Comm, Accounting Sciences, 1982; B Comm, Honours, Accounting, 1988; Diploma, Datametrics, 1992; Certified Information Systems Auditor, 1992; Certified Financial Services Auditor, 1996; Computer Professional Qualifying Examination of the Computer Society of South Africa, 1996; Certified Internal Auditor, 1998; Certified Financial Consultant, 2001; Certified Business Manager, 2001; Chartered Management Consultant, 2007. Appointments: Senior Internal Auditor, South African Post Office, 1985-88; Accountant Van Wyk and Louw, 1988-89; Manager's Assistant, Information Systems Audit Department, First National Bank, 1990-92; Manager, Computer Audit Services, SA Eagle, 1992-94; IT Audit Manager, SA Housing Trust, 1995-97; Audit Manager, Senior Auditor, Mercedes-Benz, South Africa, 1997-. Publications: Articles about computer audit, membership matters and internal audit, in Newsletter of the Institute of Internal Auditors, South Africa, 1995-96; Article on internal audit in Institute of Directors Directorship Magazine, 1997. Honours: Completed Comrades Marathon (90kms), 1984, 1986; Served on Board of Institute of Internal Auditors, South Africa, 1996-97; 21st Century Award for Achievement, IBC, 2001; Listed in Who's Who Publications and biographical dictionaries. Memberships: Information Systems Audit and Control Association; Institute of Directors; Institute of Internal Auditors; Computer Society of South Africa; Institute of Financial Consultants, The Association of Professionals in Business Management, USA; Chartered Institute of Management Consultants. Address: 26 Retha Court, Veglaer Street, Pierre Van Ryneveld Park, 0157 South Africa. E-mail: nolan.saaiman@daimler.com

SÄÄKSLAHTI Arja Kaarina, b. 24 September 1966, Lapua, Finland. Senior Departmental Researcher. m. Erkki Emil, 2 sons, 1 daughter. Education: Master of Science, 1993; PhD, 2005. Appointments: Infant Swimming Instructor and Educator, -1987; Physical Education Teacher, Kindergarten Teacher Training School, 1992-93; Researcher, University of Turku, Finland, 1993; Teacher of Didactics, 1994; Researcher, Department of Physical Education, 1994-2000, Physical Education Teacher, Researcher in Teacher Training School, -2000, Senior Lecturer, 2006, Senior Departmental Researcher, 2007-, University of Jyväskylä, Finland; Writer of books, -1997; Scriptwriter for TV programmes, 1998, 1999, 2006; Member, Editorial Board, Finnish Sport and Science. Publications: Numerous articles in professional journals; Books: Physical Education Curriculum for Preschool, Grade 1 and 2; One, Two and Dive – Theory and Practice in Infant Swimming; Baby Swimming; Numerous articles as a part of different books. Honours: Best Abstract in Sport Pedagogy in Olympic Congress, 1996; The Award of Finnish Association of Life Saving and Teaching Swimming, 1996, 2005; 2nd Prize, Poster Presentation, AIESEP World Congress, 2008. Memberships: The Finnish Association of Life Saving and Teaching Swimming; NUORI SUOMI; The Finnish Society for Research in Sport and Physical Education; International Association for Physical Education in Higher Education; International Society for Behavioral Nutrition and Physical Activity. Address: Vahverontie 16-18 B18, 40640 Jyväskylä, Finland.

SAATCHI Charles, b. 9 June 1943. Advertising Executive. m. (1) Doris Lockhart, (2) Kay, 1990, divorced 2001, 1 daughter; (3) Nigella Lawson. Education: Christ's College, Finchley, London, England. Appointments: Former junior copywriter, Benton and Bowles (US advertising agency), London; Associate Director, Collett Dickinson Pearce, 1966-68; with Ross Cramer formed freelance consultancy, Cramer Saatchi, Director, 1968-70; Co-founder (with Maurice Saatchi) of Saatchi and Saatchi (advertising agency), 1970, Saatchi & Saatchi PLC, 1984, Director, 1970-93, President, 1993-95; Co-founder, Partner, M&C Saatchi Agency, 1995-; Founder, The Saatchi Gallery, 2003-. Address: 36 Golden Square, London, W1R 4EE, England.

SAATCHI Baron (Life Peer) Maurice, b. 21 June 1946. Advertising Executive. m. Josephine Hart, 1984, 1 son, 1 stepson. Education: BSc, London School of Economics. Appointments: Co-Founder, Saatchi & Saatchi Company, 1970; Chairman, Saatchi & Saatchi Company PLC, 1984-94; Director, 1994; Co-founder, Partner, M&C Saatchi Agency, 1995-; Chairman, Megalomedia PLC, 1995-; Director (non-executive) Loot, 1998-; Shadow Cabinet Office Minister, 2001-03; Co-Chair, Conservative Party, 2003-. Publications: The Science of Politics, 2001. Memberships: Governor, LSE; Council, Royal College of Art, 1997-; Trustee, Victoria & Albert Museum, 1988-. Address: 36 Golden Square, London, W1R 4EE, England.

SACHDEV Perminder Singh, b. 27 July 1956, Ludhiana, India. Neuropsychiatrist. m. Jagdeep, 1986, 2 daughters. Education: MBBS, 1978, MD, 1981, AIIMS; FRANZCP, 1985; PhD, University of New South Wales, 1991. Appointments: Junior Resident, 1979-81, Senior Research Officer, Senior Resident, 1982, Department of Psychiatry, AIIMS; Psychiatric Registrar, Auckland Hospital Board, New Zealand, 1983-85; Consultant Psychiatrist, Otago Hospital Board, Dunedin, New Zealand, 1985-87; Clinical Lecturer, Department of Psychological Medicine, University of Otago Medical School, Dunedin, 1986; Senior Lecturer in Psychiatry, 1987-93, Associate Professor of Neuropsychiatry, 1993-98, Professor of Neuropsychiatry, 1999-, University of New South Wales; Clinical Director, Neuropsychiatric Institute, Prince of Wales Hospital, Australia; Scientia Professor of Neuropsychiatry University of New South Wales, Sydney, Australia, 2009. Publications: Numerous articles in professional medical journals; Editorial or author contributions to several respected psychiatric books. Honour: Sita Ram Jindal Gold Medal, 1972; Panjab University Gold Medal, 1973; Delhi Medical Association Diamond Jubilee Award, 1977; National Scholarship, 1972-78; Organon Senior Research Award, 1995; President Lecture, 5th Annual International Neuropsychiatry Congress, 2004; IAPA Outstanding Academician Award, 2004; Novartis Oration Award, 2004; Inaugural INA India Lecture Award, 2005. Memberships: Australian Society for Psychiatric Research; Australian Society for Biological Psychiatry; Tourette Syndrome Association; Tourette Syndrome Association of Australia; Movement Disorders Society; Sydney Movement Disorders Society; Alzheimer's

Association; International Neuropsychiatric Association; International College of Geriatric Psychopharmacology; Society of Biological Psychiatry. Address: NPI, Prince of Wales Hospital, Randwick, NSW 2031, Australia.

SACHS Leo, b. 14 October 1924, Leipzig, Germany. Scientist. m. Pnina Salkind, 1 son, 3 daughters. Education: BSc, University of Wales, Bangor, 1948; PhD, Trinity College, Cambridge University, England, 1951. Appointments: Research Scientist, Genetics, John Innes Institute, England, 1951-52; Research Scientist, 1952-, Founder, Department of Genetics and Virology, 1960, Professor, 1962, Head, Department of Genetics, 1962-89, Dean, Faculty of Biology, 1974-79, Otto Meyerhof Professor of Biology, Weizmann Institute of Science, Rehovot, Israel. Publications: Science papers in professional journals. Honours: Israel Prize, Natural Sciences, 1972; Fogarty International Scholar, National Institutes of Health, Bethesda, 1972; Harvey Lecture, Rockefeller University, New York, 1972; Rothschild Prize, Biological Sciences, 1977; Wolf Prize, Medicine, 1980; Bristol-Myers Award, Distinguished Achievement in Cancer Research, New York, 1983; Doctor Honoris Causa, Bordeaux University, France, 1985; Royal Society Wellcome Foundation Prize, London, 1986; Alfred P Sloan Prize, General Motors Cancer Research Foundation, New York, 1989; Warren Alpert Foundation Prize, Harvard Medical School, Boston, 1997; Doctor of Medicine Honoris Causa, Lund University, Sweden, 1997; Honorary Fellow, University of Wales, Bangor, 1999; Emet Prize for Life Sciences, 2002. Memberships: European Molecular Biology Organization; Israel Academy of Sciences and Humanities; Foreign Associate USA National Academy of Sciences; Fellow, Royal Society, London; Foreign Member, Academia Europaea; Honorary Life Member, International Cytokine Society. Address: Weizmann Institute of Science, Department of Molecular Genetics, Rehovot, Israel.

SACKS Jonathan Henry, b. 8 March 1948, London, England. Rabbi. m. Elaine Taylor, 1970, 1 son, 2 daughters. Education: Christ's College, Finchley; Gonville and Caius College, Cambridge; New College, Oxford; London University; Jews' College, London; Yeshivat Etz Hayyim, London. Appointments: Lecturer, Middlesex Polytechnic, 1971-73, Jew's College, London, 1973-76, 1976-82; Rabbi, Golders Green Synagogue, London, 1978-82, Marble Arch Synagogue, London, 1983-90; Chief Rabbi Lord Jakobvits Professor (1st incumbent), Modern Jewish Thought, 1982-; Director, Rabbinic Faculty, 1983-90, Principal, 1984-90, Chief Rabbi, 1991-, United Hebrew Congregations of the Commonwealth; Editor, Le'ela (journal), 1985-90; Presentation Fellow, King's College, London, 1993; Association President, Conference of European Rabbis, 2000-; Visiting Professor of Philosophy, Hebrew University, Jerusalem and of Theology and Religious Studies, King's College, London. Publications: Torah Studies, 1986; Tradition and Transition, 1986; Traditional Alternatives, 1989; Traditional in an Untraditional Age, 1990; The Persistence of Faith, 1991; Orthodoxy Confronts Modernity (Editor), 1991; Crisis and Covenant, 1992; One People? Tradition, Modernity and Jewish Unity, 1993; Will We Have Jewish Grandchildren? 1994; Faith in the Future, 1995; Community of Faith, 1995; The Politics of Hope, 1997; Morals and Markets, 1999; Celebrating Life, 2000; Radical Then Radical Now, 2001; The Dignity of Difference: How To Avoid the Clash of Civilizations, 2002; The Chief Rabbi's Haggadah, 2003; From Optimism to Hope, 2004; To Heal a Fractured World, 2005. Honours: Honorary degrees from the Universities of: Bar Ilan, Cambridge, Glasgow, Haifa, Middlesex, Yeshiva University New York, University of Liverpool, St Andrews University and Leeds Metropolitan University; Honorary Fellow, Gonville and Caius College, Cambridge, 1993; Kings College; Jerusalem Prize, 1995; Awarded Doctorate of Divinity by Archbishop of Canterbury, 2001; Knighted, Queen's Birthday Honours, 2005. Address: 735 High Road, London, N12 0US, England.

SAEKI Hiroshi, b. 9 April 1956, Ube, Yamaguchi, Japan. Accelerator Physics & Engineering. m. Jyunko Akino, 2 daughters. Education: BE, Mechanical Egg, Kyusyu University, Fukuoka, Japan, 1979; PhD, Accelerator Science, Graduate University for Advanced Studies, Kanagawa, Japan, 1992. Appointments: Engineer & Sub-section Chief, Production Engineering Laboratory, Panasonic Co Ltd, Osaka, 1980-93; Researcher, National Laboratory for High Energy Physics, Tsukuba, 1987-89; Scientist, Japan Synchrotron Radiation Research Institute, Hyogo, 1993-; Consultant, Electronic Engineering, Tohoku University, Sendai, 1997-2000. Publications: Residual currents detected with a correcting electrode in a modified Bayard-Alpert hot-cathode-ionization gauge, 2008; Vacuum seal for rectangular flange, 2011; Method to compensate radiation-induced errors in a hot-cathode-ionization gauge with correcting electrode, 2011. Memberships: American Vacuum Society; American Chemical Society; Institute of Physics. Address: Shiosaki 2-24-412, Ohoshio, Himeji, Hyogo 671-0102, Japan. E-mail: saeki@spring8.or.jp

SAFONOV Vladimir, b. 2 November 1954, St Petersburg, Russia. Computer Scientist; Educator. m. Adel. Education: MS, Mathematics, 1977, Candidate of Science, 1981, Doctor of Science, 1991, Professor, 1994, St Petersburg University. Appointments: Engineer, 1977, Junior Research Fellow, 1981; Senior Research Fellow, 1984; Head of Laboratory, 1989; Professor of Computer Science, 1994-, Department of Mathematics and Mechanics, St Petersburg University, Russia. Publications: Introduction to Java technology, 2002; Using aspect-oriented programming for trustworthy software development, 2008; Trustworthy compilers, 2010; Over 130 articles in professional journals; 4 USA software patents; 4 Russian software patents. Honours: 8 Microsoft research and teaching grant awards; Sun teaching grant award; Government of St Petersburg award; St Petersburg University award; Honoured Teacher of Russia; Listed in international biographical dictionaries. Memberships: Senior Member, Regional Chapter Chair, IEEE; Member, ACM; Member, IET (UK). E-mail: v_o_safonov@mail.ru Website: http://www.vladimirsafonov.org

SAFRONOV Alexander Yu, b. 7 December 1955, Irkutsk, Russia. Chemist. m. L L Sintsova, 1 daughter. Education: MSc, Chemistry, 1978; PhD, Chemistry, 1983; C Chem, FRSC, 1997; DSc, Chemistry, 1995; Professor, 1997. Appointments: Researcher, 1978-, Head of General and Inorganic Chemistry Chair, 1990-, Dean of Chemical Department, 1998-2008, Irkutsk State University. Publications: Over 80 articles in professional journals; Patentee in bioinorganic chemistry of gold; Contributions to 3 books. Honours: Honourable Deed of Russian Ministry of Science and Education, 1998. Membership: Fellow, Royal Society of Chemistry. Address: Irkutsk State University, Chemical Department, 1 K Marx Str, 664003 Irkutsk, Russia. E-mail: dean@chem.isu.ru

SAHA Manoranjan, b. 8 January 1952, Manikganj, Dhaka, Bangladesh. Professor of Applied Chemistry and Chemical Technology. m. Kabita, 1 son, 1 daughter. Education: BS (Hons), Chemistry, Dhaka University, 1974; MS, Chemical Engineering, Azerbaijan Institute of Petroleum and Chemistry, Baku, USSR, 1977; PhD, Petroleum and

Petrochemicals, 1982; Postdoctoral Studies, Indian Institute of Science, Bangalore, 1995, Indian Institute of Petroleum, Dehradun, 1996. Appointments: Assistant Professor, 1983-90, Associate Professor, 1990-94, Professor, 1994-, Chairman, Department of Applied Chemistry and Chemical Technology, 1998-2001, Dhaka University, Dhaka, Bangladesh. Publications: 180 publications in national and international journals. Honours: Listed in Who's Who publications and biographical dictionaries. Memberships: Asiatic Society Bangladesh; Bangladesh Association for the Advancement of Science; Bangladesh Chemical Society; Bangladesh Association of Scientists and Scientific Professions. Address: Department of Applied Chemistry and Chemical Engineering, University of Dhaka, Dhaka-1000, Bangladesh. E-mail: msaha@univdhaka.edu

SAHABDEEN Desamanya Abdul Majeed Mohamed, b. 19 May 1926, Gampola, Sri Lanka. Former Administrator; Entrepreneur. m. Ruchia Halida, 1959, 1 son, 1 daughter. Education: BA (Hons), PhD, University of Ceylon. Appointments: Founder Chairman, Majeedsons Group of Companies, 1973-; Former Administrator, Civil Service; Member, Public Service Commission; Member, Presidential Commissions on Finance and Banking, Industrialisation, Taxation, and Delimitation of Electoral Districts; Founder Chairman, AMM Sahabdeen Trust Foundation, 1991 incorporated by Act of Parliament No 03 of 1991; Established: The Mohamed Sahabdeen Institute for Advanced Studies and Research, Pahamune, 1997; Mohamed Sahabdeen International Awards for Science, Literature and Human Development; Pahamune House Rehabilitation Centre for Children in Need; Scholar; Writer. Publications: Several articles and books on philosophy and allied subjects including Sufi Doctrin in Tamil Literature, 1986; God and the Universe, 1995; The Circle of Life, 2001. Honours: Received Desamanya - highest Civil honour – 1992; Listed in Who's Who publications and biographical dictionaries. Memberships: President, Ceylon Muslim Scholarship Fund; Vice Patron, Sri Lanka-India Friendship Society; Life Member, Sri Lanka Cancer Society; Member, Royal Asiatic Society of Sri Lanka. Address: 30/12 Bagatelle Road, Colombo 03, Sri Lanka. E-mail: ammstrust@gmail.com

SAINT Dora Jessie, (Miss Read), b. 17 April 1913, Surrey, England. Novelist; Short Story Writer. Education: Homerton College, 1931-33. Publications: Village School, 1955; Village Diary, 1957; Storm in the Village, 1958; Hobby Horse Cottage, 1958; Thrush Green, 1959; Fresh From the Country, 1960; Winter in Thrush Green, 1961; Miss Clare Remembers, 1962; The Market Square, 1966; The Howards of Caxley, 1967; Country Cooking, 1969; News from Thrush Green, 1970; Tyler's Row, 1972; Christmas Mouse, 1973; Battles at Thrush Green, 1975; No Holly for Miss Quinn, 1976; Village Affairs, 1977; Return to Thrush Green, 1978; The White Robin, 1979; Village Centenary, 1980; Gossip From Thrush Green, 1981; A Fortunate Grandchild, 1982; Affairs at Thrush Green, 1983; Summer at Fairacre, 1984; At Home in Thrush Green, 1985; Time Remembered, 1986; The School at Thrush Green, 1987; The World at Thrush Green, 1988; Mrs Pringle, 1989; Friends at Thrush Green, 1990; Changes at Fairacre, 1991; Celebrations at Thrush Green, 1992; Farewell to Fairacre, 1993; Tales From a Village School, 1994; The Year at Thrush Green, 1995; A Peaceful Retirement, 1996; Chronicles of Fairacre, 2005; Village School, 2005; Village Diary, 2005; Storm in the Village, 2005; Christmas at Fairacre, 2005. Honour: Member of the Order of the British Empire, 1998. Membership: Society of Authors. Address: c/o Michael Joseph, Penguin Books Ltd, 80 Strand, London WC2R 0RL, England.

SAITO Mika, b. 19 March 1962, Japan. Veterinarian. 1 daughter. Education: PhD, Hokkaido University; Graduate School of Hokkaido University; Graduate School of Nihan Fukushi University. Appointments: Veterinarian. Publications: Flavivirus Encephalitis. Memberships: University of the Ryukyus. Address: 207 Vehara Nishihara, Nakagami, Okinawa 903-0215, Japan.

SAKAI Hirofumi, b. 28 June 1959, Chichibu City, Saitama, Japan. Associate Professor. m. Yumiko Sakai. Education: BSc, Physics, 1983, Dr Sc, 1994, Physics, The University of Tokyo. Appointments: Researcher, 1983-92, Senior researcher, 1992-99, Electrotechnical Laboratory, Tsukuba, Japan; Associate Professor, The University of Tokyo, Tokyo, Japan, 1999-. Publications: Many scientific papers published in refereed journals. Honours: Awards, The Laser Society of Japan, 1985, 1992. Memberships: Optical Society of America; Physical Society of Japan; Japan Society of Applied Physics; Laser Society of Japan; Spectroscopical Society of Japan; Society for Atomic Collision Research, Japan. Address: Department of Physics, Graduate School of Science; The University of Tokyo, 7-3-1 Hongo, Bunkyo-ku, Tokyo 113-0033, Japan. E-mail: hsakai@phys.s.u-tokyo.ac.jp

SAKAI Koji, b. 25 August 1972, Japan. Lecturer. m. Chiemi, 2 daughters. Education: BA, Tohoku University, 1995; MA, 1997, PhD, 2000, Kyoto University. Appointments: Lecturer, 2000-05, Associate Professor, 2005-, Kyoto Koka Women's University. Publications: Article, Set-size effects in simple visual search for contour curvature, 2007. Honours: Listed in international biographical dictionaries. Address: Kyoto Koka Women's University, 38 Kadono-cho, Nishikyogoku, Ukyo-ku, Kyoto 615-0882, Japan. E-mail: rb064@mail.koka.ac.jp

SAKAMOTO Yoshikazu, b. 16 September 1927, Los Angeles, California, USA. Political Scientist. m. Kikuko Ono, 2 daughters. Education: Hogakushi, Faculty of Law, University of Tokyo, 1951. Appointments: Associate Professor, Faculty of Law, 1954, Professor of International Politics, Faculty of Law, 1964-88, Professor Emeritus, 1988-, University of Tokyo; Professor, Meiji-Gakuin University, 1988-93; Senior Research Fellow, International Christian University, 1993-96. Publications: Editor: Asia: Militarization and Regional Conflict, 1988; Global Transformation, 1994; Author, The Age of Relativization, 1997; Nuclearism and Humanity, 2 volumes (editor), 1999; Selected Works, 6 Volumes, 2004-2005; Memoir, 2 volumes, 2011. Honours: Rockefeller Fellow, 1956-57; Eisenhower Fellow, 1964; Special Fellow, United Nations Institute for Research and Training; Mainichi National Book Award, 1976. Memberships: Secretary-General, International Peace Research Association, 1979-83; American Political Science Association; Japanese Political Science Association. Address: 8-29-19 Shakujii-machi, Nerimaku, Tokyo 177-0044, Japan.

SAKARI Mahyar, b. 6 September 1970, Iran. Environmental Chemist. m. Zarrintaj Aminrad, 1 son. Education: BSc, University of Lahijan, 1994; MSc, University of Lahijan, 1999; PhD, Universiti Putra Malaysia, 2009; Postdoctorate, National University of Malaysia, 2010. Appointments: Senior Lecturer, Environmental Chemistry, School of Science & Technology, Universiti Malaysia Sabah, 2010-. Publications: Numerous articles in professional journals and book chapters. Honours: Best University Lecturer, Tonekabon University, Iran, 2004-05; Gold Medal Winner, 2007, Silver Medal Winner, 2007, Bronze Medal Winner, 2007, PPPI Universiti Putra Malaysia; Best Paper Award, Journal of Environment

Asia, 2008. Memberships: Royal Society for Chemistry. Address: Private Bag 88, School of Science & Technology, Universiti Malaysia Sabah, Jalan UMS, 88400 Kota Kinabalu, Sabah, Malaysia. E-mail: mahyarsakari@gmail.com Website: http://wwwsst.ums.edu.my/lecturer/ mahyarsakari

SAKUMA Kunihiro, b. 18 February 1969, Minami-Soma City, Japan. Associate Professor. m. Yoko, 1 daughter. Education: Bachelor, 1991, MS, 1993, Physical Education, PhD, Physical Science, 1996, University of Tsukuba. Appointments: Researcher, Department of Physiology, Institute for Developmental Research, Aichi Human Service Centre, 1996-2000; Assistant Professor, Department of Legal Medicine, Kyoto Prefectural University of Medicine, 2000-05; Associate Professor, Research Centre for Physical Fitness, Sports and Health, Toyohashi University of Technology, 2005-. Publications: Numerous articles in professional journals including: Recent Research Developments in Life Sciences, 2011; Cell Aging, 2011. Honours: Research Grant-in-Aid, Ministry of Education, Culture, Sports, Science and Technology of Japan, 1999-2000, 2001-02, 2003-04, 2005-06, 2008-10. Memberships: Fellow, Japanese Society of Physical Fitness and Sports Medicine; Japanese Society of Exercise and Sports Physiology. Address: 33-1-302 Minamimatsubara, Akebono-cho, Toyohashi, 441-8151, Japan. E-mail: ksakuma@las.tut.ac.jp Website: www.health.tut.ac.jp/sakuma/index.html

SAKURADA Yutaka, b. 1 January 1933, Kyoto, Japan. Company President. m. Keiko, 2 sons. Education: BS, Petro-chemicals, 1956, MS, Polymer Chemistry, 1958, PhD, Polymer Chemistry, 1966, Kyoto University, Japan. Appointments: Research Fellow, Kuraray Company Ltd, 1958-62; International Fellow, Stanford Research Institute, 1962-64; General Manager Medical Products, Kuraray Company Ltd, 1977-88; General Manager, Corporate R&D, 1988-89; Managing Director, Kuraray Plastics, 1989-91; President, Haemonetics, Japan, 1991-2001, Chairman and Chief Executive Officer, Haemonetics, Japan, 2003-2005; Chairman, Haemonetics Japan/Asia, 2005-06. Publication: Book chapter, Impact of Medical Technology Utilizing Macromolecules on Society, in Macromolecular Concept and Strategy for Humanity in Science Technology and Industry (editors Okamura, Ranby, Ito), 1996. Honours: Chemical Technology Award, Japan Society of Polymer, 1984; Chemical Technology Award, Japanese Chemical Society, 1985; Distinguished Fellows Award, International Center for Artificial Organs and Transplantation, 1993. Memberships: Japanese Chemical Society; Japanese Society of Polymer; International Society for Artificial Organs. Address: GM Ebisunomori 1304, 23-6, 4-Chome, Ebisu, Shibuya-ku, Tokyo, Japan 150-0013. E-mail: ysakurada@star.ocn.ne.jp

SALA PARCERISAS Robert, b. 8 September 1949, Torà, Spain. Physician. Education: Student, University of Barcelona, 1966-75; Physician, 1976; Professional Degree, 1977; Master in Tropical Medicine, 1992, Medical Doctor, 1995, University of Barcelona. Appointments: Clinical Physician, Residència Sanitària, Hospital Arnau de Vilanova, Lleida, 1976; Clinical Physician: FERS (Spain), Mbini, Guinea Ecuatorial, 1997; Medicus Mundi Asturias (Spain), Ntita, Burundi, 1994; Médicos sin Fronteras (Spain), N'Giva, Angola, 1992; Ministério da Saúde, Tete and Quelimane, Moçambique, 1982-84; JOSPICE (United Kingdom), Morazán, Honduras, 1978; Assistant, Eritropathology Unity, Hospital Clínic i Provincial of Barcelona, Spain, 2003-. Publications: Functional Aspects of Granulocytic Leukocytes, Mainly Neutrophils, Related With Effects of the Heroin (doctoral thesis), 1995; Oxygen-derived germicide metabolites and ultraviolet radiation in the neutrophilic leukocyte phagosome, 1998; Concomitant factors influencing a measles epidemic in Ondgiva, 1998; Annotation concerning the initial energy in the phagosome oxidative burst of the segmented neutrophil, 1999; A Perspective on the Oxidative Burst in the Phagosome of the Leukocyte and its Neoplastic Transformation, 2002. Honours: Scholar, Fundació Catalana de Pneumologia, 1989-90; Member, Research Board of Advisors, ABI, 2006; Director General's Roll of Honour, IBC, 2010-. Address: Plaça del Pati n°5 2n 4a, 25750 Torà (Lleida), Spain. E-mail: r.sala@antics.ub.edu

SALIM Muhammad Khurram, b. 23 June 1967, Dhaka, Bangladesh. Education: BA, English and European Studies, Phillips University, 1989; Diplomas in Journalism, London School of Journalism; Diploma, Business and Office Skills, Lewisham College, 2001; Certificate, ECDL, British Computer Society, 2004. Appointments: Administration Assistant, Bon Marche Ltd, 2001-. Publications: Bangladesh Observer; Asian Times; Phillips University Publication; Buckingham University Publication; United Press; Poetry Now anthologies; Poetic Licence. Address: 116 Ewhurst Road, Crofton Park, London SE4 1SD, England.

SALISBURY-JONES Raymond Arthur, b. 31 July 1933, Camberley, England. Director of Music. Education: MA (Hons), Modern History, Christ Church, Oxford, 1953-56. Appointments: Executive, Rolls Royce Ltd/Rolls Royce Motors Ltd, 1956-75; Director, Rolls Royce Motors International, 1973-75; Chairman, Hambledon Vineyards Ltd, 1974-85; Managing Director, RSJ Aviation International Ltd, 1976-91; Non-executive Director Daniel Thwaites plc, 1974-98; Senior Consultant, Middle East Consultants Ltd, 1995-98; Consultant to mi2g Ltd (Internet Security Specialists), 1997-2000; Organist, St Mark's, Islington, 2002-. Honours: Rowe Piano Competition, 1948; Harford Lloyd Organ Prize, 1950; MA (Hons), Oxon. Memberships: Royal College of Organists. Address: The Charterhouse, Charterhouse Square, London EC1M 6AN, England. E-mail: rsj100@talk21.com

SALVADOR FERRER Carmen Maria, b. 29 September 1977, Almeria, Spain. Professor. m. Ruben Hernandez-Vaquero, 1 daughter. Education: BA, Psychology, 1999, PhD, Social Psychology, 2004, University of Almeria; Master, Human Resource Management, College of Political Science, Madrid, 2005. Appointments: Area Responsible Social Psychology; President of the Quality Assurance Unit Title of Social Work; Co-ordinator of Assessment Center Teaching and Labor Relations; Co-ordinator of International Research Projects, Mexico; International Research Project, Mexico, 2005-; Assessor, national and international journals; Professor, Psychology and Social Organizations, University of Almeria. Publications: Numerous articles in professional journals; 13 books. Honours: Research Award for Work in Villahermosa, Tabasco, Mexico; Listed in international biographical dictionaries. Memberships: Socia of Evaluation Almeriense; ULAPSIS project; European Research Project, In Other Words, 2010-13. Address: Universidad de Almeria, Facultad de Psicologia, Carretera de Sacramento, La Canada de San Urbano, S/N, CP 04120, Almeria, Spain. E-mail: cmsalva@ual.es

SAMBROOK Richard Jeremy, b. 24 April 1956, Canterbury, England. Journalist; Broadcasting Executive. m. Susan Jane Fisher, 1 son, 1 daughter. Education: BA (Hons) Reading University; MSc, Birkbeck College, London University. Appointments: Trainee Journalist, Thomson

Regional Papers, 1977-80; BBC Radio News, 1980-84; BBC TV News, 1984-92; News Editor, 1992; Head of Newsgathering, 1996-2000; Deputy Director, BBC News, 2000-2001; Director, BBC News, 2001-2004; Director, World Service and Global News, 2004-2010; Vice President, European Broadcasting Union, 2006-; Vice Chairman and Chief Content Officer, Edelman Public Relations Agency, 2010. Honours: Fellow, RTS; Fellow, RSA. Address: BBC, Bush House, The Aldwych, London WC2B 4PM, England.

SAMPRAS Pete, b. 12 August 1971, Washington DC, USA. Tennis Player. m. Brigette Wilson, 2 sons. Career: US Open Champion, 1990, 1993, 1995, 1996; Grand Slam Cup Winner, 1990; IBM/ATP Tour World Championship - Frankfurt Winner, 1991; Member, US Davis Cup Team, 1991, 1995; US Pro-Indoor Winner, 1992; Wimbledon Singles Champion, 1993, 1994, 1995, 1997, 1998, 1999, 2000; European Community Championships Winner, 1993, 1994; Ranked No 1, 1993; Winner, Australian Open, 1994; RCA Championships, 1996, ATP Tour World Championships, 1996, Australian Open, 1997; Winner, San José Open, 1997; Philadelphia Open, 1997; Cincinnati Open, 1997; Munich Open, 1997; Paris Open, 1997; Hanover Open, 1997; Advanta Championship, 1998; Winner of 63 WTA Tour singles titles and 2 doubles; Investor, Partner and Special Consultant, Tennis Magazine, 2003-. Retired, 2006. Honours: International Tennis Hall of Fame, 2007. Address: ATP Tour, 420 West 45th Street, New York, NY 10036, USA. Website: www.petesampras.com

SAMRA Jorge José H, b. 25 November 1920, Republic of Lebanon. Naturalised Argentinean. Mechanical and Electrical Engineer; Investigator. Education: Graduated as Mechanical and Electrical Engineer, La Plata National University, Argentina. Appointments: Positions in leading companies, more than 30 years, including Chief Engineer, Pilkington PLC subsidiary, 22 years; About 22 European and US visits regarding projects. Publications: Papers: Astronomical Contributions on the Solar System; Cosmic Rays Velocities Exceed Considerably the Speed of Light: Firm evidence of the Newtonian constancy of Length, Time and Mass. Honours: Best Graduate, High School (at the University entrance year); 1 of Best Graduates, La Plata National University; Letter of Congratulation for paper on Astronomical contributions to the solar system, National Research Council, Canada, 1992. Membership: COSPAR Associate. Address: Universidad Nacional de La Plata, Suipacha 1274, 1011 Buenos Aires, Argentina.

SAMUEL Valsamma M, b. 20 August 1956, Pathanamthitta, India. Educator. m. K George Varghese, 2 sons. Education: MSc, Kerala University, 1979; Postgraduate Diploma in Higher Education, IGNOU, New Delhi, 2004; PhD, MG University, Kottayam, 2008. Appointments: Associate Professor, Catholicate College, Pathanamthitta, Kerala, 1980-. Publications: Numerous articles in professional journals. Honours: Listed in international biographical dictionaries. Memberships: Material Science Research, Singapore & India; Indian Science Congress; Max Philoxenos Charitable Society; Academic Physics Teachers Association. Address: Bethania, Santhosh Junction, Pathanamthitta PO, Kerala 689645, India. E-mail: valsageorge@gmail.com

SAN DIEGO Gilbert, b. 1 November 1973, Manila, Philippines. Businessman. m. Cristina Manalad. Education: AB, Political Science; BS, Criminology; Bachelor of Law; Masters in Public Administration; Masters in Police Management; Masters in Criminology; Masters in Business Administration; Strategic Planning; Masters in Management Major in Police Management; PhD, Criminology. Appointments: Vice President, A Francisco Realty & Development Corp. Publications: Author, Dynamic Law Enforcement and Public Safety Administration. Honours: Various local and international awards. Memberships: Director, Kiwanis International; Philconman, Philippine British Society; Life Fellow, IBA; Canada Chamber of Commerce of the Philippines; Director, Rotary Club of Camp Aguinaldo (Paul Harris Fellow); Federation of Authors in Criminology & Criminal Justice Inc. Address: #83 Katipunan Road, White Plains, Quezon City 1116, Manila, Philippines. E-mail: gilbertsandiego@yahoo.com

SAN SEGUNDO MANUEL Teresa, b. 18 March 1958, Madrid, Spain. 1 son, 1 daughter. Education: Law degree, 1981, Licensure exam, 1981, Universidad Complutense de Madrid; PhD courses in law and dissertation, Universidad Carlos III de Madrid, 1994; Specialist in Real Estate Law, Universidad Complutense, Colegio de Registradores y Colegio de Abogados de Madrid, 1993-94. Appointments: College Assistant, 1994-98, Assistant, 1998-2002, Associate Professor, 2002-, College Professor, 2002-, Universidad Nacional de Educación a Distancia; Co-ordinator of Tourism Studies and Civil Law Department, 2000-08. Publications: Numerous articles in professional journals. Honours: X and XI jury prize Elisa Pérez Vera, 2008-09. E-mail: tsansegundo@der.uned.es

SANAKKAYALA Satyanarayana, b. 27 May 1982, Guntur, India. Teacher. Education: PhD. Appointments: Teacher, 1998-. Publications: 22 articles in professional journals. Honours: Editor-in-Chief. Memberships: 5 professional organisations. Address: D No 3-250, Pedakanai, Guntur 522509, India. E-mail: s.satyans1@gmail.com Website: www.ijcmi.webs.com

SANCHEZ-VICARIO Arantxa, b. 18 December 1971, Barcelona, Spain. Tennis Player. Career: Coached Juan Nunez; Winner, 1st professional title at Brussels, 1988; Winner, French Open Women's title, 1989, 1994, 1998; International Championships of Spain, 1989, 1990, Virginia Slims Tournaments, Newport, 1991, Washington, 1991; Winner, Canadian Open, 1992, Australian Open, 1992, 1993, US Open, 1994, named International Tennis Federation World Champion, 1994; Silver Medal, doubles, Bronze Medal, singles, Olympics, 1992; Silver Medal, singles, Bronze Medal, doubles, Olympics, 1996; Spanish Federal Cup team, 1986-98, 2000-01; winner of 14 Grand Slam titles, 96 WTA Tour titles and over 16 million dollars in prize money at retirement November 2002. Honours: Infiniti Commitment to Excellence Award, 1992; Tennis Magazine Comeback Player of the Year, 1998; Principe de Asturiasi Award, Spain, 1998; International Tennis Federation Award of Excellence, 2001; International Tennis Hall of Fame, 2007. Memberships: Spanish Olympic Committee, 2001. Addresss: International Management Group, 1 Erieview Plaza, Suite 1300, Cleveland, OH 4414, USA.

SANDAK-LEWIN Gloria, b. 14 November 1940, Cape Town, South Africa. Poet; Writer. m. Robert H Kaplan, 1 son. Education: BA, English and Latin, 1960, MA, English Literature, 1971, Secondary Teachers' Diploma (1962) University of Cape Town, South Africa. Appointments: Tutor, English Poetry and Fiction, University of Cape Town, 1961; Secondary School Teacher, English and Latin, Herzlia High School, Cape Town, 1963; Part-time Lecturer, Adult Education, specialising in poetry of W B Yeats, University of Cape Town, 1975; Founder, Jewish Writers' Workshop, Cape Town, 1983; Translator, Modern Hebrew Poetry Selections, with Professor I A Ben Yosef, 1987; Poet and Writer. Publications: My Father's House, 1985, 1997; My Father's House and Other

Poems 1965-85, 2000; A Separate Life: Tales of a Woman Estranged, 2006; 2 short stories on Jewish themes; 3 articles on Jewish writers. Honours: Silver medal, Good Hope Junior School, 1951; Dux Gold Medal, Good Hope Seminary Senior School, 1957; English Class Medal, University of Cape Town, 1960; Poem selected for inclusion in BBC publication, The Fate of Vultures, An Anthology of Entries from the 1988 BBC Arts and Africa Poetry Award, 1989. Address: 5 Derry Road, Rondebosch 7700, Cape Town, South Africa.

SANDER Louis Wilson, b. 31 July 1918, San Francisco, California, USA. Professor of Psychiatry. m. Betty Thorpe, 2 sons, 1 daughter. Education: AB, 1939, MD, Medical School, 1942, University of California; Intern, University of California Hospital, 1942-43. Appointments: 2nd Lieutenant to Major, USAAF Medical Corps, 1943-46; Resident in Psychiatry to Professor of Psychiatry, School of Medicine, 1947-68, Principal Investigator, Longitudinal Study in Early Personality Development, 1963-87, Professor of Psychiatry, School of Medicine, 1968-78, Boston University; Professor of Psychiatry, Senior Scholar, School of Medicine, University of Colorado, 1978-87. Publications: Contributor, over 50 articles, book chapters; reviews to professional publications, 1962-2002; Living Systems, Evolving Consciousness, The Emerging Person, 2007. Honours: Recipient, Research Career Development Award, US Public Health Service, 1963-68; Research Scientist Awards, US Public Health Service, 1968-78; Research Grantee, US Public Health Service, March of Dimes, W Grant Foundation; MacArthur Foundation, Spencer Foundation, National Council on Alcoholism; other organisations; Honorary Membership Award, American Psychoanalytic Association, 2001. Memberships: American Medical Association; American Psychiatric Association; American College of Psychoanalysts; Boston Psychoanalytic Society; American Association for the Advancement of Science; Society for Research in Child Development; American Academy of Child Psychiatry; World Association for Infant Mental Health; Boston Change Process Study Group, 1995-; San Francisco Psychoanalytic Society and Institute. Address: 2525 Madrona Ave, St Helena, CA 94574-2300, USA.

SANDER Peter, b. 9 September 1933, Budapest, Hungary. Composer; Arranger; Lecturer. Divorced, 2 sons, 1 daughter. Education: BA, History, University of Budapest, 1951-55; Music Academy, Budapest, 1955-56; LGSM, Piano and Theory, Guildhall School of Music and Drama, 1959; College of Music, Debrecen, Hungary; Trinity College of Music, London; MMus, 1987, PhD, 1992, Composition, University of London, Goldsmiths College. Appointments: Teacher of Composition, City Literary Institute, 1974-98; Composer of film, commercial, jazz and concert music Currently retired but teaching piano and composition and composing. Compositions include: String Quartet Nos 1 and 2; Wind Quintet Nos 1 and 2; Brass Quintet No 1; Exploration, for guitar; Anecdotes, Light Orchestral and Vocal Piece; Piano Pieces; Cause Célebre (opera), 1991. Recordings: String Quartet No 1; Wind Quintet No 1; Intarsii, for orchestra; Essay Nos 1 and 2, for orchestra; Exploration; String Trio; Piano Trio; Wind Trio. Publications: String Quartet No 1, Wind Quintet No 1, Brass Quintet, Exploration, Duolith, Anecdotes, Piano Pieces. Contributions to: Melody Maker; Music Maker; Into Jazz. Honour: 1st Mention, French Radio and TV International Composition Competition, 1974. Memberships: British Academy of Composers and Songwriters; PRS; MCPS. Address: 73 The Avenue, London NW6 7NS, England.

SANDERS Jeremy Keith Morris, b. 3 May 1948, London, England. Chemist. m. Louise Sanders, 1 son, 1 daughter. Education: BSc, Chemistry, Imperial College, London; PhD, Chemistry, 1972, MA, 1974, ScD, 2001, University of Cambridge; FRSC, C Chem, 1978. Appointments: Research Associate, Pharmacology, Stanford University, USA, 1972-73; Demonstrator, then Lecturer, then Reader in Chemistry, 1973-96, Professor of Chemistry, 1996-, Head, Department of Chemistry, 2000-2006, Deputy Vice-Chancellor, 2006-10; Head, School of Physical Sciences, 2009-; University of Cambridge; Chair, Chemistry sub-panel, 2008 UK Research Assessment Exercise, 2004-08. Publications: Book: Modern NMR Spectroscopy (with B K Hunter), 1987, 1992; Over 300 research papers on aspects of organic, inorganic and biological chemistry. Honours: Meldola Medal, Royal Institute of Chemistry, 1975; Hickinbottom Award, Royal Society of Chemistry, 1981; Pfizer Academic Award for work on nuclear Overhauser effect, 1984; Pfizer Academic Award for work on in vivo NMR, 1988; Josef Loschmidt Prize, Royal Society of Chemistry, 1994; Elected FRS, 1995; Elected FRSA, 1997; Pedler Medal and Prize, Royal Society of Chemistry, 1996; Visiting Fellow, Japan Society for the Promotion of Science, 2002; Izatt-Christensen Award in Macrocyclic Chemistry, USA, 2003; Davy Medal, Royal Society, 2009; President, Bürgenstock Conference, 2011; Listed in various biographical directories. Membership: The Athenaeum. Address: University Chemical Laboratory, Lensfield Road, Cambridge CB2 1EW, England. E-mail: jkms@cam.ac.uk Website: www-sanders.ch.cam.ac.uk/

SANDERSON Teresa (Tessa) Ione, b. 14 March 1956. Athlete. Career: Represented Britain in javelin, 1974-; Commonwealth Games Gold Medallist, 1978, 1986, 1990; European Championship Gold Medallist, 1978; Olympic Games Gold Medallist, Olympic Record, 1984; World Cup Gold Medallist, 1992; Other achievements: Fourth Place at Barcelona Olympics, 1992; Several records including: UK Javelin record, 1976; Presenter, Sky News Sports, 1989-92; Involvement with various charities. Publications: My Life in Athletics, 1985. Honours: British Athletics Writers Association Female Athlete of the Year, 1977, 1978, 1984; Honorary BSc University of Birmingham; MBE, 1985; OBE, 1998, CBE, 2004. Memberships: Board member, English Sports Council, 1998-. Address: c/o Derek Evans, 68 Meadowbank Road, Kingsbury, London NW9, England. E-mail: tessa@tprmplus.freeserve.co.uk

SANDLER Adam, b. 9 September 1966, Brooklyn, New York, USA. Actor; Screenwriter. m. Jackie Titone, 2003, 2 daughters. Education: New York University. Career: Actor, films include: Shakes the Clown; Coneheads; Mixed Nuts; Airheads; Billy Madison; Happy Gilmore; Bullet Proof; Guy Gets Kid, 1998; The Wedding Singer, 1998; The Water Boy, 1998; Big Daddy, 1999; Little Nicky, 2000; Punch-Drunk Love, 2002; Mr Deeds, 2002; Anger Management, 2003; Fifty First Dates, 2004; Spanglish, 2004; Longest Yard, 2005; Click, 2006; Reign Over Me, 2007; I Now Pronounce You Chuck and Larry, 2007; You Don't Mess with the Zohan, 2008; Bedtime Stories, 2008; Funny People, 2009; Grown Ups, 2010. Actor, writer, Saturday Night Live; TV appearances include: Saturday Night Live Mother's Day Special, 1992; MTV Music Video Awards, 1994; Saturday Night Live Presents President Bill Clinton's All-Time Favourites, 1994; 37th Annual Grammy Awards, 1995; ESPY Awards, 1996. Publications: Co-writer: Billy Madison; Happy Gilmore; The Water Boy; Recordings: Album: Stan and Judy's Kid; They're

All Gonna Laugh at You! 1993. Honours: Peoples Choice Award, 2000. Address: c/o Ballstein-Grey, 9150 Wilshire Boulevard, Suite 350, Beverly Hills, CA 90212, USA.

SANDS Roger Blakemore, b. 6 May 1942, London, England. Clerk of the House of Commons, now retired. m. Jennifer Ann Cattell, 2 daughters, 1 deceased. Education: University College School, Hampstead; MA, Oriel College, Oxford, 1965. Appointments: Secretary to the House of Commons Commission, 1985-87; Clerk of the Overseas Office, 1987-91; Registrar of Members Interests, 1991-94; Clerk of Public Bills, 1994-97; Clerk of Legislation, 1998-2001; Clerk Assistant, 2001-02; Clerk of the House and Chief Executive, House Commons 2003-06; Independent Chairman, Standards Committee, Mid-Sussex DC, 2007-; Independent Member, UK Public Affairs Council (UKPAC), 2010-. Honours: KCB, 2006. Membership: Holtye Golf Club. Address: 4 Woodbury House, Lewes Road, East Grinstead, West Sussex RH19 3UD, England. E-mail: rjsxrandjsands.demon.co.uk

SANNER George Elwood, b. 30 August 1929, Rockwood, Pennsylvania, USA. Electrical Engineer. m. Marjorie, 1 son, 2 daughters. Education: BS, Engineering and Physics, University of Pittsburgh, 1951; Graduate, Physics and Mathematical Studies, Johns Hopkins University, 1956; PE (Registered Professional Engineer); Computing Technology Industry Association Certification: Computer Specialist A+, 2001; Microsoft Professional Network Certifications: MCP, 2000, MCP+I, 2001 and MCSE, 2001; Numerous professional certificates include: Network Administration, 1998; Microsoft Certified System Engineering, 1999, Mercer University, Atlanta, Georgia. Appointments: Radar/Electronics Officer, US Navy, 1951-59; Supervising Microwave and Radar Design and Development Engineer, Westinghouse Electric Corporation, Baltimore, 1952-58; Space Communications Programmes Director, Engineer Manager, Bendix Corporation Radio Division, 1958-64; Chief Scientist, Consulting Engineer, Advanced Electronic Systems, Westinghouse, 1964-71; President, Chief Engineer, Electronic Control Systems, Santron Corporation, Baltimore, 1971-80; Senior Project Engineer, Bendix NASA/JPL Voyager II Program, Field Engineering Corporation, 1980-81; Senior Engineering Specialist, Air Defence Systems, Litton Data Systems, New Orleans, 1981-83; Consultant, Eaton Corporation, AIL Division, 1983-87; Senior Principal Engineer, Advanced Avionic Systems, American Electronic Laboratories Inc, Pennsylvania, 1987-92; Engineering Consultant, George E Sanner Advanced Computer Network Consultants, Georgia, 1992-; Director of Telemarketing and Electronic Systems, Regal Bank & Trust, Owings Mills, Maryland, 2007-. Publications: 17 US patents; Numerous research reports and lectures. Honours: Special Faculty Award Plaque, RETS Electronic Schools Inc, Baltimore, 1977; Eisenhower People-to-People Tour, European Crop Irrigation, 1978. Memberships: Life Member, IEEE; IEEE Computer Society; (CompTIA) Computing Technology Industry Association; Quarter Century Wireless Association; American Heritage Foundation; Judicial Watch; Life Member, National Republican Committee; National Republican Congressional and National Republican Senatorial Committees; Licensed Lay Reader in the Anglican Catholic Church. Address: 2501 Hidden Hills Drive, Marietta, GA 30066, USA. E-mail: GESTE@MSN.com

SANT CASSIA Louis Joseph, b. 19 September 1946, St Paul's Bay, Malta. Obstetrician & Gynaecologist. m. Antoinette Ferro, 1 son, 1 daughter. Education: Lyceum, Malta; MD, Royal University of Malta, 1973; DM, University of Nottingham, 1986. Appointments: Consultant Obstetrician & Gynaecologist, 1987-; Coventry District Tutor, RCOG, 1988-94; Chairman, Division of Obstetrics & Gynaecology, 1989-93; Visiting Clinical Lecturer, 1993-2002, Honorary Reader, 2008-, University of Warwick; Chairman, Coventry Research Ethics Committee, 1993-2004; Chairman, Medical Advisory Committee, Warwickshire Nuffield Hospital, 1995-2000; Leading Clinician Gynaecological Oncology, Coventry, 1997-; Honorary Lecturer, University of Malta, 1998-; Examiner Diploma, 1999-2001, Examiner, MRCOG, Royal College of Obstetricians & Gynaecologists; Lead Gynaecological Clinician, Arden Network (Warwickshire Oncology), 1999-2007; Chairman, Senior Hospital Medical Staff Committee, University Hospital Coventry & Warwickshire, 2004-09; Honorary President, Birmingham & Midlands, Obstetrical & Gynaecological Society, 2009-10; Examiner, Warwick Medical School, 2006-; Examiner, Birmingham Medical School, MBBS 1985, 1992, 2003. Publications: Numerous articles in professional journals. Memberships: Founder Member, Malta College of Obstetrics & Gynaecology; British Society for Colposcopy and Cervical Pathology; British Gynae Cancer Society. Address: Four Winds, Stoneleigh Road, Blackdown, Leamington Spa, Warwickshire CV32 6QR, England. E-mail: ljsantcassia@hotmail.co.uk

SANTANGELO Antonio, b. 20 August 1928, Udine, Italy. Doctor of Medicine. Education: Classical Studies, Milan; Doctorate in Medicine, Milan, 1952; Studies in Anthropology, 1960-. Publications include most recently: Mental Issues & Human Ontogeny, 2003; Culture Influencing Ontogeny and Adaptability of the Hominina Homo, 2004; Intellective Elements Morphotyping Homo, 2006; Some Closer Look at Mental Elements Acting Evolution Homo, 2006/07; Mental Elements and Evolution Homo, Theoretical Implications, 2008/09. Memberships: European Anthropological Association. Address: via Mac Mahon 12, 20.155 Milano, Italy; p. Giovanni dalle Bande Nere 2, 20.146 Milano, Italy. E-mail: antonio.santangelo@yahoo.it

SANTER Jacques, b. 18 May 1937, Wasserbilig, Luxembourg. Politician. m. Danièle Binot, 2 sons. Education: Athenée de Luxembourg; University of Paris; University of Strasbourg; Inst d'Etudes Politiques, Paris. Appointments: Advocate, Luxembourg Court of Appeal, 1961-65; Attaché, Officer of Minister of Labour and Social Security, 1963-65; Govt attaché, 1965-66; Parliament Secretary Parti Chrétien-Social, 1966-72, Secretary-General, 1972-74, President, 1974-82; Secretary of State for Cultural and Social Affairs, 1972-74; Member, Chamber of Deputies, 1974-79; Member, European Parliament, 1975-79, VP, 1975-77; Municipal Magistrate, City of Luxembourg, 1976-79; Minister of Finance of Labour and of Social Security, 1979-84; Prime Minister, Minister of State and Minister of Finance, 1984-89, Prime Minister, Minister of State, of Cultural Affairs and the Treasury and Financial Affairs, 1989-94; President, European Committee, 1994-99; Member, European Parliament, 1999-2004. Honour: Hon LLD (Wales), 1998. Address: 69 rue J-P Huberty, 1742 Luxembourg.

SANTOS Nunos C, b. 17 July 1972, Lisbon, Portugal. Biochemist; Researcher; Professor. m. Elisabete Santos, 2 sons. Education: Degree in Biochemistry, 1995; PhD, Biochemistry, 1999, Habilitation, Biomedical Sciences, 2010, University of Lisbon. Appointments: Researcher, Technical University of Lisbon, 1994-99; Teaching Assistant, 1999-2000, Assistant Professor, 2000-, University of Lisbon (Lisbon Medical School); Head of Unit, Institute of Molecular Medicine, 2008-. Publications: Author of more than 50 scientific articles and book chapters on molecular biophysics and biomembranes. Honour: Calouste Gulbenkian Foundation Award, 2001; Jose Luis Champalimaud Award (Basic Sciences, ex-aequo), 2004, (Applied Research and Technologies), 2005. Membership: Biophysical Society, USA. Address: Instituto de Medicina Molecular, Faculdade de Medicina da Universidade de Lisboa, Av Prof Egas Moniz, 1649-028 Lisbon, Portugal. E-mail: nsantos@fm.ul.pt

SANWARIA Hari Narayan, b. 6 April 1947, Shahar, Karauli, Raj, India. Professor. m. Shanti Devi, 1 son, 3 daughters. Education: MSc, Mathematics of Statistics; PhD, Information Theory. Appointments: Lecturer, Mathematics, R R College, Alwar; Vice-Principal/HOD, Government College, Kota; Principal, Government PG College, Kota; Principal, Government PG College, Malpura; Senior Professor, Mathematics. Publications: 15 textbooks in mathematics. Honours: Dr B R Ambedkar National Fellowship Award, 1990; Mahatma Jyoti Rao Phoole National Award, 2009. Memberships: Life Member, National Academy of Sciences, India; Life Member, Indian Society of Information Theory of Applications, India. Address: 14 Kalyan Nagar-I, Behind New Bungalow, Tonk Road, Jaipur, India. E-mail: hnsanwaria@gmail.com

SARAMAGO José, b. 16 November 1922, Azinhaga, Portugal. Author; Poet; Dramatist. Education: Principally self-educated. Publications: Fiction: Manual de Pintura e Caligrafia, 1977, (Manual of Painting and Calligraphy), 1994; Levantado do Chao (Raised from the Ground), 1980; Memorial do Convento, 1982, (Baltasar and Blimunda), 1987; A Jangada de Pedra, 1986, (The Stone Raft), 1994; O Ano da Morte de Ricardo Reis, 1984, (The Year of the Death of Ricardo Reis), 1991; Historia do Cerco de Lisboa (The History of the Siege of Lisbon), 1989; O Evangelho segundo Jesus Cristo, 1991, (The Gospel According to Jesus Christ), 1994; Ensaio Sobre A Cegueira (Blindness), 1996; Todos os nomes, All the Names, 2000; O Homeru Duplicado (The Double), 2000; La caverna, 2001; Ensaio sobre a Lucidez, 2004; Short stories: Objecto Quase, (Quasi Object), 1978; Poetica dos cinco sentidos – O ouvido, 1979; Telling Tales (charity anthology), 2004; Poetry: Os poemas posiveis, 1966; Provavelmente alegria, 1970; O ano de 1993, 1975; Plays: A noite, 1979; Que farei com este livro? 1980; A segunda vida la Francisco de Assisi, 1987; I Nomine Dei, 1993; Don Giovanni ou O dissoluto absolvido, 2005; Opera librettos: Blimunda, 1990; Diva, 1993; Il dissoluto assolto, 2005; Other writing. Contributions to: Various publications. Honours: Several literary awards and prizes, including the Nobel Prize for Literature, 1998. Address: c/o Harcourt Brace & Co, 6277 Sea Harbor Drive, Orlando, FL 32887, USA.

SARANDON Susan Abigail, b. 4 October 1946, New York, USA. Actress. m. Chris Sarandon, divorced, 1 daughter, 1 daughter with Franco Amurri, 2 sons with Tim Robbins. Education: Catholic University of America. Career: Stage appearances include: A Coupla of White Chicks Sittin' Around Talkin'; An Evening with Richard Nixon; A Stroll in the Air; Albert's Bridge; Private Ear, Public Eye; Extremities; Numerous TV appearances; Films include: Joe, 1970; Lady Liberty, 1971; The Rocky Horror Picture Show, Lovin' Molly, 1974; The Great Waldo Pepper, 1975; The Front Page, Dragon Fly, 1976; Walk Away Madden; The Other Side of Midnight, The Last of the Cowboys, 1977; Pretty Baby, King of the Gypsies, 1978; Loving Couples, 1980; Atlantic City, 1981; Tempest, 1982; The Hunger, 1983; Buddy System, 1984; Compromising Positions, 1985; The Witches of Eastwick, 1987; Bull Durham, Sweet Hearts Dance, 1988; Married to the Mob; A Dry White Season, The January Man, 1989; White Palace; Thelma and Louise, Light Sleeper, 1991; Lorenzo's Oil; The Client; Little Women, Safe Passage, 1995; Dead Man Walking, James and the Giant Peach, 1996; Illuminate, Twilight, 1998; Stepmom, Anywhere But Here, Cradle Will Rock, 1999; Rugrats in Paris, Joe Gould's Secret, 2000; Cats and Dogs, 2001; Igby Goes Down, 2002; The Banger Sisters, The Nazi Officer's Wife, Last Party 2000, 2003; Noel, Shall We Dance? Alfie, 2004; Elizabethtown, Romance & Cigarettes, 2005; Irresistible, 2006; In the Valley of Elah, Mr Woodcock, Emotional Arithmetic, Bernard and Doris, Enchanted, 2007; Middle of Nowhere, Speed Racer, 2008; Leaves of Grass, Solitary Man, The Lovely Bones, 2009; Wall Street: Money Never Sleeps, Peacock, 2010; Jeff, Who Lives at Home, Robot & Frank, That's My Boy, Arbitrage, Cloud Atlas, 2012; Snitch, 2013. Honour: Academy Award for Best Actress, 1996. Address: c/o ICM, Martha Luttrell, 8942 Wilshire Boulevard, Beverly Hills, CA 90211, USA.

SARBU Ioan, b. 31 August 1951, Timisoara, Romania. Civil Engineer; Professor. m. Eleonora Sarbu, 1 daughter. Education: Hydrotechnics, Technical University of Timisoara, 1970-75; PhD, Civil Engineering, Technical University, 1993; License in Laboratory Testing of Building Equipment, Ministry of Public Works, 2001; European Engineer, European Federation of National Engineering Associations, 2001. Appointments: Design Engineer, Water Resources Management Company, Timisoara, 1975-79; Assistant Professor, Technical University, 1979-88; Lecturer, 1988-94, Associate Professor, 1994-98, Professor, 1998-, Politechnica University; Doctoral Degree Advisor, 2004-; Head of Building Equipment Department, 2000-; Head of National Building Equipment Laboratory, 2001-; Expert Reviewer, National Board of Scientific Research for Higher Education, Bucharest, 1999-; VP, National Board of Certified Energetical Auditors Buildings, Bucharest, 2003-; Co-ordination, International Academic Research Gnomon Project, Global Gnomon Co, Madrid, 2003-; Scientific Advisor, Science Bulletin of Politechnica University, Timisoara, 2004-; Reviewer of Journal of Hydraulic Research, 2007-; Scientific Adviser, Technical Bulletin of Debrecen University, 2008-. Publications: Books (author): Hydraulics of town constructions and installations, 1989; Numerical and optimizing methods in building equipment design, 1994; Computer utility in installation engineering, 1996; Energetical optimization of water distribution systems, 1997; Refrigerating systems, 1998; Computer aided design of building equipment, 2000; Energetical optimization of buildings, 2002; Thermal building equipments, 2007; Editor: Building equipment and ambiental comfort, 2007, 2009; Contributor of over 280 articles in professional journals; Author of up to 20 computer programmes; Author of 5 patent certificates. Honours: Distinguished Professor, Ministry of Education, 1986; Award, Romanian General Association of Engineers, 1997; Excellency Diploma, Association of Building Equipment Engineer, 2001; Plaque, Great Minds of the 21st Century, ABI, 2005; Diploma, Outstanding Scientist of the 21st Century, IBC, 2005; World Medal of Freedom, ABI, 2006; Diploma, Outstanding Intellectuals of the 21st Century, IBC, 2007; Diploma, 21st Century Award for Achievement, IBC, 2007; Plaque, Gold Medal for Romania, ABI, 2007; Lifetime Achievement Award, ABI, 2008; Man of the Year in Science, ABI, 2008; Citation of Meritorious Achievement, IBC, 2008; Ultimate Achiever Award Certificate for Engineering, IBC, 2009; Hall of Fame for Distinguished Accomplishments in Science and Education, ABI, 2009; Listed in Who's Who publications and biographical dictionaries. Memberships: International Association of Hydraulic Engineering and Research; American Society of Heating, Refrigerating and Air-Conditioning Engineers; Science Academy of Romania;

Society for Computer Aided Engineering; Research Board of Advisors, ABI, 2005. Address: Piata Bisericii, No 4A, Ap 3, 300233 Timisoara, Romania. E-mail: ioan.sarbu@ct.upt.ro

SARGENT John Richard, b. 22 March 1925, Birmingham, England. Economist. m. Hester, deceased 2004, 1 son, 2 daughters. Education: BA, First Class, Christ Church, Oxford, 1948. Appointments: Fellow and Lecturer in Economics, Worcester College, Oxford, 1951-62; Economic Consultant, H M Treasury, 1963-65; Professor of Economics, Founder Member of Department of Economics, 1965-73, Pro-Vice-Chancellor, 1970-72, University of Warwick; Group Economic Advisor, Midland Bank, 1974-84; Houblon-Norman Research Fellow, Bank of England. Publications: Numerous articles in economic journals include most recently: Roads to Full Employment, 1995; Towards a New Economy? Recent Inflation and Unemployment in the UK, 2002; Book, British Transport Policy, 1958. Honours: Rockefeller Fellow, USA, 1959-60; Honorary Professor of Economics, University of Warwick, 1974-81; Visiting Professor, London School of Economics, 1981-82. Memberships: Reform Club, 1965-; Member of Council, Royal Economic Society, 1969-74; Member, Doctors and Dentists Pay Review Body, 1972-75; Member, Armed Forces Pay Review Body, 1972-85; Member, Economic and Social Research Council, 1980-85. Address: 38 The Leys, Chipping Norton, Oxfordshire OX7 5HH, England.

SARKAR Jahar, b. 25 January 1977, Murshidabad, India. Teacher; Researcher. Education: PhD, Mechanical Engineering, IIT Kharagpur, 2006. Appointments: Assistant Professor, IT-BHU, India. Publications: 65 articles in professional journals. Honours: 2 awards. Address: Department of Mechanical Engineering, IT-BHU, Varanasi, UP-221005, India. E-mail: jsarkar.mec@itbhu.ac.in

SARKAR Sunil Kumar, b. 1 February 1948, Mymensingh, Bangladesh. Medical Practitioner. m. Doli, 2 sons, 1 daughter. Education: MBBS, 1972; ECFMG, 1974; MD, 1993; PhD, 1995; DSc, 1998. Appointments: Doctor in private practice, 1973-; Emeritus Professor, College of Chest Physicians, India, 1990-; Honorary Senior Medical Consultant, Visiting Professor of Medicine, Postgraduate Institute of Medical Education and Research, New Delhi, India, 1993. Honours include: Visisht Chikitsa Medal, Gold Record of Achievement, 1997; Chikitsa Ratna honour, 20th Century Award for Achievement, Platinum Record Award, 2000 Millennium Medal of Honor, 1998; Title of Veshajachuramani, International Man of the Millennium, Outstanding Man of 20th Century, 1999; World Laureate, 2000; Outstanding Man of the 21st Century. Memberships: Society for Advanced Studies in Medical Sciences; Association of College of Chest Physicians; Leading Intellectuals of the World. Address: 166-30, 88 Ave # 3Fl, Jamaica, NY 11432, USA.

SARKER Shah-Jalal, b. 10 January 1970, Comilla, Bangladesh. University Teacher. m. Farzana P Huq, 3 sons. Education: BSc (Hons), 1990, MSc, 1991, Statistics, University of Dhaka; MSc, Epidemiology, Erasmus and Cambridge University, 1998; PhD, Statistics, University of Surrey, 2001. Appointments: Statistical Analyst, BRAC, Dhaka, 1995-96; Lecturer, Statistics, Shahjalal University of Science and Technology, Sylhet, 1996-97; Research Fellow, University of Reading, England, 2002-05; Research Fellow, King's College, London, 2005-09; Lecturer, Biostatistics, Institute of Cancer, Queen Mary University, London, 2009-. Publications: Numerous articles in professional journals. Honours: The Netherlands Fellowship Program, 1997-98; PhD Studentship, Surrey University, 1998-2001; First Prize Winner, poster competition, RSS International Conference, 2000. Memberships: Fellow, Royal Statistical Society; Academic Member, Statisticians in the Pharmaceutical Industries; Treasurer, Association of Statistics Lecturers in Universities; Life Member, Bangladesh Statistical Association; Society for Clinical Trials, USA. Address: Centre for Experimental Cancer Medicine, Barts Cancer Institute, Queen Mary University of London, Old Anatomy Building, Charterhouse Square, London EC1M 6BQ, England. E-mail: map1ms@hotmail.com

SARODE Sachin, b. 15 March 1978, Wardha, India. Oral Pathologist. m. Gargi. Education: Bachelor, Dental Surgery; Master, Dental Surgery (Oral Pathology and Microbiology); PhD, Oral Pathology, in progress. Appointments: Associate Professor, Dr D Y Patil Dental College and Hospital; Consultant Oral Pathologist. Publications: 16 international articles in indexed journals; 1 national article in indexed journals. Honours: Best Scientific Presentation, VIII National PG Convention, 2008; Reviewers' Board Member: Oral Oncology, Head & Neck Pathology, JOPM, Acta Odontol Scandinavia, and IJDR; Listed in international biographical dictionaries. Memberships: Indian Association of Oral & Maxillofacial Pathologists; Indian Dental Association; Indian Congress of Science. Address: Sriniwas Colony, Ramnagar, Wardha, Maharashtra, 442001, India. E-mail: drsachinsarode@gmail.com

SASAKI Kazutaka, b. 2 September 1957, Tokyo, Japan. Linguistics Professor. m. Kumiko Tsune-izumi, 2 sons. Education: B Ed, 1981, M Ed, 1983, English Linguistics, Tokyo Gakugei University. Appointments: Assistant Professor, Tokyo Metropolitan College of Aeronautical Engineering, 1983-87; Assistant Professor, Faculty of General Education, 1987-91, Associate Professor, 1991-94, Associate Professor, 1994-2004, Professor, 2004-, Faculty of International Studies, Utsunomiya University; Visiting Scholar, Linguistics Department, UCLA, 2000-01. Publications: 7 books including: A New Trend, 1999; Over 50 articles including: Dervied Nominals and Grammtical Dynamism: A Comparative Syntax of English and Japanese, 1997. Memberships: The English Linguistic Society of Japan; The English Literary Society of Japan; The Linguistic Society of America. Address: 1039-79 Nishikawata-machi, Utsunomiya, Tochigi 321-0151, Japan. E-mail: sasaki@cc.utsunomiya-u.ac.jp

SASIPALLI Venkata Sanyasi Rao, b. 10 June 1963, Vizianagaram, India. Researcher; Businessman. m. Guru Nageswari, 1 son, 1 daughter. Education: Doctor of Engineering, Hiroshima University, Japan, 1998; MSc nat, Kaiserlautern University, Germany, 1993; BSc, 1983, Diploma, 1986, MSc, 1987, M Phil, 1990, Andhra University, India. Appointments: Principal Advisor, RAMTEJ Gorup; Lead Researcher, CECTch; Engineer, NEC; Lecturer, Andhra University; Project Manager, RAMTEJ Technologies. Publications: Around 25 publications in the field of engineering, mathematics and social sciences; Around 10 conferences organized and delivered; A total of 50 speeches. Honours: DAAD Fellowship, German, 1991-93; Monbusho Fellowship, Japan, 1994-98. Memberships: ISIAM; ISTAM; IMS; CSI; ISTE; ISCA; CSWB; YHAI; IETE; SEMCEI; RMS; CMS; Founder Member, NSES, WIS. Address: Takeyacho 7-20-203, Naka-ku, Hiroshima City, 730-0048, Japan. drsvsrao@gmail.com

SASTRY Narasimha, b. 18 December 1951, Mudiyanur, India. m. Padma, 1 son. Professor. Education: BSc, 1970, MSc, 1972, Mysore University; PhD, Mathematics,

University of Pittsburgh, USA, 1978. Appointments: Lecturer, Mathematics, Regional College of Education, Mysore, 1974-75; Lecturer, 1983-87, Associate Professor, 1987-92, Professor, 1993-, Mathematics, Indian Statistical Institute, Bangalore. Publications: Numerous articles in professional journals; 3 books edited. Honours: Mellon Fellowship, University of Pittsburgh, USA, 1976-78. Memberships: International Directory of Mathematics. Address: Division of Theoretical Statistics and Mathematics, Indian Statistical Institute, 8th Mile, Mysore Road, RV College Post, Bangalore 560059, India.

SATO Kazuhiko, b. 14 September 1959, Natori, Japan. Assistant Professor. Education: BA, Tohoku Gakuin University, 1982; MA, English Linguistics, University of Northern Iowa, 1991. Appointments: Teacher, Tohoku Gakuin Junior and Senior High School, Sendai, Japan, 1982-89; Instructor, 1994-99, Assistant Professor, 1999-, Miyagi National College of Technology, Natori, Japan. Publications: Several articles and research reports. Memberships: Linguistic Society of America; Linguistic Association of Great Britain; Cognitive Science Society. Address: 3-1-6 Tsukinoki Higashi, Shibata-cho Shibata-gum, Miyagi 989-1757, Japan.

SATYANARAYANA Bhavanari, Professor. Appointments: Honorary Editor, Ganitha Chandrica, Ganitha Vahini, and International Journal of Computational Mathematical Ideas; Reviewer Member, Scientific Journals International, USA; Principal Investigator, 3 major research projects, UGC; Visiting Fellow, TIFR, Bombay, India, 1989; Elected President, Association for Improvement of Maths Education, 2005-09; Visiting Professor, Walt Sisulu University, South Africa, 2007; Elected Executive member, Andhra Pradesh Society for Mathematical Sciences, 2007-09; Professor, Mathematics, Acharya Nagarjuna University, India. Publications: Author/Editor, 36 books; 65 research papers. Honours: CSIR-JRF, 1980-82; CSIR-SRF, 1982-85; UGC-Research Associateship, 1985; CSIR-POOL Officer, 1988; INSA Visiting Fellowship Award, 2005; ANU-Best Research Paper Award, 2006; AP Scientist, 2009 Award; Fellow, AP Akademi of Sciences, Siksha Rattan Puraskar Award, 2011; Glory of India Award, 2011; International Achievers Award, 2011; Best Citizen of India Award, 2011. Memberships: Hungarian Academy of Sciences; Indian National Science Academy. Address: Acharya Nagarjuna University, Andhra Pradesh, India. E-mail: bhavanari2002@yahoo.co.in

SAUNDERS Ann Loreille, (Ann Cox-Johnson), b. 23 May 1930, London, England. Historian. m. Bruce Kemp Saunders, 4 June 1960, 1 son, 1 daughter, deceased. Education: Plumptre Scholar, Queen's College, London, 1946-48; BA Honours, University College, London, 1951; PhD, Leicester University, 1965. Appointments: Deputy Librarian, Lambeth Palace, 1952-55; Archivist, Marylebone Public Library, London, 1956-63; Honorary Editor, 1967-2008, Editor Emeritus, 2009-, Costume Society; Honorary Editor, London Topographical Society, 1975-. Publications: London, City and Westminster, 1975; Art and Architecture of London, 1984, St Martin-in-the-Fields, 1989; The Royal Exchange, monograph, 1991; The Royal Exchange, editor and co-author, 1997; St Paul's: the Story of the Cathedral, 2001; The History of the Merchant Taylors' Company (with Matthew Davies), 2004; Historic London Photographs from the Collection of BEC Howarth-Loomes, 2008. Contributions to: Magazines. Honours: Prize for Best Specialist Guide Book of the Year, British Tourist Board, 1984; Fellow, University College, London, 1992; MBE, 2002. Memberships: Society of Antiquaries, Fellow; Costume Society; London Topographical Society. Address: 3 Meadway Gate, London NW11 7LA, England.

SAUNDERS Jennifer, b. 6 July 1958, England. Actress; Writer. m. Adrian Edmondson, 3 daughters. Education: Central School of Speech and Drama, London. Career: Theatre: An Evening with French and Saunders (tour), 1989; Me and Mamie O'Rourke, 1993; French and Saunders Live in 2000 (tour), 2000; TV: The Comic Strip Presents …, 1990; Girls on Top; French and Saunders (5 series); Absolutely Fabulous, 1993, 1994, 995, 2001; Ab Fab The Last Shout, 1996; Let Them Eat Cake, 1999; Mirrorball, 2000; Jam & Jerusalem, 2006; A Bucker o' French & Saunders, 2007; The Life and Times of Vivienne Vyle, 2007; The Hunt for Tony Blair, 2011; Dead Boss, 2012; Blandings, 2013. Films: The Supergrass, 1984; Muppet Treasure Island, 1996; Spice World the Movie; Maybe Baby, 2000; Shrek 2 (voice), 2004; L'Entente cordiale, 2006; Coraline (voice), 2008. Publications: A Feast of French and Saunders, 1992; Absolutely Fabulous: The Scripts, 1993; Absolutely Fabulous Continuity, 2001. Honours: Emmy Award, 1993; OBE, 2001; Honorary Rose, Montreux, 2002; People's Choice Award, 2005; BAFTA Fellowship, 2009; BAFTA Television Award, 2012. Address: c/o Peters, Fraser & Dunlop, Drury House, 34-43 Russell Street, London, WC2B 5HA, England.

SAVCHENKO Alexander, b. 5 October 1958, Friazino, Moscow region, Russia. m. Olesia, 2 sons. Senior Research Worker. Education: Master, Mathematics, Novosibirsk State University, 1980; PhD, Mathematics, Computer Centre, Novosibirsk, 1998. Appointments: Researcher, Computer Centre, Novosibirsk 1982-97; Senior Research Worker, Computer Centre (now Institute of Computational Mathematics and Mathematical Geophysics, 1998-. Publications: 20 articles in professional journals. Address: PO Box 257, 630090 Novosibirsk, Russia.

SAVELYEVA Marina, b. 2 April 1962, Yaroslavl, Russia. Medical Doctor. m. Sergey Shevchenko, 1 daughter. Education: Medical diploma, Medical State Academy, Yaroslavl, 1980-86; Psychiatrist, Yaroslavl, 1987; Medical Psychologist, St Petersburg, 1992; PhD, Yaroslavl State Medical Academy, 1995; Psychotherapist, Moscow, 2000; Therapeutist, Yaroslavl, 2006; Clinical Pharmacologist, Moscow, 2007; MD, Sechenov, Moscow Medical Academy, 2009. Appointments: Psychiatrist, Yaroslavl, 1986-88; Head Doctor, Central Regional Hospital, Yaroslavl Region, 1988-90; Internist, Yaroslavl Regional Hospital, 1990-94; Executive Director, Non State Pension Foundation, 1994-95; Product Manager, Pfizer, Moscow, 1995-99; Product Manager, Beafour Ipsen, Moscow, 2000-01; Product Manager, Novartis Pharma, 2001-09; Professor, Sechenov Moscow Medical Academy, 2005-10; Head, MSW, Novartis Pharma, Moscow, 2010-. Publications: Numerous articles in professional journals, 1994-2010; Author, chapters in books on clinical pharmacology, clinical pharmacokinetics, prophylaxis of adverse events, drug interaction in sport, pylmonology drugs and psychopharmacogenetics, 2006-10. Address: 3-5-557 proezd Odoevskogo, Moscow 117574, Russian Federation. E-mail: marinasavelyeva@mail.ru

SAVKOVIC-STEVANOVIC Jelenka, 21 January 1946, Markovica, Serbia. Professor of Chemical Engineering. m. Miroljub Stevanovic. Education: BS, Degree,1970; MSc, Degree, 1975, Department of Chemical Engineering, University of Belgrade; PhD, Degree, Institut für Thermodynamik und Anlegentechnik, Technische Universität, West Berlin and

Department of Chemical Engineering, University of Belgrade, 1981. Appointments: Researcher, Department of Chemical Catalysis, Institute for Chemical Technology and Metallurgy, Belgrade, 1970; Assistant, 1972, Assistant Professor, 1982, Associate Professor, 1988, Full Professor, 1993, Department of Chemical Engineering Faculty of Technology and Metallurgy, University of Belgrade, Yugoslavia. Publications: Author and co-author: Books: Stochastic Models in Process Analysis and Optimization, 1982; Information Systems in the Process Techniques, 1987; Artificial Intelligence in Chemistry and Chemical Engineering, 1989, Process Modeling and Simulation, 1995; Process Engineering Intelligent Systems, 1999, 2008; Informatics, 2001, 2007; Light Ways, 2010; Process Plant Equipment, Operation, Reliability and Control, 2011; Over 900 articles to professional journals, patentee in field. Honours: First Prize from Belgrade City for Bachelor of Science Thesis, 1970; DAAD Prize for Research Work, 1980; 2nd Prize TI, St Petersburg, 1989; The Gold Medal, Nikola Tesla, 1993, 2004, 2006; The Silver Medals, Nikola Tesla, 2003, 2004, 2005, 2008; The Bronze Medals, 2003, 2005, 2008; Best Articles, 2009, 2010; Ambassador of Serbia for Arts, Science and Communications, 2009, 2010, 2011; Olympian Achiever, 2011; Listed in Who's Who publications and biographical dictionaries. Memberships: European Federation of Chemical Engineering; Computer Aided Process Engineering; The Institute of Chemical Engineers; The Society of Computer Simulation; The Association of Chemists and Chemical Engineers of Serbia; Modelling, Simulation and Informatics; European Federation for Simulation Modelling; Association for Modelling and Simulation of Serbia. Address: Faculty of Technology and Metallurgy, University of Belgrade, Karnegijeva, 4, 11000 Belgrade, Serbia. Website: www.tmf.bg.ac.yu

SAWA Akinobu, b. 10 August 1955, Hong Kong. Businessman. Education: Graduate, Sophia University Business Course; PhD, Empresarial University of Costa Rica. Appointments: Founder, Chairman and CEO, Ofuka International Inc; Director, Kaetsu Auto Wholesaler Company Ltd; Standing Director, Right Hand Drive Car of Industry; Founder and Director, Group of IMEC (International Man Power Educational Communication Centre); Head In-charge, Tokyo Area/District, IMEC; Founding Vice President of Asia Pacific Doctor & Fellow Alliance; Oxcel China-Judges Panel; Member, London Chamber of Commerce; Disciple of Contemporary Martial Arts Grandmaster Dr Raymond Tung (Disciple of Wing Chun Grandmaster Ip Chun); Member, Research Institute for National Policy. Address: Rm 950, 9/F, HITEC, 1 Trademart Drive, Kowloon Bay, Hong Kong. E-mail: aalphard6688@hotmail.com

SAWYER Diane, b. 22 December 1945, Glasgow, Kentucky, USA. Television Journalist. m. Mike Nichols. Education: BA, Wellesley College, 1967. Career: TV Journalist, 1967-70, 1978-; White House Press Aide, 1970-74; Literary Assistant to former President Richard Nixon, 1974-78; Anchor, CBS Morning News, 1981-84; Correspondent, 60 Minutes, 1984-89; Anchor, Primetime Live, 1989-; Anchor, Good Morning America, 1999-2010; Anchor, ABC World News, 2010-. Publications: Diane Sawyer Biography – Anchor, Good Morning America.

SAWYER Roger Martyn, b. 15 December 1931, Stroud, Gloucestershire, England. Historian. m. Daisy Harte, 30 August 1952, 2 sons. Education: BA Honours, T G James Prize in Education, Diploma in Education, University of Wales, 1958; PhD, History, University of Southampton, 1979. Appointments: Housemaster, Blue Coat School, Edgbaston, 1958-60; Deputy Head, Headmaster, Bembridge Preparatory School, 1960-83. Publications: Casement: The Flawed Hero, 1984; Slavery in the Twentieth Century, 1986; Children Enslaved, 1988; The Island from Within (editor), 1990; 'We are but Women': Women in Ireland's History, 1993; Roger Casement's Diaries 1910: The Black and The White (editor), 1997. Contributions to: Anti-Slavery Reporter; BBC History; Immigrants and Minorities; South, Symbols in Northern Ireland, UN Development Forum. Honour: Airey Neave Award, 1985. Memberships: Anti-Slavery International, council member, 1984-98; Governor, Wycliffe College; Research Fellow, Airey Neave Trust; Fellow, Royal Geographical Society; Bembridge Sailing Club; Old Wycliffian Society; Independent Association of Preparatory Schools. Address: Ducie House, Darts Lane, Bembridge, Isle of Wight PO35 5YH, England.

SAYCE Liz, b. Oxford, England. Chief Executive. Education: BA (Hons), English & French; MSc, Social Work & Social Policy. Appointments: Policy Director, Mind (National Association for Mental Health); Director, Health Action Zone, Lambeth, Southwark and Lewisham; Policy Director, Disability Rights Commission; Chief Executive, Royal Association for Disability and Rehabilitation (RADAR). Publications: From Psychiatric Patient to Citizen, 2000; Numerous articles in professional journals. Honours: Harkness Fellowship, 1995-96; OBE, 2009. Memberships: Commissioner, UK Commission for Employment & Skills; Mentor, Disability Committee, Equality and Human Rights Commission; Fellow, Royal Society of Arts. Address: RADAR, 12 City Forum, 250 City Road, London, EC1V 8AF, England. E-mail: liz.sayce@radar.org.uk

SAZONOV Sergey Nikolaevitch, b. 19 April 1962, Cherkassi, Bashkortstan Republic. Educator. m. Inga Vladimirovna Krasilnikova, 1 daughter. Education: Physics Department, Bashkirian State University. Appointments: Engineer, 1984-94; Educator, 1995-. Publications: On the Aharonov-Bohm effect in multiconnected superconductor, 1994; On the scattering of neutron on 180° Block domain wall, 2010. Address: Flat 35, Ufimian Highway 25/3, 450104, Ufa, Russia.

SCACCHI Greta, b. 18 February 1960, Milan, Italy. Actress. 1 son, 1 daughter. Education: Bristol Old Vic Drama School. Career: Films include: Second Sight; Heat and Dust; Defence of the Realm; The Cocoa-Cola Kid; A Man in Love; Good Morning Babylon; White Mischief; Paura e Amore (Three Sisters); La Donna dell Luna (Woman in the Moon); Schoolmates; Presumed Innocent; Shattered; Fires Within; Turtle Beach; Salt on Our Skins; The Browning Version; Jefferson in Paris, 1994; Country Life, 1995; Emma, 1996; Cosi; The Serpent's Kiss, 1997; The Red Violin, Cotton Mary, 1998; Ladies Room, The Manor, 1999; Tom's Midnight Garden, Looking for Anbrandi, One of the Hollywood Ten, 2000; Festival in Cannes, 2001; Baltic Storm, Il Ronzio delle mosche, 2003; Sotto falso nome, Beyond the Sea, 2004; Flightplan, 2005; Nightmares and Dreamscapes: From the Stories of Stephen King, The Book of Revelations, The Handyman, Icicle Melt, 2006; Amour cache' L', The Trojan Horse, 2007; Shoot on Sight, Brideshead Revisited, Miss Austen Regrets, The Trojan Horse, 2008; Ways to Live Forever, 2010. Theatre includes: Cider with Rosie; In Times Like These; Airbase; Uncle Vanya; The Guardsman; TV includes: The Ebony Tower; Dr Fischer of Geneva; Waterfront (series); Rasputin; The Odyssey (series), 1996; Macbeth, 1998; Christmas Glory, 2000; Jeffrey Archer: The Truth, 2002; Maigret: L'ombra cinese, 2004; Marple: By the Pricking of My Thumbs, 2006;

Broken Trail, 2006; Miss Austen Regrets, 2007. Honours: Emmy Award, 1996. Address: Susan Smith Associates, 121 San Vincente Boulevard, Beverly Hills, CA 90211, USA.

SCALES Prunella M R, b. 22nd June, 1932. Actress. m. Timothy West, 1963, 2 sons. Education: Old Vic Theatre School, London; Herbert Berghof Studio, New York, USA; Repertory in Bristol Old Vic, Oxford, Salisbury, England; Chichester and Stratford, 1967-68; London Theatre Appearances include: The Promise, 1967; The Wolf, 1975; An Evening with Queen Victoria, 1979-99; Quartermaine's Terms, 1981; When We Are Singing, 1986; Single Spies, National Theatre, 1988; School for Scandal, National Theatre, 1990; Long Day's Journey Into Night, National Theatre, 1991; At Leeds: Happy Days, 1993; The Birthday Party, 1999; The Cherry Orchard, 2000; The External, 2001; Too Far to Walk (King's Head), 2002; A Woman of No Importance, 2003; TV includes: Fawlty Towers, 1975, 1978; Mapp and Lucia (series), 1985-86; What the Butler Saw, 1987; After Henry, 1988-92; Signs and Wonders, 1995; Breaking the Code, 1997; Emma, 1997; Midsommer Murders, 1999; Silent Witness, 2000; Queen Victoria, 2003; Station Jim, 2001; A Day in the Death of Joe Egg, 2002; Looking for Victoria, 2003; Essential Poems for Christmas, 2004; The Shell Seekers, 2006. Films: An Awfully Big Adventure, 1994; Stiff Upper Lips, 1997; An Ideal Husband, 1998; The Ghost of Greville Lodge, 2000; Brank Spanking (voice), 2004; Helix, 2006. Numerous other areas of work including: Radio; Directing (Leeds, South Australia, National Theatre Studio, Nottingham Playhouse). Honours: CBE; Honorary DLitt, Bradford; Honorary DLitt, University of East Anglia. Address: c/o Conway Van Gelder, 18-21 Jermyn Street, London SW1Y 6HP, England.

SCANLON Mary Elizabeth, b. 25 May 1947, Dundee, Scotland. Member of Scottish Parliament. 1 son, 1 daughter. Education: MA, Economics, Political Science, University of Dundee; Fellow of the Institute of Professional Development. Appointments: Secretarial and administrative posts in civil service and private sector, 1962-73; Full-time Mother (Part-time Evening Class Lecturer); Student, University of Dundee, 1979-83; Lecturer, Economics, Abertay University, Dundee and Perth College, 1983-94; Lecturer in Economics and Business Management, Inverness College (University of the Highlands and Islands Network), 1994-99; Member of the Scottish Parliament, Highlands and Islands, 1999-2006, 2007-; Scottish Conservative Spokesman on Communities; Convenor of the Scottish Parliament Cross Party Group on Funerals and Bereavements; Vice Convenor of Cross Party Group on Kidney Disease. Address: (Constituency): 37 Ardconnel Terrace, Inverness IV2 3AE, Scotland. E-mail: mary.scanlon.msp@scottish.parliament.uk

SCARFE Gerald A, b. 1 June 1936, London, England. Cartoonist. m. Jane Asher, 2 sons, 1 daughter. Career: Contributor, cartoons to Punch, 1960-, Private Eye, 1961-, Daily Mail, 1966-, Sunday Times, 1967-, Time, 1967-; Animator and film director, BBC, 1969-; Group exhibitions at Grosvenor Gallery, 1969, 1970, Pavilion d'Humour, Montreal, 1969, Expo, 1970, Osaka, 1970; Solo exhibitions: Waddell Gallery, New York, 1968, 1970, Vincent Price Gallery, Chicago, 1969, Grosvenor Gallery, 1969, National Portrait Gallery, 1971, Royal Festival Hall, 1983, Langton Gallery, 1986, Chris Beetles Gallery, 1989, National Portrait Gallery, 1989-99; Comic Art Gallery, Melbourne; Gerald Scarfe in Southwark, 2000; Consultant designer and character designer for film: Hercules, 1997; Theatre design: Ubu Roi, Traverse Theatre, 1957; What the Butler Saw, Oxford Playhouse, 1980; No End of Blame, Royal Court, London, 1981; Orpheus in the Underworld, English National Opera, Coliseum, 1985; Who's A Lucky Boy, Royal Exchange, Manchester, 1985; Born Again, 1990; The Magic Flute, Los Angeles Opera, 1992; An Absolute Turkey, 1993; Mind Millie for Me, Haymarket, 1996; Fantastic Mr Fox, Los Angeles Opera, 1998; Peter and the Wolf, Holiday on Ice, Paris and world tour; Television: Director and presenter: Scarfe on Art; Scarfe on Sex; Scarfe on Class; Scarfe in Paradise; Subject of Scarfe and His Work with Disney, South Bank Special. Publications: Gerald Scarfe's People, 1966; Indecent Exposure, 1973; Expletive Deleted: The Life and Times of Richard Nixon, 1974; Gerald Scarfe, 1982; Father Kissmas and Mother Claus, 1985; Scarfe by Scarfe (autobiography), 1986; Gerald Scarfe's Seven Deadly Sins, 1987; Line of Attack, 1988; Scarfeland, 1989; Scarfe on Stage, 1992; Scarfe Face, 1993; Hades: the truth at last, 1997. Honours: Zagreb Prize for BBC film, Long Drawn Out Trip, 1973; CBE, 2008. Address: c/o ICM, Oxford House, 76 Oxford Street, London W1N 0AX, England.

SCARFE Wendy (Elizabeth), b. 21 November 1933, Adelaide, South Australia. Writer; Poet. m. Allan Scarfe, 1955, 4 children. Education: BA, 1953, BLitt, 1955, ATTC. Appointments: Teacher, Warrnambool Secondary College, retired; Writer; Poet. Publications: Novels: The Lotus Throne, 1976; Neither Here Nor There, 1978; Laura My Alter Ego, 1988; The Day They Shot Edward, 1991; Miranda, 1998; Fishing for Strawberries, 2001; Jerusha Braddon Painter, 2005; An Original Talent, 2010; Poems: Shadow and Flowers, 1964, enlarged edition, 1984; Dragonflies and Edges (with Jeff Keith), 2004; With Allan Scarfe: A Mouthful of Petals, 1967; Tiger on a Rein, 1969; People of India, 1972; The Black Australians, 1974; Hindustani Translation, 1978; Victims or Bludgers?: Case Studies in Poverty in Australia, 1974; J P: His Biography, 1975; Victims or Bludgers?: A Poverty Inquiry for Schools, 1978; J P: His Biography, abridged and revised edition, 1997; Labor's Titan: The Story of Percy Brookfield 1978-1921, 1983; All That Grief: Migrant Recollections of Greek Resistance to Fascism 1941-1949, 1994; Remembering Jayaprakash, 1997; No Taste for Carnage, Alex Sheppard: A Portrait 1913-1997, 1998. Contributions to: Several publications. Honours: With Allan Scarfe: Australia Literature Board Grants, 1980, 1988. Membership: Deakin Literary Society.

SCARGILL Arthur, b. 11 January 1938, Worsborough, Yorkshire, England. Trade Unionist. m. Anne Harper, 1961, 1 daughter. Education: White Cross Secondary School. Appointments: Former factory employee; Worked at Wolley Colliery, 1955; Member, Barnsley Young Communist League, 1955-62; Member, National Union of Mineworkers (NUM), 1955-; NUM Branch Committee, 1960; Branch delegate to NUM Yorkshire Area Council, 1964; Member, NUM National Executive, 1972-, President, Yorkshire NUM, 1972-82, President, NUM, 1981-2002, Honorary President and Consultant, 2002-; Chairman, NUM International Committee; President, International Miners Organisation, 1985-; Member, Labour Party, 1966-95; Member, TUC General Council, 1986-88; Founder, Socialist Labour Party, 1996, General Secretary, 1996-, Leader, 2006-; Contested Newport East seat, 1997, Hartlepool, 2001. Address: National Union of Mineworkers, 2 Huddersfield Road, Barnsley, S Yorks, S70 2LS England. Website: www.socialist-labour-party.org.uk

SCATENA Lorraine Borba, b. 18 February 1924, San Rafael, California, USA. Farmer-Rancher; Women's Rights Advocate. m. Louis G Scatena, 1960, deceased 1995, 1 son, 1 daughter. Education: BA, Dominican College, San Rafael, 1945; California Elementary Teacher Certificate, 1946; California School of Fine Arts, 1948; University

DICTIONARY OF INTERNATIONAL BIOGRAPHY 36th EDITION

California, Berkeley, 1956-57. Appointments: Teacher of mentally handicapped, California School District, 1946; Teacher, Fairfax Elementary School, California, 1946-53; Assistant to Mayor Fairfax City Recreation, 1948-53; Teacher, Librarian, US Dependent Schools, Mainz, Germany, 1953-56; Travel Translator, Lisbon, 1954; Bonding Secretary, American Fore Insurance Group, San Francisco, 1958-60; Rancher, Farmer, Yerington, Nevada, 1960-98; Member, Nevada State Legislative Commission, 1975; Co-ordinator, Nevadans for Equal Rights Amendment, 1975-78; Testifier, Nevada State Senate and Assembly, 1975, 1977; Member, Advisory Committee, Fleischmann College of Agriculture, University of Nevada, 1977-80, 1981-84; Speaker, Grants and Research Projects, Bishop, California, 1977, Choices for Tomorrow's Women, Fallon, Nevada, 1989; AAUW Nevada State Division President, 1981-83; Trustee, Wassuk College Hawthorne, Nevada, 1984-87; AAUW South Pacific Conferences, Hawaii and Washington DC, 1982; AAUW leadership meetings, Denver, Colorado, 1982; Participated in public panel with solo presentation, Shakespeare's Treatment of Women Characters, Nevada Theatre for the Arts hosting Ashland, Oregon Shakespearean actors local performance, 1987; Research on São Jorge history, at São Jorge and Terceira islands, Azores, 2004, 2005, 2006. Publications: Articles in professional journals. Honours include: AAUW Nevada State Humanities Award, 1975; Invitation to first all-women delegation to USA from People's Republic of China, US House of Representatives, 1979; AAUW branch travelship to Radcliffe College, 1981; NRTA State Outstanding Service Award, 1981; AAUW Future Fund National Award, 1983; Soroptimist International Women Helping Women Award, 1983; Fellow World Literary Academy, 1993; Lorraine Scatena Endowment Gift established, AAUW, 1997. Memberships include: Marin Society of Artists; American Association of University Women; Lyon County Museum Society; President, Lyon County Retired Teachers' Association; State Convention General Chairman, 1985; Rural American Women Inc; Nevada Representative for First White House Conference for Rural American Women, Washington, 1980; President, 1986-88, Italian Catholic Federation; Eleanor Roosevelt Education Fund for Women and Girls; Nevada Women's History Project, University of Nevada; Poetry presenter: World Congress on Arts and Communication, Lisbon, Portugal (1999), Washington, USA (2000), Cambridge University, St John's College (2001), Vancouver, Canada (2002); Dominican University of California, President's Circle; Charter Member, The National Museum of Women in the Arts, Washington DC; University of California, Berkeley, Bancroft, Librarian's Council; National Women's History Museum, Charter Member. Address: PO Box 247, Yerington, NV 89447-0247, USA.

SCHACHERREITER Judith, b. 2 June 1977, Linz, Austria. Researcher. Education: Magisterium and Doctorate of Law. Appointments: Specht and Partners law firm, 2000-03; Researcher, Faculty of Law, University of Vienna, 2003-. Publications: Numerous articles in professional journals. Honours: Award of the City of Vienna, 2007. Memberships: Common Core of European Private Law, Turin. Address: Juridicum, Schottenbastei 10-16, 1010 Vienna, Austria. Website: http://homepage.voivie.ac.at/judith.schacherreiter

SCHALLER Bernhard Jacob, b. 11 January 1969, Basle, Switzerland. Professor. Education: B Med, 1991, BNS (Hons), 1991, M Med, 1994, Basle Medical School, MD, Dr med, Faculty of Medicine, 1995, University of Basle, Switzerland; D MSc, Dr med sci, University of Stockholm, Karolinska Institute, Sweden, 2006, and University of Costa Rica, 2007; BME, University of Costa Rica, and University of Berne, Switzerland, 2007. Appointments: Visiting Professor, Molecular Imaging, 2003, Instructor, Spine Surgery, Faculty of Medicine, 2005, University of Zurich, Switzerland; Visiting Professor, Clinical Molecular Neurobiology, University of London, England, 2006; Guest Professor, Molecular Neurochemistry, University of Karachi, Pakistan, 2006; Visiting Professor, Neurosurgery, 2006, Instructor, Neurosurgery, Faculty of Medicine, 2007, University of Munster, Germany; Guest Professor, Molecular Biology, University of Costa Rica, 2006-; Visiting Professor, Neurosurgery, Lomonosov Moscow State University, Russia, 2007; Visiting Professor, Neurology, University of Addis Ababa, Ethiopia, 2007; University Docent in Medicine, Russian Academy of Natural Science, and Moscow State University, Moscow, 2007-. Publications: More than 400 independent citations in published manuscripts; More than 100 articles in peer-reviewed scientific journals; 22 book chapters; 15 monographies. Honours: Presidential Citation, Max Planck Society, Germany; Honorary Doctor of the University, Cuttingdon University, Monrovia, Liberia, 2005; Admiral, Great Navy of the State of Nebraska, Governor of Nebraska, USA, 2006; Honorary Citizen, Island of Eilean an Seamraig, United Kingdom, 2006; Certification of Appreciation, Harvard University, Boston, USA, 2006; Honorary Citizen of the City of Austin, Texas, USA, 2006; Honorary Doctor of the University, Moscow State University, Moscow, 2007; Listed in international biographical dictionaries. Memberships: Professional Member, Royal Society of New Zealand; Basle Academy of Science, Switzerland; New York Academy of Science, USA; American Association for the Advancement of Science; American Diabetes Association; European Committee of the Weizmann Institute of Science, Israel; Biosciences Federation, UK; Federation of European Neuroscience Societies, Germany; International Society for Cerebral Blood Flow and Metabolism, USA; Swiss Society of Neuroscience; World Association of Medical Editors, UK. Address: Raemelstrasse 12, CH-4106 Therwil, Switzerland.

SCHALLIES Michael, b. 12 June 1945, Bad Mergentheim, Germany. Professor. m. Adelheid Brandt, 1 son, 1 daughter. Education: Diploma, Biochemistry, University of Tübingen, Germany, 1971; Dr rer nat, Institute for Organic Chemistry, University of Stuttgart, Germany, 1975. Appointments: Assistant Lecturer, Chemistry Department, University of Education, Ludwigsburg, 1971-75; Senior Lecturer, 1975, Professor of Chemistry and Chemical Education, 1980, Rector, 1990-94, Director, Science-Technology Society Institute, Faculty of Mathematics and Natural Sciences, 2001-03, Dean, Faculty for Natural Sciences and Social Sciences, 2003-10, University of Education, Heidelberg; Member, Advisory Committee, Academy for Technology Assessment of the State of Baden-Württemberg, 1992-96, 2000-03. Publications: Numerous articles in professional journals. Memberships: Gesellschaft Deutscher Chemiker; Gesellschaft für Didaktik der Chemie und Physik; European Science Education Research Association. Address: Höhenweg 18, 69250 Schönau, Germany.

SCHAMA Simon Michael, b. 13 February 1945, London, England. Historian; Academic; Writer; Art Critic. m. Virginia Papaioannou, 1983, 1 son, 1 daughter. Education: Christ's College, Cambridge. Career: Fellow and Director of Studies in History, Christ's College, Cambridge, 1966-76; Fellow and Tutor in Modern History, Brasenose College, Oxford, 1976-80; Professor of History (Mellon Professor of the Social Sciences), Harvard University, 1980; University Professor, Columbia University, 1997-; Art Critic, New Yorker, 1995-;

Vice President, Poetry Society; TV: Rembrandt: The Public Eye and the Private Gaze (film), BBC, 1992; A History of Britain (series), 2000-01. Publications: Patriots and Liberators: Revolution in the Netherlands 1780-1813, 1977; Two Rothschilds and the Land of Israel, 1979; The Embarrassment of Riches: An Interpretation of Dutch Culture in the Golden Age, 1987; Citizens: A Chronicle of the French Revolution, 1989; Dead Certainties (Unwarranted Speculations), 1991; Landscape and Memory, 1995; Rembrandt's Eyes, 1999; A History of Britain Vol 1: At the Edge of the World? 3000 BC-AD 1603, 2000, Vol 2: The British Wars 1603-1776, 2001, Vol 3: The Fate of Empire 1776-2001, 2002; Hang-Ups: Essays on Painting, 2004; Rough Crossings, 2005; The Power of Art, 2006; The American Future, 2009. Honours: Wolfson Prize, 1977; Leo Gershoy Prize (American Historical Association, 1978; National Cash Register Book Prize for Non-Fiction (for Citizens), 1990; National Book Critics Circle Award, 2006. Address: Department of History, 522 Fayerweather Hall, Columbia University, New York, NY 10027, USA. Website: www.columbia.edu/cu.history

SCHEIBE Klaus Manfred, b. 27 September 1946, Berlin, Germany. Researcher. m. Annemarie. Education: Diploma, 1969; Dr rer nat, 1974; Dr sc nat (habil), 1982. Appointments: Zoo Animal Keeper, Tierpark, Berlin, 1965; Humboldt-Universitat zu Berlin; Study of Biology, Physiology of Behaviour, 1965-69; Research Student, 1969-74. Publications: Numerous articles in professional journals. Address: Werner-Seelenbinderstr 3, D-15566 Schoneiche, Germany. Website: www.scheibe-verhaltensbiologie.de

SCHELLIN Thomas Erling, b. 31 July 1939, Hamburg, Germany. Marine Engineer. m. Andrea Bielfeldt, 1984, 1 step son, 1 step daughter. Education: BS, Rensselaer Polytechnic Institute, Troy, New York, USA, 1962; MS, Massachusetts Institute of Technology, Cambridge, Massachusetts, USA 1964; PhD, Mechanical Engineering, Rice University, 1971. Appointments: Teaching Assistant, Department of Naval Architecture Massachusetts Institute of Technology, 1962-64; Mechanical Engineer, Shell Development Co, Houston, Texas, USA 1964-68; Research Assistant, Rice University, Houston, Texas, USA, 1968-71; Design Engineer, The Offshore Co, Houston, Texas, USA 1971-72; Research Scientist, GKSS, Geesthacht, Germany, 1972-75; Naval Architect, Germanischer Lloyd, Hamburg, 1976-2004; Visiting (Adjunct) Professor, Virginia Technical University, Department of Aerospace and Ocean Engineering, Blacksburg, Virginia, USA, Fall, 2004; Naval Architect (part-time after retirement in 2004), Germanischer Lloyd, Hamburg, Germany, 2005-; Lecturer, Berlin Technical University, Department of Naval Architecture and Ocean Engineering, Berlin, Germany, Spring 2005, 2006, 2007, 2008, and 2009. Publications include most recently: Status of Analysis Methods for Hull Girder Torsion of Containerships, 2010; Speed Loss in Waves and Wave-Induced Torsion of a Wide-Bodied Containership, 2010; Wave Loads – Statistical, Dynamic and Nonlinear Aspects, Ship Structural Analysis and Design, 2010; High-Frequency Ship Response Assessment of Large Containerships, 2011; Assessing the Dynamic Stability of an Offshore Supply Vessel, 2011; Wave-In-Deck Load Analysis for a Jack-Up Platform, 2011; Speed Loss in Waves and Wave-Induced Torsion of a Wide-Breadth Containership, 2011. Honours: Achievement Award, 1993, Fellow, 2007-, American Society of Mechanical Engineers; Chairman's Award for an Excellent Paper, 2010; Listed in Who's Who publications and biographical dictionaries. Memberships include: American Society of Mechanical Engineers; Society of Naval Architects and Marine Engineers; Schiffbautechnische Gesellschaft. Address: Abteistrasse 23, 20149 Hamburg, Germany. E-mail: thomas.schellin@gl-group.com

SCHENKER Joseph George, b. 20 November 1933, Krakow, Poland. Physician. m. Kitty Idels, 2 sons. Education: MD, Hebrew University, Hadassah School of Medicine, Jerusalem, Israel, 1959. Appointments include: Professor, Obstetrics and Gynaecology, Hebrew University, Jerusalem; Chairman, Department of Obstetrics and Gynaecology, Hadassah University Hospital, Jerusalem; Advisor to World Health Organization in field of reproduction; Judge, District Court of Applies, Israel, 1986-2000; Chairman, Board of Examination, Medical License and Internship, 1988-; Chairman, Committee of European Examination for Excellence in Obstetrics Gynaecology, 1993-; President, Extended European Board, Obstetrics and Gynaecology, 1994-. Publications: Over 550 in medical journals; Chapters in leading books on Infertility and Reproduction; Editor, several books on Reproduction, Obstetrics, Gynaecology. Honours: Honorary Fellow, American College; Fellow ad Eundem, Royal College; Honorary Fellow of German, Polish, Romanian, Hungarian, Macedonian, Slovak Republic, Brazilian and Israeli societies of Obstetrics and Gynaecology; Honorary Fellow: Fertility and Sterility Society of Peru; Implantation Society of Japan; Romanian Society of Assisted Reproduction; European Association of Perinatal Medicine; Medical Association of Croatia; Doctor honoris causa, University of Medicine and Pharmacy of Craiova; Honorary Citizen, The Council of the City of Jerusalem, 2005. Memberships include: European Society of Human Reproduction; International Society of the Foetus as Patient; International Society of Gynaecological Endocrinology; European Society for Gynaecological and Obstetric Investigation; International Society for the Study of Pathophysiology of Pregnancy. Address: Hadassah Hospital, Department of Obstetrics and Gynaecology, Hebrew University, Jerusalem, Israel.

SCHIFFER Claudia, b. 25 August 1970, Düsseldorf, Germany. Model. m. Matthew Vaughn, 2002, 1 son, 1 daughter. Career: Worked for Karl Lagerfeld, 1990; Revlon Contract, 1992-; Appearances on magazine covers, calendars, TV; Released own exercise video; Appeared in films: Ritchie Rich; The Blackout, 1997; Desperate But Not Serious, 1999; The Sound of Claudia Schiffer, 2000; Black and White, 2000; Chain of Fools, 2000; In Pursuit, 2000; Life Without Dick, 2001; Love Actually, 2003; Retired from modelling, 1998; Owns share in Fashion Café. Publication: Memories. Memberships: US Committee, UNICEF, 1995-98. Address: c/o Elite Model Management, 40 Parker Street, London WC2B 5BH, England.

SCHILLING (Karl Friedrich) Guenther, b. 16 August 1930, Leipzig, Germany. Agricultural Chemistry Educator. m. Gudrun Linschmann, 2 sons. Education: Studies in Agricultural Sciences and Chemistry, Friedrich-Schiller-University, Jena, Germany, 1951-56; Diploma in Agricultural Sciences, 1954, in Chemistry, 1956; Dr agr, 1957; Training in Radio Chemistry, Moscow, USSR, 1958; Dr agr habilitatus, 1960. Appointments: Lecturer, Plant Nutrition, 1960-61, Full Professor, Plant Nutrition and Soil Science, Director, Institute of Agricultural Chemistry, 1961-70, Friedrich-Schiller-University Jena, Germany; Full Professor, Physiology and Nutrition of Crop Plants, Martin-Luther-University Halle-Wittenberg, Germany, 1970-95; Professor Emeritus, 1995; Dean of Agricultural Faculty, 1983-90; Rector of Martin-Luther-University Halle-Wittenberg, 1990-93; Vice President, Rector's Conference of the Federal Republic of Germany, 1991-95.

Publications: 232 contributions to scientific journals and books; 1 monograph; 1 handbook contribution; Author and editor, Pflanzenernährung und Düngung, university textbook, revised edition, 2000. Honours include: Medal and Diploma, 8th International Fertiliser Congress, Moscow, 1976; National Prize for Science and Technology, Berlin, 1982; Dr Heinrich Baur Prize, Munich, 1994; Golden Sprengel-Liebig-Medal, Leipzig, 1997. Listed in national and international biographical dictionaries. Memberships: Deutsche Akademie der Naturforscher Leopoldina; Matica Srpska; Verband Deutscher Landwirtschaftlicher Untersuchungs-und Forschungsanstalten, Vice-President, 1993-96. Address: Institute of Agricultural and Nutritional Sciences of the Martin-Luther-University Halle-Wittenberg, Julius-Kuehn-Str 31, 06112 Halle (Saale), Germany. E-mail: guenther.schilling@landw.uni-halle.de

SCHIRRMACHER Thomas P, b. 25 June 1960, Schwelm. Professor; Publisher. m. Christine, 1 son, 1 daughter. Education: MTH STH Basel, Switzerland, 1982; Dr theol, Theologische Hogeschool, Kampen, Netherlands, 1985; Chief Editor, Verlag für Kultur und Wissenschaft, 1985-, Owner, 1987-; PhD, Cultural Anthropology, Pacific Western University, Los Angeles, 1989; ThD, Ethics, Whitefield Theological Seminary, Lakeland, Florida, 1996; Hon DD, Cranmer Theological House, Shreveport, Louisiana, 1997; Hon DD, ACTS University, Bangalore, India, 2006; Dr phil, Comparative Religions, State University of Bonn, Germany, 2007. Appointments: Lecturer, FTA Giessen, Germany, 1983-90; Lecturer, Bibelseminar Wuppertal, 1984-89; Lecturer, Bibelseminar Bonn, 1993-; General Director, Institut für Weltmission, 1984-; President, Scientific Co-ordinator, Theological Education by Distance Germany (TFU), 1986-; Chair and Head of Department, Missiology and Comparative Religions, STH Basel, Switzerland, 1991-96, STH/FST Geneva, Switzerland, 1991-96; Professor of Missiology, Philadelphia Theological Seminary, USA, 1994-1999; Professor of Ethics and Missions, Cranmer Theological House, Shreveport, USA, 1996-2000; Dean, Professor, Systematic Theology, Martin Bucer Seminar, Bonn, 1996-; Professor of Systematic Theology, Director of German Extension, Whitefield Theological Seminary, 1996-; Rector, Martin Bucer Seminar, Bonn, 1996-; External Examiner, University of South Africa, 1999-; Head of Department, SystematicTheology, FTA Giessen, 2000-03; Professor of International Development ACTS University, India, 2000-08; Vice President of Academic Affairs, Continental Net University, Zürich, 2001-04; Academic Director, Institut for Life and Family Science, Bonn, 2004-; Director, International Institute for Religious Freedom, Bonn, Cape Town and Colombo, 2005-; Professor, Sociology of Religion, State University of Oardea, Romania, 2006-09; Distinguished Professor, Global Ethics and International Development, William Carey University, Shillong, Meghalaya, India, 2009-; Professor, Sociology of Religion, State University of the West, Timisoara, 2009-. Publications: 46 scientific and 38 popular books; Approximately 240 articles. Honours include: Man of Achievement, 2002; Franz-Delitzsch-Award, 2007. Memberships include: AfeM; Deutsche Gesellschaft für Missionswissenschaft; ProMundis; Theological Commission of Hope for Europe; International Commission for Religious Freedom, World Evangelical Alliance; Commission for Religious Freedom of the German and Austrian Evangelical Alliance; Chair, Theological Commission, World Evangelical Alliance. Address: Culture and Science Publications, Friedrichstr 38, D-53111, Bonn, Germany.

SCHLECHTE Gunter B, b. 1 June 1951, Hannover, Germany. Plant Pathologist and Mycologist. m. Ute Schlechte, 2 sons, 1 daughter. Education: Diploma in Horticulture, 1974, PhD, Horticulture, 1978, University of Hannover; Certificate in Phytomedicine, DPG Giessen, 1983. Appointments: Research Assistant, University of Hannover, 1975-78; Research Associate and Project Leader, University of Hannover/ University of Göttingen, 1979-83; Assistant Professor, University of Göttingen, 1984-88; Research Associate, Institute of Industrial Microbiology and Biotechnology, Grosshansdorf, 1990-96; Visiting Lecturer, Heinz Sielmann Foundation, Duderstadt, 1998-2000; Commissary of Nature Conservancy, 1989-; Consultant, Growing Media Industry, Germany, 1994-; Business Owner, Expert and Research Office of Applied Microbiology, Bockenem, 1997-; Valuator of reed as roofing materials, 2008-. Publications: Books: Wood-inhabiting Fungi, 1986; Structure of the Basidiomycete Flora in Polluted Forests, 1991; Soil Basidiomycete Communities and Air Pollution, 1996; Wood-destroying fungi in three nature reserves of Hesse, 2009; Saprotrophic fungi in horticultural growing media, 2010; Numerous papers and articles in scientific journals. Honours: Scholarship, German Research Community, Bonn, 1989; Honorary Professor, Yorkshire University, 2003. Memberships: German Phytomedical Society (DPG). Address: Tillyschanze 9, 31167 Bockenem, Germany.

SCHMIDKUNZ Heinz, b. 3 October 1929, Graslitz, Czech Republic. Professor of Chemistry. m. Liselotte, 1 daughter. Education: Diploma, Master of Chemistry, 1959; PhD, Physical Chemistry, 1963; Professor of Chemistry, 1980. Appointments: Assistant, Physical Chemistry, University of Frankfurt/M, Germany, 1959; University Lecturer for Teacher Education at University, 1963-80; Professor of Chemistry, University of Dortmund, Germany, 1980-. Publications: 12 books; 270 articles in journals. Honour: Heinrich-Roessler-Award, German Chemical Society, 1989; Literary Award, Austrian Society of Chemistry Teachers, 2004; Honorary Member, German Chemical Society, 2005. Memberships: German Chemical Society; Austrian Society of Teachers in Chemistry. Address: Obermarkstr. 125, D-44267 Dortmund, Germany. E-mail: heinz.schmidkunz@uni-dortmund.de

SCHMITZ Anthony Francis Basil, b. 23 April 1944. Deacon. m. Judith Gail Tapson, 3 sons. Education: St George's College, Harare, Zimbabwe; PhB, Heythrop College, Oxford, 1966; BA, Divinity, Maryvale Institute, Birmingham/Pontifical University, Maynooth, 1995. Appointments: Teacher, St Ignatius College, Chishawasha, Zimbabwe, 1967; Editor, Mambo Press, Harare, 1967-70; Freelance Journalist, London, England, 1970; Manager, 1970, Director, 1973-87, Managing Director, 1987-2000, Bissets University Bookseller, Aberdeen, Scotland; Director, Russells University Bookseller, Dundee, 1973-87; Publisher, Palladio Press, 1973-; Member, Executive Committee, College & Universities Booksellers Group, Booksellers Association, 1973-78; Member, Executive Council, Scottish Branch, Booksellers Association, 1993-2000; Chairman, Board of Management, Aberdeen College of Further Education, 1993-2000; Chairman, Board of Directors, Aberdeen Skills and Enterprise Training Ltd, 1994-2002; Chairman, Board of Directors, Clinterty Estates Ltd, 1994-2002; Member, Board of Directors, Step Ahead, 1994-2002; Member, Board of Management, Union pur la culture et l'Avenir Professionel en Europe, Paris, France, 1994-; Founder Member, Federation Europeene des Centres de Formation a l'Enterprise, Brussels, Belgium, 1995; Managing Editor, Light of the North, 2005-; Editor, New Diaconal Review, 2007-; Trustee, Aberdeen City

Council, Bulawayo Trust, 2004-; Trustee, Scottish Churches Architectural Heritage Trust, 2007-; Chairman, North Europe Circle, International Diaconate Centre, 2007. Publications: A Garland of Silver, 2003. Memberships: Catenian Association; Royal Northern & University Club; Oblate, Pluscarden Abbey; Chairman, Scottish Friends of the Foyers de Charite; Member, Teams of Our Lady. Address: 77 University Road, Aberdeen AB24 3DR, Scotland.

SCHNEEWEISS Ulrich, b. 25 March 1923, Potsdam, Germany. Doctor; Medical Microbiologist. m. Sigrid Schmilinsky, 1 son, 2 daughters. Education: Student, 1946-52, Dr med, 1952, Dr med habil, 1960. Appointments: Scientific Assistant, 1952-55, Head Assistant, 1956-63, Department of Serology, University Lectureship, Medical Microbiology, Immunology, Epidemiology, 1961-68, Humboldt University, Berlin; Scientific Assistant, 1963-68, Professor, Head of Department of Diagnostic Research, 1968-88, German Academy of Sciences, Institute for Cancer Research, Robert Roessle Clinic. Publications: 90 research papers, textbooks, monographs: Reihenuntersuchung auf Syphilis..., 1963; Grundriss der Impfpraxis, 1964-68; Allgemeine/ Spezielle Mikrobiologie, 1968; Transplantations- und Tumorimmunologie, 1973; Tumorforschung am biologischen Modell, 1980; Penicillin – eine medizinhistorische Perspektive, 1999. Honour: Robert Koch Medal, German Academy of Sciences, 1982; Honorary Member, Berlin Microbiological Society, 2005. Honours: European Association for Cancer Research, 1982; German Academy of Scientists LEOPOLDINA, Halle (Saale), 1986; Listed in various international biographical dictionaries. Address: Boenkestrasse 55, D-13125 Berlin, Germany.

SCHROEDER Gerhard Fritz Kurt, b. 7 April 1944, Mossenberg, Germany. Politician. m. Doris Koepf, 2 children. Education: Degree in Law, Goettingen University, 1971. Appointments: Lawyer, Hanover, Germany, 1978-90; Chairman, Young Social Democrats, 1978-80; Legislator, German Bundestag, 1980-86; Leader of the Opposition, State Parliament of Lower Saxony, 1986-90; Prime Minister, Lower Saxony, 1990-98; Chancellor, Government of Germany, 1998-2005. Publications: Contributor of articles to numerous professional publications.

SCHUCK Otto, b. 26 August 1926, Prague, Czech Republic. Nephrologist. m. L Cizkova, 16 August 1950. Education: MD, 1950, DSc, 1966, Charles University, Prague; Research Fellow, Medical Clinic, University of Manchester, 1966-67. Appointments: Research Fellow, First Medical Clinic, Prague, 1950-51; Assistant Director, Institute for Experimental Therapy, Prague, 1962-65; Director, Clinic of Nephrology, Prague, 1967-85; Head, Department of Nephrology, Postgraduate Medical School, Prague, 1976-92; Researcher, Institute for Clinical Experimental Medicine, Prague, 1985-. Publications include: Examination of Kidney Function, 1984. Honours: Bruno Watschinger Award, Danube Symposia, 1962; Cilag Foundation Award, 1996; Purkynje Award, 1996. Memberships: Gesellschaft für Nephrologie; New York Academy of Sciences; Czech Society of Nephrology; Slovak Society of Nephrology. Address: Kratochvilova 4, 162 00 Prague, Czech Republic.

SCHULER Robert Jordan, b. 25 June 1939, California, USA. Emeritus Professor of English; Poet. m. Carol Forbis, 7 September 1963, 2 sons, 1 daughter. Education: BA, Honours, Political Science, Stanford University, 1961; MA, Comparative Literature, University of California, Berkeley, 1965; PhD, English, University of Minnesota, 1989. Appointments: Instructor in English, Menlo College, 1965-67; Instructor in Humanities, Shimer College, 1967-77; Hormel Professor, Professor of English, University of Wisconsin, 1978-2010. Emeritus Professor of English, retired 30 December 2010. Publications: Axle of the Oak, 1978; Seasonings, 1978; Where is Dancers' Hill?, 1979; Morning Raga, 1980; Red Cedar Scroll, 1981; Floating Out of Stone, 1982; Music for Monet, 1984; Grace: A Book of Days, 1995; Journeys Toward the Original Mind, 1995; Red Cedar Suite, 1999; In search of "Green Dolphin Street", 2004; Dance into Heaven, 2005; Songs of Love, Collection, 2007; Blueline Anthology; Contributions to: Caliban; Northeast; Tar River Poetry; Longhouse; Dacotah Territory; Wisconsin Academy Review; Wisconsin Review; North Stone Review; Wisconsin Poetry 1991 Transactions; Hummingbird; Abraxas; Lake Street Review; Inheriting the Earth; Mississippi Valley Review; Coal City Review; Gypsy; Imagining Home, 1995; Chiron Review; Minotaur; Free Verse; Poiesis; The Book of Jeweled Visions, 2010. Honours: Danforth Fellow, Yale, 1969-70; Wisconsin Arts Board Fellowship for Poetry, 1997; Awards from Wisconsin Humanities Council; Illinois Arts Council; NEA; New Works Award, Wisconsin Artsboard; Listed in Who's Who publications and biographical dictionaries. Membership: Phi Kappa Phi; Land Commissioner, Land Use Planner, Dunn County, Menomonie Township. Address: E4549 479th Avenue, Menomonie, WI 54751, USA. E-mail: Schulerr@uw.stout.edu

SCHULLER Gunther (Alexander), b. 22 November 1925, New York, New York, USA. Composer; Conductor; Music Educator; Publisher. m. Marjorie Black, 8 June 1948, deceased 1992, 2 sons. Education: St Thomas Choir School, New York City, 1937-40. Appointments: Teacher, Manhattan School of Music, New York City, 1950-63; Teacher, 1963-84, Artistic Co-Director, 1969-74, Director, 1974-84, Berkshire Music Center, Tanglewood, Massachusetts; Faculty, Yale School of Music, 1964-67; President, New England Conservatory of Music, Boston, 1967-77; Music Publisher, 1975-2000; Artistic Director, Festival at Sandpoint, 1985-2000. Publications: Horn Technique, 1962, 2nd edition, 1992; Early Jazz: Its Roots and Musical Development, 2 volumes, 1968-1988; Musings, 1985. Contributions to: Various publications. Honours: Guggenheim Fellowship, 1962-63; ASCAP-Deems Taylor Award, 1970; Rodgers and Hammerstein Award, 1971; William Schuman Award, Columbia University, 1989; John D and Catharine T MacArthur Foundation Fellowship, 1991; Pulitzer Prize in Music, 1994; Honorary doctorates. Memberships: American Academy of Arts and Sciences; American Academy of Arts and Letters. Address: 167 Dudley Road, Newton Centre, MA 02159, USA.

SCHULTE Michael, b. 17 July 1963, Düren, Germany. Professor. m. Ragnhild Schulte Nilsen, 1 son, 1 daughter. Education: MA (Magister), 1993, PhD, 1997, Bonn University; Integrated Studies abroad, University of Iceland, 1987-88; Certificate, German as a Foreign Language, 1998. Appointments: DAAD Lecturer, Agder University College, Norway, 1998-2002; Postdoctoral Research Fellow, 2002-2006; Professor, Volda University College, 2007-. Publications: About 100 international contributions on Germanic linguistics in profiled journals. Honours: Research Award, Volda University College, 2009. Memberships: Board Member, Human Dignity and Humiliation Studies, Columbia University, New York; Societas Linguistica Europaea; Deutsche Gesellschaft für Sprachwissenschaft; Internationale Vereiniging für Germanistik, The Philological Society; Advisory Editor, North-Western European Language

Evolution (NOWELE). Address: Volda University College, Dept of Language and Literature, PO Box 500-1, NO-6101 Volda, Norway. E-mail: michaels@hivolda.no

SCHUMACHER Joel, b. 29 August 1939, New York, USA. Film Director. Education: Parson School of Design, New York. Appointments: Work in fashion industry aged 15; Owner boutique Paraphernalia; Costume designer, Revlon, 1970s; Set and production design; Writer, director for TV; Films include: The Incredible Shrinking Woman; DC Cab (also screenplay); St Elmo's Fire (also screenplay); The Lost Boys; Cousins; Flatliners; Dying Young; Falling Down; The Client; Batman Forever; A Time to Kill; Batman and Robin; Eight Millimeter; Flawless (also screenplay and producer); Gossip; Tigerland; Phone Booth; Bad Company; Veronica Guerin, 2003; The Phantom of the Opera, 2004; The Number 23, 2007; Town Creek, 2008; Twelve, 2010. Publications: (screenplays) Sparkle; Car Wash; The Wiz. Address: Joel Schumacher Productions, 400 Warner Boulevard, Burbank, CA 91522, USA.

SCHUMACHER Michael, b. 3 January 1969. Motor Racing Driver. m. Corinna Betsch, 1995, 2 children. Appointments: Began Professional Career, 1983; 2nd Place, International German Formula 3 Championship, 1989; Driver for Mercedes, 1990; International German Champion Formula 3 Championship, 1990; European Formula 3 Champion, 1990; World Champion, Formula 3, Macau and Fiji, 1990; Formula 1 Contestant, 1991-; 1st Formula One Victory, Belgium, 1992; Other Grand Prix wins: Argentina, 1998, American, 2000, Australian, 2000, 2001, 2002, 2004, Austrian, 2002, 2003, Bahrain, 2004, Belgium, 1992, 1995, 1996, 1997, 2001, 2002, 2004, Brazil, 1994, 1995, 2000, 2002, Britain, 1998, 2002, 2004, Canadian, 1994, 1998, 2000, 2002, 2003, 2004, European, 1994, 1995, 2000, 2001, 2004, French, 1994, 1997, 1998, 2001, 2002, 2004, Germany, 1995, 2002, 2004, Hungarian, 1994, 1998, 2001, 2004, Italian, 1996, 1998, 2000, 2003, Japanese, 1995, 1997, 2000, 2001, 2002, 2004, Malaysian, 2000, 2001, 2004, Monaco, 1994, 1995, 1999, 2001, Pacific, 1994, 1995, Portuguese, 1993, San Marino, 1994, 2000, 2002, 2003, 2004, Spanish, 1995, 2001, 2002, 2003, 2004, USA, 2000, 2003, 2004; Third Place, World Motor Racing Championship, 1992, Fourth Place, 1993; Formula One World Champion, 1994, 1995, 2000, 2001, 2002, 2003, 2004. Retired, 2006; Ferrari's advisor and Jean Todt's assistant. 2007; Driver for Mercedes, 2010. Ambassador for UNESCO. Publication: Formula for Success (with Derick Allsop), 1996; Michael Schumacher (biography with Christopher Hilton), 2000. Address: c/o Weber Management GmbH, 70173 Stuttgart, Hirschstrasse 36, Germany. Website: www.mschumacher.com

SCHUNK Werner (Walter), b. 12 January 1938, Sundhausen/Gotha, Germany. Doctor; University Teacher. m. Christine Margarete Seyfert, 1 daughter. Education: Study of Medicine, Humboldt University, Berlin and Medical Academy in Erfurt; Doctor of Medicine, 1963; Dr Habilitatus, University of Halle, 1974; Specialist in Occupational Medicine. Appointments: Chief Doctor, Company Outpatients Department Gotha, 1968-72; Director of Occupational Medicine (Neurotoxicology), 1972-92, Professor of Medicine, 1976, Pro-Rector, 1976-81 Medical Academy of Erfurt; Director of Institute of Science (Private), 1992-; Private Practice; Specialist in Toxicology and Internal Medicine; Research work in Medical Schools including: London, Birmingham, Paris, Karolinska Institute, Stockholm. Publications: Numerous articles in professional journals; Poems and belletristics; 68 patents in the field of biomaterials: new polymers and your toxicology; Books: Der fröhliche Hausorzt, 2008; Selbst ist der Arzt, 2009; Selbst ist der Arzt, 2010; Das schwangere Ofchen Kongri, 2012. Honours: Title: Medizinalrat; Science Prize of Academy in Germany, 1978, 1983; Master Diploma of Literature, 2006; Hall of Fame, ABI, 2008; Ambassador, Region Gotha/Thuringia of Culture, 2010/2011; Ambassador, Thuringia-Gotha region, 2010 and 2011; The Albert Einstein Award of Excellence, 2010; The World Hall of Fame, ABI; Ambassador 2010/2011/2013 in Circle and Town Gotha, Thuringia. Membership: Gesellschaft of Arbeits und Unweltmedizin; Steinbeiss – University Berlin; Institute of Innovation. Address: Gallettistrasse 2, 99867 Gotha/Thür. Germany. E-mail: werner.schunk@web.de Website: www.werner-schunk.de

SCHUPP Ronald Irving, b. 10 December 1951, Syracuse, New York, USA. Civil and Human Rights Leader. Education: Ordained Ministry, The Old Country Church, 1972; Ordained Baptist Ministry, 1976; Certificates, Moody Bible Institute, 1986, 1988; Advanced Certificate, Evangelical Training Association, 1992; Certificates, Emmaus Bible College, 1996, 1997; Certificate, Centre for Biblical Counseling, 2001; Certificates, Henry George School of Social Science, Chicago, Illinois, 2002, 2003, 2009, 2010, 2011; Certificate, Radio Emergency Associated Communications Teams International, 2003. Appointments: Chicago Uptown Ministry (Lutheran), 1972; Missionary, Assistant Pastor, 1972-76, The Old Country Church, Chicago; Nite Pastor, Chicago, 1972-78; Southern Culture Exchange Center, 1973-76; Assistant Director, Uptown Community Organisation, Chicago, 1974-76; Field Organiser and Staff Person: Alternative Christian Training School, Chicago, 1974-78; Chicago Area Conference on Hunger and Malnutrition, 1974-78; The Great American Coffeehouse, Chicago, 1976-78; Missionary, Solid Rock Baptist Church, Chicago, 1976-89; Director, Chicago Action Centre, 1978-80; Chicago Clergy and Laity Concerned, 1981-87; National Peace Council, 1984-87; Steering Committee, Chicago Free South Africa Movement, 1984-94; Representative, Chicago Welfare Rights Organization, 1986-88; Illinois Coalition for the Homeless, 1988-99; Missionary, Marble Rock Missionary Baptist Church, Chicago, 1990-2008; TransAfrica, 1991-94; Coalition for Jobs and Income, Chicago, 1991-93; Build Illinois Transit Coalition, Chicago, 1998; International Campaign for Tibet, 1997-2003; International Campaign for Tibet, 2009-11; Chicago Coalition Against War and Racism, 2001-11; Retired Minister, 2008-; Consultant, 2009-; Organiser, Free Speech Artist's Movement, 2010-. Publications: Contributor of songs and poems to periodicals. Honours: Recipient, Letter of Commendation, Chicago Fire Department, 1983; Appreciation Award, People United to Serve Humanity, 1990; Recipient of Support Statements from Cesar Chaves (1990), Coretta Scott King (1992), Nelson Mandela (1993), Archbishop Desmond Tutu (1993), 14th Dalai Lama (1994); Best Poem Award, People's Tribune (Chicago), 1992; Appreciation Award, West Englewood United Organisation/Clara's House Shelter, Chicago, 1992; Named Wa-Kin-Ya-Wicha-Ho Thunder Voice by Traditional Lakota Elders, 1993; Named Kiyuyakki Northern Lights by Inuit Elder Etok, 1994; Appreciation Award, Nuclear Energy Information Service, 2000; Numerous proclamations, resolutions and congressional record statements. Memberships: Member, Operation Push/ Rainbow Push Coalition, 1983-2002; Member, John Brown Anti-Klan Committee, 1984-87; Chicago Peace Council, 1984-87; Illinois Nuclear Weapons Freeze Campaign/Illinois Sane/Freeze, 1984-87; Portfolio on File, National Civil Rights Museum, Birmingham Civil Rights Institute, Amistad Research Center; Board of Directors, Associate Chaplain, West Englewood United Organization/Clara's House Shelter,

1991-95; Founding Member, Chaplain, People's Campaign for Jobs, Housing and Food, Chicago, 1992-98; Founding Member, Missionary, People's Ministry Without Walls, Chicago, 1993-98; Co-founder, President, 1995-97, Member, Action Committee, Board of Directors, 1995, Chair, Steering Committee, 1995-97, 1999, Citizens Taking Action, Chicago; Defendant, Chicago Five, 1996 (acquitted, 1997); Member, United Nations Association, USA, 1996-2000; Member, Steering Committee, Raising Issues to Demand Everyone's Right to Service, 1997-98; American Association of Christian Counselors, 2001-11; Tibetan Alliance of Chicago; Founding Member, National Campaign for Tolerance; American Indian Center, Chicago, 2004-; Tibet Center, Chicago, 2009-; Students for a Free Tibet, 2010-11; Life Member: American Association of Retired Persons; The National Association for the Advancement of Colored People; The Southern Christian Leadership Conference. Address: 4541 North Sheridan Road, Apartment 409, Chicago, Illinois 60640, USA.

SCHWARZENEGGER Arnold Alois, b. 30 July 1947, Graz, Austria (US citizen, 1963). Actor; Author; Businessman; Former Bodybuilder; Former US Governor of California. m. Maria Owings Shriver, 1985, separated 2011, 2 sons, 2 daughters. Education: University of Wisconsin-Superior. Appointment: Elected Governor of California, 2003-11. Career: Film appearances include: Stay Hungry, 1976; Pumping Iron, 1977; The Jayne Mansfield Story, 1980; Conan the Barbarian, 1982; The Destroyer, 1983; The Terminator, 1984; Commando, 1985; Raw Deal, 1986; Predator, 1987; Running Man, 1987; Red Heat, 1988; Twins, 1989; Total Recall, 1990; Kindergarten Cop, 1990; Terminator II, 1991; Last Action Hero, 1993; Dave (cameo), 1993; True Lies, 1994; Junior, 1994; Eraser, 1996; Single All the Way, 1996; Batman and Robin, 1997; With Wings with Eagles, 1997; End of Days, 1999; The Sixth Day, 2001; Collateral Damage, 2002; Terminator 3: Rise of the Machines, 2003; The Rundown, 2003; Around the World in 80 Days, 2004; The Kid & I, 2005; The Expendables 2, 2012. Publications: Arnold: The Education of a Bodybuilder, 1977; Arnold's Bodyshaping for Women, 1979; Arnold's Bodybuilding for Men, 1981; Arnold's Encyclopedia of Modern Bodybuilding, 1985; Arnold's Fitness for Kids (jointly), 1993. Honours: National Weight Training Coach Special Olympics; Bodybuilding Champion, 1965-80; Junior Mr Europe, 1965; Best Built Man of Europe, 1966; Mr Europe, 1966; Mr International, 1968; Mr Universe (amateur), 1969. Memberships: Volunteer, prison rehabilitation programmes; Chairman, President's Council on Physical Fitness and Sport, 1990. Address: PMK, Suite 200, 955 South Carillo Drive, Los Angeles, CA 90048, USA.

SCHWEIZER Karl Wolfgang, b. 30 June 1946, Mannheim, Germany. Professor; Author. m. Pamela, 2008. Education: BA, Wilfrid Laurier University, 1969; MA, University of Waterloo, 1970; PhD, Cambridge, 1976. Appointments: Professor of History, Bishop's University, PQ, Canada, 1976-88; Editor, Studies in History and Politics, 1980-91; Visiting Scholar, Cambridge University, 1986; Professor, New Jersey Institute of Technology, Newark, New Jersey, 1988-; Chairman, Department of Humanities and Social Science, NJIT, 1988-93, 2000-2002; Member Graduate Faculty, Rutgers University, 1994-; Visiting Scholar, London School of Economics, 1986, 1994; Visiting Fellow, Yale University, 1994-95; Princeton University, 1994-95; Visiting Professor, Darwin College, Cambridge, 1994, 2003; Senior Research Associate, Peterhouse, Cambridge, 2003. Publications: 19 scholarly books include: The Devonshire Diary, 1982; Co-author, The Origins of War in Early Modern Europe, 1987; Multi-Culturalism in International Relations, 1998; Hanoverian Britain and Empire, 1998; Editor: Lord Bute: Essays in Re-Interpretation, 1988; Diplomatic Thought 1648-1815, 1982; Author: England, Prussia and the 7 Years War, 1989; Cobbet in His Times, 1990, paperback, 1993; Frederick the Great, William Pitt and Lord Bute, 1991; Lord Chatham, 1993; The Art of Diplomacy, 1994; Francois de Calliéres: Diplomat and Man of Letters, 1995; Herbert Butterfield: Essays on the History of Science, 1998, revised edition, 2005; Seeds of Evil: The Gray/Snyder Murder Case, 2001; War, Politics and Diplomacy, 2002; Statesmen, Diplomats and the Press: Essays on 18th Century Britain, 2003; Parliament and the Press 1689-1939, 2006; The International Thought of Herbert Butterfield, 2007; Co-author, The Seven Years War: A Transatlantic History, 2008; Oligarchy, Dissent and the Culture of Print in Georgian Britain, 2011; Contributions to: Over 200 articles, chapters and reviews in scholarly journals and reference works including Dictionary of National Biography, Oxford Encyclopaedia of the Enlightenment; Scribner's Dictionary of Modern Europe; International Military Encyclopaedia; English Literary Periodicals; Global Encyclopaedia of Historical Writing. Honours: Canada Council Doctoral Fellow, 1970-74; Mellon Fellow, Harvard University, 1978; Adelle Mellen Prize, 1990; New Jersey Writer's Conference Award, 1993; Fellow, Royal Historical Society, 1982; Medal of Merit, IBC, 2004; Congressional Order of Merit, 2005, 2006; Meritorious Decoration Certificate, IBC, 2005; Fellow, Royal Society of Arts, 2008; Member, New York Academy of Sciences, 2008; Biographical Dictionary of British Prime Ministers. Memberships: Fellow, Royal Historical Society; Honorary Chairman, US House of Representatives, Majority Trust, 2006; Member, Cambridge Historical Society; Conference on British Studies; 18th Century Studies Association; Institute of Historical Research; Republican Taskforce. Address: 120 Mt Hermon Way, Ocean Grove, NJ 07756, USA.

SCHWIMMER David, b. 2 November 1966, New York, USA. Actor; Writer; Director. Education: Beverly Hills High School; Northwestern University, Chicago. Career: Co-founder, Lookingglass Theater Co, Chicago, 1988; Actor: Theatre: West; The Odessey; Of One Blood; In the Eye of the Beholder; The Master and Margarita; Some Girl(s), 2005; Films: Flight of the Intruder, 1990; Crossing the Bridge, 1992; Twenty Bucks, 1993; The Waiter, 1993; Wolf, 1994; The Pallbearer, 1996; Shooting the Moon (executive producer), 1996; Apt Pupil, 1998; Kissing a Fool (executive producer) 1998; Six Days Seven Nights, 1998; The Thin Pink Line, 1998; All the Rage, 1999; Picking Up the Pieces, 2000; Hotel, 2001; Dogwater (also director); Duane Hopwood, 2005; Madagascar (voice), 2005; Big Nothing, 2006; Nothing But the Truth, 2008; Madagascar: Escape 2 Africa (voice), 2009; TV: The Wonder Years, 1988; Monty, 1993; NYPD Blue, 1993; Friends, 1994-2004; LA Law; The Single Guy; Happy Birthday Elizabeth: A Celebration of Life, 1997; Breast Men, 1997; Since You've Been Gone, 1998; Band of Brothers, 2001; Uprising, 2001; Director: Theatre: The Jungle; The Serpent; Alice in Wonderland. Honours: Six Joseph Jefferson Awards. Memberships: Board of Directors, Rape Foundation for Rape Treatment Center of Santa Monica. Address: c/o The Gersh Agency, PO Box 5617, Beverly Hills, CA 90210, USA.

SCORSESE Martin, b. 17 November 1942, Flushing, New York, USA. Film Director; Writer. m. (1) Laraine Marie Brennan, 1965, 1 daughter. (2) Julia Cameron, divorced, 1 daughter. (3) Isabella Rossellini, 1979, divorced 1983. (4) Barbara DeFina, 1985, divorced. (5) Helen Morris, 1999. Education: New York University. Appointments: Faculty Assistant, Instructor, Film Department, New York University,

1963-66; Instructor, 1968-70; Director, Writer of Films, including: What's a Nice Girl Like You Doing in a Place Like This?, 1963; It's Not Just You, Murray, 1964; Who's That Knocking At My Door?, 1968; The Big Shave, 1968; Director, Play, The Act, 1977-78; Director, Writer of Documentaries; Supervisor Editor, Assistant Director, Woodstock, 1970; Associate Producer, Post-Production Supervisor, Medicine Ball Caravan, 1971, Box Car Bertha, 1972; Director, Films: Mean Streets, 1973; Alice Doesn't Live Here Any More, 1974; Taxi Driver, 1976; New York, New York, 1977; King of Comedy, 1981; Actor, Director, The Last Waltz, 1978; Director, Raging Bull, 1980, After Hours, 1985, The Color of Money, 1986; Director, The Last Temptation of Christ, 1988, Goodfellas, 1989, Cape Fear, 1991, The Age of Innocence, 1993, Clockers, 1994, Casino, 1995; Kundun, 1997; Bringing Out the Dead, 1999; The Muse, 1999; The Gangs of New York, 2002; The Aviator, 2004; No Direction Home: Bob Dylan, 2005; Shine a Light, 2008; The Departed, 2006; Executive Producer, The Crew, 1989; Producer, The Grifters, 1989; Co-Producer, Mad Dog and Glory, 1993; Producer, Clockers, 1995; Executive Producer, You Can Count on Me, 2000; Executive Producer, Something to Believe in, 2004; Executive Producer, Lymelife, 2008; Producer, The Young Victoria, 2008. Publications: Scorsese on Scorsese, 1989; The Age of Innocence: The Shooting Script (with Jay Cocks), 1996; Casino (with Nicholas Pileggi), 1996; Kundun, 1997; Bringing Out the Dead, 1999; The Muse, 1999; Gangs of New York, 2002; The Aviator, 2004; No Direction Home: Bob Dylan, 2005; The Departed, 2006; Shutter Island, 2010; Hugo, 2011. Honours: Edward J Kingsley Foundation Award, 1963, 1964; 1st Prize, Rosenthal Foundation Awards of Society of Cinematologists, 1964; 1st Prize, Screen Producers Guild, 1965, Brown University Film Festival, 1965, Shared Rosellini Prize, 1990; Named Best Director, Cannes Film Festival, 1986; Courage in Filmmaking Award, Los Angeles Film Teachers Association, 1989; Award, American Museum of the Moving Image, 1996; Award for Preservation, International Federation of Film Wards, 2001; Golden Globe for Best Director, 2003; Oscar, Best Director, The Departed, 2006; Cecil B DeMille Award, 2010. Address: c/o United Artists, 10202 West Washington Blvd, Culver City, CA 90230, USA.

SCOTT James, (Dr) b. 8 December 1954, Croxdale Hall, Croxdale, Durham, England. Cleric. Education: New College, Durham, 1971-75; Certificate, 1993, Diploma, 1994, Christian Studies, Westminster College, Oxford; BA, Theology, 1999, MA, Theology (Dogma and Church History), 2002; Greenwich School of Theology; Doctor of Letters (Church Ministry), Trinity College, 1998; PhD, Theology (Dogma and Church History), Greenwich School of Theology, 2006. Appointments: Durham County Treasury, 1973-76; Novitiate, Third Order of Franciscans (Church of England), 1976; Scargill House Community, 1977-79; Life Profession, Third Order of Franciscans (Church of England), 1979; Personal Assistant to the Prior of GCA, 1979; Disabled due to the effects of a spinal cord tumour, 1978-; Pastoral Assistant, Church of England, 1980-93; Received into the Catholic Church and Life Profession, transferred to Roman Catholic Franciscan Third Order, 1993; Personal Tutor, Greenwich School of Theology, 2002-; Personal Mentor for students at Brookes, Oxford and Westminster, Oxford, 2005-. Publications: The Problem of Evil for the Religious Believer (monograph), 1997; The Meaning of the Concept of Covenant in the Holy Scriptures (BA thesis), 1998; The Life of St Francis of Assisi: Is Franciscanism Relevant Today? (MA thesis), An Evaluation of the Doctrine of Miraculous Healing, Within the Roman Catholic Tradition (PhD thesis), 2006. Honours: Serving Brother, Order of St John, 1986; Mensa Certificate of Merit, 1995; Knight of St Columba, 1995; Officer, Order of St John, 1996; Awarded Richardson Salver for exceptional service to the community in the face of great personal adversity, St John Ambulance, 1998. Memberships: St John Ambulance, 1971-2001: Divisional President, 1987-93, Area Vice-President, 1993-96, Northumbria County Vice-President, 1996-2001; Knights of St Columba, 1995-: Deputy Grand Knight, Council 549, 1996, Grand Knight, Council 549, 1997-99, Northumbrian Provincial Action Convenor, 1995, Deputy Grand Knight, Council 142, 2001-2004; Alumni: Westminster College, Oxford, 1994-, Greenwich School of Theology, 1998-, Brookes, Oxford, 2001-. Address: Wear Lodge, Manor Lane, Aisthorpe, Lincoln, LN1 2SG, England.

SCOTT Paul Henderson, b. 7 November 1920, Edinburgh, Scotland. Essayist; Historian; Critic; Former Diplomat. Education: MA, MLitt, University of Edinburgh. Publications: 1707: The Union of Scotland and England, 1979; Walter Scott and Scotland, 1981; John Galt, 1985; Towards Independence: Essays on Scotland, 1991; Scotland in Europe, 1992; Andrew Fletcher and the Treaty of Union, 1992; Scotland: A Concise Cultural History (editor), 1993; Defoe in Edinburgh, 1994; Scotland: An Unwon Cause, 1997; Still in Bed with an Elephant, 1998; The Boasted Advantages, 1999; A Twentieth Century Life, 2002; Scotland Resurgent, 2003; The Union of 1707: Why and How, 2006; The Age of Liberation, 2008; The New Scotland: A 21st Century Sequel, 2008; The Indepence Book (with Harry Reid), 2008; A Nation Again, 2011; Contributions to: Newspapers and journals. Honours: Andrew Fletcher Award, 1993; Oliver Brown Award, 2000. Memberships: International PEN, former president, Scottish Centre; Saltire Society; Association for Scottish Literary Studies; Scottish National Party. Address: 33 Drumsheugh Gardens, Edinburgh EH3 7RN, Scotland.

SCOTT Peter Richard, b. 23 March 1950, Nottingham, England. Retired Headmaster. m. Susan Margaret, 2 daughters. Education: Nottingham High School, 1957-67; St John's College, Oxford, 1968-72; Pembroke College, Oxford, 1972-74. Appointments: Housemaster, Charterhouse, Godalming, 1974-91; Deputy Head, RGS Guildford, 1991-96; Headmaster, Bancroft's School, Woodford Green, 1996-2007. Publications: 8 books on chemistry. Memberships: Chairman of Governors, Maple Walk School, Harlesden; Governor, Exeter School, Exeter. Address: 44 Slade End, Theydon Bois, Essex CM16 7EP, England. E-mail: peterscott@gmail.com

SCOTT Philip John, b. 26 June 1931, Auckland, New Zealand. Medicine; Medical Science. m. (1) Elizabeth Jane MacMillan, deceased 2001, 1 son, 3 daughters, (2) Margaret Fernie Wann, deceased 2007. Education: B Med, Science, 1952, MB ChB, 1955, University of Otago, New Zealand; MD (DM), University of Birmingham, England, 1962. Appointments: Resident/Registrar posts, Auckland, New Zealand, 1956-58, London and Birmingham, England, 1959-62; Research Fellow, University of Birmingham, 1961-62; Research Fellow, Auckland, New Zealand, 1962-69; Senior Lecturer, University of Otago, 1969-72; Honorary Senior Lecturer, University of Auckland, 1970-72; Associate Professor of Medicine, 1972-75, Professor of Medicine, Personal Chair, 1975-96, Emeritus Professor, 1996-, University of Auckland; Head, Department of Medicine, Auckland, 1979-87; Head, Department of Clinical Sciences, South Auckland, 1993-97. Publications: Over 200 papers and articles in professional journals. Honours: Fellow, 1987-, President, 1998-2008, Royal Society of New Zealand; President, New Zealand Medical Association, 1998-99; College Medal, RACP, 1992; Knight Commander of the British Empire (KBE), 1987. Memberships: Medical Research Society, London, -1988; Cardiac Society of Australia; Nutrition Society of New Zealand; International Physicians for Prevention of Nuclear War; Australia & New Zealand Society of History of Medicine. Address: 64 Temple St, Meadowbank, Auckland 1072, New Zealand.

SCOTT Sir Ridley, b. 30 November 1937, South Shields, England. Film Director. Education: Royal College of Art. Career: Director, numerous award-winning TV commercials, 1970-; Début as feature film director with The Duellists, 1978; Other films include: Alien, 1979; Blade Runner, 1982; Legend, 1985; Someone to Watch Over Me, 1987; Black Rain, 1989; Thelma and Louise, 1991; 1492: Conquest of Paradise, 1992; Monkey Trouble, 1994; The Browning Version, 1994; White Squall, 1996; G I Jane, 1997; Clay Pigeons, 1998; Where the Money Is, 2000; Gladiator, 2000; Hannibal, 2001; Black Hawk Down, 2001; Six Bullets from Now, 2002; The Hire: Hostage, 2002; The Hire: Beat the Devil, 2002; The Hire: Ticker, 2002; Matchstick Men, 2003; Kingdom of Heaven, 2005; In Her Shoes, 2005; Domino, 2005; Tristan & Isolde, A Good Year, 2006; American Gangster, 2007; Body of Lies, 2008; Robin Hood, 2010; Prometheus, 2012; TV: Z Cars, 1962; The Troubleshooters, 1965; Adam Adamant Lives! 1966; The Informer, 1966; Robert, 1967; The Hunger, 1997; RKO 281, 1999; The Last Debate, 2000; AFP: American Fighter Pilot, 2002; The Gathering Storm, 2002; Numb3rs, 2005-10; The Good Wife, 2009-; The Pillars of the Earth, 2010; Prophets of Science Fiction, 2011; Gettysburg, 2011; Britain in a Day, 2012; Coma, 2012; World Without End, 2012; Labyrinth, 2012. Honour: Honorary D Litt, Sunderland; Academy Award, Best Motion Picture, 2000; TV Emmy for Best Made-for-TV Film, 2002; Knighted, 2003; Hollywood Walk of Fame, 2011. Address: William Morris Agency, One William Morris Place, Beverly Hills, CA 90212, USA. Website: www.wma.com

SCOTT-THOMAS Kristin, b. 24 May 1960, Redruth, England. Actress. m. François Oliviennes, (divorced) 2 sons, 1 daughter. Education: Central School of Speech and Drama; Ecole National des Arts et Technique de Théâtre, Paris. Career: Resident in France from age of 18; Stage appearances include: La Terre Etrangère; Naive Hirondelles and Yves Peut-Etre; Appearances on TV in France, Germany, Australia, USA, Britain include: L'Ami d'Enfance de Maigret; Blockhaus; Chameleon La Tricheuse; Sentimental Journey; The Tenth Man; Endless Game; Framed; Titmuss Regained; Look at it This Way; Body and Soul; Actress in films: Djamel et Juliette; L'Agent Troubé; La Méridienne; Under the Cherry Moon; A Handful of Dust; Force Majeure; Bille en tête; The Bachelor; Bitter Moon; Four Weddings and a Funeral; Angels and Insects; Richard III; The English Patient; Amour et Confusions; The Horse Whisperer; Random Hearts; Up at the Villa; Gosford Park; Life As a House; Petites Coupures, 2003; Résistantes, 2003; The Three Ages of the Crime, 2004; Arsène Lupin, 2004; Man to Man, 2005; Chromophobia, 2005; Keeping Mum, 2005; La Doublure, 2006; Ne le dis à personne, 2006; Mauvaise pente, 2007; The Walker, 2007; The Other Boleyn Girl, 2008; Il y a longtemps que je t'aime, 2008; Confessions of a Shopaholic, 2009; Nowhere Boy, 2009. Honours include: BAFTA Award; Evening Stand Film Award; Chevalier, Legion d'honneur, 2005. Address: c/o PMK 85600 Wilshire Blvd, #700, Beverly Hills, CA 90211-3105, USA.

SCOWCROFT Philip Lloyd, b. 8 June 1933, Sheffield, England. Retired Solicitor. m (Elsie) Mary Robinson, deceased, 2 daughters. Education: MA, LLM Cantab., Trinity Hall, Cambridge, 1953-56; Admitted Solicitor, 1959. Appointments: Solicitor to successive Doncaster Local Authorities, 1959-93; Retired 1993. Publications include: Cricket in Doncaster and District, 1985; Lines to Doncaster, 1986; Singing for Pleasure: A Centenary History of Doncaster Choral Society, 1988; British Light Music, 1997; Railways in British Crime Fiction, 2004; Transportation and Thorne, 2009; Numerous articles on music, transport, crime fiction, military history and sport for many different periodical publications and for Grove's Dictionary 2001 edition, British Crime Writing: An Encyclopedia, and various Oxford Companions; Contributions to British Crime Writing: An Encyclopaedia. Memberships: Many societies to do with music, transport, crime fiction, military history and sport including: Committee member: Spohr Society of Great Britain, Railway and Canal Historical Society, Dorothy L Sayers Society; Chairman, Doncaster Arts and Museum Society, 1968-; Chairman, William Appleby Trust Awards; President, Doncaster Choral Society, 1992-; President, Railway and Canal Historical Society, 2008-10. Address: 8 Rowan Mount, Doncaster DN2 5PJ, England.

SCUDAMORE Peter, b. 13 June 1958, Hereford, England. Jockey. m. Marilyn, 1980, 2 sons. Career: Former point-to-point and amateur jockey; Estate agency; Professional National Hunt Jockey, 1979-93; 1,677 winners; 7 times champion National Hunt Jockey, record 221 winners, 1988-89; Retired as Jockey, 1993; Director, Chasing Promotions, 1989-; Racing Journalist, Daily Mail, 1993-; Partner with Trainer Nigel Twiston-Davis. Publications: A Share of Success (co-author), 1983; Scudamore on Steeplechasing (co-author); Scu: The Autobiography of a Champion, 1993. Membership: Joint President, Jockeys Association.

SEABORN Hugh Richard, b. 24 May 1962, York, England. Chartered Surveyor. m. Michaela, 3 sons. Education: BSc, General Practise Surveying, Newcastle upon Tyne Polytechnic, 1984. Appointments: Landmark Property Consultants, South Africa, 1985-88; Richard Ellis Fleetwood-Bird, Gabarone, Botswana, 1988-91; Richard Ellis (now CBRE), Berkeley Square, London, 1991-2000; Director, Head of Department, Investment Management Department, Richard Ellis (Property Consultants); Chief Executive Officer & Agent to the Trustees, The Portman Estate, 2000-08; Chief Executive, Cadogan Estate, 2009-. Memberships: Fellow, Royal Institution of Chartered Surveyors; Member of the Council of the Duchy of Lancaster; Non-Executive Director, TR Property Investment Trust plc; Past Chairman, Westminster Property Association, 2008; Past Member, London Board of Royal and Sun Alliance (Advisory), 2003-08.

SEAGAL Steven, b. 10 April 1951, Lansing, Michigan, USA. Actor; Martial Arts Expert. m. (1) Miyako Fujitoni, 1 son, 1 daughter, (2) Kelly Le Brock, 1 son, 2 daughters. Career: Established martial arts academies (dojo) in Japan and LA; Chief Executive Officer, Steamroller Productions; Actor in films: Above the Law, 1988; Hard to Kill, Marked for Death, 1990; Out for Justice; Under Siege/On Deadly Ground (director), 1994; Under Seige 2, 1995; The Glimmer Man; Executive Decision; Fire Down Below; The Patriot (also producer), 1998; Ticker, Exit Wounds, 2001; Half Past Dead, 2002; The Foreigner, Out for a Kill, Belly of the Beast, 2003; Clementine, Out of Reach, 2004; Into the Sun, Today You Die, Black Dawn, 2005; Shadow Man, Attack Force, 2006; Flight of Fury, Urban Justice, The Onion Movie, 2007; Pistol Whipped, 2008. Address: c/o ICM, 8942 Wilshire Blvd, Beverly Hills, CA 90211-1934, USA. Website: www.stevenseagal.com

SEAGROVE Jennifer (Jenny) Ann, b. Kuala Lumpur, Malaysia. Actress. Education: Bristol Old Vic Theatre School. Career: Theatre includes: Title role in Jane Eyre, Chichester Festival Theatre; Ilona in the Guardsman, Theatr Clwyd; Bett in King Lear in New York, Chichester Festival Theatre; Opposite Tom Conti in Present Laughter in the West End; Annie Sullivan in The Miracle Worker, UK tour and West End; Dead Guilty with Hayley Mills by Richard Harris, on tour and West End; The Dark Side, Thorndike Theatre, Leatherhead and on tour; Canaries Sometime Sing, Vertigo and Dead Certain, Theatre Royal, Windsor; Gertrude in Hamlet, Ludlow; Brief Encounter at the Apollo; The Female Odd Couple, Windsor and West End; Title role in The Constant Wife, Lyric Theatre, Shaftesbury Avenue; David Hare's The Secret Rapture, Lyric Theatre, Shaftesbury Avenue. Television includes: Emma Harte in A Woman of Substance; Paula in Hold the Dream; The title roles in Diana and Lucy Walker; Laura Fairlie in The Woman in White; The heroines of The Hitch-Hiker Killer and In Like Flynn; Leading roles in The Betrothed with Burt Lancaster, Magic Moments, Some Other Spring, The Eye of the Beholder, Incident at Victoria Falls, Deadly Games; Judge John Deed, 2001-. Films: To Hell and Back in Time for Breakfast; A Shocking Incident (Oscar for Best Film); Tattoo; Moonlighting; Sherlock Holmes' The Sign of Four; Savage Islands; Local Hero; Appointment with Death; A Chorus of Disapproval; The Guardian; Miss Beatty's Children; Don't Go Breaking My Heart; Zoe. Honour: The Michael Eliott Fellowship Award, 2004. Memberships: Equity; SAG. Address: c/o ICM, Oxford House, 76 Oxford Street, London W1N 0AX, England.

SEBALD Jama Lynn, b. 16 January 1949, Dayton, Ohio, USA. Academic Administrator. Education: Bachelor of Arts (cum laude), Ohio University, Athens, Ohio, 1971; Master of Arts, 1973, Educational Specialist, 1975, University of Northern Colorado, Greeley, Colorado. Appointments: Graduate Assistant in Financial Aid, University of Northern Colorado, Greeley, Colorado, 1974-75; Assistant Director of Financial Aid, Medical College of Georgia, Augusta, Georgia, 1975-76; Student Financial Aid Advisor, University of Idaho, Moscow, Idaho, 1976-2008; Honoured Staff Retiree, 2008. Honours: Buckeye Girls State, 1966; Daughters of the American Revolution Medal, 1967; Eta Sigma Phi Honor Society, Ohio University, 1968-71; Ohio University Upperclass Scholarship, 1968-71; Pi Gamma Mu Honor Society, Ohio University, 1970-71; Mortar Board President, Ohio University, 1970-71; Outstanding Young Woman of America Award, 1978; American Association of University Women Moscow Branch Named Gift to the American Association of University Women Educational Foundation, 1991, 1995; Circle of Excellence Team Award, University of Idaho, 2001; Student Support Services Outstanding Faculty/Staff Award, University of Idaho, 2008; College Assistance Migrant Program Faculty/Staff of the Year Award, University of Idaho, 2008; Listed in international biographical dictionaries. Memberships: American Association of University Women; Athena (University of Idaho Professional Women's Organization); Committee Membership, University of Idaho. E-mail: jama16@frontier.com

SEDAKA Neil, b. 13 March 1939. Singer; Songwriter. m. Leba Margaret Strassberg, 11 September 1962, 1 son, 1 daughter. Musical Education: Graduate, Juilliard School of Music. Career: Solo performer, worldwide, 1959-; Television appearances include: NBC-TV Special, 1976. Compositions include: Breaking Up Is Hard To Do; Stupid Cupid; Calendar Girl; Oh! Carol; Stairway To Heaven; Happy Birthday Sweet Sixteen; Laughter In The Rain; Bad Blood; Love Will Keep Us Together; Solitaire; The Hungry Years; Lonely Night (Angel Face). Recordings: Albums include: In The Pocket; Sedaka's Back; The Hungry Years; Steppin' Out; A Song; All You Need Is The Music; Come See About Me; Greatest Hits, 1988; Oh! Carol And Other Hits, 1990; Timeless, 1992; Calendar Girl, 1993; Tuneweaver, 1995; The Immaculate, 1997; Tales Of Love, 1999; The Singer and His Songs, 2000; The Very Best of Neil Sedaka: The Show Goes On, 2006; The Miracle of Christmas, 2006; Neil Sedaka: The Definitive Collection, 2007. Honours: Songwriters' Hall Of Fame, 1980; Platinum album, Timeless, 1992; Numerous Gold records; Various industry awards. Memberships: AGVA; AFofM; AFTRA. Address: c/o Neil Sedaka Music, 201 East 66th Street, Suite 3N, New York, NY 10021, USA.

SEGALL Malcolm Maurice, b. 19 December 1935, London, England. Paediatrician; Health System Analyst. m. Ivana, 1 daughter. Education: MB ChB, University of Sheffield, 1959; MRCP, Royal College of Physicians of London, 1963. Appointments: Training posts, Sheffield teaching hospitals, 1959-63; House Physician, Cardiology, Postgraduate Medical School, Hammersmith Hospital, London, 1961-62; Research Fellow, Nuffield Institute for Medical Research, University of Oxford, 1963-65; Paediatric Registrar, Radcliffe Infirmary, Oxford, 1964-65; Research Fellow, Institute of Child Health, University of London, and Senior Registrar, Great Ormond Street Hospital for Sick Children, 1966-69; Senior Paediatric Registrar, St Thomas's Hospital, London, 1969-70; Professor of Paediatrics and Child Health, University of Dar es Salaam, Tanzania, 1970-72; Fellow, Institute of Development Studies, University of Sussex, 1973-99, Head, Health Unit, 1989-98, Associate, 2000-05; Health Planner, Ministry of Health, Mozambique, 1977-79; Consultant to international agencies and governments, 1973-2005; Consultant to Minister of Health, Zimbabwe, 1980-81; European Commission-financed Special Adviser to Director General, National Department of Health, South Africa, 1995-97, 2001-04. Publications: Academic publications in neonatal physiology, paediatric lipidology, and health system policy. Honours: Gold Medal, Clinical Medicine and Surgery; Bronze Medal, Final MB ChB Examinations; Prize Medal, Mental Diseases; West Riding Panel Practitioners Prize; Distinction in Surgery; Honours in Pharmacology; Visiting Professor of Public Health, Shanghai Medical University, 1993-96; Listed in international biographical dictionaries. Memberships: Royal Society of Medicine; Editorial Board, International Journal of Health Planning and Management; Keep our NHS Public; and many others. E-mail: ivanamalc@msegall.freeserve.co.uk

SEIFINA Elena, b. 11 July 1965, Simpheropol, Russia. Astronomer. m. Igor Seifin, 1 daughter. Education: BS (Hons), 1988, MS, 1991, Physics & Astronomy, Physical Department of Moscow State University; PhD, Radio-astronomy & Astrophysics, Moscow State University, 1996. Appointments: Junior Researcher, RATAN-600 Laboratory, 1991-96, Junior Researcher, 1996-97, Researcher, 1997-2005, Senior Researcher, 2005-, Stellar Astrophysics Department, Sternberg Astronomical Institute. Publications: Numerous articles in professional journals. Honours: Keldish Fellowship for Scientific Achievements, Moscow State University, 1986-88. Address: Unviersitetsky Prospect 13, Moscow 119992, Russia. E-mail: seif@sai.msu.su

SEINFELD Jerry, b. 29 April 1955, Brooklyn, USA. Comedian. m. Jessica Sklar, 1999, 2 sons, 1 daughter. Education: Queens College, New York. Career: Former Salesman; Stand-up Comedian, 1976-; Joke-writer, Benson (TV series), 1980; Actor, Seinfeld (TV series), 1989-97, also co-writer, producer; The Ratings Game, film, 1984; The

Seinfeld Chronicles, 1990; I'm Telling You for the Last Time, 1999; Co-writer and Voice, Bee Movie, 2007. Publication: Sein Language, 1993. Honours: 2 American Comedy Awards; Emmy Award for Outstanding Comedy Series (Seinfeld), 1993. Address: c/o Lori Jonas Public Relations, 417 South Beverly Drive, Suite 201, Beverly Hills, CA 90212, USA.

SELBERG Aare, b. 11 December 1961, Saaremaa, Estonia. Chemist. Education: Diploma, Chemistry, Tartu University, 1986; MSc, 2003, PhD, 2010, Environmental Technology, University of Tartu. Appointments: Teacher, Chemistry, Biology, Mathematics, Physics, 1986-2001; Chemist, Specialist of Technology, 2002-08, Researcher, 2008-, University of Tartu. Publications: Numerous articles in professional journals. Memberships: IASWS; ACS. Address: Ravila 14A, Institute of Chemistry, University of Tartu, Tartu, 50411 Estonia. E-mail: aare.selberg@ut.ee

SELEŠ Monica, b. 2 December 1973, Novi Sad, Yugoslavia (US Citizen, 1994). Tennis Player. Career: Winner of: Sport Goofy Singles, 1984; Singles and Doubles, 1985; French Open, 1990, 1991, 1992; Virginia Slims Championships, 1990, 1991, 1992; Australian Open, 1991, 1992, 1993, 1996; US Open, 1991, 1992; Canadian Open, 1995, 1996, 1997; Los Angeles Open, 1997; Tokyo Open, 1997; Semi-finalist at: French Open, 1989; Quarter-finalist at: Wimbledon, 1990; Member, winning US Federal Cup team, 1996, 1999, 2000; 59 WTA Tour titles, 9 Grand Slam titles and over $14million in prize money, -2002; Played exhibition match Australia, 2005. Publication: Monica: From Fear to Victory, 1996. Honours: Named youngest No 1 ranked player in tennis history for women and men, at 17 years, 3 months and 9 days; Ted Tinling Diamond Award, 1990; Associated Press Athlete of the Year 1990-91; Tennis Magazine Comeback Player of the Year, 1995; Flo Hyman Award, 2000. Address: IMG, 1 Erieview Plaza, Cleveland, OH 44114, USA.

SELF Will, b. 26 September 1961. Author; Cartoonist. m. (1) Katherine Sylvia Anthony Chancellor, 1989, divorced 1996, 1 son, 1 daughter, (2) Deborah Jane Orr, 1997, 2 sons. Education: Christ's College; Exeter College, Oxford. Appointments: Cartoon illustrator, New Statesman, City Limits; Columnist: The Observer, 1995-97; The Times, 1997-; Independent on Sunday, 2000-. Publications: Fiction: Cock and Bull, 1992; My Idea of Fun, 1993; Great Apes, 1997; How the Dead Live, 2000; Dorian, an Imitation, 2002; The Book of Dave, 2006; The Butt, 2008; Walking to Hollywood, 2010; Umbrella, 2012; Short Fiction: The Quantity Theory of Insanity, 1991; Grey Area, 1994; License to Hug, 1995; The Sweet Smell of Psychosis, 1996; Design Faults in the Volvo 760 Turbo, 1998; Tough Tough Toys and Tough Tough Boys, 1998; Dr Mukti and Other Tales of Woe, 2004; Liver: A Fictional Organ with a Surface Anatomy of Four Loves, 2008; The Undivided Self: Selected Stories, 2010; Non Fiction: Junk Mail, 1996; Perfidious Man, 2000; Sore Sites, 2000; Feeding Frenzy, 2001; Psychogeography, 2007; Psycho Too, 2009; The Unbearable Lightness of Being a Prawn Cracker, 2012. Honours: Geoffrey Faber Memorial Prize, 1991; Aga Khan Prize for Fiction, 1998; Bollinger Everyman Wodehouse Prize, 2008. Address: The Wylie Agency, 17 Bedford Square, London WC1B 3BA, England.

SELKIRK OF DOUGLAS, Baron of Cramond in the City of Edinburgh, James Alexander Douglas Hamilton, b. 31 July 1942, United Kingdom. Life Peer. m. Priscilla Susan (Susie) Buchan, 4 sons. Education: MA, Balliol College, Oxford; LLB, University of Edinburgh. Appointments: Officer TA 6/7 Battalion Cameronians Scottish Rifles, 1961-66, TAVR, 1971-74, Captain, 2nd Battalion Lowland Volunteers; Advocate, 1968-76; MP, Conservative, Edinburgh West, 1974-97; Scottish Conservative Whip, 1977; A Lord Commissioner of the Treasury, 1979-81; Parliamentary Private Secretary to Malcolm Rifkind MP, as Foreign Office Minister, 1983-86, as Secretary of State for Scotland, 1986-87; Parliamentary Under Secretary of State for Home Affairs and Environment, 1987-92 (including, local government at the Scottish Office, 1987-89, additional responsibility for local government finance, 1989-90 and for the arts in Scotland, 1990-92); Parliamentary Secretary of State for Education and Housing, Scottish Office, 1992-95; Disclaimed Earldom of Selkirk, 1994 (prior to succession being determined, 1996) Heir to Earldom of Selkirk (son), John Andrew Douglas-Hamilton, Master of Selkirk); Minister of State for Home Affairs and Health (with responsibility for roads and transport and construction) Scottish Office, 1995-97; Scottish Parliament: Business Manager and Chief Whip, Conservative Group, 1999-2000, Spokesman on Home Affairs, 2001-2003, on Education, 2003-2007. Publications: Motive for a Mission: The Story Behind Hess's Flight to Britain, 1971; The Air Battle for Malta: the Diaries of a Fighter Pilot; Roof of the World: Man's First Flight Over Everest, 1983; The Truth About Rudolf Hess, 1993. Honours: Oxford Boxing Blue, 1961; President, Oxford Union, 1964; Privy Counsellor, 1996; QC (Scotland), 1996; Life Peer, 1997. Memberships: Honorary President, Scottish Amateur Boxing Association, 1975-98; President, Royal Commonwealth Society Scotland, 1979-87; Scottish National Council, UN Association, 1981-87, International Rescue Corps, 1995; Royal Company of Archers (Queen's Body Guard for Scotland); Honorary Air Commodore No 2 (City of Edinburgh) Maritime HQ Unit, 1994-99; 603 (City of Edinburgh) Squadron RAAF, 1999-; Life Member, National Trust for Scotland; Patron, Hope and Homes for Children, 2002-; President, Scottish Veterans Garden City Association Inc, 2003-. Address: c/o House of Lords, London SW1A 0PW, England.

SELLECK Tom, b. 29 January 1945, Detroit, Michigan, USA, Actor. Education: University of Southern California. m. (1) Jackie Ray, 1 step son, (2) Jillie Mack, 1 daughter. Career: Actor, films include: Myra Beckinridge; Midway; Coma; Seven Minutes; High Road to China; Runaway; Lassiter; Three Men and a Baby; Her Alibi, 1988; Quigley Down Under; An Innocent Man, 1989; Three Men and a Lady, Folks, Mr Baseball, 1991; Christopher Columbus: The Discovery, Folks!, 1992; Mr Baseball, In and Out; The Love Letter, 1999; Meet the Robinsons (voice), 2007; TV includes: Returning Home; Bracken's World; The Young and the Restless; The Rockford Files; The Sacketts; Role of Thomas Magnum in Magnum PI; Divorce Wars; Countdown at the Super Bowl; Gypsy Warriors; Boston and Kilbride; The Concrete Cowboys; Murder She Wrote; The Silver Fox; The Closer (series), 1998; Last Stand at Saber River; Friends, 1996, 2000; Ruby Jean and Joe; Broken Trust, 1995; Washington Spent Here, Louis l'Amour's Crossroads Trail, Running Mates, 2000; Monte Walsh, 12 Mile Road, 2003; Reversible Errors (TV), Ike; Countdown to D Day, 2004; Stone Cold, 2005; Jess Stone: Night Passage, Jesse Stone: Death in Paradise, Boston Legal, America's Top Sleuths, 2006; Jesse Stone: Sea Change, Las Vegas, 2007. Honours: Hon LLD, Pepperdine University, 2004; Distinguished American Award, Horatio Alger Association, 2004. Address: c/o Esme Chandlee, 2967 Hollyridge Drive, Los Angeles, CA 90068, USA.

SELTZER Gilbert L, b. 11 October 1914, Toronto, Ontario, Canada. Architect. m. Molly, deceased, 1 son, 1 daughter. Education: B Arch, University of Toronto,

Canada, 1937. Appointments: Partner, Gehron & Seltzer, New York, New York, 1952-58; Sole Proprietor, Gilbert L Seltzer Associates, New York, New York and West Orange, New Jersey, specialising in governmental and institutional projects, 1958-; Representative work includes: Projects at US Military Academy, US Merchant Marine Academy, Denison University, City College of New York, Rutgers University, William Paterson University, New Jersey City University, Kean University, University of Medicine and Dentistry of New Jersey, Utica Memorial Auditorium, Veterans Administration Medical Centers. Publications: Numerous articles in architectural journals. Honours: Numerous awards including: Henry Hering Medal of National Sculpture Society. Memberships: American Institute of Architects; New Jersey Society of Architects. Address: 80 Main Street, West Orange, NJ 07052, USA.

SEMASHKO Leo, b. 20 June 1941, Grodno, Belarus. Sociologist. Divorced, 2 sons. Education: Philosophical Faculty, 1959-65, Post-graduate course, 1967-70, PhD, 1970, Moscow State University. Appointments: Assistant and Professor, Philosophy and Sociology Departments, University, 1970-90; Deputy, St Petersburg Parliament, 1990-93; Sociology Professor, St Petersburg Universities, 1994-2005; Founder and President, Global Harmony Association, 2005-; Author of new science of social harmony since 1976: Tetrasociology. Publications: More than 300 scientific works; 14 books including Tetrasociology: Responses to Challenges, 2002; World Harmony/Peace Academy, 2008; Harmonious Civilization, 2009. Honours: State Councillor of St Petersburg. Memberships: International Association of Educators for World Peace; International Sociological Association; Human Dignity and Humiliation Studies. Address: 7-4-42 Ho-Shi-Min Street, St Petersburg 194356, Russia. E-mail: leo.semashko@gmail.com Website: www.peacefromharmony.org

SEN Amartya Kumar, b. 3 November 1933, Santiniketan, India. Professor of Economics and Philosophy; Writer. m. (1) Nabaneeta Dev, 1960, divorced 1974, 2 daughters, (2) Eva Colorni, 1977, deceased 1985, 1 son, 1 daughter, (3) Emma Rothschild, 1991. Education: BA, Presidency College, Calcutta, 1953; BA, 1955, MA, PhD, 1959, Trinity College, Cambridge. Appointments: Professor of Economics, Jadavpur University, Calcutta, 1956-58; Fellow, Trinity College, Cambridge, 1957-63, All Souls College, Oxford, 1980-88; Professor of Economics, Delhi University, 1963-71, London School of Economics and Political Science, 1971-77; Professor of Economics, 1977-80, Drummond Professor of Political Economy, 1980-88, University of Oxford; Andrew D White Professor at Large, Cornell University, 1978-85; Lamont University Professor and Professor of Economics and Philosophy, 1988-98, 2004-, Professor Emeritus, 2004-, Harvard University; Master Trinity College, Cambridge, 1998-2004. Publications: Choice of Techniques, 1960; Collective Choice and Welfare, 1970; Guidelines for Project Evaluation (with P Dasgupta and Stephen Marglin), 1972; On Economic Inequality, 1973; Employment, Technology and Development, 1975; Poverty and Famines: An Essay on Entitlement and Deprivation, 1981; Choice, Welfare and Measurement, 1982; Resources, Values and Development, 1984; Commodities and Capabilities, 1985; On Ethics and Economics, 1987; The Standard of Living (with others), 1987; Hunger and Public Action (with Jean Dreze), 1989; Jibanayatra o arthaniti, 1990; The Political Economy of Hunger (editor with Jean Dreze), 3 volumes, 1990-91; Money and Value: On the Ethics and Economics of Finance/Denaro e valore: Etica ed economia della finanza, 1991; Inequality Reexamined, 1992; The Quality of Life (editor with Martha Nussbaum), 1993; Economic Development and Social Opportunity (with Jean Dreze), 1995; Development as Freedom, 1999. Contributions to: Professional journals. Honours: Mahalanobis Prize, 1976; Honorary Doctor of Literature, University of Saskatchewan, 1979; Nobel Prize in Economic Science, 1998; Honorary CH, 2000; Grand Cross, Order of Scientific Merit, Brazil, 2000. Memberships: American Academy of Arts and Sciences; American Economic Association, president, 1994-; British Academy, fellow; Development Studies Association; Econometric Society, fellow; Indian Economic Association; International Economic Association, president, 1986-88, honorary president, 1988-; Royal Economic Society. Address: c/o Trinity College, Cambridge CB2 1TQ, England.

SEN Santanu, b. 25 December 1971, Shillong, India. Engineering Educator. m. Sonia, 1 daughter. Education: BE (CSE); MBA (IS); PhD (Engg); C Eng (I); FIETE; FIE. Appointments: Principal, Budge Budge Institute of Technology. Publications: 40 research papers; 20 technical articles. Honours: National Scholarship, 1990; Research Contributor of the Year, 2008; PhD, Recepient Award, 2008; Best Performer Award, 2010. Memberships: SMCSI; MIE; MIEEE, USA; MACM, USA; LMISTE; FIET, UK. Address: P-64, Unique Park, Behala, Kolkata – 700034, West Bengal, India. Website: www.bbit.edu.in

SEN Tapas Kumar, b. 1 March 1933, Calcutta, India. Teacher; Manager. m. Sondra Kotzin Sen, 1 son, 1 daughter. Education: MSc, Applied Psychology, Calcutta University, 1954; PhD, Psychology, Johns Hopkins University, 1963. Appointments: Member, Technical Staff, Bell Laboratories, 1963-72; Human Resources Director, AT&T, 1973-96; Executive Director, Workforce Development, Rutgers University, New Brunswick, New Jersey, USA, 1999-2006; Executive Committee Member, Governor's State Employment and Training Commission, New Jersey, 2000-06; Committee, State Employment and Training Commission, 2004-05; Chair, Strategic Planning Committee, 2009-. Publications: 15 papers in professional publications include: Building the Workplace of the Future in A Blueprint for Managing Change, A Conference Board Report; Advisory Editor, Work in America Encyclopedia, 2003. Honours: The Mayflower Group Leadership Award, 1985; Toastmasters International, Area Governor of the Year, public speaking, 1970. Memberships: Fellow, Human Factors and Ergonomics Society; American Psychological Association; The Dearborn Group. Address: 29 Arden Road, Mountain Lakes, NJ 07046, USA. E-mail: tsitsi@optonline.net

SENEVIRATNE Sri Nissanka de Silva, b. 19 January 1933, Colombo, Sri Lanka. Plant Pathologist. M. Christelle Elise, 1 son, 1 daughter. Education: BSc (Hons), University of Ceylon, Colombo; PhD, University of London. Appointments: Research Officer, Plant Pathology, Department of Agriculture, Sri Lanka, 1959-88; Plant Pathologist and Head, Division of Plant Pathology, 1969-99, Deputy Director, Research, 1984-86, Central Agricultural Research Institute, Gannoruwa, Peradeniya. Publications: On the occurrence of Pseudomonas solanacearum in the hill country of Ceylon, 1969; Identification of viruses isolated from plum trees affected by decline, line-pattern and ringspot diseases, 1970; Science, scientists and sovereignty – some considerations for the Third World, 1975. Honours: General Research Committee Award, Sri Lanka Association for the Advancement of Science, 1994; SAREC Committee Grant for Plant Virology. Memberships: Sri Lanka Association for the Advancement of Science; Fellow, National Academy of Sciences of Sri Lanka. Address: Hebron, 117 A, Christopher Road, Peradeniya, Sri Lanka.

DICTIONARY OF INTERNATIONAL BIOGRAPHY 36th EDITION

SENSIPER Samuel, b. 26 April 1919, Elmira, New York, USA. Electrical Engineer. m. Elaine Marie Zwick, 2 sons, 1 daughter. Education: BSEE, 1939, ScD, 1951, Massachusetts Institute of Technology; EE, Stanford University, 1941. Appointments: Assistant Project Engineer to Senior Project Engineer, Consultant, Sperry Gyroscope Co, New York, 1941-51; Section Head and Senior Staff Consultant, Hughes Aircraft Co, Malibu, 1951-60; Laboratory Division Manager, Space General Corp, Los Angeles, 1960-67; Laboratory Manager, TRW, Redondo Beach, 1967-70; Faculty, Electrical Engineering, University of Southern California, Los Angeles, 1955-56, 1979-80; Consulting Engineer in private practice, Los Angeles, 1970-73, 1975-95; Director of Engineering, Transco Products, Venice, 1973-75; Consultant, Los Angeles, Goleta and Santa Barbara, 1995-. Publications: Numerous articles in professional journals including: Electromagnetic Wave Propagation on Helical Conductors, 1955; Cylindrical Radio Waves, 1957; 25 issued patents. Honours: Life Fellow, Institute of Electronic and Electrical Engineers; Life Fellow, American Association for the Advancement of Science; Industrial Electronics Fellow, MIT, 1947-48; Certificate of Commendation, US Navy, 1946; Listed in international biographical dictionaries. Memberships: IEEE; AAAA; Electromagnetic Academy; Sigma Xi; Eta Kappa Nu; California Society of Professional Engineers; NSPE (retired); Alumni Associations: MIT; Stanford; UCLA. Address: 3775 Modoc Road, #117, Santa Barbara, CA 93105, USA. E-mail: sensiper1@ieee.org

SEREBRIER José, b. 3 December 1938, Montevideo, Uruguay. Musician; Conductor. m. Carole Farley, 29 March 1969, 1 daughter. Education: Diploma, National Conservatory, Montevideo, 1956; Curtis Institute of Music, 1958; BA, University of Minnesota, 1960; Studied with Aaron Copland, Antal Dorati, Pierre Monteux. Career: Debut, Carnegie Hall; Independent Composer and Conductor, 1955-; Apprentice Conductor, Minnesota Orchestra, 1958-60; Associate Conductor, American Symphony Orchestra, New York, 1962-66; Musical Director, American Shakespeare Festival, 1966; Composer-in-Residence, Cleveland Orchestra, 1968-71; Artistic Director, International Festival of Americas, Miami, 1984-; Opera Conductor, United Kingdom, USA, Australia and Mexico; Guest Conductor, numerous orchestras; International tours in USA, Latin America, Australia and New Zealand. Compositions: Published over 100 works; Variations on a Theme from Childhood, for chamber orchestra; Symphony for Percussion; Concerto for Violin and Orchestra; Concerto for Harp and Orchestra; Symphonie Mystique, 2003; Orchestration and recording of George Gershwin's Three Piano Preludes and the Lullaby; Also works for chorus, voice, keyboard; Over 250 recordings for major labels with orchestras from United Kingdom, Germany, Oslo, Spain, Italy, Sicily, Belgium, Czechoslovakia and Australia. Honours: Ford Foundation Conductors Award; Alice M Ditson Award, 1976; Deutsche Schallplatten Critics Award; Music Retailers Association Award; Guggenheim Fellow, 1958-60; 2 Guggenheim awards; Rockefeller Foundation Grants; Commissions, National Endowment for the Arts and Harvard Musical Association; BMI Award; Koussevitzky Foundation Award; 37 Grammy Nominations, 1975-2008; Subject of book by Michel Faure, 2002; 5 Grammy Nominations in 2004, including Best New Composition for 3rd symphony, Symphonie Mystique; Winner, Latin Grammy for Best Classical Album for recording of Carmen Symphony by Bizet-Serebrier with Barcelona Symphony Orchestra, 2004. Memberships: American Symphony Orchestra League; American Music Center; American Federation of Musicians. Address: 270 Riverside Drive, New York, NY 10025, USA.

SERNICKI Jan Kazimierz, b. 7 April 1943, Warsaw, Poland. Electronic Engineer - Nuclear Electronics. m. Krystyna Elzbieta Łysakowska-Sernicka. Education: Master's degree, 1969, Postgraduate training, 1971-75, Doctor of Engineering, 1976, Warsaw Technical University. Appointments: Electronic Engineer, 1969-71, Research Engineer, 1976-78, Institute of Nuclear Research, Świerk; Scientific Worker, Joint Institute of Nuclear Research, Dubna, Russia, 1978-81; Specialist, Department of Nuclear Spectroscopy and Technique, 1981-2003, Research Scientist, 2003-, Head, Department of Nuclear Spectroscopy and Technique, 2003-05, Deputy Head, 2005-08, Head, 2008-, Department of Interdyscyplinary Applications of Physics, The Andrzej Soltan Institute for Nuclear Studies, Świerk, Poland. Publications: Author, papers in Progress in Medical Physics, 2 in 1977, 3 in 1978; Co-author, paper in Nukleonika, 1981; Author, papers in Nuclear Instruments and Methods in Physics Research A, 1983, 2 in 1985, 1986, 2 in 1988, 1990, 1997, 2007 in Nukleonika, 1995, 2000; Author, papers in Nuclear Instruments and Methods in Physics Research A, 2007. Honours: Reviewer, Nuclear Instruments and Methods in Physics Research A, 2007. Address: Saska 99-4, 03-914 Warsaw, Poland.

SER-OD Sarantsatsralt, b. 12 June 1962, Ulaanbaatar, Mongolia. Painter; Sculptor. m. 2 daughters. Education: Graduate, Fine Art College, Ulaanbaatar, 1982; BA, Painting, Mongolian University of Art and Culture, Ulaanbaatar, 1987. Appointments: Solo Exhibition, Mongolia, Germany, Switzerland, France, USA and government house of Mongolia, 1991-2011; Joint Exhibition, Japan, Korea, France, Germany, Australia, Finland, USA, Hungary, Hong Kong, China, and Gallery of Cork Street, London, England, 1991-2010. Publications: Asian Art news magazine, 1993, 2010; Wochenspiegel newspaper of Germany, 1994; The News on Sunday, Australia, 1997; Japan News, 2004. Honours: Annual Committee Prize, Union of Mongolian Artists, 1994; State Prize of Mongolia, 2005; Glory of Mongolia, 2005; Best Exhibiton of UMA, 2003. Address: Chingeltei district 1-40 Myangat, 1-Khoroo, 12-2 toot, Ulaanbaatar, Mongolia. E-mail: tsatsa_serod@yahoo.com

SERVADEI Annette, b. 16 October 1945, Durban, Natal, South Africa. Pianist. m. 1972-1981, 1 son, 1 daughter. Education: Began studies with concert pianist mother, 1949; Also Violin and Organ studies, diploma level, 1964-72: Further piano studies, Europe, 1967-72, with Ilonka Deckers (Milan), Klaus Schilde (Hochschule für Musik, Detmold), Carlo Zecchi (Salzberg), Wilhelm Kempff (Positano); LTCL(T), 1964; LRSM(P), 1965; UPLM, 1965; FTCL, 1970; BMus, UNISA, 1979; HND in Sound Production, UKC, 2003; BA (Hons) in Fine Art, University of Kent, 2005. Debut: Wigmore Hall, London, 1972. Career: Radio broadcast aged 10; Concerto debut with Durban Symphony Orchestra aged 12; Recitals and concertos, UK, West Europe, Africa, USA; Frequent live radio and TV broadcasts; University Senior Piano Tutor; Lecture recitals, Masterclasses; Eisteddfod Adjudicator; Wide repertoire; Noted performer of Liszt, Ravel and 20th Century American music; World premieres: Palintropos (John Tavener), Wigmore Hall, London, 1980; Perpetual Angelus (Gordon Kerry, St John's, Smith Square), London, 1991; Mini-stroke enforced sabbatical, re-learnt LH technique and LH/RH co-ordination, 1997; Studied Mozart; Resumed career after successful valve surgery, performing and teaching. Recordings: Britten and Khachaturian Piano Concertos with London Philharmonic Orchestra; Mendelssohn, Schumann and Brahms piano pieces; Complete piano music of Sibelius, 5 CDs; 2 CDs of Dohnanyi piano music. Honours: Scholarships, Oppenheimer Trust and UNISA, 1963-70;

UNISA, 1974; Letter from Wilhelm Kempff for Beethoven interpretation, 1974; Artist of the Year, UK Sibelius Society, 1993. Membership: Incorporated Society of Musicians; EPTA. Address: 3 Bournemouth Drive, Herne Bay, Kent CT6 8HH, England. E-mail: annette.servadei@yahoo.co.uk Website: www.annetteservadei.com

SERVIEN Louis-Marc, Comte de Boisdauphin, Lord of Quendon, b. 8 January 1934, Yverdon-les-Bains, Switzerland. Businessman. Education: Master's degrees in Law and Business Administration, University of Lausanne; Doctorate, Accademia Tiberina, Rome, Italy. Appointments: Executive President of Who's Who International SA, and of the Committee of European Excellence, CEE Ltd, two Swiss based press services; President and Managing Director, Société de Financement (Genève) SA and the Compagnie des Grands Crus SA, which promotes world-wide quality wines and spirits under the brandname, Comte de Boisdauphin. Publications: Numerous contributions to professional journals as a society and arts journalist; Author: Louis XIV and Abel de Servien: Eight Centuries of the Servien Family, 2011; Les Fonds de Placement Collectif en Suisse, Investment Trusts, 1958; Les Sociétés d'Investissement ou Fonds de Placement: Nouvelle Formule d'Epargne, 1962; Mutual Funds, Why Not? A Survey of International Investment Funds, 1968. Honours: Nominated Commendatore of the Concordia Order, Brazil, 1974; Commendador de la Imperial Orden Hispanica de Carlos V, Madrid, Spain, 1992. Memberships: Club Diplomatique de Genève, Geneva; Art-Sciences-Lettres, Paris. Address: Quendon Hall, 23 chemin du Levant, CH-1005 Lausanne, Switzerland. Websites: http://www.who-s-who.com, http://www.committee-of-european-excellence.com and http://www.servien.org

SESÉ Luis M, b. 18 September 1955, Madrid, Spain. Chemistry Educator; Researcher. m. Mercedes Mejias, 1 son. Education: BS, University Complutense Madrid, 1976; MSc, honours, 1978; PhD, 1983. Appointments: Ayudante, 1978-80, Encargado, 1980-81, University Complutense; Encargado, 1981-82, Colaborador, 1982-84, Titular, 1985-87, Titular Numerario, 1987-2009, Catedrático de Universidad (Quimica-Fisica), 2010-, University National Educational Distance, Madrid. Publications: Research papers in professional journals; Books; Educational Video: Fifteen minutes in the life of the electron, 2002; Quince minutos eu la vida del election: Una mirada en detalle, 2009. Honours: Premio Extraordinario de Licenciatura, University Complutense, 1979; 3rd Prize, X Bienal Internacional de Cine y Video Cientifico, Spain, 2001; 2nd Prize, XXII Bienal Internacional de Cine Cientifico, Spain, 2002; 2nd Prize, Fisica en Acción 3 (RSEF), Spain, 2002; Scientific Radio Shows; Listed in several Who's Who and biographical publications. Memberships: New York Academy of Sciences; Planetary Society; Spanish Royal Society of Physics, 2002-; Einsteinian Chair of Science, World Academy of Letters; American Association for the Advancement of Science; American Chemical Society. Address: Facultad de Ciencias, University National Educational Distance, Senda del Rey 9, 28040 Madrid, Spain.

SETUA Dipak Kumar, b. 20 July 1956, Midnapore, India. Scientist. m. Madhuchhanda, 2 sons. Education: MSc, Physical Chemistry, 1981, PhD, Rubber Technology, 1985, Indian Institute of Technology, Kharagpur, India. Appointments: Scientist, 1984-89, Assistant Director, 1989-95, Deputy Director, 1995-2000, Joint Director, 2000-06, Additional Director, 2006-, Defence R&D Organisation, Government of India, Kanpur, India; Visiting Scientist, Polymer Engineering, University of Akron, Ohio, USA, 1989-91; Government of India Expert of Ministry of Youth Affairs and Sports, Delhi, 2000-; Guest Professor, 2001, Adjunct Professor, 2008, Indian Institute of Technology, Kharagpur; Visiting Professor, University of Pune, 2002; Member Editorial Board, Journal of Applied Polymer Science, 2002-, Journal of Chemistry and Environment, 2002-03; Reviewer of numerous professional. Publications: 62 research papers in international journals; 2 international patents; 6 book chapters; More than 100 technical papers in symposia and conferences. Honours: Dunlop Award, Ministry of Industry, Government of India, 1984; DRDO Awards, Ministry of Defence, Government of India, 1987, 1994; K M Philip Award, Ministry of Commerce and Industry, Government of India, 2000. Memberships: Editorial Board, Journal of Applied Polymer Science; Society of Plastic Engineers, USA; Governing Council, IRMRA, Ministry of Commerce & Industry; Shriram Institute for Industry, Resh, India; Indian Thermal Analysis Society; IIT Kharagpur. Address: Defence Materials & Stores R&D Establishment Post Office, GT Road, Kanpur 208 013, India. E-mail: dksetua@rediffmail.com

SEWELL Brian, Art historian; Art critic. Career: Art Critic, Evening Standard newspaper. Publications: South from Ephesus, 1988; The Review that Caused the Rumpus, 1994; An Alphabet of Villains, 1995. Honours: British Press Awards Critic of the Year, 1988; Arts Journalist of the Year, 1994; Hawthornden Prize for Art Criticism, 1995; Foreign Press Association Arts Writer of the Year, 2000; The Orwell Prize, 2003; Critic of the Year, British Press Awards, 2004. Address: The Evening Standard, Northcliffe House, 2 Derry Street, London W8 5EE, England.

SEWELL Geoffrey Leon, b. 27 January 1927, Leeds, England. Mathematical Physicist. m. Robina. Education: Mathematics, University College, Oxford; PhD, King's College, London. Appointments: Held posts at the Universities of Liverpool, Aberdeen and Hull; Professor of Mathematical Physics, Queen Mary, University of London. Publications: Quantum Theory of Collective Phenomena, 1986; Quantum Mechanics and its Emergent Macrophysics, 2002; Numerous articles on mathematical physics, quantum physics, and condensed matter physics. Membership: International Association of Mathematical Physicists. Address: Department of Physics, Queen Mary, University of London, Mile End Rd., London E1 4NS, England. E-mail: g.l.sewell@qmul.ac.uk

SEWELL Rufus Frederick, b. 29 October 1967. Actor. m. (1) Yasmin Abdallah, 1999 (divorced); (2) Amy Gardner, 2004, divorced 2009, 1 son. Career: Actor; Films include: Twenty-One, 1991; Dirty Weekend, 1993; A Man of No Importance, 1994; Carrington, Victory, 1995; Hamlet, 1996; The Woodlanders, 1997; Martha, Meet Frank, Daniel and Laurence, Illuminata, Dark City, 1998; Bless The Child, 2000; A Knight's Tale, 2001; Extreme Ops, 2002; Tristan and Isolde, The Illusionist, Amazing Grace, The Holiday, 2006; Downloading Nancy, Vinyan, 2008; The Tourist, 2010; Abraham Lincoln: Vampire Hunter, 2012; TV appearances include: Gone To Seed, 1992; Middlemarch, 1994; Cold Comfort Farm, Henry IV, Part I, 1995; Charles II: The Power and the Passion, 2003; Shakespeare Retold: The Taming of the Shrew, 2005; John Adams, 2008; Eleventh Hour, 2008-09; Pillars of the Earth, 2010; Zen, 2011; Parade's End, Restless, 2012. Stage appearances include: Royal Hunt of the Sun; Comedians; The Last Domain; Peter and the Captain; Pride and Prejudice; The Government Inspector; The Seagull; As You Like It; Making it Better; Arcadia; Translations; Rat in the Skull; Macbeth; Luther; Taste. Honours: London Critics' Circle Best Newcomer, 1992; Broadway Theatre World Award, 1995. Address: c/o Julian Belfrage Associates, 46 Albermarle Street, London, W1X 4PP, England.

SEXTON Timothy Adrian, b. 10 August 1960, South Australia. Musician. Education: B Mus, Composition, 1980, Honours degree, 1983, Dip Ed, 1988, University of Adelaide; Elder Conservatorium. Appointments: Singer; Adjudicator; Writer; Broadcaster; Music Director: Corinthian Singers of Adelaide; Adelaide Philharmonia Chorus; Adelaide Vocal Project; Chorus Master, State Opera of SA; Founder and Artistic Director & Conductor, Adelaide Art Orchestra. Publications: Multiple articles and contributions in Sing Out, to opera programmes and choral journals. Honours: Henry Krips Memorial Conducting Scholarship (twice); Centenary of Federation Medal for Services to Music, 2003; State Premier's Ruby Award for Sustained Contribution to the Arts, 2008; South Australian of the Year (Arts category), 2009. Listed in various international biographical dictionaries. Memberships: Music Arrangers Guild of Australia.

SEYMOUR David, b. 24 January 1951, Surrey, England. Lawyer. m. Elisabeth, 1 son, 2 daughters. Education: MA, Jurisprudence, The Queen's College, Oxford, 1969-72; LLB, Fitzwilliam College, Cambridge, 1973-74; Gray's Inn, Called to the Bar, 1975. Appointments: Law Clerk, Rosenfeld, Meyer & Susman (Attorneys), Beverly Hills, California, 1972-73; Legal Adviser's Branch, Home Office, 1975-97; Legal Secretary to the Attorney General, 1997-2000; Legal Adviser, Home Office and Northern Ireland Office, 2000-. Honours: Open Exhibition, The Queen's College, Oxford, 1969-72; Holt Scholar, Gray's Inn, 1974; Elected Bencher, Gray's Inn, 2001; CB, New Year Honours List, 2005. Address: Home Office, 2 Marsham Street, London SW1P 4DF, England. E-mail: david.seymour@homeoffice.gov.uk

SHABA Peter, b. 1969, Kaduna, Nigeria. Chief Lecturer. Education: DVM, Faculty of Veterinary Medicine, Ahmadu Bello University, Zaria, 1988; Advanced Training Course on Poultry Management and Farm Economics Certificate, Central Poultry Training Institute, Hessargatta, Bangalore, India, 1995; Master of Veterinary Sciences, 2002, PhD, 2007, Veterinary Medicine, Deemed University, Division of Medicine, Indian Veterinary Research Institute, Bareilly, India. Appointments: Vet-Clinician, Zanzomo Farm Estate, Sokoto State, 1988-89; Vet-Clinician, Sokoto State Veterinary Centre, Sokoto State, 1989; Private practice, Kaduna Metropolis and Environs, 1989; Assistant Manager/Vet-Clinician, Labaran Multipurpose Farm, Lagos-Kaduna Road, 1990; Lecturer, Department of Animal Helath and Production Technology, College of Agriculture, Mokwa, Niger State, late 1990s-; Representative of College of Agriculture, Mokwa, in Niger State Committee on Conflict between Arable Farmers and Herdsmen, 1994-99; Head of Department, Animal Health and Production Technology, Mokwa, 2008-. Publications: Numerous articles in professional journals. Honours: Junior Research Fellowship; Award of Honour, Indian Society of Canine Practice, 2012; Listed in international biographical dictionaries. Memberships: Association of Nigeria Veterinary Medical Association; Life Member, Indian Society of Veterinary Medicine; Association of Nigeria Teachers' Technology; Animal Production Society of Nigeria; Ethiopian Society of Animal Production; Indian Society of Parasitology; Indian Society of Veterinary Public Health Professionals; Indian Society of Canine Practice.

SHABANI Majlinda, b. 7 May 1985, Gjirokaster, Albania. Economist; Poetess; Translator. Education: Certified, Albanian Civil Society Foundation, Capacity Increase Governmental Organizations and the Rise of an Information Network among themselves in Albania, 2002; Economics Course for Journalist, Faculty of Social Sciences, University Eqrem Cabej, Gjirokaster, 2003-04; Course for Young Poets and Translators, Lnpsha Pegasi, Albania, 2008-09. Appointments: Vice Secretary, International Association of Poets, Writers and Artists, Pegasi, Albania. Publications: Sculpture of Desire in the Maneuvering Sky (poetry); Skulpture deshire ne qiell manovrimi; Scultura dipensiero nel cielo di manovra; Methmorfosi Generativa; The Anthology Korsi E Hapur; The Pegasiadal. Honours: Honour Prize (Gratitude by different manifestations), Lnpsha, IAPWA, Pegasi, Albania; The First Prize of the Year; The Prize for Translation of the Year, 2009, 2010, 2011, 2012; First Prize, Pegasi 2010; Special Prize, 2011; Prize of the International Congress, The University of Values in Literature and Art, 2012; Special Prize, Keleno literary magazine, Greece. Memberships: International Association of Poets, Writers and Artists; World Poets Society; United Poets Laureate International; Alternative Academy of the Lnpsha, Pegasi, Albania; Chair of Psycho-Analytic of the Lnpsha, Pegasi, Albania. Address: Lagjja 18 Shtatori, Pallati 1136, Gjirokaster, Albania. E-mail: aleksandra_shabani@yahoo.com

SHAFFER Peter (Levin), b. 15 May 1926, Liverpool, England. Dramatist. Education: BA, Trinity College, Cambridge, 1950. Appointments: Literary Critic, Truth, 1956-57; Music Critic, Time and Tide, 1961-62; Cameron Mackintosh Visiting Professor of Contemporary Theatre and Fellow, St Catherine's College, Oxford, 1994. Publications: Plays: Five Finger Exericse, 1958; The Private Ear, 1962; The Public Eye, 1962; The Merry Roosters Panto (with Joan Littlewood), 1963; The Royal Hunt of the Sun, 1964; Black Comedy, 1965; White Lies, 1967; The White Liars, 1968; The Battle of Shrivings, 1970; Amadeus, 1979; Yonadab, 1985; Lettice and Lovage, 1987; The Gift of Gorgon, 1992. Contributions to: Radio and television. Honours: Evening Standard Drama Awards, 1958, 1979, 1988; New York Drama Critics Cricle Awards, 1959, 1976; London Theatre Critics Award, 1979; Plays and Players Award, 1979; Tony Awards, 1979, 1980; Drama Desk Award, 1980; Academy Award, 1985; Golden Globe Award, 1985; Los Angeles Film Critics Association Award, 1985; Premi David di Donatello, 1985; Commander of the Order of the British Empire, 1987; Shakespeare Prize, Hamburg, 1989; William Inge Award for Distinguished Achievement in the American Theatre, 1992. Membership: Royal Society of Literature, fellow. Address: c/o McNaughton-Lowe Representation, 200 Fulham Road, London SW10 9PN, England.

SHAFI'I Maryam Larai, b. 20 May 1959, T/wada, Zaria, Nigeria. Retired Lecturer. m. Abdullah Ndanusa Yahaya, 1 son, 1 daughter. Education: BSc, Business Administration, 1982; MBA, Ahmadu Bello University, 1984; PhD, Public Administration, in progress. Appointments: Officer, Samaru Zaria Branch, First Bank of Nigeria Ltd, 1982; Officer, Kaduna Co-operative Bank Ltd, 1985; Lecturer, Ahmadu Bello University, Zaria, 1993-2008; Retired; Professor, 2009. Publications: Public Administration Research in Nigeria, 2002; Ethical Sentiments: The Restoration of Trust in Government and Business in Nigeria, 2008, 2009; Ethical Sentiments and the 1989 to 2009 World Financial Crisis, 2010. Honours: Listed in international biographical dictionaries; International Peace Prize, 2003; Contemporary Elite, 2004; Contemporary

Diamond Award, 2004. Memberships: Chartered Institute of Bankers, London; Professional Womens Advisory Board, 2004. Address: No 37 Benin Street, Sabon-Gari, Zaria, Nigeria.

SHAH Ashokkumar Purshottamdas, 7 September 1955, Dabhoi, India. Design Engineer. m. Darshna, 1982, 2 daughters. Education: BE, Chem, 1976, Postgraduate, Industrial Management, 1988, MS University, Baroda, India. Appointments: Deputy General Manager, Design-Process, Gujarat State Fertilizers & Chemicals Ltd, 1976-. Publications: Numerous articles in professional journals and international conferences. Honours: Award for Safety, 1992-94; 1st Prize for Best Paper, 1992. Address: Shreedhar, 50/1 Kadamnagar, Nizampura, Vadodara, 390002, Gujarat, India. E-mail: apshah@gsfcltd.com

SHAH Ira, b. 8 December 1973, Mumbai, India. Professor. Education: MBBS, MD (Pediatrics), FCPS, DNB, DCH (Gold Medallist). Appointments: Co Incharge, Pediatric Liver Clinic, Incharge, Pediatric HIV & TV Clinic, B J Wadia Hospital for Children, Mumbai. Publications: Over 83 articles in professional journals; Editor, Pediatric Oncall, 2000-; Asian Editor, Journal of Pediatric Infectious Diseases. Address: I/B Saguna, 271/B St Francis Road, Vile Parle (W), Mumbai 400 056, India.

SHAH Rikhavbhai P, b. 31 July 1929, Ranuj, Gujarat, India. Professor. m. Prabhavati, 1 son, 1 daughter. Education: MEd, Experimental Education, 1960, PhD, Test Construction, 1970, Gujarat University; DDE, Distance Education, IGNOU, 1989. Appointments: Lecturer, Gujarat Vidyapith, 1966-72; Reader, Professor, P G Department, 1972-78; Head of Department, Post Graduation, 1978-89. Publications: University textbooks: Award Winner Reports, NCERT, 1962; Planning and Evaluating Research, 1984, 1998; Concepts and Technical Terms in Education; Numerical Ability Test with Manual, Gujarat Vidyapith; Handbooks for Teachers, Mathematics State Institute, 1972. Honours: Award, NCERT National Seminar Readings Contest, 1962; International Peace Prize, UCC, ABI, 2010. Memberships: Ahmedabad Association Teacher Education; Vijaynagar Education Society. Address: 1 Geet Govind Society, Thaltej, Ahmedabad, Gujarat, 380059, India.

SHAHIN Yousef, b. 14 October 1978, Spain (National of Jordan). m. Mais Baidoun. Clinical Research Fellow. Education: Doctor of Medicine Diploma (Clinical), Damascus University, Syria, 2003; IELTS, British Council, Jordan, 2004; Jordanian Internship Exam, Jordanian Medical Council, 2004; PLAB I & II, General Medical Council, UK, 2004; PG Certificate in Critical Care, Cardiff University, 2007; MRCS Part A, Royal College of Surgeons of England, 2008; Doctor of Medicine (Research), Cardiff University, in progress. Appointments: House Officer, Arab Medical Centre, Jordan, 2003-04; Clinical Attachment, Hull & East Yorkshire Hospitals, 2004-05; House Officer, Buckinghamshire Hospitals, 2005-06; Senior House Officer, Oxford Radcliffe Hospitals, 2006-07; Core Surgical Training Year 1, Swansea Hospitals, 2007-08; Core Surgical Training Year 2, Nottingham University Hospitals, 2008-09; Clinical Research Fellow, University of Hull and Hull Royal Infirmary, 2009-10. Publications: Numerous articles in professional journals. Honours: Honour Certificate, Damascus University; Honour Certificate, Scientific College; Research Grant, Neurosurgical Research Project, 2008; Research Grant, Medical Device, 2010. Memberships: Association of Surgeons in Training; European Society of Vascular Surgeons; British Medical Association. E-mail: yousef.shahin@yahoo.co.uk

SHAKHMATOV Sergey, b. 28 November 1955, B Lozhkino village, Nizhegorodsk region, Russia. Teacher. m. Nadezhda, 1 son. Education: Krasnoyarsk Agrarian Institute, 1973-78; Candidate of Science in Engineering, 2000, Docent, 2002. Appointments: Director, Institute of Power Engineering and Energy Resource Management of Agro-Industrial Complex. Publications: More than 100 scientific papers; 15 laboratory operation manuals; 2 books. Honours: Numerous letters of gratitude and diplomas from the Rector of Krasnoyarsk State Agrarian University; Diploma of Education Ministry, Krasnoyarsk Region; Diploma of the Agriculture Ministry, Russian Federation; Listed in international biographical dictionaries. Memberships: Agroindustrial Complex Union, Krasnoyarsk Region, Trade Union Committee of Krasnoyarsk State Agrarian University. Address: 16 Slovtsova Street, apt 67, Krasnoyarsk, 660130, Russia. E-mail: etf@kgau.ru

SHAKHOVSKY Victor Ivanovich, b. 9 January 1939, Nikolaevsk, Volgograd Region, Russia. Teacher of English; Linguist. 1 daughter. Education: Graduate, Volgograd Pedagogical University, 1963; Doctor of Linguistics; Full Professor. Appointments: Chair of SLT, 1974-85; Professor and Chair of Linguistics, Head, Laboratory "Language and Personality", Volgograd State Pedagogical University, Russia, 1988-. Publications: 400 publications on language and emotions; 15 books include: Categorization of emotions by lexico-semantic system of the language; Text and its Cognitivo-emotive transformations; Emotions in Business Communication. Honour: Honoured Scientist of the Russian Federation; Honoured Doctor of Volgograd State Pedagogical University. Address: Titov Street 32, Apt 8, Volgograd 400123, Russia. E-mail: shakhovsky@inbox.ru

SHAMANIN Igor Vladimirovich, b. 16 October 1962, Rostov on the Don, Russia. Physicist. m. Evgenia Obukhova, 2 sons. Education: Engineer Physicist, 1985; Philosophy Doctor, 1987; Doctor of Physical and Mathematical Sciences, Full Professor, 1998; Academician, 2010. Appointments: Postgraduate Student, 1985-87; Assistant, 1988, Chief of Laboratory, 1990-92, Senior Lecturer, 1993, Doctoral Researcher, 1994-96, Docent, 1997, Professor, 1998, Tomsk Polytechnic University (up to 1992 - Tomsk Polytechnic Institute); Officer, Soviet Army, 1988-90; Invited Professor, Institute of Reactor Technologies Forschungszentrum Jülich, Germany, 1998-99. Publications: Monographs: The physics of interaction of pulsed beams of charged particles with matter, 2003; Thorium in nuclear fuel cycle, 2006; Electrophysics of the structured solutions of salts in liquid polar dielectrics, 2011. Honours: Certificate of Honor of State Corporation ROSATOM, 2010; Breastplate of the Honourable Worker of Higher Education of Russian Federation, 2010. Memberships: Academy of Engineering Sciences of Russian Federation. E-mail: shiva@tpu.ru

SHAMS Hoda Zaky, b. 26 January 1943, Cairo, Egypt. Professor of Organic Chemistry. m. Kadry Youssef Dimian, 2 sons. Education: BSc, Chemistry, 1963, MSc, Organic Chemistry, 1970, PhD, Organic Chemistry, Cairo University, 1977. Appointments: Demonstrator & Lecturer, 1963; Lecturer, 1971; Associate Professor, 1986; Professor, Organic & Applied Chemistry, Helwan University, Helwan, Cairo, Egypt, 1993-; Examiner, Cairo University; Visitor Researcher, Rutgers University, USA; Participator, NIH, 1990; Director, PhD and MSc students, Helwan and Cairo Universities. Publications: Pigment and Resin Technology; Phosphorus, Sulfur and Silicon; Numerous articles in scientific journals, including Molecules, 2011; Design, synthesis and structure elucidation of fused and pendant heterocyclic systems, including most recently: Synthesis and dyeing properties of new reactive dyes derived from heterocyclic pyrazolo pyrazole component, 2008; Applications as pharmaceuticals and as dyes and pigments for dyeing and printing; Formulation of photopolymers. Honours: Nominated as International Educator; Nominated as a Leading Scientist of the World; Listed in several Who's Who and biographical dictionaries. Memberships: Literati Club; MCB University, Bradford, UK. Address: Department of Chemistry, Faculty of Science, Helwan University, Helwan, Cairo, Egypt. E-mail: shamshodaz@yahoo.com

SHAND William Stewart, b. 12 October 1936, Derby, England. Surgeon. m. Caroline, deceased 2005, 2 sons, 1 stepson, 2 stepdaughters. Education: Repton School; St Johns College, Cambridge; The Medical College of St Bartholomew's Hospital London; MA, 1962; MD Cantab, 1970; FRCS, 1969; FRCS Ed, 1970. Appointments include: Consultant Surgeon, King Edward VII's Hospital for Officers, London; Honorary Consultant Surgeon, St Mark's Hospital for Diseases of the Colon and Rectum, London; Consultant Surgeon to Hackney and Homerton Hospitals, London; Honorary Consultant, St Luke's Hospital for the Clergy, London; Penrose May Tutor, Royal College of Surgeons of England, London, 1980-85; Governor of the Medical College of St Bartholomew's Hospital; Governor of the British Postgraduate Medical Federation; Member of the Court of Examiners of the Royal College of Surgeons of England, 1985-91; Consultant Surgeon, St Bartholomew's Hospital London, 1973-96; Governor of Sutton's Hospital in Charterhouse, 1989-2009; Currently: Penrose May Teacher, Royal College of Surgeons of England, London, 1985-; Trustee, 1995-2000, Vice President, 2001-, Phyllis Tuckwell Hospice, Farnham, Surrey; Member, Honorary Medical Panel of the Artists' General Benevolent Institution, 1979-; Honorary Consulting Surgeon to St Bartholomew's Hospital and the Royal London Hospital, London. Publications: Articles in various journals and contributions to books on surgery, colorectal disease, chronic inflammatory bowel disease in children and oncology; Book: The Art of Dying – The Story of Two Sculptors' Residency in a Hospice (co-author), 1989. Honour: National Art Collections Fund Award, 1992. Memberships: Member of the Court of Assistants of the Worshipful Society of Apothecaries of London, Master, 2004-2005; Member of the Court of Assistants of the Worshipful Company of Barbers of London, Master, 2001-2002; Travelling Surgical Society of Great Britain and Northern Ireland, President, 1994-97; Fellow, Association of Surgeons of Great Britain and Ireland; Fellow, Hunterian Society; Fellow, Harveian Society of London; Chairman, Homerton Hospital Artwork Committee, 1985-92; Honorary Curator of Ceramics, Royal College of Surgeons, England, 1980-. Address: Fennel Cottage, 25 Station Road, Nassington, Peterborough, PE8 6QB, England.

SHAPIRO Harvey Allan, b. 21 Apr 1941, Toledo, OH, USA. Environmental Planner. m. Fukiko N, 2 d. Education: BArch; Master Regl Plng; DAgric, Ecological Plng. Appointments: Lectr, Environ Plng (full-time), 1980; Prof, Environ Plng (tenured), 1987. Publications include: Ecological Planning in Japan, in, Hazard Waste Control, 1984. Memberships: Intl Geog Union; Pacific Sci Assn; World Conservation Union (IUCN); JEA; ACZS; JCZS; Sierra Club. Address: Department of Environmental Planning, Osaka Geijutsu University, Minami-Kawachi-Gun, Kanan-cho, Osaka Prefecture 585-8555, Japan.

SHARAPOVA Maria, b. 19 April 1987, Nyagan, Siberia, Russia. Professional Tennis Player. Education: Nick Bollettieri Tennis Academy, Florida, USA. Career: Turned professional, 2001; Youngest female to reach final of the Junior Australian Open, 2002; Reached final of the Junior Wimbledon Championships, 2002; Started playing WTA Tour events, 2003; Grand Slam Singles, Wimbledon, 2004; World No 1 ranking, US Open, 2005; Top seed, Australian Open, 2007; Fed Cup debut, 2008. Honours: Women's Tennis Association (WTA) Newcomer of the Year, 2003; WTA Player of the Year, WTA Most Improved Player of the Year, 2004; ESPY Best Female Tennis Player, Named the country's best female player for the year by Russia's tennis federation, Master of Sports of Russia, Prix de Citron Roland Garros, 2005; Named the country's best female player for the year by Russia's tennis federation, Whirlpool 6th Sense Player of the Year, 2006; ESPY Best Female Tennis Player, ESPY Best International Female Athlete, ESPY Hottest Female Athlete, 2007; Female Athlete of the Month (January), United States Sports Academy (for her performance at the Australian Open), ESPY Best Female Tennis Player, 2008.

SHARIF Omar (Michael Chalhoub), b. 10 April 1932, Cairo, Egypt. Actor. m. (1) Faten Hamama, (divorced) 1 son. Education: Victoria College, Cairo. Career: Salesman, lumber-import firm; 24 Egyptian films and 2 French co-production films; Films include: Lawrence of Arabia; The Fall of the Roman Empire; Behold a Pale Horse; Genghis Khan; The Yellow Rolls Royce; Doctor Zhivago; Night of the Generals; Mackenna's Gold; Funny Girl; Cinderella-Italian Style; Mayerling; The Appointment; Che; The Last Valley; The Horseman; The Burglars; The Island; The Tamarind Seed; Juggernaut; Funny Lady; Ace Up My Sleeve; Crime and Passion; Bloodline; Green Ice; Top Secret; Peter the Great (TV); The Possessed; Mountains of the Moon; Michaelangelo and Me; Drums of Fire; Le Guignol; The Puppet; The Rainbow Thief; 558 rue Paradis; Gulliver's Travels (TV); Heaven Before I Die; The 13th Warrior; The Parole Officer; Shaka Zulu: The Citadel (TV); Monsieur Ibrahim et les fleurs de Coran; Soyez prudents... (TV); Urban Myth Chillers (TV); Hidalgo; Benji: Off the Leash! 2004; The Search for External Egypt, 2005; The Ten Commandments, 2006; Kronprinz Rudolf, 2006; One Night with the King, 2006; 10,000 B.C. (narrator), 2008; Theatre: The Sleeping Prince, England, 1983. Publications: The Eternal Male (autobiography), 1978. Address: c/o William Morris Agency, 151 El Camino Drive, Beverly Hills, CA 90212, USA.

SHARMA J K, b. 31 July 1951. Professor. Education: MSc, Mathematics, 1974, PhD, Operations Research, 1978, Meerut University. Appointments: Lecturer, Department of Mathematics, S S V Postgraduate College, Hapur, 1978-79; Lecturer, Department of Mathematics, Kurukshetra University, 1979-81; Associate Professor, Institute of Management Technology, Ghaziabad, 1981-85; Professor, Facultyof Management Studies, University of Dehli, 1985-2006; Visiting Professor, Graduate School of Management, Cergy-Pontoise, France, 1992-94; Director, Maharishi Institute of Management, 1996-97; Director, Institute of Management Studies, 1999-2001; Professor in Charge, Faculty of Management Studies, University of Dehli, 2004-05; Director, G L Bajaj Institute of Management & Research, 2006-11; Professor, Amity Business School, Amity University, Noida, 2011-. Publications: 17 books; 91 research papers; 20 case studies. Honours: Senior Research Fellowship, Council of Scientific and Industrial Research, 1974-78; Madan Mohan Gold Medal, 1974; Meerut College Gold Medal, 1974; Merit Certificate, 1974. Memberships:

DICTIONARY OF INTERNATIONAL BIOGRAPHY 36th EDITION

Operational Research Society of India. Address: 277-A/5, Durgapuri Extension, Loni Road, Delhi 110093, India. E-mail: jks_sharma@yahoo.com

SHARMA Kal Renganathan, b. India (naturalised USA citizen). Adjunct Professor. Education: B Tech, Indian Institute of Technology, Chennai, 1985; MS, 1987, PhD, 1990, West Virginia University, USA. Appointments: Adjunct Professor, Department of Chemical Engineering, Prairie View A&M University, 2007-. Publications: 8 books; 1 book chapter; 15 journal articles; 480 conference papers; 53 preprints; 108 invited seminars/lectures and others. Honours: Listed in international biographical dictionaries. Memberships: AIChE; ACS. Address: Department of Chemical Engineering, Prairie View A&M University, Prairie View, TX 77446, USA. Website: www.pvamu.edu

SHARMA Sanjay, b. 4 August 1965, Machalpur, District of Rajgarh (Biaora), MP, India. Industrial Engineer; Educator; Researcher. m. Mamta Joshi. Education: BE, Mechanical, 1985; MTech, Engineering Materials, 1994; PhD, Industrial Engineering, 1999. Appointments: Mechanical Engineer, MMPL (LPG cylinder manufacturing industry), Pithampur, India, 1986-90; Manager (Tech), MPLUN Ltd, Bhopal, India, 1991-96; Lecturer, Mandsaur Institute of Technology, Mandsaur, India, 1997-99; Assistant Professor, NSIT, New Delhi, India, 2000-07; Associate Professor, NITIE, Mumbai, India, 2007-. Publications: Book, Mathematical modeling of production-inventory systems, 2004; Papers in professional scientific/technical/management journals. Honours: India Quality Award, 2002; Quality Culture Award, World Institution Building Programme; Best Citizens of India Award, 2005; Listed in international biographical dictionaries. Memberships: Institution of Engineers (India); Indian Institution of Industrial Engineering. Address: Operations Management, Room No 104, Training Block, National Institute of Industrial Engineering, Vihar Lake, P O NITIE, Mumbai 400087, India.

SHARMANOV Toregeldy, b. 19 October 1930, Ulytau, Kazakhstan. Doctor. Widowed, 1 son. Education: Undergraduate degree, Medical Care, 1955, Postgraduate degree, Pharmacy, 1958, Karaganda State Medical University; Candidate, Medical Sciences, 1961; Doctor of Medical Sciences, 1967. Appointments: Head, Department of Nutritional Hygiene, National Research Institute of Province Pathology, 1962-68; Rector, Aktubinsk Medical University, Chair, Department of Pharmacology, 1968-71; Minister of Healthcare of Kazakhstan, 1971-82; President, Kazakh Academy of Nutrition, 1982-. Publications: Author, over 350 publications; 23 monographs; 37 inventions; Organiser, International Conference of WHO and UNICEF on Primary Health Care, Almaty, 1978. Honours: Laureate, State Honor of the Republic of Kazakhstan; Laureate of Independent Honor, Platinum Tarbin. Memberships: Honored Science Fellow, Republic of Kazakhstan. Address: Institute of Nutrition, 050008 Almaty, 66 Klochkova Street, Kazakhstan. E-mail: sharmanov.t@mail.ru

SHARPE David Thomas, b. 14 January 1946, Kent, England. Consultant Plastic Surgeon. m. (1) Patricia Lilian Meredith, 1971, dissolved 2002, 1 son, 2 daughters, (2) Tracey Louise Bowman, 2004. Education: Grammar School for Boys, Gravesend; MA, Downing College, Cambridge; MB BChir, Clinical Medical School, Oxford; FRCS, 1975; House Surgeon, Radcliffe Infirmary, Oxford, 1970-71; Senior House Officer, Plastic Surgery, Churchill Hospital, Oxford, 1971-72; Accident Service, Radcliffe Infirmary, 1972; Pathology, Radcliffe Infirmary, 1972-73; General Surgery, Royal United Hospital, Bath, 1973-75; Plastic Surgery, Welsh Plastic Surgery Unit, Chepstow, 1976. Appointments: Registrar, Plastic Surgery, Chepstow, 1976-81; Canniesburn Hospital, Glasgow, 1978-80; Senior Registrar, Plastic Surgery, Leeds and Bradford, 1980-84; Visiting Consultant Plastic Surgeon, Yorkshire Clinic, Bradford, 1985-; BUPA Hospital Elland, West Yorkshire, 1985-; Cromwell Hospital, London, 1985-; Chairman, Breast Special Interest GP, British Association of Plastic Surgeons, 1997-; President, British Association of Aesthetic Plastic Surgeons, 1997-99; Chairman, Yorkshire Air Ambulance, 2001-03; Inventor and Designer of medical equipment and surgical instruments and devices; Exhibitor, Design Council, London, 1987. Publications: Chapters, leading articles and papers on plastic surgery topics, major burn disaster management, tissue expansion and breast reconstruction. Honours: OBE, 1986; British Design Award, 1988; Prince of Wales Award for Innovation & Production, 1988. Memberships: British Association of Plastic Surgeons; British Association of Aesthetic Plastic Surgeons; Fellow, Royal College of Surgeons of England; International Society of Aesthetic Plastic Surgeons. Address: Hazelbrae, Calverley Lane, Calverley, Leeds LS28 5QQ, England. E-mail: profsharpe@hotmail.com

SHARPE Tom (Thomas Ridley), b. 30 March 1928, London, England. Novelist. m. Nancy Anne Looper, 1969, 3 daughters. Education: Pembroke College, University of Cambridge. Appointments: Social Worker, 1952; Teacher, 1952-56; Photographer, 1956-61; Lecturer in History at Cambridge College of Arts and Technology, 1963-71; Full-time novelist, 1971-. Publications: Riotous Assembly, 1971; Indecent Exposure, 1973; Porterhouse Blue, 1974; Blott on the Landscape, 1975; Wilt, 1976; The Great Pursuit, 1977; The Throwback, 1978; The Wilt Alternative, 1979; Ancestral Vices, 1980; Vintage Stuff, 1982; Wilt on High, 1984; Grantchester Grind, 1995; The Midden, 1996; Wilt in Nowhere, 2005. Address: 38 Tunwells Lane, Great Shelford, Cambridge, CB2 5LJ, England.

SHATNER William, b. 22 March 1931, Montreal, Quebec, Canada. Actor. m. (1) Gloria Rosenberg, 1956, divorced 1969, 3 children, (2) Marcy Lafferty, 1973, divorced 1996, (3) Nerine Kidd, 1997, deceased 1999, (4) Elizabeth Anderson, 2001. Education: BA, McGill University. Career: Appeared, Montreal Playhouse, 1952, 1953; Juvenile roles, Canadian Repertory Theatre, Ottawa, 1952-53, 1953-54; Shakespeare Festival, Stratford, Ontario, 1954-56; Broadway appearances include: Tamburlaine the Great, 1956; The World of Suzie Wong, 1958; A Shot in the Dark, 1961; Numerous TV appearances; Films include: The Brothers Karamazov, 1958, The Explosive Generation, 1961, Judgement at Nuremberg, 1961, The Intruder, 1962, The Outrage, 1964, Dead of Night, 1974, The Devil's Rain, 1975, Star Trek, 1979, The Kidnapping of the President, 1979, Star Trek: The Wrath of Khan, 1982, Star Trek III, The Search for Spock, 1984, Star Trek IV: The Voyage Home, 1986, Star Trek V: The Final Frontier, 1989, Star Trek VI: The Undiscovered Country, 1991, National Lampoon's Loaded Weapon, 1993; Star Trek: Generations, 1994; Ashes of Eden, 1995; Star Trek: Avenger, 1997; Tek Net, 1997; Free Enterprise, 1999; Miss Congeniality, 2000; Groom Lake (also director and co-writer), 2002; Dodgeball, 2004; Miss Congeniality 2: Armed and Fabulous, 2005; The Wild (voice), 2006; Over the Hedge (voice), 2006. Publications: Ashes of Eden; Star Trek: Avenger, 1997; Step into Chaos, 1999; Get a Life, 1999; The Preserver, 2000; Spectre, 2000; Albums: The Transformed Man, 1968, Has Been, 2004. Honours: Emmy Award for Outstanding Guest

Actor in a Drama Series, 2004; Best Supporting Actor in a Series, Miniseries or TV Movie, Golden Globe Awards, 2005. Address: c/o Melis Productions, 760 North La Cienega Boulevard, Los Angeles, CA 90069, USA.

SHAW Fiona, b. 10 July 1958, Cork, Ireland. Actress. Education: University College, Cork; Royal Academy of Dramatic Art. Career: Stage appearances include: The Rivals; Howard Brenton's Bloody Poetry; With RSC: As You Like It; Gorky's Philistines; Les Liaisons Dangereuses; Much Ado About Nothing; The Merchant of Venice; The Taming of the Shrew; James Shirley's Hyde Park; Sophocles's Electra; Brecht's The Good Person of Sichuan; Hedda Gabler; Beckett's Footfalls; Richard II; The Waste Land, 1996; The Prime of Miss Jean Brodie, 1998; Widower's Houses, 1999; Medea, 2000, 2001; The Power Book, 2002; Happy Days, 2007, 2008; Mother Courage and her Children, 2009; London Assurance, John Gabriel Borkman, 2010; Scenes from an Execution, 2012; Films and TV include: My Left Foot; Mountains of the Moon; Three Men and a Little Lady, 1990; Super Mario Brothers, 1992; Undercover Blues, 1993; The Waste Land, Persuasion, 1995; Jane Eyre, 1996; The Avengers, The Butcher's Boy, Anna Karenina, 1997; The Last September, 1999; The Triumph of Love, 2000; Harry Potter and The Philosopher's Stone, Doctor Sleep, 2001; Harry Potter and The Chamber of Secrets, 2002; Harry Potter and the Prisoner of Azkaban, 2004; The Black Dahlia, Catch and Release, 2006; Fracture, Harry Potter and the Order of the Phoenix, 2007; Dorian Gray, 2009; Harry Potter and the Deathly Hallows, Part I, 2010; The Tree of Life, 2011; True Blood, 2011. Honours: Tree Prize, RADA, 1982; Ronson Award, RADA, 1982; Olivier Award for Best Actress, 1990; London Critics' Award for Best Actress, 1990; London Critics' Award, 1992; Olivier Award, Evening Standard Award for Machinal, 1995; Hon LLD, National University of Ireland, 1998; Honorary Professor of Drama, Trinity College, Dublin; Officier des Arts et des Lettres, 2001; Honorary CBE, 2001; Hon DUniv, Open University, 1999; Hon DLitt, Trinity College, Dublin, 2001; Evening Standard Award for Best Actress, 2001; Bancroft Gold Medal, RADA. Address: ICM, Oxford House, 76 Oxford Street, London W1N 0AX, England.

SHAW Timothy Milton, b. 27 January 1945, England. Professor. m. Jane L Parpart, 1 son, 3 daughters. Education: BA, Sussex, 1967; MA, Makerere, East Africa, 1969; PhD, Princeton, 1975. Appointments: Professor, Political Science & IDS, Dalhousie University, Nova Scotia, 1971-2000; Professor & Director, Institute of Commonwealth Studies, London, England, 2001-06; Professor & Director, Institute of International Relations, University of West Indies, 2007-11; Visiting Professor at universities in Nigeria, South Africa, Zambia, Zimbabwe, etc. Publications: Commonwealth: Inter-& Non-State Contributions to Global Governance, 2008; Ashgate Research Companion on Regionalisms, 2011; Africa & International Relations in the 21st Century, 2011; Inter-American Cooperation at a Crossroads, 2011; Many essays in International Affairs, Third World Quarterly, Global Governance, etc. Address: 318 Selby Avenue, Ottawa, K1Z 6R1, Canada. E-mail: timothy.shaw@sta.uwi.edu

SHE Jinhua, b. 23 May 1963, Jinshi, Hunan, China. University Professor. m. Yoko Miyamoto. 1 son. Education: Masters Degree, 1990, PhD, 1993, Tokyo Institute of Technology, Japan. Appointments: Lecturer, 1993-2001, Associate Professor, 2001-09, Professor, 2010-, Tokyo University of Technology, Japan; Guest Lecturer, Toyota Technical Development Corporation, Japan, 2001-; Guest Professor, Central South University, China, 2002-. Publications: Articles in scientific journals including: IEEE Transactions on Automatic Control, Automatica, Systems and Control Letters, Transactions of ASME; Control Engineering Practice; Engineering Application of Artificial Intelligence; IET Control Theory & Applications. Honour: Prize Paper Award, International Federation of Automatic Control, 1999. Memberships: IEEE; Institute of Electrical Engineers of Japan; Society of Instrument and Control Engineers; Japan Society of Mechanical Engineer; Asian Control Association. Address: School of Computer Computer Science, Tokyo University of Technology, 1404-1 Katakura, Hachioji, Tokyo 192-0982, Japan. E-mail: she@cc.teu.ac.jp Website: www.teu.ac.jp/kougi/hp037/She.htm

SHEARER Alan, b. 13 August 1970, Gosforth, Newcastle upon Tyne, England. Footballer. Career: Coached as child at Wallsend Boys' Club; Striker; Striker, played for Southampton, 1987-92, Blackburn Rovers, 1992-96; Signed by Newcastle United for world record transfer of £15 million (Captain), 1996; First played for England, 1992-2000 (63 caps, 30 goals), Captain 1996-2000; Premiership all-time leading scorer; First player to score 200 Premiership goals and first to score 100 League goals for two different clubs; Scored 400th career goal, January 2005; Pundit, Match of the Day. Address: Newcastle United Football Club, St James Park, Newcastle Upon Tyne, NE1 4ST, England. Website: www.nufc.co.uk

SHEATH Janet, b. 8 July 1952, Portsmouth, England. Artist. m. Robert John Sheath, 2 daughters. Education: Hart Plain Avenue School for Girls, Cowplain. Artist in watercolour and tempera; Solo and group exhibitions in London and Isle of Wight. Honours: Llwellyn Alexander Masters Award, 2001; Fairmans Subject Miniature Award, Royal Society of Miniatures; Llwellyn Alexander Commendation of Excellence; Honourable Mention for the Gold Bowl Memorial Award, Royal Society of Miniatures; Listed in international biographical dictionaries. Memberships: Royal Society of Miniature Painters, Sculptors and Gravers; Society of Women Artists. Address: 4 Cupressus Avenue, Winford, Sandown, Isle of Wight, PO36 0LA, England.

SHEEN Charlie, b. 3 September 1965, New York, USA. Actor. m. 1 daughter with Paula Profit, (1) Donna Peele, 1995-96, (2) Denise Richards, 2003-06, 2 daughters, (3) Brooke Mueller, 2008-11, 2 sons. Actor; Films include: Apocalypse Now; Grizzly II; The Predator; The Red Dawn; Lucas; Platoon; The Wraith; Day Off; Young Guns; Wall Street; Eight Men Out; Major League; Backtrack; Men at Work; Courage Mountain; Navy Seals; The Rookie; Stockade (director); Secret Society; Hot Shots; Dead Fall; The Three Musketeers; The Chase; Major League II, 1994; Terminal Velocity, 1994; The Shadow Conspiracy, 1995; Shockwave, 1995; All Dogs Go to Heaven (voice), The Arrival, 1996; Money Talks, 1997; No Code of Conduct, 1998; Free Money, 1998; Letter From Death Row, 1998; Being John Malkovich, 1999; Cared X; Good Advice, 2000; Lisa Picard is Famous, 2001; Scary Movie 3, 2003; Deeper Than Deep, 2003; The Big Bounce, 2004; Foodfight, 2008; Wall Street: Money Never Sleeps, Due Date, I Am, 2010; A Glimpse Inside the Mind of Charles Swan III, She Wants Me, Foodfight! 2012; Machete Kills, Scary Movie 5, 2013; TV: Amazing Stories: Book Three; Friends; Sugar Hill; Spin City, 2000-02; Two and a Half Men, 2003-11; Overhaulin', 2006; The Big Bang Theory, CSI: Crime Scene Investigation, 2008; Family Guy, 2010; Drew Carey's Improv-A-Ganza, Comedy Central Roast, 2011; Anger Management, 2012-. Honours: Golden Globe for Best Actor, 2002; Golden Icon Award, 2006; ALMA

DICTIONARY OF INTERNATIONAL BIOGRAPHY 36th EDITION

Award, 2008; WWE.com Slammy Award, 2012. Address: c/o Jeffrey Ballard Public Relations, 4814 Lemara Avenue, Sherman Oaks, CA 91403, USA.

SHEEN Martin (Ramon Estevez), b. 3 August 1940, Dayton, Ohio, USA. Actor. m. Janet Templeton, 1961, 3 sons, 1 daughter. Career: Actor, films include: The Incident; Catch 22; Rage; Badlands; Apocalypse Now; Enigma; Gandhi; The King of Prussia; The Championship Season; Man, Woman and Child; The Dead Zone; Final Countdown; Loophole; Wall Street; Night Beaker; Da, 1988; Personal Choice, 1989; Cadence (also director), 1990; Judgement in Berlin, 1990; Limited Time; The Maid, 1990; Cadence (also director), 1990; Hear No Evil; Hot Shots part Deux (cameo); Gettysburg, 1993; Trigger Fast; Hit!; Fortunes of War; Sacred Cargo; The Break; Dillinger and Capone; Captain Nuke and the Bomber Boys; Ghost Brigade; The Cradle Will Rock; Dead Presidents; Dorothy Day; Gospa; The American President; The War At Home; Spawn; Storm, Monument Avenue, Free Money; Lost & Found, 1999; Apocalypse New Redux, 2001; Catch Me If You Can, 2003; Milost mora, 2003; The Commission, 2003; Jerusalemski sindrom, 2004; Bordertown, 2006; Bobby, 2006; The Departed, 2006; Flatland: The Movie, 2007; Talk to Me, 2007; TV appearances include: The Defenders; East Side/West Side; My Three Sons; Mod Squad; Cannon; That Certain Summer; Missiles of October; The Last Survivors; Blind Ambition; Shattered Spirits; Nightbreaker; The Last POW?; Roswell; The West Wing, 1999-; Stage appearances: The Connection (New York and European tours); Never Live Over A Pretzel Factory; The Subject was Roses; The Crucible. Honours include: Honorary Mayor of Malibu, 1989-; Golden Satellite Award, 2000; Golden Globe Award, 2000. Address: c/o Jeff Ballard, 4814 Lemara Avenue, Sherman Oaks, CA 91403, USA.

SHEEN Michael, b. 5 February 1969, Newport, Wales. Actor. 1 daughter with Kate Beckinsale. Education: National Youth Theatre of Wales, Cardiff; Royal Academy of Dramatic Art. Career: Actor; Film and TV work includes: Gallowglass, 1993; Othello, 1995; Mary Reilly, 1996; Wilde, 1997; Lost in France, 1998; Heartlands, The Four Feathers, 2002; Bright Young Things, Underworld, The Deal, Timeline, 2003; Laws of Attraction, Dirty Filthy Love, The Banker, 2004; Dead Long Enough, Kingdom of Heaven, The Open Doors, The League of Gentlemen's Apocalypse, 2005; Kenneth Williams: Fantabulosa!, The Queen, Ancient Rome: The Rise and Fall of an Empire, HG Wells: War with the World, Blood Diamond, 2006; Music Within, Airlock or How to Say Goodbye in Space, Salmon Fishing in the Yemen, 2007; Frost/Nixon, 2008; Underworld: Rise of the Lycans, The Damned United, My Last Five Girlfriends, New Moon, 2009; 30 Rock; Beautiful Boy, 2011; Doctor Who; The Twilight Saga: Breaking Dawn Part 1 and 2; Resistance; Hamlet, 2011-12; Jesus Henry Christ, 2012. Honours: British Academy Television Award for Best Actor, 2006; Kansas City Film Critics Circle Award for Best Supporting Actor, 2006; Los Angeles Film Critics Association Award for Best Supporting Actor, 2006; Toronto Film Critics Association Award for Best Supporting Actor, 2006; Freedom of the Borough of Neath Port Talbot, 2008; OBE, 2009; Actor of the Year, GQ Magazine, 2009; BAFTA Britannia Award, 2010; Honorary Fellow, University of Wales, Newport, the Royal Welsh College of Music & Drama, Swansea University, Aberystwyth University and Swansea Metropolitan University; James Joyce Award, University College Dublin.

SHEERAN Ed (Edward Christopher), b. 17 February 1991, Halifax, England. Singer; Songwriter. Education: Thomas Mills High School, Framlingham. Career: Singer-Songwriter, Asylum/Atlantic Records. Publications: Singles include: The A Team, 2011; You Need Me, 2011; Lego House, 2011; EPs: The Orange Room, 2005; You Need Me, 2009; Loose Change, 2010; Ed Sheeran: Live at the Bedford, 2010; Songs I Wrote With Amy, 2010; No 5 Collaborations Project, 2011; Albums: Ed Sheeran, 2006; Want Some? 2007. Honours: British Male Solo Artist, BRIT Awards, 2012.

SHEINWALD Sir Nigel (Elton), b. 26 June 1953, London, England. Her Majesty's Diplomatic Service. m. Julia Dunne, 3 sons. Education: Harrow County Grammar School; BA, Classics, Balliol College, Oxford, 1976. Appointments: Joined HM Diplomatic Service, 1976, Japan Desk, 1976-77; British Embassy, Moscow, 1978-79; Rhodesia, Zimbabwe Dept, 1979-81; Head, FCO Anglo-Soviet Section, 1981-83; Political Section of British Embassy in Washington, 1983-87; Deputy Head, FCO's Policy Planning Staff, 1987-89; Deputy Head, FCO's European Union (Internal) Department, 1989-92; Head, UK Representation's Political and Institutional Section, Brussels, 1993-95; Head, FCO News Department, 1995-98; Europe Director, FCO, 1998-2000; Ambassador and UK Permanent Representative to European Union, Brussels, 2000-03; Foreign Policy Adviser to the Prime Minister and Head of Cabinet Office, Defence and Overseas Secretariat, 2003-; British Ambassador to the United States, 2007-. Honours: CMG, 1999; KCMG, 2001. Address: 10 Downing Street, London, SW1A 2AA, England.

SHELDRAKE Alan Leigh, b. 10 April 1944, Finchley, London, England. Electrical Power Engineering. m. Ilse. Education: ONC, 1963; HND, 1966; MSc, 1969; DIC, 1969; PhD, 1976. Appointments: Lead/Senior Electrical Engineer, major oil and gas projects worldside, 1974-98; Senior Electrical Engineer, QGPC, Doha, Qatar, 1998-2000; Author of handbook (see below), 2000-03; Consulting Electrical Power Engineer, Maersk Oil & Gas, Denmark, 2003-04; Consulting Electrical Power Engineer, Cairn Energy India, 2007-08; Managing Director, Sheldrake Engineering Pvt Ltd, India, 2008-. Publications: An algorithm to evaluate the time response of a linear biological system from its transfer function, 1973; The transient performance of an AC exciter three phase bridge rectifier when connected to an inductive load, 1973; Real-time power system simulator, 1974; Real-time simulation of power system, 1974; The cost-effective use of CAD, 1986; Harmonic suppression filter for offshore interconnected power system, 1993; Handbook of electrical engineering for practitioners in the oil, gas and petrochemical industry, 2003. Honours: Life Member, IEEE. Memberships: Institute of Engineering and Technology, UK; Institute of Electrical and Electronics Engineers Inc, USA; Institute of Directors, UK. Address: Flat FG2 Hulkul Residency, 81 Lavelle Road, Karnataka, Bangalore, South India. E-mail: leighsheldrake@gmail.com

SHENG Ching-Lai, b. 20 July 1919, Kahsing, Chekiang, China. Professor. m. Josephine Yu-Ying Chou, 2 sons, 3 daughters by 1st marriage. Education: BSc, National Chiao Tung University, Shanghai, 1941; PhD, University of Edinburgh, Scotland, 1948. Appointments: Professor, National Taiwan University, University of Ottawa, University of Windsor; President, National Chiao Tung University, Hsin-Chu, Taiwan; Chair Professor, Professor Emeritus, Tamkang University. Publications: Over 120 articles in professional journals; 8 monographs including: Threshold Logic, 1969; A New Approach to Utilitarianism, 1991; On the Regulation of Capital, 1995; A Utilitarian General Theory of Value, 1998; An Introduction to Unified Utilitarian Theory, 2000; A Defence of Utilitarianism, 2004. Honour: Sun Yat-Sen Cultural Foundation Prize for Scholarly Publication,

1972. Memberships: Philosophical Association of China, Canada, England, USA. Address: 8F 16 Lane 51, Pao-Shun Road, Yung-Ho, New Taipei, Taiwan, 234, Republic of China.

SHEPARD Sam, (Samuel Shepard Rogers), b. 5 November 1943, Fort Sheridan, Illinois, USA. Dramatist; Actor. m. O-Lan Johnson Dark, divorced, 1 son; 1 son, 1 daughter with Jessica Lange. Education: Mount San Antonio Junior College, Walnut, California, 1961-62. Career: Plays: Cowboys, Rock Garden, 1964; 4-H Club, Up to Thursday, Rocking Chair, Chicago, Icarus's Mother, 1965; Fourteen Hundred Thousand, Red Cross, Melodrama Play, 1966; La Turista, Cowboys #2, Forensic and the Navigators, 1967; The Holy Ghostly, The Unseen Hand, 1969; Operation Sidewinder, Shaved Splits, 1970; Mad Dog Blues, Terminal, Cowboy Mouth (with Patti Smith), Black Bog Beast Bait, 1971; The Tooth of Crime, 1972; Blue Bitch, Nightwalk (with Megan Terry and Jean-Claude van Itallie), 1973; Geography of a Horse Dreamer, Little Ocean, Action, Killer's Head, 1974; Suicide in B-Flat, Angel City, 1976; Curse of the Starving Class, 1977; Buried Child, 1978; Tongues, Savage/Love, Seduced, 1979; True West, 1981; Fool for Love, Superstitions, The Sad Lament of Pecos Bill on the Eve of Killing his Wife, 1983; A Lie of the Mind, 1985; States of Shock, 1991; Simpatico, 1993; TV: Lily Dale, 1996; Purgatory, 1999; Hamlet, 2000; Films: Days of Heaven; Frances; The Right Stuff; Country; Crimes of the Heart; Baby Boom; Defenceless, 1989; Voyager; Thunderheart, 1992; The Pelican Brief, 1994; Safe Passage, The Good Old Boys, 1995; Curtain Call, The Only Thrill, 1997; Snow Falling on Cedars, 1999; One Kill, 2000; Shot in the Heart, Swordfish, The Pledge, 2001; The Notebook, 2004; Don't Come Knockin', Stealth, 2005; Walker Payne, Bandidas, The Return, Charlotte's Web (narrator), 2006; Ruffian, The Assassination of Jesse James by the Coward Robert Ford, 2007; The Accidental Husband, 2008. Publications: A Murder of Crows, novel, Cruising Paradise, short stories, 1996; Great Dream of Heaven, short stories, 2002; The Rolling Thunder Logbook, 2005. Honours: Obie Awards, 1966, 1966, 1966, 1968, 1973, 1975, 1977, 1979, 1984; Rockefeller Foundation Grant, 1967; Guggenheim Fellowships, 1968, 1971; National Institute and American Academy of Arts and Letters Award, 1974; Creative Arts Award, Brandeis University, 1975; Pulitzer Prize in Drama, 1979; New York Drama Critics' Circle Award, 1986. Memberships: American Academy of Arts and Letters; Theater Hall of Fame. Address: c/o International Creative Management, 8942 Wilshire Boulevard, Beverly Hills, CA 90211, USA.

SHEPHARD Gillian Patricia (Rt Hon), b. 22 January 1940, England. Politician. m. Thomas Shephard, 1975, 2 stepsons. Education: St Hilda's College, Oxford. Appointments: Schools Inspector and Education Officer, 1963-75; Cambridge University Extra Mural Board Lecturer, 1965-87; Norfolk County Council, 1977-89; For Norfolk County Council: Chair of Social Services Committee, 1978-83; Education Committee, 1983-85; Chair, West Norfolk and Wisbech Health Authority, 1981-85; Norwich Health Authority, 1985-87; Conservative MP South West Norfolk, 1987-97, Norfolk South West, 1997-; Parliamentary Private Secretary to Economic Secretary to the Treasury, 1988-89; Parliamentary Under Secretary of State, Department of Social Security, 1989-90; Treasury Minister of State, 1990-92; Employment Secretary of State, 1992-93, for Agriculture, Fisheries and Food, 1993-94, for Education, 1995, for Education and Employment, 1995-97; Women's National Commission Co-Chair, 1990-91; Shadow Leader of the House of Commons and Shadow Chancellor of Duchy of Lancaster, 1997-99; Opposition Spokesman on Environment, Transport and the Reginos, 1998-99; Deputy Chair, Conservative Party, 1991-92, 2002-03; Vice President, Hansard Society, 1997-2003. Publication: The Future of Local Government, 1991; Shephard's Watch, 2000. Memberships: Council Member, University of Oxford, 2000-. Honour: Honorary Fellow, St Hilda's College, Oxford, 1991. Address: House of Commons, London SW1A 0AA, England.

SHEPHERD Cybill, b. 18 February 1950, Memphis, Tennessee, USA. Actress. m. (1) David Ford, 1978, divorced, 1 daughter, (2) Bruce Oppenheim, 1987, divorced 1990, 1 son, 1 daughter. Career: Former magazine cover girl; Commercials for L'Oreal Preference, 8 years; Film include: The Last Picture Show, 1971; The Heartbreak Kid, 1973; Daisy Miller, 1974; At Long Last Love, 1975; Taxi Driver, 1976; Special Delivery, 1976; Silver Bears, 1977; The Lady Vanishes, 1978; Earthquake, 1980; The Return, 1986; Chances Are, 1988; Texasville, 1990; Alice, 1990; Once Upon a Crime, 1992; Married to It, 1993; The Last Word, 1995; Due East, 2003; Open Window, 2006; Hard Luck, 2006; numerous TV films; Plays include: A Shot in the Dark, 1977; Vanities, 1981; The Muse, 1999; Marine Life, 2000; TV includes: The Yellow Rose, 1983-84; Moonlighting, 1985-89; Cybill, 1994-98; Martha Behind Bars, 2005; Detective, 2005; The L Word, 2007-08. Publication: Cybill Disobedience, 2000. Honours: Emmy Award, 1985. Website: www.cybill.com

SHEPHERD John Alan (Sir), b. 27 April 1943, Edinburgh, Scotland. m. Jessica Nichols, 1 daughter. Education: MA, Selwyn College, Cambridge, 1961-64; MA, Stanford, 1964-65. Appointments: HM Diplomatic Service, 1965-2003 including: Ambassador, Bahrain, 1988-91; Minister, Bonn, 1991-95; Director, Middle East, Foreign and Commonwealth Office, 1996-97; Deputy Under Secretary, Foreign and Commonwealth Office, Member of Boards of Foreign and Commonwealth Office, BOTB later BTI, 1997-2000; Member, Review Committee of Government Export Promotion Services, 1998-99; Ambassador to Italy, 2000-2003; Currently: Secretary-General, Global Leadership Foundation; Chairman, Norbert Brainin Foundation; Deputy-Chairman, Trustees of Prince's School for Traditional Arts. Publication: Rhine Tasting in Motor Boat and Yachting, 1996. Honours: CMG, 1988; KCVO, 2000. Membership: Oxford and Cambridge Club. Address: GLF, 14 Curzon Street, London W1J 5HN, England.

SHEPHERD Michael William, b. 24 January 1949, Cheadle Hulme, Cheshire, England. Retired Primary Headteacher; Schools Adviser & Inspector. 1 son, 2 daughters. Education: Beech Hall School, Macclesfield, 1957-62; Rydal School, Colwyn Bay, 1962-66; BA, 1970, MA, 1974, Christ's College, Cambridge; Certificate of Education, Institute of Education, Cambridge, 1971; Royal Academy of Music, London, 1972-75; Certificate in Religious Education, 1985; Ofsted Accredited Inspector, 1992. Appointments: English Teacher, Hinchingbrooke School, Huntingdon, 1971-72; Part time Home Tutor, ILEA, 1972; Part time SEN/Literacy Teacher, St Scholastica's Primary, Hackney, 1973-74, St Dominic's Primary, Hackney, 1974-75; Chorus Member, English National Opera, 1975-77; Music Co-ordinator/Class Teacher, Valley Primary, Bromley, 1978-80; Literacy Co-ordinator/Class Teacher Y6, Balgowan Primary, Bromley, 1980-82; Deputy Head, Edgebury Primary, Bromley, 1982-85; Headteacher, St Joseph's RC Primary, Southwark, 1985-90; English Adviser/ English Inspector (Primary/Secondary), London Borough of Wandsworth, 1990-93; Headteacher, Downderry Primary, Lewisham, 1993-97; Headteacher, Worsley Bridge Junior, Bromley, 1997-2005; Recitals include Wigmore Hall and St John's Smith Square; Actor, appearing with Harriet Walter, Duncan Kenworthy, etc. Publications: Poetry published in Christ's College, Cambridge Poetry Magazine, 1967; Oxford & Cambridge Poetry Magazine, Tomorrow, 1970; L'Adolescence, poem in Dr Pierre Bour's Les Racines de l'Homme, 1976; Articles: Christian Living for Change Magazine, 1989; Power to the Powerless – Life in Thatcher's Britain, 1992; Language & Learning Magazine, Pictures on the Page. Honours: Choral Exhibition, Christ's College Cambridge, 1967; Award, Countess of Munster Musical Trust, 1972; Award, Ralph Vaughan-Williams Musical Trust, 1972; Grisi Mario Opera Prize, RAM; Award, Leverhulme Trust, RAM, 1973; Hubert Khiver Prize for English Song, RAM.

SHER Sir Antony, b. 14 June 1949, Cape Town, South Africa. Actor; Artist; Author. Career: Films: Shadey; the Young Poisoner's Handbook; Alive and Kicking; Mrs Brown; Shakespeare in Love; TV appearances include: The History Man; Collision Course; The Land of Dreams; Genghis Cohn; The Moon Stone; Plays include: John, Paul, Ringo and Bert; Teeth n' Smiles; Cloud Nine; A Prayer for My Daughter; Goosepimples; King Lear; Tartuffe; Richard II; Merchant of Venice; The Revenger's Tragedy; Hello and Goodbye; Singer; Tamburlaine the Great; Travesties; Cyrano de Bergerac; The Winter's Tale; Torch Song Trilogy; True West; Arturo Ui; Uncle Vanya; Titus Andronicus; Stanley; Mahler's Conversion; ID, 2003; The Malcontent; Primo, 2005; Kean, 2007. Publications: Year of the King, 1986; Middlepost, 1988; Characters, 1989; Changing Steps (Screenplay), 1989; The Indoor Boy, 1991; Cheap Drives, 1995; Woza Shakespeare! (co-author), 1996; The Feast, 1998; Beside Myself (autobiography), 2001; Primo, 2005; Primo Time, 2005. Honours: Best Actor Awards, Drama Magazine, London Standard Awards, 1985; Olivier Award for Best Actor, Society of West End Theatres, 1985, 1997; Best Actor Award, Martini TMA Awards, 1996; Peter Sellers Evening Standard Film Award, 1998; Honorary D Litt (Liverpool) 1998, (Exeter) 2003; KBE, 2000. Address: c/o ICM, Oxford House, 76 Oxford Street, London W1N 0AX, England.

SHER Emmanuil Moiseyevich, b. 29 March 1929, Port Khorly, Ukraine. Physicist Researcher. m. Elena, 1 son. Education: BS, Moscow State University, 1951; Physicist, St Petersburg State University, 1952; PhD, Physical Electronics, 1967; DSc, Physics of Semiconductors and Dielectrics, 1983. Appointments: Senior Engineer, Vacuum Technology, 1952-59; Researcher, Senior Scientific Researcher, Leading Scientific Researcher, Physics of Thermoelectricity, Electron Emission, High Temperature Superconductors and Thin Solid Films, 1959-2009. Publications: 110 articles, 21 patents, scientific editor of 2 books. Honours: Bronze Medal, 1963, Silver Medal, 1983; Honorary Academician, International Academy of Refrigeration, 1999. Memberships: AF Ioffe Physico-Technical Institute, Russian Academy of Sciences, 1959-2009; International Thermoelectric Society, 1991; New York Academy of Sciences, 1996. Address: 20 Orbely Str, apt 73, 194223 St Petersburg, Russia. E-mail: em.sher@mail.ioffe.ru

SHETH Jayesh, b. 26 February 1957, Modasa, India. Director. m. Frenny, 1 son, 1 daughter. Education: PhD, MSc, FICMIH, Diploma Certificate in Reproductive Medicine & Reproductive Biology, Geneva University. Appointments: Junior Scientific Officer, Gujarat Cancer Hospital; Assistant Professor, Endocrinology, Associate Professor, Endocrinology and Biochemistry, Sheth V S Hospital & NHL Medical College; Director, Institute of Human Genetics; Director, Shah Pathology Laboratory & Endocrine Unit. Publications: 90 publications in peer-reviewed national and international journals; 35 abstracts at international conference; More than 100 invited lectures. Honours: Erasmus Summer Fellowship in Endocrinology; WHO Fellowship for Advance Postgraduate Study; UICC Fellowship, International Society of Newborn Screening; Travel Fellowship; ICMR Travel Fellowship. Memberships: Endocrine Society, USA; American Society of Human Genetics; Indian Society of Human Genetics; International Society of Newborn Screening; Association of Physicians of India. Address: Institute of Human Genetics, FRIGE House, Jodhpur Gam Road, Satellite, Ahmedabad 380015, Gujarat, India.

SHIBAKAWA Rinya, b. 15 February 1934, Hokkaido, Japan. Professor. m. Sachiko, 2 daughters. Education: Master Degree, Graduate School of Commerce and Management of Hitotsubashi University, 1958; PhD, Economics, Kyushu University, 1980. Appointments: Professor, Aoyama Gakuin University, 1966; Dean and Professor, Graduate School of Tsukuba University, 1979; Professor, Graduate School of Hitotsubashi University, 1990-97; Emeritus Professor, Hitotsabashi University, 1997-; Dean and Professor, Graduate School of Business, Jobu University, 2007-11. Publications: Financial Characteristics of Japanese Corporations, 1990; Corporate Governance, Cost of Capital and Financial Distress, 1994. Honours: Nikkei Economics Award, 1969. Memberships: Japanese Finance Association; Japan Society of Business Administration. Address: 2-18-14, Umezono, Tsukuba City, Ibaraki, 305-0045, Japan. E-mail: rinya@kde.biglobe.ne.jp

SHIEH Jenn-Jong, b. Taiwan. Professor of Electrical Engineering. m. Yi-Shin Lin, 1 son, 1 daughter. Education: BSc, Electrical Engineering, National Taiwan University of Science and Technology, 1989-91; MSc, Electrical Engineering, 1991-93, PhD, Electrical Engineering, 1994-98, National Tsing Hua University. Appointments: Associate Professor, 2000-2003, Office of Research and Development, Dean and Professor of Electrical Engineering, 2004-, Ta Hwa Institute of Technology, Taiwan; Patent Examiner, Intellectual Property Office, Taipei, 2001-06; Consultant, Matriteck Inc, Hsinchu, Taiwan, 2001-04; Consultant, O2 Micro Inc, Taipei, Taiwan, 2003-; Patent Agent, Taiwan, 2005-; Consultant, Grenergy Opto Inc, 2007-; Patent Attorney, Taiwan, 2008-. Publications: Electrical Machine, 3rd version, 1999; Control System, 2nd version, 2002; Power System Analysis, 3rd version, 2001; Basic Electrical Circuit Analysis, 4th version, 2002. Honours: Best Project Prize, Ministry of Education, Taiwan, 2003; Best Smart Project Prize, Control and Automation Association, 2003; Position Counseling Third Class Medal of Honor; National Youth Commission Excutive, Yuan, 2008; The Best Poster Presentation Awards, IUMRS-ICEM, Korea, 2010. Memberships: National Professional Engineer; Taiwan Power Electronic Association. Address: 1 Ta Hwa Road, Chiunglin, Hsinchu, Taiwan, ROC. E-mail: eesjj@thit.edu.tw

SHIEH Wung Yang, b. 22 September 1956, Taipei, Taiwan. Professor. m. Jiin Jiun Leu, 2 sons, 1 daughter. Education: Master's Degree, University of Tokyo, 1986; Doctor's Degree, 1989. Appointments: Associate Professor, 1989-94, Professor, 1994- Institute of Oceanography, National Taiwan University, Taipei. Publications: Contribution of articles to professional journals including International Journal of Systematic and Evolutionary Microbiology and Canadian Journal of Microbiology. Memberships: The Japanese Society of Microbial Ecology; The Taiwanese Society of Microbiology. Address: Institute of Oceanography, National Taiwan University, PO Box 23-13, Taipei, Taiwan. E-mail: winyang@ntu.edu.tw

SHIEL Derek Alexander George, b. 18 April 1939, Dublin, Ireland. Painter; Writer; Sculptor; Landscape Designer; Lecturer; Curator; Psychotherapist; Film Director. Education: Fettes College, Edinburgh; Edinburgh College of Art, 1956-61; Diploma of Art, 1960; Travelling Scholarship to USA, 1961-62. Appointments: Art Tutor, Berkshire College of Art, 1963-65; Art Tutor, West Sussex College of Art, 1964-69; Lecturer in Art Appreciation and Art Tutor, The City Literary Institute, London, 1965-77; Gardening: Landscape Gardener/Designer, 1978-98. Theatre: Writer and Director, 1980-2005; wrote stage adaptation of Gogol's The Overcoat; wrote and directed, Which One of Me?, performed in 6 European countries; wrote and directed, Landing Site; directed puppet play, The Way to St Bernard; co-directed improvised production of Bluebeard; Director and Actor/Puppeteer for Hilary Pepler Celebration, Ditchling Museum, East Sussex; Director and Actor in Celebration of Writers of Little Venice. Exhibitions: exhibitions of paintings, sound sculpture, works in theatre, landscape design, colour structures with living plants, held in Britain and Europe. Music: Originator/Percussionist with other musicians in Shiel's ensemble, Sculpted Sound, performing at museums, art galleries, theatres, festivals and for UK radio and television broadcasts; Over twenty composers have so far written for Shiel's sound sculptures; Painter/Performer with Composer Julia Usher in their duo, SoundPaint, performances at art and music festivals, universities, conferences. Psychotherapy: Psychotherapist and participant in The Men's Movement; articles in magazines, Wingspan (USA), Achilles Heel (UK); Founder of The Men's Databank. Publications: essay in Fathers and Sons, 1995; Co-author, David Jones: The Maker Unmade, 1995 (second edition, 2003); Editor, David Jones: Ten Letters, 1996; essay in The Chesterton Review, David Jones Special Issue, 1997; essay in Diversity in Unity, 2000; Editor and essay in David Jones in Ditchling, 2003; Author, Arthur Giardelli, Paintings, Constructions, Relief Sculptures, Conversations with Derek Shiel, 2001; Film: Director, In Search of David Jones, Artist, Soldier, Poet, 2007; Director, second David Jones film, David Jones Between the Wars: The Years of Achievement, 2011; Curator of exhibitions: Arthur Giardelli, National Library of Wales, 2002; David Jones in Ditchling, Ditchling Museum, 2003 (co-curator); Art Exhibition, Little Venice Music Festival, 2004. Lecturer: lectures at art galleries, museums, universities and art societies on David Jones, Arthur Giardelli or Sound Sculptures; Sculpted Sound, two radio broadcasts, Germany, 2011; Mentioned in Grove's Music Dictionary, 2001 and Peter Vergo's The Music of Painting Phaidon, 2010; Lecture, Why and How David Jones Became a Poet, 2009 and 2010. Honours: First Artist-in-Residence, Estorick Collection of Modern Italian Art, London, 2000; Elected Member, Art Workers Guild, London, 2009; Sculpted Sound concert, Central School of Speech and Drama, London, 2009. Memberships: PEN London; Friends of Tate Gallery; Friends of Royal Academy; War Poets Association; The Royal Society of Literature; The Poetry Society; English PEN. Address: 25 Randolph Crescent, London W9 1DP, England. E-mail: derek.agshiel@googlemail.com

SHIGA Atsushi, b. 24 December 1962, Ibaraki, Japan. Pathologist; Veterinarian. Education: Doctor of Veterinary Medicine, 1988; Diplomate, Japanese College of Veterinary Pathologist, 1996; Diplomate, Japanese Society of Toxicologic Pathology, 1998; Diplomate, Japanese Society of Toxicology, 2007. Appointments: Joined, 1989, Researcher, Department of Pathology, 1992, Pathology and Clinical Examination Laboratory Department, 2010, Biosafety Research Center, Foods, Drugs and Pesticides; Joined Nippon Experimental Medical Research Institute, 1997. Publications: 13 articles in professional journals including most recently: Acute toxicity of Pierisin-1, a cytotoxic protein from Pieris rapae, in the mouse and rat, 2006; Two cases of rare hepatocellular nodular lesion caused by circulatory disturbance in rat livers, 2007; Study on the pathogenesis of foreign body granulomatous inflammation in the liver of Sprague-Dawley rats, 2010. Memberships: Japanese Society of Toxicologic Pathology; Japanese Toxicology Society; Japanese Society of Pathology; Japanese Society of Veterinary Science; Society of Toxicologic Pathology, USA; Japanese Cancer Association; Japanese College of Veterinary Pathologist; Japanese Society of Veterinary Pathology; Japanese Association for Laboratory Animal Medicine. Address: Biosafety Research Center, Foods, Drugs and Pesticides, 582-2 Shioshinden, Iwata-shi, Shizuoka, 437-1213, Japan.

SHIH Tso-Min, b. 4 April 1935, Ying-Cheng, Shantung, China. Mining Engineering Educator. m. Ching-Ch'i Hsia Shih, 1 June 1961, 1 son, 2 daughters. Education: BSc, National Cheng-Kung University, Taiwan, 1958; MSc, McGill University, Montreal, Canada, 1965. Appointments: Research Assistant, Nova Scotia Technical College, Halifax, Canada, 1965-66; Lecturer, 1968-72, Associate Professor, 1972-74, Professor, Department Chairman, 1974-80, Professor, 1980-2000, Part time Professor, 2000, Retired, 2000, National Cheng-Kung University, Tainan, Taiwan, China; Director, Chinese Institute of Mining and Metal Engineering, 1976-78; Director, Mining Association of China, 1988-96; Director, Tainan Tai-Chi and Ba-Kiua-Chang Society, 2001-2003; Full Professor, 2003-06, Retired, 2006, Diwan University, Tainan County. Publications: Diamond, book (in Chinese), 1996; The Exploitation and Utilization of Graphite, book (in Chinese); This is My Life, book (in Chinese), 2011; More than 50 publications in journals and conference proceedings. Honours: Chinese Institute of Mining and Metal Engineering, Taipei, 1972, 1991; Pi Epsilon Tau National Petroleum Engineering Honor Society, Los Angeles, 1989; Department of Reconstructions, Taiwan Provincial Government, 1993; Mining Association of China, 1996; Ministry of Education, Republic of China, 1978, 1988, 1998. Memberships: Chinese Institute of Engineers; Rifacimento Inter-American Biographical Institute; Chinese Institute of Mining & Metallurgical Engineering; The Mining Association of the Republic of China. Address: Fl 1-2 No 74 Tung-Ning Road, Tainan, Taiwan, 70146, China.

SHIKHMURZAEV Yulii Damir, b. 12 September 1957, Ryazan, USSR. Mathematician. m. Zimfira Gallyamova, 1 daughter. Education: MSc, Applied Mathematics and Mechanics, 1980, PhD, Physics and Mathematics, 1985, Moscow State University. Appointments: Junior Research Scientist, 1984-88, Research Scientist, 1989-92, Senior Research Scientist, 1992-96, Moscow State University; Lecturer, University of Leeds, UK, 1996-98; Senior Lecturer, 1999-2001, Reader, 2001-2006, Professor 2006-, School of Mathematics, University of Birmingham, UK; Visiting Researcher, University of Naples, Italy, 1988-89; Visiting Professor, Purdue University, USA, 2002; Visiting Professor, University of Pierre and Marie Curie, France, 2002, University of South Australia, 2006; Associate Editor, Continuum Mechanics & Thermodynamics, 2005-11; Associate Editor, Advances in Mathematical Physics, 2008-. Publications: 1 monograph; More than 50 articles; 2 patents. Listed in various international biographical dictionaries. Memberships: International Society of Coating Science and Technology; European Mechanics Society; German Society for Applied Mathematics and Mechanics; London Mathematical Society;

American Physical Society. Address: School of Mathematics, University of Birmingham, Edgbaston, Birmingham B15 2TT, England. E-mail: yulii@for.mat.bham.ac.uk

SHIMI Sami M, b. 27 September 1954, Dammam, Saudi Arabia. Surgeon. m. Jill, 1 son. Education: BSc (Hons), 1979, MB ChB, Ninewells Hospital & Medical School, 1983, Dundee University. Appointments: Registrar, General Surgery, West of Scotland Rotational Training Scheme in Surgery, various Glasgow Hospitals, 1985-89; Research Registrar/Clinical Research Fellow in Surgery, 1989-90, Lecturer/Senior Registrar in General Surgery, 1990-93, Senior Lecturer in Surgery, Honorary Consultant Surgeon, 1993-, Ninewells Hospital & Medical School, Department of Surgery. Publications: Over 60 articles in peer reviewed journals; Over 10 chapters in authoritative textbooks. Honours: Chair, Tayside Upper GI Cancer Group and Lead Oesophago-gastric Cancer Surgeon, 1998-; Member, Tayside Cancer Network, 1998-; Member, National Panel of Specialist of Scotland, 2000-; Member, School of Medicine Board of Studies, 2000-; Health Technology Assessment Clinical Evaluation and Trials Board Member, 2009-; NICE Specialist Adviser on Hyperthermic Intraperitoneal Chemotherapy and Photodynamic Therapy for High Grade Dysplasia, 2009-; Expert Panel Member, Efficacy and Mechanism Evaluation Programme of National Institute of Health Trials and Studies Co-ordinating Centre, 2009-. Memberships: Caledonian Society of Gastroenterology; British Society of Gastroenterology; European Association of Endoscopic Surgeons; Association of Surgeons of Great Britain and Ireland; Association of Upper Gastrointestinal Surgeons; Fellowship of The Royal College of Physicians and Surgeons of Glasgow; Fellowship of The Royal College of Surgeons of Edinburgh. Address: Cidhmore House, 490 Perth Road, Dundee DD2 1LR, Scotland. E-mail: s.m.shimi@dundee.ac.uk

SHIN Dong-Hwa, b. 22 July 1943, Jeong-up, Jeonbuk, Korea. Emeritus Professor. m. Mi-Za Han, 1 daughter. Education: MSD, 1969, PhD, 1981, Dongguk University, Korea. Appointments: Professor, Chonbuk National University; Vice Director, Agriculture and Fishery Development Co-operation; President, Korean Association of Food Science & Technology; President, Korean Association of Food Safety; President, Korea Research Council for Fermented Soybean Technology. Publications: 330 articles; 13 books. Honours: Blue Ribbon Medal, Korea Government; Scholarship Award, Korea Society of Food Science & Technology. Memberships: IFT; Korean Association of Food Science & Technology; Association of Food Safety. Address: 12-201 Wooah Apt, Wooah-Dong 3 ga, Dukjin-ku, Jeonju, Korea. E-mail: dhshin@jbnu.ac.kr

SHIN Dong-Keun, b. 13 June 1959, Incheon, South Korea. Independent Researcher in Computer Science. m. Helen Chang, 2 sons. Education: Bachelor's Degree, Computer Science, University of California at Berkeley, USA, 1983; Doctor of Science, Computer Science, George Washington University, USA, 1991. Appointments: Discoverer of Shin sort, the best sorting method, 1998; Author of gospel songs, psalm and other songs; The first verifier of phenomenon of relatively good solutions; Author of the theory of massive cross-referencing; Developer of Shin Sort and Search (S^3) Database System. Publications: A Comparative Study of Hash Functions for a New Hash-Based Relational Join Algorithm, 1991; A Sorting Method by Dong-Keun Shin, 1998; In 1999, Dr Shin informed the world's press organisations of the news that he discovered the best sorting method and his overwhelming victory in the decisive battle after claiming to be the greatest computer scientist in the world in 1997. Honours: Member, International Order of Merit; Founding Member, American Order of Excellence; Several prizes and numerous nominations from international organisations; Listed in international biographical dictionaries. Address: Hwa Shin Building, Suite 701, 705-22 Yuksam-dong, Kangnam-gu, Seoul 135-080, Korea. Website: www.dkshin.com

SHIN Ho Sik, b. 25 September 1974, Daegu City, Republic of Korea. Assistant Professor. m. Jeong Hyun Kim, 1 son, 1 daughter. Education: MD, Kosin University College of Medicine, Busan, 1999; MSc, Internal Medicine, Graduate School of Kosin University, 2006. Appointments: Internship, 1999-2000, Residency, Internal Medicine, 2000-04, Fellowship, Nephrology, 2004-06, Kosin University, Gospel Hospital, Busan; Full time Instructor, 2009-11, Assistant Professor, 2011-, Nephrology, Kosin University College of Medicine. Publications: Numerous articles in professional journals. Honours: Gold Medal for Korea, 2011; Man of the Year, 2011; Listed in international biographical dictionaries. Memberships: Korean Society of Nephrology; Korean Society of Internal Medicine; Korean Society of Hypertension; Korean Society of Electrolyte & Blood Pressure Research; Korean Society of Transplantation. Address: Kosin University, College of Medicine, Gospel Hospital, 262 Gamcheon-ro, Seo-gu, Busan city, 602-702, Republic of Korea. E-mail: kidneymd@hanmail.net

SHIN Seong-Chul, b. 9 April 1963, Sowon, South Korea. Academic; Professor; Researcher. m. Young S Ra, 3 sons. Education: MEd, Korean as a Foreign Language, Yonsei University; MA, Applied Linguistics, Macquarie University; PhD, Linguistics, UNSW. Appointments: Senior Teaching Fellow, Griffith University, 1991-92; Senior Education Officer, NSW Board of Studies, 1992-93; Tenured Academic, Senior Lecturer (Associate Professor), Convenor of Korean Studies, School Postgraduate Research Convenor, University of New South Wales, 1994-. Publications: A number of books, book chapters and monographs; Numerous articles in academic journals. Honours: APA Awardee, 1992; UMAP Grant Recipient, 1998-99 Korea Foundation Fellowship, 2002, 2009; Academy of Korea Studies Fellowship, 2008-09; UNSW FASS RPG Grant Recipient, 2008-09; NALSSP Grant, 2009-10. Memberships: ICKL; KLACES Board; ALAA; KSAA; NAATI; IAKLE Board; INKLC Board; SKS Board; ARC Assessor. Address: School of International Studies, Morven Brown Building, Faculty of Arts & Social Sciences, University of New South Wales, Sydney 2052, Australia. E-mail: s.shin@unsw.edu.au Website: http://languages.arts.unsw.edu.au/staff

SHINAWATRA Thaksin, b. 26 July 1949, Chiangmai Province, Thailand. Prime Minister of Thailand. m. Khunying Potjaman Shinawatra, 1 son, 2 daughters. Education: Graduate, Police Academy, Thailand, 1973; Master Degree in Criminal Justice, Eastern Kentucky University, USA, 1975; Doctorate Degree in Criminal Justice, Sam Houston State University, USA, 1978. Appointments: Royal Thai Police Department, 1973-87; Founder, Shinawatra Computer and Communications Group, 1987-94; Founder, THAICOM Foundation, long distance satellite education programme, 1993; Established Thai Rak Thai Party and Leader of Thai Rak Tai Party, 1998-; 23rd Prime Minister of Thailand, 2001-2006. Honours: Royal Decorations: Knight Grand Cordon (Special Class) of the Most Noble Order of the Crown of Thailand, 1995; Knight Grand Cordon (Special Class), Most Exalted Order of the White Elephant, 1996; Knight Grand Cross (First Class), Most Admirable Order of the Direkgunabhorn, 2001; Knight Grand Commander, Most Illustrious Order of Chula Chom Klao, 2002; Foreign Decorations: The Royal

Order of Sahametrei (Grand Cross), Kingdom of Cambodia, 2001; Ahmed Al Fateh, Kingdom of Bahrain, 2002; The Most Blessed Order of Setia Negara Brunei (First Class), Brunei Darussalam, 2002; Commander Grand Cross of the Royal Order of the Polar Star of the Kingdom of Sweden, 2003; Numerous other awards include: Honorary Doctorate, Thammasat University, 1994; Sam Houston Humanitarian Award, Sam Houston State University, USA, 2002; Honorary Doctorate, Tokyo Institute of Technology, Japan, 2003. Memberships: President, Northerners Association of Thailand, 1998-. Address: Office of the Prime Minister, Government House, Thanon Nakhon Pathem, Bangkok 10300, Thailand.

SHIPLEY Rt Hon Jennifer Mary (Jenny), b. 1952, New Zealand. Politician. m. Burton, 1 son, 1 daughter. Appointments: Former School Teacher; Farmer, 1973-88; Joined National Party, 1975; Former Malvern County Councillor; MP for Ashburton (now Rakaia), 1987-; Minister of Social Welfare, 1990-93, Womens Affairs, 1990-98, Health, 1993-96, State Services, 1996-97, State Owned Enterprises, Transport, Accident Rehabilitation and Compensation Insurance; Minister Responsible for Radio New Zealand; Minister in Charge of New Zealand Security Intelligence Services, 1997-; Prime Minister of New Zealand, 1997-99; Leader of the Opposition, 2000-2001. Address: Parliament Buildings, Wellington, New Zealand. E-mail: hq@national.org.nz Website: www.national.org.nz

SHIPWRIGHT Adrian John, b. 2 July 1950, Southampton, England. Barrister. m. Diana Treseder, 1 son, 1 daughter. Education: BA, 1972, BCL (1st class), 1973, MA, 1977, Christ Church, Oxford. Appointments: Articled Clerk and Assistant Solicitor, Tax Department, Linklaters & Paines, 1974-77; Official Student and Tutor in Law, Christ Church, Oxford, 1977-82; Partner, Corporate Tax Group, Denton Hall Burgin & Warrens, 1982-87; Governor (appointed by University of Oxford) of King Edward VI School, Southampton, 1982-; Lecturer, Capital Gains Tax, Cambridge LLM Course, 1985-86; Partner, Tax Department (International and Corporate Tax), 1987-92, Consultant, 1992, S J Berwin & Co; Lecturer, Income Tax, Oxford BCL Tax Course, and Brunel University Erasmus European Diploma Tax Element, 1990; Visiting Professor, 1990-92, Professor of Business Law, 1992-96, King's College, London; Lecturer, Tax Aspects, Bristol University Residential Conference on Intellectual Property, 1990-2005; Professor of Business Law, Director, Tax Research Unit, King's College, London, 1992-96; Pump Court Tax Chambers, 1996-; Deputy Special Commissioner and part time VAT Tribunal Chairman, Judge of the First Tier Tribunal and Deputy Judge of the Upper Tier Tribunal, 2002-. Publications: Numerous articles in professional journals. Address: c/o Pump Court Tax Chambers, 16 Bedford Row, London WC1R 4EF, England. E-mail: ashipwright@pumptax.com

SHIRAI Yoshiaki, b. 3 August 1941, Toyota, Aichi Prefecture, Japan. Professor. m. Kuniko Hikida, 2 sons, 1 daughter. Education: B Eng, Nagoya University, 1964; M Eng, 1966, D Eng, 1969, Tokyo University. Appointments: Visiting Researcher, Artificial Intelligence Laboratory, Massachusetts Institute of Technology, 1971-72; Research Staff, Electrotechnical Laboratory, MITI, Japan, 1969-79; Chief, Computer Vision Section, 1979-85, Director, Control Division, 1985-88, Electrotechnical Laboratory; Professor, Osaka University, 1988-2005; Professor, Tokyo University, 1996-99; Professor, Ritsumeikan University, 2005-. Publications: Three-Dimensional Computer Vision, 1987; Robot Visor Research: Past and Future Role, 1999; Robust Face Recognition under Various Illumination Conditions, 2006. Honours: Best Paper Award, Pattern Recognition Society, 1948; Best Paper Award, Institute of Electrical, Information and Communication Engineers, 1976, 2005; IROS Best Paper Award, 1993; IAPR Fellow. Memberships: IEEE Computer Society; IAPR; IEICE; Japanese Society of Artificial Intelligence. Address: Department of Human Computer Intelligence, School of Information Science and Engineering, Ritsumeikan University, 1-1-1 Nojihigashi, Kusatsu 525-8577, Japan.

SHIRLEY Dame (Vera) Stephanie, (Steve), b. 16 September 1933, Dortmund, Germany. Philanthropist. m. Derek George Millington Shirley, 1 son, deceased. Education: BSc (Spec.), Sir John Cass College, London, 1956; FBCS, 1971; CEng, 1990; CITP; CIMgt. Appointments: PO Research Station, Dollis Hill, 1951-59; CDL, Subsidiary of ICL, 1959-62; Founder and Chief Executive, 1962-87, Director, 1962-93, Life President, 1993-, Xansa Plc (now part of Steria); Director, Tandem Computers Inc, 1992-97; Director, AEA Technology Plc, 1992-2000; Director, John Lewis Partnership, 1999-2001; European Advisory Board, Korn/Ferry International, 2001-2004; Member, Strategy Board, Oxford Internet Institute, 2001-; CSR Advisory Board, Steria, 2008. Publication: The Art of Prior's Court School, 2002; Designed for Disability, A History of Autism, 2010. Honours: OBE, 1980; CCMI (CBIM, 1984); Recognition of Information Technology Achievement Award, 1985; Honorary FCGI, 1989; Gold Medal Chartered Management Institute, 1991; US National Woman's Hall of Fame, 1995; Mountbatten Medal, IEE, 1999; DBE, 2000; FREng, 2001; Beacon Award for Start-ups, 2003; British Computer Society Lifetime Achievement Award, 2004; Spears, 2010; and 23 honorary Fellowships and Doctorates; Foundation Fellow, Balliol College, Oxford, 2001; Honorary Dr, Edinburgh, 2003; Open University, 2009; Honorary D Laws, Leicester, 2005; Bath, 2006; St Andrews, 2011. Memberships include: Council, Industrial Society, 1984-90; NCVQ, 1986-89; President, British Computer Society, 1989-90; Vice-President, C&G, 2000-05; Member, Council, Duke of Edinburgh's Seventh Commonwealth Study Conference, 1991-92; British-North American Committee, 1992-2001; Chairman, Women of Influence, 1993; Trustee, Help the Aged, 1987-90; Patron: Disablement Income Group, 1989-2001; Centre for Tomorrow's Co, 1997-; Honours Committee, Economy, 2001-09; Ambassdor for Philanthropy, 2009-10; CCB Fellow, 2009; Oxford University Chancellor's Court of Benefactors; Cambridge Guild of Benefactors; Founder: The Kingwood Trust, 1993, The Shirley Foundation, 1996, Prior's Court Foundation, 1998, Autism Cymru, 2001; President, Autistica, Founder, 2004; Master, Information Technologists Company, 1992, Liveryman, 1992; Freeman, City of London, 1987. Address: 47 Thames House, Phyllis Court Drive, Henley on Thames, Oxfordshire RG9 2NA, England. E-mail: steve@steveshirley.com

SHITTU Gaffar Mola, b. 24 June 1948, Kano, Nigeria. Consultant Paediatrician. m. Gabriella Hulicsko, 3 sons. Education: MD, Medical University of Debrecen, Hungary, 1970-76; Paediatric Institute, 1980-82; Member Hungarian College of Paediatricians. Appointments: Medical Officer, National Stadium, Surulere, Lagos, 1976-77; FIFA Registers Sports Medicine Doctor, 1977; Health Services Management Board, Kano, 1977-80; Medical Officer Grade I, Asmau Memorial Hospital, Kano, 1982-84; Consultant Paediatrician. Honours: National Treasurer, then Social Secretary, Guild of Medical Directors; President, Rotary Club of Bompai, Kano, Nigeria; Chairman, Kano Chapter, GM Directors and Nigerian Medical Association; Listed in numerous Who's

Who publications. Memberships: Hungarian College of Paediatricians; Nigerian Paediatric Association; Guild of Medical Directors; District Chairman, Polio Plus; Chairman, Publicity and Ethics Committee, Nigerian Medical Association. Address: Classic Clinics Ltd, 1A Abbas Road, Arakan Avenue, PO Box 244, Kano, Nigeria. E-mail: piu1948@yahoo.co

SHITTU Lukeman Adelaja Joseph, b. 6 May 1970, Lagos, Nigeria. Medical Lecturer; Medical Practitioner. m. Remilekun Keji, 2 sons, 1 daughter. Education: MBBS, College of Medicine, University of Lagos, 1998; MBA, Lagos State University, Lasu Ojo, 2005; MSc, Anatomy, Lagos State University, Lasucom, Ikeja, 2006; Certificate in Theology, Word of Faith Bible Institution, Raji-Oba, Lagos. Appointments: Housemanship, Lagos University Teaching Hospital, 1999-2000; Medical Officer, Faskari Local Government, Katsina State, 2000-01; Lecturer, Lagos State University, 2001-08; Senior Lecturer, University of Abuja, 2008-09; Associate Professor, Benue State University, 2009-; Medical Director, Jireh International Foundation Research Centre, 2009-. Publications: Over 40 papers and reviews in both national and international journals. Honours: Best Master Student, Lasucom, 2006; Associate Editor, Scientific Research and Essays, 2008-; Assistant Secretary-General, Anatomical Society of Nigeria, 2006-10; Best Science Student in Odofin Secondary School, 1987; Lagos State Scholarship, Bursary Award, 1990-97; Editor, Journal of Applied Biosciences, 2008-; Founder/President, Lagos State Medical Students' Association; WSF Minister, Living Faith Church Worldwide; NYSC Drug Free Merit Award, 2001; External examiner to some medical universities; Review of international journals. Memberships: Lasumba Heritage; Nigerian Medical Association; Anatomical Society of Nigeria; International Federation of Associations of Anatomists; Federation Association of African Anatomists; Association of Staff Union of Universities of Nigerian Universities, Abuja Chapter; West African Bioinformatics Research Initiative. Address: Department of Anatomy, College of Health Sciences, University of Abuja, PO Box 882, Gwagwalada, Abuja, Nigeria. E-mail: drlukemanjoseph@vgmail.com

SHKARA Mufadhal A, b. 1 September 1953, Baghdad, Iraq. Architect; Engineer. m. Saudi, 1 son, 1 daughter. Education: BSc, Architectural Engineering, 1975; Postgraduate Diploma, Architectural Design, 1977; MSc, Architectural Engineering, 1979. Appointments: Architect, Hisham A Munir & Partners, Iraq, 1975-80; Manager, Engineering Division, Kara Establishment, Kingdom of Saudi Arabia, 1981-87; Project Manager, 1987-92, Director, IT, 1992-94, Director, 1994-96, Assistant Vice President, 1996-2007, Senior Vice President, 2007-, Zuhair Fayez Partnership, Kingdom of Saudi Arabia. Honours: ZFP Services Award; Project Management Principles; Balanced Scorecard Forum, 2010; Strategic Finance for Non Finance Managers; Construction Project Management; Housing Symposium 3. Memberships: Project Management Institute; Iraqi Engineering Association; JCCI-IT Committee; Saudi Council of Engineers. Address: Zuhair Fayez Partnership, PO Box 5445, Jeddah 21422, Saudi Arabia. E-mail: mxhkara@zfp.com Website: www.zfp.com

SHNITKA Theodor Khyam, b. 21 November 1927, Calgary, Alberta, Canada. Physician; Pathologist. m. Toby Garfin. Education: BSc. 1948, MSc, 1952, MD, 1953, University of Alberta, Edmonton; Resident in Pathology, University of Alberta Hospital, Edmonton, 1954-58; Speciality Certification, Royal College of Physicians and Surgeons of Canada, 1958; Postdoctoral Fellow in Surgery, Histochemistry, Johns Hopkins University School of Medicine, USA, 1959-60; Fellow, Royal College of Physicians and Surgeons of Canada, 1972. Appointments: Lecturer, 1958-59, Assistant Professor, 1959-62, Associate Professor, 1962-67, Professor, 1967-87, Chairman, Department of Pathology, 1980-87, Professor Emeritus of Pathology, 1987-, Faculty of Medicine, University of Alberta, Edmonton, Canada; Director, Diagnostic Electron Microscopy Laboratory, Department of Pathology, University of Alberta, 1975-87. Publications: Enzymatic histochemistry of gastrointestinal mucous membrane, 1960; Co-author, Macroscopic identification of early myocardial infarcts, by alterations in dehydrogenase activity, 1963; Co-editor, International Symposium "Gastric Secretion - Mechanisms and Control" 1967; Author, co-author of 45 other scientific articles and 7 book chapters on diagnostic pathology and electron microscopy, cell biology and pathobiology of lysosomes and peroxisomes, and neurobiology of reactive astrocytes. Honours: Annual Outstanding Achievement Award, Medical Alumni Association, University of Alberta, Edmonton, 1983; Honorary Affiliate Membership, Canadian Society of Laboratory Technologists, 1988; Outstanding Physician Award, Edmonton Academy of Medicine, 1988; Gold Medal for Canada, 2009. Memberships: Life Member: New York Academy of Sciences; Alberta and Canadian Medical Associations; Emeritus Member: Microscopy Society of America; Histochemical Society Inc; Canadian Association of Pathologists; American Society for Cell Biology; Active, Microscopical Society of Canada, Alpha Omega Alpha Honour Medical Society. Address: 12010 87th Avenue NW, Edmonton, Alberta, T6G 0Y7, Canada.

SHOKAEVA Dina, b. 16 March 1962, Kokchetav district, USSR. Scientist; Strawberry Breeder. Education: Diploma of Agronomist, 1984, PhD, Horticulture, 1990, Timiryazev Agricultural Academy, Moscow. Appointments: Agronomist, 1984-86, Graduate Student, 1986-90, Horticultural Institute, Moscow; Junior Researcher, Institute of Irrigated Horticulture, Melitopol, Ukraine, 1990-93; Senior Researcher, Head of Laboratory of Strawberry Breeding, All Russian Institute of Horticultural Breeding, 1993-. Publications: Numerous articles in professional journals, conference proceedings and symposia; 1 brochure; 1 monograph. Honours: Listed in international biographical dictionaries. Address: Zhilina 3-17, Orel 302530, Russia. E-mail: dinashokaeva@rekom.ru

SHOR Naum Anatolievich, b. 14 July 1930, Kiev, Ukraine. Doctor; Surgeon. Education: Diploma, Medical Faculty, Kiev Medical Institute, 1953; Lugaush State Medical Institute, 1957-59. Appointments: Assistant, 1959-, Candidate of Medical Science, 1968, Docent, 1982, Dr of Medical Science, 1986, Professor, 1987, Lugansk State Medical University. Publications: 3 monographs; 225 articles. Honours: Medal of a Veteran of Labour, 1986; Honour and Medal of the President of Ukraine, 2005. Memberships: New York Academy of Sciences; Russian-Ukrainian Vascular Surgery Association.

SHORT Clare, b. 15 February 1946, Birmingham, England. Politician. m. (1) 1964, divorced 1974, (2) A Lyon, 1981, deceased 1993, 1 son. Education: BA Honours, Political Science, Universities of Leeds and Keele. Appointments: Civil Service, Home Office, 1970-75; Director, All Faith for One Race, 1976-78; Youthaid, 1979-83; Labour MP, Birmingham Ladywood, 1983-; Shadow Employment Spokesperson, 1985-89, Social Security Spokesperson, 1989-91, Environmental Protection Spokesperson, 1992-93, Spokesperson for Women, 1993-95; Shadow Secretary of State for Transport, 1995-96, for Overseas Development, 1996-97; Secretary of State for International Development, 1997-2003; Select Committee Home Affairs, 1983-85; Chair,

All Party Group on Race Relations, 1985-86; NEC, 1988-98; Vice-President, Socialist International Women, 1992-96; Chair, Women's Committee National Executive Committee, 1993-97; Chair, NEC International Committee, 1996-98; Party Representative, Social International Congress, 1996. Publication: An Honourable Deception? New Labour, Iraq and the Misuse of Power, 2005. Membership: UNISON. Address: House of Commons, London SW1A 0AA, England.

SHORT Nigel, b. 1 June 1965, Leigh, Lancashire, England. Chess Player. m. Rea Karageorgiou, 1987, 1 daughter. Appointments: At age of 12 beat Jonathan Penrose in British Championships; International Master, 1980; Grand Master, 1984; British Champion, 1984, 1987; English Champion, 1991; President, Grand Masters Association, 1992; Defeated Anatoly Karpov, 1992; Defeated by Kasparov, 1993; Ranked 7th Player in World; Chess Columnist, The Daily Telegraph, 1991; Stripped of International Ratings by World Chess Foundation, 1993, reinstated, 1994; Resigned from FIDE and formed Professional Chess Association with Gary Kasparov, 1993, left PCA, 1995; Ranked 17th in the world by FIDE, January 2003; Commonwealth Champion, 2004. Publications: Learn Chess with Nigel Short, 1993. Honours: Honorary Fellow, Bolton Institute, 1993-; Honorary MBE, 1999. Address: c/o The Daily Telegraph, 1 Canada Square, London, E14 5DT, England. E-mail: ndshort@hotmail.com

SHORTER John, b. 14 June 1926, Redhill, Surrey, England. Chemist. m. Mary Patricia Steer, 28 July 1951, 2 sons, 1 daughter. Education: BA, 1947, BSc, 1948, DPhil, 1950, Exeter College, Oxford. Appointments: Assistant Lecturer, 1950-52, Lecturer in Chemistry, 1952-54, University College, Hull; Lecturer in Chemistry, 1954-63, Senior Lecturer, 1963-72, Reader, Physical Organic Chemistry, 1972-82, Emeritus Reader in Chemistry, 1982-, University of Hull; RT French Visiting Professor, University of Rochester, New York, USA, 1966-67. Publications include: Correlation Analysis in Organic Chemistry, 1973; Correlation Analysis of Organic Reactivity, 1982; Co-editor: Advances in Linear Free Energy Relationships, 1972; Correlation Analysis in Chemistry, 1978; Similarity Models in Organic Chemistry, Biochemistry and Related Fields, 1991. Honour: 75th Anniversary Medal, Polish Chemical Society, 2001. Memberships: Fellow, Royal Society of Chemistry; Secretary, International Group for Correlation Analysis in Chemistry (formerly organic chemistry), 1982-2004; International Union of Pure and Applied Chemistry. Address: 29A Meadowfields, Whitby, North Yorkshire YO21 1QF, England.

SHRESTHA Bhanu, b. 27 April 1966, Nepal. Assistant Professor. m. Upahar, 2 sons. Education: BS, 1998, MS, 2004, PhD, 2008, Electronic Engineering, Kwangwoon University. Appointments: Adjunct Professor and Researcher, 2008-11, Assistant Professor, 2011-, Electronic Engineering, Kwangwoon University. Publications: An X-band VCOs Design using InGaP/GaAs HBT Technology, 2007; An 11.5 GHz Cascode VCO with Low Phase Noise in InGaP/GaAs HBT Technology, 2007; Double Cross Coupled Differential VCO with Low Phase Noise Using InGaP/GaAs HBT Technology, 2007; Analysis of Two Filtering Techniques in Differential LC VCO Design Using Asymmetric Tank Structure, 2007; Design of Diodes Feedback Differential Colpitts VCO with Low Phase Noise Based on InGaP/GaAs HBT Technology, 2008; Author, Practical Design of MMIC VCOs, 2009; Design of Low Phase Noise InGaP/GaAs HBT Based Differential Colpitts VCOs for Interference Cancellation System, 2010; Spurline Resonators Design and Its Implementation to Microwave Oscillators, 2011; English Course E-learning System Based on Relative Item Difficulty Using Web Component Composition, 2011; Low Phase Noise Oscillator using Spurline Resonator for I-band Applications, 2011. Honours: Bellwave Excellent Paper Award, Korean Electromagnetic Engineering Society, 2005; Nepal Vidhya Bhusan Padak 'A' Class (Gold Medal), President of Nepal, 2009; Honorary 3rd Dan Black Belt, Kukkiwon (Taekwondo Headquarter), Korea, 2009; Certificate of Commendation for Outstanding Contribution in Hapkido in Nepal and India, Korea Martial Hapkido Association, Seoul, Korea. Memberships: Nepal Engineering Council; Nepal Engineers Association; IEEE; Nepal-Korea Friendship Society; All Nepal Taekwodo Academy; Editorial Board Member of the Researchers World, Journal of Arts Science & Commerce Research, India; Chief Advisor, All India Taekwondo Association. Address: Bhimeshwor Municipality-2, Dolakha, Nepal. E-mail: bnu56@yahoo.com

SHUAIBU Aminu, b. 24 December 1985, Gombe, Nigeria. Economist; Risk Analyst. Education: BSc, Economics. Appointments: Executive Trainee, Fin Insurance Company Ltd, 2008-. Publications: Single currency in West Africa Challenges and Prospects Ahead, 2007. Honours: BSc (Hons), Economics. Memberships: Student Member, Nigeria Institute of Management. Address: c/o Fin Insurance Company ltd, No 34 Gana Street, Maitama, Abuja, Nigeria. E-mail: aminushuaibu@gmail.com

SHULGA Galia, b. 10 June 1952, St Petersburg, Russia. Polymer Chemist. 1 daughter. Education: Engineer-Chemist, Riga Polytechnical Institute, Riga, Latvia, 1974; Candidate of Sciences, Polymer Chemistry, Lomonosov Moscow State University, Moscow, Russia, 1982; Doctor of Chemistry, Latvian Academy of Sciences, Riga, Latvia, 1992; Doctor Habilitus of Chemistry (Wood Chemistry), 1998. Appointments: Junior Researcher, 1974-1981, Senior Researcher, 1981-84, State Institute of Polymeric Materials, Application in Land Reclamation and Water Management, Jelgava, Latvia; Senior Researcher, Institute of Wood Chemistry, Latvian Academy of Sciences, Riga, Latvia, 1984-93; Leading Researcher, State Institute of Wood Chemistry, Riga, Latvia, 1993-; General Manager, Eurkea E! 2622, 2002-11; Official Representative from Latvia in the Management Committee of COST Action FP0701, 2010-12; Leading Research Scientist, Head of the Project, Forest Sector Competence Centre of Latvia, 2011-. Publications: Numerous articles in scientific journals; 12 articles in edited books; Numerous abstracts; 16 inventions. Honours: Bronze Medal, Exhibition of National Economic Achievements, Moscow, USSR, 1982; Research Grant, Latvian Council of Science, 1997-2009; Financial support for participation in the IUFRO XXI Congress in Malaysia, The Scientist Assistance Programme, International Union of Forestry Research Organisations, 2000. Memberships: Society for Engineering in Agricultural, Food and Biological System, USA; American Chemical Society; The International Lignin Institute, Switzerland; The American Science Advisory Boards, Bioinformatics LLC; Deputy Director General, IBC. Address: Latvian State Institute of Wood Chemistry, 27 Dzerbenes St, LV 1006 Riga, Latvia. E-mail: shulga@junik.lv

SHUREY Richard, b. 22 September 1951, Wales. Factory Worker. m. Christine, 6 May 1972, 2 sons, 1 daughter. Educations: Pentre Grammar School. Publications: Jewels of the Imagination, 1997; By the Light of the Moon, 1997; On Reflection, 1997; Never Forget, 1998; From the Hand of a Poet, 1999; Open Minds, 1999. Contributions to: South Wales Echo; Celtic Press; Rhondda Leader. Honours: Editor's

Choice Award for Outstanding Achievement in Poetry, International Library of Poetry, 1997. Memberships: Poetry Guild. Address: 107 Tylacelyn Road, Penygraig, Tonypandy, Rhondda-Cynon-Taff CF40 1JR, South Wales.

SIDDIQUEE Ghulam Sabir, Astronomer; Astrologist; Geologist; Hydrologist. Education: MD, Kolkata; DSc, Indian Academy of Naturotherapy, Lucknow; PhD, Open International University, Sri Lanka; BCA, London. Appointments: Researcher (supported by late Dr P M Rahemany), 5 years. Publications: Research book, Shah E Mahaan; Numerous articles in professional journals. Honours: 7 awards for film making, 1971; Gold Medal for India, USA; American Order of Merit; Hall of Fame, USA; International Peace Prize, USA; Men of the Year, USA; Award for first 16mm film in Malegaon; American Excellence Highest Award, Department of Natural Science, Moberly State of Missouri, USA: Nishan-e-tib Award, Holistic Health Science Central Research Institute of Medical Science, Mumbai, India. Memberships: Rahemany Poly Clinic Research Centre, Malegaon; Naturopathy Medical Practitioner Association, Mumbai; Avicenna Research Centre, Unani Medicines, Mumbai; Indian Institute of Alternative Medicines; HUSN-E-RAQAM Education Welfare Society; Shah Nematulla Vali Research Board; Book Club, National Book Trust, Government of India; Central Research Institute of Medical Science, Mumbai; All India Talimi Wa Milli Foundation; Honorary Adviser, Indian Academy of Naturotherapeutics, Lucknow; Honorary Counsellor, Indian Board of Alternative Medicines, Kolkata; Kashmir Research Institute, Sri Nagar; All India Unani Tibbi Congress, New Delhi. Address: H No 185, Johar Chawk, Budhwar Ward, Malegaon, Dist Nasik, Maharashtra, India. E-mail: g.s.siddiquee@hotmail.com Website: http://gssiddiquee.webs.com

SIDIBE El Hassane, b. 12 May 1951, Thilene, Dagana, Saint Louis, Senegal. Doctor of Medicine; Teacher; Researcher. m. Amsatou Sow, 2 sons, 2 daughters. Education: Threefold Excellence Prize and Sevenfold registered in Honor Table, Bachelor of Science, Lycee Charles de Gaulle, St Louis, 1970; Medical Doctor, Dakar University, 1984; Internship, Dakar, 1977; Medical Assistant, Paris, 1984; Resident, Paris, 1986; Registered candidate in Academie Nationale de Medicine, 2000. Appointments: Assistant, Endocrinology Faculty of Medicine, Dakar, 1986-98; Certificate in Internal Medicine and Endocrinology, Metabolism and Nutrition, 1994; Aggregate Professor in Endocrinology, Metabolism, Nutrition, 1998; Master of Medical Sciences, 2000, Proposed Emeritus Professor, 2005, Paris VII University; Full Professor, Endocrinology, Metabolism and Nutrition, 2007. Publications: African Diabetic microangiopathy, 1979; Primary hypothyroidism in Senegal, 1984; Major diabetes mellitus complications in Africa, 2000; Sheehan disease African experience, 2000; Pheochromocytoma in Africa, 2001; Thyreopathies in Subsaharan Africa, 2007. Honours: LS Senghor Foundation Grant, 1984; Medal, Societe Medicale des Hopitaux de Paris 150th Birthday, 1999; Chevalier des Palmes Academiques Françaises, 2001. Memberships: New York Academy of Sciences, 1995; SMHP; SNFMI; ALFEDIAM; SFE; Endocrine Society; Panafrican Diabetes Study Group; MDSG; SPE; ADA; ARCOL; Societé Québecoise de l'HTA; SNFBMN; Member, European Academy of Sciences; Art and Humanities Candidate in Academie des Sciences; Full Member, Academie Française, Paris. Address: Villa 2A, Rue 1xC Point E, BP 5062, Fann, Dakar, Senegal.

SIEFKEN Hinrich Gerhard, b. 21 April 1939, Cologne, Germany. University Teacher. m. Marcia Corinne Birch, 1 son, 1 daughter. Education: German and English, University of Tübingen (Vienna and Newcastle); Dr Phil, magna cum laude, 1964; Staatsexamen, 1964. Appointments: Tutor, University of Tübingen, 1962-65; Lektor, University College of North Wales, Bangor, 1965-66; Wissenschaftlicher Assistent, University of Tübingen, 1966-67; Lecturer, Senior Lecturer, German, Saint David's University College, Lampeter, 1969-79; Professor of German, Head of Department, 1979-97, Head of School of Modern Languages, 1986-88, Dean of Faculty of Arts, 1988-91, Director, Institute of German, Austrian and Swiss Affairs, 1991-93, University of Nottingham. Publications: Books include: Kafka. Ungeduld und Lässigkeit, 1997; Thomas Mann – Goethe "Ideal der Deutschheit", 1981; Die Weisse Rose und ihre Flugblätter (editor), 1994; Theodor Haecker, Leben und Werk (co-editor), 1995; Experiencing Tradition: Essays of Discovery. For Keith Spalding, with A Bushell, 2003; Numerous articles in academic journals. Honours: D Litt, University of Nottingham, 1990; Ehrengabe zum Theodor Haecker-Preis der Stadt Esslingen, 1995; Emeritus Professor, University of Nottingham, 1997; Honorary Professor of Modern Languages, University of Wales Bangor, 1999. Address: 6 Mountsorrel Drive, West Bridgford, Nottingham NG2 6LJ, England. E-mail: hinrichsiefken@hotmail.com

SIGURDARDOTTIR Zuilma Gabriela, b. 25 February 1962, Mexico City, Mexico. Professor. 1 son, 1 daughter. Education: BA, Psychology, University of Iceland, 1985; MA, Behaviour Analysis & Therapy, SIU-Carbondale, Illinois, USA, 1989; PhD, Psychology, Northeastern University, Boston, USA, 1992. Appointments: Psychologist, Program Director, Part-time teaching at University, private practice, 1992-99; Professor, Behaviour Analysis, Psychology Department, University of Iceland, 1999-. Publications: Numerous articles in professional journals. Honours: Grants from professional organisations. Memberships: Association for Behaviour Analysis International; Icelandic Association for Behaviour Analysis; Icelandic Psychological Association. Address: Psychology Department, University of Iceland, Sudurgata Reykajavik, 101, Iceland.

SIIPOLA Olli Veikko Vihtori, b. 13 July 1945, Kalajoki, Finland. Psychiatrist. m. Anne Johansson, 2 sons, 2 daughters. Education: MD, 1973; Psychiatrist, 1982; Counselor in Psychiatry, 1983; Psychogeriatrist, 1986; BA, Theology, 1990; Administration Specialist, 1994; Psychotherapist, 1996. Appointments: Psychiatrist in mental hospitals, Oulu, 1964, Tammisaari, 1967, Niuvanniemi, 1968, Vammala, 1968-69; Psychiatrist in somatic hospitals, Lahti, 1969, Turku, 1968-72, Tampere, 1984, Pitkaniemi, 1977-84; Communal Doctor, Duumala, 1973; Communal Doctor, Maritta, 1973-75; Private practitioner, Tampere, 1975-91, Helsinki, 1989-2009; Public Service Chief Associate, Nikkila Long-Term Psychiatric Rehabilitation, 1991-99. Publications: Possible Life, autobiography, 1983; The Book of Healthy Life, 1985; Columnist in Laakariletti, 1980-99; Numerous articles in professional journals. Honours: Article Writer of the Year, 1999; Haggai Institute Award for 20 Year Contribution, 2005. Memberships: Rotary Club; Toolo Helsinki; Finnish Theological Literature Society. Address: Pasuunatie 7 D 20, 00420 Helsinki 42, Finland. E-mail: olli.siipola@welho.com

SIKDAR Malay Kanti, b. 1 January 1948, Brahmachal, Bangladesh. Writer; Scientist; Scholar; Manager. m. Susmita, 1 daughter. Education: BSc (Physics with honours), Calcutta University; MBB, Agartala College, 1969; MSc (Physics),

1971, PhD (Physics), Kalyani University. Appointments: UGC Junior, Senior Fellow, 1973-77, CSIR Senior/PD Fellow, 1977-79; District Manager, Food Corporation of India, 24-Parganas, Howrah, Kolkata, 2007; Vice President, Indian Association for the Cultivation of Science, 2010-2012. Publications: Many research papers and articles in scientific journals include: Tables of Clebsch Gordan Co-efficients of Magnetic groups, 1976; Tables of Magnetic Double Point group, 1977; Group Theoretical Analysis of second order phase transitions in Magnetic Structures, 1979; Rach co-efficients for Crystalline solids, 1980; Spin Orientations in Halides, Rare Earth & Actinide series after Magnetic Phase Transition, 1983; Higher Order of Lives in the Universe, 2002; Sym, World Forum, Oxford, 2008; Holy Bath in the Ocean of Brahman, 2007; 1 novel: Kalinga Judher Prantare, 1983 and short stories: Ghare Baire Pathe Prantare, 1989; Swarga Martya Jiban Mrityu, 2006; More publications forthcoming. Honours: Bal Sahayog Award, 2000; Bharat Excellency Award with Gold Medal, 2001; Secular India Harmony Award, 2001; UWA Lifetime Achievement Award, 2002; Indian Growing Personalities Award with Gold Medal, 2002; Man of the Year, 2002; American Medal of Honor, 2003; ABI World Lifetime Achievement Award, 2003; International Peace Prize, 2003; Eminent Personality of India, International Biographical Research Foundation, Nagpur, India, 2003; Great Indian Achievement Award Gold Medal, 2004; FFI Lifetime Achievement Award and Gold Medal, 2004; Bright Indian Citizen Award and Gold Medal, 2004; Human Excellence Award and Gold Medal, 2004; Da Vinci Diamond Award, IBC, 2004; FFI Udyog Gaurav Award, 2005; Bharat Yogyta Award, 2005; Rashtray Jyoti Award; IIFS Vijoy Rattan Award, 2005; IBC Leading Educators of the World, 2005; IISA Glory of India Award, 2006; IIFS Vijoy Shree Award, 2006; IPH Best Citizen of India Award, 2006; FFI Glory of India International Award, 2006; ABI Eminent Fellow for Magnificent and Distinguished Deed, 2006; IIEM Life Time Achievement Gold Award, 2006; ISC Jewel of India Award, 2006; IPH Best Citizen of India Award, 2006; IIEM Eminent Citizen of India Award, 2007; IBC Mother India Excellence Award, 2007; FFI Arch of Excellence Award, 2007; FFI Indian Golden Achiever Award, 2007; IIEM National Gold Star Award, 2008; IBC Roll of Honour, 2008; ABI Einstein Genius Dedication Award, 500 Greatest Genius of the 21st Century, 2008; ABI Pinnacle of Achievement, 2010. Memberships: Indian Association for the Cultivation of SC; Indian Science Congress, Nikhi; Bharat Banga Sahitya Sanmelan; Institute of Commercial Management, UK. Address: C/27, Navadarsha Co-operative Housing Society Ltd, Birati, Kolkata 700134, India.

SIKK Peetor, b. 16 October 1949, Estonia. Senior Research Scientist. m. Reet, 1 daughter. Education: Tartu University, Estonia, 1969; PhD, Chemistry, Institute of Chemistry, Estonian Academy of Science, 1978. Appointments: Senior Research Scientist. Publications: Numerous articles in professional journals on enzymology and cellular bioenergetics. Honours: Estonian Award of Science, 1978. Address: National Institute of Chemical Physics and Biophysics, Akademia 23, 12618 Tallinn, Estonia. E-mail: peetor.sikk@kbfi.ee

SILAEV Michael Mikhailovich, b. 25 February 1947, Orekhovo-Zuevo, Moscow, Russia. Chemist. Education: First Class Diploma, 1971, Postgraduate, Radiation Chemistry Laboratory, 1973-76, PhD, 1992, Chemical Department, Moscow State University. Appointments: Probationer-Researcher, 1971-73, Junior Researcher, 1976-93, Researcher, 1993-2003, Senior Researcher, 2003-, Radiation Chemistry Laboratory, Chemical Department, Moscow State University. Publications: Numerous articles in professional journals; 3 patents. Honours: IBS Foremost Scientists of the World, 2008; International Scientist of the Year, 2008; Leading Educators of the World, 2008. Address: Chemical Department, Moscow State University, Vorob'evy Gory, Moscow 119991, Russia. E-mail: mmsilaev@rc.chem.msu.ru Website: www.rc.chem.msu.ru

SILD LÖNROTH Carina, b. 26 November 1956, Malmö, Sweden. Executive Officer. m. Lars Lonröth, 1 son, 1 daughter. Education: MSc, Pedagogy/Psychology and Sociology, 1988; Programme Manager, The Nightingale Mentoring Scheme, 1997; Deputy Unit Manager, Teacher Training Department, Malmö University, 2001; Overall Co-ordinator, EU project, 2006; Consultant, Norwegian Ministry of Children and Equality; Executive Officer, Nightingale Mentoring Programme; Programme Manager, Nightingale Senior; Entrepreneur, Nightingale Youth. Publications: The Nightingale Scheme – A Song for the Heart. Honours: Malmö City Integration Award; Invited Lecturer, French Ministry of Culture and Communication; Listed in international biographical dictionaries. Memberships: Zonta International. Address: Malmö University, Nordenskioldsgatan 10, 205 06 Malmö, Sweden. E-mail: carina_sild-lonroth@mah.se

SILVERSTONE Alicia, b. 4 October 1976, California, USA. Actress. m. Christopher Jarecki, 2005, 1 son. Appointments: Stage Debut in Play, Carol's Eve, Metropolitan Theatre, Los Angeles; Stared in 3 Aerosmith Videos including: Cryin; Formed own production company, First Kiss Productions; Films: The Crush, 1993; The Babysitter, 1995; True Crime, 1995; Le Nouveau Monde, 1995; Hideaway, 1995; Clueless, 1995; Batman and Robin, 1997; Excess Baggage (also Producer), 1997; Free Money, 1998; Blast from the Past, 1999; Love's Labour Lost, 2000; Scorched, 2002; Global Heresy, 2002; Scooby Doo: Monsters Unleashed, 2004; Beauty Shop, 2005; Silence Becomes You, 2005; Stormbreaker, 2006; Tropic Thunder, 2008; The Art of Getting By, 2011; Vamps, Butter, 2012; TV: Torch Song, 1993; Shattered Dreams, 1993; The Cool and the Crazy, 1994; The Wonder Years, 1997: Miss Match, 2003-2005; Pink Collar, 2006; Candles on Bay Street, 2006; The Singles Table, 2007; The Bad Mother's Handbook, 2008; Childrens Hospital, 2011; Suburgatory, 2012. Publications: The Kind Diet, 2009. Address: c/o Premiere Artists Agency, Suite 510, 8899 Beverly Boulevard, Los Angeles, CA 90048, USA.

SIM Jae Ang, b. 8 September 1970, South Korea. Professor; Doctor. m. Shin Young Kim, 1 son, 1 daughter. Education: Bachelor, Medicine, Kyunghee University, 1996; Master, 2004, Doctor, 2007, Orthopaedics, Gachon University; Postdoctoral, Harvard Medical School, Massachusetts General Hospital, 2011. Appointments: Assistant Professor, 2006-10, Associate Professor, 2010-, Gachon University, Gil Medical Center; AO Korea Faculty, 2010-; Reviewer of Journal of Korean Orthopaedic Association; Korean Knee Society; Korean Society of Fracture. Publications: Numerous articles in professional journals. Honours: Best Paper Award, Journal of Korean Arthroscopy Society, 2010; Best Paper Award, Journal of Korean Knee Society, 2011. Memberships: AO Korea Faculty; SICOT Member; AAOA Member; AAOS Member. Address: 1198 Orthopaedic Department, Gil Hospital, Kowoldong, Namdonggu, Incheon, 405-760, Korea. E-mail: sim_ja@hanmail.net

SIM Si-Mui (Debra), b. 19 May 1958, Tawau, Sabah, Malaysia. Lecturer. Education: BSc (Hons), Pharmacology, 1980, PhD, 1984, University of Liverpool, England. Appointments: Lecturer, 1984; Associate Professor, 1993; Professor, 2006; Department of Pharmacology, University of Malaya, Malaysia. Publications: More than 48 full-length original articles in scientific journals or medical education journals. Honours: Best Lecturer Award, 1986, 1989, 1991, 1994; Excellent Service Award, 2000, 2002, 2009; Certificate of Excellent Service, 2004, 2005. Memberships: Malaysian Society of Pharmacology and Physiology; Malaysian Mensa Society; Asia Pacific Association of PBL in Health Sciences; Malaysian Society on Toxinology; Malaysian Association of Education in Medicine & Health Science. E-mail: debrasim@um.edu.my

SIMIC Charles, b. 9 May 1938, Belgrade, Yugoslavia (US citizen, 1971). Associate Professor of English; Poet; Writer. m. Helen Dubin, 1964, 1 son, 1 daughter. Education: University of Chicago, 1956-59; BA, New York University, 1967. Appointments: Faculty, California State College, Hayward, 1970-73; Associate Professor of English, University of New Hampshire, 1973-. Publications: Poetry: What the Grass Says, 1967; Somewhere Among Us a Stone is Taking Notes, 1969; Dismantling the Silence, 1971; White, 1972, revised edition, 1980; Return to a Place Lit by a Glass of Milk, 1974; Biography and a Lament, 1976; Charon's Cosmology, 1977; Brooms: Selected Poems, 1978; School for Dark Thoughts, 1978; Classic Ballroom Dances, 1980; Shaving at Night, 1982; Austerities, 1982; Weather Forecast for Utopia and Vicinity: Poems: 1967-1982, 1983; The Chicken Without a Head, 1983; Selected Poems 1963-1983, 1985, revised edition, 1990; Unending Blues, 1986; The World Doesn't End: Prose Poems, 1989; In the Room We Share, 1990; The Book of Gods and Devils, 1990; Hotel Insomnia, 1992; A Wedding in Hell, 1994; Walking the Black Cat, 1996; Jackstraws, 1999; Night Picnic, 2001; The Voice at 3:00am, 2003; Selected Poems 1963-2003, 2005; My Noiseless Entourage: Poems, 2005; Monkey Around, 2006; Sixty Poems, 2008; That Little Something: Poems, 2008; Monster Loves His Labyrinth, 2008. Other: The Uncertain Certainty: Interviews, Essays and Notes on Poetry, 1985; Wonderful Words, Silent Truth, 1990; Dimestore Alchemy, 1992; Unemployed Fortune Teller, 1994; Orphan Factory, 1998; A Fly in the Soup, 2000. Editor: Another Republic: 17 European and South American Writers (with Mark Strand), 1976; The Essential Campion, 1988. Translator: 12 books, 1970-92. Honours: PEN Awards, 1970, 1980; Guggenheim Fellowship, 1972; National Endowment for the Arts Fellowships, 1974, 1979; Edgar Allan Poe Award, 1975; American Academy of Arts and Letters Award, 1976; Harriet Monroe Poetry Award, 1980; Fulbright Fellowship, 1982; Ingram Merrill Foundation Fellowship, 1983; John D and Catharine T MacArthur Foundation Fellowship, 1984; Pulitzer Prize in Poetry, 1990; Academy of American Poets Fellowship, 1998; Poet Laureate Consultant in Poetry to the Library of Congress, 2007. Address: c/o Department of English, University of New Hampshire, Durham, NH 03824, USA. Website: www.unh.edu/english

SIMMONS David, b. 22 August 1959, Hampton Court, England. Physician. m. Denise, 2 sons. Education: Hampton Grammar School, 1970-77; St John's College, Cambridge, 1978-81; Charing Cross Hospital Medical School, London, 1981-84. Appointments: Senior House Officer, Walsgrave Hospital, Coventry, England, 1985-87; Research Registrar, Sheikh Rashid Diabetes Unit, Radcliffe Infirmary, Oxford, 1987-89; General Medical Registrar, Middlemore Hospital, Auckland, 1989-90; Diabetes Research Fellow, 1990-92, Senior Lecturer in Medicine (temporary), 1992-94, Middlemore and Auckland Hospitals; Senior Lecturer in Medicine, Middlemore Hospital, University of Auckland, 1994-99; Founder and Medical Director, South Auckland Diabetes Project (now Diabetes Projects Trust), South Auckland, New Zealand; General Physician, Diabetes Specialist and Academic Member of the Hospital Executive, Goulburn Valley Health, 1999-2003; Foundation Chair in Rural Health, 1999-2003, Acting Dean, Rural Clinical School, 2001-02, Acting Head of School of Rural Health, Acting Associate Dean of Rural Health, 2002-03, University of Melbourne; Professor of Medicine, Waikato Clinical School, University of Auckland, 2003-07; Consultant Diabetologist, Diabetes Clinical Lead, Institute of Metabolic Science, Addenbrooke's Hospital, Cambridge University Hospitals NHS Foundation Trust, Cambridge, 2007-. Publications: Over 180 refereed papers; 32 refereed letters; 9 book chapters. Honours include: National Heart Foundation Lecturer, ANZ Cardiac Society of Australia & New Zealand Annual Scientific Meeting, 2004; Simply the Best Merit Award, 2005; Honorary Member, Diabetes in Pregnancy Study Group, 2006; Honorary Professor of Medicine, University of Auckland, 2007-09; University of Melbourne Professorial Fellow, Victoria, 2008-13; Joseph Hoet Award, 2009. Memberships: Royal Geographical Society; Royal Australasian College of Physicians; Royal College of Physicians; Medical Research Society; Diabetes UK; European Association for the Study of Diabetes; American Diabetes Association; Association of British Clinical Diabetologists. Address: Braham House, The Wyches, Little Thetford, Ely, CB6 3HG, England.

SIMMONS Michael, b. 17 October 1935, Watford, England. Writer. m. Angela Thomson, 1963, 2 sons. Education: BA, Honours, Russian, Manchester University, 1960; Birkbeck College, 1998-. Appointments: Parliamentary Correspondent, Glasgow Herald, 1964-67; East Europe Correspondent, Financial Times, 1968-72; Deputy Editor, Society, East Europe Correspondent, Third World Editor, The Guardian, 1977-97; Freelance Writer and Editor, 1997-. Publications: Berlin: The Dispossessed City, 1988; The Unloved Country; A Portrait of the GDR, 1989; The Reluctant President, A Life of Vaclav Havel, 1992; Landscapes of Poverty, 1997; On the Edge, 2001; Essays on: Church and Community, 2000; Getting a Life, 2002. Membership: Trinity Cricket Club. Address: 24 Rodney Road, New Malden, Surrey KT3 5AB, England. E-mail: micsimmo@compuserve.com

SIMON Josette, Actress. Education: Central School of Speech Training and Dramatic Art. m. Mark Padmore, 1996, 1 child. Career: TV: Blake's 7; Kavanagh QC; Silent Witness; Dalziel and Pascoe; The Last Detective; Poirot; Midsomers Murders; Casualty, 2006; The Whistleblowers, 2007; Lewis, 2007; The Bill, 2008; Stage: with RSC: Measure for Measure, 1988; Arthur Miller's After the Fall; The White Devil; Ibsen's The Lady From the Sea; The Taming of the Shrew, 1995; The Maids, 1997; A Midsummer Night's Dream, 1999; several concert performances; Films: Cry Freedom; Milk and Honey; A Child from the South; Bitter Harvest; Bridge of Time. Honours: Best Actress Atlantic Film Festival, 1988; Paris Film Festival, 1990; Hon MA (Leicester), 1995. Address: Conway van Gelder Ltd, 18-21 Jermyn Street, London SW1Y 6HP, England.

SIMON Neil, b. 4 July 1927, New York, USA. Playwright. m. (1) Joan Baim, 1953-73, 2 daughters, (2) Marsha Mason, 1973-81, (3&4) Diane Lander, 1987-88, 1990-98, 1 adopted daughter, (5) Elaine Joyce. Education: New York University. Appointments: Wrote for various TV programmes including:

The Tallulah Bankhead Show, 1951; The Phil Silvers Show, 1958-59; NBC Special; The Trouble with People, 1972; Plays: Come Blow your Horn, 1961; Little Me (musical), 1962; Barefoot in the Park, 1963; The Odd Couple, 1965; Sweet Charity (musical), 1966; The Star-Spangled Girl, 1966; Plaza Suite, 1968; Promises, Promises (musical), 1968; Last of the Red Hot Lovers, 1969; The Gingerbread Lady, 1970; The Prisoner of Second Avenue, 1971; The Sunshine Boys, 1972; The Good Doctor, 1973; God's Favourite, 1974; California Suite, 1976; Chapter Two, 1977; They're Playing Our Song, 1979; I Ought to be in Pictures, 1980; Fools, 1981; Little Me (revised version), 1982; Brighton Beach Memoirs, 1983; Biloxi Blues, 1985; The Odd Couple Female Version, 1985; Broadway Bound, 1986; Rumors, 1988; Lost in Yonkers, 1991; Jake's Women, 1992; The Goodbye Girl (musical), 1993; Laughter on the 23rd Floor, 1993; London Suite, 1995; Proposals, 1997; The Dinner Party, 2000; 45 Seconds from Broadway, 2001; Rose's Dilemma, 2003; Oscar and Felix: A New Look at the Odd Couple, 2004; Screenplays include: After the Fox, 1966; Barefoot in the Park, 1967; The Odd Couple, 1968; The Out of Towners, 1970; Plaza Suite, 1971; The Last of the Red Hot Lovers, 1972; The Heartbreak Kid, 1973; The Prisoner of Second Avenue, 1975; The Sunshine Boys, 1975; Murder by Death, 1976; The Goodbye Girl, 1977; The Cheap Detective, 1978; California Suite, 1978; Chapter Two, 1979; Seems Like Old Times, 1980; Only When I Laugh, 1981; I Ought to Be in Pictures, 1982; Max Dugan Returns, 1983; The Lonely Guy, 1984; The Slugger's Wife, 1985; Brighton Beach Memoirs, 1986; Plaza Suite, 1987; Biloxi Blues, 1988; The Marrying Man, 1991; Lost in Yonkers, 1993; The Sunshine Boys, 1995; Jake's Women, London Suite, 1996; The Odd Couple II, 1998; Laughter on the 23rd Floor, 2001; The Goodbye Girl, 2004. Honours: Many awards and nominations include: Emmy Award; Antoinette Perry (Tony) Awards for The Odd Couple; Writers Guild Screen Award for the Odd Couple, 1969; American Comedy Award for Lifetime Achievement, 1989; Drama Desk Award, 1991; Pulitzer Prize, 1991; Tony Award, 1991; Kennedy Center Honoree, 1995; Helmerich Award, 1996; Mark Twain Prize, 2006. Publication: Rewrites: A Memoir, 1996; Individual Plays. Address: c/o A DaSilva, 502 Park Avenue, New York, NY 10022, USA.

SIMON Norma, b. 24 December 1927, New York City, USA. Children's Book Author. m. Edward Simon, 7 June 1951, 1 son, 2 daughters. Education: BA, Economics, Brooklyn College, 1943-47; MA, Early Childhood Education, Bank St College of Education, 1968; Graduate Work, New School of Social Research. Appointments: Clerical Worker, Frances I duPont & Co, New York City, 1943-46; Teacher, Vassar Summer Institute, Poughkeepsie, New York, Department of Welfare, Brooklyn, New York, 1948-49, Downtown Community School, New York City, 1949-52, Thomas School, Rowayton, Connecticut, 1952-53; Founder, Director, Teacher, Norwalk Community Co-operative Nursery School, Rowayton, Connecticut, 1953-54; Teacher, Norwalk Public Schools, Connecticut, 1962-63; Group Therapist, Greater Bridgeport Child Guidance Center, Connecticut, 1965-67; Special Teacher, Mid-Fairfield Child Guidance Center, Connecticut, 1967-69; Consultant, Stamford Pre-School Program, Connecticut, 1965-69; Consultant, School Division, Macmillan Publishing Co, Inc, New York City, 1968-70; Consultant, Davidson Films Inc, 1969-74, Aesop Films, San Francisco, California, 1975-79; Consultant, Children's Advertising, Dancer-Fitzgerald-Sampler Inc, New York City, 1969-79; Consultant, Fisher-Price Toys, East Aurora, New York, 1978; Consultant to Publishing Division, Bank Street College of Education, 1967-74, Follow-Through Program, 1971-72. Publications include: I Wish I Had My Father, 1983; Oh, That Cat!; The Saddest Time, 1986; Cats Do, Dogs Don't, 1986; Children Do, Grownups Don't, 1987; Wedding Days, 1988; I Am Not A Crybaby, 1989; Mama Cat's Year, 1990; Firefighters, 1995; The Baby House, 1995; Wet World, 1995; The Story of Hanukkah, 1997; The Story of Passover, 1997; Looking Back at Wellfleet, 1997; All Kinds of Children, 1999; All Families Are Special, 2003; Paperbacks: I'm Busy, Too; I Was So Mad!; Why Am I Different; The Story of Hanukkah; Translations into Japanese, German, Danish and Swedish; Books and Papers in the de Grummond Collection. McCain library and archives, university libraries, University of Southern Mississippi; Papers and books in the Kerlan Collection, Walter Library, University of Minnesota. Honours include: Jeremiah Cahir Friend of Education Award, Barnstable County Education Association, 1987; Parents' Council on Books Choice, 1998; Listed in numerous national and international biographical publications. Memberships: Authors Guild; Delta Kappa Gamma; AAUW. Address: PO Box 428, South Wellfleet, MA 02663-0428, USA.

SIMON Paul, b. 13 October 1941, Newark, New Jersey, USA. Singer; Composer. m. (1) Peggy Harper (divorced), 1 son, (2) Carrie Fisher (divorced), (3) Edie Brickell, 30 May 1992, 2 sons, 1 daughter. Education: BA, Queens College; Postgraduate, Brooklyn Law School. Career: Duo, Simon And Garfunkel, with Art Garfunkel, 1964-71; Appearances with Garfunkel include: Monterey Festival, 1967; Royal Albert Hall, 1968; Reunion concerts: Central Park, New York, 1981; US, European tours; Solo artiste, 1972-; Appearances include: Anti-war Festival, Shea Stadium, New York, 1970; Farm Aid V, 1992; Hurricane Relief concert, Miami, 1992; Born At The Right Time Tour; Tour, Europe and Russia; Television includes: Paul Simon Special, 1977; Paul Simon's Graceland - The African Concert, 1987; Paul Simon - Born At The Right Time, 1992; Film appearances: Monterey Pop, 1968; Annie Hall, 1977; All You Need Is Cash, 1978; One Trick Pony, 1980; Steve Martin Live, 1985. Compositions include: The Sound Of Silence; Homeward Bound; I Am A Rock; Mrs Robinson; The Boxer; Bridge Over Troubled Water; Cecilia; Slip Slidin' Away; Late In The Evening; You Can Call Me Al; The Boy In The Bubble; Graceland; Paul Simon - Songs From The Capeman, 1997. Albums: with Art Garfunkel: Wednesday Morning 3AM, 1964; Sounds Of Silence, 1965; Parsley Sage Rosemary And Thyme, 1967; The Graduate (film soundtrack), 1967; Bookends, 1968; Bridge Over Troubled Water, 1970; Simon and Garfunkel's Greatest Hits, 1972; Breakaway, 1975; Watermark, 1978; Collected Works, 1981; The Concert In Central Park, 1982; Various compilation albums; Solo albums: Paul Simon, 1972; There Goes Rhymin' Simon, 1973; Live Rhymin': Paul Simon In Concert, 1974; Still Crazy After All These Years, 1975; Greatest Hits Etc, 1977; One-Trick Pony, 1980; Hearts And Bones, 1983; Graceland, 1986; Negotiations and Love Songs, 1988; Rhythm Of The Saints, 1990; Paul Simon's Concert In The Park, 1991; Paul Simon 1964-1993, 1993; Paul Simon - Songs From The Capeman, 1997. Publications: The Songs of Paul Simon, 1972; New Songs, 1975; One-Trick Pony (screenplay), 1980; At The Zoo (for children), 1991. Honours include: Grammy awards: two for The Graduate soundtrack, 1968, six for Bridge Over Troubled Water, 1970, two for Still Crazy After All These Years, 1986, one for Graceland, 1987; Emmy Award, Paul Simon Special, NBC-TV, 1977; Inducted into Rock And Roll Hall Of Fame, with Art Garfunkel, 1990; Antoinette Perry Award, The Capeman, Best Original Score Written For The Theatre 1997-98; Doctorate of Music, Berklee College of Music, 1986; Doctorate of Music, Queens

College, 1995; Doctorate of Music, Yale University, 1996. Address: Paul Simon Music, 1619 Broadway, Suite 500, New York, NY 10019, USA.

SIMONENKO Sergey Victorovich, b. 2 July 1959, Uglekamensk, USSR. Engineer; Physicist. 2 daughters. Education: Engineer-Physicist diploma, Moscow Physical-Technical Institute, 1984; Post-graduate studies, Pacific Oceanological Institute, Vladivostok, 1987-92; PhD, Physical-Mathematical Sciences, USSR, Moscow, 1993. Appointments: Engineer, 1984-87, Junior Research Associate, 1992-94, Research Associate, 1994-96, Senior Scientist, 1996-2000, Pacific Oceanological Institute, Far Eastern Branch of Russian Academy of Sciences, Vladivostok; Leading Scientist, 2000-11, V I Il'ichev Pacific Oceanological Institute, Far Eastern Branch of Russian Academy of Sciences, Vladivostok; Associate Professor, Interchangeability and Quality Control, 2002-08, Pacific State University of Economics, Vladivostok. Publications: Articles: The macroscopic non-equilibrium kinetic energies of a small fluid particle, 2004; Generalization of the classical special formulation of the law of large numbers, 2005; Statistical thermohydrodynamics of irreversible strike-slip-rotational processes, 2007; Monographs: Non-Equilibrium Statistical Thermohydrodynamics, Vol II. Towards The Foundation Of The Theory Of The Non-Equilibrium Dissipative Small-Scale Turbulence And The Tolerance Theory Related With The Quality Control, 2005; Non-Equilibrium Statistical Thermohydrodynamics Of Turbulence, 2006; Non-Equilibrium Statistical Thermohydrodynamics, Foundation Of The Theory Of The Small-Scale Turbulence And The Tolerances Theory, 2006; Thermohydrogravidynamics Of The Solar System, 2007; Thermohydrogravidynamic Evolution Of The Planets And The Tolerances Theory, 2008; Fundamentals Of The Thermohydrogravidynamic Theory Of Cosmic Genesis Of The Planetary Cataclysms, 2009, 2010. Honours: Diploma, Moscow Physical-Technical Institute, 1975; Honorary Diploma, Far Eastern Mathematical Competition, Russia, 1976; Award, Presidium of the Far Eastern Branch of Russian Academy of Sciences, 1989; 2000 Outstanding Intellectuals of the 21st Century, IBC, 2007; Outstanding Scientists of the 21st Century, Inaugural Edition, IBC, 2007; Pinnacle of Achievement Award, IBC, 2007; Cambridge Blue Book, IBC, 2008; Da Vinci Diamond Award, IBC, 2008; Lifetime Achievement Award, IBC, 2008; Honorary Director General, IBC, 2008; Dedication Entry in 2000 Outstanding Intellectuals of the 21st Century, IBC, 2008; Top Two Hundred of the IBC, 2008; Dictionary of International Biography, IBC, 2008; Greatest Intellectuals of the 21st Century, IBC, 2009; Dedication Entry in Great Minds of the 21st Century, ABI, 2009; Gold Medal for Russia, ABI, 2010; The Order of International Ambassadors, ABI, 2009; International Peace Prize, The United Cultural Convention, USA, 2009; Salute to Greatness Award, IBC, 2009; Vice President, Recognition Board, World Congress of Arts, Sciences and Communications, 2009; 2000 Outstanding Scientists 2010; Lifetime Deputy Governor of the ABIRA, ABI, 2009; Inner Circle, IBC, 2009. Memberships: Fiztech Club, Moscow Physical-Technical Institute. Address: V I Il'ichev Pacific Oceanological Institute, Far Eastern Branch of Russian Academy of Sciences, 43 Baltiyskaya St, Vladivostok, 690041, Russia. E-mail: drsergeyvsimonenkohondgibc@yahoo.com Website: www.drsergeyvsimonenkohondgibc.ru

SIMONIA Irakli, b. 22 October 1961, Tbilisi, Georgia. Astrophysicist. m. Tsitsino, 1 son, 1 daughter. Education: MSc, Physics, 1985; PhD, Cometary Astrophysics, 1998. Appointments: Abastumany Astrophysical Observatory, 1988-2008; Associate Professor, School of Graduate Studies, Ilia State University, Tbilisi, Georgia, 2008-; Associate Professor, The Centre for Astronomy, James Cook University, Townsville, Australia, 2009-. Publications: 45 articles and papers in areas of meteoritics, cometary physics, interstellar and circumstellar dust physics and chemistry, cultural astronomy and archaeo-astronomy. Honours: Scholarships of DAAD, Germany, 2001, 2005. Memberships: European Astronomical Society; Astronomy in Culture Societies (European and international); IAU Consultant Commission 41. Address: Vazha-Pshavela av, 14-4, Tbilisi, 0-160, Georgia. E-mail: iraklisimonia@yahoo.com

SIMONS Peter Murray, b. 23 March 1950, Westminster, London, England. Professor. m. Susan Jane Walker, 1 son, 1 daughter. Education: BSc (Hons), Mathematics, 1971, MA, Philosophy, 1973, PhD, Philosophy, 1975, University of Manchester, Manchester, England. Appointments: Assistant Librarian, University of Manchester, 1975-77; Lecturer in Philosophy, Bolton Institute of Technology, Bolton, England, 1977-80; Lecturer in Philosophy, University of Salzburg, Austria, 1980-95; Professor of Philosophy, University of Leeds, Leeds, England, 1995-2009; Chair of Moral Philosophy, Trinity College Dublin, 2009-. Publications include: Parts 1987, 2000; Philosophy and Logic in Central Europe from Bolzano to Tarski, 1992; About 220 articles. Honours: Cultural Prize, City of Salzburg, 1986; Habilitation, University of Salzburg, 1986; Honorary Professor of Philosophy, University of Salzburg, 1996; Fellow of the British Academy, 2004; Member, Academia Europaea, 2006. Memberships include: American Philosophical Association; British Logic Colloquium; Aristotelian Society; Gesellschaft für Analytische Philosophie; Internationale Bernard Bolzano Gesellschaft. Address: Department of Philosophy, Trinity College Dublin, College Green, Dublin 2, Ireland. E-mail: psimons@tcd.ie

SIMPSON Jessica, b. 10 July 1980, Abilene, Texas, USA. Singer; Songwriter; Actress. m. Nick Lachey, 2002, divorced 2006. Career: Singer; Albums: Sweet Kisses, 1999; Irresistable, 2001; In This Skin, 2003; A Public Affair, 2006; Do You Know, 2008; Actress: Films: The Dukes of Hazzard, 2005; Employee of the Month, 2006; Blonde Ambition, 2007; The Love Guru, Private Valentine: Blonde & Dangerous, 2008; TV: Newleyweds: Nick and Jessica, 2003-05; The Price of Beauty, 2010; Numerous TV guest appearances. Honours: Teen Choice Awards, 2004, 2005, 2006; People's Choice Award, 2006.

SIMPSON John Cody Fidler, b. 9 August 1944, Cleveleys, England. Broadcaster; Writer. m. (1) Diane Jean Petteys, 1965, divorced 1995, 2 daughters, (2) Adèle Krüger, 1996. Education: MA, Magdalene College, Cambridge. Appointments: Various positions, BBC, 1966-82; BBC Diplomatic Editor, 1982-88, Foreign, later World Affairs Editor, 1988-; Associate Editor, The Spectator, 1991-95; Columnist, The Sunday Telegraph, 1995-. Publications: The Best of Granta (editor), 1966; Moscow Requiem, 1981; A Fine and Private Place, 1983; The Disappeared: Voices From a Secret War, 1985; Behind Iranian Lines, 1988; Despatches From the Barricades, 1990; From the House of War: Baghdad and the Gulf, 1991; The Darkness Crumbles: The Death of Communism, 1992; In the Forests of the Night: Drug-Running and Terrorism in Peru, 1993; The Oxford Book of Exile (editor), 1995; Lifting the Veil: Life in Revolutionary Iran, 1995; Strange Places, Questionable People (autobiography), 1998; A Mad World, My Masters, 2000; News from No Man's Land: Reporting the World, 2002; The Wars Against Saddam: Taking the Hard Road to Baghdad, 2004; Days From a Different World: A Memoir of Childhood, 2005; Not Quite World's End: A Traveller's Tales, 2007; Twenty Tales from The War Zone, 2007. Honours: Fellow, Royal Geographical Society, 1990; Commander of the Order of the British Empire, 1991; BAFTA Reporter of the Year, 1991, 2001; RTS Richard Dimbleby Award, 1991; Columnist of the Year, National Magazine Awards, 1993; Honorary DLitt, De Montfort University, 1995; RTS Foreign Report Award, 1997; Peabody Award, USA, 1997; Dr hc, Nottingham, 2000; Emmy Award, 2002; Bayeux War Correspondents' Prize, 2002; International Emmy Award, New York, 2002. Address: c/o BBC Television Centre, Wood Lane, London W12 7RJ, England.

SIMPSON O J (Orenthal James), b. 9 July 1947, San Francisco, USA. Former Professional Football Player; Actor; Sports Commentator. m. (1) Marguerite Whitley, 1967, divorced, 1 son, 1 daughter, (2) Nicole Brown, 1985, divorced 1992, deceased 1994, 2 sons. Education: University of Southern California; City College, San Francisco. Appointments: Member, World Record 440 yard relay team (38.6 sec), 1967; Downtown Athletic Club, 1968; Halfback, Buffalo Bills, 1969-75; San Francisco 49'ers, 1978-79; American Football League All-Star team, 1970; ProBowl Team, 1972-76; Sports Commentator, ABC Sports, 1979-86; Analyst, ABC Monday Night Football Broadcasts, 1984-85; co-host, NFL Live on NBC, 1990; Has appeared in several TV films; Acquitted of two charges of murder, 1995; Found responsible for the deaths of Nicole Brown Simpson and Ronald Goldman by civil jury, 1997; Films include: The Towering Inferno, 1974; Killer Force, 1976; The Cassandra Crossing, 1977; Capricorn One, 1978; Firepower, 1979; Hambone and Hillie, 1984; The Naked Gun, 1988; The Naked Gun 2 ½: The Smell of Fear, 1991; The Naked Gun 33 1/3: The Final Insult. Publication: I Want to Tell You, 1995. Honours: Recipient of various football awards.

SIMULIK Volodimir Michaylovich, b. 31 August 1957, Uzhgorod, Transkarpathia region, Ukraine. Physicist; Researcher. m. Ludmila Borisovna Dyachenko, 1988, 1 daughter. Education: Teacher of Physics, Uzhgorod State University, 1981; Candidate of Sciences in Physics and Mathematical Sciences, Kiev State University, Ukraine, 1987; Senior Research Associate, Institute of Electron Physics of Ukrainian National Academy of Sciences, Uzhgorod, 1994; Full Doctoral Sciences in Physics and Mathematical Sciences, Taras Shevchenko National University, Kiev, 2000. Appointments: Postgraduate, Institute of Nuclear Research, Kiev, 1982-84; Senior Research Associate, 1991-2000, Principal Research Associate, 2000-01, 2004-, Institute of Electron Physics, Uzhgorod; Director of Department, Transkarpathia Region, State Administration, Ukraine, 2002-04. Publications: Over 100 scientific papers; 2 books. Memberships: Ukrainian Physical Society. Address: 21 Universitetska Str, Institute of Electron Physics, 88000 Uzhgorod, Ukraine. E-mail: vsimulik@gmail.com

ŠIMUNIĆ Slavko, b. 6 December 1931, Brčko, Bosnia and Herzegovina. Professor. 1 daughter. Education: Medical Faculty, University of Zagreb, 1951-58; Intern, medical centres in Varazdin and Sisak, 1958-59; MD, Anderson Hospital, Cancer Center, Houston, Texas, USA, 1985; Grosshadernklinik, Institute of Radiology, Munich, Germany, 1987; Medical University of South Carolina, USA, 1993; Tulene University, Department of Radiology, New Orleans, USA, 1993. Appointments: Physician, 1959-64, Radiologist, 1967-68, Department of Internal Medicine, Medical Centre, Sisak; Fellowship, 1964-67, Radiologist, Assistant and Research Assistant, 1967-82, Institute of Radiology, University Hospital Centre, Zagreb; Associate Professor, 1982-87, Full Professor, 1987-97, Medical Faculty, University of Zagreb; Full Professor, Head of Chair of Radiology, 1997-2002, Professor Emeritus, 2002, Medical Faculty University, Josip Juraj Strossmamayer, Osijek; Head, Division of Angioradiology, University Hospital Center, Zagreb, 1977-87; Head, Department of Diagnostic and Interventional Radiology, University Hospital Center and Medical Faculty of University of Zagreb, 1987-97; Assistant Director, Medical Affairs, Clinical Hospital Centre, Zagreb, 1991-97; Head, Department of Radiology, University Hospital, Osijek, 1997-2002. Publications: Numerous articles in professional journals. Honours: Acknowledgements and recognition from: School of Medicine, University of Zagreb, 1983, 1984; Croatian Medical Association, Split, 1986; Jankomir Psychiatric Hospital, Zagreb, 1987; Institute for Radiology and Oncology, 1988; University Hospital Center and School of Medicine, Rijeka, 1996; Association of Radiologists of Bosnia and Herzegovina, 1996; University Hospital and School of Medicine, Split, 2002; Croatian Medical Association, 2002, 2006, 2008; many others; Listed in biographical dictionaries. Memberships: Croatian Medical Association Zagreb; Croatian Society of Radiology; European Association of Radiology; Cardiovascular and Interventional Radiological Society of Europe. Address: 21 Šubićeva, 10000 Zagreb, Croatia.

SINCLAIR Andrew Annandale, b. 21 January 1935, Oxford, England. Writer; Historian. m. Sonia Melchett, 25 July 1984, 2 sons. Education: Major Scholar, BA, PhD, Trinity College, Cambridge, 1955-59; Harkness Fellow, Harvard University,1959-61; American Council of Learned Societies Fellow, Stanford University, 1964-65. Appointments: Founding Fellow, Churchill College, 1961-63; Lecturer, University College, London, 1965-67; Publisher, Lorrimer Publishing, 1968-89; Managing Director, Timon Films Limited, 1968-2011; Films: Under Milk Wood, Dylan on Dylan, Sundance Festival, 2003. Publications: The Breaking of Bumbo, 1959; My Friend Judas, 1959; Prohibition: The Era of Excess, 1961; Gog, 1967; Magog, 1972; Jack: A Biography of Jack London, 1977; The Other Victoria, 1981; King Ludd, 1988; War Like a Wasp, 1989; The War Decade: An Anthology of the 1940's, 1989; The Need to Give, 1990; The Far Corners of the Earth, 1991; The Naked Savage, 1991; The Strength of the Hills, 1991; The Sword and the Grail, 1992; Francis Bacon: His Life and Violent Times, 1993; In Love and Anger, 1994; Jerusalem: The Endless Crusade, 1995; Arts and Cultures: The History of the 50 Years of the Arts Council of Great Britain, 1995; The Discovery of the Grail, 1998; Death by Fame: A Life of Elisabeth, Empress of Austria, 1998; Guevara, 1998; Dylan the Bard: A Life of Dylan Thomas, 1999; The Secret Scroll, 2001; Blood and Kin, 2002; An Anatomy of Terror, 2003; Rosslyn, 2005; Viva Che!, 2005; The Grail: The Quest for a Legend, 2007; Man and Horse, 2008; Contributions to: Sunday Times; Times; New York Times; Atlantic Monthly. Honours: Somerset Maugham Prize, 1967; Venice Film Festival Award for Under Milk Wood, 1971; Listed in national and international biographical dictionaries. Memberships: Society of American Historians, fellow 1970; Royal Society of Literature, fellow 1968; Royal Society of Arts, fellow, 2007. Address: Flat 20, Millennium House, 132 Grosvenor Road, London SW1V 3JY, England.

SINCLAIR Sir Clive Marles, b. 30 July 1940, London, England. Inventor; Business Executive. m. Ann Trevor-Briscoe, 1962, divorced 1985, 2 sons, 1 daughter. Education: St George's College, Weybridge. Appointments: Editor, Bernards Publishers Ltd, 1958-61; Chair, Sinclair

Radionics Ltd, 1962-79, Sinclair Research Ltd, 1979-; Sinclair Browne Ltd, 1981-85, Cambridge Computer, 1986-90; Chair, 1980-98, Honorary President, 2001-, British Mensa; Visiting Fellow, Robinson College, Cambridge, 1982-85; Visiting Professor, Imperial College, London, 1984-92; Director, Shaye Communications Ltd, 1986-91, Anamartic Ltd. Publications: Practical Transistor Receivers, 1959; British Semiconductor Survey, 1963. Honours: Hon Fellow, Imperial College, London, 1984; Hon DSc (Bath) 1983, (Warwick, Heriot Watt), 1983, (UMIST) 1984; Royal Society Mullard Award, 1984. Address: Sinclair Research Ltd, Flat A, 1-3 Spring Gardens, Trafalgar Square, London SW1A 2BB, England. Website: www.sinclair-research.co.uk

SINDEN Donald (Sir), b. 9 Oct 1923, Plymouth, Devon, England. Actor; Writer. m. Diana Mahony, 1948, 2 sons. Appointments: Professional Actor, 1942-; Films for the Rank Organisation, 1952-60; Associate Artist, Royal Shakespeare Company, 1967-. Publications: A Touch of the Memoirs, 1982; Laughter in the Second Act, 1985; Everyman Book of Theatrical Anecdotes (editor), 1987; The English Country Church, 1988; The Last Word (editor), 1994. Honour: Commander of the Order of the British Empire, 1979; Knighted, 1997. Memberships: Council of British Actors Equity, 1966-77, trustee, 1988-; Arts Council, Drama Panel, 1973-77, Advisory Board, 1982-86 Federation of Playgoers' Societies, president, 1968-93; Royal Theatrical Fund, president, 1983-; Royal Society of Arts, fellow, 1966-; Green Room Benevolent Fund, president, 1998-. Literary Agent: Vivien Green, Shiel Land, 43 Doughty Street, London WC1N 2LF. Address: Number One, NW11 6AY, England.

SINGER Nicky Margaret, b. 22 July 1956, Chalfont-St-Peter, England. Novelist. m. James King-Smith, 2 sons, 1 daughter. Education: University of Bristol. Appointments: Associate Director of Talks, ICA, 1981-83; Programme Consultant, Enigma Television, 1984-85; Chair, Brighton Festival Literature Committee, 1988-93; Member of Ace Literary Magazines Group, 1993-96; Co-Founder, Co-Director, Performing Arts Labs, 1987-96; Board Member, Printer's Devil, 1993-97; Presenter, BBC2's Labours of Eve, 1994-95; Board Member, South East Arts, 2000-03. Publications: Novels: To Still the Child, 1992; To Have and To Hold, 1993; What She Wanted, 1996; My Mother's Daughter, 1998. Non-Fiction: The Tiny Book of Time (with Kim Pickin), 1999; The Little Book of the Millennium (with Jackie Singer), 1999; Children's Fiction: Feather Boy, 2002, adapted for TV, 2004, adapted as a musical, National Theatre, 2006; Doll, 2003; The Innocent's Story, 2005; GemX, 2006; Knight Crew, 2009 (adapted for opera, Glyndebourne, 2010); The Flask, 2012; Theatre: Heartland (collaboration with Scarabeus Aerial Theatre and Candoco Dance Company), 2011. Honours: Winner, Blue Peter Book of the Year Award (Feather Boy), 2002; Winner, BAFTA Best Drama (Feather Boy), 2004); Shortlisted, Book Trust Teenage Prize (Doll), 2003. Address: c/o Conville and Walsh, 2 Ganton Street, London WIF 7QL, England.

SINGH Arjun, b. 15 June 1978, Antiyan Ka Pura, Madhya Pradesh, India. Doctor. m. Vidhyavati, 1 son, 1 daughter. Education: MBBS, MD. Appointments: Resident, G R Medical College, Gwalior, 2003-06; Assistant Professor, SLIMS, Pondicherry, 2006-08; Assistant Professor, SVMC&RC, Pondicherry, 2008-10; Associate Professor, IMCH&RC, Indore, 2011-. Publications: Numerous articles in professional journals. Honours: Paper presented at conference, Student performance and their perception of a patient-oriented problem-solving approach with audiovisual aids in teaching pathology: a comparison with traditional lectures, Vienna, 2011. Memberships: Association for Medical Education in Europe, UK. Address: HIG 1091, New Darpan Colony, Thatipur, Morar, Gwalior, MP, India. E-mail: dr_arjun12@yahoo.co.in

SINGH Hambir, b. 1 March 1963, Tapakhurd, Firozabad, UP, India. FM(SG). m. Sucheta, 2 sons, 1 daughter. Education: MSc, Physics; Computational Physics Certificate, MSW; Research work on Superconductivity, 2 years. Appointments: Chemical Engineer, Production Department, National Fertilizers Ltd, Vijaipur Unit, Guna. Publications: More than 20 publications in the field of energy efficiency, environmental issues and superconductivity. Memberships: Fellow, Society for Sciences; Fellow, Society of Environmental Sciences; Fellow, International Society for Ecological Communications; Member, Executive Council, National Environmental Science Academy, New Delhi. Address: B-253, National Fertilizers Ltd, Township, Vijaipur Unit, Guna (MP) 473111, India.

SINGH Hazara, b. 30 November 1922, Sheikhupura, India (now Pakistan). Retired University Teacher; Writer. m. Phool Kaur (deceased), 2 sons, 2 daughters. Education: BA, Punjab University, Lahore, 1945; MA, 1950, LLB, 1955, Punjab University, Chandigarh. Appointments: Lecturer of English, Khalsa College, Amritsar, 1950-53; Assistant Professor of English, Government Agricultural College, Ludhiana, 1954-66; Associate Professor of English, 1966-84, Head, Department of Languages and Journalism, 1977-82, Punjab Agricultural University, Ludhiana; Secretary to Vice-Chancellor, Guru Nanak Dev University, Amritsar, 1985-88; Versatile writer in English, Urdu and Punjabi; Participated in freedom struggle against Imperialism, jailed three times, scholarship confiscated and medal withdrawn; Migrated to India. Publications: Contributions to professional journals; Manuals for Researchers; Books in English: Poetry: Aspirations, 1981; Yearnings, 1987; Expectations, 1999; Destination, 2007; Prose: Sikhism and it's Impact on Indian Society, 1969, 1999; Lala Lajpat Rai – An Appraisal, 2003; Happy Meaningful Life, 2004, 2009; Freedom Struggle against Imperialism, 2007; Apostle of Non-Violence, 2007; Seasonal Festivals and Commemorative Days, 2010. Honours: Rattigan Gold Medal, Khalsa College, Amritsar, 1945; Tamra Patra for meritorious contribution to freedom struggle, during Silver Jubilee of Independence 1972, Government of India; Honorary degree of Doctor of Literature by the World Academy of Arts and Culture in the World Congress of Poets, Taipei, Taiwan, 2010. Memberships: Punjabi Sahitya Academy, Ludhiana; World Academy of Arts and Culture, USA; International Association of Poets, Essayists and Novelists; Guild of Indian English Writers, Editors and Critics, GIEWEC. Listed in various international biographical directories. Address: 3-C Udham Singh Nagar, Ludhiana 141001, India. Website: www.hazarasingh.com

SINGH Jaikaran, b. 16 April 1981, Etawah, India. m. Supriya, 1 daughter. Education: MSc, 2002; M Tech, 2005; PhD, in progress. Appointments: Lecturer, 2003-. Honours: M Tech with honours. Address: E-58 Siddharth Lake City, Raisen Road, Patel Nagar, Bhopal, India. E-mail: jksingh81@gmail.com

SINGH Kartar, b. 15 November 1918, Amritsar, India. Dental Surgeon. m. Narindar, 1 son, 1 daughter. Education: Bachelor, Dental Surgery, de Montmorency College of Dentistry, Lahore, India. Appointments: Dental Officer, 8th Army, World War II, Burma and Thailand; Member & Chairman, Dental Health Advisory Committee, ICMR, 1962-70; Head, Indian Armed Forces Dental Services, 1950-71; Member

& Consultant, Dental Health Advisory Committee, WHO, 1967-75; Honorary Dental Surgeon, Jaswant Kaur Charitable Dental Clinic. Publications: Maxilo Facial Surgery, 1941. Honours: Honorary Dental Surgeon to President of India, 1962-72; Param Vishisht Seva Medal, Distinguished Service of the Most Exceptional Order, 1970. Memberships: Honorary Member, Indian Dental Association, 1984; Honorary Fellow: International College of Dentists; Pierre Fauchard Academy; Academy Dentistry International. Address: 596 Sector 6, Panchkula, Haryana, PIN 134109, India.

SINGH Malvinder, b. 11 December 1951, Roorkee, Uttrakhand, India. Engineer. m. Manjeet Kaur, 1 son. Education: Master of Engineering, Mechanical Engineering, University of Roorkee, 1980. Appointments: Junior Executive, 1978-81, Engineer, 1981-85, Senior Engineer, 1985-89, Quality Control, Deputy Manager, 1989-92, Manager, 1992-97, Senior Manager, 1997-99, Deputy General Manager, 2007-08, Senior Deputy General Manager, 2008-, Heavy Electrical Equipment Plant, Bharat Heavy Electrical Ltd (BHEL), Haridwar – 249403, Uttrakhand, India; Senior Deputy General Manager, 2008-10; Additional General Manager, Heavy Electrical Equipment Plant, 2010; Bharat Heavy Electrical Ltd, Haridwar. Publications: Numerous articles in professional journals. Honours: Chartered Engineer, Institution of Engineers, India; Man of Achievement Award, 2000; Millennium Achiever Award, 2001; Bharat Excellence Award; Rashtriya Gaurav Award; Jewel of India Award; Rashtriya Udyog Ratan Award; Universal Award of Accomplishment, 2008; Man of the Year Award, 2008; Gold Medal for India, ABI; Charter Fellow, ABI; Quality Award, Institution of Engineers, India; Listed in international biographical dictionaries. Memberships: Institution of Engineers, India; Indian Institute of Welding Kolkata, India; American Welding Society, USA; Institute of Directors, New Delhi, India; National Centre for Quality Management Mumbai, India; All India Management Association, New Delhi, India; Indian Institute of Material Management (India); Computer Society of India; Quality Circle Forum of India; Indian Society of Manufacturing Engineers (India); American Society for Quality, USA. Address: Heep Bhel, Haridwar – 249403, Uttrakhand, India. E-mail: malvin@bhelhwr.co.in

SINGH Raj Kumar Prasad, b. 2 July 1947, Sheotar, Bihar, India. Metallurgical Engineer. m. Chintamani, 1 son, 1 daughter. Education: BSc, Engineering, Bihar Institute of Technology, Sindri, 1970; M Tech, Indian Institute of Technology, Bombay, 1975; PhD, Indian Institute of Technology, Madras, 1994. Appointments: Deputy Manager, Bokard Steel Plant, SAIL, 1972-79; Assistant General Manager, Research and Development Centre for Iron and Steel, Steel Authority of India, 1980-94; General Manager, Quality Control, Research and Development, Lloyds Steel Industries Ltd, 1994-99; Professor, VNIT, Nagpur, 2000-2003; Director General, Institute for Steel Development and Growth, 2003-09; Presently, Director, Kalyani Centre for Technology & Innovation. Publications: Over 50 national and international publications, including, EDD Quality Steels Al-Deoxidation Techniques; Sulphide Shape Control in HSLA Steels; Combined Blowing of Converters; Failure Analysis. Honours: Listed in several international biographical directories. Memberships: Life Fellow, Indian Institute of Metals; Life Member, Indian Society of Non-Destructive Testing. Address: Kalyani Centre for Technology & Innovation, Bharat Forge Ltd, Sur. No-15 Near Renuka Mata Mandir, Keshavnagar, Pune 411006, India. E-mail: rkpsingh@hotmail.com

SINGHAL Bhim Sen, b. 23 January 1933, Mount Abu, Rajasthan, India. Neurologist. m. Dr Asha Gupta, 1962, 1 son, 1 daughter. Education: MD, Bombay University, 1956. Appointments: Neurologist, Bombay Hospital, 1962-; Professor & Head, Department of Neurology, Grant Medical College and Sir J J Group of Hospitals, 1983-91; Neurologist, Sir J J Group of Hospitals, 1983-91; Professor & Head, Department of Neurology, 1991-2009; Director, Neurology, Bombay Hospital Institute of Medical Science, Mumbai, 2009-. Publications: Over 300 in national and international journals; Book chapters. Honours: Giants International Award for Excellence in Medicine, 1983; Karmayogi Puruskar Award, 1990; Rajasthan Ratna Award, for Service in Field of Medicine, 1993; Dr B C Roy National Award for Development of Neurology in India, 1999; Priya Darshini Academy National Award, 2004; Wockhardt Ward for Medical Excellence in Neurology, 2005; Dhanvantri Award, 2009. Memberships: American Academy of Neurology; American Neurology Association; Fellow, Royal College of Physicians; Honorary Member, French Neurological Society; Honorary Member, Association of British Neurologists. Address: Bombay Hospital Institute of Medical Sciences, 12 Marine Lines, Mumbai 400 020, India.

SINGLETON Valerie, b. 9 April 1937, England. Education: Arts Educational School London, RADA. Appointments: Broadcast Personality and Writer; Bromley Rep, 1956-57, subsequently, No 1 Tour, Cambridge Arts Theatre, Theatre work, TV appearances, Compact and Emergency Ward 10 and others, top voice over commentator for TV commercials and advertising magazines; BBC 1: Continuity Announcer, 1962-64, Presenter, Blue Peter, 1962-72, Nationwide, 1972-78, Val Meets the VIPs (3 series), Blue Peter Special Assignment (4 series), Blue Peter Royal Safari with HRH The Princess Anne, Tonight and Tonight in Town, 1978-79, Blue Peter Special Assignments Rivers Yukon and Niagara, 1980; BBC 2: Echoes of Holocaust, 1979, The Migrant Workers of Europe, 1980, The Money Programme, 1980-88; Radio 4: PM 1981-93, several appearances Midweek; Freelance Broadcaster and Travel Writer, 1993-; Channel 4: Presenter, Back-Date (daily quiz programme), 1996; Playback, History Channel, 1998, second series, 1999; Numerous appearances in TV advertising. Honour: OBE. Membership: Equity. Address: c/o Arlington Enterprises, 1-3 Charlotte Street, London W1, England.

SISSONS Peter George, b. 17 July 1942. Television Presenter. m. Sylvia Bennett, 1965, 2 sons, 1 daughter. Education: University College Oxford. Appointments: Graduate Trainee, ITN, 1964, General Reporter, 1967, Industrial Correspondent, 1970, Industrial Editor, 1972-78, Presenter, News at One, 1978-82; Presenter, Channel 4 News, 1982-89; Presenter, 6 O'Clock News, 1989-93, 9 O'Clock News, 1994-2000, 10 O'Clock News, 2000-03, News 24, 2003-, BBC TV News; Chair, BBC TV Question Time, 1989-93. Honours: Broadcasting Press Guild Award, 1984; Royal TV Society Judges' Award, 1988; Honorary Fellow, Liverpool John Moores University, 1997; Hon LLD, University of Liverpool, 2002. Address: BBC Television Centre, Wood Lane, London, W12 7RJ, England.

SIVAVAKEESAR Sivapathaingham, b. 13 December 1973, Jaffna, Sri Lanka. Senior Researcher. m. Gayathiri, 1 daughter. Education: BSc, University of Moratuwa, Sri Lanka, 1999; MSc, 2001; PhD, 2005, University of Surrey, Guildford, England. Appointments: Centre for Communication Systems Research, University of Surrey; Multiple Access Communications Ltd, Southampton; SHARP Telecommunications of Europe Ltd, Bracknell.

Publications: Numerous articles in professional journals. Honours: Motorola Award, University of Surrey, 2006; CCSR Overseas Research Scholarship, 2001; Cable & Wireless Award, 2001; Mahapola Scholarship; Academic Excellence. Memberships: IEEE Member. Address: 176A Norreys Avenue, Wokingham, Berkshire RG40 1UH, England. E-mail: s.sivavakeesar@googlemail.com

SIZOV Anatoly Alexandrovich, b. 24 November 1934, Zhukovsky, Moscow region, Russia. Hydrometeorologist. m. Ludmila Sergeevna Nikandrova, 1 son. Education: Degree, Engineering and Oceanology, Highest Marine Engineering School, Leningrad, 1957; PhD, Geophysics, Marine Hydrophysical Institute, Sevastopol, Ukraine, 1970. Appointments: Engineer, 1957-61, Junior Scientist, 1961-63, Marine Hydrophysical Institute, Moscow; Junior Scientist, 1963-71, Senior Scientist, 1971-, Marine Hydrophysical Institute, Sevastopol. Publications: 110 articles on ocean-atmosphere interaction and regional climate change. Honours: Medal, Ukrainian Academy of Sciences, Kiev, 1998; Honorary Diploma, Ukrainian Academy of Sciences, Kiev, 1999, 2004, 2009. Memberships: Chief, Museum of Marine Hydrophysical Institute, 2004-. E-mail: svk@alpha.mhi.iuf.net

SKÁRMETA Antonio, b. 7 November 1940, Antofagasta, Chile. Writer. Education: Graduated, University of Chile, 1963; MA, Columbia University, 1966. Appointments: Ambassador to Germany, 2000-01. Publications: El entusiasmo, 1967; Desnudo en el tejado, 1969; El ciclista del San Cristóbal, 1973; Tiro libre, 1973; Soñé que la nieve ardía, 1975, English translation as I Dreamt the Snow Was Burning, 1985; Novios y solitarios, 1975; La insurrección, 1980, English translation as The Insurrection, 1983; No pasó nada, 1980; Ardiente paciencia, 1985, English translation as Burning Patience, 1987; Match Ball, 1989; Watch Where the Wolf is Going, 1991; La boda del trombón, 2001; El baile de la victoria, 2003. Contributions to: Periodicals. Honours: Premio Casa de las Américas, 1969; Guggenheim Fellowship, 1986; Academy Award Nomination, 1996. Address: Chilean Embassy, 53173 Bonn, Kronprinzenstr 20, Germany.

SKARSGÅRD J Stellan, b. 13 June 1951, Goteborg, Sweden. Actor. m. (1) My Gunther, 1976, (divorced) 5 sons, 1 daughter; (2) Megan Everett, 2009, 1 son. Appointments: With Royal Dramatic Theatre, Stockholm, 1972-87; Films Include: Simple Minded Murderer, 1982; Serpent's Way, 1986; Hip Hip Hurrah, 1987; The Unbearable Lightness of Being, 1988; Good Evening Mr Wallenberg, 1990; The Ox, Wind, 1992; The Slingshot, 1993; Zero Kelvin, 1994; Breaking the Waves, 1995; Insomnia, Amistad, Good Will Hunting, 1997; Ronin, Deep Blue Sea, 1998; Passion of Mind, 1999; Kiss Kiss (Bang Bang), Signs & Wonders, Timecode, Dancer in the Dark, Aberdeen (also associate producer), 2000; The Hire: Powder Keg, Taking Sides, 2001; The House on Turk Street, City of Ghosts, 2002; Dogville, 2003; King Arthur, Eiffeltornet, Exorcist: The Beginning, 2004; Torte Bluma, 3 & 3, 2005; Pirates of the Caribbean: Dead Man's Chest, Goya's Ghosts, 2006; Pirates of the Caribbean: At World's End, 2007; Boogie Woogie, God on Trial, Mamma Mia, 2008; Angels and Demons, 2009 For TV, Hamlet, 1984; Harlan County War, 2000; Helen of Troy, 2003. Honours: Best Actor, Berlin Film Festival, 1982; Twice Best Film Actor in Sweden; Best Actor, Rouen Film Festival, 1988, 1992; Best Actor, Chicago Film Festival, 1991; Jury's Special Prize, San Sebastian Film Festival, 1995; European Film Award.

SKIFF Warner Mason, b. 11 December 1955, Oxnard, California, USA. Physical Chemist. Education: BA, Chemistry, 1977, PhD, Chemistry, 1985, Arizona State University. Appointments: Research Associate, Centre for Solid State Science, Arizona State University, 1985-88; Senior Research Chemist, Shell Oil Company, Houston, Texas, 1988-99; Assistant Professor, University of Alaska, Fairbanks, 1999-2004; Vice President, General Molecular Inc, Fort Collins, Colorado, USA, 1999-. Publications: About a dozen articles; Research contributions: Electron energy loss spectroscopy, force field development and application, theoretical catalysis. Honours: Burton Medal, Microscopy Society of America; Visiting Scientist, Shell Research and Technology Centre, Amsterdam, The Netherlands. Address: 3644 E Van Buren St, #10, Phoenix, AZ 85008, USA.

SKINNER Verna Edna, b. 5 May 1936, Gympie, Queensland, Australia. Commissioner, Salvation Army. Education: Diploma, Salvation Army Ministry and Theology, Salvation Army Training College; Certificate of Management Sales; Certificate in Public Relations; Certificate in Accounting; Certificate in Leadership; Marriage Celebrant; Justice of the Peace. Appointments: with The Salvation Army: Assistant Corps Officer, Charters Towers, Queensland, 1957; Assistant Corps Officer, Garbutt, Queensland, 1958; Corps Officer, Mount Morgan, Queensland, 1958-59; Training Officer, Training College, Sydney, 1960; Corps Officer, Gunnedah, NSW, 1961-64; Corps Officer, Ballina, NSW, 1965; Divisional Youth Secretary, Sydney West, 1965; Public Relations Secretary, East Africa, Kenya, Tanzania and Uganda, 1966-76; Public Relations Secretary, Hong Kong and Taiwan, 1976-80; Under Secretary for Public Relations, International Headquarters and Great Britain, London, England, 1980-85; Under Secretary for Africa, International Headquarters, London, 1986-88; Chief Secretary, Sri Lanka, 1988-92; Assistant Recorder, 12th High Council, London, 1993; Committee Chairman, 13th High Council, London, 1994; Territorial Commander, Sri Lanka, 1992-96; Chief Secretary, Australia Southern Territory, 1996-97; Vice President, 14th High Council, London, 1999; International Secretary for Development and Resources, International Headquarters, London, 1998-2000; Territorial Commander, Kenya and Uganda, 2000-02; Acting Territorial Commander, Ghana, 2003; ACEO, The Salvation Army Employment Plus (National), 2003-05; Acting Regional Commander, Taiwan, 2008; Administration and Leadership Consultant, Hong Kong and Macau Command, 2009-11; with Sydney Airport Corporation Limited: Volunteer Chaplain, 2006-11. Publications: Numerous contributions to global Salvation Army publications. Honours: Long Service Order, The Salvation Army Australia, 45 Years Service; Nominated for Senior Australian of the Year, 2009; Listed in international biographical dictionaries. Memberships: International Public Relations Association; Institute of Public Relations, London, England; Charity Fundraising Managers, London, England. Address: Villa 6, 8-12 Tuffy Avenue, Sans Souci 2219, NSW, Australia. E-mail: vernaski@hotmail.com

SKOROBOGATOV German, b. 10 January 1937, Datsan Cheata Region, Siberia. Physics-Chemistry Educator. m. Eugeniaja Nadeoshkeana, 2 daughters. Education: Magister, 1959, PhD, 1967, Department of Chemistry, Leningrad State University; Professor of Chemistry, St Petersburg State University, 1996. Appointments: Researcher, Institute of Silicate Chemistry, 1960-61; Researcher, Department of Physics, 1966-67, Chief of Photochemistry Laboratory, Department of Chemistry, 1968-2011, Professor, Department of Chemistry, 1984-2011, St Petersburg (Leningrad) State

University. Publications: Co-author, book: Radiochemistry and Chemistry of Nuclear Reactions, 1960; Orthodoxical and Paradoxical Chemistry, 1985; Theoretical Chemistry, 2000, 2nd edition, 2005; Take Care! Tap Water!, 2003; Foundations of Theoretical Chemistry, 2003; Kinetics and Catalysis of homogeneous Reactions, 2008; Karelian shoongites, 2008; Synthetic perovskite-like layered oxides, 2009; Scientists are discussing: how to reach 100 years, 2009; Articles in professional journals. Honours: Research Fellow, Coin, ABI, Bronze edition, 1993, Silver edition, 1996; Listed in national and international biographical dictionaries. Memberships: Mendeleev's Chemical Society (Moscow), 1975-2011; American Mathematical Society, 1988-98; Planetary Society, 1992-99. Address: Department of Chemistry, St Petersburg State University, Universitetskii prosp 26, 198504 St Petersburg, Russia. E-mail: skorgera@mail.ru Website: www.antiglobalism.ru

SKRZYPCZYNSKA Małgorzata Cecylia, b. 26 December 1940, Wadowice, Poland. Professor. m. Andrzej, 1 daughter. Education: MA, Faculty of Biology and Earth Science, Jagiellonian University, Kraków, 1958-63; Dr of Forest Sciences, 1971, Dr Sc, 1979, Professor Dr Sc, Forest Entomology, 1994, Agricultural University of Kraków. Appointments: Assistant, 1964-71, Adjunct Professor, 1971-79, Assistant Professor, 1979-94, Professor, 1994-, Agricultural University of Kraków. Publications include: 304 publications including 168 monographs, studies and dissertations; 4 books, 1 with Professor J Křistek and 2 with Professor J R Starzyk (Ed) et al; Numerous articles in magazines and journals dealing with forest entomology with particular reference to seed insect pests of conifers and zoocecidology/plant galls; Participated at 14 international congresses and meetings in Europe, USA and Asia. Honours: Stypendist, Czechoslovak Academy of Science, 1974; Stipendist, University of Bodenkultur, Vienna, Austria, 1979, 1981; Złoty Krzyż Zasługi, 1986; Krzyż Kawalerski Orderu Odrodzenia Polski, 2000; Medal Komisji Edukacji Narodowej, 2006; Diploma of the Polish Academy of Sciences, 2004. Memberships: Deputy, Working Party IUFRO, 1992-; Polish Entomological Society; Polish Forest Society. Address: Agricultural University of Kraków, Department of Forest Entomology, 31-425 Kraków, Al 29 Listopada 46, Poland. E-mail: rlwaga@cyf-kr.edu.pl

SLATER Christian, b. 18 August 1969, New York, USA. m. Ryan Haddan, 2000, divorced 2007, 1 son, 1 daughter. Actor. Appointments: Appeared at age of seven in TV series One Life to Live; Professional stage debut at age of nine in touring production of The Music Man; Stage appearances include: Macbeth; David Copperfield; Merlin; Landscape of the Body; Side Man; One Flew Over the Cuckoo's Nest, 2004-05; The Glass Menagerie, 2005; TV: Sherlock Holmes, 1981; Living Proof: The Hank Williams Jr Story, The Haunted Mansion Mystery, 1983; Ryan's Hope, 1985; Secrets, 1986; Desperate for Love, 1989; Merry Christmas, George Bailey, 1997; Prehistoric Planet, 2002; The West Wing, 2003, 2004; My Name is Earl, 2006; My Own Worst Enemy, 2008; Un-broke: What You Need to Know About Money, The Forgotten, Curb Your Enthusiasm, 2009; The Office, 2010; Breaking In, 2011-12; Entourage, 2011; Phineas and Ferb, 2012; Films: The Legend of Billie Jean, 1985; The Name of the Rose, Twisted, 1986; Tucker: The Man and his Dream, 1988; Gleaming the Cube, Heathers, Beyond the Stars, The Wizard, 1989; Tales from the Darkside: The Movie; Young Guns II: Blaze of Glory, Pump Up the Volume, 1990; Robin Hood: Prince of Thieves, Star Trek: The Undiscovered Country, 1991; Kuffs, Ferngully: The Last Rainforest, Where the Day Takes You, 1992; Untamed Heart, True Romance, 1993; Jimmy Hollywood, Interview with a Vampire, 1994; Murder in the First, 1995; Bed of Roses, Broken Arrow, 1996; Austin Powers: International Man of Mystery, Julian Po, 1997; Hard Rain (also producer), Basil (also co-producer), Very Bad Things (producer), 1998; Love Stinks, 1999; The Contender, 2000; 3000 Miles to Graceland, Who is Cletis Tout? 2001; Run for the Money, Windtalkers, 2002; Masked and Anonymous, 2003; The Good Shepherd, Mindhunters, Churchill: The Hollywood Years, Pursued, 2004; Alone in the Dark, The Deal, 2005; Bobby, 2006; Slipstream, He Was a Quiet Man, 2007; Love Lies Bleeding, Igor, 2008; Dolan's Cadillac, Lies & Illusions, 2009; Sacrifice, Soldiers of Fortune, The River Murders, Guns, Girls and Gambling, 2011; Playback, El Gringo, Dawn Rider, Rites of Passage, 2012; Bullet to the Head, The Power of Few, 2013. Honours: MTV Movie Award, 1993; Golden Slate, 1998; Broadcast Film Critics Association Award, 2001; Theatregoers' Choice Award for Best Actor, 2005. Address: c/o CAA, 9830 Wilshire Boulevard, Beverly Hills, CA 90212, USA.

SLAVITT David R(ytman), (David Benjamin, Henry Lazarus, Lynn Meyer, Henry Sutton), b. 23 March 1935, White Plains, New York, USA. Novelist; Poet; Translator; Lecturer. m. (1) Lynn Nita Meyer, 27 August 1956, divorced 1977, 2 sons, 1 daughter, (2) Janet Lee Abrahm, 16 April 1978. Education: BA, magna cum laude, Yale University, 1956; MA, Columbia University, 1957. Appointments: Instructor in English, Georgia Institute of Technology, Atlanta, 1957-58; Staff, Newsweek magazine, 1958-65; Assistant Professor, University of Maryland, College Park, 1977; Associate Professor of English, Temple University, Philadelphia, 1978-80; Lecturer in English and Comparative Literature, Columbia University, 1985-86; Lecturer, Rutgers University, 1987-; Lecturer in English and Classics, University of Pennsylvania, 1991-97; Faculty Member, Bennington College, 2000-; Visiting Professorships; Many university and college poetry readings. Publications: Novels: Rochelle, or Virtue Rewarded, 1966; Anagrams, 1970; ABCD, 1972; The Outer Mongolian, 1973; The Killing of the King, 1974; King of Hearts, 1976; Jo Stern, 1978; Cold Comfort, 1980; Alice at 80, 1984; The Agent, 1986; The Hussar, 1987; Salazar Blinks, 1988; Lives of the Saints, 1989; Turkish Delights, 1993; The Cliff, 1994; Get Thee to a Nunnery: Two Divertimentos from Shakespeare, 1999. Henry Sutton: The Exhibitionist, 1967; The Voyeur, 1969; Vector, 1970; The Liberated, 1973; The Sacrifice: A Novel of the Occult, 1978; The Proposal, 1980. As Lynn Meyer: Paperback Thriller, 1975. As Henry Lazarus: That Golden Woman, 1976. As David Benjamin: The Idol, 1979. Non-Fiction: Understanding Social Life: An Introduction to Social Psychology (with Paul F Secord and Carl W Backman), 1976; Physicians Observed, 1987; Virgil, 1991; The Persians of Aeschylus, 1998; Three Amusements of Ausonius, 1998; Re-Verse: Essays on Poets and Poetry, 2005. Other: Editor: Adrien Stoutenburg: Land of Superior Mirages: New and Selected Poems, 1986; Short Stories Are Not Real Life: Short Fiction, 1991; Crossroads, 1994; A Gift, 1996; Epigram and Epic: Two Elizabethan Entertainments, 1997; A New Pleade: Seven American Poets, 1998. Translator: The Eclogues of Virgil, 1971; The Eclogues and the Georgics of Virgil, 1972; The Tristia of Ovid, 1985; Ovid's Poetry of Exile, 1990; Seneca: The Tragedies, 1992; The Fables of Avianus, 1993; The Metamorphoses of Ovid, 1994; The Twelve Minor Prophets, 1999; The Voyage of the Argo of Valerius Flaccus, 1999; Sonnets of Love and Death of Jean de Spande, 2001; The Elegies of Propertius, 2001; The Poetry of Manuel Bandeira, 2002; The Regrets of Joachim du Bellay, 2004; The Phoenix and Other Translations, 2004;

Contributions to: Various other books as well as periodicals. Honours: Pennsylvania Council on the Arts Award, 1985; National Endowment for the Arts Fellowship, 1988; American Academy and Institute of Arts and Letters Award, 1989; Rockefeller Foundation Artist's Residence, 1989. Address: 523 South 41st Street, Philadelphia, PA 19104, USA.

SLEEP Wayne, b. 17 July 1948, Plymouth, England. Dancer; Actor; Choreographer. Education: Royal Ballet School (Leverhulme Scholar). Appointments: Joined Royal Ballet, 1966; Soloist, 1970; Principal, 1973; Roles in: Giselle; Dancers at a Gathering; The Nutcracker; Romeo and Juliet; The Grand Tour; Elite Syncopations; Swan Lake; The Four Seasons; Les Patineurs; Petroushka (title role); Cinderella; The Dream; Pineapple Poll; Mam'zelle Angot; 4th Symphony; La Fille Mal Gardee; A Month in the Country; A Good Night's Sleep; Coppelia; Also roles in operas: A Midsummer Nights Dream; Aida; Theatre Roles: Ariel in the Tempest; title role in Pinocchio; Genie in Aladdin; Soldier in The Soldiers Tale; Truffaldino in the Servant of Two Masters; Mr Mistoffelees in Cats; Choreography and lead role, The Point; co-starred in Song and Dance, 1982, 1990; Cabaret, 1986; formed own company, DASH, 1980; Dancer and Joint Choreographer, Bits and Pieces, 1989; Film: The Virgin Soldiers; The First Great Train Robbery; The Tales of Beatrix Potter; Numerous TV appearances include: Series, The Hot Summer Show, 1983; I'm a Celebrity Get Me Out of Here! 2003; Ant and Dec's Saturday Night Takeaway, 2008. Publications: Variations on Wayne Sleep, 1983; Precious Little Sleep, 1996. Honours: Show Business Personality of the Year, 1983. Address: c/o Nick Thomas Artists, Event House, Queen Margaret's Road, Scarborough, YO11 2SA, England.

SLOANE J P, b. 6 September 1942, Hollywood, California, USA. TV producer; Author; Entertainer; Biblical Scholar. Education: Purdue University, Department of Television Communications Certification, 1981; Oral Roberts University Institute of Charismatic Studies, 1985; Institute of Jewish-Christian Studies, 1992; Moody Bible Institute, 1998; IBEX Campus in Israel (The Master's College extension): Jewish Thought and Culture; Cultures and Religions of the Mideast; Physical Geography of Israel; Archaeology, 2001; BA summa cum laude, The Master's College, 2003; MABC, The Master's College, 2005; Doctor of Religious Studies, Trinity Theological Seminary, in progress; National Deans List Publication, Biographical Listing, 1998, 1999, 2000; Life Member, The National Scholars Honor Society. Appointments: Official mascot, The Flying Tigers, during WWII; TV appearances: Guest (age 5), Art Linkletter's House Party, CBS Radio Network; Played Billy Kettle, Ma and Pa Kettle movie series, Universal Studios; Appeared on: Lash La Rue Comic Books; Memory Lane TV show, Hollywood; PTL Club; Lester Sumrall Today; World Harvest; The 700 Club; Richard Roberts Live; Praise the Lord (TBN) More; Recorded High on a Mountain, 1960; Recorded Linda Darling, 1960; Lead singer, The Bros Grim, 1962-64; Featured act with Charlie Rich, 1968-69; Lead singer, JP Sloane and Co, 1973-78; Accomplished musican: Plays over 12 instruments and sings in 5 languages; Albums include: Solid Gold; TV and Radio Producer. Publications: Co-author, with Shannon Sloane, You Can Be a Virgin Again; A Christian Counselor's Guide for Restoring Virginity. Honours: CLEO Award Nominee, 1980; Angel Award for Outstanding TV Producer, 1997; Outstanding Male Vocalist; Outstanding Music Video; Medal of Merit, President Ronald Reagan; Honorary Sheriff, Los Angeles County; Honorary Kentucky Colonel; Honorary Lieutenant Govenor, State of Indiana; Honorary Citizen, Tulsa; 22nd International Angel Award, Best Multiple Character Voices, 1999; Numerous others; Key to cities of Nashville, New Orleans and Monticello; Appeared in Smithsonian and Millennium edition, Who's Who in the World and Who's Who in America and the World, 2001; 2000 Outstanding Intellectuals of the 21st Century; Excellence in Media Publication Winner (for You Can Be a Virgin Again), 2007; Angel Award (for radio programme What In The World!), 2008. Memberships: Life Member, The National Scholars Honor Society. Address: Ste 407, 2219 E Thousand Oaks Blvd, Thousand Oaks, CA 91362-2930, USA.

SLUSARSKI Ludomir Lucjan, b. 29 September 1931, Konstantynow, Poland. Scientist. m. Barbara, 1 daughter. Education: MSc, 1955; PhD, 1963; DSc, 1987; Professor, 1990. Appointments: Assistant, 1954, Director, 1989-2001, Institute of Polymers, Technical University of Lodz; Committee of Research, 1997-2000; European Access Network, 1994-2001; Council of Science, 2005-08; Textile Institute, 2008-; Technical University of Lodz, 2009-. Publications: 11 monographs and chapters in monographs; 215 articles and papers; 22 patents. Honours: Honorary Distinction of the Town of Lodz; Officer, Cross of the Order of Poland Renaissance; Medal of National Education. Memberships: American Chemical Society; Materials Science Committee; Engineering Academy in Poland. Address: Grodzienska 4/8 fl 102, 94-016 Lodz, Poland. E-mail: ludomir.slusarski@p.lodz.pl

SMALLMAN Raymond Edward, b. 4 August 1929, Wolverhampton, England. m. Joan Doreen Faulkner, 1952, 1 son, 1 daughter. Education: BSc, 1950, PhD, 1953, DSc, 1968, University of Birmingham; DSc (Hon), University of Wales, 1990, University of Novi Sad, Yugoslavia, 1990, Cranfield University, England, 2001. Appointments: Chartered Engineer, Scientific Officer, 1953-55, Senior Scientific Officer, 1955-58, Atomic Energy Research Est, Harwell, England; Lecturer, 1958-63, Senior Lecturer, 1963-65, Professor of Physical Metallurgy, 1964-69, Feeney Professor of Metallurgy and Materials Science, Head of Department, 1969-93, Dean of Faculty of Science & Engineering, Dean of Engineering, 1984-85, 1985-87, Vice Principal, 1987-92, Professor of Metallurgy and Materials Science, 1993-2000, Professor Emeritus, Metallurgy & Materials Science, 2000-, University of Birmingham. Publications: Modern Physical Metallurgy, 1962, 1985; Modern Metallography, 1966; Structure of Metals and Alloys, 1969; Defect Analysis in Electron Microscopy, 1975; Vacancies 76, Metals and Materials; Science, Processes, Applications, 1995; Modern Physical Metallurgy and Materials Engineering, 1999; Physical Metallurgy and Advances Materials, 2009; Numerous articles in professional journals. Honours: Commander of British Empire, 1992; George Beilby Gold Medal, Institute of Metals and Institute of Chemistry, London, 1969; Fellow, Institute of Materials, Platinum Medal, 1989, Rosenhain medal, 1972, Acta Materialia Gold Medal, 2004, Royal Society, Royal Academy of Engineers. Memberships: US NAE; Federation of European Materials Societies (vice president, 1992-94, president, 1994-96); Birmingham Metallurgical Society (president, 1972-73); Czech Society of Metal Science; China Ord Society. Address: University of Birmingham, B15 2TT, Birmingham, England. E-mail: ray.smallman@btopenworld.com

SMELLIE Jean McIldowie, b. 14 May 1927, Liverpool, England. Paediatrician. m. Ian Colin Stuart Normand, 1 son, 2 daughters. Education: St Hugh's College, Oxford; University College Hospital, London; Degrees and Diplomas: BA Hons Physiology Oxon, 1947; BM Oxon, 1950; DCH

England, 1953; MRCP London, 1954; MA Oxon, 1957; FRCP London, 1975; DM Oxon, 1981. Appointments include: House appointments, 1951-54; Paediatric Registrar, 1955-56, Paediatric First Assistant, 1956-60, University College Hospital, London; Lecturer, Infant Nutrition and Dietetics, Queen Elizabeth College, University of London, 1957-60; Lecturer, Paediatrics, Nuffield Department of Medicine, Oxford, 1960-61; Fellow in Pathology, Johns Hopkins Hospital, Baltimore, USA, 1964-65; Locum Consultant Paediatrician, 1968-69, Honorary Consultant Paediatrician (part-time), 1970-93, University College Hospital, London; Part-time appointments: Senior Lecturer, Paediatrics, Department of Clinical Sciences, University College, London, 1976-93; Senior Clinical Medical Officer, Southampton and SW Hampshire District, 1977-92; Honorary Senior Clinical Lecturer, University of Southampton, 1987-93; Honorary Consultant Paediatric Nephrologist, Guy's Hospital, London, 1984-93, Honorary Consultant Paediatric Nephrologist, Hospital for Sick Children, Great Ormond Street, London, 1984-; Emeritus Consultant Paediatrician, University College Hospitals, 1993-; Scientific Adviser, International Reflux Study in Children (Europe and USA), 1974-2006; Member, Medical Advisory Committee, Sir Jules Thorn Charitable Trust, 1987-97. Publications: More than 120 original articles, approximately 56 in peer reviewed journals, on urinary tract infections, vesico-ureteric reflux, renal scarring, neonatal, general and metabolic paediatric conditions including most recently: Childhood reflux and urinary infection: a follow-up of 10-41 years in 226 adults, 1998; Medical versus surgical treatment in children with severe bilateral vesicoureteric reflux and bilateral nephropathy: a randomised trial, 2001; Outcome of 10 years of severe vesicoureteric reflux managed medically or surgically: Report of the International Reflux Study in Children, 2003; 16-18 book chapters. Honours: Open Scholarship, St Hugh's College, Oxford, 1944-48; Honorary Member: European Society for Paediatric Urology, 1993; British Paediatric Association, 1995; British Association for Paediatric Nephrology, 1995; American Urological Association, 1998; Honorary Fellow, Royal College of Paediatrics and Child Health, 1996. Memberships: European Society of Paediatric Nephrology; Renal Association; International Paediatric Nephrology Association; Founder Member: British Association for Paediatric Nephrology; Neonatal Society. Address: 23 St Thomas Street, Winchester, Hampshire S023 9HJ, England. E-mail: jean.normand1@homecall.co.uk

SMETANA Karel, b. 28 October 1930, Prague, Czech Republic. Physician; Scientist. m. Vlasta Smetanova, 24 October 1953, 1 son. Education: MUDr (MD), Charles University, Prague, Czech Republic, 1955; CSc, (PhD), 1962; DrSc (DSc), 1967. Appointments: Lecturer, Dept of Histology, Charles University, Prague, 1955-62; Scientific Officer, Head, Senior Scientific Officer, Department of Blood Cytology, Laboratory of Ultrastruct Research, Czechoslovak Academy of Science, 1962-84; Research Fellow, Department of Pharmacology, Baylor College of Medicine, Houston, Texas, USA, 1962; Visiting Associate Professor, 1963; Professor, 1970; Director, Institute of Hematology and Blood Transfusion, Prague, 1984-90; Senior Scientific Officer, 1990-, Head of Laboratory, Cytology and Electron Microscopy, 1990-2000; Head, Chair of Hematology and Transfusion Service, 1985-93; Lecturer, Hematology and Transfusion Service, Institute of Postgraduate Medical Study, Prague, 1993-2007; Chairman, Board of Postgraduate Scientific Studies in Cell Biology and Pathology, Charles University, Prague, 1994-2008. Publications: 300 articles on cell nucleus, nucleolus, malignant cells; 1 monograph with H Busch, The nucleolus; 6 Monographic Chapters in various science monographs; Chapters in 7 textbooks. Honours: State Prize; Scientific Prize, Minister of Health; State Purkynje Medal; Purkynje Medal; Babak Medal; Bernhard Medal; Honorary Medals; Wilhelm Bernhard's Medal; Honorary Membership, Czech Hematological Society, Czech and Slovak Biological Society; Czech Histochemical Society; Slovak Hematological Society; Czech Medical Society; Science Prize; Many others. Memberships: Czech Histochemical Society; Czech Hematological Society; Czech Histochemical Society; Society of Clinical Cytology. Address: Prague 4, Puchovska 2, Czech Republic 141 00.

SMEU Grigore, b. 26 October 1928, Baltisoara Village, Gorj County, Romania. Scientific Researcher in Aesthetics. m. Georgeta, 1 son. Education: Graduate, 1953, PhD in Philosophy, branch of Aesthetics, 1971, Faculty of Philosophy, University of Bucharest. Appointments: Scientific Researcher, 1950-95, Retired as Principal Scientific Researcher, Head of Aesthetics Department, 1967-89, Deputy Director, 1979-89, Institute of Philosophy of the Romanian Academy. Publications: Books (in Romanian): Senses of beauty in Romanian Aesthetics, 1969; Predictable and Unpredictable in Epics, 1972; Aesthetic Marks in the Romanian Village, 1973; The Inclined Garden (novel), 1974; Pilgrimage (poetry), 1974; The Relation Social-Autonomous in Art, 1976; Introduction in Amateurs' Art Aesthetics, 1980; The Romanian Aesthetic Sensitivity, 1983; Aesthetics (main co-ordinator), 1983; The Interdependence of Values in Literature, 1987; The Daily Aesthetic in Today's World, 1992; Marin Preda – a Philosophy of Nature, 1994; The Ceremonies of Shadows (poetry), 1996; The Artistic Freedom in Romanian Literature, 2005; Vocation Transplant (novel), 2007; History of Romanian Aesthetics Vol 1, 2008, and Vol 2, 2009; At Fishing with Kant (stories), 2009; The Journey (novel), 2010; Rupester Drawings and Artistic Traditions, 2010. Over 200 published studies, articles, essays and communications in proceedings and various journals. Honour: Romanian Academy Prize for 2 papers on Industrial Aesthetics (first of the kind in Romania), 1966. Memberships: Writers' Union in Romania; Organising Committee, 7th International Aesthetics Congress, Bucharest, 1972. Address: Apt 111, 3rd Floor, Block 1, Section D, "Ion Mihalache" Boulevard 168, Bucharest 011214, Romania. E-mail: emil_smeu@physics.pub.ro

SMITH Andrew Benjamin, b. 6 February 1954, Dunoon, Scotland. Palaeontologist. m. Mary Patricia Cumming Simpson, 2 daughters. Education: BSc, Geology, 1st Class Honours, University of Edinburgh, 1976; PhD, Biological Sciences, University of Exeter, 1979; DSc, University of Edinburgh, 1989. Appointments: Lecturer, Department of Geology, University of Liverpool, 1981-82; Research Scientist, Department of Palaeontology, The Natural History Museum, London, 1982-. Publications: More than 200 monographs and scientific papers. Honours: Linnean Society Bicentennial Medal, 1993; Geological Society Bigsby Medal, 1995; Geological Society Lyell Medal, 2002; Elected Fellow of the Royal Society of Edinburgh, 1996; Elected Fellow of the Royal Society, 2002; Linnean Medal for Zoology, 2005. Memberships: Fellow of the Linnean Society; Fellow of the Geological Society; Fellow of the Royal Society of Edinburgh; Fellow of the Royal Society. Address: Department of Palaeontology, The Natural History Museum, Cromwell Road, London SW7 5BD, England. E-mail: a.smith@nhm.ac.uk

SMITH Chris(topher) Robert (Rt Hon) (Lord Smith of Finsbury), b. 24 July 1951. Politician. Education: Pembroke College, Cambridge; Harvard University (Kennedy Scholar

1975-76). Appointments: Development Secretary, Shaftesbury Society Housing Association, 1977-80; Development Co-ordinator, Society for Co-operative Dwellings, 1980-83; Councillor, London Borough of Islington, 1978-83; Chief Whip, 1978-79; Chair, Housing Committee, 1981-83; Labour, MP for Islington South and Finsbury, 1983-2005; Opposition Spokesman on Treasury and Economic Affairs, 1987-92; Principal Opposition Spokesman on Environmental Protection, 1992-94; National Heritage, 1994-95; Social Security, 1995-96; Health, 1996-97; Secretary of State for Culture, Media and Sport, 1997-2001; Chairman, Millennium Commission, 1997-2001; Created Life Peer, 2005; Member, Committee on Standards in Public Life, 2001-05; Chairman, Classic FM Consumer Panel, 2001-; Senior Adviser to The Walt Disney Company Ltd on UK film and television work; Visiting Professor in Culture and Creative Industries, University of the Arts, London, 2002-; Member of Board of Royal National Theatre; Chairman, Donmar Warehouse; Chairman of Wordsworth Trust; Member of Advisory Council of London Symphony Orchestra; Senior Associate of Judge Institute in Management Studies, Cambridge University; Honorary Fellow, Pembroke College, Cambridge, 2004-; Director of Clore Leadership Programme, 2003-; Chairman of Judges, Man Booker Prize, 2004; Chair, London Cultural Consortium, 2004-; Formerly: Chair, Labour Campaign for Criminal Justice, 1985-88; Tribune Group of MP's, 1988-89; President, Socialist Environmental and Resources Association, 1992-; Member, Executive of the Fabian Society, 1990-97 (Chair, 1996-97); Member of the Board of Shelter, 1986-92; Has held positions in several other organisations. Publication: Creative Britain, 1998. Address: House of Lords, London, SW1A 0PW, England.

SMITH David John, b. 10 October 1948, Melbourne, Australia. Physicist; Educator. m. Gwenneth Bland, 1971, divorced 1992, 2 daughters. Education: BSc, Honours, University Melbourne, 1970; PhD, University Melbourne, 1978; DSc, University Melbourne, 1988. Appointments: Postdoctoral Scholar, University Cambridge, England, 1976-78; Senior Research Associate, 1979-84; Associate Professor, 1984-87, Arizona State University; Professor, 1987-, Regents' Professor, 2000-. Publications: Author, 20 book chapters, 475 professional journal articles; Editor, 20 conference proceedings. Honours: Fellow, Institute of Physics, England, 1981; Charles Vernon Boys Prize, Institute Physics, England, 1985; Faculty Achievement Award, Burlington Resources Foundation, 1990; Director, Cambridge University High Resolution Electron Microscope, 1979-84; NSF Center for High Resolution Electron Microscopy, 1991-96; ASU Centre for High Resolution Electron Microscopy, 1996-2006; Director, Center for Solid State Science, Arizona State University, 2001-2004; Fellow, American Physical Society, 2002; President-Elect, 2008, President, 2009, Microscopy Society of America; Fellow, Materials Research Society, 2010. Memberships: American Physical Society; Microscopy Society of America; Material Research Society; Institute of Physics, UK. Address: Department of Physics, Arizona State University, Tempe, AZ 85287-1504, USA.

SMITH David Lawrence, b. 3 December 1963, London, England. Historian. Education: Eastbourne College, 1972-81; BA 1st Class Hons, 1985, MA, 1989, PhD, 1990, Selwyn College, Cambridge. Appointments: Fellow, 1988-, Director of Studies in History, 1992-, Admissions Tutor, 1992-2003, Praelector, 1996-2006, Tutor for Graduate Students, 2004-, Selwyn College, Cambridge; Affiliated Lecturer in History, 1995-, University of Cambridge; Visiting Assistant Professor, University of Chicago, 1991; Visiting Professor, Kyungpook National University, South Korea, 2004. Publications: Books: Oliver Cromwell, 1991; Louis XIV, 1992; Constitutional Royalism and the Search for Settlement, 1994; The Theatrical City (with R Strier and D Bevington), 1995; A History of the Modern British Isles, 1603-1707: The Double Crown, 1998; The Stuart Parliaments, 1603-1689, 1999; The Early Stuart Kings (with G Seel), 2001; Crown and Parliaments (with G Seel), 2001; Cromwell and the Interregnum (editor), 2003; Parliaments and Politics during the Cromwellian Protectorate (with Patrick Little), 2007; Royalists and Royalism during the English Civil Wars (with Jason McElligott), 2007; Royalists and Royalism during the Interregnum (with Jason McElligott), 2010; The Experience of Revolution in Stuart Britain and Ireland, (with Michael J Braddick), 2011; Contributions to Oxford Dictionary of National Biography, 2004, also contributions to academic journals. Honours: Alexander Prize, Royal Historical Society, 1991; Thirlwall Prize, University of Cambridge, 1991. Membership: Fellow, Royal Historical Society, 1992; President, Cambridge History Forum, 1997-. Address: Selwyn College, Cambridge CB3 9DQ, England. E-mail: dls10@cam.ac.uk

SMITH Delia, b. 18 June 1941. Cookery Writer; Broadcaster. m. Michael Wynn Jones. Appointments: Several BBC TV Series; Cookery Writer, Evening Standard, (later Standard), 1972-85; Columnist, Radio Times; Director, Norwich City Football Club; Canary Catering. Publications: How to Cheat at Cooking, 1971; Country Fare, 1973; Recipes From Country Inns and Restaurants, 1973; Family Fare, book 1, 1973, book 2, 1974; Evening Standard Cook Book, 1974; Country Recipes From "Look East", 1975; More Country Recipes From "Look East", 1976; Frugal Food, 1976; Book of Cakes, 1977; Recipes From "Look East", 1977; Food For Our Times, 1978; Cookery Course, part 1, 1978, part 2, 1979, part 3, 1981; The Complete Cookery Course, 1982; A Feast For Lent, 1983; A Feast For Advent, 1983; One is Fun, 1985. Editor: Food Aid Cookery Book, 1986, A Journey into God, 1988, Delia Smith's Christmas, 1990, Delia Smith's Summer Collection, 1993; Delia Smith's Winter Collection, 1995; Delia's Red Nose Collection, Comic Relief, 1997; How to Cook, Book 1, 1998; How to Cook Book 2, 1999; How to Cook Book 3, 2001; Delia's Chocolate Collection, Comic Relief, 2001; Delia's Vegetarian Collection, 2002; The Delia Collection: Soup, Chicken, Chocolate, Fish, 2003; The Delia Collection: Italian, Pork, 2004; The Delia Collection – Puddings, 2006; Delia's Kitchen Garden, 2007; How to Cheat at Cooking, 2008; Delia's Happy Christmas, 2009. Honours: OBE, 1995; Honorary Degree, Nottingham University, 1996; Fellowship, Royal TV Society, 1996; Honorary Degree, UEA, 1999; Honorary Fellow, Liverpool John Moores, 2000; CBE, 2009. Address: c/o Deborah Owen Ltd, 78 Narrow Street, London E14 8BP, England.

SMITH Donald Frederick, b. 30 January 1945, Chicago, Illinois, USA. m. Helle B Knudsen, 2 sons. Education: BSc, Psychology, Duke University, Durham, North Carolina, 1967; MA, Physiology and Psychology, McMaster University, Hamilton, Ontario, Canada, 1968; PhD, Biopsychology, Pritzker School of Medicine, University of Chicago, Illinois, 1971; Dr.med, University of Copenhagen, Denmark, 1980. Appointments include: Research Assistant, Division of Behavioural Sciences, Department of Psychology, University of Chicago, 1968-71; Senior Lecturer, Health Psychology and Psychobiology, University of East London, Department of Psychology, 1992-93; Consultant, Health Psychology, Committee on Social Health Services, Aarhus Municipality; Psychotherapist, Clinic for Applied Psychology, Private Practice, Arhus, 1986-; Senior Scientist, Center for

Psychiatric Research, Psychiatric Hospital of Aarhus University and PET Centre of Aarhus University Hospital, Denmark; Senior Lecturer, Postgraduate Medical Faculty, Aarhus University, Medical English Writing and Speaking; Member, Danish National University Censor Corps, Medical and Health Psychology. Publications include: Monoaminergic mechanisms in stress-induced analgesia, 1982; Stereoselective effects of tranylcypromine enantiomers on brain serotonin, 1982; Lithium and carbamazepine: Effects on locomotion of planaria, 1983; Role of 5-HT and NA in spinal dopaminergic analgesia, 1983; Handbook of Stereoisomers: Drugs in Psychopharmacology, 1984; Handbook of Stereoisomers: Therapeutic Drugs, 1989; PET neuroimaging of clomipramine challenge in humans: focus on the thalamus, Brain Research, 2001; (N-methyl-11C) Mirtazapine for positron emission tomography of antidepressant actions in humans. Memberships: Several societies and associations. Address: Center for Psychiatric Research, Psychiatric Hospital of Aarhus University, 8240 Risskov, Denmark.

SMITH Hamilton Othanel, b. 23 August 1931, New York, New York, USA. Microbiologist. m. Elizabeth Anne Bolton, 1957, 4 sons, 1 daughter. Education: Graduated, Mathematics, University of California at Berkeley, 1952; MD, Johns Hopkins University, 1956. Appointments: Junior Resident Physician, Barnes Hospital, 1956-57; Lieutenant, USNR, Senior Medical Officer, 1957-59; Resident, Henry Ford Hospital, Detroit, 1959-62; Postdoctoral Fellow, Department of Human Genetics, 1962-64, Research Associate, 1964-67, University of Michigan; Assistant Professor, 1967-69, Associate Professor, 1969-73, Professor of Microbiology, 1973-81, Professor of Molecular Biology and Genetics, 1981-, Johns Hopkins University; Sabbatical year with Institut fur Molekular-Biologie, Zurich University, 1975-76. Honour: Guggenheim Fellow, 1975-76; Joint Winner, Nobel Prize for Physiology or Medicine, 1978. Memberships: NAS; AAAS; Institute for Genomic Research, 1998. Address: Department of Molecular Biology, Johns Hopkins University School of Medicine, 720 Rutland Avenue, Baltimore, MD 21205, USA.

SMITH Ivor Ramsey, b. 8 October 1929, Birmingham, England. University Professor. m. Pamela Mary. Education: BSc, 1954, PhD, 1957, DSc, 1973, University of Bristol. Appointments: Design & Development Engineer, GEC, Witton, Birmingham, 1956-59; Lecturer, Senior Lecturer, Reader, Birmingham University, 1959-74; Professor of Electrical Engineering, 1974-, Head of Department of Electronic & Electrical Engineering, 1980-90, Dean of Engineering, 1983-86, Pro-Vice Chancellor, 1987-91, Loughborough University. Publications: More than 400 articles in learned society journals and at international conference proceedings in his field. Listed in various international biographical dictionaries. Memberships: Fellow, Institution of Engineering and Technology; Fellow, Royal Academy of Engineering. Address: Department of Electronic & Electrical Engineering, Loughborough University, Loughborough, Leicestershire, LE11 3TU, England. E-mail: i.r.smith@lboro.ac.uk

SMITH Jacqueline Mitchell, b. 7 July 1930, Reading, Pennsylvania, USA. Artist. m. Calvin E Smith, 2 sons, 1 daughter. Education: Pennsylvania State University, 1951-52; Art League of Alexandria, Virginia, 1970's-; Bachelor of Arts, Albright College, 1971; Master of Education, Temple University, 1976; Master of Education in Spanish, Millersville University, 1989. Career: Commissioned to paint local historical scenes, seascapes and figurative works, 1950's-; Works exhibited at William Ris Galleries, Stone Harbor, New Jersey, 1993-2006; Numerous exhibitions include most recently: Miniature Art Society of Florida, St Petersburg, Florida, 2005-11; Berks Art Alliance Juried Art Exhibition, Reading Museum, Pennsylvania, 2002-10; The Hilliard Society, Wells, Somerset, England, 2003-10; The Royal Miniature Society, Westminster Gallery, London, England, 2003, 2005, 2007-10; The MPSGS of Washington DC, 1998-2010; Cider Painters of America, Dallas, Pennsylvania, 2004-10; Galerie BelAge, Westhampton Beach, New York, 2005; Stone Harbor Art & Music Festival, Stone Harbor, New Jersey, 2003, 2005-09; Berks Art Council, Gallery 20, West Reading, Pennsylvania, 2002-05; Doylestown Art League Exhibition, Doylestown, Pennsylvania, 2001-05; Birdsboro Friends of the Arts, Birdsboro, Pennsylvania, 2004-2009; 3rd World Federation of Miniaturists, Smithsonian, Washington DC, 2004; SAMAP France International Exhibition, Chateau de Bernicourt, France, 2004; 4th World Federation of Miniaturists, Burnie, Australia, 2008; Art Gallery of Fells Point, Baltimore, MD, 2006-10; Seaside Art Gallery, Nags Head, NC, 2006-10; Pennsylvania Watercolor Society, Reading, PA, 2009, Warren, PA, 2010; Corporation du Presbytere Saint-Nicolas, Quebec, Canada, 2007, 2009; Parkland Gallery, Kirkland, WA, 2008-10; El Dorado Fine Arts Gallery, Colorado Springs, CO, 2008-10; Alabama Miniature Art Society, Mobile, AL, 2009, 2010; Ice House Gallery, Washington, VA, 2009-10. Publications: Articles about her works include: Berks In Focus, 1977; The Reading Eagle, 1979, 2005; The Butler Eagle, 1999; The Derrick, Venango Newspaper, 1999. Honours: Honourable Mention, Doylestown Art League Exhibition, 1999; Second Place in Portraiture Award, The Miniature Painters, Sculptors and Gravers Society of Washington, DC Exhibition, 2003; Best New Exhibitor Award, The Hilliard Society Exhibition, Somerset, England, 2003; 1st Place, Award of Excellence and Purchase Award, Boscov's, Berks Art Alliance Juried Exhibition, Reading, Pennsylvania, 2005; Honourable Mention, Art Gallery of Fells Point, Baltimore, Maryland, 2006; CPA Waterscape Award, Cider Painters of America, 2007; Second Place, Watermedia Award, The Miniature Painters, Sculptors and Gravers Society of Washington, DC Exhibiton, 2008; Purchase Award, Alabama Miniature Art Society, Mobile, Alabama, 2008; Honorable Mention, Northern California Society, Mariposa, CA, 2009; Solo Exhibition at The Hill School, Pottstown, PA, 2009; Invited Judge, MPSGS of Washington, DC, 76th International Exhibition, 2009; Third Place, Watercolor Award, Art Gallery at Fells Point, Baltimore, MD, 2010; Signature Membership Achievement, Pennsylvania Watercolor Society, Warren, PA, 2010. Memberships: Miniature Painters, Sculptors and Gravers Society of Washington, DC; World Federation of Miniaturists; Cider Painters of America; Doylestown Art League; Berks Art Alliance; The Hilliard Society; Miniature Art Society of Florida; Rhode Island Watercolor Society; Pennsylvania Watercolor Society. Address: 113 East Penn Avenue, Wernersville, PA 19565-1611, USA. E-mail: jmsces@gmail.com Website: www.jacquelinesmith.net

SMITH James Cuthbert, b. 31 December 1954, London, England. m. 3 children. Chairman; Professor. Education: First Class honours degree, Natural Sciences (Zoology), Christ's College, Cambridge, England, 1976; PhD, London University, 1979. Appointments: NATO Postdoctoral Fellow, Sidney Farber Cancer Institute and Harvard Medical School, 1979-1981; ICRF Postdoctoral Fellow, 1981-1984; National Institute for Medical Research, 1984-1990; Head, Laboratory of Developmental Biology, 1991, Head Genes and Cellular Controls Group, 1996, NIMR; Member of Zoology Department, Senior Group Leader and Chairman-designate, Wellcome/CRC Institute, Cambridge, 2000; Fellow,

Christ's College, Cambridge, 2001; Chairman, Wellcome Trust/Cancer Research UK Institute, Cambridge, 2001-; Humphrey Plummer Professor of Developmental Biology, University of Cambridge, 2001-. Publications: Numerous co-authored papers and articles to professional journals. Honours: Zoological Society's Scientific Medal, 1989; Otto Mangold Prize, German Society for Developmental Biology, 1991; Wellcome Visiting Professor, Basic Medical Sciences, 1991-1992; Elected Member, European Molecular Biology Organisation, 1992; Howard Hughes Medical Institute International Research Scholar, 1993-98; Elected Fellow, Royal Society, 1993; EMBO Medal, 1993; Honorary Senior Research Fellow, Department of Anatomy and Developmental Biology, University College, London, 1994; Jenkinson Lecture, Oxford University, 1997; Marshal R Urist Lecture and Award, 1997; Elected Fellow, Institute of Biology, 1997; Visiting Professor, Queen Mary and Westfield College, University of London, 1997-; Founder Fellow, Academy of Medical Sciences, 1998; Feldberg Foundation Award, 2000; Member, Academia Europaea, 2000; William Bate Hardy Prize, 2001. Memberships: Numerous committees including: HFSPO Review Committee – Molecular Approaches, 1997-2000; Council, Royal Society, 1997-1999; Council, Academy of Medical Sciences; 1998-2001. Address: Wellcome Trust/Cancer Research UK Institute of Cancer and Developmental Biology, University of Cambridge, Tennis Court Road, Cambridge CB2 1QR, England.

SMITH Kenneth George Valentine, b. 11 March 1929, Birmingham, England. Retired Entomologist. m. Alma Vera Thompson, 2 sons. Education: Birmingham Central College of Technology, 1945-47; University of Keele, 1952-54. Appointments: Field Assistant Entomologist, Ministry of Agriculture, Fisheries and Food, 1950-52; Senior Technician, Hope Department of Entomology, Oxford University, 1954-62; Principal Scientific Officer, British Museum (Natural History), 1962-89; Member of Editorial Board, Entomologist's Monthly Magazine, 1982-. Publications: Over 300 papers on entomology in scientific journals including books: Empididae of South Africa, 1969; Insects and Other Arthropods of Medical Importance, 1973; A Bibliography of the Entomology of the Smaller British Offshore Islands, 1983; Manual of Forensic Entomology, 1986; Darwin's Insects, 1987; An Introduction to the Immature Stages of British Flies, 1989. Memberships: Chartered Biologist; C Biol; F I Biol; FRES; FLS. Address: 31 Calais Dene, Bampton, Oxfordshire OX18 2NR, England.

SMITH Dame Maggie Natalie, b. 28 December 1934, Ilford, Essex, England. Actress. m. (1) Robert Stephens, 1967, divorced 1975, deceased 1995, 2 sons, (2) Beverley Cross, 1975, deceased 1998. Career: Theatre appearances include: With Old Vic Company, 1959-60; Rhinoceros, 1960; The Private Ear and the Public Eye, 1962; With the National Theatre played in The Recruiting Officer, 1963; Othello, 1964; Much Ado About Nothing 1965; The Beaux' Stratagem, 1970; Private Lives, 1972; 1976, 1977, 1978, 1980 seasons, Stratford Ontario Canada; Lettice and Lovage, London, 1987, New York, 1990; The Importance of Being Earnest, 1993; Three Tall Women, 1994-95; Talking Heads, 1996, Australian tour, 2004; The Lady in the Van, 1999; The Breath of Life, 2002; Talking Heads, 2004; The Lady from Dubuque, 2007; TV: Capturing Mary, 2007; Downton Abbey, 2010-; Films include: The VIP's 1963; The Pumpkin Eater, 1964; Young Cassidy, 1965; Othello, 19666; The Honey Pot, 1967; Hot Millions, 1968; The Prime of Miss Jean Brodie, 1969; Travels with My Aunt, 1972; Love and Pain and the Whole Damn Thing, 1973; Murder by Death, 1975; Death on the Nile, 1978; California Suite, 1978; Quartet, 1980; Clash of the Titans, 1981; Evil Under the Sun, 1982; The Missionary, 1982; A Private Function, 1984; A Room with a View, 1986; The Lonely Passion of Judith Hearn, 1987; Hook, 1991; The Secret Garden, 1993; Richard III, 1995; First Wives Club, 1996; Washington Square, 1998; Tea with Mussolini, 1999; The Last September, 2000; Harry Potter and the Philosopher's Stone, 2001; Gosford Park, 2002; Harry Potter and the Chamber of Secrets, 2002; Harry Potter and the Prisoner of Azkaban, 2004; Ladies in Lavender, 2004; Harry Potter and the Goblet of Fire, 2005; Keeping Mum, 2005; Becoming Jane, 2007; Harry Potter and the Order of the Phoenix, 2007; Harry Potter and the Half Blood Prince, From Time to Time, 2009; Nanny McPhee and the Big Bang, 2010; Gnomeo & Juliet, Harry Potter and the Deathly Hallows – Part 2, 2011; The Best Exotic Marigold Hotel, Quartet, 2012. Honours include: Honorary D Lit, St Andrew's and Leicester Universities, 1982, Cambridge, 1993; Academy Awards, 1969, 1978 Evening Standard Best Actress Award, 1962, 1970, 1982, 1985, 1994; Best Actress Award, Film Critics' Guild, USA, 1969; BAFTA Award, Best Actress,1984, 1987; 1989; BAFTA Award for Lifetime Achievement, 1992; Tony Award, 1990; Emmy Award, 2003, 2012; Golden Globe, 2012; Satellite Award, 2012; SAG Award, 2012. Address: c/o Write on Cue, 29 Whitcomb Street, London, WC2H 7EP, England.

SMITH Pamela M Gerrie, b. 1 February 1952, Chelsea, London. Artist. 1 son, 1 daughter, 2 step-daughters. Education: BA (Hons), Sculpture, Kingston School of Art; PGCE, Garnett College of Education. Career: Artist in Sculpture, Ceramics and Fire; Exhibitions in shows, events and studios in UK and Portugal; Work held in private collections in the UK, Europe & USA; Public collection, Bristol Oncology Centre, UK. Honours: President, Cambridge University Pottery Society, 1996; Arts Council Award, 2000; Royal Academy Summer Show, London, 2004; ING Exhibition, London, 2008; Arts Committee Member, Bristol Hospital, 2010. Memberships: Free West Papua Koteka Tribal Assembly. Address: 16 Bouverie St, Easton, Bristol, CB5 0RS England. E-mail: pamela.gerrie@gmail.com

SMITH Roland Hedley, b. 11 April 1943, Sheffield, England. HM Diplomatic Service (Retired). m. Katherine Jane Lawrence, 2 daughters. Education: King Edward VII School, Sheffield, 1954-61; Keble College, Oxford, 1961-65. Appointments: Entered Diplomatic Service, 1967; FCO, 1967-68; Moscow, 1969-71; UK Delegation to NATO, 1971-74; FCO, 1974-88; Cultural Attaché, Moscow, 1978-80; FCO, 1980-83; Political Adviser, British Military Government, Berlin, 1984-88; Head, Non-Proliferation Department, FCO, 1988-92; Minister, UK Delegation to NATO, 1992-95; Director, International Security, FCO, 1995-98; HM Ambassador, Kiev, 1999-2002; Director, St Ethelburga's Centre for Reconciliation and Peace, 2002-04; Clerk to Trustees, Wakefield and Tetley Trust, 2004-. Publications: Soviet Policy Towards West Germany, 1985. Honours: CMG, 1994. Address: Attlee House, 28 Commercial Street, London E1 6LS, England. E-mail: roland.smith@wakefield.org.uk

SMITH Stanley Desmond, b. 3 March 1931, Bristol, England. Physicist. m. Gillian Anne Parish, 1 son, 1 daughter. Education: BSc, Physics Department, University of Bristol, 1949-52, PhD, Physics Department, University of Reading, 1952-56; DSc, University of Bristol, 1966. Appointments: Senior Scientific Officer, Royal Aircraft Establishment, Farnborough, 1956-58; Research Assistant, Department of Meteorology, Imperial College, 1958-59; Research Assistant, Lecturer, Reader, Physics Department, University of Reading,

1959-70; Professor of Physics, Head of Department, Dean of Science Faculty, Heriot-Watt University, Edinburgh, 1970-96; Chairman and Chief Executive Officer, Edinburgh Instruments Ltd, 1996- (previously part-time Chairman and Founder, Director, 1971-). Publications: Books: Infrared physics, 1966; Optoelectronic Devices, 1995; Some 215 scientific papers and review articles on semiconductors, IR spectroscopy, interference filters, tunable lasers, optical computing, satellite meteorology; Chairman, Scottish Optoelectronics Association, 1996-98. Honours: C V Boys Prize, Institute of Physics, 1976; EPIC Award (Education in Partnership with Industry or Commerce) 1st Prize, 1982; TOBIE Award (Technical or Business Innovation in Electronics), Department of Trade and Industry, 1986; James Scott Prize, Royal Society of Edinburgh, 1987; OBE, 1998; Hon DSc, Heriot-Watt University, 2003. Memberships: Fellow, Royal Society of Edinburgh, 1973; Fellow, Royal Society, 1976; Fellow, Institute of Physics, 1976; Advisory Council on Science and Technology, Cabinet Office, 1985-88; Defence Scientific Advisory Council, 1985-91. Address: Treetops, 29D Gillespie Road, Edinburgh EH13 0NW, Scotland. E-mail: des.smith@edinst.com

SMITH Troy Alvin, b. 4 July 1922, Sylvatus, Virginia, USA. Aerospace Research Engineer. m. Grace Marie (Peacock) Dees, 1990. Education: BCE degree, University of Virginia, 1948; MSE degree, University of Michigan, 1952; PhD degree, University of Michigan, 1970; Registered Professional Engineer, Virginia, Alabama. Appointments: US Navy Reserve, Pacific Theatre of Operations, 1942-46; Structural Engineer, Corps of Engineers, US Army, 1948-59; Chief Structural Engineer, Brown Engineering Company Inc, Huntsville, Alabama, 1959-60; Structural Research Engineer, US Army Missile Command, Redstone Arsenal, Alabama, 1960-63; Aerospace Engineer, US Army Missile Command, 1963-80; Aerospace Research Engineer, US Army Missile Command, 1980-96; Aerospace Engineer Emeritus, US Army Aviation and Missile Command, Redstone Arsenal, Alabama, 1996-2003; Aerospace Engineer Emeritus, US Army Research, Development, and Engineering Command, Aviation and Missile Research, Development, and Engineering Center, Redstone Arsenal, Alabama, 2003-. Publications: Numerical Solution for the Dynamic Response of Rotationally Symmetric Shells of Revolution under Transient Loadings, (doctoral dissertation, University of Michigan, 1970); Articles in AIAA Journal and Journal of Sound and Vibration on analysis of shells; 18 major US Army technical reports on analysis of shells and other structures. Honours: Awarded Secretary of the Army Research and Study Fellowship for Graduate Study at the University of Michigan, 1969; IBC Leading Engineers of the World, 2006; IBC Director General's Roll of Honour, 2007; Top Two Hundred of the IBC, 2008; IBC Distinguished Service to Engineering Award, 2008; IBC Hall of Fame, 2008; IBC Lifetime Achievement Award, 2008; IBC Top 100 Engineers, 2009; ABI World Laureate, 2009; ABI Magna Cum Laude, 2009. Memberships: Sigma Xi; New York Academy of Sciences; Association of US Army. Address: 2202 Yorkshire SE, Decatur, AL 35601-3470, USA.

SMITH Will (Willard C Smith II), b. 25 September 1968, Philadelphia, Pennsylvania, USA. Singer; Rap Artist; Actor. m. (1) Sheree Zampino, 1 son, (2) Jada Pinkett, 1997, 1 son, 1 daughter. Career: Formed duo, DJ Jazzy Jeff and the Fresh Prince; Star of TV sitcom, The Fresh Prince of Bel Air; Film actor: Six Degrees of Separation, 1993, Bad Boys, 1995, Independence Day, 1996, Men in Black, 1997, Enemy of the State, 1998; Wild Wild West, 1999; Legend of Bagger Vance, 2000; Men in Black: Alien Attack, 2002; Ali, 2002; Bad Boys II, 2003; Shark Tale (voice), 2004; I, Robot, 2004; Hitch, 2005; The Pursuit of Happyness, 2006; I Am Legend, 2007; Hancock, 2008; Seven Pounds, 2008; Men in Black 3, 2012; After Earth, Winter's Tale, 2013; Producer: Lakeview Terrace, 2008; The Secret Life of Bees, 2008; Seven Pounds, 2008; Karate Kid, 2010; This Means War, 2012. Recordings: With DJ Jazzy Jeff: Singles: Parents Just Don't Understand; I Think I Could Beat Mike Tyson; Summertime, 1991; Boom! Shake the Room, 1993; Albums: Rock the House, 1997; He's the DJ, I'm the Rapper, 1988; And In This Corner..., 1989; Homebase, 1991; Code Red, 1993; Greatest Hits, 1998; Solo: Singles: Just Cruisin', 1997; Men in Black, 1997; Gettin' Jiggy With It, 1998; Miami, 1998; Wild Wild West, 1999; Albums: Big Willie Style, 1997; Willennium, 1999; Born to Reign, 2002; Lost and Found, 2005. Honours: 6 American Music Awards, 1999, 2000, 2005; 1 Saturn Award, 2008; 4 Grammys, 1989, 1992, 1998, 1999; 5 MTV Video Music Awards, 1989, 1997, 1998, 1999. Address: Ken Stovicz, Creative Artists Agency, 9830 Wilshire Boulevard, Beverly Hills, CA 90212, USA.

SMITH Zadie (Sadie Smith), b. 27 October 1975, London, England. Writer; Poet. m. Nick Laird, 2004, 1 daughter. Education: King's College, Cambridge. Career: Writer-in-Residence, Institute of Contemporary Arts, London; Radcliffe Fellow, Harvard University. Publications: White Teeth (novel), 2000; Piece of Flesh (editor), 2001; The May Anthologies (editor), 2001; The Autograph Man (novel), 2002; The Burned Children of America (editor), 2003; On Beauty, 2005; NW, 2012; Contributions to anthologies and periodicals. Honours: Rylands Prize, King's College, London; Betty Trask Prize, 2001; Guardian First Book Award, 2001; Whitbread First Novel and Book of the Year Awards, 2001; James Tait Memorial Prize for Fiction, 2001; Commonwealth Writers' Best First Book Prize, 2001. Address: A P Watt Ltd, 20 John Street, London WC1N 2DR, England. E-mail: zsmith@literati.net

SMITH OF CLIFTON (Lord), Professor Sir Trevor Arthur Smith, b. 14 June 1937, London, England. Politician. m. Julia, 2 sons, 1 daughter. Education: London School of Economics, 1955-58. Appointments: Lecturer in Politics, University of Exeter, England, 1959-60; Lecturer in Politics, University of Hull, England, 1962-67; Lecturer, Senior Lecturer, Professor of Politics, 1967-91, Deputy Principal, 1985-90, Queen Mary, London; Vice-Chancellor, University of Ulster, 1991-99; Liberal Democrat Front Bench Spokesman on Northern Ireland, 2000-. Publications: The Fixers; The Politics of Corporate Economy; Anti-Politics; Direct Action & Representative Democracy; Town & County Hall; Town Councillors; Training Managers; Numerous articles. Honours: Knighted, 1996; Life Peer, 1997; Honorary LLD, Dublin, Hull, Belfast, National University of Ireland; Honorary DHL, Alabama; Honorary DLitt, Ulster; Honorary Fellow, Queen Mary, London. Memberships: Fellow Royal Historical Society; AcSS; Vice-President, Political Studies Association. Address: House of Lords, London SW1A 0PW, England. E-mail: smitht@parliament.uk

SMITHERS Alan George, b. 20 May 1938, London, England; Professor of Education; Author; Broadcaster. 2 daughters. Education: BSc, First Class Honours, Botany, 1959, PhD, Plant Physiology, 1966 King's College London; MSc, Psychology and Sociology of Education, 1973, PhD, Education, 1974, Bradford; MEd, Manchester, 1981; Chartered Psychologist, 1988. Appointments: Lecturer in Biology, College of St Mark and St John, Chelsea, 1962-64; Lecturer in Botany, Birkbeck College, University of London, 1964-67; Research Fellow in Education, 1967-69, Senior Lecturer in

Education, 1969-76, University of Bradford; Professor of Education, University of Manchester, 1976-96; Professor of Policy Research, Brunel University, 1996-98; Sydney Jones Professor of Education, University of Liverpool, 1998-2004; Professor of Education and Director, Centre for Education and Employment Research, University of Buckingham, 2004-; Royal Society Committee on Teacher Supply, 1990-94; National Curriculum Council, 1992-93; Beaumont Committee on National Vocational Qualifications, 1995-96; Special Adviser to House of Commons Children, Education Committee, 1997-. Publications: Numerous publications include most recently: The Reality of School Staffing, 2003; England's Education, 2004; Five Years On, 2006; The Paradox of Single-Sex and Co-education, 2006; School Headship, 2007; Physics: Bucking the Trend, 2007; Blair's Education, 2007; The Diploma, 2008; Physics Teachers, 2008; HMC Schools, 2008; Specialist Science Schools, 2009; Physics Participation and Policies, 2009; Worlds Apart, 2010; The Good Teacher Training Guide, 2010; Choice and Selection, 2010; Over 100 research papers in botany, psychology and education; Columnist, Times Educational Supplement, 1995-97; Columnist, The Independent, 1997-2010; Panellist, The Times ed forum, 2001-04; Regular broadcaster, speaker and contributor to the print media. Honours: Fellow, Society for Research into Higher Education. Memberships: British Psychological Society; Society for Research into Higher Education; Listed in biographical dictionaries. Address: Centre for Education and Employment Research, Department of Education, University of Buckingham, Buckingham MK18 1EG, England. E-mail: alan.smithers@buckingham.ac.uk

SNÆDAL Magnús, b. 17 April 1952, Akureyri, Iceland. Linguist; Philologist; Educator. 1 son. Education: BA, Icelandic Language and Literature, 1978, Cand. mag. Degree, Icelandic Linguistics, 1982, University of Iceland, Reykjavík. Appointments: Language Consultant for the Terminological Committee of the Icelandic Medical Association, 1984-96; Lecturer, General Linguistics, 1989-94, Associate Professor of General Linguistics, 1994-2005; Regular Professor 2005-, University of Iceland, Reykjavík. Publications: Book: A Concordance to Biblical Gothic, Volumes I and II, 1998, 2nd edition, 2005; 30 articles, 14 of them on the Gothic language written in English; Editor of 5 books/dictionaries in the field of Icelandic medical terminology. Listed in various international biographical dictionaries. Address: Ránargata 35a, 101 Reykjavík, Iceland. E-mail: hreinn@hi.is

SNIEDZE Ojars Andrejs, b. 19 January 1930, Latvia. Inventor; Researcher. m. Janet Mary Pearce, 2 sons, 1 daughter. Education 1st Class Certificate in Wireless Telegraphy, 1958; Certificate, Marine Radar, 1959; Part of Dip Tech, Business Administration, 1969; Technical and Further Education Certificate in Occupational Health and Safety. Appointments: Chief Radio Officer, R&K Shipping, New York City, 1959-66; Project Engineer, E&C Engineering, Adelaide, South Australia, 1969-74; Senior Technical Officer, Telecom, Australia, 1987-93; Manager, Research and Development, SA Safety Engineering, Lonsdale, South Australia, 1993-97; Owner Manager, SA Safety Engineering, Tranmere, South Australia, 1997-; Director, Payneham Table Tennis Academy, Firle, South Australia, 2000-; Director, Maid for Mum, Australia Pty Ltd, Tranmere, South Australia, 2006-; CEO, Family Home Support Services Pty Ltd, Tranmere, 2007-. Publications: Various publications on occupational health and safety and on home security for neighbourhood watch schemes; Energy absorbing bollards for protection of outdoor diners, pedestrians and property from out of control vehicles (own invention). Honours: Meritorious Service Award, 1994; Member of Management Committee, Communications Workers Union, Adelaide, South Australia; Various Certificates in Occupational Health and Safety. Memberships: Life Member, IEEE; Ex-Member, Safety Institute of Australia and Ergonomics Society of Australia and New Zealand; Joined Latvian Air Force, Volunteer, October 1944. Address: 47 Hallett Avenue, Tranmere, South Australia 5073. E-mail: sniedze@picknowl.com.au

SNIPES Wesley, b. 31 July 1962, Orlando, USA. Actor. (1) April, 1985, divorced 1990, 1 child, (2) Nikki Park, 2003, 4 children. Education: High School for Performing Arts, New York; State University of New York. Appointments: Telephone Repair Man, New York; Broadway Appearances include Boys of Winter; Execution of Justice; Death and King's Horseman; Waterdance; Appeared in Martin Scorsese's video Bad, 1987; Films Include: Wildcats; Streets of Gold; Major League; Mo Better Blues, 1990; Jungle Fever, 1991; New Jack City; White Men Can't Jump; Demolition Man; Boiling Point; Sugar Hill; Drop Zone; To Wong Foo: Thanks for Everything, Julie Newmar, 1995; The Money Train; Waiting to Exhale; The Fan, 1996; One Night Stand; Murder at 1600; Blade, 1997; The Vampire Slayer, 1997; US Marshals, 1998; Down in the Delta, 1998; The Art of War, 2000; Blade 2, 2002; Undisputed, 2002; Unstoppable, 2004; Blade: Trinity, 2004; Nine Lives, 2004; 7 seconds, 2005; The Marksman, 2005; Chaos, 2005; Gallowwalker, 2009. Co-Founder, Struttin Street Stuff Puppet Theatre, mid 1980's. Honours: ACE Award for Best Actor for Vietnam War Stories, 1989. Address: Amen RA Films, 9460 Wilshire Boulevard, Beverly Hills, CA 90212, USA.

SNOW Jon (Jonathan George), b. 28 September 1947. Partner, Madeleine Colvin, 2 daughters. Education: St Edward's School, Oxford; University of Liverpool. Appointments: Voluntary Service Overseas, Uganda, 1967-68; Co-ordinator, 1970-73, Chair, 1986-, New Horizon Youth Centre, London; Journalist, Independent Radio News, LBC, 1973-76; Reporter, 1977-83, Washington Correspondent, 1983-86, Diplomatic Editor, 1986-89, ITN; Presenter, Channel Four News, 1989-; Visiting Professor of Broadcast Journalism, Nottingham Trent University, 1992-2001, University of Stirling, 2002-; Chair, Prison Reform Trust, 1992-96, Media Trust, 1995-, Tate Modern Council, 1999-; Trustee, Noel Buxton Trust, 1992-, National Gallery, 1999; Chancellor, Oxford Brookes University, 2001-. Publications: Atlas of Today, 1987; Sons and Mothers, 1996; Shooting History: A Personal Journey, 2004. Honours: Hon DLitt (Nottingham Trent), 1994; Monte Carlo Golden Nymph Award, 1979; TV Reporter of the Year, Royal Television Society, 1980; Valient for Truth Award, 1982; International Award, RTS, 1982; Home News Aard, RTS, 1989; RTS Presenter of the Year, 1994, 2002; BAFTA Richard Dimbleby Award, 2005. Address: Channel Four News, ITN, 200 Gray's Inn Road, London WC1X 8HB, England. E-mail: jon.snow@itn.co.uk

SNOW Peter John, b. 20 April 1938, Dublin, Ireland. Television Presenter; Reporter; Author. m. (1) Alison Carter, 1964, divorced 1975, 1 son, 1 daughter, (2) Ann Macmillan, 1976, 1 son, 2 daughters. Education: Wellington College and Balliol College, Oxford. Appointments: 2nd Lieutenant, Somerset Light Infantry, 1956-58; Newscaster, Reporter, ITN, 1962-79; Diplomatic and Defence Correspondent, 1966-97; Presenter, BBC Newsnight, 1979-97; Tomorrows World, 1997-2001; BBC Election Programmes, 1983-; BBC Radio 4 Mastermind, 1998-2000; Radio 4 Random Edition, 1998-; Radio 4 Masterteam, 2001; Battlefield Britain, BBC2 (jointly with son, Dan Snow), 2004. Publications: Leila's Hijack War (co-author), 1970; Hussein: a biography, 1972. Honours:

Judges Award, Royal TV Society, 1998; CBE, 2006. Address: c/o BBC TV Centre, Wood Lane, London W12 7RJ, England. E-mail: peter.snow@bbc.co.uk

SNOWDON Antony Charles Robert Armstrong-Jones (1st Earl of), b. 7 March 1930, London, England. Photographer. m. (1) HRH The Princess Margaret, 1960, divorced 1978, deceased 2002, 1 son, 1 daughter, (2) Lucy Lindsay-Hogg, 1979, 1 daughter, divorced, 2000. 1 son with Melanie Cable-Alexander. Education: Jesus College, Cambridge. Appointments: Consultant, Council of Industrial Design, 1962-89; In charge of design of Investiture of HRH the Prince of Wales, Caernarfon, 1969; Editorial Adviser, Design Magazine, 1961-67; Artistic Adviser to The Sunday Times, Sunday Times Publications Ltd, 1962-90; Photographer, Telegraph Magazine, 1990-96; Constable of Caernarfon Castle, 1963-; President, Civic Trust for Wales, Contemporary Art Society for Wales, Welsh Theatre Company; Vice President, University of Bristol Photographic Society; Senior Fellow, Royal College of Art, 1986; Provost, 1995-; Fellow, Institute of British Photographers, British Institute of Professional Photographers; Chartered Society of Design; Royal Photographic Society; Royal Society of Arts; Manchester College of Art and Design; Member, Faculty Royal Designers for Industry; South Wales Institute of Architects; Chair Snowdon Report on Integrating the Disabled, 1972; Member, Council, National Fund for Research for the Crippled Child; Founder, Snowdon Award Scheme for Disabled Students, 1980; President, International Year of Disabled People, 1981; Patron, British Disabled Water Ski Association; Member, Prince of Wales Advisory Group on Disability, 1983; Metropolitan Union of YMCAs; British Water Skiing Federation; Welsh National Rowing Club; Circle of Guide Dog Owners. Publications: London, 1958; Malta, 1958; Private View, 1965; Assignments, 1972; A View of Venice, 1972; Photographs by Snowdon: A Retrospective, 2000; Many others. Honours include: Honorary Member, North Wales Society of Architects; Dr hc, Bradford, 1989; LLD, Bath, 1989; Dr hc, Portsmouth, 1993; Art Directors Club of New York Certificate of Merit, 1969; Society of Publication Designers Certificate of Merit, 1970; The Wilson Hicks Certificate of Merit for Photocommunication, 1971; Society of Publication Designers Award of Excellence, 1973; Designers and Art Directors Award, 1978; Royal Photographic Society Hood Award, 1979. Address: 22 Launceston Place, London, W8 5RL, England.

SNOWMAN Daniel, b. 4 November 1938, United Kingdom. Writer; Lecturer; Broadcaster. m. Janet Linda Levison, 1 son, 1 daughter. Education: Double First Class Honours in History, University of Cambridge, 1958-61; Fulbright Scholarship, MA in American Government, Cornell University, USA, 1961-63. Appointments include: Lecturer in American Studies and Politics, University of Sussex, 1963-67; Visiting Professor of American History, California State University, 1972-73; Chief Producer, Features, BBC Radio, 1982-95 (joined BBC, 1967); Senior Research Fellow, Institute of Historical Research, London, 2004-2006; Principal BBC radio productions as presenter and/or producer include: A World in Common; The Vatican; Reith Lectures; Northern Lights; Victoria's Children; Spitalfields; Vaughan Williams London; TV: Plácido Domingo's Tales from the Opera, BBC Television and World Wide International Films, 1992-94. Publications: Books: America Since 1920, 1968; Eleanor Roosevelt, 1970; Britain and America: An Interpretation of their Culture, 1977; If I Had Been...Ten Historical Fantasies (editor), 1979; The Amadeus Quartet: The Men and The Music, 1981; The World of Plácido Domingo, 1985; Beyond the Tunnel of History: the 1989 BBC Reith Lectures (with Jacques Darras), 1990; Pole Positions: The Polar Regions and the Future of the Planet, 1993; Plácido Domingo's Tales From the Opera, 1994; Fins de Siècle (with Asa Briggs), 1996; Pastmasters: The Best of "History Today" (editor), 2001; The Hitler Emigres: The Cultural Impact on Britain of Refugees from Nazism, 2002; Historians, 2007; The Gilded Stage: A Social History of Opera, 2009. Book chapters articles and reviews. Address: 46 Molyneux Street, London W1H 5JD, England. E-mail: daniel@danielsnowman.org.uk Website: www.danielsnowman.org.uk

SOBOLEV, b. Moscow, Russia. Geologist. 2 daughters. Education: Diploma, 1952, PhD, 1956, DSc, 1973, Lomonosov Moscow State University. Appointments: Researcher, Geological Department, 1956, Assistant Lecturer, 1956-66, Associate Professor, 1966-74, Researcher, 1974-, Vice Dean, Geological Department, Lomonosov Moscow State University; Professor, Ecological Department, International Independent Ecologic-Politologic University, Moscow, 1995-. Publications: Over 340 articles in professional journals; Books: Geochronology of USSR, 1974; Magmatic Rocks, 1983; Using computer in Petrochemistry, 1992; Textures Magmatic Rocks and Their Genesis, 2005. Memberships: American Chemical Society; International Geological Union; Geochronologic Com; Petrographic Com; Member, Russian Academy of Natural Sciences. Address: Department of Geology, Lomonosov Moscow State University, Moscow, 119991, Russia. E-mail: sobolev2002@hotbox.ru

SODERBERGH Steven, b. 14 January 1963, Atlanta, USA. Film Director. m. (1) Elizabeth Jeanne Brantley, 1989, divorced 1994, 1 child, (2) Jules Asner, 2003. Education: high school and animation course, Louisiana State University. Appointments: Aged 15 made short film Janitor; Briefly editor, Games People Play (TV show); Made short film Rapid Eye Movement while working as coin-changer in video arcade; Produced video for Showtime for their album 90125; Author, Screenplay for Sex, Lies and Videotape, 1989; Kafka, The Last Ship, 1991; King of the Hill, 1993; The Underneath, Schizopolis, 1996; Out of Sight, 1998; Executive Producer: Suture, 1994; The Daytrippers, 1996; Writer Mimic, 1997; Nightwatch, 1998; The Limey, Erin Brockovich, 1999; Traffic, 2000; Ocean's Eleven, 2001; Solaris, 2002; Ocean's Twelve, Able Edwards, Criminal, Keane, 2004; The Big Empty, The Jacket, Bubble and Good Luck, Syriana, Rumor Has It, 2005; A Scanner Darkly, The Half Life of Timofey Berezin, 2006; Wind Chill, Michael Clayton, I'm Not There, 2007; Guerrilla, The Argentine, 2008. Honours: Academy Award for Best Director, Traffic, 2000. Address: P O Box 2000, Orange, VA 22960, USA.

SOHN Ogyu, b. 1 June 1956, Andong, Gyeongsangbuk-do, Korea. Professor. m. Younghee Seo, 1 son, 1 daughter. Education: BA, 1976, ME, 1981, Literature, Pusan National University, Busan; PhD, Sungkynkwan University, 1990. Appointments: Lecturer, 1995-97, Assistant Professor, 1997-2001, Associate Professor, 2001-06, Professor, 2006-, Jeju National University; Visiting Scholar, Chinese Classical Literature Research Center, Fudan University, China, 2003-04. Publications: 4 books: The Study on the Landscape Literature, 2000; The Study on the Aesthetics of Landscape Literature, 2006; The Study on the Toegye's Poetry, 2002; The Mountain and Water of China Travels, 2004. Honours: ToegyeHak Dissertation Award, Busan Toegye Studies Institute, 1991; ToegyeHak Science Award, Busan Toegye Studies Institute, 2011. Memberships: The Committee for Test item Review of College Scholastic Ability Test, 1993; The School General

Evaluation Committee, 2001. Address: 690-756 Jeju national University, Ara 1-dong, Jeju, Republic of Korea. E-mail: sohnogyu@jejunu.ac.kr

SOLIS Juan Caicedo, b. 18 September 1958, Buenaventura, Colombia. Pastor. m. Clementina Henao Gutierrez. Education: Bachelor's degree, Theological Education, Adventist University, Colombia, 1991; Master's degree, Family Relations, Montemorelos University, Mexico, 1995; Doctorate, Martial and Family Counseling, Rochville University, Texas, 2010; Doctorate, Pastoral Ministry, Andrews University, 2010. Appointments: Church Pastor, 1992-2002; Family Counseling, 1995-2000; International Evangelist, 1998-2010; Ministerial Secretary, 2000-04; President, Association of Seventh-Day Adventists, 2002-10;Director of Family Department, 2003-10. Publications: Technique Family Counseling; Marriage Enrichment; Freedom Behind Bars; Successful Evangelism. Honours: Certificate of Distinction, Rochville University; Award of Excellence, Rochville University; Mention of Honor, Adventist University, Colombia. Memberships: Student Council, Rochville University; Cooperative of Seventh-Day Adventists Church. Address: Carrera 45A # 94-31 Bario la Castellana, Bogotá, Colombia. E-mail: jucaso7@hotmail.com

SOLIS RAMOS Laura Yesenia, b. 21 December 1976, San Jose, Costa Rica. Biotechnology Research Scientist. Education: Bachelor, Forestry, Instituto Tecnologico de Costa Rica, 1998; Master, Forest Ecology, Universidad Veracruzana, 2002; PhD, Science and Plant Biotechnology, Centro de Investigacion Cientifica de Yucatan, 2009. Appointments: Regent Forest, 1998-2001; Instituto de Genetica Forestal, Universidad Veracruzana, 2000-02; Laboratorio de Biotecnologia y Ecologia Aplicada, 2002-05; Centro de Investigacion Cientifico de Yucatan, 2005-08; Researcher and Professor, Laboratory of Biotechnology and Plant Genetic Transformation, Escuela de Biologia, University of Costa Rica, 2008-. Publications: 2 book chapters; Numerous articles in professional journals. Honours: Listed in biographical dictionaries; Honorable Mention, Academic Performance, 1990, 1991, 1992, 1993; Antonio Mora Zuniga First Award, 1992. Address: Escuela de Biologia, Universidad de Costa Rica, PO Box 11501-2060, San Pedro, Costa Rica.

SOLO Ashu M G, Interdisciplinary Researcher; Electrical and Computer Engineer; Mathematician; Political Writer; Entrepreneur. Education: Bachelor's degree, Electrical and Computer Engineering, University of Waterloo. Appointments: Creator of multidimensional matrix mathematics and its subsets, multidimensional matrix algebra and multidimensional matrix calculus; Originator of public policy engineering, computational public policy, political engineering and computational politics; Principal/ Research and Development Engineer and Mathematician, Maverick Technologies America Inc; Intelligent Systems Instructor, Trailblazer Intelligent Systems Inc; Infantry Officer and Platoon Commander Understudy, Cdn Army Reserve. Publications: Over 400 engineering and math research and political commentary publications. Honours: Fellowship, British Computer Society; 2 Outstanding Achievement Awards; 2 Distinguished Service Awards; 2 Achievement Awards from research conferences; Listed in international biographical dictionaries. Address: Suite 808, 1220 N Market St, Wilimington, DE 19801, USA. E-mail: amgsolo@mavericktechnologies.us

SOMEKAWA Mina, Concert Pianist; Piano Teacher. Education: Bachelor of Arts, English, Sophia University, 1981; Postgraduate Musical Studies, University of Missouri-Columbia, 1990-92; Bachelor of Music in Piano Performance, 1993; Master of Music in Piano Performance, 1995, Doctor of Musical Arts in Piano Performance, in progress, University of Illinois at Urbana-Champaign. Appointments: Teaching: Teaching Assistant, University of Illinois at Urbana-Champaign, 1994-96; Faculty, Blue Lake Fine Arts Camp, Twin Lake, Michigan, 1998; Visiting Assistant Professor of Music, Millsaps College, Jackson, Mississippi, 2002; Private piano instructions, various cities in Illinois, 1996-2001, various cities in Mississippi, 2002-2008; Various cities in Washington State, 2008-. Adjudication: National Federation of Music Clubs, Illinois, 1998; Mississippi Symphony Orchestra Young Artists' Competition, 2002; Mississippi Music Teachers Association, 2004; Performance Activities: Associate Keyboardist: Civic Orchestra of Chicago, 1995-96; Principal Keyboardist: Sinfonia da Camera, Urbana, Illinois, 1995-2001; Champaign-Urbana Symphony, Illinois, 1996-2004; Illinois Symphony Orchestra, Springfield, Illinois, 1997-2006; Fresno Philharmonic, California, 1998-2008; Spokane Symphony Orchestra, 2008-10; Major Solo Piano Recitals: Artist Presentation Society Recital Series, St Louis, 1993; Dame Myra Hess Memorial Concert Series, Chicago, 1998 (live radio broadcast); Concerto Solo on Piano and Harpsichord, University of Illinois Summer Festival Orchestra, 1994; Illinois Chamber Orchestra, 2000, 2003; Fresno Philharmonic, 2004, 2008; Spokeane Symphony Orchestra, 2008, 2010. Publications: Ballet Class I played by Mina Somekawa (cassette tape), 1989; The Snowman, Easy Piano Picture Book Series, 1989; The Snowman, piano reduction score, 1987, translated Japanese editions from Zen-on, reprinted annually. Honours: Numerous prizes in piano competitions, 1991-95; Honour for Highest Academic Performance, Sophia University, 1978; Phi Beta Kappa, 1991; Sigma Alpha Iota/Ruth Melcher Allen Memorial Award, University of Missouri, 1991; Golden Key National Honor Society, 1991; University Fellowship, Music, University of Illinois, 1993-94; Recognition as an Excellent Teaching Assistant, University of Illinois, 1995, 1996, Initiation to Pi Kappa Lambda, 1996; Listed in Who's Who publications. Memberships: College Music Society; American Federation of Musicians. Address: 16122 E Valleyway Ave, #D101, Spokane Valley, WA 99037, USA. E-mail: msomekaw@msn.com

SOMMER Elke, b. 5 November 1940, Berlin, Germany. Actress. m. (1) Joe Hyams (twice), (2) Wolf Walther, 1993. Career: Films include: L'Amico del Giaguaro, 1958; The Prize; The Victors; Shot in the Dark; The Oscar; Himmelsheim; Neat and Tidy; Severed Ties; Own TV show, Painting with Elke, 1985. Honours: Golden Globe Award, 1965; Jefferson Award; Merit of Achievement Award, 1990. Address: 91080 Marloffstein, Germany.

SON Kwon, b. 6 January 1955, Seoul, Korea. Professor of Mechanical Engineering. m. Sunjoo Kim, 2 daughters. Education: Bachelor, Seoul National University, 1978; Master, Korea Advanced Institute of Science and Technology, 1980; PhD, University of Michigan, Ann Arbor, USA, 1988. Appointments: Professor, School of Mechanical Engineering, 1980-, Director, Department of Mechanical Design, 1999-2001, Pusan National University, Busan; Board Member, Kosin University Senate; Research Assistant, University of Michigan, 1986-88. Publications: Introduction to Mechanical Engineering, 2002; Engineers Can Do Writing and Presentation, 2003; Irresistible Acts of the Spirit, 2005; The Acts of Faith, 2007. Honours: McIvor Award, 1987.

Memberships: Korean Society of Mechanical Engineers; Korean Society of Medical & Biological Engineering; Korean Society of Automotive Engineers; Korean Society of Precision Engineering. Address: 103-901 Allak Apt, Allak-2-dong, Dongnae-gu, Busan 607-772, Republic of Korea. E-mail: kson@pusan.ac.kr Website: bio.me.pusan.ac.kr

SONDHEIM Stephen Joshua, b. 22 March 1930, New York, USA. Composer; Lyricist. Education: BA, Williams College, 1950. Compositions: Incidental Music: The Girls of Summer, 1956; Invitation to a March, 1961; Twigs, 1971; Lyrics: West Side Story, 1957; Gypsy, 1959; Do I Hear A Waltz?, 1965; Candide, (additional lyrics) 1973; Music and Lyrics: A Funny Thing Happened on the Way to the Forum, 1962; Anyone Can Whistle, 1964; Evening Primrose, 1966; Company, 1970; Follies, 1971; A Little Night Music, 1973; The Frogs, 1974; Pacific Overtures, 1976; Sweeney Todd, 1979; Merrily We Roll Along, 1981, 1997; Sunday in the Park With George, 1984; Into the Woods, 1987; Assassins, 1991; Passion, 1994; Bounce, 2003; The Frogs, 2004. Anthologies: Side by Side by Sondheim, 1976; Marry Me A Little, 1980; You're Gonna Love Tomorrow, 1983; Putting It Together, 1992; Company ...In Jazz, 1995; A Little Night Music, 1996. Film: Stavisky, 1974; Reds, 1981; Dick Tracy, 1990. Honours: Antoinette Perry Award, 1971, 1972, 1973, 1979; Drama Critics' Award, 1971, 1972, 1973, 1976, 1979; Evening Standard Drama Award, 1996; Grammy Award, 1984, 1986. Memberships: President, Dramatists Guild, 1973-81; American Academy and Institute of Arts and Letters. Address: c/o Flora Roberts, 157 West 57th Street, New York, NY 10019, USA.

SONG Kyo Soo, b. 28 February 1977, Gwangju, Jeollanam-do, Republic of Korea. Aeronautical Engineer; Aircraft Maintenance Armament Officer. m. KyoungMin Lee, 1 son. Education: BA, Air Force Academy, 1999; Aircraft Maintenance Armament Officer, Republic of Korea Air Force, 1999; Master, School of Material Science & Engineering, Seoul National University, 2004; Aircraft Maintenance Munition Officer, US Air Force, 2007; PhD, Material Science & Engineering, 2010. Appointments: 2nd Lieutenant, Aircraft Maintenance Officer, 17th Wing Air Base, 1999; 1st Lieutenant, Administary Officer, 2000, Quality Control Officer, 2001-02; Researcher, Aircraft Engine Division, Aero Technology Research Institute, 2005-06; Instructor, Aircraft Engine, Air Tech School in Education and Training Command, 2007; Foreign Military Sale Trainee, USAF, Wichita Falls, 2007. Publications: Numerous articles in professional journals. Honours: Listed in international biographical dictionaries; Chief of Air Force Prize. Address: Aero Technology Research Institute, Kunsa-dong, Dong-gu, Daegu, Gyeongsangbuk-do, 701-909, Republic of Korea. E-mail: sks0228@yahoo.co.kr

SONG Soon Hoo, b. 28 May 1967, Petaling Jaya, Malaysia. Consultant Physician. Education: MBChB, 1992, MD (distinction), 2000, University of Edinburgh, Scotland. Appointments: House Officer, Medicine and Surgery, Edinburgh Royal Infirmary, Scotland, 1992-93; Senior House Officer, Medicine, Sunderland City Hospitals, 1993-95; Senior House Officer, Medicine, Victoria Hospital, Kirkcaldy, 1995-97; Clinical Research Fellow, Western General Hospital, Edinburgh, 1997-99; Visiting Research Fellow, University of Southern California, Los Angeles, USA, 1999; Specialist Registrar, Diabetes/Endocrinology and General Medicine, Yorkshire Deanery, Leeds, England, 1999-2004; Consultant Physician and Diabetologist, and Honorary Senior Lecturer, Northern General Hospital, Sheffield, 2004-. Publications: Numerous articles in professional journals. Honours: Wightman Prize in Clinical Medicine, Edinburgh University, 1992; Endocrine Society/Pharmacia Corporation International Award for Excellence, 2001; HEART UK Poster Communication Prize, 2010. Memberships: Fellow, Royal College of Physicians, London; Fellow, Royal College of Physicians, Edinburgh; Diabetes UK; British Medical Association; MRCP (UK) Specialty Question Group for Metabolic Medicine, 2010. Address: Diabetes Centre, Northern General Hospital, Herries Road, Sheffield S5 7AU, England. E-mail: soon_song@hotmail.com

SONG Yong Tai, b. 6 January 1973, Seoul, Korea. Plastic Surgeon. m. Nam Hee Lee, 1 daughter. Education: Doctor of Medicine, Hanyang University, College of Medicine, 1997; Master of Medicine, Plastic and Reconstructive Surgery, Inje University, Graduate School of Medicine, 2005; PhD, Medicine, Hanyang University Graduate School of Medicine, 2009. Appointments: Intern, 1997-98, Attending Professor, Plastic & Reconstructive Surgery, 2011-, Hanyang University Medical Center; Army Surgeon, military service, 1998-2001; Resident, Plastic & Reconstructive Surgery, Inje University Seoul Paik Hospital, 2001-05; Clinical Fellowship, Hirslanden's Cranio-Facial Centre, Aarau, Switzerland, 2005; Director, Jawgak Plastic Surgery Clinic, 2006-. Publications: Numerous articles in professional journals. Memberships: The Korean Society of Plastic and Reconstructive Surgeons; The Korean Society for Aesthetic Plastic Surgery; The Korean Cleft Palate-Craniofacial Association; The Korean Association of Plastic Surgeons. Address: Jawgak Plastic Surgery Clinic, 314 Dossiervit 2-cha building (2nd), #1328-11 Seocho-dong, Seocho-gu, Seoul 137-858, Republic of Korea. E-mail: yongtaisong@gmail.com

SONG Young-Hak, b. 7 October 1974, Busan, South Korea. Senior Researcher. m. Ji-young Park, 1 daughter. Education: Bachelor, Dong-A University, Korea, 2000; Master, 2003, Doctor (Architectural Engineer), 2006, Kyushu University, Japan. Appointments: Assistant Professor, Kyushu University, 2006-07; Manager, LG Electronics, 2007-10; Senior Researcher, Korea Institute of Construction Technology, 2010-. Publications: A study on the energy performance of a cooling plant system, 2008; A development of easy-to-use tool for fault detection and diagnosis in building air-conditioning systems, 2008; Eight more publications in professional journals; Translations: The fundamental of Building HVAC control, 2012; Building Energy and the Automatic HVAC control, 2012. Honours: Award of Technical Paper, Society of Heating, Air-Conditioning and Sanitary Engineers of Japan, 2009; Excellent Award of Technical Paper, Architectural Institute of Korea, 2011. Memberships: The Society of Heating, Air-conditioning and Sanitary Engineers of Japan; Architectural Institute of Korea; Architectural Institute of Japan. Address: Korea Institute of Construction Technology, 283 Goyangdae-Ro, Ilsanseo-Gu, Gyeonggi-Do, 411-712, South Korea.

SONNENFELD Barry, b. 1 April 1953, New York. Cinematographer; Film Director. Appointments: Cinematographer, Producer and Director: m. Susan Ringo,1 child. Films: Blood Simple, 1984; Compromision Positions, 1985; Three O'Clock High, 1987; Raising Arizona, 1987; Throw Momma from the Train, 1987; Big, 1988; When Harry Met Sally..., 1989; Miller's Crossing, 1990; Misery, 1990; The Addams Family, 1991; Addams Family Values, 1993; For Love of Money, 1993; Get Shorty, 1995; Men in Black, 1997; Wild Wild West, 1999; Chippendales, 2000; Big Trouble, 2002; Men in Black II, 2002; The Ladykillers, 2004; Lemony Snicket's A Series of Unfortunate Events, 2004; Enchanted, 2007; Space

Chimps, 2008.TV: Out of Step, 1984; Fantasy Island, 1998; Secret Agent Man, 2000; The Crew, 2000; The Tick, 2001; Karen Sisco, 2003; Pushing Daisies, 2007. Honours: Emmy Award for best cinematography. Address: Gersh Agency, 232 North Canon Drive, Beverly Hills, CA 90210, USA.

SOPER Michael Courtney, b. 20 September 1941, Bournemouth, England. Researcher; Author. Education: BA (Hons), 1969, MA, 1989, Keele University; InterEurope Certificate, 1988. Appointments: Scientific Assistant, Physics, R R E Malvern, 1961-63; Elect Draughtsman, Heenan, Worcester, 1964-65; Freelance Maths Tutor, 1982-; Tutor, Open University; Lecturer II, Electronics, Oxford Polytechnic, 1984-85; Electronics, Oxford University Res Tech, 1982-84, 1986-88; Freelance Tech Author, 1988-93; PFTN Electroquantics CLB, New Marston, Oxford; Res Director, PFTN Research, Oxford, 1990-2011. Publications: Numerous articles in professional journals. Memberships: CIUFOR Research Organisation, Wheatley, Oxfordshire.

SORVINO Mira, b. 28 September 1968. Actress. m. Christopher Backus, 2004, 2 sons, 2 daughters. Education: Harvard University. Career: Film appearances include: Amongst Friends, The Second Greatest Story Ever Told, 1993; Quiz Show, Parallel Lives, Barcelona, 1994; Tarantella, Sweet Nothing, Mighty Aphrodite, The Dutch Master, Blue in the Face, 1995; Beautiful Girls, Norma Jean and Marilyn, Jake's Women, 1996; Romy and Michele's High School Reunion, The Replacement Killers, Mimic, 1997; Summer of Sam, At First Sight, 1999; Joan of Arc: The Virgin Warrior, 2000; Lisa Picard is Famous, The Great Gatsby, The Triumph of Love, 2001; Wisegirls, The Grey Zone, 2002; Gods and Generals, 2003; The Final Cut, 2004; The Reader, 2005; Reservation Road, Leningrad, 2007; Like Dandelion Dust, Multiple Sarcasms, 2008; Like Dandelion Dust, The Trouble with Cali, Attack on Leningrad, 2009; The Presence, 2010; Angels Crest, 2011; Perfect Sisters, Trade of Innocents, 2012; Television: The Great Gatsby, 2000. Honours: Academy Award, Best Supporting Actress, 1995. Address: The William Morris Agency, 1325 Avenue of the Americas, New York, NY 10019, USA.

SOU Gryphon, b. 24 September 1962, Victoria, Canada. Visiting Professor. Education: BS, Engineering, California Coast University, 1992; M of Administration, Australian Catholic University, 1995; Doctor of Management, International Management Center – Southern Cross University, 2001; Post-Doctoral A+ Enhancement Award, IMC, Revans University, 2002; Doctor of Letters, Irish International University, 2003. Appointments: Chief Executive Engineer, Sinocan Group, Canada, 1994-; Consulting Engineer, Sino-Brit (HK) Management Services & Engineering Consultancy, 1992-94; Visiting Professor, Asia International Open University (Macau), 2001-; Elite Scholar & Honorary Editor, Science Paper Online, Center for Science & Development, Ministry of Education, PRC, 2005-; Member, National Certificate Committee of Chinese Career Managers, PRC, 2005-. Memberships: Fellow: Academy of Multi-Skills; College of Preceptors; College of Teachers; Faculty of Business Administration; Institute of Incorporated Engineers; Institution of Executives & Managers; Institute of Management Specialists; Institute of Business Administration; Society of Sales & Management & Administrators; Professional Business & Technical Management; Society of Professional Engineers; International Society of Professional Engineers; Institution of Diagnostic Engineers; Institute of Leadership & Management; Hong Kong Quality Management Association; Senior Member, Chinese Mechanical Engineering Society; Life Member, Hong Kong Teachers Association; Member: Association of Business Executives; Institute of Commercial Management; Royal Institute of Navigation; American Society of Mechanical Engineers; American Society of Engineering Management; National Society of Professional Engineers; Associate Member: Royal Institution of Naval Architects; Hong Kong Institution of Engineers. Address: Unit H, 9th Floor, Block 2, 15 Kwai Yi Road, Kwai Fong, New Territories, Hong Kong.

SOUDAN Jean Pol, (Soudan Lord John's) b. 2 July 1953, Louise-Marie, Belgium. Flemish Artist; Painter. Divorced, 1 son. Education: Academy of Tournai, 1968-70; Academy of London, 1972-73; Academy of Lille, 1973-74; Academy of Brussels, 1974-76. Career to date: Painter, originally inspired by the Ardennes countryside and the North Sea; Later work in more fantastic and symbolic style, oriented towards an austral painting looking for high colours; Puts finishing touches to his paintings by scraping with a palette knife, which is an expression of excellence; Represented in many different museums in Belgium and several other countries; Architect, Industrial Design Draughtsman, concentrated on making projects concerning various ancient and new villas styles or luxury buildings; Involved with projects on Belgian power stations, Brussels Underground system and many building companies in Brussels; Signs paintings under the name of Lord John's. Publications: Featured in many reference publications and other books. Memberships: Royal Association and Royal Foundation of the Professional Belgian Artists Painters; Royal Association and Royal Foundation, Sabam of Belgium; Authors Rights Copyright and Preservations for the Belgian Artists; Member, Accadémia del Verbano. Address: 95 rue de la Lorette, The Old Memphis, Renaix 9600, Belgium. Website: www.artpartnerscenter.com

SPACEK Jiri, b. 13 August 1957, Hradec Kralove, Czech Republic. Oncogynecologist; Obstetrician. m. Maria Zubata, 1 son, 1 daughter. Education: Doctor of Medicine, School of Medicine, Charles University, Prague, 1982; 1st degree, 1985; 2nd degree, 1990; Pediatric Gynecologist, 1996; Medical Oncology, 1999; PhD, 2000; IFEPAG, 2001; Associate Professor, 2006. Appointments: Department of Obstetrics & Gynecology, NACHOD, 1982-86; Department of Obstetrics & Gynecology, University Hospital, Hradec Kralov, 1986-; Head, Gynecologic Oncology Department, 2003-. Publications: Intraconazole in this treatment of acute and recurrent candidosis, 2005; The levels of calcium, magnesium, iron and zinc in patients recurrent candidosis mycoses, 2005; Clinical aspects and uteal phase assessment in patients with recurrent vulvovaginal candidosis, 2007. Honours: IFEPAG, 2001; Best Presentation, Czech Society of Obstetrics & Gynecology, 2011. Meme; ESGO; FIGIJ; Czech Society of Obstetrics & Gynecology; Czech Society of Clinical Oncology; Czech Society of Gynecologic Oncology; Czech Society of Pediatric and Adolescent Gynecology. Address: 46 Husova, Hradec Kralove 8, 500 08, Czech Republic. E-mail: spacekj@fnhk.cz

SPACEK Mary Elizabeth (Sissy), b. 25 December 1949, Quitman, Texas, USA. Actress. m. Jack Fisk, 1974, 2 daughters. Education: Lee Strasberg Theater Institute. Career: Films: Prime Cut, Ginger in the Morning, 1972; Badlands, 1974; Carrie, 1976; Three Women, Welcome to LA, 1977; Heart Beat, Coal Miner's Daughter, 1980; Raggedy Man, 1981; Mising, 1982; The river, 1984; Marie, 1985; Violets are Blue, Crimes of the Heart, 'night Mother, 1986; JFK, 1991; The Long Walk Home; The Plastic Nightmare; Hard Promises, 1992; Trading Mom, 1994; The Grass Harp, The Streets of Laredo, 1995; If These Walls Could Talk, 1996; Affliction,

1998; Blast From the Past, 1999; In the Bedroom, 2001; Verna: USO Girl, Tuck Everlasting, 2002; Last Call, 2003; A Home at the End of the World, 2004; The Ring II, Nine Lives, The Ring Two, North Country, An American Haunting, 2005; Summer Running: The Race to Cure Breast Cancer, Gray Matters, 2006; Hot Rod, 2007; Lake City, Four Christmasses, 2008. TV: The Girls of Huntington House, The Migrants, 1973; Katherine, 1975; Verna, USO Girl, 1978; A Private Matter, 1992; A Place for Annie, 1994; The Good Old Boys, 1995; Big Love, 2010. Honours: Best Actress, National Society of Film Critics, 1976; Best Supporting Actress, New York Film Critics, 1977; Best Actress, New York and Los Angeles Film Critics, Foreign Press Association, National Society of Film Critics, 1980; Album of the Year Award, Country Music Association, 1980; Academy Award, 1981; Golden Globe Awards, 1981, 1987, 2002. Address: c/o Steve Tellez, CAA, 9830 Wilshire Boulevard, Beverly Hills, CA 90212, USA.

SPACEY Kevin, b. 26 July 1959, South Orange, New Jersey, USA. Actor; Theatre Director. Education: Juilliard Drama School, New York. Career: Stage debut in Henry IV, Part 1; Broadway debut in Ghosts, 1982; Other theatre appearances include: Hurlyburly, 1985; Long Day's Journey into Night, London, 1986; Yonkers, New York; The Iceman Cometh, London, 1998; Films: Working Girl, 1988; See No Evil, Hear No Evil, Dad, 1989; Henry and June, 1990; Glengarry Glen Ross, Consenting Adults, 1992; Hostile Hostages, 1994; Outbreak, 1995; The Usual Suspects, Seven, 1995; Looking for Richard, 1996; A Time to Kill, 1996; LA Confidential, 1997; Midnight in the Garden of Good and Evil, 1997; American Beauty, 1999; Ordinary Decent Criminal, Pay It Forward, 2000; The Shipping News, 2001; The Life of David Gale, 2003; Beyond the Sea, 2004; Edison, 2005; Superman Returns, 2006; Fred Claus, 2007; 21, Telstar, 2008; Moon (voice), Shrink, The Men Who Stare at Goats, 2009; Casino Jack, Father of Invention, 2010; Margin Call, Horrible Bosses, Inseparable, 2011; House of Cards (TV), 2013-. Director, Albino Alligator, 1997; Member, Board of Trustees, Old Vic, London, Artistic Director, 2003-. Honours: Tony Award, 1986; Academy Awards, 1996, 2000; BAFTA Award, 2000; Honorary Doctor of Letters, London South Bank University, 2005; Cameron Mackintosh Visiting Professor of Contemporary Theatre, St Catherine's College, Oxford, 2008; Honorary CBE, 2010. Address: William Morris Agency, One William Morris Place, Beverly Hills, CA 90212, USA. Website: www.wma.com

SPADER James, b. 7 February 1960, Boston, USA. Actor. m. Victoria, 1987, divorced, 2004, 2 children. Education: Phillips Academy. Career: Films: Endless Love, 1981; The New Kids, 1985; Pretty in Pink, 1986; Baby Boom, 1987; Less Than Zero, 1987; Mannequin, 1987; Jack's Back, 1988; The Rachel Papers, 1989; Sex, Lies and Videotape, 1989; Bad Influence, 1990; The Music of Chance, 1993; Dream Lover, 1994; Wolf, 1994; Stargate, 1994; Two Days in the Valley, 1996; Crash, 1997; Keys to Tulsa, 1997; Critical Care, 1997; Curtain Call, 1998; Supernova, 1998; Slow Burn, 1999; Secretary, 2002; I Witness, 2003; Alien Hunter, 2003; Shadow of Fear, 2004; TV: The Pentagon Papers, 2003; The Practice, 2003-04; Boston Legal, 2004-. Honours: Emmy Award, Outstanding Lead Actor in a Drama, 2004. Address: c/o ICM, 8942 Wilshire Boulevard, Beverly Hills, CA 90211, USA.

SPALL Timothy, b. 27 February 1957, London, England. Actor. m. Shane, 1981, 1 son, 2 daughters. Education: Battersea County Comprehensive, Kingsway and Princeton College of Further Education; Royal Academy of Dramatic Art, London. Career: TV: The Brylcream Boys, 1978; Auf Wiedersehen Pet, 1983, 1985; Roots, 1993; Frank Stubbs Promotes, Outside Edge, 1994, 1995; Neville's Island, Our Mutual Friend, 1997; Shooting the Past, 1999; The Thing About Vince, 2000; Vacuuming Completely Nude in Paradise, Perfect Strangers, 2001; Auf Wiedersehen Pet (3rd series), 2002; My House in Umbria, 2003; Cherished, Mr Harvey Lights a Candle, 2005; Mysterious Creatures, 2006; A Room with a View, Oliver Twist, 2007; Gunrush, 2008; The Fattest Man in Britain, 2009; Timothy Spall: Back at Sea, 2010-12; The Syndicate, Sinbad, 2012; Blandings, 2013; Plays: Merry Wives of Windsor; Nicholas Nickleby; The Three Sisters; The Knight of the Burning Pestle, 1978-81; St Joan, 1985; Mandragola, 1985; Le Bourgeois Gentilhomme, 1993; A Midsummer Night's Dream, 1994; This is a Chair, 1996; Films: Quadrophenia, 1978; Gothic, 1986; The Sheltering Sky, 1989; Life is Sweet, 1990; Secrets and Lies, 1996; The Wisdom of Crocodiles, Still Crazy, 1998; Topsy Turvy, Clandestine Marriage, 1999; Love's Labour's Lost, 2000; Intimacy, Lucky Break, Rock Star, Vanilla Sky, 2001; All or Nothing, Nicholas Nickleby, 2002; Gettin' Square, The Last Samurai, 2003; Harry Potter and the Prisoner of Azkaban, Lemony Snicket's A Series of Unfortunate Events, 2004; The Last Hangman, Harry Potter and the Goblet of Fire, 2005; Death Defying Acts, Enchanted, Oliver Twist, Sweeney Todd: The Demon Barber of Fleet Street, 2007; Jackboots on Whitehall, 2008; Harry Potter and the Half Blood Prince, 2009; Alice in Wonderland, Wake Wood, Reuniting the Rubins, The King's Speech, Harry Potter and the Deathly Hallows – Part I, 2010; Harry Potter and the Deathly Hallows – Part II, 2011; Comes A Bright Day, Upside Down, Love Bite, 2012. Honours: OBE, 2000. Address: c/o Markham & Froggatt, 4 Windmill Street, London W1P 1HF, England.

SPEARS Britney Jean, b. 2 December 1981, Kentwood, Louisiana, USA. Singer. m. Kevin Federline, 2004, 2 sons, divorced, 2007. Career: Presenter, Mickey Mouse Club; Solo artist, 1998-; Numerous tours, TV and radio appearances; Owner, southern grill restaurant, Nyla; Film: Crossroads, 2002; Recordings: Albums: Baby One More Time, 1999; Oops! I Did It Again, 2000; Britney, 2001; In the Zone, 2003; My Prerogative, 2004; B In The Mix: The Remixes, 2005; Blackout, 2007; Circus, 2008; The Singles Collection, 2009; Femme Fatale, 2011; Singles: Baby One More Time, Sometimes, (You Drive Me) Crazy, 1999; Born to Make You Happy, From the Bottom of My Broken Heart, Oops! I Did It Again, Lucky, Stronger, 2000; Don't Let Me Be The Last To Know, I'm A Slave For You, 2001; Overprotected, I'm Not A Girl Not Yet A Woman, I Love Rock 'n' Roll, 2002; Toxic, 2004; Do Somethin, 2005; Piece of Me, 2007; Circus, 2008; 3, 2009; Hold It Against Me, 2011. Honours: MTV Europe Music Awards for Best Female Artist, 1999, 2004; Best Breakthrough Act, 1999; Best Pop Act, 1999; Several MTV Video Music Awards, 1999; Best Female Pop Vocal Performance, 2000; Billboard Music Award, 2000; American Music Award for Favourite New Artist, 2000; Grammy Award for Best Dance Recording, 2005. Address: The Official Britney Spears International Fan Club, CS 9712, Bellingham, WA 98227, USA. Website: www.britneyspears.com

SPEDDING Sir Colin Raymond William, b. 22 March 1925. Emeritus Professor. Widower, 2 children. Education: BSc, Zoology, London, 1951; MSc, Zoology, 1953; PhD, Science, London, 1955; FZS, 1962; DSc (London), 1967; FIBiol, 1967; CBiol, 1984; FIHort, 1986; FLS, 1995. Appointments: Ilford Ltd Research Laboratory, 1940-43; RNVR, 1943-46; Allen & Hanbury Research Laboratory, 1948-49; Staff Member, later Deputy Director, Head of Ecology Division, Grassland Research Institute, 1949-75; Visiting professor, Part-time Professor, 1970-75, Head, 1975-83, Department of Agriculture and Horticulture, Dean, Faculty of Agriculture and Food, 1983-86, Professor of Agricultural Systems, Department of Agriculture, 1970-90, Director, Centre for Agricultural Strategy, 1981-90, Pro-Vice-Chancellor, 1986-90, Emeritus Professor, 1990-, University of Reading. Publications: Over 200 articles in professional journals; Books include: Fream's Principles of Food and Agriculture, 1992; Agriculture and the Citizen, 1996; Animal Welfare, 2005; The Natural History of a Garden, 2003; The Second Mouse Gets the Cheese: Proverbs and their Uses, 2005; What's in Your Garden? 2010. Honours: CBE, 1988; Kt, 1994; Hon Assoc, RCVS, 1994; Hon FIBiol, 1994; Hon DSc (Reading), 1995. Memberships: Family Farmers' Association; Honorary Life Member, British Society of Animal Science; Patron, Land Heritage; Vice President, RSPCA; Fellow, Royal Agricultural Society of England; Fellow, Royal Agricultural Societies; Fellow, Royal Society of Arts.

SPENCER Aida Besancon, b. 2 January 1947, Santo Domingo, Dominican Republic. Professor; Minister. m. William David Spencer, 1 son. Education: BA, Douglass College, 1968; ThM, MDiv, Princeton Theological Seminary, 1973, 1975; PhD, Southern Baptist Theological Seminary, 1982. Appointments: Community Organiser, 1969-70; Campus Minister, 1973-74; Adjunct Professor, New York Theological Seminary, 1974-76; Academic Dean, Professor, Alpha-Omega Community Theological School, 1976-78; Professor of New Testament, Gordon-Conwell Theological Seminary, 1982-. Publications: God through the Looking Glass: Glimpses from the Arts; Global God; Prayer Life of Jesus; Beyond the Curse: Women Called to Ministry; Paul's Literary Style; Goddess Revival; Joy through the Night; 2 Corinthians; Latino Heritage Bible; Global Voices on Biblical Equality: Women and Men Ministering in the Church; Marriage at the Crossroads: Couples in Conversation About Discipleship, Gender Roles, Decision-Making and Intimacy. Honours: Eternity Book of the Year, 1986; Christianity Today Book Award, 1996. Memberships: Society of Biblical Literature; Evangelical Theological Society; Christians for Biblical Equality; Institute for Biblical Research; Ašociacion para la Educacion Teologica Hispana. Address: Gordon-Conwell Theological Seminary, 130 Essex Street, S Hamilton, MA 01982, USA.

SPENCER Gillian Bryne White, b. 22 July 1931, London, England. Museum Curator. 1 son. Education: Selhurst Grammar School for Girls, Croydon; BA, History, 1952, MA, 1956, Newnham College, Cambridge; Academic Postgraduate Diploma in Prehistoric Archaeology, Institute of Archaeology, London University, 1954. Appointments: Curator, Saffron Walden Museum, 1958-61; Museums Education Officer, City of Norwich Museums, 1969-74; Director, Wakefield MDC Art Gallery, Museums and Castles, 1974-90; First Chairman, Wakefield Cathedral Fabric Advisory Committee, 1991-96. Publications: A Beaker Burial at Weeke, Winchester; Excavation of the Battle Ditches, Saffron Walden (co-author); Discoveries in Old World Archaeology, Encyclopaedia Britannica Year Book, 1961; Museums in Education: Trends in Education, 1974. Honours: State Scholarship, 1949-52, 1952-54; Fellow of the Museums Association, 1990. Membership: Museums Association. Address: 12 Belgrave Mount, Wakefield, West Yorkshire WF1 3SB, England.

SPICER (William) Michael (Hardy) (Sir), b. 22 January 1943, United Kingdom. Member of Parliament. m. Patricia Ann Hunter, 1 son, 2 daughters. Education: MA, Economics, Emmanuel College, Cambridge. Appointments: Assistant to Editor, The Statist, 1964-66; Conservative Research Department, 1966-68; Director, Conservative Systems Research, 1968-70; Managing Director, Economic Models Ltd, 1970-80; Member of Parliament, South Worcestershire, 1974-97, West Worcestershire, 1997-2010; PPS, Department of Trade, 1979-81; Parliamentary Under Secretary of State (Minister for Aviation, 1985-87), Department of Transport, 1984-87; Parliamentary Under Secretary of State (Minister for Coal and Power), Department of Energy, 1987-90; Minister of State (Minister for Housing and Planning), Department of the Environment, 1990; Member, Treasury Select Committee, 1997-2001; Chairman, Treasury Sub-Committee, 1999-2001. Publications: A Treaty Too Far, 1992; The Challenge from the East, 1996; Novels: Final Act, 1981; Prime Minister Spy, 1986; Cotswold Manners, 1989; Cotswold Murders, 1990; Cotswold Mistress, 1992; Cotswold Moles, 1993; Contributor, Royal Institution Public Administration. Honour: Knighted, 1996. Memberships: Vice-Chairman, Deputy Chairman, 1983-84, Conservative Party; Chairman: Parliamentary Office of Science and Technology, 1990, Parliamentary and Scientific Committee, 1996-99, European Research Group, 1994-2001, Congress for Democracy, 1998-; President, 1996-, Chairman, 1991-96, Association of Electricity Producers; Governor, Wellington College, 1992-2004; Chairman and Captain, Lords and Commons Tennis Club, 1996-; Member, 1997-99, Chairman, 2001-, 1922 Committee; Member of Board, Conservative Party, 2001. Address: House of Commons, London SW1A 0AA, England.

SPIELBERG Steven, b. 18 December 1946, Cincinnati, Ohio, USA. Film Director; Producer. m. (1) Amy Irving, 1985, divorced 1989, 1 son, (2) Kate Capshaw, 1991, 6 children. Education: California State College, Long Beach. Career: Film Director, Universal Pictures; Founder, Amblin Entertainment; Co-founder, Dreamworks SKG Inc, 1995-; Founder, Starbright Foundation. Creative Works: As Film Director: Duel (for TV), 1971; Something Evil (for TV), 1972; The Sugarland Express, 1974; Jaws, 1975; Close Encounters of the Third Kind, 1977; 1941, 1979; Raiders of the Lost Ark, 1981; E.T. (The Extra Terrestrial), 1982; Twilight Zone - The Movie, 1983; Indiana Jones and the Temple of Doom, 1984; The Color Purple (also producer), 1985; Empire of the Sun, 1988; Always, 1989; Hook, 1991; Jurassic Park, 1992; Schindler's List, 1993; Some Mother's Son, 1996; The Lost World, 1997; As Producer: I Wanna Hold Your Hand, 1978; Poltergeist (also co-writer), 1982; Gremlins, 1984; Young Sherlock Holmes (executive producer), 1985; Back to the Future (co-executive producer), 1986; The Goonies (writer, executive producer), 1986; Batteries Not Included (executive producer), 1986; The Money Pit (co-producer), 1986; An American Tail (co-executive producer), 1986; Who Framed Roger Rabbit, 1988; Gremlins II (executive producer), 1991; Joe Versus the Volcano (executive producer), 1991; Dad (executive producer) 1991; Cape Fear (co-executive producer), 1992; The Flintstones, 1994; Casper, 1995; Twister (executive producer), 1996; Men in Black, 1997; The Lost World: Jurassic Park, 1997; Amistad, 1997; Deep Impact, 1998; Saving Private Ryan, 1998; The Last Days (documentary), 1999; Semper Fi, 2000; AI: Artificial Intelligence, 2001; Taken, Minority Report, Catch Me If You Can, 2002; The Terminal, 2004; The Legend of Zorro, Memoirs of a Geisha, Munich, 2005; Monster House, Flags of Our Fathers, Letters from Iwo Jima, 2006; Transformers, 2007; Transformers: Revenge of the Fallen (executive producer), The Lovely Bones (executive producer), 2009; True Grit, 2010; Super 8, Transformers: Dark of the Moon, War Horse, Cowboys & Aliens, Real Steel, The Adventures of Tintin, 2011; Men in Black 3, Lincoln, 2012; Director/Producer, TV episodes, including Columbo; ER; Band of Brothers; Semper Fi; Taken; Into the West; United States of

Tara; The Pacific; Falling Skies; Terra Nova; Smash; The River. Publication: Close Encounters of the Third Kind (with Patrick Mann). Honours include: 4 Oscars; 4 Golden Globes; 11 Emmy Awards; Order of Merit of the Federal Republic of Germany, 1998; Honorary Knight Commander of the Order of the British Empire, 2001; Knight Grand Cross Order of Merit of the Italian Republic, 2003; Kennedy Center Honors, 2006; Liberty Medal, 2009; Commancer, Order of the Crown, Belgium, 2011. Address: CAA, 9830 Wilshire Boulevard, Beverly Hills, CA 90212, USA.

SPILIOTOPOULOS Epaminondas, b. 22 December 1925, Thessaloniki, Greece. Advocate. m. Sophia, 2 daughters. Education: Law degree, 1951, Athens University; Economics and Political Science degree, Doctor's degree, 1959, Faculté de droit de Paris, 1955; Doctor's degree, 1959; Member, Academy of Athens, 2001. Appointments: Member, Athens Bar, 1952; Professor of Law, 1973, Professor Emeritus, 1993, Athens University. Publications: Greek Administrative Law, Books in Greek and French; Numerous articles in professional journals. Honours: Doctor honoris causa, University Aix-Monseille III, Paris II, Lille II, France; Université Catholique de Louvain la Neuve, Belgium; Temple, USA; Honorary Fellow, University College, London; Honorary Professor, University of Athens. Memberships: President, Argeological Society of Athens; Various scientific institutions. Address: Omirou St, 10672, Athens, Greece.

ŠPIRIĆ Nikola, b. 4 September 1956, Drvar, Bosnia and Herzegovina. Professor. m. Nada, 1 son, 1 daughter. Education: Economist, Facultyof Economy, Sarajevo University; MSc and PhD, Monetary and Public Finance. Appointments: Researcher, Economic Institute, Sarajevo, 1980-92; Professor, Monetary and Public Finance, Facultyof Economy, Banja Luka University, 1992-; Member of Parliament, House of Representatives of Parliamentary Assembly of Bosnia and Herzegovina, 1999-2000; Deputy Minister, Human Rights and Refugees, Council of Ministers, Bosnia and Herzegovina, 2000-; Chairman, House of Peoples of Parliamentary Assembly of Bosnia and Herzegovina, 2001-02; Chairman/ Deputy Chairman, House of Representatives of Parliamentary Assembly of Bosnia and Herzegovina, 2002-06; Chairman, Council of Minister of Bosnia and Herzegovina, 2006-. Publications: 5 books; 5 scientific reports; Numerous articles in professional journals. Honours: Decoration of St Sava, I order; Decoration of Flag of Republika Srpska with Golden Wreath; Golden Medal, Parliament of Greece. Memberships: Alliance of Independent Social Democrats. Address: Trg BiH 1, 71000, Sarajevo, Bosnia and Herzegovina.

SPOONER David Eugene, b. 1 September 1941, West Kirby, Wirral, England. Writer; Naturalist. m. Marion O'Neil, 1986, 1 daughter. Education: BA, hons, University of Leeds, 1963; Diploma in Drama, University of Manchester, 1964; PhD, University of Bristol, 1968. Appointments: Lecturer, University of Kent, 1968-73; Visiting Professor, Pennsylvania State University, 1973-74; Lecturer, Manchester Polytechnic, 1974-75; Head of Publishing Borderline Press, 1976-85; Director, Butterfly Conservation, East Scotland; Academic Board, London Diplomatic Academy, 2001-. Publications: Unmakings, 1977; The Angelic Fly: The Butterfly in Art, 1992; The Metaphysics of Insect Life, 1995; Creatures of Air: Poetry 1976-98, 1998; Insect into Poem: 20th Century Hispanic Poetry, 1999, 2001; Thoreau's Insects, 2002; The Insect-Populated Mind: how insects have influenced the evolution of consciousness, 2005; Karl Spitteler: Imago, translation, 2006. Contributions to: Iron; Interactions; Tandem; Weighbauk; Revue de Littérature Comparée; Bestia (Fable Society of America); Margin; Corbie Press; Butterfly Conservation News; Butterfly News; Field Studies. Honours: American Medal of Honor for Natural History; Admitted to American Hall of Fame; Congressional Medal of Achievement in Literature. Memberships: The Welsh Academy Associate; Association Benjamin Constant; Thoreau Society; Nabokov Society; Authors Guild. Address: 96 Halbeath Road, Dunfermline, Fife KY12 7LR, Scotland. Website: members.authorsguild.net/davidspooner

SPRINGMAN Sarah Marcella, b. 26 December 1956. Professor. Education: BA, Engineering Sciences, 1978, MA, Engineering Sciences, MPhil, 1984, PhD, 1989, Soil Mechanics, Cambridge University. Appointments: Trainee, Sir Alexander Gibb & Partners, 1975-79; Engineer, Gibb Australia, Adelaide, Australia, 1979; Sir Alexander Gibb & Partners, Reading, England, 1980-83; Graduate Engineer, Gibb Australia, Fiji, 1981-82; Research Assistant, Cambridge University, 1983-89; Research Associate, 1988, Research Fellow, 1988-90, Assistant Lecturer, 1991-93, Lecturer, 1993-96, Cambridge University & Magdalene College; Professor, ETH Zurich, Switzerland, 1997-. Publications: Numerous articles in professional journals. Honours: Woman of Achievement Award, Cosmopolitan-Clairol, 1991; Global Young Leader, World Economic Forum, Geneva, 1993-96; Officer of the Order of British Empire, 1997; Life Fellow, Royal Society of Arts; Fellow, Royal Academy of Engineering, 2009. Memberships: EPSRC Peer Review College, 2006-09; Fellow, Institution of Civil Engineers; Chair, Technical Committee on Physical Modelling; International Society of Soil Mechanics and Geotechnical Engineering, 2005-10; President, 2007-, British Triathlon Federation; Member, National Olympic Committee of Great Britain, 2008-; Vice President, International Triathlon Union, 2008-. Address: ETH Zurich, Institute for Geotechnical Engineering, Department of Civil, Environmental and Geomatic Engineering, 8093 Zurich, Switzerland. E-mail: sarah.springman@igt.baug.ethz.ch

SPRINGSTEEN Bruce, b. 23 September 1949, New Jersey, USA. Singer; Songwriter; Musician. m. (1) Julianne Phillips, divorced, (2) Patti Scialfa, 1 son, 1 daughter. Appointments: Recording Artist, 1972-; Founder, The E-Street Band, 1974; Numerous national and worldwide tours. Creative Works: Albums: Greetings From Ashbury Park, 1973; The Wild The Innocent and The E Street Shuffle, 1973; Born to Run, 1975; Darkness on the Edge of Town, 1978; The River, 1980; Nebraska, 1982; Born in the USA, 1984; Live 1975-85, 1986; Tunnel of Love, 1987; Human Touch, 1992; Lucky Town, 1992; In Concert - MTV Plugged, 1993; Greatest Hits, 1995; The Ghost of Tom Joad, 1995; Bruce Springsteen Plugged, 1997; 18 Tracks, 1998; The Rising, 2002; Roll of the Dice, 2003; Devils & Dust, 2005; We Shall Overcome: The Seeger Sessions, 2006; Magic, 2007. Honours: 3 Grammy Awards, 1984, 1987, 2003; Brit Award, Best International Solo Artist, 1986; Rock'n'Roll Hall of Fame, 1988; Numerous Platinum and Gold Discs; Oscar, Best Original Song, 1994. Address: c/o Premier Talent Agency, 3 East 54th Street, New York, NY 10022, USA.

SPROT Aidan Mark, b. 17 June 1919, Lilliesleaf, Scotland. Soldier; Farmer. Education: Stowe School, Buckinghamshire. Appointments: Commissioned Scots Greys, 1940; Served in Palestine, Egypt, Libya, Italy, France, Belgium, Holland, Germany, WWII; Served Libya, Egypt, Jordan, Germany, retired as Lieutenant Colonel, 1962; Adjutant of Regiment, 1945-46, Commanding Officer, 1959-62; Inherited Haystoun Estate in Peeblesshire, 1965; Farmed 3 farms (hill sheep and cattle); Retired, 2003; County Councillor, Peeblesshire, 1963-75; County Director, 1966-74, Patron,

DICTIONARY OF INTERNATIONAL BIOGRAPHY 36th EDITION

1983-, Peeblesshire Red Cross; County Commissioner, 1968-73, President, 1973-99, Peeblesshire Scout Association. Publication: Swifter than Eagles, War Memoirs 1939-45, 1998. Honours: Military Cross, 1944; Scout Association Medal of Merit, 1993; British Red Cross Association Badge of Honour, 1998; JP, Peeblesshire, 1966-; Deputy Lieutenant, Peeblesshire, 1966-80; Lord Lieutenant, Tweeddale (formerly Peeblesshire), 1980-94; Honorary Freeman, County of Tweeddale, 1994-. Memberships: Queen's Bodyguard for Scotland, Royal Company of Archers, 1950-; Member, 1970-89, President, 1986-89, Lowlands of Scotland TA and VRA; Service Chaplains' Committee, Church of Scotland, 1974-82, 1985-92; Member, 1947-, Secretary, 1964-74, Royal Caledonian Hunt; President, 1988-96, Lothian Federation of Boys Clubs; Trustee, 1989-98, currently Honorary Vice-President, Royal Scottish Agricultural Benevolent Institution; Honorary Member, Rotary Club of Peebles, 1986-; Honorary President, 1990-, Peebles Branch, Royal British Legion; Honorary President, 1994-, Tweeddale Society. Address: Crookston, by Peebles EH45 9JQ, Scotland.

SPURWAY Marcus John, b. 28 October 1938, Surrey, England. Retired Insurance Broker and Director. m. Christine Kate Townshend, 2 sons. Appointments: National Service, 4 Regiment, Royal Horse Artillery; Insurance Broker, Director, Morgan Reid & Sharman, Ltd (Lloyd's Brokers, formerly B&C Aviation Insurance Brokers); Specialist in Aviation Insurance; Retired 1999. Publications: Aviation Insurance Abbreviations, Organisations and Institutions, 1983; Aviation Insurance. The Market and Underwriting Practice, 1991; Aviation Law and Claims, 1992. Address: Lomeer, Common Road, Sissinghurst, Kent TN17 2JR, England.

SRIVASTAVA Arvind Kumar, b. 3 January 1955, Faizabad, India. Canine Expert. m. Renu, 1 child. Education: Agra University; Chandra Shekar Azad University of Agriculture & Technology, Kanpur; PDDU University of Veterinary Science, Mathura. Appointments: Veterinary Officer Incharge, various veterinary hospitals, Animal Husbandry Department, UP, 1980-85; Officer Incharge, Veterinary Poly Clinics, Lucknow, 1985-93; Project Officer, Canine Rabies Control, Animal Husbandry Directorate, UP, 1993-99; A D Planning, UPAH Directorate, 1999-2009; Dean, COVAS, Chomu, Jaipur, 2010-. Publications: Over 100 papers in national and international symposia, seminars and conferences; More than 30 papers in professional journals worldwide; 35 popular articles; 3 books: Health Care and Management of Pet Dogs; Special Radiographic Procedures in Small Animals; Homeopathic Treatment in Livestock; 4 monographs; 3 status reports. Honours: Appreciation Award of Excellent Work, 1981-82, 1981; 16 Awards of Honour, 1984-2011; Presidents Award, 1985; National Junior Scientist Award, 1986; Appreciation Award, II World Buffalo Congress, New Delhi, 1988; Award of Merit, 1996; Prashashti Patra, 1999-2000; Eminent Personalities of India National Award, 2002; Bharat Excellence Award, 2009; Bharat Jyoti Award, 2010; Rajiv Gandhi Excellence Award, 2010; Organiser of several national and international symposia. Memberships: Indian Veterinary Association; Indian Association of Veterinary Anatomists; Indian Association for Study of Animal Reproduction; Laboratory of Animal Science Association of India; Association of Indian Zoo & Wildlife Veterinarians; Indian Association of Animal Production; Indian Society for Buffalo Development; Federal Kennel Club of India; UP Kennel Club; Oudh Kennel Club. Address: 19/51, Sector 19, Indira Nagar, Lucknow 226 016, India. E-mail: ak.srivastava55@gmail.com

SRIVASTAVA Jitendra Kumar, b. 28 February 1946, Gonda, Uttar Pradesh, India. Senior Scientist. m. Sudha, 2 sons. Education: BSc, Maharani Lal Kunwari Degree College, 1963; MSc, University of Gorakhpur, 1965; PhD, University of Bombay, 1977. Appointments: Research Training in Physics, Atomic Energy Establishment Trombay, 1965-66; Research Associate (C), 1966-73, Fellow (D), 1973-86, Reader (E), 1986-90, Associate Professor (F), 1990-2001, Professor (G), 2001-, Tata Institute of Fundamental Research; Honorary Consultant, Crystec, Mumbai, 1997-99. Publications: 3 books; 9 book chapters; 140 refereed scientific papers. Honours: Invited speaker at national and international symposia, conferences and meetings. Memberships: Indian Physics Association; Indian Mossbauer Society; Council of Scientific and Industrial Research. Address: N S Group, Tata Institute of Fundamental Research, Homi Bhabha Road, Colaba, Mumbai 400005, India. E-mail: jks@tifr.res.in

SRIVASTAVA Radhey Shyam, b. 7 June 1931, Bahadurganj (UP), India. Scientist. m. Vijay Laxmi, 1 son, 2 daughters. Education: BSc, 1951, MSc, 1953, PhD, 1963, Lucknow University; Certificate in Proficiency in French, 1957. Appointments: Research Fellow, Lecturer, 1954-58, Lucknow University; Junior Scientific Officer, 1958-61, Senior Scientific Officer, 1961-71, Principal Scientific Officer, 1971-80, Deputy Chief Scientific Officer, 1980-91, Defence Science Centre, New Delhi, India. Publications: Books: Turbulence (pipe Flows), 1977; Interaction of Shock Waves, 1994; Research papers and reports. Honours: Postdoctoral Royal Society Research Fellow, Imperial College of Science and Technology, London, 1965-67; Visiting Scientist: Institute for Aerospace Studies, University of Toronto, 1980-81; Materials Research Laboratories, Melbourne, 1983; Chiba University, Japan, 1991; Visiting Professor, Ernst Mach Institute, Freiburg, Germany, 1995; Visiting Professor, Chiba University, Japan 2000; Visiting Professor, Tohoku University, Japan, 2000; Visiting Professor, Tokyo Denki University, Japan, 2001; Visiting Professor, Aachen University, Germany, 2002; 2000 Millennium Medal of Honor, ABI, USA, 2000; Great Minds of the 21st Century, ABI, 2003; 20th Century Award for Achievement, 1998; Vijay Rattan Award, India, 2005; Rajiv Gandhi Excellence Award, 2006; Rising Personalities of India Award, 2006; Bharat Jyoti Award, India, 2008; Rashtriya Samman Puraskarand Gold Medal, India, 2008; Lifetime Achievement Award and Gold Medal, India, 2008. Listed in national and international biographical dictionaries. Memberships: Fellow, National Academy of Science, India; Life Member, Bharat Ganita Parishad, India; Indian Science Congress; Kothari Centre for Science, Ethics and Education (KCSEE); Fellow, United Writers' Association of India. Address: A-3/260, Janakpuri, New Delhi 110058, India.

ST CLEMENT Pamela, b. 12 May 1942. Actress; Presenter. m. Andrew Louis Gordon, 1967, divorced 1976. Education: The Warren, Worthing; Rolle College, Devon; Rose Bruford College of Drama, Kent. Career: Television appearances include: Wild at Heart; BBC Animal Awards: Zoo Chronicles; Adopt-a-Wild-Animal; BBC Eastenders, 1986-2010; Whipsnade, (2, 13 part wildlife series); Not for the Likes of Us (Play for Today); The Tripods; Cats Eyes; Partners in Crime; Shoestring; Emmerdale Farm; Horseman Riding By (BBC series); Shall I See You Now (BBC play); Within these Walls (2 series); Theatre includes: Joan Littlewood's Theatre Royal, Stratford; Royal Shakespeare Company; Prospect Theatre Company (Strindberg and Chekov); Thorndike Theatre (Macbeth); Yvonne Arnaud Theatre (I am a Camera); Leeds Playhouse (Once a Catholic); Victoria Theatre/Dome Brighton

(The Music from Chicago); Films include: Hedda; Dangerous Davies; The Bunker; Scrubbers. Honour: Presented Duke of Edinburgh Awards, St James' Palace, 2000. Memberships: President, West Herts RSPCA; Vice-President, Scottish Terrier Emergency Care Scheme; Patron: London Animal Day; Tusk Trust; Africat (UK); Pets as Therapy; Leicester Animal Aid Association; Ridgeway Trust for Endangered Cats; Pro-Dogs; Other charities involved with: PDSA; Blue Cross; National Animal Welfare Trust; Battersea Dogs Home; Environmental Investigation Agency; Hearing Dogs for Deaf People; International League for the Protection of Horses; Kennel Club Good Citizens Dog Scheme; Project Life Line; Earth Kind; WSPA; Humane Education Trust; Member, Institute of Advanced Motorists. Address: c/o Saraband Associates, 265 Liverpool Road, London N1 1LX, England.

ST LEGER Moya Elizabeth, b. 16 March 1938. Retired. 1 son, 2 daughters. Education: St Mary's Convent, Hampstead; Harrow County Girls' Grammar School; University of London. Appointments: Author and Freelance Journalist, 1960-; Part-time Department of English, University of Düsseldorf, 1960s; Adult Education Centre, Düsseldorf, 1975-93; External Examiner, London Chamber of Commerce, Germany, 1975-93; British Joint Services Liaison Organization, Germany, 1982-88; Legal Translator, 1993-2004; Political Activist, Campaigner for a United Ireland; President, Connolly Association, 2003-09. Publications: St Leger: the Family and the Race, 1986; Articles in: Daily Telegraph; The Tablet; Catholic Herald; The Universe; The Catholic Times; The Month; Doctrine & Life; The Furrow; Priests & People; The Irish Post; The Irish World; Sunday Business Post; Tribune; An Phoblacht; National Catholic Reporter, USA; Valley Morning Star, USA. Memberships: British-German Association; Connolly Association; European-Atlantic Group.

STADELMAN William Ralph, b. 18 July 1919, Ontario, Canada. Professional Engineer. m. Jean MacLaren, 1 daughter. Education: BASc, University of Toronto, 1941; MBA, Wharton School of Finance & Economics, University of Pennsylvania, 1949. Appointments: Chief Process Engineer, Canadian Synthetic Rubber Ltd, 1943-47; Lecturer, Marketing, University of Pennsylvania, 1948-49; Assistant to Manager, Pennsylvania Salt Manufacturing Co, 1950; Secretary-Treasurer, 1950-64, President, 1964-84, Ontario Research Foundation, Mississauga; President, WRS Associates, Toronto, 1984-; Director, Senior Executive, Institute of Chemical Science and Technology, 1985-89. Honours: Canada Medal, 1967. Memberships: Committee of Directors of Research Associations in Great Britain; Board of Trade of Metropolitan Toronto; Innovation Management Association of Canada; Club of Rome; Fellow, World Academy of Art and Science. Address: 8 The Donway East, Ste 446, Toronto, ON M3C 3R7, Canada.

STADTLÄNDER Christian Thomas Karl-Heinz, b. 8 June 1957. Microbiologist; Epidemiologist. m. Jeanne Marie Parr, 1994. Education: BS, 1982, MS, 1985, Biology, PhD, Microbiology, 1987, University of Hanover, Germany; MPH, Epidemiology, University of Alabama at Birmingham, 1997; MBA, Management, 2003, MIM, International Management, 2004, MA, Educational Leadership and Administration, 2009; University of St Thomas, Minneapolis-St Paul, Minnesota. Appointments: Medical Services Corps, German Navy, 1978-80; Postdoctoral Scientist, Progen Biotechnik GmbH, Heidelberg, Germany, 1987-88; Postdoctoral Scientist, 1988-89, Guest Lecturer, 1996, School of Veterinary Medicine, Hanover, Germany; Postdoctoral Fellow, 1989-91; Postdoctoral Research Associate, 1992-93, Scientific Marketing Assistant, UAB Research Foundation, 1996-97, Postgraduate Scholar, School of Public Health, 1996-2000, University of Alabama at Birmingham, USA; Postdoctoral Scientist, Hoechst AG, Frankfurt, Germany, 1991-92; Visiting Assistant Professor, Research Assistant Professor, Research Associate Professor, Clemson University, South Carolina, USA, 1993-95; Postgraduate Scholar, College of Business, University of St Thomas, Minneapolis-St Paul, 2001-05; Postgraduate Scholar, School of Education, University of St Thomas, Minneapolis-St Paul, 2006-09; Adjunct Faculty, Minnesota School of Business/Globe College, Richfield/Oakdale, Minnesota, 2006; Assistant Professor, University of Minnesota, College of Veterinary Medicine, 2007; Freelance Writer and Independent Researcher, 2010-. Publications: 21 original research articles; 2 review articles; 2 book chapters; 34 letters to the editor; 61 abstracts; 45 book reviews; 1 TV interview; 1 newspaper interview. Honours: Research Fellowship, German Research Council, DFG, 1989; Research Fellowship, University of Alabama at Birmingham, 1990. Memberships: American Public Health Association; American Society for Microbiology; International Organisation for Mycoplasmology; Microscopy Society of America; Minnesota Microscopy Society; International Epidemiological Association; Society for Business Ethics. Address: 3828 Fairway Terrace, Woodbury, MN 55125, USA.

STAFFORD Francis Melfort William Fitzherbert (Lord), b. 13 March 1954, Rhynie, Scotland. Landowner. m. Katharine, 2 sons, 2 daughters. Education: Reading University, England; RAC, Cirencester, England. Appointments: Non Executive Director, Tarmac Industrial Products, 1985-94; Chair, Governor, Swynnerton School, 1986-; Non Executive Director, NHS Foundation Trust, 1990-99; Vice Chairman, Harper Adams University College, 1990-; Vice Chairman, Hanley Economic Building Society, 1993-; Pro Chancellor, Keele University, 1993-; Landowner. Honours: Deputy Lieutenant, 1994-; High Sheriff of Staffordshire, 2005. Memberships: Army and Navy Club; Lord's Taverners; Sunningdale Golf Club; Patron and President various organisations mainly in Staffordshire. Address: Swynnerton Park, Stone, Staffordshire, ST15 0QE, England. E-mail: ls@lordstafford.demon.co.uk

STAFFORD-CLARK Max, b. 17 March 1941. Theatre Director. m. (1) Carole Hayman, 1971, (2) Ann Pennington, 1981, 1 daughter. Education: Trinity College, Dublin. Appointments: Artistic Director, Traverse Theatre, Edinburgh, 1968-70; Director, Traverse Workshop Company, 1970-74; Artistic Director, Joint Stock, 1974-79; English Stage Company, Royal Court Theatre, 1979-93; Out of Joint, 1993-; Visiting Professor, Royal Holloway and Bedford College, University of London, 1993-94; Maisie Glass Professor, University of Sheffield, 1995-96; Visiting Professor, University of Hertfordshire, 1999-; Visiting Professor, University of York, 2003-; Principal Productions: Fanshen; Top Girls; Tom and Viv; Rat in the Skull; Serious Money; Our Country's Good; The Libertine; The Steward of Christendom; Shopping and Fucking; Blue Heart; Drummers; Some Explicit Polaroids; Rita, Sue and Bob Too/A State Affair; A Laughing Matter; The Permanent Way; Macbeth. Publication: Letters to George 1989; The Overwhelming, 2007. Honours: Hon Fellow, Rose Bruford College, 1996; Hon DLitt, Oxford Brookes, 2000; Hon DLitt, Hertfordshire, 2000; Special Award, Evening Standard Theatre Awards, 2004. Address: Out of Joint, 7 Thane Works, Thane Villas, London N7 7PH, England.

DICTIONARY OF INTERNATIONAL BIOGRAPHY 36th EDITION

STAHL Alexander Hans Joachim, b. 27 April 1938, Netzschkau Vogtland, Germany. Official. m. Bärbel Schultheis, 2 sons. Education: Diploma in Politics, Free University, Berlin, 1965. Appointments: Adviser in informal education for the young at the Arbeitskreis deutscher Bildungsstätten, Bonn, 1965-67; Lecturer, Political Education, Jugendhof Vlotho, 1967-69; Youth Officer, Land Youth Office Westfalen-Lippe, Landschaftsverband Westfalen-Lippe, 1972-2003; Deputy-in-Chief, board of film censors, (Freiwillige Selbstkontrolle der Filmwirtschaft) Wiesbaden, 1989-. Publications: Editor, journal: Mitteilungen des Landesjugendamtes Westfalen-Lippe, Landschaftsverband Westfalen-Lippe, Landeshaus Münster, 1969-2003; Honour: Councillor, Stadt Münster, 1975-79; Honorary Member, Bavarian Association of Youth Officers. Address: Von-Humboldt-Str 33, D48159 Münster, Germany.

STÅHL Zeth Idox, b. 27 October 1949, Bunge, Gotland, Sweden. Social Psychologist. m. Kerstin Engström, 2 sons. Education: Teaching Diploma, 1974; BA, 1981; MA, 1984; PhD, 1998. Appointments: Lecturer, College University of Kristianstad, 1993-2001; Established Modus Vivendi, private counselling firm, 2002-; Guest Lecturer, Han University, Faculty of Education, Netherlands, 2008; Guest Lecturer, Roosevelt Academy, Middburg, Netherlands, 2008, 2009; Professor, Sociology and Social Psychology, University of Växjö, 2001-; Established Modus Vivendi (private counseling firm), 2002; Guest Lecturer, Han University Faculty of Education, Arnhem-Nijmegen, Netherlands, 2008; Guest Lecturer, Middleburg, Roosevelt College University, 2008. Publications: Shi Hin Cultivation ... Ethiopia, 1988; The Paradoxes of Good Intentions, 1998; Some articles in professional journals; 3 books, Book I, Book II, and Book III (subtitled More than SPSS in Social Sciences). Honours: Listed in international biographical dictionaries. Memberships: International Sociological Association; National Geographic; The Swedish Association for Treatment of Offenders; Humanisterna. Address: Stastvägen 6, S-35251 Växjö, Sweden. E-mail: zeth.stahl@lnu.se

STALLONE Sylvester Enzio, b. 6 July 1946, New York, USA. Actor; Film Director. m. (1) Sasha Czach, 1974, divorced 1985, 2 sons (1 deceased), (2) Brigitte Nielsen, 1985, divorced 1987, (3) Jennifer Flavin, 1997, 3 daughters. Education: American College of Switzerland; University of Miami. Appointments: Has had many jobs including: Usher; Bouncer; Horse Trainer; Store Detective; Physical Education Teacher; Now Actor, Producer, Director of own films; Founder, White Eagle Company; Director, Carolco Pictures Inc, 1987-; Film appearances include: Lords of Flatbush, 1973; Capone, 1974; Rocky, 1976; FIST, Paradise Alley, 1978; Rocky II, 1979; Nighthawks, Escape to Victory, 1980; Rocky III, 1981; First Blood; Rambo, 1984; Rocky IV, 1985; Cobra, Over the Top, Rambo II, 1986; Rambo III, 1988; Set Up, Tango and Cash, Rocky V, 1990; Isobar, Stop or My Mom Will Shot, Oscar, 1991; Cliffhanger, 1992; Demolition Man, 1993; Judge Dredd, The Specialist, 1994; Assassins, 1995; Firestorm, Daylight, 1996; Cop Land, 1997; An Alan Smithee Film: Burn Hollywood Burn, 1998; Get Carter, 2000; Driven, 2001; D-Tox, Avenging Angelo, 2002; Shade, Spy Kids 3-D: Game Over, 2003; Rocky Balboa, 2006; Rambo, 2008; The Expendables, 2010; Zookeeper, 2011; The Expendables 2, 2012; Bullet to the Head, The Tomb, Grudge Match, 2013; Producer, Director, Staying Alive, 1983. Publications: Paradise Alley, 1977; The Rocky Scrapbook, 1997. Honours: Oscar for best film, 1976; Golden Circle Award for best film, 1976; Donatello Award, 1976; Christopher Religious Award, 1976; Honorary Member, Stuntmans' Association; Officier Ordre des Arts et des Lettres. Memberships: Screen Actors' Guild; Writers' Guild; Directors' Guild. Address: William Morris Agency, 151 El Camino Drive, Beverly Hills, CA 90212, USA.

STAMP Terence, b. 22 July 1939, London. Actor. m. Elizabeth O Rourke, 2002 (divorced). Career: Films include: Term of Trial, 1962; The Collector, 1965; Modesty Blaise, 1966; Far From the Madding Crowd, Poor Cow, 1967; Blue, Theorem, Tales of Mystery, 1968; The Mind of Mr Soames, 1969; A Season in Hell, 1971; Hu-man, 1975; The Divine Creature, 1976; Striptease, 1977; Meetings With Remarkable Men, Superman, 1978; Superman II, 1979; Death in the Vatican, 1980; The Bloody Chamber, 1982; The Hit, 1984; Link, 1985; Legal Eagles, The Sicilian, 1986; Wall Street, Alien Nation, Young Guns, 1988; Prince of Shadows, 1991; The Real McCoy, 1992; The Adventures of Priscilla Queen of the Desert, 1994; Bliss, Limited Edition, 1995; Mindbender; Love Walked In, 1996; Kiss the Sky, 1997; The Limey, Bow Finger, 1999; Red Planet, 2000; My Wife is an Actress, 2002; My Boss's Daughter, 2003; The Haunted Mansion, Dead Fish, 2004; Elektra, 2005; September Dawn, These Foolish Things, 9/11: The Twin Towers, 2006 (voice); Get Smart, Wanted, Valkyrie, Yes Man, 2008; Ultramarines: A Warhammer 40,000 Movie, 2010; The Adjustment Bureau, 2011; Song for Marion, 2012. Publications: Stamp Album, Coming Attractions, 1988; Double Feature, 1989; The Night, 1992; Stamp Collection, 1997. Honours: Golden Globe, 1962; Hon Dr of Arts, University of East London, 1993; Seattle International Film Festival, 1994; Satellite Award, 1999. Address: c/o Markham and Froggatt, 4 Windmill Street, London, W1P 1HF, England.

STAPLETON Katharine H, b. 29 October 1919, Kansas City, Missouri, USA. Retired Food Journalist; Philanthropist. 2 sons, 1 daughter. Education: Barstow School for Girls, Kansas City; Vassar College, AB, Poughkeepsie, New York. Appointments: Retired Food Journalist; Live radio broadcasts, CBS-KOA radio, 15 years; Involved in local, national and international charities for over 60 years; Lone woman (among 16) on board to celebrate Colorado Centennial. Honours: Etoile Noire, French Government; Founder and First Chairman, Denver Debutante Ball, 1959; Girl Scout Award, 2007; Founder's Award, Denver Junior League, 2009; Listed in various international biographical dictionaries Memberships: Denver Country Club; Commandeur, Chevalier du Tastevin; Christ Episcopal Church, Denver. Address: Eight Village Road, Cherry Hills Village, Colorado 80113, USA.

STARR Kenneth Winston, b. 21 July 1946, Vernon, Texas, USA. Lawyer. m. Alice J Mendell, 1970, 1 son, 2 daughters. Education: George Washington University; Brown University; Duke University. Appointments: Law Clerk, Court of Appeals, Miami, 1973-74; Supreme Court, 1975-77; Associate, Gibson, Dunn and Crutcher, Los Angeles, 1974-75; Associate Partner, 1977-81; Counsellor to Attorney General, Justice Department, Washington, DC, 1981-83; Solicitor General, 1989-93; Judge, Court of Appeals, 1983; Partner, Kirkland and Ellis, Washington, DC, 1993-94; Independent Counsel for Whitewater Investigations as well as any collateral matters arising out of any investigation of such matters including obstruction of justice or false statements, 1994-1999; Professor and Dean, Pepperdine University School of Law, 2004-2010; President Baylor University, 2010-. Publications: Contributor, articles to legal journals. Memberships: Several law organisations. Address: Pepperdine University School of Law, 24255 Pacific Coast Highway, Malibu, CA 90263, USA. Website: www.law.pepperdine.edu

STARR Ringo (Richard Starkey), b. 7 July 1940, Dingle, Liverpool, England. Musician (drums). m. (1) Maureen Cox, 1965, divorced, 2 sons, 1 daughter; m. (2) Barbara Bach, 1981. Career: Member, Rory Storm And The Hurricanes, Liverpool; Member, The Beatles, 1962-70; Appearances, Hamburg, 1962; Worldwide tours, 1963-; Attended Transcendental Meditation Course, Maharishi's Academy, Rishkesh, India, 1968; Co-founder, Apple Corps Ltd, 1968; Solo artiste, 1969-; Narrator, childrens television series, Thomas The Tank Engine; Film appearances include: A Hard Day's Night; Help!; Candy; The Magic Christian. Recordings: Albums include: with The Beatles: Please Please Me, 1963; With The Beatles, 1963; A Hard Day's Night, 1964; Beatles For Sale, 1965; Help!, 1965; Rubber Soul, 1966; Revolver, 1966; Sgt Pepper's Lonely Hearts Club Band, 1967; The Beatles (White Album), 1968; Yellow Submarine, 1969; Abbey Road, 1969; Let It Be, 1970; Solo albums: Sentimental Journey, 1969; Beaucoups Of Blue, 1970; Ringo, 1973; Goodnight Vienna, 1974; Blasts From Your Past, 1975; Ringo's Rotogravure, 1976; Ringo The 4th, 1977; Bad Boy, 1977; Stop And Smell The Roses, 1981; Old Wave, 1985; StarrStruck - Ringo's Best (1976-83), 1989; Time Takes Time, 1992; Solo singles include: It Don't Come Easy; Back Off Boogaloo; Photograph; You're Sixteen; Oh My My; Snookeroo; Only You. Numerous honours with the Beatles include: BPI Awards: Best British Album (Sgt Pepper's Lonely Hearts Club Band), Best British Group, 1952-77, 1977; Inducted into Rock And Roll Hall Of Fame, 198. Current Management: David Fishof Presents, 252 W 71st Street, New York, NY 10023, USA.

STARY Frank E, b. 3 January 1941, St Paul, Minnesota, USA. Professor. m. Education: BChem, University of Minnesota, 1963; PhD, Inorganic Chemistry, University of Cincinnati, 1969; Appointments: Undergraduate Research, University of Minnesota, 1960-63; Graduate Research, University of Cincinnati, 1964-68; Postdoctoral Research, University of California Irvine, 1968-72; Research Associate, University of Missouri-St Louis, 1972-74; Assistant Professor, Professor, Maryville University-St Louis, Missouri, 1974-. Publications: 15 articles. Honours: Distinguished Teaching Award, 1981. Memberships: American Chemical Society; Phi Lambda Upsilon, Sigma Xi. Address: Maryville University, 650 Maryville University Drive, St Louis, MO 63141-7299, USA. E-mail: fstary@maryville.edu

STAUNTON Imelda Mary Philomena Bernadette, b. 9 January 1956. Actress. m. Jim Carter, 1983, 1 daughter. Appointments: Repertory Exeter, Nottingham, York, 1976-81; Stage appearances include: Guys and Dolls, 1982, 1996; Beggar's Opera, She Stoops to Conquer; Chorus of Disapproval, The Corn is Green, 1985; Fair Maid of the West, Wizard of Oz, 1986; Comrades, 1987; Uncle Vanya, 1988; Into the Woods, Phoenix, 1990; Life x 3, 2000; TV appearances include: The Singing Detective, 1986; Yellowbacks, Sleeping Life, Roots, Up the Garden Path, 1990; Antonia and Jane; David Copperfield, 1999; Victoria Wood Xmas Special, 2000; Murder, 2001; Cambridge Spies, Strange, 2002; Strange, 2003; Fingersmith, A Midsummer Night's Dream, Little Britain, 2005; Dog Town, The Wind in the Willows, Cranford, 2006; Big & Small, Clay, 2008; Return to Cranford, 2009; Psychoville, Dr Who, 2011; The Girl, 2012. Film appearances include: Peter's Friends, 1992; Much Ado About Nothing, 1993; Deadly Advice, 1994; Sense and Sensibility; Twelfth Night; Remember Me, 1996; Shakespeare in Love, 1998; Another Life, Rat, 1999; Crush, 2000; Bright Young Things, Virgin of Liverpool, Blackball, Family Business, 2002; Vera Drake, 2004; Nanny McPhee, 3 & 3, 2005; Freedom Writers, How About You, Harry Potter and the Order of the Phoenix, Where Have I Been All Your Life, 2007; Three and Out, 2008; Taking Woodstock, 2009; Alice in Wonderland (voice), Harry Potter and the Deathly Hallows, Part I, Another Year, 2010; The Awakening, Arthur Christmas, 2011. Honours: Oliver Award, Best Supporting Actress, 1985; Oliver Award, Best Actress in a Musical, 1990; Best Performance by an Actress, British Industry Film Awards, 2005; Best Actress, European Film Awards, 2005; Los Angeles Film Critics' Association, 2005; New York Film Critics' Circle, 2005; Evening Standard British Film Awards, 2005; Best Actress in a Leading Role, BAFTA Awards, 2005; OBE, 2006. Address: c/o ARG, 4 Great Portland Street, London W1W 4PA, England.

STAVANS Ilan, b. 7 April 1961, Mexico. Critic; Writer; Professor. m. Alison Sparks, 1988, 2 sons. Education: BA, Universidad Autónoma Metropolitana, 1984; MA, The Jewish Theological Seminary, 1987; MA, 1988, MPhil, 1989, PhD, 1990, Columbia University. Appointments: Editor-in-Chief, Hopscotch; Series Editor, Jewish-Latin America; Lewis-Sebring Professor of Latin American and Latino Culture, Amherst College, Department of Spanish, 1993-; Research Fellow, Institute of Latin American Studies, University of London, 1998-99; Exchange Professor, Deshisha University, Japan, 2010. Publications include: The Hispanic Condition; Art and Anger; The Riddle of Cantinflas; The One-handed Pianist; Mutual Impressions, The Oxford Book of Jewish Stories; The Essential Ilan Stavans; Latino USA: A Cartoon History; The Inveterate Dreamer: Essays and Conversations on Jewish Literature; On Borrowed Words: A Memoir of Language; Octavio Paz: A Meditation; The Norton Anthology of Latino Literature; The FSG Book of Twentieth-Century Latin American Poetry; What is La Hispanidad?; José Vasconcelos: the Poet of RAG; Return to Centro Historico. Honours include: National Endowment for the Humanities, 1991-92; Latino Literature Prize, 1992; Bernard M Baruch Excellence in Scholarship Award, 1993; Nomination to the Nona Balakian Excellence in Reviewing Award, National Book Critics Circle, 1994; Guggenheim Fellowship, 1998-99; Skipping Stones Honor Award; Americas Award for Children's and Young Adult Literature. Address: Department of Spanish, Amherst College, Amherst, MA 01002, USA.

STEAD C(hristian) K(arlson), b. 17 October 1932, Auckland, New Zealand. Poet; Writer; Critic; Editor; Professor of English Emeritus. m. Kathleen Elizabeth Roberts, 8 January 1955, 1 son, 2 daughters. Education: BA, 1954, MA, 1955, University of New Zealand; PhD, University of Bristol, 1961; DLitt, University of Auckland, 1982. Appointments: Lecturer in English, University of New England, Australia, 1956-57; Lecturer, 1960-61, Senior Lecturer, 1962-64, Associate Professor, 1964-67, Professor of English, 1967-86, Professor Emeritus, 1986-, University of Auckland; Chairman, New Zealand Literary Fund Advisory Committee, 1972-75, New Zealand Authors' Fund Committee, 1989-91. Publications: Poetry: Whether the Will is Free, 1964; Crossing the Bar, 1972; Quesada: Poems 1972-74, 1975; Walking Westward, 1979; Geographies, 1982; Poems of a Decade, 1983; Paris, 1984; Between, 1988; Voices, 1990; Straw Into Gold: Poems New and Selected, 1997; The Right Thing, 2000; Dog: Poems, 2002; The Red Tram, 2004. Fiction: Smith's Dream, 1971; Five for the Symbol, 1981; All Visitors Ashore, 1984; The Death of the Body, 1986; Sister Hollywood, 1989; The End of the Century at the End of the World, 1992; The Singing Whakapapa, 1994; Villa Vittoria, 1997; The Blind Blonde with Candles in her Hair (stories), 1998; Talking about O'Dwyer, 2000; The Secret History of Modernism, 2002; Mansfield, 2004; Non-fiction: The New Poetic: Yeats to Eliot, 1964, revised, 1987, 2005; In the Glass Case: Essays on New Zealand Literature, 1981; Pound, Yeats, Eliot and the Modernist Movement, 1986; Answering to the Language: Essays on Modern Writers, 1990; The Writer at Work, 2000; Kin of Place: Essays on Twenty New Zealand Writers, 2002; Mansfield, 2004; My Name Was Judas, 2006; The Black River, 2007. Editor: World's Classics: New Zealand Short Stories, 1966, 2nd edition, 1975; Measure for Measure: A Casebook, 1971, revised edition, 1973; Letters and Journals of Katherine Mansfield, 1977, 2004; Collected Stories of Maurice Duggan, 1981; The New Gramophone Room: Poetry and Fiction (with Elizabeth Smither and Kendrick Smithyman), 1985; The Faber Book of Contemporary South Pacific Stories, 1994; Werner Forman, New Zealand, 1994. Contributions to: Poetry, fiction and criticism to various anthologies and periodicals. Honours: Katherine Mansfield Prize, 1960; Nuffield Travelling Fellowship, 1965; Katherine Mansfield Menton Fellowship, 1972; Jessie Mackay Award for Poetry, 1972; New Zealand Book Award for Poetry, 1975; Honorary Research Fellow, University College, London, 1977; Commander of the Order of the British Empire, 1984; New Zealand Book Award for Fiction, 1985 and 1995; Queen Elizabeth II Arts Council Scholarship in Letters, 1988-89; Queen's Medal for services to New Zealand literature, 1990; Fellow, Royal Society of Literature, 1995; Senior Visiting Fellow, St John's College, Oxford, 1996-97; Hon DLitt, University of Bristol, 2001; Fellow, English Association, 2004; Order of New Zealand, 2007. Membership: New Zealand PEN, chairman, Auckland branch, 1986-89, national vice president, 1988-90. Address: 37 Tohunga Crescent, Auckland 1, New Zealand.

STEADMAN Alison, b. 26 August 1946, Liverpool, England. Actress. m. Mike Leigh, divorced 2002, 2 sons. Education: Drama School, Loughton, Essex. Appointments: Began career in repertory theatre, Lincoln, Bolton, Liverpool Worcester and Nottingham; Stage appearances include: Sandy in the Prime of Miss Jean Brodie; Beverley in Abigail's Party; Mae-Sister Woman in Cat on a Hot Tin Roof, National Theatre; Mari Hoff in The Rise and Fall of Little Voice; David Edgar's Maydays, Royal Shakespeare Company, Joking Apart; Kafka's Dick, Royal Court; Marvin's Room, 1993; The Plotters of Cabbage Patch Corner; The Provoked Wife, 1997; When We Are Married; The Memory of Water; Entertaining Mr Sloane; The Woman Who Cooked Her Husband; Radio: Cousin Bette; TV Appearances: Z Cars; Hard Labour; Abigail's Party; Nuts in May; The Singing Detective; Virtuoso; Newshounds; The Short and Curlies; Gone to Seed; Selling Hitler; Pride and Prejudice; The Wimbledon Poisoner; Karaoke; No Bananas; The Missing Postman; Let Them Eat Cake; Fat Friends; Adrian Mole: The Cappuccino Years; Dalziel and Pascoe; Fat Friends (series 3); The Worst Week of My Life; Bosom Pals; Gavin & Stacey. Films: Champions; Wilt; Shirley Valentine; Life is Sweet; Blame it on the Bellboy; Topsy Turvy; Happy Now; Chunky Monkey; DIY Hard; The Life and Death of Peter Sellers; The Housewife; Confetti; Dead Rich, 2006. Honours: Honorary MA, University of East London; Evening Standard Best Actress Award, 1977; Olivier Award for Best Actress, 1993; Dr hc (Essex), 2003. Address: PFD, Drury House, 34-43 Russell Street, London WC2B 5HA, England.

STEEL Danielle, b. 14 August 1947, New York, USA. Writer. m. (2) Bill Toth, 1977; (3) John A Traina Jr, 1981-1996, 5 children (4) Thomas J Perkins, 1998, separated. Education: Lycee Francais; Parsons School of Design, New York; University of New York. Appointments: Public Relations and, Advertising Executive, Manhattan, New York; Published first novel, 1973, then wrote advertising copy and poems for women's magazines; Wrote first bestseller, The Promise, 1979. Publications: Going Home, 1973; Passion's Promise, 1977; Now and Forever, Seasons of Passion, 1978; The Promise, 1979; Summer's End, 1980; The Love Again, Palomino, Loving, Rememberance, 1981; A Perfect Stranger, Once in a Lifetime, Crossings, 1982; Thurston House, 1983; Full Circle, Having a Baby, 1984; Family Album, 1985; Wanderlust, 1986; Fine Things, Kaleidoscope, 1987; Zoya, 1988; Star, Daddy, 1989; Heartbeat, Message from Nam, No Greater Love, 1991; Jewels, Mixed Blessings, 1992; Vanished, 1993; Accident, The Gift, 1994; Wings, Lightning, Five Days in Paris, Malice, 1995; Silent Honor, The Ranch, 1996; The Ghost, Special Delivery, 1997; The Ranch, The Long Road Home, The Klone and I, Mirror Image, 1998; Bittersweet, 1999; The Wedding, The House on Hope Street, Journey, 2000; Lone Eagle, 2001; Answered Prayers, 2002; Dating Game, Johnny Angel, Safe Harbour, 2003; Ransom, Second Chance, Echoes, 2004; Impossible, Miracle, Toxic Bachelors, 2005; The House, Coming Out, H.R.H. 2006; Sisters, Amazing Grace, 2007; Honour Thyself, 2008; Bungalow Two, 2008; Rogue, 2008. Eight Children's Books; One Book of Poetry. Address: c/o Dell Publishing, 1745 Broadway, New York, NY 10019, USA.

STEEL OF AIKWOOD David Martin Scott Steel (Baron) (Life Peer), b. 31 March 1938, Kirkcaldy, Scotland. Politician; Journalist; Broadcaster. m. Judith Mary MacGregor, 1962, 2 sons, 1 daughter. Education: Prince of Wales School, Nairobi, Kenya; George Watson's College; Edinburgh University. Appointments: President, Edinburgh University, Liberals, 1959; Member, Students Representative Council, 1960; Assistant Secretary, Scottish Liberal Party, 1962-64; Member of Parliament for Roxburgh, Selkirk and Peebles, 1965-83; for Tweeddale, Ettrick and Lauderdale, 1983-97; Scottish Liberal Whip, 1967-70; Liberal Chief Whip, 1970-75; Leader, Liberal Party, 1976-88; Co-Founder Social and Liberal Democrats, 1988; President, Liberal International, 1994-96; Member of Parliament delegate to UN General Assembly, 1967; Former Liberal Spokesman on Commonwealth Affairs: Sponsor, Private Member's Bill to Reform law on abortion, 1966-67; President, Anti-Apartheid Movement of UK, 1966-69; Chair, Shelter, Scotland, 1969-73; Countryside Movement, 1995-97; BBC TV Interviewer in Scotland, 1964-65; Presenter of Weekly Religious Programmes for Scottish TV, 1966-67; for Granada, 1969; for BBC, 1971-76; Director, Border TV, 1991-98; Rector, University of Edinburgh, 1982-85; Chubb Fellow, Yale University, USA, 1987; D L Ettrick and Lauderdale and Roxburghshire. Publications: Boost for the Borders, 1964; No Entry, 1969; A House Divided, 1980; Border Country, 1985; Partners in One Nation, 1985; The Time Has Come, 1987; Mary Stuart's Scotland, 1987; Against Goliath, autobiography, 1989. Honours: Freedom of Tweeddale, 1989; KBE, 1990; Ettrick and Lauderdale, 1990; Hon Dr, Stirling, 1991; German Grand Cross, 1992; Hon D Litt: Buckinghamshire, 1994, Heriot Watt, 1996; Hon LLD: Edinburgh, 1997, Strathclyde, 2000, Aberdeen, 2001; Bronze Medal, London-Cape Town Rally, 1998; D Univ, Open University, 2001; LL D (St Andrews) 2003, (Glasgow Caledonian) 2004; Legion d'Honneur, 2003; KT, 2004; LL D, Glasgow-Caledonian, 2004. Address: House of Lords, London, SW1A 0PW, England.

STEELE Tommy (Thomas Hicks), b. 17 December 1936, Bermondsey, London, England. Actor; Singer. m. Ann Donoghue, 1960, 1 daughter. Career: First stage appearance, Empire Theatre, Sunderland, 1956; First London appearance, Dominion Theatre, 1957; Major roles include: Buttons, Rodgers and Hammerstein's Cinderella, 1958; Tony Lumpkin, She Stoops To Conquer, 1960; Arthur Kipps, Half A Sixpence, 1963-64; The Same, 1965; Truffaldino, The Servant Of Two Masters, Queen's, 1969; Dick Whittington, 1969; Meet Me

In London, 1971; Jack Point, The Yeoman Of The Guard, City Of London Festival, 1978; The Tommy Steele Show, 1973; Hans Andersen, 1974, 1977; One-man show, Prince of Wales, 1979; Singing In The Rain (also director), 1983; Some Like It Hot, 1992; What A Show, 1995; Tommy Steele in Concert, 1998; Scrooge, 2003-04; Film appearances: Kill Me Tomorrow, 1956; The Tommy Steele Story; The Duke Wore Jeans; Tommy The Toreador; Light Up The Sky; It's All Happening; The Happiest Millionaire; Half A Sixpence; Finian's Rainbow; Where's Jack?; Television: Writer, actor, Quincy's Quest, 1979. Compositions: Composed, recorded, My Life My Song, 1974; A Portrait Of Pablo, 1985. Publications: Quincy, 1981; The Final Run, 1983; Rock Suite - An Elderly Person's Guide To Rock, 1987. Honour: OBE, 1979. Address: Laurie Mansfield, International Artistes, 4th Floor, 193-197 High Holborn, London WC1V 7BD, England.

STEENBURGEN Mary, b. 8 February 1953, Newport, Arkansas, USA. Film Actress. m. (1) Malcolm McDowell, 1980, divorced, 1 son, 1 daughter, (2) Ted Danson, 1995. Education: Neighborhood Playhouse. Appointments: Films include: Goin' South, 1978; Time After Time, 1979; Melvin and Howard, 1980; Ragtime, 1981; A Midsummers Night's Sex Comedy, 1982; Romantic Comedy, Cross Creek, 1983; Sanford Meidner - Theatre's Best Kept Secret, 1984; One Magic Christmas, 1985; Dead of Winter, End of the Line, The Whales of August, 1987; The Attic: The Hiding of Anne Frank, 1988; Parenthood, Back to the Future Part III, Miss Firecracker, 1989; The Long Walk Home, 1990; The Butcher's Wife, 1991; What's Eating Gilbert Grape, Philadelphia, 1993; Pontiac Moon, Clifford, It Runs in the Family, 1994; Pontiac Moon; My Family; Powder; The Grass Harp; Nixon; Gulliver's Travels, 1996; About Sarah, 1998; Trumpet of the Swan, Nobody's Baby, I Am Sam, Life as a House, The Trumpet of the Swan (voice), 2001; Sunshine State, Wish You Were Dead, 2002; Hope Springs, Casa de los babys, Elf, 2003; Marilyn Hotchkiss' Ballroom Dancing and Charm School, 2005; Inland Empire, The Dead Girl, 2006; Elvis and Anabelle, Nobel Son, Numb, The Brave One, Honeydipper, 2007; In the Electric Mist, Step Brothers, Four Christmases, 2008. Theatre appearances include: Holiday, 1987; Candida, 1993. Honours: Academy Award, 1981; Golden Globe, 1981. Address: c/o Ames Cushing, William Morris Agency Inc, 151 El Camino Drive, Beverly Hills, CA 90212, USA.

STEIN Peter Gonville, b. 29 May 1926, Liverpool, England. Professor of Law; Writer. m. (1) Divorced, 3 daughters, (2) Anne M Howard, 1978. Education: BA, 1949, LLB, 1950, Gonville and Caius College, Cambridge; Admitted as Solicitor, 1951; University of Pavia, 1951-52. Appointments: Professor of Jurisprudence, University of Aberdeen, 1956-68; Regius Professor of Civil Law, University of Cambridge, 1968-93. Publications: Regulae Iuris: From Juristic Rules to Legal Maxims, 1966; Legal Values in Western Society (with J Shand), 1974; Legal Evolution: The Story of an Idea, 1980; Legal Institutions: The Development of Dispute Settlement, 1984; The Character and Influence of the Roman Civil Law, 1988; The Teaching of Roman Law in England Around 1200 (with F de Zulueta), 1990; Roman Law in European History (translated into 6 languages), 1999. Contributions to: Professional journals. Honours: Honorary Dr Iuris, University of Göttingen, 1980; Honorary Dott Giur, University of Ferrara, 1991; Honorary QC, 1993; Honorary Fellow, Gonville and Caius College, 1999; Honorary LLD, University of Aberdeen, 2000; Hon Dr, University of Perugia, 2001; Hon Dr, University of Paris II, 2001. Memberships: British Academy, fellow; Belgian National Academy; Italian National Academy, foreign fellow; Selden Society, vice-president, 1984-87; Society of Public Teachers of Law, president, 1980-81. Address: 36 Wimpole Road, Gt Eversden, Cambridge CB23 1HR, England.

STEIN Robert A, b. 5 August 1933, Duluth, Minnesota, USA. Writer; Educator. m. Betty L Pavlik, 1955, 3 sons. Education: BSc, Industrial Management, 1956, University of Iowa; US Air Force Squadron Officers' School, 1960; US Air Force Command and Staff College, 1966; Air Force Academic Instructor School, with Honors, 1966; Permanent Professional Counselling/Teaching Certificate, Iowa Board of Public Instruction, 1968; MA, Counselling/Education, 1968; Industrial College of the Armed Forces, with Honors, 1973; MA, Writing, 1986. Appointments: Officer and Pilot, USAF, 1956-77, Retired as Colonel; Assistant Professor of Aerospace Studies, 1964-66, University of Iowa; Associate Professor, 1966-68; Professor, 1975-77; Member, Faculty Division of Writing, Kirkwood Community College, Iowa City and Cedar Rapids, Iowa, 1984-89; Instructor, Creative Writing Program, Iowa City/Johnson County Senior Center, 1994-. Publications: Novels: Apollyon: A Novel, 1985; The Chase, 1988; The Black Samaritan, 1997, 2nd edition, 2000; The Vengeance Equation, 2000, 2nd edition, 2001; Screenplays, 2001, 2008 and 2009; Two Lives to Save & GPS!; Fiction: Death Defied, 1988; Non-Fiction: Statistical Correlations, 1967; Engineers Vs. Other Students: Is There A Difference?, 1967; WhatEVER Happened to Moe Bushkin?, 1967; Quest for Viability: One Way!, 1976; Threat of Emergency, 1988. Honours: 5 Wartime Decorations, 9 Merit Awards; All-American Swimming, 1950; Outstanding Faculty Award, University of Iowa, 1967-68; Iowa Authors' Collection, 1985; Minnesota Authors' Collection, 1987; International Literary Award, 1988; Lifetime Achievement Award, University of Iowa, 1999; Entered in Iowa Athletics Hall of Fame, 2002; Letter Winner of the Year, University of Iowa, 2004; Listed in Who's Who publications and biographical dictionaries. Memberships: The Authors Guild; The Authors League of America; Alumni Association, University of Iowa; Presidents Club, University of Iowa; Daedalians; Air Force Association; Rotary International, Paul Harris Fellow; National "I" Lettermen's Club, Past President, 1978-79; National Iowa Varsity Club Hall of Fame; National Iowa Varsity (Letterwinners) Club, National Board of Directors, 1998-2005, 2006-13, Past President 2002-03, President, 2010-2011.

STEPHENS Frederick Oscar, b. 7 August 1927, Sydney, Australia. Professor of Surgery. m. Sheilagh Kelly, 2 sons, 3 daughters. Education: MBBS, The University of Sydney, 1951; FRCS (Edinburgh), 1958; FACS, 1965; FRACS, 1967; MD, 1970, MS, 1970, The University of Sydney. Appointments: Senior Professorial Registrar, The University of Aberdeen, 1958-60; Joyce Fellow in Surgical Research, Portland Oregon, USA, 1960-61; Senior Lecturer in Surgery, 1961, Associate Professor in Surgery, 1963, Professor and Head of the Department of Surgery, 1988, The University of Sydney; Currently, Emeritus Professor. Publications: Over 200 publications in medical and surgical journals; Books: Cancer Explained, 1997; All About Prostate Cancer, 2000; All About Breast Cancer, 2001; The Cancer Prevention Manual, 2002. Honours: Wellcome Travelling Fellow, 1960; Joyce Fellow in Surgical Research, 1960-61 Fulbright Fellow and Visiting Professor, San Francisco, 1969-70; US Founders Lecturer, 1972; Queen's Jubilee Medal, 1978; Foundation President, The International Society for Regional Cancer Therapy, 1991-98; Order of Australia, 1993; Surgeon to the Queen and other visiting royalty and the visiting President of the USA during their visitsis to New South Wales; Many Visiting Professorships in Australia, UK, USA, Germany, Israel and Japan. Memberships: Australian Medical Association; Edinburgh, Australian and American Colleges of Surgeons; International Society for Regional Cancer Therapy; Director, The Sporting Chance Foundation for Cancer Research. Address: 16 Inkerman Street, Mosman, NSW 2088, Australia. E-mail: sheilagh.kelly@uts.edu.au

STEPHENS Malcolm George, b. 14 July 1937. Consultant. m. Lynette Marie Caffery, 1975. Education: St Michael and All Angels and Shooters Hill Grammar School; MA, Casberd Scholar, St John's College, Oxford. Appointments: Joined Diplomatic Service, Commonwealth Relations Office, 1953, Ghana, 1959-62, Kenya, 1963-65, Exports Credits Guarantee Department, 1965-82, Principal, 1970; Seconded to Civil Service Staff College as Director of Economics and Social Administration Courses, 1971-72, Assistant Secretary, 1974, Establishment Officer, 1977, Under Secretary, 1978, Head Project Group, 1978-79, Principal Finance Officer, 1979-82; International Finance Director, Barclays Bank International, 1982; Export Finance Director and Director, Barclays Export Services with Barclays Bank, 1982-87; Chief Executive, Export Credits Guarantee Department, 1987-92; Chief Executive, London C of C and Industry, 1992-93; Secretary General, 1992-98, President, 1989-92, International Union of Credit and Investment Insurers (Berne Union); Managing Director and Deputy Chairman, Commonwealth Investment Guarantee Agency Ltd, 1998-99; Group Chairman, International Financial Consulting, 1998-; First Executive Director, International Institute for Practitioners in Credit Insurance and Surety, 2000-01; Chairman, Del Credere Insurance Services Ltd, 2001-05; Chairman, IFC Training, 2001-05; Director: European Capital, 1992-2000, Berry Palmer & Lyle, 1994-2001, Maj Projects Associates, 1996-99, Euler International, 1998-2000; Adviser, CDR International; Executive Vice-President, SGA International Florida, 1998-2000; Visiting Scholar, IMF, 1998-99; Consultant: World Bank, 1997-98, 1999, EU PHARE Prog, 1997, 1998, 1999, EU Commission, 1998, 1999, 2000, 2011; OECD (Russia), 2000, 2001; Consultant to governments of Chile, 1999, Bangladesh, 1999, Sri Lanka, 2000, Iran, 2000-01, South Africa, 2000-01, Australia, 2000-03 and 2007-08, New Zealand, 2001, Turkey, 2001, Canada, 2001, 2003, 2007-08 and 2008-09, Fiji, 2003; Singapore, 2011; Special Advisor, People's Insurance Company of China, 2000-; Zurich Emerging Markets Advisory Council, 2000-. Honours: CB, 1991; FIEx; FIB. Memberships: Overseas Project Board; British Overseas Trade Board; Institute of Credit Management; Cook Society; Australian Fine and Decorative Society; Australia Britain Society; Union, University and Schools Club, Sydney. Address: 38 Argyle Street, Bong Bong Hill, Moss Vale, NSW 2577, Australia. E-mail: malcolmstephens@hotmail.com

STEPHENS Michael Massy, b. 8 February 1951, Dublin, Ireland. Consultant Orthopaedic Surgeon. m. Juliet, 1 son, 2 daughters. Education: LRCP & SI, Royal College of Surgeons in Ireland, 1976; FRCSI, 1980; MSc (Bioeng), University of Strathclyde, Glasgow, 1984; D Obst, Royal College of Physicians in Ireland, 1978. Appointments: Clinical Fellow, Spinal Disorders, Robert Jones and Agnes Hunt Orthopaedic Hospital, Oswestry, UK, 1981-82; Lecturer, Orthopaedic Surgery, University of Hong Kong, Queen Mary and Duchess of Kent Childrens' Hospitals, 1987; Clinical Fellow, Orthopaedic Foot and Ankle Surgery, University of Cincinnati, USA, 1988; Consultant Orthopaedic Surgeon, Foot and Ankle and Paediatric Orthopaedic Surgery, Childrens University Hospital (Temple St), Mater Misericordae University Hospital, Cappagh National Orthopaedic Hospital and the Central Remedial Clinic, Dublin, Ireland; Associate Clinical Professor, University College Dublin, 2008-. Publications: Over 180 medical scientific papers in international peer reviewed journals. Honours: The Naughton Dunn Memorial Lecture, 1988; Visiting Professor, Hong Kong University, 1999; Samuel Haughton Lecture and 1st Gold Medallist, 1999; John Gibson Memorial Lecture, 2003; Visiting Professorships: University of Hannover, 1996; Australian Orthopaedic Association, 1999; Canadian Orthopaedic Association, 2000; French Orthopaedic Association, 2000; Barcelona, 2002; Bahrain, 2004; Duke University, USA, 2004; Charleston University, USA, 2004. Memberships: Senior Editor, Foot and Ankle Surgery, 1993-; President, European Foot and Ankle Society, 2000-02; President, Irish Orthopaedic Association, 2003-05; President, Irish Orthopaedic Foot and Ankle Society, 2008-; Irish Orthopaedic Association Society Membership; British Orthopaedic Association; European Foot and Ankle Society; American Orthopaedic Foot and Ankle Society; British Orthopaedic Foot and Ankle Society; British Society of Childrens Orthopaedic Surgery. Address: Suite 1, Mater Private Hospital, Eccles Street, Dublin 7, Ireland.

STEPHENS W Peter, b. 16 May 1934, Penzance, Cornwall, England. Bishop of the Gambia; Methodist Minister; Professor of Church History (Emeritus). Education: Clare College, Cambridge, 1952-57; Wesley House, Cambridge, 1955-57; University of Lund, Sweden, 1957-58; Universities of Strasbourg, France and Münster, Germany, 1965-67; MA BD (Cantab) Docteur ès Sciences Religieuses (Strasbourg). Appointments: Assistant Tutor, Hartley Victoria College, Manchester, 1958-61; Ordained as Methodist Minister, 1960; Minister and University Chaplain, Nottingham West Circuit, 1961-65; Minister, Croydon (South Norwood) Circuit, 1967-71; Ranmoor Chair of Church History, Hartley Victoria College, Manchester, 1971-73; Randles Chair of Historical and Systematic Theology, Wesley College, Bristol, 1973-80; Bristol City Councillor, 1976-83; Research Fellow, 1980-81, Lecturer, Church History, 1981-86, The Queen's College, Birmingham; Professor, Church History, 1986-99, Dean, 1987-89, Provost, 1989-90, Faculty of Divinity, University of Aberdeen; President, Methodist Conference, 1998-99; Superintendent Minister, Plymouth Methodist Mission Circuit, 1999-2000; Minister of the Mint, Exeter and Methodist Chaplain, University of Exeter, 2000-02; Superintendent Minister, Liskeard and Looe Circuit, 2002-03; Chairman and General Superintendent, Methodist Church, The Gambia, 2003-04; Minister, Mid-Sussex Circuit, 2004-06; Minister, 2006-10, Superintendent Minister, 2007-08, Camborne Circuit; Deputy Superintendent Minister, Redruth Circuit, 2008-09; Presiding Bishop, The Methodist Church, The Gambia, 2010-12. Publications: Books, papers and articles in professional and popular press. Honours: Max Geilinger Prize, 1997; Visiting Professor, University of Exeter, 2001-04; Honorary Research Fellow, University of Exeter, 2004-. Address: The Methodist Church The Gambia, PO Box 288 Banjul, The Gambia, 1 Macoumba Jallow (Dobson) Street, Banjul, The Gambia.

STEPHENSON Timothy Congreve, b. 7 March 1940, London, England. Executive Search Consultant. m. Diana-Margaret Soltmann, 5 sons, 2 daughters. Education: Harrow; London Business School. Appointments: Regular Commission, Welsh Guards, 1958-65; Gallaher Ltd, 1965-76; Managing Director, Grafton Ltd, 1980-86; Managing Director, Stephenson Cobbold Ltd, 1987-95; Chairman, Stephenson and Co, 1996-. Memberships: Clubs: Brooks's; Beefsteak; Pratts; City of London; MCC. E-mail: tcs@stephensonandco.com

STĘPNIEWSKI Alfred Daniel, b. 19 January 1939, Pająków, Poland. Mechanist Educator. Education: Master of Mechanics, 1962, Doctor of Engineering, 1974, Technical University of Szczecin; Master of Mathematics, University of Poznań, 1971. Appointment: Mechanist, Educator, Technical University of Szczecin, 1962-2004. Publications: Treaty on Fundamentals of Mechanics: D'Alembert's Supplemented and Generalised Principle as Fundamental Law of Classical Mechanics, 1984; Primary Fundamentals of Classical Mechanics, 1992; Lectures in Mechanics, 1993, 1995, 2002; Loi complétée de Newton et principe élargi d'Alembert comme lois fondamentales de la mécanique, 1982; D'Alembert's supplemented principle and Newton's five supplemented laws, 2006; D'Alembert's supplemented principle and Newton's five supplemented laws, 2007; Appell's equations as a covariant form of the motion equations in a sub-space of Riemann's space, 2008; The genesis of a vector co-ordinate with respect to an axis, 2009; Genesis of the scalar product and vector product of vectors, 2010. Honours: The Golden Cross of Merit; Foremost Educators of the World, 2008; Top 100 Educators Medal, 2011; Scientific Award of Excellence, 2011. Memberships: Polish Society of Theoretical and Applied Mechanics; Polish Society of Mathematics. Address: 70-132 Szczecin, Ruska 33c/9, Poland. E-mail: fredstep@poczta.onet.pl

STERN Howard, b. 12 January 1954, New York City, USA. Radio Disc Jockey. m. (1) Alison Berns, 1978, divorced 2001, 3 daughters, (2) Beth Ostrosky, 2008. Education: Boston University. Appointments: Disc Jockey, WNTN, Newton, Massachusetts; Disc Jockey and Programme Director, WRNW, Briarcliff Manor, New York; Disc Jockey, WCCC, Hartford, Connecticut, 1979; Disc Jockey, WWWW, Detroit, Michigan, 1980; Disc Jockey, WWDE, Washington, DC, 1981; Disc Jockey, WNBC, 1982-85; Disc Jockey, WXRK, 1985-2005, (syndicated on WYSP, Philadelphia, WJFK-FM, Washington, DC, and KLSX, Los Angeles, 1991-); Talk Show Host, The Howard Stern Show, WWOR-TV, 1990-92; Talk Show Host, Howard Stern, E!, 1994-2005; Disc Jockey, Sirius Satellite Radio, 2006-. Publications: Private Parts (autobiography), 1993; Miss America, 1995.

STEVENS Barbara Christine, b. 4 September 1939, Guildford, Surrey, England. Clinical Psychologist. m. John Ridsdale, 1974, deceased. Education: BA Honours, Sociology, London School of Economics, 1961; BA Honours, Psychology, University College London, 1962; PhD, Institute of Psychiatry, London, 1967; Academic Postgraduate Diploma, Clinical Psychology, British Psychology Society, 1982. Appointments: Medical Research Council Social Psychiatry Unit, 1962-72; Research Staff, Institute Psychiatry, 1972-77; Senior Psychologist, HM Prison Service, 1977-83; Senior Psychologist, 1983-85, Consultant Forensic Psychologist, 1985-2002, Runwell Hospital, Wickford, Essex. Publications: Marriage and Fertility of Women Suffering from Schizophrenia and Affective Disorders, 1969; Dependence of Schizophrenic Patients on Elderly Relatives, 1972; The Role of Fluphenazine Decanoate in Lessening the Burden of Chronic Schizophrenics in the Community, 1973; Numerous other scientific papers. Honours: Mapother Research Fellowship, 1962-66; Member, Medical Research Council Scientific Staff, 1962-72. Memberships: Associate Fellow, British Psychology Society, Member Criminological and Clinical Divisions, 1982; Elected, Academy of Experts, Grays Inn, London, 1996; Member of Royal Society for the Prevention of Cruelty to Animals, The Dog's Trust, Peoples Dispensary for Sick Animals, World Wildlife Fund; World Society for Protection of Animals. Address: 14 Devonshire Place, London W1G 6HX, England.

STEVENS Geoffrey, b. 4 June 1942, West Bromwich, England. Chemist; Poet. m. (1) Barbara C Smith, 1965, 1 daughter, (2) Geraldine M Wall, 1996. Education: HNC, Chemistry, Wolverhampton Polytechnic. Appointments: Director of Industrial Archaeology, Black Country Society; Editor, Purple Patch Poetry Magazine, 1976-. Publications: Ecstasy, 1992; Field Manual for Poetry Lovers, 1992; A Comparison of Myself With Ivan Blatny, 1992; The Surreal Mind Paints Poetry, 1993; The Complacency of the English, 1995; Skin Print, 1995; For Reference Only, 1999; The Phrenology of Anaglypta, 2003; A Keelhauling Through Ireland, 2005; The All Night Cafe, 2006; Reality is Not Achievable, 2006; Absinthe on Your Icecream, 2007; The Previously Uncollected Selected, Poems: 1975-2007, 2008; An Englishman's Right, 2009; The Instability of Nitro-Cellulose, 2009; Islands in the Blood, 2010; Contributions to: Magazines and periodicals. Honour: Award for Service to Poetry, Hastings Poetry Festival, 1997; Ted Slade Award for Services to Poetry, 2009. Address: 25 Griffiths Road, West Bromwich B71 2EH, England.

STEVENS Jocelyn Edward Greville (Sir), b. 14 February 1932, London, England. Publisher. m. (1) Jane Armyne Sheffield, 1956, dissolved 1979, 1 son, deceased, 2 daughters; (2) Emma Cheape, 2008. Education: Cambridge University. Appointments: Military Service, Rifle Brigade, 1950-52; Journalist, Hulton Press, 1955-56; Chair and Managing Director, Stevens Press Ltd, Editor, Queen Magazine, 1957-58; Personal Assistant to Chair, 1968, Director, 1971-81, Managing Director, 1974-77, Beaverbrook Newspapers; Managing Director, Evening Standard Co Ltd, 1969-72; Managing Director, Daily Express, 1972-74; Deputy Chair and Managing Director, Express Newspapers, 1974-81; Editor and Publisher, The Magazine, 1982-84; Director, Centaur Communications, 1982-84; Governor, Imperial College of Science, Technology and Medicine, 1985-92; Governor, Winchester School of Art, 1986-89; Rector and Vice Provost, RCA, 1984-92; Chair, The Silver Trust, 1990-93; English Heritage, 1992-2000; Deputy Chair, Independent TV Commission, 1991-96; Non Executive Director, The TV Corporation, 1996, Asprey & Co, 2002, Garrad & Co, 2002; President, The Cheyne Walk Trust, 1989-93; Trustee, Eureka! Children's Museum, 1990-2000; Chair, The Phoenix Trust; Director, The Prince's Foundation, 2000. Honours: Hon D Litt, Loughborough, 1989, Buckingham, 1998; Hon FCSD, 1990; Senior Fellow, RCA, 1990. Address: 14 Cheyne Walk, London, SW3 5RA, England.

STEVENS Shakin' (Michael Barratt), b. 4 March 1948, Ely, Cardiff, South Wales. Singer; Songwriter. Career: Enjoyed much success touring for many years with his band, the Sunsets; Starred in the multi-award-winning West End musical, Elvis, which ran for 19 months from 1977; Signed as solo artist with Epic Records world-wide in 1978; First UK Top 30 single, Hot Dog, charted in 1980; First European chart entry, Marie Marie, in 1980; First UK Number 1, later a major international hit, This Ole House, 1981; 38 hit singles, 36 of which were consecutive, throughout the 1980s and 1990s; UK hits: Four No.1s, three No.2s, 12 Top 5 hits, 15 Top 10 hits, 25 Top 20 hits, 30 Top 30 hits and 32 Top 40 hits; Musical collaborations include Bonnie Tyler, Roger Taylor, Hank Marvin and Albert Lee; Tours, personal appearances and television performances world-wide; Headlining to an audience of 200,000 in Vienna in 2003; Most successful hit-maker of the 1980s in the UK, with more weeks in the charts (254 in the 80's alone) than any other international recording artist; His work has been covered by many artists including Eddie Raven (A Letter To You) and Sylvia (Cry Just

A Little Bit), No 1 and No 9 in the Nashville charts, and Barry Manilow (Oh Julie), US hit in 1982. Recordings: Hit singles, albums and songs have sold millions of copies, earning numerous honours and awards, including many Gold and Platinum discs world-wide; Hit albums include (UK): Shakin' Stevens Take One!; This Ole House; Shakin' Stevens; Shaky; Give Me Your Heart Tonight; The Bop Won't Stop; Greatest Hits; Lipstick, Powder and Paint; Let's Boogie; A Whole Lotta Shaky; There's Two Kinds Of Music - Rock'n'Roll; The Epic Years; The Collection; UK hit singles include: Hot Dog; Marie Marie; This Ole House; You Drive Me Crazy; Green Door; It's Raining; Oh Julie; Shirley; I'll Be Satisfied; The Shakin' Stevens EP; It's Late; Cry Just A Little Bit; A Rockin' Good Way (To Mess Around And Fall In Love), duet with Bonnie Tyler; A Love Worth Waiting For; A Letter To You; Teardrops; Breaking Up My Heart; Lipstick Powder And Paint; Merry Christmas Everyone; Turning Away; Because I Love You; A Little Boogie Woogie (In The Back Of My Mind); What Do You Want To Make Those Eyes At Me For?; Love Attack; I Might; The Best Christmas Of Them All; Radio. Honours include: 30 Top 30 hits in a decade, unsurpassed by any other artist; Best singer/performer, MIDEM; Chartmaker Award for 4 simultaneous singles in the German chart; Gold and Platinum discs world-wide; First double platinum single ever to an international artist, Sweden; Most weeks in UK charts for international recording artist; Gold Badge Award from the British Academy of Composers and Song Writers; Number One Gold Award from The Guinness Book of British Hit Singles; In 2004 ranked as the 16th highest selling artist in the UK ever. Address: c/o Sue Davies, The HEC Organisation, PO Box 184, West End, Woking, Surrey GU24 9YY, England. E-mail: suedavies@shakinstevens.com

STEVENS Stuart Standish, b. 30 April 1947, Ferozepore, India. Barrister. 4 sons, 1 daughter. Education: St Josephs E H School, Bangalore; Acton County Grammar School; Royal Holloway College, London University; Inns of Court School of Law; London School of Economics, London University. Appointments: Called to the Bar, 1970; Head of Chambers, 3 Kings Bench Walk Temple, EC4, 1982; Head of Chambers, Holborn Chambers, 1994. Honours: Freeman of the City of London, 1991; Specialist in White Collar Fraud and Substantial Criminal Matters; Listed in various international biographical dictionaries. Address: The Chambers of Stuart Stevens, 6 Gate Street, Lincolns Inn Fields, London WC2A 3HP, England. E-mail: stevens@holbornchambers.co.uk

STEVENSON Juliet, b. 30 October 1956, England. Actress. 1 son, 1 daughter, 2 stepsons. Education: Hurst Lodge School, Berkshire; St Catherine's School, Surrey; Royal Academy of Dramatic Arts. Appointments: Plays include: Midsummer Night's Dream; Measure for Measure; As You Like It; Troilus and Cressida; Les Liaisons Dangerouses; No I; Footfalls; Other Worlds; Death and the Maiden; Duchess of Malfi; Hedder Gabler; The Caucasian Chalk Circle; Private Lives; A Little Night Music; Films include: Drowning by Numbers; Ladder of Swords; Truly Madly Deeply; The Trial; The Secret Rapture; Emma; The Search for John Gissing; Who Dealt?; Beckett's Play; Bend It Like Beckham; Food of Love; Nicholas Nickleby; Mona Lisa Smile; Being Julia; A Previous Engagement, 2005; Red Mercury, 2005; The Last Hangman, 2005; Infamous, 2006; Breaking and Entering, 2006; And When Did You Last See Your Father, 2007; The Secret of Moonacre, 2008; Several TV roles include: The Politician's Wife; Cider with Rosie; The Politician's Wife; A Doll's House; Life Story; Antigone; The March; Maybury; Thomas and Ruth; Aimée; The Mallens; Living With Dinosaurs; The Snow Queen, 2005; Marple: Ordeal by Innocence, 2007; 10 Days to War, 2008; Wrote and fronted BBC documentary Great Journeys; Radio includes: To the Lighthouse; Volcano; Albertina; House of Correction; Hang Up; Cigarettes and Chocolate; A Little Like Drowning; Victory; The Pallisers; Mary Poppins; The Lovers of Viorne. Publications: Clamourous Voices, 1988; Shall I See You Again?; Players of Shakespeare. Honours: Bancroft Gold Medal, Royal Academy of Dramatic Arts, 1977; Time Out Award for Best Actress, 1991; Evening Standard Film Award for Best Actress, 1992; Lawrence Olivier Theatre Award for Best Actress, 1992. Address: c/o Markham and Froggatt Ltd, Julian House, 4 Windmill Street, London, W1P 1HF, England.

STEWART Alec James, b. 8 April 1963, Merton, London, England. Cricketer. m. Lynn, 1 son, 1 daughter. Education: Tiffin Boys' School, Kingston Upon Thames. Appointments: Right-hand opening Batsman; Wicket Keeper; Surrey, 1981-2003 (Captain 1992-97); 126 Tests for England, 1989-90 to 2 Jan 2003, 14 as Captain, scoring 8187 runs (average 40.13) including 15 hundreds; Scored 25,438 first class runs (48 hundreds) to end of 2002; Held 11 catches, equaling world first-class record, for Surrey v Leicestershire, Leicester, 19-22 August, 1989; Toured Australia, 1990-91, 1994-95 and 1998-99 (captain); Overtook record (118) of Graham Gooch to become England's most-capped cricketer, Lords July 2002; 161 limited-overs internationals to 7 January 2003; Retired, 2003; Director of Business, Surrey County Cricket Club, 2003-. Publications: Alec Stewart: A Captain's Diary, 1999; Playing for Keeps, 2003. Honour: Wisden Cricketer of the Year, 1993; OBE, 2003. Address: c/o Surrey Cricket Club, Kennington Oval, London, SE11 5SS, England.

STEWART Dave, b. 9 September 1952, Sunderland, Tyne and Wear, England. Musician (guitar, keyboards); Songwriter; Composer. m. Siobhan Fahey, 1987, divorced, 1 son. Career: Musician, Harrison and Stewart (with Brian Harrison); Longdancer; The Catch, 1977; Renamed The Tourists, 1979-80; Formed Eurythmics with Annie Lennox, 1980-89; Worldwide concerts include Nelson Mandela's 70th Birthday Tribute, Wembley, 1988; As solo artiste: Nelson Mandela Tribute concert, Wembley, 1990; Amnesty International Big 30 concert, 1991; Founder, Spiritual Cowboys, 1990-92; Vegas, with Terry Hall, 1992-93; Founder, own record label Anxious Records, 1988; Owner, The Church recording studio, 1992; Producer, session musician, for artistes including Bob Dylan; Mick Jagger; Tom Petty; Daryl Hall; Bob Geldof; Boris Grebenshikov; Sinead O'Connor; Feargal Sharkey. Compositions for film and TV: Rooftops, 1989; De Kassiere (with Candy Dulfer), 1989; Jute City, BBC1, 1991; GFI (TV series with Gerry Anderson), 1992; Inside Victor Lewis-Smith (TV series), 1993; No Worries, 1993; The Ref, 1994; Showgirls, 1995; Beautiful Girls, 1996; Crimetime, 1996; TV Offal (TV series title theme), 1997; Cookie's Fortune, 1999; Honest (director), 2000; Le Pont de trieur, 2000; Chaos, 2002; Around the World in 80 Days, 2004; Alfie, 2004. Recordings: Albums: with The Tourists: The Tourists, 1979; Reality Affect, 1979; Luminous Basement, 1980; with Eurythmics: In The Garden, 1982; Sweet Dreams, 1983; Touch, 1984; Be Yourself Tonight, 1985; Revenge, 1986; Savage, 1988; We Too Are One, 1989; Eurythmics Live 1983-89, 1992; Peace, 1999; with the Spiritual Cowboys: Dave Stewart And The Spiritual Cowboys, 1990; with Vegas: Vegas, 1992; Solo: Greetings From The Gutter, 1994; Hit singles include: with the Tourists: I Only Want To Be With You, 1979; So Good To Be Back Home, 1979; with Eurythmics: Sweet Dreams, Love Is A Stranger, Who's That Girl?, Right By Your Side, 1983; Here Comes The Rain Again, Sex Crime (1984), 1984; Would I Lie To You?, There Must Be An Angel, Sisters Are Doin' It

For Themselves, 1985; It's Alright, When Tomorrow Comes, Thorn In My Side, The Miracle of Love, Missionary Man, 1986; Beethoven, Shame, 1987; I Need A Man, You Have Placed A Chill In My Heart, 1988; Revival, Don't Ask Me Why, 1989; King and Queen of America, Angel, 1990; Love Is a Stranger, Sweet Dreams, 1991; I Saved the World, 17 Again, 1999; Solo: Old Habits Die Hard (with Mick Jagger), 2004. Honours: MTV Music Awards, Best New Artist Video, 1984; 3 BRIT Awards, Best Producer, 1986, 1987, 1990; Grammy, Best Rock Performance, 1987; 2 Ivor Novello Awards, Songwriters of the Year (with Annie Lennox), 1984, 1987; Hon DMus (Westminster) 1998; BRIT Award, Outstanding Contribution, 1999; Golden Globe Award, Best Original Song, 2005. Address: 19 Management Ltd, Unit 33, Ransomes Dock, 35-37 Park Gate Road, London SW11 4NP, England. Website: www.davestewart.com

STEWART Gordon Thallon, b. 5 February 1919, Paisley, Scotland. Physician; University Professor. m. (1) Joan Kego, deceased (2) Georgina Walker, 2 sons, 2 daughters. Education: BSc, 1939, MB, ChB, 1942, MD 1949, University of Glasgow; DTM and H, University of Liverpool, 1947. Appointments: House Surgeon then House Physician, Glasgow, Scotland, 1942-43; Medical Officer, Royal Navy (Surgeon Lieutenant, RNVR), 1943-46; Hospital and research appointments in UK (Aberdeen, Liverpool, London), 1947-63; Professor of Epidemiology, Schools of Medicine and Public Health, University of North Carolina at Chapel Hill, USA, 1963-68; Watkins Professor and Head, Department of Epidemiology and Professor of Medicine, Tulane University, New Orleans Louisiana, USA, 1968-72; Consultant Physician, Epidemiology and Preventive Medicine, National Health Service, UK and Mechan Professor of Public Health, University of Glasgow, 1972-84; Emeritus Professor, 1984-. Publications: Books: Chemotherapy of Fungal Infection (with R W Riddell), 1955; Penicillin Group of Drugs, 1965; Penicillin Allergy (with J McGovern), 1970; Editor: Trends in Epidemiology, 1972; Chapters on epidemiology, control of infectious diseases and education in other books; Articles on same and on drug abuse and public health subjects in mainline medical journals, articles on liquid crystals and ordered structures in biology and medicine. Honours: High Commendation for MD Thesis, University of Glasgow, 1949; WHO Visiting Professor, Dow Medical College, Karachi, Pakistan, 1953; Senior Visiting Foreign Fellow, US National Science Foundation, 1963-64; Visiting Professor, Cornell University Medical College, New York, USA, 1971; Emeritus Fellow, Infectious Diseases Society of America; Visiting Lecturer and Consultant at various hospitals and colleges in Europe, Canada, America, India, Pakistan, Middle East, Africa; Consultant WHO; New York City Health Department; US Navy (Camp Lejeune, North Carolina). Memberships: Fellow: Royal College of Physicians, Glasgow; Royal College of Pathology, London; Faculty of Public Health of the Royal College of Physicians; Royal Statistical Society; Medical Society of London; Royal Society of Medicine. Address: 29/8 Inverleith Place, Edinburgh EH3 5QD, Scotland.

STEWART Ian, b. 28 August 1950, Blantyre, Scotland. Member of Parliament. m. 2 sons, 1 daughter. Education: Stretford Technical College; Manchester University. Appointments: Regional Office, Transport and General Workers Union, 1978-97; Member of Parliament for Eccles, 1997-2010; Fellow, Industry and Parliament Trust; Member, Deregulation Select Committee, 1998-2001; Member, Information Select Committee, 1998-2001; Backbench PLP Groups: Education and Employment, 1997-2010, Trade and Industry, 1997-2010, Foreign Affairs, 1997-2001; Treasury, 2001-; All Party Groups: Chemical Industry Group, Retail Industry Group, Regeneration Group. Occupational Health & Safety Group, Parliamentary Information Technology Committee (executive member); United Nations Association, Commonwealth Parliamentary Association, Vice-Chair, All Party China Group; Vice Chair, APPG on Kazakhstan; Chair, Group for Vaccine Damaged Children; Chair, All Party Community Media Group; Parliamentary Private Secretary to Brian Wilson MP, Minister for Industry and Energy (Stephen Timms), 2001-; PPS at DTI, 2005. Address: London Parliamentary Office, House of Commons, London SW1A 0AA, England. E-mail: ianstewartmp@parliament.uk

STEWART Martha Kostyra, b. 3 August 1941, Jersey City, New Jersey, USA. Editor; Author; Business Executive. m. Andy Stewart, 1961, divorced 1990, 1 daughter. Education: Barnard University. Career: Former model, stockbroker, caterer; Owner, Editor-in-Chief, Martha Stewart Living magazine, 1990-; Chair, CEO, 1997-2003, Member of Board, -2004, Founding Editorial Director (non-executive), 2004-, Martha Steward Living Omnimedia; Appears in cooking feature, Today Show; Member of Board, NY Stock Exchange, 2002; Member of Board, Revlon Inc, -2004; Under investigation for alleged insider trading, 2002-; Found guilty of conspiracy, making false statements and obstruction of justice, 2004. Publications: (with Elizabeth Hawes): Entertaining, 1982; Weddings, 1987; (as sole author): Martha Stewart's Hors d'Oeuvres: The Creation and Presentation of Fabulous Finger Food, 1984; Martha Stewart's Pies and Tarts, 1985; Martha Stewart's Quick Cook Menus, 1988; The Wedding Planner, 1988; Martha Stewart's Gardening: Month by Month, 1991; Martha Stewart's New Old House: Restoration, Renovation, Decoration, 1992; Martha Stewart's Christmas, 1993; Martha Stewart's Menus for Entertaining, 1994; Holidays, 1994; The Martha Rules, 2005; Martha Stewart Baking Handbook, 2005; Martha Stewart's Homekeeping Handbook, 2006. Address: Martha Stewart Living Omnimedia, 11 West 42nd Street, 25th Floor, New York, NY 10036, USA. Website: www.marthastewart.com

STEWART Miriam Joyce, Professor. Education: B Sc N, McMaster University, 1967; MN, 1976, PhD, 1988, Dalhousie University. Appointments: Instructor, Maternity Education Co-ordinator, Plummer Memorial School of Nursing, Ontario, 1967-69; Community Health Nurse, Algoma Health Unit, Ontario, 1969-74; Lecturer, 1978-80, Assistant Professor, 1980-84, Awarded Tenure, 1983, Associate Professor, 1984-89, Professor, 1990-97, School of Nursing, Assistant Dean, Faculty of Health Professions, 1980-83, Professor, Community Health and Epidemiology, Faculty of Medicine, 1991-97, Director, Atlantic Health Promotion Research Centre, 1993-97, Associate Dean, Faculty of Graduate Studies, 1996-97, Dalhousie University; Director, 1997-2001, Professor, Centre for Health Promotion Studies, Faculty of Nursing, and Faculty of Medicine, School of Public Health, University of Alberta, 1997-; Scientific Director, Institute of Gender and Health, Canadian Institutes of Health Research, 2000-07. Honours include: J Gordin Kaplan Award for Excellence in Research, University of Alberta, 2004; Women's Health Champion, Canada,' 2007; Top 40 Under 40 in Canada Award, 2008; Research Prize, Senior Scholar, Alberta Heritage Fund for Medical Research, 2008; Canadian Nurses Association Centennial Award, 2008; Plaque for Research Excellence, Celebration of Research and Innovation, 2009; Health Senior Investigator Award and Research Prize, Alberta Heritage Foundation for Medical Research, 2010; Listed in international biographical dictionaries. Memberships: Fellow, Royal Society of Canada; Canadian Academy of Health Sciences.

DICTIONARY OF INTERNATIONAL BIOGRAPHY 36th EDITION

STEWART Patrick, b. 13 July 1940, Mirfield, Yorkshire, England. Actor. m. (1) Sheila Falconer, 1966, divorced 1990, 1 son, 1 daughter, (2) Wendy Neuss, 2000, divorced 2003. Education: Bristol Old Vic Theatre School. Career: Junior Reporter, local newspaper; Actor, various repertory companies; Actor, 1966, Associate Artist, 1967-87, Royal Shakespeare Company; Founding Director, ACTER; Director, Flying Freehold Productions, Paramount Studios, LA, 1998-; Films: Hedda; Excalibur; Dune; Lady Jane; Gunmen; Robin Hood – Men in Tights; LA Story; Jeffrey; Star Trek: First Contact; Conspiracy Theory; Dad Savage; Masterminds; Star Trek: Insurrection, 1999; X-Men, 2000; Moby Dick; Star Trek: Nemesis, 2002; X-Men: X2, 2003; Boo, Zino and the Snurks (voice), 2004; Chicken Little (voice), 2005; The Game of Their Lives, 2005; X-Men: The Last Stand, 2006; TMNT (voice), 2007; X-Men Origins: Wolverine, 2009; The Captains, 2011; Ice Age: Continental Drift, Ted, 2012; Dorothy of Oz, 2013; Theatre: Antony and Cleopatra, 1979; Henry IV, 1984; Who's Afraid of Virginia Woolf?, 1987; A Christmas Carol, 1988-96; The Tempest, 1995; Othello, 1997; The Ride Down Mount Morgan, 1998; The Master Builder, 2003; Antony and Cleopatra, 2006; A Christmas Carol, 2007; Macbeth, Hamlet, 2008; Waiting for Godot, 2009; Bingo: Scenes of Money and Death, 2010; TV: Star Trek: The Next Generation; The Mozart Inquest; Maybury; I Claudius; Tinker, Tailor, Soldier, Spy; Smiley's People; The Lion in Winter, 2003; Mysterious Island, 2005; The Snow Queen, 2005; Eleventh House, 2006; Family Guy, 2005-; American Dad, 2005-10; Hamlet, 2009; Macbeth, 2010; Richard II, Futurama, The Daily Show, 2012; Music: narrative to Peter and the Wolf, 1996. Honours: Olivier Award, Society of West End Theatre Awards, 1979; London Fringe Award, 1987; OBE, 2000; Drama Desk Award, 1992; Olivier Award, 1992; Grammy Award, 1996; Knight Bachelor, 2010. Address: International Creative Management Inc, 8942 Wilshire Boulevard, Beverly Hills, CA 90211, USA.

STEWART Paul, b. 4 June 1955, London, England. Author. m. Julie, 1 son, 1 daughter. Education: BA in English, 1st class honours, Lancaster University, 1974-77; MA in Creative Writing with Malcolm Bradbury, UEA, 1978-79; German, University of Heidelberg, 1980-82. Appointments: EFL Teacher, Germany, 1980-82; EFL Teacher, Sri Lanka, 1982-83; EFL Teacher, Brighton, 1984-90; Writer, Child Carer (of own children), 1990-. Publications include: Stormchaser, 1999; The Birthday Presents, 1999; The Blobheads, series of 8 books, 2000; Midnight Over Sanctaphrax, 2000; Rabbit's Wish, 2001; The Curse of the Gloamglozer, 2001; Muddle Earth, 2003, VOX, 2003; Freeglader, 2004; Fergus Crane, 2004; The Immortals, 2009; Wyrmeweald, 2010. Honours: Gold Medal; Winner of Smarties Prize; Fergus Crane, Silver Medal, Nestle Book Prize, 2005 & 2006; Corby Flood & Hugo Pepper.

STEWART Rod (Roderick David), b. 10 January 1945, Highgate, North London, England. Singer. 1 daughter with Susannah Boffey, m. (1) Alana Collins, 1 son, 1 daughter, 1 daughter with Kelly Emberg, (2) Rachel Hunter, 1990, divorced 2006, 1 son, 1 daughter, (3) Penny Lancaster, 2007, 2 sons. Career: Singer with: Steampacket; Shotgun Express; Jeff Beck Group, 1967-69; Concerts include: UK tour with Roy Orbison, 1967; US tours, 1967, 1968; The Faces, 1969-75; Appearances include: Reading Festival, 1972; UK, US tours, 1972; Solo artiste, 1971-; Solo appearances include: Rock In Rio, Brazil, 1985; Vagabond Heart Tour, 1991-92. Recordings: Singles include: Reason To Believe; Maggie May; (I Know) I'm Losing You; Handbags And Gladrags; You Wear It Well; Angel; Farewell; Sailing; This Old Heart Of Mine; Tonight's The Night (Gonna Be All Right); The Killing Of Georgie (Parts 1 and 2); Get Back; The First Cut Is The Deepest; I Don't Want To Talk About It; You're In My Heart; Hot Legs; D'Ya Think I'm Sexy?; Passion; Young Turks; Tonight I'm Yours; Baby Jane; What Am I Gonna Do; Infatuation; Some Guys Have All The Luck; Love Touch; Every Beat Of My Heart; Downtown Train; Rhythm Of My Heart; This Old Heart Of Mine; Have I Told You Lately; Reason To Believe; Ruby Tuesday; You're The Star; Albums include: 2 with Jeff Beck; 4 with the Faces; Solo albums: Every Picture Tells A Story, 1971; Never A Dull Moment, 1972; Atlantic Crossing, 1975; A Night On The Town, 1976; Foot Loose And Fancy Free, 1977; Blondes Have More Fun, 1978; Foolish Behaviour, 1980; Tonight I'm Yours, 1981; Camouflage, 1984; Love Touch, 1986; Out Of Order, 1988; The Best Of, 1989; Downtown Train, 1990; Vagabond Heart, 1991; Lead Vocalist, 1992; Unplugged... And Seated, 1993; A Spanner In The Works, 1995; When We Were the New Boys, 1998; It Had To Be You: The Great American Songbook, 2002; Stardust: The Great American Songbook 3, 2004; Still the Same: Great Rock Classics of our Time, 2006; Numerous compilations. Honours include: First artist to top US and UK singles and album charts simultaneously, 1971; BRIT Awards, Lifetime Achievement Award, 1993; UK Music Hall of Fame, 2006; CBE, 2007. Address: c/o Warner Music, 28 Kensington Church Street, London, W8 4EP, England.

STEWARTBY Baron, Sir (Bernard Harold) Ian (Halley) Stewart, b. 10 August 1935, United Kingdom. m. Deborah Charlotte Buchan, 1 son, 2 daughters. Education: MA, Jesus College Cambridge, 1956-59; D Litt, University of Cambridge, 1978. Appointments include: National Service: Sub-Lieutenant, RNVR, 1954-56, later Lieutenant Commander, RNR; Brown Shipley & Co Ltd, Merchant Bankers, 1960-83, Director, 1971-83; MP, Conservative, North Hertfordshire (Hitchin), 1974-92; Parliamentary Private Secretary to Chancellor of the Exchequer, 1979-83; Parliamentary Under-Secretary of State for Defence Procurement, 1983; Economic Secretary to the Treasury, 1983-87; Minister of State for the Armed Forces, 1987-88; Minister of State, Northern Ireland, 1988-89; Non-Executive Director, 1990-93, Deputy Chairman, 1993-2004, Standard Chartered plc; Non-Executive Director, Diploma plc, 1990-2007; Chairman, The Throgmorton Trust PLC, 1990-2005; Member, Financial Service Authority, 1993-97; Deputy Chairman, Amlin plc, 1995-2006; Non-Executive Director, Portman Building Society, 1995-2002; Chairman, Brazilian Smaller Companies Investment Trust PLC, 1998; President, Sir Halley Stewart Trust, 2000-. Publications: The Scottish Coinage, 1955, 2nd edition, 1967; Coinage in Tenth Century England (joint author), 1989; English Coins 1180-1551, 2008. Honours: RD, 1972; FBA, 1981; FRSE, 1986; PC, 1989; Kt, 1991; Baron, 1992; K St J, 1992; Sanford Saltus Gold Medal, British Numismatic Society, 1971; Medallist, Royal Numismatic Society, 1996. Memberships: Director, British Numismatic Society, 1965-75; County Vice-President, St John Ambulance, Hertfordshire, 1978-; British Academy Committee for Sylloge of Coins of the British Isles, 1967-, Chairman, 1993-2003; Member of Council, Haileybury, 1980-95; Chairman, Treasure Valuation Committee, 1996-2001; Honorary Keeper of Medieval Coins, Fitzwilliam Museum, 2008-. Address: House of Lords, Westminster, London SW1A 0PW, England.

STEYER Rolf, b. 1 December 1950, Fulda, Germany. m. Anna-Maria, 1 son, 1 daughter. Education: Military Service, Bundesgrenzschutz border police, 1969-71; Diploma in Psychology, Göttingen, 1977; PhD, Psychology, Frankfurt am Main, 1982; Habilitation, Psychology, University of Trier, 1989. Appointments: Research Assistant, University of

Göttingen, 1977; Assistant, University of Frankfurt am Main, 1977-82; Assistant Professor, University of Trier, 1982-94; Director of Methodology Research, ZUMA, Mannheim, 1994; Associate Professor, Methodology and Assessment, University of Magdeburg, 1995; Full Professor, Methodology and Evaluation Research, University of Jena, 1996-; General Secretary, European Association of Psychological Assessment, 1996-99; Co-Editor in Chief, European Journal of Psychological Assessment, 1999-2003; Prorektor, University of Jena, 2002-04; President, Center for Human Resources Research, 2002-04, 2008-; President, European Association of Methodology, 2004-2008. Publications: Theory of causal regression models, 1992; Measuring and Testing, co-author, 1993; Probability and Regression, author, 2002; Editor of several newsletters. Memberships: German Society for Psychology; European Association of Methodolgy; European Association of Personality Psychology; European Mathematical Psychology Group; European Association of Psychological Assessment; Psychometric Society. Address: Institute of Psychology, Am Steiger 3, Haus 1, D-07743 Jena, Germany. E-mail: rolf.steyer@uni-jena.de

STICH Michael, b. 18 October 1968, Pinneberg, Germany. Former Professional Tennis Player; Business Executive. m. Jessica Stockmann, 1992, divorced 2003. Appointments: National Junior Champion, 1986; Turned professional, 1988; Semi-finalist, French Open, 1990; Member, West German Davis Cup Team, 1990; Won first professional title, Memphis, 1990; Winner, Men's Singles Championship, Wimbledon, 1991; Men's Doubles (with John McEnroe), 1992; Won ATP World Championship, 1993; Retired, 1997; Won 28 professional titles; UN Ambassador, 1999-; German Davis Cup team Captain, 2001-2002. Address: Magdalenstr 64B, 22148 Hamburg, Germany.

STIGWOOD Robert Colin, b. 16 April 1934, Adelaide, Australia. Business Executive. Education: Sacred Heart College, Adelaide. Appointments: Established Robert Stigwood Organisation (RSO), 1967; Formed RSO Records, 1973; Founder, Music for UNICEF; Producer of films: Jesus Christ Superstar; Bugsy Malone; Gallipoli; Tommy; Saturday Night Fever; Grease; Sergeant Pepper's Lonely Hearts Club Band; Moment by Moment; Times Square; The Fan; Grease 2; Staying Alive; Evita; Gallipoli; Producer of stage musicals: Hair; Oh! Calcutta; The Dirtiest Show in Town; Pippin; Jesus Christ Superstar; Evita; Grease, 1993; Saturday Night Fever; TV producer in England and USA: The Entertainer; The Prime of Miss Jean Brodie; Chair of Board, Stigwood Group of Companies. Honours: Key to City of Los Angeles; Tony Award, 1980, for Evita; International Producer of the Year, ABC Interstate Inc. Address: c/o Robert Stigwood Organization, Barton Manor, Wippingham, East Cowes, Isle of Wight, PO32 6LB, England.

STILES Frank, b. 2 April 1924, Chiswick, London, England. Composer; Conductor; Violist. m. (1) Estelle Zitnitsky, 1969, 4 daughters, (2) Elizabeth Horwood, 1988. Education: BSc, Imperial College, 1949; BMus, Durham University, 1952; Postgraduate studies, Paris Conservatoire, 1955; LGSM; AGSM. Appointments: War Service Fleet Air Arm, 1942-46; Composer; Conductor Violist; Principal Conductor, Priory Concertante of London; Director, Holland Music School, 1982-92; Composer in Residence, Protoangel Visions Festival, Normandy by Spital, Lincolnshire. Publications: 5 symphonies; Dramatic Cantata Masada; Song Cycle for Tenor and Orchestra and for Baritone and Piano Mans 4 Seasons; 7 Concertos for violin, viola (2), guitar, clarinet, cello, piano; 6 string quartets; Trios; Duos; 2 violin and piano sonatas; 3 viola and piano sonatas; among others; 3 Songs for Mezzo Soprano and Piano. Honours: City of London Award for Composition, 1955; ABI Medal of Honour, 2000; ABI Stature of Universal Accomplishment, 2001; ABI Man of the Year 2005; American Order of Merit; Listed in national and international biographical dictionaries. Memberships: Composers' Guild of Great Britain; Chairman, Association of British Music; Incorporated Society of Musicians; British Academy of Composers and Songwriters; Musicians Union; PRS; MCPS; Royal Society of Musicians. Address: 43 Beech Road, Branston, Lincoln LN4 1PP, England. E-mail: frankstiles@callnetuk.com Website: www.impulse.music.co.uk/stiles.htm

STILES Tore C, b. 1 May 1956, Trondheim, Norway. Professor. m. Ulla Rimmer, 1 son, 1 daughter. Education: MA, Candidatus Psychologiae, University of Oslo, 1984; Dr Philos, University of Trondheim, 1990. Appointments: Psychologist, Psychiatric Department, General Hospital of Trondheim, 1984; Psychologist, Inpatient treatment within Forensic Psychiatry, 1984-86, Research Assistant, 1987-89, Post Doctoral Fellow, Department of Psychiatry and Behavioural Medicine, 1990-92, Østmarka Hospital, Trondheim; Army Psychologist, Gardermoen Military Airport, 1986-87; Professor, Department of Psychology, University of Tromso, 1996-98; Head, Outpatient Clinic for Adults and the Elderly, 1997-2003, Head, Outpatient Clinic for Children and Adolescents, 1998-99, Professor, 1997-, Chief, 2000-03, Department of Psychology, Norwegian University of Science and Technology, Trondheim. Publications: Numerous articles in professional journals. Memberships: Norwegian Psychological Association; Royal Norwegian Society of Sciences and Letters; Norwegian Competence Center for Complex Disorders; Norwegian Association for Cognitive Therapy; European Association for Behaviour and Cognitive Therapies. Address: NTNU Department of Psychology, Dragroll Building 12, Level 5, Trondheim 7491, Norway. E-mail: tore.stiles@svt.ntnu.no

STILLER Ben, b. 30 November 1965, New York, USA. Actor; Film Director. m. Christine Taylor, 2000, 2 children. Education: University of California at Los Angeles. Career: Films: Empire of the Sun, 1988; Reality Bites (also director), 1994; Happy Gilmore, Flirting with Disaster, The Cable Guy (also dircctor), 1996; Zero Effect, Your Friends and Neighbors, There's Something About Mary, Permanent Midnight, 1998; Mystery Men, Black and White, 1999; Meet the Parents, Keeping the Faith, 2000; Zoolander (also director), The Royal Tenenbaums, 2001; Duplex, Nobody Knows Anything, 2003; Along Came Polly, Starsky & Hutch, Envy, Dodgeball, Meet the Fockers, Madagascar (voice), 2004; School for Scoundrels, Night at the Museum, 2006; The Heartbreak Kid, 2007; The Marc Pease Experience, Tropic Thunder, Madagascar: Escape 2 Africa, 2008; Night at the Museum: Battle of the Smithsonian, 2009; Greenberg, 2010; TV: The Ben Stiller Show, 1990-93. Honours: Emmy Award, 1990. Address: United Talent Agency, 9560 Wilshire Boulevard, Suite 500, Beverly Hills, CA 90212, USA.

STING (Gordon Matthew Sumner), 2 October 1951, Wallsend, Newcastle-Upon-Tyne, England. Singer; Musician (bass); Actor. m. (1) Frances Tomelty, 1 May 1976, divorced 1984, 1 son, 1 daughter; (2) Trudie Styler, 20th August 1992, 2 sons, 2 daughters. Career: School teacher, Newcastle, 1975-77; Singer, songwriter, bass player, The Police, 1977-86; Solo artiste, 1985-; Numerous worldwide tours, television and radio, with the Police and solo; actor in films: Quadrophenia, 1980; Secret Policeman's Other Ball, 1982; Brimstone And

DICTIONARY OF INTERNATIONAL BIOGRAPHY 36th EDITION

Treacle, 1982; Dune, 1984; The Bride, 1985; Plenty, 1985; Julia And Julia, 1988; Stormy Monday, 1988; The Adventures Of Baron Munchausen, 1989; Lock, Stock, and two Smoking Barrels, 1998; Broadway Performance, Threepenny Opera, 1989. Recordings: Hit singles include: Walking On The Moon; Message In A Bottle; So Lonely; Roxanne; De Do Do Do, De Da Da Da; Every Little Thing She Does; Every Breath You Take; Invisible Sun; Can't Stand Losing You; Don't Stand So Close To Me; If You Love Somebody; Englishman In New York; If I Ever Lose My Faith In You; Fields Of Gold; Love Is Stronger Than Justice; Cowboy Song (with Pato Banton); Let The Soul Be Your Pilot; Roxanne 97; Brand New Day; After the Rain has Gone, 2000; Albums: with the Police: Outlandos D'Armour, 1977; Regatta De Blanc, 1979; Zenyatta Mondatta, 1980; Ghost In The Machine, 1981; Synchronisity, 1983; Bring On The Night, 1986; Solo albums: The Dream Of The Blue Turtles, 1985; Nothing Like The Sun, 1987; The Soul Cages, 1991; Ten Sumner's Tales, 1994; Mercury Falling, 1996; Brand New Day, 1999; Sacred Love, 2003; Songs from the Labyrinth, 2006; If on a Winter's Night, 2009; Contributor, Tower Of Song (Leonard Cohen tribute), 1995. Publications: Jungle Stories: The Fight for the Amazon, 1989. Honours include: 10 Grammy Awards (with Police and solo); Q Award, Best Album, 1994; BRIT Award, Best Male Artist, 1994. Membership: PRS.

STIPE (John) Michael, b. 4 January 1960, Decatur, Georgia, USA. Singer; Songwriter; Record Producer. Career: Member, R.E.M., 1980-; International cocnerts include: Earth Day Concert, Maryland, 1989; Green World tour, 1989; A Performance For The Planet concert, 1990; European tour, 1992; Own film and video company C-OO; Own vegetarian restaurant, The Grit, Athens, Georgia. Recordings: Chronic Town (mini-album), 1982; Murmur, 1983; Reckoning, 1984; Fables Of The Reconstruction, 1985; Life's Rich Pageant, 1986; Dead Letter Office, 1987; Document, 1987; Eponymous, 1988; Green, 1988; Out Of Time, 1991; Monster, 1995; Up, 1998; Star Profiles, 1999; Out of Time, 1999; Singles: The One I Love, 1987; Stand, 1989; Orange Crush, 1989; Losing My Religion, 1991; Shiny Happy People, 1991; Near Wild Heaven, 1991; Radio Song, 1991; Drive, 1992; Man On The Moon, 1992; The Sidewinder Sleeps Tonite, 1993; Everybody Hurts, 1993; Nightswimming; Crush With Eyeliner; What's The Frequency Kenneth?, 1994; The Great Beyond, 2000; Tracks featured on film soundtracks: Batchelor Party, 1984; Until The End Of The World, 1991; Coneheads, 1993; Recordings with: Indigo Girls, 1988; Syd Straw, 1989; Billy Bragg, 1991; Neneh Cherry, 1991; Contributor, Disney compilation, Stay Awake, with Natalie Merchant, 1988; Tom's Album, 1991; I'm Your Fan (Leonard Cohen tribute), 1991; Producer, artistes including: Swell; Chickasaw Muddpuppies; Opal Fox Society; Co-producer, film Desperation Angels, with Oliver Stone. Honours: Earth Day Award, 1990; Numerous MTV Music Video Awards, Billboard Awards, 1991; BRIT Awards: Best International Group, 1992, 1993, 1995; Grammy Awards: Best Pop Performance, Alternative Music Album, Music Video, 1992; Atlanta Music Awards, 1992; IRMA Band of the Year, 1993; Rolling Stone Critics Awards, 1993; Q Awards: Best Album, 1991, 1992; Best Act In The World, 1991, 1995. Current Management: REM/Athens, 250 W Clayton Street, Athens, GA 30601, USA.

STIRES Midge, b. 10 April 1943, Orange, New Jersey, USA. Painter. m. Peter D Schnore, 2 sons. Education: Bachelor of Fine Art, Syracuse University, USA. Honours: Pollock and Krasner Foundation Grant; Elizabeth Foundation for the Arts Grant; Artists for the Environment Residency Grant. Publications: Painting Panoramas, The Artists Magazine, 1990. Memberships: National Association of Painters in Casein and Acrylic. Address: 144 Red Oak Dr, Boyertown, PA 19512 8963, USA.

STOCK (William) Nigel, b. 29 January 1950, Newcastle upon Tyne, England. Bishop. m. Caroline Greswell, 3 sons. Education: Durham University; Ripon College, Cuddesdon. Appointments: Curate, Stockton on Tees, 1976-79; Priest-in-Charge, Taraka, Lae, Papua New Guinea, 1979-84; Vicar, Shiremoor, 1985-91; Team Rector, North Shields, 1991-98; Rural Dean, Tynemouth, 1992-98; Honorary Canon, Newcastle Cathedral, 1997-98; Residentiary Canon, Durham Cathedral, 1998-2000; Bishop of Stockport, 2000-07; Bishop of St Edmundsbury & Ipswich, 2007-. Memberships: UK Committee Member, Papua New Guinea Church Partnership; Trustee, Melanesian Mission.

STOEV Martin, b. 2 November 1988, Bratislava, Slovakia. Entrepreneur. Education: National High School of Mathematics and Sciences, Sofia, Bulgaria, 2002-06; Lycée Louis-le-Grand, Paris, France, 2006-07; Trinity College, University of Cambridge, England, 2008-11. Appointments: Internet Entrepreneur, 2009-. Publications: Quantization of conductivity of nanotechnological point contacts. Simple derivation of the Landauer formula, 2004; Determination of the density of states in high-Tc thin films using FET-type microstructures, 2006; On the origin of solar wind. Alfven waves induced jump of coronal temperature, 2007; LCAO model for 3D Fermi surface of high-Tc cuprate $Tl_2 Ba_2 CuO_{5+\delta}$, 2010. Honours: Winner, Mlako Belkanski's Concours Generale Physics competition, 2004; First Step to Nobel Prize in Physics competition, 2006; Laureate, Young Talents international competition, 2006; Winner, National French Physics Olympiad, 2007; Multiple times winner of national physics competitions and olympiads in Bulgaria.

STOKER Dennis James, b. 22 March 1928, London, England. Consultant Radiologist (retired). m. (1) Anne Forster, 1951, deceased 1997, 2 sons, 2 daughters, (2) Sheila Mercer, 1999. Education: MB BS, Guy's Hospital Medical School University of London. Appointments: House Physician, Guy's Hospital, 1951; Commissioned, Medical Branch, RAF, 1952; RAF Brampton, 1952-53; RAF Bridgnorth, 1953-55; RAF Hospital West Kirby, 1955-56; Medical Division, RAF Hospital, Wroughton, 1956-58; I/c Medical Division, RAF Hospital, Akrotiri, Cyprus, 1958-61; Physician i/c, Chest Unit, RAF Hospital, Wroughton, 1961-64; Metabolic Unit, St Mary's Hospital, London, 1964-65; I/c Medical Division, RAF Hospital, Steamer Point, Aden, 1965-67; I/c Medical Division, RAF Hospital, Cosford, Staffordshire, 1967-68; Retired Wing Commander, 1968; Consultant Radiologist: St George's Hospital, 1972-87; Royal National Orthopaedic Hospital, 1972-93 and 1997-2002 (special trustee, 1984-2000, chairman, 1992-98); Dean, Institute of Orthopaedics, 1987-91 (director of Radiological Studies, 1975-93); Editor, Skeletal Radiology, 1984-96; Dean, Faculty of Clinical Radiology, Vice President, Royal College of Radiologists, 1990-91 (member, Faculty Board, 1983-85, Council Member, 1985-88). Publications: Numerous articles in professional journals; Books, Knee Arthrography, 1980; Orthopaedics: self assessment in radiology, 1988; Radiology of Skeletal Disorders, 2007. Honours: Knox Medal, 1992; Medal, International Skeletal Society, 1993. Memberships: International Skeletal Society; FRSM; FRCP; FRCR; FRCS. Address: 3 Pearce's Orchard, Henley-on-Thames, Oxfordshire RG9 2LF, England. E-mail: dennis.stoker@btinternet.com.

STOKER Richard, b. 8 November 1938, Castleford, Yorkshire, England. Composer; Actor; Conductor; Artist; Writer. m. Gillian Patricia Watson, 10 July 1986. Education: Huddersfield School of Art with Napier & Sugden: Huddersfield School of Music, with Harold Truscott, 1953-58; Royal Academy of Music, with Sir Lennox Berkeley, 1958-62; Composition with Nadia Boulanger, on the Mendelssohn Scholarship, Paris, 1962-63, and privately with Eric Fenby and Benjamin Britten. Career: Assistant Librarian, LSO, 1962-63; Professor, Royal Academy of Music, 1963-87; Tutor, Royal Academy of Music, 1970-81; Teacher of Composition, St Paul's School, 1972-74; Magdalen College, Cambridge, 1974-76; Visiting Professor, SUNY, USA, 1970; Lecturer, U3A Goldsmiths, 1996-98; 1957 Royal Society of Literature, 2001. Civic Activities: Member, Treasurer, Stearing Committee, Lewisham Visual Arts Festivals, 1990, 1992; MIND, 1990-91; Samaritan, 1991-94; Founder member, Atlantic Council, 1993; Founder member, Treasurer, RAM Guild, 1994; Member, European Atlantic Group, 1995; International Promotions Committee, APC, 1995-97; Magistrate (Inner London), 1995-2003, Crown Court, 1998-2003; BACS Committee, 1999-2005. Publications: Portrait of a Town, 1974; Words Without Music, 1974; Strolling Players, 1978; Open Window-Open Door, 1985; Tanglewood, 1990; Diva, 1992; Collected Short Stories, 1993; Over 36 anthologies; Appointed Advisor, 2003-, 8 commissioned entries, 2004, Oxford Dictionary of National Biography. Honours: Dove Prize, Royal Academy of Music, 1962; Mendelssohn Scholarship, 1962; Numerous awards, 1962-65, 1972-; ARCM, 1962; ARAM, 1971; FRAM, 1978; Twice winner, Editors Choice Award, National Library of Poetry, USA, 1995, 1997; Man of the Year, American Biographical Institute, 1996. Memberships: PEN International and English PEN, 1997-2004; RSL, 1997-; British Academy, 1998-, Committee member, 1999-; PRS; MCPS; Blackheath Art Society; Lewisham Society of Art; Magistrates Association, 1995-2003; Founder Member, Atlantic Council, 1994; RAM Guild; European Atlantic Group, 1995. Commissions and Creative Works: Lewisham Society of Arts, 1990; Summer exhibitions, 1992; Blackheath Art Society, 1988; Tudor Barn Eltham, 1989; Laurence House (One man shows), 1992-93; Editor, Composer magazine, 1969-80; Composed over 200 musical works; Frequent broadcasts, appeared on BBC TV 1 & 2, Channel 4, BBC Radio 3 and 4; As an actor: Over 80 films, including: Da Vinci Code; Secret Life of Mrs Beeton; Wolfman; Miss Austen Regrets; Adjudicated numerous awards including Cyprus 2002 Orchestra Composer Award; BBC Brit Composer Awards; Royal Philharmonic Society Awards; Designed many CD covers; Works in private collections including Trinity College of Music; Painted in oils by John Bratby, 1983. Memberships: Garrick Club. Address: c/o Ricordi, 210 New Kings Road, London SW6 4NZ, England. E-mail: richard.stoker@yahoo.co.uk Website: www.richardstoker.co.uk

STONE Oliver William, b. 15 September 1946, New York, USA. Screenwriter; Director. m. (1) Najwa Sarkis, 1971-77, divorced, (2) Elizabeth Stone, 1981-93, divorced, 2 sons, (3) Sun-jung Jung, 1996, 1 daughter. Education: BFA, Yale University; New York University Film School. Appointments include: Teacher, Cholon, Vietnam, 1965-66; US Merchant Marine, 1966; Served, US Army, Vietnam, 1967-68; Taxi Driver, New York City, 1971; Screenwriter, Seizure, 1973, Midnight Express, 1978, The Hand, 1981, Conan the Barbarian, with J Milius, 1982, Scarface, 1983, Year of the Dragon, with M Cimino, 1985, 8 Million Ways to Die, with D L Henry, 1986, Salvador, with R Boyle, 1986; Writer, Director, Platoon, 1986; Co-writer and Director: Wall Street, 1987; Talk Radio, 1988; The Doors, 1991; Screenwriter, Producer and Director: Born on the Fourth of July, 1989; JFK, 1991; Heaven and Earth, 1993; Natural Born Killers, 1994; Nixon, 1995; Director, U-Turn, 1997; Co-Writer, Evita, 1996; Producer: South Central, 1992; Zebrahead, 1992; The Joy Luck Club, 1993; Wild Palms, TV mini-series, 1993; New Age, 1994; Freeway, 1995; The People vs Larry Flynt, 1996; Any Given Sunday, 2000; Comandante (documentary), 2003; Alexander, 2004; South of the Border, 2009; Wall Street: Money Never Sleeps, 2010; Savages, 2012; Executive Producer: Killer: A Journal of Murder, 1995; (HBO) Indictment: The McMartin Preschool, 1995; The Corrupter, 1999; Any Given Sunday, 1999. Honours: Winner of numerous awards including: 3 Academy Awards for Midnight Express, Platoon, and Born of the Fourth of July; BAFTA Award, Directors Guild of America Award, for Platoon; Purple Heart with Oak Leaf Cluster; Bronze Star. Memberships: Writers' Guild of America; Directors' Guild of America; Academy Motion Pictures Arts and Sciences. Address: Ixtlan, 201 Santa Monica Boulevard, 6th Floor, Santa Monica, CA 90401, USA.

STONE Peter Talbot, b. 7 November 1925, London, England. University Teacher. m. Evelyn Jean Ballantyne (deceased), 1 son, 1 stepson. Education: Intermediate BSc, Chemistry, Physiology and Zoology, Chelsea Polytechnic, London University, 1947-49; Certificate in Social Science, London School of Economics, London University, 1949-51; BSc (Hons), Psychology, Birkbeck College, London University, 1951-55. Appointments: Sick Berth Branch, Royal Navy, 1944-46; Biochemistry Technician, Wellcome Physiological Research Laboratories, Beckenham, Kent, 1946-48; Social Worker, Audiology Unit, Royal National Throat, Nose & Ear Hospital, London, 1952-56; Senior Psychologist, CEPRE, Ministry of Supply, Farnborough, Hants, 1956-60; Lecturer, Senior Lecturer, Loughborough College of Technology (later Loughborough University), 1960-79; Reader in Vision and Lighting, Loughborough University, 1979-84; Consultant in Vision and Lighting, Stone Consultants, 1984-95; Retired, 1995-. Publications: Numerous articles and papers including: Discomfort glare and visual performance; Light and the eyes at work; Proposals for a practical method for evaluating complaints of eye discomfort arising from clerical work; Lighting and visual work in industry (in Textbook of Occupational Medicine); Lighting for the partially sighted; Fluorescent lighting and health; A model for the explanation of discomfort and pain in the eye caused by light, 2009. Honours: Walsh-Weston Award, The Illuminating Engineering Society, London, 1968; Owen-Aves Memorial Lecture, Yorkshire Optical Society, 1979; Honorary Fellow, Ergonomics Society, 1995. Memberships: Associate Fellow, The British Psychological Society; Fellow, The Chartered Institution of Building Services Engineers; Fellow, The Society of Light and Lighting; Fellow, The Ergonomics Society; Associate Member, Royal Society of Medicine. Address: 47 Loughborough Road, Quorn, Loughborough, Leicestershire LE12 8DU, England.

STONE Sharon, b. 10 March 1958, Meadville, USA. Actress. m. (1) Michael Greenburg, 1984, divorced 1987, (2) Phil Bronstein, 1998, divorced 2004, 3 adopted sons. Education: Edinboro College. Career: Films include: Star Dust Memories (debut); Above the Law; Action Jackson; King Solomon's Mines; Allan Quatermain and the Lost City of Gold; Irreconcilable Differences; Deadly Blessing; Personal Choice; Basic Instinct; Dairy of a hit Man; Where Sleeping Dogs Lie; Sliver; Intersection; The Specialist; The Quick and the Dead; Casino; Last Dance; Diabolique, 1996; Sphere; The Might, 1999; The Muse, 1999; Simpatico, 1999;

Gloria, 1999; Beautiful Joe, 2000; Cold Creek Manor, 2003; A Different Loyalty, 2004; Catwoman, 2004; Jiminy Glick in La La Wood, 2004; Alpha Dog, 2006; Basic Instinct 2, 2006; Bobby, 2006; If I Had Known I Was a Genius, 2007; When a Man Falls in the Forest, 2007; Democrazy, 2007; The Year of Getting in Know Us, 2008; Five Dollars a Day, 2008; TV includes: Tears in the Rain; War and Remembrance; Calendar Girl Murders; The Vegas Strip Wars. Honour: Chevalier, Ordre des Arts et des Lettres. Address: c/o Guy McElwaine, PO Box 7304, North Hollywood, CA 91603, USA.

STOPPARD Tom (Sir), (Thomas Straussler), b. 3 July 1937, Zin, Czechoslovakia (British citizen). Dramatist; Screenwriter. m. (1) Jose Ingle, 1965, divorced 1972, 2 sons, (2) Dr Miriam Moore-Robinson, 1972, divorced 1992, 2 sons. Publications: Plays: Rosencrantz and Guildenstern are Dead, 1967; The Real Inspector Hound, 1968; Albert's Bridge, 1968; Enter a Free Man, 1968; After Magritte, 1971; Jumpers, 1972; Artists Descending a Staircase, and, Where Are They Now?, 1973; Travesties, 1975; Dirty Linen, and New-Found-Land, 1976; Every Good Boy Deserves Favour, 1978; Professional Foul, 1978; Night and Day, 1978; Undiscovered Country, 1980; Dogg's Hamlet, Cahoot's Macbeth, 1980; On the Razzle, 1982; The Real Thing, 1983; The Dog It Was That Died, 1983; Squaring the Circle, 1984; Four Plays for Radio, 1984; Rough Crossing, 1984; Dalliance and Undiscovered Country, 1986; Largo Desolato, by Vaclav Havel (translator), 1987; Hapgood, 1988; In the Native State, 1991; Arcadia, 1993; Indian Ink, 1995; The Invention of Love, 1997; The Seagul, 1997; The Coast of Utopia: Ttrilogy: Part One: Voyage, Part Two: Shipwreck, Part Three: Salvage, 2002; The Television Plays 1965-1984, 1993. Fiction: Introduction 2, 1964; Lord Malquist and Mr Moon, 1965. Other: 8 screenplays; Various unpublished state, radio, and television plays. Honours: John Whiting Award, Arts Council, 1967; New York Drama Critics Award, 1968; Italia Prize, 1968; Tony Awards, 1968, 1976, 1984; Evening Standard Awards, 1968, 1972, 1974, 1978, 1993, 1997; Olivier Award, 1993; Knighted, 1997; Order of Merit, 2000.

STOREY David (Malcolm), b. 13 July 1933, Wakefield, England. Writer; Dramatist; Screenwriter; Poet. m. Barbara Rudd Hamilton, 1956, 2 sons, 2 daughters. Education: Diploma, Slade School of Art, 1956. Publications: This Sporting Life, 1960; Flight into Camden, 1960; Radcliffe, 1963; Pasmore, 1972; A Temporary Life, 1973; Edward, 1973; Saville, 1976; A Prodigal Child, 1982; Present Times, 1984; Storey's Lives: Poems 1951-1991, 1992; A Serious Man, 1998; As It Happened, 2002. Honours: Macmillan Fiction Award, 1960; John Llewellyn Memorial Prize, 1960; Somerset Maughgam Award, 1960; Evening Standard Awards, 1967, 1970; Los Angeles Drama Critics Award, 1969; Writer of the Year Award, Variety Club of Great Britain, 1969; New York Drama Critics Award, 1969, 1970, 1971; Geoffrey Faber Memorial Prize, 1973; Fellow, University College, London, 1974; Booker Prize, 1976. Address: c/o Jonathon Cape Ltd, Random House, 20 Vauxhall Bridge Road, London SW1V 2SA, England.

STOURTON Nigel John Ivo, b. 29 July 1929, Mauritius. Retired Company Director. m. Rosemary Jennifer Abbott, 3 sons, 2 daughters. Education: Ampleforth College. Appointments: National Service, Royal Armoured Corps, 1947-49; 21st Special Air Service, 1949-50; Chairman, Managing Director, British-American Tobacco Companies, Sierra Leone, Malta, Switzerland, Ghana, Zimbabwe, 1951-82; Hospitaller of the British Association of the Sovereign Military Order of Malta, 1984-90; Chairman, The Orders of St John Care Trust, 1999-2007. Publications: Recommendations to the government of Burkino Fasso to re-ignite failing medical services accepted and acted on, 1989. Honours: CBE (Civil), 1981; OBE (Civil), 2007. Memberships: Sovereign Military Order of Malta; Knight Bailiff Grand Cross of Honour and Devotion, Commander of Merit, Council Member; Various local organisations around the world. Address: Keeper's Cottage, Hornby, Bedale, North Yorkshire DL8 1NH, England. E-mail: nigelstourton@btinternet.com

STRANGE Curtis, b. 30 January 1955, Norfolk, Virginia, USA. Professional Golfer. m. Sarah Jones, 2 sons. Education: Wake Forest University. Career: Professional, 1976-; First joined PGA tour, 1977; Won Pensacola Open, 1979; Won Sammy Davis Jr Greater Hartford Open, 1983; Won LaJel Classic, 1984; Won Honda Classic, Panasonic-Las Vegas International, 1985; Won Canadian Open, 1985; Won Houston Open, 1986; Won Canadian Open, Federal Express – St Jude Classic, NEC Series of Golf, 1987; Won Sandway Cove Classic, Australia, 1988; Won Industry Insurance Agent Open, Memorial Tournament, US Open, Nabisco Championships, 1988; Won US Open, Palm Meadows Cup, Australia, 1989; Won Holden Classic, Australia, 1993. Memberships: Member, PGA Tour Charity Team, Michelob Championship, Kingsmill, 1996. Honours: Captain US Ryder Cup Team after playing on five Ryder Cup Teams, 2002; Golf Analyst, ABC Sports, 1997-; Golfer of the Year, 1986, 1987. Address: c/o IMG, 1 Erieview Plaza, Suite 1300, Cleveland, OH 44114, USA.

STRAUSS Andrew, b. 2 March 1977, Johannesburg, South Africa. Cricketer; England Captain. m. Ruth McDonald, 2003, 2 sons. Education: Caldicott School; Radley College; Hatfield College; Durham University. Career: County player, Middlesex County Cricket Club; Captain of England Cricket Team, 2009-. Honours: MBE, 2005.

STRAUSS Botho, b. 2 December 1944, Naumberg-an-der-Saale, Germany. Author; Poet; Dramatist. Education: German Language and Literature, Drama, Sociology, Cologne and Munich. Publications: Bekannte Gesichter, gemischte Gefühle (with T Bernhard and F Kroetz), 1974; Trilogie des Wiedersehens, 1976; Gross und Klein, 1978; Rumor, 1980; Kalldeway Farce, 1981; Paare, Passanten, 1981; Der Park, 1983; Der junge Mann, 1984; Diese Erinnerung an einen, der nur einen Tag zu Gast War, 1985; Die Fremdenführerin, 1986; Niemand anderes, 1987; Besucher, 1988; Kongress: Die Kette der Demütigungen, 1989; Theaterstücke in zwei Banden, 1994; Wohnen Dammern Lügen, 1994. Honours: Dramatists' Prize, Hannover, 1975; Schiller Prize, Baden-Württemberg, 1977; Literary Prize, Bavarian Academy of Fine Arts, Munich, 1981; Jean Paul Prize, 1987; Georg Büchner Prize, 1989. Membership: PEN. Address: Keithstrasse 8, D-17877, Berlin, Germany.

STREBEL Heinz, b. 23 September 1939, Munich, Germany. Professor. m. Sigrun Briesen, 1 son, 2 daughters. Education: Technical Economist, 1963; Doctorate, 1967; Habilitation, 1977. Appointments: Professor, Free University, Berlin, 1976-84; Professor, University of Oldenburg, 1984-90; Professor, Karl-Tranzens-University, Graz, 1990-2007; Professor Emeritus, 2007. Publications: About 200 articles in professional journals. Memberships: Association of University Teachers for Managerial Economy; Association of Economic Engineers. Address: Walten Dorfer Haupstr 147, A8042 Graz, Germany. E-mail: heinz.strebel@uni-graz.at

STREEP Meryl (Mary Louise), b. 22 June 1949, Summit, New Jersey, USA. Actress. m. Donald Gummer, 1978, 1 son, 3 daughters. Education: Singing Studies with Estelle Liebling; Studied Drama, Vassar; Yale School of Drama. Appointments:

Stage debut, New York, Trelawny of the Wells; 27 Wagons Full of Cotton, New York; New York Shakespeare Festival, 1976 in Henry V and Measure for Measure; Also in Happy End (musical); The Taming of the Shrew; Wonderland (musical); Taken in Marriage; Numerous other plays; Films include: Julia, 1976; The Deer Hunter, 1978; Manhattan, 1979; The Seduction of Joe Tynan, 1979; The Senator, 1979; Kramer vs Kramer, 1979; Still of the Night, 1982; Silkwood, 1983; Plenty, 1984; Falling in Love, 1984; Ironweed, 1987; A Cry in the Dark, 1988; The Lives and Loves of a She Devil, 1989; Hollywood and Me, 1989; Postcards from the Edge, 1991; Defending Your Life, 1991; Death Becomes Her, 1992; The House of the Spirits; The River Wild, 1994; The Bridges of Madison County, 1995; Before and After; Marvin's Room; One True Thing, 1998; Dancing at Lughnasa, 1999; Music of the Heart, 1999; The Hours, 2002; Adaptation, 2003; The Manchurian Candidate, 2004; Lemony Snicket's A Series of Unfortunate Events, 2004; Prime, 2005; A Prairie Home Companion, 2006; The Music of Regret, 2006; The Devil Wears Prada, 2006; The Ant Bully, (voice), 2006; Dark Matter, 2007; Evening, 2007; Rendition, 2007; Lions for Lambs, 2007; Mamma Mia! 2008; Doubt, 2008; Julie & Julia, 2009; The Fantastic Mr. Fox, 2009; It's Complicated, 2009; The Iron Lady, 2011; Hope Springs, 2012; TV appearances include: The Deadliest Season; Uncommon Women; Holocaust; Velveteen Rabbit; First Do No Harm, 1997; Angels in America, 2003; Many others. Honours: Numerous nominations and wins including: 3 Academy Awards; 2 BAFTA Awards; 2 Emmy Awards; 8 Golden Globe Awards; 2 SAG Awards. Address: c/o Creative Artists Agency, 9830 Wilshire Boulevard, Beverly Hills, CA 90212, USA.

STREET Brian Vincent, b. 24 October 1943, Manchester, England. Professor. 1 son, 2 daughters. Education: BA, Hons, London, 1966; Dip Soc Anth, 1967, D Phil, Oxon, 1970, Institute of Social Anthropology, Oxford. Appointments: Lecturer in English Language and Literature, University of Mashad, Iran, 1970-71; Lecturer in Social Anthropology, University of Sussex, 1974; Visiting Associate Professor, Graduate School of Education, University of Pennsylvania, 1988; Senior Lecturer in Social Anthropology, University of Sussex, 1989-96; Adjunct Professor of Education, Graduate School of Education, University of Pennsylvania, 1993-; Professor of Language Education, School of Education, King's College, London University, 1996-. Publications: Various books and articles on literacy and anthropology published worldwide include: The Savage in Literature, 1975; Literacy in Theory and Practice, 1984; Social Literacies: Critical Approaches to Literacy in Education, Development and Ethnography, 1995. Honours: David S Russell Award for Distinguished Research, NCTE, 1995; Shortlisted for the BAAL Annual Book Prize, 1993 and 2002; Distinguished Scholar, Lifetime of Achievement Award, NRC-USA, 2008; Awarded numerous grants in Europe and America. Memberships: Fellow of the British Institute of Persian Studies, Iran, 1969-70; Fellow, Royal Anthropological Institute, 1974-; Association of Social Anthropologists, 1974-; British Educational Research Association, 1996-; American Educational Research Association, 1996-; British Association for Applied Language Studies, 1992-. Address: Department of Education and Professional Studies, Franklin Wilkins Building, Waterloo Bridge Annex, 120 Stamford Street, London, SE1 9NN, England. E-mail: brian.street@kcl.ac.uk

STREETER Betty, b. 29 September 1967, Greene Co, Snow Hill, NC, USA. Writer; Author; Poet. Education: Graduate, Bible Study; Typing and Writing, LCC College; Creative Writing Diploma, Stratford Career School Institute. Career: Author, poet and writer in the fields of Bible study, biography and poetry. Publications: In poetry newsletters, poetry journals, newspapers, poetry magazines; Verse of greetings card, 1992; 3 published chapbooks. Honours include: Award of Merit, 1988-90, 5 in 1991; Golden Poet Award, 1989, 1990, 1991; Amherst Society, Certificate of Achievement, 1992-93; Accomplishment of Merit, 1994; Outstanding Literary Accomplishments Creative Arts and Science; Blue Ribbon Award; Certificate of Achievement, 1993-95; President's Award for Literary Excellence, 1993, 1994-95; International Poet's Hall of Fame, 1996; President's Citation, 2007; International Peace Prize, 2007; Woman of the Year, 2008; Hall of Fame for Distinguished Accomplishment, 2009; International Who's Who of Professional & Business Women Hall of Fame, 2011; Listed in international biographical dictionaries. Address: 225 Foxcroft Road, Snow Hill, NC 28580, USA.

STREET-PORTER Janet, b. 27 December 1946, England. Journalist; TV Presenter; Producer; Editor. m. (1) Tim Street-Porter, 1967, divorced 1975, (2) A M M Elliot, 1976, divorced 1978, (3) Frank Cvitanovich, divorced 1988, deceased 1995. Education: Architectural Association. Career: Petticoat Magazine Fashion Writer and Columnist, 1968; Daily Mail, 1969-71; Evening Standard, 1971-73; Own Show, LBC Radio Programme, 1973; Presenter, London Weekend Show, London Weekend Television (LWT), 1975; Producer, presenter, Saturday Night People (with Clive James and Russell Harty), The Six O'Clock Show (with Michael Aspel), Around Midnight, 1975-85; Network 7 for Channel 4, 1986-; BBC Youth and Entertainment Features Head, 1988-94; Head, Independent Production for Entertainment, 1994; Managing Director, Live TV, Mirror Group plc, 1994-95; TV Presenter, Design Awards, Travels with Pevsner, Coast to Coast, The Midnight Hour, 1996-98, As the Crow Flies (series), 1999; Cathedral Calls, 2000; J'Accuse, Internet, 1996; Janet Save the Monarchy, 2005; So You Think You Can Teach, 2004; Editor, The Independent on Sunday, 1999-2001; Editor-at-Large, 2001-; Contestant, I'm a Celebrity…. Get Me Out of Here!; The F-Word, 2006; Deadline, 2007. Publications: Scandal, 1980; The British Teapot, 1981; Coast to Coast, 1998; As the Crow Flies, 1999; Baggage, 2004. Honours: Prix Italia for the Vampyr, 1992; BAFTA award for originality for Network 7, 1998. Memberships: Vice President, Ramblers' Association; President, Globetrotters Club, 2003-; Fellow, Royal Television Society. Address: c/o Emma Hardy, Princess Television, Princess Studios, Whiteley, 151 Queensway, London WC2 4SB, England. E-mail: emma.hardy@princesstv.com

STREISAND Barbra Joan, b. 24 April 1942, Brooklyn, New York, USA. Singer; Actress; Director; Producer; Writer; Composer; Philanthropist. m. (1) Elliot Gould, 1963 (divorced 1971), 1 son; (2) James Brolin, 1998. Career: Actress since age 15; Recording artist, 1962-; Concerts include: Support to Liberace, Hollywood Bowl, 1963; Madison Square Garden (as part of first tour for 27 years), recorded for later release, 1994; Stage performances include: Nightclub debut, Greenwich Village, 1961; New York theatre debut, Another Evening With Harry Stoones, 1961; I Can Get It For You Wholesale, 1962; Funny Girl, New York 1964, London, 1966; Film appearances: Funny Girl, 1968; Hello Dolly!, 1969; On A Clear Day You Can See Forever, 1970; The Owl And The Pussycat, 1971; What's Up Doc?, 1972; Up The Sandbox, 1972; The Way We Were, 1973; For Pete's Sake, 1974; Funny Lady, 1975; A Star Is Born (also producer), 1976; The Main Event (also producer), 1979; All Night Long, 1981; Yentl (also writer, director, producer), 1984; Nuts (also producer, composer), 1987; The Prince Of Tides (also director, producer), 1990; The Mirror Has Two Faces,

1996; Meet the Fockers, 2004; Television specials: My Name Is Barbra, 1965; Color Me Barbra, 1966; Belle of 14th Street, 1967; A Happening in Central Park, 1968; Musical Instrument, 1973; One Voice, 1976; Barbra Streisand - The Concert (also producer, co-director), HBO, 1994; Executive producer, Silence: The Margarete Cammermeyer Story, NBC, 1995. Recordings: Hits include: You Don't Bring Me Flowers, duet with Neil Diamond, 1978; Enough Is Enough, duet with Donna Summer; Albums include: The Barbra Streisand Album, 1963; The Second Barbra Streisand Album, 1963; The Third Album, 1964; My Name Is Barbra, 1965; People, 1965; Color Me Barbra, 1966; Je M'Appelle Barbra, 1967; Barbra Streisand: A Happening In Central Park, 1968; What About Me?, 1969; Stoney End, 1970; Barbra Joan Streisand, 1972; Classical Barbra, 1974; The Way We Were, 1974; Lazy Afternoon, 1975; A Star Is Born, 1976; Superman, 1977; Songbird, 1978; Wet, 1979; Guilty (with Barry Gibb), 1980; Memories, 1981; Emotion, 1984; The Broadway Album, 1986; One Voice, 1986; Til I Loved You, 1989; Just For The Record, 1991; Butterfly, 1992; Back To Broadway, 1993; Barbra Streisand - The Concert (album and video), 1994; The Concert – Highlights, 1995; Mirror Has Two Faces, 1996; Higher Ground, 1997; A Love Like Ours, 1999; Timeless, 2000; Soundtracks include: Yentl, 1983; Nuts, 1987; The Prince Of Tides, 1991. Honours: NY Critics Award, Best Supporting Actress, for I Can Get It For You Wholesale, 1962; Variety Poll Award, Best Foreign Actress, for Funny Girl, UK, 1966; Academy Awards: Best Actress, Funny Girl, 1968; Best Composition (joint winner), Evergreen, 1976; Special Tony Award, for Funny Girl, 1970; Golden Globe Awards: Best Actress, Funny Girl, 1968; Best Picture and Best Director, Yentl, 1984; 5 Emmy Awards, My Name Is Barbra, 1966; 5 Emmy Awards, 3 Cable Ace Awards, Barbra Streisand: The Concert, 1994; Peabody Awards: My Name Is Barbra, 1966; Barbra Streisand: The Concert, 1994; Grammy Awards: Best Female Vocalist, 1963, 1964, 1965, 1977, 1986; Best Songwriter (with Paul Williams), 1977; Awarded 37 Gold and 21 Platinum albums; Only artist to have US Number 1 albums over 4 decades. Address: c/o Barwood Productions, 433 N Camden Drive, Suite 500, Beverly Hills, CA 90210, USA.

STRGAR KUREČIĆ Maja, b. 29 September 1972, Zagreb, Croatia. Assistant Professor; Researcher; Photographer. m. Krešimir Kurečić, 1 son, 1 daughter. Education: BA, 1996, PhD, Engineering, 2007, Faculty of Graphic Technology and Design, MA, Information Science, Faculty of Organization and Informatics, 2002, University of Zagreb. Appointments: Photographer, Vecergji List daily newspaper, Zagreb, 1994-95; Assistant, 1997-2010, Assistant Professor, 2010-, Faculty of Graphic Arts, University of Zagreb. Publications: 27 scientific papers in the field of graphic technology and photography, published in international scientific journals and proceedings of international scientific meetings; Engaged in 20 group and 10 independent photo exhibitions in Croatia and abroad. Honours: Rector's Award, University of Zagreb, 1993, 1996; 1st Fuji France Press Award for Best Photographs, 1998; Annual Award for Young Scientists and Artists, Society of University Professors and Scientists in Zagreb, 2002. Memberships: ULUPUH, Croatian Association of Artists and Applied Arts; MENSA Croatia; International Commission on Illumination, Austria. Address: Viktora Cara Emina 6, 10 000 Zagreb, Croatia. E-mail: mstrgar@grf.hr

STRITCH Elaine, b. 2 February 1926, Detroit, USA. Actress; Singer. m. John Bay, 1973, deceased 1982. Education: Sacred Heart Convent, Detroit; Drama Workshop; New School for Social Research. Career: Stage: Loco, 1946; Three Indelicate Ladies, 1947; Yes M'Lord, 1949; Pal Joey, 1952; Bus Stop, 1955; Sail Away, 1961, 1962; Who's Afraid of Virginia Woolf?1962, 1965; Company, 1970, 1971; Love Letters, 1990; Elaine Stritch At Liberty, 2002; Film: The Scarlet Hour, 1956; Three Violent People, 1956; A Farewell to Arms, 1957; The Perfect Furlough, 1958; Who Killed Teddy Bear, 1965; Pigeons, 1971; September, 1988; Cocoon: The Return; Cadillac Man, 1990; Out to Sea, 1997; Screwed, 2000; Small Time Crooks, 2000; Autumn in New York, 2001; Monster-in-Law, 2005; Romance & Cigarettes, 2005; TV: My Sister Eileen, 1962; Three's Company, 1975-76, 1979; Stranded, 1986; Elaine Stritch: At Liberty, 2004; Paradise, 2004; 30 Rock, 2007. Publications: Am I Blue? – Living with Diabetes and, Dammit, Having Fun, 1984. Honours: Emmy Awards, 1993, 2004, 2007.

STROME Robert Richard, b. 12 October 1937, New York, USA. Pediatric Eye Surgeon. m. 2 daughters. Education: BA, New York University, 1959; MD, Padua University Medical School, Italy, 1965. Appointments: Intern, 1965-66, Resident, 1966-69, Long Island Jewish Queens Hospital Center; Fellowship, Pediatric Ophthalmology, The Children's Hospital of The District of Columbia, 1969-70; Lecturer, School of Orthoptics, Pediatric Ophthalmology Consultant, NY Eye and Ear Infirmary, 1975-; Assistant Professor, Clinical Surgery, University Hospital, Health Science Center, SUNY at Stonybrook, 1978-85; Teacher, Pediatric Ophthalmology Clinic, North Shore University Hospital, 1979-2007; Clinical Assistant Professor of Ophthalmology, Cornell University Medical College, 1982-; Associate Attending, Ophthalmology, St Francis Hospital, Port Washington, 1983-; Assistant Clinical Professor, Ophthalmology, Columbia University College of Physicians & Surgeons, 2009-. Publications: Numerous articles in professional journals. Honours: Intern of the Year Award, Mary Immaculate Hospital Division Department of Medicine, Queens Hospital Center, 1965; Physician's Recognition Award, 1969; 15 Year Service Award, Mercy Medical Center, 1986-2001; Continuing Education Award, American Academy of Ophthalmology Lifelong Education for the Ophthalmologist, 2004; Certificate of Appreciation for 35 Consecutive Years of Membership, American Academy of Ophthalmology. Memberships: American Academy of Ophthalmology; American College of Surgeons; International College of Surgeons; American Medical Association; New York Academy of Medicine; American Academy of Pediatrics; Royal Society of health; Societe Francaise d'Ophtalmologie; International Strabismological Association; International Eye Foundation Society of Eye Surgeons. Address: Suite #190, 1000 Northern Blvd, Great Neck, New York 11021, USA. E-mail: rrstrome@att.net

STRONG Sir Roy (Colin), b. 23 August 1935, London, England. Writer; Historian; Lecturer. m. Julia Trevelyan Oman, 1971, deceased, 2003. Education: Queen Mary College, London; Warburg Institute, London. Appointments: Assistant Keeper, 1959, Director, Keeper and Secretary, 1967-73, National Portrait Gallery, London; Ferens Professor of Fine Art, University of Hull, 1972; Walls Lecturer, J Pierpoint Morgan Library, New York, 1974; Director, Victoria and Albert Museum, London, 1974-87; Director, Oman Publications Ltd; Andrew Carnduff Ritchie Lecturer, University of Yale, 1999; Host TV Series, The Diets That Time Forgot, 2008. Publications: Portraits of Queen Elizabeth I, 1963; Holbein and Henry the VIII, 1967; The English Icon: Elizabethan and Jacobean Portraiture, 1969; Tudor and Jacobean Portraits, 1969; Van Dyck: Charles I on Horseback, 1972; Splendour at Court: Renaissance Spectacle and the Theatre of Power, 1973; Nicholas Hilliard, 1975; The Renaissance Garden in England, 1979; Britannia Triumphans:

Inigo Jones, Rubens and Whitehall Palace, 1980; Henry, Prince of Wales and England's Lost Renaissance, 1986; Creating Small Gardens, 1986; Gloriana: Portraits of Queen Elizabeth I, 1987; A Small Garden Designer's Handbook, 1987; Cecil Beaton: The Royal Portraits, 1988; Creating Small Formal Gardens, 1989; Lost Treasures of Britain, 1990; A Celebration of Gardens (editor), 1991; The Garden Trellis, 1991; Small Period Gardens, 1992; Royal Gardens, 1992; A Country Life, 1994; Successful Small Gardens, 1994; William Larkin: Vanitù giacobite, Italy, 1994; The English Vision: Country Life 1897-1997; The Story of Britain, 1996; The Tudor and Stuart Monarchy, 3 volumes, 1995-97; The Story of Britain, 1996; The English Vision: Country Life 1897-1997, 1997; The Roy Strong Diaries 1967-1987, 1997; The Spirit of Britain. A Narrative History of the Arts, 1999, re-issued as The Arts in Britain, 2004; Garden Party, 2000; The Artist and the Garden, 2000; Ornament in the Small Garden, 2001; Feast – A History of Grand Eating, 2002; The Laskett – The Story of a Garden, 2003; Passions Past & Present, 2005; Coronation: A History of Kingshill and the British Monarchy, 2005; A Little History of the English Country Church, 2007. Co-Author: Leicester's Triumph, 1964; Elizabeth R, 1971; Mary Queen of Scots, 1972; Inigo Jones: The Theatre of the Stuart Court, 1973; An Early Victorian Album: The Hill-Adamson Collection, 1974; The English Miniature, 1981; The English Year, 1982; Artists of the Tudor Court, 1983; The Diary of John Evelyn, 2006. Honours: Fellow, Queen Mary College, 1976; Knighted, 1982; Senior Fellow, Royal College of Arts, 1983; High Bailiff and Searcher of the Sanctuary of Westminster Abbey, 2000; Honorary doctorates: Leeds 1983; Keele, 1984; Worcester, 2004; Honorary Fellow, Royal Society of Literature, 1999; President of the Royal Photographic Society's Award, 2003. Memberships: Arts Council of Great Britain, chairman, arts panel, 1983-87; British Council, Fine Arts Advisory Committee, 1974-87; Royal College of Arts Council, 1979-87; Westminster Abbey Architectural Panel, 1975-89; President, Garden History Society, 2000-. Address: The Laskett, Much Birch, Herefordshire HR2 8HZ, England.

STUART Jessica Jane, b. 20 August 1942, Ashland, Kentucky, USA. Retired; Teacher; Poet; Writer. Divorced, 2 sons. Education: AB, Western Reserve University, Cleveland, Ohio, 1964; MA, 1967, MA, 1969, PhD, 1971, Indiana University, Bloomington, Indiana. Appointments: Teaching, University of Florida, 1986-88, Santa Fe Community College, Gainesville, Florida, 1986-88; Flagler College and St Johns River Community College, St Augustine, Florida, 1989-90. Publications: Eyes of the Mole, 1968; White Barn, 1971; A Year's Harvest, 1956; Transparencies (with prose), 1986; Novels: Yellowhawk, 1973; Passerman's Hollow, 1974; Land of the Fox, 1975; A Peaceful Evening Wind, 2002; Short stories: Gideon's Children, 1976; Chapbooks: Finding Tents, 2002; Celestial Moon, 2003; Spanish Moss, 2003; Mardi Gras, 2004; The Turning Year, 2005; Along the River's Shore, 2004; Haiku, 2004; Violets, 2006; A November Moon, 2006, Pretending (a mini chap book), 2007; Spring Moon, 2007; Papyrus (I-IV) (a poetry chapbook), 2008; Translation, Edizioni Universum collections, 2011; Haiku in translation (Chinese), Haiku Page. Honours: Grand Prix, KSPS Kentucky State Poetry Society, 1993; Cameo Chapbook Contest Award (Poetry), 1998; State Poetry Contests Award; Mississippi Poetry Society First Place, 2002; CSPS; First Place Prize, Philadelphia Poets; First Place Prize, Sandcutters Poetry Prize. Memberships: MPS (Mississippi); CSPS California State Poetry Society; ASPS (Arizona). Address:The Jesse Stuart House, 225 Stuart Lane, Greenup, KY 41144, USA.

STUBBS Imogen Mary, b. 20 February 1961, Rothbury, England. Actress. m. Trevor Nunn, 1994, separated 2011, 1 son, 1 daughter. Education: Exeter College, Oxford; Royal Academy of Dramatic Arts. Appointments: Theatre: The Rover; Two Noble Kinsmen; Richard II, 1987-88; Othello, 1991; Heartbreak House, 1992; St Joan, 1994; Twelfth Night, 1996; Blast from the Past, 1998; Betrayal, 1998; The Relapse, 2001; Three Sisters, 2002; Hamlet, 2004; Duchess of Malfi, 2006; The Glass Menagerie, 2010; Private Lives, Little Eyolf, 2011; Orpheus Descending, 2012; TV: The Rainbow; Anna Lee; After the Dance; Mothertime, 1997; Blind Ambition, 2000; Big Kids, 2000; Casualty, 2005; Marple: The Moving Finger, 2006; Brief Encounters, 2006; New Tricks, 2009; Doctors, Switch, 2012; Film: Nanon; A Summer Story; Erik the Viking; True Colours; A Pin for the Butterfly; Fellow Traveller; Sandra c'est la vie; Jack and Sarah; Sense and Sensibility, 1995; Twelfth Night, 1996; Collusion, 2003; Dead Cool, 2004; Stories of Lost Souls, 2006. Honours: Gold Medal, Chicago Film Festival. Address: c/o Nick Hern Books Ltd, The Glasshouse, 49a Goldhawk Road, London W12 8QP, England.

STUCHEBNIKOV Vladimir Mikhailovich, b. 25 February 1942, Ryazan, Russia. Physicist. m. Tatyana, 1 son, 2 daughters. Education: Degree in Physics, Moscow State University, 1965; Masters degree in Physics, 1969; Doctor Degree in Technical Science, 1987. Appointments: Researcher, Physics, Moscow State University (member of working group of semiconductor – GaAs and GaSb – lasers research of tunnelling in semiconductors in high electric and magnet fields), 1963-71; Department Chief, Institute of Instrumentation Technique, Korolyev (pioneer research and development of semiconductor sensors for space technology), 1971-76; Laboratory Chief, Research Development Institute Teplopribor, Mechanical Instrumentation, Moscow, 1976-88; Professor, Ulyanovsk State University, 1988-2008; Vice Director, Integrated Sensors Institute, Ulyanovsk, 1988-91; General Director, Joint Stock Co Microelectronic Sensors and Devices, Ulyanovsk, 1991-; Vice Director, General Director, Ulyanovsk Centre for Microelectronics, 1992-2008 (research and development of mechanical sensors based on Silicon-on-Sapphire structures for industrial and special applications). Publications: Over 150 articles in professional magazines; 30 patents. Honours: Gold and Silver Medals of Russian State Exhibitions; Star of Russian Management, Russian Industrial Trade Forum, 2005. Memberships: Russian Metrological Academy; IEEE; AAAS; New York Academy of Sciences. E-mail: mida@mv.ru Website: www.midaus.com

STUMMER Peter Olaf, b. 1 June 1942, Jauernig, Czech Republic. Senior Lecturer (retired). m. Anne Stummer-Schwegmann. Education: English, Romance Philology, Philosophy, 1961-66; Teacher's Diploma, 1966; PhD, 1969; 2nd Teacher's Diploma, 1970. Appointments: Tutor Students' Hall of Residence, 1965-70; Tutor, English Department, Munich, 1967-69; Secondary School Teacher and University Lectureship, 1969-71; Assistant Professor, University of Cologne, 1971-74; Assistant Professor, 1974-78, Lecturer (tenured), 1978-2009, Senior Lecturer, Literatures Written in English, 1980-2009, University of Munich. Publications: Author and editor of several books; Author of over 30 articles on various aspects of diverse literatures written in English, especially from Africa, India and Australia; Conference Convenor; Originator of Postgraduate Programme on English Speaking Countries. Honours: German Studies Association, University of Aberdeen; Visiting Professor, University of Trento; Lectureship, University of Passau. Memberships: One-time Vice President, ASNEL; EACLALS;

DICTIONARY OF INTERNATIONAL BIOGRAPHY 36th EDITION

ACLALS; EASA; ASAL; BASA; German Association for Australian Studies. Address: Edelweiss-strasse 115, D-82178 Puchheim, Germany.

SUCHET David Courtney, b. 2 May 1946, London, England. Actor. m. Sheila Ferris, 1976, 1 son, 1 daughter. Appointments: Former Member, National Youth Theatre, Chester Repertory Company; RSC, 1973, Associate Artist. Creative Works: Roles includes: Tybalt in Romeo and Juliet, Orlando in As You Like It, Tranio in Taming of the Shrew, 1973; Zamislov in Summerfolk, The Fool in King Lear, 1974, 1975; Pisanio in Cymbeline, Wilmer in Comrades, 1974; Hubert in King John, Ferdinand King of Navarre in Love's Labour's Lost, 1975; Shylock in The Merchant of Venice, Gruio in Taming of the Shrew, Sir Nathaniel in Love's Labour's Lost, Glougauer in Once in a Lifetime, Caliban in The Tempest, Shylock in The Merchant of Venice, Sextus Pompey in Antony and Cleopatra, 1978; Angelo in Measure for Measure, 1979; Oleanna, 1993; What a Performance, 1994; Who's Afraid of Virginia Woolf?, 1997; Saturday, Sunday and Monday, 1998; Amadeus, 1998-2000; Man & Boy, 2004-05; Once in a Lifetime, 2005-06. Films include: Big Foot & The Hendersons, 1986; Crime of Honour, The Last Innocent Man, 1987; A World Apart, To Kill a Priest (also known as Popielusko), 1988; The Lucona Affair, When the Whales Came, 1990; Executive Decision, Deadly Voyage, 1995; Sunday, 1996; A Perfect Murder, Wing Commander, 1998; RKO, Sabotage, 1999; Live From Baghdad, The Wedding Party, Foolproof, 2002; The Flood, 2006; The Bank Job, Act of God, 2008; Numerous TV appearances including: Master of the Game, Reilly – Ace of Spies, 1984; Mussolini: The Untold Story, 1985; The Life of Agatha Christie, Hercule Poirot in Agatha Christie's Poirot, 8 Series including 100th Anniversary Special: The Mysterious Affair at Styles, 1990-; Days of Majesty, 1994; The Cruel Train, Moses, 1995; Solomon, Seesaw, 1997; The Way We Live Now, 2001; National Crime Squad, 2001-02; The First Lady, Henry VIII, 2003; A Bear Named Winnie, 2004; Maxwell, Flood, 2007; Diverted, 2009; Going Postal, 2010; Hidden, Great Expectations, 2011; Richard II, David Suchet: In the Footsteps of Saint Paul, 2012; Effie, 2013; Several radio drama roles, audio recordings and voice overs. Publications: Author of essays in Players of Shakespeare, 1985. Honours: Brown Belt in Aikido; 1st Master of Japanese Samurai; Best Radio Actor of the Year, 1979; Best Actor, Marseilles Film Festival, 1983; Best Actor, British Industry/ Science Film Association, 1986; Best Actor, Royal TV Society Performance Awards, 1986; Best Actor, Variety Club Award, 1998; 1994; Several BAFTA, SWET, Oliver and other nominations; Critics' Circle Award for Best Actor, 1997; Best Actor, Backstage Theatre Award, LA, 2000; Best Actor, TV, Radio and Industry, Royal Television Society, Broadcasting Press Guild, 2002; OBE, 2002; CBE, 2011. Memberships: Fellow, Royal Society of Arts; Governor, Royal Shakespeare Company; Fight Directors Association; Garrick Club, London; St James's Club, London. Address: c/o Ken McReddie, 36-40 Glasshouse Street, London W1B 5DL, England.

SUDELEY, 7th Baron, Merlin Charles Sainthill Hanbury-Tracy, b. 17 June 1939, London, England. Lecturer and Author. m (1) Elizabeth Villiers (2) Margarita Kellett. Education: History, Worcester College, Oxford, 1960-63. Appointments: Fellow of the Society of Antiquaries; Chairman, Conservative Monday Club; Lay Patron, Prayer Book Society; Patron, Bankruptcy Association; Vice-Chancellor, Monarchist League; Chairman, Constitutional Monarchy Association; Introduced debates in the House of Lords on: Export of manuscripts, 1973; Cathedral finance, 1980; Teaching and use of the Prayer Book in theological colleges, 1987; Cleared the Prayer Book (Protection) Bill on second reading in the House of Lords, 1981; Lecture tours to the USA, 1983, 1996; Occasional Lecturer, Extra-Mural Department, University of Bristol; Appearances on radio and television, 1960-. Publications: Book: The Sudeleys – Lords of Toddington (joint author), 1987; Contributor to: Contemporary Review; Family History; London Magazine; Monday World; Quarterly Review; Vogue; The Universe; John Pudney's Pick of Today's Short Stories; Montgomeryshire Collections; Salisbury Review; Transactions of the Bristol and Gloucester Archaeological Society. Honour: FSA, 1989. Address: 25 Melcombe Court, Dorset Square, London NW1 6EP, England.

SUG Hyontai, b. 5 October 1960, Busan, Republic of Korea. Professor. m. Aee-Ran Eum, 1 son, 2 daughters. Education: Bachelor of Science, Pusan National University, 1983; Master of Science, Hankuk University of Foreign Studies, 1986; PhD, University of Florida, USA, 1998. Appointments: Researcher, Agency for Defense Development, Chinhae, 1986-92; Full-time Lecturer, Pusan University of Foreign Studies, Busan, 1999-2001; Associate Professor, Dongseo University, Busan, 2001-. Publications: Reducing on the Number of Testing Items in the Branches of Decision Trees, 2004; A Comprehensively Sized Decision Tree Generation Method for Interactive Data Mining of Very Large Databases, 2005; Using Reliable Short Rules to Avoid Unnecessary Tests in Decision Trees, 2006. Honours: Knight of Justice, The Sovereign Order of the Knights of Justice, 2007; Best Software Development Award, Chinhae Machine Depot, 1990, 1991; Best Professor Award, Dongseo University, 2007; Adviser to the Director General, IBC, 2006; Deputy Director General, IBC, 2006; Diploma of Achievement Award, IBC, 2005/06, 2006/07; The Order of International Fellowship, IBC, 2006; The International Order of Merit, IBC, 2006; International Educator of the Year, IBC, 2006; 21st Century Award for Achievement, IBC, 2006, 2007; Meritorious Decoration Certificate, IBC, 2006; International Medal of Honor, IBC, 2006; Leading Scientists of the World, IBC, 2006; Leading Educators of the World, IBC, 2006; The Da Vinci Diamond, IBC, 2006; Salute to Greatness Award, IBC, 2006; Hall of Fame, IBC, 2006; The IBC Top 100 Scientists, 2007; Vice President, World Congress of Arts, Sciences and Communications, 2007; The Universal Award of Accomplishment, ABI, 2006; Outstanding Professional Award, ABI, 2006; International Commendation of Success, ABI, 2006; International Medal of Vision, ABI, 2006; American Hall of Fame, ABI, 2007; Master Diploma with Honors, World Academy of Letters, 2007; International Cultural Diploma of Honor, ABI, 2007; International Peace Prize, United Cultural Convention, 2007; American Medal of Honor, ABI, 2007; World Lifetime Achievement Award, ABI, 2007; Man of the Year, ABI, 2006, 2007, 2008; Vice Chancellor, World Academy of Letters, 2008; Lifetime of Greatness Award, IBC, 2008; Lifetime of Scientific Achievement, IBC, 2008; Lifetime Achievement Award, United Cultural Convention, 2008; Listed in national and international biographical dictionaries including Marquis, IBC and ABI. Memberships: Director, The Korea Institute of Signal Processing and Systems; The Korea Information Science Society; The Korea Contents Association. Address: Division of Computer and Information Engineering, Dongseo University, Joo-Rye-2-dong, San 69-1, Sa-Sang-gu, Busan 617-716, Republic of Korea. E-mail: hyontai@yahoo.com

SUGAR Alan, b. 24 March 1947, London, England. Business Executive. m. Ann Simons, 1968, 2 sons, 1 daughter. Education: Brooke House School, London. Appointments: Chair and Managing Director, 1968-97, CEO, -1993, Chair, 1997-2001, Chair and CEO, 2001-, Amstrad plc; Chair,

Owner, Tottenham Hotspur plc, 1991-2001; Chair, Viglen plc, 1997-; The Apprentice, 2005-. Honours: Hon Fellow, City and Guilds of London Institute; Hon DSc (City University), 1988. Address: Amstrad plc, 169 King's Road, Brentwood, Essex CM14 4EF, England. Website: www.amstrad.com

SUGISAKI Akio M, b. 6 June 1936, Yokohama, Japan. Chairman of the Board. m. Noriko, 1 son, 2 daughters. Education: Bachelor's degree, Tokyo University of Mercantile Marine, 1960; Doctor's degree, Engineering, University of Tokyo, 1989. Appointments: Lecturer, 1966, Associate Professor, 1969, Professor, 1983, Dean of Student Affairs, 1995-97, President, 1998-2002, Tokyo University of Mercantile Marine; Chairman, Japan Institute of Navigation, 1992-94; Chairman of the Board, nonprofit foundation KAIYO-KAI, 2003-. Publications: Numerous articles in professional journals. Honours: Best Thesis Award of the Year, Japan Institute of Navigation, 1967, 1977, 1979, 1982; Official Commendation, Minister of Transportation, 1989; Official Commendation, Minister of International Trade and Industry, 1998; Professor Emeritus, Dalian Maritime University, China, 1996; Professor Emeritus, Tokyo University of Mercantile Marine, 2002; Professor Emeritus, Tokyo University of Marine Science and Technology, 2003. Memberships: Japan Institute of Navigation; Institute of Electronics, Information and Communication Engineers; Information Processing Society of Japan; Japanese Society for Artificial Intelligence; Japan Society of Naval Architects and Ocean Engineering.

SUH Jeong-Kwan, b. 1 January 1972, Eung-Sung, Korea. Researcher. m. Yoo-Mi Ko, 2 daughters. Education: Bachelor, 1996, Master, 2000, Doctor course, 2003, Nuclear Engineering, Seoul National University. Appointments: Senior Researcher, KEPCO Research Institute, 2004-. Publications: Development of Human Factors Validation System for the Advanced Control Room of APR1400, 2009. Memberships: Korea Society of Simulation. Address: 65 Munjiro, YuseongGu, Daejeon 305-760, Republic of Korea. E-mail: jksuh@kepco.co.kr

SULLIVAN John William, Teacher; Professor. m. Jean Salkeld, 3 sons, 1 daughter. Education: Westcliff High School; BA, Hull University, 1970; PGCE, Liverpool University, 1971; Dip Theol, Christ's College, Liverpool, 1974; Dip Ed, London, 1977; M Litt, Lancaster University, 1981; PhD, London University, 1998. Appointments: Catholic Secondary School Teacher, 1971-83; Deputy Head, Douay Martyrs Comprehensive School, 1983-85; Vice Principal, St Francis Xavier Sixth Form College, 1985-89; Head, Professional Development & Deputy Chief Inspector/Acting Chief Inspector, Wandsworth Education Authority, 1989-93; Headteacher, Christ's School, Richmond, 1993-94; Education Management Consultant, Reader in Catholic Education, St Mary's University College, Twickenham, 1994-2002; Professor of Christian Education, Liverpool Hope University, 2002-. Publications: Catholic Schools in Contention, 2000; Catholic Education: Distinctive and Inclusive, 2001; The Idea of a Christian University, 2005; Dancing on the Edge: Chaplaincy Church & Higher Education, 2007; Communicating Faith, 2010; Learning the Language of Faith, 2010; Over 70 further chapters and articles on religion and education in books and journals in UK, Ireland, Europe, Australia and USA. Honours: Outstanding Contribution to Catholic Teacher Formation and Development, National Catholic Educational Association, 2001. Memberships: Catholic Theological Society of Great Britain; Fellow, Higher Education Academy; Association des Amis de Maurice Blondel. Address: Holly Tree Cottage, Elmcroft Lane, Hightown, Liverpool, L38 3RW, England. E-mail: sullivj@hope.ac.uk

SULLIVAN Wendy, b. 18 May 1938, London, England. Painter; Poet. Education: Notre Dame High School, London. Career: Exhibitions: Brixton Gallery, 1981-97; Royal Academy Summer Shows, 1989,1990, 1997, 1998; South Bank Picture Show, 1990; Dagmar Gallerie, East Dulwich, 1990-92; Cooltan Arts, Brixton and Camden, 1992-95; Brixton Gallery, Retrospective, 1995; 2 Solo Shows, West Norwood Library, 1997, 1999; 2 Solo Shows Ritzy Cinema, 2000, 2001, Solo Show, Brixton Library, 2000; Artist in Residence, ASC Studios, Brixton, 2000-01; Solo Show, Jacaranda Restaurant, Brixton, 2002-04; Solo Show, The Village Hall, Brixton, 2002; Brixton Open, 2003; Solo Show, Bettie Moreton Gallery, Brixton, 2004; 1st Annual Dulwich Art Fair, 2004; Transmission, New Cross, 2011; Gems of Lambeth Archives, Lambeth, 2011; Solo Show, Tom's Journey & Now Mine, Carnegie Library, Herne Hill, 2011; Art in Brixton – London Open Garden Squares, Brixton, 2011; Works in collections: St Mark's Centre, Deptford; Lambeth Archives; St John's Church, Brixton; Breast Scanning Clinic, Camberwell; Dagmar Gallerie (now private), France; Movement for Justice. Publications: Contributions to poetry magazines for 40 years. Honours: Winner, Brixton Open, 2003; Listed in Who's Who publications and biographical dictionaries. Address: 127 Crescent Lane, London SW4 8EA, England. E-mail: draw2day@hotmail.co.uk Website: www.wendysullivanartist.com

SUMIDA Masaki, b. 5 September 1969, Hiroshima, Japan. Engineer. Education: BS, Department of Materials, 1993, MS, Department of Superconductivity, 1995, DEng, Department of Metallurgy, 1998, Graduate School of Engineering, University of Tokyo. Appointments: Researcher, Department of Metallurgy, University of Tokyo, Bunkyo, 1998; Assistant, Department of Materials, Swiss Federal Institute of Technology, Lausanne, Vaud, Switzerland, 1999; Research Associate, 2002, Technical Staff, 2006-, National Institute for Materials Science, Tsukuba, Japan; Research Associate, Research Centre for Advanced Science and Technology, University of Tokyo, Meguro, 2004. Publications: 45 articles contributed to academic books; 1 book; 1 patent; Inventor of 3 metallic materials, 2 production methods, 1 software and 4 theoretical equations. Honours: Young Scientist and Engineer Awards, 1997; Best Paper Award, The Japan Society for Heat Treatment, 2010; Listed in international biographical dictionaries. Memberships: Japan Society of Powder & Powder Metallurgy; The Iron and Steel Institute of Japan; The Japan Institute of Metals; Japan Foundry Engineering Society; The Japan Institute of Light Metals; The Japan Society for Heat Treatment. E-mail: sumida-m@aist.go.jp

SUMIYOSHI Tomiki, b. 18 December 1964, Tokyo, Japan. Psychiatrist; Researcher. m. Sawako Suemasa. Education: MB, 1989, MD, 1989, PhD, 1993, Kanazawa University School of Medicine; Diplomate, National Medical Board of Japan, 1989. Appointments: Resident, Fukui Prefectural Psychiatric Hospital, Japan, 1990; Ward Administrator, Kanazawa University Hospital, Japan, 1991-93; Research Associate, Department of Psychiatry, Case Western Reserve University, Cleveland, 1993-95; Assistant Professor, Department of Psychiatry, Saitama Medical School, Japan, 1995-96; Assistant Professor, Department of Neuropsychiatry, Director, Neurochemistry Research, Toyama Medical and Pharmaceutical University, 1996-2000; Appointed Psychiatrist, Health and Welfare Ministry, Japan,

1996-; Associate Professor, Department of Neuropsychiatry, University of Toyama Graduate School of Medicine, Japan, 2000-; Visiting Professor, Department of Psychiatry, Vanderbilt University School of Medicine, Nashville, USA, 2000-2002; Clinical Professor, Department of Neuropsychiatry, University Hospital of Toyama, Japan, 2009-. Publications: Numerous articles as author and co-author in medical journals in English include most recently: Serotonin 1A receptors in memory function, 2004; Plasma glycine and serine levels in schizophrenia compared to normal controls and major depression: Relation to negative symptoms, 2004; Prediction of changes in memory performance by plasma homovanillic acid levels in clozapine-treated patients with schizophrenia, 2004; Disorganization of semantic memory underlies alogia in schizophrenia: An Analysis of verbal fluency performance in Japanese subjects, 2005; Verbal memory deficits in a preadolescent case of lesions of the left parahippocampal gyrus associated with a benign tumour, 2006; 12 book chapters in English, French and Japanese. Honours: Research Award, Saburo Matsubara Memorial Fund for Psychiatric Research, 1993; Rotary Ambassadorial Scholarship, Rotary International, 1994-95; Young Investigator Award, National Alliance for Research on Schizophrenia and Depression, Chicago, 1995, New York, 2001; Society Award, Japanese Society of Biological Psychiatry, 1996; Japan Education and Science Ministry Fellowship for Long-term Research in Foreign Countries, 2000-2002; ACNP Memorial Travel Award, American College of Neuropsychopharmacology, 2001; Academic Encouragement Award, JSCNP Dr Paul Janssen Research Award, 2008. Memberships: World Federation of Societies of Biological Psychiatry; Society for Neuroscience; Collegium Internationale Neuro-Psychopharmacologicum; Schizophrenia International Research Society; New York Academy of Sciences. Japanese Society of: Biological Psychiatry, Neuropsychopharmacology, Clinical Neuropsychopharmacology, Psychiatry and Neurology, Brain Sciences, Psychiatric Diagnosis, Clinical Neurophysiology; Schizophrenia Research. Address: Department of Neuropsychiatry, University of Toyama School of Medicine, 2630 Sugitani, Toyama, 930-0194 Japan. E-mail: tomikisumiyoshi840@yahoo.co.jp

SUMMERSCALES John, b. 9 April 1952, Wakefield, West Yorkshire, England. Lecturer. Education: BSc, University of Wales Institute of Science and Technology, 1974; MSc, Thames Polytechnic, London, 1975; PhD, Plymouth Polytechnic, Devon, 1981; Postgraduate Diploma in (Adult) Education, University of Plymouth, 1998. Appointments: Editorial Coder, Derwent Publications, London, 1976-77; Research Assistant, Plymouth Polytechnic, Plymouth, 1977-81; Materials Consultant, Diving Diseases Research Centre Ltd, Plymouth, 1982; MoD (N) Contract Materials Technologist, Western Approach (Consultants) Ltd, Torquay, 1982-84; Higher Scientific Officer, Ministry of Defence (Navy), 1984-87; Lecturer II, Senior Lecturer, Reader in Composites Engineering, University of Plymouth School of Marine Science and Engineering, 1987-. Publications: 2 books; 4 journals. Honours: FInstNDT, 1991; FIMMM, 1992; FIAQP, 1997. Listed in various international bigraphical dictionaries. Address: School of Marine Science and Engineering, University of Plymouth, Plymouth, PL4 8AA, England. E-mail: jsummerscales@plymouth.ac.uk Website: http://www.plym.ac.uk/staff/jsummerscales

SUN Jie, b. Qingdao, China. Professor. Education: MS, Chinese Academy of Science, People's Republic of China, 1981; MS, 1983, PhD, 1986, University of Washington, USA. Appointments: Assistant Professor, Northwestern University of USA, 1986-92; Senior Lecturer, 1993-97, Associate Professor, 1998-2001, Professor, 2002-, National University of Singapore. Publication: Advances in Optimisation and Approximation, 1994. Honour: Outstanding University Researcher, 1999. Membership: Mathematical Programming Society: Chair, Pacific Optimisation Activity Group; Member of 5 editorial boards. Address: Department of Decision Sciences, National University of Singapore, Republic of Singapore 119260. E-mail: jsun@nus.edu.sg

SUN Ron, b. 8 October 1960, Shanghai, China. Cognitive Scientist; Computer Scientist. Education: BSc in Computer Information Science, Fudan University, 1983; MSc in Mathematics and Computer Science, Clarkson University, USA, 1986; PhD in Computer Science, Brandeis University, 1991. Appointments: Assistant Professor of Computer Science and Psychology, 1992-98, Associate Professor of Computer Science and Psychology, 1998-99, Departments of Computer Science and Psychology, University of Alabama at Tuscaloosa; Adjunct Professor of Psychology, University of Alabama at Birmingham, 1998-2000; Visiting Scientist, NEC Research Institute, Princeton, New Jersey, 1998-2003; Associate Professor of Computer Engineering and Computer Science, Department of Computer Engineering and Computer Science, University of Missouri-Columbia, Columbia, 1999-2002; Full Professor and James C Dowell Endowed Professor of CECS, Department of CECS, University of Missouri, Columbia, 2002-2003; Full Professor, Department of Cognitive Science, Rensselaer Polytechnic Institute, 2003-. Publications: Author, Integrating Rules and Connectionism for Robust Commonsense Reasoning, 1994; Duality of the Mind, 2002; Editor: Cognition and Multi-Agent Interaction, 2006; Editor, The Cambridge Handbook of Computational Psychology, 2008; Co-editor: Computational Architectures Integrating Neural and Symbolic Processes, 1994; Connectionist Symbolic Integration, 1997; Hybrid Neural Systems, 2000; Sequence Learning: Paradigms, Algorithms, and Applications, 2001; Numerous book chapters, papers and articles in the field, especially in human and machine learning, reasoning and representation in neural networks, hybrid models, autonomous agents and multi-agent systems. Honours include: David Marr Award in Cognitive Science, Cognitive Science Society, 1991; Senior Member, Institute of Electrical and Electronics Engineers, 1998; Member, European Academy of Science, 2002; Member, Governing Board of International Neural Networks Society; Member, Governing Board of Cognitive Science Society; Hebb Award, International Neural Networks Society, 2008. Memberships: Institute of Electrical and Electronics Engineers; Cognitive Science Society; Life Member, American Association for Artificial Intelligence; International Neural Network Society; Upsilon Pi Epsilon. Address: Cognitive Science Department, Rensselaer Polytechnic Institute, 110 8th Street, Troy, NY 12180, USA.

SUN Te-Hsiung, b. 30 January 1930, Kao-hsiung, Taiwan. Professor; Government Officer. m. Chu-Chen Chao, 1 son, 2 daughters. Education: BS, Agricultural Economics, National Taiwan University, 1954; MS, 1966, PhD, 1968, Sociology, University of Michigan, USA. Appointments: Research Fellow, Director, Taiwan Population Studies Center, 1961-69; Consultant, World Health Organization, 1971-72; Committee Member, Organizations for Demographic Study in Asia, 1971-75; Member, Research Committee, International Union for the Scientific Study of Population, 1972-73; Executive Committee Member, International Committee for Applied Research on Population, 1972-82; Research Fellow, Institute of Economics, Academia Sinica, 1972-94; Consultant, World Bank, 1985; Professor, Tung-Hai University, 1973-87; National Taiwan University, 1973-79, 1989-; Advisor,

Department of Health, 1973-76, 1995-2002; Member, Population Policy Committee, Ministry of Interior, 1974-; Director, Taiwan Provincial Institute of Family Planning, 1975-87; Member, Regional Planning Committee, Ministry of Interior, 1977-92; Chairman, Planned Parenthood Association of Taiwan, 2001-07; President, Population Association of Taiwan, 1984-88; Chairman, Research, Development and Evaluation Commission, Executive Yuan, 1987-94; Professor, Chung-Cheng University, 1987-2008; Member, Mainland China Commission, Cabinet, 1991-94; Chief Editor, Journal of Population Studies, NTU, 2000-12. Publications: Numerous articles in professional journals. Honours: Fellowship, The Population Council of New York, 1964-66; Scholarship, University of Michigan, 1966-68; Research grants from National Scientific Commission, 1976-87; Outstanding Specialist of Applied Science & Technology Award of the Executive Yuan, 1986; Decoration of the National Department of Health, 1995; Medal of Honor for Research, Development and Research Commission, 2000; Distinguished Alumnus, Chang-Jung High School, 2010; Distinguished Alumnus, Department of Agricultural Economics, National Taiwan University, 2012; Life-long Accomplishment, Population Association of Taiwan, 2011. Memberships: International Union for the Scientific Study of Population; Population Association of America; Population Association of Taiwan; Chinese Association of Sustainable Development; YMCA of Taiwan; Taiwan Association for Retired Persons; Hon-tao Foundation for the Welfare of the Elderly; Planned Parents Association of Taiwan. Address: 10F No 333, Long-chiang Road, Taipei 104, Taiwan. E-mail: 53154566@so-net.net.tw

SUNDERASAN Srinivasan, b. Secunderabad, India. Economist. Education: BE, Civil Engineering, Osmania University, India, 1993; MBA, Finance, King Fahd University of Petroleum & Minerals, Saudi Arabia, 1998; PhD, Business Economics, University of Vienna, Austria, 2005. Appointments: Quantity Surveyor and Project Engineer, ITC Hotels Ltd, 1993-95; Research Assistant, College of Industrial Management, King Fahd University of Petroleum & Minerals, 1995-98; Executive Projects, TATA TeleServices Ltd, Hyderabad, 1998-2000; Head, Business & Financial Solutions, IT Power India Pvt Ltd, Pondicherry, India, 2000-05; Investment Officer, South Asian Region, Solar Development Group & Triodos Renewable Energy for Development Fund, 2000-05; Deputy Country Manager, PVMTI, India, 2000-05; Economist, Verdurous Solutions Private Ltd, Mysore, India, 2005-. Publications: 4 books; Numerous articles in professional journals. Honours: National Merit Scholarship, 1987; Syed Ali Raza Merit Scholarship, 1991-92, 1992-93; Research Assistantship, KFUPM, 1995; Listed in biographical dictionaries. Memberships: Solar Energy Society of India; Indian Institute of Architects; Institution of Engineers, India; Economist Intelligence Unit; Society of Industry Leaders; American Society of Civil Engineers. Address: 145 Navillu Road, Mysore 570023, India.

SUNKLODAS Jonas Kazys, b. 28 September 1945, Užpaliai Town, Utena District, Lithuania. Mathematician, m. Janina Survilaitė, 1 son, 3 daughters. Education: Mathematics major, Vilnius University, 1963-68; Postgraduate studies, Institute of Physics and Mathematics, Lithuanian Academy of Sciences, 1972-74; Doctors degree, Mathematics, Vilnius University, 1979; Habilitated Doctors degree of Physical Sciences, Mathematics, Institute of Mathematics and Informatics, 1999; Title of Professor, Vilnius Gediminas Technical University, 2004. Appointments: Junior Research Fellow, Institute of Physics and Mathematics, Lithuanian Academy of Sciences, 1970-71; Instructor, Faculty of Mathematics and Mechanics, Vilnius University, 1973-78; Junior Research Fellow, 1975-81, Senior Research Fellow, 1982-2002, Chief Research Fellow, 2003-10, Institute of Mathematics and Informatics, Lithuanian Academy of Sciences; Chief Research Fellow, 2010-, Institute of Mathematics and Informatics, Vilnius University; Associate Professor, 1997-99, Professor, 1999-, Faculty of Fundamental Sciences, Vilnius Gediminas Technical University. Publications: Articles in science publications on probability theory; Author, over 70 scientific publications. Memberships: Lithuanian Mathematicians' Society. Address: Institute of Mathematics and Informatics, Vilnius University, Akademijos 4, 220 cab, LT-08663 Vilnius, Lithuania.

SUPPAKUL Panuwat, b. 25 July 1971, Ranong, Thailand. Lecturer. Education: BSc (2nd Honours), 1993, MSc, 1996, Agro-Industrial Product Development, Kasetsart University, Thailand; MScTech, Engineering Materials, UNSW, Australia, 2000; PhD, Packaging Technology, VU, Australia, 2004. Appointments: Lecturer, 1997-2005, Assistant Professor, 2006-08, Associate Professor, 2009-, Kasetsart University. Publications: Natural extracts in plastic packaging, Multifunctional and Nanoreinforced Polymers for Food Packaging, 2011; Antimicrobial Packaging Material, 2011; Intelligent Packaging, Handbook of Frozen Food Processing & Packaging, 2012; Alternative technique of antimicrobial activity of lipophilic antimicrobial packaging film, 2012. Honours: Knight Commander (2nd Class), Most Noble Order of the Crown of Thailand, 2008; Second Prize, Rice Innovation Award, 2009; Third Prize, Rice Innovation Award, 2010; The Best Poster Presentation, The 25th IAPRI Symposium on Packaging, 2011; Listed in biographical dictionaries. Memberships: American Chemical Society; American Society for Testing and Materials International; International Association of Packaging Research Institutes. Address: Department of Packaging and Materials Technology, Faculty of Agro-Industry, Kasetsart University, 50 Phaholyothin Road, Ladyao, Chatuchak, Bangkok 10900, Thailand. E-mail: fagipas@ku.ac.th Website: http://sites.google.com/site/panuwatsuppakul/

SURANA Prakash Chand, b. 1 November 1955, Taranagar, Rajasthan, India. Chartered Accountant. m. Kiran, 2 sons, 2 daughters. Education: B Com (Hons), 1974; M Com, 1977; LLB, 1978; FCA, 1978; MBIM, 1979; FASM, 1979; MIIA, 1980. Appointments: Vice President, UHSJST Sabha, SJSTSCAL Trust; Secretary, Uttar Howrab Sabha, Mitra Parishad, SJST, Sabha Calcutta; Vice President, Shri JST Vidyalaya Society; Secretary, North Calcutta Jaycees; Secretary, Lions Club of Kolkata Lake Gardens; Convenor, Jain Karyavahim, Maryada Mahutsav Vyawastha Samiti Taranagar; Secretary, ISE Dealers Association of Eastern India; West Bengal Metal Market Tenants Association; Covenor, Purbanchal Chaturvas Vyawastha Samiti. Publications: Articles of various religious subjects; Biographical speeches and articles. Honours: Trophy for Individual Development, North Calcutta Jaycees; Certificate of Merit for Outstanding Social Service, Junior Chamber. Memberships: Institute of CA of India; Institute of International Auditors; Hindi Club Ltd; Tulsishanti Pratisthan; JST Mahasabha; Oswal Navywak Sumiti; W B Welfare Society; Shri Jain Swetamber Terapanthi Vidyalaya. Address: 157 Netaji Subhas Road, 2nd Floor, Room No. 143, Kolkata – 700 001, West Bengal, India. E-mail: pcsurana@cal3.vsnl.net.in

SURATWALA Narendra, b. 2 July 1955, A Nagar, India. Medical Otorhinolaryngologist. m. Daksha, 2 sons. Education: BJMC, Pune, India. Appointments: Director, VAV Clinic and R&D Centre of Sarvodaya Hospital, Surat, India;

Visiting ENT Surgeon, SDA Misson and Anand Hospital, Surat, India; Honorary Medical Advisor, AM Lokhat Hospital, Surat, India. Publications: Over 50 articles in professional journals. Honours: Top ranking in postgraduate exam in ENT, 1982; Fellowships in endoscopy, sinus surgery, basic and advanced neuro-otology, phoniatrix and endolaser surgeries; First Indian ENT surgeon invited as guest lecturer, Sydney University, 1990; 3 time recipient of SD Parikh Award, GSB-AOI; K U Shah Award; Exceptional 25 years of service award, South Guj Academy-ORL, 2010; many others. Memberships: South Guj Academy of ORL; Life Member, SGAOR, LGSB; ISOAOI; NES. Address: VAV Care E Clinic and Sarvodaya Hospital, 4/138 Haripura, Surat 395003, India. E-mail: narendra29@aim.com

SURINENAITE Birute, b. 16 May 1970, Vilnius, Lithuania. Biochemist. Education: Secondary school, 1988; Master degree, Biochemistry, Vilnius University, 1993; PhD, Physical Sciences, Biochemistry, 2001. Appointments: Science Assistant, 1993-96, Research Associate, 2001, Vilnius University; PhD student, 1996-2000; Senior Research Associate, Institute of Oncology, 2003-10; Senior Research Associate, Institute of Biotechnology, 2007-11; Managing Music Editor, Classic Rock FM radio station, Lithuania. Publications: Numerous articles in professional journals. Memberships: Lithuanian Association of Biochemistry; Lithuanian Association of Biotechnology. Address: Paribio str 28-34, LT-08103 Vilnius, Lithuania. E-mail: birute.surinenaite@rock.lt

SUTHERLAND Donald McNichol, b. 17 July 1935, St John, Canada. Actor. m. (1) Lois May Hardwick, 1959, (2) Shirley Jean Douglas, 1966, divorced, 1 son, 1 daughter, (3) Francine Racette, 1971, 3 sons. Education: University of Toronto. Appointments: Appeared on TV (BBC and ITV) in Hamlet; Man in the Suitcase; The Saint; Gideon's Way; The Avengers; Flight into Danger; Rose Tattoo; March to the Sea; Lee Harvey Oswald; Court Martial; Death of Bessie Smith; Max Dugan Returns; Crackers; Louis Malle; The Disappearance; Commander in Chief; Dirty Sexy Money; Films include: The World Ten Times Over, 1963; Castle of the Living Dead, 1964; Dr Terror's House of Horrors; Fanatic, 1965; Act of the Heart, M*A*S*H*, Kelly's Heroes, Little Murders, 1970; Don't Look Now, 1973; The Day of the Locust, 1975; 1900, 1976; The Eagle Has Landed, 1977; The Great Train Robbery, 1978; Lock Up, Apprentice to Murder, Los Angeles, 1989; The Railway Station Man, Scream from Stone, Faithful, JFK, 1991; Backdraft; Agaguk; Buffy the Vampire Slayer; Shadow of the Wolf, Benefit of the Doubt; Younger and Younger, Six Degrees of Separation, 1993; The Puppet Masters; Disclosure; Outbreak; Hollow Point; The Shadow Conspiracy; A Time To Kill; Virus, Instinct, Toscano, 1999; The Art of War, Panic, Space Cowboys, 2000; Uprising, The Big Herst, Final Fantasy: The Spirits Within, Big Shot's Funeral, 2001; Five Moons Plaza, Italian Job, Baltic Storm, Cold Mountain, 2003; Aurora Borealis, Fierce People, Pride & Prejudice, American Hun, An American Haunting, 2005; Land of the Blind, Ask the Dust, 2006; Sleepwalkers, Reign Over Me, Puffball, 2007; Fool's Gold, 2008; Astro Boy (voice), 2009; The Pillars of the Earth, 2010; The Mechanic, The Eagle, The Con Artist, Horrible Bosses, Man on the Train, Moby Dick, Jock of the Bushveld, 2011; The Hunger Games, 2012; The Hunger Games: Catching Fire, 2013; Plays: Lolita, 1981; Enigmatic Variations, 2000; President, McNichol Pictures Inc. Honours: TV Hallmark Hall of Fame; Officer, Ordre des Lettres; Order of Canada; Hon PhD; Golden Globe, 2002; Honorary Doctor of letters, Lakehead University, 2008; Hollywood Walk of Fame, 2011; Commandeur of the Ordre des Arts et des Lettres, 2012. Address: 760 N La Cienega Boulevard, Los Angeles, CA 90069, USA.

SUTHERLAND Kiefer, b. 21 December 1966, London, England. Actor. m. (1) Camelia Kath, 1987, divorced 1990, 1 daughter, 1 stepdaughter, (2) Kelly Winn, 1996-2004, divorced, 2 stepsons. Career: Debut, LA Odyssey Theatre, aged 9 years; Films: Max Dugan Returns, 1983; The Bay Boy, 1984; At Close Range, Crazy Moon, Stand By Me, 1986; The Lost Boys, The Killing Time, Promised Land, 1987; Bright Lights, Big City, Young Guns, 1988; Renegades, 1989; Chicago Joe and the Showgirl, Flashback, Flatliners, The Nutcracker Prince (voice), Young Guns II, 1990; Article 99, 1991; Twin Peaks: Fire Walk with Me, A Few Good Men, 1992; The Vanishing, 1993; The Three Musketeers; The Cowboy Way; Teresa's Tattoo; Eye for an Eye; A Time to Kill, 1996; Truth or Consequences NM (also director), Dark City, 1997; Ground Control, The Breakup, 1998; Woman Wanted, The Red Dove, Hearts and Bones, 1999; Beat, Picking up the Pieces, The Right Temptation, 2000; Cowboy Up, To End All Wars, 2001; Desert Saints, Dead Heat, Behind the Red Door, Phone Booth, 2002; Paradise Found, 2003; Taking Lives, Jiminy Glick in La La Wood, 2004; River Queen, 2005; The Wild (voice), 2006; Mirrors, 2008; 24: Redemption, 2008; Twelve, 2010; Melancholia, 2011; 24, The Reluctant Fundamentalist, 2013; TV: Amazing Stories; Trapped in Silence; Brotherhood of Justice; Last Light (also director); 24, 2001-; The Confession, 2011; Touch, 2012-. Honours: Golden Globe, Best Actor in a TV Series, 2002; 2 Satellite Awards, 2002, 2003; 2 Screen Actors Guild Awards, 2004, 2006; 2 Emmy Awards, 2006. Address: International Creative Management, 8942 Wilshire Boulevard, Beverly Hills, CA 90211, USA.

SUTHERLAND Margaret, b. 16 September 1941, Auckland, New Zealand. Writer. m. 2 sons, 2 daughters. Education: Registered Nurse; Novelist. Publications: 7 novels and 3 short story collections, titles include: The Fledgling, 1974; Hello, I'm Karen (children's book), 1974; The Love Contract, 1976; Getting Through, 1977, US edition as Dark Places, Deep Regions, 1980; The Fringe of Heaven, 1984; The City Far From Home, 1992; Is that Love?, 1999; The Sea Between, 2006; Leaving Gaza, 2007; Windsong; 2008; The Taj Mahal of Trundle, 2009. Contributions to: Journals and magazines. Honours: Katherine Mansfield Short Story Award; N Z Scholarship in Letters, Auckland University Writing Fellowship; Two Australian Council Grants; Federation of Australian Writers; National Short Story Award, 2009. Memberships: Australian Society of Authors; Federation of Australian Writers. Address: 10 Council Street, Speers Point, New South Wales 2284, Australia. Website: www.margaretsutherland.com

SUTHERLAND Peter Denis, b. 25 April 1946, Dublin, Ireland. Lawyer. m. Maria Del Pilar Cabria Valcarcel, 2 sons, 1 daughter. Education: Gonzaga College; University College, Dublin; The King's Inns; BCL. Appointments: Called to Bar, King's Inns, 1968; Middle Temple, 1976; Bencher, 1981; Attorney of New York Bar, 1981; Attorney and Counsellor of Supreme Court of USA, 1986; Tutor in Law, University College, Dublin, 1969-71; Practising Member, Irish Bar, 1969-81, 1981-82; Senior Counsel, 1980; Attorney General of Ireland, 1981-82, 1982-84; Member, Council of State, 1981-82, 1982-84; Commissioner for Competition and Commissioner for Social Affairs and Education, EEC, 1985-86, for Competition and Relations with European Parliament, 1986-89; Chairman, Allied Irish Banks, 1989-93; Director, GPA, 1989-93; Director, CRH plc, 1989-93;

Director, James Crean plc, 1989-93; Chairman, Board of Governors, European Institute of Public Administration, 1991-96; Director, Delta Air Lines Inc, 1992-93; Director General, GATT, later WTO, 1993-95; Honorary Bencher, King's Inns, Dublin, 1995; Director, Investor, 1995-2005; Chairman, Goldman Sachs International, 1995-; Director, Telefonaktiebolaget LM Ericsson, 1996-2004; Goodwill Ambassador to the United Nations Industrial Development Organisation; Chairman, BP plc, 1997-; Director, Royal Bank of Scotland Group plc, 2001-; Chairman (Europe), Special Representative of the DG of the UN for Migration and Development, 2006-, Trilateral Commission, 2001-; The Federal Trust, President; Member, Royal Irish Academy. Publications: Premier Janvier 1993 ce qui va changer en Europe, 1989; Numerous articles in law journals. Honours include: Honorary LLD: St Louis, 1986; NUI, 1990; Dublin City, 1991; Holy Cross, Massachusetts, 1994; Bath, 1995; Suffolk, USA, 1995; TCD, 1996; Reading, 1997; Nottingham, 1999; Exeter, 2000; Queens University Belfast, 2003; Koc University, Turkey, 2004; University of Notre Dame, 2004; DUniv, Open, 1995; Gold Medal, European Parliament, 1988; The First European Law Prize, Paris, 1988; Grand Cross: King Leopold II, Belgium, 1989; Grand Cross of Civil Merit, Spain, 1989; New Zealand Commemorative Medal, 1990; Chevalier, Legion d'Honneur, France, 1993; Commander, Order of Ouissam Alaouite, Morocco, 1994; Order of Rio Branco, Brazil, 1996; Order of Infante Dom Henrique, Portugal, 1998; The David Rockefeller International Leadership Award, 1998; UCD Foundation Day Medal; Honorary KCMG, 2004. Memberships: The Stephen's Green Hibernian Club, Dublin; Fitzwilliam Lawn Tennis, Dublin; Lansdowne FC, Dublin; The Athenaeum, London; Marks Club, London. Address: Goldman Sachs International, Peterborough Court, 133 Fleet Street, London, EC4A 2BB, England.

SUZMAN Dame Janet, b. 9 February 1939, Johannesburg, South Africa. Actress; Director. m. Trevor Nunn, 1969, divorced 1986, 1 son. Education: BA, University of Wittwatersrand; Graduate, London Academy of Music and Dramatic Arts, 1962. Career: For the RSC: The Wars of the Roses; Portia, Ophelia, Celia, Rosalind, Katherina; The Relapse; The Greeks, 1980; London Theatre includes: The Birthday Party; Three Sisters; Hedda Gabler; The Duchess of Malfi; Andromache; The Retreat from Moscow; Television includes: The Family Reunion; St Joan; Macbeth; Twelfth Night, Hedda Gabler; Three Men in a Boat; Clayhanger (serial), 1975-76; Mountbatten-Last Viceroy of India, 1985; The Singing Detective, 1986; The Miser, 1987; Revolutionary Witness, 1989; Masterclass on Shakespearean Comedy, 1990; Masterclass from Haymarket Theatre (Sky TV), 2001; White Clouds (BBC), 2002; Films include: A Day in the Death of Joe Egg, 1970; Nicholas & Alexandra, 1971; Nijinsky, 1978; The House on Garibaldi Street; The Priest of Love, 1981; The Black Windmill; Nuns on the Run, 1990; Leon the pig-Farmer, 1992; Max, 2001; Fairy Story, 2002; Numerous performances in South Africa; Wrote and Directed The Free State – a South African response to the Cherry Orchard, performed at the Birmingham Repertory Theatre, 1997 (revived for UK tour, 2000); The Guardsman, 2000; Television: Othello, 1988, Measure for Measure, 2004; Trial & Retribution: Sins of the Father, 2006; Lectures include: The Spencer Memorial Lecture, Harvard University, USA, 1987; The Tanner Lectures, Brasenose College, Oxford, 1995; The Judith E Wilson Annual Lecture, Trinity Hall, Cambridge, 1996; The Draper's Lecture, Queen Mary and Westfield College, University of London. 1997. Publications: Hedda Gabler: The Play in Performance, 1980; Acting with Shakespeare – Three Comedies, 1996; The Free State, 2000; A Textual Commentary on Anthony and Cleopatra, 2001. Honours: Honorary Degrees: MA, Open University; D Lit, Warwick University; D Lit, Leicester University; D Lit, Queen Mary and Westfield College, London University; D Lit, University of Southampton, 2002; Vice-President of London Academy of Music and Dramatic Arts; Dame, 2011. Address: c/o Steve Kenis & Co, Royalty House, 72-74 Dean Street, London W1D 3SG, England. E-mail: sk@sknco.com

SUZUKI Noriyasu, b. 20 October 1947, Sanjo, Nigataken, Japan. Journalist; Physician. Education: Degree in Physics, Nihon University; Degree in Journalism, University of Tokyo. Appointments: Physician; Journalist; Psychologist. Address: USFI, 1-7-4 Sanchiku, Santo City, Niigataken, 955-0041 Japan.

SUZUKI Yoshio, b. 12 October 1931, Tokyo, Japan. Economist. m. Yukiko, 3 sons, 1 daughter. Education: Graduated, 1955, Doctor of Economics, 1976, Tokyo University. Appointments: Joined Bank of Japan, 1955; Visiting Lecturer, Tokyo University, 1972; Chief Manager, Special Research Division, 1974, Chief Manager, Domestic Division, 1976, Economic Research Department, Bank of Japan; General Manager, Matumoto Branch, Bank of Japan, 1977; Visiting Lecturer, Shinshu University, 1978; Deputy Director, 1981, Director, 1984, Institute for Monetary and Economic Studies, Bank of Japan; Executive Director, Bank of Japan, 1988; Vice Chairman, 1989, Chairman, 1990, Board of Counsellors, Nomura Research Institute Ltd; Elected, Member of House of Representatives, Tokai District, Shadow Minister for Economy and Finance of the New Frontier Party, 1996; Vice Chairman, Policy Board of the Liberal Party, 1998; Re-elected, Member of the House of Representatives, Tokyo District, 2000; Chairman, Committee of Discipline, House of Representatives, 2002; Chairman, Suzuki Seikei Forum, 2004. Publications: Numerous books and papers published in English, German, Chinese and Korean. Honours: Nikkei Cultural Prize for Economic Literature, 1967; Economist's Prize, Mainichi Newspaper Company, 1975; Public Finance Fellowship, Institute of Fiscal and Monetary Policy, 1987; The Order of the Rising Sun, Gold Ray with Neck Ribbon, Emperor, 2004. Memberships: The Japanese Economic Association; The Association of Money and Banking; The Mont Pelerine Society. Address: 2-5-8 Kamitakaido, Suginami-ku, Tokyo 168-0074, Japan. E-mail: info@suzuki.org

SVENSSON Charles Robert Wilhelm, b. 11 September 1947, Göteborg, Sweden. Associate Professor; Scientist. Education: Associates Degree, Electronics, 1969; BSc, Physics, 1983, MSc, Physics, 1991, PhD, Thermionic Energy Converter Concept, 1994, Göteburg University. Appointments: Design Engineer, electronic temperature meters and heart beat monitors, -1981; Part-time teacher, 1981-83, Full-time Teacher, 1983-87, College of Applied Engineering and Maritime Studies, Chalmers University of Technology; Graduate Student, Department of Physical Chemistry, Göteburg University and Chalmers University of Technology, 1987-94; Assistant Professor, Chalmers University of Technology, 1995-96; Associate Professor, Chalmers University of Technology, 1996-; Visiting Research Professor, West Virginia University, USA, 2004, 2005, 2006, 2007. Publications: Numerous articles and papers; 2 patents. Memberships: American Institute of Aeronautics and Astronautics. Address: Dörravägen 1, SE-43893 Landvetter, Sweden. E-mail: term@chalmers.se Website: www.vison.nu/term

SVIRIDOV Andrei Valentinovitsh, b. 22 December 1946, Moscow, Russia. Entomologist. Education: Moscow Lomonosov State University, 1965-70. Appointments: Senior

Laboratory Assistant, 1970-71, Junior Researcher, 1971-86, Researcher, 1987-92, Senior Researcher, 1992-, Moscow Lomonosov State University; Scientific degree, Candidate of Biological Sciences (Dr), 1984; Academic Studies, Senior Researcher, 1995. Publications: 500 scientific publications, 1970-, include books: Types of the Biodiagnostic Keys and Their Applications, 1994; Biodiagnostical Keys: Theory and Practice, 1994; Key to the insects of Russian Far East, Vol 5, Part 4, 2003; Red Book of the Moscow Area, 2nd edition. Memberships: Russian Entomological Society; Moscow Society Naturalists; Society Europea Lepidopterology; Systematic Zoology/Biology; Hist-Genealogy Society, Moscow; Descendents Council of the Great War of 1812-1814 Vets; Commission of Red Book of Russia; Commission of Red Book of CIS. Honours: Ecologist of the Year, Moscow Region Administration, 2009; Listed in Who's Who publications and biographical dictionaries. Address: Dr A V Sviridov, Zoological Museum, Moscow State Lomonosov University, Bolshaya Nikitskaya St 6, 125009 Moscow, Russia.

SVYAZHIN Anatoly, b. 11 October 1934, Verkhnaya Tura, Russia. Metallurgist. m. Galina Kozlova, 1 son. Education: Diploma in Engineering, Moscow Steel and Alloys Institute, 1962; PhD, 1966; DSc, 1987; Professor, 1989. Appointments: Senior Research Scientist, 1967-71; Head, Division Research Laboratory, 1972-76; Head, Research Laboratory, 1976-2008, Main Researcher, 2009-, MISA; Visiting Professor, Technical University of Czestoshowa, Poland, 1994-99; Adviser, EKO Stahl GmbH, Germany, 2001-03. Publications: 2 monographs; Over 350 articles to scientific journals and conference proceedings; Patents. Honours: Awards of Minister of Education and Ferrous Metallurgy, 1980-95; Prize, Board of Ministers of USSR, 1987. Memberships: International Biographical Association; Association of Steelmakers of Commonwealth Independent States. Address: National University of Science and Technology (MISiS), Leninsky Prospect 4, 119049 Moscow, Russia.

SWALE Suzan Georgina, b. 30 April 1946, Nottingham, England. Artist; Lecturer. m. Robert Coward, 1 son, 1 daughter. Education: Foundation Course, Derby & District College of Art, 1965-66; Dip AD, BA (1st class honours), Fine Art, Bristol Polytechnic, 1969; MA, Painting, Royal College of Art, 1972. Appointments: Artist with group and solo exhibitions in UK, Poland, Greece and Austria, 1971-; Visiting lecturer, North Staffordshire Polytechnic, 1972-73; Full time Lecturer, Northern Ireland Polytechnic, Belfast, 1973-74; Full time Lecturer, Manchester Polytechnic, 1974-77; Visiting Lecturer, Maidstone College of Art, Chelsea School of Art, Bristol Polytechnic, Byam Shaw School of Art, Leeds Polytechnic and Newcastle Polytechnic, London College of Printing, 1978-79; Tutor, Morley College, 1979-; Tutor, Open University, 1980-90; Visiting Tutor, Bournemouth College of Art, 1982-84; Visiting Tutor, Goldsmiths College, London, 1984-85; Visiting Tutor, Polytechnic Central, London, 1990; Lead Tutor, Central St Martins, 1992-2001; Workshop Tutor, Tate Britain, 2002; Tutor, Open College of Arts, 2003-; Tutor, V&A Museum, 2006-. Honours: John Minton Scholarship, 1971, Burston Award, 1972, Royal College of Art; British Council Travel Award (Finland), 1983. Memberships: Royal College of Art Society; The London Group. E-mail: suzanswale@hotmail.co.uk Website: www.suzanswale.co.uk

SWAMINATHAN Monkombu Sambasivan, b. 7 August 1925, Tamil Nadu, India. Director. Education: BSc, Travancore University, 1944; BSc, Agriculture, Coimbatore Agricultural College, Madras University, 1947; Associateship, Indian Agricultural Research Institute, New Delhi, 1949; UNESCO Fellow, Agricultural University, Wageningen, The Netherlands, 1949-50; PhD, School of Agriculture, University of Cambridge, England, 1952; Research Associate, Genetics, University of Wisconsin, USA, 1952-53. Appointments: Teacher, Researcher, Research Administrator, Central Rice Research Institute, Cuttack, Indian Agricultural Research Institute, New Delhi, 1954-72; Director General, Indian Council of Agricultural Research, Secretary, Government of India, Department of Agricultural Research and Education, 1972-80; Secretary, Government of India, Ministry of Agriculture and Irrigation, 1979-80; Acting Deputy Chairman, Planning Commission, Government of India, 1980; Member, Planning Commission, Government of India, 1980-82; Director General, International Rice Research Institute, Los Banos, Philippines, 1982-88; Honorary Director, Centre for Research on Sustainable Agricultural and Rural Development, Madras, 1989-; UNESCO Chair in Ecotechnology. Publications: Numerous articles in professional journals. Honours include: World Food Prize, 1987; Tyler Prize, 1992; UNEP-Saskawa Environment Prize, 1994; V Gangadharan Award, Outstanding Contributions to National Development, 1997; BP Pal Memorial Award, Indian Science Congress Association, 1998; Volvo Environment Prize, 1999; UNESCO Gandhi Gold Medal, 1999; Franklin D Roosevelt Four Freedoms Award, 2000; Plant and Humanity Medal, 2000; Lal Bahadur Sastri National Award, 2007. Memberships: Parliament of India; National Advisory Council. Address: M S Swaminathan Research Foundation, 3rd Cross Street, Taramani Institutional Area, Chennai (Madras) 600 113, India.

SWAMY KUMARA M R, b. 23 January 1938, Mysore, India. Financial Management Researcher. m. Shaila, 1 son, 1 daughter. Education: BA (Hons), 1958, MA, 1960, PhD, 1965, Economics. Appointments: Research Fellow, Delhi School of Economics, 1960-61; Economic Investigator, National Council of Applied Economic Research, 1961-62; Advising Oil Economist, OPEC-Member Government of Qatar, 1967-69; Senior Research Officer, Commerce Research Bureau, 1969-77; Professor of Economics, Head of Finance Department, Institute of Management & Technology, Anambra State University of Technology, Nigeria, 1977-87; Director, Om Sai Ram Center for Financial Management Research, 1987-. Publications: 215 scholarly papers in professional journals. Honours: Distinguished Economist, Guest Lecturer, University of Rome, 1965-66; Member of Government of Nigeria Committee of Experts on Low-cost Housing Through Co-operative Societies, 1980-81. Memberships: Lisle Fellow; Financial Management Association International; Editorial Board Member, International Journal of Business. Address: 15 Prakash Co-op Housing Society, Relief Road, Santacruz (West), Mumbai 400054, India. E-mail: jfmaosr@gmail.com

SWANK Hilary, b. 30 July 1974, Bellingham, Washington, USA. Actress. m. Chad Lowe, 1997 (divorced). Career: Films: Buffy the Vampire Slayer, 1992; The Next Karate Kid, 1994; Sometimes They Came Back ...Again, 1996; Heartwood, 1997; Boys Don't Cry, 1999; The Gift, 2000; Affair of the Necklace, 2000; Insomnia, 2002; The Core, 2003; 11:44, 2003; Red Dust, 2004; Million Dollar Baby, 2004; The Black Dahlia, 2006; Freedom Writers, 2007; The Reaping, 2007; P.S. I Love You, 2007; Birds of America, 2008; Amelia, 2009; Conviction, 2010; The Resident, New Year's Eve, 2011; TV: Terror in the Family, 1996; Leaving LA, 1997. Academy Awards, Best Actress, 2000 and 2005; Golden Globe Awards, Best Actress, 2000 and 2005; Screen Actors Guild Awards, 2005. Address: c/o Metropolitan Talent Agency, 4526 Wilshire Boulevard, Los Angeles, CA 90010, USA.

SWEENEY Ronald Terence, b. 1 September 1932, Hull, England. Journalist; Company Director. m. Amy, 1 daughter. Education: Diplomate in Architectural Studies, Hull College (now University of Humberside); Postgraduate in Race Relations and Social Analysis, University of Bradford, 1987; Postgraduate, Church and Social Studies, Napier University, Edinburgh, 2000; MA, University of Wales/University of Leeds. Appointments: Journalist; Editor; Director of Marketing, PR Company, Leeds, Manchester, London; Head of Marketing and Communications, Bradford College; Lecturer at several universities in western-eastern Europe; Managing Director, International Travel and Conferences; Governor, Leeds Partnerships NHS Foundation Trust; Publications: Editor of Education News; Many articles in newspapers and trade professional press. Honours: Lay Preaching Commissioner for Yorkshire Synod of the United Reformed Church; Several awards for educational publications and public speaking. Memberships: Life Member, National Union of Journalists; International Federation of Journalists (Brussels); Several Travel/Conference Related Organisations. Address: "Tirconnell", 11 Endor Crescent, Burley-in-Wharfdale, West Yorkshire LS29 7QH, England.

SWETCHARNIK Sara Morris, b. 21 May 1955, Shelby, NC, USA. Artist; Sculptor; Painter; Writer. m. William Norton Swetcharnik, 1981. Education: Art Students League of New York, 1979-81; Postgraduate, Schuler School of Fine Art, Baltimore, Maryland, 1973-78; Private Study, Melvin Gerhold Studio, Frederick, Maryland, 1970-73. Appointments: Instructor, Frederick Academy for the Arts, Frederick, Maryland, 1981-82; Workshop Instructor, Landon School, Washington DC, 1991-96; Invitational Lecturer, Arts Task Force, Fulbright Conference, 2000, 2001; Guest Lecturer, The Institute, Mount Saint Mary's College, Emmitsburg, Maryland, 2001; Juror at several national and international exhibitions; Creative works: Solo Exhibitions including: Catepetl Gallery, Frederick, Maryland, 1977; Holly Hills Country Club, Frederick, Maryland, 1991; Landon School Gallery, Washington DC, 1992; Frederick Community College Art Gallery, Maryland, 1993; Showcase of Terra-cotta Animal Sculpture, Weinberg Center for the Arts, Frederick, Maryland, 1994; Komodo Dragon Yearling and other Animal Sculptures, Reptile Discovery Center, National Zoological Park, Washington DC, 1995-2001; Jungle Tails: Animal Narratives; Several group and two person exhibitions. Publications include: Glass Lizard, 1998; Marked for Life, 1998; Birthday Burro, 1998; Alfredo's Tigrillo, 1998; My Patriotic Primer, Lesson I: Patriotic Permissions. Honours include: American Collaborative Grantee in Sculpture and Research to the Fulbright Program in Spain, Commission for Cultural, Educational and Scientific Exchange between the United States and Spain: 1987-88, 1988-89; Artist in Residence Fellowship, American Numismatic Association Conference, 1994; Fellowship, Virginia Center for the Creative Arts; Linganore Distinguished Graduate Award for Achievement in Arts. Memberships: Delaplaine Visual Art Centre, Frederick, Maryland; Fulbright Association. Address: National Capitol Post Office Station, PO Box 77794, Washington, DC 20013, USA. E-mail: sara@swetcharnik.com Website: www.swetcharnik.com

SWIFT Graham Colin, b. 4 May 1949, London, England. Writer. Education: Dulwich College; Queens' College, Cambridge; University of York. Publications: The Sweet Shop Owner, 1980; Shuttlecock, 1981; Waterland, 1983; Out of This World, 1988; Ever After, 1992; Last Orders, 1996; The Light of Day, 2003; Tomorrow, 2007; Making an Elephant: Writing from Within, 2009; Short Stories: Learning to Swim and Other Stories, 1982; The Magic Wheel, 1986; Chemistry, 2008. Honours: Geoffrey Fabor Memorial Prize; Guardian Fiction Prize; Royal Society of Literature Winifred Holtby Award, 1983; Premio Grinzane Cavour, Italy, 1987; Prix du Meilleur livre etranger, France, 1994; Booker Prize, James Tait Black Memorial Prize, 1996; Hon LittD, East Anglia, 1998; Hon DUniv, York, 1998. Address: c/o A P Watt, 20 John Street, London, WC1N 2DR, England.

SWIFT Thomas, b. 17 November 1930, Oldham, England. Aeronautical Engineer. m. Irene, 1 daughter. Education: Full Technological City and Guilds of London Institute, 1950, Higher National, Mechanical Engineering, 1956, Grad I Mech E, 1957, Oldham College of Science and Technology, UK; Postgraduate Studies, Advanced Aero Structures and Metallurgy, Manchester University, UK, 1960-62; Postgraduate Studies, Theory of Elasticity, Advanced Aero Structures, Advanced Differential Equations, Newark College of Engineering, New Jersey, USA, 1962-65; Postgraduate Studies, Advanced Mathematics, Partial Differential Equations, Vector Analysis and Complex Variables, Stevens Institute of Technology, New Jersey, 1965-66; Upgrade to BSc, 1966-68, MSc, 1973, Mechanical Engineering, California State University, Long Beach, California, USA. Appointments: Engineering Apprenticeship Training, Oldham, 1947-51; Deputy Works Manager, Mellows and Co Ltd, Oldham, 1951-55; Design Engineer, Engineering Development Department, 1955-57, Stress Engineer, 1959-62, A V Roe and Co Ltd, Manchester; Stress Engineer, AVRO Aircraft, Malton, Ontario, Canada, 1957-59; Member of Technical Staff, RCA Missile Electronics and Controls, Burlington, Massachusetts, 1959; Project Engineer, Structural Analysis, X-19 VTOL Aircraft, Curtiss Wright Corp, Caldwell, New Jersey, 1962-66; Supervisor, Fuselage Fatigue, Fail-Safe Analysis and Structural Test Group, 1967-72, Stress Analysis, 1966-67, Chief, Fatigue and Fracture Mechanics Group, 1972-80, Chief Technology Engineer (Chief of Stress), C-17 Structural Analysis, 1986-87, McDonnell Douglas Corp, Long Beach, California; Lecturer, Fatigue and Damage Tolerance Technology, UCLA, 1975-; FAA National Resource Specialist, 1980-86, 1987-89, FAA Chief Scientific/Technical Advisor, 1989-97, Fracture Mechanics/Metallurgy; Aeronautical Consultant, Visiting Professor, Cranfield University, England, 1997-. Publications: Over 40 papers, articles and technical publications. Honours: John Platt Memorial Award, 1953-56; Engineer of the Month Award, Douglas Aircraft, Long Beach, California, USA, 1969; Plantema Medal, International Committee on Aeronautical Fatigue, 1987; John W Lincoln Medal, US Air Force, 1998; Wakefield Gold Medal, Royal Aeronautical Society, UK, 1999; Listed in international biographical dictionaries. Memberships: Fellow, Institution of Mechanical Engineers, UK; Chartered Engineer (C Eng), UK; Member, Council of Engineering Institutions, UK; Registered Member of Professional Engineers, Ontario, Canada; Retired Member of Fatigue Committee, Engineering Sciences Data Unit (ESDU); Retired Member, MIL-HDBK 5 Industry Co-ordinating Committee; Retired Member, FAA Technical Oversight Group-Aging Aircraft; Past Member, NASA Aeronautics Advisory Committee. Address: 3 Blencathra Gardens, Kendal, Cumbria LA9 7HL, England. E-mail: tomswiftken@aol.com

SWINBURNE Richard Granville, b. 26 December 1934, Smethwick, Staffordshire, England. Professor of Philosophy; Author. m. Monica Holmstrom, 1960, separated 1985, 2 daughters. Education: BA, 1957, BPhil, 1959, Dip Theol, 1960, MA, 1961, University of Oxford. Appointments: Fereday Fellow, St John's College, Oxford, 1958-61;

Leverhulme Research Fellow in the History and Philosophy of Science, University of Leeds, 1961-63; Lecturer to Senior Lecturer in Philosophy, University of Hull, 1963-72; Visiting Associate Professor of Philosophy, University of Maryland, 1969-70; Professor of Philosophy, University of Keele, 1972-84; Distinguished Visiting Scholar, University of Adelaide, 1982; Nolloth Professor of the Philosophy of the Christian Religion, 1985-2002, Emeritus Nolloth Professor, 2002-, University of Oxford; Visiting Professor of Philosophy, Syracuse University, 1987; Visiting Lecturer, Indian Council for Philosophical Research, 1992; Visiting Professor of Philosophy, University of Rome, 2002; Visiting Professor of Philosophy, Catholic University of Lublin, 2002; Visiting Professor of Divinity, Yale University, 2003; Visiting (Collins) Professor of Philosophy, St Louis University, USA, 2003. Publications include: Space and Time, 1968, 2nd edition, 1981; The Concept of Miracle, 1971; An Introduction to Confirmation Theory, 1973; The Coherence of Theism, 1977, revised edition, 1993; The Existence of God, 1979, 2nd edition, 2004; Faith and Reason, 1981, 2nd edition, 2005; Personal Identity (with S Shoemaker), 1984; The Evolution of the Soul, 1986, revised edition, 1997; Responsibility and Atonement, 1989; Revelation, 1992, 2nd edition, 2007; The Christian God, 1994; Is There a God?, 1996, revised edition, 2010; Providence and the Problem of Evil, 1998; Epistemic Justification, 2001; The Resurrection of God Incarnate, 2003; Was Jesus God? 2008. Honour: Fellow, British Academy, 1992. Address: 50 Butler Close, Oxford OX2 6JG, England. E-mail: richard.swinburne@oriel.ox.ac.uk

SYAL Meera, b. 27 June 1961, Wolverhampton, England. Writer; Actress. m. (1) Chandra Shekhar Bhatia, 1989, 1 daughter, (2) Sanjeev Bhaskar, 2005, 1 son. Education: Queen Mary's High School for Girls, Walsall; University of Manchester. Career: One-woman comedy, One of US; Former actress, Royal Court Theatre, London; Writer of screenplays and novels; Actress and comedienne in theatre, film and on TV; Contributions to The Guardian newspaper; Plays include: Serious Money, 1987; Stitch, 1990; Peer Gynt, 1990; Bombay Dreams, 2001; Radio: Legal Affairs, 1996; The World as We Know It, 1999; Bombay Dreams, 2002; Shirley Valentine, 2010; The Killing of Sister George, 2011; Much Ado About Nothing, 2012; Radio: Goodness Gracious Me, 1996-98; Masala FM, 1996; Woman's Hour Drama: A Small Town Murder, 2010; Films: Sammy and Rosie Get Laid, 1987; A Nice Arrangement (also writer); It's Not Unusual; Beautiful Thing, 1996; Girls' Night, 1997; Mad Sad & Bad, 2008; TV: The Real McCoy (5 series), 1990-95; My Sister Wife (also writer), 1992; Have I Got News For You, 1992, 1993, 1999; Sean's Show, 1993; The Brain Drain, 1993; Absolutely Fabulous, 1995; Soldier Soldier, 1995; Degrees of Error, 1995; Band of Gold, 1995; Drop the Dead Donkey, 1996; Ruby, 1997; Keeping Mum, 1997-98; The Book Quiz, 1998; Goodness Gracious Me (co-writer), 1998-2000; Room 101, 1999; The Kumars at No 42, 2002-2006; The All Star Comedy Show, 2004; Bad Girls, 2004; M.I.T: Murder Investigation Team, 2005; The Amazing Mrs Pritchard, 2006; Kingdom, 2007; Jekyll, 2007; Horrible Histories, 2009; Holby City, 2009; Beautiful People, 2008-2009; Dr Who, 2010; The Jury, 2011; Hunted, 2012; Written work: Bhaji on the Beach (film), 1994; Anita and Me (novel and TV adaption), 1996, 2002; Life Isn't All Ha Ha Hee Hee (novel), 1999. Honours: National Student Drama Award; Scottish Critics Award for Most Promising Performer, 1984; Best TV Drama Award, Commission for Racial Equality; Awards for Best Actress and Best Screenplay, Asian Film Academy, 1993; Woman of the Year in Performing Arts, Cosmopolitan Magazine, 1994; Betty Trask Award, 1996; Chair's Award, Asian Women of Achievement Awards, 2002. Address: Rochelle Stevens, 2 Terretts Place, Islington, London N1 1QZ, England.

SYDOW Max Von, b. 10 April 1929, Lund, Sweden. Actor. m. (1) Kerstin Olin, 1951, divorced 1979, 2 sons, (2) Catherine Brelet, 1997, 2 sons. Education: Royal Dramatic Theatre School, Stockholm; Norrköping-Linköping Theatre, 1951-53; Hälsingborg Theatre, 1953-55; Malmo Theatre, 1955-60; Royal Dramatic Theatre, Stockholm, 1960-74, 1988-94; Plays: Peer Gynt; Henry IV; The Tempest; Le misanthrope; Faust; Ett Drömspel; La valse des toréadors; Les sequestrés d'Altona; After the Fall; The Wild Duck; The Night of the Tribades, 1977; Duet for One, 1981; The Tempest, 1988; Swedenhielms, 1990; And Give US the Shadows, 1991; The Ghost Sonata, 1994; Films: Bara en mor, 1949; Miss Julie, 1950; The Seventh Seal, 1957; The Face, 1958; The Virgin Spring, 1960; Through a Glass Darkly, 1961; Winter Light, 1963; The Greatest Story Ever Told, 1963; 4x4, 1965; Hawaii, 1965; Quiller Memorandum, 1966; The Hour of the Wolf, 1966; The Shame, 1967; A Passion, 1968; The Emigrants, 1969; The New Land, 1969; The Exorcist, 1973; Steppenwolf, 1973; Heart of a Dog, 1975; Three Days of the Condor, 1975; The Voyage of the Damned, 1976; The Desert of the Tartars, 1976; Cadaveri Eccelenti, 1976; Deathwatch, 1979; Flash Gordon, 1979; Victory, 1980; The Flight of the Eagle, 1981; Hannah and Her Sisters, 1985; Duet for One, 1986; Pelle the Conqueror, 1986; Father, 1989; Until the End of the World, 1990; The Silent Touch, 1991; Time is Money, 1993; Needful Things, 1994; Judge Dredd; Hamsun, 1996; What Dreams May Come, 1997; Snow Falling on Cedars, 1999; Non ho sonno, 2000; Intacto, 2000; Minority Report, 2002; Kingdom in Twilight, 2004; Heidi, 2005; Rush Hour 3, 2007; Emotional Arithmetic, 2007; Solomon Kane, 2009; Shutter Island, 2010; Robin Hood, 2010; Extremely Loud & Incredibly Close, 2011; Truth & Treason, Branded, 2012; Director, Katinka, 1989; TV: The Last Civilian; Christopher Columbus; The Last Place on Earth, 1984; The Belarus File, 1984; Gosta Berling's Saga, 1985; The Wisdom and the Dream, 1989; Red King White Knight; Hiroshima Out of the Ashes, 1990; Best Intentions, 1991; Radetzky March, 1994; Citizen X, 1995; Confessions, 1996; Solomon, 1997; The Tudors, 2009. Publications: Loppcirkus (with Elizabeth Sörenson), 1989. Honours: Best Actor, European Film Award, Berlin, 1988. Address: London Management, 2-4 Noel Street, London W1V 3RB, England.

SYED Sabir, b. 22 July 1970, Bangalore, India. Associate Professor. m. Umma Abdullah, 2 sons, 2 daughters. Education: PhD, CCS University, India, 2002. Appointments: Assistant Professor, Chemical Engineering Department, King Saud University, Riyadh. Publications: Numerous articles in professional journals. Honours: Distinguished Research and Publication Quality Award, 2010-11. Memberships: American Nano Society; American Chemical Society; Royal Society of Chemistry, UK; International Precious Metal Institute, USA; The Electro Chemical Society of India; Life Fellow, Member, Institution of Chemists, India. Address: Chemical Engineering Department, King Saud University, PO Box 800, Riyadh, 11421, Saudi Arabia. E-mail: sabirsyed2k@yahoo.com

SYKES Richard Nesbit, b. 11 January 1942, Charlotte, North Carolina, USA. History Professor; Department Chair (retired). Education: AB, History and English, Southern Wesleyan University, 1964; MA, Social Science and Reading Specialisation, Appalachian State University, 1965; PhD, History, Greenwich University, 2001. Appointments: Instructor, History and Political Science, Gordon College,

1965-67; Assistant Professor of History and Reading, Gardner-Webb College, 1967-69; Instructor of History and Reading, Central Piedmont Community College, 1969-70; Co-ordinator, Secondary Reading, Chester County, 1971-73, Reading Specialist, Williamsburg County, 1973-74, Reading Diagnostician, Chesterfield County, 1974-79, Teacher, Reading Specialist, Lancaster County, 1979-90, South Carolina Schools; Professor of History, 1990-2005, Department Chair, 2001-05, Retired, 2006, Aiken Technical College. Publications: Saint Anselm's Life, Archbishopric and Theology: Their Contribution to Church and Society. Honours: AB summa cum laude; Faculty Member of the Year, Aiken Technical College, 1999; Educator of the Year, Aiken Technical College, 1991-92; Medal, Institute for Staff and Organisational Development, 2000; Governor's Distinguished Professor Award for Aiken Technical College, South Carolina Commission on Higher Education, 2000; International Biographical Centre Decree of Merit in History and The International Shakespeare Award for Literary Achievement in History and Reading Education; American Biographical Institute Hall of Fame for History and Man of the Year Medal; World Academy of Letters Master Diploma, with honours; Listed in international biographical dictionaries. Memberships: Certified Educator, North Carolina and South Carolina Public Schools; South Carolina Technical Education Association; South Carolina State Employees Association; National Geographic Society; Smithsonian Institution. Address: 838 Osbon Drive, Aiken, SC 29801-4154, USA.

SYMONDSON Anthony Nigel, b. 27 May 1940, Wimbledon, Surrey, England. Jesuit Priest. Education: Cuddesdon College, Oxford; Milltown Institute of Philosophy & Theology, Dublin. Appointments: Ordained in Church of England, 1976; Received into the Catholic Church, 1985; Entered Society of Jesus, 1989; Stonyhurst College, 1995-2000; Assistant Priest, Sacred Heart, Wimbledon, 2000-05; Writer, Farm Street Jesuit Community, London, 2005-. Publications: The Victorian Crisis of Faith, 1972; Sir Ninian Comper: The Last Gothic Revivalist, 1988; Sir Ninian Comper: an Introduction and Gazetter with Stephen Bucknall, 2007; Peter Favre, 2006; Paul VI, 2008; Stephen Dykes Bower, 2011. Memberships: Arts Club; Victorian Society; C20 Society; Pugin Society; London Library; Regular contributor, Catholic Herald and many other journals as critic and reviewer. Address: 114 Mount Street, London, W1K 3AH, England. E-mail: symondson@googlemail.com

SYMS Sylvia, b. 6 January 1934, London, England. Actress; Director. m. Alan Edney, 1957, divorced 1989, 1 son, 1 daughter. Education: Royal Academy of Dramatic Art. Appointments: Founder Member, Artistic Director, Arbela Production Company; Numerous lectures include: Dodo White McLarty Memorial Lecture, 1986; Member, The Actors' Centre, 1986-91; Films include: Ice Cold in Alex, 1953; The Birthday Present, 1956; The World of Suzie Wong, 1961; Run Wild Run Free, 1969; The Tamarind Seed, 1974; Chorus of Disapproval, 1988; Shirley Valentine, 1989; Shining Through, 1991; Dirty Weekend, 1992; Staggered, 1994; Food for Love, 1996; Mavis and the Mermaid, 1999; The Queen, 2006; Is There Anybody There? 2008; Booked Out, Run For Your Wife, 2012; TV includes: Love Story, 1964; The Saint, 1967; My Good Woman, 1972-73; Nancy Astor, 1982; Ruth Rendell Mysteries, 1989; Dr Who, 1989-90; May to December, 1989-90; The Last Days of Margaret Thatcher, 1991; Natural Lies; Mulberry; Peak Practice; Ruth Rendell Mysteries, 1993, 1997-98; Ghost Hour, 1995; Heartbeat, 1998; At Home with the Braithwaites, 2000-03; The Jury, 2002; Where the Heart Is, 2003; Born and Bred, 2003; Child of Mine, 2005; Judge John Deed, 2006; Dalziel and Pascoe, 2006; Doctors, 2004-06; Casualty, 2007; Eastenders, 2007, 2009, 2010; Doctors, 2010; Case Histories, Rev, 2011; Theatre includes: Dance of Death; Much Ado About Nothing; An Ideal Husband; Ghosts; Entertaining Mr Sloane, 1985; Who's Afraid of Virginia Woolf?, 1989; The Floating Lightbulb, 1990; Antony and Cleopatra, 1991; For Services Rendered, 1993; Funny Money,1996; Ugly Rumours, 1998; Radio includes: Little Dorrit; Danger in the Village; Post Mortems; Joe Orton; Love Story; The Change, 2001, 2003; Plays and TV Director: Better in my Dreams, 1988; The Price, 1991; Natural Lies, 1991-92. Honours: Variety Club Best Actress in Films Award, 1958; Ondas Award for Most Popular Foreign Actress, Spain, 1966; OBE, 2007. Address: c/o Barry Brown and Partners, 47 West Square, London, SE11 4SP, England.

SYRISTOVA Eva, b. 7 November 1928, Prague. Professor Emeritus of Psychopathology and Psychotherapy. m. Syriste Jaroslav MD, 1 son. Education: PhD, 1951, C Scientiarum in Psychopathology and Psychotherapy, Charles University, 1962. Appointments: Editor, SPN Publications, Prague, 1951-53; Clinical Psychologist, Institute of Psychiatry, Prague, 1953-57; Lecturer, 1957-67, Professor 1967-94, Prodean for Scientific Research, 1992-94, Professor Emeritus, 1994-, Psychopathology, Psychotherapy, Charles University, Prague; Pioneer of psychotherapy and art-therapy of schizophrenic psychosis in the Czech Republic. Publications: The Possibilities and Limitations of the Psychotherapy of Schizophrenic Diseases, 1965; The Imaginary World, 1973; Normality of the Personality, 1973; The Cracked Time, 1988; The Group Psychotherapy of Psychoses, 1989; Man in Crisis, 1994; The Poem as a Home in the Homelessness of Paul Celan, 1994. Honours: Honorary Appreciation Czech Medical Society for contribution to Czech Sciences, 1978; Honorary Prize for Translation of Celan's Poetry, 1983. Memberships: IAAP; IBRO; World Phenomenology Institute, International Association of Phenomenology and Sciences of Life; New York Academy of Sciences; Czech Medical, Psychiatric and Artistic Association; Director, White Rawen for Non-professional Art in Prague. Address: Sluknovska 316, 190 00 Prague 9, Czech Republic.

SYRKIN Alexander, b. 16 August 1930, Ivanovo, USSR. Philologist; Professor Emeritus. Education: Graduate (MA), Moscow State University, 1953; Candidate of History (PhD) 1962; Doctor of Philology, 1971. Appointments: Junior Research Associate, Institute of History, Academy of Science of USSR, Moscow, 1955-61; Junior Research Associate, 1961-71, Senior Research Associate, 1971-77, Institute of Oriental Studies, Academy of Science of USSR, Moscow; Research Fellow, Associate Professor, Institute of Asian and African Studies, 1978-98, Professor Emeritus, 1998-, Hebrew University, Jerusalem. Publications: Books, articles, commented translations of classical texts, essays on subjects including: Indology, Byzantine Studies, Russian Literature, etc; Examples include: Poem about Digenes Akritas, Moscow, 1964; Certain Problems Regarding the Study of the Upanishads, Moscow, 1971; To Descend in Order to Rise, Jerusalem, 1993; Upon Re-reading the Classics, Jerusalem, 2000; The Path of the Personage and the Author, Jerusalem, 2001; Upanishads, 3rd edition, Moscow, 2003. Former Memberships include: FRAS of Great Britain and Ireland; International Association of Buddhist Studies; International Association of Semiotic Studies. Address: Dov Gruner Str 236, Apt 17, Talpiot Mizrah, Jerusalem 91291 (POB 29278), Israel.

SZABÓ István, b. 18 February 1938, Budapest, Hungary. Film Director. m. Vera Gyürey. Education: Graduate, Academy of the Art of Theatre and Film, Budapest, 1961. Appointments: Film Director; Guest Professor at various film schools; University Professor, DLA. Publications: Short films: Concert, 1961; Variations upon a Theme, 1963; You, 1963; Piety, 1967; Budapest, I Love You, 1971; City Map, 1977; Feature films: The Age of Daydreaming, 1964; Father, 1966; Love Film, 1970; 25 Fireman's Street, 1973; Premiere (TV play), 1974; Budapest Tales, 1976; Confidence, 1979; The Green Bird (TV play), 1979; Mephisto, 1981; Catsplay (TV play), 1982; Bali (TV play), 1983; Colonel Redl, 1985; Hanussen, 1988; Meeting Venus, 1991; Sweet Emma, Dear Böbe (sketches and nudes), 1991; Offenbach's Secret, 1995; Steadying the Boat (TV), 1996; Sunshine, 1998; Taking Sides, 2000; Being Julia, 2004; Relatives, 2006; The Door, 2011; Director of several operas and theatre plays including: Boris Godunov, Opera Leipzig, 1993; Il Trovatore, Vienna State Opera, 1993; Chekov's Three Sisters, Staatstheater Kassel, and opera version by Péter Eötvös, Kassel Opera House, 2002. Honours include: American Academy Award; British Academy Award; David Donatello Award; Visconti Award; Silver Bear, Berlin; Fellini Award, Italy, 2002; Four times nominated for Oscar, 1981, 1983, 1986, 1989; Twice nominated for Golden Globe, 1986, 1998. Memberships: AMPAS; EFA.

SZABÓ Zoltán, b. 18 March 1957, Tirgu-Mures, Romania. Anaesthesiologist. m. Márta Harangi, 1 son, 2 daughters. Education: MD, Institutul de Medicina si Farmacie, Tirgu-Mures, Romania. 1983; Specialist in Anaesthesia and Intensive Care, Hungarian Board of Anaesthesia, Hungary, 1988; PhD, Thoracic and Cardiovascular Anaesthesia, Linköping, Sweden, 2001. Appointments: Resident, Sitalul Clinic, Judetean Mures, Romania, 1983-86; Resident 2, Sebészeti Klinika, 1986-88, Specialist in Anaesthesia, 1988-95, Debrecen University, Hungary; Doctor and Specialist in Anaesthesia, 1995-2001, Consultant Anaesthetist, 2001-, Associate Professor, Cardiothoracic and Vascular Anesthesia and Intensive Care, 2010-, University Hospital, Linköping Heart Centre. Publications: Articles in scientific journals as co-author include most recently: Neurological injury after surgery for ischemic heart disease: risk factors, outcome and role of metabolic interventions, 2001; Early postoperative outcome and medium term survival in 540 diabetic and 2239 nondiabetic patients undergoing coronary artery bypass grafting, 2002; Simple intra operative method to rapidly pass a pulmonary artery flotation catheter into the pulmonary artery, 2003; High Dose Glucose-Insulin-potassium after cardiac surgery: a retrospective analysis of clinical safety issues, 2003; Intraoperative muscle and fat metabolism in diabetic patients during coronary artery bypass grafting surgery: a parallel microdialysis and organ balance study, 2009; The Contractility of Isolated Rat atrial Tissue during Hypoxia is Better Preserved in a High-or-Zero-Glucose Environment that in a Normal Glucose Environment, 2009. Honour: First Prize for Best Poster, Congress of Cardiac Anaesthesia, Budapest, EACTA, 1990. First Prize for the best Thoracic Anesthesiological Oral presentation at the Thoracic Meeting, Linköping, 2006. Memberships: EACTA; SFTAI; Founding Member, Rotary, Debrecen; EASD; DCRA; SSRCTS; SFAI; SSAI. Address: Department of Cardiothoracic and Vascular Anaesthesia, Östergötlands Heart Centre, S-58185 Linköping, Sweden.

SZIGETI János Tamás, b. 11 October 1936, Budapest, Hungary. Physicist. m. Boglárka Gulyás, 1967, 2 daughters. Diploma, Roland Eötvös University, 1960; PhD, University of Leningrad, 1972. Appointments: Assistant Scientific Co-Worker, 1960-66, Scientific Co-Worker, Academy of Science, 1966-72, Senior Scientist, 1972-96, Central Research Institute for Physics; Senior Scientist, 1991-96, Head, Department of Laser Spectroscopy, 1991-2006, Research Institute for Particle and Nuclear Physics; Scientific Adviser, 1996-. Publications: Contributed more than 70 articles to professional journals and at international conferences. Memberships: Roland Eötvös Physics Society; European Physics Society. Address: Erzsebet u 27 app 40, 1043, Budapest, Hungary. E-mail: szigeti@remki.kfki.hu

T

TABACHNIK Eduard, b. 16 September 1947, Minsk, Belarus. Electronics Engineer. m. Lilia Leibovich, 1974, 1 son. Education: BS, Radio Technology College, 1966; MSc, 1971, Postgraduate, 1976, Byelorussian State University; PhD, Engineering, Applied Physics Institute, Byelorussian Academia of Science, 1986; Certificate, State Institute for Professional Development in Standardization and Metrology, Minsk, 1988. Appointments: Junior Researcher to Senior Researcher, Project Leader, 1971-86, Head of Department, Leader of Science and Projects, 1987-90, Byelorussian Centre of Metrology and Standardization, Minsk; Electronics Engineer, Patir R&D Ltd, Jerusalem (Israel) College of Technology, 1991-93; Electronics Engineer, 1993-98, Senior Vice President, Product Development and Engineering, 1998-, Omative Systems, Jerusalem; Omative Project Manager of two European projects. Publications: More than 50 articles to professional journals; Author, monograph, Synthesis of the Multivalued Time References, 1994. Honours: Gold Medal, Leipzig International Trade Show, 1982; Patents for CNC operated machine tools, automatic monitoring of tool status, method and system for adaptively controlling turning operation; Inventor of 8 inventions. Address: Omative Systems, Nahum Hafzadi Str 5, Jerusalem 91341, Israel. E-mail: et@omative.com

TADEUSIEWICZ Ryszard, b. 5 May 1947, Sroda Slaska, Poland. Professor of Computer Science. m. Malgonata Jaworowska, 1 daughter. Education: MSc, 1971, PhD, 1975, DSc (habilitation), 1980, Professor, 1986, Full Professor, 1986, AGH University of Science and Technology. Appointments: Professor, Computer Science, 1975-, Rector, 1996-2005, AGH University of Science and Technology. Publications: Over 70 books and more than 870 articles in international journals. Honours: Doctor Honoris Causa of 12 universities around the world. Memberships: IEEE Computational Intelligence Society; ACM; Polish Neural Networks Society. Address: AGH University, 30 av Mickiewicza, 30-059 Krakow, Poland. E-mail: rtad@agh.edu.pl

TAE Kyung, b. 9 August 1960, Korea. Head and Neck Surgeon. m. Ji-Hyeon Lee, 1 son, 1 daughter. Education: MD, 1985, PhD, 1995, Hanyang University, Seoul; Diplomate, Korean Board of Otolaryngology, 1989. Appointments: Chairman & Professor, Department of Otolaryngology, Head and Neck Surgery, Hanyang University, Seoul. Publications: 150 articles in professional journals. Honours: Best Article Award, Korean Society of Head and Neck Oncology, 2003, 2005. Address: Hanyang University Hospital, 222 Wangsimni-ro, Seongdong-gu, 133-792, Korea. E-mail: kytae@hanyang.ac.kr

TAEL Kaja, b. 24 July 1960, Tallinn, Estonia. Diplomat. Education: Estonian Language and Literature, Tartu University, 1978-83; PhD, Institute for Language and Literature of the Academy of Sciences of Tallinn, 1989. Appointments: Researcher, Department of Grammar, Institute for Language and Literature, Academy of Sciences, Tallinn, 1984-89; Guest Scholar, Chair of Finno-Ugric Languages, Uppsala University Sweden, 1990-91; Director, Estonian Institute Tallinn (non-governmental institution for informational and cultural exchange in co-operation with the Foreign Ministry), 1991-95; Lecturer, Chair of Nordic Languages, Tallinn Pedagogical University, 1995-2000; Foreign Policy Advisor to the President of Estonia, Mr Lennart Meri, 1995-98; Joined the Estonian Foreign Ministry, 1998; Executive Secretary of the Estonian-Russian Intergovernmental Commission, 1998-99; Director General, Policy Planning Department, Estonian Ministry of Foreign Affairs, 1999-2001; Ambassador Extraordinary and Plenipotentiary of the Republic of Estonia at the Court of St James, London, 2001. Publications: Computer Analysis of the Estonian Word Order (PhD thesis), 1989; An Approach to Word Order Problems in Estonian, 1990; Book chapter in The scientific Grammar of the Estonian Language, 1993, 1996; Articles on information structure and word order; Translations into Estonian: John Stuart Mill "On Liberty", 1996; Henry Kissinger "Diplomacy", 2000; Eric Hobsbawm "The Age of Extremes", 2002. Honours: Swedish Polar Star, 1995; Finnish Lion, 1995; Mexican Aguila Azteca, 1996; Estonian Order of the White Star, 2000. Memberships: Chairman of the Board, Estonian Institute; Farmers Club, London. Address: The Estonian Embassy, 16 Hyde Park Gate, London SW7 5DG, London.

TAFLA Bairu, b. 15 December 1938, Keren, Eritrea. Academic. m. Hildegard Schmidt, 1 son, 1 daughter. Education: BA, 1965; MA, 1968; Dr phil, 1979; Dr habil, 1989. Appointments: Lecturer, 1968-71, Assistant Professor, 1971-75, Addis Ababa University; Humboldt Fellow, Germany, 1975-78; Privatdozent, 1979-96, Professor, 1996-. Hamburg University. Publications: Ethiopia and Germany: Cultural, political and economic relations, 1981; Atsma Giyorgis and his Work: History of the Galla and the Kingdom of Shawa, 1987; Ethiopia and Austria: A History of their Relations, 1994; Ethiopian Records of the Menilek Era, 2000; Troubles and Travels of an Eritrean Aristocrat, 2007. Honours: Chancellor's Gold Medal, Haile Selassie I University, Addis Ababa, 1966. Memberships: German Society of Humboldt Fellows. Address: Stockflethweg 151, 22417 Hamburg, Germany. E-mail: bairu.tafla@gmx.de

TAI Weon-Pil, b. 12 December 1961, Heongsung, Republic of Korea. Materials Scientist; Researcher. m. Kyong-Hee Heo, 2 sons. Education: PhD, Kangwon National University, 1993. Appointments: Researcher, National Institute Advanced Industrial Science and Technology, Japan, 1995-2000; Professor, Inha University, Korea, 2000-05; Principal Researcher, Fine Chemical Industry Centre, Ulsan Technopark, Korea, 2005-. Publications: Numerous articles in professional journals. Honours: Listed in international biographical dictionaries; Ulsan Science and Technology Award, 2008. Address: Ulsan Industry Promotion Technopark, Ulsan Fine Chemical Industry Centre, 411 Daun-dong, Jung-gu, Ulsan, 681-340, Korea. E-mail: wptai@utp.or.kr

TAIT Andrew, b. 4 November 1958, Wallsend, nr Newcastle upon Tyne, England. Poet; Music Teacher. Education: Science A Levels, Tynemouth Sixth Form College, 1975-77; French Horn, Guildhall School of Music and Drama, 1977-81. Publications: Poetry Collections: On the Sea I Spied Him, 21 Pre-Metaphysical Poems, 2005; I've Seen Where She's Bound For, 2007; Songs: 12 albums of songs released via the music page of Viz magazine including: Songs From The Heart of the Primal Goat, 1989; Why Do Hamsters Look At You Like That? 1994; My Love is Like a Whirling Elephant, 1997; Back Off! There's a Lobster Loose! 2001; Autobiography: Me and Peter Beardsley; Poetry in periodicals: The Sunday Times, The Independent, The Big Issue, Other Poetry, Morden Tower Poets; Interviews: Features in many publications, including The Sunday Times Magazine, Time Out, Get Rhythm, Viz, The Independent, Poetry Now; Poems: Going Back Over The Wasteland; Everyone's a Fruit and Nutcase; Damson in Distress; Robert's Oriental Tea Garden; The Little Leafy Lane Off To The Left; Metaphysical Experiences; Thursdays; Suspense Account; Television and radio appearances.

Honours: Winner, Bloodaxe Poetry Competition; Winner, Iron Press 30th Anniversary Haiku Competition. Memberships: Morden Tower Poetry Society.

TAIT Marion Hooper, b. 7 October 1950, Barnet, Hertfordshire, England. Ballet Mistress. m. David Morse. Education: Royal Academy of Dance; Graduate, Royal Ballet School, 1968. Appointments: Dancer, 1968-, Principal Dancer, 1974-95, Ballet Mistress, 1995-, Royal Ballet Touring Company (later known as Sadlers Wells Royal Ballet and now Birmingham Royal Ballet). Honours: OBE, 1992; Evening Standard Ballet Award for Outstanding Performance and named Dancer of the Year, 1994; CBE, 2003; Twice nominated for Olivier Awards. Address: c/o Birmingham Royal Ballet, Birmingham Hippodrome, Thorp Street, Birmingham B5 4AU, England.

TAKAHASHI Haruka, b. 26 June 1950, Tokyo, Japan. Managing Director. m. Mariko, 2 sons. Education: Director, Tokyu Real Estate Investment Management; Director, Tokyu Libable Inc; Senior Managing Director, Tokyu Corporation. Honours: Honorable Citizen, City of Dallas, Texas. Address: 2-21-1-505 Sakurashin-Machi, Setagyaku, Tokyo 154-0015, Japan. E-mail: haruka.takahashi@tkk.tokyu.co.jp

TAKASAKI Jikido, b. 6 September 1926, Tokyo, Japan. President, Tsurumi University. m. Hiroko, 1957, 2 sons. Education: Graduate, 1950, DLitt, 1972, University of Tokyo; PhD, University of Poona, India, 1959. Appointments: Lecturer, 1957-67, Associate Professor, 1968, Komazawa University; Associate Professor, Osaka University, 1969-75; Associate Professor, University of Tokyo, 1975-76; Professor, 1977-87, Professor Emeritus, 1987, University of Tokyo; President, 1992-2004, Professor Emeritus, 2004-, Tsurumi University. Publications: A Study on the Ratnagotra Vibhaga, 1966; Formation of the Tathagatagarbha Doctrine, 1974; An Introduction to Buddhism, 1987. Honour: Imperial Prize, Japan Academy, 1975. Memberships: Scientific Council, Japan, 1991-94; Board of Directors, Toko Gakkai, Tokyo, 1991-97; Director, Japanese Association of Indian & Buddhist Studies. Address: 1-20-1 Akabane-Nishi, Kitaku, Tokyo, 115-0055, Japan.

TAKEMURA Hiroshi, b. 23 June 1962, Komagane, Nagano, Japan. Anaesthesiologist. m. Yoshiko Takemura, 1 son, 1 daughter. Education: MD, 1988, PhD, 1998, Showa University School of Medicine, Shinagawa-ku, Tokyo, Japan. Appointments: Resident, Department of Anaesthesiology, Showa University Hospital, Shinagawa-ku, 1988-90; Medical Staff, Sempo Tokyo Takanawa Hospital, Minato-ku, 1990-91; Assistant, Department of Anaesthesiology, Showa University Toyosu Hospital, Koutou-ku, 1991-93, Showa University Hospital, Shinagawa-ku, 1993; Medical Expert (Technical Co-operation), Cairo University Paediatric Hospital, Cairo, 1993-94; Assistant, Department of Anaesthesiology, Showa University Hospital, Shinagawa-ku, 1994-2003; Medical Practitioner, Pain Management Office TA, Yokohama, Japan, 2003-. Publications: Articles in medical journals: Correlation of cleft type with incidence of perioperative respiratory complications in infants with cleft lip and palate (clinical investigation, author), 2002; Mandibular nerve block treatment for trismus associated with hypoxic-ischemic encephalopathy (case report, author), 2002. Memberships: American Society of Regional Anesthesia and Pain Medicine; Japan Society of Pain Clinicians; Japanese Society of Anesthesiologists. Address: Pain Management Office TA, 13-74 Kakinokidai Aoba-ku, Yokohama, 227-0048 Japan.

TAKESHITA Takayuki, b. 9 December 1972, Aichi prefecture, Japan. Researcher. Education: Master's degree, Electrical Engineering, 1998, DSc, 2004, University of Tokyo. Appointments: Government Official, Japan's Science and Technology Agency, 1998-99; Researcher, Japan's National Institute of Science and Technology Policy, 1999-2003; Assistant Professor, School of Frontier Sciences, University of Tokyo, 2004-08; Fellow, Ritsumeikan University, 2008-09; Project Lecturer, Integrated Research System for Sustainability Science, University of Tokyo, 2009-. Publications: Lead Author, 8 articles in international journals; 3 peer-reviewed book chapters; 3 articles in peer-reviewed international conference proceedings; Expert reviewer, IPCC Fourth Assessment Report. Honours: The Tesla Award; 2010 Universal Award of Accomplishment; The Director General's Leadership Award for 2010; IBC's Salute to Greatness Award; 14th Kaya Encouragement Award; Listed in international biographical dictionaries. Memberships: Japan Society of Energy and Resources; Society for Environmental Economics and Policy Studies; Pan Pacific Association of Input-Output Studies. E-mail: takeshita@ir3s.u-tokyo.ac.jp

TALANOV Valery Michailovich, b. 20 March 1950, Russia. Chemist. m. 1 son, 2 daughters. Education: Chemical Department, Novocherkassk Polytechnic Institute, 1967; Candidate of Chemical Science, 1975; Doctor of Chemical Sciences, 2002. Appointments: Associate Professor, Professor-Lecturer, Head of Inorganic Chemistry Department. Publications: 524 scientific works including 9 monographs; 53 textbooks. Honours: Soros Associate Professor; European Teacher of Technical High School; Honoured Worker of Higher Professional Education of RF. Memberships: Full Member, Russian Academy of Natural Sciences; Foreign Member, Independent Academy of Sciences of Israel. Address: South-Russia Technical University, Prosvescheniya 132, Novocherkassk, 346400, Russia. E-mail: valtalanov@mail.ru

TALSTAD Ingebrigt, b. 23 January 1927, Fraena, Romsdal, Norway. Doctor of Medicine. m. Hjortnaes Turid, 2 sons, 1 daughter. Education: Cand Med, 1953, Doctor of Medicine, 1973, University of Bergen; Speciality in Internal Medicine, 1962, Speciality in Blood Disorders, 1982; Research Fellow, The Norwegian Research Council, 1965-69. Appointments: Resident, 1954-58, Assistent, 1962-65, Overlege, 1974-94, Medical Department B, Haukeland Hospital; Assistent, Medical Department, Namdal Hospital, 1958-59; Reservelege, Molde, 1958-62; Reservelege, Medical Department A, Rikshospitalet, 1970-73; Professor, Haematology, University of Bergen, 1974-94; Overlege, Fürst Medical Laboratory, 1994-2003. Publications: Numerous articles and papers in professional journals. Honours: His Majesty's the King's Gold Medal, University of Oslo, 1974; Fellow, International Society of Haematology. Memberships: International Society of Haematology. Address: Torjusbk 19B, 0378 Oslo, Norway. E-mail: ingebrigt.talstad@getmail.no

TALWAR Purnesh Kumar, b. 14 November 1934, Quetta, Pakistan. Scientist; Ichthyologist. m. Saroj, 1 son, 1 daughter. Education: MSc, Zoology, 1956; PhD, 1961. Appointments: Zoologist, 1965-73; Superintending Zoologist, 1973-85; Deputy Director, 1985-90; Joint Director, 1990-92. Publications: 5 books; Over 150 scientific papers in reputed national and international journals. Honours: Two merit promotions; Two advance increments by the Government of India. Memberships: Marine Biological Association of India. Address: Flat No 963, Sector A, Pocket C, Vasant Kunj, New Delhi – 110070, India. E-mail: symphonyinteriors@hotmail.com

TAN Amy, b. 19 February 1952, Oakland, California, USA. Writer. m. Lou DeMattei, 1974. Education; BA, 1973, MA, 1974, San Jose State College; Postgraduate studies, University of California at Berkeley, 1974-76. Publications: The Joy Luck Club, novel, 1989, film, 1993; The Kitchen God's Wife, novel, 1992; The Moon Lady, children's book, 1992; The Chinese Siamese Cat, children's book, 1994; The Hundred Secret Senses, novel, 1995; The Bonesetter's Daughter, 2000; Saving Fish from Drowning, 2005; Numerous short stories and essays. Contributions to: Various periodicals. Honours: Commonwealth Club Gold Award for Fiction, San Francisco, 1989; Booklist Editor's Choice, 1991; Marian McFadden Memorial Lecturer, Indianapolis-Marion County Public Library, 1996. Address: c/o Ballantine Publications Publicity, 201 East 50th Street, New York, NY 10022, USA.

TAN Chorh Chuan, b. 22 August 1959, Singapore. Doctor. m. Lee Joo Ee (Evelyn). Education: MBBS, 1983, Master of Medicine, Internal Medicine, 1987, PhD, 1993, National University of Singapore; MRCP, Royal College of Physicians, UK, 1987. Appointments: Lecturer, 1987-91, Senior Lecturer, 1991-95, Associate Professor, 1995-99, Department of Medicine, Dean, Faculty of Medicine, 1997-2000, Professor of Medicine, 1999-, Deputy President and Provost, 2004-07, President Dec, 2008, National University of Singapore; Deputy Chairman, Agency for Science, Technology & Research, 2004-; Registrar, 1987-90, Senior Registrar, 1990-93, Consultant (Standard Grade), 1994-96, Senior Consultant, 1997-, Division of Nephrology, Department of Medicine, Chairman, Medical Board, 1997-2000, National University Hospital; Registrar (on attachment), Department of Renal Medicine, Singapore General Hospital, 1988; Director of Medical Services, Ministry of Health, Singapore, 2000-04; Chief Executive, National University Health System, 2007-08; Chairman, National University Health System, Singapore Pte Ltd, 2011-14. Publications: Numerous articles in professional journals. Honours: Ministry of Education Scholarship for Junior College Studies, Singapore, 1976-77; Local Merit Scholarship, Singapore, 1978-83; Royal Free Exchange Scholarship, Singapore, 1982; Albert Lim Liat Juay Silver Medal, 1981-82; Bailey Memorial Medal, 1981-82; Book Prize, Obstetrics and Gynaecological Society of Singapore, 1982; Arthur Gordon Ransome Gold Medal, 1987; Citation Award, National University Hospital, 1989; Congress Award, European Dialysis & Transplantation/European Renal Association Congress, 1996; Singapore Youth Award, 1996; Five Year Good Service Award, Singapore Armed Forces, 1996; Long Service Award, National University of Singapore, 1996; Albert Schweitzer Gold Medal, Polish Academy of Medicine, 1999; Achievement Medal, Singapore Society of Nephrology, 2003; Public Service Star, 2003; Gold Public Administration Medal, National Day Awards, Singapore, 2004; National Science and Technology Medal, 2008; Postgraduate Fellowships: Commonwealth Medical Fellowship, Association of Commonwealth Universities, United Kingdom, 1989-90; Visiting Scholar, Wolfson College, Oxford, 1990; Welcome Fellow, University of Oxford, 1991; Honorary DSc, Loughborough University, 2009; Honorary DSc, Duke University, USA, 2011. Memberships: Fellowships: Royal Geographical Society; Royal College of Physicians (Edinburgh); Academy of Medicine, Singapore; Royal Australasian College of Physicians; Royal College of Physicians (London); American College of Physicians; Polish Academy of Medicine. Address: National University of Singapore, University Hall, Lee Kong Chian Wing, Level 4, 21 Lower Kent Ridge Road, Singapore 119077.

TAN Sinforosa, b. 7 July 1943, Lugait, Misamis Oriental, Philippines. College Professor. m. William H P Kaung. Education: BS, Chemical Engineering, University of San Carlos, Philippines, 1965; MST, Mathematics, Cornell University, USA, 1970; PhD, Curriculum Development, Syracuse University, USA, 1975. Appointments: Teacher, Iligan Capitol College, 1965-68; Mathematics Chairperson, 1967-68; Counsellor, Advanced Placement Programme, Cornell University, summer 1970; Resident Assistant, Crouse-Irving Memorial Hospital School of Nursing, 1970-73; Graduate Assistant, Syracuse University, 1973-75; Math Consultant, Mount Vernon Board of Education, 1975-76; Director, Metric Programme, Bronx Community College, 1976-77; Adjunct Mathematics Faculty, Mercy College, 1976-78; Teacher, Westchester Community College, 1977-; Professor, Mathematics, 1991-; Sophia and Joseph C Abeles Distinguished Professorial Chair in Mathematics; Visiting Professor, Nanyang Technological University, Singapore, 2009; Professor Emeritus, Westchester Community College, 2010; President, Organization of Chinese Americans, Westchester & Hudson Valley Chapter, 2011; Leadership Award in Education, Pan American Concerned Citizens Action League, 2011. Publications: Numerous articles in professional journals. Honours (most recent): Installed in YWCA Academy of Honorees of the 75th Anniversary Gala, YWCA White Plains and Central Westchester, 2004; Spring for Scholarships Award for outstanding support for scholarships, 2006; Organisation of Chinese Americans, Westchester Hudson Valley Chapter, Dynamic Achiever Award, 2006; Nominatee, Teaching Excellence Award, American Mathematical Association of America, 2007; Ulirang Guro Award in Higher Education, Association of Filipino Teachers of America, 2008; Numerous other outstanding service awards; Listed in international biographical dictionaries. Memberships: Pi Lambda Theta International Honour and Professional Association in Education; American Mathematical Association of Two Year Colleges; New York State Mathematical Association of two Year Colleges; Life member, National Council of Teachers of Mathematics; Association of Filipino Teachers of America; Life Member, Organization of Chinese Americans; Board Member, Westchester Hudson Valley Chapter; Syracuse University School of Educators Board; Numerous others. Address: Mathematics Department, Westchester Community College, 75 Grasslands Road, Valhalla, NY 10595-1636, USA.

TAN Tze Ching, b. 29 December 1966, Singapore. Neurosurgeon. m. Hung Lau. Education: MBBS, Singapore, 1990; FRCS, Edinburgh, 1996; FCSC, Hong Kong, 1996; FHKAM, Surgery, 2000. Appointments: Neurosurgeon and Senior Medical Officer, 1996-, Medical Officer, Department of Neurosurgery, Queen Elizabeth Hospital, Hong Kong; Fellow, Department of Neurosurgery, Brigham and Women's Hospital, Boston, USA, 2000. Publications: Surgery for Brain Metastases in Cancer of the Nervous System, 2004; Image-Guided Craniotomy for Brain Metastases, 2007. Honours: Ten Outstanding Young Persons of Hong Kong, 2006. Memberships: Congress of Neurological Surgeons, USA.

TAN Zheng-Hua, b. 7 October 1969, Jiangxi, China. Engineering Educator. m. Yimei Gan, 2 daughters. Education: BSc, 1990, MSc, 1996, Electrical Engineering, Hunan University; PhD, Electronic Engineering, Shanghai Jiao Tong University, 1999. Appointments: Associate Professor, Shanghai Jiao Tong University, 1999-2001; Assistant Research Professor, 2001-02, Associate Professor, 2003-, Aalborg University, Denmark. Publications: Editor (book), Automatic Speech Recognition on Mobile Devices and Communication Networks, 2008. Honours: Postdoctoral

Fellow, Korea Science and Engineering Foundation, 2000; Senior Member, Institute of Electrical and Electronic Engineers, 2006. Memberships: Institute of Electrical and Electronic Engineers; International Speech Communications Association. Address: Aalborg University, Niels Jernes Vej 12, Aalborg 9220, Denmark.

TANAKA Toshiaki, b. 28 September 1970, Wakayama, Japan. Mathematical Physicist. Education: BS, Tokyo University of Science, 1994; MS, 1996, PhD, 1999, Science, University of Tsukuba. Appointments: JSPS Research Fellow, Faculty of Integrated Human Studies, Kyoto University, 1999-2002; Research Fellow, Department of Physics, Graduate School of Science, Osaka University, 2002-03; Research Fellow, Yukawa Institute for Theoretical Physics, 2003; Research Fellow, Departamento de Fisica Teorica II, Facultad de Ciencias Fisicas, Universidad Complutense, 2003-05; Research Fellow, Department of Physics, Tamkang University, 2005-06; Research Fellow, National Center for Theoretical Sciences, National Cheng Kung University, 2006-10; Research Fellow, Institute of Particle and Nuclear Studies, High Energy Accelerator Research Organization, 2010-. Publications: Numerous articles in professional journals. Memberships: Physical Society of Japan. Address: Institute of Particle and Nuclear Studies, High Energy Accelerator Research Organization, 1-1 Oho, Tsukuba, Ibaraki 305-0801, Japan. E-mail: toshiaki@post.kek.jp

TANAKA-AZUMA Yukimasa, b. 7 March 1964, Sakai, Japan. Pharmacologist; Biochemist; Researcher. m. Hiromi Tanaka, 1991, 1 son, 1 daughter. Education: BSc, Biology, 1982-86, MSc, Biology, 1986-88, Konan University, Kobe, Japan; PhD, Pharmacology, Okayama University, Okayama, Japan, 2000. Appointments: Central Research Institute, Nissin Food Products Co Ltd, 1988-2002; Research Student, Japan Collection of Microorganisms, RIKEN, Wako, Japan, 1999-2000; Food Safety Research Institute, Nissin Food Products Co Ltd, 2002-08; Food Safety Research Institute, Nissin Foods Holdings Co Ltd, 2008-. Publications: 24 papers in scientific journals include: Cholesterol-lowering effects of NTE-122, a novel acyl-CoA: cholesterol acyltransferase (ACAT) inhibitor, on cholesterol diet-fed rats and rabbits, 1998; Effects of NTE-122, a novel acyl-CoA: cholesterol acyltransferase inhibitor, on cholesterol esterification and secretions of apolipoprotein B-containing lipoprotein and bile acids in HepG2, 1999; Effects of NTE-122, a novel acyl-CoA: cholesterol acyltransferase inhibitor, on cholesterol esterification and high-density lipoprotein-induced cholesterol efflux in macrophages, 1999; Effects of NTE-122, an acyl-CoA: cholesterol acyltransferase inhibitor, on cholesterol esterification and lipid secretion from CaCo-2, and cholesterol absorption in rats, 1999; Biological evaluation of styrene oligomers for endocrine-disrupting effects (II), 2000; Effects of NTE-122, an acyl-CoA: cholesterol acyltransferase inhibitor, prevents the progression of atherogenesis in cholesterol-fed rabbits, 2001; Lactobacillus casei NY1301 increases the adhesion of Lactobacillus gasseri NY0509 to human intestinal Caco-2 cells, 2001. Honours: Listed in Who's Who publications and biographical dictionaries. Memberships: Member, Scientific Council, The Japanese Pharmacological Society; Member, The Japanese Society for Food Science and Technology. Address: Food Safety Research Institute, Nissin Foods Holdings Co Ltd, 7-4-1 Nojihigashi, Kusatsu, Shiga 525-0058, Japan. E-mail: y-azuma@nissinfoods-holdings.co.jp

TANDBERG Erik, b. 19 October 1932, Oslo, Norway. Consultant; Writer. Divorced, 1986, 1 son, 1 daughter. Education. BSME, University of Santa Clara, California, 1957; MS, Metallurgy, Stanford University, California, 1959; Postgraduate Studies, Rocket Propulsion, Princeton University, New Jersey, 1965. Appointments: Royal Norwegian Air Force, 1959-71, Major, 1966; Consultant, Hartmark & Co, 1972-74; Chief Engineer, Director, Norconsult, 1974-80; Director of Public Relations, A/S Norske Esso, 1980-87; Established own company, working mainly for The Norwegian Space Centre, 1992-. Publications: 5 Books; Numerous articles in professional journals on Space related matters; Several TV and radio programs. Honours: Gold Medal, Norwegian Society of Chartered Technical and Scientific Professionals, 2005; Officer of The Royal Norwegian Order of St Olav, 2007. Memberships: Oslo City Council, 1971-90; Fellow, British Interplanetary Society; Norwegian Association for Chartered Engineers. Address: Sondreiveien 4K, 0378 Oslo, Norway.

TANG Czaau-Sinug, b. 28 January 1922, Nan-Tou, Taiwan. Professor. m. Pi-Yun Lin, 1 son, 2 daughters. Education: MD, Medicine, Taihoku Imperial University, Japan, 1945; PhD, Mastumoto Medical College, Japan, 1960. Appointments: Fellow, Virology, Baylor College of Medicine, Houston, USA, 1961-63; Professor, Microbiology, College of Medicine, National Taiwan University, Taipei, 1963-92; Director, Graduate Institute of Microbiology, College of Medicine, National Taiwan University, 1969-95; Consultant, USN Medical Research Unit #2, Taipei, 1974-77; Director, National Institute of Preventive Medicine, Department of Health, Taipei, 1977-81; Dean, College of Medicine, 1985-87; Professor Emeritus, College of Medicine, 1992-. Publications: Human Tumor Immunology, 1984; Epstein-Barr Virus and Human Diseases, 1990; Immunology and Infection, 1998-2001; Numerous articles in professional journals. Honours: Distinguished Scientists and Technologists Award, Cabinet, ROC, 1982; Distinguished Scientist, National Science Council, 1986; First Class Award to Health Contributors, Department of Health, 1992. Memberships: Formosan Medical Association; Taiwan Society of Microbiology; Chinese Society of Immunology; American Society for Microbiology; New York Academy of Sciences. Address: Graduate Institute of Microbiology, College of Medicine, National Taiwan University, 1-1 Jen-Ai Rd, Taipei 100, Taiwan. E-mail: taiwansom@gmail.com

TANG Tiejun, b. 13 June 1962, Heilongjiang, China. Practitioner of Chinese Medicine. m. Pinghua Bie, 1 son. Education: BSc, Heilongjiang University of Traditional Chinese Medicine, 1984; MSc, First Military Medical University, 1992; PhD, Guangzhou University of Traditional Chinese Medicine, 1998. Appointments: Assistant, Resident Doctor, Traditional Chinese Medicine Department, Xijing Hospital, The Fourth Military Medical University, China, 1984-89; Lecturer, Duty Doctor, 1992-95, Assistant Professor, 2000-05, Department of Traditional Chinese Medicine, The First Military Medical University, China; Postdoctoral Researcher, Department of Pathophysiology, Sun Yat-Sen University of Medical Sciences, China, 1998-2000; Link Tutor, Education Director, Asante Academy of Chinese Medicine, Middlesex University, England, 2005-. Publications: 40 academic papers. Memberships: Fellow and Research Executive, Association of Traditional Chinese Medicine, UK. Address: Asante Academy of Chinese Medicine, The Archway Campus, 2-10 Highgate Hill, London, N19 5LW, England. E-mail: tiejuntang@hotmail.co.uk Website: www.chinesemedicinesalon.blogspot.com

TANIKAWA Hisashi, b. 21 June 1929, Tokyo, Japan. Professor of Law. m. Keiko Hoshino, deceased 2006, 1 son, 1 daughter. Education: LLB, 1953, LLM, 1955, PhD in Law, 1958, University of Tokyo. Appointments: Associate Professor, Osaka City University, 1958-66; Professor, 1966-98, Emeritus Professor, 1998-, Seikei University, Tokyo; Corporate Auditor, Nippon Steel Corporation, 1999-2009; Managing Director, 2001-11, President, 2011-, Japan Energy Law Institute, Tokyo; President, International Commercial Law Institute, Tokyo, 2006-. Publications: System and Characteristics of Maritime Private Law, 1958; Sales of Goods, 1964; Commentary on the Security Law on Compensation for Oil Pollution Damage, 1979. Honours: Medal with Blue Ribbon, Japanese Government, 1984; Gold and Silver Star, Order of Rising Sun, 2001. Memberships: Honorary President, International Nuclear Law Association, 1992-; Honorary Vice President, International Maritime Committee, 2001-. Address: c/o Japan Energy Law Institute, Tanakayama Bldg 7F, 4-1-20 Toranomon, Minato-ku, Tokyo 105-0001, Japan.

TANN Jennifer, b. 25 February 1939, Bedford, England. Professor Emerita; Management Consultant. Education: Badminton School, Bristol; BA, Manchester University; PhD, Leicester University. Appointments: Research Assistant, Historic Towns Project, Oxford, 1964-66; Lecturer, 1969-73, Reader, 1973-86, Aston University; Director of Continuing Education, University Newcastle, 1986-89; Professor of Innovation, 1989-2008, Professor Emerita, 2008-, University of Birmingham; Management Consultant, 1992-. Publications: The Development of the Factory, 1971; Selected papers of Boulton & Watt, 1981; Children at Work, 1981; Short History of the Stock Exchange, Birmingham, 1983; Birmingham Assay Office, 1993; Many book chapters, academic papers and reports. Honours: Visiting Professor, University of Queensland, Australia, 1985; Visiting Professor, University of Newcastle upon Tyne, 1989-94; Lecture tours of USA and Canada. Memberships: General Synod of the Church of England; Bishop of Gloucester's Council; Bishops' Selection Adviser; Chair, Stroudwater Textile Trust. E-mail: innovation.jt@media-maker.com

TARANTINO Quentin, b. 1963, Los Angeles, USA. Film Director. Appointments: Worked in Video Archives, Manhattan Beach; Actor; Producer; Director; Films: My Best Friend's Birthday, 1987; Reservoir Dogs, Past Midnight, 1992; Siunin Wong Fei-hung tsi titmalau, Eddie Presley, 1993; Sleep With Me, Killing Zoe, Somebody to Love, Pulp Fiction, 1994; Destiny Tunes on the Radio, Desperado, Four Rooms, Red Rain, 1995; Girl 6, From Dusk Till Dawn, Curdled, 1996; Jackie Brown, 1997; God Said 'Ha!', 1998; 40 Lashes, Little Nicky, 2000; Kill Bill: Vol 1, 2003; Kill Bill: Vol 2, 2004; Freedom's Fury, Daltry Calhoun, 2005; Freedom's Fury, 2006; Grindhouse, Hostel: Part 11; Planet Terror, 2007; Hell Ride, 2008; Inglourious Bastards, 2008; Django Unchained, 2012; TV: ER episode, 1994; Alias episode, 2004; CSI: Crime Scene Investigation episode, 2005. Honours: Palme d'Or, 1994; Independent Spirit Award, 1994; Academy Award, 1995, 2013; BAFTA, 1995, 2013; Golden Globe, 1995, 2013; Broadcast Film Critics Association Award, 2010, 2013; Hollywood Film Festival, 2012. Address: WMA, 151 El Camino Drive, Beverly Hills, CA 90212, USA.

TARGAMADZE Aleksandras, b. 11 February 1953, Baikitas, Krasnojarsk region, Russia. Professor. m. Gene, 1 son, 1 daughter. Education: PHD, Technological Sciences, 1981; Docent, 1986; Doctor Habilitatus of Technological Sciences, 1990; Professor, 1992. Appointments: Junior Researcher, Engineering Systems, 1976-78, PhD student, 1978-80, Senior Lecturer, Docent, 1980-89, Head, Computing Centre, 1991-92, Professor, Software Engineering Department, 1991-, Vice Rector, Academic Affairs, 1992-2000, Dean, Faculty of Informatics, 2001-11, Head, Information Technology Development Centre, 2002-, Kaunas University of Technology; Doctoral student, Kaunas Polytechnic Institute, 1989-91. Publications: Over 140 articles in professional journals. Honours: Cross of the Knight of the Order of the Lithuanian Grand Duke Gediminas, 2002; Acknowledgement, Minister of Education and Science, Republic of Lithuania, 2003. Address: Studentu str 67-406, Kaunas, LT-51392, Lithuania. E-mail: aleksandras.targamadze@laba.lt

TATAI-BALTĂ Cornel, b. 5 April 1944, Sibiu, Transylvania, Romania. Professor. m. Ana, 1 daughter. Education: Iacob Mureşianu High School, Blaj, 1961; Faculty of History and Philosophy, History of Arts, 1967, PhD History of Fine Arts, 1992, Babeş-Bolyai University, Cluj-Napoca, Romania. Appointments: Head Master, History Museum, Blaj, 1967-1992; Lecturer, 1992, Senior Lecturer, 1999, Professor, 2004, December 1st 1918 University of Alba Iulia. Publications: Aspects of the Fine Arts in Blaj (18th-20th Centuries), 1993; Wood Engravers from Blaj (1750-1830), 1995; Pages of Romanian Art, 1998; On the Art and Culture of Blaj, 2000; Images of Blaj, 2002, European Culture and Artistic Interferences, 2003; Iuliu Moga (1906-1976), 2004; Writing about Art, 2005; International Art Camp Ioan Inocenţiu Micu-Klein from Blaj, 2007, Cultural and Artistic Hypostases, 2007; Big Rome and Little Rome in Teodor Răducan's Vision, 2008; Vasile Şt Crişan (1949-2003), 2009; The Iconostasis of the Greek-Catholic Cathedral of the Holy Trinity from Blaj (The 18th Century), 2011; and 90 scientific works (in Romania and abroad); Editor of the reviews 'Christian Culture', 'The Astra of Blaj' and 'Romanian Thought'; Reviewer, 'Patrimonium Apulense'. Honours: Prize for History awarded by ASTRA, Timotei Cipariu Department, Blaj, 2000; Citizen of Honour of the Municipality of Blaj, 2003; Man of the Year, ABI, 2009. Memberships: Ars Transsilvaniae Society; Member of Honour of ASTRA Society, Timotei Cipariu Department, Blaj; History Researchers' Society of the Greek-Catholic Church. Address: Str Petru Maior, nr 23, Blaj, Jud Alba, Romania. E-mail: ctataibalta@yahoo.com

TATCHELL Peter Gary, b. 25 January 1952, Melbourne, Australia. Gay Rights and Human Rights Campaigner; Journalist. Education: Mount Waverley High School, Melbourne, 1964-68; West London College, 1972-74; BSc (Hons) Sociology, Polytechnic of North London, 1977. Appointments: Secretary, Christians for Peace, 1970-71; Executive, Vietnam Moratorium Campaign, 1971; Activist, Gay Liberation Front, London, 1971-73; Student, 1972-77; Author and Freelance Journalist, 1978-; Secretary, Southwark & Bermondsey Labour Party, 1980-85; Labour candidate, Bermondsey by-election, 1983; Co-ordinator, UK AIDS Vigil Organisation, 1987-89; Co-convenor, Green & Socialist Conferences, 1987-89; Activist, ACT UP, London, 1989-91; Organiser, OutRage! 1990-; Independent Green Left candidate, London Assembly, 2000; Green Party Human Rights Spokesperson, 2007-; Director, Peter Tatchell Foundation, 2011-. Publications: The Battle for Bermondsey, 1983; Democratic Defense – A Non-Nuclear Alternative, 1985; AIDS: A Guide to Survival, 1986, 1987, 1990; Europe in the Pink – Lesbian & Gay Equality in the New Europe, 1992; Safer Sexy – The Guide to Gay Sex Safely, 1994; We Don't Want to March Straight – Masculinity, Queers and the Military, 1995; Numerous articles in magazines and journals. Honours: Campaigner of the Year, Observer Ethical Journalist, 2009; Liberal Voice of the Year, 2009; Hon DLitt, Sussex University, 2010; Southwark Blue Plaque, 2010. Memberships: Labour Party, 1978-2000; National Union of Journalists; Republic; Green Party, 2004-. E-mail: peter@petertatchell.net Website: www.petertatchell.net

TATOMIR Ion-Marius, b. 20 February 1979, Resita, Romania. PC Operator. Education: Carpenter, 1993-96, High School Graduate, 1996-99, Forestier Scholar Group, Sighetu-Marmatiei; PC Operator, Gheorghe Chivua, School of Art, Sighetu-Marmatiei, 2006-07. Appointments: Appointed Peace Representative/Volunteer for Romania, World Peace Prayer Society, 2003-; Board Member, Global Harmony Association, St Petersburg, Russia, 2008-; Member, Global Advisory Board of Human Dignity and Humiliation Studies, USA, 2008-; International Delegate, International Forum for the Literature and Culture of Peace, Haifa, Israel, 2008-. Publications: Poetry published in international journals and on the internet, including Eternal Winter, 2004. Honours: Honorary Life Member, Metverse Muse, 2004; Love Ambassador nomination, The Love Foundation, 2005; Universal Peace Ambassador nomination, University Circle of Peace Ambassadors, 2005; 1st Prize in Poetry, Bilingual Writer and Poets for Peace, 2006; Honorary Member and Author nomination. NGO Peace from Harmony, 2007; Invitee of the Week, Radio Transilvania-Sighet, 2007; Official Recognition, Sociedade Memorial Visconde de Maua, 2009; Official Invitation to Xth Historical Carnival of Savaria, 2009; Elected to Board of the International Forum for the Literature and Culture of Peace, 2010; IFLAC Poet Laureate, 2010; Listed as one of the World Harmony Persons of the Global Harmony Association, 2010. Memberships: United Religious Initiative; Association for Global New Thought; Aloha Fellowship; Citoyens du Monde; World Poets Society; Poets of the World; Romanian Society of Red Cross; many others. Website: www.peacefromharmony.org

TAUR Der-Ren, b. 26 July 1949, Canton City, China. Aerospace Engineer. m. Mei-Yu Fang, 2 sons. Education: Bachelor, Physics, National Taiwan Normal University, 1971; Master, Physics, National Tsing Hua University, 1974; PhD, Aeronautical and Astronautical Engineering, University of Illinois, USA, 1989. Appointments: Instructor, Physics, Dong-High University, Tai-Chung, Taiwan, 1974-75; Research Assistant, 1976-84, Associate Scientist, 1985-2001, Senior Scientist, 2002-11, Chung-Shan Institute of Science and Technology, Lung-Tan, Taiwan. Publications: Over 40 papers on missile guidance in national and international professional journals and conferences. Honours: Member, Phi Kappa Phi Honor Society, 1989; Academic Achievement Award, Defense Department, Taiwan Government, 1989; Listed in international biographical dictionaries. Memberships: Senior Member, American Institute of Aeronautics and Astronautics. Address: No 8-4, Alley 12, Lane 375, Chian-Kuo Road, Lung-Tan, Taoyuan, 325, Taiwan, ROC. E-mail: taur.taur@mail.tbcnet.net

TAVERNE (Lord) Dick, b. 18 October 1928, Sumatra, Indonesia. Writer. m. Janice Hennessey, 2 daughters. Education: Charterhouse School; MA, 1st class honours, Balliol College, Oxford, 1947-51. Appointments: Barrister, 1954; Queens Counsel, 1965; Member of Parliament for Lincoln, 1962-74 (Labour, 1962-72, Independent Social Democrat, 1973-74); Parliamentary Secretary, Home Office, 1966-68; Minister of State, later Financial Secretary to Treasury, 1968-70; First Director, 1971, Chairman, 1979-83, Institute for Fiscal Studies; Director, BOC Group plc, 1975-95; Director, Equity & Law plc, later Chairman, AXA Equity & Law Life Assurance plc, 1972-2000; Chairman, Founder, Sense About Science, 2002-. Publications: The Future of the Left, 1974; The March of Unreason - Science Democracy and the New Fundamentalism, 2005; Numerous articles in national newspapers. Honours: Created Baron Taverne (Life Peer), 1996. Memberships: Cruising Association. Address: 25 Tufton Court, Tufton Street, London, SW1P 3QH, England.

TAWARA Kinya, b. 31 May 1938, Yokohama, Kanagawa, Japan. Chemist; Consultant. m. Kiyomi Nishikawa, 1 son, 2 daughters. Education: B, Department of Chemical Engineering, 1961, Doctor, 2002, Kobe University, Japan. Appointments: Director, Catalyst, R&D Maruzen Oil Co Ltd, Satte, Saitama, 1981-88; Manager, Fuel Cell, R&D Cosmo Research Institute, Satte, Saitama, 1989-91; Director, Fuel Cell, R&D of Petroleum Energy Centre, Chiba, 1992-95; Senior Researcher, Cosmo Research Institute, Satte, Saitama, 1995-99; Chief Consultant, Saitama Chemical Consulting, Urawa, Saitama, 1999-. Publications: Numerous articles in professional journals. Memberships: Chemical Society of Japan; Japan Petroleum Institute. Address: 3-9-9, Maeji, Urawa, Saitama, Saitama 330-0053, Japan. E-mail: ky_tawara@ybb.ne.jp

TAYLOR Alison, b. 20 April 1944, Stockport, Cheshire, England. Author; Journalist. 1 son, 1 daughter. Education: Certificate of Qualification in Social Work; Diploma in Social Work. Appointments: Psychiatric social work and probation; Senior childcare posts, Gwynedd County Council, 1976-86; Claim for unfair dismissal settled, 1989; Author; Journalist; Conference guest speaker. Publications: 5 novels: Simeon's Bride; In Guilty Night; The House of Women; Unsafe Convictions; Child's Play; Papers on child care, ethics and social issues; Lectured and written on 18th and 19th century Welsh and German literature, music and poetry. Honours: Community Care Readers Award, 1996; Campaign for Freedom of Information Award, 1996; Pride of Britain Award, 2000. Memberships: Elected, Welsh Academy, 2001; Elected Fellow, Royal Society of Arts, 2003; Member, American Beethoven Society. Address: c/o Larinia Trevor Literary Agency, 7 The Glasshouse, 49a Goldhawk Road, London W12 8QP, England.

TAYLOR Anna, b. 14 July 1943, Preston, Lancashire, England. Teacher; Writer; Artist; Translator. m. John E Coombes, 22 December 1967, divorced 1982, 1 son. Education: BA (Honours), German and English, University of Bristol, 1965; CertEd, University of York, 1967; MA, Modern German Literature (incomplete) Manchester University, 1967-68; MA, Sociology of Literature, University of Essex, 1980. Career: Intermittent Teacher, 1964-94; Artistic Collaborator to French Sculptor, Michael Serraz, Paris, 1969-90; Since 1984, published writer of poetry, also several theatre credits; Published reviews and essays in diverse publications. Publications: Poetry: FAUSTA, 1984; Cut Some Cords, 1988; Both And: A Triptych, 1995; Out of the Blues, 1997; INTER-, 1998; Bound-un-bound, 2003; Novella: Pro Patria: a private suite, 1987; Poems selected for many anthologies. Honours: Scholarship to Manchester University, 1967; RedBeck Press Short Collection, Joint 1st Prize, 1995; 1st prize for Poem: Expressed in Your Flowers, Second Light Poetry Competition, 2002; 2nd, 3rd prizes and several short-listings in poetry competitions since 1980. Membership: Writers Guild of Great Britain; Founder Member, Yorkshire Playwrights. Address: 82 Blackhouse Road, Fartown, Huddersfield, West Yorkshire HD2 1AR, England.

DICTIONARY OF INTERNATIONAL BIOGRAPHY 36th EDITION

TAYLOR Harris C, b. 30 April 1940, Brooklyn, New York, USA. Physician; Endocrinologist. m. Diana Kahn Taylor, 1 son, 1 daughter. Education: BS, Queens College, City University of New York, 1961; MD, University of Chicago School of Medicine, 1965. Appointments: Director, Endocrinology Laboratory, 1978-96, Director, Internal Medicine Residency, 1985-94, Lutheran Hospital, Cleveland, Ohio; Currently Clinical Professor of Medicine-Endocrinology, Case Western Reserve University School of Medicine, Cleveland; Director, Resident Research, Fairview Hospital Internal Medicine Residency, Cleveland Clinic Health System, 2003-; Site Co-Principal Investigator, National Institutes of Health Accord Study, 2005-08. Publications: 43 papers in peer reviewed journals; 5 book chapters. Honours include: Phi Beta Kappa; Best Doctors in America, 1998, 2001-02, 2003-04; Master Teacher Award, American College of Physicians, 2001; Pillar of Medicine Award, Lutheran Hospital. Memberships: Fellow, American College of Physicians; Fellow, American College of Endocrinology; Endocrine Society; President, Diabetes Association of Cleveland, 1982-84. Address: Department of Medicine, Fairview General Hospital, 18101 Lorain Avenue, Cleveland, OH 44111, USA.

TAYLOR John Mark, b. 19 August 1941, Great Britain. Solicitor. Education: Solicitors Intermediate Examination, 1962, Secretary, Birmingham Law Students Society, 1964, Solicitors Final Qualifying Examination, 1965, College of Law; Admitted to Supreme Court of England and Wales, 1966. Appointments: Various positions in private practice; Elected member, Solihull County Borough Council, 1971-74; Co-founder, Solihull Duty Solicitor Scheme, 1973; Co-founder, Shirley Citizens Advice Bureau, Solihull, 1973; Elected member, West Midlands Metropolitan County Council, 1973-86; Leader, Opposition on WMCC, 1975-77; Leader, WMCC, 1977-79; Directly Elected Member, European Parliament, 1979-84; Conservative Budget Spokesman in the European Parliament, 1979-81; Deputy Leader, Conservative Group in the European Parliament, 1982-83; Member of Parliament for Solihull, 1983-2005; Member, Environment Select Committee, 1983-87; Government Whip, latterly as Vice-Chamberlain of Her Majesty's Household, 1988-92; First ever Junior Minister to the Lord Chancellor, 1992-95; Minister for Consumer Affairs, Investigations, Insider Trading, Prosecution and matters relating to Companies House, Dti, 1995-97; Various Opposition duties, 1997-2005. Address: Apartment 8, Blossomfield Gardens, 34 Blossomfield Road, Solihul, West Midlands B91 1NZ, England. E-mail: jmt@blossomfield.net

TAYLOR Judy, (Julia Marie Hough), b. 12 August 1932, Murton, Swansea, Wales. Writer. m. Richard Hough, 1980. Appointments: Bodley Head Publishers, 1951-81; Director, Bodley Head Ltd, 1967-84, Chatto, Bodley Head and Jonathan Cape Ltd, 1973-80, Chatto, Bodley Head & Jonathan Cape Australia Pty Ltd, 1977-80; Consultant to Penguin, Beatrix Potter, 1981-87, 1989-92. Publications: Sophie and Jack, 1982; My First Year: A Beatrix Potter Baby Book, 1983; Sophie and Jack in the Snow, 1984; Dudley and the Monster, 1986; Dudley Goes Flying, 1986; Dudley in a Jam, 1986; Dudley and the Strawberry Shake, 1986; That Naughty Rabbit: Beatrix Potter and Peter Rabbit, 1987; Beatrix Potter 1866-1943, 1989; Beatrix Potter's Letters: A Selection, 1989; So I Shall Tell You a Story, 1993. Play: Beatrix (with Patrick Garland), 1996; Edward Ardizzone's Sketches for Friends: A Selection, 2000. Contributions to: Numerous professional journals. Honour: Member of the Order of the British Empire, 1971. Memberships: Publishers Association Council; Book Development Council; UNICEF International Art Committee; UK UNICEF Greetings Card Committee; Beatrix Potter Society; Royal Society of Arts, fellow. Address: 31 Meadowbank, Primrose Hill Road, London NW3 3AY, England.

TAYLOR Michael Hugh, b. 8 September 1936, Northampton, England. Professor Emeritus. m. Adele May Dixon, 2 sons, 1 daughter. Education: BD, MA, STM, University of Manchester; Union Theological Seminary, New York. Appointments: Baptist Minister, North Shields, Northumberland, Hall Green, Birmingham, 1960-69; Principal, Northern Baptist College, Manchester, 1970-85; Lecturer, Theology and Ethics, University of Manchester, 1970-85; Examining Chaplain to Bishop of Manchester, 1975-85; Chairman of Trustees, Audenshaw Foundation, 1979-92; Director, Christian Aid, 1985-97; President, Selly Oak Colleges, Birmingham, 1998-2000; Chairman, Mines Advisory Group, 1999-; Chairman, Burma Campaign, UK, 1999-; Professor, 2000-, Professor Emeritus, Social Theology, University of Birmingham; Chairman, Health Unlimited, 2002-10; Chairman of Governors, Fircroft College, Birmingham, 2004-; Chairman, Responding to Conflict, 2007-09; Commissioner, High Pay Commission, 2010-. Publications: Variations on a Theme, 1973; Learning to Care, 1983; Good for the Poor, 1990; Christianity and the Persistence of Poverty, 1991; Not Angels but Agencies, 1995; Jesus and the International Financial Institutions, 1997; Christianity, Poverty and Wealth, 2003; Eat Drink and Be Merry for Tomorrow We Live, 2005; Border Crossings, 2006; Sorting Out Believing, 2011. Honours: Fulbright Travel Award, 1969; DLitt (Lambeth), 1997; OBE, 1998. Memberships: Overseas Development Institute; WCC Commissions. Address: University of Birmingham, Elmfield House, Selly Oak, Birmingham, B29 6LQ, England.

TAYLOR Wendy Ann, b. 29 July 1945, Stamford, Lincolnshire, England. Artist; Sculptor. m. Bruce Robertson, 1 son. Education: St Martin's School of Art, London. Career includes: Sculptor; Member, CNAA Fine Art Board, 1980-85; Member, Royal Fine Art Commission, 1981-99; External Assessor, London University, 1982-84; Member, Court of the Royal College, 1982-; Member, Morley College Council, 1984-88; Design Consultant, Basildon Development Corporation; 1985-88; Specialist Adviser, CNAA, 1985-93; Committee for Art and Design, CNAA, 1987-91; Design Consultant Commission for the New Towns, 1986-88; Design Consultant, London Borough of Barking and Dagenham, 1989-93, 1997-; London Docklands Advisory Panel, 1989-98; Trustee, LAMA, 1993-; Member, Council, Royal Society of British Sculptors, 1999-2000; Represented in collections world-wide; Over 60 commissioned sculptures since the early 1970's which include most recently: Globe View, Blackfriars, London, 2000; Tortoises with Triangle and Time, Holland Park, London, 2000; Millennium Fountain, New River Loop, Chase Green, Enfield, Middlesex, 2000; Voyager, Cinnibar Wharf, London, 2001; Three Reclining Rope Figures, Glaxo SmithKline, Brentford, Middlesex, 2001; Through the Loop, Pacific Place, Hong Kong, 2002; Around the Square, Pacific Place, Hong Kong, 2002; Chain Piece, Hunters Square, Warren, Ohio, USA, 2002; Knowledge, Library Square, Queen Mary University of London, 2003; Anchor Iron, Greenwich, London, 2004; Feather Piece Capital, East London, 2005; Gravesham Heritage, 2006; Silver Fountain II, Bryn Mawr, Pennsylvania; Square Chain Piece, Hillside, Bartlesville, Oklahoma, USA, 2007; Memorial to the civilians of East London, 2nd World War 1939-45 Hermitage Memorial Garden, Wapping, London, 2007; Spirit I Capital West, Royal Docks, London, 2007-08; Running Hares – A2

Pedestrian Bridges, Gravesham, Kent, 2009; Unity, Unison Centre, Euston, London, 2011. Publication: Wendy Taylor, by Edward Lucie-Smith, 1992. Honours: Walter Neurath Award, 1964; Pratt Award, 1965; Sainsbury Award, 1966; Arts Council Award, 1977; CBE, 1988; Fellow, Zoological Society, 1989; Fellow, Queen Mary and Westfield College, London University, 1993; Fellow, Royal Society of British Sculptors, 1994; Civic Trust Partnership Award, Chase Green, Enfield, 2002; Building of the Year Award, Architectural Sculpture, 2004. Address: 73 Bow Road, Bow, London E3 2AN, England. Website: www.wendytaylorsculpture.co.uk

TEBBIT, Baron of Chingford in the London Borough of Waltham, Norman Beresford Tebbit, b. 29 March 1931, Enfield, England. Politician. m. Margaret Elizabeth Daines, 1956, 2 sons, 1 daughter. Education: Edmonton County Grammar School. Appointments: RAF Officer, 1949-51; Commercial Pilot and holder of various posts, British Air Line Pilots' Association, 1953-70; Member of Parliament for Epping, 1970-74; Chingford, 1974-92; Parliamentary Private Secretary, Department of Employment, 1972-73; Under Secretary of State, Department of Trade, 1979-81; Ministry of State, Department of Industry, 1981; Secretary of State for Employment, 1981-83; Trade and Industry, 1983-85; Chancellor of the Duchy of Lancaster, 1985-87; Chairman, Conservative Party, 1985-87; Director, BET Plc, 1987-96; British Telecom Plc, 1987-96; Sears PLC, 1987-99; Spectator Ltd, 1989-2005; Advisor, JCB Excavators, 1991-; Co-Presenter, Target, Sky TV, 1989-97; Columnist, The Sun, 1995-97; Columnist, Mail on Sunday, 1997-2001. Publications: Upwardly Mobile, 1988; Unfinished Business, 1991; Weekly Columnist, The Sun, 1995-97 and The Mail on Sunday, 1997-2001; Numerous political booklets, newspapers and magazine articles. Honours: Life Peer, Baron Tebbit of Chingford; Companion of Honour. Memberships: Association of Conservative Peers; Liveryman of the Guild of Air Pilots and Navigators; Council Member of the Air League; Companion of the Royal Aeronautical Society; Chairman, Nuffield Orthopaedic Centre Appeal, 1990-2005; Chairman, Battle of Britain London Monument Appeal, 2003-. Address: House of Lords, Westminster, London, SW1A 0PW, England.

TEBBS Margaret Cecilia, b. 5 September 1948, Hillingdon, Middlesex, England. Botanical Illustrator. Education: Manor School, Ruislip, Middlesex. Appointments: Curator and Botanist, Department of Botany, Natural History Museum, London, 1967-91; Freelance Botanical Illustrator; Commissions mostly from staff and visitors to the Herbarium, Royal Botanic Gardens, Kew, England. Publications: Illustrator of books including most recently: Airplants – a study of the genus Tillandsia. New Plantsman vol 2 by A Rodriguez, 1995; Flora of Egypt, vols 1-4, by L Boulos, 1999-2005; Blepharis, a taxonomic study by K Vollesen, 2000; The Leguminosae of Madagascar by D Du Puy et al, 2002; Studies in the genus Hypericum by NKB Robson, 2002; Seedlings of Barro Colorado Island and the Neotropics, 2009; BSBI Handbook of British Grasses, 2009. Honours: Margaret Flockton Award, 2nd prize, 2006; Groves Rose Bowl, 2008; Jill Smythies Award, Linnean Society of London, 2011. Memberships: South-West Society of Botanical Artists; Institute of Analytical Plant Illustration. Address: 2 Furzey Corner, Shipton Lane, Burton Bradstock, Dorset DT6 4NQ, England. E-mail: tebbsatfurzey@aol.com

TEHAN Mary Carmel, b. 23 July 1953, Melbourne, Australia. Workplace Consultant; Educator; Researcher. Education: Graduate, Public Policy, Monash University, 2002; MPH, LaTrobe University, 2009; Grad Dip Theology (current student 2012). Appointments: Director, care services, Eastern Palliative Care, Melbourne East Palliative Care, 1996-98; Chaplain, Pastoral Care Practitioner, 2001-03; Project Leader, Palliative Care Victoria, 2003-06; Vice-Chair, Creative Ministries Network, Project Officer, 2009-10; Owner, Ultimacy, 2006-; Core Team Member, Global Dignity University; Member, Public Health Association, Australia Health Promotion Special Interest Group; Member, Compassionate Communities Network, 2011. Publications: Contributor of articles to professional peer-reviewed journals. Honours: Outstanding Service Award, National Association of Grief and Loss, Palliative Care Victoria. Memberships: ADEC USA. Address: 45 Hunter Drive, Blackburn S, Melbourne, Victoria 3130, Australia. E-mail: mctehan@hotmail.com

TEIXEIRA Paulino, b. 30 October 1960, Funchal, Portugal. Economics Professor. m. Maria da Conceição Coelho, 1 son. Education: Lic, Economics, 1984, Agreg, Economics, 2005, University of Coimbra; PhD, Economics, University of South Carolina, USA, 1992. Appointments: Teaching Assistant, 1985-87, Assistant Professor, 1993-98, Professor of Economics, 2007-, Director of Research Unit Grupo de Estudos Monetarios e Financeiros, University of Coimbra, Editor, Notas Economicas. Publications: Numerous articles in professional journals. Honours: Fulbright Grantee; Outstanding PhD Student, University of South Carolina. Memberships: Royal Economic Society, UK; European Economic Association; Research Fellow, Institute for the Study of Labor, Bonn, Germany. Address: Faculdade de Economia, University of Coimbra, Av Dias da Silva, 165, 3004-512 Coimbra, Portugal. E-mail: pteixeira@fe.uc.pt

TEMPEST Henry Roger, b. 2 April 1924, London, England. Retired. m. Janet Evelyn Mary Longton, 2 sons, 3 daughters. Education: Christ Church, Oxford. Appointments: Scots Guards, 1943-47, served North West Europe (wounded 1945); Appointed to Q Staff HQ Guards Division, 1945; Staff Captain, 1946; Britannia Rubber Co Ltd, 1947-51; Emigrated to Lusaka, Northern Rhodesia, 1952; Incorporated Cost Accountant (AACWA), South Africa, 1961; Returned to UK, 1961; Financial Officer, University of Oxford Department of Nuclear Physics, 1962-72; Inherited Broughton Hall Estate, 1970; Lord of the Manors of Broughton, Coleby, Burnsall and Thorpe in North Yorkshire, and of Coleby, Lincolnshire. Honours: Knight of Malta, 1949; A Deputy Lieutenant of North Yorkshire (retired), 1981. Memberships: North Yorkshire County Council, 1974-85; Skipton Rural District Council, 1973-74; Executive Committee, Country Landowners Association, Yorkshire, 1973-87; Council, Order of St John, North Yorkshire, 1977-97; President Skipton Branch Royal British Legion, 1974-91; Governor: Craven College of Further Education, 1974-85, Skipton Girls' High School, 1976-85; Member, Pendle Forest and Craven Harriers Hunt Committee, 1973-98; ACIS, 1958; FCIS, 1971; Member, British Computer Society, 1973-; Clubs: Boodle's; Pratt's. Address: Broughton Hall, Skipton, N Yorks BD23 3AE, England. E-mail: henrytempest@hormail.com

TENNANT David, b. 18 April 1971, Bathgate, West Lothian, Scotland. Actor. m. Georgia Moffett, 2011, 1 stepson, 1 daughter. Education: Bachelor's degree, Royal Scottish Academy of Music and Drama. Career: TV: Dramarama, 1988; Rab C Nesbitt, The Tales of Para Handy, 1993; Takin' Over the Asylum, 1994; The Bill, 1995; A Mug's Game, 1996; Holding the Baby, 1997; Duck Patrol, 1998; The Mrs Bradley Mysteries, 1999; Randall & Hopkirk (Deceased), 2000; People Like Us, 2001; Foyle's War, 2002; Post Nosh, Trust, Spine Chillers, 2003; The Deputy, He Knew He Was Right, Traffic Warden,

Old Street, Blackpool, 2004; The Quatermass Experiment, Casanova, The Secret Smile, 2005; Dr Who, 2005-10; The Romantics, The Chatterley Affair, Who Do You Think You Are? 2006; Recovery, Dead Ringers, 2007; The Human Footprint, Learners, Extras, 2007; Einstein and Eddington, 2008; The Sarah Jane Adventures, Endgame, 2009; Single Father, 2010; United, This is Jinsy, 2011; Playhouse Presents, True Love, 2012; Films: Jude, 1996; Bit, 1997; LA Without A Map, 1998; Last September, 1999; Being Considered, 2000; Sweetnight Goodheart, 2001; Nine ½ Minutes, Bright Young Things, 2003; Harry Potter and the Goblet of Fire, 2005; Free Jimmy, 2006; Glorious 39, St Trinian's II: The Legend of Fritton's Gold, 2009; Burke and Hare, How to Train Your Dragon, 2010; The Decoy Bride, Fright Night, 2011; The Pirates! In an Adventure with Scientists, Nativity 2: Danger in the Manger, 2012; Theatre includes: Twelve Angry Men; The Resistable Rise of Arturo Uri, 1991; Hay Fever, Tartuffe, 1992; Antigone, The Princess and the Goblin, 1993; What the Butler Saw, 1995; The Glass Menagerie, Long Day's Journey Into Night, Who's Afraid of Virginia Woolf? As You Like It, 1996; The Real Inspector Hound, Black Comedy, 1998; Vassa – Scenes from Family Life, Edward III, King Lear, 1999; The Comedy of Erros, The Rivals, Romeo and Juliet, 2000; A Midsummer Night's Dream, Comedians, 2001; The Pillowman, 2003; Look Back in Anger, 2005, 2006; Hamlet, Love's Labour's Lost, 2008; Much Ado About Nothing, 2011; Richard II, 2013; Appearances on numerous radio programmes and audio recordings. Honours: Critics Award, 2005; 3 TV Quick and TV Choice Awards, 2006, 2007, 2008; 3 National Television Awards, 2006, 2007, 2008; Welsh BAFTA, 2007; 2 Constellation Awards, 2007, 2008; Critics' Circle Award, 2009; Theatregoers' Choice Award, 2009; National Television Award, 2010; Constellation Award, 2010; TV Choice Award, 2011; BBC Audio Drama Awards, 2012.

TEPFERS Ralejs, b. 28 December 1933, Rezekne, Latvia. Professor Emeritus. m. Ira Majors, 1 son, 2 daughters. Education: Civ Eng (MSc), 1958, Tekn lic degree, 1966, Tekn dr, 1973, Docent, Reinforced Concrete Structures, 1973, Chalmers University of Technology, Göteborg; Dr ing hc, Latvian Academy of Sciences, 1996. Appointments: Worked on building sites, Sweden and Switzerland; Military service, 1959; Assistant, Department of Building Technology, 1960, Development of Structural Laboratory, 1967-69, Associate Professor, Building Materials and House Building Techniques, 1969, Professor, Building Technology, 1995, Professor Emeritus, 2001-, Chalmers University of Technology. Publications: Numerous articles in professional journals. Honours: JSPS Fellowship, Tohoku University, Sendai, Japan, 1988. Memberships: Swedish Concrete Association; Latvian Concrete Association; Nordic Concrete Federation; Life Honorary Membership, Comité Euro-Internationale du Béton-fédération internationale du béton; RILEM Committee; American Concrete Institute. Address: Department of Civil & Environmental Engineering, Structural Engineering and Concrete Structures, Chalmers University of Technology, SE-412 96 Goteborg, Sweden. E-mail: ralejs.tepfers@chalmers.se Website: www.chalmers.se

TERNYIK Stephen, b. 29 July 1960. Economist; Educator. m. Lisa Steven, 1988, 2 sons, 1 daughter. Education: MA, Technical University of Berlin, 1986; Postgraduate Studies, SUNY, 1997; Diploma, Jerusalem Institute of Biblical Polemics, 2000; Entrepreneurship Certificate, German Open University. Appointments: Expert, Advisor in Human Development & Monetary Learning, 1986-; Ternyik Research & Development Techno-Logos Inc; International Business Coaching. Publications: Contributor of poems to professional publications, essays, reports and abstracts; Author, Social Learning Processes, 1989; Author, Economic Heuristics, 2011. Honours: Visiting Research Fellow, Tokyo University, 1993; International Order of Merit; Pioneer Award; Deputy Governor, ABI. Memberships: Indian Sociological Society; American Consultants League; Club of Budapest; Tikkun Community; Society for Humanistic Judaism; World Congress of Jewish Scientists; Jewish Reconstructionist Federation; Listed in national and international biographical dictionaries. Address: POB 201, D-82043 Munich/Pullach, Germany. E-mail: stephenjehvcal@web.de. Website: www.jesherjehvcal.beepworld.de

TETANGCO Amando M Jr, b. 14 November 1952, Pampanga, Philippines. Central Bank Governor. m. Elvira Ma Plana, 1 son, 2 daughters. Education: MA, Public Policy and Administration (Development Economics), University of Wisconsin, Wisconsin, USA; AB, Economics, Ateneo de Manila University, Manila, Philippines. Appointments: Governor, Bangko Sentral ng Pilipinas, 2005-; Deputy Governor, 1999-2006; Managing Director, 1991-99; Director, 1986-91; Alternate Executive Director, International Monetary Fund, 1992-94. Honours: Top Six Central Bank Chiefs 2006, Global Finance Magazine. Address: Bangko Sentral ng Pilipinas, A Mabini corner P Ocampo Sts, Malate, Manila, Philippines 1004. E-mail: atetangco@bsp.gov.ph

TÉTÉNYI Péter, b. 11 May 1956, Budapest, Hungary. Assistant Professor. m. Eva Mária Kovács, 1989, 1 son. Education: BA, Pharmaceutical Faculty, Semmelweis Medical University, Budapest, 1979; PhD, Chemistry, Hungarian Academy of Sciences, 1993. Appointments: Postgraduate Fellowship, Hungarian Academy of Sciences, 1979-82, Assistant Lecturer, 1990-98, Appointed Tutor, English Language classes, Pharmacy Students, 1997-, Assistant Professor, 1998-, Department of Organic Chemistry, Semmelweis University; Researcher, Pharmacist, Pharmaceutical Works, Gedeon Richter, Budapest, 1979-90; Postdoctorate Fellowship, Research Group of Associated Professor Steven L Regen, Chemistry Department, Marquette University, Milwaukee, Wisconsin, USA, 1984-85. Publications: 5 patents in heterocyclic and polymer chemistry; 5 papers in polymer chemistry; 1 book chapter, 2006. Honours: 1st Prize, Essay competition paper on Philosophy, 1982. Memberships: American Chemical Society; Hungarian Society of Pharmacy Sciences; Society of Hungarian Chemists; Plastic Workgroup, Chemical Division of Hungarian Academy of Sciences; Chamber of Hungarian Pharmacists. Address: 27 József u, Budapest, H-1161, Hungary. E-mail: peter.tetenyi@szerves.sote.hu

THABIT JONES Peter, b. 18 May 1951, Swansea, Wales. Poet; Writer. m. Hilary, 4 sons, 2 daughters. Education: Diploma in Higher Education, University of Wales; Diploma in Office Studies; Higher National Certificate in Leisure/Conservation Management; Degree, Postgraduate Certificate in Education (Further and Higher Education). Appointment: Editor, SWAG Magazine, 1995-99; Chairman and Treasurer, Swansea Writers and Artists Group, 1996-99; Tutor, Part-time Degree Programme, University of Wales, Swansea. Publications: Tacky Brow, 1974; The Apprenticeship, 1977; Clocks Tick Differently, 1980; Visitors, 1986; The Cold Cold Corner 1995; Ballad of Kilvey Hill, 1999; The Lizard Catchers (USA), 2006; The Newspaper Birds, a bilingual collection, 2007; Walking Tour of Dylan Thomas's Greenwich Village, New York, 2008. Contributions to: 2Plus2; Poetry Wales; Poetry Review; Anglo-Welsh Review; Planet; Outposts Poetry Quarterly; Poetry Nottingham; NER/BLQ;

DICTIONARY OF INTERNATIONAL BIOGRAPHY 36th EDITION

Urbane Gorilla; Docks; Cambrensis; Orbis; White Rose; Exile; Iota; Krax; Weyfarers; Western Mail; South Wales Evening Post; Momentum; Asp; Children's poetry included in many anthologies; Work translated into Russian and published throughout Russia in a British Council Moscow schools project. Honours: Eric Gregory Award for Poetry, 1979; Grants, Royal Literary Fund, 1987, Society of Authors, 1987, Welsh Arts Council, 1990; Commendations, National Poetry Competition, 1983, 1988, Bridport Arts Festival, 1984, Welsh Arts Council (prose), 1986, (poetry), 1987; Outposts Competition Winner, 1988; Workshop Writer, St Thomas School Workshop for Prince Charles, Swansea, 1995; Invited to attend conference in Serbia by Serbian Writers' Association, 2006 and 2007; Poem incorporated into a stained glass window in New Community School, Eastside Swansea; Poem used in Secondary Schools Curriculum Exams, UK, 2006; Poetry reading tour of America with Dylan Thomas's daughter, Aeronwy Thomas, 2008. Memberships: Poetry Society, London; Swansea Writers and Artists Group, Chairman and Treasurer, 1995-99; The Welsh Academy, full member, 1995-; Founder and Editor, The Seventh Quarry, Swansea poetry magazine, 2005. Address: Dan y Bryn, 74 Cwm Level Road, Brynhyfryd, Swansea SA5 9DY, Wales.

THADANI Vinay. Marketing and Sales. Education: BSc, Chemistry, 1996, MSc, Analytical Chemistry, 1998, University of Bombay; DPBM, Bombay Institute of Technology, 1997. Appointments: Classroom Assistant, Shoreline Communtiy College, USA, 1999; Trainee Chemist, TCR Engineering Services Pvt Ltd, Mumbai, 2001-02; Analyst, GeoChem Laboratories Pvt Ltd, Mumbai, 2003; Marketing & Sales, Global Direct, Mumbai, 2003; Quality Control, 2003-04, Marketing & Sales, 2008-, CR Medisystems Pvt Ltd, Mumbai; Laboratory Analyst, Administrator, Doctor's Analytical Laboratory Pvt Ltd, Mumbai, 2004-08. Honours: Numerous elocution competitins, quizzes, oral presentations and essays in chemistry for various academic institutions and associations. Memberships: Life Member, Indian Analytical Instruments Association. Address: 1/52 Nanik Nivas, Bhulabhai Desai Road, Mumbai 400026, India. E-mail: vthadani@hotmail.com

THAMBIRATNAM David Pathmaseelan, b. 12 August 1943, Sri Lanka. Professor of Structural Engineering. m. Sulogini Vethanayagam, 2 sons, 1 daughter. Education: BSc (Engin) First Class Honours, 1968; MSc (Struct), 1975; PhD (Struct), 1978. Appointments include: District, Construction Engineer, Department of Buildings and PWD, Government of Sri Lanka, 1968-73; Chief Construction Engineer, (Colombo South) Department of Buildings, Government of Sri-Lanka, 1978-79; Senior Structural Engineer, Department of Buildings, Government of Sri Lanka, 1979-80; Lecturer, 1980-81, Senior Lecturer 1981-87, 1988-90; Department of Civil Engineering, National University of Singapore; Lecturer, 1990-91, Senior Lecturer, 1991-93, Associate Professor, 1993-96, Professor, 1996-, Structural Engineering, School of Civil Engineering/School of Urban Development, Queensland University of Technology; Major research areas: Structural dynamics, disaster mitigation and impact attenuation of structural systems, dynamics of flexible structures and health monitoring of bridges. Publications: 225 articles in international journals and conference proceedings. Honours: Canadian Commonwealth Scholarship, 1973-78; Graduate Fellowship, University of Manitoba, 1975-78; Commendation by Prime Minister of Sri Lanka, 1979; Research grants valued at more than US$4million; First Ever Australian Research Council Grant for Structural Health Monitoring of Bridges, 2008-11; Higher Degree Sujpervision Award, QUT Faculty of Engineering, 2007; QUT Vice Chancellor's Performance Award, 2008, 2010; QUT STEM (Science, Technology, Mathematics and Engineering) Award for Outstanding Supervision of Postgraduate Students, 2010; Listed in Who's Who publications; Supervised 27 PhD and 5 ME to completion. Memberships: Fellow, American Society of Civil Engineers; Fellow, Institution of Engineers, Australia, Fellow, Institution of Civil Engineers, UK. Address: School of Urban Development Faculty of Built Environment and Engineering, Queensland University of Technology, GPO Box 2434, Brisbane, QLD 4001, Australia. E-mail: d.thambiratnam@qut.edu.au

THAMRIN Yuri Octavian, b. 31 October 1961, Jambi, Sumatra, Indonesia. Ambassador of the Republic of Indonesia. m. Risandrani, 2 sons. Education: Bachelor's degree, University of Indonesia, 1986; Master's degree, Australian National University, 1999. Appointments: Spokesperson, Indonesian Task Force for the Post-Popular Consultation of East Timor, 1999; Head, Sub-Division on Disarmament and Security Council, Permanent Mission of the Republic of Indonesia, New York, 2000-02; Head, Political Division I, Permanent Mission of the Republic of Indonesia to the United Nations, New York, 2002-03; Head, Bureau of the Minister/Chef de Cabinet, 2004-05; Spokesperson, Department of Foreign Affairs, 2004-06; Director, East Asia and Pacific Affairs, 2005-08; Ambassador of the Republic of Indonesia to the Court of St James's, 2008-. Publications: Regular commentator in the Jakarta Post, The Indonesian Quarterly, Analisa, Popular and Newsweek. Honours: Satyalancana Karya Satya medal of honour awarded by President of the Republic of Indonesia. Memberships: Fellow, United Nations Institute for Disarmament Research; Association of Indonesian Civil Servants; Chatham House, London; Association of Graduates of the University of Indonesia. Address: Embassy of the Republic of Indonesia, 38 Grosvenor Square, London, W1K 2HW, England.

THAO Vo Dang, b. 8 March 1941, Saigon, Vietnam. Educator. m. Le Luu Ka, 2 sons. Education: Bachelor, Mathematics, Hanoi University, 1965; Dr rer nat, Complex Analysis, Humboldt University, Berlin, 1974. Appointments: Lecturer, Mathematics, Hanoi University of Technology, 1966-69; Head, Department of Mathematics, Ho Chi Minh City University of Technology, 1976-87, 1996-98; Associate Professor, Department of Mathematics, National University of Ho Chi Minh City, 1999-2007; Retired, 2008-. Publications: Behaviour of Schlicht Conformal Mappings of Domains Laying in Circular Rings, 1976; Estimates for Quasiconformal Mappings of Plane Domains, 1993; Estimates of Quasiconformal Mappings onto Canonical Domains, 2002. Honours: National Medal for Achievements in Education, 1995; Man of the Year representing Vietnam, ABI, 2009; Listed in international biographical dictionaries. Memberships: Vietnamese Mathematical Society. Address: 495/18/18 To Hien Thanh, P14, Q10, Ho Chi Minh City, Vietnam.

THAPPA Devinder Mohan, b. 9 March 1961, Jammu, Jak State, India. Doctor. m. Nirmal Kumari, 1 son. Education: MBBS, 1984; MD, Dermatology, 1989; Diploma in Hospital Administration, 1994; NTTC Course for Medical Teachers, 1996. Appointments: Senior Resident, Skin & VD Department, Lady Hardinge Medical College, New Delhi, 1989-92; Dermatologist, Central Government Health Scheme, Jaipur, 1992-94; Assistant Professor, 1994-96, Associate Professor and Head, 1996-2002, Professor and Head, 2002-, Skin & STD Department, Jipmer, Pondicherry. Publications: 485 articles in national and international journals; Author, 3 books; Editor of international journals. Honours: Sardarilal

Memorial Oration, 1998 and 2003; Ambady Oration, 2003; Dr R V Rajam Endowment Lecture, 2007; Award of Excellence, IASSID, 2009; Honorary Membership, University of Medicine and Dentistry, New Jersey, 2011. Memberships: IADVL; IAL; IASSTD; Indian Society of Pediatric Dermatology; IMA; NTTC; JIPMER, Pondicherry; CODFI; CSI; ISD; Society for Pediatric Dermatology; EADV. Address: Dermatology and STD Department, Jipmer, Pondicherry 605006, India. E-mail: dmthappa@gmail.com Website: www.ijdrl.com

THENUWARAGE Suresh Kumara, b. 21 January 1973, Ratnapura, Sri Lanka. Electrical Engineer. m. Niranjala Senani, 1 son, 1 daughter. Education: BSc (Hons), Engineering, University of Moratuwa, Sri Lanka, 19999; Designing & Manufacturing Panel Enclosure & Cable Management Systems, India; Powder Coating Pre-Treatment of Metal Products, ANANDA Impex Powder Courting Plant, Pune, India; CNC Engraving, Tubing & Labeling Machines, Singapore; Labour Laws, Management Conflict, Industrial Safety, Energy Management and Electrical Design. Appointments: Assistant Lecturer, Department of Electrical and Information Technology, Open University of Sri Lanka, 1999-2000; Factory Manager, Central Echo Engineering (Pvt) Ltd, 2000-01, 2003; Factory Manager, Pubudu Engineering (Pvt) Ltd, 2001-02; Design Engineer, Switch Boards, S-TEAM (Pvt) Ltd, Singapore, 2002-03; Managing Director, Electro Metal Pressings (Pvt) Ltd, 2003-. Honours: Gold Category International Star Award for World Quality Commitment, Business Initiative, 2011; Prestigious Award, CNCI Achiever Award, Ceylon National Chamber of Commerce, 2011; Order of Merit, ABI, 2011; Gold Medal for Sri Lanka, ABI, 2011; Scientific Award of Excellence, ABI, 2011. Memberships: Institute of Engineering & Technology, UK; Engineers Guild, Sri Lanka; Templeburge Industrialist Association; Chamber of Small & Medium Industries Association; National Chamber of Commerce, Sri Lanka; Federation of Chamber of Commerce and Industries of Sri Lanka; Sri Lanka Institute of Directors; Sri Lanka Institute of Builders. Address: c/o Electro Metal Pressings (Pvt) Ltd, Lot No 26, Templeburge Industrial Estate, Panagada, Sri Lanka. E-mail: suresh@emp.lk Website: www.emp.lk

THEOBALD-HICKS Barry John Frederick, b. 25 October 1945, Lockington Hall, Castle Donnington, Derbyshire. Retired Company Director & Administrator; Amateur Historian; Genealogist; Archivist; 19th Lord of the Manor of Danbury with Bretton, County of Essex. m. Sharon Ann Friend. Education: Morely College, London, 1960-65; London College of Art and Printing, 1963-66; University of London, 1986-88; Certificate of Safety Management, British Institute of Management, 1992. Appointments: Served with RAMC/v – 217 London General Hospital (City of London) Detachment, HAC, 1970-75; Deputy Manager to Lady Tara Heffler, Catalogue Department, Manager, Printing and Stationary Department, to Fire, Health and Safety Manager (UK), Sotheby's Auctioneers, Mayfair, London, 1978-93; Served with The Legion of Frontiersmen (Canadian Division) Captain (Staff), c 1989; Currently serving with The Earl Kitcheners Own (UK Command – VCF) Major (Staff), 2005, Lt Col (Staff) 2006, Chief of Staff – GHQ, 2006-11, Staff Officer to the 3rd Earl Kitchener of Khartoum, 2011; Senior Museum Assistant, Leighton House Museum and Art Gallery, Royal Borough of Kensington and Chelsea, 1993-96; Director, Parke Morrison Construction Ltd, 1994-98; Director, Consolidated Land Ltd, 1995-98; Managing Director, Theobald-Hicks, Morris & Gifford Ltd, 1999-11; Facilities Management, University of Greenwich, 2000-07; Director, The St Stanislas Trust (UK), 2004-09; Archivist to The Hon Julia Stonor Camoys, 2010; Private Archivist & Administrator to Lawrence Day, ISO, CStJ, JP, Deputy Chief Officer, St John Ambulance (UK Operation Liaison) National HQ and National General Secretary, St John Fellowship, 2010. Publications: History of the Lords of the Manor of Danbury in Essex (unpublished); History of Heather Parish Church, Leicestershire, 1986; Now I Know Where You Are Granddad, 1998; Contributor to: The Millennium Book of All Saints Church, Kent, 2000; A Theobald History (The Faversham Connection), 2004; Newsletter of the St John Historical Society. Honours include: St John Ambulance Long Service Medal, 1975 with 4 bars, 1980, 1985, 2002, 2007; Silver Medal of Merit, Sovereign Military Order of Malta, 1988; Officer, The Venerable Order of St John of Jerusalem, 1988; Commander, Orthodox Order of Hospitallers, 1989; Officer, 1992, Commander, 1995, Knight of Justice, 2000, Knight Commander, 2002, Commander, Companionate of Merit, 2010, Military & Hospitaller Order of St Lazarus; Queen's Golden Jubilee Medal, 2002; Knight Grand Cross of Justice, Order of St Stanislas, 2000; Knight Commander, Order of St Gregory the Great, 2004; Knight Commander of Justice, Order of the Collar of St Agatha of Paterno, 2002; Gentleman of the Bodyguard, Balgonie Castle, Fife, Scotland, 1995; Freeman, City of London, 1985; Liveryman of the Worshipful Company of Scriveners, 1995; Juror, The Guildable Manor of Southwark, 2006; Freeman of the Guild of Art Scholars, Dealers & Collectors, 2010; Freeman, Worshipful Company of Basketmakers, 2011. Memberships include: Fellow: Royal Microscopical Society, Royal Society of Arts, Society of Antiquaries of Scotland; Member, British Institute of Management, Institute of Administrative Management, Museums Association; Associate, Ambulance Service Institute; President, The Hospitallers' Club, 1987; Life Member, 2010, President, St John Historical Society, 1994-96; Deputy Chairman, Royal Army Medical Corps Association (City of London) Branch, 2000-06; President, The Royal British Legion (Sidcup & Foots Cray District), 2005-07, 2009-12; Life Member, Tower Ward Club, 2009; The Victory Services Club. Address: 3 Leechcroft Avenue, Blackfen, Kent DA15 8RR, England.

THEODOROU Stavroula, b. 6 March 1973, Ioannina, Greece. Physician; Radiologist. Education: MD, University of Ioannina School of Medicine, Ioannina, Greece, 1997; Speciality in Radiology, University of Ioannina Medical Centre, 1998-2003; Clinical duties and research in Musculoskeletal Imaging and Quantitative Bone Densitometry, University of California San Diego Medical Center, San Diego, California, USA, 1999, 2000-2001. Appointments: Department of Radiology, University of Ioannina Medical Centre, Ioannina, Greece, 1998-2003; Department of Radiology, University of California, San Diego, California, USA, 1999, 2000-2001; Department of Radiology, Thornton Hospital, University of California San Diego, California, USA, 1999; Department of Clinical Radiology and Bone Densitometry, University of Manchester, England, 2004-06. Publications: 57 original articles; Co-author, 8 books. Honours: Award of Excellence in University Studies, Greek National Scholarship Foundation, 1992, 1994; Award of Excellence in Pathology, University of Ioannina Medical Centre, 1996; Support in Research, Veterans Affairs, San Diego Medical Center Grant, California, USA; Certificate of Merit for Educational Exhibit, Radiological Society of North America, 1999, 2000; Certificate of Merit for Educational Exhibit, American Roentgen Ray Society, Washington DC, 2000; Best Scientific Exhibit, American Society of Spine Radiology, Florida, 2001. Memberships: American College of Radiology, Radiological Society of North America; Society for Clinical Densitometry; American Society for Bone Mineral Research; Los Angeles Radiological

Society; National Osteoporosis Foundation. Address: 13 Papadopoulos Street, Ioannina 45444, Greece. E-mail: rjtheodorou@hotmail.com

THEOTOKOGLOU Efstathios E, b. 19 January 1956, Athens, Greece. Professor. Education: MSc, 1979, PhD, 1984, National Technical University of Athens. Appointments: Research and Teaching Associate, 1979-88, Lecturer, 1988-92, Assistant Professor, 1992-99, Associate Professor, 1999-2008, Professor, 2008-, National Technical University of Athens. Publications: Numerous articles in professional journals. Honours: Postdoctoral Fellowship, NTH-Department of Marine Structures, Trondheim, Norway, 1989-91. Memberships: Technical Chamber of Greece; International Association of Computational Mechanics (IACM); International Union of Theoretical and Applied Mechanics (IUTAM). E-mail: stathis@central.ntua.gr

THERON Charlize, b. 7 August 1975, South Africa. Actress. Education: Trained as a ballet dancer. Appointments: Model, Milan, 1991; Actress, Los Angeles, 1992-; Films include: Children of the Corn III, 1994; Two Days in the Valley, That Thing You Do! 1996; Trial and Error, Hollywood Confidential, Devil's Advocate, Cop Lane/The Yards, 1997; Might Joe Young, Celebrity, 1998; The Cider House Rules, The Astronaut's Wife, 1999; The Yards, Reindeer Games, Men of Honour, The Legend of Bagger Vance, Navy Diver, 2000; Sweet November, The Curse of the Jade Scorpion, 15 Minutes, 2001; The Yards/Nightwatch, Waking Up in Reno, Trapped, 24 Hours, Executive Producer, Sweet Home Alabama, 2002; The Italian Job, Monster, 2003; The Life and Death of Peter Sellers, Head in the Clouds, 2004; North Country, Æon Flux, 2005; In the Valley of Elah, Battle in Seattle, Sleepwalking, 2007; Hancock, 2008. Honours: Golden Globe Award, Best Dramatic Actress, 2004; Critics' Choice Award, Best Actress, 2004; Screen Actors Guild, Best Actress Award, 2004; Academy Award, Best Actress, 2004. Address: c/o Spanky Taylor, 3727 West Magnolia, Burbank, CA 91505, USA.

THEROUX Paul Edward, b. 10 April 1941, Medford, Massachusetts, USA. Writer. m. (1) Anne Castle, 1967, divorced 1993, 2 sons, (2) Sheila Donnelly, 1995. Education: BA, University of Massachusetts. Appointments: Lecturer, University of Urbino, Italy, 1963, Soche Hill College, Malawi, 1963-65; Faculty, Department of English, Makerere University, Uganda, 1965-68, University of Singapore, 1968-71; Visiting Lecturer, University of Virginia, 1972-73. Publications: Fiction: Waldo, 1967; Fong and the Indians, 1968; Girls at Play, 1969; Murder in Mount Holly, 1969; Jungle Lovers, 1971; Sinning with Annie, 1972; Saint Jack, 1973; The Black House, 1974; The Family Arsenal, 1976; The Consul's File, 1977; Picture Palace, 1978; A Christmas Card, 1978; London Snow, 1980; World's End, 1980; The Mosquito Coast, 1981; The London Embassy, 1982; Half Moon Street, 1984; O-Zone, 1986; My Secret History, 1988; Chicago Loop, 1990; Millroy the Magician, 1993; My Other Life, 1996; Kowloon Tong, 1997; Collected Stories, 1997; Hotel Honolulu, 2000; Telling Tales (anthology), 2004; Blinding Light, 2006; The Elephanta Suite, 2007; Non-Fiction: V S Naipaul, 1973; The Great Patagonian Express, 1979; The Kingdom by the Sea, 1983; Sailing Through China, 1983; Sunrise with Sea Monsters, 1985; The White Man's Burden, 1987; Riding the Iron Rooster, 1988; The Happy Isles of Oceania, 1992; The Pillars of Hercules, 1995; Sir Vidia's Shadow: A Friendship Across Five Continents, 1998; Fresh Air Fiend, 2000; Nurse Wolf and Dr Sacks, 2001; Dark Star Safari, 2002. Honours: Editorial Awards, Playboy magazine, 1972, 1976, 1977, 1979; Whitbread Award, 1978; James Tait Black Award, 1982; Yorkshire Post Best Novel Award, 1982; Thomas Cook Travel Prize, 1989; Honorary doctorates. Memberships: Royal Geographical Society; Royal Society of Literature, fellow; American Academy of Arts and Letters. Address: Hamish Hamilton Ltd, 80 Strand, London WC2, England.

THEWLIS David, b. 20 March 1963. Actor. m. Sara Jocelyn Sugarman, 1992 (divorced), 1 daughter with Anna Friel. Education: Highfield High School, Blackpool; St Anne's College of Further Education; Guildhall School of Music and Drama, London. Career: Theatre: Buddy Holly at the Regal; Ice Cream; Lady and the Clarinet; The Sea; TV: Dandelion Dead; Valentine Park; Road; The Singing Detective; Bit of a Do; Skulduggery; Journey to Knock; Filipina; Dreamgirls; Frank Stubbs Promotes; Prime Suspect 3; Dinotopia (voice), 2002; The Street, 2007; Films include: Short and Curlies, 1987; Vroom, 1988; Resurrected, 1989; Afraid of the Dark, 1991; Life is Sweet, 1990; Damage, 1992; The Trial, 1993; Naked, 1993; Black Beauty, 1994; Dragonheart, 1996; Seven Year in Tibet, 1997; Divorcing Jack, 1998; The Big Lebowski, 1998; The Miracle Maker (voice), 2000; DIY Hard, 2002; Cheeky, 2003; Timeline, 2003; Harry Potter and the Prisoner of Azkaban, 2004; Kingdom of Heaven, 2005; All the Invisible Children, 2005; The New World, 2005; Basic Instinct 2, The Omen, 2006; The Inner Life of Martin Frost, 2007; Harry Potter and the Order of the Phoenix, 2007; The Boy in Striped Pyjamas, 2008; Harry Potter and the Half Blood Prince, 2009; Mr Nice, Harry Potter and the Deathly Hallows – Part I, 2010; Harry Potter and the Deathly Hallows – Part II, The Lady, Anonymous, War Horse, 2011; RED 2, The Fifth Estate, 2013. Honours: Cannes Film Festival, 1993; Evening Standard British Film Award, 1993; London Film Critics Circle Award, 1993; National Society of Film Critics Award, 1993; New York Film Critics Circle Award, 1993; BAFTA Award, 1995; British Independent Film Awards, 1998, 2008; Evening Standard British Film Award, 2010. Publication: The Late Hector Kipling, 2007.

THIERY Michel, b. 14 November 1924, Ghent, Belgium. Medical Doctor. m. Huguette Descheemaeker, 1 daughter. Education: MD, 1949, PhD, 1962, University of Ghent; Specialist in Obstetrics & Gynaecology, State University of Ghent, 1963; Fellow, College of Physicians and Surgeons, Columbia, New York, USA, 1952-53; Postgraduate, Oncology, Radiumhemmet, Stockholm, 1955. Appointments: Assistant Professor, 1963-64, Full Professor and Head, Department of Obstetrics, 1964-89, Professor Emeritus, 1989-, State University of Ghent. Publications: Numerous articles in professional journals. Memberships: Belgian Royal Academy of Medicine, Brussels; Belgian Royal Society of Obstetrics & Gynaecology; European Society of Perinatal Medicine; Royal College of Obstetricians and Gynaecologists, London. Address: 6 Aan De Bocht, B-9000 Ghent, Belgium.

THILL Georges Emile André, b. 30 November 1935, Bullange, Belgium. University Emeritus Professor. Education: Mathematics, Belgian Licence and Agrégation enseignement secondaire, University of Louvain, Philosophy, BA; Doctorate, Theological Sciences, Paris; Postgraduate Studies, High Energy Physics. Appointments: Researcher, Laboratoire de Physique Nucléaire, Collège de France, Paris, 1966-67 and Institut Interuniversitaire belge des sciences nucléaires, Laboratoire des Hautes Energies, Brussels, 1967-73; Scholar, University of Namur, Belgium, 1973-2001; Director of the interdisciplinary Department for Sciences, Philosophies, Societies, Faculty of Natural Science, Namur, 1976-88; Member of the Executive Committee,

Course Director in the Field, Science Technology Society, Inter-University Centre of Postgraduate Studies, Dubrovnik, 1986-94; Senior Fellow, EC Programme Monitor/FAST, Science Research Development, Brussels, 1991-94; Chair Professor, Professeur Ordinaire, 1986-2001, Emeritus Professor, University of Namur, 2001-; Emeritus Professor, Faculty of Human Sciences, State University of Haïti, Port-au-Prince, Haïti, 2002-; Visiting or Invited Professor in different universities: Dakar, Louvain, Brussels, Copenhagen, Donetsk National Technical University and others; Director of the Scientific Co-ordination, PRELUDE, International Networking Programme of Research and Liaison between Universities for Development, Research and Educational Network for sustainable co-development, NGO of UNESCO Collective Consultation on Higher Education implemented on the five continents (72 countries), 1985-; Responsible for the UNESCO-PRELUDE Chair of Sustainable Development, 2001-05. Publications: 26 books including: La fête scientifique, 1973; Technologies et sociétés, 1980; Plaidoyer pour des universités citoyennes et responsables, 1998; Le dialogue des savoirs, 2001; L'eau, patrimoine commun mondial, 2002; Femmes et Developpement Durable et Solidaire, Savoirs Sciences et Entrepreneuriat, 2006. Over 100 scientific articles. Honours: Director of the Scientific Co-ordination of PRELUDE; Scientific Director, UNESCO Unitwin-PRELUDE Chair; President, Institut Interuniversitaire Belge de la Vie, Sciences et Qualité de Vie, Brussels; 2003 International Peace Prize, United Cultural Convention, USA; Ambassador General, United Cultural Convention, USA. Memberships: Notably Scientific Society of Brussels; Steering Committee, International Network on the Role of the Universities for Developing Areas; Deontological Committee, Service Public Fédéral (SPF) de Belgique, Santé Publique, Sécurité de la Chaîne Alimentaire et Environement Division Bien-Être Animal et CITES; Joint Committee of Bioethics of the Centre d'études et de recherches vétérinaires et agronomiques (CERVA), Institut Pasteur, Institut Scientifique de Santé Publique (ISP), Brussels; Editing Board, La Revue Nouvelle, PRELUDE Review and Newsletter. Address: 65, Rue Saint-Quentin, B-1000, Brussels, Belgium.

THILLAINAYAGAM Chinnamanur Veluchamy, b. 10 June 1925, Chinnamanur, Tamilnadu, India. Retired Director of Public Libraries, Government of Tamilnadu. m. Gomathy, 1 son, 1 daughter. Education: Bachelor of Arts, Economics, History and Politics, 1948, Diploma in Librarianship, 1950, Madras University; Master of Arts, Economics, Nagpur University, 1955; Certificate in German, Annamalai University, 1957; Bachelor of Teaching, Madras University, 1958; Master of Library Science, Delhi University, 1962. Appointments: Non-Gazetted Librarian, Directorate of Public Libraries, 1949-62, Gazetted Librarian of Connemara (State Central) Public Library, 1962-72, Director of Public Libraries, 1972-82, Government of Tamilnadu; Chairman, Tamilnadu Library Improvement Committee, 1998-; Consulting Editor, The Contemporary Who's Who, ABI, 2002-2003. Publications: Over 21 books including: Narmarintha Ranganathan Valmai (biography), 1994; Ranganathan – Kaula Gold Medal Awardee, 1994, Vethi, 1995; Nulaga Vithagar Seventy (Vethi), 1995; New Dimensions of Library Scenario in India, 1997; S R Ranganathan and Madras Public Libraries Act, 1997; Nenchil Nirkindravargal (Life Sketches), 1998; Nulaga Padalgal (poems on library services), 2002; 654 published papers. Honours include: Madras UNESCO Mandram Awards for teaching Library Science in Tamil, 1970; Awards, Government of Tamilnadu, 1971, 1975, 1978; Honorary Doctorate, World University, 1982; Thanjavur Tamil University Award, 1989; Dr C D Sharma Award, Indian Library Association, 1994; Ranganathan-Kaula Gold Medal, 1994; Indian Library Association Abburi-Shiyali Research Award, 2001; Puravalar Mani, Mukkudai Monthly of Madras Jain Youth Forum, 2001; Tamil Pani Semmal Award, International Tamil Integration Society of Madras, 2002; Aanmiga Rathna Award, Tiruvannamalai Ashrama, 2003; Honoree of Contemporary Who's Who 2002-03 for Significant Achievement and Contributions to Society, 2004; Madurai Humanity, Tamil Monthly Award for Contributions, 2004, 2005; Sethumathi Endowment Award of Rs10,000, Cumbum, 2010; Vethiana, 2005; Listed in International Biographical Dictionaries. Memberships include: Fellow, Nagpur International Biographical Association, 2002; Foundation for Information and Communication, Madras, 2002; Fellow, Madras United Writers Association, 2003; Research Board of Advisors, ABI, 2004; Life Member: Indian Library Association; Tamilnadu Library Association; Madras Library Association; Tamilnadu Pensioners Associations at Ambasamuthram, Cumbum, Madras, Madurai and Uthamapalayam. Address: Director of Public Libraries (Retired), 48 VOC Square, Cumbum, Tamil Nadu 625 516, India.

THOMAS Donald Michael, b. 27 January 1935, Redruth, Cornwall, England. Poet; Writer; Translator. 2 sons, 1 daughter. Education: BA, 1st Class Honours, English, MA, New College, Oxford. Appointment: English teacher, Teignmouth, Devon, 1959-63; Lecturer, Hereford College of Education, 1963-78; Full-time author, 1978-. Publications: Poetry: Penguin Modern Poets 11, 1968; Two Voices, 1968; Logan Stone, 1971; Love and Other Deaths, 1975; The Honeymoon Voyage, 1978; Dreaming in Bronze, 1981; Selected Poems, 1983; Puberty Tree, 1992. Fiction: The Flute Player, 1979; Birthstone, 1980; The White Hotel, 1981; Ararat, 1983; Swallow, 1984; Sphinx, 1986; Summit, 1987; Lying Together, 1990; Flying into Love, 1992; Pictures at an Exhibition, 1993; Eating Pavlova, 1994; Lady With a Laptop, 1996; Alexander Solzhenitsyn, 1998; Charlotte, 2000. Translator: Requiem, and Poem Without a Hero, by Akhmatova, 1976; Way of All the Earth, by Akhmatova, 1979; The Bronze Horseman, by Pushkin, 1982. Honours: Gollancz/ Pan Fantasy Prize; Pen Fiction Prize; Cheltenham Prize; Los Angeles Times Fiction Prize. Address: The Coach House, Rashleigh Vale, Tregolis Road, Truro TR1 1TJ, England. E-mail: dmthomas@btconnect.com

THOMAS Iwan, b. 5 January 1974, Farnborough, Hampshire. Athlete. Education: Brunel University. Appointments: Fourth-ranked BMX rider, Europe, 1988; Fifth Olympic Games 400m, 1996; Silver Medal, 4 x 400m relay; Gold Medal Amateur Athletics Association, Championships 400m, 1997, British records, 44.36 seconds, 1998; Silver Medal World Championships 4 x 400m relay, 1997; Gold Medal European Championships 400m, 1998; Gold Medal, World Cup 400m, 1998; Gold Medal Commonwealth Games 400m, 1998; Contestant on and winner of reality show Deadline. Honours: British Athletics Writers Male Athlete of the Year, 1998; Patron Norwich Union Startract Scheme. Address: c/o UK Athletics, Athletics House, 10 Harbourne Road, Edgbaston, Birmingham, B15 3AA, England. Website: www.iwanthomas.com

THOMAS Kenneth G, b. 25 June 1944, Llanelli, Wales. Senior Vice President. m. Beth, 2 daughters. Education: BSc Honours, Metallurgy, University College, Cardiff, Wales, 1970; MSc and DIC, Management Sciences, Imperial College, University of London, 1971; PhD, Technical Sciences, Delft University of Technology, Delft, The Netherlands, 1994; Chartered Engineer, UK. Appointments:

DICTIONARY OF INTERNATIONAL BIOGRAPHY 36th EDITION

Mill Superintendent, Giant Yellowknife Mines Limited, Gold Producer, Northwest Territories, Canada, 1985-87; Vice-President, Metallurgy, 1987, Vice-President, Metallurgy and Construction, 1989, Senior Vice-President, Metallurgy and Construction, 1990, Senior Vice-President, Technical Services, 1995, Barrick Gold Corporation, Gold Producer, Ontario, Canada, 1987-2001; Managing Director, Mining and Mineral Processing, 2001, Managing Director, Western Australia, 2002-2003, Hatch, Consulting Engineers and Construction Managers, Mississauga, Ontario, Canada; Executive Vice President, Operations and Chief Operating Officer, Crystallex International Corporation, International Gold Company, Toronto, Canada, 2003-05; Global Managing Director, Hatch, Consulting Engineers and Construction Managers, Mississauga, Ontario, Canada, 2005-09; Senior Vice President, Projects, Kinross Gold Corporation, 2009-. Publications: Numerous technical and management papers internationally. Book: Research, Engineering Design and Operation of a Pressure Hydrometallurgical Facility for Gold Extraction. Honours: Mill Man of the Year Award, 1991, Airey Award, 1999, Selwyn G Blaylock Medal, 2001, Canadian Institute of Mining, Metallurgy and Petroleum. Memberships: Association of Professional Engineers of Ontario, Canada; Fellow, Institute of Mining, Metallurgy and Mining, UK; Fellow, Canadian Institute of Mining, Metallurgy and Petroleum; Fellow, Canadian Academy of Engineering. Address: 2005, Heartwood Court, Mississauga, Ontario L5C 4P7, Canada.

THOMAS Lindsey Kay Jr, b. 16 April 1931, Salt Lake City, Utah, USA. Research Ecologist Emeritus; Consultant; Educator. m. Nancy Ruth Van Dyke, 2 sons, 2 daughters. Education: BS, Utah State Agricultural College (now Utah State University), Logan, Utah, 1953; MS, Brigham Young University, Provo, Utah, 1958; PhD, Duke University, Durham, North Carolina, 1974. Appointments: Park Naturalist, National Capital Parks, National Park Service, 1957-62; Wildlife Management Consultant for Girl Scouts of America Camp 1958; Park Naturalist (Research), Region 6, 1962-63; Research Park Naturalist, National Capital Region, 1963-66; Instructor, United States Department of Agriculture Graduate School, 1964-66; Research Biologist for Southeast Temperate Forests, 1966-71; Aquatic Ecology Consultant for Fairfax County (Va) Federation of Citizen Associations 1970-71; Research Biologist, National Capital Parks, 1971-74; Research Biologist, National Capital Region, 1974-93; Guest Lecturer, Washington Technical Institute (University of the District of Columbia), 1976; Adjunct Professor, George Mason University, 1988-; Adjunct Professor, George Washington University, 1992-98; Research Biologist, Patuxent Environmental Science Center, National Biological Service (National Biological Survey, 1993-94), 1994-96; Resource Management Specialist, Baltimore-Washington Parkway, National Park Service, 1996, National Capital Parks East, 1996-98; Member, Board of Directors, Prince William County (Virginia) Service Authority, 1996-2004; Ecological and Resource Management Consultant, National Capital Region, 1998-; Research Ecologist Emeritus and Ecological and Resource Management Consultant, National Capital Region, National Park Service, 1998-; Preservation and Management Consultant for McAteean Magnolia Bogs in Charles County, Maryland, 2002-2006; Consultant for Natural Resources Division, Arlington County, Va, 2004-. Publications: Numerous articles in professional journals. Honours include: Boy Scouts of America Training Award, Superior Performance Award for Conduct and Progress in the Exotic Plant Management Research Programme; Incentive Award for Safety Feature at Overlook; Incentive Award for Interpretive Information to be placed on C&O Canal Location Map; Plaque, Virginia Native Plant Society, 2004; Certificate of Appreciation, Prince William County/Manassas, Virginia Convention & Visitors Bureau, 2007; Listed in Who's Who publications and biographical dictionaries. Memberships: American Association for the Advancement of Science; Botanical Society of Washington; Ecological Society of America; George Wright Society; The Nature Conservancy; Society for Early Historic Archaeology; Sigma Xi the Scientific Research Society; Southern Appalachian Botanical Society; Washington Biologists' Field Club; National Trust for Historic Preservation; Maryland Native Plant Society. Address: 13854 Delaney Road, Woodbridge, VA 22193-4654, USA.

THOMAS Tessamma, b. 28 May 1955, Ernakulum, India. Teacher; Researcher. m. M Ignatius, 1 son, 2 daughters. Education: MSc; M Technology; PhD. Appointments: Teaching and Research. Publications: 90 research papers in various international/national journals and conferences in fields of signal processing, image/speech processing, etc. Honours: Rashtiaya Gaurav Award, 2009; Shiksha Rattan Puraskai, 2010. Memberships: Life Member, Society of Biotechnologists; Association of Computer Electronics & Electrical Engineering. Address: Department of Electronics, Cohin University of Science & Technology, Cochin 682022, Kerala, India.

THOMPSON Daley, b. 30 July 1958, Notting Hill, London, England. Athlete. m. Tisha Quinlan, 1987, 1 child. Appointments: Sussex Schools 200m title, 1974; First competitive decathlon, Welsh Open Championship, 1975; European Junior Decathlon Champion, 1977; European Decathlon Silver Medallist, 1978; Gold Medallist, 1982, 1986; Commonwealth Decathlon Gold Medallist, 1978, 1982, 1986; Olympic Decathlon Gold Medallist, Moscow, 1980, LA, 1984; World Decathlon Champion, 1983; Established new world record for decathlon (at Olympic games, LA); Set four world records and was undefeated between 1978 and 1987; Retired, July 1992; Invited to run leg of the Olympic Torch relay at the opening of Sydney Olympic Games, 2000; Played football for Mansfield Town and Wimbledon. Publications: Going for Gold, 1987; The Greatest, 1996. Honours: MBE, 1982; OBE, 1986; BBC Sports Personality of the Year, 1982; Britain's Athlete of the Century, 1999; CBE, 2000. Address: Church Row, Wandsworth Plain, London, SW18, England.

THOMPSON Emma, b. 15 April 1959, England. Actress. m. (1) Kenneth Brannagh, 1989, divorced, (2) Greg Wise, 1 daughter. Education: Newnham College, Cambridge, England. Career: Cambridge Footlights while at University; Films include: Henry V, 1989; Howards End, Dead Again, 1991; Cheers, 1992; Peter's Friends, 1992; Much Ado About Nothing; In the Name of the Father, Remains of the Day, 1993; My Father the Hero, 1994; Junior, 1994; Sense and Sensibility, wrote screenplay and acted, 1996; The Winter Guest, 1997; Primary Colors, 1997; Judas Kiss, 1997; Imagining Argentina, 2002; Love Actually, 2003; Harry Potter and the Prisoner of Azkaban, 2004; Nanny McPhee, 2005; Stranger Than Fiction, 2006; Harry Potter and the Order of the Phoenix, 2007; I Am Legend, 2007; Brideshead Revisited, 2008; Last Chance Harvey, 2008; An Education, 2009; The Boat That Rocked, 2009; Nanny McPhee and the Big Bang, 2010; Harry Potter and the Deathly Hallows – Part II, 2011; Men in Black 3, Brave, 2012; Beautiful Creatures, Effie, Saving Mr Banks, 2013; TV includes: Carrott's Lib; Saturday Night Live; Tutti Frutti; Fortunes of War; Thompson; Knuckle; The Winslow Boy; Look Back in Anger; Blue Boy; Ellen; Wit; Angels in America, 2002; The Song of Lunch, 2010; Stage appearances include: Me and My Girl, 1984-85; Look Back in Anger,

1989; A Midsummer Night's Dream, 1990; King Lea, 1990. Publications: The Further Tale of Peter Rabbit, 2012. Honours include: Academy Awards, 1992, 1995; BAFTA Awards, 1992, 1995; Golden Globes, 1992, 1995; Writers Guild of America, 1995; Various critics awards, 1992, 1993, 1995, 2003. Address: Hamilton Hodell Ltd, 1st Floor, 24 Hanway Street, London W1T 1UH, England.

THOMPSON Richard Paul Hepworth, b. 14 April 1940, Esher, Surrey, England. Medicine. m. Eleanor Mary Hughes. Education: Epsom College, 1954-58; Worcester College, Oxford University, 1958-62; St Thomas' Hospital Medical School, 1962-64. Appointments: Consultant Physician, 1972-2005, Emeritus Consultant Physician, 2005-, Guy's & St Thomas's Hospitals; Management Committee, 1985-97, Chairman, Grants Committee, 1992-97, King Edward VII's Hospital Fund for London; Physician to HM the Queen, 1993-2005; Trustee of THRIVE, 2000-10; Visiting Professor, King's College London, 2001-; Vice Chairman of Council, British Heart Foundation, 2001-07; Treasurer, 2003-10, President, 2010-, Royal College of Physicians; Council, Royal Medical Foundation of Epsom College, 2003-10; Independent Monitoring Board, Feltham Young Offenders Institute, 2005-08. Publications: 2 medical textbooks; 250 medical and scientific publications in journals. Honours: DM, Oxon; FRCP; KCVO; Trustee, Henry Smith Charity, 2007-; Honorary Fellow, Worcester College, Oxford, 2008. Address: 36 Dealtry Road, London, SW15 6NL, England. E-mail: richard@rpht.co.uk

THOMSON John Ansel Armstrong, b. 23 November 1911, Detroit, Michigan, USA. Maufacturing Biochemist. m. June Anna Mae Hummel, deceased, 1 son, 2 daughters. Education: AA, Pasadena City College, 1935; AB (cum laude), USC, 1957; BGS (Honorary), Cal State Polytech University, 1961; MA, PhD, Columbia Pacific University, 1978-79; DA, International Institute of Advanced Studies, Clayton, Missouri, 1979; Certified Secondary Teacher, California. Appointments: Chemist, J A Thomson Bio-Organic Chemist, LA, 1938; Founder/President, Vitamin Institute, Huntington Company and North Hollywood, California, 1939-; Vocational Education Instructor, US War Manpower Commission, 1943-44. Publications: Author of booklets: Whose Are the Myths? 1949; Non-toxic Vitamins-Hormones Answers to Environmental Public Problems, 1972; Minimization of Toxics in Agriculture, 1991; Support of Pressures to Homeostasis, Normality, 1990; Need for Recognition and Reversal of Rapid Decline of Heritage of American and World Children, 1995, 1996; Contributor of articles to journals. Honours: Scouting Leadership Awards, Boy Scouts of America; Science & Industry Gold Medal, Golden Gate International Exposition, 1940; Civic Service Award, State of California, 1949; Lawn & Garden Marketing & Distribution Association Lifetime Achievement Award, 2006; Lifetime Environment Awareness Award, Sustainable Environmental Education, 2009. Memberships: Listed in international biographical dictionaries. Address: 12610 Saticoy Street South, North Hollywood, CA 91605, USA. Website: www.superthrive.com

THORLEY Virginia Gwendolen, b. 16 August 1942, Townsville, Australia. Lactation Consultant. m. Desmond Phillips (aka George Phillips), 1963, 2 sons, 2 daughters. Education: ThA, Australian College of Theology, Sydney, 1959; BA, University of Queensland, 1979; IBCLC, International Board of Lactation Consultant Examiners, 1985; Diploma in Education, University of Queensland, 1988; Graduate Certificate TESOL, University of New England, 1991; MA, University of Queensland, 2000. Appointments: Self employed Writer, Queensland, 1971, 1983-84, 1985-87; Part-time tutor, Aboriginal and Torres Strait Islander Programs, Townsville, Queensland, 1984-87; Part-time English Teacher, Townsville College of Technology and Further Education, 1986; Part-time English Language Teacher, Various Tertiary Institutes, Brisbane, Queensland, 1988-92; Part-time private lactation consultant practice, Brisbane, 1988-; English Language Teacher, Southbank Institute of Technology and Further Education, Brisbane, 1992-97. Publications: Successful Breastfeeding; Feeding your baby and young child in Australia; Establishing Breastfeeding; Chapter in, Helping One Another: Self-Help Groups in a Changing World; Over 60 papers and articles in professional journals. Honours: OAM, services in lactation and to the Australian Breastfeeding Association. Memberships: Secretary, International Lactation Consultant Association, 1999-2002; Honorary Member, Australian Breastfeeding Association; Member, Queensland Lactation College; Queensland Committee of the Baby Friendly Hospitals Initiative. Address: 4/14 Moreton Street, Norman Park, Queensland 4170, Australia. Email: vgthorley@ozemail.com.au

THORNBURG Russell C, b. 27 June 1953, Akron, Ohio, USA. Private Investigator; Security Officer. m. Linda C Blake. Education: Graduate, University of Akron, 1991. Appointments: E-6, USA Air Force Reserve, 10 years; Major, Burns Int Security System Inc; Licensed Private Investigator/ Security Officer, Stat of Ohio, 25 years; Editor, Weekly Pride Newspaper. Publications: Weekly editorial page and newspaper articles, 5 years. Honours: Law Enforcement, Arnold Air Award of Merit. Memberships: President, Ohio Chapter, American Law Enforcement Officer's Association; FBI Press Pass. Address: 600 Eastland Avenue, Akron, OH 44305, USA. E-mail: rcthorn@neo.rr.com

THORNTON Billy Bob, b. 4 August 1955, Hot Springs, Arizona, USA. Actor; Writer; Director. m. (1) Melissa Lee Gatlin, divorced 1980, 1 daughter, (2) Toni Lawrence, divorced 1988, (3) Cynda Williams, divorced 1992, (4) Pietra Dawn Chernak, divorced 1997, 2 sons, (5) Angelina Jolie, 2000, divorced 2003, 1 adopted son, 1 daughter with Connie Angland. Appointments: Films include: Sling Blade, 1996; U-Turn, 1997; A Thousand Miles, 1997; The Apostle, 1997; A Gun a Car a Blonde, 1997; Primary Colours, 1997; Homegrown, 1998; Armageddon, 1998; A Simple Plan, 1998; Pushing Tin, 1998; The Man Who Wasn't There, 2001; Bandits, 2001; Monster's Ball, 2001; Love Actually, 2003; Intolerable Cruelty, 2003; Bad Santa, 2003; The Alamo, 2004; Friday Night Lights, 2004; The Ice Harvest, 2005; Bad News Bears, 2005; School for Scoundrels, 2006; Mr Woodcock, 2007; The Astronaut Farmer, 2007; Eagle Eye, 2008; The Informers, 2008; The Smell of Success, 2009; TV: The 1,000 Chains; Don't Look Back; The Outsiders; Hearts Afire. Honours: Academy Award for Best Actor; Independent Spirit Awards. Address: c/o Miramax, 7966 Beverly Boulevard, Los Angeles, CA 90048, USA.

THORNTON Leslie Tillotson, b. 26 May 1925, Skipton, North Yorkshire, England. Sculptor; Principal Art Lecturer (Retired). m. Constance Helen Billows, 1 son, 1 daughter. Education: Keighley Art School, 1940-42; Conscripted for Mines, 1943-45; National Diploma of Art and Design, Leeds College of Art, 1945-48; Sculpture School, Royal College of Art, 1948-51; Associate of RCA. Appointments: Part-time Lecturer in London Art Colleges: Bromley, Hammersmith and Central School, 1951-65; Senior Lecturer in Charge of Sculpture, University of Sunderland, 1965-70; Principal Lecturer in Charge of Sculpture, University of Stafford,

1970-89; Exhibitions include: Arts Council Contemporary British Sculpture, 1957/58; 10 Young British Sculptors, IV Sao Paulo Biennale, Brazil, 1957; CAS Religious Theme Exhibition, Tate Gallery, 1958; 10 Young British Sculptors, British Council Touring Exhibition, Rio de Janeiro, Montevideo, Santiago, Lima, Caracas, 1958; 5th and 10th International Biennale Middleheim Park, Antwerp, 1959, 1969; British Artists Craftsmen Exhibition touring America, 1960; English Painters and Sculptors, Zurich, 1963; Art Sacre, Museum of Modern Art, Paris, 1965; Northern Sculptors Exhibition, Newcastle, 1967; One man Exhibitions, Gimpel Fils Gallery, London, 1957, 1960, 1969; Sion House, London, 1970; Royal Academy, London, 1974/76, 1978/79; Solihull Annual Exhibition, 1979; Retrospective Exhibition, Holden Gallery, Manchester, 1981; Royal Academy, 1987; 100 Years of Sculpture, Moore Institute, Leeds, 2004; Arts Council Touring Exhibition, Geometry of Fear, 2007-09; British Library Sound Archive Collections, Artists' Lives, 2009; Commissions: Daily Mirror Building, London, 1961; Crucifix, St Louis Priory, Missouri, 1965; Crucifix, St Ignatious College, Enfield, 1968; Works in collections including: Museum of Modern Art, New York; Peggy Guggenheim Collection, Venice; Arts Council of Great Britain; Victoria and Albert Museum; Leeds City Art Gallery; National Gallery of Scotland; Private collections in UK North and South America, Sweden and Belgium. Publications: Works reviewed in books and journals including: 20th Century Steel Sculptures US, 2002; Handbook of 20th Century British Sculpture, 2004. Honours: Panel Member, Council for National Academic Awards; Fellow, Royal Society of Arts; Associate, Royal Society of British Sculptors. Address: Stable Cottage, 45 Chatsworth Place, Harrogate HG1 5HR, England.

THRUSH Brian Arthur, b. 23 July 1928, Hendon, England. Retired University Professor. m. Rosemary Catherine Terry, 1 son, 1 daughter. Education: BA, MA, PhD, ScD, Emmanuel College, Cambridge. Appointments: Lecturer, Assistant Director of Research, Demonstrator in Physical Chemistry, 1953-69, Reader in Physical Chemistry, 1969-78, Professor of Physical Chemistry, 1978-95, Professor Emeritus, 1995-, University of Cambridge; Fellow, 1960, Vice Master 1986-90, Emmanuel College, Cambridge: Visiting Professor of Chinese Academy of Sciences, 1980-90. Publications: Many original papers in learned scientific journals. Honours: Tilden Lecturer, Chemical Society , 1965; Michael Polanyi Medallist, Royal Society of Chemistry, 1986; Rank Prize for Opto-Electronics, 1992. Memberships: Fellow Royal Society, 1976, Council Member, 1990-92; Fellow, Royal Society of Chemistry, 1977; Lawes Trust Committee, 1979-89; National Environment Research Council, 1985-90; Member, Academia Europaea, 1990, Council Member, 1992-98. Address: Brook Cottage, Pemberton Terrace, Cambridge, CB2 1JA, England.

THU Nguyen Van, b. 18 February 1955, Bioh Thuan Province, Vietnam. Lecturer. m. 1 son, 1 daughter. Education: BSc, Can Tho University, Vietnam, 1979; MSc, 1994, PhD, 2000, Swedish University of Agricultural Sciences, Sweden. Appointments: Assistant Lecturer, 1979-81, Lecturer, 1982-94, Senior Lecturer, 1994-2004, Associate Professor, Head of Department of Animal Sciences, Can Tho University, 2004-11. Publications: More than 100 scientific papers in Vietnam and international journals and conference proceedings. Honours: Innovative Certificate and Medal, Vietnam Labour Federation, 2003; Certificate of Merit, Vietnam Ministry of Education for Scientific Works, 2001-05. Memberships: Asian Buffalo Association; World and Asian Rabbit Association; Vietnam Animal Husbandry Association; Vietnam Milk Association. Address: Department of Animal Sciences, Faculty of Agriculture and Applied Biology, Can Tho University, Vietnam. E-mail: nvthu@etu.edu.vn

THUBRON Colin Gerald Dryden, b. 14 June 1939, London, England. Writer. Publications: Mirror to Damascus, 1967; The Hills of Adonis: A Quest in Lebanon, 1968; Jerusalem, 1969; Journey Into Cyprus, 1975; The God in the Mountain (novel), 1977; Emperor (novel), 1978; The Venetians, 1980; The Ancient Mariners, 1981; The Royal Opera House Covent Garden, 1982; Among the Russians, 1983; A Cruel Madness, 1984; Behind the Wall: A Journey Through China, 1987; Falling, 1989; Turning Back the Sun, 1991; The Lost Heart of Asia, 1994; Distance (novel), 1996; In Siberia, 1999; To the Last City (novel), 2002; Shadow of the Silk Road, 2006; To a Mountain in Tibet, 2011. Contributions to: Times; Times Literary Supplement; Independent; Sunday Times; Sunday Telegraph; New York Times; Granta; New York Review of Books. Honours: Fellow, Royal Society of Literature, 1969; Silver Pen Award, 1985; Thomas Cook Award, 1988; Hawthornden Prize, 1989; RSGS Mungo Park Medal, 2000; RSAA Lawrence of Arabia Memorial Medal, 2001; Vice-President, Royal Society of Literature, 2003; CBE, 2007; Prix Bouvier, 2009; President, Royal Society of Literature, 2010; RGS Ness Award, 2011. Membership: PEN. Address: 28 Upper Addison Gardens, London W14 8AJ, England.

THURGOOD Gwyneth Mary, b. 2 April 1938, Swansea, Wales. Artist; SciArtist; Broadcaster (Radio & TV); Teacher (Retired). m. Anthony H M Thurgood (deceased), 1 son. Education: Swansea College of Art, 1955-58; Birmingham College of Art and University Institute of Education, 1958-59. Appointments: Full-time Art Teacher, West Lawn School, Teignmouth, Devon, 1959-62; Part-time Art Tutor, Teignmouth Evening Institute, 1959-62; Full-time in charge of Art, Westwood Girls' School, Reading, Berkshire, 1962-64; Full-time Head of Art, Chatham Girls' Grammar School, 1964-69; Part-time Art Tutor: Sidcup Adult Centre, Kent, 1989-90, Sittingbourne College, 1989-90, Maidstone Adult Centre, 1991, Swadelands Adult Centre, Lenham, 1991, Holmesdale Adult Centre, East Malling, 1991-92; Supply Teacher, 1987-99; Freelance Art Tutor, 1992-99; Numerous solo exhibitions include: Hidden landscapes, University of Kent at Canterbury, 1987; Visible and Invisible Nature, University of Surrey Gallery, 1991; Invisible Nature into Art, University of Keele Art Gallery, 1993; Worlds within Worlds – Art within Science, The Science Museum, London, 1995; The Booth Museum, Brighton, 1997; Hidden Landscapes 2, University of Exeter Gallery, 1988. Publications: Articles in journals and exhibition catalogues. Honours: National Diploma in Design, 1958; Postgraduate Certificate in Education, 1959; Art teachers' Diploma, 1959; Fellowship, National Society for Education in Art and Design, 1970; The Barnard Certificate for Excellence in Photomicrography, Quekett Microscopical Club, Natural History Museum, London, 1996, 1999; Listed in international biographical dictionaries; Woman of the Year, 2006; Great Minds of the 21st Century, 2006/07; Woman of Achievement, 2007; UK Ambassador/Speaker, World Forum, Oxford, 2008; UK Ambassador/Speaker, World Forum, Washington DC, 2009; Ambassador, Speaker, Exhibitor, World Forum, Cambridge, 2010; Ambassador of Knowledge Medallion, University of Cambridge, 2010. Address: Starling Steps, Old Ashford Road, Lenham, Maidstone, Kent ME17 2PX, England. E-mail: gwyneth.thurgood@tiscali.co.uk

THURLOW, 8th Baron (Francis Edward Hovell-Thurlow-Cumming-Bruce), The Rt Hon the Lord Thurlow, b. 9 March 1912. m. Yvonne Diana, 1949, deceased 1990, 2 sons, 2 daughters. Education: Shrewsbury; MA, Trinity College, Cambridge. Appointments: Department of Agriculture for Scotland, 1935-37; Joined HM Diplomatic Service: Secretary, New Zealand, 1939-44; Secretary, Canada, 1944-45; Private Secretary to Secretary of State for Commonwealth Relations, 1947-49; Counsellor, New Delhi, 1949-52; Adviser to Governor of Gold Coast, 1955; Deputy High Commissioner, Ghana, 1957; Deputy High Commissioner, Canada, 1958; High Commissioner, New Zealand, 1959-63; High Commissioner, Nigeria, 1963-66; Deputy Under Secretary, FCO, 1964; Governor and Commander-in-Chief of Bahamas, 1968-72. Honours: KCMG, 1959; Knight of St John. Memberships: Travellers. Address: 102 Leith Mansions, Grantully Road, London W9 1LJ, England. E-mail: thurlow@btinternet.com

THURMAN Uma, b. 29 April 1970. Actress. m. (1) Gary Oldman, 1990, divorced 1992, (2) Ethan Hawke, 1998, divorced 2004, 1 son, 1 daughter. Appointments: Model; Actress; Films: The Adventures of Baron Munchhausen; Dangerous Liaisons; Even Cowgirls Get the Blues; Final Analysis; Where the Heart Is; Henry and June; Mad Dog and Glory; Pulp Fiction; Robin Hood; Dylan; A Month by the Lake; The Truth About Cats and Dogs; Batman and Robin; Gattaca; Les Miserables; Sweet and Lowdown; Vatel; The Golden Bowl; Tape; Chelsea Walls; Kill Bill Vol 1, 2003; Paycheck; Kill Bill Vol 2, 2004; Be Cool, 2005; Prime, 2005; The Producers, 2005; My Super Ex-Girlfriend, 2006; The Life Before Her Eyes, 2007; The Accidental Husband, 2008; Motherhood, 2009; Percy Jackson & The Olympians: The Lightning Thief, 2010; TV: Hysterical Blindness, 2002. Honours: Golden Globe, Best Actress in a Miniseries or TV movie, 2003. Address: c/o CAA, 9830 Wilshire Boulevard, Beverly Hills, CA 90212, USA.

THURSBY-PELHAM Vaughan Brian George, b. Wimbledon Common, London, England. Retired Chartered Accountant. m. Brigid Kathleen Doherty, 2 sons, 3 daughters. Education: Beaumont College, Old Windsor, Berkshire. Appointments: Trained with Peat Marwick Mitchell (now KPMG); Previously Board Secretary/Financial Director of various public companies; Board Secretary/Financial Controller, Engineering Construction Industry Training Board, 1990-97. Memberships: Fellow, Institute of Chartered Accountants in England & Wales; Member, Catenian Association, Provincial Counsellor. Address: Two Woodlands Avenue, New Malden, Surrey KT3 3UN, England.

THWAITE Ann, b. 4 October 1932, London, England. Writer. m. Anthony Thwaite, 1955, 4 daughters. Education: MA, Dlitt, Oxford University (St Hilda's College). Appointments: Visiting Professor, Tokyo Women's University; Contributing Editor, Editorial Board, Cricket Magazine (US). Publications: Waiting for the Party: A Life of Frances Hodgson Burnett (reissued as Frances Hodgson Burnett: Beyond the Secret Garden); Edmund Gosse: A Literary Landscape; A A Milne: His Life; Emily Tennyson: The Poet's Wife; Glimpses of the Wonderful, The Life of Philip Henry Gosse; Passageways: the Story of a New Zealand Family, 2009. Honours: Duff Cooper Prize, 1985; Whitbread Biography Award, 1990; Honorary Fellow, University of Surrey; Hon DLitt, University of East Anglia. Memberships: Fellow, Royal Society of Literature; Society of Authors. Address The Mill House, Low Tharston, Norwich NR15 2YN, England.

THWAITE Anthony Simon, b. 23 June 1930, Chester, Cheshire, England. Poet; Critic; Writer; Editor. m. Ann Barbara Harrop, 1955, 4 daughters. Education: BA, 1955, MA, 1959, Christ Church, Oxford. Appointments: Visiting Lecturer in English, 1955-57, Japan Foundation Fellow, 1985-86, University of Tokyo; Producer, BBC, 1957-62; Literary Editor, The Listener, 1962-65, New Statesman, 1968-72; Assistant Professor of English, University of Libya, 1965-67; Henfield Writing Fellow, University of East Anglia, 1972; Co-Editor, Encounter, 1973-85; Visiting Professor, Kuwait University, 1974, Chairman of the Judges, Booker Prize, 1986; Director, 1986-92, Editorial Consultant, 1992-95, André Deutsch, Ltd; Poet-in-Residence, Vanderbilt University, 1992. Publications: Poetry: Home Truths, 1957; The Owl in the Tree, 1963; The Stones of Emptiness, 1967; Inscriptions, 1973; New Confessions, 1974; A Portion for Foxes, 1977; Victorian Voices, 1980; Poems 1953-1983, 1984, enlarged edition as Poems 1953-1988, 1989; Letter from Tokyo, 1987; The Dust of the World, 1994; Selected Poems, 1956-1996, 1997; A Different Country, 2000. Other: Contemporary English Poetry, 1959; Japan (with Roloff Beny), 1968; The Deserts of Hesperides, 1969; Poetry Today, 1973, 3rd edition, revised and expanded, 1996; In Italy (with Roloff Beny and Peter Porter), 1974; Twentieth Century English Poetry, 1978; Odyssey: Mirror of the Mediterranean (with Roloff Beny), 1981; Six Centuries of Verse, 1984. Editor: The Penguin Book of Japanese Verse (with Geoffrey Bownas), 1964 revised and expanded, 1998; The English Poets (with Peter Porter), 1974; New Poetry 4 (with Fleur Adcock), 1978; Larkin at Sixty, 1982; Poetry 1945 to 1980 (with John Mole), 1983; Collected Poems of Philip Larkin, 1988; Selected Letters of Philip Larkin, 1992; Further requirements: Philip Larkin, 2001; A Move in the Weather, 2003; The Ruins of Time (Poetry of Place) (editor), 2006; Collected Poems, 2007. Honours: Richard Hillary Memorial Prize, 1968; Fellow, Royal Society of Literature, 1978; Cholmondeley Prize, 1983; Officer of the Order of the British Empire, 1990. Address: The Mill House, Low Tharston, Norfolk NR15 2YN, England.

TICHÝ Miloň, b. 28 April 1937, Praha, Czech Republic. Chemist; Toxicologist. m. Marie Karlová, 1 daughter. Education: Mgr, Charles University, Faculty of Science, 1961; PhD, Institute of Physical Chemistry, Academy of Science, 1966; Associate Professor, Analytical Chemistry, 1992; DSc, Charles University, Faculty of Pharmacy, 1990. Appointments: Research Worker in Toxicokinetics, Head of Toxicological Analysis Group, Head of Chemical Safety Group, Head of Predictive Toxicology Laboratory, National Institute of Public Health, Praha, Czech Republic, 1966-; Lecturer, Faculty of Science, Charles University, Praha. Publications: QSAR analysis and data extrapolation among mammals in a series of aliphatic alcohols, 1985; Quantitative Structure – Activity Relationships, 1976; Effect of biosolubility on pulmonary uptake and disposition of gases and vapors of lipophilic chemicals, 1984; QSAR analysis in mixture toxicity assessment, 1998; The Tubifex tubifex assay for the determination of acute toxicity, 2007; Acute toxicity estimation by calculation – Tubifex assay and quantitative structure – activity relationships, 2008; Determination of butoxyacetic acid (biomarker of ethylene glycol monobutyl ether exposure) in human urine candidate reference material, 2010; Toxicity of perfluorinated carboxylic acids for aquatic organisms, 2010. Honours: Czech Medical Society Award, 1976, 1984; Czech National Prize, 1988; Czech National Award, 2008; Honorary Member, Czech Medical Society, 2008; Czech Hunting Association Fidelity Medal. Memberships: Czech Chemical Society; Czech Medical Society; SETAC; American Chemical Society; QSAR and

Modeling Society; Slovak Toxicology Society. Address: National Institute of Public Health, Srobarova 48, 10042 Praha 10, Czech Republic.

TIJARDOVIĆ Ivica, b. 1 September 1960, Šibenik, Croatia. Shipmaster. 1 daughter. Education: Officer Certificate, Slovenia, 1980; Bachelor of Science, Navigation, Croatia, 1983; Master Mariner Certificate, Croatia, 1986; Master of Science, Technology of Transport, Croatia, 1989; Instructor for ARPA and Bridge Team Training, Norway, 1990; PhD (youngest with Shipmaster experience), Navigation, Naval Academy, Gdynia, Poland, 1994. Appointments: Sea experience: Cadet, 1979; Officer, 1981, Captain (youngest with MSc degree), 1990; Since 1998 has been sailing again as Captain (only Shipmaster with PhD); Supervisor of Commercial and Technical Management for vessels with the Shipbuilding Company of Split, Croatia, 1986-87; Assistant of Navigation, 1987, Lecturer in Navigation, 1990-98, Maritime Faculty, Split, Croatia; Assistant Professor of Navigation, 2000; Specialist for GPS and AIS receiver application in practice; Expert in Ship Stability, visited more than 300 vessels and met more than 500 Captains and Officers. Publications: More than 40 articles (over 100 pages) in Brown's Nautical Almanac (www.skipper.co.uk); 4 Articles in Journal of Navigation (www.rin.org.uk); More than 170 articles and comments in: Safety at Sea International, Solutions, Shiptalk.com, Fairplay and Lloyd's List; The Simplest and Fastest Star Finder; Nautical Tables; Articles on the commercial and technical management of ships; 15 books for students and 5 professional books in Croatia; 4 books for International Market: Draft Survey Book, Book of Differences in GPS Rhumbline Distances and Practical Ship Stability Book (www.iims.org.uk) and The Musings; Fully corrected the leading books of navigation and ship stability (over 4,000 pages). Honours: One of 3 captains nominated for Shipmaster of the Year 2004, Lloyd's List and Institute of Navigation, UK; Nominated again for Shipmaster of the Year 2005 and 2007; IBC Awards: 2000 Outstanding Intellectuals of the 21st Century for 2005 (Honours List); International Professional for 2005; Lifetime Achievement Award; Honorary and Deputy Director General; Adviser to the Director General; The Da Vinci Diamond; The IBC Hall of Fame; Decree of Excellence; Great Lives of the 21st Century; The Excellence Award; Member, Order of International Fellowship; Ambassador, International Order of Merit; Member, Order of Distinction; Life Fellow and Governor of the IBA; Lifetime Achievement Award, Vice President and Ambassador of the World Congress of Arts, Sciences and Communications; Order of American Ambassadors and Man of the Year 2008; Marquis Who's Who in the World since 2007; According to USA Notice to Mariners, the Observer No 1 with the most acknowledged reports for Safety of Navigation, 1998-2003; Recognition for contributions to navigation from HRH The Duke of Edinburgh KG KT, 2004 (www.jadranbrod.com). Memberships: Fellow, Royal Institute of Navigation; Member, Nautical Institute, UK; Life Member, US Naval Institute; Elected Chairman, Royal Institute of Navigation – Croatian Branch, 2008-10; Singer, 1st Tenor in Split, Croatia. E-mail: ivica.tijardovic@st.t-com.hr

TILLEKERATNE Herbert Walter, b. 5 March 1932, Kadugannawa, Sri Lanka. Educator. m. Elizabeth de S Gunasekera, 2 sons. Education: Specialist Science Trained Certificate, 1959; Advanced Science Trained Certificate, 1961; BSc, 1980; YMCA Secretarial Training Certificate, 1985; Asia YMCA Advanced Studies Certificate, 1985; Diploma in Business Management and Administration, 1988; MIPM, 1988; PhD, 2003. Appointments: Science Teacher, 1959; Science Lecturer, Teacher Training College, 1970; National Training Secretary, 1984; Admission to Sri Lanka Education Administrative Service, 1982; Vice-Principal, 1986, Acting Principal, 1988; Manager, Scientific Enterprise, 1989; Senior Consultant, Tertiary and Vocational Education Commission, 1991; Honorary Positions: Secretary, 1971, Vice- President, 1973, Sri Lanka Training Colleges Tutorial Staffs Union; Vice-President, Jathika Adyapana Sevaka Sangamaya, 1983; Vice-President, Colombo District Schools Football Association, 1987; Board Member, Mount Lavinia YMCA Board of Management, 1989; Director, Dehiwela YMCA, 1998; Chairman, Leadership Development Committee of the National Y, 1994; President, Sri Lanka Fellowship of YMCA Retirees, 1999; Secretary-Treasurer, South Asia Fellowship of YMCAR, 2000; President, SAFYR, 2001; Vice-Chairperson for South-SE Asia of the World Fellowship of YMCAR, 2003. Publications: Towards the Challenge of YMCA Mission (editor); Editor News Bulletins: Sapphire, Concern; Article: Sri Lanka Environment and Development. Honours: 21st Century Award for Achievement, International Illuminated Diploma of Honour, IBC, England; International Peace Prize, UCC, USA; Outstanding Intellectual of the 21st Century, IBC, England; Outstanding Old Boy of the National School, St Aloysius College, Galle. Memberships: Membership and Extension Committee, NC/YMCAs, 1994; Development, Education and Projects Committee, 1994; Child Development Committee, 1994; Environment Concerns Committee, 1994; Personal and Conferences Committee, 1994. Address: 72/6 Chakkindarama Road, Ratmalana, Sri Lanka.

TIMOFEEV Victor, b. 8 July 1950, Ermilaevo, Russia. Professor. m. Galina, 1 son, 1 daughter. Education: Graduated with honours, Krasnoyarsk Polytechnic Institute, 1974; Postgraduate studies, Leningrad Polytechnic Institute, 1975; Doctor of Technical Sciences, 1994; Certificate of Professor, 1995. Appointments: Professor; Head of Department. Publications: Application of mgd-technology in aluminium alloy productioin, 2007. Honours: Engineer of the Year. Memberships: Academy of Electrical Sciences. Address: 26 A Kirenskogo Str, 302, Krasnoyarsk, 660074, Russia. E-mail: mgd1@mail.ru

TINDLE David, b. 29 April 1932, Huddersfield, Yorkshire, England. Education: Coventry School of Art. Career: Artist: Designed and painted set for Iolanta (Tchaikovsky), Aldeburgh Festival, 1988; Visiting Tutor, 1973-83, Fellow, 1981, Honorary Fellow, 1984, Royal College of Art; Ruskin Master of Drawing, St Edmund Hall, Oxford, 1985-87; Now lives and works in Italy; Numerous exhibitions in London and the provinces, 1952-, include: First one-man exhibition, London, 1953; regular one-man shows, Piccadilly Gallery, 1954-83; Hamburg Gallerie XX, 1974-85; Los Angeles and San Francisco, 1964; Bologna and Milan, 1968; One-man show, Fischer Fine Art, 1985, 1989, 1992; Redfern Gallery, London, 1994, 1996, 1998-99, 2000, 2001, 2003, 2005, 2007, 2009; St Edmund Hall, Oxford, 1994; The Shire Hall Gallery, Stafford, 1994; Numerous group exhibitions and international biennales in Europe; Works in many public and private collections including the Tate Gallery, National Portrait Gallery. Honours: Elected Associate of the Royal Academy (ARA), 1973; Elected Full Royal Academician (RA), 1979; Honorary Fellow, St Edmund Hall, Oxford, 1988-; Honorary Member, Birmingham Society of Artists; Honorary MA, St Edmund Hall, Oxford, 1985; RA Johnson Wax Award, 1983; Listed in Who's Who publications and biographical dictionaries. Address: Via C Barsotti 194, Santa Maria del Giudice, 55058 Lucca, Italy.

TINDLE Lily Elizabeth (née Baker), b. 31 March 1939, Hebburn-on-Tyne, Co Durham, England. Psychologist. m. Robert William Tindle, 1 son, 1 daughter. Education: Jarrow Central and Grammar Schools, 1950-57; Eastbourne Training College, University of London, Institute of Education, 1957-59; University of South Australia, Diploma of Teaching, University of Adelaide, 1964-75; Bachelor of Arts, Postgraduate Diploma in Applied Psychology, Queensland University of Technology, 1993-99; Doctor of Education. Appointments: PE and Geography Teacher, Coates Endowed Secondary School, Northumberland, 1959-63; Sport and PE Teacher, Woodville High School, 1963-70; Counsellor, Plympton High School, Education Department, SA, 1970-75; Counselling Psychologist, Adelaide University, South Australia, 1975-76; Research Assistant, Charles Darwin Research Station, Galapagos Islands, 1976-79; Research Officer/Lecturer, Paisley University, Scotland; Counselling Psychologist, South Dorset Technical College, 1983-85; Lecturer, Crawley College of Technology, 1985-87; Research Officer, Griffith University, 1988-89; Tutor, Faculty of Education, University of Queensland, 1987-89; Psychologist, Queensland University of Technology, 1989-. Publications: Many articles and papers in professional journals on foetal alcohol syndrome; Articles by Elizabeth Tindle, 2007-08; Vol 1, Vol 2, Vol 3, Vol 4, Student Support Services, QUT; Serious Fears Across Cultures About the Collapse of the World Order, 2009; Chapter 19 in Meltdown: Climate Change, Natural Disasters, Editor, Kathryn Gow, QUT. Honours: Associate Fellow, British Psychological Society; Fellow, Australian Psychological Society; WOW (Wonderful Older Women) Award, 1999; Vice Chancellor's Performance Award, QUT, 2009. Memberships: Chartered Psychologist, Associate Fellow, British Psychological Society; Fellow, Australian Psychological Society; Chartered Scientist, British Science Council; College of Clinical Psychologists; College of Counselling Psychologists; Chartered Sport and Exercise Psychologists. Address: Queensland University of Technology, Gardens Point, PO Box 2434, Brisbane, Queensland 4001, Australia. E-mail: e.tindle@qut.com

TIRIMO Martino, b. 19 December 1942, Larnaca, Cyprus. Concert Pianist; Conductor. m. Mione J Teakle, 1973, 1 son, 1 daughter. Education: Royal Academy of Music, London; Vienna State Academy. Debut: Recital, Cyprus, 1949. Career: Conducted La Traviata 7 times at Italian Opera Festival, Cyprus, 1955; London debut, 1965; Concerto performances with most major orchestras, and recitals, TV, radio and festival appearances in Britain, Europe, USA, Canada, South Africa, China and the Far East from 1965; Gave public premiére of complete Schubert Sonatas, London, 1975, 1985; Public premiére of Beethoven concertos directing from the keyboard, Dresden and London, 1985, 1986; Gave several premiéres of Tippett Piano concerto since 1986; Four series of performances of complete Beethoven piano sonatas, 2000; Two series devoted to the major piano works of Robert and Clara Schumann, 2001; Six-concert series devoted to the major piano works of Chopin, 2002; Founded Rosamunde Trio 2002; Professor, Trinity College of Music, 2003-; Performed at special Athens Festival during Olympic period with Vienna Philharmonic in 2004; Mozart complete solo piano works in 8 concerts, London's Cadogan Hall, 2006; Chopin complete solo and works for piano and orchestra in series of 10 concerts, London's Kings Place, 2010. Compositions include: film score for the Odyssey in 8 episodes for Channel 4 TV, 1998. Recordings: Brahms Piano Concertos; Chopin Concertos; Mozart Concertos; Tippett Piano Concerto (with composer conducting); Rachmaninov Concertos; Complete Mozart piano works; Beethoven complete piano works; Complete Debussy piano works; Complete Janacek piano works; Complete Schubert Piano Sonatas; Various other solo recordings with mixed repertoire. Publications: Schubert: The Complete Piano Sonatas, 3 volumes, edited for Wiener Urtext Edition (with own completions to the unfinished movements), 1997-99. Honours: Gold Medal, Associated Board of the Royal Schools of Music; Liszt Scholarship, Royal Academy of Music; 11 other Prizes at Royal Academy of Music including Macfarren Medal; Boise Foundation Scholarship, 1965; Gulbenkian Foundation Scholarship, 1967-69; Joint Winner, Munich International Competition, 1971; Winner, Geneva International Competition, 1972; ARAM, 1968; FRAM, 1979; FRSAMD, 2005; Silver Disc, 1988; Gold Disc, 1994; Ran with the Olympic Torch, 2004; Nemitsas Foundation Prize, 2011. Memberships: ISM, 2005. Address: 1 Romeyn Road, London SW16 2NU, England. E-mail: martino@tirimo.fslife.co.uk

TISHKO Tatyana Vasilyevna, b. 9 December 1955, Kharkov, Ukraine. Physicist; Researcher. 1 son. Education: Physical Department, 1977, Department of Foreign Languages, 1987, Kharkov State University. Appointments: Physicist, Researcher, Holography Laboratory, 1977, Lecturer, 1991-93, Kharkov National University; Lecturer, Kharkov State Medical University, 1993-2003. Publications: Holography, 2007; Theory and Practice of Erythrocyte Microscopy; Numerous articles in professional journals. Honours: 1st Prize, Ioffee Physical Technical Institute. Memberships: European Microscopy Society. Address: 79-B Av Shironintzevst r 4, Kharkov, 61144, Ukraine. E-mail: tatyana.v.tishko@univer.kharkov.ua

TITCHMARSH Alan Fred, b. 2 May 1949, Ilkley, England. Gardener; Writer; Broadcaster. m. Alison Margaret Needs, 1975, 2 daughters. Education: Shipley Art and Technical Institute, 1964-68; National Certificate in Horticulture, Hertfordshire College of Agriculture and Horticulture, 1968-69; Diploma in Horticulture, Royal Botanic Gardens, Kew, 1969-1972. Appointments include: Apprentice Gardener, Parks Department, Ilkley, Urban District Council, 1964-68; Supervisor, Staff Training, Royal Botanic Gardens, Kew, 1972-74; Assistant Gardening Editor, Hamlyn Publishing, 1974-76; Assistant then Deputy Editor, Amateur Gardening, 1976-79; Freelance Writer and Broadcaster, 1979-; Contributor to: Daily Express; Sunday Express; Radio Times; BBC Gardeners' World Magazine; Many radio and television programmes including: Breakfast Time, Songs of Praise; Points of View; Pebble Mill; Gardeners' World; Ground Force; BBC Proms; British Isles, a Natural History; How to Be a Gardener; Royal Gardeners; 20th Century Roadshow; Vice-President, Wessex Cancer Trust, 1988-; Patron: Rainbow Trust, 1993-; Kaleidoscope Theatre; Orpheus Trust; New Winchester Theatre Royal; Seeds for Africa; CHICKS; Cowes Inshore Lifeboat; Treloar Trust; Henry Spink Foundation; Writtle College; Land Heritage; Horticap; Cowes Amateur Operatic & Dramatic Society; Ilkley Players; Yorkshire Air Ambulance; Gilbert White's House & The Oates Museum; The Calyx; Chesil Theatre Appeal, Winchester; Hampshire & Wight Trust for Maritime Archaeology; Garden Writers' Guild; Vice Patron: Jubilee Sailing Trust; President: Gardening for Disabled Trust, 1989-, Telephones for the Blind, 1993-; The London Children's Flower Society; Perennial; Vice President: Butterfly Conservation; Brent Lodge Bird & Wildlife Trust; Morriston Orpheus Choir; Ambassador, The Prince's Trust; Honorary Patron of the Friends, Castle Mey; Trustee, National Maritime Museum. Publications: More than 40 books including: Mr MacGregor (novel), 1998; The Last Lighthouse Keeper (novel), 1999; Animal Instincts (novel), 2000; Only Dad (novel), 2001; How to Be a Gardener, 2002; Trowel and Error (memoirs), 2002; Royal Gardeners, 2003; Rosie (novel), 2004; Fill My Stocking (Christmas anthology), 2005; The Gardener's Year, 2005. Honours: Freeman, City of London; RHS Gold Medal, Chelsea Flower Show, 1985; Yorkshire Man of Year, 1997; Hon DSc, Bradford, 1999; Hon DUniv, Essex, 1999, Leeds Metropolitan, 2003; Variety Club Television Personality of the Year, 1999; MBE, 2000. Deputy Lieutenant, Hampshire, 2001; Victoria Medal of Honour, Royal Horticultural Society, 2004. Memberships: Royal Horticultural Society; Garden Writers Guild; Fellow, Institute of Horticulture; Fellow, City & Guilds of London Institute; Worshipful Company of Gardeners; Royal London Yacht Club; Lord's Taverners. Address: c/o Caroline Mitchell, Colt Hill House, Colt Hill, Odiham, Hampshire RG29 1AL, England.

TIWARI Ashok Kumari, Scientist. Education: MSc, Zoology, Gorakhapur University, 1985; PhD, Zoology, JRF & SRF, Institute of Medical Sciences, Banaras Hindu University, Varanasi, 1987-92; RA (CSIR), Banaras Hindu University, Varanasi, 1993-98; CSIR Fellow, 1998-2001; Scientist E-1, 2001-06, Scientist E-II, 2006-, Indian Institute of Chemical Technology, Hyderabad. Publications: Over 50 articles and citations; Numerous lectures and abstracts in conference; More than 20 patents. Honours: 1st Prize, IUPAC international conference on biodiversity and natural products: chemistry and medical applications, 2004; 2nd Prize, Rastriya Vigyan Sangoshthi, 2005; Best Poster Award, INDO-US CCNP-2006; Listed in international biographical dictionaries. Memberships: Associate Editor, African Journal of Pharmacy and Pharmacological Research; Editorial Board Member: International Journal of Nutrition and Metabolism; Asian Journal of Experimental Biological Sciences; Pharmacologia; Faculty, African Journal of Food Science; Life Member: Indian Society for Atherosclerosis Research; Indian Society for Comparative Animal Physiology; Banaras Hindu University Old Students Association. Address: Pharmacology Division, Indian Institute of Chemical Technology, Hyderabad 500 007, India. E-mail: astiwari@yahoo.com

TJIPTOHERIJANTO Prijono, b. 3 April 1948, Malang, Indonesia. Professor. m. Yumiko Mizuno, 1978, 1 son, 1 daughter. Education: BA, Economics, University of Indonesia, 1974; MA, Economics, University of the Philippines, 1977; PhD, Economics, University of Hawaii, USA, 1981. Appointments: Professor of Economics, University of Indonesia, 1998-; Head, National Civil Service Agency, RI, 2000-02; Secretary to Vice President, RI, 2002-05. Publications: Asian Urbanization in the New Millennium, 2005; Building Trust in Government, 2010. Honours: Among 400 Distinguished Scientists in Indonesia. Memberships: Indonesian Economists Association; Philippines Economics Society. E-mail: prijonoth@yahoo.com

TOBIAS Phillip Vallentine, b. 14 October 1925, Durban, Natal, South Africa. Retired University Professor. Education: BSc, 1946, BSc Hons, 1947, MBBCh, 1950, PhD, 1953, DSc, 1967, University of Witwatersrand, Johannesburg. Appointments: Lecturer, 1951-52, Senior Lecturer, 1953-58, Professor, 1959-93, Head of Department, 1959-90, Dean of Faculty of Medicine, 1980-82, Member of Council, 1971-74, 1975-84, Professor Emeritus, 1994-; Honorary Professorial Research Fellow, 1994-, School of Anatomical Sciences, University of Witwatersrand; Past Chairman, Kalahari Research Committee; Past Director, Palaeo-Anthropology Research Unit; Past Director, Sterkfontein Research Unit; Past President, International Association of Human Biologists; Former President, Royal Society of South Africa; Founder and Sometime President, Institute for the Study of Mankind in Africa, Anatomical Society of Southern Africa, South African Society for Quaternary Research; Former President, South African Science Writers Association. Publications: Some 1200 including 40 books, 90 chapters in books; Notable works Chromosomes, sex cells and evolution in a mammal, 1956; Australopithecus boisei, 1967; The Bushmen, San Hunters and Herders of the Kalahari, 1978; Hominid Evolution Past Present and Future, 1985; The Brain in Hominid Evolution, 1971; Man's Anatomy, 1963-88; The Meaning of Race, 1961-72; Homo habilis, 1991; Humanity from African Naissance to Coming Millennia, 2001; Into the Past, 2005; Tobias in Conversation, 2008. Honours: Rivers Memorial Medal, 1978; Balzan Prize, 1987; LSB Leakey Prize, 1991; Carmel Award of Merit, 1992; Order of Meritorious Service of South Africa, 1992; Fellow of the Royal Society London, 1996; Charles Darwin Lifetime Achievement Award, 1997; Commander of the National Order of Merit of France, 1998; Order of the Southern Cross of South Africa, 1999; Hrdlicka Medal, 1999; Commander of the Order of Merit of Italy, 2000; UNESCO Medal, 2001; ISMS Medal, 2001; Honorary Cross for Science and Arts, First Class, Austrian Federal Government, 2002; Fellowship Art and Science of Medicine Gold Medal, 2007; Walter Sisulu Special Award, City of Johannesburg, 2007; Living Legends Awards, 2009; NRF President's Lifetime Achievement Award, 2010. Memberships: Academy of Science of South Africa; Royal Society, London; Royal Society of South Africa; South African Medical Association; South African Archaeological Society; American Association of Physical Anthropologists; National Academy of Sciences, USA; American Philosophical Society; American Academy of Arts and Sciences; American Anthropological Association; Royal Anthropological Institute of Great Britain and Ireland; Royal College of Physicians, London; Linnean Society, London; South African Institute of Race Relations; Anatomical Society of Southern Africa; Anatomical Societies (hon) of USA, Great Britain and Ireland, Canada, Israel; South African Dental Association (hon); Institute for Human Evolution, Wits University. Address: School of Anatomical Sciences, University of the Witwatersrand Medical School, 7 York Road, Parktown, Wits 2050, Johannesburg, South Africa. E-mail: phillip.tobias@wits.ac.za

TOLER Michael Morgan, b. 12 March 1950, Oklahoma City, Oklahoma, USA. Colonel (US Army, retired); Educator; Industrial Manager; International Defence Consultant. m. Mary Elizabeth Creagh, 3 sons. Education: Peacock Military Academy, San Antonio, Texas, 1968; BS, General Engineering and International Affairs, US Military Academy at West Point, New York, 1972; US Army Command and General Staff College, 1983; MS, Systems Management, University of Southern California, Los Angeles, 1986; MS, Strategic Studies, US Army War College, 1997. Appointments: Commissioned US Army 1972, served for 28 years active duty as an Infantry officer at every level from platoon to Department of Defence, in Europe, Africa and Pacific Theatres of Operation, selected for command 6 times, twice as colonel, decorated combat veteran; UNTAF Director of Acquisition and International Support for Operation Restore Hope in Somalia, Inspector General, charter member of the Army Acquisition Corps, Contracting Officer for over 10 years, West Point Academy Professor of Acquisition and Assistant Professor of Geography; Program Manager at General Electric Aerospace (now Lockheed Martin), Boston, Massachusetts; Adjunct Professor, Defence Acquisition Middlesex College, Massachusetts, 1988-89; North American Operations Analyst and Program Manager, Danka Services International, Canada and NYC World Trade Centre, 1999-2001; International Defence

Reform Advisor to the Ministries of Defence of Bulgaria, Bosnia-Herzegovina, and Montenegro, 2002-10; Visiting US Professor of Defence Acquisition, G S Rakovsky Defence and Staff College, Sofia, Bulgaria, 2002-05; Consultant, Centre for the Army Profession and Ethics, West Point, New York, 2010; Professional Program Manager; Contracting Manager; Systems Engineer/Analyst; Material Acquisition Manager; USMA Instructor; Deming/ISO Total Quality Manager. Publications: Numerous articles in professional journals. Honours: Ancient Order of St Barbara Medal; Secretary of the Army Procurement Savings Award; Several military medals including US Army Legion of Merit; Listed in international biographical dictionaries. Memberships: Association of Graduates, US Military Academy; Association of United States Army; Army Acquisition Corps; National Contract Management Association; Academy of Political Science; Army Athletic Association. Address: 30 Waterview Terrace, New Windsor, NY 12553, USA.

TÖLGYESI Tamás, b. 25 December 1979, Budapest, Hungary. Linguist; Language Educator. m. Ildikó Szilágyi. Education: MA, Czech Language and Literature, 2005, MA, German Language and Literature, 2005, PhD, Linguistics, 2009, Pázmány Péter Catholic University. Appointments: Assistant Professor, Pázmány Péter Catholic University, 2006-; Lecturer, University of Szeged, 2009-. Publications: Das Kasussystem im Deutschen und Tschechischen, 2009; Lexikálni germanismy v dnesni cestine, 2009. Honours: Pro Patria et Scientia Award. Memberships: Hungarian Academy of Sciences; Saint Adalbert Central Europe Research Group; Mitteleuopäischer Germanistenverband. Address: Department of West Slavic Studies, Faculty of Humanities and Social Sciences, Pázmány Péter Catholic University, Egytem utca 1, Piliscsaba, 2087, Hungary. E-mail: tolgyi@gmail.com Website: www.btk.ppke.hu/english

TOMA Stefan, b. 11 September 1937, Velke Uherce, Czechoslovakia. Chemist; Professor. m. Viera Kaliska, 1 son, 1 daughter. Education: MSc, 1960, PhD, 1965, DSc, 1982, Comenius University, Bratislava. Appointments: Assistant Professor, 1960-69, Associate Professor, 1969-83, Professor, 1983-, Dean, Faculty of Natural Sciences, 1986-91, Comenius University, Bratislava. Publications: Over 234 research papers in specialised CC journals; Over 1,700 citations. Honours: Golden Medal of Comenius University; Golden Medal of Slovak Chemical Society; Hanus Medal of Czech Chemical Society. Memberships: Slovak Chemical Society; Czech Chemical Society; American Chemical Society; The Royal Society of Chemistry. Address: H Melikovej 4, SK-84105 Bratislava, Slovakia. E-mail: toma@fns.uniba.sk

TOMALIN Claire, b. 20 June 1933, London, England. Author. m. (1) Nicholas Osborne Tomalin, deceased 1973, 2 sons (1 deceased), 3 daughters (1 deceased), (2) Michael Frayn, 1993. Education: MA, Newnham College, Cambridge, 1954. Appointment: Literary Editor, New Statesman, 1974-77; Literary Editor, The Sunday Times, London, 1979-86. Publications: The Life and Death of Mary Wollstonecroft, 1974; Shelley and His World, 1980; Parents and Children, 1981; Katherine Mansfield: A Secret Life, 1987; The Invisible Woman: The Story of Nelly Teran and Charles Dickens, 1990; The Winter Wife, 1991; Mrs Jordan's Professions, 1994; Jane Austin: A Life, 1997; Maurice by Mary Shelley, 1998; Several Strangers: writing from three decades, 1999; Samuel Pepys: The Unequalled Self, 2002; Thomas Hardy: The Time-Torn Man, 2006; Exhibitions: Mrs Jordan, English Heritage Kenwood, 1995; Hyenas in Petticoats: Mary Wollstonecraft and Mary Shelley, Wordsworth Trust and National Portrait Gallery, 1997-98; Play: The Winter Wife, 1991. Honours: Whitbread First Book Prize, 1974; James Tait Black Memorial Prize, 1990; Hawthornden Prize, 1991; NCR Prize, 1991; Los Angeles Times Book Prize, 2002; Whitbread Biography Award, 2002; Whitbread Book of the Year, 2002; British Book Awards Biography of the Year (shortlist), 2003; Samuel Pepys Award, 2003; British Book Awards Biography of the Year (shortlist), 2007. Membership: PEN, Vice-president, 1998; Member, London Library Committee, 1997-2000; Advisory Committee for the Arts, Humanities and Social Sciences, British Library, 1997-; Council, Royal Society of Literature, 1997-2000. Address: 57 Gloucester Crescent, London NW1 7EG, England. E-mail: clairetomalin@dial.pipex.com

TOMASZEWSKI Nicholas Eugene, b. 5 June 1943, Canterbury, Kent, England. Senior Lecturer. m. Muriel Rose Mogg, 1963, 1 son, 3 daughters. Education: Diploma in Welfare, Canterbury College, 1994; Certificate in Christian Theology, University of Kent, 1997; Licence to Exercise the Office of Reader, South East Institute for Theological Education, 1997; Further and Adult Education Teachers' Certificate, South Kent College, 2001; Advanced Certificate in Education, Canterbury Christ Church University, 2002. Appointments: Student Psychiatric Nurse Training, St Augustine's Psychiatric Hospital, Canterbury, 1960-61; Service with Royal Navy, 1961-64; Welfare Manager, Associated British Foods, Broadstairs, 1970-90; Senior Residential Social Worker, Resolutions (UK) Ltd, Faversham, 1990-98; Head of House, Kent Social Services Registered Care Home, Whitstable, 1998-2000; Lecturer, 2000-02, Advanced Practitioner, 2002-03, Staff Mentor, 2002-08, Senior Lecturer, 2003-, Health and Care Division, Lecturer, Personal Social Development Skills, 2011-, K College (previously known as South Kent College). Publications: The Deal Scene, 1977; Deal Before the Conquest, 1978; 800 Years of Worship at St Leonard's Church, Deal, Kent, 1980; Spruckelham: Near Deal, a lost 'ham', 1979; Numerous articles in professional journals and student course handbooks. Honours: Doctor of Arts honoris causa, USA, 1997; Member, Institute of Welfare, 1998; Member, Institute for Learning, 2004; Licentiate, City and Guilds Institute of London; Member, Institute of Leadership and Management, 2007; Listed in international biographical dictionaries. Memberships: Kent Archaeological Society; Alumni, University of Kent, Canterbury; Alumni, Canterbury Christ Church University; Member, Catholic Family History Society; Member, Guild of One Name Studies; Latin Mass Society. Address: 1 Ardent Road, Whitfield, Dover, Kent, CT16 2GH, England. E-mail: nick@tomaszewski.plus.com

TOMESCU Ioan, b. 5 November 1942, Ploiești, Romania. Professor of Computer Science. m. Marioara Tomescu, 1 son, 1 daughter. Education: BA (Hons), Computer Science and Mathematics, 1965, PhD, Computer Science, 1971, Bucharest University, Romania. Appointments: Assistant Professor, 1965-72, Senior Lecturer, 1972-90, Professor, 1990-, Department of Computer Science, Bucharest University, Romania; Visiting Professor: The University of Tirana, Albania, 1974, Auckland University, New Zealand, 1995; School of Mathematical Sciences, G C University, Lahore, Pakistan, 2005-11; Visiting Senior Research Fellow, National University of Singapore, 2002. Publications: About 140 research papers in combinatorics and graph theory published in scientific journals including: Discrete Mathematics; Journal of Combinatorial Theory (B); Combinatorica; Journal of Graph Theory; Theoretical Computer Science (A); Introduction to Combinatorics; Colette's, London and Wellingborough; Problems in Combinatorics and Graph Theory, J Wiley, New

York. Honours: Prize for Applied Mathematics, First Balkan Mathematics Competition for Young Researchers, Bucharest, 1971; Gheorghe Tzitzeica Mathematics Prize, Romanian Academy, 1975. Memberships: American Mathematical Society; Honorary President, Romanian Mathematical Society; Corresponding Member, Romanian Academy; Member, International Academy of Mathematical Chemistry. Address: Sos Colentina nr 4, Sc B, Ap. 64, 021173 Bucharest, Romania. E-mail: ioan@fmi.unibuc.ro

TOMLINSON Stephen, b. 20 December 1944, Farnworth, England. Physician; Professor; University Officer. m. Christine Margaret, 2 daughters. Education: Hayward Grammar School, Bolton; MB ChB (Hons), 1968, MD, 1976, University of Sheffield Medical School; MRCP, 1971; FRCP, 1982. Appointments: Professor of Medicine, 1985-2001, Dean of Faculty of Medicine, Dentistry & Nursing and Medical School, 1993-99, Manchester; Vice Chancellor & Provost, University of Wales College of Medicine, 2001-04; Deputy Vice Chancellor, Cardiff University, 2004-06; Provost, Cardiff University, 2006-10; Professor Emeritus, Cardiff University of Medicine, 2010-. Publications: Over 150 publications of stimulus-response coupling in endocrine cells and intracellular signalling; Papers on organisation and delivery of health care. Honours: Founder Fellow, Academy of Medical Sciences, 1998; CBE, 2007. Memberships: Association of Physicians of Great Britain & Ireland; Tropical Health & Education Trust; Ashwales. Address: Ty Gwyn, St Andrews Major, Dinas Powys, Vale of Glamorgan, CF64 4HD, Wales. E-mail: tomlinsons@cf.ac.uk

TOMLINSON, Hon Mr Justice, Hon Sir Stephen Miles, b. 29 March 1952, Wolverhampton, England. Justice of the High Court. m. Joanna Greig, 1 son, 1 daughter. Education: Scholar, Worcester College, Oxford; Eldon Law Scholar, MA; Called to the Bar, Inner Temple, 1974. Appointments: Barrister in practice, 1975-2000; QC, 1988; A Recorder of the Crown Court, 1995-2000; Judge of the High Court of Justice, 2000. Honour: Knighted, 2000. Address: Royal Courts of Justice, Strand, London WC1A 2LL, England.

TOMOHISA Kato, b. 26 September 1970, Nagoya, Japan. Researcher. m. Yukiko, 1 son, 1 daughter. Education: PhD, Osaka University, 2001. Appointments: Researcher, Takara Bio Inc, Otsu, 2001-04; Researcher, Kaneta Co, Osaka, 2004-. Publications: Numerous articles in professional journals. Memberships: Chemical Society of Japan. Address: 2-20 Nishityuzyo-cho, Ibaraki, 567-0887, Japan.

TONIOLLI Marco, b. 26 March 1932, Bressanone, Italy. Professor. m. Annacarla Rossi, 1 son, 1 daughter. Education: Degree in Political Science, 1956; Maturity Liceo Scientifico, 1961. Appointments: Unpaid Assistant, 1957-62; University Lecturer, 1964-72; Professor, Political Economics, 1972-; Professor, 2007-. Publications: L'esportazione di Industria, 1968; Econonia Politica-microeconomia, 1977; Indebitanentopubblico e soluzione scientifica, 1994; Publicist, Libero (daily paper), 1996-2002. Honours: President, Board of Director, Nuova Capica Ltd, 1980-89; Member, Ateneo Veneto, 1996-; Senator, 1996-2001; Auditor, 2005-; President, Fenice Foundation, 2007-. Address: Via Enna 2, 35100 Padova, Italy.

TONKOVICH Teresa Zenovia Maria, b. 30 July 1952, Toronto, Canada. Institutional Administrator; Gerontologist. m. John Tonkovich, deceased, 2 sons, 2 daughters. Education: BA, Psychology and Sociology, University of Toronto, Ontario; Certified Administrator, Homes for the Aged, McMaster University, Hamilton, Ontario. Appointments: Executive Administrator (Toronto), 1990-2009, Executive Director (Toronto and Mississauga), 2009-, Ivan Franko Homes (Ukrainian Home for the Aged), Toronto and Mississauga. Honours: 2000 Notable American Women; Personalities of the Americas; International Leaders in Achievement; Community Leaders in Achievement; Personalities of America; Directory of Distinguished Americans; 5000 Personalities of the World; International Book of Honour; McMaster Alumni News; Biographical Roll of Honor; Community Leader of America; Canadian Merit Award; Outstanding Young Woman of '78; International Who's Who of Business Women; Lifetime Deputy Governor, ABI; Woman of the Year, 2010. Memberships: Ontario Gerontological Association; Canadian Association of Gerontology. Address: 3584 Cherrington Cres, Mississauga, Ontario L5L 5C5, Canada. E-mail: tzmtonkovich@hotmail.com

TONTI-FILIPPINI Nicholas Antony, b. 5 July 1956, Melbourne, Australia. m. Mary Walsh, 2 sons, 2 daughters. Education: BA (Hons), MA, Monash; PhD, (Melb), FHERDSA. Appointments: Australia's First Hospital Ethicist, St Vincent's Hospital, Melbourne, 1982-90; Associate Dean and Head of Bioethics, JPII Institute. Publications: Religious and Secular Death: A Parting of the Ways, 2010; Trade in Human Tissue Products, 2011; About Bioethics, 2011. Honours: Knight Commander of St Gregory the Great. Memberships: Australian Association of Catholic Bioethicists; International Association of Catholic Bioethicists. Address: John Paul II Institute, PO Box 146, East Melbourne, VIC 3107, Australia.

TOPOLOV Vitaly Yuryevich, b. 8 November 1961, Rostov-on-Don, Russia. University Professor. Education: Physicist and Educator, Honours degree, Department of Physics, 1984, Candidate of Sciences, 1987, Doctor of Sciences, 2000, Physics and Mathematics, Rostov State University. Appointments: Research Scientist, Institute of Physics, Rostov State University, 1987-91; Senior Lecturer, 1991-92, Associate Professor, 1992-2000, Professor, 2000-, Department of Physics, Rostov State University; Visiting Scientist: Moscow State University, Russia, 1989; University of Saarland, Germany, 1994-95; Aachen University of Technology - RWTH Aachen, Germany, 1998; Karlsruhe Research Center, Germany, 2002, 2003-04; University of Bath, UK, 2006-07; University of Rome "Tor Vergata", Italy, 2008; Professor, Department of Physics, Southern Federal University (formerly Rostov State University), 2006-. Publications: Over 330 scientific publications; More than 40 teaching-methodical publications. Honours: Special award, International Science Foundation, 1993; Soros Associate Professor title and awards, International Soros Science-Educational Program and the Open Society Institute, 1997, 1998, 2000 and 2001; Excellence Award, International Symposium on Ferroelectric Domains, China, 2000; Various prizes for teaching, 2006, Best Research Work, 2008, High level of citation of scientific papers, 2009, Southern Federal University; Listed, Active Russian Scientists, 2000-06, 2001-07, 2002-08, 2003-09, 2003-09; Honorary co-worker, Higher Professional Education of the Russian Federation, 2008. Memberships: Corresponding Member, Russian Academy of Natural Science. Address: Department of Physics, Southern Federal University, 5 Zorge Street, 344090, Rostov-on-Don, Russia. E-mail: vutopolov@sfedu.ru Website: www.phys.sfedu.ru

TOPOLSKI Daniel, b. 4 June 1945, London, England. Freelance Writer; Broadcaster; Photojournalist; Motivational Speaker. m. Susan Gilbert, 1 son, 2 daughters. Education: Lycée Français, London; Westminster School; BA, Geography, 1967, DipSoc, Anthropology, 1968, MA, 1970, New College,

Oxford. Appointments: Writer and TV broadcaster on travel and sport; BBC TV Researcher and Producer, 1969-73; TV and Radio Presenter and BBC Olympics Commentator, 1982-; Expeditions: Brazil, 1963; Iran (Marco Polo), 1973-74; Travel in Africa, North and South America, India, Himalayas, China, Middle East, SE Asia, and Australia. Publications: Muzungu: One Man's Africa, 1976; Travels with my Father: Journey through South America, 1983; Boat Race, 1985; True Blue (made into feature film, 1996), 1989; Henley: the Regatta, 1989; Numerous articles in professional and popular journals. Honours: Rowing Competitor: Boat Race, Oxford, 1967, 1968; World Championships, 1969-78 (Gold Medal, 1977); 4 victories, Henley Regatta; Rowing Coach of Oxford Boat Race Crew, 1973-87 (12 victories, record 10 in a row); Oxford Coaching Consultant, 1995-; Coached World Championships and Olympics, 1979, 1980, 1982, 1984; Churchill Fellow, 1980; Sports Book of the Year (True Blue), 1991; Radio Travel Programme of the Year Award for Topolski's Travels, 1993. Memberships: Churchill Fellow; Henley Steward; Leander Club; London RC. Address: 69 Randolph Avenue, London W9 1DW, England.

TORRANCE Sam, b. 24 August 1953, Largs, Scotland. Golfer. m. Suzanne, 1 son, 2 daughters. Appointments: Professional Golfer, 1970-; Has played in 8 Ryder Cups and represented Scotland on numerous occasions; Winner, Scottish PGA Championship, 1978, 1980, 1985, 1991, 1993; Member, Dunhill Cup Team (8 times); World Cup Team (11 times); Hennessy Cognac Cup Team (5 times); Double Diamond Team (3 times); Captain, European Team in Ashai Glass Four Tours Championships, Adelaide, 1991; Captain, Ryder Cup Team, 2001; Winner of 28 tournaments world-wide since 1972 including: Italian Open, 1987; Germany Masters, 1990; Hersey Open, 1991; Kronenbourg Open, 1993; Catalan Open, 1993; Honda Open, 1993; Hamburg Open, 1993; British Masters, 1995; French Open, 1998; Played US Senior Tour, 2003-04; Returned to European Senior Tour, 2004-. Publications: Sam: The Autobiography of Sam Torrance, 2003. Honours: OBE, 2003. Address: c/o Parallel Murray Management, 56 Ennismore Gardens, Knightsbridge, London SW7 1AJ, England. Website: www.samtorrance.com

TORRES FRAGOSO Jaime, b. 7 September 1965, Puebla, Mexico. Social Studies Educator; Researcher. m. Rosa Jimenez Gonzalez, 2005, 1 daughter. Education: B, Industrial Engineering, University Cuauhtemoc, Puebla, 1989; MPA, Centre for Economic Research and Education, Mexico City, 1996; Diploma, Corporate Finance, ITAM, 1999; PhD, Public Administration, National Autonomous University of Mexico, Mexico City, 2003. Appointments: Consultant, Guaymas-integrated port authority Administration, Portuaria Integral, Mexico, 1996-97; Consultant, Vallarta Integrated Port, Puerto Vallarta, Mexico, 1996-97; Financial Studies Manager, Central Division of Ports and Merchant Navy, Mexico Coordinación, General Puertos Marina Mercante Secretaría Commission, Transports-Ministry Communication and Transport, Mexico City, 1997-99; Deputy Director, Planning Institute, National Mujeres-Nat Women's Institute, Mexico City, 2005; Professor, Researcher, University of Istmo, 2005-; Head, Research Group, Public Management, 2005-; National Researcher, National Researchers System, Consejo National Ciencia, National Technical National Council of Science and Technology, System of National Investigadores, Mexico City, 2006-; Head, Department of Public Administration, 2009-. Honours: Special Award, Colombian Association of Administration Facilities, 2007. Memberships: Active Transparency International Mexico Chapter, Mexico City; Ibero-American Network of Experts, Quality Management and Public Administration, CEDDET-MAP-INAP, Madrid; Centre of Latin American Administration; Desarrollo-Latin American Central Administration Development; Ibero-American Network of Experts in Quality Management and Public Administration. Address: University Istmo, Carretera a Chihuitán Ixtepec Oaxaca 70110, Mexico. E-mail: jaimetorres@bianni.unistmo.edu.mx

TORSHIN Alexander, b. 27 November 1953, Kamchatskykray, Russia. Senator; Lawyer. m. Nina, 2 daughters. Education: High Law School, Moscow, 1978; Moscow State University, 1989. Appointments: Senator, RF Council of Federation, 2001-. Honours: Honour Decoration. Memberships: United Russia Party. Address: 26 B Dmitrovka st, Moscow 103426, Russian Federation. E-mail: senator@umail.ru

TORTOPIDIS Ioannis, b. 25 February 1970, Thessaloniki, Greece. Electronic Engineer. Education: Department of Electrical & Computer Engineering, Aristotle University of Thessaloniki, 1994; Postgraduate course, Automation Systems, National Technical University of Athens, 2001; PhD, Dynamics and Control of Space Systems, Department of Mechanical Engineering, 2003-, National Technical University of Athens. Appointments: Teaching Assistant, Department of Automation, Alexander Technological Educational Institute, Thessaloniki, 1997-98; Programmer, B Substitution Treatment Unit, 1998-2000; Directorate General, Air Navigation, Hellenic Civil Aviation Authority, 2000-. Publications: Numerous articles in scientific journals. Honours: Scholar of State Scholarships Foundation, 2003-06; Thomaidio Award, 2005, 2006. Memberships: Technical Chamber, Greece; Life Fellow, IBA. Address: Panourgia 1, 546 29 Thessaloniki, Greece. E-mail: itortopidis@gmail.com

TORVILL Jayne, b. 7 October 1957, England. Ice Skater. m. Philip Christensen, 1990. Career: British Pair Skating Champion with M Hutchinson, 1971; Insurance Clerk, 1974-80; With Christopher Dean: British Ice Dance Champion, 1978-83, 1994; European Ice Dance Champion, 1981-82, 1984, 1994; World Ice Dance Champion, 1981-84; World Professional Ice Dance Champion, 1984, 1985, 1990, 1995, 1996; Olympic Ice Dance Champion, 1984; Olympic Ice Dance Bronze Medal, 1994; Tours include: Australia and New Zealand, 1984; Royal Variety Performance, London, 1984; World tour with own company of international skaters, 1985; Guest artists with IceCapades, 1987; World tour with company of skaters from Soviet Union, 1988; Guest of South Australian Government, 1991; Great Britain tour with company of Ukraine skaters, 1992; Torvill & Dean, Face the Music, World Tour, UK, Australia and North America, 1994; Stars on Ice Tour, USA and Canada, 1997-98; Torvill and Dean Ice Adventures, UK, 1997-98; Television: Path of Perfection, 1984; Fire & Ice, 1986; World Tour (video), 1988; Bladerunners (documentary), 1991; Great Britain Tour (TV special and video), 1992; The Artistry of Torvill and Dean, 1994; Face the Music (video), 1995; Torvill and Dean: The Story So Far (video), 1996; Bach Cello Suite (with Yo-Yo Ma), 1996; Dancing on Ice, 2006- Publications: with Christopher Dean: Torvill and Dean: Autobiography, 1984; Torvill and Dean: Facing the Music, 1995. Honours: MBE, 1981; BBC Sports Personality of the Year with Christopher Dean, 1983-84; Olympic Ice Dance Gold Medal, 1984; Figure Skating Hall of Fame with Christopher Dean, 1989; Olympic Ice Dance Bronze Medal, 1994; Hon MA, Nottingham Trent University, 1994; OBE, 2000. Address: c/o Sue Young, PO Box 32, Heathfield, East Sussex TN21 0BW, England.

TOTTERDELL Michael S, b. 21 September 1950, Woodford, Essex, England. Academic; Educationalist; Researcher. m. Rebecca Helen Burdge. Education: BA (Hons), Theology & Philosophy, 1982, PGCE, 1983, MA (Distinction), Education, 1988, University of London; MID, Historical Policy Studies, University of Strasbourg, 1998. Appointments: Military Service, HM Armed Forces, The Parachute Regiment, 1970-79; Religious Studies Teacher, Dr Challoner's Grammar School, Buckinghamshire, 1983; Religious Education Teacher, Cheshunt School, Hertfordshire, 1983-88; Senior Teacher, Henrietta Barnett School, London, 1988-90; Lecturer in Education, 1991-93; PGCE Course Director, 1993-99, Assistant Dean of Teacher Education, 1999-2001, Dean of Teacher Education, 2001-03, Institute of Education, University of London; Professor & Director, later Dean & Pro-Vice Chancellor Designate, Institute of Education, Manchester Metropolitan University, 2004-07; Professor, Executive Dean, Faculty of Education, Pro-Vice Chancellor, University of Plymouth, 2007-10; Vice Rector for Research and Graduate Studies, University of Marrin Baleti, 2010-. Publications: 20 articles in academic and professional journals; 5 chapters in edited books; 1 co-authored book. Honours: Mentioned in Dispatches, UN Peacekeeping Force, Cyprus, 2004. Memberships: American Educational Research Association; British Educational Research Association; European Educational Research Association; Churchill Fellow, 1992; Chair, Universities Council for the Education of Teachers, 2005-08; Fellow, Institute of Administrative Management; Executive Board Member, Leading Aspect Award, 2008-10; Board of Governors, Kelly College, 2010-; International Fellow at Large, Phi Delta Kappa; Fellow, Royal Society for the encouragement of the Arts, Manufactures and Commerce; Princeton Premier Business Leaders and Professionals Registry. Address: Sweet Briars, 9 Crokers Meadow, Bovey Tracey, Newton Abbot, Devon, TQ13 9HL, England. E-mail: ms.totterdell@mypostoffice.co.uk

TOWNES Charles Hard, b. 28 July 1915, Greenville, South Carolina, USA. Physicist. m. Frances Brown, 4 daughters. Education: BA, BS, Furman University, 1935; MA, Duke University, 1937; PhD, California Institute of Technology, 1939. Appointments: Bell Telephone Laboratories, 1939-47; Associate Professor, 1948-50, Professor, 1950-61, Chairman, Department of Physics, 1952-55, Columbia University; Executive Director, Columbia Radiation Laboratory, 1950-52; Vice-President, Director of Research, Institute for Defense Analyses, 1959-61; Provost, Professor of Physics, 1961-66, Institute Professor, 1966-67, Massachusetts Institute of Technology; University Professor, 1967-86, Emeritus Professor, 1986-94, Professor, Graduate School, 1994-, University of California, Berkeley. Publications: Books: Microwave Spectroscopy, 1955; Making Waves, 1995; How the Laser Happened. Adventures of a Scientist, 1999. Honours: Thomas Young Medal and Prize, Institute of Physics and The Physical Society, England, 1963; Nobel Prize for Physics, 1964; Medal of Honour, Institute of Electrical and Electronics Engineers, 1966; Wilhelm Exner Award, Austria, 1970; Niels Bohr International Gold Medal, 1979; Officier de la Légion d'Honneur, France, 1990; Rabindranath Tagore Birth Centenary Plaque of the Asiatic Society, 1999; Founders Award of the National Academy of Engineering, 2000; Lomonosov Gold Medal of the Russian Academy of Science, 2001; Templeton Prize, 2005; Vannevar Bush Award, 2006; 33 honorary doctorates, US and abroad; Numerous prizes, awards, lectureships, other honours. Memberships: Fellow, American Physical Society, Council, 1959-62, 1965-71, President, 1967; Life Fellow, Institute of Electrical and Electronics Engineers; National Academy of Sciences; American Philosophical Society; Royal Society of London; National Academy of Engineering; Many more. Address: Department of Physics, University of California, Berkeley, CA 94720, USA. E-mail: cht@ssl.berkeley.edu

TOWNSHEND Peter Dennis Blandford, 19 May 1945, Isleworth, London, England. Musician (guitar) Composer; Publisher; Author. m. Karen Astley, 1968 (divorced), 1 son, 2 daughters. Education: Ealing Art College. Career: Member, UK rock group The Who, 1964-84; Solo artiste, 1979-; Appearances include: National Jazz and Blues festival, 1965, 1966, 1969; Monterey Pop Festival, 1967; Rock At The Oval, 1972; Farewell tour, 1982-83; Live Aid, Wembley, 1985; Reunion tour, 1989; Films include: Tommy; Quadrophenia; The Kids Are Alright; Owner Eel Pie Recording Ltd, 1972-; Established Eel Pie (bookshops and publishing), 1972-; Established Meher Baba Oceanic (UK archival library), 1976-81; Editor, Faber & Faber, 1983-. Compositions include rock operas, Tommy, 1969; Quadrophenia, 1973; Numerous songs for The Who. Recordings: Albums: with The Who: My Generation, 1965; A Quick One, 1966; The Who Sell Out, 1968; Direct Hits, 1968; Tommy, 1969; Live At Leeds, 1970; Who's Next, 1971; Meaty Beefy Big And Bouncy, 1971; Quadrophenia, 1973; Odds And Sods, 1974; The Who By Numbers, 1975; The Story Of The Who, 1976; Who Are You, 1978; The Kids Are Alright (film soundtrack), 1979; Face Dances, 1981; Hooligans, 1982; It's Hard, 1982; Rarities Vols 1 and 2, 1983; The Singles, 1984; Who's Last, 1984; Who's Missing, 1987; Who's Better Who's Best, 1988; Joined Together, 1990; 30 Years of Maximum R&B, 1994; Solo albums: Who Came First, 1972; Rough Mix, 1977; Empty Glass, 1980; All The Best Cowboys Have Chinese Eyes, 1982; Scoop, 1983; White City, 1985; Another Scoop, 1987; The Iron Man, 1989; Psychoderelict, 1993; The Best Of Pete Townshend, 1996; Pete Townshend Live, 1999; Hit singles include: with The Who: I Can't Explain, 1965; Anyway Anyhow Anywhere, 1965; My Generation, 1965; Substitute, 1966; I'm A Boy, 1966; Happy Jack, 1967; Pictures Of Lily, 1967; I Can See For Miles, 1967; Pinball Wizard, 1969; See Me Feel Me, 1970; Won't Get Fooled Again, 1970; Join Together, 1972; Who Are You, 1978; You Better You Bet, 1981; Contributor, Sun City, Artists Against Apartheid, 1985. Publication: Horse's Neck, 1986. Honours include: BRIT Lifetime Achievement Award, 1983; Living Legend Award, International Rock Awards, 1991; with The Who: Gold Ticket, Madison Square Garden, 1979; Ivor Novello Award, Contribution to British Music, 1982; British Phonographic Industry Award, 1983; BRIT Award, Contribution to British Music, 1988; Inducted into Rock'n'Roll Hall of Fame, 1990; Tony Award for Tommy score, 1993; Grammy Award for original cast recording Tommy, 1993; Dora Mavor Moore Award for Tommy in Toronto, 1994; Olivier Award, Tommy, London, 1997; Q Lifetime Achievement Award for The Who. Address: Box 305, Twickenham TW1 1TT, England.

TRACEY Richard Patrick, b. 8 February 1943, Stratford-upon-Avon, England. Politican; Strategic Marketing Consultant. m. Katharine Gardner, 1 son, 3 daughters. Education: King Edward VI School, Stratford-upon-Avon; LLB (Honours), University of Birmingham. Appointments: Leader Writer, Daily Express, 1964-66; Presenter, current affairs programmes, BBC Radio and TV, 1966-78; Presenter, documentaries, BBC, 1974-76; Justice of the Peace, 1977-; Deputy Chairman, Greater London Conservative Party, 1981-83; Conservative MP, Surbiton, 1983-97; Parlimentary Under Secretary of State for Environment and Minister for Sport, 1985-87; Member, Select Committee on Televising the House of Commons, 1988-91; Committee of Selection,

1992-94; Public Accounts Committee, 1994-97; Conservative London Election Co-ordinator, 1989-93; Chairman, London Conservative MPs, 1990-97; Strategic Marketing and Media Consultant, 1997-2008; Member, Executive Committee, Association of Former MPs, 2007-; Member, London Assembly (Cons), Merton and Wandsworth, 2008-; Metropolitan Police Authority, 2008-10; Mayor's Ambassador for River Transport, 2009-; Vice-Chairman, London Fire and Emergency Planning Authority, 2010-. Publications: The World of Motor Sport (with R Hudson-Evans); Hickstead – The First Twelve Years (with M Clayton). Honours: Freeman, City of London, 1984. Memberships: Fellow, Industry and Parliament Trust, 1985; Vice-Chairman, Special Olympics, UK, 1989-93; Member, IAM, 1993; Chair, ProActive South London Sport England, 2006-08. E-mail: richard.tracey@london.gov.uk

TRAN Quoc, b. 30 April 1978, Vietnam. Martial Arts Instructor. m. Thao Lu, 1 son. Education: BS, Computer Science; PhD, Martial Arts Science. Appointments: USA Representative and Ambassador, Martial Arts Association International; Chief Advisor and USA Representative, International Martials Arts Times Magazine; Advisor for Global Taekwon-Do Federation International; Tyga Martial Arts International Representative; Founder and Chief Instructor of Tran's Combat Martial Arts Academy; Grand Master and Founder, Vietnamese Combat Martial Arts/Wushu (10th Degree Black Belt). Publications: International Martial Arts Times Magazine; International Wushu KungFu Times Magazine; Martial Arts Masters Magazine; TAO Magazine; Chuan Magazine; Taekwondo Times Magazine; Martial Arts Masters of the 21st Century Book Vol I; Martial Arts World Book Vol 2. Honours: London International Martial Arts Hall of Fame; World Head of Family Sokeship Council Hall of Fame; World Karate Union Hall of Fame; Action Martial Arts Magazine's Hall of Honors, The Academy Awards of Martial Arts; United States Martial Arts Hall of Fame; International Martial Arts Times Magazine Hall of Fame; Global Martial Arts Hall of Fame. Memberships: Martial Arts Association International, Germany; Shaolin Temple, China; Tyga Martial Arts International, England; World Head of Family Sokeship Council, USA; Shinja Martial Arts University, USA; Hawaii Martial Arts International Society, USA; United States Head of Family Martial Arts Association, USA; International Mixed Martial Arts Association, Canada. Address: 116 Lasalle Avenue, Hasbrouck Heights, NJ 07604, USA. E-mail: masterquoctran@gmail.com

TRATTNER Carola-Lotty, b. 29 May 1925, Braila, Romania. Senior University Lecturer. m. Egon, 1 son. Education: Certificate, Philology Branch, Onescu College, Bucharest, Romania, 1943-44; MA, Language and Literature, Faculty of Philology, University of Bucharest, 1944-47; Certificate, Postgraduate Pedagogical Seminar, Bucharest, 1947-48; Certificate, Second Pedagogical Seminar, Tel Aviv, Israel, 1974. Appointments: English Assistant, Faculty of Philology, University of Bucharest, 1949-52; English Assistant, Reader, Senior Lecturer, Teacher Trainer and Examiner, Institute of International Relations, Bucharest, 1952-56; English Senior Lecturer, Teacher Trainer and Examiner, Academy of Economic Studies, Bucharest, 1956-73; English Teacher for New Immigrants, Academic Recycling Institute, Ramat Gan, Israel, 1974-77; Lecturer for Communication English, French, Business French, Tel Aviv-Jaffa People's University, Tel Aviv, 1974-86; Teacher, Head of English Department, Teacher Trainer and Examiner, Shazar High School, Bat Yam, Israel, 1976-89; Recycling courses Lecturer, Organiser and Examiner for potential English Teachers, Ministry of Education and Culture, 1989-90; Senior Lecturer, Organiser, Examiner for the Tel Aviv-Jaffa Chamber of Commerce, Ministry of Labour, 1978-2002; Senior Lecturer, Academic College, Holon, 1990-2006; International interpreter (simultaneous translation) for English, French, Romanian, German (more than 100 conventions for the United Nations, FAO, governmental bodies, law/medicine/agriculture/ various technical branches/journalism/youth/women, etc from Oxford to China). Publications: Over 20 books in English, French, Romanian and Hebrew, 1952-2005, among them monolingual and bilingual Dictionaries, general and specific (English-Hebrew, Hebrew-English, Juridical and Economic; English-Romanian and English-Hebrew; Glossaries for foreign trade, banking, diplomatic activities, the textile industry, motor-car technology) and University specialised textbooks; Translation into English of 10th grade World Geography textbook; Collections of texts for translation. Memberships: English Teachers' Association in Israel. Address: 52 Eilat St, 58364 Holon, Israel. E-mail: trattner@post.com

TRATTNER Egon, b. 8 September 1923, Brasov, Romania. Economist. m. Carola Klekner, 1 son. Education: MSc, Economic, Financial and Social Studies, Academy of High Commercial and Industrial Studies, Cluj-Brasov, Romania, 1948; PhD, Economic Sciences, Academy of Economic Studies, Bucharest, Romania, 1962. Appointments: Laboratory Worker, Vacuum Oil Co, Oil Refinery, Brasov Romania, 1940-41; Forced Labourer, Romanian Army, Romania, 1941-44; Secretary, Indumin Sugar Factories, Tg-Mures & Bod, Romania, 1945-49; Section Chief, Ministry of Food Industry, Bucharest, 1950-51; Economist, Institute for Food Industry Projects, Bucharest, 1951-52; Planning Co-ordinator, Department Chief, Ministry of Consumer Goods Industry, Bucharest, 1952-1956; Head Economic Research Division, Food Technological Research Institute, Bucharest, 1956-72; Expert Instructor, Food Industry Postgraduate Study Centre, 1972-73; Senior Research Fellow, Tel-Aviv University Centre for Interdisciplinary Forecasting, Tel-Aviv, Israel, 1974-76; Project Leader, Israeli Productivity Institute, Tel-Aviv 1976-79; Senior Researcher, Institute for Development Studies, Rechovot, Israel, 1979-88. Publications: Over 100 articles published internationally on forecasting and planning, siting and sizing industrial units, measurement of labour productivity, economics of the food industry, philosophy of science published in the UK, the USA, Germany, Russia, Netherlands, Hungary and Romania; 3 books on industrialization (one in Romania, 2 in Israel); Participation in about 50 scientific conferences and seminars. Honour: Medal of Labour, 1953. Memberships: Central Board of Statistics, Scientific Methodological Council, Bucharest, 1952-57; Food Technological Research Institute, Scientific council Bucharest, 1956-72; Cybernetics Centre, Scientific Council, Bucharest, 1967-73; Israeli Association of Graduates in the Social Sciences and Humanities, Israel; Israel's Economic Association; Emeritus Member, New York Academy of Sciences; World Future Studies Federation. Address: 52 Eilat St, Holon 58364, Israel. E-mail: trattner@POBoxes.com

TRAVOLTA John, b. 18 February 1954, Englewood, New Jersey, USA. Actor. m. Kelly Preston, 1991, 1 son (deceased), 1 daughter. Appointments: Films: Carrie, The Boy in the Plastic Bubble (for TV), 1976; Saturday Night Fever, 1977; Grease, Moment by Moment, 1978; Urban Cowboy, 1980; Blow Out, 1981; Staying Alive, Two of a Kind, 1983; Perfect, 1985; The Experts, 1988; Chains of Gold, Look Who's Talking, 1989; Look Who's Talking Now, 1990; The Tender, All Shook Up, 1991; Look Who's Talking 3, Pulp Fiction, 1994; White Man's Burden, Get Shorty, 1995; Broken Arrow,

Phenomenon, 1996; Michael, Face Off, She's So Lovely, 1997; Primary Colors, A Civil Action, 1998; The General's Daughter, 1999; Battlefield Earth, Lucky Numbers, 2000; Swordfish, Domestic Disturbance, 2001; Austin Powers in Goldmember, 2002; Basic, 2003; The Punisher, A Love Song for Bobby Long, Ladder 49, 2004; Be Cool, Magnificent Desolation: Walking on the Moon (voice), 2005; Lonely Hearts, 2006; Wild Hogs, Hairspray, 2007; TV Series: Welcome Back Kotter, 1975-77; l.p. records, 1976, 1977. Publication: Staying Fit, 1984. Honours: Billboard Magazine Best New Male Vocalist Award, 1976; Best Actor Award, National Board of Review, 1978; Male Star of the Year, National Association of Theatre Owners, 1983; Alan J Pakula Prize, 1998.

TREANOR Frances, b. Penzance, Cornwall. Artist; Author. Divorced, 1 daughter. Education: Fine Art, Goldsmiths College, London University; Postgraduate Studies, Middlesex University, 1966-67; ATC (Lon); Diploma in Geriatric Art Teaching, London University, 1972; Certificate in Psychotherapy Counselling. Appointments: Taught and lectured on art and design appreciation in various ILEA and adult establishments including: Erith College of Technology; American Intercontinental University; Blackheath Conservatoire of Music and the Arts; Twice Vice Chair, Blackheath Art Society; Freelance sponsored workshops; Private and corporate commissions; 1st Artist in Residence, Royal Greenwich Park, 2005-06; Steering Group Member, Greenwich Alive Festival, 2007; Exhibitions include: The Pastel Society, Centenary Exhibition at FBA, 2000; English Heritage, Rangers House, Greenwich Artists Group, 2000; St Alphege Church, Open Studios Exhibition, 2000; Greenwich and Docklands, International Festival Open Studios, 2002, 2003, 2004; London Chamber of Commerce and Industry, selected artist, 2002; The Stephen Lawrence Gallery, University of Greenwich, mixed show, 2004. Honours: The Royal Drawing Society's Exhibit Prize, The Children's Royal Academy, London; Major County Scholarship, 1962; Twice winner, Law Society Art Group Special Prize, 1972, 1973; Dip d'Honneur, Salon d'Antony, Paris, 1975; Winner, L'Artiste Assoiffe Award, 1980; Exhibitor, The Lord Mayor's Award Exhibition, Guildhall, 1975, 1977; Represented Greenwich at twin town of Maribor, Yugoslavia, 1980; Lewisham art representative, Reinickendorf, Berlin, Germany, 1982; The George Rowney Pastel Award, Birmingham, 1982; The Frank Herring Award for Merit, 1984; Conte (UK) Award, 1986; Willi Hoffmann-Guth Award, 1988; Nominated Woman of the Year, 2006, Governing Board of Editors, ABI; Listed in international biographical dictionaries. Membership: London Press Club; Society of Women Writers & Journalists. Address: 121 Royal Hill, Greenwich, London SE10 8SS, England. E-mail: francestreanor@btinternet.com Website: www.francestreanor.com

TREBY Ivor Charles, b. Devonport, England. Poet. Education: MA, Honours, Biochemistry, Oxford. Publications: Poem Cards, 1984; Warm Bodies, 1988; Foreign Parts, 1989; Woman with Camellias, 1995; The Michael Field Catalogue: A Book of Lists, 1998; Translations From the Human, 1998; A Shorter Shīrazād, 101 poems of Michael Field chosen and annotated by Ivor C Treby, 1999; Awareness of the Sea, selected poems 1970-1995, 2000; Music and Silence, The Gamut of Michael Field, chosen and annotated by Ivor C Treby, 2000; Uncertain Rain, Sundry Spells of Michael Field chosen and annotated by Ivor C Treby, 2002; Binary Star, Leaves from the Journal and Letters of Michael Field 1846-1914, chosen and annotated by Ivor C Treby, 2006; Blanche's Last Fling, 2006. Contributions to: Windmill Book of Poetry; Bete Noire; Poetry Review; Staple; Anglo-Welsh Review; Contemporary Review; Honest Ulsterman; Literary Review; Rialto. Address: Parapets, 69 Redcliffe Close, RB Kensington and Chelsea, London SW5 9HZ, England.

TREFTS Marjorie Joan Landenberger, b. 31 January 1930, Pittsburgh, Pennsylvania, USA. Educational Administrator. m. Albert Sharpe Trefts, deceased 1998, 2 sons, 3 daughters. Education: BA, Western College for Women, 1952; Masters, John Carroll University, 1982, 1983. Appointments: Teacher and Administrator, Cleveland City Schools; Deacon and Trustee, Presbyterian Church; Consultant, Cleveland Partnership Program; President, National Society Dames of the Court of Honor, 2001-. Honour include: Teacher of the Year. Memberships: State Officer, 2000-, Daughters of the American Revolution; Board of Directors, Ohio Vocational Association; National Committee, American Vocational Association; American Home Economics Association; Trustee, Chautauqua, NY, Presbyterian Association; Dames of the Court of Honor; President General, Colonial Daughters of the 17th Century; State Officer, Daughters of American Colonists; National Officer, Chancellor, National Officers Colonial Clergy; President Chapter 18, Colonial Dames of America; US Daughters of 1912; Colonial Dames of XVII Century; Trustee, Chautauqua Literary and Scientific Circle, 1970-; Clearwater Country Club; Cleveland Skating Club; Union Clubs. Address: 20101 Malvern Road, Shaker Heights, OH 44122-2825, USA.

TRETYAKOV Mikhail, b. 15 March 1958, Gorkiy City, Russia. Scientist. m. Svetlana Evgenievna Kostigina, 1 daughter. Education: Correspondence Mathematical School Certificate, Moscow State University, 1975; MSc, Radiophysics, Gorky State University, 1980; PhD, Physics and Mathematics, Nizhniy Novgorod State University, 1995. Appointments: Research Assistant, 1980-82, Junior Research Associate, 1982-92, Research Associate, 1992-96, Senior Research Associate, 1996-2003, Leading Research Associate, 2003-05, Head, Division of Microwave Spectroscopy, 2005-, Institute of Applied Physics of Russian Academy of Sciences. Publications: About 90 papers in international peer-reviewed journals; 5 invention certificates. Honours: Award of Ministry of High Education of USSR for Best Student's Scientific Work, 1980; 5 invited lectures at international scientific conferences. Memberships: Editorial Board, Journal of Spectroscopy and Dynamics; Scientific Committee, Symposium of High Resolutioin Molecular Spectroscopy. Address: 46 Uljanova str, Nizhniy Novgorod, 603950 Russia. E-mail: trt@appl.sci-nnov.ru

TREVELYAN (Walter) Raleigh, b. 6 July 1923, Port Blair, Andaman Islands. Author. Education: Winchester. Appointment: Rifle Brigade, World War II; Publisher, 1948-88. Publications: The Fortress, 1956; A Hermit Disclosed, 1960; Italian Short Stories: Penguin Parallel Texts (editor), 1965; The Big Tomato, 1966; Princes Under the Volcano, 1972; The Shadow of Vesuvius, 1976; A Pre-Raphaelite Circle, 1978; Rome '44, 1982; Shades of the Alhambra, 1984; The Golden Oriole, 1987; La Storia dei Whitaker, 1989; Grand Dukes and Diamonds, 1991; A Clear Premonition, 1995; The Companion Guide to Sicily, 1996, revised 2009; Sir Walter Raleigh, 2002. Contributions to: Newspapers and journals. Honours: John Florio Prize for Translation, The Outlaws by Luigi Meneghello, 1967. Memberships: Anglo-Italian Society for the Protection of Animals, President; English PEN, a vice-president; Royal Society of Literature, fellow. Address: 18 Hertford Street, London W1J 7RT, England.

DICTIONARY OF INTERNATIONAL BIOGRAPHY 36th EDITION

TRICHET Jean-Claude, b. 20 December 1942, Lyon, France. President of the European Central Bank. Education: Ingénieur civil des Mines, Ecole nationale supérieure des Mines de Nancy, 1964; Economics, University of Paris, 1966; Graduate, Institut d'études politiques de Paris, 1966; Graduate, Ecole nationale d'administration, 1969-71. Appointments: Engineer in the competitive sector, 1966-68; Inspecteur adjoint de Finances, 1971; Assigned to the General Inspectorate of Finance, 1974; Assigned to the Treasury Department, 1975; Secretary General, Interministerial Committee for Improving Industrial Structures, 1976; Adviser to the Minister of Economic Affairs, 1978; Adviser to the President of the Republic on Industry, Energy and Research, 1978; Head, Development Aid Office, Deputy Director of Bilateral Affairs, 1981, Head, International Affairs, 1985, Chairman of the Paris Club - sovereign debt rescheduling (1985-93), Director, 1987, Treasury Department; Director, Private Office of the Minister for Economic Affairs, Finance and Privatisation, 1986; Alternate Governor, International Monetary Fund, -1993; Alternate Governor, World Bank, 1987; Censor, Banque de France, 1987; Chairman, European Monetary Committee, 1992-93; Governor, Banque de France, 1993; Member, Board of Directors of the Bank for International Settlements, 1993; Governor, World Bank, 1993-95; Chairman, Monetary Policy Council, Banque de France, 1994; Member, Council of the European Monetary Institute, 1994; Alternate Governor, International Monetary Fund, 1995-2003; Member, Governing Council of the European Central Bank, 1998; Governor of the Banque de France, 1999; Chairman, Group of Ten Governors, 2003; President, European Central Bank, 2003-. Honours: Officier de l'Ordre national de la Légion d'honneur, France; Officer de l'Ordre national du Mérite, France; Commander or Grand Officer, National Orders of Merit in Argentina, Austria, Belgium, Brazil, Ecuador, Germany, Ivory Coast and Yugoslavia; Policy Maker of the Year, The International Economy magazine, 1991; Prize, Zerilli Marimo, Academie des Sciences morales et politiques, 1999; International Prize, Pico della Mirandola, 2002. Address: European Central Bank, Postfach 16 03 19, D-60066 Frankfurt am Main, Germany.

TRIFU Alexandru, b. 18 June 1957, Iasi, Romania. Economist; Associate Professor. m. Carmen, 1 son. Education: Merit Diploma, Faculty of Economic Sciences, Alexandru Ioan Cuza University, 1976-80; Management and Marketing Applications in Finance and Accounting, 1981; Innovative Strategies in Risk Business Management, 2004. Appointments: Container Bureau and Chief Accountant, ROM TRANS, Iasi, 1980-91; Commercial Manager, OLTCIT Branch, Iasi, 1991-92; Chief Accountant, ADES/ARCOM Branch, Iasi, 1992-96; Audit Bureau, ASTROM, 1996-2001; Dean, Economics Faculty, Petre Andrei University, Iasi, 2001-. Publications: Internet and Impact on Market of a Specified Business, 2010; Team Building Surpasses Leadership in Higher Education System; Enhancing the Satisfaction of Consumer of Tourism Services; The relationship between development and environmental economics; Numerous articles in professional journals. Honours: Gold Medal, Euroinvent, Romania, 2011; Gold Medal, International Salon Inventica, Romania, 2011. Memberships: Romanian General Association of Economists; International Society for Intercommunication of New Ideas. Address: 91 V Lupu Street, bl L1, sc B, 1st floor, apt 1, 700139 Iasi, Romania. E-mail: alexandru.trifu@gmail.com

TRIMBLE W David (Baron Trimble of Lisnagarvey), b. 15 October 1944. Politician. m. (1) Heather McComb, divorced, (2) Daphne Elizabeth Orr, 1978, 2 sons, 2 daughters. Education: LLB, 1st class, Queens University, 1968. Appointments: Bar at Law, 1969, Lecturer, Law, Senior Lecturer, 1977, Head of Department, Commercial and Property Law, 1981-89; Convention Member, South Belfast, 1975-76; Joined Ulster Unionist Party, 1977; Vice Chairman, Lagan Valley Unionist Association, 1983-85; Chairman, 1985, 1990-96, Honorary Secretary, Ulster Unionist Council; Chairman, UUP Legal Committee, 1989-95; Member of Parliament, Upper Bann, 1990-2005; Chairman, UUP Constitutional Development Committee, 1995; Leader, Ulster Unionist Party, 1995-2005; Member of the New Northern Ireland Assembly, Upper Bann Constituency, 1998-2002; First Minister until Assembly suspended, 2002; Joined House of Lords, 2006; Joined Conservative Party, 2007. Honours: Shared Nobel Peace Prize, 1998; Honorary LLD, Queen's, 1999, New Brunswick, 2000, Wales, 2002; Life Peer, 2006. Memberships: Devolution Group, 1979-84; Founder, Chairman, Ulster Society, 1985-90; Chairman, Lisburn Ulster Club, 1985-86.

TRIPP Howard George, b. 3 July 1927, Croydon, England. Bishop. Education: The John Fisher School, Purley, Surrey, 1936-44; St Joseph's College, Mark Cross, East Sussex, 1944-47; St John's Seminary, Wonersh, Guildford, 1947-53. Appointments: Curate, Blackheath, 1953-57; Curate, East Sheen, 1957-62; Assistant Financial Secretary, Southwark Archdiocese, 1962-68; Parish Priest, Our Lady Queen of Peace, East Sheen, 1965-71; Director, Southwark Catholic Children's Society, 1971-80; Auxiliary Bishop of Southwark and Vicar General, 1980-2006. Address: 67 Haynt Walk, London, SW20 9NY, England.

TROFIMOV Boris Alexandrovich, b. 2 October 1938, Tchita, Eastern Siberia, Russia. Chemist. m. Nina Ivanovna Vodyannikova, 1 son. Education: Graduate, 1961, PhD equivalent, 1964, Irkutsk State University; DSc Degree, St Petersburg (Leningrad) University, 1970. Appointments: Head of Laboratory, 1970, Professor, 1974, Vice-Director, 1990, Irkutsk Institute of Organic Chemistry, SB, USSR Academy of Sciences; Director, A E Favorsky Irkutsk Institute of Chemistry, SB, Russian Academy of Sciences, 1994. Publications: More than 2,350 publications include: 15 monographs, 1,000 major papers, more than 500 Russian and foreign patents; Promoter of 62 PhD students, 24 D Sci (habilitations). Honours: Basic Research in Siberian Chemical Science, 1984, 1990; Applied Research in Siberian Chemical Science, 1985; Gold, 1979, Silver, 1987 and 2 Bronze Medals, 1972, 1978, Russian Exhibition for Economic Achievements; Orders: Sign of Honour, 1986, Friendship, 1999; Butlerov Prize, Russian Academy of Sciences, 1997; Medal and Diploma of Mendeleev Reader, St Petersburg, 2003. Memberships: Academician, Russian Academy of Science; Editorial Board Member: Zh.Organ.Khim (Russia), Sulfur Letters, Sulfur Reports (UK); Presidium, Irkutsk Scientific Centre, Russian Academy of Sciences; Presidium, East Siberian Scientific Centre, Russian Academy of Medical Science; Asia-Pacific Academy of Materials; Council of Experts of the Supreme Commission on Scientific Qualification; National Committee of Russian Chemists; Interdepartmental Scientific Council on Chemical and Biological Weapon Convention at the Russian Academy of Sciences and Russian Agency of Ammunition; International Council for Main Group Chemistry, The Netherlands; Honorary Fellow, Florida Center for Heterocyclic Compounds; Bureau of Scientific Council on Organic and Elemento-Organic Chemistry, Russian Academy of Sciences; Council of the section "Organic Chemistry", D I Mendeleev Russian Chemical Society; Scientific Council, Research

DICTIONARY OF INTERNATIONAL BIOGRAPHY 36th EDITION

Centre of Energy Infrastructure "Asia-Energy". Address: A E Favorsky Irkutsk Institute of Chemistry SB RAS, 1, Favorsky Str, Irkutsk 664033, Russia. Website: www.inchemistry.irk.ru

TROLLOPE Joanna, b. 9 December 1943. Author. m. (1) David Potter, 1966, 2 daughters, (2) Ian Curteis, 1985, divorced 2001, 2 step-sons. Education: MA, St Hugh's College, Oxford, 1972. Appointments: Foreign Office, 1965-67; Various teaching posts, 1967-79; Full-time writer, 1989-. Publications: Eliza Stanhope, 1978; Parson Harding's Daughter, 1979; Britannia's Daughters: A Study of Women in the British Empire, 1983, 2007; The Choir, 1988; A Village Affair, 1989; A Passionate Man, 1990; The Rector's Wife, 1991; The Men and the Girls, 1992; A Spanish Lover, 1993; The Country Habit: An Anthology, 1993; The Best of Friends, 1995; Next of Kin, 1996; Other People's Children, 1998; Marrying the Mistress, 2000; Girl From the South, 2002; Brother and Sister, 2004; Second Honeymoon, 2006; The Book Boy, 2006; Friday Nights, 2008; The Other Family, 2010; as Caroline Harvey: Leaves from the Valley, 1980; Legacy of Love: Charlotte, 1980; The City of Gems, 1981; Steps of the Sun, 1983; The Taverners' Place, 1986; A Castle in Italy, 1993; A Second Legacy, 1993; The Brass Dolphin, 1997; Contributions to newspapers and magazines. Honours: Historical Novel of the Year Award, Romantic Novelists Association, 1979; Elizabeth Goudge Historical Award, 1980; OBE, 1996; Deputy Lieutenant for the County of Gloucestershire, 2002-06. Memberships: Patron, March Foundation for Dementia; Patron, The Mulberry Bush School; Judge, Melissa Nathan Award; International PEN; Society of Authors; Romantic Novelists' Association; Vice-President, Trollope Society; West Country Writer's Association. Address: c/o United Agents, 12-26 Lexington Street, London, W1F 0LE, England. Website: www.joannatrollope.net

TROTT Laura, b. 24 April 1992, Harlow, Essex, England. Track Cyclist. Education: Turnford School, Hertfordshire. Career: Gold (team pursuit), European Championships,Pruszkow, 2010; 2 Gold medals (team pursuit and omnium), European Championships, Apeldoorn, 2011; Gold (team pursuit), World Championships, Apeldoorn, 2011; 2 Gold medals (team pursuit and omnium), World Championships, Melbourne, 2012; 2 Gold medals (team pursuit and omnium), London Olympics, 2012.

TRUBETSKOY Kliment Nikolayevich, b. 3 July 1933, Moscow, USSR. Mining Engineer. m. 2 sons. Education: Moscow Institute of Non-Ferrous Metals and Gold, 1961; Doctor of Technical Sciences, 1981; Professor, 1982; Academician, RAS, 1991. Appointments: Manager of Mines, 1953; Associate, Mining Institute A A Skochinskii, 1961; Senior Associate, Institute of Earth Physics, 1967; Head of Laboratory, 1977, Director, 1987-2003, Institute of Complex Exploitation of Mineral Resources RAS; Member, 1996-2003, Adviser, 2003-11, Presidium, RAS; Head of Chair, 2003-09, Adviser of Rectorate, 2010-11, Russian State Geological Prospecting University. Publications: 750 publications; 39 monographs; Encyclopaedia of Life Support Systems, 2002; 8 learned books; 79 patents. Honours: USSR and Russian State Prizes; 3 Prizes of the Government of Russian Federation for the field of science and technics; 2 prizes and Gold Medal, USSR and Russian Academy of Sciences; B Krupinsky Medal, WMC; 300 Years of German-Russian Friendship in Mining Medal. Memberships: Actual Member (Academician), Russian Academy of Sciences; Foreign Member, Academy of Engineering Sciences of Serbia and Montenegro. Address: Kryukovski Tupik 4, Moscow 111020, Russia. E-mail: krasavin_08@mail.ru

TRUCCO Marco, b. 30 August 1957, Savona, Italy. Neurologist. Education: Graduate, Medicine and Surgery, 1981, Specialised in Neurology, 1985, Specialised in Clinical Neurophysiology, 1990, Pavia University. Appointments: Assistant, Neurology, 1987-93, Consultant, 1993-94, Medical Director, 1995-, Neurology, Santa Corona Hospital, Pietra Ligure, Italy; Guest Researcher, Neurology, Söder Hospital, Stockholm, Sweden, 1992; Guest Researcher, Neurology, Bispebjerg Hospital, Copenhagen, Denmark, 1999. Publications: 101 articles, abstracts or chapter of books; 123 active participations in medical conferences or courses. Honours: Cicladol Award, University of Milan, 1990; Astrazeneca Award, Italian Society of Psychiatry, 2002. Memberships: International Headache Society; Italian Society for the Study of Headaches; Italian Neurological Society; Amnesty International. Address: via Costa 7/A, 17055 Toirano (SV), Italy.

TRUE Hans Christian Godskesen, b. 8 June 1936, Copenhagen, Denmark. Professor (retired); Director. m. Duda Bozena Maria, 4 sons. Education: MSME, Technical University of Denmark, 1960; PhD, Applied Mathematics, 1964; MS, Applied Mathematics, Harvard University, 1967. Appointments: Research Associate, 1960-61, Assistant Professor, 1967-69, Associate Professor, 1969-2003, Retired Professor, 2003-, Technical University of Denmark; Guest Teacher, Yale University, 1964-65; Guest Researcher, Pennsylvania State University and California Institute of Technology, 1974-75, Northwestern University and Clemson University, 1987-88; Guest Professor, University of Leeds, England, 1985; Consultant, Danish State Railways, 1991-; Senior Engineer, ES-Consult, 1992-96; Director, True Consult, 1997-; Senior Engineer, Scan Rail Consult, 1997-98. Publications: Numerous publications in professional journals; After 2000: 4 journal papers with referee; 15 conference papers with referee (2 without referee); Editor, Archive Applied Mechanics, Vehicle System Dynamics, International Journal of Vehicle Mechanics and Mobility, 2001; Chapter in book, Dynamical Analysis of Vehicle Systems, 2007; Co-editor, Proceedings of EUROMECH 500. Honours: Fulbright Fellow, 1964-67; Alexander von Humboldt Fellow, 1970-71; Anniversary Medal, Mining University, Cracow, 1989; Anniversary Medal, St Petersburg-Moscow Railway, 2001. Memberships: ASME; International Association for Vehicle System Dynamics, President, 2003-; International Society of Industrial Mathematics and Mechanics; National Railway Historical Society; Engineering Society of Denmark. Address: Dalstroget 18, DK-2870 Dyssegaard, Denmark. E-mail: truecons@gmail.com Website: www2.imm.dtu.dk/~ht

TRUMP Donald John, b. 14 June 1946, New York, USA. Property Developer. m. (1) Ivana Zelnicek, 1977, divorced 1991, 2 sons, 1 daughter, (2) Marla Maples, 1993, 1 daughter, (3) Melania Knauss, 2005, 1 son. Education: Fordham University; University of Pennsylvania. Appointments: President, Trump Organisation; Board of Directors, Police Athletic League; Advisory Board, Lenox Hill Hospital and United Cerebral Palsy; Director, Fred C Trump Foundation; Founder Member, Committee to complete construction of Cathedral of St John the Divine and Wharton Real Estate Centre; Former Co-Chair, New York Vietnam Veterans Memorial Fund; Radio: Clear Channel Radio broadcasts, 2004; TV: The Apprentice, 2004. Publications: Trump: The Art of the Deal, 1987; Trump: Surviving at the Top, 1990; The Art of the Comeback, 1997; The America We Deserve, 2000; How to Get Rich, 2004; Think Like a Billionaire, 2004; The Way to the Top, 2004; Trump World Magazine, 2004; Trump: Think Like a Billionaire, 2004; Trump: The Best Golf Advice I Ever Received, 2005; Trump:

The Best Real Estate Advice I Ever Received, 2007; Trump 101: The Way to Success, 2007; Trump Never Give Up, 2008. Honours: Hotel and Real Estate Visionary of the Century, UJA Federation, 2000. Address: Trump Organization, 725 Fifth Avenue, New York, NY 10022, USA.

TRZECIAK Henryk Ireneusz, b. 28 May 1938, Ruda Śląska, Poland. Professor. m. Jadwiga Dubicka, 1 daughter. Education: MSChE, Faculty of Chemistry, Gdansk University of Technology, 1960; MD, PhD, Faculty of Medicine, Silesian Medical University, Katowice, 1968. Appointments: Assistant Professor, 1961-68, Associate Professor, 1985-, Full Professor, 1996-, Medicine, Pharmacologist, Silesian Medical University; Head, Department of Pharmacology, 1996-2008, Head, Department of Public Health, 2008-, Cardinal August Hlond Silesian School of Pedagogy, Myslowice. Publications: 112 original publications; 7 review and handbooks; 184 reports. Honours: Medal of National Education; Gold Cross of Merit; Chivalry's Cross of Poland Renascence; Officer's Cross of Poland Renascence; Medal of the Polish Society for Pain Study; Medal of the Polish Toxicology Society. Memberships: Polish Pharmacological Society. Address: Silesian School of Pedagogy, Cardinal August Hlond, 41-40 Myslowice, ul Powstancow 19, Poland.

TSANG Marianna Wai Chun, b. 13 August 1954, Hong Kong. Chartered Secretary; Certified Tax Advisor. Education: Diploma, Secretarial Management (Distinction), Hong Kong Baptist University, 1978; MBA, Heriot-Watt University, England, 1999; Post graduate Certificate, Advanced Taxation, 2000, Post graduate Certificate, Professional Accounting, 2002, City University of Hong Kong; PhD, Empresarial University, Costa Rica, 2010. Appointments: Managing Director, TWC Management Ltd, 2000-; Hong Kong's Most Valuable Companies, 2011; Director, Chan & Wat CPA, 2000-; Audit Committee Chairman, Independent Non-Executive Director, Timeless Software Ltd, 2003-. Honours: Various scholarships, 1974-78; Placed on President's Honors Roll, Hong Kong Baptist University, 1978; Prestigious Hong Kong Best Showcase Winner Awards, 2011; Listed in international biographical dictionaries; More than 10 awards by various Chinese authorities. Memberships: Fellow, Certified Tax Adviser, The Taxation Institute of Hong Kong; Associate, The Institute of Chartered Secretaries & Administrators UK; Associate, The Hong Kong Institute of Company Secretaries; Certified Business Manager, The Association of Professionals in Business Management; Full Member, Society of Registered Financial Planners; Member, Board of Review, HK Inland Revenue Ordinance. Address: Suite A-B, and D, 19/F, Ritz Plaza, 122 Austin Road, Tsimshatsui, Kowloon, Hong Kong. E-mail: mariannatsang@twccsl.com

TSAO Vivian J Y, b. 24 April 1950, Taipei, Taiwan (American Citizen). Artist; Art Professor; Author. m. Raymond Clyde Coreil. Education: BA, Fine Arts, National Taiwan Normal University, Taiwan, 1973; Master of Fine Arts in Painting, Carnegie Mellon University, Pittsburgh, Pennsylvania, USA, 1976. Appointments: Assistant Editor, Children's Art Page, Central Daily News, Taiwan, 1971-74; Art Instructor, National Taipei University of Education, Taiwan, 1972-74; Artist and Writer on Art, Vivian Tsao Artist, 1976-; Worked on consignments for: Kingpitcher Gallery, Pittsburgh, Pennsylvania, USA, 1976-77; Nardin Galleries, New York City, USA, 1979-80; The Art Collaborative, New York City, USA, 1985-87; Correspondent, Hsiung Shih Art Monthly, Taiwan, 1980-96; Programme Auditor, Free-lance Reviewer of Exhibitions, 1990-96, Juror on Panel, 1996-99, New York State Council on the Arts, New York City; Adjunct Assistant Professor of Drawing and Design, Department of Fine Arts, Pace University, New York City, 1990-; Contributing writer in the USA, United Daily News, Literary Page, Taiwan; 15 solo and 56 group exhibitions include: American Academy of Arts and Letters; The Brooklyn Museum; Taipei Fine Arts Museum; Ceres Gallery; Biddington's Internet Gallery; National Museum of History, Taiwan. Publications: Book: The Mark of Time: Dialogues with Vivian Tsao on Art in New York, 2003; Paintings by Vivian Tsao, Museum Catalogue, 2009; Article: A Holistic Approach to Art Criticism: An Interview with Art Critic Michael Brenson, 1988; Black Velvet at Dusk (essay), 2000; Essay: Boy on the Rocking Horse: An Introduction to the Art and Life of Eugene Speicher, 2005; Paintings published in book "100 New York Painters" by Cynthia Dantzic, 2006. Honours: Artist-in-Residence, New York State Council on the Arts; Certificate of Merit, Pastel Society of America; Scholarship Grant, Carnegie Mellon University. Memberships: Inducted Fellow, Society of Fellows, Dyson College, Pace University; Elected Full Member, Pastel Society of America; National Arts Club; College Art Association of America. Address: 17 Fuller Place, Brooklyn, NY 11215-6006, USA. E-mail: viviantsao@earthlink.net

TSATSARIS Athanasios, b. 22 January 1967, Derveni, Korinthos, Greece. Sanitary Police Officer. m. Helen Kontoyianni. Education: Degree in Mechanical Engineering, National Technical University of Athens; MSc, Applied Mathematics, 1990; Degree in Medicine, University of Athens, 1995; Certificate, Naval Medicine, 1996; Degree in Mathematics, University of Athens; MSc, Functional Analysis, 2002; Certificate of Medical Speciality, GP, University of Athens, 2002; PhD, Biomedical Engineering, University of Athens and National Technical University of Athens, 2002; Degree, Cambridge, CPE, 2002. Appointments: General Practitioner, Laiko General Hospital, Athens, 1997-2002; Sanitary Police Officer, Police Academy Department of Grevena, 2003-. Publications: Effect of an Experimentally Induced Stenosis in Descending Thoracic Aorta, 2004; Effect of Experimental Stenosis on the Vibration of the Porcine Aorta Wall, 2006; Role of Chaos in Atherosclerosis, 2006; Changes in Aortic Function after the interposition of a tubular graft in the Descending Thoracic Aorta, 2006; Impact of pressure prop on PWV along experimental stenosis, 2007; Role of infrasound waves in atherosclerotic plaque rupture; A theoretical approach, 2007; Yielding criterion of porcine thoracic aorta, 2007; Recent patents on cardiovascular drug discovery, 2007; Current development in tissue-engineered vascular grafts, 2007; Gene Expression and Chaos Theory: A Theoretical Approach, 2008; Reviewer of professional journals. Honours: Listed in international biographical dictionaries. Memberships: Editorial Board Member, The Open Biomedical Engineering Journal; Reviewer, Artificial Organs. Address: Police Academy Department of Grevena, 83 Megalexandrou, 51100, Grevena, Greece. E-mail: tsapol@otenet.gr

TSAY Jyh-Shen, b. 25 October 1969, Kinmen, Taiwan. Professor. Education: BSc, 1992, PhD, 1997, National Taiwan Normal University. Appointments: Postdoctoral Research Fellow, Academia Sinica, 1997-99; Visiting Research Fellow, Institute for Physical and Theoretical Chemistry, Bonn University, 1999-2000; Assistant Professor, Tunghai University, 2000-04; Associate Professor, National Chung-Cheng University, 2004-06; Associate Professor, 2006-2007, Professor, 2007-, National Taiwan Normal University. Publications: 70 articles in scientific journals. Honours: Best Dissertation Award, Physical Society of Republic of China, 1998; Research Award, Taiwan

DICTIONARY OF INTERNATIONAL BIOGRAPHY 36th EDITION

Association for Magnetic Technology, 2003; Best Poster Award, Physical Society, Republic of China, 1997. Address: Department of Physics, National Taiwan Normal University, 88 Sec 4, Ting-Chou Road, Taipei 116, Taiwan, ROC. E-mail: jstsay@phy.ntnu.edu.tw

TSIFRINOVICH Vladimir, b. December 1950, Sverdlovsk, Russia. Physicist. m. Tatyana, 1 son, 1 daughter. Education: MS, Physics, Krasnoyarsk University, 1972; PhD, Physics, 1977, Dr of Sciences, Physics, 1992, Institute of Physics, Russian Academy of Sciences, Krasnoyarsk. Appointments: Senior Research Scientist, Leading Research Scientist, 1987-93, Institute of Physics, Russian Academy of Sciences; Adjunct Professor, 1994-98, Instructor of Physics, 1999-2002, Lecturer of Physics, 2002-10, Industry Associate Professor of Physics, 2010-, Polytechnic Institute of NYU. Publications: Introduction to Quantum Computers, 1998; Modern Physics and Technology for Undergraduates, 2003; Perturbation Theory for Solid-State Quantum Computation with Many Quantum Bits, 2005; Magnetic Resonance Force Microscopy and a Single-Spin Measurement, 2006. Honours: Listed in international biographical directories. Memberships: American Physics Society. Address: Department of Physics, Polytechnic Institute of NYU, 6 MetroTech Center, Brooklyn, NY 11201, USA.

TSITVERBLIT Naftali Anatol, b. 29 October 1963, Kiev, Ukraine. Researcher. Education: MSc, Control Systems in Heat and Power Engineering, Kiev Polytechnic Institute, 1987; PhD, Fluid Mechanics and Heat Transfer, Tel Aviv University, 1995. Appointments: Engineer, Scientific Research Institute of Robotics, Kiev, 1985-87; Teaching Assistant, Instructor, Tel-Aviv University, 1988-94; Visiting Scientist, Cornell University, 1994; Postdoctoral Research Fellow, Lamont-Doherty Earth Observatory, Columbia University, 1995-97; Postdoctoral Fellow, 1996 Geophysical Fluid Dynamics Summer Programme, Woods Hole Oceanographic Institution; Visiting Department of Fluid Mechanics and Heat Transfer, Tel Aviv University, 1997-. Publications: Contributed articles to professional journals; including, Finite-Amplitude double-component convection due to different boundary conditions for two compensating horizontal gradients, 2000; Mechanism of finite-amplitude double-component convection due to different boundary conditions, 2004; Double-component convection due to different boundary conditions in an infinite slot diversely oriented to the gravity, 2007; Double-Component Convection due to Different Boundary Conditions with Broken Reflection Symmetry for a Component, 2011. Honours: Scholarship, Salim and Rahel Benin; Post Doctoral Fellowship, Lamont-Doherty Earth Observatory; Geophysical Fluid Dynamics Summer School Fellowship; Who's Who in Science and Engineering; Who's Who in the World; Who's Who in America; others. Memberships: New York Academy of Sciences; American Physical Society; American Geophysical Union; American Association for the Advancement of Science. Address: 1 Yanosh Korkhak Street, Apt 6, Kiryat Nordau, Netanya 42495, Israel.

TSUCHIYA Masa, b. 24 October 1958, Osaka, Japan. Associate Professor. m. Takako, 2 daughters. Education: BSc, Biophysical Engineering, Osaka University, 1983; MSc, 1987, PhD, 1995, Physics, West Virginia University, USA. Appointments: Research Fellow, National Laboraotry of High Energy Physics and Department of Physics, Osaka University graduate school, 1983-84; Postdoctoral Fellow, Department of Chemistry, West Virginia University, 1995-96; Postdoctoral Fellow, Department of Chemistry and Chemical Biology, Cornell University, 1996-99; Research Associate, Department of Chemistry, 1999-2001, Research Associate, Senior Staff, Stanford Genome Technology Center, Stanford Medical School, 2001-04, Stanford University; Senior Research Scientist, Cancer Biology Group, Bioinformatics Institute Singapore, 2004-06; Associate Professor, Systems Immunology Group, Institute for Advance Biosciences, Keio University, 2006-. Publications: Numerous articles in professional journals. Honours: Outstanding Student, Biophysical Engineering, Osaka University, 1983; Full Scholarship, Los Alamos National Laboratory, USA, 1985; Full Scholarship, Georgetown University, USA, 1985; Phi Lambda Upsilon National Chemistry Honor Society, 1992; Sigma Phi Sigma National Physics Honor Society, 1994; Listed in international biographical dictionaries. Memberships: American Chemical Society; American Physical Society; American Association for the Advancement of Science.

TSUDA Nobuo, b. 20 April 1936, Kobe, Japan. Physicist; Emeritus Professor. m. Akiko, 2 daughters. Education: BSc, 1959, MSc, 1961, Doctor of Science, 1964, University of Tokyo. Appointments: Assistant, Institute for Solid State Physics, University of Tokyo, 1964; Researcher in Charge, 1969, Leader, Research Group, 1974, National Institute for Research in Inorganic Materials; Professor, Faculty of Science, 1982, Part-time Professor, 2002, Emeritus Professor, 2008, Tokyo University of Science. Publications: Electronic Conduction in Oxides, 1st edition, 1983. Memberships: Physical Society of Japan. Address: Minami 3-1-30, Higashikaigan, Chigasaki, Kanagawa, 253-0054, Japan.

TSUKAMOTO Daniel, b. 18 April 1970, Encarnacion, Paraguay (American citizen). Church Organist. Education: BA, Piano Performance, Asbury College, Wilmore, Kentucky, 1994; Master of Music, Piano Performance, University of South Dakota, Vermillion, 1995. Appointments: Church Organist, First United Methodist Church, Watertown, South Dakota; Church Organist, Hillside Community Church, Vermillion, South Dakota, 1994-95; Church Organist, Bethel Baptist Church, Brookings, South Dakota, 1997-99; Praise Band Keyboardist, Cornerstone United Methodist Church, Watertown, 1999-2000; Church Organist, Romeo United Methodist Church, Michigan, 2000-. Publications: Book, Music Performance, in progress. Honours: National Honor Society, 1987, National School Orchestra Award, 1988, Rapid City Central High School; First Chair All-State Orchestra, South Dakota High Schools, 1988; 2 Perfect Attendance Faculty Awards, Watertown Senior High, 1988-89; First Chair All-State Band, Dakota High Schools, 1989; Outstanding Musician Plaque, Watertown Senior High, 1989; Era Wilder Peniston Award, Asbury College, 1993; Graduate Assistantship, University of South Dakota, 1994-95; Annual Music Competition, University of South Dakota, 1994; Dean's Honor Roll, South Dakota State University, 1997; Republican National Committee Certificate, 1997; Certificate of Appreciation, 1998, Certificate of Achievement, 2nd place, 1998, Music Business Internet Guide; Outstanding Young Americans Certificate, 1998; Certificate of Accomplishment 2007, Poetry.com, 2008; National Safety Council certificate, 2011; Listed in international biographical dictionaries. Memberships: American Guild of Organists, Detroit Chapter. Address: 42221 Toddmark Lane, Apt 124, Clinton Township, MI 48038, USA. E-mail: z5aj@sbcglobal.net

TSURKO Elena Nikolajevna, b. 9 October 1967, Moscow, Russia. Chemist. Education: Courses in Journalism, 1986-88; Courses in English Language, 1988-90; MSc, Chemist, 1990, Dr Sc, PhD, Chemistry, 1994, Kharkiv (later National) State University, USSR; Courses in German as a Foreign Language,

University of Regensburg, 1997-98; Courses in German Language, Kharkiv National University, Ukraine, 1999-; Advanced Course of German Language, Goethe-Institut, Kiev, Ukraine, 2005. Appointments: Laboratory Assistant, 1990, Graduate School, 1990-94, Junior Scientific Researcher, 1994-95, Scientific Researcher, 1995-2000, Senior Scientific Researcher, 2000-04, Physical Chemistry Department, Senior Scientific Researcher, Scientific-Research Institute of Chemistry, 2004-, Kharkiv National University. Publications: 96 scientific works including: 3 textbooks; 1 book edition; 41 articles; 6 deposited papers. Honours: PhD, 1994; DAAD Scholar, University of Regensburg, Germany, 1997-99; Senior Scientific Researcher, 2007-. Memberships: Ukrainian High School Union of Germanists; European Molecular Liquids Group. Address: Scientific-Research Institute of Chemistry, V N Karasin National University Kharkiv, Svoboda Pl 4, 61022 Kharkiv, Ukraine. E-mail: jelena.n.tsurko@univer.kharkov.ua

TSVETKOV Oleg Boris, b. 7 September 1939, Leningrad, USSR. Professor of Thermophysical Properties of Fluids. m. Marianna Konstantin Utkina, 2 daughters. Education: Diploma in Engineering, Technological Institute of Refrigeration (TIR), Leningrad, 1961; PhD, TIR, 1965; DSc, TIR, 1983; Postgraduate, Northwestern University, Evanston, Illinois, USA, 1979-80; TIR, Leningrad, 1980-83; University of Maryland, Washington DC, 1987-88. Appointments: Research Assistant Professor, TIR, 1964-68; Associate Professor, Royal University, Phnom-Penh, Cambodia, 1968-70; Acting Director, Research Department, TIR, 1970-79; Pro Rector of Research, State Academy of Refrigeration and Food Technology (SARFT former TIR), St Petersburg, Russia, 1983-98, Head of Department, State University of Refrigeration and Food Engineering (formerly SARFT), St Petersburg, 1991-. Publications: Numerous articles in professional journals. Honours include: Vice Chairman, 14th World Congress of Refrigeration, Moscow, 1975; Vice-President Com B1, International Institute of Refrigeration, 1972-75, 1995-; Medal, USSR Ministry of Higher Education, Moscow, 1981; President, Science and Technology Society of Food Industry, St Petersburg, 1990-98; Recipient, Excellence in Teaching and Research, 1993; Vice-President, International Academy of Refrigeration, 1998; Research Grantee, International Science Foundation, 1994; Medal, Fifty Years of Victory in Second World War, 1995; Deputy editor-in-chief Proc. of the International Academy of Refrigeration, 1997; Research Grantee, EU Contract, 1998-2002; Professor Emeritus, 1999; Medal, 300 Years of St Petersburg, 2003; Vice President, Programm Committee of XI Russian Thermophysical Properties Conference, 2004; Medal, 60 Years of the Liberation of Leningrad from the Blockade, 2004; Medal, Sixty Years of Victory in Second World War, 2005; Medal, 100 Years of Russian Trade Unions, 2006; Laureat 2007 of State Russia prize; Medal, 50 Years of Space Flight of Yuri Gagarin, 2011. Memberships: International Academy of Sciences in Higher Education, 1992-; Member, Editorial Board, Kholodilnaya Teknika, Moscow, 1992-; Member, International Academy of Refrigeration, 1993; Member, International Union of Pure and Applied Chemistry, 1994-; Member, Editorial Board, Refrigeration Business, 1995-; Member, National Committee on Thermophysics, Russian Academy of Sciences, 1997-. Address: 31 Moika Embankment, Apt 54, 191186 St Petersburg, Russia. E-mail: obereg@softrex.com

TSYGANOV Vladimir, b. 5 September 1949, Kiev, USSR. Researcher; Professor. m. Alla, 1 daughter. Education: Magister, Moscow Physico-Technical Institute, 1972; Magister, Patent Institute, Moscow, 1973; Dr Sci, PhD,1979, 2nd PhD, 2000, Professor, 2005, Institute of Control Sciences. Appointments: Engineer, 1972-79, Researcher, 1979-81, Senior Researcher, 1981-99, Leading Researcher, 2000-09, Head Researcher, 2010-, Institute of Chemical Physics, Russian Academy of Sciences; Bank Consultant, 2003, 2006. Publications: 11 books including Adaptive Control Mechanisms of Branch of Industry, 1991; Information Management, 2009; Adaptive Organization of Railway Complex, 2010; Upgrade of National Security System, 2010. Honours: Best Book of the Year (Intellectual Enterprise: Mastering Capital and Power) , 2004; Honour List, President of Russia Adviser for Designing Pechenga Sea Port, 2010. Memberships: Russian Academy of Natural Sciences; Russian Academy of Creopolitics; Russian Academy of Security. Address: dom 40-42, kv 185, Kosmodamianskaya Nab, 115035, Moscow, Russia. E-mail: av188958@akado.ru

TU Ming-Shium, b. 19 February 1956, Hsing-Chu, Taiwan. Physician. m. Wei-Jen Yeh, 1 son, 2 daughters. Education: B Med, National Yang-Ming Medical College, Taipei, 1975-82. Appointments: Head, Kaohsiung Veterans General Hospital, Kaohsiung, Taiwan, 1993-2010; Visiting Scholar, College of Medicine, University Medical Center and Affiliated Hospitals, University of Arizona, USA, 1996. Publications: Illness: An opportunity for Spiritual Growth, 2006; Perceptual Consistency of Pain and Quality of Life Between Hospice Cancer Patients and Family Caregivers: A Pilot Study, 2007. Honours: Awards, Exemplar Public Servant, Veterans Affairs Commission, Executive Yuan, ROC, 1999; People of Benevolence, Association of Benevolent People Promotion, 2000; Listed in Who's Who in the World, 2009-2010 and other international biographical dictionaries. Memberships: American Society of Teachers of Family Medicine; Taiwan Society of Internal Medicine; Taiwan Academy of Hospice Palliative Medicines; Taiwan Association of Family Medicine. Address: 386 Ta-Chung 1st Road, Tso-Ying District, Kaohsiung, 81362, Taiwan. E-mail: mstu@isca.vghks.gov.tw

TUCKER Eva Marie, b. 18 April 1929, Berlin, Germany. Writer. m. 11 March 1950 (widowed 1987), 3 daughters. Education: BA, Honours, German, English, University of London. Appointments: C Day-Lewis Writing Fellow, Vauxhall Manor School, London, 1978-79; Hawthornden Writing Fellowship, 1991. Publications: Novels: Contact, 1966; Drowning, 1969; Berlin Mosaic, 2005; Becoming English, 2009; Translator, Radetzkymarch by Joseph Roth, 1974; Contributions to: BBC Radio 3 and 4; Encounter; London Magazine; Woman's Journal; Vogue; Harper's; Spectator; Listener; Times Literary Supplement; PEN International. Memberships: English PEN; FRLS, 2009; Dorothy Richardson Society. Address: 63B Belsize Park Gardens, London NW3 4JN, England.

TUĞLACI Pars, b. 1 April 1933, Istanbul, Turkey. Linguist; Historian; Lexicographer. Education: Graduate, Melconian Education Institute, Cyprus, 1951; English Language and Literature, Michigan University, Ann Arbor, USA, 1955. Appointments: English Teacher, Gulhane Military Medical Academy, Ankara, Turkey; School Teacher, Secondary Schools in Istanbul; Freelance Scholar. Publications include: An English-Turkish Dictionary of Idioms, 1961 16th edition, 1993; An English-Turkish Medical Dictionary, 1964, 8th edition, 1990; Okyanus Encyclopedic Turkish Dictionary, 1974; Modern Turkey, 3 volumes, 1987-90; Armenian Churches of Istanbul, 1991; Selections from the Armenian Literature, 1992; The Role of the Dadian Family in Ottoman Social, Economic and Political Life, 1993. Honours: Gold Medal, 1300th Anniversary of the creation of the Bulgarian

State, 1982; Order of Universal Knighthood, Supreme Council of International Knights Union of Spain; Turkish Ambassador to the International Parliament for Safety and Peace, Italy. Memberships: International Parliament for Safety and Peace; Maison International des Intellectuals, Paris; Institut des Affaires Internationales, Paris; Academia Argentina Diplomatia, Buenos Aires; World Institute of Achievement, USA; International Order of Merit. Address: PO Box 37, Levent, Istanbul, Turkey.

TULASIEWICZ Witold, b. Berlin, Germany. Part time Professor of Language Education; Researcher. m. 1 son. Appointments: Fellow, Wolfson College Cambridge; Former Full-time University Teacher, University of Cambridge; Director and Co-director of several national and international projects including: Education as Dialogue, Europe East and West; Intercultural Education in a multicultural and multilingual context; Currently researching and practising the application of a language awareness approach to the study of language and intercultural education; Visiting Chairs in Calgary and Montreal, Canada, Warsaw and Bialystok, Poland, Canton and Hong Kong, China, Mainz, Germany and other. Publications include: Index Verborum zur deutschen Kaiserchronik (author); Teaching the Mother Tongue in a Multilingual Europe (co-author); Education in a Single Europe (co-author); The Crisis in Teacher Education: A European Concern? (co-author); Language Awareness: A History and Implementations (co-author); Articles and translations into English of several short stories by Johannes Bobrowski and Anna Seghers; Editorial Adviser, Compare, Recherche et Formation, Kwartalnik Pedagogiczny. Memberships: Comparative Education Society in Europe; Association of Language Awareness; Committee for Russian and East European Studies in Cambridge; Polish Academy of Sciences Abroad; Belarus Academy of Educational Studies; Corresponding Member, Brandenburg Berlin Academy; Consultant to EU Committee of the Regions. Address: Wolfson College, Barton Road, Cambridge CB3 9BB, England. E-mail: wft20@cam.ac.uk

TULEEV Aman Gumirovich, b. 13 May 1944, Krasnovodsk, Turkmenian Republic. Politician. m. Elvira Solovyeva, 2 sons, 1 deceased. Education: Novosibirsk Institute of Railway Engineering, 1973; Academy of Social Studies, 1989. Appointments: Assistant Station Master, 1964-69, Station Master, 1969-73, Railway Station, Moundebash; Station Master, Railway Station, Mezhdurechensk, 1973-78; Head, Novokuznetsk Line, Kemerovo Railway, 1978-85; Head, Transport Department, Kemorovo's Regional Committee of the CPSU, 1985-88; Head, Kemerovo Railway, 1988-90; Chairman, Kemerovo's Regional Council of People's Deputies, People's Deputy of RSFSR, 1991; Peoples' Deputy of Russian Federation, 1990-93; Candidate for Presidency, 1991, 1996, 2000; Supported coup d'etat attempt, 1991; Member, CP of Russian Federation, 1993-2003; Yedinaya Rossiya party, 2003-; Chair, Legislative Assembly, Kemerovo Region, 1994-96; Minister of Co-operation with CIS, 1996-97; Governor, Kemerovo Region, 1997-; Member, Council of Federation, 1993-95, 1997-2001; Candidate, Russian presidential elections, 2000; Supported Putin's regional party, 2003; Joined United Russia, 2005. Publications: Author of more than 100 articles and books including: Power in hands of a man and man in hands of the power, 1993; State power in region: personal factor, social contacts, 1998; To remain yourself, 1999; Political leader and political leadership in regional conflicts, 1999; We have the only Russia, 1999; Political leadership in modern Russia, 2000. Honours: Medal for Labour Valour, 1976; Medal, Labour Veteran of USSR, 1992; Medal, 300th Anniversary of Russian Navy, 1998; The Order of Honor, 1999; The Order of the North Star; Peter the Great International Award, 2002; International Millennium Award for Service to Humanity, 2003; Order for Outstanding Country Service IV degree, 2003; Andrey Pervozvanny International Award for Faith and Loyalty, 2003. Memberships: Honorary Railwayman; Freeman of Kemerovo and Novokuznetsk; Honorary Doctor of Sciences, Ulan-Bator University of Mongolian Academy of Sciences; Full Member, International Academy of Informatization; Full Member, International Engineering Academy. Address: pr Sovetskiy, 62, 650099 Kemerovo, Russia. Website: www.mediakuzbass.ru

TULLY (William) Mark, b. 24 Oct 1935, Calcutta, India. Journalist; Broadcaster. m. Margaret Frances Butler, 13 Aug 1960, 2 sons, 2 daughters. Education: Marlborough College; MA, Trinity Hall, Cambridge, 1959. Appointments: Regional Director, Abbeyfield Society, 1960-64; Assistant, Appointments Department, 1964-65, Assistant, later Acting Representative, New Delhi, 1955-69, Programme Organiser and Talks Writer, Eastern Service, 1969-71, Chief of Bureau, Delhi, 1972-93, South Asia Correspondent, 1993-94, BBC; Presenter, The Lives of Jesus, BBC TV, 1996. Publications: Amritsar: Mrs Gandhi's Last Battle (with Satish Jacob), 1985; From Raj to Rajiv (with Z Masani), 1988; No Full Stops in India, 1991; The Heart of India, 1995; The Lives of Jesus, 1996. Honours: Officer of the Order of the British Empire, 1985; Padma Shri, India, 1992; Honorary Fellow, Trinity Hall, Cambridge, 1994; Honorary Doctor of Letters, University of Strathclyde, 1997. Address: 1 Nizamuddin East, New Delhi 110 013, India.

TUNG Raymond Hong Nin, b. 1 April 1959, Hong Kong. Education: PhD, Empresarial University, Costa Rica; Chartered Marketer, CIM UK; Hon Fellow of OXCEL & SBP respectively, UK. Appointments: Founder and Chairman, Natural Talent Holding Club Ltd; Founder, RT Wing Chun Self Defense Technique Fast Track Program; Master Trainer, Leadership and Potential Development Course. Honours: A Patriot of Merit, People's Republic of China; Honorary Chairman, China International Economic Development Research Center; Top 100 Organizer with Strong Impact of the Year, China; Distinguished Entrepreneur Award, Hong Kong, 2008; Prime Awards for Best Brand Enterprise in Greater China, 2008; Award for Most Creative Chinese Entrepreneurial Leaders of Great China, 2008; National Logistics Industry Renowned Experts Award; Senior Fellow, Logistics Industry Award; Great Wall of China Outstanding People Contribution Award; 2010 Asia-Pacific Chinese Entrepreneurial Leaders with the Strongest Social Responsibility Award; Contemporary Martial Arts Grandmaster Achievement Award; Honorary President of China Experts Investigation and Research Committee; Top Ten Experts with Breakthrough Contributions in Chinese Industry Award; The Most Influential Person in China Award; The Outstanding Charity Person in Moving China Award; The Asia-Pacific Chinese Entrepreneurial Leaders Forum, Outstanding Contribution Award, 2008; Vice Chairman, Executive Council of Industry. Address: Room 407, Empire Centre, No 68, Mody Road, Tsimshatsui East, Kowloon, Hong Kong. E-mail: raymond@ntcl.com.hk

TURCAN Robert Alain, b. 22 June 1929, Paris, France. Professor. m. Marie Deleani, 1 son, 2 daughters. Education: Bachelor's degree in Arts, 1953; Diploma of Higher Studies, 1954; Aggregation of Letters, 1955; D Litt, Paris, Sorbonne, 1966. Appointments: Ecole Normale Supérieure, Paris-Ulm,

1952-55; Ecole Française de Rome, 1955-57; Assistant, 1957-63, Master of Conferences, 1963-69, Professor, University of Lyon, 1969-87, University of Paris-Sorbonne, 1988-94; Member, Institute of France, 1990-. Publications: Numerous books, papers and articles in professional journals. Honours: Prix Jeanbernat, 1958; Prix Th Reinach, 1967; Prix Saintour, 1981; Chevalier de la Légion d'Honneur; Officier des Arts et des Lettres; Commandeur des Palmes Académiques. Memberships: Académie des Inscriptions et Belles-Lettres, Institut de France; Académie Centrale Européenne de Science et Art; Institut Archéologique de Berlin. Address: 3 residence du Tourillon, F-69290 Craponne, France.

TURCOTTE Paul-André Gaëtan, b. 10 July 1943, Saint-Cuthbert, Canada. Professor; Researcher. Education: Baccalaureate of Arts, Collège de Joliette, 1964; Baccalaureate in Education, Laval University, Quebec, 1970; Licence and Master in Theology, University of Montreal, 1970; Doctorate in Sociology, École des Hautes Études en Sciences Sociales, 1979; Doctorate in Theology, Institut Catholique de Paris, 1987. Appointments: Professor, University of Haiti, 1971-75; Associate Researcher, French National Research Centre, 1977-; Professor, Saint-Paul's University, Ottawa, 1980-98; Professor, University of Montreal, 1984; Visiting Researcher, IRESCO, Paris, 1986-87; Fellow, School of Graduate Studies and Research, University of Ottawa, 1987-2000; Professor of Sociology, Institut Catholique de Paris, 1993-2006; Visiting Researcher, Instituto de Investigacion en Ciencias Sociales (INCIS), Valencia, Spain, 1996-2002; Visiting Professor, UCAC, Yaoundé, Cameroon, 2000-2005; University of Roma Tre, 2003, 2006; University St Joseph, Beirut, Lebanon, 2003, 2006; Visiting Researcher, University of Valencia, Valencia, Spain, 2005; Director of Research, French Association for the Formation and Research in Social Sciences, Paris, 2006-; Director of Research, International Agency for Diplomacy and Public Opinion, Paris, 2008-. Publications: Réconciliation et Libération, 1972; L'Éclatement d'un monde, 1981; Les Chemins de la différence, 1985; L'Enseignement secondaire public des frères éducateurs, 1988; Intransigeance ou Compromis, 1994; Sociologie du Christianisme, 1996; La Religion dans la modernité, 1997; Compromis religieux et mutation du croire, 1998; Sociologia e Storia della Vita Consecrata, 2000; Le Phénomène des sectes, 2002; Handbook of Early Christianity, 2002; Médiation et Compromis, 2006; Editor of 8 collective works and 19 issues of Social Compass, Retm Le Supplément, Pastoral Sciences, Claretianum; Over 250 papers and articles in 27 different journals or chapters of collective works (50 as co-author). Honours: Prize of the Provincial Bank, Faculty of Theology, University of Montreal, 1970; Cafe-Best Publication, Canadian Society for the Study of Education, 1989; IBC Top 100 Educators, 2005; Man of the Year, 2005; Genius Laureate of France, 2006. Memberships: International Council of Museums, UNESCO, 1998-; Institute of Canadian Studies, 1998-; Association Internationale des Sociologues de Langue Francaise, 1980; Association for the Sociology of Religion, 1980-; Society for the Scientific Study of Religion, 1980-; 10 other professional associations. Address: 170 Blvd du Montparnasse, 75014 Paris, France.

TURK Austin Theodore, b. 28 May 1934, Gainesville, Georgia, USA. Sociologist; Criminologist. m. Ruth-Ellen Marie Grimes. Education: BA, cum laude, University of Georgia, 1956; MA, University of Kentucky, 1959; PhD, University of Wisconsin, 1962. Appointments: Instructor, to Professor, Indiana University, 1962-74; Professor of Sociology, University of Toronto, 1974-88; Professor of Sociology, 1988-, Chair, 1989-94, University of California at Riverside. Publications: Criminality and Legal Order, 1969; Political Criminality: The Defiance and Defense of Authority, 1982. Honours: President, American Society of Criminology, 1984-85; Fellow, American Society of Criminology, 1978. Memberships: American Society of Criminology; American Sociological Association; Academy of Criminal Justice Sciences; Law and Society Association. Address: Department of Sociology, University of California, Riverside, CA 92521, USA.

TÜRK Danilo, b. 19 February 1952, Maribor, Slovenia. President of Slovenia. m. Barbara. Education: MA, University of Ljubljana; PhD, 1982. Appointments: Assistant Professor, 1978, Professor of International Law and Dean of Student Affairs, 2005, Faculty of Law, University of Ljubljana; Director, Institute for International Law, University of Ljubljana, 1983; UN Special Rapporteur on Realization of Economic, Social and Cultural Rights, 1986-92; Member, Constitutional Commission, Slovenian National Assembly, 1990; First Slovenian Permanent Representative to the United Nations, 1992-2000; President, United Nations Security Council, 1998-99; UN Assistant Secretary-General for Political Affairs, 2000-05; Elected third President of Slovenia, 2007. Publications: Co-author, chapter of human rights in the 19th Slovenian Constitution. Address: Office of the President of the Republic, Erjavceva 17, SI-1000 Ljubljana, Slovenia. E-mail: gp.uprs@up-rs.si

TURNER Amédée Edward, b. 26 March 1929, London, England. Queens Counsel. m. Deborah Dudley Owen, 1 son, 1 daughter. Education: BA, 1951, MA, 1953, Christ Church, Oxford. Appointments: Practised at Patent Bar, Inner Temple, London, 1954-57; Counsel at Kenyon & Kenyon (Patent Attorneys) New York, USA, 1957-60; Practice at Patent Bar, London, 1960-; Contested General Elections (Conservative) Norwich North, 1964, 1966, 1970; Appointed Queens Counsel, 1976-; Elected to European Parliament for Suffolk and Harwich and Suffolk and Cambridgeshire (Conservative), European Democratic Group, European People's Party, 1979-94; Chief Whip, 1989-2002, Chairman, 2002-04, Civil Liberties Committee; Counsel, Oppenheimer Wolff & Donnelly, Brussels, 1994-2001; Senior Counsel, Apco Europe, 1995-98; Member Executive Committee European League for Economic Co-operation, 1996-; Director, CJA Consultants, 2001-, Chairman, 2005-; Phare Advisor to Macedonian Parliament on approximation of EU legislation, 2001-2002; Member, Advisory Council to the Anglican Observer to UN, 2002-. Publications: The Law of Trade Secrets, 1964; The Law of the New European Patent, 1979; Reports for the European Commission including Intellectual Property Law and the Single Market, 1997; Manuals for the Macedonian Parliament on the Approximation of EU Laws and on Democratic Procedures, 2002; Numerous political articles on behalf of the Conservative Party; Numerous studies for the European Commission. Honours: Queens Counsel, 1976; Honorary Member of the European Parliament, 1994. Memberships: Carlton Club; The European Network; Conservative Group for Europe; Tory Reform Group; Kenya Society; African Society; International Association for the Protection of Industrial Property; Bar Association for Commerce and Industry. Address: Penthouse 7, Bickenhall Mansions, London W1U 6BS, England. E-mail: amedee.turner@btinternet.com

TURNER (Jonathan) Adair, b. 5 October 1955, Ipswich, England. Business Executive, Public Policy Specialist. m Orna ni Chionna, 2 daughters. Education: Degree, Economics and History, Cambridge University, 1974-78. Appointments: McKinsey and Company, 1982-95; Director-General, Confederation of British Industry, 1995-99; Director,

United Business Media, 2000-08; Chairman UK Low Pay Commission, 2003-06; Chairman, UK Pension Commission, 2003-06; Vice-Chairman, Merrill Lynch Europe, 2000-06. Director, Standard Chartered plc 2006-08; Director, Patemoster Ltd 2006-08; Director Siemens plc 2006-08; Chairman, Economic and Social Research Council, 2007-08; Chairman, Committee on Climate Change, 2008; Chairman, FSA, 2008. Publication: Just Capital, The Liberal Economy, 2004. Honours: Non Party Peerage, UK House of Lords, Lord Turner of Ecchinswell, 2005; Honorary Doctorate, City University, 2004. Memberships: Fellow of the World-Wide Fund for Nature, WWF, UK.

TURNER Kathleen, b. 19 June 1954, Springfield, Missouri, USA. Actress. m. (1) David Guc, divorced 1982, (2) Jay Weiss, 1984, divorced, 1 daughter. Education: Central School of Speech and Drama, London; SW Missouri State University; University of Maryland. Career: Theatre: various roles including: Gemini, 1978; The Graduate, London, 2000; TV includes: The Doctors, 1977; Leslie's Folly, 1995; Style and Substance, 1996; Legalese, 1998; Cinderella; King of the Hill; Friends; Law & Order; Nip/Tuck Films: Body Heat, 1981; The Man With Two Brains, 1983; Crimes of Passion, 1984; Romancing the Stone, 1984; Prizzi's Honour, 1985; The Jewel of the Nile, 1985; Peggy Sue Got Married, 1986; Julia and Julia, 1988; Switching Channels, 1988; The Accidental Tourist, 1989; The War of the Roses, 1990; V I Warzhawski, 1991; House of Cards; Undercover Blues, 1993; Serial Mom, 1994; Naked in New York, 1994; Moonlight and Valentino, 1995; A Simple Wish, 1997; The Real Blonde, 1997; The Virgin Suicides, 1999; Love and Action in Chicago, 1999; Baby Geniuses, 1999; Prince of Central Park, 2000; Beautiful, 2000; Without Love, 2004; Monster House, 2006; Marley & Me, 2008. Address: c/o Chris Andrews, ICM, 8942 Wilshire Boulevard, Beverly Hills, CA 90211, USA.

TURNER Lynette, b. 28 May 1945, London, England. Graphic Artist. Education: BSc (Hons) Zoology, Manchester University, 1965-68; Etching, City and Guilds Art School, 1968-69; HNDD, Graphic Design, Manchester Polytechnic, 1970-71. Career: Set up etching workshop at home at the Oval in London and sold prints at Heal's and Liberty's, 1975-94; Moved to Cornwall 1994-; Exhibitions: Century Gallery, Henley, 1976; Margaret Fisher Gallery, 1976; RA, 1977; SE London Art Group, YMCA, Great Russell Street, 1983; RA Summer Show, 1987; Etchings and watercolours, The Crypt of St Martin-in-the-Fields, 1989. Publications: Works featured in the Observer, 1989; Currently working on comic strip adventures. Honour: 2nd Prize for Etching, City and Guilds Art School, 1969. Membership: Royal Cornwall Polytechnic Society. Address: 2 Doctors Hill, St Keverne, Cornwall TR12 6UX, England.

TURNER Neil Clifford, b. 13 March 1940, Preston, England. Research Scientist. m. Jennifer Gibson, 3 sons. Education: BSc (Hons), 1962; PhD, 1968; DSc, 1983. Appointments: Plant Physiologist, CT Agricultural Experimental Station, New Haven, USA, 1967-74; Senior Research Scientist, 1974-84, Research Leader, 1984-93, Chief Research Scientist, 1993-2005, CSIRO Plant Industry, Canberra and Perth, Australia; Adjunct Professor, University of Western Australia, Perth, Australia, 1998-2006; Director, Centre for Legumes in Mediterranean Agriculture, The University of Western Australia, Perth, 2006-07; Winthrop Research Professor, Centre for Legumes in Mediterranean Agriculture, University of Western Australia, Perth, 2008-; Sustainability of Agricultural Ecosystems in Arid Regions in Response to Climate Change, 2011; Climate Change and Agricultural Ecosystem Management in Dry Areas, 2011. Publications: Adaption of Plants to Water and High Temperature Stress, 1980; Plant Growth, Drought and Salinity, 1986; Crop Production on Duplex Soils, 1992; The Role of Agroforestry and Perennial Pasture in Mitigating Waterlogging and Secondary Salinity, Special Issue, Agricultural Water Management, 2002; Water Scarcity: Challenges and Opportunities for Crop Science, Special Issue, Agricultural Water Management, 2006; Ground-breaking Stuff, Special Issue, Field Crops Research, 2007. Honours: Fellow, American Society of Agronomy, 1982; Fellow, Crop Science Society of America, 1985; Fellow, Australian Academy of Technology Sciences and Engineering, 1992; Medallist, 1993, Fellow, 1995, Australian Institute of Agricultural Science and Technology; Institute for Scientific Information Australian Citation Laureate, 2001; Foreign Fellow, Indian Academy of Agricultural Sciences, 2003; Centenary Medal, Australia, 2003. Memberships: Australian Academy of Technology Sciences and Engineering; Australian Institute of Agricultural Science and Technology, ACT President, 1978-79. Address: Centre for Legumes in Mediterranean Agriculture, M080, The University of Western Australia, 35 Stirling Highway, Crawley, Western Australia 6009, Australia.

TURNER Roger Burton, b. 28 July 1947, England. Solicitor; Consultant. m. Jennifer Bound, 1998. Education: Graduate Certificate in Education, University of London Institute of Education, 1971; MA, University of Kent, 1976; Bachelor of Divinity, 1970, Master of Theology, 1972, King's College, London; Diploma in Law, Polytechnic of Central London, 1981; Bar Final, Inns of Court School of Law, 1982; Qualified Lawyers' Transfer Test, College of Law, 1999; Diploma, History of Art and Architecture, 2009, Birkbeck College, University of London; M Phil candidate, School of Architecture and Construction, University of Greenwich, 2011-. Appointments: Teacher, preparatory school, secondary schools and college of higher education, 1966-67, 1972-80; Practised at criminal bar, 1983-98; Part-time Tutor, Inns of Court School of Law, 1993-96; Visiting Research Fellow, Institute of Historical Research, University of London, 1995-96; Solicitor Advocate, 1999-; Consultant, Foreman Young (now Julian Young & Co), London; Consultant, Dalton Holmes Gray, London, 2003-; President, West London Law Society, 2003; London Arts Correspondent, Guernsey Press and Star. Publications: Manchester and the '45: a study of Jacobitism in context, 1996; Proper Missionaries: Clergymen in the Household of Lord Burlington during the period 1715-1753 in Lord Burlington - the Man and his Politics: Questions of Loyalty, 1998; Contributor, Oxford Dictionary of National Biography; Various reviews of London art exhibitions. Honours: Listed in international biographical dictionaries. Memberships: Solicitors' Association of Higher Court Advocates; London Criminal Courts Solicitors' Association; The Lansdowne Club; Affiliate Member, RIBA. Address: 26 Evesham Road, London N11 2RN, England. E-mail: roger.turner@googlemail.com

TURNER Simon Paul, b. 21 March 1959, Richmond, Surrey, England. Educator; Manager; Consultant. Education: Academic and professional qualifications in the fields of: Astronomy and Planetary Science; Health & Safety; Electrical; Engineering (Electronic & Mechanical); Computing; Science; Life/Key Skills; Teaching and Learning; Management; and others. Appointments: Junior Technician, 1980-84, Corporal, 1984-85, RAF General Technician Electrical, Royal Air Force West Raynham; Flying Officer, RAF Engineering Officer, Royal Military College of Science, Swindon, and RAF (Cranwell, Chivenor, Marham and Cottesmore) 1985-89; Sole Proprietor, Eastern Office Equipment, Norfolk, 1989-93; Part time Private Tuition, Norfolk Home Tutor Agency, 1991-93; Part time Lecturer, Adult Education Centre, Litcham, Norfolk, 1992-93; Lecturer, 1993-95, Head of Section Engineering, 1995-99, Head of Technology (Construction, IT and Engineering), 1999-2001, Deputy Head of Faculty (Design & Technology), 2001-03, Director of Operations, 2003-06, Isle College, Wisbech, Cambridgeshire; Part time Electrical & Electronic Private Work, Kings Lynn, Norfolk, 1993-98; Part time External Verifier, City and Guilds, 2005-; Part time Educational Consultant, Huntingdonshire Regional College, 2006-07; Part time Technical Author, Part time Examination Auditor, Part time Lead Consultant Investigator, City & Guilds, 2008-. Publications: Introduction of Foundation Provision for Vocational Programmes. Honours: RAF Certificate of Merit; Norfolk Circle Electrical Prize; Royal Military College of Science College Prize; Listed in international biographical dictionaries. Memberships: Institute of Electrical Engineers; Institution of Engineering and Technology; Institute of Incorporated Engineers; Institute for Learning; Institute of Motor Industries; Institute of Physics; Institute of Leadership and Management; British Astronomical Association; City & Guilds Association; The Association of Managers in Education; Association of External Verifiers; Uganda Association for the Promotion of Science; Graduate, City and Guilds Institute; Engineering Council registered Incorporated Engineer; Institute of Assessors and Verifiers; City & Guilds Institute; Affiliate Member, Computer Society. Address: 27 Lovat Road, Kinlochleven, Argyll, PH50 4RQ, Scotland.

TURNER Ted (Robert Edward II), b. 19 November 1938. American Broadcasting Executive; Yachtsman. m. (1) Judy Nye, divorced, 1 son, 1 daughter, (2) Jane S Smith, 1965, divorced 1988, 1 son, 2 daughters, (3) Jane Fonda, 1991, divorced 2001. Education: Brown University. Appointments: General Manager, Turner Advertising, Macon, Georgia, 1960-63; President, CEO, various Turner companies, Atlanta, 1963-70; Chair of Board, President, Turner Broadcasting System Inc, 1970-96; Established Cable News Network (CNN), 1980, Headline News Network, 1992, CNN International, 1985; Chair, Better World Society, Washington, DC, 1985-90; Acquired MGM library of film and TV properties, 1986; Founder, Turner Foundation Inc, 1991; Launched Cartoon Network, 1992; TBS merged with New Line Cinema, 1994; Vice Chair, Time Warner Inc (after TBS merger with Time Warner Inc), 1996-2001; Founder, UN Foundation, 1997; Founder, Nuclear Threat Initiative, 2001; Vice Chair, AOL Time Warner (after Time Warner Inc merger with AOL), 2001-03; Founder, Ted Turner Pictures and Ted Turner Documentaries, 2001; Founder, Ted's Montana Grill restaurant chain, 2002; Former owner and President, Atlanta Braves professional baseball team; Former owner and Chair of Board, Atlanta Hawks professional basketball team; Director, Martin Luther King Center, Atlanta. Publication: The Racing Edge, 1979. Honours: Fastnet Trophy, 1979; Man of the Year, Time Magazine, 1991; Cable and Broadcasting's Man of the Century, 1999; Cable TV Hall of Fame, 1999; U Thant Peace Award, 1999; World Ecology Award, University of Missouri, 2000; Named Yachtsman of the Year 4 times. Address: c/o Ted's Montana Grill, 133 Luckie Street, NW, Atlanta, GA 30303, USA. Website: www.tedturner.com

TURNER Tina (Annie Mae Bullock), b. 26 November 1939, Nutbush, Tennessee, USA. Singer. Songwriter. m. Ike Turner, 1958, divorced 1978. Career: Member, Ike & Tina Turner, 1958-76; Worldwide tours include: Support to Rolling Stones, UK tour, 1966, US tour, 1969; European tour, 1971; Newport Festival, 1969; Solo artiste, 1978-; US tour, 1981; Support to Lionel Richie, UK tour, 1984; Rock In Rio Festival, Brazil, 1985; Live Aid, Philadelphia, 1985; European tour, 1985; Prince's Trust Gala, London, 1986; World tours, 1987, 1990; Record 182,000 audience attend concert, Rio De Janeiro, 1988; First woman to play Palace of Versailles, France, 1990; Film appearances: Tommy, 1974; Mad Max - Beyond Thunderdome, 1985; Life story documented in film What's Love Got To Do With It?, 1992. Compositions include: Nutbush City Limits; Recordings: Albums with Ike Turner: Live! The Ike And Tina Turner Show, 1965; River Deep, Mountain High, 1966; Outa Season, 1969; The Hunter, 1969; Come Together, 1970; Workin' Together, 1971; Live At Carnegie Hall, 1971; 'Nuff Said, 1971; Feel Good, 1972; Nutbush City Limits, 1974; Solo albums: The Acid Queen, 1975; Private Dancer, 1984; Mad Max - Beyond The Thunderdome, 1985; Break Every Rule (Number 1 in nine countries), 1986; Live In Europe, 1988; Foreign Affair (Number 1, UK), 1989; Simply The Best, 1991; What's Love Got To With It (film soundtrack), 1993; Wildest Dreams, 1996; Dues Paid, 1999; Twenty Four Seven, 1999; Hit singles include: with Ike Turner: It's Gonna Work Out Fine, 1961; Poor Fool, 1962; River Deep, Mountain High, 1966; I Want To Take You Higher, 1970; Proud Mary, 1971; Nutbush City Limits, 1973; Solo: Let's Stay Together, 1983; What's Love Got To Do With It? (Number 1, US), 1984; Better Be Good To Me, 1984; Private Dancer, 1984; We Don't Need Another Hero, theme for film Thunderdome (Number 2, US), 1985; One Of The Living, 1985; It's Only Love, with Bryan Adams, 1985; Typical Male (Number 2, US), 1986; The Best, 1989; I Don't Wanna Lose You, 1989; Be Tender With Me Baby, 1990; It Takes Two, duet with Rod Stewart, 1990; Way Of The World, 1991; I Don't Wanna Fight, 1993; Goldeneye (film theme), 1995; Missing You, 1996; In Your Wildest Dreams, 1996; When the Heartache is Over, 1999; Whatever You Need, 2000; Contributor, We Are The World, USA For Africa, 1985. Publications: I Tina (autobiography). Honours include: Grammy Awards: Record of the Year; Song of the Year; Best Female Vocal Performance; Best Female Rock Vocal, 1985; American Music Awards: Favourite Soul/R&B Female Artist, and Video Artist, 1985; Best Female Pop/Rock Artist, 1986; MTV Music Video award, 1985; Star on Hollywood Walk of Fame, 1986; Rock And Roll Hall Of Fame, with Ike Turner, 1991; World Music Award, Outstanding Contribution To The Music Industry, 1993; Kennedy Center Honors, 2005. Address: c/o Roger Davies Management, 15030 Ventura Blvd, Suite 772, Sherman Oaks, CA 91403, USA.

TURNER WARWICK Margaret Elizabeth, b. 19 November 1924, London, England. Emeritus Professor of Medicine. m. Richard, 2 daughters. Education: Lady Margaret Hall, Oxford, England; University College Hospital, University of London, England. Appointments: Casualty Medical Officer, University College Hospital, London, England; Registrar and House Officer appointments, University College Hospital and the Royal Brompton Hospital, London; Consultant Physician, Elizabeth Garrett Anderson Hospital, London; Consultant Physician, London Chest Hospital, London, 1967-72; Consultant Physician, Royal Brompton Hospital, 1967-89; Senior Lecturer, 1967-72, Professor of Medicine, 1972-87, Cardiothoracic Institute, University of London; Dean, National Heart and Lung Institute, University of London, 1984-87; President, Royal College of Physicians, 1989-92; Chairman, Royal Devon and Exeter Health Trust, 1992-95; Consulting Physician, Royal Brompton Hospital, London; Emeritus Professor of Medicine, University of London. Publications: Immunology of the Lung, 1978; Occupational Lung Disease, co-editor Professor Hans Weill; Papers and chapters on asthma, interstitial lung disease, occupational lung disease. Honours: Dame of the British Empire, 1991; Honorary DSc: New York,

Sussex, Exeter, Oxford, Cambridge, London, Hull, Leicester; Honorary Fellowships: FRCS, LMH, Oxford, Girton College, Cambridge; Green College, Oxford. Fellowships: F Acad Med Sci, FRACP, FRCGP, FRCP (Edin), FRCPS (Glasgow), FRCP Canada, FRCR, FRCPath, FUCL, F Imp Coll; Osler medal for Medicine, Oxford; President's Medal, British Thoracic Society; President's Award, European Respiratory Society, Hon Bencher, Middle Temple. Memberships: Doctor of Medicine, Oxford; PhD, London; FRCP; Previously Member, Board of Governors, Royal Brompton Hospital; Chairman, Academy of Royal Medical Colleges; Chairman, UCCR; Member, Round Table on Sustainable Development; Member, Nuffield Bioethics Council; Member, National Employers Liaison Committee. Address: Pynes House, Silver Street, Thiorverton, Exeter, Devon EX5 5LT, England.

TURTURRO John, b. 28 February 1957, Brooklyn, USA. Actor. m. Katherine Borowitz, 2 sons. Education: State University of New York at New Paltz; Yale Drama School. Career: Former labourer; Films: Raging Bull; Desperately Seeking Susan; Exterminator III; The Flamingo Kid; To Live and Die in LA; Hannah and Her Sisters; Gung Ho; Offbeat; The Color of Money; The Italian Five Corners; Do the Right Thing; Miller's Crossing; Men of Respect; Mo' Better Blues; Jungle Fever; Barton Fink; Brain Doctors; Mac; Being Human; Quiz Show; Fearless; Clockers; Search and Destroy; Unstrung Heroes; Sugartime; Grace of My Heart; Box of Moonlight; The Truce; The Big Lebowski, 1997; Animals, 1997; Lesser Prophets, 1998; Rounders, 1998; Illuminata, 1998; The Source, 1999; The Cradle Will Rock, 1999; Company Men, 1999; Two Thousand and None, 1999; Oh Brother, Where Art Thou?, 1999; The Man Who Cried, 1999; The Luzhin Defense, 1999; Thirteen Conversations About One Thing, 2000; Collateral Damage, 2001; Mr Deeds, 2002; Fear X, 2003; Anger Management, 2003; 2B Perfectly Honest, 2004; Secret Passage, 2004; Secret Window, 2004; She Hate Me, 2004; The Moon and the Son: An Imagined Conversation (voice), 2005; Romance & Cigarettes, 2005; Quelques jours en Septembre, 2006; The Good Shepherd, 2006; Slipstream, 2007; Transformers, 2007; Margot at the Wedding, 2007; Joulutarina (voice), 2007; What Just Happened? 2008; You Don't Mess with the Zohan, 2008; Miracle at St. Anna, 2008; The Taking of Pelham 1 2 3, 2009; Transformers 2: Revenge of the Fallen, 2009; Nutcracker and the Rat King, 2010 . Address: c/o ICM, 40 West 57th Street, New York, NY 10019, USA.

TUTT Sylvia Irene Maud, b. London, England. Chartered Secretary and Administrator. Appointments: Chartered Secretary and Administrator in private practice; Writer; Senior Examiner, Chartered Insurance Institute, 1975-2004; Examiner, Society of Financial Advisers, 1992-2004. Publications: Author of numerous technical articles in professional and financial journals; Author or joint author of the following books: Private Pension Scheme Finance, 1970; Pensions and Employee Benefits, 1973; Pension Law and Taxation, 1981; Financial Aspects of Pension Business, 1985; Financial Aspects of Life Business, 1987; A Mastership of a Livery Company, 1988; Financial Aspects of Long Term Business, 1991; Pension Law and Administration, 2002. Memberships: Fellow and Past Member of Council, The Publications and Public Relations Committee, Education Committee, Benevolent Management Committee and Crossways Trust, Past President of its Women's Society and Past Chairman of London Branch, Institute of Chartered Secretaries and Administrators; Fellow Royal Statistical Society; Fellow Royal Society of Arts; Member of Court of City University London; Past President, Soroptimist International of Central London; Past President, United Wards Club of the City of London; Past President, Farringdon Ward Club, London; President, City Livery Club, London, 2001-2002; Past Chairman and currently Vice-President, Royal Society of St George, City of London Branch; Master, The Scriveners Company, 2007-08; Master, 1983-84, Worshipful Company of Chartered Secretaries and Administrators, Member of its Finance and General Purposes Committee, 1995-2004, Managing Trustee of its Charitable Trust, 1978-; Freeman, Guild of Freemen of the City of London. Address: 21 Sandilands, Croydon, Surrey CR0 5DF, England.

TUTU Desmond Mpilo, (Most Rev), b. 7 October 1931, Klerksdorp, South Africa. Archbishop Emeritus. m. Leah Nomalizo Tutu, 1955, 1 son, 3 daughters. Education: Bantu Normal College; University of South Africa; St Peter's Theological College, Rosettenville; King's College, University of London; LTh; MTh. Appointments: Schoolmaster, 1954-57; Parish priest, 1960-; Theology Seminary Lecturer, 1967-69; University Lecturer, 1970-71; Associate Director, Theology Education Fund, World Council of Churches, 1972-75; Dean of Johannesburg, 1975-76; Bishop of Lesotho, 1977-78; Bishop of Johannesburg, 1984-86; Archbishop of Cape Town, Metropolitan of the Church of the Province of Southern Africa, 1986-96; Chancellor, University of Western Cape, 1988-; President, All Africa Conference of Churches, 1987-; Secretary-General, South Africa Council of Churches, 1979-84; Visiting Professor, Anglican Studies, New York General Theology Seminary, 1984; Elected to Harvard University Board of Overseers, 1989; Director, Coca Cola, 1986-; Visiting Professor, Emory University, Atlanta, 1996-; Leader, Truth and Reconciliation Commission, 1995-; Archbishop Emeritus, Cape Town, 1996-; Robert R Woodruff Visiting Distinguished Professor, Candler School of Theology, 1998-99; William R Cannon Distinguished Visiting Professor, Emory University, 1999-2000; Visiting Professor, King's College, London, 2004. Publications: Crying in the Wilderness, 1982; Hope and Suffering, 1983; The Rainbow People of God, 1994; An African Prayer Book, 1996; The Essential Desmond Tutu, 1997; No Future without Forgiveness, 1999. Honours include: Numerous Honorary Degrees; Nobel Peace Prize, 1984; Carter-Menil; Human Rights Prize, 1986; Martin Luther King Junior Peace Award, 1986; Third World Prize, 1989; Order of Jamaica; Freedom of Borough of Merthyr Tydfil, Wales; Order of Meritorious Service, South Africa, 1996; Order of Grand Cross, Germany; Nelson Mandela Award for Health and Human Rights, Florida, USA, 1998; Monismanien Prize, Uppsala University Sweden, 1999; MESB Service Award, Medical Education for South African Blacks, 1999; Athenagoras Award for Human Rights, 2000. Memberships: Third Order of Society of St Francis; President, All Africa Conference of Churches; Council for National Orders, Republic of South Africa. Address: c/o Truth and Reconciliation Commission, PO Box 3162, Cape Town 8000, South Africa.

TWAIN Shania, b. 28 August 1965, Windsor, Toronto, Canada. Country Singer; Songwriter. m. Robert John Lange, 1 son. Appointments: Several TV performances on CMT and TNN; Songwriter with husband. Creative Works: Albums: Shania Twain, 1993; The Woman in Me, 1995; Come On Over, 1997; On The Way, 1999; Beginnings 1989-90, 1999; Wild and Wicked, 2000; Complete Limelight Sessions, 2001; Up! 2002; Greatest Hits, 2004; Singles: What Made You Say That, 1993; Dance With The One That Brought You, 1993; You Lay A Whole Lotta Love On Me, 1993; Whose Bed Have Your Boots Been Under, 1995; Any Man of Mine, 1995; Woman In Me, 1995; You Win My Love, 1996; God Bless The Child, 1996; I'm Outta Here, 1996; Love Gets

Me Every Time, 1997; Don't Be Stupid, 1997; You're Still The One, 1998; From This Moment On, 1998; When, 1998; That Don't Impress Me Much, 1998; Man, I Feel Like a Woman, 1999; You've Got A Way, 1999; Don't Be Stupid (You Know I Love You), 2000; I'm Gonna Get You Good, 2002; Ka-Ching! 2003; Up, 2003; Forever & Always, 2003; Thank You Baby For Making Someday Come So Soon, 2003; When You Kiss Me, 2003; Party For Two, 2005; Don't! 2005; I Ain't No Quitter, 2005; Shoes, 2005. Honours: CMT Europe, Rising Video Star Of The Year, 1993; Entertainer of the Year, Academy of Country Music and Country Music Association, 1999; 5 Grammy Awards including Best Female Country Vocal Performance, 2000 and Best Country Song, 2000; 27 BMI Songwriter Awards; First non-US citizen to win the CMA award; Canada's Walk of Fame, 2003; Officer in the Order of Canada, 2005. Address: Mercury Nashville, 54 Music Square E, Nashville, TN 37203, USA. Website: www.shaniatwain.com

TWEDDLE Beth, b. 1 April 1985, Johannesburg, South Africa (British citizen). Gymnast. Education: Queens School, Chester; Degree in Sports Science, Liverpool John Moores University, 2007. Career: World Championships, Ghent, 2001; World Championships, Debrecen, 2002; Continental Championships/Games, Patras, 2002; World Championships, Anaheim, 2003; World Cup/Series, Stuttgart, 2003; World Cup/Series, Paris, 2003; World Cup/Series, Cottbus (win on Uneven Bar), 2003; World Cup/Series, Glasgow (win on Uneven Bar), 2003; Olympic Games, Athens, 2004; Continental Championships/Games, Amsterdam, 2004; World Cup/Series,Cottbus (win on Uneven Bar), 2004; World Cup/Series, Lyon (win on Uneven Bar), 2004; World Cup/Series Final, Birmingham, 2004; World Championships, Melbourne, 2005; World Cup/Series, Paris, 2005; Continental Championships/Games, Debrecen, 2005; World Cup/Series (win on Uneven Bar), Ghent, 2005; World Cup/Series, New York, 2005; World Cup/Series, Glasgow (win on Uneven Bar and Floor Exercise), 2005; World Championships, Aarhus (win on Uneven Bar), 2006; World Cup/Series, Glasgow (win on Uneven Bar), 2006; Continental Championships/Games, Volos (win on Uneven Bar), 2006; World Cup/Series, Sao Paulo (win on Uneven Bar), 2006; World Championships, Stuttgart, 2007; World Cup/Series, Glasgow (win on Floor Exercise), 2007; Continental Championships/Games, Amsterdam, 2007; Olympic Games, Beijing, 2008; Continental Championships/Games, Clermont-Ferrand, 2008; Continental Championships/Games, Milan (win on Uneven Bar and Floor Exercise), 2009; World Cup/Series, Glasgow (win on Uneven Bar and Floor Exercise), 2009; World Championships, London (win on Floor Exercise), 2009. Honours: 3rd place, BBC Sports Personality of the Year, 2006.

TYERS Anthony Gordon, b. 14 September 1944, Romsey, England. Consultant Ophthalmic Surgeon. m. Renée De Waard, 2 sons, 2 daughters. Education: Hampton School, Middlesex; Charing Cross Hospital Medical School, University of London, 1963-70; Resident, 1978-81, Fellow, 1982-86, Moorfields Eye Hospital, London; Fellow, Massachusetts Eye & Ear Infirmary, Boston, USA, 1981-82; Fellow, University Eye Department, Amsterdam, 1982. Appointments: Visiting Consultant, St John Eye Hospital, Jerusalem, 1995-; Consultant Ophthalmic (Plastic) Surgeon, Moorfields Eye Hospital, London, 1997-99; Consultant Ophthalmic Surgeon, Salisbury District Hospital (NHS), 1986-; New Hall Hospital, Salisbury & Sarum Road Hospital, Winchester (Private). Publications: Colour Atlas of Ophthalmic Plastic Surgery, 2008; 6 chapters in other Ophthalmic Plastic Surgery publications. Honours: Medical Book of the Year, Royal Society of Medicine, Society of Authors, 2008; Officer of the Most Venerable Order of the Hospital of St John of Jerusalem. Memberships: European Society of Ophthalmic Plastic and Reconstructive Surgery (President 2009-11); British Oculo-Plastic Surgery Society (President, 2005-07); British Association of Aesthetic Plastic Surgeons; British Medical Association; Royal Society of Medicine. Address: Huckleberry, Bouverie Close, Salisbury SP2 8DY, England. E-mail: anthony.tyers@salisbury.nhs.uk

TYLER Anne, b. 25 October 1941, Minneapolis, Minnesota, USA. Writer. m. Taghi M Modaressi, 1963, 2 children. Education: BA, Duke University, 1961; Postgraduate Studies, Columbia University, 1962. Publications: If Morning Ever Comes, 1964; The Tin Can Tree, 1965; A Slipping Down Life, 1970; The Clock Winder, 1972; Celestial Navigation, 1974; Searching for Caleb, 1976; Earthly Possessions, 1977; Morgan's Passing, 1980; Dinner at the Homesick Restaurant, 1982; The Best American Short Stories, 1983 (editor with Shannon Ravenel), 1983; The Accidental Tourist, 1985; Breathing Lessons, 1988; Saint Maybe, 1991; Tumble Tower (juvenile), 1993; Ladder of Years, 1995; A Patchwork Planet, 1998; Back When We Were Grown-ups, 2001; The Amateur Marriage, 2004; Digging to America, 2006; Short stories in magazines. Honours: PEN/Faulkner Prize for Fiction, 1983; National Book Critics Circle Award for Fiction, 1985; Pulitzer Prize for Fiction, 1989; Orange Broadband Prize for Fiction, 1996, 2007. Memberships: American Academy of Arts and Letters; American Academy of Arts and Sciences. Address: 222 Tunbridge Road, Baltimore, MD 21212, USA. E-mail: atmBaltimore@aol.com

TYLER Liv, b. 1 July 1977, Portland, Maine, USA. Actress. m. Royston Langdon, 2003 (divorced), 1 son. Career: Film appearances include: Silent Fall; Empire Records; Heavy; Stealing Beauty; That Thing You Do!; Inventing the Abbotts; Plunkett and Macleane, 1999; Armageddon, 1998; Cookie's Fortune, 1999; Onegin, 1999; The Little Black Book, 1999; Dr T and the Women, 2000; The Lord of the Rings: The Fellowship of the Ring, 2001; One Night at McCool's, 2001; The Lord of the Rings: The Two Towers, 2002; The Lord of the Rings: The Return of the King, 2003; Jersey Girl, 2004; Lonesome Jim, 2004; Reign Over Me, 2007; Smother, 2007; The Strangers, 2008; The Incredible Hulk, 2008. Address: c/o CAA, 9830 Wilshire Boulevard, Beverly Hills, CA 90212, USA.

TYSON Mike G, b. 30 June 1966, New York, USA. Boxer. m. (1) Robin Givens, 1988, divorced 1989, (2) Monica Turner, 1997, divorced 2003, 2 children, (3) Lakiha Spicer, 2009, 2 children, 4 children from previous relationships (1 daughter deceased). Appointments: Defeated Trevor Berbick to win WBC Heavyweight Title, 1986; Winner WBA Heavyweight Title, 1987; IBF Heavyweight Title, 1987; Former Undefeated World Champion, winner all 32 bouts, lost to James Buster Douglas, 1990; Defeated Donovan Ruddock, 1991; Sentenced to 6 years imprisonment for rape and two counts of deviant sexual practice, 1992; Appealed against sentence; Appeal rejected by US Supreme Court, 1994; released, 1995; Regained title of Heavyweight World Champion after defeating Frank Bruno, 1996; Lost to Evander Holyfield, 1996; License revoked by Nevada State Athletics Commission after disqualification from rematch against Holyfield, 1996; reinstated on appeal 1998; Sentenced to a years imprisonment for assault, 1999; released on probation, 1999; Fought Lennox Lewis, 2002 for the WBC and IBF titles, knocked out in eighth round; Defeated Clifford Etienne, 2003; Lost to Danny Williams, 2004; Retired, 2005. Honours:

Honorary Chair Cystic Fibrosis Association, 1987; Young Adult Institute, 1987. Address: Don King Productions, 501 Fairway Drive, Deerfield Beach, FL 33441, USA.

DICTIONARY OF INTERNATIONAL BIOGRAPHY 36th EDITION

U

UCHINO Akira, b. 28 May 1952, Fukuoka, Japan. Professor. m. Machiko Osada, 3 daughters. Education: Faculty of Medicine, Kyushu University. Appointments: Associate Professor, Radiology, Saga Medical School, 1994-2007; Professor, Diagnostic Radiology, Saitama Medical University, International Medical Center, 2007-. Publications: Scientific papers in professional journals. Honours: Japan Radiological Society; Japanese Society for Magnetic Resonance in Medicine; Radiological Society of North America. Memberships: Japan Radiological Society; Japanese Society of Neuroradiology; Japanese Society for Magnetic Resonance in Medicine; Japanese Society of Interventional Radiology; American Society of Neuroradiology; European Society of Neuroradiology. Address: 336-7-502, Harajuku, Hidaka, Saitama 350-1205, Japan.

UCHIUMI Fumiaki, b. 12 April 1962, Haboro-cho, Hokkaido, Japan. Associate Professor. m. Hongmei Shan, 1 daughter. Education: BSc, 1987, PhD, Pharmaceutical Science, 1999, Tokyo University of Science; MSc, Tokyo Institute of Technology, 1989; PhD, Medical Science, Tokyo University, 1993. Appointments: Research Associate, 1993-2000, Lecturer, 2000-10, Associate Professor, 2010-, Tokyo University of Science; Postdoctoral Exchange Researcher, Dr E Fanning's Laboratory, Vanderbilt University, US-Japan Cooperative Cancer Research Program, 2000-01. Publications: Regulations of telomerase activity and WRN gene expression, 2010; The effect of Resveratrol on the Werner Syndrome RecQ helicase gene and Telomerase activity, 2011. Memberships: Japan Cancer Association; Japan Biochemical Society; Molecular Biological Society of Japan; Pharmaceutical Society of Japan. E-mail: uchiumi@rs.noda.tus.ac.jp

UDEH Kenneth Ogbonna, b. 26 May 1959, Naze-Owerri, Nigeria. Food Biotechnologist. m. Zofia Urszula Udeh, 1989, 2 daughters. Education: Diploma, Cold Storage Technology, College of Food Technology, Sandomierz, Poland, 1981; MSc, Lublin Agriculture University, 1986; PhD, Lublin Agriculture University, 1996; PhD in Food Biotechnology. Appointments: Doctoral Student, 1991-96, Research Fellow, 1996, Reader, 2001- Department of Biotechnology, Human Nutrition and Food Quality Sciences, University of Life Science; Deputy Director General, IBC, England, 1999. Publications: Several articles in professional journals; Patentee in field. Honours: International Man of the Year, IBC, 1998-99, 1999-2000; Listed in several biographical publications. Memberships: New York Academy of Sciences; Polish Food Technology Society. Address: Przy Stawie Street 4/3, Lublin 20-067, Poland.

UDRISTE Constantin, b. 22 January 1940, Turceni, Gorj, Romania. Professor. m. Aneta, 2 sons. Education: Professor of Mathematics, University of Timisoara, 1963; Doctor in Mathematics, University of Cluj-Napoca, 1971. Appointments: Teacher, High School, Bucharest, 1963-64; Assistant, 1964-70, Lecturer, 1970-76; Professor, 1976-90, Full Professor, Dean, Director, Chair, 1990-, University Politehnica of Bucharest. Publications: Over 45 books; 270 papers; 270 communications. Honours: D Hurmuzescu Prize, Romanian Academy, 1985; Award MEI, 1988; Stefan Hepites Prize, Romanian Academy, 2010; Correspondent Member, Academia Peloritana, Messina, 1997; Titular Member, Academy of Romanian Scientists, 2007; Anassilaos International, 2000; Prize COPIRO – 2000 for Exact Sciences; Honorary Member, World Scientific and Engineering Academy and Society, 2008-. Memberships: Society of Mathematical Scientists of Romania, 1963; AMS, 1987; Tensor Society, 1985; Balkan Society of Geometers, President, 1994. Address: University Politehnica of Bucharest, Department of Mathematics I, Splaiul Independentei 313, 060042 Bucharest, Romania. E-mail: udriste@mathem.pub.ro

UESUGI Takamichi, b. 15 September 1935, Kyoto Prefecture, Japan. Professor. m. Mitsuyo, 3 daughters. Education: MA, Graduate School, Kyoto University, 1961. Appointments: Associate Professor, Nara Women's University, 1973; Associate Professor, 1978, Professor, 1987, Emeritus Professor, 1999, Kyoto University; Professor, Ryukoku University, 1999; Professor, Kio University, 2006. Publications: Modern Culture and Education (Kobundo-Shuppansha), 1989; Development of Community Education (Shorai-Sha), 1993. Memberships: Director, Japan Society for the Study of Education: President, Director, Japan Society for the Study of Adult and Community Education. Address: 2-38-10 Yuyamadai, Kawanishi, Hyogo, Japan. E-mail: uesugi15@bea.hi-ho.ne.jp

UKAEGBU David Okwukanmanihu, b. 28 January 1939, Umuahia, Nigeria. Professional Accountant; MGT Scientist. Education: General Certificate of Education, Wolsey Hall, Oxford, Kings College, Lagos University College, Ibadan, 1958-66; Taxation, Foulks Lynch & Co Ltd, London; Chartered Secretaries and Administration, Metropolitan College, St Albans and Manchester College, England, 1962-70; Doctorate thesis, at Harvard University, Massachusetts Institute of Technology and Alexander Hamilton Institute Inc, University of Cambridge, Department of Applied Economics, through the Institute for International Research, London and New York, 1975-79; Degree in Management Sciences, MBIM, from the Institute of Management, UK and American Management Association, USA, 1975-79; BSc/MBA, Business Administration, California Coast University, Santa Ana, USA, 1982; Diploma, Kings College, Cambridge, 2000-01; Graduated with honours, Crossroads Bible Institute, USA, 2003; World Bible School, USA, 2004. Appointments: Chief Audit Clerk, 1958-60, Assistant Audit Manager, 1961-64, Audit Manager, 1964-66, Articled Clerk, 1967-70, Firms of Chartered Accountants; Professional Accountant, MGT Consultant, Charter House, 1971-2008; Chief Accountant, Consultant, Silver Shoes Manufacturing Company Ltd, 1974-99; Honorary Treasurer, Employers Association of Leather Footwear and Rubber Industries of Nigeria, 1990-94. Publications: Unpublished work in investment financing, 1986; Articles in professional financial journals, industrial and general management. Honours: IBC Outstanding Speaker Award; ABI World Laureate; Recommended as Decision Maker in International Finance, Currencies and Foreign Exchange, International Reports, London; 2000 Scholars of the 20th Century; 2000 Scholars of the 21st Century; Who's Who in the World, 1995-2005; Who's Who in Finance & Industry, 1998/1999; Who's Who in America, 2003; ABI International Peace Prize, 2003; 1000 Leaders of World Influence, Ambassador of Grand Eminence, Leading Intellectuals of the World, ABI; The Da Vinci Diamond for Inspirational Excellence, IBC; Certificate of Achievement, Crossroads Bible Institute, 2003; Certificate of Recognition, World Bible School, USA, 2004; World Medal of Freedom, ABI, 2005; Living Legends 2004/2005; Who's Who in Finance & Business, 2004/2005; International Professional of the Year, 2005; International Educator of the Year, 2006; Gold Medal for Nigeria, ABI; 4th Distinguished Nation Builders Merit Award, 2007; International Profiles of Accomplished Leaders, ABI, 2011. Memberships: New York Academy of Sciences; American Association for the Advancement of Science; Planetary Society; British Institute of Securities Laws; FFA; FCEA; AIPA, Dublin, Ireland; London Diplomatic Academy; IBC Salute to Greatness Award, 2005. Address: Charter House Auditors, PO Box 998, No 5, Ojike St, Umuahia, Abia State, Nigeria.

ULLMAN Susanne, b. 15 May 1938, Copenhagen, Denmark. Physician; Professor of Dermatology; Doctor of Medical Science. Education: Medical Degree, University of Copenhagen, 1965; Postgraduate Training in Dermatology, Rigshospital, University of Copenhagen. Appointments: Visiting Professor, University of Minnesota, Minneapolis, USA, 1974-76; Professor of Dermatology, Rigshospital, University of Copenhagen, 1979; Visiting Professor, King Faisal University, Dahran, Saudi Arabia, 1981; Visiting Professor, Hunan Medical University, Changsa, Hunan, China, 1989; Professor of Dermatology, Bispebjerg Hospital and Rigshospital, University of Copenhagen, 1996; Co-ordinator, Education of Dermatologists in Denmark, 1983-90; Member, National Board of Health's Advisory Group on AIDS, 1984-89; Member, National Board of Health's Advisory Group on Sexually Transmitted Diseases, 1987-1996; Member, Committee for The Robert J Gorlin Conference on Dysmorphology, Minneapolis, 1996-2005. Publications: Author and Co-author, 110 publications in international and Danish journals. Honours: Schering-Plough Prize in Dermatology, 2001. Memberships: Listed in Who's Who publications and biographical dictionaries. Address: Bispebjerg Hospital, Department of Dermatology, DK 2400, Copenhagen, Denmark.

ULMANIS Guntis, b. 13 September 1939, Riga, Latvia. Economist. m. Aina, 1 son, 1 daughter. Education: Diploma of Highest Education in Economy, The State University of Latvia, 1963. Appointments: Riga Public Transportation Board, 1965-71; Various positions and eventually Manager of Riga's Municipal Services, 1971-92; Member of the Board of the Bank of Latvia, 1992-93; Member of Parliament, 1993; President of Latvia, 1993-99; Director General of 2006 IIHF World Championship Organising Committee, 2002-2006; Co-Founder, Chairman of the Board, 2008-10, Dihamo Righ ice-hockey club; Member of Parliament, 2010-. Publication: Autobiographical book: No tevis Jau Neprasa Daudz (subsequently translated into Russian). Honours: 14 Highest Decorations of various states, Honorary Doctor of Charleston University, USA and Latvia University; East-West Studies Institutes, 1996 Award; Ceeli 1997 award; Anti-Defamation League award, 1998, etc. Membership: National Library of Latvia Support Foundation. Address: President's Chancery, Pils Laukums 3, Riga LV-1900, Latvia. E-mail: eva.eihmane@president.lv

ULMANU Vlad, b. 17 March 1944, Taratel, Brad, Romania. University Professor. m. Mihaela Teodorescu, 2 daughters. Education: Diploma of Baccalaureat, 1961; Diploma of Engineer, Petroleum, Gas and Geology Institute of Bucharest, 1966; PhD, Doctor Engineer, 1974. Appointments: Assistant Professor, Petroleum, Gas and Geology Institute of Bucharest, 1966-70; Assistant Professor, 1970-72, Lecturer, 1972-78, Associated Professor, 1978-90, University Professor, 1990-, Petroleum and Gas Institute of Ploiesti. Publications: Books: Construction and Exploitation of the Drill String, 1986; Tubulars for Oil and Gas Fields, 1992; Submarine Pipelines for Oil-based Products Transporting, 2001; Construction and Repair Technology of Petroleum Equipment, 2001; 150 technical papers. Honours: Traian Vuia Award, Romanian Academy; Doctor honoris causa, University of Petrosani University Lucian Blaga of Sibiu and University Ovidius of Constanta. Memberships: Romanian Association for Fracture Mechanics; European Structure Integrity Society; General Association of Engineering in Romania; Society of Petroleum Engineers. Address: B-dul Bucuresti 39, 100680 Ploiesti, Romania. E-mail: vulmanu@upg-ploiesti.ro

UNDE Madhavji (Mark), b. 28 June 1934, Pune, India. Welding Scientist; Engineer. 1 son, 2 daughters (adopted). Education: MS, Welding Engineering, The Ohio State University, Columbus, Ohio, USA, 1978. Appointments: Senior Scientific Officer (1), Defence R&D, Government of India, 1965-74; Division Welding Engineer, Fruehauf Corporation; Tool Design Engineer, Danly Machines/Ingersol Milling Machines Inc; Mechanical Engineer, Sacramento Army Depot, Sacramento, California, USA; President, California Consulting Engineers. Publications include: Effect of back-up on Welding of Thin Sections of Aluminium Alloy; Mathematical Theory of Heat Diffusion, 1994; A Brief on IPSR technology for weld-joints, 2nd revision, 2003; Several other professional articles; Patented processes in casting, non-destructive testing, mechanisms and welding; IPSR, the in process stress relief of welds (US patent 1983); EHS the equivalent heat sink process for in process production of welds without defects and reduced residual stress (US patent 1991); Mind Engineering; US Patents: Covered Trailing Edge of Weld, 2000; Trailing Edge Stress Relief, 2001; Total of 4 processes in IPSR technology to produce a metal joint without defect and known value residual stress during welding; IPSR technology eliminates 70% of the welding labour. Honour: Presidential Award, ARPA, for development of IPSR process. Memberships: Chartered Engineer, UK; MIProdE, London; MIE, India; AWS; ASM International. Address: California Consulting Engineers, 1980 Watt Avenue, Sacramento, CA 98825-2151, USA.

UNOSAWA Kazuko, b. 8 November 1955, Japan. University Lecturer. m. Noboru Unosawa, 1 son. Education: BA, Liberal Arts, International Christian University, 1981; MA, International Studies, Tsukuba University, 1983; MA, TESOL, Teachers College, Columbia University, 1989; Teaching of Japanese as a Second Language course, Asahi Culture Center, 2006. Appointments: Secretary, Japanese Journal of Ethnology, 1983-86; Instructor, English Program for Returnee Children, 1983-89, Executive Committee, Speech Contest for Returnee Children, 1983-85, Program Co-ordinator, English Proram for Returnee Children, 1988-89, Japan Overseas Educational Services; Instructor, Kanda Institute of Foreign Languages, 1984-88; Translator, Bulletin of the National Museum of History, 1983-86; Examiner, 1987-, Chief Examiner, 2001, STEP Hitotsubashi University Site; Part-time Lecturer, Tamagawa University, 1988-91; Judge, 16th Annual Contest, Yokohama Mayor's Cup, 1989; Part-time Lecturer, Toyo Eiwa Women's University, 1990-91; Part-time Assistant, Division of Social Sciences, International Christian University, 1991-93; Part-time Lecturer, Shukutoku Junior College, 1993-95; Part-time Lecturer, Shukutoku University, 1995-2009; Part-time Lecturer, Tokyo Metropolitan Institute of Technology (now Tokyo Metropolitan University), 1998-2009; Tutor, Teachers College, Columbia University Writing Center, 2009-. Publications: Numerous articles in professional journals; 3 essays; 1 book review; 3 newspaper articles; Several presentations. Memberships: Japan Association of Language Teachers; Intercultural Education Society of Japan; Japan Association of College English Teachers; Japan Association for Current English Studies; Society of Children's Books Writers and Illustrators. Address: The Square A-1202, 1-1-5 Sekido, Tama-shi, Tokyo, 206-0011, Japan. E-mail: k-unosawa@msa.biglobe.ne.jp

UNSWORTH Barry (Forster), b. 10 August 1930, Durham, England. Novelist. m. (1) Valerie Moor, 1959, divorced, 1991, 3 daughters, (2) Aira Pohjanvaara-Buffa, 1992. Education: BA, University of Manchester, 1951. Appointments: Lectureships in English; Writer-in-Residence, University of Liverpool, 1984-85, University of Lund, Sweden, 1988. Publications: The Partnership, 1966; The Greeks Have a Word for It, 1967; The Hide, 1970; Mooncrankers Gift, 1973; The Big Day, 1976; Pascalis Island, 1980, US edition as The Idol Hunter, 1980; The Rage of the Vulture, 1982; Stone Virgin, 1985; Sugar and Rum, 1988; Sacred Hunger, 1992; Morality Play, 1995; After Hannibal, 1996; Losing Nelson, 1999; The Songs of the Kings, 2002; The Ruby in her Navel, 2006; Land of Marvels, 2009. Honours: Heinemann Award, Royal Society of Literature, 1974; Arts Council Creative Writing Fellowship, 1978-79; Literary Fellow, University of Durham and University of Newcastle upon Tyne, 1983-84; Co-Winner, Booker Prize, 1992; Hon LittD, Manchester, 1998. Address: c/o Hamish Hamilton, 22 Wrights Lane, London W8 5TZ, England.

UPADHYAY R K, b. 17 May 1978, Assam, India. Scientific Researcher. Education: MSc, 2002; DCSc, 2003; MPhil, 2006; PhD, 2009. Appointments: UGC Research Fellow; Teaching Assistant; etc. Publications: 10 international and 7 national scientific research publications. Honours: UGC Research Fellowship, Government of India, 2006; Research Scholarship, Government of Assam; Best Research Articles citation, Aquatic Plant Information Retrieval System database bibliographic collection, Florida; Diploma in Computer Science, Neo-World Computer Education, Assam; Life Member, Indian Botanical Society; and others. Memberships: Indian Botanical Society; and others. Address: Bhanjang Basti, Songpijang Road, Haflong 788819, Assam, India. E-mail: rishik.upadhyay@yahoo.com

UPPER OSSORY and CASTLETOWN, the Rt Hon the Earl of, please see under **FITZPATRICK, Horace**.

UPTON Graham, b. 30 April 1944, Birmingham, England. Educationalist. m. (1) Jennifer Clark, 1 son, 1 daughter, (2) Bebe Speed. Education: BA, 1966, Dip Ed, 1966, MA, 1979, University of Sydney, Australia; M Ed, University of New South Wales, 1973; PhD, University of Wales, 1978. Appointments: Schoolteacher, New South Wales Department of Education, Australia, 1966-70; Lecturer in Education, Sydney Teachers' College, Australia, 1971; Temporary Lecturer in Education, Chester College of Education, 1972; Lecturer in Special Education, Leeds Polytechnic, 1972-74; Variously Lecturer, Senior Lecturer and Reader in Education, Head of Department of Education, Dean of Collegiate Faculty of Education and Dean of Faculty of Education and Related Professional Studies, University College, Cardiff, 1974-88; Professor, Educational Psychology and Special Educational Needs and Head, School of Education, 1988-93, Pro Vice-Chancellor, 1993-97, University of Birmingham; Vice Chancellor, 1997-2007, Emeritus Professor, Oxford Brookes University; Chairman, Development Committee, Oxford Playhouse; Educational Consultant, Ministry of Education, Brunei; Chair of Board of Directors, Oxford Expressions Technologies, 2009-; Member, Board of Governors, University of West of England, 2009-; President, Oxford Playhouse, 2010-; Vice Chancellor, University of Cumbria, 2010-. Publications: Over 100 books, chapters in books and articles in learned and professional journals; Key publications: Special Educational Needs, 1992; Emotional and Behavioural Difficulties in Schools: From Theory to Practice, 1994; The Voice of the Child: A Handbook for Professionals, 1996; Effective Schooling for Children with Emotional and Behavioural Difficulties, 1998. Honours: Honorary DUniv, Oxford Brookes University, 2009; Hon DUniv, Oxford Brookes University. Memberships: Chartered Psychologist; Fellow, British Psychological Society; Fellow, Royal Society of Arts; Academician, Learned Society for the Social Sciences; Honorary Fellow, Birmingham College of Food, Tourism and Leisure. Address: Brock Leys, Pullens Lane, Oxford OX3 0BX, England. E-mail: grahamupton@aol.com

URBIKAIN Miren Karmele, b. Bilbao, Spain. Engineer. Education: Mechanical Engineer degree, PhD, Thermal Engineering, School of Engineering of Bilbao, University of the Basque Country; Degree of Musical Studies (Piano), Conservatory of Bilbao. Appointments: Researcher, 2003-08, Lecturer, 2008-09, 2011, School of Engineering, Bilbao; Lecturer, University College of Technical Mining and Civil Engineering, Barakaldo, 2009-10; Lecturer, School of Engineering, Bilbao, 2011. Publications: One-dimensional solutions to Fourier's Equation and Measures of Heat Transmission Through Walls: The Role of Wall Decay Times, 2008; Analysis of Different Models to Estimate Energy Savings Related to Windows in Residential Buildings, 2009; Determination of wall decay times by use of a polynomial equation, 2010. E-mail: mirenkarmele.urbicain@ehu.es

URCH David Selway, b. 10 February 1933, London, England. University Reader Emeritus. m. Patricia Maria Erszebet Hair, 4 sons, 1 daughter. Education: Drapers' Company's Scholar, 1951; BSc, 1st Class Honours, Chemistry, 1954, PhD, 1957, Queen Mary College, University of London. Appointments: Research Fellow, Yale University, USA, 1957-59; Lecturer, Birmingham University, England, 1960; Lecturer, Reader, Chemistry, Queen Mary and Westfield College, University of London, 1961-98; Senior Lecturer, Chemistry, Brunel University, 1998-2000; Adjunct Professor, Organic Chemistry, New York University in London, 2000-. Publications: Over 200 papers in scientific literature; Book: Orbitals and Symmetry, 1970, revised, 1979. Honours: Fellow Royal Society of Chemistry; Chartered Chemist. Memberships: Royal Society of Chemistry; American Chemical Society; Association of University Teachers; Catenian Association. Address: 56 Mount Ararat Road, Richmond, Surrey TW10 6PJ, England. E-mail: du3@nyu.edu

URSU Ioan, b. 22 April 1946, Tartaria-Alba, Romania. Mathematician. m. Felicia, 1 daughter. Education: BS, Fluid Mechanics, University of Bucharest, 1969; Postgraduate studies, Polytechnic Institute of Bucharest, 1985-86; Doctorate studies, 1995-2000, PhD, Mathematics, 2000, Institute of Mathematics, Romanian Academy. Appointments: Scientific Researcher, 1969-, Head of Systems Analysis Department, 1995-2008, Head, Mechatronic Systems Department, 2008-, Elie Carafoli National Institute for Aerospace Research, Bucharest. Publications: Numerous articles in professional journals. Honours: Award for Excellence for Outstanding Paper, 1999; Aurel Vlaicu Prize, Romanian Academy, 2000 and 2004. Memberships: Literati Club, Bradford, England; Gesellschaft für Angewandte Mathematik und Mechanic, Germany; Romanian Society of Applied Industrial Mathematics. Address: Elie Carafoli National Institute for Aerospace Research, Boulevard Iuliu Maniu 220, Bucharest, 061126, Romania. E-mail: iursu@incas.ro Website: www.incas.ro/english/people/iursu/iursu.htm

URUSHADZE Levan Z, b. 7 February 1964, Tbilisi, Georgia. Historian. Education: MSc, History, Tbilisi State University, 1986; PhD, History, Georgian Academy of Sciences, 1990; Doctor of Historical Sciences, The Council

DICTIONARY OF INTERNATIONAL BIOGRAPHY 36th EDITION

of Scientific Experts of Georgia, 2006. Appointments: Post-graduate student, 1986-89, Research Fellow, 1989-95, Senior Research Fellow, 2003-06, Javakhishvili Institute of History and Ethnology, Georgian Academy of Sciences; Editor in Chief, Independent Newspaper, Adamianis Uplebebi (Human Rights), 1995-2003; Senior Research Fellow, Georgian National Museum, Curator of the Museum of the Soviet Occupation, 2006-. Publications: More than 130 scientific research works; 8 monographs. Honours: Grants, Westminister Foundation for Democracy, 1997; Certificate of Merit of the Chairman of the Parliament of Georgia, 2010. Memberships: World Academy of Art & Science; Royal Society of Great Britain and Ireland; Royal Society of New Zealand; Georgian Historical Society. Address: G Rcheulishvili Street, Build 7, Flat 6, Tbilisi 0179, Republic of Georgia. Website: http://lurushadze.tripod.com

USHARANI S, b. 7 December 1965, Chennai, India. Assistant Professor. m. P Sukumar, 1 son. Education: MSc, 1989, M Phil, 1990, PhD, 2009, Central Leather Research Institute, Adyar, Chennai. Appointments: Lecturer, Anna Adarsh College for Women, Chennai, 1991-2000; Assistant Professor, SIVET College, Gowrivakkam, 2000-. Publications: Numerous articles in professional journals; Reference book for undergraduate chemistry course. Honours: Listed in biographical dictionaries. Address: No 41 First Main Road, L H Ngr, First Lay Out, Adambakkam, Chennai 600088, Tamil Nadu, India. Address: sivetur@rediffmail.com

UTKU Senol, b. 23 November 1931, Suruc, Turkey. Professor (Mathematics, Computer Science, Civil Engineering). m. Bisulay Bereket, 1 son, 1 daughter. Education: Dipl Ing, Faculty of Civil Engineering, Istanbul Technical University, Turkey, 1954; SM, 1959, ScD, 1960, Massachusetts Institute of Technology, USA. Appointments include: Site Engineer, Andolu Ltd Construction Firm, Turkey, 1955, 1957; Lieutenant, Reserve Officer and Technical Translator, Corps of Engineers, Turkish Army, 1955-57; Research Assistant, Structural Mechanics, 1958-60, Assistant Professor, Civil Engineering, 1960-62, Technical Consultant, 1960-61, 1961-62, Massachusetts Institute of Technology, Cambridge, USA; Research Engineer, 1959-60, Consultant, 1960-65, International Business Machines Corporation, USA; Associate Professor, 1962-63, Head, Computation Center Founding Committee, 1962-63, Visiting Professor, 1980, Fulbright Professor of Computer Science, 1998, Middle East Technical University, Turkey; Engineer & Partner, PENTA Engineering Firm, Ankara, Turkey, 1963-65; Technical Staff, 1965-70, Technical Consultant, 1975-97, Jet Propulsion Laboratory, NASA, USA; Lecturer, University of Southern California, Los Angeles, USA, 1966-70; Visiting Lecturer, University of Washington, USA, 1968; Technical Consultant, Westinghouse R&D Center, Pittsburgh, USA, 1970; CEO, Dr Utku & Associates, Durham, NC, USA, 1970-; Associate Professor, 1970-72, Professor, 1972-2001, Civil Engineering, Professor of Computer Science, 1972-2001, Director of Undergraduate Studies, 1980-85, Director of Graduate Studies, 1987-89, Duke University, Durham; Professor of Numerical Analysis, Mathematics Department, 1977-, Executive Committee Member, Alumni Association (Mezunlar Konseyi), Istanbul Technical University, 2007-11; Technical Consultant, NASA Langley Research Center, USA, 1971; Technical Consultant, DBA Systems, Melbourne, Florida, USA, 1971; Technical Consultant, ITT Communications, Mackay Marine Division, Raleigh, USA, 1974-77; Visiting professor in universities in Turkey, Romania, USA and Saudi Arabia, 1977-91; Fulbright Professor, Scientific and Technical Council of Turkey, 1998; Fulbright Professor, Selcuk University, Turkey, 1998; Invited Seminar Speaker for Adaptive Structures, Cambridge University, England, 2004. Publications: Author, 4 books; Co-author, 4 books; Numerous articles in professional journals. Honours: NASA Awards, 1969, 1971, 1977, 1984, 1986-87; CalTech President's Award, 1981; NSF's International Joint Research Award for Japan, 1991; Fulbright Lectures to Turkey Award, 1998; Listed in biographical dictionaries. Memberships: American Association of University Professors; American Academy of Mechanics; Association of Turkish American Scientists; Fulbright Association, USA; American Society of Civil Engineers (fellow); Structural Engineering Institute (charter), USA; Turkish Society of Civil Engineers; American Society of Engineering Education; Civil Engineering Honor Society of Chi Epsilon; many others. Address: M1 Blok K:4, D:8, 2-5-6 Mah Atakoy, Bakirkoy 34158, Istanbul, Turkey.

UYKAN Zekeriya, b. 10 November 1971, Istanbul, Turkey. Electrical Engineer. Education: BSc, Electronics and Communications Engineering, 1993, MSc, Control and Computer Engineering, 1996, Istanbul Technical University; Licentiate of Technology, 1998, PhD, 2001, Helsinki University of Technology, Finland. Appointments: Research and Teaching Assistant, Istanbul Technical University, 1994-96; Research Scientist, Helsinki University of Technology, 1996-2001; Visiting Researcher, Sabanci University, Turkey, 2000; Research Engineer, Nokia Research Center, 2000-07; Nokia Siemens Networks, Finland, 2007-; Visiting Scholar, Electrical Engineering, Stanford University, California, 2002; Visiting Scientist, Harvard University, MA, 2008-09; Nokia-Siemens Networks, 2007-10; Dogus University, Istanbul, Turkey, 2009-. Publications: Author and co-author, over 20 journal and conference papers. Honours: Awards from Academy of Finland Graduate School, GETA, 1999, 2000, 2002; Center for International Mobility, CIMO, 1996, 1997; Imatran Voiman Found, 1999; Telia Sonera, 1999; Elisa, 2000; Listed in Who's Who in the World, 2006 and Who's Who in Science and Engineering, 2006-07. Memberships: Istanbul Technical University Alumni Foundation, 1993-; Finnish Association of Graduate Engineers, TEK, 1999-; Senior Member IEEE; Life Fellow, International Biographical Association. Address: Nokia Siemens Networks, Espoo, Finland. E-mail: zekeriya.uykan@nsn.com

UYSAL Gurhan, b. 9 May 1970, Unye, Ordu, Turkey. Academic. Education: BSc, 1991, PhD, 2005, Hacettepe University, Ankara; MBA, Adelphi University, New York, USA, 1998. Appointments: Head, Department of Business Administration, 2010, Member, Faculty Board of School of Business, 2010, MBA Director, School of Business, 2011, Ondokuz Mayis University; Member, Harvard Business Review Advisory Council, 2012. Publications: Europe 2020 Strategy: PPP-model to Cobweb Theorem in Clisteral Innovation; Program and Curriculum Development of Hem Program in Business Schools; Taylor, HRM, Strategic HRM with Jobs, Employee Performance, Business Performance Relationship: HR Governance through 100 years; Linear Programs in Cost Accounting: A Unit Cost Model. Memberships: EMAB Euromed Academy of Business. Address: Ondokuz Mayis University, School of Business, 55139, Kurupelit - Samsun, Turkey.

UZUNIDIS Dimitri Nicolas, b. 24 May 1960, Alexandropolis, Greece. Professor; Economist. m. Sophie Boutillier, 1 son, 1 daughter. Education: Diploma, Journalism, Athens, Greece, 1979; Master in Sociology, 1985, PhD, Economics, 1987, University of Paris 10. Appointments: Associate Professor, Institute of Political Studies, Lille, France, 1991-96;

Professor, University of Littoral, Dunkirque, France, 1992-; Professor, Postgraduate School, University of Littoral, Invited Professor, Institute of Social Management, Paris, 2002-; Director, Research Unit: Industry and Innovation, 1994-; Editor: Innovations, Journal of Innovation Economics, L'esprit economique. Publications: Le Travail brade, 1997; La Legende de l'entrepreneur, 1999; Mondialisation et Citoyennete, 1999; L'histoire des entrepreneurs, 2002; L'innovation et l'economie contemporaine, 2004: Firm Power In "Contemporary Post-Keynsian Analysis", 2005; John Kenneth Galbraith and the Future of Economics; Innovation, Evolution and Economic Change; Cluster of Entrepreneurs; The Capitalism; Power Finance and Innovation Trends in a High-Risk Economy; Genesis of Innovation. Honours: Ministry of Industry, Athens, Greece, 1989; Ministry of National Education, Paris, 1999; Palmes Academiques, 2004. Memberships: French Council of Universities; Association of French Economists; The Society of Advancement of Socio-Economics; Observatory of Globalization; Vice-President, European Citizenship Association; Resp of Research on Innovation (Paris, Seattle). Address: MRSH-Lab Network RII, 21 Quai de la Citadelle, F-59140 Dunkirque, France. E-mail: Uzunidis@univ-littoral.fr Website: rri.univ-littoral.fr

V

VAGNORIUS Gediminas, b. 10 June 1957, Plunge District, Lithuania. Politician. m. Nijole Vagnorienė, 1 son, 1 daughter. Education: D Econ Science, Institute of Engineering and Construction, Vilnius, Lithuania. Appointments: Engineer-Economist, Junior Researcher, Researcher, Institute of Economics, Lithuanian Academy of Sciences, 1989-90; Deputy to Lithuanian Supreme Soviet, Member, Presidium, 1990-91; Prime Minister of Lithuania, 1991-92, 1996-99; Member of Parliament, 1992-; Chair, Council of Ministers of Lithuania, 1991-92, 1996-99; Chair, Board, Homeland Union/ Lithuanian Conservative Party, 1993-2000; Chair, Moderate Conservative Union, 2000-; Chair, Christian Conservative Social Union (CCSU). Address: CCSU, Odminiu Str 5, 01122 Vilnius, Lithuania. E-mail: sekretoriatas@nks.lt

VAGUNDA Vaclav, b. 16 December 1959, Uherske Hradiste, Czech Republic. Medical Doctor; Pathologist; Researcher. m. Marcela, 1 son, 1 daughter. Education: MD (General Medicine), Faculty of Medicine, Purkyne University, Brno, 1985; Pathology, degree I, 1988, Pathology, degree II, 1992, Institute for Postgraduate Study in Health Care, Prague; PhD (Oncology), Faculty of Medicine, Masaryk University, Brno, 2004. Appointments: Resident, 2nd Institute of Pathology, Faculty Children Hospital, Brno, 1985-88; Medical Researcher, Pathology Department, Research Institute of Clinical and Experimental Oncology, Brno, 1988-93; Consultant Pathologist, 1993-95, 1st Institute of Pathology, Faculty Hospital, Brno, 1993-95; Lecturer, Faculty of Medicine, Masaryk University, Brno, 1993-2004; Head, Department of Pathology, Masaryk Memorial Cancer Institute, Brno, 1995-2003; Cytopathologist, Department of Cytology, 2004; Sanatorium Helios Ltd, Brno; Head, CEDELAB Ltd, Laboratory of Pathology and Clinical Cytology, Hospital St Zdislava, Velke Mezirici, Czech Republic, 2005-. Publications: 32 articles in professional journals. Honours: International Scientist of the Year, IBC, 2003. Memberships: The Czech Medical Society, Society of Pathologists, 1986; Founding President, Vice-Chairman, League Against Cancer, Brno, 1990; Pathology Group, Organisation of European Cancer Institutes, 1995; The Czech Medical Society, Society of Clinical Cytology, 1996; International Academy of Pathology, Czech section, 1996; WHO, Melanoma Programme, 1997; European Society of Pathology, 2003; Society for Melanoma Research, 2004. Address: CEDELAB Ltd, Laboratory of Pathology & Cytology, Hosp St Zdislava, Mostiste 105, 594 01 Velke Mezirici, Czech Republic. E-mail: vagunda@cedelab.cz Website: www.cedelab.cz

VAISEY David George, b. 15 March 1935, Tetbury, England. Librarian; Archivist. m. Maureen Anne Mansell, 1965, 2 daughters. Education: BA, 1959, MA, 1962, Oxford University, England. Appointments: Served to 2nd Lieutenant, British Army, 1954-56; Archivist, Staffordshire County Council, Stafford, England, 1960-63; From Assistant to Senior Assistant Librarian, 1963-75, Keeper of Western Manuscripts, 1975-86, Bodley's Librarian, 1986-96, Bodley's Librarian Emeritus, 1997-, Bodleian Library, Oxford, England; Deputy Keeper, 1966-75, Keeper, 1995-2000, Oxford University Archives; Visiting Professor, Department of Library Studies, UCLA, 1985; Commissioner, Royal Commission of Historical Manuscripts, 1987-98; Founding Chairman, National Council Archives, 1988-91. Honours: Decorated encomienda Order of Isabel la Catholica (Spain); Commander, Order of the British Empire; Fellow, 1975, Emeritus Fellow, 2000, Exeter College, Oxford; Honorary Research Fellow, University College, London, 1987; Honorary Fellow, Kellogg College, Oxford, 1996. Memberships: Fellow, Society of Antiquaries, Royal Historical Society; Society of Archivists (president, 1999-2002); British Records Association (vice president, 1998-2006). Address: Bodleian Library, Broad Street, Oxford, OX1 3BG, England. E-mail: david.vaisey@bodleian.ox.ac.uk

VAJPAYEE Atal Bihari, b. 25 December 1924, Gwalior, Madhya Pradesh, India. 11th Prime Minister of India; Poet. Education: Student of political science and law. Career: Journalist; Joined Bharatiya Jana Sangh, now Bharatiya Janata Party, 1951-; Elected to the Lok Sabha, House of the People, 9 times; Elected to the Rajya Sabha, House of the States, twice; Foreign Minister; Leader of the Opposition; Prime Minister of India, 1996, 1998-2004; Minister of Health and Family Welfare, Atomic Energy and Agriculture, 1998-2004; Chair, National Security Council, 1998-2004; Senior Leader, Bharatjiya Janata Party; Retired from politics, 2005. Publications: New Dimensions of India's Foreign Policy; Jan Sangh Aur Musalmans; Three Decades in Parliament; collections of poems and numerous articles. Honours: Hon PhD, Kanpur University, 1993; Padma Vibhushan; Best Parliamentarian, 1994. Memberships: Chair, National Security Council, 1998-; Member, National Integration Council, 1961-. Address: 7 Race Course Road, New Delhi 110011, India.

VAKARIN Sergey, b. 25 May 1952, Chita, Russia. Physicist. Education: Student studies, Physics Department, Urals State University, 1970-75; PhD, Physics and Mathematics, High-Temperature Electrochemistry Institute, Russian Academy of Sciences, 1997. Appointments: Research Scientist, 1991-2011, Junior Research Scientist, 1983-91, Engineer, 1975-83, Senior Technician, 1975, High-Temperature Electrochemistry Institute, Russian Academy of Sciences. Publications: 1 monograph; 29 articles; 13 inventions; 11 scientific reports. Honours: Inventor of the USSR Medal, 1991; Veteran of Work, 2001; Archimedes Award, 2006; Vernadsky Medal (Russian Academy of Natural History), 2006; American Hall of Fame, ABI, 2008; Listed in international biographical dictionaries. Memberships: Corresponding Member, International Personnel Academy, Council of Europe/UNESCO; Professor of Russian Academy of Natural History; An Active Working Partnership, European Academy of Natural History. Address: Aviatorov Street 7, Apartment 21, Ekaterinburg 620910, Russia. E-mail: s.vakarin@ihte.uran.ru

VALLER Rachel, b. 14 September 1929, Sydney, Australia. Pianist; Teacher; Examiner; Adjudicator. m. Walter Travers, 1965. Education: BA, 1952; DipEd, 1960; LTCL, 1947; Conservatorium of Music, Sydney; University of Sydney; Pupil of Ignaz Friedman. Debut: Sydney, 1940. Career: Soloist, Associate Artist Chamber Ensembles, ABC Radio, TV; Appearances with Sydney, Melbourne and Queensland Symphony Orchestras; Toured with Cellist André Navarra, with Violinists Wanda Wilkomirska, Stoika Milanova, Zvi Zeitlin, Erick Friedman, Erich Gruenberg, Thomas Zehetmair and Bassoonist George Zukerman. Recordings: Lesser known piano works of Beethoven issued to mark Beethoven bicentenary, 1970; Schubert's Sonatinas with violinist Susanne Lautenbacher to commemorate 150th anniversary of his death, Germany, 1978. Publications: Music and Drama Critic, Wentworth Courier; Articles for 2MBS. Honours: Harriet Cohen Commonwealth Medal, 1956; OAM, 1995. Memberships: Amateur Chamber Music Society; Australian Musicians Academy. Address: 22 Allen's Parade, Bondi Junction, New South Wales 2022, Australia.

VÁMOS Tibor, b. 1 June 1926, Budapest, Hungary. Research Professor. Noémi Stenczer, 1 son. Education: Diploma, Electrical Engineering, Budapest Technical University, 1950; PhD, Technical Sciences, Automatic Control, 1958, DSc, Technical Sciences, Computer Control, 1964, Hungarian Academy of Sciences, Budapest. Appointments: Director, 1964-85, Chair, 1986-, Computer and Automation Research Institute, Hungarian Academy of Sciences; Professor, Budapest Technical University, 1969-; Corresponding Member, 1973, Member, 1979, Member of Governing Board, 1980-, Hungarian Academy of Sciences; President, 1981-84, Lifetime Advisor, 1987-, International Federation of Automatic Control; Distinguished Visiting Professor, George Mason University, 1992-93; Editorial board member of 4 international scientific journals. Publications: Numerous articles in professional journals. Honours: Honorary Member, Austrian Computer Society; Honorary Member, Austrian Society for Cybernetic Studies; Honorary President, J von Neumann Society of Computer Science, 1986-; Dr hc, Tallinn University; IEEE Fellow, 1986-; State Prize, 1983; Chorafas Prize, Swiss Acads, 1994; Order of Hungarian Republic, 1996; ECCAI Fellow, 2004; IFAC Fellow, 2005; WAC Congress Dedication, 2006; Széchenyi Prize, Hungarian Government, 2008. Memberships: Chairman and board member of various philanthropic foundations. Address: Lágymányosi u 11, 1111 Budapest, Hungary. E-mail: vamos@sztaki.hu

VAN CAEKENBERGHE Koen A P A, b. 3 July 1979, Vilvoorde, Belgium. Mixed signal/RFIC Designer. m. Cindy Callens. Education: MSc (cum laude), Electrical Engineering, Katholieke Universiteit, Leuven, Belgium, 2002; PhD, Electrical Engineering, University of Michigan, Ann Arbor, USA, 2007. Appointments: Antenna Designer, Thales Air Systems, Netherlands, 2007-08; MMIC Designer, TNO Defence & Security, Netherlands, 2008-09; RF Design Engineer, NXP, Netherlands, 2010; RF IC Designer, M4S, Belgium, 2011-. Publications: An Analog RF MEMS Slotline True-Time-Delay Phase Shifter, 2008; RF MEMS on the Radar, 2009; A 3-14.5 GHz 0.15µm InGaAs pHEMT Low Noise Pseudo-Differential Distributed Amplifier, 2010; Patent, OFDM Frequency Scanning Radar, 2008; Short courses and tutorials: RF MEMS for Radar, 2010; Electronically Scanned Reflectarrays, 2011; Behavioral Modeling of Timing and Frequency Control Circuits using Verilog-AMS. Memberships: IET; IEEE; KIVI-NIRIA. Address: Kapellelaan 361, 1860 Meise, Belgium. E-mail: vcaeken@umich.edu Website: http://www-personal.umich.edu/~vcaeken

VAN DAMME Jean-Claude, b. 18 October 1961, Brussels, Belgium. Actor. m. (1) Maria Rodriguez, 1980, divorced 1984, (2) Cynthia Derderian, 1985, divorced 1986, (3) Gladys Portugues, 1987, divorced 1992, re-married 1999, 1 son, 1 daughter, (4) Darcy LaPier, 1994, divorced 1997, 1 son. Career: Former European Professional Karate Association Middleweight Champion; Films: Bloodsport; Death Warrant; Kickboxer; Cyborg; AWOL; Universal Soldier; No Retreat; No Surrender; Nowhere to Run; Monaco Forever; Hard Target; Streetfighter; Time Cop; Sudden Death; The Quest; Maximum Risk; Double Team; Universal Soldier: The Return, 1999; The Order, 2001; Replicant, 2001; Derailed, 2002; The Savage, 2003; In Hell, 2003; Narco, 2004; Wake of Death, 2004; Kumite, 2005; Second in Command, 2006; The Hard Corps, 2006; Sinave, 2006; Until Death, 2007; The Shepherd: Border Patrol, 2008; Universal Soldier: Regeneration, 2009. Address: United Talent Agency, Suite 500, 9560 Wilshire Boulevard, Beverly Hills, CA 90212, USA.

VAN PRAAG Herman Meir, b. 17 October 1929, Schiedam, The Netherlands. Psychiatrist. m. Cornelia Eikens, 3 sons, 1 daughter. Education: MD, State University, Leiden, The Netherlands, 1948-56; PhD, University of Utrecht, 1958-62; 4 years Psychiatry and Psychotherapy, 1 year, Neurobiology, Foundation for Advanced Clinical Training, Rotterdam, 1958-63. Appointments: Chief of Staff, Department of Psychiatry, Dijkzigt Hospital, Rotterdam, 1963-66; Founder, 1st Head of Department of Biological Psychiatry State University of Gronigen, 1966-77; Associate Professor, 1968, Professor, 1970, Biological Psychiatry, State University Groningen; Lady Davis Visiting Professor, Hebrew University, Jerusalem, Israel, 1976-77; Professor and Head of Department of Psychiatry, Academic Hospital, State University, Utrecht, 1977-82; Professor, Chairman, Department of Psychiatry, Albert Einstein College of Medicine, Bronx, New York; Psychiatrist-in-Chief, Montefiore Medical Center, Bronx, 1982-92; Professor and Chairman, Department of Psychiatry and Neuropsychology, Maastricht University, 1992-97; Interim Head of Department of Psychiatry and Neuropsychology, Academic Hospital, Maastricht, 1997-99; Scientific Advisor, Department of Psychiatry and Neuropsychology, Academic Hospital, Maastricht, 1999-. Publications: 600 in international professional journals. Honours: Recipient of many honours and distinctions; Knighted by Queen Beatrix of the Netherlands, 1989; Guest speaker, lecturer, in many countries; Visiting professorships including: H B Williams Travelling Professor of the Royal Australian and New Zealand College of Psychiatrists, 1997. Memberships include: Fellow, New York Academy of Medicine, 1983; Fellow, American Psychopathological Association, 1984; Fellow, American College of Neuropsychopharmacology, 1987; Fellow, American Psychiatric Association, 1992; Member, Royal Society of Arts and Scientists of the Netherlands, 1996; Founding Member, Foundation for Psychiatry and Religion; Chairman, Section Religion, Spirituality and Psychiatry, World Psychiatric Association. Address: University Hospital Maastricht, Department of Psychiatry, PO Box 5800, 6202 AZ Maastricht, The Netherlands.

VAN SANT Gus Jr, b. 1952, Louisville, Kentucky, USA. Film Director; Screenwriter. Education: Rhode Island School of Design. Appointments: Former Production Assistant to Ken Shapiro. Films include: Mala Noche; Drugstore Cowboy, 1989; My Own Private Idaho, 1991; Even Cowgirls Get the Blues, 1993; To Die For, 1995; Kids, 1995; Ballad of the Skeletons, 1996; Good Will Hunting, 1997; Psycho, 1998; Finding Forrester, 2000; Gerry, 2002; Elephant, 2003; Red Hot Chili Peppers: Greatest Videos, 2003; Last Days, 2005; Paris, j t'aime, 2006; To Each His Cinema, 2007; Paranoid Park, 2007; Milk, 2008. Publications: 108 Portraits, 1995; Pink, 1997. Honours: National Society of Film Critics Awards for Best Director and Screenplay, 1990; New York Film Critics and Los Angeles Film Critics Award for Best Screenplay, 1989; PEN Literary Award for Best Screenplay Adaptation, 1989; American Civil Liberties Union of Oregon, Freedom of Expression Award, 1992; Palme d'Or and Best Director, Cannes Film Festival, 2003. Address: c/o William Morris Agency Inc, 151 South El Camino Drive, Beverly Hills, CA 90212, USA. Website: www.wma.com

VAN ZWIETEN Pieter A, b. 20 May 1937, The Netherlands. Emeritus Professor of Clinical Pharmacology. Education: PhD, Amsterdam, 1961; MD, University of Kiel, 1968. Appointments: Military Service, NATO, 1961-63; Postdoctoral, University of Vienna, 1963-65; Associate Professor, University of Kiel, 1965-71; Professor, Chairman, Department of Pharmacotherapy, University of Amsterdam,

Clinical Consultant, Cardiology, Cardiac Surgery, 1971-. Publications: Over 1500 papers in professional medical journals. Honours: Elected member, German National Academy of Sciences, 2008; Honorary Fellow, British Pharmacological Society, 2008; Honorary Member, European Society of Hypertension, 2009; Knight in the Order of the Netherlands' Lion. Memberships: 20 learned societies. Address: Academic Medical Centre, Department of Pharmacotherapy, University of Amsterdam, Meibergdreef 15, 1105 AZ Amsterdam, The Netherlands.

VANDERHAEGEN Frédéric Bernard Michel, b. Lille, France. Professor. 1 son, 1 daughter. Education: Diploma in Computer Science, University of Lille, France, 1986; Degree in Industrial Automation, 1987, Master's Degree, Industrial Automation, 1988, Postgraduate Diploma, Industrial Automation, 1989, Doctorate Diploma, Industrial and Human Automation, 1993, Habilitation to manage research on Industrial and Human Automation, 2003, University of Valenciennes, France. Appointments: Postdoctoral Researcher, Joint Research Centre of the European Commission, Ispra, Italy, 1994-95; Researcher, Engineering Department, Researcher and Scientific Project Co-ordinator, Laboratory of Automated, Mechanical and Computer Science Studies integrating Industrial and Human Aspects (LAMIH), CNRS, 1995-2005; Professor, University of Valenciennes and Head, Human-Machine System Group of the LAMIH, 2005-. Publications: Book: Analysis and Control of Human Error; Articles in scientific journals including: IEEE Transactions on Reliability; International Journal on Human-Computer Interaction; Interacting with Computers; Reliability and System Safety; Le Travail Humain; Control Engineering Practice; Safety Science. Honour: Third Prize for the best doctoral thesis on Automation between 1993 and 1994, AFCET, CNRS and MESR, 1995. Memberships include: Regional Research Group on Transport; Regional Research Group on Integrated Automation and Human-Machine System; National Research Group on Modelling, Analysis and Control of Systems; Civil Activity Organiser, Eclaireuses et Eclaireurs de France, 1984-93; Co-Chairman, Fretttt Production Association to promote the regional music group Tante Adèle et La Famille, 1996-. Address: 36 rue Claudin Le Jeune, 59300 Valenciennes, France. E-mail: frederic.vanderhaegen@univ-valeniennes.fr

VANGELIS (Evangelos Papathanassiou), b. 29 March 1943, Volos, Greece. Musician (keyboards); Composer. Education: Academy of Fine Arts, Athens. Musical Education: Studied Classical music with Aristotelis Coudourof. Career: Member, Formynx, 1960s; Member, Aphrodite's Child, with Demis Roussos; Composer, Paris, 1972; Built Nemo recording studio, London, 1974; Partnership with Jon Anderson as Jon & Vangelis, 1980-1984. Compositions: Music scores for French wildlife films, 1972; Heaven and Hell, Third Movement, theme for Carl Sagan's TV series Cosmos, BBC1, 1981; Film scores: Chariots Of Fire; Blade Runner; Missing; Mutiny On The Bounty; City; 1492 - Conquest Of Paradise; De Nuremberg a Nuremberg, 1994; Rangeela, 1995; Kavafis, 1996; I Hope, 2001; Alexander, 2004; Blade Runner Trilogy: 25th Anniversary, 2007; All tracks on solo albums self-composed, played and produced. Recordings: Albums: with Aphrodite's Child: Aphrodite's Child, 1968; Rain & Tears, 1968; End of the World, 1969; It's Five O'Clock, 1970; 666, 1972; Solo albums: Terra, Dragon, 1971; L'Apocalypse des animaux, 1972; Earth, 1972; Heaven And Hell, 1975; Albedo 0.39, 1976; The Vangelis Radio Special, 1976; Spiral, 1977; Beauborg, 1978; Hypothesis, 1978; China, 1979; Odes, 1979; See You Later, 1980; To The Unknown Man, 1981; Soil Festivities, 1984; Invisible Connections, 1985; Magic Moments, 1985; Mask, 1985; Direct, 1988; The City, 1990; Themes, 1989; Voices, 1995; El Greco, 1995; Oceanic, 1997; Reprise 1990-1999, 2000; Mythodea: Music for the NASA Mission – 2001 Mars Odyssey, 2001; As Jon & Vangelis: Short Stories, 1980; The Friends Of Mr Cairo, 1981; Private Collection, 1983; The Best Of Jon & Vangelis, 1984; Page Of Life, 1991. Honour: Oscar, Best Original Score, Chariots Of Fire, 1982. Address: c/o Sony Classical, 550 Madison Avenue, New York, NY 10022-3211, USA. Website: www.vangelisworld.com

VANSTONE Joan Eleanor, b. 1933, Vancouver, Canada. Adoption Reform Advocate. m. S Martin, 2 sons, 1 daughter. Education: Fenton Business College, 1951-52; Women's Royal Canadian Navy (R), 1952-58; Langara College, 1974-75. Appointments: Professional Model, Fashion Commentator; Secretary, Marsh and McLennan Ltd, British American Oil and Forest Industrial Relations; Flight Attendant, Canadian Pacific Air Lines and Wardair; Proprietor, Leanne Imports; Founder, National Director, Parent Finders of Canada; Secretary, Member, Board of Directors, Liberty Technology Inc. Publications: Columnist, Ladner Optimist, 1962-64; Parent Finders in-house newsletter; Reunion Research Report; Others. Honours: Founders Award, Canadian Adoption Reform Association, 1981; Nomination for Women of Distinction Award, YWCA Community and Human Services, 1990; Adoptee Activist Award, Adoption Council of Canada; Legislation Reform Award, American Adoption Congress, 1996; Distinguished Services to Families Award, British Columbia Council for the Family, 1996; Victoria Leach Award, 1998; Queen Elizabeth II Diamond Jubilee Medal, 2012. Memberships: Tree International Soundex Reunion Register; American Adoption Congress; International Wings; Families for Children; Adoption Council of Canada; Adopting Families Association of British Columbia; Reproductive Technology Workshop; Adoption Advisory and Consultative Committee; Adoption Council of British Columbia. Address: 1264 Pacific Drive, Delta, BC V4M 4B1, Canada.

VARADAN T R, b. 10 January 1941, Chennai, India. Co-op Sub Registrar (retired). m. R Shiamala. Education: BSc; DOM; DFM; DMM; DAPR; DCA; DEM; DOPD; DPMIR; DIMR; DICS; DIBA; DGDBA; DIHRD; MDBA; DAA; DMSM; DLW & LL; DMIT; DJ; DCM; DISS; DMJ. Appointments: Co-op Sub Registrar (retired), Co-op Department, State Government. Honours: MDH, MSc, (H) Gold Medallist, Hemopathy Institution, Jammu & Kashmeer; UWA Lifetime Achievement Award, United Writers Association, Valasarawakkam, Chennai; Lifetime Achievement Award, International Institute of Education and Management, Delhi; Genius Millennium Award, All India Management Council, New Delhi, 2000; Appreciation Award, Manas Institute of Management and Technology, Modi Nagar; National Award for Excellence, All India Freelance Journalists Association, Chennai; MSPI Gold Medalist, MSPI Excellence Award, Medal of Achievement; Gems of New Millennium 2000 Award, Gold Medal of Honour, Educational Excellence Award, Management Excellence Award, Medal of Membership, Medal of Achievement, Gold Medal of Achievement Award, Three Gold Medals, Three Medal of Membership, Patron Membership Award, Fellow Patron Membership Award, Global Personality Award, Medal of Achievement, Medal of Membership, 6 Medals of Achievement, and Super Gem Award, Management Studies Promotion Institute, New Delhi; UWA Lifetime Achievement Award; National Award for Excellence. Memberships: MSPI;

FMSPI; AMSPI; Management Studies Promotion Institute, New Delhi. Address: 16 Raghava Chetty Street, Choolai, Chennai 600112, India.

VARLEY Peter Ashley Clifford, b. 13 June 1957, United Kingdom. Researcher. Education: MA, Chemistry, St Peter's College, Oxford, 1985; MSc, Energy, 1996, PhD, Computer Science, 2003, University of Wales, Cardiff. Appointments: JSPS Research Fellow, Department of Precision Machinery and Engineering, University of Tokyo, Japan, 2003-05; Ramón y Cajal, Department of Engineering and Mechanical Construction, Universitat Jaume I, Spain, 2006-11. Publications: Numerous articles in professional journals. Address: Departemento de Ingenieria Mecánica y Construcción, Universitat Jaume I, Campus del Riu Sec, Castellón de la Plana, E-12080, Castellón, Spain. E-mail: varley@emc.uji.es Website: http://pacvarley.110mb.com/

VASANIA Kaizad Rusi, b. 5 October 1977, Surat, India. Research Scientist. Education: MSc, PhD, Chemistry. Appointments: Lecturer, Chemistry, V S Patel College; Research Scientist, Sabero Organics Limited. Publications: Many research articles in national and international journals. Honours: Listed in international biographical dictionaries. Memberships: Life Member, National Environmental Science Academy. Address: Jawahar Road, Bazar Street, Next to Jeevandoep Clinic, Bilimora – 396321, Gujarat, India. E-mail: vasania_kaizad@yahoo.com

VASHADZE Grigol, b. 19 July 1958, Tbilisi, Georgia. Diplomat. m. Nino Ananiashuili, 1 son, 1 daughter. Education: Graduate (Honours), Faculty of International Law, Moscow State Institute of International Relations, 1981; Postgraduate student, Diplomatic Academy, 1988-90. Appointments: Ministry of Foreign Affairs of the Soviet Union, 1981-88; Head, Georgia Arts Management, and Gregory Vashadze and BR, 1990-2008; Deputy Minister, Foreign Affairs of Georgia, 2008; Minister of Culture, Georgia, 2008; Minister of Foreign Affairs, Georgia, 2008-. Publications: Several publications on foreign policy. Address: Ministry of Foreign Affairs of Georgia, #4 Chitadze st, Tbilisi, Georgia. Website: www.mfa.gov.ge

VASILEVICH Fyodor, b. 1 October 1949, Sunaii, Kopylsk, Minsk region, Russia. Veterinary Surgeon. m. Lidiya Balashova, 1 son. Education: Graduate, Moscow Veterinary Academy, 1976; Dr Sc (Vet), 1998; Professor, 1999. Appointments: Assistant, 1982-86, Lecturer, 1986-98, Department of Parasitology, Veterinary Academy, Moscow; Pro-Rector on Education, 1998-2008, Rector, 2008-, K I Skryabin, Moscow State Academy of Veterinary Medicine. Publications: 4 monographs; 12 manuals; Over 200 research papers. Honours: Merited Professor, Higher School of RF, 1999; Honoured Professor, Higher Professional Education of RF, 2005. Memberships: Russian Academy of Agricultural Sciences; International Association of Parasitocenologists; RF Ministry of Education and Science. Address: Tashkentskaya str 34, building 5, flat 78, 109472, Moscow, Russia. E-mail: rector@mgavm.ru Website: www.magvm.ru

VATS Nitin, b. 15 October, Meerut, UP, India. Researcher; Businessman. Education: B Tech, Mechanical Engineering, 2002; MS, Computer Science, 2007. Appointments: Researcher, Microsoft Research Lab, Bangalore; Researcher, Indian Institute of Science, Bangalore, India, 2007-09; CEO, Brain Programmers, 2009-. Publications: NNRU, a non-commutative analogue of NTRU; Algebraic Cryptanalysis of CTRU cryptosystem; A new approximation of factorial function for natural numbers. Honours: World Record Holder for mental calculation; Numerous articles in professional journals in more than 45 countries worldwide. Memberships: American Chemical Society. Address: 41/26, J-23, Punch Sheil St N5, Nehru Nagar, Meerut, UP, 250001, India. E-mail: nitinvatsa@gmail.com Website: www.nitinvats.com

VEERAKYATHIAH V D, b. 25 June 1926, Vaddagere, India. Retired. m. V Rajamma, 25 June 1955, 2 sons. Education: BSc, Agriculture. Appointments: Village Level Worker, 1954-55; Agricultural Extension Officer, 1955-57; Block Development Officer, 1957-65; Principal, State Level Young Farmers Training Centre, 1 year; Instructor, Orientation and Study Centre, Government of India, Poona, 1 year; Assistant Development Commissioner, 1967-71; Assistant Director, Land Army, 1971-72; Principal, Rural Development Training Centre, Mandya, Karnataka, 1972-75; Secretary, Chief Executive Officer, State Khadi and Village Industries Board, Bangalore, 1976-77; Project Director, SFDA, Government of Karnataka, 1977-80; Selected for Indian Administrative Service, Government of India; Director, Special Economic Programmes, IRDP, Government of Karnataka, 1980-82; Director, Backward Classes and Other Weaker Sections, 1982-84. Publications: 3 professional papers in the Indian Science Congress Sessions. Memberships: Honorary Director, Asian Institute for Urban Development; Advisor, Ganga Rural Development Trust; Bangalore Zilla Aadhar Member, Age Foundation, Ministry of Social Welfare, Government of India; Honorary President, Vaddagere Temple Development Committee; Founder-President, Akhila Kunchitigara Mahal Mardal, Bangalore. Address: 596 IInd Stage 1 E Block, Rajajinagar, Bangalore 560010, India.

VELINOV Milen T, b. 29 July 1959, Bulgaria. Physician; Researcher. m. Milena Velinova, 1 son, 1 daughter. Education: MD, Higher Medical Institute, Sofia, 1986; PhD, Biomedical Institute, Sofia, 1995. Appointments: Postdoctoral Fellow, University of Connecticut Health Centre, USA, 1991-95; Resident in Paediatrics, New York Methodist Hospital, 1995-98; Staff Research Scientist, New York State Institute for Basic Research, Staten Island, 1998-; Fellow in Clinical Genetics, Maimonides Medical Centre, 1999-2003; Assistant Professor of Paediatrics, State University of New York, College of Medicine, 2004; Program Director, Comprehensive Genetic Services, Assistant Director, Speciality Clinical Laboratories, 2004-, NYS Institute for Basic Research; Assistant Professor, State University of New York, 2004-06; Assistant Professor, Department of Human Genetics, Mount Sinai Medical Center, 2006-09; Assistant Professor, Albert Einstein College of Medicine, 2009-. Publications: Co-author: Connective Tissue Research, 29:13, 1993; American Journal of Medical Genetics, 47:294, 1993; Nature Genetics, 6(3):314, 1994; Molecular Genetics and Metabolism, 69:81, 2000. Honours: Fellow's Clinical Research Award, Society for Paediatric Research, 1994; Resident Research Grant, American Academy of Paediatrics, 1997. Memberships: American Society of Human Genetics; American Academy of Paediatrics; American College of Medical Genetics. Address: New York State Institute for Basic Research, 1050 Forest Hill Road, Staten Island, NY 10314, USA. E-mail: velinovm@aol.com

VELT Ivan D, b. 8 May 1929, Moscow, Russia. Engineering. m. Lidia, 2 sons. Education: Diploma, Technical Education, 1954; Cand Tech Sci, 1968; Dr Sci Tech, 1988. Appointments: Scientific-Researchers Institute, NIIteplopribor, Moscow, 1955-. Publications: 80 patents for inventions; Around 200 scientific publications. Honours: Many honourable diplomas and medals from international organisations. Memberships: Academy of Electrotechnical Sciences of Russia. Address: 2/102 Kirova Proezd, Moscow 109382, Russia. E-mail: vellt@rol.ru

VENABLES Terry Frederick, b. 6 January 1943. Professional Football Manager; Commentator. m. Yvette, 2 daughters. Education: Dagenham High School. Career: Professional Footballer, Chelsea, 1958-66 (Captain, 1962), Tottenham Hotspur, 1966-68 (FA Cup winners, 1967), Queens Park Rangers, 1968-73; Coach, Crystal Palace, 1973-76, Manchester, 1976-80; Manager, Queens Park Rangers, 1980-84; Manager, Barcelona, 1984-87 (winners, Spanish Championship, 1984, European Cup finalists, 1985); Manager, Tottenham Hotspur, 1987-91 (FA Cup winners, 1991); Chief Executive, Tottenham Hotspur plc, 1991-93; Coach, England National Team, 1994-96; Director of Football, Portsmouth Football Club, 1996-98; Coach, Australian National Team, 1996-98; Head Coach, Crystal Palace, 1998; Coach, Middlesborough, 2001; Manager, Leeds United, 2002-03; Assistant to Manager Steve McClaren, England, 2006-07; Only player to have represented England at all levels. Publications: They Used to Play on Grass, 1971; Terry Venables: The Autobiography, 1994; The Best Game in the World, 1996; Venables' England – The Making of the Team, 1996. Honours: Honorary Fellow, University of Wolverhampton; English Football Hall of Fame, 2007. Address: Terry Venables Holdings Ltd, 213 Putney Bridge Road, London, SW15 2NY, England.

VENDLER Helen, (Helen Hennessy), b. 30 April 1933, Boston, Massachusetts, USA. Professor; Poetry Critic. 1 son. Education: AB, Emmanuel College, 1954; PhD, Harvard University, 1960. Appointments: Instructor, Cornell University, 1960-63; Lecturer, Swarthmore College and Haverford College, Pennsylvania, 1963-64; Associate Professor, 1966-68, Professor, 1968-85, Boston University; Fulbright Lecturer, University of Bordeaux, 1968-69; Poetry Critic, The New Yorker, 1978-99; Overseas Fellow, Churchill College, Cambridge, 1980; Senior Fellow, Harvard Society of Fellows, 1981-93; Visiting Professor, 1981-85, Kenan Professor, 1985-90, Associate Academic Dean, 1987-92, Porter University Professor, 1990-, Harvard University; Charles Stewart Parnell Fellow, 1996, Honorary Fellow, 1996-, Magdalene College, Cambridge. Publications: Yeats's Vision and the Later Plays, 1963; On Extended Wings: Wallace Stevens' Longer Poems, 1969; The Poetry of George Herbert, 1975; Part of Nature, Part of Us: Modern American Poets, 1980; The Odes of John Keats, 1983; Wallace Stevens: Words Chosen Out of Desire, 1984; The Harvard Book of Contemporary American Poetry (editor), 1985; Voices and Visions: The Poet in America, 1987; The Music of What Happens, 1988; Soul Says, 1995; The Given and the Made, 1995; The Breaking of Style, 1995; Poems, Poets, Poetry, 1995; The Art of Shakespeare's Sonnets, 1997; Seamus Heaney, 1998; Coming of Age as a Poet, 2003; Poets Thinking, 2004; Invisible Listeners, 2005; Our Secret Discipline, 2007. Contributions to: Professional journals. Honours: Lowell Prize, 1969; Guggenheim Fellowship, 1971-72; American Council of Learned Societies Fellow, 1971-72; National Institute of Arts and Letters Award, 1975; Radcliffe College Graduate Society Medal, 1978; National Book Critics Award, 1980; National Endowment for the Humanities Fellowships, 1980, 1985, 1994, 2005; Keats-Shelley Association Award, 1994; Truman Capote Award, 1996; Jefferson Medal, American Philosophical Society, 2002; Jefferson Lecturer, NEH, 2004; Many honorary doctorates; Phi Beta Kappa. Memberships: American Academy of Arts and Letters; American Academy of Arts and Sciences, vice-president, 1992-95; American Philosophical Society; English Institute; Modern Language Association, president, 1980. Address: Harvard University, Department of English, Barker Center, Cambridge, MA 02138, USA.

VENGATESAN Balasubramanian, b. 4 June 1962, Villupuram, India. Materials Scientist. m. Kusuma, 1 son, 1 daughter. Education: BSc, 1982; MSc, 1984; PhD, 1990. Appointments: Researcher, 1984-89; Lecturer, Anna University, 1989-93; Research and Development Manager, 1993-2002, Deputy Director, NanoTech Laboratory, 2002-05, Director, 2005-, Canare Electric Co Ltd, Japan. Publications: Several research papers in international reputed journals. Honours: Visiting Professor, University of Madras, India, 2007-; Distinguished Professor, Nanotechnology, Anna University, India, 2008-; Visiting Professor (Overseas), Anna University, Chennai, India, 2009-; Numerous national and international awards. Memberships: IEEE, USA; IET, UK. Address: Canare Electric Co Ltd, NanoTech Laboratory, 2888-1 Rikka, Kumabari, Nagakute-cho, Aichi-gun, Aichi-ken, 480-1101, Japan. E-mail: cbsvenki@canare.co.jp

VENKATA KRISHNA Parimala, b. 1 February 1977, Gudur, Nellore, AP, India. Professor. m. Saritha, 1 son, 1 daughter. Education: Bachelor, Technology in Electronics and Electrical Engineering; Master, Technology in Computer Science and Engineering; PhD, Computer Science and Engineering. Appointments: Associate Professor; Assistant Professor; Division Leader. Publications: Over 50 articles in professional journals and at conference. Honours: VIT Best Research Award, 2009; VIT Research Award, 2010. Memberships: IEEE; CSI; DMTF. Address: School of Computing Science and Engineering, VIT University, Vellore, TN 632014, India. Website: www.vit.ac.in

VENKATESH Yeldur P, b. 2 December 1953, Kalale, Karnataka State, India. Biochemist; Researcher. m. Poornima, 1 son. Education: BS, Chemistry, Biology, Bangalore University, India, 1970; MS, Biochemistry, University of Mysore, 1974; PhD, Biochemistry, Indian Institute of Science, Bangalore, 1981; Scientist, 1997-2011; Senior Scientist, 2011-. Appointments: Lecturer, Biochemistry, Kasturaba Medical College, Manipal, 1974-75; Postdoctoral Fellow, Washington University School of Medicine, St Louis, 1981-83; NIH Trainee, Immunology, 1984-85; Research Associate, Smith Kline and French Laboratories, King of Prussia, USA, 1985-87; Research Scientist, ImmunoGen Inc, Cambridge, USA, 1987-92; Senior Research Scientist, 1992-95; Scientist Fellow, Central Food Technological Research Institute, Mysore, India, 1996-97; Scientist, 1997-. Publications: Many articles in biochemistry, immunology and allergy journals including: First report of allergy to eggplant, 2004. Honours: CFTRI Foundation Day Awards, 2005; Professor P B Rama Rao Memorial Award, 2009; Overseas Associateship, DBT, 2002-03. Memberships: Society of Biological Chemists, India; Indian Immunology Society; Indian Academy of Allergy; Association of Food Scientists and Technologists, India; Indian College of Allergy and Applied Immunology; World Allergy Organization; Board of Studies in Bioscience, University of Mysore; Fellow, Indian College of Allergy, Asthma & Applied Immunology. Address: Department of Biochemistry and Nutrition, Central Food Technological Research Institute, Mysore 570 020, India.

VENKITACHALAM Gangsan, b. 19 February 1945, Nagercoil, India. Teacher; Researcher. m. P Rajalakshmi, 1 son, 1 daughter. Education: BE, 1967; MTech, 1970;

PhD, 1975. Appointments: Professor, 1977-2010; Emeritus Professor, 2010-. Publications: More than 300 technical papers in national and international conferences and journals. Honours: 45 awards to date. Memberships: Fellow and Member of many professional bodies. Address: Department of Mechanical Engineering, IIT Madras, Chennai 600 036, India. E-mail: vganesan@iitm.ac.in

VENN George Andrew Fyfe, b. 12 October 1943, Tacoma, Washington, USA. Professor; Writer; Editor; Poet; Critic. m. (1) Elizabeth Cheney, divorced, 1 son, 1 daughter, (2) Marie Balaban. Education: BA, College of Idaho, 1967; MFA, Creative Writing, University of Montana, 1970; Central University, Quito, Ecuador; University of Salamanca, Spain; City Literary Institute, London. Appointments: Writer-on-Tour, Western States Arts Foundation, 1977; Foreign Expert, Changsha Railway University, Hunan, China, 1981-82; General Editor, Oregon Literature Series, 1989-94; Writer-in-Residence, Eastern Oregon University. Publications: Sunday Afternoon: Grande Ronde, 1975; Off the Main Road, 1978; Marking the Magic Circle, 1988; Oregon Literature Series, 1992-94; West of Paradise: New Poems, 1999; Soldier to Advocate: CES Wood's 1877 Legacy, 2006; Darkroom Soldier: Photographs and Letters from the Pacific Theater WWII, 2007. Many other poems, essays and stories. Contributions to: Oregon Humanities; Northwest Review; Northwest Reprint Series; Poetry Northwest; Willow Springs; Oregon East; Oregon Historical Quarterly; Idaho Yesterdays; Worldviews and the American West (book). Honours: Pushcart Prize, 1980; Oregon Book Award, 1988; Stewart Holbrook Award, 1994; Andres Berger Poetry Prize, Northwest Writers, 1995; Listed in Who's Who publications and biographical dictionaries. Memberships: Authors Guild, Western Writers of America. Address: Department of English, Eastern Oregon University, La Grande, OR 97850, USA. E-mail: gvenn@eou.edu Website: www.georgevenn.com

VERBEKE Lutgarde Romanie Cesar, b. 20 February 1960, Sint-Niklaas, Belgium. Professor. 1 daughter. Education: MusM, Music and Pedagogie, Music Theory, 1982, MusM, Music and Recorder, 1982, MusM, Music and Chamber Music, 1983, University of Science and Arts, Department Lemmensinstituut, Leuven. Appointments: Professor, Recorder and Chamber Music, University of Science and Arts, Department Lemmensinstituut, Leuven, and Academy of Music of Sint-Niklaas, 1982-90; Professor, Music Theory, 1985, Co-ordinator, 1995-, Pastiche Composition and Harmony, University of Science and Arts, Department Lemmensinstituut, Leuven. Publications: 4 articles in professional journals; Book, Principals of Western tonal-functional harmony, Compendium of the traditional harmony education in Flanders, 2009. Honours: 25 Years of Dedication, Laureate of the Lemmens Institute, 2007. Memberships: Permanente Onderwijscommissie; Departementaal Onderhandelingscomité; Jury Member, Academy of Music for Lebbeke; Ti Solèy Leve, Belgium. Address: Lemmensinstituut, Herestraat 53, Belgium.

VERBINSKI Gore, b. 16 March 1964, Oak Ridge, Tennessee, USA. Film Director; Screenwriter; Producer; Musician. Education: BFA, UCLA Film School, 1987. Career: Member of several rock bands; Film Director, screenwriter and producer of music videos, commercials and films; Commercials: Budweiser; Nike; Coca-Cola; Canon; Skittles; United Airlines; Films: Mouse Hunt, 1997; The Mexican, 2001; The Ring, 2002; Pirates of the Caribbean: The Curse of the Black Pearl, 2003; The Weather Man, 2005; Pirates of the Caribbean: Dead Man's Chest, 2006; Pirates of the Caribbean: At World's End, 2007; Rango, 2011; The Lone Ranger, BioShock, Clue, 2013. Honours: 4 Clio Awards; Cannes Advertising Silver Lion; 2 Academy Awards, 2002, 2011.

VEREKER John (Michael Medlicott) (Sir), b. 9 August 1944, UK. Governor of Bermuda. m. Judith Diane Rowen, 1 son, 1 daughter. Education: BA (Hons), University of Keele, 1967. Appointments: World Bank, Washington, 1970-72; Principal, Ministry of Overseas Development, 1972; Private Secretary to successive Ministers of Overseas Development, 1977-78; Prime Minister's Office, 1980-83; Under Secretary, 1983-88, Principal Finance Officer, 1986-88, Overseas Development Administration, Foreign and Commonwealth Office; Deputy Secretary, Department for Education, 1988-93; Permanent Secretary, Department for International Development, 1994-2002; Governor and Commander-in-Chief of Bermuda, 2002-07. Publication: Blazing the Trail (Journal of Development Studies), 2002. Honours: CB, 1992; CIMgt, 1995; Hon D Litt, University of Keele; KCB, 1999; FRSA, 1999, KStJ, 2001. Memberships: Chairman, Student Loans Co Ltd, 1989-91; Board Member, British Council, 1994-2001; Board Member, Institute of Development Studies, 1994-2000. Address: Government House, Hamilton, Bermuda.

VERESCHIAGHIN Boris, b. 20 April 1924, Barnaul, Russia. Entomologist. Widower, 1 daughter. Education: Institut of Agriculture, Barnaul, USSR, 1946; Doctor hab, Agriculture, 1972; Professor of Entomology, 1990. Appointments: Leading Researcher, Institute of Zoology; Entomologist, Academy of Sciences of Moldova, 1957-2010. Publications: Over 170 articles in professional journals; 8 books including: Insects, in Animal Life of Moldova, 1983; The Aphids of Moldova, 1985. Honours: Laureat of Premium of State of Moldova in Science and Technology. Memberships: Leader, Entomological Society of Moldova, 25 years. Address: 19 ap 250, str Decebal, Kishinev, 2002, Republic of Moldova.

VERITY Colin, b. 7 March 1924, Darwen, Lancashire, England. Marine Artist; Architect (retired). m. (1) Stella Elizabeth Smale, 1 son, 3 daughters, (2) Sonya Josephine Raven Ainley. Education: Malet Lambert High School, Hull; Hull University School of Architecture. Appointments: RAF Pilot, Second World War; Principal Architect, Hull City Architects Department; Principal Architect, Humberside County Council. Publications: Articles in Royal Society of Marine Artist's Celebration of Marine Art, 1996; A Glance Astern – a Retrospective, 2003. Honours: RIBA; RSMA; Finalist, prestigious Hunting Group Art Awards; Winner, 3 international art awards, Mystic Seaport Museum, USA; Winner, World Ship Society, Design for a Poster Award, 1980s; Paints in oils and watercolours; Work held in private and corporate collections in 17 countries; Clients include HRH Duke of Gloucester, the Sultan of Oman, the Sultan of Brunei, John Betjeman, Lloyds of London, the National Maritime Museum and Shipping Companies throughout the world. Memberships: Life Member, RSMA; The Fylingdales Group of Artists; President, Hornsea Art Society. Address: c/o Mr M Atkin, Fylingdales Group of Artists, Byways, Low Street, Scalby, YO13 0QW, England.

VERSACE Donatella, b. 2 May 1955, Reggio Calabria, Italy. Vice-President and Chief Designer of the Versace Group. m. Paul Beck, 1 son, 1 daughter. Appointments: Joined Versace, 1978; Formerly overseer of advertising and public relations, accessories designer, children's collection designer, solo designer, Versus and Isante Lines; Creative Director, Gianni Versace Group, 1997-; Launched own fragrance, Versace

DICTIONARY OF INTERNATIONAL BIOGRAPHY 36th EDITION

Woman, 2001. Address: c/o Keeble Cavaco and Duka Inc, 450 West 15th Street, Suite 604, New York, NY 10011, USA. Website: ww.versace.com

VIERTL Reinhard, b. 25 March 1946, Hall in Tirol, Austria. Professor of Applied Statistics. m. Dorothea, 2 sons. Education: Dipl Ing, 1972; Dr techn. 1974. Appointments: Assistant, 1972-79; University Docent, 1979-80; Research Fellow, University of California, Berkeley, 1980-81; Visiting Docent, University of Klagenfurt, 1981-82; Full Professor, Vienna University of Technology, 1982-; Visiting Professor, University of Innsbruck, 1991-93; Seasonal Instructor, University of Calgary, summer 2003; Visiting Professor, University of Salatiga, Indonesia, 2010. Publications: 11 books, including Statistical Methods for Fuzzy Data, 2011; Over 100 scientific papers in mathematics, probability theory, life testing, regional statistics, Bayesian statistics, and statistics with non-precise data. Honours: Max Kade Fellow, 1980; Honorary Member, Austrian Statistical Society, 2008. Memberships: Royal Statistical Society, London; Austrian Statistical Society; International Statistical Institute; German Statistical Society; New York Academy of Sciences; Austrian Mathematical Society. Address: Department of Statistics, Vienna University of Technology, Wiedner Hauptstr 8/107, A-1040 Vienna, Austria. E-mail: r.viertl@tuwien.ac.at

VIGDERGAUZ Vladimir, b. 31 July 1953, Luga, Russia. Scientist. m. Maria Teplyakova. Education: MSc, Physical Chemistry, Lomonosov University, 1975; PhD, 1980, DrSc, 1991, Mineral Processing, Russian Academy of Sciences, Moscow. Appointments: Institute of Complex Exploitation of Mineral Resources, Russian Academy of Sciences, Moscow; Scientist; Postdoctoral; Staff Scientist; Head of Mineral Processing Laboratory, Chief Research Scientist, 1975-; Professor in Mineral Processing. Publications: Electrochemistry of Sulfides: Theory and Practice of Flotation, 2009. Honours: Plaksin Prize, Russian Academy of Mining Sciences, 1997. Memberships: Russian Academy of Mining Sciences; Council of International Mining Processing Congress.

VIKBERG Veli Valtteri, b. 2 November 1936, Pyhäjärvi, Ul, Finland. Retired Physician; Amateur Entomologist. m. Marjatta Kurkela, 1 son, 3 daughters. Education: Licenciate of Medicine, 1961, Specialising in medical microbiology, 1967, University of Helsinki. Appointments: Senior Physician, Laboratory Department, Central Hospital of North Karelia, Joensuu, 1967-74; Senior Physician, Laboratory Department, 1974-87, Senior Physician, Department of Clinical Microbiology, 1988-95, Central Hospital of Kanta-Häme, Hämeenlinna; Retired, 1995. Publications: Numerous entomological articles in scientific journals, 1960-2011. Honours: Silvery Saalas-medal, The Entomological Society of Finland, 2007. Memberships: The Entomological Society of Finland, 1989; The International Society of Hymenopterists, 1991. Address: Liinalammintie 11 as. 6, FI-14200 Turenki, Finland.

VILLANO Raimondo, b. 24 June 1960, Torre Annunziata, Italy. Pharmacist; Editor; Historian. m. Maria Rosaria Giordano, 1 son. Education: Degree, Pharmacy, Naples, 1985; Diploma, Employer Corporate Safety Expert, 2000; Certificate of Advanced Training Course, Quality Management Systems, 2001; Certificate of Course in Technique and Cosmetic Legislation, Department of Medicinal Chemistry, 2002; Certificate of Advanced Course in Medicinal Plants, Department of Experimental Pharmacology, 2009; Honorary Doctorate, Humanities and Social Sciences, Ruggero II University, USA, 2009; Honorary Member, JS Bach Academy of Music, Arts, Sciences and Letters, 2010; Diploma of Merit, Center for Bioethics, Nobilis Theodorae Imperatricis Academia Sanctae, 2010; Honorary MSc, Medical Ethics, ASAM University, 2010; Diploma of Honorary Member, Center for Bioethics Institution, 2010; Honorary Degree, History Philosophy, Republic of Gambia, 2010 and Universitas Studiorum Roger, USA, 2011. Appointments: Assistant, Faculty of Pharmacy, 1985-90, Chemist, 1985-2010, Torre Annunziata; Founder and President, Foundation's Social Care and Humanitarian Chiron, 2006-; Historical, Essayist, Institutional Consultant, Writer, Director of Chiron's Editor, Naples, 2007-; Member, 2008-, Secretary, 2009-, International Commission of Biothecnologie Virosphere; Ordinary, Pontifical Academy Tiberina of University Culture and Higher Education, Rome, 2009-; District President, Campania Region Aerec, 2011-; Aerec Diplomatic Adviser, Department for the Enhancement of the Industry, Commerce and Handicrafts ENVA, 2011-; Chairman in numerous professional conferences and Rotary; Dozens of conferences in provincial and national professional meetings and conferences in more than 30 Rotary district and local levels. Publications: 30 books; Over 30 media; Over 320 articles in national and international journals. Honours: Medal Aesculapius, 1987; Diploma Honour International President Rotary, 2001; Certificate of Merit, Rotary International, 2001; Piccinini National Award for Scientific Research, 2006; Wisdom and Professional Ethics International Prize, 2007; Stramezzi National Prize Foundation, 2007; Award for Industriousness Labour Aristocracy, 2010; Award, Norman Academy, 2010. Memberships: WABT; AERC; Academy of Medical History; Noble College of Chemical and Pharmaceutical; Sovereign Military Order of Malta; International Society of History of Pharmacy. Address: Via Maresca, 12-ScA, 80058 Torre Annunziata (NA), Italy. E-mail: farmavillano@gmail.com Website: www.chiron-found.org

VILLENEUVE Jacques, b. 9 April 1971, Canada. Racing Car Driver. Appointments: Started racing in Italian Touring Car Championship Italian Formula 3, 1989, 1990; With Reynaud and Alfa Romeo, 1992; Japanese Formula 3, 1993; Formula Atlantic, 1993; IndyCar Driver, 1994-95; IndyCar Racing Champion, 1995; Drove Formula One Cars with Williams Renault Team, then British American Racing team, now with BAR-Honda; Grand Prix Winner, Britain, 1996, 1997, Brazil, 1997; Argentina, 1997; Spain, 1997; Hungary, 1997, Austria, 1997; Luxembourg, 1997; Formula One Champion, 1997; Owns restaurant/bar, Newtown in Montreal; Guest driver, Renault, last three races, 2004; Driver, Formula 1 with Sauber team, 2005-06; Driver, Peugeot, 2007; Driver, NASCAR, 2007; Driver, Speedcar, 2008. Publications: Album, Private Paradise. Website: www.jv-world.com

VINCENT John James, b. 29 December 1929, Sunderland, England. Writer; Community Activist; Broadcaster; Methodist Minister. m. Grace Johnston Stafford, 1958, 2 sons, 1 daughter. Education: BD, Richmond College, London University, 1954; STM, Drew University, 1955; DTheol, Basel University, 1960. Appointments: Ordained Minister, Methodist Church, 1956; Leader, Ashram Community, 1967-; Founder and Director, Urban Theology Unit, 1969-97; Director Emeritus 1997-; Adjunct Professor, New York Theological Seminary, 1979-87; President, Methodist Church of Great Britain, 1989-90; Honorary Lecturer, Sheffield University, 1990-, Birmingham University, 2003-; Centenary Award, Sheffield University, 2005. Publications: Christ and Methodism, 1964; Here I Stand, 1967; Secular Christ, 1968; The Race Race, 1970; The Jesus Thing, 1973; Stirrings, Essays Christian and Radical, 1975; Alternative Church, 1976; Disciple and Lord, 1976; Starting all over Again, 1981; Into the City, 1982; OK

- 1045 -

DICTIONARY OF INTERNATIONAL BIOGRAPHY 36th EDITION

Let's Be Methodists, 1984; Radical Jesus, 1986; Mark at Work, 1986; Britain in the 90's, 1989; Liberation Theology from the Inner City, 1992; A Petition of Distress from the Cities, 1993; A British Liberation Theology, bi-annual volumes, editor,1995-; The Cities: A Methodist Report, 1997; Hope from the City, 2000; Faithfulness in the City, 2003; Methodist and Radical, 2004; Mark: Gospel of Action, 2006; A Lifestyle of Sharing, 2009; Biblical Perspectives on the City, 2009; Stilling the Storm, 2011. Memberships: Studiorum Novi Testamenti Societas; Alliance of Radical Methodists; Urban Theologians International, Joint Chair, 1995-. Address: 178 Abbeyfield Road, Sheffield S4 7AY, England.

VINE Jeremy, b. 17 May 1965, Epsom, Surrey, England. Broadcaster. m. Rachel Schofield, 2 daughters. Education: Epsom College; First Class honours degree, English, University of Durham. Appointments: Journalist, Coventry Evening Telegraph, 1986-87; New Trainee, 1987-89, Programme Reporter, Today, 1989-93, Political Correspondent, 1993-97, Africa Correspondent, 1997-99, Presenter, Newsnight, 1996-2002 (full-time 1999-2002), BBC; Presenter, The Jeremy Vine Show, BBC Radio 2, 2003-. Honours: Best Speech Broadcaster, Sony Radio Academy Award, 2005. Address: c/o Room G680, BBC Television Centre, Wood Lane, London W12 7RJ, England. Website: www.bbc.co.uk

VINGT-TROIS André, b. 7 November 1942, Paris, France. Cardinal. Education: Bachelor's degree, Theology, Institut Catholique of Paris, 1962; Military Service, Germany, 1964-65; Ordination for the Archdiocese of Paris, 1969. Appointments: Assistant Pastor, St Jeanne de Chantal's Parish, Paris, 1969-74; Director, St Sulpice Seminary of Issy-les-Moulineaux, Professor of Sacramental and Moral Theology, 1974-81; Vicar General, Archdiocese of Paris, 1981-99; Auxiliary Bishop of Paris, ordained, 1988; Metropolitan Archbishop of Tours, 1999; Appointed to succeed Jean-Marie Cardinal Lustiger as Archbishop of Paris and Ordinary of Oriental Rite Catholics in France, 2005; Created Cardinal with the see of St Louis of the French in Rome, 2007; President, French Bishops' Conference, 2007-10. Publications: Numerous articles in professional journals. Honours: Knight of the Legion of Honor; Officer of the National Order of Merit. Memberships: Presidency Committee, Pontifical Council for the Family and of the Congregation for Bishops.

VINH Thoson, b. 28 June 1944, Hue, France. Medical Educator; Surgeon. m. Josianne, 2 daughters. Education: MD, Paris, 1972; PhD, Paris, 1987. Appointments: Internship, Hospital Fellowship, Paris, 1970-76; Head of Clinic Educator, Faculty of Medicine, 1976; Plastic Surgery in a Burns Unit, 1978-82; Professor Assistant, Maitre de Conferences des Universites, 1980; Professor of Universities, 1982-; Orthopaedic Surgeon, Hospital Practitioner, 1982-. Publications: Numerous articles in professional journals. Honours: Charles Neer Award, New Orleans, USA, 1990. Memberships: International Society for Orthopaedic Surgery & Traumatology; French Society of Orthopaedic Surgery & Traumatology; European Association of Clinical Anatomy; Hand Surgery Society; Society of Anatomists in France; Institute of Anatomy; College of Professors of Anatomy in France; Collegiate of Orthopaedic Professors. E-mail: thoson.vinh@gmail.com

VINOT Valliappan, b. 7 October 1985, Pudukkottai, Tamilnadu, India. Geotechnical Engineer. Education: Master in Technology, IIT Guwahati; BE, Anna University Affiliated College; Diploma, Murugappa Polytechnic College. Appointments: Project Officer, IIT Madras; Assistant Engineer, Tata Consulting Engineers Ltd; Geotechnical Engineer, AECOM. Publications: Numerous articles in professional journals. Honours: Undergraduate University Rank Holder; Undergraduate College Medalist; Diploma College Topper; Postgraduate MHRD Scholarship holder. Memberships: Life Member, IGS; 4-year annual subscription member, ISSMG. Address: Plot No 5A, Vasuki Nilayam, Srinagar Colony, Velacherry West, Chennai 600042, India. E-mail: vinot.valli@gmail.com

VIOVICENTE-MAGGAY Gemma, b. 1 May 1965, Cebu City, Philippines. Physician. m. Domingo B Maggay Jr, 1 daughter. Education: Leyte State College, 1971-78; Leyte National High School, 1978-82; BSc, Biology, University of the Philippines, 1986; D Med, Remedios Trinidad Romualdez College of Medicine, Tacloban City, Philippines, 1990. Appointments: Postgraduate Internship, 1990-91, Resident Physician, 1992-93, Cebu City Medical Center; Resident Physician, Pasay City General Hospital, 1994; Resident Physician in Paediatric Medicine, 1995-97, Fellowship Training, Pediatric Intensive Care, 1998-2000, Philippine Childrens Medical Center; Critical Care Specialist, Asian Hospital and Medical Center, Alabang Medical Center, Divine Mercy Hospital; Family Care Hospital, San Pedro Doctors Hospital, Binan Doctors Hospital, University of Perpetual Help and Medical Center Hospital, St James Hospital, Santa Rosa Hospital and Medical Center, Southern Luzon Hospital and Medical Center, MDI Sinai Hospital, Calamba Doctors Hospital, Calamba Medical Center, Balibago Polyclinic, Santa Rosa Community Hospital, Tagaytay Hospital and Medical Center, 2001-; Training Pediatric Intensive Care Fellow, Department of Pediatrics, National University Hospital, Singapore, 2007. Publications: Utilization of the Emergency Division of the Philippine Childrens Medical Center; Use of Human Albumin in Dengue Shock Syndrome; Chronic Bullous Disease of Childhood; Renal Therapies in the Intensive Care Unit; Rabies; Acute Renal Failure; Fulminant Hepatitis A. Honours: Assistant Chief Resident in Pediatric Medicine, Philippine Childrens Medical Center, 1997; First Prize Winner, Residents Research Paper Contest and Representative to National Level Research Contest. Memberships: Philippine Pediatric Society, National Level and Southern Tagalog Chapter; Philippine Medical Association; Singapore Medical Council. Address: Pediatric Intensive Care Unit & Neonatal Intensive Care Unit, St James Hospital, Dita, Cabuyao, Santa Rosa, Laguna, Philippines.

VIRTANEN Vesa Oiva, b. 21 April 1956, Laitila, Finland. Principal Lecturer; Entrepreneur. m. Maileena Kariniemi, 1 son, 2 daughters. Education: MSc, 1982, Licentiate, Structural Engineering, 1998, Technology, Tampere University of Technology; Master, Economic Sciences, Entrepreneurship, Jyvaskyla University, 2000; M Ed, Adult Education, Tampere University, 2007; Doctor, Structural Engineering, Technology, Tampere University of Technology, 2009. Appointments: Designer, Engineering Office Pertti Piirta Inc, Lahti, 1983-84; Project Engineer, Juva Inc, Turku, 1984-92; Line Manager, Turun Juva Inc, Turku, 1992-2000; Lecturer, 2001-02, Principal Lecturer, Structural Engineering, 2002-, Turku University of Applied Sciences; Leader of own consulting firm, 2009-. Publications: Structural Engineering design specifications of the Concrete Element Building, 1982; Structural Engineering Moved on the 20th Century, 1997; Entrepreneurship in Project Team of Expert Service Organization, 2000; Learning Procedure in unexpected situations of Working Life and Tasks, 2007; Production Prerequisites for the Modern Wooden Town Project, 2009. Honours: Winner (with students), Span 2010 Timber

Bridge Competition; Listed in biographical dictionaries. Memberships: Association of Finnish Construction Engineers; Association of Finnish Consultants; Association of Project Consultants; Association of Structural Mechanics; Association of Finnish Welding Work; Association of Goods Inspectors; Concrete Association of Finland; Taxpayers Association of Finland. Address: Kappakuja 1 D 18, 20540 Turku, Finland. E-mail: vesa.virtanen@turkuamk.fi

VISCO Guiseppe, b. 28 October 1927, Sorrento, Italy. Senior Consultant. Education: MD, 1950, Masters, Medical Clinics, 1955, Haematology, 1958, Hygiene and Hospital Technology, 1963, Clinical Toxicology, 1968, Rome University. Appointments: Resident, Medical Clinics Institute, Rome University, 1948-61; Professor, Infectious Diseases, 1960-2005; Teaching Courses in Infectious Diseases, Postgraduate Schools of Medical Clinics, Tropical Medicine, Hepatology, Medical Genetics, Cardio-Surgery; Medical Assistant and Resident, Cardiology Department, S Giovanni Hospital, Rome, 1961-62; Senior Registrar, Infectious Diseases Department, Spedali Civili, Brescia, 1962-63; Sub-Chief Medical Officer, Hospital Direction, Hygiene and Toxicology; Consultant, Internal Medicine, Urology, Neurology, Obstetrics and Gynaecology, Orthopedics and Intensive Care Unit, S Camillo Hospital, Rome, 1963-71; Chief Medical Officer, Infectious Diseases, L Spallanzani Hospital, 1972-95; Chief Medical Officer, Hepatology, 1972-95; Chief Medical Officer, Epidemiology and Hygiene, Public Health and Labour Departments, 1972-95; Senior Consultant, Hepatology, Regional Liver Transplant Unit, Rome, 1996-2010; Sanitary (Health) Director, S Famiglia Hospital, 1996-2000, Clinica Parioli Hospital, Rome, 2000-. Publications: About 400 scientific papers; 5 books. Memberships: Italian Ministry of Health; many other international scientific societies. Address: via Flaminia 195, 00196 Rome, Italy.

VISNJIC Goran, b. 9 September 1972, Sibenik, Croatia. Actor. m. Ivana Vrdoljak, 1999, 1 adopted son, 1 daughter with Mirela Rupic. Education: Academy of Dramatic Arts, Zagreb. Career: Films: Braca Po Materi, 1988; Welcome to Sarajevo, 1997; The Peacemaker, 1997; Rounders, 1998; Practical Magic, 1998; Committed, 2000; The Deep End, 2001; Ice Age (voice), 2002; Doctor Sleep, 2002; Duga mracna noc, 2004; Elektra, 2005; TV: ER, 1999-2008; Spartacus, 2004. Honours: Best Croatian Actor, 2004; Vladimir Nazor Award for Best Realization of a Theatrical Performance – Film, 2005.

VISWANATHA Borlinge Gowda, b. 2 May 1962, Bangalore, India. m. Thriveri, 1 daughter. Education: MBBS; DLO; MS. Appointments: Professor, Otorhinolaryngology, Bangalore Medical College & Research Institute. Publications: 30 articles in national and international journals. Honours: Editorial board member of a few national and international journals. Memberships: Association of Otolaryngologists of India; Indian Medical Association; Indian Society of Otology. Address: #716, 10th Cross, 5th Main, MC Layout, Vijayanagar, Bangalore 560040, India. E-mail: drbviswanatha@yahoo.co.in

VITHARANA Vini, b. 2 June 1928, Tangalla, Sri Lanka. Professor Emeritus. m. Tilaka Abeysiriwardana, 1 son, 1 daughter. Education: BA, 1956, BA (Hons), 1958, MA, 1959, PhD, 1968, University of London, England; PhD, University of Ceylon, Sri Lanka, 1966. Appointments: Assistant Teacher, Mahinda College, Galle, Sri Lanka, 1949-53; Assistant Teacher, St Thomas' College, Mt Lavinia, Sri Lanka, 1954-57; Assistant Editor, Sinhala Encyclopaedia, Ministry of Cultural Affairs, 1957-60; Lecturer, Senior Lecturer, Associate Professor of Sinhala, Vidyodaya (later Jayawardenepura) University, Nugegoda, Sri Lanka, 1960-81; Professor of Sinhala, Ruhuna University, Matara, Sri Lanka, 1981-93; Visiting Professor: University of Kelaniya, 1993-, Buddhist & Pali University, 1996-97, University of Sri Jayawardenepura University, 1996-2006, University of Sabaragamuwa, 1997-98; Editor in Chief, Sinhala Dictionary, 2001-04; Discipline Specialist, Maritime Archaeology, Central Cultural Fund. Publications: Dictionary of Geography, 1961; Eight Essays on the History of Sinhala Literature, 1975; Totagamuva, 1986; The Curative Dance Ritual, 1992; The Oru and the Yatra, 1992; Sun and Moon in Sinhala Culture, 1993; Common Errors & Literary Composition, 1993, revised 2007; Sri Lankan-Maldivian Cultural Affinities, 1997; Sri Lanka – the Geographical Vision, 1999; Numerous articles in learned journals; Translation into Sinhala Verse: Godamanela (a few English poems), 1978; Light of Asia, 2000; Rubaiyat, 2002; Gitanjali, 2004; Padaya, Vakaya saha Chedaya, 2008; Translation into Sinhala Prose: Light of Asia, 1955; Translation of Sinhala Classical Works into English: Muvadevdavata & Sasadavata (12th century poems); Saddharmaratnavaliya (13th century prose work); Mayūra Sandesa (14th century poem) Sinhala poetry: Megharagaya, 1978, revised 2008; A Discriptive Sinhala Grammar, 2011; Translation of Sinhala Classical Works into English; Parevi Sandesa (15th century poem). Honours: UNESCO Award for Sinhala Literature, 1962; Sri Lanka Sahitya Mandala Award, 1978; Kala Kirti National Presidential Award, 1993; All Ceylon Buddhist Congress Award, 1997; Sinhala Institute of Culture Award, 2001; Rohana Ransilu Award, Southern Provincial Council, 2004; Sarvodaya Trust Award for Research, 2002; Sri Lanka Kala Mandala Award for Best Translation, 2003; Sri Lanka Arts Society Award, 2005. Memberships: Vice Patron, Sri Lanka Arts Society; Vice President, Royal Asiatic Society of Sri Lanka; Sri Lanka Archaeological Society; Mahinda College Old Boys' Association; President, Sri Lanka Archaeological Society, 2008-. Address: 67/1 Samudrasanna Road, Mt Lavinia and Lilavasa, Tangalla, Sri Lanka.

VITOVEC Jiri, b. 1 January 1940, Tabor, Czech Republic. Veterinary Medicine. m. Ludmila Cerhova, 2 daughters. Education: MVD, 1963, Dr Sc, 2001, Veterinary and Pharmaceutical University, Brno; Professor, University of South Bohemia, České Budějovice, Czech Republic, 1998. Appointments: State Veterinary Institute, České Budějovice, 1967-; Member, FAO Veterinary Team, Mogadishu, Somalia, 1977; Institute of Parasitology, Czechoslovak Academy of Science, České Budějovice, 1980; University of South Bohemia, České Budějovice, 1995. Publications: More than 600 citations in 151 web of science. Honours: S E Purkyne Award, Czechoslovak Academy of Science, 1986. Memberships: Czech Societies of Pathology and Parasitology. Address: Jana Stursy 34, 37010 České Budějovice, Czech Republic. E-mail: jirkavitovec@seznam.cz

VIVEKANANDAN Bhagavathi Panicker, b. 21 May 1939, Trivandrum, Kerala, India. Professor of European Studies. m. Vimala Vivekanandan, 9 December 1977, 1 daughter. Education: University College, Trivandrum; MA, Department of Politics, Kerala University, 1961; PhD, School of International Studies, Jawaharlal Nehru University, 1972. Appointments: Assistant Professor of European Studies, Associate Professor of European Studies, Professor of European Studies, Chairman of Centre for American and West European Studies, School of International Studies, Jawarlal Nehru University, New Delhi. Publications: The Shrinking Circle: The Commonwealth in British Foreign

Policy, 1945-1974, 1983; Pathfinders: Social Democrats of Scandinavia, 1991; International Concerns of European Social Democrats, 1997; In Retrospect: Reflections on Select Issues in World Politics, 1975-2000, 2000; Editor: Issues of Our Times, 1991; As The Mind Unfolds, 1993; Echoes in Parliament, 1995; Building on Solidarity: Social Democracy and the New Millennium, 2000; Co-editor: Contemporary Europe and South Asia, 2001; Author, co-author or editor, 17 other books; Numerous research papers on international affairs, world politics, international security, British foreign and security policies, American foreign policy, India's foreign and security policies, European Community, European Social Democracy, European Security, Welfare States, other topics, in international research journals; Numerous articles in national newspapers and periodicals. Honours: Several scholarships and fellowships; President, Jayaprakash Foundation, New Delhi; Chairman, Executive Council, Centre for International Strategic and Development Studies, Bombay. Memberships: Executive Committee, Indian Centre for Democratic Socialism; Executive Committee, Indian Centre for International Cupertino; Editorial Board Member, quarterly journals. Address: Centre for American and West European Studies, School of International Studies, Jawaharlal Nehru University, New Delhi 110067, India.

VLADYKINA Tatiana Fedorovna, b. 6 March 1954, Rostov region, USSR. Scientist. m. Alexander Vladikin, 1 daughter. Education: School No 12, Krasny Sulin, Rostov region, 1961-71; College of Meat and Milk, Rossosh, Voronezh region, 1972-75; St Petersburg State University of Refrigeration and Food Engineering, 1975-80; Diploma of Cand Tech Science, 1988. Appointments: Researcher, 1980-88, High Researcher, 1988-89, Lithuanian Branch, All-Union Research Institute for Butter and Cheese Industry; Leading Researcher, All-Russia Dairy Research Institute, 1989-93. Publications: 70 articles in professional journals; 2 monographs. Address: Mitinskaya str 52 – 460, Moscow 125430, Russia. E-mail: tatiana543@yandex.ru

VLASTARAKOS Petros V, b. 3 June 1974, Athens, Greece. ENT Surgeon. m. Evangelia-Filothei Tavoulari. Education: Degree, Medicine, 1999, MSc, Healthcare Administration, 2005, ENT Board Exams, Greek Ministry of Health, 2008; PhD, ENT, 2009, University of Athens. Appointments: Specialist ENT Surgeon, Lister Hospital, UK. Publications: 30 peer reviewed articles in professional journals; 3 book chapters. Honours: Annual Awards, Minister of Education for Outstanding High School and Lyceum Performance, 1987-92; Letter of Recognition for Excellent Services, Greek Air Force, 2003; Scholarship, Healthcare Administration, Alexandros S Onassis, 2004-05; Scholarship of Excellence, Healthcare Administration, Greek State Scholarship Foundation, 2005 and 2006. Memberships: General Medical Council, UK; Athens Medical Association, Greece; Association of ENT Specialists, Greece; Editorial Board Member, 3 peer-reviewed journals. Address: 29 Dardanellion str, 16562, Glyfada, Athens, Greece. E-mail: pevlast@hotmail.com

VODICKA Mark Andrew John, b. 1959, Melbourne, Australia. Legal Author; Independent Counsel; Barrister; Head, Median Chambers. Education: St John's School Hawthorn, Camberwell High School, HSC Taylors' College, Melbourne, 1978; BA, Art History and Russian, Australian National University, 1982; LLB, University of Sydney, 1986; LLM, by dissertation, University of New South Wales, 1990; Languages: Czech, Russian and French. Appointments: Para-Legal, Allen, Allen & Hemmsley, Sydney, 1985; Clerk, Department of the Attorney-General for NSW, 1986; Barrister, 1986-; Voluntary Barrister, Redfern Legal Centre, 1986-91; Research Academic, University of Sydney, 1987; Law Lecturer, University of Western Sydney, 1988-89; Legal Advisor, Australian Stock Exchange, Sydney, 1990-91; Legal Consultant, Prague, Czechoslovakia, 1992-94; Independent Counsel, and Barrister, Melbourne, Australia, 1995-; Head, Median Chambers, 2008-. Publications: Article, The Extraterritorial Operation of Australian Securities Laws, Company and Securities Law Journal, Sydney, 1991; Textbook, International Securities Trading, Legal Books/Pearson Publishing (Penguin), Melbourne, 1992. Memberships: Australian Bar Association; International Law and Bar Association; Hawthorn FC. Address: Levels 13 & 14, 200 Queen Street, Melbourne, VIC 3000, Australia. E-mail: markvodicka@medianchambers.com Website: www.markvodicka.com

VOGEL Gerth R, b. 26 April 1946, Augsburg, Germany. Top Management Consultant. m. Anna, 2 daughters. Education: Diploma, Business Administration and Psychology, University of Munich, Germany, Ohio State University and University of Maryland, USA, 1966-71. Appointments: Head, Business Administration, Frisch GmbH, 1971-73; CFO Industri AB EUROC, 1973-75; CFO Randstad, 1975-80; CEO, Zentrum für Unternehmensentwicklung, 1980-; CEO, FECON Consulting Group, 2000-; CEO, Teubl Private Foundation, 2002-; President, Advisory Board, Profiles International, 2005-; Board Member, Oxanto AG, 2010-. Publications: Numerous articles in professional journals. Honours: Listed in international biographical dictionaries. Memberships: FECON Consulting Group; IBCG International Business Consultants Group; LinkedIn; Pool of Experts; OSEC Business Network Switzerland; Swiss Venture Club; VS-link. Address: Zentrum für Unternehmensentwicklung, Chalet Suisse, CH-3924 St Niklaus VS, Switzerland. E-mail: gerth.vogel@zfu-vs.com Website: www.zfu-vs.com

VOHRALIK Martin, b. 22 May 1977, Pardubice, Czech Republic. Mathematician; Consultant; Educator. Education: Master degree (honours), Mathematical Modeling, Faculty of Nuclear Sciences and Physical Engineering, Czech Technical University in Prague, 2000; PhD, 2004, Czech Technical University in Prague and University of Paris-South, France. Appointments: Part-time Research and Teaching Assistant, Czech Technical University in Prague, 2001; Part-time Research Assistant, Technical University of Liberec, Czech Republic, 2002-06; Society HydroExpert, Paris, France, 2002-04; Postdoctoral Fellow, University of Paris-South, French National Center for Scientific Research, 2005-06; Associate Professor, Jacques-Louis Lions Laboratory, Pierre and Marie Curie (Paris 6) University, France, 2006-. Publications: Numerous articles in professional journals. Honours: Vice President, 1996-99, Student Union, Faculty of Nuclear Sciences and Physical Engineering, Czech Technical University in Prague; President, 1997-98, Student Union, Czech Technical University in Prague; Rector's Award for Excellent Achievements, 1998, 1999; Honorary Prize, Foundation of Marie, Zdenka and Josef Hlavka, 2000; Siemens Main Prize for Research, 2000; Scholar, French Government, 2001-04; Fellow, French National Center for Scientific Research, 2005-06. Memberships: Society for Industrial and Applied Mathematics; French Society for Industrial and Applied Mathematics. E-mail: vohralik@ann.jussieu.fr Website: www.ann.jussieu.fr/~vohralik

VOIGHT Jon, b. 29 December 1938, Yonkers, New York, USA. Actor. m. (1) Lauri Peters, 1962, divorced 1967, (2) Marcheline Bertrand, 1971, divorced, 1 son, 1 daughter.

DICTIONARY OF INTERNATIONAL BIOGRAPHY 36th EDITION

Education: Catholic University. Career: Theatre: A View From The Bridge; That Summer That Fall, 1966; San Diego Shakespeare Festival; A Streetcar Named Desire, 1973; Hamlet, 1975; Films: Hour of the Gun, 1967; Fearless Frank, 1968; Out of It, 1969; Midnight Cowboy, 1969; The Revolutionary, 1970; The All-American Boy, 1970; Catch 22, 1970; Deliverance, 1972; Conrack, 1974; The Odessa File, 1974; Coming Home, 1978; The Champ, 1979; Lookin' to Get Out, 1982; Table for Five, 1983; Runaway Train, 1985; Desert Bloom, 1986; Eternity; Heat; Rosewood; Mission Impossible, 1996; U-Turn, 1997; The Rainmaker, 1997; Varsity Blues, 1998; The General, 1998; Enemy of the State, 1998; Dog of Flanders, 1999; Lara Croft: Tomb Raider, 2001; Pearl Harbour, 2001; Ali, 2001; Zoolander, 2002; Holes, 2003; Superbabies, 2003; The Manchurian Candidate, Superbabies: Baby Geniuses 2, National Treasure, 2004; Glory Road, 2006; September Dawn, Transformers, Bratz: The Movie, National Treasure: Book of Secrets, 2007; Pride and Glory, An American Carol, Tropic Thunder, Four Christmases, 2008; TV: End of the Game, 1976; Gunsmoke and Cimarron Strip; Chernobyl: The Final Warning, 1991; The Last of His Tribe, 1992; The Tin Soldier; Convict Cowboy, 1995; The Fixer, 1998; Noah's Ark, 1999; Second String, 2000; Jasper Texas, Karate Dog, 2003; The Five People You Meet in Heaven, 2004; Pope John Paul II, 2005; September Dawn, Glory Road, The Legend of Simon Conjurer, 2006; Transformers, Bratz, 2007; 24: Redemption, 2008; 24, 2009; Lone Star, 2010. Honours: Academy Award, Best Actor, 1979; Best Actor Awards, 1969, 1979; Cannes International Film Festival, Golden Globe Award, Best Actor, 1979; Montreal World Film Festival, 2007; CineVegas Marquee Award, 2009. Address: c/o Martin Baum and Patrick Whitesell, CAA 9830 Wilshire Boulevard, Beverly Hills, CA 90212, USA.

VOLKOVA Maya A, b. 20 March 1932, Smolensk, Russia. Professor. m. Sigidin Yakov, 1 daughter. Education: 2nd Moscow Medical Institute, 1950-56; Postgraduate, -1961. Appointments: Institute of Clinical Emergency, 1961-64; Clinical Researcher, Institute of Internal Medicine, 1964-71; Professor, Hematology Department, N W Blokhin Cancer Research Centre, 1971-. Publications: Over 300 articles in professional journals; Out-patients treatment of chronic leukemias, 1979; Clinical oncohematology, 2001; Rare hematological diseases and syndromes, 2011. Honours: First Prize, Competition of best books of the Cancer Research Center, 2008. Memberships: Russian Hematological Society; American Society of Hematology. Address: 5/3-2-132 Kuturov prosp, Moscow 121248, Russia.

VOLLMAR James Anthony, b. 8 January 1952, Wellingborough, Northamptonshire, England. Writer; Poet; Playwright. Education: Queen Mary College, University of London, 1970-72. Appointment: Founder, Editor, Greylag Press, 1977-. Publications: Circles and Spaces; Orkney Poems; Hoy: The Seven Postcards; Warming the Stones; Explorers Log Book; Notes from Café Bizarre; Play, Clearing the Colours; Contributions to: Agenda; Iron; Oasis; Joe Soaps Canoe; Ally; Pacific Quarterly; Ambit. Memberships: Writers' Guild of Great Britain. Address: c/o The Sharland Organisation, The Manor House, Raunds, Northamptonshire NN9 6JW, England.

VON BLÜCHER HSH Prince Dennis Wilhelm, b. 21 August 1944, Rostock, Germany. International Diplomat. Education: Bachelors degree, Theatre Arts, Royal Academy of Dramatic Arts; Doctorate, Homeopathy, London College of Homeopathy; Masters degree, International Relations, Vienna Diplomatic Academy; Doctorate, International Diplomatic Relations, Belford University. Appointments: Contract Player, Universal Studios, Hollywood, USA, 1974-84; Instructor/Director, Pasadena Playhouse, 1984-88; Head of Production, D W Productions Inc, California, 1988-92; Established Homeopathic Practitioners Clinic, Palm Springs, 1992-99; Consultant & Executive Vice President, In-Home Assistance Service; Consultant to the Sovereign Nation of the Kingdom of Hawai'i, 2004-; Consultant to the Council of the European Union, 2004-. Honours include: International Professional of the Year 2006; Chevalier of Malta St John of Jerusalem; Chevalier Grand Cross of Justice; Chevalier of the Order of Victory; Chevalier Grand Cross of the Imperial Order of St Constantine the Great; Chevalier of the Order of San Firminus de Gabales, Grand Cross of Justice; Order of Merit, Outstanding Service to the Diplomatic Community; Outstanding Contribution to Special Olympics, Kennedy Foundation; City of Hope Award; United Way Award; Hollywood Heritage Award; Men & Women of Distinction, Diploma of Distinction Permanent Roll of Honour; Outstanding Achievement and Leadership; Humanitarian of the Year, Southern California Motion Picture Council. Memberships: World Affairs Council; English Speaking Union of the Desert; Austrian-American Council West; Traditions und Leben, German Monarchist Society; The Prince's Council on Cultural Preservation; International Monarchist League; Order of the Golden Fleece; Fellow of the Augustan Society, First Class; Associate Member, Charles F Menninger Society; Member, Royal Society of North America; Prinz Blücher von Wahlstatt Principe de Narcea, Cantabria, Spain; Chevalier of the Order of Victory; Chevalier of the Order of San Firminus de Gabales, Grand Cross of Justice; Chevalier of the Order of Santa Maria of Buenos Aires (also Ambassador/Prior); Order of Merit – Outstanding Service to the Diplomatic Community; Order of the Prussian Crown, First Class; Member of Students' Council, Belford University; Organiser of Summer Party for the Jubilee Celebration of Queen Elizabeth II and participant of same; Member, Freelance Consulting Team of Diplomaticnet.com; Southwest Blue Book, Society Register of Southern California; Regent/Member of International Fraternity of Nobles of Titled Houses; Listed in the Imperial College of Princes and Counts of the Holy Roman Empire. Address: 2701 E Mesquite Avenue #S-85, Palm Springs, California 92264, USA. E-mail: dvblucher@juno.com

VON DER DUNK Hermann Walther, b. 9 October 1928, Bonn, Germany. Historian; Professor Emeritus. m. Goverdina Schuurmans Stekhoven, 2 sons, 1 daughter. Education: Masters Degree, 1957; Promotion Dr degree, 1966. Appointments: Teacher in secondary schools, 1956-57, 1961-63; Research Fellow and Assistant, Institut für Europäische Geschichte/ Mainz, 1957-61; Assistant Professor, Modern History, 1963-67, Professor, Contemporary History, 1967-88, Professor, Cultural History, 1988-90, University of Utrecht; Visiting Professor, Cultural History, University of Nymegen, 1993-95. Publications: Conservatisme, 1976; De organisatie von het Verleden, 1982; De verboder drempel de Shoah, 1990; Cultuurgeschiedenis 20ᵉ eenw, 2000; Jengdherinneriugen, 2008; I n het huis van de herinnering, 2007; Op schuivende planken, 2007; De glimlachende Sfinx, kernproblemen in de gerschiedenis, 2011; Bundles (compilations) of essays; Articles and essays in scientific and general journals; Contributions to textbooks and anthologies. Honours: Grosse Bundesverdienst Kreuz, 1989; Ridder Nederlandse Leeuw, 1991; Vondel-Prÿs, 1994; Goethe medaille, 1995. Memberships: Academia Europaea; Koninklijke Nederlandse Academie vor Kunsten/Wetenshappen; Hollandse Maatschapji der Wetenschappen. Address: Nicolailaan 20, 3723 HS Bilthoven, The Netherlands.

VON HAUSEN Michael Anthony, b. 19 June 1955, Ottawa, Ontario, Canada. Urban Designer; Planner and Landscape Architect+. m. Laura von Hausen, 1 daughter. Education: Bachelor of Landscape Architecture, Honours, University of Guelph, Ontario, 1978; Master of Landscape Architecture in Urban Design, Harvard University, USA, 1980. Appointments: Senior Design Planner, Proctor and Redfern Group, Ottawa; Project Manager, Design Workshop, Denver, Colorado, USA; Senior Planner and Senior Landscape Architect, City of Vancouver Planning Department, Vancouver, British Columbia, Canada; President, MVH Urban Planning & Design Inc, Surrey, British Columbia, Canada; Adjunct Professor, Urban Studies Program, Simon Fraser University, Vancouver, British Columbia, Canada; Curriculum Co-ordinator and Chief Instructor, Urban Design Certificate Program, Simon Fraser University. Past Civic Activities: Surrey Foundation Board of Directors Member and Executive Director; City of Surrey Urban Design Panel. Publications: Dynamic Urban Design: Place, Process and Plans, 2011; Eco-Plan: Community Ecological Planning and Design, 2010; 100 Timeless Urban Design Principles, 2008; Urban Design and Planning Graphics Resource Book, 2004; Real Estate Economics in Urban Design, 2004; Leading Edges: Alternative Development Standards in British Columbia Municipalities, 2002. Honours: Selected by Canada Mortgage and Housing Corporation to represent Canada as a sustainable urban design expert for missions to China and Russia; Numerous Awards of Excellence in Planning by the Planning Institute of British Columbia; Commendation for Design Excellence, US Department of Transportation and National Endowment for the Arts; Honours Award, Canadian Institute of Planners; Special Achievement Award, International Downtown Association; Master Planned Community of the Year Award, Urban Development Institute (Pacific Region); Award of Excellence, Canadian Association for University Continuing Education for the Simon Fraser University Urban Design Certificate Program. Memberships: British Columbia Society of Landscape Architects, Past President; Canadian Society of Landscape Architects; Planning Institute of British Columbia; Canadian Institute of Planners. Commissions and Creative Works: Vancouver Greenways Plan, Vancouver; Vancouver City Plan; City of Langley Downtown Master Plan, BC; City of Medicine Hat Downtown Redevelopment Plan, Alberta; 100 Year Midtown Plan, City of Calgary, Alberta; City of Chilliwack Downtown Neighbourhoods Plan, BC; City of Leduc, Downtown Master Plan, Alberta; Elita Community Master Plan, Krasnoyarsk, Russia, Cambrian Crossing Master Plan, Strathcona County, Alberta; Garrison Crossing Master Plan, Chilliwack, BC; Liberty Crossing and Gasoline Alley Urban Design Plan, Red Deer, Alberta. Address: 12601 19A Avenue, South Surrey, British Columbia, V4A 7M1, Canada. Email: vhausen@telus.net Website: www.mvhinc.com

VONKA Vladimir, b. 31 July 1930, Prague, Czech Republic. Physician; Scientific Worker. m. Jarmila, 1 son. Education: MD, Charles University, Prague, 1955; PhD, 1963; DSc, 1981; WHO Senior Researcher Training Grant, Department of Virology and Epidemiology, Baylor College of Medicine, Houston, Texas, 1964-65. Appointments: Clinical Physician, 1955-56; Postdoctoral Fellow, Virology, 1956-60; Head, Department of Virus Biology, Research Institute of Immunology, Prague, 1961-70; Visiting Professor of Virology, Baylor College of Medicine, Houston, Texas, USA, 1968-69; Head, Department of Experimental Virology, Institute of Sera and Vaccines, Prague, 1971-91; Visiting Scientist, Pennsylvania State University, Hershey, Pennsylvania, USA, 1983-84; Head, Department of Experimental Virology, Institute of Hematology and Blood Transfusion, Prague, 1991-2001; Head, Laboratory of Gene Therapy & Tumour Immunology, 2001-, Institute of Hematology and Blood Transfusion, Prague; Professor of Microbiology, Charles University, 1992. Publications: More than 300 scientific publications; Quoted more than 3,000 times; 2 text books; 20 monographs or chapters in monographs. Honours: G Mendel Medal, 1991; American Academy of Microbiology, 1992; Academia Scient Artium Europea, 1997; WHO Certificate of Appreciation, 2003; State Medal for Merit, 2005; Award of the Year, International Society of Papillomavirus, 2006; Praemium Bohemiae, 2007; and others. Memberships: Learned Society of theCzech Republic; Czech Medical Academy; American Academy of Microbiology; Academia Scientiarum et Artium Europea; Czech Medical Society; and others. Address: Institute of Hematology & Blood Transfusion, U Nemocnice 1, 128 20 Prague 2, Czech Republic. E-mail: vonka@uhkt.cz

VOROBYEVA Natalya Mikhaylovna, b. 2 August 1976, Tyumen, Russian Federation. Cardiologist. Education: MD, Tyumen State Medical Academy, 1999; Cardiology Residency, 1999-2001; PhD, Cardiology, 2004; Cardiology Doctoral Studies, 2007-10. Appointments: Cardiologist, Department of Urgent Cardiology, Tyumen Cardiology Center, 2001-06; Doctoral Candidate, Department of Angiology, Russian Cardiology Research and Production Complex, 2007-10; Senior Research Assistant, Laboratory of Medical Genetics, Russian Cardiology Research and Production Complex, 2010-. Publications: 62 articles in professional journals. Honours: Young Investigator Award, XXII Congress of the International Society on Thrombosis and Haemostasis, 2009; Listed in international biographical dictionaries. Memberships: Heart Failure Association of the European Society of Cardiology. Address: 15A, 3-d Cherepkovskaya street, Moscow 121552, Russia. E-mail: natalyavorobjeva@mail.ru

VRANA Ivan, b. 12 June 1941, Myjava, Czech Republic. University Professor. m. Hana, 1 son, 1 daughter. Education: MSc, Radioelectronics, 1963; PhD, Radioelectronics, 1973; Dr Sc, Radioelectronics, 1990, Associate Professor, Radioelectronics, 1991. Full Professor, Informatics, 1992. Appointments: Senior Research Fellow, 1974; Principal Research Fellow, 1990; Head, Department of Informatics, 1991; Vice Rector, 1993; Head, Department of Information Engineering, 1997. Publications: On a Direct Method of Analysis of the SPRT, 1982; Optimum Statistical Estimates in Conditions of Ambiguity, 1993; Fuzzy Aggregation and Averaging for Group Decision Making, 2009; 3 books. Honours: Master of Sports, 1987; President, EUNIS-CZ, 1997; General Secretary, EUNIS, 1999. Memberships: IEEE; ACM; ECAR; EUNIS. Address: Czech University of Life Sciences, Prague 16521, Czech Republic. E-mail: vrana@pef.czu.cz

VUJIČIĆ Mile, Senior Thermal Engineer. Education: Dip Ing, Mechanical Engineering, University of Sarajevo, Yugoslavia, 1989; MSc, Mechanical Engineering, University of Belgrade, Serbia and Montenegro, 2001; PhD, Mechanical Engineering, University of Wales, Swansea, UK, 2005. Appointments: Designer of Heat Exchangers, 1989-92, Senior Designer, 1989-92, Energoinvest, Sarajevo; Assistant Professor, Electrotechnical Faculty, 1994-2002, Visiting Assistant Professor, Faculty of Mechanical Engineering, 1995-2002, University of East Sarajevo; Head of Executive Board, Bosnia and Herzegovina, 1997-2000; Research Engineer, University of Wales, School of Engineering, Swansea, 2002-05; Mechanical Design Engineer, Unit Superheater Engineering, Swansea, 2006-07; Senior Thermal Engineer, Davy Process Technology, London, 2007-. Publications: Over

50 articles in professional journals. Memberships: CEng; IMechE; Heat Transfer Society. Address: Davy Process Technology, 10 Eastbourne Terrace, London W2 6LG, England. E-mail: mile.vujicic@davyprotech.com Website: www.davyprotech.com

W

WÄCHTLER Martin, b. 9 May 1958, Idstein, Germany. Internist. Education: Diplomate, University of Frankfurt Main, 1983; D, University of Frankfurt, 1984; Specialist, Internal Medicine, Bavarian Medical Association, 1993; Specialist, Infectious Diseases, German Society for Infectious Diseases, 2003. Appointments: Resident, German Heart Centre, Munich, 1985-87; Munich Schwabing Hospital, Academic Teaching Hospital, University of Munich, 1988-; Specialist, Infectious Diseases, Bavarian Medical Association, 2006. Publications: Articles in professional journals. Honours: Certificate in Hepatology, 2008. Memberships: German Society of Infectious Diseases; Deutsche Gesellschaft für Verdauungs und Stoffwechselkrankheiten. Address: Munich Schwabing City Hospital, Kölner Platz 1, 80804, Munich, Germany. E-mail: martin.waechtler@klinikum-muenchen.de

WADDELL Heather, b. 11 July 1950, Scotland. Author; Art Critic; Artist; Photographer; Publisher. Partner: Roger Wilson, deceased 1999. Education: Westbourne School, Glasgow; St Leonard's School, St Andrews; MA, University of St Andrews; Diploma in Fine Art, Leverhulme Bursary, Byam Shaw School of Art, University of London. Career: Lecturer, Paddington College, London, 1978; Researcher, International Artists Exchange Programme, Australia and New Zealand, 1979; London Correspondent, Vie des Arts, 1979-89; International Administrator, Artists Exchange Programme, ACME Gallery, London, 1980; Founder and Managing Director, Art Guide Publications Ltd, 1980-87; Publisher, Art Guide Publications, 1987-90; Company Director, 1987-, Company Secretary, 1992-, 27 Holland Park Avenue Ltd; Visual Arts Editor, Time Out Publications, 1989-93; Arts Editor, The European, 1990-91; Lecturer, American University Summer School, Paris, 1995; Artist/ Photographer: 5 photographs in National Portrait Gallery Photography Collection; Exhibitions: Battersea Arts Centre, 1979; SH NSW House Gallery, London, 1980; Morley Gallery, 1984. Publications: Numerous articles in newspapers and magazines; London Art and Artist's Guide, 11 editions, 1979-2012; The Artist's Directory, 3 editions, 1981, 1983, 1987; The London Art World 1979-99, 2000; Henri Goetz: 50 Years of Painting; Art Snakes and London Ladders, 2012; Contributor: Londres, 1990; L'Ecosse Lumiere, Granit et Vent, 1988; Blue Guide Spain; London Encyclopedia; many others. Memberships: Honorary Member, Royal Over-Seas League; Independent Publishers' Guild; AICA UK; DACS; Society of Authors; Serpentine Swimming Club. Address: 27 Holland Park Avenue, Campden Hill, London W11 3RW, England. E-mail: hw.artlondon1@virginmedia.com Website: www.hwlondonartandartistsguide.com

WAGNER Robert, b. 10 February 1930, Detroit, Michigan, USA. Actor. m. (1) Natalie Wood, 1957, divorced 1962, re-married 1972, deceased 1981, 1 daughter, 1 stepdaughter, (2) Marion Marshall Donen, 1 daughter, (3) Jill St John, 1991. Career: Films: Halls of Montezuma, The Frogmen, Let's Make It Legal, 1951; With a Song in My Heart, What Price Glory? Stars and Strips Forever, 1952; The Silver Whip, Titantic, Star of Tomorrow: Beneath the 12-Mile Reef, 1953; Prince Valiant, Broken Lance, 1954; White Feather, 1955; A Kiss Before Dying, The Mountain, 1956; The True Story of Jesse James, Stopover Tokyo, 1957; The Hunters, In Love and War, Mardi Gras, 1958; Say One For Me, 1959; Between Heaven and Hell; All the Fine Young Cannibals, 1960; Sail a Crooked Ship, 1961; The Longest Day, The War Lover, The Condemned of Altona, 1962; The Pink Panther, 1963; Harper, 1966; Banning, 1967; The Biggest Bundle of Them All, Don't Just Stand There! 1968; Winning, 1969; Madame Sin, Journey Through Rosebud, 1972; The Towering Inferno, 1974; Midway, 1976; The Concorde: Airport '79, 1979; The Curse of the Pink Panther, 1983; Dragon: The Bruce Lee Story, 1993; Overdrive, Austin Powers: International Man of Mystery, 1997; Wild Things, Something to Believe In, 1998; The Kidnapping of Chris Burden, Dill Scallion, Crazy in Alabama, No Vacancy, Love and Fear; Austin Powers: The Spy Who Shagged Me, Play It to the Bone, 1999; Forever Fabulous, The Mercury Project, 2000; The Retrievers, Sol Goode, Jungle Juice, 2001; Nancy and Frank – A Manhattan Love Story, Austin Powers in Goldmember, The Calling, 2002; El Padrino, 2004; Little Victim, 2005; The Wild Stallion, Hoot, 2006; Man in the Chair, Netherbeast Incorporated, 2007; TV: numerous TV series including Hart to Hart, 1979-. Honours: 6 Golden Globes. Address: c/o William Morris Agency, One William Morris Place, Beverly Hills, CA 90212, USA. Website: www.robert-wagner.com

WAGONER David (Russell), b. 5 June 1926, Massillon, Ohio, USA. Professor of English; Poet; Author. m. (1) Patricia Parrott, 1961, divorced 1982, (2) Robin Heather Seyfried, 1982, 2 daughters. Education: BA, Pennsylvania State University, 1947; MA, Indiana University, 1949. Appointments: Instructor, DePauw University, 1949-50, Pennsylvania State University, 1950-53; Assistant Professor, 1954-57, Associate Professor, 1958-66, Professor of English, 1966-, University of Washington, Seattle; Editor, Poetry Northwest, 1966-; Elliston Professor of Poetry, University of Cincinnati, 1968. Publications: Poetry: Dry Sun, Dry Wind, 1953; A Place to Stand, 1958; Poems, 1959; The Nesting Ground, 1963; Staying Alive, 1966; New and Selected Poems, 1969; Working Against Time, 1970; Riverbed, 1972; Sleeping in the Woods, 1974; A Guide to Dungeness Spit, 1975; Travelling Light, 1976; Collected Poems, 1956-1976, 1976; Who Shall be the Sun?: Poems Based on the Love, Legends, and Myths of Northwest Coast and Plateau Indians, 1978; In Broken Country, 1979; Landfall, 1981; First Light, 1983; Through the Forest: New and Selected Poems, 1977-1987, 1987; Traveling Light: Collected and New Poems, 1999. Fiction: The Man in the Middle, 1954; Money, Money, Money, 1955; Rock, 1958; The Escape Artist, 1965; Baby, Come on Inside, 1968; Where Is My Wandering Boy Tonight?, 1970; The Road to Many a Wonder, 1974; Tracker, 1975; Whole Hog, 1976; The Hanging Garden, 1980. Editor: Straw for the Fire: From the Notebooks of Theodore Roethke 1943-1963, 1972. Honours: Guggenheim Fellowship, 1956; Ford Foundation Fellowship, 1964; American Academy of Arts and Letters Grant, 1967; National Endowment for the Arts Grant, 1969; Morton Dauwen Zabel Prize, 1967; Oscar Blumenthal Prize, 1974; Fels Prize, 1975; Eunice Tietjens Memorial Prize, 1977; English-Speaking Union Prize, 1980; Sherwood Anderson Prize, 1980; Pacific Northwest Booksellers Award, 2000. Membership: Academy of American Poets, chancellor, 1978. Address: University of Washington, 4045 Brooklyn Avenue NE, Seattle, WA 98105, USA.

WAHEED Abdul, b. 9 October 1958, Lahore, Pakistan. Librarian. m. Shakeela Akhtar, 2 sons. Education: LLB, 1982; MA, Dol Sc, 1983; MA, Urdu, 1984; Diploma, Library Science, 1985; MA, Library Science, 1986; Postgraduate Diploma, ILS, 1994; MA, Information and Library Studies, 1995. Appointments: RD, Urdu Board, Lahore; Librarian, Punjab Education Department, 1984-86; Librarian, MMU, UK, 1986-; Senior Librarian, 1992-93, Chief Librarian, 1997-2000, 2000-02, Government College of Lahore; Chief Librarian, University of the Punjab, 2002-04; Professor, Chief Librarian, Government College University, 2004-.

Publications: Author, 3 books; Contributor, around 200 articles in national newspapers and magazines of Pakistan. Honours: International Information Issues Special Interest Group (Sig-III) Awards, American Society for Information Science and Technology, 2009; All Pakistan Uni Best Library Website Awards, 73rd IFLA conference, Seoul; Selected CL with status of Professor in any university in Pakistan. Memberships: PLA; PAL; AMIInfSoc, UK. Address: 67, Afzal Street, Rustam Park, PO Multan Road, Lahore, Pakistan. E-mail: waheed2834@yahoo.com

WAHEED Magdi M Abdelrahman, b. 4 May 1968, Damitta, Egypt. Professor. m. Narmeen El-Wishy, 2 sons. Education: Doctorate, 2001. Appointments: Professor of Theriogenology, King Faisal University. Publications: 24 articles in professional journals. Memberships: 6 societies. Address: 1757 Al-Hufof 31982, College of Veterinary Medicine, King Faisal University, Al-Hasa, Saudi Arabia. E-mail: mmwaheed@kfu.edu.sa

WAHLBERG Mark, b. 5 June 1971, Dorchester, Massachusetts, USA. Actor. m. Rhea Durham, 2 sons, 2 daughters. Career: Films: Renaissance man, 1994; The Basketball Diaries, 1995; Fear, 1996; Traveller, 1997; Boogie Nights, 1997; The Big Hit, 1998; The Corruptor, 1999; Three Kings, 1999; The Yards, 2000; The Perfect Storm, 2000; Metal God, 2000; Planet of the Apes, 2001; Rock Star, 2001; The Truth About Charlie, 2003; The Italian Job, 2003; I Heart Huckabees, 2004; Four Brothers, 2005; Invincible, 2006; The Departed, 2006; Shooter, 2007; We Own the Night, 2007; The Happening, 2008; Max Payne, 2008; The Lovely Bones, 2009; Date Night, The Other Guys, The Fighter, 2010; Contraband, Ted, 2012; Broken City, Pain & Gain, 2 Guns, 2013; TV: Teen Vid II, 1991; The Substitute, 1993. Recordings: Albums: Music for the People, 1991; You Gotta Believe, 1992. Address: c/o United Talent Agency, 9560 Wilshire Boulevard, Suite 500, Beverly Hills, CA 90212, USA. Website: www.markwahlberg.com

WAINWRIGHT Geoffrey, b. 16 July 1939, Yorkshire, England. Professor of Systematic Theology; Methodist Minister. m. Margaret Wiles, 1965, 1 son, 2 daughters. Education: BA, 1960, MA, 1964, BD, 1972, DD, 1987, University of Cambridge; DrThéol, University of Geneva, 1969. Appointments: Editor, Studia Liturgica, 1974-87; Professor of Systematic Theology, The Divinity School, Duke University, Durham, North Carolina, 1983-. Publications: Christian Initiation, 1969; Eucharist and Eschatology, 1971, 2nd edition, 1981; The Study of Liturgy (co-editor), 1978, 2nd edition, 1992; Doxology, 1980; The Ecumenical Moment, 1983; The Study of Spirituality (co-editor), 1986; On Wesley and Calvin, 1987; Keeping the Faith: Essays to Mark the Centenary of Lux Mundi (editor), 1989; The Dictionary of the Ecumenical Movement (co-editor), 1991; Methodists in Dialogue, 1995; Worship With One Accord, 1997; For Our Salvation, 1997; Is the Reformation Over? Catholics and Protestants at the Turn of the Millennia, 2000; Lesslie Newbigin: A Theological Life, 2000; The Oxford History of Christian Worship (co-editor), 2006; Embracing Purpose: Essays on God, the World and the Church, 2007. Contributions to: Reference books and theological journals. Honours: Numerous named lectureships world-wide; Berakah Award, North American Academy of Liturgy, 1999; Received a Festschrift: Ecumenical Theology in Worship, Doctrine, and Life: Essays Presented to Geoffrey Wainwright on his 60th Birthday, 1999; Outstanding Ecumenist Award, Washington Theological Consortium, 2003; Johannes Quasten Medal, 2005. Memberships: American Theological Society, secretary, 1988-95, president, 1996-97; International Dialogue Between the World Methodist Council and the Roman Catholic Church, chairman; Societas Liturgica, president, 1983-85; World Council of Churches Faith and Order Commission, 1976-91. Address: The Divinity School, Duke University, Durham, NC 27708, USA.

WAITE Terence Hardy, b. 31 May 1939, Bollington, England. Writer and Broadcaster. m. Helen Frances Watters, 1964, 1 son, 3 daughters. Education: Church Army College, London. Appointments: Lay Training Advisor to Bishop and Diocese of Bristol, 1964-68; Advisor to Archbishop of Uganda, Rwanda and Burundi, 1968-71; International Consultant with Roman Catholic Church, 1972-79; Advisor, Archbishop of Canterbury on Anglican Communion Affairs, 1980-92; Iranian Hostages Mission, 1981; Libyan Hostages Mission, 1985; Kidnapped in Beirut, 1987, Released, 1991. Publications: Taken on Trust, 1993; Footfalls in Memory, 1995; Travels with a Primate, 2000. Honours include: Hon DCL, Kent, 1986, City of London, Durham, 1992; Hon DLL, Liverpool; Hon LLD, Sussex, 1992; Hon LHD, Wittenberg University, 1992; Hon Dr International Law, Florida Southern University, 1992; Dr hc, Yale University Divinity School, 1992; Roosevelt Freedom Medal, 1992; Man of the Year, England, 1985; Freeman, City of Canterbury, 1992, Borough of Lewisham, 1992; Hon DPhil, Anglia Polytechnic, 2001; Hon DLitt, Nottingham Trent, 2001. Memberships: Church of England National Association, 1966-68; Co-ordinator, Southern Sudan Relief Project, 1969-71; Butler Trust, Prison Officers Award Programme; President, Y-Care International (YMCA International Development Committee); President, Emmaus UK (for the Homeless), 1996-; Founder Chair, Friends of Victim Support, 1992-; Patron, Strode Park Foundation for the Disabled; Rainbow Trust; Fellow Commoner, Trinity Hall, Cambridge, 1992-; Honorary Chancellor, Florida Southern University, 1992; Chairman, Prison Video Trust; Trustee Freeplay Foundation. Address: Trinity Hall, Cambridge, CB2 1TJ, England.

WAITS Tom, b. 7 December 1949, Pomona, California, USA. Singer; Songwriter; Musician (piano, accordion); Actor. m. Kathleen Brennan, 1981, 1 son, 1 daughter. Career: Recording artist, 1973-; Concerts include: Ronnie Scott's jazz club, 1976; London Palladium, 1979; The Black and White Night - Roy Orbison And Friends, 1987; Actor, films including: Paradise Alley, 1978; Wolfen, 1981; Stone Boy; One From The Heart, 1982; The Outsiders, 1983; Rumblefish, 1983; The Cotton Club, 1984; Down By Law, 1986; Cold Feet, 1989; The Fisher King, 1991; At Play In The Fields Of The Lord, 1991; Queen's Logic, 1991; Bram Stoker's Dracula, 1992; Short Cuts, 1993; Mystery Men, 1999; Coffee And Cigarettes, 2003; Domino. Compositions include: Ol' 55, The Eagles, 1974; Angel Wings, Rickie Lee Jones, 1983; Downtown Train, Rod Stewart, 1990; The Long Way Home, Norah Jones, 2004; Temptatino, Diana Krall, 2004; Jersey Girl, Bruce Springsteen. One From The Heart (film soundtrack), 1981; Co-writer (with wife), musical Frank's Wild Years, 1986; Score, Alice In Wonderland, Hamburg, 1992. Recordings: Albums: Closing Time, 1973; The Heart Of Saturday Night, 1974; Nighthawks At The Diner, 1975; Small Change, 1976; Foreign Affairs, 1977; Blue Valentine, 1978; Heartattack And Vine, 1980; One From The Heart, 1982; The Asylum Years - Bounced Check, 1983; Anthology, 1983; Swordfishtrombones, 1983; Raindogs, 1985; Frank's Wild Years, 1987; Big Time, 1988; Stay Awake, 1988; Bone Machine, 1992; Black Rider, 1993; Mule Variations, 1999; Used Songs 1973-80, 2001; Alice, 2002; Blood Money, 2002; Real Gone, 2004; The Orphans Tour, 2006; Contributor, compilation albums: Lost In The Stars, 1984; Stay Awake, 1988; Contributor, Night On Earth (film soundtrack), 1992. Honours: Oscar Nomination, One From The Heart, 1982; Grammy Award, Best Alternative Music, Bone Machine, 1993. Address: c/o Anti-Inc, 2798 Sunset Blvd, Los Angeles, CA 90026, USA.

WAKAGI Masatoshi, b. 18 September 1957, Tokyo, Japan. Businessman. m. Minako, 1 daughter. Education: Bachelor's degree, 1980, Master's degree, 1982, University of Tokyo; PhD, Tokyo Institute of Technology, 1996. Appointments: Researcher, 1982-94, Senior Researcher, 1994-, Hitachi Research Laboratory; Visiting Researcher, Pennsylvania State University, 1993-94. Publications: Structural Study of a Si and a SiiH Films by EXAFS and Raman Scattering Spectroscopy, 1994; Structural Study of Crystallization of a Ge Using Extended X-ray Absorption Fine Structure, 1994; Real Time Spectroscopic Ellipsometry for Characterization of the Crystallization of Amorphous Silicon by Thermal Amealing, 1998; Development of Transparent Conductive Films II, 2002; and others. Honours: Koan-Hyosho, Kanto Electric Association. Memberships: Japan Society of Applied Physics. Address: 7-1-1 Omika-Cho, Hitachi-shi, Ibaraki-ken, 319-1292, Japan. E-mail: masatoshi.wakagi.vd@hitachi.com

WAKEHAM John (Baron Wakeham of Malden), b. 1932. Chartered Accountant; Politician. m. (1) Roberta, deceased 1984, 2 sons, (2) Alison Ward, 1985, 1 son. Appointments: Chartered Accountant with own practice; Retired from business, 1977; Elected Conservative Member of Parliament for Maldon and Rochford, 1974, South Colchester and Maldon, 1983; Ministerial Appointments: Assistant Government Whip, 1979; Lord Commissioner of the Treasury, 1981; Parliamentary Under Secretary of State, Department of Industry, 1981; Minister of State, Treasury, 1982; Government Chief Whip, 1983; Appointed Member of the Privy Council, Lord Privy Seal and Leader of the House of Commons, 1987; Lord President of the Council and Leader of the House of Commons, 1988; Secretary of State for Energy, 1989; Lord Privy Seal and Leader of the House of Lords, 1992; Retired from Government, 1994; 6 Non-Executive Directorships; Chairman, Cothill House, 1998; Chairman, Alexandra Rose Day, 1998; Chairman, Vosper Thorneycroft Holdings Plc, 1995; Chairman, Press Complaints Commission, 1995-2002; Non-Executive Director, Enron Corporation, 1994-2002; Bristol and West PLC, 1995-2002; NM Rothschild & Sons Ltd, 1995-2002; Chairman, Royal Commission on House of Lords Reform, 1999-2000; Chairman, Michael Page International Plc, 2001-02. Honours: JP; DL; FLA; Honorary PhD; Honorary D Univ. Memberships: Director, National Association for Gambling Care, Educational Resources and Training; Trustee and Committee of Management, RNLI; Trustee, HMS Warrior 1860; Clubs: Garrick, Carlton, Royal Yacht Squadron, Royal Southern Yacht Club. Address: House of Lords, London SW1, England.

WAKELEY Amanda, b. 15 September 1962, England. Fashion Designer. m. Neil David Gillon, 1992. Appointments: Fashion industry, New York, 1983-85; Designing, private clients, England, 1986; Launched own label, 1990; Retail, wholesale world-wide, bridal, high street brand Amanda Wakeley for Principles and corporate-wear consultancy; Co-chair of Fashion Targets Breast Cancer Campaign and raised over £5 million for Breakthrough in 1996, 1998, 2000, 2002 and 2004. Honours: Glamour Award, British Fashion Awards, 1992, 1993, 1996. Membership: Co-Chair, Fashion Targets Breast Cancer Campaign, 1996, 1998, 2000, 2002. Address: Amanda Wakeley Ltd, 26-28 Conway Street, London W1T 6BQ, England. Website: www.amandawakeley.com

WAKOSKI Diane, b. 3 August 1937, Whittier, California, USA. Poet; Professor of English. m. Robert J Turney, 1982. Education: BA, English, University of California at Berkeley, 1960. Appointments: Poet-in-Residence, Professor of English, 1975-, University Distinguished Professor, 1990-, Michigan State University; Many visiting writer-in-residencies. Publications: Poetry: Coins and Coffins, 1962; Discrepancies and Apparitions, 1966; The George Washington Poems, 1967; Inside the Blood Factory, 1968; The Magellanic Clouds, 1970; The Motorcycle Betrayal Poems, 1971; Smudging, 1972; Dancing on the Grave of a Son of a Bitch, 1973; Virtuoso Literature for Two and Four Hands, 1975; Waiting for the King of Spain, 1976; The Man Who Shook Hands, 1978; Cap of Darkness, 1980; The Magician's Feastletters, 1982; The Collected Greed, 1984; The Rings of Saturn, 1986; Emerald Ice: Selected Poems 1962-1987, 1988; Medea the Sorceress, 1991; Jason the Sailor, 1993; The Emerald City of Las Vegas, 1995; Argonaut Rose, 1998; The Butcher's Apron: New and Selected Poems, 2000. Criticism: Towards a New Poetry, 1980. Contributions to: Anthologies and other publications. Honours: Cassandra Foundation Grant, 1970; Guggenheim Fellowship, 1972; National Endowment for the Arts Grant, 1973; CAPS Grant, 1988, New York State, 1974; Writer's Fulbright Award, 1984; Michigan Arts Council Grant, 1988; William Carlos Williams Prize, 1989; Distinguished Artist Award, Michigan Arts Foundation, 1989; Michigan Library Association Author of the Year, 2004. Memberships: Author's Guild; PEN; Poetry Society of America. Address: 607 Division Street, East Lansing, MI 48823, USA.

WALCOTT Derek (Alton), b. 23 January 1930, Castries, St Lucia, West Indies. Poet; Dramatist; Visiting Professor. m. (1) Fay Moyston, 1954, divorced 1959, 1 son, (2) Margaret Ruth Maillard, 1962, divorced, 2 daughters, (3) Norline Metivier, 1982, divorced 1993. Education: St Mary's College, Castries, 1941-47; BA, University College of the West Indies, Mona, Jamaica, 1953. Appointments: Teacher, St Mary's College, Castries, 1947-50, 1954, Grenada Boy's Secondary School, St George's, 1953-54, Jamaica College, Kingston, 1955; Feature Writer, Public Opinion, Kingston, 1956-57; Founder-Director, Little Carib Theatre Workshop, later Trinidad Theatre Workshop, 1959-76; Feature Writer, 1960-62, Drama Critic, 1963-68, Trinidad Guardian, Port-of-Spain; Visiting Professor, Columbia University, 1981, Harvard University, 1982, 1987; Assistant Professor of Creative Writing, 1981, Visiting Professor, 1985-, Brown University. Publications: Poetry: 25 Poems, 1948; Epitaph for the Young: XII Cantos, 1949; Poems, 1951; In a Green Night: Poems 1948-1960, 1962; Selected Poems, 1964; The Castaway and Other Poems, 1965; The Gulf and Other Poems, 1969; Another Life, 1973; Sea Grapes, 1976; The Star-Apple Kingdom, 1979; Selected Poems, 1981; The Fortunate Traveller, 1981; The Caribbean Poetry of Derek Walcott and the Art of Romare Bearden, 1983; Midsummer, 1984; Collected Poems 1948-1984, 1986; The Arkansas Testament, 1987; Omeros, 1989; Collected Poems, 1990; Poems 1965-1980, 1992; Derek Walcott: Selected Poems, 1993. Plays: Cry for a Leader, 1950; Senza Alcun Sospetto or Paolo and Francesca, 1950; Henri Christophe: A Chronicle, 1950; Robin and Andrea or Bim, 1950; Three Assassins, 1951; The Price of Mercy, 1951; Harry Dernier, 1952; The Sea at Dauphin, 1954; Crossroads, 1954; The Charlatan, 1954, 4th version, 1977; The Wine of the Country, 1956; The Golden Lions, 1956; Ione: A Play with Music, 1957; Ti-Jear and His Brothers, 1957; Drums and Colours,

1958; Malcochon, or, The Six in the Rain, 1959; Jourmard, or, A Comedy till the Last Minute, 1959; Batai, 1965; Dream on Monkey Mountain, 1967; Franklin: A Tale of the Islands, 1969, 2nd version, 1973; In a Fine Castle, 1970; The Joker of Seville, 1974; O Babylon!, 1976; Remembrance, 1977; The Snow Queen, 1977; Pantomime, 1978; Marie Laveau, 1979; The Isle is Full of Noises, 1982; Beef, No Chicken, 1982; The Odyssey: A Stage Version, 1993; Tiepolo's Hound, 2000; The Prodigal: A Poem, 2005; Selected Poems, 2007. Non-Fiction: The Antilles: Fragments of Epic Memory: The Nobel Lecture, 1993; What the Twilight Says (essays), 1998. Honours: Rockefeller Foundation Grants, 1957, 1966, and Fellowship, 1958; Arts Advisory Council of Jamaica Prize, 1960; Guinness Award, 1961; Ingram Merrill Foundation Grant, 1962; Borestone Mountain Awards, 1964, 1977; Heinemann Awards, Royal Society of Literature, 1966, 1983; Cholmondeley Award, 1969; Eugene O'Neill Foundation Fellowship, 1969; Gold Hummingbird Medal, Trinidad, 1969; Obie Award, 1971; Officer of the Order of the British Empire, 1972; Guggenheim Fellowship, 1977; Welsh Arts Council International Writers Prize, 1980; John D and Catharine T MacArthur Foundation Fellowship, 1981; Los Angeles Times Book Prize, 1986; Queen's Gold Medal for Poetry, 1988; Nobel Prize for Literature, 1992. Memberships: American Academy of Arts and Letters, honorary member; Royal Society of Literature, fellow. Address: c/o Faber & Faber, 3 Queen Square, London, WC1N 3AU, England.

WALDEN Rotraut, b. 1956, Gelhausen, Germany. m. Hans-Jurgen Hutter. Senior Lecturer. Education: Dr phil, Paderborn; Dr habil, Koblenz. Appointments: PD Dr, Senior Lecturer, Architectural Psychology, Work & Organizational Psychology. Publications: Author and co-author, 8 books; Editor, Schools for the Future; 7 books in German. Memberships: Environmental Design Research Association; German Association of Psychology, Work & Organizational Psychology; Environmental Psychology. Address: University of Koblenz, Universitaets str 1, 56070 Koblenz, Germany.

WALES HRH The Prince of, Charles Philip Arthur George, Duke of Cornwall, Duke of Rothsay, Earl of Carrick, Baron of Renfrew, Lord of the Isles and Prince and Great Steward of Scotland, b. 14 November 1948. m. (1) Lady Diana Spencer, 1981 (divorced 1996, deceased 1997), 2 sons; (2) Camilla Parker Bowles, 2005. Education: Gordonstoun; Geelong GS, Australia; MA, Trinity College, Cambridge; UCW, Aberystwyth. Appointments: RN: HMS Norfolk, 1971-72, HMS Minerva, 1972-73 and HMS Jupiter, 1974; Helicopter pilot training, RNAS Yeovilton, 1974-75; Pilot, 845 NAS, HMS Hermes, 1975; Commander, HMS Bronington, 1975; Captain, 1988, Rear Admiral, 1998, Vice Admiral, 2002, Admiral, 2006, Commodore-in-Chief, Plymouth, 2006-; General, 2006; Colonel-in-Chief (UK): 1st Queen's Dragoon Guards, 2003-, Royal Dragoon Guards, 1992-, Parachute Regiment, 1977-, Royal Gurkha Rifles, 1994-, Army Air Corps, 1992-; Royal Colonel: The Black Watch 3rd Battalion, 2006-, The Royal Regiment of Scotland, 51st Highland 7th Battalion, The Royal Regiment of Scotland, 2006-, The Mercian Regiment, 2007-, Colonel-in-Chief (Commonwealth): Royal Canadian Dragoons 1985-, Lord Strathcona's Horse, 1977-, Royal Regiment of Canada, 1977-, Royal Winnipeg Rifles, 1977-, Royal Australian Armoured Corps, 1977-, 2nd Battalion, Royal Pacific Islands Regiment, 1984-, Black Watch (Royal Highland Regiment) Canada, 2004-; Toronto Canada Regiment, 1977-, Air Reserve Group Air Command, Canada, 1977-, Toronto Scottish Regiment (Queen Elizabeth The Queen Mother's Own), 2005-; Deputy Colonel-in-Chief: Highlanders, 1994-; Personal ADC to HM The Queen, 1973-; Colonel, Welsh Guards, 1975-; Royal Honorary Colonel Queen's Own Yeomanry, 2000-; RAF: Air Chief Marshal, 2006, Honorary Air Commodore RAF Valley, 1977; Air Commodore-in-Chief, RNZAF, 1993-. Publications: The Old Man of Lochnagar, 1980; A Vision of Britain, 1989; TV productions for Channel 4, DVD, 1999. Honours: Coronation Medal, 1953; KG, 1958; GCB and Great Master Order of the Bath, 1975; Honorary Bencher, Gray's Inn, 1975; KT, 1977; PC, 1977; Queen's Silver Jubilee Medal, 1977; AK, 1981; CD, 1982; QSO, 1983; Honorary Fellow, Trinity College, Cambridge, 1988; OM, 2002; Queen's Golden Jubilee Medal, 2002; New Zealand Commemoration Medal, 1990; RHS Medal of Honour, 2009. Address: Clarence House, London SW1A 1BA, England. Website: www.princeofwales.gov.uk

WALES Prince Harry of, Henry Charles Albert David (Harry), b. 15 September 1984. Education: Eton; RMA Sandhurst. Appointments: Commodore-in-Chief, Small Ships and Diving, 2006-; 2nd Lieutenant, Blues and Royals, 2006; Lieutenant, 2008; Honorary Air Commandant, RAF Honington, 2008-; Patron, Sentebale, 2006-, Dolen Cymru, 2007-, MapAction, 2007-, WellChild, 2007-, Khumbu Challenge 09, 2008-; Joint Patron, City Salute Appeal, 2008, Henry van Straugenzee Memorial Fund, 2009-. Honours: Queen's Golden Jubilee Medal, 2002; Afghanistan Operational Service Medal, 2008.

WALES HRH Prince William of, William Arthur Philip Louis, b. 21 June 1982. m. Catherine Middleton, 2011. Education: Eton; MA, University of St Andrews; RMA Sandhurst. Appointments: Commodore-in-Chief, Scotland and Submarines, 2006-; 2nd Lieutenant, 2006, Lieutenant, 2007, Blues and Royals; Flying Officer, RAF, 2008; Sub-Lieutenant, RN, 2008; Honorary Air Commandant, RAF Coningsby, 2008. Honours: Queen's Golden Jubilee Medal, 2002; KG, 2008; Honorary barr and bencher, Middle Temple, 2009. Memberships: President, The Football Association, 2006; Patron, Centrepoint, 2005-, The Tusk Trust, 2005-, English Swimming School's Association, 2007-, Mountain Rescue, 2007-, Royal Marsden Hospital, 2007-, Lord Mayor's Appeal, 2008, HMS Alliance Conservation Appeal, 2008-, A Positive View 2010, 2008-, RAF Battle of Britain Memorial Flight, 2008-, Still Force, 2009, Child Bereavement Charity, 2009, National Memorial Arboretum Future Foundations Appeal Fund, 2009-; Vice-Patron, Welsh Rugby Union, 2007-; Joint Patron: City Salute, 2008, Henry van Straubenzee Memorial Fund, 2009-.

WAŁĘSA Lech, b. 29 September 1943, Popowo, Poland. Former Politician; Trade Union Activist. m. Danuta, 1969, 4 sons, 4 daughters. Appointments: Electrician, Lenin Shipyard, Gdańsk, 1966-76, 1983-; Chair, Strike Committee in Lenin Shipyard, 1970; Employed Zremb and Elektromontaz, 1976-80; Chair, Inter-institutional Strike Committee, Gdańsk, 1980; Co-Founder and Chair, Solidarity Industry Trade Union, 1980-90; Chair, National Executive Committee of Solidarity, 1987-90; Interned, 1981-82; Founder, Civic Committee attached to Chair of Solidarity, 1988-90; Participant and Co-chair, Round Table debates, 1989; President, Polish Republic, 1990-95; Chair, Country Defence Committee, 1990-95, Supreme Commander of Armed Forces of Polish Republic for Wartime, 1990-95; Founder, Lech Wałęsa Institute Foundation, 1995; Founder, Christian Democratic Party of the Third Republic, 1997; Appointed President, 1998, Chair, -2000, Honorary Chair, 2000-; Retired from politics. Publications: Autobiographies: A Path of Hope, 1987; The Road to Freedom, 1991; The

Struggle and the Triumph, 1992; Everything I Do, I Do for Poland, 1995. Honours include: Order of the Bath, 1991; Grand Cross of Legion d'honneur, 1991; Grand Order of Merit (Italy), 1991; Order of Merit (FRG), 1991; Great Order of the White Lion, 1999; Orden Heraldica do Cristobal Colon, 2001; 100 honorary doctorates: Man of the Year, Financial Times, 1980, The Observer, 1980, Die Welt, 1980, Die Zeit, 1981, L'Express, 1981, Le Soir, 1981, Time, 1981, Le Point, 1981; Let Us Live in Peace Prize of Swedish journal, Arbetet, 1981; Love International Award (Athens), 1981; Freedom Medal (Philadelphia), 1981; Medal of Merit (Polish American Congress), 1981; Free World Prize (Norway), 1982; International Democracy Award, 1982; Social Justice Award, 1983; Nobel Peace Prize, 1983; Humanitarian Public Service Medal, 1984; International Integrity Award, 1986; Phila Liberty Medal, 1989; Human Rights Prize, Council of Europe, 1989; White Eagle Order (Poland), 1989; US Medal of Freedom, 1989; Meeting-90 Award (Rimini), 1990; Path for Peace Award, Apostolic Nuncio to the UN, 1996; Freedom Medal of National Endowment for Democracy (Washington, USA), 1999; International Freedom Award (Memphis, USA). Address: Lech Wałęsa Institute Foundation, Al Jerozolimskie 11/19, 00 508 Warsaw, Poland. Website: www.ilw.org.pl

WALKEN Christopher, b. 31 March 1943, Astoria, New York, USA. Actor. m. Georgianne, 1969. Education: Hofstra University. Career: Films: Me and My Brother, 1969; The Anderson Tapes, 1971; The Happiness Cage, 1972; Next Stop Greenwich Village, 1976; Roseland, The Sentinel, Annie Hall, 1977; The Deer Hunter, 1978; Last Embrace, 1979; Heaven's Gate, 1980; Shoot the Sun Down, The Dogs of War, Pennies From Heaven, 1981; The Dead Zone, Brainstorm, 1983; A View to a Kill, 1984; At Close Range, 1986; Deadline, 1987; The Milagro Beanfield War, Biloxi Blues, Homeboy, 1988; Communion, The Comfort of Strangers, 1989; King of New York, 1990; McBain, 1991; Mistress, Batman Returns, Day of Atonement, 1992; True Romance, Wayne's World II, 1993; A Business Affair, Scam, Pulp Fiction, 1994; Wild Side, Search and Destroy, Things to do in Denver when You're Dead, The Prophecy, The Addiction, Nick of Time, 1995; Celluloide, Basquiat, The Funeral, Last Man Standing, 1996; Touch, Excess Baggage, Suicide Kings, Mousehunt, 1997; Illuminata, New Rose Hotel, Trance, Antz (voice), 1998; Blast from the Past, Sleepy Hollow, Kiss Toledo Goodbye, 1999; The Opportunists, 2000; Jungle Juice, Scotland, Pa, Joe Dirt, America's Sweethearts, The Affairs of the Necklace, Popcorn Shrimp, 2001; Poolhall Junkies, The Country Bears, Plots with a View, 2002; Catch Me If You Can, Kangaroo Jack, Gigli, The Rundown, 2003; Man on Fire, Envoy, The Stepford Wives, Around the Bend, 2004; Romance & Cigarettes, Domino, 2005; Click, Fade to Black, Man of the Year, 2006; Hairspray, Balls of Fury, 2007; Evil Calls: The Raven, Five Dollars a Day, 2008; The Maiden Heist, 2009; Kill the Irishman, Dark Horse, 2011; Seven Psychopaths, A Late Quartet, 2012; Stand Up Guys, The Power of Few, 2013; Theatre: West Side Story; Macbeth; The Lion in Winter; The Night Thoreau Spent in Jail, 1970-71; Cinders, 1984; A Bill of Divorcement, 1985; The Seagull, 2001; A Behanding in Spokane, 2010. Honours: Clarence Derwent Award, 1966; Joseph Jefferson Award, 1970; New York Film Critics and Academy Awards, Best Supporting Actor, 1978; Oscar, 1979; BAFTA Award for Best Supporting Actor, 2003; Montreal World Film Festival, Best Actor, 2004; Hollywood Film Award, Ensemble of the Year, 2007. Address: William Morris Agency, 151 El Camino Drive, Beverly Hills, CA 90212, USA.

WALKER Alice (Malsenior), b. 9 February 1944, Eatonton, Georgia, USA. Author; Poet. m. Melvyn R Leventhal, 1967, divorced 1976, 1 daughter. Education: BA, Sarah Lawrence College, 1966. Appointments: Writer-in-Residence and Teacher of Black Studies, Jackson State College, 1968-69, Tougaloo College, 1970-71; Lecturer in Literature, Wellesley College, 1972-73, University of Massachusetts at Boston, 1972-73; Distinguished Writer, Afro-American Studies Department, University of California at Berkeley, 1982; Fannie Hurst Professor of Literature, Brandeis University, 1982; Co-Founder and Publisher, Wild Trees Press, Navarro, California, 1984-88. Publications: Once, 1968; The Third Life of Grange Copeland, 1970; Five Poems, 1972; Revolutionary Petunias and Other Poems, 1973; In Love and Trouble, 1973; Langston Hughes: American Poet, 1973; Meridian, 1976; Goodnight, Willie Lee, I'll See You in the Morning, 1979; I Love Myself When I'm Laughing..., 1979; You Can't Keep a Good Woman Down, 1981; The Color Purple, 1982; In Search of Our Mother's Gardens, 1983; Horses Make a Landscape Look More Beautiful, 1984; To Hell With Dying, 1988; Living by the Word: Selected Writings, 1973-1987, 1988; The Temple of My Familiar, 1989; Her Blue Body Everything We Know: Earthling Poems, 1965-1990, 1991; Finding the Green Stone, 1991; Possessing the Secret of Joy, 1992; Warrior Marks (with Pratibha Parmar), 1993; Double Stitch: Black Women Write About Mothers and Daughters (with others), 1993; Everyday Use, 1994; By the Light of My Father's Smile, 1998; The Way Forward is with a Broken Heart, 2000; A Long Walk of Freedom, 2001; Sent By Earth: A Message from the Grandmother Spirit After the Bombing of the World Trade Center and Pentagon, 2001; Woman; Absolute Trust in the Goodness of the Earth: New Poems, 2003; The Third Life of Grange Copeland, 2003; A Poem Traveled Down My Arm: Poems And Drawings, 2003; Now is the Time to Open Your Heart, 2004; Collected Poems, 2005; We Are the Ones We Have Been Waiting For, 2006; Mississippi Winter IV. Honours: Bread Loaf Writer's Conference Scholar, 1966; Ingram Merrill Foundation Fellowship, 1967; McDowell Colony Fellowships, 1967, 1977-78; National Endowment for the Arts Grants, 1969, 1977; Richard and Hinda Rosenthal Pound Award, American Academy and Institute of Arts and Letters, 1974; Guggenheim Fellowship, 1977-78; Pulitzer Prize for Fiction, 1983; American Book Award, 1983; O Henry Award, 1986; Nora Astorga Leadership Award, 1989; Freedom to Write Award, PEN Center, West, 1990; Honorary doctorates. Address: c/o Random House, 201 E 50th Street, New York, NY 10022, USA.

WALKER Edward Donald, b. 2 August 1937. Marine Artist. m. Susan, 1 son, 1 daughter. Education: Liverpool College of Art. Appointments: Commissions for Cunard, Queen Victoria, Queen Mary, Queen Elizabeth II, Royal Mail (1st class stamp); Official Artist to RMS Titanic Artefacts exhibitions; Exhibitions worldwide; Paintings in private & public collections. Publications: Illustrated countless nautical books; Numerous articles in magazines; Work used in TV documentaries; Book, Sea Liverpool. Address: 1 Richmond Grove, Lydiate, Merseyside L31 0BL, England. E-mail: ed_walker@sumarpubl.fsnet.co.uk Website: www.edwalkermarine.com

WALKER Michael John, b. 24 November 1955. Headmaster. m. (1) Rita Bridget Carpenter (dissolved), 1 son, 2 daughters, (2) Corinne Anne Francis, 2007. Education: BA (Hons), History, 1977, Cert Ed, 1979, MA, 1980, PhD, 1985, Corpus Christi College, Cambridge. Appointments: Assistant Professor, History, Birmingham-Southern College, Birmingham, Alabama, 1977-78; Assistant Master, Dulwich

DICTIONARY OF INTERNATIONAL BIOGRAPHY 36th EDITION

College, 1982-86; Head of History, Gresham's School, Norfolk, 1986-89; Senior Teacher, 1989-90, Deputy Head (Middle School), 1990-92, Deputy Head (Sixth Form), 1992-99, Headmaster, 1999-2008, King Edward VI Grammar School, Chelmsford; Headmaster, Felsted School, 2008-; Member, Leading Edge National Steering Group, 2003-05; Forum for Learning and Research Enquiry in Essex, 2003-05; Evaluation and Knowledge Transfer Working Groups, 2003-04; Working with DFES Innovation Unit; Leading National Heads' Group, 2004-07; Leading Next Practice Project on Higher Order Teaching Skills, 2005-06; Member, Steering Group of ARIA Project (UK Wide Assessment Reform Group on Evaluation of Assessment Development), 2006-08. Memberships: HMC; Helen Rollason Cancer Care Trust; FRSA; Essex Club. Address: Felsted School, Felsted, Essex CM6 3LL, England.

WALKER Miles Rawstron, b. 13 November 1940, Colby, Isle of Man. Politician; Company Director. m. Mary L Cowell, 1966, 1 son, 1 daughter. Education: Shropshire College of Agriculture, 1959-60. Appointments: Member and Chairman, Arbory Parish Commissioners, 1970-76; Member of House of Keys, Isle of Man Government, 1976-; Elected to Chief Ministry, 1986-96, Member of Treasury, 1996-, Isle of Man Government. Publications: Isle of Man Government Policy Documents, 1987-96. Honours: CBE, 1991; Awarded LLD, Liverpool University, 1994; KB, 1997. Memberships: Member, Isle of Man Treasury, 1996-2000; Chair, Isle of Man Swimming Association; President, Rotary Club, 2000-01; Port St Mary Rifle Club. Address: Magher Feailley, Main Road, Colby, IM9 4AD, Isle of Man. E-mail: miles.walker@talk21.com

WALL Charles Terence Clegg, b. 14 December 1936, Bristol, England. Mathematician. m. Alexandra Joy Hearnshaw, 2 sons, 2 daughters. Education: BA, 1957, PhD, 1960, Trinity College, Cambridge. Appointments: Fellow, Trinity College Cambridge, 1959-64; Harkness Fellow, IAS Princeton, 1960-61; Lecturer, Cambridge University, 1961-64; Reader, Oxford University, Fellow St Catherine's College, 1964-65; Professor of Pure Mathematics, 1965-99, Senior Fellow, 1999-2003, Emeritus Professor, 1999-, University of Liverpool; Royal Society Leverhulme Visiting Professor, Mexico, 1967; SERC Senior Fellow, 1983-88; JSPS Fellow, Tokyo Institute of Technology, 1987; Invited speaker at numerous international conferences. Publications: Books: Surgery on compact manifolds, 1970; A geometric introduction to topology, 1972; The geometry of topological stability (with A A du Plessis), 1995; Singular points of plane curves, 2004; About 170 papers in scientific journals. Honours: Numerous academic awards at school and university; Junior Berwick Prize, 1965, Whitehead Prize, 1976, Polya Prize, 1988, London Mathematical Society; Sylvester Medal, Royal Society, 1988. Memberships: Cambridge Philosophical Society; American Mathematical Society; London Mathematical Society; Fellow of the Royal Society, Council, 1974-76; Foreign Member, Royal Danish Academy; Honorary Member, Irish Mathematical Society. Address: 5 Kirby Park, West Kirby, Wirral, Merseyside CH48 2HA, England. E-mail: ctcw@liv.ac.uk

WALLACE-CRABBE Chris(topher Keith), b. 6 May 1934, Richmond, Victoria, Australia. Poet; Writer. m. (1) Helen Margaret Wiltshire, 1957, 1 son, 1 daughter, (2) Marianne Sophie Feil, 2 sons. Education: BA, 1956, MA, 1964, University of Melbourne; Reader in English, 1976-87, Professor of English, 1987-, Personal Chair, 1987-97, Professor Emeritus, 1998-, University of Melbourne; Visiting Chair in Australian Studies, Harvard University, 1987-88, USA. Publications: Poetry: No Glass Houses, 1956; The Music of Division, 1959; Eight Metropolitan Poems, 1962; In Light and Darkness, 1964; The Rebel General, 1967; Where the Wind Came, 1971; Act in the Noon, 1974; The Shapes of Gallipoli, 1975; The Foundations of Joy, 1976; The Emotions Are Not Skilled Workers, 1979; The Amorous Cannibal and Other Poems, 1985; I'm Deadly Serious, 1988; For Crying out Loud, 1990; Falling into Language, 1990; From the Republic of Conscience, 1992; Rungs of Time, 1993; Whirling, 1998; By and Large, 2001; Next, 2004; The Universe Looks Down, 2005; Then, 2006; Selected Poems 1956-1994, 1995. Novel: Splinters, 1981. Other: Melbourne or the Bush: Essays on Australian Literature and Society, 1973; Falling into Language, 1990; Author! Author!, 1999. Editor: Volumes of Australian poetry and criticism. Honour: Masefield Prize for Poetry, 1957; Farmer's Poetry Prize, 1964; Grace Leven Prize, 1986; Dublin Prize, 1987; Christopher Brennan Award, 1990; Age Book of the Year Prize, 1995; Philip Hodgins Memorial Medal, 2002; Centenary Medal, 2003. Address: c/o The Australian Centre, University of Melbourne, Melbourne, Victoria 3010, Australia.

WALLIAMS David, b. 20 August 1971, Surrey, England. Comedian; Actor. m. Lara Stone, 2010. Education: Reigate Grammar School, Surrey; Drama, Bristol University; National Youth Theatre. Career: TV: Rock Profile, 1999; Sir Bernard's Stately Homes, 1999; Coming Soon, 1999; The Web of Caves, 1999; The Pitch of Fear, 1999; The Kidnappers, 1999; Attachents, 2000; Ted and Alice, 2002; Cruise of the Gods, 2002; Little Britain, 2003; Comic Relief 2003: The Big Hair Do, 2003; The All Star Comedy Show, 2004; Marple: The Body in the Library, 2004; My Life with James Bond, 2006; Capturing Mary, 2007; Rather You Than Me, 2008; Film: Plunkett & Macleane, 1999; Tristram Shandy: A Cock and Bull Story, 2005; Decameron: Angels & Virgins, 2006; Virgin Territory, forthcoming. Publications: Yeah but No But: The Biography of Matt Lucas and David Walliams, 2006; Inside Little Britain, 2006; The Boy in the Dress, 2008; Mr Stink, 2009. Honours: The Mirror's Pride of Britain Award for the Most Influential Public Figure, 2006; Children's Award, People Book Prize, 2010.

WALLINGER Alexander Wolfgang, b. 29 April 1971, Schwanenstadt, Austria. Director. Education: Commercial Sciences, 1990-97, Business Administration, 1991-2000, University of Economics and Business Administration, Vienna; MIM-CEMS, International Management, HEC in Paris, LSE in London, University of Economics and Business Administration in Vienna, 1993-99; MIB, NHH Bergen, Norway, 1994; MBA, Coventry University, England, 1997; International Law, University of Law, Vienna, 1998; MoD program, Military Academy, Austria, 2004-06. Appointments: Enterprise/real estate, 1991-96, Trust/Property Management, 1997-98, Dr Kohut, Vienna; Marketing & Sales Management, Henkel Central Eastern Europe, Vienna, 1998-2003; Information and Press Officer, Austrian Army, Vienna, 2003-06; Sales & Marketing Manager, Siemens AG/FSC, Vienna and London, 2006-08; Director, SMN Investment Services, Austria and Bermuda, 2008-. Publications: Numerous articles in professional journals; Book, Convergence Criteria – a critical analysis, 1998. Honours include: Cross of Merit, Black Cross, 2006; Grand Cross with Star, Albert Schweitzer Society, 2007; Grand Cross with Swords and Star, Gaming Officers Association, 2007; Honorary Commanders Cross, Order of St Lazarus of Jerusalem, 2007; Knights Cross, Order of St George, 2008; Grand Cross with Star, Royal House of Georgia, Order of the

DICTIONARY OF INTERNATIONAL BIOGRAPHY 36th EDITION

Eagle of Georgia, 2010; Hungarian National Defence Cross, Hungarian Ministry of Defence, 2011; many other awards. Memberships: Order of the Eagle of Georgia; Vice Rector for Austria. Address: Hietzinger Hauptstrasse 62, 1130 Vienna, Austria. E-mail: a_w_wallinger@hotmail.com

WALLIS Kenneth Horatio, b. 26 April 1916, Ely, Cambridgeshire, England. RAF Retired; Autogyro Designer, Operator and Consultant. m. Peggy Mary Stapley, deceased, 1 son, 2 daughters. Education: Ely High School, 1921-25; King's School, Ely, 1926-32. Appointments: Father's motorcycle and cycle business, Ely and Soham; Operational Pilot, RAF, during World War 2; Specialist Armament Officer, RAF; Retired, 1964; Participation in military trials and exercises with autogyros, UK and overseas; Film-making and Special Aerial Photography and other sensing for archaeology; MOD contracts, British Aircraft Corporation, Guided Weapons Division, Plessey Radar Research Center and Police Contracts, etc; Autogyro flight and demonstrations. Publications: Many articles in professional and popular journals. Honours: Alan Marsh Medal, 1963; Segrave Trophy, 1969 & 1985; Breguet Trophy, 1973; Royal Aero Club Silver Medal, 1975; Rose Trophy, The Helicopter Club of Great Britain, 1975 & 1984; Honorary Fellowship, Manchester Polytechnic, 1980; Reginald Mitchell Medal, 1982; Salomon Trophy, 1989; Rotocraft Gold Medal, 1995; Member of the British Empire (MBE); Honorary Doctorate, University of Birmingham, 1997; Honorary Fellowship, Society of Experimental Test Pilots, 1998; Special Award, The Air League, 1999; Sir Barnes Wallis Medal, 1998; Oldest Pilot to have achieved an Aviation World Record, Guinness Book of Records, 1999; Honorary Doctorate of Philosophy, Hofstra University, New York, USA, 2003; Honorary President, Skywatch Civil Air Patrol. Memberships: Bomber Command Association; Aircrew Association; Aircraft Owners & Pilots Association; GASCO; President, Norfolk-Suffolk Aviation Museum; President, RAFA Wymondham Branch; Range Officers Association; Vintage Arms Association; Society of Experimental Test Pilots; Fellow, Royal Aeronautical Society; Fellow, Institute of Transport Administration; Chartered Engineer; President, Norfolk Austin 7 Club. Address: Reymerston Hall, Norfolk, NR9 4QY, England.

WALSH Louis, b. 5 August 1952, Kiltimagh, Co Mayo, Ireland. Music Manager. Career: Manager of numerous music groups/singers including: Boyzone, 1993-2000, 2007-; Westlife, 1998-; Ronan Keating, 2000-; Girls Aloud, 2002-06; Shayne Ward, 2005-; Eton Road, 2006-; JLS, 2008-; Judge of TV talent shows: Popstars: The Rivals; You're A Star; The X Factor.

WALTER Hugo, b. 12 March 1959, Philadelphia, Pennsylvania, USA. Professor. Education: BA, Princeton University, 1981; PhD, Literature, Yale University, 1985; MA, Humanities, Old Dominion University, 1989; PhD, Humanities, Drew University, 1996. Appointments: Assistant Professor, Washington and Jefferson College, 1989-92; Assistant Professor, Fairleigh Dickinson University, 1992-96; Assistant Professor, Humanities, Kettering University, 1996-99; Associate Professor, Humanities, Berkeley College, 1999-. Publications: The Apostrophic Moment in 19th and 20th Century Lyric Poetry, 1988; Evening Shadows, 1990; Golden Thorns of Light and Sterling Silhouettes, 1990; Waiting for Babel Prophesies of Sunflower Dreams, 1992; Along the Maroon Prismed Threshold of Bronze Pealing Eternity, 1992; The Light of the Dance is the Music of Eternity, 1993; Dusk, Gloaming Mirrors and Castle Winding Dreams, 1994; Amaranth Sage Epiphanies of Dusk Weaving Paradise, 1995; Amaranth Sage Epiphanies of Dusk Weaving Paradise, 1996; Space and Time on the Magic Mountain: Studies in European Literature, 1999; A Purple-Golden Renascence of Eden-Exalting Rainbows, 2001; Sanctuaries of Light in Nineteenth Century European Literature, 2010. Honours: Outstanding Achievement in Poetry, 1992, 1993, 1994, 1995, 1996, 1997; Faculty of the Year Award for Outstanding Teaching in Berkeley College's Online Program. Listed in Who's Who publications and biographical dictionaries. Memberships: International Society of Poets; American Poetry Association. Address: 157 Loomis Court, Princeton, NJ 08540, USA.

WALTERS Julie, b. 22 February 1950, Birmingham, England. Actress. m. Grant Roffey, 1998, 1 daughter. Education: Manchester Polytechnic; School Governor, Open University. Creative Works: Films include: Educating Rita, 1983; She'll Be Wearing Pink Pyjamas, 1984; Personal Services, 1986; Prick Up Your Ears, 1986; Buster, 1987; Mack the Knife, 1988; Killing Dad, 1989; Stepping Out, 1991; Just Like a Woman, 1992; Sister My Sister, 1994; Intimate Relations, 1996; Titanic Town, 1997; Girls Night, 1997; All Forgotten, 1999; Dancer, 1999; Billy Elliot, 2000; Harry Potter and the Philosopher's Stone, 2001; Before You Go, 2002; Harry Potter and the Chamber of Secrets, 2002; Calendar Girls, 2003; Harry Potter and the Prisoner of Azkaban, 2004; Mickybo and Me, 2004; Wah-Wah, 2005; Driving Lessons, 2006; Becoming Jane, 2007; Harry Potter and the Order of the Phoenix, 2007; TV includes: Talent, 1980; Wood and Walters, 1981; Boys From the Blackstuff, 1982; Say Something Happened, 1982; Victoria Wood as Seen on TV, 1984, 1986, 1987; The Birthday Party, 1986; Her Big Chance, 1987; GBH, 1991; Stepping Out, 1991; Julie Walters and Friends, 1991; Clothes in the Wardrobe, 1992; Wide Eyed and Legless, 1993; Bambino Mio, 1993; Pat and Margaret, 1994; Jake's Progress, 1995; Little Red Riding Hood, 1995; Intimate Relations, 1996; Julie Walters in an Alien, 1997; Dinner Ladies, 1998-99; Jack and the Beanstalk, 1998; Oliver Twist, 1999; My Beautiful Son, 2001; Murder, 2002; The Canterbury Tales, mini-series, 2003; The Return, 2003; Ahead of the Class, 2005; The Ruby in the Smoke, 2006; Several stage appearances; Acorn Antiques: The Musical, 2006. Publication: Baby Talk, 1990; Julie Walters: Seriously Funny, 2003. Honours: Variety Club Best Newcomer Award, 1980; Best Actress Award, 1984; British Academy Award for Best Actress, 1984; Golden Globe Award, 1984; Variety Club Award for Best Actress, 1991; Olivier Award, 2001; CBE, 2008. Address: c/o ICM, 76 Oxford Street, London W1N 0AX, England.

WALTON James Stephen, b. 27 November 1946, Kingston upon Thames, Surrey, England. Research Scientist. m. Dorcas Ann Graham, 1 son, 1 daughter. Education: Diploma in Physical Education, 1968, Certificate of Education, 1968, Carnegie College of Physical Education, Leeds, England; MA, Education, Michigan State University, USA, 1970; MS, Applied Mechanics, Stanford University, California, USA, 1976; PhD, Physical Education, Biomechanics, Pennsylvania State University, USA, 1981. Appointments: Graduate Teaching Assistant, Michigan State University, 1968-69; Teacher, Gaynesford High School, Carshalton, Surrey, England, 1969-70; Graduate Teaching and Research Assistant, Pennsylvania State University, 1970-74; Graduate Teaching Assistant, Stanford University, California, 1974-76; Director of Engineering, Computerised Biomechanical Analysis, Amherst, Massachusetts, 1979; Associate Senior Research Scientist, 1979-81, Senior Research Scientist, 1981-85, Biomedical Science Department, General Motors Research Laboratories; Vice-President Applications Engineering, Motion Analysis Corporation, 1987-88; President/Owner, 4D

Video, Sebastopol, California, 1988-; US National Delegate to the International Congress on High-Speed Photography and Photonics, 2005-2011. Publications: Numerous papers in scientific journals and presented at conferences including: Image-Based Motion Measurement: The Camera as a Transducer, 1997; Image-Based Motion Measurement: An Introduction to the Elements of the Technology, 1998; Calibration and Processing of Images as an After Thought, 2000; A High-Speed Video Tracking System for Generic Applications, 2000; The Camera as a Transducer, 2000. Honours: Fellow, Society of Photo-optical Instrumentation Engineers (SPIE) Honorary Fellow, British Association for Physical Training; Professional Achievement Award, Deptof Kinesiology, Michigan State University, 2010. Memberships include: American Association for the Advancement of Science; American Society for Photogrammetry and Remote Sensing; Sigma Xi; Society of Photo-Optical Instrumentation Engineers Address: 4D Video, 825 Gravenstein Highway North, Suite #4, Sebastopol, California 95472-2844, USA.

WALTON OF DETCHANT, Baron of Detchant (1989) in the County of Northumberland, Sir John Nicholas Walton, b. 16 September 1922. m. Elizabeth (Betty) Harrison, deceased 2003, 1 son, 2 daughters. Education: Alderman Wraith GS; MD, King's College Medical School, University of Durham; DSc, University of Newcastle upon Tyne. Appointments: Consultant Neurologist, University of Newcastle Hospitals, 1958-83; Professor of Neurology, 1968-83, Dean of Medicine, 1971-81, University of Newcastle upon Tyne; Col (late RAMC) CO I (N) General Hospital (TA), 1963-66, Hon Col 201 (N) General Hospital (T&AVR), 1968-73; Chairman, 1970-95, Life President, 2000-, Muscular Dystrophy Gp, Great Britain; Member, 1971-90, Chairman, 1975-82, President, 1982-89, Education Committee, GMC; PresL BMA, 1980-82; ASME, 1982-94; RSM, 1984-86; ABN, 1987-88; First Vice President, 1981-89, President, 1989-97, World Federation of Neurology; Warden, Green College, Oxford, 1983-89; Chairman, Hamlyn National Commission on Education, 1991-93. Publications: Subarachnoid Haemorrhage; Polymyositis; Essentials of Neurology; Disorders of Voluntary Muscle; Brain's Diseases of the Nervous System; The Spice of Life, autobiography. Honours: Honorary DUniv, Aix Marseille, Laurea (hc), Genoa; Honorary MD, University of Sheffield; Hon MD, Mahidol University, Thailand; Hon DSc: University of Leeds, University of Leicester, University of Hull, Oxford Brookes University, University of Durham; Hon DCL, University of Newcastle upon Tyne; Hewitt Lifetime Achievement Award, Royal Society of Medicine, 2006. Memberships: Honorary Fellow, Institute of Education, University of London; Norwegian Academy of Arts and Science; FRCP; Hon FRCPE; FRCPath; FRCPsych; FRCPCH; FMedSci. Address: 15 Croft Way, Belford, Northumberland, NE70 7ET, England. E-mail: waldetch@aol.com

WANAMAKER Zoë, b. 13 May 1949, New York, USA (British citizen, 2000). Actress. m. Gawn Grainger, 1994, 1 stepson, 1 stepdaughter. Education: Hornsey College of Art; Central School of Speech and Drama. Appointments: Actor; Theatre: A Midsummer Night's Dream, 1970; Guys and Dolls, 1972; The Cherry Orchard, 1970-71; Dick Whittington, 1971-72; Tom Thumb, Much Ado About Nothing, 1974; A Streetcar Named Desire, Pygmalion, The Beggar's Opera, Trumpets and Drums, 1975-76; Wild Oats, 1977; Once in a Lifetime, 1970-80; The Devil's Disciple; Wild Oats; Ivanov; The Taming of the Shrew; Captain Swing; Piaf; A Comedy of Errors, Twelfth Night and The Time of Your Life, 1983-85; Mother Courage; Othello; The Importance of Being Earnest 1982-83; The Bay at Nice and Wrecked Eggs, 1986-87; Mrs Klein; The Crucible; Twelfth Night, 1973-74; Cabaret, 1974; Kiss Me Kate, 1974; The Taming of the Shrew, 1975; Loot; Made in Bangkok, 1988; The Last Yankee, 1993; Dead Funny, 1994; The Glass Menagerie; Sylvia, 1996; Electra, 1997; The Old Neighbourhood, 1998; Electra, New York, 1998; Battle Royal, 1999; Boston Marriage, Donmar Warehouse, 2001; Boston Marriage, New Ambassadors, 2002; Hildy in His Girl Friday, National Theatre, 2003; TV: Sally for Keeps, 1970; The Eagle Has Landed, 1972; Between the Wars, 1973; The Silver Mask, 1973; Lorna and Ted, 1973; The Confederacy of Wives, 1974; The Village Hall, 1975; Danton's Death, 1977; Beaux Stratagem, 1977; The Devil's Crown, 1978-79; Strike, 1981; Baal, 1981; All the World's A Stage, 1982; Richard III, 1982; Enemies of the State, 1982; Edge of Darkness, 1985; Paradise Postponed, 1985; Poor Little Rich Girl, 1987; Once in a Lifetime, 1987; The Dog It Was That Died, 1988; Ball Trap on the Cote Sauvage, 1989; Othello, 1989; Prime Suspect, 1990; Love Hurts, 1991-93; Dance to the Music of Time, 1997; Gormenghast, Leprechauns, David Copperfield, 1999; Adrian Mole, The Cappuccino Years, 2001; My Family, BBC Series 1-5, 2000-04; Miss Marple: A Murder is Announced, 2004; Commentary, Someone to Watch Over Me, 2004; Dr Who: The End of the World, 2005; Film: Harry Potter and the Philosopher's Stone, 2001; Five Children & It, 2003; Radio including: The Golden Bowl, Plenty, 1979; Bay at Nice, 1987; A February Morning, 1990; Carol, book reading, 1990; Such Rotten Luck, 1991, series I and TV films: The Blackheath Poisonings, Central, 1991; Memento Mori, BBC, 1991; Countess Alice, BBC, 1991; The English Wife, 1994; The Widowing of Mrs Holroyd, BBC, 1995; Wilde; Swept in By the Sea. Honours: SWET Award, 1979; Numerous Tony nominations; Drama Award, Mother Courage, 1985; Honorary DLitt, Southbank University, 1995; Variety Club of Great Britain Award, Best Actress, Electra, 1997; Olivier Awards including Best Actress for Electra, 1997; Calaway Award, New York, Best Actress, Electra; Best Actress, BAFTA for Love Hurts, Prime Suspects and Wilde; Honorary Doctorate Richmond American University of London; CBE; Boston Marriage, Oliver Nomination, Best Actress, 2002; Patron, Prisoners of Conscience; UK TV Mummies: Favourite UK TV Mum, 2004; Award for Excellence in the Arts, DePaul University, Chicago, 2004; Rose d'Or, Best Comedy Actress, My Family, 2005. Membership: Honorary Member, Voluntary Euthanasia Society; Trustee, Honorary President, Shakespeare's Globe. Address: c/o Conway Van Gelder, 18/21 Jermyn Street, London SW1Y 6HP, England. Website: www.geocities.com/zwsite

WANSELL (Stephen) Geoffrey, b. 9 July 1945, Greenock, Scotland. Author; Journalist. Divorced, 1 son, 1 daughter. Education: BSc, Econ, London School of Economics, 1962-66; MA Student and Tutorial Assistant, University of Sheffield, 1966-67. Appointments: Reporter, Columnist, News Editor, Times Educational Supplement, 1967-70; Reporter, Feature Writer, The Times, 1970-73; Programme Controller, London Broadcasting Company and Independent Radio News, 1973-75; Pendennis Columnist, The Observer, 1977-78; Columnist, Now! Magazine, 1979-81; Columnist, Sunday Telegraph Magazine, 1981-85; Executive Producer, Motion Picture, When The Whales Came, 1989; Columnist, Sunday Express, 1993; Feature Writer, Daily Mail, 1999-2011. Publications: Author of 10 books. Honour: Shortlisted for the Whitbread Book of the Year, 1995. Membership: Garrick Club; Society of Authors. Address: 28B Bedford Place, London WC1B 5JH, England. E-mail: geoffreywansell@aol.com

WARD Eric Thomas, b. 20 November 1945, St Ives, Cornwall, England. Artist. m. Karen, 2 sons. Education: Hayle Grammar School. Appointments: Fisherman, -1985; St Ives Harbour Master, 1985-2000; Artist, 1987-; Solo exhibitions: London, Cornwall and Japan, 1989-; Group exhibitions throughout UK, 1988-; Work held in private and public collections; Subject of 'Oils and Oilskins', BBC2 television, 1996. Publications: Eric Ward's St Ives: From His Studio and Beyond, 2010. Honours: 2 Royal National Lifeboat Institution Bronze Medals. Memberships: Chelsea Arts Club, London; St Ives Society of Artists, Cornwall. Address: 5 Ocean View Terrace, St Ives, Cornwall TR26 1RQ, England. E-mail: wardthp@aol.com

WARD Simon, b. 19 October 1941, Beckenham, England. Actor. m. Alexandra Malcolm, 3 daughters. Education: Royal Academy of Dramatic Art. Creative Works: Stage appearances include: Konstantin in The Seagull, Birmingham Repertory, 1964; Abel Drugger in The Alchemist and Hippolytus in Phèdre, Playhouse, Oxford, 1965-66; Dennis in Loot, Jeannetta Cochrane and Criterion, 1966; The Unknown Soldier in the Unknown Soldier and His Wife, Ferdinand in The Tempest and Henry in The Skin of Our Teen, Chichester Festival, 1968; Donald in Spoiled, Haymarket, 1971; Romeo in Romeo and Juliet, Shaw, 1972; Troilus in Troilus and Cressida, Young Vic; Films include: I Start Counting, 1970; Young Winston, 1971; Hitler - The Last Ten Days, 1972; The Three Musketeers, 1973; The Four Musketeers, Deadly Strangers, All Creatures Great and Small, 1974-75; Aces High, 1975; Battle Flag, 1976; The Four Feathers, 1978; Zulu Dawn, 1979; Supergirl, Around the World in 80 Days, Double X, 1992; Wuthering Heights, 1992; Ghost Writers; TV includes: The Black Tulip; The Roads to Freedom; Holocaust (serial). Address: c/o Shepherd & Ford Associates Ltd, 13 Radner Walk, London SW3 4BP, England.

WARDAK Ghulam Farooq, b. 5 March 1959, Wardak, Afghanistan. Minister of Education. m. Zarlashta, 1 son. Education: Bachelor of Pharmacy, Punjab University, Lahore, Pakistan, 1986; Master, Business Administration, Project Management, Preston University, 2001. Appointments: Director of Health, Swedish Committee for Afghanistan, 1986-96; Director, COAP/UNDP, 1996-2001; Assistant Resident Respresentative, UNDP, 2001-02; Director, Secretariat Constitutional Commission, 2002-03; Chief Election Officer, 2004-05; Chief de Cabinet, Director of Administrative Office of the President and State Minister for Parliamentary Affairs, 2005-08; Director, Afghan-Pak Joint Peace Jirga Secretariat and National Consultative Peace Jirga Director, Director of International Affairs of High Peace Council and Minister of Education, 2009-. Honours: Ghazi Amanullah Khan State Medal; Sayed Jamaluddin Afghan State Medal. Address: Minister of Education, Mohammad Jan Khan Watt, Kabul, 0093-20-2100484, Afghanistan. E-mail: info@moe.gov.af Website: www.moe.gov.af

WARDEN Peter Campbell, b. 19 March 1950, Vancouver, Canada. Artist. Divorced, 1 daughter. Education: Diploma in Drawing and Painting, 1976, Post-diploma in Printmaking, 1977, Glasgow School of Art. Appointments: Freelance Artist, 1977-; Regular exhibitor at The Royal Academy; Exhibitions include: Royal Society of British Artists; Royal Scottish Academy; RSW, Edinburgh; RWA, Bristol; New English Art Club; Many one-man shows in Scotland, England and Spain. Honours: Special Award, Robert Colquhoun Competition, 1976; First Prize, Devon & Cornwall Figurative Arts, 1992. Memberships: Associate and Member, Royal Society of British Artists. Address: 62 St Annes Drive, Llantwit Fardre, Pontypridd, RCT, Wales. E-mail: peterwardenpear@yahoo.com

WARNE Shane Keith, b. 13 September 1969, Ferntree Gully, Melbourne, Australia. Cricketer. m. Simone, 1 son, 2 daughters. Appointments: Leg-Break and Googly Bowler; Right-Hand Lower-Order Batsman; 183 first-class matches for Hampshire took 70 wickets (average 23.1), 2000; Highest ever Australian wicket taker in Tests; 107 Tests for Australia, 1991-92 to 2002, taking 491 wickets (average 25.71) and scoring 2,238 runs, took hat-trick v England, Melbourne, 1994; Took 850 wickets and scored 4,103 runs in 1st class cricket, to 2003; Toured England, 1993, 1997, 2001; 191 limited-overs internationals (11 as Captain), to 2003; Captain Victoria Sheffield Shield Team (Bushrangers), 1996-99; received 12 month ban for testing positive for a banned substance, 2003; Captain of Hampshire, 2004-; Retirement from limited-overs internationals, 2004. Publications: Shane Warne: The Autobiography, 2001. Honours: Wisden Cricketer of the Year, 1994; Selected as one of five Wisden Cricketers of the Century, 2000. Address: c/o Victorian Cricket Association, 86 Jolimont Street, Victoria 3002, Australia.

WARNECKE Hans-Jürgen, b. 2 April 1934, Braunschweig, Germany. Engineer. m. Elisabeth, 2 daughters. Education: PhD, Mechanical Engineering, TH Braunschweig, 1963. Appointments: Director, Rollerwerke, Braunschweig; Professor, University of Stuttgart, 1971-93; President, Fraunhofer Gesellschaft, München, 1993-2002. Publications: Several books, including The Fractal Company; Schiffstriebe; Serienschiffe. Honours: Several Honorary Doctorates; Cross of Merit, Germany. Memberships: VDI (German Association of Engineers); SME. Address: Max-Caspar str 77, D-71263, Weil der Stadt, Germany.

WARNER Margaret Anne (Megan), b. 4 September 1943, Epsom, Surrey, England. Educator. Education includes: Teacher's Certificate, Mathematics, Froebel Educational Institute, London, 1964; Diploma, English as a Second Language, 1976, Diploma, School Management Studies, 1979, College of Preceptors; Master's Degree, Educational Studies, University of Surrey at Roehampton, 1990; OFSTED Registered Inspector, 1996; Performance Management Consultant, DfES/NPQH/Consortium, 2000. Appointments include: Assistant Teacher various schools, ILEA and Australia, 1964-72; Deputy Headteacher, Church of England Primary School, Oxfordshire, 1973-79; Headteacher, Church of England Primary School, ILEA, 1979-89; Teaching Practice Supervisor, primary and nursery classes, London Boroughs, 1990-91; SEN Co-ordinator, Mathematics Teacher, Girls' High School, Merton, 1991-92; Assistant Teacher, Merton Middle School, 1992-93; Head of Religious Education Departments, Wandsworth, 1993, 1994-95, i/c Pupils with Statements, 1994, Wandsworth Comprehensive School; Team Inspector, Primary, Secondary, Special, 1994-2005; Registered Primary Inspector, 1996-2005; DfES Trained Performance Management Consultant, 2000-; Assessor of HLTAs, 2005-; International Teacher Trainer, Inspector, Consultant, Qatar, India, Algeria, Dubai (UAE), 2006-11; Sole Trader trading as MAW Education, 1999-; Life Coach, 2007-. Publications: Headteachers' perceptions of their role in spiritual education (book chapter, editor R Best), 1996; Reflections on Inspection (book chapter, editor R Best), 2000; 81 Ofsted Inspection Reports, 1996-2004; Developing Multiple Intelligences, 2008; Bring Mutiple Intelligences into the Classroom, 2008; Changing Education, 2011. Honours include: International Peace Prize, 2005, Legion of Honor,

2006, United Cultural Convention; Woman of the Year, ABI, 2005, 2006; World Achievement Award, ABI, 2006; Deputy Governor, Research Board, ABI, 2006; Professional of the Year, 2006-07, 2007-08, 2008-09; President's Citation, ABI, 2007; Fellowship, ABI, 2007; Fellow, College of Teachers (UK), 2008; Distinguished Service Order and Cross, ABI, 2008; Founding Member, Women's Review Board, ABI, 2008; International Ambassador, World Forum, Washington DC, 2009; ABI World Laureate, 2009. Memberships: Association of Professionals in Education and Children's Trusts; Council for Education in the Commonwealth; Association for Supervision and Curriculum Development; Royal Commonwealth Society; Associate, College of Preceptors. Address: 27 Old Gloucester Street, London WC1N 3XX, England. E-mail: maweducation@easynet.co.uk

WARNER Marina (Sarah), b. 9 November 1946, London, England. Author; Critic. m. (1) William Shawcross, 1971, divorced 1980, 1 son, (2) John Dewe Mathews, 1981, divorced 1998. Education: MA, Modern Languages, French and Italian, Lady Margaret Hall, Oxford. Appointments: Getty Scholar, Getty Centre for the History of Art and the Humanities, California, 1987-88; Tinbergen Professor, Erasmus University, Rotterdam, 1991; Visiting Fellow, British Film Institute, 1992; Visiting Professor, University of Ulster, 1995, Queen Mary and Westfield College, London, 1995-, University of York, 1996-2000; Reith Lecturer, 1994; Whitney J Oakes Fellow, Princeton University, 1996; Mellon Professor, University of Pittsburgh, 1997; Visiting Fellow Commoner, Trinity College, Cambridge, 1998; Tanner Lecturer, 1999; Visiting Professor, University of Stanford, California, USA, 2000; Clarendon Lecturer, Oxford, 2001; Visiting Fellow, All Souls' College, Oxford, 2001; Visiting Fellow, Italian Academy, Columbia University, New York, 2003; Professor, Department of Literature, Film and Theatre Studies, University of Essex, 2004-; Robb Lecturer, University of Auckland, 2004; Senior Fellow, Remarque Institute, New York University, 2006; Janina Tammes Professor (Visiting), University of Groningen, 2007. Publications: The Dragon Empress, 1972; Alone of All Her Sex: The Myth and the Cult of the Virgin Mary, 1976; Queen Victoria's Sketchbook, 1980; Joan of Arc: The Image of Female Heroism, 1981; Monuments and Maidens: The Allegory of the Female Form, 1985; L'Atalante, 1993; Managing Monsters: Six Myths of Our Time, 1994; From the Beast to the Blonde: On Fairy Tales and Their Tellers, 1994; No Go the Bogeyman: Scaring, Lulling and Making Mock, 1998; Fantastic Metamorphoses, Other Worlds, 2002; Signs and Wonders: Essays on Literature and Culture, 2003; Phantasmagoria: Spirit Visions, Metaphors, and Media, 2006. Fiction: In a Dark Wood, 1977; The Skating Party, 1983; The Lost Father, 1988; Indigo, 1992; The Mermaids in the Basement, 1993; Wonder Tales (editor), 1994; The Leto Bundle, 2001; Murderers I Have Known, 2004; Cancellanda, 2004; Libretti: The Legs of the Queen of Sheba, 1991; In the House of Crossed Desires 1996. Other: Children's and juvenile books; Contributions to various publications, artists' catalogues, radio and television; Exhibitions (curator): The Inner Eye, South Bank Touring, Manchester, Swansea, Dulwich, 1996; Metamorphing, Wellcome Trust, Science Museum, London, 2002-03; Eyes, Lies & Illusions (curatorial advisor), Hayward Gallery, London, 2005; Only Make-Believe: Ways of Playing, Compton Verney, 2005. Honours: Fellow, Royal Society of Literature, 1985; Honorary D Litt, University of Exeter, 1995; Hon Dr, Sheffield Hallam University, 1995; Hon D Litt, University of York, 1997; Hon D Litt, University of St Andrew's, 1998; Hon Dr, Tavistock Institute, University of East London, 1999; Katharine Briggs Award, 1999; Rosemary Crawshay Prize, British Academy, 2000; Fellow, British Academy, 2005; Hon D Litt, University of Kent; Hon D Litt, University of Oxford, 2006; Hon D Litt, University of Leicester, 2006. Memberships: Arts Council, literature panel, 1992-97; British Library, advisory council, 1992-97; Charter 88, council member, 1990-97; PEN; Trustee, Artangel; Chevalier des Arts et des Lettres, 2000; Stella di Solidareità dell'Ordine delle Arti e Lettere, 2005. Address: c/o Rogers, Coleridge and White, 20 Powis Mews, London W11 1NJ, England. Website: www.marinawarner.com

WARNOCK Helen Mary, (Baroness), b. 14 April 1924, England. Philosopher; Writer. m. Sir Geoffrey Warnock, 1949, deceased 1995, 2 sons, 3 daughters. Education: MA, BPhil, Lady Margaret Hall, Oxford. Appointments: Fellow and Tutor in Philosophy, 1949-66, Senior Research Fellow, 1976-84, St Hugh's College, Oxford; Headmistress, Oxford High School, 1966-72; Talbot Research Fellow, Lady Margaret Hall, Oxford, 1972-76; Mistress, Girton College, Cambridge, 1985-91; Visiting Professor of Rhetoric, Gresham College, 2000-2001; Several visiting lectureships. Publications: Ethics Since 1900, 1960, 3rd edition, 1978; J-P Sartre, 1963; Existentialist Ethics, 1966; Existentialism, 1970; Imagination, 1976; Schools of Thought, 1977; What Must We Teach? (with T Devlin), 1977; Education: A Way Forward, 1979; A Question of Life, 1985; Teacher Teach Thyself, 1985; Memory, 1987; A Common Policy for Education, 1988; Universities: Knowing Our Minds, 1989; The Uses of Philosophy, 1992; Imagination and Time, 1994; Women Philosophers (editor), 1996; An Intelligent Person's Guide to Ethics, 1998; A Memoir: People and Places, 2000; Making Babies, 2002; Nature and Mortality, 2003; Utilitarianism (editor), 2003. Honours: 15 honorary doctorates; Honorary Fellow, Lady Margaret Hall, Oxford, 1984, St Hugh's College, Oxford, 1985, Hertford College, Oxford, 1997; Dame Commander of the Order of the British Empire, 1984; Life Peer, 1985; Albert Medal, RSA; Honorary Fellowship, British Academy, 2000. Address: 60 Church Street, Great Bedwyn, Wiltshire SN8 3PF, England.

WARWICK Kevin, b. 9 February 1954, Coventry, England. University Professor. m. Irena Voračkova, 1 son, 1 daughter. Education: BSc (1st), Electrical and Electronic Engineering, Aston University, 1979; PhD, DIC, 1982, DSc, 1993, Computer Control, Imperial College, London; DrSc, Technical Cybernetics, Czech Academy of Science, Prague, 1994. Appointments: Telecomms Engineer, BT, 1970-76; Lecturer, University of Newcastle on Tyne, 1982-85; Research Lecturer, Oxford University, 1985-87; Senior Lecturer, Warwick University, 1987-88; Professor of Cybernetics, University of Reading, 1988-. Publications: March of the Machines, 1997; QI: the Quest for Intelligence, 2000; I Cyborg, 2002; Artificial Intelligence: The Basics, 2011. Honours: Honorary Member, Academy of Science, St Petersburg, 1999; Future of Health Technology Award, MIT, 2000; IEE (IET) Achievement Award, 2004; Mountbatten Medal, 2008; Ellison-Cliffe Medal, 2011; Honorary DSc, Aston University, 2008; Honorary DSc, Coventry University, 2008; Honorary DSc, Bradford University, 2010; Honorary DTech, Robert Gordon University, 2011. Memberships: Chartered Engineer (C Eng); Fellow, Institute of Engineering & Technology (FIET); Fellow, City & Guilds of London Institute (FCGI).

WARWICK (Marie) Dionne, b. 12 December 1940, East Orange, New Jersey, USA. Singer. m. Bill Elliott, deceased, 2 sons. Education: Hartt College Of Music, Hartford, Connecticut. Music Education: Masters degree, Music. Career: Singer, gospel groups The Drinkard Singers; The Gospelaires; Solo singer, 1962-; Association with songwriters Bacharach and David, originally as demo and backing singer, 1961-72;

Numerous concerts, tours and benefit shows worldwide; Television includes: Top Of The Pops; Thank Your Lucky Stars; Ready Steady Goes Live!; The Bacharach Sound; It's What's Happening Baby; The Divine Dionne Warwick; Ed Sullivan Show; Host, Solid Gold, 1980, 1984-86; Host, A Gift Of Music, 1981; Sisters In The Name Of Love, 1986; Dionne And Friends, 1990; Actress, film Slaves, 1969. Recordings: Albums: Presenting Dionne Warwick, 1964; Make Way For Dionne Warwick, 1964; The Sensitive Sound Of Dionne Warwick, 1965; Dionne Warwick In Paris, 1966; Here Where There Is Love, 1967; On Stage And In The Movies, 1967; The Windows Of The World, 1967; Valley Of The Dolls, 1968; Promises Promises, 1969; Soulful, 1969; Dionne, 1972; From Within, 1972; Just Being Myself, 1973; Then Came You, 1975; Track Of The Cat, 1976; A Man And A Woman, with Isaac Hayes, 1977; No Night So Long, 1980; Hot, Live And Otherwise, 1981; Friends In Love, 1982; Heartbreaker, 1982; So Amazing, 1983; Without Your Love, 1985; Reservations For Two, 1987; Dionne Warwick Sings Cole Porter, 1990; Friends Can Be Lovers, 1993; Aquarela Do Brazil, 1995; Hits from Stage and Screen, 1997; Dionne Sings Dionne, 1998; Numerous compilation albums; Hit singles include: Anyone Who Had A Heart, 1964; Walk On By, 1964; A Message To Michael, 1966; Alfie, 1967; I Say A Little Prayer, 1967; Do You Know The Way To San José, 1968; This Girl's In Love With You, 1969; I'll Never Fall In Love Again, 1970; Then Came You, with The Spinners (Number 1, US), 1974; I'll Never Love This Way Again, 1979; Heartbreaker, with Barry Gibb (Number 2, UK), 1982; All The Love In The World, 1983; That's What Friends Are For (AIDS charity record), with Stevie Wonder, Gladys Knight, Elton John (Number 1, US), 1985; Featured on numerous film soundtracks including: A House Is Not A Home, 1964; What's New Pussycat?, 1965; Valley Of The Dolls, 1968; The April Fools, 1969; Slaves, 1969; The Love Machine, 1971; After You, 1980; The Woman In Red, 1984; Contributor, charity records: We Are The World, USA For Africa, 1985; Forgotten Eyes, 1990; Lift Up Every Voice And Sing, 1990; That's What Friends Are For, 1993; Sunny Weather Lover, 1993; What the World Needs Now, 1998. Honours: Top Selling Female Artist, NARM, 1964; Grammy Awards: Best Female Pop Vocal Performance, 1969, 1970, 1980; Best Contemporary Vocal Performance, 1971; Best Female R&B Vocal Performance, 1980; Best Pop Performance, Duo or Group, 1987; Song Of The Year, 1987; Star on Hollywood's Walk Of Fame, 1985; NAACP Key Of Life Award, 1990; CORE Humanitarian Award, 1992; Nosotros Golden Eagle Humanitarian Award, 1992; Award from City of New York for contributions to AIDS research, 1987; DIVA Award, 1992; Platinum and Gold discs. Address: c/o Brokaw Company, 9255 Sunset Blvd, Suite 804, Los Angeles, CA 90069, USA.

WASHINGTON Denzel, b. 28 December 1954, Mount Vernon, New York, USA. Film Actor. m. Pauletta Pearson, 1983, 2 sons, 2 daughters. Education: Fordham University; American Conservatory Theatre, San Francisco. Creative Works: Theatre: Ceremonies in Dark Old Men; When the Chickens Come Home to Roost; A Soldier's Play; Richard III, 1990; Julius Caesar, 2005; Fences, 2010; Films include: A Soldier's Story, 1984; The Mighty Quinn, 1987; Cry Freedom, 1987; Heart Condition, 1989; Glory, 1990; Love Supreme, 1990; Mo' Better Blues, 1990; Ricochet, 1991; Mississippi Masala, 1991; Much Ado About Nothing, 1992; Malcolm X, 1992; The Pelican Brief, 1993; Philadelphia, 1993; Devil in a Blue Dress, 1995; Courage Under Fire, 1996; The Preachers Wife, 1996; Fallen, 1997; He Got Game, 1998; The Siege, 1998; The Bone Collector, 1999; The Hurricane, 1999; Remember the Titans, 2001; Training Day, 2001; John Q, 2002; Antwone Fisher, 2002; Out of Time, 2003; Man on Fire, 2004; Manchurian Candidate, 2004; Inside Man, 2006; Déjà vu, 2006; American Gangster, 2007; The Great Debaters, 2007; The Taking of Pelham 123, 2009; The Book of Eli, Unstoppable, 2010; Safe House, Flight, 2012; 2 Guns, 2013. Honours: 2 Golden Globe Awards, 1989, 1999; 1 Tony Award, 2010; 2 Academy Awards, 1989, 2001. Address: c/o ICM, 8942 Wilshire Boulevard, Beverly Hills, CA 90211, USA.

WASTERLAIN Claude, b. 15 April 1935, Courcelles, Belgium. Neurologist. m. Anne Thomsin, 1 son. Education: CSc, 1957, MD, 1961, University of Liege; LSc, Molecular Biology, Free University of Brussels, 1969. Appointments: Resident, 1964-66, Chief Resident, 1966-67, Medical College, New York City; Assistant Professor, Cornell University, 1970-75; Associate Professor, Cornell University Medical College, 1975-76; Associate Professor, 1976-79, Professor of Neurology, 1979-, University of California, Los Angeles School of Medicine; Chair, VA Greater Los Angeles Health Care System, 1997-. Publications: Over 400 articles; Many books and book chapters: Status Epilepticus (book), 1984; Neonated Seizures (book). Honours: Milken Award for Basic Research in Epilepsy, American Epilepsy Association, 1992; Golden Hammer Teaching Award, University of California, Los Angeles. Memberships include: American Neurological Association; Fellow, American Academy of Neurology; American Epilepsy Society; American and International Societies for Neurochemistry. Address: Neurology Department (127), VA Medical Center, 11301 Wilshire Boulevard, West Los Angeles, CA 90073, USA.

WATANABE Toru, b. 2 May 1960, Niigata, Japan. Medical Doctor; Paediatrician. m. Chieko Hoshi, 2 sons, 2 daughters. Education: MD, Niigata University, 1985; PhD, Niigata University Graduate School of Medicine and Dental Science, 2002. Appointments: Resident, 1985-90, Staff, 1991-, Department of Paediatrics, Niigata City General Hospital. Publications: 78 articles in medical journals including: Pediatric Nephrology; Nephron; Clinical Nephrology; Journal of Clinical Endocrinology and Metabolism; Pediatrics International; Pediatrics; European Journal of Pediatrics. Honours: Plenary Presentation Award, 1994, Best Clinical Research Award, 1999, Japanese Society for Pediatric Nephrology; Top 100 Health Professionals Pinnacle of Achievement Award, 2005, Salute to Greatness, 2005, Leading Health Professionals of the World, 2005, Diploma of Achievement in Medicine and Healthcare Award, 2005, International Biographical Centre; American Medal of Honor, 2005, American Biographical Association; Listed in Who's Who publications and biographical dictionaries. Memberships: Japanese Society for Paediatric Nephrology; International Pediatric Nephrology Association; Editorial Board of Pediatric Nephrology; Japan Pediatric Society; Japanese Society of Nephrology. Address: Department of Paediatrics, Niigata City General Hospital, 463-7 Shumoku, Chuoku, Niigata 950-1197, Japan. E-mail: twata@hosp.niigata.niigata.jp

WATERS General Sir (Charles) John, b. 2 September 1935, Rangoon, Burma. Retired Army Officer. m. Hilary Doyle Nettleton, 3 sons. Education: Oundle; Royal Military Academy, Sandhurst; Army Staff College, Camberley, 1967; Royal College of Defence Studies, 1982. Appointments: Commissioned into Gloucestershire Regiment, 1955; Instructor Army Staff College, 1973-75; Commanding Officer, 1 Battalion The Gloucestershire Regiment, 1975-77; Colonel General Staff, 1 Armoured Division, 1977-79; Commanded 3 Infantry Brigade, 1979-81; Royal College of Defence Studies,

DICTIONARY OF INTERNATIONAL BIOGRAPHY 36th EDITION

1982; Deputy Commander, Land Forces, Falklands, 1982; Commander 4 Armoured Division, 1983-85; Commandant, Staff College, Camberley, 1986-88; General Officer Commanding and Director of Operations, Northern Ireland, 1988-90 (dispatches 1990); Colonel, The Gloucestershire Regiment, 1985-91; Colonel Commandant, Prince of Wales Division, 1988-92; Commander-in-Chief, United Kingdom Land Forces, 1990-93; Deputy Supreme Allied Commander Europe, 1993-94; ADC General to HM The Queen, 1992-94; Magistrate 1998-2006. Honours: OBE, 1977; CBE, 1981; KCB, 1988; GCB, 1995; Honorary Colonel, Royal Devon Yeomanry, 1991-97; Wessex Yeomanry, 1991-97; Kermit Roosevelt Lecturer, 1992; Deputy Lieutenant, Devon, 2001-. Memberships: Advisory Council, Victory Memorial Museum, Arlon, Belgium, 1988-97; Chairman of the Council, National Army Museum, 2002-05; President, Officers' Association, 1997-2006; County President, Devon Royal British Legion, 1997-2002; Admiral: Army Sailing Association, 1990-93; Infantry Sailing Association, 1990-93; Member of the Council, Cheltenham College, 1990-97; Governor, Colyton Primary School, 1996-2002; President, Honiton and District Agricultural Society, 2004; Patron, Royal Albert Memorial Museum, 2006-. Address: c/o Lloyds Bank, Colyton, Devon EX23 6JS, England.

WATERS Brian Richard Anthony, b. 27 March 1944, Liverpool, England. Architect. m. Myriam Leiva Arenas. Education: City of London School, 1958-63; Degree and Diploma in Architecture, St Johns, Cambridge, 1963-68; PCL Diploma in Town Planning, 1969-71; RIBA, 1972; MRTPI, 1973. Appointments: City Corporation Planning Department, 1968-70; Greater London Council Architects Department, 1969-70; Shankland Cox & Associates, 1970-72; Founder, The Boisot Waters Cohen Partnership, 1972; Solo exhibition, Leighton House, 2002. Publications: Joint Publishing Editor, Planning in London; Planning correspondent of Architects' Journal. Honours: Master, Worshipful Company of Chartered Architects, 2002-03; International Building Press Magazine of the Year Award, 2008; 4 commendations for articles in Architect's Journal, Building, RIBA Journal. Memberships: RIBA Council; Association of Consultant Architects; London Planning & Development Forum; National Planning Forum; Society of Architect Artists; Old Citizens' Association; City of London School Alumni. Address: 17 Lexham Mews, London W8 6JW, England. E-mail: brian@bwcp.co.uk

WATSON Emily, b. 14 January 1967, London, England. Actress. m. Jack Waters, 1 son, 1 daughter. Education: London Drama Studio; University of Bristol. Appointments: Films include: Breaking the Waves, 1996; Mill on the Floss, 1997; Metroland, 1997; The Boxer, 1997; Hilary & Jackie, 1998; Angela's Ashes, 1999; Trixie, 2000; The Luzhin Defense, 2000; In Search of the Assassin, 2001; Gosford Park, 2001; Red Dragon, 2002; Punch-Drunk Love, 2002; Equilibrium, 2002; Boo, Zino & The Snurks (voice), 2004; The Life & Death of Peter Sellers, 2004; The Proposition, 2004; Separate Lies, 2005; Corpse Bride (voice), 2005; Crusade in Jean, 2005; Miss Potter, 2006; The Waterhorse, 2007; Fireflies in the Garden, 2008; Synecdoche, New York, 2008; Within the Whirlwind, 2008; Cold Souls, 2009; Oranges & Sunshine, 2010; Cemetery Junction, 2010; Theatre includes: Uncle Vanya; Twelfth Night, London, 2002, and New York, 2003; TV includes: The Memory Keeper's Daughter, 2008. Honours: New York Society of Film Critics Award, 1996; National Society of Film Critics Award, 1996; European Film Awards, 1996; LA Film Critics Association Awards, 1996; Evening Standard Film Awards, 1996; London Film Critics Association Awards, 1996, 2002; British Independent Film Awards, 1998; London Critics Circle Film Awards, 1998; Toronot Film Critics Association Awards, 2002. Address: c/o Independent Talent Group, Oxford House, 76 Oxford Street, London, W1D 1BS, England.

WATSON Emma, b. 15 April 1990, Paris, France. Actress. Career: Films: Harry Potter and the Philosopher's Stone, 2001; Harry Potter and the Chamber of Secrets, 2002; Harry Potter and the Prisoner of Azkaban, 2004; Harry Potter and the Goblet of Fire, 2005; Harry Potter and the Order of the Phoenix, Ballet Shoes, 2007; The Tale of Despereaux (voice), 2008; Harry Potter and the Half-Blood Prince, 2009; Harry Potter and the Deathly Hallows: Part 1, 2010; Harry Potter and the Deathly Hallows: Part 2, 2011. Honours: Young Artist Award, 2002; Best Female Film Star, Otto Awards, 2003, 2004, 2005, 2006, 2008; Child Performance of the Year, 2004; Best Female Performance, ITV National Film Awards, 2007; Best Movie Actress, UK Nickelodeon Kids' Choice Awards, 2007; Best Female Performance, Constellation Award, 2008; Best Actress, SyFy Genre Awards, 2008.

WATSON James Dewey, b. 6 April 1928, Chicago, Illinois, USA. m. Elizabeth Lewis, 1968, 2 sons. Education: Graduated, Zoology, University of Chicago, 1947; Postgraduate Research, University of Indiana, PhD, 1950. Appointments: Research into viruses, University of Copenhagen, 1950; Cavendish Laboratory, Cambridge University, 1951; Senior Research Fellow, Biology, California Institute of Technology, 1953-55; Several positions, Department of Biology, Harvard University; Assistant Professor, 1955-58, Associate Professor, 1958-61, Professor, 1961-68; Director, 1968, President, 1994-, Quantitative Biology, Cold Spring Harbor Laboratory; Associate Director, NIH (USA), 1988-89; Director, National Center for Human Genome Research, NIH, 1989-92; Newton Abraham Visiting Professor, Oxford University, England, 1994; Research to help determine the structure of DNA. Publications: Molecular Biology of the Gene, 1965, 1970, 1976; The Double Helix, 1968; The DNA Story, 1981; Recombinant DNA: A Short Course, 1983; The Molecular Biology of the Cell, 1986; Recombinant DNA, 1992; Avoid Boring People: Lessons from a Life in Science; Papers on the structure of DNA, on protein synthesis and on the induction of cancer by viruses. Honours: Joint Winner, Nobel Prize for Physiology or Medicine, 1962; John J Carty Gold Medal, 1971; Medal of Freedom, 1977; Gold Medal Award, National Institute of Social Sciences, 1984; Kaul Foundation Award for Excellence, 1992; Capley Medal of Royal Society, 1993; National Biotechnology Venture Award, 1993; Lomosonov Medal, 1994; National Medal of Science, 1997; Liberty Medal Award, 2000; Benjamin Franklin Medal, 2001; Gairdner Award, 2002; Lotos Club Medal of Merit, 2004; Othmer Gold Medal, Chemical Heritage Foundation, 2005. Address: Cold Spring Harbor Laboratory, PO Box 100, Cold Spring Harbor, New York NY 11724, USA.

WATSON Peter Gordon, b. 30 April 1930, Newport, Monmouth, Wales. Eye Surgeon. m. Ann Macintosh, 3 sons, 2 daughters. Education: Queen's College, Cambridge; University College Hospital, London; Moorfields Eye Hospital, London. Appointments: Senior Lecturer, University of London, Moorfields Eye Hospital, London, 1960-65; Consultant Ophthalmic Surgeon, Moorfields Eye Hospital, 1970-95; Consultant Ophthalmic Surgeon, Addenbrookes University Hospital, Cambridge, 1965-95; Boerhaave Professor, University of Leiden, Netherlands, 1999-2005; Council & Chairman/Organiser, Assessments, International Council of Ophthalmology, 1995-2008; President, Academia Ophthalmologica Internationalis, 2006-. Publications: 4

books; 23 book chapters; Over 200 articles in refereed journals. Honours: Doyne Memorial Medal, 1982; Royal College of Ophthalmologists Honoris Causi Fellowship, 1995; Duke Elder International Medal, 2002; Honor Award, Achievement Award, Honorary Membership, American Academy of Ophthalmology; Krawicz Gold Medal, Poland, 2000. Memberships: Royal College of Ophthalmologists; Society of Apothecaries, London; Master, Oxford Ophthalmological Congress. Address: 7 Richmond Terrace, Cambridge, CB5 8AJ, England.

WATSON Thomas Sturges (Tom), b. 4 September 1949, Kansas City, USA. Golfer. m. Linda Tova Rubin, 1973, 1 son, 1 daughter. Education: Stanford University. Appointments: Professional, 1971-; British Open Champion, 1975, 1977, 1980, 1982, 1983; Record low aggregate for British Open of 268, record two single round scores of 65, lowest final 36-hole score of 130, Turnberry, 1977; Won US Masters Title, 1977, 1981; Won US Open, 1982; Won World Series, 1975, 1977, 1980; Winner, numerous other open championships, 1974-; First player ever to win in excess of $500,000 in prize money in one season, 1980; Ryder Cup Player, Captain, 1993-; Senior Tour victories: 1999 Bank One Championship; 2000 IR Senior Tour Championship; 2001 Senior PGA Championship; 2002 Senior Tour Championship; Senior British Open 2003. Publication: Getting Back into Basics (jointly), 1992; Tom Watson's Strategic Golf. Honours include: Top Money Winner on US PGA Circuit, 1977, 1978, 1979, 1980; US PGA Player of the Year, 1977, 1978, 1979, 1980, 1982; PGA World Golf Hall of Fame, 1988; Payne Stewart Award, 2003. Address: PGA America, PO Box 109801, 100 Avenue of the Champions, Palm Beach Gardens, FL 33410, USA.

WATTS Charlie, b. 2 June 1941, Islington, London, England. Musician (drums). Career: Member, Blues Incorporated; Member, Rolling Stones, 1962-; Numerous tours and concerts include: National Jazz & Blues Festival, 1963; First UK tour, 1963; Group Scene UK tour, 1964; Debut US tour, 1964; Free concert, Hyde Park, 1969; Free concert, Altamont Speedway, 1969; Knebworth Festival, 1976; Steel Wheels North American Tour, 1989; Films include: Ladies And Gentlemen The Rolling Stones, 1976; Let's Spend The Night Together, 1983; Co-founder, record label, Rolling Stones Records, 1971. Recordings: Albums include: The Rolling Stones, 1965; The Rolling Stones No 2, 1965; Out Of Our Heads, 1965; Aftermath, 1966; Between The Buttons, 1967; Their Satanic Majesties Request, 1967; Beggar's Banquet, 1968; Let It Bleed, 1969; Get Yer Ya-Ya's Out, 1969; Sticky Fingers, 1971; Exile On Main Street, 1972; Goat's Head Soup, 1973; It's Only Rock And Roll, 1974; Black And Blue, 1976; Some Girls, 1978; Emotional Rescue, 1980; Tattoo You, 1981; Still Life, 1982; Steel Wheels, 1989; Flashpoint, 1991; Stripped, 1995; Long Ago and Far Away, 1996; Hit singles include: It's All Over Now; Little Red Rooster; Get Off Of My Cloud; (I Can't Get No) Satisfaction; 19th Nervous Breakdown; Ruby Tuesday; Jumping Jack Flash; Honky Tonk Women; Let's Spend The Night Together; Brown Sugar; Miss You; Start Me Up; Emotional Rescue; Harlem Shuffle; Going To A Go-Go; Paint It Black; Angie; Undercover Of The Night; She's So Cold. Honours: with Rolling Stones include: Silver Clef, Nordoff-Robbins Therapy, 1982; Grammy Award, Lifetime Achievement Award, 1986; Inducted into Rock And Roll Hall Of Fame, 1989; Q Award, Best Live Act, 1990; Ivor Novello Award, Outstanding Contribution to British Music, 1991. Current Management: Rupert Loewenstein, 2 King Street, London SW1Y 6QL, England.

WAX Ruby, b. 19 April 1953, Illinois, USA. Comedienne; Actress. m. Edward Richard Morison Bye, 1988, 1 son, 2 daughters. Education: Berkeley University; Royal Scottish Academy of Music and Drama. Appointments: With Crucible Theatre, 1976, Royal Shakespeare Company, 1978-82. Creative Works: TV includes: Not the Nine O'Clock News, 1982-83; Girls on Top, 1983-85; Don't Miss Wax, 1985-87; Hit and Run, 1988; Full Wax, 1987-92; Ruby Wax Meets..., 1996, 1997, 1998; Ruby, 1997, 1998, 1999; Ruby's American Pie, 1999, 2000; Hot Wax, 2001; The Waiting Game, 2001, 2002; Ruby, 2002; Films include: Miami Memoirs, 1987; East Meets Wax, 1988; Class of '69; Ruby Takes a Trip, 1992; Tara Road, 2005; Ruby Wax with ..., 2003; Popetown (series), 2003; Plays include: Wax Acts (one woman show), 1992; Stressed (one woman show), 2000. Publication: How Do You Want Me? (autobiography), 2002. Honours: Performer of the Year, British Comedy Awards, 1993. Address: c/o ICM, Oxford House, 76 Oxford Street, London W1N 0AY, England.

WAY Danny, b. 15 April 1974, Portland, Oregon, USA. Professional Skateboarder. m. Kari Way, 2 sons. Career: Started skateboarding 1988, Turned professional for Alein Workshop 1989. Film appearances include: The DC video, 2002; Alien Workshop – mosaic, 2003. TV appearances include: Legends or the Extreme, 2003. Honours: MTV Sports and Music Festival 1st Place in highest air, 1999; Holds the Guinness Book of World Records highest air on a skateboard at 18'+, and longest air on a skateboard at 79'; Thrasher Magazine Skater of the Year, 1992 and 2004; Big Air Gold Medal, 2004, 2005; First person to jump the Great Wall of China on a skateboard or any other non-motorized vehicle, 2005. Address: Carlsbad, California, USA.

WEAVER Sigourney, b. 8 October 1949, New York, USA. Actress. m. James Simpson, 1984, 1 daughter. Creative Works: Films include: Annie Hall, 1977; Tribute to a Madman, 1977; Camp 708, 1978; Alien, 1979; Eyewitness, 1981; The Year of Living Dangerously, 1982; Deal of the Century, 1983; Ghostbusters, 1984; Une Femme ou Deux, 1985; Half Moon Street, 1986; Aliens, 1986; Gorillas in the Mist, 1988; Ghostbusters II, 1989; Aliens 3, 1992; 1492: Conquest of Paradise, 1993; Dave, 1993; Death and the Maiden, 1994; Jeffrey, 1995; Copycat, 1996; Snow White in the Black Forest, 1996; Ice Storm, 1996; Alien Resurrection, 1997; A Map of the World, 1999; Galaxy Quest, 1999; Get Bruce, 1999; Company Man, 1999; Airframe, 1999; Heartbreakers, 2001; Tadpole, 2002; The Guys, 2002; Holes, 2003; The Village, 2004; Snow Cake, 2006; The TV Set, 2006; Infamous, 2006; Happily N'Ever After, 2006; The Girl in the Park, 2007; Be Kind Rewind, 2008; Vantage Point, 2008; Prayers for Bobby, 2009; Avatar, 2009; Crazy on the Outside, You Again, 2010; Cedar Rapids, Paul, Abduction, Rampart, 2011; The Cabin in the Woods, Red Lights, The Cold Light of Day, Vamps, 2012. Honours include: Golden Globe Best Actress Award, 1988; Best Supporting Actress Golden Globe Award, 1988. Address: c/o ICM, 8942 Wilshire Boulevard, Beverly Hills, CA 90211, USA.

WEBB David John, b. 1 September 1953. Professor. m. (1) Margaret Jane Cullen, 1984 (dissolved 2007), 3 sons, (2) Louise Eleanor Bath, 2009. Education: MB BS, 1977, MD, 1990, University of London; DSc, University of Edinburgh, 2000. Appointments: House Officer Posts, Royal London Hospital scheme, 1977-78; Senior House Officer, Chelmsford Hospitals, 1978-79; Senior House Officer, Stoke Mandeville Hospital, 1979-80; Registrar, Royal London Hospital, 1980-82; Registrar, 1982-85, MRC Clinical Scientist, MRC BP Unit, 1982-85, Western Infirmary, Glasgow; Lecturer, Clinical Pharmacology, St George's Medical School,

1985-89; Senior Registrar in Medicine, St George's Hospital, London, 1985-89; Consultant Physician, Lothian University Hospitals NHS Trust, 1990-; Senior Lecturer, Medicine, 1990-95, Christison Professor of Therapeutics and Clinical Pharmacology, 1995-, Director, Clinical Research Centre, 1990-96, Head, University Department of Medicine, 1997-98, Head, Department of Medical Sciences, 1998-2001, Wellcome Trust Research Leave Fellowship, and Leader, Wellcome Trust Cardiovascular Research Initiative, 1998-2001, Convenor, Cardiovascular Interdisciplinary Group, 1999-2000, Head, Centre for Cardiovascular Science, 2000-04, University of Edinburgh; Director, Education Programme, Wellcome Trust Clinical Research Facility, Edinburgh, 1998-; Chairman, New Drugs Committee, 2001-05, Chairman, Scottish Medicines Consortium, 2005-08; Leader, Wellcome Trust, Scottish Translational Medicine and Therapeutics Initiative, 2008-; President, European Association of Clinical Pharmacology & Therapeutics, 2009; Honorary EACPT President; Vice-President, Royal College of Physicians of Edinburgh, 2006-09; Deputy Director and Lead for Clinical Pharmacology, Medical Research Council, Scottish Clinical Pharmacology and Pathology Programme, 2010-; President, Scottish Society of Physicians, 2010. Publications: The Molecular Biology & Pharmacology of the Endothelins, 1995; The Endothelium in Hypertension, 1996; Vascular Endothelium in Human Physiology and Pathophysiology, 1999; The Year in Therapeutics Vol 1, 2005. Memberships: Royal College of Physicians Edinburgh; British Hypertension Society; British Pharmacological Society; High Blood Pressure Foundation; International Union for Pharmacology. Address: British Heart Foundation, Centre of Research Excellence, Queen's Medical Research Institute, Centre for Cardiovascular Science, University of Edinburgh, E3.22, 47 Little France Crescent, Edinburgh EH16 4TJ, Scotland. E-mail: d.j.webb@ed.ac.uk

WEBSTER Henry de Forest, b. 22 April 1927, New York, USA. Neuroscientist. m. Marion Havas Webster, 4 sons, 1 daughter. Education: BA, Chemistry (cum laude), Amherst College, Massachusetts, 1948; MD, Harvard Medical School, Boston, Massachusetts, 1952. Appointments: Postgraduate training, Internal Medicine, Neurology, Neuropathology, 1952-59, Instructor, Neurology to Assistant Professor, Neuropathology, Harvard Medical School, 1959-66; Associate Professor, Professor, Neurology, University of Miami Medical School, 1966-69; Head, Section Cell Neuropathology, 1969-97, Chief, Laboratory of Experimental Neuropathology, 1984-97, Emeritus Scientist, 1997-, NINDS, National Institute of Health, Bethesda, Maryland, USA. Publications: Co-author : Fine Structure of the Nervous System, 1970, 1976, 1991; Gliogenesis: Historical Perspectives, 1839-85, 2009; Author: Cellular Neuroscience: Projects and Images 1957-1997, 2006; Book chapters, reviews and scientific articles. Honours: Weil Award, American Association of Neuropathologists, 1960; Superior Service Award, US Public Health Service, 1977; Alexander von Humboldt Foundation (Germany) Senior US Scientist Award, 1985; Honorary Professor, Norman Bethune University Medical Science, 1991; Scientific Award, Peripheral Neuropathy Association, 1994; Award for Meritorious Contributions to Neuropathology; American Association of Neuropathologists, 2001. Memberships: American Association of Neuropathologists, President, 1978-79; International Society of Neuropathology, President, 1986-90; Honorary Member, International Society of Neuropathology and Japanese Society of Neuropathology; Fellow, Royal College of Medicine. Address: 4515 Willard Avenue, Apt 2303 South, Chevy Chase, MD 20815-3622, USA. E-mail: mhwebster@verizon.net

WEBSTER John Barron, (Jack Webster), b. 8 July 1931, Maud, Aberdeenshire, Scotland. Journalist. m. Eden Keith, 17 February 1956, 3 sons. Education: Maud School; Robert Gordon's College, Aberdeen. Publications: The Dons, 1978; A Grain of Truth, 1981; Gordon Strachan, 1984; Another Grain of Truth, 1988; Alistair MacLean: A Life, 1991; Famous Ships of the Clyde, 1993; The Flying Scots, 1994; The Express Years, 1994; In the Driving Seat, 1996; The Herald Years, 1996; Webster's World, 1997; From Dali to Burrell, 1997; Reo Stakis Story, 1999; The Auld Hoose, 2005; Jack Webster's Aberdeen, 2007. Television Films: The Webster Trilogy, 1992; John Brown: The Man Who Drew a Legend, 1994; Walking Back to Happiness, 1996; Play: The Life of Grassic Gibbon, 2008. Honours: Bank of Scotland Awards, Columnist of the Year, 1996; UK Speaker of the Year, 1996; Honorary M University, Aberdeen University, 2000; Honorary Doctor of Letters, Robert Gordon University, 2009. Address: 58 Netherhill Avenue, Glasgow G44 3XG, Scotland.

WEBSTER John Morrison, b. 3 November 1932, Sri Lanka. Artist. Widower, 2 daughters. Appointments: 40 years in Royal Navy; Vice Admiral, KCB; Chairman of Governors, Pangbourne College, 1992-2000; Chairman, Armed Forces Art Society, 1990-96; Marine and Landscape Painter in oil and pastel; President, Royal Naval Benevolent Trust, 1991-98. Solo and group exhibitions: Work held in private collections worldwide; Commissions include Royal Cruising Club, Corporation of Trinity House; Principal works include: Silver Jubilee Fleet Review 1977; International Fleet Review 2005; HMY Britannia on Decommissioning Day. Publication: HMY Britannia on Decommissioning (collection of HM The Queen). Memberships: Royal Society of Marine Artists, Royal Cruising Club. Address: Old School House, Soberton, Southampton, SO32 3PF, England. Website: www.johnwebster.org.uk

WEBSTER Richard, b. 6 May 1933, Derby, England. Scientist. m. Mary Buxton, 1 son, 2 daughters. Education: BSc, Chemistry, University of Sheffield, 1954; D Phil, Oxford University, 1966; DSc, Sheffield University, 1983. Appointments: Soil Chemist, Northern Rhodesia (Zambia) Government, 1957-61; Research Associate, Oxford University, 1961-68; Senior Scientific Officer, 1968-71, Principal Scientific Officer, 1971-79, Soil Survey of England and Wales; Senior Research Scientist, CSIRO Division of Soils, Australia, 1973-74; Senior Principal Scientific Officer, Soils Department, Rothamsted Experimental Station, 1979-90; Maître de Recherche, Ecole Nationale Supérieure des Mines de Paris, 1990; Chief Editor of Catena, 1990-95; Directeur de Recherche, Institut National de la Recherche Agronomique, France, 1990-91; Visiting Scientist, Rothamsted Experimental Station, 1991-92, 1993-94; Guest Professor, Swiss Federal Institute of Technology, 1992-94; Professor, Eidgenössische Forschungsanstalt für Wald, Schnee und Landschaft (WSL), Switzerland, 1994-95; Editor-in Chief, European Journal of Soil Science, 1995-2003; Visiting Professor in Soil Science, University of Reading, 1997-2003; Lawes Trust Senior Fellow, Rothamsted, 2003-; Visiting Professor, Universidad Nacional Autónoma de México, 2006-. Publications: Author of more than 220 papers in scientific journals, conference proceedings and other collected works; 4 text books; 3 atlases; 20 technical reports. Honour: Docteur Honoris Causa, Louvain, 1995. Membership: British Society of Soil Science; International Association of Mathematical Geology. Address: Rothamsted Research, Harpenden, Hertfordshire AL5 2JQ, England. E-mail: richard.webster@rothamsted.ac.uk

WEERAPERUMA Claudia Valentine, b. 1 April 1961, Berne, Switzerland. Writer; Poet; Painter; Book Illustrator. m. Susunaga Weeraperuma. Education: Ecole des Beaux-Arts, Toulouse; Feusi Rüedi Schulen, Berne; Kunstgewerbeschule, Berne; Neue Mädchenschule, Berne; Licentiate, University of Berne; PhD, Comparative Religion, Somerset University. Publications: Contemplative Prayer in Christianity and Islam; Ocean of Compassion, poems; Hunt of Hera, novella; Jiddu Krishnamurti: Begegnungen und Gespräche, translation; Bamboo Grove: Buddhist Poems. Memberships: The Theosophical Society. Address: Villa Claudia, 338 Chemin du Colombier, 83460 Les Arcs sur Argens, France. Website: www.weeraperuma.com

WEERAPERUMA Susunaga, b. 19 May 1934, Galle, Sri Lanka. Author. m. Claudia Valentine Weeraperuma. Education: Mahinda College, Galle; Ananda College, Colombo; MSc (Economics), London University; D Litt; Associate of the Library Association. Appointments: Senior Librarian, British Library; Senior Librarian, Parliamentary Library of South Australia. Publications: Religion and Philosophy: Major Religions of India; Divine Messengers of Our Time; Homage to Yogaswami; The Pure in Heart; Miraculous Waters of Lourdes; Servant of God: Sayings of a Self-Realised Sage Swami Ramdas; My Philosophy of Life; Autobiographical Writings: So You Want to Emigrate to England, Mohandas; Memoirs of an Oriental Philosopher; Library Science: Staff Exchanges in Librarianship; In-Service Training in Librarianship; The Role of Conferences in the Further Education of Librarians; Drama: The Pleasures of Life; Short Stories: The Holy Guru and Other Stories; The Stranger and Other Stories; Mysterious Stories of Sri Lanka; The Homeless Life and Other Stories; J Krishnamurti: J Krishnamurti As I Knew Him; Living and Dying from Moment to Moment; That Pathless Land; Bliss of Reality; Sayings of J Krishnamurti; A Bibliography of the Life and Teachings of Jiddu Krishnamurti; Jiddu Krishnamurti: A Bibliographical Guide; Buddhism: New Insights into Buddhism; Nirvana the Highest Happiness; The First and Best Buddhist Teachings; Serenity Here and Now: The Buddha's Sutta-Nipata Sermons; Saida of Marrakesh; Enrich Your Inner Life; Sunil the Struggling Student; Saida of Marrakesh; Enrich Your Inner Life. Memberships: Life Member, Vegetarian Society of the UK; Life Member, Indian Vegetarian Congress; Member, The Theosophical Society. Address: Villa Claudia, 338 chemin du Colombier, 83460 Les Arcs-sur-Argens, France.

WEHBE Jahida, b. 20 September 1969, Ana, Bekaa, Lebanon. Singer; Composer; Songwriter; Actress. Education: Opera in Arabic Language Studies, 1998-2002, Diploma, Oriental Songs, Syriac and Byzantine Chant, Qura'nic Recitals and 'ud (Middle Eastern lute), 2003, Lebanese National Conservatory of Music, Lebanon; Bachelor degree, Psychology, 2002, Master's degree, Acting & Directing, Institute of Fine Arts, 2003, Lebanese University, Lebanon. Appointments: President, Committee of Culture and Programs, Lebanese Council for Authors and Composers; Freelance Poet, Orator, Singer, Songwriter and Actress (theatre, television and film); Representative of Lebanon in several seminars and events around the world. Publications: CDs: Angham fil Bal; Takatik Al Echrinat; Ya Maryamou; Yadaya Dariaatan; Katabtany, 2007; Ayyoha Nmesyan habni Kobla tak, 2009; Books: Al Azrak Wal Huduhud – Passion on Facebook. Honours: 1st Prize (for film, Void Bullet), Lebanese University; Arab Pioneers and Innovators Festival Award; Honoured by: Lebanese Ministry of Culture; Lebanese Ministry of Health; Bahraini Ministry of Culture; Jordanian Ministry of Culture; Arab Music Festival in Cairo – Opera House; Many Arab and Lebanese Poetry Festivals; Many international and Lebanese Cultural Associations. Memberships: Professional Musicians Syndicate in Lebanon; French Society of Authors, Composers and Music Publishers (Sacem); Professional Artists Syndicate in Lebanon. Address: 4th Floor, Bloc E, Atef Aoun Building, Mar Roukoz Monastery Street, Mar Roukoz, Beirut, Lebanon. E-mail: jahidawehbenews@gmail.com Website: www.jahidawehbe.com

WEIDNER Stanislaw Marian, b. 22 March 1947, Wrzesnia. Biochemist; Plant Physiologist. Educator. m. Maria Minakowska, 1 son, 1 daughter. Education: Master, Olsztyn University of Agricultural Technology, Poland, 1971; Doctor, 1980; Teaching: Biochemistry, Enzymology, Proteomics. Appointments: Assistant, 1971-80, Adjunct, 1980-89, Assistant Professor, 1989-92, Associate Professor, 1992-2001, Olsztyn University of Agricultural Technology; Visiting Professor, Okayama University, 1998-99; Professor, 2001-, Head of Department of Biochemistry, 2005-, University of Warmia and Mazury, Olsztyn; Achievements include research in possible involvement of cytoskeleton in regulation of cereal caryopses dormancy and germination. Publications: 78 refereed journal publications; 80 conference papers; Co-Editor, Biochemistry of Vertebrates, 1998, 2005, 2007 and 2010. Honours: Silver and Gold Cross for Achievements in Science and Educational Fields, President of Poland, 1994, 2003; Awards of the Minister of Education: 1990, 1999, 2006; The Antoni Dmochowski Award for the book Biochemistry of Vertebrates, 2008; The National Education Commission Medal, 2009; State Commission for Scientific Research Grantee, 1993-96, 1997-01, 2004-07, 2008-09, 2008-10; COST project European Co-op, 1996-2001, 2003-09, 2007-11, 2009-13, 2010-14; Recipient of several research fellowships. Memberships: Federation of European Biochemical Societies; Federation of European Societies of Plant Biology; International Society for Seed Science; Polish Society for Experimental Biology; Polish Botanical Society; Editorial Council, Acta Physiologiae Plantarum, 2000-. Address: Iwaszkiewicza Street 41/3, PL-10089 Olsztyn, Poland. E-mail: weidner@uwm.edu.pl Website: www.uwm.edu.pl/edu/stanislawweidner/

WEINBERG Steven, b. 3 May 1933, New York, New York, USA. Professor of Science; Author. m. Louise Goldwasser, 1954, 1 daughter. Education: BA, Cornell University, 1954; Postgraduate Studies, Copenhagen Institute of Theoretical Physics, 1954-55; PhD, Princeton University, 1957. Appointments: Research Associate and Instructor, Columbia University, 1957-59; Research Physicist, Lawrence Radiation Laboratory, Berkeley, 1959-60; Faculty, 1960-64, Professor of Physics, 1964-69, University of California at Berkeley; Visiting Professor, 1967-69, Professor of Physics, 1979-83, Massachusetts Institute of Technology; Higgins Professor of Physics, Harvard University, 1973-83; Senior Scientist, Smithsonian Astrophysics Laboratory, 1973-83; Josey Professor of Science, University of Texas at Austin, 1982-; Senior Consultant, Smithsonian Astrophysics Observatory, 1983-; Various visiting professorships and lectureships. Publications: Gravitation and Cosmology: Principles and Application of the General Theory of Relativity, 1972; The First Three Minutes: A Modern View of the Origin of the Universe, 1977; The Discovery of Subatomic Particles, 1982; Elementary Particles and the Laws of Physics (with R Feynman), 1987; Dreams of a Final Theory, 1992; The Quantum Theory of Fields, Vol I, Foundations, 1995, Vol II, Modern Applications, 1996, Vol III, Supersymmetry, 2000; Facing Up, 2001. Contributions to: Books, periodicals and professional journals. Honours: J Robert

Oppenheimer Memorial Prize, 1973; Dannie Heineman Prize in Mathematical Physics, 1977; American Institute of Physics-US Steel Foundation Science Writing Award, 1977; Nobel Prize in Physics, 1979; Elliott Cresson Medal, Franklin Institute, 1979; Madison Medal, Princeton University, 1991; National Medal of Science, National Science Foundation, 1991; Andrew Gemant Prize, American Institute of Physics, 1997; Piazzi Prize, Governments of Sicily and Palermo, 1998; Lewis Thomas Price for the Scientist as Poet, Rockefeller University, 1999. Memberships: American Academy of Arts and Sciences; American Mediaeval Academy; American Philosophical Society; American Physical Society; Council on Foreign Relations; History of Science Society; International Astronomical Union; National Academy of Science; Phi Beta Kappa; Philosophical Society of Texas, president, 1994; Royal Society; Texas Institute of Letters. Address: c/o Department of Physics, University of Texas at Austin, Austin, TX 78712, USA.

WEINSTEIN Harvey, b. USA. Film Company Executive. Appointment: Co-Chair, Miramax Films Corporation, New York. Creative Works: Films produced jointly include: Playing for Keeps, 1986; Scandal, 1989; Strike it Rich, Hardware, 1990; A Rage in Harlem, 1991; The Crying Game, 1992; The Night We Never Met, Benefit of the Doubt, True Romance, 1993; Mother's Boys, Like Water for Chocolate, Pulp Fiction, Pret-A-Porter, 1994; Smoke, A Month by the Lake, The Crossing Guard, The Journey of August King, Things To Do In Denver When You're Dead, The Englishman Who Went Up A Hill But Came Down A Mountain, Blue in the Face, Restoration, 1995; Scream, The Pallbearer, The Last of the High Kings, Jane Eyre, Flirting with Disaster, The English Patient, Emma, The Crow; City of Angels, Beautiful Girls, 1996; Addicted to Love, 1997; Shakespeare in Love, 1998; Allied Forces, She's All That, My Life So Far, The Yards, 1999; Bounce, Scary Movie, Boys and Girls, Love's Labour Lost, Scream 3, About Adam, Chocolat, 2000; Spy Kids, Scary Movie 2, The Others, Lord of the Rings: The Fellowship of the Ring, Iris, 2001; Halloween: Resurrection, Spy Kids 2: Island of Lost Dreams, Lord of the Rings: The Two Towers, Gangs of New York, Chicago, 2002; Spy Kids 3-D: Game Over, Kill Bill: Vol 1, Scary Movie 3, Lord of the Rings: Return of The King, Cold Mountain, 2003; Kill Bill: Vol 2, Paper Clips, Fahrenheit 9/11, Shall We Dance, Cursed, The Aviator, 2004; Cursed, Sin City, The Adventures of Sharkboy and Lavagirl 3-D, Dracula III: Legacy, The Great Raid, An Unfinished Life, The Brothers Grimm, Underclassman, Proof, The Prophecy: Forsaken, Venom, Feast, Curandero, Derailed, 2005; Project Jay, Scary Movie 4, Clerks II, Pulse, Breaking and Entering, School for Scoundrels, Factory Girl, 2006; Grindhouse, Sicko, Killshot, Death Proof, 1408, Planet Terror, Who's Your Caddy? The Nanny Diaries, Halloween, Rogue, The Mist, Awake, 2007; Hell Ride, Rambo, The Promotion, The No 1 Ladies' Detective Agency, Superhero Movie, 2008. Honour: Fellow, British Film Institute. Address: Miramax Films Corporation, 375 Greenwich Street, New York, NY 10013, USA.

WEINSTEIN Robert, b. 1954, USA. Film Producer; Executive. Appointment: Co-Chair, Miramax Films Corporation. Creative Works: Films produced include: Playing for Keeps (with Alan Brewer), 1986; Scandal (with Joe Boyd and Nik Powell), 1989; Strike it Rich, Hardware (with Nik Powell, Stephen Wooley, Trix Worrell), 1990; A Rage in Harlem (with Terry Glinwood, William Horberg, Nik Powell), 1991; The Night We Never Met (with Sidney Kimmel), Benefit of the Doubt, True Romance (with Gary Barber, Stanley Margolis, James G Robinson), 1993; Mother's Boys (with Randall Poster), Pulp Fiction (with Richard N Gladstein), Pret-A-Porter (with Ian Jessel), 1994; Smoke (with Satoru Iseki), A Month By the Lake (with Donna Gigliotti), The Crossing Guard (with Richard N Gladstein), The Journey of August King, Things To Do in Denver When You're Dead (with Marie Cantin), The Englishman Who Went Up a Hill But Came Down a Mountain (with Sally Hibbin, Robert Jones), Blue in the Face (with Harvey Keitel), Restoration (with Donna Gigliotti), 1995; Velvet Goldmine, Shakespeare in Love, 1998; Allied Forces, My Life So Far, The Yards, Music of the Heart, The Cider House Rules, 1999; Down To You, Boys and Girls, Scream 3, Love's Labour's Lost, Scary Movie, Chocolat, 2000; Spy Kids, Scary Movie 2, The Others, Lord of the Rings: The Fellowship of the Ring, Iris, 2001; Halloween: Resurrection, Spy Kids 2: Island of Lost Dreams, Lord of the Rings: The Two Towers, Gangs of New York, Chicago, 2002; Spy Kids 3-D: Game Over, Kill Bill: Vol 1, Scary Movie 2, Lord of the Rings: Return of the King, Cold Mountain, 2003; Kill Bill: Vol 2, Paper Clips, Fahrenheit 9/11, Shall We Dance, Cursed, The Aviator, 2004; Cursed, Sin City, The Adventures of Sharkboy and Lavagirl 3-D, Dracula III: Legacy, The Great Raid, An Unfinished Life, The Brothers Grimm, Underclassman, Proof, The Prophecy: Forsaken, Venom, Feast, Curandero, Derailed, 2005; Project Jay, Scary Movie 4, Clerks II, Pulse, 2006; Breaking and Entering, School for Scoundrels, Factory Girl, 2006; Grindhouse, Sicko, Killshot, Death Proof, 1408, Planet Terror, Who's Your Caddy? The Nanny Diaries, Halloween, Rogue, The Mist, Awake, 2007; Hell Ride, Rambo, The Promotion, Superhero Movie, 2008. Honour: Fellow, British Film Institute. Address: Miramax Films Corporation, 375 Greenwich Street, New York, NY 10013, USA.

WEIR Peter Lindsay, b. 21 August 1944, Sydney, Australia. Film Director. m. Wendy Stites, 1966, 1 son, 1 daughter. Education: Sydney University. Appointments: Real Estate, 1965; Stagehand, TV, Sydney, 1967; Director, Film Sequences, Variety Show, 1968; Director, Amateur University Reviews, 1967-69; Director, Film Australia, 1969-73; Made Own Short Films, 1969-73; Independent Feature-Film Director, Writer, 1973-. Creative Works: Films: Cars That Ate Paris, 1973; Picnic at Hanging Rock, 1975; The Last Wave, 1977; The Plumber (TV), 1978; Gallipoli, 1980; The Year of Living Dangerously, 1982; Witness, 1985; The Mosquito Coast, 1986; The Dead Poets Society, 1989; Green Card, 1991; Fearless, 1994; The Truman Show, 1997; Master and Commander: The Far Side of the World, 2003. Honours include: BAFTA Award, Best Director, 1997; BAFTA Award, Best Director, 2004. Address: Salt Pan Films Pty Ltd, PO Box 29, Palm Beach, NSW 2108, Australia.

WEISS Simona, b. 8 September 1929, Brooklyn, New York, USA. Retired Paralegal. Divorced, 1 son, 1 daughter. Education: Columbia University, New York, 1968-70; BA (cum laude), Fairleigh Dickinson University, Teaneck, New Jersey, 1974; Postgraduate, New York University, New York City; Graduate School of Public Administration, 1974-76; Certified Paralegal, Upsala College, East Orange, New Jersey, 1980; William Patterson University, Wayne, New Jersey, Graduate School of Art and Communication, 2003. Appointments: Vice President of Fundraising, Haworth (New Jersey) Home and School Association, 1967-69; Financial and Corresponding Secretary, Temple Beth El, Closter (New Jersey), 1968-72; Program and Publicity Chairman, 1st Bergen County Women's Center, Teaneck (New Jersey), 1972-74; Chairman, Haworth (New Jersey) Parks & Playgrounds Committee, 1972-78; Candidate, Non-Partisan Bergen County (New Jersey) Charter Study Commission, 1973-74; County Committee Municipal Chairman, Haworth

(New Jersey) Republican Organization, 1973-79; Primary Candidate, Bergen County (New Jersey) Board of Chosen Freeholders, 1977; Paralegal: Witco Chemical Corp, 1980-81; Pitney, Hardin, Kipp & Szuch, 1982; Willkie Farr & Gallagher, 1983-84; Robinson Silverman Pearce Aronsohn & Berman, 1984-90; Freddie Mac, 1991; The Prudential Insurance Company of America, 1992-94; Cleary, Gottlieb, Steen & Hamilton, 1994-96; Hannoch Weisman, 1996-98; Unilever Bestfoods, 1998-2002; Temple Sholom, 2007. Publications: Numerous articles in professional journals. Honours: Mayor's Certificate, Borough of Haworth, 1979; Scholar, Fairleigh Dickinson University, 1971-74; Phi Omega Epsilon Honor Society. Memberships: Legal Assistant Management Association; National Paralegal Association; Industrial Commercial Real Estate Women; Association of Real Estate Women; National Council of Jewish Women; Dazzling Damsels; Dizzy Dames; Mingle and Meet; National Network of Commercial Real Estate Women. Address: 2000 Linwood Ave, Apt 19U, Fort Lee, NJ 07024, USA. E-mail: simona_wei@msn.com

WEISZ Rachel, b. 7 March 1971, London, England. Actress. 1 son with Darren Aronofsky, m. Daniel Craig, 2011. Education: English, Cambridge University. Career: Model, age 14; Formed theatre company, Talking Tongues, 1991; Face of Revlon, 2005-; Acted on stage, film and television;Theatre: Design for Living, 1994; A Streetcar Named Desire, 2009; Films include: Stealing Beauty, 1996; Bent, 1997; The Land Girls, 1998; The Mummy, 1999; The Mummy Returns, 2001; Enemy at the Gates, 2001; About a Boy, 2002; The Shape of Things, 2003; Confidence, 2003; Runaway Jury, 2003; Envy, 2004; Constantine, 2005; The Constant Gardener, 2005; The Fountain, 2006; Eragon (voice), 2006; My Blueberry Nights, 2007; Fred Claus, 2007; Definitely, Maybe, The Brothers Bloom, 2008; The Lovely Bones, Agora, 2009; The Whistleblower, 2010; 360, Page Eight, Dream House, The Deep Blue Sea, 2011; The Bourne Legacy, 2013; Oz: The Great and Powerful, 2013. Honours include: Academy Award, 2005; British Independent Film Award, 2005; Golden Globe Award, 2005; London Film Critic's Circle Award, 2005; Screen Actors Guild Award, 2005; New York Film Critics Circle Award, 2011; many others. Memberships: Patron, The X Appeal, Royal College of Radiologists.

WEIZSÄCKER Carl Friedrich von, b. 28 June 1912, Kiel, Germany. Theoretical Physicist. Education: PhD, University of Leipzig, 1933. Appointments: Assistant, Institute of Theoretical Physics, University of Leipzig, 1934-36; Kaiser Wilhelm Institute of Physics, Berlin-Dahlem; Lecturer, University of Berlin, 1936-42; Chair, University of Strasbourg, 1942; Kaiser Wilhelm Institute, 1944; Member of German research team investigating feasibility of nuclear weapons, but feared that such weapons may be used by the Nazi government; Director, Department, Max Planck Institute of Physics, Göttingen, 1946, with Honorary Professorship; Professor of Philosophy, University of Hamburg, 1957-69; Honorary Chair, University of Munich, 1969; Director, Max Planck Institute, 1970; Investigated the way in which energy is generated in the centre of stars; Devised theory on the origin of the solar system. Publications include: Bedingungen der Freiheit, 1990; Der Mensch in seiner Geschichte, 1991; Zeit und Wissen, 1992; Der bedrohte Friede-heute, 1994; Wohin gehen wir?, 1997. Address: Alpenstrasse 15, 82319 Starnberg, Germany.

WELCH Raquel, b. 5 September 1940, Chicago, Illinois, USA. Actress. m. (1) James Westley Welch, 1959, divorced, 1 son, 1 daughter, (2) Patrick Curtis, divorced, (3) Andre Weinfeld, 1980, divorced, (4) Richard Palmer, 1999, divorced 2003. Career: Former model for Neiman-Marcus stores; Films include: Fantastic Voyage, 1966; One Million Years BC, 1967; Fathom, 1967; The Biggest Bundle of Them All, 1968; Magic Christian, 1970; Myra Breckinridge, 1970; Fuzz, 1972; Bluebeard, 1972; Hannie Caulder, 1972; Kansas City Bomber, 1972; The Last of Sheila, 1973; The Three Muskateers, 1974; The Wild Party, 1975; The Four Musketeers, 1975; Mother, Jugs and Speed, 1976; Crossed Swords, 1978; L'Animal, 1979; Right to Die, 1987; Scandal in a Small Town, 1988; Trouble in Paradise, 1989; Naked Gun 33 1/3, 1993; Folle d'Elle, 1998; Chairman of the Board, 1998; The Complete Musketeers, 1999; Tortilla Soup, 2001; Legally Blonde, 2001; Plays include: Woman of the Year, 1982; Torch Song, 1993; Videos: Raquel: Total Beauty and Fitness, 1984; A Week with Raquel, 1987; Raquel: Lose 10lbs in 3 Weeks, 1989. Publication: The Raquel Welch Total Beauty and Fitness Program, 1984. Address: Innovative Artists, 1999 Avenue of the Stars, Suite 2850, Los Angeles, CA 90067, USA.

WELCOME Menizibeya Osain, b. 12 June 1981, Yenagoa, Nigeria. Medical Researcher. Education: Leadership Training Course, Citizenship and Leadership Training Centre, Aluu, 1999; College Education, College of Arts and Science, Yenagoa, 2000-01; University of Port Harcourt, College of Health Sciences, Department of Human Anatomy, 2002-03; Diploma, Russian Language Preparatory Course, Belarusian State University, 2004-05; Latin course, Department of Foreign Languages, Belarusian State Medical University, Minsk, Belarus, 2005-08; MD course, 2005-, Experience in Fundamental Research with Professor V A Pereverzev, 2006-, Belarusian State Medical University, Minsk. Publications: 1 book, How Tom Became Rich, 2010; Numerous articles in professional journals. Honours: Award of Success, Award for Active Participation in Social Life, and First Prize for Best Essay entitled My Life and Studies in Minsk, Russian Language Preparatory Course, 2005; Award for Excellence, 2008; Travel Grant, 2008; First Prize, Republican Science Competition, Belarus, 2008. Memberships: Science Circle, Department of Normal Physiology; Belarusian State Medical University; American Academy of Addiction Psychiatry; New York Academy of Sciences; Christian Medical and Dental Association. Address: Pr, Dzerjinsky 83, Minsk 220116, Belarus. E-mail: menimed1@yahoo.com

WELD Tuesday Ker, b. 27 August 1943, New York City, USA. Actress. m. (1) Claude Harz, 1965, divorced 1971, 1 daughter, (2) Dudley Moore, 1975, divorced, 1 son, (3) Pinchas Zukerman, 1985. Education: Hollywood Professional School. Career: Fashion and catalogue model, aged 3 years; Magazine cover-girl and in child roles on TV by age 12; Numerous TV programmes and TV films including: The Many Loves of Dobie Gillis, 1959; Cimarron Strip; Playhouse 90; Climax; Ozzie and Harriet; 77 Sunset Strip; The Millionaire; Tab Hunter Show; Dick Powell Theatre; Adventures in Paradise; Naked City; The Greatest Show on Earth; Mr Broadway; Fugitive; Films include: Rock Rock, 1956; Serial; Rally Round the Flag Boys; The Five Pennies; The Private Lives of Adam and Eve; Return to Peyton Place; Wild in the Country; Bachelor Flat; Lord Love a Duck; Pretty Poison; I Walk The Line; A Safe Place; Play It As It Lays; Because They're Young; High Time; Sex Kittens Go To College; The Cincinnati Kid; Soldier in the Rain; Looking for Mr Goodbar; Thief; Author!; Once Upon A Time in America; Heartbreak Hotel; Falling Down; Feeling Minnesota, 1996; Chelsea Walls, 2001; Investigating Sex, 2001.

WELDON Fay, b. 22 September 1931, Alvechurch, Worcestershire, England. Writer. m. (1) Ron Weldon, 1961, 4 daughters, (2) Nick Fox, 1994. Education: MA, St Andrews University, 1952; CBE. Career: Numerous theatre plays and over 30 television plays, dramatizations and radio plays. Publications: Fat Woman's Joke, 1968; Down Among the Women, 1971; Female Friends, 1975; Remember Me, 1976; Praxis, 1978; Puffball, 1980; The President's Child, 1982; Letters to Alice, 1984; Life and Loves of a She Devil, 1984; Rebecca West, 1985; The Shrapnel Academy, 1986; The Hearts and Lives of Men, 1987; Leader of the Band, 1988; Wolf of the Mechanical Dog, 1989; The Cloning of Joanna May, 1989; Party Puddle, 1989; Moon Over Minneapolis or Why She Couldn't Stay, (short stories), 1991; Life Force, 1992; Growing Rich, 1992; Affliction, 1994; Splitting, 1995; Worst Fears, 1996; Wicked Women, (short stories), 1996; Big Women, 1998; A Hard Time to be a Father (short stories), 1998; Rhode Island Blues, 2000; Godless in Eden (essays), 2000; Nothing to Wear, Nowhere to Hide, 2002; Auto-da-Fay (autobiography), 2002; Mantrapped, 2004; She May Not Leave, 2005; What Makes Women Happy, 2006; The Spa Decameron, 2007; Contributor to numerous journals and magazines. Honours: DLitt, Universities of Bath, 1989 and St Andrews, 1992; PEN/Macmillan Silver Pen Award, 1996: Women in Publishing, Pandora Award, 1997; CBE, 2001. Memberships: Royal Society of Authors. Address: c/o Curtis Brown, 5th Floor, Haymarket House, 28-29 Haymarket, London SW1Y 4SP, England.

WELLBER Omer Meir, b. 28 October 1981, Beer Sheva, Israel. Conductor. Education: BA, 2005, MA, 2007, Jerusalem Academy of Music & Dance. Appointments: Resident Conductor, 2002-09, General Music Director, 2009-, Symphonette Orchestra, Raanana, Israel; Resident Conductor, Israeli Opera, 2008; Assistant Conductor to Danel Barenboim, 2008-10; General Music Director, Valencia Opera House (Palau de les Arts Reina Sofia), 2011-14. Compositions: Suite for Strings Orchestra; Bassoon and Clarinet; Piano Concerto No 1; Mandolin Concerto; Music for Ten Instruments; Oboe Quintet, The Last Leaf; Piano Trio and Accordion; Viola Concerto. Honours: American Israel Foundation, 2000-08; Classic Voice, Conductor of the Year in Italy, 2008.

WELLER Paul, b. 25 May 1958, Woking, Surrey, England. Singer; Songwriter; Musician (guitar, piano). m. Dee C Lee, 1986. Career: Founder, singer, guitarist, The Jam, 1976-1982; Concerts include: Reading Festival, 1978; Great British Music Festival, 1978; Pink Pop Festival, 1980; Loch Lomond Festival, 1980; Founder, The Style Council, 1983-89; Appearances include: Miners benefit concert, Royal Albert Hall, London, 1984; Live Aid, Wembley Arena, 1985; Film: JerUSAlem, 1987; Founder, The Paul Weller Movement, 1990; Solo artiste, 1990-; UK and international tours; Phoenix Festival, 1995; T In The Park Festival, Glasgow, 1995; Own record label, Freedom High. Compositions include: My Ever Changing Moods; Shout To The Top; The Walls Come Tumbling Down; Have You Ever Had It Blue, for film Absolute Beginners; It Didn't Matter; Wanted; Sunflower; Wild Wood; The Weaver. Recordings: Albums: with the Jam: In The City, 1977; This Is The Modern World, 1977; All Mod Cons, 1978; Setting Sons, 1979; Sound Affects, 1980; The Gift, 1982; Dig The New Breed, 1982; Snap!, 1983; Greatest Hits, 1991; Extras, 1992; Live Jam, 1993; with Style Council: Introducing The Style Council, 1983; Café Bleu, 1984; Our Favourite Shop, 1985; Home And Abroad, 1986; The Cost Of Loving, 1987; Confessions Of A Pop Group, 1988; The Singular Adventures Of The Style Council, 1989; Here's Some That Got Away, 1993; Solo albums: Paul Weller, 1992; Wild Wood, 1993; Live Wood, 1994; Stanley Road, 1995; Heavy Soul, 1997; Helioscentric, 2000; EPs and Singles: Broken Stones, 1998; Brushed, 1998; Friday Street, 1998; Mermaids, 1998; Brand New Start, 1999; Wild Wood (remixes), 1999; Hung Up, 1999. Honours include: Ivor Novello Award; BRIT Awards: Best Male Artist, 1995, 1996. Current Management: Solid Bond Management, 45-53 Sinclair Road, London W14 0NS, England.

WELLER Roy Oliver, b. 27 May 1938, London, England. Medical Practitioner; Emeritus Professor; Emeritus Consultant. m. Francine Michelle Cranley, 1 son (deceased), 1 daughter. Education: BSc, Guy's Hospital Medical School, 1959; MB BS (London), 1962; PhD (London), 1967; MRCPath, 1970; MD (London), 1971; FRCPath, 1982. Appointments: Consultant Neuropathologist, Institute of Psychiatry and Guy's Maudsley, London, 1971-72; House Officer, Junior Lecturer in Anatomy and Pathology, Lecturer in Pathology, 1961-67, Lecturer and Senior Lecturer, Pathology, 1968-72, Guy's Hospital Medical School, London; Consultant Neuropathologist to Wessex Neurological Centre, Southampton University Hospitals Trust, 1973-2003; Professor, 1978-2003, Emeritus Professor, 2003-, Neuropathology, Southampton School of Medicine. Publications: Around 200 articles in professional journals and books, 1965-2011; Editor, Neurodegeneration: Molecular Pathology, 2011. Memberships: British Neuropathological Society; Pathological Society of Great Britain; French Neuropathological Society; Swiss Neuropathological Society; German Neuropathological Society; International Society of Neuropathology; Association of American Neuropathologists. Address: Qazvin, 22 Abbey Hill Road, Winchester, SO23 7AT, England. E-mail: row@soton.ac.uk

WELLS Peter George, b. 27 April 1925, Sheffield, England. Medical Doctor. m. Finola Fidelma Ginty, deceased 2000, 1 son, 1 daughter. Education: University of Sheffield Medical School; Numerous Postgraduate Institutes from 1955-1970. Appointments: Sub-Lieutenant RNVR, Royal Navy, 1943-46; House Physician, Royal Postgraduate Medical School, Hammersmith Hospital; London Chest Hospital; Resident Medical Officer, Maida Vale Hospital for Nervous Diseases; RMO, National Heart Hospital; Registrar, General Medical Unit, West Middlesex Hospital; General Practice, West Kirby, Cheshire; Registrar, 1963, Senior Registrar, 1966-69, Deva Hospital, Chester; Senior Registrar, United Liverpool Hospitals; Senior Registrar, Walton Hospital, Tavistock Clinic, London; Consultant, Adolescent Psychiatry, Mersey and NWRHA's, 1970-1992; Seconded to create a brief for services for disturbed adolescents in the Hunter Valley, New South Wales, Australia, 1980-81; Locum Consultant, Isle of Wight, 1992, 1993; Psychiatric Adviser to Visyon, 1994-2008; Founder five mental after-care clubs and mental after-care home in Chester. Publications: Numerous articles in medical journals including: Are Adolescent Units Satisfactory, 1982; Cut Price Adolescent units that Meet All Needs and None?, 1986; Whatever Happened to the Nursing Process?, 1986; Another Big Bang, 1986; Management of The Disturbed Adolescent, 1987; Why admit to a bed? Disposal of 1000 referrals to a Regional Adolescent Service, 1989; Survival in a cold climate, 1992; Inpatient treatment of 165 adolescents with emotional and conduct disorders – a study of outcome, 1993; Henbury: History of a Village, 2003; Co-author, Two Lost Water Corn Mills, 2004; Henbury Deeds, 2004; Poetry in various poetry journals; 4 Psychiatric Films. Honours: BMA Silver Medal for film, 1969; Fellow, Royal College of Psychiatrists, 1979; Fellow, Royal Australian and New Zealand College, 1983; 'C' Merit Award, 1979; Cheadle

Royal Prize for Research Paper, 1992. Memberships: British Medical Association; Association for Professionals in Service for Adolescents; Poetry Society. Address: High Trees, Dark Lane, Henbury, Macclesfield, SK11 9PE.

WENDT Albert, b. 27 October 1939, Apia, Western Samoa. Professor of English; Writer; Poet; Dramatist. 1 son, 2 daughters. Education: MA, History, Victoria University, Wellington, 1964. Appointments: Professor of Pacific Literature, University of the South Pacific, Suva, Fiji, 1982-87; Professor of English, University of Auckland, 1988-; Visiting Professor of Asian and Pacific Studies, University of Hawaii, 1999. Publications: Comes the Revolution, 1972; The Contract, 1972; Sons for the Return Home, 1973; Flying-Fox in a Freedom Tree, 1974; Inside Us the Dead: Poems 1961-74, 1975; Pouliuli, 1977; Leaves of the Banyan Tree, 1979; Shaman of Visions, 1984; The Birth and Death of the Miracle Man, 1986; Ola, 1990; Black Rainbow, 1992; Photographs, 1995; The Best of Albert Wendt's Short Stories, 1999; The Book of the Black Star, 2002; Whetu Moana: A Collection of Pacific Poems, 2002; The Mango's Kiss: a Novel, 2003; The Songmaker's Chair, 2004. Honours: Landfall Prize, 1963; Wattie Award, 1980; Commonwealth Book Prize, South East Asia and the Pacific, 1991; Companion of the New Zealand Order of Merit, 2001. Address: c/o Department of English, University of Auckland, Private Bag 92019, Auckland 1, New Zealand. Website: www.auckland.ac.nz

WENG Yu-Chi, b. 4 November 1976, Taipei City, Taiwan. Assistant Professor. m. Wen-Ying Li. Education: Bachelor, Environmental Engineering, 1999, Master, Engineering, 2001, National Cheng Kung University, Taiwan; PhD, Engineering, Kyoto University, Japan, 2009. Appointments: Assistant Engineer, Department of Environmental Protection, Taipei City Government, 2003-04; Assistant Researcher, Taiwan Institute of Economic Research, 2004-05; Specially Appointed Assistant Professor, Graduate School of Environmental Science, Okayama University, 2004-11; Assistant Professor, Graduate School of Engineering, Hokkaido University, 2011-. Publications: Book, Towards Sustainable Municipal Solid Waste Management: An Integral Economic-Environmental Modeling Approach with a Case Study in Taiwan, 2010; Examining the Effectiveness of Municipal Solid Waste Management Systems: An Integrated Cost-Benefit Analysis Perspective with a Financial Cost Modeling in Taiwan, 2011. Honours: Excellent Paper Award, 30th Symposium of the Association of Environmental & Sanitary Engineering Research, Kyoto; Listed in international biographical dictionaries. Memberships: Japan Society of Material Cycles and Waste Management; Association of Environmental & Sanitary Engineering Research; International Society for Environmental Information Sciences; Japan Society of Civil Engineers. E-mail: clyde.weng@gmail.com

WENG Yueh-Sheng, b. 1 July 1932, Chaiyi, Taiwan. Professor of Law. m. Chuan Shu-Chen, 3 daughters. Education: LLB, National Taiwan University, 1960; Dr Jur, Heidelberg University, Germany, 1966. Appointments: Associate Professor of Law, 1966-70, Professor of Law, 1970-72, National Taiwan University; Commissioner of the Legal Commission, Executive Yuan, 1971-72; Commissioner of Research, Development and Evaluation Commission, Executive Yuan, 1972; Justice, Council of the Grand Justices, Judicial Yuan, 1972-99; Commissioner & Convenor of Administrative Procedure Act Research Commission, Judicial Yuan, 1981-92; Member, 1988-99, Standing Member, 1996-99, Council of Academic Reviewal Evaluation, Ministry of Education; Visiting Professor, School of Law, University of Washington, Seattle, 1991; Commissioner of Academic Consultation Commission, 1991-2001, Convenor, 1998-2001, Sun Yat-Sen Institute of Social Sciences and Philosophy, Academica Sinica; Presiding Justice of the Constitutional Court, 1992-99; President, Judicial Yuan & Chairman, Council of the Grand Justices, 1999-2003; Chief Justice of Constitutional Court & President of Judicial Yuan, 2003-07; Professor of Law, National Taiwan University, College of Law. Publications: Die Stellung der Justiz im Verfassungsrecht der Republik China, 1970; Administrative Law and Rule of Law, 1976; Administrative Law and Judiciary in a State Under the Rule of Law, 1994; Administrative Law I and II, 2000; Annotation of Administrative Procedure Act, 2003. Honours: Judicial Medal of the First Grade, Merit and Achievement Medal of the First Grade, Judicial Yuan, Republic of China, 1994; President, 1999-2004, Honorary President, 2004-, Chinese Society of Constitutional Law, Republic of China; President, 1998-2004, Honorary President, 2004-07, Taiwan Administrative Law Association, Republic of China; Golden Medal of the Distinguished Justice, Supreme Court of the Republic of Guatemala, 2000; Order of Propitious Clouds with Special Grand Cordon, President of the Republic of China, 2000; Chung-Cheng Medal of Honour, President of the Republic of China, 2007; Honorary President, German Academic Exchange Service, Republic of China, 2003-07; Honorary President, Taiwan Jurist Association, Republic of China, 2003-06. Memberships: Director, Chiang Ching-kuo Foundation for International Scholarly Exchange, Taiwan, 2001-2013; Society of Comparative Law, Germany; East Asia Administrative Law Association. Address: 19 Alley 9, Lane 143, Jun-Gong Road, Taipei 11655, Taiwan.

WESKER Arnold, b. 24 May 1932, London, England. Dramatist; Playwright; Director. m. Dusty Bicker, 2 sons, 2 daughters. Appointments: Founder-Director, Centre Fortytwo, 1961-70. Publications: Chicken Soup with Barley, 1959; Roots, 1959; I'm Talking About Jerusalem, 1960; The Wesker Trilogy, 1960; The Kitchen, 1961; Chips with Everything, 1962; The Four Seasons, 1966; Their Very Own and Golden City, 1966; The Friends, 1970; Fears of Fragmentation (essays), 1971; Six Sundays in January (stories), 1971; The Old Ones, 1972; The Journalists, 1974; Love Letters on Blue Paper (stories), 1974, 2nd edition, 1990; Say Goodbye!: You May Never See Them Again (with John Allin), 1974; Words--As Definitions of Experience, 1976; The Wedding Feast, 1977; Journey Into Journalism, 1977; Said the Old Man to the Young Man (stories), 1978; The Merchant (renamed Shylock), 1978; Fatlips, 1978; The Journalists: A Triptych, 1979; Caritas, 1981; Distinctions (essays), 1985; Yardsale, 1987; Whatever Happened to Betty Lemon, 1987; Little Old Lady, 1988; Shoeshine, 1989; Collected Plays, 7 volumes, 1989-97; As Much As I Dare (autobiography), 1994; Circles of Perception, 1996; Break, My Heart, 1997; Denial, 1997; The Birth of Shylock and the Death of Zero Mostel (diaries), 1997; The King's Daughters (stories), 1998; Barabbas (play for TV), 2000; Groupie (play for radio), 2001; The Wesker Trilogy, 2001; One Woman Plays, 2001; Longitude, 2002; Letter to Myself, 2004; Contributions to: Stage, film, radio and television. Honours: Fellow, Royal Society of Literature, 1985; Honorary DLitt, University of East Anglia, 1989; Honorary Fellow, Queen Mary and Westfield College, London, 1995; Honorary DHL, Denison University, Ohio, 1997; Evening Standard Award, Most Promising Playwright, 1959; Premio Marzotto Drama Prize, 1964; Gold Medal, Premios el Espectador y la Critica, 1973, 1979; The Goldie Award, 1986; Last Frontier Award for Lifetime Achievement, Valdez, Alaska, 1999; Annual pension and award for lifetime achievement, Royal Literary Fund, 2003. Memberships:

International Playwrights Committee, president, 1979-83; International Theatre Institute, chairman, British Centre, 1978-82. Address: Hay on Wye, Hereford HR3 5RJ, England. Website: www.arnoldwesker.com

WESSAPAN Teerapot, b. 8 April 1980, Thailand. Lecturer. Education: B Eng, Mechanical Engineering, Srinakhapinwirot University, Thailand, 2002; M Eng, Mechanical Engineering, Kasetsart University, Thailand, 2005; PhD, Engineering, Thammasat University, Thailand, 2011. Appointments: Lecturer, Department of Mechanical Engineering, Eastern Asia University, Thailand, 2005-. Publications: International Journal of Heat Transfer; ASME Journal of Heat Transfer; Applied Thermal Engineering; many others. Honours: Outstanding Paper Award, 23rd Conference of Mechanical Engineering Network of Thailand. Memberships: Thai Society of Mechanical Engineers. Address: 200 Eastern Asia University, Rangsit-Nakhonnayok Road, Rangsit, Thanyaburi, Pathumthani, 12110, Thailand.

WESSEX HRH The Earl of Wessex; Viscount Severn, Prince Edward Antony Richard Louis, b. 10 March 1964. m. Sophie Rhys-Jones, 1999, 1 son, 1 daughter. Education: BA, History, Jesus College, Cambridge, 1986. Appointments: Second Lieutenant, Royal Marines; Theatre production, Really Useful Group; Founder, Ardent Productions Ltd, 1993; Opened Commonwealth Games, Auckland and Malaysia, 1998; President, Commonwealth Games Federation; UK and International Trustee, The Duke of Edinburgh's Award; Chair, International Council, The Duke of Edinburgh's Award International Association; Patron, National Youth Music Theatre, National Youth Theatre, Royal Exchange Theatre Co, Manchester; Haddo Arts Trust; National Youth Orchestras of Scotland, City of Birmingham Symphony Orchestra and Chorus; London Mozart Players; Cheetham School of Music; Orpheus Trust; State Management Association; Scottish Badminton; Globe Theatre, Saskatchewan, Canada; Friends of Wanganui Opera House, New Zealand; British Ski and Snowboard Federation; Central Caribbean Marine Institute. Publications: Crown and Country, 1999. Honours: Queen Elizabeth II Silver Jubilee Medal, 1977; Commander of the Royal Victorian Order, 1989; Commemorative Medal (150th anniversary of Treaty of Waitangi), 1990; Honorary Degree, University of Victoria, Canada, 1994; Queen Elizabeth II Golden Jubilee Medal, 2002; Knight Commander of the Royal Victorian Order, 2003; Personal Aide-de-Camp to the Queen, 2004; Honorary Member, Saskatchewan Order of Merit, 2005; Commemorative Medal, Centennial of Saskatchewan, 2005; Knight of the Garter, 2006; Honorary Degree, University of Prince Edward Island, 2007; Royal Honorary Colonel, of the Royal Wessex Yeomanry; Royal Colonel, of the 2nd Battalion, The Rifles; Commodore-in-Chief, Royal Fleet Auxiliary; Colonel-in-Chief, The Hastings and Prince Edward Regiment; Colonel-in-Chief, The Prince Edward Island Regiment; Colonel-in-Chief, Saskatchewan Dragons.

WEST Bill, b. Chicago, Illinois, USA. Artist; Writer; Composer. Education: AB, English, Loyola University of Chicago; MA, English, PhD, English and American Literature, Northwestern University. Appointments: Teaching Assistant, Northwestern University; Instructor in English, The Illinois Institute of Technology and Georgetown University; Assistant Professor, English, The Illinois Institute of Technology and Loyola University of Chicago; Professor Emeritus, Loyola University of Chicago. Publications: Sacred Numbers (Great Britain); American Summer Suite, The Sparrow with the Slit Tongue, The Heians, Kaimami, The Coming of the Calling: A Tale of Christmas, Revolting Portraits; Over 1,000 poems in magazines in many countries; Poems translated into Japanese, Chinese, Korean, Bengali, Hindi, Serbian and Slovene. Honours: Conroy Memorial Essay Award; Scholarship and Assistantship, Northwestern University; Listed in numerous biographical publications. Memberships: Poets and Writers; WGA; International Artists and Writers Association.

WEST Peter Christopher, b. 4 December 1951, Kent, England. Professor. m. Susan Amanda, 1 son, 1 daughter. Education: BSc, ARCS, Theoretical Physics, 1973, PhD, 1976, Imperial College. Appointments: Academic Visitor, 1976-77, Visiting Professor, 1999, Ecole Normale Superieure, Paris, France; Postdoctoral Fellowship, Imperial College, 1977-78; Lecturer, 1978-85, Professor, 1986, King's College, London; Visiting Associate, Theoretical Physics, California Institute of Technology, Pasadena, California, 1984-85; Paid Scientific Associate, CERN, Geneva, Switzerland, 1985, 1986-89, 2000; Chalmers 150th Anniversary Professor, The Chalmers Institute of Technology, Goteborg, Sweden, 1992, 1993; Programme Organiser, Newton Institute, Cambridge University, 1997; PPARC Senior Research Fellow, 2003-06. Publications: Numerous articles in professional journals. Honours: Imperial College Scholarship, 1971-74; Governors Prize, 1973; Granville Scholarship, London University, 1973-74. Memberships: Royal Society; Fellow, Institute of Physics; Fellow, King's College, London. Address: Department of Mathematics, King's College, Strand, London WC2R 2LS, England. E-mail: peter.west@kcl.ac.uk

WEST Timothy Lancaster, b. 20 October 1934. Actor; Director. m. (1) Jacqueline Boyer, 1956, dissolved, 1 daughter, (2) Prunella Scales, 1963, 2 sons. Education: Regent Street Polytechnic, London, 1951-52. Appointments: Freelance Actor and Director, 1956-, Member, various times, Royal Shakespeare Company, National Theatre, Old Vic Company and Prospect Theatre Company; Artistic Director, Billingham Theatre Company, 1974-76, Old Vic Company, 1980-82; Director in Residence, University of Washington, 1982; Associate Director, Bristol Old Vic, 1991-; Theatre: The External King Lear, Edinburgh Festival, 1971; The Merchant of Venice, Royal Flemish Theatre Brussels, 1981; King Lear, English Touring Theatre Company, 2003; Coriolanus, Royal Shakespeare Company, Stratford-upon-Avon, 2007; Opening of St Pancras railway station as William Henry Barlow, 2007; The Lover/The Collection, 2008; The Winslow Boy, 2009; Uncle Vanya, 2012; Film appearances include: The Looking Glass War; The Day of the Jackal; Oliver Twist; Cry Freedom; 102 Dalmatians; The Fourth Angel; Villa des Roses; Iris; Beyond Borders; Endgame; TV appearances include: Why Lockerbie?; Framed; Smokescreen; Reith to the Nation; Eleven Men Against Eleven; Cuts; Place of the Dear; Midsomer Murders; Murder in Mind; Bedtime; Dickens; The Alan Clark Diaries; The Inspector Lynley Mysteries; Essential Poems for Christmas; Waking the Dead; Bleak House; Not Going Out; Going Postal; Exile; Titanic; Coronation Street; Numerous theatre appearances. Publications: I'm Here I Think, Where Are You? 1997; A Moment Towards the End of the Play, 2001; Various articles in national newspapers, National Trust magazine, Times Literary Supplement. Honours: CBE, 1984; Honorary DUniv, Bradford, 1993; Honorary DLitt, West of England, 1994; East Anglia, 1995; Honorary DLitt, University of Westminster, 1999. Memberships: FRSA, 1992-; Chairman, London Academy of Music and Dramatic Art, 1992-; Chairman, All Change Arts, 1986-99; At various times, member of Arts Council Drama and Touring Panels, various Theatre Boards; Director, National Student Drama Festival; President, Society for Theatrical Research.

WESTBROOK Roger, b. 26 May 1941, Surrey, England. Retired Diplomat. Education: MA, Modern History, Hertford College, Oxford. Appointments: Foreign Office, 1964: Assistant Private Secretary to the Chancellor of the Duchy of Lancaster and Minister of State, Foreign Office, 1965; Yaoundé, 1967; Rio de Janeiro, 1971; Brasilia, 1972; Private Secretary to Minister of State, Foreign Office, 1975; Head of Chancery, Lisbon, 1977; Deputy Head, News Department, 1980, Deputy Head, Falkland Islands Department, 1982, Overseas Inspectorate, Foreign and Commonwealth Office, 1984; High Commissioner, Brunei, 1986-91; Ambassador to Zaire, 1991-92; High Commissioner, Tanzania, 1992-95; Ambassador to Portugal, 1995-99, UK Commissioner, Expo 98, Lisbon; Chairman, Spencer House, 2000-06; Chairman, 2000-03, Vice President, 2006-, Anglo Portuguese Society; Council, Book Aid International, 2002-11; Chairman, Foreign and Commonwealth Office Association, 2003-09; Chief Honorary Steward, Westminster Abbey, 2006-; President, Hertford Society, 2009-. Honour: CMG, 1990. Address: 33 Marsham Court, Marsham Street, London, SW1P 7JY, England.

WESTERBERG Siv, b. 11 June 1932, Borås, Sweden. Lawyer. m. Per Westerberg, 2 sons, 1 daughter. Education: Medicine Kandidat, 1954, Medicine Licentiat, 1960, University Uppsala; Juris kandidat, 1982, University of Lund. Appointments: Hospital Doctor, University Clinics in Gothenburg, Sweden, 1960-63; GP, Gothenburg, 1964-79; Lawyer, Gothenburg, 1982-; Specialised in medical and sociomedical cases; Tried and won several cases in the European Court of Human Rights. Publication: Books, To be a Physician, 1977; Punishment Without Crime, 2004. Address: Skårsgatan 45, SE-412 69, Göteborg, Sweden.

WESTMINSTER, Archbishop of (RC), His Eminence Cardinal Cormac Murphy-O'Connor, b. 24 August 1932, Reading Berkshire, England. Education: The Venerable English College Rome; PhL, STL, Gregorian University, Rome. Appointments: Ordained Priest, 1956; Assistant Priest, Corpus Christi Parish, Portsmouth, 1956-63; Sacred Heart Parish, Fareham, 1963-66; Private Secretary, Chaplain to Bishop of Portsmouth, 1966-70; Parish Priest, Parish of the Immaculate Conception, Southampton, 1970-71; Rector, The Venerable English College, Rome, 1971-77; Bishop of Arundel and Brighton, West Sussex, 1977-2000; Archbishop of Westminster, 2000-; Created Cardinal Priest of the title Santa Maria sopra Minerva, 2001; Chairman: Bishops' Committee for Europe, 1978-83; Committee for Christian Unity, 1983-2000; Department for Mission and Unity Bishops' Conference of England and Wales, 1993-; Joint Chairman, ARCIC-II, 1983-2000; President, Catholic Bishops' Conference of England and Wales, 2000-; Vice-President, Council of the Episcopal Conferences of Europe, 2001-. Publications: The Family of the Church, 1984; At the Heart of the World, 2004. Honours: Honorary DD, Lambeth, 1999; Freeman of the City of London, 2001; Honorary Bencher of the Inner Temple, 2001; Bailiff Grand Cross of Sovereign Military Order of Malta, 2002; Prior of British and Irish Delegation of Constantine Order, 2002. Memberships: Presidential Committee of the Pontifical Council for the Family, 2001-; Congregation for Divine Worship and the Discipline of the Sacraments, 2001-; Administration of the Patrimony of the Holy See, 2001; Pontifical Council for Culture, 2002-; Pontifical Commission for the Cultural Heritage of the Church, 2002-; Pontifical Council for Promoting Christian Unity, 2002. Address: Archbishop's House, Westminster, London SW1P 1QJ, England. E-mail: archbishop@rcdow.org.uk Website: www.rcdow.org.uk/archbishop.

WESTWOOD Vivienne Isabel, b. 8 April 1941, England. Fashion Designer. 2 sons. Career: Developed Punk fashion in partnership with Malcolm McLaren, Chelsea, London, 1970-83; Work produced for musicians including: Boy George; The Sex Pistols; Bananarama; Adam and the Ants; Bow Wow Wow; Solo avant-garde designer, 1984-; Also worked with S Galeotti, Italy, 1984; Launched Mini Crini, 1985; Produced collection featuring Harris tweed suits and princess coats; Pagan 5, 1989; Opened own shop in Mayfair, London, 1990; Launch of debut fragrance, Boudoir, 1998; Launch of Red Label, USA, 1999; First shop in New York, 1999; Vivienne Westwood: the Collection of Romilly McAlpine exhibition, Museum of London, 2000; Launch of second fragrance, Libertine, Europe, 2000; Shop opens in Hong Kong, 2002; Shop opens in Milan, 2003; Shop opens in Liverpool, 2003; Vivienne Westwood retrospective, Victoria and Albert Museum, London, 2004; Numerous fashion shows including: London; Paris Tokyo; New York. Honours: Professor of Fashion, Academy of Applied Arts, Vienna, 1989-91; Hochschule der Künste, Berlin, 1993-; Senior FRCA, 1992; British Designer of the Year, 1990, 1991; OBE, 1992; Queen's Award for Export, 1998; Moët & Chandon Fashion Tribute, V&A, 2001; UK fashion Export Award for Design, 2003. Address: Westwood Studios, 9-15 Elcho Street, London SW11 4AU, England.

WETHMAR-LEMMER Marlene Muriel, b. 22 May 1979, Durban, South Africa. Senior Lecturer. m. Jurie Lemmer. Education: B Com Law (cum laude), 2000; LLB (cum laude), 2003; MA, Latin (cum laude), 2003; LLM International Commercial Law (cum laude), 2006; LLD Private International Law, 2011. Appointments: Tutor and Lecturer, Roman Law, University of Pretoria, 1999-2004; Senior Lecturer, Private International Law, University of South Africa, 2004-. Publications: Numerous articles in professional journals. Honours: Adams & Adams Prize, 2003; Grotius Medal of the Pretoria Bar Council, 2003; The Law Society of the Northern Provinces Prize, 2003; First Publication Award, University of South Africa Research Directorate, 2008; Listed in international biographical dictionaries. Memberships: Southern African Society of Legal Historians; Golden Key International Honour Society. Address: Postnet Suite 32, Private Bag X 025, Lynnwood Ridge, Pretoria, Gauteng, 0040, South Africa. E-mail: wethmm@unisa.ac.za

WHALLEY Joanne, b. 25 August 1964, Salford, England. Actress. m. Val Kilmer, 1988, divorced 1996, 1 son, 1 daughter. Career: Stage: Began acting during teenage years; Season of Edward Bond plays, Royal Court Theatre, London; The Three Sisters; What the Butler Saw; Lulu; TV includes: The Singing Detective; A Kind of Loving; A Quiet Life; The Gentle Touch; Bergerac; Reilly; Edge of Darkness; A Christmas Carol; Save Your Kisses; Will You Love Me Tomorrow?; Scarlett; 40, 2003; Criminal Minds, 2005; Child of Mine, 2005; The Virgin Queen, 2005; Far from Home, 2006; Justice League, 2006; Life Line, 2007; Films: Pink Floyd – The Wall; Dance With a Stranger; No Surrender; The Good Father; To Kill A Priest; Willow; Scandal; Kill Me Again; The Big Man; Navy Seals; Miss Helen; Shattered; Crossing the Line; Storyville; Mother's Boys; A Good Man in Africa; Trial By Jury; The Man Who Knew Too Little; The Guilty, 1999; Run the Wild Fields, 2000; Jacqueline Kennedy Onassis: A Life, 2000; Virginia's Run, 2001; Before You Go, 2002; The Californians, 2005; Played, 2006; Flood, 2007. Address: Creative Artists Agency, 9830 Wilshire Boulevard, Beverly Hills, CA 90212, USA.

WHATELY Kevin, b. 6 February 1951, Northumberland, England. Actor. m. Madelaine Newton, 1 son, 1 daughter. Education: Newcastle Polytechnic; The Central School of Speech and Drama, 1972-75. Career: Extensive television work including: Neville Hope in Auf Wiedersehen Pet, 1982-2004; Sergeant Lewis in Inspector Morse, 1986-2001; Steve in B & B, 1992; Dr Jack Kerruish in Peak Practice, 1992-95; Skallagrig, 1994; Trip Trap (BBC), 1996; Gobble, 1996; Jimmy Griffin in the Broker's Man, 1997-98; Pure Wickedness (BBC), 1999; What Katy Did (Tetra), 1999; Plain Jane (Carlton), 2001; Nightmare Neighbour (BBC), 2001; Hurst in Promoted to Glory, 2003; Dad, 2005; Belonging, ITV 2005; Footprints in the Snow, 2005; Lewis, 2006-13; New Tricks, 2006; Dogtown, 2006; Who Gets the Dog? 2007; The Children, 2008; Silent Cry; Theatre includes: Prince Hal in Henry IV Part 1 (Newcastle), 1981; Andy in Accounts (Edinburgh and London), 1982; Title Role in Billy Liar (national tour), 1983; John Proctor in The Crucible (Leicester), 1989; Daines in Our Own Kind (Bush), 1991; Twelve Angry Men (Comedy), 1996; Snake in the Grass (Pert Hall Co, Old Vic), 1997; How I Learned to Drive (Donmar), 1998; White Rabbit, Red Rabbit, 2013; Film: The English Patient, 1996; Paranoid, 1999; Purely Belter, 2000; Silent Cry, 2001; The Legend of the Tamworth Two, 2003. Honours: Pye Comedy Performance of the Year Award, 1983; Variety Club Northern Personality of the Year, 1990; Honorary Doctor of Civil Law, Northumbria University. Memberships: Ambassador for the Prince's Trust; Ambassador for Newcastle and Gateshead; Ambassador for Sunderland; Vice-President, NCH; Patron, SPARKS; Patron, The Rose at Kingston Theatre; Patron, Oesophageal Patients Association. Address: c/o CDA, 125 Gloucester Road, London SW7 4TE, England.

WHEATER Roger John, b. 24 November 1933, Brighton, Sussex, England. Conservationist. m. Jean Ord Troup, 1 son, 1 daughter. Education: Brighton, Hove & Sussex Grammar School, 1945-50; Brighton Technical College, 1950-51. Appointments: Assistant Superintendent of Police, Uganda, 1956-61; Chief Warden, Murchison Falls National Park, 1961-70; Director, Uganda National Parks, 1970-72; Director, Royal Zoological Society of Scotland, 1972-98; Chairman: Federation of Zoological Gardens of Great Britain & Ireland, 1993-96; Anthropoid Ape Advisory Panel, 1977-91; Editorial Board, World Zoo Conservation Strategy, 1991-93; European Association of Zoos & Aquaria, 1994-97; Access Forum, 1996-2000; Tourism and Environment Forum, 1999-2003; Beaver-Salmonia Working Group, 2009-; National Trust for Scotland, 2000-05; Heather Trust, 1999-2003; Deputy Chairman, Scottish Natural Heritage, 1997-99; President: Association of British Wild Animal Keepers, 1984-99; International Union of Zoo Directors (now World Association of Zoos and Aquaria), 1988-91; Cockburn Trout Angling Club, 1997-; President, The Scottish Wildlife Trust, 2006-08; President, The Tweeddale Society, 2007-; Chairman, The Gorilla Organisation, 2008-. Publications: Wide range of publications on national park management, environmental education, captive breeding, animal welfare, access to countryside, National Trust for Scotland Properties, etc. Honours: OBE, 1991; Honorary Professor, Edinburgh University, 1993; Honorary Doctorate, DUniv, 2004; Honorary Fellow, RSGS, 1995; Honorary Fellow, RZSS, 1999; Awards for outstanding achievement, World Association of Zoos and Aquaria, 2001; National Federation of Zoos in Great Britain and Ireland, 1998; European Association of Zoos and Aquaria, 2004. Memberships: Fellow: Royal Society, Edinburgh, 1985-; Royal Society of Arts, 1991-, Institute of Biology, 1987-; Trustee: The Gorilla Organisation, 1993-2010; Dynamic Earth, Edinburgh, 1998-; Tweed Foundation, 2007-. Address: 17 Kirklands, Innerleithen, Peeblesshire, EH44 6NA, Scotland. E-mail: roger.wheater@btinternet.com

WHICKER Alan Donald, b. 2 August 1925. Television Broadcaster; Journalist; Author. Education: Haberdasher's Aske's School. Career: Director, Army Film and Photo Unit, 8th Army and US 5th Army; War Correspondent, Korea; Foreign Correspondent, Exchange Telegraph, 1947-57, BBC TV, 1957-68; Founder Member, Yorkshire TV, 1968; TV appearances include: Whicker's World, 1959-60; Whicker Down Under, 1961; Whicker in Sweden, 1963; Whicker's World, 1965-67; 122 documentaries for Yorkshire TV; Whicker's World – The First Million Miles! 1982; Whicker's World, A Fast Boat to China, 1983; Whicker! 1984; Whicker's World – Living with Uncle Sam, 1985; Whicker's World – Living with Waltzing Matilda, 1988; Whicker's World – Hong Kong, 1990; Whicker's World – A Taste of Spain, 1992; Around Whicker's World, 1992; Whicker's World – The Sultan of Brunei, 1992; South Africa: Whicker's Miss World and Whicker's World – The Sun King, 1993; South-East Asia: Whicker's World Aboard the Real Orient Express, Whicker's World – Pavarotti in Paradise, 1994; Travel Channel, 1996; Whicker's Week, BBC Choice, 1999; Travel Ambassador on the Internet for AOL, 2000; One on One, 2002; Whicker's War Series, 2004; Radio includes: Whicker's Wireless World, 1983; Around Whicker's World, 1998; Whicker's New World, 1999; Whicker's World Down Under, 2000; Fabulous Fifties, 2000; It'll Never Last – The History of Television, 2001; Fifty Royal Years; Around Whicker's World, 2002. Publications: Some Rise by Sin, 1949; Away – with Alan Whicker, 1963; Best of Everything, 1980; Within Whicker's World (autobiography), 1982; Whicker's Business Travellers Guide, 1983; Whicker's New World, 1985; Whicker's World Down Under, 1988; Whicker's World – Take 2! 2000; Whicker's War, 2005. Honours: Various awards including: Guild of TV Producers and Directors; Personality of the Year, 1964; Silver Medal, Royal TV Society; Dimbleby Award, BAFTA, 1978; TV Times Special Award, 1978; First inductee, Royal TV Society's Hall of Fame, 1993; Travel Writers' Special Award, 1998; BAFTA Grierson Documentary Tribute Award, 2001; National Film Theatre tribute; 6th TV Festival, 2002. Address: Trinity, Jersey, JE3 5BA, Channel Islands.

WHITAKER (Baroness of Beeston in the County of Nottinghamshire); Janet Alison Whitaker, Life Peer; Member of the House of Lords. Education: Major Scholar BA, Girton College, Cambridge; Farley Graduate Scholar, MA, Brynmawr College, USA; Radcliffe Fellow, Harvard, USA. Appointments: Commissioning Editor, André Deutsch Ltd, 1961-66; Speechwriter to Chairman of the Health and Safety Commission, 1976; Head of Gas Safety, Health and Safety Executive, 1983-86, Head of Nuclear Safety Administration, 1986-88; Head of Health and Safety, Department of Employment, 1988-92; Head of Sex Equality, 1992-96; Member, Employment Tribunals, 1995-2000; Consultant, CRE and Commonwealth Secretariat, 1996-99; Member: Immigration Complaints Audit Committee, 1998-99, European Union Select Committee Sub-Committee on Education, Social Affairs and Home Affairs, 1999-2003, Joint Committee on Human Rights, 2000-03, Joint Parliamentary Committee on the Draft Corruption Bill, 2003-, Friends Provident Committee of Reference; Chair, Camden Racial Equality Council, 1999; Chair, Working Men's College, 1998-2001; Non Executive Director, Tavistock and Portman NHS Trust, 1997-2001; Deputy Chair, Independent Television Commission, 2001-2003; Vice President, British Humanist Association, One World Trust; Trustee: UNICEF; Patron, British Stammering

Association; SoS Sahel; Runnymede Trust. Memberships: Overseas Development Institute Council; Opportunity International; Advisory Council, Transparency International (UK); Interact Worldwide; Reform Club. Address: The House of Lords, London SW1A 0PW, England.

WHITE Edmund (Valentine III), b. 13 January 1940, Cincinnati, Ohio, USA. Writer. Education: BA, University of Michigan, 1962. Appointments: Writer, Time-Life Books, New York City, 1962-70; Senior Editor, Saturday Review, New York City, 1972-73; Assistant Professor of Writing Seminars, Johns Hopkins University, 1977-79; Adjunct Professor, Columbia University School of the Arts, 1981-83; Executive Director, New York Institute for the Humanities, 1982-83; Professor, Brown University, 1990-92; Professor of Humanities, Princeton University, 1999-. Publications: Fiction: Forgetting Elena, 1973; Nocturnes for the King of Naples, 1978; A Boy's Own Story, 1982; Aphrodisiac (with others), stories, 1984; Caracole, 1985; The Darker Proof: Stories from a Crisis (with Adam Mars-Jones), 1987; The Beautiful Room is Empty, 1988; Skinned Alive, stories, 1995; The Farewell Symphony, 1997; The Married Man, 2000; Fanny: A Fiction, 2003; Chaos: A Novella and Stories, 2007; Hotel de Dream, 2007; Non-Fiction: The Joy of Gay Sex: An Intimate Guide for Gay Men to the Pleasures of a Gay Lifestyle (with Charles Silverstein), 1977; States of Desire: Travels in Gay America, 1980; The Faber Book of Gay Short Fiction (editor), 1991; Genet: A Biography, 1993; The Selected Writings of Jean Genet (editor), 1993; The Burning Library, essays, 1994; Our Paris, 1995; Proust, 1998; The Flâneur: A Stroll Through the Paradoxes of Paris, 2000; Arts and Letters, 2004; Plays: Terre Haute, 2006; Contributions to: Many periodicals. Honours: Ingram Merrill Foundation Grants, 1973, 1978; Guggenheim Fellowship, 1983; American Academy and Institute of Arts and Letters Award, 1983; Chevalier de l'ordre des arts et lettres, France, 1993; Officier Ordre des Arts et des Lettres, 1999. Memberships: American Academy of Arts and Letters; American Academy of Arts and Sciences. Address: c/o Amanda Urban, International Creative Management, 40 West 57th Street, New York, NY 10019, USA.

WHITE George Edward, b. 19 March 1941, Northampton, Massachusetts, USA. Professor. m. Susan Davis White, 2 daughters. Education: BA, Amherst College, 1963; MA, PhD, Yale University, 1967; JD, Harvard Law School, 1970. Appointments: Law Clerk, Chief Justice Earl Warren, Supreme Court of United States, 1971-72; Assistant Professor of Law, University of Virginia Law School, 1972-74; Associate Professor, 1974-77; Professor, 1977-86; John B Minor Professor of Law and History, 1986-2003; University Professor, 1992-2003; David and Mary Harrison Distinguished Professor of Law, 2003-. Publications: The Eastern Establishment and the Western Experience, 1968; The American Judicial Tradition, 1976; Patterns of American Legal Thought, 1978; Tort Law in America, 1980; Earl Warren: A Public Life, 1982; The Marshall Court and Cultural Change, 1987; Justice Oliver Wendell Holmes: Law and the Inner Self, 1993; Intervention and Detachment: Essays in Legal History and Jurisprudence, 1994; Creating the National Pastime, 1996; The Constitution and the New Deal, 2000; Alger Hiss's Looking-Glass Wars, 2004; Oliver Wendell Holmes Jr, 2006; History and the Constitution: Collected Essays, 2007; Editor, Oliver Wendell Holmes, The Common Law, 2009; Law in American History, Volume One, From the Colonial Years Through the Civil War, 2012. Honours: Fellow, National Endowment for the Humanities, 1977-78, 1982-83; Fellow, Guggenheim Foundation, 1982-83; Triennial Award for Distinguished Scholarship, Association of American Law Schools, 1996. Memberships: Phi Beta Kappa; American Academy of Arts and Sciences; Society of American Historians; American Law Institute. Address: School of Law, University of Virginia, 580 Massie Road, Charlottesville, VA 22903, USA.

WHITE Marco Pierre, b. 11 December 1961, Leeds, England. Chef; Restaurateur. m. (1) Alexandra McArthur, 1988, divorced 1990, 1 daughter, (2) Lisa Butcher, 1992, divorced 1994, (3) Matilda Conejero-Caldera, 2000, divorced 2007, 2 sons, 1 daughter. Appointments: Commis Chef, The Box Tree, Ilkley, 1978; Commis Chef de Partie, Le Gavroche, 1981, Tante Claire, 1983; Sous Chef, Le Manoir aux Quat' Saisons, 1984; Chef, Proprietor, Harveys, 1987-, The Restaurant, 1993-; Co-Owner, The Canteen, 1992-96; Founder, Criterion Restaurant with Sir Rocco Forte, 1995-; Re-opened Quo Vadis, 1996-; Oak Room, Le Meridien, 1997-99; MPW Canary Wharf, 1997-; Café Royal Grill Room, 1997-; Mirabelle Restaurant, Curzon Street, 1998-; L'Escargot Belvedere, 1999; Wheeler of St James, 2002; Head Chef, Hell's Kitchen, ITV, 2007; Publications: White Heat, 1990; White Heat II, 1994; Wild Food From Land and Sea, 1994; Canteen Cuisine, 1995; The Mirabelle Cookbook, 1999. Honours include: Restaurant of the Year, Egon Ronay (for The Restaurant), 1997. Address: Mirabelle Restaurant, 56 Curson Street, London W1Y 7PF, England.

WHITEN (David) Andrew, b. 20 April 1948. Professor. m. Susie Challoner, 1973, 2 daughters. Education: BSc (1st class honours), Zoology, Sheffield University, 1969; PhD, Bristol University, 1973. Appointments: SSRC Conversion Fellow, Queen's College, Oxford, 1972-75; Lecturer, Psychology, 1975-90, Reader, 1991-97, Leverhulme Research Fellow, 1997, 2003-06, St Andrew's University; Royal Society Leverhulme Trust Senior Research Fellow, 2006-07; Visiting Professor, Zurich University, 1992; F M Bird Professor, Emory University, 1995-96; British Academy Research Reader, 1999-2001; FBPsS, 1991; FBA, 2000; FRSE, 2001; AcSS, 2003. Publications: Books and numerous articles in professional journals (http://risweb.st-andrews.ac.uk/portal/en/browse.html). Honours: Jean-Marie Delwart International Scientific Prize, Academy Royale des Sciences de Belgique, 2001; Rivers Memorial Medal, RAI, 2007; Osman Hill Memorial Medal, PSGB, 2010. Address: School of Psychology, University of St Andrews, St Andrews, Fife KY16 9JP, Scotland. E-mail: a.whiten@st-and.ac.uk

WHITNEY Stewart Bowman, b. 15 November 1938, Buffalo, New York, USA. Professor Emeritus; Expedition Leader. m. Joan Noel Conti, 2 sons, 2 daughters. Education: BA, University of Buffalo, 1961; MA, 1965, PhD, 1972, SUNY, Buffalo. Appointments: Study Director, School of Medicine, SUNY, Buffalo, 1962-65; Assistant Professor, Ithaca College, 1965-69; Assistant Professor, Antioch College, 1970-73; Professor, Niagara University, 1973-2006; Director, Niagara Research Institute, 2006-. Publications: Several book and numerous articles in professional journals. Honours: Outstanding Achievement, International Wildlife; CFLE, National Council on Family Relations; FAACS, American Board of Sexology; Alpha Kappa Delta. Memberships: National Council on Family Relations; American Board of Sexology; American Sociological Association; World Future Society; Society for Scientific Study of Sexuality. Address: Niagara Research Institute, 73 Niagara Falls Blvd, Buffalo, NY 14214, USA.

WHITTINGDALE John, b. 1959. Member of Parliament. m. Ancilla, 2 children. Education: Economics Degree, University College, London. Appointments: Head, Political

Section, Conservative Research Department, 1982-84; Special Advisor to three consecutive Secretaries of State for Trade and Industry, 1984-85; Political Secretary to the Prime Minister, 1988-90; Private Secretary to Baroness Thatcher, 1990-92; Elected Member of Parliament for South Colchester and Maldon, 1992; Member, House of Commons Select Committee on Health, 1993-97; Parliamentary Private Secretary to the Minister of State for Education and Employment, 1994-96; Elected Member of Parliament for Maldon and East Chelmsford, 1997; Opposition Whip, 1997; Frontbench Treasury Spokesman, 1998; Parliamentary Private Secretary to the Leader of the Opposition, 1999; Shadow Secretary of State for Trade and Industry, 2001; Shadow Secretary of State for Culture, Media and Sport, 2002, 2004-05; Shadow Secretary of State for Agriculture, Fisheries and Food, 2003-04; Chairman of the House of Commons Culture, Media and Sport Select Committee, 2005-; Parliamentary representative, Board of the Conservative Party, 2006; Vice Chairman, Conservative Parliamentary Party 1922 Committee, 2006. Memberships: President, Maldon District Chamber of Commerce; Patron, Dawn Sailing Barge Trust; Patron, Home-Start, Maldon; Vice-Patron, Helen Rollason Cancer Care Centre Appeal; President, Maldon Branch, Parkinson's Disease Society; Patron, Friends of St Lawrence Newland Church Trust; Honorary 'Friend of Swans', SWANS, Maldon (Sometimes We All Need Support); Patron, East Coast Sail Trust; Patron, Victoria County History of Essex Appeal Fund; Patron, Friends of St Mary's Church, Burnham. Address: House of Commons, London SW1A 0AA, England. E-mail: jwhittingdale.mp@tory.org.uk

WHITTINGTON Ralph Edward, b. 13 January 1945, Washington, DC, USA. Retired Curator. Divorced, 1 daughter. Education: High school, Surrattsville, Clinton, Maryland, 1963. Appointments: Curator, Library of Congress, retired; Consultant, The Museum of Sex in New York, 2004-; Consultant, Erotic Heritage Museum in Las Vegas, NV, 2011-. Publications: The Library of Sexual Congress, Washington City Paper, 1997; Working Girls (radio), 1997; The Daily Show with Jon Stewart, Comedy Central (Cable TV), 1999; The Librarian of Sexual Congress, Spin Magazine, 1999; Extra TV, 1999; The King of Porn: The World's Foremost Collector of Fine Tart, Penthouse.com, 2000; TV2, Hungary, 2002; King of Porn Empties out his Castle, Washington Post, 2002; The Librarian of Sleaze, Details magazine, 2002; As It Happens (radio), Canadian Broadcast Corporation, 2002; World's Largest Professionally Catalogued Collection of Pornography, Time Magazine, 2002. Honours: Who's Who in America, 2004-2009; Who's Who in the World, 2009. Memberships: Consultant, The Museum of Sex in New York. Address: 9204 Greenfield Lane, Clinton, MD 20735, USA.

WHITWELL Katherine Elsa, b. 24 May 1942, Southampton, England. Veterinary Surgeon. Education: Bachelor of Veterinary Science, Liverpool Veterinary School, 1965; Member, Royal College of Veterinary Surgeons. Appointments: Assistant Veterinary Clinician, four large animal practices in Gloucester, Herefordshire, Montgomery and Alnwick, Northumberland, 1965-68; Assistant Veterinary Pathologist, later Senior Pathologist and Section Head of Pathology, Animal Health Trust, Newmarket, Suffolk, 1968-92; Self-employed Consultant, Equine Pathology Consultancy, Newmarket, 1993-. Publications: Nearly 100 items as author or co-author including book chapters and articles in scientific refereed journals, including: Equine diagnostic and research work: Morphological studies on the fetal membranes of the normal foal at term, 1975; Causes of ataxia in horses, 1980; The collection and evaluation of tracheobronchial washes in the horse, 1984; The cervical vertebrae, 1986; Atypical myoglobinuria: an acute myopathy in grazing horses, 1988; An immuno-peroxidase method applied to the diagnosis of equine herpesvirus abortion, using conventional and rapid microwave techniques, 1992; A survey of equine abortion, stillbirth and neonatal death in the UK from 1988 to 1997, 2003; Equine herpesvirus-1 abortion: atypical cases with lesions largely or wholly restricted to the placenta, 2004; Postmortem examination of horses, 2009; Two cases of equine pregnancy loss associated with Leptospira infection in England, 2009; Abortion and stillbirths: A pathologist's overview (in book, Equine Reproduction), 2011; Palaeopathology and horse domestication: the case of some Iron Age horses from the Altain mountains, Siberia, 2000; On hares and rabbits: More cases of leporine dysautonomia, 1994; Mucoid enteropathy in UK rabbits: dysautonomia confirmed, 1996; Histopathology of grass sickness – comparative aspects of dysautonomia in various species (equine, feline, canine, leporids), 1997; Rabbits and hares (in book, BSAVA Manual of Wildlife Casualties), 2003; Neuropathological lesions resembling equine grass sickness in rabbits, 2005; Other: Glanders. (in book, OIE Manual of Standards for diagnostic Tests and Vaccines), 1996; Skeletal and dental changes in the Old Lady of Richmond Park, 1998. Honours: RCVS Specialist in Veterinary Pathology (equine), 1993, 1998, 2003, 2008; FRCVS Diploma, 1994; Diplomate, Member of the European College of Veterinary Pathologists, 1998, 2003, 2008; Richard Hartley Pet Plan Lecture and Prize, 1993; Blount Memorial Scholarship, 1995-97. Memberships: Royal College of Veterinary Surgeons; British Veterinary Association; British Equine Veterinary Association; Veterinary Defence Society; European Society of Veterinary Pathology; European College of Veterinary Pathology; CL Davis Foundation; British Society of Veterinary Pathology; Association of Veterinary Teachers and Research Workers; Royal Society of Medicine; British Mammal Society; British Veterinary Zoological Society; many others. Address: Newmarket, Suffolk, England.

WIDDECOMBE Rt Hon Ann Noreen, b. 4 October 1947, Bath, Somerset, England. Conservative Party Politician; TV Presenter; Novelist. Education: BA (Hons) Latin, University of Birmingham, 1966-69; BA (Hons) Politics, Philosophy and Economics, University of Oxford, Lady Margaret Hall, 1976. Appointments: Marketing, Unilever, 1973-75; Senior Administrator, London University, 1975-87; Member of Parliament, Maidstone, 1987-97, Maidstone and The Weald, 1997-2010; Parliamentary Under Secretary (1) Social Security (2) Employment, 1990-94; Minister of State, Employment, 1994-95; Minister of State, Home Office, 1995-97; Shadow Health Secretary, 1998-99; Shadow Home Secretary, 1999-2001. Publications: The Clematis Tree, 2000; An Act of Treachery, 2002; Father Figure, 2005; An Act of Peace, 2005. Honour: Privy Counsellor, 1997. Address: House of Commons, London SW1, England.

WIDDICOMBE (Mary Josephine) Catherine, b. 22 May 1928, Montreux, Switzerland. Educator; Consultant. Education: Certificate of Education, St Mary's College, Newcastle upon Tyne, 1948; Community Development and Extension Course, 1970, Diploma in Education, 1978; Master of Philosophy, 1984, Institute of Education, University of London. Appointments: Teacher, St Benedict's Boys School, Ealing, London, 1948-49; Various posts including: Sales and Publicity for Grail Publications, Grail Youth Movement, Ecumenical Centre Work in London, Training Officer - as a Member of the Grail Society (a Roman Catholic lay community), 1949-69; Project 70-75 (action research), 1970-76; Co-Founder and Associate Director, Avec (a service agency for church and Christian community work based in Chelsea, work with church and community organisation leaders in UK and Ireland and people from overseas), 1976-92; Freelance Consultant, Trainer and Facilitator in church and community development, Researcher and Writer, Work in UK, Ireland, Italy and Nigeria, 1992-; President of the Grail Society, 1993-96; Co-Founder, Avec Resources (resources for people working and consulting in church and community), 1993-. Publications: Churches and Communities: An Approach to Development in the Local Church (co-author with George Lovell), 1978, reprinted, 1986; Meetings that Work: A Practical Guide to Teamworking in Groups, 1994, 2000; Small Communities in Religious Life: Making Them Work, 2001; Book chapter: Practicalities of Creative Collaborative Community Living in "Creating Harmony: Conflict Resolution in Community" (ed. Hilda Jackson), 1999; Working with People for Development: a Study and Training Manual for Community Workers and Trainers, 2009; Many articles in In Touch, the magazine of the Grail. Honour: Awarded the Cross of St Augustine by Rowan William, Archbishop of Canterbury for advancing friendly relations between various Christian communities and churches, 2006. Memberships: The Grail Society; Pinner Association of Churches; Christians for a New Awareness; The Bede Griffiths Sangha; The Three Faiths Dialogue, Pinner; The Church's Community Work Alliance; Living Spirituality Network; World Community of Christian Meditation. Address: 125 Waxwell Lane, Pinner, Middlesex HA5 3ER, England. E-mail: mjc.widdicombe@grailsociety.org.uk

WIĘCEK Tomasz Kazimierz, b. 21 February 1953, Jarosław, Poland. Mechanical Engineer. m. Maria, 3 daughters. Education: MS, Rzeszów University of Technology, 1978; PhD, Military University of Technology, Warsaw, 1986. Appointments: Assistant, 1978-86, Post-doctoral position, 1986-, Rzeszów University of Technology; President, Foundation Science for Industry and Environment, 1992-; Editor-in-Chief, Informatics Control Measurement in Economy and Environment Protection, 2008-. Publications: Research works reports in professional international journals. Honours: Listed in international biographical dictionaries. Memberships: Polish Physical Association; Photonics Society of Poland; Poland Society for Measurement; Automatic Control and Robotics. E-mail: ftkwiece@prz.edu.pl

WIENER Marvin S, b. 16 March 1925, New York City, USA. Rabbi; Editor; Executive. m. Sylvia Bodek, 1 son, 1 daughter. Education: BS, 1944; MS, 1945; BHL, 1947; MHL and Ordination, 1951; DD (Hon), 1977. Appointments: Registrar, Rabbinical School, Jewish Theological Seminary of America, 1951-57; Consultant, Frontiers of Faith, television series, NBC, 1951-57; Director, Instructor Liturgy, Cantors Institute-Seminary College Jewish Music, Jewish Theological Seminary of America, 1954-58; Faculty Co-ordinator, Seminary School and Womens Institute, 1958-64; Director, National Academy for Adult Jewish Studies, United Synagogue, New York City, 1958-78; Editor, Burning Bush Press, 1958-78, United Synagogue Review, 1978-86; Director, Committee on Congregational Standards, United Synagogue, 1976-86; Consultant, Community Relations and Social Action, 1981-82, Editor, Executive, Joint Retirement Board, 1986-2009. Publications: Editor of numerous volumes of Judaica; Author of articles in professional journals. Memberships include: American Academy of Jewish Research; Association of Jewish Studies; Rabbinical Assembly, New York Board of Rabbis. Address: 67-66 108th Street, Apt D-46, Forest Hills, NY 11375-2974, USA.

WIESEL Elie(zer), b. 30 September 1928, Sighet, Romania (US citizen, 1963). Author; Professor in the Humanities Religion and Philosophy. m. Marion Erster Rose, 1969, 1 son. Education: Sorbonne, University of Paris, 1948-51. Appointments: Distinguished Professor, City College of the City University of New York, 1972-76; Andrew W Mellon Professor in the Humanities, 1976-, Professor of Philosophy, 1988-, Boston University; Distinguished Visiting Professor of Literature and Philosophy, Florida International University, Miami, 1982; Henry Luce Visiting Scholar in the Humanities and Social Thought, Yale University, 1982-83. Publications include: La Nuit (Night), 1958; Le Mendiant de Jerusalem (A beggar in Jerusalem), 1968; Célébration Hassidique (Souls on Fire), 1972; Célébration Biblique (Messengers of God: Biblical Portraits and Legends), 1976; Le Mal et l'Exil (Evil and Exile), 1988; L'Oublié (The Forgotten), 1989. Honours: Numerous, including: Prix Medicis, 1969; Prix Bordin, 1972; US Congressional Gold Medal, 1985; Nobel Prize for Peace, 1986; US Presidential Medal of Freedom, 1992; Grand-Croix of the French Legion of Honor, 2001. Memberships: American Academy of Arts and Sciences; Amnesty International; Author's Guild; European Academy of Arts and Sciences; Foreign Press Association, honorary lifetime member; Jewish Academy of Arts and Sciences; PEN; Writers Guild of America; The Royal Norwegian Society of Sciences and Letters; Founding President, Universal Academy of Cultures, Paris, 1993-; PEN New England Council, 1993-; Fellow, American Academy of Arts and Letters, Department of Literature, 1996-; Honorary Fellow, Modern Language Association of America, 1998; Honorary Member, Romanian Academy, 2001. Address: Boston University, 147 Bay State Road, Boston, MA 02215, USA.

WIGGINS Bradley, b. 28 April 1980, Ghent, Belgium (British citizen). Track and Road Racing Cyclist. m. Catherine, 2004, 2 children. Education: St Augustine's Church of England High School, Kilburn, London. Career: Bronze (team pursuit) Sydney Olympics, 2000; Linda McCartney Racing Team, 2001; Francaise de Jeux, 2002; Credit Agricole, 2004; Gold (pursuit), Silver (team pursuit) and Bronze (madison), Athens Olympics, 2004; Winner (individual and team pursuit), UCI World Cup and Track Cycling Championships, 2007; Winner (prologue), Criterium du Dauphine Libere, 2007; 3 Gold medals (pursuit, team pursuit and madison), UCI Track Cycling World Championships, 2008; 2 Gold medals (pursuit and team pursuit), Beijing Olympics, 2008; Garmin-Slipstream, 2009; Winner, British National Time Trial Championships, 2009; Winner, Herald Sun tour, 2009; Team Sky, 2010; Winner, ITT Stage 4, Bayern-Rundfahrt, 2011; Winner, British National Road Race Championships, 2011; Silver Medal (time trial), UCI Road World Championships, 2011; Winner, Tour de France, 2012; Gold Medal, Men's Individual Time Trial Cycling, London Olympics, 2012. Publications: In Pursuit of Glory, 2008. Honours: OBE, 2005; CBE, 2009.

WIGGINS Christopher David, b. 1 February 1956, Leamington Spa, England. Composer; Music Teacher. m. Karin Czok, 1985, divorced 1995. Education: University of Liverpool, 1974-77, Postgraduate, 1978-79; Bretton Hall College, University of Leeds, 1977-78; Goldsmiths College, London (part-time), 1980-82; University of Surrey (part-time), 1991-97; BA honours, Music, 1977, BMus, 1979, Liverpool University; PGCE, Bretton Hall, University of Leeds, 1978; MMus, London, 1982; FTCL, Composition, 1986; MPhil, Surrey, 1997. Career: Teacher of Music, Putteridge High School, Icknield High School, Luton Sixth Form College, Luton, 1979-95; GCSE Examiner, Music, 1989-95; Conducted various broadcast concerts by Central Music

School String Orchestra, Tallinn, Estonia, 1990-93; Education Director, Classical Music Show, London, 1993-94; A Level Examiner, Music, 1995-; Head of Music and Examinations Co-ordinator, International School, Berlin-Potsdam, 1995-98; Co-founder and Vice Principal, Erasmus International School, Potsdam, 1999-2003; Co-ordinator, with Berliner Landesmusikakademie, visit to Berlin by string ensemble from University of Surrey, 2001; Member of Senior Leadership Team, Schiller Academy, Potsdam, Germany, 2003-2004; Teacher of Music and English, Neues Gymnasium Potsdam, 2004; Inspector for Examination Centres, 2004-; I B Music Examiner, 2005-; IGCSE Music Examiner, 2006-; House Composer, Freiburg Cathedral, Freiburg, Germany. Major Compositions: About 150 compositions, over 110 performed including St-Johannes Passion, op 145, Concerto for 4 horns, op 93, Kleine Freiburger Messe, op 111, Triple Concerto, op 134; Over 90 published in total in USA, Netherlands, Germany, Sweden and UK, including music for strings, horn ensemble and choir. Recordings include: Missa Brevis op 69,Germany; Ave Maria op 70, Germany; Soliloquy IX op 94 no 9; In Einem Kripplein Lag Ein Kind op 72, Germany; Elegy op 83, Estonia; Five Miniatures for 4 horns op 85, USA; Fanfare for Quadré, op 139A, USA; Missa Cantabrica op 123; Quem Quaeritis op 160, Germany; Three Pieces for Hand-Horn & Piano op 88, USA. Honours: Allsop Prize, Composition, Liverpool, 1977; Wangford Composers' Prize, 1991. Memberships: International Horn Society; British Horn Society; Schools Music Association; PRS; MCPS; ESTA, UK; ABCD, Member of Convocation, University of London. Address: c/o Tilsdown Lodge, Dursley, Gloucestershire GL11 5QQ, England.

WIKNER Johan Nils Pontus, b. 18 June 1956, Stockholm, Sweden. Consultant. m. Birgitta Norstedt, 1985, 2 sons, 1 daughter. Education: MD, 1982, PhD, 1998, Karolinska Institute, Stockholm. Appointments: Resident, Cardiology, Karolinska Hospital, 1985-88; Resident, 1989-91, Consultant, 1991-, Endocrinology and Internal Medicine, Sodersjukhuset. Publications: Contributed articles to professional journals. Honours: Tutor of the Year, Student Union, School of Medicine, 1997, Teacher of the Year, 2007, Karolinska Institute. Memberships: Swedish Society of Cardiology; Swedish Society of Endocrinology; Swedish Society of Diabetrology. Address: Department of Internal Medicine, Sodersjukhuset, 118 83 Stockholm, Sweden. E-mail: johan.wikner@sodersjukhuset.se

WILBUR Richard (Purdy), b. 1 March 1921, New York, New York, USA. Poet; Writer; Translator; Editor; Professor. m. Mary Charlotte Hayes Ward, 20 June 1942, 3 sons, 1 daughter. Education: AB, Amherst College, 1942; AM, Harvard University, 1947. Appointments: Assistant Professor of English, Harvard University, 1950-54; Associate Professor of English, Wellesley College, 1955-57; Professor of English, Wesleyan University, 1957-77; Writer-in-Residence, Smith College, 1977-86; Poet Laureate of the USA, 1987-88; Visiting Lecturer at various colleges and universities. Publications: Poetry: The Beautiful Changes and Other Poems, 1947; Ceremony and Other Poems, 1950; Things of This World, 1956; Poems, 1943-1956, 1957; Advice to a Prophet and Other Poems, 1961; The Poems of Richard Wilbur, 1963; Walking to Sleep: New Poems and Translations, 1969; Digging to China, 1970; Seed Leaves: Homage to R F, 1974; The Mind-Reader: New Poems, 1976; Seven Poems, 1981; New and Collected Poems, 1988; Bone Key and other poems, 1998; Mayflies: New Poems and Translations, 2000; Collected Poems, 1943—2004, 2004; For Children: Loudmouse, 1963; Opposites, 1973; More Opposites, 1991; A Game of Catch, 1994; Runaway Opposites, 1995; Opposites, More Opposites and Some Differences, 2000; The Pig in the Spigot, 2000. Non-Fiction: Anniversary Lectures (with Robert Hillyer and Cleanth Brooks), 1959; Emily Dickinson: Three Views (with Louise Bogan and Archibald MacLeish), 1960; Responses: Prose Pieces, 1953-1976, 1976. Editor: Modern American and Modern British Poetry (with Louis Untermeyer and Karl Shapiro), 1955; A Bestiary, 1955; Poe: Complete Poems, 1959; Shakespeare: Poems (with Alfred Harbage), 1966, revised edition, 1974; Poe: The Narrative of Arthur Gordon Pym, 1974; Witter Bynner: Selected Poems, 1978. Translator: Molière: The Misanthrope, 1955; Molière: Tartuffe, 1963; Molière: The School for Wives, 1971; Molière: The Learned Ladies, 1978; Racine: Andromache, 1982; Racine: Phaedra, 1986; Molière: The School for Husbands, 1992; Molière: The Imaginary Cuckold, 1993; Molière: Amphitryon, 1995; Molière: Don Juan, 2000; Molière: The Bungler, 2000. Honours include: Edna St Vincent Millay Memorial Award, 1957; Pulitzer Prizes in Poetry, 1957, 1989; National Book Award for Poetry, 1957; Ford Foundation Fellowship, 1960; Bollingen Prizes, 1963, 1971; Chevalier, Ordre des Palmes Academiques, 1983; 2nd US Poet Laureate; Ruth Lilly Poetry Prize, 2006. Memberships: Academy of American Poets, chancellor; American Academy of Arts and Letters, president, 1974-76, chancellor, 1976-78, 1980-81; American Academy of Arts and Sciences; American Society of Composers, Authors and Publishers; Authors League of America; Dramatists Guild; Modern Language Association, honorary fellow. Address: 87 Dodwells Road, Cummington, MA 01206, USA.

WILBY Basil Leslie, (Gareth Knight), b. 1930, Colchester, England. Writer. Education, BA, Hons, French, Royal Holloway College, University of London, 2000; Postgraduate Diploma, Imperialism and Culture, Sheffield Hallam University, 2002. Publications: A Practical Guide to Qabalistic Symbolism, 1965; The New Dimensions Red Book, 1968; The Practice of Ritual Magic, 1969; Occult Exercises and Practices, 1969; Meeting the Occult, 1973; Experience of the Inner Worlds, 1975; The Occult: An Introduction, 1975; A History of White Magic, 1978; The Secret Tradition in Arthurian Legend, 1983; The Rose Cross and the Goddess, 1985; The Treasure House of Images, 1986; The Magical World of the Inklings, 1990; The Magical World of the Tarot, 1991; Magic and the Western Mind, 1991; Tarot and Magic, 1991; Evoking the Goddess, 1993; Dion Fortune's Magical Battle of Britain, 1993; Introduction to Ritual Magic (with Dion Fortune), 1997; The Circuit of Force (with Dion Fortune) 1998; Magical Images and the Magical Imagination, 1998; Principles of Hermetic Philosophy (with Dion Fortune), 1999; Merlin and the Grail Tradition, 1999; Dion Fortune and the Inner Light, 2000; Spiritualism and Occultism (with Dion Fortune), 2000; Pythoness, the Life and Work of Margaret Lumley Brown, 2000; Dion Fortune and the Threefold Way, 2002; The Wells of Vision, 2002; The Abbey Papers, 2002; Granny's Magic Cards, 2004; Dion Fortune and the Lost Secrets of the West, 2005; The Occult Fiction of Dion Fortune, 2007; The Arthurian Formula (with Dion Fortune & Margaret Lumley Brown), 2007; Magic and the Power of the Goddess, 2008; The Faery Gates of Avalon, 2008; Melusine of Lusignan and the Cult of the Faery Woman, 2010; Yours Very Truly, Gareth Knight, 2011; I Called It Magic (autobiography), 2011; Contributions to: Inner Light Journal, 1993-2009. Address: c/o 38 Steeles Road, London NW3 4RG, England.

WILBY David Christopher, b. 14 June 1952, Leeds, England. Barrister at Law; Queen's Counsel. m. Susan Christine, 1 son, 3 daughters. Education: Roundhay School, Leeds; BA (Hons), MA, Downing College, Cambridge. Appointments: Called to the Bar, Inner Temple, 1974;

Chairman, Criminal Injuries Appeal Panel, 2007; Bencher, 2002; Silk, 1998; Recorder, 2000; Recorder in Civil, 2001; Deputy High Court Judge, 2008. Publications: Editor, Professor Negligence and Liability Law Reports, 1996-; Professional Negligence Key Cases, 1996; Author, The Law of Damages, Butterworths Common Law Series, 2002, 2007 (online, 2010); Editor, Atkins Court Forms, Health and Safety, 2001, 2006, 2011; Munkman Employer's Liability, 2006, 2009. Honours: Member, Bar Council, 1997-99; Executive Committee, PNBA, 1995-; Chairman, North America Bar Council, 1998-2000; Chairman, Millennium Bar Conference, 2000; Judicial Studies Board Civil Committee, 2005-09. Memberships: Royal Overseas League; Pannal Golf Club; American Bar Association; International Association of Defense Counsel, USA. Address: 4 Dickens Mews, Britton Street, Clerkenwell, London EC1M 5SZ, England.

WILDASH Richard James, b. 24 December 1955, Ealing, London, England. Member of HM Diplomatic Service. m. Elizabeth Jane, 2 daughters. Education: St Paul's School, Barnes; Corpus Christi College, Cambridge. Appointments: Desk Officer, European Community Development (External), 1977-79, Desk Officer, UN Department, 1984-86, Head of AIDS Section, Narcotics and Control and AIDS Department, 1987-88, Head of Multilateral Policy Section, Eastern Department, 1992-94, Foreign and Commonwealth Office; Third Secretary, British Embassy, Bahrain, 1979-80; Third Secretary, British Embassy, East Berlin, 1980-82; Third Secretary (later Second Secretary), British Embassy, Abidjan, 1982-84; First Secretary, British High Commission, Harare, 1988-92; First Secretary, British High Commission, New Delhi, 1994-98; Deputy British High Commissioner to Malaysia, 1998-2002; British High Commissioner to Cameroon, and non-resident Ambassador to Gabon, Chad, Central African Republic and Equatorial Guinea, 2002-06; British High Commissioner to Malawi, 2006-09; British Ambassador to Angola and non-resident Ambassador to Sao Tome and Principe, 2010-. Honours: Lieutenant of the Royal Victorian Order. Memberships: Member, Chartered Institute of Linguists; Fellow, Royal Geographical Society. Address: Flat 5, 26 Medway Street, London SW1P 2BD, England. E-mail: wildash@tusker.co.uk

WILDER Gene, b. 11 June 1935, Milwaukee, Wisconsin, USA. Film Actor; Director; Producer. m. (1) Mary Joan Schutz, 1967, divorced 1974, 1 daughter, (2) Gilda Radner, 1984, deceased, (3) Karen Boyer, 1991. Education: University of Iowa; Bristol Old Vic Theatre School. Appointment: US Army, 1956-58. Creative Works: Films include: Bonnie and Clyde, 1966; The Producers, 1967; Start the Revolution Without Me, 1968; Quackser Fortune Has a Cousin in the Bronx, 1969; Willy Wonka and the Chocolate Factory, 1970; The Scarecrow, 1972; Everything You Always Wanted to Know About Sex, But Were Afraid to Ask, 1971; Rhinoceros, 1972; Blazing Saddles, 1973; Young Frankenstein, 1974; The Little Prince, 1974; Thursday's Game, 1974; The Adventure of Sherlock Holmes's Smarter Brother, 1975; Silver Streak, 1976; The World's Greatest Lover, 1977; The Frisco Kid, 1979; Stir Crazy, 1980; Sunday Lovers, 1980; Hanky Panky, 1982; The Woman in Red, 1984; Haunted Honeymoon, 1986; See No Evil, Hear No Evil, 1989; Funny About Love, 1990; Another You, 1991; Stuart Little (voice), 1999; Murder in a Small Town, 1999; Instant Karma, 2005; Will & Grace, 2002-03; TV appearances include: The Scarecrow, 1972; The Trouble With People, 1973; Marlo Thomas Special, 1973; Thursday's Games, 1973; Something Wilder, 1994-; Alice in Wonderland (film), 1999; The Lady in Question (film), 1999. Publications: Kiss Me Like a Stranger: My Search for Love and Art, 2005; My French Whore, 2007. Address: Ames Cushing, William Morris Agency, 151 El Camino Drive, Beverly Hills, CA 90212, USA.

WILDHABER Luzius, b. 18 January 1937, Basel, Switzerland. Professor; Judge. m. Simonè Creux, deceased 1994, 2 daughters. Education: Dr iur, Basel, 1961; Bar Exam, Basel, 1964; LLM, 1965; JSD, Yale, 1968. Appointments: Professor, International Constitutional and Comparative Law, Fribourg, 1971-77; Judge, Constitutional Court of Liechtenstein, 1975-88; Professor, International Constitutional and Comparative Law, Basel, 1977-98; Administrative Tribunals of Inter-American Development Bank, 1988-94 and of Council of Europe, 2009-11; Judge, 1991-2007, President, 1998-2002, European Court of Human Rights. Publications: 9 books; Co-editor, 10 books; Around 200 articles. Honours: 13 Honorary Doctorates; Award of Merit, Yale Law School; Order of Merit of Lithuania; Commander of the Order of Oranje-Nassau, Netherlands; Great Gold Badge of Honor with Sash, Austria; Star of Romania. Memberships: Honorary Bencher of the Inner Temple, London; Society of Kings Inn, Dublin; Institute of International Law. Address: Auf der Wacht 21, CH-4104 Oberwil, Switzerland.

WILES Gillian, b. 25 September 1946, Johannesburg, South Africa. Artist. m. Robin Catchpole. Education: University of Cape Town; Heatherley Art School, London; British Horse Society Instructor. Appointments: Sculptor; Group and solo exhibitions in UK, South Africa, USA and Japan; Numerous commissions and work held in public and private collections around the world. Honours: Listed in international biographical dictionaries. Memberships: Royal Society of British Sculptors; NADFAS (Arts Society). Address: 9 Sterndale Close, Girton, Cambridge CB3 0PR, England.

WILKINSON Jonny Peter, b. 25 May 1979, Surrey, England. Rugby Player. Education: Lord Wandsworth College. Career: Selected for English under-16 team, 1995; Selected for English under 18 team tour of Australia, 1997; Player, Newcastle Falcons; Selected to play for England; International debut, 1998; British Lions Tour, 2001; Player, Rugby World Cup, 2003; Irish Lions Tour, 2005. Publications: Lions and Falcons: My Diary of a Remarkable Year, 2002; My World, 2004; How to Play Rugby My Way, 2005; DVDs: Jonny Wilkinson: The Perfect 10; Jonny Wilkinson - The Real Story. Honours: MBE, 2003; International Rugby Board, International Player of the Year, 2003; BBC Sports Personality of the Year, 2003; OBE, 2004; Honorary Doctorate in Civil Law, Northumbria University, 2005.

WILLCOCKS Michael (Sir), b. 27 July 1944, Kent, England. Lieutenant General Retired; Gentleman Usher of the Black Rod. m. Jean, 1 son, 2 daughters. Education: Royal Military Academy, Sandhurst, 1962-64; BSc (Hons), London University, 1965-68; Army Staff College, 1975-76; Higher Command and Staff Course, 1988; Royal College of Defence Studies, 1991. Appointments: Regimental and Staff Appointments, 1965-83; Commanding Officer, 1st Regiment Royal Horse Artillery, 1983-85; Staff Posts, UK, 1985-89; Commander, Royal Artillery 4th Armoured Division, 1989-90; Chief of Staff, Land Operations, Gulf War, 1991; Director, Army Plans and Programme, 1991-93; Director General, Land Warfare, 1993-94; Chief of Staff, Allied Command Europe Rapid Reaction Corps, 1994-96; Chief of Staff, Land Component Implementation Force, Bosnia-Herzegovina, 1995-96; Assistant Chief, UK Army, 1996-99; Deputy Commander (Operations) Stabilisation Force, Bosnia-Herzegovina, 1999-2000; UK Military

Representative to NATO, the EU and WEU, 2000-2001; Retired 2001; Gentleman Usher of the Black Rod, Secretary to the Lord Great Chamberlain and Serjeant at Arms of the House of Lords, 2001-. Publication: Airmobility and the Armoured Experience, 1989. Honours: Meritorious Service Medal (USA), 1996, 2000; CB (Companion Order of Bath), 1997; KCB (Knight Commander Order of Bath), 2000. Memberships: Pilgrims; European Atlantic Group; Honourable Artillery Company; Honorary Colonel 1st Regiment Royal Horse Artillery; Colonel Commandant Royal Artillery; Commissioner, Royal Hospital Chelsea, 1996-99; Clubs: National Liberal, Pitt. Address: House of Lords, London SW1A 0PW, England. E-mail: willcocksm@parliament.uk

WILLIAM SCOTT Seann, b. 3 October 1976, Cottage Grove, Minnesota, USA. Actor. Films include: Born into Exile, 1997; American Pie, 1999; Final Destination, Road Trip, Dude, where's my car?, 2000; Evolution, American Pie 2, Jay and Silent Bob Strike Back; 2001; Stark Raving Mad, 2002; Old School, Bulletproof Monk, American Wedding, The Rundown, 2003; The Dukes of Hazzard, 2005; Ice Age 2: The Meltdown, Southland Tales, Lost Historical Films on the Ice Age Period, 2006; Trainwreck: My Life as an Idiot, Mr Woodcock, 2007; Ball's Out: The Gary Houseman Story, The Promotion, 2008; TV Appearances include: Unhappily Ever After, 1996; Something So Right, 1998; The Big Breakfast, 2001; The Tonight Show with Jay Leno, 2001; Diary, 2003. Honours: MTV Movie Award, 2002; MTV Movie Award, 2004.

WILLIAMS C(harles) K(enneth), b. 4 November 1936, Newark, New Jersey, USA. Poet; Professor. m. (1) Sarah Dean Jones, 1966, divorced 1975, 1 daughter, (2) Catherine Justine Mauger, April 1975, 1 son. Education: BA, University of Pennsylvania, 1959. Appointments: Visiting Professor, Franklin and Marshall College, Lancaster, Pennsylvania, 1977, University of California at Irvine, 1978, Boston University, 1979-80; Professor of English, George Mason University, 1982; Visiting Professor, Brooklyn College, 1982-83; Lecturer, Columbia University, 1982-85; Holloway Lecturer, University of California at Berkeley, 1986; Professor, Princeton University, 1996-. Publications: A Day for Anne Frank, 1968; Lies, 1969; I Am the Bitter Name, 1972; With Ignorance, 1977; The Women of Trachis (co-translator), 1978; The Lark, the Thrush, the Starling, 1983; Tar, 1983; Flesh and Blood, 1987; Poems 1963-1983, 1988; The Bacchae of Euripides (translator), 1990; A Dream of Mind, 1992; Selected Poems, 1994; The Vigil, 1997; Poetry and Consciousness (selected essays), 1998; Repair (poems), 1999; Misgivings, A Memoir, 2000; Love About Love, 2001; The Singing, 2003; Collected Poems, 2006; Contributions to: Akzent; Atlantic; Carleton Miscellany; Crazyhorse; Grand Street; Iowa Review; Madison Review; New England Review; New Yorker; Seneca Review; Transpacific Review; TriQuarterly; Yale Review; Threepenny Review. Honours: Guggenheim Fellowship; Pushcart Press Prizes, 1982, 1983, 1987; National Book Critics Circle Award, 1983; National Endowment for the Arts Fellowship, 1985; Morton Dawen Zabel Prize, 1988; Lila Wallace Writers Award, 1993; Berlin Prize Fellowship, 1998; PEN Voelker Prize, 1998; Pulitzer Prize, 2000; Los Angeles Times Book Prize, 2000; National Book Award, 2003; Ruth Lilly Prize, 2005. Memberships: PEN; American Academy of Arts and Science. Address: 245 Moore St, Princeton, NJ 08540, USA.

WILLIAMS Cynthia Ann, b. 8 December 1959, Portsmouth, Virginia, USA. Nurse. 2 sons, 2 daughters. Education: Medical Specialist Diploma, 1982; Primary Leadership Development Diploma, 1984; Licensed Practical Nurse Diploma, 1986; Basic Non-Commissioned Officers Course Diploma, 1993; Associate Arts Degree, 1994; Bachelor of Arts in Theology Degree, 2004; Nutrition and Wellness Certification, American Fitness Professional Association. Appointments: United States Army, 1981-2001; LPN, Home Health Care Pediatrics; Equal Opportunities Representative, 1996; Ordained Minister, Victory New Testament Fellowship, 2001-; Independent Distributor, Zija International; President, It's a New Day Productions; Nutrition and Wellness Counselor; CEO, KBI. Publications: Marriage – Not Just a Simple "I Do" (commentary), 1999; One of Those Women (book), 2001; Monthly articles, Freewill Fellowship Ministry On-line, 2000-2001; Relationships On-line Producer Romauld Wells; Online blog, Let's Talk About Life (www.getreadytogrow.wordpress.com), 2011-. Honours: 21st Century Universal Award of Achievement for Theology and Spiritual Healing, 2004; 2004 Female Executive Award for Theology and Spiritual Healing; Lifetime Achievement Award for Spiritual Healing and Theology; 2007 Woman of the Year in the field of Theology and Spiritual Healing; FABI; Woman of the Year 2007; Ambassador of Poetry, 2007; New Face Model for Model Productions. Memberships: Living Waters Christian Fellowship, Presidential Prayer Team; Concerned Women of America; Hampton Reads Medical Reserve Corp; Non-Commissioned Officers Association; Partner, Aaron's Army, Paula White Ministries, KCM Ministries, BELL Ministries; Life Member, IBA; Fellow, ABI; Member, Veterans of Foreign Wars; Deputy Director General, IBC; Millionaire 300; The Elite Network; 8th Wonder Medallion Club; Mentor to Millions. Address: 87 Deer Run Trail, Newport News, VA 23602, USA. E-mail: oneofthosewomen@yahoo.com Website: www.oneofthosewomen.myzija.com

WILLIAMS Gerald (Ged) Francis, b. 11 January 1964, Melbourne, Australia. Nursing. m. Grace Anne, 2 sons, 2 daughters. Education: Diploma, Applied Science (Nursing); Bachelor, Applied Science (Midwifery); Critical Care Nursing Certificate; Graduate Diploma, Public Sector Management; Master, Health Administration; Master of Laws; Diploma, Australian Institute of Company Directors. Appointments: Executive Director of Nursing, Alice Springs Hospital, 1996-2003; Principal Nurse Advisor, Northern Territory, 2000-03; Director of Nursing, Maroonday Hospital, Melbourne, 2004-07; Executive Director, Nursing & Midwifery Gold Coast Health, 2007-. Publications: 1 textbook; 7 book chapters; Over 40 articles in peer reviewed journals; Invited conference speaker at 50 occasions, 2000-10. Honours: Fellow, Australian College of Health Service Managers; Royal Australian College of Nursing; Australian Institute of Company Directors; American Academy of Nursing; Life Member, Australian College of Critical Care Nurses; Alumni, Wharton School, University of Pennsylvania, USA. Address: Nursing Administration, Gold Coast Health Service Executives, 8 Little High Street, Southport, Queensland 4215, Australia. E-mail: ged_williams@health.qld.gov.au

WILLIAMS Herbert Lloyd, b. 8 September 1932, Aberystwyth, Wales. Writer; Poet; Historian; Biographer; Novelist. m. Dorothy Maud Edwards, 1954, 4 sons, 1 daughter. Publications: The Trophy, 1967; A Lethal Kind of Love, 1968; Battles in Wales, 1975; Come Out Wherever You Are, 1976, new edition 2004; Stage Coaches in Wales, 1977; The Welsh Quiz Book, 1978; Railways in Wales, 1981; The Pembrokeshire Coast National Park, 1987; Stories of King Arthur, 1990; Ghost Country, 1991; Davies the Ocean, 1991; The Stars in Their Courses, 1992; John Cowper Powys, 1997; Looking Through Time, 1998; A Severe Case of Dandruff, 1999; Voices of Wales, 1999; The Woman in Back Row, 2000;

Punters, 2002; Wrestling in Mud, 2007; The Marionettes, 2008; Tiger in the Dark, 2010; Love Child, 2011. Television Dramas and Documentaries: Taff Acre, 1981; A Solitary Mister, 1983; Alone in a Crowd, 1984; Calvert in Camera, 1990; The Great Powys, 1994; Arouse All Wales, 1996. Radio Dramas: Doing the Bard, 1986; Bodyline, 1991; Adaptations: A Child's Christmas in Wales, 1994; The Citadel, 1997. Contributions to: Reviews and journals. Honours: Welsh Arts Council Short Story Prize, 1972, and Bursary, 1988; Aberystwyth Open Poetry Competition, 1990; Hawthornden Poetry Fellowship, 1992; Rhys Davies Short Story Award, 1995; Cinnamon Press Novella Award, 2007. Memberships: Welsh Academy, fellow; The Society of Authors. Address: 63 Bwlch Road, Fairwater, Cardiff CF5 3BX, Wales

WILLIAMS Hermine Weigel, b. 4 February 1933, Sellersville, Pennsylvania, USA. College Teacher; Writer and Editor. Performing Musician. m. Jay Gomer Williams, 2 sons, 2 daughters. Education: AB, 1954, MA, 1956, Vassar College; PhD, Musicology, Columbia University, 1964. Appointments: Teacher of Music History: Vassar College, 1954-59; Hamilton College, 1964-65; Teacher, Religion and Arts, Hamilton College, 1972-93; Scholar in Residence, Hamilton College, 1994-; Assistant to Donald Jay Grout, The Operas of Scarlatti, 1980-87; Member, international editorial board for complete works edition of G B Pergolesi; Professional accompanist, organist, choral director, area churches; Organ soloist with Utica Symphony; Solo and ensemble recitals; Freelance writer and editor. Publications: The Operas of Scarlatti, vol 6, 1980; The Symphony 1720-1840, series B, 1983; Co-author, A Short History of Opera, 3rd edition, 1988, 4th edition (greatly expanded and revised), 2003; Co-author, Giovanni Battista Pergolesi: A Guide to Research, 1989; Sibelius and His Masonic Music, 1998, 2nd editino 2008; Francesco Bartolomeo Conti: His Life and Music, 1999; Thomas Hastings: An Introduction To His Life and Music, 2005; Therese von Jakob Robinson: A Biographical Portrait, 2007; Robinson's Letter – Journal (1826-1829), 2009; Contributor to music books and journals. Honours: Maarston Fellowship; Theodore Presser Award, Composition; Commission from San Francisco Opera, 1982; Fulbright Lecturer in Musicology; Council of International Exchange of Scholars, New Zealand, 1987; Dewitt Clinton Masonic Award for Community Service. Memberships: American Musicological Society; Fulbright Association; Member, Board of Directors for the William Lincer Foundation, 1999-. Address: 7153 College Hill Road, Clinton, New York 13323, USA.

WILLIAMS John Towner, b. 8 February 1932, Long Island, New York, USA. Composer; Conductor; Pianist. m. (1) Barbara Ruick, 1956 (deceased 1974), 2 sons, 1 daughter, (2) Samantha Winslow, 1980. Education: North Hollywood High Schoo; University of California at Los Angeles; Private studies with Mario Castelnuovo-Tedesco; Juilliard School. Career: Jazz pianist in New York clubs and studios; Film scores include: The Cowboys, 1972; Jaws, 1975; Close Encounters of the Third Kind, 1977; Star Wars, 1977; Superman, 1978; The Empire Strikes Back, 1980; Raiders of the Lost Ark, 1981; The Witches of Eastwick, 1987; Indiana Jones and Last Crusade, 1989; Schindler's List, 1993; AI, 2001; Harry Potter and the Sorcerer's Stone, 2001; Harry Potter and the Prisoner of Azkaban, 2004; Munich, 2007; Indiana Jones and the Kingdom of the Crystal Skull, 2009; War Horse, 2011; many others. Honours: 5 Academy Awards; 4 Golden Globe Awards; 7 BAFTA Awards; 21 Grammy Awards; Richard Kirk Award, 1999; Hollywood Bowl Hall of Fame, 2000; Kennedy Center Honors, 2004.

WILLIAMS Michelle, b. 9 September 1980, Kalispell, Montana, USA. Actress. 1 daughter with Heath Ledger. Career: TV and film actress. TV: Baywatch, 1993; Step by Step, 1994; Home Improvement, 1995; Dawson's Creek, 1998-2003; If These Walls Could Talk 2, 2000; Films: Lassie, 1994; Species, 1995; Killing Mr Griffin, 1997; A Thousand Acres, 1997; Halloween H20: 20 Years Later, 1998; Dick, 1999; Me Without You, 2001; Prozac Nation, 2001; The United States of Leland, 2003; The Station Agent, 2003; Land of Plenty, 2004; Imaginary Heroes, 2004; A Hole in One, 2005; The Baxter, 2005; Brokeback Mountain, 2005; The Hawk is Dying, 2006; The Hottest State, I'm Not There, 2007; Deception, Incendiary, Synedoche New York, Wendy and Lucy, 2008; Mammoth, 2009; Shutter Island, Blue Valentine, 2010; Meek's Cutoff, My Week with Marylin, 2011. Honours: Lucy Award, 2000; Broadcast Film Critics Association Award, 2005; Robert Altman Award, 2008; Toronto Film Critics Association Award, 2008; Hollywood Film Festival Award, 2011; Golden Globe, 2011; many other awards.

WILLIAMS Nadine, Journalist; Author; Public Speaker; Freelance Travel Writer. m. (3) Olivier Foubert, 3 children from previous marriages. Education: Certificate in Public Relations; Bachelor of Arts in Journalism. Appointments: Journalist, The Advertiser, Adelaide, Australia, 1989-2009; Editor, PS (now Adelaide Confidential), 2 years; Editor, Looking Forward magazine, 2005. Publications: Book, From France with Love, 2007; Numerous articles on women's issues. Honours: Prime Minister's Centenary Award; Mitchell Media Award; Archbishop of Adelaide's Media Citation for Print Journalism Excellence; Runner Up, Justice Reporter of the Year and Youth Reporter of the Year Awards. Address: 18 Hawker Ave, Belair, SA 5052, Australia. E-mail: nadinefwilliams@gmail.com

WILLIAMS Robbie (Robert Peter), b. 13 February 1974, Stoke-on-Trent, Staffordshire, England. Singer. m. Ayda Field, 2010, 1 daughter. Career: Member, UK all-male vocal group Take That, 1990-95; Solo artiste, 1995-; Television includes: Take That And Party, C4, Take That Away documentary, BBC2, 1993; Take That In Berlin, 1994. Recordings: Albums: Take That And Party, 1992; Everything Changes, 1993; Greatest Hits, 1996; Solo album: Life Thru A Lens, 1997; I've Been Expecting You, 1998; The Ego Has Landed, 1999; Sing When You're Winning, 2000; Swing When You're Winning, 2001; Escapology, 2002; Live at Knebworth, Greatest Hits, 2004; Intensive Care, 2005; Rudebox, 2006; Reality Killed the Video Star, 2009; Take the Crown, 2012; Hit singles: with Take That: It Only Takes A Minute, I Found Heaven, A Million Love Songs, 1992; Could It Be Magic, Why Can't I Wake Up With You, Pray, Relight My Fire (with Lulu), Babe, 1993; Everything Changes, Sure, Love Ain't Here Anymore, 1994; Never Forget, Back For Good, 1995; Solo hit singles: Freedom, 1996; Old Before I Die, Lazy Days, South of the Border, Angels, 1997; I've Been Expecting You, Millennium, Let Me Entertain You, 1998; No Regrets, She's The One/It's Only Us, Strong, 1999; Rock DJ, Kids, with Kylie Minogue, Supreme, 2000; Let Love Be Your Energy, Eternity/Road To Mandalay, Better Man, Somethin' Stupid (with Nicole Kirman), 2001; Feel, My Culture, 2002; Come Undone, Something Beautiful, Sexed Up, 2003; Radio, Misunderstood, 2004; Tripping, Make Me Pure, Advertising Space, 2005; Sin Sin Sin, Rudebox, Kiss Me, Lovelight, 2006; Bongo Bong and Je Ne T'aime Plus, She's Madonna, 2007; Bodies, You Know Me, 2009; Morning Sun, Shame, 2010; Candy, Different, 2012. Publications: F for English, 2000; Numerous videos, books, magazines. Honours include: 7 Smash Hit Awards, 1992; 1 Smash Hit Award, 1996; BRIT

Awards: Best Male Artist, Best Single, Best Video, 1998; MTV Award, Best Male, 1998; Smash Hits, Best Male, 1998; Nordoff-Robbins Music Therapy Original Talen Award, 1998; BRIT Awards: Best Video, Best Single, 1999; Echo Award, Best International Male Rock and Pop Artist, Germany, 2005. Memberships: Equity; Musicians' Union; MCPS; PRS; ADAMI; GVC; AURA. Address: c/o IE Music Ltd, 59 A Chesson Road, London, W14 9QS, England. Website: www.robbiewilliams.com

WILLIAMS Robert Joseph Paton, b. 25 February 1926, Wallasey, Cheshire, England. Scientist; Academic. m. Jelly Klara Büchli, 2 sons. Education: BA, 1948, DPhil, 1951, Chemistry, Merton College, Oxford University. Appointments: Junior Research Fellow, Merton College, Oxford, 1951-55; Tutor, Chemistry, Wadham College, Oxford, 1955-66; Lecturer, Chemistry, Oxford University, 1955-72; Commonwealth Fellow, Harvard Medical School, USA, 1965-66; Tutor, Biochemistry, Wadham College Oxford, 1966-72; Reader, Chemistry, 1972-74, Royal Society Napier Research Professor, 1974-91; Senior Research Fellow, 1991-93, Emeritus Fellow, 1993-, Wadham College, Oxford; Visiting Professor, Royal Free Hospital, London University, 1991-95. Publications: Books: Inorganic Chemistry (with C S G Phillips) volume 1 and 2, 1966; The Natural Selection of the Chemical Elements (with J R R Fràusto da Silva), 1996; Bringing Chemistry to Life (with J R R Fràusto da Silva), 1999; The Biological Chemistry of the Elements (with J R R Fràusto da Silva), 2nd edition, 2001; Editor of several books; Over 600 articles in chemical and biological journals. Honours include: Fellow of the Royal Society, 1972; Twice Medallist of the Biochemical Society; Twice Medallist of the Royal Society; Three times Medallist of the Royal Chemical Society; Twice Medallist of the European Biochemical Societies and the International Union of Biochemistry; Named Lecturer at Numerous colleges and universities in the UK, USA and Europe; Honorary Doctorates: Universities of Leicester, Keele, East Anglia and Lisbon. Memberships: Fellow Royal Society of Chemistry; Honorary Member, British Biophysics Society, Society for Biological Inorganic Chemistry, Society for the Study of Calcium Proteins; Member, Biochemical Society; Editor of several journals; Foreign Member, Academies of Belgium, Sweden, Portugal and Czechoslovakia. Address: Inorganic Chemistry Laboratory, Oxford University, South Parks Road, Oxford, OX1 3QR, England. E-mail: bob.williams@chem.ox.ac.uk

WILLIAMS Robin, b. 21 July 1951, Chicago, USA. Actor; Comedian. m. (1) Valerie Velardi, 1978, 1 son, (2) Marsha Garces, 1989, 1 son, 1 daughter. Education: Juillard School, New York. Creative Works: TV appearances include: Laugh-In; The Richard Pryor Show; America 2-Night; Happy Days; Mork and Mindy, 1978-82; Carol and Carl and Whoopi and Robin; Stage appearances include: Waiting for Godot; Films include: Popeye, 1980; The World According to Garp, 1982; The Survivors, 1983; Moscow on the Hudson, 1984; Club Paradise, 1986; Good Morning Vietnam, 1987; Dead Poets' Society, 1989; Awakenings, 1990; The Fisher King, Hook, Dead Again, 1991; Toys, 1992; Being Human, Aladdin (voice), Mrs Doubtfire, 1993; Jumanji, The Birdcage, Jack, Hamlet, Joseph Conrad's The Secret Agent, 1996; Good Will Hunting, Flubber, 1997; What Dreams May Come, Patch Adams, 1998; Jakob the Liar, Bicentennial Man, Get Bruce, 1999; One Hour Photo, 2001; Insomnia, Death to Smoochy, 2002; The Final Cut, House of D, Noel, 2004; Robots, The Big White, 2005; The Night Listener, RV, Everyone's Hero, Man of the Year, Happy Feet, Night at the Museum, 2006; License to Wed, August Rush, 2007. Recordings: Reality, What a Concept, 1979; Throbbing Python of Love; A Night at the Met. Honours include: Several Emmy Awards; Several Grammy Awards; Golden Globe Award, 1988, 1991; Academy Award, 1998; Cecil B DeMille Award, Golden Globe Awards, 2005. Address: CAA, Creative Artists Agency, 9830 Wilshire Boulevard, Beverly Hills, CA 90212, USA.

WILLIAMS Rowan Douglas (Most Reverend and Right Honourable the Lord Archbishop of Canterbury), b. 14 June 1950, Swansea, Wales. Archbishop. m. Jane Paul, 1 son, 1 daughter. Education: BA, 1971, MA, 1975, Christ's College, Cambridge; D Phil, Wadham College, Oxford, 1975; College of the Resurrection, Mirfield, 1975; Deacon, 1977, Priest, 1978; DD, 1989. Appointments: Tutor, Westcott House, Cambridge, 1977-80; Honorary Curate, Chesterton St George, Ely, 1980-83; Lecturer in Divinity, Cambridge, 1980-86; Dean and Chaplain, Clare College, Cambridge, 1984-86; Canon Theologian, Leicester Cathedral, 1981-82; Canon Residentiary, Christ Church, Oxford, 1986-92; Lady Margaret Professor of Divinity, Oxford, 1986-92; Enthroned as Bishop of Monmouth, 1992; Enthroned as Archbishop of Wales, 2000; Enthroned as Archbishop of Canterbury, 2003-12. Publications: The Wound of Knowledge, 1979; Resurrection, 1982; The Truce of God, 1983; Arius, Heresy and Tradition, 1987, 2nd edition, 2001; Teresa of Avila, 1991; Open to Judgement (sermons), 1994; After Silent Centuries (poetry), 1994; On Christian Theology (essays), 2000; Lost Icons: Reflections on Cultural Bereavement, 2000; Christ on Trial, 2000; Remembering Jerusalem (poetry) 2001; Ponder These Things, 2002; Writing in the Dust, 2002; The Dwelling of the Light: praying with icons of Christ, 2003; Silence and Honey Cakes, 2003; Anglican Identities, 2004; Christian Imagination in Poetry and Polity, 2004; Grace and Necessity, 2005; Why Study the Past? 2005; The Worlds We Live In: dialogues with Rowan Williams on global economics and politics, 2005; Tokens of Trust: An Introduction to Christian Belief, 2007; Wrestling with Angels: Conversations in Modern Theology, 2007; Dostoevsky: Language, Faith and Fiction, forthcoming. Membership: Fellow of the British Academy. Address: Lambeth Palace, London SE1 7JU, England.

WILLIAMS Serena, b. 26 September 1981, Saginaw, Michigan, USA. Professional Tennis Player. Education: Coached by father, Richard Williams. Career: Turned professional, 1994; Won mixed doubles (with Max Mirnyi), Wimbledon and US Open, 1998; Doubles winner (with Venus Williams), Oklahoma City, 1998, French Open, 1999, Hanover, 1999, Wimbledon, 2000, 2002, Australian Open, 2001, 2003; Single semi-finalist, Sydney Open, 1997, Chicago, 1998; Singles finalist, Wimbledon, 2000; Winner, US Open, 1999, 2002, Paris Indoors, 1999, 2003, Indian Wells, 1999, 2001, LA, 1999, 2000, Grand Slam Cup, 1999; Hanover, 2000, Tokyo, 2000, Canadian Open, 2001, French Open, 2002, Wimbledon, 2002, 2003, Australian Open, 2003, 2005, Miami, 2003; US Federation Cup Team, 1999; US Olympic Team (won doubles gold medal with Venus Williams), 2000; Ranked world No 1 in 2002; 25 WTA Tour singles titles (including 7 Grand Slam titles) and US $14,789,661 prize money; Debuted The Serena Williams Collection by Nike, 2005; Numerous appearances on TV. Honours: Sanex WTA Tour Most Impressive Newcomer Award, 1998; Most Improved Player, 1999; Teen Awards Achievement Award (shared with Venus Williams), 2000; Associated Press Female Athlete of the Year, 2002. Address: c/o William Morris Agency, One William Morris Place, Beverly Hills, CA 90212, USA. Website: www.serenawilliams.com

WILLIAMS Venus Ebone Starr, b. 17 June 1980, Lynwood, California, USA. Professional Tennis Player. Education: Associate Degree in Fashion Design, Art Institute of Fort Lauderdale, 2007. Career: Professional debut, Bank of West Classic, Oakland, California, 1994; Bausch & Lomb Championships, 1996; Winner, numerous singles titles (WTA Tour) including Oklahoma City, 1998, Lipton, 1998, 1999, Hamburg, 1999, Italian Open, 1999; Grand Slam Cup, 1998; 5 Grand Slam doubles titles (with Serena Williams): French Open, 1999, US Open, 1999, Wimbledon, 2000, 2002, Australian Open, 2001, 2003; Singles finalist, Wimbledon, 2000, 2001, 2005, 2007, US Open, 2000, 2001, French Open, 2002, Australian Open, 2003; with Serena Williams, first sisters in tennis history to have each won a Grand Slam singles title; First sisters to win Olympic Gold Medal in doubles, 2000; Olympic Gold Medal in doubles, 2000; Olympic Gold Medal in singles, 2000; only sisters in 20th Century to win a Grand Slam doubles title together; US Federation Cup Team, 1995, 1999; Awarded largest-ever endorsement contract for a female athlete by Reebok, 2002; Founder, V Starr Interiors, 2002; Launched fashion line, EleVen, 2007. Honours: Sports Image Foundation Award, 1995; Tennis Magazine Most Impressive Newcomer, 1997; Most Improved Player, 1998; Sanex WTA Tour Player of the Year and Doubles Team of the Year (with Serena Williams), 2000; Women's Sports Foundation Athlete of the Year, 2000; ESPY Awards for Best Female Athlete and Best Female Tennis Player of 2001, 2002, Certificate of Achievement Howard University, 2002. Address: V Starr Interiors, 1102 West Indiantown Road, Suite 11, Jupiter, FL 33458, USA. Website: www.venuswilliams.com

WILLIS Bruce Walter, b. 19 March 1955, Germany. Actor; Singer. m. (1) Demi Moore, divorced 2000, 3 daughters, (2) Emma Heming, 2009, 1 daughter. Education: Montclair State College; Moved to USA, 1957; Studied with Stella Adler. Creative Works: Stage appearances: (off Broadway): Heaven and Earth, 1977; Fool for Love, 1984; The Bullpen; The Bayside Boys; The Ballad of Railroad William; Films: Prince of the City, 1981; The Verdict, 1982; Blind Date, 1987; Sunset, Die Hard, 1988; In Country, 1989; Die Hard 2: Die Harder, Bonfire of the Vanities, 1990; Hudson Hawk, The Last Boy Scout, 1991; Death Becomes Her, Distance, Color of Night, North, Nobody's Fool, Pulp Fiction, 1994; Die Hard with a Vengeance, 12 Monkeys, 1995; Four Rooms, Last Man Standing, 1996; The Jackal, The Fifth Element, 1997; Mercury Rising, Armageddon, Breakfast of Champions, 1998; The Story of US, The Sixth Sense, 1999; Unbreakable, Disney's The Kid, 2000; Bandits, 2001; Hart's War, Grand Champion, True West, 2002; Tears of the Sun, Rugrats Go Wild! (voice), Charlie's Angels: Full Throttle, 2003; The Whole Ten Yards, 2004; Hostage, Sin City, 2005; Alpha Dog, Lucky Number Slevin, 16 Blocks, Over the Hedge, Fast Food Nation, The Astronaut Farmer, Hammy's Boomerang Adventure, 2006; Grindhouse, Perfect Stranger, Die Hard 4.0, Nancy Drew, Planet Terror, 2007; Assassination of a High School President, 2008; Surrogates, 2009; Cop Out, 2010; The Expendables, 2010; Catch.44, 2011; Moonrise Kingdom, Lay The Favorite, The Expendables 2, The Cold Light of Day, Looper, Fire with Fire, 2012; A Good Day to Die Hard, GI Joe: Retaliation, RED 2, 2013; TV: Trackdown (film); Miami Vice (series); The Twilight Zone (series); Moonlighting (series), 1985-89; Friends (guest), 2000; That '70s Show, 2005; Recordings: The Return of Bruno, 1987; If It Don't Kill You, It Just Makes You Stronger, 1989. Honours include: People's Choice Award, 1986; Emmy Award, 1987; Golden Globe Award, 1987.

WILLMOT William Clarence, b. 26 June 1925, Elizabeth, New Jersey, USA. Technical Writer; Editor. m. Florence C Veverka, 1948, deceased 2009. Education: LLB, Blackstone School of Law, 1958; BGS, Rollins College, Florida, 1967; MS, Florida Institute of Technology, 1970; MEd, Stetson University, Florida, 1972; PhD, Hawaii University, Hawaii, 1997; PhD, Chapel Christian University, 1998. Appointments: US Army, World War II, 1943-46; Small Arms Disassembler, Small Arms Assembler, Small Arms Inspector, Weapons Specialist, Technical Writer, Systems Improvement Officer, Chief, Program Management Office, Raritan Arsenal, Metuchen, New Jersey, 1947-61; Technical Writer, Ordnance, Picatinny Arsenal, Dover, New Jersey, 1961-62; Technical Writer, Supervisory Technical Editor, Program Management Specialist, Emergency Preparedness Officer, John F Kennedy Space Center, 1962-79; Technical Editor, Pan Am World Services, Florida, 1983-88; Technical Editor, Computer Sciences Raytheon (CSR), Florida, 1988-95; Communication Consultant, Merritt Island, Florida, 1995-; Adjunct Instructor, Brevard Community College, Cocoa, Florida, 1988-2001; Adjunct Instructor, University Central Florida, 1998-2001. Honours: Bronze Star Medal, US Army, New Guinea Campaign, World War II, 1944; Superior Achievement Award, NASA, 1970; Group Achievement Award, NASA, 1972; Distinguished Service Medal, State of New Jersey, Trenton, 1994; International Man of Year Award, IBC, 1997-98; Man of Year Award, ABI, 1998. Memberships: Fellow, ABI, Radio Club of America; Life Member, Society of Wireless Pioneers, Quarter Century Wireless Association, US Army Signal Corps Association; Psi Chi; Board of Directors, Chapel Christian University; Member, Board of Directors, Military Society of the Blue Badge. Address: 1630 Venus Street, Merritt Island, FL 32953-3162, USA.

WILSON A(ndrew) N(orman), b. 27 October 1950, England. Author. m. (1) Katherine Duncan-Jones, 2 daughters, (2) Ruth Alexander Guilding, 1991, 1 daughter. Education: MA, New College, Oxford. Appointments: Lecturer, St Hugh's College and New College, Oxford, 1976-81; Literary Editor, The Spectator, 1981-83. Publications: The Sweets of Pimlico (novel), 1977; Unguarded Hours (novel), 1978; Kindly Light (novel), 1979; The Laird of Abbotsford, 1980; The Healing Art (novel), 1980; Who Was Oswald Fish (novel), 1981; Wise Virgin (novel), 1982; A Life of John Milton, 1983; Scandal (novel), 1983; Hilaire Belloc, 1984; Gentlemen in England (novel), 1985; Love Unknown (novel), 1986; The Church in Crisis (co-author), 1986; Stray (novel), 1987; Landscape in France, 1987; Incline Our Hearts (novel), 1987; Penfriends from Porlock: Essays and Reviews, 1977-86, 1988; Tolstoy: A Biography, 1988; Eminent Victorians, 1989; C S Lewis: A Biography, 1990; A Bottle in the Smoke (novel), 1990; Against Religion, 1991; Daughters of Albion (novel), 1991; Jesus, 1992; The Vicar of Sorrows (novel), 1993; The Faber Book of Church and Clergy, 1992; The Rise and Fall of the House of Windsor, 1993; The Faber Book of London (editor), 1993; Hearing Voices (novel), 1995; Paul: The Mind of the Apostle, 1997; Dream Children (novel), 1998; God's Funeral, 1999; The Victorians, 2002; Beautiful Shadow: A Life of Patricia Highsmith, 2003; My Name is Legion, 2004; Iris Murdoch as I Knew Her, 2004; London: A Short History, 2004; A Jealous Ghost, 2005; After the Victorians, 2005; Betjeman, 2006; Winnie and Wolf, 2007; Columnist for London Evening Standard; Occasional contributor to Daily Mail, Times Literary Supplement; New Statesman, The Spectator and The Observer. Honours: Royal Society of Literature, fellow, 1981; Whitbread Biography Award, 1988. Address: 5 Regent's Park Terrace, London, NW1 7EE, England.

DICTIONARY OF INTERNATIONAL BIOGRAPHY 36th EDITION

WILSON Arnold Perken, b. 15 February 1932, Dulwich, England. Retired Art Gallery Director. m. (1) 2 daughters, (2) Alexandra. Education: Selwyn College, Cambridge University; Courtauld Institute of Art, London. Appointments: Curator, William Morris Gallery, London; Curator of Art, Director, Bristol City Art Gallery. Publications: Dictionary of British Marine Painters; Dictionary of British Military Painters; Exploring Museums: South West England; Numerous articles in professional journals. Honours: Fellow, Society of Antiquaries of London; Fellow, Museums Association. Memberships: Past Chairman of Trustees, Holburne Museum of Art, Bath; Past Trustee, Bath Preservation Trust. Address: St Winifred's Well Cottage, Winifred's Lane, Bath, BA1 5SE, England.

WILSON Brian, b. 20 June 1942, Inglewood, California, USA. Musician (bass, keyboards); Singer; Composer. Founder member, the Beach Boys, 1961-; Retired from live performance, to concentrate on composing and recording, 1964-; Appearances include: Australian tour, 1964; Headlines Million Dollar Party, Honolulu, 1964; US tour, 1964; Established Brother Records label, 1967; Concert at International Center, Honolulu, 1967; Plays with Beach Boys, Whiskey-A-Go-Go, Los Angeles, 1970; Filmed for NBC Special, 1976; Presenter, Don Kirshner's Second Annual Rock Music Awards, Hollywood, 1976; 15th Anniversary Beach Boys show, 1976; Rejoins band for US concerts, 1989; Solo appearance, China Club, Hollywood, 1991; Documentaries include: Prime Time Live, ABC, 1991; I Just Wasn't Made For These Times, BBC, 1995; Performed at Live 8, Germany, 2005; Debut of That Lucky Old Sun (Narrative), Royal Festival Hall, London, 2007; Free concert, Sydney Festival, Australia, 2008. Compositions: Many hit songs include: Caroline No; Co-writer, California Girls; Good Vibrations; Fun Fun Fun. Recordings: Albums include: Surfin' Safari, 1962; Surfer Girl, 1963; Little Deuce Coupe, 1963; Shut Down Vol 2, 1964; All Summer Long, 1964; Surfin' USA, 1965; Beach Boys Party, 1966; Pet Sounds, 1966; Beach Boys Today!, 1966; Smile, 1967; Surfer Girl, 1967; Smiley Smile, 1967; Wild Honey, 1968; 15 Big Ones, 1976; The Beach Boys Love You, 1977; Solo albums: Brian Wilson, 1988; I Just Wasn't Made For These Times, 1995; Imagination, 1998; Gettin' in Over My Head, 2004; SMiLE, 2004; What I Really Want for Christmas, 2005; Contributor, vocals for film soundtrack Shell Life; Singles include: Surfin' USA; Surfer Girl; Little Deuce Coupe; In My Room; I Get Around; When I Grow Up To Be A Man; Dance Dance Dance; Producer: Help Me Rhonda; Barbara Ann; Caroline No; Sloop John B; God Only Knows; Good Vibrations; Wouldn't It Be Nice; Friends; Do It Again; I Can Hear Music; Brian Wilson, 1988; Sweet Insanity, 1990; I Just Wasn't Made for These Times, 1995; Orange Crate Art, 1995. Honours include: Rock And Roll Hall Of Fame, 1988; Special Award Of Merit, 1988; Grammy Award, Best Rock Instrumental Performance, 2005; UK Hall of Fame, 2006; Lifetime of Contributions to American culture through the performing arts in music, Kennedy Center Honors, 2007. Current Management: Elliott Lott, Boulder Creek Entertainment Corp, 4860 San Jacinto Circle West, Fallbrook, CA 92028, USA.

WILSON Colin Henry, b. 26 July 1931, Leicester, England. Author. m. (1) Dorothy Betty Troop, 1 son, (2) Joy Stewart, 2 sons, 1 daughter. Appointments: Visiting Professor, Hollins College, Virginia, 1966-67, University of Washington, Seattle, 1967, Dowling College, Majorca, 1969, Rutgers University, New Jersey, 1974. Publications: The Outsider, 1956; Religion and the Rebel, 1957; The Age of Defeat, 1959; Ritual in the Dark, 1960; The Strength to Dream, 1962; Origins of the Sexual Impulse, 1963; Necessary Doubt, 1964; Eagle and the Earwig, 1965; The Glass Cage, 1966; Sex and the Intelligent Teenager, 1966; Voyage to a Beginning, 1969; Hermann Hesse, 1973; Strange Powers, 1973; The Space Vampires, 1976; Mysteries, 1978; Starseekers, 1980; Access to Inner Worlds, 1982; Psychic Detectives, 1983; The Essential Colin Wilson, 1984; Rudolf Steiner: The Man and His Work, 1985; An Encyclopedia of Scandal (with Donald Seaman), 1986; Spider World: The Tower, 1987; Aleister Crowley - The Man and the Myth, 1987; An Encyclopedia of Unsolved Mysteries (with Damon Wilson), 1987; Marx Refuted, 1987; Written in Blood (with Donald Seaman), 1989; The Misfits - A Study of Sexual Outsiders, 1988; Beyond the Occult, 1988; The Serial Killers, 1990; Spiderworld: The Magician, 1991; The Strange Life of P D Ouspensky, 1993; Unsolved Mysteries Past and Present (with Damon Wilson), 1993; Atlas of Holy Places and Sacred Sites, 1996; From Atlantis to the Sphinx, 1996; Alien Dawn, 1998; The Devil's Party, 2000; Atlantis Blueprint (with Rand Fle'math), 2000; Spiderworld: Shadowland, 2003; Autobiography Dreaming to some Purpose, 2004; Atlantis and the Kingdom of the Neanderthals, 2006; Crimes of Passion: The Thin Line Between Love and Hate, 2006; The Rise and Fall of the Angry Young Men, 2007; Serial Killer Investigations, 2007. Contributions to: The Times; Daily Mail. Membership: Society of Authors. Address: Tetherdown, Trewallock Lane, Gorran Haven, Cornwall, PL26 6NT, England.

WILSON OF TILLYORN, Baron (Life Peer) of Finzean in the District of Kincardine and Deeside and of Fanling in Hong Kong, Sir David Clive Wilson, b. 14 February 1935. m. Natasha Helen Mary Alexander, 2 sons. Education: Scholar, MA, Keble College, Oxford; University of Hong Kong; Visiting Scholar, Columbia University New York, USA; PhD, University of London. Appointments: HM Diplomatic Service: Joined SE Asia Department, Foreign Office, 1958; Third Secretary, Vientiane, 1959-60; Language Student, Hong Kong, 1960-62; Third then Second Secretary, Peking, 1963-65; First Secretary, Far Eastern Department, 1965-68, resigned 1968; Editor, The China Quarterly, Contemporary China Institute SOAS, University of London, 1968-74; Rejoined HM Diplomatic Service, 1974; Cabinet Office, 1974-77; Political Adviser, Hong Kong, 1977-81; Head, Southern European Department, Foreign and Commonwealth Office 1981-84; Assistant Under Secretary of State responsible for Asia and the Pacific, Foreign and Commonwealth Office, 1984-87; Governor and Commander in Chief of Hong Kong, 1987-92; Member of the Board, British Council, 1993-2002, Chairman, Scottish Committee, 1993-2002; Council, CBI Scotland, 1993-92; Prime Minister's Advisory Committee on Business Appointments, 2000-; Chairman, Scottish and Southern Energy (formerly Scottish Hydro-Electric), 1993-2000; Director, Martin Currie Pacific Trust plc, 1993-2003; Chancellor, University of Aberdeen, 1997-; Master, Peterhouse, Cambridge, 2002-. Honours: CMG, 1985; KCMG, 1987; GCMG, 1991; Life Peer, 1992; KT, 2000; Honorary Fellow, Keble College, Oxford, 1987; KStJ, 1987; Honorary LLD, University of Aberdeen, 1990, University of Abertay Dundee, 1995, Chinese University of Hong Kong, 1996; Honorary DLitt, University of Sydney, 1991; FRSE, 2000; Burgess, Guild of City of Aberdeen, 2004; Honorary degree, University on Hong Kong, 2006. Memberships: President: Bhutan Society of the UK, 1993-, Hong Kong Society, 1994-, Hong Kong Association, 1994-; Vice-President, RSGS, 1996; Chairman of Trustees, National Museums of Scotland, 2002-; Chairman, Council of Glenalmond College, 2000-05, Scottish Peers' Association, 2000-2002; Member, Carnegie Trust for the Universities of Scotland, 2000-; Registrar, Order of St Michael and St George, 2001-. Address: House of Lords, London SW1A 0PW, England or The Master's Lodge, Peterhouse, Cambridge, CB2 1QY, England.

WILSON George Douglas, b. 8 November 1936. Painter. m. Heather Hildersley Brown, 1 son. Education: Ruskin School of Fine Art; Oxford University, 1959-62. Appointments: Painter in oil and watercolour; Solo and group exhibitions include: RA, RBA, ROI, R Cam A, Vis Art I, Edinburgh Festival, National Library of Wales and galleries in London and the UK; Works held in public and private collections in Britain and abroad. Publications: Author, Wirral Visions. Memberships: Royal Cambrian Academy. Address: 123 Masons Place, Newport, Shropshire, TF10 7JX, England. Website: www.oddyart.com

WILSON Jim C, b. 16 July 1948, Edinburgh, Scotland. Writer; Poet. m. Mik Kerr, 1971. Education: MA, Honours, English Language and Literature, University of Edinburgh, 1971. Appointments: Lecturer, English Telford College, Edinburgh, 1972-81; Writer-in-Residence, Stirling District, 1989-91; Creative Writing Tutor, University of Edinburgh, 1994-; Royal Literary Fund Fellow, 2001-07. Publications: The Loutra Hotel, 1988; Six Twentieth Century Poets; Cellos in Hell, 1993; A Book of Scottish Verse, 2001; Poems in The Edinburgh Book of Twentieth-Century Scottish Poetry, 2005; Paper Run, 2007; Contributions to: Scotsman; The Herald; Chapman; Lines Review; Radical Scotland; Times Educational Supplement; Cencrastus; Outposts; Orbis; Acumen; Rialto; Poetry Canada Review; Envoi; 2 Plus 2; Poet's Voice; Iron; Stand; Encounter; Literary Review; Imago (Australia); Prose Publications: The Happy Land, 1991; Spalebone Days, 2002. Honours: Scottish Arts Council Writer's Bursary, 1987, 1994; 1st Prize Scottish International Open Poetry Competition, 1997, 2005; 1st Prize, Swanage Arts Festival Literary Competition, 1988, 1989, 1997; Hugh MacDiarmid Trophy for Poetry, 1997, 2005; 1st Prize, Scottish National Galleries Competition, 2006. Memberships: Edinburgh's Shore Poets. Address: 25 Muirfield Park, Gullane, East Lothian EH31 2DY, Scotland. Website: www.jimcwilson.com

WILSON Peter Robert Russell, b. 15 September 1986, Dorset, England. Sport Shooter. Education: Millfield School, Somerset; The Arts University College, Bournemouth. Career: European Junior Champion, Slovenia, 2006; 4th, European Shooting Championships, Belgrade, 2011; Silver, World Cup, Chile, 2012; Silver (team double trap), European Championship, Belgrade, 2011; Gold medal (double trap), London Olympics, 2012.

WILSON Robert Woodrow, b. 10 January 1936, USA. Radioastronomer. m. Elizabeth Rhoads Sawin, 1958, 2 sons, 1 daughter. Education: Bachelor's Degree, Rice University, 1957; PhD, California Institute of Technology, 1962. Appointments: Technical Staff, Bell Telephone Laboratory, Holmdel, New Jersey, 1963, Head, Radiophysics Department, 1976-94; Senior Scientist, Harvard-Smithsonian Center for Astrophysics, 1994-; Detected cosmic microwave background radiation, supposedly a residue of the Big Bang. Publications: Numerous articles in scientific journals. Memberships: NAS; American Astronomical Society; American Physical Society; International Astronomical Union. Honours: Henry Draper Award, National Academy of Sciences, 1977; Herschel Award, Royal Astronomical Society, 1977; Joint Winner, Nobel Prize for Physics, 1978. Address: Harvard-Smithsonian Center for Astrophysics, 60 Garden Street #42, Cambridge, MA 02138, USA.

WILTON James Andrew Rutley, b. Farnham, Surrey, England. Visiting Research Fellow, Tate. Education: Dulwich College, 1953-60; Trinity College, Cambridge, 1960-64. Appointments: Assistant Keeper, Walker Art Gallery, Liverpool, 1965-67; Assistant Keeper, Prints & Drawings, British Museum, 1967-76, 1981-85; Curator of Prints & Drawings, Yale Center for British Art, New Haven, Connecticut, USA, 1976-80; Curator, Turner Collection, Clore Gallery, 1986-89; Keeper, British Collection, Tate Gallery, 1989-98; Senior Research Fellow, Tate, 1998-2002, Visiting Research Fellow, Tate, London, 2003-. Publications: Turner Bicentenary Exhibition, 1974-75; British Watercolours 1750-1850, 1977; The Life and Works of J M W Turner, 1979; The Age of Rossetti, Burne-Jones & Watts, 1997; American Sublime, 2002; Five Centuries of British Painting, 2001; Turner as Draughtsman, 2006. Honours: Axa Prize, 2002; Henry Russell Hitchcock Prize, 2002-03. Memberships: Fellow, Society of Antiquaries; Honorary Curator of Prints & Drawings, Royal Academy, London; Honorary Curator & Honorary Liveryman, Worshipful Company of Painter-Stainers; Honorary Member, RWS.

WIMBUSH Stuart Christopher, b. 6 August 1976, Bellshill, Scotland. Research Scientist. m. Makiko Moroto. Education: M Phys, University of Salford, England, 1998; Dr rer nat, TU Dresden, Germany, 2004. Appointments: ICYS Research Fellow, National Institute for Materials Science, Japan, 2004-06; Research Fellow, University of Cambridge, England, 2006-. Publications: Over 50 scientific papers. Memberships: Institute of Physics; Chartered Physicist; Associate of the High Education Academy; Member, St John's College, Cambridge. Address: Department of Materials Science & Metallurgy, University of Cambridge, Pembroke Street, Cambridge, CB2 3QZ, England, E-mail: scw42@cam.ac.uk

WINCH Donald Norman, b. 15 April 1935, London, England. Professor of the History of Economics. m. Doreen Lidster, 1983. Education: BSc, London School of Economics and Political Science, 1956; PhD, Princeton University, 1960. Appointments: Visiting Lecturer, University of California, Berkeley, 1959-60; Lecturer in Economics, University of Edinburgh, 1960-63; Lecturer, 1963-66, Reader, 1966-69, Dean, School of Social Sciences, 1968-74, Professor of the History of Economics, 1969-, Pro-Vice-Chancellor, Arts and Social Studies, 1986-89, University of Sussex; Publications Secretary, Royal Economic Society, 1971-; Visiting Fellow, Institute for Advanced Study, Princeton, New Jersey, 1974-75, King's College, Cambridge, 1983, Australian National University, 1983, St Catharine's College, Cambridge, 1989, All Souls College, Oxford, 1994; Review Editor, Economic Journal, 1976-83; British Council Distinguished Visiting Fellow, Kyoto University, 1992; Carlyle Lecturer, University of Oxford, 1995. Publications: Classical Political Economy and Colonies, 1965; James Mill: Selected Economic Writings (editor), 1966; Economics and Policy, 1969; The Economic Advisory Council 1930-1939 (with S K Howson), 1976; Adam Smith's Politics, 1978; That Noble Science of Politics (with S Collini and J W Burrow), 1983; Malthus, 1987; Riches and Poverty, 1996. Contributions to: Many learned journals. Honours: British Academy, fellow, 1986-, vice president, 1993-94; Royal Historical Society, fellow, 1987-. Address: c/o Arts B, University of Sussex, Brighton BN1 9QN, England.

WINEGARTEN Renee, b. 23 June 1922, London, England. Literary Critic; Author. m. Asher Winegarten, deceased, 1946. Education: BA, 1943, PhD, 1950, Girton College, Cambridge. Publications: French Lyric Poetry in the Age of Malherbe, 1954; Writers and Revolution, 1974; The Double Life of George Sand, 1978; Madame de Staël, 1985; Simone de Beauvoir: A Critical View, 1988; Accursed Politics: Some French Women Writers and Political Life 1715-1850, 2003; Germaine de Staël and Benjamin Constant, 2008;

DICTIONARY OF INTERNATIONAL BIOGRAPHY 36th EDITION

Contributions to: Journals. Memberships: George Sand Association; Society of Authors; Authors Guild. Address: 12 Heather Walk, Edgware, Middlesex HA8 9TS, England.

WINFREY Oprah, b. 29 January 1954, Missouri, USA. Talk Show Host; Actress. Education: Tennessee State University. Career: Radio WVOL while at University in Tennessee, then on TV Stations: WTVF-TV Nashville as Reporter and Anchor, WJZ-TV Balt News, Co-anchor, 1976; People are Talking, Co-host, 1978; AM Chicago, Host, show re-named The Oprah Winfrey Show, 1985-; formed Harpo Productions, Owner/Producer, 1986; Founder, Editing Director, The Oprah Magazines, 2000-; Partner, Oxygen Media, 2000-; Producer of several TV films; Actress: The Color Purple, 1985; Native Son, 1986; The Woman of Brewster Place, TV, 1989; Throw Momma From the Train, 1988; Listen Up: The Lives of Quincy Jones, 1990; Beloved, 1998; Their Eyes Were Watching God, 2005; Charlotte's Web (voice), 2006; Bee Movie (voice), 2007. Publications: Oprah, 1993; In the Kitchen with Rosie, 1996; Make the Connection, 1996. Honours: Numerous awards including: International Radio and Television Society's Broadcaster of the Year Award, 1988; Lifetime Achievement Award, National Academy of TV Arts and Sciences, 1998. Address: Harpo Productions, 110 N Carpenter Street, Chicago, IL 60607, USA.

WING Robert Farquhar, b. 31 October 1939, New Haven, Connecticut, USA. Astronomer. m. Ingrid McCowen Wing, deceased, 2 sons, 1 daughter. Education: BS, Yale University, 1961; Attended Cambridge University, 1961-62; PhD, University of California, Berkeley, 1967. Appointments: Assistant Professor, 1967-71, Associate Professor, 1971-76, Professor, 1976-2002, Professor Emeritus, 2002-, Astronomy Department, Ohio State University. Publications: Approximately 150 research articles in journals of astronomy and astrophysics; The Carbon Star Phenomenon (editor), 2000. Honours: Various research grants from the NSF and NASA. Memberships: International Astronomical Union; Royal Astronomical Society; American Astronomical Society; Astronomical Society of the Pacific; American Association of Variable Star Observers; International Dark Sky Association. Address: 400 Lenappe Drive, Columbus, OH 43214, USA. E-mail: wing@astronomy.ohio-state.edu

WINGER Debra, b. 16 May 1955, Cleveland, USA. Actress. m. (1) Timothy Hutton, 1986, divorced 1990, 1 son, (2) Arliss Howard, 1996, 1 son. Education: California University, Northridge. Appointments: Served, Israel Army, 1972; First Professional Appearance, Wonder Woman, tv series, 1976-77. Creative Works: Films include: Thank God Its Friday, 1978; French Postcards, 1979; Urban Cowboy, 1980; Cannery Row, 1982; An Officer and a Gentleman, 1982; Terms of Endearment, 1983; Mike's Murder, 1984; Legal Eagles, 1986; Black Widow, 1987; Made in Heaven, 1987; Betrayed, 1988; The Sheltering Sky, 1990; Everybody Wins, 1990; Leap of Faith, 1992; Shadowlands, 1993; A Dangerous Woman, 1993; Forget Paris, 1995; Big Bad Love, 2002; Radio, 2003; Eulogy, 2004; TV includes: Dawn Anna, 2005; Sometimes in April, 2005. Address: c/o CAA, 9830 Wilshire Boulevard, Beverly Hills, CA 90212, USA.

WINIARCZYK Marek, b. 30 June 1947, Wrocław, Poland. Historian. Education: MA, 1970, PhD, 1976, Doctor habilitatus, 1982, Department of Classics, University of Wrocław, Poland. Appointments: Librarian, 1970-73, Lecturer, Department of Foreign Languages, 1973-83, Associate Professor of Classical Languages, 1983-93, Professor of Ancient History, 1993-, University of Wrocław.

Publications: Diagorae Melii et Theodori Cyrenaei reliquiae, 1981; Euhemeri Messenii reliquiae, 1991; Bibliographie zum antiken Atheismus, 1994; Co-editor: Abkürzungen aus Personalschriften des XVI bis XVIII Jahrhunderts, 1993 (second edition, 2002); Author, dictionary: Sigla Latina in libris impressis occurrentia, 1995; Euhemeros von Messene. Leben, Werk und Nachwirkung, 2002; Utopie im Grecji hellenistycrnej, 2010; Die hellenistischen Utopien, 2011. Honours: Listed in Who's Who publications and biographical dictionaries. Memberships: Wrocławskie Towarzystwo Naukowe; Polskie Towarzystwo Filologiczne; Polskie Towarzystwo Historyczne; American School of Classical Studies at Athens, 1995. Address: Mianowskiego 25/2, 51-605, Wrocław, Poland.

WINKEL Wolfgang, b. 15 June 1941, Danzig, Germany. Zoologist. m. Doris Laux, 1 daughter. Education: Graduation (Dr rer nat), University Brunswick, 1968. Scientific Assistant, Institute of Avian Research, Wilhelmshaven, Germany, 1970-77; Head, working group population ecology of Vogelwarte Helgoland, Brunswick, 1978-2006. Publications: Over 200 in scientific journals; Co-author, Eco-ornithological Glossary, 1983; Co-author, Die Vogelfamilien der Westpaläarktis, 1995; Editor-in-Chief, Die Vogelwelt, 1971-87; Co-editor, Die Vogelwarte, 1972-2004. Honours: Silberne Ehrennadel, Deutscher Bund für Vogelschutz, 1984; Förderpreis der Werner-Sunkel-Stiftung, Deutsche Ornithologen-Gesellschaft, 2001. Memberships: Deutsche Ornithologen-Gesellschaft. Address: Bauernstr 14/15, D-38162 Cremlingen-Weddel, Germany.

WINKELMAN Joseph William, b. 20 September 1941, Keokuk, Iowa, USA. Artist; Printmaker. m. Harriet Lowell Belin, 2 daughters. Education: BA, English, University of the South, Sewanee, Tennessee, 1964; CFA, University of Oxford, 1971. Appointments: President, Royal Society of Painter-Printmakers, 1989-95; Artist-in-Residence, St John's College, Oxford, 2004. Honours: Honorary Member: Royal Watercolour Society, Oxford Art Society, Printmaker's Council of Great Britain. Memberships: Royal Society of Painter-Printmakers. Address: The Hermitage, 69 Old High Street, Headington, Oxford OX3 9HT, England. Website: www.winkelman.co.uk

WINSLET Kate, b. October 1975, Reading, England. Actress. m. (1) Jim Threapleton, 1998, divorced 2001, 1 daughter, (2) Sam Mendes, 2003, divorced 2010, 1 son, (3) Ned Rocknroll, 2012. Education: Theatre School, Maidenhead. Creative Works: TV appearances: Get Back; Casualty; Anglo-Saxon Attitudes; Films: A Kid in King Arthur's Court; Heavenly Creatures, 1994; Sense and Sensibility, 1996; Jude, 1996; Hamlet, 1996; Titanic, 1997; Hideous Kinky, 1997; Holy Smoke, 1998; Quills, 1999; Enigma, 2000; Iris, 2001; The Life of David Gale, 2002; Plunge: The Movie, 2003; Eternal Sunshine of the Spotless Mine, 2004; Finding Neverland, 2004; Pride (voice), 2004; Romance & Cigarettes, 2005; All the King's Men, 2005; Flushed Away (voice), 2006; The Holiday, 2006; The Reader, 2008; Revolutionary Road, 2008; Mildred Pierce (TV), Carnage, Contagion, 2011; Movie 43, Labor Day, 2014. Honours include: BAFTA Award; 5 Golden Globes; Best European Actress, European Film Academy, 1998; Film Actress of the Year, Variety Club of Great Britain, 1998; CBE, 2012.

WINTERBOTTOM Michael John Jude, b. 15 June 1959. Journalist. Education: The Grammar School, Ashton-under-Lyne. Appointments: Columnist, Universe Catholic Weekly; Assistant Editor, Church Building & Heritage

Review; Archivist, Universal Media Group. Publications: Numerous articles on ecclesiatical art and architecture and heritage generally; Weekly column in Universe Catholic Weekly; Pius XII – a Saint in the Making, 2010. Memberships: The Monachist League; The Constitutional Monarchy Association; Society of St Vincent de Paul; Catholic Family History Society; Catholic Archive Society. Address: 15 Harper Place, Ashton-under-Lyne, Lancashire OL6 6LR, England. E-mail: michael.winterbottom@btopenworld.com

WINTERTON Rosie, b. 10 August 1958, Leicester, England. Member of Parliament. Education: BA (Hons) History, University of Hull, England, 1979. Appointments: Assistant to John Prescott MP, 1980-86; Parliamentary Officer, London Borough of Southwark, 1986-88; Parliamentary Officer, Royal College of Nursing, 1988-90; Managing Director, Connect Public Affairs, 1990-94; Head of Private office of John Prescott MP, Deputy Leader of the Labour Party; Entered Parliament as MP for Doncaster Central, 1997-; Elected representative of Parliamentary Labour Party on the National Policy Forum of the Labour Party, 1997-2001; Chair of Transport and General Worker's Parliamentary Group, 1998-99; Leader of Leadership Campaign Team, 1998-99; Member on Standing Committee of Transport Bill, 2000; Intelligence and Security Committee, 2000; Member on Standing Committee of Finance Bill, 2000; Standing Committee of the Local Government Finance (Supplementary Credit Approvals) Bill and the Regional Development Agencies Bill; Member of the Labour Party Strategic Campaign; Parliamentary Secretary at the Lord Chancellor's Department, 2001-03; Minister of State, Department of Health, 2003-07; Minister of State for Transport, 2007-. Address: Guildhall Advice Centre, Old Guildhall Yard, Doncaster, South Yorkshire, DN1 1OW, England.

WINTHER Morten, b. 9 August 1967, Roskilde, Denmark. Senior Adviser. m. Charlotte Bligaard, 2 sons. Education: MSc, Civil Engineering (Mechanical), Technical University of Denmark, 1993. Appointments: Researcher, 1994-2006, Senior Adviser, 2006-, Department of Environmental Science, University of Aarhus; Member, Management Committee, COST319, 1996-98; Member, Working Group under ECAC/ANCAT/EMCAL, 1998-2001; Partner, thematic network AERONET I-II, 2000-04; Member, Danish Innovation Network for Land, Sea and Air Transport, 2010-. Publications: Numerous articles in professional journals. Honours: Nominated Expert Reviewer for emission inventories under UNECE LRTAP convention; Nominated TAIEX expert for EU Commission in field of air pollution monitoring; Listed in international biographical dictionaries. Address: Department of Environmental Science, University of Aarhus, Frederiksborgvej 399, Roskilde 4000, Denmark. E-mail: mwi@dmu.dk

WINWOOD Steve, b. 12 May 1948, Birmingham, Warwickshire, England. Musician (keyboards, guitar); Vocalist. Career: Founder member, Spencer Davis Group, 1963-67; Performances include: National Jazz And Blues Festival, 1965, 1966; Grand Gala du Disques, Amsterdam, 1966; UK tours with The Rolling Stones, 1965; The Who, 1966; The Hollies, 1967; Traffic, 1967-68; Blind Faith, 1969; Concerts include: Hyde Park, 1969; Madison Square Garden, 1969; Rejoined Traffic, 1970-75; Concerts include: Zurich Rock Festival, 1968; Hollywood Festival, 1970; Headliners, Reading Festival, 1973; Solo artiste, 1977-; ARMS benefit concert, Royal Albert Hall, 1983; US tour, with Robert Cray, 1991. Recordings: Albums: with The Spencer Davis Group: Their First LP, 1966; The Second Album, 1966; Autumn '66, 1966; with Traffic: Mr Fantasy, 1968; Traffic, 1968; John Barleycorn Must Die, 1970; The Low Spark Of High Heeled Boys, 1972; When The Eagle Flies, 1974; with Blind Faith: Blind Faith (Number 1, UK and US), 1969; Solo albums: Steve Winwood, 1977; Arc Of A Diver, 1981; Talking Back To The Night, 1982; Back In The High Life, 1986; Refugees Of The Heart, 1990; Junction Seven, 1997; Singles include: with Spencer Davis Group: Keep On Running (Number 1, UK), 1966; Somebody Help Me, 1966; Gimme Some Lovin', 1966; I'm A Man, 1967; with Traffic: Paper Sun, 1967; Hole In My Shoe, 1967; Solo: Freedom Overspill, 1986; Roll With It, 1989; One and Only Man, 1990; I Will Be Here, 1991; Reach for the Light, 1995; Spy in the House of Love, 1997; Solo include: Higher Love, 1986; The Finer Things, 1987; Valerie, 1987; Roll With It (Number 1, US), 1988; Don't You Know What The Night Can Do, 1988; Holding On, 1989; One And Only Man, 1989. Honours include: Grammy Awards: Record of the Year, Best Pop Vocal Performance, Higher Love, 1987; Gold discs. Address: Helter Skelter, 3rd Floor, 18 Bond Street, Brighton BN1 1RD, England.

WIRTZ Stefan, b. 17 January 1982, Saarbruecken, Germany. Lecturer. Education: Paratrooper, German Army, 2001-02; Student, Trier University, 2002-07. Appointments: PhD grant, 2007-10; Member, Trier University, 2010-. Publications: Numerous articles in professional journals. Memberships: European Geoscience Union; Deutsche Bodenkundliche Gesellschaft; Deutscher Arbeitskreis fuer Geomorphologie. Address: Trier University, Campus II, Physical Geography, Behringstr, 54286 Trier, Germany.

WISLOWSKA Margaret, b. 10 March 1949, Warsaw, Poland. Professor. m. Janusz Wislowski, 1 son, 1 daughter. Education: Medical Academy, Warsaw, 1966-72; Physician diploma, 1972; I degree, 1977, II degree, 2006, Internal Medicine specialization; II degree, Rheumatology specialization, 1981; PhD, 1986; Professor, 2006; II degree, Rehabilitation Medicine specialization, 2011. Appointments: Head, Internal and Rheumatology Department, Central Clinical Hospital, Warsaw, 2003-. Publications: Around 100 articles in professional journals. Honours: Academy of Polish Success. Memberships: Polish Society of Rheumatology; Polish Society of Osteoarthritis; Polish Society of Osteoporosis; Polish Society of Internal Medicine; New York Society of Medicine; OARSI. Address: Woloska 25 Street, Warsaw, 02-583, Poland.

WISZNIEWSKI Leslaw, b. 6 February 1936. Professor; Colonel CAF (USA) (Retired). m. (1) 1 son, (2) Kathleen Margaret, 1982. Education: Xaverian College, Manchester; Saltley College of St Peter, Birmingham; Studied Psychology at universities of Manchester, Birmingham and Somerset, Louisiana. Appointments: Retired from Junior Secondary and Special Education, 1985; Instructor, Lecturer, Technical Advisor with several police forces; Writer. Publications: The Martial Arts Instructor, 1975; Practical Psychology, 1980; Evasion Techniques, 1980; Dynamic Baton Techniques, 1980; Practical Hypnosis, 1981; Control of Self: Sequences and Situation; Spiritual Aspects of Kung Fu, 1987; Practical Hypnosis, 1988; Fic-Choy-Sau (Self Defence), 1989; Psychology: The Subtle Approach, 1997; A Thought and other Poems, 1998; End of Century Reflections, 1999; The Spider's World, 1999; New Poems for a New Millennium, 2000; We, The Rats, 2000; From My Memoirs, 2000; The Gorilla and The Snail, 2001; The Way, 2001; In Vino Veritas, 2002; The Gift, 2003; A Book of Selected Verse, 2004; Several publications in Polish. Honours: CF Medal, Ministry of Defence, 1983; Police Award for Services Rendered, 2004. Memberships: Fellow, College of Preceptors; Fellow, Institute of Linguists; Numerous sports organisations of

DICTIONARY OF INTERNATIONAL BIOGRAPHY 36th EDITION

Oriental derivation; President, Self Defence Society; Chief advisor to several organisations. Address: 7 Ambleside Court, Congleton, Cheshire CW12 4HZ, England.

WITHERSPOON Reese, b. 22 March 1976, Baton Rouge, Louisiana, USA. Actress. m. (1) Ryan Phillippe, 1999, divorced 2007, 1 son, 1 daughter, (2) Jim Toth, 2011, 1 son. Education: English Literature, Stanford University. Career: Model, age 7; Appeared in TV commercials; First place in Ten-State Talent Fair, age 11; Own production company, Type A Films; Films include: The Man in the Moon, 1991; Jack the Bear, 1993; A Far Off Place, 1993; Fear, 1996; Freeway, 1996; Pleasantville, 1998; Election, 1999; Cruel Intentions, 1999; Legally Blonde, 2001; Sweet Home Alabama, 2002; The Importance of Being Earnest, 2002; Legally Blonde 2: Red, White & Blonde, 2003; Vanity Fair, 2004; Walk the Line, 2005; Just Like Heaven, 2005; Penelope, 2006; Rendition, 2007; Penelope, 2008; Four Christmases, 2008; Monsters vs Aliens (voice), 2009; How Do You Know, 2010; Water for Elephants, 2011; This Means War, Mud, 2012; Devil's Knot, 2013. Membership: Gamma Phi Beta Sorority. Honours: Academy Award, Best Actress, and numerous other awards for Walk the Line, 2006.

WITKOWSKI Jacek Maciej, b. 10 September 1953, Gdansk, Poland. Scientist; Academic Professor. m. (1) Elzbieta, (2) Ewa Bryl, 3 daughters. Education: MD, 1978, PhD, 1983, DSc, 1991, Medical University of Gdansk; Full Professor Titularius, President of the Republic of Poland, 2009. Appointments: Research Assistant, 1978-83, Assistant Professor, 1984-91, Department of Histology, Associate Professor, Department of Histology and Immunology, 1992-96, Associate Professor, Department of Biology and Genetics, 1996-97, Associate Professor, 1998-2002, Professor, 2002-, Head, 2003-, Department of Pathophysiology, Vice-Dean, Faculty of Medicine, 2003-08, Medical University of Gdansk; Wellcome Trust Postdoctoral Research Fellow, University of Edinburgh, Scotland, 1984-85; Post-doctoral Research Fellow, 1991-92, Assistant Research Scientist, 1992-94, 1996-97, University of Michigan, USA; Senior Research Fellow, Department of Internal Medicine and Immunology, Mayo Clinic, USA, 1999-2000; Faculty of Medicine Co-ordinator, ERASMUS Programme, 2006-08; Professor titularius, President of the Republic of Poland, 2009. Publications: Numerous articles in professional journals. Honours: 5 Scientific Awards, Ministry of Health and Social Services of the Republic of Poland, 1986, 2002, 2005, 2006, 2008. Memberships: American Association of Immunologists; Scientific Society of Gdansk; Polish Society of Cytometry; Polish Gerontological Society; Polish Immunological Society; Polish Medical Society; Polish Histochemistry and Cytobiology Society. Address

WITTNER Michal, b. 29 January 1968, Karlovy Vary, Czech Republic. Science Educator. Education: MD, 1993, MSc, Biology, 2000, PhD, Human Physiology, 2005, Charles University in Prague. Appointments: Assistant Professor, Physiology Department, Charles University, Prague, 1994-; University of Kuopio, Finland, 1995-96; Humboldt University, Berlin, Germany, 1996-97. Publications: 3 articles in professional journals. Memberships: Czech Neuroscience Society; Czech Physiology Society; Czech Society for Cybernetics and Informatics. Address: Krizikova 7, 360 01 Karlovy Vary, Czech Republic.

WOGAN Sir Terry (Michael Terence), b. 3 August 1938, Ireland. Broadcaster. m. Helen Joyce, 1965, 2 sons, 1 daughter. Education: Crescent College, Limerick; Belvedere College, Dublin. Appointments: Announcer, RTE, 1963, Senior Announcer, 1964-66; Various programmes for BBC Radio, 1965-67; Late Night Extra, BBC Radio, 1967-69; The Terry Wogan Show, BBC Radio 1, 1969-72, BBC Radio 2, 1972-84; Wake Up to Wogan, BBC Radio 2, 1993-2009; Weekend Wogan, 2010-. Creative Works: TV shows include: Lunchtime with Wogan, ATV; BBC: Come Dancing; Song for Europe; The Eurovision Song Contest; Children in Need; Wogan's Guide to the BBC; Blankety Blank; Wogan; Terry Wogan's Friday Night; Auntie's Bloomers; Wogan's Web; Points of View, 2000-01. Publications: Banjaxed, 1979; The Day Job, 1981; To Horse, To Horse, 1982; Wogan on Wogan, 1987; Wogan's Ireland, 1988; Bumper Book of Togs, 1995; Is It Me?, autobiography, 2000. Honours include: Radio Award, 1980; Radio Industry Award, 1982, 1985, 1987; Carl Alan Award, 3 times; Variety Club of Great Britain Special Award, 1982; Showbusiness Personality, 1984; Radio Personality of Last 21 years, Daily Mail National Radio Awards, 1988; Sony Radio Award, Barcelona Olympics, 1993; Sony Radio Award, Best Breakfast Show, 1994; Honorary OBE, 1997 New Year's Honours List; Radio Broadcaster of the Year, Broadcasting Press Guild Awards, 2005; Honorary Knighthood, 2005. Address: c/o Jo Gurnett, 2 New Kings Road, London SW6 4SA, England.

WOHLHAUSER René Claude, b. 24 March 1954, Zurich, Switzerland. Composer. Divorced, 2 sons, 2 daughters. Education: Diploma, Teacher of Music Theory, Basel Conservatory, 1975-79; Composition courses with Kazimierz Serocki, Mauricio Kagel, Herbert Brun and Heinz Holliger; Study with Klaus Huber, Staatliche Musikhochschule, Freiburg, 1980-81; Composition with Brian Ferneyhough, 1982-87. Appointments: Many performances in Switzerland and abroad; Works played by Arditti String Quartet, Symphony Orchestras from Basel, Biel, Lucerne, Bayerischer Rundfunk, Basel Sinfonietta and many international ensembles and soloists; Lecturer on own works; Freelance composer. Publications: Numerous compositions and recordings including: Carpe diem in beschleunigter Zeit for string quartet, 1989-99; Die Auflösung der Zeit im Raum for saxophone, piano and percussion, 2000-01; Klavierstück, 2001-02; Opera "Gantenbein" for 4 soloists and orchestra, 2002-04. Honours: Valentino Bucchi Composition Prize, Rome, 1978; Association of German Music Schools' Composition Prize, Bonn, 1981; VJMZ Composition Prize, Zurich, 1983; City and Canton Fribourg Composition Prize, 1984; Salzburg Cathedral Chapter Composition Prize, 1987; Kranichsteiner Stipendienpreis, Internationale Ferienkurse für Neue Musik Darmstadt, 1988; Eastern Swiss Foundation for Music and Theatre Composition Prize, St Gallen, 1990; Bursary, Luzern Department of Education, 1991; Commendation Prize, Swiss Society for Furtherance of Musical Education, Zurich, 1992; Selection Prize, Swiss Radio International, 1996; Bursary, Basel-Landschaft Department of Education, 1998. Address: Schillerstrasse 5, 4053 Basel, Switzerland.

WOHLLEBEN Rudolf, b. 4 June 1936, Bad Kreuznach, Germany. Retired Telecommunications and Antenna Engineer; Writer. m. Rosemarie, 2 sons, 1 stepson, 1 stepdaughter. Education: BSEE, University of Karlsruhe, 1957; MSEE, Dipl-Ing, Technical University, Munich; Dr Ing, 1969; RWTH, Aachen. Appointments: Lecturer, Radar, Antennas, Radioastronomy, Microwaves, Technical University of Kaiserslautern, Germany, 1980-2006; Forschungsinst f HF-Physik, Rolandseck, 1961-64; Institut f Techn Elektronik, RWTH Aachen, 1964-70; Writer, 1968-; Max-Planck Institute fuer Radioastronomie, Electronics Division, Bonn, 1971-99; Retired, 1999-; Archiver, WSC-Sammlung, Institut fuer Hochschulkunde, University Library of Wuerzburg, Germany, 2003-; Opened Faust Museum, Bad Kreuznach,

2011. Publications: 70 articles in professional journals; 8 books, including Interferometry in Radioastronomy and Radar Techniques, 1991; Fruehe Spaetlese, poems, 1997; (The Poet) Stefan George, for enthusiasts and scholars (in German), 2004; Co-author (with K E Wild and A P Faust), Literatur-Geschichte des Nahelands u Hunsruecks, 2011. Honours: Sport Medal, town of Bonn, 2002; Theodor Heuss Medal, FDP, 1990. Listed in national and international biographical dictionaries. Memberships include: Verband deutscher Schriftsteller, Stefan-George-Gesellschaft/ Bingen, 4 WSC-Corps; Chairman, Verein für corpsstudent. Geschichtsforschung. Address: Kurhausstr 1A, D-55543 Bad Kreuznach, Germany. E-mail: r.wohlleben@freenet.de

WOLFE Larry E, b. 10 February 1949, Knoxville, Tennessee, USA. Medical Doctor. m. Susan Chumley, 5 sons, 1 daughter. Education: Physics, University of Tennessee, 1971; MD, University of Tennessee Center for Health Sciences, 1977; Partial residency in Psychiatry, Residency in Family Medicine and Surgery, East Tennessee State University, -1982. Appointments: Private practice, Union County, Tennessee, 1982- 92; Private practice, Scott County, Tennessee, 1992-. Honours: Consumers Research Council of America Top American Physicians, 2006, 2007, 2008, 2009, 2010; Listed in biographical dictionaries. Memberships: National Astronomy Association.

WOLFE Tom, (Thomas Kennerly Wolfe Jr), b. 2 March 1930, Richmond, Virginia, USA. Writer; Journalist; Artist. m. Sheila Berger, 1 son, 1 daughter. Education: AB, Washington and Lee University, 1951; PhD, American Studies, Yale University, 1957. Appointments: Reporter, Springfield Union, Massachusetts, 1956-59; Reporter and Latin American Correspondent, Washington Post, 1959-62; Writer, New York Sunday Magazine, 1962-66; City Reporter, New York Herald Tribune, 1962-66; Magazine Writer, New York World Journal Tribune, 1966-67; Contributing Editor, New York magazine, 1968-76, Esquire magazine, 1977-; Contributing Artist, Harper's magazine, 1978-81. Publications: The Kandy-Kolored Tangerine-Flake Streamline Baby, 1965; The Electric Kool-Aid Acid Test, 1968; The Pump House Gang, 1968; Radical Chic and Mau-mauing the Flak Catchers, 1970; The Painted Word, 1975; Mauve Gloves and Madmen, Clutter and Vine, 1976; The Right Stuff, 1979; In Our Time, 1980; From Bauhaus to Our House, 1981; The Purple Decades: A Reader, 1982; The Bonfire of the Vanities, 1987; A Man in Full, 1998; Hooking Up, 2000; I am Charlotte Simmons, 2004. Contributions to: Newspapers and magazines. Honours: Various honorary doctorates; American Book Award, 1980; Harold D Vursell Memorial Award, American Academy of Arts and Letters, 1980; John Dos Passos Award, 1984; Theodore Roosevelt Medal, Theodore Roosevelt Association, 1990; St Louis Literary Award, 1990. Membership: American Academy of Arts and Letters. Address: c/o Janklow & Nesbit Associates, 445 Park Avenue, New York, NY 10022, USA.

WOLFF Tobias J A, b. 19 June 1945, Birmingham, USA. Writer. m. Catherine Dolores Spohn, 1975, 2 sons, 1 daughter. Education: BA, Oxford University, 1972; MA, Stanford University, 1975; LHD (hon), Santa Clara University, 1996. Appointments: US Army, 1964-68; Reporter, Washington Post, 1972; Writing Fellow, Stanford University, 1975-78; Writer-in-Residence, Arizona State University, 1978-80, Syracuse University, 1980-97, Stanford University, 1997-; Director, creative writing programme, 2000-02. Publications: Hunters in the Snow, 1981; The Barracks Thief, 1984; Back in the World, 1985; This Boy's Life, 1989; In Pharaoh's Army: Memories of a Lost War, 1994; The Vintage Book of Contemporary American Short Stories, 1994; The Best American Short Stories, 1994; The Night in Question, 1996; Old School, 2003; Our Story Begins: New and Selected Stories, 2008. Honours include: O Henry Award, 1981, 1982, 1985; Guggenheim Fellow, 1983; National Endowment Fellow, 1978, 1984; PEN/Faulkner Award for Fiction, 1985; Rea Award, 1989; Whiting Foundation Award, 1989; Los Angeles Times Book Prize, 1989; Ambassador Book Award, 1990; Lila Wallace/Readers Digest Award, 1993; Esquire-Volvo-Waterstone Award for Non-Fiction, 1994; Exceptional Achievement Award, American Academy of Arts and Letters, 2001; Fairfax Prize for Literature, 2003; PEN/ Faulkner Award for Fiction nominee, 2004. Address: English Department, Stanford University, CA 94305-2087, USA.

WONDER Stevie (Steveland Morris), b. 13 May 1950, Saginaw, Michigan, USA. Singer; Musician (multi-instrumentalist); Composer. m. Syreeta Wright, 1970, divorced, 3 children. Education: Michigan State School for the Blind, 1963-68. Musical Education: Self-taught harmonica, piano. Career: Motown recording artist (initially as Stephen Judkins), 1963-70; Founder, president, music publishing company, Black Bull Music Inc; Founder, Wonderdirection Records Inc; Taurus Productions; Numerous concerts include: Midem Festival, France, 1974; Night Of The Hurricane II (hurricane relief concert), Houston, 1976; Peace Sunday, Rose Bowl, 1982; Nelson Mandela's Birthday Tribute, Wembley, 1988; Film appearances include: Bikini Beach, 1964; Muscle Beach Party, 1964. Compositions include: Lovin' You, Minnie Riperton, 1975; Recordings: Hit singles include: Fingertips Part 2 (Number 1, US), 1963; Uptight (Everything's Alright), 1966; I Was Made To Love Her, 1967; For Once In My Life, 1968; My Cherie Amour, 1969; Yester-Me, Yester-You, Yesterday, 1969; Signed Sealed Delivered I'm Yours, 1970; Superstition (Number 1, US), 1973; You Are The Sunshine Of My Life (Number 1, US), 1973; Higher Ground, 1974; Living For The City, 1974; You Haven't Done Nothin' (Number 1, US), 1974; Boogie On Reggae Woman, 1975; I Wish (Number 1, US), 1977; Sir Duke (Number 1, US), 1977; Master Blaster, 1980; Lately, 1981; Happy Birthday, 1981; Ebony And Ivory, duet with Paul McCartney (Number 1, US and UK), 1982; I Just Called To Say I Love You (Number 1, US and UK), 1984; Part-Time Lover, 1985; Don't Drive Drunk, 1985; Get It, 1988; Keep Our Love Alive, 1990; Gotta Have You, 1991; Fun Day, 1991; These Three Words, 1991; For Your Love, 1995; Tomorrow Robins Will Sing, 1995; Treat Myself, 1995; Kiss Away Your Tears, 1996; Albums include: The 12 Year Old Genius, 1963; Up Tight Everything's Alright, 1966; Down To Earth, 1967; I Was Made To Love Her, 1967; Greatest Hits, 1968; For Once In My Life, 1969; My Cherie Amour, 1969; Signed Sealed And Delivered, 1969; Greatest Hits Vol.2, 1971; Music Of My Mind, 1972; Talking Book, 1972; Innervisions, 1973; Fulfillingness' First Finale, 1974; Songs In The Key Of Life, 1976; Journey Through The Secret Life Of Plants, 1979; Hotter Than July, 1980; Woman In Red (soundtrack), 1984; Love Songs, 1984; In Square Circle, 1985; Characters, 1987; Music From The Music Jungle Fever (soundtrack), 1991; Conversation Peace, 1995; Natural Wonder, 1996; Contributor, I Feel For You, Chaka Khan, 1984; There Must Be An Angel, The Eurythmics, 1985; That's What Friends Are For, Dionne Warwick And Friends, 1986; Hallelujah!, Quincy Jones, 1992. Honours include: Numerous Grammy Awards, including Lifetime Achievement Award, 1990; Edison Award, 1973; NARM Presidential Award, 1975; Inducted into Songwriters Hall Of Fame, 1983; Numerous American Music Awards, including Special Award of Merit, 1982; Oscar, Best Song, 1984; Gold Ticket, Madison Square Garden, 1986; Soul Train Heritage Award, 1987; Inducted into Rock'n'Roll Hall Of

Fame, 1989; Nelson Mandela Courage Award, 1991; IAAAM Diamond Award for Excellence, 1991; Lifetime Achievement Award, National Academy Of Songwriters, 1992; NAACP Image Award, 1992; Numerous other charity and civil rights awards. Current Management: Stevland Morris Music, 4616 Magnolia Blvd., Burbank, CA 91505, USA.

WOO John, b. 1948, Guangzhou, China. Film Director. m. Annie Woo Ngau Chun-lung, 3 children. Education: Matteo Ricci College, Hong Kong. Appointments: Production Assistant, Assistant Director, Cathay Film Co, 1971; Assistant Director to Zhang Che, Shaw Bros. Creative Works: Films: The Young Dragons, 1973; The Dragon Tamers; Countdown in Kung Fu; Princess Chang Ping; From Riches to Rags; Money Crazy; Follow the Star; Last Hurrah for Chivalry; To Hell with the Devil; Laughing Times; Plain Jane to the Rescue; Sunset Warriors (Heroes Shed No Tears); The Time You Need a Friend; Run Tiger Run; A Better Tomorrow; A Better Tomorrow II; Just Heroes; The Killer; Bullet in the Head; Once a Thief; Hard Boiled; Hard Target; Broken Arrow; Face/Off; Kings Ransom; Mission Impossible II; The Last Word; Windtalkers, 2000; The Hire: Hostage, 2002; Red Skies (producer), 2002; Paycheck, 2003; Bullet Proof Monk, 2003; All the Invisible Children, 2005; Appleseed Ex Machina, 2007; Stranglehold, 2007; Red Cliff, 2008. Address: c/o MGM Studios Inc, 2500 Broadway Street, Santa Monica, CA 90404, USA.

WOOD David Bernard, b. 21 February 1944, Sutton, England. Playwright; Director; Actor; Magician. m. Jacqueline Stanbury, 2 daughters. Education: Chichester High School for Boys; BA (Hons) in English, Worcester College, Oxford, 1963-66. Appointments: Freelance actor, playwright, director, magician, children's book author. Publications: Many plays; Children's books. Honours: OBE, 2004; Honorary MA, University of Chichester, 2005. Memberships: Society of Authors; British Actors' Equity; The Magic Circle (MIMC); International Brotherhood of Magicians; Chair, Action for Children's Arts; Trustee, The Story Museum. Address: c/o Casarotto Ramsay Ltd, Waverley House, 7-12 Noel Street, London, W1F 8GQ, England. E-mail: info@casarotto.co.uk

WOOD Elijah, b. 28 January 1981, Ceder Rapids, Iowa, USA. Actor. Education: Avent Studios, Modelling school. Films include: Back to the Future Part II, 1989; Internal Affairs, 1990; The Adventures of Huck Finn, 1993; The War, 1994; The Ice Storm, 1997; Oliver Twist, 1997; Deep Impact, 1998; The Faculty, 1998; Chains of Fools, 2000; The Lord of the Rings: The Fellowship of the Ring, 2001; The Adventures of Tom Thumb and Thumbelina, 2002; The Lord of the Rings: The Two Towers, 2002; The Lord of the Rings: The Return of the King, 2003; Eternal Sunshine of the Spotless Mind, 2004; Christmas on Mars, 2005; Hooligans, 2005; Sin City, 2005; Everything is Illuminated, 2005; Paris, je t'aime, 2006; Bobby, 2006; Happy Feet (voice), 2006; Day Zero, 2007; Legend of Spyro: The Eternal Night (voice), 2007; The Oxford Murders, 2008; 9, Beyond All Boundaries, 2009; The Romantics, 2010; Fight For Your Right: Revisited, Happy Feet Two, The Death and Return of Superman, 2011; Celeste and Jesse Forever, Revenge for Jolly, Maniac, The Hobbit: An Unexpected Journey, 2012; Black Wings Has My Angel, 2013; TV Appearances include: Frasier, 1994; Adventures from the Book of Virtues, 1996; SM:TV Live, 2001; The Osbournes, The Buzz, Player$, 2002; The Tonight Show with Jay Leno, Saturday Night Live, 2003; NY Graham Norton, King of the Hill (voice), 2004; Robot Chicken (voice), American Dad, 2006; Glen Martin DDS, 2010; Funny or Die Presents, Robot Chicken, 2011; Wilfred, 2011-; Treasure Island, Red vs Blue, 2012; Tron: Uprising, 2012-. Honours: Young Artist Award, 1991; Saturn Award, 1994; Young Star Award, 1998; Empire Award, 2002; Young Hollywood Award, 2002; MTV Movie Award, 2003; National Board of Review, USA, 2003; Saturn Award, 2004; Broadcast Film Critics Association Award, 2004; Screen Actors Guild Award, 2004; Visual Effects Society Awards, 2003. Address: c/o Nicole David 151 S El Camino Drive, Beverly Hills, CA 90212-2775, USA.

WOOD Larry (Mary Laird), b. Sandpoint, Idaho, USA. Journalist; Author; University Educator; Public Relations Executive; Environmental Consultant. m. Wilbur Byron, deceased, 1 son, 2 daughters. Education: BA, summa cum laude, University of Washington, 1939; MA, summa cum laude, 1940; Postgraduate, Stanford University, 1940-43; University of California, Berkeley, 1946-47; Certificate, Photography, 1971; Postgraduate, Journalism, University of Wisconsin, 1971-72; University of Georgia, 1972-73; University of Minnesota, 1973-74; Postgraduate, Art, Architecture, Marine Biology, University of California, Berkeley and Santa Cruz and Stanford Hopkins Marine Station, 1974-78. Appointments: Internationally and nationally syndicated by-lined feature writer, by-lined columnist, 1939-; Environmental, Real Estate, Fashion, Business, Travel and Feature Writer; Teaching Fellow, Stanford University, 1940-43; Public Relations Director, 65-park, 100,000 acre East Bay Regional Parks and California Children's Home Society Adoptive Agency; President, Larry Wood Public Relations, 1946-: accounts included American Red Cross, American Cancer Society, Girl Scouts, Boy Scouts, California Spring Garden Show, Bay Area Hospitals and others; Associate Professor Journalism and Public Relations (tenure), 1974, 1975; Distinguished Visiting Professor, California State Universities, 1976; Associate Professor, Science and Environmental Journalism, University of California Berkeley, 1979-. Publications: By-lined award-winning author of more than 5000 articles on various topics; Author and co-author of 21 books including Focus on Science texts, Fodor's Travel Guides; State of California's Golden State Travel Guide, 1998. Honours: Citations for Environmental Writing, National Park Service and Bureau of Land Management; Magazine writer awards, Social Issues Resources Series, California Writer's Club; California Publishers Association and National Headliners Award; USA Treasury War Bond fund-raising award; Hall of Fame and Distinguished Alumnus Awards, Seattle, Washington. Memberships: Smithsonian; Audubon Society; California Academy of Sciences; Phi Betta Kappa; Mortar Board; San Francisco Press Club; National Press Club; Society of American Travel Writers; Society of Environmental Journalists; National Press Photographers Association; Society of Professional Journalists; Women in Communications; American Medical Writers Association; American Board of Forensic Experts; American Association of Investigative Reporters and Editors, Public Relations Society of America; National Association of Science Writers; American Association for Education in Journalism and Mass Communications; American Association for Advancement in Science Writing; others. Address: 6161 Castle Drive, Oakland, CA 94611, USA.

WOOD Mary Elizabeth, b. 15 April 1929, Berwyn, Illinois, USA. Retired High School Teacher; Church Musician. m. Harvey E Wood (deceased), 4 sons, 5 daughters. Education: BA, Marycrest College, Davenport, Iowa; MA, Michigan State University, East Lansing, Michigan; Associate, Lansing Community College. Appointments: Teacher, English, various high schools in Michigan and Iowa, 17 years; Director of Music, St Jude Parish, DeWitt, Michigan, 10 years;

Accompanist to congregational singing at Saturday Mass, Church of the Resurrection. Publications: 2 poems: Strips of Cloth; On An Old-fashioned Christmas Card; Children's musical, The Country Cousin; Original liturgical music used at several local parishes; Mass of St Peter. Honours: Summa cum laude, Lansing Community College; Soprano soloist, Lucien Deiss' album, Jesus Lives. Memberships: National Pastoral Musicians, Lansing Chapter Co-chairman; Michigan Education Association; American Association of Retired Persons. Address: 5102 Killarney Drive, Holt, MI 48842-2909, USA.

WOOD Ron, b. 1 June 1947, Hillingdon, London, England. Musician (guitar, bass). 1 son. Career: Musician, Jeff Beck Group, 1967-69; Concerts include: National Jazz And Blues Festival, 1967, 1968; Newport Jazz Festival, 1969; Member, The Faces, 1969-75; Reading Jazz Festival, 1972; Buxton Festival, 1974; Member, The Rolling Stones, 1975-; US tour, 1975; Knebworth Festival, 1976; The Band's Last Waltz Farewell Concert, San Francisco, 1976; Film, Ladies And Gentlemen, The Rolling Stones, 1977; Played Knebworth Festival as The New Barbarians (with Keith Richards), 1979; Live Aid, JFK Stadium, Philadelphia, 1985; Played with Bo Diddley as the Gunslingers; Tours: North America, 1987; Japan, 1988; Germany, Italy, Spain, 1988; Sang at Bob Dylan 30th Anniversary Tribute, Madison Square Garden, 1992. Recordings: Albums with The Faces: First Step, 1970; Long Player, 1971; A Nod's As Good As A Wink...To A Blind Horse, 1971; Coast To Coast Overture And Beginners, 1974; with The Rolling Stones: Made In The Shade, 1975; Black And Blue, 1976; Love You Live, 1977; Emotional Rescue, 1980; Tattoo You, 1981; Still Life, 1982; Undercover, 1983; Dirty Work, 1986; Steel Wheels, 1989; Forty Licks, 2002; Live Licks, 2004; Solo: I've Got My Own Album to Do; Now Look; Mahoney's Last Stand; 1234; Live at the Ritz; Slide on This; Slide on Live; Singles: with The Faces: Stay With Me, 1972; Cindy Incidentally, 1973; Pool Hall Richard, 1974; You Can Make Me Dance Or Sing Or Everything, 1974; with The Rolling Stones: Fool To Cry, 1976; Miss You (Number 1 US), 1978; Emotional Rescue, 1980; Start Me Up, 1981; Going To a Go-GO; Undercover Of The Night; Dancing In The Street (Number 1 UK), 1985; Mixed Emotions, 1989. Honours include: Silver Clef, Nordoff-Robbins Music Therapy, 1982; Madison Square Garden Hall Of Fame, 1984; Grammy, Lifetime Achievement Award, 1986; Ivor Novello, Outstanding Contribution To British Music, 1991. Current Management: Rupert Loewenstein, 2 King Street, London SW1Y 6QL, England.

WOODHOUSE Christopher Richard James, b. 20 September 1946, Knebworth, Hertfordshire, England. Urologist. m. Anna Philipps, 1 son, 1 daughter. Education: Winchester College, 1960-64; Guy's Hospital Medical School, 1965-70. Appointments: Consultant, Royal Marsden Hospital, London, 1981-; Consultant and Senior Lecturer, The Institute of Urology, London, 1981-2005; Chairman, BJU International Journal, 2000-10; Consultant Urologist, University College London Hospitals, 2005-; Professor of Adolescent Urology, University College, London, 2005-. Publications: More than 200 peer reviewed articles in learned journals; 3 books; 57 book chapters. Honours: MB BS, 1970; FRCS (Eng), 1975; FEBU, 1993; St Peter's Medal, British Association of Urological Surgeons, 2007; Chairman, BJU International Journal. Memberships: British Association of Urological Surgeons; American Association of Genito-Urinary Surgeons; American Urological Association; Urological Society of Australia and New Zealand (Honorary); German Urological Association (Honorary). Address: 31 Eustace Building, 372 Queenstown Road, London SW8 4NT, England. E-mail: christopher@crjwoodhouse.fsnet.co.uk

WOODS Brian, b. 22 March 1938, Loughborough, England. Artist; Teacher. m. June Margaret, 1 son, 1 daughter. Education: Loughborough College School, 1949-54; Youth in Training, GPO Telephones, 1954-56; RAF National Service, 1956-58; Dip A D Hons, Loughborough College of Art,1963-67. Appointments: Telephone Engineer, GPO Telephones, 1958-63; Lecturer, Drawing and Painting, Rochdale College of Art, then Hopwood Hall College, 1967-92; Part time Artist in schools, projects in Bolton, Bury and Rochdale schools, 2001-04; Part time Painting Host, SAGA Special Interest Painting Holidays, 1996-2005; Group and solo exhibitions in and around Rochdale, Bury and Manchester; Singer & Friedlander/Sunday Times Watercolour Exhibitions, 2003-09; Some Royal Academy Summer Exhibitions, RWS 21st Century Watercolour, 2008-09. Honours: Shared 1st Prize, MAFA Open Exhibition, 1986; Edward Oldham Trust Travel Bursary to Study in Venice, 1995 and 2001; Siemens Figure Painting Award, 1997; Royal Watercolour Society Award, 21st Century Watercolour Exhibition, Bankside Gallery, London, 2008. Memberships: Manchester Academy of Fine Arts; Rochdale Sculptors Group. Address: 7 North Court, Rossall Beach, Thornton Cleveleys, Lancashire FY5 1JA, England.

WOODS Michael, b. 6 December 1933, Norwich, England. Artist. m. Jacqueline, 1 son, 2 daughters. Education: Norwich School of Art; Diploma in Fine Art, The Slade School of Fine Art, University College, London, 1957. Appointments: Chairman, The Young Contemporaries, 1956-57; Tutor, Open College of the Arts; Assistant Artmaster, 1957-70, Director of Art, 1970-94, Charterhouse, Surrey. Publications: Author, 9 books; Illustrator, 10 books; Paintings exhibited around UK; Work in public and private collections. Honours: Prize for Anatomy, 1955; Listed in international biographical dictionaries. Memberships: British Craft Centre; Crafts Council; Society of Authors. Address: 2 Alan Road, King Street, Norwich, Norfolk NR1 2BX, England.

WOODS Philip Wells, b. 2 November 1931, Springfield, Massachusetts, USA. Musician (Alto Saxophone, Clarinet); Composer. m. Jill Goodwin, 20 December 1985, 1 son, 2 daughters. Education: Lessons with Harvey Larose, Springfield; Manhattan School, New York, 1948; Juilliard Conservatory, 1948-52. Career: Appearances with Benny Goodman, Buddy Rich, Quincy Jones, Thelonious Monk, Michel Legrand, Dizzy Gillespie and others; Appearing with own bands, Phil Woods Quintet, Phil Woods Little Big Band, Phil Woods Big Band; Featured, soundtracks of films including It's My Turn; Bandleader, Composer, Arranger and Soloist. Compositions include: Three Improvisations for Saxophone Quartet; Sonata for Alto and Piano; Rights of Swing; The Sun Suite; Fill the Woods with Light; I Remember; Deer Head Sketches. Recordings include: Images, with Michel Legrand, 1976; I Remember, Phil Woods Quartet, 1979; Dizzy Gillespie Meets Phil Woods Quintet; Evolution, Phil Woods Little Big Band; An Affair to Remember, Phil Woods Quintet; The Rev & I, with Johnny Griffin; Elsa, 1998; Porgy and Bess, 1999; Phil Woods in Italy, 2000; Giants at Play, 2001; The Thrill is Gone, 2002; Big Encounter at Umbria, 2003; Woodlands, 2004; Blues for New Orleans, 2005; American Songbook II, 2006. Honours: Down Beat Magazine New Star Award, 1956; Critics' Poll Winner, alto saxophone, 1975-79, 1981-90, 1992, Readers' Poll Winner, alto saxophone, 1976-95; Grammy Award, Images with Michel Legrand, 1976, for More Live, Phil Woods Quartet, 1982, 1983; National Association of Jazz

Educators Poll Winner, alto saxophone, 1987, Phil Woods Quintet, 1987; East Stroudsburg University Honorary Degree, 1994; Induction into American Jazz Hall of Fame, 1994; Officier des Arts et des Lettres; Beacon in Jazz Award, 2001; Swing Journal Readers' Poll, 2004; Jazz Times Readers' Poll, 2004-2006; Alto Saxophonist of the Year, Jazz Journalists Association Jazz Awards, 2005-06; National Endowment for the Arts Jazz Master Fellowship, 2007; President's Merit Award from the Grammy Foundation, 2007; Kennedy Center Living Legends in Jazz Award, 2007. Memberships: Delaware Water Gap Celebration of the Arts; Board of Directors, Al Cohn Memorial Jazz Collection; American Federation of Musicians; International Association of Jazz Educators. Address: Box 278, Delaware Water Gap, PA 18327, USA.

WOODS Tiger (Eldrick), b. 30 December 1975, Cypress, California, USA. Golfer. Education: Stanford University. Career: 11 amateur wins; 64 official PGA Tour wins; 7 European Tour wins; 22 individual professional titles; 2 team titles, two-man WGC World Cup; Winner, inaugural FedEx Cup playoffs; Successfully defended a title 21 times on PGA Tour; Member, US Team World Amateur Team Championship, 1994; Member, US Walker Cup Team, 1995; Member, Ryder Cup 1997, 1999, 2002, 2004; Winner, The Masters, 1997, 2001, 2002, 2005; Winner, PGA Championship, 1999, 2000, 2006, 2007; Winner, US Open, 2000, 2002; Winner, The Open Championship, 2000, 2005, 2006; Winner, WGC American Express Championship, 2006; Winner, Buick International, 2007; Winner, Arnold Palmer Invitational, 2008. Publications: Columnist, Golf Digest, 2001-; Book, How I Play Golf. Honours include: 9 times, PGA Player of the Year; 8 times, PGA Tour Money Leader; 7 times, Vardon Trophy winner; 8 times, Byron Nelson Award; One of five players (and youngest) to have won all four professional major championships in his career; Associated Press Male Athlete of the Year, 1997, 1999, 2000, 2006; Sports Illustrated Sportsman of the Year, 2000; World Sportsman of the Year, 2001, 2002; California Hall of Fame, 2006; California Museum for History, Women and the Arts, 2007. Address: PGA, PO Box 109601, 100 Avenue of the Champions, Palm Beach Gardens, FL 33418, USA.

WOOLFSON Michael Mark, b. 9 January 1927, London, England. Emeritus Professor. m. Margaret Frohlich, 2 sons, 1 daughter. Education: Jesus College, Oxford, 1944-47; UMIST, 1949-52; MA (Oxon), 1951; PhD (Man), 1952; DSc (Man), 1961. Appointments: 2nd Lieutenant, Royal Engineers, National Service, 1947-49; Research Fellow, Cambridge, 1952-54; ICI Fellow, Cambridge, 1954-55; Lecturer, 1955-61, Reader, 1961-65, UMIST; Professor of Theoretical Physics, York, 1964-94, Emeritus Professor, 1994-. Publications: Direct Methods in Crystallography, 1960; An Introduction to X-ray Crystallography, 1970, 2nd edition, 1997; The Origin of the Solar System: The Capture Theory, 1989; Physical and non-physical methods of solving crystal structures, 1995; An introduction to computer simulation, 1999; The origin and evolution of the Solar System, 2000; Planetary Science, 2002; Mathematics for Physics, 2007; The Formation of the Solar System: Theories old and new, 2007; Everyday Probability and Statistics: Health, elections, gambling and war, 2008; Time, Space, Stars & Man: The story of the Big Bang, 2009; On the Origin of Plants: By means of natural simple processes, 2011; The Fundamentals of Imaging: From particles to galaxies, 2011; Articles in learned journals. Honours: C.Phys, 1961; FRAS, 1966; FRS, 1984; Hughes Medal, Royal Society, 1986; Patterson Award, American Crystallographic Association, 1990; Gregori Aminoff Medal, Royal Swedish Academy, 1992; Dorothy Hodgkin Prize, British Crystallographic Association, 1997; Honorary Fellow, Jesus College, Oxford, 2001; Ewald Prize, International Union of Crystallography, 2002. Memberships: Institute of Physics; Royal Astronomical Society; Royal Society; Yorkshire Philosophical Society, President, 1985-99. Address: Physics Department, University of York, York YO10 5DD, England. E-mail: mmw1@york.ac.uk

WOOSNAM Ian Harold, b. 2 March 1958, England. Golfer. m. Glendryth Pugh, 1983, 1 son, 2 daughters. Education: St Martin's Modern School. Appointments: Professional Golfer, 1976-. Creative Works: Tournament Victories: News of the World Under-23 Matchplay, 1979; Cacharel Under-25 Championship, 1982; Swiss Open, 1982; Silk Cut Masters, 1983; Scandinavian Enterprise Open, 1984; Zambian Open, 1985; Lawrence Batley TPC, 1986; 555 Kenya Open, 1986; Hong Kong Open, 1987; Jersey Open, 1987; Cepsa Madrid Open, 1987; Bell's Scottish Open, 1987, 1990; Lancome Trophy, 1987; Suntory World Match-Play Championship, 1987, 1990; Volvo PGA Championship, 1988; Million Dollar Challenge, 1988; Carrolls Irish Open, 1988, 1989; Panasonic Euro Open, 1988; Welsh Pro Championship, 1988; American Express Mediterranean Open, 1990; Torras Monte Carlo Open, 1990; Epson Grand Prix, 1990; World Cup Team and Individual Winner, 1987; World Cup Individual Winner, 1991; US Masters, 1991; USF+G Lassic, 1991; PGA Grand Slam, 1991; Fujitsu Mediterranean Open, 1991; Torras Monte Carlo Open, 1991; European Monte Carlo Open, 1992; Lancome Trophy, 1993; Murphy's English Open, 1993; British Masters, 1994; Cannes Open, 1994; Heineken Classic, 1996; Scottish Open, 1996; German Open, 1996; Johnnie Walker Classic, 1996; Volvo PGA Championships, 1997; Hyundai Motor Masters, 1997; Ryder Cup Member, 1983, 1985, 1987, 1989, 1991, 1993, 1995, 1997; European Ryder Cup Team Captain, 2006; Numerous team events. Publications: Ian Woosnam's Golf Masterpieces (with Peter Grosvenor), 1991; Golf Made Simple: The Woosie Way, 1997. Membership: President, World Snooker Associate, 2000-. Address: c/o IMG, McCormack House, Burlington Lane, London W4 2TH, England. Website: www.woosie.com

WORCESTER Sir Robert, Deputy Lieutenant of the County of Kent; Professor. Appointments: Founder, MORI (Market & Opinion Research International), London, 1969-; Past-President, World Association for Public Opinion Research (WAPOR), 1983-84; Vice President, Social Science Council, UNESCO, 1989-94; Member of Council, 2002-, Chancellor, 2006-, University of Kent; Visiting Professor of Government, 1992-, Govenor, 1995-2010, Honorary Fellow, 2005, London School of Economics and Political Science; Honorary Professor, Department of Politics, University of Kent, 2002-; Honorary Professor, Department of Politics and International Studies, Warwick University, 2005-; Visiting Professor, Graduate Centre for Journalism, City University, London, 1990-2002; Governor, UK-UK Fulbright Committee, 1995-2005; Visiting Professor, Department of Marketing, University of Strathclyde, Glasgow, 1996-2001; Specialist Advisor, House of Commons Librarian, 2007-; Former Specialist Advisor, Treasury Select Committee, 2004-07; Deputy Lieutenant, County of Kent, 2004; Kent Ambassador, Kent County Council; Co-chairman, Jamestown 2007 British Committee, 2004-07; Former Non-Executive Director, Kent Messenger Group, 2004-08; Chairman, Maidstone Radio Ltd, 2004-06; Former Trustee, Kent Foundation; Former Non-Executive Director, Medway Maritime Hospital NHS Trust; Advisory Board, GovNet, 2008-; Chairman, Magna Carta 2015 800th Anniversary Committee, 2010-. Publications: More than a dozen books including: Co-author, Explaining Cameron's Coalition, 2011; Articles in newspapers, magazines and in professional journals. Honours: Doctor of Science, University of Buckingham, 1998; Doctor of Letters, University of Bradford, 2001; Doctor of the University, Middlesex University, 2001; Doctor of Law, University of Greenwich, 2002; KBE, 2005; Honorary Fellow, London School of Economics and Political Science, 2005; Distinguished Graduate, University of Kansas, 2006; Doctor of Civil Law, University of Kent, 2006; Honorary Fellow, Kings College, University of London, 2007; Doctor of Laws, The American International University in London, Richmond, 2009. Memberships: Chairman, 1993-2010, Vice President, 2010, Pilgrims Society; Governor, English-Speaking Union, 2005-; Trustee, Magna Carta Trust, 1995-; Freeman of the City of London, 2001; Governor, Ditchley Foundation, Vice President, Royal Society for Nature Conservation/Wildlife Trusts, 1995-; Vice President, United Nations Association, 1999-; Vice President, European Atlantic Group; Advisory Board Member: Institute of Business Ethics, President, IBE, 2010-; Media Standards Trust; Camelot Corporate Responsibility Advisory Board, 2006-11; President, ENCAMS, 2002-06; Trustee, WWT, 2002-08; Fellow, MRS, 1997; Royal Statistical Society, 2004; Founding Co-Editor, International Journal of Public Opinion Research. Address: 79-81 Borough Road, London SE1 1FY, England. E-mail: rmworcester@yahoo.com

WORKMAN Robert Peter, b. 27 January 1961, Chicago, Illinois, USA. Artist; Author. Education: Art Institute of Chicago; Doctoral, Ecole Du Louvre; Docteur, Faculte De Medecine Clermont Ferrand, France. Appointments: Maitre de Conferences, Paris; Adjunct Lecturer, University Arizona; Graphic Artist, Cartoonist, Columnist, Village View Publications, Oak Lawn, 1983-98; Founder, Librarian, Kennedy Park Library, Chicago; Professor, Histoire de l'Art, Spéialité, Archeologie Egyptienne, France. Publications: 10 children's books under Sesqui-Squirrel; Angels of Doom (graphic novel); Contribution, Journey to Infinity. Honours: Resolution, City Council of Chicago, 1992, Illinois House of Representatives, 1994; Pulitzer Prize Nomination, 1983; First American artist accepted into collection of Musee de Louvre for 21st Century; Youngest artist accepted into Musee de Louvre, 2001; CPS Alumni Site; Included, Congressional Record, USA, 2010; Nominated National Medal of Arts, USA, 2011. Memberships: Knights of Columbus; Mensa; Alumni School, Art Institute of Chicago; Working Press of Chicago; Registration with General Medical Council, England; American Society of Portrait Artists; Listed in several biographical publications. Address: 2509 W 111th Street, Apt #1E, Chicago, IL 60655, USA. Website: www.myspace.com/workmanmuseum

WORRICKER Julian Gordon, b. 6 January 1963, Woking, Surrey, England. Journalist; Broadcaster. Education: Epsom College, Epsom, Surrey, 1976-81; BA (Hons), English, Leicester University, 1981-84; Diploma in Radio Journalism, Cornwall College, Falmouth, 1984-85. Appointments: BBC Radio Leicester; BBC Midlands Today; Presenter, Five Aside, Radio Five, 1991-94; Presenter, Weekend Breakfast, Five Live, 1994-97; Presenter, Nationwide, Radio Five Live, 1997-98; Presenter, Breakfast, Radio Five Live, 1998-2003; Presenter, Worricker on Sunday, BBC Radio Five Live and on other BBC radio and TV outlets until 2007 when he took a career break and travelled for 6 months; Presenter, You and Yours, BBC Radio 4, and The World Today, BBC World Service; TV Presenter, BBC News channel. Publications: Articles on media and travel published in Independent and Guardian newspapers. Honours: 3 Sony Gold Radio Awards for programmes on BBC Radio Five Live; 1 TRIC (TV & Radio Industry Club Award) for Five Live Breakfast. E-mail: jgwo@aol.com

WORSLEY Sir (William) Marcus John, 5th Baronet, b. 6 April 1925, Hovingham, Yorkshire, England. Retired Landowner. m. Bridget Assheton, deceased 2004, 3 sons, 1 daughter. Education: New College Oxford. Appointments: JP, 1957-90 (Chairman, Malton Bench 1983-90); Member of Parliament for Keighley, 1959-64; Member of Parliament for Chelsea, 1966-74; Second Church Estates Commissioner, 1970-74; Church Commissioner, 1976-84; Deputy Chairman, National Trust, 1986-92; High Sheriff, North Yorkshire, 1982; Lord Lieutenant, North Yorkshire,1987-99. Address: Park House, Hovingham, York, YO62 4JZ, England.

WORSLEY William Ralph, 12 September 1956, York, England. Chartered Surveyor. m. Marie-Noelle Dreesmann, 1 son, 2 daughters. Education: Royal Agricultural College. Appointments: Chairman, Hovingham Estates; Vice-Chairman, Scarborough Building Society; Director, The Brunner Investment Trust plc; President, Country Land and Business Association; Member, Forestry Commission's Advisory Panel; Vice-Chairman, Howardian Hills AONB JAC. Honour: Fellow, Royal Institution of Chartered Surveyors. Address: Hovingham Hall, York, England. E-mail: office@hovingham.co.uk.

WORSTHORNE Sir Peregrine (Gerard), b. 22 Dec 1923, London, England. Journalist; Editor; Writer. m. (1) Claude Bertrand de Colasse, 1950, dec 1990, 1 daughter, (2) Lady Lucinda Lambton, 1991. Education: BA, Peterhouse, Cambridge; Magdalen College, Oxford. Appointments: Sub-editor, Glasgow Herald, 1946; Editorial Staff, The Times, 1948-53; Daily Telegraph, 1953-61; Deputy Editor, 1961-76, Associate Editor, 1976-86, Editor, 1986-89, Editor, Comment Section, 1989-91, Sunday Telegraph. Publications: The Socialist Myth, 1972; Peregrinations: Selected Pieces, 1980; By the Right, 1987; Tricks of Memory (autobiography), 1993; In Defence of Aristocracy, 2004. Contributions to: Newspapers and journals. Honours: Granada Columnist of the Year, 1980; Knighted, 1991. Address: The Old Rectory, Hedgerley, Buckinghamshire SL2 3VY, England.

WORTHINGTON Sam, b. 2 August 1976, Godalming, England. Actor. Education: National Institute of Dramatic Art. Career: TV: JAG, Water Rats, Blue Heelers, 2000; Love My Way, 2004; The Surgeon, 2005; Two Twisted, 2006; Films: Bootmen, 2000; Hart's War, Dirty Deeds, 2002; Gettin' Square, 2003; Somersault, Thunderstruck, 2004; The Great Raid, 2005; Macbeth, 2006; Rogue, 2007; Terminator Salvation, Avatar, 2009; Clash of the Titans, Last Night, 2010; The Debt, Texas Killing Fields, 2011; Drift, Man on a Ledge, Wrath of the Titans, 2012. Honours: AFI Award for Best Lead Actor, 2004; GQ Australia Actor, 2009; Saturn Award, International Award, Giffoni Award, ShoWest Award, Teen Choice Award, 2010.

WÓRUM Ferenc, b. 15 March 1936, Hungary. Professor of Medicine; Cardiologist. m. Erzsébet Mészáros, 2 sons. Education: MD, University Medical School of Debrecen, 1960; Specialist of Internal Diseases, 1965; Specialist of Cardiac Diseases, 1988; PhD, Hungarian Academy of Sciences, 1980; Széchenyi Professorial Scholarship, 1998. Appointments: Assistant Professor, Lecturer, Associate Professor, 1960-92, Professor, 1992-, Departments of Internal Medicine, Medical and Health Science Centre, University of Debrecen; Pioneer of Clinical Cardiac Electrophysiology and modern Arrhythmology in Hungary (His-Bundle ECG, Programmed Electro-stimulation); Head of the Research Working Group of Cardiac Arrthythmias, Cardiac Electrophysiology, Pacemaker and Implantable Defibrillator

Therapy; Developed several new cardiologic instruments and methods; Reader of 4 medical journals. Publications: 186 publications (45 passages in books); 231 lectures in 18 countries; 69 European, World and International Congresses, 10 in USA, Canada, Australia and Hong Kong. Honours: 3 Governmental Awards: Award for Sporting Activity, 1976; Awards for University Teaching, 1980, 1986; Listed in national and international biographical dictionaries. Memberships: Hungarian Society of Internal Medicine, 1965-; Hungarian Society of Cardiology, 1975-; European Society of Cardiology, 1975-; Board, Hungarian Society of Cardiology, 1990-98; Board, Hungarian Arrhythmia's and Pacemaker Working Group, 1990-98; Fellow of European Society of Cardiology, 2008-. Address: 1st Department of Medicine, Medical and Health Science Centre, University of Debrecen, Nagyerdei krt. 98, PO Box 19, H-4012 Debrecen, Hungary. E-mail: worum@internal.med.unideb.hu

WRIGHT George T(haddeus), b. 17 December 1925, Staten Island, New York, USA. Professor Emeritus; Author; Poet. m. Jerry Honeywell, 1955. Education: BA, Columbia College, 1946; MA, Columbia University, 1947; University of Geneva, 1947-48; PhD, University of California, 1957. Appointments: Teaching Assistant, 1954-55; Lecturer, 1956-57, University of California; Visiting Assistant Professor, New Mexico Highlands University, 1957; Instructor-Assistant Professor, University of Kentucky, 1957-60; Assistant Professor, San Francisco State College, 1960-61; Associate Professor, University of Tennessee, 1961-68; Fulbright Lecturer, University of Aix-Marseilles, 1964-66, University of Thessaloniki, 1977-78; Visiting Lecturer, University of Nice, 1965; Professor, 1968-89, Chairman, English Department, 1974-77, Regents' Professor, 1989-93, Regents' Professor Emeritus, 1993-, University of Minnesota. Publications: Author: The Poet in the Poem: The Personae of Eliot, Yeats and Pound, 1960; W H Auden, 1969, revised edition, 1981; Shakespeare's Metrical Art, 1988; Hearing the Measures: Shakespearean and Other Inflections, 2002; Poetic Craft and Authorial Design, 2011. Editor: Seven American Literary Stylists from Poe to Mailer: An Introduction, 1973; Aimless Life: Poems 1961-1995, 1999. Contributions to: Articles, reviews, poems and translations in many periodicals and books. Honours: Guggenheim Fellowship, 1981-82; National Endowment for the Humanities Fellowship, 1984-85; Phi Kappa Phi; William Riley Parker Prize, Modern Language Association, 1974, 1981; T S Eliot Memorial Lecturer, 2007. Memberships: Minnesota Humanities Commission, 1985-88; Modern Language Association; Shakespeare Association of America. Address: 2617 West Crown King Drive, Tucson, AZ 85741, USA.

WRIGHT John Robert, b. 20 October 1936, Carbondale, Illinois, USA. Priest; Professor. Education: BA optime merens, University of the South, Sewanee, Tennessee, 1958; MA Honours, Mediaeval History, Emory University, Atlanta, Georgia, 1959; MDiv cum laude, General Theological Seminary, New York City, 1963; DPhil, Oxford University, England, 1967. Appointments: Ordained, 1963; Instructor in Church History, Episcopal Divinity School, Cambridge, Massachusetts, 1966-68; Assistant Professor of Church History, 1968-71, Professor of Church History, 1971-, St Mark's Professor of Ecclesiastical History, 1974-, General Theological Seminary, New York City; Several visiting positions including Visiting Professor, St George's College, Jerusalem, 1982, 1992, 1995, 1996; Provost's Visiting Professor in Divinity, Trinity College, University of Toronto, 1989. Publications: Author, co-author, editor, co-author, 16 books including: Episcopalians and Roman Catholics: Can They Ever Get Together?, 1972; Handbook of American Orthodoxy, 1972; A Communion of Communions: One Eucharistic Fellowship, 1979; The Church and the English Crown, 1305-1334: A Study based on the Register of Archbishop Walter Reynolds, 1980; Called to Full Unity: Documents on Anglican-Roman Catholic Relations 1966-1983, 1986; Prayer Book Spirituality, 1989; Readings for the Daily Office from the Early Church, 1991; The Anglican Tradition: A Handbook of Sources, 1991; On Being a Bishop: Papers on Episcopacy from the Moscow Consultation 1992, 1993; Saint Thomas Church Firth Avenue, 2001; Russo-Greek papers 1863-1874, 2002; Ancient Christian Commentary on Scripture: Proverbs, Ecclesiastes, and Song of Solomon, 2005; A Companion to Bede, 2008; Forthcoming: Anglican Commentaries on the 39 Articles; The Privilege of England 1231-1530; 3 booklets; 169 papers and articles. Honours include: Phi Beta Kappa, Pi Gamma Mu and Omicron Delta Kappa, 1958; Life Fellow, Royal Historical Society, London, 1981-; DD hc, Episcopal Theological Seminary of the Southwest, Austin, Texas, 1983; Honorary Canon Theologian to Bishop of New York, 1990-; DD hc, Trinity Lutheran Seminary, 1991; DCnL hc, University of the South, 1996; Dr Theol hc, University of Bern (Switzerland), 2000; Holy Crosses of the Orthodox Patriarchs of Constantinople, Jerusalem, Antioch and Moscow; Historiographer of the Episcopal Church, 2000-; Life Fellow, Society of Antiquaries, London, 2001; One Lord, One Faith, One Baptism: Studies in Christian Ecclesiality and Ecumenism in Honor of J Robert Wright, 2006; Cross of St Augustine of Canterbury, 2007. Memberships include: The Anglican Society, President, 1994-; North American Academy of Ecumenists, President, 1989-91; Conference of Anglican Church Historians, Convenor, 1995-; American Catholic Historical Association; American Society of Church History; Medieval Academy of America. Address: c/o General Theological Seminary, 177 Ninth Avenue #2H, New York, NY10011, USA. E-mail: wright@gts.edu

WRIGHT Robert Alfred (Air Marshal Sir), b. 10 June 1947, Hamble, Hampshire, England. Military Representative. m. Margaret, 1 son, 1 daughter. Education: Graduate, Royal Air Force Staff College, 1982. Appointments: Operational Requirements Division, Ministry of Defence, 1982-84; Directing Staff, Royal Air Force Staff College, 1984-87; Officer Commanding IX Squadron, RAF Brueggen, 1987-89; Personal Staff Officer to Chief of Air Staff, 1989-91; Station Commander, RAF Brueggen, 1992-94; Assistant Chief of Staff, Policy & Plans, NATO HQ, High Wycombe, 1994-95; Air Commander, Operations Headquarters Strike Command, 1995-97; Promoted to Air Vice Marshal, 1997; Military Advisor to High Representative, Sarajevo, 1997-98; Chief of Staff to Air Member for Personnel and Deputy Commander-in-Chief, Personnel & Training Command, RAF Innsworth, 1998-2000; Assistant Chief of Staff, Policy & Requirements, Supreme Headquarters Allied Powers Europe, 2000-02; Promoted to Air Marshal, 2002; UK Military Representative to NATO and EU Military Committees, 2002-. Honours: Air Force Cross, 1982; KBE, 2004. Memberships: Fellow, Royal Aeronautical Society; President: Combined Services Winter Sports Association; RAF Winter Sports Federation; RAF Athletics Association; Naval 8/208 Squadron Association. Address: UKMILREP, HQ NATO, Boulevard Leopold III, 1110 Brussels, Belgium.

WRIGHT Theodore Paul Jr, b. 12 April 1926, Port Washington, New York, USA. Professor. m. Susan J Standfast, 1 son, 2 daughters. Education: BA, Swarthmore College, 1949; MA, 1951, PhD, 1957, Yale University. Appointments:

Instructor to Associate Professor, Bates College, Lewiston, Maine, USA, 1955-65; Associate Professor, Professor, Graduate School of Public Affairs, State University of New York at Albany, Albany, New York, 1965-95; Emeritus Professor, 1995-. Publications: American Support of Free Elections Abroad, 1963; 78 articles and chapters in books on Muslim politics, India and Pakistan, 1963-2010; Affirmative Action vs Reservaton in the Private Sector: The United States and India; Return of the Diaspora to the Homeland: Israel and Pakistan compared, 2009; Alliances of Sentiment vs Allicance of Interests: A cooperation study, 2010. Honours: Phi Beta Kappa, 1949; BA with high honours, Swarthmore College; Fulbright Awards to India, 1961, 1963-64, to Pakistan, 1983, 1990; SSRC/ACLS to London, 1974-75; AIIS to India, 1969-70. Memberships: Association for Asian Studies; Board Member, American Council for the Study of Islamic Societies; Past President, now Newsletter Editor, South Asian Muslim Studies Association; Columbia University Faculty Seminar on South Asia, 1967-; Past President, New York Conference on Asian Studies; European Conference on Modern South Asian Studies, 1974-; Board Member, New Netherland Institute; Past President, The Dutch Settler's Society of Albany; Secretary, New Netherland Institute, 2007-. Address: 17 Wellington Way, Niskayuna, NY 12309, USA. E-mail: wright15@Juno.com

WRONG Dennis Hume, b. 22 November 1923, Toronto, Ontario, Canada. Emeritus Professor of Sociology. Education: BA, University of Toronto, 1945; PhD, Columbia University, New York City, 1956. Appointments: Instructor, Department of Economics and Social Institutions, Princeton University, 1949-50; Instructor in Sociology, The Newark Colleges, Rutgers University, Newark, New Jersey, 1950-51; Research Assistant to George F Kennan and Robert Strunsky, Institute for Advanced Studies, 1951-53; Research Associate and Lecturer, Department of Political Economy, University of Toronto, 1954-56; Assistant Professor and Associate Professor, Department of Sociology, Brown University, 1956-61; Associate Professor of Sociology, Graduate Faculty, The New School for Social Research, 1961-63; Professor and Chairman, Department of Sociology, University College, New York University, 1963-65; Professor of Sociology, University of Nevada, Reno, 1965-66; Professor of Sociology, 1966-94, Emeritus Professor of Sociology, 1994-, New York University. Publications: Author and editor: 13 books; Numerous articles in professional, intellectual and political journals. Honours: Visiting Fellow, Nuffield College, Oxford University, 1978; Guggenheim Fellow, 1984-85; Visiting Fellow, European University Institute, Florence, Italy, 1996-97. Listed in Who's Who publications and biographical dictionaries. Memberships: Pre-doctoral Fellow, Canadian Social Science Research Council; Fellow, Woodrow Wilson International Center for Scholars, Washington DC, 1991-92. Address: 144 Drakes Corner Road, Princeton, NJ 08540, USA.

WRONG Oliver Murray, b. 7 February 1925, Oxford, England. Clinical Medicine. m. Marilda Musacchio, 2 daughters. Education: Edinburgh Academy, 1938-41; Magdalen College, Oxford University, 1942-47. Appointments: Junior Hospital Posts, Oxford & RAMC, 1947-51; Senior Intern in Medicine, Toronto General Hospital, 1951-52; Clinical and Research Fellow, Massachusetts General Hospital, Boston, 1952-53; Tutor, Medicine, University of Manchester, 1954-58; Lecturer, Medicine, 1959-61, Professor of Medicine, 1972-90, University College London; Senior Lecturer, Royal Postgraduate Medical School, London, 1961-69; Professor of Medicine, Dundee University, 1969-72. Publications: Approximately 150, on renal function and salt and water metabolism, in peer reviewed journals and books. Honours: Demyship, Magdalen College, Oxford, 1943; George Herbert Hunt Travelling Scholarship, University of Oxford, 1951; James Howard Means Visiting Physician, Massachusetts General Hospital, 1973; Chairman, National Kidney Research Fund, 1976-80. Memberships: Renal Association; Association of Physicians, Great Britain & Ireland. Address: Flat 8, 96-100 New Cavendish Street, London W1W 6XN, England. E-mail: oliverwrong@aol.com

WULSTAN David, b. 18 January 1937, Birmingham, England. Research Professor. m. Susan Graham, 1 son. Education: Royal Masonic School, Bushey; BSc (Lond), College of Technology, Birmingham; MA, Magdalen College, Oxford (pupils include Professors David Riley, John Deathridge, Jan Smacny, Nicola le Fanu, also Jane Glover, Geoffrey Skidmore, Harry Christophers & Peter Philips); Studied under Egon Wellesz and Bernard Rose, also Lennox Berkeley and Peter Wishart; Composition: Clarence Raybould and Sir Adrian Boult (conducting). Appointments: Fellow and Lecturer, Magdalen College, Oxford, 1964-78; Visiting Professor, Department of N E Studies, Berkeley, USA, 1979; Statutory Lecturer and Professor of Music, University College, Cork (pupils include Mary O'Neill, Professors Desmond Hunter & Noel O'Regan), 1979-83; Gregynog Professor of Music, University of Wales, Aberystwyth, 1983-90; Research Professor, 1990-, Honorary Professor, 2010; Director, The Clerkes of Oxenford (founded 1961). Publications: Tudor Music, 1985; Editions of Gibbons & Sheppard; The Emperor's Old Clothes, 2001; The Poetic and Musical Legacy of Heloise and Abelard, 2003; The Play of Daniel (new edition), 2006; Music from the Paraclete, 2007; St Peter's Chant Book, 2011; Appearances at BBC Proms and many festivals in Britain and Europe; Broadcasts and TV appearances. Memberships: Member of Council, Plainsong & Medieval Music Society; Consulting Editor, Spanish Academic Press; Fellow, Royal Society of Musicians; Musical Consultant, Centre for the Study of the Cantigas de Santa Maria, Oxford; Instructor, British Aikido Federation. Address: Hillview Croft, Lon Tyllwyd, Llanfarian, Aberystwyth, Cardiganshire, SY23 4UH, Wales.

WYATT Harold Vivian, Chartered Biologist. Education: BSc, General, 1951, BSc (2nd class Hons), Zoology, 1952, PhD, Microbiology, 1957, University of London; Appointments: HM Army, 1944-48; Research Assistant, Department of Bacteriology, St Bartholomew's Hospital, London, 1954-57; Postdoctoral Fellow, Johns Hopkins, Baltimore, USA, 1957-59; ICI Fellow, University of Leeds, 1959-62; Fellow, Institute of Biology, 1964-; Visiting Scientist, National Cancer Institute, Maryland, USA, 1969-71; Honorary Research Associate, Manchester University, 1980-81; Reader in Microbiology, University of Bradford, 1962-82; Director, School of Sciences, West Bank, 1982-83; Guest Worker, Indian Institute of Chemical Biology, Calcutta, 1985; Independent research, Malta, India, Bangladesh & Pakistan, 1983-; Honorary Research Fellow, University of Leeds, 1986-2002; WHO Expert, 2002-; Visiting Lecturer, Philosophy, University of Leeds, 2004-. Publications: Over 300 papers, letters chapters and books; More than 150 book reviews; Over 150 abstracts at meetings, pieces in newsletters, reports, etc. Honours: Honorary Lecturer, Bradford College of Art, 1962-69; Honorary Demonstrator, Leeds University, 1962-69; Visiting Scientist Award, National Institutes of Health, USA, 1969-71; Guest Lecturer, British Society for Parasitology, 1980; Invited speaker at many conferences around the world; Listed in international biographical dictionaries; Numerous grants for research. Memberships: European Association of Science Editors; Society for General

Microbiology; Royal Society for Tropical Medicine and Hygiene; British Society for Medical Anthropology; Society of Biology; British Infection Society; Sickle Cell Society; Marine Biological Association. Address: 1 Hollyshaw Terrace, Leeds LS15 7BG, England. E-mail: nurhvw@leeds.ac.uk Website: http://sites.google.com/site/vivianwyatt/

WYMAN Bill (William George Perks), b. 24 Oct 1936, Lewisham, London, England. Musician (bass). m. (1) Diane Cory, 1959, divorced, 1 son, (2) Mandy Smith, 1989, divorced 1991, m. (3) Suzanne Accosta, 1993, 1 son, 1 daughter. Career: Member, The Rolling Stones, 1962-93; Owner, Ripple Records; Ripple Music; Ripple Publications; Ripple Productions; Sticky Fingers Restaurants; Numerous tours, concerts include: Rolling Stones '66 tour, 1966; Sunday Night At The London Palladium, 1967; Free concert, Altamont Speedway, 1969; Knebworth Festival, 1976; Prince's Trust charity concert, 1986; Steel Wheels North American Tour, 1989. Recordings: Albums include: The Rolling Stones, 1964; The Rolling Stones, No 2, 1965; Out Of Our Heads, 1965; Aftermath, 1966; Between The Buttons, 1967; Their Satanic Majesties Request, 1967; Beggar's Banquet, 1968; Let It Bleed, 1969; Get Yer Ya-Ya's Out, 1969; Sticky Fingers, 1971; Exile On Main Street, 1972; Goat's Head Group, 1973; It's Only Rock and Roll, 1974; Black And Blue, 1976; Some Girls, 1978; Emotional Rescue, 1980; Still Life, 1982; Primitive Cool, 1987; Steel Wheels, 1989; Flashpoint, 1991; Solo: Stone Alone; Monkey Grip; Bill Wyman; Digital Dreams; Struttin' Our Stuff; Anyway the Wind Blows; Singles include: Come On; I Wanna Be Your Man; Get Off Of My Cloud; 19th Nervous Breakdown; Let's Spend The Night Together; It's All Over Now; Little Red Rooster; (I Can't Get No) Satisfaction; Jumping Jack Flash; Honky Tonk Women; Brown Sugar; Miss You; Ruby Tuesday; Paint It Black; Going To A Go-Go; Emotional Rescue; It's Only Rock'n'Roll; Harlem Shuffle; Start Me Up; Angie; Undercover Of The Night. Publications: The Story Of A Rock And Roll Band (with Ray Coleman), 1990; Stone Alone. Honours include: Silver Clef Award, Nordoff-Robbins Music Therapy, 1982; Grammy Lifetime Achievement Award, 1986; Inducted into Rock And Roll Hall Of Fame, 1989; Q Award, Best Live Act, 1990; Ivor Novello Awards, Outstanding Contribution To British Music, 1991. Address: c/o Ripple Productions, 344 Kings Road, London SW3 5UR, England.

X

XIAO Jianhua, b. 29 May 1962, Jiangxi, China. Professor. m. Hao Caikong, 1 son. Education: BA, Applied Geophysics, China Institute of Mining & Technology, 1978-82; Master, Applied Geophysics, 1988-91, Dr, Mechanics, 1997-2000, China University of Mining & Technology; Visitor, Geology & Geophysics, Edinburgh University, 1994-95. Appointments: Technician, Geophysical Prospecting Group of Coal Industry Ministry, 1982-87; Engineer, 1987-91, Senior Engineer, 1991-99, Researcher, 1999-2004, Geophysical Prospecting Group of Coal Geology of China; Researcher, Shanghai Jiaotong University, Basic Science Research Group, 2004-06; Professor, Henan Polytechnic University, 2006-. Publications: About 20 papers on geophysical prospecting; Around 10 papers on physics; Approximately 60 papers on rational mechanics and its application. Memberships: Society of Geophysist of China; Society of Physics of China; Society of Mechanics of China; Society of Materials Science of China. Address: Measurement Institute, Henan Polytechnic University, Jiaozuo, Henan, 454000, China. E-mail: jhxiao@hpu.edu.cn

XIAO Wenjia, b. 21 August 1979, China. Scientist. m. Xiuyin He, 1 daughter. Education: PhD, Physics, Sun Yat-sen University, 2008. Appointments: Postdoctoral Scientist, TU Darmstadt, Germany, 2009-. Publications: More than 10 academic papers on international journals and/ or conferences. Honours: Permanent Resident of Germany as Highly Qualified Young Scientist. Address: Center of Smart Interfaces, TU Darmstadt, Petersenstr 32, 64287 Darmstadt, Germany. E-mail: wenjiaxiao@gmail.com

XIE Baohui, b. August 1943, Tianjin, China. Senior Physician. Education: 4th Military Medicine University; Chinese Traditional Medicine Research Class, Tianjin Traditional Medicine University. Appointments: Physician in Chief, Acupuncture Department, First Teaching Hospital, Tianjin Traditional Medicine University, National Clinical Research Centre of Acupuncture and Moxibustion, China Centre of Acupuncture and Moxibustion; Dr of Medicine, Visiting Professor, The Open University for Complementary Medicine; Standing Councillor, Chinese Famous Physician Association. Publications: Numerous articles in professional journals. Honours: Honourship of Outstanding Contribution and Achievement, 1997; Excellent Essay Prize, 2nd Shanghai International Symposium on Clinical Acupuncture, 1998; Excellent Essay Prize, Shanghai Journal of Acupuncture and Moxibustion, 1998; Honourable title of The Famous Doctor of China, and First Prize for Science and Technology Contributions, Co-operative Centre for Characteristic Medicine of China, Academy of Chinese Medical Sciences and General Editorial Committee of Library for Excellent Academic Achievements of Traditional Chinese Medicine, 1998; Contemporary Great Figure in World Traditional Medicine by Board of Committee of Grand System of World Traditional Medicine, 1999; First Prize, Golden Cup Award, Chinese Famous Physician, 2000; Great Anton Medal, Indian 46th World Traditional Medicine Conference, 2008; Distinguished Award of Excellence, Open International University for Complementary Medicine, 2008; Title of Health Ambassador and Distinguished Award of Excellence, World Traditional Medicine & Culture Protection and Development Committee, 2008; Chinese Famous Figure, 2009; Listed in international biographical dictionaries. Memberships: Senior Member, Chinese Acupuncture Society. Address: Unit 301, Bldg 13, No 1800 DongFang Rd, PuDong District, Shanghai 200127, P R China.

XIE Christina Xinyan, b. 4 October 1962, Beijing, China. Language Educator. 2 daughters. Education: BA, Language Education, Middle South University of China, 1982; MA, Language Education, University of Cincinnati, Ohio, USA, 1988; Doctor of Education, University of Leicester, England, 2010. Appointments: Language Instructor, Department of Chinese and Bilingual Studies, Hong Kong Polytechnic University, 1998-2011. Publications: Mainland Chinese Students' Adjustment to Studying and Living in Hong Kong, 2010; Seeking Educational Opportunities in Hong Kong, 2011. Honours: Listed in international biographical dictionaries; Putonghua Proficiency Test National Examiner, PRC National Committee of Chinese Languages, 2004-11; Examiner of Putonghua Oral Subject for Teacher Assessment Hong Kong Examinations Assessment Authority, Hong Kong, 2008-11; Chairperson, Session on Education and Globalization, 2010; Member, International Scientific Advisory Board, 2011; Life Member, International Biographical Association, Cambridge; Member, International Technology, Education and Development Conference, 2011. Address: Hong Kong Polytechnic University, Department of Chinese and Bilingual Studies, Hung Hom, Kowloon, Hong Kong. E-mail: chxyxie@polyu.edu.hk

XIONG Yu, b. 7 April 1981. Professor. Education: BSc, Chongqing University; PhD, Nottingham Trent University. Appointments: EPSRC Research Fellow, 2009-10; Lecturer, Operations Management; Director, China Management Research Institute, Queen's University, Belfast. Publications: 2 books; 1 book chapter; Numerous articles in professional journals. Honours: Chinese Government Awards for Outstanding Overseas Student; London Olympic Torch Bearer, 2012. Memberships: FSRA; MIEI; CEng. E-mail: xyu2000@gmail.com

DICTIONARY OF INTERNATIONAL BIOGRAPHY 36th EDITION

Y

YADLIN Aharon, b. 17 April 1926, Ben Shemen, Tel Aviv, Israel. Chairman. m. (1) Ada Hacohen, 1950, deceased 1998, 3 sons, (2) Adina Lindborg, 2008. Education: Graduate, Reali High School, Haifa, 1944; BA, 1954, MA, 1964, Hebrew University of Jerusalem. Appointments: National Leader, Boy Scout Movement, 1945-46; Founder Member, Kibbutz Hatzerim, 1946-; Educational Attache, Palmach (Hagana Forces), 1948-49; Member, Executive Council of the Histadrut (Israel Federation of Labour), 1950-52; Lecturer, Director, Beit Berl, 1955-57; Member, Israeli Parliament (Knesset), 1959-79; Deputy Minister of Education, Chairman of Public Council on Youth, Chairman of Zionist Council in Israel, Chairman of the Board of Directors of Beit Berl, 1964-72; Secretary, Israeli Labour Party, 1972-74; Minister of Education and Culture, 1974-77; Chairman, Educational and Cultural Committee, Israeli Parliament, 1977-79; Chairman, Scientific Council of the Ben Gurion Institute and Archives, 1979-85; Chairman, Beer Sheva Theatre, 1980-82; Chairman, Beit Berl, College of Education, 1981-82; Member, Faculty of Efal College and of Yad Tabenkin Institute for Kibbutz Studies, 1981-84; Visiting Scholar, Jewish Studies, Harvard University, Boston, USA, 1982; General Secretary, United Kibbutz Movement, 1985-89; Chairman, Bialik Institute, 1990-; Chairman, World Labour Zionist Movement, 1992-2002; Chairman, Efal College and Yad Tabenkin Research Center, 2002-; Deputy Chairman, Executive Council of Ben Gurion University of the Negev, 1990-; Chairman, Beit Yatziv Educational Center, Beer Sheva, 1992-. Publications: Understanding the Social System, 1957; The Aim and the Movement, On Humanistic Socialism/Articles of Israeli Sociology, the Labour Movement, Education, Youth Problems and Kibbutz issues, 1979. Honours: Doctor Honoris, Ben Gurion University of the Negev, 1988; Israel Prize, 2010. Address: Kibbutz Hatzerim, M P Hanegev 85420, Israel.

YAKOVLEV Valery Petrovitch, b. 28 September 1940, Volgograd, Russia. Physicist. m. Margarita Yakovleva, 2 daughters. Education: MS, Distinction, 1963, PhD, 1967, DSc, 1987, Moscow Engineering Physics Institute. Appointments: Assistant Professor, 1967-69, Senior Lecturer, 1969-75, Associate Professor, 1975-88, Full Professor, 1988-, Moscow Engineering Physics Institute; Heraeus Professor, Universität Ulm, Germany, 1994-1996. Publications: Over 180 scientific papers on quantum electrodynamics of strong fields, physics of semiconductors, interferometry of atomic states and matter waves, subrecoil laser cooling and atom optics and strange kinetics; Monograph, Mechanical Action of Light on Atoms, 1990. Memberships: Affiliate, Institute of Physics, London. Address: Theoretical Nuclear Physics Department, National Research Nuclear University, Kashirskoe shosse 31, 115409 Moscow, Russia. E-mail: yakovlev@theor.mephi.ru

YALCINKAYA Ozgur, b. 14 November 1978, Turkey. Industrial Engineer. m. Esen Gun. Education: BSc, 2000, MSc, 2004, PhD, 2010, Industrial Engineer. Appointments: Research Assistant. Publications: Modelling and optimization of average travel time for a metro line by simulation and response surface methodology, 2009; An Integrated Decision Support Approach for Project Investors in Risky and Uncertain Environments, 2010. Honours: Excellence Success Award, Rank of First Department. Memberships: UCTEA Chamber of Mechanical Engineers; Graduates Association of Kyrykkale Anatolia High School; Operational Research Society, Turkey. Address: DEÜ Mühendislik Fakültesi Endüstri Mühendislioi Bölümü, Týnaztepe Kampüsü 35160 Buca, Ismir, Turkey. E-mail: ozgur.yalcinkaya@deu.edu.tr Website: http://kisi.deu.edu.tr/ozgur.yalcinkaya

YALE-LOEHR Stephen, b. 10 June 1954, Newport News, Virginia, USA. Lawyer. m. Amy, 2 sons, 1 daughter. Education: BA, Archaeology, Japanese, Photography, Cornell University, 1977; JD (cum laude), International Legal Affairs, Cornell Law School, 1981. Appointments: Special Prosecutor's Office, New York State Department of Law, 1979; Olwine, Connelly, Chase, O'Donnell & Weyher, New York, 1980; Law Clerk to Chief Judge Howard G Munson, Syracuse, 1981-82; Associate, Sutherland, Asbill & Brennan, 1982-86; Immigration Columnist, New York Law Journal, 1997-2007; Of counsel, Miller Mayer, 1990-; Adjunct Professor, Georgetown University Law Center, Washington, 1988-90; Adjunct Professor, Cornell Law School, 1991-; Executive Editor, Immigration Briefings, Co-Editor, Interpreter Releases, Federal Publications Inc, 1986-94; Co-author, Immigration Law and Procedure, Matthew Bender & Company, 1994-. Publications: Editor, Green Card Stories, 2011; Author or co-author of over 200 books and articles. Honours: American Immigration Lawyers Association (AILA)'s Elmer Fried Award for Excellence in Teaching, 2001; AILA's Edith Lowenstein Award for Excellence in Advancing the Practice of Immigration Law, 2004; Annually listed in Chambers USA and Chambers Global as one of the top immigration lawyers in the USA. Memberships: ABA; Alliance of Business Immigration Lawyers; American Immigration Lawyers Association; DC Bar Association; New York Bar Association; Amnesty International; Phi Beta Kappa; Founder and initial Executive Director, Invest In the USA; AILA, EB-5 Committee; AILA Business Immigration. Address: 301 Highgate Road, Ithaca, NY 14850, USA. E-mail: swy1@cornell.edu

YALOW Rosalyn, b. 19 July 1921, New York, New York, USA. Medical Physicist. m. Aaron Yalow, 1943, 1 son, 1 daughter. Education: Graduated, Physics, Hunter College, New York, 1941; PhD, Experimental Nuclear Physics, University of Illinois, 1945. Appointments: Assistant in Physics, University of Illinois, 1941-43; Instructor, 1944-45; Lecturer and temporary Assistant Professor in Physics, Hunter College, New York, 1946-50; Physicist and Assistant Chief, 1950-70, Acting Chief, 1968-70, Chief Radioimmunoassay Reference Laboratory, 1969, Chief Nuclear Medicine Service, 1970-80, Senior Medical Investigator, 1972-92, Senior Medical Investigator Emeritus, 1992-, Director, Solomon A Berson Research Laboratory, Veterans Administration Medical Center, 1973-92, Radioisotope Service, Veterans Administration Hospital, Bronx, New York; Research Professor, 1968-74, Distinguished Service Professor, 1974-79, Department of Medicine, Mount Sinai School of Medicine, New York; Distinguished Professor at Large, 1979-85, Professor Emeritus, 1985-, Albert Einstein College of Medicine, Yeshiva University; Chair, Department of Clinical Sciences, Montefiore Hospital, Bronx, 1980-85; Solomon A Berson Distinguished Professor at Large, Mt Sinai School of Medicine, New York, 1986-; Harvey Lecturer, 1966; American Gastroenterology Association Memorial Lecturer, 1972; Joslyn Lecturer, New England Diabetes Association, 1972; Franklin I Harris Memorial Lecturer, 1973; 1st Hagedorn Memorial Lecturer, Acta Endocrinologia Congress, 1973; President, Endocrine Society, 1978-79; Honours: Over 60 honorary doctorates; Joint Winner, Nobel Prize for Physiology or Medicine, 1977; More than 30 other awards. Memberships: NAS; American Physics Society; Radiation Research Society; American Association of Physicists in Medicine; Biophysics Society; American Academy of Arts and Sciences; American Physiology Society; Foreign Associate, French Academy of Medicine; Fellow, New York Academy of Science; Radiation Research Society; American Association of Physicists in Medicine; Associate Fellow in Physics, American College of Radiology; American Diabetes Association; Endocrine Society; Society of Nuclear Medicine. Address: Veterans Administration Medical Center, 130 West Kingsbridge Road, Bronx, New York, NY 10468, USA.

YAMADA Yoshiro, b. 23 January 1942, Miwa-cho, Ono City, Hyogo Prefecture, Japan. Technical Advisor; Lecturer; Licensed Professional Engineer in Japan; Licensed Industry Safety Consultant. m. Keiko Kanemoto, 1 daughter. Education: Bachelor of Engineering, Metallurgical Department, Faculty of Engineering, 1964, Master of Engineering, Graduate School, 1966, Doctor of Engineering, 1976, Osaka University. Appointments: Researcher, Research Leader, Central Research Laboratory, 1966-78, Senior Researcher, 1979-85, Section Manager, 1986-89, General Manager, Wire Rod and Bar Development Department, 1989-91, General Manager, Wire Rod and Bar Technology Department, 1992-93, Kobe Steel Ltd; Director, Suncall Corporation, Japan, 1993-99; Technical Advisor, Suncall Corporation, 1999-2003; Part-time Lecturer, Graduate School, Kansai University, 2002-; Representative, Yamada Technoresearch & Consultant Office, 2003-; Lecturer, Setsunan University, 2006-. Publications: Guide to Fastening Technology of Bolted Joints, Part 1, Strength, 1992; Spring Materials and their Characteristics, 2000; Materials for Springs, 2007. Honours: Allan B Dove Awards, 1986, 1992; Honourable Mention, Wire Association International, 1976; Aida Technology Award, 1977; Nishiyama Memorial Award, 1994; American Medal of Honor, 2002; Various invention awards. Memberships: ASM International; Wire Association International; Iron and Steel Institute of Japan; Japan Society of Spring Engineers; Japan Society for Technology of Plasticity; The Institution of Professional Engineers, Japan; The Japan Society for Heat Treatment; American Society for Engineering Education; Japan Association of Fine Particle Bombardment Surface Modification Technology; Society of Materials Science, Japan; Japanese Society for Engineering Education. Address: 968-5 Fujie, Akashi-City, Hyogo-Prefecture, 673-0044, Japan.

YAMAGATA Hideo, b. 13 September 1930, Osaka city, Japan. Mathematician. m. Reiko Kusakabe, 2 daughters. Education: Bachelor, 1953, Master, 1955, Osaka University; Doctorate, Kyoto University, Japan, 1981. Appointments: Assistant, Osaka University, Toyonaka, 1962-64; Full time Lecturer, 1964-88, Associate Professor, 1988-94, University of Osaka Prefecture, Sakai; Reviewer, Zentralblatt für Math, Berlin, 1963-; Math Revs, Ann Arbor, Michigan, USA, 1988-; Commuting Editor (Referee), Scienticae Mathematicae Japonicae, Sakai, 2002-. Publications: The Riemann Lebesgue's Theorem and its Application to Cut-off Process, 1964; Singular Cut-off Process and Lorentz Properties, 1965; On c-solitons, 1977; Prime Numbers and Random Numbers, 1988; Comment for a Work on the Generalized Fourier Transform, 2007. Memberships: Mathematical Society of Japan; American Mathematical Society; Society of Systems, Control and Information.

YAMAGATA Toshio, b. 25 March 1948, Utsunomiya City, Japan. Physical Oceanographer. m. Yoko Yamagata, 1 son, 1 daughter. Education: Bachelor of Science, 1971, Master of Science, 1973, Doctor of Science, 1977, University of Tokyo. Appointments: Associate Professor, Research Institute for Applied Mechanics, Kyushu University, 1979; Associate Professor, 1991, Professor, 1995-, Dean, 2009-, Graduate School of Science, University of Tokyo. Publications: About 160 publications in professional scientific journals including: Philosophical Transactions, Royal Society London, 1989; Bulletin of the American Meteorological Society, 1997; Nature, 1999. Honours: Okada Prize and Society Prize, Japan Oceanographic Society; Society Prize, Japan Meteorological Society; Burr Steinbach Scholar of Woods Hole Oceanographic Institution; The Sverdrup Gold Medal, American Meteorological Society; Medal with Purple Ribbon, The Emperor of Japan; Techno-Ocean Award, Techno-Ocean Network. Memberships: Japan Oceanographic Society; Japan Meteorological Society; Fellow, American Geophysical Union; Fellow, American Meteorological Society; Charter member, The Oceanographic Society of the United States of America. Address: Department of Earth and Planetary Science, Graduate School of Science, The University of Tokyo, Tokyo 113-0033, Japan. Website: http://www-aos/ eps.s.u-tokyo.ac.jp/~yamagata/indexj.html

YAMAGUCHI Kenji, b. 19 July 1933, Yamagata, Japan. Economist. m. Momoe Matsumoto, 1 son, 1 daughter. Education: BA, Economics, Tokyo University, 1956; Equivalent MA, Academy of Theoretical Economics, 1962-63. Appointments: Director, National Property Division, Ministry of Finance, 1977-81; Director General, North East Japan, Ministry of Finance, 1981-82; Executive Director, World Bank Group, 1982-87; Senior Executive, Water Development Corporation, 1987-92; Executive Advisor, Mitsui Trust Bank, Tokyo; Chairman for Mitsui Trust International (London), Mitsui Trust Bank, (Zurich), 1992-96; Executive Advisor, Chiyoda Mutual Life, 1996-98; Director, World Economy & Land Laboratory, WELL, 2006-. Publications include: The World Bank, 1990; Land is Public Property, 1992; Land is owned by the Public, 1998; Cool Observation of Japanese Economy, 2006; Foundation for New Prosperity of Japanese Economy, 2008. Honours: Life Rescue Award, 1955; Zuihou-Chuu-Jushou, awarded by the Emperor of of Japan, 2003. Memberships: Ookura-Douyuu-Kai (MOF Old Boys Club). Address: 3-16-43, Utukusiga-oka, Aoba-ku, Yokohama City, 225-0002, Japan. E-mail: well@mx7.ttcn.ne.jp

YAMAGUCHI Masashi, b. 1 September 1948, Yamagata, Japan. Associate Professor. m. Naoko Terakawa, 2 sons, 1 daughter. Education: BS, Yamagata University, Yamagata, Japan, 1971; MS, Tokyo Metropolitan University, Tokyo, Japan, 1974; DSc, 1978. Appointments: Visiting Research Fellow, Memorial Sloan-Kettering Cancer Center, New York, USA 1979; Associate Researcher, 1980; Staff Scientist, Monell Chemical Senses Center, Philadelphia, USA, 1980-81; Research Associate, The Jikei University School of Medicine, Tokyo, Japan, 1981-88; Lecturer, 1988-96; Associate Professor, 1996-, Chiba University, Chiba, Japan. Publications: Articles in medical journals include: Guide Book for Electron Microscopy (in Japanese), 2004; Structome of Exophiala yeast cells determined by freeze-substitution and serial ultrathim sectioning electron microscopy, 2006; Zernike phase contrast electron microscopy of ice-embedded influenza A virus, 2008; Dynamics of the spindle pole body of the pathogenic yeast Cryptococcus neoformance examined by freeze-substitution electron microscopy, 2009. Honours: Best Paper Award, Japanese Society of Electron Microscopy, 1996; Best Paper Award, Japanese Society of Microscopy, 2005; Skill testimonial, Japanese Society of Microscopy, 2010. Memberships: Japanese Society of Microscopy; Japanese Society of Medical Mycology. Address: Medical Mycology Research Centre, Chiba University, 1-8-1 Inohana, Chuo-ku, Chiba 260-8673, Japan. Website: http://www.pf.chiba-u.ac.jp/

DICTIONARY OF INTERNATIONAL BIOGRAPHY 36th EDITION

YAMAGUCHI Masayoshi, b. 15 June 1947, Atami, Japan. Professor. m. Eiko Yamaguchi, 1 son, 1 daughter. Education: Bachelor, 1971, Master, 1973, PhD, 1976, Pharmaceutical Sciences, Shizuoka College of Pharmacy. Appointments: Research Associate, 1973-86, Assistant Professor, 1986-87, Shizuoka College of Pharmacy; Visiting Lecturer, University of Pennsylvania, 1981; Visiting Assistant Professor, Texas Tech University, 1985-86; Visiting Assistant Professor, University of Texas, 1988-89; Faculty, 1987-91, Associate Professor, 1991-93, Professor, 1993-2007, Life and Health Sciences, University of Shizuoka; Scientific Advisor, Kemin Health L C, 2005-10; Visiting Professor, Emory University School of Medicine, 2007-; President, Institute of Bone Health and Nutrition, 2007-; Scientific Advisor, Primus Pharmaceuticals Inc, 2007-. Publications: Over 500 original scientific papers; Books including: Calcium Signaling, Nutritional Factors and Osteoporosis Prevention; Calcium and Life; Biometals; Prevention of Osteoporosis and Nutrition; Discoverer of regucalcin as a regulatory protein in intercellular signalling and a novel protein RGPR-p117 as transcription factor; 90 reviews and books; 8 international and 15 national patents. Honours include: Salute to Greatness Award, IBC, 2006; American Medal of Honour, ABI, 2006; Distinguished Service to Science Award, IBC, 2007; Award, Japan Society for Biomedical Research on Trace Elements, 2007; Gold Medal for Japan, ABI, 2008. Memberships: New York Academy of Sciences; American Society of Cell Biology; American Society for Bone and Mineral Research; International Society for Bone and Mineral; American Society for Biochemistry and Molecular Biology; Japan Society of Biochemistry (councillor); The Japan Endocrine Society (councillor); Japanese Society for Bone and Mineral Research (councillor); Japan Society of Pharmacology (councillor); Japan Society for Biomedical Research on Trace Elements (councillor); Japan Society for Osteoporosis (councillor); Editor, Biomedical Research on Trace Elements, Japan; Editorial Academy Member of the International Journal of Molecular Medicine; Editorial Member, Molecular Medicine Reports, Journal of Osteoporosis; Biotechnology Research International; Jounral of Diabetes and Metabolism; Molecular and Cellular Biochemistry; Endocrinology Studies; Experimental and Therapeutic Medicine; Alternative Medicine Studies; Stem Cell Discovery; Endocrinology & Metabolic Syndrome; Deputy Director General, IBC; Research Board Advisor, ABI; Deputy Governor, ABI; Listed in international biographical dictionaries. Address: Senagawa 1-chome, 15-5, Aoi-ku, Shizuoka City 420-0913, Japan. E-mail: yamamasa1155@yahoo.co.jp

YAMANAKA Einosuke, b. 12 December 1928, Sakai City, Osaka, Japan. Legal History Educator; Professor Emeritus. m. Hideko Nishio. Education: LLB, 1953, LLD, 1975, Osaka University. Appointments: From Assistant to Professor, 1957-92, Professor Emeritus, 1992-, Japanese Legal History, Faculty of Law, Osaka University; Professor, Otemon Gakuin University, 1992-2001; Visiting Professor, Asian Research Institute, Osaka University of Economics and Law, 2002-10; Research Associate, East Asian Studies, Harvard University, 1976; Dean, Faculty of Law Osaka University, 1983-85; Member, Science Council of Japan, 1988-97. Publications: The Formation of the Modern State in Japan and the Bureaucracy, 1974; The Formation of the Modern State in Japan and the Village Law, 1975; The Formation of the Modern State in Japan and the Family System, 1988; Local Government and Local Notables in Modern Japan, 1989; The Rule of The State and Law: From The Tokugawa Shogunate Through The Meiji Restoration Era, 1991; State and Local Government in Modern Japan, 1994; City System and City Notables in Modern Japan, 1995; Modern Local Government System and State in Japan, 1999; Studies in Legal History: A New Perspective on Civil Procedure, 2005. Honours: Fujita Prize, Tokyo Institute for Municipal Research, 1975; Order of Sacred Treasure, Goldrays with Neck Ribbon, Japanese Emperor, 2008. Memberships: Legal History Association, Japan; Japanese Association of Sociology of Law; Comparative Family History Association, Japan. Address: 8-9 4cho Takakuradai, MinamiKu, Sakai City, Osaka, 590-0117 Japan.

YAN Liu, b. 12 October 1969, Shanghai, China. Education: BS, Harbin Institute of Technology, 1991; MS, Qinghai Institute of Environmental Science, 1996; PhD, Qinghai University, 1999. Appointments: Water Engineer, Qinghai Institute of Environmental Science, 1991-96; Research Fellow, Qinghai University, 1996-. Publications: Shanghai Environmental Science, 1990; Modern Chemical Industry, 1994; Water Research, 1995; Spectroscopy and Spectral Analysis, 2000; Acta Physico-Chimica Sinica, 2001; Chinese Journal of Inorganic Chemistry, 2007. Honours: Nobel Prize Nomination, 1996; Listed in international biographical dictionaries; Associate Editor of Environmental Chemistry Letters. Memberships: International Water Association; American Chemical Society; American Physical Society; New York Academy of Sciences; The Chemical Society of Japan; AAAS. Address: School of Chemical Engineering, Qinghai University, Xining, 810016, China. E-mail: liuyan_qhu@163.com

YANAGIHARA Takehiko, b. 10 February 1936, Kobe, Japan. Professor. Education: MD, Osaka University Medical School, Japan, 1960; Neurology, Mayo Graduate School of Medicine, Rochester, USA, 1966. Appointments: Research Fellow, Institute of Neurology, University of London, UK, 1966-67; Research Fellow, Institute of Neurobiology, University of Goteborg, Sweden, 1968-70; Consultant, Neurology, Mayo Clinic, Rochester, USA, 1971-91; Professor, Neurology, Mayo Clinic School of Medicine, Rochester, USA, 1978-91; Professor and Chair, Department of Neurology, Osaka University Medical School, Osaka, Japan, 1991-99. Publications: Over 200 original articles in English; Monographs, Memory Disorders, 1991; Subarachnoid Hemorrhage, 1998. Honours: Special Research Fellowship, Mayo Foundation, 1966-71; Emeritus Professor of Neurology, Mayo Clinic Graduate School of Medicine, 1991-; Emeritus Professor, Osaka University, 1999-. Memberships: American Neurological Association; American Academy of Neurology; American Heart Association; Japanese Neurological Society; Japanese Stroke Society. Address: 1-6-18-202 Minami-ichioka, Minato-ku, Osaka 552-0011, Japan.

YÁÑEZ MORALES María de Jesús, b. 21 September 1952, Madero City, Tamaulipas, Mexico. Plant Pathologist; Professor. Education: Diploma, Shorthand Typist and Accountant Technician, Instituto Comercial Latino, Madero City, 1968; Diploma, Laboratory Technician, Instituto Tecnologico de Ciudad Madero, 1978; BSc, Biology, Universidad del Noreste, Tampico, 1983; MSc, Plant Pathology, Colegio de Postgraduados, Estado de Mexico, 1989; PhD, Plant Pathology, Cornell University, New York, USA, 2000. Appointments: Secretary and Accountant Technician, Pepsi-cola Company, Tampico, 1970-78; Laboratory Technician, 1978-83, Researcher, 1984-91, INIFAP-CEH, Tamaulipas; Researcher, Colegio de Postgraduados, Estado de Mexico, 1991-; Professor/Educator, Universidad del Noreste, Tampico, 1984-85; Professor/Educator, Colegio de Postgraduados, 1992, 2001-; Teaching Assistant, Plant Pathology, Cornell University, 1998.

DICTIONARY OF INTERNATIONAL BIOGRAPHY 36th EDITION

Publications: Numerous articles in professional journals. Honours: Honorific Mention (BSc), Universidad del Noreste, 1983; Honorific Mention (MSc), Colegio de Postgraduados, Estado de Mexico, 1989; National Researcher Level One, SNI and CONACYT, 1989-95, 2000-; Listed in international biographical dictionaries. Memberships: Agrociencia; Revista Mexicana de Fitopatologia; World Federation for Culture Collection in Europe. Address: Colegio de Postgraduados, Fitosanidad, Carretera Federal Mexico-Texcoco Km 36.5, Montecillo, Municipio de Texcoco, Estado de Mexico, CP 56230, Mexico. E-mail: yanezmj@colpos.mx

YANG Victor Ting Hsun, b. 9 April 1931, Peikang, Taiwan. Physician. Education: MB, National Taiwan University, Taipei, 1957. Appointments: Intern, 1959, Resident, 1959-63, Fellow, Gastroenterology, 1963-66, Staff Physician, 1966-92, Department of Medicine, National Taiwan University Hospital, Taipei; Instructor, Medicine, National Taiwan University College of Medicine, 1969-92; Fellow, Gastroenterology, Hospital of the University of Pennsylvania, Department of Medicine, University of Pennsylvania School of Medicine, Philadelphia, USA, 1971-72; Retired, 1992.

YANG Xinjian (Sam), b. 15 November 1954, Hunan, China. Environmental Engineer. m. Bing Shui, 1 son. Education: Bachelor of Engineering, Xiangtan University, China, 1982; Master of Science, University of Cincinnati, Cincinnati, Ohio, 1991. Appointments: Lecturer, Xiangtan University, China, 1982-86; Research Scholar, University of Cambridge, England, 1987-88; Research Assistant, Graduate Student, University of Cincinnati, part-time USEPA Contractor, Cincinnati, 1988-91; Senior Engineer, Process and Development, Preussag Noell Inc, Long Beach, California, 1991-97; Senior Engineer: Mitsubishi, 1997-2000, ABB-ALSTOM Inc, 2000-2001, ERM Inc, 2004-05, City of Los Angeles, 2005-. Publications: Many published papers in China, England and United States authorised textbooks; Invented 7 patent applications and one privately owned patent. Honours: Chinese Education Committee Scholarship; Honorary Fellowship, Salford University; Visiting Scholar, University of Cambridge, England; Listed in national and international biographical dictionaries. Memberships: Air and Waste Management Association, USA; Chinese Science and Technology Association, China. Address: 12001 Cherry Street, Los Alamitos, CA 90720, USA.

YANG Yong-Eui, b. 27 December 1955, Gu-Rye, Junranam Do, Republic of Korea. Professor. m. Hyun-Ja Park, 2 sons, 2 daughters. Education: BA (Honours), 1986, MA (Distinction), 1992, London Bible College; PhD, Wycliffe Hall, Oxford, 1995. Appointments: Paster, Korea General Assembly of Presbyterian Church, 1990; Assistant Professor, Reformed Theological Seminary, Republic of Korea, 1995-2000; Associate Professor, Kukje Theological Seminary, Seoul, 2000-03; Associate Professor, 2003-07, Professor, 2007-, Ezra Bible Institute for Graduate Studies, Goyang Shi. Publications: Jesus and the Sabbath in Matthew's Gospel, 1997; Jesus, the Sabbath, and the Lord's Day, 2000; The Kingdom of God, 2005; How to Read Matthew's Gospel, 2005; How to Read Mark's Gospel, 2010. Honours: Best Book of the Year in the Theology Area Award, Korea Christian Publishers Association, 2000; Most Distinguished Theologian of the Year Award, Korea Evangelical Theological Society, 2007; Best Book of the Year in the Theology Area Award, Korea Christian Publishers Association, 2010. Memberships: Society of Biblical Literature; Tyndale Fellowship; Korea Evangelical Theological Society; Korean Evangelical Society of New Testament Studies. Address: Ezra Bible Institute for Graduate Studies, 292 Goyang Dong, Duckyang Gu, Goyang Shi, Gyunggi Do, 412-801, Republic of Korea. E-mail: ezrayang@hanmail.net

YANNOU Demetre, b. 19 May 1946, Athens, Greece. Musicologist; Educator. Education: MA, History and Archaeology, University of Athens, 1972; Diploma, Viola, Conservatory of Athens, 1972; Musicology, Linguistics, Philosophy, PhD (Musicology), University of Cologne, Germany, 1980. Appointments: Viola Player, 1980-85, Member, Administration Council, 1982-83, Greek National Opera, Athens; Professor, Aristotle University of Thessaloniki, 1985-; Head, Department of Music Studies, Dean of Faculty of Fine Arts, Aristotle University, 1985-. Publications: Articles and communications in musicological journals and conferences in Greek, French, German and English; Musicology books in Greek and German. Memberships: Deutsche Viola Gesellschaft; Gesellschaft für Musik-Forschung; Historic Brass Society, EA. E-mail: yannou@mus.auth.gr

YAO Kui, b. 14 October 1967, Huainan, China. Senior Scientist. Education: BEng, Xi'an Jiaotong University, China, 1989; MEng, Xidian University, China, 1992; PhD, Xi'an Jiaotong University, China, 1995. Appointments: Post Doctoral Fellow, 1995-97, Research Fellow, assigned to Institute of Materials Research and Engineering, 1997-98, Nanyang Technological University, Singapore; Research Associate, Pennsylvania State University, USA, 1998-99; Research Fellow, 1997-2001, Senior Research Fellow, 2002-2003, Senior Scientist, 2003-, Institute of Materials Research and Engineering (IMRE), Singapore. Publications: Invention patents, technical services and publications on functional materials and devices, including ferroelectric, piezoelectric, photovoltaic and chemical sensor materials and their applications. Memberships: Senior member, IEEE; MRS; American Ceramic Society. Address: Institute of Materials Research and Engineering, 3 Research Link, Singapore 117602, Singapore.

YARICHIN Evgeny Mikhailovich, b. 13 June 1950, Krasnoyarsk, Russia. Operational System of Video Information Technology; Researcher. m. Galina Fedorovna, 1 son, 1 daughter. Education: Diploma of Engineer, Krasnoyarsk Polytechnical Institute, 1972; PhD, Leningrad Electrotechnical Institute, 1977. Appointments: Senior Lecturer, Supervisor of research of Laboratory of Systems of Artificial Intellect, Krasnoyarsk technical universities and Siberian Federal University, 1973-2008; General Director, Innovative Research and Production Enterprises, Intron, Sibem and Sem, 1986-98; Senior Scientific Employee, Institute of Petroleum Geology and Geophysics, Siberian branch of Russian Academy of Sciences, 2008-10. Publications: 79 scientific articles; 2 monographs. Honours: Various certificates of honour. Address: Apartment 36, House 13a, Kirenskogo Street, Krasnoyarsk, 660074, Russia. E-mail: intron@yandex.ru

YASUFUKU Sachio, b. 11 November 1929, Qingdao, China. Retired Electrical Engineer. m. Yoko Kikutani, 16 December 1958. Education: BSc, 1952, DEng, 1979, Nagoya University. Appointments: Engineer, Furukawa Electric Co Ltd, Japan, 1952-72; Senior and Chief Specialists, Toshiba Corporation, Japan, 1972-89; Adjunct Professor, Tokyo Denki University, 1989-2005. Publications: 13 papers, on IEEE Transactions Electrical Insulation; 10 papers on IEEE Electrical Insulation Magazine; 13 papers on IEEE DEIS Sponsored Conference Proceedings; Altogether over 60 papers published; Over 10 patents (including US patents). Honours: National Award Invention, Japan, 1963; 23rd National Award for JEMA, about Progress of Electric Machinery, 1974; IEEE Fellow Award, 1993; Distinguished Service Award, IEEE DEIS, 1997; IEEE Life Fellow, 2001; Da Vinci Diamond, 2009; IBC Lifetime Achievement Award, 2010. Memberships: Society Polymer Science, Japan, 1952; IEEE, 1972; IEEJ, 1974. Address: 603, 2-5 2-chome, Katase, Fujisawa City, 251-0032 Japan.

YASUOKA Yoshinori, b. 22 January 1971, Osaka, Japan. Medical Doctor; Cardiovascular Clinician. m. Yuriko, 2 sons, 1 daughter. Education: MD, Kinki University School of Medicine, 1995; Diplomate, Japanese Board of Internal Medicine, 1999; Diplomate, Japanese Board of Circulation Society, 2008. Appointments: Medical Staff, Osaka National Hospital, 2000-04; Assistant Researcher, Victor Chang Cardiac Resesarch Institute, Sydney, Australia, 2004-06; Medical Staff, Osaka Mirami Medical Center, 2006-; Fellow, Japanese Association of Cardiovascular Intervention and Therapeutics, 2008. Publications: Numerous articles in professional journals. Honours: Listed Marquis Who's Who in the World, 2010, 2011. Memberships: Japanese Society of Internal Medicine; Japanese Circulation Society; Japanese College of Cardiology; Japanese Association of Cardiovascular Intervention and Therapeutics. Address: Osaka Minami Medical Center, 2-1 Kidohigashi-machi, Kawachinagano, Osaka 586-8521, Japan.

YATES Alan, b. 30 November 1947, Bishop Auckland, England. Sculptor. Education: Leeholme School; Bishop Auckland Grammar School; Bede College, Durham University. Career: Sculptor in cast bronze; Exhibited at RA, RSA, RCA, RGI, RWA, Paris Salon, Durham University, York, Grantham, Darlington, Perth, Newcastle University, Edinburgh, Cheltenham, Swansea University, Stratford, Northern Open Touring Exhibition, Chelsea Harbour, Manchester Academy, Mall Galleries London, Burlington House, London, Kowalsky Gallery London; Commissions for St James' Youth Centre, Coundon; Grey College, Durham University. Publications: Artists in Britain since 1945; Artists of Northumbria. Address: Leaside, Frosterley, Bishop Auckland, Co Durham, DL13 2RH, England. E-mail: enquiries@sculpturestudio-alanyates.com Website: www.alanyates-sculpture.com

YATUSEVICH Anton Ivanovich, b. 2 January 1947, Brest Region, Belarus. Veterinary Surgeon. m. Valentina P Yatusevich, 1 son, 1 daughter. Education: Zoo-Vet, Technical School, Pinsk, 1967; Veterinarian, 1972; Vitebsk State Veterinary Medicine Institute, 1972; PhD, Veterinary Science, 1978; Doctor of Veterinary Medicine, 1989; Associate Professor, 1980; Professor, 1990. Appointments: Farm Veterinary Surgeon, 1972-73; Assistant, 1973-80, Associate Professor, 1980-84, Pro-rector for Academic Affairs, 1984-89, Parasitology Department, Vitebsk Veterinary Medicine Academy; Head, Parasitology Department, 1990-; Rector, Vitebsk Veterinary Medicine Academy, 1998-; Chief Editor, Veterinarnaya Gazeta, 1995-99; Chief Editor, Veterinary Medicine, 2001-; Scientific Editor, Veterinarnaya Encyclopedia; Editor, Vestnik VSAVM. Publications: 52 textbooks and monographs; 30 invention patents; 665 articles. Honours: Honorary Scientist of the Republic of Belarus; Leading Educator of Belarus; Honorary Inventor; Order of The Badge of Honour; Honorary medals for: Achievements in Veterinary; Exhibition of Economic Achievements; Memorable medals for: Cristianity 2000; 60 Years to the Victory in the Great Patriotic War 1941-1945; Order of Honour; Order of Sts Cyril and Methodius. Memberships: Deputy of the National Parliament; National Assembly of the Republic of Belarus; Chairman, Belarusian Society of Protozoologists; Vice President, International Society of Parasitocenologists; Member, Petrovskaya Academy of Sciences and Arts; Russian Agrarian Education Academy; Russian Academy of Agri-Sci. Address: 1 Dovatora Street 7/11, Vitebsk 210026, Republic of Belarus. E-mail: vetlib@vitebsk.by

YAURA Yukki, Artist. m. Leom Woodal. Education: M Phil, MA, Royal College of Art (Kyoto City University of Art. Appointments: Lecturer and Artist; Group and solo exhibitions and performances throughout the UK and in Spain, Italy, France and Japan; Appearances on film, radio, television and on stage. Publications: Haiga: Illustrated Haiku Poems, 2000; Suiboku-ga: Japanese Ink Painting, 2000; Flowers: Japanese Ink Painting, 2003; Haiga: Illustrated Haiku Poems, 2005; Sho: Japanese Calligraphy, 2006; Haiku Poems E-Book, 2008; Haiku Poems Ilustrados E-book, 2008; Artwork for several books; Numerous articles in professional journals. Honours: New Wave Award, Japan; Holbein Award, Japan; Folio Society Award; Faber-Castel and Letteraset Award; Sheila Robinson Drawing Award; Ray Finnis Scholarship Award; Dunhill Project Award; Kyoto Exchange Award. Address: PO Box 26052, London, SW10 9GW, England. E-mail: info@yaura.net Website: www.yukkiyaura.com

YE Minglu, b. 13 April 1936, Fujian Province, China. Professor of Chemistry. m. Jingjuan Tang, 1 son, 1 daughter. Education: Graduated, Chemistry Department, Fudan University, Shanghai, China, 1958. Appointments: Worked in Department of Nuclear Science, 1958-96, then Department of Environmental Science and Engineering, 1996-98, Fudan University, Shanghai, 1958-98; Professor and Director of the Nuclear Chemistry Section, Fudan University; Lectures, Nuclear Chemistry and Application of Nuclear Technology and completed many science research projects; Visiting Scholar, Freie Universitat Berlin (Free University, Berlin), West Germany, 1984-85; Visiting Researcher, Japan Atomic Energy Research Institute, 1994; Retired, 1998. Publications: 5 books include: Radiochemistry Experiments, 1991; Introduction of Environmental Chemistry, 1997; 62 scientific papers. Honours: 5 science and technology prizes awarded by Shanghai Science Commission and Ministry of Nuclear Industry of China, 1984-96; Biography listed in several national and international biographical publications. Memberships: Council Member: Isotope Society of China, 1985-98, Nuclear and Radiochemistry Society of China, 1991-98; President, 2001-03, Honourable President, 2003-, Australia Alumni Association of Fudan University. Address: 14 Sydney Road, Lindfield, NSW 2070, Australia. E-mail: mingluye@yahoo.com.au

YE Sheng-Long, b. 6 December 1945, Zhejiang, China. m. Wen-Di Zhao, 1 daughter. Education: MD, 1969, MSc, 1982, PhD, 1992, Shanghai Medical University. Appointments: Professor, Medicine and Oncology, Liver Cancer Institute, Zhongshan Hospital, Fudan University, Shanghai; Deputy Director of Institute and Chairman of Department of Hepatic Oncology. Publications: 377 papers, 1983-. Honours: First Prize, 2006, Second Prize, 2008, Achievement in Science & Technology, China. Memberships: Governing Board Member, International Liver Cancer Association; Executive Councilor, Chinese Anti-Cancer Association; Honorary President, Chinese Society of Liver Cancer. Address: 180 Fenglin Road, Shanghai 200032, China.

YELTON Michael Paul, b. 21 April 1950, Birkenhead, England. Circuit Judge. m. Judith Sara, 2 sons, 1 daughter. Education: Colchester Royal Grammar School; BA, 1971, MA, 1974, Corpus Christi College, Cambridge. Appointments: Fellow of Corpus Christi College, Cambridge, 1977-81; Barrister in Practice, 1973-98; Circuit Judge, 1998-. Publications: Fatal Accidents: A Practical Guide to Compensation, 1998; Martin Travers (1886-1948): An Appreciation, written with Rodney Warrener, 2003; Trams Trolleybuses Buses and the Law, 2004; Peter Anson, Monk, Writer and Artist, 2005; Anglican Papalism 1900-1960, 2005 and 2008; Alfred Hope Patten and the Shrine of Our Lady of Walsingham, 2006; Empty Tabernacles: Twelve Lost Churches of London, 2006; Anglican Churchbuilding in London 1915-45, written with John Salmon, 2007; Alfred Hope Patten: His Life and Times in Pictures, 2007; West Mon, written with Chris Taylor, 2008; The Twenty One, an Anglo-Catholic Rebellion in London, 1929, 2009; The South India Controversy and the Converts of 1955-56, 2010; An Anglo-Catholic Scrapbook , 2010; Bedwas and Macher, 2010. Address: Cambridge County Court, 197 East Road, Cambridge, CB1 1BA, England.

YENTOB Alan, b. 11 March 1947, London, England. Television Administrator. 1 son, 1 daughter, by Philippa Walker. Education: University of Grenoble, France; University of Leeds. Appointments: BBC General Trainee, 1968; Producer, Director, 1970-, Head of Music & Arts, 1985-88, BBC TV; Controller, BBC 2, 1988-93, BBC 1, 1993-96; BBC Director of Programmes, 1997-2000, Director of Drama, Entertainment and Children's Programmes, 2002-, Creative Director, 2004-, BBC Television; Presenter, Imagine, arts series, BBC1, 2003-. Honours: Honorary Fellow, RCA; RIBA; Royal TV Society. Memberships: Board of Directors, Riverside Studios, 1984-88, British Film Institute Production Board, 1985-93; British Screen Advisory Council; Advisory Committee, Institute of Contemporary Arts; Council, Royal Court Theatre; Governor, National Film School, 1998-; South Bank Board, International Academy of Television Arts and Sciences, 1999-. Timebank, 2001-. Address: BBC Television, Television Centre, Wood Lane, London W12 7RJ, England.

YI Jae-Woo, b. 29 November 1973, Seoul, Korea. Assistant Professor; Medical Educator. m. Hyo-Kyung Chae, 1 son. Education: Bachelor's degree, 1999, Master's degree, 2003, Doctor's degree, 2005, Medicine, Kyung Hee University. Appointments: Intern & Resident, 1999-2004, Clinical Assistant Professor, 2006-09, Assistant Professor, 2009-, Kyung Hee University Hospital, Gangdong; Instructor, Eul-ji Hospital, College of Medicine, Eul-gi University, 2004-06. Publications: Over 30 articles in professional journals including most recently: Remifentail alleviates transient cerebral ischemia-induced memory impairment through suppression of apoptotic neuronal cell death in gerbils, 2011; Anesthetic management of an adult patient with Rett syndrome and limited mouth opening, 2011; Anesthetic management of penetrating neck injury patient with embedded knife, 2012. Memberships: Korea Society of Obstetric Anesthesia; Korean Society of Anesthesiologists; Korean Society of Critical Care Medicine. Address: Department of Anesthesiology and Pain Medicine; #149 Sangil-dong, Gangdong-Gu, Seoul 134-727, Republic of Korea. E-mail: mdyjwchk@khu.ac.kr

YI Sang Wook, b. 13 November 1970, Seoul, Korea. Doctor; Professor. m. Sun Mi Park, 1 son. Education: MD, College of Medicine, 1995, MS, Graduate School, 2000, KyungHee University; PhD, University of Ulsan Graduate School, 2009. Appointments: Rotating Intern, 1995-96, Resident, 1996-2000, KyungHee University Hospital, Seoul; Physician, ROK Army, 2000-03; Faculty, Wonju Medical Centre, Wonju-si, 2003-05; Lecturer, 2005, Assistant Professor, 2005-10, Associate Professor, 2010-, Department of Obstetrics and Gynecology, Gangneung Asan Hospital, University of Ulsan. Publications: Two-part total laparoscopic hysterectomy with a multichannel port, 2009; Two-part laparoscopic adnexal surgery with a multichannel port using a wound retractor: is it safe and minimally scarring? 2009; Endometrioid adenocarcinoma arising from endometriosis of the uterine cervix: a case report, 2009; Secondary postpartum hemorrhage due to a pseudoaneurysm rupture at the fundal area of the uterus: A case treated with selective urterine arterial embolization, 2010; A modified intracorporeal knot-tying technique using an endoknot cannula during laparoscopy: Coiling and snaring method, 2011. Honours: Listed in international biographical dictionaries. Memberships: Korean Medical Association; Korean Association of Obstetricians & Gynaecologists; Korean Society of Gynecologic Endoscopy and Minimally Invasive Surgery; Korean Society of Gynecologic Oncology and Colposcopy; American Association of Gynecologic Laparoscopists; European Society for Gynecological Endoscopy; Korean Society of Gynecologic Endocrinology; Korean Society of Perinatology; Korean Cancer Association; Korean Urogynecologic Society. Address: Department of Obstetrics & Gynaecology, Gangneung Asan Hospital, University of Ulsan College of Medicine, 38 Bangdong street, Sacheon-myeon, Gangneung-si, Gangwon-do, 210-711, Korea. E-mail: buzzmi@chol.com

YLITALO Pauli Henrik, b. 27 April 1944, Lavia, Finland. m. Liisa Holma, 1 daughter. Education: MD, 1970, PhD, 1973, Docent, Pharmacology, 1975, Physician, Clinical Pharmacology, 1979, University of Helsinki; Professorship in Pharmacology, Clinical Pharmacology or Toxicology in all five Medical Schools and two Pharmacy Schools in Finland, 1979-92. Appointments: Resident Associate, Pharmacology, University of Helsinki and University of Heidelberg, Germany, 1970-74; Chief Assistant, biomedical Science, University of Tampere, 1974-82; Professor, Toxicology and Pharmacokinetics, University of Kuopio, 1983-91; Professor, Clinical Pharmacology and Toxicology, University of Tampere, 1992-2005; Director, Medical School, University of Tampere, 2001-04, Retired, 2005-; Part-time Chief Physician, Clinical Pharmacology, Tampere University Hospital District, 1992-2005. Publications: Over 500 scientific articles and contributions to professional journals; Editor: Textbooks of Clinical Pharmacology, 1994; Clinical Pharmacology and Drug Treatment, 2002; The Century of Health Care, 1998; 30 Years War – The History of Medical School of University of Tampere, 2003; Abstract Book of 10th International Congress of Toxicology, 2004; Proceedings of 10th International Congress of Toxicology, 2005. Honours: Sanitary Captain to Finnish Army; Several national and military decorations; Tampere Medical Society, 2008; Finnish Society of Toxicology, 2009; Ski Runner, Pirkan-Hiihto, 2001. Memberships: Finnish Society of Toxicology; Finnish Pharmacological Society; Tampere Medical Society; Finnish Society of Clinical Pharmacology; Finnish Medical Society; Ethics Committee, Tampere University Hospital District. Address: Liutuntie 15 A 5,m FIN-36240 Kangasala, Finland.

YOKOTA Takashi, b. 29 January 1953, Tokyo, Japan. Molecular Biology. m. Kyoko Kambegawa, 2 daughters. Education: BA, 1975, MS, 1977, PhD, 1980, Science, University of Tokyo. Appointments: Research Associate, 1980, Associate Professor, 1990-95, Visiting Professor, 1995-2003, University of Tokyo; Research Scientist, Toray Industries Inc,

DICTIONARY OF INTERNATIONAL BIOGRAPHY 36th EDITION

Kamakura, 1980-84; Postdoctoral Fellow, Stanford University, Palo Alto, 1982-83; Postdoctoral Fellow, 1983-84, Staff Scientist, 1984-88, Senior Scientific Staff, 1988-90, DNAX Research Institute; Professor, Kanazawa University, 2001-. Publications: IgE production by normal human lymphocytes is induced by interleukin 4, 1988; Cytokines: Co-ordinators of immune and inflammatory responses, 1990. Memberships: Japanese Biochemical Society. Address: 13-1 Takara-machi, Kanazawa, Ishikawa 920-8640, Japan.

YONG Othman, b. 25 August 1961, Kuala Terengganu, Malaysia. Professor. m. Noraini Man, 2 sons, 1 daughter. Education: BA, Statistics, California State University, 1981; MBA, Missouri State University, 1983; DBA, Finance, Mississppi State University, 1987. Appointments: Instructor, Business Statistics, Mississippi State University, Starkville, 1983-86; Assistant Professor, Finance, University of Wisconsin-River Falls, 1986-87; Head, 1987-89, Associate Professor, Finance, 1991-94, Professor, 1994-, Finance Department, Deputy Dean, Faculty of Business, 1992-96, National University of Malaysia. Publications: Author of 30 books and around 100 articles. Honours: Gold Award for Academic Excellence, Majlis Amanah Rakyat, Malaysia; Excellent Service Award, National University of Malaysia, 2006; Listed in international biographical dictionaries; Youngest Full Professor (aged 32), Malaysian Book of Records. Memberships: Asian Finance Association; Chief Editor, Journal Pengurusan. Address: National University of Malaysia, Graduate School of Business, UKM Bangi, Selangor 43600, Malaysia. E-mail: othmanyo@ukm.my

YOON Sang Pil, b. 18 February 1973, Jeollanam-Do, Korea. m. Ju Won Ku, 1 son. Education: BS, 1997, MS, 1999, PhD, 2005, Medicine, Chosun University. Appointments: MD, 1997; Assistant Professor, Seonam University, 2005-10; Associate Professor, Jeju National University, 2010-. Memberships: Editor, Islets. Address: Department of Anatomy, School of Medicine, Jeju National University, 66 Jejudaehakno, Jeju-Si, Jeju-Do, 690-756, Republic of Korea.

YOON Yang Ho, b. 1 August 1957, Jeju, Korea. Professor. m. Yoon Ok Kim (Yoon), 1 son, 1 daughter. Education: B Fisheries, Jeju National University, Korea, 1980; M Fisheries, Nagasaki University, Japan, 1986; PhD, Graduate School of Biosphere Science, Hiroshima University, Japan, 1989. Appointments: Instructor, Assistant, Associate Professor, Professor, 1990-2006, Chief Professor, Department of Oceanography, 1992, 1994, Director, Institute of Fisheries Science, 2000-01, Director of Library, 2004-05, Yosu National University; Director, Yeosu Campus Industry Liaison (Associate Vice President for Research Affairs), 2010-, Professor, 2006-, Chief Professor, Faculty of Marine Technology, 2006-07, Chonnam National University; Visiting Professor, Nagasaki University, Japan, 2009. Publications: 130 articles in professional journals; 18 books. Honours: Best Paper Awards, Korean Society for Marine Environmental Engineering, 2005, 2007. Memberships: American Society of Limnology and Oceanography; Plankton Society of Japan; Korean Society of Oceanography; Korean Fisheries Society; Korean Society of Phycology; Vice President of the Korean Society for Marine Environmental Engineering. Address: Faculty of Marine Technology, Chonnam National University, No 386 Mipyeong-ro, Yeosu 550-749, Republic of Korea. E-mail: yoonyh@chonnam.ac.kr

YORK HRH The Duke of York, Prince Andrew Albert Christian Edward, Earl of Inverness and Baron Killyleagh, b. 19 February 1960, London, England. m. Sarah Ferguson, 1986, divorced 1996, 2 daughters. Education: Lakefield College School, Ontario, Canada; Britannia Royal Naval College, Dartmouth. Appointments: Seaman Officer, Pilot, 1979, Royal Navy; Flying training with RAF Leeming, Yorkshire; Helicopter training at Royal Naval Air Station Culrose, Cornwall; Received Wings, 1981; Front-line unit 820 Naval Air Squadron, Anti-Submarine Warfare Carrier HMS Invincible; Participated in Falklands conflict; Rank of Lieutenant, 1984; Personal ADC to HM The Queen, 1984; Flight Pilot in NAS, Type 22 Frigate HMS Brazen, 1984-86; Helicopter Warfare Instructor, 702 NAS, 1987; Officer of the Watch, Type 42 Destroyer HMS Edinburgh, 1988-89; Formed HMS Campbeltown Flight, RNAS Portland; Flight Commander, 829 NAS, 1989-91; Army Command and Staff Course, Staff College, Camberley, 1992; Rank of Lt Commander, 1992; Commanded Hunt Class Minehunter HMS Cottesmore, 1993-94; Senior Pilot, 815 NAS, RNAS Portland, 1995-96; Staff Officer, Ministry of Defence, London, Directorate of Naval Operations, 1997-99; Rank of Commander, Diplomacy Section of Naval Staff, London, 1999-2001; Special Representative for International Trade and Investment, 2001-; Admiral of the Sea Cadet Corps, 1992-; Colonel-in-Chief, Staffordshire Regiment, 1989-; Royal Irish Regiment, 1992-; Royal New Zealand Army Logistic Regiment, Small Arms School Corps, Royal Highland Fusiliers (Princess Margaret's Own and Ayrshire Regiment), 9th/12th Royal Lancers (Prince of Wales's); Honorary Air Commodore RAF Lossiemouth, Morayshire; Patron of over 90 organisations including: Greenwich Hospital, Fight for Sight, Defeating Deafness, Jubilee Sailing Trust, Royal Aero Club; Trustee, National Maritime Museum, Greenwich; Chair, Trustees Outward Bound Trust; Captain, Royal and Ancient Golf Club of St Andrews; Member, Advisory Board of Governors, Lakefield College School; Commodore Royal Thames Yacht Club; Elder Brother, Trinity House.

YORK Michael (Michael York-Johnson), b. 27 March 1942, Fulmer, England, Actor. m. Patricia McCallum, 1968. Education: University College, Oxford. Appointments: Dundee Repertory Co, 1964, National Theatre Company, 1965; Guest Lecturer, Chair, CA Youth Theatre. Creative Works: TV appearances include: The Forsyte Saga; Rebel in the Grave; True Patriot; Much Ado About Nothing; Jesus of Nazareth; A Man Called Intrepid; For Those I Loved; The Weather in the Streets; The Master of Ballantrae; Space; The Far Country; Are You My Mother, 1986; Ponce de Leon, Knot's Landing, 1987; The Four Minute Mile, The Lady and the Highwayman, The Heat of the Day, 1988; A Duel of Love, The Road to Avonlea, 1990; Teklab, 1994; September, A Young Connecticut Yankee in King Arthur's Court, Not of This Earth, 1995; The Ring, True Women, 1996; The Haunting of Hall House, 2000; The Lot, 2001; Founding Fathers, Founding Brothers; La Femme Musketeer, 2004; Radio: Jane Eyre, Alice in Wonderland, 2002; The Trial of Walter Raleigh, 2003; Films include: The Return of the Musketeers, 1988; Till We Meet Again, The Heat of the Day, 1989; The Night of the Fox, Eline Vere, Duel of Hearts, 1990; The Wanderer, The Long Shadow, Wide Sargasso Sea, Rochade, 1991; Discretion Assured, 1993; The Shadow of a Kiss, Fall From Grace, 1994; Gospa, 1995; Goodbye America, Austin Powers, Dark Planet, 1996; The Ripper, 1997; A Knight in Camelot, Perfect Little Angels, Wrongfully Accused, One Hell of a Guy, 1998; The Omega Code, 1999; Borstal Boy, 2000; Megiddo, 2001; Austin Powers in Goldmember, 2002; Moscow Heat, 2004; Scarface: The World is Yours (voice), 2006; Flatland: The Movie, 2007; Transformers, Revenge of the Fallen (voice), 2009; Numerous TV appearances; Music: Christopher Columbus: A Musical Journey, 2002; Enoch

Arden, 2003. Publications: The Courage of Conviction, 1986; Voices of Survival, 1987; Travelling Player (autobiography), 1991; Accidentally on Purpose (autobiography), 1992; A Shakespearian Actor Prepares, 2000; Dispatches From Armageddon, 2002. Honours: Numerous. Address: c/o Andrew Manson, 288 Munster Road, London SW6 6BQ, England. Website: www.michaelyork.net

YORKE Margaret, (Margaret Beda Nicholson), b. 30 January 1924, Surrey, England. Writer. 1 son, 1 daughter. Appointments: Assistant Librarian, St Hilda's College, Oxford, 1959-60; Library Assistant, Christ Church, Oxford, 1963-65; Chairman, Crime Writers Association, 1979-80. Publications: Summer Flight, 1957; Pray Love Remember, 1958; Christopher, 1959; Deceiving Mirror, 1960; The China Doll, 1961; Once a Stranger, 1962; The Birthday, 1963; Full Circle, 1965; No Fury, 1967; The Apricot Bed, 1968; The Limbo Ladies, 1969; Dead in the Morning, 1970; Silent Witness, 1972; Grave Matters, 1973; No Medals for the Major, 1974; Mortal Remains, 1974; The Small Hours of the Morning, 1975; Cast for Death, 1976; The Cost of Silence, 1977; The Point of Murder, 1978; Death on Account, 1979; The Scent of Fear, 1980; The Hand of Death, 1981; Devil's Work, 1982; Find Me a Villain, 1983; The Smooth Face of Evil, 1984; Intimate Kill, 1985; Safely to the Grave, 1986; Evidence to Destroy, 1987; Speak for the Dead, 1988; Crime in Question, 1989; Admit to Murder, 1990; A Small Deceit, 1991; Criminal Damage, 1992; Dangerous to Know, 1993; Almost the Truth, 1994; Pieces of Justice, 1994; Serious Intent, 1995; A Question of Belief, 1996; Act of Violence, 1997; False Pretences, 1998; The Price of Guilt, 1999; A Case to Answer, 2000; Cause for Concern, 2001. Honours: Swedish Academy of Detection, 1982; Cartier Diamond Dagger, Crime Writers Association, 1999 Address: c/o Curtis Brown Ltd, Haymarket House, 28/29 Haymarket, London SW1Y 4SP, England.

YOSHIDA Tsuguo, b. 12 September 1952, Yokosuka City, Japan. Physician. m. Shizue Komori, 1 son, 2 daughters. Education: Bachelor of Science, Tokyo University of Education, Tokyo, 1971-76; Doctor of Medicine, University of Tsukuba, Tsukuba City, 1979-86; MS in Education, Meisei University, Tokyo, 2004-2006. Appointments: Systems Engineer, IBM, Tokyo, Japan, 1976-79; Physician Tsukuba University Hospital, 1986-92; Part-time Radiologist, Tsukuba Municipal Hospital Tsukuba City, 1986-2006; Associate Professor, Tsukuba College of Technology, Tsukuba City, 1992-2004; Professor, Tsukuba University of Technology, Ibaraki Prefecture, Japan, 2005-09; Radiooncologist, Kamagoya General Hospital, Kamagaya City, Japan, 2009-. Publications: Articles in medical journals conference proceedings include: Evaluation on Surface and Deep Temperature of Phantom Irradiated by Pulsed or Continuous Microwaves, 1997; Mental health of the visually and hearing impaired students from the viewpoint of University Personality Inventory, 1998; Making Tactile Charts on a Personal Computer for Blind Students in the Allied Health Professions, 2002; MRI of Testicular Epidermoid Cyst, 2004. Honours: Life Science Foundation, 1992, The Telecommunication Advancement Foundation, 1999. Memberships: MENSA International, London; Consultant, Tsukuba City Office, Tsukuba City, Ibaraki Prefecture, Japan, 2001-2006; Address: 2-15-30 Higashi, Tsukuba City, Ibaraki Prefecture, Japan 305-0046. E-mail: tyoshida@k.tsukuba-tech.ac.jp

YOUNG Ian George, b. 5 January 1945, London, England. Poet; Writer; Editor. Appointments: Director, Catalyst Press, 1969-80, Director, TMW Communications, 1990-. Publications: Poetry: White Garland, 1969; Year of the Quiet Sun, 1969; Double Exposure, 1970; Cool Fire, 1970; Lions in the Stream, 1971; Some Green Moths, 1972; The Male Muse, 1973; Invisible Words, 1974; Common-or-Garden Gods, 1976; The Son of the Male Muse, 1983; Sex Magick, 1986. Fiction: On the Line, 1981. Non-Fiction: The Male Homosexual in Literature, 1975, 2nd edition, 1982; Overlooked and Underrated, 1981; Gay Resistance, 1985; The AIDS Dissidents, 1993; The Stonewall Experiment, 1995; The Aids Cult, 1997; The Beginnings of Gay Liberation in Canada, 2005; Out in Paperback, 2007. Honours: Several Canada Council and Ontario Arts Council Awards. Membership: International Psychohistory Association. Address: 2483 Gerrard Street East, Scarborough, Ontario M1N 1W7, Canada.

YOUSSEF Ahmad Mohamad Kamal, b. 9 March 1975, Assiut, Egypt. Lecturer. Education: BSc, Special Chemistry, 1997, MSc, 2003, PhD, 2009, Analytical Chemistry, Faculty of Science, Assiut University. Appointments: Demonstrator, 1997-, Assistant Lecturer, 2003-, Lecturer, 2009-, Analytical Chemistry, Faculty of Science, Assiut University. Publications: Several articles on analytical chemistry, food and pharmaceutical analysis. Honours: Assiut University Award, 2007. Memberships: American Chemical Society. Address: Chemistry Department, Faculty of Science, Assiut University, Assiut, Egypt.

YOUSSEF Eman M Kamal, b. 21 December 1972, Assiut, Egypt. Lecturer. m. Eng A Galal, 1 daughter. Education: BSc, Medicine & Surgery, 1996, MSc, 2001, MD, 2008, Dermatology, Venereology & Andrology, Assiut University. Appointments: Resident Doctor, Dermatology, 1998-2002, Assiut University Hospital, Demonstrator, Dermatology, 2001, Assistant Lecturer, Dermatology, 2002-08, Lecturer, Dermatology & Andrology, 2008-, Faculty of Medicine, Assiut University. Publications: Several articles on dermatology. Honours: Excellent 1st Honours, 1996; Faculty of Medicine Award, 2009. Memberships: Egyptian Society of Dermatology and Andrology. Address: Department of Dermatology, Venereology & Andrology, Assiut University Hospital, Faculty of Medicine, Assiut, Egypt.

YU Sang Joun, b. 13 October 1978, Suncheon, South Korea. Dentist. m. Hee Jung Kim, 1 son. Education: Bachelor, Dentistry, 2004, MSc, Peridontology, 2007, Chosun University. Appointments: Intern, 2004, Resident, 2005-08, Chosun Dental Hospital; Army Dentist, Gaeyongdae Jigu Hospital, 2008-11. Publications: Histomorphometric Analysis of Sinus Augmentation Using the ICB and MBCP; Key Engineering Materials; Bioceramics. Honours: Dental Licence, South Korea, 2004; Achievement Award, Chosun Dental Hospital, 2006; Excellence Award in field of Dental Research, Korean Academy of Periodontology, 2007; Periodontal Specialist Licence, South Korea, 2008. Memberships: Korean Academy of Periodontology; American Academy of Periodontology. Address: 520-26 Sansu Dong, Dong Gu, Gwang-Ju Si, 501-090, South Korea. E-mail: bluemandu78@hanmail.net

YU Zhiming, b. 3 February 1956, Hebei, China. Professor. m. ShengYing Bai, 1 son. Education: BS, Department of Machine Manufacture, Jiangsu Institute of Technology, Zhenjiang, 1983; Trainee, Thir Research Department, Institute for Super Materials, Tsukuba, Japan, 1988; PhD, Molecular Chemistry, Graduate School of Engineering, Hokkaido University, Sapporo, Japan, 2002. Appointments: Researcher Assistant, Associate Professor, Institute of Corrosion and Protection of Metals, Chinese Academy of Science, P R China, 1983-96; Senior Visiting Scholar, Department of Engineering, Hokkaido University, 1996; Associate Professor, Professor,

State Key Laboratory for Corrosion and Protection, Institute of Metal Research, Chinese Academy of Science, P R China, 2002-. Publications: More than 70 papers in professional journals; 16 Chinese patents. Honours: 3rd Class Award, Science & Technology Progress, Chinese Academy of Sciences; Excellent Project Award for Co-operation Research, CAS-Shenyang City; Listed in biographical dictionaries. Memberships: American Association for the Advancement of Science; American Chemical Society; Editorial Board Member, Global Journal of Nanotechnology. Address: 62 Wencui Road, Shenyang 110016, China.

YUAN Bing Sheng, b. September 1971, China. Traditional Chinese Medicine Practitioner. Education: Acupuncture, Sichuan MianYang TCM College, 1987-90; China National Self-Education Examination, Bachelor degree, Tradiational Chinese Medicine; Tradiational Chinese & Western Medicine Master lessons, Chengdu TCM University, Mian Yang Station, 2005-06; Tradiational Chinese Medicine and Acupuncture Clinical Practices under Professor Li Kong King and Yang Jie Bin. Appointments: Traditional Chinese Medicine Therapist, Chinese TCM Hospital, -2007; Traditional Chinese Medicine Practitioner, United Kingdom, 2007-. Publications: Numerous Traditional Chinese Medicine articles in professional journals. Honours: Excellent Thesis Award, 1997. Memberships: Association of Tradiational Chinese Medicine, UK; China Association of Acupuncture & Moxibustion; Chinese Medical Association; Chinese Association of the Integration of Traditional & Western Medicine. Address: Dr TCM Ltd, 51 Upper South mall, Frenchgate, Interchang Shopping Centre, Doncaster, DN1 1TT, England. E-mail: yswcxl@126.com

YUKI Nobukazu, b. 28 November 1959, Osaka, Japan. Gastroenterologist. Education: MD, Osaka University Graduate School of Medicine, Suita, Japan, 1984; Diplomate, Japanese Government, 1984. Appointments: Research Fellow, Osaka University Graduate School of Medicine, 1984-98; Assistant Director, Department of Gastroenterology, Osaka National Hospital, 1998-. Publications: Numerous articles in professional journals. Address: Osaka National Hospital, Hoenzaka 2-1-14, Chuo-ku, Osaka 540-0006, Japan. E-mail: yuki@onh.go.jp

YURCHENKO Eugene (Yauheni), b. 8 July 1974, Minsk, Belarus. Mycologist. Education: Secondary School certificate, 1991; Higher Education Diploma, Belarusian State University, 1996; Candidate of Biological Sciences degree, V F Kuprevich Institute of Experimental Botany, Minsk, 2001. Appointments: Junior Research Officer, 1999-2002, Research Officer, 2002-04, Senior Research Officer, 2004-10, Leading Research Officer, V F Kuprevich Institute of Experimental Botany, 2010. Publications: Books: The basics of fungal DNA molecular marking, 2007; The genus Peniophora of Eastern Europe, 2010; Main web-publication: History of taxonomic mycology in Belarus: a bibliographic survey, 2007; Private editorial & publish activity: Mycena: An independent mycological journal, 2001-08; many others. Honours: International Soros Science Educational Program grant, 1995. Memberships: European Mycological Association. Address: Laboratory of Mycology, V F Kuprevich Institute of Experimental Botany, Akademichnay str, 27, BY-220072, Belarus. E-mail: eugene_yu@tut.by

Z

ZACHARIASSON Toini Maria, b. 14 March 1943, Hedenaeset, Sweden. Director; Business Owner. Education: Computer Degree, Scandinavian School, Gothenburg, Sweden, 1974; Degree, Philosophy, Stockholm University, Sweden, 1980. Appointments: Clerk, Executive, The Defence Office, Stockholm, 1962-64; Secretary of Business, Eriksson, Stockholm, 1964-79; Secretary of Parliament, 1979-82; Director of Business, Stockholm, Sweden, 1982-88; Taxation Professional, The Central Party, Stockholm, 1977-88. Memberships: Volunteer, Marine Defence, Sweden; Member, The Central Party. Address: Tingshusvagen 1F, SE-95731, Overtornea, Norrbotten, Sweden.

ZAHRAN Samah Khaled Abd El Kawy, b. 7 September 1972, Cairo, Egypt. Associate Professor. Education: BSc, 1994, Diploma in Education, 1996, Master Degree, 1998, PhD, 2001, Psychology, Department of Child Education, College of Women, Ain Shams University. Appointments: Demonstrator, 1995, University Teacher Assistant, 1998, University Teacher, 2001, Associate Professor, 2007, Department of Child Education, College of Women, Ain Shams University. Publications: Author, Social Perception: How to understand yourself and others, for better humanity relationships, 2004; The Psychometry of Pre-School Child Psychocharacteristics, 2005; Science for a Better Human Society, 2006; Adelinquent Victim Child: A social psychological study of the crime in society, 2010; Authorised books: Psychological Researches in Social Psychology; 15 scientific researches on Psychology including: A Perceived Type of Egyptian Personality among Parents and its Effect on Young Education, 2010; Translated books: Entangled Minds by Dean Radin (translated from English to Arabic, first Arabic translation all over the world), in progress; Global Shift (first translation all over the world, in progress); Society Responsibility Towards Violence Against Children. A subject analysis study, 2009; A Factor Analysis Study about some Aspects of Juvenile Delinquency in Egyptian Society; Roll of the Sixth Sense in Decision Making and Interpersonal Relationships; Some Personal and Social Variables that Affect the Sixth Sense; The Impact of Some Variables on Parenting Styles across Cultures; Translated book, Global Shift by Edmund J Bourne; Translated (English to Arabic), Global Shift by Edmund J Bourne. Honours: Institute of Heart Math Certificate of Appreciation; Listed in international biographical directories. Memberships: American Psychological Association; APA Division 40, 52; Egyptian Association of the Friends of Biblotheca Alexandria; Egyptian Association of Psychological Studies; Parapsychological Association; El Sawy Culture Wheel; Global Coherence Initiative; Institute of Heart Math; Associate Member, Paranormal Study & Investigative Research Organisation (PSIRO), 2010; Free Membership, Institute of Noetic Sciences; APADiv 10. Address: Flat 302, Bldg No 9, Ramo Bldg, Nasr Road, Nasr City, Cairo, Egypt. E-mail: skhaekz@yahoo.com Website: http://humanbehavior.wetpaint.com

ZAIKOV Gennady Efremovich, b. 7 January 1935, Omsk, Siberia, Russia. Professor. m. Olga, 1 son. Education: BS, Chemistry, Moscow State University, 1957; PhD, Chemistry, 1964, DSc, Chemistry, 1968, Full Professor, 1970, Institute of Chemical Physics. Appointments: Research Associate, 1958-66, Head of Laboratory, 1966-, Deputy Head of Department, 1989-, Institute of Chemical Physics, N M Emanuel Institute of Biochemical Physics, Russian Academy of Sciences; Full Professor, Moscow State Academy of Fine Chemical Technology, 1970-; Full Professor, Kazan State Chemical Technological University, 2010-. Publications: Over 200 books; More than 3000 papers in professional journals. Honours: 1 Order; 5 medals (USSR and Russia); The World Medal of Freedom; Diploma of International Fund of Scientific Partnership, 2005. Memberships: International Academy of Sciences; Academy of Creation; American Chemical Society; American Society of Plastics; Royal Chemical Society, UK. Address: Leninskii prospect 64-188, 119296 Moscow, Russia.

ZAITSEV Oleg, b. 30 March 1935, Moscow, Russia. Teacher; Professor. m. Olga, 2 sons. Education: ScD, 1965; PhD, 1986. Appointments: Assistant to Professor, 1961-70; Head of Laboratory, Education Methods in Chemistry, 1970; Assistant Professor, 1971-90; Professor, 1991. Publications: Graduate and undergraduate textbooks: Methods of Chemistry Education, 1999; Chemistry, 2008; About 300 articles; 30 textbooks. Honours: Honoured Scientist of Russian Federation, 1996; Lomonsov Prize Winner for Pedagogical Achievements, 1998. Memberships: Member of councils giving scientific degress (PhD).

ZAMBERLAN Stefano, b. 30 November 1977, Vicenza, Italy. Editor in Chief. Education: Economics, 2002, PhD, Bioeconomics and Environmental Economics, 2006, University of Verona. Appointments: Teaching Assistant, 2005-, Contracted Professor, Environmental Economics and Policy, 2006-07, University of Verona; Editor in Chiev, Rev Economia e Ambiente, 2009-; Municipal Councilor, Isola Vicentina, 2009-; Editor in Chief, Rev Studi Economici e Sociali, 2010-. Publications: Numerous articles in professional journals. Honours: Listed in international biographical dictionaries. Memberships: ANEAT; Fondazione Studi Tonioliani; ASCA; Centro Nazionale Documentazione e studi sull'ambiente; AISEP; Centro Studi Tocqueville-Acton. Address: Via All'Acqua 25, 36033 Isola Vicentina (VI), Italy. E-mail: stefano.zamberlan@univr.it Website: www.economiaeambiente.it

ZANE Billy, b. 24 February 1966, Chicago, Illinois, USA. m. Lisa Collins, 1988, divorced 1995. Education: American School, Switzerland. Career: Stage: American Music, New York; The Boys in the Backroom, Chicago; Films: Back to the Future, 1985; Critters, 1986; Dead Calm, Back to the Future Part II, 1989; Megaville, Memphis Belle, 1990; Blood and Concrete: A Love Story, Millions, Femme Fatale, 1991; Posse, Orlando, Sniper, Flashfire; Tombstone, 1993; The Silence of the Hams, Cyborg Agent; Only You, 1994; Tales from the Crypt Presents: Demon Knight, Reflections in the Dark; Danger Zone, 1995; The Phantom, This World – Then the Fireworks, Head Above Water, 1996; Titanic, 1998; Taxman, Morgan's Ferry, Cleopatra, 1999; Hendrix, 2000; Invincible, The Diamond of Jeru, The Believer, 2001; Sea Devils, 2002; Vlad, Imaginary Grace, 2003; Silver City, Three, Dead Fish, Big Kiss, Kingdom Hearts: Chain of Memories, 2004; The Pleasure Drivers, The Last Drop, BloodRayne, Three, 2005; Valley of the Wolves, Memory, 2006; The Mad, Alien Agent, Fishtales, 2007; Perfect Hideout, 2008; The Man Who Came Back, 2008; Love N' Dancing, 2009; Mama, I Want to Sing!, 2009; Surviving Evil, 2009; To Kako – Stin epohi ton iroon, 2009; Magic Man, 2009; Darfur, 2009; TV: Twin Peaks; Cleopatra; Brotherhood of Justice; The Case of the Hillside Stranglers, 1989; Lake Consequence; Running Delilah; The Set Up; Blue Seduction, 2009; Samantha Who?, 2009. Address: Creative Artist Agency, 9830 Wilshire Boulevard, Beverly Hills, CA 90212, USA.

ZARDARI Asif Ali, b. 26 July 1955, Karachi, Pakistan. President of Pakistan. Widower of Benazir Bhutto, 1 son. Education: Graduate, Cadet College Petaro, Dadu, 1972;

DICTIONARY OF INTERNATIONAL BIOGRAPHY 36th EDITION

Business & Economics, Pedinton School, London, 1976. Appointments: Director of M/s Zardari Group (Pvt.) Ltd; Member, National Assembly, 1990-93; Member, National Assembly, 1993-96; Federal Minister, 1993; Federal Minister, 1995-96; Senator, 1997-99; President of Pakistan, 2008-.

ZAREMBKA Paul, b. 17 April 1942, St Louis, Missouri, USA. Economist. m. Beata Banas, 1 daughter. Education: BS, Mathematics, Purdue University, 1964; MS, PhD, Economics, 1967, University of Wisconsin. Appointments: Assistant Professor, Department of Economics, University of California, Berkeley, 1967-72; Visiting Professorships: Heidelberg University, 1970-71; Goettingen University, 1971-72; Associate Professor, then Professor, Department of Economics, State University of New York at Buffalo, 1973-; Senior Research Officer, World Employment Program, International Labor Office, Geneva, Switzerland, 1974-77; Researcher, Group for Research on Science, Louis Pasteur University, Strasbourg, 1978-79. Publications: Author, Toward a Theory of Economic Development, 1972; Editor, Frontiers in Econometrics, 1974; The Hidden History of 9-11, 2008; Co-editor with M Brown and K Sato, Essays in Modern Capital Theory, 1976; General Editor, Research in Political Economy, to date, 27 volumes, 1977-, including: Why Capitalism Survives Crises, 2009; The National Question and the Question of Crisis, 2010; Revitalizing Marxist Theory for Today's Captialism, 2011; Numerous articles and book chapters. Honours: Fulbright-Hayes Lecturer, Poznan, Poland, 1979; Listed in numerous biographical dictionaries. Address: Department of Economics, 415 Fronczak Hall, State University of New York at Buffalo, Buffalo, New York 14260, USA. E-mail: zarembka@buffalo.edu. Website: http://www.buffalo.edu/~zarembka

ZAVATI Constantin C, b. 7 July 1923, Bacau, Romania. Teacher. m. Iulia Bucur, 1 daughter. Education: Scoala de Baieti No 2, Bacau; Scholarship, Stefan Cel Mare Military Boarding College; Baccalauréat, Distinction, 1942; Private Merit Regiment 10; Chemistry Faculty, University Alexandru Ioan Cuza, 1947-51; MSc, chemistry, 1951. Appointments: Various Military Positions; Assistant Lecturer, University Alexandru Ioan Cuza and Academy Iasi, Romania; High school teacher, Chemistry and Physics, Ferdinand I Boarding College, Bacau; High school teacher, Chemistry and Physics, Head of Chemistry, Vasile Alecsandri Boarding College, Bacau; Schools Inspector for Chemistry, county/City of Bacau. Publications: Numerous scientific papers at various national conferences; Many scientific articles in newspapers and magazines under the pen name, A Tom; Co-author, 1 book on applied sciences; Organised the first modern school science laboratories in the county/City of Bacau. Honours: Citation for great bravery during the Second World War; Several Orders and Medals for Bravery in Battle; Professor Fruntas, 1964; Professor Grade 1, 1972; Advanced Captain, Major and Colonel in the Army Reserves. Memberships: Societatea de Stiinte Fizice Si Chimice; Societatea Stiintelor Medicale; First President, Radio Club, Bacau. Address: c/o Mariana Zavati Gardner, 14 Andrew Goodall Close, East Dereham, Norfolk, NR19 1SR, England.

ZAVATI Iulia Bucur, b. 19 July 1921, Racova-Bacau, Romania. Pharmacist. m. Constantin C Zavati, 26 January 1947, 1 daughter. Education: Baccalauréat with Distinct; MSc, Pharmacy, 1st class honours, University of Bucharest, Romania. Appointments: Opened own pharmacy at Valea Rea-Târgu Ocna, Romania; Pharmacist, State Pharmacy in Bacau, Romania; Appointed Principal Pharmacist; Deputy Director, Director, Oficiul Farmaceutic, City and Region Judet of Bacau-Romania; Directed, re-organised and modernised all pharmacies in Bacau; Established links with western pharmacy companies; Lecturer, Scoala Sanitara for nurses and pharmacy assistants in Bacau. Honours: Medals and Orders for modernising and re-organising pharmacies in Bacau. Membership: Romanian Society of Pharmacists. Address: c/o Andrew Goodall Close, East Dereham, Norfolk NR19 1SR, England.

ZEČEVIĆ Miodrag Dj, b. 4 September 1930, Topola, Serbia. University Professor Emeritus. m. Ljubica, 1 son, 1 daughter. Education: BA, Faculty of Law, 1956, BA, Faculty of Philosophy, 1961, MA, Faculty of Political Science, 1967, PhD, Faculty of Law, 1970, University of Belgrade. Appointments: Federal Secretariat for Internal Affairs and Institute of Social Sciences in Belgrade; Secretary, Political Council of the Serbian Assembly, 1960; Teacher, University of Belgrade Law School, 1961-70; President, Legislative and Juridical Committee of Parliament, Republic of Serbia, 1969-74; Professor, University of Belgrade's Faculty of Political Science, 1973-97; President, Legislative and Juridical Committee of Parliament, SFR Yugoslavia, 1974-82; High Official, Parliament of Yugoslavia, 1982-85; Federal Counsellor, Government of Federal Republic of Yugoslavia, 1985-87; Director, Archives of Yugoslavia, 1987-95; President, Committee for International Co-operation; Deputy President, Serbian SUBNOR (organisation for WWII veterans); President of SUBNOR (Association of Veterans of WWII of Serbia, 2010. Publications: 20 books and numerous articles and studies in the field of history and law; Constitutional Law, 1975; Creation of General Enactments, 1978; Joint Interests in the Federation, 1984; The Contradictions of the Yugoslav Law, 1987; Yugoslavia 1918-1992, 1994; The Beginning of The End of the SFR Yugoslavia, 1998; Documents from Ravna Gora Trial, 2001; Hunting in Yugoslavia, Serbia and Montenegro from 1818 to 2000 – Laws, Politics and Ethics, 2002; That's the Way it Was (Memoirs); That is the Way it Was, 2010; Memoralis Liber. Memberships: General Secretary, 1997-2003, President, 2004-, Yugoslav War Veterans Organisation; Former President, Yugoslav Ecology Organisation; Former President, Scientific Association of Science and Society; Member, Association for Constitutional Law; Member, Association for Political Sciences; Secretary General, Yugoslav Hunting Organisation; President, Serbian Association of World War Two Veterans, 2010. Address: Njegoševa 56, 11000 Belgrade, Serbia.

ZEFFIRELLI G Franco, b. 12 February 1923, Florence, Italy. Opera & Film Producer; Designer. Education: Liceo Artistico, Florence; School of Agriculture, Florence. Appointments: Designer, University Productions, Florence; Actor, Morelli Stoppa Co; Collaborated with Salvador Dali on sets for As You Like It, 1948; Designed sets for A Streetcar Named Desire, Troilus, Cressida, Three Sisters; Producer, Designer, numerous operas. Creative Works: Operas: Lucia di Lammermoor,1959, 1973; Falstaff, 1961; L'elisir d'amore, 1961; Don Giovanni, 1962, 1972, 1990; Tosca, 1964, 1966, 1973, 1985, 2000; Otello, 1972, 1976; Antony and Cleopatra, 1973; La Bohème, 1981, 2003; Turandot, 1983, 1985, 1987; Don Carlos, 1992; Carmen, 1996, 2003; Aida, 1997, 2000, 2002; La Traviata, 1998; Il Trovatore, 2001; I Pagliacci, 2003, 2005; Madame Butterfly, 2004; Theatre: Romeo and Juliet, 1960; Othello, 1961; Amleto, 1964; After the Fall, 1964; Who's Afraid of Virginia Woolf, 1964, 1965; Much Ado About Nothing, 1966; Black Comedy, 1967; A Delicate Balance, 1967; Saturday, Sunday, Monday, 1973; Filumena, 1977; Six Characters in Search of an Author, 1992; Absolutely Perhaps! 2002; Films: The Taming of the Shrew, 1966; Florence, Days of Destruction, 1966; Romeo and Juliet, 1967; Brother Sun and Sister Moon, 1973; Jesus of Nazareth, 1977; The Champ, 1979; Endless Love, 1981; La Traviata, 1983; Cavalleria Rusticana, 1983; Otello, 1986; The Young Toscanini, 1987; Hamlet, 1990; Sparrow, 1994; Jane Eyre, 1995; Tea With Mussolini, 1998; Callas Forever, 2002; Omaggio a Roma, 2009; Ballet: Swan Lake, 1985; Producer, Beethoven's Missa Solemnis, San Pietro, Rome, 1971. Publication: Zeffirelli by Zeffirelli (autobiog), 1986. Honours: Prix des Nations, 1976; Senator Forza Italia, 1994-2002, Cultural Collaborator, 1976, Italian Ministry of Culture and Arts; Honorary KBE, 2005. Address: Via Lucio Volumnio 45, 00178 Rome, Italy.

ZEINOUN Toni, b. 24 January 1961, Deir Jennine, Lebanon. Oral and Maxillo-Facial Surgeon; Periodontologist. m. Carla Moussali, 1 daughter. Education: Oral Surgeon, Lebanese University, 1985; Laser Therapy in Dental Medicine certificate, 1992, Oral Surgery and Implantology certificate, 1993, Free University of Brussel, Belgium; PhD, Dental Sciences, 1995, MS, Periodontology, 1997, ULB, Belgium. Appointments: Chairman, Department of Oral and Maxillo Facial Surgery, 1994-95, Chairman, Post Graduate Program, 1995-96, Dental Faculty, Lebanese University; President, Lebanese Dental Association, 2000-03; Chairman, Middle East and Africa division, World Federation of Laser in Dentistry, 2006-12; Organizing Chairman, WFLD congress, Dubai, 2010; Professor, Dental Sciences, Lebanese University, 2011. Publications: Myofibroblasts in healing Laser excision wounds, 2001; Eosinophils and mastocyts in healing Laser excision wounds, 2009; Pulp temperature increase during photo-activated disinfection (PAD) of periodontal pockets, 2010; Evaluation of dental pulp temperature rise during photo-activated decontamination (PAD) of caries, 2010. Honours: President, League of Lebanese Dentists diplomate, Lebanese University, 1996-2000; President, Lebanese Dental Association, 2000-03; President, Lebanese Order of Liberal Profession, 2002; Organising Chairman, World Federation Congress of Laser in Dentistry, Dubai, 2010. Memberships: Belgium Society of Periodontology; Lebanese Dental Association; World Federation of Laser in Dentistry. Address: 1 Avenue de la petite Cigue, 1970 Wezembeek Oppem, Belgium. E-mail: toni.zeinoun@telenet.be

ZELLWEGER Renée, b. 25 April 1969, Texas, USA. Actress. m. Kenny Chesney, 2005, annulled December 2005. Education: University of Texas at Austin. Appointments: Films: Dazed and Confused, 1993; Reality Bites, Love and a .45, 8 Seconds, 1994; The Low Life, Empire Records, 1995; The Whole Wide World, Jerry Maguire, 1996; Texas Chainsaw Massacre: The Next Generation, Deceiver, 1997; One True Thing, A Price Above Rubies, 1998; The Bachelor, 1999; Me, Myself and Irene, Nurse Betty, 2000; Bridget Jones' Diary, 2001; Chicago, 2002; Down With Love, Cold Mountain, 2003; Bridget Jones: The Edge of Reason, 2004; Cinderella Man, 2005; Miss Potter, 2006; Bee Movie (voice), 2007; Leatherheads, Appaloosa, 2008; New in Town, My One and Only, Monsters vs Aliens (voice), Case 39, 2009; My Own Love Song, 2010; TV: Shake, Rattle and Rock Movie, 1993; Murder in the Heartland, 1994. Honours: Golden Globe Best Comedy Film Actress Award for Nurse Betty, 2001; Golden Globe Best Actress in a Musical for Chicago, 2003; Screen Actors Guild Award for Best Actress for Chicago, 2003; BAFTA Award for Best Supporting Actress, 2004; Best Supporting Actress Oscar for Cold Mountain, 2004. Memberships: Patron, The GREAT Initiative.

ZEMECKIS Robert, b. May 1952, Chicago, USA. Film Director; Producer; Writer. m. Mary Ellen Trainor, 1980, divorced 2000, 1 son, (2) Lesley Harter, 2001-, 2 sons. Education: University South California. Creative Works: Films: The Life, 1972; Field of Honor, 1973; I Wanna Hold Your Hand, 1978; Used Cars, 1980; Romancing the Stone, 1984; Back to the Future, 1985; Who Framed Roger Rabbit, 1988; Back to the Future II, 1989; Back to the Future III, 1990; Death Becomes Her, 1992; Forrest Gump, 1994; Bordello of Blood, 1996; Contact, 1997; The House on Haunted Hill, 1999; What Lies Beneath, 2000; Cast Away, 2000; 13 Ghosts, 2001; Ghost Ship, 2002; Matchstick Men, 2003; Gothika, 2003; Clink Inc, 2003; Polar Express, 2004; House of Wax, 2005; Monster House, 2006; Beowulf, 2007; A Christmas Carol, 2009; Behind the Burly Q, 2010; Mars Needs Moms, Real Steel, 2011; Flight, 2012; TV: Tales from the Crypt, 1989; Two-Fisted Tales, 1991; Johnny Bago, 1993; WEIRD World, 1995; Perversions of Science, 1997. Honours: Academy Award for Best Director, 1995. Address: c/o CAA, 9830 Wilshire Boulevard, Beverly Hills, CA 90212, USA.

ZENKIEWICZ Marian, b. 17 March 1945, Torun, Poland. Scientist. m. Wieslawa, 2 daughters. Education: Graduate, 1971, PhD, Technical Science, 1979, University of Technology, Gdansk; Nicolaus Copernicus University, Torun, 1977; Assistant Professor, Materials Science, University of Technology, Gliwice, 1990; Full Professor, Technical Sciences, President of Poland, 2002. Appointments: Director, Research Centre, Torun, 1981; Member of Polish Sejm, 1989-97; Professor, Academy of Bydgoszcz, 1992; Member of Polish Senat, 1997-2005; Member of EU Parliament, 2003-04; Vice-Rector, Kazimierz Wielki University, Bydgoszcz, 2005; Head, Department of Materials Engineering, Kazimierz Wielki University, 2004-. Publications: More than 320 scientific papers; 5 books; 20 patents. Honours: 4 Ministerial awards; 6 Rector awards; President of Poland honours: Golden Cross of Merit, 1985; Knight's Cross of the Order of the Renaissance, 1990; Officer's Cross of the Renaissance of Poland, 2005. Memberships: World Academy of Material and Manufacturing Engineering; Polymer Processing Society; Committee of Materials Science of the Polish Academy of Sciences. E-mail: marzenk@ukw.edu.pl

ZENKOVA Claudia, b. 14 July 1972, Chernivtsi, Ukraine. Optician; University Lecturer. m. Andriy Mudriy. Education: Engineering-Technical Faculty, 1994, PhD, 1997, Chernivtsi National University. Appointments: University Lecturer, 1997; Vice-Dean, Engineering-Technical Faculty, 2004; Associated Professor, 2004. Publications: Numerous articles in professional journals. Honours: Six state diplomas for scientific and pedagogical work. Memberships: SPIE; OSA; American Nano Society. Address: 9 Pivdenno-Kiltseva Str, Apt 16, Chernivtsy, 58013, Ukraine. E-mail: zenkova@itf.cv.ua

ZEPPELIN Helga von, b. Berlin, Germany. Architect; Sculpture. 1 son, 1 daughter. Education: Architect, 1966; Artist, 1972. Civic Activities: Founded the Forum of Integration for Culture, Economics and Society, 1986; Integration Management. Honours: Grand Prix du Prestige Européen, Foundation Européenne. Memberships: Alliance of Women Artists, USA; Accademia Internationale; Foundation Européenne. Commissions and Creative Works: Exhibitions: Germany, 1978, 1982, 1990; Switzerland, 1981, 1988, 1995, 1996; Japan, 1984, 1985; Ireland, 1986; France, 1992, 1994; USA, 1996. Address: Glockenacker 68, 8053 Zurich, Switzerland.

DICTIONARY OF INTERNATIONAL BIOGRAPHY 36th EDITION

ZHANG De-Wen, b. 5 April 1937, Wuhan, Hubei, China. Senior Research Fellow. m. Kangling Huang, 28 September 1968, 1 daughter. Education: BTech, 1962; MTech, 1965; PhD, 1967. Appointments: Assistant Engineer, Shenyang (China) Aerocraft Manufacturing Corporation, 1962-64; Associate Engineer, Aerocraft Strength Institute, Xian, 1968-69; Engineer, Seaplane Institute, Jingmen, 1970-80; Senior Engineer, Beijing Institute of Structure and Environment, 1981-96; Professor, China Academy of Launch Vehicle Technology, 1997-. Publications include: System Identification for Flight Vehicle; Model Updating and Damage Detection; Processing of Pseudo-Structure Modal Testing of Launch-Vehicle; Over 120 articles published in AIAAJ and Mechanical System and Signal Processing, and others. Honours: Award, Progress in Science and Technology, Chinese Ministry of Aeronautics, 1982; Award, Progress of Science and Technology, National Committee of Science and Technology, 1985; Award, Progress in Science and Technology, Chinese Ministry of Astronautics, 1996. Memberships: Fellow, Chinese Society of Aeronautics and Astronautics; AIAA; Chinese Society of Astronautics; Chinese Society of Vibration Engineering. Address: Beijing Institute of Structure and Environment, PO Box 9210, Beijing 100076, China. E-mail: zh1de2wen3@sina.com

ZHANG Jingguo, b. 7 October 1940, Shanghai, China. Materials Scientist; Engineer. m. Ninghua Zhu, 1 son. Education: Graduate, Department of Physical Metallurgy, University of Science and Technology, Beijing, China, 1964. Appointments: Research Assistant, 1964-74, Research Engineer, 1974-80, 1980-1982 in USA, Director of Testing Centre, 1983-84, Deputy Director of Institute, Senior Engineer, 1984-87, Vice-President, Academic Committee, Associate Chief Engineer, Professor of Materials Science and Engineering, 1987-2000, Shanghai Iron and Steel Research Institute; Senior Specialist, Professor of Materials Science and Engineering, Shanghai Bao Steel Research Institute, 2000-2003; Visiting Professor, Tongji University, 2004-05; Visiting Scholar, Columbia University, USA, 1980; Assistant Professor, University of Connecticut, USA, 1980-82; Senior Expert on Materials, Science & Engineering, Shanghai Society of Metals, Shanghai, China, 2005-11; Senior Expert on Advanced Materials, Shanghai HuiZhi Advanced Materials & Technology Co Ltd, 2012-. Publications: 38 and 48 papers published in scientific and engineering journals in English and Chinese respectively; Co-author 2 books in Chinese; Recently published papers: Structure of Amorphous Fe-Zr-B powders obtained by chemical reduction, 2002; Microstructure and CCT Thermograms of Spray Formed G Cr15 Steel, 2002; Superplastic Ultra-high Carbon Steels Processed by Spray Forming, 2003; Microstructure and Mechanical Properties of Spray Formed Ultrahigh-Carbon Steels, 2004; Co-author "Recent New Development of Spray Formed Ultrahigh-Carbon Steels", 2005. Honours: Honours and Prize for distinct achievements and contribution in engineering, The State Council of China, 1993; Li Xun Prize, Acta Metallurgica Sinica, 1993; Special Prize for Scientists in the fields of applied basic research, Science and Technology Commission of Shanghai Municipality, 1994-95, 1998-99. Memberships: Institute of Materials Science, University of Connecticut, USA, 1980-82; SAMPE, Japan, 1993-95; Board of Directors: Chinese Society of Metals, 1991-94, Chinese Materials Research Society, 1991-2003, Chinese Stereology Society, 1991-2004. Address: Room 2603, No 12, Lane 300, Wu Ning Road, Shanghai 200063, PR China. E-mail: jgz2010new@163.com

ZHAO Wenming, b. 24 January 1938, Xi-Xiang County, Shaanxi province, China. Professor. m. Zhi-Hui Hu, 1963, 1 son, 1 daughter. Education: BS, 1960, MSc, 1964, Northwestern College of Agriculture; Visitor, Department of Botany, University of Durham, UK, 1981-83; Visiting Professor, Department of Biological Science, University of Calgary, Canada, 1991. Appointments: Assistant, 1960-61, Lecturer and Professor, 1974-94, Northwestern College of Agriculture, China; Teacher and Vice Dean, Shanxi Labour University, Dai-yuan, Chain, 1965-70; Teacher, Zhou-zhi Middle School, China, 1971-73; Professor and Adviser, Xian Jiaotong University, China, 1995-. Publications: Numerous articles in professional journals; Author, Gene Engineering of Seed Proteins, 1995. Honours: Prize, State Council of China, 1992. Memberships: Chinese Society of Biochemistry and Molecular Biology; Chinese Society of Cell Biology. Address: 1 Cun 34 She 151 Hao, Xian Jiaotong University, Xian 710049, China.

ZHAO Yun, b. 24 October 1974, Zhejiang, P R China. Education. m. Yonghui Bian, 2 sons. Education: LLB, 1995, LLM, 1998, China University of Political Science and Law, Beijing; LLM, Leiden University, Netherlands, 1999; PhD, Law, Erasmus University, Rotterdam, Netherlands, 2003. Appointments: Researcher, Erasmus University, 2000-02; Associate Professor, LLM Program Leader, City University of Hong Kong, 2002-07; Associate Professor, The University of Hong Kong, 2008-. Publications: More than 80 publications including 5 books, 16 book chapters and 41 refereed journal articles. Honours: Dr Isa Diederiks-Verschool Prize; Listed in international biographical dictionaries. Memberships: Founding Council Member, Hong Kong Internet Forum; Elected Member, International Institute of Space Law; Member, Asia Pacific Law Association; Arbitrator, Hong Kong International Arbitration Centre; Arbitrator, Guangzhou Arbitration Commission; Panelist, Asian Domain Name Dispute Resolution Center. Address: Faculty of Law, The University of Hong Kong, Pokfulam, Hong Kong. E-mail: zhaoy@hku.hk

ZHENG Min, b. 18 July 1920, Beijing, China. Professor of English and American Literature; Poet; Writer; Translator. m. Shi Bai Tong, 1952, 1 son, 1 daughter. Education: BA, Philosophy, National South-West Associated University, 1943; MA, English Literature, Brown University, Providence, Rhode Island, 1952. Appointments: Editor, Department of Translation, Central News Agency, 1945-48; Assistant Research Fellow, Chinese Academy of Social Sciences, 1956-61; Professor of English and American Literature, Beijing Normal University, 1961-; Visiting Professor, University of California at San Diego, 1985. Publications: Books of poetry, criticism, and translations, 1949-91. Contributions to: Journals and periodicals. Honours: Stars Poetry Writing Award, 1982-83; Best Poetry Award, Poetry Monthly and the Writer's Association, 1986; Honorary Citizen, San Jose, California, 1986. Memberships: Shakespearean Society, Shanghai; Society of Comparative Literature; Writer's Association of China. Address: c/o Department of Foreign Languages, Beijing Normal University, Beijing 100875, China.

ZHMAILO Alexander, b. 1954, Samarkand, Uzbekistan. Artist; Writer; Teacher. Divorced, 1 son. Education: Art College, Siktivkar, Russia, 1980; Graphic Artist, Pedagogical Institute, Khabarovsk, Russia, 1987. Appointments: Responsible Secretary, Youth Association, Union of the Artists of Samarkand, 1986-88; Founder, Art Manager, Gallery of Modern and Ethno-Decorative Art, Intouris Hotel, Uzbekistan, 1993-95; Founder, Co-ordinator, Alexander International

Art Centre, Samarkand, 1994, Crimea, 2012. Publications: Numerous articles in professional journals. Honours: Komsomol Award, Uzbekistan, 1988; Laureate, Satirical Graphics international contest, Japan, 1987, Italy (Ancona), 1987, 1989, 1991, 1993, Italy (Foligno), 1990; Laudable Opinion, Marostik, Italy, 2002. Memberships: National Artists Union of Ukraine; Professional Union of Artists of Russia. Address: Tereshkovoy 15, SkalistoeBahchisaray R-N, 98440, Crimea, Ukraine. E-mail: zhmailoart@yandex.ua

ZHOU Xiaochuan, b. January 1948, Beijing, P R China. Governor, People's Bank of China. Education: Bachelor, Beijing Institute of Chemical Technology, 1975; PhD, Economic Systematic Engineering, Tsinghua University, 1985. Appointments: Member, State Economic Restructuring Commission, 1986-91; Member, Leading Group of Economic Structural Reform, State Council, 1986-87; Deputy Director, Research Institute of Economic Structural Reform, 1986-87; Assistant Minister, Ministry of Foreign Trade and Economic Co-operation (now Ministry of Commerce), 1986-89; Various senior policy making positions including: Vice President, Bank of China, Administrator, State Administration of Foreign Exchange, Deputy Governor, People's Bank of China; President, China Construction Bank, Chairman, China Securities Regulatory Commission, 1991-2002; Governor, People's Bank of China, 2002-. Publications: Author of over 100 academic papers; More than 10 books. Honours: SUN Yefang Economics Essay Award, 1994 and 1997; Ann Tse-kai International Trade Essays Award, 1994. Memberships: Chinese Governor, IMF; Chinese Governor, African Development Bank; Board of Directors, Bank for International Settlements; Chairman, BIS Asian Consultative Committee; Member, Commisson on Growth and Development of the World Bank; Member, Group of Thirty; Member, Chinese Economists 50 Forum. Address: People's Bank of China, 32 Chengfang Street, Xicheng District, Beijing, 100800, P R China.

ZHOU Yuming, b. 23 June 1934, Hebei, China. Senior Translator. m. Shuying Li, 2 sons. Education: Graduate, Faculty of Foreign Languages and Literature, University of Central China, 1956. Appointments: Assistant Professor, University of Central China, 1956; English Translator, Chinese Ministry of the Petroleum Industry, 1974; Senior Translator, China National Offshore Oil Corporation, 1984; Retired 1994; Senior Translator, Enron Oil and Gas China Ltd, 1994-1999; Retired from Enron Oil and Gas, China, 1999. Publications: Books of modern lyrics: Flowing Bunch of Flowers; Kiss of Wings; Love of Dolphin; The Tenderly Grown Green; Selected Poems of Yuming; Earth Newborn; Selected Verses by Yuming; Books of long epic poems: Liang Shanbo and Zhu Yingtai – Chinese Romeo and Juliet; Love Between a Human Being and a Serpentine Being; Far Away Off the Milky Way (extracts in book: Eternal Motherlove, 2005); Two Verse Dramas ("Moses" and "Salem"); Verse Dramas: Wordless Longing and Wedding Date; Three Verse Dramas; General Yue; A Journey on the Train; The Separated Love. Honours: Gold Prize of the Chinese Long "Dragon" Culture; Award, International Poet of Merit, International Society of Poets, America; Honorary Doctor of Literature of the World Academy of Arts and Culture; Distinguished Leadership Award, ABI; Man of the Year 2002, ABI; The Founders Award, IBC; Universal Award of Accomplishment; American Medal of Honor; ABI World Laureate of China; Worldwide Honours List, IBC; First Class Award for Far Away Off the Milky Way, Chinese Ministry of Culture, 2005; International Shakespeare Award for Literary Achievement, IBC, 2009. Memberships: China Poetry Association; Life Member, World Congress of Poets; Distinguished Member, International Society of Poets; Vice-Chair, China Association of Contemporary Arts. Address: 233, Building 7, Ruyili, Western District, Beijing 100035, China.

ZHU Hua, b. 10 August 1970, Heilongjiang, China. Professor. m. Li Wei, 2 sons. Education: BSc, Telecommunication & English, Beijing University of Post and Telecommunication, 1992; MA, Linguistics for TESOL (Distinction), British Council/Beijing Normal (Teachers) University, 1995; PhD, Speech and Language Sciences, Department of Speech, University of Newcastle upon Tyne, 2000. Appointments: Research Associate, Department of Speech, 1998, Sir James Knott Fellow, 2000-03, Lecturer, 2003-05, Senior Lecturer, 2005-06, School of Education, Communication & Language Sciences, Newcastle University; Senior Lecturer, 2007-09, Reader, 2009-, School of Languages, Linguistics & Culture, Birkbeck, University of London. Publications: 5 books; Numerous articles in professional journals. Honours: International Visiting Research Fellowship, MARCS Auditory Laboratories, College of Arts, Education & Social Sciences, University of Western Sydney, Australia, 2004, 2010. Memberships: International Association of Applied Linguistics; British Association of Applied Linguistics; International Pragmatics Association; International Association for the Study of Child Language. Address: Department of Applied Linguistics & Communication, University of London, Birkbeck College, 26 Russell Square, Bloomsbury, London WC1B 5DQ, England.

ZICCARDI CAPALDO Giuliana, b. 9 March 1940, Terni, Italy. Professor. m. Gerardo Capaldo, 1 son, 1 daughter. Education: Degree in Law, University of Naples Federico II, 1964. Appointments: Founder and Director, Department for International Studies, 1991-95, Director, PhD Program in International Law, 1995-2006, Professor, General Public Law, 2009-10, University of Salerno, Italy; General Editor, The Global Community YILJ, Oxford, 2001-20; Scientific Director, Research Programs, Italian Ministry of University and Research, Italian National Research Council, University of Salerno. Publications: Le situazioni territoriali illegitime nel diritto internazionale, 1977; Repertory of decisions of the international court of justice 1947-1992, 1995; The Global Community YILJ, 2001-06; The Pillars of Global Law, 2008; Diritto Globale – il Nuovo Diritto Internazionale, 2010. Honours: Honorary Member, The Border Legion 11th Armored Cavalry Regiment Border of West Germany, 1998; Listed in international biographical dictionaries. Memberships: American Society of International Law; Italian Society of International Law; Italian Bar Association. Address: Via de Renzi 38, 83100 Avellino, Italy. E-mail: globalcommunity@tin.it

ZILBER Nelly, b. 3 February 1941, Montpellier, France. Research Scientist. 1 daughter. Education: BA, 1962, MA, 1963, Aggregation, 1964, D ès Sc, 1970, Certificate in Epidemiology & Statistics, 1978, University of Paris, France. Appointments: Scientific Researcher, CNRS, 1964-2007; Scientific Researcher, Falk Institute for Mental Health Studies, Jerusalem, 1984-; Counselor, Epidemiology & Statistics, Jerusalem, 1984-. Publications: Over 100 articles in professional journals. Address: Falk Institute for Mental Health Studies, Kfar Shaul Hospital, Givat Shaul, 91060 Jerusalem, Israel.

ZIMMERMANN Karel, b. 2 March 1941, Prague, Czech Republic. University Teacher. m. Olga, 2 sons. Education: Diploma, Mathematics, Moscow State University, 1963; RNDr, 1966, DrSc, 1986, Charles University, Prague,

Czech Republic; PhD, Czech Academy of Sciences, 1968. Appointments: Professor of Mathematics, Faculty of Mathematics and Physics, Charles University, Prague, 1996-. Publications: Numerous articles in professional journals. Honours: Gold Medal, Faculty of Natural Sciences, University of P J Šafařík, Košice, Slovakia. Memberships: Union of Czech Mathematicians and Physicists; GAMM; AMS; Czech Society of Operatins Research. Address: Faculty of Mathematics and Physics, Charles University, Malostranske nam 25, CZ-118 00, Praha 1, Czech Republic.

ZINCK Philippe, b. 11 December 1972, France. Lecturer. m. Virginie, 2 daughters. Education: Engineer and Master Degree, 1995, PhD, Polymer Science, 1999, INSA Lyon. Appointments: Postdoctoral Research, The Weizman Institute of Science, 2000; Polytechnic Federal School of Lausanne, 2001; Ecole Superieure de Physique et Chimie Industrielles de la Ville de Paris, 2002; Lecturer, Chemistry and Polymer Science, University of Lille, Nord de France. Publications: 35 articles in professional journals; 3 book chapters; 1 book. Honours: Marie Curie Individual Fellowship, 2000. Memberships: Marie Curie Fellowship Association (Advisory Board); French Group of Polymer (North Section Board); French Chemistry Society. Address: UCCS, ENSCL, Bat C7, Cite Scientifique, 59652 Villeneuve d'Ascq, France. E-mail: philippe.zinck@ensc-lille.fr

ŽIVKO-BABIĆ Jasenka, b. 10 August 1949, Velika Pisanica, Croatia. Dentist. m. Davor, 1 son. Education: DMD, 1968-73; Reward for Scientific Research, University of Zagreb, 1972; Postgraduate, School of Dental Medicine, 1973; Master Thesis, 1980; PhD, School of Dental Medicine, University of Zagreb, 1987; Principal Investigator, Prosthetic Materials, 2001. Appointments: Scientific Assistant, 1982; Scientific Associate, 1987; Assistant Professor of Prosthodontics, 1988; Higher Scientific Associate, 1997; Associate Professor, 2002; Full Professor, 2007; Full Professor of Prosthodontics, Permanent, 2007; Subject Lecturer, Dental Materials. Publications: Anodic sampling of Titanium by thin layer chromatography, 2003; Estimation of chemical resistance of dental ceramics by neural network, 2008; Book, Metals in Prosthodontics, 2005. Honours: Award of Croatian Medical Association, 1974, 1999; Award of Yugoslav Medical Association, 1986; Award of Medical Centre, Vukovar, 1999. Memberships: Croatian Medical Association; Croatian Society for Prosthodontics; European Prosthodontics Association; International College of Prosthodontics; Croatian Association for Chemical Engineering; Croatian Association for Materials and Tribology; Medical Academy of Science. Address: School of Dental Medicine, 10000 Zagreb, Gunduliceva 5, Croatia. E-mail: zivko@stzg.hr

ZLOCHEVSKAYA Alla, b. 10 November 1951, Moscow, Russia. Literary Critic; Researcher. Education: MA, Philology, Moscow State University; Defended and published 2 literary research theses: PhD equivalent, 1982 and 2002. Appointments: Research Worker, 1985-2000, Senior Researcher, 2000-, Department of Philology, Moscow State University, Russia. Publications: Published more than 100 research articles concerning Russian literature of XIX-XX centuries and Czech and Slovak Rusistik; In-depth study of F Dostoyevsky, V Nabokov, M Bulgakov; Monograph: Artistic World of V Nabokov and Russian Literature of XIX Century, 2002. Membership: F M Dostoyevsky Society, Moscow. Address: Olympic Village 8, Flat 153, Mitchurinsky Pr. Moscow 119602, Russia. E-mail: zlocevskaya@mail.ru

ZNAK Vladimir, b. 22 December 1937, Kracnoiarsk city, Russia. Mathematician. m. Lubov Karpova, 2 daughters. Education: Navigator diploma, 1960; Physicist diploma, Radioelectronics, 1963; PhD, Technical Cybernetics, 1980. Appointments: Probationer-Researcher, 1964-65; Junior Researcher, 1965-92; Senior Researcher, 1993-2010. Publications: Around 60 papers, conference proceedings, journal articles and inventor's certificates. Address: Tereshkova Street 6, Apartment 50, Novosibirsk 630090, Russia.

ZOLBERG Vera L, b. 22 September 1932, Vienna, Austria. Sociology Professor. m. Aristide R Zolberg, 1 son, 1 daughter. Education: AB, Hunter College, 1953; MA, Boston University, 1956; PhD, University of Chicago, 1974. Appointments: Edgewood College, Madison, Wisconsin, 1962-64; St Xavier College, Chicago, 1964-67; Purdue University, 1974-84; Professor, New School for Social Research, 1984-. Publications include: After Bourdieu: Influence, Critique, Elaboration; Outsider Art: Contested Boundaries in Contemporary Culture; The Happy Few-en Masse: Franco-American Comparisons in Cultural Democratization; Constructing a Sociology of the Arts. Honours: Rockefeller Humanities Fellowship; ACLS Fellowship; Many travel grants; Listed in Who's Who publications and biographical dictionaries. Memberships: American Sociological Association; Society for Social Theory, Politics and the Arts; International Sociological Association; Association Internationale des Sociologues de Langue Francaise; Eastern Sociological Society. Address: New School for Social Research, 65 5th Avenue, New York City, NY 10003, USA.

ZOLOTAREVSKAYA Dina Isaakovna, b. 2 February 1937, Zhitomir, Ukraine, USSR. Professor; Scientific Researcher. m. Victor Iosifovich Zolotarevskii, 2 sons. Education: Mechanics Engineer Diploma, 1960, Postgraduate Student, Theoretical Mechanics Chair, 1965, Candidate of Engineering Science, 1972, Moscow Auto-Mechanical Institute, Moscow; Docent of High Mathematics Chair, Resolution of High Certifying Commission of Council of Ministers, USSR, 1978; Doctor of Engineering Science, 1998, Professor of High Mathematics Chair, 2000, Resolution of State High Certifying Committee of Russia Federation. Appointments: Designer Engineer, State Bearing Factory, Moscow, 1960-62; Theoretical Mechanics Chair, Moscow Auto-Mechanical Institute, Moscow, 1962-65; Assistant, 1966-78, Docent, 1978-98, High Mathematics Chair, K A Timiryazev Moscow Agricultural Academy, Moscow; Professor, High Mathematics Chair, Russian State Agrarian University - Moscow, 1998-; High Mathematics Chair Professor, Russian State Agrarian University, Moscow Timiryazev Agricultural Academy. Publications: More than 120 scientific articles in Russian and foreign journals and educational mathematics books for high school students: Theory of Probabilities. Problems and Solutions, 2002; Book of Linear Algebra Problems, 2004; Analytic Geometry, 2010. Honours: Soros Professor, International Soros Education Program; Competition Laureate of International Soros Education Program in the Field of Exact Sciences and Moscow Government, 2000, 2001, 2002; Honorary Worker Professional High Education of Russia Federation. Memberships: G V Vinogradov Reology Society, Petrochemical Institute of Russia Academy of Science; Academic Council of Finance Faculty, Russian State Agrarian University - Moscow Timiryazev Agricultural Academy; Soros Professor Club. Address: Academician Anokhin ul, 12-3-215, 119602, Moscow, Russia. E-mail: zolot@gagarinclub.ru

ZUBRITSKY Alexander, b. 14 March 1949, Severo-Kurilsk, Sakhalin Region, Russia. Pathologist. 2 sons. Education: Curative and Preventative Faculty, Sverdlovsk Medical Institute, 1968-74; 1 year specialism in Pathological Anatomy, Sverdlovsk Regional Clinical Hospital No 1, 1975; Advanced Training Course for Pathological Anatomy, Kharkov, Ukraine Institute of Advanced Medical Studies, 1977; Advanced Training Course for Perinatal Pathology, Moscow Institute for Postgraduate Medical Training, 1986; PhD, 1991; Advanced Training Course for Cytology, Moscow Regional Research Clinical Institute, 1994; Pathological Anatomy, Russian Medical Academy for Postgraduate Training, 2000, 2006; Advanced Training Course for Histological Diagnostics of Endometrium Scrape, Research Centre of Obstetrics, Gynaecology and Perinatology, Russian Academy of Medical Sciences, 2004; Advanced Training Course for Diagnostics of Soft Tissue Tumors, 2008. Appointments: Hospital Attendant, Department of Pathology, City Hospital No 21, Sverdlovsk, 1965-67; Hospital Attendant, Medico-Legal Morgue No 1, Sverdlovsk, 1967-68; Chief of Pathology Department, Central Regional Hospital in Neviyansk, Sverdlovsk Region, 1975-76; Chief of Pathology Department, Head Pathologist, Sverdlovsk Road, 1976-83; Lecturer, Pathological Anatomy, Medical School of Sverdlovsk Road, 1976-77; Chief of Department of Pathology, Municipal Institution, Taldom Central Regional Hospital, Taldom, Moscow Region, 1983-; Pathologist, Pathology Department, City Clinical Hospital No 81, Moscow, 2004. Publications: 4 rationalisation proposals; 190 published works as sole author. Honours: Certificate, A Finalist, Marvin I Dunn Award, Best Poster Presentation in Cardiology, American College of Chest Physicians, 1990; Pathology Research Practice Award for the Expert Quiz, Innsbruck, MD Taldom, 1993; International Man of the Year, 1994-95; Certificate, Researcher of the Year, ABI, 2001; International Peace Prize Winner, UCC, 2003; 21st Century Award for Achievement (Bronze Medal), IBC, 2003; Gold Medal International Scientist of the Year 2004, IBC; The World Medal of Freedom for significant accomplishments in the field of Pathological Anatomy, ABI, 2005; 2005 Man of Achievement Award for Outstanding Contributions to Pathological Anatomy of Cor Pulmonale, ABI, 2005; The Best People of Russia Medal, 2006; Gold Medal for Russia, ABI, 2007. Memberships: European Society of Pathology, 1989; International Union Against Tuberculosis and Lung Disease, 1990; European Section, International Society for Heart Research, 1992; International Society on Diagnostic Quantitative Pathology, 1994; New York Academy of Sciences, 1995; Research Board of Advisors, ABI, 2000; Honorary Member, IBC Advisory Council, 2000; American Association for the Advancement of Science, 2003; Research Fellow, ABI, 2005; Atlantic-Euro-Mediterranean Academy of Medical Sciences, 2006; Academic Board, Atlantic-Euro-Mediterranean Academy of Medical Sciences, 2008. Address: Prospekt Mira 101B/79, Moscow 129085, Russia. E-mail: alex_26zubr@yahoo.com

ZUCKER-FRANKLIN Dorothea, b. 9 August 1930, Berlin, Germany. Physician, Scientist. m. Edward C Franklin, deceased, 1 daughter. Education: BA, Hunter College, New York, 1952; MD, New York Medical College, New York, 1956; Post-Doctoral Fellowships: Department of Hematology, Montefiore Hospital, Bronx, 1959-61; Department of Anatomy, New York University School of Medicine, 1961-63. Appointments include: Assistant Professor of Medicine 1963-68, Associate Professor of Medicine 1968-74, Professor of Medicine 1974-, Department of Medicine, New York University School of Medicine. Publications include: Numerous articles in professional journals. Honours include: Phi Beta Kappa; AOA; Henry Moses Prize for Research, 1973, 1985; Elected member, Institute of Medicine of the National Academy of Sciences, 1995; Woman of the Year Award, American Women in Science, 1996; Fellow, American Association for the Advancement of Science, 1997; Doctor of Science, honoris causa, City University of New York, 1996; Elected, American Academy of Arts and Sciences, 2001; Listed in several biographical dictionaries. Memberships include: Numerous scientific societies including: FASEB, 1966-; American Society of Clinical Investigations, 1973; American Association of Physicians, 1974; American Association of Immunologists, 1979-; Greater New York Blood Program Ad Hoc committee for donor notification, criteria and protocols AIDS study, 1982-84; IV International Symposium on Amyloid-Organizing Committee, 1983-84; VA AIDS Center Grant Review Panel, 1988 and 1989; Member of Board of Directors, Henry M and Lillian Stratton Foundation Inc, 1987-95; Many other Ad Hoc NIH and academic committees at various institutions; Institute of Medicine, National Academy of Science, 1995; President, American Society of Hematology, 1995. Address: New York University School of Medicine, Department of Medicine, 550 First Avenue, New York, NY 10016, USA.

ZUHDI Nazih, b. 19 May 1925, Beirut, Lebanon (naturalized US citizen, 1960). Surgeon (retired). m. (1) 2 sons, (2) Annette, 2 sons, 1 daughter. Education: BA, American University of Beirut, 1946; MD, 1950; Diplomate, American Board of Surgery, American Board of Thoracic Surgery. Appointments: Intern, St Vincent's Hospital, SI, New York, 1950-51, Presbyterian-Columbia Medical Center, New York City, 1951-52; Resident, Kings County SUNY Medical Center, New York City, 1952-56; Fellow, SUNY Downstate Medical Center, Brooklyn, 1953-54; Resident, University Hospital, Minneapolis, 1956, Oklahoma City, 1957-58, Practice surgery specialising in cardiovascular and thoracic, 1958-87, Nazih Zuhdi Transplant Institute, Administrator, 1985-99, Retired, 1999; Co-founder, Chairman, laboratories of Mercy Heart and Research Institute, 1958-65; Founder, Chairman, Director, Surgeon-in-Chief, Oklahoma Transplantation Institute (now Nazih Zuhdi Transplant Institute), Baptist Medical Center, 1984-99, Chairman, Department of Transplantation, Baptist Hospital, Oklahoma City, 1994-99; Co-founder, Chairman, Oklahoma Cardiovascular Institute, Oklahoma City, 1983-84, Oklahoma Heart Center, 1984-85. Publications: Numerous articles in professional medical journals around the world. Honours: Oklahoma Hall of Fame, 1994; Fellow, ACS; Humanitarian Award, 1996. Memberships: American Thoracic Society; Oklahoma Thoracic Society; Southern Medical Association; Oklahoma Medical Association; International College of Angiology; American College of Chest Physicians; American College of Cardiology; American Society of Artificial Internal Organs; Society of Thoracic Surgeons; American Association for Thoracic Surgery; International Cardiovascular Society; Oklahoma State Heart Association; Milestones of Cardiovascular Medicine of the American College of Cardiology; Dwight Harken Founders Group of Heart Surgery; Stephen Westaby Pioneers of Cardiac Surgery; many others. Achievements include: first to used banked citrated blood for cardiopulmonary bypass for open heart surgery; orignation and completion of experiments leading to and first clinical non-hemic primes of heart-lung machines producing total intentional hemodilution; laid the foundation and opened the gateway for bloodless surgery for all patients. Address: 7305 Lancet Court, Nichols Hills, Oklahoma 73120 1430, USA. E-mail: anz70@aol.com

ZUK Carmen Veiga, b. 5 March 1939, Buenos Aires, Argentina. Child Psychiatry. m. Gerald H Zuk, 2 daughters. Education: MD, University of Buenos Aires; Residency, Medical College of Pennsylvania, USA. Appointments: Part-time worker in psychiatric clinics in several California counties, Los Angeles, Ventura, Santa Barbara, USA; Partner, Kaiser-Permanente, Southern California, USA; Private practice, Buenos Aires, Argentina. Publications: Co-author, articles in Contemporary Family Therapy; Co-author, articles in Argentine psychiatric journals; Co-author, Psychology of Delusion; Co-author, Unique Tranformation in a Dali Painting of the Female Cycle, 2010. Honours: Diplomate, American Board of Psychiatry and Neurology; Listed in international biographical dictionaries. Memberships: American Medical Association; International Society for Adolescent Psychiatry. Address: 2140 Santa Cruz Ave, Apt E-102, Henlo Park, CA 94025, USA. E-mail: carmenzuk@msn.com

ZWARTJES Otto, b. 12 November 1958, Amsterdam, Holland. Associate Professor. m. Anne Van Mechelen, 2 sons, 1 daughter. Education: MA (cum laude), Department of Spanish, University of Amsterdam, 1986; PhD, Department of Arabic/Department of Spanish, Radbond University, Nymegen, 1995. Appointments: Assistant Professor, Radbond University, Nymegen, 1991-98; Post-doctoral Researcher, 1997-98; Full Professor, Spanish Linguistics, University of Oslo, 1998-2003; Assistant Professor, 2003-07, Associate Professor, 2007-, University of Amsterdam. Publications: Missionary Linguistics Vols I-IV. Honours: Fellow, Netherlands Institute for Advanced Studies in the Humanities and Social Sciences, 2007-08; Invited Visiting Scholar, Tokyo University of Foreign Studies, 2010. Memberships: Associate Editor, Historiographia Linguistica; Editorial Board, Studies in the History of Language Sciences. Address: Raadhuisstraat 7, 2022 DK Haarlem, The Netherlands. E-mail: o.j.zwartjes@uva.nl Website: http://home.medewerker.uva.nl/o.j.zwartes/index.html

ZWIERZCHOWSKI Henryk, b. 24 October 1926, Łódź, Poland. Orthopaedic Surgeon. m. Danuta Anna Zuchowicz, 2 sons. Education: MD, Medical University, Łódź, 1952; PhD, 1964; DSc, 1974; Specialist of Orthopaedics and Traumatology, 1957. Appointments: From Assistant to Senior Assistant, 1952-63, Consultant, Outpatient Clinic, 1958-74, Orthopaedic Hospital, Łódź; From Lecturer to Assistant Professor, Orthopaedic Clinic, 1964-78, Head of Orthopaedic Clinic, 1979-83, Associate Professor, 1984-91, Professor, 1991-, Head of Orthopaedic Department, 1984-97, Medical University, Łódź; Active Member, Scientific Council of the Surgical Institute, Łódź, 1976-87; Member of Editorial Committee, Chirurgia Narządów Ruchu i Ortopedia Polska (Journal of the Polish Society of Orthopaedics and Traumatology, 1984-; Regional Consultant, Orthopaedics and Traumatology, Łódź, 1995-98. Publications: Author or co-author of 176 research articles, clinical reviews and research reports published in various scientific periodicals as well as 5 books all related to the area of orthopaedics, traumatology and rehabilitation of the motor system; patentee prosthese of crutiate ligament, 1993. Honours: Cavalier Cross of the Order Polonia Restituta, 1984; Golden Badge, Polish Society for Fight with Cripleness Award, 1984; Ministers Award, 1985, 1987, 1995; Honorary Member, Polish Orthopaedics and Traumatology Society, 1996; Consulting Editor, Contemporary Who's Who, ABI, 2003. Memberships: Polish Society for Fight with Cripleness, 1964-90; Polish Orthopaedics and Traumatology Society, 1952-, Vice-President, 1982-86, Chairman Łódź Branch, 1979-82, 1987-90. Address: Zachodnia 12, Apt 63, 91-058 Łódź, Poland.

ZWOLINSKA-BRZESKI Teresa, b. 17 June 1934, Poland. Architect; Artist. m. Z Brzeski. Education: Primary education in Persia and Lebanon; Ignacy Paderewski High School for Girls; Basingstoke High School for Girls; Architectural Education, Bournemouth College of Arts; Architectural Association School; Brixton School of Building. Appointments: Senior Architect, Croydon Borough and NAW; Retired Architect; Self-styled and employed Artist; Fellow of Royal Society of Arts; Owner, TZB Southbourne Gallery. Publications: Articles in professional and popular journals. Honours: Several prizes for paintings and photography; Cyril Flisher Prize (Architecture), 1962/63. Memberships: Chartered Architect; Member, Royal Institute of British Architects; National Society of Painters, Sculptors and Printmakers; Society of Women Artists; Society of Floral Painters; Christchurch Arts Guild; Highcliffe Art Fellowship; Southbourne Art Society; Royal Horticultural Society; Amici di Verdi Society; Federation of British-Artists; Great London Architecture Club. Address: 2 Carbery Row, Off Southbourne Road, Bournemouth, BH6 3QR, England.

21st CENTURY HONOURS LIST

DICTIONARY OF INTERNATIONAL BIOGRAPHY 35th EDITION

NAME: Dorothy W. Bertine

ADDRESS: PO Box 2965
Denton
TX 76202
USA

OCCUPATION: Artist, Writer and Teacher

YEAR OF ENTRY: 2005

CITATION: For your Outstanding Contribution to Art and Teaching

---

NAME: Lady of Soul Eleonora Hajdar Bregu MOIF DDG

ADDRESS: Holy Mission Eleonore
Ru. "Komuna e Parisit" #4
PO Box 7435
Tirana
Albania

OCCUPATION: Missionary

YEAR OF ENTRY: 2006

CITATION: For your Outstanding Contribution to Improving Life

---

NAME: Daniel D Brunda DDG LPIBA MOIF AIOM AdVSci DO HonDG

ADDRESS: 106 West Upper Ferry Road
Ewing
NJ 08628
USA

OCCUPATION: Consultant: Mechanical/Electromagnetic Powerline Radiation/Engineer/Scientist

YEAR OF ENTRY: 2002

CITATION: For your Outstanding Contribution to the Design and Control of Electrical Transmission, Distribution and Service Lines

---

HONOURS LIST

NAME: Dr Barry Lloyd Chapman LFIBA

ADDRESS: 31 Elbrook Drive
Rankin Park
NSW 2287
Australia

OCCUPATION: Consultant Cardiologist (Retired)

YEAR OF ENTRY: 2006

CITATION: For your Outstanding Contribution to Medical Research, Teaching and Treatment

---

NAME: Dr C Juliana Ching LPIBA DDG AIOM MOIF AdVBus DO HonDG

ADDRESS: 4 Mount Butler Drive
Jardine's Lookout
Hong Kong

OCCUPATION: Businesswoman

YEAR OF ENTRY: 2000

CITATION: For your Outstanding Contribution to Business & Medicine

---

NAME: Christodoulos Christodoulou HonDG DDG

ADDRESS: 12 Pritagora Street
2406 Engomi
Nicosia
Cyprus

OCCUPATION: Governor of Central Bank of Cyprus

YEAR OF ENTRY: 2006

CITATION: For your Outstanding Contribution to Central Banking

DICTIONARY OF INTERNATIONAL BIOGRAPHY 35th EDITION

NAME: Dr Miss Sara Ciampi WCOIM

ADDRESS: Via San Fruttuoso 7/4
16143 Genova
Italy

OCCUPATION: Writer

YEAR OF ENTRY: 2006

CITATION: For your Outstanding Contribution to Literature and Philosophy

---

NAME: Donald Mercer Cormie LLM. Q.C. IOM

ADDRESS: 9369 Rockwood Drive
Scottsdale
AZ 85255-9255
USA

OCCUPATION: Barrister

YEAR OF ENTRY: 2001

CITATION: For your Outstanding Contribution to Law

NAME: Sandra Lynn Daves LFIBA DDG MOIF

ADDRESS: 6825 Susanna Ct
Citrus Hts
CA 95621
USA

OCCUPATION: Poet Laureate and Lyricist

YEAR OF ENTRY: 2006

CITATION: For your Outstanding Contribution to Poetry and Music

---

HONOURS LIST

NAME: Dr Tarun Kumar De, Scientific (H) VECC DAE

ADDRESS: 22a Motilal Nehru Road
Calcutta
700029
India

OCCUPATION: Scientist, Engineer & Researcher

YEAR OF ENTRY: 2000

CITATION: For your Outstanding Contribution to Engineering Research

---

NAME: Joan E Hirsh Emma

ADDRESS: 23 Pheasant Lane
E Setauket
NY 11733
USA

OCCUPATION: Teacher, Writer

YEAR OF ENTRY: 2000

CITATION: For your Outstanding Contribution to College Teaching and Manuscript Development

---

NAME: Professor Dr James M Fragomeni Ph.D. LPIBA MOIF AdVSci HonDG IOM

ADDRESS: PO Box 1446
Royal Oak
MI 48068-1446
USA

OCCUPATION: Educator and Researcher

YEAR OF ENTRY: 2006

CITATION: For your Outstanding Contribution to Mechanical Engineering and Engineering Education

---

DICTIONARY OF INTERNATIONAL BIOGRAPHY 35th EDITION

NAME: Bruce Alan Grindley LFIBA

ADDRESS: Tenerife Property Shop S.L.
117 Puerto Colon
Playa De Las Americas, Adeje, Tenerife
Canary Islands
Spain

OCCUPATION: Estate Agent

YEAR OF ENTRY: 2001

CITATION: For your Outstanding Contribution to International Business Integrity in Property Conveyancing

---

NAME: Rev Dr Prof Tzu-Yang Hwang LPIBA AdVAh AIOM MOIF CH DO DDG HonDG AWCASC WCOIM

ADDRESS: 11768 Roseglen Street
El Monte
CA 91732
USA

OCCUPATION: Supreme Grand Master; Chair; CEO; Chancellor

YEAR OF ENTRY: 2008

CITATION: For your Outstanding Contribution to Multi-Religio-Philo-Cultu-Theo-Arts-Educa

---

NAME: Neil Herman Jacoby Jr LPIBA IOM AdVSci CH DO DDG

ADDRESS: 1434 Midvale Avenue
Los Angeles
CA 90024
USA

OCCUPATION: Astrodynamic Scientist

YEAR OF ENTRY: 2000

CITATION: For your Outstanding Contribution to Astrodynamics

HONOURS LIST

NAME: Dr Tien-Ming Jen MD

ADDRESS: Clinical Mycology Study
No 24-5 3rd Floor
Lane 24 Kinmen Road
Taipei 100-17
Taiwan ROC

OCCUPATION: Educator, Consultant and Physician

YEAR OF ENTRY: 2002

CITATION: For your Outstanding Contribution to Medical Research

---

NAME: Dr Sci Nella Kacergiene MOIF DDG LFIBA DO

ADDRESS: Virsuliskiu 89-22
Vilnius
LT-2056
Lithuania

OCCUPATION: Physician, Paediatrician

YEAR OF ENTRY: 2000

CITATION: For your Outstanding Contribution to Paediatrics and Human Ecology

---

NAME: Tetsuo Kaneko LPIBA DDG AdVSci IOM

ADDRESS: Kogane Kazusacho 16-1
Matsudo-shi
270-0015
Japan

OCCUPATION: Physicist

YEAR OF ENTRY: 2000

CITATION: For your Outstanding Contribution to Scientific Research

---

DICTIONARY OF INTERNATIONAL BIOGRAPHY 35th EDITION

NAME: Dr Khoo Boo-Chai AdVMed DDG IOM MOIF HonDG

ADDRESS: Parkway Parade Medical Centre # 05-12
80 Marine Parade
Singapore 449269

OCCUPATION: Medical Doctor

YEAR OF ENTRY: 2001

CITATION: For your Outstanding Contribution to Reconstructive Plastic Surgery

---

NAME: Prof Kwang Seog Kim LFIBA MOIF HonDG

ADDRESS: Dept of Plastic & Recon. Surgery
Chonnam Nat Univ Medical School
8 Hak-dong
Dong-gu Gwangju
501-757 Korea

OCCUPATION: Plastic and Reconstructive Surgeon, Biomedical Researcher and Educator

YEAR OF ENTRY: 2005

CITATION: For your Outstanding Contribution to Plastic Reconstructive Surgery, Biomedical Research and Education

---

NAME: Dr Kyoung Soo Kim LPIBA IOM MOIF HonDG DDG AdVSci

ADDRESS: Chirogenix Co Ltd
801 Kowoon Inst of Tech Innovation, Suwon Univ
Whasung City, Kyunggi-do 445-743
Korea

OCCUPATION: Researcher, CEO

YEAR OF ENTRY: 2006

CITATION: For your Outstanding Contribution to Medicinal Chemistry

HONOURS LIST

NAME: Professor Pill Soo Kim LPIBA DDG IOM AdVSci CH

ADDRESS: Dept of Automotive Engineering
Daelim College
526-9 Bisan-dong, Dongan-ku
Anyang-si. Kyunggi-do
431-715 Korea

OCCUPATION: Professor

YEAR OF ENTRY: 2001

CITATION: For your Outstanding Contribution to Engineering

NAME: Mr Masashi Kimura MOIF DDG IOM DO HonDG AdVSci

ADDRESS: Dept of Molecular Pathobiochemistry
Gifu University School of Medicine
Yanagido 1-1
Gifu 501-1194
Japan

OCCUPATION: Researcher

YEAR OF ENTRY: 2005

CITATION: For your Outstanding Contribution to Cell Biology

NAME: Professor Eliezer I Klainman LPIBA IOM AdVMed DDG

ADDRESS: 86 Pardess-Meshutaf St
Raanana
Israel 43350

OCCUPATION: Cardiologist

YEAR OF ENTRY: 2000

CITATION: For your Outstanding Contribution to Cardiology

DICTIONARY OF INTERNATIONAL BIOGRAPHY 35*th* EDITION

NAME: Dr Vladimir Kozlovskiy

ADDRESS: Saarmunder Str. 85
14478 Potsdam
Germany

OCCUPATION: Technical Physics

YEAR OF ENTRY: 2008

CITATION: For your Outstanding Contribution to Physics of Dielectric Crystals

---

NAME: Professor Distinguished Soji Kurimoto IOM AdVMed DDG

ADDRESS: Asthma Institute
1-17 Tamondori-2 chome
Chuoku, Kobe 650
Japan

OCCUPATION: Physician

YEAR OF ENTRY: 2000

CITATION: For your Outstanding Contribution to Education and Professional Training in Medicine

---

NAME: Professor Chul Lee IOM

ADDRESS: Department of Chemistry
Hanyang University
133-791 Seoul
Korea

OCCUPATION: Professor

YEAR OF ENTRY: 2000

CITATION: For your Outstanding Contribution to Chemistry

NAME:	Dr.-Ing. Paul Ih-Fei Liu
ADDRESS:	1715 Oak Street Santa Monica CA 90405 USA
OCCUPATION:	Engineer, Educator and Writer
YEAR OF ENTRY:	2006
CITATION:	For your Outstanding Contribution to Engineering Education

---

NAME:	Associate Professor Cornelis A Los
ADDRESS:	Block B Nanyang Avenue 10-04 Singapore 639611 Singapore
OCCUPATION:	Economist
YEAR OF ENTRY:	2000
CITATION:	For your Outstanding Contribution to Financial Economics

---

NAME:	The Revd Prof. John Warwick Montgomery, Ph.D., D.Théol., LL.D.
ADDRESS:	55 rue de Rountzenheim 67620 Soufflenheim France
OCCUPATION:	Christian Apologetics
YEAR OF ENTRY:	2006
CITATION:	For your Outstanding Contribution to The International Law of Human Rights

---

DICTIONARY OF INTERNATIONAL BIOGRAPHY 35th EDITION

NAME: Dr Tadeusz K Murawski DDG MOIF LFIBA IOM

ADDRESS: ul. Szkoly Orlat 4
Apt 59
03-984 Warsaw
Poland

OCCUPATION: Economist

YEAR OF ENTRY: 2001

CITATION: For your Outstanding Contribution to Environmental Economics

----

NAME: Dr Shoichi Nakakuki

ADDRESS: 281-2 Oosonoki
Shimotsuma-city
Ibaraki
304-0801
Japan

OCCUPATION: Researcher and Educator

YEAR OF ENTRY: 2006

CITATION: For your Outstanding Contribution to Comparative Anatomy and Veterinary Medicine

----

NAME: Professor Shiro Nii, MD, PhD

ADDRESS: Famir Okayama 206
Hama 372-1
Okayama 703-8256
Japan

OCCUPATION: Researcher and Educator

YEAR OF ENTRY: 2005

CITATION: For your Outstanding Contribution to Research and Education

----

HONOURS LIST

NAME: Dr Tanya Niyamapa

ADDRESS: Agricultural Machinery & Management
Dept of Agricultural Eng
Kasetsart Univ Kampaeng Saen
Campus Nakornpathom 73140
Thailand

OCCUPATION: Agricultural Engineer

YEAR OF ENTRY: 2000

CITATION: For your Outstanding Contribution to Agricultural Engineering

---

NAME: Dr Takashi Oguchi DDG AIOM DO HonDG AdVSci MOIF LPIBA

ADDRESS: Center for Spatial Info Science
Univ of Tokyo
5-1-5 Kashiwanoha
Kashiwa 277-8568
Japan

OCCUPATION: Scientist and Educator

YEAR OF ENTRY: 2006

CITATION: For your Outstanding Contribution to Geomorphology and Geography

---

NAME: Joyce A. Oliver IOM MOIF CH DO

ADDRESS: 904 Silver Spur Rd
Suite 449
Rolling Hills Estate
CA 90274
USA

OCCUPATION: Author/Journalist

YEAR OF ENTRY: 2001

CITATION: For your Outstanding Contribution to Commercial Journalism

DICTIONARY OF INTERNATIONAL BIOGRAPHY 35th EDITION

NAME: Thresia Pierce LFIBA DDG AdVAh

ADDRESS: 1600 So. Valley View Blvd
Bldg 6, Apt 1106
Las Vegas
NV 89102
USA

OCCUPATION: Teacher

YEAR OF ENTRY: 2001

CITATION: For your Outstanding Contribution to Teaching and Writing

---

NAME: Professor Naseem Rahman HonDG

ADDRESS: Department of Chemistry
University of Trieste
Via Giorgieri No 1
34100 Trieste
Italy

OCCUPATION: Professor

YEAR OF ENTRY: 2001

CITATION: For your Outstanding Contribution to Chemistry

NAME: Luis B Rosario MD, FESC

ADDRESS: R Quinta Grande 8 r/c
2780-156 Oeiras
Portugal

OCCUPATION: Physician

YEAR OF ENTRY: 2001

CITATION: For your Outstanding Contribution to Cardiology

HONOURS LIST

NAME:	Honorable Dr Kazuo Sato DDG
ADDRESS:	3-11-21 Yabe Sagamihara-shi Kanagawa-ken 229-0032 Japan
OCCUPATION:	University Professor
YEAR OF ENTRY:	2001
CITATION:	For your Outstanding Contribution to Engineering

NAME:	Dr Mika Sato-Ilic
ADDRESS:	Institute of Policy & Planning Sciences University of Tsukuba Tenodai 1-1-1 Tsukuba, Ibaraki 305-8573 Japan
OCCUPATION:	Assistant Professor
YEAR OF ENTRY:	2000
CITATION:	For your Outstanding Contribution to Engineering

NAME:	Count Hans C von Seherr-Thoss LFIBA AdVSci DO
ADDRESS:	Habichtstr 39 D 82008 Unterhaching Germany
OCCUPATION:	Mechanical Engineer
YEAR OF ENTRY:	2000
CITATION:	For your Outstanding Contribution to Mechanical Engineering

DICTIONARY OF INTERNATIONAL BIOGRAPHY 35th EDITION

NAME: Dr Ingeborg Hildegard Solbrig

ADDRESS: 1126 Pine Street
Iowa City
IA 52240
USA

OCCUPATION: Educator

YEAR OF ENTRY: 2004

CITATION: For your Outstanding Contribution to Writing, Education and Research

---

NAME: Mary Goldacre Spencer

ADDRESS: Tenerife Property Shop SL
117 Puerto Colon
Playas De Las Americas
Adeje Tenerife
Canary Islands, Spain

OCCUPATION: Real Estate Agent

YEAR OF ENTRY: 2001

CITATION: For your Outstanding Contribution to International Business Integrity

---

NAME: Professor Dr Andy Sun IOM MOIF LPIBA DDG CH AdVMed HonDG

ADDRESS: National Taiwan University Hospital
Taipei
Taiwan
Republic of China

OCCUPATION: Immunologist

YEAR OF ENTRY: 2001

CITATION: For your Outstanding Contribution to Immunology and Medical Science

HONOURS LIST

NAME: Dr Manfred Thiel IOM LPIBA DDG MOIF AAAS CH DO

ADDRESS: Rohrbacherstr 20
69115 Heidelberg
Germany

OCCUPATION: Philosopher, Poet

YEAR OF ENTRY: 2000

CITATION: For your Outstanding Contribution to Philosophy and Poetry

- - - - - - - - - - - - - - - - - - - -

NAME: Captain Dr Ivica Tijardović DDG LFIBA MOIF AIOM HonDG AdVSci DO

ADDRESS: Nazorov Prilaz 37
Split 21000
Croatia

OCCUPATION: Shipmaster and Scientist

YEAR OF ENTRY: 2006

CITATION: For your Outstanding Contribution to Maritime Navigation

- - - - - - - - - - - - - - - - - - - -

NAME: J E Vander Naald LFIBA DDG IOM

ADDRESS: 44 Darby Creek Ct.
Bluffton
SC 29909-6222
USA

OCCUPATION: Educator

YEAR OF ENTRY: 2000

CITATION: For your Outstanding Contribution to Education

- - - - - - - - - - - - - - - - - - - -

NAME:	Dr Ruslana Vernickaite DDG LFIBA IOM MOIF
ADDRESS:	Rambyno 7-5 LT-93173 Klaipeda Lithuania
OCCUPATION:	Physician, Obstetrician-Gynaeologist
YEAR OF ENTRY:	2000
CITATION:	For your Outstanding Contribution to Obstetrics, Gynaecology and Ecology

---

NAME:	Dr Veniamin Volkov MD
ADDRESS:	Rileeva Str. 11/3 St. Petersburg 191014 Russia
OCCUPATION:	Ophthalmosurgeon
YEAR OF ENTRY:	2006
CITATION:	For your Outstanding Contribution to Ophthalmology

NAME:	Professor Hugo Walter
ADDRESS:	157 Loomis Court Princeton NJ 08540 USA
OCCUPATION:	College Professor
YEAR OF ENTRY:	2000
CITATION:	For your Outstanding Contribution to Humanities and Poetry

HONOURS LIST

NAME: Professor Masayoshi Yamaguchi IOM DDG

ADDRESS: Senagawa 1-chome 15-5, Aoi-ku
Shizuoka City 420-0913
Japan

OCCUPATION: University Professor

YEAR OF ENTRY: 2005

CITATION: For your Outstanding Contribution to Life Sciences

NAME: Professor Michiru Yasuhara LFIBA IOM AdVSci

ADDRESS: 34-18 Neura Iwasaki
Nissin-city
Aichi 470-0131
Japan

OCCUPATION: Professor

YEAR OF ENTRY: 2000

CITATION: For your Outstanding Contribution to Education

NAME: Dr Vak Yeong Yoo MOIF DDG LPIBA AdVMed IOM DO HonDG

ADDRESS: Cheong-Vak Antiaging Hospital
582 Shinsa Dong Kangnam Gu
Seoul 135-892
Korea

OCCUPATION: Physician

YEAR OF ENTRY: 2001

CITATION: For your Outstanding Contribution to Medicine